A CONCORDANCE TO THE POETRY OF
D. H. LAWRENCE

A Concordance to the Poetry of

D.H. LAWRENCE

Edited by

Reloy Garcia and James Karabatsos

UNIVERSITY OF NEBRASKA PRESS • LINCOLN

This concordance is dedicated to the memory of
Vivian de Sola Pinto (1895–1969).

CONTENTS

Acknowledgments — vii

Introduction — ix

Table of Symbols — xvi

Word Index — 1

Appendices

    I.   Lawrence's Persona — 499

    II.   Familial References — 512

    III.   Nature

        A. Topography — 512

        B. Animals — 512

        C. Fruits, Flowers, and Trees — 512

        D. Time, Seasons, and Cycles — 513

        E. Elements and Minerals — 513

    IV.   Anatomy, Physiology, and Senses — 514

    V.   Science and Technology — 514

    VI.   Religion, Mythology, and Metaphysics — 514

    VII. Politics and Social Commentary — 515

    VIII. Dialect and Archaisms — 516

    IX.   Miscellaneous

        A. Names — 517

        B. Numbers and Colors — 517

        C. Foreign Words and Expressions — 518

Page-Line Index — 519

ACKNOWLEDGMENTS

The Complete Poems of D. H. Lawrence, used as the text for this concordance, is reprinted by kind permission of The Viking Press, Inc. Grateful acknowledgment is extended to Alfred A. Knopf, Inc., for permission to use the poems from *The Plumed Serpent*.

We also wish to thank Father Edward Sharp, S. J., our close friend, who programmed the entire project for us, and who graciously tolerated the presence of two humanists among his computers; Father Clement Schneider, S. J., Academic Vice-President of Creighton University, who unhesitatingly provided the seed money to begin our work; the United States Office of Education, which provided the necessary funds to complete the concordance; and Miss Teresa Heise, our efficient typist.

INTRODUCTION

A Concordance to the Poetry of D. H. Lawrence consists of three main divisions: a Word Index; nine appendices classifying predominant interests in Lawrence's poetry; and a Page-Line Index. A table of symbols, discussed below, appears opposite the first page of the Word Index.

The text used is *The Complete Poems of D. H. Lawrence,* edited by Vivian de Sola Pinto and Warren Roberts (New York: Viking Press, 1964), which is generally accepted as the standard edition.[1] Employing an 1130 computer, we key-punched the entire body of Lawrence's verse, exclusive of poem titles, on IBM computer cards, one line per card, coding each card by page and line. To facilitate the preparation and use of this concordance, we numbered each page sequentially from the first line to the last, rather than re-numbering with the first line of each successive poem. Thus the numbering begins with each new page, and the page is the basic counting unit, not the poem. This numbering system, it seems to us, most efficiently resolves problems occasioned by Lawrence's particular use of free verse, and from the many long pieces. But because our counting unit is the page, we have provided a Page-Line Index which gives the beginning and ending page and line of each poem. This index should serve as a useful complement to the index of titles in the standard edition.

The Word Index includes the nine prefatory prose pieces in the section entitled "Unrhyming Poems": "Fruits" (*CP*, 277), "Trees" (*CP*, 295), "Flowers" (*CP*, 303), "The Evangelistic Beasts" (*CP*, 319), "Creatures" (*CP*, 331), "Reptiles" (*CP*, 348), "Birds" (*CP*, 368), "Animals" (*CP*, 376), and "Ghosts" (*CP*, 406). We felt that their inclusion would not create an imbalance in the basic vocabulary of the poetry; indeed, their vocabulary mirrors that of the poems. The Word Index also in-

---

1. All references to the poetry in this Introduction are to this edition, which is indicated by the abbreviation *CP*.

ix

cludes the variant poems and early drafts which Pinto and Roberts collected in Appendix III of the standard text.

We first typed the entire text exactly as it appears, and checked our copy to make sure it included no typographical errors. We then programmed the computer to give us an alphabetical print-out of the entire vocabulary, excluding certain common words—A, AT, BY, IS, THE, etc.—which comprise almost half the text. In compiling deletion lists, concordance makers generally follow an arbitrary frequency policy, excluding words appearing more than one hundred times; yet there is no logical rationale for such a policy. We preferred to mold the formula to fit the poet. The alternative would have been to eliminate such key words as SUN (appearing 376 times), EARTH (213 times), GOD (361 times), and many other fundamental concepts.[2] In addition, we listed in Appendix I: Lawrence's Persona all references to I, I'D, I'LL, I'M, and I'VE. Conversely, some words which occurred less than one hundred times—DIDN'T (27), THOSE (80), MAY (61), etc.—were eliminated because their retention would have needlessly inflated the Word Index. In sum, the Word Index lists every word in the two volumes of Lawrence's poetry except the following one hundred and ninety-six entries, whose frequencies are listed parenthetically:

A (3675)	AROUND (34)	CAN (337)
AH (135)	AS (1049)	CANNOT (77)
ABOUT (149)	ASIDE (20)	CAN'T (97)
ABOVE (76)	AT (839)	COME (321)
ACROSS (92)	AWAY (224)	COMES (112)
AFTER (131)	BACK (248)	COMING (54)
AGAINST (116)	BE (761)	COULD (140)
ALL (1001)	BECAUSE (94)	DID (108)
ALONG (79)	BEEN (102)	DIDN'T (27)
ALWAYS (101)	BEFORE (126)	DO (367)
AM (423)	BEHIND (74)	DOES (82)
AN (279)	BELOW (53)	DOESN'T (31)
AND (6909)	BETWEEN (170)	DON'T (193)
ANOTHER (108)	BUT (904)	DOWN (450)
ANY (145)	BY (245)	EACH (103)
ANYTHING (46)	BEYOND (106)	EVEN (276)
ARE (1135)	CAME (79)	EVER (90)

2. These counts take in all variant forms, including compound words.

EVERY (109)   LONG (200)   SAYS (38)
FAR (92)   MADE (69)   SAYING (26)
FOR (1047)   MAKE (158)   SHALL (201)
FORTH (98)   MAKES (64)   SHE (451)
FROM (817)   MAKING (27)   SHOULD (181)
GET (89)   MANY (77)   SINCE (76)
GIVE (95)   MAY (61)   SMALL (86)
GO (240)   ME (1352)   SO (798)
GOES (110)   MIGHT (51)   SOME (127)
GOING (85)   MINE (67)   SOMETHING (94)
GONE (130)   MORE (305)   STILL (309)
GOT (110)   MOST (63)   SUCH (107)
HAD (166)   MUCH (121)   THAN (216)
HAS (390)   MUST (202)   THAT (1590)
HAVE (721)   MY (1595)   THAT'S (49)
HAVING (42)   MYSELF (113)   THE (11,907)
HE (730)   NEVER (278)   THEIR (554)
HER (863)   NO (509)   THEM (493)
HERE (174)   NOT (763)   THEMSELVES (71)
HIM (347)   O (131)   THEN (452)
HIMSELF (90)   OF (5627)   THERE (455)
HIS (789)   OFF (161)   THERE'S (38)
HOW (296)   OH (381)   THEY'RE (37)
IF (517)   ON (1189)   THEY'VE (21)
IN (3118)   ONLY (326)   THEREFORE (21)
INTO (391)   OR (465)   THESE (119)
IS (2246)   OTHER (141)   THEY (961)
ISN'T (40)   OUR (390)   THIS (504)
IT (1557)   OUT (609)   THOSE (80)
ITS (290)   OVER (309)   THOUGH (104)
IT'S (130)   PERHAPS (59)   THROUGH (304)
ITSELF (57)   PUT (136)   TILL (176)
JUST (125)   QUITE (88)   TO (3210)
LEAVE (80)   RATHER (44)   TOO (121)
LEFT (75)   REALLY (62)   TOWARDS (94)
LET (245)   ROUND (211)   UNDER (127)
LIKE (1088)   SAID (107)   UP (510)
LITTLE (390)   SAY (194)   UPON (181)

US (436)	WHILE (112)	WOULD (210)
VERY (138)	WHO (353)	YES (56)
WAS (478)	WHOM (34)	YET (243)
WAY (145)	WHOSE (58)	YOU (2054)
WELL (92)	WHY (189)	YOUR (803)
WERE (205)	WILL (456)	YOURSELF (48)
WHAT (524)	WITH (1521)	YOU'D (20)
WHEN (535)	WITHIN (87)	YOU'LL (26)
WHERE (328)	WITHOUT (106)	YOU'RE (52)
WHICH (253)	WON'T (44)	YOU'VE (55)

In the second print-out, which excluded the foregoing words, the entire line was reproduced unless it was more than fifty-five spaces long. In such cases a plus sign followed to indicate that the line was not reproduced in its entirety. Also, if a word appeared more than once in a line, the line was given only once. Each of us proofread the print-out to provide a cross-check. Next we programmed the computer to indicate "gaps" in the text; that is, places where lines were either not in proper sequence or omitted altogether. The third print-out, proofread in turn, comprises this concordance. Theoretically, a computer renders error-free copy when perfect data is fed into it. Although we are sure that there are still errors in this volume, we hope that we have done all we can to reduce their number.

Some minor problems were posed by the limited storing capacity of the 1130 computer and the number of Lawrence's inconsistencies. As one consequence, we were unable to indicate capitalization, diacritical marks, and punctuation; to ascertain these features it will be necessary to consult the primary works. Further, we have linked all names, certain Biblical and foreign expressions, and concepts which Lawrence clearly considered units. Thus, in this concordance, such phrases and names as SON OF MAN, TREE OF LIFE, APRES MOI LE DELUGE, JOHN THOMAS, etc., are treated as units. Such units are listed according to the first letter of the lead element; SON OF MAN, for example, appears in the s's. In addition, because the apostrophe was read into the computer as a separate symbol following the twenty-six alphabetical characters, such clipped forms as 'AN, AN', 'AD, TH', etc., are indexed after words containing the same alphabetical characters, but which do not have an apostrophe. For example, 'AN and AN' follow ANYWHERE; 'AD follows

ADVOCATE; and TH' follows THY-SEN. Our last technical consideration concerned Lawrence's extensive use of foreign expressions, which normally appear in italic type. In Appendix IX, we chose not to indicate italicization by underlining, since it seemed to us redundant both to isolate and to underline. When foreign expressions appear in any of the other appendices, however, they are underlined. It should be noted that while a plus sign at the end of a line in the Word Index indicates that the line is not completely reproduced, a plus sign in the appendices signals that the derivational and inflectional affixes of various form classes and the variant spellings are not incorporated. On occasion we departed from this rule to give particularly interesting variants. The asterisks preceding the notations in the Word Index mark all variant lines collected in the *Complete Poems*, Appendix III.

No Lawrentian can be unaware of the irony in our use of a computer to compile this work. We hope, however, that far from seeming a victory of the machine over Lawrence and his poetry, our computer concordance is tangible proof that machines can be subjugated to the higher interests of art and the human imagination, so long as the tool does not turn the hand.

R. G.

J. K.

Creighton University

xiii

A CONCORDANCE TO THE POETRY OF

D. H. LAWRENCE

SYMBOLS

Word Index

+ indicates that the line is not reproduced in its entirety.

* indicates variant lines collected in *CP*, Appendix III.

Appendices

+ indicates that the derivational and inflectional affixes of various form classes are not incorporated.

ABAHT
  ABAHT IT YES I'M A GENT AN' LIZ   434 23
  WELL WHAT ABAHT IT   546 26
  ALL RIGHT GUVNOR WHAT ABAHT IT   547 16
  RIGHT CH'ARE BOSS AN' WHAT ABAHT IT   547 25

ABANDON
  TASSELS IN ABANDON   170 20
  YET SEE HIM FLING HIMSELF ABROAD IN FRESH ABANDON   305 6
  YOU'D BETTER ABANDON ALL IDEA OF FEELINGS ALTOGETHER   501 15

ABANDONED
  DOWN THE ABANDONED HEAVEN   455 13
  BE WELL IF THESE OLD FATHERS ABANDONED THEIR FOOLISH   777 30

ABANDONMENT
  YOU WITH LOOSE HANDS OF ABANDONMENT HANGING DOWN   58 23
  OF ABANDONMENT   367 4

ABASH
  THAT DAY IS HALF GROWN OVER IT NEED NOT ABASH   91 4

ABATE
  DO YOU THINK IF YOU TAKE ME THAT THAT WILL ABATE YOU *932 12

ABBREVIATION
  OR THE ABBREVIATION OF NICOLAS   404 10

ABEYANCE
  YOUTH IN ABEYANCE   503 10

ABHORRENT
  ABHORRENT GREEN SLIPPERY CITY   278 10

ABIDE
  TO ABIDE   464 22
  TOO GREAT A SKUNK TO ABIDE BY HIS OWN SELF   *949 2

ABJECTLY
  SUBMIT ABJECTLY TO THE BLIND MECHANICAL TRAFFIC-STREAMS+ 666 6

ABLAZE
  YOUR YOUNG HUSHED LOOK THAT THEN SAW GOD ABLAZE   157 23
  MOON ALL ABLAZE   755 13

ABLE
  GOODNESS KNOWS IF THEY'LL BE ABLE   45 15
  STOIC ABLE TO WAIT THROUGH AGES   292 29
  TO BE ABLE TO STAND FOR ALL THESE   317 26
  YET NEVER ABLE TO PASS THE WHITENESS OF LIGHT INTO   345 17
  ARE YOU ABLE TO WONDER   353 16
  AS TIME HAS NOT DARED TO AVOUCH NOR ETERNITY BEEN ABLE + 370 31
  THE FULL DOOM OF LOVING AND NOT BEING ABLE TO TAKE BACK 410 16
  YET NOT SUFFICIENTLY CONSCIOUS TO BE ABLE TO FORGET OUR+ 496 20
  INSTEAD OF GETTING ON AND NOT BEING ABLE TO GET OFF AGA+ 518 25
  THEY'LL NEVER BE ABLE TO SAY   534 10
  AT LAST IN SHEER HORROR OF NOT BEING ABLE TO LEAVE OFF 701 31
  TO BE ABLE TO FORGET IS TO BE ABLE TO YIELD   725 20
  THEN THEY'D BE ABLE TO LOVE DESPAIR CAN'T LOVE IT CAN O+ 838 13

ABOARD
  SHALL TAKE THEM ABOARD TOWARDS THE GREAT GOAL OF OBLIVI+ *958 13

ABOLISH
  BUT TO ABOLISH THE WORKING CLASSES FOR EVER   453 11
  LET'S ABOLISH LABOUR LET'S HAVE DONE WITH LABOURING   517 19
  TO ABOLISH THE TYRANNY OF MONEY   838 4

ABOLISHED
  THE MACHINE SHALL BE ABOLISHED FROM THE EARTH AGAIN   666 15

ABOMINATION
  FOR THE ABOMINATION OF OUR OLD RIGHTEOUSNESS   232 8
  FOR THE ABOMINATION OF OUR PAST RIGHTEOUSNESS   232 13
  GOBBLE UP FILTH YOU HORROR SWALLOW UTTER ABOMINATION   398 28

ABOMINATIONS
  THE SILENCED RACES AND ALL THEIR ABOMINATIONS   298 2

ABORIGINAL
  DARK ABORIGINAL EYES   292 28

ABORIGINALITY
  YOUR ABORIGINALITY   369 8

ABORIGINALLY
  HE IS THE ONE THING THAT IS ABORIGINALLY AMERICAN   776 21

ABORIGINES
  THE ABORIGINES OF THEIR COUNTRY   776 4
  TOLD THE OLD AMERICAN ABORIGINES THAT IT WOULD   777 29

ABOUND
  WHO ABOUND   235 8

ABRAHAM
  AS ABRAHAM WHOSE SEED SHALL MULTIPLY   126 16
  THE ANGELS CAME TO ABRAHAM AND THEY STAYED   234 5

ABREAST
  SUDDEN DEMONIC DAUNTLESSNESS FULL ABREAST   371 10
  CHIEFTAINS THREE OF THEM ABREAST ON FOOT   388 16

ABROAD
  THE WOODBINE CREEPS ABROAD   42 9
  AND OUT OF THE CHAMBERED WILDERNESS WANDERS A SPIRIT AB+ 70 6
  ABROAD I IN THIS NAKED BERRY   107 17
  THEN A LAUNCH ABROAD OF SHRINKING DOVES   179 13

ABROAD
  FEAR WAS ABROAD WE WHISPERED NO ONE KNOWS US   217 6
  YET SEE HIM FLING HIMSELF ABROAD IN FRESH ABANDON   305 6
  THEN THE PROUD LION STALKS ABROAD ALONE   325 19
  THOSE THAT GO GLITTERING ABROAD   523 24
  ABROAD IN MY HANDS LIKE WAVES AMONG THE ROCKS OF SUBSTA+ 705 6
  AND GOD ABROAD AND ALIGHT ON US EVERYWHERE   742 30
  AND ALL MY DOVES ARE LAUNCHED ABROAD AND LOST   875 24
  AND OUT OF THE CHAMBERED WEARINESS WANDERS A PERFUME AB+ *916 14

ABRUPT
  BUT I ABRUPT   884 1

ABSENCE
  CEASE THEN FROM MUSIC DOES ANGUISH OF ABSENCE BEQUEATH 85 23
  AND THE ABSENCE OF COTTON-WOOD LEAVES OR OF ASPEN   404 1
  EVEN THE ABSENCE OF DARK-CROSSED DONKEYS   404 2
  AND A COMPLETE ABSENCE OF CONSEQUENCE TO THE MURDERER 532 23

ABSENT
  AND NOT BE ALLOWED TO ABSENT THEMSELVES   779 3

ABSOLUTE
  I IN THE SOUR BLACK TOMB TRODDEN TO ABSOLUTE DEATH   259 1
  I FEEL ABSOLUTE REVERENCE TO NOBODY AND TO NOTHING HUMAN 622 6
  I FEEL ABSOLUTE REVERENCE SAY NO MORE   622 13
  AND THE WHEEL OF THE CONSCIOUS SELF SPINS ON IN ABSOLUT+ 712 15
  ABSOLUTE ABSOLVED FROM THE SUN AND THE EARTH AND THE MO+ 712 16
  ABSOLUTE CONSCIOUSNESS ABSOLVED FROM STRIFE AND KISSES 712 17
  ABSOLUTE SELF-AWARENESS ABSOLVED FROM THE MEDDLING OF C+ 712 18
  ABSOLUTE FREEDOM ABSOLVED FROM THE GREAT NECESSITIES OF+ 712 19
  SING THEN THE CORE OF DARK AND ABSOLUTE   724 8
  IF THERE WERE NOT AN UTTER AND ABSOLUTE DARK   724 12
  AND IF THERE WERE NOT AN ABSOLUTE UTTER FORGETTING   724 20
  AN ABSOLUTE NOTHING   *948 18
  TO MAKE THEM FEEL ABSOLUTE WORMS   *948 26

ABSOLUTELY
  ABSOLUTELY TO NOTHING   258 21
  AND FEEL ABSOLUTELY IT   414 4
  WHILE THEIR HEARTS BECOME ABSOLUTELY EMPTY   502 10
  BECAUSE HE IS SO ABSOLUTELY IN YOUR POWER THAT   776 15
  HE IS SO ABSOLUTELY AT YOUR MERCY   776 33

ABSOLUTE ONE
  AND THE GLOWING THRONE OF THE ABSOLUTE ONE   823 14

ABSOLUTION
  AND THE WHEEL OF THE CONSCIOUS SELF SPINS ON IN ABSOLUT+ 712 15

ABSOLUTISM
  ABSOLUTISM IS FINISHED IN THE HUMAN CONSCIOUSNESS TOO 473 14

ABSOLVED
  I SIT ABSOLVED ASSURED I AM BETTER OFF   36 7
  ABSOLVED   643 17
  ABSOLUTE ABSOLVED FROM THE SUN AND THE EARTH AND THE MO+ 712 16
  ABSOLUTE CONSCIOUSNESS ABSOLVED FROM STRIFE AND KISSES 712 17
  ABSOLUTE SELF-AWARENESS ABSOLVED FROM THE MEDDLING OF C+ 712 18
  ABSOLUTE FREEDOM ABSOLVED FROM THE GREAT NECESSITIES OF+ 712 19
  ONLY THE HUMAN BEING ABSOLVED FROM KISSING AND STRIFE 713 27

ABSORB
  IF IT DOESN'T ABSORB YOU   450 21
  AND ABSORB HER IN ME   605 10
  I MUST SEE IF I CAN'T ABSORB THIS SAMSON OF SELF-ABSORP+ 605 14

ABSORBED
  THEIR STILL SOULS ABSORBED   451 4
  OF THE BODY'S MEMORIES SLIPS AND IS ABSORBED   *959 25

ABSORBING
  LIKE AN ABSORBING GAME   450 20

ABSORBS
  UNLESS IT ABSORBS YOU   450 19

ABSTAIN
  YOU ABSTAIN FROM FURTHER INTERFERENCE   779 32

ABSTRACT
  FALTERS A STATEMENT ABOUT AN ABSTRACT NOUN   76 8
  TO THINK OUT IN THE ABSTRACT WHEN ALL WAS TWILIT GREEN + 690 29

ABSTRACTION
  ABSTRACTION   619 11
  ALL FORMS OF ABSTRACTION ARE EVIL   716 7
  FINANCE IS A GREAT EVIL ABSTRACTION   716 8
  SCIENCE HAS NOW BECOME AN EVIL ABSTRACTION   716 9
  EDUCATION IS AN EVIL ABSTRACTION   716 10
  AND POLITICS NOW ARE AN EVIL ABSTRACTION FROM LIFE   716 13

ABSTRACTIONS
  OH THESE ARE ABSTRACTIONS TO YOUR NASTY LITTLE BELLY   399 20
  ARE ALL EVIL ABSTRACTIONS FROM LIFE   716 12

ABSURD
  SO ABSURD   397 11
  IT IS ABSURD FOR ME TO DISPLAY MY NAKED SOUL AT THE TEA+ 608 11

ABUNDANCE
  THERE WOULD BE ABUNDANCE IN THE WORLD   488 5
  I SEE IT HAS A NATURAL ABUNDANCE   498 20
  I WANT TO BE LIKE THAT TO HAVE A NATURAL ABUNDANCE   498 24

ABUNDANT
    OF DARKNESS ABUNDANT WHICH SHAKEN MYSTERIOUSLY   136 18
    THEIR ABUNDANT SUMMERY WORDAGE SILENCED CAUGHT   142 2

ABUTTING
    LIKE CLIFFS ABUTTING IN SHADOW A DEAD GREY SEA   164 19

ABYSS
    LEARNING OF THEIRS IT ALL GOES DOWN THE SAME ABYSS   74 26
    SINKING IN THE ENDLESS UNDOING THE AWFUL KATABOLISM INT+   699 26
    INTO HIMSELF ALONE DOWN THE GODLESS PLUNGE OF THE ABYSS   700 24
    WHICH HE CAN NEVER REACH TILL HE TOUCH THE BOTTOM OF TH+   700 28
    WHICH HE CAN NEVER TOUCH FOR THE ABYSS IS BOTTOMLESS   700 29
    BUT THE ABYSS WHICH IS BOTTOMLESS   701 2
    FOR THE ABYSS IS BOTTOMLESS   701 4
    IT IS THE ABYSS OF THE IMMORTALITY   701 8
    INTO THE ABYSS OF SELF-KNOWLEDGE   701 15
    IS AN ABYSS DOWN WHICH THE SOUL CAN SLIP   701 18

ABYSSES
    THE MOON FROM FAR ABYSSES   37 16

ACANTHUS
    HANDS TO EAT THE ACANTHUS OR BITE AT THE ALMOND BUDS   385 10
    THE UNROLLING OF FERNS WHITE TONGUES OF THE ACANTHUS LA+   623 27
    THE UNROLLING OF FERNS WHILE TONGUES OF ACANTHUS LAPPIN+   *953 15

ACAUSE
    AN' I COME AWAY ACAUSE O' TH' TEEMIN' RAIN   61 16

ACCENT
    THAT EVERY SYLLABLE EVERY ACCENT EVERY INTONATION AND E+   655 4

ACCENTS
    DO YOU HEAR THE CHEMICAL ACCENTS OF THE SUN   301 9

ACCEPT
    AND ACCEPT OBLITERATION   430 6
    IS THAT THEY ACCEPT LIES   504 2
    YOU MIGHT AS WELL ACCEPT THE THUNDERBOLT   559 14
    AND THEN TRUTH MUCH MORE BITTER TO ACCEPT   636 7
    CEASE TO ACCEPT THEM AS BROTHERS   639 5
    I SHALL HAVE TO REFUSE ENTIRELY TO ACCEPT EITHER OF THEM   645 13
    SO THEY ACCEPT COVERED DISLIKE AS THE NORMAL FEELING BE+   832 15
    I COULD ACCEPT MEN   840 3

ACCEPTANCE
    AND LIVE IN THE ACCEPTANCE OF IT   636 27

ACCEPTED
    OF THE MAN I'VE ACCEPTED AS MINE   59 14
    LIVED UNDAUNTED AND UNSOURED WITH ACCEPTED LIES   503 18

ACCEPTING
    MY FEAR IN ACCEPTING THE PORTENT THE TRAIN CAN NOW   88 27
    IF PEOPLE LIVED WITHOUT ACCEPTING LIES   503 19

ACCESS
    TO HAVE ACCESS TO THE KNOWLEDGE THAT THE GREAT DEAD   263 22
    ONE SMALL WAY OF ACCESS ONLY AND THIS CLOSE-CURTAINED F+   283 16

ACCIDENT
    YOUR MESTER'S 'AD A ACCIDENT   45 5
    AN' THERE'S COMPENSATION SIN' IT'S ACCIDENT   45 32
    THE SEED IS PURPOSE BLOSSOM ACCIDENT   218 26

ACCIDENTS
    'E'S 'AD TWENTY ACCIDENTS IF 'E'S 'AD ONE   45 27

ACCOMMODATION
    LET THERE BE NO ACCOMMODATION AT THIS ISSUE   608 7

ACCOMPLISHED
    TO AN UNBORN FUTURE THAN TO AN ACCOMPLISHED PAST   775 17

ACCOMPLISHING
    RISEN ACCOMPLISHING A RESURRECTION   258 28

ACCOMPLISHMENT
    AND SO IN THE GREAT AEONS OF ACCOMPLISHMENT AND DEBACLE   682 19

ACCORDING
    FOR ACCORDING TO SOME THE BEANS WERE THE BEANS OF VOTES+   303 17
    ACCORDING TO THE SOUL'S DESIRE   652 17
    AND STEER ACCORDING TO THE CURRENTS AND WINDS AND TIDES+   *953 10

ACCOUNT
    AND THE MAN AND THE CHILD OF NO MORE ACCOUNT   202 7
    OF NO ACCOUNT WHATEVER   269 16
    BUT OF WHAT ACCOUNT DO I HOLD THEM   269 21
    ACCOUNT TOO   607 16

ACCOUNTS
    WITH BANK ACCOUNTS AND INSURANCE POLICIES   442 4

ACCOUTREMENTS
    AND LITTLE DISHES AND ALL ACCOUTREMENTS   718 25
    AND LITTLE DISHES AND ALL ACCOUTREMENTS   *958 21

ACCUMULATED
    AND THE ACCUMULATED SPLASHING OF A GONG   623 9

ACCURSED
    YOU PILLAR OF SALT ACCURSED   207 35
    ACCURSED BASE MOTHERHOOD   207 37
    THEY ARE ACCURSED AND THE CURSE IS NOT TAKEN OFF   208 20
    ONLY YOUR ACCURSED HAIRY FRAILTY   334 6
    I DESPISED MYSELF AND THE VOICES OF MY ACCURSED HUMAN   351 20

ACCUSED
    AND MY HEART ACCUSED ITSELF   339 11

ACCUSING
    AND CHRIST I HAVE MET HIS ACCUSING EYES AGAIN   225 22

ACH ACH
    ACH ACH NOW INDEED GOD IS BORN HE TWINKLES WITHIN   682 28

ACHE
    THIS ACHE WAS SHED   35 25
    AND I WAS NUMB WITH A BITTER DEATHLY ACHE   98 27
    FOR I ACHE MOST EARNESTLY FOR YOUR TOUCH   117 15
    THAT YOU COULD DISCHARGE THE ACHE   117 26
    THE TURGID ELECTRIC ACHE AWAY   117 29
    GOOD IT WOULD LET THE ACHE COME THROUGH   122 20
    THE PAIN THAT IS HER SIMPLE ACHE FOR ME   128 26
    WITH ACHE OF DREAMS THAT BODY FORTH THE SLEEP   195 30
    AND DEATH WOULD ACHE STILL I AM SURE   205 18
    THE LONELINESS DAUNTS THEM THEIR STIFF THROATS ACHE   228 12
    THIS ACHE FOR BEING IS THE ULTIMATE HUNGER   265 26
    THE URGE THE MASSIVE BURNING ACHE   326 20
    FOR WHAT DOES HE ACHE AND GROAN   326 23
    ACHE AND WANT OF BEING   362 29
    AND IT RANKLES THEY ACHE WHEN THEY SEE THE YOUNG   502 24
    A STRANGE ACHE POSSESSED HIM AND HE ENTERED THE STRUGGLE   690 5
    AND HEALED FROM ALL THIS ACHE OF BEING   724 30
    AND WHAT I'VE UNDERSTOOD AND THEN THE UTTER ACHE   738 11
    I WOULD NOT MISS IT FOR YOUR ACHE OF WONDER   876 16
    WHO ACHE WITH AN ANGUISH OF MUSIC TO MAKE FOR YOU   884 19
    FOR I ACHE MOST EARNESTLY FOR YOUR TOUCH   *931 19
    I AM ASHAMED THAT I ACHE SO MUCH   *931 20

ACHES
    OH MY GOD HOW IT ACHES   212 19
    IT ACHES IN ME   213 4
    IT ACHES IN ME FOR HER   213 8

ACHIEVE
    I AM MYSELF AT LAST NOW I ACHIEVE   218 5
    FLOWERS ACHIEVE THEIR OWN FLOWERINESS AND IT IS A MIRAC+   683 22
    MEN DON'T ACHIEVE THEIR OWN MANHOOD ALAS OH ALAS ALAS   683 23
    IS THAT YOU SHALL ACHIEVE YOUR BEAUTY   683 26

ACHIEVED
    YOU HAVE SURELY ACHIEVED YOUR FATE   168 29
    SHALL SING OF HEAVEN ACHIEVED WHERE EVERY BRIGHT   872 15

ACHILLES
    LEST HER HEEL OF ACHILLES SHOULD BE REVEALED   577 14

ACHING
    THE REDDENED ACHING EYES OF THE BAR-MAN WITH THIN ARMS   72 2
    WILL YOU OPEN THE AMOROUS ACHING BUD   117 22
    AND I DO LIFT MY ACHING ARMS TO YOU   129 19
    LIKE THE AGONY OF LIMBS CUT OFF AND ACHING   213 9
    THEN THE DUMB ACHING BITTER HELPLESS NEED   263 20
    AT THE WOUND'S ACHING CICATRICE   869 2
    MY BREAST'S ACHING CICATRICE   869 9

ACHINGS
    WITH VIOLENT ACHINGS HEAVING TO BURST THE SLEEP THAT IS+   149 23

ACID
    STIRRING THE FIRES TO ACID OF BITTERNESS   795 25

ACID-BLUE
    YOU ACID-BLUE METALLIC BIRD   375 29

ACKNOWLEDGE
    TO ACKNOWLEDGE US   881 15

ACKNOWLEDGEMENT
    OF BIGGER LIVES WITH DUE REVERENCE AND ACKNOWLEDGEMENT   679 22

ACONITE
    ABOUT YOUR FEET SPONTANEOUS ACONITE   308 30

ACORNS
    AND IDEAS ARE HARD LIKE ACORNS READY TO FALL   608 23

ACQUAINTANCE
    OR THE MENTAL EFFORT OF MAKING HER ACQUAINTANCE   506 18

ACQUAINTANCES
    EXCEPT THAT PAPA AND MAMA ARE OLD ACQUAINTANCES OF   357 21

ACQUIESCE
    WHY SHOULD AMERICANS IMMEDIATELY ACQUIESCE   775 31

ACQUIESCED
    I ACQUIESCED AGAIN   207 4

ACQUIESCENCE
    ACQUIESCENCE OF WATCHFUL LIONS   770 17

ACQUITTED
    AND GET ACQUITTED   563 8

ACRID
    THE ACRID SCENTS OF AUTUMN   107 5
    AND ACRID NIGHT OF AUTUMN   107 21
    THEY ARE THE ISSUE OF ACRID WINTER THESE FIRST-FLOWER Y+   270 15
    WHERE FLOWERS SPROUT IN THE ACRID HUMUS AND FADE INTO H+   321 11

ACRIDITY
  RAISING DUSK AND ACRIDITY OF GOATS AND BLEATING   384 3

ACROBAT
  THEY TOUCH IN MID-HEAVEN LIKE AN ACROBAT   820 15

ACT
  HOW CAN YOU SHAME TO ACT THIS PART   55 8
  O ACT OF FEARFUL TEMERITY   310 4
  I THOUGHT HOW PALTRY HOW VULGAR WHAT A MEAN ACT   351 19
  WHY DON'T THEY PREPARE TO ACT ON THEM   520 30
  AND YOU HAVE TO ACT UP LIKE THEY DO   549 29
  WE'LL TRY TO ACT UP SUBLIME   573 4
  BEING AN ACT OF ONE   715 9
  AND SO WHEN THE OUTSIDE WORLD CALLS UPON AMERICA TO ACT+   775 29

ACTED
  AND ACTED ON IT   504 5

ACTION
  THE HARVEST THE SPENT ACTION TO ITSELF   195 3
  OR OIL OR COPPER OR GOLD A CAUSE FOR POLITICAL ACTION   779 19
  THERE IS NO ACTION IT IS ALMOST A SLEEP   856 23

ACTIVE
  SKY CEASED TO QUIVER AND LOST ITS ACTIVE SHEEN   35 15
  ALONG THE RAILWAY ACTIVE FIGURES OF MEN   174 9
  STILL AND SENSITIVE AND ACTIVE   285 25
  ACTIVE WITH CAPTIVE ACTIVITY   484 26
  PASSES THE EVER-CHANGING JOY OF HIS ACTIVE BODY   868 4
  FLUENT ACTIVE FIGURES OF MEN PASS ALONG THE RAILWAY   *906 16
  BEATS THE ACTIVE ECSTASY SUDDENLY LIFTING MY EYES   *906 21
  FLUENT ACTIVE FIGURES OF MEN PASS ALONG THE RAILWAY AND+   *908 11
  ALONG THE RAILWAY ACTIVE FIGURES OF MEN   *908 13
  BEATS THE ACTIVE ECSTASY   *908 17

ACTIVITIES
  FULL OF INORDINATE ACTIVITIES   510 27

ACTIVITY
  MY CONFIDENT ACTIVITY   64 24
  ACTIVE WITH CAPTIVE ACTIVITY   484 26
  OUR ACTIVITY HAS LOST ITS MEANING   510 22
  ONE FREE CHEERFUL ACTIVITY STIMULATES ANOTHER   520 26
  AS NORMAL ACTIVITY   832 17
  THE GREAT ACTIVITY SWELLING THROUGH THE ROUND FLESH PUL+   *907 14
  HERE IN THE SWELLING FLESH THE GREAT ACTIVITY WORKING   *909 11

ACT OF FAITH
  THEY WANT TO MAKE AN ACT OF FAITH AND BURN MY PRETTY   633 9

ACTS
  CHILDREN ACTS UTTERANCE   247 21

ACTUAL
  BUT ACTUAL FULFILMENT   265 18
  AND A MONSTER WHEN YOU'RE PINCHED FOR ACTUAL NECESSITIES   498 14
  CURIOUSLY ENOUGH ACTUAL REVOLUTIONS ARE MADE BY ROBOTS   647 21

ACTUALLY
  ACTUALLY GROWING   278 16
  OR WHETHER IT ACTUALLY IS AN EAGLE YOU ARE   414 13
  TILL WE ACTUALLY FEEL AS BLANK AS WE REALLY ARE   513 10
  OF THE FEMALE FORM TECHNICALLY BEAUTIFUL ACTUALLY A WHI+   619 12

ACUTE-DELIGHT
  WAR-CRY TRIUMPH ACUTE-DELIGHT DEATH-SCREAM REPTILIAN   364 22

ACUTELY
  RONALD SHE RESUMED DOESN'T LIKE WOMEN JUST ACUTELY   447 11

ADAM
  I ADAM FORM THE VEINS OF ME   240 11
  ADAM   358 10

ADAMANT
  AGAINST THE SILVERY ADAMANT WALLS OF LIFE'S EXCLUSIVE C+   722 3
  AGAINST THE SILVERY ADAMANT WALLS OF THIS OUR EXCLUSIVE+   *958 3
  OVER THE ADAMANT WALLS OF THIS OUR BY-NO-MEANS IMPREGNA+   *958 7

ADD
  HE CAN ADD THE RECKONING UP   199 1
  SERVE THEN I TELL YOU ADD YOUR STRENGTH TO MINE   235 1
  ADD YOURSELF UP AND YOUR SEED TO THE NOUGHT   235 15
  SO THAT THE RAMBLING SKY-DROPPED GRAPE CAN ADD ITS SAVO+   281 25
  SELF-EXPOSURE HARD HUMILIATION NEED TO ADD HIMSELF ON TO   362 31
  IS NOT TO ADD OUR LOVE TOGETHER OR OUR GOOD-WILL   506 2
  TO ADD THE MYSTERY OF JOY-IN-RESURRECTION TO THE MASS   609 20
  YET A WOMAN CAN ADD HER FLAME TO A MAN'S   680 3
  OR A MAN CAN ADD HIS FLAME TO THE FLAME OF ANOTHER MAN   680 4

ADDED
  THEY HAVE ADDED BLUENESS TO BLUENESS UNTIL   *954 21

ADDER
  NOR THE ADDER WE SAW ASLEEP WITH HER HEAD ON HER SHOULD+   255 26
  WHERE THE ADDER DARTS HORIZONTAL   321 15

ADDING
  SWIFTER AND HIGHER AND BRIGHTER OR THE YIELDING AND THE+   680 6

ADDITION
  AND IN ADDITION THE GREAT MUSCULAR PYTHON-STRETCH OF HER   393 22

ADDLED
  THAT ADDLED GOLDEN EGG   414 34

ADDRESS
  PLEASE ADDRESS THESE QUESTIONS TO THE PROPER PERSON   604 15

ADDS
  THE VEINS OF LIVING SPACE AND ADDS A GLISTEN   505 3

ADEPT
  FLOATING ABOVE MY SILVER SO THAT THE ADEPT   874 5

ADHERENCE
  HAVING NO ADHERENCE NO ADHESION ANYWHERE   267 19

ADHERENTS
  COME NOW TO US YOUR ADHERENTS WHO CANNOT FLOWER FROM   273 10

ADHERING
  A BIT OF SLAG STILL ADHERING AFTER YOUR FIRING IN THE F+   370 2

ADHESION
  HAVING NO ADHERENCE NO ADHESION ANYWHERE   267 19

ADHESIVE
  AND GLISTENING ADHESIVE MUZZLE   325 29

ADIOS
  ANSWER ADIOS   798 32
  SAY ADIOS MY CHILDREN   798 33

ADJUNCT
  MERE FEMALE ADJUNCT OF WHAT I WAS   264 22

ADMIRABLE
  BIOLOGICALLY ADMIRABLE   828 8

ADMIRATION
  IS THE GORGEOUSNESS THAT EVOKES MY MOST PUZZLED ADMIRAT+   369 7

ADMIRE
  I ADMIRE YOU SO YOU ARE BEAUTIFUL THIS CLEAN SWEEP OF   255 11
  AH HOW I ADMIRE YOUR FIDELITY   296 12
  COMPELLED TO ADMIRE THE BRIGHT RHYTHMS OF MOVING BODIES   445 25

ADMISSION
  WHICH IS PERHAPS THE LAST ADMISSION THAT LIFE HAS TO WR+   338 16

ADMIT
  IN A LITTLE THRONG AT YOUR DOOR AND ADMIT THE ONE WHO IS   179 6
  ADMIT THEM ADMIT THEM   250 32
  ADMIT THAT APPLES AND STRAWBERRIES AND PEACHES AND PEAR+   285 5
  I ADMIT A GOD IN EVERY CREVICE   346 15
  YOU ADMIT WE ARE   434 12
  AT PRESENT I AM A BLANK AND I ADMIT IT   501 16
  EXCEPT ADMIT IT AND LEAVE IT TO THE MOON   510 6
  TILL WE ADMIT HOW DEAD WE ARE   513 9
  YOU MUST ADMIT I'VE RISEN   626 15
  YOU MUST ADMIT I'VE RISEN   626 17
  NOW WE HAVE TO ADMIT WE CAN'T KNOW OURSELVES WE CAN ONL+   674 11
  MUST WE OPEN THE DOORS AND ADMIT THEM RECEIVE THEM HOME   740 13
  EVEN WHILE WE ADMIT THE GHASTLY IMPORTANCE OF MONEY   831 15
  BUT HE'S FAR TOO GREAT A COWARD EVER TO ADMIT HIS INSTI+   *948 32
  TOO DIRTY A HYPOCRITE TO ADMIT HIS OWN NATURE   *949 3

ADMITTED
  ADMITTED   262 26
  ADMITTED THEY SWARM IN COMPANIES   337 14
  WITH KNOWLEDGE OF THINGS THAT SHALL NEVER BE ADMITTED   656 18

ADMITTING
  GO BRAVELY ACROSS THE BORDER ADMITTING YOUR MISTAKE   809 7

ADMONITION
  OF ADMONITION   198 28

ADOLESCENCE
  HIS ADOLESCENCE SAW HIM CRUCIFIED INTO SEX   361 2
  THE MYSTERIOUS BULL TORE HIM AT ADOLESCENCE INTO PIECES   361 11

ADOLPH
  AND THOSE OVER-PROLIFIC WHITE MICE AND ADOLPH AND REX   395 9

ADONIS
  FOR A MOMENT GODLY LIKE BAAL OR KRISHNA OR ADONIS OR BA+   675 16

ADOPT
  WHOM SOME RECALCITRANT OLD MAID WILL ADOPT AS A HOBBY   665 15

ADORABLE
  YET SHE HAS SUCH ADORABLE SPURTY KIDS LIKE SPURTS OF BL+   386 17

ADORATION
  SUCH ADORATION PIERCES THE LOINS AND PERISHES THE MAN   538 13

ADORE
  HOW I ADORE YOU FOR YOUR SIMPLE PRIDE   221 14
  THEY THINK THAT WE ADORE THEM ALAS WOULD IT WERE TRUE   270 1
  PROBABLY THEY THINK ALL MEN ADORE THEM   270 2
  HOW I ADORE YOU FOR YOUR SIMPLE PRIDE   *944 28
  HOW I ADORE YOU YOU HAPPY THINGS YOU DEARS   *945 6

ADORED
  ALL THE WOMEN WHO ADORED THE SHADOW OF THE MAN ON   538 10
  SO THEY SIMPLY ADORED ONE ANOTHER   605 15

ADORN
    BUT NOW THEY STITCH TO ADORN THE BURSTEN FIG NOT TO COV+   284 14

ADORNED
    YOU ARE SHAPELY YOU ARE ADORNED   111 28
    THOU ART SHAPELY THOU ART ADORNED   *927 16
    YOU ARE SHAPELY YOU ARE ADORNED   *928 16

ADORNMENT
    NAKED OF WORSHIP OF LOVE OR OF ADORNMENT   197 14

ADOWN
    ADOWN THE PALE-GREEN GLACIER RIVER FLOATS   209 1

ADREAM
    ASLEEP AND ADREAM   70 13
    AND SLOWLY VERY SLOWLY AS IF THRICE ADREAM   350 30

ADRIFT
    I AM ADRIFT AS A MOONBEAM AND WITHOUT FORM   86 10
    YOU ALWAYS LOOSE ME ADRIFT   875 6

ADULTRESS'
    KEEP THEN THE KISS FROM THE ADULTRESS' THEFT   *916 8

ADVANCE
    THE GREY PLASM-LIMPID PELLUCID ADVANCE   68 9
    THEN WE ALL ADVANCE TO MEET   401 11
    WHICH SEEMS TO ME A GREAT ADVANCE   828 27
    THE GREY PHOSPHORESCENT PELLUCID ADVANCE   *914 24

ADVANCES
    MAKING HIS ADVANCES   362 12
    HE ADVANCES ABOVE YOU   387 11

ADVANCING
    SOFTLY-IMPULSIVE ADVANCING AS WATER TOWARDS A WEIR FROM+   66 19
    GREY FOAM-MIST OF ADVANCING TIME   68 14
    OF DARKNESS ADVANCING STEADILY OVER US ALL   164 24
    ELEPHANT ADVANCING HIS FRONTAL BONE HIS TRUNK CURLED   387 7
    ADVANCING WITH THE SLOW-SWIFTNESS OF A SHIP BACKING HER+ 672 21
    GREY FOAM-FRINGE OF ADVANCING GOD   *914 29

ADVANTAGE
    NOT TOO NICE OF COURSE THEY TAKE ADVANTAGE   660 17

ADVENT
    IF YOU ARE EXPECTING A SECOND ADVENT IN THE SHAPE OF A   531 19

ADVENTURE
    TO THE ADVENTURE OF DEATH IN EAGERNESS   676 21
    IN A GREAT ADVENTURE   677 7
    OH THE GREAT ADVENTURE OF DEATH WHERE THOMAS COOK CANNO+ 677 8

ADVENTURING
    ADVENTURING AMONG THEM   256 17

ADVENTUROUS
    THE BRAVE ADVENTUROUS ROSACEAE   283 9

ADVERSITY
    GRITTING AGAINST THE GREAT ADVERSITY   485 5

ADVICE
    HE USED TO GIVE KIND ADVICE TO THE PROSTITUTES ON PICCA+ 582 2

ADVOCATE
    I SHOULD ADVOCATE REFORM   609 15

'AD
    YOUR MESTER'S 'AD A ACCIDENT   45 5
    'E'S 'AD TWENTY ACCIDENTS IF 'E'S 'AD ONE   45 27
    AND WATCHED WHAT 'ER 'AD ON   61 4
    AH'VE 'AD A' AS I CAN CARRY   84 15
    EVEN THOUGH I'VE 'AD   84 22
    I DIDN'T KNOW IT WAS SO LATE NO SIR I 'AD TO BECAUSE   866 10
    AN' WATCHED WHAT 'ER 'AD ON   *911 20

AEGEAN
    IT IS AEGEAN SHIPS AND MEN WITH ARCHAIC POINTED BEARDS   687 6

AEONS
    BACK TO THOSE CHILDREN YOU HAD LEFT BEHIND TO ALL THE A+ 206 24
    YOUR PRISTINE ISOLATE INTEGRITY LOST AEONS AGO   290 13
    DRIVEN AFTER AEONS OF PRISTINE FORE-GOD-LIKE SINGLENESS+ 363 14
    HAVE AEONS OF WEARINESS ROUND THEIR EYES   425 20
    IT TOOK AEONS TO MAKE A SAPPHIRE AEONS FOR IT TO PASS A+ 477 5
    AND SO IN THE GREAT AEONS OF ACCOMPLISHMENT AND DEBACLE 682 19
    THROUGHOUT THE AEONS AS THE LIZARD SWIRLS HIS TAIL FINE+ 683 7

AEROLANES
    TRAINS AND CAMIONS AUTOMOBILES AND AEROLANES   794 12

AEROPLANES
    SOUND OF ARTILLERY AEROPLANES PRESENCES   169 15
    THEY SEND AEROPLANES ACROSS THE SKY   441 18

AESTHETIC
    BUT BRAINY ROBOT OR AESTHETIC ROBOT OR MERELY MUSCULAR + 637 23

AFAR
    THAT IS MY HOME WHERE THE LAMP GLEAMS AFAR   857 27
    AND I IN IMMEASURABLE NIGHT LOOKED ON FROM AFAR AFAR   865 10

AFFAIR
    OF THIS EARTHLY AFFAIR   176 25
    TOWARDS THE END OF HER PARTICUALR AFFAIR WITH HIM   446 27
    AFTER AN AFFAIR WITH THIS NOBLE ENGLISHMAN   *948 9

AFFAIRS
    WITH YOUR LIFE AND AFFAIRS DON'T THRUST   561 16

AFFECTED
    IT WAS ONLY AFFECTED AND MEAN   554 14

AFFECTION
    BIBBLING AFFECTION   395 30
    YOU LOVE TO LAP UP AFFECTION TO WALLOW IN IT   396 22
    IN YOUR APPETITE FOR AFFECTION   399 3
    THEY MAY EVEN ONE DAY DISCOVER SIMPLE AFFECTION AS A GR+ 832 18
    THE SHADOW DANCES UP IN AFFECTION   887 21

AFFIRMATION
    BECOMES AN AFFIRMATION THROUGH MOIST SCARLET LIPS   284 18
    LET US BURST INTO AFFIRMATION   284 23

'AFFLE
    TO THINK I SHOULD 'AVE TER 'AFFLE AN' CAFFLE   82 9

AFFLUENCE
    A WOMAN HAS GIVEN ME STRENGTH AND AFFLUENCE   262 25

AFFORD
    THE MORNING SMILE SURE THAT IT WILL AFFORD HER   583 15
    TO AFFORD HER   749 15

AFFRIGHT
    AND SET US AFFRIGHT   *929 25

AFIRE
    AFIRE AT A MYRIAD SCARLET POINTS   315 24
    AND FLARE OF A TROPICAL ENERGY TIRELESS AFIRE IN THE DA+ 389 16
    AND ROUND EYES AFIRE   861 24
    TO CATCH AFIRE WITH LIFE   888 6

AFLAME
    AFLAME WITH BLOSSOM   244 3

AFLOAT
    BUT HELD MY HAND AFLOAT TOWARDS THE SLIPS   125 21
    WHAT BREAD AFLOAT ON THE WATERS   171 21
    OF SILVER SINGING AFLOAT   253 2
    BUT HELD MY HAND AFLOAT STILL TOWARDS THE SLIPS   *936 20

AFLOW
    A TALL WOMAN WITH HER LONG WHITE GOWN AFLOW   155 13
    WITH HER SILKEN STEAM LIKE A BANNER BEHIND HER AFLOW   *894 30

AFLOWER
    NOW AT LAST WE LIFT OUR FACES AND OUR FACES COME AFLOWER   70 3
    NOW AT LAST WE LIFT OUR FACES AND OUR FACES COME AFLOWER *916 11
    THE GOLDEN GRAINED NIGHT AFLOWER ACROSS THE SKY   *916 17

AFLUTTER
    THE FIGURE OF SONG AFLUTTER IN A BLACK-WINGED REVELRY   *918 2

AFORE
    AFORE I CAN TA'E THEE I'VE GOT A WIDDER O' FORTY-FIVE T+   83 8
    HOW LONG IT'LL BE AFORE THA'LT BE   139 32

AFRAID
    THOUGHTFUL AND HALF AFRAID   178 19
    I AM AFRAID OF YOU I AM AFRAID AFRAID   210 27
    ARE YOU AFRAID OF GOD   231 21
    I'M NOT AFRAID OF GOD   231 23
    YOU ARE AFRAID IF HE RISES TO HIS FEET   255 34
    AND A THING TO BE AFRAID OF   264 24
    I CONFESS I AM AFRAID OF YOU   290 8
    DO YOU WONDER THAT I AM AFRAID TO COME   291 1
    IF YOU WERE NOT AFRAID YOU WOULD KILL HIM   350 18
    AND TRULY I WAS AFRAID I WAS MOST AFRAID   350 19
    TO TRAVEL TO BURROW INTO A LITTLE LOOSE EARTH AFRAID OF+ 358 2
    SOMNAMBULIST WIDE-EYED AFRAID   407 27
    NOR YET THAT PALE YOUNG MAN AFRAID OF FATHERHOOD   437 2
    THE PURITAN IS AFRAID   516 17
    AND THE PROFLIGATE IS AFRAID   516 18
    THE WEALTHY ARE AFRAID   516 19
    AND THE POVERTY-STRICKEN ARE AFRAID   516 20
    THEY ARE AFRAID WITH HORRIBLE AND OPPOSING FEARS   516 21
    IN ALL CREATION ONLY MAN COWERS AND IS AFRAID OF LIFE   529 11
    AFRAID OF THE WORLD BUT TO SALLY FORTH   550 23
    APPLICANT I'M AFRAID I DON'T   582 11
    APPLICANT I DON'T THINK SO SIR I'M AFRAID NOT   582 18
    THEY ARE AFRAID OF CLIMBING DOWN FROM THIS IDIOTIC TIN-+ 667 19
    AND ANXIOUSLY LIKE A BOY AFRAID TO BE FOUND OUT   734 4
    THEY AREN'T AFRAID OF LOSING SOMETHING AS THE OLDER ONE+ 828 25
    BUT I WAS AFRAID HENCEFORTH   881 14
    I WAS AFRAID   883 23
    THE SEA AFRAID   883 27
    OF A SECOND AFRAID OF THE CLIPS   *912 17

AFRESH
    WHO SHALL TAKE YOU AFRESH   112 5
    SOUGHT HER AFRESH   120 31
    THEN SWERVING AND STEERING AFRESH   380 25
    HAS OPENED HIS EYES AFRESH   459 26
    WITH WHICH TO MANURE AFRESH THE ROOTS OF THE TREE OF LI+ 616 15
    THE WORLD IS CREATED AFRESH   725 10
    TO START MY HEART AFRESH GIVE ME THE SOFT SMALL STRESS   738 31
    AFRESH   817 12
    WHO SHALL TAKE YOU AFRESH   *928 25
    SINCE THE MONTH OF CHILDHOOD IS OVER AND WE START AFRESH *938 8

AFRICAN
THE AFRICAN QUEER ONES AND SCANDINAVIAN QUEER ONES 671 15

AFRICA'S
AND SOME OF AFRICA'S IMPERTURBABLE SANG-FROID 296 22

AFT
BRIGHT AND NAKED AFT AND FORE 574 20
IN YOUR FIFTIES WITH A SHORT FROCK SHOWING YOUR FORE AN+ 835 10

AFTER-DAMP
WHEN THE AFTER-DAMP IS AROUND IT 619 6

AFTER-ECHO
TO HEAR ON ITS MOCKING TRIUMPHANCE UNWITTING THE AFTER-+ 58 6

AFTER-GLADNES
THERE COMES AN AFTER-GLADNES A STRANGE JOY 677 6

AFTERGLOW
IN THE AFTERGLOW 770 5

AFTER-LIFE
I DIED THE FIRST I IN THE AFTER-LIFE 156 17
ON THE WATERS OF THE AFTER-LIFE 786 9

AFTER-NIGHT
BETWEEN THE BITTER KNEES OF THE AFTER-NIGHT 160 12

AFTERNOON
WHERE THE SUNLIGHT SOAKS IN THE STONE THE AFTERNOON 52 13
OF THE AFTERNOON GLOWS STILL THE OLD ROMANCE OF DAVID A+ 53 3
AND YOU REMEMBER IN THE AFTERNOON 98 11
ONE LONELY BELL ONE ONLY THE STORM-TOSSED AFTERNOON IS 137 1
THE BIG MOUNTAINS SIT STILL IN THE AFTERNOON LIGHT 223 13
FLUSHING THE AFTERNOON THEY ARE UNCOMFORTABLE 228 11
I MUST BE PUT DOWN LORD IN THE AFTERNOON 321 26
BUT LATER IN THE SUN OF THE AFTERNOON 324 10
AND OLEANDER IS HOT WITH PERFUME UNDER THE AFTERNOON SUN 630 3
ON SUNDAY AFTERNOON 755 25
PARADISAL THROUGH THE LONG AFTERNOON 768 29
THE DELICATE AFTERNOON 769 22
OF STILLNESS AND AFTERNOON 770 26
BETWEEN THE MORNING AND THE AFTERNOON STAND I HERE WITH+ 803 6
WHERE THE SUNLIGHT SOAKS IN THE STONE THE AFTERNOON *905 2
OF THE AFTERNOON GLOWS ONLY THE OLD ROMANCE OF DAVID AN+ *905 18
THROUGH THE WAKENED AFTERNOON RIDING DOWN MY DREAMS *906 15

AFTER-PAIN
WITH AFTER-PAIN MY SLEEPING BABY HANGS UPON MY LIFE 73 27

AFTER-SHOW
WAITING FOR THE FIREWORKS OF THE AFTER-SHOW 391 11

AFTERTHOUGHT
COMING MY WAY WITHOUT FORETHOUGHT OR AFTERTHOUGHT 288 27
THAT SPANGLED GLISTEN IS GONE THAT AT-ONENESS WITHOUT A+ 656 16
FOR A MOMENT FREE FROM ALL CONCEIT OF YOURSELF AND ALL + 674 3

AFTER-THOUGHT
TREES BIRDS AND EARTH ARRESTED IN THE AFTER-THOUGHT 142 15
AND SLY WITH A LOT OF AFTER-THOUGHT 556 11

AFTERWARD
EVE IN THE AFTERWARD 768 25

AFTERWARDS
AY IT DID BUT AFTERWARDS 00 21
AFTERWARDS HOW MANY TIMES AFTERWARDS 80 23
FOWLS OF THE AFTERWARDS 171 20
AFTERWARDS AFTERWARDS 322 25
DOWN TO THE OCEAN OF THE AFTERWARDS WHERE IT REMAINS 495 5
AND AFTERWARDS LEAVE ME ALONE 602 15
ABOUT THE AFTERWARDS 676 26
THE WINDS OF THE AFTERWARDS KISS US INTO BLOSSOM OF MAN+ 677 19
EVE OF THE AFTERWARDS 769 1
WHERE ONLY THE WOMEN OF THE AFTERWARDS 769 24
IN TONES OF THE AFTERWARDS PARADISAL 769 29
TALL VIRGINS OF THE AFTERWARDS 770 2
WITH MEN OF THE AFTERWARDS WALKING TO MEET US FROM 770 9
TOWARDS THE WOMEN WHO ARE VIRGINS OF THE AFTERWARDS 770 20
IT IS FINISHED THE REST IS AFTERWARDS 816 21
AY I DID BUT AFTERWARDS *922 21
AFTERWARDS AN' AFTER HOW LONG *922 23

AGAIN
THEY HAVE TRIUMPHED AGAIN O'ER THE AGES THEIR SCREAMING+ 33 4
HIS BENT COURSE MILDLY HERE WAKES AGAIN LEAPS LAUGHS AN+ 33 14
NOW AND AGAIN 38 29
I SH'D THINK 'E'LL GET RIGHT AGAIN 46 4
AND THEN HE TURNS AGAIN WITH A LITTLE GLAD 51 17
THRILL OF HIS WORK HE TURNS AGAIN FROM ME 51 18
RIGHT IN 'EM AN' SCRAIGHTED A BIT AGAIN 61 14
WHEN SHALL I SEE THE HALF-MOON SINK AGAIN 62 25
FALLS AGAIN AND AGAIN ON MY HEART WITH A HEAVY REPROACH 63 3
AND ASKING NOTHING PATIENTLY STEALS BACK AGAIN 63 29
LOVE WILL YET AGAIN RETURN TO HER AND MAKE ALL GOOD 65 22
A TEAR WHICH I HAD HOPED THAT EVEN HELL HELD NOT AGAIN + 67 17
THEM AGAIN ON A QUARRY OF KNOWLEDGE THEY HATE TO HUNT 74 10
NOW I AM COME AGAIN TO YOU WHO HAVE SO DESIRED 85 17
AGAIN FROM EARTH LIKE LILIES FLAGGED AND SERE 87 28
GIVES US ALL FORTH THAT WE MAY GIVE AGAIN 89 9
THE ANGEL OF JUDGMENT HAS DEPARTED AGAIN TO THE NEARNESS 94 22
AS YOU PLEASE SHALL GO AGAIN 95 7
THAT MY LOVE CAN DAWN IN WARMTH AGAIN UNAFRAID 99 15
SWEEP PAST THE WINDOW AGAIN 100 4
OF MEMORY UNROLLS AGAIN TO ME 100 17
RARE PASSION AND NEVER AGAIN 104 15

AGAIN
AND RETURNS AGAIN BELOW 105 12
TO SIP THEM ALL UP AGAIN 109 26
KIND ON THE WEIGHT OF SUFFERING SMILES AGAIN 113 16
OF AUTUMN TELL THE WITHERED TALE AGAIN 119 14
CLUCK MY MARIGOLD BIRD AND AGAIN 119 17
NOW BEING COME AGAIN HOW MAKE THE BEST 122 15
AGAIN I SAW A BROWN BIRD HOVER 124 23
SHE MOVED HER HAND AND AGAIN 124 32
TO QUICKEN THE SPHERES SPRING-VIRGIN AGAIN IN THE SKY 127 10
AGAIN I TELL YOU I BLEED I AM BOUND WITH WITHIES 131 11
THE EARTH AGAIN LIKE A SHIP STEAMS OUT OF THE DARK SEA + 132 27
DOST WANT ME TER WANT THEE AGAIN NAY THOUGH 138 17
BUT THA'LT COME AGAIN BECAUSE WHEN A MAN'S 139 25
AND AGAIN AT ME 143 16
AND SO AGAIN ON THE RECREATION GROUND 153 9
I WILL NOT AGAIN REPROACH YOU LIE BACK 153 16
YET SOON TOO SOON SHE HAD HIM HOME AGAIN 155 9
BUT YOU ARE GIVEN BACK AGAIN TO ME 157 9
NEVER AGAIN 162 28
THE PIVOT AGAIN 169 17
TIME SLEEPS AGAIN 169 23
GIVE US AIR WE CRY OH LET US BUT BREATHE AGAIN 175 18
I WILL TRAIL MY HANDS AGAIN THROUGH THE DRENCHED COLD L+ 180 34
LEAVES ME UNBURDENED TO BEGIN AGAIN 195 4
AGAIN IN HER BLUE BLUE MANTLE 201 5
GIVE ME THE CHILD AGAIN 202 4
THEN YOU PUT YOUR HAND IN MINE AGAIN KISSED ME AND WE 206 13
FOR YOU WERE STRAINING WITH A WILD HEART BACK BACK AGAIN 206 23
I ACQUIESCED AGAIN 207 4
AND IF I NEVER SEE HER AGAIN 213 15
WHAT SHOULD I DO IF YOU WERE GONE AGAIN 214 4
AND CHRIST I HAVE MET HIS ACCUSING EYES AGAIN 225 22
FULL IN MY OWN AND THE TORMENT STARTS AGAIN 225 24
ALONE ON THE OPEN ROAD AGAIN 228 9
MOVES AT HER EASE AGAIN 228 20
AGAIN THE LOVE SO FULL 229 13
AGAIN MY DARLING BUT NEW 239 14
AGAIN UNDEFILED 239 18
YOU ARE BORN AGAIN OF ME 240 10
TO START AGAIN 244 24
CONTACTS AND BOUNCING OFF AGAIN BOUNCE BOUNCE LIKE A 249 19
BOUNCE OFF AGAIN MEANING NOTHING ASSERTIONS ASSERTIONS 249 24
AGAIN ON THE WONTED SKIES 253 22
RISEN NOT BORN AGAIN BUT RISEN BODY THE SAME AS BEFORE 258 29
HERE AGAIN MAN HAS BEEN GOOD IN HIS LEGACY TO US IN THE+ 263 18
FALLING I HEAR AGAIN 268 23
OR ELSE BEFORE THEY HAD BEEN LET DOWN AGAIN IN NOAH'S F+ 285 21
GONE AGAIN IN THE BRIGHT TRAIL OF LAVA 293 23
TO SET AGAIN INTO ROCK 294 4
TO BRING THEIR MEANING BACK INTO LIFE AGAIN 298 11
AH YES AH YES WOULD I MIGHT SEE IT AGAIN 303 7
NEW BODY AGAIN LIKE ALMOND BLOSSOM IN JANUARY 303 11
SO THAT THE FAITH IN HIS HEART SMILES AGAIN 306 1
SO HE COULD TRACK HER DOWN AGAIN WHITE VICTIM 308 23
OUT ON EARTH AGAIN 308 26
LISTEN AGAIN 313 12
NEVER OF COURSE TO PUT ANYTHING UP AGAIN 317 32
BUT PUT ME DOWN AGAIN IN TIME MASTER 321 8
PUT ME DOWN AGAIN ON THE EARTH JESUS ON THE BROWN SOIL 321 10
AGAIN 321 12
BUT BLEW BACK AS IF AN INCOMING WIND BLEW HIM IN AGAIN 343 17
AGAIN HE SWERVED INTO THE WINDOW BAY 344 3
HE FELL AGAIN WITH A LITTLE THUD 346 26
AND CLIMB AGAIN THE BROKEN BANK OF MY WALL-FACE 350 32
FOR HE SEEMED TO ME AGAIN LIKE A KING 351 24
NOW DUE TO BE CROWNED AGAIN 351 26
OR IS SLEEP COMING OVER YOU AGAIN 353 13
FIVE AND FIVE AGAIN AND FIVE AGAIN 355 7
AND THERE AGAIN ON HIS SHELL-TENDER EARTH-TOUCHING BELLY 355 29
SO TURN HIM OVER ON HIS TOES AGAIN 356 5
IN HIS EFFORT TOWARD COMPLETION AGAIN 361 9
SINGING AND CALLING AND SINGING AGAIN BEING ANSWERED 366 36
TORN TO BECOME WHOLE AGAIN AFTER LONG SEEKING FOR WHAT 367 1
THAT WHICH IS IN PART FINDING ITS WHOLE AGAIN THROUGHOUT 367 6
AND IN A MONTH AGAIN IS AS IF SHE HAD NEVER HAD THEM 386 19
STOPS AGAIN HALF TURNS INQUISITIVE TO LOOK BACK 393 29
ONLY TO DISAPPEAR AGAIN QUICKLY AWAY FROM THE SIGHT OF 394 2
AND START PRANCING AND LICKING AND CUDDLING AGAIN 396 24
AIMING AGAIN AT BEING LOVED 398 14
SO SHE WILL NEVER LEAP IN THAT WAY AGAIN WITH THE YELLOW 402 15
AGAIN FOR OH THE DEAD ARE DISCONSOLATE SINCE EVEN DEATH+ 406 8
THEN CAME THE HUSH AGAIN LIKE A HUSH OF FEAR 444 23
AND SO IT WILL BE AGAIN MEN WILL SMASH THE MACHINES 451 20
THEN TRYING AGAIN 457 16
IN THE TOMB AND WAS NOT I HAVE RISEN AGAIN 460 23
NO ANSWER MAN RISES AGAIN 461 14
AGAIN MAN AMONG MAN 461 16
CAN DENIAL DENY THEM AGAIN 461 20
UNLOCKS THE FOUNTAINS OF PEACE AGAIN 461 24
THE DIRTY MIND LIKE A URINAL AGAIN 463 3
SUPPRESS IT AGAIN 464 16
WHEN AGAIN IN US 471 14
LET IT DIE RIGHT AWAY TILL IT RISES OF ITSELF AGAIN 471 20
AND GET HIS ROOTS IN EARTH AGAIN 475 4
FOR A DAY FOR TWO DAYS AND WITHDRAW SLOWLY VANISH AGAIN 476 14
FOR THE FIERCE CURVE OF OUR LIVES IS MOVING AGAIN TO THE 478 1
AND GET INTO THE FOREST AGAIN 482 18
YOU'RE A CAGED MONKEY AGAIN IN FIVE MINUTES 486 5
THEN SOMETIMES I FEEL DEFEATED AND THEN AGAIN I KNOW 508 22
SHALL I TELL YOU AGAIN THE NEW WORD 513 1
AND THEN COULD NEVER GET OFF AGAIN 518 22
INSTEAD OF GETTING ON AND NOT BEING ABLE TO GET OFF AGA+ 518 25
THEIR CHILDREN BROUGHT UP EASY LET IT SLIP AWAY AGAIN 535 24
AND YOU CLAPPED YOUR HANDS AND SAID SAY IT AGAIN 550 26
BUT NOW I AM SLITHERING DOWN AGAIN 552 5
GOD LET ME DOWN TO EARTH AGAIN 552 13
TO SCRAMBLE BACK AGAIN 554 4

AGAIN
    YOU'D BETTER GET DOWN AGAIN   555 8
    ONE ANOTHER AGAIN   561 2
    AGAIN AND ENTWINES   562 3
    AND YOU WILL BE AGAIN THEREFORE WHY LOOK BLUE   577 12
    EDITOR GOOD MORNING DON'T TROUBLE TO CALL AGAIN WE   582 19
    MEN AGAIN   585 5
    THEN I SAW HIM TURN TO GLANCE AGAIN SURREPTITIOUSLY   604 4
    THE SWAN WILL LIFT UP AGAIN HIS FLATTENED SMITTEN HEAD   625 2
    AND THE LARK WILL FOLLOW TRILLING ANGERLESS AGAIN   625 6
    NOW AGAIN AND NOW FOR EVER BREAKS THE GREAT ILLUSION   635 9
    UNLESS MEN SWIFTLY DIVIDE AGAIN AND THE BASE ARE THRUST   637 14
    TAKE ME SOUTH AGAIN TO THE OLIVE TREES   652 22
    AGAIN AND AGAIN SOME GOD OF EVENING LEANS OUT OF IT   656 2
    TILL THEY ARE SOFTENED BACK TO LIFE-STUFF AGAIN AGAINST+   663 7
    THE MACHINE SHALL BE ABOLISHED FROM THE EARTH AGAIN   666 15
    LO AGAIN THE SHUDDER OR BLISS THROUGH ALL THE ATOMS   682 15
    OF THOSE THAT WILL WITHOUT FAIL COME BACK AGAIN   688 14
    AND SET ME AGAIN ON MOON-REMEMBERING FEET   696 6
    THEN THE BRIGHT DAWNING OF DELIGHT AGAIN   708 26
    A FLUSH OF ROSE AND THE WHOLE THING STARTS AGAIN   720 11
    AND THE FRAIL SOUL STEPS OUT INTO HER HOUSE AGAIN   720 16
    THEN I HAVE BEEN DIPPED AGAIN IN GOD AND NEW-CREATED   726 25
    THE ISAR WHISPERS AGAIN IN THE VALLEY THE CHILDREN   732 18
    CAREFULLY AGAIN AND AGAIN TO STOP THE BLEEDING   734 10
    AND AGAIN ROLLING IN HIS HEAVY HIGH BOOTS   734 12
    AND LOOKS AROUND AGAIN AT HIS HEEL THE BRIGHT SPUR   734 14
    AND BENDS AGAIN AND LOOKS AT THE BELLY OF THE HORSE   734 15
    SWUNG STRONG AND HEAVY TO SADDLE AGAIN   735 13
    LAST TWILIGHT OF THE GODS TO FIND AGAIN   737 8
    NOT ANYTHING NOR EVER AGAIN ASK WHY   738 26
    MULTITUDINOUS ENDLESS THE GHOSTS COMING HOME AGAIN   739 15
    SINCE FROM BLOOD POURED OUT RISE ONLY GHOSTS AGAIN   740 10
    THEN WE SHALL TURN US HOME AGAIN TO LIFE   740 22
    TO THE TRENCHES I SEE AGAIN A FACE WITH BLUE EYES   742 6
    LIKE BLOOD IN THE EARTH AGAIN WE WALK THE EARTH   743 26
    I WHO HAVE BEEN AND NOW AM RISEN AGAIN   744 18
    HE WHO RETURNS AGAIN FROM OUT THE TOMB   745 16
    IN ME AGAIN   747 11
    SET FREE AGAIN   747 20
    OF MORNING IS BACK WE SHALL CHANGE AGAIN AND ESSAY   748 11
    NOTHING AGAIN   748 30
    DO NOT ASK ME ALMIGHTY GOD TO PART FROM HER AGAIN   749 20
    EACH EVENING BITTER AGAIN   758 9
    BROTHER LET ME DIE DOWN AGAIN   759 4
    HOME AT LAST IN THE OPEN AGAIN AND UNHOUSELED   770 8
    ONLY TO WRECK ON THE SHORES OF NIGHT AGAIN   771 26
    AND AGAIN   771 27
    OF SHARING THE NIGHT WITH GOD OF MINGLING UP AGAIN   772 25
    WILL YOU STRIKE THE SUN'S HEART OUT AGAIN   783 19
    WHO BREATHED YOU OUT AND BREATHES YOU IN AGAIN   784 8
    OF EXPIRATION TURNED INTO THE WORLD AGAIN   784 15
    I ROSE AGAIN TO SEE A STAR FALLING AND FEEL A BREATH ON   786 10
    AND THE BREATH BLEW UPON ME AGAIN   787 1
    THEY SEE ME AND LOSE ME AGAIN   787 30
    THE DRAGONS IN THE COSMOS ARE STIRRING WITH ANGER AGAIN   795 11
    AGAIN   795 34
    BACK AGAIN NOW ON HIGH   798 24
    OF FIRE BENT BACK AGAIN   805 11
    READY AGAIN FOR THE BUSINESS OF BEING A MAN   809 18
    NEVER AN ANGEL WILL SOAR AGAIN   823 11
    OH LET US NEVER BEGIN AGAIN   826 8
    EVER AGAIN LYING PRONE LYING SLACK   827 12
    IT IS ODD AGAIN ABOUT THE YOUNG   829 11
    IT SHOWS AGAIN HOW HIGHLY DEVELOPED THE SOCIAL CONSCIEN+   829 16
    FOR ALL THAT LIFE WILL ONLY BE GOOD AGAIN WHEN THERE IS+   838 1
    WITH GUSTO BEGIN AGAIN THE BRISK FIGHT   865 31
    BUT DISSIPATED DISSOLVED AGAIN   870 15
    SIEGMUND LIFT UP YOUR FACE AGAIN OFF THE TURF   871 36
    EVER AGAIN AND LAUGHING LOOK AT ME   876 24
    AND ONCE AGAIN AS MANY A TIME BEFORE   877 35
    SHAKE AND SINK DOWN TO REST THEN SHAKE AGAIN   878 26
    I KISSED HER ONCE AGAIN UPON THE MOUTH   881 1
    THEN LOOKED AGAIN WITHIN HER EYES   881 3
    SO GLAD TO FIND MYSELF AGAIN   882 12
    YET LOOKING AGAIN AT THE NIGHT   882 14
    AND RANK AND DRIPPED WITH BLOOD AND DRIPPED AGAIN   884 27
    AT YOUR COTTAGE-END IT FALLS BACK AGAIN   885 29
    ITS CURIOUS COURSE MILDLY HERE IT WAKES AGAIN LEAPS LAU+   *891 15
    NOW AND AGAIN   *893 11
    THEM AGAIN ON A QUARRY OF KNOWLEDGE THEY HATE TO HUNT   *895 18
    THEN HE TURNS AGAIN TO HIS WORK WITH GLEE   *898 28
    THEN HE TURNS AGAIN TO HIS WORK WITH GLEE   *902 12
    THEM AGAIN ON A QUARRY OF KNOWLEDGE THEY HATE TO HUNT   *904 7
    AN' 'ER BODY FAIR SHOOK AGAIN   *910 13
    BY A HEAD-STUN SOBBIN' AN' SOBBIN' AGAIN   *911 1
    RIGHT UNTIL 'EM AND SCRAIGHTED OUT AGAIN   *911 30
    A MOMENT AND SHE WAS TAKEN AGAIN IN THE MERCIFUL DARK   *912 24
    AN' GI'E HER THEE BACK AGAIN   *922 28
    MY SOUL AGAIN   *929 29
    CLUCK MY MARIGOLD BIRD AND AGAIN   *932 26
    AGAIN AND I FELT A BROWN BIRD HOVER   *935 31
    IS DELIVERED FROM US HERSELF BORN AGAIN AMID THE MOAN   *938 10
    AND ONCE AGAIN A SUAVE YOUNG GOD   *946 18
    IT WILL BE SO AGAIN FOR MAN WILL SMASH ALL HIS MACHINES+   *950 6
    HE WILL CANCEL AGAIN THESE MACHINES WE HAVE GOT   *950 11
    THAT CONVULSES AND TREMBLES AGAIN WITH THE SYMPATHY OF +   *952 7
    OF THE ARMS OF PLUTO AS HE RAVISHES HER ONCE AGAIN   *956 17

AGAPE
    ALWAYS AGAPE   465 6
    THE MEN STOOD AROUND LIKE CROCUSES AGAPE IN THE SUN   540 4

AGE
    THIS IS THE IRON AGE   304 3
    AND THE ALMOND-TREE IN EXILE IN THE IRON AGE   305 11
    AND APART IN THIS CEREBRAL AGE   469 7
    IN THIS MIND-MISCHIEVOUS AGE   470 3

AGE
    I DO NOT WANT A WOMAN WHOM AGE CANNOT WITHER   478 27
    IN THEIR OLD AGE   503 21
    OR THE MOST HIGH DURING THE COAL AGE CUDGELLING HIS MIG+   690 26
    OH AGE THAT IS HOAR AS ANEMONE BUDS   814 19
    THE AGE IS A JOKE AND SURELY TOMORROW   815 4
    THAT IS THE MEN OF MY AGE AND I AM FORTY-THREE   828 15
    WHAT ABOUT GIRLY-WIRLY AT HER AGE   834 19
    AT HER AGE WHY I'LL BE EARNING A JOLLY GOOD SCREW   834 20
    ITS MOTHER DID SOMETHING TO IT AT ABOUT THE AGE OF TWEL+   841 13
    AND BORN HIM A SON OR SO WHO AT THE AGE OF SEVEN IS SO +   842 7
    SEVEN IS STILL A SAFE-ISH AGE   842 27
    AND A BOY AS HE REACHES THE AGE OF FOURTEEN WHEN HE SHO+   843 2
    THE BURDENED AGE SEVENTY-NINE THE VICAR   859 2
    WITH AGE DECLARING   862 3

AGE-AFTER-AGE
    COLD VOICELESS AGE-AFTER-AGE BEHIND HIM SERPENTS' LONG   360 15

AGEING
    IF YOU CAN ONLY SIT WITH A MIRROR IN YOUR HAND AN AGEING   478 20

AGELESS
    THE EXQUISITE AND AGELESS ARISTOCRACY   314 14
    EXCEPT THAT YOU MAKE SLOW AGELESS PROGRESS   352 31
    HIS STEEL-TRAP STOIC AGELESS HANDSOME FACE   360 25
    AND THEY ROCK AND THEY ROCK THROUGH THE SENSUAL AGELESS+   694 8

AGELESSLY
    AGELESSLY SILENT   360 13
    ONLY AGELESSLY SILENT WITH A REPTILE'S AWFUL PERSISTENCY   362 25

AGE-LONG
    AGE-LONG REPTILIAN PERSISTENCE   365 26

AGES
    THEY HAVE TRIUMPHED AGAIN O'ER THE AGES THEIR SCREAMING+   33 4
    WINGS AND FEATHERS ON THE CRYING MYSTERIOUS AGES PEEWIT+   34 26
    FOR AGES I DON'T CARE A FIG FOR IT MEN SAY BUT WHY A FI+   277 5
    STOIC ABLE TO WAIT THROUGH AGES   292 29
    AND HAS BEEN LAUGHING THROUGH SO MANY AGES   299 15
    TREES SUFFER LIKE RACES DOWN THE LONG AGES   304 25
    LONG AGES   304 27
    EXILE AGAINST THE AGES   305 19
    THAT NOBLE BLOOD HAS BROUGHT US DOWN THE AGES   313 31
    AND THE LONG AGES AND THE LINGERING CHILL   353 2
    AGES   354 13
    AND WHAT AGES OF TIME   426 2
    AS SHADOWS FROM THE AGES GONE AND PERISHED   426 18
    WATCH SILENT THE LOOMING OF THE HOARY FAR-GONE AGES   426 21
    AND THEY ROCK AND THEY ROCK THROUGH THE SENSUAL AGELESS+   694 8
    FAR-OFF FAR-OFF IN THE HYACINTH AGES   814 4
    THE WISDOM OF AGES DROOPS IT IS FOLLY   814 22
    THE WISDOM OF AGES DROOPS AIN'T IT JOLLY   814 25

AGHAST
    IT SHUT BEHIND HER LEAVING THE STREET AGHAST   122 8

AGITATING
    IT IS RATHER AGITATING SLEEPING WITH A LITTLE VESUVIUS   539 6

AGITATION
    FLEES IN ITS AGITATION   242 14

AGLANCE
    AGLANCE   57 12

AGLOW
    AND YOU MY LASS WITH YOUR RICH WARM FACE AGLOW   126 28
    HE HAD A SHOVEL AND A BRUSH ON HIS SHOULDER HIS FACE WA+   866 18

AGO
    A MOMENT AGO   37 12
    AGO   48 4
    LONG AGO LONG AGO WOOED   105 8
    VENTURED SO LONG AGO IN THE DEEPS OF REFLECTION   161 19
    WHAT HAS BEEN LONG AGO   240 13
    WHOM I MARRIED YEARS AGO   260 5
    BUT LONG AGO OH LONG AGO   285 15
    BUT IT'S SO LONG AGO THE ANCIENT BUSHMAN HAS FORGOTTEN   286 17
    YOUR PRISTINE ISOLATE INTEGRITY LOST AEONS AGO   290 13
    AND LONG AGO THE ALMOND WAS THE SYMBOL OF RESURRECTION   303 1
    BUT I CONSIDER I WAS SUFFICIENTLY CIRCUMCISED LONG AGO   541 22
    THE MOST PART LONG AGO ENTERED THE ROMAN CATHOLIC   776 25
    TODAY IS EASTER SUNDAY CHRIST RISEN TWO DAYS AGO WAS   777 22
    LONG AGO ONCE BEFORE   817 17
    HIS OWN SONG-MEASURE MANY MONTHS AGO   877 24
    THE WITHERING FLOWERS THAT DAYS AGO YOU BROUGHT ME   880 11

AGOG
    ALL AGOG AND CURLING UP HER TRUNK   426 12

AGONISED
    IS DRUNK FROM AN AGONISED SKY BY THE EARTH   117 32
    IT IS LIKE THE AGONISED PERVERSENESS OF A CHILD HEAVY W+   287 2
    SO ENDING ON A GRUNT OF AGONISED RELIEF   377 16
    ONLY IS MAN AGONISED IN FRONT OF THE NECESSITY TO BE SO+   529 14
    PAST THE LURKING OCTOPUS ARMS OF AGONISED MEMORY   *959 6

AGONIZED
    A BLANCHED FACE FIXED AND AGONIZED   742 7

AGONY
    AN' WALKIN' IN AGONY   80 8
    TO THE LODE OF HER AGONY   99 28
    THE RED REFLECTION OF HER AGONY   103 17
    LIKE THE AGONY OF LIMBS CUT OFF AND ACHING   213 9
    IT IS ONLY AGONY   213 11

AGONY

I THINK I COULD ALTER THE FRAME OF THINGS IN MY AGONY	213 18
ONE MOMENT I SEE THE STILLNESS OF AGONY	225 26
AND HEART LIKE A CROSS THAT BEARS DEAD AGONY	226 6
A CURIOUS AGONY AND A RELIEF WHEN I TOUCH THAT WHICH IS+	266 14
HENCE HE UNCOVERS HIS BIG ASS-TEETH AND HOWLS IN THAT A+	378 24
THE WAVE OF AGONY BURSTS IN THE STONE THAT HE WAS	379 20
MY GOD WHAT AGONY THEY ARE TO ME	741 18
STARTLED AND FULL OF AGONY TO FIND HE HAD BUT SLEPT	859 18
AN' WALKIN' IN AGONY	*922 8
YOUR FACE TOWARD MY AGONY	*930 19
STILL I MUST SIT IN AGONY	*931 1

AGREE

BUT WHEN YOU COME TO KNOW IT BETTER YOU AGREE WITH THE	282 15
QUITE I QUITE AGREE	435 9
DON'T YOU THINK OR DON'T YOU AGREE	552 4
AND TRYING TO MAKE YOU AGREE	555 2
OH WHAT A PITY OH DON'T YOU AGREE	579 7
USUALLY WANT TO FORCE SOMEBODY TO AGREE WITH THEM	626 5

AGREEING

IN US LIFE UNTO DEATH AGREEING	243 7
AND AGREEING WITH ALL THE MEALY-MOUTHED MEALY-MOUTHED	458 18

AGUARDIENTE

HE SAW THE MEN THAT WERE BLIND REELING WITH AGUARDIENTE	790 12

AHA

AHA THE STRIPE-CHEEKED WHELPS WHIPPET-SLIM CROCUSES	309 5
AHA THERE'S SOMEBODY IN THE KNOW	338 5

AHEAD

IF SO LET US FORGE AHEAD STRAIGHT ON	164 13
LOOKING BLEAK AHEAD SHE RODE	202 6
IN THE WORLD WHERE THE HUMMING-BIRD FLASHED AHEAD OF	372 15
SNIFFING FOREVER AHEAD OF HIM AT THE REAR OF THE GOATS +	380 21
TOWARDS A SHOCK AND A CRASH AND A SMITING OF HORNS AHEAD	381 22
AND GO AHEAD WITH WHAT IS HUMAN NATURE	429 15
AHEAD OF THE MULTITUDE	440 11
BUT SOMETIMES WE RUN AHEAD TOO FAST	543 16
WHICH GET US AHEAD SO MUCH FASTER THAN OUR FEET COULD	543 21
AHEAD	543 24
TO THE FATHOMLESS DEEPS AHEAD FAR FAR FROM THE GREY SHO+	723 24
FATHOMLESS DEEP AHEAD FAR FAR FROM THE GREY SHORES	*959 1

AHEM

SOME SMALL VOICE WENT AHEM	554 20
AHEM THEY WENT THIS FELLOW	554 21
PRIVATELY COUGHING AHEM	554 26
THAT WAS WHAT THEIR AHEM MEANT	556 8

AH'N

AH'N PUT MY-SEN I' TH' WRONG LIZ	83 26

AH'VE

AH'VE 'AD A' AS I CAN CARRY	84 15

AILED

IF ANYTHING AILED 'IM AT ANY RATE	45 19

AILS

WHAT AILS THEE THEN WOMAN WHAT AILS THEE	540 12

AIMING

AIMING AGAIN AT BEING LOVED	398 14
OF ENGLAND WITH THE GUTS TO TURN ROUND ON HIM AIMING	494 11

AIMLESS

WHY DO I WANDER AIMLESS AMONG THEM DESIROUS FOOL	180 23
AND ALL RAMBLING AIMLESS LIKE LITTLE PERAMBULATING PEBB+	357 18
WHERE THE BLUE CRABS RUSTLED IN QUEST OF HER AIMLESS WI+	864 6
SHE MAY COVER HER EYES YET THE AIMLESS BREEZE OF MY WOR+	868 29
SO SHE CLOSES HER EYES BUT THE AIMLESS BREEZE OF THE WO+	*942 1

AIN'T

THE WISDOM OF AGES DROOPS AIN'T IT JOLLY	814 25
SLIPPED LIKE ANYTHING BUT DON'T YOU LIKE IT AIN'T IT FI+	865 23
WE AIN'T GOT NO FARVER ONLY A MOVVER AN' SHE 'AS TER GO	866 20

AIR-AIR

OVER MY SKIN IN THE SUNSHINE THE WARM CLINGING AIR	34 13
WHERE THE GLASS IS DOMED ON THE SILENT AIR	52 19
WARM AS A FLAME IN THE CLOSE NIGHT AIR	61 29
A SODOM SMOULDRING IN THE DENSE SOILED AIR	72 14
MELTS IN THE AIR WHILE TWO BLACK BIRDS	100 3
AS THE AIR MOVES IN	112 18
FOR THE MOON ON MY BREAST AND THE AIR ON MY LIMBS	130 11
LIKE VIVID THOUGHT THE AIR SPINS BRIGHT AND ALL	142 14
BLOTCHING THE THICK SOILED AIR	142 18
HANGS IN THE AIR	147 22
THE AIR IS DARK WITH NORTH AND WITH SULPHUR THE GRASS IS	148 24
VIOLET AIR	149 18
OF RED GOES DOWN THE BILLOWING AIR	149 31
WITH HIS WAN SPIRIT SOMEWHERE IN THE AIR	158 23
AS IF MOVING IN AIR TOWARDS US TALL ANGELS	164 23
BEATS THE NEW FRESH AIR OF LIFE THEY COME FOR STRIFE	174 14
WE ASPHYXIATE IN A SLEEP OF DREAMS REBREATHING THE IMPU+	174 26
THE AIR IS ALL CLOSE AND POISONOUS IT HAS DRUGGED OUR S+	175 12
GIVE US AIR WE CRY OH LET US BUT BREATHE AGAIN	175 18
LET US BREATHE FRESH AIR AND WAKE FROM FOUL DREAMS IN W+	175 19
TO FEEL FRESH AIR IN OUR THROATS TO HAVE FRESH BREATH I+	175 21
THE FAINT FINE SEETHE IN THE AIR	216 6
SOME FIREFLIES DRIFT THROUGH THE MIDDLE AIR	221 19
RIDING THE AIR AND CARRYING ALL THE TIME	221 21
THE BREATH OF THE BULLOCK STAINS THE HARD CHILL AIR	225 13
ROCKS SEEM AND EARTH AND AIR UNEASY AND WATERS STILL	249 15
MADE OF SWEET UNTARNISHED SILVER IN THE SEA-SOUTHERN AIR	298 21

AIR

LIKE STEEL LIKE SENSITIVE STEEL IN THE AIR	300 29
DO YOU FEEL THE AIR FOR ELECTRIC INFLUENCES	301 3
DO YOU TAKE THE WHISPER OF SULPHUR FROM THE AIR	301 8
UPON THE FRIGHTENED AIR	315 17
THAT GNASH THE AIR	315 19
UPON THE SMOULDERING AIR	317 10
RAMPING UP THROUGH THE AIR LIKE A KESTREL	324 30
AND WEIGH NO MORE THAN AIR AS YOU ALIGHT UPON ME	332 7
HOW YOU SAIL LIKE A HERON OR A DULL CLOT OF AIR	332 16
QUEER HOW YOU STALK AND PROWL THE AIR	332 25
I HATE THE WAY YOU LURCH OFF SIDEWAYS INTO THE AIR	333 5
AND TO SPRING AWAY WITH A CURVETTING CLICK IN THE AIR	337 2
LUNGING IN THE AIR ON THE LINE	339 5
A SUDDEN TURNING UPON ITSELF OF A THING IN THE AIR	341 4
LITTLE LUMPS THAT FLY IN AIR AND HAVE VOICES INDEFINITE+	341 26
TO THE FREE CALM UPPER AIR	343 2
FUMBLING A BEAST IN AIR	343 10
ALWAYS REFUSING TO GO OUT INTO THE AIR	343 13
DROPPING ABOUT THE AIR	344 9
SEEMING TO STUMBLE TO FALL IN AIR	345 15
WINGS DARK SKINNY AND FLAPPING THE AIR	346 23
AND FLICKERED HIS TONGUE LIKE A FORKED NIGHT ON THE AIR+	350 21
AND LOOKED AROUND LIKE A GOD UNSEEING INTO THE AIR	350 28
AND HOWLS HIS PANDEMONIUM ON THE INDIGNANT AIR	379 23
GREY BIRD IN THE AIR ON THE BOUGH OF THE LEANING	385 17
AIR VAST BEAST	385 24
LIFE SEEMS TO LEAP AT THE AIR OR SKIM UNDER THE WIND	392 15
SO SHE WISTFULLY SENSITIVELY SNIFFS THE AIR AND THEN TU+	393 25
WILL THERE BE A WHISTLE OF WINGS IN THE AIR AND AN ICY	439 6
AIR	445 5
THAT YOU'VE LET IN A LITTLE AIR	459 16
A LITTLE FRESH AIR IN THE MONEY STY	459 17
AND ITS PLUMES LOOK LIKE GREEN CUPS HELD UP TO THE SUN +	498 22
FIRE AND RAIN AND AIR AND LIVE LOAM	505 13
HAD BLASTED THE SICKLY AIR	536 15
AND IF THEY'RE OVER FORTY-FIVE HURL GREAT STONES INTO T+	541 4
WE'RE NOT FIT FOR THE AIR WE BREATHE	553 30
BELONGS TO THE BAMBOO THICKET AND THE DRAKE IN THE AIR +	623 12
AND THE AIR IS ALIVE AND CAN DENY US AS A WOMAN CAN	625 15
SONS OF EARTH SONS OF FIRE SONS OF AIR AND WATER	635 3
AT THE STILLNESS OF THE AIR	646 18
AH IN THE THUNDER AIR	646 19
IN THE THUNDER AIR ALL STRANGERS TO ONE ANOTHER	647 6
AND GOLD-BRONZE FLUTTERS BENT THROUGH THE THICK UPPER A+	647 12
THAT MAKES THE AIR SO STILL AND LOVELY TO ME	652 5
TRAFFICKING MYSTERIOUSLY THROUGH THE AIR	655 19
I FEEL GODDESSES TRAFFICKING MYSTERIOUSLY THROUGH THE A+	655 27
OF THE UNKNOWN AIR AND EYES SO SOFT	667 8
IT IS ENOUGH I SAW YOU VANISH INTO AIR	696 28
THE DEAD THREADED THE AIR LINGERING	704 3
THE DEAD TREAD HEAVILY THROUGH THE MUDDY AIR	704 8
OF FIRE AND THE WET EARTH AND THE WIDE AIR OF THE WORLD	706 5
AND DEATH IS ON THE AIR LIKE A SMELL OF ASHES	717 5
UPON THE OUTER AIR	784 18
AND THE AIR THAT BLOWS GOOD BREATH IN THE NOSTRILS OF P+	792 14
SEEKING THE OFFAL AND GARBAGE OF LIFE IN THE INVISIBLE +	796 6
CRAWL LIKE MASTERLESS DOGS IN THE BACK STREETS OF THE A+	796 12
LO IN THE BACK STREETS OF THE AIR DEAD ONES ARE CRAWLIN+	798 29
THE EARTH AND AIR	800 37
AND I QUETZALCOATL THE EAGLE OF THE AIR AM BRUSHING YOU+	802 1
IN THE WHITE AIR	827 24
THE AIR AND THE FLOWING SUNSHINE AND BRIGHT DUST	870 9
OR WHETHER IT RANG IN THE AIR	881 25
STREAMED REDNESS DOWN THE AIR SHOT RED ON HIS EYES	884 24
OVER MY SUNLIT SKIN THE WARM CLINGING AIR	*892 1
LIKE A GLITTERING OF SHADOWS WITHIN THE MORNING AIR	*895 6
TO FOLLOW MY LIFE ALOFT TO THE FINE WILD AIR OF LIFE AN+	*900 8
TO FOLLOW MY LIFE ALOFT TO THE FINE WILD AIR OF LIFE AN+	*903 22
WARM AS A FLAME IN THE CLOSE NIGHT AIR	*912 8
ON THE AIR FOR OUR NOURISHMENT WHO FROM THESE WEAVE FAI+	*938 24
A WOMAN IS SINGING ME A WILD HUNGARIAN AIR	*940 19
RIDING THE AIR AND CARRYING ALL THE TIME	*945 7

AIR-BOMBS

ARE POISON GASES AND AIR-BOMBS	715 17

AIREDALE

SO NOW WHAT WITH GREAT AIREDALE DOGS	400 20

AIR-LIFE

DARK AIR-LIFE LOOPING	341 9

AIRS

FROM AIRS AND FROM FALSE MODESTY	470 8
IT'S YOUR WIFE WI' HER AIRS AN' GRACES	493 20

AIR-SHIP

WHILE YOU READ ABOUT THE AIR-SHIP CROSSING THE WILD ATL+	441 22

AIRY

AND THE AIRY PRIMULAS OBLIVIOUS	243 28

ALARMS

BUT MY HEART STANDS STILL AS A NEW STRONG DREAD ALARMS	132 5
THAT STARTLES ME ALARMS ME STIRS UP A REPULSION	270 14
MY HEART DISTURBED IN ITS DREAM SLOW-STEPPING ALARMS	*937 32

ALAS

WAVE FRIGHTENED WHO COMES A LABOURER ALAS	41 4
SOUTHWARDS ALAS	50 18
THE HUNGER FOR THE WOMAN ALAS	264 14
THEY THINK THAT WE ADORE THEM ALAS WOULD IT WERE TRUE	270 1
ALAS SALVIA AND HIBISCUS FLOWERS	313 10
ALAS THE SUNDAY COATS OF SICILIAN BOLSHEVISTS	313 34
MEANWHILE ALAS	317 6
RED ANGRY MEN ARE A RACE EXTINCT ALAS	317 12
ALAS ALAS I HAVE GOT TO LEAVE IT ALL	317 27

ALAS
    ALAS WHAT A FOOL HE LOOKS IN THIS SCUFFLE   360 26
    ALAS THE SPEAR IS THROUGH THE SIDE OF HIS ISOLATION   361 1
    SOMEHOW ALAS HE FELL IN LOVE   378 8
    ALAS LOVE DID IT   379 8
    AND SEX ALAS GETS DIRTIER AND DIRTIER WORKED FROM THE   464 1
    O EAGLE OF THE MIND ALAS YOU ARE MORE LIKE A BUZZARD   473 9
    BUT OUR CIVILISATION ALAS   524 7
    WHEN ALAS IT'S ONLY PART OF OUR CLEVER LITTLE SELF THAT+   543 23
    ALAS MY POOR YOUNG MEN   558 15
    TO CONFIRM WHAT HE SAID BUT ALAS HE MEANT   579 21
    ALAS THEY HAVE SAVED YOU FROM YOURSELF   585 13
    ALAS THEY HAVE SAVED YOU FROM YOURSELF FROM YOUR OWN   630 14
    MEN DON'T ACHIEVE THEIR OWN MANHOOD ALAS OH ALAS ALAS   683 23
    BUT ALAS THIS IS NOT WHAT I CAME FOR I HAVE FALLEN SHORT   751 8
    ALAS BUT THE ROPE IS GNAWING   751 17
    ALAS MY LAND IS ENGLAND AND I KNOW NOT HOW NOR WHENCE   757 3
    ALAS TOSSED BACK IN MY HEARTS SWIRL   862 16

A-LAUGHING
    THE HOT DARK BLOOD OF ITSELF A-LAUGHING WET HALF-DEVILI+   389 20

ALBATROSS
    AND I THOUGHT OF THE ALBATROSS   351 22

ALERT
    SUCH FAIR FRESH ALERT FIRST-FLOWER FACES   270 5
    HO GOLDEN-SPANIEL SWEET ALERT NARCISSUS   309 7
    SHE IS SUCH AN ALERT LISTENER WITH HER EARS WIDE TO KNOW   384 15

ALGEBRA
    AND ALGEBRA IN THE EYES OF DESIROUS MEN   118 23
    A CUNNING ALGEBRA IN THE FACES OF MEN   *932 1

ALIEN
    THE ALIEN TREES IN ALIEN LANDS AND YET   305 1
    WITH ITS OWN ALIEN AURA   780 30

ALIGHT
    NOT EVEN THE MOTHS CAN ALIGHT   114 6
    SINCE THE BELOVED FADED MOTHER THAT SET US ALIGHT   132 17
    BACKWARD INTO SPACE TO ALIGHT   162 27
    WHITE AND ALIGHT THE NIGHT WAS   165 11
    SEEKING WHERE TO ALIGHT   253 7
    AND WEIGH NO MORE THAN AIR AS YOU ALIGHT UPON ME   332 7
    WHERE THE ANGELS USED TO ALIGHT   725 19
    AND GOD ABROAD AND ALIGHT ON US EVERYWHERE   742 30
    EVERYWHERE MEN AND WOMEN ALIGHT WITH GOD   742 31
    WE MUST KEEP YOUR LAMP ALIGHT NEVERTHELESS JEANNETTE   859 27
    AND THE WORLD WAS ALIGHT   884 7
    THE MOON OF SLEEP IS ALIGHT   *917 16
    AND STRIP ME NAKED TOUCH ME ALIGHT   *931 17
    BUT LEAVES ALIGHT AND LOVELY ETERNALLY   *937 6
    SINCE THE BELOVED FADED MOON THAT SET US ALIGHT   *938 9

ALIGHTS
    SHE ALIGHTS A STRANGER WONDERING UNUSED TO THE SCENE   153 10

ALIKE
    THE RICH AND THE POOR ALIKE DREAMING AND WRITHING ALL I+   175 15
    THE PAIR OF THEM ALIKE IN THAT   378 12
    GODS AND LOVE ALIKE ARE BUT AN IDEA   474 13
    BUT THEY'RE ALL ALIKE AN' IT MAKES YOU   550 9
    MEN ARE NOT ALIKE IN THE SIGHT OF GOD   638 7
    MEN ARE ANYTHING BUT ALIKE IN THE SIGHT OF GOD   638 9
    ALL MORE OR LESS ALIKE   657 4

ALIVE
    THE SHORES OF THIS INNERMOST OCEAN ALIVE AND ILLUSORY   71 12
    IN SCARLET ALIVE WITH THE BIRDS' BRIGHT TWITTERING   72 22
    ALIVE WITHIN THE OOZY UNDER-MIRE   89 19
    TRACK OF THE RAILWAY ALIVE AND WITH SOMETHING TO DO   174 8
    HOW QUAVERINGLY I DEPEND ON YOU TO KEEP ME ALIVE   246 2
    NEW BEYOND KNOWLEDGE OF NEWNESS ALIVE BEYOND LIFE   258 30
    NOT QUITE ALIVE   352 7
    A YARD OF INDIA MUSLIN IS ALIVE WITH HINDU LIFE   448 21
    HE IS ALIVE LIKE A TREE IN SPRING   450 25
    FOR SPACE IS ALIVE   505 5
    FOR IT IS ALL ALIVE   515 20
    THE ONLY REASON FOR LIVING IS BEING FULLY ALIVE   522 9
    AND YOU CAN'T BE FULLY ALIVE IF YOU ARE CRUSHED BY SECR+   522 10
    TO BE ALIVE YOU'VE GOT TO FEEL A GENEROUS FLOW   522 24
    SPACE OF COURSE IS ALIVE   525 1
    THAT THING'S ALIVE IT'S DANGEROUS MAKE AWAY   528 16
    ESPECIALLY IF I SEE THEIR ALONENESS ALIVE IN THEM   602 5
    THOSE THAT ARE FRESH AND ALIVE ARE THE SAME IN EVERY   612 10
    LET ME TELL YOU THAT THE SUN IS ALIVE AND CAN BE ANGRY   625 13
    AND THE SEA IS ALIVE AND CAN SULK   625 14
    LET ME TELL YOU THAT THE SUN IS ALIVE AND CAN BE ANGRY   625 15
    I AM MORE ALIVE MORE AWARE AND MORE WISE   655 24
    ALL THE GODS AND YOU SEE THEM ALL IF YOU LOOK ALIVE AND+   671 20
    AND ALIVE AND MOVING TOMORROW MANY TOMORROWS AS YESTERD+   671 21
    ONLY WHEN SHE IS BURNT ALIVE BURNT DOWN   728 7
    ALIVE AND YET DRAINED OF LIFE   767 16
    FOR THE SUN AND THE MOON ARE ALIVE AND WATCHING WITH GL+   792 10
    AND THE EARTH IS ALIVE AND READY TO SHAKE OFF HIS FLEAS   792 12
    THE BONE IS WHITE AND ALIVE   808 27
    WHILE THE BLOOD IS ALIVE   857 16
    ARE THEY ASLEEP ARE THEY ALIVE NOW SEE WHEN I   *891 9
    ALL MY BODY SPRINGS ALIVE   *893 12

ALL-BUT-NAKED
    REDDENS STILL MORE ON THE BLATANT BODIES OF THESE ALL-B+   625 11

ALL-CREATIVE
    THE POWER OF THE RISING GOLDEN ALL-CREATIVE SAP COULD T+   272 22

ALLEGIANCE
    YOUR LAST ALLEGIANCE   168 33
    OLD ALLEGIANCE   374 4

ALLERS
    AS THA ALLERS HAST BUT LET ME TELL THEE   *922 5

ALL-FORE-ORDAINING
    OF THE ALL-SEEING ALL-FORE-ORDAINING IDEAL   329 18

ALL-KNOWING
    HUNG ALL THE TIME DID WE BUT KNOW IT THE ALL-KNOWING SH+   328 8

ALLOW
    ALOOF MY FLAMING HEART WILL NOT ALLOW   122 22
    AND ALLOW THE SOUL TO FIND ITS LEVEL   428 7

ALLOWED
    AND NOT BE ALLOWED TO ABSENT THEMSELVES   779 3
    THE GOLD SUN SHINES IN HEAVEN ONLY BECAUSE HE'S ALLOWED   783 1

ALLOWS
    I WONDER IF GOD ALLOWS   104 9
    THE SYSTEM ALLOWS US TO BE   520 32

ALL-PENETRATING
    AND THE DEEP SECRET ALL-PENETRATING TAIL CURVED BENEATH   365 3

ALL-SEEING
    ALL-SEEN AND THEN ALL-SEEING   243 6
    OF THE ALL-SEEING ALL-FORE-ORDAINING IDEAL   329 18

ALL-SEEN
    ALL-SEEN AND THEN ALL-SEEING   243 6

ALL SOULS' DAY
    IT IS MY OFFERING TO YOU EVERY DAY IS ALL SOULS' DAY   233 17

ALLURE
    ALLURE ME TILL I AM BESIDE MYSELF   293 9
    THIS IS NO WISTFUL ALLURE   *907 6

ALLURING
    ALLURING MY EYES FOR I AM I NOT ALSO DREAM-STUFF   *909 3

ALLUS
    AS THA ALLUS 'AST BUT LET ME TELL THEE   80 5

ALL-WISE
    THE ALL-WISE HAS TIRED US OF WISDOM   439 28

ALMIGHTY
    AND THE WORD WAS THE FIRST OFFSPRING OF THE ALMIGHTY JO+   329 11
    FOR THE ALMIGHTY EAGLE OF THE FORE-ORDAINING MIND   329 21
    ALMIGHTY MACHINE   643 22

ALMIGHTY GOD
    DO NOT ASK ME ALMIGHTY GOD TO PART FROM HER AGAIN   749 20

ALMIGHTY MAMMON
    ALMIGHTY MAMMON MAKE ME RICH   584 5

ALMIGHTY NULLUS
    IT WAS WON BY THE ONE ALMIGHTY NULLUS   824 6

ALMOND
    ALMOND AND APPLE AND PEAR DIFFUSE WITH LIGHT THAT VERY   179 3
    OF THE SKY AND THE ALMOND FLOWERS   244 6
    BLACK ALMOND TRUNKS IN THE RAIN   300 20
    ALMOND TRUNKS CURVING BLACKLY IRON-DARK CLIMBING THE   300 24
    AND LONG AGO THE ALMOND WAS THE SYMBOL OF RESURRECTION   303 1
    BUT TELL ME TELL ME WHY SHOULD THE ALMOND BE THE SYMBOL+   303 2
    IN JANUARY AND IN FEBRUARY THE RE-BIRTH OF THE ALMOND T+   303 5
    CALLED THE ALMOND BONE IN THE BODY THE LAST BONE OF THE+   303 9
    SOMETHING MUST BE REASSURING TO THE ALMOND IN THE EVENI+   303 31
    AND ALMOND HONEY-STILL   316 4
    HANDS TO EAT THE ACANTHUS OR BITE AT THE ALMOND BUDS   385 10

ALMOND-TREES
    WET ALMOND-TREES IN THE RAIN   300 18
    THE RUSTY SWORDS OF ALMOND-TREES   304 24
    BRISTLING NOW WITH THE IRON OF ALMOND-TREES   305 15

ALMOND-TREE
    HERE THERE'S AN ALMOND-TREE YOU HAVE NEVER SEEN   58 12
    UNDER THE ALMOND-TREE THE HAPPY LANDS   58 16
    IS THERE AN ALMOND-TREE   244 2
    ALMOND-TREE BENEATH THE TERRACE RAIL   300 26
    THE ALMOND-TREE   304 7
    THE ALMOND-TREE   304 9
    AND THE ALMOND-TREE IN EXILE IN THE IRON AGE   305 11
    ALMOND-TREE   385 18
    COME DOWN CRAPA OUT OF THAT ALMOND-TREE   385 22

ALMOND-
    UPON US AND APPLE- AND ALMOND- AND APRICOT- AND QUINCE-+   271 26

ALMOST
    YOUR STUFF ALL GONE YOUR MENACE ALMOST RASED   53 23
    ALMOST I HATED HER SACRIFICED   62 21
    THROUGH THE FILM I CAN ALMOST TOUCH YOU   194 3
    THIS IS ALMOST BLISS   203 11
    IS ALMOST MORE THAN I CAN BEAR   215 15
    IS ALMOST MORE THAN I CAN BEAR   216 12
    ALMOST THE FLOWER IN THE BUD   239 17

ALMOST
    TILL IT IS ALMOST ENOUGH TILL I AM REDUCED PERHAPS   258   7
    AND FOR MYSELF I CAN SAY ALMOST ALMOST OH VERY NEARLY   265 27
    FLOWERS SCENTLESS OR PUNGENT AMMONIACAL ALMOST   270 11
    RARE ALMOST AS BEAMS YET OVERWHELMINGLY POTENT   271 19
    FAR-OFF KINGS PAINTED THEIR FACES VERMILION AND WERE AL+   303 22
    THAT THE OLD BIRD IS WEARY AND ALMOST WILLING   329 27
    A RUSH THAT ALMOST SCREAMS   336 15
    ALMOST FISH-VOICE   336 16
    GREAT HASTE AND STRAIGHT ALMOST BIRD STRAIGHT ABOVE THE   347 12
    YOU ARE ALMOST TOO LARGE I AM ALMOST FRIGHTENED   359 29
    HIS POOR DARLING IS ALMOST FIERY   359 34
    UNTIL YOUR VEILED HEAD ALMOST TOUCHES BACKWARD   370 14
    HAVE ALMOST ALL FORGOT   379 32
    AN OBSTINATE OLD WITCH ALMOST JERKING THE ROPE FROM MY   385   9
    REAL LITTLE DUST-PIG EARS ALMOST BLOWN AWAY   397 16
    YET THE STRANGE ALMOST FRIGHTENED SHOUT OF DELIGHT THAT   446 14
    WE ARE ALMOST ANYTHING   480   3
    AS THE VULTURE THAT SCREAMS HIGH UP ALMOST INAUDIBLE   500 16
    MY SOUL IS ALMOST BLANK MY SPIRIT QUITE   501 20
    THEY HAVE HIGH BLOOD-PRESSURE AND ALMOST BURST   502   5
    ALMOST EVERY SCRAP OF THE LIVING EARTH YOU STROLL UP AND   521 15
    AUNT LOUIE IS ALMOST BOUND TO COME   572 11
    BUT IT WAS NOT ENOUGH HE LOOKED AT ME ALMOST WITH HATE   603   5
    THEN DIED OUT ALMOST AS SWIFTLY   618   5
    SHE HAS A SECRET ALMOST ECSTASIED HATRED OF MALENESS IN+   619 20
    AND I ALMOST CEASE TO EXIST WEIGHED DOWN TO EXTINCTION   629 20
    AND SUNK INTO DEPRESSION THAT ALMOST BLOTS ME OUT   629 21
    I TOO AM ALMOST DEAD   629 25
    NOW IT IS ALMOST NIGHT FROM THE BRONZEY SOFT SKY   647   8
    AND CHIRRUP THEIR ALMOST INDECENT NOISES   681   6
    ALMOST AS EMPTY AS BELCHING OR HICCUP   681   7
    THICK ALMOST THUNDROUS ON THE HARDENED EARTH   717   4
    ALMOST AN INSTINCT   829 21
    WE HAVE LEARNED THAT ANOTHER MAN'S LIBERTY IS AS ESSENT+   833   1
    AMOUNTING ALMOST TO LOVE   834 12
    I LOVE LIFE I LOVE LIFE SO DEARLY I COULD ALMOST DIE   837 10
    HAVE NO EXPERIENCE OF SEX AT ALL IT IS ALMOST NOTHING T+   843 20
    THERE IS NO ACTION IT IS ALMOST A SLEEP   856 23
    LIKE ALMOST ALL ENGLISHMEN   *948 31

ALOFT
    OF GLASS PALACE ALOFT THERE AMONG MISTY INDEFINITE THIN+   52 24
    SO I HELD MY HEART ALOFT   124   3
    HOLDING ALOFT THEIR UMBRELLAS THAT FLASH AND ARE BRIGHT   146 19
    CAUGHT UP ALOFT   269   4
    THERE NEVER WAS ANY STANDING ALOFT AND UNFOLDED ON A BO+   283   3
    AND AT LAST THE PERA-HERA PROCESSION FLAMBEAUX ALOFT IN   387 25
    HE IS ROYALTY PALE AND DEJECTED FRAGMENT UP ALOFT   388 13
    THAT I HAD BEEN HE IN THE PAVILION AS IN A PEPPER-BOX A+   392   2
    ARE YOU SO PURE AND LOFTY UP ALOFT   710 14
    LIFE HAS ITS PLACE OF BLUE DAY ALOFT   711   1
    ALOFT BY ONE GREAT BENDING RAFTER DUSTY   876 13
    THAT BEARS ALOFT TOWARD RARER SKIES   *899 28
    TO FOLLOW MY LIFE ALOFT TO THE FINE WILD AIR OF LIFE AN+   *900   8
    THAT BEARS ALOFT TOWARDS RARER SKIES   *903   7
    TO FOLLOW MY LIFE ALOFT TO THE FINE WILD AIR OF LIFE AN+   *903 20
    OF BLUE PALACE ALOFT THERE AMONG THE MISTY INDEFINITE D+   *905 13
    AND AH I HELD MY HEART ALOFT   *936   9

ALONE
    ALONE UNDERSTANDS   39 24
    I MUST SIT ALONE AND WAIT AND NEVER KNOW   48   7
    AS I SIT ON THE SHORES OF THE CLASS ALONE   51 10
    IN THE RIPENING MORNING TO SIT ALONE WITH THE CLASS   51 22
    THAT STRUGGLES ALONE IN THE DARK   63 28
    LEANS ALL ALONE ABOVE MY WINDOW ON NIGHT'S WINTRY BOWER   67 19
    WHO STAND ALONE IN DESPAIR LIKE A GUTTERING LIGHT   73 16
    ALONE WITHIN THE DIM AND HOARSE SILENCE   76 21
    I IN THE FUR OF THE WORLD ALONE BUT THIS HELEN CLOSE BY   98   6
    ALONE MY DEAR   102 18
    BUT I AM ALONE AND WAVERING HOME   106 15
    TO LIVE ALONE IS MY DOOM   106 22
    ALONE ON THE PERFECT SILENCE   110 23
    SURELY AH NOT IN WORDS ALONE I'D SPILL   127 16
    HE SITS LIKE A SHADE BY THE FLOOD ALONE   130   5
    WHAT CAN I DO BUT DANCE ALONE   130   9
    SINCE THE MONTH OF CHILDHOOD IS OVER AND WE STAND ALONE   132 16
    RIGID SLEEPS THE HOUSE IN DARKNESS I ALONE   140   7
    ALONE ON A SEAT   143   4
    PLAYING YOUR GREAT GAME AROUND THE WORLD ALONE   197   7
    FULFILLED AND ALONE   198 18
    AND YOU STOOD ALONE WATCHING THEM GO   206   1
    TO-NIGHT I HAVE LEFT HER ALONE   212 17
    I HAVE BEEN SO INNERLY PROUD AND SO LONG ALONE   214   1
    THE HOUSE IS SILENT IT IS LATE AT NIGHT I AM ALONE   220 21
    BOAT DOWN THERE ALL ALONE   226 18
    ALONE ON THE OPEN ROAD AGAIN   228   9
    DO YOU THINK IT IS BLISS ALONE   235 32
    WHEN HE THINKS HIMSELF ALONE   244 10
    I AM VERY GLAD AND ALL ALONE IN THE WORLD   256   7
    ALL ALONE AND VERY GLAD IN A NEW WORLD   256   8
    NOT BREAD ALONE NOT THE BELLY NOR THE THIRSTY THROAT   263   8
    THEN ALONG THE DAMP ROAD ALONE TILL THE NEXT TURNING   280 29
    INTENSELY ALONE   281   5
    IT ALONE   299 30
    THEN THE PROUD LION STALKS ABROAD ALONE   325 19
    ALONE WITH THE ELEMENT   336 26
    EACH ONE ALONE WITH THE WATERS UPON ONE WAVE WITH THE   337 21
    YOU KNOW WHAT IT IS TO BE BORN ALONE   352   1
    ALONE SMALL INSECT   352 15
    AND YOU ARE SLOWLY MOVING PIONEER YOU ALONE   354   3
    ALONE WITH NO SENSE OF BEING ALONE   354 10
    HE DOESN'T KNOW HE IS ALONE   357 31
    BORN TO WALK ALONE   363   1
    AS HE CERTAINLY BEGAN SO PERFECTLY ALONE   364 10
    AND ALONE   392   3
    BUT IT IS THE SOVIET STATE ALONE WHICH COUNTS   443   5

ALONE
    WHEN IT'S LEFT ALONE AS IT STIRS AND ROUSES AND SLEEPS   464 31
    LEAVE ME ALONE LET ME BE   469 29
    LEAVE SEX ALONE LEAVE SEX ALONE LET IT DIE RIGHT AWAY   471 19
    LET US LEAVE IT ALONE PHYSICALLY KEEP APART   471 26
    AND ALSO ALONE   480 13
    I CANNOT HELP BUT BE ALONE   507 16
    THE DEEP INSTINCTS WHEN LEFT ALONE ARE QUITE MORAL   529   3
    NOW THEN YOU LEAVE A MAN'S MISFORTUNES ALONE   545 11
    AND LEAVE ME ALONE AWHILE   580 16
    LEAVE ME ALONE NOW FOR MY SOUL IS BURNING   580 19
    IS TO BE ALONE TO POSSESS ONE'S SOUL IN SILENCE   601   3
    NAKEDLY TO BE ALONE UNSEEN   601   4
    IF THEY WILL ONLY LEAVE ME ALONE   602   7
    AND AFTERWARDS LEAVE ME ALONE   602 15
    EXCEPT TO BE LEFT IN THE LAST RESORT ALONE QUITE ALONE   602 24
    YET I CAN'T BE ALONE I WANT SOMEBODY TO KEEP ME WARM   603 20
    I AM NOT YET ALONE   607 29
    ONLY WHEN I AM STRIPPED STARK NAKED I AM ALONE   607 30
    TO BE ALONE IS ONE OF LIFE'S GREATEST DELIGHTS THINKING+   610   3
    I KNOW NO GREATER DELIGHT THAN THE SHEER DELIGHT OF BEI+   610 19
    ALONE ON A HILL-SIDE IN THE NORTH HUMMING IN THE WIND   610 23
    NO MAN UNLESS HE HAS DIED AND LEARNED TO BE ALONE   612 17
    WHY SEEK TO ALTER PEOPLE WHY NOT LEAVE THEM ALONE   614 17
    DEATH ALONE THROUGH THE LONG PROCESS OF DISINTEGRATION   617   8
    AND TO LEAVE ONE ANOTHER ALONE   620   4
    ON AND ON LIKE A DARK-FACED BIRD SINGING ALONE   623 19
    AND THAT WHICH IS CHOICE ALONE MATTERS   639 27
    DO THEY MEAN THEY ARE A GREAT DEAL ALONE   646   4
    BUT WHAT IS LOVELIER THAN TO BE ALONE   646   5
    AND BE ALONE   646   8
    BE ALONE AND FEEL THE TREES SILENTLY GROWING   646   9
    BE ALONE AND SEE THE MOONLIGHT OUTSIDE WHITE AND BUSY   646 10
    BE QUITE ALONE AND FEEL THE LIVING COSMOS SOFTLY ROCKING   646 12
    WHEN I AM ALONE WITH THE SILENT GREAT COSMOS   646 15
    BUT A WOMAN SHY AND ALONE WAS WASHING HERSELF UNDER A T+   651   4
    BUT LEAVE ME ALONE LEAVE ME ALONE TO MYSELF   652   3
    I TELL YOU IT IS NO WOMAN IT IS NO MAN FOR I AM ALONE   652 14
    ALONE SATISFIES US IN THE END   653 14
    PONDERING FOR HE WAS A GREEK THAT GOD IS ONE AND ALL AL+   692 23
    BREATHE ALL ALONE IN SILENCE IN THE DARK   698   4
    INTO HIMSELF ALONE DOWN THE GODLESS PLUNGE OF THE ABYSS   700 24
    HOLDING THEIR BREATH NAKED AND DARKLY ALONE   711   5
    THERE AND THERE ALONE LIES THE PIVOT OF PURE EVIL   712 11
    AND SHOW US NOTHING LEAVE US QUITE ALONE   737 27
    OF WHAT WAS GODLY LEAVE US QUITE ALONE   738   7
    OR LEAVE ME ALONE   752   8
    BUT NOT ALONE NOR FORLORN   770   6
    I TELL YOU YOU ARE NOT MEN ALONE   800 16
    NOW I AM ALONE ON EARTH AND THIS IS MINE   801 15
    MAN ALONE IS IMMORAL   836   7
    FIRST AND LAST MAN IS ALONE   843 24
    HE IS BORN ALONE AND ALONE HE DIES   843 25
    AND ALONE HE IS WHILE HE LIVES IN HIS DEEPEST SELF   843 26
    BUT UNDERNEATH ARE THE DEEP ROCKS THE LIVING ROCK THAT +   844   2
    AND ALONE   844   4
    BUT UNDERNEATH ANY TWONESS MAN IS ALONE   844   6
    I AM OUT ALONE ON THE ROAD   857   9
    EVE ALONE UNSATISFIED AMONG THE ORANGE AND GUAVA TREES   864   1
    SCATTER OVER THE WHITENESS ONE BOY ALONE IN THE CLASSRO+   865 20
    AND THE HOUSE IS EMPTY AND I AM ALONE   871 11
    I AM ALONE ALONE THERE IS NO MORE SIEGMUND FOR ME   871 13
    GONE AND I AM ALONE ALONE   871 16
    SHAPE SHINES ALONE LIKE A MELODY AND WHERE   872 16
    AS IF FOR HIM ALONE OF ALL OUR MEN   877 29
    AH SURE TO VENTURE ALL ALONE IN DEATH   879 26
    WERE WORSE THAN BEING LEFT ALONE IN LIFE   879 27
    AS I SIT ON THE BEACH OF THE CLASS ALONE   *898 22
    ALONE   *900 13
    I ALONE AM LIVING THEN IT KEEPS   *900 22
    AS I SIT ON THE BEACH OF THE CLASS ALONE   *902   6
    ALONE   *903 25
    I ALONE AM LIVING THEN IT KEEPS   *903 34
    AND FEARFUL TO FILE FORTH NOW FOR THE FIRST TIME ALONE   *938 12
    SINGING LOVE'S FIRST SURPRISED GLADNESS ALONE IN THE GL+   *940 15
    FIRST AND LAST MAN IS ALONE   *951   3
    BORN ALONE DIES ALONE   *951   4
    LIVES WHILE HE LIVES MOST OF HIS TIME ALONE   *951   5
    AND IN HIS DEEPEST SELF NEVER CEASES TO BE ALONE   *951   6
    BUT UNDERNEATH MAN IS ALONE EACH ONE A ROCK TO HIMSELF   *951 10
    AND ALSO ALONE   *951 26
    FRIGHTENED AND ALONE THE SOUL SLIPS OUT OF THE HOUSE   *957 12

ALONENESS
    ESPECIALLY IF I SEE THEIR ALONENESS ALIVE IN THEM   602   5
    KEEP YOUR ALONENESS LEAVE ME MY ALONENESS   602 16
    FIRST COMES THE DEATH THEN THE PURE ALONENESS WHICH IS +   611 12

ALONGSIDE
    ALONGSIDE GOING   110 16
    COCKING YOUR EYES AT ME AS YOU COME ALONGSIDE TO SEE IF   397 23

ALOOF
    ALOOF MY FLAMING HEART WILL NOT ALLOW   122 22
    LIKE A RED INDIAN DARKLY UNFINISHED AND ALOOF   369 10

ALOOFNESS
    BUT BARBED ALOOFNESS WHEN I WOULD DRAW NEAR   85 24

ALOUD
    BY BRIGHT LEAVES UTTERED ALOUD AND STRIFE   68   7
    WHEN THEY LIFT THEIR TRUNKS AND SCREAM ALOUD   70 11
    AND I CRY ALOUD IN THE MOMENTS THAT INTERVENE   100 23
    ALOUD SUDDENLY ON MY MIND   140 16
    SO THAT THEY SEEM TO UTTER THEMSELVES ALOUD   197 25
    AS CARRIES ME YOU WOULD WONDER ALOUD THAT HE   251 29
    NOT TO BE SPOKEN ALOUD   264 17
    I SPEAK ALOUD TO FLEETING HOSTS OF RED   745 25

9

ALREADY
  SINCE ALREADY I AM IMPLICATED WITH YOU   242   6
  WHEN EVERYTHING WAS ME I KNEW IT ALL ALREADY I ANTICIPA+   257 11
  FOR THE MAIN ALREADY IS FULFILMENT   265 30
  ARE THE VIOLETS ALREADY HERE   273 27
  RUN PERSEPHONE HE IS AFTER YOU ALREADY   309 15
  ARE WE NOTHING ALREADY BUT THE LAPSING OF A GREAT DEAD   429   1
  ALREADY THE WHITENESS OF FALSE DAWN IS ON MY INNER OCEAN   513 13
  BUT NOT THE JAGGLING AND TWISTING OF ALREADY EXISTENT I+   673   8
  ALREADY IT IS OCTOBER AND THE WIND BLOWS STRONG TO THE +   696 15
  ALREADY OUR BODIES ARE FALLEN BRUISED BADLY BRUISED   718   3
  ALREADY OUR SOULS ARE OOZING THROUGH THE EXIT   718   4
  ALREADY THE DARK AND ENDLESS OCEAN OF THE END   718   6
  ALREADY THE FLOOD IS UPON US   718   8
  ALREADY I SEE THE SHELLED MOON LIE   747 28

ALSO
  THE DISGRACE IS ALSO MINE   111   9
  OF A MOMENT SEE SHE LAUGHED IF YOU ALSO   125   8
  AND WISH I COULD GO ALSO   134   2
  STILL THE JOY WAS THERE ALSO YOU SPOKE TRULY   207 10
  THE FROGS HELPED ALSO WHIRRING AWAY   207 14
  I TRY TO REMEMBER IT IS ALSO WELL BETWEEN US   208 10
  AND GOD OF HORROR I WAS KISSING ALSO MYSELF   257 19
  ALSO SHE WHO IS THE OTHER HAS STRANGE=MOUNDED BREASTS A+   261   8
  AND SHE ALSO PURE ISOLATED COMPLETE   267 21
  WERE POLITICS BUT OTHERS SAY IT WAS A FOOD-TABOO OTHERS+   303 18
  IS HE TO BE A BIRD ALSO   323 26
  AND ALSO TO ENCOURAGE THE RED-CROSS LAMB   325 21
  AND ALSO TO ENSURE A GOODLY INCREASE IN THE WORLD   325 22
  NAY ONCE IT WAS ALSO A FORTRESS WALL AND THE WEIGHT OF +   326 25
  BUT ALSO IT WAS A FIERY FORTRESS FROWNING SHAGGILY ON T+   327   1
  FEAR ALSO   336 12
  I ALSO REALISED   344 16
  AND CLEAVE IN A HIGH CORNER FOR A SECOND LIKE A CLOT AL+   345 23
  I MUST FOLLOW ALSO HER TREND   461 12
  BUT ALSO HE IS INSTINCTIVE INTUITIVE AND IN TOUCH   473 18
  AND THE DARK MOON DRAWS THE TIDES ALSO   473 28
  BUT THOU ART ALSO LIKE THE NIGHT   474   1
  FOR THE STRONGEST LIGHT THROWS ALSO THE DARKEST SHADOW   474   4
  THE BLOOD ALSO KNOWS RELIGIOUSLY   474   7
  AND ALSO ALONE   480 13
  THE SOUL OF MAN ALSO LEANS IN THE UNCONSCIOUS INCLINATI+   480 12
  BUT THERE IS ALSO A THIRD THING THAT MAKES IT WATER   515 12
  YOU MUSTN'T EXPECT IT ALSO TO WAIT FOR YOUR CONVENIENCE   531 21
  BUT WHAT WE ALSO ARE AND WE NEED TO KNOW IT   544   3
  ARE ALSO POOR BLIND CYCLOPS MOANING   544 27
  BUT ALSO THE COMELY   562 30
  THEN I SAY TO MYSELF AM I ALSO DEAD IS THAT THE TRUTH   629 22
  AND THE MASSES ARE ALSO SUPERIOR   641 15
  THE BOLSHEVIST GETS OPENLY MORE IMPUDENT ALSO KNOWING H+   663 22
  ALSO I KNOW SO MUCH ABOUT YOU   677   2
  AND ALSO WE SEE   683 17
  WHERE GOD IS ALSO LOVE BUT WITHOUT WORDS   695   6
  BUT ALSO THE SUNDERERS THE ANGELS WITH BLACK SHARP WING+   706 23
  ALSO THE LIVES THAT STILL HE MAY REQUIRE   736 17
  BUT ALSO IT IS NOT A TERM OF REPROACH   776 12
  CHEW ALSO YOUNG HEIFERS YOUR JUICIER CUDS   814 21
  SETS MY HEART ALSO THROBBING WITH PAIN   862 22
  FOR AM I NOT ALSO DREAM-STUFF DIFFUSING MYSELF IN THE P+   *907   7
  ALLURING MY EYES FOR I AM I NOT ALSO DREAM-STUFF   *909   3
  OF A MOMENT SEE SHE LAUGHED IF YOU ALSO   *935 24
  AND ALSO ALONE   *951 26
  BUT CAN IT BE THAT ALSO IT IS PROCREATION   *960   6

ALTAIR
  VEGA AND SIRIUS AND ALTAIR   713 21

ALTAR
  DEED AN' I WISH I C'D 'A' STOOD AT TH' ALTAR WI' THEE A+   83 11
  THE ALTAR I   96 24
  ALL ALL ON THE ALTAR AND DEATH SWOOPING DOWN   239   4
  MASSIVE OLD ALTAR OF HIS OWN BURNT OFFERING   326 28
  IT WAS ALWAYS AN ALTAR OF BURNT OFFERING   326 29
  IF YOU WANT TO MAKE HER AN OFFERING LET THE DOVES FLY F+   678   9
  AND GUTTER TO EXTINCTION LIKE A TAPER ON A FORGOTTEN AL+   859   4
  DEED AN' I WISH AS I COULD STOOD AT THE ALTAR WI' THEE +   *925 15

ALTARS
  ALTARS BARBAROUS BELOW   95 30
  MY ALTARS SULLIED I BEREFT REMAIN   151 20

ALTER
  TO ALTER MY ONE SPECK OF DOOM WHEN ROUND ME BURNS   195 25
  BUT IT DOES NOT ALTER ME NOR HELP ME   205 17
  I THINK I COULD ALTER THE FRAME OF THINGS IN MY AGONY   213 18
  WHY SEEK TO ALTER PEOPLE WHY NOT LEAVE THEM ALONE   614 17
  TO ALTER THE PRESENT FRAME OF CIVILISATION   838   3

ALTERATION
  ALTERATION   511 25

ALTERING
  SEE NO HOPE OF ALTERING   750   7

ALTERNATE
  AND FLAMES OF KATABOLISTIC ENERGY ALTERNATE   616 11

ALTERNATELY
  ALTERNATELY PALPITANT   667 11

ALTERNATING
  MAN IS AN ALTERNATING CONSCIOUSNESS   474 15
  MAN IS AN ALTERNATING CONSCIOUSNESS   474 16

ALTERNATIVE
  OR PERISH THERE IS NOT ALTERNATIVE   264 20

ALTHOUGH
  REMOTE ALTHOUGH I HEAR THE BEGGAR'S COUGH   36   5
  ALTHOUGH BEREAVED OF YOU   109   8
  LOVE YOU ALTHOUGH I WOULD   111 19
  ALTHOUGH YOU WATCH   359 12

ALTOGETHER
  AND THEY GRUDGE THEM THEIR CIRCUS=LIFE ALTOGETHER   446 13
  OLDER THAN PLASM ALTOGETHER IS THE SOUL OF A MAN UNDERN+   477 11
  YOU'D BETTER ABANDON ALL IDEA OF FEELINGS ALTOGETHER   501 15
  YOU'RE NOT ALTOGETHER   564   7
  ALTOGETHER   842 30
  WAS SHATTERED ALTOGETHER   880 25
  ALTOGETHER   *950 21

ALUMINA
  THINK THAT THE SAPPHIRE IS ONLY ALUMINA LIKE KITCHEN PA+   530   1

ALYOSHAS
  AND THE ALYOSHAS AND DMITRIS AND MYSHKINS AND STAVROGINS   533 14

AMATEUR
  ALL RIGHT THEN HE'S JUST AN AMATEUR   452 33
  FLAUTIST OR JUST AN AMATEUR   453   2

AMAZE
  EMERGING WHITE AND EXQUISITE AND I IN AMAZE   67   9

AMAZED
  I AM AMAZED AT THIS SPRING THIS CONFLAGRATION   116   6
  ME WHO AM ISSUED AMAZED FROM THE DARKNESS STRIPPED   133   2
  DELIVERED HELPLESS AND AMAZED   262 19
  AND SHOOT ONE ANOTHER AMAZED AND MAD WITH SOMNAMBULISM   408 12

AMAZING
  AND ALL THE MANIFOLD BLUE AMAZING EYES   136 14
  BUT ONLY YOU HAVE THROWN THIS AMAZING MANTILLA OF   369 19
  IS TO DIE THE AMAZING DEATH   512 24
  AND YOU STIR UP THE MOST AMAZING MUD   830 15
  ARE AN AMAZING PUTRESCENT SLUSH   830 18

AMAZINGLY
  BUT IT SOUNDS SO AMAZINGLY LIKE A SLOGAN   333 23

AMAZON
  WHEN DARKER STILL THAN CONGO OR AMAZON   607   7
  WITH EVE AND THE AMAZON THE LIZARD AND THE FRAIL   633   3

AMBASSADOR
  AMBASSADOR FROM HALLS OF NOISELESS DEATH   745 15

AMBASSADORS
  LIKE AMBASSADORS   268   9

AMBER
  AS A FIELD-BEE BLACK AND AMBER   46   6

AMBITION
  SUCH SUBURBAN AMBITION SO MESSILY GORING   494 23

AMBULANCE
  AN' THEY TA'EIN' 'IM I' TH' AMBULANCE   45   6

AMEN
  IN THE WORLD WITHOUT END AMEN   823 12
  TIME WITHOUT END AMEN AMEN   826   7

AMENITIES
  AMONG SOFT AMENITIES   462 26

AMERICA
  WHICH I SUPPOSE IS WHY AMERICA HAS GONE DRY   286 20
  OH AMERICA   289 24
  AMERICA   290   5
  IN A NEW PROUD SINGLENESS AMERICA   290 20
  I AM SO TERRIFIED AMERICA   291   9
  YET AMERICA   291 22
  AMERICA AMERICA   292 25
  MODERN UNISSUED UNCANNY AMERICA   293   6
  AND MECHANICAL AMERICA MONTEZUMA STILL   298 18
  IN AMERICA STILL   374 10
  AMERICA   409 25
  AMERICANS ARE THE PEOPLE OF AMERICA   774 22
  THE DESTINY OF AMERICA IS IN THEIR HANDS   774 23
  THE LIVING AMERICA IS IN THE HEARTS OF AMERICANS   774 24
  WHAT THE AMERICA OF THE FUTURE WILL BE WE DON'T KNOW   774 25
  WHAT WE KNOW IS THAT THE FUTURE AMERICA   774 26
  WE CAN'T KNOW WHAT THE FUTURE OF AMERICA WILL BE   775   1
  AMERICA STILL HAS ONLY AN UNREVEALED FUTURE   775 15
  AND SO WHEN THE OUTSIDE WORLD CALLS UPON AMERICA TO ACT+   775 29
  AMERICA WILL HAVE TO FIND HER OWN WAY INTO THE FUTURE   775 32
  AMERICA THAT IS IN YOU   780 22
  OH VINDICTIVE EAGLE OF AMERICA   783 21

AMERICAN
  MACHINE AMERICAN   290 29
  AMERICAN   291   6
  AND WHITE WORDS WHITE-WASH AMERICAN   292 32
  NASCENT AMERICAN   293   1
  A RAW AMERICAN WILL THAT HAS NEVER BEEN TEMPERED BY LIFE   370 34
  TAKE UP THE TRAIL OF THE VANISHED AMERICAN   371 26
  AMERICAN EAGLE   374   2
  AND I I SIT ON THIS HIGH AMERICAN DESERT   410 27
  I'M AMERICAN FROM NEW ORLEANS   435 12
  OR IN AMERICAN LONESOME   646   2

AMERICAN
```
BUT THE GERM OF THAT FUTURE IS INSIDE THE AMERICAN PEOP+      775   2
AND YET THERE IS A SPECK A GERM OF AMERICAN FUTURE           775   7
IN THE HEART OF EVERY INTELLIGENT AMERICAN WHETHER           775   8
AMERICAN FUTURE                                              775  11
THERE IS I BELIEVE SCARCELY ONE INTELLIGENT AMERICAN WHO     775  12
BUT IF TAKEN AT ITS VERY BEST THE TITLE AMERICAN             775  34
AMERICAN                                                     776  20
HE IS THE LAST OF THE ORIGINALLY AMERICAN RACE               776  34
TOLD THE OLD AMERICAN ABORIGINES THAT IT WOULD               777  29
SUBMIT TO IT AND LET YOUR AMERICAN NOBLESSE COMPEL YOU       779  30
OR TRANSFER THE CONTROL TO THE AMERICAN INSTITUTE            780   9
SILENT UPON THE AMERICAN CEDAR-BUSH                          783  13
```

AMERICAN EAGLE
```
TILL THE AMERICAN EAGLE WAS THE ONLY EAGLE LEFT IN THE       413  10
SO BETTER MAKE UP YOUR MIND AMERICAN EAGLE                   414   5
IS THAT YOU AMERICAN EAGLE                                   414  29
```

AMERICAN GOVERNMENT
```
AMERICAN GOVERNMENT                                          776   6
LET THEM LEASE THEIR LAND TO THE AMERICAN GOVERNMENT         778  27
```

AMERICAN INDIAN
```
THE AMERICAN INDIAN LINGERS HERE WARD OF THE                 776   5
THE AMERICAN INDIAN IS BASICALLY A SAVAGE                    776  13
```

AMERICANS
```
AMERICANS AND FRENCH AND GERMANS AND SO ON                   660   4
AMERICANS                                                    774  19
AMERICANS ARE THE PEOPLE OF AMERICA                          774  22
THE LIVING AMERICA IS IN THE HEARTS OF AMERICANS             774  24
IS A GERM LYING IN THE HEARTS OF AMERICANS                   774  27
BUT A GERM IN THE HEARTS OF MEN AND WOMEN AMERICANS          774  31
WHY SHOULD AMERICANS IMMEDIATELY ACQUIESCE                   775  31
YOU ARE AMERICANS                                            776  35
TURN THEM INTO HUNDRED-PER-CENT AMERICANS                    777   3
IT WAS YOU WHO CAME AMERICANS                                777   6
ON YOUR HONOUR AMERICANS WHAT ARE YOU DOING                  777  11
NOW AMERICANS WHAT ABOUT IT                                  779  12
IT IS YOUR TEST AMERICANS                                    779  21
IT IS A TEST AMERICANS                                       780  13
AS HUNDRED-PER-CENT AMERICANS WELL-EDUCATED                  780  18
```

AMERINDIAN
```
THE BIG BIRD OF THE AMERINDIAN BEING THE EAGLE               414   2
```

AMERINDIANS
```
AMERINDIANS                                                  371  34
```

AMETHYST
```
UNDER WHOSE BROWN THE AMETHYST                               123  26
WITH THE AMETHYST IN HER CUP                                 123  30
UNDER WHOSE BROWN THE AMETHYST                              *934  32
```

AMID
```
SAVE IN A BROKEN PATTERN AMID PURPLE AND GOLD AND SABLE       90   6
YOU AMID THE DOG-END'S YELLOW INCANTATION                     90  13
AMID THE AUTUMN RUSHING RED ABOUT                            744  22
THE BITTER WORLD AMID THE SMOKE                              744  23
BEWILDERED AMID THE MOVING IMMENSITY                         875  16
DARK GLITTER OF LIFE AMID A SKY THAT TEEMS                  *895   7
AMID THE HIGH WIND'S ENTERPRISE                             *899  30
AMID THE HIGH WIND'S ENTERPRISE                             *903   9
IS DELIVERED FROM US HERSELF BORN AGAIN AMID THE MOAN       *938  10
```

AMISS
```
WHAT DO I CARE FOR ALL THAT THEY DO AMISS                    74  24
```

AMMONIACAL
```
FLOWERS SCENTLESS OR PUNGENT AMMONIACAL ALMOST              270  11
```

AMMONITES
```
AND CURLING THEIR PRECIOUS LIVE TRUNKS LIKE AMMONITES       445  14
```

AMNESIA
```
BUT IF YOU DON'T YOU ARE SUFFERING FROM AN AMNESIA          655  13
```

AM-NOT
```
ALL THAT I AM-NOT IN SOFTNESS SWEET SOFTNESS FOR SHE IS+    250   3
```

AMOEBA
```
WHEN THE LITTLE EGGY AMOEBA EMERGED OUT OF FOAM AND NOW+    682  26
```

AMONG
```
OF GLASS PALACE ALOFT THERE AMONG MISTY INDEFINITE THIN+     52  24
A SIGH AMONG THE SHADOWS THUS RETRIEVING                     66   3
AND AMONG THE WRECK OF THE THEATRE CROWD                     71  28
AMONG THE CRUMPLED BEECH-LEAVES PHOSPHORESCENT               86  22
MY FALLEN STAR AMONG THE LEAVES MY DEAR                      86  24
I MOVE AMONG A TOWNFOLK CLAD                                109  10
MY DEAR AMONG IT ALL                                        110   2
AND I WHAT SORT OF FIRE AM I AMONG                          116  10
AN UNCHARTED WAY AMONG THE MYRIAD THICK                     132  11
AMONG CROWDS OF THINGS IN THE SUNSHINE JOSTLED AND RACK+    133   8
THE WHITE MOON GOING AMONG THEM LIKE A WHITE BIRD           134  16
AMONG SNOW-BERRIES                                         134  17
NOW LAMPS LIKE YELLOW ECHOES GLIMMER AMONG                 135   9
ITSELF AMONG EVERYTHING ELSE HERE HUNGRILY STEALING        141  18
UNNOTICED AMONG THEM A STILL QUEEN LOST IN THE MAZE        176  24
YOU WOULD AMONG THE LAUGHING HILLS                         178   5
WAIT AMONG THE BEECHES                                     178  30
WHY DO I WANDER AIMLESS AMONG THEM DESIROUS FOOL           180  23
WE SITTING HERE AMONG THE CRANBERRIES                     223  16
HERE AMONG ALL THIS SILENCE CROUCHING FORWARD             225  19
THEN AMONG THE AVERTED PANSIES BENEATH THE HIGH           225  29
AMONG THE EAGER CORDIAL MEN                                228  18
AMONG THE PINK AND BLUE                                    244   5
```

AMONG
```
ADVENTURING AMONG THEM                                     256  17
I HAVE CHOSEN AMONG THE BRIGHT AND MARVELLOUS BOOKS        264   3
IT IS NOT LONG SINCE HERE AMONG ALL THESE FOLK            269  14
AND HEAVE IT OFF AMONG THE STARS INTO THE INVISIBLE       272  24
A NEW INTOXICATION OF LONELINESS AMONG DECAYING FROST-C+  281   2
DROPPING AMONG HIS LEAVES HANGS THE DARK GRAPE            286  10
ONLY I GROPE AMONG YOU PALE-FACES CARYATIDS AS AMONG A    287  27
SIGHTLESS AMONG ALL YOUR VISUALITY                        289   9
DEMONISH LURKING AMONG THE UNDERGROWTH                    293   2
LURKING AMONG THE DEEPS OF YOUR INDUSTRIAL THICKET        293   8
AMONG THE SINUOUS FLAME-TALL CYPRESSES                    296  17
AMONG SQUAT TOAD-LEAVES SPRINKLING THE UNBORN             312   2
FRAIL-FILIGREED AMONG THE REST                            314   3
AMONG MUCH OTHER AIR                                      315   9
THEIR DROPPINGS AMONG THE TURF                            321  14
AND RABBITS MAKE PILLS AMONG THE SHORT GRASS              321  23
AND LET IT MOULT THERE AMONG THE STONES OF THE BITTER S+  329  20
AWAY FROM AMONG GODS AND MEN HE DID NOT SEE THAT HE WAS+  348   2
AS HE CHARGES SLOW AMONG THE HERD                         380  17
AND ROWS AMONG THE FEMALES LIKE A SHIP PERTINACIOUSLY     380  18
SOCKETS AMONG BARE FEET OF ELEPHANTS AND MEN ON THE       388  31
PERPETUAL FIRE-LAUGHING MOTION AMONG THE SLOW SHUFFLE     389  18
PLAYING AMONG THE ELEMENTS NEATLY BEYOND COMPETITION      445  33
THEY KNOW THEY HAVE NO BODIES THAT COULD PLAY AMONG THE   446   2
AGAIN MAN AMONG MAN                                       461  16
AND NEVER A ONE AMONG US ALL                              462   3
AMONG SOFT AMENITIES                                      462  26
AMONG MEN                                                 486  17
BEING BORN AMONG THE WORKING PEOPLE                       498  12
AND THE YOUNG AMONG THE OLD                               504  10
I WISH MEN WOULD GET BACK THEIR BALANCE AMONG THE ELEME+  505  17
AMONG ALL THE SMASHED DEBRIS OF MYSELF                    514   6
THERE ISN'T A MAN AMONG 'EM                               550   1
THERE'S NOT A COCK BIRD AMONG 'EM                         550  15
LAMBS FRISK AMONG THE DAISIES OF HIS BRAIN                624   9
WHAT ARE YOU GOING TO DO ENTANGLED AMONG ALL THE ENGINES  635  26
THREADING HIS WAY AMONG THE ROBOT MACHINE-PEOPLE          645  20
WHITE IVORY WHITE AMONG THE RAMBLING GREENS               646  24
A STILL BRIGHTER WHITE SNAKE WRIGGLES AMONG IT SPILLED    647  14
BUT AMONG THE BOURGEOIS AND THE BOLSHEVIST BOUNDERS       665  22
THERE AMONG THE DARK SUN-RAYS OF DEATH                    677  14
TO THINK AMONG THE MOSS AND MUD OF LIZARDS AND MASTODONS  690  28
BUT IMAGINE AMONG THE MUD AND THE MASTODONS               691   1
AND VENUS AMONG THE FISHES SKIPS AND IS A SHE-DOLPHIN     695   9
SHE IS THE FEMALE TUNNY-FISH ROUND AND HAPPY AMONG THE +  695  11
AMONG THE SPLENDOUR OF TORCHES OF DARKNESS SHEDDING DAR+  697  21
ABROAD IN MY HANDS LIKE WAVES AMONG THE ROCKS OF SUBSTA+  705   6
AMONG SPINNING WHEELS IN AN APOTHEOSIS OF WHEELS          711  27
AND STILL AMONG IT ALL SNATCHES OF LOVELY OBLIVION AND +  727  22
SO MANY GHOSTS AMONG US                                   739   7
OUR BRIDE AMONG THE RUSTLING CHORUS OF SHELLS             743   9
ANOTHER RACE ANOTHER SPEECH AMONG                         746   5
HOW THOU DOST POKE UP AMONG THE SPOKES OF MY              760   4
AMONG THE NEGROES                                         780  17
IN EVERY WAY AND THE LORDS AMONG MEN                      787  28
CHATTERING AMONG THE ICE                                  795  22
BUT YOU WHAT HAVE YOU MASTERED AMONG THE DRAGON HOSTS O+  796  16
QUETZALCOATL IS AMONG THE TREES                           802  17
CREEPING AMONG THE SLEEPING AND THE DREAMING WHO ARE LA+  807   6
OF THE MEN AND THE WOMEN WHO WALK AMONG YOU               807  24
THE GREY DOG CREEPS AMONG YOU                             807  29
BUT THE GREY DOGS ARE AMONG THE ASHES                     809   2
AND ONE GREEN LEAF SPRANG AMONG THE BLACK                 809  20
DETERMINED EFFORT AMONG MEN                               838   2
BUT OF THOSE LIFE-LOVING CARELESS OF THEIR RANK AMONG T+  855  12
LEFT OF THEIR LIGHT AMONG THE MEAN FLOWERS' THRONG        855  16
LIFE LOVERS WHO COULD HOPE FOR NO RANK AMONG THE PALLID+  855  20
EVE ALONE UNSATISFIED AMONG THE ORANGE AND GUAVA TREES    864   1
AMONG THE SHADOWS OF BLOSSOMS AND TREES AND RUSHES        867  26
HIS BLUE SHIRT GLIMMERING ON THE WATER AMONG THE SHADOW+  867  29
THERE AMONG THE FLOWERS OF THE BOAT-ROOF                  868   3
I SAW THE PAIN AMONG THE IRIS THERE                       880  28
BUT I WHERE AMONG THEM ALL AM I                           882  19
THE PSALMS AND FURTIVELY FROM AMONG THE TEXTS            *894  17
OF BLUE PALACE ALOFT THERE AMONG THE MISTY INDEFINITE D+ *905  13
HIS WICKEDNESS AMONG                                     *911  11
THE SIGHT OF THEIR WHITE PLAY AMONG THE GRASS            *913   1
AND THE SIGHT OF THEIR WHITE PLAY AMONG THE GRASS        *914   2
OUR CHARTERED WAY AMONG THE MYRIAD THICK                 *938   3
AND LAMPS LIKE VENTUROUS GLOW-WORMS STEAL AMONG          *939   9
AMONG THE SPLENDOUR OF BLACK-BLUE TORCHES SHEDDING FATH+ *956  19
```

AMONGST
```
AS SHE STRODE HER LIMBS AMONGST IT ONCE MORE             155  14
```

AMOROUS
```
WILL YOU OPEN THE AMOROUS ACHING BUD                     117  22
ALWAYS GLADDEN MY AMOROUS FINGERS WITH THE TOUCH OF THE+ 180  25
AMOROUS CATS                                             366   9
```

AMORPHOUS
```
THERE IS HOWEVER THE VAST THIRD HOMOGENEOUS AMORPHOUS    649  24
```

A'MOST
```
WAS A'MOST BURSTIN' MAD O' MY-SEN                         80   7
WAS A'MOST BURSTIN' MAD O' MY-SEN                       *922   7
```

AMOUNT
```
THE PROCESS WILL AMOUNT TO THE SAME IN THE END           317  35
AND THEN IF YOU AMOUNT TO A HILL O' BEANS                457   9
I HAVE A CERTAIN AMOUNT OF MONEY SO MY ANXIETIES ARE BL+ 501  21
AND AN AMOUNT OF FUNGOID AND PARASITIC GROWTH            677  23
```

AMOUNTING
  AMOUNTING ALMOST TO LOVE   834 12

AMOUNTS
  OR THE EXPERIENCE AMOUNTS TO NOTHING   466 7
  AND AMOUNTS TO VERY MUCH THE SAME THING   523 7
  AND IT ALL AMOUNTS TO THE SAME THING FURNITURE   657 9

AMPHORAS
  BAKED AMPHORAS CRATERS CANTHARUS OENOCHOE AND   305 13

AMPUTATE
  OR MUST HE TRY TO AMPUTATE HIMSELF FROM THE IRON-ENTANG+   632 3

AMUSED
  IS AMUSED   426 7
  SPEAKING OF PERVERTS HE TAKES ON AN AMUSED BUT ICY   *948 4
  HE SHOWS AN AMUSED SUPERIOR CONTEMPT AT THE PREVALENCE +   *949 4

AMUSES
  WHAT HURTS FROM WHAT AMUSES   131 6
  WHILE THE MACHINE AMUSES US THE RADIO OR FILM OR   450 15

AMUSING
  GAY AND AMUSING TOGETHER AND FREE   470 7

ANACONDA
  AND SNAPS THEM SHARP WITH A LITTLE TWIST OF HER ANACONDA   385 28

ANAESTHETIC
  INVISIBILITY AND THE ANAESTHETIC POWER   332 22

ANALYSIS
  NOR IN ANALYSIS   833 33

ANALYST
  FOR THE ANALYST IS TANGLED IN AN ESPECIALLY TANGLED BUN+   833 34

ANAPO
  I SAW A WATER-SERPENT SWIM ACROSS THE ANAPO   337 24

ANARCHY
  WORK RECREATION GOVERNING ANARCHY   256 28
  AND YOU'VE INTRODUCED ANARCHY INTO YOUR COUNTRY   536 5
  CLASS OF ANARCHY   649 25

ANATHEMA
  THIS RED ANATHEMA   302 15

ANATOMISED
  SPECIMENS TO BE ANATOMISED   619 23

ANAXAGORAS
  WHEN ANAXAGORAS SAYS EVEN THE SNOW IS BLACK   708 12

ANAXAGORAS'
  BUT NEVER THE GHOST OF A GLIMPSE OF ANAXAGORAS' FUNERAL+   708 30

ANCHOR
  AS WHEN A GREAT SHIP MOVES TO ANCHOR   445 16

ANCHORS
  CAST YOUR LITTLE ANCHORS IN PORTS OF ETERNITY   542 13

ANCIENT
  AND ALL DAY LONG THAT RAW AND ANCIENT COLD   98 21
  THIS RARE ANCIENT NIGHT FOR IN HERE   114 1
  OF THIS ANCIENT PLACE OF MY ANCIENT CURSE   131 21
  NOW I OFFER HER UP TO THE ANCIENT INEXORABLE GOD   238 23
  WHOSE DOGES WERE OLD AND HAD ANCIENT EYES   278 11
  BUT IT'S SO LONG AGO THE ANCIENT BUSHMAN HAS FORGOTTEN   286 17
  THIS IS THE ANCIENT SOUTHERN EARTH WHENCE THE VASES WERE   305 12
  TRIUMPH THE ANCIENT PIG-TAILED MONSTER   426 14
  SLOWLY A GEM FORMS IN THE ANCIENT ONCE-MORE-MOLTEN   477 13
  OF TWO HUMAN HEARTS TWO ANCIENT ROCKS A MAN'S HEART   477 15
  OF THE ANCIENT CAVE SMASHING INTO ONE ANOTHER   544 15
  THAT ANCIENT EYES HAVE LEFT ON YOU WHERE OBSCENE EYES   581 3
  THE ANCIENT RIVER WEEK THE OLD ONE   702 20
  IN ANCIENT ROME DOWN THE THRONGED STREETS   703 24
  OH CHEW OLD COWS AT YOUR ANCIENT CUDS   814 20
  WAITING WAITING TILL AT LAST THE ANCIENT BOATMAN WITH T+   *958 11

'ANDFUL
  OVER A DOUBLE 'ANDFUL O' VIOLETS A' IN A PACK   61 11
  OVER A DOUBLE 'ANDFUL OF VIOLETS ALL IN A PACK   *911 27

ANDREW
  THE MAN ANDREW KEEP HIM SAFE IN THE WAR   751 10

ANEMONE
  THE BLUE ANEMONE WITH A DARK CORE   814 1
  BUDS A BLUE ANEMONE STILL BLUER   814 14
  OH AGE THAT IS HOAR AS ANEMONE BUDS   814 19

ANEMONES
  THE WILD ANEMONES LIE   126 10
  PASS THE MEN WHOSE EYES ARE SHUT LIKE ANEMONES IN A DAR+   180 20
  SCYLLAS AND YELLOW-HAIRED HELLEBORE JONQUILS DIM ANEMON+   270 7
  BUT OPENED AROUND HER PURPLE ANEMONES   308 12
  DARK BLUE ANEMONES   309 12
  AND NO MORE ANEMONES RISE FROM THE DEAD   815 12

ANEW
  BURST IT WITH GERMINATION WITH WORLD ANEW   273 9
  BLUE SILKEN SKY BEFORE THEY BEND ANEW   *895 4
  OUR DRAUGHT OF FAITH THAT SENT US ON ANEW   *941 12

ANGEL
  THE ANGEL OF CHILDHOOD KISSED ME AND WENT I EXPECTED   48 5
  ANGEL IN DISGUISE   234 10
  I MIGHT BE A SOUL IN BLISS AN ANGEL APPROXIMATING TO THE   321 2
  NEVER AN ANGEL WILL SOAR AGAIN   823 11

ANGEL-GUARDED
  BUT WE STORM THE ANGEL-GUARDED   243 9

ANGELIC
  AND I AM NOT THAT OTHER ANGELIC MATTER   321 6

ANGEL OF JUDGMENT
  THE ANGEL OF JUDGMENT HAS DEPARTED AGAIN TO THE NEARNESS   94 22

ANGELS
  AS IF MOVING IN AIR TOWARDS US TALL ANGELS   164 23
  THE ANGELS CAME TO ABRAHAM AND THEY STAYED   234 5
  NO ANGELS HERE FOR ME NO GODDESSES   234 19
  QUEENS LADIES ANGELS WOMEN RARE   234 25
  WHERE THE BRANDS OF THE ANGELS LIKE TORCHES   242 25
  NO NO IT IS THE THREE STRANGE ANGELS   250 31
  THEN WE SHALL BE FREE FREER THAN ANGELS AH PERFECT   267 23
  ANGELS   267 27
  MAN IS LOP-SIDED ON THE SIDE OF THE ANGELS   505 16
  A LITTLE LOWER THAN THE ANGELS   528 26
  FOR THOU HAST MADE HIM A LITTLE LOWER THAN THE ANGELS   548 33
  LIKE MONKEYS OR ANGELS OR SOMETHING IN A LIMITED   550 3
  ANGELS ARE BRIGHT STILL THOUGH THE BRIGHTEST FELL   614 12
  HE ONLY FELL OUT OF YOUR KEN YOU ORTHODOX ANGELS   614 15
  YOU DULL ANGELS TARNISHED WITH CENTURIES OF CONVENTIONA+   614 16
  WHAT LOUSY ARCHANGELS AND ANGELS YOU HAVE TO SURROUND   643 27
  HENCE THE RIDICULOUS WAY THEY RUSH IN WHERE ANGELS FEAR+   665 20
  AND THE FEED OF PAP THAT WE NURSES AND GUARDIAN ANGELS +   670 16
  ANGELS ARE BRIGHT STILL THOUGH THE BRIGHTEST FELL   697 23
  FOR THE UNSEEN WITNESSES ARE THE ANGELS OF CREATION   706 22
  BUT ALSO THE SUNDERERS THE ANGELS WITH BLACK SHARP WING+   706 23
  THE ANGELS ARE STANDING BACK THE ANGELS OF THE KISS   707 6
  AND THE ANGELS ARE STANDING BACK   707 25
  LIFE IS FOR THE ANGELS AND THE SUNDERERS   709 26
  THE ANGELS AND THE SUNDERERS   710 2
  WHERE THE ANGELS USED TO ALIGHT   725 19
  THOU NEWCOMER TO THE ANGELS   753 15
  PAST SALUTING SWORDS OF THE ANGELS   770 16
  THE ANGELS HAVE SOMEWHERE FOUGHT AND LOST   823 1
  THE ANGELS HAVE EVERYWHERE FOUGHT AND LOST   823 6
  THE ANGELS ARE GONE ALL THE HEAVENLY HOST   823 18
  THE BATTLE THAT THE ANGELS FOUGHT   824 4
  WHERE THRONGS OF ANGELS HASTENING UPON   872 18

ANGEL-STERN
  STANDING ANGEL-STERN AND TALL   140 10

ANGEL'S
  AS FREE AS THE RUNNING OF ANGEL'S FEET   746 18

ANGER
  AND I WANT TO SMITE IN ANGER THE BARREN ROCK OF EACH WA+   57 30
  SUCH ANGER AS SETS YOUR MOUTH UNWONTEDLY   85 20
  MYSELF IN ANGER AND YOU HAVE BENT   104 19
  SAVES YOU WAFTS YOU AWAY ON THE VERY DRAUGHT MY ANGER   334 8
  THEY EXCHANGE NO WORD NO SPASM NOT EVEN ANGER   337 18
  IN PURE BRILLIANCE OF ANGER SEA-IMMERSED ANGER   453 26
  A WAVE BURSTS IN ANGER ON A ROCK BROKEN UP   467 12
  BURNS THE SMALL FLAME OF ANGER GNAWING   601 9
  EITHER IN ANGER OR TENDERNESS OR DESIRE OR SADNESS OR W+   672 4
  AND THE SHUDDER OF ELECTRIC ANGER   707 10
  OH NOW THEY MOAN AND THRONG IN ANGER AND PRESS BACK   722 24
  WOMANLESS SHOUTING IN ANGER   759 3
  STONE OF ANGER AT THE BOTTOM   790 15
  THE DRAGONS IN THE COSMOS ARE STIRRING WITH ANGER AGAIN   795 11
  OF THE ANGER OF THE MANHOOD OF MEN   805 9
  I CARRY MY ANGER SULLENLY 'CROSS THESE WASTE LANDS   *896 21
  AND THEY SEND ARROWS OF ANGER BULLETS AND BOMBS OF FRUS+   *958 6

ANGERLESS
  AND THE LARK WILL FOLLOW TRILLING ANGERLESS AGAIN   625 6

ANGER-REDDENED
  THE ANGER-REDDENED GOLDEN-THROATED SALVIA   315 15

ANGLER
  WHEN THE EVIL ANGLER HAS PLAYED THEM LONG ENOUGH   586 17
  WHISTLING AND SEETHING AND PULLING THE ANGLER DOWN INTO   586 27

ANGRILY
  NOT ROAMING HERE DISCONSOLATE ANGRILY   740 24

ANGRY
  AND FROM THE SWIRLING ANGRY FOLK THAT TRY   89 24
  ANGRY AT THE SIMPLEST DOOR   95 13
  AND THROAT OF BRIMSTONE-MOLTEN ANGRY GOLD   317 11
  RED ANGRY MEN ARE A RACE EXTINCT ALAS   317 12
  SO NINE-TENTHS ASLEEP MOTIONLESS BORED AND STATICALLY A+   324 15
  IS SO ANGRY   374 22
  OF ETERNAL SALT RAGE ANGRY IS OLD OCEAN WITHIN A MAN   454 11
  LET ME TELL YOU THAT THE SUN IS ALIVE AND CAN BE ANGRY   625 13
  I SAW AN ANGRY ITALIAN SEIZE AN IRRITATING LITTLE OFFIC+   674 20
  ANGRY MAN   674 23
  DARKLY FROM THE FECUND COSMOS FROM THE ANGRY RED SUN FR+   675 11
  OH BUT BEWARE BEWARE THE ANGRY DEAD   723 3
  IS DUE TO THE ANGRY UNAPPEASED DEAD   723 5
  OF ELSE BEWARE THEIR ANGRY PRESENCE NOW   723 14
  OH THEY CAN LAY YOU WASTE THE ANGRY DEAD   723 16
  THEIR GHOSTS ARE ANGRY UNAPPEASED   739 6
  THEY ARE ANGRY WITH US   739 18
  GREY STERN ANGRY UNSATISFIED   739 26
  THE DEAD UNASSUAGED AND ANGRY SILENCING US   740 5

ANGRY
    FOR ONE YEAR'S SPACE ATTEND ON OUR ANGRY DEAD   740 16
    OR FLUFFED UP RATHER ANGRY AS A CAT DOES   836 15

ANGUISH
    AND MY HEART REBELS WITH ANGUISH AS NIGHT DRAWS NIGHER   48 13
    THE MOON WALKS HER LONELY WAY WITHOUT ANGUISH   63 20
    CEASE THEN FROM MUSIC DOES ANGUISH OF ABSENCE BEQUEATH   85 23
    THE THORN-LEAVES CRACKLED AND TWISTED AND SWEATED IN AN+   94 26
    FULL ANGUISH PERHAPS HAD BEEN CAST   111 31
    OF MORDANT ANGUISH TILL SHE CEASED TO LAUGH   125 17
    CAN KNOW THE FEARFUL ANGUISH THAT THIS IS SO   173 12
    WHEN TEARING THROUGH THE ANGUISH OF THIS LIFE   195 22
    OF SUDDEN ANGUISH SUDDEN OVER AND SPENT   196 4
    I STAND IN A CHILL OF ANGUISH TRYING TO SAY   225 31
    REACHING OUT IN ANGUISH YET UNABLE QUITE TO TOUCH THEM   233 4
    REACHING AND GRIPPING TENSE MORE REACHING ANGUISH IN   365 5
    NOR EVE FOR YOUR HEAVY ANGUISH OF EMBRACE   876 17
    WHO ACHE WITH AN ANGUISH OF MUSIC TO MAKE FOR YOU   884 19
    THE THORN-LEAVES CRACKLED AND TWISTED AND SWEATED IN AN+   *897 14
    FIRE-THRESHING ANGUISH HAD BEEN FUSED AND CAST   *927 19
    ANGUISH THEN I SUFFERED A BALK   *928 10
    FIRE-THRESHING ANGUISH WERE FUSED AND CAST   *928 19
    OF ANGUISH TILL SHE CEASED TO LAUGH TILL DOWN   *936 16
    YOUR TRIUMPH OF ANGUISH ABOVE YOU THEY WOULD SAY   *941 8

ANGUISHED
    TURNS BACK HER LIQUID ANGUISHED EYES   43 6
    AND I DO LIFT MY ANGUISHED AVID BREAST   129 20
    BUT THE UTTER ANGUISHED SPRINGING FORTH OF ME   880 5

ANIMAL
    INDISCRIMINATING ANIMAL   396 2
    MEN THE ONLY ANIMAL IN THE WORLD TO FEAR   401 6
    NO ANIMAL NO BEAST NOR CREEPING THING   701 12
    LET HIM HAVE NO ANIMAL WALK ON HIS BODY NOR THROUGH THE+   791 24
    NOR EVEN LIKE AN ANIMAL BULL RAM OR LION OR LAMB   840 26

ANIMALS
    THE ASS WAS THE FIRST OF ALL ANIMALS TO FALL FINALLY IN+   378 16
    AND THINK HOW WILD ANIMALS TROT WITH SPLENDOUR   530 12
    AND THE ANIMALS CURL DOWN ON THE DEAR EARTH TO SLEEP   834 3

ANIMATE
    ALL ANIMATE CREATION ON YOUR SHOULDER   353 32
    THE IMMUNE THE ANIMATE   360 30

ANIMATED
    THEY STOLE YOUR BODY FROM YOU AND LEFT YOU AN ANIMATED   630 26

ANIMATION
    BRISTLING WITH ANIMATION OH PLEASE SIR HOW D'YOU LIKE T+   865 21

ANKLE
    SCALY ANKLE   360 21
    SUDDENLY SEIZING THE UGLY ANKLE AS SHE STRETCHES OUT TO   361 17

ANKLES
    AT HER WHITE ANKLES   309 19
    AT HER ANKLES AND CATCHING HER BY THE HAIR   309 19
    NIPPING HER ANKLES   360 10
    O LET MY ANKLES BE BATHED IN MOONLIGHT THAT I   684 10
    AND PUTTING HIS STRENGTH IN YOUR HEELS AND ANKLES HIS F+   801 24
    EASY EASY AND EASY DOWN TO MY ANKLES   835 33
    YOUR FEET AND TOUCHING YOUR ANKLES TRY   887 16

ANNA
    OF REBELS LIKE ANNA AND VRONSKY   536 14
    ALL MY SAINTS AND ANNA TERESA   798 7

ANNA KARENIN
    IF VRONSKY AND ANNA KARENIN   536 8

ANNAS
    IT IS STRANGE TO THINK OF THE ANNAS THE VRONSKYS THE   533 11

ANNIHILATE
    I WISH WITH MY BREAST I HERE COULD ANNIHILATE IT ALL   173 16
    I DON'T AT ALL WANT TO ANNIHILATE THEM   316 14

ANNIHILATES
    ENDS THIS DARKNESS THAT ANNIHILATES ME   221 4

ANNIHILATION
    WILL THE DARK FLOOD OF OUR DAY'S ANNIHILATION   428 24
    TO THE PIT OF ANNIHILATION   468 8

ANNOUNCE
    AND ROARS TO ANNOUNCE HIMSELF TO THE WOLVES   325 20

ANNOUNCEMENT
    GROUND WITH A SUDDEN ROCK-HAMMER ANNOUNCEMENT   381 14

ANNOUNCING
    AND ANNOUNCING BATTLE READY   327 2
    ANNOUNCING HE'S HERE   405 12

ANNUNCIATION
    SETTING SUPREME ANNUNCIATION TO THE WORLD   304 21
    WITH HIS OWN ANNUNCIATION TOWARDS US   697 31
    AND HONKING WITH A HORN-LIKE ANNUNCIATION OF LIFE FROM +   841 6

ANOINT
    THEY ANOINT THEIR BROWS WITH YOUR PAIN AS A PERFECT   168 19
    WREATHE AND ENLAP AND ANOINT THEM   229 3

ANON
    AND EVER AND ANON THE GREAT BREATHS COME   878 32

ANSWER
    SHOULD I NOT ANSWER TO HIS TALK   43 16
    OLD QUESTION WITHOUT ANSWER STRANGE AND FAIN   69 27
    HOW CAN I ANSWER THE CHALLENGE OF SO MANY EYES   76 5
    THEM AN ANSWER BACK IT IS MORE THAN I CAN BEAR   76 13
    THA'S GOTTEN THY ANSWER PAT   80 4
    I SHALL GET NO ANSWER IN ANY HOUR   106 21
    TO ME THAT I ANSWER YES   109 6
    THE ANSWER THEY DID DEVISE   124 22
    YOU WOULD NOT TURN AND ANSWER ME   130 27
    YOU ARE THE CALL AND I AM THE ANSWER   203 22
    AND ANSWER THE FIRST MACHINE-CUT QUESTION FROM THE LIPS+   291 2
    HE DOES NOT EVEN TROUBLE TO ANSWER WOMAN WHAT HAVE   357 3
    A SCORCHED BREAST BREASTING THE SUN LIKE AN ANSWER   372 27
    THAT BEING HER WAY OF ANSWER IF I SPEAK TO HER SELF-CON+   385 5
    AND LEAVE HIM FOREVER LISTENING FOR THE ANSWER   439 10
    NO ANSWER MAN RISES AGAIN   461 14
    ANSWER WITHOUT A RIGMAROLE   545 7
    EH ANSWER ME THAT   547 24
    BECAUSE I COULD NOT ANSWER THE RIDDLE OF HER OWN SELF-I+   604 12
    OH WHAT IN YOU CAN ANSWER TO THIS BLUENESS   684 3
    HE LOOKED AT ME WITHOUT ANSWER BUT SUCH A LOVELINESS   692 15
    ANSWER ADIOS   798 32
    THERE IS NO ANSWER   816 14
    STILL TO ANSWER ME JUST THE SAME   873 8
    HOW CAN I ANSWER THE CHALLENGE OF SO MANY EYES   *897 32
    THEM AN ANSWER BACK IT IS MORE THAN I CAN BEAR   *898 7
    HOW CAN I ANSWER THE CHALLENGE OF SO MANY EYES   *901 9
    THEM AN ANSWER BACK IT IS MORE THAN I CAN BEAR   *901 16
    HERE HAVE I FOUND AN ANSWER FOR MY HOLLOW YEARNING   *907 10
    HERE IN MY CLASS IS THE ANSWER FOR THE GREAT YEARNING   *909 6
    THA'S GOTTEN THY ANSWER PAT   *922 4
    AN' ANSWER ME FOR I'VE SAID MY SAY AN' THERE'S NO MORE +   *925 22
    THE ANSWER THEY DID DEVISE   *935 22
    MY QUIVERING ANSWER AND KISSES LIKE FRAGRANCE OF FLOWERS   *942 3

ANSWERED
    ITS RAINY SWILL ABOUT US SHE ANSWERED ME   180 14
    SINGING AND CALLING AND SINGING AGAIN BEING ANSWERED   366 36
    THEY ASK AND THEY MUST BE ANSWERED THEY   461 9
    HE ANSWERED DEAR BRITANNIA WHY   577 9
    CHALLENGES ME AND IS ANSWERED   *906 25

ANSWERS
    LO THE GREAT ONE ANSWERS TRACK HIM DOWN   808 7
    ANSWERS THE QUESTION AS HE PUTS IT IN HIS STRIDE   816 8
    HER QUIVERING ANSWERS AND KISSES LIKE THIEVING BIRDS   868 31
    SHAPE ANSWERS SHAPE IN CHORUS TO THE SIGHT   872 17
    THE MAN ANSWERS AND SHE MOCKS   *945 16

ANT
    NO COBRA NOR HYAENA NOR SCORPION NOR HIDEOUS WHITE ANT   701 13

ANTENNAE
    WITH ITS LONG ANTENNAE OF RAGE PUT OUT   315 16
    NO GALVIA FRENZIED COMRADES ANTENNAE   317 8

ANT-EYES
    FOR SPECTACLES AND BULGING CLEVER ANT-EYES ARE NO GOOD +   544 7

ANTHONY
    ANTHONY MIGHT HAVE MADE A SPLENDID THING OF THE EAST   479 24
    JOAQUIN FRANCIS AND ANTHONY   798 13

ANTHROPOLOGISTS
    ANTHROPOLOGISTS HISTORIANS AND MEN OF LETTERS   780 8

ANTICIPATED
    WHEN EVERYTHING WAS ME I KNEW IT ALL ALREADY I ANTICIPA+   257 11

ANTICIPATION
    AH DO NOT LET ME DIE ON THE BRINK OF SUCH ANTICIPATION   274 7

ANTI-CLIMAX
    AND NAKED EMBRACE AN ANTI-CLIMAX HUMILIATING AND RIDICU+   608 19

ANTICS
    PERFORMING OUR ANTICS   544 2

ANTI-LIFE
    THERE IS ONLY LIFE AND ANTI-LIFE   679 19

ANTIPODAL
    BUT THE YELLOW ANTIPODAL KANGAROO WHEN SHE SITS UP   392 27
    HER FULL ANTIPODAL EYES SO DARK   393 11

ANTIPODES
    TO THE DARK ZENITH OF THINE ANTIPODES   322 19

ANTIQUITY
    AND SMILES THE VASTNESS OF HER ELEPHANT ANTIQUITY   426 6

ANTLERED
    ANTLERED   222 18

ANTLERS
    AND THE EXTINCT GIANT ELK TOO BIG IN ANTLERS   529 18

ANT-MEN
    AH CYCLOPS THE LITTLE ANT-MEN CAN NEVER ENLIGHTEN YOU   544 20

ANTS
    THREADING LIKE ANTS THAT CAN NEVER RELENT   50 29
    CLEVER LITTLE ANTS IN SPECTACLES WE ARE   544 1
    AS LITTLE SOCIAL ANTS PERHAPS WE FUNCTION ALL RIGHT   544 14
    MOST MEN DON'T MATTER AT ALL ANY MORE THAN ANTS MATTER   638 11
ANVIL
    ON YOUR BODY THE BEATEN ANVIL   168 21
    THINGS OF IRON ARE BEATEN ON THE ANVIL   381 31
    AND HE-GOAT IS ANVIL TO HE-GOAT AND HAMMER TO HE-GOAT   381 32
ANXIETIES
    ALL THE TROUBLES AND ANXIETIES AND PAIN   203 13
    TROUBLES ANXIETIES AND PAINS   203 21
    I HAVE A CERTAIN AMOUNT OF MONEY SO MY ANXIETIES ARE BL+   501 21
ANXIETY
    IN A THAW OF ANXIETY FOR THE BOY   100 7
    BURNS LIKE A BLOT OF ANXIETY   103 11
    MY ANXIETY IN A HEAT OF LOVE   *936 8
ANXIOUS
    INTO THE EVENING'S ANXIOUS BREAST   42 7
    TALL AND DARK THE CHURCH MOVES ANXIOUS TO KEEP   48 21
    WELL YOU ANXIOUS INQUISITIVE LOVER   95 14
    THAT WHIRL AND SWEEP LIKE ANXIOUS LEAVES AWAY   744 14
    THE CATTLE RUN ANXIOUS IN QUEST AS THE TIME DRAWS NIGH   749 25
    WHY ARE YOU SO ANXIOUS LEAVE ME PEACEFUL WITH MY DEAD   756 17
ANXIOUSLY
    PEER ANXIOUSLY FORTH AS IF FOR A BOAT TO CARRY THEM OUT+   71 26
    THIS TRAIN BEATS ANXIOUSLY OUTWARD BOUND   169 4
    AND ANXIOUSLY LIKE A BOY AFRAID TO BE FOUND OUT   734 4
ANYBODY
    WHO ARE YOU WHO IS ANYBODY TO TELL ME I AM WRONG   278 2
    YOU DON'T CARE A RAP FOR ANYBODY   396 18
    TO ALL AND ANYBODY ALL AND ANYBODY ALL OVER THE WORLD   487 10
    NOR ANYBODY ELSE   508 24
    THAN TO SHELTER ANYBODY FROM THE COLD BLAST   540 30
    NEED TO KNOW ABOUT ANYBODY AND DO YOU KNOW I'VE NEVER B+ 546 18
    AND WHOEVER FORCES HIMSELF TO LOVE ANYBODY   653 3
    FOR WE CAN'T LOVE ANYBODY NEIGHBOUR OR NO NEIGHBOUR TO + 654 8
    AND TO SACRIFICE THAT TO ANYTHING OR ANYBODY WHATSOEVER   680 1
    I WOULD WARN ANYBODY AGAINST A CULTURE   763 13
    AS RICH AS ANYBODY ELSE ON THE SAME TERMS   778 15
ANYHOW
    ANYHOW A CARPENTER AND JOINER   452 26
    THE THOUGHT IS UNTHINKABLE ANYHOW   479 15
    ANYHOW THEY NEVER WILL EXCEPT FOR SECONDARY MOTIVES   485 22
    LET PEOPLE BE WISE FOR THEMSELVES AND ANYHOW   495 23
    IS THEIR MONEY BUT I DOUBT IF I'D FIGHT FOR MINE ANYHOW   497 20
    DON'T DO IT ANYHOW FOR INTERNATIONAL LABOUR   517 17
    ANYHOW   518 20
    ANYHOW GONE FROM WHAT THEY WERE ENTIRELY   533 20
    ANYHOW THE TOLSTOYAN LOT SIMPLY ASKED FOR EXTINCTION   533 24
    ANYHOW   547 12
    ANYHOW SHE DESPISES   565 1
    THE MILLS OF GOD WILL GRIND THEM SMALL ANYHOW THERE IS + 614 18
    AND ANYHOW THEY CAN'T DO ANY HURT   634 12
    OH HE'S AN HONEST MAN ANYHOW   659 21
ANYONE
    IF I COULD IF ANYONE COULD   118 27
    WHICH IS JUST A STONE TO ANYONE ASKING FOR MEAT   414 31
    BUT ANYONE WHO SHALL ASCRIBE ATTRIBUTES TO GOD OR   726 12
    IF I CAN IF ANYONE COULD   *932 5
ANYTHING
    IF ANYTHING AILED 'IM AT ANY RATE   45 19
    I AM LISTENING IS ANYTHING SAID   140 22
    ANYTHING IN SUCH IMMENSITY I AM TOO   223 11
    NEVER OF COURSE TO PUT ANYTHING UP AGAIN   317 32
    HER BRIGHT EYE SEES BUT NOT ME NOT ANYTHING   359 16
    BEFORE ANYTHING HAD A SOUL   372 9
    SO I CAN'T SEE WHERE THE WORM THAT HAS TURNED PUTS ANYT+ 432 34
    MEANS ANYTHING FURTHER AND PHYSICAL   470 12
    WE ARE ALMOST ANYTHING   480 3
    HEAVIER AND HOTTER THAN ANYTHING KNOWN   480 12
    SO IF YOU WANT EITHER OF US TO FEEL ANYTHING AT 'ALL   501 14
    AND I CAN'T DO ANYTHING ABOUT IT EVEN THERE I AM BLANK   501 22
    WANTS US OR CAN HAVE ANYTHING TO DO WITH US   514 21
    WHY ISN'T ANYTHING FREE WHY IS IT ALWAYS PAY PAY PAY   518 3
    HE REPLIED TO THRILL TO ANYTHING   532 4
    OH SAFER THAN ANYTHING ELSE IN A WELL-CORKED GLASSY EGO   543 2
    IF THERE'S ANYTHING GOT TO BE DONE WHY   553 21
    FEELING ANYTHING BUT GAY   569 20
    IS BETTER THAN ANYTHING ELSE IN THE WORLD   601 5
    I CAN'T SEE THAT I REFUSE ANYTHING   611 4
    MEN ARE ANYTHING BUT ALIKE IN THE SIGHT OF GOD   638 9
    YOU CAN COUNT ON ANYTHING BUT YOU CAN'T COUNT ON   639 14
    THEY NEVER DID ANYTHING   658 21
    YOU CAN JUST SAY ANYTHING TO THEM   660 13
    YOU WILL REALISE THERE WAS NEVER ANYTHING TO SEEK FOR   661 2
    IT CANNOT BE ANYTHING BUT WRONG TO SACRIFICE   678 2
    JUST AS IT CANNOT BE ANYTHING BUT WRONG TO CUT THE THRO+ 678 4
    ANYTHING THAT BELONGS TO US AND IS UGLY AND AN IMPEDIME+ 678 15
    AND TO SACRIFICE THAT TO ANYTHING OR ANYBODY WHATSOEVER   680 1
    AS IF THE REDNESS OF A RED GERANIUM COULD BE ANYTHING B+ 690 15
    BECAUSE NAKED YOU ARE MORE WONDERFUL THAN ANYTHING WE C+ 695 18
    NOT ANYTHING NOR EVER AGAIN ASK WHY   738 26
    DO ANYTHING BUT DO SOMETHING TO DRAW THIS ONE   780 11
    THEY DON'T MIND BEING DEPRAVED IMMORAL OR ANYTHING OF T+ 829 12
    ANYTHING RATHER THAN THAT CERTAIN BACK OF A NECK   836 3
    ANYTHING THAT EXPRESSED LIFE   837 17
    SLIPPED LIKE ANYTHING BUT DON'T YOU LIKE IT AIN'T IT FI+ 865 23
    DON JUAN WAS NEVER ANYTHING BUT A SELF-THWARTED SODOMIST *949 17

ANYTHING
    AND GREATER HEAT INTO FIRE MORE HEAVY AND HOTTER THAN A+ *951 21
    SO PONDEROUSLY CENTRAL HEAVIER AND HOTTER THAN ANYTHING+ *951 25
ANYTHINK
    FOR ANYTHINK OF HIS   *924 20
ANYWHERE
    THAT ENDS NOT ANYWHERE   203 6
    HAVING NO ADHERENCE NO ADHESION ANYWHERE   267 19
    AND HAS NO HOME NO HOME ANYWHERE   712 4
    ANYWHERE NOWHERE THE DEAD ROAD GOES   858 4
    ANYWHERE   867 18
'AN
    'AN 'APPEN YOU MIGHT GUESS WHAT I'VE COME FOR   *923 23
AN'
    MOTHER COME DOWN AN' SEE   44 11
    SHOUT AN' AX WHAT 'E WANTS   44 18
    COME OUT O' TH' WAY AN' LET ME SEE   45 1
    AN' STOP THY SCRAIGHTIN' CHILDT   45 3
    AN' THEY TA'EIN' 'IM I' TH' AMBULANCE   45 6
    'AVE I PUT 'IS CLEAN STOCKIN'S AN' SHIRT   45 14
    AN' WHAT A MOAN 'E'LL MAKE THERE NIVER   45 17
    AN' OTHERS 'AS REAMS   45 24
    OWT BAD AN' IT'S HIS   45 28
    AN' THERE'S COMPENSATION SIN' IT'S ACCIDENT   45 32
    AN' CLUB-MONEY I WON'T GROWSE   45 33
    AN' A FORK AN' A SPOON 'E'LL WANT AN' WHAT ELSE   46 1
    ASIDE O' T' GRAVE AN' TH' COFFIN SET   60 12
    AN' T' PARSON MAKIN' HASTE AN' A' T' BLACK   60 15
    HOVERIN' LOOKIN' POOR AN' PLAIN   60 18
    AN' ME STANDIN' THERE ON TH' PLANK   60 20
    AN' OUR TED'S COFFIN SET ON TH' GROUND   60 21
    THAT YOUNG AN' A' THE FAULT OF DRINK   60 25
    AN' CARRYIN'S ON   60 26
    THA SHOULD HA' SEED 'ER KNEEL AN' LOOK IN   61 6
    AT TH' SLOPPY GRAVE AN' 'ER LITTLE NECK SHONE   61 7
    THAT WHITE AN' 'ER CRIED THAT MUCH I'D LIKE TO BEGIN   61 8
    JACKET AT TH' BOSOM AN' TOOK OUT   61 10
    AN' WHITE AN' BLUE IN A RAVEL LIKE A CLOUT   61 12
    AN' WARM FOR TH' SMELL COME WAFTIN' TO ME 'ER PUT 'ER F+   61 13
    RIGHT IN 'EM AN' SCRAIGHTED A BIT AGAIN   61 14
    AN' I COME AWAY ACAUSE O' TH' TEEMIN' RAIN   61 16
    AY AN' YALLER AS A CROWFLOWER AN' YET I' TH' DARK   77 7
    AN' 'IM TO 'AVE BEEN TOOK IN   77 16
    ATWEEN A LAD AN' 'IS WIFE   77 20
    WITCH TEETH AN' 'ER BLACK HAWK-EYES AS I'VE   77 23
    AN' ME AS 'AS KEP' MY-SEN   77 25
    CLEAN AN' NEW AN' NICE SO'S WHEN   77 27
    AN' 'IM AS NICE AN' FRESH   77 29
    TO HA' GONE AN' GIVEN HIS CLEAN YOUNG FLESH   77 31
    WHY YOUR YOUNG MAN AN' WIDOW NAYLOR   78 9
    AN' IF IT'S NOT TRUE YOU MAY BACK YOUR LIFE   78 15
    AN' WHEN I KNOW FOR SURE MISSIS   78 19
    LARROPIN' NECK AN' CROP   78 30
    AS STOUT AS THE TRUTH MY SIRS AN' 'IS FACE   79 6
    FOR THIS NICE OLD SHAME AN' DISGRACE   79 8
    YI AN' 'IS FACE GOES WHITE OH YES   79 10
    DONE I SHOULD THINK SO AN' MIGHT I ASK   79 31
    SO THERE AN' I TELL THEE FLAT   80 2
    AN' WALKIN' IN AGONY   80 8
    AN' THA'S LAID AGAINST ME AN' MELTED   80 10
    AN' IF MY LANDLADY SEED ME LIKE IT   80 13
    AN' IF 'ER CLAWKIN' EYES   80 14
    AFTER KISSIN' AN' CUDDLIN' WI' ME THA COULD   80 18
    AN' 'ER MAUN TA'E 'ER LUCK   81 2
    'E UP AN' FIRED 'IS PISTOL   81 7
    AN' THEN AWAY 'E RAN   81 8
    AM' THERE'S THE DARK-BLUE TIE I BOUGHT 'IM   81 14
    AN' THESE IS THE WOMAN'S KIDS 'E'S SO FOND ON   81 15
    AN' 'ERE COMES THE CAT AS CAUGHT 'IM   81 16
    AN' 'APPEN YOU'D GUESS THEN WHAT I'VE COME FOR   81 23
    AN' YET YER'VE BIN CARRYIN' ON WI' 'IM   81 27
    AY AN' 'IM WI' ME   81 28
    I'M NOT 'AVIN' YOUR ORTS AN' SLARTS   82 3
    THOUGH I'LL SEE AS 'E PAYS YOU AN' DOES WHAT'S RIGHT   82 7
    TO THINK I SHOULD 'AVE TER 'AFFLE AN' CAFFLE   82 9
    WI' A WOMAN AN' NAME 'ER A PRICE   82 10
    TER MARRY WI' CABS AN' RICE   82 12
    AN' GIVE 'ER THE MONEY THERE IS   82 14
    AN' COME IN 'ERE WI' ME   82 18
    AN' LOOK AT ME   82 20
    I DO AN' THAT I DO   82 22
    TWENTY POUND O' THY OWN THA HAST AN' FIFTY POUND HA'E I   83 1
    THINE SHALL GO TER PAY THE WOMAN AN' WI' MY BIT WE'LL B+   83 2
    AN' WE'LL BE MARRIED AT TH' REGISTRAR NOW LIFT THY FACE   83 4
    LIFT THY FACE AN' LOOK AT ME MAN CANNA TER LOOK AT ME   83 5
    SORRY I AM FOR THIS BUSINESS AN' SORRY IF EVER I'VE DRI+   83 6
    AN' 'DEED AN' I WISH AS THIS TALE O' THINE WOR NIVER MY+   83 10
    DEED AN' I WISH I C'D 'A' STOOD AT TH' ALTAR WI' THEE A+   83 11
    BUT WE MAUN MA'E THE BEST ON'T SO NOW ROUSE UP AN' LOOK+   83 14
    LOOK UP AN' SAY THA'RT SORRY THA DID IT SAY THA'RT SORR+   83 15
    AN' 'ER AS WELL   83 27
    AN' THA'RT THAT RIGHT THA KNOWS 'TIS   83 28
    FROM YOU AN' FROM 'ER   84 16
    SO I S'LL GO AN' LEAVE YER   84 17
    AN' I REALLY LIKE 'ER NEITHER   84 21
    AN' 'S NOT GOOD ENOUGH IT ISN'T   84 31
    AN' WI' 'ER SOMEHOW IT ISN'T RIGHT   85 3
    SO GOOD-BYE AN' LET'S BE   85 4
    AN' MIST IS SUCKIN' AT TH' SPOTS O' SNOW   137 21
    AN' OWER A' THE THAW AN' MESS   137 22
    WHILE T' CLOCKS 'AS A' RUN DOWN AN' STOPPED   137 28
    AN' T' SHORT DAYS GOIN' UNKNOWN TER THEE   137 29
    ON THY FACE AS THA GOT MORE WHITE AN' WAN   138 5
    THA COME TER HA' FINISHED AN' DONE WI' ME   138 10

AN'

AN' OFF TO A GEL AS WOR YOUNGER THAN ME	138 11
AN' FRESH AN' MORE NICER FOR MARRYIN' WI'	138 12
THERE'S HARDLY OWT LEFT O' THEE GET UP AN' GO	138 18
AS 'UD MAKE THEE A WIFE AN' LOOK UP TER THEE	138 30
AS 'UD WINCE WHEN THAT TOUCHED 'ER CLOSE AN'	138 31
AN' LIE FRIGHTENED TER DEATH UNDER THEE	138 33
'APPEN THA DID AN' A'	139 2
THA THOUGHT THA WANTED TER MARRY AN' SEE	139 3
IF TER COULDNA BE MASTER AN' TH' WOMAN'S BOSS	139 4
AN' THA KNOWED IT AY YET THA COMES ACROSS	139 6
TER SAY GOOD-BYE AN' A'	139 7
O' THY SPUNK AN' THA'RT EMPTY AN' MORTIFIED	139 12
EMPTY AN' EMPTY FROM BOTTOM TO TOP	139 13
AN' I'VE LOVED THEE FOR IT	139 16
AN' A WOMAN LIKE ME LOVES THEE FOR IT	139 20
AY AN' THA MAUN	139 22
NOW GO AN' MARRY THAT WENCH AN' SEE	139 31
WEARY AN' SICK O' THE LIKES O' SHE	139 33
AN' HANKERIN' FOR ME BUT GO	139 34
HE IS AN' ALL YOU BET 'E IS	434 21
ABAHT IT YES I'M A GENT AN' LIZ	434 23
ALL THE HINGLISH IS GENTLEMAN AN' LIDIES	434 27
LIKE THE KING AN' QUEEN THOUGH THEY'RE	434 28
'ARK 'ERE LAD ATWEEN THEE AN' ME	490 28
AN' I RECKON IT'S NOWT BUT RIGHT	491 2
WE SHOULD START AN' KICK THEIR -SES FOR 'EM	491 3
AN' TELL 'EM TO	491 4
AN' MAKING US COME UNCURLED	493 8
AN' LIFE SEEMS TO BEGIN	493 10
AN' THEN HE LEADS YOU BY THE NOSE	493 13
AN' LEAVES YOU NEVER A TRIMMIN'	493 16
AN' THEN SOMEBODY HAS TER MARRY YOU	493 17
IT'S YOUR WIFE WI' HER AIRS AN' GRACES	493 20
COME AN' BE STILL WI' ME MY OWN BIT OF A WENCH	540 10
IF THA CANNA SAY'T COME THEN AN' SCRAIGHT IT OUT ON MY	540 14
AN' THA'LT FEEL BETTER	540 19
RIGHT CH'ARE BOSS AN' WHAT ABAHT IT	547 25
BUT THEY'RE ALL ALIKE AN' IT MAKES YOU	550 9
WANT TO GET UP AN' SHOUT	550 10
AN' BLAST 'EM FOREVER BUT THEY'D ONLY	550 17
AN' YOU COULD NO MORE GET 'EM A MOVE ON	550 17
UP I ROSE MY LADS AN' I HEARD YER	552 17
AN' IF YOU DID YOU'D FIND	552 28
GOIN' UP AN' BEIN' REFINED	553 2
AN' ALL THEY CAN THINK OF IS SINS	553 12
GET UP AN' DO IT YOURSELVES	553 22
AN' IF YOU'RE NOT ANY BETTER	553 25
WE'D BETTER GET OUT AN' MAKE WAY FOR	553 31
WE'RE GETTING TO BE BIG LADS NOW AN' SOON	573 19
PLEASE SIR I WAS SWEEPING SNOW AN' I NEVER HEARD THE BE+	866 9
TILL HE SAW ME BUT PLEASE SIR MY MOVVER SAID I COULD AN'	866 19
WE AIN'T GOT NO FARVER ONLY A MOVVER AN' SHE 'AS TER GO	866 20
NAY I SAW NOWT BUT TH' COFFIN AN' TH' YELLER CLAY AN' '+	*909 31
WHILE TH' PARSON WAS PRAYIN' I WATCHES 'ER AN' SHE WOR +	*910 1
I COULD THINK O' NOWT BUT OUR TED AN' 'IM TAKEN	*910 3
YOU SHOULD 'A SEEN HER KNEEL AN' LOOK DOWN	*910 10
WHITE WHEN THE WIND SHIFTED HER HAIR THAT WAS SOFT AN' +	*910 12
AN' 'ER BODY FAIR SHOOK AGAIN	*910 13
AN' SHE UNDID 'ER JACKET NECK AN' THEN	*910 15
BECAUSE THEY WAS WARM AN' THE WIND BLEW	*910 18
US A LITTLE WIFT AN' I KNEW THE SMELL	*910 19
THEN SHE RUMMAGED HER HAND IN 'ER BOSOM AN' KISSED THE +	*910 20
THA KNOWS 'E 'D A WINSOME WAY WI 'IM AN' SHE	*910 24
ON TH' YALLER CLAY AN' TH' WHITE FLOWERS TOP OF IT	*910 28
AN' PARSON MAKIN' HASTE AN' A' THE BLACK	*911 1
BY A HEAD-STUN SOBBIN' AN' SOBBIN' AGAIN	*911 4
AN' ME STANDIN' ON THE PLANK	*911 6
YI AN' 'IM THAT YOUNG	*911 9
LIKE BETTER NOR ALL YOUR GOOD AN' 'E WAS ONE	*911 14
AN' COS I LIKED HIM BEST YI BETT'R NOR THEE	*911 15
AN' WATCHED WHAT 'ER 'AD ON	*911 20
THA SHOULD HA' SEED HER KNEEL AN' LOOK IN	*911 22
AT TH' SLOPPY WET GRAVE AN' 'ER LITTLE NECK SHONE	*911 23
THAT WHITE AN' 'ER SHOOK THAT MUCH I'D LIKE TO BEGIN	*911 24
JACKET AT TH' BOSOM AN' TOOK FROM OUT OF IT	*911 31
AN' I COME AWAY BECAUSE O' THE TEEMIN' RAIN	*911 32
AY AN' YALLER AS A CROWFLOWER AN' YET I' THE DARK	*918 25
AN' 'IM TO HAVE BEEN TOOK IN	*919 4
ATWEEN A LAD AN' 'IS WIFE	*919 8
WITCH TEETH AN' 'ER BLACK HAWK-EYES AS I'VE	*919 11
AN' ME AS 'AS KEP MY-SEN	*919 13
CLEAN NEW AN' NICE SO'S WHEN	*919 15
AN' 'IM AS NICE AN' FRESH	*919 17
TO HA'E GONE AN' GIVEN HIS WHITE YOUNG FLESH	*919 19
WHY YOUR YOUNG MAN AN' WIDOW NAYLOR	*920 1
AN' IF IT'S NOT TRUE I'D BACK MY LIFE	*920 7
AN' WHEN I KNOW FOR SURE MISSIS	*920 11
LARROPIN' NECK AN' CROP	*920 22
AS STOUT AS THE TRUTH MY SIRS AN' 'IS FACE	*921 5
YES AN' 'IS FACE GOES WHITE OH YES	*921 6
AN' 'ER'S WANTIN IT I HEAR	*921 16
AN' WALKIN' IN AGONY	*922 8
THA'S LAIN RIGHT UP TO ME LIZZIE AN' MELTED	*922 10
AN' IF MY LANDLADY SEED ME LIKE IT	*922 13
AN' IF 'ER CLAWKIN' TIGER'S EYES	*922 14
AFTERWARDS AN' AFTER HOW LONG	*922 23
AN' GI'E HER THEE BACK AGAIN	*922 28
AN' SHE MAUN TA'E HER LUCK	*923 2
HE UP AN' FIRED OFF HIS PISTOL	*923 7
AN' THEN AWAY HE RAN	*923 8
AN' THAT'S THE DARK BLUE TIE I BOUGHT 'IM	*923 14
AN' THESE IS THE WOMAN'S KIDS HE'S SO FOND ON	*923 15
AN' 'ERE COMES THE CAT THAT CAUGHT 'IM	*923 23
AN' YET YOU'VE BEEN CARRYIN' ON WI' HIM	*923 27
AY AN' 'IM WI' ME	*923 32
AN' IF I HAN WHAT'S THAT TO THEE	*924 2
IS IT A TOSS-UP 'TWIXT THEE AN' ME	*924 4

IT'S NO TOSS-UP 'TWIXT THEE AN' ME	*924 5
I'M NOT HAVIN' YOUR ORTS AN' SLARTS	*924 7
THOUGH I'LL SEE AS 'E PAYS YOU AN' COMES TO THE SCRATCH	*924 11
TO THINK I SHOULD HA'E TO HAFFLE AN' CAFFLE	*924 13
WI' A WOMAN AN' PAY 'ER A PRICE	*924 14
TO MARRY WI' CABS AN' RICE	*924 16
AN' GIVE 'ER WHAT MONEY THERE IS	*924 18
AN' COME WI' ME IN HERE	*924 22
AN' LOOK ME CLEAR	*924 24
I DO AN' THAT I DO	*924 26
THINE SHALL GO TO PAY THE WOMAN AN' WI' MY BIT WE'LL BUY	*925 6
AN' WE'LL BE MARRIED AT TH' REGISTRAR NOW LIFT THY FACE	*925 8
LIFT THY FACE AN' LOOK AT ME MAN UP AN' LOOK AT ME	*925 9
SORRY I AM FOR THIS BUSINESS AN' SORRY IF I HA'E DRIVEN+	*925 13
BUT 'DEED AN' I WISH AS THIS TALE O' THINE WOR NIVER MY+	*925 14
DEED AN' I WISH AS I COULD STOOD AT THE ALTAR WI' THEE +	*925 15
AN' THEN WI' THAT TWENTY POUND WE GI'E 'ER I S'D THINK +	*925 20
SO VERY MUCH WORSER OFF THAN 'ER WOR BEFORE AN' NOW LOO+	*925 21
AN' ANSWER ME FOR I'VE SAID MY SAY AN' THERE'S NO MORE +	*925 22
AS SULKY AN' ORMIN' AS THINE HAST OWT TO SAY OTHERWISE	*925 25
HIS SCYTHE STONE AN' OVER THE GRASS TO ME	*944 13
AN' A MAN AN' A FATHER THA'LT HA'E TO BE	*944 15
MY YOUNG SLIM LAD AN' I'M SORRY FOR THEE	*944 16

APACE

THE FIRE ROSE UP IN THE BUSH AND BLAZED APACE	94 25

APART

HOW LONG HAVE THEY TUGGED THE LEASH AND STRAINED APART	74 8
BUT WHOEVER WOULD PLUCK APART MY FLOWERING WILL BURN TH+	93 29
WILL YOU PLUCK IT APART	117 21
A BROWN BEE PULLING APART	124 29
IS LOST SINCE WE FALL APART	163 6
MANY SUSPENDED TOGETHER FOREVER APART	337 20
EACH ONE APART AND INSTANT	371 12
TURN FEET APART	389 10
THE BODY INTO IT LET US STAY APART	469 5
AND APART IN THIS CEREBRAL AGE	469 7
AND QUITE APART	470 17
PERSONALITIES EXIST APART	471 10
LET US LEAVE IT ALONE PHYSICALLY KEEP APART	471 26
QUITE APART FROM SODOM	562 23
FOR WE ENGLISH ARE REALLY A RACE APART	576 12
APART FROM POPPIES AND THE FLYING FISH	691 15
LET ME NEVER KNOW MYSELF APART FROM THE LIVING GOD	699 29
OF SELF-AWARENESS NOW APART FROM GOD FALLING	701 21
KNOWING ITSELF KNOWING ITSELF APART FROM GOD FALLING	701 32
THE CLEAVERS THAT CLEAVE US FOREVER APART FROM ONE ANOT+	707 17
AND JERKED BACK THEIR BRIDLES PUSHING THEIR HEADS APART	735 9
HAS DEATH SET ME APART	749 9
KEEPS DAY AND NIGHT APART	809 24
AND WIDE WIDE APART	819 11
THESE THINGS APART	870 11
HOW LONG HAVE THEY TUGGED THE LEASH AND STRAINED APART	*895 16
HOW LONG HAVE THEY TUGGED THE LEASH AND STRAINED APART	*904 5
AND LIPS APART WITH DUMB CRIES	*911 23
WILL YOU PLUCK IT APART	*931 25
A BROWN BEE PULL APART	*935 35

APATHETIC

WHICH SHE DRAGS APATHETIC AWAY THOUGH WITHOUT RETREATING	360 11
SHE SEEMS EARTHILY APATHETIC	361 29

APATHY

EACH WITH THE UTMOST APATHY	357 7

APHRODITE

AND THAT POOR LATE MAKESHIFT APHRODITE EMERGING IN A	439 31
GODLY AND LOVELY COMES APHRODITE OUT OF THE SEA	693 19
AND APHRODITE IS THE WIFE OF WHALES	695 7
BY HERMES AND APHRODITE FLASHING WHITE GLITTERING WORDS	702 10
AND KILL APHRODITE DON'T SPEAK DO NOT TALK	750 23

APOCALYPTIC

HEAVENS WHERE THEY BELONG THE APOCALYPTIC BEASTS FOR WI+	319 2

APOLLO

OR SUN-BRIGHT APOLLO HIM SO MUSICAL	307 25
WHEN GOETHE BECOMES AN APOLLO HE BECOMES A PLASTER CAST	673 1

APOLLO BELVEDERE

AT FIFTY YOU'RE NOT GOING TO BE THE APOLLO BELVEDERE DO+	835 23

APOLOGISE

AND HEREBY I APOLOGISE	492 23

APOTHEOSIS

AMONG SPINNING WHEELS IN AN APOTHEOSIS OF WHEELS	711 27

APPALLING

THE LESBIAN PASSION IS THE MOST APPALLING	475 18

APPARATUS

LIKE SOME STRANGE MAGNETIC APPARATUS	301 4

APPAREL

SLOWLY SAILING IN GORGEOUS APPAREL THROUGH THE FLAME-LI+	387 30

APPARENTLY

SETTING OFF SOMEWHERE APPARENTLY	356 22

APPASSIONATO

WITH THE GREAT BLACK PIANO APPASSIONATO THE GLAMOUR	148 16

APPEAL
    IN PROMISCUOUS INTIMATE APPEAL   608 17
    APPEAL FROM THE GARDEN   758 1

APPEALING
    AND THE WHITE DOG SNUFFS THE WARMTH APPEALING   41 10

APPEARANCE
    UNDER A SMOOTH SKIN AND AN UPRIGHT APPEARANCE   431 21
    WITH THIS APPEARANCE OF FALTERING   750 5

APPEARANCES
    STANDING IN THEIR THOUSANDS THESE APPEARANCES IN DAMP   431 25
    FOR I CANNOT BE BULLIED BACK INTO THE APPEARANCES OF LO+   478 10
    BUT APPEARANCES ARE DECEPTIVE NOWADAYS AREN'T THEY   548 17

APPEARED
    YOU'VE SOLD EVERY GREAT MAN THAT EVER APPEARED   762 18

APPEARING
    THE LIGHTNING AND THE RAINBOW APPEARING IN US UNBIDDEN +   268 8

APPEARS
    WE ENGLISH ARE SO SENSITIVE MUCH MORE THAN APPEARS   576 5

APPEASE
    HOW ARE WE GOING TO APPEASE HER MAIDEN AND MOTHER   539 19
    SEEKING TO APPEASE WITH BLOOD THE INSISTENT GHOSTS   739 24
    HOW SHALL WE NOW APPEASE WHOM WE HAVE RAISED UP   740 9

APPEASED
    AND MY BODY'S BODY WAS APPEASED   265 9

'APPEN
    DID T' 'APPEN TER NOTICE A BIT OF A LASS WAY BACK   60 17
    LET THAT BE 'APPEN IT WORNA TH' DRINK NEITHER   60 27
    NO 'APPEN NOT   60 29
    'APPEN THEN YOU'VE 'EERED   78 6
    WHAT'S THAT AS 'APPEN I'VE 'EERED ON MISSIS   78 7
    AN' 'APPEN YOU'D GUESS THEN WHAT I'VE COME FOR   81 23
    'APPEN I MIGHTN'T 'APPEN I MIGHT   81 24
    'APPEN I CAN IF I TRY   82 26
    'APPEN THA DID AN' A'   139 2
    EH MEN DOESNA HA'E BOSOMS 'APPEN NOT ON'Y THA KNOWS   540 16
    DID T' 'APPEN TER NOTICE A BIT OF A LASS AWAY BACK   *911 3
    'APPEN THEN YOU'VE 'EERED   *919 26
    WHAT'S THAT AS 'APPEN I'VE 'EERED-ON MISSIS   *919 27
    'AN 'APPEN YOU MIGHT GUESS WHAT I'VE COME FOR   *923 23
    'APPEN I MIGHTN'T 'APPEN I MIGHT   *923 24

APPETITE
    IN YOUR APPETITE FOR AFFECTION   399 3
    NOR THE BRITISH LION HIS APPETITE   413 29
    APPETITE   762 28

APPLAUD
    BLADE OF HIS GLANCE THAT ASKS ME TO APPLAUD   43 25
    LET HIM SHOW IT TO THE CROWD PROBABLY THEY WILL APPLAUD   634 11

APPLAUDED
    AND THE PEOPLE APPLAUDED WITH HOLLOW FRIGHTENED   445 8

APPLAUSE
    APPLAUSE   445 9

APPLE
    WE HAVE BIT NO FORBIDDEN APPLE   37 24
    OH EARTH YOU ROTTEN APPLE ROLLING DOWNWARD   73 3
    ALMOND AND APPLE AND PEAR DIFFUSE WITH LIGHT THAT VERY   179 3
    AND SEE ITS SECRETS SO IT IS THAT THE POMEGRANATE IS TH+   277 3
    FOR AGES I DON'T CARE A FIG FOR IT MEN SAY BUT WHY A FI+   277 5
    BUT TILL THEN TILL THAT APPLE OF KNOWLEDGE SHE HADN'T H+   284 10
    EVEN IF IT IS A WOMAN MAKING AN APPLE DUMPLING OR A MAN   449 10
    SO AN APPLE BECOMES MYSTIC WHEN I TASTE IT IN   707 28
    ALL OF WHICH THINGS I CAN SURELY TASTE IN A GOOD APPLE   708 3
    IF I SAY I TASTE THESE THINGS IN AN APPLE I AM CALLED M+   708 5
    THE ONLY WAY TO EAT AN APPLE IS TO HOG IT DOWN LIKE A P+   708 7
    BUT IF I EAT AN APPLE I LIKE TO EAT IT WITH ALL MY SENS+   708 10
    THE WHOLE APPLE   817 30
    WE HAVE BIT NO FORBIDDEN APPLE   *892 12

APPLE-BLOSSOM
    BUT WHEN THE APPLE-BLOSSOM OPENS WIDE   129 11

APPLE-CART
    AND IT WOULD BE FUN TO UPSET THE APPLE-CART   517 11

APPLE-GREEN
    THE DAWN WAS APPLE-GREEN   216 13

APPLE-OF-SODOM
    HE HAS A VERY NICE APPLE-OF-SODOM RIND   830 8

APPLE-PIE
    BUST UP THE HOLY APPLE-PIE   458 7

APPLES
    O THE GREEN GLIMMER OF APPLES IN THE ORCHARD   119 7
    NOTHING NOW WILL RIPEN THE BRIGHT GREEN APPLES   119 11
    O THE GREY GARNER THAT IS FULL OF HALF-GROWN APPLES   120 5
    IS IT MORE THAN THE APPLES OF SODOM YOU SCORN SO THE MEN 235 7
    THE GREAT GOLD APPLES OF NIGHT   252 13
    THE RIPENESS OF THESE APPLES OF NIGHT   252 20
    IT TO THE MAN EVEN THE APPLES OF KNOWLEDGE ARE EVE'S FR+ 277 7
    WOMAN'S BUT THE APPLES OF LIFE THE DRAGON GUARDS AND NO+ 277 8
    ADMIT THAT APPLES AND STRAWBERRIES AND PEACHES AND PEAR+ 285 5
    THEY WOULD RIPEN LIKE APPLES AND BE SCENTED LIKE PIPPINS 503 20
    SOOTHING OLD PEOPLE SHOULD BE LIKE APPLES   503 22

APPLES
    AND SEE WHICH WAY THE APPLES WOULD GO A-ROLLING   517 12
    THOUGH SOME APPLES TASTE PREPONDERANTLY OF WATER WET AN+ 708 2
    THE APPLES FALLING LIKE GREAT DROPS OF DEW   716 20
    THE GRIM FROST IS AT HAND WHEN THE APPLES WILL FALL   717 3
    AND ON THE TREES HANG THE APPLES OF GOLD   770 22
    ALL YOU WHO HATE APPLES   816 25
    DOWN APPLES LIE   817 2
    WANT APPLES   817 5
    REVIVE ME WITH APPLES   817 9
    REVIVE WITH APPLES   817 14
    DOWN APPLES   817 23
    OR THE BUTTER OR THE APPLES OR PEACHES FROM THE BASKET   828 19
    WE HAVE FORGOTTEN THE SUNNY APPLES OF DAY THAT WE CRAVE+ *917 15
    OH THE GREEN GLIMMER OF APPLES IN THE ORCHARD   *932 16
    NOTHING NOW WILL RIPEN THE BRIGHT GREEN APPLES   *932 20
    RATTLE THE RAIN-DROPS RUIN THE APPLES   *933 9
    THE APPLES FALLING LIKE GREAT DROPS OF DEW   *956 26

APPLE-TREES
    WHEN SNOW FELL ON THE APPLE-TREES   248 17

APPLE-
    UPON US AND APPLE- AND ALMOND- AND APRICOT- AND QUINCE-+ 271 26

APPLICANT
    APPLICANT FOR POST AS LITERARY CRITIC HERE ARE MY   582 7
    APPLICANT I'M AFRAID I DON'T   582 11
    APPLICANT IN WHAT WAY QUITE   582 15
    APPLICANT I DON'T THINK SO SIR I'M AFRAID NOT   582 18

APPOINTED
    I QUAILED AT MY APPOINTED FUNCTION TURNED POLTROON   194 29

APPRECIATE
    DON'T TOUCH ME AND APPRECIATE ME   255 20
    BECAUSE WE ENGLISH DO APPRECIATE A REAL GENTLEMAN OR A   548 15

APPRECIATION
    SLOWLY THE RAINDROPS OF APPRECIATION   495 2

APPREHENDING
    AND OH MY HEART CEASE APPREHENDING   150 17

APPREHENSION
    HE IS FAR TOO FEW TO CAUSE ANY APPREHENSION   777 10

APPRENTICE
    DO THOU OH TRAVELLING APPRENTICE LIKEWISE   872 5

APPROACH
    APPROACH   66 24
    TO APPROACH YOU   172 3
    WE APPROACH THE GATE   242 19
    HEARING MAN APPROACH   321 25
    COMES A STRIDENT LAUGH AS WE APPROACH THIS LITTLE BLACK 375 8
    AS THEY APPROACH AND SALAAM UNDER THE DRIPPING FIRE OF   388 3
    WATCHING AND HARDLY SEEING THE TRUNK-CURL APPROACH AND   388 9
    PLEASE APPROACH THE SUPREME AUTHORITY DIRECT   604 18
    AND IF STARK NAKED I APPROACH A FELLOW-MAN OR FELLOW-WO+ 608 1
    FROM HER FLUTTERED FAREWELLS AT THE APPROACH OF MY WELL+ 865 14

APPROACHED
    APPROACHED AND PASSED BY   242 23
    SAVE IT HAD FIRST APPROACHED HIM AND CAJOLED HIS SOUL   290 3

APPROACHES
    TELEGRAM-BICYCLE APPROACHES I WAIT   100 6

APPROACHING
    AND EVE APPROACHING OVER THE GROUND   262 7
    APPROACHING UNDER THAT SMALL PAVILION AND TROPICAL EYES 389 22
    I SAW A DARK FIGURE APPROACHING A RAGGED SOLITARY CROW   866 17

APPROPRIATE
    I'D NEVER HAVE LET YOU APPROPRIATE ME HAD I KNOWN   395 16

APPROPRIATED
    APPROPRIATED ME NOT I YOU   395 12
    AS BENJAMIN FRANKLIN APPROPRIATED PROVIDENCE TO HIS   395 13

APPROVAL
    APPROVAL GOGGLE-EYED FOWL   170 24

APPROVE
    SOLEMNLY USED TO APPROVE CHIME CHIMING   170 23
    OR EVEN WHAT WE LIKE OR DISLIKE OR APPROVE OR DISAPPROVE 531 24

APPROXIMATE
    THEN GRADUALLY I APPROXIMATE TO THE DOG   645 3

APPROXIMATED
    AND I HAD BETTER EVEN HAVE APPROXIMATED TO THE DOG   645 9

APPROXIMATING
    I MIGHT BE A SOUL IN BLISS AN ANGEL APPROXIMATING TO THE 321 2

APRES MOI LE DELUGE
    THEY SAY APRES MOI LE DELUGE AND CALMLY EXPECT   531 8

APRICOT-
    UPON US AND APPLE- AND ALMOND- AND APRICOT- AND QUINCE-+ 271 26

APRON
    HER APRON WAS BROWN WITH BLOOD SHE PRAYED   753 10

APT
IS APT TO PROVE A GREAT DEAL TOO STRONG   576   2
AS THE ELDER GENERATIONS ARE APT TO DO   828 21

AQUA REGIA
IN WHAT STRONG AQUA REGIA NOW ARE YOU STEEPED   53 27

AQUEOUS
AQUEOUS SUBAQUEOUS   334 25
AQUEOUS   340   4

ARAB
TO THE ARAB AND THE FIG HAS BEEN A CATCH-WORD FOR THE F+   277   4

ARABIC
THIS IS THE AUTHENTIC ARABIC INTERPRETATION OF THE BRAY+   377 17

ARABS
AND ARABS SHOULD KNOW   377 19
THE ARABS WERE ONLY HALF RIGHT THOUGH THEY HINTED THE   378 28

ARARAT
AT THIS MOMENT SCRAPING TARDY ARARAT   429 10

ARC
HAVE YOU TRAVELLED YOUR DOWNWARD ARC   764 26
BURSTS LIKE AN ARC LAMP INTO LIGHT   773   2

ARCH
SOFTLY-IMPULSIVE ADVANCING AS WATER TOWARDS A WEIR FROM+   66 19
OH WEIRD DEMOS WHERE EVERY TWIG IS THE ARCH TWIG   300   7
THE SCALES ARE LOCKED IN AN ARCH LIKE A BRIDGE   355   2
WHY DO YOU ARCH YOUR NAKED-SET EYE WITH A MORE-THAN-COM+   369 16
YOU ARCH YOURSELF AS AN ARCHER'S BOW   370 12
WHILST BETWEEN THE TWO ALONG THE TENSE ARCH OF YOUR BACK   370 22
AS UP AN INVISIBLE RAINBOW AN ARCH   696 23
THE FEET OF THE ARCH   819   9
IN THE ARCH   819 29

ARCHAIC
IT IS AEGEAN SHIPS AND MEN WITH ARCHAIC POINTED BEARDS   687   6
SLIM NAKED MEN FROM CNOSSOS SMILING THE ARCHAIC SMILE   688 13

ARCHANGELS
AND SO THE OFFICIAL ARCHANGELS   614   6
WHAT LOUSY ARCHANGELS AND ANGELS YOU HAVE TO SURROUND   643 27
THE BURNING ARCHANGELS UNDER THE SEA KEEP PASSING BACK +   694 18
KEEP PASSING ARCHANGELS OF BLISS   694 24

ARCH-CREST
TILL THE WIND SLIDES YOU SHEER FROM THE ARCH-CREST   696 24

ARCHED
OR WHETHER I WAS THE DARKNESS WITH ARCHED WINGS   882   1

ARCHER'S
YOU ARCH YOURSELF AS AN ARCHER'S BOW   370 12

ARCHES
WHEN UNDER THE ARCHES OF THE PONTE VECCHIO   340 24
ARCHES   341   2
THE WORN ARCHES OF THEIR SPINES SUPPORT   426   3

ARCHIBALD
IF THIS IS WHAT ARCHIBALD THINKS I AM   489 19

ARCHIE
WITH A MARVELLOUS OUTFIT HOW DID ARCHIE SEE   489 27
SAYING YOU KNOW I ALWAYS HAVE TO SAY THAT ARCHIE LOOKS +   842 20
I CAN NEVER EVEN THINK THAT IT'S BABY WHO LOOKS LIKE AR+   842 21

ARCHING
THE RAINBOW ARCHING OVER IN THE SKIES   136 15
ARCHING   311   4

ARCHITECTURE
AND IS AN ARCHITECTURE OF GLISTENING ATOMS   692   3

ARCHWAY
WHERE AN ARCHWAY TORN AND GLITTERING   201 23
GONE UNDER THE ARCHWAY HOME HE CAN JOIN   228 15

ARC-LAMP
EACH ARC-LAMP GOLDEN DOES EXPOSE   104 26

ARDOUR
BUSHED IN AN UNCOUTH ARDOUR COILED AT CORE   160 13

'ARD
HOW 'ARD 'E KNOCKS   44 15
YI THA MUST HA' BIN 'ARD TER WEAN   79 24

A-REEL
SHOWING THE ROCKING DARKNESS NOW A-REEL   136 10

ARENA
I'M SCRAIGHTIN' MY-SEN BUT ARENA GOIN'   78 27
THA ARENA VERY FLIG TER GO   138 16

ARE-NA
I'M SCREETIN' MY-SEN BUT ARE-NA GOIN'   *920 19

AREN'T
AREN'T TER HEARIN' SUMMAT   138   7
SEE IF YOUR SKIES AREN'T FALLING   289 16
AND AREN'T YOUR FEELINGS VIOLATED YOU HIGH-BRED LITTLE +   400 13
'ERE SHE'S A LIDY AREN'T YER OLD QUIZZ   434 24
THE OLD ONES WANT TO BE YOUNG AND THEY AREN'T YOUNG   502 23

AREN'T
THAT'S WHY WOMEN AREN'T MUCH FUN YOU'RE ALWAYS HAVING   517 27
THE YOUNG AREN'T VITALLY INTERESTED IN IT ANY MORE   518 16
HAPPY AS PERHAPS KINGS USED TO BE BUT CERTAINLY AREN'T   520 18
BUT APPEARANCES ARE DECEPTIVE NOWADAYS AREN'T THEY   548 17
THEY AREN'T EVEN FIT TO CURSE   553   8
OH AREN'T THEY GREEN OH HAVEN'T WE HAVEN'T WE SPENT   569 11
AREN'T THEY MADE QUITE THE SAME THEN AS YOU AND I   578 15
WHAT'S THE MATTER WITH THEM AREN'T THEY WOMEN AND   578 18
THAT FIGS AREN'T FOUND IN THE LAND OF THE FREE   579   8
AREN'T YOU PINING TO BE CLASSY SUPERIOR UPPER   774 17
THEY AREN'T AFRAID OF LOSING SOMETHING AS THE OLDER ONE+   828 25
AND THEY AREN'T OUT ON THE MAKE   828 26

ARES
BY ARES AND KRONOS AND ZEUS   702 11

ARGONAUTS'
NOW THE SEA IS THE ARGONAUTS' SEA AND IN THE DAWN   687 19

ARGOSY
OR IS OUR SHATTERED ARGOSY OUR LEAKING ARK   429   9

ARID
TO FIND HIMSELF ON THE CROWDED ARID MARGINS OF EXISTENCE *957 14

ARISEN
ARISEN   632 31
FROM THE SURF HAS ARISEN THE BOYS ARE MUTTERING   *894 16

ARISTOCRACIES
DO IT SO THAT WE CAN ALL OF US BE LITTLE ARISTOCRACIES +   517 14

ARISTOCRACY
THE EXQUISITE AND AGELESS ARISTOCRACY   314 14
THAT PUTS FORTH ITS OWN ARISTOCRACY   627   7

ARISTOCRAT
AND AN ARISTOCRAT IN SO FAR AS I DETEST NARROW-GUTTED   526   8
TO BE AN ARISTOCRAT OF THE SUN   526 25
A BLOOMING ARISTOCRAT ALL ROUND   587 26

ARISTOCRATIC
AND I FEEL ARISTOCRATIC NOBLE WHEN I FEEL A PULSE GO   525   7
THEY WOULDN'T SUDDENLY BECOME THEMSELVES ARISTOCRATIC   527 24
HOW ARISTOCRATIC IT IS   587 19

ARITHMETIC
ONLY A MEAN ARITHMETIC ON THE FACE OF THINGS   *931 32

ARK
A MOMENT THEN DARKNESS SHUT THE LID OF THE SACRED ARK   62 18
OR IS OUR SHATTERED ARGOSY OUR LEAKING ARK   429   9
OH BUILD YOUR SHIP OF DEATH YOUR LITTLE ARK   718   9
IN THE FRAGILE SHIP OF COURAGE THE ARK OF FAITH   719   3
FOR YOU SET WIDE THE DOORS OF MY VENTURESOME ARK   875 23
SO BIG AND WORTHY IN MY OWN SMALL ARK   876   3
THE BONNY FLOATING ARK OF THIS FAIR WORLD   876 10

ARK OF THE COVENANT
UNKNOWN THAT LIES BEFORE US BEARING THE ARK OF THE COVE+   132 24

'ARK
BUT 'ARK THEE 'ERE THAT WIDDER WOMAN   84   3
'ARK THA'RT FOR HEARIN' SUMMAT   137 26
'ARK 'ERE LAD ATWEEN THEE AN' ME   490 28

ARM
HER SOFT WHITE LEGS HANGING HEAVILY OVER MY ARM   73 25
THIS IS WHY I TUG AT THEM INDIVIDUALLY WITH MY ARM ROUND   288   8
WITH HIS CLOAK OVER HIS ARM WAITING TO BE ASKED IN   692 11
AND WE WALKED DARK SO HE HELD HIS ARM CLOSE ROUND ME   732 15
HER SOFT WHITE LEGS HANGING HEAVILY OVER MY ARM   *913 17
SWAYS ON MY ARM LIKE SORROWFUL STORM-HEAVY BOUGHS   *913 23

ARMADA
GULPING UP SCIENCE'S SMART ARMADA   824 11

ARMADAS
THAT PUT TO SEA AND BOLDLY SINK ARMADAS   542   9

ARM-CHAIRS
THE UPHOLSTERED DEAD THAT SIT IN DEEP ARM-CHAIRS   440 20

ARMFUL
SWEET AS AN ARMFUL OF WHEAT   198 14

ARMFULS
YOU ARMFULS OF SUNSHINE AND YOU WON'T LET ME LIVE   211   6
IN RAPID ARMFULS FROM THE LINE TOSSING IT IN THE BASKET   672 15

ARMIES
NATIONS ARMIES WAR PEACE-TALKING   256 27

ARMOUR
TEARS AND SWORDS TO MY HEART ARROWS NO ARMOUR WILL TURN+   57 23
IS THIS ARMOUR OF STIFF RELUCTANCY   117   9

ARMS
LIFT MY ARMS THE HILL BURSTS AND HEAVES UNDER THEIR SPU+   33   9
REPEATING WITH TIGHTENED ARMS AND THE HOT BLOOD'S BLIND+   61 26
WHERE HER ARMS AND MY NECK'S THICK PULSE COULD MEET   62   2
AND MY ARMS FELL LOOSE AND I WAS DUMB   62 20
THE REDDENED ACHING EYES OF THE BAR-MAN WITH THIN ARMS   72   2
OH YOU WHO FLASH YOUR ARMS LIKE ROCKETS TO HEAVEN   73 10
THE SLENDER BARE ARMS OF THE BRANCHES YOUR TIRE-MAIDENS   86 17
WHO LIFT SWART ARMS TO FEND ME OFF BUT I COME   86 18
THEM DOWN TO MY ARMS   105 19

ARMS
    TO MY ARMS WITH HER WELCOME LOAD   106 18
    ROUND CLOUDS ROLL IN THE ARMS OF THE WIND   126 7
    AND SOMETIMES HOW SHE GRASPS HER ARMS WITH HER   128 20
    BIG HANDS AS IF SURELY HER ARMS DID HURT   128 22
    CLOSES HER ARMS THAT SHOULD FOLD ON ME IN SLEEP   128 30
    AND I DO LIFT MY ACHING ARMS TO YOU   129 19
    AND FALLING WAVES IN HIS ARMS AND THE LOST SOUL'S KISS 130 20
    THE DEAD MOON HEAPED WITHIN THE NEW MOON'S ARMS   132 2
    SLIPPED THROUGH MY ARMS ON THE THRESHING FLOOR   198 11
    HIS ARMS SO SHE LIGHTS FROM HER PALFREY   200 11
    AH YES YOUR OPEN ARMS AH YES AH YES   230 20
    HERE IN MY ARMS MY NAKED SACRIFICE   238 19
    DEATH DO YOU HEAR IN MY ARMS I AM BRINGING   238 20
    WHICH MOUNTS UP MY ARMS   241 19
    ARMS   245 22
    AND SIT BESIDE THE STEEL-STRAIGHT ARMS OF YOUR FAIR WOM+ 291 5
    NAKED DARK MEN WITH ORNAMENTS ON ON THEIR NAKED ARMS   389 7
    AND CATCH FLESH LIKE THE NIGHT IN ONE'S ARMS   428 5
    OCTOPUS ARMS   451 31
    SAFER THAN IN THE ARMS OF JESUS   543 1
    BECAUSE THEY ARE THE ARMS AND LEGS OF THE MACHINE   641 16
    OF THE ARMS PLUTONIC AND PIERCED WITH THE PASSION OF DE+ 697 20
    THE TIDE IN MY ARMS   705 4
    WHOSE POWER RUNS TO THE SHORES ALONG MY ARMS   705 15
    MY ARMS LET ME COVER HIM UP IN MY SKIRT   750 20
    THAT I MAY HOLD THEM LIKE MEMORIES IN MY ARMS WHEN I GO+ 789 20
    NOW THE TREES WITH INTERLOCKED HANDS AND ARMS UPLIFTED + 854 4
    OVERHEAD THE REDDEST SHE LIFTED HER LONG ARMS AND TRIED 864 9
    FLASHING HIS BRIGHT BROWN ARMS AS HE LEANS ON THE POLE 867 28
    HIS RUDDY ARMS GLOW ACROSS HER   868 8
    SIEGMUND WITH YOUR ARMS AND YOUR HEART YOU ARE CHOKING + 870 20
    HIS COAT AND HIS ARMS AND HIS LABOURING HEART ARE STRAN+ 871 25
    LEAN TOGETHER AND LIFT WILD ARMS TO EMBRACE   883 9
    HOLDING DOWN MY LEAPING ARMS   883 11
    MOVE MY ARMS THE HILL BURSTS AND HEAVES UNDER THEIR SPU+ *891 10
    AND MY DOCILE FLUENT ARMS   *893 23
    DARK WAVING OF THEIR ARMS AGAINST THE BLAND   *895 3
    REPEATING WITH TIGHTENED ARMS AND THE HOT BLOOD'S BLIND+ *912 6
    WHERE HER ARMS AND MY NECK'S BLOOD-SURGE COULD MEET   *912 10
    OF MY ARMS INERT WITH DREAD WILTED IN FEAR OF MY KISS *912 18
    IS LIKE WHEN TWO WHITE BUTTERFLIES SETTLE IN THE ARMS O+ *913 3
    THE DEAD MOON HEAPED WITHIN THE YOUNG MOON'S ARMS   *937 29
    AND HER ARMS AND HER BOSOM AND THE WHOLE OF HER SOUL IS+ *940 20
    OF THE ARMS OF PLUTO AS HE RAVISHES HER ONCE AGAIN   *956 17
    PAST THE LURKING OCTOPUS ARMS OF AGONISED MEMORY   *959 6

ARNO
    AGAINST THE CURRENT OF OBSCURE ARNO   340 26

A-ROLLING
    AND SEE WHICH WAY THE APPLES WOULD GO A-ROLLING   517 12

AROMA
    SUCH AN AROMA OF LOST HUMAN LIFE   298 7

AROMATIC
    AROMATIC AS FRANKINCENSE   301 26

AROSE
    WITHIN THE HOUSE TWO VOICES AROSE A SLENDER LASH   36 13

AROUSED
    SHOWING A GLINT OF TEETH AND GLANCING TROPICAL EYES ARO+ 391 14

ARRANGE
    FIXED ARRANGE YOU UNDERSTAND WHAT I MEAN   582 10

ARRANGED
    AS ALL DRAWING-ROOMS ARE ARRANGED   657 5
    FROM WHAT I'VE ARRANGED WI' THEE EH MAN WHAT A STUBBORN+ *925 26

ARRANGEMENT
    STAND UP FOR A NEW ARRANGEMENT   560 29
    IS FOR SOME MORE NATURAL MORE DECENT SOCIAL ARRANGEMENT 837 24

ARRANGES
    SHE SMILING WITH GOATY MUNCH-MOUTH MONA LISA ARRANGES 382 26

ARRAS
    I FEEL THICK WALLS OF STONE BEHIND THE ARRAS   173 26
    THE SURFACE OF DREAMS IS BROKEN THE ARRAS IS TORN   174 5
    FOR THE RIPPING OF ARRAS AND SMASHING OF WALLS AND THE + 174 15
    THE ARRAS IS ALL ILLUSION OH COME AND TEAR IT AWAY   174 18

ARRAS-FOLD
    DEADENS THIS DAY'S GREY-DROPPING ARRAS-FOLD   141 12

ARREST
    ARREST HIM HE'S INDECENT HE'S OBSCENE WHAT'S MORE   574 24

ARRESTED
    TREES BIRDS AND EARTH ARRESTED IN THE AFTER-THOUGHT   142 15
    ARRESTED LISTENING   165 20
    ARRESTED STATIC   255 36
    POLICEMEN AND ARRESTED THEM AND HAULED THEM OFF TO GAOL 632 33
    AN UNHOLY INQUISITION HAS ARRESTED ALL MY PICTURES   633 14

ARRIVED
    NOW I AM ARRIVED   224 22

ARRIVING
    ARRIVING ACROSS THE SKY   71 6
    ARRIVING GREY FROM THE DARKNESS ABOVE SUDDENLY INTO THE+ 179 22
    AND NEVER NEVER ARRIVING AT JOURNEY'S END AT THE REAR OF 380 26
    THE LUMINOUS MIST WHICH THE POOR THINGS WIST WAS DAWN A+ *917 23

ARROGANCE
    FLOURISHING FROM THE ROCK IN A MYSTERIOUS ARROGANCE   299 8
    ARROGANCE   369 17
    YOUR BRITTLE SUPER-SENSUAL ARROGANCE   370 26

ARROGANTLY
    AND BITING THE FRAIL GRASS ARROGANTLY   358 20

ARROGANTY
    DECIDEDLY ARROGANTY   358 21

ARROW
    CAN THIS SHOT ARROW OF TRAVEL FLY   116 15
    IS JUST BEYOND RANGE OF THE ARROW HE SHOOTS   382 22
    AN ARROW ON THE BED AT THE PILLOW   397 3
    CAN THIS SHOT ARROW OF TRAVEL FLY   *930 14

ARROWS
    TEARS AND SWORDS TO MY HEART ARROWS NO ARMOUR WILL TURN+ 57 23
    AND DARKER THAN EVEN THE ARROWS OF VIOLENTEST WILL   383 10
    THE TRILLING LARK IN A WILD DESPAIR WILL TRILL DOWN ARR+ 624 14
    AND CLEAN AS ARROWS THEY SPED AT THE MARK   688 24
    REFUSED TO BE MOULDED IN ARROWS OF ENGLISH WORDS   859 12
    AND THEY SEND ARROWS OF ANGER BULLETS AND BOMBS OF FRUS+ *958 6

ARSE
    ARSE PERHAPS YOU'LL REMEMBER   563 14

ART
    WHO THEN ART THOU   39 14
    WHO ART THOU WHAT HAST   39 17
    FOR THE REST WHEN THOU ART WEDDED   44 6
    ART   61 27
    PLANTED THEE UPRIGHT ART PROUD TO SEE   69 15
    THA ART SMOCK-RAVELLED BUNNY   78 29
    THEN WHAT ART COLLEYFOGLIN' FOR   82 2
    THA ART SO SURE THA'RT RIGHT LIZ   84 1
    A WOMAN'S MAN THA ART MA LAD   140 1
    AND CALL TO GOD WHERE ART THOU   231 29
    AND THOU ART JESUS SON OF MAN   323 7
    THEIR HANDS AND PRODUCE WORKS OF ART AS MEN DO HORSES W+ 376 2
    KNOW THYSELF AND THAT THOU ART MORTAL   473 22
    AND THEREFORE THAT THOU ART FOREVER UNKNOWABLE   473 23
    THOU ART LIKE THE MOON   473 25
    THOU ART LIKE THE DAY   474 1
    BUT THOU ART ALSO LIKE THE NIGHT   474 2
    WHAT IS MAN THAT THOU ART MINDFUL OF HIM   548 31
    NOR WOVEN WITH ITALIAN ART   575 18
    WHAT IS MAN THAT THOU ART NO LONGER MINDFUL OF HIM   629 12
    UNDER THE GREAT COMMAND KNOW THYSELF AND THAT THOU ART + 674 8
    UGLY OLD FURNITURE UGLY OLD BOOKS UGLY OLD BUILDINGS UG+ 678 14
    THOU WHO ART NAMELESS   704 14
    KNOW THYSELF AND THAT THOU ART MORTAL   714 5
    BUT OH WIND WHAT A KNAVE THOU ART   731 15
    AS THOU ART SHOWN AND HAVING DONE SO MUCH   872 8
    REPEATING WITH TIGHTENED ARMS AND THE HOT BLOOD'S BLIND+ *912 6
    PLANTED THEE UPRIGHT ART NOT PROUD TO SEE   *915 27
    THA ART SMOCK-RAVELLED BUNNY   *920 21
    THEN WHAT ART COLLEYFOGLIN' FOR   *924 6
    THOU ART   *925 27
    THOU ART SHAPELY THOU ART ADORNED   *927 16

ARTEMIS
    AND BY ARTEMIS THE WHITEST   702 9

ARTHUR HOLLIDAY'S
    'E SAYS IS IT ARTHUR HOLLIDAY'S   44 20

ARTICLE
    YOU MUST CHOP UP EACH ARTICLE MAKE IT PAPPY   583 18

ARTICLES
    THE ARTICLES PASSING BENEATH YOUR SCRAWL   583 4

ARTIFICIAL
    IT'S EITHER AN ARTIFICIAL RAG BLOSSOM OR AN IMMORTELLE + 472 26
    ALL OTHER CLASS IS ARTIFICIAL   649 23
    NAPOLEON THEY SOLD TO MADAME TUSSAUDS AND TO THE ARTIFI+ 763 4

ARTILLERY
    SOUND OF ARTILLERY AEROPLANES PRESENCES   169 15

ARTIST
    EVEN AN ARTIST KNOWS THAT HIS WORK WAS NEVER IN HIS MIND 690 3

ARTISTS
    THAT ENGLISH ARTISTS MIGHT FINALLY LEARN   579 24
    THAT THE OLD DARK FATHERS SHOULD NOT TRUST THESE ARTISTS 778 4
    THEIR CAUSE BECAUSE THEY THE ARTISTS AND LONG-HAIRED   778 6
    BECAUSE THEY LIVE ON HIM ARTISTS AND   778 9

A-SAIL
    OF SOMETHING COMING SHIPS A-SAIL FROM OVER THE RIM OF T+ 687 3

ASBESTOS
    LIKE INDIA-RUBBER AND ASBESTOS   765 15

ASCENDANT
    THAT MOON-LIKE SWORD THE ASCENDANT DEAD UNSHEATHE   168 23

ASCENDING
    A RED ROSE GOES ON THE WIND ASCENDING   150 9

ASCENT
    AND BONES AND TWIGS AND A PERILOUS ASCENT   402 14
    WE CLIMBED THE STEEP ASCENT TO HEAVEN   554 1
    IN SPITE OF MY ASCENT   626 14

ASCRIBE
   BUT ANYONE WHO SHALL ASCRIBE ATTRIBUTES TO GOD OR   726 12

A SGHEMBO
   AND HE LUNGED FLIGHT-HEAVY AWAY FROM ME SIDEWAYS A SGHE+   346 19

ASH
   OF THE ASH   36 18
   WHERE ASH ON THE DYING COALS GROWS SWIFTLY LIKE HEAVY   47 6
   THE LAST YEAR'S FIRE IS GONE AND YOUR FACE IS ASH   91 2
   PUT SACKCLOTH ON BE CROWNED WITH POWDERY ASH   234 27
   AND FEED THE YOUNG NEW FIELDS OF LIFE WITH ASH   315 5
   WITH ASH I SAY   315 6
   AMONG MUCH OTHER ASH   315 9
   TO BURN THE WORLD BACK TO MANURE-GOOD ASH   315 11
   BURNT BACK TO ASH   315 30
   INSTEAD OF FLAME AND FLAME-CLEAN ASH   318 1
   ASH FLUTTERS FLOCCULENT LIKE DOWN ON A BLUE WAN FLEDGEL+   330 8
   TO DUST TO ASH ON THE TWILIT FLOOR OF THE DESERT   403 23
   WITH GREY REPENTANT ASH   492 30
   TO REDUCE THE WORLD TO GREY ASH   716 3
   TO HOT AND FLOCCULENT ASH   728 8
   WITH STRANDS OF DOWN LIKE FLOATING ASH   728 10
   IN THE FLOCCULENT ASH OF THE SAGE-GREY DESERT   780 24
   BUT THE GREY DOG BELONGS TO THE ASH OF THE WORLD   808 20
   AND BLOW THE ASH AWAY   811 26
   IS HEAVY IS CLOGGED AND HEAVY WITH WASTED ASH   *897 17

ASHAKE
   SOMETHING WHICH SETS THE BLACK POPLARS ASHAKE WITH HYST+   102 26

ASHAMED
   I AM ASHAMED YOU WANTED ME NOT TO-NIGHT   87 14
   AND NOW I KNOW SO I MUST BE ASHAMED   87 18
   A BULLOCK WAGON COMES SO I AM ASHAMED   225 10
   SHE SAID AS WELL TO ME WHY ARE YOU ASHAMED   254 8
   ASHAMED AND SHAMEFUL AND VICIOUS   264 31
   EVEN IT IS A TRICK BUT SHE IS NOT ASHAMED   654 12
   I AM ASHAMED THAT I ACHE SO MUCH   *931 20
   SILENT TONGUED I AM ASHAMED   *946 6

ASHES
   LIKE SOFT HOT ASHES ON MY HELPLESS CLAY   87 13
   PUT ASHES ON YOUR HEAD PUT SACKCLOTH ON   234 21
   YOUR ASHES EVEN MY FRIENDS   315 8
   CAN RISE FROM THE ASHES   329 34
   THOUGH HIS ASHES MIGHT   545 23
   WITH ASHES OF UTTER BOREDOM ENNUI AND DISGUST   616 12
   AND DEATH IS ON THE AIR LIKE A SMELL OF ASHES   717 5
   AND LICK UP THY ASHES WITH A REPENTANT TONGUE   760 17
   I'LL SEND FIRE AND ASHES UPON THEM AND SMOTHER THEM ALL   792 5
   BUT THE GREY DOGS ARE AMONG THE ASHES   809 2
   FOR MYSELF A HEAP OF ASHES OF WEARINESS TILL SLEEP   *896 1
   FOR MYSELF A HEAP OF ASHES OF WEARINESS TILL SLEEP   *904 22

ASH-GREY
   AN ASH-GREY PELT   408 28
   THERE ARE DEAD THAT SIT UNDER THE TREES WATCHING WITH A+   795 26

ASHRINK
   WITH ALL YOUR SENSES ASHRINK   *931 14

ASH-SCARRED
   BUT FORM THE ASH-SCARRED FALLOW   315 33

ASHTAROTH
   BUT PERHAPS ASHTAROTH PERHAPS SIVA PERHAPS HUITZILOPOCH+   674 25

ASH-TREES
   THE ASH-TREES OF THE VALLEY-ROAD WILL RAISE   176 15
   THE SHADOWS OF THE ASH-TREES STRIDE ACROSS THE HAY   858 9
   THE ASH-TREES OF THE VALLEY ROAD SHOULD RAISE   *941 2

ASH-TREE
   OUTSIDE THE HOUSE AN ASH-TREE HUNG ITS TERRIBLE WHIPS   36 9
   OR THE SPLENDID GROWING OF AN ASH-TREE   610 22

ASH-WHITE
   ROUND THE ASH-WHITE HEARTH OF THE DESERT   408 20

ASHY
   DRIFTING BENEATH THE DEATHLY ASHY GREY   720 7

ASINELLO
   ASINELLO CIUCO   979 2

ASK
   THE SUN AND THE RAIN DO NOT ASK THE SECRET   63 18
   DONE I SHOULD THINK SO AN' MIGHT I ASK   79 31
   YOU ASK ME DO THE HEALING DAYS CLOSE UP   90 22
   BEGGED ME TO ASK NOT FOR THE DOOR   104 2
   I OUGHT TO BE PROUD THAT SHE SHOULD ASK IT   152 4
   WHOM SHALL WE ASK ABOUT HIM   286 12
   I WOULD NOT EVEN ASK TO LEAVE A FOSSIL CLAW EXTANT   430 7
   AND IN PRIVATE BOASTS HIS EXPLOITS EVEN LOUDER IF YOU A+   432 30
   GODS DO YOU ASK FOR GODS   438 16
   THEY ASK AND THEY MUST BE ANSWERED THEY   461 9
   ALL I ASK OF A WOMAN IS THAT SHE SHALL FEEL GENTLY TOWA+   479 1
   IT IS ALL I ASK   479 6
   TILL YOU ASK FOR LIGHTNING INSTEAD OF LOVE   484 15
   ELDERLY DISCONTENTED WOMEN ASK FOR INTIMATE COMPANIONSH+   502 1
   ASK BUT THE LEAGUE INSISTS THANK YOU SO MUCH NO SIGN HE+   546 14
   MAY I ASK IF YOU ARE REALLY SUPERIOR   548 13
   THOUGH WHAT IT WAS YOU CAN ASK ME   555 13
   BUT WHY I ASK YOU OH TELL ME WHY   578 14
   THE ONLY QUESTION TO ASK TODAY ABOUT MAN OR WOMAN   603 15
   AH BUT THE SIMPLE ASK FOR IMAGES   651 10
   MAY I ASK YOU THEN WHERE INSINCERITY AND DISHONESTY BEG+   659 13

ASK
   AND THE FIRST QUESTION TO ASK YOURSELF IS   661 14
   NOT ANYTHING NOR EVER AGAIN ASK WHY   738 26
   OF JUST ONE TOUCH EVEN SO DO I ASK TOO MUCH   738 32
   DO NOT ASK ME ALMIGHTY GOD TO PART FROM HER AGAIN   749 20
   YOU LAD WILL YOU ASK THE BOSS   759 6
   I HEAR THE VOICE OF MY FIRST MAN ASK ME WHY I AM LAUGHI+   791 14
   THERE IS NOTHING MORE TO ASK FOR   802 8
   I ASK FOR NOTHING EXCEPT TO SLIP   812 25
   ASK IN THE SPACE OF THEIR EYES   816 10
   WE ASK MORE AND MORE TO BE DIMINISHED   826 1
   WHAT A BITTER SHAME THAT SHE SHOULD ASK IT   874 17
   I ASK WHEN THA BEGUN   *921 28
   BUT ASK THE WOMEN   *949 7
   ASK ALL THE WOMEN HE'S EVER HAD   *949 8
   DON JUAN IF YOU ASK ME   *949 16

ASKED
   FATHER YOU ARE NOT ASKED   405 8
   ANYHOW THE TOLSTOYAN LOT SIMPLY ASKED FOR EXTINCTION   533 24
   AN EARL ONCE ASKED ME DOWN TO STAY   551 27
   WITH HIS CLOAK OVER HIS ARM WAITING TO BE ASKED IN   692 11
   WHY ARE YOU LAUGHING ASKED THE FIRST MAN OF QUETZALCOATL   791 13

ASKER
   LOVE IS THE GREAT ASKER   63 17

ASKING
   AND ASKING NOTHING PATIENTLY STEALS BACK AGAIN   63 29
   ASKING SOMETHING MORE OF ME   64 27
   YOU ARE ALWAYS ASKING DO I REMEMBER REMEMBER   90 19
   FOR ALL YOUR LIFE OF ASKING AND DESPAIR   100 27
   IT WAS ASKING TOO MUCH OF HIS NATURE   344 22
   WHICH IS JUST A STONE TO ANYONE ASKING FOR MEAT   414 31
   NO GOOD ASKING THE REASON WHY   458 3
   ONLY HERE AND THERE A PAIR OF EYES HAUNTED LOOKS OUT AS+   625 25
   SEEM ALWAYS TO BE ASKING ASKING SOMETHING   816 4

ASKS
   BLADE OF HIS GLANCE THAT ASKS ME TO APPLAUD   43 25
   ASKS TO BE HIDDEN AND WISHES NOTHING TO TELL   64 13
   'TIS THE SUN THAT ASKS THE QUESTION IN A LOVELY HASTE F+   119 29
   AS THE WIND ASKS WHITHER THE WAN ROAD GOES   163 24
   AND ASKS IF SHE SEES THE LAND THE LAND   201 3
   AS THE WIND ASKS WHITHER THE DARK ROAD GOES   857 24

ASLANT
   AND SKYWARDS HIS FACE IS IMMOBILE EYELIDS ASLANT   66 11
   NOR RUN ASLANT HIS RAYS   806 9

ASLEEP
   ARE THEY ASLEEP ARE THEY LIVING NOW SEE WHEN I   33 8
   LIKE DROWSY CREATURES THE HOUSES FALL ASLEEP   48 19
   ASLEEP AND ADREAM   70 13
   ASLEEP STILL SHAKES IN THE CLUTCH OF A SOB   136 25
   ASLEEP MY FINGERS CREEP   143 10
   BARE AND ASLEEP   144 27
   MOANS AND BOOMS THE SOUL OF A PEOPLE IMPRISONED ASLEEP   149 11
   AND ASLEEP ON THE SNOW'S LAST SHADOW   226 19
   NOR THE ADDER WE SAW ASLEEP WITH HER HEAD ON HER SHOULD+   255 26
   SO NINE-TENTHS ASLEEP MOTIONLESS BORED AND STATICALLY A+   324 15
   NOT ASLEEP   379 5
   AND INSTEAD THE WHITE MEN SCRAMBLE ASLEEP IN THE   408 9
   AND RIDE ON HORSEBACK ASLEEP FOREVER THROUGH THE DESERT   408 11
   THE PALE-GOLD FLESH OF PRIAPUS DROPPING ASLEEP   651 19
   AND I FALL ASLEEP WITH THE GODS THE GODS   652 15
   LIKE A CAT ASLEEP ON A CHAIR   700 3
   ARE THEY ASLEEP ARE THEY ALIVE NOW SEE WHEN I   *891 9

'ASN'T
   IT 'ASN'T NOTHIN' TO DO WITH ME   82 1

ASP
   SHE MIGHT HAVE SAVED HERSELF THE ASP   479 25

ASPECT
   THE SHAKING ASPECT OF THE SEA   310 26
   WHAT IS THIS AWFUL ASPECT OF MAN   628 25

ASPECTS
   AFTER THAT OF COURSE THERE'S SUICIDE CERTAIN ASPECTS   532 26

ASPEN
   NOW THAT THE SUN HAS GONE AND THE ASPEN LEAVES   403 14
   AND THE ABSENCE OF COTTON-WOOD LEAVES OR OF ASPEN   404 1
   TIGRESS BRINDLED WITH ASPEN   409 23

ASPENS
   OVER THE ROUNDED SIDES OF THE ROCKIES THE ASPENS OF   408 23
   THE ASPENS OF AUTUMN   408 25

ASPEN-TREES
   WHEN I TROT MY LITTLE PONY THROUGH THE ASPEN-TREES OF T+   409 4
   ON THE YELLOW POINTED ASPEN-TREES LAID ONE ON ANOTHER L+   409 14

ASPHALT
   ALL THE FLOWERS ARE FADED FROM THE ASPHALT ISLE IN THE +   71 10
   THEY WILL HEAR THE FAINT RENDING OF THE ASPHALT ROADS   *954 8

ASPHYXIATE
   WE ASPHYXIATE IN A SLEEP OF DREAMS REBREATHING THE IMPU+   174 26

ASPIRE
   THE HEAVENS ABOVE THAT WE YEARN TO AND ASPIRE TO   287 24
   I DO NOT YEARN NOR ASPIRE FOR I AM A BLIND SAMSON   287 25
   WHOM THE INDIANS ASPIRE TO   374 19

ASS
THE LONG-DRAWN BRAY OF THE ASS   377 1
OF THE ASS   377 18
SUCH AN ASS   377 28
POOR ASS LIKE MAN ALWAYS IN RUT   378 11
THE ASS WAS THE FIRST OF ALL ANIMALS TO FALL FINALLY IN+   378 16
LOVE ON A SUBMISSIVE ASS   379 27
BUT THE ASS NEVER FORGETS   379 29
BUT THE ASS IS A PRIMAL CREATURE AND NEVER FORGETS   379 33
OR EVEN AN ASS   563 20

ASSAIL
DO YOU RUSH TO ASSAIL ME   140 29

ASS-COLT
AND JESUS ON A MEEK ASS-COLT MARES MARY ESCAPING TO   380 2

ASSEMBLY
I AM NOT A MECHANISM AN ASSEMBLY OF VARIOUS SECTIONS   620 10

ASSENTED
IT SHALL BE IT SHALL BE ASSENTED SEVEN TIMES   702 7

ASSERT
WE SHALL DO AS WE LIKE SIN IS OBSOLETE THE YOUNG ASSERT   463 26
YOU DON'T HAVE TO ASSERT THAT YOU FEEL IT   500 25
ONLY EGOISTICALLY WE ASSERT OURSELVES   513 6
IS THAT THEY CALMLY ASSERT WE ONLY THRILL TO PERVERSITY   531 3
BUT MUST EVER STRUGGLE ON TO ASSERT THEMSELVES   612 20

ASSERTING
LIBIDINOUS DESIRE RUNS BACK AND FORTH ASSERTING ITSELF +   386 15

ASSERTION
THE EXQUISITE ASSERTION OF NEW DELICATE LIFE   314 19
PERHAPS IT IS YOUR ASSERTION IN ALL THIS OSTENTATION OF+   369 27
SO EVERYBODY MAKES AN ASSERTION OF HIMSELF   496 22
HOW VIVIDLY THEY MAKE THEIR ASSERTION OF LIFE   530 14

ASSERTIONS
BOUNCE OFF AGAIN MEANING NOTHING ASSERTIONS ASSERTIONS   249 24

ASSERTIVENESS
THE INWARD COCKY ASSERTIVENESS OF THE SPANIARD SEEMS TO+   618 9

ASSERTS
THE BOURGEOIS ASSERTS THAT HE OWNS HIS PROPERTY BY DIVI+   663 13
AND THE BOLSHEVIST ASSERTS THAT BY HUMAN RIGHT NO MAN S+   663 14

ASSES
AND KICK OUR HEELS LIKE JOLLY ESCAPED ASSES   517 16
AND THE INTELLECTUAL ASSES   534 17
A WORSE LOT O' JUJUBEY ASSES   553 15

ASSIST
TO ASSIST US DISASTROUSLY SILENCE-BOUND   166 15

ASSOCIATIONS
MANY UNDESIRABLE ASSOCIATIONS   581 13
IT SAVES HIM FROM SO MANY UNDESIRABLE ASSOCIATIONS   581 16
TO SAVE THEM FROM UNDESIRABLE ASSOCIATIONS   581 22

ASS'S
BARES HIS LONG ASS'S TEETH FLATTENS HIS LONG ASS'S EARS   379 21

ASS-TEETH
HENCE HE UNCOVERS HIS BIG ASS-TEETH AND HOWLS IN THAT A+   378 24

ASSUME
WHO SAID THEY MIGHT ASSUME THESE BLOSSOMS   313 25
FROM WHICH WE ARE LED TO ASSUME   329 26

ASSUMES
OR THE PERSONALITY ASSUMES IT AS AN ATTRIBUTE OR THE EGO   473 3

ASSUMING
FLATLY ASSUMING THE SUN   50 24

ASSURANCE
WITH MARVELLOUS NAKED ASSURANCE EACH SINGLE TWIG   299 26
WITH SUCH INSUPERABLE SUBTLY-SMILING ASSURANCE   306 31
WHERE BEFORE THE ASSURANCE CHUCKLED   767 18
THE SKY WITH A WEALTH OF EASE AND ASSURANCE   772 5

ASSURE
AND HIS ATTEMPT TO ASSURE HIMSELF THAT WHAT IS SO IS NO+   299 17

ASSURED
I SIT ABSOLVED ASSURED I AM BETTER OFF   36 7
THEY KEEP ME ASSURED AND WHEN MY SOUL FEELS LONELY   *900 20
THEY KEEP ME ASSURED AND WHEN MY SOUL FEELS LONELY   *903 32

ASSYRIAN-WISE
ASSYRIAN-WISE   326 7.

ASTART
GLOW LIKE BLOSSOMS ASTART   887 2

ASTARTE
MADE HER HALF MADONNA HALF ASTARTE   617 22

ASTIR
SHAKEN ASTIR   57 20

ASTOUNDED
I CANNOT TELL YOU THE MAD ASTOUNDED RAPTURE OF ITS DISC+   260 20

ASTRIDE
ASTRIDE ABOVE ME   409 9

'AST
AS THA ALLUS 'AST BUT LET ME TELL THEE   80 5

ASUNDER
WONDERING MOUNT AND PUT THE FLOWERS ASUNDER   176 17
THE HEAVENS LIKE SPECKS OF DUST THAT ARE FLOATING ASUND+   223 3
THAT WHICH IS WHOLE TORN ASUNDER   367 5
SHAKING ASUNDER AND FLICKING AT HIS RIBS   453 15
STARK ASUNDER   839 9
SHOULD CLIMB THE HILL AND PUT THE FLOWERS ASUNDER   *941 4

AS-YET-UNKNOWABLE
AND FOR THE SAKE OF THIS NASCENT UNBORN AS-YET-UNKNOWAB+   775 10

'AS
AN' OTHERS 'AS REAMS   45 24
AS 'AS SLUDGED LIKE A HORSE ALL 'ER LIFE   77 18
AN' ME AS 'AS KEP' MY-SEN   77 25
IT'S THEE AS 'AS DONE IT AS MUCH AS ME   80 1
WHILE T' CLOCKS 'AS A' RUN DOWN AN' STOPPED   137 28
WE AIN'T GOT NO FARVER ONLY A MOVVER AN' SHE 'AS TER GO   866 20
WAS TH' LITTLE LOVIN' SORT AS 'AS NOWT TER SCREEN 'EM   *910 25
AN' ME AS 'AS KEP MY-SEN   *919 13
IT'S THEE AS 'AS DONE IT AS MUCH AS ME   *922 1

ATE
I AM THINKING OF COURSE OF THE PEACH BEFORE I ATE IT   279 13
EAT ME UP DEAR PEASANT SO THE PEASANT ATE HIM   533 25
TILL HE WAS BORN FROM A WOMB AND ATE SOUP AND BREAD   689 28
PROBABLY AS SHE GREW OLDER SHE ATE HER RIVALS   836 6

ATHWART
WHO RUNS ATHWART MY SERPENT-FLAME   805 6
WHERE THE LOFTY TREES ATHWART STREAM PERCHANCE   *914 26

ATHWART-STREAM
WHERE LOFTY TREES ATHWART-STREAM CHANCE   68 11

ATLANTIC
WHILE YOU READ ABOUT THE AIR-SHIP CROSSING THE WILD ATL+   441 22

ATMOSPHERE
TO YOU EARTH OF MY ATMOSPHERE STONE   118 4
EARTH OF MY SWAYING ATMOSPHERE   118 7
RAGE OF THE SULLEN-STAGNATING ATMOSPHERE OF GOATS   381 24
ATMOSPHERE   444 4
AND DANGLED THEM IN THE ATMOSPHERE   683 3

ATOM
THAT CRUSHES ME TO AN UNSEEN ATOM OF FIRE   195 36
STOIC ULYSSEAN ATOM   354 5
THIS ATOM   357 33
AND FLUTTERS AT THE CORE OF THE ATOM   440 4
OR IN EVERY ATOM   480 27
THAT SHINES SOMEWHERE IN THE ATOM SOMEWHERE PIVOTS THE   481 14
PEACE I HAVE FROM THE CORE OF THE ATOM FROM THE CORE OF+   499 4
TO THE ATOM TO THE BODY OF IMMORTAL CHAOS   505 4
AND IN THE MIDDLE OF EVERY ATOM WHICH IS THE SAME THING   512 6
AND FURTHER THE SUN WITHIN THE ATOM   513 19
WHICH IS GOD IN THE ATOM   513 20
IN DEATH THE ATOM TAKES US UP   514 17
THE ATOM LOCKS UP TWO ENERGIES   515 14
BUT IT IS A THIRD THING PRESENT WHICH MAKES IT AN ATOM   515 15
ONE MIGHT TALK OF THE SANITY OF THE ATOM   515 16
AND AS IF THE ATOM WERE AN IMPULSIVE THING   524 24
THEN EVERY ATOM OF THE COSMOS TREMBLED WITH DELIGHT   682 8

ATOMS
NOR IS HE NESTING PASSIVE UPON THE ATOMS   436 5
WHERE THE FORCES TIE THEMSELVES UP INTO KNOTS OF ATOMS   437 29
WHERE THE FATHER OF ALL THINGS SWIMS IN A MIST OF ATOMS   438 4
THERE IS A SPIRAL FLAME-TIP THAT CAN LICK OUR LITTLE AT+   440 5
AND SENDS OFF MILLIONS OF SPARKS OF NEW ATOMS   506 9
LO AGAIN THE SHUDDER OR BLISS THROUGH ALL THE ATOMS   682 15
AND IS AN ARCHITECTURE OF GLISTENING ATOMS   692 3
WHENCE ISSUE UNBLEMISHED THE ATOMS WHICH SOFT BESTOWED   *938 17
AND FORCES TIE THEMSELVES UP INTO KNOTS OF ATOMS THEN C+   *947 6
THE FATHER OF ALL THINGS SWIMS IN THE VAST DUSK OF ALL +   *947 17

AT-ONENESS
THAT SPANGLED GLISTEN IS GONE THAT AT-ONENESS WITHOUT A+   656 16

ATROPHY
AND YOUR SENSUAL ATROPHY   655 16
HYPERTROPHY OF THE MIND ATROPHY OF THE SENSES   841 21

ATTACHMENT
FIDELITY LOYALTY ATTACHMENT   399 19
A CLUTCH OF ATTACHMENT LIKE PARENTHOOD   *899 33
A CLUTCH OF ATTACHMENT LIKE PARENTHOOD   *903 12

ATTACK
THERE ARE DEAD THAT ATTACK THE SUN LIKE SWARMS OF BLACK+   795 28
EVER TO SUFFER LOVE'S WILD ATTACK   854 18

ATTACKED
IT IS SAID A DISEASE HAS ATTACKED THE CYPRESS TREES OF +   295 1

ATTAIN
  THE DEATH THEY WILL ATTAIN TO WHERE THEY GO   744 17
  GOAL TO TRAVEL TOWARDS YET IT'S SOMETHING TO ATTAIN YOU+   761 15

ATTAINMENT
  ALL HOPE OF MY ATTAINMENT THENCE SERENE   877 16

ATTEMPT
  AND HIS ATTEMPT TO ASSURE HIMSELF THAT WHAT IS SO IS NO+   299 17

ATTEND
  ONLY ATTEND TO THE NOISELESS MULTITUDES   736 2
  FOR ONE YEAR'S SPACE ATTEND ON OUR ANGRY DEAD   740 16

ATTENDING
  BUT THE MOON IS WENDING HER WAY ATTENDING   456 3
  TRUE YOU CAN'T PRODUCE THE BEST WITHOUT ATTENDING TO TH+   668 2
  THOUGHT IS A MAN IN HIS WHOLENESS WHOLLY ATTENDING   673 15

ATTENTION
  OUR ATTENTION OUT OF THE VOID WHEREIN WE ARE CRUSHED   165 33
  TO DEADEN MY ATTENTION IN YOUR DIRECTION   332 23
  METAL HITTING ON METAL TO ENFORCE OUR ATTENTION   623 3
  ATTENTION   818 29
  AND SUPERFICIAL ATTENTION AND CARE AND FULFILMENT OF DU+   832 16
  WHERE THE ATTENTION WILL BE LIFTED OFF MATERIAL THINGS   833 14
  WHEN MEN WOVE WITH THEIR HANDS AND THEIR SOUL'S ATTENTI+   *949 26

ATTEST
  SOUL'S NAKED LIGHTNING WHICH SHOULD SURE ATTEST   87 24

ATTESTS
  AND WHAT OF GOOD I HAVE GIVEN THE DAY MY PEACE ATTESTS   *946 3

ATTILA
  I WOULD CALL ATTILA ON HIS LITTLE HORSE   497 1
  SO THAT I WOULD CALL ATTILA ON HIS LITTLE HORSE   497 11

ATTIS
  AND LIKE PERSEPHONE OR ATTIS   711 17

ATTRACTIVE
  BUT ON WHAT THEY FIND DISTASTEFUL REPULSIVE OR ATTRACTI+   831 19

ATTRIBUTE
  OR THE PERSONALITY ASSUMES IT AS AN ATTRIBUTE OR THE EGO   473 3

ATTRIBUTES
  BUT ANYONE WHO SHALL ASCRIBE ATTRIBUTES TO GOD OR   726 12

ATWEEN
  ATWEEN A LAD AN' 'IS WIFE   77 20
  'ARK 'ERE LAD ATWEEN THEE AN' ME   490 28
  ATWEEN A LAD AN' 'IS WIFE   *919 8

AUBURN
  COIFFING UP YOUR AUBURN HAIR   178 8
  PLAITING A HEAVY AUBURN BRAID   178 20

AUDIENCE
  AND HEARD THE AUDIENCE SIGHING AND SOBBING WITH ALL THE   443 24
  BUT THE AUDIENCE COMPELLED TO WONDER   445 24

AUDILE
  AUDILE TACTILE SENSITIVENESS AS OF A TENDRIL WHICH ORIE+   285 26

AUGHT
  AS IF HE KNEW AUGHT   54 16

AUGUST
  US OUT AS DREAMS YOU AUGUST SLEEP   194 22
  ANY MORE THAN AUGUST CAN BE BULLIED TO LOOK LIKE MARCH   478 11

AUNT
  WHAT IS THE POINT TO US BOTH IT IS ALL MY AUNT   74 29
  TO THEIR LEVELS MY HOLY AUNT   555 24

AUNT GWENDOLINE
  INSTEAD OF AUNT GWENDOLINE   571 18
  SO WELL BROUGHT UP AS AUNT GWENDOLINE IS   571 21

AUNT GWEN
  AUNT GWEN WAS A POOR ONE BUT AUNT MAUD YOU SEE   571 25

AUNTIE
  GO A BANGING LITTLE TATTAH WITH ITS AUNTIE   571 2
  THEN WHEN SUNDAY COMES IT SHALL GO TATTAH WITH ITS AUNT+   571 5
  AND TO GO A BANGING TATTAH WITH ITS AUNTIE   571 9
  SUCH A DEAR KIND AUNTIE ISN'T SHE TO A LUCKY LITTLE   571 11
  HOLD MY HAND AUNTIE AUNTIE   572 17
  AUNTIE HOLD MY HAND   572 18
  I FEEL I'M GOING TO BE NAUGHTY AUNTIE   572 19
  HOLD MY HAND AND LOVE ME AUNTIE   572 21
  WE WANT TO BE LOVED ESPECIALLY AUNTIE   572 23
  IDLE WE STAND BY THE KERB-EDGE AUNTIE   572 25
  THAT AUNTIE UNDERSTANDS   572 29
  BUT WAGES GO DOWN AND REALLY AUNTIE   573 1
  BUT SO LONG AS WE KNOW THAT AUNTIE LOVES US   573 3
  HOLD MY HAND AUNTIE AUNTIE   573 5
  AUNTIE HOLD MY HAND   573 6
  PERHAPS I'M GOING TO BE NAUGHTY AUNTIE   573 7
  OH AUNTIE ISN'T HE A BEAUTY AND IS HE A GENTLEMAN OR   581 10
  IF AUNTIE DOESN'T LOVE ME   670 24
  AUNTIE IS ONLY MY HOUSEKEEPER   671 3
  SO IF AUNTIE DOESN'T LOVE ME   671 5

AUNTIE MAUD
  AUNTIE MAUD HAS COME TO KEEP HOUSE   571 17
  THEY SAY THAT AUNTIE MAUD YOU KNOW   571 19

AUNTIES
  AND NOW ALL THE AUNTIES LIKE HIM SO MUCH   581 17
  AUNTIES   581 20

AUNT LIBBY'S
  AUNT LIBBY'S REALLY A FEEBLE LOT   571 29

AUNT LOUIE'S
  OH AUNT LOUIE'S THE ONE I DREAD   572 16

AUNT LOUIE
  AUNT LOUIE IS ALMOST BOUND TO COME   572 11

AUNT LOU
  AND I SIMPLY DAREN'T THINK OF AUNT LOU   571 30

AUNT MAUD
  AUNT GWEN WAS A POOR ONE BUT AUNT MAUD YOU SEE   571 25
  OH I DO HOPE AUNT MAUD WILL MANAGE ALL RIGHT   572 9

AUNTY'S
  WRINKLED OLD AUNTY'S FACE   400 19

AURA
  YET WHAT AN AURA SURROUNDS YOU   332 18
  YOUR EVIL LITTLE AURA PROWLING AND CASTING NUMBNESS ON   332 19
  A MANGO-FLESHED AURA NAUSEOUSLY STEAMING   760 9
  WITH ITS OWN ALIEN AURA   780 30

AUREOLED
  YOUR HORRIBLE SKELETON AUREOLED IDEAL   292 7

AURICULAS
  EVEN THE SULPHUR AURICULAS   270 8

AUSTERE
  FINALLY RIDGED WITH THE AUSTERE LINE OF THE DEAD   155 5

AUSTRALIA
  EMPTY DAWNS IN SILENT AUSTRALIA   393 13

AUSTRALIAN
  OF AN AUSTRALIAN BLACK-BOY   394 7

AUSTRIA
  OVER THERE IS RUSSIA AUSTRIA SWITZERLAND FRANCE IN A   213 1
  FROM AUSTRIA THERE LIES THE WORLD AND HERE   231 6

AUTHENTIC
  THIS IS THE AUTHENTIC ARABIC INTERPRETATION OF THE BRAY+   377 17

AUTHOR
  BECAUSE I WAS THE AUTHOR AND THE RESULT   257 13

AUTHORITIES
  PALE-FACE AUTHORITIES LOITERING TEPIDLY   316 27

AUTHORITY
  LOOK AT THEM STANDING THERE IN AUTHORITY   287 11
  PALE-FACE AUTHORITY   287 14
  PLEASE APPROACH THE SUPREME AUTHORITY DIRECT   604 18

AUTO-DA-FE
  THEY WANT TO MAKE AN AUTO-DA-FE   633 8
  THROUGH THE AUTO-DA-FE OF LOVE   769 6
  LOVE'S LONG MOILED MADDENED AUTO-DA-FE   769 7

AUTOMAT
  THE AUTOMAT HAS NO SOUL TO LOSE   638 18

AUTOMATA
  OR SITTING STUCK LIKE AUTOMATA IN AUTOMOBILES   530 17

AUTOMATIC-MACHINE
  LIKE SLITS IN AN AUTOMATIC-MACHINE YOU COLUMNS OF GIVE-+   288 25

AUTOMATON
  AUTOMATON OF YOUR UPRISEN SELF   290 28

AUTOMOBILE
  THICKEN MIASMA THE FUMES OF THE AUTOMOBILE   703 22

AUTOMOBILES
  OR SITTING STUCK LIKE AUTOMATA IN AUTOMOBILES   530 17
  AT HER TRAINS AT HER RAILWAYS AND HER AUTOMOBILES   790 7
  YEA LORD EVEN TRAINS AND CAMIONS AND AUTOMOBILES   794 11
  TRAINS AND CAMIONS AUTOMOBILES AND AEROLANES   794 12
  FACTORIES AND THE AUTOMOBILES   794 22

AUTUMM
  AND LIKE HAZEL-NUTS IN AUTUMM AT LAST   504 8

AUTUMN
  LIGHTING THESE AUTUMN LEAVES LIKE A STAR DROPPED THROUGH   86 16
  UPON YOU AS AN AUTUMN WIND ON SOME   86 19
  THE PINE-TREES BEND TO LISTEN TO THE AUTUMN WIND AS IT +   102 25
  WHEN IT WAS AWFUL AUTUMN TO ME   103 15
  THE ACRID SCENTS OF AUTUMN   107 5
  EVERYTHING TEAR-TREMBLING STARS OF AUTUMN   107 7
  AND ACRID NIGHT OF AUTUMN   107 21
  OF AUTUMN TELL THE WITHERED TALE AGAIN   119 14
  AND O BEHIND THE CLOUD-LEAVES LIKE YELLOW AUTUMN   120 7
  THE FIELDS OF AUTUMN   120 12
  IN THE AUTUMN FIELDS THE STUBBLE   152 18

AUTUMN
THE TREES IN TROUBLE BECAUSE OF AUTUMN	160	5
THE SUN SETS OUT THE AUTUMN CROCUSES	177	1
WHEN THE AUTUMN ROSES	178	1
WHEN THE AUTUMN ROSES	178	12
WHEN IN THE AUTUMN ROSES	178	23
FLUX OF AUTUMN	281	22
OVER THE CLODS OF THE AUTUMN WIND-CHILLED SUNSHINE	357	27
AUTUMN	408	24
STILLNESS AND SATISFACTION OF AUTUMN	503	25
AS HE BITES AT THE STEMS OF LEAVES IN AUTUMN TO MAKE TH+	609	3
ARE TORN DOWN BY DISMEMBERING AUTUMN	709	19
NOW IT IS AUTUMN AND THE FALLING FRUIT	716	18
AND IF AS AUTUMN DEEPENS AND DARKENS	727	6
NOW LIKE A CROCUS IN THE AUTUMN TIME	744	4
OF WINDY AUTUMN WHEN THE WINDS ALL SWEEP	744	7
IN AUTUMN LIKE TO A MESSENGER COME BACK	744	20
AMID THE AUTUMN RUSHING RED ABOUT	744	22
IN PUTRID AUTUMN ISSUING THROUGH THE FALL	745	22
CALLS TO THE AUTUMN RESURRECTION	745	28
IN THE AUTUMN I'LL LOOK FOR IMMORTAL FRUIT	855	9
IN THE GARNERING AUTUMN A GLOW OF IMMORTAL FRUIT	855	17
I SING OF AUTUMN AND THE FALLING FRUIT	*956	24

AUTUMNAL
MOAN SOFTLY WITH AUTUMNAL PARTURITION	160	9
AUTUMNAL EXCREMENTA	280	17
AUTUMNAL	311	32

AUTUMN-BROWN
HIS LITTLE PUNT AN AUTUMN-BROWN BEECH-LEAF	867	15

AUTUMNUS
AH THE FALLEN STILLNESS OF GOD AUTUMNUS AND IT IS ONLY +	651	18

AVAIL
WHAT SHOULD IT AVAIL ME	140	31
DARKNESS OF FAILURE WAS IN THEM WITHOUT AVAIL	156	4

AVENGE
IF THE JOY THAT THEY ARE LIFTED TO AVENGE	126	3
IF THE JOY WHICH THEY ARE LIFTED TO AVENGE	*937	3

AVENUE
ALONG THE GLAMOROUS BIRCH-TREE AVENUE	206	5
ALONG THE AVENUE OF CYPRESSES	232	16
BETWEEN THE AVENUE OF CYPRESSES	232	29

AVENUES
VISTAS DOWN DARK AVENUES	286	30
THE GRAPE IS SWART THE AVENUES DUSKY AND TENDRILLED SUB+	286	32
DUSKY ARE THE AVENUES OF WINE	287	5
DOWN THE TENDRILLED AVENUES OF WINE AND THE OTHERWORLD	287	10
IN THE AVENUES WHERE THE BAT HANGS SLEEPING UPSIDE-DOWN	322	33
HUMMING-BIRDS RACED DOWN THE AVENUES	372	8

AVERTED
THEN AMONG THE AVERTED PANSIES BENEATH THE HIGH	225	29
AND I AS I STAND IN THE COLD AVERTED FLOWERS	226	9
TO HAVE YOU SITTING AVERTED THERE	*931	13

'AVE
'AVE I PUT 'IS CLEAN STOCKIN'S AN' SHIRT	45	14
I SHAN'T 'AVE 'IM TO NUSS	45	20
THERE'S ONE THING WE S'LL 'AVE A PEACEFUL 'OUSE	45	29
AN' 'IM TO 'AVE BEEN TOOK IN	77	16
YER NEDN'T 'AVE SWORE	81	12
TO THINK I SHOULD 'AVE TER 'AFFLE AN' CAFFLE	82	9

AVID
AND I DO LIFT MY ANGUISHED AVID BREAST	129	20
AVID AND TERRIBLE	241	23

'AVIN'
I'M NOT 'AVIN' YOUR ORTS AN' SLARTS	82	3

AVOCATION
TRAVEL THINE AVOCATION HERE AND LEARN	872	2

AVOID
PRETENDING TO AVOID US YET ALL THE TIME	269	27
AND SHE'LL AVOID IT SHE'LL GO AND ORDER	583	14

AVOIDING
AVOIDING EACH OTHER YET INCURRING ECLIPSES	823	28

AVOUCH
AS TIME HAS NOT DARED TO AVOUCH NOR ETERNITY BEEN ABLE +	370	31

A-WAGGLE
YOU MUST ALWAYS BE A-WAGGLE WITH LOVE	399	21

AWAIT
AND DO YOU AWAIT US WATTLED FATHER WESTWARD	371	24
WHERE MY DARLING PICTURES PRISONERS AWAIT HIS DEADLY	633	23

AWAITING
AWAITING THE SENTENCE OUT FROM THE WELKIN BROUGHT	142	16
AWAITING THE FIRE	155	18
AWAITING THE CRY OF THE TURKEY-COCK	371	37
ALL MY PRETTY PICTURES HUDDLED IN THE DARK AWAITING	634	1

AWAITS
THE NEMESIS THAT AWAITS OUR CIVILISATION	514	25
FOR THE VOYAGE OF OBLIVION AWAITS YOU	720	22

AWAKE
QUIVERING AWAKE WITH ONE IMPULSE AND ONE WILL	39	8
YOU HAVE DREAMED AND ARE NOT AWAKE COME HERE TO ME	211	1
YET WE'RE AWAKE	229	8
ARE YOU AWAKE	230	7
BUT WE AS WE START AWAKE CLUTCH AT OUR VISTAS DEMOCRATIC	286	34
SLEEP YET FIGHTING FIGHTING TO KEEP AWAKE	287	3
NOT YET AWAKE	352	5
EVEN WHEN THE MIND HAS FLICKERED AWAKE	407	24
IN THEIR EFFORTS TO COME AWAKE FOR ONE MOMENT	408	5
THE INDIANS THOUGHT THE WHITE MAN WOULD AWAKE THEM	408	8
THOUGH THE MIND IS AWAKE	408	18
ARE AWAKE THROUGH YEARS WITH TRANSFERRED TOUCH AND GO	448	3
TO THE SIGHTLESS REALM WHERE DARKNESS IS AWAKE UPON THE+	697	17
BUT IF I EAT AN APPLE I LIKE TO EAT IT WITH ALL MY SENS+	708	10
ARE THERE TWO OF YOU AWAKE	791	11
I RUN AWAKE TO THE HOUSE OF MY SOUL AND FIND IT EMPTY	871	9
AND ALL THEIR FACES LIKE BRIGHT FLOWERS AWAKE	872	21
QUIVERING AWAKE WITH ONE IMPULSE OF DESIRE	*893	21

AWAKEN
THINKING DEATH WILL AWAKEN SOMETHING	408	13

AWAKENED
AND I AM JUST AWAKENED FROM THE TOMB	744	1

AWAKENING
AND FEEL THE STREAM OF AWAKENING RIPPLE AND PASS	51	23
HAVE STOLEN THE TREASURE OF AWAKENING	878	30

AWARE
HE IS WELL AWARE OF HIMSELF	325	5
AWARE	333	3
THE GOAT IS AN EGOIST AWARE OF HIMSELF DEVILISH AWARE OF	382	10
FOR WE'RE ALL SELF-CONSCIOUSLY AWARE OF OURSELVES	496	19
I AM AWARE I FEEL NOTHING EVEN AT DAWN	509	24
AWARE AT LAST THAT OUR MANHOOD IS UTTERLY LOST	585	7
I AM MORE ALIVE MORE AWARE AND MORE WISE	655	24
BECOME AWARE AS LEAVES ARE AWARE	667	26
I WASN'T AWARE OF THE THINGS I COULD DO	761	9
HOW HIGHLY AWARE WE ARE OF ONE ANOTHER SOCIALLY	829	17

AWARENESS
AWARENESS THEN I SUFFERED A BALK	111	17
IN CLEAN NEW AWARENESS BUT NOW	112	4
YET YOU CANNOT GET BEYOND YOUR AWARENESS OF ME	235	30
AND FEARLESS FACE-TO-FACE AWARENESS OF NOW-NAKED LIFE	667	4
AND A SILENT SHEER CESSATION OF ALL AWARENESS	724	22

AWE
INTO AWE	165	30

AWED
DEATH IN OUR AWED EMBRACES	242	22

AWFUL
THE NIGHT IS IMMENSE AND AWFUL YET TO ME IT IS NOTHING +	98	1
WHEN IT WAS AWFUL AUTUMN TO ME	103	15
AND HE HAS A REPTILE'S AWFUL PERSISTENCE	361	30
ONLY AGELESSLY SILENT WITH A REPTILE'S AWFUL PERSISTENCY	362	25
THE AWFUL CONCUSSION	363	11
AND THE STILL MORE AWFUL NEED TO PERSIST TO FOLLOW FOLL+	363	12
IN THAT MOST AWFUL STILLNESS THAT ONLY GASPED AND HUMMED	372	7
I NEVER DREAMED TILL NOW OF THE AWFUL TIME THE LORD MUST	395	17
WITH PERFECTLY AWFUL THINGS IN IT	491	14
AND IN THESE AWFUL PAUSES THE EVOLUTIONARY CHANGE TAKES	510	10
WON'T IT BE AWFUL WHAT SHALL WE DO	571	28
WHAT IS THIS AWFUL ASPECT OF MAN	628	25
AND WHAT AN AWFUL CONCATENATION OF SOUND IT IS	657	12
THAT AWFUL AND SICKENING ENDLESS SINKING SINKING	699	21
SINKING IN THE ENDLESS UNDOING THE AWFUL KATABOLISM INT+	699	26
THE KIND OF HELL THAT IS REAL GREY AND AWFUL	714	1
AWFUL JOB	865	24
UPON THESE AWFUL WATERS OF LIFE AND DEATH	875	27
BY A SLOW GASPING PUMP THAT HAS AWFUL INTERVALS	878	34

AWFULLY
AWFULLY MUST I CALL BACK A HUNDRED EYES A VOICE	76	7
HOW AWFULLY DISTINCT AND FAR OFF FROM EACH OTHER'S BEING	248	3
SO AWFULLY NICE	659	25
AWFULLY SORRY DEAR BUT I CAN'T COME BECAUSE OF THE CHIL+	832	11
AWFULLY MUST I CALL BACK THOSE HUNDRED EYES A VOICE	*898	2
AWFULLY MUST I CALL BACK THOSE HUNDRED EYES A VOICE	*901	11

AWHILE
YET WAIT AWHILE FOR HENCEFORTH I WILL LOVE WHEN A BLOSS+	94	5
MY LOVE WHERE IT IS WANTED YET WAIT AWHILE MY FALL	94	7
HER HAIR FOR WOMANHOOD AND PLAY AWHILE WITH HER THEN	179	8
IN HIS HOUSE AWHILE	234	6
AND LEAVE ME ALONE AWHILE	580	16
OF DEATH BUT I WAIT AWHILE IN THIS TABERNACLE	772	20
SO HE TOSSED IT AWHILE IN HIS HAND AND PLAYED WITH IT	791	6
AND WAIT WAIT AWHILE	*947	22

A-WHORING
THE BONNIE BONNIE BOURGEOIS GOES A-WHORING UP BACK	432	22

AWKWARD
AND HIS HANDS ARE AWKWARD AND WANT TO HIDE	228	3
THIS AWKWARD HARROWING PURSUIT	363	4
A BIT AWKWARD AND WITH A FUNNY SQUAWK IN HIS VOICE	413	21
AND IN MY FRAGILE AWKWARD BOAT BETWEEN	875	28
THY BODY FROM ITS TERRORS AWKWARD LEASH	*927	25

AWKWARDLY
  BENDING BACKWARDS AWKWARDLY   734 3

AWOKE
  WHEN I AWOKE THIS MORNING   46 25
  I AWOKE WITH THE YOUNG NETTLES ON MY WRISTS   882 5

AWRY
  OF DESIRE IS DISTORTED AND TWISTED AWRY   485 3

AX
  SHOUT AN' AX WHAT 'E WANTS   44 18
  AX 'IM THY-SEN WENCH A WIDDER'S LODGER   77 11
  AX HIM THY-SEN WENCH A WIDDER'S LODGER   *918 29

AXE
  WITH AXE IN HAND AND THE HAMMER AND THE PICK-AXE OVER-A+   174 16
  OH MEN WITH THE AXE AND THE PICK-AXE BREAK THE WALLS OF+   175 26

AXIN'
  NOW LAD I'M AXIN' THEE SUMMAT   138 2

AXIS
  THERE WHERE THE PIVOT IS THE AXIS   169 7
  THERE AT THE AXIS   169 18

AXLE
  WHILE THE POLE STAR LIES ASIDE LIKE AN OLD AXLE TAKEN F+   616 30

AY
  OH AY HE'LL COME AN TELL THEE HIS-SEN   76 25
  AY AN' YALLER AS A CROWFLOWER AN' YET I' TH' DARK   77 7
  AY IT DID BUT AFTERWARDS   80 21
  AY AN' 'IM WI' ME   81 28
  AY I'M SORRY I'M SORRY   83 18
  AY I'M SORRY THA NEDNA WORRY   83 20
  I'M SORRY FOR TH' TROUBLE AY   84 9
  AY LAD I'LL TELL THEE THY MIND   138 28
  AN' THA KNOWED IT AY YET THA COMES ACROSS   139 6
  AY AN' THA MAUN   139 22
  AY IT'S A RUM UN   140 6
  NOW AT THIS MOMENT AY   788 27
  NOW AT THIS MOMENT AY   789 2
  AY IN A MOMENT AY   789 6
  OH AY HE'LL BE COMIN' TO TELL THEE HIS-SEN   *918 17
  AY AN' YALLER AS A CROWFLOWER AN' YET I' THE DARK   *918 25
  AY I DID BUT AFTERWARDS   *922 21
  AY AN' 'IM WI' ME   *923 28

AYE
  AYE BUSY WITH A FEW HARD TASKS AND WRATH   875 31
  AYE SUFFOCATED WITH A DRUNK SURFEIT   877 10

AZALEA
  AZALEA AND CAMELLIA SINGLE PEONY   313 28

AZTEC
  DO YOU LIFT IT TO THE SUN AS THE AZTEC PRIESTS USED TO +   374 7
  THE GREEK BEAUTIFUL ONES THE PHOENICIAN UGLY ONES THE A+   671 16
  WILL YOU LIKE AN AZTEC SACRIFICE REVERSED   783 20

AZTECS
  AND THOSE SOMBRE DEAD FEATHER-LUSTROUS AZTECS   371 33

'A
  YOU SHOULD 'A SEEN HER SLIVE UP WHEN WE'D GO   *910 9
  YOU SHOULD 'A SEEN HER KNEEL AN' LOOK DOWN   *910 10
  WOR IT THA'D LIKED TO 'A KILLED HER   *922 24

A'
  AN' T' PARSON MAKIN' HASTE AN' A' T' BLACK   60 15
  THAT YOUNG AN' A' THE FAULT OF DRINK   60 25
  OVER A DOUBLE 'ANDFUL O' VIOLETS A' IN A PACK   61 11
  IN A' THIS DEPTH O' SNOW   79 14
  I'M SORRY F'R US A'   83 23
  AFTER A'   83 25
  AS COMES ON US A'   84 10
  I'M NOT THAT'S A'   84 12
  AH'VE 'AD A' AS I CAN CARRY   84 15
  LET'S A' HA' DONE   84 26
  AN' OWER A' THE THAW AN' MESS   137 22
  WHILE T' CLOCKS 'AS A' RUN DOWN AN' STOPPED   137 28
  'APPEN THA DID AN' A'   139 2
  TER SAY GOOD-BYE AN' A'   139 7
  THEY'RE A' A D-D LOT O' -3   491 1
  AN' PARSON MAKIN' HASTE AN' A' THE BLACK   *911 1
  IN A' THIS DEPTH O' SNOW   *921 10

'A'
  DEED AN' I WISH I C'D 'A' STOOD AT TH' ALTAR WI' THEE A+   83 11
  THAT I COULD 'A' BIN FIRST WOMAN TER THEE AS THA'RT FIR+   83 13
  THA MUST 'A' BEEN HARD TO WEAN   *921 20

BAA-BAA
  BAA-BAA BLACK SHEEP   669 19

BAAL
  FOR A MOMENT GODLY LIKE BAAL OR KRISHNA OR ADONIS OR BA+   675 16

BABEL
  SOLEMNLY AND DISTINCTLY CRIES DOWN THE BABEL OF CHILDREN   48 15

BABES
  THE BABES JUST BEGINNING TO TEETHE   553 32

BABIES
  BABIES   438 19
  THERE'LL BE BABIES BORN THAT ARE CYGNETS O MY SOUL   438 21
  AND BABIES OF WOMEN WILL COME OUT YOUNG WILD GEESE   438 23
  DON'T SYMPATHISE OR YOU TAINT THE UNBORN BABIES   442 5
  AND HYGIENIC BABIES IN HUGE HULKS OF COFFIN-LIKE PERAMB+   522 5
  DON'T YOU THINK LITTLE MAN YOU'LL BE FATHER OF HUMAN BA+   *947 23
  THERE'LL BE BABIES BORN THAT ARE YOUNG WILD SWANS O MY +   *947 24

BABY
  WHEN THE WHITE FEET OF THE BABY BEAT ACROSS THE GRASS   64 29
  AND I WISH THAT THE BABY WOULD TACK ACROSS HERE TO ME   65 5
  MY BABY HER BROWN HAIR BRUSHED WITH WET TEARS   73 23
  WITH AFTER-PAIN MY SLEEPING BABY HANGS UPON MY LIFE   73 27
  BABY TORTOISE   352 2
  UNDER ITS SLOW LID TINY BABY TORTOISE   352 22
  AND A BABY MAKES NONE   352 32
  YOUR FACE BABY TORTOISE   353 9
  ALONG THE BACK OF THE BABY TORTOISE   355 1
  THE SECTIONS OF THE BABY TORTOISE SHELL   355 9
  OF THE BABY TORTOISE   355 16
  OF THE BABY TORTOISE   356 10
  OH BRITANNIA'S GOT A BABY A BABY A BABY   570 12
  BRITANNIA'S GOT A BABY AND SHE GOT IT BY AND BY   570 13
  IT'S SUCH A BONNY BABY A BABY A BABY   570 16
  TO FEED THE BONNY BABY AND KEEP ITS TARA DRY   570 19
  PROPERTY IS NOW SOLOMON'S BABY   664 14
  AND WHOEVER GETS IT IT'LL BE A DEAD BABY   664 15
  HUSHABY BABY ON A TREE TOP   669 7
  DARLING YOU LOOK SO LIKE BABY   842 14
  YOU LOOK SO LIKE BABY IT WRINGS MY HEART   842 15
  SAYING YOU KNOW I ALWAYS HAVE TO SAY THAT ARCHIE LOOKS +   842 20
  I CAN NEVER EVEN THINK THAT IT'S BABY WHO LOOKS LIKE AR+   842 21
  BABY WAS HER LITTLE BOY OF SEVEN   842 23
  AND WE STILL HAVE TO SEE WHAT BABY WILL BE LIKE AT THIR+   842 26
  MY OWN BABY   863 18
  WHEN THE WHITE FEET OF THE BABY BEAT ACROSS THE GRASS   *912 25
  I WAIT FOR THE BABY TO WANDER HITHER TO ME   *913 6
  MY BABY HER BROWN HAIR BRUSHED WITH WET TEARS   *913 13
  MY SLEEPING BABY HANGS UPON MY LIFE   *913 19
  WHEN THE BARE FEET OF THE BABY BEAT ACROSS THE GRASS   *913 28
  I LONG FOR THE BABY TO WANDER HITHER TO ME   *914 6
  YI' THA'RT A MAN THA'RT A FINE BIG MAN BUT NIVER A BABY+   *925 24

BABYLON
  JESUS BUDDHA JEHOVAH AND RA EGYPT AND BABYLON   671 19

BABYLON'S
  NOT TO SPEAK OF BABYLON'S WHOREDOM   328 6

BACCHAE
  TALL BLACK BACCHAE OF MIDNIGHT WHY THEN WHY   140 28

BACCHANTE
  ME UP I PRAY OH YOU WHO ARE NIGHT'S BACCHANTE   86 7

BACCHUS
  BACCHUS IS A DREAM'S DREAM   286 15

BACHELOR OF CASH ARTS
  IT WILL BE BACHELOR OF CASH ARTS MASTER OF CASH SCIENCE   *950 23

BACK-BOARD
  BENEATH THE LOW-DROPPING BACK-BOARD OF HER SHELL   361 21

BACKBONE
  HER BACKBONE SHARP AS A ROCK   386 10

BACK-BONE
  AT THE END OF A BACK-BONE RIDGE LIKE A STRAIGHT SIERRA +   381 3

BACKGROUND
  THE BACKGROUND   835 2

BACKING
  ADVANCING WITH THE SLOW-SWIFTNESS OF A SHIP BACKING HER+   672 21

BACKWARD
  IN A BACKWARD RIPPLE THE WAVE-LENGTH REVEAL   68 26
  BACKWARD INTO SPACE TO ALIGHT   162 27
  UNTIL YOUR VEILED HEAD ALMOST TOUCHES BACKWARD   370 14
  BACKWARD AND FORWARD FROM WALL TO WALL   746 11
  IN A BACKWARD RIPPLE GOD'S PROGRESS REVEAL   *915 10

BACKWARD-CURVING
  AND ONE INTENSE AND BACKWARD-CURVING FRISSON   370 16

BACKWARDS
  AND THE STREAM IS TOWARDS THE GODS NOT BACKWARDS TOWARD+   650 11
  BENDING BACKWARDS AWKWARDLY   734 3

BACK-YARD
  HOW SMELLY THEY MAKE THE GREAT BACK-YARD   493 27

BAD
  THEY ON'Y TOWD ME IT WOR BAD   45 11
  I DO 'OPE AS IT'S NOT VERY BAD   45 21
  OWT BAD AN' IT'S HIS   45 28
  THA WANTS 'IM THY-SEN TOO BAD   82 6
  THA WANTED TER LEAVE ME THAT BAD THA KNOWS   138 20
  A GO AT T'OTHER FOR I'M A BAD   140 4
  THIS BOUNDLESS LOVE IS LIKE THE BAD SMELL   291 17
  JUST A BAD SMELL   291 21
  SURELY IT IS BAD POLICY   333 19
  SO DO BAD HUSBANDS JUST AS OFTEN   456 6

BAD
    THAN THE UNHAPPINESS OF A WIFE WITH A BAD HUSBAND   456   9
    BAD INSIDE LIKE FRUIT   462   20
    MEN ARE NOT BAD WHEN THEY ARE FREE   488   1
    PRISON MAKES MEN BAD AND THE MONEY COMPULSION MAKES   488   2
    MEN BAD   488   3
    IT'S BAD TASTE TO BE WISE ALL THE TIME LIKE BEING A PER+   496   1
    WHEN THINGS GET VERY BAD THEY PASS BEYOND TRAGEDY   514   10
    YES I KNOW IT'S TOO BAD OF COURSE IT'S PERFECTLY SUPERF+   546   13
    LIKE A BAD SMELL   687   11
    POLITICIANS MAY BE BAD INDUSTRIAL MAGNATES MAY BE AT FA+   775   5
    IS READY TO BLOW BAD BREATH UPON THEM TO PERISH THEM ALL   792   16
    WHAT YET ANOTHER BAD END OF THE WORLD   814   27
    MIND AND SPIRIT BAD AND GOOD   824   14
    BAD YESTERDAYS UNSURE TOMORROWS   825   3
    BAD AND THE GOOD   826   19
    AND NO MORE THAN THE BARON DID EH NO OLD GIRL AND NOT S+   859   32
    LET BE THAT THERE'S SOME O' TH' BAD AS WE   *911   13
    THA WANTS 'IM THY-SEN TOO BAD   *924   10
    AND WHORING ON THE BRAIN AS BAD AS SYPHILIS INCIPIENT I+   *952   20

BADE
    LIKE A SUDDEN CHUCKLING OF MUSIC I BADE HER EYES   125   26
    SHE BADE ME FOLLOW TO HER GARDEN WHERE   *934   1
    LIKE A SUDDEN CHUCKLING OF MUSIC I BADE HER EYES   *936   25

BADGE
    YOU ARE ONLY KNOWN TO US NOW AS THE BADGE OF AN INSURAN+   330   3

BADGERS
    ONLY MICE AND MOLES AND RATS AND BADGERS AND BEAVERS   392   22

BADLY
    THE TREE OF HUMANITY NEEDS PRUNING BADLY   677   24
    THE TREE OF HUMAN EXISTENCE NEEDS BADLY PRUNING   677   28
    ALREADY OUR BODIES ARE FALLEN BRUISED BADLY BRUISED   718   3

BAFFLE
    TANGLING HIS CIRCLES TO BAFFLE YOU AND ME   118   25

BAFFLING
    THE BAFFLING LIGHT OR THE STRANGE STILL GLEAM OF THE GO+   656   13

BAGS
    SANS BEARDS SANS BAGS   313   2
    THREE BAGS FULL   669   22

BAH
    BUT BAH HOW CAN HE POOR DOMESTICATED BEAST   383   26

BAIL
    O SOMEBODY BAIL THEM OUT   632   29

BAIT
    DON'T SWALLOW THE CULTURE BAIT   459   10

BAITING
    I KNEW THAT SHE WAS BAITING   885   20
    FOR ALL HER SHYNESS BAITING   885   22

BAKED
    BAKED AMPHORAS CRATERS CANTHARUS OENOCHOE AND   305   13
    IS LIKE BISCUITS BAKED FOR A FEAST   758   20

BALAAM'S ASS
    DOES NOT THAT PASSION STAND IN YOUR WAY LIKE A BALAAM'S+   236   8
    AND AM I NOT BALAAM'S ASS   236   9

BALANCE
    WHICH SLIPS DOWN LIKE A PENDULUM TO BALANCE THE THROBBI+   370   6
    THE OVER-DRIP OF A GREAT PASSION HANGING IN THE BALANCE   370   8
    TO ANOTHER BALANCE TRIPPED ROUND POISED AND SLOWLY SANK   444   30
    SPINNING WITH THE HEAVINESS OF BALANCE   480   16
    BACK AND FORTH GOES THE BALANCE AND THE ELECTRIC BREATH   480   21
    WHEN A BIRD FLIPS HIS TAIL IN GETTING HIS BALANCE ON A +   496   6
    I WISH MEN WOULD GET BACK THEIR BALANCE AMONG THE ELEME+   505   17
    SO SATAN ONLY FELL TO KEEP A BALANCE   710   12
    AND HELL AND HEAVEN ARE THE SCALES OF THE BALANCE OF LI+   710   21
    HEAVY WITH THE HEAVINESS OF BALANCE   *951   29
    BALANCE WITH THE OTHER THE VAST UNKNOWABLE FIRE   *951   30

BALANCED
    HAS SOME HAND BALANCED MORE LEAVES IN THE DEPTHS OF THE   142   5
    THE MOUNTAINS ARE BALANCED   204   20
    EACH OF US TO THE BALANCED ETERNAL ORBIT   236   18
    BALANCED IN GLORIOUS EQUILIBRIUM   251   17
    AND THE SWEET CONSTANT BALANCED HEAT   263   15

BALANCES
    A MAN BALANCES BONE UNTO BONE   251   4
    BALANCES EVERYTHING THROWN   251   5
    THAT CENTRES AND BALANCES ALL THINGS   *951   31

BALANCING
    YOU FEET OF THE RAINBOW BALANCING THE SKY   73   9
    HE SAW IN A SHAFT OF LIGHT A LAMB ON A PINNACLE BALANCI+   324   16

BALCONIES
    THE BALCONIES   205   3

BALCONY
    HERE THE BALCONY   209   15
    HERE FROM THE BALCONY   209   19
    FROM THE BALCONY   220   22

BALCONY'S
    AND THROUGH THE SCENT OF THE BALCONY'S NAKED TIMBER   208   29

BALD
    THE VULTURE IS BALD SO IS THE CONDOR OBSCENELY   369   18
    OH MY BALD HEAD   760   1
    BALD AND PRICKLY PATE   760   16

BALDER
    FOR A MOMENT GODLY LIKE BAAL OR KRISHNA OR ADONIS OR BA+   675   16

BALD-HEADED
    THE KNELL OF OUR BALD-HEADED CONSCIOUSNESS   512   10

BALE-FIRE
    A BALE-FIRE MOUNTING MOUNTING UP IN ME   241   12

BALK
    AWARENESS THEN I SUFFERED A BALK   111   17
    FLESH-ANGUISH THEN I SUFFERED A BALK   *927   10
    ANGUISH THEN I SUFFERED A BALK   *928   10

BALKING
    AT THE GATE THE NETS HUNG BALKING   152   16
    BALKING HIS OWN NATURE   *949   11

BALL
    HER OUT OF THE NEST'S WARM BUSY BALL   42   28
    PITEOUS BROWN BALL OF QUIVERING FEARS   43   11
    WHO TOOK A HANDFUL OF LIGHT AND ROLLED A BALL   69   18
    ALL THE BIRDS ARE FOLDED IN A SILENT BALL OF SLEEP   71   9
    AND THE SAME FIRE THAT BOILS WITHIN THIS BALL   89   1
    HERE THIS ROUND BALL OF EARTH   196   7
    BALL   249   20
    TO TOSS THE GLOBE OF EARTH LIKE A BALL ON A WATER-JET   272   14
    AS YOU SEE A TINY CELLULOID BALL TOSSING ON A SQUIRT OF+   272   16
    TO PLAY WITH THE GLOBE OF EARTH LIKE A BALL ON A FOUNTA+   272   19
    BALL   279   22
    BUT IT WASN'T ROUND AND FINISHED LIKE A BILLIARD BALL   279   25
    HURTLING LIKE A BLACK BALL THROUGH THE SNOW   397   8
    AFTER PARTRIDGES OR A LITTLE RUBBER BALL   430   23
    HE TOOK A HANDFUL OF LIGHT AND ROLLED A BALL   *916   1
    ALL THE BIRDS ARE FOLDED IN A SILENT BALL OF SLEEP   *917   27
    BEFORE THE STOUT SWART BEETLE HAD A BALL OF DUNG TO ROL+   *946   26

BALLOON
    IN THE NET OF THE NIGHT'S BALLOON   54   11
    OF THE WIND SHE IS LIFTED AND CARRIED AWAY AS IN A BALL+   153   2

BALLS
    THE BALLS OF FIVE RED TOES   145   22
    LIKE BALLS OF THISTLEDOWN   253   4

BALSAM
    DARK GROW THE SPRUCE-TREES BLUE IS THE BALSAM WATER   401   2

BALSAM-PINES
    AND THE BALSAM-PINES THAT ARE BLUE WITH THE GREY-BLUE B+   647   2

BALTIC
    I COME TO THE NORTH SEA OR THE BALTIC   212   25

BAMBOO
    BELONGS TO THE BAMBOO THICKET AND THE DRAKE IN THE AIR +   623   12

BAN
    YOUR CURT PRIDE'S BAN   55   6
    NOR PUT ME UNDER A BAN   534   22

BANANA-SKIN
    MIND THE BANANA-SKIN   829   30

BAND
    THE BAND IS ACROSS ITS BROW AND IT SCARCELY SEEMS   225   14
    THERE IS A BAND OF DULL GOLD IN THE WEST AND SAY WHAT Y+   656   1
    THERE IS A BAND PLAYING IN THE EARLY NIGHT   656   5
    STRESS OF COMPULSION REMAINS AND A BAND THAT GIRTS   746   16

BANDED
    SHE LOOKED AT HIM AS HE LAY WITH BANDED CHEEK   156   11

BANDS
    LAMPS IS RAYED WITH GOLDEN BANDS   144   4
    TO OPEN MY BLOSSOM-FULL BREAST FROM ITS DREARY BANDS   *896   24
    BANDS   *940   18

BANG
    OR IS HE DRIVEN AGAINST HER WITH A BANG LIKE A BIRD FLY+   363   8

BANGING
    GO A BANGING LITTLE TATTAH WITH ITS AUNTIE   571   2
    AND TO GO A BANGING TATTAH WITH ITS AUNTIE   571   9

BANISH
    UTTERLY DEAD WHO LIVED BUT TO BANISH   855   7

BANK
    I ON THE BANK ALL SUBSTANCE MY SHADOW ALL SHADOW LOOKIN+   34   2
    IF MY FATHER CAN GET THEE A JOB ON T' BANK SAY THA'RT S+   83   17
    AS ONE STANDS ON A BANK AND LOOKS IN   338   31
    AND CLIMB AGAIN THE BROKEN BANK OF MY WALL-FACE   350   32
    SO YOU STEP DOWN THE BANK TO MAKE WAY   387   9
    WITH BANK ACCOUNTS AND INSURANCE POLICIES   442   4
    HE DOESN'T PUT MY BLOOD IN THE BANK   466   22
    THEN YOU WILL SHATTER THE BANK   484   20
    THAN PAPER MONEY WHEN THE BANK IS BROKE   528   4
    A MAN'S BUSINESS IS ONE OF HIS POCKETS HIS BANK   607   15
    CLERKS OF THE BANK   618   19

BANK
    ON THE LITTLE BANK BELOW THE ORCHARD   886 22
    ON THE LITTLE BANK OUR TWO SOULS   887 1
    ON THE LITTLE BANK WHERE BLUEBELLS DROOP   887 10
    OF THE BANK I STAND WATCHING MY OWN WHITE SHADOW QUIVER+   *891 21
BANK-BOOK
    LIFTING A BANK-BOOK TO BLESS US   456 25
BANK-CLERKS
    THEY ARE GOING TO BE SCHOOL-TEACHERS OR BANK-CLERKS   774 2
    WHOSE FATHERS WERE SCHOOL-MASTERS OR BANK-CLERKS   774 4
BANK-CLERK
    DO YOU WANT TO LOOK LIKE A BANK-CLERK   773 16
    DEAR DEAR BANK-CLERK   773 17
BANK-DIRECTORS
    CLERGYMEN PROFESSORS BANK-DIRECTORS AND STOCK-BROKERS   774 6
BANKED
    HIS FIRES OF WRATH ARE BANKED DOWN   327 5
    WHO HAD SPREAD WHITE WASHING ON THE GRAVEL BANKED ABOVE+   693 3
BANK-MANAGER
    DO YOU WANT TO LOOK LIKE A BANK-MANAGER   773 18
BANK-NOTES
    AND BANK-NOTES ARE POETRY PURER THAN GOLD   814 10
BANKRUPT
    FIND OUT IF I'M SOUND OR BANKRUPT   237 3
BANKS
    THE COLTSFOOT FLOWERS ALONG THE RAILWAY BANKS   162 2
    NOT IN DOLLARS NOR IN BANKS NOR IN SYNDICATES   774 29
BANK-TELLERS
    AND BANK-TELLERS TELL THE ONE TALE THAT IS TOLD   814 9
BANNER
    WATCH AT THE BANNER OF DEATH AND THE MYSTERY   232 23
    WITH HER SILKEN STEAM LIKE A BANNER BEHIND HER AFLOW   *894 30
BAPTISED
    AND I BAPTISED MYSELF IN THE WELL   104 13
BAR
    THROUGH THE RED DOORS BEYOND THE BLACK-PURPLE BAR   134 3
    THE DARK BAR HORIZONTAL   355 33
    THE BASE THOSE THAT ARE BELOW THE BAR OF THE CROSS   637 4
BARBARIC
    ITS TREASURES OF CONSCIOUSNESS ITS SUBTLE BARBARIC   776 9
BARBAROUS
    ALTARS BARBAROUS BELOW   95 30
    IN HER BARBAROUS SOUL TO GROPE WITH ECSTASY   *936 35
BARBED
    BUT BARBED ALOOFNESS WHEN I WOULD DRAW NEAR   85 24
    AND BARBED BARBED WITH A CROWN   278 14
BARBED-WIRE
    OH WHEN MAN ESCAPED FROM THE BARBED-WIRE ENTANGLEMENT   667 1
    WHEN AT LAST WE ESCAPE THE BARBED-WIRE ENCLOSURE   667 12
BARE
    WATCHING THE DOOR OPEN HE FLASHES BARE   43 19
    BARE STEMS OF STREET LAMPS STIFFLY STAND   51 1
    WITH TWO LITTLE BARE WHITE FEET UPON MY KNEE   65 7
    THE SLENDER BARE ARMS OF THE BRANCHES YOUR TIRE-MAIDENS   86 17
    SCOOPED OUT AND BARE WHERE A SPIDER   112 20
    STRETCHING BARE   120 13
    BARE AND ASLEEP   144 27
    THE WHITE BARE BONE OF OUR SHAMS   145 7
    ON THE THIN BARE SHINS OF A MAN WHO UNEASILY LIES   145 21
    AS RED AND DIRTY BARE   145 23
    BENEATH BARE JUDGMENT STARS   202 14
    IN SYRACUSE ROCK LEFT BARE BY THE VICIOUSNESS OF GREEK   278 4
    THE SECRET IS LAID BARE   284 4
    DECEMBER'S BARE IRON HOOKS STICKING OUT OF EARTH   304 8
    WHEN THEY FELT THEIR FOREHEADS BARE NAKED TO HEAVEN THE+   310 5
    AND MAN'S DEFENCELESS BARE FACE   310 27
    THAT LITTLE LIFTED BARE HAND   386 16
    SOCKETS AMONG BARE FEET OF ELEPHANTS AND MEN ON THE   388 21
    FRIGHTENED OF THE BARE EARTH AND THE TEMPORARY CANVAS   444 12
    GOES BEHIND ITS MOTHER ON BLITHE BARE FOOT   466 11
    AND STRIPPED IT BARE   507 23
    I AM HERE YET MY HEART IS BARE AND UTTERLY EMPTY   509 7
    ARE SEA-BED STILL THROUGH THEIR HOUR OF BARE DENUDING   509 19
    LOVE CANNOT LIVE BUT ONLY BARE SALT SPLINTERS   693 22
    WITH A BARE BODKIN   717 11
    GOES BEHIND HIS MOTHER WITH BARE BLITHE FOOT   757 10
    WITH HER TWO BARE FEET ON MY HANDS   *913 9
    WHEN THE BARE FEET OF THE BABY BEAT ACROSS THE GRASS   *913 28
    WITH HER LITTLE BARE FEET IN MY HANDS   *914 9
    EFFLUENCE FROM SUFFERING FOLK-STUFF WHICH DEATH HAS LAI+ *938 23
    AND HER ARMS AND HER BOSOM AND THE WHOLE OF HER SOUL IS+ *940 20
    AND MAKES OUR BARE MANYNESS INTO A ONENESS   *951 9
    WITH A BARE BODKIN   *957 2
BARE-FOOT
    AND DOWN BELOW HUGE HOMAGE OF SHADOWY BEASTS BARE-FOOT   388 14

BARELY
    FORE-RUNNERS HAVE BARELY LANDED ON THE SHORE   607 4
BARES
    BARES HIS LONG ASS'S TEETH FLATTENS HIS LONG ASS'S EARS 379 21
BARGAIN
    FOR A BARGAIN   483 3
    I'M PERFECTLY WILLING TO STRIKE A DECENT BARGAIN   483 22
BARGAINING
    AND SEE SATAN BARGAINING THE WORLD AWAY   483 12
    BARGAINING TRUST   561 5
BARGE
    OF MISTINESS COMPLICATED INTO KNOTS AND CLOTS THAT BARGE 437 32
    THAT EVERYTHING TIES ITSELF UP INTO COMPLICATED LITTLE +*947 8
    BARGE   *958 12
BARK
    MOUTH-HAIR OF SOLDIERS PASSING ABOVE US OVER THE WRECK + 66 29
    UNSEEN MY HANDS EXPLORE THE SILENCE DRAWING THE BARK   147 2
    THE DOGS DO BARK   312 5
    THE DOGS DO BARK   312 26
    THE DOGS DO BARK   313 17
    HE DOESN'T BARK AT HIMSELF LIKE A DOG DOES   528 23
    THE BARK OF THEIR DELIVERANCE FROM THE DILEMMA   722 14
    HE DOESN'T BARK AT HIMSELF AS A DOG DOES   836 11
    HE DOESN'T BARK AT IT LIKE A DOG DOES   *950 26
    WAFT NEARER TO THEM THE BARK OF DELIVERY   *958 18
BARKED
    NO LEOPARD SCREECHED NO LION COUGHED NO DOG BARKED   394 17
    IT WOULD BE SO MUCH NICER IF HE JUST BARKED AT HIMSELF   836 14
BARKING
    SO FIERCE WHEN THE COYOTES HOWL BARKING LIKE A WHOLE   396 29
BARKLED
    AND NOW THE SKY WITH DREARY DIRT IS BARKLED   *933 16
BARKS
    FRIGATES BARKS AND PINNACES YAWLS   542 7
    BUT ONCE AND FOREVER BARKS THE OLD DOG   580 13
BAR-MAN
    THE REDDENED ACHING EYES OF THE BAR-MAN WITH THIN ARMS   72 2
BARNYARD
    THE EAGLE THE DOVE AND THE BARNYARD ROOSTER DO THEY CALL 371 22
    SWINE WASH IN MIRE AND BARNYARD FOWLS IN DUST   376 8
BARON
    HE WAS A SOLDIER ONCE OUR FIERCE LITTLE BARON A POLE   859 5
    AND NO MORE THAN THE BARON DID EH NO OLD GIRL AND NOT S+ 859 32
BARRED
    LEAVING THEM SHADOW STRIPES BARRED ON A FIELD OF GREY   858 12
BARREL
    THAT UNNATURAL BARREL BODY THAT LONG GHOUL NOSE   338 8
    WE LEAK LIKE A BARREL THAT IS SPRUNG BUT YET   750 6
BARREN
    AND I WANT TO SMITE IN ANGER THE BARREN ROCK OF EACH WA+ 57 30
BARRIERS
    TO WIPE AWAY THE MYSTIC BARRIERS OF SEX   636 19
BARS
    DRIFTS OVER THE GULF THAT BARS   144 12
    COMES LICKING THROUGH THE BARS OF YOUR LIPS   151 7
    COMES LICKING IN FLAME THROUGH THE BARS OF YOUR LIPS   873 17
BASE
    ROUND HIS BASE HIS DARK LIGHT ROLLS   39 32
    ACCURSED BASE MOTHERHOOD   207 37
    TO LIFT THE UPPER HAWK-BEAK FROM THE LOWER BASE   352 12
    AT THE BASE OF THE LOWER BRAIN   455 16
    AND AFTER ALL LYING AND BASE HYPOCRISY AND TREACHERY   497 6
    AND THE BASE THINGS LIKE HYAENAS OR BED-BUGS HAVE LEAST+ 621 18
    BECAUSE THEY WERE SUCH BASE AND SORDID OPTIMISTS   627 26
    THE ETERNAL DIVISION BETWEEN THE BASE AND THE BEAUTIFUL 637 3
    THE BASE THOSE THAT ARE BELOW THE BAR OF THE CROSS   637 4
    UNLESS MEN SWIFTLY DIVIDE AGAIN AND THE BASE ARE THRUST 637 14
    FOR TODAY THE BASE THE ROBOTS SIT ON THE THRONES OF THE 637 17
    BUT THAT WHICH IS MEAN AND BASE AND SQUALID AND DEGENER+ 679 3
    IS BASE TO US AND DISTASTEFUL   831 16
    I HAVE SUCH SWARMING SENSE OF LIVES AT THE BASE OF ME S+*900 5
    I HAVE SUCH SWARMING SENSE OF LIVES AT THE BASE OF ME S+*903 17
BASED
    BASED ON THE MYSTERY OF PRIDE   414 18
    NOT BASED ON WAGES NOR PROFITS NOR ANY SORT OF BUYING A+ 483 26
    FOR OUR SOCIETY IS BASED ON GRAB AND DEVIL TAKE THE HIN+ 829 24
BASER
    TO DEFEAT YOUR BASER STUFF   157 8
BASICALLY
    HE IS BASICALLY A SAVAGE IT IS A TERM OF REPROACH   776 11
    THE AMERICAN INDIAN IS BASICALLY A SAVAGE   776 13
BASK
    THAT BASK AND WAKE OH HIGH AND DRY   824 19

BASKET
    YOUR PASSION IN THE BASKET OF YOUR SOUL   151 13
    ME THAT I FLICKER IN THE BASKET   151 36
    IN RAPID ARMFULS FROM THE LINE TOSSING IT IN THE BASKET   672 15
    OR THE BUTTER OR THE APPLES OR PEACHES FROM THE BASKET   828 19
    YOUR BEAUTY IN THE BASKET OF YOUR SOUL   873 23
    ME THAT I FLICKER IN THE BASKET   874 14

BASKETS
    BASKETS   613 9

BASTA
    BASTA   358 6

BASTION
    A WALL A BASTION   325 26
    SEAL UP HIS FOREHEAD ONCE MORE TO A BASTION   327 22

BAT
    HER ROOM WHERE THE NIGHT STILL HANGS LIKE A HALF-FOLDED+   129 29
    IN THE AVENUES WHERE THE BAT HANGS SLEEPING UPSIDE-DOWN   322 33
    IN CHINA THE BAT IS SYMBOL OF HAPPINESS   342 6
    A BAT   342 17
    A BAT BIG AS A SWALLOW   342 25

BAT-EARED
    BUBSEY BAT-EARED DOG   395 5

BATH
    SUNBEAMS LUSTY AND CLEAN FROM THE BATH OF NIGHT   856 16
    AS I PAUSE AT THE SIDE OF THE BATH   870 1

BATH-CLOTH
    SHE SPREADS THE BATH-CLOTH UNDERNEATH THE WINDOW   217 11

BATHED
    O LET MY ANKLES BE BATHED IN MOONLIGHT THAT I   684 10

BATHERS
    BUT THE BLATANT BATHERS DON'T KNOW THEY KNOW NOTHING   625 16

BATHING
    A NAKED TREE OF BLOSSOM LIKE A BRIDEGROOM BATHING IN DEW   306 8
    PEOPLE WERE BATHING AND POSTURING THEMSELVES ON THE BEA+   651 1

BATHING-SUIT
    BATHING-SUIT FROM OUR MODERN SEA-SIDE FOAM   439 32

BATHROOM
    OR THAN IF HE'D JUST BUILT HIMSELF A NEST WITH A BATHRO+   496 8
    AS THE SUN COMES IN THE BATHROOM   870 3

BATS
    BEFORE ALL THE BATS HAVE DROPPED FROM THE BOUGH   35 9
    OF THE NEW-BORN AND THEN THE OLD OWL THEN THE BATS THAT+   38 11
    ON FANS OF UNSUSPECTED TISSUE LIKE BATS   322 17
    BATS   341 16
    AT A WAVERING INSTANT THE SWALLOWS GIVE WAY TO BATS   341 18
    BATS AND AN UNEASY CREEPING IN ONE'S SCALP   341 21
    AS THE BATS SWOOP OVERHEAD   341 22
    BATS   341 29
    BATS   342 5
    LET THE GOD WHO IS MAKER OF BATS WATCH WITH THEM IN   346 13
    BUT NOT BATS IN MY ROOM   346 16
    NOR THE GOD OF BATS WHILE THE SUN SHINES   346 17
    BATS MUST BE BATS   346 31
    OF THE NEW-BORN AND THE UNBORN AND THE OLD OWL AND THE +   *892 26
    TO THE HUSHED GREY-WINGED MINISTRANTS THE BATS OF NIGHT+   *916 12
    ONLY THE BATS ARE FLICKERING ROUND AND ROUND AND KEEP   *918 1
    THE BATS DEPRAVED ARE DROPPING GAILY FROM OFF THE TREE   *918 13

BATTEN
    MY GRIEFS AND ON NEW YORK NEWSPAPERS BATTEN   815 16

BATTENING
    I KNOW HE IS EITHER A BED-BUG BATTENING ON SLEEPING PEO+   621 23

BATTERY
    BATTERY   326 26

BATTLE
    DEFEAT IN SUCH A BATTLE IN THE DARK OF HER EYES   125 29
    PROUD KNIGHTS TO BATTLE SWEET HOW I WARM   221 28
    WERE RANKED TO BLUE BATTLE AND YOU AND I   248 22
    AND ANNOUNCING BATTLE READY   327 2
    THE BATTLE IS NOT TO THE STRONG   658 8
    AND THERE'S A BATTLE THAT'S STILL TO BE BATTLED   669 5
    NO BATTLE NO WILL-TO-LIVE   769 20
    THE BATTLE THAT THE ANGELS FOUGHT   824 4
    FOR WITH THE REDNESS OF LAUGHTER THE BATTLE IS WAGING I+   854 19
    IN BATTLE OF HEATED WORDS HARDLY STILLED BY MY REITERAT+   865 32
    DEFEAT IN SUCH A BATTLE IN THE DARK OF HER EYES   *936 28

BATTLECRY
    BATTLECRY   495 17

BATTLED
    AND THERE'S A BATTLE THAT'S STILL TO BE BATTLED   669 5

BATTLES
    OF THE DAY THAT BATTLES ITS JOURNEY   771 24

BATTLE-SHIELD
    SET FORTH LITTLE TITAN UNDER YOUR BATTLE-SHIELD   353 33

BATTLE-TWIG
    THEY HAVEN'T THE SPUNK OF A BATTLE-TWIG   553 11

BATTLING
    OF BATTLING FOR A LITTLE FOOD   105 6

BAT-WINGED
    BAT-WINGED HEART OF MAN   322 21

BAT-WINGS
    I CAN NO MORE DENY THE BAT-WINGS OF MY FATHOM-FLICKERIN+   323 2

BAVARIA
    NEVERTHELESS ONCE THE FROGS THE GLOBE-FLOWERS OF BAVARIA   208 4

BAVARIAN
    I HERE IN THE UNDERMIST ON THE BAVARIAN ROAD   213 3
    BAVARIAN GENTIANS BIG AND DARK ONLY DARK   697 3
    OH BAVARIAN GENTIANS TALL ONES   *954 18
    BAVARIAN GENTIANS   *954 24
    BAVARIAN GENTIANS TALL AND DARK BUT DARK   *956 1

BAVARIAN GASTHAUS
    OF THE OLD BAVARIAN GASTHAUS   206 28

BAWDY
    BAWDY CAN BE SANE AND WHOLESOME   844 29
    IN FACT A LITTLE BAWDY IS NECESSARY IN EVERY LIFE   844 30
    BAWDY ON THE BRAIN BECOMES OBSCENITY VICIOUS   845 7
    AND RIGID SUPPRESSION OF ALL BAWDY WHORING OR OTHER SUC+   845 13
    BAWDY CAN BE SAND AND WHOLESOME   *952 10
    IN FACT A LITTLE BAWDY IS NECESSARY IN EVERY LIFE   *952 19
    BUT BAWDY ON THE BRAIN IS LEWD AND NAUSEOUS A SORT OF I+   *952 19

BAY
    COOL LONELY NIGHT HER BREASTS WILL KEEP THE NIGHT AT BAY   91 11
    A GREAT BAY STALLION DANCES SKIRTS   126 25
    AT LAST HE SWERVED INTO THE WINDOW BAY   343 16
    AGAIN HE SWERVED INTO THE WINDOW BAY   344 3
    WHO HAD SPREAD WHITE WASHING ON THE GRAVEL BANKED ABOVE+   693 3

BAYING
    BAYING EPITHALAMION   306 19

BAYONET
    LIKE A BRIDE HE TOOK MY BAYONET WANTING IT   742 9
    LIKE A VIRGIN THE BLADE OF MY BAYONET WANTING IT   742 10

BAYONETS'
    SMOULDERING WITH DARKENED BUSBIES BENEATH THE BAYONETS'+   66 8

B-D
    THEY'RE A' A B-D LOT O' -S   491 1

BEACH
    BEACH   520 14
    PEOPLE WERE BATHING AND POSTURING THEMSELVES ON THE BEA+   651 1
    CRAWL OUT OF THE WATER AND LIE ON THE BEACH   827 17
    AS I SIT ON THE BEACH OF THE CLASS ALONE   *898 22
    AS I SIT ON THE BEACH OF THE CLASS ALONE   *902 6

BEACHED
    OUR BEACHED VESSEL DARKENED RENCONTRE INHUMAN AND CLOSE+   66 27

BEACHES
    THE BEACHES CAN DO NOTHING ABOUT IT   509 21
    THE MARGINS THE GREY BEACHES OF SHADOW   *957 15
    THRUST OUT ON TO THE GREY GREY BEACHES OF SHADOW   *957 22
    ONCE OUTSIDE UPON THE GREY MARSH BEACHES WHERE LOST SOU+   *957 28
    AND CROWD THERE ON THE GREY MUD BEACHES OF THE MARGINS   *958 9

BEAD
    THE MIND FUSED DOWN LIKE A BEAD   242 13

BEAD-BERRY
    WITH STICKING-OUT BEAD-BERRY EYES BLACK   345 29

BEADS
    LIKE BEADS THEY GO AROUND AND NOT ONE MISSES   154 5

BEADY
    IF I STRING THE PLANETS AND THE BEADY STARS   735 18

BEAK
    BEAK   329 24
    BEAK   359 25
    AND DRAGS AT THESE WITH HIS BEAK   362 8
    AND CATCHES HER TROUSER-LEGS IN HIS BEAK   362 21
    BEAK   372 18
    AND YOU GREAT BIRD SUN-STARER HEAVY BLACK BEAK   374 34
    AND SEA-TOUCH TIP OF A BEAK   436 24
    BEAK   783 12
    BEAK   783 18

BEAKED
    BEAKED EAGLE   373 32
    BEAKED EAGLE   782 8

BEAK-MOUTH
    TO OPEN YOUR TINY BEAK-MOUTH THAT LOOKS AS IF IT WOULD   352 9

BEAKS
    FANGS AND CLAWS AND TALONS AND BEAKS AND HAWK-EYES   409 29

BEAK-SHAPED
    SUDDENLY BEAK-SHAPED AND VERY WIDE LIKE SOME SUDDENLY   353   5

BEAM
    COMPRESSED IT TILL ITS BEAM GREW WONDROUS DARK   69 19
    PASSES THE GALLIVANT BEAM OF THE TRAMS   145   5
    YET IS UPLIFTED IN ME THE PURE BEAM   745 30
    THOU SILVER BEAM IN THE PRESENCE   753 16
    COMPRESSED IT TILL ITS BEAM GREW WONDROUS DARK   *916   2

BEAMING
    BEAMING   396   4

BEAMS
    OUT OF EACH FACE STRANGE DARK BEAMS THAT DISQUIET   76   1
    STRANGE BEAMS MUST TRAVEL STILL FOR I FEEL THAT   115   3
    FINE THRILLS TO THE NEIGHBOUR STARS FINE HIDDEN BEAMS   127   7
    RARE ALMOST AS BEAMS YET OVERWHELMINGLY POTENT   271 19
    SO QUEENLY SHAKING HER GLISTENING BEAMS   702 26
    OUT OF EACH STAR DARK STRANGE BEAMS THAT DISQUIET   *897 28
    OUT OF EACH STAR DARK STRANGE BEAMS THAT DISQUIET   *901   5

BEAN
    BEAN WAS ONE OF THE OLDEST SYMBOLS OF THE MALE ORGAN FO+   303 19
    A TINY FRAGILE HALF-ANIMATE BEAN   352   8

BEAN-O
    WHAT A BEAN-O   668   6

BEAN-POD
    AND ROT LIKE A BEAN-POD WHAT ARE YOU OH MULTIFORM   73 19

BEANS
    WRETCHES UTTER WRETCHES KEEP YOUR HANDS FROM BEANS SAITH   303 15
    FOR ACCORDING TO SOME THE BEANS WERE THE BEANS OF VOTES+   303 17

BEANS-COD
    IS LATER THAN THE BEANS-COD   303 20

BEAR
    WHERE THAT LUMBERING BEE WHO CAN HARDLY BEAR   50 11
    THEM AN ANSWER BACK IT IS MORE THAN I CAN BEAR   76 13
    HEAVY TO BEAR EVEN HEAVY TO UPREAR   87 27
    AND THIS HELEN BESIDE ME I AM BLANK BEING NOTHING I BEA+   97 12
    OPPRESSES ME SO I CAN HARDLY BEAR   116 26
    TO BEAR BUT RETALIATE NOTHING GIVEN TO GAVE   160 27
    WHO CANNOT BEAR TO THINK BACK TO THE DEPARTURE   169 11
    I WOULD BEAR THE PAIN   214 25
    IS ALMOST MORE THAN I CAN BEAR   215 15
    IS ALMOST MORE THAN I CAN BEAR   216 12
    IF ONLY I LET IT BEAR ME CARRY ME IF ONLY IT CARRY ME   250 15
    AND STILL I CANNOT BEAR IT   318   5
    I CAN'T BEAR IT I CAN'T BEAR IT   377   8
    AS UNDER THE HAIRY BELLY OF A GREAT BLACK BEAR   409 12
    WE CAN'T BEAR TO TOUCH OR BE TOUCHED   468 13
    OR THEY BEAR EVERYBODY A GRIM AND GRISLY GRUDGE   502 19
    I BEAR THE HOPE   772 24
    AND I COULD NOT BEAR HER LOOK UPON ME   869   7
    BEAR THE THOUGHT OF MY MOTHER'S PAIN-DARKENED BLUE EYES   869 14
    THERE I CANNOT BEAR TO SEE THE SOBS IN YOUR THROAT   871 19
    NO MORE CAN I ENDURE TO BEAR THE BRUNT   *895 20
    THEM AN ANSWER BACK IT IS MORE THAN I CAN BEAR   *898   7
    THEM AN ANSWER BACK IT IS MORE THAN I CAN BEAR   *901 16
    NO MORE CAN I ENDURE TO BEAR THE BRUNT   *904   9
    FAR AND WIDE RUN THE EASY ROOTS THAT BEAR THE LEAVES OF+   *926 12
    OPPRESSES ME I CAN SCARCELY BEAR   *930 25
    IT IS ONLY I FIND IT HARD TO BEAR   *931 12

BEARD
    MY BEARD IS RED   405   2
    LAUGHING IN HIS BLACK BEARD   689   8
    THERE ARE FOXES IN THE COVER OF HIS BEARD   *953 29

BEARDED
    A LITTLE BEARDED MAN PEAKED IN SLEEPING   145   8
    THE PEASANTS ARE BENDING CUTTING THE BEARDED WHEAT   605 22
    LIKE BEARDED WHEAT IN EAR   627   8
    HARK THE LOW AND SHATTERING LAUGHTER OF BEARDED MEN   689   2

BEARDS
    SANS BEARDS SANS BAGS   313   2
    IT IS AEGEAN SHIPS AND MEN WITH ARCHAIC POINTED BEARDS   687   6

BEARING
    UNKNOWN THAT LIES BEFORE US BEARING THE ARK OF THE COVE+   132 24
    AS FOR BEARING MY CHILDREN WHY THERE   541 17
    HER LOOKS HER BEARING TO ME   885 21

BEARS
    AND HEART LIKE A CROSS THAT BEARS DEAD AGONY   226   6
    AND PERHAPS BEARS   392 23
    THAT BEARS ALOFT TOWARD RARER SKIES   *899 28
    THAT BEARS ALOFT TOWARDS RARER SKIES   *903   7

BEAST
    BEAST CROUCHED ACROSS THE GLOBE READY IF NEED BE TO POU+   97 21
    FLUTTER FOR A MOMENT OH THE BEAST IS QUICK AND KEEN   119 21
    ROARS LIKE A BEAST IN A CAVE   159   2
    MONEY FROM OUT OF THE EARTH OR THE BEAST OR THE MAN AS +   175 24
    FUMBLING A BEAST IN AIR   343 10
    OUT YOU BEAST   345 26
    JESUS RODE ON HIM THE FIRST BURDEN ON THE FIRST BEAST OF   379 31
    BUT BAH HOW CAN HE POOR DOMESTICATED BEAST   383 26
    AIR VAST BEAST   385 24
    SUBTLY TO THE TWIGS OVERHEAD FAR UP VAST BEAST   385 27
    THE SLOW BEAST CURIOUSLY SPREADING HIS ROUND FEET FOR T+   387 12
    AND THE SLIM NAKED MAN SLIPS DOWN AND THE BEAST DEPOSITS   387 14
    WOMAN WHERE GOT YOU THIS LITTLE BEAST   439   5

BEAST
    TOWARDS WOMAN OR MAN BIRD BEAST OR CREATURE OR THING   454 13
    THE ELEPHANT THE HUGE OLD BEAST   465   7
    HE'S A BEAST OF PREY   466 19
    NO ANIMAL NO BEAST NOR CREEPING THING   701 12
    BECAUSE MAN POOR BEAST CAN LOOK AT HIMSELF   836   9
    MONEY IS THE VAST STINKING BEAST   843   7

BEASTLY
    HOW BEASTLY THE BOURGEOIS IS   430 15
    HOW BEASTLY THE BOURGEOIS IS   431 11
    HOW BEASTLY THE BOURGEOIS IS   431 24
    BECAUSE OF THE BEASTLY EXPENSE   518   5

BEASTS
    TAKE WRITHING FORMS OF ALL BEASTS THAT SWEAT AND THAT F+   73 15
    REMINISCENT OF SLINKING BEASTS MAKE ME FEAR   107   6
    BEASTS THAT SLEEP WILL COVER   144 20
    HEAVENS WHERE THEY BELONG THE APOCALYPTIC BEASTS FOR WI+   319   2
    FOUR GREAT BEASTS THE FOUR NATURES THE FOUR WINDS THE F+   319   9
    THEY ARE NOT ALL BEASTS   320   1
    WHERE BEASTS DROP THEIR UNLICKED YOUNG AND PASTURE AND +   321 13
    AND CEASES TO BE A BLOOD-THIRSTY KING OF BEASTS   325   7
    OF THE HUGEST OLDEST OF BEASTS IN THE NIGHT AND THE FIR+   388 11
    AND DOWN BELOW HUGE HOMAGE OF SHADOWY BEASTS BARE-FOOT   388 14
    VAST-BLOODED BEASTS   390 15
    LOOMING GALLOP OF THE BEASTS   390 36
    FIRST GREAT BEASTS OF THE EARTH   392 10
    AT ALL THESE SKINS OF WILD BEASTS   409 27
    AND THE SMELL OF HORSES AND OTHER BEASTS   444 13
    THE MYSTERY THAT LIES IN BEASTS   445 18
    THEY HAVE WITH THEIR CIRCUS BEASTS   446 12
    AND THE GREAT BEASTS MATE IN SECRET AT LAST   465 21
    OLDEST THEY ARE AND THE WISEST OF BEASTS   465 23
    BEASTS   792 15
    DEEP PANTING BREATHS LIKE GREAT BEASTS READY FOR   827   8
    NEITHER BEASTS NOR FLOWERS ARE   836   8
    MAN IS ONE OF THOSE BEASTS THAT WILL BREED IN A CAGE   843 14

BEASTS'
    BEASTS' LIMBS AND THE BREATH FROM THEIR FEET THAT THEY +   406   2

BEAT
    OR A BEAT OF WINGS AT THE WINDOW THERE   37 11
    WHEN THE WHITE FEET OF THE BABY BEAT ACROSS THE GRASS   64 29
    WHY SHOULD WE BEAT OUR HEADS AGAINST THE WALL   75   5
    BEAT THROUGH THE FLESH   94 21
    KNOWLEDGE I SET YOUR HEART TO ITS STRONGER BEAT   156 28
    BEAT AFTER BEAT FALLS SOMBRE AND DULL   164   1
    I BEAT MY WAY TO BE LOST IMMEDIATELY   223   9
    AS AN INSOLENT MISTRESS TELLING MY PULSE'S BEAT   230 27
    AS I AM IF MY HEART IN UPLIFTING CEASED TO BEAT TO TOSS+   320 27
    AND FELT HIM BEAT IN MY HAND WITH HIS MUCOUS LEAPING   339   9
    TO ROAM AND FEEL THE SLOW HEART BEAT   358 12
    HE SPOKE THIS WORD STOP DON'T BEAT IT FOR IT IS THE SOU+   376   6
    FORTH TO THE TOM-TOM'S BEAT IN THE TORCH-LIGHT   387 29
    ON A NARROW BEAT ABOUT THE SAME AS A PRISONER TAKING HIS   521 17
    THE POLICEMAN ON HIS BEAT   570   7
    THE SWAN WILL BEAT THE WATERS IN RAGE WHITE RAGE OF AN I   624 15
    THE JOURNEY STILL THEY MOAN AND BEAT   722   2
    BUT IT MAKES THE SUNLIGHT BEAT   746 10
    THE HEART HEART THAT HAS BEAT   746 17
    I BEAT MY WINGS TOWARD IT NEVER   876 29
    AND ITS BEAT OF PAIN IS DISTRIBUTED ON THE WIND   883   7
    WHEN THE WHITE FEET OF THE BABY BEAT ACROSS THE GRASS   *912 25
    WHEN THE BARE FEET OF THE BABY BEAT ACROSS THE GRASS   *913 28
    THE JOURNEY STILL THEY MOAN AND BEAT   *958   2
    THEY MOAN AND BEAT THEY GNASH THEY RAGE   *958   4

BEATEN
    ON YOUR BODY THE BEATEN ANVIL   168 21
    ONCE THEY SAY HE WAS PASSING BY WHEN A DOG WAS BEING BE+   376   5
    THINGS OF IRON ARE BEATEN ON THE ANVIL   381 31

BEATING
    NEXT TO MY BREAST WHERE MY OWN HEART WAS BEATING   61 22
    AND MY BREAST TO HER BEATING   120 20
    BEATING LIKE SOBS I COME TO MYSELF AND STAND   143 21
    NEW FEET ON THE EARTH BEATING WITH IMPATIENCE   272   3
    BEFORE MY HEART STOPS BEATING AND I BECOME WHAT I AM NOT   321   9
    IN THE BUSINESS OF BEATING THE METTLE OF GOATS TO A GOD+   381 33
    MY GOD IT TAKES SOME BEATING   547 18
    AND BEATING THEIR GREAT WINGS IN OUR PANTING FACES   707   5
    AND BEATING DOWN RESISTANCES   714 28
    HOW CAN MY HEART KEEP BEATING IN THIS PALLOR OF WHITISH   766 28
    DRUMS FOR THE BEATING HEART   804   2
    SIEGMUND THE STRONG BEATING OF YOUR HEART HURTS ME   870 19
    NEXT MY BREAST WHERE MY OWN HEART WAS BEATING   *912   2

BEATS
    A FEW QUICK BEATS FROM A WOOD-PIGEON'S HEART AND WHEN I+   38 14
    RISEN UP HE BEATS ME   39 12
    INTO OUR SOOTY GARDEN HE DRAGS AND BEATS   47 16
    SO EVEN IT BEATS LIKE SILENCE AND SKY AND EARTH IN ONE +   88   3
    THE TRAIN BEATS FRANTIC IN HASTE AND STRUGGLES AWAY   88 23
    IS HEAVY AND MY HEART BEATS SLOWLY LABORIOUSLY   95   2
    YOUR VIOLENT HEART BEATS TO AND FRO   122 12
    THIS TRAIN BEATS ANXIOUSLY OUTWARD BOUND   169   4
    BEATS THE NEW FRESH AIR OF LIFE THEY COME FOR STRIFE   174 14
    AND LAND THAT BEATS WITH A PULSE   261   4
    HOW MY HEART BEATS   320 19
    I AM MAN AND THEREFORE MY HEART BEATS AND THROWS THE DA+   320 21
    BEATS   435 25
    SO THAT MY HEART BEATS SOOTHED SOOTHED SOOTHED AND AT P+   652   8
    OR BEATS THEM OR CHEATS THEM   828 11
    SHARPLY BEATS OUT A THRICE-TOLD FUNERAL KNELL   858 24
    A FEW QUICK BEATS OF A WOODPIGEON'S HEART THEN RISE   *892 30
    BEATS THE ACTIVE ECSTASY SUDDENLY LIFTING MY EYES   *906 21

BEATS
   BEATS THE ACTIVE ECSTASY   *908 17

BE-AUREOLED
   LIKE A BE-AUREOLED BLEACHED SKELETON HOVERING   290 22

BEAUTIES
   HE PAINTED SOME PICTURES REAL BEAUTIES   577 4
   BEAUTIES SO SLEEK   861 8

BEAUTIFUL
   HOW BEAUTIFUL HE IS WITHOUT SOUND   39 19
   A MUTE NEARLY BEAUTIFUL THING   112 11
   OF MY EYES I SEE YOU BEAUTIFUL AND DEAR   118 13
   BEAUTIFUL PASSIVE AND STRONG AS THE BREATH   118 14
   THE OLD DREAMS ARE BEAUTIFUL BELOVED SOFT-TONED AND SURE   174 21
   I AM BEAUTIFUL I LOOK AT THE RUMPLED YOUNG ROSES   218 2
   CHRIST ON THE CROSS HIS BEAUTIFUL YOUNG MAN'S BODY   225 5
   BEAUTIFUL CANDID LOVERS   243 1
   I DON'T CARE WHETHER I AM BEAUTIFUL TO YOU   251 1
   I ADMIRE YOU SO YOU ARE BEAUTIFUL THIS CLEAN SWEEP OF   255 11
   THOUGH SHE LOOKED RARELY BEAUTIFUL   255 30
   OH HONEY-BODIED BEAUTIFUL ONE   306 20
   BEAUTIFUL   310 21
   HENCE HIS BEAUTIFUL EYES   378 21
   WITH THE HALF-VEILED BEAUTIFUL EYES AND THE PENSIVE FACE   379 4
   AND LIFTING HER BEAUTIFUL SLENDER FACE OH SO MUCH MORE   393 6
   BEAUTIFUL DEAD EYES   402 7
   WOMEN WITH THE BEAUTIFUL EYES OF THE OLD DAYS   410 11
   THE TRAPEZE MAN SLIM AND BEAUTIFUL AND LIKE A FISH IN T+   445 4
   QUITE BEAUTIFUL CHAIRS   452 23
   IT IS A WONDER FOAM IS SO BEAUTIFUL   467 11
   WITH FRUSTRATION HOW BEAUTIFUL   467 15
   TOO NICE TOO BEAUTIFUL   490 6
   BEAUTIFUL THINGS   540 3
   OF THE FEMALE FORM TECHNICALLY BEAUTIFUL ACTUALLY A WHI+   619 12
   BUT IF HE PRODUCES SOMETHING BEAUTIFUL WITH THE FRAIL   634 13
   THE ETERNAL DIVISION BETWEEN THE BASE AND THE BEAUTIFUL   637 3
   THE GREEK BEAUTIFUL ONES THE PHOENICIAN UGLY ONES THE A+   671 16
   WAS A GOD IN GODLINESS PURE AS CHRIST BEAUTIFUL   674 24
   AT HER BEST AND HER MOST BEAUTIFUL BEING GOD MADE MANIF+   691 20
   KISSES OF FOUR GREAT LORDS BEAUTIFUL AS THEY HELD ME TO+   695 29
   A CREATURE OF BEAUTIFUL PEACE LIKE A RIVER   714 14
   THEY HAVE TAKEN OFF THE BEAUTIFUL RED LILLY   845 24
   MINT ME BEAUTIFUL MEDALS AND HAND THEM ME HOT   873 1
   AND GATHER MY BURNING BEAUTIFUL DREAMS FOR HER SHARE   874 8
   AND OH OH BEAUTIFUL   879 5
   BACK FROM MY BEAUTIFUL LONELY BODY   *893 31
   THE OLD DREAMS ARE BEAUTIFUL BELOVED SOFT-TONED AND SURE *907 1
   THE OLD DREAMS ARE BEAUTIFUL BELOVED SOFT-TONED AND SURE *909 1
   A MUTE NEARLY BEAUTIFUL THING IS THY FACE   *927 28
   A MUTE NEARLY BEAUTIFUL THING   *929 1
   SO BEAUTIFUL OVER THE LAST OF SEAS   *960 16

BEAUTIFULLY
   AND BEAUTIFULLY LAID IN BLACK ON A GOLD-GREY SKY   146 29
   BEAUTIFULLY BEFOREHAND WITH IT ALL   337 13
   EVEN MICE PLAY QUITE BEAUTIFULLY AT SHADOWS   523 26
   ALL BEAUTIFULLY RIGGED AND BOTTLED UP   542 8
   NATURE RESPONDS SO BEAUTIFULLY   831 1

BEAUTY
   THOU DARK ONE THOU PROUD CURVED BEAUTY I   40 17
   I LOVED BUT THERE SHE GOES AND HER BEAUTY HURTS MY HEART   67 11
   AND THEN YOU LAMP YOU LEMON-COLOURED BEAUTY   73 2
   THEN BRILLIANT EARTH FROM THE BURR OF NIGHT IN BEAUTY   73 4
   OVER EVERY SINGLE BEAUTY   95 20
   THEIR BEAUTY FOR HIS TAKING BOON FOR BOON   129 18
   OF FIRE AND BEAUTY LOOSE NO MORE   151 11
   OF BLISS TILL ALL HER LAMBENT BEAUTY SHAKES TOWARDS US   193 7
   THAT BEAUTY IS A THING BEYOND THE GRAVE   193 9
   GLISTENING WITH ALL THE MOMENT AND ALL YOUR BEAUTY   210 4
   IS NOT EVEN THE BEAUTY AND PEACE OF AN ORBIT   236 14
   THE LISTLESS BEAUTY OF THE HOUR   248 16
   THERE'S THE BEAUTY YOU CANNOT SEE MYSELF AND HIM   251 16
   THE SWINGING BEAUTY OF EQUILIBRIUM   251 18
   THERE'S THIS OTHER BEAUTY THE WAY OF THE STARS   251 20
   AND THIS IS BEAUTY TO ME TO BE LIFTED AND GONE   252 9
   IN SIGHTLESS BEAUTY AND THE FEW   262 5
   WOOING BOYS AND BEAUTY   437 7
   BEAUTY OF COURSE BEAUTY IS STILL A DELICIOUS ESCAPE   532 8
   BUT OF COURSE ONE KNOWS THAT BOTH BEAUTY AND PURE   532 11
   OH AUNTIE ISN'T HE A BEAUTY AND IS HE A GENTLEMAN OR   581 10
   BEAUTY OF LIFE   634 14
   WILL DEFILE IT AND SPOIL ITS BEAUTY   634 17
   THERE IS A MARVELLOUS RICH WORLD OF CONTACT AND SHEER F+   667 3
   WITH THE DARK AND GLEAMING BEAUTY OF THE MESSAGELESS GO+   674 26
   TURNING TO DEATH AS I TURN TO BEAUTY   676 22
   TO THE BREATH THAT IS OF NEW BEAUTY UNFOLDING IN DEATH   676 23
   IS THAT YOU SHALL ACHIEVE YOUR BEAUTY   683 26
   TELL ME TELL ME IS THERE IN YOU A BEAUTY TO COMPARE   684 5
   OH FOR SOME OTHER BEAUTY SOME OTHER BEAUTY   691 4
   EVERYTHING THAT HAS BEAUTY HAS A BODY AND IS A BODY   691 6
   YOU BEAUTY O YOU BEAUTY   695 13
   YOU GLISTENING GARMENTLESS BEAUTY   695 14
   NOW I AM AT YOUR GATE YOU BEAUTY YOU LADY OF ALL NAKEDN+   695 22
   PUT SLEEP AS BLACK AS BEAUTY IN THE SECRET OF MY BELLY   803 2
   AND THE WHITE NAPE OF HER NECK WAS THE BEAUTY OF THE ST+   865 9
   RETURN WHERE ALL IN BEAUTY STAND ERECT   872 9
   MARRIED MAKE PERFECT BEAUTY NO DEFECT   872 11
   WITH BEAUTY SHINE AND BOW IN GOD'S GREAT WAKE   872 22
   OF LOVE AND BEAUTY LOOSE NO MORE   873 21
   YOUR BEAUTY IN THE BASKET OF YOUR SOUL   873 23
   WOOING BOYS AND BEAUTY   *946 19
   IT IS DARK BEAUTY   *954 22

BEAVERS
   ONLY MICE AND MOLES AND RATS AND BADGERS AND BEAVERS   392 22

BEAVER'S
   AND DWELLING IN HIS OWN BOWERY HOUSE LIKE A BEAVER'S   451 24

BECAME
   I BECAME A STRANGE BEING   222 11
   HENCE HE BECAME A CURLY SHEEP-DOG WITH DANGEROUS PROPEN+   324 26
   SO THEY BECAME LIKE MACHINES   640 26
   AND GREW UP AND BECAME IN THE WONDER OF CREATION JESUS   689 29

BECKON
   AND SINISTER BEINGS WILL BECKON BETWEEN   748 4

BECKONING
   THEY SEEM TO BE BECKONING RUSHING AWAY AND   140 24
   BECKONING   140 25

BECOME
   IS THIS WHAT'S BECOME OF YOU   57 9
   MUST HAVE SUNK AND BECOME EXTINCT   193 15
   AND BECOME UNIQUE   267 25
   BEFORE MY HEART STOPS BEATING AND I BECOME WHAT I AM NOT   321 9
   TORN TO BECOME WHOLE AGAIN AFTER LONG SEEKING FOR WHAT   367 1
   CAN YOU AFTER DARK BECOME A DARKIE   428 1
   SINCE WE HAVE BECOME SO CEREBRAL   468 12
   WE BECOME VICIOUS   468 21
   AND THAT FEAR CAN BECOME A DELIRIUM   487 2
   WHILE THEIR HEARTS BECOME ABSOLUTELY EMPTY   502 10
   THEY WOULDN'T SUDDENLY BECOME THEMSELVES ARISTOCRATIC   527 24
   THEY'D BECOME NOTHING   527 25
   CHANGE FROM BEING SINGLE AND BECOME GRADUALLY DOUBLE   534 26
   AND LIKE TO BECOME INCURABLY DISEASED INSIDE   535 22
   I DARE DO ALL THAT MAY BECOME A MAN   606 9
   THE UNHAPPY SOULS ARE THOSE THAT CAN'T DIE AND BECOME S+   612 19
   AND THE PERSON HAS BECOME FINALLY SELF-CENTRED   617 7
   OR ELSE TO SEVER THE CONNECTION TO BECOME SELF-CENTRED +   617 15
   UNLESS THEY HAVE FALLEN AND BECOME ROBOTS   649 2
   WHEREAS IF YOU RIDE AWAY AND BECOME DEEPLY CONCERNED IN+   665 12
   BECOME AWARE AS LEAVES ARE AWARE   667 26
   WE HAVE BECOME FATALLY SELF-CONSCIOUS FATALLY SELF-IMPO+   674 9
   THOSE THINGS THAT HAVE BECOME THEMSELVES   689 22
   AND EVERY MAN WHO HAS BECOME A DETACHED AND SELF-ACTIVA+   713 4
   SCIENCE HAS NOW BECOME AN EVIL ABSTRACTION   716 9
   TO TWIST AND GROVEL AND BECOME A HEAP OF DIRT   742 2
   AND STONES SHALL MAKE PLACE FOR THY FOOT BECOME EASY TO+   750 1
   THE INDIAN QUESTION HAS WORSE LUCK BECOME A POLITICAL   777 13
   HE WOULD GO OUT INTO THE WORLD AND BECOME   778 14
   NEW LIFE BUBBLES IN WE BECOME SOMETHING ELSE   832 22
   AND A BOY AS HE REACHES THE AGE OF FOURTEEN WHEN HE SHO+   843 2
   BUT GET ANY OF THEM ON THE BRAIN AND THEY BECOME PERNIC+   845 6
   NOR WHAT HAD BECOME OF ME   881 19
   AND WHAT HAS BECOME OF THE FLUFFY YELLOW STARS   *933 24

BECOMES
   BECOMES PAIN   40 8
   BUT THE SHADE ON HER FOREHEAD ILL BECOMES   201 11
   BECOMES AN AFFIRMATION THROUGH MOIST SCARLET LIPS   284 18
   AND BECOMES THE FAITHFUL SHEEP-DOG OF THE SHEPHERD THIN+   325 8
   IS VERY NORMAL AS BECOMES AN ENGLISHMAN   446 23
   AS A PLANT BECOMES POT-BOUND   474 23
   MAN BECOMES EGO-BOUND   474 24
   SLOWLY THE SALT OF THE EARTH BECOMES SALT OF THE SEA   495 1
   SLOWLY THE SALT OF THE EARTH BECOMES SALT OF THE SEA   495 9
   AND CEASES TO BE A ROBOT AND BECOMES A SERVANT OF LIFE   648 19
   THE TRUTH OF YESTERDAY BECOMES A LIE TOMORROW   661 17
   THE MORE DEADLY AND DANGEROUS IT BECOMES   665 11
   WHEN GOETHE BECOMES AN APOLLO HE BECOMES A PLASTER CAST   673 1
   AND BECOMES AT LAST A CLOVE CARNATION LO THAT IS GOD   691 17
   AND BECOMES AT LAST HELEN OR NINON ANY LOVELY AND GENER+   691 18
   SO AN APPLE BECOMES MYSTIC WHEN I TASTE IT IN   707 28
   BECOMES POINTLESS AND SILLY   723 28
   BAWDY ON THE BRAIN BECOMES OBSCENITY VICIOUS   845 7
   WHORING ON THE BRAIN BECOMES REALLY SYPHILITIC   845 8
   AND SODOMY ON THE BRAIN BECOMES A MISSION   845 9
   BECOMES POINTLESS AND SILLY   *961 10

BECOMING
   BUT TELL ME OH TELL ME WHAT IS BECOMING TO A MAN   606 10
   AND BECOMING LIGHT   681 29
   IS THE HISTORY OF THE STRUGGLE OF BECOMING   682 2
   PREVENT HIS BECOMING A HUNDRED-PER-CENT AMERICAN   778 8

BECOMINGLY
   THEY TAKE TRAGEDY SO BECOMINGLY   71 30

BED
   NO-ONE NEAR THE BED   37 8
   WHERE THE SWALLOW HAS HUNG HER MARRIAGE BED   42 22
   WHITENING ACROSS THE BED   58 27
   BESIDE YOUR BED   102 24
   THE SICK GRAPES ON THE CHAIR BY THE BED LIE PRONE AT TH+   112 16
   FOLDED IN ITS LEGS AS IN A BED   112 21
   OF DARKNESS WHEREON SHE SLEEPS ON HER PERFECT BED   133 25
   WHY CONTINUALLY DO THEY CROSS THE BED   140 20
   EVER THE LONG BLACK FIGURES SWOOP BY THE BED   140 23
   THE WHITE RUGS ON THE FLOOR NOR THE SILENT BED   155 3
   UPRAISED ON THE BED WITH FEET ERECT AS A BOW   155 19
   HER HEAD ASIDE BUT STRAIGHT TOWARDS THE BED   156 9
   COME BACK TO BED LET US SLEEP ON OUR MYSTERIES   211 25
   AND SUNSHINE FILLS ONE HIGH VALLEY BED   224 12
   SLIPPING INTO ITS BED OF DEAD LEAVES YOU HURRY INTO YOUR   254 16
   AN ARROW ON THE BED AT THE PILLOW   397 3
   TERRIBLE AND STRANGE THE GOD LIES ON THE BED WISTFUL CO+   676 9
   IN THE BLUE DEEP BED OF THE SEA   694 14
   CLEANSED AND IN CONCORD FROM THE BED OF DEATH   743 28
   AND WHEN SHE HAS MOST UNSATISFACTORILY SHARED HIS LITTL+   842 5

BED
    AS I LAY ON THE BED AND YOU SAT WITH THE FLOWERS ON YOU+   886 11
    YOU WEPT AND THE BED TREMBLED UNDER ME   886 14
    THE WEALD THE ENORMOUS BED   886 26

BED-BUGS
    AND THE BASE THINGS LIKE HYAENAS OR BED-BUGS HAVE LEAST+   621 18

BED-BUG
    I KNOW HE IS EITHER A BED-BUG BATTENING ON SLEEPING PEO+   621 23

BEDROCK
    AND DEEPER EVEN THAN THE BEDROCK OF PRIDE   844 11
    BUT BELOW ALL ROOTS OF LOVE LIES THE BEDROCK OF NAKED P+   844 19
    AND DEEPER THAN THE BEDROCK OF PRIDE IS THE PRIMORDIAL +   844 20

BED-ROCKED
    BED-ROCKED IN HIS OWN PRIMORDIAL PRIDE   *951 17

BED-ROCK
    THERE MUST BE A BED-ROCK SOMEWHERE OF PEOPLE WHO ARE   548 3

BEDROOM
    AH THEN UPON THE BEDROOM I DO DRAW   129 15
    AT HOME WE LEANED IN THE BEDROOM WINDOW   206 27
    AND IN THE MORNING WHEN THE BEDROOM DOOR IS OPENED   397 1

BEDS
    AND THROUGH TO THE MOWIE ONLY THE DEAD IN THEIR BEDS   173 11

BED-SHEETS
    WHO IS IT SMOOTHS THE BED-SHEETS LIKE THE COOL   652 9

BEE
    OF THE BEE BEFORE HE FLIES   46 12
    IN HER EYES AS A YOUNG BEE STUMBLETH   46 16
    WHERE THAT LUMBERING BEE WHO CAN HARDLY BEAR   50 11
    AS A DRENCHED DROWNED BEE   73 20
    AS THE WINGS OF A DRENCHED DROWNED BEE   74 5
    A BROWN BEE PULLING APART   124 29
    CREEPS A BEE   178 24
    FOR YOUR LATE BEE WHO BESEECHES   178 31
    ARE SINNERS STRANGE THE BEE THAT BLUNDERS   223 19
    AND A HAIRY BIG BEE HUNG OVER THE PRIMULAS   243 23
    OF THE IMPENDING BEE THEY WERE FAIR ENOUGH SIGHTS   243 29
    MY PICTURES EAGER AS THE HONEY BEE   577 25
    BETTER LITTLE BEE   668 10
    AS A BEE WAXES OVER A WOUND   824 28
    LIKE A BEE THAT PLAYS WITH THE REFLECTION OF FLOWERS   867 12
    HIS ROUND BROWN HEAD BENDS LIKE A BEE ABOVE A BLOSSOM   868 5
    AS A DRENCHED DROWNED BEE   *913 12
    AS A SILENT BEE AT THE END OF A SHOWER   *913 20
    AS THE WINGS OF A DRENCHED DROWNED BEE   *913 26
    A BROWN BEE PULL APART   *935 35

BEECH
    AND THE YOUNG COPPER BEECH ITS LEAVES RED-ROSY AT THE E+   647 4

BEECHEN
    UNDER THE BEECHEN HEDGE   886 24

BEECHES
    WAIT AMONG THE BEECHES   178 30

BEECH-GREEN
    LOOK NOW THROUGH THE WOOD WHERE THE BEECH-GREEN   126 22

BEECH-LEAF
    HIS LITTLE PUNT AN AUTUMN-BROWN BEECH-LEAF   867 15

BEECH-LEAVES
    YOU WHO ARE TWISTED IN GRIEF LIKE CRUMPLING BEECH-LEAVES   73 16
    AMONG THE CRUMPLED BEECH-LEAVES PHOSPHORESCENT   86 22
    YOU UPON THE DRY DEAD BEECH-LEAVES ONCE MORE ONLY ONCE   90 25

BEERIER
    DON'T DRINK DON'T DRINK AND GET BEERIER AND BEERIER   459 11

BEES
    OF BEES THAT VIBRATE WITH REVOLT WHO FALL TO EARTH   73 18
    IT IS STORMY AND RAINDROPS CLING LIKE SILVER BEES TO TH+   92 1
    THE BEES ROLL ROUND IN THE WILD-THYME WITH DELIGHT   223 15
    AND EVENING HAS TAKEN ALL THE BEES FROM THE THYME   224 26
    LIKE BEES ABOVE THEM AND FEELS FOR THEIR WEALS   824 26
    CLINGING TO THE RADIATORS LIKE NUMBED BEES TO THE DRENC+   866 1
    THE HUM OF THE BEES IN THE PEAR-TREE BLOOM   885 14
    AND THE BUSTLE OF BEES IN THE PEAR-TREE BLOOM   885 24
    IT IS STORMY AND RAIN-DROPS CLING LIKE SILVER BEES TO T+   *926 1

BEE'S
    OR A BEE'S   355 4

BEETHOVEN
    AND BEETHOVEN THEY SOLD TO CERTAIN CONDUCTORS TO BE CON+   763 8

BEETLE
    THE KICKING LITTLE BEETLE   355 28
    OR THE STOUT SWART BEETLE ROLLED THE GLOBE OF DUNG IN W+   437 16
    AND AN OCEAN LINER GOING EAST LIKE A SMALL BEETLE WALKI+   687 9
    THE SUN HAS CREPT LIKE A SCARLET BEETLE IN THE HUSK   757 15
    BEFORE THE STOUT SWART BEETLE HAD A BALL OF DUNG TO ROL+   *946 26

BEFOREHAND
    BEAUTIFULLY BEFOREHAND WITH IT ALL   337 13
    BUT HE KNOWS NOTHING BEFOREHAND   690 9
    THUS BEFOREHAND   749 7
    BEFOREHAND   749 10

BEG
    POLTROON AND BEG THE SILENT OUTSPREAD GOD   195 24
    I BEG YOUR PARDON   546 6
    SO NOW WE BEG YOU MR SQUIRE   681 9
    NOW I MUST ENTER YOUR MANSION AND BEG YOUR GIFT   695 23
    BE GOOD TO ME NOW AS I BEG YOU AS YOU'VE ALWAYS BEEN GO+   696 9
    WASTE ME NOT I BEG YOU WASTE   *930 1

BEGAN
    SO THAT I BEGAN TO WONDER OVER MYSELF AND WHAT I WAS   254 23
    BEFORE THE ROSE BEGAN TO SIMPER SUPREME   285 16
    AH MEDITERRANEAN MORNING WHEN OUR WORLD BEGAN   311 14
    AS WE BEGAN   364 9
    AS HE CERTAINLY BEGAN SO PERFECTLY ALONE   364 10
    SO THE TALE BEGAN   379 28
    AND DOWN ALL EAGLES BEGAN TO FLUTTER REELING FROM THEIR   413 5
    THEN IT BEGAN TO FIDGET SHIFTING FROM ONE LEG TO THE OT+   413 12
    IT BEGAN WITH JUDAS AND GOES ON IN THE WAGE-SYSTEM   483 1
    BUT BRITANNIA TURNED PALE AND BEGAN TO FAINT   577 7
    WHEN AT A CERTAIN POINT A DROP OF WATER BEGAN TO DRIP D+   682 13
    AND A BREATH OF VAPOUR BEGAN TO WREATHE UP   682 14
    SUDDENLY HIS HORSES BEGAN TO START   735 7
    SHE WATCHED MY HAND AND THE SKIES BEGAN TO THRILL   *935 28

BEGET
    TO BRING TOGETHER TWO STRANGE SPARKS BEGET   218 20
    WHAT I BEGET MUST I BEGET OF BLOOD   742 24
    HE CAN COPULATE AND BEGET CHILDREN   843 15

BEGETS
    BEGETS A MURDERER IN HIS OWN BODY   653 4

BEGETTER
    I WAS A FATHER AND A BEGETTER OF CHILDREN   257 20

BEGETTING
    TO START A BIRTH FROM JOY OF THE BEGETTING   89 7
    AND PANGS OF BIRTH AND JOY OF THE BEGETTING   89 12
    THE SHARP BEGETTING OR THE CHILD BEGOT   219 11
    AND OH OH HORROR I WAS BEGETTING AND CONCEIVING IN MY   257 21
    HOW CAN THEY COMMIT THE INDECENCY OF BEGETTING CHILDREN   521 22
    WITHOUT FIRST BEGETTING A NEW HOPE FOR THE CHILDREN TO   521 23
    AND WHAT IS DEATH TO US BUT A BEGETTING   880 1

BEGGAR
    I'E THINK ITIS NOBBUT A BEGGAR   44 12
    IT'S NOT A BEGGAR MOTHER HARK   44 14
    TILL A BEGGAR SPOKE TO JOSEPH   202 9
    THE BEGGAR HAD GATHERED AT NIGHT   202 18

BEGGAR'S
    REMOTE ALTHOUGH I HEAR THE BEGGAR'S COUGH   36 5

BEGGAR-WOMAN
    THE BEGGAR-WOMAN THE YEARNING-EYED   64 5

BEGGED
    BEGGED ME TO ASK NOT FOR THE DOOR   104 2
    WHO BEGGED OF YOU AND GAVE YOU HOMAGE   696 10

BEGGING
    I FOLLOW HER DOWN THE NIGHT BEGGING HER NOT TO DEPART   67 12

BEGIN
    MY UNKNOWN BREASTS BEGIN   39 2
    THAT WHITE AN' 'ER CRIED THAT MUCH I'D LIKE TO BEGIN   61 8
    SLOWLY BEGIN TO PLASH   149 28
    LEAVES UNBURDENED TO BEGIN AGAIN   195 4
    WE MUST BEGIN   229 12
    BUT THIS TIME WE BEGIN TO DO RIGHT   232 11
    THEY BEGIN TO UNDERSTAND   390 1
    THE RICKSHAW BOYS BEGIN TO UNDERSTAND   390 2
    NOW TO BEGIN TO DISAPPEAR   429 23
    THEY BEGIN TO BE SOOTHED AND SOOTHING THEN WE THROW   448 12
    TILL THE WALLS BEGIN TO LOOSEN AND CRACK   462 13
    THAT IT ALWAYS HAS TO BEGIN WITH AND BY WHICH YOU OUGHT   464 21
    THAT MOMENT I BEGIN TO HATE HER   472 18
    AN' LIFE SEEMS TO BEGIN   493 10
    NOW BEGIN TO STEAM OMINOUSLY   541 3
    MAY I ASK YOU THEN WHERE INSINCERITY AND DISHONESTY BEG+   659 13
    AND THOU SHALT BEGIN TO SPIN ROUND ON THE HUB OF THE   714 17
    OH LET US NEVER BEGIN AGAIN   826 9
    AND WHERE WE CAN BEGIN TO LEARN OUR GREAT EMOTIONAL LES+   833 16
    I BEGIN TO HATE HER   834 9
    WITH GUSTO BEGIN AGAIN THE BRISK FIGHT   865 31
    THAT WHITE AN' 'ER SHOOK THAT MUCH I'D LIKE TO BEGIN   *911 24

BEGINNING
    I WILL TEACH THEM THE BEGINNING OF THE LESSON AT THE RO+   93 24
    A FEW TIMES ONLY AT THE BEGINNING   106 29
    THAT MY COMPLETION OF MANHOOD SHOULD BE THE BEGINNING   218 24
    THE END CRACKS OPEN WITH THE BEGINNING   278 25
    EVEN THE VERY BEGINNING   328 11
    IN THE BEGINNING WAS THE WORD   328 12
    IN THE BEGINNING WAS THE WORD   328 24
    IN THE BEGINNING WAS THE WORD OF COURSE   329 10
    SO THAT A NEW CONCEPTION OF THE BEGINNING AND END   329 33
    IN THE BEGINNING   340 14
    THE BABES JUST BEGINNING TO TEETHE   553 32
    IF EVER THERE WAS A BEGINNING   681 12
    ALL WE CAN HONESTLY IMAGINE IN THE BEGINNING   681 26
    THE BEGINNING AND THE END   694 32
    AND HIS SINGING SOUND AS THEY ALWAYS DO AT THE BEGINNIN+   865 17

BEGINNINGS
  YEA WHAT GOOD BEGINNINGS   152 22
  THOUGH FAMILY FEELING THERE IS NONE NOT EVEN THE BEGINN+   357 23
  UNCONTAMINATED BY EVEN THE BEGINNINGS OF A LIE   481 30

BEGINS
  AND SO MY HEART BEGINS TO CRY AND CALL   174 3
  AND WHEN THE HERD GOES BY AT DAWN SHE BEGINS TO BLEAT F+   384 6
  AH WHEN HE BEGINS TO DRAW THE LINE IN TIGHT TO LAND HIS   586 21
  AND THE MACHINE BEGINS TO WOBBLE   676 2
  WHY THE MODERN YOUNG WIFE OF THE LITTLE-BOY BRILLIANT B+   842 9

BEGONE
  A CACHE SEXE A CACHE SEXE OR ELSE BEGONE   580 2

BEGOT
  THE SHARP BEGETTING OR THE CHILD BEGOT   219 11
  YET I HAVE LAIN IN HIS LOINS ERE HE BEGOT ME IN MOTHER +   801 14
  CRUCIBLE WHERE NEW BLOSSOMS OF SHAPE ARE BEGOT   873 5

BEGOTTEN
  WERE BOTH BEGOTTEN   562 25

BEGRUDGE
  THEY DON'T BEGRUDGE YOU A DRINK   828 18

BEGUILE
  I NEED NOT LOOK AFTER MY SOUL BEGUILE MY FEAR   *945 27

BEGUN
  WHEN THA BEGUN   79 32
  BUT LET ME FINISH WHAT I HAVE BEGUN   154 18
  FLOWER THE DAY HAS BEGUN   166 27
  THE DAY HAS BEGUN   230 10
  WHERE THE END IS BEGUN   253 33
  NOW THAT THE WAVES OF OUR UNDOING HAVE BEGUN TO STRIKE   513 22
  TOUCH HAS BEGUN   612 2
  IN HEAVEN HAS BEGUN   758 14
  WE HAVE NOT BEGUN   825 30
  I ASK WHEN THA BEGUN   *921 28

BEHALF
  BEHALF   291 20

BEHAVE
  AND LET ME NOTICE IT BEHAVE ITSELF   299 23

BEHAVED
  BUT IT CAN'T BE SO FOR THEY BEHAVED   579 1

BEHAVES
  AND BEHAVES LIKE THE REST OF MEN   38 32
  WHERE THE ELECTRON BEHAVES AND MISBEHAVES AS IT WILL   477 28
  ONLY THE ELECTRON BEHAVES AND MISBEHAVES INCOMPREHENSIB+   *947 5

BEHAVIOUR
  DROP YOUR SLOPPY BEHAVIOUR   564 15

BEHOLD
  BEHOLD MY HAIR TWISTING AND GOING BLACK   301 21
  BEHOLD MY EYES TURN TAWNY YELLOW   301 22
  I BEHOLD YOU STAND   333 28
  AND SO BEHOLD HIM FOLLOWING THE TAIL   361 13
  BEHOLD HOW YOU CAN'T BEHOLD ME   403 12
  BEHOLD ME TROTTING AT EASE BETWIXT THE SLOPES OF THE GO+   409 6
  AND THEY SAY NOW BEHOLD YOU ARE LIVING THE GREAT LIFE   441 19
  BEHOLD YOU ARE LIVING THE GREAT LIFE THE STUPENDOUS LIFE   441 23
  IS A FEARFUL THING TO BEHOLD   475 10
  FEARFUL TO BEHOLD   502 18
  BEHOLD THE GULF IMPASSABLE   635 27
  BEHOLD YOUR CROSS CHRISTIANS   636 1
  BEHOLD GOD IS BORN   682 9
  BEHOLD HE IS BORN WET   682 17
  BEHOLD NOW VERY GOD IS BORN   683 13
  AND THE EYE CANNOT BEHOLD HIM   692 8
  AND THE EYE CANNOT BEHOLD HIM   692 19
  ONLY BEHOLD THE GHOSTS THE GHOSTS OF THE SLAIN   736 4
  BEHOLD THEM HOMELESS AND HOUSELESS WITHOUT COMPLAINT   736 5
  ICHABOD ICHABOD LO AND BEHOLD   814 18
  AND BEHOLD THEM DEPLORABLY DEAD BY WRONG USAGE DEFACED   859 24

BEHOLDEN
  FOR I WON'T BE BEHOLDEN TO SUCH AS 'ER   82 15
  SO HE PAUSES AND IS BEHOLDEN AND STRAIGHTWAY IS GONE   403 8
  FROM ALL SORTS OF MEN DON'T BE BEHOLDEN   458 28
  FOR I WON'T BE BEHOLDEN TO SUCH AS HER   *924 19

BEHOLDS
  HIS BLACK SAD-LIDDED EYE SEES BUT BEHOLDS NOT   362 4

BEING
  IN THE NIGHT WHERE WE FIRST HAVE BEING BEFORE WE RISE O+   92 15
  WHERE THE FIGHT THAT IS FIGHT FOR BEING IS FOUGHT THROU+   93 4
  AT LAST INTO BLOSSOM OF BEING EACH ONE HIS OWN FLOWER O+   93 15
  AND THIS HELEN BESIDE ME I AM BLANK BEING NOTHING I BEA+   97 12
  YOUR HEAD THROUGH BEING LONELY   104 20
  NOW BEING COME AGAIN HOW MAKE THE BEST   122 15
  THEN WILL SOMEBODY SQUARE THIS SHADE WITH THE BEING I   141 22
  AND ALL YOUR BEING IS GIVEN TO ME SO NONE   157 19
  THE PULSE THROUGH THE WHOLE BLAND BEING   165 13
  OF RIDING AND BEING ENVIED SUCH ENVY AS HAS NO END   175 9
  ONLY TO DANCE TOGETHER IN TRIUMPH OF BEING TOGETHER   210 15
  BY ALL THE BLOOD OF THE ROSE-BUSH INTO BEING   218 17
  AND WHIRLING IN BLOSSOM OF FLAME AND BEING UPON ME   218 23
  TILL ALL YOUR BEING SMOKES WITH FINE DESIRE   219 4
  I BECAME A STRANGE BEING   222 11
  AH YES BEING MALE IS NOT MY HEAD HARD-BALANCED   222 17
  YOU WOMEN MOST HOLY YOU MOTHER YOU BEING BEYOND   235 13

BEING
  YOU ARE HELD BACK BY MY BEING IN THE SAME WORLD WITH YOU   235 31
  THERE SURE IN SINLESS BEING   243 5
  WHERE I TOUCH YOU I FLAME INTO BEING BUT IS IT ME OR   245 12
  AM A SUNLIGHT UPON THEM THAT SHINES THEM INTO BEING   245 19
  THE VERY QUICK OF MY BEING   246 6
  HOW AWFULLY DISTINCT AND FAR OFF FROM EACH OTHER'S BEING   248 3
  AND YET HOW HIS SEPARATE BEING LIBERATES ME   252 3
  BEING BURNED WITH OIL AND CONSUMED IN CORRUPT THICK   258 10
  BEING MAD WITH VORACIOUS DESIRE   264 36
  THIS ACHE FOR BEING IS THE ULTIMATE HUNGER   265 26
  IT IS THE MAJOR PART OF BEING THIS HAVING SURPASSED ONE+   266 20
  SEPARATE BEING   266 32
  IT IS IN PURE UNUTTERABLE RESOLVEDNESS DISTINCTION OF B+   267 3
  BEING PRESSED UP AGAINST THE OTHER   267 16
  ONE CLEAR BURNISHED ISOLATED BEING UNIQUE   267 20
  CONDITIONED ONLY BY OUR OWN PURE SINGLE BEING   267 28
  HAVING NO LAWS BUT THE LAWS OF OUR OWN BEING   267 29
  EVERY HUMAN BEING WILL THEN BE LIKE A FLOWER UNTRAMMELL+   267 30
  WHICH I BEING A LITTLE WEARY OF ROMAN VIRTUE   297 32
  NO BOUNDS BEING SET   306 34
  THE TREE BEING LIFE-DIVINE   307 1
  PROFITEERS HERE BEING CALLED DOG-FISH STINKING DOG-FISH+   316 25
  I MATTHEW BEING A MAN   320 10
  WHICH IS MY WAY BEING MAN   323 13
  BUT I MATTHEW BEING A MAN   323 16
  I STAND AT THE PALE OF MY BEING   338 28
  THINGS HAVE THEIR BEING   348 5
  BEING EARTH-BROWN EARTH-GOLDEN FROM THE BURNING BOWELS   349 26
  ALONE WITH NO SENSE OF BEING ALONE   354 10
  BEING TOUCHED WITH LOVE AND DEVOID OF FATHERLINESS   357 15
  MOVING AND BEING HIMSELF   358 15
  AND DOOMED TO PARTIALITY PARTIAL BEING   362 28
  ACHE AND WANT OF BEING   362 29
  SINGING AND CALLING AND SINGING AGAIN BEING ANSWERED   366 36
  ONCE THEY SAY HE WAS PASSING BY WHEN A DOG WAS BEING BE+   376 5
  THE HORSE BEING NOTHING BUT A NAG WILL FORGET   379 30
  AND MEN BEING MOSTLY GELDINGS AND KNACKER-BONED HACKS   379 31
  ESPECIALLY IF BEING GIVEN A NEEDLE'S EYE OF EGRESS ELSE+   381 6
  AT DUSK THEY PATTER BACK LIKE A BOUGH BEING DRAGGED ON   384 1
  THAT BEING HER WAY OF ANSWER IF I SPEAK TO HER SELF-CON+   385 5
  WITH HAIR ON THEM ARE BEING IDLE   386 30
  WRINKLED PILLARS OF THEIR LEGS AS THEY WERE BEING   390 17
  BEING ROYAL OF THE GODS   392 8
  HOW YOU HATE BEING BRUSHED WITH THE BOOT-BRUSH TO BRUSH   397 30
  HOW YOU HATE BEING MADE TO LOOK UNDIGNIFIED MA'AM   397 33
  HOW YOU HATE BEING LAUGHED AT MISS SUPERB   397 34
  AIMING AGAIN AT BEING LOVED   398 14
  YOUR SENSITIVE LOVE-PRIDE BEING ALL HURT   400 29
  THE FULL DOOM OF LOVING AND NOT BEING ABLE TO TAKE BACK   410 16
  THE BIG BIRD OF THE AMERINDIAN BEING THE EAGLE   414 2
  BUT IF IT IS THUMBS UP AND MANKIND MUST GO ON BEING MAN+   430 10
  AND FLUTTERING AND BEING BIRDS   443 20
  IT WAS LIKE BEING IN HEAVEN WHICH I AM SURE HAS A WHITE   444 3
  RATHER PROUD OF BEING A BIT OF A DON JUAN   446 24
  BEING AS GOOD AS YOU CAN   458 17
  IS THERE A GEM WHICH CAME INTO BEING BETWEEN US   478 5
  IS THERE A RUBY OF FUSED BEING MINE AND YOURS AN INWARD   478 7
  ON BEING LOVED WHEN THERE IS NO LOVE IN THEM   479 8
  IF ONLY CLEOPATRA HAD LEFT OFF BEING SO CLEOPATRA-ISH   479 20
  THE PASSION OF JUSTICE BEING PROFOUND AND SUBTLE   482 8
  AND IGNOBLE HASTE FOR FEAR OF BEING LATE   484 7
  IT IS A FORM OF WAR EVEN SELF-ASSERTION AND BEING WISE +   495 21
  IT'S BAD TASTE TO BE WISE ALL THE TIME LIKE BEING A PER+   496 1
  BEING BORN AMONG THE WORKING PEOPLE   498 12
  SO I AM JUST GOING TO GO ON BEING A BLANK TILL SOMETHIN+   501 23
  EFFORT OF BEING YOUNG   502 15
  WHY DON'T PEOPLE LEAVE OFF BEING LOVABLE   505 9
  IN MY VERY BEING   508 10
  WHICH IS ONLY A SLOPPY WAY OF BEING IN LOVE WITH YOURSE+   508 15
  AND A MAN CAN NO LONGER FEEL HEROIC ABOUT BEING A HAMLET   508 26
  INSTEAD OF GETTING ON AND NOT BEING ABLE TO GET OFF AGA+   518 25
  THE ONLY REASON FOR LIVING IS BEING FULLY ALIVE   522 9
  IT IS THE PENALTY OF FEAR AND MEANNESS BEING MEANER THAN   522 22
  HE CAN'T HELP BEING A SLAVE A WAGE-SLAVE   524 11
  BUT CENSORS BEING DEAD MEN   528 14
  OR BEING RAPED EITHER WAY SO LONG AS IT WAS CONSCIOUSLY   532 17
  CHANGE FROM BEING SINGLE AND BECOME GRADUALLY DOUBLE   534 26
  I SUPPOSE WHEN THE MEN ALL STARTED BEING WILLY WET-LEGS   537 28
  WOMEN FELT IT WAS NO LONGER ANY USE BEING A LINGER-LONG+   537 29
  SKIRTING THE POLES OF BEING AND OF NOT-BEING   542 15
  FROM BEING MARY   558 14
  WHEN YOU'VE BEEN BEING   564 1
  BEING CRUDE AND STRAIGHTFORWARD YOU'LL ONLY PROVE   576 14
  LIKE FEARFUL AND CORPSE-LIKE FISHES HOOKED AND BEING PL+   586 9
  AND I LOATHE THE THOUGHT OF BEING A PILFERER   610 19
  I KNOW NO GREATER DELIGHT THAN THE SHEER DELIGHT OF BEI+   610 19
  BEING   621 19
  LIKE FEARFUL AND CORPSE-LIKE FISHES HOOKED AND BEING PL+   632 24
  ARE DEFLOWERED BY BEING LOOKED AT BY SO MANY UNCLEAN   634 19
  AND RULERS OF MILLIONS OF ROBOTS BEING ROBOTS THEMSELVES   637 20
  BEING GROUND EXCEEDING SMALL   642 4
  WHEN I HEAR SOMEBODY COMPLAIN OF BEING LONELY   646 1
  AND SHARES BEING WITH ME SILKILY   656 3
  BEING TRAMPLED TO MUD   658 12
  AND WHAT'S MORE THEY'RE VERY NICE ABOUT BEING NICE   660 1
  ABOUT YOUR BEING NICE AS WELL   660 2
  IT IS ALL A QUESTION OF BEING PROFOUNDLY INTERESTED IN +   665 16
  AND ALL THINGS AND NOTHING AND BEING AND NOT-BEING   667 10
  BUT OFF SHE WENT BEING REALLY RATTLED   669 4
  BEING CONCEITED FOOLS   673 6
  NOW LET ME BE MYSELF IN THE BEING ONE OF THE GODS   674 17
  THE KNOWLEDGE IS WITHIN ME WITHOUT BEING A MATTER OF FA+   677 3
  MEN PREVENT ONE ANOTHER FROM BEING MEN   677 17
  ON A DAY OF SPLENDOUR FOR THE FURTHER SPLENDOUR OF BEIN+   679 14
  THAT PURE BEING IS BODILESS   689 16
  EVERYTHING THAT HAS BEING HAS BEING IN THE FLESH   691 7
  AT HER BEST AND HER MOST BEAUTIFUL BEING GOD MADE MANIF+   691 20

BEING
    ANY CLEAR AND FEARLESS AND BEING GOD VERY GOD   691 21
    IN HIS OWN AND GREATER BEING   700 15
    AT LAST IN SHEER HORROR OF NOT BEING ABLE TO LEAVE OFF   701 31
    IN THE CENTRE OF YOUR BEING GROAN NOT   703 12
    IN THE CENTRE OF YOUR BEING GROAN NOT DO NOT GROAN   703 13
    CONCEIT OF BEING IMMUNE   709 32
    AND BEING WHICH IS NOT   711 31
    ABSOLUTE FREEDOM ABSOLVED FROM THE GREAT NECESSITIES OF+   712 19
    ONLY THE HUMAN BEING ABSOLVED FROM KISSING AND STRIFE   713 27
    BEING AN ACT OF ONE   715 9
    AND HEALED FROM ALL THIS ACHE OF BEING   724 30
    MAY CEASE FROM BEING   726 20
    YET THROUGH THE TEARS STEALS A SENSE OF PEACE AND GREAT+   768 1
    THAT THE INDIANS COMPLAINED OF BEING POOR   778 18
    AND BEING DEAD YOU SHALL NOT BE REFRESHED   796 3
    BEING DEAD YOU SHALL ROVE LIKE DOGS WITH THE BROKEN HAU+   796 5
    READY AGAIN FOR THE BUSINESS OF BEING A MAN   809 18
    THEY DON'T MIND BEING DEPRAVED IMMORAL OR ANYTHING OF T+   829 12
    BUT THEY DO MIND BEING UNJUST UNFAIR   829 13
    WHICH IS VERY ODD BEING THE EXACT REVERSE OF THEIR FATH+   829 14
    ANOTHER HUMAN BEING   834 5
    WHEREAS TO THE ORDINARY MORAL HUMAN BEING THE WORD   837 3
    OF CHAGRIN AT BEING A MAN   837 11
    WHEREIN A MAN CAN LIVE HIS LIFE WITHOUT BEING A SLAVE T+   837 25
    WHEN ALL MY SUBSTANCE IS BEING SPENT   874 16
    WERE WORSE THAN BEING LEFT ALONE IN LIFE   879 27
    MY EYES BEING DOWNCAST   880 17
    BEING TOO MIRTHLESS TO MOVE THE LILT OF SINGING   884 13
    AND MAKES A POINT OF BEING VERY GENTLE VERY TENDER   *948 12

BEINGS
    THRONG OF STARTLED BEINGS SUDDENLY THROWN   140 12
    THE MOANING OF SLEEP-BOUND BEINGS IN TRAVAIL THAT TOIL +   149 19
    AND BETWEEN THEM THE LAST LIVING HUMAN BEINGS   642 3
    AND SINISTER BEINGS WILL BECKON BETWEEN   748 4

BEIN'
    OF 'IM BEIN' GONE   60 24
    GOIN' UP AN' BEIN' REFINED   553 2

BELATED
    AND SLOWLY DOWN THE MOUNTAIN ROAD BELATED   225 9

BELCHING
    ALMOST AS EMPTY AS BELCHING OR HICCUP   681 7

BELFRY
    MAKES OF HIMSELF A BELFRY OF THROBBING SOUND   530 10

BELIAL
    THE FEAR OF HUNGER IS MOLOCH BELIAL THE HORRIBLE GOD   263 6

BELIEF
    UNBLEMISHED BELIEF IN YOUR OWN PERFECTION   398 3
    BELIEF IN LOVE AND SORROW OF SUCH BELIEF   410 12
    WOMEN WITH EYES THAT WERE GENTLE IN OLDEN BELIEF IN LOVE   410 23

BELIEFS
    REELING IN THE BLACK END OF ALL BELIEFS   542 24

BELIES
    IT ALL BELIES   166 9

BELIEVE
    IF THAT IS SO THEN I BELIEVE A LITTLE IN PROVIDENCE PRO+   333 21
    I BELIEVE HE CHIRPS PIPISTRELLO SEEING ME HERE ON THIS   347 19
    I BELIEVE THERE WERE NO FLOWERS THEN   372 14
    I BELIEVE HE PIERCED THE SLOW VEGETABLE VEINS WITH HIS +   372 17
    BELIEVE IN THE ONE IDENTITY DON'T YOU   395 25
    DON'T EVER BELIEVE THEM   441 4
    SHE SAYS SHE WANTS A LOVER BUT DON'T YOU BELIEVE HER   539 13
    IF YOU ARE A MAN AND BELIEVE IN THE DESTINY OF MANKIND   666 10
    AND IN DEATH I BELIEVE I SHALL BE AS THE FLOWERS ARE   677 12
    PROGRESS YOU KNOW WE BELIEVE IN PROGRESS   773 23
    THERE IS I BELIEVE SCARCELY ONE INTELLIGENT AMERICAN WHO   775 12

BELIEVES
    THA NIVER BELIEVES IT DOES TER MOTHER   77 9
    THA NIVER BELIEVES IT MOTHER DOES TER   *918 27

BELIEVING
    OF THE SHE-DOVE IN THE BLOSSOM STILL BELIEVING   65 21
    AND FEARFUL YET OF BELIEVING   168 35
    HALF BELIEVING 'EM TILL ONE DAY   556 14

BELIEVIN'
    WELL I'M BELIEVIN' NO TALE MISSIS   78 17
    WELL I'M BELIEVIN' NO TALE MISSIS   *920 9

BELITTLE
    BUT WHY GO ON HAVING THEM IF THEY BELITTLE US   452 12

BELITTLED
    WHY SHOULD WE BE BELITTLED ANY LONGER   452 13

BELL
    WHY IS IT THE LONG SLOW STROKE OF THE MIDNIGHT BELL   63 1
    THE MOON-MIST IS OVER THE VILLAGE OUT OF THE MIST SPEAK+   63 4
    WHEN WILL THE BELL RING AND END THIS WEARINESS   74 7
    OF EACH OTHER I SHALL SIT AND WAIT FOR THE BELL   75 6
    ONE LONELY BELL ONE ONLY THE STORM-TOSSED AFTERNOON IS   137 1
    I WAS LAST NIGHT WHEN MY SOUL RANG CLEAR AS A BELL   141 24
    THE WILD-FLOWER SHAKES ITS BELL   216 9
    THIS THEN AT LAST IS THE DAWN AND THE BELL   220 12
    LIKE A BELL THAT IS CHIMING EACH STROKE AS A STROKE FAL+   251 12
    TORTOISE-WISE THE FIRST BELL SOUNDING   358 13
    RINGING THE SOUNDLESS BELL OF HIS PRESENCE IN CHAOS   358 19

BELL
    AS THE ELEPHANT BELLS SOUNDED TONG-TONG-TONG BELL OF THE   390 32
    A TINY BELL OF CONCLUSION HAS SOUNDED   512 7
    WHO STRUCK THE BELL   512 12
    MY BODY GLAD AS THE BELL OF A FLOWER   742 32
    I START FROM THE DROOP OF FORGETFULNESS AS THE SOUND OF+   858 21
    I HOLD HER STILL AND WAIT TILL THE BELL SHALL FALTER   859 1
    PLEASE SIR I WAS SWEEPING SNOW AN' I NEVER HEARD THE BE+   866 9
    WHEN WILL THE BELL RING AND END THIS WEARINESS   *895 15
    I WILL SIT AND WAIT FOR THE BELL   *896 5
    WHEN WILL THE BELL RING AND END THIS WEARINESS   *904 4
    I WILL SIT AND WAIT FOR THE BELL   *904 26

BELLE
    LIKE A BELLE AT HER WINDOW   384 21

BELLIES
    NO WISTFUL BELLIES   335 19
    AND SHOW VAST BELLIES TO THE CHILDREN   425 22
    SUCH LUMPS SUCH FROGS WITH STONES IN THEIR BELLIES   791 29
    TELL THEM THEY ARE LIKE FROGS WITH STONES IN THEIR BELL+   791 30
    TELL THEM THEY MUST GET THE STONES OUT OF THEIR BELLIES   791 31
    TO ROLL THE GRAVE-STONE OFF THEIR SOULS FROM THE CAVE O+   793 7
    SERPENT IN THE BELLIES OF MEN   806 12
    BELLIES THAT SHRINK NOT   827 23

BELLOW
    AND HEAR HIM BELLOW AFTER MANY YEARS THE BULL THAT SERV+   327 8

BELLOWED
    BEYOND THE GREAT BULL THAT BELLOWED THROUGH SPACE AND   437 10
    A GREAT BULL BELLOWED THROUGH SPACE CALLING TO THE MILK+   *946 21

BELLOWING
    SQUEAKILY BELLOWING FOR ALL HE WAS WORTH   492 1

BELLOWS
    WHY THE OLD CHURCH BELLOWS AND BRAGS   54 20

BELL-ROPE
    AT A WIRE AT A BELL-ROPE   343 22

BELLS
    THE CHIME OF THE BELLS AND THE CHURCH CLOCK STRIKING FI+   48 14
    THE FIVE OLD BELLS   54 1
    THE DAMNED BELLS CEASE AND WE ARE EXEMPT   54 28
    THE ELEPHANT BELLS STRIKING SLOW TONG-TONG TONG-TONG   387 33
    AS THE ELEPHANT BELLS SOUNDED TONG-TONG-TONG BELL OF THE   390 32
    THEIR BELLS SOUNDING FRUSTRATE AND SINISTER   391 4
    AND THERE SHALL BE THE SOFT SWIFT TREMOR AS OF UNHEARD B+   479 4
    THE MOHAMMEDANS SAY THAT THE SOUND OF BELLS   622 19
    YET BELLS CALL THE CHRISTIANS TO GOD   623 1
    ESPECIALLY CLAPPER BELLS HARD TONGUES WAGGING IN HARD M+   623 2
    AND LET ME COME PAST THE SILVER BELLS OF YOUR FLOWERS A+   696 2
    WITH A HINT OF THE FROZEN BELLS OF THE SCYLLA FLOWER   708 29
    STARTLING THE THICK-SPUN TWILIGHT THE BELLS SHAKE OUT   858 26

BELLS'
    MAKES TITTERING JESTS AT THE BELLS' OBSCENITY   54 15

BELL-WIRES
    AND STUMBLING LUNGING AND TOUCHING THE WALLS THE BELL-W+   343 11

BELLY
    RHYTHM STARTS AND MY SILENT AND SLUMBEROUS BELLY   39 5
    MY SOFT SLUMBERING BELLY   39 7
    BELLY   207 22
    AND IN HIS BELLY THE SMOULDERING HATE OF ME   226 8
    NOT BREAD ALONE NOT THE BELLY NOR THE THIRSTY THROAT   263 8
    I HAVE NEVER YET BEEN SMITTEN THROUGH THE BELLY WITH THE   263 9
    AND DESIROUS BELLY GULPING   336 11
    DART AND TWIST STILL HE MUST GO WITH HIS BELLY ON THE G+   348 12
    AND THERE GOES ON HIS SHELL-TENDER EARTH-TOUCHING BELLY   355 29
    ALL HER GREAT HAIRY-SHAGGY BELLY OPEN AGAINST THE MORNI+   385 30
    BELLY   393 16
    LIKE A FUNNY TRIMMING TO THE MIDDLE OF HER BELLY THIN   393 19
    HER BELLY HER BIG HAUNCHES   393 21
    WHILE SOMETHING STIRS QUICKLY IN HER BELLY AND A LEAN   393 30
    BELLY   394 24
    OH THESE ARE ABSTRACTIONS TO YOUR NASTY LITTLE BELLY   399 20
    AS UNDER THE HAIRY BELLY OF A GREAT BLACK BEAR   409 12
    AND THE FLOOD STRIKES THE BELLY AND WE ARE GONE   425 18
    INTO THE MARSH-SOFT BELLY   436 26
    AND HE GOES AND WASHES THE BELLY OF THE HORSE   734 5
    SOILING THE CLEAN WHITE DUST HE RUBS THE BELLY   734 9
    AND BENDS AGAIN AND LOOKS AT THE BELLY OF THE HORSE   734 15
    ON THE HORSE'S BELLY HURT HIM FOR HE WAS RATHER GENTLE   734 20
    MY LEGS MY BREAST MY BELLY   741 17
    BETWEEN YOUR BREAST AND BELLY IS A STAR   800 2
    YOUR BELLY   800 6
    BELLY   801 26
    YOUR BELLY   801 29
    PUT SLEEP AS BLACK AS BEAUTY IN THE SECRET OF MY BELLY   803 2
    SUN AND INERTIA ON THE BELLY ON THE BACK   827 14
    RUNS ECSTATIC OVER THE PLIANT FOLDS RIPPLING DOWN TO MY+   *891 32
    AND MY SOFT SLUMBERING BELLY   *893 20

BELLY-ACHE
    YET ITS BELLY-ACHE SEEMS TO GET BIGGER TOO   670 19

BELLYFUL
    HE ONLY TAKES HIS BELLYFUL   466 21

BELLY-PLUMBED
    SEEM BELLY-PLUMBED TO THE EARTH'S MID-NAVEL   392 24

BELONG
　BELONG .　　　　　　　　　　　　　　　　　　　　　　　　　93　3
　BETRAYS ME BACK TILL THE HEART OF ME WEEPS TO BELONG　　148　11
　HEAVENS WHERE THEY BELONG THE APOCALYPTIC BEASTS FOR WI+　319　2
　DOWN ON THE DAMP UNCEASING GROUND WHERE MY FEET BELONG　321　16
　NOR YET COMRADES FOR I DON'T BELONG TO ANY CAUSE　　499　22
　WE BELONG NEITHER TO MEN NOR OUR CHILDREN NOR　　525　25
　WHERE I BELONG YOU SEE　　　　　　　　　　　　552　8
　WITH MY FELLOW-COUNTRYMEN OR ELSE I DON'T BELONG　　579　6
　THERE IS THE ORGANIC CONNECTION LIKE LEAVES THAT BELONG+　615　1
　YOU BELONG TO THE NIGHT　　　　　　　　　　　803　23
　AND SURELY THE HEART THAT IS IN ME MUST BELONG　　*940　10

BELONGED
　OF EDEN EVEN WAS EVE'S FRUIT TO HER IT BELONGED AND SHE+　277　6

BELONGS
　HE'S A RARE ONE BUT HE BELONGS　　　　　　　337　27
　BELONGS TO THE BAMBOO THICKET AND THE DRAKE IN THE AIR +　623　12
　IT ALL BELONGS TO ME　　　　　　　　　　　671　2
　ANYTHING THAT BELONGS TO US AND IS UGLY AND AN IMPEDIME+　678　15
　BUT THE GREY DOG BELONGS TO THE ASH OF THE WORLD　　808　20

BELOVED
　MY BELOVED SMELTING DOWN IN THE BLAZE　　　　103　18
　SINCE THE BELOVED FADED MOTHER THAT SET US ALIGHT　　132　17
　THE OLD DREAMS ARE BEAUTIFUL BELOVED SOFT-TONED AND SURE　174　21
　WHAT THE BELOVED SEVEN　　　　　　　　　196　19
　HE'S THE STAR OF MY FIRST BELOVED　　　　　　198　21
　I BURIED MY BELOVED IT WAS GOOD I BURIED MYSELF AND WAS　257　25
　AND MOUNT LIKE A LARK BELOVED　　　　　　　322　28
　CHASTITY BELOVED CHASTITY　　　　　　　　469　11
　O BELOVED CHASTITY　　　　　　　　　　469　12
　CHASTITY BELOVED CHASTITY　　　　　　　　469　14
　THE OLD DREAMS ARE BEAUTIFUL BELOVED SOFT-TONED AND SURE　*907　4
　THE OLD DREAMS ARE BEAUTIFUL BELOVED SOFT-TONED AND SURE　*909　1
　SINCE THE BELOVED FADED MOON THAT SET US ALIGHT　　*938　9

BELOVEDS
　BUT ONE OF HIS BELOVEDS LOOKING A LITTLE PEAKED　　446　26
　ONE OF HIS BELOVEDS LOOKING RATHER A WRECK　　　*948　8

BEND
　THE PINE-TREES BEND TO LISTEN TO THE AUTUMN WIND AS IT +　102　25
　BEND OVER THEM WITH MY SOUL TO CHERISH THE WET　　180　10
　ROUND THE BEND　　　　　　　　　　　　476　9
　NOW BEND YOU DOWN　　　　　　　　　　563　9
　OH YOU WHO BEND YOUR HEAD DOWN AND　　　　762　8
　SHY OF YOUR FACE STILL BEND TO WOO　　　　　887　15
　BLUE SILKEN SKY BEFORE THEY BEND ANEW　　　　*895　4
　AND ROUND THE GREAT FINAL BEND OF UNBROKEN DARK　　*959　27

BENDED
　TO SEE THE CLASS'S LIFTED AND BENDED FACES　　　90　5

BENDING
　HANGS NUMB AND HEAVY FROM A BENDING FLOWER　　　73　21
　THE DAISIES IN THE GRASS ARE BENDING　　　　150　4
　BENDING THEIR ROSY MUZZLES PENSIVE DOWN　　　311　11
　SCUFFING BESIDE HER BENDING DOWN CATCHING HIS OPPORTUNI+　360　19
　THE PEASANTS ARE BENDING CUTTING THE BEARDED WHEAT　　605　22
　BENDING BACKWARDS AWKWARDLY　　　　　　　734　3
　HIS FULL FINE BODY BENDING AND URGING LIKE THE STRESS O+　867　24
　ACROSS THE RIVER BENDING LOW　　　　　　　868　1
　ALOFT BY ONE GREAT BENDING RAFTER DUSTY　　　876　13
　OH MY BOYS BENDING OVER YOUR BOOKS　　　　*907　1
　OH MY BOYS BENDING OVER YOUR BOOKS　　　　*908　22
　HANGS NUMB AND HEAVY FROM THE BENDING FLOWER　　*913　13

BENDS
　AND BENDS AGAIN AND LOOKS AT THE BELLY OF THE HORSE　　734　15
　HIS ROUND BROWN HEAD BENDS LIKE A BEE ABOVE A BLOSSOM　　868　5

BENEATH
　BLOOD-DROPS BENEATH EACH CURL　　　　　　36　22
　AS THE HEART BENEATH DID WIELD　　　　　　55　29
　PATENT AND OPEN BENEATH MY EYE　　　　　　59　27
　SMOULDERING WITH DARKENED BUSBIES BENEATH THE BAYONETS'+　66　8
　UPON US DARK EYES AS HERE BENEATH THE BUSBIES GLITTERIN+　66　25
　AND SO IT IS EBB-TIME THEY TURN THE EYES BENEATH THE BU+　67　1
　FOOTSTEPPING TAP OF MEN BENEATH　　　　　　68　23
　A SPARK BENEATH THE WHEEL　　　　　　　68　28
　NOW HERE I SIT WHILE YOU BREAK THE MUSIC BENEATH　　85　21
　AM LIT BENEATH MY HEART WITH A HALF-MOON WEIRD AND BLUE　115　4
　IN UNDULATING SHIVERS BENEATH THE WIND　　　126　11
　BENEATH THIS POWERFUL TREE MY WHOLE SOUL'S FLUID　　131　8
　BENEATH THE OAK　　　　　　　　　　　131　18
　AT CHARING CROSS HERE BENEATH THE BRIDGE　　　144　14
　THE SANDY DESERT BENEATH HER THE DREARY PLATOON　　153　4
　SHE KNOWS THE WASTE ALL DRY BENEATH HER IN ONE PLACE　　153　5
　SPARKLE BENEATH LUMINOUS HILLS　　　　　　162　7
　SLUMBER BENEATH　　　　　　　　　　　172　17
　FIELDS BENEATH　　　　　　　　　　　199　16
　BENEATH BARE JUDGMENT STARS　　　　　　　202　14
　HELD STILL BENEATH THE SUNSHINE　　　　　　204　18
　A BLOTCH OF PALLOR STIRS BENEATH THE HIGH　　　210　19
　THEN AMONG THE AVERTED PANSIES BENEATH THE HIGH　　225　29
　IS SHATTERED AT LAST BENEATH THE STRIPE　　　253　25
　COMES LIKE A PUNGENT SCENT A VIBRATION BENEATH　　270　13
　LET ME SIT DOWN BENEATH THE MANY-BRANCHING CANDELABRUM　299　9
　LET ME SIT DOWN BENEATH THIS MANY-BRANCHING CANDELABRUM　299　19
　ALMOND-TREE BENEATH THE TERRACE RAIL　　　　300　26
　WHEN THE TIRED FLOWER OF FLORENCE IS IN GLOOM BENEATH T+　340　21
　BENEATH THE LOW-DROPPING BACK-BOARD OF HER SHELL　　361　21
　NAIL-STUDDED THAT SHAKE BENEATH HER SHELL　　　362　7
　THAT WORK BENEATH HER WHILE SHE SPRAWLS ALONG　　362　16
　BENEATH THE EARTH-SOILED HOVEL IN WHICH SHE MOVES　　362　19
　AND SO HE STRAINS BENEATH HER HOUSEY WALLS　　362　20

BENEATH
　AND THE DEEP SECRET ALL-PENETRATING TAIL CURVED BENEATH　365　3
　NAKED DARK MEN BENEATH　　　　　　　　387　27
　MUST CREEP HER GREAT BULK BENEATH THE BRIDGE OF HIM　　426　10
　BENEATH THE WEIGHT OF MUCK　　　　　　　491　24
　BENEATH ENGLAND'S GARDEN STONES　　　　　492　14
　BENEATH THE COTTON　　　　　　　　　562　27
　THE ARTICLES PASSING BENEATH YOUR SCRAWL　　　583　4
　MEN ARE UNSEEN BENEATH THE SHADING HATS　　　606　5
　ON AND ON AND DIVE BENEATH THE ICEBERGS　　　694　4
　DRIFTING BENEATH THE DEATHLY ASHY GREY　　　720　7
　BENEATH THE STEPS OF ST PAUL'S CATCH SEVERAL　　750　22
　THE GOD-THRUST THRUSTING YOU SILENT AND DARK FROM BENEA+　782　9
　TILL I SAW BENEATH ME　　　　　　　　787　5
　AND HAVING PASSED THE YELLOW LINE HE SAW THE EARTH BENE+　790　4
　LIE DOWN BENEATH THE TREE　　　　　　　818　13
　MYSELF AND GATHER THE WATERS BENEATH ME AND LOSE　　*894　22
　FOOTSTEPPING TAP OF MEN BENEATH　　　　　*915　7
　A SPARK BENEATH HIS WHEEL　　　　　　　*915　12
　THIRTEEN LAY THE YELLOW CHICKS BENEATH THE JOIST OF WOOD　*933　3
　SOMEWHERE BENEATH THAT PIANO'S SUPERB SLEEK BLACK　　*940　1

BENEFICENT
　ITS CAGE-RIBS IN THE SOCIAL HEAVEN BENEFICENT　　290　23

BENEVOLENCE
　ALL THIS PHILANTHROPY AND BENEVOLENCE ON OTHER PEOPLE'S　291　19

BENJAMIN FRANKLIN
　AS BENJAMIN FRANKLIN APPROPRIATED PROVIDENCE TO HIS　　395　13

BENT
　HIS BENT COURSE MILDLY HERE WAKES AGAIN LEAPS LAUGHS AN+　33　14
　BENT IF WE DID BUT KNOW IT ON A WEARY AND BITTER GRIMACE　54　23
　BENT ON MY PURSUITS　　　　　　　　　63　16
　MYSELF IN ANGER AND YOU HAVE BENT　　　　　104　19
　ON A NIGHT-SKY BENT WITH A LOAD　　　　　104　24
　HER FACE IS BENT IN THE BITTER STEAM　　　　202　27
　AND RUN TOWARDS IT BENT　　　　　　　462　33
　AND GOLD-BRONZE FLUTTERS BENT THROUGH THE THICK UPPER A+　647　12
　OF FIRE BENT BACK AGAIN　　　　　　　805　11
　DREW HER LIPS OVER THE MOON-PALE PETALS SOFTLY BENT　　856　20
　WHEREAS PURITANISM IS BENT ON SUPPRESSING THE FACT　　*953　4

BENZINE
　THE WEATHER IN TOWN IS ALWAYS BENZINE OR ELSE PETROL　　703　18

BEOUT
　BEOUT A THOUGHT　　　　　　　　　　84　6

BEQUEATH
　CEASE THEN FROM MUSIC DOES ANGUISH OF ABSENCE BEQUEATH　85　23

BEREAVED
　ALTHOUGH BEREAVED OF YOU　　　　　　　109　8

BEREAVEMENT
　PURSUED BY NO SIGH OF BEREAVEMENT　　　　63　33
　I FORGET MY BEREAVEMENT　　　　　　　115　16
　I FORGET MY BEREAVEMENT　　　　　　　115　26

BEREFT
　LIKE AN EMPTY DANDELION STALK BEREFT OF CONNECTION SMALL　98　3
　MY ALTARS SULLIED I BEREFT REMAIN　　　　　151　20
　OF ALL FEELING BEREFT　　　　　　　　230　4
　SHALL WE LAMENT FOR WHAT IS BEREFT US　　　*916　18

BERG
　THAT RIDES THE ROOM LIKE A FROZEN BERG ITS CREST　　155　4

BERRIES
　AS MISTLETOE BERRIES BURNING IN A BLACK TREE　　　86　2
　AND SCARLET BERRIES FALLING FROM THE BUSH　　　160　6
　AND SHE WOKE TO DISTIL THE BERRIES　　　　202　17
　JUST ORTS AND SLARTS BERRIES THAT SMOULDER IN THE BUSH　219　15

BERRY
　LIKE A NEWLY-NAKED BERRY SHRINK　　　　　107　14
　ABROAD I IN THIS NAKED BERRY　　　　　　107　17
　A NEWLY-NAKED BERRY OF FLESH　　　　　　108　?

BESEECHES
　FOR YOUR LATE BEE WHO BESEECHES　　　　　178　31

BESEECHING
　AND ALL THE LITTLE ROOFS OF THE VILLAGE BOW LOW PITIFUL+　63　5
　THE SOUL BESEECHING　　　　　　　　　861　28

BESIDE
　OH WATER-HEN BESIDE THE RUSHES　　　　　43　1
　SET LIKE ROCKS BESIDE A SEA OF GLOOM　　　　56　14
　THAT SHINES BLOOD-RED BESIDE THE RAILWAY SIDING　　72　5
　AND THIS HELEN BESIDE ME I AM BLANK BEING NOTHING I BEA+　97　12
　BESIDE YOUR BED　　　　　　　　　　　102　24
　WHITE EARTH AND RUINS OURSELVES AND NOTHING BESIDE　　166　8
　THE CANDLE-FLAMES BESIDE THE SURPLICES　　　232　31
　AND SIT BESIDE THE STEEL-STRAIGHT ARMS OF YOUR FAIR WOM+　291　5
　ALLURE ME TILL I AM BESIDE MYSELF　　　　　293　9
　BESIDE THE INFINITESIMAL FAINT SMEAR OF YOU　　　334　17
　DAPPER BESIDE HER　　　　　　　　　　359　31
　RUNNING BESIDE HER LIKE A DOG BITING HER EARTHY SPLAY　　360　8
　SCUFFING BESIDE HER BENDING DOWN CATCHING HIS OPPORTUNI+　360　19
　BESIDE THE HIGH ROAD PAST THE DEATHLY DUST　　　605　24
　OR THAT HARD-BOILED YOUNG WOMAN BESIDE HIM　　645　12
　IT IS VERY FITTING THERE IS NAUGHT BESIDE　　　699　2
　NATIONS BESIDE THE SEA ARE OLD　　　　　814　15
　AND BESIDE IT ON THE TABLE HER GLOVES AND MY WILTED WIL+　856　15
　WOODSTACKS BESIDE THE RAILWAY GLISTEN AND GLOW　　*894　26

BESIDE
  BESIDE THE OPEN GROUND   *911 7
  THE WHITE DOG NIPPED THE MOTHER RAT THE FATHER RAT BESI+   *933 7

BESIDES
  BESIDES SHE'S HAD TWENTY LOVERS ONLY TO FIND SHE DIDN'T   539 16
  BESIDES MY DAILY BREAD   704 16

BEST
  ME SO DISTINCTLY FROM SLEEPING THE SLEEP I'D LOVE BEST   48 26
  BUT WE MAUN MA'E THE BEST ON'T SO NOW ROUSE UP AN' LOOK+   83 14
  HUMILIATION DEEP TO ME THAT ALL MY BEST   87 23
  LIKE A PAINTED WINDOW THE BEST   112 1
  THOUGH SURELY MY SOUL'S BEST DREAM IS STILL   117 4
  NOW BEING COME AGAIN HOW MAKE THE BEST   122 15
  ARE JOINED TOGETHER FOR EVER AS IS BEST   231 4
  OR A POOR THING AT BEST   237 4
  AND BEST   281 19
  BUT THE BEST IS THE PERA-HERA AT MIDNIGHT UNDER THE   387 19
  IS THE BEST THAT WE ARE BUT SPERM LOOSE SPERM LIKE THE   429 3
  THEY HAVE ONLY THEIR PERSONALITIES THAT ARE BEST SEEN F+   446 4
  AND THE BEST WON'T BREED THOUGH THEY DON'T KNOW WHY   484 27
  HE DID HIS BEST THE GOOD OLD DOG   492 7
  SHE'S A HOLY TERROR SHE TAKES YOUR BEST FROCK   572 2
  AND ALL YOUR BEST THINGS AND JUST GIVES THEM AWAY   572 3
  I LOVE MY NATIVE LAND THE BEST ETC ETC   575 14
  I LOVE MY NATIVE TONGUE THE BEST   575 16
  AND STILL SPEAK HIS NATIVE LANGUAGE THE BEST   575 23
  ONLY THE BEST MATTERS EVEN THE COW KNOWS IT   587 11
  LEAVES OF GRASS WHAT ARE LEAVES OF GRASS WHEN AT ITS BE+   587 16
  THE BEST OF ALL   601 2
  BUT TO THE FRAIL WHO KNOW BEST   658 9
  ONLY THE BEST MATTERS IN MAN ESPECIALLY   668 2
  TRUE YOU CAN'T PRODUCE THE BEST WITHOUT ATTENDING TO TH+   668 2
  IN SO FAR AS IT GOES TO THE BRINGING FORTH OF THE BEST   668 4
  THAT FLICKERED FORTH IN THE BRIGHT HOURS OF LIFE   676 11
  SHE WHO AT HER BEST HOURS WAS HERSELF WARM FLICKERING H+   676 16
  O SLAY NOT THE BEST BRIGHT PROUD LIFE THAT IS IN YOU TH+   678 24
  THE SELF THAT WE ARE AT ITS BEST IS ALL THAT WE ARE   679 24
  WERE BEST NOT DONE AT ALL   689 12
  AT HER BEST AND HER MOST BEAUTIFUL BEING GOD MADE MANIF+   691 20
  AND SERVE THE BEST OF FOOD THE FONDEST WINE   723 11
  BE BRIDEGROOM OR BEST MAN AS THE CASE TURNS OUT   743 20
  MY ROSY RIVER MY BEST   766 22
  ROSY BEST OF THE BLOOD GONE OUT OF THE BODY   767 33
  BUT IF TAKEN AT ITS VERY BEST THE TITLE AMERICAN   775 34
  AS IT MUST BE TAKEN AT ITS VERY BEST   775 36
  FOR I AM SWEET I AM THE LAST AND THE BEST THE POOL OF N+   796 24
  AN' COS I LIKED HIM BEST YI BETT'R NOR THEE   *911 15
  BUT WE MAUN MA'E THE BEST ON'T I'LL REAR THY CHILDT IF +   *925 18
  LIKE A PAINTED WINDOW THE BEST   *928 21

BESTOWED
  WHENCE ISSUE UNBLEMISHED THE ATOMS WHICH SOFT BESTOWED   *938 17

BET
  HE IS AN' ALL YOU BET 'E IS   434 21
  I BET I AM YOU CAN 'OLD YER PHIZ   434 22

BETE
  DEAFNESS BETE   385 2

BETELGEUSE
  THE MOON AND THE EARTH THE SUN SATURN AND BETELGEUSE   713 20

BETHINKS
  THE CLEAR COLD SKY COLDLY BETHINKS ITSELF   142 13

BETIDE
  AND WOE BETIDE   201 8
  BETIDE   464 7
  AND WOE BETIDE YOU   563 25

BETRAY
  LEST OUR FACES BETRAY US TO SOME UNTIMELY FIEND   267 34
  WHO SO BRILLIANTLY BETRAY   534 12
  I'D BETRAY THE MIDDLE CLASSES   534 15
  SO OUR GOODY-GOOD MEN BETRAY US   537 7

BETRAYED
  AND QUAILING HERE IN THE SUNSHINE BETRAYED FROM HAUNTING   133 3
  I SEE THE STRONG SOUND EARTH BETRAYED AS A FLOATING   874 30

BETRAYS
  EXCEPT HER KISS BETRAYS ME THIS THIS ONLY   127 25
  BETRAYS ME BACK TILL THE HEART OF ME WEEPS TO BELONG   148 11
  AND BETRAYS ITS CANDOUR IN THE ROUND WHITE STRAWBERRY F+   272 28

BETROTHED
  BETROTHED YOUNG LADY WHO LOVES ME AND TAKES GOOD   129 4
  I AND MY BETROTHED ARE TOGETHER IN THE SHED   756 15

BETTER
  I SIT ABSOLVED ASSURED I AM BETTER OFF   36 7
  COMMUNION OFFERING A BETTER THING   104 3
  AND DEATH I KNOW IS BETTER THAN NOT-TO-BE   126 6
  WHAT THING BETTER ARE YOU WHAT WORSE   131 19
  OH BETTER THERE THAN IN ANY BOOK   151 3
  AND OH I WISH IT WAS BETTER   208 22
  IT WERE BETTER SO   230 23
  BUT WHEN YOU COME TO KNOW IT BETTER YOU AGREE WITH THE   282 15
  YOU THINK YOU'D BETTER MIND YOUR P'S AND Q'S FOR A BIT   400 28
  SO BETTER MAKE UP YOUR MIND AMERICAN EAGLE   414 5
  WHO WOULD BE SO MUCH BETTER WITHOUT PICKLING   495 8
  YOU'D BETTER ABANDON ALL IDEA OF FEELINGS ALTOGETHER   501 15
  GETTING THE BETTER OF OTHER PEOPLE WHO CARES   518 18
  GETTING THE BETTER OF THEM WHICH BETTER WHAT BETTER   518 19
  AS A MATTER OF FACT WE ARE BETTER THAN WE KNOW   519 10

BETTER
  THEN THEY'D BE HAPPY FOR WE ARE ALL SO MUCH BETTER THAN   520 31
  BETTER THAN HE IS   529 15
  HOW MUCH BETTER IT WOULD HAVE BEEN   536 7
  AN' THA'LT FEEL BETTER   540 19
  TO USE THEY'D BETTER BE USED   553 20
  THOUGH GOD KNOWS IF YOU'RE ANY BETTER   553 23
  AN' IF YOU'RE NOT ANY BETTER   553 25
  WE'D BETTER GET OUT AN' MAKE WAY FOR   553 31
  YOU'D BETTER GET DOWN AGAIN   555 8
  BETTER DO HIM JUSTICE   563 27
  A BETTER MANAGER FOR OH DEAR ME   571 24
  IS BETTER THAN ANYTHING ELSE IN THE WORLD   601 5
  THOUGH YOU BLOODY OUTSIDERS HAD BETTER NOT TRY IT ON   618 13
  AND I HAD BETTER EVEN HAVE APPROXIMATED TO THE DOG   645 9
  BETTER LITTLE BEE   668 10
  YOU'RE NO BETTER THAN A CROOK   668 22
  YOU'D BETTER OMIT THAT TOO COMMUNISTIC   669 26
  RELIGION KNOWS BETTER THAN PHILOSOPHY   689 26
  FOR THE DEAD VANITY OF KNOWING BETTER NOR THE BLANK   709 30
  AND BETTER YET   747 10
  WERE IT BETTER   749 1
  I WANT MY SON TO BE SOMETHING BETTER THAN HIS FATHER WAS   773 26
  LAND BETTER INSTEAD OF WASTING TIME   777 32
  THAT IT WOULD BE FAR FAR BETTER FOR THE INDIAN YOUTH   778 1
  TILL THEN I LIKE BETTER THIS SEA I MUST SAY   815 17
  BETTER MAN OF THE TWO   842 8
  OH BETTER THERE THAN IN ANY BOOK   873 13
  LIKE BETTER NOR ALL YOUR GOOD AN' 'E WAS ONE   *911 14

BETT'R
  AN' COS I LIKED HIM BEST YI BETT'R NOR THEE   *911 15
  AH KNOW THA LIKED 'IM BETT'R NOR ME BUT LET   *911 17

BETWITCHED
  SINCE THE LAMB BETWITCHED HIM WITH THAT RED-STRUCK FLAG   327 3

BETWIXT
  BEHOLD ME TROTTING AT EASE BETWIXT THE SLOPES OF THE GO+   409 6

BEWAIL
  FROM THE WOES I BEWAIL   133 30

BEWARE
  BEWARE O MY DEAR YOUNG MEN OF GOING ROTTEN   463 17
  AND BEWARE AND TAKE CARE   565 15
  WITH METAL THORNS BEWARE   634 25
  BUT BEWARE   675 5
  BEWARE THE UNHAPPY DEAD THRUST OUT OF LIFE   722 16
  OH BUT BEWARE BEWARE THE ANGRY DEAD   723 2
  OF ELSE BEWARE THEIR ANGRY PRESENCE NOW   723 14
  OH BEWARE OF HIM   805 4
  OH BEWARE OF ME   805 5
  BEWARE BEWARE   807 23

BEWILDER
  ROSE-LEAVES TO BEWILDER THE CLEVER FOOLS   634 29

BEWILDERED
  ABOUT OUR BEWILDERED FACES   271 28
  THE CLUMSY BEWILDERED RUSSIA   536 20
  BEWILDERED AMID THE MOVING IMMENSITY   875 16

BEWILDERING
  AND BE OUT IN THE BEWILDERING DARKNESS WHICH IS ALWAYS +   179 25

BEWILDERMENT
  IN SORROW SINCE WE STAND IN BEWILDERMENT STRANGE   192 19
  CLANGING AT THE FARM SUCH BEWILDERMENT   220 13
  YOUR DEEP BEWILDERMENT FILTERS THROUGH   *894 3

BEWILDERS
  EVEN NOW THE THOUGHT OF IT BEWILDERS ME SUCH GENTLENESS   447 19

BIBBLES
  OH BIBBLES LITTLE BLACK BITCH IN THE SNOW   375 16
  BIBBLES   394 27
  NOT PURE BIBBLES   395 4
  AND EVEN NOW BIBBLES LITTLE MA'AM IT'S YOU WHO   395 11
  OH BIBBLES BLACK LITTLE BITCH   395 15
  OH BIBBLES OH PIPS OH PIPSEY   395 20
  WITH INDISCRIMINATE LOVE BIBBLES   396 6
  YELLING PIPS PIPS BIBBLES   396 9
  PLENTY OF GAME OLD SPIRIT IN YOU BIBBLES   397 28

BIBBLING
  BIBBLING AFFECTION   395 30

BIBBLINGS
  WITH MOANS AND HOLLOW BIBBLINGS   492 6

BIBLE
  AND ALL THE HEROES OF THE BIBLE THEY SOLD FOR CATS-MEAT+   763 1

BIBS
  IT'S THE BLUE JAY JEERING AT US BIBS   375 21

BICKERING
  BETWEEN THE BICKERING FIRE   242 9

BID
  BID HER DEPART   179 9
  AND IT IS TIME TO GO TO BID FAREWELL   716 22
  AND BID FAREWELL OF STATELY TRAVELLERS   740 20

BIDDING
    AND THEN RUN LIKE SURLY DOGS AT THE BIDDING OF PALEFACE+   795   4
BIDE
    I CANNA BIDE TO THINK WHERE HE IS GONE   *911 16
BIDING
    AS IF THE BUTCHER WERE BIDING HIS TIME   828   1
BIDS
    JESUS THE SON OF GOD BIDS YOU FAREWELL   798 29
    MARY THE MOTHER OF GOD BIDS YOU FAREWELL   798 30
BIER
    SWEET AND STILL ON YOUR BIER   102 16
BIG
    AT THE WINDOW SO BIG AND RED   37   6
    BIG HANDS AS IF SURELY HER ARMS DID HURT   128 22
    PRESSES THEM THERE AND KISSES HER BIG DARK HANDS   128 32
    THE BIG SOFT COUNTRY LASS   198   9
    I HOLD MYSELF UP AND FEEL A BIG WIND BLOWING   223   4
    THE BIG MOUNTAINS SIT STILL IN THE AFTERNOON LIGHT   223 13
    AND A HAIRY BIG BEE HUNG OVER THE PRIMULAS   243 23
    HOW FULL AND BIG LIKE A ROBUST HAPPY FLAME   246 13
    MY LITTLE ONE MY BIG ONE   246 17
    MY LITTLE ONE MY BIG ONE   246 22
    MY LITTLE ONE MY BIG ONE   247 14
    QUEER WHAT A BIG STAIN MY SUCKED BLOOD MAKES   334 16
    ONCE A BIG PIKE RUSH   338 19
    A BAT BIG AS A SWALLOW   342 25
    PROBABLY HE WAS BIG   372 19
    AND ARE YOU HIS PRIEST BIG EAGLE   374 18
    I DON'T YIELD TO YOU BIG JOWL-FACED EAGLE   374 25
    FLY OFF BIG BIRD WITH A BIG BLACK BACK   374 29
    HIS BIG FURRY HEAD   377 23
    HIS BIG REGRETFUL EYES   377 24
    HENCE HE UNCOVERS HIS BIG ASS-TEETH AND HOWLS IN THAT A+   378 24
    LIKE A BIG SHIP PUSHING HER BOWSPRIT OVER THE LITTLE SH+   380 24
    SO BIG AND QUIET AND REMOTE HAVING WATCHED SO MANY   393 12
    HER BELLY HER BIG HAUNCHES   393 21
    MAKE BIG EYES LITTLE PONY   409 26
    STARTLING BIG BIRD   413 19
    THE BIG BIRD OF THE AMERINDIAN BEING THE EAGLE   414   2
    WITH WHICH WE SHALL DO BIG BUSINESS   442 25
    AND TACKLE THE BLOWSY BIG BLOW-FLY   458 11
    IN RHYTHMS TOO BIG AND TOO SMALL FOR US TO KNOW   479 10
    THOUGH MAYBE THE MAMMOTH GOT TOO BIG IN TUSK AND TEETH   529 17
    AND THE EXTINCT GIANT ELK TOO BIG IN ANTLERS   529 18
    THE BIG FLAMBOYANT RUSSIA   536 12
    AND BLINDED HIM IN HIS ONE BIG EYE   543 27
    WE'RE GETTING TO BE BIG LADS NOW AN' SOON   573 19
    IN THE BIG MIRROR AT HIS OWN FASCINATING SHADOW   604   5
    ESPECIALLY BIG ONES IS OBSCENE   622 20
    AND SOON EVEN GOD WON'T BE BIG ENOUGH TO HANDLE THAT IN+   670 20
    WAS A GREAT BIG HYDROCEPHALOUS WATER-IN-THE-BRAIN INFANT   670 22
    LIFTING YOUR VEINED WINGS LIFTING THEM BIG WHITE BUTTER+   696 14
    WILL YOU CLIMB ON YOUR BIG SOFT WINGS BLACK-DOTTED   696 22
    BAVARIAN GENTIANS BIG AND DARK ONLY DARK   697   3
    HOW BIG AND WHITE THE NIGHT IS   731   1
    NOW I TAKE THE BIG STONE JUG OF WATER   734 24
    IT DOES NOT SHRIVEL LIKE BIG HERBAGE   746   9
    ON GOOD FRIDAY THE BIG WHITE MEN OF THE INDIAN BUREAU   777 24
    AND THE BIG WHITE MEN FROM WASHINGTON DROVE OUT TO   777 25
    THEN THE BIG MEN OF THE WHITE AMERICANS   777 28
    OH SOLDIER-ERECT BIG BIRD   781 13
    STRETCHING THEIR BIG FULL LIMBS TO SEEK   827 13
    IT HAS GROWN UP OFTEN A BIG AND OFTEN INTERESTING-LOOKI+   841 16
    A HAT QUAINTLY CURIOUSLY WOVEN LUXURIOUS WITH BIG ROSES   856 12
    THE NIGHT A BIG BLACK STAIN   862 20
    SO BIG AND WORTHY IN MY OWN SMALL ARK   876   3
    MY JOY-BLOSSOMS SHAPING AM BIG   888 15
    YI' THA'RT A MAN THA'RT A FINE BIG MAN BUT NIVER A BABY+   *925 24
    A BIG BUD OF MOON HANGS OUT OF THE TWILIGHT   *929   6
BIGGER
    NO BIGGER THAN MY THUMB-NAIL   353 30
    BUT A BIGGER TRUST   561   2
    IT GETS BIGGER AND BIGGER   670   9
    AND ITS PERAMBULATOR HAS TO GET BIGGER AND BIGGER   670 10
    AND ITS DUMMY-TEAT HAS TO BE MADE BIGGER AND BIGGER AND+   670 11
    AND THE JOB OF CHANGING ITS DIAPERS GETS BIGGER AND BIG+   670 12
    AND BIGGER   670 13
    BIGGER AND BIGGER   670 15
    GETS BIGGER AND BIGGER AND BIGGER AND BIGGER AND BIGGER+   670 18
    YET ITS BELLY-ACHE SEEMS TO GET BIGGER TOO   670 19
    INTO THE DANCE AND SPLENDOUR OF A BIGGER LIFE   679 17
    OF BIGGER LIVES WITH DUE REVERENCE AND ACKNOWLEDGEMENT   679 22
BIGGEST
    AND IN THE BIGGEST HOUSES THEY KEEP THEIR MACHINES THAT+   793 24
BIG-MEN
    FURTHERMORE THE WHITE BIG-MEN SAID TO THE OLD INDIANS   778 17
BILIOUS
    A BILIOUS BLAST   760   8
BILLIARD
    WHY WAS NOT MY PEACH ROUND AND FINISHED LIKE A BILLIARD   279 21
    BUT IT WASN'T ROUND AND FINISHED LIKE A BILLIARD BALL   279 25
BILLOWING
    OF RED GOES DOWN THE BILLOWING AIR   149 31

BILLY GOAT
    AND WHEN THE BILLY GOAT MOUNTS HER   386 20
BIMMEL-BAMMEL
    RIDICULOUS BIMMEL-BAMMEL   492 10
BIN
    YI THA MUST HA' BIN 'ARD TER WEAN   79 24
    AN' YET YER'VE BIN CARRYIN' ON WI' 'IM   81 27
    DEED AN' I WISH I C'D 'A' STOOD AT TH' ALTAR WI' THEE A+   83 11
    THAT I COULD 'A' BIN FIRST WOMAN TER THEE AS THA'RT FIR+   83 13
    THA'S BIN SNOWED UP I' THIS COTTAGE WI' ME   137 25
    THA'S BIN SNOWED UP I' THIS COTTAGE WI' ME   137 27
BIND
    ANY COMMUNION WHATEVER BUT THEY BIND THEMSELVES ON TO T+   92 18
    STAND STILL AND BIND AND BLIND MYSELF   215   5
    BIND HIM WITH SHADOW WHILE I PASS   786 21
    BIND HIM WITH SHADOW WHILE I PASS   789 14
BINDERS
    AND BINDERS IN EXCHANGE   779 10
BINDING
    INFLAMED WITH BINDING UP THE SHEAVES OF THE DEAD   135 23
    INFLAMED WITH BINDING UP THE SHEAVES OF DEAD   *939 23
BINDS
    A WOMAN BINDS HER HAIR   200 18
BIOLOGICALLY
    EDITOR ER QUITE BUT ER BIOLOGICALLY HAVE YOU BEEN   582   9
    BIOLOGICALLY ADMIRABLE   828   8
BIRCH
    THEIR DUST FROM THE BIRCH ON THE BLUE   126 31
    BIRCH   142   8
    BREEZE OF THE MORNING THROUGH A NARROW WHITE BIRCH   209 28
BIRCH-TREES
    GO BY WITH THEIR LOADS OF GREEN AND SILVER BIRCH-TREES   209 17
BIRCH-TREE
    ALONG THE GLAMOROUS BIRCH-TREE AVENUE   206   5
BIRD
    THE BIRD LIES WARM AGAINST THE WALL   42 23
    LIKE A THIN WHITE BIRD BLOWN OUT OF THE NORTHERN SEAS   47 14
    LIKE A BIRD FROM THE FAR NORTH BLOWN WITH A BROKEN WING   47 15
    THAT SILENCE SHOULD TAKE THE SONG AND THE BIRD   110 11
    CLUCK MY MARIGOLD BIRD AND AGAIN   119 17
    SHE SUNK INTO MY SIGHT LIKE A SETTLING BIRD   123   8
    BIRD WHO WAS WEARY TO HAVE FURLED   124   8
    THIS BIRD THIS RICH   124 11
    AGAIN I SAW A BROWN BIRD HOVER   124 23
    I FELT A BROWN BIRD HOVER   124 25
    I FELT THE BROWN BIRD COVER   124 33
    THE BIRD CAME DOWN ON MY HEART   124 35
    THE WHITE MOON GOING AMONG THEM LIKE A WHITE BIRD   134 16
    BIRD I HEAR   134 19
    A WET BIRD WALKS ON THE LAWN CALL TO THE BOY TO COME   137   7
    ONE BIRD ONE BLOT FOLDED AND STILL AT THE TOP   147 24
    CRY OF A BIRD   150   8
    A DARK BIRD FALLS FROM THE SUN   166 25
    AS IF A BIRD IN DIFFICULTY UP THE VALLEY STEERS   210 22
    SEE THE BIRD IN THE FLOWERS HE'S MAKING   244 27
    MY BIRD MY BROWN SPARROW IN MY BREAST   246 18
    SINGING AGAINST THE BLACK BIRD   272 26
    ONE IS A MAN FOR EXAMPLE AND ONE IS A BIRD   320   2
    IS HE TO BE A BIRD ALSO   323 26
    THOU HONOURABLE BIRD   328   2
    THE SLY BIRD OF JOHN   329   2
    LIKE A KING EAGLE BIRD OF THE MOST HIGH SWEEPING THE RO+ 329   4
    YET PUT SALT ON THE TAIL OF THE JOHANNINE BIRD   329 14
    THAT THE OLD BIRD IS WEARY AND ALMOST WILLING   329 27
    WITH HIS HEAD UP STEERING LIKE A BIRD   337 26
    WHY A BIRD   342 13
    A BIRD   342 14
    A BIRD WOULD HAVE DASHED THROUGH COME WHAT MIGHT   345 19
    GREAT HASTE AND STRAIGHT ALMOST BIRD STRAIGHT ABOVE THE 347 12
    WHITHER AWAY SMALL BIRD   352 29
    VOICELESS LITTLE BIRD   354   7
    SMALL BIRD   354 16
    ON THIS SMALL BIRD THIS RUDIMENT   356 15
    OR IS HE DRIVEN AGAINST HER WITH A BANG LIKE A BIRD FLY+ 363   8
    BIRD FLIES SO NEAR   368   3
    YOU SHALL KNOW A BIRD BY HIS CRY AND GREAT BIRDS CRY. LO+ 368   9
    YOU BRITTLE WILL-TENSE BIRD WITH A FOOLISH EYE   370 35
    ARE YOU THE BIRD OF THE NEXT DAWN   371 19
    BLOOD-THIRSTY BIRD   373 35
    LIGHT-BLOODED BIRD   374   6
    DOES THE SUN IN NEW MEXICO SAIL LIKE A FIERY BIRD OF PR+ 374 12
    BLOOD-THIRSTY BIRD   374 17
    FLY OFF BIG BIRD WITH A BIG BLACK BACK   374 29
    AND YOU GREAT BIRD SUN-STARER HEAVY BLACK BEAK   374 34
    YOU ACID-BLUE METALLIC BIRD   375 29
    YOU THICK BIRD WITH A STRONG CREST   375 30
    YOU COPPER-SULPHATE BLUE BIRD   375 33
    GREY BIRD IN THE AIR ON THE BOUGH OF THE LEANING   385 17
    BUT DIDN'T DISOWN THE BIRD   413   3
    STARTLING BIG BIRD   413 19
    THE BIG BIRD OF THE AMERINDIAN BEING THE EAGLE   414   2
    EAGLE OF THE ROCKIES BIRD OF MEN THAT ARE MASTERS   414 21
    FOR EVERY BLOOMING BIRD IS AN OXFORD CUCKOO NOWADAYS   434   1
    AS THE VAST WHITE BIRD   436 15
    A BIRD   443 12
    MEN MIGHT PUT THEM FORTH AS A SNAIL ITS SHELL AS A BIRD+ 451 12
    I'D SAY IT WAS JUST A BIRD   453   3

BIRD
    TOWARDS WOMAN OR MAN BIRD BEAST OR CREATURE OR THING   454 13
    A SMALL BIRD WILL DROP FROZEN DEAD FROM A BOUGH   467 3
    LIKE A BIRD   487 25
    WHEN A BIRD FLIPS HIS TAIL IN GETTING HIS BALANCE ON A +   496 6
    LIVING SHOULD BE AS FREE TO A MAN AS TO A BIRD   520 2
    A DRAB AND DINGY BIRD   523 29
    THERE'S NOT A COCK BIRD AMONG 'EM   550 15
    SUCH A HUMAN BIRD   564 8
    ON AND ON LIKE A DARK-FACED BIRD SINGING ALONE   623 19
    IMMORTAL BIRD   728 12
    THE BIRD GAVE A CLUCK THE COW GAVE A COO   761 4
    OH SOLDIER-ERECT BIG BIRD   781 13
    I HEARD THE STAR SINGING LIKE A DYING BIRD   786 15
    AS A BIRD THAT LIFTS ITS WINGS AND STANDS   787 17
    AND THE BRANCHES ARE MINE IN THE PATHS OF THE SKY AND T+   801 17
    THERE WAS A GAY BIRD NAMED CHRISTINE   845 17
    LIKE A BIRD AM I   860 27
    MY WHITE BIRD   863 14
    CLUCK MY MARIGOLD BIRD AND AGAIN   *932 26
    SHE SUNK INTO MY SIGHT LIKE A SETTLING BIRD   *934 14
    LIKE A HEAVY BIRD DISTURBED AND HER SHOULDERS STIRRED   *934 16
    BIRD WHO WAS WEARY TO HAVE FURLED   *935 8
    THIS BIRD THIS RICH   *935 10
    AND THEN I SAW A BROWN BIRD HOVER   *935 29
    AGAIN AND I FELT A BROWN BIRD HOVER   *935 31
    BIRD ABOVE MY HEART   *936 2
    TO THE CUCKOO BIRD AS SHE FLUTTERED ABOVE   *936 10
    AND DWELLING IN HIS OWN BOWERY HOUSE LIKE A BIRD IN A B+   *950 9

BIRD-BLITHE
    I SEE YOU ALL THE TIME YOU BIRD-BLITHE LOVELY   234 9

BIRD-CRY
    OR WHEN IT UTTERS THAT UNDAUNTED LITTLE BIRD-CRY   439 1

BIRDS
    THREE DEAD BIRDS LIE   36 24
    DISCOVERY LIKE BIRDS THAT STEAL AND FLEE   51 30
    ALL THE BIRDS ARE FOLDED IN A SILENT BALL OF SLEEP   71 9
    ON THE SHORES OF THIS CEASELESS OCEAN GAY BIRDS FLY   71 18
    STEPPING LIKE BIRDS WITH THEIR BRIGHT AND POINTED FEET   71 25
    AND SO FROM OUT THE SCREAMING BIRDS THAT FLY   89 22
    DUST AS THE PUFF-BALL DOES AND BIRDS THAT CHAFF   89 28
    BLOWING LITTLE FLOCKS OF BIRDS   99 17
    MELTS IN THE AIR WHILE TWO BLACK BIRDS   100 3
    LIKE HEAVY BIRDS AT REST THERE SOFTLY STIRRED   123 10
    LIKE HEAVY BIRDS FROM THE MORNING STUBBLE TO SETTLE   128 11
    UPON ME LIKE SLEEPING BIRDS LIKE BIRDS THAT SHIFT   128 12
    TREES BIRDS AND EARTH ARRESTED IN THE AFTER-THOUGHT   142 15
    YOUNG BIRDS FORSAKEN AND LEFT IN A NEST OF MUD   145 24
    BUT OH MY HEART WHAT BIRDS ARE PIPING   150 14
    OF INCENSE-SMOKE THAT RISES LIKE BIRDS   151 30
    CARESSES NEVER FLEW TO YOU LIKE BIRDS   158 9
    DRIFT THEN FOR THE SIGHTLESS BIRDS   172 1
    SKIES TREES FLOWERS BIRDS WATER   256 25
    BIRDS ARE THE LIFE OF THE SKIES AND WHEN THEY FLY THEY +   368 1
    YOU SHALL KNOW A BIRD BY HIS CRY AND GREAT BIRDS CRY LO+   368 3
    BIRDS HAVE THEIR VOICES EACH MEANS A DIFFERENT THING   368 12
    AND ALL THE UNSPEAKABLE CHARM OF BIRDS HOPPING   443 19
    AND FLUTTERING AND BEING BIRDS   443 20
    THOUGH MOST BIRDS HAVE TO PAY WITH THEIR LIVES WHERE MEN   520 3
    THE EFFORTS OF MEN LIKE THE EFFORTS OF BIRDS IN SPRING   520 9
    THE MULTITUDES ARE LIKE DROPPINGS OF BIRDS LIKE DUNG OF+   614 21
    THEY TELL ME THAT THESE BRITISH MORAL BIRDS   659 7
    LIKE THE PIGEONS AND THE OTHER LITTLE BIRDS   668 16
    EVEN DOVES EVEN SMALL BIRDS   679 16
    LIKE SCREAMING BIRDS OF FATE   741 12
    IT IS THE LOUD CRIES OF THESE BIRDS OF PAIN   741 14
    WHOSE BIRDS THEY ARE   743 10
    THEY ARE TOLLING HIS FAILURE AFTER ALL THESE YEARS TO T+   859 9
    INTO THE GLOOM-WOVEN FOREST WHERE THE BIRDS AND CICALAS+   864 5
    HER QUIVERING ANSWERS AND KISSES LIKE THIEVING BIRDS   868 31
    AND WHAT WAS THE SOUND OF THE BIRDS AND THE WATER BUT S+   870 26
    RARE BIRDS THAT NO   *894 6
    DEFENDING THE MEMORY OF BIRDS THAT USED TO NEST   *896 16
    AS BIRDS WHO ARE STEALING TURN AND FLEE   *899 13
    AS BIRDS WHO ARE STEALING TURN AND FLEE   *902 25
    THE MUSIC OF MUSIC IS STILLNESS YOU BIRDS   *914 12
    BY NOISE OF SMALL BIRDS SINGING FIFE   *914 22
    OF NOISY BIRDS BE YOU CHIDDEN   *914 23
    ALL THE BIRDS ARE FOLDED IN A SILENT BALL OF SLEEP   *917 27
    THE SMALL BIRDS THAT LIFTED THEIR HEADS WHEN MORNING LO+   *918 3
    BLACK BIRDS WHOSE SONGS ARE UNUTTERABLE SPINNING FANTAS+   *918 14

BIRD'S-EYE
    MAY-BLOSSOM AND BLUE BIRD'S-EYE FLOWERS FALLING   65 15
    TAKING A BIRD'S-EYE VIEW   328 4

BIRD-SPATTERED
    MAKE IT ROOST ON BIRD-SPATTERED ROCKY PATMOS   329 19

BIRDS'
    IN SCARLET ALIVE WITH THE BIRDS' BRIGHT TWITTERING   72 22

BIRMINGHAM
    AND WHEN THIS CASH-CHEMIST UNIVERSITY GRANTS DEGREES LI+   *950 22

BIRTH
    IN A NEW NIGHT-SPASM OF BIRTH AND GIVEN US THIS NEW RED+   88 20
    FROM THIS ROSY TERROR OF BIRTH THAT HAS SLID DOWN   88 24
    TO START A BIRTH FROM JOY OF THE BEGETTING   89 7
    AND PANGS OF BIRTH AND JOY OF THE BEGETTING   89 12
    NOR DEATH WHICH QUIVERS WITH BIRTH   205 13
    HE CAUSALLY GIVES BIRTH TO ANOTHER YOUNG BUD FROM HIS   300 1
    BIRTH OF THE SUN   616 22
    EVEN THE FACT OF BIRTH EVEN LITTLE CHILDREN   656 19
    THERE IS NO END TO THE BIRTH OF GOD   683 18

BIRTH-CRY
    A BIRTH-CRY   364 19

BIRTHDAY
    AND SEEING IT IS YOUR BIRTHDAY   *941 5

BIRTHRIGHT
    ISOLATION IS HIS BIRTHRIGHT   357 32
    ARE OF THEIR BIRTHRIGHT   446 17

BISCUITS
    IS LIKE BISCUITS BAKED FOR A FEAST   758 20

BISON
    EVEN THE BISON KNEW IT   587 7

BISONS
    LIKE BULLS OR BISONS OR WILD PIGS   392 19

BIT
    WE HAVE BIT NO FORBIDDEN APPLE   37 24
    F'R A BIT   45 30
    DID T' 'APPEN TER NOTICE A BIT OF A LASS WAY BACK   60 17
    RIGHT IN 'EM AN' SCRAIGHTED A BIT AGAIN   61 14
    THEN AFTER A BIT 'ER DROPPED 'EM DOWN THAT PLACE   61 15
    BUT I THOWT TER MYSEN AS THAT WOR TH' ONLY BIT   61 17
    FROM THAT BIT OF A WENCH'S BOSOM 'E'D BE GLAD OF IT   61 19
    THINE SHALL GO TER PAY THE WOMAN AN' WI' MY BIT WE'LL B+   83 2
    WHAT BIT O' CUNT I HAD WI' 'ER   84 29
    IS MUCH LESS THAN THE BIT OF BLUE EGG   244 30
    THAT LITTLE BIT OF YOUR CHEST THAT SHOWS BETWEEN   254 9
    THE BIT OF HUSBAND-TILTH SHE IS   309 26
    THAT IS YOUR TRICK YOUR BIT OF FILTHY MAGIC   332 21
    AND TAKE YOUR FIRST BITE AT SOME DIM BIT OF HERBAGE   352 14
    JUST AS HE SNAPS WHEN I POKE A BIT OF STICK AT HIM   357 13
    A BIT OF SLAG STILL ADHERING AFTER YOUR FIRING IN THE F+   370 2
    THIS LITTLE BIT CHIPPED OFF IN BRILLIANCE   372 11
    HE RUNS IN THE SNOW LIKE A BIT OF BLUE METAL   375 3
    AND THE WIND IN HIS TEETH FOR A BIT   378 2
    MOTIONLESS LIKE A BIT OF ROCK   379 6
    FORGET THE FEMALE HERD FOR A BIT   383 20
    WAIT WAIT A BIT I'LL COME WHEN I'VE LIT THE FIRE   384 9
    PEAKED AND A BIT DISMAYED   394 1
    WITH YOUR IMBECILE BIT OF A TAIL IN A LOVE-FLUTTER   396 14
    THEN WHEN I DUST YOU A BIT WITH A JUNIPER TWIG   399 12
    YOU THINK YOU'D BETTER MIND YOUR P'S AND Q'S FOR A BIT   400 28
    A BIT AWKWARD AND WITH A FUNNY SQUAWK IN HIS VOICE   413 21
    LET HIM COME HOME TO A BIT OF MORAL DIFFICULTY LET LIFE+   431 4
    RATHER PROUD OF BEING A BIT OF A DON JUAN   446 24
    DONE YOUR OWN LITTLE BIT MADE YOUR OWN LITTLE TRY   459 19
    ON SMELLING IT ALL BEFORE YOUR BIT OF VITALITY SPENT IS   462 34
    AND THAT IS MY BIT OF INWARD PEACE WHERE I AM AT ONE   497 23
    AND BE A BIT ELEMENTAL INSTEAD   505 11
    AND BE A BIT MORE FIERY AS INCAPABLE OF TELLING LIES   505 18
    IF ONLY WE COULD MAKE LIFE A BIT MORE JUST   518 23
    WITHOUT A BIT OF COMMON TRUST IN ONE ANOTHER WE CAN'T   522 19
    WITH A BIT OF SPLENDOUR   523 25
    AND I SUPPOSE MOST GIRLS ARE A BIT TARTY TODAY   530 20
    FOR THEIR VERY PALTRY LITTLE BIT OF MONEY   531 18
    THE LAST BIT OF SANITY   537 4
    POOR LASS POOR BIT OF A WENCH   540 8
    COME AN' BE STILL WI' ME MY OWN BIT OF A WENCH   540 10
    FOR IT WASN'T A BIT SUPERIOR   554 13
    YOU DON'T MIND A BIT   557 16
    NOW THEN PRIME MINISTER HOLD ON A BIT   573 25
    GOING A BIT FURTHER THAN HIS POCKET WHAT   659 16
    BECAUSE THE LORD ALMIGHTY ROSE A BIT TOO HIGH   710 10
    A BIT BEYOND HIMSELF   710 11
    BUT OF WHICH HE HAD A BIT INSIDE HIM   714 4
    OH YOU COME COME COME FOR HERE IS A BIT   762 11
    THE BIT OF LAND IN QUESTION IS A FLEA-BITE   779 13
    TO MAKE THIS BIT OF LAND AND WATER-RIGHTS   779 18
    WE HAVE BIT NO FORBIDDEN APPLE   *892 12
    TRYIN' TO KEEP OFF 'N HIM A BIT O' TH' WET   *910 29
    DID T' 'APPEN TER NOTICE A BIT OF A LASS AWAY BACK   *911 3
    RAVELLED BLUE AND WHITE WARM FOR A BIT   *911 28
    THEN AFTER A BIT 'ER DROPPED 'EM DOWN THAT PLACE   *911 31
    THINE SHALL GO TO PAY THE WOMAN AN' WI' MY BIT WE'LL BUY *925 6
    TILL HE'S GOT A WOMAN A BIT SOFT AND TRUSTFUL   *948 15

BITCH
    SO HALTS THE LITTLE BLACK BITCH ON FOUR SPREAD PAWS IN +   375 10
    OH BIBBLES LITTLE BLACK BITCH IN THE SNOW   375 16
    LITTLE BLACK SNUB-NOSED BITCH WITH A SHOVED-OUT JAW   394 29
    OH BIBBLES BLACK LITTLE BITCH   395 15
    YOU LITTLE WALT-WHITMANESQUE BITCH   395 26
    PLENTY OF GAME OLD SPUNK LITTLE BITCH   397 29
    SELF-CONSCIOUS LITTLE BITCH   398 13
    YOU MISERABLE LITTLE BITCH OF LOVE-TRICKS   398 21
    TRICK ON THEM DIRTY BITCH   399 18
    OF YOU MY BITCH TILL YOU GET SO FAR YOU EAT FILTH   400 17
    ALL RIGHT MY LITTLE BITCH   400 30

BITCHES
    LIKE DELICATE VERY-YOUNG GREYHOUND BITCHES   311 6
    GREYHOUND BITCHES   311 10

BITE
    IN ONE BITE   282 10
    WELL COVERED LEST HE SHOULD BITE ME   347 5
    AND TAKE YOUR FIRST BITE AT SOME DIM BIT OF HERBAGE   352 14
    TO TAKE YOUR FIRST SOLITARY BITE   352 18
    HANDS TO EAT THE ACANTHUS OR BITE AT THE ALMOND BUDS   385 10
    HE COULDN'T BITE 'EM HE WAS MUCH TOO OLD   492 7
    AND THE LAMBS WILL BITE OFF THE HEADS OF THE DAISIES FO+   625 7
    MEANWHILE WE BITE OURSELVES AND EVERYONE NEAR US   833 30

BITES
DRAGS AND DRAGS AND BITES   362   9
WHERE NOTHING BITES BUT INSECTS AND SNAKES AND THE SUN   394 14
SHE BITES HIM IN THE NECK AND PASSES ON   539 22
AND BITES AT OUR THROATS AND CHESTS   609   2
AS HE BITES AT THE STEMS OF LEAVES IN AUTUMN TO MAKE TH+   609   3
RUNS INTO THE SHADOW WITH HER CAPTURE A FEW LITTLE BITE+   864 17

BITING
THE MOSQUITOES ARE BITING TO-NIGHT   302   9
AND BITING THE FRAIL GRASS ARROGANTLY   358 20
POOR DARLING BITING AT HER FEET   360   7
RUNNING BESIDE HER LIKE A DOG BITING HER EARTHY SPLAY   360   8
CREEPING FOR THE GARBAGE OF LIFE AND BITING WITH VENOMO+   796 13

BITS
THEY ARE A CLICKETING OF BITS OF DISJOINTED METAL   288 32
ODD FLAKES AS IF OF SNOW ODD BITS OF SNOW   304 13
CURVETTING BITS OF TIN IN THE EVENING LIGHT   335 24
WINGS LIKE BITS OF UMBRELLA   341 28
NOT KNOWING EACH OTHER FROM BITS OF EARTH OR OLD TINS   357 20
BITS   375 24
WITH BITS OF BRINDLE COMING THROUGH LIKE RUST TO SHOW   395   2
RED MEN STILL STICK THEMSELVES OVER WITH BITS OF HIS FL+   414   3
WE SHALL ALL BE CUT TO BITS   663 17
DO YOU SEE THE SEA BREAKING ITSELF TO BITS AGAINST THE +   705   1
BITS OF RESERVED LAND IT WERE A FLEA-BITE   779 16
TO BITS   *910   2
YOU'VE DISCOVERED SO MANY BITS WITH YOUR CLEVER EYES   *932   7

BITTED
AND THEY ARE BRIDLED WITH CUNNING AND BITTED   656 17

BITTEN
LOW-ROUNDED ON THE MOURNFUL TURF THEY HAVE BITTEN DOWN +   33   6
YET CLOSELY BITTEN IN TO ME   117   8
FOR I WOULD HAVE HAD TO KILL HIM IF HE'D BITTEN ME THE   347   6
GETS BITTEN AND MUST DIE   805   7
WHO IS BITTEN DIES   806 10
LOW-ROUNDED ON THE MOURNFUL GRASS THEY HAVE BITTEN DOWN+   *891   7

BITTER
BITTER SCIENCE THE EXAMS ARE NEAR   41 13
BENT IF WE DID BUT KNOW IT ON A WEARY AND BITTER GRIMACE   54 23
ONLY I AND THE CLASS MUST WRANGLE THIS WORK IS A BITTER+   76 22
WI' A BITTER DIRTY SKIN   77 14
AND I WAS NUMB WITH A BITTER DEATHLY ACHE   98 27
EVEN TO MYSELF HOW BITTER THE SEPARATION   122 14
AND SITS IN HER OWN DARK NIGHT OF HER BITTER HAIR   129   1
BETWEEN THE BITTER KNEES OF THE AFTER-NIGHT   160 12
BITTER TO FOLD THE ISSUE AND MAKE NO SALLY   160 25
HER FACE IS BENT IN THE BITTER STEAM   202 27
MY HEART IS BITTER   232   2
IT WOULD BE SO BITTER NEVER MIND   244 17
THEN THE DUMB ACHING BITTER HELPLESS NEED   263 20
AND LET IT MOULT THERE AMONG THE STONES OF THE BITTER S+   329 20
AND SO WITH BITTER PERVERSITY   485   4
IS SOUR BITTER FRUITS CANKERED BY LIES   504 14
AND HOW BITTER IT IS TO COME DOWN   551   3
AND THEN TRUTH MUCH MORE BITTER TO ACCEPT   636   7
TREES RAISED FROM SEED HAVE WILD AND BITTER FRUITS   640 21
AFTER THE BITTER PASSAGE OF OBLIVION   721   7
THE BITTER WORLD AMID THE SMOKE   744 23
ALL BITTER AND CORRODING TO THE GRAVE   744 25
I TURN TOWARDS THE BITTER BLACKENING WIND   745 24
SWEEP ON TO BITTER TO CORROSIVE DEATH   745 34
AND EXULTS IN ITS BITTER USAGE OF US ALL   746 12
BITTER TO ME IS THIS EVENING HOUR   758   8
EACH EVENING BITTER AGAIN   758   9
THERE ARE DEAD THAT WEEP IN BITTER RAINS   795 20
THE BITTER AND SWEET RAW AND THE ROTTEN   825   2
HER FRUIT IS UNRIPE AND HER SOFT MOUTH IS BITTER AND RO+   864 18
OH MY GOD WHAT A BITTER SHAME   873   6
BUT OH MY GOD WHAT A BITTER SHAME   874   2
OH MY GOD WHAT A BITTER SHAME   874 10
WHAT A BITTER SHAME THAT SHE SHOULD ASK IT   874 17
AS HE DID SIP THE BITTER MILK OF SLEEP   878 14
IN RECKLESSNESS HE DRANK WITH A BITTER MOUTH   878 17
BITTER AND PAINFUL FLOWERS   888   2
EARNESTLY AND OH FOR ME THIS CLASS IS A BITTER ROOD   *898 16
EARNESTLY AND OH FOR ME THIS CLASS IS A BITTER ROOD   *901 25
WITH A BITTER SWARTHY SKIN   *919   2
AH AND MY HAIR IS HANGING WET AND BITTER ON MY FACE   *933 31
AND AH MY BITTER BREASTS THAT SULK AND FRET   *933 32

BITTERLY
FALL ALL THE FRUITS MOST BITTERLY INTO EARTH   160 15
BITTERLY INTO CORROSION BITTERLY TRAVEL   160 16
DON'T YOU CARE FOR MY LOVE SHE SAID BITTERLY   604 13
I HATE THEM BITTERLY   741 20
SHE WEPT BITTERLY HIDING HER FACE IN HER KERCHIEF I SAI+   749 16

BITTERNESS
STILL THE KISS WAS A TOUCH OF BITTERNESS ON MY MOUTH   206 20
IN SUPREME BITTERNESS   304 11
AND DELIVER OUR LIPS OF THEIR PRAISE AND THEIR BITTERNE+   753 18
AND HIS MOUTH WIPED CLEAN OF THE BITTERNESS OF REPROACH   770 19
STIRRING THE FIRES TO ACID OF BITTERNESS   795 25
RECKLESS ABOUT THE BITTERNESS OF THE DRAUGHT   878 12
HE WATERS OUR FACE WITH TEARS OUR YOUNG FRUITS FILLS WI+   *926 29

BITTER-STINGING
BITTER-STINGING WHITE WORLD THAT BORE US   302 12

BITTER-SWEET
THE WITNESS OF ALL THAT BITTER-SWEET   198 23

BIURET
HUSH NOW HUSH WHERE AM I BIURET   40 30

BIVALVE
TO ESCAPE IN SLEEP THE TERROR OF THIS GREAT BIVALVE DAR+   88 14
WHY THE LOVELY BIVALVE ROUNDNESSES   279 18

BLACK
AS A FIELD-BEE BLACK AND AMBER   46   6
AN' T' PARSON MAKIN' HASTE AN' A' T' BLACK   60 15
SCRAIGHTIN' MYSEN AS WELL 'ER UNDID 'ER BLACK   61   9
THAT THE BLACK NIGHT HID HER FROM ME BLOTTED OUT EVERY   62   4
BEHIND THE BLACK SYCAMORE AT THE END OF THE GARDEN   62 26
BETWEEN THE SCHOOLS SWEEPS ONE BLACK ROOK   76 16
WITCH TEETH AN' 'ER BLACK HAWK-EYES AS I'VE   77 23
AS MISTLETOE BERRIES BURNING IN A BLACK TREE   86   2
WASTEFUL INTO THE NIGHT'S BLACK NOSTRILS DRINK   86   6
MELTS IN THE AIR WHILE TWO BLACK BIRDS   100   3
SOMETHING WHICH SETS THE BLACK POPLARS ASHAKE WITH HYST+   102 26
WHOSE BLACK BOUGHS FLAP THE GROUND   113 26
THEN LETS HER BLACK HAIR LOOSE THE DARKNESS FALL   128 33
BUT OH THE PALMS OF HIS TWO BLACK HANDS ARE RED   135 22
EVER THE LONG BLACK FIGURES SWOOP BY THE BED   140 23
TALL BLACK BACCHAE OF MIDNIGHT WHY THEN WHY   140 28
BLACK AND PHANTASMAL   141   4
PALE-BLURRED WITH TWO ROUND BLACK DROPS AS IF IT MISSED   141 17
IT IS ONLY THE SPARROWS LIKE DEAD BLACK LEAVES ON THE   142   9
IN THE BLACK WET NIGHT AS THE FURTIVE RAIN SLINKS DOWN   143   2
AND GLEAM AS OF SUNSHINE CROSSING THE LOW BLACK HEAP   144 25
TOSSED ON THE LOW BLACK RUFFLED HEAP   145 13
AND BEAUTIFULLY LAID IN BLACK ON A GOLD-GREY SKY   146 29
OF CRYSTAL HEAVEN FALLS ONE FULL BLACK DROP   147 26
WITH THE GREAT BLACK PIANO APPASSIONATO THE GLAMOUR   148 16
IN ANOTHER COUNTRY BLACK POPLARS SHAKE THEMSELVES OVER A   148 20
MY IVORY AND MARBLE BLACK WITH STAIN   151 18
WITH WONDER EVERY BLACK TREE   165 23
THROUGH THE BLACK FRAME   204   5
AND IT WOULD BE THICK BLACK DARK FOR EVER   205 11
SHE PRICKED A FINE BLACK BLOTCH   222   7
THREE OF THEM BLACK IN SHADOW TWO OF THEM BRIGHT   224 10
THE BROWN EYES BLACK WITH MISERY AND HATE THAT LOOK   225 23
HAVE ALL GONE DARK GONE BLACK   226 22
SHADING HIS FACE IN HIS BLACK FELT HAT   228   6
HER PROUD HEAD HELD IN ITS BLACK SILK SCARF   228 14
THE PRIESTS IN GOLD AND BLACK THE VILLAGERS   232 19
THE GREAT BLACK NIGHT SCOOPED OUT   238   2
THIS INTERMINGLING OF THE BLACK AND MONSTROUS FINGERS OF   242   2
IN THE WINDOW HIS BODY BLACK FUR AND THE SOUND OF   243 24
DEAD AND TRODDEN TO NOUGHT IN THE SOUR BLACK EARTH   258 16
I IN THE SOUR BLACK TOMB TRODDEN TO ABSOLUTE DEATH   259   1
YET RISING FROM THE TOMB FROM THE BLACK OBLIVION   260   9
FALL BLACK AND WET   268 15
SINGING AGAINST THE BLACK BIRD   272 26
HONEY-WHITE FIGS OF THE NORTH BLACK FIGS WITH SCARLET I+   284 26
LOOK HOW BLACK HOW BLUE-BLACK HOW GLOBED IN EGYPTIAN   286   8
PEACE BLACK PEACE CONGEALED   293 15
PEACE CONGEALED IN BLACK LAVA ON THE DOORSTEP   294   1
BLACK ALMOND TRUNKS IN THE RAIN   300 20
BLACK RUSTED IRON TRUNK   300 27
SUN OF BLACK VOID HEAT   301 19
BEHOLD MY HAIR TWISTING AND GOING BLACK   301 21
COAGULATING AND GOING BLACK IN MY VEINS   301 25
COMPARED TO THE FLOOD OF BLACK HEAT THAT ROLLS UPWARDS   302   5
LIKE DRAWN BLADES NEVER SHEATHED HACKED AND GONE BLACK   304 28
WHEN HE PUSHED HIS BUSH OF BLACK HAIR OFF HIS BROW   310   1
AND THE ROAR OF BLACK BULL'S BLOOD IN THE MIGHTY PASSAG+   326 15
HIS OWN BLACK BLOOD POURED OUT LIKE A SHEET OF FLAME OV+   326 30
MASSIVE BLACK BLOOD   327 15
LIKE A GLOVE A BLACK GLOVE THROWN UP AT THE LIGHT   341 13
BLACK PIPER ON AN INFINITESIMAL PIPE   341 25
WITH STICKING-OUT BEAD-BERRY EYES BLACK   345 29
FOR IN SICILY THE BLACK BLACK SNAKES ARE INNOCENT THE G+   350   3
BLACK   350 26
INTO THAT HORRID BLACK HOLE   351   5
INTO THE BLACK HOLE THE EARTH-LIPPED FISSURE IN THE WAL+   351 16
AND LOOK WITH LACONIC BLACK EYES   353 12
HIS BLACK SAD-LIDDED EYE SEES BUT BEHOLDS NOT   362   4
YOU RUFFLED BLACK BLOSSOM   369   1
SEEMS LIKE THE BLACK AND GLOSSY SEEDS OF COUNTLESS CENT+   369 11
RUFFLING BLACK SHINING FEATHERS LIKE LIFTED MAIL   370 24
FLY OFF BIG BIRD WITH A BIG BLACK BACK   374 29
AND YOU GREAT BIRD SUN-STARER HEAVY BLACK BEAK   374 34
COMES A STRIDENT LAUGH AS WE APPROACH THIS LITTLE BLACK   375   8
SO HALTS THE LITTLE BLACK BITCH ON FOUR SPREAD PAWS IN +   375 10
OH BIBBLES LITTLE BLACK BITCH IN THE SNOW   375 16
HENCE THE BLACK CROSS ON HIS SHOULDERS   378 27
SEE HIS BLACK NOSE SNUBBED BACK PRESSED OVER LIKE A WHA+   380 13
AND THEN YOU SEE THE GOD THAT HE IS IN A CLOUD OF BLACK   381 10
BLACK PROCREANT MALE OF THE SELFISH WILL AND LIBIDINOUS   383 14
GOD IN BLACK CLOUD WITH CURVING HORNS OF BRONZE   383 16
YET SHE HAS SUCH ADORABLE SPURTY KIDS LIKE SPURTS OF BL+   386 17
FACES DARK AS BLACK RICE GROWING   391 13
LITTLE BLACK DOG IN NEW MEXICO   394 28
LITTLE BLACK SNUB-NOSED BITCH WITH A SHOVED-OUT JAW   394 29
NOT BLACK ENOUGH   395   6
OH BIBBLES BLACK LITTLE BITCH   395 15
YOU LITTLE BLACK LOVE-BIRD   395 21
ALL YOUR WRINKLED MISERERE CHINESE BLACK LITTLE FACE   396   3
AND YOUR BLACK LITTLE BODY BOUNCING AND WRIGGLING   396   5
SO QUICK LIKE A LITTLE BLACK DRAGON   396 28
AND STARTING FORWARD IN THE DUSK WITH YOUR LITTLE BLACK   396 31
RUSHING IN LIKE A LITTLE BLACK WHIRLWIND LEAPING STRAIG+   397   1
AND TURNING THE DAY SUDDENLY INTO A BLACK TORNADO OF JO+   397   4
HURTLING LIKE A BLACK BALL THROUGH THE SNOW   397   8
LITTLE BLACK SPOT IN THE LANDSCAPE   397 10

BLACK
    AND BLACK EYES BULGING BRIGHT IN A DUST-MASK   397 17
    AND CRAWL AWAY LIKE A BLACK SNAIL   400 11
    AND A BLACK CRUCIFIX LIKE A DEAD TREE SPREADING WINGS   403 24
    MAYBE A BLACK EAGLE WITH ITS WINGS OUT   403 25
    A MEMBRANE OF SLEEP LIKE A BLACK BLANKET   407 25
    A BLACK MEMBRANE OVER THE FACE   408 16
    AS UNDER THE HAIRY BELLY OF A GREAT BLACK BEAR   409 12
    FROM WOUNDS BELOW THE DEEP BLACK WAVE   428 13
    UNDER THE COLD BLACK WAVE   428 15
    AND STAMPS HIS BLACK MARSH-FEET ON THEIR WHITE AND   436 18
    ARE CAST IN BLACK AND WHITE AND MOVE   444 6
    WHITE AND SLIPPERY AS ON THE BLACK WATER IN A PORT   453 14
    SO FATHOMLESSLY BLACK   454 6
    REELING IN THE BLACK END OF ALL BELIEFS   542 24
    BOILING BLACK DEATH   586 28
    THE WISP OF MODERN BLACK MANTILLA   617 21
    EVEN THE OLD PRIEST IN HIS LONG BLACK ROBE AND SILVERY +   618 16
    WHEN A BLACK PRIEST BLOWS ON A CONCH   623 14
    BAA-BAA BLACK SHEEP   669 19
    AND LET THE SLIM BLACK SHIP OF DIONYSOS COME SAILING IN   688 4
    LAUGHING IN HIS BLACK BEARD   689 8
    AND THE DIM NOTCH OF BLACK MAIDENHAIR LIKE AN INDICATOR   693 14
    BLACK LAMPS FROM THE HALLS OF DIS BURNING DARK BLUE   697 9
    BUT ALSO THE SUNDERERS THE ANGELS WITH BLACK SHARP WING+   706 23
    THE ONES WITH THE SHARP BLACK WINGS   707 9
    WHEN ANAXAGORAS SAYS EVEN THE SNOW IS BLACK   708 12
    BUT NEVER THE GHOST OF A GLIMPSE OF ANAXAGORAS' FUNERAL+   708 30
    TILL NOT A VESTIGE IS LEFT AND BLACK WINTER HAS NO TRACE   709 20
    LIKE SAYING SNOW IS BLACK OR DESIRE IS EVIL   709 34
    UPON THE FLOOD'S BLACK WASTE   719 6
    I CAN SEE HIS RAGING BLACK EYES BLAZE AT ME   733 3
    WITH SAVAGE BLACK EYES IS SULKY AND ALL THE TIME   734 18
    TO THE THING AND RATHER FRETTED AND HIS THICK BLACK HAIR   734 21
    FLINGS OUT ITS VIVID BLACK NOTES   772 32
    IGNORING OUR MOTOR-CAR BLACK AND ALWAYS HURRYING   780 25
    HE SAW THE HEARTS OF THEM ALL THAT WERE BLACK AND HEAVY+   790 14
    AND BLACK MEN   792 30
    THERE ARE DEAD THAT ATTACK THE SUN LIKE SWARMS OF BLACK+   795 28
    PUT SLEEP AS BLACK AS BEAUTY IN THE SECRET OF MY BELLY   803 2
    HUITZILOPOCHTLI GIVES THE BLACK BLADE OF DEATH   809 4
    AND ONE GREEN LEAF SPRANG AMONG THE BLACK   809 20
    BLACK HUITZILOPOCHTLI   810 13
    BEYOND THE BLACKNESS OF BLACK   810 24
    FROM THE BLACK OIL AND THE WHITE   811 1
    HUITZILOPOCHTLI HAS THROWN HIS BLACK MANTLE   811 18
    BLACK FOR THE FUNERAL WOW WALY AND WORROW   815 2
    TINY BLACK MOTHS FLUTTER OUT AT THE TOUCH OF THE FORK   858 13
    THE FIERCE BLACK EYES ARE CLOSED THEY WILL OPEN NO MORE   859 17
    THE NIGHT A BIG BLACK STAIN   862 20
    AND WHEN BLACK LEAVES STREAM OUT IN A TRAIL DOWN THE WI+   883 12
    LIKE A TRESS OF BLACK HAIR   883 14
    LIKE IVORY AND GOLDEN MARBLE TWO BLACK CROWS HOLD   *894 27
    BETWEEN THE RUDDY SCHOOLS SWEEPS ONE BLACK ROOK   *898 10
    BETWEEN THE RUDDY SCHOOLS SWEEPS ONE BLACK ROOK   *901 19
    NAY I SAW NOWT BUT TH' COFFIN AN' TH' YELLER CLAY AN' '+   *909 31
    AN' PARSON MAKIN' HASTE AN' A' THE BLACK   *911 1
    SCRAIGHTIN' MY-SEN AS WELL 'EN UNDID HER BLACK   *911 25
    THAT THE BLACK NIGHT HID HER FROM ME BLOTTED OUT EVERY +   *912 12
    BLACK BIRDS WHOSE SONGS ARE UNUTTERABLE SPINNING FANTAS+   *918 14
    WITCH TEETH AN' 'ER BLACK HAWK-EYES AS I'VE   *919 11
    WHERE BLACK BOUGHS FLAP THE GROUND   *929 15
    BUT OH THE PALMS OF HER TWO BLACK HANDS ARE RED   *938 26
    BUT OH THE PALMS OF HIS BLACK HANDS ARE RED   *939 22
    SOMEWHERE BENEATH THAT PIANO'S SUPERB SLEEK BLACK   *940 1
    AND THE GREAT BLACK PIANO IS CLAMOURING AS MY MOTHER'S +   *940 21
    AND IN THE DARK I FEEL HIS COLD WEBBED FEET MUD BLACK   *947 19
    BLACK LAMPS FROM THE HALLS OF DIS SMOKING DARK BLUE   *956 7

BLACK-AND-WHITE
    WHEN I WENT TO THE FILM AND SAW ALL THE BLACK-AND-WHITE   443 22
    AND CAUGHT THEM MOANING FROM CLOSE-UP KISSES BLACK-AND-+   444 1

BLACKBERRIES
    BLACKBERRIES   285 6

BLACKBERRY
    BLACKBERRY FACE   398 1

BLACKBIRD
    PALE-BREASTED THROSTLES AND A BLACKBIRD ROBBERLINGS   36 25
    SOMEWHERE THE LONG MELLOW NOTE OF THE BLACKBIRD   40 25

BLACK-BLUE
    AMONG THE SPLENDOUR OF BLACK-BLUE TORCHES SHEDDING FATH+   *956 19

BLACK-BOUGHED
    PUT TRUST THEN NOW IN THE BLACK-BOUGHED TREE   114 9

BLACK-BOY
    OF AN AUSTRALIAN BLACK-BOY   394 7

BLACK COUNTRY
    AND THE DEATH OF THE BLACK COUNTRY IS UPON ME   630 6

BLACK-DOTTED
    WILL YOU CLIMB ON YOUR BIG SOFT WINGS BLACK-DOTTED   696 22

BLACKENED
    OF WEED THAT BLACKENED THE SHORE SO THAT I RECOILED   98 17
    BLACKENED EDGE OF THE SKIES   103 27

BLACKENING
    OR STORMS OF TEARS OR RAGE OR BLACKENING RAIN   745 12
    THAT POUR CASCADE-LIKE DOWN THE BLACKENING WIND   745 19
    I TURN TOWARDS THE BITTER BLACKENING WIND   745 24

BLACKENS
    AND TAINTS AND BLACKENS THE SKY TILL AT LAST IT IS DARK+   258 12

BLACKER
    BLACKER UPON THE SOUNDLESS UNGURGLING FLOOD   719 12

BLACKFACES
    PALEFACES YELLOWFACES BLACKFACES THESE ARE NO MEXICANS   793 11

BLACK-GREEN
    AFTER THE BLACK-GREEN SKIRTS OF A YELLOW-GREEN OLD MEXI+   395 31

BLACK-HEADED
    YET WHEN I THINK OF THE WILD SWAN OR THE RIPPLE-MARKED +   841 1

BLACKISH
    BLACKISH THEY WILL TASTE OF TEARS WHEN THE YELLOW DAPPL+   119 13

BLACKLY
    ALMOND TRUNKS CURVING BLACKLY IRON-DARK CLIMBING THE   300 24
    WITH IRON BRANCHING BLACKLY RUSTED LIKE OLD TWISTED   301 13

BLACKNESS
    DELIBERATELY GOING INTO THE BLACKNESS AND SLOWLY DRAWING   351 6
    BLACKNESS   398 12
    WITH A SHOCK AS AGAINST THE BLACKNESS OF A NEGRO   428 4
    HAS IN IT AN ELEMENT OF BLACKNESS   708 16
    AND YET THE ROOTS BELOW THE BLACKNESS ARE INTACT   709 22
    ONLY THE DEEPENING BLACKNESS DARKENING STILL   719 11
    SEPARATES ITSELF ON THE BLACKNESS   719 28
    BEYOND THE BLACKNESS OF BLACK   810 24

BLACK-PAPER
    WITH LONG BLACK-PAPER EARS   345 35

BLACK PRINCE
    PROUDER THAN THE BLACK PRINCE   587 22

BLACK-PURPLE
    THROUGH THE RED DOORS BEYOND THE BLACK-PURPLE BAR   134 3

BLACK-SCARVED
    AND BLACK-SCARVED FACES OF WOMEN FOLK WISTFULLY   232 22

BLACK-STRIPED
    AND REACHES HER BLACK-STRIPED FACE UP LIKE A SNAKE FAR +   385 26

BLACK-WINGED
    THE FIGURE OF SONG AFLUTTER IN A BLACK-WINGED REVELRY   *918 2

BLADDER
    BLADDER   438 8
    LIKE A WILD SWAN OR A GOOSE WHOSE HONK GOES THROUGH MY +   *947 18

BLADDERS
    SUCKED OUT OF YOUR EMPTY BLADDERS   281 23

BLADE
    BLADE OF HIS GLANCE THAT ASKS ME TO APPLAUD   43 25
    WHICH RUSHES UPWARD BLADE BEYOND BLADE   49 23
    SHE SEES THE BLADE OF THE SEA   200 6
    AND THE SEA LIKE A BLADE AT THEIR FACE   310 9
    LIKE A VIRGIN THE BLADE OF MY BAYONET WANTING IT   742 10
    A BLADE ON THE WHEEL THEN THE SLUMBERING NIGHT   773 4
    WITH A BLADE OF GRASS BETWEEN MY TEETH   804 14
    WITH A BLADE OF GREEN GRASS BETWEEN HIS TEETH   805 22
    AND BETWEEN OUR FINGERS ROSE A BLADE OF GREEN GRASS   806 27
    HUITZILOPOCHTLI GIVES THE BLACK BLADE OF DEATH   809 4
    IS MALINTZI'S BLADE OF GRASS   810 20
    HIS SCYTHE BLADE BRIGHT UNHOOKS   *944 12

BLADES
    NO MORE NARCISSUS PERFUME LILY HARLOTS THE BLADES OF SE+   273 16
    LIKE DRAWN BLADES NEVER SHEATHED HACKED AND GONE BLACK   304 28
    AND BETWEEN THE TWO BLADES OF THIS PAIR OF SHEARS PROPE+   663 16
    IN SHOWERS OF MINUTE RUDDY DROPS FROM THEIR BLADES   884 29

BLAKE
    THE DARK SATANIC MILLS OF BLAKE   628 13

BLAME
    YET WARM HERSELF AT THE FIRE THEN BLAME   151 35
    THAT LITTLE BLIGHTER'S TO BLAME   493 4
    YET WARM HERSELF AT THE FIRE AND BLAME   874 15

BLANCH
    TO BLANCH SLOWLY   766 20

BLANCHED
    I SEE YOUR BLANCHED FACE AT MY BREAST AND HIDE   129 13
    GODS NUDE AS BLANCHED NUT-KERNELS   280 19
    A BLANCHED FACE FIXED AND AGONIZED   742 7

BLAND
    AND SITS WITH A SMOOTH BLAND SMILE UP THERE IN THE SKY   54 12
    THE PULSE THROUGH THE WHOLE BLAND BEING   165 13
    ALL OF SHADOW AND OF BLAND   261 27
    MONKEYS WITH A BLAND GRIN ON OUR FACES   450 17
    DARK WAVING OF THEIR ARMS AGAINST THE BLAND   *895 3

BLANDISHMENT
    WITH SHELTER NOW AND WITH BLANDISHMENT SINCE THE WINDS +   75 14

BLANDLY
    AND GOING BLANDLY ON TO HIS NEXT SPITE   *949 14

BLANK
    AND THE FLESH OF THE STALK HOLDS UP FOR NOTHING A BLANK+   97   8
    AND THIS HELEN BESIDE ME I AM BLANK BEING NOTHING I BEA+   97 12
    NO NOT EVEN SNIFF AT HER HIS NOSE IS BLANK   362 14
    A WOODEN BLANK ON HER FACE   384 24
    AT PRESENT I AM A BLANK AND I ADMIT IT   501 16
    IN FEELING I AM JUST A BLANK   501 17
    MY MIND IF FAIRLY NIMBLE AND IS NOT BLANK   501 18
    MY BODY LIKES ITS DINNER AND THE WARM SUN BUT OTHERWISE+   501 19
    MY SOUL IS ALMOST BLANK MY SPIRIT QUITE   501 20
    I HAVE A CERTAIN AMOUNT OF MONEY SO MY ANXIETIES ARE BL+   501 21
    AND I CAN'T DO ANYTHING ABOUT IT EVEN THERE I AM BLANK   501 22
    SO I AM JUST GOING TO GO ON BEING A BLANK TILL SOMETHIN+   501 23
    AND MAKES ME KNOW I AM NOT BLANK ANY LONGER   501 25
    TILL WE ARE BLANK   512 26
    TILL WE ACTUALLY FEEL AS BLANK AS WE REALLY ARE   513 10
    IS A BLANK AT THE GAME   564 32
    FOR THE DEAD VANITY OF KNOWING BETTER NOR THE BLANK   709 30

BLANKET
    A MEMBRANE OF SLEEP LIKE A BLACK BLANKET   407 25
    THEY CAN'T GET UP THEY ARE UNDER THE BLANKET   408 22

BLANKET-WRAPPED
    MOUNTAINS BLANKET-WRAPPED   407   1
    MOUNTAINS BLANKET-WRAPPED   408 19

BLANK-IT-OUT
    THAN THE BLANK-IT-OUT GIRL   565 28

BLANKNESS
    AND DISDAIN AND BLANKNESS AND ONRUSH AND PRISE OPEN THE   371 30

BLASPHEME
    WHICH WISHES TO BLASPHEME THE WORLD INTO GREYNESS   713   7

BLASPHEMIES
    EVEN THROUGH THE GREATEST BLASPHEMIES THE HANDS OF THE +   700 20

BLASPHEMY
    LET HIM BE CAST OUT FOR BLASPHEMY   726 14
    AND ALL DESCRIPTION IS A BLASPHEMY   726 16

BLAST
    ANY MORE THAN I COULD ENTER THE WHITE-HOT DOOR OF A BLA+   344 18
    THAN TO SHELTER ANYBODY FROM THE COLD BLAST   540 30
    AN' BLAST 'EM FOREVER BUT THEY'D ONLY   550 11
    AND THE SOUND OF A BLAST THROUGH THE SEA-CURVED CORE OF+   623 13
    A BILIOUS BLAST   760   8

BLASTED
    HAD BLASTED THE SICKLY AIR   536 15

BLASTING
    IT NEEDS THOROUGHLY PRUNING NOT AS IN THE LATE WAR BLAS+   677 25

BLASTS
    BLOWS THE MAGNETIC CURRENT IN FIERCE BLASTS   370 23

BLATANT
    REDDENS STILL MORE ON THE BLATANT BODIES OF THESE ALL-B+   625 11
    BUT THE BLATANT BATHERS DON'T KNOW THEY KNOW NOTHING   625 16

BLAZE
    FACE FREED OF THE WAVERING BLAZE   59   8
    MY BELOVED SMELTING DOWN IN THE BLAZE   103 18
    OF GREEN FIRES LIT ON THE SOIL OF EARTH THIS BLAZE   116   7
    WHERE I HAD BEEN WAS A SUDDEN BLAZE   259   5
    A SUDDEN FLARING BLAZE   259   6
    HA I WAS A BLAZE LEAPING UP   259 11
    SO THAT IT RUSHES UP IN A HUGE BLAZE LIKE A PHALLUS   506   6
    RIBBED AND TORCH-LIKE WITH THEIR BLAZE OF DARKNESS SPRE+   697   6
    I CAN SEE HIS RAGING BLACK EYES BLAZE AT ME   733   3
    A SCORCHED BREAST BREASTING THE BLAZE   781   3
    RIBBED HELLISH FLOWERS ERECT WITH THEIR BLAZE OF DARKNE+   *956   4
    TORCH-FLOWERS OF THE BLUE-SMOKING DARKNESS PLUTO'S DARK+   *956   6

BLAZED
    THE FIRE ROSE UP IN THE BUSH AND BLAZED APACE   94 25
    THE FIRE ROSE UP AND THE BUSH BLAZED FORTH GOD'S GRACE   *897 13

BLAZES
    I WANT TO GO THERE'S A GOLD ROAD BLAZES BEFORE   230 12
    AND SEND MANKIND TO ITS INFERIOR BLAZES   316 29
    MANKIND'S INFERIOR BLAZES   316 30

BLAZING
    THE BLAZING TIGER WILL SPRING UPON THE DEER UNDIMMED   268   3
    THE TROPICAL NIGHT OF BLAZING COCOA-NUT   387 26
    IS THE PYRE OF BLAZING GAS   702 24

BLAZONED
    IS BLAZONED HERE SO WHITE AND SO BLOODILY RED   176 19

BLEACHED
    LIKE A BE-AUREOLED BLEACHED SKELETON HOVERING   290 22
    EVEN THE WINGED SKELETON OF YOUR BLEACHED IDEAL   290 26

BLEAK
    LOOKING BLEAK AHEAD SHE RODE   202   6

BLEAT
    TO BLEAT   130 16
    AND LISTENING INWARDLY TO THE FIRST BLEAT OF A LAMB   366 14
    AND WHEN THE HERD GOES BY AT DAWN SHE BEGINS TO BLEAT F+ 384   6

BLEATING
    RAISING DUSK AND ACRIDITY OF GOATS AND BLEATING   384   3

BLED
    HANG STRINGS OF CRIMSON CHERRIES AS IF HAD BLED   36 21
    HAD BLED   88 19
    AND TATTERED AND RED WITH THE LIFE THAT HAS BLED   823   4

BLEED
    THE STREET-LAMPS IN THE TWILIGHT HAVE SUDDENLY STARTED + 102 31
    AGAIN I TELL YOU I BLEED I AM BOUND WITH WITHIES   131 11
    AND WE STILL BLEED AND WE GROPE AND ROAR   544   6
    THEY WILL BLEED ROTTEN BLOOD IN PESTILENCE   792   7
    HE IS BREATHING COLD CORRUPTION UPON YOU YOU SHALL BLEE+ 796 32

BLEEDER
    THAT LITTLE BLEEDER COMES BUSTIN' IN   493 11
    IF POOR LITTLE BLEEDER   564 19

BLEEDING
    ALL FEARFUL LEST I FIND THE LAST WORDS BLEEDING   135 19
    THE SUN IS BLEEDING ITS FIRES UPON THE MIST   164 17
    AND RISK BLEEDING TO DEATH BUT PERHAPS ESCAPE INTO SOME 632   5
    CAREFULLY AGAIN AND AGAIN TO STOP THE BLEEDING   734 10
    BLEEDING AND SHOUTING AND DYING   739   2
    AH NO NOT BLEEDING AWAY   768   9
    NOT BLEEDING AWAY TO LEAVE ME WITH WHITENED GUMS   768 10
    ALL FEARFUL LEST I FIND SOME NEXT WORD BLEEDING   *939   3

BLEEDING-HEART
    FLOWERS OF THE BLEEDING-HEART FALL TO THE THROB   137   5

BLEEDS
    AND HOPE BLEEDS RIGHT AWAY   639 24

BLEMISH
    NIGHT AFTER NIGHT WITH A BLEMISH OF DAY   117 18
    LOOK SHE'S A WONDERFUL DOVE WITHOUT BLEMISH OR SPOT   239   1
    O SPILL THE BLOOD NOT OF YOUR FIRSTLING LAMB WITHOUT SP+ 678 22
    FOR NIGHT AFTER NIGHT WITH A BLEMISH OF DAY   *931 22

BLENCH
    NOR BLENCH IT WITH NOISE   110 22
    BLENCH   138 32

BLENCHED
    NIGHT BLENCHED WITH A THOUSAND SNOWS   104 28

BLENCHES
    AS HE BLENCHES AND TURNS AWAY AND MY HEART STANDS STILL 47 27

BLENT
    MEDICINAL OF THE ELDER-FLOWERS WITH MEADOW-SWEET IS BLE+ 858 19

BLESS
    OF THE HOT-BORN INFANT BLESS THE FOLLY WHICH HAD   88 30
    AND BLESS THE WOUND   113 28
    LIFTING A BANK-BOOK TO BLESS US   456 25
    WHEN THOU RUNNEST THE RACE WITH THE FOREMOST GOD BLESS + 750   2
    WE PRAY FOR THEE MARY DELIGHTFUL THAT GOD MAY BLESS THEE 753   2
    FOR THE LAST TIME THEY BLESS YOU AS THEY LEAVE YOU   798 31

BLESSED
    NAY YO' BLESSED PEE-WHIPS   78 25
    BLESSED ARE THE PURE IN HEART AND THE FATHOMLESS IN BRI+ 314 16
    BLESSED IN ALL THINGS   768 24
    NAY YOU BLESSED PEE-WHIPS   *920 17
    UNDROSSED IT AND BLESSED IT WITH A QUIVERING   *927 23

BLESSING
    CHILD DEAR TO MY EYE GOD'S BLESSING IS ON THY SERVICE 749 21
    AH WITH HIS BLESSING BRIGHT ON THY MOUTH AND THY BROW 872   1

BLEST
    UNDROSSED IT AND LEFT IT BLEST   112   3
    SHADOWS TO COVER OUR STRICKEN MANHOOD AND BLEST   167 18
    UNDROSSED IT AND LEFT IT BLEST   *928 23

BLETHER
    DAY OF THE MENTAL WELTER AND BLETHER   471 17
    SO SHUT UP PIE-JAW BLETHER   564 11

BLEW
    AND I SLEPT TILL DAWN AT THE WINDOW BLEW IN LIKE DUST 99   1
    AGAINST THE WIND AND IF WHERE THE LAMPLIGHT BLEW   180 13
    NOISELESS THEIR WONDER NOISELESS BLEW   262   3
    BUT BLEW BACK AS IF AN INCOMING WIND BLEW HIM IN AGAIN 343 17
    AND THE BREATH BLEW UPON ME AGAIN   787   1
    SO HE BLEW DOWN ON THEM TO BLOW HIS BREATH IN THEIR FAC+ 790 24
    BECAUSE THEY WAS WARM AN' THE WIND BLEW   *910 18

BLIGHT
    TO TESTIFY TO A BLIGHT ON THE LAND   51   3
    FIRE ENTERS YOU LIKE FROST LIKE A CRUEL BLIGHT   87 17
    TO THIS HUMAN BLIGHT   146 16

BLIGHTERS
    CAN'T YOU GIVE IT THEM BLIGHTERS   457 27
    HAVE YOU GOT ONE LITTLE BLIGHTERS   457 29
    I WAS ONE OF THE LITTLE BLIGHTERS   534 11

BLIGHTER'S
    THAT LITTLE BLIGHTER'S TO BLAME   493   4

BLIND

MAKES BLIND   75 19
THE TASSEL OF THE BLIND SWINGS CONSTANTLY TAPPING THE P+   112 17
CLOSE YOUR EYES MY LOVE LET ME MAKE YOU BLIND   118 20
I WOULD KISS YOU OVER THE EYES TILL I KISSED YOU BLIND   118 26
AND STILL MY BLIND FACE   120 30
OVER MY EYES AND I WAS BLIND   123 19
AND I WAS BLIND IN A TAWNY-GOLD DAY   123 32
THE BLIND TO HIDE THE GARDEN WHERE THE MOON   129 16
FEELING THE SHADOWS LIKE A BLIND MAN READING   135 18
BREAKS AND SOBS IN THE BLIND   140 18
IN A WORM THAT IS BLIND YET STRIVES   170   5
STAND STILL AND BIND AND BLIND MYSELF   215   5
I DO NOT YEARN NOR ASPIRE FOR I AM A BLIND SAMSON   287 25
THEY ARE NOT STRONGER THAN I AM BLIND SAMSON   288 11
AM I NOT BLIND AT THE ROUND-TURNING MILL   288 17
AND I AM BLIND   289   8
GOING BLIND AT LAST   325 25
YET BLIND WITH FRENZY WITH CLUTTERED FEAR   343 15
AND I HAVE TO CLEAN UP AFTER YOU FILTH WHICH EVEN BLIND   399   6
BUT OH OUR HUMAN LIVES THE LUNGING BLIND CYCLOPS WE ARE   544 12
AND NEVER KNOWING WHAT WE ARE DOING ROARING BLIND WITH   544 18
ARE ALSO POOR BLIND CYCLOPS MOANING   544 27
AND GRIEVING WITH PUPPY-LIKE BLIND CRYING   544 29
THE BOURGEOIS AND THE BOLSHEVIST ARE BOTH QUITE BLIND   665 19
SUBMIT ABJECTLY TO THE BLIND MECHANICAL TRAFFIC-STREAMS+   666   6
THE DIVIDERS THE THUNDERERS THE SWIFT ONES BLIND WITH S+   707 20
BLIND WITH THE GOSSAMER OF PREVALENT DEATH   737   3
THE SECRET IN THE BLIND MOUTH OF THE WORM   744 28
WORK HAS MADE US BLIND AND NOW THE DUSK   757 13
HE SAW THE MEN THAT WERE BLIND REELING WITH AGUARDIENTE   790 12
BACK AND FORTH IN A BLIND MOVEMENT   825 19
WHEREIN WE ARE NOW BLIND UGLY BOORS   833 17
CLOSE YOUR EYES MY LOVE LET ME MAKE YOU BLIND   *931 30
I'LL KISS YOU OVER THE EYES TILL I KISS YOU BLIND   *932   4
OVER MY EYES AND I WAS BLIND   *934 25
FEELING THE SHADOWS LIKE A BLIND MAN READING   *939   2

BLINDED

AND BLINDED HIM IN HIS ONE BIG EYE   543 27
PUT OUT A LIGHT OF CONSCIOUSNESS AND LEFT A BLINDED BRU+   543 28
IS BLINDED BRUTES OF CYCLOPS WITH OUR CYCLOPEAN EYE PUT   544   4

BLINDFOLD

REPEATING WITH TIGHTENED ARMS AND THE HOT BLOOD'S BLIND+   61 26
REPEATING WITH TIGHTENED ARMS AND THE HOT BLOOD'S BLIND+   *912   6

BLINDING

INVISIBLE BLINDING MY FACE AND MY EYES WHAT IF IN   147   5
TILL IT BURST FORTH BLINDING WITHERING THE EARTH   294   3

BLINDLY

LUNGING BLINDLY   345   6

BLINDNESS

AND STRIKE WITH A BLINDNESS OF FURY AGAINST ME CAN I CA+   *926 24

BLINDS

THE BLINDS ARE DRAWN BECAUSE OF THE SUN   51   5
ACROSS THE WALLS AS THE BLINDS ARE BLOWN   51   8
DRAWS DOWN THE BLINDS WHOSE SHADOWS SCARCELY STAIN   155   2
THE BLINDS ARE DRAWN BECAUSE OF THE SUN   *898 17
ACROSS THE WALLS AS THE BLINDS ARE BLOWN   *898 20
THE BLINDS ARE DRAWN BECAUSE OF THE SUN   *902   1
ACROSS THE WALLS AS THE BLINDS ARE BLOWN   *902   4

BLIND-WEARY

BLIND-WEARY   345 16

BLINKING

WITH WHITE PLUMES BLINKING UNDER THE EVENING GREY SKY   66 14

BLINKS

AND IMMEDIATELY SHE SEES ME SHE BLINKS STARES DOESN'T   384 22

BLISS

OF FIERY COLDNESS TO BE GONE IN A LOST SOUL'S BLISS   130 23
WITH A KNOT OF LIFE THAT ONLY BLISS CAN UNRAVEL   160 14
OF BLISS TILL ALL HER LAMBENT BEAUTY SHAKES TOWARDS US   193   7
THIS IS ALMOST BLISS   203 11
DO YOU THINK IT IS BLISS ALONE   235 32
THE SWINGING BLISS NO SHATTERING EVER DESTROYS   251 24
LAYING BACK HER LONG EARS WITH UNWINKING BLISS   311 19
I MIGHT BE A SOUL IN BLISS AN ANGEL APPROXIMATING TO THE   321   2
LO AGAIN THE SHUDDER OR BLISS THROUGH ALL THE ATOMS   682 15
KEEP PASSING ARCHANGELS OF BLISS   694 24
AND DENSE WITH HAPPY BLOOD DARK RAINBOW BLISS IN THE SEA   695 12
HAVE AN EXPERIENCE OF BLISS   708 23
AND LIFE IS FOR DELIGHT AND FOR BLISS   708 24
AND FOR BLISS   709   4
AND LIFE IS FOR DELIGHT AND BLISS   709   8
NEW JOY TO GIVE MORE LIFE NEW BLISS TO LIVE   740 26

BLISS-DRENCHED

YOUR HAIR FOR THE BLISS-DRENCHED REVEL   243 19

BLISS-FULL

SOUNDLESS BLISS-FULL WIDE-RAYED HONEY-BODIED   307   6

BLISTER

BLISTER   751 25

BLISTERED

A COOL OINTMENT OVER THE EARTH BLISTERED IN THE FLIGHT +   855 31

BLITHE

WE HOLD THEM PROUD AND BLITHE   204 23
AND YOUR BLITHE GLAD MIEN   234 18
SHE TROTS ON BLITHE TOES   386   3
GOES BEHIND ITS MOTHER ON BLITHE BARE FOOT   466 11
GOES BEHIND HIS MOTHER WITH BARE BLITHE FOOT   757 10

BLITHER

MY SIRS BUT I SAY 'TWAS FOR A BLITHER   60 30

BLOCK

DO THEY BLOCK THE WAY   765   9

BLOCKS

IN HOLLOW BLOCKS AND CUBES DEFORMED AND HEAPED   53 25
AND BLOCKS UP THE DOOR   515   9

BLOKES

YE SWINDLED LITTLE BLOKES   560 18

BLOND

PLUMS THE BLOND ONES ARE GOLD WITH LESS GLISTEN   827   5

BLONDE

IN BLONDE AND WHITE ON THE FLOOR NOR EVEN TURNED   156   8
THE TIGHT-ROPE LADY PINK AND BLONDE AND NUDE-LOOKING   444 24

BLOOD

THE OTHER VOICE IN A SILENCE OF BLOOD 'NEATH THE NOISE   36 17
AND SLOWLY BACK IN MY BLOOD   37 20
WHO SNIFFS WITH JOY BEFORE HE DRINKS THE BLOOD   43 32
TO PUT HER EARS TO THE PAINFUL SOB OF MY BLOOD   64 17
OF SHADOW EMERGING AS BLOOD EMERGES FROM INWARD SHADES +   66 20
BUT THE BLOOD HAS SUSPENDED ITS TIMBRE THE HEART FROM O+   67   3
FOR I THOUGHT YOU WERE WARM AS A SUDDEN JET OF BLOOD   99   7
LIKE FLAGS IN PALE BLOOD NEWLY WET   105   3
BLOOD SHED IN THE SILENT FIGHT   105   4
HAVE RISEN FLOATING ON MY BLOOD THE RARE   113   3
SINCE FROM OUT OF MY BLOOD AND BONE   118   2
DISSOLVED IN THE BLOOD   118 30
THE GORGE OF THE GAPING FLOWER TILL THE BLOOD DID FLOAT   123 18
I LONGED TO FEEL MY HOT BLOOD BURN   123 29
CONSOLATION THAT IN HER LIPS HER BLOOD AT CLIMAX CLIPS   127 26
THEIR DUMB CONFESSION OF WHAT HER BLOOD MUST FEEL   128   9
I TELL YOU MY BLOOD RUNS OUT ON THE FLOOR OF THIS OAK   131 13
THEIR BLOOD IN A WOMAN TO THE VERY LAST VEIN   139 17
HEART'S BLOOD   157 32
THE HEART OF THE LIVE WORLD PULSES AND THE BLOOD OF THE+   176   4
THERE IS SOMETHING I WANT TO FEEL IN MY RUNNING BLOOD   180 30
BY ALL THE BLOOD OF THE ROSE-BUSH INTO BEING   218 17
WHICH THE SWEET BLOOD FEEDS   240   6
NEW SUNNY STREAMS OF BLOOD   240   8
SMASHED ALL OOZING WITH BLOOD AND BURNED IN HEAPS   258   2
OH IF IT BE TRUE AND THE LIVING DARKNESS OF THE BLOOD O+   273 31
BUT BLOOD IS RED AND BLOOD IS LIFE RED WAS THE COLOUR O+   303 21
SWEATING HIS DROPS OF BLOOD THROUGH THE LONG-NIGHTED   305 25
AND HIS BLOOD RIPPLES WITH THAT UNTELLABLE DELIGHT OF O+   306   2
AND THE GETHSEMANE BLOOD AT THE IRON PORES UNFOLDS UNFO+   306   4
WHO SMEARED THEIR DOORS WITH BLOOD   313 19
THAT NOBLE BLOOD HAS BROUGHT US DOWN THE AGES   313 31
PURE BLOOD AND NOBLE BLOOD IN THE FINE AND ROSE-RED VEI+   314   1
BLOOD FROM SIDE TO SIDE   320 22
BLOOD FROM SIDE TO SIDE CAUSING MY MYRIAD SECRET STREAMS   320 28
BREAK INTO DROPS BURN INTO DROPS OF BLOOD AND DROPPING   322 14
THROWS STILL THE DARK BLOOD BACK AND FORTH   322 32
EVEN OF BLOOD   324   9
AND THE ROAR OF BLACK BULL'S BLOOD IN THE MIGHTY PASSAG+   326 15
HIS OWN BLACK BLOOD POURED OUT LIKE A SHEET OF FLAME OV+   326 30
MASSIVE BLACK BLOOD   327 15
BLOOD   327 27
WHICH SHAKES MY SUDDEN BLOOD TO HATRED OF YOU   333 16
BLOOD RED BLOOD   333 25
SUCKING LIVE BLOOD   333 31
MY BLOOD   333 32
QUEER WHAT A BIG STAIN MY SUCKED BLOOD MAKES   334 16
FROM THE WARM BLOOD IN THE DARK-CREATION MORNING   358 14
THE SUN BUT ALL CREATURES OF THE SUN MUST DIP THEIR MOU+   368   6
BLOOD   368   8
YOU'VE DIPPED IT IN BLOOD SO MANY TIMES   373 33
DOES THE SUN NEED STEAM OF BLOOD DO YOU THINK   374   9
DOES HE SHRIEK FOR BLOOD   374 15
IS THE BLOOD OF YOUR CONTINENT SOMEWHAT REPTILIAN STILL   374 23
THAT SUCKS UP BLOOD   374 27
BLOOD   382   0
THE CAT WHO LAPS BLOOD AND KNOWS   383   3
THE SOFT WELLING OF BLOOD INVINCIBLE EVEN BEYOND BONE OR   383   4
THE SOFT THE SECRET THE UNFATHOMABLE BLOOD   383   6
THE HOT DARK BLOOD OF ITSELF A-LAUGHING WET HALF-DEVILI+   389 20
AS IF THE HOMAGE OF THE KINDLED BLOOD OF THE EAST   389 28
THE MYSTERY OF THE DARK MOUNTAIN OF BLOOD REEKING IN   390   6
SERVE VAST MOUNTAINOUS BLOOD IN SUBMISSION AND SPLENDOUR   390 23
TEMPLE OF BLOOD IN THE NIGHT SWIFT-STRIKING   390 33
AND ALL HER WEIGHT ALL HER BLOOD DRIPPING SACK-WISE DOWN   394 21
THE PENITENTES LASH THEMSELVES TILL THEY RUN WITH BLOOD   408   4
DRINK A LITTLE BLOOD AND LOSING ANOTHER ROYALTY UNTO   414 27
WHEN THE MOON FALLS ON A MAN'S BLOOD   453 13
LO I AM FLESH AND BLOOD THAT RACES   460 25
THE KNOCK OF THE BLOOD IN MY WRISTS   461   2
THEIR MASSIVE BLOOD   465 28
HE DOESN'T PUT MY BLOOD IN THE BANK   466 22
SLOWLY UP IN THE BLOOD OF MEN   470 26
OF THE BLOOD IN ME OF THE BLOOD IN THEE   471   2
TOUCH IS OF THE BLOOD   471 12
THE SOFT BLOOD SOFTLY FLOWS TOGETHER   471 15
THE BLOOD KNOWS IN DARKNESS AND FOREVER DARK   474   5
THE BLOOD ALSO KNOWS RELIGIOUSLY   474   7
IN MY BLOOD   474 20
WHICH ROTS THE BRAIN THE BLOOD THE BONES THE STONES THE   487 16

BLOOD
    YET ALL OF THESE DRINK BLOOD   496 17
    NOT TO SHED A LOT OF BLOOD OVER IT   497 21
    AND THAT SENT THE BLOOD RUSHING TO THE SURFACE OF THE B+   502 7
    WILL BE BRIGHT RED WITH BLOOD   515 6
    AND SUCKIN' YOUR BLOOD   557 1
    A COLUMN OF BLOOD   563 4
    MY BRITISH BLOOD THE WORLD SHALL KNOW   576 21
    AND HIS BRITISH BLOOD THE WORLD IT KNEW   576 25
    IF HIS BLOOD WAS BRITISH OR TIMBUCTOOT   577 1
    BUT WITH THAT BRITISH BLOOD OF HIS   577 3
    TO BRITAIN WHERE HIS BLOOD CAME FROM   577 6
    THE SPARK FELL AND KINDLED INSTANTLY ON MY BLOOD   618 4
    IN COLD BLOOD I CANNOT FEEL GODDESSES IN THE SUMMER EVE+   655 18
    BUT WHAT RIGHT HAS MY BLOOD TO BE COLD   655 20
    IF I CUT MY FINGER MY BLOOD IS HOT NOT COLD   655 22
    AND EVEN IN COLD BLOOD I KNOW THIS   655 23
    WHEN MY BLOOD IS KINDLED   655 25
    WITHOUT SHEDDING OF BLOOD THERE IS NO REMISSION OF SIN   678 18
    AND THE BLOOD OF IT MUST BE SPILT   678 21
    O SPILL THE BLOOD NOT OF YOUR FIRSTLING LAMB WITHOUT SP+   678 22
    DESTROY IT SHED ITS UNCLEAN BLOOD KILL IT PUT IT OUT OF+   679 4
    BLOOD   679 6
    THAT BLOOD OF THE LOWER LIFE MUST BE SHED   679 9
    OH AND THEIR FACES SCARLET LIKE THE DOLPHIN'S BLOOD   689 5
    THE HOTTEST BLOOD OF ALL AND THE WILDEST THE MOST URGENT   694 2
    AND OUT OF THE INWARD ROARING OF THE INNER RED OCEAN OF+   694 16
    AND DENSE WITH HAPPY BLOOD DARK RAINBOW BLISS IN THE SEA   695 12
    IT IS SET UP AS A BOUNDARY AND BLOOD AND SWEAT   706 13
    A CALLING COLUMN OF BLOOD   714 9
    JESUS HIS SPURS ARE RED WITH SHINING BLOOD   733 34
    CRYING POUR OUT THE BLOOD OF THE FOE   739 23
    SEEKING TO APPEASE WITH BLOOD THE INSISTENT GHOSTS   739 24
    OUT OF BLOOD RISE UP NEW GHOSTS   739 25
    SINCE FROM BLOOD POURED OUT RISE ONLY GHOSTS AGAIN   740 10
    FOR THE LORD TO COME FORTH AT LARGE ON THE SCENT OF BLO+   742 19
    WHAT I BEGET MUST I BEGET OF BLOOD   742 24
    WHAT IS THE CRIME THAT MY SEED IS TURNED TO BLOOD   742 37
    FEED ON OUR WOUNDS LIKE BREAD RECEIVE OUR BLOOD   743 4
    LIKE BLOOD IN THE EARTH AGAIN WE WALK THE EARTH   743 26
    SCARLET AND CRIMSON AND A RUST OF BLOOD   744 30
    HER APRON WAS BROWN WITH BLOOD SHE PRAYED   753 10
    THE BLOOD FROM OUR HEARTS OH YOU WHO STAND BEHIND US   756 7
    IT IS VERY DARK OH KINDRED DEARER THAN BLOOD   765 1
    OUT OF THE BLOOD   766 13
    WHERE ONCE THE BLOOD SANG   767 3
    DON'T TAKE THE BLOOD OF MY BODY   767 7
    ROSY BEST OF THE BLOOD GONE OUT OF THE BODY   767 22
    THIS BLOOD THAT WAS ONCE MY OWN   768 7
    THAT'S BEEN WHETTED AND WHETTED IN BLOOD   782 3
    I'LL TURN THEIR BLOOD LIKE SOUR MILK ROTTEN WITH THUNDER   792 6
    THEY WILL BLEED ROTTEN BLOOD IN PESTILENCE   792 7
    AND DART HIS ELECTRIC NEEDLES INTO YOUR BONES AND CURDL+   797 10
    SUN IN THE BLOOD   804 9
    BONE IN THE BLOOD   804 12
    SUN IN THE BLOOD   805 17
    BONE IN THE BLOOD   805 20
    AND RED AS BLOOD   806 25
    RED IS HUITZILOPOCHTLI'S BLOOD   808 19
    RED IS THE BLOOD AND THE FIRE   808 25
    THE RAIN OF BLOOD IS FALLEN IS GONE INTO THE EARTH   811 13
    SOUL AND BODY BONE AND BLOOD   824 13
    AND FALLS WINGLESS BLOOD STREAMING THROUGH ITS YELLOW H+   855 25
    MY CHAFED CURBED BLOOD NO LONGER BROKS   857 3
    WHILE THE BLOOD IS ALIVE   857 6
    HAS THE WARMTH OF A NIGHT KISS SPREAD THROUGH THEIR BLO+   860 22
    DRIFTED WITH THE BLOOD OF THE FLOWERS ON HER FEET AND K+   864 3
    OF THEIR DANCING BLOOD LADS SUCKING THE COLD MOISTURE F+   865 29
    BY MY OWN BONDS OF BLOOD AND MUSIC-LESS   884 18
    AND RANK AND DRIPPED WITH BLOOD AND DRIPPED AGAIN   884 27
    RED ON MY MEMORY HEAVY WITH OUR OWN BLOOD   885 1
    AND AH WITH ALL HIS BLOOD FOR ERE THE STAIN   885 4
    PENETRATED MY BLOOD   885 15
    PASSED INTO MY BLOOD   885 27
    AND THE SOUL OF THE WIND AND MY BLOOD COMPARE   *892 4
    LIVING BLOOD   *892 9
    MOVES THE BLOOD   *909 10
    THIRTEEN TIMES THE TEETH FLASHED IN A FIRE OF BLOOD   *933 1
    THE GORGE OF THE GAPING FLOWER TILL THE BLOOD DID FLOAT   *934 24
    OF MY BLOOD IN HER DARKENED CUP   *935 2
    THAT WE HAVE BLOOD AND BOWELS AND LIVELY GENITALS   *953 3

BLOOD-BORN
    ABOVE ME SPRINGS THE BLOOD-BORN MISTLETOE   131 15

BLOOD-BROWN
    AND BLOOD-BROWN FLUX OF LIVES THAT SWEEP THEIR WAY   745 8
    AND CRIMSON AND THE BLOOD-BROWN HEAPS OF SLAIN   745 26

BLOOD-DARK
    UNFOLD SLOWLY UPWARDS BLOOD-DARK   302 17

BLOOD-DROPS
    BLOOD-DROPS BENEATH EACH CURL   36 22

BLOOD-DROP
    YOU WINGED BLOOD-DROP   334 11

BLOODILY
    IS BLAZONED HERE SO WHITE AND SO BLOODILY RED   176 19

BLOOD-JETS
    IN THE BLOOD-JETS OF YOUR THROAT   242 4

BLOODLESS
    MAKING US PALE AND BLOODLESS WITHOUT RESISTANCE   740 6

BLOOD-MOUNTAINS
    BLOOD-MOUNTAINS   392 12

BLOOD-ORANGE
    A HOLE IN THE BLOOD-ORANGE BRILLIANT ROCKS THAT STICK U+   402 12
    MORE OUT OF THE SHADOW OF THE CAVE IN THE BLOOD-ORANGE   402 18

BLOOD-POISONING
    THEY WILL TEAR YOU TERRIBLY AND GIVE YOU BLOOD-POISONING   675 8

BLOOD-PRESSURE
    THEY HAVE HIGH BLOOD-PRESSURE AND ALMOST BURST   502 5
    WHY AS THEY GROW OLDER DO THEY SUFFER FROM BLOOD-PRESSU+   537 24

BLOOD-RED
    THAT SHINES BLOOD-RED BESIDE THE RAILWAY SIDING   72 5
    BLOOD-RED DEEP   279 5
    THE BLOOD-RED   804 6
    THE BLOOD-RED   805 14
    YOU HIGHLY EVERY BLOOD-RED ROSE DISPLAY   *941 7

BLOOD-SACRIFICES
    IN ALL THE SINISTER SPLENDOUR OF THEIR RED BLOOD-SACRIF+   371 35

BLOODSHED
    IS THERE A BOND OF BLOODSHED BETWEEN YOU   374 20
    BLOODSHED   497 8

BLOOD-STAIN
    IRON WASHES AWAY LIKE AN OLD BLOOD-STAIN   455 5

BLOOD-SURGE
    WHERE HER ARMS AND MY NECK'S BLOOD-SURGE COULD MEET   *912 10

BLOOD-SWEPT
    AND STRANGE IN MY BLOOD-SWEPT EARS WAS THE SOUND   61 24
    AND STRANGE IN MY BLOOD-SWEPT EARS WAS THE SOUND   *912 4

BLOOD'S
    REPEATING WITH TIGHTENED ARMS AND THE HOT BLOOD'S BLIND+   61 26
    REPEATING WITH TIGHTENED ARMS AND THE HOT BLOOD'S BLIND+   *912 6

BLOOD-THIRSTY
    AND CEASES TO BE A BLOOD-THIRSTY KING OF BEASTS   325 7
    BLOOD-THIRSTY BIRD   373 35
    BLOOD-THIRSTY BIRD   374 17
    NOR YOU NOR YOUR BLOOD-THIRSTY SUN   374 26

BLOOD-VEINED
    MEMBRANED BLOOD-VEINED WINGS   322 16

BLOOD-WELDED
    WILL YOU STRIKE AT THE HEART OF THE SUN WITH YOUR BLOOD+   783 17

BLOODY
    THEY WERE JUST A BLOODY SHAM   556 4
    THEY WERE JUST A BLOODY COLLECTIVE FRAUD   556 7
    THOUGH YOU BLOODY OUTSIDERS HAD BETTER NOT TRY IT ON   618 13
    AND BLOODY WATER FALLS UPON THE ROAD   734 8
    EXTINCT ONE YELLOW BLOODY SPARK   *932 31
    NOT THIS GRAY BOOK BUT THE RED AND BLOODY SCENES   *938 28

BLOODY-WHITE
    RED ONES A BLOODY-WHITE FLAG OVER YOU   *940 28

BLOOM
    NO TREE IN BLOOM   56 4
    ON THE COMFORTED POOL LIKE BLOOM   56 18
    LAST EVENING AND SHE WHO WAS SOFTLY IN BLOOM   141 7
    'TWAS I WHO PLACED THE BLOOM OF MANHOOD ON   156 25
    BLOOM ALONG THE CORSO ON THE LIVING PERAMBULATING BUSH   313 24
    AND POMEGRANATE BLOOM AND SCARLET MALLOW-FLOWER   313 29
    EVEN THE STUPIDEST FARMER GATHERS HIS HAY IN BLOOM IN   587 8
    WITH A LOVELY BLOOM OF WHITENESS UPON WHITE   708 21
    THE HUM OF THE BEES IN THE PEAR-TREE BLOOM   885 14
    AND THE BUSTLE OF BEES IN THE PEAR-TREE BLOOM   885 24
    SETTLE UPON US MAGNETIC SO WE WAX AND BLOOM   *938 18

BLOOMED
    SO THEY BLOOMED OUT AND FILLED THEMSELVES WITH COLOURED+   831 3

BLOOMING
    FOR EVERY BLOOMING BIRD IS AN OXFORD CUCKOO NOWADAYS   434 1
    A BLOOMING ARISTOCRAT ALL ROUND   587 26
    YOU'LL STOP THAT BLOOMING   755 20

BLOOMIN'
    AND FOR EVERY BLOOMIN' MORTAL THING   493 3
    UP LIKE A BLOOMIN' LITTLE EXCELSIOR   552 19
    UP HE GOES UP THE BLOOMIN' LADDER   552 21
    SUCH BLOOMIN' FAT-ARSED DOOL-OWLS   553 7
    MY THE BLOOMIN' POMPOMS   557 5

BLOOMS
    TO FLOURISH THERE AS PALE MOULD BLOOMS ON A CRUST   99 5

BLORTING
    I REMEMBER THE HEIFER IN HER HEAT BLORTING AND BLORTING   366 6

BLOSSOM
    OF THE SHE-DOVE IN THE BLOSSOM STILL BELIEVING   65 21
    LIQUID AS LIME-TREE BLOSSOM SOFT AS BRILLIANT WATER OR +   67 20
    WHO CROWD IN CROWDS LIKE RHODODENDRONS IN BLOSSOM   73 12
    AT LAST INTO BLOSSOM OF BEING EACH ONE HIS OWN FLOWER O+   93 15
    OF THE BLOSSOM ARE ROSES TO LOOK AT BUT FLAMES WHEN THE+   93 32

BLOSSOM
YET WAIT AWHILE FOR HENCEFORTH I WILL LOVE WHEN A BLOSS+   94   5
TO MY BLOSSOM IN PERFUME AND SEED-DUST AND ONLY THEN I +   94   6
GHOST BEYOND GHOST OF BLOSSOM SHOWS   104 27
BLOSSOM ME STALK BY STALK   111 14
AND SLOWLY ALL THE BLOSSOM SHUTS IN PAIN   113 13
WHAT THEN IS THERE HIDDEN IN THE SKIRTS OF ALL THE BLOS+   119 27
YEA BUT IT IS CRUEL WHEN UNDRESSED IS ALL THE BLOSSOM   120   1
OF BLOSSOM SHE FINGERED AND MY FINGERS ALL   125 22
AND WHIRLING IN BLOSSOM OF FLAME AND BEING UPON ME   218 23
THE SEED IS PURPOSE BLOSSOM ACCIDENT   218 26
THE SEED IS ALL IN ALL THE BLOSSOM LENT   218 27
BLOSSOM MY DARLING BLOSSOM BE A ROSE   219 17
MY LOVE MY BLOSSOM A CHILD   239 16
IN ONE BLOSSOM BLOWING   239 21
AFLAME WITH BLOSSOM   244   3
STORMS AND CUMULUS CLOUDS OF ALL IMAGINABLE BLOSSOM   271 27
COME AND LIFT US TO OUR END TO BLOSSOM BRING US TO OUR +   272 33
PIERCING THE FLESH TO BLOSSOM OF DEATH   273 17
AFTER YOU HAVE TAKEN OFF THE BLOSSOM WITH YOUR LIPS   282   7
SEEING RUSTY IRON PUFF WITH CLOUDS OF BLOSSOM   304   6
THE HEART OF BLOSSOM   305   2
THE UNQUENCHABLE HEART OF BLOSSOM   305   3
SEE IT COME FORTH IN BLOSSOM   305 20
INTO BLOSSOM INTO PRIDE INTO HONEY-TRIUMPH INTO MOST   305 27
OH GIVE ME THE TREE OF LIFE IN BLOSSOM   305 29
A NAKED TREE OF BLOSSOM LIKE A BRIDEGROOM BATHING IN DEW   306   8
BLOSSOM BEYOND THE SWORD-RUST   306 16
YOU RUFFLED BLACK BLOSSOM   369   1
THAT WILL BLOSSOM FORTH THE WHOLE OF HUMAN NATURE   429 13
IT'S EITHER AN ARTIFICIAL RAG BLOSSOM OR AN IMMORTELLE +   472 26
THAT WOULD RISE AT LAST AND BLOSSOM OUT   488 21
BLOSSOM   587   9
GRASS IN BLOSSOM BLOSSOMING GRASS RISEN TO ITS HEIGHT A+   587 12
OF THE GRASS IN BLOSSOM   587 25
I SHALL BLOSSOM LIKE A DARK PANSY AND BE DELIGHTED   677 13
THE WINDS OF THE AFTERWARDS KISS US INTO BLOSSOM OF MAN+   677 19
HIS ROUND BROWN HEAD BENDS LIKE A BEE ABOVE A BLOSSOM   868   5
BEYOND THE GAY PINK BLOSSOM   886 23
IS SWELLING AND SHAPING A BUD INTO BLOSSOM   *907 26
AS IT SWELLS AND SHAPES A BUD INTO BLOSSOM   *909 17
BLOSSOM YOU STALK BY STALK   *927   7
BLOSSOM YOU STALK BY STALK   *928   7
OF BLOSSOM SHE FINGERED AND MY POISED FINGERS ALL   *936 21

BLOSSOMED
BLOSSOMED OUTRIGHT   165 24
THAT BLOSSOMED AT LAST RED GERANIUM AND MIGNONETTE   691   5

BLOSSOM-FULL
TO OPEN MY BLOSSOM-FULL BREAST FROM ITS DREARY BANDS   *896 24

BLOSSOMING
CROWDS OF GLITTERING KING-CUPS SURGE TO CHALLENGE THE B+   33 11
AND NEVER A BLOSSOMING WOMAN WILL ROAM   106 17
AND SENSITIVE BUD-LIKE BLOSSOMING OF PASSION   113   6
CARRY INTO YOUR ROOM THE BLOSSOMING BOUGHS OF CHERRY   179   2
PRAY NOT TO DIE ON THIS PISGAH BLOSSOMING WITH VIOLETS   273 36
GRASS IN BLOSSOM BLOSSOMING GRASS RISEN TO ITS HEIGHT A+   587 12
LET HIM HIDE IT AWAY SO IT CAN GO ON BLOSSOMING   634 15
PROLIFIC I AM A BLOSSOMING TWIG   888 17
CROWDS OF GLITTERING KING-CUPS SURGE TO CHALLENGE THE B+ *891 12

BLOSSOMLESS
AS I CAME HOME IN THE DUSK DESPOILED BY SCHOOL A MERE B+   864 27

BLOSSOMS
ENJOYS THE OPEN BLOSSOMS AS THEY STRAW   129 17
THAW-COLD ICE-CORRUPT BLOSSOMS   270 25
WHO SAID THEY MIGHT ASSUME THESE BLOSSOMS   313 25
GRASS BLOSSOMS GRASS HAS FLOWERS FLOWERS OF GRASS   587   2
EVEN THE BLUE-GRASS BLOSSOMS   587   6
GRASS BLOSSOMS   587 17
SUCH AS MY LIFE HAS NOT BROUGHT FORTH BEFORE NEW BLOSSO+   727 26
AMONG THE SHADOWS OF BLOSSOMS AND TREES AND RUSHES   867 26
CRUCIBLE WHERE NEW BLOSSOMS OF SHAPE ARE BEGOT   873   5
GLOW LIKE BLOSSOMS ASTART   887   2

BLOT
BURNS LIKE A BLOT OF ANXIETY   103 11
ONE BIRD ONE BLOT FOLDED AND STILL AT THE TOP   147 24
NOT ONE INSTANT CLEAVE CLING LIKE A BLOT WITH HIS BREAS+ 343 29

BLOTCH
HOW TOWARDS THE NORTH A RED BLOTCH ON THE SKY   103 10
A BLOTCH OF PALLOR STIRS BENEATH THE HIGH   210 19
SHE PRICKED A FINE BLACK BLOTCH   222   7

BLOTCHING
BLOTCHING THE THICK SOILED AIR   142 18

BLOTS
AND SUNK INTO DEPRESSION THAT ALMOST BLOTS ME OUT.   629 21

BLOTTED
THAT THE BLACK NIGHT HID HER FROM ME BLOTTED OUT EVERY   62   4
OF SEVERAL INSULTS OF BLOTTED PAGES AND SCRAWL   74 14
OF SEVERAL INSULTS OF BLOTTED PAGES AND SCRAWL   *895 22
OF SEVERAL INSULTS OF BLOTTED PAGES AND SCRAWL   *904 11
THAT THE BLACK NIGHT HID HER FROM ME BLOTTED OUT EVERY + *912 12

BLOUSES
WATCH THE BOYS IN THEIR SUMMER BLOUSES   51 11
WATCH THE BOYS IN THEIR SUMMER BLOUSES   *898 23
WATCH THE BOYS IN THEIR SUMMER BLOUSES   *902   7

BLOW
WHOSE LOFTY ROSES BREAK AND BLOW   104 23
SO WIDE AS YOU WATCH THE CATKINS BLOW   126 30
THERE'S A MOON FULL BLOW   137 23
AND MY QUESTIONS BLOW   168   5
WHERE STRANGE WINDS BLOW   202 24
ON THE FACES THAT DRIFT AND BLOW   252 17
CAN BLOW ACROSS THE DARK SEAS TO OUR USUAL WORLD   261   3
THEN BLOW THEM OVER WITH GOLD   273   3
AND IT IS DAY THEN FROM THE FOUR QUARTERS THE FOUR WIND+ 319   7
SOMETHING SEEMED TO BLOW HIM BACK FROM THE WINDOW   344 11
INTO WHICH THE CREATIVE FUTURE SHALL BLOW STRANGE UNKNO+ 428 29
COME BLOW UP YOUR HORN   659   6
THERE THEY BLOW THERE THEY BLOW HOT WILD WHITE BREATH O+ 694   6
SO HE BLEW DOWN ON THEM TO BLOW HIS BREATH IN THEIR FAC+ 790 24
IS READY TO BLOW BAD BREATH UPON THEM TO PERISH THEM ALL 792 16
AND BLOW THE ASH AWAY   811 26
HISSES THROUGH THE FLOWERS THE TIMID NIGHT-AIRS BLOW   855 30
SHE LOVES ME AND I BLOW A LITTLE BOAT   *943 15

BLOW-FLY
AND TACKLE THE BLOWSY BIG BLOW-FLY   458 11

BLOW-HOLES
BLOW-HOLES   380 14

BLOWING
BLOWING LITTLE FLOCKS OF BIRDS   99 17
FACES OF PEOPLE BLOWING ACROSS MY GAZE   116   9
THE SOFT WIND BLOWING COOL   194   7
THE GREAT BREATH BLOWING A TINY SEED OF FIRE   219   2
I HOLD MYSELF UP AND FEEL A BIG WIND BLOWING   223   4
IN ONE BLOSSOM BLOWING   239 21
A FINE WIND IS BLOWING THE NEW DIRECTION OF TIME   250 14
CUNNINGLY BLOWING ON THE FALLEN SPARKS ODDS AND ENDS OF+ 271 31
TO FEEL A FINE FINE BREEZE BLOWING THROUGH THE NAVEL AND 481 21
SO MEAN AND SELF-CONSCIOUS BLOWING AND SNORING   494 20
BLOWING DOWN YOUR NECK AND YOUR EARS   506 23

BLOWN
LIKE A THIN WHITE BIRD BLOWN OUT OF THE NORTHERN SEAS   47 14
LIKE A BIRD FROM THE FAR NORTH BLOWN WITH A BROKEN WING 47 15
ACROSS THE WALLS AS THE BLINDS ARE BLOWN   51   8
IS BLOWN OUT LIKE A CANDLE   115 20
LARGE SHADOWS FROM THE OUTSIDE STREET-LAMP BLOWN   140 14
TRAMS THAT PASS BLOWN RUDDILY DOWN THE NIGHT   146 13
TO BE BLOWN OUT TO LET NIGHT DOWSE THE SPARK   212   9
OF SEED-SPECKS KINDLED LATELY AND SOFTLY BLOWN   218 16
LIKE A FLAME BLOWN WHITER AND WHITER   281   9
REAL LITTLE DUST-PIG EARS ALMOST BLOWN AWAY   397 16
ON THE GARDENER WHOSE SHIRT'S BLOWN BACK   633 27
ACROSS THE WALLS AS THE BLINDS ARE BLOWN   *898 20
ACROSS THE WALLS AS THE BLINDS ARE BLOWN   *902   4
WAS BLOWN   *909 32
BLOWN FLAT INTO POINTS BY THE HEAVY WHITE DRAUGHT OF TH+ *956 5

BLOWS
THE BRANCHES INVISIBLE SEED OF EXPERIENCE BLOWS   89 30
OF MY YEARNING BLOWS OVER YOU   118 15
WHEN THE WIND BLOWS HER VEIL   133 26
WHEN THE WIND BLOWS HER VEIL   133 29
WHEN THE WIND BLOWS HER VEIL   133 32
THE WINDOW-SASH AS THE WEST WIND BLOWS   150 19
THROUGH THE POPLARS THE NIGHT-WIND BLOWS   163 22
NOT I NOT I BUT THE WIND THAT BLOWS THROUGH ME   250 13
DRIVEN BY INVISIBLE BLOWS   250 22
BLOWS THE MAGNETIC CURRENT IN FIERCE BLASTS   370 23
SOFTLY BLOWS OUT ITS THIN LITTLE MALE SIAMENS   535   3
WHEN A BLACK PRIEST BLOWS ON A CONCH   623 14
WHEN THE WIND BLOWS THE CRADLE SHALL ROCK   669   8
BUTTERFLY THE WIND BLOWS SEA-WARD STRONG BEYOND THE GAR+ 696 12
ALREADY IT IS OCTOBER AND THE WIND BLOWS STRONG TO THE + 696 15
BUT THE WIND BLOWS STRONG TO SEA-WARD WHITE BUTTERFLY C+ 696 19
AND BLOWS THAT ARE CARESSES   709 12
A WIND THAT BLOWS BACK AND FORTH   714 13
THAT BLOWS UPON IT THROUGH THE ORIFICES   717   9
AND THE AIR THAT BLOWS GOOD BREATH IN THE NOSTRILS OF P+ 792 14
WEARILY THROUGH THE OAKS THE NIGHT WIND BLOWS   857 22
IN TERRIBLE RHYTHM LIKE BLOWS THAT ARE STRUCK TILL THE + 879 2

BLOWSY
AND TACKLE THE BLOWSY BIG BLOW-FLY   458 11

BLUE
BELOW THE LAWN IN SOFT BLUE SHADE IS KEEPING   35 28
ALL BE SWEET WITH WHITE AND BLUE VIOLET   40 29
IN ONE BLUE STOOP FROM OUT THE SKIES   42 30
PIERCING THE BLUE WITH THEIR CROCKETED SPIRES   49 25
ON THE GREAT BLUE PALACE AT SYDENHAM LIGHTS STIR AND SH+ 52 18
WHITE ONES AND BLUE ONES FROM UNDER THE ORCHARD HEDGE   58   9
AT REST IN THE BLUE AND WONDER AT WHAT THEY MEAN   58 15
AN' WHITE AN' BLUE IN A RAVEL LIKE A CLOUT   61 12
MAY-BLOSSOM AND BLUE BIRD'S-EYE FLOWERS FALLING   65 15
COLOSSAL IN NEARNESS A BLUE POLICE SITS STILL ON HIS HO+ 66 9
TREMBLING BLUE IN HER PALLOR A TEAR THAT SURELY I HAVE + 67 16
SEEM TO BE MAKING OUT OF THE BLUE OF THE MORNING   72   6
TO-DAY A THICKET OF SUNSHINE WITH BLUE SMOKE-WREATHS   72 15
OH LABOURERS OH SHUTTLES ACROSS THE BLUE FRAME OF MORNI+ 73 8
THA CAN STARE AT ME WI' THY FIERCE BLUE EYES   79 11
AND THOUGH IT BE LOVE'S WET BLUE EYES THAT CRY   89 32
EVEN THERE I SEE A BLUE SPARK THAT WILL FLY   89 34
KILLING THE BLUE DUSK WITH HARSH SCENT UNNERVING   91 14
AND WAITING THROUGH THE BLUE   91 20
BLUE RECESSES   96 14
AM LIT BENEATH MY HEART WITH A HALF-MOON WEIRD AND BLUE 115 4
BLUE SHADOW WITHIN ME A PRESENCE WHICH LIVES CONTAINED 115 7
IS WASHED FROM THE BLUE   118 12
OVER THE BLUE OF THE DUCK-POND PLY   126 12

BLUE

THEIR DUST FROM THE BIRCH ON THE BLUE	126	31
ALL WITH A FLASH OF BLUE WHEN WILL SHE BE LEAVING	129	28
FRAIL AS A SCAR UPON THE PALE BLUE SKY	131	24
THE EDGE OF THE BLUE AND THE SUN STANDS UP TO SEE US GL+	132	28
JETS OF SPARKS IN FOUNTAINS OF BLUE COME LEAPING	136	6
RUNS INTO SPEED LIKE A DREAM THE BLUE OF THE STEEL	136	9
AND OUT OF THE INVISIBLE STREAMS OF BRIGHT BLUE DROPS	136	11
RAIN FROM THE SHOWERY HEAVENS AND BRIGHT BLUE CROPS	136	12
AND ALL THE MANIFOLD BLUE AMAZING EYES	136	14
LIKE A GLOWING BRAZIER FAINTLY BLUE OF FLAME	151	25
UNDER AN OAK WHOSE YELLOW BUDS DOT THE PALE BLUE SKY	152	27
THAT SAVES THE BLUE GRAIN OF ETERNAL FIRE	161	3
WHEN THE BLUE MIST UNCLOSES	178	14
AGAIN IN HER BLUE BLUE MANTLE	201	5
WALLS OF BLUE SHADOW	204	14
AND THE SKYLARK TWINKLES BLUE	216	10
ALL OVER THE DIM CORN'S MOTION AGAINST THE BLUE	221	25
AGAINST THE HARD AND PALE BLUE EVENING SKY	225	1
AMONG THE PINK AND BLUE	244	5
HE THINKS THE WHOLE BLUE SKY	244	29
IS MUCH LESS THAN THE BIT OF BLUE EGG	244	30
WERE RANKED TO BLUE BATTLE AND YOU AND I	248	22
IN HEAVEN IN BLUE BLUE HEAVEN	307	5
DARK BLUE ANEMONES	309	12
ASH FLUTTERS FLOCCULENT LIKE DOWN ON A BLUE WAN FLEDGEL+	330	8
THIS QUEER DROSS SHAWL OF BLUE AND VERMILION	369	22
HE RUNS IN THE SNOW LIKE A BIT OF BLUE METAL	375	3
YOU COPPER-SULPHATE BLUE BIRD	375	33
HIGH HIGH UP IN FLAKES SHIMMERING FLAKES OF BLUE FIRE	391	18
HAUNTED BLUE BUSH	394	19
DARK GROW THE SPRUCE-TREES BLUE IS THE BALSAM WATER	401	2
EARTH SMOKES BLUE	467	8
IS THERE A SAPPHIRE OF MUTUAL TRUST A BLUE SPARK	478	6
CLEAR AND FLOWERY BLUE	530	4
AND YOU WILL BE AGAIN THEREFORE WHY LOOK BLUE	577	12
AND BURN BLUE AND COLD LIKE THE FLAME IN A MINER'S LAMP	619	5
TURNING THE BLUE WHEELS OF YOUR OWN HEAVEN	643	21
AND THE BALSAM-PINES THAT ARE BLUE WITH THE GREY-BLUE B+	647	2
LITTLE BOY BLUE	659	5
THE YOUNG TRAM-CONDUCTOR IN A BLUE UNIFORM TO HIMSELF F+	672	8
AND LIFTED HIS FACE UP WITH BLUE EYES LOOKING AT THE EL+	672	9
SEE GOD IS BORN HE IS BLUE HE IS DEEP BLUE HE IS FOREVE+	682	23
NOR CEASE TO BE BLUE NOR IN THE DAWN	688	2
IN THE BLUE DEEP BED OF THE SEA	694	14
RIBBED AND TORCH-LIKE WITH THEIR BLAZE OF DARKNESS SPRE+	697	7
BLACK LAMPS FROM THE HALLS OF DIS BURNING DARK BLUE	697	9
GIVING OFF DARKNESS BLUE DARKNESS AS DEMETER'S PALE LAM+	697	10
LET ME GUIDE MYSELF WITH THE BLUE FORKED TORCH OF THIS +	697	14
DOWN THE DARKER AND DARKER STAIRS WHERE BLUE IS DARKENE+	697	15
AND IN THE SHADOW OF THE SUN THE SNOW IS BLUE SO BLUE-A+	708	28
LIFE HAS ITS PLACE OF BLUE DAY ALOFT	711	1
IT GONE BY OUR FARM TO THE MOUNTAINS THAT STAND BACK BL+	732	7
AND THEIR UNIFORMS ARE THE SAME OF WHITE AND BLUE	732	13
THREADS OF BLUE WIND FAR AND DOWN THE ROAD	732	22
BUT HIS HANDKERCHIEF IS WHITE WITH A BROAD BLUE BORDER	733	28
AND CALLED TO HIS HORSES AND HIS STRONG BLUE BODY	735	14
TO THE TRENCHES I SEE AGAIN A FACE WITH BLUE EYES	742	6
BLUE AT THE CORE AND WHEN IS WHETTED	773	3
BLUE DAYLIGHT SINKS IN MY HAIR	802	26
BLUE IS THE BREATH OF QUETZALCOATL	808	18
BLUE IS THE DEEP SKY AND THE DEEP WATER	808	24
INTO BLUE DAY PAST HUITZILOPOCHTLI	810	10
WHEN THE BLUE WIND OF QUETZALCOATL	811	20
THE BLUE ANEMONE WITH A DARK CORE	814	1
BUDS A BLUE ANEMONE STILL BLUER	814	14
BRAGGADOCCIOS AROUND THE BLUE RIMS OF THE WORLD	814	30
HIDDEN BLUE WITH THE BLUENESS OF ONE MORE DAY	815	9
WHICH IS BLUE WITH THE BLUENESS OF ONE MORE DAY	815	18
DARK BLUE THE WHOLE DESIRE LEAPS	819	24
WHERE THE BLUE CRABS RUSTLED IN QUEST OF HER AIMLESS WI+	864	6
IN THE DEEP CART-RUTS GLEAMED THROUGH THE BLUE OF THE D+	864	30
THE BOYS FROM THE HOME BLUE AND INANIMATE	866	2
UNDER AN OAK TREE WHOSE YELLOW BUDS DOTTED THE PALE BLU+	866	23
HIS BLUE SHIRT GLIMMERING ON THE WATER AMONG THE SHADOW+	867	29
WHEN I SEE THE SKY'S BLUE DARKEN	869	4
MY MOTHER HAD BLUE EYES	869	5
WHEN THE SKY'S BLUE DARKENS AT NIGHTFALL	869	8
AH BUT MY MOTHER HAD BLUE EYES	870	17
LIKE A GLOWING BRAZIER FAINTLY BLUE OF FLAME	874	4
ME AS A DARK BLUE WATER BETWEEN THE HILLS	874	28
ALWAYS BEFORE YOU GO THE HEAVY BLUE	875	12
TO THE VAST OF SPACE WHERE BRIGHTNESS RACES THE BLUE	875	14
OF SEED TO LOSE MYSELF IN THE BODY OF THIS BLUE	876	19
BLUE DARKNESSES OF WONDER THAT HOLD ALL	876	27
HOW CAN I TEACH YOU WHEN YOUR BLUE	*894	1
BLUE SILKEN SKY BEFORE THEY BEND ANEW	*895	4
ON THE UPLIFTED BLUE PALACE LIGHT POOLS STIR AND SHINE	*905	7
WHERE THE GLASS IS DOMED BY THE BLUE SOFT DAY	*905	8
OF BLUE PALACE ALOFT THERE AMONG THE MISTY INDEFINITE D+	*905	13
THEY WAS WILD ONES WHITE AND BLUE I COULD TELL	*910	17
RAVELLED BLUE AND WHITE WARM FOR A BIT	*911	28
THA CAN STARE AT ME WI' THY FIERCE BLUE EYES	*921	7
AN' THAT'S THE DARK BLUE TIE I BOUGHT 'IM	*923	14
THROUGH THE WHOLE BLUE SKY AND THE NOON	*937	11
FRAIL AS A SCAR UPON THE PALE BLUE SKY	*937	23
ALL OVER THE CORN'S DIM MOTION AGAINST THE BLUE	*945·11	
BLUE AND DARK	*954	17
BLUE JOY OF MY SOUL	*954	23
YOUR DARK BLUE GLOOM IS SO NOBLE	*954	25
SINCE I EMBARKED ON YOUR DARK BLUE FRINGES	*954	28
IN THE DARK BLUE GLOOM	*955	2
IT IS SO BLUE IT IS SO DARK	*955	7
DOWN THE BLUE DEPTHS OF MOUNTAIN GENTIAN FLOWERS	*955	19
DOWN THE DARK BLUE PATH	*955	22
RIBBED HELLISH FLOWERS ERECT WITH THEIR BLAZE OF DARKNE+	*956	4
BLACK LAMPS FROM THE HALLS OF DIS SMOKING DARK BLUE	*956	7
GIVING OFF DARKNESS BLUE DARKNESS UPON DEMETER'S YELLOW+	*956	8

BLUE

LET ME GUIDE MYSELF WITH THE BLUE FORKED TORCH OF A FLO+	*956	11
DOWN THE DARKER AND DARKER STAIRS WHERE BLUE IS DARKENE+	*956	12

BLUE-ALOOF

AND IN THE SHADOW OF THE SUN THE SNOW IS BLUE SO BLUE-A+	708	28

BLUE-ARSED

BLUE-ARSED WITH THE MONEY-BRUISE	485	25

BLUEBELL

OH IN THE SPRING THE BLUEBELL BOWS HIM DOWN FOR VERY	272	9

BLUEBELLS

THE UNCLOUDED SEAS OF BLUEBELLS HAVE EBBED AND PASSED	854	1
ON THE LITTLE BANK WHERE BLUEBELLS DROOP	887	10

BLUE-BLACK

LOOK HOW BLACK HOW BLUE-BLACK HOW GLOBED IN EGYPTIAN	286	8

BLUE-BRILLIANT

AND STRUTS BLUE-BRILLIANT OUT OF THE FAR EAST	371	2

BLUE-COPED

AH THERE WITHIN THAT BLUE-COPED WELL AH THERE	877	1

BLUE-GLEAMED

THE BLUE-GLEAMED DRAKE STEMS PROUD	126	15

BLUE-GRASS

EVEN THE BLUE-GRASS BLOSSOMS	587	6

BLUE-GREY

AND UNDERNEATH A BLUE-GREY TWILIGHT HEAPED	135	5
UNDER THE BLUE-GREY TWILIGHT HEAPED	*939	5

BLUE-HOT

IN THE WILD DAYS WHEN LIFE WAS SLIDING WHIRLWINDS BLUE-+	529	23

BLUE JAY

THE BLUE JAY WITH A CREST ON HIS HEAD	375	1
IT'S THE BLUE JAY LAUGHING AT US	375	20
IT'S THE BLUE JAY JEERING AT US BIBS	375	21
THE BLUE JAY PACES ROUND THE CABIN VERY BUSY PICKING UP	375	23

BLUENESS

STAND IN THEIR BLUENESS FLASHING WITH SNOW AND THE	209	24
THE DAWN COMES UP WITH A GLITTER AND A BLUENESS AND I S+	509	25
SHIMMERS IN A STREAM OF BLUENESS AND LONG-TRESSED	530	6
AND THE BALSAM-PINES THAT ARE BLUE WITH THE GREY-BLUE B+	647	2
OH WHAT IN YOU CAN ANSWER TO THIS BLUENESS	684	3
DARKENING THE DAY-TIME TORCH-LIKE WITH THE SMOKING BLUE+	697	4
DOWN THE DARKER AND DARKER STAIRS WHERE BLUE IS DARKENE+	697	15
HIDDEN BLUE WITH THE BLUENESS OF ONE MORE DAY	815	9
WHICH IS BLUE WITH THE BLUENESS OF ONE MORE DAY	815	18
WITH LIGHT AND LUXURIOUS BLUENESS	*895	8
OF BLUENESS MINGLED WITH A FUME OF GOLD	*939	14
THEY HAVE ADDED BLUENESS TO BLUENESS UNTIL	*954	21
DARKENING THE DAYTIME TORCH-LIKE WITH THE SMOKING BLUEN+	*956	2
DOWN THE DARKER AND DARKER STAIRS WHERE BLUE IS DARKENE+	*956	12

BLUER

BUDS A BLUE ANEMONE STILL BLUER	814	14

BLUE-SKY

BUT THERE WITHIN THE BLUE-SKY RIMS THAT COPE	876	34

BLUE-SMOKING

TORCH-FLOWER OF THE BLUE-SMOKING DARKNESS DARK-BLUE DAZE	697	8
TORCH-FLOWERS OF THE BLUE-SMOKING DARKNESS PLUTO'S DARK+	*956	6

BLUE-TINTED

WHERE THE TREES RISE LIKE CLIFFS PROUD AND BLUE-TINTED +	66	5

BLUEY-BROWN

OH THE HANDSOME BLUEY-BROWN BODIES THEY MIGHT JUST AS W+	625	19

BLUFF

AND SEE WHO WINS IN THIS SLY GAME OF BLUFF	333	8
AND THEIR LAST REFINEMENT BLUFF A HATE DISGUISED	644	12

BLUISH

AND THE BLUISH MOUNTAINS BEYOND WOULD BE CRUSHED OUT	205	4

BLUNDERING

BLUNDERING MORE INSANE AND LEAPING IN THROBS TO CLUTCH +	343	20

BLUNDERS

ARE SINNERS STRANGE THE BEE THAT BLUNDERS	223	19

BLUNT-PROWED

HIS WIMPLE HIS BLUNT-PROWED FACE	360	1

BLUR

WOULD BLUR NO WHISPER SPOIL NO EXPRESSON	250	27

BLURRED

OF OLD SPENT LIVES LINGER BLURRED AND WARM	173	18
OF OLD INEFFECTUAL LIVES LINGER BLURRED AND WARM	*906	12
OF OLD INEFFECTUAL LIVES LINGER BLURRED AND WARM	*908	6

BLUSHED

AND THEY BLUSHED THEY GIGGLED THEY SNIGGERED THEY	578	7

BLUSHES
    HIDE YOUR QUAINTLY SCARLET BLUSHES   43   2
    THE NEW MOON IN COOL HEIGHT ABOVE THE BLUSHES   467   9
    BLUSHES AND FLAUNTS IN THE SUNSHINE ABOVE   858   7

BLUSHING
    SHE WILL START WHEN SHE SEES ME AND BLUSHING SPREAD OUT+   *940 16

BOARD
    HE FLINGS THE RABBIT SOFT ON THE TABLE BOARD   43 22
    ARE ON THE BOARD ARE OVER-FILLED   177   6
    STRAIGHT AS A BOARD ON THE BOUGH LOOKING DOWN LIKE SOME   385 19
    AS OF THE MASTER SITTING AT THE BOARD   700 14

BOARDS
    BOARDS INTO THE DAY   384 20

BOARD-SCHOOLS
    IN THE HOT-BEDS OF THE BOARD-SCHOOLS AND THE FILM   644   7

BOARD-SCHOOL
    AND GAVE A BOARD-SCHOOL EDUCATION NEWSPAPERS AND THE   630 24
    AND A BOARD-SCHOOL BRAIN STUFFED UP WITH THE HA'PENNY   630 30
    OH CARCASS WITH A BOARD-SCHOOL MIND AND A HA'PENNY NEWS+   631   3

BOASTS
    AND IN PRIVATE BOASTS HIS EXPLOITS EVEN LOUDER IF YOU A+   432 30
    THE TURNED WORM BOASTS I COPULATE   433   4
    NOR THE DEAR OLD MATER WHO SO PROUDLY BOASTS   458 24

BOAT
    DRIFTS MY BOAT WISTFULLY LAPSING AFTER   53 18
    PEER ANXIOUSLY FORTH AS IF FOR A BOAT TO CARRY THEM OUT+   71 26
    LIKE THE PROW OF A BOAT HIS HEAD LAID BACK LIKE THE STE+   155 20
    TO WHERE A MAN IN A HEAVING BOAT   201 19
    A DARK BOAT THROUGH THE GLOOM AND WHITHER   209   2
    THE BOAT HAS GONE   209   6
    LIKE A MAN IN A BOAT ON VERY CLEAR DEEP WATER SPACE FRI+   222 24
    BOAT DOWN THERE ALL ALONE   226 18
    BUT SITTING IN A BOAT ON THE ZELLER LAKE   337 28
    HE THREW THE FISH IN THE BOAT   802 10
    IN A BOAT ON A ROUGH SEA WHEN WE WERE ALL NEARLY SEA-SI+   842 13
    AND IN MY FRAGILE AWKWARD BOAT BETWEEN   875 28
    DRIFTS MY BOAT WISTFULLY LAPSING AFTER   *906   9
    SHE LOVES ME AND I BLOW A LITTLE BOAT   *943 15
    HAVING NO BOAT TO LAUNCH UPON THE SHAKEN SOUNDLESS   *957 30
    THE OARS HAVE GONE FROM THE BOAT AND THE LITTLE DISHES   *959 29
    GONE GONE AND THE BOAT DISSOLVES LIKE PEARL   *959 30

BOATMAN
    WAITING WAITING TILL AT LAST THE ANCIENT BOATMAN WITH T+   *958 11

BOAT-ROOF
    THERE AMONG THE FLOWERS OF THE BOAT-ROOF   868   3

BOATS
    FLOAT LIKE BOATS ON A RIVER WHILE OTHER   217 29
    THEIR TWO SHELLS LIKE DOMED BOATS BUMPING   361 22
    FLOAT LIKE BOATS ON A RIVER WAITING   *943 12

BOB
    WHITE FLOWERS IN THE WIND BOB UP AND DOWN   *912 26

BOBBED
    WITH HAIR THAT WAS BOBBED SO EARLY   834 15

BOBBIES
    SIX FAT SMALLER BOBBIES ARE THE INQUISITORS MINOR   633 16
    WITH A SET OF CANKERED MAGISTRATES AND BUSY-BUSY BOBBIES   634   8

BOBBING
    WETLY BOBBING AND DRIFTING AWAY ON OUR SIGHT   146 22
    AND BOBBING HIS THICK DARK CREST ABOUT THE SNOW AS IF   375 26

BOCCACCIO
    O MY BOCCACCIO O HOW GOES YOUR PRETTY TALE   633   1
    WHO'VE DECIDED THAT BOCCACCIO MUST BURN   633 17

BODIES
    THE HIDDEN BODIES MATING EVERYWHERE   .   126 21
    THEY HAVE NO HANDS THEY HAVE NO BODIES ALL   174   1
    AND THE BODIES OF MEN AND WOMEN ARE MOLTEN MATTER OF DR+   176   2
    AND OUR BODIES MOLTEN DROPS OF DREAM-BLOOD THAT SWIRL A+   176   7
    THE MURDERED BODIES OF YOUTHS AND MEN IN HEAPS   258   5
    BODIES IN THE IMAGE OF THEIR SEVERAL KINDS   376   4
    COMPELLED TO ADMIRE THE BRIGHT RHYTHMS OF MOVING BODIES   445 25
    BODIES   445 27
    THEY KNOW THEY HAVE NO BODIES THAT COULD PLAY AMONG THE   446   2
    FROM THE BUSY BODIES OF PEOPLE   451 19
    THE KEY OF LIFE ON THE BODIES OF MEN   461 23
    O YOU WITH MENTAL BODIES STAY A LITTLE DISTANCE FROM ME   468 25
    AND PASSION WILL MAKE OUR BODIES TAUT WITH POWER   482   3
    ON TO THEIR POOR DERANGED BODIES   500 20
    AND EMERGE AS SQUEAKY GLOBULES WITH NO BODIES TO SPEAK +   501   1
    LEFT IN THE HEFTY BODIES   537   5
    OUR BODIES BEFORE WE DIE   584 10
    GIVE US BACK OUR BODIES FOR A DAY FOR A SINGLE DAY   585   3
    GIVE US BACK OUR BODIES FOR ONE DAY   585   8
    REDDENS STILL MORE ON THE BLATANT BODIES OF THESE ALL-B+   625 11
    OH THE HANDSOME BLUEY-BROWN BODIES THEY MIGHT JUST AS W+   625 19
    NONE IN THEIR LITTLE THROATS OR CLASS-ROOM BODIES   657 14
    AND NOW THAT THE MOON WHO GIVES MEN GLISTENING BODIES   688 10
    BODIES AND PRESENCES HERE AND NOW CREATURES WITH A FOOT+   689 23
    AND DREAMS ARE ONLY DRAWN FROM THE BODIES THAT ARE   691   8
    ALREADY OUR BODIES ARE FALLEN BRUISED BADLY BRUISED   718   3
    WE ARE DYING WE ARE DYING PIECEMEAL OUR BODIES ARE DYING   718 17
    WE GIVE UP O LORD OUR BODIES TO DEADLY HATE   743 11
    OUR BODIES TO THE EXPIATION LORD   743 16

BODIES'
    FORGET EACH OTHER AND THE BRUISE OF OUR BODIES' CLASH   91   6
    WE EXPIATE IN OUR BODIES' RENTS AND RAGS   743   7

BODILESS
    AND LISTEN TO BODILESS NOISES   558 23
    BODILESS AS WE LIVED   584 20
    THAT PURE BEING IS BODILESS   689 16

BODILY
    BE BODILY THERE   813   2

BODKIN
    WITH A BARE BODKIN   717 11
    WITH A BARE BODKIN   *957   2

BODKINS
    WITH DAGGERS BODKINS BULLETS MAN CAN MAKE   717 12
    WITH DAGGERS BODKINS BULLETS MAN CAN MAKE   *957   3

BODY
    LIKE MOONBEAMS KISSING YOU BUT THE BODY OF ME   87 20
    YOUR BODY WITH THEIR NIPPLE-THRUST UNTIL   91 15
    WHITE BODY DRIPS   96 21
    ME OVER AND DRIVE FROM OUT OF MY BODY THE DEEP   98 24
    BODY TO BODY I COULD NOT   111 18
    LIKE A CANDLE-FLAME ON THIS BODY BUT I ENCLOSE   115   6
    OF MY BODY AND LOOSE THE ESSENTIAL FLOOD   117 23
    OF YOUR SOFT WHITE BODY AS LIGHTNING   117 31
    AND SEEING MY CAST-OFF BODY LYING LIKE LUMBER   134 12
    AS THE BODY CORRODES WHEN DEATH INVADES   142 23
    OF MY BODY SLOWLY BEHIND   147   3
    PLANT OF YOUR BODY TO ME YOU LOOKED ERE SPRUNG   156 20
    HIS BODY DOWN IN WEIGHT TO REST IN YOU   158 11
    ON YOUR BODY THE BEATEN ANVIL   168 21
    WE ARE AND BODY OF SLEEP LET IT NEVER BE SAID   194 28
    HAVE SAID THAT I THIS MOTE IN THE BODY OF SLEEP   195 18
    LAPPED LIKE A BODY CLOSE UPON A SLEEP   195 27
    WITH ACHE OF DREAMS THAT BODY FORTH THE SLEEP   195 30
    WITHIN MY BODY CRY OUT TO THE DREAMING SOUL   195 32
    COME TO ME HERE AND LAY YOUR BODY BY MINE   211 26
    THE THING WITH MY BODY THAT WOULD GO ON LIVING   214 28
    CHRIST ON THE CROSS HIS BEAUTIFUL YOUNG MAN'S BODY   225   5
    AND MY NAKED BODY STANDING ON YOUR GRAVE   233 14
    ON THE BODY OF FIERCE DESIRE   242 11
    IN THE WINDOW HIS BODY BLACK FUR AND THE SOUND OF   243 24
    THE BODY OF A MAN   254 19
    SHE SAID TO ME WHAT AN INSTRUMENT YOUR BODY   254 24
    BODY   257   8
    OWN BODY   257 22
    RISEN NOT BORN AGAIN BUT RISEN BODY THE SAME AS BEFORE   258 29
    I AM BURROWING MY BODY INTO THE SOIL   259 32
    BETWEEN THE BODY OF LIFE AND ME   262 14
    HAS NOT SO MUCH OF STRENGTH AS THE BODY OF ONE WOMAN   263   2
    OF THE SUAVE SENSITIVE BODY THE HUNGER FOR THIS   263 16
    I HAVE EATEN AND DRUNK AND WARMED AND CLOTHED MY BODY   264   1
    THE VERY BODY'S BODY CRYING OUT   264 10
    AND MY BODY'S BODY WAS APPEASED   265   9
    CALLED THE ALMOND BONE IN THE BODY THE LAST BONE OF THE+   303   9
    WAS THE SEED OF THE BODY AND FROM THE GRAVE IT COULD GR+   303 10
    CALLED THE ALMOND BONE IN THE BODY THE LAST BONE OF THE+   303   9
    WITH A BODY LIKE SPRAY DAWN-TENDER AND LOOKING ABOUT   306 30
    THAT UNNATURAL BARREL BODY THAT LONG GHOUL NOSE   338   8
    AND BROWN FURRY BODY   345 32
    BODY   349 17
    AND SO ON TILL THE LAST PLASM OF MY BODY WAS MELTED BACK   365 20
    AND YOUR BLACK LITTLE BODY BOUNCING AND WRIGGLING   396   5
    ALL YOUR GAME LITTLE BODY DUST-SMOOTH LIKE A LITTLE PIG   397 26
    BECAUSE HIS BODY CAN'T WAKE UP   407 21
    ON THE SEA WITH NO MESSAGE IN IT AND THE BODY SUBMERGED   428 11
    SPLENDID BODY ON THE ROPE   444 32
    WHEN MODERN PEOPLE SEE THE CARNAL BODY DAUNTLESS AND   445 31
    THE BODY OF ITSELF IS CLEAN BUT THE CAGED MIND   463 19
    THE BODY INTO IT LET US STAY APART   469   5
    THAT MY BODY NEED NOT ME   469 15
    THE BODY OF ANOTHER UNTO MINE   469 27
    THE BODY   471 28
    AND IN THE BODY WE CAN ONLY MENTALLY FORNICATE   472   8
    AND THEN TURN ROUND AND EMBRACE THE EXTANT BODY OF LIFE   482   4
    MY BODY LIKES ITS DINNER AND THE WARM SUN BUT OTHERWISE+   501 19
    AND THAT SENT THE BLOOD RUSHING TO THE SURFACE OF THE B+   502   7
    TO THE ATOM TO THE BODY OF IMMORTAL CHAOS   505   4
    BODY AND SOUL   546   1
    FROM YOUR OWN BODY SAVED YOU FROM LIVING YOUR OWN   585 14
    THAT POSSESS THE WHOLE BODY   627 19
    SUCCESSFULLY CASTRATING THE BODY POLITIC   627 27
    THAT DABBLES ITS BODY IN ME   628   5
    THEY STOLE YOUR BODY FROM YOU AND LEFT YOU AN ANIMATED   630 26
    BODY OF MANKIND   632   4
    BODY   642 23
    WITH HIS EARS PRICKED AND HIS BODY WINCING   645 19
    AH THE GODS THE SWAYING BODY OF GOD   651 17
    BEGETS A MURDERER IN HIS OWN BODY   653   4
    WITH A BODY AND WITH NEEDS AND A LOVELY SPIRIT   689 30
    EVERYTHING THAT HAS BEAUTY HAS A BODY AND IS A BODY   691   6
    UNLESS GOD HAS A BODY HOW CAN HE HAVE A VOICE   691 10
    GOD IS THE GREAT URGE THAT HAS NOT YET FOUND A BODY   691 15
    EVEN THE RAINBOW HAS A BODY   692   1
    BODY   694 20
    TILL ALL IS SOUNDLESS AND SENSELESS A TREMENDOUS BODY O+   698 22
    AND IS MY BODY OCEAN OCEAN   705 14
    AND IN THE BRUISED BODY THE FRIGHTENED SOUL   717   7
    PIECEMEAL THE BODY DIES AND THE TIMID SOUL   718 12
    NOW LAUNCH THE SMALL SHIP NOW AS THE BODY DIES   719   1
    AND EVERYTHING IS GONE THE BODY IS GONE   719 20
    THE FLOOD SUBSIDES AND THE BODY LIKE A WORN SEA-SHELL   720 12
    AND SILVERY CITY OF THE NOW HOPELESS BODY   721 12
    AND CALLED TO HIS HORSES AND HIS STRONG BLUE BODY   735 14

BODY
    HOW I HATE MYSELF THIS BODY WHICH IS ME   741   1
    WHEELING TO LACERATE AND RIP UP THIS MY BODY   741 13
    FOR I HATE THIS BODY WHICH IS SO DEAR TO ME   741 16
    MY BODY GLAD AS THE BELL OF A FLOWER   742 32
    SHALL I OFFER TO HIM MY BROTHERLY BODY TO KILL   743 19
    WHY IF YOU SAW MY LIMBS HOW THEY SHINE ON MY BODY   755   6
    HEAL ME FOR BODY AND SOUL I AM NOT WELL   759 15
    DON'T TAKE THE BLOOD OF MY BODY   767   7
    ROSY BEST OF THE BLOOD GONE OUT OF THE BODY   767 22
    THERE IS A BREAST OF A VAST AND UNKNOWN BODY   784   9
    LET HIM HAVE NO ANIMAL WALK ON HIS BODY NOR THROUGH THE+   791 24
    FOR MEN UPON THE BODY OF THE EARTH ARE LIKE LICE   793   1
    WITH MY REDNESS STAINING THE BODY OF THE DARK   804 16
    WITH HIS REDNESS STAINING THE BODY OF THE NIGHT   805 24
    SOUL AND BODY BONE AND BLOOD   824 13
    BUT THE LIMBS OF MAN LONG TO FOLD AND CLOSE UPON THE LI+   834   4
    BUT PRESSING HER SUPPLE BODY INTO THE COOL DARK LEAVES   864 11
    HIS BODY PULSING WITH PLAY   867 23
    HIS FULL FINE BODY BENDING AND URGING LIKE THE STRESS O+   867 24
    PASSES THE EVER-CHANGING JOY OF HIS ACTIVE BODY   868   4
    ROUND HIS BRIGHT JOYFUL BODY   868 12
    OF SEED TO LOSE MYSELF IN THE HUE OF THIS BLUE   876 19
    HIS BODY THAT DOES SHAKE LIKE THE WIRE OF A HARP   877 13
    AND WHEN I SEE THE THICK WHITE BODY OF TRAIN-SMOKE BREAK   883 16
    OWNING MY SUPPLE BODY A RARE GLAD THING SUPREMELY GOOD   *892 11
    ALL MY BODY SPRINGS ALIVE   *893 12
    FLIES LIKE A WILD THING ACROSS MY BODY   *893 15
    UNDER THE WILD STRANGE TYRANNY OF MY BODY   *893 27
    BACK FROM MY BEAUTIFUL LONELY BODY   *893 31
    AN' 'ER BODY FAIR SHOOK AGAIN   *910 13
    THY BODY FROM ITS TERRORS AWKWARD LEASH   *927 25
    YOUR BODY QUAILED AT MY STROKE   *928 13
    LIKE A CANDLE FLAME ON THIS BODY BUT I ENSHRINE   *930   6
    COMES UP UNNAMED FROM HER BODY AND SURELY   *945   5
    IT IS EASY TO BE PUSHED OUT OF THE SILVERY CITY OF THE +   *957 20

BODY'S
    FROM YOUR BODY'S DEADNESS AND DROSS   112   7
    THE VERY BODY'S BODY CRYING OUT   264 10
    AND MY BODY'S BODY WAS APPEASED   265   9
    FROM YOUR BODY'S TERRORS AND DROSS   *928 27
    MANTLE OF THE BODY'S STILL MORTAL MEMORIES   *957 11
    THAT LIE OUTSIDE THE SILVERY WALLS OF OUR BODY'S BUILDE+   *957 17
    WRAPPED IN THE DARK-RED MANTLE OF THE BODY'S MEMORIES   *958 31
    OF THE BODY'S MEMORIES SLIPS AND IS ABSORBED   *959 25

BOG-END'S
    YOU AMID THE BOG-END'S YELLOW INCANTATION   90 13

BOG-END
    I CAN SMELL THE BOG-END GORGEOUS IN ITS BREATHLESS   90   7
    THE BUTTERCUP BOG-END WHERE THE FLOWERS ROSE UP   90 20

BOG-FLAME
    ME YOUR SHADOW ON THE BOG-FLAME FLOWERY MAY-BLOBS   90 15

BOILED
    OR THEY BOILED AND THEY FUMED IN FURY THEY SNEERED   578   9

BOILING
    LIKE A BOILING POT THE POND CRACKLED WITH HAPPINESS   206 30
    BOILING BLACK DEATH   586 28

BOILS
    AND THE SAME FIRE THAT BOILS WITHIN THIS BALL   89   1
    FROM THE FIRE THAT BOILS IN THE MOLTEN HEART OF THE WOR+   782 15

BOISTEROUS
    OH BOISTEROUS THE CUCKOO SHOUTS FORESTALLING   65 27

BOLD
    AS BOLD AS A ROBIN IT'S MUCH HE CARES   79   7
    AS BOLD AS A ROBIN IT'S MUCH HE CARES   *921   3

BOLDLY
    THAT PUT TO SEA AND BOLDLY SINK ARMADAS   542   9

BOLSHEVISM
    DON'T YOU SEE HOW YOU MAKE BOLSHEVISM INEVITABLE   664 13

BOLSHEVIST
    I LONG TO BE A BOLSHEVIST   315 22
    A BOLSHEVIST A SALVIA-FACE   315 25
    TO BE A BOLSHEVIST   317 14
    TO HIM WORSE THAN A BOLSHEVIST JEW OR AN UTTER   576   8
    THE BOURGEOIS PRODUCES THE BOLSHEVIST INEVITABLY   663   9
    AND THE BOLSHEVIST ASSERTS THAT BY HUMAN RIGHT NO MAN S+   663 14
    BOURGEOIS COWARDICE PRODUCES BOLSHEVIST IMPUDENCE   663 18
    THE BOLSHEVIST GETS OPENLY MORE IMPUDENT ALSO KNOWING H+   663 22
    IF I HAVE TO CHOOSE BETWEEN THE BOURGEOIS AND THE BOLSH+   664   5
    ONLY MORE INEVITABLY THE BOLSHEVIST   664   9
    SINCE THE BOURGEOIS IS THE DIRECT CAUSE OF THE BOLSHEVI+   664 10
    BOURGEOIS AND BOLSHEVIST   664 18
    THE BOURGEOIS AND THE BOLSHEVIST ARE BOTH QUITE BLIND   665 19
    BUT AMONG THE BOURGEOIS AND THE BOLSHEVIST BOUNDERS   665 22
    THOSE WHO ARE NEITHER BOURGEOIS NOR BOLSHEVIST BUT TRUE+   666   2
    THE STONE-BLIND BOURGEOIS AND THE STONE-BLIND BOLSHEVIST   666   8

BOLSHEVISTICALLY
    NEVER BOLSHEVISTICALLY   317 25

BOLSHEVISTS
    BOLSHEVISTS   313   5
    ALAS THE SUNDAY COATS OF SICILIAN BOLSHEVISTS   313 34
    SICILIAN BOLSHEVISTS   314 10
    BOLSHEVISTS   315   7
    IF THERE WERE SALVIA-SAVAGE BOLSHEVISTS   315 10

BOLSHEVISTS
    THESE BOLSHEVISTS   316 32
    UPON THE BREASTS OF LOUTISH BOLSHEVISTS   317   2
    DAMNED LOUTISH BOLSHEVISTS   317   3

BOMBS
    AND THEY SEND ARROWS OF ANGER BULLETS AND BOMBS OF FRUS+   *958   6

BOND
    I'LL SAY YOUR BOND OF UGLINESS IS VAIN   72 23
    IS THERE A BOND OF BLOODSHED BETWEEN YOU   374 20

BONDS
    ME NOW FROM THE STUNTING BONDS OF MY CHASTITY   180 17
    BY MY OWN BONDS OF BLOOD AND MUSIC-LESS   884 18

BONE
    SINCE FROM OUT OF MY BLOOD AND BONE   118   2
    IN MY FLESH AND MY BONE AND FORAGES INTO ME   128 16
    THE WHITE BARE BONE OF OUR SHAMS   145   7
    AND KNOW THE DEAD CHRIST WEIGHING ON MY BONE   226 12
    I AM CHILLED TO THE BONE   229 28
    I AM PURE LIKE BONE   230   3
    A MAN BALANCES BONE UNTO BONE   251   4
    CALLED THE ALMOND BONE IN THE BODY THE LAST BONE OF THE+   303   9
    AND THROUGH THE BONE   354 27
    AND SUDDENLY LOWERING HIS HEAD THE WHORLS OF BONE AND   381 16
    THE SOFT WELLING OF BLOOD INVINCIBLE EVEN BEYOND BONE OR   383   4
    METAL OF BONE   383   5
    STRONGER THAN MULTIPLICITY OF BONE ON BONE   383   9
    ELEPHANT ADVANCING HIS FRONTAL BONE HIS TRUNK CURLED   387   7
    WILL BE BONE   797 20
    WHITE OF THE BONE   804 11
    BONE IN THE BLOOD   804 12
    WHITE OF THE BONE   805 19
    BONE IN THE BLOOD   805 20
    AND WHITE AS BONE   806 24
    THE BONE IS WHITE AND ALIVE   808 27
    IS WASHED BONE   810 18
    SOUL AND BODY BONE AND BLOOD   824 13

BONES
    AND BONES AND TWIGS AND A PERILOUS ASCENT   402 14
    LEAVING A FEW BONES   414 24
    WHICH ROTS THE BRAIN THE BLOOD THE BONES THE STONES THE   487 16
    THE OLD DOG'S GREENEST BONES   492 12
    OH THEY ARE GRIST FOR THE MILLS OF GOD THEIR BONES GROU+   614 23
    AND THE DULL BREAKING OF BONES   640 12
    EVEN THEIR BONES SHALL CRUMBLE   792   8
    THEY SHALL CRUNCH YOUR BONES   796 26
    AND DART HIS ELECTRIC NEEDLES INTO YOUR BONES AND CURDL+   797 10
    AND BUILDING MY NEST OF PEACE IN YOUR BONES   802   4

BONFIRE
    ARE A BONFIRE OF ONENESS ME FLAME FLUNG LEAPING ROUND Y+   245 24

BONFIRES
    THIS SPRING AS IT COMES BURSTS UP IN BONFIRES GREEN   116   1
    SO WE ROAR UP LIKE BONFIRES OF VITALITY   440   7

BONNIE
    THE BONNIE BONNIE BOURGEOIS GOES A-WHORING UP BACK   432 22
    BUT BONNIE AND BRIGHT WERE THE CHICKENS   *933 10

BONNY
    BE ALL YOURSELF ONE BONNY BURNING COAL   151 14
    IT'S SUCH A BONNY BABY A BABY A BABY   570 16
    TO FEED THE BONNY BABY AND KEEP ITS TARA DRY   570 19
    HE'S LIKE A BONNY ROSY SEA-CRAB WITH HEALTHY CLAWS   830 19
    BE ALL YOURSELF ONE BONNY BURNING COAL   873 24
    THE BONNY FLOATING ARK OF THIS FAIR WORLD   876 10

BOOBS
    NOT YOU POOR BOOBS   794 29

BOOING
    MOANING BOOING ROARING HOLLOW   327 10

BOOK
    THE OPEN BOOK OF LANDSCAPE NO MORE FOR THE COVERS OF DA+   88   8
    MY MISSAL BOOK OF FINE FLAMBOYANT HOURS   135   2
    MY BOOK OF TURRETS AND OF RED-THORN BOWERS   135   3
    AND SO I SIT AND SCAN THE BOOK OF GREY   135 17
    NAY TAKE THIS WEARY BOOK OF HOURS AWAY   135 20
    OH BETTER THERE THAN IN ANY BOOK   151   3
    THEY SAY I WROTE A NAUGHTY BOOK   491 13
    YET IF PUT IN A BOOK   551 15
    BY PUBLISHING SUCH A BOOK   668 19
    DID YOU EVER OPEN THE BOOK   668 25
    DO OPEN THE BOOK AND LOOK   669   7
    OH BETTER THERE THAN IN ANY BOOK   873 13
    NOT THIS GRAY BOOK BUT THE RED AND BLOODY SCENES   *938 28
    AND SO I SIT AND TURN THE BOOK OF GRAY   *939   1
    NAY TAKE MY PAINTED MISSAL BOOK AWAY   *939   4

BOOKS
    OF THE BOOKS THAT LIE OUT ON THE DESKS A FULL THREESCORE   74 13
    I CAN ALWAYS LINGER OVER THE HUDDLED BOOKS ON THE STALLS   180 24
    BOOKS   263 26
    I HAVE CHOSEN AMONG THE BRIGHT AND MARVELLOUS BOOKS   264   3
    UGLY OLD FURNITURE UGLY OLD BOOKS UGLY OLD BUILDINGS UG+   678 14
    DESTROY AT LAST THE HEAVY BOOKS OF STONE   737 25
    I AM QUITE SICK OF BOOKS   857   1
    THE BOOKS THAT YOU HAVE TOUCHED CLEAVE CLOSE TO ME   880 10
    OF THE BOOKS THAT LIE OUT ON THE DESKS A FULL THREE SCO+   *895 21
    OF THE BOOKS THAT LIE OUT ON THE DESKS A FULL THREE SCO+   *904 10
    OH MY BOYS BENDING OVER YOUR BOOKS   *907   1
    OH MY BOYS BENDING OVER YOUR BOOKS   *908 22

BOOM
    A CHILD SITTING UNDER THE PIANO IN THE BOOM OF THE TING+   148 6
    SLOW BOOM   149 4
    A CHILD SITTING UNDER THE PIANO IN THE BOOM OF THE SHAK+ *940 7

BOOMING
    OF A MALE THONG BOOMING AND BRUISING UNTIL IT HAD   36 15
    OF THE STRONG MACHINE THAT RUNS MESMERIC BOOMING THE   149 13
    AND THEIR SUBTLE EAGER BOOMING   885 25

BOOMS
    MOANS AND BOOMS THE SOUL OF A PEOPLE IMPRISONED ASLEEP   149 11

BOON
    THEIR BEAUTY FOR HIS TAKING BOON FOR BOON   129 18

BOOR
    TOO GREAT A BOOR TO REALISE HIS TRUE FEELINGS   *949 1

BOORS
    WHEREIN WE ARE NOW BLIND UGLY BOORS   833 17

BOOT
    WEARING NO BOOT MY CHILDREN   757 11

BOOT-BRUSH
    HOW YOU HATE BEING BRUSHED WITH THE BOOT-BRUSH TO BRUSH 397 30

BOOTH
    FOR MEN TO SHOOT AT PENNY-A-TIME IN A BOOTH AT A FAIR   272 17

BOOTS
    IN SUNDAY SUITS AND YELLOW BOOTS ALONG THE CORSO   314 33
    BY BOOTS I AM M A   489 4
    IS A LAST OFFSHOOT OF BOOTS   489 8
    AND AGAIN ROLLING IN HIS HEAVY HIGH BOOTS   734 12
    SHUFFLING HIS RAGGED BOOTS THERE COMES ONE BOY LATE   866 6
    AND SHUFFLE OF BROKEN SODDENED BOOTS YET SINGING GOES R+ 866 14
    BY NATURE THAN BY BOOTS AND WET FEET OFTEN CARRY MERRY + 866 15

BOOT-SOLE
    UNDER HIS NOBLE BOOT-SOLE   *948 27

BOOT'S
    OVER ON BOOT'S CASH CHEMIST'S COUNTER   488 17

BOOZE
    I BOOZE AND FORNICATE AND USE FOUL LANGUAGE AND DESPISE 432 18
    THE TURNED WORM SHOUTS I BRAVELY BOOZE   433 2
    FOR A DREARY LITTLE BOOZE   560 24

BORDER
    BUT HIS HANDKERCHIEF IS WHITE WITH A BROAD BLUE BORDER 733 28
    THAT BORDER   749 12
    GO BRAVELY ACROSS THE BORDER ADMITTING YOUR MISTAKE   809 7

BORE
    I WAS WATCHING THE WOMAN THAT BORE ME   111 1
    YOU WOKE MY SPIRIT AND BORE ME   111 15
    YOU NEVER BORE HIS CHILDREN NEVER DREW   158 10
    BITTER-STINGING WHITE WORLD THAT BORE US   302 12
    ONE CAN BE TOLERANT WITH A BORE   499 12
    THAT YOU BORE ME   602 26
    TILL THY FULL-FED FIRE OF CURIOSITY BORE YOU   *927 8
    TILL MY FIRE OF CREATION BORE YOU   *928 8

BORED
    SO NINE-TENTHS ASLEEP MOTIONLESS BORED AND STATICALLY A+ 324 15
    AS IF SHE WERE A WORM OR A HIRED WHORE WHO BORED HIM   *948 17

BOREDOM
    WITH ASHES OF UTTER BOREDOM ENNUI AND DISGUST   616 12
    AND BOREDOM ENNUI DEPRESSION   627 17

BORGO SAN JACOPO
    TOWARDS THE BORGO SAN JACOPO   347 15

BORING
    THAT'S WHAT'S SO BORING PEOPLE ARE SO BORING   435 12
    AND HAMLET HOW BORING HOW BORING TO LIVE WITH   494 19
    HOW BORING HOW SMALL SHAKESPEARE'S PEOPLE ARE   494 25

BORN
    TWICE I AM BORN MY DEAREST   102 3
    THE PLACE IS PALPABLE ME FOR HERE I WAS BORN   172 22
    YOU ARE BORN AGAIN OF ME   240 10
    TO-NIGHT IS A WOMAN BORN   240 20
    RISEN NOT BORN AGAIN BUT RISEN BODY THE SAME AS BEFORE 258 29
    SWORD-BLADE BORN   306 32
    AND CABBAGES BORN TO BE CUT AND EAT   317 20
    BORN BEFORE GOD WAS LOVE   337 11
    HE WAS BORN IN FRONT OF MY SUNRISE   339 20
    YOU KNOW WHAT IT IS TO BE BORN ALONE   352 1
    BORN TO WALK ALONE   363 1
    BORN WITH A CAUL   408 15
    THERE'LL BE BABIES BORN THAT ARE CYGNETS O MY SOUL   438 21
    ARE BORN DEAD THEY ARE SHROUDS THEY SOAK LIFE OUT OF US 448 9
    BEING BORN AMONG THE WORKING PEOPLE   498 12
    THAT ARE BORN IN THEIR MINDS AND FORCED DOWN BY THE WILL 500 19
    SO THAT WHEN WE ARE RE-BORN WE CAN BE BORN INTO A FRESH 512 29
    THE YOUNG TODAY ARE BORN PRISONERS   518 7
    BORN IN A UNIVERSAL WORKHOUSE   518 19
    TO SEE THAT A CHILD AS SOON AS IT IS BORN   521 26
    O I WAS BORN LOW AND INFERIOR   554 5
    WHERE I WAS BORN   644 15
    BEHOLD GOD IS BORN   682 9
    OH GOD IS BORN   682 16
    BEHOLD HE IS BORN WET   682 17

BORN
    LO GOD IS BORN   682 21
    SEE GOD IS BORN HE IS BLUE HE IS DEEP BLUE HE IS FOREVE+ 682 23
    GOD IS BORN GOD IS BORN BRIGHT YELLOW AND DUCTILE HE IS+ 682 25
    ACH ACH NOW INDEED GOD IS BORN HE TWINKLES WITHIN   682 28
    GOD IS BORN GOD IS BORN PERFUMED AND DANGLING AND WITH + 683 5
    THE UNIVERSE TREMBLES GOD IS BORN GOD IS HERE   683 10
    BEHOLD NOW VERY GOD IS BORN   683 13
    GOD HIMSELF IS BORN   683 14
    UNTIL HE IS BORN   683 16
    TILL HE WAS BORN FROM A WOMB AND ATE SOUP AND BREAD   689 28
    UNBORN AND UNPRODUCED YET TO BE BORN   746 7
    IN THE STILLNESS WHERE WATERS ARE BORN   786 3
    THERE THE WINDS ARE BORN   786 8
    AND THEY DART TO HER WOMB THEY FIGHT FOR THE CHANCE TO + 795 31
    THEY GNASH WHEN IT CLOSES AND HATE THE ONE THAT GOT IN + 795 33
    AND BORN HIM A SON OR SO WHO AT THE AGE OF SEVEN IS SO + 842 7
    HE IS BORN ALONE AND ALONE HE DIES   843 25
    LATE BORN   860 19
    IS DELIVERED FROM US HERSELF BORN AGAIN AMID THE MOAN *938 10
    THERE'LL BE BABIES BORN THAT ARE YOUNG WILD SWANS O MY + *947 24
    BORN ALONE DIES ALONE   *951 4

BORNE
    ALL MY LIFE I HAVE BORNE THE BURDEN OF MYSELF   47 29
    LOVE WHO HAD BORNE AND NOW WAS LEAVING ME   103 20
    SO HIGH AND MIGHTY LOOK HOW THE HEADS ARE BORNE   221 7
    I'D HAVE TORN THEM UP HAD THEY BORNE AWAY THE PATIENT B+ *926 13
    IT IS YOU WHO HAVE BORNE THE SHAME AND SORROW   *927 1
    SO HIGH AND MIGHTY LOOK HOW ITS HEADS ARE BORNE   *944 20

BORROW
    TILL I COULD BORROW   38 13
    THE WORLD IS ENDING LET'S HURRY TO BORROW   815 2
    TILL YOU CAN BORROW   *892 29

BORROWED
    IF ONLY MOST LOVELY OF ALL IS YIELD MYSELF AND AM BORRO+ 250 17

BOSOM
    OF HIS HAND AGAINST MY BOSOM AND OH THE BROAD   43 24
    WHITE BOSOM   56 6
    JACKET AT TH' BOSOM AN' TOOK OUT   61 10
    FROM THAT BIT OF A WENCH'S BOSOM 'E'D BE GLAD OF IT   61 19
    AND HER BOSOM COUCHED IN THE CONFINES OF HER GOWN   123 9
    TO HER SHE CRUSHES THEM INTO HER BOSOM DEEP   128 28
    HOW MY SOUL CLEAVES TO YOUR BOSOM AS I CLASP YOU   246 5
    WHERE HER BOSOM SOFTENS TOWARDS ME AND THE TURMOIL HAS 250 7
    AND THE LAST FIRES OF DISSOLUTION BURN IN THE BOSOM OF + 270 23
    BOSOM   540 15
    OR YOUR MANLY BOSOM EITHER   540 24
    KISSES OF FOUR GREAT LORDS BEAUTIFUL AS THEY HELD ME TO+ 695 29
    NOR IS HE A WOMAN WITH A BOSOM OF SORROW AND CONSOLATION 840 21
    ITS COOL WEIGHT LAY FULL ON HER BOSOM NOW IT ROLLS TO R+ 864 15
    PRESSES HER HAND TO HER BOSOM WHERE THE FRUIT HAS LAIN 864 20
    AND LOOKING AT HER BOSOM   880 22
    KNOWING THEN I HAD TAKEN MY BOSOM FROM HER CRUCIFIED BREA+ 882 9
    ROUND AND WHITE AS A SMALL BOSOM   886 17
    A LOT O' VIOLETS FELL OUT OF 'ER BOSOM ON 'IM DOWN THEER *910 16
    THEN SHE RUMMAGED HER HAND IN 'ER BOSOM AN' KISSED THE + *910 21
    JACKET AT TH' BOSOM AN' TOOK FROM OUT OF IT   *911 26
    TO WITHER ON THE BOSOM OF THE MERCIFUL SO MANY SEEDS TH+ *926 27
    FROM MY BREAST TO YOUR BOSOM ECLIPSE   *929 28
    AND I SAW HER BOSOM COUCH IN THE NEST OF HER GOWN   *934 15
    AND HER ARMS AND HER BOSOM AND THE WHOLE OF HER SOUL IS+ *940 20

BOSOMS
    EH MEN DOESNA HA'E BOSOMS 'APPEN NOT ON'Y THA KNOWS   540 16

BOSS
    IF TER COULDNA BE MASTER AN' TH' WOMAN'S BOSS   139 4
    WHOSE BOSS ARE YOU WITH ALL YOUR BULLY WAY   375 32
    WITH A BOSS PILING LOADS ON HIS BACK   379 10
    AND FIGHT TO BE BOSS OF THE WORLD   383 21
    RIGHT CH'ARE BOSS AN' WHAT ABAHT IT   547 25
    NOT A BOSS BUT THE GLEAM OF LIFE ON THE FACE OF A MAN 650 15
    YOU LAD WILL YOU ASK THE BOSS   759 6
    THAN MY BOSS   762 7

BOSSY
    WE'LL SHOW THESE OLD UNCLES WHO'S GOING TO BE BOSSY   573 24

BOTH
    WHAT IS THE POINT TO US BOTH IT IS ALL MY AUNT   74 29
    BOTH ON YER   84 18
    OF YOUR LOVE WE BOTH HAVE ENTERED THEN THE RIGHT   104 4
    AND LOSE THEM BOTH   110 12
    'TWAS YOU WHO KILLED HIM WHEN YOU BOTH CAROUSED   158 3
    WITH ME BOTH IN ONE HURT   160 4
    WE WRITHE AND LUST IN BOTH   177 20
    WHAT GHOST OF US BOTH DO YOU THINK HE SAW   227 11
    ALL GOOD EVIL BOTH   239 20
    GROWS DIMMER WE BOTH FORGET   240 14
    BUT OF BOTH OF US   247 17
    WELL YOU CAN'T HAVE IT BOTH ROADS   379 18
    OR IS IT EVEN POSSIBLE WE MUST DO BOTH   429 30
    THE FEELINGS YOU WOULD LIKE US BOTH TO HAVE WE   501 5
    BUT OF COURSE ONE KNOWS THAT BOTH BEAUTY AND PURE   532 11
    TILL WE BOTH OF US   562 5
    WERE BOTH BEGOTTEN   562 25
    OH A MAN MAY TRAVEL BOTH EAST AND WEST   575 22
    THEY HAVE BORN NERVOUS WRECKS BECAUSE   605 17
    BUT THE MACHINE IT IS THAT HAS INVENTED THEM BOTH   641 12
    THE BOURGEOIS AND THE BOLSHEVIST ARE BOTH QUITE BLIND 665 19
    BOTH BREASTS DIM AND MYSTERIOUS WITH THE GLAMOROUS KIND+ 693 12
    THERE ARE SOULS THAT ARE AT HOME IN BOTH HOMES   711 18
    THE WHEAT ON BOTH SIDES OF THE ROAD STANDS GREEN   732 5
    BUT THE STAR IS THE SAME FOR BOTH OF US   812 7

BOTH (CONT.) BOW

BOTH
LAST TIME WE WERE BOTH 817 31
THAT STOOD CLOSE TO THE WALL AND THE FRONT'S FADED SILK+ *940 3

BOTHER
STILL IF YOU DON'T WANT TO BOTHER 557 7
THAT DOES NOT BOTHER 561 10
THEY NEEDN'T BOTHER MOST OF THEM WILL NEVER GET DOWN AT+ 667 22
FOR THE REST DON'T BOTHER 818 24

BOTHERED
FOR YEARS AND YEARS IT BOTHERED ME 556 1

BOTTLE
TILL THE HEAD FLOATS TILTED LIKE A BOTTLE FORWARD TILTED 428 10
O SHIP IN A BOTTLE 542 1

BOTTLED
FROM THE SOURCE NOT OUT OF BOTTLES AND BOTTLED PERSONAL 481 4
NOT BOTTLED IN HUMAN BOTTLES 481 8
ALL BEAUTIFULLY RIGGED AND BOTTLED UP 542 8

BOTTLES
FROM THE SOURCE NOT OUT OF BOTTLES AND BOTTLED PERSONAL 481 4
NOT BOTTLED IN HUMAN BOTTLES 481 8
WHEN WE GET OUT OF THE GLASS BOTTLES OF OUR OWN EGO 482 15
WHEN MEN ARE MADE IN BOTTLES 501 1
O SHIPS IN BOTTLES 542 4
SAFE INSIDE THEIR BOTTLES 542 28
SAFE INSIDE THEIR BOTTLES 542 32
WEEKLY OR TWICE-WEEKLY WHISTLE ROUND YOUR BOTTLES 543 9
THE STORM IS WORDS THE BOTTLES NEVER BREAK 543 11

BOTTOM
EMPTY AN' EMPTY FROM BOTTOM TO TOP 139 13
LIKE A FISH SEEKING THE BOTTOM JESUS 321 31
AND RESTED HIS THROAT UPON THE STONE BOTTOM 349 12
AT THE BOTTOM THEY MUST KNOW WE ARE REALLY SUPERIOR 435 14
I'VE NEVER GOT TO THE BOTTOM OF SUPERIORITY 435 19
THAT A PRETTY BOTTOM 562 21
WHICH HE CAN NEVER REACH TILL HE TOUCH THE BOTTOM OF TH+ 700 28
YET NEVER NEVER COMING TO THE BOTTOM FOR THERE IS NO BO+ 701 25
STONE OF ANGER AT THE BOTTOM 790 15

BOTTOMLESS
INTO THE FATHOMLESS BOTTOMLESS PIT 322 2
WHERE MY SOUL FALLS IN THE LAST THROES OF BOTTOMLESS CO+ 322 3
SHUDDERING A STRANGE WAY DOWN THE BOTTOMLESS PIT 322 23
WHICH HE CAN NEVER TOUCH FOR THE ABYSS IS BOTTOMLESS 700 29
BUT THE ABYSS WHICH IS BOTTOMLESS 701 2
FOR THE ABYSS IS BOTTOMLESS 701 4
FOR THE DEPTH IS BOTTOMLESS 701 29

BOTTOMS
MAYBE THEIR LITTLE BOTTOMS 560 1
THE VIBRATION OF THE MOTOR-CAR HAS BRUISED THEIR INSENS+ 625 17

BOUGH
BEFORE ALL THE BATS HAVE DROPPED FROM THE BOUGH 35 9
HANG FROM THE STREET'S LONG BOUGH 252 14
THE SAME SETS THE THROSTLE AT SUNSET ON A BOUGH 272 25
THERE NEVER WAS ANY STANDING ALOFT AND UNFOLDED ON A BO+ 283 3
AT DUSK THEY PATTER BACK LIKE A BOUGH BEING DRAGGED ON 384 1
GREY BIRD IN THE AIR ON THE BOUGH OF THE LEANING 385 17
STRAIGHT AS A BOARD ON THE BOUGH LOOKING DOWN LIKE SOME 385 19
A SMALL BIRD WILL DROP FROZEN DEAD FROM A BOUGH 467 3
WHEN THE BOUGH BREAKS 669 9
FROM THE RED-FIBRED BOUGH OF THE CEDAR FROM THE CEDAR-R+ 782 11
SHAKE THE BOUGH 817 15
DOWN THE DARK BOUGH HAVE FLED 861 11
TO PULL DOWN THE BOUGH THE LEAVES BROKE AND THE FRUIT S+ 864 10

BOUGHS
UNDER THE LONG DARK BOUGHS LIKE JEWELS RED 36 19
THAT LEAVES THE BOUGHS 56 19
WHOSE BLACK BOUGHS FLAP THE GROUND 113 26
CARRY INTO YOUR ROOM THE BLOSSOMING BOUGHS OF CHERRY 179 2
JESUS' PALE AND LAMBENT DOVE COOING IN THE LOWER BOUGHS 329 8
YOU SIT IN THE BOUGHS AND GIBBER 549 17
AND THE BOUGHS OF THE LIME TREE SHAKE AND TOSS THE LIGHT 878 5
SWAYS ON MY ARM LIKE SORROWFUL STORM-HEAVY BOUGHS *913 23
WHERE BLACK BOUGHS FLAP THE GROUND *929 15
MEN USED TO PUT THEM FORTH SENSITIVELY LIKE BOUGHS LEAV+ *950 2

BOUGHT
AN' THERE'S THE DARK-BLUE TIE I BOUGHT 'IM 81 14
THE JOY I BOUGHT WAS NOT TOO HIGHLY PRICED 225 32
YOU'RE A DOVE I HAVE BOUGHT FOR SACRIFICE 238 17
MY OFFERING BOUGHT AT A GREAT PRICE 238 21
SHE WAS BOUGHT AT GIARDINI FAIR ON THE SANDS FOR SIX HU+ 385 7
AND EMPLOYERS ARE BOUGHT BY FINANCIERS AND FINANCIERS A+ 483 4
BOUGHT SECOND-HAND FROM MRS JUSTICE ENNIS 760 13
AND A MAN WHEN HE ISN'T BOUGHT FEELS SOLD 814 12
NOTHING TO SELL IN THEE NOUGHT TO BE BOUGHT 824 10
AN' THAT'S THE DARK BLUE TIE I BOUGHT 'IM *923 14

BOULDERS
BOULDERS 130 4

BOULEVARD
THE TREES DOWN THE BOULEVARD STAND NAKED IN THOUGHT 142 1

BOULEVARDS
BOULEVARDS TRAM-CARS POLICEMEN 286 35

BOUNCE
CONTACTS AND BOUNCING OFF AGAIN BOUNCE BOUNCE LIKE A 249 19
MY FLESH IS WEARY WITH BOUNCE ON THEM AND 249 21
MY EARS ARE WEARY WITH WORDS THAT BOUNCE ON THEM AND 249 22
BOUNCE OFF AGAIN MEANING NOTHING ASSERTIONS ASSERTIONS 249 24
THREE SIDES SET ON ME CHAOS AND BOUNCE BUT THE FOURTH 249 27

BOUNCED
I AM NOR WILL I BE BOUNCED OUT OF IT SO AT LAST I TOUCH 250 2
WHILE YOU PRANCED AND BOUNCED WITH LOVE OF HER YOU 396 1

BOUNCES
AND THE CHAOS THAT BOUNCES AND RATTLES LIKE SHRAPNEL AT 250 4

BOUNCING
CONTACTS AND BOUNCING OFF AGAIN BOUNCE BOUNCE LIKE A 249 19
AND YOUR BLACK LITTLE BODY BOUNCING AND WRIGGLING 396 5
IN THE BOUNCING OF THESE SMALL AND HAPPY WHALES 693 30

BOUND
AM HELPLESSLY BOUND 40 10
AND I LAUGHED TO FEEL IT PLUNGE AND BOUND 61 23
TO DO SUCH A THING THOUGH IT'S A POOR TALE IT IS THAT I+ 83 7
BREAST WAS BOUND 120 21
HEARTBEAT BOUND 121 10
AGAIN I TELL YOU I BLEED I AM BOUND WITH WITHIES 131 11
THIS TRAIN BEATS ANXIOUSLY OUTWARD BOUND 169 4
DRAWING ALL MEN UNTO THEE BUT BOUND TO RELEASE THEM WHEN 323 8
WRAPPED TO THE EYES THE SHEET BOUND CLOSE ON HIS BROWS 403 10
AUNT LOUIE IS ALMOST BOUND TO COME 572 11
I BOUND THE BRIGHT FANGS OF THE SUN 786 23
LADS IN THEIR WARM LIGHT SLIPPERS BOUND DOWN THE HALL T+ 865 28
IN ONE SWIFT BOUND TO THE HOUSE-BOAT 868 2
AND I LAUGHED TO FEEL IT PLUNGE AND BOUND *912 3
TO SUCH A THING BUT IT'S A POOR TALE THAT I'M BOUND TO + *925 11
TO COVER MY MOUTH'S RAILLERY TILL I'M BOUND IN HER SHAM+ *940 17

BOUNDARY
SO SALT IS THE BOUNDARY MARK BETWEEN FIRE THAT BURNS AN+ 706 10
IT IS SET UP AS A BOUNDARY AND BLOOD AND SWEAT 706 13
ARE MARKED OUT WITH THE BOUNDARY OF SALT BETWEEN FIRE A+ 706 14

BOUNDERS
BUT AMONG THE BOURGEOIS AND THE BOLSHEVIST BOUNDERS 665 22

BOUNDING
UP FROM THE BOUNDING EARTH STRANGE PREGNANT STREAMS IN + 675 13

BOUNDLESS
BOUNDLESS LOVE 291 13
NOT BOUNDLESS 291 16

BOUNDS
ALL BOUNDS THE GREAT OLD CITY 159 9
BROKE THE BOUNDS AND BEYOND DIM RECOLLECTION 161 21
IS OUT OF BOUNDS AND ONLY THE OLD GHOSTS KNOW 172 24
BRUSHING THE STARS GOES MY SOUL THAT SKIMS THE BOUNDS 193 25
IT IS GOING A LITTLE BEYOND THE BOUNDS 266 9
YOUR BOUNDS OF ISOLATION 290 17
NO BOUNDS BEING SET 306 34
THIS IS GOING BEYOND THE BOUNDS OF PRESENT HONOUR 779 20

BOUNTY
LET THEM DISENCUMBER YOUR BOUNTY LET THEM ALL SHARE 168 12

BOURGEOIS
HOW BEASTLY THE BOURGEOIS IS 430 15
HOW BEASTLY THE BOURGEOIS IS 431 11
HOW BEASTLY THE BOURGEOIS IS 431 24
I DO ALL THE THINGS THE BOURGEOIS DAREN'T DO 432 17
THE BONNIE BONNIE BOURGEOIS GOES A-WHORING UP BACK 432 22
THE BUSY BUSY BOURGEOIS IMBIBES HIS LITTLE SHARE 432 25
THE PRETTY PRETTY BOURGEOIS PINKS HIS LANGUAGE JUST AS + 432 28
YOU ARE NO LONGER MEN THAT IS BOURGEOIS 443 2
NOTHING THAT TRANSCENDS THE BOURGEOIS MIDDLINGNESS 528 2
THE BOURGEOIS PRODUCES THE BOLSHEVIST INEVITABLY 663 9
THE BOURGEOIS ASSERTS THAT HE OWNS HIS PROPERTY BY DIVI+ 663 13
BOURGEOIS COWARDICE PRODUCES BOLSHEVIST IMPUDENCE 663 18
AS THE BOURGEOIS GETS SECRETLY MORE COWARDLY KNOWING HE+ 663 20
IF I HAVE TO CHOOSE BETWEEN THE BOURGEOIS AND THE BOLSH+ 664 5
I CHOOSE THE BOURGEOIS 664 6
BUT IN CHOOSING THE BOURGEOIS ONE BRINGS TO PASS 664 8
SINCE THE BOURGEOIS IS THE DIRECT CAUSE OF THE BOLSHEVI+ 664 10
BOURGEOIS AND BOLSHEVIST 664 18
THE BOURGEOIS AND THE BOLSHEVIST ARE BOTH QUITE BLIND 665 19
BUT AMONG THE BOURGEOIS AND THE BOLSHEVIST BOUNDERS 665 22
THOSE WHO ARE NEITHER BOURGEOIS NOR BOLSHEVIST BUT TRUE+ 666 2
THE STONE-BLIND BOURGEOIS AND THE STONE-BLIND BOLSHEVIST 666 8

BOURGEOISIE
IN THE GOD-DAMN BOURGEOISIE 490 16
O I AM A MEMBER OF THE BOURGEOISIE 490 25

BOUTS
AND A FEW VOMITING BOUTS 400 22

BOVINE
BUT WITH MORE THAN BOVINE GRIM EARTH-DANK PERSISTENCE 361 16

BOW
AND ALL THE LITTLE ROOFS OF THE VILLAGE BOW LOW PITIFUL+ 63 5
YOUR BOW FOR BROKEN IT IS AND HURTING TO HEAR 85 22
UPRAISED ON THE BED WITH FEET ERECT AS A BOW 155 19
YOU ARCH YOURSELF AS AN ARCHER'S BOW 370 12
TO BOW BEFORE ROYALTY IN THE LAND OF ELEPHANTS BOW DEEP 391 28
BOW DEEP 391 29
BOW DEEP FOR IT'S GOOD AS A DRAUGHT OF COOL WATER TO BOW 391 30
AND ALL THERE WAS TO BOW TO A WEARY DIFFIDENT BOY WHOSE 391 32

BOW
MUST BOW   636 26
WITH BEAUTY SHINE AND BOW IN GOD'S GREAT WAKE   872 22
THEN HE LAID DOWN THE BOW OF HIS VIOLIN   884 8
I STAND RELUCTANT TO ENTER TO DREAM NO MORE BUT TO BOW   *894 21

BOW-CORD
WHEN THE BOW-CORD TWANGED   688 25

BOWED
AS THEY WRITE THEIR ROUND HEADS BUSILY BOWED   51 12
FRAIL AND SAD WITH GREY BOWED HEAD   64 4
A STRICKEN WIFE SO SUNK IN OBLIVION BOWED   155 50
BOWED DOWN WITH HIS INNER MAGNIFICENCE   272 12
BOWED AND LIFTED HER FOOT IN HER HAND SMILED SWUNG HER   444 28
AS THEY WRITE THEIR ROUND HEADS BUSILY BOWED   *898 24
AS THEY WRITE THEIR ROUND HEADS BUSILY BOWED   *902 8

BOWELS
WITH BOWELS OF STEEL   56 28
BEING EARTH-BROWN EARTH-GOLDEN FROM THE BURNING BOWELS   349 26
INTO THE BURNING BOWELS OF THIS EARTH   350 12
THERE ARE DEAD THAT CREEP THROUGH THE BURNING BOWELS OF+   795 24
OUT OF THE BOWELS OF THE EARTH LIKE A SNAKE   801 7
AND KNEES AND THIGHS AND LOINS AND THE BOWELS OF STRENG+   801 20
IT HAS NEITHER HEART NOR BOWELS NOR GENITALS   830 28
THAT WE HAVE BLOOD AND BOWELS AND LIVELY GENITALS   *953 3

BOWER
LEANS ALL ALONE ABOVE MY WINDOW ON NIGHT'S WINTRY BOWER   67 19
YOU FORTY LADIES IN THE HAREM BOWER   758 6

BOWERS
MY BOOK OF TURRETS AND OF RED-THORN BOWERS   135 3
AND CITIES MIGHT BE AS ONCE THEY WERE BOWERS GROWN OUT   451 18
BOWERS OF MEN   *950 5

BOWERY
AND DWELLING IN HIS OWN BOWERY HOUSE LIKE A BEAVER'S   451 24
AND DWELLING IN HIS OWN BOWERY HOUSE LIKE A BIRD IN A B+   *950 9

BOWING
GRACIOUSLY BOWING DOWN   556 26

BOWL
HOW MANY STARS IN YOUR BOWL   49 2
YOU SURELY SEEING I AM A BOWL OF KISSES   86 3
HOW CAN YOU FROM MY BOWL OF KISSES SHRINK   86 8
WITH GENTLENESS CAME I WITH MY HEART 'TWIXT MY HANDS LI+   92 22
ONE BOWL OF KISSES   96 6
MY BOWL OF KISSES   96 12
EXALT THE BOWL   96 25
MY GRAIL A BROWN BOWL TWINED   123 24
MY GRAIL WHOSE BOWL WAS TWINED   *934 30

BOW-LEGGED
ONE THING THAT IS BOW-LEGGED   818 25
BUT THE ONE THING THAT IS BOW-LEGGED   820 5

BOWLER
OF MEN IN BOWLER HATS HURRYING   484 4

BOWS
GOD BOWS HIS HEAD AND GRANTS ME THIS SUPREME   157 16
OH IN THE SPRING THE BLUEBELL BOWS HIM DOWN FOR VERY   272 9
SHE BOWS QUITE HUMBLE SUCH A SUBTLE DESTROYING MIND MUS+   841 28

BOWSPRIT
LIKE A BIG SHIP PUSHING HER BOWSPRIT OVER THE LITTLE SH+   380 24

BOW-WOW
IN SILENCE FROM THE GREAT BOW-WOW   494 8

BOX
I WILL ESCAPE FROM THE HOLLOW ROOM THE BOX OF LIGHT   179 24
IN THE BOX AND FOUR HOT HORSES GOING DREARILY   733 7

BOY
IN A THAW OF ANXIETY FOR THE BOY   100 7
A WET BIRD WALKS ON THE LAWN CALL TO THE BOY TO COME   137 7
I REMEMBER WHEN I WAS A BOY   365 29
SHATTERED BOY UP THERE   390 26
AND ALL THERE WAS TO BOW TO A WEARY DIFFIDENT BOY WHOSE   391 32
LIKE SOME MALICIOUS INDECENT LITTLE BOY   447 31
FIGHT YOUR LITTLE FIGHT MY BOY   458 14
DON'T BE A GOOD LITTLE GOOD LITTLE BOY   458 16
IF YOU'VE GOT THE GOODS COME FORWARD BOY AND LET'S SEE   483 20
WITH HELLO BOY WHAT ABOUT SIN   493 12
LOVE YOUR LITTLE BOY   572 22
OH I'M A BRITISH BOY SIR   576 16
FOR I'M A BRITISH BOY SIR   576 22
I'M YOUR BRITISH BOY AND I DID BUT TRY   577 10
BUT THE BRITISH BOY HE TURNED AND FLED   577 20
AND SAID OH BOY I TELL YOU WHAT   578 10
LITTLE BOY BLUE   659 5
AND ONE FOR THE LITTLE BOY THAT LIVES DOWN THE   669 24
AND ANXIOUSLY LIKE A BOY AFRAID TO BE FOUND OUT   734 4
CLOSE FRIEND IN EVERYTHING IS OUR LORD MY BOY   749 23
LIKE A BOY IN A MEADOW PLAYING   782 30
YOU LOOK LIKE THE TOPPINGEST TOPPING FIFTH-FORM ETON BO+   835 17
BABY WAS HER LITTLE BOY OF SEVEN   842 23
AND A BOY AS HE REACHES THE AGE OF FOURTEEN WHEN HE SHO+   843 2
SCATTER OVER THE WHITENESS ONE BOY ALONE IN THE CLASSRO+   865 20
SHUFFLING HIS RAGGED BOOTS THERE COMES ONE BOY LATE   866 6

BOYS
AND THE BOYS AND THE ROOM IN A COLOURLESS GLOOM   51 6
WATCH THE BOYS IN THEIR SUMMER BLOUSES   51 11
FROM ME TO THE BOYS WHOSE BRIGHTENING SOULS IT LAVES   51 24
IS FULL OF DREAMS MY LOVE THE BOYS ARE ALL STILL   52 14
BUT THE FACES OF THE BOYS IN THE BROODING YELLOW LIGHT   75 25
THE HEADS OF THE BOYS MOVE DIMLY THROUGH A YELLOW GLOOM+   92 4
I CAME TO THE BOYS WITH LOVE DEAR AND ONLY THEY TURNED +   92 21
LET THEM LIVE THE BOYS AND LEARN NOT TO TRESPASS I HAD +   93 11
OF THE DAY BUT IT'S NOTHING TO DO WITH THE BOYS SO LET +   93 27
I WATCHED THE TEARS ON THE GUILTY CHEEKS OF THE BOYS   94 14
IN THE CHOIR THE BOYS ARE SINGING THE HYMN   147 18
AT 'EM BOYS AT 'EM   309 6
THE RICKSHAW BOYS BEGIN TO UNDERSTAND   390 2
WOOING BOYS AND BEAUTY   437 7
DON'T LONG TO HAVE DEAR LITTLE DEAR LITTLE BOYS   459 1
THEY'LL NEVER DO A THING BOYS   553 17
ALL THE LITTLE BOYS WHOSE FATHERS WERE COLLIERS OR FARM+   774 1
AND ALL THE LITTLE BOYS   774 3
THAT THE BOYS MUST STAY AT SCHOOL NOT BE KEPT AWAY   777 33
THAT OUR BOYS MUST STAY AT SCHOOL TILL THEY ARE EIGHTEEN   779 2
THE BOYS FROM THE HOME BLUE AND INANIMATE   866 2
FROM THE SURF HAS ARISEN THE BOYS ARE MUTTERING   *894 16
OF THE BOYS WITH ME   *895 14
I WATCHED THE TEARS ON THE FRUITED CHEEKS OF THE BOYS   *897 2
BUT THE FACES OF THE BOYS IN THE BROODING YELLOW LIGHT   *897 24
AND THE BOYS AND THE ROOM IN A COLOURLESS GLOOM   *898 18
WATCH THE BOYS IN THEIR SUMMER BLOUSES   *898 23
A TEACHER OF THESE YOUNG BOYS MY SLAVES   *899 6
AND THOUGH I SCARCELY SEE THE BOYS OR KNOW THAT THEY AR+   *900 10
BUT THE FACES OF THE BOYS IN THE BROODING YELLOW LIGHT   *901 1
AND THE BOYS AND THE ROOM IN A COLOURLESS GLOOM   *902 2
WATCH THE BOYS IN THEIR SUMMER BLOUSES   *902 7
A TEACHER OF THESE YOUNG BOYS MY SLAVES   *902 18
AND THOUGH I SCARCELY SEE THE BOYS OR KNOW THAT THEY AR+   *903 22
IS FULL OF DREAMS MY LOVE THE BOYS ARE ALL STILL   *905 3
OH MY BOYS BENDING OVER YOUR BOOKS   *907 1
OH MY BOYS BENDING OVER YOUR BOOKS   *908 22
THE HEADS OF MY BOYS MOVE DIMLY THROUGH THE YELLOW GLOO+   *926 4
WITH THE LUSTY SOULS OF MY BOYS YET THEY HIDE THEIR FAC+   *926 23
WOOING BOYS AND BEAUTY   *946 19

BOY'S
THROUGH THE POOR BOY'S PICTURES YOU SEE WHAT I   577 18

BRACE
SHALL A MAN BRACE HIMSELF UP   420 17
WHY SHOULD WE BRACE OURSELVES UP WITH MEAN EMULATION   520 5
IF WE BRACE OURSELVES UP IT SHOULD BE FOR SOMETHING WE   520 6

BRACES
AS I LEAVE OFF MY BRACES   321 28

BRACKISH
AND SOME OF TOO MUCH SUN BRACKISH SWEET   708 3
BRACKISH THEY WILL TASTE OF TEARS WHEN THE YELLOW DAPPL+ *932 22

BRACTS
AND I THE SWIFT BRACTS THAT SHEATHE IT THOSE BREASTS TH+   845 16

BRAGGADOCCIOS
BRAGGADOCCIOS AROUND THE BLUE RIMS OF THE WORLD   814 30

BRAGGING
BRAGGING A LITTLE REALLY   531 5

BRAGS
WHY THE OLD CHURCH BELLOWS AND BRAGS   54 20

BRAID
PLAITING A HEAVY AUBURN BRAID   178 20

BRAIDS
A LILAC THERE LIKE A LADY WHO BRAIDS   105 25

BRAIN
IN THE BRAIN   97 25
TO STEADY MY BRAIN IN THIS PHANTOM SHOW   105 10
AT THE BASE OF THE LOWER BRAIN   455 16
WHICH ROTS THE BRAIN THE BLOOD THE BONES THE STONES THE   487 16
IT IS AS IF MODERN WOMEN HAD ALL GOT THEMSELVES ON THE +   502 6
LAMBS FRISK AMONG THE DAISIES OF HIS BRAIN   624 9
AND THE MACHINE HAS ENTANGLED THE BRAIN AND GOT IT FAST   629 7
AND A BOARD-SCHOOL BRAIN STUFFED UP WITH THE HA'PENNY   630 30
THE BRAIN OF THE MACHINE KNOWS THE LIMBS AND TRUNK OF   635 21
IS BRITISH HYPOCRISY A FORM OF SOFTENING OF THE BRAIN   659 22
THAT WE'VE HAD ENOUGH THE BRAIN IS STRETCHED TILL IT PA+ 756 5
EVEN ITS BRAIN SEEMS UPSIDE DOWN   830 29
BUT GET ANY OF THEM ON THE BRAIN AND THEY BECOME PERNIC+ 845 6
BAWDY ON THE BRAIN BECOMES OBSCENITY VICIOUS   845 7
WHORING ON THE BRAIN BECOMES REALLY SYPHILITIC   845 8
AND SODOMY ON THE BRAIN BECOMES A MISSION   845 9
BUT CHASTITY ON THE BRAIN IS A VICE A PERVERSION   845 12
BUT BAWDY ON THE BRAIN IS LEWD AND NAUSEOUS A SORT OF I+ *952 19
AND WHORING ON THE BRAIN AS BAD AS SYPHILIS INCIPIENT I+ *952 20
AND SODOMY ON THE BRAIN IS A SORT OF MISSION AND WHAT I+ *952 21
BUT CHASTITY ON THE BRAIN IS ANOTHER VICE IT ENDS IN LU+ *952 26

BRAINS
GENITALS BRAINS AND SOULS   631 22
BECAUSE THEY ARE THE BRAINS OF THE MACHINE   641 14
OR THE MOST HIGH DURING THE COAL AGE CUDGELLING HIS MIG+ 690 26
EVEN IF HE HAD ANY BRAINS STRAINING HIS MIGHTY MIND   690 27

BRAINY
    ONLY THE BRAINY SORT   637 22
    BUT BRAINY ROBOT OR AESTHETIC ROBOT OR MERELY MUSCULAR +   637 23

BRAKE
    AND DASH IN PANIC THROUGH THE BRAKE   465 15

BRANCH
    BRANCH AND ENCHAIN   *937 9

BRANCHES
    THE SLENDER BARE ARMS OF THE BRANCHES YOUR TIRE-MAIDENS   86 17
    THE BRANCHES INVISIBLE SEED OF EXPERIENCE BLOWS   89 30
    WILL FLOURISH ITS BRANCHES IN HEAVEN WHEN WE   172 16
    IF SOMETHING STIRS IN THE BRANCHES   231 16
    SAY THROUGH THE BRANCHES   292 24
    COWERING IN THE LAST BRANCHES OF THE TREE OF OUR LIFE   718 20
    AND THE BRANCHES ARE MINE IN THE PATHS OF THE SKY AND T+   801 17

BRANCHING
    TIMELESS AS BRANCHING LICHENS PALE AS MUST   135 15
    WITH IRON BRANCHING BLACKLY RUSTED LIKE OLD TWISTED   301 13

BRAND
    THE BRAND IS UPON HIM LOOK YOU   228 23

BRANDISHING
    AND BRANDISHING AND STOOPING OVER EARTH'S WINTRY FLEDGE   301 15
    WHEN THEY FELT THE LIGHT OF HEAVEN BRANDISHING LIKE A K+   310 7

BRANDS
    BUT SOMETIMES THE OPENING PETALS ARE FIRE AND THE SCARL+   93 31
    WHERE THE BRANDS OF THE ANGELS LIKE TORCHES   242 25
    OH BRANDS   784 19

BRASS
    AND THE HALF-HIDDEN PRIVATE PARTS JUST A LITTLE BRASS T+   625 22
    OH MY WIFE'S BRASS INCENSE-BOWL   760 12

BRASS-RESONANT
    AND YET AS HIS BRASS-RESONANT HOWLING YELL RESOUNDS   377 20

BRASSY
    ME WORDS THAT RANG WITH A BRASSY SHALLOW CHIME   98 20
    AND ONE TRAPPED ONE'S FINGERS IN THEIR BRASSY POLISHED   644 13

BRAVE
    OF THE SORREL'S CRESSET A GREEN BRAVE TOWN   49 27
    YOU'RE STOUT TO BRAVE THIS SNOW MISS STAINWRIGHT   78 1
    VERY BRAVE OF YOU SIR   80 32
    WITH MULTITUDE OF WHITE ROSES AND SINCE YOU WERE BRAVE   176 12
    IS DIGNIFIED IN THE FOXGLOVE LIKE A RED INDIAN BRAVE   272 29
    THE BRAVE ADVENTUROUS ROSACEAE   283 9
    BUT THE FEAR OF LIFE IS STILL HERE I AM BRAVE   460 31
    AND HAD A BRAVE DESTINY EVEN WHEN SHE WENT WRONG   535 16
    BUT STILL MORE BRAVE AND STILL MORE RARE   634 26
    THUNDERS IN HEAVEN TILL THE BRAVE WORLDS REEL   773 8
    WHEN YOU TURN TO YOUR WIVES AS BRAVE MEN TURN TO THEIR +   800 12
    BRAVE MEN HAVE PEACE AT NIGHTFALL   810 7
    YOU'RE STOUT TO BRAVE THIS SNOW MISS STAINWRIGHT   *919 21
    AND EATING THE BRAVE BREAD OF A WHOLESOME KNOWLEDGE   *959 14

BRAVELY
    THE COMMON FLAUNTS BRAVELY BUT BELOW FROM THE RUSHES   33 10
    THE TURNED WORM SHOUTS I BRAVELY BOOZE   433 2
    TAKE IT BRAVELY   809 5
    TAKE DEATH BRAVELY   809 6
    GO BRAVELY ACROSS THE BORDER ADMITTING YOUR MISTAKE   809 7
    THE COMMON FLAUNTS BRAVELY BUT BELOW FROM THE RUSHES   *891 11

BRAVERY
    WHEN YOU LIFT YOUR HANDS IN COURAGE AND BRAVERY ITS GLO+   800 10

BRAVES
    SHE BRAVES IT OUT SINCE SHE MUST BE SEEN   228 4

BRAVING
    BRAVING   137 2

BRAY
    BUT MOSTLY DO YOU NOT DETEST MY BRAY   236 11
    THE LONG-DRAWN BRAY OF THE ASS   377 1

BRAYING
    THIS IS THE AUTHENTIC ARABIC INTERPRETATION OF THE BRAY+   377 17

BRAZIER
    LIKE A GLOWING BRAZIER FAINTLY BLUE OF FLAME   151 25
    LIKE A GLOWING BRAZIER FAINTLY BLUE OF FLAME   874 4

BREACH
    THERE'S A BREACH IN THE WALLS OF THE PAST LETS THE DAYL+   174 6
    THROUGH ANY BREACH IN THE WALL   *957 21

BREACHES
    IS WASHING IN THROUGH THE BREACHES OF OUR WOUNDS   718 7
    THROUGH BREACHES IN THE WALLS OF THIS OUR BY-NO-MEANS I+   722 25

BREAD
    WHAT BREAD AFLOAT ON THE WATERS   171 23
    NOT BREAD ALONE NOT THE BELLY NOR THE THIRSTY THROAT   263 8
    LACK OF BREAD   263 10
    I HAD EATEN OF THE BREAD THAT SATISFIES   265 8
    WHAT PRICE HIS BREAD UPON THE WATERS   335 30
    SHE SNAPS THE SOFT BREAD FROM MY HAND IN GREAT MOUTHFULS   359 1
    AND HAVING THE BREAD HANGING OVER HER CHIN   359 7
    TAKING BREAD IN HER CURVED GAPING TOOTHLESS MOUTH   359 19
    YOU KNOW WHICH SIDE YOUR BREAD IS BUTTERED   396 17

BREAD
    THEY SAY CAN'T WE HAVE A LOAF OF COMMON BREAD   442 17
    AND MEN AND THE BREAD OF MEN   483 13
    AND IF I HAVE NO MONEY THEY WILL GIVE ME A LITTLE BREAD   486 22
    BREAD SHOULD BE FREE   487 7
    WITH ITS ROOTS IT HAS A GRAND GRIP ON ITS DAILY BREAD   498 21
    TILL HE WAS BORN FROM A WOMB AND ATE SOUP AND BREAD   689 28
    BESIDES MY DAILY BREAD   704 16
    FEED ON OUR WOUNDS LIKE BREAD RECEIVE OUR BLOOD   743 4
    AND EATING THE BRAVE BREAD OF A WHOLESOME KNOWLEDGE   *959 14

BREAD-FRUIT
    AND THROUGH THE SHADOW OF BREAD-FRUIT TREES WITH THEIR   383 30
    AND THROUGH THE SHADOW OF BREAD-FRUIT TREES WITH THEIR   387 1

BREADTH
    IF I GO ON WALKING THROUGH THE WHOLE BREADTH OF GERMANY   212 24

BREAK
    TO BREAK MY HEART   55 11
    WHAT WAS MY QUESTION MY GOD MUST I BREAK THIS   76 9
    NOW HERE I SIT WHILE YOU BREAK THE MUSIC BENEATH   85 21
    AND TRIED TO BREAK THE VESSEL AND VIOLATE MY SOUL   92 24
    WHOSE LOFTY ROSES BREAK AND BLOW   104 23
    TO BREAK AND POUR HER OUT ITS PRECIOUS DEW   113 12
    OF FLESH DOES CRACKLE AND SHIVER AND BREAK IN PAIN   151 17
    BREAK IN BY MAKING ANY REPLY   152 9
    OH COME AND BREAK THIS PRISON THIS HOUSE OF YESTERDAY   174 17
    AND BREAK THE WALLS OF POSSESSION OF ALL THE WIDE WORLD   175 17
    OH MEN WITH THE AXE AND THE PICK-AXE BREAK THE WALLS OF+ 175 26
    TO BREAK THIS SICK AND NAUSEOUS DREAM   177 19
    BREAK OUT OF THIS FOUL HAS-BEEN   177 24
    I THINK I COULD BREAK THE SYSTEM WITH MY HEART   213 19
    I THINK IN MY CONVULSION THE SKIES WOULD BREAK   213 20
    DO NOT LEAVE ME OR I SHALL BREAK   214 2
    WHEN THEY BREAK AND SHOW THE SEED THEN WE LOOK INTO THE+ 277 2
    YOU WHO IN LOVING BREAK DOWN   290 15
    AND BREAK FURTHER AND FURTHER DOWN   290 16
    SEEING IRON BREAK AND BUD   304 5
    BREAK INTO DROPS BURN INTO DROPS OF BLOOD AND DROPPING   322 14
    YOU WOULD TAKE A STICK AND BREAK HIM NOW AND FINISH   350 6
    I REMEMBER WHEN I FIRST HEARD BULL-FROGS BREAK INTO SOU+ 365 32
    BREAK THE DRUMS OF HIS EARS   439 9
    MUST RUN THE PATTERN OUT IN A LITTLE BREAK AT THE END   448 24
    LET US LOSE SIGHT OF OURSELVES AND BREAK THE MIRRORS   477 27
    BREAK THE CAGE THEN START IN AND TRY   485 9
    THE STORM IS WORDS THE BOTTLES NEVER BREAK   543 11
    IF YOU DON'T WANT TO BREAK THE SWEET ENGLISH SPELL   576 11
    I MUST SEE IF I CAN'T BREAK THROUGH IT   605 9
    OR THEY BREAK DOWN   639 10
    AND STILL THROUGH KNOWLEDGE AND WILL HE CAN BREAK AWAY   700 22
    MAN CAN BREAK AWAY AND FALL FROM THE HANDS OF GOD   700 23
    TO BREAK AGAINST THE GROUND   705 12
    THAT STRIP US AND DESTROY US AND BREAK US DOWN   709 17
    A BRUISE OR BREAK OF EXIT FOR HIS LIFE   717 13
    I FEEL THE PAIN OF FALLING LEAVES AND STEMS THAT BREAK + 727 7
    AND FEEL HIM GRIPPING MY WRIST AS IF HE WOULD BREAK IT   733 4
    WHICH YOU CAN ONLY BREAK   794 27
    AND WHEN I SEE THE THICK WHITE BODY OF TRAIN-SMOKE BREAK 883 16
    MY QUESTION MY GOD I MUST BREAK FROM THIS HOARSE SILENCE *898 4
    MY QUESTION MY GOD I MUST BREAK FROM THIS HOARSE SILENCE *901 13
    ARE OPEN FOR THEM THEY ARE MOPING OR THEY BREAK WITH LI+ *918 7
    A BRUISE OR BREAK OF EXIT FOR HIS LIFE   *957 4

BREAKER
    FROM THE CREST OF A FALLING BREAKER   200 23

BREAKERS
    IN THE FLAT RECURRENT BREAKERS OF MY TWO FEET   705 13

BREAKING
    AND THE DULL BREAKING OF BONES   640 12
    DO YOU SEE THE SEA BREAKING ITSELF TO BITS AGAINST THE + 705 1
    HE IS BREAKING ME DOWN TO HIS OWN OBLIVION   727 29
    NOW LIKE A STRANGE LIGHT BREAKING FROM THE GROUND   744 10
    ONLY BREAKING CAMP AND ENTERING   768 11
    OF MY BREAKING HAD DIED UPON HIM ERE THE STAIN   885 5

BREAKS
    BREAKS FROM THE WINTER-CELL TO CLAMBER   46 7
    THE MORNING BREAKS LIKE A POMEGRANATE   58 24
    BREAKS INTO DAZZLE OF LIVING AS DOLPHINS LEAP FROM THE + 136 19
    BREAKS AND SOBS IN THE BLIND   140 18
    BREAKS LIGHT INTO GEMS AND DEAD BREASTS WHITER   188 17
    SEX WHICH BREAKS UP OUR INTEGRITY OUR SINGLE INVIOLABIL+ 366 31
    SEX WHICH BREAKS US INTO VOICE SETS US CALLING ACROSS T+ 366 34
    NOW AGAIN AND NOW FOR EVER BREAKS THE GREAT ILLUSION   635 1
    IT IS MERELY A MACHINE BREAKS DOWN   638 22
    BREAKS DOWN   640 9
    THEN HE REPENTS AND HIS WILL BREAKS AND A GREAT LOVE OF+ 648 16
    WHEN THE BOUGH BREAKS   669 9
    THE WORN-OUT MACHINE AT LAST BREAKS DOWN   676 4
    THAT RUNS DOWN TO THE SHALLOWS OF MY WRISTS AND BREAKS 705 5
    AND BREAKS IN THE FOAMY HANDS WHOSE POWER ROLLS OUT   705 16
    AS THE MACHINE BREAKS FINALLY DOWN   *954 12

BREAST
    RIPPLES BELOW THE BREAST AN URGENT   39 4
    INTO THE EVENING'S ANXIOUS BREAST   42 7
    THEN HER BRIGHT BREAST SHE WILL UNCOVER   42 17
    THE WHITE MOON SHOW LIKE A BREAST REVEALED   55 26
    NEXT TO MY BREAST WHERE MY OWN HEART WAS BEATING   61 22
    HER FACE LAY PALE AGAINST MY BREAST   62 14
    WHILE HER TEARS SOAK THROUGH TO MY BREAST   64 18
    THE WAVE OF SOLDIERS THE COMING WAVE THE THROBBING RED + 66 23
    MY CONSTABLE WI' 'IS BUTTONED BREAST   79 5
    RELIEF THAT STARTS IN MY BREAST   100 10
    SO I LAY ON YOUR BREAST FOR AN OBSCURE HOUR   104 4

BREAST
   ON THE BREAST OF MY COAT AND ONE BY ONE   107 3
   AND MY BREAST TO HER BEATING   120 20
   BREAST WAS BOUND   120 21
   AND GLADLY I'D OFFERED MY BREAST TO THE TREAD OF HER   123 6
   HUNGRY FOR LOVE YET IF I LAY MY HAND IN HER BREAST   128 2
   I SEE YOUR BLANCHED FACE AT MY BREAST AND HIDE   129 13
   AND I DO LIFT MY ANGUISHED AVID BREAST   129 20
   FEELING YOUR STRONG BREAST CARRY ME ON INTO   129 25
   FOR THE MOON ON MY BREAST AND THE AIR ON MY LIMBS   130 11
   SOME MONEY HER HAND SLIPS OUT OF THE BREAST OF HER   143 8
   FULL MID-BETWEEN THE CHAMPAIGN OF YOUR BREAST   154 8
   LEAVES AN EMPTY BREAST   155 12
   I WISH WITH MY BREAST I HERE COULD ANNIHILATE IT ALL   173 16
   FALL ON MY SHALLOW BREAST   194 5
   OF RIPPLES ACROSS MY BREAST   194 9
   WITH A HEAVY CHILD AT HER BREAST   200 2
   MY BREAST WHICH IS SO SORE   230 13
   YOU WOULD TAKE ME TO YOUR BREAST BUT NO   230 21
   OF MY MANLY BREAST   237 2
   CREEP RIGHT UP WITH YOUR ROUND HEAD PUSHED IN MY BREAST   245 6
   MY BIRD MY BROWN SPARROW IN MY BREAST   246 18
   IF YOU START AWAY FROM MY BREAST AND LEAVE ME   246 24
   OF THE BULL'S BREAST   326 21
   IS HIS BREAST A WALL   326 24
   NOT ONE INSTANT CLEAVE CLING LIKE A BLOT WITH HIS BREAS+   343 29
   YOUR WATTLES DRIP DOWN LIKE A SHAWL TO YOUR BREAST   369 29
   MASS OF A GENEROUS BREAST   370 7
   BREAST   370 28
   A SCORCHED BREAST   372 26
   A SCORCHED BREAST BREASTING THE SUN LIKE AN ANSWER   372 27
   REFLECTING THE SCORCH OF THE SUN FROM HIS BREAST   373 3
   ONLY THE INNER EYE OF YOUR SCORCHED BROAD BREAST   373 24
   AT YOUR SCORCHED BREAST   373 30
   FEATHER OVER FEATHER ON THE BREAST OF THE GREAT AND GOL+   409 16
   AND LIFT HIS FACE AND SET HIS BREAST   428 18
   ITS BREAST AGAINST ITS NEST TO MAKE IT ROUND   451 14
   EACH ONE TURNING HIS BREAST STRAIGHT TO THE SUN OF SUNS   525 12
   AND THROUGH THE WIDE PRAIRIES OF HIS BREAST A YOUNG BUL+   624 7
   WHO IS IT THAT SOFTLY TOUCHES THE SIDES OF MY BREAST   652 6
   AND MY LOST WHITE FEARLESS BREAST   696 5
   UNKNOWN WITHIN YOUR BREAST AND YOUR DEADENED LOINS   723 18
   MY LEGS MY BREAST MY BELLY   741 17
   A SCORCHED BREAST SUN-TURNED FOREVER   781 2
   A SCORCHED BREAST BREASTING THE BLAZE   781 3
   BREAST   781 30
   AT THE SUN OF YOUR BREAST   782 6
   FROM A RED BREAST   783 27
   THERE IS A BREAST OF A VAST AND UNKNOWN BODY   784 9
   INTO THAT BREAST   784 24
   TO LEAN OVER MY HEAD AND MY NECK AND MY BREAST   799 18
   BETWEEN YOUR BREAST AND BELLY IS A STAR   800 2
   WHEN YOU WALK THE STAR WALKS WITH YOU BETWEEN YOUR BREA+   800 5
   EVE WITH HER RESTLESS VIRGIN-BUDDED BREAST   864 13
   THAT LIFT UP HIGH THEN DROP HIS STRANGE HARSH BREAST   879 1
   AND HANDS AND FACE AND BREAST WITH THAT HOT CLOAK   879 10
   CLEAVES FROZEN TO THE WALLS OF MY COLD BREAST   879 20
   AND I RAISED MY BREAST   882 8
   OF THE CREEPER ON THE BREAST OF THE HOUSE OPPOSITE   883 2
   ON THE BREAST OF A ROBIN THAT IS FLUTTERED WITH PAIN   883 5
   AND MY OWN BREAST OPENS IN QUICK RESPONSE   883 6
   I LIFT MY BREAST AND LEAN FORWARD   883 10
   DUG FIRM IN MY BREAST AS YOU REACHED OUT RIGHT   886 8
   AS MY WILD SOUL SHRINKS AND THE SONGS ARE DRIVEN FROM M+   *896 12
   TO OPEN MY BLOSSOM-FULL BREAST FROM ITS DREARY BANDS   *896 24
   NEXT MY BREAST WHERE MY OWN HEART WAS BEATING   *912 2
   HER FACE LAY THERE BEFORE MY BREAST   *912 20
   MY CONSTABLE WI' 'IS BUTTONED BREAST   *921 1
   FROM MY BREAST TO YOUR BOSOM ECLIPSE   *929 28
   WOULD GLADLY HAVE OFFERED MY BREAST FOR HER TREAD TO TRY   *934 12
   CAME DOWN ON MY BREAST SHOVING OVER   *936 3
   ON MY BREAST WITH HER WINGS AND HER FEATHERS TO DROWN   *936 7
   DEER CRASH THEIR HORNS IN THE MOUNTAINS OF HIS BREAST   *953 28

BREAST-FEATHERS
   HANDING OUT A FEW LOOSE GOLDEN BREAST-FEATHERS AT MOULT+   414 9

BREASTING
   A SCORCHED BREAST BREASTING THE SUN LIKE AN ANSWER   372 27
   A SCORCHED BREAST BREASTING THE BLAZE   781 3

BREAST-LIGHTS
   THE BREAST-LIGHTS ABOVE   *891 33

BREASTS
   MY UNKNOWN BREASTS BEGIN   39 2
   COOL LONELY NIGHT HER BREASTS WILL KEEP THE NIGHT AT BAY   91 11
   PRESSING HER SPREAD HANDS OVER HER BREASTS AS SHE   128 24
   CATCH MY HANDS MY DARLING BETWEEN YOUR BREASTS   147 15
   BREAKS LIGHT INTO GEMS AND DEAD BREASTS WHITER   168 17
   TO FEEL FRESH AIR IN OUR THROATS TO HAVE FRESH BREATH I+   175 21
   BREASTS   207 2
   A SHADOW OVER MY BREASTS THAT WILL KILL ME AT LAST   211 4
   KISS ME HOW COLD YOU ARE YOUR LTTTLE BREASTS   212 6
   SHE STOOPS TO THE SPONGE AND HER SWUNG BREASTS   217 16
   YOUR BREASTS YOUR NAKEDNESS   238 11
   AND I THE SWIFT BRACTS THAT SHEATHE IT THOSE BREASTS TH+   245 16
   YOUR BREASTS YOUR KNEES AND FEET I FEEL THAT WE   245 23
   BETWEEN HER BREASTS IS MY HOME BETWEEN HER BREASTS   249 9
   SURE AND A TOWER OF STRENGTH 'TWIXT THE WALLS OF HER BR+   249 12
   BETWEEN HER BREASTS IS MY HOME BETWEEN HER BREASTS   249 26
   BREASTS   249 30
   WITH MY FACE DOWN BURIED BETWEEN HER BREASTS   250 10
   AND MY STILL HANDS FULL OF HER BREASTS   250 12
   BREASTS   254 31
   ALSO SHE WHO IS THE OTHER HAS STRANGE-MOUNDED BREASTS A+   261 8
   I COULD PUT MY FACE AT LAST BETWEEN HER BREASTS   265 4
   WHO ON THEIR BREASTS   313 20

BREASTS
   UPON THE BREASTS OF LOUTISH BOLSHEVISTS   317 2
   AND THEIR NAKED BREASTS THE GROOVED LOINS   389 8
   SOBBING IN DARK SWEAT-SHINING BREASTS   389 12
   SLIM LIMBS AND BREASTS   389 17
   WENT UP IN WAVELETS TO HIM FROM THE BREASTS AND EYES   389 29
   AND ALL WAS DREARY GREAT ROBOT LIMBS ROBOT BREASTS   651 2
   BOTH BREASTS DIM AND MYSTERIOUS WITH THE GLAMOROUS KIND+   693 12
   OUR HANDS OUR BREASTS REBEL AGAINST US   746 13
   I AM FANNING YOUR BREASTS WITH MY BREATH   802 2
   BREASTS THAT WINK NOT   827 21
   HER BREASTS UPLIFTED IN ENDEAVOR SHE TOUCHES SHE REEVES   864 12
   KNOWING THEN I HAD TAKEN MY BOSOM FROM HER CRUSHED BREA+   882 9
   YOUR SMALL BREASTS CLUMPS OF WHITE   886 6
   IF MY VEINS AND MY BREASTS WITH LOVE EMBOSSED   *891 26
   FILLING MY STILL BREASTS WITH A FLUSH AND A FLAME   *893 17
   GATHERING THE SOFT RIPPLES BELOW MY BREASTS   *893 18
   AND AH MY BITTER BREASTS THAT SULK AND FRET   *933 32
   GOLDEN SHADOW GLOWS AND HER BREASTS   *942 25
   BETWEEN HER BREASTS IS MY HOME BETWEEN HER BREASTS   *945 21
   WARM IN A CITY OF STRENGTH BETWEEN HER BREASTS   *945 23
   MY FACE BETWEEN HER BREASTS   *946 2
   WITH MY FACE DOWN-BURIED BETWEEN HER BREASTS   *946 8
   AND MY STILL HANDS FULL OF HER BREASTS   *946 10

BREAST'S
   MY BREAST'S AS RED AS THINE I RECKON   78 23
   MY BREAST'S ACHING CICATRICE   869 9
   MY BREAST'S AS RED AS THINE I RECKON   *920 15

BREAST-TIPS
   WHITE BREAST-TIPS OF MY MEXICO   787 6
   AND HE SAW MEXICO LYING LIKE A DARK WOMAN WITH WHITE BR+   790 5

BREATH
   WHO WITH A RUFFLING CAREFUL BREATH   46 13
   IT HAS NO BREATH   55 19
   HER BREATH FLEW WARM AGAINST MY NECK   61 28
   AS THE BREATH WHICH UPWARDS FROM THE NOSTRILS OF AN IMM+   97 20
   FOR THE NIGHT WITH A GREAT BREATH TAKEN   107 25
   SUBSTANCE OF MY INCONSISTENT BREATH   118 8
   BEAUTIFUL PASSIVE AND STRONG AS THE BREATH   118 14
   TO FALL LIKE A BREATH WITHIN THE BREATHING WIND   134 26
   ALL SHAPES OF WONDER WITH SUSPENDED BREATH   165 19
   YOUR CARGO OUT BREATH FROM BREATH   168 11
   FOR THE HOUSE IS SHUT AND SEALED AND THE BREATH OF THE +   174 27
   TO FEEL FRESH AIR IN OUR THROATS TO HAVE FRESH BREATH I+   175 21
   LIKE A BREATH IN A BUBBLE SPINNING   193 24
   THE GREAT BREATH BLOWING A TINY SEED OF FIRE   219 2
   THE BREATH OF THE BULLOCK STAINS THE HARD CHILL AIR   225 13
   STILL IN HIS NOSTRILS THE FROZEN BREATH OF DESPAIR   226 5
   LOOK FOR LIKE THE BREATH OF LIFE AS LONG AS I LIVE   248 10
   DARK BREATH OF THE EARTH THE SERPENT SLID FORTH LAY REV+   348 7
   AND DANCE AND DANCE FOREVER DANCE WITH BREATH HALF   389 11
   BEASTS' LIMBS AND THE BREATH FROM THEIR FEET THAT THEY +   406 2
   YOUR VERY BREATH   456 13
   YFT I FFAR MY OWN BREATH   460 32
   THF BREATH THAT RUSHES THROUGH MY NOSE THE STRIFE   461 3
   AND FALLS BACK DRAWING IN ITS BREATH IN RAGE   467 14
   IF HIS PRESENCE AND HIS BREATH ARE POISON TO ME   468 4
   BACK AND FORTH GOES THE BALANCE AND THE ELECTRIC BREATH   480 21
   TOWARDS THE SUN OF SUNS AND BACK AND FORTH GOES THE BRE+   480 24
   AND MY LEAVES ARE GREEN WITH THE BREATH OF HUMAN EXPERI+   499 11
   NOT BY TIME BUT BY UNCLEAN BREATH AND EYES   580 24
   AWAY THE EVIL STARINGS AND THE BREATH   581 7
   THE BREATH OF LIFE   615 13
   BUT THE LIVING LEAVES IN THE BREATH OF THE WIND ARE MOR+   615 14
   THE BREATH OF LIFE AND THE SHARP WINDS OF CHANGE ARE TH+   615 16
   AND THE BREATH OF LIFE NEVER COMES TO NOURISH THEM   615 20
   IF HE SHOW IT THE EYES AND THE BREATH OF THE CROWD   634 16
   HARDLY LOOSES EVEN A LAST BREATH OF PERFUME   646 22
   YOU MAY SMELL THE BREATH OF THE GODS IN THE COMMON ROSES   655 7
   TO THE BREATH THAT IS OF NEW BEAUTY UNFOLDING IN DEATH   676 23
   AND A BREATH OF VAPOUR BEGAN TO WREATHE UP   682 14
   THEN ALL THE ELECTRONS HELD THEIR BREATH   682 27
   POURING OUT HIS BREATH   684 7
   THERE THEY BLOW THERE THEY BLOW HOT WILD WHITE BREATH O+   694 6
   THE BREATH OF LIFE IS IN THE SHARP WINDS OF CHANGE   698 1
   MINGLED WITH THE BREATH OF DESTRUCTION   698 2
   THE DIVIDERS ARE CLOSE UPON US DOGGING OUR EVERY BREATH   707 3
   HOLDING THEIR BREATH NAKED AND DARKLY ALONE   711 5
   PUSHED UP ON END AND THE BREATH SIGHING   733 25
   WHERE FLAMES WHEEL IN LIKE BREATH   784 10
   AND THE FLAME OF YOU SWEPT BACK IN A NEW BREATH OF LIFE   784 26
   I ROSE AGAIN TO SEE A STAR FALLING AND FEEL A BREATH ON   786 10
   THE BREATH SAID GO AND LO   786 12
   AND THE BREATH BLEW UPON ME AGAIN   787 1
   SO HE BLEW DOWN ON THEM TO BLOW HIS BREATH IN THEIR FAC+   790 24
   AND THE AIR THAT BLOWS GOOD BREATH IN THE NOSTRILS OF P+   792 14
   IS READY TO BLOW BAD BREATH UPON THEM TO PERISH THEM ALL   792 16
   I AM FANNING YOUR BREASTS WITH MY BREATH   802 3
   BLUE IS THE BREATH OF QUETZALCOATL   808 18
   WHERE THE BREATH AND THE FOUNTAINS COMMINGLE   811 4
   A THRILL THROUGH THE LISTENING TREES AND HOLD THE BREATH   858 26
   FOR HIS MISSION HAD CRUELLY FAILED WHILE HIS PASSIONATE+   859 11
   THE BREATH OF MY DREAM IS FADED FROM OFF THE MIRROR   871 10
   HE DRAWS A DEEP HARD BREATH FROM SPACE TO SPACE   878 23
   FROM SPACE TO LONGER SPACE LIFTS A HARSH BREATH   878 24
   AND STILL THE LONG HARSH BREATH SINKS HOARSELY OUT   878 27
   HER BREATH FLEW WARM AGAINST MY NECK   *912 7

BREATHE
   BREATHE LARGELY THE LUMINOUS BREEZE   69 8
   SWORD THAT SEVERS THE QUESTION FROM US WHO BREATHE   168 26
   GIVE US AIR WE CRY OH LET US BUT BREATHE   175 18
   LET US BREATHE FRESH AIR AND WAKE FROM FOUL DREAMS IN W+   175 19
   AND RELEASE US POOR ONES AND RICH ONES LET US BREATHE A+   175 28
   AND BREATHE DESPAIR THAT TURNS MY LUNGS TO STONE   226 11

BREATHE
TO BREATHE FROM THE FLOOD AT THE GILLS   336 30
WE'RE NOT FIT FOR THE AIR WE BREATHE   553 30
BUT IF YOU WANT TO BREATHE DEEP SUMPTUOUS LIFE   698 3
BREATHE ALL ALONE IN SILENCE IN THE DARK   698 4
TO COME AT IT TO BREATHE IT IN THIS DARK   876 30
BREATHE LARGELY THE LUMINOUS BREEZE   *915 20

BREATHED
BREATHED QUIET ABOVE ME AND THE CROP   35 19
IN THE OLD DAYS WHEN SAPPHIRES WERE BREATHED UPON AND   477 1
CRUSHED UTTERLY AND BREATHED THROUGH AND THROUGH   530 2
WHO BREATHED YOU OUT AND BREATHES YOU IN AGAIN   784 8
SHE KISSED THEIR COOLNESS LAST NIGHT BREATHED THEIR CLE+   856 19
I BREATHED MY DREAMS UPON YOU I LAID MY MOUTH ON YOUR M+   871 1
AND BREATHED ON YOU THE PICTURE-MIST OF MY DREAMS   871 2

BREATHES
BUT IT BREATHES GENTLY AND LANGUISHINGLY IN THE BACK OF+   434 3
WHO BREATHED YOU OUT AND BREATHES YOU IN AGAIN   784 8

BREATHING
OF THE BREATHING HOSTS   108 19
TO FALL LIKE A BREATH WITHIN THE BREATHING WIND   134 26
AND BREATHING THE FROZEN MEMORY OF HIS WRONG   226 4
SO CLOSE BREATHING SO STILL   246 21
AND BREATHING SOFT UNWILLING TO WAKE TO THE NEW DAY   311 12
AND WATCHING THE FISHES IN THE BREATHING WATERS   337 29
AND THEY WHISPER IT OUT AND THEY TITTER IT OUT BREATHING   462 25
TOWARDS THE BREATHING STARS AND THE CENTRAL OF ALL SUNN+   480 18
BREATHING OF THE DEAD MEN   528 20
THE CENSORS BREATHING WITH RELIEF   528 21
LOOKING DIRT ON THEM AND BREATHING ON THEM LIES   580 26
BREATHING ON HIS SMALL FRAIL SAIL AND HELPING HIM ON   723 23
HE IS BREATHING COLD CORRUPTION UPON YOU YOU SHALL BLEE+   796 32

BREATHLESS
I CAN SMELL THE BOG-END GORGEOUS IN ITS BREATHLESS   90 7
AND A GIRL RAN SWIFTLY LAUGHING BREATHLESS TAKING IN HE+   672 13
BREATHLESS SOUNDS OF SATISFACTION CLAMOUR OF DELIGHT   865 27

BREATHS
ON HIS LIPS WHERE THE LIGHT BREATHS COME AND GO   60 5
BY HER MEASURED BREATHS I LIKE TO SEE SAID SHE   123 11
SHARP BREATHS TAKEN YEA AND I   219 23
DEEP PANTING BREATHS LIKE GREAT BEASTS READY FOR   827 8
AND EVER AND ANON THE GREAT BREATHS COME   878 32
AT THESE WIDE-SPACED TORN ENORMOUS BREATHS   878 36
SHARP BREATHS SWISHING YEA BUT I   *944 3

BREATH'S
LIFE IN THY MOUTH AND DIM BREATH'S HASTENING HISS   69 24

BRED
IN MANY WAYS VERY FINELY BRED   400 15
BUT BRED IN CONCEIT THAT THE WORLD IS ALL FOR LOVE   400 16

BREED
WON'T BREED THEY MOPE THEY DIE   484 24
AND THE BEST WON'T BREED THOUGH THEY DON'T KNOW WHY   484 27
MAN IS ONE OF THOSE BEASTS THAT WILL BREED IN A CAGE   843 14

BREEZE
WITH THAT UNFELT BREEZE THAT EBBS OVER THE SEAS WHERE T+   53 13
A BREEZE   58 5
BREATHE LARGELY THE LUMINOUS BREEZE   69 8
LIKE A RHYTHMIC BREEZE   104 6
BREEZE   133 21
PAST WITH THE NOISE OF A BREEZE   144 24
BREEZE OF THE MORNING THROUGH A NARROW WHITE BIRCH   209 28
TO FEEL A FINE FINE BREEZE BLOWING THROUGH THE NAVEL AND   481 21
IN A BREEZE OF KNOWLEDGE   742 34
THE BREEZE WAKES UP A MUSIC IN THE SALLOW   868 21
SHE MAY COVER HER EYES YET THE AIMLESS BREEZE OF MY WOR+   868 29
WITH THE UNFELT BREEZE THAT EBBS OVER THE SEAS WHEN THE+   *906 5
BREATHE LARGELY THE LUMINOUS BREEZE   *915 20
THE BREEZE WAKES UP A MUSIC IN THE SALLOW   *941 21
THEN DOWN THE BREEZE LIGHT WAFTING O'ER THE FALLOW   *941 23
SO SHE CLOSES HER EYES BUT THE AIMLESS BREEZE OF THE WO+   *942 1
THAT WILL SPREAD IN DEATH TO THE BREEZE   *961 2

BRETHREN
PAUSE BRETHREN PAUSE   510 15

BREWING
SHE IS BREWING HOPE FROM DESPAIR   203 8

BRICK
AND LOOSEN THE BRICK AND THE HARD CEMENT   462 11

BRICK-STUFF
THAT YOU LOSE THE BRICK-STUFF OUT OF YOU   53 28

BRIDAL
YOUR OWN DARK MOUTH WITH THE BRIDAL FAINT LADY-SMOCKS   90 11
HAD BEEN WOVEN INTO A GLORIOUS MESH LIKE A BRIDAL LACE   860 14

BRIDE
BRIDE TO YOUR GROOM   56 3
NAY BUT SHE SLEEPS LIKE A BRIDE AND DREAMS HER DREAMS   101 12
BUT I WHOM THE YEARS HAD REARED TO BE YOUR BRIDE   157 1
WHO FOR ONE STRANGE YEAR WAS AS A BRIDE TO YOU YOU SET +   157 4
THEN THE GREAT BULL LIES UP AGAINST HIS BRIDE   694 13
THE LOST BRIDE AND HER GROOM   697 22
GREAT BRIDE OF ALL CREATION   698 7
LIKE A BRIDE HE TOOK MY BAYONET WANTING IT   742 9
AND HE IS THE BRIDE I HAVE SOWN HIM WITH THE SEED   742 13
OUR FLESH THE BRIDE   742 26

BRIDE
OUR BRIDE AMONG THE RUSTLING CHORUS OF SHELLS   743 9
WE TAKE THE BRIDE O GOD AND OUR SEED OF LIFE   743 12
IT MAY BE I SHALL GIVE THE BRIDE   743 22
MY BRIDE   787 7
MY BRIDE BETWEEN THE SEAS   787 12
STOOPING OVER HIS BRIDE   *946 13
AND PERSEPHONE HERSELF IS BUT A VOICE AS A BRIDE   *956 15

BRIDEGROOM
OF FINISHED BRIDEGROOM SEEN HER RISE AND THROW   193 4
A NAKED TREE OF BLOSSOM LIKE A BRIDEGROOM BATHING IN DEW   306 8
ARE THE GUNS AND THE STEEL THE BRIDEGROOM   742 25
WHY AM I BRIDEGROOM OF WAR WAR'S PARAMOUR   742 36
BE BRIDEGROOM OR BEST MAN AS THE CASE TURNS OUT   743 20
TO HER BRIDEGROOM IN THE DARK   *955 15

BRIDE'S
ALONG THY LIMBS DELIGHTED AS A BRIDE'S   69 12
ALONG THY LIMBS DELIGHTED THINE HIS BRIDE'S   *915 24

BRIDGE
UNDER THE BRIDGE   144 7
AT CHARING CROSS HERE BENEATH THE BRIDGE   144 14
THE BRIDGE ON ITS STANCHIONS   146 14
A CIRCLE SWOOP AND A QUICK PARABOLA UNDER THE BRIDGE   341 1
THE SCALES ARE LOCKED IN AN ARCH LIKE A BRIDGE   355 2
MUST CREEP HER GREAT BULK BENEATH THE BRIDGE OF HIM   426 10
AND OVER THE BRIDGE OF THE WHALE'S STRONG PHALLUS LINKI+   694 21

BRIDGES
AT THE BRIDGES   146 34
FORESTS CITIES BRIDGES   293 22

BRIDLE
AND JOSEPH HOLDING THE BRIDLE   200 3

BRIDLED
AND THEY ARE BRIDLED WITH CUNNING AND BITTED   656 17

BRIDLES
AND JERKED BACK THEIR BRIDLES PUSHING THEIR HEADS APART   735 9

BRIEF
THE BRIEF MATERIAL CONTROL OF THE HOUR LEAVE THEM FREE +   93 8

BRIGHT
THEN HER BRIGHT BREAST SHE WILL UNCOVER   42 17
HIS BRIGHT DARK EYES COME OVER ME LIKE A HOOD   43 34
THE PINK YOUNG HORSES SHOW ONE SIDE BRIGHT   50 23
OF UNDERWATER FLOAT BRIGHT RIPPLES RUN   51 7
THEN BACK IN A SWIFT BRIGHT FLUTTER TO WORK   51 28
BY BRIGHT LEAVES UTTERED ALOUD AND STRIFE   68 7
STEPPING LIKE BIRDS WITH THEIR BRIGHT AND POINTED FEET   71 25
IN SCARLET ALIVE WITH THE BIRDS' BRIGHT TWITTERING   72 22
GOD STEPPING THROUGH OUR LOINS IN ONE BRIGHT STRIDE   87 25
BRIGHT CRIMSON RIM   96 18
NOTHING NOW WILL RIPEN THE BRIGHT GREEN APPLES   119 11
ONCE I HAD A LOVER BRIGHT LIKE RUNNING WATER   119 23
LEST HER BRIGHT EYES LIKE SPARROWS SHOULD FLY IN   122 29
BRIGHT   128 21
OF MY MOCKERY MOCKS AT HIM OVER THE WAVES' BRIGHT   130 7
AND SKIES OF GOLD AND LADIES IN BRIGHT TISSUE   135 4
AND OUT OF THE INVISIBLE STREAMS OF BRIGHT BLUE DROPS   136 11
RAIN FROM THE SHOWERY HEAVENS AND BRIGHT BLUE CROPS   136 12
LIKE VIVID THOUGHT THE AIR SPINS BRIGHT AND ALL   142 14
HOLDING ALOFT THEIR UMBRELLAS THAT FLASH AND ARE BRIGHT   146 19
IT WAS SO FAIR THE BRIGHT   165 2
ONE BRIGHT RED RAY   176 13
THAT PERFECT BRIGHT EXPERIENCE NEVER FALLS   193 10
AND THE BRIGHT RIVERS FLIT   196 10
MANY BRIGHT PEOPLE PASS   196 16
CROWDING THE BRIGHT DOORWAY   201 26
HIS SCYTHE-BLADE BRIGHT UNHOOKS   220 4
AGAINST ME AND BRIGHT PEAK SHINING TO PEAK   224 4
THREE OF THEM BLACK IN SHADOW TWO OF THEM BRIGHT   224 10
I HAVE MADE THE FIRE UP BRIGHT   237 20
BRIGHT GLANCING EXQUISITE CORN OF MANY A STUBBORN   263 27
I HAVE CHOSEN AMONG THE BRIGHT AND MARVELLOUS BOOKS   264 3
POMEGRANATES LIKE BRIGHT GREEN STONE   278 13
YOUR WEIRD BRIGHT MOTOR-PRODUCTIVE MECHANISM   292 8
GONE AGAIN IN THE BRIGHT TRAIL OF LAVA   293 23
HIS RED-GOLD WATER-PRECIOUS MIRROR-FLAT BRIGHT EYE   339 8
ONLY IN THE BRIGHT DAY I WILL NOT HAVE THIS CLOT IN MY   346 11
YOUR BRIGHT DARK LITTLE EYE   352 20
YOUR EYE IS VERY DARK VERY BRIGHT   359 10
HER BRIGHT EYE SEES BUT NOT ME NOT ANYTHING   359 16
AND BLACK EYES BULGING BRIGHT IN A DUST-MASK   397 17
HER ROUND BRIGHT FACE BRIGHT AS FROST   402 2
AND HER BRIGHT STRIPED FROST-FACE WILL NEVER WATCH ANY   402 17
COMPELLED TO ADMIRE THE BRIGHT RHYTHMS OF MOVING BODIES   445 25
IN THE BRIGHT WILD CIRCUS FLESH   446 18
SEA-BEASTS IMMERSED LEAN SIDEWAYS AND FLASH BRIGHT   453 25
WILL BE BRIGHT RED WITH BLOOD   515 6
WITH BRIGHT LEGS AND UNCRINGING BUTTOCKS   525 21
ON WHAT A BRIGHT LITTLE ISLAND   574 15
BRIGHT AND NAKED AFT AND FORE   574 20
OH WHAT A BRIGHT LITTLE ISLAND   575 11
ANGELS ARE BRIGHT STILL THOUGH THE BRIGHTEST FELL   614 12
JUGFULL AFTER JUGFULL OF PURE WHITE LIQUID FIRE BRIGHT + 647 9
SACRIFICE THAT TO THE BRIGHT GODS AND SATISFY THE DESTR+ 678 17
O SLAY NOT THE BEST BRIGHT PROUD LIFE THAT IS IN YOU TH+ 678 24
AND LET MANKIND MAKE NEW BLOOD FRESH AND BRIGHT   679 7
HE IS BRIGHT LIGHT   682 10
GOD IS BORN GOD IS BORN BRIGHT YELLOW AND DUCTILE HE IS+ 682 25
THAT WE SHOULD BE LOVELY IN THE FLESH WITH BRIGHT CRESC+ 687 16
ANGELS ARE BRIGHT STILL THOUGH THE BRIGHTEST FELL   697 23
THEN THE BRIGHT DAWNING OF DELIGHT AGAIN   708 26

BRIGHT
AND THERE ARE THE BRIGHT DOORS WHERE SOULS GO GAILY IN   711   3
AND LOOKS AROUND AGAIN AT HIS HEEL THE BRIGHT SPUR   734 14
LOOK IN THE SKY AT THE BRIGHT   755 12
WITH HIS BROW WIPED BRIGHT OF THE TOIL OF SWEAT   770 18
IN PEACE BEYOND THE LASHING OF THE SUN'S BRIGHT TAIL   786   2
I BOUND THE BRIGHT FANGS OF THE SUN   786 23
WITH THE BRIGHT WING ON THE RIGHT   787 18
FLARE BRIGHT TO WANDER AND DO NOTHING   794 16
WHEN YOU SPEAK TRUE AND TRUE IT IS BRIGHT ON YOUR LIPS +   800   8
IN-WEAVING THE BRIGHT THREAD OF HIS JOY   867 27
FLASHING HIS BRIGHT BROWN ARMS AS HE LEANS ON THE POLE   867 28
ROUND HIS BRIGHT JOYFUL BODY   868 12
THE AIR AND THE FLOWING SUNSHINE AND BRIGHT DUST   870   9
AH WITH HIS BLESSING BRIGHT ON THY MOUTH AND THY BROW   872   1
SHALL SING OF HEAVEN ACHIEVED WHERE EVERY BRIGHT   872 15
AND ALL THEIR FACES LIKE BRIGHT FLOWERS AWAKE   872 21
OF UNDER-WATER FLOAT BRIGHT RIPPLES RUN   *898 19
THEN BACK IN A SWIFT BRIGHT FLUTTER TO WORK   *899 12
OF UNDER-WATER FLOAT BRIGHT RIPPLES RUN   *902   3
THEN BACK IN A SWIFT BRIGHT FLUTTER TO WORK   *902 24
BRIGHT TORTURE THOU DIDST DESERVE   *927 15
NOTHING NOW WILL RIPEN THE BRIGHT GREEN APPLES   *932 20
BUT BONNIE AND BRIGHT WERE THE CHICKENS   *933 10
ONCE I HAD A LOVER BRIGHT LIKE RUNNING WATER   *933 13
MY SIGHT BUT THEN WHO HAS STOLE THE BRIGHT WHITE HEN OF+   *933 23
LEST HER BRIGHT EYES LIKE SPARROWS SHOULD FLY IN   *934   5
THEIR EYES TO YOUR BRIGHT PLACE AND THEN IN WONDER   *941   3
HIS SCYTHE BLADE BRIGHT UNHOOKS   *944 12
AND THOSE BRIGHT FIREFLIES WAFTING IN BETWEEN   *945   1

BRIGHT-BOSOMED
WHILE NORTH OF THEM ALL AT THE FARTHEST ENDS STANDS ONE+   57 11

BRIGHTENING
FROM ME TO THE BOYS WHOSE BRIGHTENING SOULS IT LAVES   51 24

BRIGHTER
IN THE WATER MUCH CLEARER AND BRIGHTER   48 28
I IMAGINE DEAD HANDS ARE BRIGHTER   168 13
A STILL BRIGHTER WHITE SNAKE WRIGGLES AMONG IT SPILLED   647 14
SWIFTER AND HIGHER AND BRIGHTER OR THE YIELDING AND THE+   680   6

BRIGHTEST
THE SUN IS FOREVER THIRSTY THIRSTING FOR THE BRIGHTEST +   368   7
AS ONE OF OUR BRIGHTEST YOUNG INTELLECTUALS SAID TO ME   441 22
SO ONE OF THE BRIGHTEST YOUNG INTELLECTUALS PUT IT TO ME   533   4
ANGELS ARE BRIGHT STILL THOUGH THE BRIGHTEST FELL   614 12
ANGELS ARE BRIGHT STILL THOUGH THE BRIGHTEST FELL   697 23
BY THE GREAT SEVEN BY HELIOS THE BRIGHTEST   702   8

BRIGHT-EYE
TINY BRIGHT-EYE   352 16

BRIGHT-FOOTED
SURE AND MOON-SHOD COOL AND BRIGHT-FOOTED   684 12

BRIGHT-GREY
DOWN THE BRIGHT-GREY RUIN OF THINGS   150 23

BRIGHTLY
LOOK BRIGHTLY ON A CONFUSION OF MUD AND SAND AND MORTAR   864 26

BRIGHTNESS
YOUR BRIGHTNESS DIMS WHEN I DRAW TOO NEAR AND MY FREE   87 16
GOLD AND OF INCONCEIVABLY FINE QUINTESSENTIAL BRIGHTNESS   271 18
THAT HE LOST ANY OF HIS BRIGHTNESS IN FALLING   614 14
HE LOST ANY OF HIS BRIGHTNESS IN THE FALLING   697 25
TO THE VAST OF SPACE WHERE BRIGHTNESS RACES THE BLUE   875 14

BRIGHT-PRIDE
BLESSED ARE THE PURE IN HEART AND THE FATHOMLESS IN BRI+   314 16

BRILLIANCE
AND THE FINE BRILLIANCE OF YOUR SO TINY EYE   353 22
THIS LITTLE BIT CHIPPED OFF IN BRILLIANCE   372 11
IN PURE BRILLIANCE OF ANGER SEA-IMMERSED ANGER   453 26

BRILLIANT
LIQUID AS LIME-TREE BLOSSOM SOFT AS BRILLIANT WATER OR +   67 20
THEN BRILLIANT EARTH FROM THE BURR OF NIGHT IN BEAUTY   73   4
OF QUESTING BRILLIANT SOULS GOING OUT WITH THEIR TRUE   221 27
BRILLIANT INTOLERABLE LAVA   293 18
BRILLIANT AS A POWERFUL BURNING-GLASS   293 19
AND STRIPES IN THE BRILLIANT FROST OF HER FACE SHARP FI+ 402   4
DARK KEEN FINE RAYS IN THE BRILLIANT FROST OF HER FACE   402   6
A HOLE IN THE BLOOD-ORANGE BRILLIANT ROCKS THAT STICK U+ 402 12
CALM WITH THE CALM OF SCIMITARS AND BRILLIANT REAPING H+ 609 11
IS THE LITTLE-BOY BRILLIANT   841 12
AND QUITE CLEVER BRILLIANT IS THE MODERN WORD   841 17
IF YOU HEAR A MAN CALLED BRILLIANT YOU MAY BE PRETTY SU+ 841 18
AND DESTRUCTIVE IN SHORT BRILLIANT   841 23
THE MODERN YOUNG WOMAN THINKS IT WONDERFUL TO BE SO BRI+ 841 26
WHY THE MODERN YOUNG WIFE OF THE LITTLE-BOY BRILLIANT B+ 842   9
I HEARD HER SAY TO HER BRILLIANT YOUNG HUSBAND   842 12
AND THE BRILLIANT YOUNG HUSBAND MADE A LITTLE MOVE POUT+ 842 16
YET THE HUSBAND WAS MOST BRILLIANT AND FAMOUS   842 25
A BRILLIANT STATION THE CHASE   862 28
OF QUESTING BRILLIANT THINGS YOU JOY YOU TRUE   *945 13

BRILLIANTEST
EVEN OUR BRILLIANTEST YOUNG INTELLECTUALS   544 26

BRILLIANTLY
AND SOME OF THEM ARE BRILLIANTLY PIEBALD   523 27
WHO SO BRILLIANTLY BETRAY   534 12

BRILLIANTS
SO SHE MARRIES ONE OF THESE LITTLE-BOY BRILLIANTS   842   1

BRIM
THE BRIM EACH CAREFUL PART   125   3

BRIMFUL
BRIMFUL AND CRY   96 26
TO FILL THEM UP A BRIMFUL MEASURE   868 18

BRIMMING
TO FILL THEM UP THEIR BRIMMING MEASURES   *941 18

BRIMSTONE
AS FRICTIONAL AS PERILOUS EXPLOSIVE AS BRIMSTONE   301 31
SHE IS BRITTLE AS BRIMSTONE   386 21

BRIMSTONE-MOLTEN
AND THROAT OF BRIMSTONE-MOLTEN ANGRY GOLD   317 11

BRINDLE
WITH BITS OF BRINDLE COMING THROUGH LIKE RUST TO SHOW   395   2

BRINDLED
AND I IN THE STEALTHY BRINDLED ODOURS   107 19
STRETCHED IN THE BRINDLED DARKNESS   111   2
A BRISK BRINDLED LITTLE TORTOISE ALL TO HIMSELF   358   9
LIKE YELLOW HAIR OF A TIGRESS BRINDLED WITH PINES   408 26
TIGRESS BRINDLED WITH ASPEN   409 23
BRINDLED WITH RAYS   819 25

BRINE
NOT TEARS BUT WHITE SHARP BRINE   207 19
AS BRINE   495   6
AND HOTNESS AND THEN MORE CRUSTED BRINE IN OUR HEARTS   707 23
BRINE   766 29
NOR EVEN A LOVELY WOMAN FOAMY TO STING ME LIKE BRINE   840 23

BRING
I SHOULD HAVE BEEN CRUEL ENOUGH TO BRING   112 14
TO BRING TOGETHER TWO STRANGE SPARKS BEGET   218 20
AND BRING THEM TO YOU   227 16
BRING FORTH THE SONS OF YOUR WOMB THEN AND PUT THEM   235   9
OF SODOM THAT COVERS THE EARTH BRING THEM FORTH   235 11
COME AND LIFT US TO OUR END TO BLOSSOM BRING US TO OUR + 272 33
SEE IF I DON'T BRING YOU DOWN AND ALL YOUR HIGH OPINION 289 11
TO BRING BACK THE RARE AND ORCHID-LIKE   297 20
TO BRING THEIR MEANING BACK INTO LIFE AGAIN   298 11
OH PERSEPHONE PERSEPHONE BRING BACK TO ME FROM HADES TH+ 303 13
AND BRING IT HURTLING TO A HEAD WITH CRASH OF HORNS AGA+ 381 25
UPON THE WORLD TO BRING A CHANGE TO PASS   428 22
TO BRING FORTH CREATURES THAT ARE AN IMPROVEMNT ON   429 25
FOR WE'RE SURE TO BRING IN A LOT OF LIES   506   4
AND BRING US TO GOD   623   4
WAIT WAIT DON'T BRING THE COFFEE YET NOR THE PAIN GRILLE 687 21
OH BRING HIM TO ME I SAID OH LAY HIM BETWEEN   750 19
BRING ALL YOUR SIGNS   798 20
ALONG THE TABLE AT NOON OR WHEN YOU BRING   875   8
SWELLING MANKIND LIKE ONE BUD TO BRING FORTH THE FRUIT + *909 20
HELPED TO BRING   *910   8

BRINGER
CAN BE PUT OUT OF OFFICE AS SACRIFICE BRINGER   374 35

BRINGING
AS HE SEES ME BRINGING THE DINNER HE LIFTS   220   1
DEATH DO YOU HEAR IN MY ARMS I AM BRINGING   238 20
LIKE SOME FIERCE MAGNET BRINGING ITS POLES TOGETHER   370 18
SO CULTURED EVEN BRINGING LITTLE GIFTS   500   3
IN SO FAR AS IT GOES TO THE BRINGING FORTH OF THE BEST   668   4
BRINGING NIGHT ONCE MORE AND THE MAN WITH THE KEYS   758   4

BRINGIN'
AS HE SEES ME BRINGIN' THE DINNER HE LIFTS   *944   9

BRINGS
AND A GLINT OF COLOURED IRIS BRINGS   46 10
WHATIVER BRINGS THEE OUT SO FAR   79 13
SO HE BRINGS DOWN THE LIFE OF THE SUN AND THE POWER OF + 368   4
WON'T IT BE STRANGE WHEN THE NURSE BRINGS THE NEW-BORN   438 26
BRINGS A FRESH FRAGRANCE OF HEAVEN TO OUR SENSES   467 10
AND MAN AND WOMAN ARE LIKE THE EARTH THAT BRINGS FORTH   477   7
AND A SERVANT-MAID BRINGS ME MY TEA   490 26
BRINGS HIM TO HIS KNEES IN HOMAGE AND PURE PASSION OF S+ 648 17
BUT IN CHOOSING THE BOURGEOIS ONE BRINGS TO PASS   664   8
IN A DAY THEY ARE LOST IN THE NOTHINGNESS PURITY BRINGS 855   4
WHATIVER BRINGS THEE OUT SO FAR   *921   9

BRINK
IN THE SHADOW OF THE CART-SHED MUST WE HOVER ON THE BRI+ 173   7
PLUNGING AS I HAVE DONE OVER OVER THE BRINK   266   1
AH DO NOT LET ME DIE ON THE BRINK OF SUCH ANTICIPATION   274   7
FOR WE ARE ON THE BRINK OF RE-REMEMBRANCE   286 19

BRINSLEY
ARE YOU MAKIN' BRINSLEY WAY   78   2
ARE YOU MAKIN' BRINSLEY WAY   *919 22

BRISK
WHITHER AWAY BRISK EGG   356 23
A BRISK BRINDLED LITTLE TORTOISE ALL TO HIMSELF   358   9
WITH GUSTO BEGIN AGAIN THE BRISK FIGHT   865 31

BRISTLE
OH YOU WHO MAKE MY FEATHERS BRISTLE WITH   762   1
BRISTLE AND FLY IN SHADOWS ACROSS THE WALLS   879   3

BRISTLES
OF REDDISH HERBAGE THAT BRISTLES AND SLANTS   50 21
SHE LAYS AN EGG HE BRISTLES LIKE A DOUBLE WHITE POPPY A+   761 19

BRISTLING
BRISTLING NOW WITH THE IRON OF ALMOND-TREES   305 15
AS FROM THE STEM OF HIS BRISTLING LIGHTNING-CONDUCTOR T+   381 19
FUR ALL BRISTLING LIKE PLUSH   396 32
BRISTLING WITH ANIMATION OH PLEASE SIR HOW D'YOU LIKE T+   865 21

BRITAIN
THE SPOT I SHOULD HIT ON WOULD BE LITTLE BRITAIN   574 13
TO BRITAIN WHERE HIS BLOOD CAME FROM   577 6

BRITANNIA
BUT BRITANNIA TURNED PALE AND BEGAN TO FAINT   577 7
HE ANSWERED DEAR BRITANNIA WHY   577 9
BRITANNIA HID BEHIND HER SHIELD   577 13
PLEASING BRITANNIA IS NO LIGHT WORK   577 23

BRITANNIA'S
OH BRITANNIA'S GOT A BABY A BABY A BABY   570 12
BRITANNIA'S GOT A BABY AND SHE GOT IT BY AND BY   570 13

BRITISH
NOR THE BRITISH LION HIS APPETITE   413 29
SO SPOKE THE BRITISH GENTLEMAN   433 14
POLICEMEN AND THE BRITISH NATION   575 1
OH I'M A BRITISH BOY SIR   576 16
MY BRITISH BLOOD THE WORLD SHALL KNOW   576 21
FOR I'M A BRITISH BOY SIR   576 22
AND HIS BRITISH BLOOD THE WORLD IT KNEW   576 25
IF HIS BLOOD WAS BRITISH OR TIMBUCTOOT   577 2
BUT WITH THAT BRITISH BLOOD OF HIS   577 3
I'M YOUR BRITISH BOY AND I DID BUT TRY   577 10
AND SHE JABBED HER BRITISH TRIDENT CLEAN   577 17
BUT THE BRITISH BOY HE TURNED AND FLED   577 20
SO THAT ALL OUR DADDIES WERE QUITE BRITISH PURE   658 20
THEY TELL ME THAT THESE BRITISH MORAL BIRDS   659 7
IS BRITISH HYPOCRISY A FORM OF SOFTENING OF THE BRAIN   659 22

BRITISH PUBLIC
A MEMBER OF THE BRITISH PUBLIC DON'T YOU SEE   570 6
IT'S CALLED THE BRITISH PUBLIC THE PUBLIC THE PUBLIC   570 14
IT'S CALLED THE BRITISH PUBLIC INCLUDING YOU AND I   570 15
FOR OH THE BRITISH PUBLIC THE PUBLIC THE PUBLIC   571 13
FOR OH THE BRITISH PUBLIC IS A LUCKY LITTLE MAN   571 14
BRITISH PUBLIC HAS EVERYTHING OBJECTIONABLE BEEN   582 13
HAVE THE WELFARE OF THE BRITISH PUBLIC AT HEART   582 20
FOR THE BRITISH PUBLIC ONCE MORE BE IT SAID   584 3
REMEMBER THE BRITISH PUBLIC   669 18
REMEMBER THE STATE OF MIND OF THE BRITISH PUBLIC   669 27
ABOUT THE BRITISH PUBLIC   670 8
OH YOU'D THINK THE BRITISH PUBLIC   670 21

BRITTLE
I WISH THESE BRITTLE FROST-LOVELY FLOWERS OF PASSIONATE+   272 6
YOUR BRITTLE SUPER-SENSUAL ARROGANCE   370 26
YOU BRITTLE WILL-TENSE BIRD WITH A FOOLISH EYE   370 35
SHE IS BRITTLE AS BRIMSTONE   386 21

BRITTLY
GREY LAVENDER SENSITIVE STEEL CURVING THINLY AND BRITTLY   300 30

BROACH
THREATS THAT BROACH   66 26
SECRETS THAT YOU MAY NOT BROACH   95 27

BROAD
OF HIS HAND AGAINST MY BOSOM AND OH THE BROAD   43 24
ONLY THE INNER EYE OF YOUR SCORCHED BROAD BREAST   373 24
AND FUSE IN A BROAD HARD FLAME OF MANY MEN IN A ONENESS   440 8
INTO BROAD SWEET PETALS   535 4
PONDERING YET EAGER THE BROAD AND THICK-SET ITALIAN WHO+   672 26
BUT HIS HANDKERCHIEF IS WHITE WITH A BROAD BLUE BORDER   733 28
YOU ONLY STARE AT THE SUN WITH THE ONE BROAD EYE OF YOUR   781 29

BROKE
YOU ONLY ENDURED AND IT BROKE   111 23
BROKE THE BOUNDS AND BEYOND DIM RECOLLECTION   161 21
BROKE IN HER LAIR   171 12
WHEN SHE BROKE FORTH FROM BELOW   308 5
THAN PAPER MONEY WHEN THE BANK IS BROKE   528 4
AND BROKE AT LAST INTO LIGHT AND DARK   682 5
TO PULL DOWN THE BOUGH THE LEAVES BROKE AND THE FRUIT S+   864 10
BROKE INTO THE PRIVACY   884 2
I HEARD THY CRIES OF PAIN AND THEY BROKE   *927 11
I KNEW YOUR PAIN AND IT BROKE   *928 11

BROKEN
LIKE A BIRD FROM THE FAR NORTH BLOWN WITH A BROKEN WING   47 15
YOUR BOW FOR BROKEN IT IS AND HURTING TO HEAR   85 22
SAVE IN A BROKEN PATTERN AMID PURPLE AND GOLD AND SABLE   90 6
NOW I AM BROKEN DOWN LIKE A PLANT IN WINTER AND ALL   94 2
THE MOON IS BROKEN IN TWAIN AND HALF A MOON   114 17
THE OTHER HALF OF THE BROKEN COIN OF TROTH   114 19
TURNING ITS BROKEN EDGE TO THE DARK ITS SHINE   114 27
ENDS LIKE A BROKEN LOVE THAT TURNS TO THE DARK OF SLEEP   114 28
THEIR FEET IN A BROKEN RIDGE   144 17
WITH JEWELS OF PASSION ONCE BROKEN THROUGH YOU AS A   168 15
HAS BROKEN HER SPELL   171 16
THE SURFACE OF DREAMS IS BROKEN THE ARRAS IS TORN   174 5
AT THRESHING-TIME BROKEN WAS BROKEN   198 15
A THICK MIST-SHEET LIES OVER THE BROKEN WHEAT   212 12
DRAWN ON HIS MOUTH EYES BROKEN AT LAST BY HIS PANGS   225 8
IS BROKEN AT LAST AND DONE   253 16
FOR MY PART I PREFER MY HEART TO BE BROKEN   279 1
BROKEN IN HEAVINESS   345 5

BROKEN
AND CLIMB AGAIN THE BROKEN BANK OF MY WALL-FACE   350 32
HE SO FINISHED AND IMMUNE NOW BROKEN INTO DESIROUS   361 6
THE WHEEL ON WHICH OUR SILENCE FIRST IS BROKEN   366 30
THE BROKEN GREEK TOMB IN THE GARDEN   384 5
A WAVE BURSTS IN ANGER ON A ROCK BROKEN UP   467 12
THE SPELL IS NEVER BROKEN   575 20
THE SPELL IS NEVER BROKEN   575 21
AND SHE WOULD HAVE BROKEN IT OVER MY HEAD   604 20
AFTER OUR INDUSTRIAL CIVILISATION HAS BROKEN AND THE CI+   612 1
ONCE THE CONNECTION HAS BEEN BROKEN   617 6
SHAKING THE LARK'S NEST TILL THE EGGS HAVE BROKEN   623 31
MY WRISTS SEEM BROKEN AND MY HEART SEEMS DEAD   727 19
BEING DEAD YOU SHALL ROVE LIKE DOGS WITH THE BROKEN HAU+   796 5
AT THE MOMENT WE TEND TO RUN INSANE THE MIND HAVING BRO+   838 21
WERE BROKEN AGAINST HER THIGHS SHE SHATTERED THE HIBISC+   863 25
AND SHUFFLE OF BROKEN SODDENED BOOTS YET SINGING GOES R+   866 14
MY TEMPLES BROKEN THEN I SHOULD REMAIN   873 31
I SAW THE BROKEN VIOLETS   880 23
AND BROKEN BY MY WEIGHT AND THE PURPLE STEAM   881 8
ONE BROKEN THORN-TREE STILL IN THE TWILIGHT STANDS   *896 14
THE SURFACE OF DREAMS IS BROKEN   *908 9
AND I TWISTED THEN OVER THE BROKEN LEAVES INTO UNBREAKA+   *926 17
HARDENED THE EARTH SHAKING THE LARK'S NEST TILL THE EGG+   *953 18

BROKEN-HAUNCHED
AND EVEN THEN THEY SHALL SPIT YOU OUT AS BROKEN-HAUNCHE+   796 27

BROKEN-HEARTED
AND EVER I SEE YOUR TRACES BROKEN-HEARTED   880 15

BRONZE
PILLARS OF WHITE BRONZE STANDING RIGID LEST THE SKIES F+   287 16
NOT IN STONE LIKE THE JUDEAN LORD OR BRONZE BUT IN LIFE+   355 18
THE PEACOCK LIFTS HIS RODS OF BRONZE   371 1
ALL THE BRONZE GLOSS OF ALL HIS MYRIAD PETALS   371 11
YET THE BRONZE WIND-BELL SUDDENLY CLASHING   371 16
YET IF YOU HAD WHORLED HORNS OF BRONZE IN A FRONTAL DARK   381 1
GOD IN BLACK CLOUD WITH CURVING HORNS OF BRONZE   383 16
WHERE TISSUE PLUNGES INTO BRONZE WITH WIDE WILD CIRCLES+   623 10

BRONZES
THEN WE SUFFER AND THOUGH THE SUN BRONZES US   609 4

BRONZEY
NOW IT IS ALMOST NIGHT FROM THE BRONZEY SOFT SKY   647 8
A ROSE TREE BRONZEY WITH THORNS   714 10

BROOD
HARDLY A MURMUR COMES FROM THE SLEEPING BROOD   48 23
AND ALL THINGS ARE IN SILENCE THEY CAN BROOD   76 20
MY BROOD IN RETREAT   766 10
AND ALL THINGS ARE POSSESSED BY SILENCE AND THEY CAN BR+   *898 14
AND ALL THINGS ARE POSSESSED BY SILENCE AND THEY CAN BR+   *901 23
THEN THE DAYS RAN ROUND ME IN A GOLDEN BROOD   *933 17

BROODING
BUT THE FACES OF THE BOYS IN THE BROODING YELLOW LIGHT   75 25
OF BROODING AND DELIGHTING IN THE SECRET OF LIFE'S GOIN+   197 17
VICIOUS YOU SUPPLE BROODING SOFTLY-SWAYING PILLARS OF   297 10
WHERE THE SLOW TOADS SAT BROODING ON THE PAST   310 15
HENCE HIS PONDEROUS HEAD BROODING OVER DESIRE AND DOWNF+ 378 22
BUT THE FACES OF THE BOYS IN THE BROODING YELLOW LIGHT   *897 24
BUT THE FACES OF THE BOYS IN THE BROODING YELLOW LIGHT   *901 1

BROOD-SOUL
IN MY BROOD-SOUL WITHERING   766 18

BROODY
MY LIFE MY BROODY SELF   766 23

BROOK
DARK OVERGROWN WITH WILLOWS COOL WITH THE BROOK EBBING +   33 16
A GLINTING WEB QUICK HID IN THE GLOOM OF THE BROOK   161 7
LIKE GRASS IN A BROOK   194 12
DARK OVERGROWN WITH WILLOWS COOL WITH THE BROOK EBBING + *891 18
OF THE BROOK   *891 25

BROOKS
MY CHAFED CURBED BLOOD NO LONGER BROOKS   857 3

BROOMS
NEW BROOMS SWEEP CLEAN   536 1

BROTHER
THE ENEMY MY BROTHER   743 18
OH BROTHER PUT ME IN YOUR POUCH   752 13
OH BROTHER AND I AM THE GOLDEN RING   752 17
MY BROTHER DIED IN THE HEAT   754 17
BROTHER THE SCENT OF YOUR CLOTHING   758 19
BROTHER I LIKE YOUR FRAGRANCE   759 1
BROTHER LET ME DIE DOWN AGAIN   759 4
OH BROTHER QUETZALCOATL   786 19
SLEEP SLEEP MY BROTHER SLEEP   787 11
BROTHER QUETZALCOATL   789 12
QUETZALCOATL MY BROTHER HE CALLED SEND ME MY IMAGES   789 17

BROTHERHOOD
THE EMOTION OF BROTHERHOOD   611 8
ONCE DISILLUSION FALLS ON LIVING MEN AND ILLUSION OF BR+   639 23

BROTHERLESS
FATHERLESS MOTHERLESS BROTHERLESS SISTERLESS   357 24

BROTHERLY
    SHALL I OFFER TO HIM MY BROTHERLY BODY TO KILL   743 19

BROTHERS
    AND THREE LITTLE BROTHERS   357 17
    NOR YET BROTHERS IT'S SO CONCEITED   499 23
    CEASE TO ACCEPT THEM AS BROTHERS   639 5
    WITH THE WHITE MEN HIS BROTHERS   778 16

BROTHER'S
    AND THE MARRIAGE SHALL BE MY BROTHER'S IT MAY BE SO   743 23

BROUGHT
    AWAITING THE SENTENCE OUT FROM THE WELKIN BROUGHT   142 16
    ITS LIMPID SAP TO CULMINATION HAS BROUGHT   218 10
    IN STARK-CLEAR ROSES THAN I TO MYSELF AM BROUGHT   218 12
    ONLY GOD COULD HAVE BROUGHT IT TO ITS SHAPE   254 27
    AND BROUGHT YOU TO THE VERY QUICK OF YOUR FORM   254 32
    THAT NOBLE BLOOD HAS BROUGHT US DOWN THE AGES   313 31
    BROUGHT FORTH   477 2
    THEIR CHILDREN BROUGHT UP EASY LET IT SLIP AWAY AGAIN   535 24
    SO WELL BROUGHT UP AS AUNT GWENDOLINE IS   571 21
    WAS BROUGHT UP POOR SO SHE'LL HAVE TO BE   571 26
    MY LITTLE CRITICS MUST ALL HAVE BEEN BROUGHT UP BY THEIR 581 19
    WHICH HAS BROUGHT TO PASS THE FEARFUL THING CALLED EVIL 712 25
    SUCH AS MY LIFE HAS NOT BROUGHT FORTH BEFORE NEW BLOSSO+ 727 26
    AH MASTER MASTER YOU WHO HAVE BROUGHT US HITHER   757 14
    HAS BROUGHT DOWN A RIPE FRUIT HEAVILY TO HER FEET   864 14
    I BROUGHT FOR HIM AND WAITED WHILE HE DRANK   878 15
    THE WITHERING FLOWERS THAT DAYS AGO YOU BROUGHT ME   880 11

BROW
    I'LL WET MY BROW FOR THEE   44 7
    IN MY SOUL FROM UNDER THE SUDDEN FROWN OF HIS BROW   47 26
    BROW   57 31
    ON HIS BROW WHERE THE CURVED WISPS CLOT AND TWINE   60 3
    GLAD AS THE MAGI WHEN THEY SAW THE BROW   88 29
    WITH FIRE ON YOUR CHEEKS AND YOUR BROW AND YOUR CHIN AS+ 90 9
    SHE LOOKS LIKE A YOUNG MAIDEN SINCE HER BROW   101 7
    THE BAND IS ACROSS ITS BROW AND IT SCARCELY SEEMS   225 14
    WHEN HE PUSHED HIS BUSH OF BLACK HAIR OFF HIS BROW   310 1
    TOSSES THE CRAPE OF RED ACROSS YOUR BROW AND DOWN YOUR 370 27
    WITH HIS BROW WIPED BRIGHT OF THE TOIL OF SWEAT   770 18
    FROM THE BROW A GOLD   819 21
    ALL WITH HIS BLESSING BRIGHT ON THY MOUTH AND THY BROW 872 1

BROW-METALLED
    AND NEVER AN ENEMY BROW-METALLED TO THRESH IT OUT WITH 382 30

BROWN
    RABBITS HANDFULS OF BROWN EARTH LIE   33 5
    PITEOUS BROWN BALL OF QUIVERING FEARS   43 11
    AND READY TO OPEN IN BROWN SURPRISE   43 15
    MY BABY HER BROWN HAIR BRUSHED WITH WET TEARS   73 23
    O THE WET WALK OF MY BROWN HEN THROUGH THE STACKYARD   119 9
    ALL ROUND THE YEAR IT IS CLUCK MY BROWN HEN   119 15
    TWO BROWN PONIES TROTTING SLOWLY   121 28
    HER LARGE BROWN HAND STRETCHED OVER   123 20
    MY GRAIL A BROWN BOWL TWINED   123 24
    UNDER WHOSE BROWN THE AMETHYST   123 26
    AGAIN I SAW A BROWN BIRD HOVER   124 23
    I FELT A BROWN BIRD HOVER   124 25
    A BROWN BEE PULLING APART   124 29
    I FELT THE BROWN BIRD COVER   124 33
    THE LEAF'S BROWN HUE   178 4
    THE BROWN EYES BLACK WITH MISERY AND HATE THAT LOOK   225 23
    MY BIRD MY BROWN SPARROW IN MY BREAST   246 18
    SO BROWN AND SOFT AND COMING SUAVE   280 4
    WINESKINS OF BROWN MORBIDITY   280 16
    PUT ME DOWN AGAIN ON THE EARTH JESUS ON THE BROWN SOIL 321 10
    BROWN HILLS SURROUNDING   340 23
    THE OUTSIDE WILL SEEM BROWN   344 27
    THE OUTSIDE DID NOT SEEM BROWN   344 29
    AND BROWN FURRY BODY   345 32
    BROWN NUT-BROWN FINE FUR   345 33
    FLAT BROWN ROCKS TO WATCH THE FERRY IN THE SUN   386 24
    THEY'VE DONE YOU BROWN   556 28
    AND RUBS THE SILVER CLEAN WITH HIS THICK BROWN FINGERS 734 2
    HER APRON WAS BROWN WITH BLOOD SHE PRAYED   753 10
    THESE WHITE MEN AND RED MEN AND YELLOW MEN AND BROWN MEN 792 29
    THAT ARE NEITHER WHITE NOR RED NOR YELLOW NOR BROWN NOR+ 792 31
    THEY ARE GOLD THEY ARE BROWN THEY ARE PURPLISH THEY   827 1
    FULL INSIDE OF WEIRD BROWN SLUSHY CRAB-MEAT   830 20
    SOFT TICKLING BROWN   863 8
    FLASHING HIS BRIGHT BROWN ARMS AS HE LEANS ON THE POLE 867 28
    HIS ROUND BROWN HEAD BENDS LIKE A BEE ABOVE A BLOSSOM   868 5
    RABBITS HANDFULS OF BROWN EARTH LIE   *891 6
    WHITE WHEN THE WIND SHIFTED HER HAIR THAT WAS SOFT AN' + *910 12
    MY BABY HER BROWN HAIR BRUSHED WITH WET TEARS   *913 15
    OH THE WET WALK OF MY BROWN HEN THROUGH THE STACKYARD *932 18
    ALL ROUND THE YARD IT IS CLUCK MY BROWN HEN   *932 24
    AND THE BROWN DOG SETTLED THE REST   *933 8
    HER LARGE BROWN HAND LOOMED OVER   *934 26
    UNDER WHOSE BROWN THE AMETHYST   *934 32
    THIS BROWN CORE OF NIGHT   *935 16
    AND THEN I SAW A BROWN BIRD HOVER   *935 29
    AGAIN AND I FELT A BROWN BIRD HOVER   *935 31
    A BROWN BEE PULL APART   *935 35
    MUST HIDE MY MOTHER'S PIANO LITTLE AND BROWN WITH THE B+ *940 2

BROWNING
    WITH A CIGARETTE BROWNING YOUR FINGERS   651 23

BROWS
    I SAW YOUR BROWS   56 13
    OVER MY HAIR AND TRACING MY BROWS   104 7
    THEY ANOINT THEIR BROWS WITH YOUR PAIN AS A PERFECT   168 19
    AND COILING IT ROUND THE WISE BROWS OF A MAID   178 21

BROWS
    WRAPPED TO THE EYES THE SHEET BOUND CLOSE ON HIS BROWS 403 10
    WHEN I SEE IT BETWEEN HIS BROWS   526 11
    AND LOOKED SULKY UNDER HER THICK STRAIGHT BROWS   617 20
    HE LOOKED AT ME AND HIS HEAVY BROWS CAME OVER   735 1

BROWSE
    AND DRINK AND BROWSE   465 14
    THAT PRICK THEIR EARS LIKE A RABBIT OR BROWSE IN THE DA+ 807 14

BROWSING
    ON THE DREAM-SLOPES BROWSING LIKE A DEER IN THE DUSK   807 10
    I SEE THE GREY DOGS CREEPING OUT WHERE MY DEER ARE BROW+ 807 18

BRUISE
    FORGET EACH OTHER AND THE BRUISE OF OUR BODIES' CLASH   91 6
    OR A DEEPER BRUISE OF KNOWING THAT STILL   100 11
    TO BRUISE THEMSELVES AN EXIT FROM THEMSELVES   716 21
    A BRUISE OR BREAK OF EXIT FOR HIS LIFE   717 13
    OF THE CRUEL BRUISE   718 5
    TO BRUISE THEMSELVES AN EXIT FROM THEMSELVES   *956 27
    A BRUISE OR BREAK OF EXIT FOR HIS LIFE   *957 4

BRUISED
    WHAT YOUR THROAT IS BRUISED BRUISED WITH MY KISSES   230 14
    I AM BRUISED RIGHT THROUGH   230 16
    YOUR SHOULDERS YOUR BRUISED THROAT   238 10
    THE VIBRATION OF THE MOTOR-CAR HAS BRUISED THEIR INSENS+ 625 17
    AND IN THE BRUISED BODY THE FRIGHTENED SOUL   717 7
    ALREADY OUR BODIES ARE FALLEN BRUISED BADLY BRUISED   718 3

BRUISES
    BRUISES ON MY INWARD FLESH   601 11

BRUISING
    OF A MALE THONG BOOMING AND BRUISING UNTIL IT HAD   36 15

BRUNT
    NO LONGER NOW CAN I ENDURE THE BRUNT   74 12
    BRUNT   97 13
    IMPLACABLE WINTER'S LONG CROSS-QUESTIONING BRUNT   142 4
    NO MORE CAN I ENDURE TO BEAR THE BRUNT   *895 20
    NO MORE CAN I ENDURE TO BEAR THE BRUNT   *904 9

BRUSH
    HOW YOU HATE BEING BRUSHED WITH THE BOOT-BRUSH TO BRUSH 397 30
    BRUSH OVER MY FACE AS HE GOES   438 12
    I BRUSH THE WING OF THE DAY   787 23
    HE HAD A SHOVEL AND A BRUSH ON HIS SHOULDER HIS FACE WA+ 866 18
    BRUSH OVER MY FACE AS HE GOES TO TREAD OUR WEIRD WOMEN *947 20

BRUSHED
    MY BABY HER BROWN HAIR BRUSHED WITH WET TEARS   73 23
    HOW YOU HATE BEING BRUSHED WITH THE BOOT-BRUSH TO BRUSH 397 30
    MY BABY HER BROWN HAIR BRUSHED WITH WET TEARS   *913 15

BRUSHES
    A SHARP SKY BRUSHES UPON   166 19
    THE OTHER WING BRUSHES THE DARK   787 25

BRUSHING
    BRUSHING THE STARS GOES MY SOUL THAT SKIMS THE BOUNDS 193 25
    MEN SINGING SONGS AND WOMEN BRUSHING THEIR HAIR IN THE + 691 24
    AND I QUETZALCOATL THE EAGLE OF THE AIR AM BRUSHING YOU+ 802 1
    PAST AND WE'RE BRUSHING   862 27

BRUSHWOOD
    OH WITHERED CRACKLING TWIGS OF BRUSHWOOD PEOPLE   784 20

BRUTAL
    AND THE UGLY BRUTAL YEARS   240 1
    YOUR WESTERN BRUTAL FAERY QUALITY   291 25

BRUTE
    SO OUT OUT YOU BRUTE   346 18
    PUT OUT A LIGHT OF CONSCIOUSNESS AND LEFT A BLINDED BRU+ 543 28

BRUTES
    AND IF IT BE NOT SO BRUTES TO PULL DOWN HIBISCUS FLOWERS 314 24
    OF MAQUILLAGE AND POSE AND MALICE TO SHAME THE BRUTES 463 23
    I THINK OF ALL THE LITTLE BRUTES   493 21
    IS BLINDED BRUTES OF CYCLOPS WITH OUR CYCLOPEAN EYE PUT 544 4

B SC
    EACH-CHEMICALLY B SC   489 2

BUB
    THEN THE SMALL STIRRING OF A NEW SMALL BUB IN THE NEST 728 9

BUBBLE
    WITH A BUBBLE OF LAUGHTER AND SHRILLY SHOUT   179 18
    THE BUBBLE HEMMING THIS EMPTY EXISTENCE WITH LIGHTS   193 22
    LIKE A BREATH IN A BUBBLE SPINNING   193 24
    THE FILM OF THE BUBBLE NIGHT TO WHERE YOU ARE   194 2
    BUT THEY BUBBLE UNDER THE HEAVY WALL   461 27
    THEY BUBBLE UNDER THE HEAVY WALL   462 1
    A LITTLE WILD BUBBLE IS LOOSENING HOLD   868 28
    A LITTLE WILD BUBBLE IS LOOSING HOLD   *941 28

BUBBLED
    LIKE LUNATICS LOOKING THEY BUBBLED AND RAVED   579 2

BUBBLES
    BUBBLES RAVELLED IN THE DARK GREEN GRASS   204 17
    THE PALE BUBBLES   205 23
    ARE BUBBLES OF ICE KISS ME YOU KNOW HOW IT RESTS   212 7
    OH FOR THE WONDER THAT BUBBLES INTO MY SOUL   250 25
    NEW LIFE BUBBLES IN WE BECOME SOMETHING ELSE   832 22

BUBBLES
    TWIN BUBBLES SHADOW-FULL OF MYSTERY AND CHALLENGE IN TH+   *897 30
    TWIN BUBBLES SHADOW-FULL OF MYSTERY AND CHALLENGE IN TH+   *901 7

BUBBLING
    ON THE SLOW BUBBLING OF YOUR RHYTHMIC HEART   154 11
    COME BUBBLING SURGING TIDE OF SAP   270 31

BUB-EAGLE
    AND THE BUB-EAGLE THAT LIBERTY HAD HATCHED WAS GROWING A   413 18

BUBSEY
    BUBSEY BAT-EARED DOG   395 5

BUCKLE
    THE GLITTER OF THE BUCKLE OF YOUR SHOE   887 13

BUD
    SHUT LIKE A DAISY BUD   77 26
    WILL YOU OPEN THE AMOROUS ACHING BUD   117 22
    ALMOST THE FLOWER IN THE BUD   239 17
    LIKE A FLOWER IN BUD   240 17
    BUD   285 18
    HE CAUSALLY GIVES BIRTH TO ANOTHER YOUNG BUD FROM HIS   300 1
    SEEING IRON BREAK AND BUD   304 5
    PEARLS ITSELF INTO TENDERNESS OF BUD   306 5
    BUD OF THE UNIVERSE   356 20
    ARE STILL IN BUD AND EAGER   627 3
    INSTEAD OF A FLOWER THAT DIES AND OPENS A DIFFERENT BUD   662 6
    SHOWS ONE BUD MORE   814 3
    IS SWELLING AND SHAPING A BUD INTO BLOSSOM   *907 16
    INTO ONE BUD ON THE STALK OF ETERNITY   *908 3
    AS IT SWELLS AND SHAPES A BUD INTO BLOSSOM   *909 17
    SWELLING MANKIND LIKE ONE BUD TO BRING FORTH THE FRUIT +   *909 20
    SHUT LIKE A DAISY BUD   *919 14
    A BIG BUD OF MOON HANGS OUT OF THE TWILIGHT   *929 6
    WILL YOU LOOSE THE HEAVY WEARY BUD   *931 26
    NOW LIKE A ROSE COME TIP-TOE OUT OF BUD   *943 18
    AND DAY BY DAY OUT OF THE ENVIOUS BUD   *943 22

BUDDED
    ARE BUDDED AS SHE   862 11

BUDDHA
    JESUS BUDDHA JEHOVAH AND RA EGYPT AND BABYLON   671 19

BUDDING
    THE BUDDING TREES   58 2
    AND SEE WHERE THE BUDDING HAZELS ARE THINNED   126 9
    THE HEART OF MAN IN SO FAR AS IT IS BUDDING IS BUDDING +   612 4
    AND BUDDING TOWARDS INFINITE VARIETY VARIEGATION   612 5
    IN MY BURSTING AND BUDDING I FEEL   888 14

BUD-LIKE
    AND SENSITIVE BUD-LIKE BLOSSOMING OF PASSION   113 6

BUD-LIPS
    THE SEA HAS ITS BUD-LIPS SMILINGLY CURLED   814 26

BUDS
    COOL AS SYRINGA BUDS IN MORNING HOURS   65 9
    AND ALL THE LOTUS BUDS OF LOVE SINK OVER   113 14
    UNDER AN OAK WHOSE YELLOW BUDS DOT THE PALE BLUE SKY   152 27
    OF THE WIND IN THE KNOTTED BUDS MAKES A CANOPY   152 29
    COME AND SOFTEN THE WILLOW BUDS TILL THEY ARE PUFFED AN+   273 2
    LONG PENSIVE SLIM-MUZZLED GREYHOUND BUDS   310 29
    HANDS TO EAT THE ACANTHUS OR BITE AT THE ALMOND BUDS   385 10
    AND PUT SCARLET BUDS IN THEIR HAIR ON THE WAY TO HELL   710 19
    BUDS A BLUE ANEMONE STILL BLUER   814 14
    OH AGE THAT IS HOAR AS ANEMONE BUDS   814 19
    UNDER AN OAK TREE WHOSE YELLOW BUDS DOTTED THE PALE BLU+   866 23
    OF THE WIND ROUND THE KNOTTED BUDS LIKE A CANOPY   866 25
    MY TOP OF LIFE THAT BUDS ON HIGH   *899 29
    MY TOP OF LIFE THAT BUDS ON HIGH   *903 8
    COOL AS SYRINGA BUDS   *913 10
    COOL LIKE SYRINGA BUDS   *914 10

BUFFER
    LEAR THE OLD BUFFER YOU WONDER HIS DAUGHTERS   494 16

BUGLE
    IT IS YOUR SMALL HIGH HATEFUL BUGLE IN MY EAR   333 17
    LOVE-FIRE IS DRIFTING THOUGH THE BUGLE IS PRIM AND DEMU+   854 16

BUILD
    O BUILD YOUR SHIP OF DEATH FOR YOU WILL NEED IT   717 2
    BUILD THEN THE SHIP OF DEATH FOR YOU MUST TAKE   717 21
    OH BUILD YOUR SHIP OF DEATH YOUR LITTLE ARK   718 9
    IS NOW TO BE WILLING TO DIE AND TO BUILD THE SHIP   718 22
    OH BUILD YOUR SHIP OF DEATH OH BUILD IT   720 20
    SO BUILD YOUR SHIP OF DEATH AND LET THE SOUL DRIFT   721 4
    AND HELP THEM TO BUILD THEIR LITTLE SHIP OF DEATH   721 19
    SET FOOD FOR THEM AND ENCOURAGE THEM TO BUILD   722 11
    COME LET US BUILD A TEMPLE TO OBLIVION   726 7
    THEY BUILD UPON AS MICE ARE SLAVES   *899 8
    THEY BUILD UPON AS MICE ARE SLAVES   *902 20
    BUILD THEN YOUR SHIP OF DEATH FOR YOU WILL NEED IT   *956 29
    OH BUILD YOUR SHIP OF DEATH OH BUILD IT IN TIME   *957 25
    AND BUILD IT LOVINGLY AND PUT IT BETWEEN THE HANDS OF Y+ *957 26
    LET ME BUILD A LITTLE SHIP WITH OARS AND FOOD   *958 20
    OH BUILD YOUR SHIP OF DEATH   *960 7
    OH BUILD IT   *960 8
    OH BUILD YOUR SHIP OF DEATH FOR YOU WILL NEED IT   *960 11
    OF PEACE AND BUILD YOUR LITTLE SHIP   *960 13
    OH BUILD YOUR SHIP OF DEATH BE BUILDING IT NOW   *960 27
    THEN BUILD YOUR SHIP OF DEATH IN READINESS   *961 6

BUILDED
    THAT LIE OUTSIDE THE SILVERY WALLS OF OUR BODY'S BUILDE+ *957 17

BUILDER
    AND SING IN THIS SPACE THAT THE BUILDER NOW DEMANDS   *896 16

BUILDER'S
    INTO MUD THE SPACE FAST SHRINKS IN THE BUILDER'S HANDS   *896 11

BUILDING
    THEN YOU WILL HIT THE FLAT-IRON BUILDING AND FLATTEN IT+ 484 19
    AND BUILDING MY NEST OF PEACE IN YOUR BONES   802 4
    OH BUILD YOUR SHIP OF DEATH BE BUILDING IT NOW   *960 27

BUILDINGS
    UGLY OLD FURNITURE UGLY OLD BOOKS UGLY OLD BUILDINGS UG+ 678 14

BUILDS
    THE OPTIMIST BUILDS HIMSELF SAFE INSIDE A CELL   515 7

BUILT
    AND BUILT UP THE WAY I SALUTE THEE   40 22
    THEY'VE BUILT A NEW UNIVERSITY   488 9
    BUILT IT MOST GRAND AND CAKEILY   488 11
    OR THAN IF HE'D JUST BUILT HIMSELF A NEST WITH A BATHRO+ 496 8
    BUILT UP BUILT UP   692 4
    HAVE YOU BUILT YOUR SHIP OF DEATH O HAVE YOU   717 1
    THEY HAVE BUILT A NEW AND CAKEY UNIVERSITY   *950 13
    HAVE YOU BUILT YOUR SHIP OF DEATH OH HAVE YOU   *956 28
    HAVE YOU BUILT YOUR SHIP OF DEATH OH HAVE YOU   *960 10

BULBS
    I'D HAVE TORN THEM UP HAD THEY BORNE AWAY THE PATIENT B+ *926 13

BULGING
    SHALLOW WINE-CUPS ON SHORT BULGING STEMS   283 6
    AND BLACK EYES BULGING BRIGHT IN A DUST-MASK   397 17
    LOOK UP AT ME WITH MISGIVING IN YOUR BULGING EYES   400 25
    FOR SPECTACLES AND BULGING CLEVER ANT-EYES ARE NO GOOD + 544 7
    WITH THEIR BULGING POLICEMAN'S-LAMP EYES   544 21

BULK
    MUST CREEP HER GREAT BULK BENEATH THE BRIDGE OF HIM   426 10
    THE ELEPHANTS HUGE AND GREY LOOMED THEIR CURVED BULK   445 10
    WHAT HAS KILLED MANKIND FOR THE BULK OF MANKIND IS DEAD 654 3

BULKS
    IT WAS AS IF THE GREAT BULKS OF ELEPHANTS IN THE OBSCURE 391 1

BULL
    AND THE YOUNG BULL IN THE FIELD WITH HIS WRINKLED SAD F+ 255 33
    SLEEPS FOUR SLEEPS THE SLEEP OF THE LION THE SLEEP ON T+ 319 5
    AND THE BULL NOR WAKES FROM THE LIGHT-EYED EAGLE SLEEP   319 11
    AND HEAR HIM BELLOW AFTER MANY YEARS THE BULL THAT SERV+ 327 8
    LUKE THE BULL THE FATHER OF SUBSTANCE THE PROVIDENCE BU+ 327 16
    THE BULL OF THE PROLETARIAT HAS GOT HIS HEAD DOWN   327 30
    THE MYSTERIOUS BULL TORE HIM AT ADOLESCENCE INTO PIECES 361 11
    LIKE SOME UNHAPPY BULL AT THE TAIL OF A COW   361 15
    HE IS NOT FATHERLY LIKE THE BULL MASSIVE PROVIDENCE OF + 382 8
    WHERE NO BULL ROARED NO COW EVER LOWED NO STAG CRIED   394 16
    LITTLE BLACK FEMALE PUP SORT OF FRENCH BULL THEY SAY   395 1
    BEYOND THE GREAT BULL THAT BELLOWED THROUGH SPACE AND   437 10
    AND THROUGH THE WIDE PRAIRIES OF HIS BREAST A YOUNG BUL+ 624 7
    THEN THE GREAT BULL LIES UP AGAINST HIS BRIDE   694 13
    NOR EVEN LIKE AN ANIMAL BULL RAM OR LION OR LAMB   840 26
    A GREAT BULL BELLOWED THROUGH SPACE CALLING TO THE MILK+ *946 21

BULL-BITCH
    DEMOCRATIC LITTLE BULL-BITCH DIRT-EATING LITTLE SWINE   399 26

BULLETS
    WITH DAGGERS BODKINS BULLETS MAN CAN MAKE   717 12
    WITH DAGGERS BODKINS BULLETS MAN CAN MAKE   *957 3
    AND THEY SEND ARROWS OF ANGER BULLETS AND BOMBS OF FRUS+ *958 6

BULL-FROGS
    I REMEMBER WHEN I FIRST HEARD BULL-FROGS BREAK INTO SOU+ 365 32

BULLIED
    FOR I CANNOT BE BULLIED BACK INTO THE APPEARANCES OF LO+ 478 10
    ANY MORE THAN AUGUST CAN BE BULLIED TO LOOK LIKE MARCH 478 11
    AND BULLIED WITH THE THREAT GET MONEY OR EAT DIRT   522 12

BULLIES
    HOW HE BULLIES THE FLOWERS   244 11

BULL-MONGREL
    WHEN A LOW BULL-MONGREL STARTS DECLAIMING   494 9

BULLOCK
    A BULLOCK WAGON COMES SO I AM ASHAMED   225 10
    THE BREATH OF THE BULLOCK STAINS THE HARD CHILL AIR   225 13
    DREAMING AND LETTING THE BULLOCK TAKE ITS WILL   225 20

BULLOCK-WAGONS
    OVERHANGS THE STREET WHERE THE BULLOCK-WAGONS SLOWLY   209 16

BULLS
    LIKE BULLS OR BISONS OR WILD PIGS   392 19

BULL'S
    AND A BULL'S LARGE SOMBRE GLANCING EYE   325 28
    AND THE ROAR OF BLACK BULL'S BLOOD IN THE MIGHTY PASSAG+ 326 15
    OF THE BULL'S BREAST   326 21
    OF PERHAPS THERE IS SOMETHING IN YOUR WATTLES OF A BULL+ 370 4

BULL-WHALES
    AND BULL-WHALES GATHER THEIR WOMEN AND WHALE-CALVES IN +   695   1

BULLY
    WHOSE BOSS ARE YOU WITH ALL YOUR BULLY WAY   375 32
    WATCH HIM TURN INTO A MESS EITHER A FOOL OR A BULLY   431   7
    NOT TO WANT TO BULLY THOSE WEAKER THAN OURSELVES   833   5

BUMP
    AND BUMP ON ONE ANOTHER AND EXPLODE INTO MORE MIST   437 34
    AND BUMP ON ONE ANOTHER AND COME UNTIED   *947 10

BUMPING
    THEIR TWO SHELLS LIKE DOMED BOATS BUMPING   361 22

BUNCH
    YOUR FACE IN THE MARIGOLD BUNCH TO TOUCH AND CONTRAST Y+   90 10
    YES BUNCH YOURSELF BETWEEN   240 26
    BEFORE THE GLACIERS WERE GATHERED UP IN A BUNCH OUT OF +   285 19
    AND SHOW A TINY BUNCH OF WHITE TEETH IN YOUR UNDERHUNG   398 11
    FOR THE ANALYST IS TANGLED IN AN ESPECIALLY TANGLED BUN+   833 34
    THE HEAVY PURPLE PERFUMED BUNCH   880 24

BUNCHED-UP
    A GUN AND A BUNCHED-UP DEER ITS FOUR LITTLE FEET   220 18

BUNCHES
    IN LITTLE BUNCHES LIKE BUNCHES OF WILD HARES   311 23

BUNGLED
    NAY LEONARDO ONLY BUNGLED THE PURE ETRUSCAN SMILE   297 26

BUNK
    WHY LET'S ALL OF US DO A BUNK   553 28
    ALL THE SILLY BUNK   556 18
    THAT SHUT ME UP IN MY BUNK   758   5

BUNNY
    THA ART SMOCK-RAVELLED BUNNY   78 29
    LIKE THAT BUNNY   240 23
    YOU BUNNY   240 25
    YOU HAVE A HOT UNTHINKABLE DESIRE OF ME BUNNY   241   4
    OF YOUR EYE BUNNY   241   7
    'TIS NOT OF ME BUNNY   241 13
    THA ART SMOCK-RAVELLED BUNNY   *920 21
    I' TH' SNOW BUT I'S WARANT THEE BUNNY   *920 23

B JON VIAGGIO
    BUON VIAGGIO   353 31

BUOYANT
    AS BUOYANT AS A SEA-BIRD ON THE SEA   876   5

BUOYANTLY
    DO YOU SEE THE GOLD SUN FLUTTERING BUOYANTLY IN HEAVEN   782 29

BUOYS
    THE STARS ARE BUOYS   110 24

BURDEN
    LOVE MAKES THE BURDEN OF HER VOICE   46 17
    ALL MY LIFE I HAVE BORNE THE BURDEN OF MYSELF   47 29
    HIS BURDEN ABOVE ME NEVER HAS CLOMB   50 12
    LIKE A BURDEN SHE HANGS ON ME   73 28
    MEANS BUT TO YOU A BURDEN OF DEAD FLESH   87 26
    THE GRASS DEEP DOWN WITH THE ROYAL BURDEN OF HER   123   3
    THE BURDEN OF SELF-ACCOMPLISHMENT   215   9
    JESUS RODE ON HIM THE FIRST BURDEN ON THE FIRST BEAST OF 379 25
    BURDEN   379 26
    NO LONGER OR CARRY THE BURDEN OF A MAN ON YOUR HEART   411 12
    OR THE BURDEN OF MAN WRIT LARGE   411 13
    HAS COME DOWN ON THE HEART IN A BURDEN OF LOCUSTS   507 22
    DON'T BURDEN ME   561 15
    THE GRASS DEEP DOWN WITH HER ROYAL BURDEN AND I   *934 11

BURDENED
    TOO HEAVILY BURDENED TO MOUNT THE HEAVENS SO   132   4
    THE BURDENED AGE SEVENTY-NINE THE VICAR   859   2
    DRAWS DOWN THE BURDENED FLOWER   *913 21
    TOO HEAVILY BURDENED TO MOUNT THE HEAVENS SO   *937 31

BURIED
    WAITIN' TER BE BURIED OUT O' TH' WET   60 14
    IS BURIED AWAY IN THE DARK WHERE THE DEAD ALL LIE   114 20
    THEY BURIED HER HALF IN THE GRAVE WHEN THEY LAID HER AW+ 114 21
    WITH MY FACE DOWN BURIED BETWEEN HER BREASTS   250 10
    I BURIED MY BELOVED IT WAS GOOD I BURIED MYSELF AND WAS   257 25
    FOR OH I KNOW IN THE DUST WHERE WE HAVE BURIED   298   1
    WE HAVE BURIED SO MUCH OF THE DELICATE MAGIC OF LIFE   298   3
    NOW THAT THE WIFE AND MOTHER AND MISTRESS IS BURIED IN   412 23
    THAT HE'S BURIED NOW FOR CENTURIES   492 13
    TO THE END FOR THEY ARE NOT YET BURIED   703   5

BURN
    WHERE THEY BURN AND CAUTERISE   64 19
    CRUEL SELF THE FIGHT IS NOT FOR EXISTENCE THE FIGHT IS +   93 14
    BUT WHOEVER WOULD PLUCK APART MY FLOWERING WILL BURN TH+   93 29
    NOW WHO WILL BURN YOU FREE   112   6
    MANY YEARS HAVE I STILL TO BURN DETAINED   115   5
    SO THROUGH THESE DAYS WHILE BURN ON THE FUEL OF LIFE   115   9
    I LONGED TO FEEL MY HOT BLOOD BURN   123 29
    LEAVING A BURN AND AN UGLY SMART   151   9
    LIKE A DEEP DEEP BURN   208 16
    IT BURNS WITHIN ME LIKE A DEEP OLD BURN   208 21
    WHERE THE CANDLES BURN IN THE DAYLIGHT AND THE PAINTED   233   6
    THE NAKED CANDLES BURN ON EVERY GRAVE   233   9
    AND THE LAST FIRES OF DISSOLUTION BURN IN THE BOSOM OF + 270 23
    AND BURN IT DOWN THE GLUTTED STUFFY WORLD   315   4

BURN
    TO BURN THE WORLD BACK TO MANURE-GOOD ASH   315 11
    BUT THESE THEMSELVES MUST BURN THESE LOUTS   315 13
    BREAK INTO DROPS BURN INTO DROPS OF BLOOD AND DROPPING   322 14
    FOR THE FIRE TO BURN IT UP FEATHERS AND ALL   329 32
    BURN THE HOUSE DOWN   440 16
    THAT BURN INWARDLY   511 13
    MAY BURN FOR LONG YEARS   511 16
    THE UPSHOT WAS MY PICTURE MUST BURN   579 23
    AND BURN BLUE AND COLD LIKE THE FLAME IN A MINER'S LAMP   619   5
    HELP HELP THEY WANT TO BURN MY PICTURES   633   7
    THEY WANT TO MAKE AN ACT OF FAITH AND BURN MY PRETTY   633   9
    WHO'VE DECIDED THAT BOCCACCIO MUST BURN   633 17
    BURN THAT HE SEES EVE RUNNING FROM THE LIKES OF HIM I   633 28
    BUT THE DAY THEY BURN MY PICTURES THEY BURN THE ROSE OF   634   3
    HELP OH HELP THEY WANT TO BURN MY PICTURES   634   6
    EARTH-CLODS AND NIGHT TO FLOWERS THAT PRAISE AND BURN   872   4
    LEAVING A BURN AND A SMART   873 19
    EVEN WHILE IN HIS INNERMOST EYES THERE BURN   876 26
    THEIR DROSS OF INDIFFERENCE AND BURN THE SCROLL   *895 29
    THEIR DROSS OF INDIFFERENCE AND BURN THE SCROLL   *904 18
    NOW WHO WILL BURN YOU FREE   *928 26
    MANY YEARS HAVE I STILL TO BURN DETAINED   *930   5
    AND THROUGH THESE YEARS WHILE I BURN ON THE FUEL OF LIFE *930   9

BURNED
    MOVED WITH SLOW FEET AND HER EYES' FLAME STEADILY BURNED 156 10
    BURNED CLEAN BY REMORSELESS HATE   242 17
    SMASHED ALL OOZING WITH BLOOD AND BURNED IN HEAPS   258   3
    BEING BURNED WITH OIL AND CONSUMED IN CORRUPT THICK   258 10

BURNING
    KNOWS BUT THE RETREAT OF THE BURNING SHOULDERS THE RED-+   67   4
    AS MISTLETOE BERRIES BURNING IN A BLACK TREE   86   2
    BE ALL YOURSELF ONE BONNY BURNING COAL   151 14
    I PLACE A GREAT AND BURNING SEAL OF LOVE   154   9
    LIKE SALT BURNING IN   206 21
    BURNING OF POWERFUL SALT BURNING EATING THROUGH MY   207 23
    SNOW OF SALT WHITE BURNING EATING SALT   207 31
    BUT I AM YOUR NAKED CANDLE BURNING   233 11
    UPRIGHT TOWARDS HEAVEN IS BURNING OFF TO YOU   233 15
    I AM BUSY ONLY AT MY BURNING   233 19
    I AM A NAKED CANDLE BURNING ON YOUR GRAVE   233 26
    A SOFT MOST UNWARRANTABLE BURNING   241 11
    IT SMELLS OF BURNING SNOW OF HOT-ACHE   270 18
    THE ONCE THE MASSIVE BURNING ACHE   276 20
    BUT NOW IT IS A BURNING HEARTHSTONE ONLY   326 27
    THAT THE SUN IS MORE THAN BURNING MORE THAN THE BURNING+ 331   6
    BEING EARTH-BROWN EARTH-GOLDEN FROM THE BURNING BOWELS   349 26
    INTO THE BURNING BOWELS OF THIS EARTH   350 12
    BURNING PALE POSITIVE POLE OF YOUR WATTLED HEAD   370 19
    MOST OF HIS TIME THE TIGER PADS AND SLOUCHES IN A BURNI+ 496 13
    LEAVE ME ALONE NOW FOR MY SOUL IS BURNING   580 19
    THE BURNING ARCHANGELS UNDER THE SEA KEEP PASSING BACK + 694 23
    BLACK LAMPS FROM THE HALLS OF DIS BURNING DARK BLUE   697   8
    THE DEAD ARE BURNING IN THE FUNERAL WIND   744   9
    FROM BURNING FIRES OF MANY SMOULDERING LIVES   744 24
    THERE ARE DEAD THAT CREEP THROUGH THE BURNING BOWELS OF+ 793 24
    BE ALL YOURSELF ONE BONNY BURNING COAL   873 24
    AND GATHER MY BURNING BEAUTIFUL DREAMS FOR HER SHARE   874   8
    BURNING LIKE DIVES IN HELL TO HER   874 20
    I LONGED TO POUR THE BURNING STORE   *935   1

BURNING-GLASS
    BRILLIANT AS A POWERFUL BURNING-GLASS   293 19

BURNISHED
    I SHALL BE CLEARED DISTINCT SINGLE AS IF BURNISHED IN S+ 267 18
    ONE CLEAR BURNISHED ISOLATED BEING UNIQUE   267 20

BURNS
    WHILE THAT VETCH-CLUMP STILL BURNS RED   35   8
    I TREMBLE IN HIS SHADOW AS HE BURNS   39 29
    SCHOOL NOW IS THE ROCK IN THIS WEARY LAND THE WINTER BU+   75 18
    WHY BURNS YOUR CHEEK AGAINST ME HOW HAVE I INSPIRED   85 19
    BURNS LIKE A BLOT OF ANXIETY   103 11
    OUT OF DEATH AND IT BURNS IN THE DRAUGHT   108 18
    A LOOK OF HATRED ON THE FLOWER THAT BURNS   113 11
    TO ALTER MY ONE SPECK OF DOOM WHEN ROUND ME BURNS   195 25
    IT BURNS WITHIN ME LIKE A DEEP OLD BURN   208 21
    ACROSS THERE A DISCOLOURED MOON BURNS ITSELF OUT   212 14
    HOT HURRYING YET IT BURNS IF YOU TOUCH IT   505 26
    AND SINGES US AND BURNS THE HOUSE DOWN   506 10
    BURNS THE SMALL FLAME OF ANGER GNAWING   601   9
    SO SALT IS THE BOUNDARY MARK BETWEEN FIRE THAT BURNS AN+ 706 10
    WONDER I CRAVE FOR THAT BURNS STRONG IN HIM   876 31
    FOR MYSELF IN MY OWN EYES' LAUGHTER BURNS   *891 31

BURNT
    RAIN THAT BURNT ON MY RAGE SAYING COME   62 23
    HIS MIND UNTIL IT BURNT HIS HEART AWAY   158   2
    WHICH BURNT JUST NOW WITH MARVELLOUS IMMANENCE   219 16
    BURNT OUT OF OUR EARTHLY COVERS   243   2
    BURNT BACK TO ASH   315 30
    MASSIVE OLD ALTAR OF HIS OWN BURNT OFFERING   326 28
    IT WAS ALWAYS AN ALTAR OF BURNT OFFERING   326 29
    IN BURNT DARK FEATHERS   373   9
    WE SHALL LAUGH THE INSTITUTIONS WILL CURL UP LIKE BURNT 482 26
    ONLY WHEN SHE IS BURNT ALIVE BURNT DOWN   728   7
    IN BURNT DARK FEATHERS   781 15
    SUFFERING BURNT THROUGH YOUR FLESH   *928 22

BURR
    THEN BRILLIANT EARTH FROM THE BURR OF NIGHT IN BEAUTY   73   4

BURRO
NOW HE'S A JACKASS A PACK-ASS A DONKEY SOMARO BURRO　379　9

BURROW
TO TRAVEL TO BURROW INTO A LITTLE LOOSE EARTH AFRAID OF+　358　2

BURROWING
AND BURROWING IN ITS HEART　124　31
I AM BURROWING MY BODY INTO THE SOIL　259　32

BURST
I AM HERE I AM HERE SCREAMS THE PEEWIT THE MAY-BLOBS BU+　34　9
AS IF IT WOULD BURST ITS WINE-SKIN IN MY THROAT　123　16
SO NOW IT IS VAIN FOR THE SINGER TO BURST INTO CLAMOUR　148　15
WITH VIOLENT ACHINGS HEAVING TO BURST THE SLEEP THAT IS+　149　23
BURST　159　24
WITHIN THE RAGE WE SHALL NOT KNOW TILL IT BURST　160　19
TINY LIGHTHOUSES LITTLE SOULS OF LANTERNS COURAGE BURST+　206　16
BURST IT WITH GERMINATION WITH WORLD ANEW　273　9
TILL IT'S FINISHED AND YOU'RE OVER-RIPE AND YOU BURST T+　283　23
LET US BURST INTO AFFIRMATION　284　23
TILL IT BURST FORTH BLINDING WITHERING THE EARTH　294　3
BURST THE NIGHT'S MEMBRANE OF TRANQUIL STARS　302　18
CAN BE KEPT DOWN BUT HE'LL BURST LIKE A POLYP INTO　305　9
ACROSS THE HISS OF WONDERS AS THE ROCKET BURST　391　17
AND THE EGO WILL HAVE TO BURST LIKE THE SWOLLEN FROG　472　12
THEN HE CAN BURST THE POT　475　2
THEY HAVE HIGH BLOOD-PRESSURE AND ALMOST BURST　502　5
TILL THEY GROW HOT AND BURST AS EVEN STONE CAN　642　14
THEN THE MILL-STONES BURST WITH THE INTERNAL HEAT OF TH+　648　12
AS IF IT WOULD BURST ITS WINESKIN IN MY THROAT　*934　22

BURSTEN
LIKE A PROSTITUTE THE BURSTEN FIG MAKING A SHOW OF HER +　283　33
BUT NOW THEY STITCH TO ADORN THE BURSTEN FIG NOT TO COV+　284　14
WHAT THEN WHEN WOMEN THE WORLD OVER HAVE ALL BURSTEN IN+　284　29
AND BURSTEN FIGS WON'T KEEP　284　31
IN THE BURSTEN CITIES　704　7
TILL THE BURSTEN FLOOD OF LIFE EBBS BACK TO MY EYES　*893　30

BURSTING
I WAS A TIGER BURSTING INTO SUNLIGHT　259　12
WHY ARE THEY SO BURSTING FLINGING THEMSELVES ABOUT　537　23
IN MY BURSTING AND BUDDING I FEEL　888　14

BURSTIN'
WAS A'MOST BURSTIN' MAD 'O' MY-SEN　80　7
WAS A'MOST BURSTIN' MAD O' MY-SEN　*922　7

BURSTS
LIFT MY ARMS THE HILL BURSTS AND HEAVES UNDER THEIR SPU+　33　9
THIS SPRING AS IT COMES BURSTS UP IN BONFIRES GREEN　116　1
TILL THE HILL BURSTS　293　17
THE WAVE OF AGONY BURSTS IN THE STONE THAT HE WAS　379　20
A WAVE BURSTS IN ANGER ON A ROCK BROKEN UP　467　12
BURSTS LIKE AN ARC LAMP INTO LIGHT　773　2
THE SUBSTANCE OF SHADOW THAT BURSTS AND EXPLODES　788　13
MOVE MY ARMS THE HILL BURSTS AND HEAVES UNDER THEIR SPU+　*891　10

BURY
TO BURY ITS WEARY SPARK　253　32
LET THE DEAD GO BURY THEIR DEAD　440　21
BURY A MAN GENTLY IF HE HAS LAIN DOWN AND DIED　442　1

BURYING-GROUND
AND THE VILLAGE FOLK OUTSIDE IN THE BURYING-GROUND　233　2

BUS
YOU CAN'T SIT ON A BUS NOR IN THE TUBE　434　2

BUSBIES
SMOULDERING WITH DARKENED BUSBIES BENEATH THE BAYONETS'+　66　8
UPON US DARK EYES AS HERE BENEATH THE BUSBIES GLITTERIN+　66　25
AND SO IT IS EBB-TIME THEY TURN THE EYES BENEATH THE BU+　67　1

BUSH
THE FIRE ROSE UP IN THE BUSH AND BLAZED APACE　94　25
NAKED EXPOSED ON THE BUSH　107　12
I ON THE BUSH OF THE GLOBE　107　13
OF FLESH THAT STANDS DISMAYED ON THE BUSH　107　18
HERE ON THE BUSH OF THE GLOBE　108　2
IN EVERY BUSH IS GIVEN YOU BACK AND WE　157　24
AND SCARLET BERRIES FALLING FROM THE BUSH　160　6
JUST ORTS AND SLARTS BERRIES THAT SMOULDER IN THE BUSH　219　15
WHEN HE PUSHED HIS BUSH OF BLACK HAIR OFF HIS BROW　310　1
BLOOM ALONG THE CORSO ON THE LIVING PERAMBULATING BUSH　313　24
I REMEMBER THE FIRST TIME OUT OF A BUSH IN THE DARKNESS+　366　1
HAUNTED BLUE BUSH　394　19
AS THE TURNIP MODELS HIS ROUND ROOT AS THE BUSH MAKES　451　19
PEOPLE ARE LIKE LEAVES FLUTTERING AND GAY ON THE BUSH　615　7
SO HERE WE GO ROUND THE MULBERRY BUSH　658　1
MULBERRY BUSH MULBERRY BUSH　658　2
HERE WE GO ROUND THE MULBERRY BUSH　658　3
NEVER HAVING SEEN A MULBERRY BUSH IN OUR LIVES　658　4
OLD ONE ERECT ON A BUSH　782　28
THE FIRE ROSE UP AND THE BUSH BLAZED FORTH GOD'S GRACE　*897　13
AND DWELLING IN HIS OWN BOWERY HOUSE LIKE A BIRD IN A B+　*950　9

BUSHED
BUSHED IN AN UNCOUTH ARDOUR COILED AT CORE　160　13

BUSHES
BUSHES　33　12
WILD PUFFING OF GREEN-FIRE TREES AND FLAME-GREEN BUSHES　116　2
THE BUSHES SUMPTUOUSLY　126　26
COFFEE FROM THE BUSHES IN THE HOT LANDS EVEN THE JUICY +　793　22
THE QUICK SPARKS ON THE GORSE BUSHES ARE LEAPING　*891　1
BUSHES　*891　13

BUSHMAN
BUT IT'S SO LONG AGO THE ANCIENT BUSHMAN HAS FORGOTTEN　286　17

BUSILY
AS THEY WRITE THEIR ROUND HEADS BUSILY BOWED　51　12
AS THEY WRITE THEIR ROUND HEADS BUSILY BOWED　*898　24
AS THEY WRITE THEIR ROUND HEADS BUSILY BOWED　*902　8

BUSINESS
SORRY I AM FOR THIS BUSINESS AN' SORRY IF EVER I'VE DRI+　83　6
HAVE DONE HAVE DONE WITH THIS SHUDDERING DELICIOUS BUSI+　273　18
ABOUT A FORGOTTEN BUSINESS　296　23
WHAT BUSINESS THEN　296　24
WHO PERHAPS WILL DO THE BUSINESS AFTER ALL　317　4
IN THE BUSINESS OF BEATING THE METTLE OF GOATS TO A GOD+　381　33
WITH WHICH WE SHALL DO BIG BUSINESS　442　25
THEN YOU WILL SETTLE THE HASH OF BUSINESS FINALLY　484　21
IS IT THE QUOS VULT PERDERE DEUS BUSINESS　533　23
AND DO YOU THINK IT'S MY BUSINESS TO BE HANDING OUT MON+　547　22
THIS BUSINESS OF SPEAKING FROM HEART TO HEART　575　25
A MAN'S BUSINESS IS ONE OF HIS POCKETS HIS BANK　607　15
THAT IS WHY BUSINESS SEEMS TO ME DESPICABLE　607　21
READY AGAIN FOR THE BUSINESS OF BEING A MAN　809　18
SORRY I AM FOR THIS BUSINESS AN' SORRY IF I HA'E DRIVEN+　*925　10

BUST
I WISH I WAS ONLY A BUST　41　18
START IN AND BUST IT ALL　457　10
BUST UP THE HOLY APPLE-PIE　458　7
DOESN'T SOON GO BUST　519　20
BUST IN AND HOLD THE GROUND　560　32

BUSTIN'
THAT LITTLE BLEEDER COMES BUSTIN' IN　493　11

BUSTLE
IN A BUSTLE　231　15
AND THE BUSTLE OF BEES IN THE PEAR-TREE BLOOM　885　24

BUSY
HER OUT OF THE NEST'S WARM BUSY BALL　42　28
SAY I'M BUSY　44　13
AND PERHAPS THEY WERE RIGHT FOR THE YOUNG ARE BUSY DEEP+　92　25
I AM BUSY ONLY AT MY BURNING　233　19
I AM BUSY ONLY AT MY LIFE　233　20
THE BLUE JAY PACES ROUND THE CABIN VERY BUSY PICKING UP　375　23
THE BUSY BUSY BOURGEOIS IMBIBES HIS LITTLE SHARE　432　25
FROM THE BUSY BODIES OF PEOPLE　451　19
ULTIMATELY WE ARE ALL BUSY BUYING AND SELLING ONE ANOTH+　482　29
AND BUSY PUTTING OUT THE SUN　528　8
WE THOUGHT WE'D ELECT YOU TO KEEP YOU ALL BUSY　574　4
BE ALONE AND SEE THE MOONLIGHT OUTSIDE WHITE AND BUSY　646　10
BUSY　818　16
AYE BUSY WITH A FEW HARD TASKS AND WRATH　875　31
ALL DAY LONG I AM BUSY AND HAPPY AT MY WORK　*945　24

BUSY-BUSY
WITH A SET OF CANKERED MAGISTRATES AND BUSY-BUSY BOBBIES　634　8

BUTCHER
AS IF THE BUTCHER WERE BIDING HIS TIME　828　1

BUTS
AND BUTTER YOUR SLIPPERY BUTS　549　12

BUTT
SUDDENLY BUTT　381　9

BUTTER
AND BUTTER YOUR SLIPPERY BUTS　549　12
OR THE BUTTER OR THE APPLES OR PEACHES FROM THE BASKET　828　19

BUTTERCUP
THE BUTTERCUP BOG-END WHERE THE FLOWERS ROSE UP　90　20

BUTTERCUPS
ON THE BUTTERCUPS AND THE BUTTERCUPS WAS I　119　26

BUTTERED
YOU KNOW WHICH SIDE YOUR BREAD IS BUTTERED　396　17

BUTTERFLIES
OR LIKE TWO BUTTERFLIES THAT SETTLE ON A GLASS　65　3
IS LIKE WHEN TWO WHITE BUTTERFLIES SETTLE IN THE ARMS O+　*913　3
OR AS TWO WHITE BUTTERFLIES SETTLE IN THE CUP OF ONE FL+　*914　4

BUTTERFLY
BUTTERFLY THE WIND BLOWS SEA-WARD STRONG BEYOND THE GAR+　696　12
BUTTERFLY WHY DO YOU SETTLE ON MY SHOE AND SIP THE DIRT+　696　13
LIFTING YOUR VEINED WINGS LIFTING THEM BIG WHITE BUTTER+　696　14
BUT THE WIND BLOWS STRONG TO SEA-WARD WHITE BUTTERFLY C+　696　19
MY PALE WET BUTTERFLY FLUFFY CHICKEN　863　6

BUTTOCKS
WOULD WORSHIP THEE LETTING MY BUTTOCKS PRANCE　40　18
AND SPLASHES WARM BETWEEN THE BUTTOCKS　427　6
WITH BRIGHT LEGS AND UNCRINGING BUTTOCKS　525　21

BUTTONED
MY CONSTABLE WI' 'IS BUTTONED BREAST　79　5
MY CONSTABLE WI' 'IS BUTTONED BREAST　*921　1

BUTTONHOLES
WITH HIBISCUS FLOWERS IN THE BUTTONHOLES OF YOUR SUNDAY+　314　11

BUY
  TAKE THEM AND BUY THEE A SILVER RING   44   4
  THINE SHALL GO TER PAY THE WOMAN AN' WI' MY BIT WE'LL B+   83   2
  THE ROOT OF OUR PRESENT EVIL IS THAT WE BUY AND SELL   482 28
  THINE SHALL GO TO PAY THE WOMAN AN' WI' MY BIT WE'LL BUY   *925   6

BUYING
  ULTIMATELY WE ARE ALL BUSY BUYING AND SELLING ONE ANOTH+   482 29
  NOT BASED ON WAGES NOR PROFITS NOR ANY SORT OF BUYING A+   483 26

BUZZARD
  O EAGLE OF THE MIND ALAS YOU ARE MORE LIKE A BUZZARD   473   9

BUZZING
  AND WHITE PEOPLE IN EVENING DRESS BUZZING AND CROWDING   387 23

BYE-BYE
  DOES IT WANT TO GO TO BYE-BYE THERE THEN TAKE ITS LITTLE   570 22
  TAKE ITS DUMMY GO TO BYE-BYE LIKE A MAN LITTLE MAN   570 24

BYGONE
  ALL THE BYGONE HUSHED YEARS   53   9
  AND LIKE A FUNGUS LIVING ON THE REMAINS OF BYGONE LIFE   431 15
  OVER THE BYGONE HUSHED YEARS   *906   1

BY-NO-MEANS
  THROUGH BREACHES IN THE WALLS OF THIS OUR BY-NO-MEANS I+   722 25
  OVER THE ADAMANT WALLS OF THIS OUR BY-NO-MEANS IMPREGNA+   *958   7

BY-PATHS
  BY-PATHS WHERE THE WANTON-HEADED FLOWERS DOFF THEIR HOOD   65 30

B-
  LIKE B- AND F- AND SH-   491 16

CA-A-A
  CA-A-A COMES THE SCRAPE OF RIDICULE OUT OF THE TREE   375 14

CABAGE
  AND PUT A DIRTY GREEN LARGE CABAGE   845 25

CABAGES
  BUT NOW THEY ARE LIKE CABAGES   848   9

CABBAGE
  NOT THIS VAST ROTTING CABBAGE PATCH WE CALL THE WORLD   315 32
  YOU NEED NOT CLEAR THE WORLD LIKE A CABBAGE PATCH FOR ME   316   9
  WHAT ROT TO SEE THE CABBAGE AND HIBISCUS-TREE   316 18
  NO MATTER OF WHAT SORT THE CABBAGE BE   569 14
  THE COURAGE OF ROSINESS IN A CABBAGE WORLD   634 27

CABBAGE-IDEALISTIC
  BUT I WON'T BE PUT ON A CABBAGE-IDEALISTIC LEVEL OF EQU+   316 16

CABBAGES
  AND CABBAGES BORN TO BE CUT AND EAT   317 20
  BUT THE CABBAGES OF ENGLAND LEAVE ME COLD   569   2
  OH THE CABBAGES OF ENGLAND LEAVE ME COLD   569   3
  BUT LOOK AT THE CABBAGES OH COUNT THEM BY THE SCORE   569 10
  YET THE CABBAGES OF ENGLAND LEAVE ME COLD   569 13

CABIN
  COMES ROUND THE CABIN IN THE SNOW   375   2
  IMMENSE ABOVE THE CABIN   375   7
  THE BLUE JAY PACES ROUND THE CABIN VERY BUSY PICKING UP   375 23

CABINET
  THERE YOU ARE THEN HE'S A CABINET MAKER   452 24

CABOT
  CORTES PISARRO COLUMBUS CABOT THEY ARE NOTHING   259 23

CABS
  TER MARRY WI' CABS AN' RICE   82 12
  TO MARRY WI' CABS AN' RICE   *924 16

CACHE SEXE
  WHEN THEY PAINTED A NUDE TO PUT A CACHE SEXE ON   580   1
  A CACHE SEXE A CACHE SEXE OR ELSE BEGONE   580   2
  AS A CACHE SEXE I'D HAVE PUT A WHOLE FOG   580 12

CACHINNATE
  AND EAT AND CACHINNATE AND EVEN SEEM TO SMILE   644 19

CACHINNATION
  THEIR ROBOT CACHINNATION COMES RATTLING OUT OF MY THROAT   645   8

CACKLE
  AND THEN THE HEAVENS CACKLE WITH UNCOUTH SOUNDS   647 16
  ECHO OF HER I'VE-LAID-AN-EGG CACKLE IS RICH AND RESONAN+   761 21
  OH YOU WHOSE CACKLE MAKES MY THROAT GO   762   3

CACOPHONY
  TO DROWN THEIR INNER CACOPHONY AND OURS   656   7

CACTUS
  THE CACTUS SHARPENS HIS THORN   804 20

CACTUSES
  WE WHO HAVE NEVER FLOWERED LIKE PATIENT CACTUSES   272 32
  CACTUSES SHARPEN THEIR THORNS   806   2

CADENCE
  CADENCE IS A LIE   655   5

CAESAR
  IMMORTAL CAESAR DEAD AND TURNED TO CLAY   545 24

CAFFLE
  TO THINK I SHOULD 'AVE TER 'AFFLE AN' CAFFLE   82   9
  TO THINK I SHOULD HA'E TO HAFFLE AN' CAFFLE   *924 13

CAGE
  THE GREAT CAGE OF OUR DOMESTICITY   485   1
  IN A CAGE IT CAN'T TAKE PLACE   485   8
  BREAK THE CAGE THEN START IN AND TRY   485   9
  THE WOMEN ARE IN THE CAGE AS MUCH AS YOU ARE   485 19
  THERE IS NO WAY OUT THE CAGE HAS NO DOOR IT'S RUSTED   486   1
  THEREFORE BE PREPARED TO TACKLE THE CAGE   486   6
  MAN IS ONE OF THOSE BEASTS THAT WILL BREED IN A CAGE   843 14
  THE CAGE WHICH DOES NOT KILL THE MECHANISM OF SEX   843 17
  THEY ARE IN THE CAGE   843 21

CAGED
  THE BODY OF ITSELF IS CLEAN BUT THE CAGED MIND   463 19
  THEY LOOK AT YOU THEY SEE A CAGED MONKEY   485 20
  THERE IS NO WAY OUT WE ARE ALL CAGED MONKEYS   485 24
  YOU'RE A CAGED MONKEY AGAIN IN FIVE MINUTES   486   5
  HAVE BEEN CAGED AND COVERED WITH DARKNESS ALL DAY AND N+   *918   5

CAGE-RIBS
  ITS CAGE-RIBS IN THE SOCIAL HEAVEN BENEFICENT   290 23

CAGES
  CAGES OF OUR PERSONALITY   482 17

CAJOLE
  COME AND CAJOLE THE GAWKY COLT'S-FOOT FLOWERS   273   4
  WHY WON'T YOU CAJOLE MY SOUL   290   6
  AND STRIKE WITH A BLINDNESS OF FURY AGAINST ME CAN I CA+   *926 24

CAJOLED
  AND MEMORIES CLUSTERED ME CLOSE AND SLEEP WAS CAJOLED   98 30
  SAVE IT HAD FIRST APPROACHED HIM AND CAJOLED HIS SOUL   290   3
  YOU HAVE CAJOLED THE SOULS OF MILLIONS OF US   290   4

CAKE
  HE SAYS THE SOONER WILL YOU EAT IMAGINARY CAKE IN THE   442 15
  MARVELLOUS CAKE   442 19

CAKEILY
  BUILT IT MOST GRAND AND CAKEILY   488 11

CAKES
  AND FURNISH IT WITH FOOD WITH LITTLE CAKES AND WINE   718 10

CAKEY
  IN GRAND AND CAKEY STYLE   488 22
  THEY HAVE BUILT A NEW AND CAKEY UNIVERSITY   *950 13

CALCULATING
  CALCULATING   269 28

CALCULATIONS
  AND FROM ALL THIS DO YOU MAKE CALCULATIONS   301 11

CALF
  THE GAZELLE CALF O MY CHILDREN   466   9
  AS THE LEOPARD SMITES THE SMALL CALF WITH A SPANGLED PA+   683   9

CALL
  AWFULLY MUST I CALL BACK A HUNDRED EYES A VOICE   76   7
  OF THE LEAVES AS THOUGH THEY WOULD LEAP SHOULD I CALL   105 18
  LESS THAN THE WIND THAT RUNS TO THE FLAMY CALL   116 13
  A WET BIRD WALKS ON THE LAWN CALL TO THE BOY TO COME   137   7
  CALL TO HIM OUT OF THE SILENCE CALL HIM TO SEE   137 10
  ITS HEAD AS IT WALKED I CAN NEVER CALL HIM TO ME   137 15
  AND SO MY HEART BEGINS TO CRY AND CALL   174   3
  YOU ARE THE CALL AND I AM THE ANSWER   203 22
  AND CALL TO GOD WHERE ART THOU   231 29
  WHAT WE CALL HUMAN   291 29
  WHAT WE CALL HUMAN AND WHAT WE DON'T CALL HUMAN   292   2
  CALL IT PEACE   294   6
  CALL IT MOONRISE   302 14
  NOT THIS VAST ROTTING CABBAGE PATCH WE CALL THE WORLD   315 32
  I HEARD A WOMAN CALL YOU THE WINGED VICTORY   332   9
  THE DAWN ROOKS CALL AT EVENING WHEN THE NIGHTINGALE SIN+   368 11
  HAS THE PEACOCK HAD HIS DAY DOES HE CALL IN VAIN SCREEC+   371 20
  THE EAGLE THE DOVE AND THE BARNYARD ROOSTER DO THEY CALL   371 22
  CALL ME HARRY IF YOU WILL   404   8
  CALL ME OLD HARRY SAYS HE   404   9
  I CALL HIM NO NAMES   405 22
  WE CALL RELIGION   480 23
  WHAT THE OLD PEOPLE CALL IMMEDIATE CONTACT WITH GOD   481   6
  I WOULD CALL ATTILA ON HIS LITTLE HORSE   497   1
  SO THAT I WOULD CALL ATTILA ON HIS LITTLE HORSE   497 11
  WE CALL SANITY IN OURSELVES   515 22
  WE CALL FREE COMPETITION AND INDIVIDUAL ENTERPRISE AND   519 29
  AND I CALL IT THE SUN   525   6
  FROM THE WILD HEART OF SPACE THAT I CALL THE SUN OF SUNS   525   9
  EDITOR GOOD MORNING DON'T TROUBLE TO CALL AGAIN WE   582 19
  YET BELLS CALL THE CHRISTIANS TO GOD   623   1
  THEY CALL IT HEALTH IT LOOKS LIKE NULLITY   625 24
  THIS I CALL A SHOCKING HUMILIATION   645   5
  BUT WHAT WE MAY SACRIFICE IF WE CALL IT SACRIFICE FROM +   678 10
  THEY CALL ALL EXPERIENCE OF THE SENSES MYSTIC WHEN THE +   707 26
  HOGGING IT DOWN LIKE A PIG I CALL THE FEEDING OF CORPSES   708 11
  THAT THEY CALL SCIENCE AND REALITY   708 17
  I CALL IT MENTAL CONCEIT AND MYSTIFICATION   708 18
  I WILL CALL TO THEM   790 18

CALL
    LET US CALL THE ELEVEN   798   4
    FROM THE PLACE WHICH I CALL MY FATHER   801   3
    GIVE HIM TREES CALL BACK THE TREES   802   15
    CALL ME A MAN   803   4
    THEN CALL ON HUITZILOPOCHTLI   808   1
    HUITZILOPOCHTLI CALL HIM OFF   808   6
    CALL OH COME   812   6
    I CANNOT CALL HER SWEET JOY NOW   863   9
    WHEN SOFTLY I CALL AT HER DOOR AND ENTER THE ROOM   868   25
    THERE IS SOMETHING ABOUT THAT THEY CALL THE WIND   882   16
    AWFULLY MUST I CALL BACK THOSE HUNDRED EYES A VOICE   *898   2
    AWFULLY MUST I CALL BACK THOSE HUNDRED EYES A VOICE   *901   11
    PALS WORSE N'R ONY NAME AS YOU COULD CALL   *911   12
    WHEN SOFTLY I CALL AT HER DOOR AND ENTER THE ROOM   *941   25
    LEANING IN THE MASSIVE UNCONSCIOUS INCLINATION WE CALL +   *952   4

CALLED
    AND CLUSTERED STAR CALLED DOWN TO ME TO-NIGHT   86   15
    WHOM ROME CALLED VICIOUS   297   8
    COME UP AND BE CALLED A MOON   302   8
    CALLED THE ALMOND BONE IN THE BODY THE LAST BONE OF THE+   303   9
    PROFITEERS HERE BEING CALLED DOG-FISH STINKING DOG-FISH+   316   25
    JESUS WAS CALLED THE FISH   340   15
    INDOORS WE CALLED EACH OTHER YOU   490   19
    THIS IS CALLED UNIVERSAL FREEDOM   521   19
    IN THE DAYS CALLED CHAOS WHICH LEFT US ROCKS AND GEMS   529   25
    I SUPPOSE TARTS ARE CALLED TARTS BECAUSE THEY'RE TART   530   18
    IT'S CALLED THE BRITISH PUBLIC THE PUBLIC THE PUBLIC   570   14
    IT'S CALLED THE BRITISH PUBLIC INCLUDING YOU AND I   570   15
    CALLED HIM OLD DADDY DO NOTHING   582   4
    SO I CALLED HIM COME IN IF YOU WILL   692   12
    IF I SAY I TASTE THESE THINGS IN AN APPLE I AM CALLED M+   708   5
    WHICH HAS BROUGHT TO PASS THE FEARFUL THING CALLED EVIL   712   25
    AND CALLED TO HIS HORSES AND HIS STRONG BLUE BODY   735   14
    IN THE CAVE WHICH IS CALLED DARK EYE   786   5
    QUETZALCOATL MY BROTHER HE CALLED SEND ME MY IMAGES   789   17
    AND QUETZALCOATL CALLED BACK I WILL DO IT   789   21
    IF YOU HEAR A MAN CALLED BRILLIANT YOU MAY BE PRETTY SU+   841   18
    AND THAT A PEEWIT CALLED   881   23
    BUT WHETHER IT CALLED IN MY SOUL   881   24

CALLING
    IS HE CALLING THE LONE ONE IS HIS DEEP   40   1
    CALLING LOW TO HER LOVER   42   10
    ARE HURRYING AND STRIDENTLY CALLING   54   2
    THE CUCKOO AND THE COO-DOVE'S CEASELESS CALLING   65   11
    CALLING   65   12
    SEX WHICH BREAKS US INTO VOICE SETS US CALLING ACROSS T+   366   34
    DEEPS CALLING CALLING FOR THE COMPLEMENT   366   35
    SINGING AND CALLING AND SINGING AGAIN BEING ANSWERED   366   36
    AND THE CALLING OF THE OLD RED INDIAN HIGH ON THE PUEBL+   623   16
    WHOSE VOICE FLIES ON AND ON CALLING LIKE A SWAN   623   17
    HELP HELP I AM CALLING IN ENGLISH   633   12
    AND I A NAKED MAN CALLING   704   27
    CALLING TO THEE FOR MY MANA   704   28
    A CALLING COLUMN OF BLOOD   714   9
    CALLING ANOTHER ONE   825   13
    A GREAT BULL BELLOWED THROUGH SPACE CALLING TO THE MILK+   *946   21

CALLOUS
    CALLOUS AND DOUR   145   11
    CALLOUS   197   13
    SHAMELESS AND CALLOUS I LOVE YOU   210   5

CALLOUSLY
    CALLOUSLY CONTINUOUS   427   4

CALLS
    IN THE VALLEY A CORNCRAKE CALLS   64   21
    YET WAIT AWHILE FOR HENCEFORTH I WILL LOVE WHEN A BLOSS+   94   5
    DISCREETLY YET RECKLESSLY CALLS   105   32
    AND WOLF HE CALLS ME AND RED   405   21
    THE MODERN MIND CALLS LOVE   469   22
    ODYSSEUS CALLS THE COMMANDS AS HE STEERS PAST THOSE FOA+   687   20
    CALLS TO THE AUTUMN RESURRECTION   745   28
    AND SO WHEN THE OUTSIDE WORLD CALLS UPON AMERICA TO ACT+   775   29

CALM
    YET CALM AND KINDLY ARE HIS EYES   43   14
    OH IF I WERE CALM AS YOU ARE   102   15
    AT LAST TO CALM INCANDESCENCE   242   16
    TO THE FREE CALM UPPER AIR   343   2
    CALM WITH THE CALM OF SCIMITARS AND BRILLIANT REAPING H+   609   11
    A DEEP CALM IN THE HEART   700   12
    WITH DIM CALM THOUGHTS AND QUIET HANDS   *960   28

CALMLY
    NO LONGER HE SWIMS CALMLY   436   2
    IS THAT THEY CALMLY ASSERT WE ONLY THRILL TO PERVERSITY   531   3
    AND AT THE SAME TIME EXPECT TO GO ON CALMLY EATING GOOD   531   6
    THEY SAY APRES MOI LE DELUGE AND CALMLY EXPECT   531   8

CALVARY
    EVEN OF CALVARY AND RESURRECTION   328   5

CALVE
    SHE WILL CALVE TOMORROW   38   7
    SHE WILL CALVE TOMORROW   *892   23

CALVES
    OF THE DARK-GREEN HILLS NEW CALVES IN SHED PEEWITS TURN+   57   27
    CURIOUS LONG-LEGGED FOALS AND WIDE-EARED CALVES AND NAK+   271   34

CALYX
    WHICH IS JUST LIKE A FOUR-SEPALLED CALYX   282   6
    NOW AT LAST THE CLOSED CALYX OPENS FROM OUR TIRED EYES   *916   13

CAMBREE
    CAMBREE MY WORD CAMBREE   835   12

CAMEL
    TO SUPPORT HER THE HYSTERICAL CAMEL   492   8
    TO THE CAMEL AND THE DOG   492   20

CAMELLIA
    AZALEA AND CAMELLIA SINGLE PEONY   313   28

CAMEL'S
    I'D LOADED THE CAMEL'S BACK BEFORE   491   19
    I HEARD THE CAMEL'S BACK GO CRACK   491   23
    SUCH WORDS TO THE CAMEL'S CHARGE   492   16

CAMION
    HOW NICE TO GET IN THE CAMION AND FOR TWENTY CENTAVOS T+   794   14

CAMIONS
    YEA LORD EVEN TRAINS AND CAMIONS AND AUTOMOBILES   794   11
    TRAINS AND CAMIONS AUTOMOBILES AND AEROLANES   794   12

CAMP
    ONLY BREAKING CAMP AND ENTERING   768   11

CAMPED
    THEY CAMPED AND WENT TO SLEEP   407   7

CAMP-FIRE
    ROUND THE LOST MAN'S CAMP-FIRE   816   18

CAMPIONS
    THE CAMPIONS DRIFT IN FRAGILE ROSY MIST   854   11

CAMPIONS'
    FOR WITH THE REDNESS OF LAUGHTER THE BATTLE IS WAGING I+   854   19

CANADA
    ALL THE ROCKING WHEAT OF CANADA RIPENING NOW   263   1

CANAILLE
    YOU CULTURED CANAILLE   762   19
    OH THE CANAILLE OF CULTURE THE CHRISTIAN CANAILLE   762   20

CANARY
    CANARY   398   10

CANCEL
    HE WILL CANCEL THE MACHINES WE HAVE GOT   451   28
    HE WILL CANCEL AGAIN THESE MACHINES WE HAVE GOT   *950   11

CANCELLED
    ARE YOU WILLING TO BE SPONGED OUT ERASED CANCELLED   728   1

CANCERS
    LIKE FLICKERING CANCERS   511   14

CANDELABRUM
    LET ME SIT DOWN BENEATH THE MANY-BRANCHING CANDELABRUM   299   9
    LET ME SIT DOWN BENEATH THIS MANY-BRANCHING CANDELABRUM   299   19
    OH MANY-BRANCHING CANDELABRUM OH STRANGE UP-STARTING   300   5

CANDID
    WISTFUL AND CANDID WATCHING ME WISTFULLY FROM HER DISTA+   67   14
    LIKE CANDID GHOSTS   108   22
    BEAUTIFUL CANDID LOVERS   243   1
    THE CANDID REVELATION   285   14

CANDLE
    IS BLOWN OUT LIKE A CANDLE   115   20
    TO THE LEFT THIS GHOST LIKE A CANDLE SWEALING   141   16
    BUT I AM YOUR NAKED CANDLE BURNING   233   11
    I AM A NAKED CANDLE BURNING ON YOUR GRAVE   233   26
    INTENT TO HOLD THE CANDLE OF THE SUN UPON ITS SOCKET-TIP   299   29
    TO HOLD THE ONE AND ONLY LIGHTED CANDLE OF THE SUN IN H+   299   34
    AND HOLD THE LIGHTED CANDLE OF THE SUN   300   4
    LIKE THE FLAME OF A CANDLE SLOW AND QUICK   460   7
    SO IS A CANDLE EVEN AS A MATCH   724   19
    LIKE A CANDLE FLAME ON THIS BODY BUT I ENSHRINE   *930   6

CANDLE-FLAMES
    THE CANDLE-FLAMES BESIDE THE SURPLICES   232   31

CANDLE-FLAME
    LIKE A CANDLE-FLAME ON THIS BODY BUT I ENCLOSE   115   6
    ISSUING LIKE A GREAT CLOVEN CANDLE-FLAME   780   29

CANDLE-LIGHT
    HOW MANY TIMES HAS T' CANDLE-LIGHT SHONE   138   4

CANDLES
    WHERE THE CANDLES BURN IN THE DAYLIGHT AND THE PAINTED   233   6
    THE NAKED CANDLES BURN ON EVERY GRAVE   233   9
    PAIN YET THE LIGHT OF LAMPS AND CANDLES HAS NO FEARS FO+   331   4
    LIKE THE GREEN CANDLES OF MALINTZI   811   13

CANDLESTICK
    THERE'S 'IS COLLAR ROUND TH' CANDLESTICK   81   13
    THE JEWISH SEVEN-BRANCHED TALLOW-STINKING CANDLESTICK   299   20

CANDLE-STICK
    THAT'S HIS COLLAR ROUND THE CANDLE-STICK   *923 13

CANDOUR
    AND BETRAYS ITS CANDOUR IN THE ROUND WHITE STRAWBERRY F+   272 28

CANE
    THEY TAKE SUGAR FROM THE TALL TUBES OF THE CANE   793 20

CANE-BRAKE
    SO IN THE CANE-BRAKE HE CLASPED HIS HAND IN DELIGHT   693 16

CANKERED
    IS SOUR BITTER FRUITS CANKERED BY LIES   504 14
    WITH A SET OF CANKERED MAGISTRATES AND BUSY-BUSY BOBBIES   634 8

CANNA
    I CANNA COME DOWN   44 19
    LIFT THY FACE AN' LOOK AT ME MAN CANNA TER LOOK AT ME   83* 5
    IF THA CANNA SAY'T COME THEN AN' SCRAIGHT IT OUT ON MY   540 14
    I CANNA BIDE TO THINK WHERE HE IS GONE   *911 16

CANNON
    WHEN I HEARD THE CANNON OF THE WAR I LISTENED WITH MY   257 5

CANNY
    SUCH A CANNY LISTENER FROM A DISTANCE LOOKING UPWARDS   384 17

CANOPY
    OF THE WIND IN THE KNOTTED BUDS MAKES A CANOPY   152 29
    SO SITTING UNDER THE KNOTTED CANOPY   153 1
    MY CASHMERE SHAWL I'LL HANG FOR A CANOPY   754 24
    OF THE WIND HUNG ROUND THE KNOTTED BUDS LIKE A CANOPY   866 25

CANST
    THEN LEAVES THEE AND THOU CANST NOT BUT COMPLAIN   69 29
    BUT EVEN THOU SON OF MAN CANST NOT QUAFF OUT THE DREGS +   322 9

CANTERS
    SO SO GAILY A GENERAL CANTERS ACROSS THE SPACE   66 13
    DOST THA HEAR MY HORSE'S FEET AS HE CANTERS AWAY   664 1

CANTHARUS
    BAKED AMPHORAS CRATERS CANTHARUS OENOCHOE AND   305 13

CAN'T-HELP-IT
    AND THE HOLY CAN'T-HELP-IT TOUCH   537 14

CANVAS
    FRIGHTENED OF THE BARE EARTH AND THE TEMPORARY CANVAS   444 12

CANYON
    CANYON   409 5

CAPABLE
    HE IS CAPABLE OF AN ENDLESS GRINDING NIHILISTIC HATE   648 3
    THAT IS THE ONLY STRONG FEELING HE IS CAPABLE OF   648 4

CAPITAL
    THEREFORE YOU ARE OUR SAVINGS OUR CAPITAL   442 24

CAPITALS
    THEIR POOR IDEALIST FOREHEADS NAKED CAPITALS   287 18

CAPSICUM
    NOR A DOSE OF CAPSICUM ESSENCE GIVING AN ORGASM   837 9

CAPTIVE
    STRANGE TO ME LIKE A CAPTIVE IN A FOREIGN COUNTRY HAUNT+   47 9
    ACTIVE WITH CAPTIVE ACTIVITY   484 26

CAPTIVITY
    WILD THINGS IN CAPTIVITY   484 22
    ALL MEN ARE IN CAPTIVITY   484 25
    SEX WON'T WORK IN CAPTIVITY   843 13

CAPTURE
    EVERY SIN-MOUSE YOU COULD CAPTURE   95 23
    RUNS INTO THE SHADOW WITH HER CAPTURE A FEW LITTLE BITE+   864 17

CAR
    A CAR AT THE END OF THE STREET GOES BY WITH A LAUGH   54 26
    A SUDDEN CAR GOES SWEEPING PAST AND I STRAIN MY SOUL TO+   58 3
    THE LAST CAR TRAILED THE NIGHT BEHIND   121 24
    A HASTENING CAR SWEPT SHAMEFUL PAST   122 1
    DRIVE THE CAR   441 21
    WHO GETS INTO THE CAR   565 29
    SIT SIT SIT CORPSE-BODY IN THE CAR   584 13
    HAVE A GAME OF TENNIS GO OUT IN THE CAR DO SOME SHOPPIN+   651 21

CARCASS
    CARCASS   630 27
    OH CARCASS WITH A BOARD-SCHOOL MIND AND A HA'PENNY NEWS+   631 3

CARE
    DO YOU CARE NO LONGER HOW   56 23
    HOLDING HER THUS COULD I CARE   62 3
    WHAT DO I CARE FOR ALL THAT THEY DO AMISS   74 24
    AND YET I'M SUPPOSED TO CARE WITH ALL MY MIGHT   74 30
    AND I DO NOT CARE THOUGH THE LARGE HANDS OF REVENGE   126 1
    CARE   129 5
    AND WHAT DO I CARE THOUGH THE VERY STONES SHOULD CRY ME   133 10
    THE NIGHT'S SLOW CARE   142 20
    WHO FOR THE REST OF LIFE WALK OUT OF CARE   157 11
    WHEN WE DID NOT KNOW DID NOT CARE   172 12
    AS THEY DREAM CORRUPTED DREAMS ALL POISONED WITH CARE   174 28
    HAS CEASED TO CARE   199 22
    HOW MUCH DO I CARE   199 26

CARE
    OF MY CARE   209 11
    I DON'T CARE   237 16
    I DON'T CARE WHETHER I AM BEAUTIFUL TO YOU   251 1
    FOR AGES I DON'T CARE A FIG FOR IT MEN SAY BUT WHY A FI+   277 5
    WHAT DO I CARE FOR HER THE UGLY FEMALE STANDING UP THERE   384 25
    YOU DON'T CARE A RAP FOR ANYBODY   396 18
    I CAN'T VERY MUCH CARE ABOUT THE WOES AND TRAGEDIES   508 16
    ALL I CARE ABOUT IN A MAN   524 1
    I DON'T CARE MYSELF A WHALE   557 8
    AND BEWARE AND TAKE CARE   565 15
    WITH THEIR CATERPILLARS AND THE CARE WITH WHICH THEY FO+   569 5
    DON'T YOU CARE FOR MY LOVE SHE SAID BITTERLY   604 13
    A MAN CAN'T FULLY LIVE UNLESS HE DIES AND CEASES TO CARE   613 1
    CEASES TO CARE   613 2
    THERE IS NO SINNING AGAINST GOD WHAT DOES GOD CARE ABOU+   621 1
    CARE   632 13
    THEN SAY TO YOURSELF WE WILL CEASE TO CARE   666 11
    WHAT DO I CARE IF THE SMOKING SHIPS   688 6
    MEN SLIMLY WENT LIKE FISHES AND DIDN'T CARE   688 22
    AND WE DO NOT CARE   713 14
    I WONDER WILL HE CARE   734 23
    AND WHAT DO I CARE   771 18
    WHAT DO I CARE THOUGH THE VERY STONES   771 21
    WHAT DO I CARE THOUGH FROM THE DAY'S WHITE ENVELOPE   772 22
    OH MEN TAKE CARE TAKE CARE   806 7
    TAKE CARE OF HIM AND IT   806 8
    THEY DON'T REALLY CARE VASTLY   828 23
    AT THE SAME TIME THEY TAKE THE GREATEST POSSIBLE CARE O+   832 4
    THE GREATEST POSSIBLE CARE   832 6
    AND SUPERFICIAL ATTENTION AND CARE AND FULFILMENT OF DU+   832 16
    WHY SHOULD I CARE WHERE THE OLD ROAD GOES   858 8
    HOLDING HER THUS DID I CARE   *912 11
    AND I DO NOT CARE THOUGH THE LARGE HANDS OF REVENGE   *937 1

CARED
    THEY CARED SO EXCESSIVELY THEMSELVES   508 18
    THE CHILDREN OF COURSE KNOW THAT THEY ARE CARED FOR   832 12

CAREFUL
    WHO WITH A RUFFLING CAREFUL BREATH   46 13
    THE BRIM EACH CAREFUL PART   125 3
    I WHO AM WORN AND CAREFUL   199 25
    WITH SUCH PEOPLE ONE HAS TO BE CAREFUL   554 29
    MORE CAREFUL THOUGH IF SHE'S NOT   571 27
    WE CAN'T BE TOO CAREFUL   670 7
    WALK WARILY WALK WARILY BE CAREFUL WHAT YOU SAY   707 1
    BE CAREFUL THEN AND BE GENTLE ABOUT DEATH   721 8
    BUT BE CAREFUL HOW YOU DESTROY HIM   776 14
    BEFORE GOD YOU MUST BE CAREFUL   776 16
    BE CAREFUL BEFORE YOU DESTROY HIM   776 18
    BE CAREFUL HOW YOU TURN HIM INTO A HUNDRED-PER-CENT   776 19
    BUT BE CAREFUL HOW YOU UTTERLY QUASH THEM   776 32

CAREFULLY
    CAREFULLY OVER THE SWEET   143 11
    THE LUMP OF WOOD CAREFULLY   387 15
    TOUCH ME CAREFULLY OLD FATHER   405 1
    HAVE ALL BY MR WATTS AND THE VICTORIANS BEEN CAREFULLY   658 18
    CAREFULLY AGAIN AND AGAIN TO STOP THE BLEEDING   734 10

CAREFULNESS
    WITH WHAT SHADOW-LIKE SLOW CAREFULNESS   426 16

CARELESS
    BUT OF THOSE LIFE-LOVING CARELESS OF THEIR RANK AMONG T+   855 12
    SPIRIT OF CARELESS JOY AH HOW I WARM   *945 14

CARELESSLY
    CARELESSLY   60 4
    YOU HAVE STEPPED ACROSS YOUR PEOPLE CARELESSLY HURTING   209 8
    OF GODHEAD IN MAN DESPISED CARELESSLY THROWN OVER   859 22

CARELESSNESS
    A CERTAIN CARELESSNESS A CERTAIN TENDERNESS A CERTAIN   612 12

CARELESS-WISE
    IN A SMILE LIKE TRIUMPH UPON ME THEN CARELESS-WISE   43 21

CARES
    SHE NEITHER KNOWS NOR CARES   54 19
    AS BOLD AS A ROBIN IT'S MUCH HE CARES   79 7
    AND CARES NOT A STRAW FOR THE PUT-UP HUMAN FIGMENTS   481 16
    GETTING THE BETTER OF OTHER PEOPLE WHO CARES   518 18
    INTO YOUR CARES   561 18
    NOW THAT THE MOON WHO REMEMBERS AND ONLY CARES   687 15
    AS BOLD AS A ROBIN IT'S MUCH HE CARES   *921 3
    THE CARES AND THE RESTLESS SMART   *936 4

CARESS
    YEA AND HER MOUTH'S PRUDENT AND CRUDE CARESS   127 23
    YOU DID NOT STRETCH FORWARD TO CARESS HER   255 29
    WHILE THE SOFT CARESS OF HER HIDDEN LAUGHTER   868 10
    LIVE THINGS CARESS ME AND ENTREAT MY FONDLING   876 33
    ME UP CARESS AND CLOTHE WITH FREE   *899 24
    ME UP CARESS AND CLOTHE WITH FREE   *903 3

CARESSES
    WE SOUGHT YOU SUBSTANTIAL YOU TOUCHSTONE OF CARESSES YO+   34 17
    AND CARESSES ME WITH HIS FINGERS THAT STILL SMELL GRIM   43 27
    IN WILD CARESSES   96 16
    CARESSES NEVER FLEW TO YOU LIKE BIRDS   158 9
    NOT WITH CARESSES   436 21
    AND SEPARATE HEART FROM HEART AND CUT AWAY ALL CARESSES   707 18
    AND BLOWS THAT ARE CARESSES   709 12

CARESSING
UNDER THE CARESSING LEAVES AND FELT WHERE THE ROOTS WER+ *926 10

CARESSINGLY
HOW CARESSINGLY SHE LAYS HER HAND ON MY KNEE   128 14

CARESSIVE
WITH HIS MOUTH OF CARESSIVE FIRE   801 23

CARGO
YOUR CARGO OUT BREATH FROM BREATH   168 11
HEAVY WITH A RANCID CARGO THROUGH THE LESSER SHIPS   380 19

CARNAL
WHEN MODERN PEOPLE SEE THE CARNAL BODY DAUNTLESS AND   445 31

CARNATION
AND BECOMES AT LAST A CLOVE CARNATION LO THAT IS GOD   691 17

CARNATIONS
THERE WERE NO POPPIES OR CARNATIONS   286 3

CAROB-TREE
IN THE DEEP STRANGE-SCENTED SHADE OF THE GREAT DARK CAR+   349 4

CAROUSED
'TWAS YOU WHO KILLED HIM WHEN YOU BOTH CAROUSED   158 3

CARPACCIO
AS CARPACCIO WILL TELL YOU   324 27

CARPENTER
ANYHOW A CARPENTER AND JOINER   452 26
THAT HE MADE CHAIRS AND WAS A JOINER AND CARPENTER   452 30
CARPENTER   452 32

CARPING
NOW STOP CARPING AT ME DO YOU WANT ME TO HATE YOU   119 1
NOW STOP CARPING AT ME BUT GOD HOW I HATE YOU   *932 10

CARRARA
MOUNTAINS OF CARRARA   340 19

CARRIED
WHEN I CARRIED MY MOTHER DOWNSTAIRS   106 28
WHEN YOU WENT HOW WAS IT YOU CARRIED WITH YOU   135 1
OF THE WIND SHE IS LIFTED AND CARRIED AWAY AS IN A BALL+   153 2
INTO THE WORLD OF SHADOW CARRIED DOWN   160 11
I TOUCHED HER FLANK AND KNEW I WAS CARRIED BY THE CURRE+   260 12
CARRIES ME WHERE I WANT TO BE CARRIED   291 30
ALL LIFE CARRIED ON YOUR SHOULDER   354 21
WHILE THEY CARRIED THE SHAMELESS THINGS AWAY   579 15
THEY'VE SEIZED AND CARRIED THEM AWAY   633 11
TO BE CARRIED AT LAST FROM THE FIRE   769 12
SUNDAY AFTER SUNDAY THEY CARRIED HIM TREMBLING TO HIS P+   859 13

CARRIES
THAT CARRIES MOONS ALONG AND SPARE THE STRESS   195 35
AS CARRIES ME YOU WOULD WONDER ALOUD THAT HE   251 29
SOMETHING IN YOU WHICH CARRIES ME BEYOND   291 27
CARRIES ME WHERE I WANT TO BE CARRIED   291 30
THE INDIVIDUAL CARRIES HIS OWN GRAIN OF INSANITY AROUND+   486 9
LIKE A SHUTTLE THAT CARRIES THE WEFT   746 24
LIKE THE WOOF THE SHUTTLE CARRIES   747 2
CARRIES ITS OWN PATENT AND ITS OWN OBLIGATION   774 21
CARRIES A DIM LOW SONG THAT STIRS   868 30
THAT CARRIES A HEAVY RICH LIQUOR   869 24
AND WHAT THE SOUL CARRIES WITH HIM AND WHAT HE LEAVES B+   *961 12

CARRION
AND FIR-WORT STINKING FOR THE CARRION WASP   316 5
THEY HATE LIFE THEY ONLY LIKE CARRION   500 12
THEY ARE HUMBLE WITH A CREEPING HUMILITY BEING PARASITE+   621 20

CARRION-CROW
YOU WORSE THAN A CARRION-CROW   398 31

CARRION-GREEDY
CARRION-GREEDY IN ITS SENSATIONS   830 21

CARRY
PEER ANXIOUSLY FORTH AS IF FOR A BOAT TO CARRY THEM OUT+   71 26
AH'VE 'AD A' AS I CAN CARRY   84 15
FEELING YOUR STRONG BREAST CARRY ME ON INTO   129 25
I CARRY MY PATIENCE SULLENLY THROUGH THE WASTE LANDS   167 3
I CARRY MY PATIENCE SULLENLY THROUGH THE WASTE LANDS   167 16
CARRY INTO YOUR ROOM THE BLOSSOMING BOUGHS OF CHERRY   179 2
MAGNIFICENT GHOSTS OF THE DARKNESS CARRY OFF HER DECISI+   213 26
IF ONLY I LET IT BEAR ME CARRY ME IF ONLY IT CARRY ME   250 15
NO LONGER OR CARRY THE BURDEN OF A MAN ON YOUR HEART   411 12
CARRY THE SALT OF THE EARTH THE WISDOM OF WISE MEN   495 3
EVER CARRY US   543 22
OF DEATH TO CARRY THE SOUL ON THE LONGEST JOURNEY   718 22
BY NATURE THAN BY BOOTS AND WET FEET OFTEN CARRY MERRY +   866 15
I CARRY MY ANGER SULLENLY 'CROSS THESE WASTE LANDS   *896 21
OF DEATH THAT WILL CARRY THE SOUL   *960 14

CARRYING
RIDING THE AIR AND CARRYING ALL THE TIME   221 21
WHAT IS HE CARRYING   401 15
RIDING THE AIR AND CARRYING ALL THE TIME   *945 7

CARRYIN'S
AN' CARRYIN'S ON   60 26

CARRYIN'
NOR TH' CARRYIN' ON AS KILLED 'IM   60 28
AN' YET YER'VE BIN CARRYIN' ON WI' 'IM   81 27
AN' YET YOU'VE BEEN CARRYIN' ON WI' HIM   *923 27

CARS
GREAT ELECTRIC CARS   144 8
TWO PALE CLOTS SWEPT BY THE LIGHT OF THE CARS   144 28
THEN THE MOUNTAINS LIKE CHARIOT CARS   248 21
IN THOSE UGLY GREEN LARGE CARS   846 3

CART
I FORCE MY CART THROUGH THE SODDEN FILTH THAT IS PRESSED   167 5
IN MOTHER ENGLISH OR YOU'RE IN THE CART   575 26
LET HIS OLD CART   751 24

CART-RUTS
IN THE DEEP CART-RUTS GLEAMED THROUGH THE BLUE OF THE D+   864 30

CART-SHED
IN THE SHADOW OF THE CART-SHED MUST WE HOVER ON THE BRI+   173 7

CARYATIDS
CARYATIDS   287 15
ONLY I GROPE AMONG YOU PALE-FACES CARYATIDS AS AMONG A   287 27
YOU STARING CARYATIDS   289 10
CARYATIDS PALE-FACES   289 21

CASCADE
IN A CASCADE OF SOULS TO SORROWFUL DEATH   743 31

CASCADE-LIKE
THAT POUR CASCADE-LIKE DOWN THE BLACKENING WIND   745 19

CASE
IN EITHER CASE A WORM   432 5
BE BRIDEGROOM OR BEST MAN AS THE CASE TURNS OUT   743 20

CASH
OVER ON BOOT'S CASH CHEMIST'S COUNTER   488 17
IN THE DEEP DUNG OF CASH AND LORE   489 7
THE WAGES OF WORK IS CASH   521 1
THE WAGES OF CASH IS WANT MORE CASH   521 2
THE WAGES OF WANT MORE CASH IS VICIOUS COMPETITION   521 3
AND CASH CHRISTIANITY   534 18

CASH-CHEMICALLY
CASH-CHEMICALLY B SC   489 2

CASH-CHEMISTRY
DERIVED FROM SHREWD CASH-CHEMISTRY   488 13
DOSES OF SMART CASH-CHEMISTRY   488 25
BUT CASH-CHEMISTRY CASH-PHYSICS CASH CLASSICS AND CASH +   *950 20

CASH-CHEMIST
THE WHOLE THING HAS RISEN OUT OF THIS CASH-CHEMIST MONEY   *950 17
IN SUCH A CASH-CHEMIST UNIVERSITY WHAT CAN THEY TEACH   *950 19
AND WHEN THIS CASH-CHEMIST UNIVERSITY GRANTS DEGREES LI+   *950 22

CASH CHEMIST
VERY SUMPTUOUS WITH THE MONEY OF SIR JESSE BOOT OF CASH+   *950 14

CASH CLASSICS
BUT CASH-CHEMISTRY CASH-PHYSICS CASH CLASSICS AND CASH +   *950 20

CASH CULTURE
BUT CASH-CHEMISTRY CASH-PHYSICS CASH CLASSICS AND CASH +   *950 20

CASHMERE
MY CASHMERE SHAWL I'LL HANG FOR A CANOPY   754 24

CASH-PHYSICS
BUT CASH-CHEMISTRY CASH-PHYSICS CASH CLASSICS AND CASH +   *950 20

'CASIONS
THA'S NO 'CASIONS TER HA'E ME ON   79 29

CAST
AND LEAF FOR ITS PASSAGE A SHADOW CAST   69 3
YOU YIELDED WE THREW THE LAST CAST   111 21
FULL ANGUISH PERHAPS HAD BEEN CAST   111 31
ENTERED AND QUICKLY CAST   122 7
IF I COULD CAST THIS CLOTHING OFF FROM ME   122 17
AND CAST US FORTH LIKE THIN SHORN MOONS TO TRAVEL   132 10
OF CHILDISH DAYS IS UPON ME MY MANHOOD IS CAST   148 17
CAST OUT BY THE HAND THAT SCATTERS   171 22
MY DEAR YES YES YOU ARE CRUEL TO ME YOU CAST   211 3
WISE TORTOISE LAID HIS EARTHY PART AROUND HIM HE CAST I+   348 13
ARE CAST IN BLACK AND WHITE AND MOVE   444 6
CAST YOUR LITTLE ANCHORS IN PORTS OF ETERNITY   542 13
AND THERE IS THE MECHANICAL CONNECTION LIKE LEAVES THAT+   615 2
WHEN GOETHE BECOMES AN APOLLO HE BECOMES A PLASTER CAST   673 1
LET HIM BE CAST OUT FOR BLASPHEMY   726 14
THE DEAD TRIUMPHANT AND THE QUICK CAST DOWN   740 4
AND CAST ME SCORN   772 6
FROM THE FIERY HAMMERING OF YOUR HEART I CAST   873 2
OR LEAF AND HIS PASSING SHADOW IS CAST   *915 15
FIRE-THRESHING ANGUISH HAD BEEN FUSED AND CAST   *927 19
FIRE-THRESHING ANGUISH WERE FUSED AND CAST   *928 19
AND CAST US FORTH LIKE SHORN THIN MOONS TO TRAVEL   *938 2

CASTEST
HOW THOU CASTEST UP A SICKLY GLARE   760 7

CASTING
CASTING A SHADOW OF SCORN UPON ME FOR MY SHARE IN DEATH   133 17
AND CASTING THE CYCLES OF CREATION   329 6
YOUR EVIL LITTLE AURA PROWLING AND CASTING NUMBNESS ON   332 19

CASTLE
THEIR CASTLE IS IMPREGNABLE THEIR CAVE   325 16
NEVER A MOUNTAIN PEAK TO BE KING OF THE CASTLE   382 32

CAST-OFF
AND SEEING MY CAST-OFF BODY LYING LIKE LUMBER   134 12

CASTRATED
ON OUR CASTRATED SOCIETY   628 12

CASTRATING
SUCCESSFULLY CASTRATING THE BODY POLITIC   627 27

CASTS
STRETCHED OUT ON THE WAY AND A LOUT CASTS   144 18
THAT CASTS ITS SPERM UPON THE WATERS AND KNOWS NO INTER+   616 25
OH HE KNOWS ALL ABOUT IT HE CASTS A YELLOW EYE   633 26

CASUS BELLI
IT HAS BEEN MADE A CAUSE FOR STRIFE A CASUS BELLI   777 15
THE INDIAN SHOULD NEVER HAVE BEEN MADE A CASUS BELLI   777 17

CAT
AN' 'ERE COMES THE CAT AS CAUGHT 'IM   81 16
ACROSS THE SPACE ON THE CAT IN HEAVEN'S HOSTILE EMINENCE   97 22
THE INVOLVED VOLUPTUOUSNESS OF THE SOFT-FOOTED CAT   383 1
THE CAT WHO LAPS BLOOD AND KNOWS   383 3
THE CAT HAS LAPPED   383 7
A LONG LONG SLIM CAT YELLOW LIKE A LIONESS   401 24
I'M ABOUT AS MUCH LIKE A PERSIAN CAT   489 23
OR FLUFF UP IN INDIGNANT FURY LIKE A CAT   528 24
THE OLD DRAGON WILL DWINDLE DOWN TO THE SIZE OF A STRAY+   665 14
LIKE A CAT ASLEEP ON A CHAIR   700 3
OR FLUFFED UP RATHER ANGRY AS A CAT DOES   836 15
AN' 'ERE COMES THE CAT THAT CAUGHT 'IM   *923 16
OR FLUFF UP IN INDIGNANT FURY LIKE A CAT   *950 27

CATAPULT
LET HIM CHARGE LIKE A MIGHTY CATAPULT ON THE RED-CROSS +   327 24

CATARACT
OVER THE EDGE OF THE SOUNDLESS CATARACT   322 1
AND A CREATURE OF CONFLICT LIKE A CATARACT   714 15

CATASTROPHE
THE CATASTROPHE OF YOUR EXAGGERATE LOVE   290 9

CATCH
I S'LL NEVER CATCH THAT TRAIN   46 2
FOR WHAT CAN ALL SHARP-RIMMED SUBSTANCE BUT CATCH   68 25
HER FACE AND FORWARD LEANS TO CATCH THE SIGHT   105 27
CATCH MY HANDS MY DARLING BETWEEN YOUR BREASTS   147 15
TO CATCH AND KEEP ME WITH YOU THERE   178 10
HOLD MY HAND TO CATCH THE RAINDROPS THAT SLANT INTO SIG+   179 21
I WILL CATCH IN MY EYES' QUICK NET   180 8
HE SAID DO YOU CATCH WHAT THEY SAY   201 28
YOU GLOW AT LAST LIKE THE MOUNTAIN TOPS WHEN THEY CATCH   209 29
AND THE SUNBEAMS CATCH HER   217 12
CAN I CATCH LIKE A MOTH BETWEEN MY HANDS   227 23
IF YOU CATCH A WHIFF OF VIOLETS FROM THE DARKNESS OF TH+   274 1
TO CATCH SIGHT OF HER STANDING LIKE SOME HUGE GHOULISH   385 16
COMING UP ON FIERCE LITTLE LEGS TEARING FAST TO CATCH U+   397 15
AND CATCH FLESH LIKE THE NIGHT IN ONE'S ARMS   428 5
SO WHEN I CATCH MYSELF THINKING AH IF I WAS RICH   498 7
BENEATH THE STEPS OF ST PAUL'S CATCH SEVERAL   750 22
YOU WILL NEVER CATCH FIRE   784 22
BUT I WILL CATCH THEE UP AT A STRIDE OF DEATH   879 28
TO CATCH AFIRE WITH LIFE   888 6
AND STRIVING TO CATCH A GLIMPSE OF THE SHAPE OF THE COM+   *909 25
CATCH THE SCENT AND THE COLOUR OF THE COMING DREAM   *909 27
FOR WHAT CAN ALL THAT SHARP-RIMMED SUBSTANCE BUT CATCH   *915 9
AND THE SUNBEAMS CATCH HER   *942 22

CATCHES
SHE HAS NO QUALM WHEN SHE CATCHES MY FINGER IN HER STEEL   359 20
BUT HE CATCHES THE FOLDS OF VULNERABLE LEATHERY SKIN   362 6
AND CATCHES HER TROUSER-LEGS IN HIS BEAK   362 21

CATCHING
WEARILY CATCHING   146 8
AT HER ANKLES AND CATCHING HER BY THE HAIR   309 19
SCUFFING BESIDE HER BENDING DOWN CATCHING HIS OPPORTUNI+   360 19

CATCH-WORD
TO THE ARAB AND THE FIG HAS BEEN A CATCH-WORD FOR THE F+   277 4

CATERPILLARS
WITH THEIR CATERPILLARS AND THE CARE WITH WHICH THEY FO+   569 5

CATHEDRAL
AS A PIGEON LETS ITSELF OFF FROM A CATHEDRAL DOME   134 21

CATKINS
SO WIDE AS YOU WATCH THE CATKINS BLOW   126 30

CATS
CATS AND THE NEAPOLITANS   340 6
AMOROUS CATS   366 9
THEY ARE LIKE CATS WITH UNCLEAN CLAWS TANGLED UP IN NETS   675 6

CATS-MEAT
AND ALL THE HEROES OF THE BIBLE THEY SOLD FOR CATS-MEAT+   763 1

CAT'S
LIKE A CAT'S DISTENDED PUPIL THAT SPARKLES WITH LITTLE +   97 15

CATTLE
WOULD GOD THEY WERE SHATTERED QUICKLY THE CATTLE WOULD   159 21
HE LIFTED HIS HEAD FROM HIS DRINKING AS CATTLE DO   349 21
AND LOOKED AT ME VAGUELY AS DRINKING CATTLE DO   349 22
THE CATTLE RUN ANXIOUS IN QUEST AS THE TIME DRAWS NIGH   749 25
WHEN THE CATTLE ARE FED   756 11
SLOW CATTLE STIR ON THE STEEP MEADOW NEAR BY   886 28

CATTLE-SHED
TO AND FROM THE CATTLE-SHED   756 9

CAUGHT
OF THE RABBIT'S FUR GOD I AM CAUGHT IN A SNARE   43 28
NOW I AM CAUGHT YOU ARE HOPELESSLY LOST O SELF   47 32
TO SETTLE THE QUESTION HEADS OR TAILS HAS CAUGHT   54 10
LIKE FLOWERS I FELL TO BE CAUGHT   56 17
LIKE THE SOUGH OF A WIND THAT IS CAUGHT UP HIGH IN THE +   58 1
AN' 'ERE COMES THE CAT AS CAUGHT 'IM   81 16
HEAVIER THAN MINE YET LIKE LEVERETS CAUGHT IN STEEL   128 7
THEIR ABUNDANT SUMMERY WORDAGE SILENCED CAUGHT   142 2
CAUGHT DUST FROM THE SEA'S LONG SWATHS   152 13
CAUGHT UP ALOFT   269 4
I HEARD THE SCREAM OF A FROG WHICH WAS CAUGHT WITH HIS   365 30
HE SMILES FOOLISHLY AS IF HE WERE CAUGHT DOING WRONG   401 20
AND CAUGHT THEM MOANING FROM CLOSE-UP KISSES BLACK-AND-+   444 1
THESE ARE NO SPIRITS CAUGHT AND SORE   460 3
CAUGHT BETWEEN GREAT ICEBERGS OF DOUBT   542 18
BUT SHE CAUGHT SIGHT OF HER OWN REFLECTION   604 21
WHEN THE VAST MASSES OF MEN HAVE BEEN CAUGHT BY THE   631 11
HAVE I CAUGHT FROM IT   705 3
THE GREY DOG CAUGHT ME AT THE CROSS-ROADS   808 2
CAUGHT WHEN MY HEART WOULD LEAP IN A NET OF LIVES   884 11
AM CAUGHT IN THE MESH   *897 9
AN' 'ERE COMES THE CAT THAT CAUGHT 'IM   *923 16

CAUL
BORN WITH A CAUL   408 15

CAUSALLY
HE CAUSALLY GIVES BIRTH TO ANOTHER YOUNG BUD FROM HIS   300 1

CAUSE
IS IT ANY CAUSE FOR SURPRISE   80 16
NO CAUSE FOR SURPRISE AT ALL MY LAD   80 17
NOR YET COMRADES FOR I DON'T BELONG TO ANY CAUSE   499 22
SINCE THE BOURGEOIS IS THE DIRECT CAUSE OF THE BOLSHEVI+   664 10
HE IS FAR TOO FEW TO CAUSE ANY APPREHENSION   777 10
IT HAS BEEN MADE A CAUSE FOR STRIFE A CASUS BELLI   777 15
THEIR CAUSE BECAUSE THEY THE ARTISTS AND LONG-HAIRED   778 6
OR OIL OR COPPER OR GOLD A CAUSE FOR POLITICAL ACTION   779 19
HUDDLIN' CLOSE TOGETHER A CAUSE O' TH' RAIN   *911 2
IS IT ANY CAUSE FOR SURPRISE   *922 16
NO CAUSE FOR SURPRISE AT ALL MY LAD   *922 17

CAUSES
AS A HALF-LIE CAUSES THE IMMEDIATE CONTRADICTION OF THE+   664 11
THERE FOR THE HEAT OF IT CAUSES A SMART   863 19

CAUSING
BLOOD FROM SIDE TO SIDE CAUSING MY MYRIAD SECRET STREAMS   320 28

CAUTERISE
WHERE THEY BURN AND CAUTERISE   64 19

CAUTION
ON HER KNEES IN UTMOST CAUTION   426 11

CAUTIOUS
CAUTIOUS PEOPLE   445 2
SOMEHOW SO SAD SO INTRINSIC SO SPIRITUAL YET SO CAUTIOU+   *932 13

CAUTIOUSLY
CAUTIOUSLY I SHALL RAISE   59 2
FOOTED CAUTIOUSLY OUT ON THE ROPE TURNED PRETTILY SPUN   444 26
YET I KNOW HE DOES IT DELIBERATELY AS CAUTIOUSLY AND   447 20
CAUTIOUSLY SWALLOWING THEIR PHLEGM   554 28

CAVE
OF DAY TROLLS AT THE CAVE OF RINGING CERULEAN MINING   72 10
AS I STAND ON THIS HILL WITH THE WHITENING CAVE OF THE +   97 11
BUT A GREY CAVE WITH GREAT GREY SPIDER-CLOTHS HANGING   112 25
THE SPIDERS WITH WHITE FACES THAT SCUTTLE ON THE FLOOR +   112 28
ROARS LIKE A BEAST IN A CAVE   159 2
ONCE HE LAY IN THE MOUTH OF A CAVE   324 5
THEIR CASTLE IS IMPREGNABLE THEIR CAVE   325 16
LITTLE CAVE   402 13
MORE OUT OF THE SHADOW OF THE CAVE IN THE BLOOD-ORANGE   402 18
OF THE ANCIENT CAVE SMASHING INTO ONE ANOTHER   544 15
IN THE CAVE WHICH IS CALLED DARK EYE   786 5
TO ROLL THE GRAVE-STONE OFF THEIR SOULS FROM THE CAVE O+   793 7

CAVERN
CAVERN AND THE PORTENT   544 10
INSTINCT IN THE CAVERN   544 23

CAVERNOUS
WITH CAVERNOUS NOSTRILS WHERE THE WINDS RUN HOT   325 30

CAVERNS
    CAVERNS   308 13

CAVES
    LITTLE HELLS OF COLOUR CAVES OF DARKNESS   308 14
    CAVES INWARD KNOWING THE OUTSIDE WORLD   843 4

CAVIL
    THERE IS NOTHING TO WONDER OR CAVIL AT   228 8

CAVITIES
    RUSH IN AND FILL THE LIVING CAVITIES   784 11

C'D
    DEED AN' I WISH I C'D 'A' STOOD AT TH' ALTAR WI' THEE A+   83 11

CEASE
    THE DAMNED BELLS CEASE AND WE ARE EXEMPT   54 28
    CEASE THEN FROM MUSIC DOES ANGUISH OF ABSENCE BEQUEATH   85 23
    I CEASE I TURN PALE   133 28
    I CEASE I TURN PALE   133 33
    AND OH MY HEART CEASE APPREHENDING   150 17
    I SHALL NEVER CEASE TO BE FILLED WITH NEWNESS   248 14
    O CEASE TO LISTEN TO THE LIVING DEAD   441 28
    O CEASE TO LABOUR FOR THE GOLD-TOOTHED DEAD   441 30
    WILL BE PASSING AWAY WE SHALL CEASE TO FUSS   471 18
    OF COURSE IT WOULD CEASE TO EXIST   479 14
    AND UNIVERSALISM AND COSMOPOLITANISM WILL CEASE   611 16
    WAR WILL CEASE THERE WILL BE NO MORE WARS   612 3
    AND I ALMOST CEASE TO EXIST WEIGHED DOWN TO EXTINCTION   629 20
    CEASE TO ACCEPT THEM AS BROTHERS   639 5
    AND THE TIME HAS COME TO CEASE TO BE KIND ANY MORE   640 16
    CEASE TO SEE   662 13
    IS TO CEASE TO BE INTERESTED IN IT TO BE SO INTERESTED +   665 7
    THEN SAY TO YOURSELF WE WILL CEASE TO CARE   666 11
    MONEY SHALL CEASE TO BE AND PROPERTY SHALL CEASE TO PER+   666 17
    CEASE TO LIFT UP ITS HILLS   688 3
    THE KISSING AND COMMUNING CANNOT CEASE   710 7
    SWEET DARK OBLIVION WHEN I CEASE   726 5
    WHERE WE MAY CEASE FROM KNOWING AND AS FAR AS WE KNOW   726 19
    MAY CEASE FROM BEING   726 20
    NOR CEASE TO BE DARK ON THE DARKNESS STAY   738 20
    MAKE IT CEASE TO BE A POLITICAL QUESTION FOR EVER   780 2
    AND THIS SUN CEASE SHINING OVERHEAD   815 11
    BEFORE THE LIFE SHALL CEASE TO URGE AND STRIDE   879 6
    CEASE FOR A MOMENT IN REVERENCE   *914 13

CEASED
    WHAT IF THE WATERS CEASED WHERE WERE THE MARIGOLDS THEN+   33 22
    SKY CEASED TO QUIVER AND LOST ITS ACTIVE SHEEN   35 15
    AND COLDNESS CLOGGED THE SEA TILL IT CEASED TO CROON   98 15
    OF MORDANT ANGUISH TILL SHE CEASED TO LAUGH   125 17
    HAVE I CEASED TO GRIEVE THAT I WAS NOT GREAT ENOUGH   157 7
    THE HOURS HAVE CEASED TO FALL AND A STAR COMMANDS   167 17
    HAS CEASED TO CARE   199 22
    CEASED   250 8
    DIED AS IT WERE CEASED FROM KNOWING SURPASSED MYSELF   266 5
    AND IF IT CEASED   320 25
    AS I AM IF MY HEART IN UPLIFTING CEASED TO BEAT TO TOSS+   320 27
    IF ONCE FOR A SECOND THE UNIVERSE CEASED TO FLOW   479 13
    THE TRAGEDY IS OVER IT HAS CEASED TO BE TRAGIC THE LAST+   510 13
    THE HOURS HAVE CEASED TO FALL AND A STAR COMMANDS   *896 22
    OF ANGUISH TILL SHE CEASED TO LAUGH TILL DOWN   *936 16

CEASELESS
    THE CUCKOO AND THE COO-DOVE'S CEASELESS CALLING   65 11
    ON THE SHORES OF THIS CEASELESS OCEAN GAY BIRDS OF THE   71 18
    THE CRUMBLING DAMP FRESH LAND LIFE HORIZONTAL AND CEASE+   321 18
    AND SO STRANGLE OFF THEIR CONNECTION WITH THE CEASELESS+   616 5
    WHEN DANGER THREATENS ON THE SURFACE OF THE CEASELESS F+   695 2

CEASELESSLY
    CEASELESSLY   75 24
    DOWN THE SOILED STREET WE HAVE PATTERED THE LESSONS CEA+   *897 23
    CEASELESSLY   *900 32

CEASES
    AND CEASES TO BE A BLOOD-THIRSTY KING OF BEASTS   325 7
    HE IS NO LONGER MY CONCERN HE CEASES TO BE   468 10
    A MAN CAN'T FULLY LIVE UNLESS HE DIES AND CEASES TO CARE   613 1
    CEASES TO CARE   613 2
    AND CEASES TO BE A ROBOT AND BECOMES A SERVANT OF LIFE   648 16
    THE HEART CEASES NOT   804 3
    AND IN HIS DEEPEST SELF NEVER CEASES TO BE ALONE   *951 6

CEASING
    AND CEASING TO SEE   660 24
    AND A CEASING TO KNOW A PERFECT CEASING TO KNOW   724 21

CEDAR
    ERECT SCORCHED-PALLID OUT OF THE HAIR OF THE CEDAR   373 5
    EAGLE SCORCHED-PALLID OUT OF THE HAIR OF THE CEDAR   781 10
    FROM THE RED-FIBRED BOUGH OF THE CEDAR FROM THE CEDAR-R+   782 11
    INTO THE ROOTS OF THE CEDAR INTO THE CEDAR-BOUGHS   782 21
    ERECT SCORCHED-PALLID OUT OF THE HAIR OF THE CEDAR   783 6

CEDAR-BOUGHS
    INTO THE ROOTS OF THE CEDAR INTO THE CEDAR-BOUGHS   782 21

CEDAR-BUSH
    AN EAGLE AT THE TOP OF A LOW CEDAR-BUSH   373 1
    ON A LOW CEDAR-BUSH   780 23
    FROM THE TOP OF A DARK-HAIRED CEDAR-BUSH   780 28
    SILENT UPON THE AMERICAN CEDAR-BUSH   783 13

CEDAR-MOTTLED
    TROT-TROT TO THE MOTTLED FOOT-HILLS CEDAR-MOTTLED AND P+   409 1

CEDAR-ROOTS
    FROM THE RED-FIBRED BOUGH OF THE CEDAR FROM THE CEDAR-R+   782 11

CEILING
    WITH DARK SLEEP THAT ONCE COVERED THE CEILING   38 5
    SOMEWHERE THE LAMP HANGING LOW FROM THE CEILING   41 6
    CEILING   141 21
    NEAR THE CEILING AS IF IN A WEB   345 2
    ROOFED WITH A DAY'S NEAR CEILING AND A DARK   876 11
    LOW NAKED CEILING OF THE NIGHT-SKY HELD   876 12
    WITH THE DARK SLEEP THAT ONCE COVERED THE CEILING   *892 21

CELIBATE
    YOU ARE CELIBATE AND SINGLE SCORNING A COMRADE EVEN   197 3

CELL
    THE OPTIMIST BUILDS HIMSELF SAFE INSIDE A CELL   515 7
    LOCKED UP IN A DUNGEON CELL   633 2
    TO THE POLICE-STATION CELL   633 22

CELLAR
    AND SHE SHUTS YOU IN THE CELLAR FOR THE LEAST LITTLE TI+   572 7

CELLS
    IN A TISSUE AS ALL THE MOLTEN CELLS IN THE LIVING MESH   176 8

CELLULOID
    AS YOU SEE A TINY CELLULOID BALL TOSSING ON A SQUIRT OF+   272 16

CEMENT
    AND LOOSEN THE BRICK AND THE HARD CEMENT   462 11
    MADE OF CEMENT POURED INTO A MOULD AROUND IRON STICKS   673 3

CEMETERY
    AND ALL ALONG THE PATH TO THE CEMETERY   232 20
    THE CEMETERY   472 27
    THAT YOUR SLEEP BE NOT AS A CEMETERY   808 15

CENOTAPH
    TOWARDS ITS CENOTAPH   54 32

CENSERS
    WHILE THE STREET LAMP CENSERS SWINGING HIGH   *916 19

CENSOR
    FOR NO LIVE SUNNY MAN WOULD BE A CENSOR   528 12

CENSORS
    CENSORS ARE DEAD MEN   528 10
    BUT CENSORS BEING DEAD MEN   528 14
    THE CENSORS BREATHING WITH RELIEF   528 21

CENSUS
    OH I'M SURE YOU'LL UNDERSTAND WE'RE MAKING A CENSUS OF +   546 7

CENT
    TO GIVE THE INDIANS ONE SINGLE THING NOT ONE CENT   778 25

CENTAUR
    FOR A MOMENT HE WAS THE CENTAUR THE WISE YET HORSE-HOOF+   672 28

CENTAVOS
    HOW NICE TO GET IN THE CAMION AND FOR TWENTY CENTAVOS T+   794 14

CENTRAL
    SUMPTUOUS CENTRAL GRAIN   124 12
    SO PONDEROUSLY CENTRAL   480 11
    TOWARDS THE BREATHING STARS AND THE CENTRAL OF ALL SUNN+   480 18
    SUMPTUOUS CENTRAL GRAIN   *935 11
    CENTRAL PRIMORDIAL FIRE OF THE SOUL HEAVIER THAN IRON   *951 24
    SO PONDEROUSLY CENTRAL HEAVIER AND HOTTER THAN ANYTHING+   *951 25
    CENTRAL PRIMORDIAL FIRE OF THE SOUL HEAVIER THAN IRON   *952 1
    SO PONDEROUSLY CENTRAL YET LEANING ITS WEIGHT TOWARDS   *952 2
    CENTRAL PRIMORDIAL FIRE OF THE SOUL THAT LEANS AND YEAR+   *952 6

CENTRALISING
    THE GREAT MOVEMENT OF CENTRALISING INTO ONENESS WILL ST+   611 17

CENTRAL PARK
    AND DEEP IN CENTRAL PARK I'LL FATTEN   815 15

CENTRE
    BUT MY HEART AT THE CENTRE   120 22
    BUT FIRM AT THE CENTRE   121 7
    THE WONDERFUL MOIST CONDUCTIVITY TOWARDS THE CENTRE   282 20
    IS IT SO THAT YOU SHALL LIFT YOUR CENTRE OF GRAVITY UPW+   332 6
    CENTRE OF THE EARTH   392 26
    TOWARDS THE EARTH'S CENTRE   394 22
    EARTH'S DEEP HEAVY CENTRE   394 26
    THERE IS A SWAN-LIKE FLAME THAT CURLS ROUND THE CENTRE +   440 2
    IN THE CENTRE OF ALL THINGS   525 13
    WITH THE CENTRE OF ALL THINGS   610 7
    IN THE CENTRE OF YOUR BEING GROAN NOT   703 12
    IN THE CENTRE OF YOUR BEING GROAN NOT DO NOT GROAN   703 13
    A CENTRE OF THE EVIL WORLD   714 21
    AND FAR AT THE CENTRE WITH ONE UNBLINKING EYE THE DRAGO+   796 21
    DOWN IN THE CENTRE OF THE EARTH   805 2
    DOWN IN THE CENTRE OF THE EARTH   806 5
    DEEP INTO THE HEART OF THE LIGHT THE CENTRE OF A STAR   865 6
    WITH A NIPPLE CENTRE OF RED   886 18

CENTRES
    IS CENTRES HERE AND THERE OF SILENCE AND FORGETTING   726 18
    THAT CENTRES AND BALANCES ALL THINGS   *951 31

CENTRIFUGAL
    WHY ARE THEY SO CENTRIFUGAL   537 22

CENTS
    PUT THE FIRST CENTS INTO METALLIC FINGERS OF YOUR OFFIC+   291 4
    PAY A FEW CENTS   387 18

CENTURIES
    MAN'S SWEETEST HARVEST OF THE CENTURIES SWEET PRINTED   263 25
    SEEMS LIKE THE BLACK AND GLOSSY SEEDS OF COUNTLESS CENT+   369 11
    WHO HAS BEEN LOST SO MANY CENTURIES ON THE MARGINS OF   394 8
    UNTOLD CENTURIES OF WATCHING FOR SOMETHING TO COME   394 11
    THAT HE'S BURIED NOW FOR CENTURIES   492 13
    AND THROUGH THE CENTURIES GOES ON AND ON   535 5
    YOU DULL ANGELS TARNISHED WITH CENTURIES OF CONVENTIONA+   614 16
    OUT OF THE THOUSANDS AND THOUSANDS OF CENTURIES OF MAN   623 26
    THOUGH THEIR SHOULD HAVE BEEN GROWING HEAVY FOR CENTURI+   778 37
    OUT OF THE THOUSANDS AND THOUSANDS OF CENTURIES OF MAN   *953 14

CENTURY
    FOR ONE SAD CENTURY   623 29
    FOR ONE SAD CENTURY   *953 16

CEREBRAL
    SINCE WE HAVE BECOME SO CEREBRAL   468 12
    SINCE WE ARE SO CEREBRAL   468 14
    AND APART IN THIS CEREBRAL AGE   469 7
    CONTACT OF CEREBRAL FLESH   469 18
    WE HAVE ONLY CEREBRAL EXCITATIONS   472 10
    HE IS CEREBRAL INTELLECTUAL MENTAL SPIRITUAL   473 17
    I AM SICK OF PEOPLE'S CEREBRAL EMOTIONS   500 18

CEREBRALLY
    FOR IF CEREBRALLY WE FORCE OURSELVES INTO TOUCH   468 17

CEREMENTS
    WINDING ABOUT THEIR DIMNESS THE MIST'S GREY CEREMENTS A+   102 30

CEREMONIAL
    IN THESE USELESS PRACTICES OF CEREMONIAL   111 35
    FOR CEREMONIES AND CEREMONIAL PREPARATIONS   779 4

CEREMONIES
    HEATHEN DANCES AND CEREMONIES AND TILLED THEIR   777 31
    FOR CEREMONIES AND CEREMONIAL PREPARATIONS   779 4

CERES
    CERES KISS YOUR GIRL YOU THINK YOU'VE GOT HER BACK   309 25

CERTAIN
    BUT NOW I AM FULL AND STRONG AND CERTAIN   247 1
    THEIR GUTS WITH A CERTAIN FAT AND OFTEN   460 15
    THEIR GUTS WITH A CERTAIN FAT AND OFTEN   460 19
    THE MOMENT I SWEAR TO LOVE A WOMAN A CERTAIN WOMAN   472 16
    EVEN ITS OWN NULLITY BEYOND A CERTAIN POINT   473 21
    A CERTAIN PEACE A CERTAIN GRACE   499 2
    I HAVE A CERTAIN AMOUNT OF MONEY SO MY ANXIETIES ARE BL+   501 21
    AFTER THAT OF COURSE THERE'S SUICIDE CERTAIN ASPECTS   532 26
    THAT PUT TO SEA ON CERTAIN EVENINGS   542 6
    IN A PUB PARLOUR IN LITERARY LONDON ON CERTAIN EVENINGS   542 10
    A CERTAIN CARELESSNESS A CERTAIN TENDERNESS A CERTAIN   612 12
    A CERTAIN WARLESSNESS EVEN MONEYLESSNESS   612 15
    AND PATIENCE AND A CERTAIN DIFFICULT REPENTANCE   620 17
    WHEN AT A CERTAIN POINT A DROP OF WATER BEGAN TO DRIP D+   682 13
    AND BEETHOVEN THEY SOLD TO CERTAIN CONDUCTORS TO BE CON+   763 8
    CERTAIN WAYS PERFORM CERTAIN SACRIFICES   775 30
    ONE THING IS CERTAIN WE'VE GOT TO TAKE HANDS OFF LOVE   834 7
    ANYTHING RATHER THAN THAT CERTAIN BACK OF A NECK   836 3

CERTAINLY
    AS HE CERTAINLY BEGAN SO PERFECTLY ALONE   364 10
    HAPPY AS PERHAPS KINGS USED TO BE BUT CERTAINLY AREN'T   520 18
    HE WOULD CERTAINLY BE MUCH MORE INVISIBLE IF HE WERE   523 14
    AND IF I DID I CERTAINLY COULDN'T SCRAIGHT IT OUT   540 21
    I DON'T KNOW WHAT YOU WANT BUT I CERTAINLY HAVEN'T GOT   541 11
    CERTAINLY THE GOD IN THE MACHINE CANNOT   641 19

CERTAINTY
    SLEEP ON SPEED IN DEAD CERTAINTY   169 20

CERULEAN
    OF DAY TROLLS AT THE CAVE OF RINGING CERULEAN MINING   72 10
    SITTING HUDDLED AGAINST THE CERULEAN ONE FLESH WITH THE+   142 11

CESSATION
    AFTER THE CESSATION   321 1
    AND A SILENT SHEER CESSATION OF ALL AWARENESS   724 22

CHAFED
    AND SELF-SAME DARKNESS CHAFED TO IRE   773 7
    MY CHAFED CURBED BLOOD NO LONGER BROOKS   857 3

CHAFES
    TILL HE CHAFES AT MY CROUCHING PERSISTENCE AND A SHARP   47 24

CHAFF
    AND THE STARS CAN CHAFF   54 29
    DUST AS THE PUFF-BALL DOES AND BIRDS THAT CHAFF   89 28

CHAFFINCH
    COME MAKING THE CHAFFINCH NESTS HOLLOW AND COSY   273 1
    I WOULD SAY THE SAME IF I WERE A CHAFFINCH OR TREE   499 3

CHAFING
    MYRIAD MYRIAD DEAD TWIGS OF PALLID AND CHAFING PEOPLE   784 21

CHAGRIN
    OF CHAGRIN AT BEING A MAN   837 11

CHAIN
    DRAGGING THE LINKS OF MY SHORTENING CHAIN   50 17
    NAY LET ME WORK A DELICATE CHAIN OF KISSES   154 4
    CHAIN OF MY MYSTIC WILL WRAPPED PERFECTLY   154 25

CHAINED
    CHAINED SUBJUGATED TO HIS USE   647 19
    A FIERY SIGN OF THE CHAINED POWER THAT WASTED HIM TO TH+ 859 20

CHAIR
    I HEAR HIS HAND ON THE LATCH AND RISE FROM MY CHAIR   43 18
    THE SICK GRAPES ON THE CHAIR BY THE BED LIE PRONE AT TH+ 112 16
    LIKE A CAT ASLEEP ON A CHAIR   700 3

CHAIRS
    QUITE BEAUTIFUL CHAIRS   452 23
    THAT HE MADE CHAIRS AND WAS A JOINER AND CARPENTER   452 30
    I SAID HE MADE CHAIRS BUT I DID NOT SAY HE WAS A   452 31

CHALICES
    RUNS WASTE DOWN THEIR CHALICES   177 4
    AND DEEP IN THE GLOWING WINE-FILLED CHALICES   868 19
    AND DEEP IN THE GOLDEN WINE OF THEIR CHALICES   *941 19

CHALK
    FROM THE TULIPS COLOURED WITH CHALK AND THE DULL GRASS'+ 867 4

CHALK-COLOURED
    HURT AT THE CHALK-COLOURED TULIPS AND THE EVENING-GREEN   153 12

CHALLENGE
    CROWDS OF GLITTERING KING-CUPS SURGE TO CHALLENGE THE B+   33 11
    TWIN-BUBBLING CHALLENGE AND MYSTERY IN THE FOAM'S   76 3
    HOW CAN I ANSWER THE CHALLENGE OF SO MANY EYES   76 5
    CHALLENGE ME I KEEP ASIDE   95 26
    LET HIM ROAR OUT CHALLENGE ON THE WORLD   327 25
    SOMETIMES HE TURNS WITH A START TO FIGHT TO CHALLENGE TO 381 8
    AND WHICH WHEN DAY CROWS CHALLENGE   112 31
    CROWDS OF GLITTERING KING-CUPS SURGE TO CHALLENGE THE B+ *891 12
    TWIN BUBBLES SHADOW-FULL OF MYSTERY AND CHALLENGE IN TH+ *897 30
    HOW CAN I ANSWER THE CHALLENGE OF SO MANY EYES   *897 32
    TWIN BUBBLES SHADOW-FULL OF MYSTERY AND CHALLENGE IN TH+ *901 7
    HOW CAN I ANSWER THE CHALLENGE OF SO MANY EYES   *901 9

CHALLENGED
    I WAITED AND MY SILENCE CHALLENGED HIM   878 16

CHALLENGER
    CHALLENGER   353 23
    CHALLENGER   353 28

CHALLENGES
    CHALLENGES ME AND IS ANSWERED   *906 25

CHAMBER
    INTO THE SHADOW-WHITE CHAMBER SILTS THE WHITE   154 27
    HER RISE FROM OUT OF THE CHAMBER OF THE DEEP   193 2
    FLUSHED AND GRAND AND NAKED AS FROM THE CHAMBER   193 3
    TO HIS GUEST CHAMBER KNOWING EACH SINEW AND VEIN   877 37

CHAMBERED
    AND OUT OF THE CHAMBERED WILDERNESS WANDERS A SPIRIT AB+   70 6
    AND OUT OF THE CHAMBERED WEARINESS WANDERS A PERFUME AB+ *916 14

CHAMBERS
    ALL THE CHAMBERS OF MY SOUL   95 9

CHAMOIS
    CHAMOIS GLOVES   433 10
    PULLING ON HIS CHAMOIS GLOVES   433 15
    ONLY IF YOU INSIST ON PULLING ON THOSE CHAMOIS GLOVES   433 19

CHAMPAIGN
    FULL MID-BETWEEN THE CHAMPAIGN OF YOUR BREAST   154 8

CHAMPING
    MORDANT CORROSION GNASHING AND CHAMPING HARD   160 23
    CHAMPING IT TOSSING A MOUTHFUL   397 9

CHAMPION
    CHAMPION HER ALL YOU WOMEN MEN MENFOLK   228 27
    WOMEN ANOTHER CHAMPION   229 1

CHANCE
    ME THE CHANCE   40 20
    WHERE LOFTY TREES ATHWART-STREAM CHANCE   68 11
    GIVE US OUR TURN GIVE US A CHANCE LET OUR HOUR STRIKE   273 21
    AND SO I MISSED MY CHANCE WITH ONE OF THE LORDS   351 27
    A JOB YOU DON'T LIKE AND A SCANTY CHANCE   560 23
    FOR A CHANCE OF LIFE ALL ROUND   560 30
    BUT WHAT IF MY LOVE SHOULD CHANCE TO HEAR   752 2
    AND THEY DART TO HER WOMB THEY FIGHT FOR THE CHANCE TO + 795 31
    ROSES ARE ONLY ONCE-WILD ROSES THAT WERE GIVEN AN EXTRA+ 831 2

CHANCED
    FOR WHEN FIRE IN ITS DOWNWARD PATH CHANCED TO MINGLE WI+ 348 6
    TILL THEY CHANCED TO MEET IN THE LORD'S GREEN ZOO   761 3

CHANGE
WITH FEELINGS THAT CHANGE AND QUIVER   38 25
O STIFFLY SHAPEN HOUSES THAT CHANGE NOT   53 20
YET THEY NEVER CHANGE THE DARKNESS   110 21
AND THE LEOPARD CANNOT CHANGE HIS SPOTS   413 28
AND GO FORTH TO CHANGE THE WORLD   428 19
UPON THE WORLD TO BRING A CHANGE TO PASS   428 22
IT CHANGES AND WITH IT CHANGE   460 10
WITH THE RIPPLING FRESHLY CHANGE   460 12
AND LOVE LIKE A FLOWER WILL FADE WILL CHANGE INTO SOMET+   476   3
AND CHANGING IN A FLOW AS ALL PASSIONS CHANGE   482   9
OR EXCEPT YOU CHANGE   485 23
AND IN THESE AWFUL PAUSES THE EVOLUTIONARY CHANGE TAKES   510 10
IS THAT YOU CAN'T PREVENT CHANGE   511 22
WE MUST CHANGE THE SYSTEM AND MAKE LIVING FREE TO ALL   522 29
CHANGE FROM BEING SINGLE AND BECOME GRADUALLY DOUBLE   534 26
THEY WANT TO CHANGE THE MAN HIMSELF   538 21
WE'VE GOT A CHANGE OF GOVERNMENT   571 15
THE WINDS OF CHANGE THAT WILL NOT BE STILL   615 12
THE BREATH OF LIFE AND THE SHARP WINDS OF CHANGE ARE TH+   615 16
FEEL THE WINDS OF CHANGE GRIND THEM DOWN   615 19
THE GODS WHO ARE LIFE AND THE FLUIDITY OF LIVING CHANGE   662 22
THE BREATH OF LIFE IS IN THE SHARP WINDS OF CHANGE   698   1
AND CHANGE OF CLOTHES   719   5
THAT CANNOT FIND THE WAY ACROSS THE SEA OF CHANGE   721 16
DO YOU THINK IT IS EASY TO CHANGE   727 31
AH IT IS VERY HARD TO CHANGE AND BE DIFFERENT   727 32
IF NOT YOU WILL NEVER REALLY CHANGE   728   5
OF MORNING IS BACK WE SHALL CHANGE AGAIN AND ESSAY   748 11
THE WOMAN WEEPS HER CHANGE OF LIFE   766   7
THIS CHANGE   767   6
IT IS CHANGE THAT IS COMING UPON ME   768   4
IT WAS THE STONE OF CHANGE   791   4
THIS IS THE STONE OF CHANGE HE SAID   791   5
VISIBLE THERE IN THE CHANGE OF EYES AND THE MOBILE FEAT+   *909 12

CHANGED
TO SHOW YOU THUS TRANSFIGURED CHANGED   53 22
ONLY INSTEAD OF CHANGING THINGS THAT MIGHT BE CHANGED   538 20
AND IN ONE INSTANT'S PAUSE ARE REVOLVED ROUND AND CHANG+   784 12
TO BE REVOLVED AND IN ONE INSTANT CHANGED   784 25

CHANGELESS
RISEN NOT TO THE OLD WORLD THE OLD CHANGELESS I THE OLD+   260 15

CHANGES
LIFE HAS ITS CHANGES BUT WHEN THE HEAVENS ARE EMPTY EMP+   319   8
IT CHANGES AND WITH IT CHANGE   460 10
WOMEN START IN TO MAKE CHANGES   538 19
YOU WHO HAVE NO FEELING OF THE MOON AS SHE CHANGES HER   643 10
THEY ONLY CROSS THE DISTANCE NEVER CHANGES   688   9

CHANGING
CHANGING GUARD   341 20
AND CHANGING IN A FLOW AS ALL PASSIONS CHANGE   482   9
ALWAYS CHANGING ITS MIND   524 25
ONLY INSTEAD OF CHANGING THINGS THAT MIGHT BE CHANGED   538 20
AND THE JOB OF CHANGING ITS DIAPERS GETS BIGGER AND BIG+   670 12
AND IF IN THE CHANGING PHASES OF MAN'S LIFE   727 17
VISIBLE UNDER THE CHANGING EYES   *907 16

CHANNEL
SEAL UP EACH CHANNEL OUT OF WHICH MIGHT SLIP   153 22
DEEPER DOWN THE CHANNEL THEN ROSE SHALLOWER SHALLOWER   693   9

CHANNELLED
CREATING THE CHANNELLED VEIN OF MAN   69   2
DOWN EVERY CHANNELLED VEIN OF MAN   *915 14

CHANTING
OF LINEN GO THE CHANTING CHORISTERS   232 18
THE COMING OF THE CHANTING CHORISTERS   232 28
THEY ARE CHANTING NOW THE SERVICE OF ALL THE DEAD   233   1
TO MUSIC AND QUEER CHANTING   387 34

CHAOS
WHAT IS CHAOS MY LOVE   236 21
THREE SIDES SET ON ME CHAOS AND BOUNCE BUT THE FOURTH   249 27
AND THE CHAOS THAT BOUNCES AND RATTLES LIKE SHRAPNEL AT   250   4
CHAOS OF THE WORLD   250 19
YOUR LITTLE ROUND HOUSE IN THE MIDST OF CHAOS   354 14
RINGING THE SOUNDLESS BELL OF HIS PRESENCE IN CHAOS   358 19
CHAOS   360 29
THAT DRIFTS UPON TIME AND CHAOS TILL SOME UNKNOWN FUTURE   429   5
LEAVING IT TO THE VAST REVOLUTIONS OF CREATIVE CHAOS   429 24
THE SWAN WITHIN VAST CHAOS WITHIN THE ELECTRON   435 28
DURING THE WILD ORGASMS OF CHAOS   477   3
THE GEM OF MUTUAL PEACE EMERGING FROM THE WILD CHAOS   477 19
TO THE ATOM TO THE BODY OF IMMORTAL CHAOS   505   4
DISTINCT FROM CHAOS   514 16
IN THE DAYS CALLED CHAOS WHICH LEFT US ROCKS AND GEMS   529 25
AND A CHAOS OF IMPULSE SUPERVENES   640 10
AND IN THE GREAT STRUGGLE OF INTANGIBLE CHAOS   682 12
WHEN SAPPHIRES COOLED OUT OF MOLTEN CHAOS   682 22
OF CHAOS   841   7

CHAPLETS
PALE DREAMY CHAPLETS A GREY NUN-SISTER SETS   854 23
CHAPLETS OF CREAM AND DISTANT GREEN   854 25

CHAR
TO THE CHAR WHO'S AS GOOD AS YOU ARE ANY DAY   572   4

CHARACTERS
IN WHICH ONE OF THE CHARACTERS WAS ME   489 10

CH'ARE
RIGHT CH'ARE BOSS AN' WHAT ABAHT IT   547 25

CHARGE
THE CHARGE OF FULFILMENT   215 10
LET HIM CHARGE LIKE A MIGHTY CATAPULT ON THE RED-CROSS +   327 24
OR ELSE RUSH HORIZONTAL TO CHARGE AT THE SKY'S HORIZON   392 18
SUCH WORDS TO THE CAMEL'S CHARGE   492 16

CHARGED
SO THEN THEY CHARGED HIM WITH DEFAMATION   575   6

CHARGES
AS HE CHARGES SLOW AMONG THE HERD   380 17

CHARING CROSS
AT CHARING CROSS HERE BENEATH THE BRIDGE   144 14

CHARIOT
THEN THE MOUNTAINS LIKE CHARIOT CARS   248 21

CHARIOTS
NO WHEELS MIGHT RUN NO INSOLENT CHARIOTS   703 25

CHARLATAN
UPON A ROCK FROM WHENCE AH CHARLATAN   877   6

CHARM
BE ALL YOURSELF FOR OH THE CHARM   151   1
AND ALL THE UNSPEAKABLE CHARM OF BIRDS HOPPING   443 19
I HAVE A CHARM LIKE LAUGHTER THROUGH A VEIL   860 15
THE STEADY GLOW FOR OH THE CHARM   873 11

CHARMS
YOUR LITTLE CHARMS   105 21

CHARRED
AS A FLOWER ABOVE CHARRED REMAINS   769 11
AS ONE DYING WITH THE CHARRED RAGS FALLING AWAY   769 13

CHART
AND NOW THE CHART   100 16

CHARTED
A VOYAGE TO SAIL BEYOND THE CHARTED SEAS   168   3
TOES AND THE DOME OF HIS HOUSE IS HIS HEAVEN THEREFORE +   348 15

CHARTERED
OUR CHARTERED WAY AMONG THE MYRIAD THICK   *938   3

CHARTING
DOWN THE SKY'S STEEP STAIRS CHARTING NO TRACK FOR HER   *937 27

CHASE
YET WARM THE CHASE   165   6
A BRILLIANT STATION THE CHASE   862 28

CHASES
THE WIND CHASES BY US AND OVER THE CORN   163 17
THE WIND CHASES BY ME AND OVER THE CORN   857 17

CHASING
OF HIS VOLUPTUOUS PLEASURE OF CHASING THE SHEEP TO THE +   325   9
AND FOUND YOU AFTER ENDLESS CHASING   395 28

CHASM
CROSS THE CHASM   146 33
ACROSS THE CHASM   763 16
LIES A CHASM   763 22

CHASTE
IN A PURITAN FILLET A CHASTE WHITE SNARE   178   9
GREAT IS MY NEED TO BE CHASTE   469   6
MORE THAN THE CHASTE SHORT DASH   492 28
LOVE-LIGHT IS GLOWING THOUGH THE GUELDER-ROSE IS TOO CH+   854 17

CHASTENED
EVEN THE SUN IN HEAVEN CAN BE CURBED AND CHASTENED AT L+   374 32

CHASTITY
ME NOW FROM THE STUNTING BONDS OF MY CHASTITY   180 17
CHASTITY BELOVED CHASTITY   469 11
O BELOVED CHASTITY   469 12
CHASTITY BELOVED CHASTITY   469 14
CHASTITY DEARER FAR TO ME   470   1
CHASTITY IS INSANE AND DEBAUCHERY IS INSANE   516   4
SUCCESS FAILURE LOVE CHASTITY DEBAUCHERY MONEY OR SOVIE+   839 19
IN THE SAME WAY CHASTITY IN ITS HOUR IS SWEET AND WHOLE+   845 11
BUT CHASTITY ON THE BRAIN IS A VICE A PERVERSION   845 12
CHASTITY IN ITS HOUR IS SWEET AND WHOLESOME   *952 23
IN FACT QUITE A LOT OF CHASTITY IS NECESSARY IN LIFE TO+   *952 24
BUT CHASTITY ON THE BRAIN IS ANOTHER VICE IT ENDS IN LU+ *952 26

CHATELAINE
YOU SHALL BE MY CHATELAINE   95   5

CHATTER
AND PASSING FEET ARE CHATTER AND CLAPPING OF THOSE   58 18
THEY ALL GIBBER AND GIBBER AND CHATTER   549 19

CHATTERING
THE HORSES ARE UNTACKLED THE CHATTERING MACHINE   35 11
CHATTERING THOUGH NOT WITH GLEE   552 10
AND LORD BUT HARK AT THE PIGEONS WHAT ARE THEY CHATTERI+   751 12
CHATTERING AMONG THE ICE   795 22

CHATTING
   ARE HEARD SOFTLY LAUGHING AND CHATTING AS EVER   688 18

CHAUNTING
   ALWAYS ON THE DISTANCE AS IF HIS SOUL WERE CHAUNTING   47 12
   AND DIAPERED ABOVE THE CHAUNTING FLOWERS   135 28
   AND DIAPERED ABOVE THE CHAUNTING FLOWERS   *939 20

CHAVEL
   OF LIVES WHICH SORROWS LIKE MISCHIEVOUS DARK MICE CHAVEL 132 13
   OF LIVES THAT SORROWS LIKE MISCHIEVOUS STRANGE MICE CHA+ *938 5

CHEAP
   IN JAPANESE HENNA OR WHATEVER IT IS CHEAP AT THE PRICE 835 8

CHEAT
   I KNOW I KNOW YOU ARE WINSOME SO BUT YOU CHEAT 872 25

CHEATED
   SHOWS THAT THE CHILDREN VAGUELY KNOW HOW CHEATED THEY 446 16

CHEATING
   TOO MUCH YOU MINT ME THAT CHEATING COUNTERFEIT 872 23

CHEATS
   OR BEATS THEM OR CHEATS THEM 828 11

CHEEK
   AND LAID AGAINST HER CHEEK 73 24
   WHY BURNS YOUR CHEEK AGAINST ME HOW HAVE I INSPIRED 85 19
   SHE LOOKED AT HIM AS HE LAY WITH BANDED CHEEK 156 11
   AND YOU LEANED YOUR CHEEK TO MINE 206 33
   LITTLE RED CRANBERRIES CHEEK TO CHEEK 224 1
   COLD ON MY CHEEK 861 6
   THERE PRESS YOUR HOT RED CHEEK AGAINST MINE 863 17
   AND LAID LAUGHTERLESS ON HER CHEEK *913 16

CHEEKS
   WITH FIRE ON YOUR CHEEKS AND YOUR BROW AND YOUR CHIN AS+ 90 9
   I WATCHED THE TEARS ON THE GUILTY CHEEKS OF THE BOYS 94 14
   HER CHEEKS ARE VERY SMOOTH HER EYES ARE CLOSED 101 9
   CHEEKS AND HAIR A MOMENT SAYING IS IT YOU 180 11
   I WATCHED THE TEARS ON THE FRUITED CHEEKS OF THE BOYS *897 2

CHEEK'S
   THE TEARS ARE DRY AND THE CHEEK'S YOUNG FRUITS ARE FRESH 94 19

CHEEKS'
   THE TEARS ARE DRY THE CHEEKS' YOUNG FRUITS ARE FRESH *897 7

CHEER
   COMFORT AND CHEER SURE THAT IT WILL TELL HER 583 16

CHEERED
   THEY CHEERED BUT NERVOUSLY 445 3

CHEERFUL
   ONE FREE CHEERFUL ACTIVITY STIMULATES ANOTHER 520 26

CHEERFULLY
   RESPECTABLY UNSEEN AND CHEERFULLY GNAWS AWAY AT THE 432 7

CHEERS
   YOUR LITTLE LANTERNS BEHIND YOU AH IT CHEERS 221 22
   YOUR LITTLE LANTERNS BEHIND YOU IT CHEERS *945 8

CHEMICAL
   DO YOU HEAR THE CHEMICAL ACCENTS OF THE SUN 301 9

CHEMICALISED
   FLAT-CHESTED CROP-HEADED CHEMICALISED WOMEN OF INDETERM+ 522 2
   WHEN I SEE THE MESSED-UP CHEMICALISED WOMEN 837 14

CHEMIST'S
   OVER ON BOOT'S CASH CHEMIST'S COUNTER 488 17

CHERISH
   BEND OVER THEM WITH MY SOUL TO CHERISH THE WET 180 10
   WITHOUT PLAYMATE OR HELPMATE HAVING NO ONE TO CHERISH 197 8
   FOLD HIM BE GOOD TO HIM CHERISH HIM 228 31
   CHERISH ME MY TINY ONE CHERISH ME WHO ENFOLD YOU 246 10
   CHERISH LIKE A CHILD 411 8
   LORD CHERISH AND COMFORT 751 9

CHERISHED
   WOMEN I LOVED AND CHERISHED LIKE MY MOTHER 410 3

CHERISHES
   AND HE CHERISHES VOLUPTUOUS DELIGHTS AND THINKS ABOUT T+ 325 6

CHERRIES
   HANG STRINGS OF CRIMSON CHERRIES AS IF HAD BLED 36 21
   UNDER THE GLISTENING CHERRIES WITH FOLDED WINGS 36 23
   CHERRIES HUNG ROUND HER EARS 37 2

CHERRY
   CARRY INTO YOUR ROOM THE BLOSSOMING BOUGHS OF CHERRY 179 2
   SCARLET AND CHERRY RED 861 9

CHERRY-PIE
   YOU CAN'T IMAGINE THE HOLY GHOST SNIFFING AT CHERRY-PIE+ 690 25

CHERRY-TREE
   SWINGING CHERRY-TREE 860 26

CHERUBIM
   FROM HIM TO HER FROM HER TO HIM GREAT CHERUBIM 694 25

CHERUBIM OF JUDGMENT
   THE CHERUBIM OF JUDGMENT HAVE DEPARTED FROM ME *897 10

CHERUBS
   OF CRITICAL CHERUBS THAT CHIRRUP AND PIPE 680 22

CHEST
   I HAVE SEEN IT FELT IT IN MY MOUTH MY THROAT MY CHEST MY 207 21
   THAT ROUND HEAD PUSHED IN MY CHEST LIKE A NUT IN ITS 245 14
   THAT LITTLE BIT OF YOUR CHEST THAT SHOWS BETWEEN 254 9
   THE MASSIVE THUNDER OF HIS DEW-LAPPED CHEST 326 10
   HIS CHEST 326 16
   MY CHEST GAPES OPEN SOMETIMES 869 1
   I CAN ALWAYS FEEL IT ON MY CHEST 869 19
   LINEN WITHIN MY OWN OLD FRAGRANT CHEST 877 31

CHESTNUT
   AND NEVER A GIRL LIKE A CHESTNUT FLOWER 106 19

CHESTS
   AND BITES AT OUR THROATS AND CHESTS 609 2
   CHESTS 796 33

CHEVELURE
   DARLING I SEE YOUR IRON-GREY CHEVELURE 835 5

CHEW
   NOR YO' SO CHEW IT NO MORE 81 10
   CHEW CHEW CHEW CORPSE-BODY AT THE MEAL 584 12
   OH CHEW OLD COWS AT YOUR ANCIENT CUDS 814 20
   CHEW ALSO YOUNG HEIFERS YOUR JUICIER CUDS 814 21
   SO CHEW AT IT NO MORE *923 10

CHEWING
   THE GREY DOG IS CHEWING YOUR ENTRAILS 807 31

CHICK
   CHICK OF THE INTELLECTUAL EAGLE 329 13
   THAT A NEW CHICK SHOULD CHIP THE EXTENSIVE SHELL 329 28

CHICKEN
   I HEARD A LITTLE CHICKEN CHIRP 680 8
   FOR I AM A CHICKEN AND I CAN CHIRP 680 14
   MY PALE WET BUTTERFLY FLUFFY CHICKEN 863 6
   THEN UP COMES A GREY RAT A FLOSS-GOLD CHICKEN GRAPPLES+ *933 11

CHICKEN-HOUSE
   MEET HER AS SHE FLOUNDERS DOWN FROM THE CHICKEN-HOUSE A+ 761 20

CHICKENS
   THE HEN WILL NESTLE OVER HER CHICKENS 268 4
   BUT BONNIE AND BRIGHT WERE THE CHICKENS *933 10
   THEN LIKE CHICKENS MOUNTED IN MY HAND *933 18

CHICKS
   THIRTEEN LAY THE YELLOW CHICKS BENEATH THE JOIST OF WOOD *933 3
   WITH GOLDEN CHICKS OF CLOUD AND A SKY OF RUNNING LAUGHT+ *933 15

CHICKWEED
   WITH A FACE LIKE A CHICKWEED FLOWER 145 9

CHIDDEN
   OF NOISY BIRDS BE YOU CHIDDEN *914 23

CHIEFLY
   WRECKED CHIEFLY ME *897 12

CHIEFTAINS
   CHIEFTAINS THREE OF THEM ABREAST ON FOOT 388 16

CHIGNON
   BACK IN A GRECIAN KNOT OR A JUG HANDLE OR A CHIGNON 836 2

CHILD
   BUT CHILD YOU'RE TOO SMALL FOR ME TOO SMALL 105 20
   THE RAIN-BRUISED LEAVES ARE SUDDENLY SHAKEN AS A CHILD 136 24
   A CHILD SITTING UNDER THE PIANO IN THE BOOM OF THE TING+ 148 6
   DOWN IN THE FLOOD OF REMEMBRANCE I WEEP LIKE A CHILD FOR 148 18
   THE CHILD LIKE MUSTARD SEED 172 5
   WITH A HEAVY CHILD AT HER BREAST 200 2
   SHE HAS GIVEN THE CHILD TO JOSEPH 200 13
   THAT HOLDS THE PERFECT CHILD 201 10
   GIVE ME THE CHILD AGAIN 202 4
   AND THE MAN AND THE CHILD OF NO MORE ACCOUNT 202 7
   NO CHILD AND NO PALFREY SLOW 202 22
   LIKE A RATTLE A CHILD SPINS ROUND FOR JOY THE NIGHT RAT+ 206 31
   THE SHARP BEGETTING OR THE CHILD BEGOT 219 11
   LAD THOU HAST GOTTEN A CHILD IN ME 220 6
   AND WINSOME CHILD OF INNOCENCE NOR 230 26
   MY LOVE MY BLOSSOM A CHILD 239 16
   WHEN I WAS A CHILD I LOVED MY FATHER'S RIDING-WHIP 255 1
   IT IS LIKE THE AGONISED PERVERSENESS OF A CHILD HEAVY W+ 287 2
   CHERISH LIKE A CHILD 411 8
   TO SEE THAT A CHILD AS SOON AS IT IS BORN 521 26
   MY CHILD I CANNOT TELL A LIE 681 23
   I AM WITH CHILD BY YOU 734 34
   CHILD DEAR TO MY EYE GOD'S BLESSING IS ON THY SERVICE 749 21
   ME TOO AT LAST ERE THOU GOEST CHILD DEAR TO MY EYE 750 3
   CHILD OF THE LIVING DEAD THE DEAD THAT LIVE AND ARE NOT+ 796 1
   I AM THE SON OF THE MORNING STAR AND CHILD OF THE DEEPS 799 14
   THERE IS NO MEANS OF REALLY DECEIVING A CHILD 832 14
   NO MY DARLING CHILD 835 16
   CHILD EYES SO CLEAR 866 30
   A CHILD SITTING UNDER THE PIANO IN THE BOOM OF THE SHAK+ *940 7

CHILDHOOD
    THE ANGEL OF CHILDHOOD KISSED ME AND WENT I EXPECTED   48   5
    SINCE THE MONTH OF CHILDHOOD IS OVER AND WE STAND ALONE   132 16
    SINCE THE MONTH OF CHILDHOOD IS OVER AND WE START AFRESH   *938   8

CHILDISH
    OF CHILDISH DAYS IS UPON ME MY MANHOOD IS CAST   148 17

CHILDREN
    THE CHILDREN HAVE FORSAKEN THEIR PLAY   41 28
    SOLEMNLY AND DISTINCTLY CRIES DOWN THE BABEL OF CHILDREN   48 15
    SUFFERING AT SIGHT OF THE CHILDREN PLAYING AROUND   153 11
    YOU NEVER BORE HIS CHILDREN NEVER DREW   158 10
    AND SHE DREAMED OF HER CHILDREN AND JOSEPH   202 15
    BACK TO THOSE CHILDREN YOU HAD LEFT BEHIND TO ALL THE A+   206 24
    YEARNING TOWARDS ENGLAND TOWARDS YOUR YOUNG CHILDREN   207   8
    CHILDREN ACTS UTTERANCE   247 21
    I WAS A FATHER AND A BEGETTER OF CHILDREN   257 20
    NO MORE CHILDREN TO LAUNCH IN A WORLD YOU MISTRUST   411 10
    AND SHOW VAST BELLIES TO THE CHILDREN   425 22
    WHILE THE WISPY MODERN CHILDREN HALF-AFRAID   426 20
    AND THE CHILDREN UTTERED A LITTLE CRY   444 17
    AND THE CHILDREN SUDDENLY SHOUTED OUT   444 22
    COMES NOW AND THEN FROM THE CHILDREN   446 15
    SHOWS THAT THE CHILDREN VAGUELY KNOW HOW CHEATED THEY   446 16
    THE GAZELLE CALF O MY CHILDREN   466   9
    REQUIRING NO SHOES O MY CHILDREN   466 12
    WE CHILDREN WERE THE IN-BETWEENS   490 17
    NOR MY CHILDREN NOR MY COUNTRY NOR MY FELLOW-MAN   497 17
    HOW CAN THEY COMMIT THE INDECENCY OF BEGETTING CHILDREN   521 22
    WITHOUT FIRST BEGETTING A NEW HOPE FOR THE CHILDREN TO   521 23
    WE BELONG NEITHER TO MEN NOR OUR CHILDREN NOR   525 25
    PERHAPS IF WE STARTED RIGHT ALL THE CHILDREN COULD GROW+   527   4
    THEIR CHILDREN BROUGHT UP EASY LET IT SLIP AWAY AGAIN   535 24
    AS FOR BEARING MY CHILDREN WHY THERE   541 17
    EVEN FROM THE FACE OF THE CHILDREN NOW   656 15
    EVEN THE FACT OF BIRTH EVEN LITTLE CHILDREN   656 19
    CHILDREN OF DADDY-DO-NOTHING   659   4
    THE ISAR WHISPERS AGAIN IN THE VALLEY THE CHILDREN   732 18
    AND CHILDREN BEHIND YOU TAUNTING YOU IN TEARS   755   5
    THE GAZELLE-CALF OH MY CHILDREN   757   8
    WEARING NO BOOT MY CHILDREN   757 11
    SAY ADIOS MY CHILDREN   798 33
    IS HOW THEY HATE THEIR CHILDREN   831 21
    THEY INSTINCTIVELY HATE THEIR OWN CHILDREN   832   2
    THEY SEEM TO FEEL THE CHILDREN A GHASTLY LIMITATION   832   8
    BUT FOR THESE CHILDREN I SHOULD BE FREE   832   9
    AWFULLY SORRY DEAR BUT I CAN'T COME BECAUSE OF THE CHIL+   832 11
    THE CHILDREN OF COURSE KNOW THAT THEY ARE CARED FOR   832 12
    HE CAN COPULATE AND BEGET CHILDREN   843 15
    FROM THE NOISE OF CHILDREN PLAYING AROUND   867   3
    AND HIS CHILDREN STIRRED IN THEIR SLEEP AND WHEN THEY W+   885 12

CHILDREN'S
    FROM THE HAY COMES THE CLAMOUR OF CHILDREN'S MIRTH   41 22

CHILDT
    AN' STOP THY SCRAIGHTIN' CHILDT   45   3
    OUT O' MY WAY CHILDT DEAR O' ME WHEER   45 13
    THEY SAY HE'S GOT 'ER WI' CHILDT BUT THERE   78 11
    ME GOTTEN A CHILDT TER THY LANDLADY   80   3
    T' CHILDT MAUN TA'E ITS LUCK IT MUN   81   1
    THEY SAY HE'S GOT HER WI' CHILDT BUT THERE   *920   3
    ME GOTTEN A CHILDT TO THY LANDLADY   *922   3
    THE CHILDT MAUN TA'E ITS LUCK IT MAUN   *923   1
    BUT WE MAUN MA'E THE BEST ON'T I'LL REAR THY CHILDT IF +   *925 18
    LAD THA'S GOTTEN A CHILDT IN ME   *944 14

CHILL
    CHILL DUSK FOR YOU AND GLADLY GLEAMING   91 21
    CLEAN PAIN SENDING ON US A CHILL DOWN HERE   225   4
    THE BREATH OF THE BULLOCK STAINS THE HARD CHILL AIR   225 13
    I STAND IN A CHILL OF ANGUISH TRYING TO SAY   225 31
    TO DESTROY THE CHILL LENT LILIES   271 14
    AND THE LONG AGES AND THE LINGERING CHILL   353   2
    WITHOUT HAVING TO TAKE A CHILL TALKING TO HER   506 19
    I AM TIRED OF THIS JOURNEY IT IS STUPID AND CHILL   858   1
    AND WHEN MY HEART IS CHILL WITH LONELINESS   *900 25
    AND WHEN MY HEART IS CHILL WITH LONELINESS   *904   1

CHILLED
    I AM CHILLED TO THE BONE   229 28
    AND STRANGELY O CHILLED WAN SOUL A FLUSH OF ROSE   720 10

CHILLNESS
    TILL MY HANDS ARE FULL OF THE CHILLNESS AND TOUCH OF LE+   180 35

CHILLY
    THE EAR PERHAPS IS CHILLY UNDERNEATH   87   8

CHIMAERA
    MOST PEOPLE TODAY ARE CHIMAERA   603 21

CHIME
    THE CHIME OF THE BELLS AND THE CHURCH CLOCK STRIKING EI+   48 14
    ME WORDS THAT RANG WITH A BRASSY SHALLOW CHIME   98 20
    SOLEMNLY USED TO APPROVE CHIME CHIMING   170 23
    MOODS THOUGHTS DESIRES AND DEEDS THAT CHIME   460 11

CHIMERICAL
    CHIMERICAL   603 22

CHIMES
    OF OUR ERA HAS STRUCK AND IT CHIMES   512 17
    FROM THE QUIET CHURCH-TOWER THAT KNOWS NO PRATTLE OF CH+   858 22

CHIMING
    SOLEMNLY USED TO APPROVE CHIME CHIMING   170 23
    LIKE A BELL THAT IS CHIMING EACH STROKE AS A STROKE FAL+   251 12

CHIMNEY
    I WATCHED THEM FLOAT UP THE DARK CHIMNEY   107   4
    UP MY VEINS AS UP A CHIMNEY   241 30

CHIMNEY-POTS
    SALLY GO ROUND THE CHIMNEY-POTS   755 24

CHIMNEYS
    OF MANY-STEMMED MACHINES AND CHIMNEYS THAT SMOKE LIKE   293   3
    THEY PUT UP TALL CHIMNEYS THAT SMOKE   793 23

CHIMNEY-TIPS
    THE MYRIAD GLITTERING CHIMNEY-TIPS   166 20

CHIN
    WITH FIRE ON YOUR CHEEKS AND YOUR BROW AND YOUR CHIN AS+   90   9
    AND HAVING THE BREAD HANGING OVER HER CHIN   359   7
    PALE DISPIRITED PRINCE WITH HIS CHIN ON HIS HANDS HIS   388   7
    THE IDIOT WITH HIS CHIN ALL WET   463 16
    AND WHAT A DANDY FELLOW THE RIGHT TOSS OF A CHIN FOR YOU   524 15
    AND NESTING HIS CHIN IN HIS HAND   842 18

CHINA
    IN CHINA THE BAT IS SYMBOL OF HAPPINESS   342   6

CHINESE
    ROSE-RED PRINCESS HIBISCUS ROLLING HER POINTED CHINESE +   313 27
    ALL YOUR WRINKLED MISERERE CHINESE BLACK LITTLE FACE   396   3
    CHINESE DRAGON   397   5
    CHINESE PUZZLE-FACE   398   5

CHINESE-DRAGON-WRINKLED
    CHINESE-DRAGON-WRINKLED WITH A PINK MOUTH GRINNING   397 18

CHINKING
    ME OUT OF MY PROPER DUES WITH YOUR CHINKING JESTS   872 26

CHIP
    THAT A NEW CHICK SHOULD CHIP THE EXTENSIVE SHELL   329 28

CHIPPED
    THIS LITTLE BIT CHIPPED OFF IN BRILLIANCE   372 11
    IS HAS SHE CHIPPED THE SHELL OF HER OWN EGO   603 16
    HAS HE CHIPPED THE SHELL OF HIS OWN EGO   603 17
    WHEN THE CUCKOO THE COW AND THE COFFEE-PLANT CHIPPED THE   760 22

CHIRP
    I HEARD A LITTLE CHICKEN CHIRP   680   8
    FOR I AM A CHICKEN AND I CAN CHIRP   680 14

CHIRPS
    I BELIEVE HE CHIRPS PIPISTRELLO SEEING ME HERE ON THIS   347 19

CHIRRUP
    OF CRITICAL CHERUBS THAT CHIRRUP AND PIPE   680 22
    AND CHIRRUP THEIR ALMOST INDECENT NOISES   681   6

CHIRRUPING
    SONG AND CHIRRUPING GAY FEATHERS FLUFF-SHADOWED   443 17

CHISEL
    LIKE A FINE AN EXQUISITE CHISEL A WEDGE-BLADE INSERTED   250 20

CHITS
    WHITE-NIGHTGOWNED LITTLE CHITS I SEE   105 16

CHITTER
    AND CHITTER AND WIND THAT SHAKES AND CUFFS   89 29

CHOCK-FULL
    I LONG TO SEE ITS CHOCK-FULL CROWDEDNESS   315 27

CHOICE
    SHE HAS NOT CHOSEN ME FINALLY SHE SUSPENDS HER CHOICE   213 24
    LEAVE HER NO CHOICE MAKE HER LAPSE ME-WARD MAKE HER   213 28
    GOD THAT I HAVE NO CHOICE   215   6
    NECESSARY AND I HAVE NO CHOICE   215 12
    AND OF COURSE THRILLING IS LIKE LOVING YOU HAVE NO CHOI+   531 28
    THEN THEN COMES THE GREAT MOMENT OF CHOICE   639 25
    OH LIFE IS NOTHING IF NOT CHOICE   639 26
    AND THAT WHICH IS CHOICE ALONE MATTERS   639 27
    IN THE MOMENT OF CHOICE THE SOUL ROLLS BACK   640   1
    TODAY LIFE IS A CHOICE OF INSANITIES   839 18

CHOIR
    IN THE CHOIR THE BOYS ARE SINGING THE HYMN   147 18
    SO LONG AS YOU LEAD THE GAWKY CHOIR   680 21

CHOKE
    CHOKE ME IN MY OWN CRIMSON I WATCHED HER PULL   123 17
    THAT THEY CHOKE THE SWEEPER   536   3
    AND CHOKE ME IN MY OWN CRIMSON I WATCHED HER PULL   *934 23

CHOKED
    TO BE CHOKED BACK THE WIRE RING   43   9
    AND I HELD THE CHOKED FLOWER-SERPENT IN ITS PANGS   125 16
    FROM OUT OF MY HEART AND LOINS CHOKED AND SHACKLED   884 17
    AND I KEPT THE CHOKED SNAKE FLOWER IN ITS PANGS   *936 15

CHOKING
    SIEGMUND WITH YOUR ARMS AND YOUR HEART YOU ARE CHOKING +   870 20

CHOOSE
    AND IF I COULD THE LAST PLACE I SHOULD CHOOSE   540 22
    WHERE HE DOES NOT CHOOSE TO LAND THEM YET HOOKED FISHES   586 11
    THE HUMAN WILL IS FREE ULTIMATELY TO CHOOSE ONE OF TWO +   617 12
    WHERE HE DOES NOT CHOOSE TO LAND THEM YET HOOKED FISHES   632 26
    IF I HAVE TO CHOOSE BETWEEN THE BOURGEOIS AND THE BOLSH+   664 5
    I CHOOSE THE BOURGEOIS   664 6
    IS IDIOT SO YOU'VE GOT TO CHOOSE   845 16

CHOOSING
    BUT IN CHOOSING THE BOURGEOIS ONE BRINGS TO PASS   664 8

CHOP
    ME OR THE MEXICAN WHO COMES TO CHOP WOOD   398 23
    YOU MUST CHOP UP EACH ARTICLE MAKE IT PAPPY   583 18

CHORALE
    IN GRAND CHORALE TO YOUR MONTHLY KICK-UP   681 8

CHORING
    AND MACBETH AND HIS LADY WHO SHOULD HAVE BEEN CHORING   494 22

CHORISTERS
    OF LINEN GO THE CHANTING CHORISTERS   232 18
    THE COMING OF THE CHANTING CHORISTERS   232 28

CHORUS
    OUR BRIDE AMONG THE RUSTLING CHORUS OF SHELLS   743 9
    SHAPE ANSWERS SHAPE IN CHORUS TO THE SIGHT   872 17
    SING LIKE A CHORUS SOME DAY   *938 20

CHOSE
    BUT WHO COULD COMPEL HER IF SHE CHOSE ME AGAINST THEM   213 22

CHOSEN
    SHE HAS NOT CHOSEN ME FINALLY SHE SUSPENDS HER CHOICE   213 24
    THEY ARE CHOSEN AH THEY ARE FATED   228 25
    I HAVE CHOSEN AMONG THE BRIGHT AND MARVELLOUS BOOKS   264 3
    WHICH MANKIND AT LARGE HAS CHOSEN TO SANCTIFY   620 21
    THE FULL THROATED WOMAN HAS CHOSEN A WINNING LIVING SONG *940 9

CHOUGH
    THE OLD CHOUGH THE OLD CHUFFER   494 18

CHRISM
    IN PERFECT CHRISM   164 16
    CHRISM   168 20

CHRIST
    CHRIST ON THE CROSS HIS BEAUTIFUL YOUNG MAN'S BODY   225 5
    TO GAZE ANY MORE AT THE CHRIST WHOM THE MOUNTAIN SNOWS   225 11
    AND CHRIST I HAVE MET HIS ACCUSING EYES AGAIN   225 22
    WHITE PEAKS OF SNOW AT THE FOOT OF THE SUNKEN CHRIST   225 30
    WITH A PALE DEAD CHRIST ON THE CRUCIFIX OF HIS HEART   226 3
    AND KNOW THE DEAD CHRIST WEIGHING ON MY BONE   226 12
    THE SAME CRY FROM THE TORTOISE AS FROM CHRIST THE OSIRI+ 367 3
    THAT THE RISEN CHRIST SHOULD BE RISEN   459 20
    AND NO ONE NOT GOD NOR CHRIST NOR ANY OTHER   617 3
    CHRIST THE HUMAN CONSCIOUSNESS   636 15
    WAS A GOD IN GODLINESS PURE AS CHRIST BEAUTIFUL   674 24

CHRIST CRUCIFIED
    GOOD FRIDAY CHRIST CRUCIFIED   777 23

CHRISTIAN
    OH THE CANAILLE OF CULTURE THE CHRISTIAN CANAILLE   762 20

CHRISTIANITY
    AND CASH CHRISTIANITY   534 18
    WITH HIS SHAM CHRISTIANITY   537 2

CHRISTIANS
    YET BELLS CALL THE CHRISTIANS TO GOD   623 1
    BEHOLD YOUR CROSS CHRISTIANS   636 1

CHRISTINE
    THERE WAS A GAY BIRD NAMED CHRISTINE   845 17

CHRISTMAS
    I DANCE AT THE CHRISTMAS PARTY   198 5
    MOTIONLESS STANDING IN SNOW LIKE A CHRISTMAS TOY   402 26
    FOR ME WHO AM COLD AS A CHRISTMAS ROSE   877 34

CHRIST RISEN
    TODAY IS EASTER SUNDAY CHRIST RISEN TWO DAYS AGO WAS   777 22

CHRISTUS
    LIKE A WHITE CHRISTUS FALLEN TO DUST FROM A CROSS   403 22

CHUCK
    I'LL CHUCK THE FLAMIN' LOT O' YOU   81 11
    OR I'LL CHUCK THE FLAMIN' LOT OF YOU   *923 11

CHUCKED
    I'VE CHUCKED HIM I'VE REPENTED   493 24

CHUCKLE
    HOW IS IT I GRIN THEN AND CHUCKLE   199 27

CHUCKLED
    WHERE BEFORE THE ASSURANCE CHUCKLED   767 18

CHUCKLES
    AND THE SUAVE SEA CHUCKLES AND TURNS TO THE MOON   130 2

CHUCKLING
    LIKE A SUDDEN CHUCKLING OF MUSIC I BADE HER EYES   125 26
    LIKE A SUDDEN CHUCKLING OF MUSIC I BADE HER EYES   *936 25

CHUFF
    THEY MAKE TRAINS CHUFF MOTOR-CARS TITTER SHIPS LURCH   441 6

CHUFFER
    THE OLD CHOUGH THE OLD CHUFFER   494 18

CHURCH
    THE CHIME OF THE BELLS AND THE CHURCH CLOCK STRIKING EI+ 48 14
    THE CHURCH DRAWS NEARER UPON US GENTLE AND GREAT   48 17
    TALL AND DARK THE CHURCH MOVES ANXIOUS TO KEEP   48 21
    I WISH THE CHURCH HAD COVERED ME UP WITH THE REST   48 24
    WHY THE OLD CHURCH BELLOWS AND BRAGS   54 20
    THE COOL HIGH MOON AT THEIR EASE WHILE THE DRONING CHUR+ 54 30
    FOREVER OUT OF THE MIST THE CHURCH LIFTS UP A REPROACHF+ 63 24
    DESOLATE I AM AS A CHURCH WHOSE LIGHTS ARE PUT OUT   94 23
    CHURCH   776 26
    HE WAS A SOLDIER ALWAYS IN CHURCH IT WAS A SIGHT   859 7

CHURCHES
    CHURCHES   763 2

CHURCH OF ROME
    IF I WAS A MEMBER OF THE CHURCH OF ROME   609 14

CHURCH-TOWER
    FROM THE QUIET CHURCH-TOWER THAT KNOWS NO PRATTLE OF CH+ 858 22

CHURCHYARD
    THE TOWN IS LIKE A CHURCHYARD ALL SO STILL   136 2
    THE TOWN IS LIKE A CHURCHYARD ALL SO STILL   *938 30

CHURN
    THAT CHURN THE FRANKINCENSE AND OOZE THE MYRRH   298 5

CHURNS
    HE STANDS LIKE A LIGHTHOUSE NIGHT CHURNS   39 31

CHUTE
    IN A GREAT CHUTE AND RUSH OF DEBACLE DOWNWARDS   287 21

CICALAS
    INTO THE GLOOM-WOVEN FOREST WHERE THE BIRDS AND CICALA+ 864 5

CICATRICE
    AT THE WOUND'S ACHING CICATRICE   869 2
    MY BREAST'S ACHING CICATRICE   869 9

CIDEVANTS
    OR NAPOLEON SAYS SINCE I HAVE SAVED YOU FROM THE CIDEVA+ 442 20

CIGARETTE
    CIGARETTE BETWEEN MY FINGERS   106 25
    WITH A CIGARETTE BROWNING YOUR FINGERS   651 23

CIGARETTES
    AND KINDLY HAND ME THE CIGARETTES   540 27

CINE
    HOW NICE TO SIT IN THE CINE WHERE THE PICTURE OF ALL TH+ 794 17

CINEMA
    THE DEAD GIVE SHIPS AND ENGINES CINEMA RADIO AND GRAMOP+ 441 17
    CINEMA   630 25

CIRCE-DOM
    THE MODERN CIRCE-DOM   538 26

CIRCLE
    AND DREW THE CIRCLE OF HIS GRASP O MAN   69 11
    CIRCLE   213 2
    WHEREIN WE CIRCLE ON OUR FATE   236 19
    A CIRCLE SWOOP AND A QUICK PARABOLA UNDER THE BRIDGE   341 1
    THE WORK-CASH-WANT CIRCLE IS THE VICIOUSEST CIRCLE   521 5
    ENCLOSED CIRCLE OF SELF   637 6
    CIRCLE WHILE I PRANCE IN THE UPPER   762 10
    HALF-WAY ROUND THE CIRCLE NOW   764 11
    OPPOSITE WAYS ROUND THE CIRCLE   764 13
    I WENT THE OPPOSITE WAY ROUND THE CIRCLE   764 23
    KNEES AND YOUR LEGS AND YOUR LOINS HIS CIRCLE OF REST I+ 801 25
    AND I AM NOT WITH YOU TILL MY SERPENT HAS COILED HIS CI+ 801 28
    BUT THEY CAN'T OR THERE'D BE THE VICIOUS CIRCLE   819 15
    AND DREW THE CIRCLE OF HIS GRASP O MAN   *915 23

CIRCLES
    TANGLING HIS CIRCLES TO BAFFLE YOU AND ME   118 25
    IN CIRCLES AND EVASIONS ENVELOPING ME   332 26
    THEY MOVE IN OTHER CIRCLES   339 30
    FLYING ROUND THE ROOM IN INSANE CIRCLES   342 15
    IN INSANE CIRCLES   342 16
    CIRCLES AN EAGLE   403 2
    IN TERRIBLE RIPPLING CIRCLES BETWEEN THE STARS   512 18
    WHERE TISSUE PLUNGES INTO BRONZE WITH WIDE WILD CIRCLES+ 623 10
    COMPLETING HIS CIRCLES AND WORKING CLEVERLY   *932 3
    IN WIDE AND WIDER CIRCLES ROUND THE WORLD   *943 25

CIRCULATES
    AS IT CIRCULATES ROUND OUR FIRE   238 8

CIRCULATING
    INTO THE CIRCULATING SAP ONCE MORE OF THE TREE OF LIFE 617 11

CIRCUMCISED
    BUT I CONSIDER I WAS SUFFICIENTLY CIRCUMCISED LONG AGO   541 22

CIRCUMSTANCE
    SINCE THERE WAS NO CIRCUMSTANCE REQUIRING TRUST BETWEEN   603 7

CIRCUS
    ELEPHANTS IN THE CIRCUS   425 19
    WHEN I WENT TO THE CIRCUS THAT HAD PITCHED ON THE WASTE   444 9
    IN THE CIRCUS WITH THEIR CIRCUS PEOPLE   445 23
    AND THEY GRUDGE THE CIRCUS PEOPLE THE SWOOPING GAY   446 8
    THEY HAVE WITH THEIR CIRCUS BEASTS   446 12
    IN THE BRIGHT WILD CIRCUS FLESH   446 18
    AND THE PROSTITUTES ON PICCADILLY OR IN THE CIRCUS   582 3

CIRCUS-LIFE
    AND THEY GRUDGE THEM THEIR CIRCUS-LIFE ALTOGETHER   446 13

CITADEL
    THAT CITADEL OF DELIGHT   142 24

CITIES
    FORESTS CITIES BRIDGES   293 22
    AND CITIES MIGHT BE AS ONCE THEY WERE BOWERS GROWN OUT   451 18
    CITIES DISSOLVE LIKE ROCK-SALT   455 3
    OH OVER THE FACTORY CITIES THERE SEEMS TO HOVER A DOOM   586 13
    WHEN I SEE THE GREAT CITIES   632 10
    IN THE CITIES   703 16
    DENSELY THICKEN IN THE CITIES   703 23
    IN ALL THE CITIES WITH LION GATES   704 2
    IN THE BURSTEN CITIES   704 7
    THEN DESTROY THEM THROW THEM OUT INTO THE CITIES   780 16
    AT HER CITIES OF STONE AND HER HUTS OF STRAW   790 8
    I'LL SHAKE THE EARTH AND SWALLOW THEM UP WITH THEIR CIT+   792 4
    HOW NICE IN THE GREAT CITIES WHERE ALL THINGS RUSH AND +   794 15
    FROM THEIR TREE OF LIFE AND VILLAGES WHOLE CITIES LIVED+   *950 4

CITIZEN
    IF HE WERE A HUNDRED-PER-CENT AMERICAN CITIZEN   778 13
    NOW FIRST CITIZEN OF NOTTINGHAM   *950 16

CITIZENS
    IT IS THE OBLIGATION OF THE CITIZENS OF THIS COUNTRY TO+   776 3

CITY
    LIKE A WEEDED CITY IN SHADOW UNDER THE SEA   72 17
    AS I STAND ON THIS HILL WITH THE WHITENING CAVE OF THE +   97 11
    OF LEAVES AND LAMPS AND THE CITY STREET MINGLED   111 6
    AND CITY STARS SO DIM AND HOLY   121 31
    THE CITY CORRODES OUT OF SIGHT   142 22
    ALL BOUNDS THE GREAT OLD CITY   159 9
    ABHORRENT GREEN SLIPPERY CITY   278 10
    SEA-BATHING CITY PEOPLE   625 12
    WHEN I AM IN A GREAT CITY I KNOW THAT I DESPAIR   632 11
    AND SILVERY CITY OF THE NOW HOPELESS BODY   721 12
    AGAINST THE SILVERY ADAMANT WALLS OF LIFE'S EXCLUSIVE C+   722 3
    IN THE CITY SOMETHING OF YOU   887 8
    WARM IN A CITY OF STRENGTH BETWEEN HER BREASTS   *945 23
    THAT LIE OUTSIDE THE SILVERY WALLS OF OUR BODY'S BUILDE+   *957 17
    IT IS EASY TO BE PUSHED OUT OF THE SILVERY CITY OF THE +   *957 20

CITYWARDS
    CITYWARDS IN LITTLE RIVERS THAT SWELL TO A GREAT STREAM   484 3

CIUCO
    ASINELLO CIUCO   379 2

CIVILISATION
    TO KEEP ON HOLDING UP THIS IDEAL CIVILISATION   288 5
    OF A SWAMPED CIVILISATION AND START A NEW WORLD OF MAN   429 12
    CIVILISATION   508 20
    THE TOCSIN OF THIS OUR CIVILISATION   512 11
    THE NEMESIS THAT AWAITS OUR CIVILISATION   514 25
    BUT OUR CIVILISATION ALAS   524 7
    FORM OF MACHINE CIVILISATION WILL MELT AWAY   611 15
    AFTER OUR INDUSTRIAL CIVILISATION HAS BROKEN AND THE CI+   612 1
    WORD OF OUR CIVILISATION   620 26
    FORMS OF CIVILISATION   776 10
    SAY WHAT WE LIKE OUR CIVILISATION HAS LEARNT A GREAT LE+   831 5
    TO ALTER THE PRESENT FRAME OF CIVILISATION   838 3
    AN ESCAPE FROM THEIR HORROR OF IMPRISONMENT IN OUR CIVI+   838 8

CLACKS
    NOR CLACKS ACROSS THE FORCES FURROWING A GREAT GAY TRAIL   436 3

CLAD
    I MOVE AMONG A TOWNFOLK CLAD   109 10

CLAIM
    THIS LAST ONE TO CLAIM ME AND NOW MY SON O MY SON   48 6
    AND CLAIM HER UTTERLY IN A KISS   62 7
    LIFE COMES TO THEE ON WHICH THOU HAST NO CLAIM   69 28
    AT SUCH AN HOUR TO LAY HER CLAIM ABOVE   155 29
    IS MINE I CLAIM HIM ONCE AND FOR ALL   219 26
    THEIR CLASS-SUPERIOR CLAIM   554 32
    THEY PRESS THEIR CLAIM UPON US   739 17
    AND CLAIM HER UTTERLY IN A KISS   *912 14
    IS MINE I MUN CLAIM HIM ONCE FOR ALL   *944 6

CLAIMED
    NOW CLAIMED THE HOST   156 6

CLAMBER
    BREAKS FROM THE WINTER-CELL TO CLAMBER   46 7

CLAMMILY
    SLOW SLOW FUNGOID CLAMMILY DECAY   784 28

CLAMOROUS
    REDDER THAN DEATH MORE CLAMOROUS   264 13
    LEAVING MY EYES HALF EMPTY AND CLAMOROUS   *893 16

CLAMOROUSLY
    THEY ARE RIGHT YET CLAMOROUSLY FALLING   54 4

CLAMOUR
    FROM THE HAY COMES THE CLAMOUR OF CHILDREN'S MIRTH   41 22
    SO NOW IT IS VAIN FOR THE SINGER TO BURST INTO CLAMOUR   148 15
    WILL CLAMOUR FORTH FROM THE FLESH AND NEVER   461 19
    CLAMOUR OF DEATH   739 3
    BREATHLESS SOUNDS OF SATISFACTION CLAMOUR OF DELIGHT   865 27
    CLAMOUR   *940 22

CLAMOURING
    AND THE GREAT BLACK PIANO IS CLAMOURING AS MY MOTHER'S + *940 21

CLANGING
    CLANGING AT THE FARM SUCH BEWILDERMENT   220 13

CLANK
    ALL DAY HAS THE CLANK OF IRON ON IRON DISTRESSED   167 13

CLAPPED
    AND YOU CLAPPED YOUR HANDS AND SAID SAY IT AGAIN   550 26
    THEN EVERY MOLECULE OF CREATION JUMPED AND CLAPPED ITS + 683 4

CLAPPER
    THAT HARD CLAPPER STRIKING IN A HARD MOUTH   622 21
    ESPECIALLY CLAPPER BELLS HARD TONGUES WAGGING IN HARD M+ 623 2

CLAPPING
    AND PASSING FEET ARE CHATTER AND CLAPPING OF THOSE   58 18
    WHO PLAY AROUND US COUNTRY GIRLS CLAPPING THEIR HANDS   58 19

CLARINDA
    THANK YOU DEAR CLARINDA   550 19

CLASH
    AND CLASH AND YET SEEM TO TALLY   38 26
    LIKE ALL THE CLASH OF A RIVER   38 27
    FORGET EACH OTHER AND THE BRUISE OF OUR BODIES' CLASH   91 6
    FIND AN ENEMY EGOIST AND CLASH THE CYMBALS IN FACE-TO-F+ 383 17
    YET THE CLASH HAS BEEN STARTED THE INDIAN IS ABOUT TO BE 777 20

CLASHES
    AND EVERY SELF-ASSERTION CLASHES ON EVERY OTHER   496 23

CLASHING
    YET THE BRONZE WIND-BELL SUDDENLY CLASHING   371 16

CLASP
    TOUCHES THE CLASP WITH TREMBLING FINGERS AND TRIES   64 16
    HOW MY SOUL CLEAVES TO YOUR BOSOM AS I CLASP YOU   246 5
    IN THE CLASP AND THE SOFT WILD CLUTCH OF A SHE-WHALE'S + 694 19
    TO CLASP WHAT THEY HAVE NEVER CLASPED   *893 25
    WITH A RICH A THRILLED YOUNG CLASP OF LIFE   *899 32
    WITH A RICH A THRILLED YOUNG CLASP OF LIFE   *903 11

CLASPED
    SO IN THE CANE-BRAKE HE CLASPED HIS HAND IN DELIGHT   693 16
    WE LEAP LIKE TWO CLASPED FLAMES FROM OFF THE FIRE   879 30
    TO CLASP WHAT THEY HAVE NEVER CLASPED   *893 25

CLASPS
    WHO IS IT THAT CLASPS AND KNEADS MY NAKED FEET TILL THE+ 652 12

CLASS
    AS I SIT ON THE SHORES OF THE CLASS ALONE   51 10
    IN THE RIPENING MORNING TO SIT ALONE WITH THE CLASS   51 22
    ALL THE LONG SCHOOL-HOURS ROUND THE IRREGULAR HUM OF TH+ 75 20
    ONLY I AND THE CLASS MUST WRANGLE THIS WORK IS A BITTER+ 76 22
    THE CLASS OVER THEM ALL THE DARK NET OF MY DISCIPLINE W+ 92 6
    OUTSIDE ALL CLASS   563 18
    OH I HAVE LOVED THE WORKING CLASS   644 4
    ALL OTHER CLASS IS ARTIFICIAL   649 23
    CLASS OF ANARCHY   649 25
    TO GATHER AND FORTIFY THEMSELVES IN EVERY CLASS IN EVER+ 666 3
    NOT A MOB THING NOR A MASS THING NOR A CLASS THING NOR   775 23
    THEY ARE REALLY LOW CLASS PEOPLE OUT ON THE MAKE   831 8
    THE HUM AND WHISPER OF THE CLASS LIKE A LITTLE WIND   *894 15
    THE SURGE AND TIDE OF LIFE IN THE TURBULENT CLASS   *895 10
    ALL THE SLOW SCHOOL HOURS ROUND THE IRREGULAR HUM OF TH+ *897 20
    EARNESTLY AND OH FOR ME THIS CLASS IS A BITTER ROOD   *898 16
    AS I SIT ON THE BEACH OF THE CLASS ALONE   *898 22
    AND ALL THE CLASS   *899 17
    ALL THE SLOW SCHOOL HOURS ROUND THE IRREGULAR HUM OF TH+ *900 28
    EARNESTLY AND OH FOR ME THIS CLASS IS A BITTER ROOD   *901 25
    AS I SIT ON THE BEACH OF THE CLASS ALONE   *902 6
    AND ALL THE CLASS   *902 29
    HERE IN MY CLASS IS THE ANSWER FOR THE GREAT YEARNING   *909 6
    THE CLASS OVER THEM ALL THE DARK NET OF MY DISCIPLINE W+ *926 6

CLASS-CHILDREN
    CLASS-CHILDREN ARE SINGING IN SCHOOL   657 11

CLASSES
    WHY HAVE WORKING CLASSES AT ALL AS IF MEN WERE ONLY   452 5
    WORKING CLASSES   452 11
    BECAUSE OBVIOUSLY HE'S NOT ONE OF THE LEISURED CLASSES   452 21
    NOT TO INSTALL THE WORKING CLASSES   453 10
    BUT TO ABOLISH THE WORKING CLASSES FOR EVER   453 11
    DON'T DO IT FOR THE WORKING CLASSES   517 13
    FOR THESE MASSES AND CLASSES OF MEN   639 22

CLASSES
OF CLASSES AND MASSES   640 6
THEN AT ONCE THE IMPULSE OF THE GREEDY CLASSES AND MASS+   640 8
FOR THE ROBOT CLASSES AND MASSES ARE ONLY KEPT SANE   640 13
TO THE ROBOT CLASSES AND MASSES   640 17
THERE ARE MASSES AND THERE ARE CLASSES   641 11
THE CLASSES ARE SO SUPERIOR   641 13
NOR ITS MECHANISED ROBOTS ROBOT CLASSES AND MASSES   643 4
THERE ARE TWO CLASSES OF MEN   649 19
THE SUPERIOR CLASSES   762 23
WHICH THE SUPERIOR CLASSES ARE MAKING MONEY OUT OF   763 14

CLASSROOM
SCATTER OVER THE WHITENESS ONE BOY ALONE IN THE CLASSRO+   865 20

CLASS-ROOM
RISING UP IN THE CLASS-ROOM LITTER MAKES ME UNABLE   90 4
NONE IN THEIR LITTLE THROATS OR CLASS-ROOM BODIES   657 14

CLASS-SUPERIOR
THEIR CLASS-SUPERIOR CLAIM   554 32

CLASS'S
TO SEE THE CLASS'S LIFTED AND BENDED FACES   90 5

CLASSY
CLASSY   774 16
AREN'T YOU PINING TO BE CLASSY SUPERIOR UPPER   774 17

CLATCH
SO WE FOUND THE DEAD CLATCH SIDE BY SIDE   *933 5

CLATTER
AND THREW IT AT THE WATER-TROUGH WITH A CLATTER   351 11
IN A COG-WHEEL CLATTER OF VIOLATION   839 7
THE INRUSH THE CLATTER THE STAMPING EYES LAUGHING WIDE +   865 25

CLATTERING
WE ALL MARCH OUT TO PRAYERS SOFT SLIPPERED FEET AND CLA+   866 13

CLAW
I WOULD NOT EVEN ASK TO LEAVE A FOSSIL CLAW EXTANT   430 7
DOZING IN THE UNDER-DEEPS THEN REACHING OUT A SAVAGE AN+   889 20

CLAWING
HIGH AND CLAWING WITH RAGE AT THE CLIFFS OF THE SOUL   454 9

CLAWKIN'
AN' IF 'ER CLAWKIN' EYES   80 14
AN' IF 'ER CLAWKIN' TIGER'S EYES   *922 14

CLAWS
FANGS AND CLAWS AND TALONS AND BEAKS AND HAWK-EYES   409 29
AND CLAWS NOT MADE TO SHAKE HANDS WITH   414 15
BEFORE SHE COULD SET THE CLAWS OF HER SELF-CONSCIOUS QU+   604 9
THEY ARE LIKE CATS WITH UNCLEAN CLAWS TANGLED UP IN NETS   675 6
AND HOLD MYRIAD THREADS FROM THEIR CLAWS   793 26
HE'S LIKE A BUNNY ROSY SEA-CRAB WITH HEALTHY CLAWS   830 19

CLAY
ON TH' YALLER CLAY WI' TH' WHITE FLOWERS TOP OF IT   60 13
LIKE SOFT HOT ASHES ON MY HELPLESS CLAY   87 13
IS WOMB-FIRE IN THE STIFFENED CLAY OF US   89 3
CLAY   509 18
AND LEAVES MEN LIVING CLAY   524 9
IMMORTAL CAESAR DEAD AND TURNED TO CLAY   545 24
OF CLAY   545 28
NAY I SAW NOWT BUT TH' COFFIN AN' TH' YELLER CLAY AN' '+   *909 31
ON TH' YALLER CLAY AN' TH' WHITE FLOWERS TOP OF IT   *910 28

CLAY-COLOURED
CLAY-COLOURED WHO ROLL IN FATIGUE   162 14

CLEAN
ALONG THE FLAGGED CLEAN PAVEMENT SUMMER-WHITE   36 2
'AVE I PUT 'IS CLEAN STOCKIN'S AN' SHIRT   45 14
AS I HEAR THE SHARP CLEAN TROT OF A PONY DOWN THE ROAD   63 9
CLEAN AN' NEW AN' NICE SO'S WHEN   77 27
TO HA' GONE AN' GIVEN HIS CLEAN YOUNG FLESH   77 31
CLEAN OF THE COLD AND THE MUST WITH MY HAND ON THE LATCH   99 9
AND CAME BACK TINGLING CLEAN BUT WORN AND FRAYED   99 13
IN CLEAN NEW AWARENESS BUT NOW   112 4
CLEAN PAIN SENDING ON US A CHILL DOWN HERE   225 4
AND WASH QUITE CLEAN   229 18
I AM WASHED QUITE CLEAN   229 22
QUITE CLEAN OF IT ALL   229 23
SO COLD SO COLD AND CLEAN   229 25
BURNED CLEAN BY REMORSELESS HATE   242 17
AND I LOVE YOU SO STRAIGHT AND CLEAN AND ALL OF A PIECE+   254 18
LOOK YOU ARE CLEAN AND FINE AND SINGLED OUT   255 10
I ADMIRE YOU SO YOU ARE BEAUTIFUL THIS CLEAN SWEEP OF   255 11
IS NOT SO FRIGHTENING AS THAT CLEAN SMOOTH   290 27
TO LICK THE WORLD WITH FLAME THAT LICKS IT CLEAN   315 26
AND I HAVE TO CLEAN UP AFTER YOU FILTH WHICH EVEN BLIND   399 6
DOESN'T HE LOOK THE FRESH CLEAN ENGLISHMAN OUTSIDE   430 21
THE BODY OF ITSELF IS CLEAN BUT THE CAGED MIND   463 19
O LEAVE ME CLEAN FROM MENTAL FINGERING   469 19
VIVID AND CLEAN   524 6
NEW BROOMS SWEEP CLEAN   536 1
AND SHE JABBED HER BRITISH TRIDENT CLEAN   577 17
GIVE ME A SPONGE AND SOME CLEAR CLEAN WATER   580 15
AH THE CLEAN WATERS OF THE SKY AH CAN YOU WASH   581 6
IF THE ROBOT CAN RECOGNISE THE CLEAN FLAME OF LIFE   648 16
SOME MEN CAN SEE LIFE CLEAN AND FLICKERING ALL ROUND   649 7
WHEN THEY ARE PURE WHICH MEANS WHEN THEY ARE QUITE CLEA+   672 2
AND CLEAN AS ARROWS THEY SPED AT THE MARK   688 24
AND RUBS THE SILVER CLEAN WITH HIS THICK BROWN FINGERS   734 2
SOILING THE CLEAN WHITE DUST HE RUBS THE BELLY   734 9

CLEAN
WORKED WITH CLEAN SWEAT FOR YEAST   758 22
AND HIS MOUTH WIPED CLEAN OF THE BITTERNESS OF REPROACH   770 19
HE SAW THE WOMEN THAT WERE NOT CLEAN   790 13
TO MAKE THEMSELVES CLEAN INSIDE AND OUT   793 6
WILL WAKE AT LAST FROM THE CLEAN FORGETTING   809 16
FRESH CLEAN WELL-GROOMED ENGLISHMAN   830 9
HE HAS FRESH CLEAN WELL-GROOMED EMOTIONS   830 11
QUITE THE FRESH CLEAN MANLY FELLOW   830 13
SUNBEAMS LUSTY AND CLEAN FROM THE BATH OF NIGHT   856 16
SHE KISSED THEIR COOLNESS LAST NIGHT BREATHED THEIR CLE+   856 19
CLEAN AN' NEW AN' NICE SO'S WHEN   *919 15

CLEANED
KEEP HIS PATH WELL CLEANED   563 28

CLEANING
LET US HAVE A SPRING CLEANING IN THE WORLD   792 33

CLEANIN'
CLEANIN' YES SIR A SHILLN BY MYSELF ALL RIGHT SIR   866 21

CLEANNESS
THE COOL THE CLEANNESS OF THE SEA   747 7

CLEANSED
CLEANSED AND IN CONCORD FROM THE BED OF DEATH   743 28

CLEAR
TO THE SUN AND THE SWALLOWS CUT CLEAR   35 4
CLEAR UPON THE LONG-DRAWN HOARSENESS OF A TRAIN ACROSS +   63 11
WITH LAUGHTER AND CLEAR THE EXONERATED EYES SINCE PAIN   94 20
BY ITS SHAPE LIKE THRUSHES IN CLEAR EVENINGS   101 16
I WAS LAST NIGHT WHEN MY SOUL RANG CLEAR AS A BELL   141 24
THE CLEAR COLD SKY COLDLY BETHINKS ITSELF   142 13
THEY SHONE CLEAR LIKE FLOWERS UNDONE   216 17
FULL OF FINE WARMTH I ISSUE FORTH IN CLEAR   218 7
LIKE A MAN IN A BOAT ON VERY CLEAR DEEP WATER SPACE FRI+   222 24
THE MOUNTAIN'S NEW-DROPPED SUMMER SNOW IS CLEAR   225 2
ONE CLEAR BURNISHED ISOLATED BEING UNIQUE   267 20
YOU NEED NOT CLEAR THE WORLD LIKE A CABBAGE PATCH FOR ME   316 9
HAVE WE GOT TO GET DOWN AND CLEAR AWAY THE DEBRIS   429 11
CLEAR AND FEARLESS EVEN IF TINY   526 12
AND CLEAR INTUITION IS MORE THAN MORAL   529 4
CLEAR AND FLOWERY BLUE   530 4
HENCEFORTH HE'LL KEEP CLEAR OF HER TOASTING-FORK   577 22
GIVE ME A SPONGE AND SOME CLEAR CLEAN WATER   580 15
BECAUSE I'VE RISEN CLEAR   626 26
ANY CLEAR AND FEARLESS AND BEING GOD VERY GOD   691 21
WHEN YOU LIFT YOUR HANDS IN COURAGE AND BRAVERY ITS GLO+   800 10
CHILD EYES SO CLEAR   866 30
EMERGING AND CROSSING THE CLEAR SKY UNPERCEIVED   874 24
THROUGH THE CLOSE THICKETS TO THE CLEAR OF DEATH   879 14
SHALL HAVE RAKED THE EMBERS CLEAR I WILL KEEP   *896 2
SHALL HAVE RAKED THE EMBERS CLEAR I WILL KEEP   *904 23
AN' LOOK ME CLEAR   *924 24

CLEARED
I SHALL BE CLEARED DISTINCT SINGLE AS IF BURNISHED IN S+   267 18

CLEARER
IN THE WATER MUCH CLEARER AND BRIGHTER   48 28
IN THE SUDDEN LIFTING MY EYES IT IS CLEARER   *908 18

CLEARLY
AND CLEARLY   826 28

CLEARNESS
CLEARNESS   349 14

CLEARS
SO HE CLEARS HIS THROAT THE YOUNG COCK-EAGLE   413 26

CLEAVAGE
THE LONE CLEAVAGE OF DIVISION UPRIGHT OF THE ETERNAL CR+   355 30
AND THE SUDDEN DRIPPING OF THE KNIFE-EDGE CLEAVAGE OF T+   707 13

CLEAVE
THAT THEY CLEAVE UNTO AND UP WHICH THEY CLIMB   52 6
I FEEL THEM CLING AND CLEAVE TO ME   52 8
I CANNOT BUT CLEAVE TO YOU HELEN   118 9
NOT ONE INSTANT CLEAVE CLING LIKE A BLOT WITH HIS BREAS+   343 29
CLUTCH CLEAVE STAGGER   344 8
AND CLEAVE IN A HIGH CORNER FOR A SECOND LIKE A CLOT AL+   345 23
THE CLEAVERS THAT CLEAVE US FOREVER APART FROM ONE ANOT+   707 17
THE BOOKS THAT YOU HAVE TOUCHED CLEAVE CLOSE TO ME   880 10
THAT THEY CLEAVE UNTO THAT THEY LEAP ALONG   *899 20
SO DO THEY CLEAVE AND CLING TO ME   *899 22
THAT THEY CLEAVE UNTO THAT THEY LEAP ALONG   *902 32
SO DO THEY CLEAVE AND CLING TO ME   *903 1

CLEAVED
UNTIL HER PRIDE'S FLAG SMITTEN CLEAVED DOWN TO THE STAFF   125 18

CLEAVERS
THE CLEAVERS THAT CLEAVE US FOREVER APART FROM ONE ANOT+   707 17

CLEAVES
HOW MY SOUL CLEAVES TO YOUR BOSOM AS I CLASP YOU   246 5
AND DARK CLEAVES DOWN AND WEAPON-HARD DOWNWARD   373 28
THE DARK CLEAVES DOWN AND WEAPON-HARD DOWNWARDS CURVING   782 4
CLEAVES FROZEN TO THE WALLS OF MY COLD BREAST   879 20

CLEAVING
HOW GORGEOUS THAT SHOCK OF RED LILIES AND LARKSPUR CLEA+   129 27
MALE TORTOISE CLEAVING BEHIND THE HOVEL-WALL OF THAT DE+   364 28
CLEAVING CLEAVING   707 15

CLEFT
    FROM HIS PINK CLEFT OLD-MAN'S MOUTH   365 12

CLENCH
    AND OFTEN I SEE HER CLENCH HER FINGERS TIGHT   128 18
    WHICH QUIVERS INDRAWN AS YOU CLENCH YOUR SPINE   370 13
    SEIZES YOU AS YOU CLENCH YOURSELF TOGETHER   370 17
    OF MEN THEY CLENCH FEAR IN THEIR FISTS   460 28

CLENCHED
    OF NAKED LOVE CLENCHED IN HIS FISTS THE SHAME   226 7
    OPENING ITS CLENCHED FACE FROM HIS OUTSTRETCHED NECK   365 9
    THOU OF THE DARK CLENCHED TOMB   753 14

CLEOPATRA
    IF ONLY CLEOPATRA HAD LEFT OFF BEING SO CLEOPATRA-ISH   479 20

CLEOPATRA-ISH
    IF ONLY CLEOPATRA HAD LEFT OFF BEING SO CLEOPATRA-ISH   479 20

CLERGYMEN
    SPINNING A GLAMOUR ROUND MONEY AND CLERGYMEN   456 24
    CLERGYMEN PROFESSORS BANK-DIRECTORS AND STOCK-BROKERS   774 6

CLERKS
    CLERKS OF THE BANK   618 19

CLEVER
    HE'S INSTINCTIVELY FRIGHTFULLY CLEVER   447 16
    OR TO PUT UP WITH THE CLEVER MESS-MAKERS   499 17
    YES I SHOULD SAY THE CONTEMPLATION OF CLEVER SUICIDE IS   532 28
    WE THINK WE'RE SUCH CLEVER LITTLE JOHNNIES   543 19
    WHEN ALAS IT'S ONLY PART OF OUR CLEVER LITTLE SELF THAT+   543 23
    AH CLEVER ODYSSEUS WHO OUTWITTED THE CYCLOP   543 26
    CLEVER LITTLE ANTS IN SPECTACLES WE ARE   544 1
    FOR SPECTACLES AND BULGING CLEVER ANT-EYES ARE NO GOOD +   544 7
    ROSE-LEAVES TO BEWILDER THE CLEVER FOOLS   634 29
    THAT SHONE AND DARKENED THEY WERE ALL TOO CLEVER   737 26
    THEY ARE THE CLEVER ONES   794 4
    AND QUITE CLEVER BRILLIANT IS THE MODERN WORD   841 17
    YOU'VE DISCOVERED SO MANY BITS WITH YOUR CLEVER EYES   *932 7
    SAID RONALD YOU SEE IS QUITE A CLEVER SADIST   *948 10

CLEVERLY
    SO HE VERY CLEVERLY TORTURES WOMEN WITH HIS SORT OF LOVE   447 15
    COMPLETING HIS CIRCLES AND WORKING CLEVERLY   *932 3
    SO HE CLEVERLY PLAYS THE NORMAL THE DON JUAN   *948 25

CLICHE
    CLICHE   509 28

CLICK
    OF THE IRON CLICK OF YOUR HUMAN CONTACT   291 10
    AND TO SPRING AWAY WITH A CURVETTING CLICK IN THE AIR   337 2

CLICKETING
    THEY ARE A CLICKETING OF BITS OF DISJOINTED METAL   288 32

CLIFF
    THE ENORMOUS CLIFF OF HORSE-CHESTNUT TREES   105 13
    TILL THEY HALT AT A CLIFF ON THE EDGE OF THE LAND   201 15
    KICKED OVER THE CLIFF   299 21

CLIFFS
    WHERE THE TREES RISE LIKE CLIFFS PROUD AND BLUE-TINTED +   66 5
    BETWEEN THE CLIFFS OF THE TREES ON THE GREY-GREEN PARK   66 6
    AND THE MOON SIGNIFICANT SMILES AT THE CLIFFS AND THE   130 3
    LIKE CLIFFS ABUTTING IN SHADOW A DEAD GREY SEA   164 19
    HIGH AND CLAWING WITH RAGE AT THE CLIFFS OF THE SOUL   454 9

CLIMAX
    CONSOLATION THAT IN HER LIPS HER BLOOD AT CLIMAX CLIPS   127 26

CLIMB
    THAT THEY CLEAVE UNTO AND UP WHICH THEY CLIMB   52 6
    AND CLIMB THE STAIRS TO FIND THE GROUP OF DOORS   140 9
    MY SOUL TO SEE YOU SETTLING AND TRYING TO CLIMB   221 23
    AND CLIMB AGAIN THE BROKEN BANK OF MY WALL-FACE   350 32
    WHEN HER TRICK IS TO CLIMB OVER HIM   426 15
    CLIMB DOWN O LORDLY MIND   473 8
    WHEN YOU CLIMB UP TO THE MIDDLE CLASSES   549 1
    IF YOU CLIMB UP THE TREE   549 14
    WILL YOU CLIMB ON YOUR BIG SOFT WINGS BLACK-DOTTED   696 22
    OF ALL THE STRAYS OF LIFE THAT CLIMB MY LIFE   *900 27
    OF ALL THE STRAYS OF LIFE THAT CLIMB MY LIFE   *904 3
    SHOULD CLIMB THE HILL AND PUT THE FLOWERS ASUNDER   *941 4
    MY HEART TO SEE YOU SETTLING AND TRYING TO CLIMB   *945 9

CLIMBED
    WE CLIMBED THE HUNTSMAN'S LADDER AND SAT SWINGING   216 22
    GOD MAY STAY IN MID-HEAVEN THE SON OF MAN HAS CLIMBED TO   323 14
    WE CLIMBED THE STEEP ASCENT TO HEAVEN   554 1
    THE NAKED ONE CLIMBED IN   802 12
    THE SUN HAS CLIMBED THE HILL THE DAY IS ON THE DOWNWARD+   803 5
    AND THE PALE STARS OF FORGET-ME-NOTS HAVE CLIMBED TO TH+   854 2
    AND YOU CLIMBED BACK NAKED OVER ME   886 10
    WE CLIMBED THE HUNTSMAN'S LADDER AND SAT SWINGING   *942 8

CLIMBING
    OVER TO THE NEW WORLD AND WAS CLIMBING OUT ON THE SHORE   260 14
    ALMOND TRUNKS CURVING BLACKLY IRON-DARK CLIMBING THE   300 24
    CLIMBING THE SLOPES   301 16
    CLIMBING THROUGH THE JANUARY SNOW INTO THE LOBO CANYON   401 1
    SO UP I STARTED CLIMBING   554 9
    THEY ARE AFRAID OF CLIMBING DOWN FROM THIS IDIOTIC TIN-+   667 19
    PAUSES NEAR THE CREST OF THE HILL CLIMBING SLOWLY LIKE +   687 17

CLIME
    RIPE FIGS WON'T KEEP WON'T KEEP IN ANY CLIME   284 28

CLING
    I FEEL THEM CLING AND CLEAVE TO ME   52 8
    SOME FEW DARK-CLEAVING THE DOORWAY SOULS THAT CLING AS +   75 10
    IT IS STORMY AND RAINDROPS CLING LIKE SILVER BEES TO TH+   92 1
    MAUN THA CLING TO THE WA' AS THA STAN'S   139 21
    NOT ONE INSTANT CLEAVE CLING LIKE A BLOT WITH HIS BREAS+   343 29
    AND CLING TO THEIR THIN YOUNG WOMEN   558 24
    SO DO THEY CLEAVE AND CLING TO ME   *899 22
    THOUGH THEY CLING FORGOTTEN THE MOST PART NOT COMPANION+ *900 14
    SO DO THEY CLEAVE AND CLING TO ME   *903 1
    THOUGH THEY CLING FORGOTTEN THE MOST PART NOT COMPANIONS *903 26
    IT IS STORMY AND RAIN-DROPS CLING LIKE SILVER BEES TO T+ *926 1

CLINGING
    OVER MY SKIN IN THE SUNSHINE THE WARM CLINGING AIR   34 13
    AND THE SENSE OF HER CLINGING FLESH WAS SWEET   62 1
    CLINGING MERRILY   860 28
    CLINGING TO THE RADIATORS LIKE NUMBED BEES TO THE DRENC+ 866 1
    OVER MY SUNLIT SKIN THE WARM CLINGING AIR   *892 1
    TO ME YET STILL BECAUSE OF THE SENSE OF THEIR CLOSENESS+ *900 16
    TO ME YET STILL BECAUSE OF THE SENSE OF THEIR CLOSENESS+ *903 28
    AND THE SENSE OF HER CLINGING FLESH WAS SWEET   *912 9

CLINGS
    SO CLINGS TO ME   73 22
    SO CLINGS TO ME   *913 14

CLINK
    THE CLINK OF THE SHUNTING ENGINES IS SHARP AND FINE   52 16
    ALL DAY THE CLINK OF THE HAMMERS HAS OPPRESSED   *896 18
    THE CLINK OF THE SHUNTING ENGINES IS SHARP AND FINE   *905 5

CLIPS
    CONSOLATION THAT IN HER LIPS HER BLOOD AT CLIMAX CLIPS   127 26
    WHEN THE THREAD CLIPS   155 25
    WITH A QUICK KISS CLIPS   862 12
    OF A SECOND AFRAID OF THE CLIPS   *912 17

CLOAK
    BUT WHEN I DRAW THE SCANTY CLOAK OF SILENCE OVER MY EYES   64 14
    TAKE OFF YOUR CLOAK AND YOUR HAT   237 17
    WITH HIS CLOAK OVER HIS ARM WAITING TO BE ASKED IN   692 11
    IT WAS COLD AND HE PUT HIS CLOAK RIGHT ROUND ME   732 14
    HE'S GOING TO WEAR THE SKY-BLUE CLOAK   797 15
    THE STREAM AND CLOAK ME OVER WITH THY RED   879 9
    AND HANDS AND FACE AND BREAST WITH THAT HOT CLOAK   879 10

CLOAKS
    ALL IN THEIR SCARLET CLOAKS AND SURPLICES   232 17

CLOCK
    THE CHIME OF THE BELLS AND THE CHURCH CLOCK STRIKING EI+   48 14
    A TWO-EYED CLOCK LIKE AN OWL   170 22
    NO GOGGLING CLOCK   170 26

CLOCKS
    WHILE T' CLOCKS 'AS A' RUN DOWN AN' STOPPED   137 28
    THE TIME WITHOUT CLOCKS   825 23

CLOCK-WORK
    CROSS LIKE CLOCK-WORK THE MINOAN DISTANCE   688 8

CLOD
    OH EARTH YOU SPINNING CLOD OF EARTH   73 1
    I EXPECT THE DODO LOOKED LIKE A CLOD   523 28

CLODS
    OVER THE CLODS OF THE AUTUMN WIND-CHILLED SUNSHINE   357 27
    THINK OF IT IN A GARDEN OF INERT CLODS   358 8

CLOG
    AND PAST LIVES HAMPER ME CLOG AND EMBARRASS   173 28

CLOGGED
    AND COLDNESS CLOGGED THE SEA TILL IT CEASED TO CROON   98 15
    IS HEAVY IS CLOGGED AND HEAVY WITH WASTED ASH   *897 17

CLOMB
    HIS BURDEN ABOVE ME NEVER HAS CLOMB   50 12

CLOSE
    CLOSE AND IT ROLLS ME ENFOLDS ME TOUCHES ME AS IF NEVER+   34 23
    WARM AS A FLAME IN THE CLOSE NIGHT AIR   61 29
    AND WE ARE CRUSHED BETWEEN THE COVERS WE CLOSE OUR EYES+   88 12
    YOU ASK ME DO THE HEALING DAYS CLOSE UP   90 22
    THE HEALING DAYS SHALL CLOSE THE DARK GULF UP   90 29
    IN YOUR CLOSE HOUSEKEEPING ROLE   95 11
    I IN THE FUR OF THE WORLD ALONE BUT THIS HELEN CLOSE BY   98 6
    AND MEMORIES CLUSTERED ME CLOSE AND SLEEP WAS CAJOLED   98 30
    CLOSE YOUR EYES MY LOVE LET ME MAKE YOU BLIND   118 20
    AS 'UD WINCE WHEN THAT TOUCHED 'ER CLOSE AN'   138 31
    I CLOSE YOUR EARS WITH KISSES   154 1
    WITH SHUTTERS OF SOMBRE CLOUD WILL CLOSE   163 14
    THE AIR IS ALL CLOSE AND POISONOUS IT HAS DRUGGED OUR S+   175 12
    LAPPED LIKE A BODY CLOSE UPON A SLEEP   195 27
    I THE MAN WHO ENFOLDS YOU AND HOLDS YOU CLOSE   246 4
    SO CLOSE BREATHING SO STILL   246 21
    AND VALLEYS THAT DRAW CLOSE IN LOVE   261 5
    IF I PASS THEM CLOSE OR ANY MAN   269 25
    CLOSE THE EYES AND GO   287 9
    THEN CLOSE THE WEDGE OF YOUR LITTLE MOUNTAIN FRONT   353 8
    WRAPPED TO THE EYES THE SHEET BOUND CLOSE ON HIS BROWS   403 10
    THE DIVIDERS ARE CLOSE UPON US DOGGING OUR EVERY BREATH   707 3
    WITH GOD WE ARE CLOSE TOGETHER NOW THE MOON'S IN SHADOW   727 5
    AND WE WALKED DARK SO HE HELD HIS ARM CLOSE ROUND ME   732 15

CLOSE

CLOSE FRIEND IN EVERYTHING IS OUR LORD MY BOY   749 23
IN WHOSE CLOSE FOLDS ABOVE YOU NEAR ABOVE   750 11
THAT IS MY SPIRIT HOVERING CLOSE ABOVE   750 13
A NEW THING COMES TO PASS EYES CLOSE   834 2
BUT THE LIMBS OF MAN LONG TO FOLD AND CLOSE UPON THE LI+   834 4
WITH SHUTTERS OF CLOUDED NIGHT WILL CLOSE   857 14
AND NOW HANGS LIKE THE FRAGRANT CLOSE OF THE MEASURE   868 15
YEA I WOULD SHUT MY EYES I WOULD CLOSE MY WINDOWS   875 26
THROUGH THE CLOSE THICKETS TO THE CLEAR OF DEATH   879 14
THE BOOKS THAT YOU HAVE TOUCHED CLEAVE CLOSE TO ME   880 10
AND I LAY CLOSE DOWN   882 22
AND WHEN I SEE THE TREES SWAY CLOSE   883 8
HUDDLIN' CLOSE TOGETHER A CAUSE O' TH' RAIN   *911 2
WARM AS A FLAME IN THE CLOSE NIGHT AIR   *912 8
CLOSE YOUR EYES MY LOVE LET ME MAKE YOU BLIND   *931 30
SINCE DEATH FROM THE MOTHER MOON HAS PARED CLOSE TO THE+   *938 1
THAT STOOD CLOSE TO THE WALL AND THE FRONT'S FADED SILK+   *940 3

CLOSE-CURTAINED

ONE SMALL WAY OF ACCESS ONLY AND THIS CLOSE-CURTAINED F+   283 16

CLOSED

NEVER HAVE I SAID TO MYSELF AS HE CLOSED THE DOOR   47 31
OUR BEACHED VESSEL DARKENED RENCONTRE INHUMAN AND CLOSE+   66 27
AND LITTERED LETTERING OF TREES AND HILLS AND HOUSES CL+   88 6
ITS FIGURED PAGES AND SKY AND EARTH AND ALL BETWEEN ARE+   88 10
HER CHEEKS ARE VERY SMOOTH HER EYES ARE CLOSED   101 9
SHE SPOKE AND I CLOSED MY EYES   124 18
THE CLOSED FLESH OF THE CLOVER   124 30
THE NIGHT YOU CLOSED YOUR EYES FOR EVER AGAINST ME   193 16
HELD A MEETING BEHIND CLOSED DOORS   777 27
BEHIND CLOSED DOORS   778 32
THE FIERCE BLACK EYES ARE CLOSED THEY WILL OPEN NO MORE   859 17
HAVE CLOSED IN LOVE LIKE VERY DEATH FOR STRESS   875 19
THOUGH WE HAVE CLOSED TOGETHER THROUGH THE NIGHTS   875 21
NOW AT LAST THE CLOSED CALYX OPENS FROM OUR TIRED EYES   *916 13
SHE SPOKE AND I CLOSED MY EYES   *935 18
THE CLOSED FLESH OF THE CLOVER   *935 36

CLOSELY

YET CLOSELY BITTEN IN TO ME   117 8

CLOSENESS

TO ME YET STILL BECAUSE OF THE SENSE OF THEIR CLOSENESS+   *903 28

CLOSENESS'

TO ME YET STILL BECAUSE OF THE SENSE OF THEIR CLOSENESS+   *900 16

CLOSER

COME MY LITTLE ONE CLOSER UP AGAINST ME   245 5
BUT HOW LOVELY TO BE YOU CREEP CLOSER IN THAT I AM MORE   245 20
FUSING CLOSER AND CLOSER WITH LOVE   249 7
BUT WATCHING CLOSER   338 6

CLOSES

CLOSES HER ARMS THAT SHOULD FOLD ON ME IN SLEEP   128 30
FROGS WERE SINGING AND OVER THE RIVER CLOSES   217 4
THE STARS IN THEIR SUN-DIMMED CLOSES   242 29
AS THE DARK CLOSES ROUND HIM HE DRAWS NEARER   455 14
THEY GNASH WHEN IT CLOSES AND HATE THE ONE THAT GOT IN +   795 33
SO SHE CLOSES HER EYES BUT THE AIMLESS BREEZE OF THE WO+   *942 1
FROGS WERE SINGING AND OVER THE RIVER CLOSES   *942 15
SO THAT WHEN THE HOUR COMES AND THE LAST DOOR CLOSES BE+   *958 24

CLOSE-SHUT

WHY EVEN NOW YOU SPEAK THROUGH CLOSE-SHUT TEETH   87 5

CLOSE-UP

AND CAUGHT THEM MOANING FROM CLOSE-UP KISSES BLACK-AND-+   444 1

CLOSING

CLOSING UPON YOU IN THE LIGHTNING-FLAMED   87 21
AS SLOWLY THE HOUSE OF DAY IS CLOSING ITS EASTERN SHUTT+   102 28
CLOSING THE ROUND   121 12
CLOSING ITS CRIMSON THROAT MY OWN THROAT IN HER POWER   123 14
AND CLOSING HIS STEEL-TRAP FACE   360 24
CLOSING ITS CRIMSON THROAT MY OWN THROAT IN HER POWER   *934 20

CLOT

ON HIS BROW WHERE THE CURVED WISPS CLOT AND TWINE   60 3
THIS CLOT OF NIGHT   124 16
HOW YOU SAIL LIKE A HERON OR A DULL CLOT OF AIR   332 16
AND CLEAVE IN A HIGH CORNER FOR A SECOND LIKE A CLOT AL+   345 23
AND THERE A CLOT HE SQUATTED AND LOOKED AT ME   345 28
ONLY IN THE BRIGHT DAY I WILL NOT HAVE THIS CLOT IN MY   346 11
AND ROUND AND ROUND AND ROUND MY ROOM A CLOT WITH   346 20
THIS CLOT OF LIGHT   *935 15

CLOTH

WHAT CONJURER'S CLOTH WAS THROWN ACROSS YOU AND RAISED   53 21
OF THE SKY SAGGED DUSTY AS SPIDER CLOTH   98 14
ARE FALLEN AND THEIR MAUVE-RED PETALS ON THE CLOTH   217 28
AS WITH CLOTH SO WITH HOUSES SHIPS SHOES WAGONS OR CUPS   451 10
CLOTH   451 22
ARE FALLEN AND THEIR MAUVE-RED PETALS ON THE CLOTH   *943 11
CLOTH THEY WORE   *949 27
AND IT MADE THEM HAPPY AND THE WOVEN CLOTH OF THEIR HAN+   *949 29
AND AS WITH CLOTH SO WITH ALL THINGS HOUSES SHOES WAGON+   *950 1
AT LAST AND FOR THE SAKE OF CLOTHING HIMSELF IN HIS OWN+   *950 7

CLOTHE

AND THEY CLOTHE THEMSELVES IN WHITE AS A TREE CLOTHES I+   451 8
ME UP CARESS AND CLOTHE WITH FREE   *899 24
THEY ALL DO CLOTHE MY UNGROWING LIFE   *899 31
ME UP CARESS AND CLOTHE WITH FREE   *903 3
THEY ALL DO CLOTHE MY UNGROWING LIFE   *903 10

CLOTHED

SO I AM CLOTHED ALL OVER WITH THE LIGHT   113 5
I HAVE EATEN AND DRUNK AND WARMED AND CLOTHED MY BODY   264 1
CLOTHED VISION CAN NEVER COMMUNICATE   286 29
WHEN I AM CLOTHED I AM A MORAL MAN   607 9
BUT STILL MY NAKEDNESS IS CLOTHED WITH RESPONSIBILITY   607 26
IF WE ARE PROPERLY CLOTHED AND DISCIPLINED IN THE DININ+   608 12
AND CLOTHED THEM WITH LIVING LEAVES   *949 31

CLOTHES

CLOTHES   254 17
NEW HOUSES NEW FURNITURE NEW STREETS NEW CLOTHES NEW   448 14
AND THEY CLOTHE THEMSELVES IN WHITE AS A TREE CLOTHES I+   451 8
IN HIS SUNDAY CLOTHES   552 20
AS WE HAVE CLOTHES   608 10
AND A WOMAN WHO HAS BEEN WASHING CLOTHES IN THE POOL OF+   693 1
AND CHANGE OF CLOTHES   719 5
TO EASE HIMSELF IN HIS CLOTHES IT MAKES   733 22
DOWN THE GLAD STREETS PINCHED WAIFS IN ILL-ASSORTED CLO+   866 5
WHICH CLOTHES OUR NAKEDNESS LIKE GRASS THE PLAINS AND T+   *951 8

CLOTHING

IF I COULD CAST THIS CLOTHING OFF FROM ME   122 17
AT LAST FOR THE SAKE OF CLOTHING HIMSELF IN HIS OWN LEA+   451 21
TO TAKE IT OFF THIS CLOTHING OF A MAN   738 13
BROTHER THE SCENT OF YOUR CLOTHING   758 19
ONLY STARK WITHOUT CLOTHING   825 10
AT LAST AND FOR THE SAKE OF CLOTHING HIMSELF IN HIS OWN+   *950 7

CLOTHS

TO WHERE THE SUNSET HUNG ITS WAN GOLD CLOTHS   205 27

CLOTS

TWO PALE CLOTS SWEPT BY THE LIGHT OF THE CARS   144 28
OF MISTINESS COMPLICATED INTO KNOTS AND CLOTS THAT BARGE   437 32
WHAT IS IT THAT CLOTS ME HOLDS ME TOGETHER OUT OF THESE   870 10

CLOTTED

IN A GREAT SWARM CLOTTED AND SINGLE   205 25
HOW AM I CLOTTED TOGETHER   870 7
WHY SHOULD I GRIEVE THAT MY MOTHER IS NO LONGER CLOTTED   870 12

CLOTTING

CLOTTING TO ONE DEAD MASS IN THE SINKING FIRE   47 5

CLOUD

A CLOUD COMES UP LIKE THE SURGE OF A FOUNTAIN   50 3
GREET THE CLOUD   52 23
OF CLOUD THE RAIN-SKIES YIELD   68 20
TWO STREAMING PEACOCKS GONE IN A CLOUD   70 17
WHITE DUCKS A QUACKING FLOTILLA OF CLOUD   126 13
WITH SHUTTERS OF SOMBRE CLOUD WILL CLOSE   163 14
FROM OUT THE CLOUD OF SLEEP LOOKS ROUND ABOUT   195 13
THE CLOUD SHEAVES   268 17
SHAGGY CLOUD   375 6
AND LOOKS UP INQUIRINGLY INTO THE PILLAR OF CLOUD   375 12
AND THEN YOU SEE THE GOD THAT HE IS IN A CLOUD OF BLACK   383 10
GOD IN BLACK CLOUD WITH CURVING HORNS OF BRONZE   383 16
THE UNSEEN CLOUD   748 28
HE SAT WITHIN THE HOLLOW OF A CLOUD AND SAW THE MEN THA+   790 10
SO LEANING FORWARD ON HIS CLOUD HE SAID TO HIMSELF   790 17
THE REST IS A CLOUD OF THISTLE DOWN   863 7
THOUGH YOU MOVE WITH A QUIET GRACE LIKE A CLOUD   874 23
CLOUD   *905 12
OF CLOUD THE MORN SKIES YIELD   *915 4
WITH GOLDEN CHICKS OF CLOUD AND A SKY OF RUNNING LAUGHT+   *933 15

CLOUDED

GOES CLOUDED HAVING MISUNDERSTOOD   37 19
TO THE ENTABLATURE OF CLOUDED HEAVEN   287 19
WITH SHUTTERS OF CLOUDED NIGHT WILL CLOSE   857 14

CLOUD-LEAVES

AND O BEHIND THE CLOUD-LEAVES LIKE YELLOW AUTUMN   120 7

CLOUDS

THE CLOUDS ARE PUSHING IN GREY RELUCTANCE SLOWLY NORTHW+   57 10
ROUND CLOUDS ROLL IN THE ARMS OF THE WIND   126 7
UNREAL THOUGH THE CLOUDS   133 11
THE CLOUDS GO DOWN THE SKY WITH A WEALTHY EASE   133 16
YEA THOUGH THE VERY CLOUDS HAVE VANTAGE OVER ME   133 22
STORMS AND CUMULUS CLOUDS OF ALL IMAGINABLE BLOSSOM   271 26
ALL STANDING IN CLOUDS OF GLORY   303 6
SEEING RUSTY IRON PUFF WITH CLOUDS OF BLOSSOM   304 6
WHAT THOUGH THE CLOUDS SHOULD SHINE   772 1
WHAT THOUGH THE CLOUDS GO GLANCING DOWN   772 4
YEA THOUGH THE VERY CLOUDS HAVE VANTAGE OVER ME   772 9
AND SCATTERED WITH HER HAIR CLOUDS OF PALE MIMOSA SANDS   863 27
IS A TRACK OF CLOUDS ACROSS THE MOON   882 18

CLOUT

AN' WHITE AN' BLUE IN A RAVEL LIKE A CLOUT   61 12

CLOUTS

HE CLOUTS THE TUFTS OF FLOWERS   244 14

CLOVE

AND BECOMES AT LAST A CLOVE CARNATION LO THAT IS GOD   691 17

CLOVEN

YOU SENT ME A CLOVEN FIRE   108 17
THERE CAME A CLOVEN GLEAM   169 27
THROUGH HIS CROSS-WISE CLOVEN PSYCHE   356 3
ISSUING LIKE A GREAT CLOVEN CANDLE-FLAME   780 29
OH YOU IN THE TENT OF THE CLOVEN FLAME   812 11
AND BE THERE IN THE HOUSE OF THE CLOVEN FLAME   812 27

CLOVER
THERE'S A SCENT OF CLOVER CREPT THROUGH MY HAIR   50 9
I THOUGHT I SAW ON THE CLOVER   124 28
THE CLOSED FLESH OF THE CLOVER   124 30
I THOUGHT I SAW ON THE CLOVER   *935 34
THE CLOSED FLESH OF THE CLOVER   *935 36

CLOWN
SAY YES THA CLOWN   44 21
FLESH FLAMEY AND A LITTLE HEROIC EVEN IN A TUMBLING CLO+ 445 28

CLUB
BUT WHILE FLOWERS CLUB THEIR PETALS AT EVENING   321 22

CLUB-MONEY
AN' CLUB-MONEY I WON'T GROWSE   45 33

CLUCK
ALL ROUND THE YEAR IT IS CLUCK MY BROWN HEN   119 15
CLUCK AND THE RAIN-WET WINGS   119 16
CLUCK MY MARIGOLD BIRD AND AGAIN   119 17
CLUCK FOR YOUR YELLOW DARLINGS   119 18
THE BIRD GAVE A CLUCK THE COW GAVE A COO   761 4
ALL ROUND THE YARD IT IS CLUCK MY BROWN HEN   *932 24
CLUCK AND THE RAIN-WET WINGS   *932 25
CLUCK MY MARIGOLD BIRD AND AGAIN   *932 26
CLUCK TO YOUR YELLOW DARLINGS   *932 27

CLUCKING
AND A HIDDEN VOICE LIKE WATER CLUCKING   427 3

CLUE
FOUR AND ONE MAKES FIVE WHICH IS THE CLUE TO ALL MATHEM+ 356 8
NOR A THUMB-MARK LIKE A CLUE   430 8
WORK IS THE CLUE TO A MAN'S LIFE   520 19

CLUMPS
YOUR SMALL BREASTS CLUMPS OF WHITE   886 6

CLUMSY
I PICKED UP A CLUMSY LOG   351 10
CLUMSY KNEE-LIFTING SALAAM   388 10
THE CLUMSY BEWILDERED RUSSIA   536 20

CLUNG
A RED ROCK SILENT AND SHADOWLESS CLUNG ROUND WITH CLUST+ 75 8
SHE CLUNG TO THE DOOR IN HER HASTE TO ENTER   122 6

CLUSTER
TO FIND THE NEW HOUSES A CLUSTER OF LILIES GLITTERING   72 21
THE TOWN WILL CLUSTER HER HERBAGE THEN   748 3
THERE ARE DEAD THAT CLUSTER IN THE FROZEN NORTH SHUDDER+ 795 21

CLUSTERED
AND CLUSTERED STAR CALLED DOWN TO ME TO-NIGHT   86 15
AND MEMORIES CLUSTERED ME CLOSE AND SLEEP WAS CAJOLED   98 30
FARTHER DOWN THE VALLEY THE CLUSTERED TOMBSTONES RECEDE 102 29
CLUSTERED DEAD AND THIS IS THE DAWN   220 19
THE SOFT CLUSTERED SHOULDER-FEATHERS IN ROSY CONFUSION + 855 23
THE ROSY PERIWINKLES THAT CLUSTERED AND LEANED ACROSS   863 24

CLUSTERING
CLUSTERING UPON ME REACHING UP AS EACH AFTER THE OTHER + *900 7
CLUSTERING UPON ME REACHING UP AS EACH AFTER THE OTHER + *903 19

CLUSTERS
A RED ROCK SILENT AND SHADOWLESS CLUNG ROUND WITH CLUST+ 75 8
ONE ON ANOTHER AND THEN IN CLUSTERS TOGETHER   258 2
HEAVY NODDING CLUSTERS OF CRIMSON RED   855 10
HEAVY HANGING CLUSTERS OF CRIMSON RED   855 18
LIKE A PICTURE BY THAULOW DARK CLUSTERS OF SHOUTING LADS 865 19

CLUTCH
ASLEEP STILL SHAKES IN THE CLUTCH OF A SOB   136 25
BUT WE AS WE START AWAKE CLUTCH AT OUR VISTAS DEMOCRATIC 286 34
BLUNDERING MORE INSANE AND LEAPING IN THROBS TO CLUTCH + 343 20
CLUTCH CLEAVE STAGGER   344 8
AND FORCED TO CLUTCH ON TO POSSESSIONS IN THE HOPE THEY+ 522 15
THEN MUST A SINGLE MAN DIE WITH THEM IN THE CLUTCH OF   632 1
IN THE CLASP AND THE SOFT WILD CLUTCH OF A SHE-WHALE'S + 694 19
A CLUTCH OF ATTACHMENT LIKE PARENTHOOD   *899 33
A CLUTCH OF ATTACHMENT LIKE PARENTHOOD   *903 12

CLUTCHED
I TOUCHED WITH MY HAND I CLUTCHED WITH MY HAND   260 2

CLUTCHES
CLUTCHES IN MID-AIR   447 28
CLUTCHES FOR ME   862 15

CLUTCHING
MY SQUIRREL CLUTCHING IN TO ME   246 19
AND CLUTCHING CLUTCHING FOR ONE SECOND'S PAUSE   345 8
CLUTCHING TASTING DROPPING   861 27

CLUTTERED
YET BLIND WITH FRENZY WITH CLUTTERED FEAR   343 15

CNOSSOS
IT IS SHIPS OF CNOSSOS COMING OUT OF THE MORNING END OF+ 687 5
SLIM NAKED MEN FROM CNOSSOS SMILING THE ARCHAIC SMILE 688 13

COAGULATING
COAGULATING AND GOING BLACK IN MY VEINS   301 25

COAL
BE ALL YOURSELF ONE BONNY BURNING COAL   151 14
LIKE FIRE-TONGS A LIVE COAL   427 17
BUT THE COAL COAL COAL   545 13
OR THE MOST HIGH DURING THE COAL AGE CUDGELLING HIS MIG+ 690 26
BE ALL YOURSELF ONE BONNY BURNING COAL   873 24

COALS
WHERE ASH ON THE DYING COALS GROWS SWIFTLY LIKE HEAVY   47 6
I AM INCLINED TO HEAP THY COALS OF FIRE ON MY OWN   760 15
LOOKED WHERE THE RED FRUIT HUNG LIKE COALS OF FIRE   864 8

COARSE
TO A WOMAN THAT COARSE   77 32
SAID GROSS COARSE HIDEOUS AND I LIKE A SILLY   579 18
TELL ME IS THE GENTIAN SAVAGE AT THE TOP OF ITS COARSE + 684 2
TO A WOMAN THAT COARSE   *919 20

COAST
ALONG THE COAST TO HEAR THE HUSH   747 3
WAY DOWN THE COAST THEN COMES UP FLUSH   747 6
TO HEAR THE LONG WAVES STRIKE THE COAST   747 11
AND OIL MUCH OIL FROM THE COAST   793 19
THEIR DEBRIS IS FLOTSAM AND FLUNG ON THE COAST   823 8

COAT
ON THE BREAST OF MY COAT AND ONE BY ONE   107 3
THIS FIERY COAT   238 12
WOULDN'T I STICK THE SALVIA IN MY COAT   315 12
LIKE A GENTLEMAN IN A LONG-SKIRTED COAT   354 20
WHEN I PUT ON MY COAT MY COAT HAS POCKETS   607 11
WITH YOUR TAILORED CUT-AWAY COAT   835 18
HIS COAT AND HIS ARMS AND HIS LABOURING HEART ARE STRAN+ 871 25

COATS
ALAS THE SUNDAY COATS OF SICILIAN BOLSHEVISTS   313 34

COBBLE-STONES
OF WALKING OVER THE FACES OF MEN LIKE COBBLE-STONES   175 8

COBRA
NO COBRA NOR HYAENA NOR SCORPION NOR HIDEOUS WHITE ANT 701 13

COCAINE
MILD FORMS OF COCAINE THEY'RE NOT LIFE EXACTLY   532 13

COCK
AND THE FIGHTING COCK   457 26
THE FIGHTING COCK THE FIGHTING COCK   457 28
THERE'S NOT A COCK BIRD AMONG 'EM   550 15
BECAUSE FLAT-FOOT IS THE FAVOURITE OF THE WHITE LEGHORN+ 761 17
THE COCK ROSE AND CREW OVER THE WATERS   802 11

COCK-CRESTED
COCK-CRESTED CROWING YOUR ORANGE SCARLET LIKE A TOCSIN 314 28

COCK-EAGLE
SO HE CLEARS HIS THROAT THE YOUNG COCK-EAGLE   413 26
NEITHER CAN A YOUNG COCK-EAGLE SIT SIMPERING   413 30

COCKED
AND HATS COCKED UP AND DOWN   312 17
STILL SHE WATCHES WITH ETERNAL COCKED WISTFULNESS   394 5

COCKING
COCKING YOUR EYES AT ME AS YOU COME ALONGSIDE TO SEE IF 397 23

COCKLES
WHO WARMED THE COCKLES OF MY HEART   507 9
I'D REJOICE OVER THE WOMAN AND THE WARMED COCKLES OF MY 507 10

COCKLESHELLS
AND LET ME COME PAST THE SILVER BELLS OF YOUR FLOWERS A+ 696 2

COCKS
A SQUIRREL COCKS HIS HEAD ON THE FENCE AND WONDERS   223 21
THESE COCKS THAT CAN'T CROW   792 24

COCK'S-FOOT
COCK'S-FOOT FOX-TAIL FESCUE AND TOTTERING-GRASS   587 20

COCKY
THE INWARD COCKY ASSERTIVENESS OF THE SPANIARD SEEMS TO+ 618 9

COCOA-NUT
THE TROPICAL NIGHT OF BLAZING COCOA-NUT   387 26
IN THE FUME OF COCOA-NUT OIL IN THE SWEATING TROPICAL N+ 387 36
COCOA-NUT CRESSETS   388 28

CODE
DO YOU TAKE IN MESSAGES IN SOME STRANGE CODE   301 5

COD'S
THAT LITTLE COD'S THE HOLY WORST   493 23

COFFEE
WAIT WAIT DON'T BRING THE COFFEE YET NOR THE PAIN GRILLE 687 21
COFFEE FROM THE BUSHES IN THE HOT LANDS EVEN THE JUICY + 793 22

COFFEE-PLANT
WHEN THE CUCKOO THE COW AND THE COFFEE-PLANT CHIPPED THE 760 22
AND THE COFFEE-PLANT STARTED COFFING THREE VERY DISTINC+ 760 27

COFFIN
ASIDE O' T' GRAVE AN' TH' COFFIN SET   60 12
AN' OUR TED'S COFFIN SET ON TH' GROUND   60 21
IS PUT BY ITS PARENTS INTO ITS COFFIN   521 27
SHUT-UP COFFIN OF A THING WITH A SOLDIER WEARY   733 6

COFFIN
    NAY I SAW NOWT BUT TH' COFFIN AN' TH' YELLER CLAY AN' '+   *909 31
    ASIDE O' TH' GRAVE WHILE TH' COFFIN WOR LYIN' YET   *910 27

COFFING
    AND THE COFFEE-PLANT STARTED COFFING THREE VERY DISTINC+   760 27

COFFIN-LIFE
    AND THE COFFIN-LIFE SLIT WHERE THE INDIAN'S EYES ARE   403 30

COFFIN-LIKE
    AND HYGIENIC BABIES IN HUGE HULKS OF COFFIN-LIKE PERAMB+   522 5

COFFIN-LINING
    AND I AM WRAPPED IN THE LEAD OF A COFFIN-LINING THE LIV+   630 7

COFFINS
    COFFINS   629 19
    IN THE HEARSE OF NIGHT YOU SEE THEIR TARNISHED COFFINS   703 3

COGGED
    LEAVE THE OLD ONES FIXED TO THEIR UGLY COGGED SELF-WILL   662 23

COGITO ERGO SUM
    COGITO ERGO SUM   474 18

COGNISANCE
    WITHOUT COGNISANCE OR COMMUNION   715 11

COG-WHEEL
    ONLY THEY ARE MADE TO UTTER THESE COG-WHEEL SOUNDS   657 15
    IN A COG-WHEEL CLATTER OF VIOLATION   839 7

COIFFING
    COIFFING UP YOUR AUBURN HAIR   178 8

COILED
    BUSHED IN AN UNCOUTH ARDOUR COILED AT CORE   160 13
    ALONG IN THE COILED CONVULSIVE THROES   164 6
    UNFOLDING ALL HER COILED AND LOVELY SELF   317 23
    AND I AM NOT WITH YOU TILL MY SERPENT HAS COILED HIS CI+   801 28
    EMOTIONS WHICH WOULD COME UP LIKE FLOWERS WERE THEY NOT+   833 27

COILING
    THAT HUDDLES IN GREY HEAPS COILING AND HOLDING BACK   164 18
    AND COILING IT ROUND THE WISE BROWS OF A MAID   178 21

COILS
    ENTANGLED IN THE LAOCOON COILS OF OUR CONCEIT   674 10
    COILS AND RECOILS SENSITIVE TO LIFE AND CONSCIOUS OF TR+   *952 8

COIN
    SEE THE WOMAN'S TRINKLING FINGERS TEND HIM A COIN   36 6
    MY LOVE THAT SPINNING COIN LAID STILL   59 21
    THE OTHER HALF OF THE BROKEN COIN OF TROTH   114 19
    SHINE LIKE FLAT COIN WHICH JOVE IN THANKS   162 3
    AS IF IT WERE COIN WITH A FIXED VALUE   662 8
    AH COIN ME SPEECH OF YOUR HEART'S GOLD FURNACE HEAT   872 27

COINCIDES
    THE WHICH SINCE IT COINCIDES WITH MY DAY   815 19

COITION
    AM I DOOMED IN A LONG COITION OF WORDS TO MATE YOU   119 4
    TILL SUDDENLY IN THE SPASM OF COITION TUPPING LIKE A JE+   365 7
    JERK OF COITION AND AT ONCE   365 18
    STRANGE FAINT COITION YELL   366 25
    COITION   481 25
    IN THE SHEER COITION OF THE LIFE-FLOW STARK AND UNLYING   482 14

COLD
    AH STERN COLD MAN   55 1
    COLD INSENSATE   56 30
    COLD METAL-COLD   57 6
    O' WARMTH AS 'E GOT DOWN THEER TH' REST WOR STONE COLD   61 18
    BUT SHE'S WAITING I KNOW IMPATIENT AND COLD HALF   85 11
    YOUR PALLOR INTO RADIANCE FLUSH YOUR COLD   86 12
    THE HARSH COLD WIND OF MY WORDS DROVE ON AND STILL   94 13
    FEELING THE RAW COLD DUN ME AND ALL THE TIME   98 18
    AND ALL DAY LONG THAT RAW AND ANCIENT COLD   98 21
    COLD THAT HAD SUNK TO MY SOUL AND THERE KEPT HOLD   98 25
    BUT STILL TO ME ALL EVENING LONG YOU WERE COLD   98 26
    CLEAN OF THE COLD AND THE MUST WITH MY HAND ON THE LATCH   99 9
    WITH COLD LIKE THE SHELL OF THE MOON AND STRANGE IT SEE+   99 14
    AND UNCANNY COLD   101 6
    BUT THAT YOU HOLD ME STILL SO KINDLY COLD   122 21
    SINCE ALL THE SKY HAS WITHERED AND GONE COLD   135 16
    THE CLEAR COLD SKY COLDLY BETHINKS ITSELF   142 13
    IS SOFT THOUGH IT IS COLD DO NOT SEEM   158 20
    A COLD HAND I PEEP BETWEEN THE FINGERS   162 18
    THROUGH THE LOW WEST WINDOW A COLD LIGHT FLOWS   162 18
    I WILL TRAIL MY HANDS AGAIN THROUGH THE DRENCHED COLD L+   180 34
    YOU ARE SINGLE YOU ARE FRUITLESS PHOSPHORESCENT COLD AND   197 12
    COME YOU ARE COLD THE NIGHT HAS FRIGHTENED YOU   212 1
    KISS ME HOW COLD YOU ARE YOUR LITTLE BREASTS   212 6
    AND ALL THE SCENT IS SHED AWAY BY THE COLD   224 27
    AND I AS I STAND IN THE COLD AVERTED FLOWERS   226 9
    SO COLD SO COLD AND CLEAN   229 25
    FLOWERS THAT COME FIRST FROM THE DARKNESS AND FEEL COLD+   270 9
    WAS MOIST AND COLD THE SUN IN HIM DARTED UNEASY HELD DO+   348 8
    COLD VOICELESS AGE-AFTER-AGE BEHIND HIM SERPENTS' LONG   360 15
    AND IS GOING COLD   369 13
    IS YOUR CONTINENT COLD FROM THE ICE-AGE STILL THAT THE +   374 21
    AND IF YOU LOOK AT HER SHE LOOKS BACK WITH A COLD SARDO+   386 4
    SARDONIC SARDONYX ROCK OF COLD FIRE   386 6
    BUT A DIFFERENT SORT A COLD REBELLIOUS JEERING DEVIL   390 4
    UNDER THE COLD BLACK WAVE   428 15
    AND THE DRIP OF HIS COLD WEBBED FEET MUD-BLACK   438 11

COLD
    AND MAKES US COLD MAKES US LIFELESS   448 17
    FROM THE COLD COPULATION OF THE WILL   469 20
    IT'S A COLD EGG IT ISN'T LOVE ANY MORE   472 23
    WE SHALL SHIVER WITH COLD AND FRIGHT   482 19
    HAS HE NO MONEY THEN LET HIM EAT DIRT AND GO COLD   486 21
    BETWEEN THE DEVIL AND THE DEEP COLD SEA   490 24
    AND GIVING YOU A COLD IN YOUR INSIDE   506 24
    FROM THE HEART AND LEAVING STRANGE COLD STRETCHES OF SA+   509 4
    SLOW CREEPING COLD ONES   511 12
    AND THE SLOW COLD FLAMES   511 15
    AND WANT TO BE COLD AND DEVILISH HARD   537 17
    THAN TO SHELTER ANYBODY FROM THE COLD BLAST   540 30
    BUT THE CABBAGES OF ENGLAND LEAVE ME COLD   569 2
    OH THE CABBAGES OF ENGLAND LEAVE ME COLD   569 3
    YET THE CABBAGES OF ENGLAND LEAVE ME COLD   569 13
    IN COLD BLUE AND COLD LIKE THE FLAME IN A MINER'S LAMP   619 5
    IN COLD BLOOD I CANNOT FEEL GODDESSES IN THE SUMMER EVE+   655 18
    BUT WHAT RIGHT HAS MY BLOOD TO BE COLD   655 20
    IF I CUT MY FINGER MY BLOOD IS HOT NOT COLD   655 22
    AND EVEN IN COLD BLOOD I KNOW THIS   655 23
    AND WHO NOW DRAWS SLOWLY AWAY COLD THE WISTFUL GODDESS +   676 18
    CAME INTO EXISTENCE AS COLD SHADOW   682 7
    HE IS PITCH DARK AND COLD   682 11
    THEY SAY THE SEA IS COLD BUT THE SEA CONTAINS   694 1
    COLD SUPERIORITY NOR SILLY   709 31
    FINDS ITSELF SHRINKING WINCING FROM THE COLD   717 8
    SEEKING THEIR OLD HAUNTS WITH COLD GHOSTLY RAGE   722 27
    IT WAS COLD AND HE PUT HIS CLOAK RIGHT ROUND ME   732 14
    SAVE THE COLD GHOSTS THAT HOMELESS FLOCK ABOUT   736 8
    ONLY COLD INSTEAD OF QUICK   784 31
    THE COLD AND THE HOT   788 4
    IS LASHING HIS TAIL IN HIS SLEEP THE WINDS HOWL THE COL+   795 14
    THE SPIRITS OF THE COLD DEAD WHISTLE IN THE EARS OF THE+   795 15
    HE IS BREATHING COLD CORRUPTION UPON YOU YOU SHALL BLEE+   796 32
    TO WITHDRAW HIS WARMTH FROM YOUR FEET SO YOUR FEET TURN+   797 3
    FOLK-FLOWERS HAVE FADED MEN HAVE GROWN COLD   814 16
    FROM THE LOW WEST WINDOWS THE COLD LIGHT FLOWS   857 10
    COLD ON MY CHEEK   861 6
    OF THEIR DANCING BLOOD LADS SUCKING THE COLD MOISTURE F+   865 29
    FOR ME WHO AM COLD AS A CHRISTMAS ROSE   877 34
    MIGHT FOLLOW WARM AND GLAD WHO SIT HERE COLD   879 15
    CLEAVES FROZEN TO THE WALLS OF MY COLD BREAST   879 20
    THE HARSH COLD WRATH OF MY WORDS DROVE ON AND STILL   *897 1
    AND PALE HOT SKIES HAVE DARKENED AND GONE COLD   *939 15
    AND IN THE DARK I FEEL HIS COLD WEBBED FEET MUD BLACK   *947 19
    AND THE ROCK GOES DOWN DOWN DEEPER FROM COLD INTO HEAT *951 20
    COLD COLD   *955 20

COLD-BLOODED
    SO MUCH DENSER THAN COLD-BLOODED FROGS   393 3
    QUITE COLD-BLOODED INTELLECTUAL MURDER WITH A SUFFICIENT 532 21

COLDER
    COLDER   754 6

COLDLY
    AH BUT I AM ILL AND IT IS STILL RAINING COLDLY RAINING   112 29
    THE CLEAR COLD SKY COLDLY BETHINKS ITSELF   142 13
    TERRIBLE AND STRANGE THE GOD LIES ON THE BED WISTFUL CO+ 676 9

COLDNESS
    AND COLDNESS CLOGGED THE SEA TILL IT CEASED TO CROON   98 15
    OF FIERY COLDNESS TO BE GONE IN A LOST SOUL'S BLISS   130 23

COLLAPSE
    THEY WOULD THEMSELVES AT ONCE COLLAPSE INTO NULLITY   527 22
    UNTIL THEY COLLAPSE INTO EGOISM THE MECHANICAL SELF-CEN+ 649 4

COLLAR
    THERE'S 'IS COLLAR ROUND TH' CANDLESTICK   81 13
    WHERE THE MEADOW-LARK WEARS HIS COLLAR OF SUBMISSION   768 21
    COME ON LET'S TAKE OFF YOUR COLLAR AND DON'T REPROACH ME 859 30
    BUT SHE PUT HER FINGERS ON MY NECK UNDER MY COLLAR   882 30
    THAT'S HIS COLLAR ROUND THE CANDLE-STICK   *923 13

COLLECTING
    COLLECTING FORESKINS   541 21

COLLECTIVE
    MONEY IS OUR MADNESS OUR VAST COLLECTIVE MADNESS   486 7
    IT IS THE COLLECTIVE MONEY-MADNESS OF MANKIND   486 19
    THEY WERE JUST A BLOODY COLLECTIVE FRAUD   556 7
    AND EVEN OUR COLLECTIVE SANITY   839 11
    OF COLLECTIVE INSANITY   839 14

COLLEGE
    GOES TREMBLING PAST ME UP THE COLLEGE WALL   35 27
    WHERE I WENT TO SCHOOL AND COLLEGE   488 8
    IN NOTTINGHAM WHERE I WENT TO SCHOOL AND COLLEGE   *950 12

COLLEYFOGLIN'
    THEN WHAT ART COLLEYFOGLIN' FOR   82 2
    THEN WHAT ART COLLEYFOGLIN' FOR   *924 6

COLLIER
    YOUNG COLLIER WHO HAS LONG SINCE DRUNK HIMSELF TO   366 18
    AND A COLLIER WAS HE   490 10

COLLIERS
    ALL THE LITTLE BOYS WHOSE FATHERS WERE COLLIERS OR FARM+ 774 1

COLLISION
    TRAFFIC WILL TANGLE UP IN A LONG DRAWN-OUT CRASH OF COL+ 624 27

COLONEL
  OH COLONEL YOU FROM EMBABA   754 21

COLORATION
  COLORATION   523 19

COLOSSAL
  COLOSSAL IN NEARNESS A BLUE POLICE SITS STILL ON HIS HO+   66 9

COLOUR
  YOU WHO STEEP FROM OUT THE DAYS THEIR COLOUR   197 26
  ROSE-LEAVES THAT WHIRL IN COLOUR ROUND A CORE   218 15
  BEFORE PETALS SPREAD BEFORE COLOUR MADE ITS DISTURBANCE   285 31
  BUT BLOOD IS RED AND BLOOD IS LIFE RED WAS THE COLOUR O+   303 21
  LITTLE HELLS OF COLOUR CAVES OF DARKNESS   308 14
  YOUR WATTLES ARE THE COLOUR OF STEEL-SLAG WHICH HAS BEE+   369 12
  CATCH THE SCENT AND THE COLOUR OF THE COMING DREAM   *909 27

COLOUR-BLIND
  NOT LIKE GREY DANTE COLOUR-BLIND   711 19

COLOURED
  AND A GLINT OF COLOURED IRIS BRINGS   46 10
  THE WORLD IS A PAINTED MEMORY WHERE COLOURED SHAPES   173 17
  FLOWERS ARE JUST A MOTION A SWIFT MOTION A COLOURED   476 18
  AND THE GHOSTLY CREAMY COLOURED LITTLE TREES OF LEAVES   646 23
  SO THEY BLOOMED OUT AND FILLED THEMSELVES WITH COLOURED+   831 3
  FROM THE TULIPS COLOURED WITH CHALK AND THE DULL GRASS'+   867 4
  UNDER THE COLOURED FADING-OFF OF THE SKY   884 32
  THROUGH THE COLOURED IRIDESCENCE THAT SWIMS IN THE WARM   *906 7
  MY WORLD IS A PAINTED FRESCO WHERE COLOURED SHAPES   *906 11
  MY WORLD IS A PAINTED FRESCO WHERE COLOURED SHAPES   *908 5

COLOURLESS
  AND THE BOYS AND THE ROOM IN A COLOURLESS GLOOM   51 6
  AND THE BOYS AND THE ROOM IN A COLOURLESS GLOOM   *898 18
  AND THE BOYS AND THE ROOM IN A COLOURLESS GLOOM   *902 2

COLOUR-RIPPLES
  PLAYS ROUND HIM AS COLOUR-RIPPLES PLAYED   868 11

COLOURS
  MANY VIVID SMALL STATES LIKE A KALEIDOSCOPE ALL COLOURS   611 19
  ALL OF THE COLOURS   819 26
  PLAYING WITH THE SHADOW COLOURS AND THE WAVING REFLECTE+   867 20

COLTSFOOT
  THE COLTSFOOT FLOWERS ALONG THE RAILWAY BANKS   162 2

COLT'S-FOOT
  COME AND CAJOLE THE GAWKY COLT'S-FOOT FLOWERS   273 4

COLUMBINE
  AS A COLUMBINE FLOWER HAS OR EVEN A STARLING WALKING AN+   621 16

COLUMBUS
  CORTES PISARRO COLUMBUS CABOT THEY ARE NOTHING   259 23

COLUMN
  HE STANDS THE COLUMN OF FIRE BY NIGHT   39 22
  TRAVELLER COLUMN OF FIRE   40 5
  THE PILLAR OF SALT THE WHIRLING HORRIBLE COLUMN OF SALT+   207 28
  A COLUMN OF BLOOD   563 4
  AND THE LARCH THAT IS ONLY A COLUMN IT GOES UP TOO TALL+   647 1
  A CALLING COLUMN OF BLOOD   714 9

COLUMNS
  LIKE SLITS IN AN AUTOMATIC-MACHINE YOU COLUMNS OF GIVE-+   288 25
  COLUMNS DARK AND SOFT   301 27

COMB
  WHICH THEY COULD COMB BY THE HOUR IN LUXURIOUS QUIET   537 27
  ARE A POPPY-SHOW PEEP WHILE YOU COMB   886 2

COMBAT
  WE TRAIL BEHIND US AN ENDLESS TRADITION OF COMBAT   519 11
  IMBECILE STRUGGLE OF COMBAT   519 16
  WE ARE FED UP WITH COMBAT   519 18
  TO GET A LIVING IN THE DASTARDLY MEAN COMBAT   519 28
  IS LIFE STRIFE IS IT THE LONG COMBAT   606 13
  YET I AM NOT INTERESTED IN FIGHT IN STRIFE IN COMBAT   606 16

COMBATING
  AND WE FEEL WE'VE GOT TO KEEP IT UP KEEP ON COMBATING   519 13

COMBATIVE
  WE FEEL THAT IF THE WHOLE COMBATIVE COMPETITIVE SYSTEM   519 19

COMBING
  IS COMBING HER DARK HAIR   787 13

COME-BACK
  AND THEY FEAR THE COME-BACK   626 3

COMELY
  YET ARE SHAPELY AND COMELY TO SEE   101 22
  BUT ALSO THE COMELY   562 30

COMER
  I AM THE FIRST COMER   259 22
  I AM THE FIRST COMER   259 25
  AND I LIKE A SECOND COMER WAITING   349 20
  AND THEN TURN TAIL TO THE NEXT COMER FOR A NEW DOLLOP   396 23

COMET
  SINKS AND IS GONE LIKE A COMET CURVING INTO THE INVISIB+   476 11

COMETH
  WHENCE COMETH THIS THAT THOU MUST GUARD FROM THEFT   69 25
  WHENCE COMETH WHITHER GOETH STILL THE SAME   69 26

COMETS
  LIKE COMETS AND THEY COME INTO OUR KEN   476 13

COMFORT
  NO ONE TO COMFORT AND REFUSING ANY COMFORTER   197 9
  POURING COMFORT AND CONDOLING   457 23
  SPLENDIDLY AND IT IS A COMFORT ISN'T IT   546 21
  COMFORT AND CHEER SURE THAT IT WILL TELL HER   583 16
  SHE SAID TO ME STAY THREE HOURS TO COMFORT ME SUCH IS A+   749 19
  LORD CHERISH AND COMFORT   751 9
  OF LIVING MY LIFE WERE DOUBLED I STILL HAVE THIS TO COM+   *900 3
  OF LIVING MY LIFE WERE DOUBLED I STILL HAVE THIS TO COM+   *903 16

COMFORTABLE
  AND A COMFORTABLE FEELING AT NIGHT   459 15

COMFORTED
  ON THE COMFORTED POOL LIKE BLOOM   56 18
  SHE WEEPS AND CANNOT BE COMFORTED   767 8
  ME COMFORTED TO FEEL THE WARMTH THAT CREEPS   *900 23
  ME COMFORTED TO FEEL THE WARMTH THAT CREEPS   *903 35

COMFORTER
  NO ONE TO COMFORT AND REFUSING ANY COMFORTER   197 9

COMFORTLESS
  THIS IS COMFORTLESS AND UNLOVELY WITH CUSHIONS AND THOS+   856 9

COMFORTS
  THEN COMFORTS IT THE CREEPING TENDERNESS   *900 26
  THEN COMFORTS IT THE CREEPING TENDERNESS   *904 2

COMIN'
  OH AY HE'LL BE COMIN' TO TELL THEE HIS-SEN   *918 17

COMMAND
  UNDER THE GREAT COMMAND KNOW THYSELF AND THAT THOU ART +   674 8
  THE GREAT COMMAND WILL NEVER BE OBSOLETE   832 20

COMMANDED
  WHEN JESUS COMMANDED US TO LOVE OUR NEIGHBOUR   654 6

COMMANDING
  OVERWEENING MEN FULL OF POWER OF LIFE COMMANDING A   414 19
  OUT OF THE DISTANCE NEARER COMMANDING MY DREAMY WORLD   *908 15

COMMANDS
  THE HOURS HAVE CEASED TO FALL AND A STAR COMMANDS   167 17
  ODYSSEUS CALLS THE COMMANDS AS HE STEERS PAST THOSE FOA+   687 20
  IN BATTLE OF HEATED WORDS HARDLY STILLED BY MY REITERAT+   865 32
  THE HOURS HAVE CEASED TO FALL AND A STAR COMMANDS   *896 22

COMMAS
  LET'S HAVE NO FULL STOPS LET'S JUST MANAGE WITH COMMAS   550 28

COMMERCE
  AND RIGID SUPPRESSION OF ALL BAWDY WHORING OR OTHER SUC+   845 13

COMMINGLE
  WHERE THE BREATH AND THE FOUNTAINS COMMINGLE   811 4

COMMINGLED
  COMMINGLED WINES   97 3

COMMINGLES
  OF DEATH COMMINGLES IN GOD'S MIGHTY GLOOM   *938 16

COMMISSION
  THIS LAST COMMISSION   198 26

COMMIT
  HOW CAN THEY COMMIT THE INDECENCY OF BEGETTING CHILDREN   521 22

COMMITTED
  WITHIN ITS QUICK COMMITTED TO HOLD AND WAIT   161 4

COMMON
  THE COMMON FLAUNTS BRAVELY BUT BELOW FROM THE RUSHES   33 10
  SETS QUIVERING WITH WISDOM THE COMMON THINGS   46 19
  IN THE COMMON PRISON-LIKE DRESS   109 4
  MINE IS A COMMON DEVIL'S   234 15
  BE COMMON STUFF   234 28
  THEY SAY CAN'T WE HAVE A LOAF OF COMMON BREAD   442 17
  WITHOUT A BIT OF COMMON TRUST IN ONE ANOTHER WE CAN'T   522 19
  IS RATHER COMMON SHE'S NOT   571 20
  ABOVE THE COMMON RUN   626 18
  YOU MAY SMELL THE BREATH OF THE GODS IN THE COMMON ROSES 655 7
  GIRDLING WITH JEWELS THE MEANNESS OF COMMON THINGS   855 2
  THE COMMON FLAUNTS BRAVELY BUT BELOW FROM THE RUSHES   *891 11
  WAITING WAITING TILL AT LAST THE ANCIENT BOATMAN WITH T+ *958 11

COMMONNESS
  SANS ANY DISTINCTION AT ALL EXCEPT LOUTISH COMMONNESS   313 3

COMMONPLACE
  I THOUGHT IT WAS A COMMONPLACE   578 24

COMMON-SENSE
    IN LANGUAGE OF COMMON-SENSE   488 26

COMMOTION
    COMMOTION   698 12

COMMUNE
    STAND A WAY OFF AND IF YOU LIKE COMMUNE   158 22

COMMUNES
    FOR THE GOLDEN MOON COMMUNES   883 24

COMMUNICATE
    CLOTHED VISION CAN NEVER COMMUNICATE   286 29

COMMUNICATING
    AND ALL IN NAKED COMMUNION COMMUNICATING AS NOW OUR   286 28

COMMUNICATION
    YOUR EYES TAKE ALL OF ME IN AS A COMMUNICATION   210 12
    THAT STRANGE ESSENTIAL COMMUNICATION OF LIFE   481 7

COMMUNING
    IN THE DISTANCE LIKE HOAR-FROST LIKE SILVERY GHOSTS COM+   306 26
    THE KISSING AND COMMUNING CANNOT CEASE   710 7

COMMUNION
    ANY COMMUNION WHATEVER BUT THEY BIND THEMSELVES ON TO T+   92 18
    COMMUNION OFFERING A BETTER THING   104 3
    AND ALL IN NAKED COMMUNION COMMUNICATING AS NOW OUR   286 28
    COMMUNION WITH THE GODHEAD THEY USED TO SAY IN THE   481 17
    TOWARDS OTHER WOMEN IN COMMUNION   619 3
    ENTERING INTO THE OTHER COMMUNION   711 6
    AND THE CONFLICT IS A COMMUNION   714 24
    AND THAT IS PASSION AND COMMUNION   715 7
    WITHOUT COGNISANCE OR COMMUNION   715 11

COMMUNISM
    WHAT WE WANT IS SOME SORT OF COMMUNISM   483 25
    COMMUNISM   829 9

COMMUNISTIC
    YOU'D BETTER OMIT THAT TOO COMMUNISTIC   669 26

COMMUNISTS
    COMMUNISTS   313 7

COMPACT
    I WHO AM SUBSTANCE OF SHADOW I ALL COMPACT   133 6
    NO GLITTERING COMPACT DROPS OF DAWN   278 28

COMPANIES
    ADMITTED THEY SWARM IN COMPANIES   337 14

COMPANION
    DOES HE LOOK FOR A COMPANION   357 29

COMPANIONS
    STRANGEST OF ALL STRANGE COMPANIONS   281 18
    COMPANIONS TO A MAN   539 24
    THOUGH THEY CLING FORGOTTEN THE MOST PART NOT COMPANION+   *900 14
    THOUGH THEY CLING FORGOTTEN THE MOST PART NOT COMPANIONS   *903 26

COMPANIONSHIP
    AND DIM HOPES CROWDED ME WARM WITH COMPANIONSHIP   98 29
    ELDERLY DISCONTENTED WOMEN ASK FOR INTIMATE COMPANIONSH+   502 1

COMPANY
    UNLESS THE LITTLE STAR THAT KEEPS HER COMPANY   54 14
    COMPANY   330 4
    AS IF FOR OUR COMPANY   455 15
    LIABILITY COMPANY   550 4
    LIKE A LIMITED LIABILITY COMPANY   550 5

COMPARABLE
    AND HAS SOMETHING COMPARABLE TO THAT WHICH   515 21

COMPARATIVELY
    BUT THE FEATHERS WERE COMPARATIVELY A MERE FLEA-BITE   413 17

COMPARE
    BEYOND COMPARE   251 27
    TELL ME TELL ME IS THERE IN YOU A BEAUTY TO COMPARE   684 5
    AND THE SOUL OF THE WIND AND MY BLOOD COMPARE   *892 4

COMPARED
    COMPARED TO THE FLOOD OF BLACK HEAT THAT ROLLS UPWARDS   302 5

COMPASSES
    ON TWO WINGS LIKE A PAIR OF COMPASSES   329 7

COMPASSION
    HE IS NOT A PALE MAN FILLED WITH LOVE AND COMPASSION AN+   840 13
    LOVE NOR COMPASSION NOR PITY NOR DEARNESS NOR PAIN MAKE+   840 14

COMPEL
    BUT WHO COULD COMPEL HER IF SHE CHOSE ME AGAINST THEM   213 22
    FOR A RHYTHM TO COMPEL ME BACK FOR PEACE   747 23
    SUBMIT TO IT AND LET YOUR AMERICAN NOBLESSE COMPEL YOU   779 30

COMPELLED
    BUT THE AUDIENCE COMPELLED TO WONDER   445 24
    COMPELLED TO ADMIRE THE BRIGHT RHYTHMS OF MOVING BODIES   445 25
    COMPELLED TO SEE THE DELICATE SKILL OF FLICKERING HUMAN   445 26

COMPELLING
    THE HALLS OF MY MIND COMPELLING MY LIFE TO CONFORM   173 20
    THE HALLS OF MY LIFE COMPELLING MY SOUL TO CONFORM   *908 8

COMPELS
    THE HALLS OF MY LIFE AND COMPELS MY SOUL TO CONFORM   *906 14

COMPENSATE
    LIFE STILL MORE LIFE RUSHES INTO US TO COMPENSATE TO BE   449 7

COMPENSATION
    AN' THERE'S COMPENSATION SIN' IT'S ACCIDENT   45 32
    COMPENSATION   842 3

COMPETE
    WHY SHOULD WE COMPETE WITH ONE ANOTHER   520 22

COMPETENT
    AND CONTROLLED BY MEN OF SCIENCE COMPETENT   780 7

COMPETITION
    PLAYING AMONG THE ELEMENTS NEATLY BEYOND COMPETITION   445 33
    WE CALL FREE COMPETITION AND INDIVIDUAL ENTERPRISE AND   519 29
    THE WAGES OF WANT MORE CASH IS VICIOUS COMPETITION   521 3
    THE WAGES OF VICIOUS COMPETITION IS THE WORLD WE LIVE IN   521 4

COMPETITIVE
    WE FEEL THAT IF THE WHOLE COMBATIVE COMPETITIVE SYSTEM   519 19
    AND UNDER A COMPETITIVE SYSTEM THAT IS IMPOSSIBLE REALLY   522 25

COMPLAIN
    THEN LEAVES THEE AND THOU CANST NOT BUT COMPLAIN   69 29
    COMPLAIN OF WHAT THE DAY HAS HAD THEM DO   195 7
    NO ONE EVER HEARD YOU COMPLAIN   352 24
    YOU WHO COMPLAIN YOU KNOW NO JOY IN YOUR LIVES   484 13
    I NEVER KNOW WHAT PEOPLE MEAN WHEN THEY COMPLAIN OF   610 1
    PEOPLE WHO COMPLAIN OF LONELINESS MUST HAVE LOST SOMETH+   610 8
    WHEN I HEAR SOMEBODY COMPLAIN OF BEING LONELY   646 1
    LISTEN FOR I WILL COMPLAIN   758 7

COMPLAINED
    THAT THE INDIANS COMPLAINED OF BEING POOR   778 18

COMPLAINING
    BELOW ME COMPLAINING THAT NEVER NEVER YET   860 21

COMPLAINT
    DO TREMBLE UNDER MY COMPLAINT   680 13
    BEHOLD THEM HOMELESS AND HOUSELESS WITHOUT COMPLAINT   736 5

COMPLEMENT
    DEEPS CALLING CALLING FOR THE COMPLEMENT   366 35

COMPLEMENTAL
    NEW LIFE FOR YOURSELVES AND YOUR WOMEN COMPLEMENTAL   463 12

COMPLETE
    IS COMPLETE FOR THE MOMENT YET WAIT AND YOU'LL SEE THAT+   94 8
    IT IS PERFECTLY COMPLETE   203 26
    AND SHE ALSO PURE ISOLATED COMPLETE   267 21
    AS YOU KNOW IT IS A COMPLETE LIE   441 24
    AND A COMPLETE ABSENCE OF CONSEQUENCE TO THE MURDERER   532 23
    THERE IS ENOUGH OF GREAT SOULS TO COMPLETE AN EFFICIEN+   859 23
    PEACE COMPLETE PEACE   *960 5

COMPLETELY
    I WISH IT WOULD BE COMPLETELY DARK EVERYWHERE   205 20
    I WOULD BE WILLING TO VANISH COMPLETELY COMPLETELY   430 9
    COMPLETELY UNDER GONE ENTIRELY GONE   719 21
    WHEN I AM GONE COMPLETELY LAPSED AND GONE   724 29
    THEN OUR LIFE IS FINISHED OUR DAY IS OVER COMPLETELY   779 5

COMPLETENESS
    IN ITS LAST COMPLETENESS DRINKING   109 27
    THE WRINKLED SMILE OF COMPLETENESS THAT FOLLOWS A LIFE   503 17

COMPLETING
    COMPLETING HIS CIRCLES AND WORKING CLEVERLY   *932 3

COMPLETION
    THAT MY COMPLETION OF MANHOOD SHOULD BE THE BEGINNING   218 24
    IN HIS EFFORT TOWARD COMPLETION AGAIN   361 9

COMPLEX
    THE COMPLEX MANIFOLD INVOLVEDNESS OF AN INDIVIDUAL   356 12
    AND RUINS OUR COMPLEX HARMONY   529 10
    THE EGO RUNNING IN ITS OWN COMPLEX AND DISCONNECTED   635 9

COMPLEX-NATURE
    THROUGH HIS FIVE-FOLD COMPLEX-NATURE   356 4

COMPLICATED
    GREAT COMPLICATED NUDE FIG-TREE STEMLESS FLOWER-MESH   299 3
    OF MISTINESS COMPLICATED INTO KNOTS AND CLOTS THAT BARGE   437 32
    THAT EVERYTHING TIES ITSELF UP INTO COMPLICATED LITTLE + *947 8

COMPOSED
    STILL WINSOME SLEEP SO STILL AND SO COMPOSED   101 11
    IT STANDS SO STILL IN THE HUSH COMPOSED OF TREES AND IN+ 159 27

COMPREHENSION
    SINCE MAN IS JUST MIDDLING AND HIS COMPREHENSION JUST   479 11

COMPRESSED
    COMPRESSED IT TILL ITS BEAM GREW WONDROUS DARK   69 19
    AND A GASP OF RELIEF BUT THE SOUL IS STILL COMPRESSED   167 15
    HOW IT IMPRESSES ME HOW HARD AND COMPRESSED   249 14
    INTO ROLLICKING SUNS AND THEIR LOST GOLD ROTS COMPRESSED *896 20

COMPRESSED
    COMPRESSED IT TILL ITS BEAM GREW WONDROUS DARK   *916   2

COMPULSION
    PRISON MAKES MEN BAD AND THE MONEY COMPULSION MAKES   488   2
    STRESS OF COMPULSION REMAINS AND A BAND THAT GIRTS   746 16

COMPULSORY
    THE RED RANGE HEAVES AND COMPULSORY SWAYS AH SEE IN THE+   66 17

COMPUNCTION
    INSTANTLY FEEL A PANG OF COMPUNCTION   834 11

COMPUTED
    TODAY WHEN THE SUN IS COMPUTED OLD   814   7

COMRADE
    YOU ARE CELIBATE AND SINGLE SCORNING A COMRADE EVEN   197   3

COMRADES
    NO SALVIA-FRENZIED COMRADES ANTENNAE   317   8
    NOR YET COMRADES FOR I DON'T BELONG TO ANY CAUSE   499 22

CONCATENATION
    AND WHAT AN AWFUL CONCATENATION OF SOUND IT IS   657 12

CONCAVE
    AND COMING DOWN UPON US OUT OF THE DARK CONCAVE   403 28
    TO FOLD IN A SHINING CONCAVE THE PALE NIGHT   882   3

CONCEIT
    SHINE IN CONCEIT OF SUBSTANCE UPON ME WHO AM LESS THAN   133 12
    BUT ANOTHER WORD CONCEIT AND VANITY   158 14
    PLENTY OF CONCEIT IN YOU   398   2
    BUT BRED IN CONCEIT THAT THE WORLD IS ALL FOR LOVE   400 16
    DOWN THE SINK OF THE MALE CONCEIT   457 24
    IN THE POT OF HIS OWN CONCEIT   474 30
    CONCEIT   479 18
    AND SOUNDER THAN ALL INSURANCE IS A SHINY MENTAL CONCEIT   543   3
    FOR A MOMENT FREE FROM ALL CONCEIT OF YOURSELF AND ALL +   674   3
    IT IS CONCEIT THAT KILLS US   674   6
    ENTANGLED IN THE LAOCOON COILS OF OUR CONCEIT   674 10
    IS JUST CONCEIT   681 20
    JUST MAN'S CONCEIT   681 21
    I CALL IT MENTAL CONCEIT AND MYSTIFICATION   708 18
    CONCEIT OF BEING IMMUNE   709 32
    IN CONCEIT OF SUBSTANCE UPON ME   772   2

CONCEITED
    NOR YET BROTHERS IT'S SO CONCEITED   499 23
    SOME MEN LIVE FOR THE CONCEITED FURNITURE OF THEIR MINDS   657   7
    BEING CONCEITED FOOLS   673   6

CONCEIVED
    IMMACULATELY CONCEIVED   659   2
    THOUGH THE YEAR IS RIPENING LIKE A WOMAN WHO HAS CONCEI+   854   8

CONCEIVING
    AND OH OH HORROR I WAS BEGETTING AND CONCEIVING IN MY   257 21

CONCENTRATE
    YET MORE I SEE YOU DARKLY CONCENTRATE   297   1

CONCENTRATES
    CONCENTRATES HER GOLDEN SHADOW   217 24

CONCENTRATION
    IS SWELLING WITH WIDESPREAD LABOURING CONCENTRATION   *908   2
    OH THE MIRACLE OF THE WHOLE THE WIDESPREAD LABOURING CO+ *909 19

CONCEPTION
    PROUD BEYOND INKLING OR FURTHEST CONCEPTION OF PRIDE   258 31
    SO THAT A NEW CONCEPTION OF THE BEGINNING AND END   329 33
    TO INCULCATE THE NEW CONCEPTION OF THE RISEN MAN   609 21

CONCEPTIONLESS
    CONCEPTIONLESS   362   3

CONCERN
    HE IS NO LONGER MY CONCERN HE CEASES TO BE   468 10

CONCERNED
    BUT I AM NOT CONCERNED WITH YOU   233 24
    WHEREAS IF YOU RIDE AWAY AND BECOME DEEPLY CONCERNED IN+ 665 12

CONCH
    WHEN A BLACK PRIEST BLOWS ON A CONCH   623 14

CONCLUSION
    A TINY BELL OF CONCLUSION HAS SOUNDED   512   7
    THOUGHT IS PONDERING OVER EXPERIENCE AND COMING TO CONC+ 673 13

CONCORD
    CLEANSED AND IN CONCORD FROM THE BED OF DEATH   743 28

CONCRETE
    EACH ONE FOR ITS HOLD ON THE CONCRETE DARKNESS I KNOW T+ 92 14
    AND FEARFUL CONTIGUOUS AND CONCRETE   267 12

CONCUSSION
    THE AWFUL CONCUSSION   363 11

CONDESCEND
    CONDESCEND TO BE VILE   234   8

CONDITION
    YOU LOVE ONE AFTER ANOTHER ON ONE CONDITION THAT EACH   399 24
    BUT THE REAL FAULT LIES IN THE EGO-BOUND CONDITION OF   475 24
    AND FED ON CONDITION THEY DANCE THIS DANCE OF CORPSES   631 15

CONDITIONED
    CONDITIONED ONLY BY OUR OWN PURE SINGLE BEING   267 28

CONDOLING
    POURING COMFORT AND CONDOLING   457 23

CONDOR
    THE VULTURE IS BALD SO IS THE CONDOR OBSCENELY   369 18

CONDUCTED
    AND BEETHOVEN THEY SOLD TO CERTAIN CONDUCTORS TO BE CON+ 763   8

CONDUCTIVITY
    THE WONDERFUL MOIST CONDUCTIVITY TOWARDS THE CENTRE   282 20

CONDUCTORS
    AND BEETHOVEN THEY SOLD TO CERTAIN CONDUCTORS TO BE CON+ 763   8

CONFESS
    I CONFESS I AM AFRAID OF YOU   290   8
    BUT MUST I CONFESS HOW I LIKED HIM   350   8

CONFESSED
    LONG HAVE I WAITED NEVER ONCE CONFESSED   122 13
    HAVING KNOWN THE WORLD SO LONG I HAVE NERVER CONFESSED 249 13
    THE GREAT SOCIAL IDIOT IT MUST BE CONFESSED   522   6

CONFESSION
    THEIR DUMB CONFESSION OF WHAT HER BLOOD MUST FEEL   128   9
    CONFESSION OF DELIGHT UPON THE WAVE   193   5
    INTO A DARING SHORT-BREATH'D CONFESSION   854 13

CONFIDENT
    MY CONFIDENT ACTIVITY   64 24
    DRINKING THE CONFIDENT WATER FROM THE LITTLE JUG   *959 13

CONFINED
    SINCE YOU ARE CONFINED IN THE ORBIT OF ME   236 12

CONFINEMENT
    DO YOU NOT LOATHE THE CONFINEMENT   236 13
    INHERITING A SORT OF CONFINEMENT   518 11

CONFINES
    THE CONFINES GAZING OUT BEYOND WHERE THE WINDS GO FREE 47 10
    YOU LET ME OUT OF THE CONFINES   101 19
    AND HER BOSOM COUCHED IN THE CONFINES OF HER GOWN   123   9

CONFIRM
    TO CONFIRM WHAT HE SAID BUT ALAS HE MEANT   579 21

CONFIRMATION
    IN CONFIRMATION I HEAR SEVENFOLD LARK-SONGS PEALING   34 29

CONFLAGRATION
    I AM AMAZED AT THIS SPRING THIS CONFLAGRATION   116   6
    THIS CONFLAGRATION OF SPRING THE GAP IN IT ALL   116 11
    THE WHOLE GREAT CONFLAGRATION OF ALL LIFE   195 26

CONFLAGRATIONS
    AND KINDLING SHAPELY LITTLE CONFLAGRATIONS   271 33

CONFLICT
    AND A CREATURE OF CONFLICT LIKE A CATARACT   714 15
    AND THE CONFLICT IS A COMMUNION   714 24

CONFLICTING
    BETWEEN CONFLICTING POLITICAL PARTIES AND   777 18

CONFORM
    THE HALLS OF MY MIND COMPELLING MY LIFE TO CONFORM   173 20
    AND ARE JUST LIKE THEM AND CONFORM AND ARE NICE   431 31
    CONFORM   432   3
    THE HALLS OF MY LIFE AND COMPELS MY SOUL TO CONFORM   *906 14
    THE HALLS OF MY LIFE COMPELLING MY SOUL TO CONFORM   *908   8

CONFORMING
    THE CONFORMING WORM STAYS JUST INSIDE THE SKIN   432   6

CONFOUNDS
    AND CONFOUNDS ME   222 25

CONFRONT
    IN THE GRIM UNDERTOW NAKED THE TREES CONFRONT   142   3
    WHITELY CONFRONT I WAIT ON THE GRASS AM LAMED   225 12

CONFRONTED
    JUST WATCH THE DISPLAY OF HIM CONFRONTED WITH A NEW   431   8

CONFRONTING
    I ON THE DECK AM STARTLED BY THIS DAWN CONFRONTING   133   1

CONFUSE
    O DON'T CONFUSE   469   4

CONFUSED
    TILL THEN WE ARE CONFUSED A MIXTURE UNRESOLVED UNEXTRIC+ 267   1
    THEN I SHALL BE GLAD I SHALL NOT BE CONFUSED WITH HER 267 17

CONFUSING
AND CONFUSING YOU AND FEEDING ITSELF ON YOUR LIFE			642 21

CONFUSION
INTO GABBLING CONFUSION WITHOUT RESTING				54 5
IN CONFUSION AGAINST MY ENTRY IS IT ONLY THE TREES'		140 13
AND OUR LOVE WAS A CONFUSION					204 8
THE SOFT CLUSTERED SHOULDER-FEATHERS IN ROSY CONFUSION +	855 23
LOOK BRIGHTLY ON A CONFUSION OF MUD AND SAND AND MORTAR		864 26

CONGEALED
PEACE BLACK PEACE CONGEALED					293 15
PEACE CONGEALED IN BLACK LAVA ON THE DOORSTEP			294 1

CONGERIE
LEAVING THIS CONGERIE BEHIND AND IN DANGER			767 24

CONGO
WHEN DARKER STILL THAN CONGO OR AMAZON				607 7

CONICAL
THE EARTH'S LONG CONICAL SHADOW IS FULL OF SOULS		721 15

CONJUNCTION
IN STRANGE CONJUNCTION						236 20
TWO OF US UNUTTERABLY DISTINGUISHED AND IN UNUTTERABLE +	267 22

CONJURER'S
WHAT CONJURER'S CLOTH WAS THROWN ACROSS YOU AND RAISED		53 21

CONNECTED
LOST AND YET STILL CONNECTED AND BETWEEN THE TWO		115 2
EITHER TO STAY CONNECTED WITH THE TREE OF LIFE AND SUBM+	617 13

CONNECTION
LIKE AN EMPTY DANDELION STALK BEREFT OF CONNECTION SMALL	98 3
TO THE ALL AND SEVERED THE CONNECTION				262 18
REELING WITH CONNECTION						480 15
AND FEELING ONESELF UNINTERRUPTED IN THE ROOTED CONNECT+	610 6
LOST SOME LIVING CONNECTION WITH THE COSMOS OUT OF THEM+	610 9
ROOTED CONNECTION						610 14
THERE IS THE ORGANIC CONNECTION LIKE LEAVES THAT BELONG+	615 1
AND THERE IS THE MECHANICAL CONNECTION LIKE LEAVES THAT+	615 2
BUT PEOPLE WHO ARE FALLEN FROM THE ORGANIC CONNECTION W+	615 17
AND SO STRANGLE OFF THEIR CONNECTION WITH THE CEASELESS+	616 5
CAN PUT BACK A HUMAN LIFE INTO CONNECTION WITH THE LIVI+	617 4
ONCE THE CONNECTION HAS BEEN BROKEN				617 6
OR ELSE TO SEVER THE CONNECTION TO BECOME SELF-CENTRED +	617 15
FROM ANY OTHER CONNECTION					643 18
AND ITS PRIMORDIAL CONSCIOUSNESS OF CONNECTION			844 14
CONNECTION WITH STILL DEEPER STILL MORE TERRIBLE LIFE-F+	844 15
WHICH RESTS IN CONNECTION WITH THE FURTHER FOREVER UNKN+	844 22
AND WHICH ROCKS WITH A SENSE OF CONNECTION RELIGION		844 24
AND TWO ARE ONE IN SWEET CONNECTION				887 22
REELING WITH CONNECTION						*951 28

CONNIE
AND YOU DEAR LADY JEAN ARE YOU CONNIE				889 2

CONQUER
NOW I MUST CONQUER THE FEAR OF LIFE				461 1
CONQUER SAYS THE MORNING STAR PASS THE DRAGONS AND PASS+	796 23
HE HAD HOPED TO DIE IN THE PULPIT TO CONQUER IN DEATH		859 10

CONQUERED
I HAVE CONQUERED THE FEAR OF DEATH				460 30

CONQUERING
TRIUMPHING CONQUERING						519 14

CONQUEST
TRIUMPH CONQUEST						519 12

CONSCIENCE
CONSCIENCE							527 9
THOUGHT IS THE TESTING OF STATEMENTS ON THE TOUCHSTONE +	673 11
IT SHOWS AGAIN HOW HIGHLY DEVELOPED THE SOCIAL CONSCIEN+	829 16
WHICH SHOWS ONCE MORE THAT OUR SOCIAL CONSCIENCE IS DEV+	829 22
AND DISLOCATED THE INTUITIVE CONSCIENCE				838 23

CONSCIOUS
EYEING ME SIDEWAYS AND CUNNINGLY CONSCIOUS THAT I AM		333 2
THEY ARE ROYALTY DARK-FACED ROYALTY SHOWING THE CONSCIO+	388 22
OVER THE CONSCIOUS PERSONALITY					471 4
YET NOT SUFFICIENTLY CONSCIOUS TO BE ABLE TO FORGET OUR+	496 20
AND OUR SOCIETY IS ONLY PART CONSCIOUS LIKE AN IDIOT		515 2
AND THE WHEEL OF THE CONSCIOUS SELF SPINS ON IN ABSOLUT+	712 15
COILS AND RECOILS SENSITIVE TO LIFE AND CONSCIOUS OF TR+	*952 8

CONSCIOUSLY
OR BEING RAPED EITHER WAY SO LONG AS IT WAS CONSCIOUSLY	532 17

CONSCIOUSNESS
ALL ROUND ME ABOVE AND BELOW THE NIGHT'S TWIN CONSCIOUS+	97 23
ME TILL I REEL WITH DISSEMINATED CONSCIOUSNESS			107 27
TO CONSCIOUSNESS YOU GAVE ME THE DOUR				111 16
OR A SOARING CONSCIOUSNESS					323 29
IS NOT EACH SOUL A VIVID THOUGHT IN THE GREAT CONSCIOUS+	328 27
ABSOLUTISM IS FINISHED IN THE HUMAN CONSCIOUSNESS TOO		473 14
BUT IN HIS CONSCIOUSNESS HE IS TWO-FOLD AT LEAST		473 16
MAN IS AN ALTERNATING CONSCIOUSNESS				474 15
MAN IS AN ALTERNATING CONSCIOUSNESS				474 16
ONLY THAT EXISTS WHICH EXISTS IN MY OWN CONSCIOUSNESS		474 17
ENCLOSED IN HIS OWN LIMITED MENTAL CONSCIOUSNESS		474 25
MY WHOLE CONSCIOUSNESS IS CLICHE				510 1
THE KNELL OF OUR BALD-HEADED CONSCIOUSNESS			512 10
SANITY MEANS THE WHOLENESS OF THE CONSCIOUSNESS			515 1
IF WE DO NOT RAPIDLY OPEN ALL THE DOORS OF CONSCIOUSNESS	515 3

CONSCIOUSNESS
TODAY THE SOCIAL CONSCIOUSNESS IS MUTILATED			516 1
A FEARFUL THING IS THE MUTILATED SOCIAL CONSCIOUSNESS		516 6
PUT OUT A LIGHT OF CONSCIOUSNESS AND LEFT A BLINDED BRU+	543 28
WHEN THE DAYTIME CONSCIOUSNESS HAS GOT OVERWEENING		608 21
IN THE FLESH IS PART OF OUR CONSCIOUSNESS			621 4
THE HOLY GHOST IS THE DEEPEST PART OF OUR OWN CONSCIOUS+	621 5
SO IF WE GO COUNTER TO OUR OWN DEEPEST CONSCIOUSNESS		621 8
OF OUR OWN CONSCIOUSNESS						621 14
CHRIST THE HUMAN CONSCIOUSNESS					636 15
THE GODS THAT MADE US ARE GREATER THAN OUR CONSCIOUSNESS	636 29
AND OUR CONSCIOUSNESS IS A SPOT OF LIGHT IN A GREAT BUT	636 31
AND OPEN OUR CONSCIOUSNESS TO THE DEEP MYSTERIOUS LIFE		666 13
THERE ARE VAST REALMS OF CONSCIOUSNESS STILL UNDREAMED +	666 24
THOUGHT IS THE WELLING UP OF UNKNOWN LIFE INTO CONSCIOU+	673 10
AND SINKING STILL IN DEPTH AFTER DEPTH OF DISINTEGRATIV+	699 25
ABSOLUTE CONSCIOUSNESS ABSOLVED FROM STRIFE AND KISSES		712 17
HOW TERRIBLE IT WOULD BE TO THINK AND KNOW TO HAVE CONS+	724 24
THIS CONTENT OF MY CONSCIOUSNESS THIS VERY ME			738 14
ITS TREASURES OF CONSCIOUSNESS ITS SUBTLE BARBARIC		776 9
HE IS A SAVAGE WITH HIS OWN PECULIAR CONSCIOUSNESS HIS +	776 28
DON'T SENTIMENTALIZE HIS SAVAGE CONSCIOUSNESS			776 30
IN ALL HONESTY A WORD IS NEITHER A GAP IN THE CONSCIOUS+	837 8
CONSCIOUSNESS							837 19
FOR AT PRESENT IN THE WHIRRING INSANITY OF THE MENTAL C+	839 5
WITH ITS STRANGE PRIMORDIAL CONSCIOUSNESS OF JUSTICE		844 13
AND ITS PRIMORDIAL CONSCIOUSNESS OF CONNECTION			844 14
AND TREMBLES WITH A SENSE OF TRUTH PRIMORDIAL CONSCIOUS+	844 25
OH THE TERRIBLE ECSTASY OF THE CONSCIOUSNESS THAT I AM +	*909 18
THEN HE TURNS AWAY AND WIPES HER FROM HIS CONSCIOUSNESS		*948 16
PRIDE PRISTINE AND DEEPER THAN CONSCIOUSNESS THE NATIVE+	*951 18

CONSECRATE
COME I WILL CONSECRATE YOU FOR THE JOURNEY			153 14

CONSEQUENCE
AND A COMPLETE ABSENCE OF CONSEQUENCE TO THE MURDERER		532 23

CONSERVATIVES
O YOU HARD-BOILED CONSERVATIVES AND YOU SOFT-BOILED LIB+	664 12

CONSIDER
THEY WILL CONSIDER HOW YOU WENT YOUR WAYS			176 23
BUT I CONSIDER I WAS SUFFICIENTLY CIRCUMCISED LONG AGO		541 22
CONSIDER MISS WILKS OR DEPART FORTHWITH				584 2
AND CONSIDER THE LILY NOT THE PAWPAW NOR THE MANGO-FLESH	760 18

CONSIDERABLE
NOT FAR FROM THE LILY THE CONSIDERABLE LILY			587 5
AND MAKE THE CONSIDERABLE MESS THAT ISN'T EVEN WORTH TH+	*947 12

CONSIDERABLY
MY LOVE DIES DOWN CONSIDERABLY					472 20

CONSIDERED
IS CONSIDERED							707 27

CONSIDERS
WHO CONSIDERS HIMSELF A GENTLEMAN				830 5
HE CONSIDERS HIMSELF SUCH IF YOU PLEASE				830 6

CONSOLATION
CONSOLATION THAT IN HER LIPS HER BLOOD AT CLIMAX CLIPS		127 26
NOR IS HE A WOMAN WITH A BOSOM OF SORROW AND CONSOLATION	840 21

CONSOLE
HOW HASTEN AND WHAT WILL CONSOLE				757 6

CONSOLED
IT HAS ALL THE TIME TO BE SOOTHED AND CONSOLED BY		641 20
I HAVE NO DESIRE IN THE LEAST TO BE SORROWED OVER OR CO+	840 22

CONSOLING
WOMEN ARE SICK OF CONSOLING					457 21

CONSTABLE
MY CONSTABLE WI' 'IS BUTTONED BREAST				79 5
MY CONSTABLE WI' 'IS BUTTONED BREAST				*921 1

CONSTANT
HER CONSTANT TREAD						64 2
OF THE MOURNFUL CONSTANT HEART THAT WHILE SHE'S WEAVING		65 25
AND THE SWEET CONSTANT BALANCED HEAT				263 15

CONSTANTLY
THE TASSEL OF THE BLIND SWINGS CONSTANTLY TAPPING THE P+	112 17
SO CONSTANTLY ROUND ETNA					301 7

CONSTELLATION
HAVE BEEN FOR ME LIKE A DAZED CONSTELLATION OF STARS		75 26
THE GAP IN MY LIFE'S CONSTELLATION				115 17
HAVE SHONE FOR ME LIKE A CROWDED CONSTELLATION OF STARS		*897 25
HAVE SHONE FOR ME LIKE A CROWDED CONSTELLATION OF STARS		*901 2

CONSTELLATIONS
THE CONSTELLATIONS YOUR GREAT HEART THE SUN			194 24
TOWNS CONSTELLATIONS RACE					862 26

CONSTERNATION
THE SEA-GOD SAID IN CONSTERNATION				575 4

CONSTRAINED
CONSTRAINED TO POUR FORTH ALL HIS FIRE DOWN THE NARROW +	327 11

CONSULT
MEET MINE I OPENED HER HELPLESS EYES TO CONSULT   125 27
WHAT GOD DID THEY CONSULT   313 26
TO MINE I OPENED HER HELPLESS EYES TO CONSULT   *936 26

CONSUME
AND KINDLE MY WILL TO A FLAME THAT SHALL CONSUME   74 20
ONE OF YOU KINDLE A FIRE TO CONSUME THEM WITHAL   750 24
TILL I ROUSE MY WILL LIKE A FIRE TO CONSUME   *895 28
TILL I ROUSE MY WILL LIKE A FIRE TO CONSUME   *904 17

CONSUMED
BEING BURNED WITH OIL AND CONSUMED IN CORRUPT THICK   258 10

CONSUMES
AND YELLOW AS THE FIRE THAT CONSUMES   806 23

CONSUMMATE
AND I THE LOVER AM CONSUMMATE   742 12

CONSUMMATED
EVEN FROM MYSELF AND AM CONSUMMATED   726 6

CONSUMMATION
SOONER THAN OUR FULL CONSUMMATION HERE   193 12
OUR CONSUMMATION MATTERS OR DOES IT NOT   219 12
DOOMED IN THE LONG CRUCIFIXION OF DESIRE TO SEEK HIS CO+ 361 3
IT IS A CONSUMMATION DEVOUTLY TO BE WISHED   511 4
IN DEATH THE CONSUMMATION   742 23

CONSUMMATUM EST
CONSUMMATUM EST   779 6
CONSUMMATUM EST OH GOD AND ON GOOD FRIDAY   779 7

CONTACT
OF THE IRON CLICK OF YOUR HUMAN CONTACT   291 10
BUT SOUNDLESS AND OUT OF CONTACT   337 17
INTO CONTACT   468 18
IN MENTAL CONTACT GAY AND SAD   469 2
CONTACT OF CEREBRAL FLESH   469 18
THAN ANY CONTACT THAT CAN BE   470 2
WHAT THE OLD PEOPLE CALL IMMEDIATE CONTACT WITH GOD   481 6
CONTACT WITH THE SUN OF SUNS   481 13
POURING INTO THE VEINS FROM THE DIRECT CONTACT WITH THE 481 28
SAFE FROM EVERY CONTACT   543 5
AND OUR NAKED CONTACT WILL BE RARE AND VIVID AND TREMEN+ 608 15
FROM THE ROBOT CONTACT ON EVERY HAND   645 24
AND WE WILL FIND THE WAY TO IMMEDIATE CONTACT WITH LIFE 666 18
THERE IS A MARVELLOUS RICH WORLD OF CONTACT AND SHEER F+ 667 3

CONTACTS
CONTACTS AND BOUNCING OFF AGAIN BOUNCE BOUNCE LIKE A   249 19
FROM TRESPASSED CONTACTS FROM RED-HOT FINGER   601 10

CONTAGION
BUT KILL THE SCABBED AND UGLY LAMB THAT SPREADS CONTAGI+ 678 23

CONTAIN
FIRE AND WATER THEY CONTAIN THE PROPORTION OF MALE AND + 295 7
IS TO CONTAIN OURSELVES   513 24
BECAUSE ALL THE FACES CONTAIN SETS OF EMOTIONAL AND   657 2
IS TO LEARN TO CONTAIN HIMSELF   838 15
TO LEARN TO CONTAIN OURSELVES   839 2
LET US CONTAIN OURSELVES   839 15
WHY NOT STAY OUT AND LEARN TO CONTAIN ONESELF   839 22

CONTAINED
BLUE SHADOW WITHIN ME A PRESENCE WHICH LIVES CONTAINED 115 7
A DARKNESS WITHIN ME A PRESENCE WHICH SLEEPS CONTAINED *930 7

CONTAINS
THEY SAY THE SEA IS COLD BUT THE SEA CONTAINS   694 1

CONTEMPLATE
RATHER THRILLING TO CONTEMPLATE   532 25
QUITE THRILLING I SHOULD SAY AT LEAST TO CONTEMPLATE   533 1

CONTEMPLATION
YES I SHOULD SAY THE CONTEMPLATION OF CLEVER SUICIDE IS 532 28

CONTEMPT
DROP THEIR LEAVES WITH A FAINT SHARP HISS OF CONTEMPT   54 25
INSTINCTIVE CONTEMPT   612 13
CONTEMPT   *948 5
HE SHOWS AN AMUSED SUPERIOR CONTEMPT AT THE PREVALENCE + *949 4

CONTENDING
CONTENDING INTERESTS   777 19

CONTENT
ME THAT I GLOW NOT WITH CONTENT   152 1
CONTENT IS THE WOMAN WITH FRESH LIFE RIPPLING IN TO HER 449 14
CONTENT IS THE MAN   449 15
BUT THE WIND BLOWS STRONG TO SEA-WARD WHITE BUTTERFLY C+ 696 19
THIS CONTENT OF MY CONSCIOUSNESS THIS VERY ME   738 14
BACK AND FORTH WITHOUT CONTENT   826 6
ME THAT I GLOW NOT STILL IN CONTENT   874 15

CONTENTMENT
DESIRE COMES UP AND CONTENTMENT   199 23

CONTIGUOUS
AND FEARFUL CONTIGUOUS AND CONCRETE   267 12

CONTINENT
I DON'T MIND THIS CONTINENT STRETCHING THE SEA FAR AWAY 213 7
GREEN STREAMS THAT FLOW FROM THE INNERMOST CONTINENT OF 260 24
CONTINENT   260 29
IS YOUR CONTINENT COLD FROM THE ICE-AGE STILL THAT THE + 374 21
IS THE BLOOD OF YOUR CONTINENT SOMEWHAT REPTILIAN STILL 374 23
OUR PALE MIND STILL FROM THE PULSING CONTINENT   607 2

CONTINUALLY
WHY CONTINUALLY DO THEY CROSS THE BED   140 20

CONTINUE
CONTINUE   363 13
STILL CONTINUE TO CRADLE HIM   700 21
TO CONTINUE ON THE LONGEST JOURNEY   722 18

CONTINUING
AND YET THE SOUL CONTINUING NAKED-FOOTED EVER MORE VIVI+ 281 7

CONTINUOUS
CALLOUSLY CONTINUOUS   427 4

CONTORTED
BUT WE ARE MAIMED CRIPPLED CONTORTED AND SICK   833 8

CONTOUR
AND THE WATER-SUAVE CONTOUR DIMS   339 18

CONTOURS
FROM OUT YOUR FACE'S FAIR FORGETFUL CONTOURS   875 2

CONTRACT
WHY DOES MY SOUL CONTRACT WITH UNNATURAL FEAR   140 21
YOU CONTRACT YOURSELF   370 11

CONTRADICTION
AS EVERY HALF-TRUTH AT LENGTH PRODUCES THE CONTRADICTION 663 10
AS A HALF-LIE CAUSES THE IMMEDIATE CONTRADICTION OF THE+ 664 11

CONTRADICTIONS
NOR PUERILITY OF CONTRADICTIONS   709 33

CONTRADICTORINESS
CONTRADICTORINESS   369 28

CONTRADICTS
WHO CONTRADICTS   308 4

CONTRARY
ON THE CONTRARY HE MERELY GIVES HIMSELF AWAY   433 1
NAY ON THE VERY CONTRARY   470 13
BE SO CONTRARY   558 11

CONTRAST
YOUR FACE IN THE MARIGOLD BUNCH TO TOUCH AND CONTRAST Y+ 90 10

CONTROL
FIXED IN THE DARKNESS GRAPPLING FOR THE DEEP SOIL'S CRO+ 92 11
THE BRIEF MATERIAL CONTROL OF THE HOUR LEAVE THEM FREE + 93 8
OR TRANSFER THE CONTROL TO THE AMERICAN INSTITUTE   780 9
FIXED IN THE DARKNESS GRAPPLING FOR THE DEEP SOIL'S LIT+ *926 11

CONTROLLED
AND CONTROLLED BY MEN OF SCIENCE COMPETENT   780 7

CONVENIENCE
YOU MUSTN'T EXPECT IT ALSO TO WAIT FOR YOUR CONVENIENCE 531 21

CONVENTIONALITY
YOU DULL ANGELS TARNISHED WITH CENTURIES OF CONVENTIONA+ 614 16

CONVENTIONALLY
BUT WITH THE WALKING AND TALKING AND CONVENTIONALLY PER+ 442 2

CONVERSATION
WOULDN'T THINK IT NECESSARY TO MAKE CONVERSATION   506 21
WHELMED IN PROFUNDITIES OF PROFOUND CONVERSATION   542 29
ESCAPING THE PETROL FUMES OF HUMAN CONVERSATION   646 6

CONVERT
FIG FRUIT OF THE FEMALE MYSTERY CONVERT AND INWARD   283 18

CONVEYED
HAS CONVEYED THIS THING THAT SITS AND WRITES   887 6

CONVOLUTED
INTO THE SHELL-LIKE WOMB-LIKE CONVOLUTED SHADOW   *959 26

CONVOLUTIONS
LIKE THE CONVOLUTIONS OF SHADOW-SHELL   *959 20

CONVULSE
I COULD CONVULSE THE HEAVENS WITH MY HORROR   213 17

CONVULSED
BUT SUDDENLY THAT PART OF HIM THAT WAS LEFT BEHIND CONV+ 351 13
STRUGGLED CONVULSED BACK AND FORTH UPON ITSELF   682 4

CONVULSES
THAT CONVULSES AND TREMBLES AGAIN WITH THE SYMPATHY OF + *952 7

CONVULSION
I THINK IN MY CONVULSION THE SKIES WOULD BREAK   213 20
WHERE MY SOUL FALLS IN THE LAST THROES OF BOTTOMLESS CO+ 322 3

CONVULSIVE
TILL HER DARK DEEPS SHOOK WITH CONVULSIVE THRILLS AND T+ 125 31
IN THE SPELLBOUND NORTH CONVULSIVE NOW WITH A DREAM NEAR 149 21
ALONG IN THE COILED CONVULSIVE THROES 164 6
TILL HER DARK DEEPS SHOOK WITH CONVULSIVE THRILLS AND T+ *936 30

COO
HIS MOTHER LIBERTY TRYING ALWAYS TO TEACH HIM TO COO 413 22
COO COO COO COO-ARK COO-ARK QUARK QUARK 413 24
THE BIRD GAVE A CLUCK THE COW GAVE A COO 761 4

COO-ARK
COO COO COO COO-ARK COO-ARK QUARK QUARK 413 24

COO-DOVE'S
THE CUCKOO AND THE COO-DOVE'S CEASELESS CALLING 65 11

COOED
DOWN WITH ALL EAGLES COOED THE DOVE 413 4

COOING
JESUS' PALE AND LAMBENT DOVE COOING IN THE LOWER BOUGHS 329 8
AND HOOING AND COOING AND SIDLING THROUGH THE FRONT TEE+ 433 22
WHOOING AND COOING AND FADING AWAY WITH WONDERFUL 830 24

COOL
DARK OVERGROWN WITH WILLOWS COOL WITH THE BROOK EBBING + 33 16
TO COOL IN THE NIGHT IF SHE CAME TO ME NOW 35 10
THE COOL OF AN OAK'S UNCHEQUERED SHADE 49 21
THE COOL HIGH MOON AT THEIR EASE WHILE THE DRONING CHUR+ 54 30
COOL AS SYRINGA BUDS IN MORNING HOURS 65 9
ON A SUBTLE RUSH OF COOL GREY FLAME 68 2
COOL LONELY NIGHT HER BREASTS WILL KEEP THE NIGHT AT BAY 91 11
YOU UNDINE-CLEAR AND PEARLY SOULLESSLY COOL 161 15
THE SOFT WIND BLOWING COOL 194 7
NOW IN THE COOL OF THE DAY 231 27
COME THAW DOWN THEIR COOL PORTENTOUSNESS DISSOLVE THEM 271 5
BUT FISHES ARE VERY FIERY AND TAKE TO THE WATER TO COOL 331 1
BOW DEEP FOR IT'S GOOD AS A DRAUGHT OF COOL WATER TO BOW 391 30
THE NEW MOON IN COOL HEIGHT ABOVE THE BLUSHES 467 9
AND HAVE A COOL SENSE OF TRUTH INHUMAN TRUTH AT LAST 481 23
THE COOL COOL TRUTH OF PURE VITALITY 481 27
COOL UNLYING LIFE WILL RUSH IN 482 22
COOL MOTIVE 532 22
THEN ONLY UNDER THE MOON COOL AND UNCONCERNED 609 10
WHO IS IT SMOOTHS THE BED-SHEETS LIKE THE COOL 652 9
SURE AND MOON-SHOD COOL AND BRIGHT-FOOTED 684 12
THE COOL THE CLEANNESS OF THE SEA 747 7
A COOL OINTMENT OVER THE EARTH BLISTERED IN THE FLIGHT + 855 31
COOL ON MY MOUTH 861 4
BUT PRESSING HER SUPPLE BODY INTO THE COOL DARK LEAVES 864 11
ITS COOL WEIGHT LAY FULL ON HER BOSOM NOW IT ROLLS TO R+ 864 15
AND HER FINGERS WERE COOL 882 31
DARK OVERGROWN WITH WILLOWS COOL WITH THE BROOK EBBING + *891 18
COOL AS SYRINGA BUDS *913 10
COOL AND FIRM AND SILKEN AS PINK YOUNG PEONY FLOWERS *913 11
COOL LIKE SYRINGA BUDS *914 10
ON THE SUBTLE RUSH OF THE COOL GREY FLAME *914 17

COOL-DROOPING
THOUGH WHITE YOU ARE COOL-DROOPING AND RICH 874 25

COOLED
WHEN SAPPHIRES COOLED OUT OF MOLTEN CHAOS 682 22

COOLED-OFF
WHEN GOLD LAY SHINING THREADING THE COOLED-OFF ROCK 682 24

COOLING
COOLING TO A POWDERY PALE-OXYDISED SKY-BLUE 369 14
WITH ITS STORE OF FOOD AND THE LITTLE COOLING PANS 719 4

COOLNESS
YOU THIRST FOR COOLNESS WITH A HUSKY THIRST 91 16
SHE KISSED THEIR COOLNESS LAST NIGHT BREATHED THEIR CLE+ 856 19
AND ALONG THE SCENT AND THE COOLNESS A DROWSE OF SLEEP + 858 20

COOLS
TILL MY PARCHED VISION COOLS 754 15

COPE
BUT THERE WITHIN THE BLUE-SKY RIMS THAT COPE 876 34

COPPER
AND THE YOUNG COPPER BEECH ITS LEAVES RED-ROSY AT THE C+ 647 4
EVEN IF THERE WERE OIL COPPER GOLD UPON THESE 779 15
OR OIL OR COPPER OR GOLD A CAUSE FOR POLITICAL ACTION 779 19

COPPER-SULPHATE
YOU COPPER-SULPHATE BLUE BIRD 375 33

COPULATE
THE TURNED WORM BOASTS I COPULATE 433 4
THE YOUNG ONES COPULATE HATE IT AND WANT TO CRY 485 6
IF YOU COPULATE WITH THE FINEST WOMAN ON EARTH 486 3
HE CAN COPULATE AND BEGET CHILDREN 843 15
WHICH IS WHY THE YOUNG WHO COPULATE SO FREELY 843 19

COPULATION
FROM THE COLD COPULATION OF THE WILL 469 20

CORD
AND THE WHITE DOG DANCES AND QUIVERS I AM HOLDING HIS C+ 34 5

CORDED
KILOSSA SWEET WELL OF MY STRENGTH THOU CORDED WITH SILK 759 14

CORDIAL
AMONG THE EAGER CORDIAL MEN 228 18

CORDS
LAPPED PRISONER IN THE CORDS OF LOVE I HAVE SPUN 884 16

CORE
OPEN THE CORE OF GLOAMING TASTE 114 15
SEEING THE CORE IS A SHADOW INVIOLATE 115 11
BUSHED IN AN UNCOUTH ARDOUR COILED AT CORE 160 13
ROSE-LEAVES THAT WHIRL IN COLOUR ROUND A CORE 218 15
THIS FIREGLOW THE CORE 238 4
YOU THE CORE OF THE FIRE CREPT INTO ME 245 25
WITH YOU THERE FIRM AT THE CORE OF ME 247 2
AND KINDLES IT FURTHER AT THE CORE OF UTTER MYSTERY 261 16
FEARING NOTHING LIFE-BLISSFUL AT THE CORE 307 2
RED AT THE CORE 307 7
RED AT THE CORE 307 8
AND RED AT THE CORE WITH THE LAST SORE-HEARTEDNESS 307 15
AT THE CORE OF SPACE 435 22
AND FLUTTERS AT THE CORE OF THE ATOM 440 4
AT THE CORE OF YOUR HEART THE OTHER CREATURE 466 2
THE HOT WILD CORE OF THE EARTH HEAVIER THAN WE CAN EVEN 480 8
PIVOTAL CORE OF THE SOUL HEAVIER THAN IRON 480 10
PEACE I HAVE FROM THE CORE OF THE ATOM FROM THE CORE OF+ 499 4
AT THE CORE OF SPACE THE FINAL KNELL 512 16
YOUR HEART'S QUICK CORE 561 25
AT THE CORE OF ME 601 8
AND THE SOUND OF A BLAST THROUGH THE SEA-CURVED CORE OF+ 623 13
BUT A TINY CORE OF STILLNESS IN THE HEART 658 14
THEN THERE WAS A HUSH OF SUSPENSE AT THE CORE OF EVERY + 683 12
WHOSE WHORLS FOLD ROUND TO THE CORE OF SOUNDLESS SILENC+ 724 5
SING THEN THE CORE OF DARK AND ABSOLUTE 724 8
AT THE CORE OF EVERYTHING 724 14
UPON A CORE OF PURE OBLIVION 724 18
BLUE AT THE CORE AND WHEN IS WHETTED 773 5
THE BLUE ANEMONE WITH A DARK CORE 814 1
NOW LET'S EAT UP THE CORE 817 20
TO KEEP A SANE CORE TO LIFE 839 17
A FIERY SIGN OF THE CHAINED POWER THAT WASTED HIM TO TH+ 859 20
WAYS OF ST PETERSBURG I HAVE DWELLED IN THE CORE 866 28
THIS BROWN CORE OF NIGHT *935 16
AND THIS IS THE CORE OF A MAN *951 23
AND DEEPER TO A CORE OF SHEER OBLIVION *959 19
AS THE SOUL AT LAST SLIPS PERFECT INTO THE GOAL THE CORE *959 31

CORN
THE WIND CHASES BY US AND OVER THE CORN 163 17
AH YOU YOU EAR OF CORN STRAIGHT LYING 171 18
MY FATHER SUDDENLY DIED IN THE HARVESTING CORN 173 1
SHOULDER-DEEP OUT OF THE CORN AND WIPES 220 3
LOOK AT THE LITTLE DARLINGS IN THE CORN 221 5
A DOE SPRANG OUT OF THE CORN 222 2
BRIGHT GLANCING EXQUISITE CORN OF MANY A STUBBORN 263 27
THE MAN WHO IS MOWING THE TALL WHITE CORN 651 13
THE WIND CHASES BY ME AND OVER THE CORN 857 17
SHOULDER-DEEP OUT O' TH' CORN AND WIPES *944 11
LOOK AT THE LITTLE DARLINGS IN THE CORN *944 18

CORNCRAKE
IN THE VALLEY A CORNCRAKE CALLS 64 21

CORNER
A CORNER 343 21
IN AN OBSCURE CORNER 343 31
AND CLEAVE IN A HIGH CORNER FOR A SECOND LIKE A CLOT AL+ 345 23
TILL HE FELL IN A CORNER PALPITATING SPENT 345 27
CAME UPON YOU PRANCING ROUND THE CORNER IN EXUBERANT 395 29
AS I RUSHED LIKE AN IDIOT ROUND THE CORNER AFTER YOU 396 8

CORNERS
OH PUT THEM BACK PUT THEM BACK IN THE FOUR CORNERS OF T+ 319 1
THEIR UNCLEAN CORNERS 346 14
INTO THE UTTERMOST CORNERS OF THE SOUL 624 12
ALL THE CREATURES THAT WERE DRIVEN BACK INTO THE UTTERM+ *954 14

CORNSTALKS
AND OVER THE SWAYING CORNSTALKS JUST ABOVE *945 2

CORN-STALKS
AND OVER THE SWAYING CORN-STALKS JUST ABOVE 221 16
THE CORN-STALKS TIPPING WITH FIRE THE SPEARS 221 24
THE CORN-STALKS TIPPING WITH FIRE THEIR SPEARS *945 10

CORN'S
ALL OVER THE DIM CORN'S MOTION AGAINST THE BLUE 221 25
ALL OVER THE CORN'S DIM MOTION AGAINST THE BLUE *945 11

CORONETS
THE GUELDER ROSE-BUSH IS HUNG WITH CORONETS 854 21

CORPORAL
THAT CORPORAL EXISTENCE IS A KIND OF DEATH 689 15

CORPSE
WHY ARE YOU HERE WHAT IS HIS CORPSE TO YOU 158 27
AND ENSHROUDED IN THE VAST CORPSE OF THE INDUSTRIAL MIL+ 629 30
A CORPSE EVEN OF PROPERTY 664 16
THEY CANNOT DIE THEIR CORPSE STILL RUNS ON 675 19
IS DEAD WE RUN WHEELS ACROSS HER CORPSE 703 8

CORPSE-ANATOMIES
  CORPSE-ANATOMIES WITH READY-MADE SENSATIONS   584 21
  CORPSE-ANATOMIES THAT CAN WORK   584 22

CORPSE-BODY
  TROT TROT TROT CORPSE-BODY TO WORK   584 11
  CHEW CHEW CHEW CORPSE-BODY AT THE MEAL   584 12
  SIT SIT SIT CORPSE-BODY IN THE CAR   584 13
  STARE STARE STARE CORPSE-BODY AT THE FILM   584 14
  LISTEN LISTEN LISTEN CORPSE-BODY TO THE WIRELESS   584 15
  TALK TALK TALK CORPSE-BODY NEWSPAPER TALK   584 16
  SLEEP SLEEP SLEEP CORPSE-BODY FACTORY-HAND SLEEP   584 17
  DIE DIE DIE CORPSE-BODY DOESN'T MATTER   584 18

CORPSE-EATERS
  THE GREY VULTURE THE GREY HYAENA CORPSE-EATERS   711 23

CORPSE-LIKE
  SO HIDEOUS AND CORPSE-LIKE UTTERLY SUNLESS   526 14
  LIKE FEARFUL AND CORPSE-LIKE FISHES HOOKED AND BEING PL+ 586 9
  LIKE FEARFUL AND CORPSE-LIKE FISHES HOOKED AND BEING PL+ 632 24

CORPSE-PALE
  YOU ARE ALL GOING DEAD AND CORPSE-PALE   441 25

CORPSES
  IT IS PANDERING TO CORPSES   441 34
  OR A HYAENA EATING CORPSES   621 24
  AND FED ON CONDITION THEY DANCE THIS DANCE OF CORPSES   631 15
  CORPSES ENTANGLED IN IRON   631 20
  HOGGING IT DOWN LIKE A PIG I CALL THE FEEDING OF CORPSES 708 11

CORPUS
  OF A FRAIL CORPUS   332 14
  FOR MANKIND IS A SINGLE CORPUS WE ARE ALL ONE FLESH   631 24
  OUR CORPUS WITH FOOD   826 13

CORPUS CHRISTI
  FOR THE FEAST OF CORPUS CHRISTI   209 18

CORRAL
  AND THE PONIES ARE IN CORRAL   403 16

CORRESPOND
  WHO IS SO STRANGE SHOULD CORRESPOND WITH ME   251 30

CORRIDOR
  I STEAL ACROSS THE HUSHED CORRIDOR   877 36

CORRODES
  THE CITY CORRODES OUT OF SIGHT   142 22
  AS THE BODY CORRODES WHEN DEATH INVADES   142 23

CORRODING
  ALL BITTER AND CORRODING TO THE GRAVE   744 25

CORROSION
  BITTERLY INTO CORROSION BITTERLY TRAVEL   160 16
  OUT OF CORROSION INTO NEW FLORESCENCE   160 20
  MORDANT CORROSION GNASHING AND CHAMPING HARD   160 23
  THE SPARK FROM STORMS OF CORROSION AS SEEDS   160 28

CORROSIONS
  AND SPUE OUT CORROSIONS INTO YOUR STREAMS ON YOUR RAINS 797 6

CORROSIVE
  HOW I KNOW THAT GLITTER OF SALT DRY STERILE SHARP CORRO+ 207 17
  SWEEP ON TO BITTER TO CORROSIVE DEATH   745 34

CORRUPT
  BEING BURNED WITH OIL AND CONSUMED IN CORRUPT THICK   258 10
  AND SINKS SEETHING AND SINKING CORRUPT   699 24

CORRUPTED
  AS THEY DREAM CORRUPTED DREAMS ALL POISONED WITH CARE   174 28

CORRUPTION
  OF EARTH WINTER-PRESSED STRANGLED IN CORRUPTION   270 19
  IT IS THE SCENT OF THE FIERY-COLD DREGS OF CORRUPTION   270 20
  FLOWERS OF THE PENUMBRA ISSUE OF CORRUPTION NOURISHED IN 271 8
  CORRUPTION   272 7
  PERFUME OF CORRUPTION   273 15
  HE IS BREATHING COLD CORRUPTION UPON YOU YOU SHALL BLEE+ 796 32

CORRUPTIVE
  THROUGH THE SLOW CORRUPTIVE LEVELS OF DISINTEGRATIVE KN+ 699 22

CORSO
  STROLLING IN GANGS AND STARING ALONG THE CORSO   312 19
  BLOOM ALONG THE CORSO ON THE LIVING PERAMBULATING BUSH   313 24
  ALONG THE CORSO ALL THIS SUNDAY MORNING   314 29
  IN SUNDAY SUITS AND YELLOW BOOTS ALONG THE CORSO   314 33
  WHAT ROT TO SAY THE LOUTS ALONG THE CORSO   316 20

CORTES
  CORTES PISARRO COLUMBUS CABOT THEY ARE NOTHING   259 23

COS
  AN' COS I LIKED HIM BEST YI BETT'R NOR THEE   *911 15

COSMIC
  TO THIS SPRING OF COSMIC GOLD   162 10
  THAT STIRS WITH A STIR WHICH IS COSMIC AS EVER INVISIBLY 176 3

COSMOPOLITANISM
  AND UNIVERSALISM AND COSMOPOLITANISM WILL CEASE   611 16

COSMOS
  LOST SOME LIVING CONNECTION WITH THE COSMOS OUT OF THEM+ 610 9
  COSMOS   615 18
  COSMOS   617 5
  BE QUITE ALONE AND FEEL THE LIVING COSMOS SOFTLY ROCKING 646 12
  WHEN I AM ALONE WITH THE SILENT GREAT COSMOS   646 15
  DARKLY FROM THE FECUND COSMOS FROM THE ANGRY RED SUN FR+ 675 11
  THE HISTORY OF THE COSMOS   682 1
  THEN EVERY ATOM OF THE COSMOS TREMBLED WITH DELIGHT   682 8
  FOR THE COSMOS EVEN IN DEATH IS LIKE A DARK WHORLED SHE+ 724 4
  THE DRAGONS IN THE COSMOS ARE STIRRING WITH ANGER AGAIN 795 11
  COSMOS   796 17
  OF THE KINDNESS OF THE COSMOS THAT WILL WAFT   *961 3

COST
  NOR A DEAR LITTLE HOME WITH ITS COST ITS COST   459 5
  LORD GOD ABOVE WOULD IT COST ME DEAR   759 10
  DEPARTS WITHOUT COUNTING THE COST   823 10

COSTS
  DON'T LIVE UP TO THE DEAR LITTLE GIRL WHO COSTS   458 22
  AND WHATEVER COSTS YOU MONEY MONEY MONEY IS REALLY   517 25

COSY
  AND HYMNS IN THE COSY PARLOUR THE TINKLING PIANO OUR   148 13
  COME MAKING THE CHAFFINCH NESTS HOLLOW AND COSY   273 1

COTTAGE
  THA'S BIN SNOWED UP I' THIS COTTAGE WI' ME   137 25
  THA'S BIN SNOWED UP I' THIS COTTAGE WI' ME   137 27

COTTAGE-END
  AT YOUR COTTAGE-END IT FALLS BACK AGAIN   885 29

COTTAGES
  THEY SAVED YOU FROM SQUALID COTTAGES AND POVERTY OF HAND 630 17

COTTON
  BENEATH THE COTTON   562 27

COTTON-WOOD
  AND THE COTTON-WOOD LEAVES ARE FALLEN AS GOOD AS FALLEN 403 15
  AND THE ABSENCE OF COTTON-WOOD LEAVES OR OF ASPEN   404 1

COTTON-WRAPPED
  AND ALL THE DARK-FACED COTTON-WRAPPED PEOPLE MORE   391 5
  ALL THE DARK-FACED COTTON-WRAPPED PEOPLE A COUNTLESS   391 8
  COTTON-WRAPPED PEOPLE   391 26

COUCH
  AND I SAW HER BOSOM COUCH IN THE NEST OF HER GOWN   *934 15

COUCHED
  AND HER BOSOM COUCHED IN THE CONFINES OF HER GOWN   123 9

COUGH
  REMOTE ALTHOUGH I HEAR THE BEGGAR'S COUGH   36 5

COUGHED
  NO LEOPARD SCREECHED NO LION COUGHED NO DOG BARKED   394 17

COUGHING
  PRIVATELY COUGHING AHEM   554 26

COULDNA
  IF TER COULDNA BE MASTER AN' TH' WOMAN'S BOSS   139 4

COULDNA'
  I COULDNA' SEE HER FACE BUT HER LITTLE NECK SHONE   *910 11

COULDN'T
  THINK I COULDN'T LOOK TOWARDS DEATH   215 1
  AND MY HEART COULDN'T OWN THEM   337 32
  YOU TRIED TO LOOK BACK TO IT AND COULDN'T   381 7
  AND HE COULDN'T TAKE IT   389 31
  I COULDN'T SAY   435 18
  WITH DIRT THEY COULDN'T FORGET   491 20
  HE COULDN'T BITE 'EM HE WAS MUCH TOO OLD   492 3
  AND IF I DID I CERTAINLY COULDN'T SCRAIGHT IT OUT   540 21
  AND THEY THOUGHT YOU COULDN'T HEAR THEM   554 25
  AND THEY THOUGHT YOU COULDN'T SEE THEM   554 27
  WHICH FOR MYSELF I COULDN'T   555 3
  THAT I COULDN'T FEEL ONE OF THEM   556 2
  THEN IF WE REALISE THAT WE NEVER WERE LOST WE REALISE W+ 613 15
  COULDN'T HAVE BEEN A   668 9
  WE KNOW IT COULDN'T BE DONE   690 32
  IT COULDN'T PUT ITS FEET TOGETHER   818 30

COUNT
  AND I SHALL COUNT THE STAMP AND WORTH   59 13
  LITTLE TO COUNT IN THE WIND THAT DRIFTS ME THROUGH   223 12
  AND ON EITHER SIDE COUNT FIVE   355 31
  AS IF IT WERE YOUR DUES AND I DIDN'T COUNT AT ALL   547 15
  BUT LOOK AT THE CABBAGES OH COUNT THEM BY THE SCORE   569 10
  YOU CAN COUNT ON ANYTHING BUT YOU CAN'T COUNT ON   639 14
  YOU CAN'T EVEN COUNT ON THE MECHANICAL IMPULSE FOR   639 16
  FOR HOW CAN I COUNT IN YOUR THREE TIME THREE   702 3
  COUNT THE RED GRAINS OF THE HUITZILOPOCHTLI   811 24

COUNTED
  COUNTED OUR SCARS   248 23

COUNTENANCE
  STARING CREATION OUT OF COUNTENANCE   328 20
  YOU GO ABOUT IN A DREAM WITH YOUR COUNTENANCE SUNK   755 4

COUNTER
  THEM DOWN ON THE COUNTER ROUNDLY   236 26
  OVER ON BOOT'S CASH CHEMIST'S COUNTER   488 17
  CAME TO THE COUNTER WITH HIS HAT OFF HUMBLE AT THE SHRI+   618 17
  SO IF WE GO COUNTER TO OUR OWN DEEPEST CONSCIOUSNESS   621 8

COUNTERFEIT
  TOO MUCH YOU MINT ME THAT CHEATING COUNTERFEIT   872 23

COUNTERS
  IT NEEDED PYTHAGORAS TO SEE LIFE PLAYING WITH COUNTERS +   355 14

COUNTERSIGN
  PLEASE AND THERE I COUNTERSIGN THAT'S RIGHT YES THAT'S +   546 15
  COUNTERSIGN YOUR DECLARATION IT'S SO SIMPLE AND REALLY +   546 17

COUNTIES
  SOUNDLESSLY DOWN ACROSS THE COUNTIES OUT OF THE RESONANT   149 1

COUNTING
  DEPARTS WITHOUT COUNTING THE COST   823 10

COUNTLESS
  SEEMS LIKE THE BLACK AND GLOSSY SEEDS OF COUNTLESS CENT+   369 11
  ALL THE DARK-FACED COTTON-WRAPPED PEOPLE A COUNTLESS   391 8
  AS THE ROCKETS WENT UP AND THE GLARE PASSED OVER COUNTL+   391 12

COUNTRIE
  INTO THIS STRANGE COUNTRIE   101 20

COUNTRIES
  THE OLD COUNTRIES HAVE A PAST TO BE FAITHFUL TO   775 14

COUNTRY
  STRANGE TO ME LIKE A CAPTIVE IN A FOREIGN COUNTRY HAUNT+   47 9
  WHO PLAY AROUND US COUNTRY GIRLS CLAPPING THEIR HANDS   58 19
  IN ANOTHER COUNTRY BLACK POPLARS SHAKE THEMSELVES OVER A   148 20
  ALONG WITH A RIPE SLACK COUNTRY LASS   198 7
  THE BIG SOFT COUNTRY LASS   198 9
  THE WARM SOFT COUNTRY LASS   198 13
  AND IN MY COUNTRY JUST OVER THE WAY   455 5
  NOR MY CHILDREN NOR MY COUNTRY NOR MY FELLOW-MAN   497 17
  ENGLAND WAS ALWAYS A COUNTRY OF MEN   535 15
  NOW IT'S A COUNTRY OF FRIGHTENED OLD MONGRELS   535 17
  AND YOU'VE INTRODUCED ANARCHY INTO YOUR COUNTRY   536 5
  COUNTRY   612 11
  TO GATHER AND FORTIFY THEMSELVES IN EVERY CLASS IN EVER+   666 3
  IT IS THE OBLIGATION OF THE CITIZENS OF THIS COUNTRY TO+   776 3
  THE ABORIGINES OF THEIR COUNTRY   776 4
  WHAT ELSE HAVE THEY COME TO THIS COUNTRY FOR   777 4
  I SEE DARK THINGS RUSHING ACROSS THE COUNTRY   794 10

COUNTS
  WITH A TOUCH THE DEAD AND THE LIVING WHILE TIME COUNTS +   174 12
  BUT IT IS THE SOVIET STATE ALONE WHICH COUNTS   443 5

COUPLE
  AND GAVE YOU A COUPLE OF NUTS   549 10

COURAGE
  TINY LIGHTHOUSES LITTLE SOULS OF LANTERNS COURAGE BURST+   206 16
  YET NOTHING ON EARTH WILL GIVE HIM COURAGE TO PASS THE   346 4
  O RIPPLING HARD FIRE OF COURAGE O FUSING OF HOT TRUST   440 13
  WE MUST HAVE THE COURAGE OF MUTUAL TRUST   487 21
  IF PEOPLE HAD COURAGE AND REFUSED LIES   504 3
  THE COURAGE OF ROSINESS IN A CABBAGE WORLD   634 27
  IN THE FRAGILE SHIP OF COURAGE THE ARK OF FAITH   719 3
  WHEN YOU LIFT YOUR HANDS IN COURAGE AND BRAVERY ITS GLO+   800 10
  FLAWED MY DELICATE COURAGE IN ITS STROKE   *927 13
  AND MY COURAGE FAILED TO GIVE YOU THE LAST   *928 14
  PULLING THE LONG OARS OF A LIFE-TIME'S COURAGE   *959 12

COUREUR DE FEMMES
  A GREAT COUREUR DE FEMMES   *948 3

COURSE
  HIS BENT COURSE MILDLY HERE WAKES AGAIN LEAPS LAUGHS AN+   33 14
  THE COURSE OF OUR JOURNEY HERE HERE WHERE WE PART   100 18
  YOUR FOUNTAINS AS HEAVEN DRINKS FROM OUT THEIR COURSE   153 30
  THAT MAN HAS A COURSE TO GO   168 2
  BY THE FINE FINE WIND THAT TAKES ITS COURSE THROUGH THE   250 18
  I AM THINKING OF COURSE OF THE PEACH BEFORE I ATE IT   279 13
  NEVER OF COURSE TO PUT ANYTHING UP AGAIN   317 32
  IN THE BEGINNING WAS THE WORD OF COURSE   329 10
  FOOD OF COURSE   336 7
  COURSE   357 22
  AND THERE OF COURSE YOU MEET A HUGE AND MUD-GREY   387 6
  OF COURSE I'M A LIDY WHAT D'YER THINK   434 25
  OF COURSE YOU ARE BUT LET ME SAY   435 1
  A MAN OF COURSE   452 15
  OF COURSE IT WOULD CEASE TO EXIST   479 14
  EXCEPT OF COURSE FOR SECONDARY MOTIVES   485 18
  AND OF COURSE IF THE MULTITUDE IS MAD   486 8
  OF COURSE IF YOU MAKE NAUGHTINESS NASTY   491 5
  SPICILY NASTY OF COURSE   491 6
  AND OF COURSE ONE HAS NO RIGHT TO LAY   492 15
  FOR OF COURSE IF YOU REALLY FEEL SOMETHING   500 24
  SPACE OF COURSE IS ALIVE   525 1
  AND OF COURSE THRILLING IS LIKE LOVING YOU HAVE NO CHOI+   531 18
  BEAUTY OF COURSE BEAUTY IS STILL A DELICIOUS ESCAPE   532 8
  BUT OF COURSE ONE KNOWS THAT BOTH BEAUTY AND PURE   532 11
  AFTER THAT OF COURSE THERE'S SUICIDE CERTAIN ASPECTS   532 26
  SO OF COURSE THE NATION IS SWOLLEN WITH INSOLUBLE PROBL+   535 21
  COURSE YOU UNDERSTAND WHAT I MEAN SO WOULD YOU MIND GIV+   546 9

COURSE
  YES I KNOW IT'S TOO BAD OF COURSE IT'S PERFECTLY SUPERF+   546 13
  THOUGH OF COURSE WE WON'T LET HIM SEE   554 24
  BUT OF COURSE I ALWAYS HEARD THEM   554 29
  WANT TO GO A LITTLE TATTAH SO IT SHALL OF COURSE IT SHA+   571 1
  WE MUST BE NICE TO THEM OF COURSE   660 9
  OF COURSE NATURALLY   660 10
  NOT TOO NICE OF COURSE THEY TAKE ADVANTAGE   660 17
  AT NIGHT TEMPORARILY OF COURSE   761 30
  THE CHILDREN OF COURSE KNOW THAT THEY ARE CARED FOR   832 12
  BUT OF COURSE THIS MEANS SMASHING THE PRESENT SYSTEM OF+   837 27
  ITS CURIOUS COURSE MILDLY HERE IT WAKES AGAIN LEAPS LAU+   *891 15

COURSED
  COURSED ROUND BY RHYTHMIC MOVEMENT OF ALL TIME   194 23

COURT
  SNEAKING COURT OF RAVENNA   497 5
  AND FOUND GREY DOVES IN THE FOUNTAIN COURT   751 2

COURTIN'
  YER KNOWED AS I WAS COURTIN' TIM MERFIN   81 25
  YIS I KNOWED 'E WOR COURTIN' THEE   81 26
  YOU KNOWED AS I WAS COURTIN' TIM MERFIN   *923 25
  YIS I KNOWED 'E WOR COURTIN' THEE   *923 26

COURTSHIP
  ALWAYS KNEEL IN COURTSHIP TO THE SHELVES IN THE DOORWAY+   180 26

COUSINS
  WITH ALL OUR HORRIBLE COUSINS   572 12

COVER
  THEIR SLEEPING COVER THEM SOFT UNSEEN   48 22
  TAKE COVER IN DEATH   55 24
  JEALOUS OF THE SMALLEST COVER   95 12
  I FELT THE BROWN BIRD COVER   124 33
  BEASTS THAT SLEEP WILL COVER   144 20
  BETWEEN THE FINGERS THAT COVER MY FACE   162 22
  SHADOWS TO COVER OUR STRICKEN MANHOOD AND BLEST   167 18
  I SHALL PUT ROSES ON ROSES AND COVER YOUR GRAVE   176 11
  DOES NOT MY FEAR COVER HER FEAR   222 21
  IF HE IS HIDING IN THE COVER   231 25
  THE GAP OF YOUR SHIRT WHY COVER IT UP   254 10
  ONLY TO BE WILL BE SUCH DELIGHT WE COVER OUR FACES WHEN+   267 92
  BUT NOW THEY STITCH TO ADORN THE BURSTEN FIG NOT TO COV+   284 14
  DIVESTED OF COVER   306 9
  WHETHER THE WATERS RISE AND COVER THE EARTH   334 22
  DRAWING NEAR THEY COVER THE MUNCHEN ROAD   732 26
  WE COVER THE HOUSELESS DEAD SO THEY SLEEP IN PEACE   736 25
  MY ARMS LET ME COVER HIM UP IN MY SKIRT   750 20
  ALL MEN COVER THEIR EYES   811 9
  SHE MAY COVER HER EYES YET THE AIMLESS BREEZE OF MY WOR+   868 29
  TO COVER MY MOUTH'S RAILLERY TILL I'M BOUND IN HER SHAM+   940 17
  I WOULD PUT ROSES ON ROSES AND COVER YOUR GRAVE   940 26
  THERE ARE FOXES IN THE COVER OF HIS BEARD   *953 29

COVERED
  WITH DARK SLEEP THAT ONCE COVERED THE CEILING   38 5
  I WISH THE CHURCH HAD COVERED ME UP WITH THE REST   48 24
  AND I COVERED THE EARTH AND ALL SPACE   248 27
  WELL COVERED LEST HE SHOULD BITE ME   347 5
  ENGLAND SEEMS COVERED WITH GRAVES TO ME   410 5
  NOW THAT THE GRAVES ARE MADE AND COVERED   410 18
  NOW THEN THAT ALL THEIR YEARNING IS HUSHED AND COVERED   410 24
  SO THEY ACCEPT COVERED DISLIKE AS THE NORMAL FEELING BE+   832 15
  WITH THE DARK SLEEP THAT ONCE COVERED THE CEILING   *892 21
  HAVE BEEN CAGED AND COVERED WITH DARKNESS ALL DAY AND N+   *918 5

COVERING
  IN SHADOW COVERING US UP WITH HER GREY   48 18
  HIDING AND COVERING IN THE ETERNAL SLEEP   195 28
  I AM COVERING MYSELF WITH THE SAND   259 30

COVERS
  AT HER TATTERED SILENCE AS SHE CROUCHES AND COVERS HER +   54 22
  THE OPEN BOOK OF LANDSCAPE NO MORE FOR THE COVERS OF DA+   88 8
  AND WE ARE CRUSHED BETWEEN THE COVERS WE CLOSE OUR EYES+   88 12
  OF SODOM THAT COVERS THE EARTH BRING THEM FORTH   235 11
  BURNT OUT OF OUR EARTHLY COVERS   243 2
  OUT OF THEIR COVERS LIKE ANY SNAKE   254 15
  OF EACH OF US AND COVERS US   471 5
  COVERS   521 14
  AND THE FOUNTAIN COVERS YOUR FACE FOREVER   809 13
  THIS IS COMFORTLESS AND UNLOVELY WITH CUSHIONS AND THUS+   856 9

COVERT
  MEDITERRANEAN FRUIT WITH YOUR COVERT NAKEDNESS   283 19
  COMES OVER TO ME WITH A COVERT MUSIC THAT STIRS   *942 2

COW
  LIKE SOME UNHAPPY BULL AT THE TAIL OF A COW   361 15
  WHERE NO BULL ROARED NO COW EVER LOWED NO STAG CRIED   394 16
  ONLY THE BEST MATTERS EVEN THE COW KNOWS IT   587 11
  WHEN THE CUCKOO THE COW AND THE COFFEE-PLANT CHIPPED THE   760 22
  DIMENSION THE CUCKOO WENT CUCKOO-WARDS THE COW WENT COW+   760 26
  THE COW WAS DUMB AND THE CUCKOO TOO   761 1
  THE BIRD GAVE A CLUCK THE COW GAVE A COO   761 4

COWARD
  IN THE NIGHT THE SOUL OF A COWARD CREEPS OUT OF HIM   807 4
  BUT HE'S FAR TOO GREAT A COWARD EVER TO ADMIT HIS INSTI+   *948 32

COWARDICE
  WAS IT COWARDICE THAT I DARED NOT KILL HIM   350 13
  COWARDICE EVERY OLD LOUT   458 21
  BOURGEOIS COWARDICE PRODUCES BOLSHEVIST IMPUDENCE   663 18
  AND BETWEEN THE COWARDICE AND IMPUDENCE OF THIS PAIR WH+   663 24

COWARDICE
  IS THE VILEST COWARDICE AND TREACHERY   680 2
  AND I FAILED IN MY COWARDICE TO GIVE THEE THE LAST   *927 14

COWARDLY
  AS THE BOURGEOIS GETS SECRETLY MORE COWARDLY KNOWING HE+   663 20
  BUT THE CRAVEN THE COWARDLY THE CREEPING YOU THAT CAN O+   678 25
  O SHED THE UNCLEAN MEAN COWARDLY GREEDY EGOISTIC DEGENE+   679 5

COWARDS
  OR COWARDS   654 15
  AND MAKES US COWARDS INSTEAD OF GODS   674 7
  WHO ARE COWARDS WHO ARE LIARS WHO ARE TRAITORS WHO HAVE+   807 12
  NO GREY-DOGS COWARDS PASS HIM   810 3

COWERING
  COWERING IN THE LAST BRANCHES OF THE TREE OF OUR LIFE   718 20

COWERS
  IN ALL CREATION ONLY MAN COWERS AND IS AFRAID OF LIFE   529 11
  AND OUR SOUL COWERS NAKED IN THE DARK RAIN OVER THE FLO+   718 19

COWS
  OR GREEDILY SNUFFING BEHIND THE COWS   325 32
  COWS   624 8
  OH CHEW OLD COWS AT YOUR ANCIENT CUDS   814 20
  A GREAT BULL BELLOWED THROUGH SPACE CALLING TO THE MILK+   *946 21

COWSLIPS
  YOU SITTING IN THE COWSLIPS OF THE MEADOW ABOVE   90 14
  ME FULL LENGTH IN THE COWSLIPS MUTTERING YOU LOVE   90 16

COW-WISE
  DIMENSION THE CUCKOO WENT CUCKOO-WARDS THE COW WENT COW+   760 26

COYOTES
  SO FIERCE WHEN THE COYOTES HOWL BARKING LIKE A WHOLE   396 29
  AGAINST THOSE COYOTES WHO WOULD SWALLOW YOU LIKE AN   396 33

CRAB-MEAT
  FULL INSIDE OF WEIRD BROWN SLUSHY CRAB-MEAT   830 20

CRABS
  WHERE THE BLUE CRABS RUSTLED IN QUEST OF HER AIMLESS WI+   864 6

CRACK
  IN A SHINING CRACK OF RED   58 25
  IT IS SO LOVELY DAWN-KALEIDOSCOPIC WITHIN THE CRACK   279 2
  IS JUST TO PUT YOUR MOUTH TO THE CRACK AND TAKE OUT THE+   282 9
  TILL THE WALLS BEGIN TO LOOSEN AND CRACK   462 13
  I HEARD THE CAMEL'S BACK GO CRACK   491 23
  FOR HER TO MUMBLE AND HIM TO CRACK   492 21
  OF FLESH WOULD CRACK AND SHIVER WITH KEEN PAIN   873 29

CRACKLE
  AS WITH THOUGHTS THAT FLASH AND CRACKLE IN FAR-OFF MALI+   97 16
  OF FLESH DOES CRACKLE AND SHIVER AND BREAK IN PAIN   151 17
  AND THE THICK FALLEN CROWDS CRACKLE AND CRUMBLE UNDER T+   615 10

CRACKLED
  THE THORN-LEAVES CRACKLED AND TWISTED AND SWEATED IN AN+   94 26
  LIKE A BOILING POT THE POND CRACKLED WITH HAPPINESS   206 30
  THE THORN-LEAVES CRACKLED AND TWISTED AND SWEATED IN AN+   *897 14

CRACKLING
  OH WITHERED CRACKLING TWIGS OF BRUSHWOOD PEOPLE   784 20

CRACKS
  THE END CRACKS OPEN WITH THE BEGINNING   278 25

CRADLE
  HER HEART IS A SWINGING CRADLE   201 9
  WHEN THE WIND BLOWS THE CRADLE SHALL ROCK   669 8
  THEY ARE SO LARGE AND THEY CRADLE SO MUCH OF A MAN   700 18
  STILL CONTINUE TO CRADLE HIM   700 21

CRAFTSMAN'S
  MY CRAFTSMAN'S NERVE   111 24
  MY FINE CRAFTSMAN'S NERVE   *927 12
  MY FINE CRAFTSMAN'S NERVE   *928 12

CRAMMED
  ALL THAT WE KNOW IS NOTHING WE ARE MERELY CRAMMED WASTE+   613 8

CRANBERRIES
  WE SITTING HERE AMONG THE CRANBERRIES   223 16
  LITTLE RED CRANBERRIES CHEEK TO CHEEK   224 1

CRANING
  WATER-EYES CRANING   336 14

CRANIUM
  CRANIUM   760 2

CRAPA
  COME ON YOU CRAPA I'M NOT YOUR SERVANT   384 33
  COME DOWN CRAPA OUT OF THAT ALMOND-TREE   385 22

CRAPE
  TOSSES THE CRAPE OF RED ACROSS YOUR BROW AND DOWN YOUR   370 27

CRASH
  WAVES CRASH LIKE THUNDER THROUGH   159 16
  FORCED TO CRASH AGAINST HER   363 18
  TOWARDS A SHOCK AND A CRASH AND A SMITING OF HORNS AHEAD   381 22
  AND BRING IT HURTLING TO A HEAD WITH CRASH OF HORNS AGA+   381 25
  AND RUIN ABOVE US AND THE CRASH OF RELEASE   462 15
  CRASH   511 20

CRASH
  TRAFFIC WILL TANGLE UP IN A LONG DRAWN-OUT CRASH OF COL+   624 27
  DEER CRASH THEIR HORNS IN THE MOUNTAINS OF HIS BREAST   *953 28

CRASH-BOX
  MY ROOM A CRASH-BOX OVER THAT GREAT STONE RATTLE   342 10

CRASH-GULF
  ABOVE THAT CRASH-GULF OF THE VIA DE' BARDI   343 14
  ABOVE THAT CRASH-GULF OF EXPLODING WHIPS   347 14

CRASHING
  HITTING OURSELVES AGAINST UNSEEN ROCK CRASHING OUR HEAD   544 13
  IN WHICH IS HEARD THE CRASHING SPLINTER OF MACHINES   640 11

CRATERS
  BAKED AMPHORAS CRATERS CANTHARUS OENOCHOE AND   305 13
  ARE ONLY SITTING TIGHT ON THE CRATERS OF THEIR VOLCANO   539 25

CRAVE
  WONDER I CRAVE FOR THAT BURNS STRONG IN HIM   876 31

CRAVED
  WE HAVE FORGOTTEN THE SUNNY APPLES OF DAY THAT WE CRAVE+ *917 15

CRAVEN
  FEAR CRAVEN IN HIS TAIL   347 11
  BUT THE CRAVEN THE COWARDLY THE CREEPING YOU THAT CAN O+ 678 25

CRAWL
  WHY DO I CRAWL ABOUT THIS POT THIS OUBLIETTE   224 17
  AND CRAWL AWAY LIKE A BLACK SNAIL   400 11
  CRAWL LIKE MASTERLESS DOGS IN THE BACK STREETS OF THE A+ 796 12
  NO SPOTTED TRAITORS CRAWL BY   810 4
  CRAWL OUT OF THE WATER AND LIE ON THE BEACH   827 17

CRAWLED
  HAVE CRAWLED   581 4
  AS YOU CRAWLED NAKED OVER ME   886 5

CRAWLING
  LO IN THE BACK STREETS OF THE AIR DEAD ONES ARE CRAWLIN+ 796 29

CRAWLS
  CRAWLS THE FIRST LOAD INTO SIGHT AND NOW THERE ARE SOME   732 25

CRAZED
  LIFE TWISTING ITS CRAZED MACHINERY   887 5

CRAZY
  CRAZY   *952 22

CREAM
  AND SLEEP THEREBY IS ONE MORE CREAM ENRICHENED   195 16
  I LICK THE CREAM OFF PROPERTY THAT'S WHAT IT SEEMS TO S+ 664 4
  CHAPLETS OF CREAM AND DISTANT GREEN   854 25

CREAMY
  AND THE GHOSTLY CREAMY COLOURED LITTLE TREES OF LEAVES   646 23

CREATE
  POWER TO KILL POWER TO CREATE   326 3
  I DIDN'T CREATE HIM   346 9

CREATED
  CREATED I LOOKED AT MYSELF THE CREATOR   257 16
  LET THE GOD THAT CREATED HIM BE RESPONSIBLE FOR HIS DEA+ 346 10
  THE WORLD IS CREATED AFRESH   725 10

CREATES
  HE CREATES WITH HIS SHINE   *928 5

CREATING
  CREATING THE CHANNELLED VEIN OF MAN   69 2

CREATION
  I WAS THE GOD AND THE CREATION AT ONCE   257 14
  CREATOR I LOOKED AT MY CREATION   257 15
  COME RUSH OF CREATION   271 1
  STARING CREATION OUT OF COUNTENANCE   328 20
  AND CASTING THE CYCLES OF CREATION   329 6
  THINKING I AM NOT THE MEASURE OF CREATION   339 12
  ALL ANIMATE CREATION ON YOUR SHOULDER   353 32
  OF ALL CREATION   356 17
  OF CREATION   370 3
  CREATION   372 16
  IN ALL CREATION ONLY MAN COWERS AND IS AFRAID OF LIFE   529 11
  IS THE INCOMPREHENSIBLE PLASM OF LIFE OF CREATION   681 27
  THEN EVERY MOLECULE OF CREATION JUMPED AND CLAPPED ITS + 683 4
  CREATION   689 24
  AND GREW UP AND BECAME IN THE WONDER OF CREATION JESUS   689 29
  THE MYSTERY OF CREATION IS THE DIVINE URGE OF CREATION   690 1
  IT IS CREATION GOD LOOKS HIMSELF ON IT IN WONDER FOR TH+ 690 11
  GREAT BRIDE OF ALL CREATION   698 7
  LO THE LAST OF THE SEVEN GREAT LAUGHS OF CREATION   698 17
  FOR THE UNSEEN WITNESSES ARE THE ANGELS OF CREATION   706 22
  ABSOLUTE SELF-AWARENESS ABSOLVED FROM THE MEDDLING OF C+ 712 18
  TIME BUT DIFFERENT DIRECTIONS IN CREATION WITHIN THE FO+ 760 25
  THEY STARTLED CREATION AND WHEN THEY WERE THROUGH   761 7
  THE CREATION OF A NEW-PATTERNED DREAM DREAM OF A GENERA+ *907 3
  THE CREATION OF A NEW-PATTERNED DREAM DREAM OF A GENERA+ *908 24
  GOD LONELY PUT DOWN HIS MOUTH IN A KISS OF CREATION   *916 5
  TILL MY FIRE OF CREATION BORE YOU   *928 8

CREATIVE
INTO WHICH THE CREATIVE FUTURE SHALL BLOW STRANGE UNKNO+   428 29
LEAVING IT TO THE VAST REVOLUTIONS OF CREATIVE CHAOS   429 24
THERE ARE SAID TO BE CREATIVE PAUSES   510 7
AND KNOW OUR DEPENDENCE ON THE CREATIVE BEYOND   621 7
BUT TO SOMETHING UNSEEN UNKNOWN CREATIVE   622 11
GOD SIGHING AND YEARNING WITH TREMENDOUS CREATIVE YEARN+   691 2
BUT URGES TOWARDS INCARNATION WITH THE GREAT CREATIVE U+   691 16

CREATIVE GODHEAD
BUT NOW WE HAVE TO GO BACK TO THE CREATIVE GODHEAD   609 25

CREATOR
CREATOR I LOOKED AT MY CREATION   257 15
CREATED I LOOKED AT MYSELF THE CREATOR   257 16
LO THE LAUGH OF THE CREATOR   698 15
THE FASCINATION OF THE RESTLESS CREATOR THROUGH THE MES+   *906 23
THE FASCINATION OF THE QUICK RESTLESS CREATOR MOVING TH+   *908 19
AND I WATCH TO SEE THE CREATOR THAT PATTERNS +   *908 25

CREATURE
CREATURE   356 13
BUT THE ASS IS A PRIMAL CREATURE AND NEVER FORGETS   379 33
THE KEEPER HOODS THE VAST KNEE THE CREATURE SALAAMS   387 16
CREATURE WENT EAST   405 27
TOWARDS WOMAN OR MAN BIRD BEAST OR CREATURE OR THING   454 13
AT THE CORE OF YOUR HEART THE OTHER CREATURE   466 2
THE OTHER CREATURE THE OTHER CREATURE   466 3
BUT THE CREATURE THERE THAT HAS COME TO MEET YOU   466 5
HOVERING TO PECK OUT THE EYES OF THE STILL-LIVING CREAT+   500 17
LO THERE IS A CREATURE FORMED HOW STRANGE   690 12
TO BE A CREATURE IN THE HOUSE OF THE GOD OF LIFE   700 2
A GOD-LOST CREATURE TURNING UPON HIMSELF   700 25
A CREATURE OF BEAUTIFUL PEACE LIKE A RIVER   714 14
AND A CREATURE OF CONFLICT LIKE A CATARACT   714 15
AND DRINKS HIMSELF LIKE A SOAKED GORGED CREATURE DULL   877 9
DO YOU THINK I'D HAVE A CREATURE LIKE YOU AT MY SIDE   *944 25

CREATURES
LIKE DROWSY CREATURES THE HOUSES FALL ASLEEP   48 19
WHERE HASTENING CREATURES PASS INTENT   50 27
ONLY WE HARD-FACED CREATURES GO ROUND AND ROUND AND KEEP   71 11
AND NAKEDLY NOTHING 'TWIXT WORLD AND HEAVEN TWO CREATUR+   90 4
US CREATURES PEOPLE AND FLOWERS UNDONE   127 3
HURRYING CREATURES RUN   166 22
I THANK YOU I DO YOU HAPPY CREATURES YOU DEARS   221 20
MEN ARE THE SHYEST CREATURES THEY NEVER WILL COME   254 14
AND CREATURES WEBBED AND MARSHY   285 23
EMPEDOKLES SAYS TREES WERE THE FIRST LIVING CREATURES T+   295 4
THE SHINING OF LAMPS BECAUSE WITH HIS RAYS HE HURTS THE+   331 7
CREATURES THAT HANG THEMSELVES UP LIKE AN OLD RAG TO SL+   342 1
AND FOUND HIS FEET SO HE IS THE FIRST OF CREATURES TO S+   348 14
THE SUN SO THAT ALL CREATURES OF THE SUN MUST DIP THEIR MOU+ 368 6
AND IS FECUND WITH A NEW DAY OF NEW CREATURES DIFFERENT   429 7
TO BRING FORTH CREATURES THAT ARE AN IMPROVEMNT ON   429 25
ALL THE CREATURES SEEMED TO ENJOY THE GAME   445 22
O YOU CREATURES OF MIND DON'T TOUCH ME   468 23
AS A MATTER OF FACT THE ONLY CREATURES THAT SEEM TO SUR+   523 21
CREATURES   621 21
ALL THESE CREATURES THAT CANNOT DIE DRIVEN BACK   624 11
AND AGAINST THIS INWARD REVOLT OF THE NATIVE CREATURES +   624 20
BODIES AND PRESENCES HERE AND NOW CREATURES WITH A FOOT+   689 23
THEY WENT THEIR WAYS AS CREATURES DO   761 2
AND DRUNK WITH THE DEATH OF THE SOOTHING GREY-WINGED CR+ *918 11
ALL THE CREATURES THAT CANNOT DIE WHILE ONE HEART HARBO+ *954 5
ALL THE CREATURES THAT WERE DRIVEN BACK INTO THE UTTERM+ *954 14

CREATURE'S
LIES THE LIVING ROCK OF A SINGLE CREATURE'S PRIDE   844 9

CREDENTIALS
CREDENTIALS SIR   582 8

CREDIT
AND I HAD TO GIVE HIM CREDIT FOR HIS RATHER EXHIBITIONI+   533 5
HIS CREDIT HIS NAME HIS WIFE EVEN MAY BE JUST ANOTHER   607 17

CREEP
CREEP UP THE WALL TO ME AND IN AT MY OPEN WINDOW   62 28
ASLEEP MY FINGERS CREEP   143 10
TO CREEP THROUGH YOUR LOOSENED HAIR TILL HE REACHES   178 32
CREEP RIGHT UP WITH YOUR ROUND HEAD PUSHED IN MY BREAST   245 6
BUT HOW LOVELY TO BE YOU CREEP CLOSER IN THAT I AM MORE   245 20
WHEN I ENFOLD YOU AND YOU CREEP INTO ME   246 14
MUST CREEP HER GREAT BULK BENEATH THE BRIDGE OF HIM   426 10
THERE ARE DEAD THAT CREEP THROUGH THE BURNING BOWELS OF+   795 24
WHERE DOGS CREEP UNCLEAN   808 16
AND MEN ARE THE LICE THAT CREEP ON IT   843 8
CREEP ON THE VAST MONEY-BEAST   843 11

CREEPER
OF THE CREEPER ON THE BREAST OF THE HOUSE OPPOSITE   883 2

CREEPING
AND WHEN THE DAWN COMES CREEPING IN   59 1
BATS AND AN UNEASY CREEPING IN ONE'S SCALP   341 21
SLOW CREEPING COLD ONES   511 12
CREEPING BACK AND FORTH TO WORK   585 10
THEY ARE HUMBLE WITH A CREEPING HUMILITY BEING PARASITE+   621 20
WHAT HAVE THEY DONE TO YOU MEN OF THE MASSES CREEPING   630 9
BUT THE CRAVEN THE COWARDLY THE CREEPING YOU THAT CAN O+   678 25
NO ANIMAL NO BEAST NOR CREEPING THING   701 12
CREEPING FOR THE GARBAGE OF LIFE AND BITING WITH VENOMO+   796 13
CREEPING AMONG THE SLEEPING AND THE DREAMING WHO ARE LA+   807 6
IN THE NIGHT I SEE THE GREY DOGS CREEPING OUT OF THE SL+   807 11
I SEE THE GREY DOGS CREEPING OUT WHERE MY DEER ARE BROW+   807 18
THEN COMFORTS IT THE CREEPING TENDERNESS   *900 26
THEN COMFORTS IT THE CREEPING TENDERNESS   *904 2

CREEPS
THE WOODBINE CREEPS ABROAD   42 9
FROM ME FROM THE HAND OF MY LOVE WHICH CREEPS UP   47 18
OH BUT THE RAIN CREEPS DOWN TO WET THE GRAIN   63 27
CREEPS UPON HER THEN AND RAVISHES HER STORE   120 4
SHE CREEPS PERSISTENT DOWN THE SKY'S LONG STAIRS   131 28
CREEPS A BEE   178 24
IN THE NIGHT THE SOUL OF A COWARD CREEPS OUT OF HIM   807 4
THE GREY DOG CREEPS AMONG YOU   807 29
ME COMFORTED TO FEEL THE WARMTH THAT CREEPS   *900 23
ME COMFORTED TO FEEL THE WARMTH THAT CREEPS   *903 35

CREPE DE CHINE
FULL FORE-AND-AFT IN GOOD GREY CREPE DE CHINE   835 28

CREPT
LOVE HAS CREPT OUT OF HER SEALED HEART   46 5
THERE'S A SCENT OF CLOVER CREPT THROUGH MY HAIR   50 9
YOU THE CORE OF THE FIRE CREPT INTO ME   245 25
THE SUN HAS CREPT LIKE A SCARLET BEETLE IN THE HUSK   757 15
QUIETLY THROUGH THE YEARS I HAVE CREPT BACK TO SEE   *940 6

CRESCENT
DELICATE FRAIL CRESCENT OF THE GENTLE OUTLINE OF WHITE   371 13
PUT MY FEET UPON THE CRESCENT LIKE A LORD   684 9
THAT WE SHOULD BE LOVELY IN THE FLESH WITH BRIGHT CRESC+ 687 16

CRESSET
OF THE SORREL'S CRESSET A GREEN BRAVE TOWN   49 27

CRESSETS
COCOA-NUT CRESSETS   388 28

CREST
THAT RIDES THE ROOM LIKE A FROZEN BERG ITS CREST   155 4
LAPS LITTLE CREST AFTER CREST   194 8
FROM THE CREST OF A FALLING BREAKER   200 23
THE BLUE JAY WITH A CREST ON HIS HEAD   375 1
AND BOBBING HIS THICK DARK CREST ABOUT THE SNOW AS IF   375 26
YOU THICK BIRD WITH A STRONG CREST   375 30
WITH THE CREST OF THE DIRTY DRAB WORLD DOWN BELOW   551 2
PAUSES NEAR THE CREST OF THE HILL CLIMBING SLOWLY LIKE + 687 17

CREVICE
I ADMIT A GOD IN EVERY CREVICE   346 15

CREW
THE COCK ROSE AND CREW OVER THE WATERS   802 11

CRIBBED
AND FRESHEN THE PUTRID LITTLE SPACE IN WHICH WE ARE CRI+ 515 4

CRIED
I CRIED BUT NO ONE HEARD ME   46 23
THAT WHITE AN' 'ER CRIED THAT MUCH I'D LIKE TO BEGIN   61 8
WHERE NO BULL ROARED NO COW EVER LOWED NO STAG CRIED   394 16
AND YOU CRIED 'OORAY PLAY UP JOHN THOMAS   550 27
WAS UNAWARE BUT HIS WIFE CRIED IN HER DREAM   885 11

CRIES
WITH SNARLING RED JAWS AND I HEARD THE CRIES   38 10
SOLEMNLY AND DISTINCTLY CRIES DOWN THE BABEL OF CHILDREN 48 15
YET NOW EVERY FIBRE OF ME CRIES IN PAIN   117 2
NIGHTINGALE'S PIERCING CRIES AND GURGLES STARTLED THE   366 2
IT IS THE LOUD CRIES OF THESE BIRDS OF PAIN   741 14
WITH RED SNARLING JAWS LET YOURSELF LISTEN TO THE CRIES *892 25
AND LIPS APART WITH DUMB CRIES   *912 23
ARE OPEN FOR THEM THEY ARE MOPING OR THEY BREAK WITH LI+ *918 7
I HEARD THY CRIES OF PAIN AND THEY BROKE   *927 11
YET EVERY FIBRE OF ME CRIES IN PAIN   *931 6

CRIME
WHAT IS THE CRIME THAT MY SEED IS TURNED TO BLOOD   742 37
WHO IS IT WILL HAVE IT SO WHO DID THE CRIME   743 2
WE EXPIATE IT THUS THE UNKNOWABLE CRIME   743 14
THE CRIME FULL-EXPIATE THE ERINNYES SUNK   743 25

CRIMSON
HANG STRINGS OF CRIMSON CHERRIES AS IF HAD BLED   36 21
BRIGHT CRIMSON RIM   96 18
CLOSING ITS CRIMSON THROAT MY OWN THROAT IN HER POWER   123 14
CHOKE ME IN MY OWN CRIMSON I WATCHED HER PULL   123 17
ITS SOFTLY-STIRRING CRIMSON WELLING-UP   153 27
THAT'S HOW THE FIG DIES SHOWING HER CRIMSON THROUGH THE 283 30
SCARLET AND CRIMSON AND A RUST OF BLOOD   744 30
AND CRIMSON AND THE BLOOD-BROWN HEAPS OF SLAIN   745 26
HEAVY NODDING CLUSTERS OF CRIMSON RED   855 10
HEAVY HANGING CLUSTERS OF CRIMSON RED   855 18
THE CRIMSON SHEAF OF THE WEST THE DEEP FETCHED SIGH   885 6
CLOSING ITS CRIMSON THROAT MY OWN THROAT IN HER POWER *934 20
AND CHOKE ME IN MY OWN CRIMSON I WATCHED HER PULL   *934 23

CRINGE
AND DIDN'T YOU CRINGE ON THE FLOOR LIKE ANY INKSPOT   400 10

CRINGING
LIKE A CRINGING DOG AT HIS HEELS OFFEND HIM NOW   47 22
CRINGING PITY AND LOVE WHITE-HANDED CAME   94 16
CRINGING PITY AND MY SELF WHITE-HANDED CAME   *897 4

CRIPPLE
A CRIPPLE   213 12
TO BE A CRIPPLE   213 14

CRIPPLED
  BUT WE ARE MAIMED CRIPPLED CONTORTED AND SICK   833   8

CRISIS
  ENCROACHING TOWARDS A CRISIS A MEETING A SPASM AND THRO+   66 22
  RUSSIA ACROSS HER CRISIS   536 10

CRISP
  THE CRISP FLESH   817 27

CRISPED
  CRISPED WITH INTENSE DESIRE   861 22

CRISPING
  THE CRISPING STEAM OF A TRAIN   100   2

CRITIC
  APPLICANT FOR POST AS LITERARY CRITIC HERE ARE MY   582   7

CRITICAL
  AND THE CRITICAL GRASSHOPPER   507 21
  OF CRITICAL CHERUBS THAT CHIRRUP AND PIPE   680 22
  AND LEAVE THE CRITICAL PIGGY-WIGGIES   681 11

CRITICISING
  WITH FINGER-NAILS OF SEPTIC CRITICISING   533 10

CRITICS
  MY LITTLE CRITICS MUST ALL HAVE BEEN BROUGHT UP BY THEIR   581 19
  MY LITTLE CRITICS DEAR SAFE LITTLE PETS   581 26

CROAK
  CROAK   500   5

CROCKETED
  PIERCING THE BLUE WITH THEIR CROCKETED SPIRES   49 25

CROCUS
  NOW LIKE A CROCUS IN THE AUTUMN TIME   744   4
  OF DEATH A CYCLAMEN A CROCUS FLOWER   744   6
  NOW LIKE A CYCLAMEN A CROCUS FLOWER   744 19
  SO LIKE A CYCLAMEN A CROCUS FLOWER   745   1
  NOW LIKE A CYCLAMEN A CROCUS FLOWER   745 21
  JUST AS A CYCLAMEN OR CROCUS FLOWER   745 27

CROCUSES
  THE SUN SETS OUT THE AUTUMN CROCUSES   177   1
  LIKE LAVENDER CROCUSES SNOWDROPS LIKE ROMAN HYACINTHS   270   6
  PURPLE CROCUSES   271   7
  AHA THE STRIPE-CHEEKED WHELPS WHIPPET-SLIM CROCUSES   309   5
  THE MEN STOOD AROUND LIKE CROCUSES AGAPE IN THE SUN   540   4
  THE SUN SETS WIDE THE YELLOW CROCUSES   868 17
  THE SUN SETS WIDE THE YELLOW CROCUSES   *941 17

CROFT
  ON A MOUNTAIN CROFT   240 18

CROOK
  CROOK THE KNEE AND BE GLAD   392 13
  YOU'RE NO BETTER THAN A CROOK   668 22

CROOKED
  NEITHER STRAIGHT NOR CROOKED NEITHER HERE NOR THERE   *959 17

CROOK-LEGGED
  STIFF GALLANT IRASCIBLE CROOK-LEGGED REPTILE   363 19

CROON
  AND COLDNESS CLOGGED THE SEA TILL IT CEASED TO CROON   98 15
  WHILE I DANCE A TARANTELLA ON THE ROCKS AND THE CROON   130   6

CROP
  BREATHED QUIET ABOVE ME AND THE CROP   35 19
  LARROPIN' NECK AN' CROP   78 30
  TO CROP A LITTLE SUBSTANCE   358   4
  LARROPIN' NECK AN' CROP   *920 22

CROP-HEADED
  FLAT-CHESTED CROP-HEADED CHEMICALISED WOMEN OF INDETERM+   522   2

CROPS
  RAIN FROM THE SHOWERY HEAVENS AND BRIGHT BLUE CROPS   136 12
  OF HAVING SHORT CROPS   778 19

CROSS
  AND I AT THE FOOT OF HER CROSS DID SUFFER   103 21
  THE SHRIEKING CROSS   112 10
  LIKE A THING UNWARRANTABLE CROSS THE HALL   140   8
  WHY CONTINUALLY DO THEY CROSS THE BED   140 20
  CROSS THE CHASM   146 33
  MY DEAR WHEN YOU CROSS THE STREET IN THE SUNSHINE SURELY   211 13
  CHRIST ON THE CROSS HIS BEAUTIFUL YOUNG MAN'S BODY   225   5
  AND HEART LIKE A CROSS THAT BEARS DEAD AGONY   226   6
  HIM CROSS   243 25
  AS THEY CROSS AND PART AND MEET   253 13
  AND SO I CROSS INTO ANOTHER WORLD   256   4
  AND WE MUST CROSS THE FRONTIERS THOUGH WE WILL NOT   287   6
  AND THE CROSS SPROUTING ITS SUPERB AND FEARLESS FLOWERS   305 30
  THE CROSS THE CROSS   354 23
  THE LONE CLEAVAGE OF DIVISION UPRIGHT OF THE ETERNAL CR+   355 30
  THE CROSS   356   1
  THE CROSS   366 29
  HENCE THE BLACK CROSS ON HIS SHOULDERS   378 27
  AND YOU CROSS THE FERRY WITH THE NAKED PEOPLE GO UP THE   386 25
  LIKE A WHITE CHRISTUS FALLEN TO DUST FROM A CROSS   403 22
  HOW CROSS YOU WERE   557 11
  AND THE FOOT OF THE CROSS NO LONGER IS PLANTED IN THE P+   616 21
  THE CROSS THE VIRGIN PISCES THE SACRED FISH   616 24

CROSS
  BEHOLD YOUR CROSS CHRISTIANS   636   1
  ON THIS CROSS OF DIVISION DIVISION INTO SEX   636 13
  THE BASE THOSE THAT ARE BELOW THE BAR OF THE CROSS   637   4
  CROSS LIKE CLOCK-WORK THE MINOAN DISTANCE   688   8
  THEY ONLY CROSS THE DISTANCE NEVER CHANGES   688   9
  THOSE THAT FOLLOW ME MUST CROSS THE MOUNTAINS OF THE SKY   799   8
  THE SHRIEKING CROSS   *928 30

CROSSE AND BLACKWELLS
  SHAKESPEARE THEY SOLD TO CROSSE AND BLACKWELLS TO BE JA+   763   6

CROSSED
  HAVE I CROSSED   749 11
  HOW GAVE THESE PALEFACES YELLOWFACES CROSSED THE WATERS+   794 30
  AND CROSSED THE ROAD OF THE UNEASY   808   4
  BUT WHEN I CROSSED THE DUNES   883 21
  AS WE CROSSED THE MOW-FIELDS DOWN THE GLOWING HILL   884 28

CROSSING
  THE NIGHT WITH SILENCE CROSSING THE LAMP-TOUCHED TIDE   144 13
  AND GLEAM AS OF SUNSHINE CROSSING THE LOW BLACK HEAP   144 25
  NAY WE FIND OURSELVES CROSSING THE FERN-SCENTED FRONTIE+   286 24
  WHILE YOU READ ABOUT THE AIR-SHIP CROSSING THE WILD ATL+   441 22
  OR WE SHOULD NEVER KNOW WHEN WE WERE CROSSING THE   548 29
  FLOWERS NOW AS WE'RE CROSSING THE DREARY STAGES   814   6
  LIKE GRAINS OF MUSIC CROSSING THE FERTILE FALLOW   868 23
  EMERGING AND CROSSING THE CLEAR SKY UNPERCEIVED   874 24

CROSSIN'
  NOW SITHEE THEER AT TH' REELROAD CROSSIN'   79   1
  NOW SITHEE THEER AT TH' RAILROAD CROSSIN'   *920 25

CROSS-QUESTIONING
  IMPLACABLE WINTER'S LONG CROSS-QUESTIONING BRUNT   142   4

CROSS-ROADS
  THE GREY DOG CAUGHT ME AT THE CROSS-ROADS   808   2

CROSSWAYS
  THEN CROSSWAYS DOWN HIS SIDES   355   5

CROSS-WISE
  THROUGH HIS CROSS-WISE CLOVEN PSYCHE   356   3

'CROSS
  I CARRY MY ANGER SULLENLY 'CROSS THESE WASTE LANDS   *896 21

CROUCH
  CROUCHING AS LITTLE HOUSES CROUCH UNDER THE MIST WHEN I+   63 23
  AS YOU CROUCH AND TURN AWAY FROM ME   *931   2

CROUCHED
  BEAST CROUCHED ACROSS THE GLOBE READY IF NEED BE TO POU+   97 21
  I LIKE TO SEE SHE SAID AND SHE CROUCHED HER DOWN   123   7
  WHILE THE DRIVER ON THE SHAFT SITS CROUCHED IN DREAMS   225 16
  I LIKE TO SEE SHE SAID AND SHE CROUCHED HER DOWN   *934 13

CROUCHES
  AND CROUCHES LOW THEN WITH WILD SPRING   43   7
  AT HER TATTERED SILENCE AS SHE CROUCHES AND COVERS HER +   54 22
  A WOMAN CROUCHES   143   5
  AND THEN INVARIABLY SHE CROUCHES HER REAR AND MAKES   385   3

CROUCHING
  TILL HE CHAFES AT MY CROUCHING PERSISTENCE AND A SHARP   47 24
  CROUCHING AS LITTLE HOUSES CROUCH UNDER THE MIST WHEN I+   63 23
  WHO CROUCHING PUT HIS MOUTH DOWN IN A KISS   69 22
  HERE AMONG ALL THIS SILENCE CROUCHING FORWARD   225 19
  AND CROUCHING AND SPEAKING THE MUSIC OF LOST LANGUAGES   688 16

CROW
  SUDDEN OUTSIDE THE HIGH WINDOW ONE CROW   147 21
  A CROW FLOATS PAST ON LEVEL WINGS   166   1
  AND SALVIA FIERCE TO CROW AND SHOUT FOR FIGHT   317 21
  LET IT CROW THEN LIKE ONE O'CLOCK   457 30
  THESE COCKS THAT CAN'T CROW   792 24
  I SAW A DARK FIGURE APPROACHING A RAGGED SOLITARY CROW   866 17

CROWD
  THE OLD LIVES CROWD   52 27
  OUT OF THE STRESS OF THE CROWD   70   9
  AND AMONG THE WRECK OF THE THEATRE CROWD   71 28
  WHO CROWD IN CROWDS LIKE RHODODENDRONS IN BLOSSOM   73 12
  THE ROUND DARK HEADS OF MEN CROWD SILENTLY   232 21
  AND THE CROWD LIKE A FIELD OF RICE IN THE DARK GAVE WAY   390 34
  LET HIM SHOW IT TO THE CROWD PROBABLY THEY WILL APPLAUD   634 11
  IF HE SHOW IT THE EYES AND THE BREATH OF THE CROWD   634 16
  GAUNT GAUNT THEY CROWD THE GREY MUD-BEACHES OF SHADOW   722   6
  LIVES CROWD   *905 16
  AND CROWD THERE ON THE GREY MUD BEACHES OF THE MARGINS   958   9

CROWDED
  FIXED IN THE DARKNESS GRAPPLING FOR THE DEEP SOIL'S CRO+   92 11
  AND DIM HOPES CROWDED ME WARM WITH COMPANIONSHIP   98 29
  WHERE PEOPLE ARE CROWDED LIKE THISTLES   101 21
  THE HEART ALL CROWDED WITH SLAVES MOST WORKING SOME FEW+ 174 20
  ARE CROWDED WITH LOST SOULS THE UNEASY DEAD   722 22
  THOUGH ALL THE CROWDED SUNLIGHT JOSTLING   771 19
  HAVE SHONE FOR ME LIKE A CROWDED CONSTELLATION OF STARS *897 25
  HAVE SHONE FOR ME LIKE A CROWDED CONSTELLATION OF STARS *901   2
  TO FIND HIMSELF ON THE CROWDED ARID MARGINS OF EXISTENCE *957 14
  STREWN WITH DIM WRECKAGE AND CROWDED WITH CRYING SOULS   *957 16
  THE LONG MARGINAL STRETCHES OF EXISTENCE CROWDED WITH L+ *957 23

CROWDEDNESS
  I LONG TO SEE ITS CHOCK-FULL CROWDEDNESS   315 27

CROWDING
  CROWDING THE BRIGHT DOORWAY   201 26
  AND WHITE PEOPLE IN EVENING DRESS BUZZING AND CROWDING   387 23

CROWDS
  CROWDS OF GLITTERING KING-CUPS SURGE TO CHALLENGE THE B+   33 11
  WHO CROWD IN CROWDS LIKE RHODODENDRONS IN BLOSSOM   73 12
  AMONG CROWDS OF THINGS IN THE SUNSHINE JOSTLED AND RACK+   133 8
  OR THEY ARE LIKE LEAVES RUSTLING THICK IN THE CROWDS ON+   615 8
  AND THE THICK FALLEN CROWDS CRACKLE AND CRUMBLE UNDER T+   615 10
  CROWDS OF GLITTERING KING-CUPS SURGE TO CHALLENGE THE B+   *891 12

CROWFLOWER
  AY AN' YALLER AS A CROWFLOWER AN' YET I' TH' DARK   77 7
  AY AN' YALLER AS A CROWFLOWER AN' YET I' THE DARK   *918 25

CROWING
  COCK-CRESTED CROWING YOUR ORANGE SCARLET LIKE A TOCSIN   314 28

CROWN
  HE GAVE HER NO CROWN OF FLOWERS   202 21
  TO CROWN THE TRIUMPH OF THIS NEW DESCENT   218 28
  AND BARBED BARBED WITH A CROWN   278 14
  OH CROWN OF SPIKED GREEN METAL   278 15
  IF WE TOUCH THE SOB-STUFF CROWN   537 10
  I WEAR FRAILITY AS A CROWN   772 8
  HER SOUL'S FLAG SANK AND HER PRIDE PUT OFF ITS CROWN   *936 17

CROWNED
  PUT SACKCLOTH ON BE CROWNED WITH POWDERY ASH   234 27
  NOW DUE TO BE CROWNED AGAIN   351 26

CROWNLESS
  CROWNLESS AND JEWELLESS AND GARMENTLESS   695 17

CROWNS
  AND CROWNS KINGLY GENEROUS TILTING CROWNS   278 19
  SORB-APPLES MEDLARS WITH DEAD CROWNS   280 23

CROWS
  AND WHICH WHEN DAY CROWS CHALLENGE   772 31
  LIKE IVORY AND GOLDEN MARBLE TWO BLACK CROWS HOLD   *894 27

CRUCIBLE
  CRUCIBLE WHERE NEW BLOSSOMS OF SHAPE ARE BEGOT   873 5

CRUCIFIED
  AND I TAKE THE WINGS OF THE MORNING TO THEE CRUCIFIED   321 20
  HIS ADOLESCENCE SAW HIM CRUCIFIED INTO SEX   361 2
  WHY WERE WE CRUCIFIED INTO SEX   364 7
  WAS CRUCIFIED   636 16
  AFTER YOUR MASTER THE CRUCIFIED   798 19

CRUCIFIX
  WITH A PALE DEAD CHRIST ON THE CRUCIFIX OF HIS HEART   226 3
  WHERE IT DISAPPEARED AT THE FOOT OF THE CRUCIFIX   371 27
  AND A BLACK CRUCIFIX LIKE A DEAD TREE SPREADING WINGS   403 24

CRUCIFIXION
  DOOMED IN THE LONG CRUCIFIXION OF DESIRE TO SEEK HIS CO+   361 3
  CRUCIFIXION   364 27
  THIS HORRIFIC CRUCIFIXION   636 21
  RISEN FROM THE DEAD AFTER THIS CRUCIFIXION   636 23

CRUDE
  YFA AND HER MOUTH'S PRUDENT AND CRUDE CARESS   127 23
  TWO HARD CRUDE PAWS IN HUNGER ON THE LONELY   127 27
  BEING CRUDE AND STRAIGHTFORWARD YOU'LL ONLY PROVE   576 14

CRUEL
  FIRE ENTERS YOU LIKE FROST LIKE A CRUEL BLIGHT   87 17
  CRUEL SELF THE FIGHT IS NOT FOR EXISTENCE THE FIGHT IS +   93 14
  I SHOULD HAVE BEEN CRUEL ENOUGH TO BRING   112 14
  YEA BUT IT IS CRUEL WHEN UNDRESSED IS ALL THE BLOSSOM   120 1
  SO SHE FOLLOWS THE CRUEL JOURNEY   203 5
  NO I HAVE WAKENED IT IS YOU YOU ARE CRUEL TO ME   211 2
  MY DEAR YES YES YOU ARE CRUEL TO ME YOU CAST   211 3
  NOW HOW CRUEL YOU ARE YOU PEOPLE THE SUNSHINE   211 18
  AH BUT IF I AM CRUEL WHAT THEN ARE YOU   230 15
  TO THOSE THINGS THAT LOVE DARKNESS THE LIGHT OF DAY IS +   331 3
  AND HE HAS A CRUEL SCAR ON HIS SHELL   360 6
  AND NO WONDER FOR MONEY HAS A FEARFUL CRUEL POWER   486 16
  AND THEN RISEN WE MUST LEARN THE MOST CRUEL LESSON   637 1
  OF THE CRUEL BRUISE   718 5
  THE CRUEL DAWN OF COMING BACK TO LIKE   720 4
  HEAVY WITH DROPS OF THE FIRST CRUEL RAIN   863 15

CRUELLY
  FOR HIS MISSION HAD CRUELLY FAILED WHILE HIS PASSIONATE+   859 11
  YOU SOUND SO DREADFUL SO CRUELLY HURT MY DEAR   871 18
  THAT ARE DEAD YOU HAVE LEFT ME CRUELLY SIEGMUND   871 30
  HIS RECKLESS RED MOUTH LAUGHING CRUELLY   876 25

CRUELTY
  AND THIS TERROR IS THE ROOT OF ALL CRUELTY   264 33
  HE JIGS ALONG IN THE IMBECILE CRUELTY OF THE MACHINE   645 15

CRUMBLE
  AND THE THICK FALLEN CROWDS CRACKLE AND CRUMBLE UNDER T+   615 10
  I SHOT MY MAN I SAW HIM CRUMBLE AND HANG   741 27
  EVEN THEIR BONES SHALL CRUMBLE   792 8

CRUMBLES
  THE HOAR-FROST CRUMBLES IN THE SUN   100 1

CRUMBLING
  THE CRUMBLING DAMP FRESH LAND LIFE HORIZONTAL AND CEASE+   321 18

CRUMBS
  ODD CRUMBS OF MELTING SNOW   304 14

CRUMPLE
  GLISTEN AS SILVER THEY CRUMPLE UP   217 20
  GLISTEN AS SILVER THEY CRUMPLE UP   *943 3

CRUMPLED
  THE THICK SNOW IS CRUMPLED ON THE ROOF IT PLUNGES DOWN   76 6
  AMONG THE CRUMPLED BEECH-LEAVES PHOSPHORESCENT   86 22
  THE THICK SNOW IS CRUMPLED ON THE ROOF IT PLUNGES DOWN   *898 1
  THE THICK SNOW IS CRUMPLED ON THE ROOF IT PLUNGES DOWN   *901 10

CRUMPLING
  YOU WHO ARE TWISTED IN GRIEF LIKE CRUMPLING BEECH-LEAVES   73 16

CRUNCH
  THEY SHALL CRUNCH YOUR BONES   796 26

CRUSH
  AND DRAWING THE DARKNESS TOGETHER CRUSH FROM IT A TWILI+   92 19
  WOULD CRUSH THEIR MOUNDS ON HER HEART TO KILL IN THERE   128 25
  I THINK SOMETIMES IT WILL CRUSH MY HEART INWARD   869 22

CRUSHED
  EMBRACE OF DARKNESS LIE AROUND AND CRUSHED BETWEEN THEM+   88 4
  AND WE ARE CRUSHED BETWEEN THE COVERS WE CLOSE OUR EYES+   88 12
  OUR ATTENTION OUT OF THE VOID WHEREIN WE ARE CRUSHED   165 33
  AND THE BLUISH MOUNTAINS BEYOND WOULD BE CRUSHED OUT   205 4
  AND YOU CAN'T BE FULLY ALIVE IF YOU ARE CRUSHED BY SECR+   522 10
  BECAUSE WHEN THE SPARK IS CRUSHED IN A MAN   524 10
  CRUSHED UTTERLY AND BREATHED THROUGH AND THROUGH   530 2
  THEY ARE ALL BUT CRUSHED   542 19
  TO RISE AN ODOUR OF PURPLE VIOLETS CRUSHED   881 7
  KNOWING THEN I HAD TAKEN MY BOSOM FROM HER CRUSHED BREA+ 882 9
  LEAVING THEM CRUSHED WORMS   *949 13

CRUSHES
  TO HER SHE CRUSHES THEM INTO HER BOSOM DEEP   128 28
  THAT CRUSHES ME TO AN UNSEEN ATOM OF FIRE   195 36
  WITH LUST CRUSHES OUT THE SPARK   524 8

CRUSHING
  CRUSHING OUT THE NATURAL HUMAN LIFE   508 21
  STRAYED DOWN THE HILL CRUSHING THE SILKEN MOSS   863 22
  YOU ARE CRUSHING ME LET ME GO LET ME GO   870 21

CRUST
  TO FLOURISH THERE AS PALE MOULD BLOOMS ON A CRUST   99 5

CRUSTED
  AND HOTNESS AND THEN MORE CRUSTED BRINE IN OUR HEARTS 707 23

CRUTCHES
  BUT I'VE HAD SUCH A JOB MY CRUTCHES I FAIRLY DRAGGED TH+ 865 22

CRY
  WE CRY IN THE WILDERNESS FORGIVE ME I   40 13
  WHOSE PLAINTIVE CRY IS HEARD AS SHE FLIES   42 29
  AND THOUGH IT BE LOVE'S WET BLUE EYES THAT CRY   89 32
  CRY OUT AND FEND HER OFF AS SHE SEEKS HER PROCREANT GRO+ 91 27
  CRY OUT TO YOU   96 15
  BRIMFUL AND CRY   96 26
  AND I CRY ALOUD IN THE MOMENTS THAT INTERVENE   100 23
  LET US NOT CRY TO HER STILL TO SUSTAIN US HERE   132 21
  AND WHAT DO I CARE THOUGH THE VERY STONES SHOULD CRY ME 133 10
  CRY OF A BIRD   150 8
  AND SO MY HEART BEGINS TO CRY AND CALL   174 3
  GIVE US AIR WE CRY OH LET US BUT BREATHE AGAIN   175 18
  WITHIN MY BODY CRY OUT TO THE DREAMING SOUL   195 32
  WHY DO YOU CRY   231 9
  WHY SHOULD YOU CRY THEN   231 20
  WHY DO YOU CRY   232 1
  WHY DO YOU CRY   232 5
  I COULD CRY WITH JOY BECAUSE I AM IN THE NEW WORLD JUST 256 10
  I COULD CRY WITH JOY AND QUITE FREELY THERE IS NOBODY TO 256 12
  WHAT THEN GOOD LORD CRY THE WOMEN   284 20
  YET I'VE HEARD HIM CRY   363 27
  WORSE THAN THE CRY OF THE NEW-BORN   364 13
  CRY LOUDLY BEYOND THE LAKE OF WATERS   365 35
  TEARING A CRY FROM US   366 33
  THE SAME CRY FROM THE TORTOISE AS FROM CHRIST THE OSIRI+ 367 3
  YOU SHALL KNOW A BIRD BY HIS CRY AND GREAT BIRDS CRY LO+ 368 9
  AWAITING THE CRY OF THE TURKEY-COCK   371 37
  AND SOME CRY OUT   388 2
  AND THE CHILDREN UTTERED A LITTLE CRY   444 17
  THE YOUNG ONES COPULATE HATE IT AND WANT TO CRY   485 6
  I HAD TO SIT DOWN AND CRY   554 12
  IT'S SUCH A BONNY BABY WE DAREN'T LET IT CRY   570 17
  AND THE DAWN CRY FROM A MINARET GOD IS GREAT   623 15
  WILL SEND UP THE WILD CRY OF DESPAIR   624 13
  ME WANT TO CRY TO SEE HIM SO STRONG AND EASY   733 23
  CRY FOR THEE OUT OF THE NIGHT WHEREIN WE ARE PRONE   753 5
  AND THE CHURCHES CRY PUSS PUSS COME AND BE FED   763 3
  THE SUN IS IN THE OUTER PORCH CRY TO HIM THANKS OH THAN+ 803 21
  NOT TO UTTER ONE CRY TO HER   874 21
  I STIFLE A CRY OF DESPAIR   883 18
  CRY OUT AND FEND HER OFF AS SHE SEEKS HER PROCREANT GRO+ *926 20
  WITH DREAMS AND THRUSTS THAT MAKE THEM CRY IN THEIR SLE+ *947 13
  SEND UP THE LAST WILD CRY OF DESPAIR   *954 11

CRYING
    WINGS AND FEATHERS ON THE CRYING MYSTERIOUS AGES PEEWIT+   34 26
    THE VERY BODY'S BODY CRYING OUT   264 10
    AND GRIEVING WITH PUPPY-LIKE BLIND CRYING   544 29
    AND THEY ARE CRYING LIKE PLANTS WHOSE ROOTS ARE CUT   610 12
    THERE ARE OTHER WAYS OF SUMMONS CRYING LISTEN LISTEN CO+   623 23
    FROM TIME TO TIME THE WILD CRYING OF EVERY ELECTRON   682 20
    CRYING POUR OUT THE BLOOD OF THE FOE   739 23
    CRYING HUITZILOPOCHTLI IS THIS WELL DONE   808 14
    STREWN WITH DIM WRECKAGE AND CROWDED WITH CRYING SOULS   *957 16

CRYSTAL
    OF CRYSTAL HEAVEN FALLS ONE FULL BLACK DROP   147 26
    TAKE AWAY ALL THIS CRYSTAL AND SILVER   427 11
    THAT IS THE CRYSTAL OF PEACE THE SLOW HARD JEWEL OF TRU+   477 17

CRYSTALLINE
    HITHER AND THITHER ACROSS THE HIGH CRYSTALLINE FRAME   72 9
    YOU HAVE MELTED IN THE CRYSTALLINE DISTANCE   696 27

CRYSTAL PALACE
    WHEN PEOPLE POSE AS GODS THEY ARE CRYSTAL PALACE STATUES   673 2

CRYSTALS
    I HAVE BEEN THRUST INTO WHITE SHARP CRYSTALS   207 25
    LIKE QUARTZ CRYSTALS   224 14

CUB
    AND GREY-STRIPED SUIT A YOUNG CUB OF A PIKE   338 2

CUBES
    IN HOLLOW BLOCKS AND CUBES DEFORMED AND HEAPED   53 25

CUBS
    AND PLAYS WITH THE WAVELETS LIKE A PANTHER PLAYING WITH+   709 10

CUCKOO
    THE CUCKOO AND THE COO-DOVE'S CEASELESS CALLING   65 11
    OH BOISTEROUS THE CUCKOO SHOUTS FORESTALLING   65 27
    TO THE CUCKOO THAT HUNG LIKE A DOVE   124 4
    CUCKOO COMES AND SHOVES OVER   125 2
    QUITE SAYS THE OTHER CUCKOO   433 8
    FOR EVERY BLOOMING BIRD IS AN OXFORD CUCKOO NOWADAYS   434 1
    WHEN THE CUCKOO THE COW AND THE COFFEE-PLANT CHIPPED THE   760 26
    DIMENSION THE CUCKOO WENT CUCKOO-WARDS THE COW WENT COW+   760 26
    THE COW WAS DUMB AND THE CUCKOO TOO   761 1
    CUCKOO   761 10
    CUCKOO   761 12
    LIKE A REIVING CUCKOO SHE SETTLED DOWN   *936 6
    TO THE CUCKOO BIRD AS SHE FLUTTERED ABOVE   *936 10

CUCKOO-WARDS
    DIMENSION THE CUCKOO WENT CUCKOO-WARDS THE COW WENT COW+   760 26

CUDDLING
    AND START PRANCING AND LICKING AND CUDDLING AGAIN   396 24
    AND SAW THEM CUDDLING WITH RISING PASSIONS THEY NONE OF   443 26

CUDDLIN'
    AFTER KISSIN' AN' CUDDLIN' WI' ME THA COULD   80 18

CUDGEL
    EGYPT JOSEPH'S CUDGEL   380 3

CUDGELLING
    OR THE MOST HIGH DURING THE COAL AGE CUDGELLING HIS MIG+   690 26

CUDS
    OH CHEW OLD COWS AT YOUR ANCIENT CUDS   814 20
    CHEW ALSO YOUNG HEIFERS YOUR JUICIER CUDS   814 21

CUFFING
    CUFFING THEM WITH SOFT PAWS   709 11

CUFFS
    AND CHITTER AND WIND THAT SHAKES AND CUFFS   89 29

CULMINATING
    AND OBVIOUSLY IT IS THE CULMINATING POINT OF HIS EXISTE+   523 12

CULMINATION
    ITS LIMPID SAP TO CULMINATION HAS BROUGHT   218 10
    COME AND LIFT US TOWARDS OUR CULMINATION WE MYRIADS   272 31

CULTURE
    DON'T SWALLOW THE CULTURE BAIT   459 10
    THAT CULTURE HAS HER ROOTS   489 6
    OH THE CANAILLE OF CULTURE THE CHRISTIAN CANAILLE   762 20
    EVERYTHING IN THE WORLD OF CULTURE AND SUPERIORITY   763 10
    I WOULD WARN ANYBODY AGAINST A CULTURE   763 13

CULTURED
    THE LIES THE TREACHERY THE SLIPPERY CULTURED SQUALOR OF+   497 4
    SO CULTURED EVEN BRINGING LITTLE GIFTS   500 3
    YOU CULTURED CANAILLE   762 19
    WHERE NOW THEY DEAL OUT SLICES OF PLATO-SAUSAGE TO THE +   762 27

CUMULUS
    STORMS AND CUMULUS CLOUDS OF ALL IMAGINABLE BLOSSOM   271 27

CUNNING
    THEN THE LITTLE CUNNING PIG-DEVIL OF THE ELEPHANT'S LUR+   390 9
    THE WORM THAT IS TOO CUNNING TO TURN   432 36
    THEY WERE CUNNING ABOUT THE GOODS   556 10
    AND THEY ARE BRIDLED WITH CUNNING AND BITTED   656 17
    A CUNNING ALGEBRA IN THE FACES OF MEN   *932 1

CUNNINGLY
    CUNNINGLY BLOWING ON THE FALLEN SPARKS ODDS AND ENDS OF+   271 31
    EYEING ME SIDEWAYS AND CUNNINGLY CONSCIOUS THAT I AM   333 2

CUNT
    WHAT BIT O' CUNT I HAD WI' 'ER   84 29

CUP
    CUP FOR A MOMENT SOFT LITTLE WING-BEATS UTTERING   65 4
    WHO SHOOK THY ROUNDNESS IN HIS FINGER'S CUP   69 9
    WITHIN YOUR CUP   96 31
    THE MELLOW SUNLIGHT STOOD AS IN A CUP   122 26
    MY HEART'S RED MEASURE IN HER CUP   123 28
    WITH THE AMETHYST IN HER CUP   123 30
    OUT OF THE HELL-QUEEN'S CUP THE HEAVEN'S PALE WINE   177 13
    THEY LIE SPILT ROUND THE CUP   216 4
    LIKE A POPPY IN ITS CUP   239 12
    CUP   683 6
    THE MIST IS A CUP OF WINE AND THE NEW AND OLD   *894 25
    OR AS TWO WHITE BUTTERFLIES SETTLE IN THE CUP OF ONE FL+ *914 4
    GOD SHOOK THY ROUNDNESS IN HIS FINGER'S CUP   *915 21
    THE MELLOW SUNLIGHT STOOD AS IN A CUP   *934 2
    MY HEART'S RED MEASURE IN THE CUP   *934 34
    OF MY BLOOD IN HER DARKENED CUP   *935 2

CUPBOARD
    AWAY IN SOME PRIVATE CUPBOARD   554 19
    WHY SHOULDN'T WE STEAL THE JAM IN THE CUPBOARD   573 11
    WHY SHOULDN'T I STEAL THE JAM IN THE CUPBOARD   670 26

CUPS
    ALL ALL PERSEPHONE'S PALE CUPS OF MOULD   177 5
    SWEAR IN THE PALE WINE POURED FROM THE CUPS OF THE QUEEN 177 21
    CUPS LET THEM BE DARK   427 7
    I WANT TO DRINK OUT OF DARK CUPS THAT DRIP DOWN ON   427 9
    AS WITH CLOTH SO WITH HOUSES SHIPS SHOES WAGONS OR CUPS   451 10
    AND DRINKING FROM CUPS THAT CAME OFF HIS FINGERS LIKE   451 26
    AND ITS PLUMES LOOK LIKE GREEN CUPS HELD UP TO THE SUN + 498 22
    TOUCH CUPS AND DRINK   *931 11
    AND AS WITH CLOTH SO WITH ALL THINGS HOUSES SHOES WAGON+ *950 1
    AND DRINKING FROM THE CUPS THAT HAVE FLOWERED FROM HIS + *950 10

CUP-SHAPE
    WERE PRESSED CUP-SHAPE TO TAKE THIS REIVER   124 7
    WERE PRESSED CUP-SHAPE TO TAKE THIS REIVER   *935 7

CURBED
    EVEN THE SUN IN HEAVEN CAN BE CURBED AND CHASTENED AT L+ 374 32
    MY CHAFED CURBED BLOOD NO LONGER BROOKS   857 3

CURDLE
    AND DART HIS ELECTRIC NEEDLES INTO YOUR BONES AND CURDL+ 797 10

CURDLES
    AND MILKY-SAPPED SAP THAT CURDLES MILK AND MAKES RICOTTA 283 11

CURDS
    SOUTH WITH FLYING CURDS   99 21

CURFEW
    THE CURFEW OF OUR GREAT DAY   512 8

CURIOSITY
    TILL THY FULL-FED FIRE OF CURIOSITY BORE YOU   *927 8

CURIOUS
    AND A CURIOUS DEARTH OF SOUND   145 31
    WHENCE HE DREW THE CURIOUS LIQUORS   202 19
    A CURIOUS AGONY AND A RELIEF WHEN I TOUCH THAT WHICH IS+ 266 14
    CURIOUS LONG-LEGGED FOALS AND WIDE-EARED CALVES AND NAK+ 271 34
    IT IS CURIOUS TOO THAT THOUGH THE MODERN MAN IN THE STR+ 648 1
    AND HE SAID SURELY THIS LOOKS VERY CURIOUS   790 9
    SURELY HE SAID THIS IS A CURIOUS PEOPLE I HAVE FOUND   790 16
    ANOTHER CURIOUS THING ABOUT THE ENGLISH MIDDLE CLASSES   831 20
    A KEEN FAR-REACHING CURIOUS MIND CYNICAL WITH LITTLE-BO+ 841 22
    AND CURIOUS SMILING EYES   878 18
    ITS CURIOUS COURSE MILDLY HERE IT WAKES AGAIN LEAPS LAU+ *891 15

CURIOUSLY
    HAVE YOU NOT MOST CURIOUSLY   95 17
    THE SLOW BEAST CURIOUSLY SPREADING HIS ROUND FEET FOR T+ 387 12
    CURIOUSLY ENOUGH ACTUAL REVOLUTIONS ARE MADE BY ROBOTS   647 21
    THE DARK ONES ARE CURIOUSLY PURPLISH LIKE FRESH   827 4
    A HAT QUAINTLY CURIOUSLY WOVEN LUXURIOUS WITH BIG ROSES 856 12
    AND SMILING CURIOUSLY WITH WATCHFUL EYES   878 13

CURL
    BLOOD-DROPS BENEATH EACH CURL   36 22
    WHO CURL IN SLEEP LIKE KITTENS WHO MASS AS A SWARM   73 17
    ELEPHANTS AFTER ELEPHANTS CURL THEIR TRUNKS VAST SHADOWS 388 1
    WE SHALL LAUGH THE INSTITUTIONS WILL CURL UP LIKE BURNT 482 26
    AND THE ANIMALS CURL DOWN ON THE DEAR EARTH TO SLEEP   834 3
    HER HAIR'S LIVE CURL   862 14

CURLED
    CURLED UP IN THE SUNSHINE LIKE A PRINCESS   255 27
    ELEPHANT ADVANCING HIS FRONTAL BONE HIS TRUNK CURLED   387 7
    FURTHER STILL BEFORE THE CURLED HORNS OF THE RAM STEPPED 437 14
    OR SITTING WITH OUR TAILS CURLED   450 14
    THE SEA HAS ITS BUD-LIPS SMILINGLY CURLED   445 26
    AND FURTHER STILL BEFORE THE CURLED HORNS OF THE RAM ST+ *946 25

CURLING
    DEFIANT CURLING THE LEAF OF HER TAIL AS IF SHE WERE CUR+ 386 13
    ALL AGOG AND CURLING UP HER TRUNK   426 12
    AND CURLING THEIR PRECIOUS LIVE TRUNKS LIKE AMMONITES   445 14

CURLS
AT SEASONS SHE CURLS BACK HER TAIL LIKE A GREEN LEAF IN+   385 31
THERE IS A SWAN-LIKE FLAME THAT CURLS ROUND THE CENTRE +   440 2
CURLS   574 7
IN CURLS AND FLAPS BETWEEN WORLDS THAT PLOD   823 26

CURLY
HENCE HE BECAME A CURLY SHEEP-DOG WITH DANGEROUS PROPEN+   324 26
ON CURLY PLUMP PIEBALD PONIES   444 16

CURRENT
I TOUCHED HER FLANK AND KNEW I WAS CARRIED BY THE CURRE+   260 12
THE UNKNOWN STRONG CURRENT OF LIFE SUPREME   261 12
AGAINST THE CURRENT OF OBSCURE ARNO   340 26
BLOWS THE MAGNETIC CURRENT IN FIERCE BLASTS   370 23
AS THE CURRENT   425 15
DO THEY PREVENT THE CURRENT   765 16

CURRENTS
AND CURRENTS OF EXCITEMENT IN OUR LIMBS   707 22
AND STEER ACCORDING TO THE CURRENTS AND WINDS AND TIDES+ *953 10

CURS
LO IN THE BACK STREETS OF THE AIR DEAD ONES ARE CRAWLIN+ 796 29

CURSE
OF THIS ANCIENT PLACE OF MY ANCIENT CURSE   131 21
I HAVE LEARNED TO CURSE YOUR MOTHERHOOD   207 34
I LONG FOR THE TIME TO COME WHEN THE CURSE AGAINST YOU + 208 1
NEVERTHELESS THE CURSE AGAINST YOU IS STILL IN MY HEART   208 15
THE CURSE AGAINST ALL MOTHERS   208 17
THEY ARE ACCURSED AND THE CURSE IS NOT TAKEN OFF   208 20
THEY AREN'T EVEN FIT TO CURSE   553 8

CURSED
I HAVE CURSED MOTHERHOOD BECAUSE OF YOU   207 36
AND CURSED BE HE THAT REMOVETH HIS NEIGHBOUR'S LANDMARK   706 16

CURSING
WHO HATED YOU AND KEPT LOOKING ROUND AT YOU AND CURSING   395 33

CURT
YOUR CURT PRIDE'S BAN   55 6

CURTAIN
CURTAIN US IN SO DARK   113 22
NEAR THE CURTAIN ON THE FLOOR   340 27
CURTAIN US IN SO DARK   *929 11

CURTAINS
LOOP BACK THE CURTAINS   343 3

CURVE
CURVE SWEEP TOWARDS A WOMAN'S   40 4
SLOPES ROUND THE HEAVENS IN ONE SMOOTH CURVE   172 19
AS IF HIS NOSTRILS WERE GOING TO CURVE BACK TO THE ROOT+ 380 15
FOR THE FIERCE CURVE OF OUR LIVES IS MOVING AGAIN TO THE 478 1
SWEEPING THE CURVE OF SPACE AND MOVING THE SILENCE   609 12
HAVE YOU COME ROUND THE CURVE YOUR WAY   764 18
FOR I HAVE TRAVERSED MY UPWARD CURVE   764 28
AND THEY CURVE OVER   819 19
SOME SHAPELESS DARK TO THE LOVELY CURVE OF LIGHT   872 7
IN THE CURVE OF THINE EXQUISITE FORM THE JOY OF THE   *915 28

CURVED
THOU DARK ONE THOU PROUD CURVED BEAUTY I   40 17
ON HIS BROW WHERE THE CURVED WISPS CLOT AND TWINE   60 3
CURVED THY MOUTH FOR THEE AND WHAT STRONG SHOULDER   69 14
LIKE SUDDEN CURVED SCISSORS   359 4
TAKING DREAD IN HER CURVED GAPING TOOTHLESS MOUTH   359 19
SHE DOES NOT EVEN KNOW SHE IS NIPPING ME WITH HER CURVED 359 24
AND THE DEEP SECRET ALL-PENETRATING TAIL CURVED BENEATH 365 3
THE ELEPHANTS HUGE AND GREY LOOMED THEIR CURVED BULK   445 10
OF THE PARABOLA OF CURVED FLIGHT   476 10
CURVED SPACE   481 15
CURVED CUT THE LAST THREADS   816 20
CURVED THY MOUTH FOR THEE AND HIS STRONG SHOULDER   *915 26

CURVES
IN THE CURVES OF THY FORM THE TRACE OF THE UNKNOWN   69 16
IT CURVES IN A RUSH TO THE HEART OF THE VAST   166 26
SWUNG GREAT CURVES THROUGH THE UPPER SPACE AND CAME   445 6
SUDDENLY IT CURVES AS IT YIELDS THE WHITE WHEAT   651 14
WHOSE EDGE OF HAIR CURVES THICKLY TO THE RED   878 21

CURVETTING
CURVETTING BITS OF TIN IN THE EVENING LIGHT   335 24
AND TO SPRING AWAY WITH A CURVETTING CLICK IN THE AIR   337 2

CURVING
LEANING IN YOUR ROOM LIKE TWO TIGER-LILIES CURVING   91 12
ALMOND TRUNKS CURVING BLACKLY IRON-DARK CLIMBING THE   300 24
GREY LAVENDER SENSITIVE STEEL CURVING THINLY AND BRITTLY 300 30
PROCEEDED TO DRAW HIS SLOW LENGTH CURVING ROUND   350 31
CURVING   373 29
GOD IN BLACK CLOUD WITH CURVING HORNS OF BRONZE   383 16
SINKS AND IS GONE LIKE A COMET CURVING INTO THE INVISIB+ 476 11
CURVING THEIR FEET AND DANCING AND FLUTTERING IN SPORT   751 4
ARE YOU CURVING UP TO ME   764 27
THE DARK CLEAVES DOWN AND WEAPON-HARD DOWNWARDS CURVING 782 4

CUSHION
SET A PLACE FOR THE DEAD WITH A CUSHION AND SOFT SEAT   723 9

CUSHIONS
THIS IS COMFORTLESS AND UNLOVELY WITH CUSHIONS AND THOS+ 856 9

CUSTOMS
PECULIAR CUSTOMS AND OBSERVANCES   776 29
CUSTOMS AND OBSERVANCES   776 31

CUSTOMS-OFFICIAL
BUT HERE EVEN A CUSTOMS-OFFICIAL IS STILL VULNERABLE   291 8

CUT
TO THE SUN AND THE SWALLOWS CUT CLEAR   35 4
WHERE SHE IS CUT OFF FROM ME   212 20
LIKE THE AGONY OF LIMBS CUT OFF AND ACHING   213 9
AND CABBAGES BORN TO BE CUT AND EAT   317 20
GOT HIS THROAT CUT   437 11
CUT OUT TO PLAY A SUPERIOR ROLE   490 15
AND WOMEN EVEN CUT THEIR SHIMMERY HAIR   530 8
WHY DID THEY CUT OFF THEIR LONG HAIR   537 26
HE CUT ME VERY DEAD   570 1
CUT THE IRON HOOK OUT OF THEIR FACES THAT MAKES THEM SO 586 4
NOR CUT THE INVISIBLE WIRES OF STEEL THAT PULL THEM   586 6
LIKE A PLANT WHOSE ROOTS ARE CUT   610 11
AND THEY ARE CRYING LIKE PLANTS WHOSE ROOTS ARE CUT   610 12
NOR CUT THE INVISIBLE WIRES OF STEEL THAT PULL THEM   632 21
IF I CUT MY FINGER MY BLOOD IS HOT NOT COLD   655 22
WE SHALL ALL BE CUT TO BITS   663 17
THAT WE ARE NOW CUT OFF FROM   666 14
JUST AS IT CANNOT BE ANYTHING BUT WRONG TO CUT THE THRO+ 678 4
AND SEPARATE HEART FROM HEART AND CUT AWAY ALL CARESSES 707 18
HOW I WOULD LIKE TO CUT OFF MY HANDS   741 3
CURVED CUT THE LAST THREADS   816 20

CUT-AWAY
WITH YOUR TAILORED CUT-AWAY COAT   835 18

CUTTING
THE PEASANTS ARE BENDING CUTTING THE BEARDED WHEAT   605 22
CUTTING YOU OFF FROM YOUR JOY   706 21

CYCLAMEN
SLOW TOADS AND CYCLAMEN LEAVES   310 16
CYCLAMEN LEAVES   310 19
ROSE CYCLAMEN ECSTATIC FORE-RUNNER   311 21
THE CYCLAMEN   311 29
OF DEATH A CYCLAMEN A CROCUS FLOWER   744 6
NOW LIKE A CYCLAMEN A CROCUS FLOWER   744 19
SO LIKE A CYCLAMEN A CROCUS FLOWER   745 1
NOW LIKE A CYCLAMEN A CROCUS FLOWER   745 21
JUST AS A CYCLAMEN OR CROCUS FLOWER   745 27

CYCLAMENS
THEY SAW TINY ROSE CYCLAMENS BETWEEN THEIR TOES GROWING 310 14
AND CYCLAMENS PUTTING THEIR EARS BACK   310 28
CYCLAMENS YOUNG CYCLAMENS   311 3
AND UNBUDDING CYCLAMENS   311 17
CYCLAMENS RUDDY-MUZZLED CYCLAMENS   311 22

CYCLE
A CYCLE OF EVOLUTION IS FINISHED   510 21

CYCLES
AND CASTING THE CYCLES OF CREATION   329 6

CYCLOP
AH CLEVER ODYSSEUS WHO OUTWITTED THE CYCLOP   543 26
THE CYCLOP   544 8

CYCLOPAEAN
THE ONE EYE OF OUR CYCLOPAEAN INSTINCT PUT OUT   833 18

CYCLOPEAN
IS BLINDED BRUTES OF CYCLOPS WITH OUR CYCLOPEAN EYE PUT 544 4
OVER THEIR MUTILATED CYCLOPEAN EYE   544 30

CYCLOPS
IS BLINDED BRUTES OF CYCLOPS WITH OUR CYCLOPEAN EYE PUT 544 4
BUT OH OUR HUMAN LIVES THE LUNGING BLIND CYCLOPS WE ARE 544 12
AH CYCLOPS THE LITTLE ANT-MEN CAN NEVER ENLIGHTEN YOU   544 20
ARE ALSO POOR BLIND CYCLOPS MOANING   544 27

CYGNETS
THERE'LL BE BABIES BORN THAT ARE CYGNETS O MY SOUL   438 21

CYLIX
OPEN-HEARTED CYLIX   305 14

CYMBALS
FIND AN ENEMY EGOIST AND CLASH THE CYMBALS IN FACE-TO-F+ 383 17

CYNICAL
A KEEN FAR-REACHING CURIOUS MIND CYNICAL WITH LITTLE-BO+ 841 22
CYNICAL EVEN ABOUT CYNICISM   842 10

CYNICISM
A KEEN FAR-REACHING CURIOUS MIND CYNICAL WITH LITTLE-BO+ 841 22
AND FINDS THAT THE SUBTLE DESTRUCTIVE CYNICISM IS ONLY + 842 2
CYNICAL EVEN ABOUT CYNICISM   842 10

CYPRESS
IT IS SAID A DISEASE HAS ATTACKED THE CYPRESS TREES OF + 295 1
WHO MADE SO LITTLE NOISE OUTSIDE THE CYPRESS GROVES   296 16
CYPRESS SHADOWY   298 6

CYPRESSES
  ALONG THE AVENUE OF CYPRESSES   232 16
  BETWEEN THE AVENUE OF CYPRESSES   232 29
  TUSCAN CYPRESSES   296 1
  TUSCAN CYPRESSES   296 5
  ETRUSCAN CYPRESSES   296 11
  DARK CYPRESSES   296 13
  AMONG THE SINUOUS FLAME-TALL CYPRESSES   296 17
  TUSCAN CYPRESSES   297 2
  ETRUSCAN CYPRESSES   297 5
  VICIOUS DARK CYPRESSES   297 9
  IS THE SHADOWY MONOMANIA OF SOME CYPRESSES   297 20
  ETRUSCAN CYPRESSES   297 24
  ETRUSCAN CYPRESSES   298 14

CYPRESS-TREES
  CYPRESS-TREES IN A WIND   297 17
  AND WRAPT INVIOLABLE IN SOFT CYPRESS-TREES   298 13

CYPRIAN'S
  AND THE CYPRIAN'S PAVEMENT-ROSES ARE GONE AND NOW   71 15

CYTHERA
  SHE SAYS I WENT TO CYTHERA   201 7

DABBLE
  SEEMS TO DABBLE IN ME   194 11

DABBLES
  THAT DABBLES ITS BODY IN ME   628 5

DADDIES
  OUR POOR OLD DADDIES GOT ON   518 21
  SO THAT ALL OUR DADDIES WERE QUITE BRITISH PURE   658 20

DADDY
  WAS YOUR'S A DADDY   582 5

DADDY-DO-NOTHINGS
  ALL DEAR DADDY-DO-NOTHINGS   658 22

DADDY-DO-NOTHING
  OR A DADDY-DO-NOTHING   582 6
  CHILDREN OF DADDY-DO-NOTHING   659 4

DADDY DO NOTHING
  CALLED HIM OLD DADDY DO NOTHING   582 4

DADDYLESS
  DADDYLESS   659 3

DAFFODIL
  LIKE A WILD DAFFODIL DOWN-DREAMING   91 19
  I WANT YOU TO BE AS SAVAGE AS THE GENTIAN AND THE DAFFO+   684 4

DAFFODILS
  IN PURPLE ELMS DAFFODILS   162 6
  WALK INNOCENT IN THE DAFFODILS   178 7
  OUT OF THE WITHERING DAFFODILS   178 18
  FOR WHETHER I SEE YOU SET THE DAFFODILS   875 7

DAGGER
  WITH A DAGGER OF DARK LIVE IRON   782 2

DAGGERS
  OLD DUNCAN WITH DAGGERS   494 24
  WITH DAGGERS BODKINS BULLETS MAN CAN MAKE   717 12
  WITH DAGGERS BODKINS BULLETS MAN CAN MAKE   *957 3

DAILY
  WHAT MATTER THE STUFF I LICK UP IN MY DAILY FLAME   115 10
  WITH ITS ROOTS IT HAS A GRAND GRIP ON ITS DAILY BREAD   498 21
  BESIDES MY DAILY BREAD   704 16
  AT LOVE SHOULD SPRINKLE ME DAILY WITH A RARE   874 6

DAIMONS
  LIFE IS FOR THE DAIMONS AND THE DEMONS   709 27

DAINTY
  AND ALL THE DAINTY FOOD   573 12
  FOR OUR DAINTY OUR DELICATE ENGLISH EARS   576 3
  AND ALL THE DAINTY FOOD   670 27
  DAINTY AND READY FOR THE DEPARTING SOUL   *958 22

DAISIES
  YOU TELL ME THE LAMBS HAVE COME THEY LIE LIKE DAISIES W+   57 25
  DAISIES THAT WAKEN ALL MISTAKEN WHITE-SPREAD IN EXPECTA+   71 1
  THE DAISIES IN THE GRASS ARE BENDING   150 4
  EASILY DOWN THE SKY THE DAISIES SENDING   150 11
  LAMBS FRISK AMONG THE DAISIES OF HIS BRAIN   624 9
  AND THE LAMBS WILL BITE OFF THE HEADS OF THE DAISIES FO+   625 7
  DAISIES THAT WAKEN ALL MISTAKEN WHITE-SPREAD IN EXPECTA+   *917 22

DAISY
  SHUT LIKE A DAISY BUD   77 26
  SHUT LIKE A DAISY BUD   *919 14

DAISY-FROTH
  THE DAISY-FROTH QUIESCENT SOFTLY IN THRALL   35 29

DAMAGE
  AND THE SIN IS TO DAMAGE THE FLOW FORCE IT OR DIRTY IT +   464 15
  AND DAMAGE ONCE MORE THE FRAIL QUICK OF THE FUTURE   780 21
  ROARING AND DOING DAMAGE   833 21

DAMASKED
  AND DAMASKED RED AND WHITE   534 24

DAME
  ONE FOR THE MASTER AND ONE FOR THE DAME   669 23

DAMMED-UP
  IS HE NOT OVER-CHARGED BY THE DAMMED-UP PRESSURE OF HIS+   327 14

DAMN
  I DAMN WELL SHANNA MARRY 'ER   81 9
  WELL DAMN MY EYES I SAID TO MYSELF   489 17
  WELL DAMN MY LITTLE EYES   489 18
  A DAMN FOR THEIR DIRTY KENNELS   494 2
  IT DAMN WELL WASN'T WORTH IT   553 1
  A DAMN FRAUD UNDERLINED   553 4
  THERE ISN'T A DAMN THING IN 'EM   553 9
  IT DAWNS ON THEM THAT THE WHOLE DAMN SWINDLE   560 11
  I DAMN WELL SHANNA MARRY 'ER   *923 9

DAMNED
  THE DAMNED BELLS CEASE AND WE ARE EXEMPT   54 28
  THAT DAMNED SURE   84 2
  DAMNED LOUTISH BOLSHEVISTS   317 3
  DO IT AND BE DAMNED TO THE MONEY   517 8
  HAIL AND BE DAMNED TO THEE EMPTY MOST EMPTILY   824 9
  HAIL AND BE DAMNED TO THEE WINNING THE GAME   824 17

DAMOCLES
  LIKE A SWORD OF DAMOCLES   373 31

DAMP
  AND DAMP OLD WEB OF MISERY'S HEIRLOOM   141 11
  THEN ALONG THE DAMP ROAD ALONE TILL THE NEXT TURNING   280 29
  DOWN ON THE DAMP UNCEASING GROUND WHERE MY FEET BELONG   321 16
  THE CRUMBLING DAMP FRESH LAND LIFE HORIZONTAL AND CEASE+   321 18
  STANDING IN THEIR THOUSANDS THESE APPEARANCES IN DAMP   431 25
  SWARTHY AND STRONG WITH HIS DAMP THICK HAIR   733 24

DANAE
  ENGLAND O DANAE   162 9
  FOR A MOMENT SHE WAS IO IO WHO FLED FROM ZEUS OR THE DA+   672 17

DANCE
  THY TWOFOLD DANCE   40 16
  AND FROM THE MEN THAT DANCE AND THE GIRLS THAT LAUGH   89 26
  LIKE THE DANCE OF A DERVISH   121 3
  WHILE I DANCE A TARANTELLA ON THE ROCKS AND THE CROON   130 6
  WHAT CAN I DO BUT DANCE ALONE   130 9
  DANCE TO THE SLIDING SEA AND THE MOON   130 10
  DANCE IN AND OUT   179 16
  I DANCE AT THE CHRISTMAS PARTY   198 5
  OUT OF MOCKERY WE DANCE TOGETHER   210 7
  AS WE DANCE   210 11
  AS WE DANCE   210 13
  ONLY TO DANCE TOGETHER IN TRIUMPH OF BEING TOGETHER   210 15
  NO NO I DANCE IN THE SUN I'M A THING OF LIFE   211 16
  AND DANCE BUT I CAN'T LIFT UP   216 2
  AND DANCE AND DANCE FOREVER DANCE WITH BREATH HALF   389 11
  INDIANS DANCE AND RUN AND STAMP   407 11
  AND THE SAME FLAME THAT FILLS US WITH LIFE IT WILL DANC+   440 15
  INTO THE INDUSTRIAL DANCE OF THE LIVING DEATH THE JIGGI+   631 13
  AND FED ON CONDITION THEY DANCE THIS DANCE OF CORPSES   631 15
  THEY DANCE DANCE DANCE THIS DRY INDUSTRIAL JIG OF THE   631 19
  INTO THE DANCE AND SPLENDOUR OF A BIGGER LIFE   679 17
  ARE ABOUT TO DANCE THE WAR DANCE ROUND YOU MEN   792 18

DANCERS
  IN THE LONG HOT NIGHT MORE DANCERS FROM INSIGNIFICANT   389 2
  OF MOON-LIT DANCERS   689 4

DANCES
  AND THE WHITE DOG DANCES AND QUIVERS I AM HOLDING HIS C+   34 5
  A GREAT BAY STALLION DANCES SKIRTS   126 25
  HEATHEN DANCES AND CEREMONIES AND TILLED THEIR   777 31
  DANCES BEFORE THE EYES   794 18
  THE SHADOW DANCES UP IN AFFECTION   887 21

DANCING
  DANCING SPORTFULLY   272 15
  AND DEVIL-DANCERS LUMINOUS WITH SWEAT DANCING ON TO THE   388 33
  MEN-PEASANTS FROM JUNGLE VILLAGES DANCING AND RUNNING   389 5
  SPINNING AND DANCING LIKE FLAMEY FIRE-SPOUTS IN THE DARK   440 10
  THEY ARE DANCING THEY RETURN AS THEY WENT DANCING   689 9
  CURVING THEIR FEET AND DANCING AND FLUTTERING IN SPORT   751 4
  THAN TO REMAIN A DANCING SAVAGE   778 3
  TIE MY SPOTTED SHOES FOR DANCING   802 22
  OF THEIR DANCING BLOOD LADS SUCKING THE COLD MOISTURE F+   865 29

DANDELION
  THE LAST SILK-FLOATING THOUGHT HAS GONE FROM THE DANDEL+   97 7
  LIKE AN EMPTY DANDELION STALK BEREFT OF CONNECTION SMALL   98 3
  MYRIADS OF DANDELION PAPPUS   204 16
  THE DANDELION SEEDS STAY HALF-SUBMERGED IN THE GRASS   204 21

DANDELIONS
  THE POOR SHUT DANDELIONS WHOM SMALL WARMTH EXPANDS   *896 19

DANDY
  AND WHAT A DANDY FELLOW THE RIGHT TOSS OF A CHIN FOR YOU   524 15

DANGER
  AND THEREIN LIES THE DANGER OF ROBOT-DEMOCRACY AND ALL +   648 5
  FULL OF FRICTION FULL OF GRINDING FULL OF DANGER TO THE+   675 27
  WHEN DANGER THREATENS ON THE SURFACE OF THE CEASELESS F+   695 2
  OF DANGER I FIND HER EVEN WORSE THAN THE FIELDS WHERE W+   752 12
  LEAVING THIS CONGERIE BEHIND AND IN DANGER   767 24

DANGEROUS
        YOU SEE HE IS DIFFERENT HE IS DANGEROUS   252 1
        IN SIGN OF LIFE OF LOVELY DANGEROUS LIFE   317 16
        HENCE HE BECAME A CURLY SHEEP-DOG WITH DANGEROUS PROPEN+   324 26
        THAT THING'S ALIVE IT'S DANGEROUS MAKE AWAY   528 16
        JUST TO SHOW HOW DANGEROUS THEY ARE   572 15
        THE MORE DEADLY AND DANGEROUS IT BECOMES   665 11
        AND SO HIDEOUSLY DANGEROUS TO BE AT THE MERCY   839 13

DANGERS
        WHAT DANGERS AH WHAT DANGERS   542 17
        FRAIL DANGERS   630 15

DANGLE
        LITTLE DANGLE OF AN IMMATURE PAW AND ONE THIN EAR   393 20
        AND DANGLE IN A LAST FASTIDIOUS FINE DELIGHT   667 15

DANGLED
        AND DANGLED THEM IN THE ATMOSPHERE   683 3

DANGLES
        THE SAME THAT DANGLES THE GLOBE-SHAPED PLEIADS OF FRUIT   271 23

DANGLING
        DANGLING OUR USELESS HANDS   572 26
        AS THE FUCHSIA DOES DANGLING HER RECKLESS DROP   667 16
        GOD IS BORN GOD IS BORN PERFUMED AND DANGLING AND WITH +   683 5

DANIELE MANIN
        EVEN AS LATE AS DANIELE MANIN   323 24

DANK
        A DANK SICKENING SCENT CAME UP FROM THE GRIME   98 16

DANS L'EAU
        DANS L'EAU   336 25

DANTE
        NOT LIKE GREY DANTE COLOUR-BLIND   711 19
        THE KIND OF HELL GREY DANTE NEVER SAW   714 3

DAPPER
        DAPPER BESIDE HER   359 31

DAPPLE
        FALLING ROUND US NO LONGER DAPPLE   37 27
        FALLING ROUND US NO LONGER DAPPLE   *892 15

DAPPLED
        WHERE ROSES' SHADOWS DAPPLED HER   753 9

DAPPLES
        BLACKISH THEY WILL TASTE OF TEARS WHEN THE YELLOW DAPPL+   119 13
        DAPPLES   120 8
        LAST RED LIGHT DAPPLES   816 26
        BRACKISH THEY WILL TASTE OF TEARS WHEN THE YELLOW DAPPL+   *932 22

DARE
        HOW DID YOU DARE   55 23
        BETWEEN THE OLD GREY WALLS I DID NOT DARE   122 27
        TO RAISE MY FACE I DID NOT DARE LOOK UP   122 28
        IS SOFT THOUGH IT IS COLD DO NOT DARE   158 20
        I DARE NOT TURN ROUND   212 16
        SOMETHING FROZEN IN THE SILENCE THAT DARE NOT BE   225 27
        AND IF YOU DARE THE FISSURE   278 21
        SUDDENLY TO DARE TO COME OUT NAKED IN PERFECTION OF   306 15
        NOT THIS HYENA TAME PEACE WHERE NO MAN DARE TELL ANOTHER   519 23
        AND SHE SAID DON'T DARE YOU WRETCH TO BE LEWD   577 15
        DON'T YOU DARE TO SUGGEST SUCH A THING   580 8
        I DARE DO ALL THAT MAY BECOME A MAN   606 9
        THAT WE KNOW NOTHING OF THAT WE DARE NOT EXPLORE   606 22
        AND WHO DARE NOT DIE FOR FEAR THEY SHOULD BE NOTHING AT+   613 4
        AND STILL I LOOK FOR THE MEN WHO WILL DARE TO BE   634 21
        THAT'S WHY THE DOGGED RESISTANT OLD ONES DARE NOT DIE   662 26
        DARE NOT DIE THEY DAREN'T GO THROUGH THE DOOR   662 27
        THEY DARE NOT DIE BECAUSE THEY KNOW   663 1
        DARE NOT DIE BECAUSE IN DEATH   663 5
        IF THE STAR SHONE THEY DARE NOT THEY COULD NOT   800 28
        OH IF YOU DARE   861 20
        I DARE NOT LOOK AT HIS EYES   871 28
        BETWEEN THE OLD RED WALLS I DID NOT DARE   *934 3
        TO RAISE MY FACE I DID NOT DARE LOOK UP   *934 4

DARED
        AND I DARED NOT ENTER FEELING SUDDENLY DISMAYED   99 11
        THE DARK GRAVE-EYED MISTRESS WHO THUS DARED   155 28
        WAS IT COWARDICE THAT I DARED NOT KILL HIM   350 13
        AS TIME HAS NOT DARED TO AVOUCH NOR ETERNITY BEEN ABLE +   370 31
        NO RAT OF THE DARK DARED GNAW YOU   800 31

DAREN'T
        THINK I DAREN'T DIE   214 21
        AND I DAREN'T LIVE   214 21
        I DO ALL THE THINGS THE BOURGEOIS DAREN'T DO   432 17
        IT'S SUCH A BONNY BABY WE DAREN'T LET IT CRY   570 17
        AND I SIMPLY DAREN'T THINK OF AUNT LOU   571 30
        PEOPLE KEEP IT UP BECAUSE THEY DAREN'T STOP   657 20
        DARE NOT DIE THEY DAREN'T GO THROUGH THE DOOR   662 27

DARES
        THAT HE DARES DEMAND   749 5

DARING
        INTO A DARING SHORT-BREATH'D CONFESSION   854 13

DARK
        DARK OVERGROWN WITH WILLOWS COOL WITH THE BROOK EBBING +   33 16
        UNDER THE LONG DARK BOUGHS LIKE JEWELS RED   36 19
        WITH DARK SLEEP THAT ONCE COVERED THE CEILING   38 5
        FOR THE DARK GOAL   39 30
        ROUND HIS BASE HIS DARK LIGHT ROLLS   39 32
        DARK RUDDY PILLAR FORGIVE ME I   40 9
        THOU DARK ONE THOU PROUD CURVED BEAUTY I   40 17
        WHAT LARGE DARK HANDS ARE THOSE AT THE WINDOW   42 1
        HIS BRIGHT DARK EYES COME OVER ME LIKE A HOOD   43 34
        AND STRUCK AT ME WITH SOMETHING DARK   46 22
        TALL AND DARK THE CHURCH MOVES ANXIOUS TO KEEP   48 21
        SWEET DARK PURPLE AND WHITE ONES MIXED FOR A PLEDGE   58 10
        A MOMENT THERE LIKE SNOW IN THE DARK   62 13
        OF THE TIME WHEN THE GRAIN STRUGGLES DOWN IN THE DARK   63 19
        THAT STRUGGLES ALONE IN THE DARK   63 28
        UPON US DARK EYES AS HERE BENEATH THE BUSBIES GLITTERIN+   66 25
        LIPS AND DARK   66 28
        COMPRESSED IT TILL ITS BEAM GREW WONDROUS DARK   69 19
        THEN GAVE THEE THY DARK EYES O MAN THAT ALL   69 20
        IN STUPOR PERSIST AT THE GATES OF LIFE OBSTINATE DARK M+   75 12
        OUT OF EACH FACE STRANGE DARK BEAMS THAT DISQUIET   76 1
        IN THE OPEN DEPTHS OF EACH FLOWER DARK RESTLESS DROPS   76 2
        MY GEL OWT'LL DO FOR A MAN I' TH' DARK   77 3
        AY AN' YALLER AS A CROWFLOWER AN' YET I' TH' DARK   77 7
        OBSCURES THE DARK WOOD AND THE DULL ORANGE SKY   85 10
        YOUR OWN DARK MOUTH WITH THE BRIDAL FAINT LADY-SMOCKS   90 11
        THE HEALING DAYS SHALL CLOSE THE DARK GULF UP   90 29
        THE CLASS OVER THEM ALL THE DARK NET OF MY DISCIPLINE W+   92 6
        I HAVE PUSHED MY HANDS IN THE DARK SOIL UNDER THE FLOWE+   92 8
        AND THERE IN THE DARK MY DARLING WHERE THE ROOTS ARE EN+   92 12
        AND IN THE ORIGINAL DARK THE ROOTS CANNOT KEEP CANNOT K+   92 17
        ANY COMMUNION WHATEVER BUT THEY BIND THEMSELVES ON TO T+   92 18
        MYSELF BUT A KNOWLEDGE OF ROOTS OF ROOTS IN THE DARK TH+   94 3
        THROUGH INVISIBLE PULSES SLOWLY FILLING THE NIGHT'S DAR+   97 28
        WHEN ONLY THERE GLOWED ON THE DARK OF THE SKY   103 16
        HER FORTH FROM THE DARK MY STRENGTH HAS FAILED   106 1
        I WATCHED THEM FLOAT UP THE DARK CHIMNEY   107 4
        UP IN THE DARK   110 8
        OVER THE WET DARK ROCKS THE HOUSES AND OVER   112 27
        CURTAIN US IN SO DARK   113 22
        THE INNER DARK OF THE MYSTERY   114 11
        THE LAST DARK DELIGHT   114 16
        IS BURIED AWAY IN THE DARK WHERE THE DEAD ALL LIE   114 20
        TURNING ITS BROKEN EDGE TO THE DARK ITS SHINE   114 27
        ENDS LIKE A BROKEN LOVE THAT TURNS TO THE DARK OF SLEEP   114 29
        AND HALF LIES THERE IN THE DARK WHERE THE DEAD ALL LIE   115 1
        THEN PERHAPS IN THE DARK YOU'D GET WHAT YOU WANT TO FIND   118 28
        HUDDLED AWAY IN THE DARK   119 20
        THE DARK VAN DRUMMED DOWN THE DISTANCE LOWLY   121 30
        AND THERE IN THE DARK I DID DISCOVER   123 22
        THEN I LAUGHED IN THE DARK OF MY HEART I DID EXULT   125 25
        DEFEAT IN SUCH A BATTLE IN THE DARK OF HER EYES   125 29
        TILL HER DARK DEEPS SHOOK WITH CONVULSIVE THRILLS AND T+   125 31
        PRESSES THEM THERE AND KISSES HER BIG DARK HANDS   128 32
        AND SITS IN HER OWN DARK NIGHT OF HER BITTER HAIR   129 1
        OF LIVES WHICH SORROWS LIKE MISCHIEVOUS DARK MICE CHAVEL   132 13
        LET US NOT HOLD HER SHADOW BACK FROM THE DARK   132 21
        THE EARTH AGAIN LIKE A SHIP STEAMS OUT OF THE DARK SEA +   132 27
        WAVING SLOWLY BEFORE ME PUSHED INTO THE DARK   147 1
        THE AIR IS DARK WITH NORTH AND WITH SULPHUR THE GRASS IS   148 24
        LIKE A DARK ROSE A MYSTERY OF REST   154 10
        THE DARK GRAVE-EYED MISTRESS WHO THUS DARED   155 28
        THE STRANGER'S HAIR WAS SHORN LIKE A LAD'S DARK POLL   156 1
        DARK IN INDOMITABLE FAILURE SHE WHO HAD LOST   156 5
        A DARK BIRD FALLS FROM THE SUN   166 25
        NO SOUND FROM THE STRANGERS THE PLACE IS DARK AND FEAR   173 3
        LOOKING EARNESTLY UNDER THE DARK UMBRELLAS HELD FAST   180 12
        PASS THE MEN WHOSE EYES ARE SHUT LIKE ANEMONES IN A DAR+   180 20
        THE GREAT DARK GLITTERY WINDOW   193 21
        AND DARK GRASS UNDER MY FEET   194 10
        THIS ME WHICH RISES FROM THE DARK OF SLEEP   195 10
        AND LOOKED FAR DOWN THE DARK   201 22
        HIS DARK EYES FULL OF PAIN   202 2
        BUBBLES RAVELLED IN THE DARK GREEN GRASS   204 17
        AND IT WOULD BE THICK BLACK DARK FOR EVER   205 11
        I WISH IT WOULD BE COMPLETELY DARK EVERYWHERE   205 20
        INSIDE ME AND OUT HEAVILY DARK   205 21
        STAND LIKE DARK STUMPS STILL IN THE GREEN WHEAT   208 27
        A DARK BOAT THROUGH THE GLOOM AND WHITHER   209 2
        SQUARE PICTURE-DUSK THE WINDOW OF DARK SKY   210 20
        YOU LOVE IT IT IS DARK IT KILLS ME I AM PUT OUT   211 12
        EVEN THEN IT IS DARK BEHIND YOU TURN ROUND MY WIFE   211 17
        ONE TO BE QUENCHED TO BE GIVEN UP TO BE GONE IN THE DARK   212 8
        NIGHT FOLK TUATHA DE DANAAN DARK GODS GOVERN HER SLEEP   213 25
        MY EYES FROM THE SHADOWS DARK   216 3
        WE FOUND THE DARK WILD ROSES   217 2
        DARK AND PROUD ON THE SKY LIKE A NUMBER OF KNIGHTS   221 8
        OF THESE DARK KNIGHTS SHEDDING THEIR DELICATE SHEEN   221 19
        DARK SKY OF NIGHT A WANDERING GLITTER A SWARM   221 26
        HAVE ALL GONE DARK GONE BLACK   226 22
        AND NOW IN THE DARK MY SOUL TO YOU   226 23
        IN THE DARK   231 22
        THE ROUND DARK HEADS OF MEN CROWD SILENTLY   232 21
        LET US LEAVE THE REST IN THE DARK   237 21
        TO SETTLE AT LAST IN THE DARK   253 31
        AND TAINTS AND BLACKENS THE SKY TILL AT LAST IT IS DARK+   258 12
        CAN BLOW ACROSS THE DARK SEAS TO OUR USUAL WORLD   261 3
        EVEN THEN IN THE DARK I WAS TORTURED RAVENING UNFREE   264 30
        DROPPING AMONG HIS LEAVES HANGS THE DARK GRAPE   286 10
        OF THE WORLD BEFORE THE FLOODS WHERE MAN WAS DARK AND   286 25
        VISTAS DOWN DARK AVENUES   286 30
        TO ME ALL FACES ARE DARK   288 21
        TO ME MEN ARE PALPABLE INVISIBLE NEARNESSES IN THE DARK   289 1
        SEE IF I DON'T MOVE UNDER A DARK AND NUDE VAST HEAVEN   289 19
        SEE IF I AM NOT LORD OF THE DARK AND MOVING HOSTS   289 22
        A DARK UNFATHOMED WILL THAT IS NOT UN-JEWISH   292 11
        DARK ABORIGINAL EYES   292 28

DARK

DARK ELVISH   293   5
FOLDED IN LIKE A DARK THOUGHT   296   3
DARK CYPRESSES   296 13
VICIOUS DARK CYPRESSES   297   9
DARK FLAME   297 11
OR WAS THEIR WAY ONLY EVASIVE AND DIFFERENT DARK LIKE   297 16
SUN DARK SUN   301 18
COLUMNS DARK AND SOFT   301 27
ROCK WAVES OF DARK HEAT   302   1
WAVES OF DARK HEAT ROCK SWAY UPWARDS   302   2
IN THE LONG DARK NIGHTS OF THE EVENING STAR AND SIRIUS +   305 23
THE DARK ONE   308   2
DIS THE DARK THE JEALOUS GOD THE HUSBAND   308   7
DARK BLUE ANEMONES   309 12
I AM MAN AND THEREFORE MY HEART BEATS AND THROWS THE DA+   320 21
AS I AM IF MY HEART IN UPLIFTING CEASED TO BEAT TO TOSS+   320 27
AND LONG SNAKES QUICKLY GLIDE INTO THE DARK HOLE IN THE+   321 24
DARK REVERSION OF NIGHT   321 30
TO THE DARK ZENITH OF THINE ANTIPODES   322 19
THROWS STILL THE DARK BLOOD BACK AND FORTH   322 32
QUEER WHAT A DIM DARK SMUDGE YOU HAVE DISAPPEARED   334 18
SWALLOWS WITH SPOOLS OF DARK THREAD SEWING THE SHADOWS   340 29
DARK AIR-LIFE LOOPING   341   9
WINGS DARK SKINNY AND FLAPPING THE AIR   346 23
DARK BREATH OF THE EARTH THE SERPENT SLID FORTH LAY REV+   348   7
IN THE DEEP STRANGE-SCENTED SHADE OF THE GREAT DARK CAR+   349   4
FROM OUT THE DARK DOOR OF THE SECRET EARTH   350 22
YOUR BRIGHT DARK LITTLE EYE   352 20
YOUR EYE OF A DARK DISTURBED NIGHT   352 21
THE DARK BAR HORIZONTAL   355 33
YOUR EYE IS VERY DARK VERY BRIGHT   359 10
IN THE DARK AGAINST A WINDOW   363   9
ON WILD DARK LIPS   366 21
YOU GLOSSY DARK WIND   369   2
DARK AND LUSTROUS   369   4
IN BURNT DARK FEATHERS   373   9
YOU ARE DARK   373 26
AND DARK CLEAVES DOWN AND WEAPON-HARD DOWNWARD   373 28
THAT DARK FACE-WEAPON TO TEMPER IT WELL   373 34
DARK AS YOU ARE ON YOUR DARK SIDE EAGLE OF HEAVEN   374 31
AND BOBBING HIS THICK DARK CREST ABOUT THE SNOW AS IF   375 26
YET IF YOU HAD WHORLED HORNS OF BRONZE IN A FRONTAL DARK   381   1
WITH A NEEDLE OF LONG RED FLINT HE STABS IN THE DARK   382 16
DARK GREEN GLOSSY FANGED LEAVES   383 31
DARK GREEN GLOSSY FANGED LEAVES   387   2
NAKED DARK MEN BENEATH   387   7
AND THEIR FACES ARE DARK AND FAT AND IMPORTANT   388 21
PATH IN THE DARK   388 32
NAKED DARK MEN WITH ORNAMENTS ON ON THEIR NAKED ARMS   389   7
SOBBING IN DARK SWEAT-SHINING BREASTS   389 12
A NAKED GLEAMING DARK LAUGH LIKE A SECRET OUT IN THE DA+   389 15
AND FLARE OF A TROPICAL ENERGY TIRELESS AFIRE IN THE DA+   389 16
THE HOT DARK BLOOD OF ITSELF A-LAUGHING WET HALF-DEVILI+   389 20
WITH THE STRANGE DARK LAUGH IN THEIR EYES GLANCING UP   389 33
THE MYSTERY OF THE DARK MOUNTAIN OF BLOOD REEKING IN   390   6
AND THE CROWD LIKE A FIELD OF RICE IN THE DARK GAVE WAY   390 34
LIKE LIQUID TO THE DARK   390 35
FACES DARK AS BLACK RICE GROWING   391 13
HER FULL ANTIPODAL EYES SO DARK   393 11
DARK GROW THE SPRUCE-TREES BLUE IS THE BALSAM WATER   401   2
TWO MEXICANS STRANGERS EMERGING OUT OF THE DARK AND   401 12
DARK RAYS   402   5
DARK KEEN FINE RAYS IN THE BRILLIANT FROST OF HER FACE   402   6
ABOVE THE TREES OF THE LOBO DARK VALLEY-MOUTH   402 20
AND IT'S DARK BETWEEN ME AND HIM   403   3
A RED WOLF STANDS ON THE SHADOW'S DARK RED RIM   403 20
AND COMING DOWN UPON US OUT OF THE DARK CONCAVE   403 28
WELL YOU'RE A DARK OLD DEMON   404 12
AND LEFT ME HOMELESS HERE IN THE DARK AT YOUR DOOR   404 17
THE DOGS OF THE DARK PUEBLO   405 13
THAT DARK OLD DEMON AND I   405 19
I'M THE RED WOLF SAYS THE DARK OLD FATHER   405 31
A DARK MEMBRANE OVER THE WILL HOLING A MAN DOWN   407 23
CUPS LET THEM BE DARK   427   7
I WANT TO DRINK OUT OF DARK CUPS THAT DRIP DOWN ON   427   9
CAN YOU AFTER DARK BECOME A DARKIE   428   1
WILL THE DARK FLOOD OF OUR DAY'S ANNIHILATION   428 24
IN THE DARK   436 11
AND IN THE DARK UNSCIENTIFIC I FEEL THE DRUM-WINDS OF H+   438   9
TO SEEK THE WOMEN IN THE DARK OUR WOMEN OUR WEIRD   438 13
SPINNING AND DANCING LIKE FLAMEY FIRE-SPOUTS IN THE DARK 440 10
WITH THEIR THIN DARK HANDS AND THEIR WIDE DARK EYES AND   451   3
ON HIS SOUL THAT IS DARK OCEAN WITHIN HIM   453 22
AS THE DARK CLOSES ROUND HIM HE DRAWS NEARER   455 14
THE WIDE SEA WINS AND THE DARK   455 25
OF DESIRES IN THE LOINS' DARK TWISTS   461   4
BUT THE OTHER SIDE IS DARK FOREVER   473 27
AND THE DARK MOON DRAWS THE TIDES ALSO   473 28
THE BLOOD KNOWS IN DARKNESS AND FOREVER DARK   474   5
TO MY DARK HEART GODS ARE   474 10
IN MY DARK HEART LOVE IS AND IS NOT   474 11
OUT OF SIGHT IN THE DEEP DARK LIFTING HEART   478   3
BUT SAY IN THE DARK WILD METAL OF YOUR HEART   478   4
AND GLEAMS ON THE WORLD WITH THE WARM DARK VISION OF   544 24
AND GOES DARK BUT SHINES   562   2
SO DARK SO DARK THE MIND IS LOST IN IT   586 14
AND NOON IS SUDDENLY DARK IS LUSTROUS IS SILENT AND DARK 606   4
THROUGH THE DARK HADES AT THE ROOTS OF THE TREE   617 10
THE DARK SATANIC MILLS OF BLAKE   628 13
ALL MY PRETTY PICTURES HUDDLED IN THE DARK AWAITING   634   1
WITH THE DARK AND GLEAMING BEAUTY OF THE MESSAGELESS GO+ 674 26
I SHALL BLOSSOM LIKE A DARK PANSY AND BE DELIGHTED   677 13
THERE AMONG THE DARK SUN-RAYS OF DEATH   677 14
I CAN FEEL MYSELF UNFOLDING IN THE DARK SUNSHINE OF DEA+ 677 15
AND BROKE AT LAST INTO LIGHT AND DARK   682   5
HE IS PITCH DARK AND COLD   682 11
IS LEAVING A LONG THREAD OF DARK SMOKE   687 10

DARK

THAT DARK GREEN MESS   691   3
OH LOVELY LOVELY WITH THE DARK HAIR PILED UP AS SHE WEN+ 693   8
AND UP THEY COME WITH THE PURPLE DARK OF RAINBOWS   693 27
AND DENSE WITH HAPPY BLOOD DARK RAINBOW BLISS IN THE SEA 695 12
BAVARIAN GENTIANS BIG AND DARK ONLY DARK   697   3
BLACK LAMPS FROM THE HALLS OF DIS BURNING DARK BLUE   697   9
TO THE SIGHTLESS REALM WHERE DARKNESS IS AWAKE UPON THE+ 697 17
OR A DARKNESS INVISIBLE ENFOLDED IN THE DEEPER DARK   697 19
COMING LIKE THE RUBY IN THE INVISIBLE DARK GLOWING   697 30
BREATHE ALL ALONE IN SILENCE IN THE DARK   698   4
LIKE THE KINGDOM OF THE FOX IN THE DARK   704 22
AND THE WATCHERS THE DIVIDERS THOSE SWIFT ONES WITH DAR+ 706 17
AND DREAD AND THE DARK ROLLING OMINOUSNESS OF DOOM   708 25
ON THE WAY TO DARK PERDITION   710 20
WITH HIS KEY TO THE TWO DARK DOORS   710 26
AND ITS HALLS OF THE GREAT DARK BELOW   711   2
AND THERE ARE THE DARK DOORS WHERE SOULS PASS SILENTLY 711   4
BUT OTHERS THE DARK DOORS OH HUSH HUSH   711   9
DARK   712   3
ALREADY THE DARK AND ENDLESS OCEAN OF THE END   718   6
FOR THE DARK FLIGHT DOWN OBLIVION   718 11
HAS HER FOOTING WASHED AWAY AS THE DARK FLOOD RISES   718 13
AND OUR SOUL COWERS NAKED IN THE DARK RAIN OVER THE FLO+ 718 19
THAT FUMES A LITTLE WITH PALLOR UPON THE DARK   719 30
TO DARK OBLIVION   721   5
AND DRAWS AWAY AWAY TOWARDS DARK DEPTHS   723 21
FOR THE COSMOS EVEN IN DEATH IS LIKE A DARK WHORLED SHE+ 724   4
SING THEN THE CORE OF DARK AND ABSOLUTE   724   8
IF THERE WERE NOT AN UTTER AND ABSOLUTE DARK   724 12
BUT DIPPED ONCE DIPPED IN DARK OBLIVION   724 25
DARK DREAMLESS SLEEP IN DEEP OBLIVION   725   4
SWEET DARK OBLIVION WHEN I CEASE   726   5
AND IF AS WEEKS GO ROUND IN THE DARK OF THE MOON   727   1
WITH THE DARK EARTH AND DRENCHED   727 15
IS IT ME THE DARK FIRS MEAN   731   6
AND WE WALKED DARK SO HE HELD HIS ARM CLOSE ROUND ME 732 15
OF ANY GODHEAD LEAVE US IN THE DARK   738   2
AND LET THE DARK BE SOUNDLESS WITHOUT FACE   738   3
NOR CEASE TO BE DARK ON THE DARKNESS STAY   738 20
INTO THE UTTER DARK THEY CANNOT HEAR   744 31
AND STILL AGAINST THE DARK AND VIOLENT WIND   745   6
HAVE I NOTHING IN THIS DARK LAND   749 13
THOU OF THE DARK CLENCHED TOMB   753 14
IN THE DARK   763 17
IT IS VERY DARK   764 15
IT IS VERY DARK OH KINDRED DEARER THAN BLOOD   765   1
REACH OUT REACH OUT IN THIS DARK   765   8
ITS WAY ACROSS THE DARK SHOULD MOCK MY NAKEDNESS   771 20
OVER THE FACE OF THE DARK   771 25
TO SINK UNCONSCIOUS IN THE ROCKING DARK   771 28
LIFE IS DARK AND RIPPLING BUT FRETTED   773   1
THAT THE OLD DARK FATHERS SHOULD NOT TRUST THESE ARTISTS 778   4
IN BURNT DARK FEATHERS   781 15
WITH A DAGGER OF DARK LIVE IRON   782   2
THE DARK CLEAVES DOWN AND WEAPON-HARD DOWNWARDS CURVING 782   4
THE DARK DRIPS DOWN SUSPENDED   782   5
THE GOD-THRUST THRUSTING YOU SILENT AND DARK FROM BENEA+ 782   9
FROM THE DARK EARTH OVER THE ROCK FROM THE DARK ROCK OV+ 782 13
TRANSMUTED THE DARK REDNESS TAKEN OUT   784 13
MY MOTHER THE MOON IS DARK   786 18
IS COMBING HER DARK HAIR   787 13
AND THE WING OF THE DARK ON THE LEFT   787 19
THE OTHER WING BRUSHES THE DARK   787 25
THE PATH BETWEEN GULFS OF THE DARK AND THE STEEPS OF 788   9
MY MOTHER THE MOON IS DARK   789 11
JESUS HAD GONE FAR UP THE DARK SLOPE WHEN HE LOOKED BACK 789 16
AND HE SAW MEXICO LYING LIKE A DARK WOMAN WITH WHITE BR+ 790   7
IN HIS HAND IT LAY AND WENT DARK   791   3
I SEE DARK THINGS RUSHING ACROSS THE COUNTRY   794 10
WAITING FOR THE RATS OF THE DARK TO COME AND GNAW YOUR + 800 24
NO RAT OF THE DARK DARED GNAW YOU   800 31
BEYOND ME IS A LORD WHO IS TERRIBLE AND WONDERFUL AND D+ 801 12
THE ROOTS ARE MINE DOWN THE DARK MOIST PATH OF THE SNAKE 801 16
THE DARK IS DIVIDING THE SUN IS COMING PAST THE WALL 803 12
I AM HUITZILOPOCHTLI SITTING IN THE DARK   804 15
WITH MY REDNESS STAINING THE BODY OF THE DARK   804 16
HE IS HUITZILOPOCHTLI SITTING IN THE DARK   805 23
I AM DARK AS THE SUNLESS UNDER-EARTH   806 22
MY DARK   807   7
THAT PRICK THEIR EARS LIKE A RABBIT OR BROWSE IN THE DA+ 807 14
DARK   807 19
THE HAIR OF NIGHT IS DARK OVER OUR FACES   809   1
THE DEAD ARE ON THEIR JOURNEY THE WAY IS DARK   810 21
THE BLUE ANEMONE WITH A DARK CORE   814   1
DARK BLUE THE WHOLE DESIRE LEAPS   819 24
THE DARK ONES ARE CURIOUSLY PURPLISH LIKE FRESH   827   4
THE DARK NAIF PRIDE   844 10
AS THE WIND ASKS WHITHER THE DARK ROAD GOES   857 24
BUT IT'S THE OTHER WAY THAT MY DARK ROAD NOW GOES 857 28
WHAT LIES OVER THE NEXT DARK HILL   858   3
AND THE FLUSH FADED AND IT CAME DARK I SLEPT STILL IGNO+ 860   7
DOWN THE DARK BOUGH HAVE FLED   861 11
AND DARK NOW IS THE SKY THAT SHE CAME THROUGH   863 13
BUT PRESSING HER SUPPLE BODY INTO THE COOL DARK LEAVES 864 11
LEANS OVER TO READ HIS WORK AND HER DARK HEAD DIPS 865   5
LIKE A PICTURE BY THAULOW DARK CLUSTERS OF SHOUTING LADS 865 19
I SAW A DARK FIGURE APPROACHING A RAGGED SOLITARY CROW 866 17
NO A LONG SEASON I HAVE BEEN WITH DOSTOIEVSKY IN THE DA+ 866 27
SOME SHAPELESS DARK TO THE LOVELY CURVE OF LIGHT   872   7
ME AS A DARK BLUE WATER BETWEEN THE HILLS   874 28
ROOFED WITH A DAY'S NEAR CEILING AND A DARK   876 11
TO COME AT IT TO BREATHE IT IN THIS DARK   876 30
UP THE DARK SHAFT TO DEATH AND WHAT IF I   879 23
OF THE DARK SHAFT THAT ISSUES TO THE NIGHT   879 35
DARK INCENSE DID I FEEL HER OFFER UP   881 12
I SAID THIS IS GRASS THAT TWINKLES IN THE DARK   882 15
INTO THE DARKNESS SIGHING ON DARK AND I   885 10

DARK
    DARK OVERGROWN WITH WILLOWS COOL WITH THE BROOK EBBING +   *891 18
    WITH THE DARK SLEEP THAT ONCE COVERED THE CEILING   *892 21
    DARK WAVING OF THEIR ARMS AGAINST THE BLAND   *895 3
    DARK GLITTER OF LIFE AMID A SKY THAT TEEMS   *895 7
    OUT OF EACH STAR DARK STRANGE BEAMS THAT DISQUIET   *897 28
    IN THE OPEN DEPTHS OF EACH FLOWER DARK RESTLESS DROPS   *897 29
    OUT OF EACH STAR DARK STRANGE BEAMS THAT DISQUIET   *901 5
    IN THE OPEN DEPTHS OF EACH FLOWER DARK RESTLESS DROPS   *901 6
    A MOMENT AND SHE WAS TAKEN AGAIN IN THE MERCIFUL DARK   *912 24
    COMPRESSED IT TILL ITS BEAM GREW WONDROUS DARK   *916 2
    THEN GAVE THEE THY DARK EYES O MAN THAT ALL   *916 3
    THEY SIGH JUST ONCE ROUND OUR FEET AND ARE STILL HEAVY +   *917 11
    MY GEL OWT'LL DO FOR A MAN I' THE DARK   *918 21
    AY AN' YALLER AS A CROWFLOWER AN' YET I' THE DARK   *918 25
    AN' THAT'S THE DARK BLUE TIE I BOUGHT 'IM   *923 14
    THE CLASS OVER THEM ALL THE DARK NET OF MY DISCIPLINE W+   *926 6
    I HAVE PUSHED MY HANDS IN THE DARK LOAM UNDER THE FLOWE+   *926 8
    YOUR LOVE WAS DARK AND THOROUGH   *928 3
    CURTAIN US IN SO DARK   *929 11
    THEN PERHAPS IN THE DARK YOU'LL HAVE GOT WHAT YOU WANT +   *932 6
    HUDDLED AWAY IN THE DARK   *932 29
    AND IN THE DARK I DID DISCOVER   *934 28
    THEN I LAUGHED IN THE DARK OF MY HEART I DID EXULT   *936 24
    DEFEAT IN SUCH A BATTLE IN THE DARK OF HER EYES   *936 28
    TILL HER DARK DEEPS SHOOK WITH CONVULSIVE THRILLS AND T+   *936 30
    DARK AND PROUD ON THE SKY LIKE A NUMBER OF KNIGHTS   *944 21
    OF THIS DARK EARTH AND WANDERING ALL SERENE   *945 5
    DARK SKY OF NIGHT THE WANDERING GLITTER THE SWARM   *945 12
    AND IN THE DARK I FEEL HIS COLD WEBBED FEET MUD BLACK   *947 19
    BLUE AND DARK   *954 17
    IT IS DARK BEAUTY   *954 22
    YOUR DARK BLUE GLOOM IS SO NOBLE   *954 25
    DARK GENTIANS   *954 27
    IN THE DARK BLUE GLOOM   *955 2
    IT IS DARK   *955 4
    IT IS SO BLUE IT IS SO DARK   *955 7
    IN THE DARK DOORWAY   *955 8
    TO HER BRIDEGROOM IN THE DARK   *955 15
    AND ALL THE DARK GREAT ONES OF THE UNDERWORLD   *955 17
    ARE GATHERING TO A WEDDING IN THE WINTER DARK   *955 21
    DOWN THE DARK BLUE PATH   *955 22
    BAVARIAN GENTIANS TALL AND DARK BUT DARK   *956 1
    BLACK LAMPS FROM THE HALLS OF DIS SMOKING DARK BLUE   *956 7
    TO THE SIGHTLESS REALM WHERE DARKNESS IS MARRIED TO DARK *956 14
    A GLOOM INVISIBLE ENFOLDED IN THE DEEPER DARK   *956 16
    AND PIERCES HER ONCE MORE WITH HIS PASSION OF THE UTTER+ *956 18
    GIVE ME A FLOWER ON A TALL STEM AND THREE DARK FLAMES   *956 21
    AT THE MARRIAGE OF THE LIVING DARK   *956 23
    AND DRAWS AWAY AWAY AWAY TOWARDS THE DARK DEPTHS   *958 33
    MOST DARK OBLIVION   *959 23
    AND ROUND THE GREAT FINAL BEND OF UNBROKEN DARK   *959 27

DARK-BLUE
    AN' THERE'S THE DARK-BLUE TIE I BOUGHT 'IM   81 14
    TORCH-FLOWER OF THE BLUE-SMOKING DARKNESS DARK-BLUE DAZE 697 8
    IN THE DARK-BLUE DEPTHS UNDER LAYERS AND LAYERS OF   697 26
    HAVE POURED FOR THE HORSES A DARK-BLUE STAGGERING   733 18
    MAKE A DARK-BLUE GLOOM   *954 19
    OF DARK-BLUE GENTIANS TO PLUTO   *955 14
    WHAT A DARK-BLUE GLOOM   *955 23
    TORCH-FLOWERS OF THE BLUE-SMOKING DARKNESS PLUTO'S DARK+ *956 6

DARK-CLEAVING
    SOME FEW DARK-CLEAVING THE DOORWAY SOULS THAT CLING AS +   75 10

DARK-CREATION
    FROM THE WARM BLOOD IN THE DARK-CREATION MORNING   358 14

DARK-CROSSED
    EVEN THE ABSENCE OF DARK-CROSSED DONKEYS   404 2

DARKEN
    YOU SHOULD BE OUT BY THE ORCHARD WHERE VIOLETS SECRETLY+   57 17
    DARKEN THE SHINING GRASS   196 13
    OUR EYES DARKEN AND IMPOTENCE HURTS   746 14
    WHEN I SEE THE SKY'S BLUE DARKEN   869 4
    HAVE FELT THE DAY DARKEN AND SHUDDER   *937 14

DARKENED
    YOU WHO DARKENED AND SHONE   56 34
    SMOULDERING WITH DARKENED BUSBIES BENEATH THE BAYONETS'+   66 8
    OUR BEACHED VESSEL DARKENED RENCONTRE INHUMAN AND CLOSE+   66 27
    OF A TRAIL OF OUR SMALL FIRE ON THE DARKENED SKY   89 15
    LIKE A TONGUE OF DARKENED FLAME   169 28
    HERE BY THE DARKENED LAKE   227 6
    NOW FROM THE DARKENED SPACES   242 20
    IN THE GREEN GARDEN DARKENED THE SHADOW OF COMING RAIN   672 12
    DOWN THE DARKER AND DARKER STAIRS WHERE BLUE IS DARKENE+ 697 15
    THAT SHONE AND DARKENED THEY WERE ALL TOO CLEVER   737 22
    OF MY BLOOD IN HER DARKENED CUP   *935 2
    AND PALE HOT SKIES HAVE DARKENED AND GONE COLD   *939 15
    DOWN THE DARKER AND DARKER STAIRS WHERE BLUE IS DARKENE+ *956 12

DARKENING
    OF STEAM FROM THE DARKENING NORTH   99 22
    KINDLES THE DARKENING PYRE   108 20
    DARKENING THE DAY-TIME TORCH-LIKE WITH THE SMOKING BLUE+ 697 4
    ONLY THE DEEPENING BLACKNESS DARKENING STILL   719 11
    OF DARKENING NIGHT AND THE QUIVERING LIGHT   823 9
    IN THE DEEP CART-RUTS GLEAMED THROUGH THE BLUE OF THE D+ 864 30
    AND DARKENING MY ETERNAL FAME   *929 5
    DARKENING THE DAYTIME TORCH-LIKE WITH THE SMOKING BLUEN+ *956 2

DARKENS
    FOR DOOM THAT DARKENS AND THE SUNDERERS   709 15
    MY SPIRIT DARKENS AND GOES OUT AND SOFT STRANGE GLOOM   727 2
    AND IF AS AUTUMN DEEPENS AND DARKENS   727 6
    WHEN THE SKY'S BLUE DARKENS AT NIGHTFALL   869 8

DARKER
    A DARKER GREEN   148 25
    AND DARKER THAN EVEN THE ARROWS OF VIOLENTEST WILL   383 10
    WHEN DARKER STILL THAN CONGO OR AMAZON   607 7
    HOW MUCH DARKER AND MORE SATANIC THEY ARE NOW   628 14
    DOWN THE DARKER AND DARKER STAIRS WHERE BLUE IS DARKENE+ 697 15
    SINGING DARKER THAN THE NIGHTINGALE ON ON TO THE SOLSTI+ 727 12
    THEY SEEMED TO GROW DARKER AS SHE CAME TO THE EDGE OF D+ 869 6
    DOWN THE DARKER AND DARKER STAIRS WHERE BLUE IS DARKENE+ *956 12

DARKEST
    WHEN SHE HAS PUT HER HAND ON MY SECRET DARKEST SOURCES + 267 6
    DARKEST OUTGOINGS   267 7
    FOR THE STRONGEST LIGHT THROWS ALSO THE DARKEST SHADOW 474 4

DARK EYE
    IN THE CAVE WHICH IS CALLED DARK EYE   786 5

DARK-FACED
    SUDDEN A DARK-FACED STRANGER   200 9
    THEY ARE ROYALTY DARK-FACED ROYALTY SHOWING THE CONSCIO+ 388 22
    AND ALL THE DARK-FACED COTTON-WRAPPED PEOPLE MORE   391 5
    ALL THE DARK-FACED COTTON-WRAPPED PEOPLE A COUNTLESS   391 8
    THEY WERE FOILED THE MYRIAD WHISPERING DARK-FACED   391 25
    HE IS QUITE GENTLE AND DARK-FACED   401 22
    ON AND ON LIKE A DARK-FACED BIRD SINGING ALONE   623 19
    AND THE OLD DARK-FACED MEN CAME OUT HEAVILY WITH A   778 35

DARK-FEATHERED
    ALL THE DARK-FEATHERED HELMETS LIKE LITTLE GREEN   221 17
    ALL THEIR DARK-FEATHERED HELMETS LIKE LITTLE GREEN   *945 3

DARK-GREEN
    OF THE DARK-GREEN HILLS NEW CALVES IN SHED PEEWITS TURN+ 57 27

DARK-HAIRED
    FROM THE TOP OF A DARK-HAIRED CEDAR-BUSH   780 28

DARKIE
    CAN YOU AFTER DARK BECOME A DARKIE   679 1

DARKLING
    HOLD MY OWN IN THE MIDST OF THEM DARKLING DEFY   133 19

DARKLY
    INTO DARKNESS AND DARKLY RETURNS   39 33
    AND PEOPLE DARKLY INVESTED WITH PURPLE MOVE PALPABLE   148 26
    WHAT FOOD IS THIS FOR THE DARKLY FLYING   171 19
    COMES DARKLY INTO SIGHT   227 2
    DARKLY MONUMENTAL IN YOU   296 10
    YET MORE I SEE YOU DARKLY CONCENTRATE   297 1
    THOSE THAT HAVE NOT SURVIVED THE DARKLY LUST   298 10
    LIKE A RED INDIAN DARKLY UNFINISHED AND ALOOF   369 10
    EAGLE WITH THE SICKLE DRIPPING DARKLY ABOVE   373 4
    DARKLY SAYING   375 27
    DARKLY FROM THE FECUND COSMOS FROM THE ANGRY RED SUN FR+ 675 11
    HOLDING THEIR BREATH NAKED AND DARKLY ALONE   711 5
    DARKLY FOR WE CANNOT STEER AND HAVE NO PORT   719 9
    EAGLE WITH THE SICKLE DRIPPING DARKLY ABOVE   781 7
    AND SEE YOURSELF AS IN A GLASS DARKLY   834 18

DARK-MASKED-ONE
    DARK-MASKED-ONE DAY-STARER THREATENING THE SUN WITH YOUR 703 11

DARKNESS
    INTO DARKNESS AND DARKLY RETURNS   39 33
    DARKNESS COMES OUT OF THE EARTH   41 20
    WOULD THE DARKNESS LOOK LIKE A GRAVE   49 19
    I LEANED IN THE DARKNESS TO FIND HER LIPS   62 6
    A MOMENT THEN DARKNESS SHUT THE LID OF THE SACRED ARK   62 18
    EMBRACE OF DARKNESS LIE AROUND AND CRUSHED BETWEEN THEM+ 88 4
    THE OPEN BOOK OF LANDSCAPE NO MORE FOR THE COVERS OF DA+ 88 8
    TO ESCAPE IN SLEEP THE TERROR OF THIS GREAT BIVALVE DAR+ 88 14
    THE DARKNESS RED   88 17
    ONLY THE DARKNESS AND THE SCENT OF YOU   90 27
    FIXED IN THE DARKNESS GRAPPLING FOR THE DEEP SOIL'S CRO+ 92 11
    EACH ONE FOR ITS HOLD ON THE CONCRETE DARKNESS I KNOW T+ 92 14
    AND DRAWING THE DARKNESS TOGETHER CRUSH FROM IT A TWILI+ 92 19
    I THROW FROM OUT OF THE DARKNESS MYSELF LIKE A FLOWER I+ 93 26
    IN FRONT OF ME YES UP THE DARKNESS GOES THE GUSH OF THE+ 97 18
    YET THEY NEVER CHANGE THE DARKNESS   110 21
    A YELLOW LEAF FROM THE DARKNESS   110 25
    STRETCHED IN THE BRINDLED DARKNESS   111 2
    THE DARKNESS IS SECRET AND I COULD SEAR   114 3
    A DARKNESS THAT DREAMS MY DREAM FOR ME EVER THE SAME   115 12
    AND I IN THE DARKNESS WANDERED ABOUT   121 25
    THEN LETS HER BLACK HAIR LOOSE THE DARKNESS FALL   128 33
    AND PASSION UNBEARABLE SEETHES IN THE DARKNESS LIKE MUST 129 30
    HOW THIS DARKNESS SOAKS ME THROUGH AND THROUGH   131 2
    VESSEL OF DARKNESS TAKES THE RISING TIDE   132 30
    ME WHO AM ISSUED AMAZED FROM THE DARKNESS STRIPPED   133 2
    DO I NOT KNOW THE DARKNESS WITHIN THEM WHAT ARE THEY   133 14
    OF DARKNESS WHEREON SHE SLEEPS ON HER PERFECT BED   133 25
    THE DARKNESS STEALS THE FORMS OF ALL THE QUEENS   135 21
    OUT OF THE DARKNESS FRETTED SOMETIMES IN ITS SLEEPING   136 5
    SOMETIMES THE DARKNESS TRAPPED WITHIN A WHEEL   136 8
    SHOWING THE ROCKING DARKNESS NOW A-REEL   136 10
    OF DARKNESS ABUNDANT WHICH SHAKEN MYSTERIOUSLY   136 18
    RIGID SLEEPS THE HOUSE IN DARKNESS I ALONE   140 7
    LIKE A SOFT FULL DROP OF DARKNESS IT SEEMS TO SWAY   148 1
    DARKNESS OF FAILURE WAS IN THEM WITHOUT AVAIL   156 4
    OF DARKNESS ADVANCING STEADILY OVER US ALL   164 24

DARKNESS
  OUR DARKNESS DO YOU UNDERSTAND   170 15
  DARKNESS AND SKIN-WRAPPED   171 2
  LIKE A FOREST DARKNESS LIKE A MARSH   171 10
  OF THIS SELF-SAME DARKNESS YET THE SHADOWY HOUSE BELOW   172 23
  ARRIVING GREY FROM THE DARKNESS ABOVE SUDDENLY INTO THE+   179 22
  AND BE OUT IN THE BEWILDERING DARKNESS WHICH IS ALWAYS +   179 25
  THE STREAM OF MY LIFE IN THE DARKNESS   199 19
  IN THE DARKNESS   204 3
  BETWEEN TWO VALVES OF DARKNESS   205 5
  THE DARKNESS FALLING THE DARKNESS RISING WITH MUFFLED   205 6
  WOULD FALL AND DARKNESS WOULD COME HURLING HEAVILY DOWN   205 10
  BUT HEAVY SEALING DARKNESS SILENCE ALL IMMOVABLE   205 14
  SO THEN THERE SHONE WITHIN THE JUNGLE DARKNESS   206 8
  DARKNESS   206 12
  EVERYWHERE DOWN IN THE GRASS WHERE DARKNESS WAS RAVELLED   206 18
  IN DARKNESS   206 19
  A SOUND SUBDUED IN THE DARKNESS TEARS   210 21
  YOU STAND BEFORE ME LIKE GHOSTS LIKE A DARKNESS UPRIGHT   211 8
  IN THE DARKNESS WE ALL ARE GONE WE ARE GONE WITH THE TR+   211 21
  MAGNIFICENT GHOSTS OF THE DARKNESS CARRY OFF HER DECISI+   213 26
  OH GODS OF THE LIVING DARKNESS POWERS OF NIGHT   213 29
  THE DARKNESS STARTS UP WHERE   215 17
  ENDS THIS DARKNESS THAT ANNIHILATES ME   221 4
  LOOSED ONE MOMENT THE DARKNESS FRIGHTENS ME   225 28
  IN HEAVEN NOW THAT THE DARKNESS   226 15
  I KNOW YOU HERE IN THE DARKNESS   227 29
  LISTEN THE DARKNESS RINGS   238 7
  AS THE DARKNESS FLICKERS AND DIPS   238 13
  GLITTERING AT ME ON THE UNUTTERABLE DARKNESS   241 6
  DARKNESS AND DEPTH OF SLEEP   254 1
  GLEBE IN THE UPTURNED DARKNESS   263 28
  MY DARKNESS   266 29
  WHEN SHE KNOWS THE FEARFUL OTHER FLESH AH DARKNESS UNFA+   267 11
  FLOWERS THAT COME FIRST FROM THE DARKNESS AND FEEL COLD+   270 9
  LET THE DARKNESS TURN VIOLET WITH RICH DAWN   273 23
  LET THE DARKNESS BE WARMED WARMED THROUGH TO A RUDDY VI+   273 24
  OH IF IT BE TRUE AND THE LIVING DARKNESS OF THE BLOOD O+   273 31
  IF YOU CATCH A WHIFF OF VIOLETS FROM THE DARKNESS OF TH+   274 1
  IN A DEEPER AND DEEPER DARKNESS   281 10
  DARKNESS   286 9
  THAT SWAYED THEIR LENGTH OF DARKNESS ALL AROUND   296 18
  SUN OF THE TORRID MID-DAY'S HORRIFIC DARKNESS   *   301 20
  LITTLE HELLS OF COLOUR CAVES OF DARKNESS   308 14
  DOWN BETWEEN THE STEEP SLOPES OF DARKNESS FUCUS-DARK SE+   321 35
  OF DARKNESS   323 3
  TO THOSE THINGS THAT LOVE DARKNESS THE LIGHT OF DAY IS +   331 3
  I REMEMBER THE FIRST TIME OUT OF A BUSH IN THE DARKNESS+   366 1
  AND FROM THE DARKNESS OF THAT OPPOSITE ONE   370 20
  WE WADE WE WADE WE STAGGER DARKNESS RUSHED   425 6
  WREATHE STRONG WEED ROUND THE KNEES AS THE DARKNESS   425 13
  WHILE DARKNESS SUBMERGES THE STONES   427 5
  AND THY DARKNESS IS FOREVER INVISIBLE   474 3
  THE BLOOD KNOWS IN DARKNESS AND FOREVER DARK   474 5
  LIVING DARKNESS   636 32
  ONLY FROM DARKNESS   660 23
  RIBBED AND TORCH-LIKE WITH THEIR BLAZE OF DARKNESS SPRE+   697 6
  TORCH-FLOWER OF THE BLUE-SMOKING DARKNESS DARK-BLUE DAZE   697 8
  GIVING OFF DARKNESS BLUE DARKNESS AS DEMETER'S PALE LAM+   697 10
  TO THE SIGHTLESS REALM WHERE DARKNESS IS AWAKE UPON THE+   697 17
  OR A DARKNESS INVISIBLE ENFOLDED IN THE DEEPER DARK   697 19
  AMONG THE SPLENDOUR OF TORCHES OF DARKNESS SHEDDING DAR+   697 21
  DARKNESS   697 27
  WHEN THE MOON FROM OUT OF THE DARKNESS   702 13
  HELL IS THE HOME OF SOULS LOST IN DARKNESS   711 15
  DARKNESS AT ONE WITH DARKNESS UP AND DOWN   719 13
  THE UPPER DARKNESS IS HEAVY AS THE LOWER   719 22
  AND HOW HE ENTERS FOLD AFTER FOLD OF DEEPENING DARKNESS   724 3
  AND AFTER DARKNESS OF HER PEACE   725 16
  TOWARDS THE DARKNESS AND THE SHADOW OF DEATH   737 11
  NOR CEASE TO BE DARK ON THE DARKNESS STAY   738 20
  STRUCK DOWN DO THOU PART US THE DARKNESS THAT WE SEE TH+   753 6
  OH MEN DUMB IN THE DARKNESS   765 1
  I HAVE A DARKNESS INTACT WITHIN ME GLOWING SECURE   772 10
  I HAVE A TENT OF DARKNESS BY DAY   772 14
  WITH ALL THE UNQUENCHABLE DARKNESS   772 26
  THE MINUTE SPARKING OF DARKNESS WHICH   772 29
  AND DARKNESS RUNS THE RACING WHEEL   773 6
  AND SELF-SAME DARKNESS CHAFED TO IRE   773 7
  EAGLE WITH EGYPTIAN DARKNESS JUTTING IN FRONT OF YOUR F+   782 20
  DO YOU HEAR THE RATS OF THE DARKNESS GNAWING AT YOUR IN+   800 25
  THE SNAKE OF MY LEFT-HAND OUT OF THE DARKNESS IS KISSIN+   801 22
  LET THE DARKNESS LEAVE YOU LET THE LIGHT COME INTO YOU   803 16
  AS IT COMES OVER THE MILK-BLUE SEA HINTING AT GOLD AND +   840 5
  AND THE IGNOBLE PRAYERS OF THE PANIC-STRICKEN WHOM DARK+   856 1
  TO HELP HIM LIFT THE WELTERING DARKNESS TURN   872 3
  INTO THE FERTILE DARKNESS AFTER DEATH   880 2
  OR WHETHER I WAS THE DARKNESS WITH ARCHED WINGS   882 1
  WITH THE DARKNESS OPPOSITE   883 25
  INTO THE DARKNESS SIGHING ON DARK AND I   885 10
  DARKNESS TO RAISE THE STRICKEN DIGNITY AND REST   *896 23
  HAVE BEEN CAGED AND COVERED WITH DARKNESS ALL DAY AND N+   *918 5
  FIXED IN THE DARKNESS GRAPPLING FOR THE DEEP SOIL'S LIT+   *926 11
  THE DARKNESS IS LOVELIEST WHERE I COULD SEAR   *929 20
  A DARKNESS WITHIN ME A PRESENCE WHICH SLEEPS CONTAINED   *930 7
  A DARKNESS THAT DREAMS MY DREAMS FOR ME EVER THE SAME   *930 12
  INTO DARKNESS OPEN AND EAGER FOR THE THRUST OF THE   *937 20
  THE DARKNESS STEALS THE FORMS OF ALL THE QUEENS   *938 25
  THE DARKNESS STEALS THE FORMS OF ALL THE QUEENS   *939 21
  TO THE OLD SUNDAY EVENINGS WHEN DARKNESS WANDERED OUTSI+   *940 11
  RIBBED HELLISH FLOWERS ERECT WITH THEIR BLAZE OF DARKNE+   *956 4
  TORCH-FLOWERS OF THE BLUE-SMOKING DARKNESS PLUTO'S DARK+   *956 6
  GIVING OFF DARKNESS BLUE DARKNESS UPON DEMETER'S PALE +   *956 8
  TO THE SIGHTLESS REALM WHERE DARKNESS IS MARRIED TO DARK   *956 14
  AMONG THE SPLENDOUR OF BLACK-BLUE TORCHES SHEDDING FATH+   *956 19
  AND HOW HE FINDS THE DARKNESS THAT ENFOLDS HIM INTO UTT+   *961 13

DARKNESSES
  MALE AND FEMALE DARKNESSES   171 15
  STILL AND THE DARKNESSES STEEP   254 6
  BLUE DARKNESSES OF WONDER THAT HOLD ALL   876 27

DARK-PURE
  KEEPS ME PROUD IN SHAME PLEDGE OF THE NIGHT DARK-PURE   772 13

DARK-RED
  WRAPPED IN THE DARK-RED MANTLE OF WARM MEMORIES   723 19
  AND FOLDED IN THE DARK-RED UNSEEN   *957 10
  WRAPPED IN THE DARK-RED MANTLE OF THE BODY'S MEMORIES   *958 31
  AND AT THE PENULTIMATE PORCHES THE DARK-RED MANTLE   *959 24

DARK-SKINNED
  WHEN THE VINE WAS ROSE GODS WERE DARK-SKINNED   286 14

DARK'S
  WITH TOO MUCH TINCTURE OF ME INSTEAD OF THE DARK'S DEEP+   92 29

DARK-VISAGED
  DARK-VISAGED   373 15

DARK-WEDGED
  DARK-WEDGED   781 21

DARK-WINGED
  AFTER THEM ISSUES A DARK-WINGED FLUTTERING SPRITE   858 15

DARK-WRAPPED
  WITH DARK-WRAPPED ROCKY MOUNTAINS MOTIONLESS SQUATTING   410 28

DARLING
  THERE LIES THE WORLD MY DARLING FULL OF WONDER AND WIST+   52 20
  AH MY DARLING WHEN OVER THE PURPLE HORIZON SHALL LOOM   91 25
  AND THERE IN THE DARK MY DARLING WHERE THE ROOTS ARE EN+   92 12
  WE ARE NOT LOVERS MY DARLING WE FIGHT AND WE DO NOT SPA+   92 16
  THERE ARE DEPTHS BELOW DEPTHS MY DARLING WHERE LOVE DOE+   93 2
  SHE LIES AT LAST THE DARLING IN THE SHAPE OF HER DREAM   101 14
  MY LITTLE LOVE MY DARLING   101 17
  FREE OF ALL HEARTS MY DARLING   101 27
  I KISS YOU GOOD-BYE MY DARLING   102 7
  OUT OF MY REACH MY DARLING   108 6
  SINCE I LOST YOU MY DARLING THE SKY HAS COME NEAR   134 14
  DON'T DISTURB IT DARLING   137 14
  CATCH MY HANDS MY DARLING BETWEEN YOUR BREASTS   147 15
  BLOSSOM MY DARLING BLOSSOM BE A ROSE   219 17
  MOANING FOR ME TO LOVE HIM O DARLING RYE   221 13
  TO YOU MY LITTLE DARLING   226 25
  WHAT DOES HE SEE MY DARLING   227 5
  BUT NEVER NOW MY DARLING   227 17
  AGAIN MY DARLING BUT NEW   239 14
  HIS POOR DARLING IS ALMOST FIERY   359 34
  POOR DARLING BITING AT HER FEET   360 7
  HOW ROUGH THAT WOULD BE ON YOU DARLING   433 18
  NOW THE PROUSTIAN LOT DEAR DARLING DEATH LET ME WRIGGLE   534 3
  WHERE MY DARLING PICTURES PRISONERS AWAIT HIS DEADLY   633 23
  DARLING I SEE YOUR IRON-GREY CHEVELURE   835 5
  NO MY DARLING ONION   835 16
  DARLING YOU LOOK SO LIKE BABY   842 14
  THERE LIES THE WORLD MY DARLING FULL OF WONDER AND WIST+   *905 9
  AH MY DARLING WHEN OVER THE PURPLE HORIZON SHALL LOOM   *926 18
  O DARLING RYE   *944 27

DARLINGS
  CLUCK FOR YOUR YELLOW DARLINGS   119 18
  LOOK AT THE LITTLE DARLINGS IN THE CORN   221 5
  CLUCK TO YOUR YELLOW DARLINGS   *932 27
  LOOK AT THE LITTLE DARLINGS IN THE CORN   *944 18

DARN
  NO MORE STOCKINGS TO DARN FOR THE FLOWER-ROOTS DOWN   309 2

DARNING
  THE SAME WITH THE FISHERMEN SITTING DARNING THEIR NETS   520 17

DART
  AS THEY DART AND FLASH   269 23
  DART AND TWIST STILL HE MUST GO WITH HIS BELLY ON THE G+   348 12
  THEN HE LAUGHED SEEING THE SUN DART FIERCELY AT HIM   790 1
  AND THEY DART TO HER WOMB THEY FIGHT FOR THE CHANCE TO +   795 31
  AND DART HIS ELECTRIC NEEDLES INTO YOUR BONES AND CURDL+   797 10

DARTED
  WAS MOIST AND COLD THE SUN IN HIM DARTED UNEASY HELD DO+   348 8

DARTING
  WHILE HIGHER THE DARTING GRASS-FLOWERS PASS   49 24
  EACH ONE DARTING AWAY WITH HIS   51 29
  DARTING HIS LIGHT PUNT WITH THE QUICK-SHIFTING FANCY OF+   867 25

DARTS
  WHERE THE ADDER DARTS HORIZONTAL   321 15
  AND DARTS A FEW GOLD RAYS   455 18
  DARTS A MAN AT PLAY   867 13

DASH
  AND DASH IN PANIC THROUGH THE BRAKE   465 15
  MORE THAN THE CHASTE SHORT DASH   492 28

DASHED
  A BIRD WOULD HAVE DASHED THROUGH COME WHAT MIGHT   345 19

DASTARDLY
  TO GET A LIVING IN THE DASTARDLY MEAN COMBAT   519 28

DAUBS
AND DAUBS THE SAND WITH ITS FLESH   628   6

DAUGHTER
DO YOU SET YOUR FACE AGAINST THE DAUGHTER   55   4
YOU THOUGHT YOUR DAUGHTER HAD ESCAPED   309   1
NO MORE HE SENDS HIS DAUGHTER   541 20
TO PRETEND THAT YOUR DAUGHTER   564 31
THE DAUGHTER OF THE GREAT MAN ROLLS HER KHAKI WOOL   752   9

DAUGHTERS
LEAR THE OLD BUFFER YOU WONDER HIS DAUGHTERS   494 16

DAUNTED
YET THEIR DAUNTED LOOKING FLICKERS   109   5
THA'RT DAUNTED OR SUMMAT   138 15
OUR DAUNTED EYES   166   7

DAUNTLESS
IN SIGN OF DAUNTLESS SILENT VIOLETS   317 18
WHEN MODERN PEOPLE SEE THE CARNAL BODY DAUNTLESS AND   445 31
GIVE VITALITY STILL TO THE DAUNTLESS   559   3

DAUNTLESSNESS
SUDDEN DEMONIC DAUNTLESSNESS FULL ABREAST   371 10

DAUNTS
THE LONELINESS DAUNTS THEM THEIR STIFF THROATS ACHE   228 12

DAVID
OF THE AFTERNOON GLOWS STILL THE OLD ROMANCE OF DAVID A+   53   3
OF THE AFTERNOON GLOWS ONLY THE OLD ROMANCE OF DAVID AN+   *905 18

DAWN
AH WHEN TO-MORROW THE DAWN COMES LATE   58 26
AND WHEN THE DAWN COMES CREEPING IN   59   1
SHALL WATCH THE DAWN LIGHT UP FOR ME   59 31
THE LUMINOUS MIST WHICH THE POOR THINGS WIST WAS DAWN   71   5
WHEN DAWN IS FAR BEHIND THE STAR THE DUST-LIT TOWN HAS   71   7
AND I SLEPT TILL DAWN AT THE WINDOW BLEW IN LIKE DUST   99   1
THAT MY LOVE CAN DAWN IN WARMTH AGAIN UNAFRAID   99 15
I ON THE DECK AM STARTLED BY THIS DAWN CONFRONTING   133   1
OPEN AND A GREAT GREY DAWN SWIRLS OVER MY FEET BEFORE   147   9
AND AM SWEPT AWAY IN THE HORRIBLE DAWN AM GONE   147 12
FLUX OF ANOTHER DAWN THE WIND THAT ALL NIGHT   154 28
TO DRAW HIS NET THROUGH THE SURF'S THIN LINE AT THE DAW+   180   2
WITH THE PALE DAWN SEETHING AT THE WINDOW   204   4
THE DAWN WAS APPLE-GREEN   216 13
THIS THEN AT LAST IS THE DAWN AND THE BELL   220 12
CLUSTERED DEAD AND THIS IS THE DAWN   220 19
HAS FOR ME A DOOR INTO PEACE WARM DAWN IN THE EAST   250   6
LET THE DARKNESS TURN VIOLET WITH RICH DAWN   273 23
NO GLITTERING COMPACT DROPS OF DAWN   278 28
NEW THROB LIKE A STIRRING UNDER THE FALSE DAWN THAT PRE+   292 34
OUT OF LIFE'S UNFATHOMABLE DAWN   364   2
ALL TINY FAR AWAY REPTILE UNDER THE FIRST DAWN   364 21
THE DAWN ROOKS CALL AT EVENING WHEN THE NIGHTINGALE SIN+   368 11
ARE YOU THE BIRD OF THE NEXT DAWN   371 19
DO THEY STAND UNDER THE DAWN HALF-GODLY HALF-DEMON   371 36
DAWN   383 28
AND WHEN THE HERD GOES BY AT DAWN SHE BEGINS TO BLEAT F+   384   6
THAT HAS FOLLOWED THE SUN FROM THE DAWN THROUGH THE EAST   404 14
I AM AWARE I FEEL NOTHING EVEN AT DAWN   509 24
THE DAWN COMES UP WITH A GLITTER AND A BLUENESS AND I S+   509 25
ALREADY THE WHITENESS OF FALSE DAWN IS ON MY INNER OCEAN   513 13
DAWN IS NO LONGER IN THE HOUSE OF THE FISH   616 18
AND THE DAWN CRY FROM A MINARET GOD IS GREAT   623 15
NOW THE SEA IS THE 'ARGONAUTS' SEA AND IN THE DAWN   687 19
THE DAWN IS NOT OFF THE SEA AND ODYSSEUS' SHIPS   687 22
I SEE DESCENDING FROM THE SHIPS AT DAWN   688 12
AH WAIT WAIT FOR THERE'S THE DAWN   720   3
THE CRUEL DAWN OF COMING BACK TO LIKE   720   4
TRUE MEN LOOK UP AT THE DAWN   810   8
WITH THE FIRST DAWN I ROSE TO LOOK IN THE GLASS   860 11
MY HEART HAS A WARMTH LIKE THIS SEA WHERE THE DAWN   860 17
SENDING THEM RIOTING AT DAWN DOWN THE LANE OF SCARLET P+   860 23
OF DUSTY GRASSES LIKE THE STARS THAT DAWN   884 31
THE LUMINOUS MIST WHICH THE POOR THINGS WIST WAS DAWN A+   *917 23
WHEN THE DAWN IS FAR BEHIND THE STAR THAT THE LAMP-LIT +   *917 25
SWIMS THE MALLARD DUCK AT DAWN IN THAT QUICK JOY   *953 27

DAWN-COCK'S-COMB
WARRIOR-LIKE DAWN-COCK'S-COMB FLARING FLOWER   315   1

DAWNED
OF A DAWNED TO-MORROW   116 17

DAWN-FOUNTAIN
LIKE WOMEN AT A WELL THE DAWN-FOUNTAIN   311 26

DAWN-HEARTED
IRON DAWN-HEARTED   305 17

DAWN-HEART
EVER-BEATING DAWN-HEART ENVELOPED IN IRON AGAINST THE   305 18

DAWNING
MISCHIEF HAS COME IN HER DAWNING EYES   46   9
A NURSE IN WHITE AT THE DAWNING FLOWER-FOAMED PANE   155   1
FAR OFF SO FAR LIKE A MADNESS UNDER THE HORIZON'S DAWNI+   364   3
THEN THE BRIGHT DAWNING OF DELIGHT AGAIN   708 26

DAWNINGS
GREY DAYS AND WAN DREE DAWNINGS   193 17

DAWN-KALEIDOSCOPIC
IT IS SO LOVELY DAWN-KALEIDOSCOPIC WITHIN THE CRACK   279   2

DAWN-PALE
DAWN-PALE   312   1

DAWN-PINK
DAWN-PINK   311 33

DAWN-ROSE
DAWN-ROSE   311   1

DAWNS
DAWNS MY INSURGENT DAY   176 29
EMPTY DAWNS IN SILENT AUSTRALIA   393 13
IT DAWNS ON THEM THAT THE WHOLE DAMN SWINDLE   560 11

DAWN STAR
THE DAWN STAR STOOD INTO SIGHT   787 20

DAWN'S
INTO THE NIGHT AND ARE LOST TO SADDEN WITH JETSAM THE D+   *918   8

DAWN-TENDER
WITH A BODY LIKE SPRAY DAWN-TENDER AND LOOKING ABOUT   306 30

DAY
YET THE SPLASHES OF DAY AND NIGHT   37 26
BUT DAY SHOWS IT VIVID WITH FEELING   38   3
ALL THAT THE WORLDLY DAY HAS MEANT   41 26
GLIMMERS LITTER OF DAY   41 30
EVERY DAY BY THE FENCE TO LOOK UP AT THE FLOWERS THAT E+   58 14
OF DAY TROLLS AT THE CAVE OF RINGING CERULEAN MINING   72 10
THIS NEW RED ROCK IN A WASTE OF WHITE RISES AGAINST THE+   75 13
THAT DAY IS HALF GROWN OVER IT NEED NOT ABASH   91   4
ONE DAY A HEAVY-BREASTED JUNE-HOT WOMAN   91   8
OF THE DAY BUT IT'S NOTHING TO DO WITH THE BOYS SO LET +   93 27
AND ALL DAY LONG THAT RAW AND ANCIENT COLD   98 21
AS SLOWLY THE HOUSE OF DAY IS CLOSING ITS EASTERN SHUTT+   102 28
AND ALL DAY LONG THE TOWN   109   1
AND IF THE DAY OUTSIDE WERE MINE WHAT IS THE DAY   112 24
WHERE IT GATHERED TOWARDS THE PLAIT ON THAT VERY LAST D+   114 23
NIGHT AFTER NIGHT WITH A BLEMISH OF DAY   117 18
AND I WAS BLIND IN A TAWNY-GOLD DAY   123 32
SLOWLY INTO ANOTHER DAY SLOWLY THE ROVER   132 29
THE WHOLE OF THE DAY TO EXTINGUISH THE SHADOW I LIFT ON+   133 20
I STILL AM NOT HOMELESS HERE I'VE A TENT BY DAY   133 24
OF OUR SABBATH SUFFUSING OUR SACRED DAY   148   3
I KNEW THAT SOME DAY SOON I SHOULD FIND YOU THUS   156 14
FLOWER THE DAY HAS BEGUN   166 27
ALL DAY HAS THE CLANK OF IRON ON IRON DISTRESSED   167 13
ON THAT DAY   176 10
DAWNS MY INSURGENT DAY   176 29
DAY WEARIES ME WITH ITS OSTENTATION AND FAWNINGS   193 19
COMPLAIN OF WHAT THE DAY HAS HAD THEM DO   195   7
YOU ARE THE NIGHT AND I THE DAY   209 21
DAY AND MAKE MAGIC IN HEAVEN   209 30
HOW LOVELY IS THE SELF THIS DAY DISCLOSES   218   4
THE DAY HAS BEGUN   230 10
NOW IN THE COOL OF THE DAY   231 27
IT IS MY OFFERING TO YOU EVERY DAY IS ALL SOULS' DAY   233 17
IS THE ORB OF DAY   253 17
THE GLOBE OF THE DAY OVER-RIPE   253 24
LIKE A WOUND THE EXPOSURE OF HER SECRET ON THE OPEN DAY   283 32
OUR PALE DAY IS SINKING INTO TWILIGHT   286 21
ARE YOU THE GRAVE OF OUR DAY   289 26
OUT OF THE EARTH BEFORE THE SUN WAS SPREAD OUT AND BEFO+   295   5
VISTA OF DAY   311   8
AND BREATHING SOFT UNWILLING TO WAKE TO THE NEW DAY   311 12
AND IT IS DAY THEN FROM THE FOUR QUARTERS THE FOUR WIND+   319   7
TO THOSE THINGS THAT LOVE DARKNESS THE LIGHT OF DAY IS +   331   3
BEFORE MY DAY   339 21
BETWEEN THE DAY AND THE NIGHT   340 28
IT WAS THE LIGHT OF DAY WHICH HE COULD NOT ENTER   344 17
SWEET FIRE OF DAY   346   5
ONLY IN THE BRIGHT DAY I WILL NOT HAVE THIS CLOT IN MY   346 11
ON A HOT HOT DAY AND I IN PYJAMAS FOR THE HEAT   349   2
ON THE DAY OF SICILIAN JULY WITH ETNA SMOKING   349 28
THE FIRST DAY TO HEAVE YOUR FEET LITTLE BY LITTLE FROM +   352   3
HAS THE PEACOCK HAD HIS DAY DOES HE CALL IN VAIN SCREEC+   371 20
NEW DAY WITH THEM   371 31
EVERY DAY SINCE THE SNOW IS HERE   375 22
BOARDS INTO THE DAY   384 20
AND TURNING THE DAY SUDDENLY INTO A BLACK TORNADO OF JO+   397   4
DAY HAS GONE TO DUST ON THE SAGE-GREY DESERT   403 21
FROM THE FAR FAR OTHER END OF THE DAY   405 16
OUR DAY IS OVER NIGHT COMES UP   425   1
OUR DAY IS DONE   425   5
OUR DAY IS OVER   425   9
AND IS FECUND WITH A NEW DAY OF NEW CREATURES DIFFERENT   429   7
ISN'T IT GOD'S OWN IMAGE TRAMPING HIS THIRTY MILES A DAY   430 22
AT THE TRASHY MOTOR-DRIVEN TRANSIT OF DIRTY DAY   453 27
ALL DAY LONG I FEEL THE TIDE ROCKING ROCKING   454 14
THE DAY IS ENDING THE NIGHT DESCENDING   456   1
AND DULL DEATH COMES IN A DAY   459   8
DAY OF THE MENTAL WELTER AND BLETHER   471 17
YOUR UNIQUE DAY IS OVER   473 13
THOU ART LIKE THE DAY   474   1
FOR A DAY FOR TWO DAYS AND WITHDRAW SLOWLY VANISH AGAIN   476 14
THE CURFEW OF OUR GREAT DAY   512   8
DAY DIE WITH US   512 28
THE NEW WORD OF THE UNBORN DAY   513   2
I SEE THE TIN-MAN THE TINKER SITTING DAY AFTER DAY ON T+   520 13
AND SO THERE CAME THE SADDEST DAY   555   5
HALF BELIEVING 'EM TILL ONE DAY   556 14
WILL RISE IN THEM ONE DAY   560   6
TO THE CHAR WHO'S AS GOOD AS YOU ARE ANY DAY   572   4

DAY

FATHER NEPTUNE ONE DAY TO FREEDOM DID SAY   574 11
TO GAOL TO BE HID FROM THE LIGHT OF DAY   579 16
GIVE US BACK OUR BODIES FOR A DAY FOR A SINGLE DAY   585 3
GIVE US BACK OUR BODIES FOR ONE DAY   585 6
THE PROTESTANT CHURCHES HAVE HAD THEIR DAY   609 22
AND SHE WAS SO PLEASED WITH IT SHE THOUGHT ONE DAY IT W+   619 14
WILL BE DRIVEN MAD FROM HIMSELF AND SIGHTLESS AND ON TH+   624 25
NEW DAY   625 5
SISTER THE WHOLE DAY LONG   628 2
BUT THE DAY THEY BURN MY PICTURES THEY BURN THE ROSE OF   634 3
BUT WE DO IT EVERY DAY   668 15
ON A DAY OF SPLENDOUR FOR THE FURTHER SPLENDOUR OF BEIN+   679 14
ALL THAT STORY OF MR GOD SWITCHING ON DAY   681 19
DOWN FLATTENING INTO POINTS FLATTENED UNDER THE SWEEP O+   697 7
IT IS THE DAY OF THE SUNDERERS   707 24
LIFE HAS ITS PLACE OF BLUE DAY ALOFT   711 1
OH ON THIS DAY FOR THE DEAD NOW NOVEMBER IS HERE   723 8
MY SOUL HAS HAD A LONG HARD DAY   725 11
DO THOU O VIRGIN AT DAY WHEN WE RISE FROM OUR SLEEPING   753 3
WHO LABOURS ALL DAY IN THE SUN   758 12
OF THE DAY THAT BATTLES ITS JOURNEY   771 24
THE DAY SHALL MOCK ME INEFFICACIOUS WHAT THEN   771 30
I HAVE A TENT OF DARKNESS BY DAY   772 14
AND WHICH WHEN DAY CROWS CHALLENGE   772 31
THEN OUR LIFE IS FINISHED OUR DAY IS OVER COMPLETELY   779 5
STOOD BETWEEN THE DAY AND THE NIGHT   787 16
I BRUSH THE WING OF THE DAY   787 23
THE TREMORS OF NIGHT AND THE DAY   788 6
ON THE SEVENTH DAY LET EVERY MAN WASH HIMSELF AND PUT O+   791 22
AND I WAIT FOR THE FINAL DAY WHEN THE DRAGON OF THUNDER+   797 7
BETWEEN NIGHT AND DAY MY SOUL-STAR IN ONE   799 23
I TELL YOU THE DAY SHOULD NOT TURN INTO GLORY   799 25
NIGHT TURNS UPON ME AND DAY WHO AM THE STAR BETWEEN   800 1
THE SUN HAS CLIMBED THE HILL THE DAY IS ON THE DOWNWARD+   803 9
DAY IS AT HAND   803 13
KEEPS DAY AND NIGHT APART   809 24
INTO BLUE DAY PAST HUITZILOPOCHTLI   810 10
BEYOND SPOKEN DAY   810 25
HIDDEN BLUE WITH THE BLUENESS OF ONE MORE DAY   815 9
WHICH IS BLUE WITH THE BLUENESS OF ONE MORE DAY   815 18
THE WHICH SINCE IT COINCIDES WITH MY DAY   815 19
THEY MAY EVEN ONE DAY DISCOVER SIMPLE AFFECTION AS A GR+   832 18
THE NEXT DAY IS THE DAY OF THE GOOSE THE WILD SWAN'S DAY   841 9
IN A DAY THEY ARE LOST IN THE NOTHINGNESS PURITY BRINGS   855 5
AT THE END OF A SWEET SPRING DAY THEY WILL VANISH   855 5
AT THE END OF THE SWEET SPRING DAY THEY ARE YOURS   855 13
HELPLESS ANOTHER DAY HAS FLOWN TOO HIGH   855 24
SLOWLY THE WINGS OF DAY ARE EDDYING LOWER   855 27
A COOL OINTMENT OVER THE EARTH BLISTERED IN THE FLIGHT +   855 31
SNOW AND THE SILENCE OF SNOW HEAVY ON THE ROUSING DAY   865 11
WHERE THIS FRAIL SHADOWY HUSK OF A DAY IS LOST   875 15
WHICH YIELDS THE DAY TO DEATH ERE YET THE LIGHT   885 7
YET THE SPLASHES OF DAY AND NIGHT   *892 14
BUT THE DAY SHOWS IT VIVID WITH FEELING   *892 19
ALL DAY THE CLINK OF THE HAMMERS HAS OPPRESSED   *896 16
WHERE THE GLASS IS DOMED BY THE BLUE SOFT DAY   *905 8
WE HAVE FORGOTTEN THE SUNNY APPLES OF DAY THAT WE CRAVE+   *917 15
HAVE BEEN CAGED AND COVERED WITH DARKNESS ALL DAY AND N+   *918 5
FOR NIGHT AFTER NIGHT WITH A BLEMISH OF DAY   *931 22
HAVE FELT THE DAY DARKEN AND SHUDDER   *937 14
SING LIKE A CHORUS SOME DAY   *938 20
AND DAY BY DAY OUT OF THE ENVIOUS BUD   *943 22
AND DAY BY DAY MY HAPPINESS VIBRATES   *943 24
ALL DAY LONG I AM BUSY AND HAPPY AT MY WORK   *945 24
AND WHAT OF GOOD I HAVE GIVEN THE DAY MY PEACE ATTESTS   *946 3
BLOWN FLAT INTO POINTS BY THE HEAVY WHITE DRAUGHT OF TH+   *956 5
GIVING OFF DARKNESS BLUE DARKNESS UPON DEMETER'S YELLOW+   *956 8
WHOM HAVE YOU COME FOR HERE IN THE WHITE-CAST DAY   *956 9
WHEN THE DAY COMES THAT WILL COME   *960 17
THE LAST DAY AND THE SETTING FORTH   *960 19

DAYBREAK
MAKE THE DAYBREAK SHIVER   109 24

DAYLIGHT
MYSELF TO WATCH THE DAYLIGHT WIN   59 3
THERE'S A BREACH IN THE WALLS OF THE PAST LETS THE DAYL+   174 6
OF REAL DAYLIGHT UPON US RELEASED FROM THE FOUL DREAM'S+   175 30
WHERE THE CANDLES BURN IN THE DAYLIGHT AND THE PAINTED   233 6
AND WHAT IS DAYLIGHT TO ME THAT I SHOULD LOOK SKYWARD   287 26
AND I A MANY-FINGERED HORROR OF DAYLIGHT TO HIM   339 23
HE COULD NOT PLUNGE INTO THE DAYLIGHT THAT STREAMED AT +   344 20
WAS THE HORROR OF WHITE DAYLIGHT IN THE WINDOW   344 25
BLUE DAYLIGHT SINKS IN MY HAIR   802 26

DAYS
AND WATCH MY DEAD DAYS FUSING TOGETHER IN DROSS   47 3
ON MY FIRST OF DAYS   59 4
YOU ASK ME DO THE HEALING DAYS CLOSE UP   90 22
THE HEALING DAYS SHALL CLOSE THE DARK GULF UP   90 29
TILL OLD DAYS DREW ME BACK INTO THEIR FOLD   98 28
THOSE WERE THE DAYS   103 14
SO THROUGH THESE DAYS WHILE BURN ON THE FUEL OF LIFE   115 9
THE DAYS PERCEIVE OUR MARRIAGE AND REJOICE   129 10
THE SOUNDLESS NIGHT WHEREON OUR DAYS ARE SHIPPED   133 4
AN' T' SHORT DAYS GOIN' UNKNOWN TER THEE   137 29
HOW MANY DAYS DOST THINK HAS GONE   138 1
HOW MANY DAYS DOST THINK HAS GONE   138 3
SEVEN DAYS MY LAD OR NONE   138 4
IT'S TA'EN THEE SEVEN DAYS TER SAY IT TER ME   139 30
OF CHILDISH DAYS IS UPON ME MY MANHOOD IS CAST   148 17
ARE MET AT LENGTH TO FINISH OUR REST OF DAYS   157 25
WHILE DAYS RUSH WAVE AFTER WAVE   159 5
AFTER MANY DAYS MY HEART YEARNS   171 25
WILL YOU RETURN AFTER MANY DAYS   171 27
WHO HAS REMEMBERED HER AFTER MANY DAYS   176 21
GREY DAYS AND WAN DREE DAWNINGS   193 17

DAYS
YOU WHO STEEP FROM OUT THE DAYS THEIR COLOUR   197 26
SHE'D BEEN NAKED ALL HER DAYS BEFORE   284 9
IS LOOKING RATHER SHABBY AND ISLAND-BOUND THESE DAYS   329 22
WOMEN WITH THE BEAUTIFUL EYES OF THE OLD DAYS   410 11
AND WE RIPPLE WITH LIFE THROUGH THE DAYS   449 9
FOR A DAY FOR TWO DAYS AND WITHDRAW SLOWLY VANISH AGAIN   476 14
IN THE OLD DAYS WHEN SAPPHIRES WERE BREATHED UPON AND   477 1
IN THE WILD DAYS WHEN LIFE WAS SLIDING WHIRLWINDS BLUE-+   529 23
IN THE DAYS CALLED CHAOS WHICH LEFT US ROCKS AND GEMS   529 25
AND THE SILENCE OF SHORT DAYS THE SILENCE OF THE YEAR T+   727 13
TO MAKE SPORT OF ME WHEN THE DAYS OF MY HEART   731 16
GOD WHAT SHALL I DO IN THE WHITE DAYS   766 25
TODAY IS EASTER SUNDAY CHRIST RISEN TWO DAYS AGO WAS   777 22
THE LAST OF MY DAYS IS GONE   797 18
OUR OVERWEENING DAYS STRIVE TOO FAR TILL THE HEAT AND T+   856 1
AND THEN ALL OUR DAYS IN A PLUNGE OF DEATH PAY THE DEBT   856 3
SHE IS NO LONGER TWO DAYS OLD   863 11
THE WITHERING FLOWERS THAT DAYS AGO YOU BROUGHT ME   880 11
THEN THE DAYS RAN ROUND ME IN A GOLDEN BROOD   *933 17
WAFTING LIKE SOLACE DOWN THEIR LENGTH OF DAYS   *941 16
ONCE OUTSIDE THE GATE OF THE WALLED SILVERY LIFE OF DAYS   *957 27

DAY-SEED
SEED AFTER DAY-SEED WENDS   253 19

DAY-STARER
DARK-MASKED-ONE DAY-STARER THREATENING THE SUN WITH YOUR   783 11

DAY-SUN
WINTER AND THE GREAT DAY-SUN AND THE SUN IN MY SOUL   455 26

DAY'S
FEELING MYSELF UNDAWNING THE DAY'S LIGHT PLAYING UPON ME   133 5
DEADENS THIS DAY'S GREY-DROPPING ARRAS-FOLD   141 12
OF A DAY'S EXPERIENCE SLEEP DOES SLOWLY DRAW   195 2
NOW AT THE DAY'S RENASCENCE   242 18
AND THE DAY'S NOW DEAD   404 30
WILL THE DARK FLOOD OF OUR DAY'S ANNIHILATION   428 24
GLOWING AFTER THE DAY'S RESTLESS DRAUGHTS   506 13
WHAT DO I CARE THOUGH FROM THE DAY'S WHITE ENVELOPE   772 22
ROOFED WITH A DAY'S NEAR CEILING AND A DARK   876 11

DAYTIME
WHEN THE DAYTIME CONSCIOUSNESS HAS GOT OVERWEENING   608 21
DARKENING THE DAYTIME TORCH-LIKE WITH THE SMOKING BLUEN+   *956 2

DAY-TIME
DARKENING THE DAY-TIME TORCH-LIKE WITH THE SMOKING BLUE+   697 4

DAY-WORLD
THEN THE NOISY DIRTY DAY-WORLD   453 16

DAZE
TORCH-FLOWER OF THE BLUE-SMOKING DARKNESS DARK-BLUE DAZE   697 8

DAZED
HAVE BEEN FOR ME LIKE A DAZED CONSTELLATION OF STARS   75 26
I AM DAZED WITH THE FAREWELL   108 11
FROM THE WOMB OF THE ALL I AM WAITING DAZED   262 20
WHEN I SAW HER STRAYING A LITTLE DAZED THROUGH HER UNTI+   618 21
AND I AM DAZED   875 5
AND DAZED WITH A TAWNY-GOLD DISPLAY   *935 4

DAZZLE
DAZZLE OF MAY-BLOBS WHERE THE MARIGOLD GLARE OVERCAST Y+   90 8
BREAKS INTO DAZZLE OF LIVING AS DOLPHINS LEAP FROM THE +   136 19
EVEN THE SHAKING WHITE POPLAR WILL DAZZLE LIKE SPLINTER+   624 18

D B B P BB
YOU'RE A D B B B P BB SAYS THE WORM   433 6

DEAD
BEFORE THE LAST-MOWN HAREBELLS ARE DEAD   35 7
AND LIE DEAD STILL WHILE SHE   35 18
AS IF I WAS DEAD BUT FEELING   35 22
THREE DEAD BIRDS LIE   36 24
THOUGH IT'S ALL THE SAME WHEN WE ARE DEAD   41 17
STILL YOUR QUICK TAIL LIE STILL AS DEAD   43 3
AND WATCH MY DEAD DAYS FUSING TOGETHER IN DROSS   47 3
CLOTTING TO ONE DEAD MASS IN THE SINKING FIRE   47 5
OF THE DEAD   75 11
MEANS BUT TO YOU A BURDEN OF DEAD FLESH   87 26
YOU UPON THE DRY DEAD BEECH-LEAVES ONCE MORE ONLY ONCE   90 25
MY SPIRIT IS DEAD   95 3
TO NUMBNESS AND NOTHINGNESS I DEAD SHE REFUSING TO DIE   98 8
I OWN THAT SOME OF ME IS DEAD TONIGHT   100 28
AND HER DEAD MOUTH SINGS   101 15
NOW YOU ARE DEAD   102 22
IS BURIED AWAY IN THE DARK WHERE THE DEAD ALL LIE   114 20
OF THE TROTH WITH THE DEAD THAT WE ARE PLEDGED TO KEEP   114 26
AND HALF LIES THERE IN THE DARK WHERE THE DEAD ALL LIE   115 1
THE DEAD MOON HEAPED WITHIN THE NEW MOON'S ARMS   132 2
ENJOYING THEIR GLANCING FLIGHT THOUGH LOVE IS DEAD   133 23
INFLAMED WITH BINDING UP THE SHEAVES OF THE DEAD   135 23
IT IS ONLY THE SPARROWS LIKE DEAD BLACK LEAVES ON THE   142 9
FINALLY RIDGED WITH THE AUSTERE LINE OF THE DEAD   155 5
PURE LOOK OF YOUR LAST DEAD FACE WHENCE NOW IS GONE   157 17
SO YOU HAVE COME TO GET HIM NOW HE'S DEAD   157 28
EVEN DEAD HE STILL IS MORTAL AND HIS HAIR   158 19
THAT HE IS DEAD AND YOU ARE NOT BUT STAND   158 29
WHEN WE FIND THE PLACE WHERE THIS DEAD ROAD GOES   164 4
LIKE CLIFFS ABUTTING IN SHADOW A DEAD GREY SEA   164 19
AND GLAD ARE THE EAGER DEAD TO RECEIVE YOU THERE   168 9
LET THE DEAD SORT   168 10
I IMAGINE DEAD HANDS ARE BRIGHTER   168 13
BREAKS LIGHT INTO GEMS AND DEAD BREASTS WHITER   168 17
THAT MOON-LIKE SWORD THE ASCENDANT DEAD UNSHEATHE   168 23

DEAD
    AND THE PERFECT DEAD ARE ELATE   168 30
    NOW TO THE DEAD YOU ARE GIVING   168 32
    SLEEP ON SPEED IN DEAD CERTAINTY   169 20
    SOFT-FOOTED DEAD   171   4
    AND THROUGH TO THE MOWIE ONLY THE DEAD IN THEIR BEDS   173 11
    WHERE DEAD MEN'S LIVES GLOW GENTLY AND IRON HURTS   173 22
    WITH A TOUCH THE DEAD AND THE LIVING WHILE TIME COUNTS +   174 12
    THEN THEY WILL SAY 'TIS LONG SINCE SHE IS DEAD   176 20
    DOES MY SLOW HEART REBEL DO MY DEAD HANDS   195   6
    CLUSTERED DEAD AND THIS IS THE DAWN   220 19
    HAS FALLEN DEAD UPON THE NAILS AND HANGS   225   6
    WITH A PALE DEAD CHRIST ON THE CRUCIFIX OF HIS HEART   226   3
    AND HEART LIKE A CROSS THAT BEARS DEAD AGONY   226   6
    AND KNOW THE DEAD CHRIST WEIGHING ON MY BONE   226 12
    THEY ARE CHANTING NOW THE SERVICE OF ALL THE DEAD   233   1
    LISTEN EXCEPT THOSE WHO STRIVE WITH THEIR DEAD   233   3
    NO DOUBT IF I WERE DEAD YOU MUST   236   1
    SLIPPING INTO ITS BED OF DEAD LEAVES YOU HURRY INTO YOUR   254 16
    WHEN I SAW THE TORN DEAD I KNEW IT WAS MY OWN TORN DEAD   257   7
    THOUSANDS AND THOUSANDS OF GAPING HIDEOUS FOUL DEAD   258   8
    AND I AM DEAD AND TRODDEN TO NOUGHT IN THE SMOKE-SODDEN   258 14
    DEAD AND TRODDEN TO NOUGHT IN THE SOUR BLACK EARTH   258 16
    OF THE TOMB DEAD AND TRODDEN TO NOUGHT TRODDEN TO NOUGHT   258 17
    TRODDEN TO NOUGHT IN SOUR DEAD EARTH   258 19
    TO HAVE ACCESS TO THE KNOWLEDGE THAT THE GREAT DEAD   263 23
    THE SHEAVES OF DEAD   269   5
    SORB-APPLES MEDLARS WITH DEAD CROWNS   280 23
    DEAD WITH A DEAD RACE AND A DEAD SPEECH AND YET   296   9
    NAY TONGUES ARE DEAD AND WORDS ARE HOLLOW AS HOLLOW   296 25
    MONUMENTAL TO A DEAD DEAD RACE   297 12
    THEY ARE DEAD WITH ALL THEIR VICES   297 18
    OF A DEAD MAN   303 14
    THE EAST A DEAD LETTER AND EUROPE MORIBUND IS THAT SO   371 32
    AND THOSE SOMBRE DEAD FEATHER-LUSTROUS AZTECS   371 33
    ALL MARES ARE DEAD   377   3
    ALL MARES ARE DEAD   377   4
    ALL MARES ARE DEAD   380   5
    OR ELSE I AM DEAD   380   6
    DEAD   401 25
    HER ROUND FINE-FASHIONED HEAD WITH TWO DEAD EARS   402   3
    BEAUTIFUL DEAD EYES   402   7
    AND A BLACK CRUCIFIX LIKE A DEAD TREE SPREADING WINGS   403 24
    AND THE DAY'S NOW DEAD   404 30
    FOLLOW THE TRAIL OF THE DEAD ACROSS GREAT SPACES FOR TH+   406   4
    FAR ONE TO SLEEP AND A FORGETTING AND OFTEN THE DEAD LO+   406   5
    AGAIN FOR OH THE DEAD ARE DISCONSOLATE SINCE EVEN DEATH+   406   8
    FELL FROM THE HOOKS AND WERE DEAD   413   9
    LIKE SPERM OF WHALES LIKE GERMS OF THE GREAT DEAD PAST   428 24
    ARE WE NOTHING ALREADY BUT THE LAPSING OF A GREAT DEAD   429   1
    SUCKING HIS LIFE OUT OF THE DEAD LEAVES OF GREATER LIFE+   431 16
    THE UPHOLSTERED DEAD THAT SIT IN DEEP ARM-CHAIRS   440 20
    LET THE DEAD GO BURY THEIR DEAD   440 21
    LET THE DEAD LOOK AFTER THE DEAD   440 23
    THE DEAD IN THEIR NASTY DEAD HANDS   440 26
    THE DEAD IN THEIR SEETHING MINDS   441   1
    THE DEAD ARE IN MYRIADS THEY SEEM MIGHTY   441   5
    IT IS THE GREAT LIE OF THE DEAD   441 10
    THE DEAD GIVE SHIPS AND ENGINES CINEMA RADIO AND GRAMOP+   441 17
    YOU ARE ALL GOING DEAD AND CORPSE-PALE   441 25
    O CEASE TO LISTEN TO THE LIVING DEAD   441 28
    O CEASE TO LABOUR FOR THE GOLD-TOOTHED DEAD   441 30
    DON'T EVER BE KIND TO THE SMILING TOOTH-MOUTHED DEAD   441 32
    DON'T EVER BE KIND TO THE DEAD   441 33
    THE REPULSIVE LIVING FAT DEAD   441 35
    DEAD   442   3
    ARE BORN DEAD THEY ARE SHROUDS THEY SOAK LIFE OUT OF US   448   9
    LETTING THE LIVING DEAD EAT YOU UP   449 20
    THE HEART IS FROZEN THE SPIRIT DEAD   456   2
    A SMALL BIRD WILL DROP FROZEN DEAD FROM A BOUGH   467   3
    BUT TIME HAS FLED OUR PARENTS ARE DEAD   490 21
    TO GIVE OF MY LIFE TO THE DEAD   500   9
    WHEN PEOPLE ARE DEAD AND PEACELESS   500 11
    WHEN PEOPLE ARE DEAD AND PEACELESS   500 13
    DESIRE MAY BE DEAD   504 15
    WHEN LOVE IS GONE AND DESIRE IS DEAD AND TRAGEDY HAS LE+   509   1
    PAUSES THAT ARE AS GOOD AS DEATH EMPTY AND DEAD AS DEATH   510   8
    AND DESIRE IS DEAD   510 18
    FOR OUR WORD IS DEAD   510 24
    FOR OUR FLESH IS DEAD   513   5
    TILL WE ADMIT HOW DEAD WE ARE   513   9
    AND EVEN THE SEA OF SEAS WILL HAVE TO GIVE UP ITS DEAD   514   9
    WE NEED HAVE NO DEAD PEOPLE MONEY-SLAVES AND SOCIAL   527   7
    CENSORS ARE DEAD MEN   528 10
    BUT CENSORS BEING DEAD MEN   528 14
    BREATHING OF THE DEAD MEN   528 20
    GONE DEAD OR WANDERING IN EXILE WITH THEIR FEATHERS   533 18
    IMMORTAL CAESAR DEAD AND TURNED TO CLAY   545 24
    HE CUT ME VERY DEAD   570   1
    THEN I SAY TO MYSELF AM I ALSO DEAD IS THAT THE TRUTH   629 22
    THAT WITH SO MANY DEAD MEN IN MILLS   629 24
    I TOO AM ALMOST DEAD   629 25
    I WITH THEM AM LIVING DEAD MECHANICAL ENSLAVED AT THE   629 28
    DEAD   631   2
    IS THE LANGUAGE DEAD AND EMPTY OF REPLY   633 13
    RISEN FROM THE DEAD AFTER THIS CRUCIFIXION   636 23
    WHAT HAS KILLED MANKIND FOR THE BULK OF MANKIND IS DEAD   654   3
    BEFORE I AM DEAD   655 21
    AND WHOEVER GETS IT IT'LL BE A DEAD BABY   664 15
    IT IS LIKE A VAST GREAT TREE WITH A VAST GREAT LOT OF S+   677 21
    VENUS WOULD RATHER HAVE LIVE DOVES THAN DEAD IF YOU WAN+   678   7
    THEY ARE NOT DEAD THEY ARE NOT DEAD   687 12
    FOR THE SUN IS DEAD AND ALL THAT IS IN HEAVEN   702 23
    IS DEAD TOO A DEAD ORB WHEELED ONCE A MONTH ROUND THE P+   702 27
    THEY ARE ALL DEAD   703   2
    IS DEAD WE RUN WHEELS ACROSS HER CORPSE   703   8
    THE DEAD THREADED THE AIR LINGERING   704   3
    THE DEAD TREAD HEAVILY THROUGH THE MUDDY AIR   704   8

DEAD
    FOR THE DEAD VANITY OF KNOWING BETTER NOR THE BLANK   709 30
    AND THE POOR DEAD WHEN THEY HAVE LEFT THE WALLED   721 11
    BE KIND OH BE KIND TO YOUR DEAD   721 17
    PROVIDE FOR YOUR DEAD ONCE MORE EQUIP THEM   721 25
    OH PITY THE DEAD THAT ARE DEAD BUT CANNOT TAKE   722   1
    OH PITY THE DEAD THAT WERE OUSTED OUT OF LIFE   722   4
    THE POOR GAUNT DEAD THAT CANNOT DIE   722   9
    BEWARE THE UNHAPPY DEAD THRUST OUT OF LIFE   722 16
    ARE CROWDED WITH LOST SOULS THE UNEASY DEAD   722 22
    OH BUT BEWARE BEWARE THE ANGRY DEAD   723   3
    IS DUE TO THE ANGRY UNAPPEASED DEAD   723   5
    OH ON THIS DAY FOR THE DEAD NOW NOVEMBER IS HERE   723   8
    SET A PLACE FOR THE DEAD WITH A CUSHION AND SOFT SEAT   723   9
    FOR YOUR DEAD YOUR UNSEEN DEAD AND WITH YOUR HEARTS   723 12
    OH THEY CAN LAY YOU WASTE THE ANGRY DEAD   723 16
    MY WRISTS SEEM BROKEN AND MY HEART SEEMS DEAD   727 19
    WE COVER THE HOUSELESS DEAD SO THEY SLEEP IN PEACE   736 25
    THERE ARE SO MANY DEAD   739   4
    THE DEAD TRIUMPHANT AND THE QUICK CAST DOWN   740   4
    THE DEAD UNASSUAGED AND ANGRY SILENCING US   740   5
    FOR ONE YEAR'S SPACE ATTEND ON OUR ANGRY DEAD   740 16
    KNOWING OUR DEAD ARE FITLY HOUSED IN DEATH   740 22
    SURE OF OUR DEAD IN THE PROUD HALLS OF DEATH   740 27
    THE DEAD ARE BURNING IN THE FUNERAL WIND   744   9
    OF PURE AND LAMBENT HOSTAGE FROM THE DEAD   745 14
    WHY ARE YOU SO ANXIOUS LEAVE ME PEACEFUL WITH MY DEAD   756 17
    THEY ARE DEAD SO GOD AS BETWEEN YOU YOU SEE   759 19
    INTO THE DEAD SEA FALLING   766 21
    MYRIAD MYRIAD DEAD TWIGS OF PALLID AND CHAFING PEOPLE   784 21
    THE DRAGON OF THE DISAPPOINTED DEAD THAT SLEEPS IN THE +   795 12
    THE SPIRITS OF THE COLD DEAD WHISTLE IN THE EARS OF THE+   795 15
    FOR I TELL YOU THERE ARE NO DEAD DEAD NOT EVEN YOUR DEAD   795 17
    THERE ARE DEAD THAT SLEEP IN THE WAVES OF THE MORNING S+   795 18
    THERE ARE DEAD THAT WEEP IN BITTER RAINS   795 20
    THERE ARE DEAD THAT CLUSTER IN THE FROZEN NORTH SHUDDER+   795 21
    THERE ARE DEAD THAT CREEP THROUGH THE BURNING BOWELS OF+   795 24
    THERE ARE DEAD THAT SIT UNDER THE TREES WATCHING WITH A+   795 26
    THERE ARE DEAD THAT ATTACK THE SUN LIKE SWARMS OF BLACK+   795 28
    THERE ARE DEAD THAT STAND UPON YOU WHEN YOU GO IN TO YO+   795 30
    CHILD OF THE LIVING DEAD THE DEAD THAT LIVE AND ARE NOT+   796   1
    AND BEING DEAD YOU SHALL NOT BE REFRESHED   796   3
    THERE ARE NO DEAD DEAD   796   4
    BEING DEAD YOU SHALL ROVE LIKE DOGS WITH THE BROKEN HAU+   796   5
    THE DEAD THAT HAVE MASTERED FIRE LIVE ON SALAMANDERS IN+   796   7
    THE DEAD OF THE WATER-LORDS ROCK AND GLIMMER IN THE SEAS   796   8
    THE DEAD OF THE STEEL MACHINES GO UP IN MOTION AWAY   796   9
    THE DEAD OF ELECTRIC MASTERS ARE ELECTRICITY ITSELF   796 10
    BUT THE DEAD OF THOSE WHO HAVE MASTERED NOTHING NOTHING+   796 11
    LO IN THE BACK STREETS OF THE AIR DEAD ONES ARE CRAWLIN+   796 29
    HIM OF THE DISAPPOINTED DEAD HE IS LASHING AND TURNING +   796 31
    HE WHO HOUSELS THE DEAD OF THE GUNS   797   2
    BUT HAVE YOU SEEN A DEAD MAN HOW HIS STAR HAS GONE OUT +   800 18
    DEAD ARE THE GREY DOGS   808 22
    THE DEAD ARE ON THEIR JOURNEY THE WAY IS DARK   810 21
    WHERE THE DEAD ARE LIVING AND THE LIVING ARE DEAD   811   5
    THE DEAD HAVE GONE THE LONG JOURNEY   811 16
    AND THE DEAD DIE   811 28
    WHEN I SEE THIS SEA LOOKING SHODDY AND DEAD   815 10
    AND NO MORE ANEMONES RISE FROM THE DEAD   815 12
    AND WE ARE NOT DEAD   825 27
    SUCH ON THE VIRGIN HAIR OF DEAD SIXTEEN   854 24
    UTTERLY DEAD LIVED BUT TO BANISH   855   7
    BUT OF THOSE LIFE-LOVING CARELESS OF THEIR RANK AMONG T+   855 12
    LIFE LOVERS WHO COULD HOPE FOR NO RANK AMONG THE PALLID+   855 20
    GIVE THEM TO THE DEAD   857   2
    ANYWHERE NOWHERE THE DEAD ROAD GOES   858   4
    IS DEAD AT LAST THEN HIS POOR SUNK FLAME MUST FLICKER   859   3
    AND BEHOLD THEM DEPLORABLY DEAD BY WRONG USAGE DEFACED   859 24
    THAT ARE DEAD YOU HAVE LEFT ME CRUELLY SIEGMUND   871 30
    I AM TERRIFIED YOU ARE DEAD   886 21
    SENTRY UPON THE DEAD OAK WHILE ANOTHER BELOW   *894 28
    SO WE FOUND THE DEAD CLATCH SIDE BY SIDE   *933   5
    THE DEAD MOON HEAPED WITHIN THE YOUNG MOON'S ARMS   *937 29
    THAT IS DEAD THE MOTHER-LOVE LIKE LIGHT THAT FLOWED   *938 14
    IT IS DEATH I FEAR SO MUCH IT IS NOT THE DEAD   *938 27
    INFLAMED WITH BINDING UP THE SHEAVES OF DEAD   *939 23
    AND ALL THE DEAD   *955 16
    OH PITY THE DEAD THAT ARE DEAD BUT CANNOT TAKE   *958   1
    PITY OH PITY THE POOR DEAD THAT ARE ONLY OUSTED FROM LI+   *958   8
    PITY THE POOR GAUNT DEAD THAT CANNOT DIE   *958 14
    THROUGH THE DEAD WEED OF A LIFE-TIME'S FALSITY   *959   8

DEAD-ALIVE
    TO BE DEAD-ALIVE   528   6

DEAD-BEAT
    INCONSOLABLE YOUTH DEAD-BEAT   457 22

DEAD-BLACK
    OVER THE DEAD-BLACK RIVER   109 22

DEADEN
    TO DEADEN MY ATTENTION IN YOUR DIRECTION   332 23

DEADENED
    DEADENED ME THROUGH TILL THE GREY DOWNS DULLED TO SLEEP   98 22
    SO I WENT AND WASHED MY DEADENED FLESH IN THE SEA   99 12
    UNKNOWN WITHIN YOUR BREAST AND YOUR DEADENED LOINS   723 18

DEADENING
    ARE THEY JUST THE DEADENING FUNGUS   765 20

DEADENS
    WITH A PLAINTIVE UNALTERABLE VOICE THAT DEADENS   64 23
    DEADENS THIS DAY'S GREY-DROPPING ARRAS-FOLD   141 12

DEADLIEST
   THAT KNOWS THE DEADLIEST POISON LIKE A SNAKE   304 10

DEAD-LOCKED
   AND TIED IN A KNOT INSIDE DEAD-LOCKED BETWEEN TWO DESIR+   379 12

DEADLY
   THAT MOTIONLESS DEADLY MOTION   338 7
   UP WITH THEM AND GREAT IS THE PAIN OF GREETING AND DEAD+   406 7
   DON'T DO IT IN DEADLY EARNEST   517 3
   WITH DEADLY LOATHING   538 9
   WHERE MY DARLING PICTURES PRISONERS AWAIT HIS DEADLY   633 23
   THE MORE DEADLY AND DANGEROUS IT BECOMES   665 11
   IRON GIVES THE DEADLY WOUND   712 6
   WE GIVE UP O LORD OUR BODIES TO DEADLY HATE   743 11

DEADNESS
   FROM YOUR BODY'S DEADNESS AND DROSS   112 7
   INTO RUBBER-LIKE DEADNESS DUNLOP INFLATED UNCONCERN   625 18

DEAD-SURE
   AND MORE THAN ALL THE DEAD-SURE SILENCE   169 16

DEAF
   THEY HAVE GONE STONE DEAF HE SAID   790 23

DEAFNESS
   DEAFNESS BETE   385 2

DEAL
   AND IT WORRIED ME A GOOD DEAL   555 28
   IS APT TO PROVE A GREAT DEAL TOO STRONG   576 2
   WE WERE MEANT TO MEAN A GREAT DEAL TO ONE ANOTHER   603 10
   DO THEY MEAN THEY ARE A GREAT DEAL ALONE   646 4
   HAVE TO DEAL OUT TO IT   670 17
   WHERE NOW THEY DEAL OUT SLICES OF PLATO-SAUSAGE TO THE +   762 27

DEAR
   I WISH YOU DID NOT WAIT MY DEAR   41 15
   TER NOTTINGHAM EH DEAR O' ME   45 7
   OUT O' MY WAY CHILDT DEAR O' ME WHEER   45 13
   MY LAST DEAR FUEL OF LIFE TO HEAP ON MY SOUL   74 19
   MY FALLEN STAR AMONG THE LEAVES MY DEAR   86 24
   IS IT WITH PAIN MY DEAR THAT YOU SHUDDER SO   87 1
   IS IT BECAUSE I HURT YOU WITH PAIN MY DEAR   87 2
   NAY DEAR BE STILL   87 7
   THE LEAVES AND DEAR YOU HAVE HAD YOUR WILL   87 9
   IT IS NO GOOD DEAR GENTLENESS AND FORBEARANCE I ENDURED+   92 7
   I CAME TO THE BOYS WITH LOVE DEAR AND ONLY THEY TURNED +   92 21
   ALONE MY DEAR   102 18
   MY DEAR AMONG IT ALL   110 2
   OF MY EYES I SEE YOU BEAUTIFUL AND DEAR   118 13
   AND I AM WILLING TO COME TO YOU NOW MY DEAR   134 20
   FOR I AM TIRED MY DEAR AND IF I COULD LIFT MY FEET   134 24
   WHAT DID YOU SAY MY DEAR   136 23
   OR DEAR O' ME SAY SUMMAT   138 19
   MY DEAR YES YES YOU ARE CRUEL TO ME YOU CAST   211 3
   MY DEAR THE NIGHT IS SOFT AND ETERNAL NO DOUBT   211 11
   MY DEAR WHEN YOU CROSS THE STREET IN THE SUNSHINE SURELY   211 13
   AND THE DEAR DEAR FIREFLIES WAFTING IN BETWEEN   221 15
   BUT AH MY DEAR   309 4
   SUCH A DEAR   377 27
   NOT THAT YOU'RE MERELY A SOFTY OH DEAR ME NO   396 16
   EVERYBODY SO DEAR AND YOURSELF SO ULTRA-BELOVED   398 26
   HUSH AND DIE MY DEAR   410 14
   AND THE WOMAN SAID DEAR ME   433 17
   BUT MY DEAR FELLOW MY DEAR FELLOW   434 17
   DON'T LIVE UP TO THE DEAR LITTLE GIRL WHO COSTS   458 22
   NOR THE DEAR OLD MATER WHO SO PROUDLY BOASTS   458 24
   DON'T LONG TO HAVE DEAR LITTLE DEAR LITTLE BOYS   459 1
   NOR A DEAR LITTLE HOME WITH ITS COST ITS COST   459 5
   BEWARE O' MY DEAR YOUNG MEN OF GOING ROTTEN   462 17
   AND IT'S FUNNY MY DEAR YOUNG MEN THAT YOU IN YOUR   462 29
   FOR OBSCENITY AFTER ALL MY DEAR YOUNG MEN   463 1
   AND I THOUGHT YOU WANTED LIFE AND EXPERIENCE DEAR YOUNG   463 5
   HOW INFINITELY DEAR TO ME   469 13
   EAT ME UP DEAR PEASANT SO THE PEASANT ATE HIM   533 25
   NOW THE PROUSTIAN LOT DEAR DARLING DEATH LET ME WRIGGLE   534 3
   DEAR LADIES NONE WHATSOEVER   541 14
   YOU MUSTN'T EXPECT MY DEAR TO GET AWAY WITH IT   548 21
   AND IF YOU'RE NOT ON THE LIST WHY THERE YOU ARE MY DEAR   548 23
   THANK YOU DEAR CLARINDA   550 19
   DEAR LORD OF DELIGHT   558 4
   DEAR LORD OF RIGHT   558 10
   SUCH A DEAR KIND AUNTIE ISN'T SHE TO A LUCKY LITTLE   571 11
   A BETTER MANAGER FOR OH DEAR ME   571 24
   HE ANSWERED DEAR BRITANNIA WHY   577 9
   NEITHER MY DEAR I HAD HIM FIXED IT SAVES HIM FROM SO   581 12
   BECAUSE YOU SEE HE IS NEITHER MY DEAR   581 18
   MY LITTLE CRITICS DEAR SAFE LITTLE PETS   581 26
   TOWARDS THOSE NEAR AND DEAR TO ME MY VERY NEXT   607 27
   ALL DEAR DADDY-DO-NOTHINGS   658 22
   AND DEAR OLD LADY JEAN   668 17
   WAIT DEAR LADY JEAN WAIT A MINUTE   668 23
   AND YOU DEAR LADY JEAN ARE YOU CONNIE   669 2
   FOR I HATE THIS BODY WHICH IS SO DEAR TO ME   741 16
   CHILD DEAR TO MY EYE GOD'S BLESSING IS ON THY SERVICE   749 21
   ME TOO AT LAST ERE THOU GOEST CHILD DEAR TO MY EYE   750 3
   AH MY LOVE MY DEAR   752 1
   LORD GOD ABOVE WOULD IT COST ME DEAR   759 10
   DEAR DEAR WORKING-MAN   773 15
   DEAR DEAR BANK-CLERK   773 17
   DEAR DEAR DEAR DEAR THEY'RE ALL ON THE RISE   773 19
   BUT WATCH YOUR SEXUAL STEP OH DEAR MY DEAR   829 29
   AWFULLY SORRY DEAR BUT I CAN'T COME BECAUSE OF THE CHIL+   832 11
   AND THE ANIMALS CURL DOWN ON THE DEAR EARTH TO SLEEP   834 3
   IT'S NO GOOD MY DEAR   834 13
   MY DEAR LITTLE GIRLY-WIRLY   834 14

DEAR
   A JOLLY GOOD SCREW WHEN THE DEAR LITTLE GIRLY-WIRLY'S O+   834 21
   OH MY DEAR LITTLE GIRLY-WIRLY   835 9
   DEAR LITTLE GIRLY-WIRLY   835 13
   MY DEAR YOU WON'T GET AWAY WITH IT   835 30
   OH DEAR WHAT'S HAPPENING   846 2
   OH DEAR WHAT'S HAPPENING TO TUSCANS   846 12
   YOU SOUND SO DREADFUL SO CRUELLY HURT MY DEAR   871 18
   SIEGMUND DEAR KISS ME KISS ME   871 20
   WHY DEAR   871 31
   SIEGMUND DEAR WHAT ARE YOU DOING LYING WITH YOUR FACE O+   871 33
   THE LAST DEAR FUEL AND HEAP IT ON MY SOUL   *895 27
   THE WAY THAT I HAVE GONE AND NOW AM LEADING THEY ARE DE+   *900 19
   THE WAY THAT I HAVE GONE AND NOW AM LEADING THEY ARE DE+   *903 31
   THE LAST DEAR FUEL AND HEAP IT ON MY SOUL   *904 16
   IT IS NO GOOD DEAR MEEKNESS AND FORBEARANCE I ENDURED T+   *926 7
   BUT MY DEAR LOVE WHEN ANOTHER NIGHT   *931 15
   LORD DEAR LORD DO YOU THINK HE EVER CAN SHINE   *945 20
   WITH PRAYER I NEED ONLY COME HOME EACH NIGHT TO FIND TH+   *945 28
   BUT FOR MYSELF BUT FOR MY SOUL DEAR SOUL   *958 19

DEARER
   CHASTITY DEARER FAR TO ME   470 1
   FIRE IS DEARER TO US THAN LOVE OR FOOD   505 25
   AND DEARER TO ME   764 1
   IT IS VERY DARK OH KINDRED DEARER THAN BLOOD   765 1
   AND DEARLY DEARER THAN MONEY   765 2
   OH MEN DEARER THAN SUCCESS TO ME   765 4
   MEN DEARER TO ME THAN PEACE   765 5
   DEARER THAN LOVE   765 6
   DEARER THAN TRIUMPH   765 7

DEAREST
   MY LITTLE LOVE MY DEAREST   101 23
   TWICE I AM BORN MY DEAREST   102 3
   I KISS YOU GOOD-BYE MY DEAREST   102 13
   OF DEATH MY DEAREST   103 19
   YOUR VERY DEAREST LOVE AT HIM   398 16
   AND SAY BE WELCOME DEAREST FRIEND   754 25
   BUT MY DEAREST DEAREST LADDIE-LASS   835 21

DEARLY
   YOU HEAR A WOMAN SAY I LOVE MY HUSBAND DEARLY   654 10
   AND DEARLY DEARER THAN MONEY   765 2
   THE LAST TWO THINGS WE CAN STILL HOLD DEARLY   826 25
   I LOVE LIFE I LOVE LIFE SO DEARLY I COULD ALMOST DIE   837 10

DEARLY-BELOVED
   IF THERE ISN'T MY DEARLY-BELOVED LIAR   79 4
   DEARLY-BELOVED MR SQUIRE   680 20
   IF THERE ISN'T MY DEARLY-BELOVED LIAR   *920 28

DEARNESS
   LOVE NOR COMPASSION NOR PITY NOR DEARNESS NOR PAIN MAKE+   840 14

DEARS
   I THANK YOU I DO YOU HAPPY CREATURES YOU DEARS   221 20
   POST ME NIHIL BUT PERHAPS MY DEARS   531 11
   MY DEARS DON'T LOOK AT ME I AM MERELY TERRIFIED OF YOU   541 10
   MY DEARS IF YOU WANT THE SKIES TO FALL   541 23
   OH TOUCH THE HARP TOUCH THE HARP GENTLY MY DEARS   576 4
   HOW I ADORE YOU YOU HAPPY THINGS YOU DEARS   *945 6

DEARTH
   AND A CURIOUS DEARTH OF SOUND   145 31

DEATH
   AGAINST HIM DIE AND FIND DEATH GOOD   43 37
   THE LOSS OF MYSELF TILL DEATH COMES WHO CANNOT FAIL   48 8
   DEATH IN WHOSE SERVICE IS NOTHING OF GLADNESS TAKES ME   48 9
   TAKE COVER IN DEATH   55 24
   FROM A ROOF INERT WITH DEATH WEEPING NOT THIS NOT   62 11
   TO LIFE AND TO DEATH IN YOU   102 4
   OF DEATH MY DEAREST   103 19
   OUT OF DEATH AND IT BURNS IN THE DRAUGHT   108 18
   DEATH-DARKENED STORM AND DEATH   118 11
   WHICH EVEN DEATH CAN ONLY PUT OUT FOR ME   126 5
   AND DEATH I KNOW IS BETTER THAN NOT-TO-BE   126 6
   SINCE DEATH FROM THE MOTHER MOON HAS PARED US DOWN TO   132 8
   SINCE DEATH HAS DELIVERED US UTTERLY STRIPPED AND WHITE   132 15
   I WITH THE NIGHT ON MY LIPS I SIGH WITH THE SILENCE OF +   133 9
   CASTING A SHADOW OF SCORN UPON ME FOR MY SHARE IN DEATH   133 17
   AN' LIE FRIGHTENED TER DEATH UNDER THEE   138 33
   AS THE BODY CORRODES WHEN DEATH INVADES   142 23
   IN FRONT OF THE TERRIBLE RAGE THE DEATH   165 17
   YOU UNLADE YOUR RICHES INTO DEATH   168 8
   ROLLS OUT OF THE HUSK OF DEATH   172 6
   NO MORE AND MONEY STINKS NOT AND DEATH AT LAST   173 23
   SEA YOU SHADOW OF ALL THINGS NOW MOCK US TO DEATH WITH   197 32
   FIELDS OF DEATH   199 14
   NOR DEATH WHICH QUIVERS WITH BIRTH   205 13
   AND DEATH WOULD ACHE STILL I AM SURE   205 18
   WHAT SHOULD I THINK OF DEATH   214 13
   THE SAME WANT LIFE OR DEATH   214 17
   FOR FEAR OF THE LACK IN DEATH   214 22
   NEITHER LIFE NOR DEATH COULD HELP   214 30
   THINK I COULDN'T LOOK TOWARDS DEATH   215 1
   IT IS DEATH STILL SEETHING WHERE   216 8
   WATCH AT THE BANNER OF DEATH AND THE MYSTERY   232 23
   REACH INTO DEATH AFTER ME   236 2
   DEATH DO YOU HEAR IN MY ARMS I AM BRINGING   238 20
   ALL ALL ON THE ALTAR AND DEATH SWOOPING DOWN   239 4
   YOU DEATH IN THE GAME   239 9
   DEATH IN OUR AWED EMBRACES   242 22
   IN US LIFE UNTO DEATH AGREEING   243 7
   AT LAST CAME DEATH SUFFICIENCY OF DEATH   257 23
   NIGHT OR DEATH OR HELL   258 13
   I IN THE SOUR BLACK TOMB TRODDEN TO ABSOLUTE DEATH   259 1

DEATH
IN DEATH   260 13
REDDER THAN DEATH MORE CLAMOROUS   264 13
IT IS A KIND OF DEATH WHICH IS NOT DEATH   266 8
IT WOUNDS ME TO DEATH WITH MY OWN NOT-BEING DEFINITE IN+   266 16
WHEN IT HAS STRUCK HOME TO HER LIKE A DEATH THIS IS HIM   267 8
AGAINST TOO MUCH DEATH   273 6
ALL THE WORLD GLEAMS WITH THE LILIES OF DEATH THE UNCON+   273 12
PIERCING THE FLESH TO BLOSSOM OF DEATH   273 17
LET THE GOD THAT CREATED HIM BE RESPONSIBLE FOR HIS DEA+   346 10
AH DEATH DEATH   346 29
DEATH   366 19
AGAIN FOR OH THE DEAD ARE DISCONSOLATE SINCE EVEN DEATH+   406 8
THINKING DEATH WILL AWAKEN SOMETHING   408 13
INTO SLOW DEATH   456 11
AND DULL DEATH COMES IN A DAY   459 8
I HAVE CONQUERED THE FEAR OF DEATH   460 30
DEATH NO NOT DEATH FOR YOUR LOT   461 8
I DIED AND DEATH IS NEUTER IT SPEAKS NOT IT GIVES   461 13
IS DEATH TO US ALL IN THE MARSHES OF PEACE   462 16
PAUSES THAT ARE AS GOOD AS DEATH EMPTY AND DEAD AS DEATH   510 8
IS TO DIE THE AMAZING DEATH   512 24
IN DEATH THE ATOM TAKES US UP   514 17
OR FOR A GREAT WAVE OF DEATH   522 28
SET UP TO JUDGE BETWEEN LIFE AND DEATH   528 11
NOW THE PROUSTIAN LOT DEAR DARLING DEATH LET ME WRIGGLE   534 3
AND YOUNG WASH-OUTS PRETENDING TO BE IN LOVE WITH DEATH   535 19
THEM NOW FROM ALL THIS TOUCH OF TAINTED DEATH   581 9
BOILING BLACK DEATH   586 28
A RELIEF LIKE DEATH   601 6
FIRST COMES THE DEATH THEN THE PURE ALONENESS WHICH IS +   611 12
DEATH ALONE THROUGH THE LONG PROCESS OF DISINTEGRATION   617 8
MACHINE-DRAWING MORE NULL THAN DEATH   619 13
HOW WELCOME DEATH WOULD BE   628 10
AND THE DEATH OF THE BLACK COUNTRY IS UPON ME   630 6
DEATH OF MY FELLOW MEN   630 8
INTO THE INDUSTRIAL DANCE OF THE LIVING DEATH THE JIGGI+   631 13
AND RISK BLEEDING TO DEATH BUT PERHAPS ESCAPE INTO SOME   632 5
I KNOW THERE IS NO HOPE FOR US DEATH WAITS IT IS USELES+   632 12
WHEN MERCURY AND LOVE AND DEATH   658 16
EVERYTHING HAS BEEN SEEN TO DEATH   660 27
DEATH IS NO ESCAPE AH NO ONLY A DOORWAY TO THE INEVITAB+   662 25
IN DEATH THEY CANNOT ANY MORE ESCAPE   663 2
DARE NOT DIE BECAUSE IN DEATH   663 5
RESURRECTED FROM THE DEATH OF MECHANICAL MOTION AND EMO+   667 33
THE DEATH OF NOTHINGNESS WORN OUT MACHINES KAPUT   670 7
GLEAMING HER HOUR IN LIFE AS SHE NOW GLEAMS IN DEATH   676 14
TO THE ADVENTURE OF DEATH IN EAGERNESS   676 21
TURNING TO DEATH AS I TURN TO BEAUTY   676 22
TO THE BREATH THAT IS OF NEW BEAUTY UNFOLDING IN DEATH   676 23
OH DEATH   676 24
YET OH DEATH OH DEATH   677 1
OH THE GREAT ADVENTURE OF DEATH WHERE THOMAS COOK CANNO+   677 8
AND IN DEATH I BELIEVE I SHALL BE AS THE FLOWERS ARE   677 12
THERE AMONG THE DARK SUN-RAYS OF DEATH   677 14
I CAN FEEL MYSELF UNFOLDING IN THE DARK SUNSHINE OF DEA+   677 15
BUT IN THE GREAT SPACES OF DEATH   677 18
THAT CORPOREAL EXISTENCE IS A KIND OF DEATH   689 15
IS THIS ILLUSION OF THE DEATH OF THE UNDYING   703 15
WHICH IS DEATH TO THE GOOSE   704 24
AND PERHAPS IN UNKNOWN DEATH WE PERHAPS SHALL KNOW   710 3
A MAN MAY BE MY ENEMY TO THE DEATH   715 6
THEY LET DEATH UPON UNSEEN MEN   715 14
HAVE YOU BUILT YOUR SHIP OF DEATH O HAVE YOU   717 1
O BUILD YOUR SHIP OF DEATH FOR YOU WILL NEED IT   717 2
AND DEATH IS ON THE AIR LIKE A SMELL OF ASHES   717 5
BUILD THEN THE SHIP OF DEATH FOR YOU MUST TAKE   717 21
AND DIE THE DEATH THE LONG AND PAINFUL DEATH   718 1
OH BUILD YOUR SHIP OF DEATH YOUR LITTLE ARK   718 9
OF DEATH TO CARRY THE SOUL ON THE LONGEST JOURNEY   718 23
UPON THE SEA OF DEATH WHERE WE STILL SAIL   719 8
OH BUILD YOUR SHIP OF DEATH OH BUILD IT   720 20
TO DIE THE DEATH   720 24
FOR DEATH COMES WHEN HE WILL   720 25
YET DEATH WILL NOT COME   721 1
SO BUILD YOUR SHIP OF DEATH AND LET THE SOUL DRIFT   721 4
BE CAREFUL THEN AND BE GENTLE ABOUT DEATH   721 8
AND HELP THEM TO BUILD THEIR LITTLE SHIP OF DEATH   721 19
FOR THE SOUL HAS A LONG JOURNEY AFTER DEATH   721 20
SING THE SONG OF DEATH O SING IT   723 26
FOR WITHOUT THE SONG OF DEATH THE SONG OF LIFE   723 27
SING THEN THE SONG OF DEATH AND THE LONGEST JOURNEY   724 1
FOR THE COSMOS EVEN IN DEATH IS LIKE A DARK WHORLED SHE+   724 4
SING THE SONG OF DEATH O SING IT   724 11
SLEEP IS THE SHADOW OF DEATH BUT NOT ONLY THAT   724 27
BLIND WITH THE GOSSAMER OF PREVALENT DEATH   737 3
THIS SERRIED ECSTASY OF PREVALENT DEATH   737 5
TOWARDS THE DARKNESS AND THE SHADOW OF DEATH   737 11
CLAMOUR OF DEATH   739 3
KNOWING OUR DEAD ARE FITLY HOUSED IN DEATH   740 23
SURE OF OUR DEAD IN THE PROUD HALLS OF DEATH   740 27
IN DEATH THIS DEATH HIS DEATH MY DEATH   742 3
IT IS THE SAME THIS DEATH   742 4
IS MARRIAGE ONLY WITH DEATH   742 22
IN DEATH THE CONSUMMATION   742 23
BUT SHALL I TOUCH HANDS WITH DEATH IN KILLING THAT OTHER   743 17
CLEANSED AND IN CONCORD FROM THE BED OF DEATH   743 28
IN A CASCADE OF SOULS TO SORROWFUL DEATH   743 31
IN TIMELESSNESS LAID BY IN NOISELESS DEATH   744 3
OF DEATH A CYCLAMEN A CROCUS FLOWER   744 6
THE HOSTS AWAY TO DEATH WHERE HEAP ON HEAP   744 8
I VENTURE FROM THE HALLS OF SHADOWY DEATH   744 11
OF NOISELESS DEATH I KNOW IT WELL   744 14
THE DEATH THEY WILL ATTAIN TO WHERE THEY GO   744 17
FROM EMBASSY IN DEATH I ISSUE FORTH   744 21
OF SWEET RETURNING FROM THE SLEEP OF DEATH   745 5
UNQUENCHABLE OF WIND OR HOSTS OF DEATH   745 11
AMBASSADOR FROM HALLS OF NOISELESS DEATH   745 15

DEATH
SWEEP ON TO BITTER TO CORROSIVE DEATH   745 34
IS DEATH SO PROUD   749 4
HAS DEATH SET ME APART   749 9
DEATH DEATH TAKE ME WITH YOU TO SPARE ME THIS LAST   767 27
A LOVELY SHADOW OF DEATH   772 11
OF DEATH BUT I WAIT AWHILE IN THIS TABERNACLE   772 20
THEY HAVE HOMES IN DEATH   796 15
DEATH   797 4
HUITZILOPOCHTLI GIVES THE BLACK BLADE OF DEATH   809 4
TAKE DEATH BRAVELY   809 6
GUARDS LIFE FROM DEATH AND DEATH FROM LIFE   810 2
ONLY THAT IT IS AND ITS LIFE IS OUR LIFE AND OUR DEATH   811 8
AND THEN ALL OUR DAYS IN A PLUNGE OF DEATH PAY THE DEBT   856 3
OF THE DYING GRASS WITH A THRICE-TOLD TALE OF DEATH   858 27
HE HAD HOPED TO DIE IN THE PULPIT TO CONQUER IN DEATH   859 10
SLOW INFIRM DEATH HAS AT LAST GATHERED UP THE WASTE   859 21
THEY SEEMED TO GROW DARKER AS SHE CAME TO THE EDGE OF D+   869 6
HAVE CLOSED IN LOVE LIKE VERY DEATH FOR STRESS   875 19
UPON THESE AWFUL WATERS OF LIFE AND DEATH   875 27
THROUGH THE CLOSE THICKETS TO THE CLEAR OF DEATH   879 14
UP THE DARK SHAFT TO DEATH AND WHAT IF I   879 23
AH SURE TO VENTURE ALL ALONE IN DEATH   879 26
BUT I WILL CATCH THEE UP AT A STRIDE OF DEATH   879 28
AND WHAT IS DEATH TO US BUT A BEGETTING   880 1
TWIN FLESH AND WHAT IS DEATH FOR ME WHAT IS IT   880 4
INTO THE FERTILE DARKNESS AFTER DEATH   880 8
WHICH YIELDS THE DAY TO DEATH ERE YET THE LIGHT   885 7
AND DRUNK WITH THE DEATH OF THE SOOTHING GREY-WINGED CR+ *918 11
WHICH EVEN DEATH CAN NOT PUT OUT FROM ME   *937 5
SINCE DEATH FROM THE MOTHER MOON HAS PARED CLOSE TO THE+ *938 1
SINCE DEATH HAS DELIVERED NAKED AND THIN AND WHITE   *938 7
OF DEATH COMMINGLES IN GOD'S MIGHTY GLOOM   *938 16
EFFLUENCE FROM SUFFERING FOLK-STUFF WHICH DEATH HAS LAI+ *938 23
IT IS DEATH I FEAR SO MUCH IT IS NOT THE DEAD   *938 27
HAVE YOU BUILT YOUR SHIP OF DEATH OH HAVE YOU   *956 28
BUILD THEN YOUR SHIP OF DEATH FOR YOU WILL NEED IT   *956 29
OH BUILD YOUR SHIP OF DEATH OH BUILD IT IN TIME   *957 25
OH LOVELY LAST LAST LAPSE OF DEATH INTO PURE OBLIVION   *960 3
OH BUILD YOUR SHIP OF DEATH   *960 7
HAVE YOU BUILT YOUR SHIP OF DEATH OH HAVE YOU   *960 10
OH BUILD YOUR SHIP OF DEATH FOR YOU WILL NEED IT   *960 11
OF DEATH THAT WILL CARRY THE SOUL   *960 14
OUT OF OUR LITTLE SHIPS OF DEATH   *960 25
OH BUILD YOUR SHIP OF DEATH BE BUILDING IT NOW   *960 27
THAT WILL SPREAD IN DEATH TO THE BREEZE   *961 2
THEN BUILD YOUR SHIP OF DEATH IN READINESS   *961 6
SING THE SONG OF DEATH OH SING IT   *961 8
FOR WITHOUT THE SONG OF DEATH THE SONG OF LIFE   *961 9
SING THEN THE SONG OF DEATH AND THE LONGEST JOURNEY   *961 11

DEATH-AGONY
A DEATH-AGONY   364 18

DEATH-DARKENED
DEATH-DARKENED STORM AND DEATH   118 11

DEATH EDGED
OF THRILLING RUIN IN THE FLESH OF PUNGENT PASSION OF RA+   273 19

DEATH-FLOOD
AND NOTHING WILL STAY THE DEATH-FLOOD RISING WITHIN US   718 15

DEATHLESS
TO SHARE THE RHYTHM OF THE DEATHLESS WAVE   772 19

DEATHLY
AND I WAS NUMB WITH A BITTER DEATHLY ACHE   98 27
BESIDE THE HIGH ROAD PAST THE DEATHLY DUST   605 24
DRIFTING BENEATH THE DEATHLY ASHY GREY   720 7

DEATH-PRODUCING
OF DEATH-PRODUCING WINE TILL TREASURE   177 3

DEATH-SCREAM
WAR-CRY TRIUMPH ACUTE-DELIGHT DEATH-SCREAM REPTILIAN   364 22

DEATH-VEINED
SNOWDROPS STRAIGHT DEATH-VEINED EXHALATIONS OF WHITE AND   271 6

DEATHWARD
DEATHWARD SET   199 20

DEBACLE
IN A GREAT CHUTE AND RUSH OF DEBACLE DOWNWARDS   287 21
AND SO IN THE GREAT AEONS OF ACCOMPLISHMENT AND DEBACLE   682 19

DEBAUCHED
THE FIFTH GENERATION OF PURITANS WHEN IT ISN'T DEBAUCHED *953 7

DEBAUCHERY
CHASTITY IS INSANE AND DEBAUCHERY IS INSANE   516 4
SUCCESS FAILURE LOVE CHASTITY DEBAUCHERY MONEY OR SOVIE+   839 19

DEBONAIR
IS DEBONAIR   199 24

DEBRIS
HAVE WE GOT TO GET DOWN AND CLEAR AWAY THE DEBRIS   429 11
AMONG ALL THE SMASHED DEBRIS OF MYSELF   514 6
THEIR DEBRIS IS FLOTSAM AND FLUNG ON THE COAST   823 8

DEBT
AND THEN ALL OUR DAYS IN A PLUNGE OF DEATH PAY THE DEBT   856 3

DECAY
  COMES OUT OF YOUR FALLING THROUGH THE STAGES OF DECAY   280   7
  SLOW SLOW FUNGOID CLAMMILY DECAY   784 28

DECAYING
  A NEW INTOXICATION OF LONELINESS AMONG DECAYING FROST-C+ 281   2
  ON THE DECAYING EFFORT OF MANKIND   765 21

DECEIVE
  WORSE LET ME NOT DECEIVE MYSELF   274   8

DECEIVING
  WHEN I KNOW THAT THERE MUST EVER BE DECEIVING   65 23
  DECEIVING   65 24
  THERE IS NO MEANS OF REALLY DECEIVING A CHILD   832 14

DECEMBER
  WHAT ARE YOU DOING IN THE DECEMBER RAIN   301   1

DECEMBER'S
  SICILY DECEMBER'S SICILY IN A MASS OF RAIN   301 12
  DECEMBER'S BARE IRON HOOKS STICKING OUT OF EARTH   304   8

DECENCY
  JUSTICE HUMAN DECENCY IN MATERIAL THINGS   833 24

DECENT
  A DECENT SHORT REGRET FOR THAT WHICH ONCE WAS VERY GOOD   66   4
  AND THE RUIN OF ANY DECENT RELATION   470 21
  I'M PERFECTLY WILLING TO STRIKE A DECENT BARGAIN   483 22
  TO A DECENT MAN   565 14
  IT SEEMS TO ME THAT SOME SORT OF DECENT SOCIALIZATION E+ 829   8
  HOW DECENT IS OUR DESIRE TOWARDS ONE ANOTHER SOCIALLY   829 18
  THE LATENT DESIRE IN ALL DECENT MEN TODAY   837 23
  IS FOR SOME MORE NATURAL MORE DECENT SOCIAL ARRANGEMENT 837 24

DECEPTIVE
  BUT APPEARANCES ARE DECEPTIVE NOWADAYS AREN'T THEY   548 17

DECIDE
  DECIDE WHETHER YOU CAN BECAUSE IT IS A TEST   779 27

DECIDED
  WHO'VE DECIDED THAT BOCCACCIO MUST BURN   633 17

DECIDEDLY
  DECIDEDLY ARROGANTY   358 21

DECIMALS
  ALL THE VOLTE FACE OF DECIMALS   355 25

DECISION
  MAGNIFICENT GHOSTS OF THE DARKNESS CARRY OFF HER DECISI+ 213 26
  O STEP ASIDE WITH DECISION SONS OF MEN WITH DECISION   642 29

DECK
  I ON THE DECK AM STARTLED BY THIS DAWN CONFRONTING   133   1

DECKS
  THE SHAPELINESS THAT DECKS US HERE-BELOW   88 34

DECLAIMING
  WHEN A LOW BULL-MONGREL STARTS DECLAIMING   494   9

DECLARATION
  IT IS A DECLARATION OF SUCH TENSION IN WILL   370 30
  COUNTERSIGN YOUR DECLARATION IT'S SO SIMPLE AND REALLY + 546 17

DECLARE
  I DECLARE I AM A SUPERIOR PERSON YES EXACTLY AND HERE I 546 16

DECLARING
  WITH AGE DECLARING   862   3

DECLINE
  DOWNWARD THEY RACE IN DECLINE   455 28

DECLINES
  THE SUN IN ME DECLINES TO HIS WINTER SOLSTICE   455 17

DECLINING
  FIRE HORIZONTAL DECLINING AND EBBING THE TWILIT EBB OF + 67   6

DECOMPOSING
  WHEN DESTRUCTION SOAKS THROUGH THE MORTIFIED DECOMPOSING 270 21
  BUT ONLY LOSE YOURSELF FURTHER DECOMPOSING   290 11

DECORATION
  PERHAPS IT IS A SORT OF UNCANNY DECORATION A VEIL OF LO+ 369 25

DEED
  DEED AN' I WISH I C'D 'A' STOOD AT TH' ALTAR WI' THEE A+ 83 11
  A WAITING FOR THE PROPER TOUCH NOT FOR ANY WORD OR DEED 612 16
  SELF-SACRIFICE IS PERHAPS THE VILEST DEED A MAN CAN DO 679 23
  DEED AN' I WISH AS I COULD STOOD AT THE ALTAR WI' THEE + *925 15

DEEDS
  MOODS THOUGHTS DESIRES AND DEEDS THAT CHIME   460 11

'DEED
  AN' 'DEED AN' I WISH AS THIS TALE O' THINE WOR NIVER MY+ 83 10
  BUT 'DEED AN' I WISH AS THIS TALE O' THINE WOR NIVER MY+ *925 14

DEEP
  INTO A DEEP POND AN OLD SHEEP-DIP   33 15
  IS HE CALLING THE LONE ONE IS HIS DEEP   40   1
  FALLS ON ME AS I LIE IN DEEP GRASS   49 22
  YET HER DEEP FOOTSTEPS MARK THE SNOW AND GO   85   7

DEEP
  HUMILIATION DEEP TO ME THAT ALL MY BEST   87 23
  FIXED IN THE DARKNESS GRAPPLING FOR THE DEEP SOIL'S CRO+ 92 11
  AND PERHAPS THEY WERE RIGHT FOR THE YOUNG ARE BUSY DEEP+ 92 25
  WITH TOO MUCH TINCTURE OF ME INSTEAD OF THE DARK'S DEEP+ 92 29
  ME OVER AND DRIVE FROM OUT OF MY BODY THE DEEP   98 24
  THE SOLUTION THAT EVER IS MUCH TOO DEEP FOR THE MIND   118 29
  THE GRASS DEEP DOWN WITH THE ROYAL BURDEN OF HER   123   5
  FROM OFF MY MEASURE TO TOUCH YOU DEEP AND FILL   127 18
  TO HER SHE CRUSHES THEM INTO HER BOSOM DEEP   128 28
  THUMB-MOUND INTO THE PALM'S DEEP POUCHES   143 12
  OUT OF THE DEEP   145 15
  LIKE MEN WHO ARE DROWNED BUT FLOAT ERECT IN THE DEEP   146 10
  THAT WRAPS THE NORTH IN STUPOR AND PURPLE TRAVELS THE D+ 149   3
  HER RISE FROM OUT OF THE CHAMBER OF THE DEEP   193   2
  LIKE A DEEP DEEP BURN   208 16
  IT BURNS WITHIN ME LIKE A DEEP OLD BURN   208 21
  LIKE A MAN IN A BOAT ON VERY CLEAR DEEP WATER SPACE FRI+ 222 24
  VERY DEEP AND RAVENING   264   9
  IT IS SO DEEP A MOLOCH RUTHLESS AND STRONG   264 15
  BLOOD-RED DEEP   279   5
  SAY IN THE DEEP SOCKETS OF YOUR IDEALISTIC SKULL   292 27
  DEEP PULSING OF A STRANGE HEART   292 33
  OUT OF THE DEEP SOFT FLEDGE OF SICILIAN WINTER-GREEN   300 22
  DEEP AND REVERBERATING   326 11
  IN THE DEEP STRANGE-SCENTED SHADE OF THE GREAT DARK CAR+ 349   4
  AND THE DEEP SECRET ALL-PENETRATING TAIL CURVED BENEATH 365   3
  OUR DEEP SILENCE   366 32
  DEEP UNEXPLAINED   369   9
  TO BOW BEFORE ROYALTY IN THE LAND OF ELEPHANTS BOW DEEP 391 28
  BOW DEEP   391 29
  BOW DEEP FOR IT'S GOOD AS A DRAUGHT OF COOL WATER TO BOW 391 30
  EARTH'S DEEP HEAVY CENTRE   394 26
  LOBBING WILDLY THROUGH DEEP SNOW LIKE A RABBIT   397   7
  FROM WOUNDS BELOW THE DEEP BLACK WAVE   428 13
  THE UPHOLSTERED DEAD THAT SIT IN DEEP ARM-CHAIRS   440 16
  SWAYING SWAYING O SO DEEP   454   5
  LOVE IS LIKE THE GRASS BUT THE HEART IS DEEP WILD ROCK 477 22
  GO DOWN TO YOUR DEEP OLD HEART WOMAN AND LOSE SIGHT OF 477 24
  OUT OF SIGHT IN THE DEEP DARK LIFTING HEART   478   3
  HAVE YOU NO DEEP OLD HEART OF WILD WOMANHOOD   478 15
  IN THE DEEP DUNG OF CASH AND LORE   489   7
  BETWEEN THE DEVIL AND THE DEEP COLD SEA   490 24
  DEEP BEYOND THE WORLD OF MAN   499   7
  AND OUR DEEP INSTINCT   527 11
  THE DEEP INSTINCTS WHEN LEFT ALONE ARE QUITE MORAL   529   3
  I AM ILL BECAUSE OF WOUNDS TO THE SOUL TO THE DEEP EMOT+ 620 13
  I SUDDENLY SAW DEEP INTO THE EYES OF GOD   650 22
  AND OPEN OUR CONSCIOUSNESS TO THE DEEP MYSTERIOUS LIFE 666 13
  SEE GOD IS BORN HE IS BLUE HE IS DEEP BLUE HE IS FOREVE+ 682 22
  IN THE BLUE DEEP BED OF THE SEA   694 14
  BUT IF YOU WANT TO BREATHE DEEP SUMPTUOUS LIFE   698   3
  A DEEP CALM IN THE HEART   700 12
  THAT WE CAN KNOW THE DEEP AND LOVELY QUIET   717 18
  OH THINK OF THEM AND WITH THE SOUL'S DEEP SIGH   722 12
  DARK DREAMLESS SLEEP IN DEEP OBLIVION   725   4
  TO GOD WHO DWELLS IN DEEP OBLIVION   725 21
  AND THEN THE SOFTNESS OF DEEP SHADOWS FOLDING FOLDING   727   9
  WITH THE DEEP OBLIVION OF EARTH'S LAPSE AND RENEWAL   727 16
  AND LAY THEM DEEP IN LOVE LAY THEM TO SLEEP   736 15
  DEEP IN THE MOISTURES OF PEACE   788 18
  MY FATHER IS DEEP WITHIN THE DEEPS WHENCE HE SENT ME FO+ 799 16
  AND THE NIGHT SHOULD NOT TURN DEEP   799 26
  NAKED I COME FROM OUT OF THE DEEP   801   2
  BLUE IS THE DEEP SKY AND THE DEEP WATER   808 24
  AND DEEP IN CENTRAL PARK I'LL FATTEN   815 15
  DEEP PANTING BREATHS LIKE GREAT BEASTS READY FOR   827   8
  DEEP INSTINCTS   838 22
  THERE IS LOVE AND IT IS A DEEP THING   843 22
  BUT UNDERNEATH ARE THE DEEP ROCKS THE LIVING ROCK THAT + 844   2
  IN THE DEEP CART-RUTS GLEAMED THROUGH THE BLUE OF THE D+ 864 30
  DEEP INTO THE HEART OF THE LIGHT THE CENTRE OF A STAR   865   6
  AND DEEP IN THE GLOWING WINE-FILLED CHALICES   868 19
  AND TREMBLING SOMEWHERE DEEP IN THEIR SUNKIST GLOOM   868 27
  HE DRAWS A DEEP HARD BREATH FROM SPACE TO SPACE   878 23
  LIKE WATER SUCKED FROM DEEP DOWN UNDERGROUND   878 33
  THE CRIMSON SHEAF OF THE WEST THE DEEP FETCHED SIGH   885   6
  A SHADOW WAS DEEP IN THEIR EYES   885 13
  INTO A DEEP POND AN OLD SHEEP-DIP   *891 17
  YOUR DEEP BEWILDERMENT FILTERS THROUGH   *894   3
  FIXED IN THE DARKNESS GRAPPLING FOR THE DEEP SOIL'S LIT+ *926 11
  SEEING I DEEP IN THE FIRE-CORE INVIOLATE   *930 11
  THE GRASS DEEP DOWN WITH HER ROYAL BURDEN AND I   *934 11
  AND DEEP IN THE GOLDEN WINE OF THEIR CHALICES   *941 19
  GOLD GOLD DEEP GOLD HER GLOWING EYES UNFOLD   *941 26
  O LOVE IS A DEEP THING   *951   1
  HOW DEEP I HAVE GONE   *954 26
  HOW DEEP HOW DEEP HOW HAPPY   *954 29
  AND THINK OF THEM AND WITH THE SOUL'S DEEP SIGH   *958 17
  FATHOMLESS DEEP AHEAD FAR FAR FROM THE GREY SHORES   *959   1

DEEPENING
  ONLY THE DEEPENING BLACKNESS DARKENING STILL   719 11
  AND HOW HE ENTERS FOLD AFTER FOLD OF DEEPENING DARKNESS 724   3

DEEPENS
  AND IF AS AUTUMN DEEPENS AND DARKENS   727   6

DEEPER
  OR A DEEPER BRUISE OF KNOWING THAT STILL   100 11
  IN A DEEPER AND DEEPER DARKNESS   281 10
  GOES DEEPER IN THAN WE KNOW   354 24
  DEEPER INTO LIFE   354 25
  SWIM DEEPER DEEPER TILL IT LEAVES NO PEAK EMERGING   428 25
  GO DEEPER THAN LOVE FOR THE SOUL HAS GREATER DEPTHS   477 21
  IF ONLY SHE HAD GONE DOWN TO A DEEPER SELF IN HERSELF   479 22
  OH LOVELY LOVELY WITH THE DARK HAIR PILED UP AS SHE WEN+ 693   8
  DEEPER DOWN THE CHANNEL THEN ROSE SHALLOWER SHALLOWER   693   9

DEEPER
    OR A DARKNESS INVISIBLE ENFOLDED IN THE DEEPER DARK   697 19
    WRITHING DEEPER AND DEEPER IN ALL THE MINUTIAE OF SELF-+   701 23
    FOR GOD IS DEEPER FORGETTING FAR THAN SLEEP   726 15
    DEEPER THAN THE ROOTS OF THE MANGO TREE   805 1
    DEEPER THAN THE ROOTS OF THE MANGO TREE   806 4
    AGAINST ALL YOUR DEEPER INSTINCTS AND YOUR INTUITION   836 19
    BUT THERE ARE DEEPER THINGS THAN LOVE   843 23
    AND DEEPER STILL THE UNKNOWN FIRE UNKNOWN AND HEAVY HEA+   844 3
    AND DEEPER EVEN THAN THE BEDROCK OF PRIDE   844 11
    CONNECTION WITH STILL DEEPER STILL MORE TERRIBLE LIFE-F+   844 15
    AND DEEPER THAN THE BEDROCK OF PRIDE IS THE PRIMORDIAL +   844 20
    ALL THIS IS DEEPER THAN LOVE   844 27
    DEEPER THAN LOVE   844 28
    BUT THERE ARE DEEPER THINGS THAN LOVE   *951 2
    PRIDE PRISTINE AND DEEPER THAN CONSCIOUSNESS THE NATIVE+   *951 18
    AND THE ROCK GOES DOWN DOWN DEEPER FROM COLD INTO HEAT   *951 20
    A GLOOM INVISIBLE ENFOLDED IN THE DEEPER DARK   *956 16
    BUT SHADOWS FOLDED ON DEEPER SHADOWS   *959 18
    AND DEEPER TO A CORE OF SHEER OBLIVION   *959 19
    OR DEEPER LIKE THE FOLDINGS AND INVOLVINGS OF A WOMB   *959 21

DEEPEST
    THEREFORE EVEN IN THE HOUR OF MY DEEPEST PASSIONATE MALE   208 8
    YOU MUST KNOW SEX IN ORDER TO SAVE IT YOUR DEEPEST SELF   465 3
    THE HOLY GHOST IS THE DEEPEST PART OF OUR OWN CONSCIOUS+   621 5
    SO IF WE GO COUNTER TO OUR OWN DEEPEST CONSCIOUSNESS   621 8
    AND THE NEXT DEEPEST SENSUAL EXPERIENCE   653 7
    AND ALONE HE IS WHILE HE LIVES IN HIS DEEPEST SELF   843 26
    AND IN HIS DEEPEST SELF NEVER CEASES TO BE ALONE   *951 6
    DEEPEST AND LONGEST OF SEAS   *957 31

DEEPLY
    MOST OF MY FRIENDS WERE DEEPLY HURT   491 17
    WE DON'T EXIST UNLESS WE ARE DEEPLY AND SENSUALLY IN TO+   613 6
    WHEREAS IF YOU RIDE AWAY AND BECOME DEEPLY CONCERNED IN+   665 12

DEEPS
    TILL HER DARK DEEPS SHOOK WITH CONVULSIVE THRILLS AND T+   125 31
    VENTURED SO LONG AGO IN THE DEEPS OF REFLECTION   161 19
    LURKING AMONG THE DEEPS OF YOUR INDUSTRIAL THICKET   293 8
    THERE IN THE DEEPS   298 4
    DEEPS CALLING CALLING FOR THE COMPLEMENT   366 35
    ITS DEEPS   464 29
    ALL THE WHALES IN THE WIDER DEEPS HOT ARE THEY AS THEY +   694 3
    TO THE FATHOMLESS DEEPS AHEAD FAR FAR FROM THE GREY SHO+   723 24
    I AM THE SON OF THE MORNING STAR AND CHILD OF THE DEEPS   799 14
    MY FATHER IS DEEP WITHIN THE DEEPS WHENCE HE SENT ME FO+   799 16
    THE DEEPS THAT LIFE CANNOT FATHOM   811 6
    TILL HER DARK DEEPS SHOOK WITH CONVULSIVE THRILLS AND T+   *936 30

DEER
    HIS HEAD AS PROUD AS A DEER THAT LOOKS   220 2
    A GUN AND A BUNCHED-UP DEER ITS FOUR LITTLE FEET   220 18
    THE BLAZING TIGER WILL SPRING UPON THE DEER UNDIMMED   268 3
    A DEER   401 17
    ON THE DREAM SLOPES BROWSING LIKE A DEER IN THE DUSK   807 10
    THAT PRICK THEIR EARS LIKE A RABBIT OR BROWSE IN THE DA+   807 14
    I SEE THE GREY DOGS CREEPING OUT WHERE MY DEER ARE BROW+   807 18
    HIS HEAD AS PROUD AS A DEER THAT LOOKS   *944 10
    DEER CRASH THEIR HORNS IN THE MOUNTAINS OF HIS BREAST   *953 28

DEFACED
    AND BEHOLD THEM DEPLORABLY DEAD BY WRONG USAGE DEFACED   859 24

DEFAMATION
    SO THEN THEY CHARGED HIM WITH DEFAMATION   575 6

DEFEAT
    DEFEAT IN SUCH A BATTLE IN THE DARK OF HER EYES   125 29
    TO DEFEAT YOUR BASER STUFF   157 8
    IN LOVE WITH HIS OWN DEFEAT   508 14
    MY SHABBY LITTLE DEFEAT WOULD DO NEITHER ME ANY GOOD   508 23
    DEFEAT IN SUCH A BATTLE IN THE DARK OF HER EYES   *936 28

DEFEATED
    THEN SOMETIMES I FEEL DEFEATED AND THEN AGAIN I KNOW   508 22
    I HAVE BEEN DEFEATED AND DRAGGED DOWN BY PAIN   709 1

DEFECT
    MARRIED MAKE PERFECT BEAUTY NO DEFECT   872 11

DEFECTION
    FOR THE DEFECTION OF THE SELF-CENTRED ONES   616 17

DEFENCELESS
    DEFENCELESS NAKEDNESS   207 24
    AT THEIR DEFENCELESS EYES   310 8
    AND MAN'S DEFENCELESS BARE FACE   310 27

DEFENDING
    DEFENDING THE MEMORY OF LEAVES AND THE HAPPY ROUND NEST   167 10
    DEFENDING THE MEMORY OF BIRDS THAT USED TO NEST   *896 15

DEFERRED
    TO ITS WILL DEFERRED   149 16

DEFIANCE
    POINTING MY EYES IN WRETCHED DEFIANCE WHERE LOVE HIDES +   63 25
    SNORTING DEFIANCE   325 31
    DEFIANCE   383 18
    STRONG WITH EYES OF DEFIANCE EVE WALKS WITH SORROWS   864 23

DEFIANT
    DEFIANT CURLING THE LEAF OF HER TAIL AS IF SHE WERE CUR+   386 13

DEFICIENCY
    FOR HIS OWN DEFICIENCY MOST MAWKISH IN ITS INVERTED SEN+   842 4

DEFILE
    WILL DEFILE IT AND SPOIL ITS BEAUTY   634 17

DEFINITE
    IT WOUNDS ME TO DEATH WITH MY OWN NOT-BEING DEFINITE IN+   266 16

DEFLOWER
    BUT TO DEFLOWER THEE THY TOWER IMPINGES   40 23

DEFLOWERED
    ARE DEFLOWERED BY BEING LOOKED AT BY SO MANY UNCLEAN   634 19

DEFORMED
    IN HOLLOW BLOCKS AND CUBES DEFORMED AND HEAPED   53 25

DEFT
    LIKE A HARPIST THAT STRIKES HIS DEFT   746 25

DEFY
    HOLD MY OWN IN THE MIDST OF THEM DARKLING DEFY   133 19

DEGENERATE
    BUT THAT WHICH IS MEAN AND BASE AND SQUALID AND DEGENER+   679 3
    O SHED THE UNCLEAN MEAN COWARDLY GREEDY EGOISTIC DEGENE+   679 5

DEGENERATED
    BEFORE IT DEGENERATED   481 10

DEGRADING
    FIGHT THEN POOR DUFFERS DEGRADING   456 12
    TO BE HUMBLE BEFORE OTHER MEN IS DEGRADING I AM HUMBLE +   622 1

DEGREE
    WHERE SHAPE ON SPIRIT IN SUPERB DEGREE   872 10

DEGREES
    AS BY DEGREES   54 27
    AND WHEN THIS CASH-CHEMIST UNIVERSITY GRANTS DEGREES LI+   *950 22

DEJECTED
    HE IS ROYALTY PALE AND DEJECTED FRAGMENT UP ALOFT   388 13
    THEN I KNEW THEY WERE DEJECTED HAVING COME TO HEAR THE   390 19

DEJECTEDLY
    DEJECTEDLY A HUNTSMAN GOES BY WITH HIS LOAD   220 17

DELETE
    FORGETTING TILL FATE SHALL DELETE   146 26

DELIBERATE
    A DELIBERATE GENEROSITY NON-ORIENTAL   292 14
    OF DELIBERATE LOVE-MAKING   469 24
    TODAY IF A MAN DOES SOMETHING PRETENTIOUS AND DELIBERATE   634 10

DELIBERATELY
    DELIBERATELY GOING INTO THE BLACKNESS AND SLOWLY DRAWING   351 6
    YET I KNOW HE DOES IT DELIBERATELY AS CAUTIOUSLY AND   447 20
    DELIBERATELY AS WHEN HE SHAVES HIMSELF   447 21
    OF DELIBERATELY TAKING   469 26

DELICACY
    THE SENSITIVE DELICACY OF YOUR SEX IN ITS EBBING TO AND+   464 25

DELICATE
    AT JUST THE SAME OLD DELICATE GAME   150 25
    SO THAT THE DELICATE LOVE-ADEPT   151 26
    NAY LET ME WORK A DELICATE CHAIN OF KISSES   154 4
    OF A ROSE-TREE MOVE TO ROSES AND THORNS AND A DELICATE +   176 9
    OF THESE DARK KNIGHTS SHEDDING THEIR DELICATE SHEEN   221 19
    IF ONLY I AM SENSITIVE SUBTLE OH DELICATE A WINGED GIFT   250 16
    WHEN SHE LIFTED HER HEAD IN DELICATE STARTLED WONDER   255 28
    DELICATE TENDER SPRING   272 5
    ORPHIC DELICATE   280 25
    REACHING OUT AND GRASPING BY AN INSTINCT MORE DELICATE +   285 28
    WE HAVE BURIED SO MUCH OF THE DELICATE MAGIC OF LIFE   298 3
    NAY WHAT A HEART OF DELICATE SUPER-FAITH   304 22
    LIKE DELICATE VERY-YOUNG GREYHOUND BITCHES   311 6
    THE EXQUISITE ASSERTION OF NEW DELICATE LIFE   314 19
    AND ROSY DELICATE HIBISCUS FLOWERS   317 30
    ARE ALL MORE DELICATE THAN SHE   360 5
    DELICATE FRAIL CRESCENT OF THE GENTLE OUTLINE OF WHITE   371 13
    SO DELICATE   371 15
    AND STRANGELY PAWS THE AIR DELICATE   385 25
    DELICATE MOTHER KANGAROO   393 4
    COME DELICATE OVERLOOKED VIRGIN COME BACK TO ME   411 29
    COMPELLED TO SEE THE DELICATE SKILL OF FLICKERING HUMAN   445 26
    SO DELICATE IN HIS LOVE-MAKING   447 18
    SEX ISN'T SIN IT'S A DELICATE FLOW BETWEEN WOMEN AND MEN   464 14
    FOR OUR DAINTY OUR DELICATE ENGLISH EARS   576 3
    FLASHING OF DELICATE WRATH   735 23
    THE DELICATE AFTERNOON   769 22
    AND IT IS MUCH MORE DIFFICULT AND DELICATE TO BE TRUE   775 16
    DELICATE LINE OF NON-INTERFERENCE   780 12
    FLAWED MY DELICATE COURAGE IN ITS STROKE   *927 13

DELICATELY
    AND A MIRACLE AS SHE GLIDED DELICATELY AWAY WITH SUCH   255 31

DELICIOUS
    HAVE DONE HAVE DONE WITH THIS SHUDDERING DELICIOUS BUSI+   273 18
    DELICIOUS ROTTENNESS   280 2
    AND HOW DELICIOUS IT IS TO FEEL SUNSHINE UPON ONE   526 1
    AND HOW DELICIOUS TO OPEN LIKE A MARIGOLD   526 2
    BEAUTY OF COURSE BEAUTY IS STILL A DELICIOUS ESCAPE   532 8
    SHE'S A MARV'LOUS DELICIOUS HIGH-SPIRITED FELLER   583 17

DELICIOUS
   IT MAKES ME REALISE THE DELICIOUS PLEASURE OF THE MOON   610 20
   YOU'VE A DELICIOUS TENDENCY TO EMBONPOINT   835 26

DELICIOUSLY
   KISSED HER DELICIOUSLY   884 6

DELIGHT
   AT MY HEART'S DELIGHT   42 4
   ENCROACHING TOWARDS A CRISIS A MEETING A SPASM AND THRO+   66 22
   THE LAST DARK DELIGHT   114 16
   THIS FIELD OF DELIGHT   124 17
   WITHIN HER SPACIOUS SOUL TO FIND DELIGHT   125 35
   THAT CITADEL OF DELIGHT   142 24
   CONFESSION OF DELIGHT UPON THE WAVE   193 5
   HE HELD IN DELIGHT   202 20
   THE BEES ROLL ROUND IN THE WILD-THYME WITH DELIGHT   223 15
   I SHALL BE MAD WITH DELIGHT BEFORE I HAVE DONE   260 21
   ONLY TO BE WILL BE SUCH DELIGHT WE COVER OUR FACES WHEN+   267 32
   AND HIS BLOOD RIPPLES WITH THAT UNTELLABLE DELIGHT OF O+   306 2
   YET THE STRANGE ALMOST FRIGHTENED SHOUT OF DELIGHT THAT   446 14
   AND REALLY TAKE DELIGHT IN HER   506 16
   DELIGHT   529 13
   DEAR LORD OF DELIGHT   558 4
   I KNOW NO GREATER DELIGHT THAN THE SHEER DELIGHT OF BEI+   610 19
   SERVING WITH DELIGHT AND WITH REVERENCE THOSE MEN WHOSE+   648 20
   AND DANGLE IN A LAST FASTIDIOUS FINE DELIGHT   667 15
   THEN EVERY ATOM OF THE COSMOS TREMBLED WITH DELIGHT   682 8
   SO IN THE CANE-BRAKE HE CLASPED HIS HAND IN DELIGHT   693 16
   AND FLIP THEY GO WITH THE NOSE-DIVE OF SHEER DELIGHT   693 28
   AND THROUGH THE SALT THEY REEL WITH DRUNK DELIGHT   694 10
   OPENING TILL THE ROUND WHITE DOORWAY OF DELIGHT   702 15
   WITH THE WHITE TRIUMPHANCE OF LIGHTNING AND ELECTRIC DE+   707 19
   AND LIFE IS FOR DELIGHT AND FOR BLISS   708 24
   THEN THE BRIGHT DAWNING OF DELIGHT AGAIN   708 26
   BUT STILL I KNOW THAT LIFE IS FOR DELIGHT   709 1
   TIP THE MORNING LIGHT ON EDGE AND SPILL IT WITH DELIGHT   709 6
   AND LIFE IS FOR DELIGHT AND BLISS   709 8
   AND I WOKE WONDERING WHO TOUCHED ME WITH SUCH FEAR AND +   860 10
   BREATHLESS SOUNDS OF SATISFACTION CLAMOUR OF DELIGHT   865 27
   THAT YEAR WHEN THE PEAR WAS OUT MY DELIGHT   886 4
   THIS SUM OF DELIGHT   *935 17

DELIGHTED
   ALONG THY LIMBS DELIGHTED AS A BRIDE'S   69 12
   I HAVE LIVED DELIGHTED IN THE HALLS OF THE PAST   173 21
   I SHALL BLOSSOM LIKE A DARK PANSY AND BE DELIGHTED   677 13
   SHE IS THE GAY DELIGHTED PORPOISE SPORTING WITH LOVE AN+   695 10
   ALONG THY LIMBS DELIGHTED THINE HIS BRIDE'S   *915 24
   THE HOURS PECKED PLEASURE FROM ME AND THE SUN DELIGHTED+   *933 19

DELIGHTEDLY
   OF RIGOUR THEY TASTE DELIGHTEDLY   52 3
   OF RIGOUR THEY TASTE DELIGHTEDLY   *899 16
   OF RIGOUR THEY TASTE DELIGHTEDLY   *902 28

DELIGHTFUL
   WE PRAY FOR THEE MARY DELIGHTFUL THAT GOD MAY BLESS THEE   753 2

DELIGHTING
   OF BROODING AND DELIGHTING IN THE SECRET OF LIFE'S GOIN+   197 17

DELIGHTS
   AND HE CHERISHES VOLUPTUOUS DELIGHTS AND THINKS ABOUT T+   325 6
   TO BE ALONE IS ONE OF LIFE'S GREATEST DELIGHTS THINKING+   610 3
   OF LIFE UNDIMMED DELIGHTS HIM SO EVEN HE IS LIT UP   648 21
   IN WHICH THE SOUL DELIGHTS AND THE SENSES   708 22

DELIRIOUS
   TOWARDS TOUCH THEN THIS DELIRIOUS   471 16

DELIRIUM
   AND INCREASING DELIRIUM   343 26
   AND THAT FEAR CAN BECOME A DELIRIUM   487 2
   OH FOR A DELIRIUM OF LOVE OR OF STRIFE   856 24

DELIVER
   O GOD DELIVER ME   469 28
   AND DELIVER OUR LIPS OF THEIR PRAISE AND THEIR BITTERNE+   753 18

DELIVERANCE
   THE BARK OF THEIR DELIVERANCE FROM THE DILEMMA   722 14

DELIVERED
   SINCE DEATH HAS DELIVERED US UTTERLY STRIPPED AND WHITE   132 15
   IS DELIVERED OUT AND PAYS NO HEED THOUGH WE MOAN   132 18
   DELIVERED HELPLESS AND AMAZED   262 19
   SINCE DEATH HAS DELIVERED NAKED AND THIN AND WHITE   *938 7
   IS DELIVERED FROM US HERSELF BORN AGAIN AMID THE MOAN   *938 10

DELIVERING
   WITHOUT EVER SLEEP DELIVERING US   116 18
   WITHOUT DELIVERING ONCE MY EYE   *930 17

DELIVERY
   WAFT NEARER TO THEM THE BARK OF DELIVERY   *958 18

DELUGE
   THAT THE DELUGE WILL NEVER BE TURNED ON THEM ONLY AFTER   531 9
   WHY SHOULD THE DELUGE WAIT WHILE THESE YOUNG GENTRY GO   531 13
   DELUGE   531 20

DEMAND
   HIM WITH A NEW DEMAND ON HIS UNDERSTANDING   431 5
   DEMAND ON HIS INTELLIGENCE   431 9
   MEN SHOULD DEMAND TO WORK FOR THEMSELVES OF THEMSELVES   450 8
   THEY DEMAND AS THEY STAND IN MENACE OVER AGAINST US   740 8
   THAT HE DARES DEMAND   749 5

DEMANDS
   WE YIELD THE ENEMY HIS LAST DEMANDS   736 26
   MAKES NO DEMANDS   754 12
   AND SING IN THIS SPACE THAT THE BUILDER NOW DEMANDS   *896 16

DEMEANED
   IF HE FEELS DEMEANED   563 26

DEMETER'S
   GIVING OFF DARKNESS BLUE DARKNESS AS DEMETER'S PALE LAM+   697 10
   GIVING OFF DARKNESS BLUE DARKNESS UPON DEMETER'S YELLOW+   *956 8

DEMI-URGE
   THE REST THE UNDISCOVERABLE IS THE DEMI-URGE   691 26

DEMOCRACY
   THE WORLD IS MOVING MOVING STILL TOWARDS FURTHER DEMOCR+   611 6
   BUT NOT A DEMOCRACY OF IDEA OR IDEAL NOR OF PROPERTY NO+   611 7
   BUT A DEMOCRACY OF MEN A DEMOCRACY OF TOUCH   611 9
   AND SO I SING A DEMOCRACY   627 5
   A DEMOCRACY A DEMOCRACY   627 6
   AND DEMOCRACY IS GROUND INTO DUST   648 11
   DEMOCRACY IS SERVICE BUT NOT THE SERVICE OF DEMOS   650 1
   DEMOCRACY IS DEMOS SERVING LIFE   650 2

DEMOCRAT
   I AM A DEMOCRAT IN SO FAR AS I LOVE THE FREE SUN IN MEN   526 7
   OH I AM A DEMOCRAT   587 24

DEMOCRATIC
   BUT WE AS WE START AWAKE CLUTCH AT OUR VISTAS DEMOCRATIC   286 34
   ESPECIALLY DEMOCRATIC LIVE-BY-LOVE HUMANITY   395 19
   DEMOCRATIC LITTLE BULL-BITCH DIRT-EATING LITTLE SWINE   399 26

DEMON
   AND THAT MOTHER-LOVE LIKE A DEMON DREW YOU FROM ME   206 2
   YOUR NASCENT DEMON PEOPLE   293 7
   DEMON TOO   300 15
   I AM VERY WELL OLD DEMON   404 6
   WELL YOU'RE A DARK OLD DEMON   404 12
   OLD DEMON YOU AND I   404 19
   THAT DARK OLD DEMON AND I   405 19
   LET IT BE DEMON JUSTICE   562 9
   TO DEMON JUSTICE   563 10
   OH BE A DEMON   563 17
   STILL BE A DEMON   563 21
   AND YOUR DEMON STARTS LASHING OUT   564 3
   LET YOUR DEMON BE HEARD   564 12
   YOUR DEMON RUMP TWINKLING   564 17
   THEN FOLLOW YOUR DEMON   564 23

DEMONIACAL
   WITH THAT FINE DEMONIACAL SPARK   241 15
   NOT EVEN THE HOME OF DEMONIACAL HELL   711 14

DEMONIC
   SUDDEN DEMONIC DAUNTLESSNESS FULL ABREAST   371 10

DEMONISH
   THE STRANGE UNACCUSTOMED GESTE OF YOUR DEMONISH NEW WOR+   292 15
   DEMONISH LURKING AMONG THE UNDERGROWTH   293 2

DEMONS
   COME TALL OLD DEMONS SMILING   404 3
   LIFE IS FOR THE DAIMONS AND THE DEMONS   709 27
   NO NOT THE ITHYPHALLIC DEMONS   710 24

DEMOS
   OH WEIRD DEMOS WHERE EVERY TWIG IS THE ARCH TWIG   300 7
   DEMOS DEMOS DEMOS   300 14
   DEMOCRACY IS SERVICE BUT NOT THE SERVICE OF DEMOS   650 1
   DEMOCRACY IS DEMOS SERVING LIFE   650 2
   AND DEMOS SERVES LIFE AS IT GLEAMS ON THE FACE OF THE F+   650 3

DEMURE
   LOVE-FIRE IS DRIFTING THOUGH THE BUGLE IS PRIM AND DEMU+   854 16

DEN
   BUT TO GET OUT FROM THIS DIM DREADFUL DEN   174 4
   ENVELOP OUR DEN   748 6

DENIAL
   CAN DENIAL DENY THEM AGAIN   461 20
   AND THE ROBOT IS DENIAL OF THE SAME   649 17
   EVEN THE DENIAL THAT THERE IS ANY GLEAM   649 18
   KNOW THYSELF IN DENIAL OF ALL THESE THINGS   714 16

DENIED
   OUR EXISTENCE WE WAIT AND ARE STILL DENIED   166 10
   AS ROME DENIED ETRURIA   298 17
   DENIED A SIGNATURE WE ENGLISH ARE A SOLID PEOPLE AFTER +   546 19
   AND JESUS HIMSELF COULD NOT HAVE DENIED THAT AT THAT MO+   674 22

DENIES
   WAS SET TO SONG AND NEVER YOUR SONG DENIES   156 23
   I GIVE WHOEVER DENIES   202 12

DENSE
   A SODOM SMOULDERING IN THE DENSE SOILED AIR   72 14
   AS IT SPINS TO SLEEP ON ITS MOTION DRUGGED DENSE IN THE   149 7
   IN THE DENSE FOLIAGE OF THE INNER GARDEN   278 12
   STRANGE STORMING UP FROM THE DENSE UNDER-EARTH   304 18
   MALE TORTOISE CLEAVING BEHIND THE HOVEL-WALL OF THAT DE+   364 28
   THE MORE THAN HUMAN DENSE INSISTENCE OF WILL   371 29
   MOLTEN YET DENSE AND PERMANENT   477 23
   AND DENSE WITH HAPPY BLOOD DARK RAINBOW BLISS IN THE SEA   695 12
   OF THE ARMS PLUTONIC AND PIERCED WITH THE PASSION OF DE+   697 20
   AS OVER SOME DENSE MARSH THE FUMES   703 21

DENSELY
  DENSELY THICKEN IN THE CITIES   703 23
  DENSELY TO ME   *900 17
  DENSELY TO ME   *903 29

DENSER
  SO MUCH DENSER THAN COLD-BLOODED FROGS   393 3

DENTY
  THEY WERE SO SMALL AND DENTY   846 4

DENUDING
  ARE SEA-BED STILL THROUGH THEIR HOUR OF BARE DENUDING   509 19

DENY
  BUT THE HOSTS OF MEN WITH ONE VOICE DENY   40 19
  THERE IS ONLY ONE EVIL TO DENY LIFE   298 16
  I CAN NO MORE DENY THE BAT-WINGS OF MY FATHOM-FLICKERIN+   323 2
  CAN DENIAL DENY THEM AGAIN   461 20
  AND THE AIR IS ALIVE AND CAN DENY US AS A WOMAN CAN   625 15
  THE ROBOTS THOSE WHO DENY THE GLEAM   649 26
  IF IT IS PERFECTLY SINCERE TO DENY YOUR OWN MAKE-UP   659 11
  THE HATE OF TERROR OR DENY THE FECUND SOUL HER EMBRACES *926 25

DENYING
  WOUNDING THEMSELVES AGAINST HER DENYING HER FECUND   91 28
  BUT KNOW THYSELF DENYING THAT THOU ARE MORTAL   -714 6
  WOUNDING THEMSELVES AGAINST HER DENYING HER GREAT EMBRA+ *926 21

DEPART
  I FOLLOW HER DOWN THE NIGHT BEGGING HER NOT TO DEPART   67 12
  SINCE YOU DID DEPART   108 5
  ENDLESSLY IN ONE MOTION DEPART   163 7
  BID HER DEPART   179 9
  AND DEPART PEACEFUL PACIFIED AND THANKLESS   350 11
  CONSIDER MISS WILKS OR DEPART FORTHWITH   584 2
  NOW SOME MEN MUST GET UP AND DEPART   715 19
  MEN MUST DEPART FROM IT OR ALL IS LOST   716 15
  WHEN IN THE MORNING I ROSE TO DEPART MY LOVE CAME TO SA+ 749 17
  IN MILLIONS UNABLE TO DEPART   *957 29

DEPARTED
  THE ANGEL OF JUDGMENT HAS DEPARTED AGAIN TO THE NEARNESS   94 22
  LIKE LUGGAGE OF SOME DEPARTED TRAVELLER   134 9
  EVEN THE POLE ITSELF HAS DEPARTED NOW FROM THE POLE STAR 616 28
  YOU WILL HAVE DEPARTED FOREVER FROM YOUR MISTAKE   809 14
  AND EVER ERE I COME YOU HAVE DEPARTED   880 13
  THE CHERUBIM OF JUDGMENT HAVE DEPARTED FROM ME   *897 10

DEPARTING
  EACH SOUL DEPARTING WITH ITS OWN ISOLATION   281 17
  BEYOND US NOW BEYOND DEPARTING WITH THAT PURITY   676 16
  AND DEPARTING INVIOLATE NOTHING CAN LAY HANDS ON HER   676 15
  FITTING AND READY FOR THE DEPARTING SOUL   718 26
  LIKE DEPARTING MARINERS LOVINGLY   721 26
  DEPARTING DEPARTING DEPARTING   766 12
  DEPARTING   766 16
  AND KNOWS DEPARTING IN SILENCE   769 27
  DAINTY AND READY FOR THE DEPARTING SOUL   *958 22

DEPARTS
  DEPARTS AND THE WORLD IS TAKEN BY SURPRISE   340 20
  AND LIFE DEPARTS LAUNCH OUT THE FRAGILE SOUL   719 2
  DEPARTS WITHOUT COUNTING THE COST   823 10

DEPARTURE
  A MONOTONOUS WEIRD OF DEPARTURE AWAY FROM ME   47 13
  BECAUSE NO ONE GRIEVES OVER HER DEPARTURE   63 21
  WHO CANNOT BEAR TO THINK BACK TO THE DEPARTURE   169 11
  THE SUN'S DEPARTURE   347 18
  IF YOU INSIST ON IT I INSIST ON DEPARTURE   478 14

DEPEND
  HOW QUAVERINGLY I DEPEND ON YOU TO KEEP ME ALIVE   246 2
  HOW I DEPEND ON YOU UTTERLY   247 13

DEPENDENCE
  AND KNOW OUR DEPENDENCE ON THE CREATIVE BEYOND   621 7

DEPENDS
  IT ALL DEPENDS WHETHER I FOUND THEM WORTH FIGHTING FOR   497 18
  AND THE DESTINY OF MANKIND DEPENDS AT LAST   831 17

DEPLORABLY
  AND BEHOLD THEM DEPLORABLY DEAD BY WRONG USAGE DEFACED   859 24

DEPLORE
  AND I CAN'T DEPLORE HIM   39 16

DEPLOYED
  DEPLOYED AROUND ME AND I SEE   115 23

DEPOSITED
  HIS MOTHER DEPOSITED HIM ON THE SOIL AS IF HE WERE NO M+ 356 24

DEPOSITS
  AND THE SLIM NAKED MAN SLIPS DOWN AND THE BEAST DEPOSITS 387 14

DEPRAVED
  THEY DON'T MIND BEING DEPRAVED IMMORAL OR ANYTHING OF T+ 829 12
  THE BATS DEPRAVED ARE DROPPING GAILY FROM OFF THE TREE   *918 13

DEPRECATINGLY
  DEPRECATINGLY   434 7

DEPRECATION
  GENTEEL DEPRECATION   830 25

DEPRESSED
  MODERN PEOPLE ARE DEPRESSED   445 35

DEPRESSION
  AND BOREDOM ENNUI DEPRESSION   627 17
  AND SUNK INTO DEPRESSION THAT ALMOST BLOTS ME OUT   629 21

DEPRIVES
  SHADOWS YET IT DEPRIVES   170 8

DEPTH
  IN A' THIS DEPTH O' SNOW   79 14
  DARKNESS AND DEPTH OF SLEEP   254 1
  TO THE GREAT DEPTH OF ITS REVERSED ZENITH   322 24
  AND SINKING STILL IN DEPTH AFTER DEPTH OF DISINTEGRATIV+ 699 25
  NEITHER CAN IT REACH THE DEPTH   701 28
  FOR THE DEPTH IS BOTTOMLESS   701 29
  IN A' THIS DEPTH O' SNOW   *921 10

DEPTHS
  AND HE KNOWS FROM THE DEPTHS HE QUITE   39 23
  IN THE OPEN DEPTHS OF EACH FLOWER DARK RESTLESS DROPS   76 2
  THERE ARE DEPTHS BELOW DEPTHS MY DARLING WHERE LOVE DOE+   93 2
  HAS SOME HAND BALANCED MORE LEAVES IN THE DEPTHS OF THE   142 5
  TO THE SOURCES OF MYSTERY IN THE DEPTHS   261 14
  HELL ON EARTH AND DIS WITHIN THE DEPTHS   309 14
  DEPTHS OF MY SOUL   366 3
  DEPTHS BELOW   464 27
  GO DEEPER THAN LOVE FOR THE SOUL HAS GREATER DEPTHS   477 21
  DEPTHS   478 2
  TO THE DEPTHS TO THE DEPTHS   551 7
  DEPTHS OF A MAN   624 23
  ON THE DEPTHS OF THE SEVEN SEAS   694 9
  IN THE DARK-BLUE DEPTHS UNDER LAYERS AND LAYERS OF   697 26
  AND DRAWS AWAY AWAY TOWARDS DARK DEPTHS   723 21
  AT THE DEPTHS OF THE PEACE AND THE FLIGHT   788 17
  OUT OF THE DEPTHS OF THE SKY I CAME LIKE AN EAGLE   801 6
  FAR OFF UPON THE MISTY WATERS OF THE DEPTHS OF SPACE   841 3
  IN THE OPEN DEPTHS OF EACH FLOWER DARK RESTLESS DROPS   *897 29
  IN THE OPEN DEPTHS OF EACH FLOWER DARK RESTLESS DROPS   *901 6
  TO THE DEPTHS   *955 6
  DOWN THE BLUE DEPTHS OF MOUNTAIN GENTIAN FLOWERS   *955 19
  AND DRAWS AWAY AWAY AWAY TOWARDS THE DARK DEPTHS   *958 33

DERANGED
  ON TO THEIR POOR DERANGED BODIES   500 20

DERISION
  AWAY WITH A PAEAN OF DERISION   334 10

DERISIVE
  AND IMPROPER DERISIVE EARS   345 30

DERIVATIVE
  FROM WHICH I FEEL I AM A DERIVATIVE   622 12

DERIVED
  DERIVED FROM SHREWD CASH-CHEMISTRY   488 13

DERVISH
  LIKE THE DANCE OF A DERVISH   121 3

DESCEND
  AND THOSE THAT DO DESCEND HAVE GOT TO SUFFER A SENSE-CH+ 667 24

DESCENDING
  THE DAY IS ENDING THE NIGHT DESCENDING   456 1
  I SEE DESCENDING FROM THE SHIPS AT DAWN   688 12

DESCENDS
  THE SNOW DESCENDS AS IF THE SLOW SKY SHOOK   76 14
  THE SNOW DESCENDS AS IF THE DULL SKY SHOOK   *898 8
  THE SNOW DESCENDS AS IF THE DULL SKY SHOOK   *901 17

DESCENT
  TO CROWN THE TRIUMPH OF THIS NEW DESCENT   218 28
  AND PROUD OF MY DESCENT   626 10

DESCRIBE
  I REFUSE TO DESCRIBE THE GODS BECAUSE THEY HAVE NO FORM+ 651 8
  NOR VOICE DESCRIBE HIM   692 9
  NOR THE VOICE DESCRIBE HIM   692 20

DESCRIBED
  WHICH DESCRIBED IN A STORY   551 19

DESCRIPTION
  A DESCRIPTION OF A DOG OR IF THEY CAN'T   74 28
  AND ALL DESCRIPTION IS A BLASPHEMY   726 16

DESCRY
  A GRAIN OF THIS SAME FIRE WE CAN DESCRY   89 20
  ON OUR MYSTERY NOUGHT CAN DESCRY US   114 7

DESERT
  AND LAID THE DESERT HORRIFIC OF SILENCE AND SNOW ON THE+ 75 16
  THE SANDY DESERT BENEATH HER THE DREARY PLATOON   153 4
  ON THE SAGE-ASH DESERT   373 2
  AND OUT TO THE DIM OF THE DESERT LIKE A DREAM NEVER REAL 402 22
  OVER THE HEART OF THE WEST THE TAOS DESERT   403 1
  DAY HAS GONE TO DUST ON THE SAGE-GREY DESERT   403 21
  TO DUST TO ASH ON THE TWILIT FLOOR OF THE DESERT   403 23
  ROUND A WHITE HEARTH OF DESERT   407 2
  AND ROUND AND ROUND THE DESERT   407 4
  AND RIDE ON HORSEBACK ASLEEP FOREVER THROUGH THE DESERT 408 11

DESERT
     ROUND THE ASH-WHITE HEARTH OF THE DESERT   408 20
     DOWN ON MY HEARTH-RUG OF DESERT SAGE OF THE MESA   408 27
     AND I I SIT ON THIS HIGH AMERICAN DESERT   410 27
     GOES BEHIND ITS MOTHER ACROSS THE DESERT   466 10
     THEY NIBBLE THE FACE OF THE EARTH TO A DESERT   606 20
     IN THE FLOCCULENT ASH OF THE SAGE-GREY DESERT   780 24
     THE SUN-BLAZE OF THE DESERT   781 4
     ON THE RIM OF THE DESERT   816 17
     WITH GREY ON THE FLOOR OF THE DESERT   816 22

DESERTER
     DESERTER   767 23

DESERTS
     GOING OUT IN SPRING TO THE ROUND OF HIS TAME DESERTS   126 27

DESERVE
     FINE TORTURE YOU DID DESERVE   111 27
     AS I DESERVE   234 24
     BRIGHT TORTURE THOU DIDST DESERVE   *927 15
     FINE TORTURE YOU DID DESERVE   *928 15

DESIRABLE
     THAT YOU'RE NOT DESIRABLE   485 16

DESIRABLY
     HORIZONTAL AND MEANINGLESS DESIRABLY DULL   827 18

DESIRE
     THE GLOW OF THY FULL DESIRE   40 7
     WITH DREAD AND FILLS MY HEART WITH THE TEARS OF DESIRE   48 12
     SPURTING TO SOOTHE THE WOMB'S UNSLAKED DESIRE   89 21
     TO THE OTHER LOVE TO RELINQUISH HIS DESIRE   89 33
     SO NIGHT'S FLOOD-WINDS HAVE LIFTED MY LAST DESIRE FROM +   97 9
     SOFT GLIMMERS OF DESIRE ESCAPED FROM PRISON   113 4
     OF MY STEEL LOVELY WHITE FLINT OF DESIRE   118 5
     YOU ARE LOVELIER THAN LIFE ITSELF TILL DESIRE   151 6
     HE NEVER LOVED YOU NEVER WITH DESIRE   158 5
     DESIRE COMES UP AND CONTENTMENT   199 23
     TILL ALL YOUR BEING SMOKES WITH FINE DESIRE   219 4
     OF DESIRE   228 24
     FROM THE WOMB OF YOUR PRECIOUS DESIRE   235 12
     WHAT IS THE HOT PLUMB WEIGHT OF YOUR DESIRE ON ME   241 3
     YOU HAVE A HOT UNTHINKABLE DESIRE OF ME BUNNY   241 4
     IT MUST BE YOU WHO DESIRE   242 1
     COME YOU SHALL HAVE YOUR DESIRE   242 5
     ON THE BODY OF FIERCE DESIRE   242 11
     BEING MAD WITH VORACIOUS DESIRE   264 36
     LET THEM PRAISE DESIRE WHO WILL   265 12
     NO LOINS OF DESIRE   335 20
     DOOMED IN THE LONG CRUCIFIXION OF DESIRE TO SEEK HIS CO+   361 3
     AND HIS HEAD GONE HEAVY WITH THE KNOWLEDGE OF DESIRE   378 14
     HENCE HIS PONDEROUS HEAD BROODING OVER DESIRE AND DOWNF+   378 22
     THAT IS HALF INSATIABLE DESIRE AND HALF UNQUENCHABLE   378 25
     EVERLASTING LAMENT IN EVERLASTING DESIRE   378 30
     DESIRE   383 15
     LIBIDINOUS DESIRE RUNS BACK AND FORTH ASSERTING ITSELF +   386 15
     HAS SUCCESSFULLY KILLED ALL DESIRE IN US WHATSOEVER   439 33
     I HAVE NO DESIRE ANY MORE   454 12
     GROW FULL OF DESIRE   465 20
     YOU WILL FIND YOU HAVE A GREAT DESIRE TO DRINK LIFE DIR+   481 3
     OF DESIRE IS DISTORTED AND TWISTED AWRY   485 3
     THAT NO WOMAN WILL EVER DESIRE YOU AS YOU ARE   485 17
     HOW DO YOU EXPECT THEM EVER TO DESIRE YOU   485 21
     DESIRE MAY BE DEAD   504 12
     FOR DESIRE HAS DIED IN ME SILENCE HAS GROWN   507 17
     DESIRE HAS FAILED DESIRE HAS FAILED   507 20
     AND DESIRE HAS FAILED   508 3
     WHEN LOVE IS GONE AND DESIRE IS DEAD AND TRAGEDY HAS LE+   509 1
     AND DESIRE IS DEAD   510 18
     I HAVE FELT THE PULL OF DESIRE   602 11
     SO NOW I HAVE NO DESIRE ANY MORE   602 23
     FLOW THE HEART'S RIVERS OF FULNESS DESIRE AND DISTRESS   607 8
     ACCORDING TO THE SOUL'S DESIRE   652 17
     EITHER IN ANGER OR TENDERNESS OR DESIRE OR SADNESS OR W+   672 4
     AND ROLL WITH MASSIVE STRONG DESIRE LIKE GODS   694 12
     LIKE SAYING SNOW IS BLACK OR DESIRE IS EVIL   709 34
     AND HARK TO THE WORDS OF THEIR HEART'S DESIRE   789 3
     WITH NOTHING BUT DESIRE BETWEEN THEM   819 10
     DARK BLUE THE WHOLE DESIRE LEAPS   819 24
     LIES LATENT IN THE SOULS OF THE YOUNG A LATENT DESIRE   829 10
     HOW DECENT IS OUR DESIRE TOWARDS ONE ANOTHER SOCIALLY   829 18
     EVEN IN THE MOST IMMORAL SETS THERE IS STILL THIS DESIR+   829 20
     OUT OF SHEER DESIRE TO BE SPLENDID AND MORE SPLENDID   831 4
     THE LATENT DESIRE IN ALL DECENT MEN TODAY   837 23
     I HAVE NO DESIRE IN THE LEAST TO BE SORROWED OVER OR CO+   840 22
     WITH SHARP DESIRE I AM NOT EAGER FOR SHARP DESIRE ANY M+   840 24
     BUT WITHOUT DESIRE WITHOUT JOY WITHOUT RELEASE   843 16
     CRISPED WITH INTENSE DESIRE   861 22
     AND MY SOUL'S DESIRE AND MADE YOU REAL   871 3
     RICHER THAN LIFE ITSELF TILL DESIRE   873 16
     BUT DO NOT SEEK TO TAKE ME BY DESIRE   873 26
     OF LOVE NOT TO DESIRE   874 18
     HER LOOKS WITH DESIRE   885 23
     QUIVERING AWAKE WITH ONE IMPULSE OF DESIRE   *893 21

DESIRED
     NOW I AM COME AGAIN TO YOU WHO HAVE SO DESIRED   85 17

DESIRES
     AND TIED IN A KNOT INSIDE DEAD-LOCKED BETWEEN TWO DESIR+   379 12
     MOODS THOUGHTS DESIRES AND DEEDS THAT CHIME   460 11
     OF DESIRES IN THE LOINS' DARK TWISTS   461 4
     GOOD HEALTHY NATURAL FEELINGS INSTINCTS PASSIONS OR DES+   678 3
     AND EMOTIONS AND DESIRES AND STRENGTH GLORY OR HONOUR   691 11

DESIROUS
     AND ALGEBRA IN THE EYES OF DESIROUS MEN   118 23
     WHY DO I WANDER AIMLESS AMONG THEM DESIROUS FOOL   180 23
     THERE IS A NEW ECSTASY IN HIS ROAR OF DESIROUS LOVE   325 3
     AND DESIROUS BELLY GULPING   336 11
     HE SO FINISHED AND IMMUNE NOW BROKEN INTO DESIROUS   361 6
     AND DO I NOT SEEK TO MATE MY GROWN DESIROUS SOUL   *926 22

DESKS
     OF THE BOOKS THAT LIE OUT ON THE DESKS A FULL THREESCORE   74 13
     OF THE BOOKS THAT LIE OUT ON THE DESKS A FULL THREE SCO+   *895 21
     OF THE BOOKS THAT LIE OUT ON THE DESKS A FULL THREE SCO+   *904 10

DESOLATE
     AT RANDOM DESOLATE TWIGS   51 2
     DESOLATE I AM AS A CHURCH WHOSE LIGHTS ARE PUT OUT   94 23
     THEY ARE LORDS OF THE DESOLATE WASTES OF SADNESS THEIR +   *891 4
     DESOLATE AND DESPOILED AM I FOR THEIR FLAMING STORM   *897 11

DESOLATIVE
     NOR FLYING NORTH DESOLATIVE ICEWARDS   436 6

DESPAIR
     WHO STAND ALONE IN DESPAIR LIKE A GUTTERING LIGHT   73 13
     FOR ALL YOUR LIFE OF ASKING AND DESPAIR   100 27
     OVER DESPAIR   199 28
     SHE IS BREWING HOPE FROM DESPAIR   203 8
     STILL IN HIS NOSTRILS THE FROZEN BREATH OF DESPAIR   226 5
     AND BREATHE DESPAIR THAT TURNS MY LUNGS TO STONE   226 11
     IF NOT THEN DESPAIR   237 12
     IF DESPAIR IS OUR PORTION   237 13
     THEN LET US DESPAIR   237 14
     NIPPED UPON THE FROZEN FLOODS OF PHILOSOPHIC DESPAIR   542 21
     OH EVEN TO KNOW THE LAST WILD WINCING OF DESPAIR   585 6
     WILL SEND UP THE WILD CRY OF DESPAIR   624 13
     THE TRILLING LARK IN A WILD DESPAIR WILL TRILL DOWN ARR+   624 14
     WHEN I AM IN A GREAT CITY I KNOW THAT I DESPAIR   632 11
     OF FULL DESPAIR I LIFT MY TENDER FLAME   745 13
     THEN THEY'D BE ABLE TO LOVE DESPAIR CAN'T LOVE IT CAN O+   838 13
     NO MORE AND WE LAY AT HOME UNUTTERABLE DESPAIR IN HIS F+   859 16
     AND LEAVE ME TORTURE AND WRATH AND A DROSSED DESPAIR   874 9
     I STIFLE A CRY OF DESPAIR   883 18
     SEND UP THE LAST WILD CRY OF DESPAIR   *954 11

DESPAIRING
     STIFF AND DESPAIRING   862 1

DESPEDIDA
     FAREWELL FAREWELL DESPEDIDA   797 17

DESPERATENESS
     AN ULTIMATE DESPERATENESS UN-AFRICAN   292 13

DESPERATION
     JUST IN DESPERATION   558 26

DESPICABLE
     THAT IS WHY BUSINESS SEEMS TO ME DESPICABLE   607 21

DESPISE
     I BOOZE AND FORNICATE AND USE FOUL LANGUAGE AND DESPISE   432 18
     I DESPISE THAT SELF-IMPORTANT GAME   673 9

DESPISED
     I DESPISED MYSELF AND THE VOICES OF MY ACCURSED HUMAN   351 20
     OF GODHEAD IN MAN DESPISED CARELESSLY THROWN OVER   859 22

DESPISES
     ANYHOW SHE DESPISES   565 1

DESPOILED
     AS I CAME HOME IN THE DUSK DESPOILED BY SCHOOL A MERE B+   864 27
     DESOLATE AND DESPOILED AM I FOR THEIR FLAMING STORM   *897 11

DESTINIES
     TOUCH ME OH TOUCH ME GIVE ME DESTINIES   738 23

DESTINY
     FROM OUR DESTINY   162 16
     YOUR HEART OF DESTINY   178 33
     O DESTINY DESTINY   430 1
     O DESTINY   430 3
     ONLY O DESTINY   430 13
     NOT EVEN THE MOST MASSIVE WAVE OF DESTINY   514 5
     AND HAD A BRAVE DESTINY EVEN WHEN SHE WENT WRONG   535 16
     MAYBE A SENSE OF DESTINY   560 5
     IF YOU ARE A MAN AND BELIEVE IN THE DESTINY OF MANKIND   666 10
     THE DESTINY OF AMERICA IS IN THEIR HANDS   774 23
     AND THE DESTINY OF MANKIND DEPENDS AT LAST   831 17

DESTROY
     DID DESTROY   121 4
     OF PASSION PARCH IT UP DESTROY REMOVE   153 26
     TO DESTROY THE CHILL LENT LILIES   271 14
     DESTROY SHE MOANED THESE HORRORS IN PAINT   577 8
     NATURALLY WE DESTROY THE MOST ESSENTIAL SELF IN US   621 9
     ORDER YOU DESTROY THE WHOLE VILE PACK   633 29
     AND THEY WILL DESTROY ALL UNLESS THEY ARE MADE TO SUBMIT   637 9
     THEY'LL MERELY DESTROY ALL PROPERTY AND A GREAT MANY PE+   665 1
     DESTROY IT SHED ITS UNCLEAN BLOOD KILL IT PUT IT OUT OF+   679 4
     THAT STRIP US AND DESTROY US AND BREAK US DOWN   709 17
     DESTROY AT LAST THE HEAVY BOOKS OF STONE   737 25
     SCANDALS MAY DESTROY EVERY MAN'S FAITH IN MAN   775 6
     BUT BE CAREFUL HOW YOU DESTROY HIM   776 14
     BE CAREFUL BEFORE YOU DESTROY HIM   776 18
     THEN DESTROY THEM THROW THEM OUT INTO THE CITIES   780 16

DESTROYED
    MOMENT DESTROYS YOU YOU ARE JUST DESTROYED   87 22

DESTROYING
    SHE BOWS QUITE HUMBLE SUCH A SUBTLE DESTROYING MIND MUS+   841 28

DESTROYS
    MOMENT DESTROYS YOU YOU ARE JUST DESTROYED   87 22
    THERE IS SOMETHING IN YOU DESTROYS ME   210 28
    THE SWINGING BLISS NO SHATTERING EVER DESTROYS   251 24
    TILL MAN DESTROYS THEM   530 13

DESTRUCTION
    OWN EARS TO MY OWN DESTRUCTION   257 6
    WHEN DESTRUCTION SOAKS THROUGH THE MORTIFIED DECOMPOSING   270 21
    FOR THE DESTRUCTION OF THE UNIVERSE FOR IF HIS PRAYER W+   348 3
    WITH UNINTELLIGENT AND EVIL DESTRUCTION   677 26
    MINGLED WITH THE BREATH OF DESTRUCTION   698 2
    NOR DESTRUCTION DIFFERENT QUITE   788 21

DESTRUCTIVE
    STRONGER THAN FEAR OR DESTRUCTIVE MOTHER-LOVE IT STOOD   207 12
    SACRIFICE THAT TO THE BRIGHT GODS AND SATISFY THE DESTR+   678 17
    AND DESTRUCTIVE IN SHORT BRILLIANT   841 23
    DESTRUCTIVE   841 27
    AND FINDS THAT THE SUBTLE DESTRUCTIVE CYNICISM IS ONLY +   842 2

DETACH
    AND STRIVE TO DETACH HERSELF FROM THE RAW   103 26
    AFTER THAT THERE WILL ONLY REMAIN THAT ALL MEN DETACH T+   267 24

DETACHED
    THAT WE ARE ALL DETACHED MOVING IN FREEDOM MORE THAN THE   267 26
    CAN MELT THE DETACHED LIFE BACK   617 9
    AND EVERY MAN WHO HAS BECOME A DETACHED AND SELF-ACTIVA+   713 4

DETAINED
    MANY YEARS HAVE I STILL TO BURN DETAINED   115 5
    MANY YEARS HAVE I STILL TO BURN DETAINED   *930 5

DETECTION
    AH WITH A FEARFUL STRANGE DETECTION   262 16

DETER
    DETER   57 24

DETERMINATION
    AND WITH A GRIM REPTILE DETERMINATION   360 14

DETERMINE
    DETERMINE TO GO ON AND ON TILL YOU ENTER THE MORNING ST+   809 8

DETERMINED
    AND FULL OF MALICE PREPENSE AND OVERWEENING DETERMINED   382 12
    WE ARE ULTIMATELY DETERMINED BY WHAT WE THRILL TO   531 27
    HAST THOU DETERMINED TO STRANGLE ME O GOD   751 14
    DETERMINED EFFORT AMONG MEN   890 2

DETEST
    TO-MORROW WILL POUR THEM ALL BACK THE DULL HOURS I DETE+   167 4
    TO-MORROW WILL POUR THEM ALL BACK THE DULL HOURS I DETE+   167 20
    BUT MOSTLY DO YOU NOT DETEST MY BRAY   236 11
    THE MOMENT I REALLY DETEST HER   385 14
    AND AN ARISTOCRAT IN SO FAR AS I DETEST NARROW-GUTTED   526 8
    FOR TOMORROW WILL POUR THEM ALL BACK THE SCHOOL HOURS I+   *896 9
    TOMORROW WILL POUR THEM ALL BACK THE DULL HOURS I DETEST   *896 25

DETESTATION
    I HAD A MOMENT'S PURE DETESTATION OF YOU   396 7
    EARNS MY UNDYING DETESTATION   507 15

DETESTED
    AND DETESTED ME   557 14

DEVASTATING
    INSISTING UPON YOUR MOTHERHOOD DEVASTATING   207 9
    ALL MOTHERS WHO FORTIFY THEMSELVES IN MOTHERHOOD DEVAST+   208 18
    IS MUCH MORE DEVASTATING   456 8

DEVELOPED
    IT SHOWS AGAIN HOW HIGHLY DEVELOPED THE SOCIAL CONSCIEN+   829 16
    WHICH SHOWS ONCE MORE THAT OUR SOCIAL CONSCIENCE IS DEV+   829 22
    HIS MIND DEVELOPED AT THE EXPENSE OF HIS MALE SELF   841 20

DEVICES
    ABOUT PROPERTY AND MONEY AND MECHANICAL DEVICES   666 12
    OF HIS OWN IDEAS AND HIS OWN MECHANICAL DEVICES   667 2
    AND MOST MURDEROUS OF ALL DEVICES   715 16

DEVIL
    THE LORD OF HOSTS AND THE DEVIL   243 13
    LIKE THE DEVIL AND LOOK ON THE WORLD AS HIS OWN   382 14
    FIGHT TO BE THE DEVIL ON THE TIP OF THE PEAK   383 24
    TOM-TOMS WEIRD MUSIC OF THE DEVIL VOICES OF MEN FROM   388 35
    AND THEN THE DEVIL COMES INTO THEIR FACES   390 3
    BUT A DIFFERENT SORT A COLD REBELLIOUS JEERING DEVIL   390 4
    SOLD TO THE DEVIL   483 5
    BETWEEN THE DEVIL AND THE DEEP COLD SEA   490 24
    NOT EVEN THE DOUBLE PHALLUS OF THE DEVIL HIMSELF   710 25
    FOR OUR SOCIETY IS BASED ON GRAB AND DEVIL TAKE THE HIN+   829 24
    AND DEVIL TAKE THE HINDMOST   829 28
    DEVIL TAKE THE HINDMOST   837 28
    IF THE MEAN DEVIL HAS ANY SEX-FEELING AT ALL   *948 29

DEVIL-DANCERS
    AND DEVIL-DANCERS LUMINOUS WITH SWEAT DANCING ON TO THE   388 33

DEVILISH
    THE GOAT IS AN EGOIST AWARE OF HIMSELF DEVILISH AWARE OF   382 10
    AND WANT TO BE COLD AND DEVILISH HARD   537 17

DEVILRY
    HOW CAN YOU PUT SO MUCH DEVILRY   332 12

DEVILS
    IN ELEPHANTS AND THE EAST ARE TWO DEVILS IN ALL MEN MAY+   390 5

DEVIL'S
    MINE IS A COMMON DEVIL'S   234 15

DEVISE
    THE ANSWER THEY DID DEVISE   124 22
    THE ANSWER THEY DID DEVISE   *935 22

DEVOID
    BEING TOUCHED WITH LOVE AND DEVOID OF FATHERLINESS   357 15

DEVOTED
    WOMEN MIGHT BE DEVOTED AND GENTLE   538 16
    AND DEVOTED HERSELF TO HER HUSBAND   619 8

DEVOUR
    PROWLING TO DEVOUR THE DREAM   807 3
    TO THE HUSHED GREY-WINGED MINISTRANTS THE BATS OF NIGHT+   *916 12

DEVOURED
    AND DEVOURED YOU WITH THE MACHINE THE VAST MAW OF IRON   630 16
    LIKE THE TWO LIONS WHO DEVOURED ONE ANOTHER AND LEFT TH+   665 2
    AND MY MOTHER'S TUNES ARE DEVOURED OF THIS MUSIC'S RAVA+   *940 23

DEVOURING
    STARVED FROM A LIFE OF DEVOURING ALWAYS MYSELF   259 15
    DEVOURING THE EARTH INTO SORES   793 2

DEVOURS
    FLAME DEVOURS THE WORLD   511 9

DEVOUTLY
    IT IS A CONSUMMATION DEVOUTLY TO BE WISHED   511 4

DEW
    WHEREIN WE FAINTED LIKE A SMOKE OR DEW   90 30
    LIKE VAPOUR DEW OR POISON NOW THANK GOD   91 1
    TO BREAK AND POUR HER OUT ITS PRECIOUS DEW   113 12
    ARE HEAVY WITH DEW   178 2
    TRICKLES THE DEW   178 13
    A NAKED TREE OF BLOSSOM LIKE A BRIDEGROOM BATHING IN DEW   306 8
    THE APPLES FALLING LIKE GREAT DROPS OF DEW   716 20
    THE APPLES FALLING LIKE GREAT DROPS OF DEW   *956 26

DEWBERRIES
    AND FAR AWAY ON THE SAND-HILLS DEWBERRIES   152 12

DEWDROP
    SOME DEWDROP MAYBE SPLASHED MY FACE DOWN HERE   87 4

DEWLAP
    AH THE DEWLAP SWINGS PENDULOUS WITH EXCESS   326 17

DEW-LAPPED
    THE MASSIVE THUNDER OF HIS DEW-LAPPED CHEST   326 10

DEW-LAP
    DEW-LAP   370 5

DEWS
    MORNING COMES AND I SHAKE THE DEWS OF NIGHT FROM THE WI+   322 26

DEXTEROUS
    A SWIFT DEXTEROUS MAN PLYING THE SLENDER POLE   867 22

DIABLERETS
    UP THERE AT THAT HEIGHT IN THE DIABLERETS   550 30

DIADEM
    AND THE FLESH OF THE STALK HOLDS UP FOR NOTHING A BLANK+   97 8
    WHEREAS THE PEACOCK HAS A DIADEM   369 23

DIAPERED
    AND DIAPERED ABOVE THE CHAUNTING FLOWERS   135 28
    AND DIAPERED ABOVE THE CHAUNTING FLOWERS   *939 20

DIAPERS
    AND THE JOB OF CHANGING ITS DIAPERS GETS BIGGER AND BIG+   670 12

DIASTOLE
    SYSTOLE DIASTOLE   55 30

DICKLETS
    TOMLETS DICKLETS HARRYLETS WHINEY   457 19

DICTATORIAL
    BUT NOT GOD GREY-BEARDED AND DICTATORIAL   437 1

DIDON DINA DIT-ON DU DOS D'UN
    DIDON DINA DIT-ON DU DOS D'UN DODU DINDON   836 5

DIDST
    BRIGHT TORTURE THOU DIDST DESERVE   *927 15

DIE
AGAINST HIM DIE AND FIND DEATH GOOD   43 37
TILL I DIE   82 28
TO NUMBNESS AND NOTHINGNESS I DEAD SHE REFUSING TO DIE   98   8
TO DIE AND THE QUICK LEAF TORE ME   111   4
TO DIE UNOPENED WHEN THIS MOON-FACED LOVER   113 15
IN A DRIFT DIE THERE   154 32
THINK I DAREN'T DIE   214 21
I WOULD DIE RATHER THAN HAVE IT INJURED WITH ONE SCAR   255 13
ON THE THRESHOLD OF SPRING I FEAR I SHALL DIE   273 29
PRAY NOT TO DIE ON THIS PISGAH BLOSSOMING WITH VIOLETS   273 36
AH DO NOT LET ME DIE ON THE BRINK OF SUCH ANTICIPATION   274   7
THAT'S HOW WOMEN DIE TOO   283 34
BEFORE I DIE   289 23
THE SUN LIVES IN HIS SHINING AND IS NOT LIKE FIRES THAT+   331   9
HAVE MADE HIM DIE   339 24
YET I HAD TO TELL THEM TO DIE   410   4
AND TOLD TO DIE   410 10
HUSH AND DIE MY DEAR   410 14
WHO UNDERSTOOD AT LAST WHAT IT WAS TO BE TOLD TO DIE   410 17
REMEMBERING I TOLD THEM TO DIE TO SINK INTO THE GRAVE IN   410 30
WOMEN WHOM I LOVED AND TOLD TO DIE   411   4
COME BACK THEN MOTHER MY LOVE WHOM I TOLD TO DIE   411 21
I DIDN'T TELL YOU TO DIE FOR NOTHING   412   1
SO I TOLD YOU TO DIE   412 13
YOU ARE MY PROPERTY BE PREPARED TO DIE FOR ME AND TO   442 21
IT'S EITHER YOU FIGHT OR YOU DIE   458   1
IT'S EITHER YOU FIGHT OR YOU DIE   458   4
DIE DIE LILY-LIVEREDLY DIE   458   5
OF MONEY DO IT OR DIE   458 12
LEAVE SEX ALONE LEAVE SEX ALONE LET IT DIE RIGHT AWAY   471 19
LET IT DIE RIGHT AWAY TILL IT RISES OF ITSELF AGAIN   471 20
AND HE CAN ONLY SLOWLY DIE   474 31
WON'T BREED THEY MOPE THEY DIE   484 24
SO I DO NOT DIE   486 23
WE ARE NOT GOING TO MAKE WAY WE ARE NOT GOING TO DIE   503   2
WHEN FULFILLED PEOPLE DIE   505   1
IS TO DIE THE AMAZING DEATH   512 24
AND YET AS WE DIE WHY SHOULD NOT OUR VAST MECHANISED   512 27
DAY DIE WITH US   512 28
KILLS US WE ARE SICK OF IT TO DIE   519 17
OR WE MUST SEE MEN DIE AND THEN DIE OURSELVES   522 31
FINALLY OUR LITTLE LOT I DON'T WANT TO DIE BUT BY JINGO+   534   6
OUR BODIES BEFORE WE DIE   584 10
DIE DIE DIE CORPSE-BODY DOESN'T MATTER   584 18
MUST WE DIE MUST WE DIE   584 19
AH NO AH NO BEFORE WE FINALLY DIE   585   1
THE UNHAPPY SOULS ARE THOSE THAT CAN'T DIE AND BECOME S+   612 19
AND WHO DARE NOT DIE FOR FEAR THEY SHOULD BE NOTHING AT+   613   4
ALL THESE CREATURES THAT CANNOT DIE DRIVEN BACK   624 11
THEN MUST A SINGLE MAN DIE WITH THEM IN THE CLUTCH OF   632   1
WHEN MOST MEN DIE TODAY   638 20
WHEN MOST WOMEN DIE   638 21
YOU ARE LIKE TO DIE OF MALNUTRITION OF THE SENSES   655 15
WHOM THE GODS LOVE DIE YOUNG   662 14
THE RANCID OLD MEN THAT DON'T DIE   662 16
THAT'S WHY THE DOGGED RESISTANT OLD ONES DARE NOT DIE   662 26
DARE NOT DIE THEY DAREN'T GO THROUGH THE DOOR   662 27
THEY DARE NOT DIE BECAUSE THEY KNOW   663   1
DARE NOT DIE BECAUSE IN DEATH   663   5
THEY CANNOT DIE THEIR CORPSE STILL RUNS ON   675 19
SO SELF-WILLED SELF-CENTRED SELF-CONSCIOUS PEOPLE DIE   676   6
BUT WHEN LIVING PEOPLE DIE IN THE RIPENESS OF THEIR TIME   676   8
SO LET ME LIVE THAT I MAY DIE   676 19
THIS SEA WILL NEVER DIE NEITHER WILL IT EVER GROW OLD   688   1
BUT WHY THEN SHOULD WE DIE WHILE WE CAN LIVE   710   5
AND DIE THE DEATH THE LONG AND PAINFUL DEATH   718   1
IS NOW TO BE WILLING TO DIE AND TO BUILD THE SHIP   718 22
IT IS NOT EASY TO DIE O IT IS NOT EASY   720 23
TO DIE THE DEATH   720 24
AND LONGING UTTERLY TO DIE   721   2
FOR IT IS HARD TO DIE IT IS DIFFICULT TO GO THROUGH   721   9
THE POOR GAUNT DEAD THAT CANNOT DIE   722   9
TOUCH ME THEN TOUCH ME TOUCH ME I DID NOT DIE   738 28
I DO NOT DIE I AM NOT EVEN HURT   741 24
A MOMENT AS HE FELL AND GROVEL AND DIE   741 28
AND GOD IS GOOD FOR I WANTED HIM TO DIE   742   1
OF DANGER I FIND HER EVEN WORSE THAN THE FIELDS WHERE W+   752 12
AND DIE LIKE A DOG IN A HOLE 'TIS STRANGE WHAT A SHODDY   755   8
BROTHER LET ME DIE DOWN AGAIN   759   4
I TELL YOU SORROW UPON YOU YOU SHALL ALL DIE   796   2
THOSE THAT HAVE MASTERED THE FORCES OF THE WORLD DIE IN+   796 14
YOU SHALL HAVE NOWHERE TO DIE INTO   796 28
GETS BITTEN AND MUST DIE   805   7
AND THE DEAD DIE   811 28
I LOVE LIFE I LOVE LIFE SO DEARLY I COULD ALMOST DIE   837 10
HE HAD HOPED TO DIE IN THE PULPIT TO CONQUER IN DEATH   859 10
ALL THE CREATURES THAT CANNOT DIE WHILE ONE HEART HARBO+   *954   5
PITY THE POOR GAUNT DEAD THAT CANNOT DIE   *958 14

DIED
LIKE A MAN WHO HAS DIED   107 28
I DIED THE FIRST I IN THE AFTER-LIFE   156 17
MY FATHER SUDDENLY DIED IN THE HARVESTING CORN   173   1
IF I DIED IT WOULD NOT BE YOU   214 14
WE HAVE DIED WE HAVE SLAIN AND BEEN SLAIN   244 21
AND THAT AT LAST RELIEVED ME I DIED   257 24
GOD BUT IT IS GOOD TO HAVE DIED AND BEEN TRODDEN OUT   258 18
DIED AS IT WERE CEASED FROM KNOWING SURPASSED MYSELF   266   5
AS THE ROCKET-CORUSCATION DIED AND SHADOW WAS THE   391 31
BURY A MAN GENTLY IF HE HAS LAIN DOWN AND DIED   442   1
I DIED AND DEATH IS NEUTER IT SPEAKS NOT IT GIVES   461 13
FOR DESIRE HAS DIED IN ME SILENCE HAS GROWN   507 17
SO PERHAPS THEY TOO DIED OUT FROM FEAR   529 20
NO MAN UNLESS HE HAS DIED AND LEARNED TO BE ALONE   612 17
THEN DIED OUT ALMOST AS SWIFTLY   618   5
MANY HAVE DIED UNCONSENTING   739   5
MY BROTHER DIED IN THE HEAT   754 17

DIED
MEXICANS LIKE PEOPLE WHO HAVE DIED   816   9
OF MY BREAKING HAD DIED UPON HIM ERE THE STAIN   885   5

DIENT IHR DIENT
AND SAY TO THEM DIENT IHR DIENT   392   5

DIENT IHR
ROYAL SUMMONS DIENT IHR   390 21

DIES
AH SOON IN HIS LARGE HARD HANDS SHE DIES   43 12
THAT'S HOW THE FIG DIES SHOWING HER CRIMSON THROUGH THE   283 30
AND THE RED-GOLD MIRROR-EYE STARES AND DIES   339 17
MY LOVE DIES DOWN CONSIDERABLY   472 20
A MAN CAN'T FULLY LIVE UNLESS HE DIES AND CEASES TO CARE   613   1
OH IF THE HUGE TREE DIES   640 18
INSTEAD OF A FLOWER THAT DIES AND OPENS A DIFFERENT BUD   662   6
PIECEMEAL THE BODY DIES AND THE TIMID SOUL   718 12
NOW LAUNCH THE SMALL SHIP NOW AS THE BODY DIES   719   1
WHO IS BITTEN DIES   806 10
HE IS BORN ALONE AND ALONE HE DIES   843 25
BORN ALONE DIES ALONE   *951   4

DIES IRAE DIES ILLA
DIES IRAE DIES ILLA   511   6

DIFFERENCE
DIVIDED IN THE MYSTIC TANGIBLE AND INTANGIBLE DIFFERENCE   636   6
BUT EVEN IN PRISTINE MEN THERE IS THE DIFFERENCE   649   6

DIFFERENCES
AND ALL THE DIFFERENCES GIVEN EXPRESSION   611 20
ONLY DIFFERENCES   636   5

DIFFERENT
HOW DIFFERENT IN THE MIDST OF SNOW THE GREAT SCHOOL 'RIS+   75   7
OUR WAYS ARE DIFFERENT NOW   102   8
YOU HAD TAKEN ME THEN HOW DIFFERENT   104 17
THA'D NEED A WOMAN DIFFERENT FROM ME   139   5
TO BE DIFFERENT   251 15
YOU SEE HE IS DIFFERENT HE IS DANGEROUS   252   1
OR WAS THEIR WAY ONLY EVASIVE AND DIFFERENT DARK LIKE   297 16
BIRDS HAVE THEIR VOICES EACH MEANS A DIFFERENT THING   368 12
BUT A DIFFERENT SORT A COLD REBELLIOUS JEERING DEVIL   390   4
LEAVING THE TRAIL OF A DIFFERENT PAW HANGING OUT   394   4
AND IS FECUND WITH A NEW DAY OF NEW CREATURES DIFFERENT   429   7
FIDELITY AND LOVE ARE TWO DIFFERENT THINGS LIKE A FLOWER   476   1
BUT A GEM IS DIFFERENT IT LASTS SO MUCH LONGER THAN WE +   476 21
THAT SOCIETY MUST ESTABLISH ITSELF UPON A DIFFERENT PRI+   487 19
STAND UP FOR SOMETHING DIFFERENT   560 25
TURNED ON FOR DIFFERENT PURPOSES   625 23
IS DIFFERENT FROM THE LOVE I FELT LAST YEAR   662   2
INSTEAD OF A FLOWER THAT DIES AND OPENS A DIFFERENT BUD   662   6
THEY WANDER THEIR STRANGE AND DIFFERENT WAYS IN HEAVEN   713 22
AH IT IS VERY HARD TO CHANGE AND BE DIFFERENT   727 32
SET OFF IN DIFFERENT DIRECTIONS NOT DIFFERENT DIRECTION+   760 24
TIME BUT DIFFERENT DIRECTIONS IN CREATION WITHIN THE FO+   760 25
NOR DESTRUCTION DIFFERENT QUITE   788 21
HOW DIFFERENT IN THE MIDDLE OF SNOWS THE GREAT SCHOOL R+   865 18
DIFFERENT YES SHALL THE POSIES BE   888   3

DIFFICULT
THE DIFFICULT GLEBE OF THE FUTURE   102 11
HAVING WALKED HIMSELF IN THE THORNY DIFFICULT   199   2
TO THAT DIFFICULT INNERMOST PLACE IN A MAN   412   8
THEY SAY IT IS VERY DIFFICULT   495 10
PERHAPS THAT'S WHY IT IS SO DIFFICULT   495 12
I SUPPOSE AS A MATTER OF FACT IT'S GETTING A LITTLE DIF+   532   3
AND PATIENCE AND A CERTAIN DIFFICULT REPENTANCE   620 17
LONG DIFFICULT REPENTANCE REALISATION OF LIFE'S MISTAKE+   620 18
FOR IT IS HARD TO DIE IT IS DIFFICULT TO GO THROUGH   721   9
AND IT IS MUCH MORE DIFFICULT AND DELICATE TO BE TRUE   775 16
THAT IS A DIFFICULT THING TO BE FAITHFUL TO   775 27

DIFFICULTY
AS IF A BIRD IN DIFFICULTY UP THE VALLEY STEERS   210 22
LET HIM COME HOME TO A BIT OF MORAL DIFFICULTY LET LIFE+   431   4

DIFFIDENT
WITH A PALE LITTLE WISP OF A PRINCE OF WALES DIFFIDENT +   387 21
AND ALL THERE WAS TO BOW TO A WEARY DIFFIDENT BOY WHOSE   391 32

DIFFUSE
ALMOND AND APPLE AND PEAR DIFFUSE WITH LIGHT THAT VERY   179   3

DIFFUSING
FOR AM I NOT ALSO DREAM-STUFF DIFFUSING MYSELF IN THE P+   *907   7
AM I NOT QUICKENING DIFFUSING MYSELF IN THE PATTERN SHA+   *909   4

DIGGING-IN
FROM HOT DIGGING-IN FINGERS OF LOVE   601 12

DIGNIFIED
IS DIGNIFIED IN THE FOXGLOVE LIKE A RED INDIAN BRAVE   272 29
THE LONELY RAMBLER THE STOIC DIGNIFIED STALKER THROUGH   360 28

DIGNITY
DIGNITY   255 32
IN THE SLOW DIGNITY OF YOUR ETERNAL PAUSE   354   9
DARKNESS TO RAISE THE STRICKEN DIGNITY AND REST   *896 23

DILATED
DILATED LOOK UP   389 23

DILEMMA
  SO A DILEMMA   346   1
  THE BARK OF THEIR DELIVERANCE FROM THE DILEMMA   722 14

DILIGENT
  I WAS DILIGENT TO EXPLORE YOU   *928   6

DIM
  WHEN WILL THE SCENT OF THE DIM WHITE PHLOX   62 27
  DIM TREES SO HUGE AND TALL   68 24
  SINCE LIFE SWEEPS WHIRLING DIM AND VAST   69   1
  LIFE IN THY MOUTH AND DIM BREATH'S HASTENING HISS   69 24
  TO-MORROW SWIMMING IN EVENING'S VAGUE DIM VAPOUR   72 16
  ALONE WITHIN THE DIM AND HOARSE SILENCE   76 21
  DIM SELF THAT RISES SLOWLY TO LEAVES AND THE FLOWER'S G+   92 20
  AND DIM HOPES CROWDED ME WARM WITH COMPANIONSHIP   98 29
  AND CITY STARS SO DIM AND HOLY   121 31
  DIM SPRING THAT INTERWEAVES   126 20
  SOME DIM LITTLE EFFORTS PLACED IN THE THREADS OF THE   142   7
  BROKE THE BOUNDS AND BEYOND DIM RECOLLECTION   161 21
  BUT TO GET OUT FROM THIS DIM DREADFUL DEN   174   4
  TO NOTHINGNESS AND TIME WILL DIM THE MOON   193 11
  THE INNERMOST FIRE OF MY OWN DIM SOUL OUT-SPINNING   218 22
  ALL OVER THE DIM CORN'S MOTION AGAINST THE BLUE   221 25
  SCYLLAS AND YELLOW-HAIRED HELLEBORE JONQUILS DIM ANEMON+   270   7
  GREEN DIM INVISIBLE FLOURISHING OF VINES   286   5
  NUDE WITH THE DIM LIGHT OF FULL HEALTHY LIFE   298 26
  QUEER WHAT A DIM DARK SMUDGE YOU HAVE DISAPPEARED   334 18
  AND TAKE YOUR FIRST BITE AT SOME DIM BIT OF HERBAGE   352 14
  AND OUT TO THE DIM OF THE DESERT LIKE A DREAM NEVER REAL   402 22
  FRAGRANT LIKE YELLOWING LEAVES AND DIM WITH THE SOFT   503 24
  WITH THE PATHOS OF THOSE WHO CAN SEE BUT WHOSE SIGHT IS+   665 24
  WHEN THE DIM FLUX OF UNFORMED LIFE   682   3
  BOTH BREASTS DIM AND MYSTERIOUS WITH THE GLAMOROUS KIND+   693 12
  AND THE DIM NOTCH OF BLACK MAIDENHAIR LIKE AN INDICATOR   693 14
  CARRIES A DIM LOW SONG THAT STIRS   868 30
  WITH DIM LIGHT SHOWING THE HEADS OF THE SILVER NAILS   876 14
  A RED FLOWER FALLS TO ITS DIM REFLECTION   887 18
  WRAPPED UP IN THE SKY'S DIM SPACE OF HOARSE SILENCE   *898 15
  WRAPPED UP IN THE SKY'S DIM SPACE OF HOARSE SILENCE   *901 24
  SINCE GOD SWEEPS ONWARD DIM AND VAST   *915 13
  ALL OVER THE CORN'S DIM MOTION AGAINST THE BLUE   *945 11
  STREWN WITH DIM WRECKAGE AND CROWDED WITH CRYING SOULS   *957 16
  WITH DIM CALM THOUGHTS AND QUIET HANDS   *960 28

DIMENSION
  DIMENSION THE CUCKOO WENT CUCKOO-WARDS THE COW WENT COW+   760 26
  ACROSS THE FOURTH DIMENSION   760 28
  FOURTH DIMENSION NOT IN YARDS AND MILES LIKE THE ETERNA+   761 16

DIMENSIONS
  FLAT PERSONALITIES IN TWO DIMENSIONS IMPONDERABLE AND   446   6

DIMINISH
  FINISH FINISH DIMINISH DIMINISH   826 10
  TO STREW ROUND OUR WAY TO DIMINISH EACH FULL STAR'S GLI+   *938   6

DIMINISHED
  HIS DIMINISHED DROOPING HINDQUARTERS   377 25
  WE ASK MORE AND MORE TO BE DIMINISHED   826   1
  THEE A GOD-JOY DIMINISHED   *927 30
  IT TRUELY A GOD-THOUGHT DIMINISHED   *927 31

DIMINISHING
  TO NOUGHT DIMINISHING EACH STAR'S GLITTER   132 14

DIMINUTION
  QUESTION OR DIMINUTION   235 14

DIM-LIT
  STOPPED AT A DIM-LIT TROUGH TO DRINK   121 29

DIMLY
  DRIFTS DIMLY FORWARD EASILY HIDDEN   68   6
  LIKE HALF-BLOWN FLOWERS DIMLY SHAKING AT THE NIGHT   75 27
  THE HEADS OF THE BOYS MOVE DIMLY THROUGH A YELLOW GLOOM+   92   4
  I SAW DIMLY   338 18
  HOLD THE STARS STILL LEST WE HEAR THE HEAVENS DIMLY RIN+   698 11
  LIKE FULL-BLOWN FLOWERS DIMLY SHAKING AT THE NIGHT   *897 26
  UP DIMLY FROM THEIR STRIVING IT HEARTENS MY STRIFE   *900 24
  LIKE FULL-BLOWN FLOWERS DIMLY SHAKING AT THE NIGHT   *901   3
  UP DIMLY FROM THEIR STRIVING IT HEARTENS MY STRIFE   *903 36
  DRIFTS DIMLY FORWARD EASILY HIDDEN   *914 21
  THE HEADS OF MY BOYS MOVE DIMLY THROUGH THE YELLOW GLOO+   *926   4

DIMMED
  OF THE MORNING THE ELMS ARE LOFTILY DIMMED AND TALL   164 22

DIMMER
  GROWS DIMMER WE BOTH FORGET   240 14

DIMNESS
  WINDING ABOUT THEIR DIMNESS THE MIST'S GREY CEREMENTS A+   102 30

DIMS
  YOUR BRIGHTNESS DIMS WHEN I DRAW TOO NEAR AND MY FREE   87 16
  AND THE WATER-SUAVE CONTOUR DIMS   339 18

DINGY
  A DRAB AND DINGY BIRD   523 29
  BUT HOW PALTRY MINGY AND DINGY AND SQUALID PEOPLE LOOK   530 15

DINING-ROOM
  IF WE ARE PROPERLY CLOTHED AND DISCIPLINED IN THE DININ+   608 12

DINNER
  AS HE SEES ME BRINGING THE DINNER HE LIFTS   220   1
  MY BODY LIKES ITS DINNER AND THE WARM SUN BUT OTHERWISE+   501 19
  AS HE SEES ME BRINGIN' THE DINNER HE LIFTS   *944   9

DINNERS
  DINNERS FOR THE NEXT FIFTY YEARS   531   7
  GOOD DINNERS FOR FIFTY MORE LONG YEARS   531 15

DINT
  CAN MAKE THEM YAWN I PUT MY HAND TO THE DINT   125   9
  CAN MAKE THEM YAWN I STRETCHED MY HAND TO THE DINT   *935 25

DIONYSOS
  AND THE EGO SUM OF DIONYSOS   281 28
  AND LET THE SLIM BLACK SHIP OF DIONYSOS COME SAILING IN   688   4
  AND DIONYSOS YOUNG AND A STRANGER   688 19
  AND THE SEA IS MAKING LOVE TO DIONYSOS   693 29

DIONYSOS OF THE UNDERWORLD
  DIONYSOS OF THE UNDERWORLD   280 26

DIONYSOS'
  THE DOLPHINS LEAP ROUND DIONYSOS' SHIP   693 25

DIP
  AND SWALLOWS DIP INTO THE PALLOR OF THE WEST   41 21
  A DIP TO THE WATER   341   5
  THE SUN BUT ALL CREATURES OF THE SUN MUST DIP THEIR MOU+   368   6
  I WISH THAT I MIGHT DIP MYSELF WITHIN   879   8
  AND DIP IN THE HEART   *935 37

DIPPED
  WITH FIRE ON YOUR CHEEKS AND YOUR BROW AND YOUR CHIN AS+   90   9
  YOU'VE DIPPED IT IN BLOOD SO MANY TIMES   373 33
  BUT DIPPED ONCE DIPPED IN DARK OBLIVION   724 25
  THEN I HAVE BEEN DIPPED AGAIN IN GOD AND NEW-CREATED   726 25
  DIPPED INTO OBLIVION   728   4

DIPPING
  DIPPING WITH PETTY TRIUMPHANT FLIGHT AND TITTERING OVER   347 17

DIPS
  AS THE DARKNESS FLICKERS AND DIPS   238 13
  LEANS OVER TO READ HIS WORK AND HER DARK HEAD DIPS   865   5

DIRECT
  EVERY MOVEMENT WILL BE DIRECT   267 31
  OR DID IT SOUND ON THE PLASM DIRECT   364 12
  YOU WILL FIND YOU HAVE A GREAT DESIRE TO DRINK LIFE DIR+   481   3
  POURING INTO THE VEINS FROM THE DIRECT CONTACT WITH THE   481 28
  YOU DRAW YOUR NOBILITY DIRECT FROM THE SUN   526 27
  PLEASE APPROACH THE SUPREME AUTHORITY DIRECT   604 18
  IN DIRECT RATIO   663 19
  SINCE THE BOURGEOIS IS THE DIRECT CAUSE OF THE BOLSHEVI+   664 10
  AND SUPPRESSION OF SUCH FACT LEADS AS WE KNOW DIRECT TO+ *953   5

DIRECTION
  FOR A MOMENT THE MIGHTY DIRECTION SNATCH   68 27
  SOUNDLESSLY MOVING IN HEAVEN'S OTHER DIRECTION   161 23
  A FINE WIND IS BLOWING THE NEW DIRECTION OF TIME   250 14
  TO DEADEN MY ATTENTION IN YOUR DIRECTION   332 23
  THE FIGHT'S GOT TO GO IN SOME DIRECTION   538 17
  AND SIDEWAYS UTTERLY DARK SO THERE IS NO DIRECTION ANY +   719 14
  IN ANY DIRECTION   777 11
  AND OUR INTUITION CAN COME TO LIFE AND GIVE US DIRECTION   839   4
  FOR A MOMENT HIS GREAT DIRECTION SCRATCH   *915 11

DIRECTIONS
  SET OFF IN DIFFERENT DIRECTIONS NOT DIFFERENT DIRECTION+   760 24
  TIME BUT DIFFERENT DIRECTIONS IN CREATION WITHIN THE FO+   760 25

DIRT
  FOUNTAINS OF DIRT   160   2
  INTO OOZE AND THE SOMBRE DIRT SPOUTS UP AT MY HANDS   167   6
  IS ONLY MENTAL DIRT   463   2
  SIN IS OBSOLETE SIN IS OBSOLETE BUT NOT SO DIRT   463 27
  AND DIRT IF IT ISN'T SIN IS WORSE ESPECIALLY DIRT INSIDE   464   5
  HAS HE NO MONEY THEN LET HIM EAT DIRT AND GO COLD   486 21
  BUT THEY WILL MAKE ME EAT DIRT WITH IT   486 24
  I SHALL HAVE TO EAT DIRT I SHALL HAVE TO EAT DIRT   486 25
  TO SAVE US FROM EATING DIRT   487   5
  WITH DIRT THEY COULDN'T FORGET   491 20
  AND BULLIED WITH THE THREAT GET MONEY OR EAT DIRT   522 12
  LOOKING DIRT ON THEM AND BREATHING ON THEM LIES   580 26
  GODDESSES OF LOVE GODDESSES OF DIRT EXCREMENT-EATERS OR+   671 18
  BUTTERFLY WHY DO YOU SETTLE ON MY SHOE AND SIP THE DIRT+   696 13
  TO TWIST AND GROVEL AND BECOME A HEAP OF DIRT   742   2
  AND NOW THE SKY WITH DREARY DIRT IS BARKLED   *933 16

DIRT-EATING
  DEMOCRATIC LITTLE BULL-BITCH DIRT-EATING LITTLE SWINE   399 26

DIRTIED
  AH MY NICE PICTURES THEY ARE FOULED THEY ARE DIRTIED   580 23

DIRTIER
  AND SEX ALAS GETS DIRTIER AND DIRTIER WORKED FROM THE   464   1
  SEX GETS DIRTIER AND DIRTIER THE MORE IT IS FOOLED WITH+   464   3

DIRTIEST
  AND EVEN THE DIRTIEST SCALLYWAG IS TAKEN IN   398 19

DIRTY
  WI' A BITTER DIRTY SKIN   77 14
  OF EVERY DIRTY MUST-BESPRINKLED MOULD   141 10
  AS RED AND DIRTY BARE   145 23
  RATHER DIRTY ON DUNG-WHITENED PATMOS   329 25

DIRTY
    AND RATHER DIRTY   358 23
    TRICK ON THEM DIRTY BITCH   399 18
    THEN THE NOISY DIRTY DAY-WORLD   453 16
    AT THE TRASHY MOTOR-DRIVEN TRANSIT OF DIRTY DAY   453 27
    THE DIRTY MIND LIKE A URINAL AGAIN   463 3
    NOR IS IT DIRTY NOT UNTIL THE DIRTY MIND POKES IN   463 25
    IF YOU'RE DIRTY INSIDE YOU GO ROTTEN AND ONCE ROTTEN WOE   464 6
    SEX ISN'T SIN BUT DIRTY SEX IS WORSE SO THERE YOU ARE   464 8
    AND THE SIN IS TO DAMAGE THE FLOW FORCE IT OR DIRTY IT +   464 15
    A DAMN FOR THEIR DIRTY KENNELS   494 2
    A GOOD KICK AT HIS DIRTY OLD HOLE   494 12
    WITH THE CREST OF THE DIRTY DRAB WORLD DOWN BELOW   551 2
    TO THE DIRTY DRAB WORLD   551 4
    IT WAS NOWT BUT A DIRTY SELL THAT'S ALL   553 3
    YOU LIARS YOU DIRTY LOT   762 17
    THE DIRTY DOGS OF WISDOM   762 21
    AND PUT A DIRTY GREEN LARGE CABAGE   845 25
    TOO DIRTY A HYPOCRITE TO ADMIT HIS OWN NATURE   *949 3
    THE DIRTY LITTLE DON JUAN   *949 10

DIRTYISH
    BUT EVERYONE OF THEM DIRTYISH   792 32

DIS
    INFERNAL DIS   307 22
    DIS   308 1
    DIS THE DARK THE JEALOUS GOD THE HUSBAND   308 7
    HELL ON EARTH AND DIS WITHIN THE DEPTHS   309 14
    BLACK LAMPS FROM THE HALLS OF DIS BURNING DARK BLUE   697 9
    BLACK LAMPS FROM THE HALLS OF DIS SMOKING DARK BLUE   *956 7

DISADVANTAGE
    MODERN PEOPLE FEEL THEMSELVES AT A DISADVANTAGE   446 1

DISAPPEAR
    AND DISAPPEAR WHAT HAVE WE BUT EACH OTHER   209 5
    ONLY TO DISAPPEAR AGAIN QUICKLY AWAY FROM THE SIGHT OF   394 2
    NOW TO BEGIN TO DISAPPEAR   429 23
    AS IF IN ANOTHER MOMENT SHE WOULD DISAPPEAR   646 26

DISAPPEARED
    QUEER WHAT A DIM DARK SMUDGE YOU HAVE DISAPPEARED   334 18
    WHERE IT DISAPPEARED AT THE FOOT OF THE CRUCIFIX   371 27

DISAPPEARING
    THEN DISAPPEARING BACK WITH A HISS   454 10

DISAPPOINTED
    THE DRAGON OF THE DISAPPOINTED DEAD THAT SLEEPS IN THE +   795 12
    HIM OF THE DISAPPOINTED DEAD HE IS LASHING AND TURNING +   796 31

DISAPPOINTMENT
    FULL OF DISAPPOINTMENT AND OF RAIN   119 12
    AND THE SHADOW OF A JEER OF UNDERNEATH DISAPPOINTMENT   391 22
    OR TEAR ME WITH THE FANGS OF DISAPPOINTMENT   604 11
    FULL OF DISAPPOINTMENT AND OF RAIN   *932 21

DISAPPROVE
    OR EVEN WHAT WE LIKE OR DISLIKE OR APPROVE OR DISAPPROVE   531 24

DISARRAY
    AND ALL THE HEAVENS ARE WANDERING IN DISARRAY   115 21
    IN DISARRAY   145 17
    A DISARRAY OF FALLING STARS COMING TO NOUGHT   236 23

DISASTROUSLY
    TO ASSIST US DISASTROUSLY SILENCE-BOUND   166 15
    DISASTROUSLY REMINISCENT OF HAMMERS AND FILES AND DOOR-+   835 6
    OR STILL MORE DISASTROUSLY REMINISCENT OF THAT-WILL-BE-+   835 7

DISCARD
    OF LIFE CAN YOU NEVER DISCARD   55 5

DISCARDED
    AND LEAVE MY FLESH DISCARDED LYING   134 8
    PUSHED THEM ALL ASIDE DISCARDED THEM MAKE WAY NOW FOR S+   616 26
    AND I AM DRIFTING LIKE A SHELL DISCARDED   875 25

DISCHARGE
    THAT YOU COULD DISCHARGE THE ACHE   117 26

DISCIPLINE
    THE CLASS OVER THEM ALL THE DARK NET OF MY DISCIPLINE W+   92 6
    LEARN THEY MUST TO OBEY FOR ALL HARMONY IS DISCIPLINE   93 9
    THE CLASS OVER THEM ALL THE DARK NET OF MY DISCIPLINE W+   *926 6

DISCIPLINED
    IT IS WELL TO BE DISCIPLINED IN ALL THE SOCIAL USAGES   608 8
    IF WE ARE PROPERLY CLOTHED AND DISCIPLINED IN THE DININ+   608 12

DISCIPLINE'S
    WHAT'S BEYOND THEM AND FIGHT WITH ME IN DISCIPLINE'S LI+   93 28

DISCLOSE
    DISCLOSE   818 3

DISCLOSED
    DISCLOSED BUT 'TIS I WHO AM PROWLING   107 15

DISCLOSES
    BEFORE THE MIST DISCLOSES   178 3
    HOW LOVELY IS THE SELF THIS DAY DISCLOSES   218 4
    SHAKE DOWN THEIR GOLDEN LITTER THAT DISCLOSES   *916 22

DISCOLOURED
    WHITE LILAC SHOWS DISCOLOURED NIGHT   104 30
    ACROSS THERE A DISCOLOURED MOON BURNS ITSELF OUT   212 14

DISCONNECTED
    THE EGO RUNNING IN ITS OWN COMPLEX AND DISCONNECTED   635 9

DISCONSOLATE
    AGAIN FOR OH THE DEAD ARE DISCONSOLATE SINCE EVEN DEATH+   406 8
    NOT ROAMING HERE DISCONSOLATE ANGRILY   740 24
    EVE SWINGING HER DUSKY LIMBS DISCONSOLATE   863 21

DISCONTENT
    COME DRAW THE THORN FROM MY DISCONTENT   113 27
    WERE NOT YET TO COME STILL MORE FROM THE STILL-FLICKERI+   272 8
    NOW THAT THE WINTER OF OUR DISCONTENT   569 7
    HUNGRY AND DISCONTENT IN THE FRUITFUL SHADE   864 2
    YOU SHALL DRAW THE THORN FROM MY DISCONTENT   *929 16

DISCONTENTED
    ELDERLY DISCONTENTED WOMEN ASK FOR INTIMATE COMPANIONSH+   502 1
    ELDERLY DISCONTENTED WOMEN ARE SO FULL OF THEMSELVES   502 4

DISCOVER
    AND THERE IN THE DARK I DID DISCOVER   123 22
    THEY MAY EVEN ONE DAY DISCOVER SIMPLE AFFECTION AS A GR+   832 18
    AND IN THE DARK I DID DISCOVER   *934 28

DISCOVERED
    SHOULD SCOFF ME DISCOVERED   771 22
    YOU'VE DISCOVERED SO MANY BITS WITH YOUR CLEVER EYES   *932 7

DISCOVERER
    I AM THE DISCOVERER   259 26

DISCOVERY
    DISCOVERY LIKE BIRDS THAT STEAL AND FLEE   51 30
    MY WINDOWS OF DISCOVERY AND SHRILL SIN   122 30
    I CANNOT TELL YOU THE MAD ASTOUNDED RAPTURE OF ITS DISC+   260 20
    DISCOVERY   832 19
    MY WINDOWS OF DISCOVERY AND SHRILL SIN   *934 6

DISCREETLY
    DISCREETLY YET RECKLESSLY CALLS   105 32

DISCRIMINATE
    DO LEARN TO DISCRIMINATE   459 12

DISCRIMINATION
    YOU LOOK AT ME FOR DISCRIMINATION DON'T YOU   400 24

DISCUSSING
    ARE DISCUSSING WITH ONE ANOTHER THEY ARE MAKING READY T+   793 4

DISDAIN
    AND DISDAIN AND BLANKNESS AND ONRUSH AND PRISE OPEN THE   371 30
    OVERSET IN DISDAIN   823 15

DISDAINFUL
    AND SO MUCH PROUDER SO DISDAINFUL OF RELUCTANCES   306 25

DISEASE
    IT IS SAID A DISEASE HAS ATTACKED THE CYPRESS TREES OF +   295 1

DISEASED
    AND LIKE TO BECOME INCURABLY DISEASED INSIDE   535 22

DISEMBARKED
    WHERE I AM DISEMBARKED AT LAST   256 9

DISEMBODIED
    AND CAN BUT HAUNT IN DISEMBODIED RAGE   723 2

DISEMBURDENED
    NOW YOU ARE DISEMBURDENED OF MAN AND A MAN   411 14

DISENCUMBER
    LET THEM DISENCUMBER YOUR BOUNTY LET THEM ALL SHARE   168 12

DISGRACE
    FOR THIS NICE OLD SHAME AN' DISGRACE   79 8
    THE DISGRACE IS ALSO MINE   111 9
    DODGING BEHIND IN DISGRACE   731 12
    FOR THIS NICE OLD SHAME AND DISGRACE   *921 4
    BUT THE DISGRACE IS MINE   *927 2
    AND WHO WILL REMOVE FROM ME THE DISGRACE   *927 26
    BUT THE DISGRACE IS MINE   *928 2
    ALL THE TREES ARE HANGING WITH DISHONOURED FLAGS' DISGR+   *933 29

DISGRACES
    ELSEWHERE HALLS OF HIGH DISGRACES   95 31

DISGUISE
    ANGEL IN DISGUISE   234 10

DISGUISED
    AND THEIR LAST REFINEMENT BLUFF A HATE DISGUISED   644 12
    LIKE A MUD FROM WINTER DISGUISED IN GREY   815 8

DISGUST
    WITH ASHES OF UTTER BOREDOM ENNUI AND DISGUST   616 12
    AND ALL THE FLOWERS ARE FALLEN IN DISGUST   *939 16

DISGUSTING
    AND EVERYTHING ELSE TO THEIR DISGUSTING LEVEL   317 31
    HANGING UPSIDE DOWN LIKE ROWS OF DISGUSTING OLD RAGS   342 3
    A DISGUSTING BAT   342 18
    TELLS DULL MEANINGLESS DISGUSTING TALES   522 7

DISGUSTING
HOW DISGUSTING HOW INFINITELY SORDID THIS HUMANITY IS   628   4
I THINK IDIOTS TELL DULL STUPID DISGUSTING TALES   837 21

DISGUSTINGLY
AND DISGUSTINGLY UPSIDE DOWN   342   2

DISHES
AND LITTLE DISHES AND ALL ACCOUTREMENTS   718 25
AND LITTLE DISHES AND ALL ACCOUTREMENTS   *958 21
THE OARS HAVE GONE FROM THE BOAT AND THE LITTLE DISHES   *959 29

DISHEVEL
RETURN WE EVEN DISHEVEL   243 18

DISHONESTY
MAY I ASK YOU THEN WHERE INSINCERITY AND DISHONESTY BEG+   659 13

DISHONOURED
ALL THE TREES ARE HANGING WITH DISHONOURED FLAGS' DISGR+   *933 29

DISILLUSION
ONCE DISILLUSION FALLS ON LIVING MEN AND THEY FEEL THE   639 19
ONCE DISILLUSION FALLS ON LIVING MEN AND ILLUSION OF BR+   639 23

DISINTEGRATES
DISINTEGRATES   616 10

DISINTEGRATION
DEATH ALONE THROUGH THE LONG PROCESS OF DISINTEGRATION   617   8

DISINTEGRATIVE
THROUGH THE SLOW CORRUPTIVE LEVELS OF DISINTEGRATIVE KN+   699 22
AND SINKING STILL IN DEPTH AFTER DEPTH OF DISINTEGRATIV+   699 25

DISJOINTED
THEY ARE A CLICKETING OF BITS OF DISJOINTED METAL   288 32

DISLIKE
OR EVEN WHAT WE LIKE OR DISLIKE OR APPROVE OR DISAPPROVE   531 24
DO IT BECAUSE THEY DISLIKE SUCCESS IN ITSELF   829   3
SO THEY ACCEPT COVERED DISLIKE AS THE NORMAL FEELING BE+   832 15

DISLIKED
AND DISLIKED   832 13

DISLIKES
DISLIKES THEM   447 12

DISLOCATED
AND DISLOCATED THE INTUITIVE CONSCIENCE   838 23

DISLOYAL
ARE ALWAYS THEMSELVES BY NATURE DISLOYAL   626   2

DISMAL
SUBURBAN DISMAL   141   2
IN NOTTINGHAM THAT DISMAL TOWN   499   7

DISMANTLED
HIS FORTRESS IS DISMANTLED   327   4
DISMANTLED   390 18

DISMAY
THE WALLS ARE THICK AND THE INNER ROOMS ARE SUCH THEY D+   174 19
PAIN AND DISMAY   544 19

DISMAYED
AND I DARED NOT ENTER FEELING SUDDENLY DISMAYED   99 11
OF FLESH THAT STANDS DISMAYED ON THE BUSH   107 18
PEAKED AND A BIT DISMAYED   394   1

DISMEMBERING
ARE TORN DOWN BY DISMEMBERING AUTUMN   709 19

DISOBEY
HE FORCED US TO LIVE A GREAT LIE OR TO DISOBEY   654   7

DISOWN
HOW STRANGELY SHE TRIES TO DISOWN IT AS IT SINKS   128 15
BUT DIDN'T DISOWN THE BIRD   413   3
AND ESSAY TO DISOWN OURSELVES AND THEN WHEN THE LIGHT   748 10
TO DISOWN THE NIGHT   748 12

DISPENSATION
FOR A NEW DISPENSATION OF KNOWLEDGE   488 10

DISPENSE
WHERE SMART MEN WOULD DISPENSE   488 24

DISPIRITED
PALE DISPIRITED PRINCE WITH HIS CHIN ON HIS HANDS HIS   388   7

DISPLAY
HER SMALL HEAD MAKING WARM DISPLAY   42 26
JUST WATCH THE DISPLAY OF HIM CONFRONTED WITH A NEW   431   8
IT IS ABSURD FOR ME TO DISPLAY MY NAKED SOUL AT THE TEA+   608 11
AND DAZED WITH A TAWNY-GOLD DISPLAY   *935   4
YOU HIGHLY EVERY BLOOD-RED ROSE DISPLAY   *941   7

DISPLAYING
AND DISPLAYING NO PERSONALITY   445 34

DISPLEASURE
HIS HAPPINESS WHILST HE IN DISPLEASURE RETREATS   47 20

DISPOSES
LET IT BE AS THE SNAKE DISPOSES   217   7

DISQUALITY
AND PASSIONATE DISQUALITY OF MEN   317 17

DISQUIET
OUT OF EACH FACE STRANGE DARK BEAMS THAT DISQUIET   76   1
OUT OF EACH STAR DARK STRANGE BEAMS THAT DISQUIET   *897 28
OUT OF EACH STAR DARK STRANGE BEAMS THAT DISQUIET   *901   5

DISSATISFACTION
OF YOUR DISSATISFACTION AND MISPRISION   230 18

DISSATISFIED
DISSATISFIED AND WEARY   200   5

DISSEMBLE
ONE SHADOW AND WE NEED NOT DISSEMBLE   170 14

DISSEMINATED
DISSEMINATED OUT   107 24
ME TILL I REEL WITH DISSEMINATED CONSCIOUSNESS   107 27

DISSIPATED
BUT DISSIPATED DISSOLVED AGAIN   870 15

DISSOLUTION
AND THE LAST FIRES OF DISSOLUTION BURN IN THE BOSOM OF +   270 23
AND TROUBLE AND DISSOLUTION AND DISTRESS   727   8

DISSOLVE
COME THAW DOWN THEIR COOL PORTENTOUSNESS DISSOLVE THEM   271   5
CITIES DISSOLVE LIKE ROCK-SALT   455   3

DISSOLVED
DISSOLVED IN THE BLOOD   118 30
DISSOLVED WITH THE MYSTERY OF THE INNERMOST HEART OF THE   260 28
BUT DISSIPATED DISSOLVED AGAIN   870 15

DISSOLVES
THE SEA DISSOLVES SO MUCH   454 18
GONE GONE AND THE BOAT DISSOLVES LIKE PEARL   *959 30

DISSOLVING
ARE DISSOLVING OUT OF YOU   240   2

DISTANCE
TILL THE DISTANCE FOLDS OVER HIS OMINOUS TREAD   43   4
ALWAYS ON THE DISTANCE AS IF HIS SOUL WERE CHAUNTING   47 12
WHERE THE TREES RISE LIKE CLIFFS PROUD AND BLUE-TINTED +   66   5
WISTFUL AND CANDID WATCHING ME WISTFULLY FROM HER DISTA+   67 14
THE DARK VAN DRUMMED DOWN THE DISTANCE LOWLY   121 30
AWAY IN THE DISTANCE WAKES A LAMP   163 25
OUT OF THE DISTANCE NEARER COMING TO PROVE   174 11
STILL IN THE PURPLE DISTANCE   253 11
IN THE DISTANCE LIKE HOAR-FROST LIKE SILVERY GHOSTS COM+   306 26
SUCH A CANNY LISTENER FROM A DISTANCE LOOKING UPWARDS   384 17
O YOU WITH MENTAL BODIES STAY A LITTLE DISTANCE FROM ME   468 25
AT A LITTLE DISTANCE   602   2
A STRANGE GREY DISTANCE SEPARATES   607   1
CROSS LIKE CLOCK-WORK THE MINOAN DISTANCE   688   8
THEY ONLY CROSS THE DISTANCE NEVER CHANGES   688   9
YOU HAVE MELTED IN THE CRYSTALLINE DISTANCE   696 27
INTO THE DISTANCE WITH RECEDING OARS   722 10
TO THE DISTANCE THE WAVE THAT TARRIES   747   5
THE GOOD GHOST OF ME GOES DOWN THE DISTANCE   812   9
OUT OF THE DISTANCE NEARER   *906 19
FROM THE DREAMS THAT THE DISTANCE FLATTERED   *908 12
OUT OF THE DISTANCE NEARER COMMANDING MY DREAMY WORLD   *908 15
INTO THE DISTANCE WITH RECEDING OARS   *958 15

DISTANCES
THE SUN OF IMMENSE DISTANCES THAT FOLD THEMSELVES TOGET+   513 17

DISTANT
SO DISTANT THEY CANNOT TOUCH ME WHOM NOW NOTHING MARS   97 17
WITH DISTANT SUNSHINE   224 11
AND KISS OF THE FAR-OFF LINGERING LADY WHO LOOKS OVER T+   695 31
CHAPLETS OF CREAM AND DISTANT GREEN   854 25

DISTASTEFUL
AND TO THE YOUNG THIS IS REALLY IMMORAL AND DISTASTEFUL   829 25
THAT IS THE IMPORTANT POINT REALLY DISTASTEFUL   829 26
IS BASE TO US AND DISTASTEFUL   831 16
BUT ON WHAT THEY FIND DISTASTEFUL REPULSIVE OR ATTRACTI+   831 19

DISTENDED
LIKE A CAT'S DISTENDED PUPIL THAT SPARKLES WITH LITTLE +   97 15

DISTIL
STREAMING BACK WHERE THE MISTS DISTIL   53 10
IS LOST IN THIS SHADOWED SILENCE THE SKIES DISTIL   76 19
AND SHE WOKE TO DISTIL THE BERRIES   202 17
TO DISTIL SEA-WATER INTO SWEET   495 11
THEY WOULD DISTIL THE ESSENTIAL OIL OUT OF EVERY   504   6
IS LOST IN THE SHADOWED SILENCE THE SKIES DISTIL   *898 13
IS LOST IN THE SHADOWED SILENCE THE SKIES DISTIL   *901 22

DISTILLED
EVER MORE EXQUISITE DISTILLED IN SEPARATION   281 11
THE DISTILLED ESSENCE OF HELL   281 13
SILKY WITH OIL OF DISTILLED EXPERIENCE   505   8

DISTILLING
  OF ROCK DISTILLING OUR MEMORIES   223 18
  DISTILLING OVER ME   252 21

DISTILS
  ITS SWEETNESS DISTILS AND TRICKLES AWAY INTO   504 21
  STREAMING BACK WHERE THE MIST DISTILS   *906 2

DISTINCT
  HE GROWS DISTINCT AND I SEE HIS HOT   59 7
  LITTLE BUT DISTINCT A WAY OFF   224 15
  HOW AWFULLY DISTINCT AND FAR OFF FROM EACH OTHER'S BEING   248 3
  SINGLE AND PERFECTLY DISTINCT FROM EVERYTHING ELSE   254 25
  THEN WE SHALL BE TWO AND DISTINCT WE SHALL HAVE EACH OUR   266 31
  I SHALL BE CLEARED DISTINCT SINGLE AS IF BURNISHED IN S+   267 18
  DISTINCT FROM CHAOS   514 16
  AND THE COFFEE-PLANT STARTED COFFING THREE VERY DISTINC+   760 27

DISTINCTION
  IT IS IN PURE UNUTTERABLE RESOLVEDNESS DISTINCTION OF B+   267 3
  SANS ANY DISTINCTION AT ALL EXCEPT LOUTISH COMMONNESS   313 3

DISTINCTIVE
  NOR BY ANY DISTINCTIVE GOWN   312 15

DISTINCTLY
  SOLEMNLY AND DISTINCTLY CRIES DOWN THE BABEL OF CHILDREN   48 15
  ME SO DISTINCTLY FROM SLEEPING THE SLEEP I'D LOVE BEST   48 26

DISTINGUISH
  DISTINGUISH   131 5
  I DISTINGUISH THE SCENT OF YOUR HAIR SO NOW THE LIMBER   208 30
  SUCH A WAGGLE OF LOVE YOU CAN HARDLY DISTINGUISH ONE   399 22
  STILL I COULD NOT DISTINGUISH MYSELF   882 14

DISTINGUISHED
  TWO OF US UNUTTERABLY DISTINGUISHED AND IN UNUTTERABLE +   267 22
  NIGHT WERE DISTINGUISHED FROM THE SYMMETRY OF THEIR MIX+   295 6
  AND IF YOU ONLY LOOK SO DISTINGUISHED AND SUPERIOR   548 18

DISTORTED
  DISTORTED EVEN LOST   49 7
  OF DESIRE IS DISTORTED AND TWISTED AWRY   485 3

DISTRACTED
  NOW SUDDENLY DISTRACTED INTO THIS MAZY SIDE-TRACK   363 3

DISTRAUGHT
  THE WILD YOUNG HEIFER GLANCING DISTRAUGHT   64 7
  DISTRAUGHT   *900 11
  DISTRAUGHT   *903 23

DISTRESS
  NEVER A LAMP DISTRESS   261 22
  FLOW THE HEART'S RIVERS OF FULNESS DESIRE AND DISTRESS   607 8
  AND TROUBLE AND DISSOLUTION AND DISTRESS   727 8
  THE WILLOW SHALL LIFT HER LEAVES TO SOOTHE THY DISTRESS   749 24
  SPEAK SOOTHINGLY FOR US TO GOD AND WHEN IN DISTRESS WE   753 4

DISTRESSED
  AND OPEN LIPS DISTRESSED   62 17
  ALL DAY HAS THE CLANK OF IRON ON IRON DISTRESSED   167 13

DISTRESSES
  THE NOISE DISTRESSES HER EARS AND TEARS   54 21

DISTRIBUTED
  AND ITS BEAT OF PAIN IS DISTRIBUTED ON THE WIND   883 7

DISTURB
  DON'T DISTURB IT DARLING   137 14

DISTURBANCE
  BEFORE PETALS SPREAD BEFORE COLOUR MADE ITS DISTURBANCE   285 31

DISTURBED
  LIKE A LINTY RAW-COLD DUST DISTURBED FROM THE FLOOR   99 2
  UNEASILY DISTURBED BY THE STRESS   231 18
  YOUR EYE OF A DARK DISTURBED NIGHT   352 21
  LIKE A HEAVY BIRD DISTURBED AND HER SHOULDERS STIRRED   *934 16
  MY HEART DISTURBED IN ITS DREAM SLOW-STEPPING ALARMS   *937 32

DISTURBING
  UNEASILY IN THEIR SLEEP DISTURBING MY METTLE   128 13
  AND HARDLY DISTURBING WAVERING SHIMMER   860 4

DISTURBS
  SHAKES O'ER HIS WALLS WHEN THE WIND DISTURBS THE NIGHT   878 4

DITCH
  IN MY FINE PROSPERITY KICK THOSE IN THE DITCH   584 7

DITHER
  THE NAKED LIGHTNINGS IN THE HEAVENS DITHER   209 4
  OF THE HILLS AND THE HEARTS WITHIN US DITHER   757 16

DITHERING
  ROUND AND ROUND AND DITHERING WITH TIREDNESS AND HASTE   343 25

DIVE
  ON AND ON AND DIVE BENEATH THE ICEBERGS   694 4

DIVERSELY
  FLOWERS AND SAPPHIRES AND US DIVERSELY STREAMING   476 28

DIVERT
  TO HALT THE HEART DIVERT THE STREAMING FLOW   195 34

DIVES
  BURNING LIKE DIVES IN HELL TO HER   874 20

DIVESTED
  DIVESTED OF COVER   306 9

DIVESTING
  DIVESTING HERSELF OF HER GOLDEN SHIFT AND SO   67 8

DIVIDE
  PATIENTLY TO DIVIDE AND SELF-DIVIDE   64 12
  AND THEY DIVIDE THE WORLD   516 13
  UNLESS MEN SWIFTLY DIVIDE AGAIN AND THE BASE ARE THRUST   637 14

DIVIDED
  DIVIDED INTO PASSIONATE DUALITY   361 5
  NOW THE DIVIDED YEARNING IS OVER   411 6
  DIVIDED IN THE MYSTIC TANGIBLE AND INTANGIBLE DIFFERENCE   636 6

DIVIDERS
  AND THE WATCHERS THE DIVIDERS THOSE SWIFT ONES WITH DAR+   706 17
  THE DIVIDERS ARE CLOSE UPON US DOGGING OUR EVERY BREATH   707 3
  THE DIVIDERS THE THUNDERERS THE SWIFT ONES BLIND WITH S+   707 20

DIVIDING
  DIVIDING EARTH AND HEAVEN   200 7
  THE DARK IS DIVIDING THE SUN IS COMING PAST THE WALL   803 12

DIVINE
  FOR DIVINE EXCESSES   96 10
  THE BOURGEOIS ASSERTS THAT HE OWNS HIS PROPERTY BY DIVI+   663 13
  THE MYSTERY OF CREATION IS THE DIVINE URGE OF CREATION   690 1

DIVINELY
  THE RIM OF THE MOON DIVINELY RISE   103 25
  RUNS A RAGE DRAWN IN FROM THE ETHER DIVINELY THROUGH HIM   381 21

DIVISIBLE
  FINELY DIVISIBLE   269 12

DIVISION
  THE LONE CLEAVAGE OF DIVISION UPRIGHT OF THE ETERNAL CR+   355 30
  WITH THE UPRIGHT DIVISION INTO SEX   636 2
  WITHOUT ANY DIVISION INTO INFERIORITY AND SUPERIORITY   636 4
  THE HORIZONTAL DIVISION OF MANKIND   636 8
  ON THIS CROSS OF DIVISION DIVISION INTO SEX   636 13
  DIVISION INTO SLAVE AND FREEMAN   636 14
  THAT SEX IS AN ETERNAL UPRIGHT DIVISION BEFORE WHICH WE   636 25
  OF THE HORIZONTAL DIVISION OF MANKIND   637 2
  THE ETERNAL DIVISION BETWEEN THE BASE AND THE BEAUTIFUL   637 3
  IN THE SUSPENSION OF WHOLENESS IN THE MOMENT OF DIVISIO+   699 7

DIZZY
  BACK ON A STRANGE PARABOLA THEN ROUND ROUND DIZZY IN   344 13

DMITRIS
  AND THE ALYOSHAS AND DMITRIS AND MYSHKINS AND STAVROGINS   533 14

DOCILE
  AND MY DOCILE FLUENT ARMS   *893 23

DOCTOR
  WHEN I WENT TO THE SCIENTIFIC DOCTOR   620 5

DOCTORS
  NURSES DOCTORS PROPER FOOD HYGIENE SCHOOLS ALL THAT   832 5

DODGED
  WE DODGED WHEN THE PERA-HERA WAS FINISHED UNDER THE   390 11

DODGES
  THOUGHT IS NOT A TRICK OR AN EXERCISE OR A SET OF DODGES   673 14

DODGING
  MYSELF SO LITTLE DODGING RATHER SCARED AGAINST THE ETER+   390 16
  COME SATAN DON'T GO DODGING BEHIND MY BACK ANY LONGER   483 19
  BUT I'M NOT HAVING ANY DODGING GOING ON BEHIND MY   483 23
  DODGING BEHIND IN DISGRACE   731 12

DODO
  I EXPECT THE DODO LOOKED LIKE A CLOD   523 28

DOE
  A DOE SPRANG OUT OF THE CORN   222 2

DOESNA
  THA DOESNA MEAN TER SAY TER ME MOTHER   77 1
  'ER DOESNA WANT NO WEDDIN'-DRESS   79 21
  EH MEN DOESNA HA'E BOSOMS 'APPEN NOT ON'Y THA KNOWS   540 16
  THA DOESNA MEAN TO SAY TO ME MOTHER   *918 19
  BUT THA DOESNA STARE ME OUT I GUESS   *921 8
  'ER DOESNA WANT NO WEDDIN'-DRESS   *921 17

DOFF
  BY-PATHS WHERE THE WANTON-HEADED FLOWERS DOFF THEIR HOOD   65 30

DOG
  WHITE ON THE WATER WIMPLES MY SHADOW STRAINS LIKE A DOG+   33 25
  HOW IT LOOKS BACK LIKE A WHITE DOG TO ITS MASTER   34 1
  AND THE WHITE DOG DANCES AND QUIVERS I AM HOLDING HIS C+   34 5
  AND THE WHITE DOG SNUFFS THE WARMTH APPEALING   41 10
  LIKE A CRINGING DOG AT HIS HEELS OFFEND HIM NOW   47 22
  A DESCRIPTION OF A DOG OR IF THEY CAN'T   74 28
  RUNNING BESIDE HER LIKE A DOG BITING HER EARTHY SPLAY   360 8
  LIKE A DOG   362 24

DOG
DOG AND I 375 9
ONCE THEY SAY HE WAS PASSING BY WHEN A DOG WAS BEING BE+ 376 5
NO LEOPARD SCREECHED NO LION COUGHED NO DOG BARKED 394 17
LITTLE BLACK DOG IN NEW MEXICO 394 28
BUBSEY RAT-EARED DOG 395 5
THINKING THIS DOG SURE HAS TAKEN A FANCY TO ME 398 20
AND I'M A PALE-FACE LIKE A HOMELESS DOG 404 27
THEN YOU'RE A LOST WHITE DOG OF A PALE-FACE 404 29
AND AS THE DOG WITH ITS NOSTRILS TRACKING OUT THE FRAGM+ 406 1
OR A DOG WITH A HARROWING FLEA 489 24
HE DID HIS BEST THE GOOD OLD DOG 492 7
TO THE CAMEL AND THE DOG 492 20
HE DOESN'T BARK AT HIMSELF LIKE A DOG DOES 528 23
BUT ONCE AND FOREVER BARKS THE OLD DOG 580 13
THEN GRADUALLY I APPROXIMATE TO THE DOG 645 3
WRIGGLE AND WAG AND SLAVER AND GET THE MENTALITY OF A D+ 645 4
AND I HAD BETTER EVEN HAVE APPROXIMATED TO THE DOG 645 9
AND DIE LIKE A DOG IN A HOLE 'TIS STRANGE WHAT A SHODDY 755 8
A FALLING STAR WAS RUNNING LIKE A WHITE DOG OVER A PLAIN 791 9
LIKE A GREY DOG WHOSE MOUTH IS FOUL WITH RABIES 807 5
THEN I TAKE MY KNIFE AND THROW IT UPON THE GREY DOG 807 20
THE HOUSE OF THE GREY DOG 807 22
MAYBE THEY KENNEL THE GREY DOG 807 27
THE GREY DOG CREEPS AMONG YOU 807 29
THE GREY DOG IS CHEWING YOUR ENTRAILS 807 31
THE GREY DOG CAUGHT ME AT THE CROSS-ROADS 808 2
THE GREY DOG LEAPT AT MY ENTRAILS 808 5
YOU TRACK THE GREY DOG HOME 808 10
BUT THE GREY DOG BELONGS TO THE ASH OF THE WORLD 808 20
HE DOESN'T BARK AT HIMSELF AS A DOG DOES 836 11
THE WHITE DOG NIPPED THE MOTHER RAT THE FATHER RAT BESI+ *933 7
AND THE BROWN DOG SETTLED THE REST *933 8
HE DOESN'T BARK AT IT LIKE A DOG DOES *950 26

DOGES
WHOSE DOGES WERE OLD AND HAD ANCIENT EYES 278 11

DOG-FISH
PROFITEERS HERE BEING CALLED DOG-FISH STINKING DOG-FISH+ 316 25
THESE DOG-FISH 316 33

DOGGED
THAT'S WHY THE DOGGED RESISTANT OLD ONES DARE NOT DIE 662 26

DOGGIE
THAT MILDEWED PUP GOOD DOGGIE 491 26

DOGGING
THE DIVIDERS ARE CLOSE UPON US DOGGING OUR EVERY BREATH 707 3

DOGS
THE DOGS DO BARK 312 5
THE DOGS DO BARK 312 26
THE DOGS DO BARK 313 17
AS FOXES STOATS AND WOLVES AND PRAIRIE DOGS 392 21
OUT AND THE DOGS ARE AFTER YOU 400 5
SO NOW WHAT WITH GREAT AIREDALE DOGS 400 20
THE DOGS OF THE DARK PUEBLO 405 13
AND DOGS JUMPED THROUGH HOOPS AND TURNED SOMERSAULTS 444 18
O THE STALE OLD DOGS WHO PRETEND TO GUARD 493 25
OF THE YELLOW DOGS HOW THEY SLINK AWAY 494 7
SUPPOSING I SAY DOGS ARE MY NEIGHBOURS 645 1
I WILL LOVE DOGS AS MYSELF 645 2
BUT MUST ROAM LIKE OUTCAST DOGS ON THE MARGINS OF LIFE 722 11
HOW IT DOGS ME WHAT A GALLING SHADOW 741 2
THE DIRTY DOGS OF WISDOM 762 21
AND THEN RUN LIKE SURLY DOGS AT THE BIDDING OF PALEFACE+ 795 4
OH DOGS AND FOOLS MEXICANS AND PEONS 795 5
BEING DEAD YOU SHALL ROVE LIKE DOGS WITH THE BROKEN HAU+ 796 5
CRAWL LIKE MASTERLESS DOGS IN THE BACK STREETS OF THE A+ 796 12
AND EVEN THEN THEY SHALL SPIT YOU OUT AS BROKEN-HAUNCHE+ 796 27
IN THE DREAM OF THE NIGHT I SEE THE GREY DOGS PROWLING 807 2
IN THE NIGHT I SEE THE GREY DOGS CREEPING OUT OF THE SL+ 807 11
BUT WHOSE DREAMS ARE DOGS GREY DOGS WITH YELLOW MOUTHS 807 15
I SEE THE GREY DOGS CREEPING OUT WHERE MY DEER ARE BROW+ 807 18
YOU KNOW NOT HOW MANY ARE HOUSES OF GREY DOGS 807 25
WHERE DOGS CREEP UNCLEAN 808 16
DEAD ARE THE GREY DOGS 808 22
BUT THE GREY DOGS ARE AMONG THE ASHES 809 2
BUT MUST ROAM LIKE OUTCAST DOGS ON THE MARGINS OF LIFE *958 16

DOG-STAR
TO THE GREEN NIGHT-BAYING OF THE DOG-STAR ETNA'S SNOW-E+ 306 11
WITH ALL THE SNOW-WIND AND THE SUN-GLARE AND THE DOG-ST+ 306 18

DOG'S
THE OLD DOG'S GREENEST BONES 492 12

DOING
WHAT ARE YOU DOING IN THE DECEMBER RAIN 301 1
WHAT ARE THEY DOING HERE ON THIS VANISHING TRAIL 401 14
HE SMILES FOOLISHLY AS IF HE WERE CAUGHT DOING WRONG 401 20
AND WE FEEL IS WORTH DOING 520 8
AND NEVER KNOWING WHAT WE ARE DOING ROARING BLIND WITH 544 18
DOING ONE'S OWN LITTLE JOBS SEEING THE WORLD BEYOND 610 5
AND DOING WHICH DOES NOT 711 30
ON YOUR HONOUR AMERICANS WHAT ARE YOU DOING 777 16
ONLY KNOW THAT DOING IT YOU FAIL IN POINT OF HONOUR 780 20
THEY DON'T EVEN MIND DOING THINGS FOR YOU IN REASON 828 24
ROARING AND DOING DAMAGE 833 21
SIEGMUND DEAR WHAT ARE YOU DOING LYING WITH YOUR FACE O+ 871 33

DOIN'
THA'RT FOR DOIN' A LOT WI' T' LAD 82 8
THA'RT FOR DOIN' A LOT WI' TH' LAD *924 12

DOLE
WELL LET HIM GET ON THE DOLE 545 2
DOLE DOLE DOLE 545 3
ON THE DOLE DOLE DOLE 545 8
SO THE DOLE DOLE DOLE'S 545 16
AND ON THE DOLE DOLE DOLE 545 18
YOUR WAGE IS THE DOLE OF WORK AND THE DOLE IS YOUR 630 20

DOLE'S
SO THE DOLE DOLE DOLE'S 545 16

DOLLARS
NOT IN DOLLARS NOR IN BANKS NOR IN SYNDICATES 774 29

DOLLOP
AND THEN TURN TAIL TO THE NEXT COMER FOR A NEW DOLLOP 396 23

DOLOROUS
FROM EACH OTHER OR LOSING THE DOLOROUS 116 19

DOLPHINS
BREAKS INTO DAZZLE OF LIVING AS DOLPHINS LEAP FROM THE + 136 19
WITH GRAPE-VINES UP THE MAST AND DOLPHINS LEAPING 688 5
THE DOLPHINS LEAP ROUND DIONYSOS' SHIP 693 25

DOLPHIN'S
OH AND THEIR FACES SCARLET LIKE THE DOLPHIN'S BLOOD 689 5

DOME
HEAVING AND PILING A ROUND WHITE DOME 50 5
FROM THE FULL RESOURCE OF SOME PURPLE DOME 50 10
AS A PIGEON LETS ITSELF OFF FROM A CATHEDRAL DOME 134 21
MY TENACIOUS FEET FROM OFF THE DOME OF THE EARTH 134 25
FOREST OF PILLARS THAT HOLD UP THE DOME OF HIGH IDEAL 287 28
TOES AND THE DOME OF HIS HOUSE IS HIS HEAVEN THEREFORE + 348 15
UNDER ALL THE ETERNAL DOME OF MATHEMATICAL LAW 355 22
THIS LITTLE DOME THIS PEDIMENT 356 16

DOMED
WHERE THE GLASS IS DOMED ON THE SILENT AIR 52 19
THEIR TWO SHELLS LIKE DOMED BOATS BUMPING 361 22
WHERE THE GLASS IS DOMED BY THE BLUE SOFT DAY *905 8

DOMESTICATED
BUT BAH HOW CAN HE POOR DOMESTICATED BEAST 383 26

DOMESTICITY
A LITTLE SARDONIC-LOOKING AS IF DOMESTICITY HAD DRIVEN + 358 24
THE GREAT CAGE OF OUR DOMESTICITY 485 1

DOMINANT
THE GREAT AND DOMINANT HUNGER OF THE MIND 263 24
DOMINANT WOMEN ARE AS A RULE SO SUBTLY AND FIENDISHLY D+ 619 24

DOMINATED
IT IS A FEARFUL THING TO BE DOMINATED BY THE FEAR OF HU+ 263 7

DOMINEERING
DOMINANT WOMEN ARE AS A RULE SO SUBTLY AND FIENDISHLY D+ 619 24
BUT IF YOU CANNOT KEEP POLITICAL DOMINEERING HANDS 780 14

DONA CARLOTA
DONA CARLOTA WISHED HE WOULD 797 14

DONE
WHERE ARE YOU WHAT HAVE YOU DONE 55 21
LIZZIE WHAT'S DONE IS DONE 79 30
DONE I SHOULD THINK SO AN' MIGHT I ASK 79 31
IT'S THEE AS 'AS DONE IT AS MUCH AS ME 80 1
I WISH THA HADNA DONE IT TIM 82 21
LET'S A' HA' DONE 84 26
THA COME TER HA' FINISHED AN' DONE WI' ME 138 10
WITH WET FLAT LIGHTS WHAT I'VE DONE 143 23
NOW IT IS DONE THE MORT 154 16
HE HAS DONE AS I HAVE DONE 199 5
I HAVE DONE A QUIVER OF EXULTATION GOES THROUGH ME LIKE 209 26
WE HAVE DONE WRONG 232 9
IS BROKEN AT LAST AND DONE 253 16
TO SINK AND HAVE DONE 253 30
IT WAS ALL ME I HAD DONE IT ALL IN MY OWN FLESH 257 9
I SHALL BE MAD WITH DELIGHT BEFORE I HAVE DONE 260 21
PLUNGING AS I HAVE DONE OVER OVER THE BRINK 266 1
HAVE DONE HAVE DONE WITH THIS SHUDDERING DELICIOUS BUSI+ 273 18
WRINKLED UNDERHUNG PHYSIOG THAT LOOKS AS IF IT HAD DONE 398 6
OUR DAY IS DONE 425 5
DONE YOUR OWN LITTLE BIT MADE YOUR OWN LITTLE TRY 459 19
THE ONLY THING TO BE DONE NOW 513 21
LET'S ABOLISH LABOUR LET'S HAVE DONE WITH LABOURING 517 19
BUT IT MUST BE FREE WORK NOT DONE JUST FOR MONEY BUT FOR 520 20
DONE AND SLIGHTLY SUBTLE 532 18
SO LONG AS THE THING IS DONE NEATLY AND THE WORLD IS LE+ 532 30
AND THAT'S WHAT WE'VE DONE TODAY 543 18
I TELL YOU SOMETHING'S BEEN DONE TO 'EM 550 13
AND THE DUCHESS HAS DONE WITH ME 552 2
IF THERE'S ANYTHING GOT TO BE DONE WHY 553 21
ONCE AND FOR ALL HAVE DONE WITH IT 556 17
THEY'VE DONE YOU BROWN 556 28
BEFORE YOU'VE DONE 560 28
AND NOW LOOK HERE WHAT YOU'VE GONE AND DONE 583 5
WHAT HAVE THEY DONE TO YOU MEN OF THE MASSES 585 9
WHAT HAVE THEY DONE TO YOU THE SAVIOURS OF THE PEOPLE 585 11
AND ONCE DONE THERE IS NO REMEDY NO SALVATION FOR THIS 621 10
WHAT HAVE THEY DONE TO YOU WHITE-FACED MILLIONS 628 22
WHAT HAVE THEY DONE TO YOU WHAT HAVE THEY DONE TO YOU 628 24
WHAT HAVE THEY DONE TO YOU MEN OF THE MASSES CREEPING 630 9
WHAT HAVE THEY DONE TO YOU THE SAVIOURS OF THE PEOPLE OH 630 11
WHAT HAVE THEY DONE TO YOU WHAT HAVE THEY DONE TO YOU 631 5
OH WHAT HAVE THEY DONE TO YOU 631 6

DONE
THE MASSES OH WHAT HAS BEEN DONE TO THEM   631   8
I DON'T KNOW WHAT THEY'VE DONE POOR THINGS BUT JUSTICE +   632 30
FOR THE THING THAT IS DONE WITHOUT THE GLOWING AS OF GOD   689 10
WERE BEST NOT DONE AT ALL   689 12
WE KNOW IT COULDN'T BE DONE   690 32
LORD WHAT WE HAVE DONE WE HEREBY EXPIATE   743   6
BE NEAR US AND GOD'S WILL BE DONE   753   7
WE ARE SO LET US HAVE DONE AH MASTER WE WAIT   757 18
TO LET US HAVE DONE FOR TODAY WE ARE   759   7
AS THE OKLAHOMA INDIANS HAVE DONE   778 28
CRYING HUITZILOPOCHTLI IS THIS WELL DONE   808 14
AND NOTHING IS DONE   825 26
AND HAVE STILL NOT DONE   825 33
AS THOU ART SHOWN AND HAVING DONE SO MUCH   872   8
TO OPEN ERE THE THIEF HAVE DONE HIS WORK   878 29
LIZZIE WHAT'S DONE IS DONE   *921 26
DONE I SHOULD THINK SO DONE BUT MIGHT   *921 27
IT'S THEE AS 'AS DONE IT AS MUCH AS ME   *922   1
I WISH THA HADNA DONE IT TIM   *924 25

DON JUAN
RATHER PROUD OF BEING A BIT OF A DON JUAN   446 24
OH COME SAID I THAT DON JUAN OF A RONALD   447   1
EXACTLY SHE SAID DON JUAN WAS ANOTHER OF THEM IN LOVE   447   2
SO HE CLEVERLY PLAYS THE NORMAL THE DON JUAN   *948 25
THE DIRTY LITTLE DON JUAN   *949 10
DON JUAN IF YOU ASK ME   *949 16
DON JUAN WAS NEVER ANYTHING BUT A SELF-THWARTED SODOMIST   *949 17

DONKEY
NOW HE'S A JACKASS A PACK-ASS A DONKEY SOMARO BURRO   379   9
STRAIGHTENS HIS DONKEY NECK   379 22

DONKEYS
EVEN THE ABSENCE OF DARK-CROSSED DONKEYS   404   2

DON RAMON
DON RAMON DON'T DRINK DON'T SMOKE   797 13

DOOL-OWLS
SUCH BLOOMIN' FAT-ARSED DOOL-OWLS   553   7

DOOM
TO LIVE ALONE IS MY DOOM   106 22
TO ALTER MY ONE SPECK OF DOOM WHEN ROUND ME BURNS   195 25
TAKE ON THIS DOOM   235   2
ON YOUR DOOM   239 24
THE FULL DOOM OF LOVING AND NOT BEING ABLE TO TAKE BACK   410 16
OH OVER THE FACTORY CITIES THERE SEEMS TO HOVER A DOOM   586 13
THEIR DOOM AT THE HANDS OF MR MEADE   634   2
IT IS THEIR HEAVEN AND THEIR DOOM   643   7
AND DREAD AND THE DARK ROLLING OMINOUSNESS OF DOOM   708 25
FOR DOOM THAT DARKENS AND THE SUNDERERS   709 15
PREPARE FOR DOOM   795 16
IS DOOM   810 14

DOOMED
AM I DOOMED IN A LONG COITION OF WORDS TO MATE YOU   119   4
DOOMED IN THE LONG CRUCIFIXION OF DESIRE TO SEEK HIS CO+ 361   3
DOOMED TO MAKE AN INTOLERABLE FOOL OF HIMSELF   361   8
GRIM GRUESOME GALLANTRY TO WHICH HE IS DOOMED   362 26
AND DOOMED TO PARTIALITY PARTIAL BEING   362 28

DOOR
WATCHING THE DOOR OPEN HE FLASHES BARE   43 19
SOMEBODY'S KNOCKIN' AT TH' DOOR   44 10
NEVER HAVE I SAID TO MYSELF AS HE CLOSED THE DOOR   47 31
THE LIGHT HAS GONE OUT FROM UNDER MY MOTHER'S DOOR   63 12
WILL ENTER AND SHUT THE DOOR TO STAY   91   9
ANGRY AT THE SIMPLEST DOOR   95 13
HOLLOW RANG THE HOUSE WHEN I KNOCKED AT THE DOOR   121 13
RUN TO THE SILENT DOOR WHERE LAST   122   4
SHE CLUNG TO THE DOOR IN HER HASTE TO ENTER   122   6
MY HANDS SHOULD TOUCH THE DOOR   147   7
WHAT IF I SUDDENLY STUMBLE AND PUSH THE DOOR   147   8
WHAT IF UNWITTING I SET THE DOOR OF ETERNITY WIDE   147 11
WILL SET A GUARD OF HONOUR AT EACH DOOR   153 21
YOU INTEGRAL TO ME EACH DOOR EACH MYSTIC PORT   154 13
AS SHE LISTENED IN SILENCE OUTSIDE THE SILENT DOOR   155 16
TO THE VERY DOOR   167 22
TO THE VERY DOOR   168 28
CAN I GO NO NEARER NEVER TOWARDS THE DOOR   173   5
IN A LITTLE THRONG AT YOUR DOOR AND ADMIT THE ONE WHO IS 179   6
AT THE OPEN DOOR OF THE ROOM I STAND AND LOOK AT THE NI+ 179 20
AH THROUGH THE OPEN DOOR   244   1
OUTSIDE THE DOOR   245   4
HAS FOR ME A DOOR INTO PEACE WARM DAWN IN THE EAST   250   6
WHAT IS THE KNOCKING AT THE DOOR IN THE NIGHT   250 29
ANY MORE THAN I COULD ENTER THE WHITE-HOT DOOR OF A BLA+ 344 18
FROM OUT THE DARK DOOR OF THE SECRET EARTH   350 22
LIKE SOME IRON DOOR   352 11
THEY LIFT THE LITTLE DOOR   380 22
AND THE LIVE LITTLE-ONE TAKING IN ITS PAW AT THE DOOR O+ 394 23
AND IN THE MORNING WHEN THE BEDROOM DOOR IS OPENED   397   1
LET THE MEREST SCALLYWAG COME TO THE DOOR AND YOU LEAP 398 15
AND LEFT ME HOMELESS HERE IN THE DARK AT YOUR DOOR   404 17
THERE IS NO WAY OUT THE CAGE HAS NO DOOR IT'S RUSTED   486   1
AND BLOCKS UP THE DOOR   515   9
DARE NOT DIE THEY DAREN'T GO THROUGH THE DOOR   662 27
HAS COME LIKE A THREAD LIKE A DOOR JUST OPENING   702 14
THEN WHEN THE DOOR IS HALF OPEN   702 18
THE DOOR EVEN WHEN IT OPENS   721 10
THE WIND THE RASCAL KNOCKED AT MY DOOR AND I SAID   731 13
AT THE DOOR OF THE GASTHAUS DOWN THE ROAD GREAT   732 21
THOU DOOR INTO HEAVEN SISTER   753 13
AS HE SLOWLY WALKS FROM THE WESTERN DOOR TO THE WORLD 770 14
SOME ONE WILL KNOCK WHEN THE DOOR IS SHUT   789   5

DOOR
MALINTZI OF THE GREEN DRESS WILL OPEN THE DOOR   809 10
WHEN SOFTLY I CALL AT HER DOOR AND ENTER THE ROOM   868 25
OR SOFTLY TAPPING AT MY STUDY DOOR   875 10
WHEN SOFTLY I CALL AT HER DOOR AND ENTER THE ROOM   *941 25
DOOR ON THE LATCH AND SHUT MYSELF IN SHUT OUT FEAR   *945 29
AND THE DOOR IS OPEN   *955   5
SO THAT WHEN THE HOUR COMES AND THE LAST DOOR CLOSES BE+ *958 24

DOOR-KNOBS
DISASTROUSLY REMINISCENT OF HAMMERS AND FILES AND DOOR-+ 835 6

DOORS
THOU SHALT SHUT DOORS ON ME   44   9
WE HAVE SHUT THE DOORS BEHIND US AND THE VELVET FLOWERS+ 70 1
AND FLING MYSELF AT THE DOORS OF SLEEP FOR REST   129 22
THROUGH THE RED DOORS BEYOND THE BLACK-PURPLE BAR   134   3
THROUGH THE RED DOORS WHERE I COULD PUT OFF   134   5
AND CLIMB THE STAIRS TO FIND THE GROUP OF DOORS   140   9
BEHIND SEPARATE DOORS   229   4
WHO SMEARED THEIR DOORS WITH BLOOD   313 19
IF WE DO NOT RAPIDLY OPEN ALL THE DOORS OF CONSCIOUSNESS 515 3
IN THE SILENCE OF PASSING THROUGH DOORS   699   5
WITH HIS KEY TO THE TWO DARK DOORS   710 26
AND THERE ARE THE BRIGHT DOORS WHERE SOULS GO GAILY IN 711 3
AND THERE ARE THE DARK DOORS WHERE SOULS PASS SILENTLY 711 4
THERE IS A DOUBLE SACREDNESS OF DOORS   711   7
BUT OTHERS THE DARK DOORS OH HUSH HUSH   711   9
TO THE SCARLET AND PURPLE FLOWERS AT THE DOORS OF HELL 711 20
MUST WE OPEN THE DOORS AND ADMIT THEM RECEIVE THEM HOME 740 13
TOWARDS THE SILENT DOORS OF THE WEST   769 31
THE DOORS OF THE WEST   770 10
HELD A MEETING BEHIND CLOSED DOORS   777 27
BEHIND CLOSED DOORS   778 32
AND WHEN THE DOORS WERE OPENED   778 33
YE EVERLASTING DOORS   818   7
OF YOUR EYES DRAWS OPEN MY SHELTERING FLIMSY DOORS   875 13
FOR YOU SET WIDE THE DOORS OF MY VENTURESOME ARK   875 23
WE HAVE SHUT THE DOORS BEHIND US AND THE VELVET FLOWERS+ *916 9
THE DOORS   *918   6

DOORSTEP
PEACE IS WRITTEN ON THE DOORSTEP   293 13
PEACE CONGEALED IN BLACK LAVA ON THE DOORSTEP   294   1

DOORWAY
THE REST HAD DOORWAY TO THEE THROUGH THAT SPARK   69 21
SOME FEW DARK-CLEAVING THE DOORWAY SOULS THAT CLING AS + 75 10
YOU WERE A DOORWAY TO ME   101 18
CROWDING THE BRIGHT DOORWAY   201 26
DEATH IS NO ESCAPE AH NO ONLY A DOORWAY TO THE INEVITAB+ 662 25
OPENING TILL THE ROUND WHITE DOORWAY OF DELIGHT   702 15
WHEN I STAND IN THE DOORWAY SHAMEFULLY   735 28
HE MADE HAD DOORWAY TO THEE THROUGH THAT SPARK   *916   4
IN THE DARK DOORWAY   *955   8

DOORWAYS
ALWAYS KNEEL IN COURTSHIP TO THE SHELVES IN THE DOORWAY+ 180 26
STREAMING FORTH FROM LITTLE DOORWAYS   484   2
SHE LINGERS IN THE DOORWAYS   756 10

DORA
DORA   53   4
OF THE AFTERNOON GLOWS ONLY THE OLD ROMANCE OF DAVID AN+ *905 18

DOSE
NOR A DOSE OF CAPSICUM ESSENCE GIVING AN ORGASM   837   9

DOSES
DOSES OF SMART CASH-CHEMISTRY   488 25

DOST
WHY BUT WHAT DOST MEAN   79 22
HOW MANY DAYS DOST THINK HAS GONE   138   1
HOW MANY DAYS DOST THINK HAS GONE   138   3
DOST WANT ME TER WANT THEE AGAIN NAY THOUGH   138 17
DOST THA HEAR MY HORSE'S FEET AS HE CANTERS AWAY   664   1
HOW THOU DOST POKE UP AMONG THE SPOKES OF MY   760   4
ME WATCHIN' DOST THINK THERE WAS OWT BETWEEN 'EM *910 23
WHAT BUT WHAT DOST MEAN   *921 18

DOSTOEVSKY
THE DOSTOEVSKY LOT   533 15
AND THE DOSTOEVSKY LOT WALLOWED IN THE THOUGHT   533 26
OF DOSTOEVSKY AND TCHEKOV   536 16
DOSTOEVSKY THE JUDAS   537   1

DOSTOIEVSKY
NO A LONG SEASON I HAVE BEEN WITH DOSTOIEVSKY IN THE DA+ 866 27

DOT
UNDER AN OAK WHOSE YELLOW BUDS DOT THE PALE BLUE SKY 152 27
OR THEY THINK YOU'RE OFF YOUR DOT   549 30

DOTE
FOR I DOTE ON THEM WITH TENDERNESS AND I HATE THEM 741 19

DOTTED
UNDER AN OAK TREE WHOSE YELLOW BUDS DOTTED THE PALE BLU+ 866 23

DOUBLE
OVER A DOUBLE 'ANDFUL O' VIOLETS A' IN A PACK   61 11
CHANGE FROM BEING SINGLE AND BECOME GRADUALLY DOUBLE 534 26
THEY ARE ALL DOUBLE ROSES   535 11
NOT EVEN THE DOUBLE PHALLUS OF THE DEVIL HIMSELF   710 25
THERE IS A DOUBLE SACREDNESS OF DOORS   711   7
SHE LAYS AN EGG HE BRISTLES LIKE A DOUBLE WHITE POPPY A+ 761 19
OVER A DOUBLE 'ANDFUL OF VIOLETS ALL IN A PACK   *911 27

DOUBLED
    THEN DOUBLED AND BACK WITH A FUNNY UP-FLUTTER OF WINGS   444 21
    OF LIVING MY LIFE WERE DOUBLED I STILL HAVE THIS TO COM+ *900 3
    OF LIVING MY LIFE WERE DOUBLED I STILL HAVE THIS TO COM+ *903 16

DOUBT
    THEY'LL TURN THEE OUT O' TH' FORCE I DOUBT ME IF THEY D+   83 16
    AND DOUBT ENTERS IN DREARNESS   94 24
    WITH A FLUTTER OF HOPE AND A QUENCHING DOUBT   121 26
    THE SLEEP NO DREAM NOR DOUBT CAN UNDERMINE   129 26
    NO DOUBT   .   199 6
    MY DEAR THE NIGHT IS SOFT AND ETERNAL NO DOUBT   211 11
    NO DOUBT IF I WERE DEAD YOU MUST   236 1
    NO DOUBT YOU HAVE FORGOTTEN THE POMEGRANATE-TREES IN   278 6
    STILL NO DOUBT EVERY ONE OF YOU CAN BE THE SUN-SOCKET AS 300 12
    HE WAS ONE OF NATURE'S PHENOMENA NO DOUBT   328 18
    I DOUBT IF ANY MAN LIVING HANDS OUT A POUND NOTE WITHOUT 486 11
    IS THEIR MONEY BUT I DOUBT IF I'D FIGHT FOR MINE ANYHOW 497 20
    NO DOUBT HE WAS KHAKI-COLOURED WITH MUDDY PROTECTIVE   523 18
    NO DOUBT TO THE SOUNDING OF THE SPHERES   524 14
    CAUGHT BETWEEN GREAT ICEBERGS OF DOUBT   542 18
    WE'LL SHOW 'EM A THING OR TWO NEVER YOU DOUBT   573 22
    WITH YOUR GLOOM AND YOUR DOUBT THAT YOU LOVE ME   *944 26

DOUBTFUL
    NO SAND IN MY DOUBTFUL SUGAR   236 30
    IN A DOUBTFUL WORLD   317 24
    STRUGGLING IN DOUBTFUL EMBRACES   457 15

DOUR
    BEGGED ME TO ASK NOT FOR THE DOUR   104 2
    TO CONSCIOUSNESS YOU GAVE ME THE DOUR   111 16
    CALLOUS AND DOUR   145 11
    SHRIVELLING DOWN IN THE FINAL DOUR   *927 9
    SHRIVELLING DOWN IN THE FINAL DOUR   *928 9

DOVE
    YOU WITH YOUR FACE ALL RICH LIKE THE SHEEN ON A DOVE   90 18
    TO THE CUCKOO THAT HUNG LIKE A DOVE   124 4
    YOU'RE A DOVE I HAVE BOUGHT FOR SACRIFICE   238 17
    SHE'S A SILVERY DOVE WORTH MORE THAN ALL I'VE GOT   238 22
    LOOK SHE'S A WONDERFUL DOVE WITHOUT BLEMISH OR SPOT   239 1
    HIGH OVER THE MILD EFFULGENCE OF THE DOVE   328 7
    JESUS' PALE AND LAMBENT DOVE COOING IN THE LOWER BOUGHS 329 8
    THE EAGLE THE DOVE AND THE BARNYARD ROOSTER DO THEY CALL 371 22
    THE DOVE OF LIBERTY SAT ON AN EGG   413 1
    DOWN WITH ALL EAGLES COOED THE DOVE   413 4
    WHETHER YOU'RE A SUCKING DOVE ROO COO OOO QUARK   414 6

DOVE OF THE SPIRIT
    UTTERLY BEYOND THEE DOVE OF THE SPIRIT   322 5

DOVES
    A FLUTTERING IN OF DOVES   179 12
    THEN A LAUNCH ABROAD OF SHRINKING DOVES   179 13
    OF DOVES FOR VENUS OR STEERS FOR HERMES   678 5
    VENUS WOULD RATHER HAVE LIVE DOVES THAN DEAD IF YOU WAN+ 678 7
    IF YOU WANT TO MAKE HER AN OFFERING LET THE DOVES FLY F+ 678 9
    EVEN DOVES EVEN SMALL BIRDS   679 16
    AND YOU OH SEE THE MYRIAD DOVES THAT WALK   750 21
    AND FOUND GREY DOVES IN THE FOUNTAIN COURT   751 2
    AND ALL MY DOVES ARE LAUNCHED ABROAD AND LOST   875 24

DOWNARD
    DRAWS TOWARDS THE DOWNARD SLOPE SOME SORROW HATH   131 25

DOWN-BURIED
    WITH MY FACE DOWN-BURIED BETWEEN HER BREASTS   *946 8

DOWNCAST
    SO WITH A DOWNCAST MIEN AND LAUGHING VOICE   123 1
    MY EYES BEING DOWNCAST   880 17
    SO WITH A DOWNCAST MIEN AND LAUGHING VOICE   *934 7

DOWN-CURVED
    LIKE A DOWN-CURVED SWORD OF DAMOCLES   782 7

DOWN-DREAMING
    LIKE A WILD DAFFODIL DOWN-DREAMING   91 19

DOWNFALL
    HENCE HIS PONDEROUS HEAD BROODING OVER DESIRE AND DOWNF+ 378 22

DOWNS
    MIDST OF THE DOWNS   70 23
    DEADENED ME THROUGH TILL THE GREY DOWNS DULLED TO SLEEP 90 22
    BETWEEN THE DOWNS GROWS HAZY WITH SUNSHINE   886 27
    THE DOWNS   *917 20

DOWNSTAIRS
    WHEN I CARRIED MY MOTHER DOWNSTAIRS   106 28
    UPSTAIRS DOWNSTAIRS   669 14

DOWN-URGE
    THE DOWN-URGE   393 2

DOWNWARD
    OH EARTH YOU ROTTEN APPLE ROLLING DOWNWARD   73 3
    DOWNWARD TRACK   322 13
    THEY THREAD AND THRILL AND FLICKER EVER DOWNWARD   322 18
    FOR WHEN FIRE IN ITS DOWNWARD PATH CHANCED TO MINGLE WI+ 348 14
    AND DARK CLEAVES DOWN AND WEAPON-HARD DOWNWARD   373 28
    THE DOWNWARD DRIP   393 1
    DOWNWARD THEY RACE IN DECLINE   455 28
    HAVE YOU TRAVELLED YOUR DOWNWARD ARC   764 26
    THE SUN HAS CLIMBED THE HILL THE DAY IS ON THE DOWNWARD+ 803 5
    DRAWS TOWARDS THE DOWNWARD SLOPE SOME SICKNESS HATH *937 24

DOWNWARD-DROPPING
    IN THE DOWNWARD-DROPPING OF FLIMSY SHEAVES   68 19

DOWNWARDS
    REACHING DOWNWARDS   74 4
    IN A GREAT CHUTE AND RUSH OF DEBACLE DOWNWARDS   287 21
    FACE DOWNWARDS   321 33
    DOWNWARDS EBBING DOWNWARDS EBBING DOWNWARDS TO THE   428 8
    WHEN AT A CERTAIN POINT A DROP OF WATER BEGAN TO DRIP D+ 682 13
    DOWNWARDS EXHAUSTIVE   701 24
    THE DARK CLEAVES DOWN AND WEAPON-HARD DOWNWARDS CURVING 782 4
    GRASS FEELS DOWNWARDS WITH HIS ROOTS   806 3
    REACHING DOWNWARDS   *913 25

DOWN-WARD
    IN THE DOWN-WARD DROOPING FLIMSY SHEAVES   *915 3

DOWSE
    TO BE BLOWN OUT TO LET NIGHT DOWSE THE SPARK   212 9

DOZENS
    THE WHIRLIGIG OF DOZENS AND THE PINNACLE OF SEVEN   355 26

DOZING
    DOZING IN THE UNDER-DEEPS THEN REACHING OUT A SAVAGE AN+ 689 20

DRAB
    A DRAB AND DINGY BIRD   523 29
    WITH THE CREST OF THE DIRTY DRAB WORLD DOWN BELOW   551 2
    TO THE DIRTY DRAB WORLD   551 4

DRAG
    SNAKE-LIKE SHE DRAWS AT MY FINGER WHILE I DRAG IN HORROR 359 26
    AND DON'T WITH THE NASTY PRYING MIND DRAG IT OUT FROM 464 28

DRAGGED
    DRAGGED OUT OF AN ETERNITY OF SILENT ISOLATION   362 27
    AT DUSK THEY PATTER BACK LIKE A BOUGH BEING DRAGGED ON 384 1
    I HAVE BEEN DEFEATED AND DRAGGED DOWN BY PAIN   709 1
    BUT I'VE HAD SUCH A JOB MY CRUTCHES I FAIRLY DRAGGED TH+ 865 22

DRAGGING
    DRAGGING THE LINKS OF MY SHORTENING CHAIN   50 17

DRAGON
    WOMAN'S BUT THE APPLES OF LIFE THE DRAGON GUARDS AND NO+ 277 8
    SO QUICK LIKE A LITTLE BLACK DRAGON   396 28
    CHINESE DRAGON   397 5
    FROM THE DRAGON OF THE MODERN FEMALE   619 27
    THE MORE YOU TACKLE THE PROPERTY DRAGON   665 10
    THE OLD DRAGON WILL DWINDLE DOWN TO THE SIZE OF A STRAY+ 665 14
    HOLD BACK THE DRAGON OF THE SUN   786 20
    SO HE PASSED THE YELLOW LINE WHO LASHED LIKE A DRAGON I+ 790 3
    THE DRAGON OF THE DISAPPOINTED DEAD THAT SLEEPS IN THE + 795 12
    BUT YOU WHAT HAVE YOU MASTERED AMONG THE DRAGON HOSTS O+ 796 16
    THERE IS THE SPANGLED DRAGON OF THE STARS AT LARGE   796 20
    AND FAR AT THE CENTRE WITH ONE UNBLINKING EYE THE DRAGO+ 796 21
    I AM GOING TO SPEAK TO THE DRAGON OF THE INNER FIRES 797 1
    I AM ABOUT TO TELL THE DRAGON OF THE WATERS TO TURN ROU+ 797 5
    AND I WAIT FOR THE FINAL DAY WHEN THE DRAGON OF THUNDER+ 797 7

DRAGON-FACED
    THE DRAGON-FACED   315 14

DRAGON-FLIES
    TWO GREAT DRAGON-FLIES WRESTLING   224 2

DRAGON-GRIN
    AND WHITE TEETH SHOWING IN YOUR DRAGON-GRIN AS YOU RACE 397 20

DRAGON-MOUTHED
    OR DRAGON-MOUTHED SALVIA WITH GOLD THROAT OF WRATH   314 26

DRAGONS
    LO THE UNIVERSE TANGLES ITS GREAT DRAGONS   795 10
    THE DRAGONS IN THE COSMOS ARE STIRRING WITH ANGER AGAIN 795 11
    THERE ARE DRAGONS OF SUN AND ICE DRAGONS OF THE MOON AN+ 796 18
    DRAGONS OF SALTY WATERS DRAGONS OF THUNDER   796 19
    CONQUER SAYS THE MORNING STAR PASS THE DRAGONS AND PASS+ 796 23
    BUT LO YOU INERT ONES I WILL SET THE DRAGONS UPON YOU 796 25
    LO I RELEASE THE DRAGONS THE GREAT WHITE ONE OF THE NOR+ 796 30

DRAGS
    INTO OUR SOOTY GARDEN HE DRAGS AND BEATS   47 16
    WHICH SHE DRAGS APATHETIC AWAY THOUGH WITHOUT RETREATING 360 11
    LETTING GO AT LAST AS SHE DRAGS AWAY   360 23
    AND DRAGS AT THESE WITH HIS BEAK   362 8
    DRAGS AND DRAGS AND BITES   362 9
    AND STRANGE AND GRIMLY DRAGS AT HER   362 23

DRAIN
    THA'RT ONE O' TH' MEN AS HAS GOT TO DRAIN   139 15

DRAINED
    ALIVE AND YET DRAINED OF LIFE   767 16

DRAKE
    THE BLUE-GLEAMED DRAKE STEMS PROUD   126 15
    BELONGS TO THE BAMBOO THICKET AND THE DRAKE IN THE AIR + 623 12

DRAMAS
    GLOW AND ENACT THE DRAMAS AND DREAMS   151 4
    GLOW AND ENACT THE DRAMAS AND DREAMS   873 14

DRANK

SOFTLY DRANK THROUGH HIS STRAIGHT GUMS INTO HIS SLACK L+	349	16
AND STOOPED AND DRANK A LITTLE MORE	349	25
HE DRANK ENOUGH	350	23
I BROUGHT FOR HIM AND WAITED WHILE HE DRANK	878	15
IN RECKLESSNESS HE DRANK WITH A BITTER MOUTH	878	17

DRAPE

IN WHITE FLESH ROBED TO DRAPE ANOTHER DREAM	195	11

DRAPERIES

HER DRAPERIES DOWN	106	4

DRAPES

AN ENDLESS TAPESTRY THE PAST, HAS WOVEN DRAPES	173	19
AN ENDLESS TAPESTRY THE PAST HAS WOVEN DRAPES	*906	13
AN ENDLESS TAPESTRY THE PAST HAS WOVEN DRAPES	*908	7

DRAUGHT

OUT OF DEATH AND IT BURNS IN THE DRAUGHT	108	18
WHIRLING IN THE DRAUGHT OF LIFE	110	18
THAT HAS DRAWN THIS TERRIBLE DRAUGHT OF WHITE FIRE	241	29
SAVES YOU WAFTS YOU AWAY ON THE VERY DRAUGHT MY ANGER	334	8
BOW DEEP FOR IT'S GOOD AS A DRAUGHT OF COOL WATER TO BOW	391	30
DRAUGHT	439	7
AND SUBJECT REALLY TO THE DRAUGHT OF EVERY MOTOR-CAR OR+	617	17
AND A DRAUGHT OF THEE IS STRENGTH TO A SOUL IN HELL	759	13
RECKLESS ABOUT THE BITTERNESS OF THE DRAUGHT	878	12
OUR DRAUGHT OF FAITH THAT SENT US ON ANEW	*941	12
BLOWN FLAT INTO POINTS BY THE HEAVY WHITE DRAUGHT OF TH+	*956	5

DRAUGHT-HORSE

AND A SOLDIER IN THE SADDLE OF THE LEFT-HAND DRAUGHT-HO+	733	8

DRAUGHT-MADDENED

THIS FURNACE THIS DRAUGHT-MADDENED FIRE	241	18

DRAUGHTS

GLOWING AFTER THE DAY'S RESTLESS DRAUGHTS	506	13
AND SEND THIN DRAUGHTS OF WORDS	506	22

DRAW

BUT WHEN I DRAW THE SCANTY CLOAK OF SILENCE OVER MY EYES	64	14
BUT BARBED ALOOFNESS WHEN I WOULD DRAW NEAR	85	24
YOUR BRIGHTNESS DIMS WHEN I DRAW TOO NEAR AND MY FREE	87	16
THEY DRAW THEIR SAP FROM THE GODHEAD NOT FROM ME BUT TH+	93	20
COME DRAW THE THORN FROM MY DISCONTENT	113	27
AH THEN UPON THE BEDROOM I DO DRAW	129	15
DRAW IT OUT OF 'IM DID TER KNOW IT	138	26
I CAN DRAW BACK	147	10
'TWAS I WHOSE FINGERS DID DRAW UP THE YOUNG	156	19
VIBRATION TO DRAW	165	32
TO DRAW HIS NET THROUGH THE SURF'S THIN LINE AT THE DAW+	180	2
OF A DAY'S EXPERIENCE SLEEP DOES SLOWLY DRAW	195	2
TO DRAW THE LOAD SO STILL AND SLOW IT MOVES	225	15
AND YOUR SHOES AND DRAW UP AT MY HEARTH	237	18
YOU WOULD DRAW YOUR MIRROR TOWARDS YOU YOU WOULD WISH	251	14
AND VALLEYS THAT DRAW CLOSE IN LOVE	261	5
AND I IF I BE LIFTED UP WILL DRAW ALL MEN UNTO ME	320	4
TO DRAW ALL MEN UNTO ME	320	12
THEY DRAW NEAR TO TASTE IT AS IF SAYING NOW WHAT IS THI+	331	5
PROCEEDED TO DRAW HIS SLOW LENGTH CURVING ROUND	350	31
YOU DRAW YOUR HEAD FORWARD SLOWLY FROM YOUR LITTLE	352	25
AS YOU DRAW YOURSELF UPON YOURSELF IN INSISTENCE	370	29
SO THAT ONE COULD DRAW NEAR HER	506	14
AND NOTHING NOW REACHES OUT TO DRAW	507	18
YOU DRAW YOUR NOBILITY DIRECT FROM THE SUN	526	27
WE MUST DRAW A LINE SOMEWHERE	548	28
AH WHEN HE BEGINS TO DRAW THE LINE IN TIGHT TO LAND HIS	586	21
DRAW IT AWAY DRAW IT AWAY FOR THESE HORRIBLE MACHINE-PE+	639	3
TO DRAW A LINE AROUND THE INDIANS BEYOND WHICH LINE	779	31
DO ANYTHING BUT DO SOMETHING TO DRAW THIS ONE	780	11
DRAW NEARER REDDEN AND LAUGH LIKE YOUNG GIRLS KISSED	854	12
YOU SHALL DRAW THE THORN FROM MY DISCONTENT	*929	16
BUT DRAW THE TURGID PAIN	*929	27

DRAWING

AND DRAWING THE DARKNESS TOGETHER CRUSH FROM IT A TWILI+	92	19
UNSEEN MY HANDS EXPLORE THE SILENCE DRAWING THE BARK	147	2
I'D LIE FOR EVER DRINKING AND DRAWING IN	153	29
DRAWING ALL MEN UNTO THEE BUT BOUND TO RELEASE THEM WHEN	323	8
DELIBERATELY GOING INTO THE BLACKNESS AND SLOWLY DRAWING	351	6
AND FALLS BACK DRAWING IN ITS BREATH WITH RAGE	467	14
DRAWING NEAR THEY COVER THE MUNCHEN ROAD	732	26

DRAWING-ROOMS

AS ALL DRAWING-ROOMS ARE ARRANGED	657	5

DRAWN

THE BLINDS ARE DRAWN BECAUSE OF THE SUN	51	5
HAS DRAWN MY SPIRIT OUTSIDE	107	26
TILL A WOMAN HAS DRAWN THE LAST LAST DROP	139	11
DRAWN ON HIS MOUTH EYES BROKEN AT LAST BY HIS PANGS	225	8
THAT HAS DRAWN THIS TERRIBLE DRAUGHT OF WHITE FIRE	241	29
DROOP AND ARE DRAWN	268	19
LIKE DRAWN BLADES NEVER SHEATHED HACKED AND GONE BLACK	304	28
DRAWN OUT OF EARTH	310	10
AM DRAWN TO THE UPLIFTED AS ALL MEN ARE DRAWN	320	15
RUNS A RAGE DRAWN IN FROM THE ETHER DIVINELY THROUGH HIM	381	21
DRAWN	586	5
DRAWN	632	20
AND DREAMS ARE ONLY DRAWN FROM THE BODIES THAT ARE	691	8
THE BLINDS ARE DRAWN BECAUSE OF THE SUN	*898	17
THE BLINDS ARE DRAWN BECAUSE OF THE SUN	*902	1

DRAWN-OUT

TRAFFIC WILL TANGLE UP IN A LONG DRAWN-OUT CRASH OF COL+	624	27

DRAWS

AND MY HEART REBELS WITH ANGUISH AS NIGHT DRAWS NIGHER	48	13
THE CHURCH DRAWS NEARER UPON US GENTLE AND GREAT	48	17
THE LITTLE GRAIN DRAWS DOWN THE EARTH TO HIDE	64	10
DRAWS TOWARDS THE DOWNWARD SLOPE SOME SORROW HATH	131	25
DRAWS DOWN THE BLINDS WHOSE SHADOWS SCARCELY STAIN	155	2
SNAKE-LIKE SHE DRAWS AT MY FINGER WHILE I DRAG IN HORROR	359	26
LEAP THEN AND COME DOWN ON THE LINE THAT DRAWS TO THE	394	25
AS THE DARK CLOSES ROUND HIM HE DRAWS NEARER	455	14
AND THE DARK MOON DRAWS THE TIDES ALSO	473	28
AND WHO NOW DRAWS SLOWLY AWAY COLD THE WISTFUL GODDESS +	676	18
OH NOW AS NOVEMBER DRAWS NEAR	722	19
AND DRAWS AWAY AWAY TOWARDS DARK DEPTHS	723	21
THE CATTLE RUN ANXIOUS IN QUEST AS THE TIME DRAWS NIGH	749	25
OF YOUR EYES DRAWS OPEN MY SHELTERING FLIMSY DOORS	875	13
HE DRAWS A DEEP HARD BREATH FROM SPACE TO SPACE	878	23
DRAWS DOWN THE BURDENED FLOWER	*913	21
DRAWS TOWARDS THE DOWNWARD SLOPE SOME SICKNESS HATH	*937	24
WHAT A PITY HE TAKES HIMSELF SERIOUSLY AND DRAWS A	*950	28
AND DRAWS AWAY AWAY AWAY TOWARDS THE DARK DEPTHS	*958	33

DREAD

WITH DREAD AND FILLS MY HEART WITH THE TEARS OF DESIRE	48	12
BUT MY HEART STANDS STILL AS A NEW STRONG DREAD ALARMS	132	5
'TIS LIKE THE UNUTTERABLE NAME OF THE DREAD LORD	264	16
OH AUNT LOUIE'S THE ONE I DREAD	572	16
AND DREAD AND THE DARK ROLLING OMINOUSNESS OF DOOM	708	25
AND LIFE IS FOR DREAD	709	14
I DREAD HIM COMING I WONDER HOW HE WILL TAKE IT	733	2
EVE RUNNING WITH SWIFT LIMBS QUICKENED BY DREAD	864	19
OF MY ARMS INERT WITH DREAD WILTED IN FEAR OF MY KISS	*912	18

DREADFUL

WHISTLING SHE-DELIRIOUS RAGE AND THE DREADFUL SOUND	36	14
DREADFUL	130	26
BUT TO GET OUT FROM THIS DIM DREADFUL DEN	174	4
AND GIVING OFF DREADFUL EFFLUVIA IN A GHASTLY EFFORT OF+	175	4
AND AS HE PUT HIS HEAD INTO THAT DREADFUL HOLE	351	1
DREADFUL GUSH	628	17
YOU SOUND SO DREADFUL SO CRUELLY HURT MY DEAR	871	18
TO FOUNDER AT LAST WITHIN THE DREADFUL FLOOD	875	33

DREAM

PERHAPS 'TWAS A DREAM OF WARNING	46	27
IN A WISTFUL DREAM OF LORNA DOONE	52	15
SHE LIES AT LAST THE DARLING IN THE SHAPE OF HER DREAM	101	14
A DARKNESS THAT DREAMS MY DREAM FOR ME EVER THE SAME	115	12
THOUGH SURELY MY SOUL'S BEST DREAM IS STILL	117	4
AND MY DREAM IS ILL-FOUNDED	117	10
THE SLEEP NO DREAM NOR DOUBT CAN UNDERMINE	129	26
RUNS INTO SPEED LIKE A DREAM THE BLUE OF THE STEEL	136	9
IN THE SPELLBOUND NORTH CONVULSIVE NOW WITH A DREAM NEAR	149	21
YOUR WIDOW AM I AND ONLY I DREAM	157	15
THAN A DREAM OF YOURS 'TWAS ALL YOU EVER COULD	157	30
SEE IN HIM YOUR SELF'S DREAM IN HIS SORE	157	31
OH COME AND WAKE US UP FROM THE GHASTLY DREAM OF TO-DAY	174	25
AS THEY DREAM CORRUPTED DREAMS ALL POISONED WITH CARE	174	28
THE GHASTLY DREAM OF LABOUR AND THE STENCH OF STEEL AND+	175	1
UNFINISHED FOR EVER BUT GASPING FOR MONEY AS THEY DREAM+	175	5
THE GHASTLY DREAM OF RICHES OF MASSES OF MONEY TO SPEND	175	7
TO MAKE NEW WORDS WITH OUR LIPS TO ESCAPE THE FOUL DREAM	175	22
DREAM	175	27
AND WHAT IS LIFE BUT THE SWELLING AND SHAPING THE DREAM+	176	6
TO BREAK THIS SICK AND NAUSEOUS DREAM	177	19
THAT DOES INFORM THIS VARIOUS DREAM OF LIVING	194	20
AT THIS MY TASK OF LIVING THIS MY DREAM	195	9
IN WHITE FLESH ROBED TO DRAPE ANOTHER DREAM	195	11
ONE MOMENT SEES AND SWIFT ITS DREAM IS OVER	195	14
MUST BE A DREAM OF ALL THROUGH PAIN	195	20
RISING TO DREAM IN ME A SMALL KEEN DREAM	196	3
BUT DID YOU DREAM	244	16
BACCHUS IS A DREAM'S DREAM	286	15
AND OUT TO THE DIM OF THE DESERT LIKE A DREAM NEVER REAL	402	22
HER DREAM	448	23
OH DON'T FOR AN INSTANT EVER DREAM	576	6
IN THEIR OWN DREAM	652	11
NOT EVEN DREAM NOT EVEN PASS AWAY	738	19
YOU GO ABOUT IN A DREAM WITH YOUR COUNTENANCE SUNK	755	4
AND THE DREAM OF THE NIGHT RISES FROM ME LIKE A RED FEA+	806	30
I AM THE WATCHER AND MASTER OF THE DREAM	807	1
IN THE DREAM OF THE NIGHT I SEE THE GREY DOGS PROWLING	807	2
PROWLING TO DEVOUR THE DREAM	807	3
AND IN WHOM THE DREAM SITS UP LIKE A RABBIT LIFTING LON+	807	8
TILL A DREAM CAME TREMBLING THROUGH MY FLESH IN THE NIG+	860	9
THE BREATH OF MY DREAM IS FADED FROM OFF THE MIRROR	871	10
WILL DREAM INTO THE FUTURE DID HE GUESS	878	10
SPEAK IN HALF-BITTER SCENT YOUR DREAM OF ME	880	12
WAS UNAWARE BUT HIS WIFE CRIED IN HER DREAM	885	11
I STAND RELUCTANT TO ENTER TO DREAM NO MORE BUT TO BOW	*894	21
IN A WISHFUL DREAM OF LORNA DOONE	*905	4
THE CREATION OF A NEW-PATTERNED DREAM DREAM OF A GENERA+	*907	3
IMPELLING SHAPING THE COMING DREAM	*907	15
ROUNDED AND SWELLING TOWARDS THE FRUIT OF A DREAM	*908	4
THE CREATION OF A NEW-PATTERNED DREAM DREAM OF A GENERA+	*908	24
AND I WATCH TO SEE THE CREATOR THE POWER THAT PATTERNS +	*908	25
DREAM IN THE FLESH	*909	16
SWELLING MANKIND LIKE ONE BUD TO BRING FORTH THE FRUIT	*909	20
AND STRIVING TO CATCH A GLIMPSE OF THE SHAPE OF THE COM+	*909	25
CATCH THE SCENT AND THE COLOUR OF THE COMING DREAM	*909	27
MY HEART DISTURBED IN ITS DREAM SLOW-STEPPING ALARMS	*937	32

DREAM-BLOOD
  AND OUR BODIES MOLTEN DROPS OF DREAM-BLOOD THAT SWIRL A+   176   7

DREAMED
  OF THE SHIP OF THE SOUL OVER SEAS WHERE DREAMED DREAMS   53   7
  AND SHE DREAMED OF HER CHILDREN AND JOSEPH   202 15
  YOU HAVE DREAMED AND ARE NOT AWAKE COME HERE TO ME   211   1
  LIVING WHERE LIFE WAS NEVER YET DREAMED OF NOR HINTED AT 258 32
  I NEVER DREAMED TILL NOW OF THE AWFUL TIME THE LORD MUST 395 17
  I HAD DREAMED OF LOVE OH LOVE I HAD DREAMED OF LOVE   742 27
  OF THE SHIP OF THE SOUL OVER SEAS WHERE DREAMED DREAMS + *905 20

DREAMERS
  INTERIOR A HOUSE OF DREAMS WHERE THE DREAMERS WRITHE AN+ 174 24

DREAM-HEAVY
  POOR DREAM-HEAVY SLAVES AT THE MILL WHAT WE HAVE TO DO + 859 28

DREAMILY
  AND LIFTED HIS HEAD DREAMILY AS ONE WHO HAS DRUNKEN   350 24
  OF EVERYTHING I'VE KNOWN EVEN DREAMILY   738 12

DREAMING
  DREAMING GOD KNOWS OF WHAT FOR TO ME SHE'S THE   129   2
  DREAMING YOUR YIELDED MOUTH IS GIVEN TO MINE   129 24
  THE WRITHING OF MYRIADS OF WORKMEN ALL DREAMING THEY AR+ 175   2
  THE RICH AND THE POOR ALIKE DREAMING AND WRITHING ALL I+ 175 15
  WITHIN MY BODY CRY OUT TO THE DREAMING SOUL   195 32
  DREAMING   223 26
  DREAMING AND LETTING THE BULLOCK TAKE ITS WILL   225 20
  AND ENORMOUS WHALES LIE DREAMING SUCKLING THEIR WHALE-T+ 694 29
  AND DREAMING WITH STRANGE WHALE EYES WIDE OPEN IN THE W+ 694 31
  CREEPING AMONG THE SLEEPING AND THE DREAMING WHO ARE LA+ 807   6

DREAMLESS
  DARK DREAMLESS SLEEP IN DEEP OBLIVION   725   4

DREAMLETS
  AND THE GLIMMERING DREAMLETS OF THE MORNING ARE PALLID + 854   7

DREAMS
  TEARS AND DREAMS FOR THEM FOR ME   41 12
  IS FULL OF DREAMS MY LOVE THE BOYS ARE ALL STILL   52 14
  AT THE BACK OF MY LIFE'S EXPERIENCE WHERE DREAMS FROM   52 26
  OF THE SHIP OF THE SOUL OVER SEAS WHERE DREAMED DREAMS   53   7
  NAY BUT SHE SLEEPS LIKE A BRIDE AND DREAMS HER DREAMS   101 12
  A DARKNESS THAT DREAMS MY DREAM FOR ME EVER THE SAME   115 12
  AND FECUND GLOBE OF DREAMS   127   9
  GLOW AND ENACT THE DRAMAS AND DREAMS   151   4
  THESE SHAPES THAT NOW ARE DREAMS AND ONCE WERE MEN   174   2
  THE SURFACE OF DREAMS IS BROKEN THE ARRAS IS TORN   174   5
  THE OLD DREAMS ARE BEAUTIFUL BELOVED SOFT-TONED AND SURE 174 21
  INTERIOR A HOUSE OF DREAMS WHERE THE DREAMERS WRITHE AN+ 174 24
  WE ASPHYXIATE IN A SLEEP OF DREAMS REBREATHING THE IMPU+ 174 26
  AS THEY DREAM CORRUPTED DREAMS ALL POISONED WITH CARE   174 28
  LET US BREATHE FRESH AIR AND WAKE FROM FOUL DREAMS IN W+ 175 19
  AND THE BODIES OF MEN AND WOMEN ARE MOLTEN MATTER OF DR+ 176   2
  US OUT AS DREAMS YOU AUGUST SLEEP   194 22
  PERMIT OF NO BEYOND AH YOU WHOSE DREAMS   194 27
  WITH ACHE OF DREAMS THAT BODY FORTH THE SLEEP   195 30
  FINISHING YOUR DREAMS FOR YOUR OWN SAKE ONLY   197   6
  AND DREAMS AS SHE STIRS THE MIXING-POT   203   7
  NOT SLEEP WHICH IS GREY WITH DREAMS   205 10
  NO SHADOW OF US ON THEIR SNOWY FOREHEAD OF DREAMS   223 24
  WHILE THE DRIVER ON THE SHAFT SITS CROUCHED IN DREAMS   225 16
  AND IF WE SIP THE WINE WE FIND DREAMS COMING UPON US   286 22
  WITH DREAMS AND THRUSTS THAT MAKE THEM DRY IN THEIR SLE+ 438 15
  AND DREAMS ARE ONLY DRAWN FROM THE BODIES THAT ARE   691   8
  DREAMS   807 13
  BUT WHOSE DREAMS ARE DOGS GREY DOGS WITH YELLOW MOUTHS   807 15
  A THIEF A MURDERER OF DREAMS   808 12
  THOUGH THE PURPLE DREAMS OF THE INNOCENT SPRING HAVE GO+ 854   6
  I BREATHED MY DREAMS UPON YOU I LAID MY MOUTH ON YOUR M+ 871   1
  AND BREATHED ON YOU THE PICTURE-MIST OF MY DREAMS   871   2
  AND NOW THE MIST OF MY DREAMS HAS DRIED FROM YOU   871   5
  GLOW AND ENACT THE DRAMAS AND DREAMS   873 14
  AND GATHER MY BURNING BEAUTIFUL DREAMS FOR HER SHARE   874   8
  AS IF THE SOUTHERN-WOOD SHOULD SOOTHE HIS DREAMS   877 32
  IS FULL OF DREAMS MY LOVE THE BOYS ARE ALL STILL   *905   3
  OF BLUE PALACE ALOFT THERE AMONG THE MISTY INDEFINITE D+ *905 13
  AT THE BACK OF MY LIFE'S HORIZON WHERE THE DREAMS FROM + *905 15
  OF THE SHIP OF THE SOUL OVER SEAS WHERE DREAMED DREAMS + *905 20
  THROUGH THE WAKENED AFTERNOON RIDING DOWN MY DREAMS   *906 15
  THE OLD DREAMS ARE BELOVED BEAUTIFUL SOFT-TONED AND SURE *907   4
  EYES WHERE I CAN WATCH THE SWIM OF OLD DREAMS REFLECTED+ *907 11
  MOLTEN METAL OF DREAMS   *907 12
  THE GREAT MYSTERIOUS ONE IS SWELLING AND SHAPING THE DR+ *907 24
  THE SURFACE OF DREAMS IS BROKEN   *908   9
  FROM THE DREAMS THAT THE DISTANCE FLATTERED   *908 12
  THE OLD DREAMS ARE BEAUTIFUL BELOVED SOFT-TONED AND SURE *909   1
  EYES WHERE I CAN WATCH THE SWIM OF OLD DREAMS REFLECTED+ *909   7
  MOLTEN METAL OF DREAMS   *909   8
  A DARKNESS THAT DREAMS MY DREAMS FOR ME EVER THE SAME   *930 12
  WITH DREAMS AND THRUSTS THAT MAKE THEM CRY IN THEIR SLE+ *947 21

DREAM-SLOPES
  ON THE DREAM-SLOPES BROWSING LIKE A DEER IN THE DUSK   807 10

DREAM-STUFF
  FOR THE PROPER DREAM-STUFF IS MOLTEN AND MOVING MYSTERI+ 176   1
  BUT THE DREAM-STUFF IS MOLTEN AND MOVING MYSTERIOUSLY   *907   5
  FOR AM I NOT ALSO DREAM-STUFF DIFFUSING MYSELF IN THE P+ *907   7
  BUT THE DREAM-STUFF IS MOLTEN AND MOVING MYSTERIOUSLY   *909   2
  ALLURING MY EYES FOR I AM I NOT ALSO DREAM-STUFF   *909   3

DREAM'S
  OF REAL DAYLIGHT UPON US RELEASED FROM THE FOUL DREAM'S+ 175 30
  BACCHUS IS A DREAM'S DREAM   286 15

DREAMY
  DREAMY NOT YET PRESENT   310 30
  PALE DREAMY CHAPLETS A GREY NUN-SISTER SETS   854 23
  OUT OF THE DISTANCE NEARER COMMANDING MY DREAMY WORLD   *908 15

DREAR
  SINCE YOU HAVE DRUNKEN UP THE DREAR   118 10

DREARILY
  AND SO DREARILY ENJOYS ITSELF   628   8
  IN THE BOX AND FOUR HOT HORSES GOING DREARILY   733   7

DREARINESS
  AND THE NOISE AND THE STENCH AND THE DREARINESS   510 28

DREARISOME
  ARE DREARISOME   731 17

DREARNESS
  AND DOUBT ENTERS IN DREARNESS   94 24

DREARY
  THE SANDY DESERT BENEATH HER THE DREARY PLATOON   153   4
  AND US FROM THE DREARY INHERITANCE OF ROMAN STUPIDITY   479 27
  FOR A DREARY LITTLE BOOZE   560 24
  AND ALL WAS DREARY GREAT ROBOT LIMBS ROBOT BREASTS   651   2
  HERE COMES THE FIRST OF THE WAGONS A GREY A DREARY   733   5
  FLOWERS NOW AS WE'RE CROSSING THE DREARY STAGES   814   6
  TO OPEN MY BLOSSOM-FULL BREAST FROM ITS DREARY BANDS   *896 24
  AND NOW THE SKY WITH DREARY DIRT IS BARKLED   *933 16

DREDGED
  DREDGED DOWN TO THE ZENITH'S REVERSAL   323 12

DREE
  GREY DAYS AND WAN DREE DAWNINGS   193 17
  DREE IT   463 18
  OR PROSTITUTED BY THE DREE   469 17

DREGS
  IT IS THE SCENT OF THE FIERY-COLD DREGS OF CORRUPTION   270 20
  BUT EVEN THOU SON OF MAN CANST NOT QUAFF OUT THE DREGS + 322   9

DRENCHED
  AS A DRENCHED DROWNED BEE   73 20
  AS THE WINGS OF A DRENCHED DROWNED BEE   74   5
  I WILL TRAIL MY HANDS AGAIN THROUGH THE DRENCHED COLD L+ 180 34
  AND DRENCHED WITH MYSTERY   280 22
  WITH THE DARK EARTH AND DRENCHED   727 15
  CLINGING TO THE RADIATORS LIKE NUMBED BEES TO THE DRENC+ 866   1
  AS A DRENCHED DROWNED BEE   *913 12
  AS THE WINGS OF A DRENCHED DROWNED BEE   *913 26

DRESS
  WI' A DRESS AS IS WANTED TO-DAY   78   4
  IN THE COMMON PRISON-LIKE DRESS   109   4
  I FOLLOWED FOLLOWED THE SWING OF HER WHITE DRESS   123   2
  AND WHITE PEOPLE IN EVENING DRESS BUZZING AND CROWDING 387 23
  MALINTZI OF THE GREEN DRESS WILL OPEN THE DOOR   809 10
  WI' A DRESS AS IS WANTED TODAY   *919 24
  I'M TAKIN' 'OME A WEDDIN' DRESS   *921 11
  AS 'ER'LL BE WANTIN' MY WEDDIN' DRESS   *921 23
  I FOLLOWED FOLLOWED THE SWING OF HER WHITE DRESS   *934   8

DRESSED
  DRESSED IN THE GRACE OF IMMORTALITY   745 17

DRESSED-UP
  OF DRESSED-UP PEOPLE   607 23

DREW
  AND DREW THE CIRCLE OF HIS GRASP O MAN   69 11
  THE GULF THAT CAME BETWEEN US AND DREW US IN   90 23
  TILL OLD DAYS DREW ME BACK INTO THEIR FOLD   98 28
  YOU NEVER BORE HIS CHILDREN NEVER DREW   158 10
  WHENCE HE DREW THE CURIOUS LIQUORS   202 19
  AND THAT MOTHER-LOVE LIKE A DEMON DREW YOU FROM ME   206   2
  THAT DREW THIS RED GUSH IN ME   241 26
  AND AS HE SLOWLY DREW UP SNAKE-EASING HIS SHOULDERS AND 351   2
  DREW HER LIPS OVER THE MOON-PALE PETALS SOFTLY BENT   856 20
  AND DREW THE CIRCLE OF HIS GRASP O MAN   *915 23
  THAT SHE WAS AS THE WINE-JAR WHENCE WE DREW   *941 11

DRIBBLING
  DRIBBLING OVER THE LAKE   229   6

DRIBBLINGS
  BUT HE MADE A POOL OF DRIBBLINGS   492   4

DRIED
  AND NOW THE MIST OF MY DREAMS HAS DRIED FROM YOU   871   5

DRIFT
  ME THEIR DRIFT   108 16
  IN A DRIFT DIE THERE   154 32
  DRIFT THEN FOR THE SIGHTLESS BIRDS   172   1
  SOME FIREFLIES DRIFT THROUGH THE MIDDLE AIR   221   1
  ON THE FACES THAT DRIFT BELOW   252 16
  ON THE FACES THAT DRIFT AND BLOW   252 17
  SO BUILD YOUR SHIP OF DEATH AND LET THE SOUL DRIFT   721   4
  BUT BY THE HEAVY DRIFT OF HIS UNPERVERTED INSTINCTS   838 17
  THE CAMPIONS DRIFT IN FRAGILE ROSY MIST   854 11
  WITH A FEW SWIFT PASSIONS WOULD I DRIFT AWAY   875 32
  DRIFT ON DRIFT ON MY SOUL TOWARDS THE MOST PURE   *959 22

DRIFTED
AND ALONG THE SCENT AND THE COOLNESS A DROWSE OF SLEEP +   858 20
DRIFTED WITH THE BLOOD OF THE FLOWERS ON HER FEET AND K+   864 3

DRIFTING
WETLY BOBBING AND DRIFTING AWAY ON OUR SIGHT   146 22
THE SILENT DRIFTING HOURS   249 1
AND NIGHT DRIFTING UP TO THE NIGHT   249 3
DRIFTING IN FLIGHT   253 10
DRIFTING BENEATH THE DEATHLY ASHY GREY   720 7
OUR SERRIED WANDERING HEARTS DRIFTING WITHOUT A PLACE   736 9
LOVE-FIRE IS DRIFTING THOUGH THE BUGLE IS PRIM AND DEMU+ 854 16
AND I AM DRIFTING LIKE A SHELL DISCARDED   875 25

DRIFTS
DRIFTS MY BOAT WISTFULLY LAPSING AFTER   53 18
DRIFTS DIMLY FORWARD EASILY HIDDEN   68 6
DRIFTS OVER THE GULF THAT BARS   144 12
LITTLE TO COUNT IN THE WIND THAT DRIFTS ME THROUGH   223 12
DRIFTS OVER THE TOWN IN ITS NEED   253 29
THAT DRIFTS UPON TIME AND CHAOS TILL SOME UNKNOWN FUTURE 429 5
THEIR WANDERING HAPPINESS AND THE WIND WASTED IN LIBERT+ *892 5
DRIFTS MY BOAT WISTFULLY, LAPSING AFTER   *906 9
DRIFTS DIMLY FORWARD EASILY HIDDEN   *914 21

DRINK
THAT YOUNG AN' A' THE FAULT OF DRINK   60 25
LET THAT BE 'APPEN IT WORNA TH' DRINK NEITHER   60 27
SHOULD PUT YOUR MOUTH TO MINE AND DRINK OF ME   86 4
WASTEFUL INTO THE NIGHT'S BLACK NOSTRILS DRINK   86 6
AND DRINK MOST HIGH   96 28
AH DRINK ME UP   96 29
DRINK IT UP IN THE GROUND   117 30
STOPPED AT A DIM-LIT TROUGH TO DRINK   121 29
THE DRINK AND A LONG STRONG PULL   177 12
DRINK THEN INVISIBLE HEROES DRINK   177 14
NO SIN IS IT TO DRINK AS MUCH AS A MAN CAN TAKE AND GET+ 277 10
TO DRINK THERE   349 3
HOW GLAD I WAS HE HAD COME LIKE A GUEST IN QUIET TO DRI+ 350 9
DRINK A LITTLE BLOOD AND LOSING ANOTHER ROYALTY UNTO   414 27
I WANT TO DRINK OUT OF DARK CUPS THAT DRIP DOWN ON   427 9
DON'T DRINK DON'T DRINK AND GET BEERIER AND BEERIER   459 11
AND DRINK AND BROWSE   465 14
YOU WILL FIND YOU HAVE A GREAT DESIRE TO DRINK LIFE DIR+ 481 3
TO GET A REFRESHING DRINK OUT OF OLD WISDOM   495 13
YET ALL OF THESE DRINK BLOOD   496 17
DRINK ITS MINKY-WINKY THEN LIKE A MAN   570 21
WHERE THE LEOPARD PAUSING TO DRINK   771 1
AND DRINK FIRE-WATERS AND QUARREL AND STAB   795 3
DON RAMON DON'T DRINK DON'T SMOKE   797 13
AS THEY DRINK THROUGH THEIR HUSK   824 24
THEY DON'T BEGRUDGE YOU A DRINK   828 18
TOUCH CUPS AND DRINK   *931 11

DRINKING
IN ITS LAST COMPLETENESS DRINKING   109 27
I'D LIE FOR EVER DRINKING AND DRAWING IN   153 29
HE LIFTED HIS HEAD FROM HIS DRINKING AS CATTLE DO   349 21
AND LOOKED AT ME VAGUELY AS DRINKING CATTLE DO   349 22
AND DRINKING FROM CUPS THAT CAME OFF HIS FINGERS LIKE   451 26
AND DRINKING FROM THE CUPS THAT HAVE FLOWERED FROM HIS + *950 10
DRINKING THE CONFIDENT WATER FROM THE LITTLE JUG   *959 13

DRINKS
WHO SNIFFS WITH JOY BEFORE HE DRINKS THE BLOOD   43 32
YOUR FOUNTAINS AS HEAVEN DRINKS FROM OUT THEIR COURSE   153 30
HE DRINKS AND DRINKS THEN TURNS AWAY HIS HEAD   734 29
THAT DRINKS ME UP AS IF I WERE A SPECK   876 18
AND DRINKS HIMSELF LIKE A SOAKED GORGED CREATURE DULL   877 9

DRIP
IN ONE RICH DRIP IT SINKS TO ANOTHER SLEEP   195 15
LIKE A FURNACE DRIPPING A MOLTEN DRIP   326 19
YOUR WATTLES DRIP DOWN LIKE A SHAWL TO YOUR BREAST   369 29
THE DOWNWARD DRIP   393 1
I WANT TO DRINK OUT OF DARK CUPS THAT DRIP DOWN ON   427 9
AND THE DRIP OF HIS COLD WEBBED FEET MUD-BLACK   438 11
WHEN AT A CERTAIN POINT A DROP OF WATER BEGAN TO DRIP D+ 682 13

DRIPPED
AND WHERE THE WATER HAD DRIPPED FROM THE TAP IN A SMALL 349 13
AND RANK AND DRIPPED WITH BLOOD AND DRIPPED AGAIN   884 27

DRIPPIN
AH STOPPED BEHIND ON T' PAD I' TH' DRIPPIN WET   *911 19

DRIPPING
DRIPPING OVER THE RUNNELS   94 12
DRIPPING WITH ALL THE GOLDEN LEES   104 31
THE NIGHT RAIN DRIPPING UNSEEN   144 1
OF MIRTH THEN THE DRIPPING OF TEARS ON YOUR GLOVE   179 19
DRIPPING THEIR LIGHT   252 15
THEY FALL BACK AND LIKE A DRIPPING OF QUICKSILVER TAKIN+ 322 12
LIKE A FURNACE DRIPPING A MOLTEN DRIP   326 19
EAGLE WITH THE SICKLE DRIPPING DARKLY ABOVE   373 4
SICKLE-OVERSWEPT SICKLE DRIPPING OVER AND ABOVE   373 11
AS THEY APPROACH AND SALAAM UNDER THE DRIPPING FIRE OF   388 3
HUGE MORE TASSELS SWINGING MORE DRIPPING FIRE OF NEW   388 27
AND ALL HER WEIGHT ALL HER BLOOD DRIPPING SACK-WISE DOWN 394 21
AND THE SUDDEN DRIPPING OF THE KNIFE-EDGE CLEAVAGE OF T+ 707 13
EAGLE WITH THE SICKLE DRIPPING DARKLY ABOVE   781 7
SICKLE-OVERSWEPT SICKLE DRIPPING OVER AND ABOVE   781 17
ALL SICKLE-OVERSWEPT SICKLE DRIPPING OVER AND ABOVE   783 7
DRIPPING OVER THE RUNNELS   *896 28

DRIPS
WHITE BODY DRIPS   96 21
SHE DRIPS HERSELF WITH WATER AND HER SHOULDERS   217 19
IT DRIPS SLOWLY AWAY   767 12
THE DARK DRIPS DOWN SUSPENDED   782 5
SHE DRIPS HERSELF WITH WATER   *943 1

DRIVE
ME OVER AND DRIVE FROM OUT OF MY BODY THE DEEP   98 24
THEY DRIVE IN SHOALS   337 16
SO TO DRIVE HIM OUT FLICKING WITH MY WHITE HANDKERCHIEF 343 5
TRYING TO DRIVE HIM THROUGH THE WINDOW   344 2
DRIVE THE CAR   441 21
AND TWENTIETH WAGON AND HE WILL NOT DRIVE PAST   733 12
HE PULLS UP FOR OUR WATER WOULD HE DRIVE   733 13

DRIVEN
DRIVEN SO HIGH   71 8
SORRY I AM FOR THIS BUSINESS AN' SORRY IF EVER I'VE DRI+ 83 6
I WAS JUST DRIVEN   196 21
THE JOY WAS NOT TO BE DRIVEN OFF SO EASILY   207 11
DRIVEN BY INVISIBLE BLOWS   250 22
A LITTLE SARDONIC-LOOKING AS IF DOMESTICITY HAD DRIVEN + 358 24
OR IS HE DRIVEN AGAINST HER WITH A BANG LIKE A BIRD FLY+ 363 8
DRIVEN AFTER AEONS OF PRISTINE FORE-GOD-LIKE SINGLENESS+ 363 14
DRIVEN AWAY FROM HIMSELF INTO HER TRACKS   363 17
AND YET EVERY MAN IS DRIVEN INTO ROBBING EVERY OTHER MAN 519 25
ALL THESE CREATURES THAT CANNOT DIE DRIVEN BACK   624 11
WILL BE DRIVEN MAD FROM HIMSELF AND SIGHTLESS AND ON TH+ 624 25
DRIVEN BY STEAM   631 16
WE ARE DRIVEN MAD   739 20
THEN DRIVEN BACK IN A NEW SILENT RUSH   784 14
AS MY WILD SOUL SHRINKS AND THE SONGS ARE DRIVEN FROM M+ *896 12
DRIVEN SO HIGH   *917 26
SORRY I AM FOR THIS BUSINESS AN' SORRY IF I HA'E DRIVEN+ *925 10
ALL THE CREATURES THAT WERE DRIVEN BACK INTO THE UTTERM+ *954 14

DRIVER
WHILE THE DRIVER ON THE SHAFT SITS CROUCHED IN DREAMS   225 16

DRIVES
DRIVES THEM ON AND ON LIKE MACHINES   675 24

DRIVING
AND STRONG SPINE URGING DRIVING   336 10
AND DRIVING THEM AROUND IN FRENZIED ENERGY   502 8

DRIZZLING
MADE OF THE DRIZZLING RAIN   692 2

DRONING
THE COOL HIGH MOON AT THEIR EASE WHILE THE DRONING CHUR+ 54 30
YET ALL THE WHILE COMES THE DRONING INAUDIBLE OUT OF THE 149 17
DRONING OVER THREATENING ME   741 10

DROOP
DROOP AND ARE DRAWN   268 19
I START FROM THE DROOP OF FORGETFULNESS AS THE SOUND OF+ 858 21
ON THE LITTLE BANK WHERE BLUEBELLS DROOP   887 10

DROOPED
WITH FROZEN RIGGING SHE SAW HIM SHE DROOPED LIKE A FERN 155 22

DROOPING
HIS DIMINISHED DROOPING HINDQUARTERS   377 25
HER LITTLE LOOSE HANDS AND DROOPING VICTORIAN SHOULDERS 393 14
AS WILD WHITE FOX GLOVES DROOPING WITH FULNESS   874 26
IN THE DOWN-WARD DROOPING FLIMSY SHEAVES   *915 3

DROOPS
THE WISDOM OF AGES DROOPS IT IS FOLLY   814 22
THE WISDOM OF AGES DROOPS AIN'T IT JOLLY   814 25

DROP
I SHOULD LIKE TO DROP   35 16
DROP THEIR LEAVES WITH A FAINT SHARP HISS OF CONTEMPT   54 25
DROP A LITTLE LOWER WITHOUTEN RESPITE   113 19
TILL A WOMAN HAS DRAWN THE LAST LAST DROP   139 11
OF CRYSTAL HEAVEN FALLS ONE FULL BLACK DROP   147 26
LIKE A SOFT FULL DROP OF DARKNESS IT SEEMS TO SWAY   148 1
TILL THE DROP OF RIPENESS EXUDES   283 25
WHERE BEASTS DROP THEIR UNLICKED YOUNG AND PASTURE AND + 321 13
ALWAYS AS IF FOR ONE DROP OF REST   345 9
ONE LITTLE DROP   345 10
WHO CAN UNSEAT HER LIKE A LIQUID DROP THAT IS HEAVY AND 392 28
DROP WHICH SHE LOVES SENSITIVE MOTHER KANGAROO   393 9
A SMALL BIRD WILL DROP FROZEN DEAD FROM A BOUGH   467 3
DROP YOUR SLOPPY BEHAVIOUR   564 15
DROP OF WHISKEY IN ITS MINKY WELL IT SHALL YET IT SHALL 570 25
AS THE FUCHSIA DOES DANGLING HER RECKLESS DROP   667 16
WHEN AT A CERTAIN POINT A DROP OF WATER BEGAN TO DRIP D+ 682 13
MUST WE GO ON TILL WE DROP OH YOU WHO STAND BEHIND US   756 3
AS WE DROP THROUGH THE NIGHT   862 19
THAT LIFT UP HIGH THEN DROP HIS STRANGE HARSH BREAST   879 1

DROPPED
BEFORE ALL THE BATS HAVE DROPPED FROM THE BOUGH   35 9
THEN AFTER A BIT 'ER DROPPED 'EM DOWN THAT PLACE   61 15
LIGHTING THESE AUTUMN LEAVES LIKE A STAR DROPPED THROUGH 86 16
UNBEKNOWN HAS DROPPED   137 30
THE HAWK HAS DROPPED THE WIND IS SPENDING   150 5
I HAVE DROPPED AT LAST HEADLONG INTO NOUGHT PLUNGING UP+ 266 2
THEN AFTER A BIT 'ER DROPPED 'EM DOWN THAT PLACE   *911 31

DROPPING
    LIKE SPATTERING SHOUTS OF AN ORATOR ENDLESSLY DROPPING   54   6
    SUCCEEDING SHARP LITTLE SOUNDS DROPPING INTO SILENCE   63 10
    DROPPING AND STARTING FROM SLEEP   143   3
    THIS ROLLING DROPPING HEAVY GLOBULE   279 12
    DROPPING AMONG HIS LEAVES HANGS THE DARK GRAPE   286 10
    BREAK INTO DROPS BURN INTO DROPS OF BLOOD AND DROPPING   322 14
    DROPPING TAKE WING   322 15
    DROPPING BACK WITH A SLAP ON THE FACE OF THE FLOOD   337   4
    DROPPING ABOUT THE AIR   344   9
    THE PALE-GOLD FLESH OF PRIAPUS DROPPING ASLEEP   651 19
    THE FRIZZLING FALLING FIRE THAT CANNOT GO OUT DROPPING +   701 27
    CLUTCHING TASTING DROPPING   861 27
    LIKE A LONELY STAR DROPPING THROUGH SPACE   862 24
    THE BATS DEPRAVED ARE DROPPING GAILY FROM OFF THE TREE   *918 13

DROPPINGS
    THEIR DROPPINGS AMONG THE TURF   321 14
    THAN DROPPINGS   356 25
    THE MULTITUDES ARE LIKE DROPPINGS OF BIRDS LIKE DUNG OF+   614 21

DROPS
    IN THE OPEN DEPTHS OF EACH FLOWER DARK RESTLESS DROPS   76   2
    OH BUT 'E DROPS 'IS FLAG WHEN 'E SEES ME   79   9
    AND OUT OF THE INVISIBLE STREAMS OF BRIGHT BLUE DROPS   136 11
    PALE-BLURRED WITH TWO ROUND BLACK DROPS AS IF IT MISSED   141 17
    AND OUR BODIES MOLTEN DROPS OF DREAM-BLOOD THAT SWIRL A+   176   7
    HE TAKES THE FLAME-WILD DROPS   203   2
    WHEN SOME ONE PASSES HE DROPS HIS HEAD   228   5
    NO GLITTERING COMPACT DROPS OF DAWN   278 28
    SWEATING HIS DROPS OF BLOOD THROUGH THE LONG-NIGHTED   305 25
    BREAK INTO DROPS BURN INTO DROPS OF BLOOD AND DROPPING   322 14
    AND THE POINT OF YOUR MANTILLA DROPS ACROSS YOUR NOSE   369 30
    THERE SHE SHAN'T HAVE ANY MORE PEPPERMINT DROPS   393 24
    THE APPLES FALLING LIKE GREAT DROPS OF DEW   716 20
    HEAVY WITH DROPS OF THE FIRST CRUEL RAIN   863 15
    IN SHOWERS OF MINUTE RUDDY DROPS FROM THEIR BLADES   884 29
    IN THE OPEN DEPTHS OF EACH FLOWER DARK RESTLESS DROPS   *897 29
    IN THE OPEN DEPTHS OF EACH FLOWER DARK RESTLESS DROPS   *901   6
    OH BUT HE DROPS HIS FLAG WHEN 'E SEES ME   *921   5
    THE APPLES FALLING LIKE GREAT DROPS OF DEW   *956 26

DROSS
    AND WATCH MY DEAD DAYS FUSING TOGETHER IN DROSS   47   3
    THEIR DROSS OF INDIFFERENCE AND TAKE THE TOLL   74 21
    FROM YOUR BODY'S DEADNESS AND DROSS   112   7
    THIS QUEER DROSS SHAWL OF BLUE AND VERMILION   369 22
    NOT QUITE FUSE FROM THE DROSS   370 10
    THEIR DROSS OF INDIFFERENCE AND BURN THE SCROLL   *895 29
    THEIR DROSS OF INDIFFERENCE AND BURN THE SCROLL   *904 18
    FROM YOUR BODY'S TERRORS AND DROSS   *928 27

DROSSED
    AND LEAVE ME TORTURE AND WRATH AND A DROSSED DESPAIR   874   9

DROSS-JABOT
    DROSS-JABOT   372   4

DROUTH
    I KISS IT IN DROUTH   55 18

DROVE
    THE HARSH COLD WIND OF MY WORDS DROVE ON AND STILL   94 13
    AND THE BIG WHITE MEN FROM WASHINGTON DROVE OUT TO   777 25
    THE WHITE MEN DROVE AWAY   778 34
    THE HARSH COLD WRATH OF MY WORDS DROVE ON AND STILL   *897   1

DROWN
    OF SWEET FIRE SWEEPS ACROSS ME SO I DROWN   43 30
    LIKE A PORTENT BUT LORD I AM GLAD SO GLAD I DROWN   88 26
    WITH HER WINGS AND HER FEATHERS TO DROWN   125   5
    AND LIKE TO DROWN   159   4
    WE SHALL DROWN   425   8
    AND SLOWLY FEEL YOURSELF DROWN   551   5
    TO DROWN THEIR INNER CACOPHONY AND OURS   656   7
    TILL ALL MY MEMORIES DROWN   754 16
    I WISH TO DROWN MYSELF   877   2
    ON MY BREAST WITH HER WINGS AND HER FEATHERS TO DROWN   *936   7

DROWNED
    DROWNED   36 16
    AS A DRENCHED DROWNED BEE   73 20
    AS THE WINGS OF A DRENCHED DROWNED BEE   74   5
    LIKE MEN WHO ARE DROWNED BUT FLOAT ERECT IN THE DEEP   146 10
    STRETCHING OUT MY HAND MY HAND FLUNG LIKE A DROWNED   260 10
    AS A DRENCHED DROWNED BEE   *913 12
    AS THE WINGS OF A DRENCHED DROWNED BEE   *913 26

DROWNING
    FROM SEEKING THE UTTER DROWNING   772 18

DROWNS
    DROWNS ME AND SWEEPS ME AWAY AND HOLDS ME DOWN   261 13

DROWSE
    FROM THE DROWSE OF LIFE WAKE UP ANOTHER WILL   127 15
    SO SWEET LIKE A SWOON OR MORE LIKE THE DROWSE OF A LOW +   727 11
    AND ALONG THE SCENT AND THE COOLNESS A DROWSE OF SLEEP +   858 20

DROWSY
    LIKE DROWSY CREATURES THE HOUSES FALL ASLEEP   48 19

DRUDGE
    DRUDGE TO THE PUBLIC   391 36

DRUG
    UNLESS THERE WERE A MORPHINE OR A DRUG   214 24

DRUGGED
    AS IT SPINS TO SLEEP ON ITS MOTION DRUGGED DENSE IN THE   149   7
    THE AIR IS ALL CLOSE AND POISONOUS IT HAS DRUGGED OUR S+   175 12

DRUID
    AT THE KNIFE OF A DRUID   131 10

DRUM
    DRUMMING HIS VAULTED WINGS AS SAVAGES DRUM   371   4
    THE PONDEROUS SOMBRE SOUND OF THE GREAT DRUM OF   371   6
    DRUM AND THE TURKEY ONRUSH   371   9
    THE HUGE OLD FEMALE ON THE DRUM   426   4
    HE STANDS WITH HIS FOREFEET ON THE DRUM   426   8

DRUMMED
    THE DARK VAN DRUMMED DOWN THE DISTANCE LOWLY   121 30

DRUMMING
    BEHIND ME ON THE LAKE I HEAR THE STEAMER DRUMMING   231   5
    DRUMMING HIS VAULTED WINGS AS SAVAGES DRUM   371   4
    AND THE DRUMMING OF PINIONS OF THUNDER   707 11

DRUMS
    THEIR RHYTHMS ON LONG-DRAWN HOLLOW SINISTER DRUMS   371   5
    SHUDDER OF DRUMS   388 34
    BREAK THE DRUMS OF HIS EARS   439   9
    THE SOFT THUDDING OF DRUMS   623   5
    DRUMS FOR THE BEATING HEART   804   2

DRUM-WINDS
    AND IN THE DARK UNSCIENTIFIC I FEEL THE DRUM-WINDS OF H+   438   9

DRUNK
    IS DRUNK FROM AN AGONISED SKY BY THE EARTH   117 32
    I HAVE EATEN AND DRUNK AND WARMED AND CLOTHED MY BODY   264   1
    YOUNG COLLIER WHO HAS LONG SINCE DRUNK HIMSELF TO   366 18
    AND THROUGH THE SALT THEY REEL WITH DRUNK DELIGHT   694 10
    WHAT SORT OF TIMOROUS POTION OF LOVE HAVE YOU DRUNK   755   2
    AYE SUFFOCATED WITH A DRUNK SURFEIT   877 10
    FOR HE HAS DRUNK THE MORSELS WHITE OF SLEEP   878 11
    AND DRUNK WITH THE DEATH OF THE SOOTHING GREY-WINGED CR+ *918 11

DRUNKEN
    SINCE YOU HAVE DRUNKEN UP THE DREAR   118 10
    AND LIFTED HIS HEAD DREAMILY AS ONE WHO HAS DRUNKEN   350 24

DRUNKENNESS
    THE SONO IO OF PERFECT DRUNKENNESS   281 29

DRY
    WE COULD GATHER UP THE DRY HAY FROM   35 13
    YOU UPON THE DRY DEAD BEECH-LEAVES ONCE MORE ONLY ONCE   90 25
    THE TEARS ARE DRY AND THE CHEEK'S YOUNG FRUITS ARE FRESH   94 19
    SHE KNOWS THE WASTE ALL DRY BENEATH HER IN ONE PLACE   153   5
    HOW I KNOW THAT GLITTER OF SALT DRY STERILE SHARP CORRO+   207 17
    WHICH I SUPPOSE IS WHY AMERICA HAS GONE DRY   286 20
    GOATS GO PAST THE BACK OF THE HOUSE LIKE DRY LEAVES IN +   383 27
    AND JUMPS STACCATO TO EARTH A SHARP DRY JUMP STILL   384 30
    WITH DREAMS AND THRUSTS THAT MAKE THEM DRY IN THEIR SLE+   438 15
    THEY LIE HIGH AND DRY   542 22
    HIGH AND DRY   542 23
    TO FEED THE BONNY BABY AND KEEP ITS TARA DRY   570 19
    IF EVER I LIVED UPON DRY LAND   574 12
    THEY DANCE DANCE DANCE THIS DRY INDUSTRIAL JIG OF THE   631 19
    THAT BASK AND WAKE OH HIGH AND DRY   824 19
    HIGH AND DRY   824 20
    WET AND DRY WET AND DRY   825 14
    NOW WET NOW DRY   825 17
    FROM WET TO DRY   826   3
    THE TEARS ARE DRY THE CHEEKS' YOUNG FRUITS ARE FRESH   *897   7
    DRY FEVER IN HER POOL OF FULL TWILIGHT   *936 33

DUALITY
    DIVIDED INTO PASSIONATE DUALITY   361   5

DUBIOUS
    TO YOUR DUBIOUS STATE   237   6

DUCHESS
    AND A DUCHESS ONCE CAME TO TEA   551 28
    AND THE DUCHESS HAS DONE WITH ME   552   2

DUCK
    SWIMS THE MALLARD DUCK AT DAWN IN THAT QUICK JOY   *953 27

DUCK-EGG
    DUCK-EGG   760   3

DUCKING
    ARE DUCKING THEIR HEADS IN THE WATER TUBS AT THE GATE   732 19

DUCK-POND
    OVER THE BLUE OF THE DUCK-POND PLY   126 12

DUCKS
    WHITE DUCKS A QUACKING FLOTILLA OF CLOUD   126 13

DUCT
    IN A RUSH UP THE SHRIEKING DUCT OF HIS VERTEBRAL WAY   381 20

DUCTILE
    GOD IS BORN GOD IS BORN BRIGHT YELLOW AND DUCTILE HE IS+   682 25

DUDGEON
NOW AT LAST THE INK AND DUDGEON PASSES FROM OUR FERVENT+			70 5

DUDS
AND THEY PUT IT OVER US THE DUDS			556 12

DUE
LIKE A BELL THAT IS CHIMING EACH STROKE AS A STROKE FAL+			251 12
NOW DUE TO BE CROWNED AGAIN			351 26
ARE DUE			464 19
OF BIGGER LIVES WITH DUE REVERENCE AND ACKNOWLEDGEMENT			679 22
IS DUE TO THE ANGRY UNAPPEASED DEAD			723 5

DUES
AS IF IT WERE YOUR DUES AND I DIDN'T COUNT AT ALL			547 15
WE GIVE HATE HER DUES O GOD WE YIELD HER UP			743 15
ME OUT OF MY PROPER DUES WITH YOUR CHINKING JESTS			872 26

DUFFERS
FIGHT THEN POOR DUFFERS DEGRADING			456 12

DUG
DUG FIRM IN MY BREAST AS YOU REACHED OUT RIGHT			886 8

DULL
OBSCURES THE DARK WOOD AND THE DULL ORANGE SKY			85 10
WITH DULL FACE LEANING TO FACE			106 14
BEAT AFTER BEAT FALLS SOMBRE AND DULL			164 1
AND PILED THEM UP IN A DULL GREY HEAP IN THE WEST			167 2
TO-MORROW WILL POUR THEM ALL BACK THE DULL HOURS I DETE+			167 4
AND PILED THEM UP IN A DULL GREY HEAP IN THE WEST			167 12
TO-MORROW WILL POUR THEM ALL BACK THE DULL HOURS I DETE+			167 20
DULL METEORITE FLASH ONLY INTO LIGHT			195 21
TO ME MEN'S FOOTFALLS FALL WITH A DULL SOFT RUMBLE			288 28
THICK SMOOTH-FLESHED SILVER DULL ONLY AS HUMAN LIMBS ARE			298 23
DULL			298 24
AND LAUGH AT TIME AND LAUGH AT DULL ETERNITY			299 11
HOW YOU SAIL LIKE A HERON OR A DULL CLOT OF AIR			332 16
WHILE SHE PULLS HERSELF FREE AND ROWS HER DULL MOUND			362 10
AND DULL DEATH COMES IN A DAY			459 8
IT'S REALLY RATHER DULL			490 8
TELLS DULL MEANINGLESS DISGUSTING TALES			522 7
YOU DULL ANGELS TARNISHED WITH CENTURIES OF CONVENTIONA+			614 16
AND THE DULL BREAKING OF BONES			640 12
THERE IS A BAND OF DULL GOLD IN THE WEST AND SAY WHAT Y+			656 1
HORIZONTAL AND MEANINGLESS DESIRABLY DULL			827 18
I THINK IDIOTS TELL DULL STUPID DISGUSTING TALES			837 21
FROM THE TULIPS COLOURED WITH CHALK AND THE DULL GRASS'+			867 4
AND DRINKS HIMSELF LIKE A SOAKED GORGED CREATURE DULL			877 9
THERE LIES THE DULL RED HEAP OF THEIR SAND IN THE WEST			*896 7
THERE LIES A DULL RED HEAP OF HIS SAND IN THE WEST			*896 17
TOMORROW WILL POUR THEM ALL BACK THE DULL HOURS I DETEST			*896 25
THE SNOW DESCENDS AS IF THE DULL SKY SHOOK			*898 8
THE SNOW DESCENDS AS IF THE DULL SKY SHOOK			*901 17
BUT OPAQUE AND DULL IN THE FLESH			*927 17
BUT OPAQUE AND DULL IN THE FLESH			*928 17

DULLED
DEADENED ME THROUGH TILL THE GREY DOWNS DULLED TO SLEEP			98 22

DULLER
DULLER THAN YOUR GRANDMOTHERS BUT LEAVE THAT ASIDE			464 11

DUMB
THE WARM DUMB WISDOM			38 19
I LAY DUMB AND STARK			46 24
AND MY ARMS FELL LOOSE AND I WAS DUMB			62 20
THEIR DUMB CONFESSION OF WHAT HER BLOOD MUST FEEL			128 9
WHO VOICE THE DUMB NIGHT FITTINGLY			197 31
THEN THE DUMB ACHING BITTER HELPLESS NEED			263 20
HE IS DUMB HE IS VISIONLESS			362 2
I THOUGHT HE WAS DUMB			363 25
I SAID HE WAS DUMB			363 26
THE COW WAS DUMB AND THE CUCKOO TOO			761 1
MEN DUMB IN THE DUSK			763 28
DUMB			764 5
OH MEN DUMB IN THE DARKNESS			765 3
TOGETHER WHEREVER THE DUMB ROAD GOES			857 16
THIS WARM DUMB WISDOM			*893 2
AND LIPS APART WITH DUMB CRIES			*912 23

DUMBNESS
HOW CAN ONE SPEAK WHERE THERE IS A DUMBNESS ON ONE'S MO+			266 10

DUMMY
DUMMY			570 23

DUMMY-TEAT
AND ITS DUMMY-TEAT HAS TO BE MADE BIGGER AND BIGGER AND+			670 11

DUMPLING
EVEN IF IT IS A WOMAN MAKING AN APPLE DUMPLING OR A MAN			449 10

DUN
FEELING THE RAW COLD DUN ME AND ALL THE TIME			98 18

DUNCAN
OLD DUNCAN WITH DAGGERS			494 24

DUNES
BUT WHEN I CROSSED THE DUNES			883 21

DUNG
AND FRESH-DROPPED DUNG			398 29
OR THE STOUT SWART BEETLE ROLLED THE GLOBE OF DUNG IN W+			437 16
DUNG			449 25
AND STANDS THERE A PIECE OF DUNG			450 4
MEN SHOULD REFUSE TO BE HEAPS OF WAGE-EARNING DUNG			450 6

DUNG
OF DUNG			450 11
OR A DUNG SQUIRT			463 4
IN THE DEEP DUNG OF CASH AND LORE			489 7
THE MULTITUDES ARE LIKE DROPPINGS OF BIRDS LIKE DUNG OF+			614 21
BEFORE THE STOUT SWART BEETLE HAD A BALL OF DUNG TO ROL+			*946 26

DUNGEON
LOCKED UP IN A DUNGEON CELL			633 2

DUNG-MOUTH
REEKING DUNG-MOUTH			398 32

DUNG-WHITENED
RATHER DIRTY ON DUNG-WHITENED PATMOS			329 25

DUNLOP
INTO RUBBER-LIKE DEADNESS DUNLOP INFLATED UNCONCERN			625 18

DUNNA
I DUNNA KNOW			45 10
DUNNA THEE TELL ME IT'S HIS'N MOTHER			76 23
DUNNA THEE DUNNA THEE			76 24
SAY NO MORE LIZ DUNNA THEE			80 25
DUNNA THEE TELL ME IT'S HIS'N MOTHER			*918 15
DUNNA THEE DUNNA THEE			*918 16
SAY NO MORE LIZ DUNNA THEE			*922 25

DUNNAT
DUNNAT THEE THINK BUT WHAT I'VE LOVED THEE I'VE LOVED T+			83 9
DUNNAT THEE THINK BUT WHAT I LOVE THEE I LOVE THEE WELL			*925 13

DUNNO
I DUNNO WHEER 'IS EYES WAS A GRET			81 17
I DUNNO WHERE HIS EYES WAS A GRET			*923 17

DUPLICATED
AND THE WOMAN WAS HERSELF NEVER TO BE DUPLICATED A GODD+			676 13

DURANCE
FROM DURANCE VILE			580 18

DURING
YES EVEN DURING MY UPLIFTING			320 24
IN PYRAMID MEXICO DURING SACRIFICE			371 8
AND IF YOU DON'T LIVE DURING YOUR LIFE YOU ARE A PIECE +			449 24
DURING THE WILD ORGASMS OF CHAOS			477 3
DURING MY MINORITY			671 4
OR THE MOST HIGH DURING THE COAL AGE CUDGELLING HIS MIG+			690 26

DUSK
KILLING THE BLUE DUSK WITH HARSH SCENT UNNERVING			91 14
CHILL DUSK FOR YOU AND GLADLY GLEAMING			91 21
SEVEN TOADS THAT MOVE IN THE DUSK TO SHARE			126 19
SOFTLY IN THE DUSK A WOMAN IS SINGING TO ME			148 4
WENT ROLLING IN THE DUSK TOWARDS THE RIVER			205 26
ME LIKE A GADFLY INTO THE DUSK WITHOUT MY KNOWING			223 5
AND LET THE LIGHTNING OUT OF YOUR SMOTHERED DUSK			383 19
AT DUSK THEY PATTER BACK LIKE A BOUGH BEING DRAGGED ON			384 1
RAISING DUSK AND ACRIDITY OF GOATS AND BLEATING			384 3
AND STARTING FORWARD IN THE DUSK WITH YOUR LITTLE BLACK			396 31
HARK IN THE DUSK			425 11
THROUGH THE DUSK			445 11
IN THE RED STILLNESS OF THE DUSK			506 15
WORK HAS MADE US BLIND AND NOW THE DUSK			757 13
MEN DUMB IN THE DUSK			763 28
MEN IN THE DUSK			764 4
ON THE DREAM-SLOPES BROWSING LIKE A DEER IN THE DUSK			807 10
SOME TURNING PINK SOME TURNING PURPLE DUSK			824 23
AS I CAME HOME IN THE DUSK DESPOILED BY SCHOOL A MERE B+			864 27
IN THE DEEP CART-RUTS GLEAMED THROUGH THE BLUE OF THE D+			864 30
THE FATHER OF ALL THINGS SWIMS IN THE VAST DUSK OF ALL +			*947 17
PUTTING ITS TIMBERS TOGETHER IN THE DUSK			*960 29

DUSKY
TO WALK THE LONELY DUSKY HEIGHTS			63 31
LIES ON THE DUST WATCHING WHERE THERE IS NOTHING TO SEE+			112 22
THERE WAS ANOTHER WORLD A DUSKY FLOWERLESS TENDRILLED W+			285 22
THE GRAPE IS SWART THE AVENUES DUSKY AND TENDRILLED SUB+			286 32
DUSKY ARE THE AVENUES OF WINE			287 5
ALL LIPS ARE DUSKY AND VALVED			288 22
DUSKY SLIM MARROW-THOUGHT OF SLENDER FLICKERING MEN OF			297 6
EVE SWINGING HER DUSKY LIMBS DISCONSOLATE			863 21

DUST
MESSAGES OF TRUE-LOVE DOWN THE DUST OF THE HIGHROAD			65 18
OF GOLDEN DUST WITH STAR AFTER STAR			70 18
WHEN INTO THE NIGHT THE YELLOW LIGHT IS ROUSED LIKE DUST			70 20
DUST AS THE PUFF-BALL DOES AND BIRDS THAT CHAFF			89 28
A FLOCCULENT DUST ON THE FLOOR OF THE WORLD THE FESTOON			98 13
AND I SLEPT TILL DAWN AT THE WINDOW BLEW IN LIKE DUST			99 1
LIKE A LINTY RAW-COLD DUST DISTURBED FROM THE FLOOR			99 2
LIES ON THE DUST WATCHING WHERE THERE IS NOTHING TO SEE+			112 22
LOW FROM THE ROOF AND THE WET DUST FALLING SOFTLY FROM +			112 26
THEIR DUST FROM THE BIRCH ON THE BLUE			126 31
AND ALL THE EARTH IS GONE INTO A DUST			135 13
CAUGHT DUST FROM THE SEA'S LONG SWATHS			152 13
THE HEAVENS LIKE SPECKS OF DUST THAT ARE FLOATING ASUND+			223 3
FOR OH I KNOW IN THE DUST WHERE WE HAVE BURIED			298 1
SWINE WASH IN MIRE AND BARNYARD FOWLS IN DUST			376 8
DUST			387 13
LEFT IN THE DUST BEHIND LIKE A DUST-BALL TEARING ALONG			397 14
ALL THAT DUST OUT OF YOUR WRINKLED FACE			397 31
THEN WHEN I DUST YOU A BIT WITH A JUNIPER TWIG			399 12
DAY HAS GONE TO DUST ON THE SAGE-GREY DESERT			403 21
LIKE A WHITE CHRISTUS FALLEN TO DUST FROM A CROSS			403 22
TO DUST TO ASH ON THE TWILIT FLOOR OF THE DESERT			403 23
HE FELL TO DUST AS THE TWILIGHT FELL			404 26

DUST
    TILL AT LAST IT'S A FULL FULL ROSE AND HAS NO MALE DUST+   535   7
    BUT THEY OFTEN RAISE SUCH A DUST IN THE SWEEPING   536   2
    BESIDE THE HIGH ROAD PAST THE DEATHLY DUST   605 24
    TILL THE SOUL OF THE STIFF-NECKED IS GROUND TO DUST TO +   616 14
    AND DEMOCRACY IS GROUND INTO DUST   648 11
    SOILING THE CLEAN WHITE DUST HE RUBS THE BELLY   734   9
    AND KICKS DUST OVER THE RED STAIN IN THE ROAD   734 16
    YOU ARE EMPTY GOURD-SHELLS FILLED WITH DUST AND WIND   800   4
    NOW THE WORLD IS ENDING IN DUST AND IN SORROW   815   1
    ELOQUENT PURITY VOICELESS IN THE DUST   855   6
    THE AIR AND THE FLOWING SUNSHINE AND BRIGHT DUST   870   9
    WHEN INTO THE NIGHT THE YELLOW LIGHT IS ROUSED LIKE DUS+   *917 17
    KISS BUT THEN THE DUST FROM OFF MY LIPS   *929 26
    AND ALL THE TOWN IS GONE INTO A DUST   *939 13

DUST-BALL
    LEFT IN THE DUST BEHIND LIKE A DUST-BALL TEARING ALONG   397 14

DUST-HEAP
    THE DUST-HEAP OF MAN'S FILTHY WORLD ON FIRE   315   3

DUST-LIT
    WHEN DAWN IS FAR BEHIND THE STAR THE DUST-LIT TOWN HAS   71   7

DUST-MASK
    AND BLACK EYES BULGING BRIGHT IN A DUST-MASK   397 17

DUST-PIG
    REAL LITTLE DUST-PIG EARS ALMOST BLOWN AWAY   397 16

DUST-SMOOTH
    ALL YOUR GAME LITTLE BODY DUST-SMOOTH LIKE A LITTLE PIG   397 26

DUSTY
    OF THE SKY SAGGED DUSTY AS SPIDER CLOTH   98 14
    OF THE MIRROR TOWARDS THE DUSTY GRATE AS IF FEELING   141 14
    PELTING BEHIND ON THE DUSTY TRAIL WHEN THE HORSE SETS O+   397 12
    DUSTY POLLEN OF GRASS TALL GRASS IN ITS MIDSUMMER MALEN+   587   3
    WITH HER SUAVE FORM DUSTY WITH SPICES HONEY SWEET STRAY+   864   4
    ALOFT BY ONE GREAT BENDING RAFTER DUSTY   876 13
    OF DUSTY GRASSES LIKE THE STARS THAT DAWN   884 31

DUTEOUS
    MY EYES FROM DUTEOUS WORK MALINGERING   129 14

DUTY
    YOU ARE ALL THESE AND ON ME LIES THE DUTY   73   6
    TA'E OFF THY DUTY STRIPES TIM   82 17
    YOU HAVE SLAIN AS WAS YOUR DUTY   95 22
    AND SUPERFICIAL ATTENTION AND CARE AND FULFILMENT OF DU+   832 16
    TAKE OFF THY DUTY STRIPES TIM   *924 21

DWELL
    THEY DWELL IN THE OUTSKIRT FRINGES OF NOWHERE   711 24

DWELLED
    WAYS OF ST PETERSBURG I HAVE DWELLED IN THE CORE   866 28

DWELLEST
    THOU OUR MAIDEN THOU WHO DWELLEST IN HEAVEN   753   1

DWELLING
    AND DWELLING IN HIS OWN BOWERY HOUSE LIKE A BEAVER'S   451 24
    AND DWELLING IN HIS OWN BOWERY HOUSE LIKE A BIRD IN A B+   *950   9

DWELLING-PLACE
    EVIL HAS NO DWELLING-PLACE   711 22

DWELLINGS
    AND EMBEDDED YOU IN THE WORKMEN'S DWELLINGS WHERE   630 19

DWELLS
    TO GOD WHO DWELLS IN DEEP OBLIVION   725 21
    AND THERE OBLIVION DWELLS AND THE SILENT SOUL   726 10

DWELT
    THEY DWELT IN A HUGE HOARSE SEA-CAVE   201 21

DWINDLE
    THE OLD DRAGON WILL DWINDLE DOWN TO THE SIZE OF A STRAY+   665 14

DYE
    STAINED WITH RED DYE   36 26

DYED
    SHE IS A MADE-UP LIE A DYED IMMORTELLE   478 28

D'YER
    OF COURSE I'M A LIDY WHAT D'YER THINK   434 25

DYES
    REVEAL THE UNIVERSAL TINT THAT DYES   197 27
    YET THE LANGUAGE SO LOVELY LIKE THE DYES FROM GAS-TAR   494 26

DYING
    WHERE ASH ON THE DYING COALS GROWS SWIFTLY LIKE HEAVY   47   6
    IN THE DYING LAMP OF MY LOVE   121 27
    THEY ARE ALL DYING   295   2
    MARRIED OR DYING   495 25
    OUR ERA IS DYING   512   1
    AFTER THE PAINFUL PAINFUL EXPERIENCE OF DYING   677   5
    SO UNHAMPERED IN THEIR LIVING AND DYING   677 11
    WE ARE DYING WE ARE DYING WE ARE ALL OF US DYING   718 14
    WE ARE DYING WE ARE DYING PIECEMEAL OUR BODIES ARE DYING   718 17
    WE ARE DYING WE ARE DYING SO ALL WE CAN DO   718 21
    AND WE CAN BE DYING DYING DYING   721   1
    BLEEDING AND SHOUTING AND DYING   739   2

DYING
    AS ONE DYING WITH THE CHARRED RAGS FALLING AWAY   769 13
    THE STAR THAT WAS FALLING WAS FADING WAS DYING   786 14
    I HEARD THE STAR SINGING LIKE A DYING BIRD   786 15
    OF THE DYING GRASS WITH A THRICE-TOLD TALE OF DEATH   858 27

DYKE
    DYKE BETWEEN PADDY-FIELDS   387   5

DYNAMICALLY
    ONLY THAT EXISTS WHICH EXISTS DYNAMICALLY AND UNMENTALI+   474 19

DYNAMO
    GOD THE FATHER IS A DYNAMO   641   3
    AND THE WILL THE LIVING DYNAMO GIVES THE MOTION AND THE+   712 14

DYNAMOS
    AND MEN HAVE PERFORCE TO BE LITTLE DYNAMOS   641   6

D'YOU
    BRISTLING WITH ANIMATION OH PLEASE SIR HOW D'YOU LIKE T+   865 21

'D
    THA KNOWS 'E 'D A WINSOME WAY WI 'IM AN' SHE   *910 24

EAGER
    AND GLAD ARE THE EAGER DEAD TO RECEIVE YOU THERE   168   9
    AMONG THE EAGER CORDIAL MEN   228 18
    I FEEL NEW AND EAGER   244 23
    THERE IS THAT WHICH MAKES US EAGER   439 16
    WHILE WE ARE EAGER WE THINK NOTHING OF IT   439 17
    THEY WERE ONLY TOO EAGER TO GRANT   555 22
    MY PICTURES EAGER AS THE HONEY BEE   577 25
    ARE STILL IN BUD AND EAGER   627   3
    PONDERING YET EAGER THE BROAD AND THICK-SET ITALIAN WHO+   672 26
    BUT THE FATHER OF ALL THINGS IS HE WHO MAKES US EAGER   840 11
    EAGER AT ALL   840 15
    WITH SHARP DESIRE I AM NOT EAGER FOR SHARP DESIRE ANY M+   840 24
    AND THEIR SUBTLE EAGER BOOMING   885 25
    INTO DARKNESS OPEN AND EAGER FOR THE THRUST OF THE   *937 20

EAGERLY
    AS VINES GOING EAGERLY UP THEY TWINE   52   9
    EAGERLY PASSING OVER FROM THE ENTANGLEMENT OF LIFE   676 20

EAGERNESS
    BUT WHEN OUR EAGERNESS LEAVES US WE ARE GODLESS AND FULL   439 19
    TO THE ADVENTURE OF DEATH IN EAGERNESS   676 21
    RULING THE EARTH ROUSES NO EAGERNESS IN ME AT ALL   840 17

EAGLE
    AND THE BULL NOR WAKES FROM THE LIGHT-EYED EAGLE SLEEP   319 11
    SUN-PEERING EAGLE   328   3
    OF JOHN'S GREAT GOLD-BARRED EAGLE   328   9
    OH THAT MIND-SOARING EAGLE OF AN EVANGELIST   328 19
    AS AN EAGLE STARING DOWN ON THE SUN   328 22
    LIKE A KING EAGLE BIRD OF THE MOST HIGH SWEEPING THE RO+   329   4
    CHICK OF THE INTELLECTUAL EAGLE   329 13
    JOHN'S EAGLE   329 16
    FOR THE ALMIGHTY EAGLE OF THE FORE-ORDAINING MIND   329 21
    THE POOR OLD GOLDEN EAGLE OF THE WORD-FLEDGED SPIRIT   329 30
    JOHN'S EAGLE   330   2
    THE THOUGHTS OF THE SKIES THE EAGLE FLIES NEAREST TO TH+   368   2
    NOT THE EAGLE SCREAMS WHEN THE SUN IS HIGH THE PEACOCK +   368 10
    THE EAGLE THE DOVE AND THE BARNYARD ROOSTER DO THEY CALL   371 22
    AN EAGLE AT THE TOP OF A LOW CEDAR-BUSH   373   1
    EAGLE WITH THE SICKLE DRIPPING DARKLY ABOVE   373   4
    EAGLE GLOVED IN FEATHERS   373 16
    BEAKED EAGLE   373 32
    AMERICAN EAGLE   374   2
    OLD EAGLE   374 11
    AND ARE YOU HIS PRIEST BIG EAGLE   374 18
    I DON'T YIELD TO YOU BIG JOWL-FACED EAGLE   374 25
    DARK AS YOU ARE ON YOUR DARK SIDE EAGLE OF HEAVEN   374 31
    CIRCLES AN EAGLE   403   2
    MAYBE A BLACK EAGLE WITH ITS WINGS OUT   403 25
    AND HATCHED ANOTHER EAGLE   413   2
    TILL THE AMERICAN EAGLE WAS THE ONLY EAGLE LEFT IN THE   413 10
    THE BIG BIRD OF THE AMERINDIAN BEING THE EAGLE   414   2
    OR WHETHER IT ACTUALLY IS AN EAGLE YOU ARE   414 13
    EAGLE OF THE ROCKIES BIRD OF MEN THAT ARE MASTERS   414 21
    BEYOND EVEN THAT EAGLE THAT PHOENIX HANGING OVER THE   437 12
    O EAGLE OF THE MIND ALAS YOU ARE MORE LIKE A BUZZARD   473   9
    SHOWS THAT SHE IS RENEWING HER YOUTH LIKE THE EAGLE   728 11
    SITS AN EAGLE ERECT AND SCORCH-BREASTED   780 27
    EAGLE IN THE SCORCH FOREVER   781   5
    EAGLE SOUTH-WESTWARD FACING   781   6
    EAGLE WITH THE SICKLE DRIPPING DARKLY ABOVE   781   7
    EAGLE SCORCHED-PALLID OUT OF THE HAIR OF THE CEDAR   781 10
    EAGLE GLOVED IN FEATHERS   781 12
    BEAKED EAGLE   782   8
    AND UP THE IRON FEET OF THE EAGLE IN THRILLS OF FIERY P+   782 22
    EAGLE WITH EGYPTIAN DARKNESS JUTTING IN FRONT OF YOUR F+   782 27
    AND SENT THE EAGLE TO KEEP AN EYE ON HIM   783   5
    SOLDIER-ERECT FROM THE GOD-THRUST EAGLE   783   8
    OH VINDICTIVE EAGLE OF AMERICA   783 21
    OH SINISTER INDIAN EAGLE   783 22
    OH EAGLE OF KINGS AND EMPERORS   783 23
    HE SENDS THE EAGLE OF SILENCE DOWN ON WIDE WINGS   799 17
    I AM QUETZALCOATL OF THE EAGLE AND THE SNAKE   800 36
    OUT OF THE DEPTHS OF THE SKY I CAME LIKE AN EAGLE   801   6
    AND I QUETZALCOATL THE EAGLE OF THE AIR AM BRUSHING YOU+ 802   1
    OVER MY HEAD HIS NOISELESS EAGLE   802 20
    AND BEYOND THE EAGLE ROSE AND THE PHOENIX PARENT SOARIN+ *946 23

EAGLES
  DOWN WITH ALL EAGLES COOED THE DOVE   413   4
  AND DOWN ALL EAGLES BEGAN TO FLUTTER REELING FROM THEIR   413   5
  EAGLES WITH TWO HEADS EAGLES WITH ONE PRESENTLY EAGLES   413   7

EAGLE'S
  SLEEP OF THE MAN AND THE EAGLE'S SLEEP AFTER WHICH THE +   319   6
  OF THE EAGLE'S WINGS   403 29

EAR
  THE EAR PERHAPS IS CHILLY UNDERNEATH   87   8
  AND THE SNORE OF THE NIGHT IN MY EAR   107   8
  AH YOU YOU EAR OF CORN STRAIGHT LYING   171 18
  SWEET IN EAR NOR SO MUCH TO GIVE   263   3
  WITH A HIBISCUS FLOWER BEHIND MY EAR   317 15
  IT IS YOUR SMALL HIGH HATEFUL BUGLE IN MY EAR   333 17
  LENDING FIRST ONE EAR THEN ANOTHER   304 18
  STRAGGLE OF A LONG THIN EAR LIKE RIBBON   393 18
  LITTLE DANGLE OF AN IMMATURE PAW AND ONE THIN EAR   393 20
  AND TURN THE POOR SILK GLOVE INTO A LUSTY SOW'S EAR   538 22
  LIKE BEARDED WHEAT IN EAR   627   8
  I SHOULD LEAN AND WHISPER IN HIS EAR   752   5
  THAT IS HER SMALL EAR AGAINST MY EYES   882 24
  AND I TOOK HER EAR LIKE THE LEAF OF A WATER-FLOWER BETW+   882 27

EAR-APRICK
  MUZZLES TOGETHER EAR-APRICK   311 24

EARL
  AN EARL ONCE ASKED ME DOWN TO STAY   551 27
  I DIDN'T STAY VERY LONG WITH THE EARL   552   1

EARLY
  OF OUR EARLY LOVE THAT HARDLY HAS OPENED YET   58 11
  THERE IS A BAND PLAYING IN THE EARLY NIGHT   656   5
  WITH HAIR THAT WAS BOBBED SO EARLY   834 15

EARN
  A MAN SHOULD NEVER EARN HIS LIVING   443 10
  DON'T EARN GOLDEN OPINIONS OPINIONS GOLDEN   458 26
  TO EARN THEIR LIVINGS NOR YET GIRLS SWEET JOYS   459   3

EARNEST
  FOR SURELY THIS EARNEST MAN HAS NONE   130 13
  DON'T DO IT IN DEADLY EARNEST   517   3

EARNESTLY
  FOR I ACHE MOST EARNESTLY FOR YOUR TOUCH   117 15
  LOOKING EARNESTLY UNDER THE DARK UMBRELLAS HELD FAST   180 12
  EARNESTLY AND OH FOR ME THIS CLASS IS A BITTER ROOD   *898 16
  EARNESTLY AND OH FOR ME THIS CLASS IS A BITTER ROOD   *901 25
  FOR I ACHE MOST EARNESTLY FOR YOUR TOUCH   *931 19

EARNESTNESS
  YOU SIT TALKING IN ALL EARNESTNESS TO A WOMAN   655   1
  YET YOU GO ON TALKING IN ALL EARNESTNESS   655   6
  AS I AM WITH LIVING MY LIFE IN EARNESTNESS STILL PROGRE+ *900 12
  AS I AM WITH LIVING MY LIFE IN EARNESTNESS STILL PROGRE+ *903 24

EARNING
  EARNING YOUR LIVING WHILE YOUR LIFE IS LOST   459   7
  IF MEN WERE FREE FROM THE TERROR OF EARNING A LIVING   488   4
  EARNING A WAGE IS A PRISON OCCUPATION   521   7
  EARNING A SALARY IS A PRISON OVERSEER'S JOB   521   9
  AT HER AGE WHY I'LL BE EARNING A JOLLY GOOD SCREW   834 20
  WHEREIN A MAN CAN LIVE HIS LIFE WITHOUT BEING A SLAVE T+ 837 25

EARNINGS
  EARNINGS   44   3

EARNS
  IF HE EARNS HIS LIFE HE'LL BE LOVELY   443 11
  EARNS MY UNDYING DETESTATION   507 15

EARS
  CHERRIES HUNG ROUND HER EARS   37   2
  THE RABBIT PRESSES BACK HER EARS   43   5
  THE NOISE DISTRESSES HER EARS AND TEARS   54 21
  AND STRANGE IN MY BLOOD-SWEPT EARS WAS THE SOUND   61 24
  TO PUT HER EARS TO THE PAINFUL SOB OF MY BLOOD   64 17
  I CLOSE YOUR EARS WITH KISSES   154   1
  MY EARS ARE WEARY WITH WORDS THAT BOUNCE ON THEM AND   249 22
  OWN EARS TO MY OWN DESTRUCTION   257   6
  AND CYCLAMENS PUTTING THEIR EARS BACK   310 28
  WAKING PRICKING THEIR EARS   311   5
  FOLDING BACK THEIR SOUNDLESS PETALLED EARS   311   9
  LAYING BACK HER LONG EARS WITH UNWINKING BLISS   311 19
  AND IMPROPER DERISIVE EARS   345 30
  WITH LONG BLACK-PAPER EARS   345 35
  BARES HIS LONG ASS'S TEETH FLATTENS HIS LONG ASS'S EARS 379 21
  SHE IS SUCH AN ALERT LISTENER WITH HER EARS WIDE TO KNOW 384 15
  WHILE HIS SLITTED EYES SQUINT BACK TO THE ROOTS OF HIS + 386 22
  REAL LITTLE DUST-PIG EARS ALMOST BLOWN AWAY   397 16
  HER ROUND FINE-FASHIONED HEAD WITH TWO DEAD EARS   402   3
  BREAK THE DRUMS OF HIS EARS   439   9
  BLOWING DOWN YOUR NECK AND YOUR EARS   506 23
  INTO SOW'S EARS   538 25
  FOR OUR DAINTY OUR DELICATE ENGLISH EARS   576   3
  WITH HIS EARS PRICKED AND HIS BODY WINCING   645 19
  IF YOU SEE MY RINGS HOW THEY SPARKLE WITHIN MY EARS   755   3
  THE SPIRITS OF THE COLD DEAD WHISTLE IN THE EARS OF THE+ 795 15
  AND IN WHOM THE DREAM SITS UP LIKE A RABBIT LIFTING LON+ 807   8
  THAT PRICK THEIR EARS LIKE A RABBIT OR BROWSE IN THE DA+ 807 14
  AND HER FINGERS MOVE IN THE RUTS OF MY EARS   863   3
  PERHAPS THE TINY YOUNG NETTLES HAVE STUNG HER EARS   882 26
  AND STRANGE IN MY BLOOD-SWEPT EARS WAS THE SOUND   *912   4

EARTH
  RABBITS HANDFULS OF BROWN EARTH LIE   33   5
  DARKNESS COMES OUT OF THE EARTH   41 20
  THE EARTH   57 18
  SHALL SEE AN IMAGE OF HEAVEN OR OF EARTH   59 15
  THE LITTLE GRAIN DRAWS DOWN THE EARTH TO HIDE   64 10
  OH EARTH YOU SPINNING CLOD OF EARTH   73   1
  OH EARTH YOU ROTTEN APPLE ROLLING DOWNWARD   73   3
  THEN BRILLIANT EARTH FROM THE BURR OF NIGHT IN BEAUTY   73   4
  OF BEES THAT VIBRATE WITH REVOLT WHO FALL TO EARTH   73 18
  I AM SICK AND WHAT ON EARTH IS THE GOOD OF IT ALL   74 16
  AGAIN FROM EARTH LIKE LILIES FLAGGED AND SERE   87 28
  SO EVEN IT BEATS LIKE SILENCE AND SKY AND EARTH IN ONE + 88   3
  ITS FIGURED PAGES AND SKY AND EARTH AND ALL BETWEEN ARE+ 88 10
  OF EARTH AND QUICKENS ALL HERSELF WITH FLOWERS   89   2
  BUT NOW I AM TRODDEN TO EARTH AND MY FIRES ARE LOW   94   1
  OF GREEN FIRES LIT ON THE SOIL OF EARTH THIS BLAZE   116   7
  IS DRUNK FROM AN AGONISED SKY BY THE EARTH   117 32
  TO YOU EARTH OF MY ATMOSPHERE STONE   118   4
  EARTH OF MY SWAYING ATMOSPHERE   118   7
  ARE THE EARTH I HOVER OVER   118 19
  THE ROUND EARTH ROLLS LIKE A GERM IN THE SKY   126   8
  WHY I SHOULD THINK THAT FROM THE EARTH THERE FLY   127   6
  THE EARTH AGAIN LIKE A SHIP STEAMS OUT OF THE DARK SEA + 132 27
  MY TENACIOUS FEET FROM OUT THE DOME OF THE EARTH   134 25
  AND ALL THE EARTH IS GONE INTO A DUST   135 13
  TREES BIRDS AND EARTH ARRESTED IN THE AFTER-THOUGHT   142 15
  FALL ALL THE FRUITS MOST BITTERLY INTO EARTH   160 15
  WHITE EARTH AND RUINS OURSELVES AND NOTHING BESIDE   166   8
  MONEY FROM OUT OF THE EARTH OR THE BEAST OR THE MAN AS + 175 24
  BY HEAVEN AND EARTH AND HELLISH STREAM   177 18
  HERE THIS ROUND BALL OF EARTH   196   7
  NOT LIKE THE EARTH THE SPOUSE ALL FULL OF INCREASE   197 10
  DIVIDING EARTH AND HEAVEN   200   7
  THAN THE EARTH THE PALFREY TRODE   202   8
  OF SODOM THAT COVERS THE EARTH BRING THEM FORTH   235 11
  AND I COVERED THE EARTH AND ALL SPACE   248 27
  ROCKS SEEM AND EARTH AND AIR UNEASY AND WATERS STILL   249 15
  TO THE EARTH OF THE UNDER-NIGHT   254   4
  DEAD AND TRODDEN TO NOUGHT IN THE SOUR BLACK EARTH   258 16
  TRODDEN TO NOUGHT IN SOUR DEAD EARTH   258 19
  I AM FILLING MY MOUTH WITH THE EARTH   259 31
  BUT TO A NEW EARTH A NEW I A NEW KNOWLEDGE A NEW WORLD   260 17
  OF EARTH WINTER-PRESSED STRANGLED IN CORRUPTION   270 19
  EARTH   270 22
  NEW FEET ON THE EARTH BEATING WITH IMPATIENCE   272   3
  TO TOSS THE GLOBE OF EARTH LIKE A BALL ON A WATER-JET   272 14
  TO PLAY WITH THE GLOBE OF EARTH LIKE A BALL ON A FOUNTA+ 272 19
  EARTH   272 23
  TO ME THE EARTH ROLLS PONDEROUSLY SUPERBLY   288 26
  TILL IT BURST FORTH BLINDING WITHERING THE EARTH   294   3
  NOW EVEN THE SHADOW OF THE LOST SECRET IS VANISHING FRO+ 295   3
  OUT OF THE EARTH BEFORE THE SUN WAS SPREAD OUT AND BEFO+ 295   5
  GROW RISING UP OWING TO THE HEAT WHICH IS IN THE EARTH + 295   8
  ARE PARTS OF THE EARTH JUST AS EMBRYOS ARE PARTS OF THE+ 295   9
  LIKE IRON STICKING GRIMLY OUT OF EARTH   300 19
  LIKE IRON IMPLEMENTS TWISTED HIDEOUS OUT OF THE EARTH   300 21
  DO YOU TELEPHONE THE ROAR OF THE WATERS OVER THE EARTH   301 10
  DECEMBER'S BARE IRON HOOKS STICKING OUT OF EARTH   304   8
  THIS IS THE ANCIENT SOUTHERN EARTH WHENCE THE VASES WERE 305 12
  WITHIN IRON AND EARTH   307   3
  OUT ON EARTH AGAIN   308 26
  HELL ON EARTH AND DIS WITHIN THE DEPTHS   309 14
  AND POMP OF HUSBAND-STRATEGY ON EARTH   309 24
  KEEPING TO EARTH   310 18
  DRAWN OUT OF EARTH   310 31
  PUT ME DOWN AGAIN ON THE EARTH JESUS ON THE BROWN SOIL   321 10
  WHETHER THE WATERS RISE AND COVER THE EARTH   334 22
  FISH IN THE WATERS UNDER THE EARTH   335 29
  YET NOTHING ON EARTH WILL GIVE HIM COURAGE TO PASS THE   346   4
  DARK BREATH OF THE EARTH THE SERPENT SLID FORTH LAY REV+ 348   7
  MOIST EARTH NEVER COULD HE MISS ON HIS FEET AND THIS IS+ 348   9
  AND MOVE ON FEET BUT MOIST EARTH WEIGHS HIM DOWN THOUGH+ 348 11
  OF THE EARTH   349 27
  INTO THE BURNING BOWELS OF THIS EARTH   350 12
  FROM OUT THE DARK DOOR OF THE SECRET EARTH   350 22
  AND REMAIN LAPSED ON EARTH   352   6
  OVER THE GARDEN EARTH   354 15
  NOT KNOWING EACH OTHER FROM BITS OF EARTH OR OLD TINS   357 20
  TO TRAVEL TO BURROW INTO A LITTLE LOOSE EARTH AFRAID OF+ 358   2
  BUT WATCH A TURKEY PRANCING LOW ON EARTH   371   3
  AND JUMPS STACCATO TO EARTH A SHARP DRY JUMP STILL   384 30
  FIRST GREAT BEASTS OF THE EARTH   392 10
  CENTRE OF THE EARTH   392 26
  JUST TOUCHES EARTH   392 29
  OVER WITH EARTH   410 25
  EARTH   412 24
  SHADOWS STEAL OUT OF THE EARTH   425   2
  THE EARTH TO THINK   437 19
  BETWEEN HEEDLESS EARTH AND HEAVEN   443 14
  FRIGHTENED OF THE BARE EARTH AND THE TEMPORARY CANVAS   444 12
  AND TREADS THE EARTH TO FEEL THE SOIL   459 23
  EARTH SMOKES BLUE   467   8
  AND GET HIS ROOTS IN EARTH AGAIN   475   4
  RAW EARTH   475   5
  AND MAN AND WOMAN ARE LIKE THE EARTH THAT BRINGS FORTH   477   7
  THE HOT WILD CORE OF THE EARTH HEAVIER THAN WE CAN EVEN 480   8
  THE EARTH LEANS ITS WEIGHT ON THE SUN AND THE SUN ON THE 480 19
  BETWEEN MEN AND MEN MEN AND WOMEN AND EARTH AND   482   6
  IF YOU COPULATE WITH THE FINEST WOMAN ON EARTH   486   3
  SLOWLY THE SALT OF THE EARTH BECOMES SALT OF THE SEA   495   1
  CARRY THE SALT OF THE EARTH THE WISDOM OF WISE MEN   495   3
  SLOWLY THE SALT OF THE EARTH BECOMES SALT OF THE SEA   495   9
  THE VEINS OF THE EARTH   504 22
  ALMOST EVERY SCRAP OF THE LIVING EARTH YOU STROLL UP AND 521 15
  NO SUN NO EARTH   528   1
  OFF THE FACE OF THE EARTH   533 28
  YOU'VE NO MORE USE FOR THE SOLID EARTH   549 15

EARTH
  I FIND I'D RATHER GET BACK TO EARTH   552   7
  GOD LET ME DOWN TO EARTH AGAIN   552 13
  WE'RE NOT FIT FOR THE EARTH WE LIVE ON   553 29
  TO STAMP THE EARTH AND FEEL THE WIND LIKE WAKEFUL   585   4
  THERE ARE TOO MANY PEOPLE ON EARTH   606 18
  THEY NIBBLE THE FACE OF THE EARTH TO A DESERT   606 20
  TO SWAY THE EARTH OF MEN   614 10
  THE HEAVENS ARE THE NETHER MILL-STONE AND OUR HEAVY EAR+   614 19
  UPON THE EARTH   615   3
  THE EARTH   615   9
  HARD HARD ON THE EARTH THE MACHINES ARE ROLLING   624   3
  BUT OVER THE MIDDLE OF THE EARTH WILL BE THE SMOKY RUIN+   625   8
  SONS OF FIRE SONS OF FIRE SONS OF AIR AND WATER   635   3
  THAT SPRAWLS ACROSS THE EARTH IN IRON IMBECILITY   642 26
  LEAVE THEM TO STALE ON EARTH   662 19
  WHICH TURNS ON AND ON THE SAME AND IS HELL ON EARTH   662 24
  THE MACHINE SHALL BE ABOLISHED FROM THE EARTH AGAIN   666 15
  UP FROM THE BOUNDING EARTH STRANGE PREGNANT STREAMS IN +   675 13
  WHILE NOTHING COMES FROM THE OPEN HEAVEN FROM EARTH FRO+   675 20
  GROAN THEN FOR EVEN THE MAIDEN EARTH   703   7
  OF FIRE AND THE WET EARTH AND THE WIDE AIR OF THE WORLD   706   5
  THE SUMMER AND THE SNOWS THE WILD WELTER OF EARTH   707 29
  ABSOLUTE ABSOLVED FROM THE SUN AND THE EARTH AND THE MO+   712 16
  FOR EVERY REVOLUTION OF THE EARTH AROUND THE SUN   713 12
  FOR THE EARTH LIKE THE SUN IS A WANDERER   713 16
  THE MOON AND THE EARTH THE SUN SATURN AND BETELGEUSE   713 20
  THICK ALMOST THUNDROUS ON THE HARDENED EARTH   717   4
  THEY LINGER IN THE SHADOW OF THE EARTH   721 14
  FOR MAN HAS KILLED THE SILENCE OF THE EARTH   725 17
  OH WHAT WE WANT ON EARTH   726 17
  WITH THE DARK EARTH AND DRENCHED   727 15
  I WALK THE EARTH INTACT HEREAFTERWARDS   743 24
  LIKE BLOOD IN THE EARTH AGAIN WE WALK THE EARTH   743 26
  ANOTHER TRIUMPH ON THE FACE OF EARTH   746   4
  FROM THE EARTH   782 12
  THE HEART OF THE WORLD IS THE HEART OF THE EARTH WHERE +   782 16
  AT THE MIDDLE OF THE EARTH THIS EARTH   783   3
  AND HAVING PASSED THE YELLOW LINE HE SAW THE EARTH BENE+   790   4
  I'LL SHAKE THE EARTH AND SWALLOW THEM UP WITH THEIR CIT+   792   4
  AND THE EARTH IS ALIVE AND READY TO SHAKE OFF HIS FLEAS   792 12
  THE STARS AND THE EARTH AND THE SUN AND THE MOON AND TH+   792 17
  FOR SUN AND STARS AND EARTH AND THE VERY RAINS ARE WEARY   792 20
  FOR MEN UPON THE BODY OF THE EARTH ARE LIKE LICE   793   1
  DEVOURING THE EARTH INTO SORES   793   2
  THIS IS WHAT STARS AND SUN AND EARTH AND MOON AND WINDS+   793   3
  THERE ARE DEAD THAT CREEP THROUGH THE BURNING BOWELS OF   795 24
  THERE ARE DRAGONS OF SUN AND ICE DRAGONS OF THE MOON AN+   796 18
  THE EARTH AND AIR   800 37
  OUT OF THE BOWELS OF THE EARTH LIKE A SNAKE   801   7
  ALL THINGS THAT LIFT IN THE LIFT OF LIVING BETWEEN EART+   801   8
  NOW I AM ALONE ON EARTH AND THIS IS MINE   801 15
  DOWN IN THE CENTRE OF THE EARTH   805   2
  DOWN IN THE CENTRE OF THE EARTH   806   5
  AND FROM MIDDLE EARTH   806 20
  THE RAIN OF BLOOD IS FALLEN IS GONE INTO THE EARTH   811 15
  AND THE ANIMALS CURL DOWN ON THE DEAR EARTH TO SLEEP   834   3
  NOR IS HE A STRONG MAN RULING THE EARTH   840 16
  RULING THE EARTH ROUSES NO EAGERNESS IN ME AT ALL   840 17
  LIKE THE LIVING LIFE ON THE EARTH   844 18
  WHICH OPENS EARTH AND HEAVEN TO LOVE'S FUGITIVE GLOWING   854 14
  A COOL OINTMENT OVER THE EARTH BLISTERED IN THE FLIGHT +   855 31
  REVEALING THE SKY THROUGH THE RAGGED EARTH AND SUDDEN   874 29
  I SEE THE STRONG SOUND EARTH BETRAYED AS A FLOATING   874 30
  I SAW ON THE RED EARTH   880 18
  OVER THE WITHERED MOSSES AND RED EARTH   880 20
  RABBITS HANDFULS OF BROWN EARTH LIE   *891   6
  OF FLOWERS AND THE SWELTERING EARTH   *937 12
  WITH LIFE TILL THE EARTH AND THE SKY HAVE TUMBLED   *937 18
  OF THIS DARK EARTH AND WANDERING ALL SERENE   *945   5
  BEFORE THE GOLDEN FATHERLY SERPENT LIFTED HIS HEAD OFF +   *946 27
  AS EARTH LEANS ON THE SUN   *952   5
  HARDENED THE EARTH SHAKING THE LARK'S NEST TILL THE EGG+   *953 18
  HARD HARD ON THE EARTH THE MACHINES ARE ROLLING   *953 21
  AH IF YOU WANT TO LIVE IN PEACE ON THE FACE OF THE EARTH   *961   5

EARTH-BROWN
  BEING EARTH-BROWN EARTH-GOLDEN FROM THE BURNING BOWELS   349 26

EARTH-CLODS
  EARTH-CLODS AND NIGHT TO FLOWERS THAT PRAISE AND BURN   872   4

EARTH-COLOURED
  STIRRING WITH EARTH-COLOURED LIFE EVER TURNING AND STIR+   153   6

EARTH-DANK
  BUT WITH MORE THAN BOVINE GRIM EARTH-DANK PERSISTENCE   361 16

EARTHEN
  AS HER EARTHEN MOUND MOVES ON   362   5

EARTH-GOLDEN
  BEING EARTH-BROWN EARTH-GOLDEN FROM THE BURNING BOWELS   349 26

EARTH-GRASS
  EARTH-GRASS UNEATABLE   300 23

EARTHILY
  SHE SEEMS EARTHILY APATHETIC   361 29

EARTH-IRIDESCENT
  TOAD-FILMY EARTH-IRIDESCENT   310 20

EARTH-LIPPED
  INTO THE BLACK HOLE THE EARTH-LIPPED FISSURE IN THE WAL+   351 16

EARTHLY
  OF THIS EARTHLY AFFAIR   176 25
  BURNT OUT OF OUR EARTHLY COVERS   243   2

EARTHQUAKE
  AND NEVER KNOWING WHEN YOU'LL PROVOKE AN EARTHQUAKE   539   9

EARTH-SOILED
  BENEATH THE EARTH-SOILED HOVEL IN WHICH SHE MOVES   362 19

EARTH'S
  AND BRANDISHING AND STOOPING OVER EARTH'S WINTRY FLEDGE   301 15
  SEEM BELLY-PLUMBED TO THE EARTH'S MID-NAVEL   392 24
  TOWARDS THE EARTH'S CENTRE   394 22
  EARTH'S DEEP HEAVY CENTRE   394 26
  GRINDING THEM SMALL TO HUMUS ON EARTH'S NETHER MILL-STO+   615   6
  LINGERING IN THE EARTH'S SHADOW   704   4
  THE EARTH'S LONG CONICAL SHADOW IS FULL OF SOULS   721 15
  THE GREY GREY REACHES OF EARTH'S SHADOW   722 20
  WITH THE DEEP OBLIVION OF EARTH'S LAPSE AND RENEWAL   727 16

EARTH-TOUCHING
  AND THERE AGAIN ON HIS SHELL-TENDER EARTH-TOUCHING BELLY   355 29

EARTH-WALL
  HE REACHED DOWN FROM A FISSURE IN THE EARTH-WALL IN THE   349   8

EARTHY
  WISE TORTOISE LAID HIS EARTHY PART AROUND HIM HE CAST I+   348 13
  HER LACONIC EYE HAS AN EARTHY MATERIALISTIC LOOK   359 33
  RUNNING BESIDE HER LIKE A DOG BITING HER EARTHY SPLAY   360   8
  POOR LITTLE EARTHY HOUSE-INHABITING OSIRIS   361 10

'EAR
  'ER'LL BE WANTIN' IT I 'EAR   79 20

EASE
  AND WED ME TO EASE MY YEARNINGS   44   5
  THE COOL HIGH MOON AT THEIR EASE WHILE THE DRONING CHUR+   54 30
  THE CLOUDS GO DOWN THE SKY WITH A WEALTHY EASE   133 16
  MOVES AT HER EASE AGAIN   228 20
  BEHOLD ME TROTTING AT EASE BETWIXT THE SLOPES OF THE GO+   409   6
  AND IT'S NO GOOD MOONING FOR SLOPPY EASE   559   9
  TO EASE HIMSELF IN HIS CLOTHES IT MAKES   733 22
  THE SKY WITH A WEALTH OF EASE AND ASSURANCE   772   5

EASIER
  IT IS EASIER TO STAND STOCK RIGID THAN TO MOVE   288   7

EASIEST
  THE ONE THING EASIEST TO LOSE IS SAVINGS   614   5

EASILY
  DRIFTS DIMLY FORWARD EASILY HIDDEN   68   6
  I SEE THE SILENCE EASILY SIP THEM   110   7
  IF UNDER YOUR SLIPPING WORDS THAT EASILY FLOW   122 10
  ABOUT YOU AS A GARMENT EASILY   122 11
  EASILY DOWN THE SKY THE DAISIES SENDING   150 11
  THE JOY WAS NOT TO BE DRIVEN OFF SO EASILY   207 11
  AND I THINK IN THE WORLD BEYOND HOW EASILY WE MIGHT   402 29
  A THRILL RATHER EASILY EXHAUSTS ITSELF TAKE EVEN THE WAR   532   5
  HE STRIKES THE GUSH OF PASSION EASILY   877   7
  DRIFTS DIMLY FORWARD EASILY HIDDEN   *914 21

EAST
  THAT ISSUING OUT OF THE EAST HAS SIFTED   68   3
  HAS FOR ME A DOOR INTO PEACE WARM DAWN IN THE EAST   250   6
  AND STRUTS BLUE-BRILLIANT OUT OF THE FAR EAST   371   2
  THE EAST A DEAD LETTER AND EUROPE MORIBUND IS THAT   371 32
  HIGH HIGH FLAMBEAUX SMOKING OF THE EAST   388 29
  AS IF THE HOMAGE OF THE KINDLED BLOOD OF THE EAST   389 28
  IN ELEPHANTS AND THE EAST ARE TWO DEVILS IN ALL MEN MAY+   390   5
  THAT HAS FOLLOWED THE SUN FROM THE DAWN THROUGH THE EAST   404 14
  TROTTING EAST AND EAST AND EAST TILL THE SUN HIMSELF WE+   404 15
  THE LAST STEP OUT OF THE EAST   404 28
  HAS THE RED WOLF TROTTED EAST AND EAST AND EAST   405 15
  CREATURE WENT EAST   405 27
  ANTHONY MIGHT HAVE MADE A SPLENDID THING OF THE EAST   479 24
  OF EVERY LAND OR EAST OR WEST   575 13
  OF EVERY TONGUE OR EAST OR WEST   575 15
  OH A MAN MAY TRAVEL BOTH EAST AND WEST   575 22
  AND AN OCEAN LINER GOING EAST LIKE A SMALL BEETLE WALKI+   687   9
  SAUNTERING DOWN THE LONG SLOPE FROM THE EAST   770 21
  FROM THE EAST TO THE WEST IN THE UPPER VALLEY   770 25
  THE WOMEN BY THE GATE OF THE EAST   771 11

EASTERN
  IN THE HAIR OF AN EASTERN GIRL   36 20
  AS SLOWLY THE HOUSE OF DAY IS CLOSING ITS EASTERN SHUTT+   102 28
  AND ALL THE EASTERN EXQUISITE ROYAL PLANTS   313 30
  COMING OUT OF THE EASTERN END   687   7

EASTER SUNDAY
  TO START THE YEAR ON EASTER SUNDAY   609 19
  TODAY IS EASTER SUNDAY CHRIST RISEN TWO DAYS AGO WAS   777 22

EASY
  OF EASY SAILING ODD RED WICKS SERVE   172 20
  YOUR HAND WOULD NOT BE SO FLIG AND EASY   255 25
  SO BE EASY   409 31
  BUT GIVING LIFE IS NOT SO EASY   449 18
  IT'S SO EASY TO FOLLOW SUIT   462 18
  THEIR CHILDREN BROUGHT UP EASY LET IT SLIP AWAY AGAIN   535 14
  AH LOVE SWEET LOVE NOT SO EASY   559   5
  AND EASY TO SWALLOW ALWAYS TELL THEM THEY'RE HAPPY   583 19
  IT IS NOT EASY TO FALL OUT OF THE HANDS OF THE LIVING G+   700 17
  IT IS NOT EASY TO DIE O IT IS NOT EASY   720 23
  DO YOU THINK IT IS EASY TO CHANGE   727 31

EASY
    ME WANT TO CRY TO SEE HIM SO STRONG AND EASY   733 23
    AND STONES SHALL MAKE PLACE FOR THY FOOT BECOME EASY TO+   750 1
    TRADITION TRADITION TRADITION IT IS EASY ENOUGH   775 18
    EASY EASY AND EASY DOWN TO MY ANKLES   835 33
    FAR AND WIDE RUN THE EASY ROOTS THAT BEAR THE LEAVES OF+   *926 12
    OH IT IS NOT SO EASY I TELL YOU IT IS NOT SO EASY   *957 18
    IT IS EASY TO BE PUSHED OUT OF THE SILVERY CITY OF THE +   *957 20

EAT
    THE PROPER WAY TO EAT A FIG IN SOCIETY   282 1
    AND CABBAGES BORN TO BE CUT AND EAT   317 20
    SHE LIKES TO EAT   358 30
    HANDS TO EAT THE ACANTHUS OR BITE AT THE ALMOND BUDS   385 10
    THAT YOU HAVE TO RUN OUT AT LAST AND EAT FILTH   398 27
    SO YOU YOU GO OUT AT LAST AND EAT THE UNMENTIONABLE   399 2
    YOU MUST EAT EVEN THAT   399 11
    OF YOU MY BITCH TILL YOU GET SO FAR YOU EAT FILTH   400 17
    HE SAYS THE SOONER WILL YOU EAT IMAGINARY CAKE IN THE   442 15
    HE SAYS NO YOU MUST GO TO HEAVEN AND EAT THE MOST   442 18
    LETTING THE LIVING DEAD EAT YOU UP   449 20
    HAS HE NO MONEY THEN LET HIM EAT DIRT AND GO COLD   486 21
    BUT THEY WILL MAKE ME EAT DIRT WITH IT   486 24
    I SHALL HAVE TO EAT DIRT I SHALL HAVE TO EAT DIRT   486 25
    AND BULLIED WITH THE THREAT GET MONEY OR EAT DIRT   522 12
    EAT.ME UP DEAR PEASANT SO THE PEASANT ATE HIM   533 25
    EAT YOUR PAP LITTLE MAN LIKE A MAN   570 20
    AND EAT AND CACHINNATE AND EVEN SEEM TO SMILE   644 19
    THE ONLY WAY TO EAT AN APPLE IS TO HOG IT DOWN LIKE A P+   708 7
    BUT IF I EAT AN APPLE I LIKE TO EAT IT WITH ALL MY SENS+   708 10
    SO THAT LOST SOULS MAY EAT GRAPES   710 17
    NO MORE WOULD I LET HIM EAT   754 20
    LET US EAT THE LAST MEAL   756 2
    NOW LET'S EAT UP THE CORE   817 20
    EAT WOMAN EAT MORE   817 26
    EAT IT ALL OH   817 29
    EAT AND LIE DOWN   818 1
    THEY'D BE GOOD TO EAT   828 9
    WE HAVE FORGOTTEN THE SUNNY APPLES OF DAY THAT WE CRAVE+ *917 15

EATEN
    I HAVE EATEN AND DRUNK AND WARMED AND CLOTHED MY BODY   264 1
    I HAD EATEN OF THE BREAD THAT SATISFIES   265 8
    THOUGH I'VE EATEN IT NOW   279 24
    BEFORE THEY'VE EATEN THROUGH THE JOISTS AND   511 17
    THAT LITTLE LIVES MUST BE EATEN UP INTO THE DANCE AND S+   679 21
    HAVE EATEN THE NARCOTICS OF NIGHT   *917 14

EATING
    BURNING OF POWERFUL SALT BURNING EATING THROUGH MY   207 23
    SNOW OF SALT WHITE BURNING EATING SALT   207 31
    TO SAVE US FROM EATING DIRT   487 5
    AND AT THE SAME TIME EXPECT TO GO ON CALMLY EATING GOOD   531 6
    ON EATING   531 14
    OR A HYAENA EATING CORPSES   621 24
    STEP ASIDE STEP OUT OF IT IT IS EATING YOU UP   642 28
    IT WAS THE EATING UP OF LITTLE LIVES   679 15
    AND EATING THE BRAVE BREAD OF A WHOLESOME KNOWLEDGE   *959 14

EATS
    THAT NOBODY EATS AND NOBODY WANTS SO IT ROTS BUT IS NOT   462 21
    THE FATHER EATS THE PEAR AND THE SON'S TEETH ARE SET ON+   530 22
    BUT IF NOBODY EATS THEM   828 10

EAVES
    ONLY AS SWALLOWS ARE SLAVES TO THE EAVES   *899 7
    ONLY AS SWALLOWS ARE SLAVES TO THE EAVES   *902 19

EBB
    FIRE HORIZONTAL DECLINING AND EBBING THE TWILIT EBB OF +   67 6
    WHEN THE SLEEPER STIRS OR TURNS ON THE EBB OF THE FLOOD   145 27
    MOVING ALONG IN THE MYSTERIOUS EBB OF THE NIGHT   180 19
    ABOVE THE EBB OF FEET   253 9
    ILLUSION EBB AWAY   639 20
    WHERE THE EBB OF LIFE SLIPS BY   *917 8

EBBED
    THE UNCLOUDED SEAS OF BLUEBELLS HAVE EBBED AND PASSED   854 1

EBBING
    DARK OVERGROWN WITH WILLOWS COOL WITH THE BROOK EBBING +   33 16
    OF LIVING HAS PASSED EBBING ON   53 15
    FIRE HORIZONTAL DECLINING AND EBBING THE TWILIT EBB OF +   67 6
    LIKE HALF-SEEN FROTH ON AN EBBING SHORE IN THE MOON   75 28
    EBBING WEST   249 16
    DOWNWARDS EBBING DOWNWARDS EBBING DOWNWARDS TO THE   428 8
    THE SENSITIVE DELICACY OF YOUR SEX IN ITS EBBING TO AND+   464 25
    DARK OVERGROWN WITH WILLOWS COOL WITH THE BROOK EBBING + *891 18
    LIKE FLOATING FROTH ON AN EBBING SHORE IN THE MOON   *897 27
    LIKE FLOATING FROTH ON AN EBBING SHORE IN THE MOON   *901 4

EBBS
    WITH THAT UNFELT BREEZE THAT EBBS OVER THE SEAS WHERE T+   53 13
    TWITCHES AND EBBS HITTING WASHING INWARDLY SILVERILY   453 20
    MINUTE BY MINUTE EBBS   766 9
    TILL THE BURSTEN FLOOD OF LIFE EBBS BACK TO MY EYES   *893 30
    WITH THE UNFELT BREEZE THAT EBBS OVER THE SEAS WHEN THE+ *906 5

EBB-TIME
    AND SO IT IS EBB-TIME THEY TURN THE EYES BENEATH THE BU+   67 1

ECHO
    ECHO OF HER I'VE-LAID-AN-EGG CACKLE IS RICH AND RESONAN+   761 21
    THE MISTS OF RECEDING TEARS AND THE ECHO OF LAUGHTER   *906 10

ECHOED
    I ECHOED WITH SURPRISE   124 20

ECHOES
    THE SILENCE OF VANISHING TEARS AND THE ECHOES OF LAUGHT+   53 19
    NOW LAMPS LIKE YELLOW ECHOES GLIMMER AMONG   135 9
    LIKE ECHOES EVEN   268 24
    WITHIN THE SILENCE VOID OF ECHOES EVEN   738 8

ECHOING
    HAVING SHED THEIR SOUND AND FINISHED ALL THEIR ECHOING   296 27

ECHOINGS
    OR LAST NIGHT'S ECHOINGS   109 23

ECLIPSE
    FROM MY BREAST TO YOUR BOSOM ECLIPSE   *929 28

ECLIPSES
    AVOIDING EACH OTHER YET INCURRING ECLIPSES   823 28

ECSTASIED
    OBSCENELY ECSTASIED   333 30
    SHE HAS A SECRET ALMOST ECSTASIED HATRED OF MALENESS IN+   619 20

ECSTASY
    IN ECSTASY   96 34
    IN ECSTASY   97 2
    HIS ECSTASY   178 26
    IN A GLITTER OF ECSTASY   200 8
    BUT THE RESIDUUM OF THE ECSTASY   219 8
    TO ECSTASY   235 20
    ECSTASY   273 20
    THERE IS A NEW ECSTASY IN HIS ROAR OF DESIROUS LOVE   325 3
    IN FLAT ECSTASY SUPREMELY UNFELT   444 7
    THIS SERRIED ECSTASY OF PREVALENT DEATH   737 5
    ECSTASY OF WORK HE TURNS FROM ME   *899 2
    AN ECSTASY SURELY SWEET TO BE HAD   *899 3
    ECSTASY OF WORK HE TURNS FROM ME   *902 14
    AN ECSTASY SURELY SWEET TO BE HAD   *902 15
    BEATS THE ACTIVE ECSTASY SUDDENLY LIFTING MY EYES   *906 21
    BEATS THE ACTIVE ECSTASY   *908 17
    OF MEN VIBRATING IN ECSTASY THROUGH THE ROUNDED FLESH   *908 21
    OH THE TERRIBLE ECSTASY OF THE CONSCIOUSNESS THAT I AM + *909 18
    IN HER BARBAROUS SOUL TO GROPE WITH ECSTASY   *936 35
    AND WIDE IN ECSTASY I SIT AND WATCH   *943 20

ECSTATIC
    IN ECSTATIC REVERIE   165 21
    ROSE CYCLAMEN ECSTATIC FORE-RUNNER   311 21
    RUNS ECSTATIC OVER THE PLIANT FOLDS RIPPLING DOWN TO MY+ *891 32

ECZEMA
    THEY MUST GO ON SCRATCHING THE ECZEMA OF THEIR MENTAL I+   533 9

EDDIES
    PLAYING WITH THE EDDIES   867 16

EDDYING
    SLOWLY THE WINGS OF DAY ARE EDDYING LOWER   855 27

EDEN
    OUR EDEN OUR HOME   38 2
    TO EDEN HOME   243 16
    OF EDEN EVEN WAS EVE'S FRUIT TO HER IT BELONGED AND SHE+   277 6
    OUT OF EDEN WEARY WITH THE WISTFULNESS OF HER SILENT TO+   864 24
    THE SAME EDEN WITH PURPLE AND WHITE   *892 16
    MY EDEN MY HOME   *892 18

EDGE
    ON THE GREEN WOOD'S EDGE A SHY GIRL HOVERS   41 1
    OVER THE TREE'S EDGE AS OVER A MOUNTAIN   50 1
    BLACKENED EDGE OF THE SKIES   103 27
    TURNING ITS BROKEN EDGE TO THE DARK ITS SHINE   114 27
    THE EDGE OF THE BLUE AND THE SUN STANDS UP TO SEE US GL+   132 28
    A LOOK AS HE STANDS ON THE EDGE OF THIS NAKED STALL   144 19
    TREAD OVER THE EDGE OF THE PIT AND WE'RE GONE   164 11
    TILL THEY HALT AT A CLIFF ON THE EDGE OF THE LAND   201 15
    THIS HAVING TOUCHED THE EDGE OF THE BEYOND AND PERISHED+   266 21
    BEFORE THE SHOPS LIKE WAGTAILS ON THE EDGE OF A POOL   269 24
    OVER THE EDGE OF THE SOUNDLESS CATARACT   322 1
    OVER THE EDGE OF THE STONE TROUGH   349 11
    OVER THE EDGE OF ALL THINGS   354 17
    TINY FROM UNDER THE VERY EDGE OF THE FARTHEST FAR-OFF   366 27
    THE WATER'S EDGE   391 10
    THE SEA'S EDGE   467 7
    THE FATHER EATS THE PEAR AND THE SON'S TEETH ARE SET ON+   530 22
    SMOOTH OCEAN WHERE THE FISHES REST ON EDGE   652 10
    AND AN OCEAN LINER GOING EAST LIKE A SMALL BEETLE WALKI+   687 9
    BETWEEN YOU AND YOUR PURPOSE LIKE A KNIFE'S EDGE SHADOW   706 20
    TIP THE MORNING LIGHT ON EDGE AND SPILL IT WITH DELIGHT   709 6
    THE HOSTS ARE LEAPING FROM THE EDGE OF LIFE   743 30
    THEY SEEMED TO GROW DARKER AS SHE CAME TO THE EDGE OF D+   869 6
    WHOSE EDGE OF HAIR CURVES THICKLY TO THE RED   878 21

EDGES
    AND THEY PEEP AT ME OVER THE EDGES   105 17
    I WILL SIFT THE SURF THAT EDGES THE NIGHT WITH MY NET T+   180 4
    AND ROUND THE EDGES TWENTY-FIVE LITTLE ONES   355 8
    SHE EDGES THROUGH WITHOUT UPSETTING HIM   426 13
    ENVELOPING EVEN THE EDGES OF THE THOUGHT-WAVES   698 23

EDIFICE
    AND ENGINES WILL RUSH AT THE SOLID HOUSES THE EDIFICE O+   624 28

EDITOR
    EDITOR ER QUITE BUT ER BIOLOGICALLY HAVE YOU BEEN   582   9
    EDITOR STERNLY HAVE YOU BEEN MADE SAFE FOR THE GREAT   582 12
    EDITOR BY SURGICAL OPERATION DID YOUR PARENTS HAVE YOU   582 16
    EDITOR GOOD MORNING DON'T TROUBLE TO CALL AGAIN WE   582 19

EDUCATE
    WHOM YOU'LL HAVE TO EDUCATE   459   2

EDUCATION
    THE VOICE OF MY EDUCATION SAID TO ME   350   1
    EDUCATION   351 21
    AND GAVE A BOARD-SCHOOL EDUCATION NEWSPAPERS AND THE   630 24
    STOP WHERE'S YOUR EDUCATION   669 16
    EDUCATION IS AN EVIL ABSTRACTION   716 10
    THE PURVEYORS OF EDUCATION   762 22

'E'D
    FROM THAT BIT OF A WENCH'S BOSOM 'E'D BE GLAD OF IT   61 19

E'EN
    BUT E'EN   229 24

'EERED-ON
    WHAT'S THAT AS 'APPEN I'VE 'EERED-ON MISSIS   *919 27

'EERED
    'APPEN THEN YOU'VE 'EERED   78   6
    WHAT'S THAT AS 'APPEN I'VE 'EERED ON MISSIS   78   7
    'APPEN THEN YOU'VE 'EERED   *919 26

EERILY
    RIFT OF THE RIVER EERILY BETWEEN THE PINES UNDER A   220 25

EFFACE
    HOW TO EFFACE THEMSELVES   658 10

EFFECT
    WHAT EFFECT I CAN HAVE MY HANDS WAVE UNDER   223   2
    AS IF IT COULD HAVE ANY EFFECT ANY MORE   287 13
    THINK OF THE EFFECT ON MISS HARRISON   583 10

EFFICIENT
    THERE ARE ENOUGH OF GREAT SOULS TO COMPLETE AN EFFICIEN+   859 23

EFFLUENCE
    EFFLUENCE FROM SUFFERING FOLK-STUFF WHICH DEATH HAS LAI+ *938 23

EFFLUVIA
    AND GIVING OFF DREADFUL EFFLUVIA IN A GHASTLY EFFORT OF+   175   4

EFFORT
    HER FRANTIC EFFORT THROTTLING   43 10
    AND GIVING OFF DREADFUL EFFLUVIA IN A GHASTLY EFFORT OF+   175   4
    YOU GREAT YOU PATIENT EFFORT AND YOU SLEEP   194 19
    WERE NOT WORTH WHILE NOR SPINNING WORTH THE EFFORT   197 21
    I AM HERE MYSELF AS THOUGH THIS HEAVE OF EFFORT   218 13
    IN HIS EFFORT TOWARD COMPLETION AGAIN   361   9
    AND FLING HIMSELF IN EFFORT AFTER EFFORT   428 21
    EFFORT OF BEING YOUNG   502 15
    WITHOUT HAVING TO MAKE THE POLITE EFFORT OF LOVING HER   506 17
    OR THE MENTAL EFFORT OF MAKING HER ACQUAINTANCE   506 18
    WITH THE EFFORT OF TRYING TO LOVE PEOPLE   506 26
    AND EFFORT IS THE RUIN OF ALL THINGS   613 14
    WE CAN BUT TOUCH AND WONDER AND PONDER AND MAKE OUR EFF+   667 14
    ON THE DECAYING EFFORT OF MANKIND   765 21
    THE UPRIGHT IS TEMPORAL IS EFFORT OUTREACH   827 15
    DETERMINED EFFORT AMONG MEN   838   2
    BUT LAYING FOREVER OUR EFFORT AT MUSIC BY   884 22
    THE FIRST EFFORT TO THINK   *946 28

EFFORTS
    SOME DIM LITTLE EFFORTS PLACED IN THE THREADS OF THE   142   7
    IN THEIR EFFORTS TO COME AWAKE FOR ONE MOMENT   408   5
    THE EFFORTS OF MEN LIKE THE EFFORTS OF BIRDS IN SPRING   520   9
    HOW THEY HATE THE WOMEN'S EFFORTS TO TURN THEM   538 24

EFFULGENCE
    OR LOVE THE EFFULGENCE OF THEIR HOLY LIGHT   288 19
    HIGH OVER THE MILD EFFULGENCE OF THE DOVE   328   7
    A PAWPAW EFFULGENCE   760 10

EFFULGENT
    TO THE EFFULGENT LANDSCAPE OF OUR IMMORTAL GIRLY-WIRLY   835   4

EGG
    NAY EVEN THE SLUMBEROUS EGG AS IT LABOURS UNDER THE SHE+   64 11
    IS MUCH LESS THAN THE BIT OF BLUE EGG   244 30
    WHITHER AWAY BRISK EGG   356 23
    THIS IS YOUR MOTHER SHE LAID YOU WHEN YOU WERE AN EGG   357   2
    THE DOVE OF LIBERTY SAT ON AN EGG   413   1
    OR ARE YOU THE GOOSE THAT LAYS THE GOLDEN EGG   414 30
    LAYING THAT GOLDEN EGG   414 33
    THAT ADDLED GOLDEN EGG   414 34
    GOLD EGG OF ALL THINGS   437 13
    IT'S A COLD EGG IT ISN'T LOVE ANY MORE   472 12
    AS A FINE GREY EGG OR A SLENDER ROD   752 16
    SHE LAYS AN EGG HE BRISTLES LIKE A DOUBLE WHITE POPPY A+   761 19
    SHE'S LAID AN EGG   761 23
    I'VE LAID AN EGG   761 24
    I'VE LAID AN EGG   761 26
    OVER THE GREAT EGG   *946 24

EGGS
    THOUGH WHAT SHE DOES EXCEPT LAY FOUR EGGS AT RANDOM IN   358 26
    FATHERING ENDLESS TEN-DOLLAR GOLDEN EGGS   414 12
    AND GONE LIKE WEED LIKE WEED LIKE EGGS OF FISHES   428 27
    THEY ARE ALL PERAMBULATING EGGS   603 18

EGGS
    SHAKING THE LARK'S NEST TILL THE EGGS HAVE BROKEN   623 31
    HARDENED THE EARTH SHAKING THE LARK'S NEST TILL THE EGG+ *953 18

EGGY
    WHEN THE LITTLE EGGY AMOEBA EMERGED OUT OF FOAM AND NOW+   682 26

EGO
    AND THE EGO WILL HAVE TO BURST LIKE THE SWOLLEN FROG   472 12
    OR THE PERSONALITY ASSUMES IT AS AN ATTRIBUTE OR THE EGO   473   3
    SHELL OFF HIS EGO   475   3
    THE EGO REVEALED IN ALL ITS MONSTROUS INHUMANITY   475 11
    TAINTED WITH THE EGO AND THE PERSONALITY   481 20
    WHEN WE GET OUT OF THE GLASS BOTTLES OF OUR OWN EGO   482 15
    OH SAFER THAN ANYTHING ELSE IN A WELL-CORKED GLASSY EGO   543   2
    IS HAS SHE CHIPPED THE SHELL OF HER OWN EGO   603 16
    HAS HE CHIPPED THE SHELL OF HIS OWN EGO   603 17
    THE EGO RUNNING IN ITS OWN COMPLEX AND DISCONNECTED   635   9
    ONLY IN THE SOUL OF MAN WHEN IT PIVOTS UPON THE EGO   712 12
    WHEN THE MIND MAKES A WHEEL WHICH TURNS ON THE HUB OF T+   712 13
    EGO   713   5
    FIXED UPON THE HUB OF THE EGO   713 29
    OBSCENE EGO   714 18
    A SINGLE EGO STRIVING FOR ITS OWN ENDS   714 27

EGO-BOUND
    MAN BECOMES EGO-BOUND   474 24
    HE IS EGO-BOUND   474 28
    THE JEALOUSY OF AN EGO-BOUND WOMAN   475   6
    THE JEALOUSY OF AN EGO-BOUND WOMAN   475   9
    EGO-BOUND WOMEN ARE OFTEN LESBIAN   475 12
    PERHAPS THE EGO-BOUND CAN ONLY LOVE THEIR OWN   475 14
    BUT THE REAL FAULT LIES IN THE EGO-BOUND CONDITION OF   475 24
    THE EGO-BOUND   636 12
    THE SMALL ONES EGO-BOUND LITTLE MACHINES RUNNING IN AN   637   5
    FROM THE ROBOT MASS OF RICH AND POOR MECHANICAL EGO-BOU+   637 29

EGOCENTRIC
    POWERS TO REPEAT ITS OWN EGOCENTRIC MOTIONS   635 12

EGO-CENTRIC
    THE HORDES OF THE EGO-CENTRIC THE ROBOTS   635   7
    FOR LISTEN THE EGO-CENTRIC SELF IS THE SAME AS THE MACH+   635   8

EGOISM
    UNTIL THEY COLLAPSE INTO EGOISM THE MECHANICAL SELF-CEN+   649   4

EGOIST
    THE GOAT IS AN EGOIST AWARE OF HIMSELF DEVILISH AWARE OF   382 10
    FIND AN ENEMY EGOIST AND CLASH THE CYMBALS IN FACE-TO-F+   383 17

EGOISTIC
    AND EGOISTIC   447 14
    ARE ALL THE OBSTRUCTIONS TO LIFE SELF-IMPORTANCE SELF-C+   678 11
    O SHED THE UNCLEAN MEAN COWARDLY GREEDY EGOISTIC DEGENE+   679   5

EGOISTICALLY
    ONLY EGOISTICALLY WE ACCENT OURSELVES   513   6

EGO-PERVERTED
    EGO-PERVERTED LOVE   473   7

EGO SUM
    AND THE EGO SUM OF DIONYSOS   281 28

EGRESS
    OF EGRESS FROM YOU I WILL SEAL AND STEEP   154 14
    ESPECIALLY IF BEING GIVEN A NEEDLE'S EYE OF EGRESS ELSE+   381   6

EGYPT
    OF EGYPT FILLED   96   9
    EGYPT JOSEPH'S CUDGEL   380   2
    JESUS BUDDHA JEHOVAH AND RA EGYPT AND BABYLON   671 19

EGYPTIAN
    LOOK HOW BLACK HOW BLUE-BLACK HOW GLOBED IN EGYPTIAN   286   8
    EAGLE WITH EGYPTIAN DARKNESS JUTTING IN FRONT OF YOUR F+   782 27

EH
    EH THA'RT A MARD-ARSED KID   44 16
    EH THERE'S NO PEACE   45   2
    TER NOTTINGHAM EH DEAR O' ME   45   7
    EH WHAT A SHAME IT SEEMS   45 22
    EH MEN DOESNA HA'E BOSOMS 'APPEN NOT ON'Y THA KNOWS   540 16
    EH ANSWER ME THAT   547 24
    AND NO MORE THAN THE BARON DID EH NO OLD GIRL AND NOT S+   859 32
    FROM WHAT I'VE ARRANGED WI' THEE EH MAN WHAT A STUBBORN+ *925 26

EHAW
    HEE HEE EHEE EHOW EHAW OH OH OH-H-H   379 19

EHEE
    HEE HEE EHEE EHOW EHAW OH OH OH-H-H   379 19
    HEE HEE EHEE EHOW-OW-OW-AW-AW-AW   380   4

EHOW
    HEE HEE EHEE EHOW EHAW OH OH OH-H-H   379 19

EHOW-OW-OW-AW-AW-AW
    HEE HEE EHEE EHOW-OW-OW-AW-AW-AW   380   4

EIGHT
    THE CHIME OF THE BELLS AND THE CHURCH CLOCK STRIKING EI+   48 14
    THE SERGEANT SAYS THAT EIGHT AND TWENTY WAGONS   732   1

EIGHT AND TWENTY
  I WAIT FOR THE EIGHT AND TWENTY WAGONS TO COME   732 23

EIGHTEEN
  THAT OUR BOYS MUST STAY AT SCHOOL TILL THEY ARE EIGHTEEN   779 2

EIGHTY
  EIGHTY SUMMERS   502 21

EITHER
  AND I COULD FEEL HER FEET IN EITHER HAND   65 8
  MORE FROM 'ER THAN FROM YOU BUT EITHER   84 23
  EITHER OF US ANY MORE HENCEFORTH WE CAN   91 5
  THE SUN FROM THEIR NEIGHBOUR EITHER NOR BE SMOTHERED IN+   93 22
  TO TOUCH ITS FELLOW ON EITHER SIDE   154 6
  NOT AS A VISITOR EITHER NOR A SWEET   230 25
  WITH PALE SHUT FACE NOR EITHER HEARS NOR FEELS   232 27
  NOR OF EITHER OF US   247 16
  AND ON EITHER SIDE COUNT FIVE   355 31
  WATCH HIM TURN INTO A MESS EITHER A FOOL OR A BULLY   431 7
  IN EITHER CASE A WORM   432 5
  IT'S EITHER YOU FIGHT OR YOU DIE   458 1
  IT'S EITHER YOU FIGHT OR YOU DIE   458 4
  IT'S EITHER AN ARTIFICIAL RAG BLOSSOM OR AN IMMORTELLE +   472 26
  SO IF YOU WANT EITHER OF US TO FEEL ANYTHING AT ALL   501 14
  AS FOR THOSE OVER FIFTY EITHER THEY RUSH FORWARD   502 16
  AND IF THEY HAD NO UPPER CLASSES EITHER TO BE INFERIOR +   527 23
  OR BEING RAPED EITHER WAY SO LONG AS IT WAS CONSCIOUSLY   532 17
  WELL IT WON'T MATTER SO VERY MUCH EITHER   534 8
  OR YOUR MANLY BOSOM EITHER   540 24
  EITHER TO STAY CONNECTED WITH THE TREE OF LIFE AND SUBM+   617 13
  I KNOW HE IS EITHER A BED-BUG BATTENING ON SLEEPING PEO+   621 23
  I SHALL HAVE TO REFUSE ENTIRELY TO ACCEPT EITHER OF THEM   645 13
  EITHER IN ANGER OR TENDERNESS OR DESIRE OR SADNESS OR W+   672 4
  EITHER MAKE THE INDIAN BUREAU INTO A PERMANENT OFFICE   780 5
  THEY ARE EITHER IMMORALLY GOOD THE WORD DOES NOT AND   836 22
  AND EITHER RELEASE ENERGY OR SWALLOW IT UP   *947 11

EJECTS
  WHO IS IT EJECTS HIS SPERM TO THE NAKED FLOOD   335 25

EKED
  EKED OUT BY HIS TAILOR AND HIS HATTER   *947 30

EKKE
  IS EKKE SIR CLIFFORD IT'S REALLY FUNNY   669 1

EKKERHART
  ME AND EKKERHART AND SOMERS AND PAMELIE   668 21

ELABORATE
  ALL THE FITTINGS AND ELABORATE FURNISHINGS   440 17

ELASTIC
  A TWITCH A TWITTER AN ELASTIC SHUDDER IN FLIGHT   341 11

ELATE
  AND THE PERFECT DEAD ARE ELATE   168 30

ELATION
  WINGS AND MEN WHO SEE HIM WHEELING ARE FILLED WITH THE +   368 5

ELBOW
  HIS MOUSTACHE WITH AN ELBOW LIFTED AND HURLED   814 29

ELBOWS
  OF LINKING ELBOWS AND THEY TALK   106 13
  AND WORK IRON ELBOWS UP AND DOWN   793 25

ELDER
  HOW EVANESCENT VARIEGATED ELDER SHE HESITATES ON THE GR+   646 25
  TO THE NEXT FARM PULLS UP WHERE THE ELDER FLOWERS FALL   732 4
  AS THE ELDER GENERATIONS ARE APT TO DO   828 21

ELDER-FLOWERS
  MEDICINAL OF THE ELDER-FLOWERS WITH MEADOW-SWEET IS BLE+   858 19

ELDERLY
  ELDERLY DISCONTENTED WOMEN ASK FOR INTIMATE COMPANIONSH+   502 1
  ELDERLY DISCONTENTED WOMEN ARE SO FULL OF THEMSELVES   502 4

ELDER-TREES
  I WISH THE ELDER-TREES IN FLOWER COULD SUDDENLY HEAVE A+   159 23

ELECT
  WE THOUGHT WE'D ELECT YOU TO KEEP YOU ALL BUSY   574 4

ELECTRIC
  THE TURGID ELECTRIC ACHE AWAY   117 29
  GREAT ELECTRIC CARS   144 8
  AND THE LITTLE ELECTRIC FLASHES WENT WITH US IN THE GRA+   206 15
  HAVE YOU A STRANGE ELECTRIC SENSITIVENESS IN YOUR STEEL+   301 2
  DO YOU FEEL THE AIR FOR ELECTRIC INFLUENCES   301 3
  SO I SWITCHED ON THE ELECTRIC LIGHT THINKING NOW   344 26
  AND HE DID NOT MIND THE YELLOW ELECTRIC LIGHT   344 30
  BACK AND FORTH GOES THE BALANCE AND THE ELECTRIC BREATH   480 21
  AND AS THE ELECTRIC LIQUID POURS OUT SOMETIMES   647 13
  AND LIFTED HIS FACE UP WITH BLUE EYES LOOKING AT THE EL+   672 9
  AND THE SHUDDER OF ELECTRIC ANGER   707 10
  WITH THE WHITE TRIUMPHANCE OF LIGHTNING AND ELECTRIC DE+   707 19
  THE DEAD OF ELECTRIC MASTERS ARE ELECTRICITY ITSELF   796 10
  AND DART HIS ELECTRIC NEEDLES INTO YOUR BONES AND CURDL+   797 10
  LIKE MILK WITH ELECTRIC VENOM   797 11

ELECTRICITY
  FROM HEAVEN'S WOLFISH WANDERING ELECTRICITY THAT PROWLS   301 6
  AND STEEL HAS TWISTED THE LOINS OF MAN ELECTRICITY HAS   629 8
  THIS IS THE ELECTRICITY THAT MAN IS SUPPOSED TO HAVE MA+   647 18
  THE DEAD OF ELECTRIC MASTERS ARE ELECTRICITY ITSELF   796 10

ELECTRON
  THE SWAN WITHIN VAST CHAOS WITHIN THE ELECTRON   435 28
  WHERE THE ELECTRON BEHAVES AND MISBEHAVES AS IT WILL   437 28
  THE SANITY OF THE ELECTRON   515 18
  FROM TIME TO TIME THE WILD CRYING OF EVERY ELECTRON   682 20
  THEN THERE WAS A HUSH OF SUSPENSE AT THE CORE OF EVERY +   683 12
  ONLY THE ELECTRON BEHAVES AND MISBEHAVES INCOMPREHENSIB+   *947 5

ELECTRONS
  ELECTRONS AND ENERGIES QUANTUMS AND RELATIVITIES   438 5
  THEN ALL THE ELECTRONS HELD THEIR BREATH   682 27

ELEGANT
  THE SAME I SAY TO THE PALE AND ELEGANT PERSONS   316 26

ELEMENT
  YOU AND THE NAKED ELEMENT   335 22
  IN THE ELEMENT   336 2
  AND THE ELEMENT   336 6
  ALONE WITH THE ELEMENT   336 27
  TO HAVE THE ELEMENT UNDER ONE LIKE A LOVER   337 1
  THINGS OF ONE ELEMENT   340 3
  HAS IN IT AN ELEMENT OF BLACKNESS   708 16
  FROM ELEMENT TO ELEMENT   825 16
  FROM ELEMENT TO ELEMENT   826 5

ELEMENTAL
  AND BE A BIT ELEMENTAL INSTEAD   505 11
  BUT ELEMENTAL   505 15
  BUT OUR FIRE OUR ELEMENTAL FIRE   506 5
  THAT WHICH IS ELEMENTAL AND OF THE SUBSTANTIAL GODS IN +   637 12

ELEMENTS
  THE FIRST ELEMENTS OF FOREIGN SPEECH   366 20
  PLAYING AMONG THE ELEMENTS NEATLY BEYOND COMPETITION   445 33
  ELEMENTS   446 3
  SINCE MAN IS MADE UP OF THE ELEMENTS   505 12
  I WISH MEN WOULD GET BACK THEIR BALANCE AMONG THE ELEME+   505 17
  SONS OF THE LIVING ELEMENTS SONS OF THE UNTHINKING GODS   635 4
  SONS OF THE ELEMENTS AND THE UNSPEAKING GODS   635 24
  TO OUR SENSES THE ELEMENTS ARE FOUR   706 1
  FOR THEY ARE THE ELEMENTS OF LIFE OF POETRY AND OF PERC+   706 3
  TO FIND THE OTHER MANY ELEMENTS YOU MUST GO TO THE LABO+   706 6
  WE DON'T KNOW HOW LOVELY THE ELEMENTS ARE   839 23

ELEPHANT
  ELEPHANT ADVANCING HIS FRONTAL BONE HIS TRUNK CURLED   387 7
  THE ELEPHANT BELLS STRIKING SLOW TONG-TONG TONG-TONG   387 33
  AS THE ELEPHANT BELLS SOUNDED TONG-TONG-TONG BELL OF THE   390 32
  AND SMILES THE VASTNESS OF HER ELEPHANT ANTIQUITY   426 6
  THE ELEPHANT THE HUGE OLD BEAST   465 7
  SO SLOWLY THE GREAT HOT ELEPHANT HEARTS   465 19

ELEPHANTS
  MUSIC SCREAMS AS ELEPHANTS SCREAM   70 10
  AND THE HUGE FRONTAL OF THREE GREAT ELEPHANTS STEPPING   387 28
  ELEPHANTS AFTER ELEPHANTS CURL THEIR TRUNKS VAST SHADOWS   388 1
  MORE ELEPHANTS TONG TONG-TONG LOOM UP   388 26
  SOCKETS AMONG BARE FEET OF ELEPHANTS AND MEN ON THE   388 31
  AND SMALLER MORE FRIGHTENED ELEPHANTS   389 4
  OF ELEPHANTS   389 19
  AND THE SPARSE-HAIRED ELEPHANTS SLOWLY FOLLOWING   389 34
  IN ELEPHANTS AND THE EAST ARE TWO DEVILS IN ALL MEN MAY+   390 5
  THAT'S WHY AS THE ELEPHANTS PONDEROUSLY WITH UNSEEMING   390 29
  IT WAS AS IF THE GREAT BULKS OF ELEPHANTS IN THE OBSCURE   391 1
  TO BOW BEFORE ROYALTY IN THE LAND OF ELEPHANTS BOW DEEP   391 28
  AND TO THE ELEPHANTS   392 9
  ELEPHANTS IN THE CIRCUS   425 19
  THE ELEPHANTS HUGE AND GREY LOOMED THEIR CURVED BULK   445 10

ELEPHANT'S
  THEN THE LITTLE CUNNING PIG-DEVIL OF THE ELEPHANT'S LUR+   390 9

ELEPHANTS'
  AND THE FLAT FLACCID MOUNTAINS OF THE ELEPHANTS' STANDI+   390 13

ELEVEN
  LET US CALL THE ELEVEN   798 4

ELIMINATE
  AND THUS ELIMINATE US   429 21

ELK
  AND THE EXTINCT GIANT ELK TOO BIG IN ANTLERS   529 18

ELLIPSES
  PATIENTLY ROUND AND ROUND IN ELLIPSES   823 27

'E'LL
  'E'LL GIE THEE SOCKS   44 17
  AN' WHAT A MOAN 'E'LL MAKE THERE NIVER   45 17
  AN' A FORK AN' A SPOON 'E'LL WANT AN' WHAT ELSE   46 1
  I SH'D THINK 'E'LL GET RIGHT AGAIN   46 4

ELMS
  IN PURPLE ELMS DAFFODILS   162 6
  OF THE MORNING THE ELMS ARE LOFTILY DIMMED AND TALL   164 22

ELM-TREE
    IN A LITTER THROUGH THE ELM-TREE SHADE ARE SCRAWLING   65 17

ELOQUENCE
    THEY WERE THE HALO THE ELOQUENCE NOW IS NONE   855 15

ELOQUENT
    ELOQUENT LIMBS   145 16
    ELOQUENT PURITY VOICELESS IN THE DUST   855 6

ELSE
    AN' A FORK AN' A SPOON 'E'LL WANT AN' WHAT ELSE   46 1
    THA WANTS IT AND EVERYTHING ELSE IS IN VAIN   139 19
    ITSELF AMONG EVERYTHING ELSE HERE HUNGRILY STEALING   141 18
    WHAT ELSE IT IS PERFECT ENOUGH   203 25
    SINGLE AND PERFECTLY DISTINCT FROM EVERYTHING ELSE   254 25
    OR ELSE BEFORE THEY HAD BEEN LET DOWN AGAIN IN NOAH'S F+   285 21
    AND EVERYTHING ELSE TO THEIR DISGUSTING LEVEL   317 31
    OR ELSE I AM DEAD   380 6
    OR ELSE RUSH HORIZONTAL TO CHARGE AT THE SKY'S HORIZON   392 18
    YOU RUN STRAIGHT AWAY TO LIVE WITH SOMEBODY ELSE   399 13
    OR ELSE OR ELSE   428 16
    GIVE US SOMETHING ELSE   437 9
    ELSE   476 4
    WE ARE SOMETHING ELSE   480 2
    AS THEY TRY TO SCREW EVERYBODY ELSE DOWN WITH THEIR WILL   502 12
    NOR ANYBODY ELSE   508 24
    OR ELSE POOR THINGS THEY'RE HAVING TO PAY FOR THEMSELVES   518 11
    WHATEVER ELSE THEY SAY OF ME   534 9
    IT'S SOMETHING ELSE YOU ARE AFTER IF YOU COULD BUT   541 15
    OH SAFER THAN ANYTHING ELSE IN A WELL-CORKED GLASSY EGO   543 2
    SUPERIOR TO EVERYONE ELSE SO DON'T START   576 13
    WITH MY FELLOW-COUNTRYMEN OR ELSE I DON'T BELONG   579 6
    A CACHE SEXE A CACHE SEXE OR ELSE BEGONE   580 2
    IS BETTER THAN ANYTHING ELSE IN THE WORLD   601 5
    I LIKE HIM WHAT ELSE IS THERE   611 5
    ELSE   616 27
    OR ELSE TO SEVER THE CONNECTION TO BECOME SELF-CENTRED +   617 15
    NOBODY ELSE DID   619 17
    TO WORK WITH AND NOTHING ELSE   630 28
    SOMETHING ELSE   665 8
    ELSE   665 13
    AND THERE IS NOTHING ELSE THROUGHOUT TIME AND ETERNITY   701 1
    THE WEATHER IN TOWN IS ALWAYS BENZINE OR ELSE PETROL   703 18
    OF ELSE BEWARE THEIR ANGRY PRESENCE NOW   723 14
    THAN EVERYTHING ELSE   764 2
    WHICH ELSE WERE A SILENT GRASP THAT HELD THE SKIES   773 9
    THERE AND NOWHERE ELSE   774 28
    IN INDIVIDUAL HEARTS AND NOWHERE ELSE   775 26
    WHAT ELSE HAVE THEY COME TO THIS COUNTRY FOR   777 4
    AS RICH AS ANYBODY ELSE ON THE SAME TERMS   778 15
    OR ELSE PREPARE FOR THE OTHER THINGS   793 9
    NEW LIFE BUBBLES IN WE BECOME SOMETHING ELSE   832 22
    LIES IN FORCING YOURSELF OR SOMEBODY ELSE   836 18
    OR ELSE THEY ARE IMMORALLY NASTY AND THE WORD LOOMS   837 1
    WE VIOLATE OURSELVES EVERY MOMENT AND VIOLATE EVERYBODY+   839 6
    AND NOTHING ELSE BUT THIS   *947 7

ELSEWHERE
    ELSEWHERE HALLS OF HIGH DISGRACES   95 31
    AT VENICE AND ELSEWHERE   325 24
    ESPECIALLY IF BEING GIVEN A NEEDLE'S EYE OF EGRESS ELSE+   381 6

ELVISH
    DARK ELVISH   293 5

ELVISHNESS
    YOUR ELVISHNESS   291 23

ELYSIUM
    THEN I SHALL KNOW THE ELYSIUM   262 22

EMASCULATED
    EMASCULATED   658 19

EMBABA
    OH COLONEL YOU FROM EMBABA   754 21

EMBALMED
    EMBALMED FLOWERS ARE NOT FLOWERS IMMORTELLES ARE NOT   476 16

EMBANKMENT
    DOWN THE EMBANKMENT RUN FOR MY LIFE   143 18

EMBARK
    THAT CANNOT EMBARK ON THE SLINKING SEA BEYOND   722 23

EMBARKED
    SINCE I EMBARKED ON YOUR DARK BLUE FRINGES   *954 28

EMBARRASS
    AND PAST LIVES HAMPER ME CLOG AND EMBARRASS   173 28

EMBASSY
    FROM EMBASSY IN DEATH I ISSUE FORTH   744 21

EMBEDDED
    EMBEDDED IN THEM I LOOK OUT ON THE SUNSHINE OF THE SOUTH   629 31
    AND EMBEDDED YOU IN THE WORKMEN'S DWELLINGS WHERE   630 19
    WHO AM EMBEDDED IN A SHELL OF SILENCE   698 25
    I WAS EMBEDDED IN THE REST OF THINGS   881 30

EMBER
    LIKE GHOSTS ON THE GLOWING OF THE EMBER   103 13

EMBERS
    AND SCARLET HOT EMBERS OF TORCHES KNOCKED OUT OF THE   388 30
    I WILL NOT WASTE MYSELF TO EMBERS FOR THEM   *895 31
    SHALL HAVE RAKED THE EMBERS CLEAR I WILL KEEP   *896 2
    I WILL NOT WASTE MYSELF TO EMBERS FOR THEM   *904 20
    SHALL HAVE RAKED THE EMBERS CLEAR I WILL KEEP   *904 23

EMBODIED
    EMBODIED   281 8
    EMBODIED JOBS   452 6

EMBONPOINT
    YOU'VE A DELICIOUS TENDENCY TO EMBONPOINT   835 26

EMBOSOMED
    BUT SLEEPS THE LONG WEEK OUT EMBOSOMED IN MURMURING LIM+   858 23

EMBOSSED
    IF MY VEINS AND MY BREASTS WITH LOVE EMBOSSED   *891 26

EMBOWERED
    EMBOWERED IN YOU   297 13

EMBRACE
    EMBRACE OF DARKNESS LIE AROUND AND CRUSHED BETWEEN THEM+   88 4
    THEY PASS IN A HALF EMBRACE   106 12
    PERFECTING NOW OUR UNFINISHED FIRST EMBRACE   157 22
    I WISH I COULD TAKE IT ALL IN A LAST EMBRACE   173 15
    TO YOU WHOEVER YOU ARE WITH ENDLESS EMBRACE   396 12
    AND THEN TURN ROUND AND EMBRACE THE EXTANT BODY OF LIFE   482 4
    WITH THE THRUSTING EMBRACE OF NEW JUSTICE NEW JUSTICE   482 5
    BUT THE PASSION OF JUSTICE IS A PRIMAL EMBRACE   482 10
    AND THE PASSION OF TRUTH IS THE EMBRACE BETWEEN MAN AND   482 12
    AND NAKED EMBRACE AN ANTI-CLIMAX HUMILIATING AND RIDICU+   608 19
    AND LET US EMBRACE   764 9
    NOR EVE FOR YOUR HEAVY ANGUISH OF EMBRACE   876 17
    LEAN TOGETHER AND LIFT WILD ARMS TO EMBRACE   883 9

EMBRACES
    EMBRACES   91 29
    DEATH IN OUR AWED EMBRACES   242 22
    STRUGGLING IN DOUBTFUL EMBRACES   457 15
    WOUNDING THEMSELVES AGAINST HER DENYING HER GREAT EMBRA+   *926 21
    THE HATE OF TERROR OR DENY THE FECUND SOUL HER EMBRACES   *926 25

EMBRYOS
    ARE PARTS OF THE EARTH JUST AS EMBRYOS ARE PARTS OF THE+   295 9

EMERALD
    LIKE A STORM OF EMERALD SNOW NOW SEE   126 24

EMERGE
    AND NOW THE LONGEST GRASS-LEAVES HARDLY EMERGE   85 6
    AND NEVER EMERGE   335 5
    GLAD TO EMERGE AND LOOK BACK   409 13
    AND EMERGE AS SQUEAKY GLOBULES WITH NO BODIES TO SPEAK +   501 2
    AND TO EMERGE AT LAST   769 9

EMERGED
    WHEN THE LITTLE EGGY AMOEBA EMERGED OUT OF FOAM AND NOW+   682 26

EMERGES
    OF SHADOW EMERGING AS BLOOD EMERGES FROM INWARD SHADES +   66 20
    EMERGES STRANGE AND LOVELY   720 13

EMERGING
    OF SHADOW EMERGING AS BLOOD EMERGES FROM INWARD SHADES +   66 20
    EMERGING WHITE AND EXQUISITE AND I IN AMAZE   67 9
    TWO MEXICANS STRANGERS EMERGING OUT OF THE DARK AND   401 12
    SWIM DEEPER DEEPER TILL IT LEAVES NO PEAK EMERGING   428 25
    AND THAT POOR LATE MAKESHIFT APHRODITE EMERGING IN A   439 31
    THE GEM OF MUTUAL PEACE EMERGING FROM THE WILD CHAOS   477 19
    EMERGING AND CROSSING THE CLEAR SKY UNPERCEIVED   874 24

EMINENCE
    ACROSS THE SPACE ON THE CAT IN HEAVEN'S HOSTILE EMINENCE   97 22

EMINENTLY
    PRESENTABLE EMINENTLY PRESENTABLE   430 17

EMISSION
    INSTEAD OF WHICH THE SILENT FATAL EMISSION FROM THAT PA+   390 25

EMOTION
    LIFT LOOKS OF SHOCKED AND MOMENTOUS EMOTION UP AT ME   71 22
    LET HIM MEET A NEW EMOTION LET HIM BE FACED WITH ANOTHER   431 3
    THE EMOTION OF BROTHERHOOD   611 8
    RESURRECTED FROM THE DEATH OF MECHANICAL MOTION AND EMO+   667 33
    WITH SNAKE-BITES OF TANGLED UNCONSCIOUS EMOTION   833 31

EMOTIONAL
    IT IS NO USE MY SAYING TO HIM IN AN EMOTIONAL VOICE   357 1
    WITH ALL THE HURT TO THEIR INSTINCTIVE AND EMOTIONAL SE+   544 28
    IN ALL MATTERS OF EMOTIONAL IMPORTANCE   604 17
    I AM ILL BECAUSE OF WOUNDS TO THE SOUL TO THE DEEP EMOT+   620 13
    BECAUSE ALL THE FACES CONTAIN SETS OF EMOTIONAL AND   657 2
    SOME ONLY LIVE FOR THEIR EMOTIONAL FURNISHING   657 8
    WHEN IT COMES TO OUR EMOTIONAL SELVES   833 9
    AND WHERE WE CAN BEGIN TO LEARN OUR GREAT EMOTIONAL LES+   833 16

EMOTIONS
    EMOTIONS THEY NONE OF THEM FELT   443 25
    I AM SICK OF PEOPLE'S CEREBRAL EMOTIONS   500 18
    EVEN THE OLD EMOTIONS ARE FINISHED   510 16
    EMOTIONS TO MUD   544 17
    AND EMOTIONS AND DESIRES AND STRENGTH GLORY OR HONOUR   691 11
    HE HAS FRESH CLEAN WELL-GROOMED EMOTIONS   830 11
    ALL HIS EMOTIONS HIS FEELINGS THAT ARE NOT SUPERFICIAL +   830 16

EMOTIONS
WE CAN UNCOIL THE GHASTLY SNAKE-TANGLE OF OUR UNCONSCIO+   833 26
EMOTIONS WHICH WOULD COME UP LIKE FLOWERS WERE THEY NOT+   833 27
AND UNDERNEATH THE GREAT TURBULENT EMOTIONS OF LOVE THE+   844   7

EMPEDOKLES
EMPEDOKLES SAYS TREES WERE THE FIRST LIVING CREATURES T+   295   4
EMPEDOKLES   303 16

EMPERORS
OH EAGLE OF KINGS AND EMPERORS   783 23

EMPLOY
US WHOM YOU CAN'T EMPLOY   572 24

EMPLOYERS
MEN SELL THEMSELVES FOR A WAGE AND EMPLOYERS LOOK OUT   483   2
AND EMPLOYERS ARE BOUGHT BY FINANCIERS AND FINANCIERS A+   483   4

EMPTIED
AND EMPTIED MY HEART OF LOVE   124   2

EMPTILY
HAIL AND BE DAMNED TO THEE EMPTY MOST EMPTILY   824   9

EMPTY
INTO THE TWILIGHT'S EMPTY HALL   42 31
LIKE AN EMPTY DANDELION STALK BEREFT OF CONNECTION SMALL   98   3
O' THY SPUNK AN' THA'RT EMPTY AN' MORTIFIED   139 12
EMPTY AN' EMPTY FROM BOTTOM TO TOP   139 13
LEAVES AN EMPTY BREAST   155 12
THE BUBBLE HEMMING THIS EMPTY EXISTENCE WITH LIGHTS   193 22
SUCKED OUT OF YOUR EMPTY BLADDERS   281 23
LIFE HAS ITS CHANGES BUT WHEN THE HEAVENS ARE EMPTY EMP+ 319   8
QUARTERS THEN SLEEP IS EMPTY TOO MAN SLEEPS NO MORE LIK+ 319 10
EMPTY DAWNS IN SILENT AUSTRALIA   393 13
AND I THINK IN THIS EMPTY WORLD THERE WAS ROOM FOR ME   402 27
WHILE THEIR HEARTS BECOME ABSOLUTELY EMPTY   502 10
I AM HERE YET MY HEART IS BARE AND UTTERLY EMPTY   509   7
PAUSES THAT ARE AS GOOD AS DEATH EMPTY AND DEAD AS DEATH 510   8
THEY'RE AS EMPTY AS EMPTY TINS   553 10
IS THE LANGUAGE DEAD AND EMPTY OF REPLY   633 13
ALMOST AS EMPTY AS BELCHING OR HICCUP   681   7
WOULD YOU PEEP IN THE EMPTY HOUSE LIKE A PILFERER   742 17
YOU ARE EMPTY GOURD-SHELLS FILLED WITH DUST AND WIND   800   4
TILL YOU ARE AS EMPTY AS RAT-GNAWED POMEGRANATES HANGIN+ 800 26
THE VASTNESS IS EMPTY EXCEPT THAT THERE PLY   823 20
HAIL AND BE DAMNED TO THEE EMPTY MOST EMPTILY   824   9
I RUN AWAKE TO THE HOUSE OF MY SOUL AND FIND IT EMPTY   871   9
AND THE HOUSE IS EMPTY AND I AM ALONE   871 12
LEAVING MY EYES HALF EMPTY AND CLAMOROUS   *893 16
WHEN YOU ARE ONLY OCCUPIED YOU ARE AN EMPTY SHELL   *949 21

EMPYREAN
SHOO IT DOWN OUT OF THE EMPYREAN   329 17
LIFTS HIM FANNING IN THE HIGH EMPYREAN   782 23

EMULATION
WHY SHOULD WE BRACE OURSELVES UP WITH MEAN EMULATION   520   5

'EM
RIGHT IN 'EM AN' SCRAIGHTED A BIT AGAIN   61 14
THEN AFTER A BIT 'ER DROPPED 'EM DOWN THAT PLACE   61 15
AT 'EM BOYS AT 'EM   309   6
SMELL 'EM SMELL 'EM OUT   309   8
YOU LOVE 'EM ALL   395 24
YOU LOVED 'EM ALL SO MUCH BEFORE DIDN'T YOU LOVED 'EM   399 31
YOU DON'T LOVE 'EM NOW   400   1
'EM   483 21
WE SHOULD START AN' KICK THEIR -SES FOR 'EM   491   3
AN' TELL 'EM TO   491   4
HE COULDN'T BITE 'EM HE WAS MUCH TOO OLD   492   3
THERE ISN'T A MAN AMONG 'EM   550   1
AN' BLAST 'EM FOREVER BUT THEY'D ONLY   550 11
I TELL YOU SOMETHING'S BEEN DONE TO 'EM   550 13
THERE'S NOT A COCK BIRD AMONG 'EM   550 15
AN' YOU COULD NO MORE GET 'EM A MOVE ON   550 17
MILLIONS FOR THERE'S MILLIONS OF 'EM   552 15
THERE ISN'T A DAMN THING IN 'EM   553   9
HALF BELIEVING 'EM TILL ONE DAY   556 14
GIVE 'EM A FEW HARD POKES   560 20
WE VOTED 'EM IN AND WE'LL VOTE 'EM OUT   573 21
WE'LL SHOW 'EM A THING OR TWO NEVER YOU DOUBT   573 22
LOOK OUT MY LAD YOU'VE GOT 'EM ON YOUR TRACK   634   9
ME WATCHIN' DOST THINK THERE WAS OWT BETWEEN 'EM   *910 23
WAS TH' LITTLE LOVIN' SORT AS 'AS NOWT TER SCREEN 'EM   *910 25
RIGHT UNTIL 'EM AND SCRAIGHTED OUT AGAIN   *911 30
THEN AFTER A BIT 'ER DROPPED 'EM DOWN THAT PLACE   *911 31

ENACT
GLOW AND ENACT THE DRAMAS AND DREAMS   151   4
GLOW AND ENACT THE DRAMAS AND DREAMS   873 14

ENACTS
AND SACRIFICE IS THE LAW OF LIFE WHICH ENACTS   679 20

ENCHAIN
BRANCH AND ENCHAIN   *937   9

ENCHANTED
IN THE WHITE MORNING WHERE IS THE ENCHANTED ROOM OF THE+ 856   7

ENCIRCLING
ENCIRCLING THEIR HUDDLED MONSTERS OF LOVE   695   4

ENCLOSE
LIKE A CANDLE-FLAME ON THIS BODY BUT I ENCLOSE   115   6
NEWSPAPER SHEETS ENCLOSE   145 25

ENCLOSED
I AM LIKE A SEED WITH A PERFECT FLOWER ENCLOSED   247   6
FOLDED UPON ITSELF ENCLOSED LIKE ANY MOHAMMEDAN WOMAN   283 14
ENCLOSED IN HIS OWN LIMITED MENTAL CONSCIOUSNESS   474 25
ENCLOSED CIRCLE OF SELF   637   6

ENCLOSES
AND A TREMBLING FLOWER ENCLOSES   178 25
OF THIS HOUSE OF LIFE THAT ENCLOSES US ALL   461 28
OF THE PRISON HOUSE THAT ENCLOSES US ALL   462   8

ENCLOSURE
WHEN AT LAST WE ESCAPE THE BARBED-WIRE ENCLOSURE   667 12

ENCOMPASSED
ENCOMPASSED AND MANY REDUCED TO NONE   252 11

ENCOURAGE
AND ALSO TO ENCOURAGE THE RED-CROSS LAMB   325 21
JUST VOTE US SOME PIN-MONEY TO ENCOURAGE OUR   574   6
SET FOOD FOR THEM AND ENCOURAGE THEM TO BUILD   722 13

ENCOURAGED
AND ALL ARE ENCOURAGED INTO THE SIN   620 24

ENCOURAGEMENT
AND ROBOTS MUST HAVE ENCOURAGEMENT FROM MEN OF THE   639   8
AND GIVE THEM A LITTLE ENCOURAGEMENT   721 18

ENCROACHING
ENCROACHING TOWARDS A CRISIS A MEETING A SPASM AND THRO+ 66 22

END
A CAR AT THE END OF THE STREET GOES BY WITH A LAUGH   54 26
BEHIND THE BLACK SYCAMORE AT THE END OF THE GARDEN   62 26
WHEN WILL THE BELL RING AND END THIS WEARINESS   74   7
TO THIS SAD END   152 23
OF RIDING AND BEING ENVIED SUCH ENVY AS HAS NO END   175   9
THAT YOU ARE WITH ME IN THE END   208 11
AT LAST I CAN THROW AWAY WORLD WITHOUT END AND MEET YOU 210   1
ARE PROPPED ON END THERE WHERE THE MYSTERY STARTS   233   8
ITS FLAME OF LIFE NOW AND ALWAYS TILL THE END   233 16
WHERE THE END IS BEGUN   253 33
I SHALL NEVER FORGET THE MANIACAL HORROR OF IT ALL IN T+ 257 10
IT WAS A MANIACAL HORROR IN THE END   257 17
COME AND LIFT US TO OUR END TO BLOSSOM BRING US TO OUR + 272 33
THE END CRACKS OPEN WITH THE BEGINNING   278 25
THE PROCESS WILL AMOUNT TO THE SAME IN THE END   317 35
SO THAT A NEW CONCEPTION OF THE BEGINNING AND END   329 33
AND IN THE END   340 16
AT THE END OF SOME MYSTERIOUS RED-HOT IRON   363 16
WE WILL GO ON TO THE END   363   2
WE LOOK AT HIM THROUGH THE WRONG END OF THE LONG TELESC+ 372 22
AND THERE END   379 17
AND NEVER NEVER ARRIVING AT JOURNEY'S END AT THE REAR OF 380 26
AT THE END OF A BACK-BONE RIDGE LIKE A STRAIGHT SIERRA + 381   3
OR LIKE A LIFTED HAND HAILING AT HER WRONG END   385 33
FROM THE FAR FAR OTHER END OF THE DAY   405 16
WHERE THE WATERS END IN MARSHES   437 22
TOWARDS THE END OF HER PARTICUALR AFFAIR WITH HIM   446 27
MUST RUN THE PATTERN OUT IN A LITTLE BREAK AT THE END   448 24
ARE AND THEY SHALL TO THE END   461 10
STRAIGHT TO THE VERY END   471 23
LOVE OUT OF SEASON ESPECIALLY AT THE END OF THE SEASON 478 12
AND THE END OF ALL THINGS IS INSIDE US   510 19
WHICH IN THE END IS ALWAYS HOMICIDAL   514 27
IN THE END WE GO INSANE   522 21
REELING IN THE BLACK END OF ALL BELIEFS   542 24
AND IN THE END   605 16
ALONE SATISFIES US IN THE END   653 14
THERE IS NO END TO THE BIRTH OF GOD   683 18
IT IS SHIPS OF CNOSSOS COMING OUT OF THE MORNING END OF+ 687   5
COMING OUT OF THE EASTERN END   687   7
THE BEGINNING AND THE END   694 32
WHICH GOES FURTHER AND FURTHER AND YET NEVER FINDS AN E+ 701   6
FOR THERE IS NO END   701   7
TO THE END FOR THEY ARE NOT YET BURIED   703   5
ALREADY THE DARK AND ENDLESS OCEAN OF THE END   718   6
UPON THE WATERS OF THE END   719   7
IT IS THE END IT IS OBLIVION   719 26
THE END OF ALL KNOWLEDGE IS OBLIVION   726   4
TO WOLFRATSHAUSEN LAST WINTER'S END COMES THROUGH   732 10
PUSHED UP ON END AND THE BREATH SIGHING   733 25
HOW SHE FARES AT HER END   748 16
TO MAKE AN END OF THE MALICE OF THIS OVERSEER   759 11
THEY ARE SAYING TO ONE ANOTHER LET US MAKE AN END   792 22
THE SOURCE AND THE END OF WHICH WE KNOW   811   7
WHEN THE END OF THE WORLD WE ARE TOLD IS SCROLLED   814 11
WHAT YET ANOTHER BAD END OF THE WORLD   814 27
IN THE WORLD WITHOUT END AMEN   823 12
WORLDS WITHOUT END WITHOUT REASON WHY   823 21
TIME WITHOUT END AMEN AMEN   826   7
FOREVER AND EVER AND NEVER COME TO THE END   832 25
THE MEN IN THE END ONLY HATE THEM BECAUSE THE ESCAPE WA+ 838 10
AT THE END OF A SWEET SPRING DAY THEY WILL VANISH   855   5
AT THE END OF THE SWEET SPRING DAY THEY ARE YOURS   855 13
FLEEING IN EXILE TO ENGLAND AT THE END OF THE FIGHT   859   6
WHEN WILL THE BELL RING AND END THIS WEARINESS   *895 15
WHEN WILL THE BELL RING AND END THIS WEARINESS   *904   1
AS A SILENT BEE AT THE END OF A SHOWER   *913 20
AT THE END OF THE LONGEST JOURNEY   *960   4

ENDANGERED
    ENDANGERED BY THE PILFERER ON HIS QUEST   128 4

ENDEAVER
    HER BREASTS UPLIFTED IN ENDEAVER SHE TOUCHES SHE REEVES   864 12

ENDED
    THAT ENDED HER LIFE AND MINE   198 4
    THAT ENDED HER LIFE AND MINE   199 12
    UPON THE WATERS THAT ENDED IN MARSHES   *947 1

ENDING
    TO THEE I ROSE LIKE A ROCKET ENDING IN MID-HEAVEN   322 8
    SO ENDING ON A GRUNT OF AGONISED RELIEF   377 16
    AND HIM ALWAYS ENDING WITH A YAWP   413 23
    THE DAY IS ENDING THE NIGHT DESCENDING   456 1
    NOW THE WORLD IS ENDING IN DUST AND IN SORROW   815 1
    THE WORLD IS ENDING LET'S HURRY TO BORROW   815 2

ENDINGS
    THE GREAT SWAN UPON THE WATERS OF ALL ENDINGS   435 27

ENDLESS
    DOWN THE ENDLESS SLOPE WHERE THE LAST ROAD GOES   164 12
    AN ENDLESS TAPESTRY THE PAST HAS WOVEN DRAPES   173 19
    TO SPEAK ENDLESS INAUDIBLE WAVELETS INTO THE WAVE   336 29
    ENDLESS UNDER THE PRINCE   388 37
    AND FOUND YOU AFTER ENDLESS CHASING   395 28
    TO YOU WHOEVER YOU ARE WITH ENDLESS EMBRACE   396 12
    FATHERING ENDLESS TEN-DOLLAR GOLDEN EGGS   414 12
    WE TRAIL BEHIND US AN ENDLESS TRADITION OF COMBAT   519 11
    WHEN AS A MATTER OF FACT THE THOUGHT OF THIS ENDLESS   519 15
    FROM THE ENDLESS REPETITION OF THE MISTAKE   620 20
    HE IS CAPABLE OF AN ENDLESS GRINDING NIHILISTIC HATE   648 3
    OF ENDLESS AND LIVING SILENCE   698 27
    THAT AWFUL AND SICKENING ENDLESS SINKING SINKING   699 21
    SINKING IN THE ENDLESS UNDOING THE AWFUL KATABOLISM INT+   699 26
    IN THE ENDLESS WRITHE OF THE LAST THE LAST SELF-KNOWLED+   700 27
    ALREADY THE DARK AND ENDLESS OCEAN OF THE END   718 6
    MULTITUDINOUS ENDLESS THE GHOSTS COMING HOME AGAIN   739 15
    MY SOUL COMES LAMBENT FROM THE ENDLESS NIGHT   744 5
    OF RESURRECTION FROM THE ENDLESS GRAVE   745 4
    BETWEEN WINGS OF THE ENDLESS FLIGHT   788 16
    IS SWEPT FROM OUT OF THE ENDLESS SKY   823 19
    HEY WITH THIS ENDLESS LABOUR AND LITTLE-SOULED FRET   859 26
    AN ENDLESS TAPESTRY THE PAST HAS WOVEN DRAPES   *906 13
    AN ENDLESS TAPESTRY THE PAST HAS WOVEN DRAPES   *908 1
    ENDLESS WHISPER OF PASSING FEET   *917 6

ENDLESSLY
    LIKE SPATTERING SHOUTS OF AN ORATOR ENDLESSLY DROPPING   54 6
    FROM THE TOWER ON THE TOWN BUT ENDLESSLY NEVER STOPPING   54 7
    WITH SOUNDS THAT ENDLESSLY SWELL AND SINK LIKE THE STOR+   97 24
    THAT AT THE WINDOW ENDLESSLY   116 22
    COMES ENDLESSLY KISSING MY FACE AND MY HANDS   144 2
    ENDLESSLY IN ONE MOTION DEPART   163 7
    THEM ENDLESSLY ENDLESSLY BY   252 24
    INSIPID UNSALTED RABBITY ENDLESSLY HOPPING   606 19
    ENDLESSLY RETURNING ON THE UNEASY SEA   739 12
    MOVING VIBRATING ENDLESSLY IN THE ROUNDED FLESH   *906 24
    AS AT THE WINDOW ENDLESSLY   *930 21

ENDOW
    FOR SEED TO ENDOW   102 12

ENDOWED
    ENDOWED WITH A SUFFICIENT ENDOWMENT   780 6

ENDOWMENT
    ENDOWED WITH A SUFFICIENT ENDOWMENT   780 6

ENDS
    WHILE NORTH OF THEM ALL AT THE FARTHEST ENDS STANDS ONE+   57 11
    ENDS LIKE A BROKEN LOVE THAT TURNS TO THE DARK OF SLEEP   114 28
    BACK FROM THE STRAIGHT HORIZON THAT ENDS ALL ONE SEES   168 6
    THAT ENDS NOT ANYWHERE   203 6
    ENDS THIS DARKNESS THAT ANNIHILATES ME   221 4
    NOW TO THEIR SEPARATE ENDS   253 18
    CUNNINGLY BLOWING ON THE FALLEN SPARKS ODDS AND ENDS OF+   271 31
    OR SLIP LIKE WATER SLIPPERY TOWARDS ITS ENDS   392 20
    FOR THEIR OWN IMMORTAL ENDS   492 26
    AND THE YOUNG COPPER BEECH ITS LEAVES RED-ROSY AT THE E+   647 4
    A SINGLE EGO STRIVING FOR ITS OWN ENDS   714 27
    TO LIVE THEIR OWN LIFE FULFIL THEIR OWN ENDS   779 24
    BUT CHASTITY ON THE BRAIN IS ANOTHER VICE IT ENDS IN LU+   *952 26

ENDUE
    NOURISH ME AND ENDUE ME I AM ONLY OF YOU   246 11

ENDURANCE
    MYSTERY BEYOND KNOWLEDGE OR ENDURANCE SO SUMPTUOUS   260 30
    A SET STOIC ENDURANCE NON-EUROPEAN   292 12

ENDURE
    NO LONGER NOW CAN I ENDURE THE BRUNT   74 12
    OR TO ENDURE THE JAZZY PERSON   499 18
    NO MORE CAN I ENDURE TO BEAR THE BRUNT   *895 20
    NO MORE CAN I ENDURE TO BEAR THE BRUNT   *904 9

ENDURED
    IT IS NO GOOD DEAR GENTLENESS AND FORBEARANCE I ENDURED+   92 7
    YOU ONLY ENDURED AND IT BROKE   111 23
    IT IS NO GOOD DEAR MEEKNESS AND FORBEARANCE I ENDURED T+   *926 7

ENEMY
    YOU MADAME CERES MIND YOURSELF THE ENEMY IS UPON   308 28
    HIS HORNS TURN AWAY FROM THE ENEMY   327 6
    OF THE OPPOSITE ENEMY GOAT   381 27
    BUT THEY'VE TAKEN HIS ENEMY FROM HIM   382 1
    SO IT IS WHEN THEY TAKE THE ENEMY FROM US   382 6
    AND NEVER AN ENEMY BROW-METALLED TO THRESH IT OUT WITH   382 30
    FIND AN ENEMY EGOIST AND CLASH THE CYMBALS IN FACE-TO-F+   383 17
    MY ENEMY   468 11
    OUT OF FEAR OF THE UNKNOWN ENEMY   529 19
    A MAN MAY BE MY ENEMY TO THE DEATH   715 6
    WE YIELD THE ENEMY HIS LAST DEMANDS   736 26
    THE ENEMY   741 8
    THE ENEMY MY BROTHER   743 18

ENERGETIC
    OF INCIPIENT ENERGETIC LIFE   480 25
    WHY ARE WOMEN SO ENERGETIC   537 19

ENERGIES
    ELECTRONS AND ENERGIES QUANTUMS AND RELATIVITIES   438 5
    THE ATOM LOCKS UP TWO ENERGIES   515 14

ENERGY
    AND FLARE OF A TROPICAL ENERGY TIRELESS AFIRE IN THE DA+   389 16
    GATHER HIS WILL AND HIS ENERGY TOGETHER   428 20
    OF HAPPY ENERGY   436 4
    MIST OF ENERGY MOST SCIENTIFIC   438 1
    WITH THE GODHEAD OF ENERGY THAT CANNOT TELL LIES   481 26
    AND DRIVING THEM AROUND IN FRENZIED ENERGY   502 8
    WE HAVE MORE ENERGY AND OUR GRIP ON LIFE IS HARDER   503 6
    ALL OF THEM WHO WIND THEIR ENERGY ROUND THE IDEA OF THE+   616 4
    AND FLAMES OF KATABOLISTIC ENERGY ALTERNATE   616 11
    ONLY THE MECHANICAL POWER OF SELF-DIRECTED ENERGY   675 23
    AND EITHER RELEASE ENERGY OR SWALLOW IT UP   *947 11

ENFEEBLE
    THEIR HOLD ON REALITY ENFEEBLE THEIR RISING SHOOTS   92 28

ENFEEBLED
    WITH ENFEEBLED VITALITY   457 8

ENFOLD
    AND OH MY LITTLE ONE YOU WHOM I ENFOLD   246 1
    CHERISH ME MY TINY ONE CHERISH ME WHO ENFOLD YOU   246 10
    WHEN I ENFOLD YOU AND YOU CREEP INTO ME   246 16

ENFOLDED
    OR A DARKNESS INVISIBLE ENFOLDED IN THE DEEPER DARK   697 19
    A GLOOM INVISIBLE ENFOLDED IN THE DEEPER DARK   *956 16

ENFOLDING
    I WHO AM SO FIERCE AND STRONG ENFOLDING YOU   246 23

ENFOLDS
    CLOSE AND IT ROLLS ME ENFOLDS ME TOUCHES ME AS IF NEVER+   34 23
    I THE MAN WHO ENFOLDS YOU AND HOLDS YOU CLOSE   246 4
    AND HOW HE FINDS THE DARKNESS THAT ENFOLDS HIM INTO UTT+   *961 17

ENFORCE
    METAL HITTING ON METAL TO ENFORCE OUR ATTENTION   623 3

ENFRANCHISED
    THOSE TWO ENFRANCHISED WOMEN   309 9

ENGENDERED
    IT WAS YOU ENGENDERED IT   241 14

ENGINE
    THE VOICE OF THE FURTIVE TRIUMPHANT ENGINE AS IT RUSHES+   58 4
    WILL BE POWERLESS FOR NO ENGINE CAN REACH INTO THE MARS+   624 22
    USING ALL LIFE ONLY AS POWER AS AN ENGINE USES STEAM OR+   635 11
    AN ENGINE OF FLESH USELESS UNLESS HE IS A TOOL   635 17

ENGINES
    THE CLINK OF THE SHUNTING ENGINES IS SHARP AND FINE   52 16
    THE DEAD GIVE SHIPS AND ENGINES CINEMA RADIO AND GRAMOP+   441 17
    AND ENGINES WILL RUSH AT THE SOLID HOUSES THE EDIFICE O+   624 28
    WHAT ARE YOU GOING TO DO ENTANGLED AMONG ALL THE ENGINES   635 26
    THE CLINK OF THE SHUNTING ENGINES IS SHARP AND FINE   *905 5

ENGLAND
    ENGLAND O DANAE   162 9
    TOWARDS ENGLAND   206 3
    WE WENT IN SILENCE AND YOU STARING TO ENGLAND   206 7
    ENGLAND   207 7
    YEARNING TOWARDS ENGLAND TOWARDS YOUR YOUNG CHILDREN   207 8
    PERHAPS SHE WILL GO BACK TO ENGLAND   212 21
    WHAT IS ENGLAND OR FRANCE FAR OFF   213 5
    ON YOUR GRAVE IN ENGLAND THE WEEDS GROW   233 10
    AND THAT IS NOT YOUR GRAVE IN ENGLAND   233 12
    ENGLAND SEEMS FULL OF GRAVES TO ME   410 1
    ENGLAND SEEMS COVERED WITH GRAVES TO ME   410 5
    NOW THAT IN ENGLAND PANSIES AND SUCH-LIKE GROW ON THE   410 19
    NOW THAT IN ENGLAND IS SILENCE WHERE BEFORE WAS A MOVING   410 21
    ENGLAND SEEMS LIKE ONE GRAVE TO ME   410 26
    ENGLAND   410 31
    ENGLAND   431 26
    INTO THE SOIL OF ENGLAND   431 29
    OF ENGLAND WITH THE GUTS TO TURN ROUND ON HIM AIMING   494 11
    THE TOUGH OLD ENGLAND THAT MADE US   534 13
    BUT NOT THE ENGLAND THAT MADE ME   534 19
    THE OLD ENGLAND THAT DOESN'T UPBRAID ME   534 21
    OH THE ROSE OF ENGLAND IS A SINGLE ROSE   534 23
    OH THE ROSE OF ENGLAND IS A SINGLE ROSE   535 13
    ENGLAND WAS ALWAYS A COUNTRY OF MEN   535 15
    AND STILL IN SPITE OF ALL THEY DO I LOVE THE ROSE OF EN+   569 1
    BUT THE CABBAGES OF ENGLAND LEAVE ME COLD   569 2

ENGLAND
    OH THE CABBAGES OF ENGLAND LEAVE ME COLD   569   3
    IS SETTLED ON THE LAND ROSES ARE SCARCE IN ENGLAND VERY   569   8
    YET THE CABBAGES OF ENGLAND LEAVE ME COLD   569   13
    ENGLAND   634   4
    ROSES OF ENGLAND   634   22
    WILD ROSES OF ENGLAND   634   23
    MEN WHO ARE WILD ROSES OF ENGLAND   634   24
    ALAS MY LAND IS ENGLAND AND I KNOW NOT HOW NOR WHENCE   757   3
    ANOTHER TYPE THAT ENGLAND HAS PRODUCED   841   10
    FLEEING IN EXILE TO ENGLAND AT THE END OF THE FIGHT   859   6

ENGLAND'S
    BENEATH ENGLAND'S GARDEN STONES   492   14

ENGLISH
    IN ENGLISH EARTH   412   25
    AND THEN OUR ENGLISH IMITATION INTELLIGENTSIA   533   22
    AND THAT'S WHAT'S HAPPENED TO THE ENGLISH ROSE   534   27
    DENIED A SIGNATURE WE ENGLISH ARE A SOLID PEOPLE AFTER +   546   19
    BECAUSE WE ENGLISH DO APPRECIATE A REAL GENTLEMAN OR A   548   15
    EVEN THOUGH THEY GROW ON GENUINE ENGLISH MOULD   569   4
    IN MOTHER ENGLISH OR YOU'RE IN THE CART   575   26
    FOR OUR HONEST AND HEALTHY ENGLISH TONGUE   576   1
    FOR OUR DAINTY OUR DELICATE ENGLISH EARS   576   3
    WE ENGLISH ARE SO SENSITIVE MUCH MORE THAN APPEARS   576   5
    OF SPEAKING PLAIN ENGLISH TO AN ENGLISHMAN YOU'LL SEEM   576   7
    IF YOU DON'T WANT TO BREAK THE SWEET ENGLISH SPELL   576   11
    FOR WE ENGLISH ARE REALLY A RACE APART   576   12
    THAT ENGLISH ARTISTS MIGHT FINALLY LEARN   579   24
    A WREATH OF ENGLISH MIST WOULD DO   580   11
    HELP HELP I AM CALLING IN ENGLISH   633   12
    THE ENGLISH ARE SO NICE   659   24
    TURN THE POLES THE GERMS THE ENGLISH THE ITALIANS   777   1
    IS WHERE DOES IT COME FROM THIS LOVELY ENGLISH VOICE   830   23
    THE LOVELY ENGLISH VOICE   830   32
    ANOTHER CURIOUS THING ABOUT THE ENGLISH MIDDLE CLASSES   831   20
    REFUSED TO BE MOULDED IN ARROWS OF ENGLISH WORDS   859   12

ENGLISHMAN
    DOESN'T HE LOOK THE FRESH CLEAN ENGLISHMAN OUTSIDE   430   21
    I KNOW A NOBLE ENGLISHMAN   446   1
    IS VERY NORMAL AS BECOMES AN ENGLISHMAN   446   23
    OF SPEAKING PLAIN ENGLISH TO AN ENGLISHMAN YOU'LL SEEM   576   7
    AND BY GENTLEMAN I MEAN THAT UBIQUITOUS ENGLISHMAN   830   4
    FRESH CLEAN WELL-GROOMED ENGLISHMAN   830   9
    I KNOW A NOBLE ENGLISHMAN   *947   27
    AFTER AN AFFAIR WITH THIS NOBLE ENGLISHMAN   *948   9

ENGLISHMEN
    SAID RONALD YOU KNOW IS LIKE MOST ENGLISHMEN   446   28
    NO DON'T TALK TO ME ABOUT THE LOVE OF ENGLISHMEN   447   32
    SO IT IS WITH ENGLISHMEN   535   10
    LIKE ALMOST ALL ENGLISHMEN   *948   31

ENJOY
    ALL THE CREATURES SEEMED TO ENJOY THE GAME   445   22
    THE TINY FISH ENJOY THEMSELVES   466   13
    WORK CAN BE FUN AND MEN CAN ENJOY IT THEN IT'S NOT   517   20
    AND ENJOY MYSELF FINE   671   8

ENJOYED
    THEY WERE HAPPY THEY ENJOYED IT   445   21

ENJOYING
    ENJOYING THEIR GLANCING FLIGHT THOUGH LOVE IS DEAD   133   23
    AND ENJOYING THE SENSATION OF HEAVEN AND RIGHTEOUSNESS +   324   32

ENJOYMENTS
    FORLORN ENJOYMENTS FORLORNER SORROW   825   5

ENJOYS
    ENJOYS THE OPEN BLOSSOMS AS THEY STRAW   129   17
    WITH THE MAN IF YOU KNEW HOW MY FLESH ENJOYS   251   23
    AND SO DREARILY ENJOYS ITSELF   628   8

ENLAP
    WREATHE AND ENLAP AND ANOINT THEM   229   3

ENLARGE
    AND YOU WANT TO ENLARGE YOURSELF WITH THIS FRIEND OF MI+   235   28

ENLIGHTEN
    AH CYCLOPS THE LITTLE ANT-MEN CAN NEVER ENLIGHTEN YOU   544   20

EN MASSE
    SO THAT ALL MAY BE LOST TOGETHER EN MASSE THE GREAT   620   25

ENNA
    AND IN SICILY ON THE MEADOWS OF ENNA   308   10

ENNUI
    WITH ASHES OF UTTER BOREDOM ENNUI AND DISGUST   616   12
    AND BOREDOM ENNUI DEPRESSION   627   17

ENORMOUS
    THE ENORMOUS CLIFF OF HORSE-CHESTNUT TREES   105   13
    ENORMOUS SHADOW-PROCESSIONS FILING ON IN THE FLARE OF F+   387   35
    AND ENORMOUS WHALES LIE DREAMING SUCKLING THEIR WHALE-T+   694   29
    AT THESE WIDE-SPACED TORN ENORMOUS BREATHS   878   36
    THE WEALD THE ENORMOUS BED   886   26

ENORMOUSLY
    INTO AN ENORMOUSLY SIDE-BEAKED MOUTH   359   3

ENOUGH
    TOUCH ME ENOUGH   34   24
    AN' 'S NOT GOOD ENOUGH IT ISN'T   84   31
    I SHOULD HAVE BEEN CRUEL ENOUGH TO BRING   112   14
    HAVE I CEASED TO GRIEVE THAT I WAS NOT GREAT ENOUGH   157   7
    BUT OH IT IS NOT ENOUGH IT IS ALL NO GOOD   180   29
    WHAT ELSE IT IS PERFECT ENOUGH   203   25
    IT IS ENOUGH YOU ARE NEAR   204   19
    FOR ME IT IS MORE THAN ENOUGH IF THE FLOWER UNCLOSE   219   20
    I HAVE HAD ENOUGH   234   26
    OF THE IMPENDING BEE THEY WERE FAIR ENOUGH SIGHTS   243   29
    TILL IT IS ALMOST ENOUGH TILL I AM REDUCED PERHAPS   258   7
    AH THAT WAS TORMENT HARD ENOUGH   264   23
    OH YES THE GUSH OF SPRING IS STRONG ENOUGH   272   13
    THE GUSH OF SPRING IS STRONG ENOUGH   272   18
    ENOUGH OF THE VIRGINS AND LILIES OF PASSIONATE SUFFOCAT+   273   14
    AND THEN THE FIG HAS KEPT HER SECRET LONG ENOUGH   283   27
    WE HAVE KEPT OUR SECRET LONG ENOUGH   284   21
    AND MY HEAD AT LEAST IS THICK ENOUGH TO STAND IT THE   289   17
    AM I NOT MOSQUITO ENOUGH TO OUT-MOSQUITO YOU   334   15
    HE DRANK ENOUGH   350   23
    SHE KNOWS WELL ENOUGH TO COME FOR FOOD   359   14
    THE MARK FAR ENOUGH   382   24
    BUT SHE PUTS HER NOSE DOWN SHREWDLY ENOUGH WHEN THE   384   28
    NOT BLACK ENOUGH   395   6
    BECAUSE TO TELL THE TRUTH I HAVE ENOUGH AS I AM   498   6
    THAT'S QUITE ENOUGH FOR ME   507   7
    YOU'D HAVE MONEY YOU'D HAVE IT ENOUGH TO SUPPORT YOURSE+   547   11
    THEY'VE SAT LONG ENOUGH ON THE FENCE   559   24
    WHEN THE EVIL ANGLER HAS PLAYED THEM LONG ENOUGH   586   17
    I CAN STILL HAVE THE ILLUSION THAT THERE IS ROOM ENOUGH   602   8
    BUT IT WAS NOT ENOUGH HE LOOKED AT ME ALMOST WITH HATE   603   5
    CURIOUSLY ENOUGH ACTUAL REVOLUTIONS ARE MADE BY ROBOTS   647   21
    IT IS ENOUGH   650   23
    BUT NICE ENOUGH JUST NICE ENOUGH   660   18
    AND SOON EVEN GOD WON'T BE BIG ENOUGH TO HANDLE THAT IN+   670   20
    IT IS ENOUGH I SAW YOU VANISH INTO AIR   696   28
    THAT WE'VE HAD ENOUGH THE BRAIN IS STRETCHED TILL IT PA+   756   5
    OH MASTER LET IT BE LOOSE-ALL IT IS ENOUGH   757   12
    STEEPED ENOUGH TELL HIM TO COME ACROSS   759   8
    TRADITION TRADITION TRADITION IT IS EASY ENOUGH   775   18
    AND TRUE ENOUGH HE WAS INFINITELY THE MORE MANLY FELLOW   842   26
    THERE ARE ENOUGH OF GREAT SOULS TO COMPLETE AN EFFICIEN+   859   23
    RUNS INTO THE SHADOW WITH HER CAPTURE A FEW LITTLE BITE+   864   17
    YEA I WAS FINE ENOUGH TO EXPLORE YOU   *927   6
    FOR ME IT'S NOT GOOD ENOUGH   *947   14
    NOT GOOD ENOUGH TO BE LOVED BY THIS EXPERT   *948   20

ENRAGED
    FLAME-FLUSHED ENRAGED SPLENDID SALVIA   314   27
    THE SWAN WILL BEAT THE WATERS IN RAGE WHITE RAGE OF AN +   624   15

ENRICHENED
    AND SLEEP THEREBY IS ONE MORE CREAM ENRICHENED   195   16

ENRINGS
    ENRINGS   856   6

ENSHEATHED
    ENSHEATHED INVULNERABLE WITH ME WITH SEVEN   154   23

ENSHRINE
    LIKE A CANDLE FLAME ON THIS BODY BUT I ENSHRINE   *930   6

ENSHROUDED
    AND ENSHROUDED IN THE VAST CORPSE OF THE INDUSTRIAL MIL+   629   30

ENSLAVED
    I WITH THEM AM LIVING DEAD MECHANICAL ENSLAVED AT THE   629   28

ENSPASMED
    FOR A SECOND ENSPASMED IN OBLIVION   333   29

ENSURE
    AND ALSO TO ENSURE A GOODLY INCREASE IN THE WORLD   325   22

ENTABLATURE
    TO THE ENTABLATURE OF CLOUDED HEAVEN   287   19

ENTANGLE
    I ONLY ENTANGLE MYSELF IN THE KNOWING   674   14

ENTANGLED
    AND THERE IN THE DARK MY DARLING WHERE THE ROOTS ARE EN+   92   12
    AND THE MACHINE HAS ENTANGLED THE BRAIN AND GOT IT FAST   629   7
    CORPSES ENTANGLED IN IRON   631   20
    AND LEAVE THE FEARFUL LAOCOON OF HIS FELLOW-MAN ENTANGL+   632   7
    WHAT ARE YOU GOING TO DO ENTANGLED AMONG ALL THE ENGINES   635   26
    ENTANGLED IN THE LAOCOON COILS OF OUR CONCEIT   674   10

ENTANGLEMENT
    FROM THE ENTANGLEMENT OF THE GIGGLING MACHINE   642   25
    OH WHEN MAN ESCAPED FROM THE BARBED-WIRE ENTANGLEMENT   667   1
    EAGERLY PASSING OVER FROM THE ENTANGLEMENT OF LIFE   676   20

ENTER
    WITH SWEAT I'LL ENTER A HOUSE FOR THY SAKE   44   8
    WILL ENTER AND SHUT THE DOOR TO STAY   91   9
    YOU SHALL ENTER AS YOU PLEASE   95   6
    AND I DARED NOT ENTER FEELING SUDDENLY DISMAYED   99   11
    SHE CLUNG TO THE DOOR IN HER HASTE TO ENTER   122   6
    FOR EVER AND NEVER ENTER THE HOMESTEAD ANY MORE   173   8
    IT WAS THE LIGHT OF DAY WHICH HE COULD NOT ENTER   344   17
    ANY MORE THAN I COULD ENTER THE WHITE-HOT DOOR OF A BLA+   344   18
    AND ROWING ON UNARRIVED NO MATTER HOW OFTEN HE ENTER   380   23
    BUT IN VIRGINITY JEALOUSY DOES NOT ENTER   412   31
    NOW I MUST ENTER YOUR MANSION AND BEG YOUR GIFT   695   23
    NOT FOR THE THIEVES TO ENTER THE PILFERERS   742   20

ENTER
    SOMEONE WILL ENTER BETWEEN THE GATES   788 26
    DETERMINE TO GO ON AND ON TILL YOU ENTER THE MORNING ST+   809 8
    WHEN SOFTLY I CALL AT HER DOOR AND ENTER THE ROOM   868 25
    I STAND RELUCTANT TO ENTER TO DREAM NO MORE BUT TO BOW   *894 21
    WHEN SOFTLY I CALL AT HER DOOR AND ENTER THE ROOM   *941 25

ENTERED
    OF YOUR LOVE WE BOTH HAVE ENTERED THEN THE RIGHT   104 14
    ENTERED AND QUICKLY CAST   122 7
    ENTERED FARTHER   351 3
    AND NOW THE IRON HAS ENTERED INTO THE SOUL   629 6
    A STRANGE ACHE POSSESSED HIM AND HE ENTERED THE STRUGGLE   690 5
    ENTERED ME I SMILED TO MYSELF SAYING HE IS GOD   692 16
    THE GREY NURSE ENTERED A ROSE GARDEN   753 8
    THE MOST PART LONG AGO ENTERED THE ROMAN CATHOLIC   776 25

ENTERING
    ENTERING SHE SAW HIM IN OUTLINE RAISED ON A PYRE   155 17
    ERECT WITH THE GOD-THRUST ENTERING HIM FROM BELOW   373 6
    THE GOD-THRUST ENTERING YOU STEADILY FROM BELOW   373 22
    ENTERING IN SHOCKS OF TRUTH UNFOULED BY LIES   482 2
    ENTERING INTO THE OTHER COMMUNION   711 6
    ONLY BREAKING CAMP AND ENTERING   768 11
    ERECT WITH THE GOD-THRUST ENTERING FROM BELOW   781 11

ENTERPRISE
    ENTERPRISE   70 7
    WE CALL FREE COMPETITION AND INDIVIDUAL ENTERPRISE AND   519 29
    ENTERPRISE   *894 12
    AMID THE HIGH WIND'S ENTERPRISE   *899 30
    AMID THE HIGH WIND'S ENTERPRISE   *903 9
    ITS ENTERPRISE   *916 15

ENTERS
    FIRE ENTERS YOU LIKE FROST LIKE A CRUEL BLIGHT   87 17
    AND DOUBT ENTERS IN DREARNESS   94 24
    A GREEN LIGHT ENTERS AGAINST STREAM FLUSH FROM THE WEST   340 25
    THE ESSENTIAL OIL OF THEIR EXPERIENCE ENTERS   505 2
    AND HOW HE ENTERS FOLD AFTER FOLD OF DEEPENING DARKNESS   724 3

ENTERTAIN
    OF THIS OLD HOUSE WHOSE STRANGERS I NOW ENTERTAIN   877 38

ENTHRALLING
    A PROGRESS DOWN THE INTRICATE ENTHRALLING   65 29

ENTICING
    ENTICING WILL RECALL WHEN I   *894 7

ENTIRE
    ENTIRE   *937 19

ENTIRELY
    ANYHOW GONE FROM WHAT THEY WERE ENTIRELY   533 20
    I MEAN THEY WERE NEVER ENTIRELY   554 17
    AND I FAILED ENTIRELY TO SEE WHAT HE MEANT   603 6
    I SHALL HAVE TO REFUSE ENTIRELY TO ACCEPT EITHER OF THEM   645 13
    CAN SLIP ENTIRELY THROUGH THE FINGERS OF THE HANDS OF G+   701 14
    COMPLETELY UNDER GONE ENTIRELY GONE   719 21
    IS LOST ENTIRELY YOU CANNOT FOOL US   824 5
    KILLS ENTIRELY THE TRUE EXPERIENCE OF SEX   843 18
    WHEN WE HAVE TRUSTED OURSELVES ENTIRELY   *960 23

ENTRAILS
    THE GREY DOG IS CHEWING YOUR ENTRAILS   807 31
    THE GREY DOG LEAPT AT MY ENTRAILS   808 5

ENTRANCE
    OF EACH HEART'S ENTRANCE FEE   101 28

ENTREAT
    LIVE THINGS CARESS ME AND ENTREAT MY FONDLING   876 33

ENTRY
    IN CONFUSION AGAINST MY ENTRY IS IT ONLY THE TREES'   140 13
    THE OMINOUS ENTRY NOR SAW THE OTHER LOVE   155 27
    HENCE JESUS RODE HIM IN THE TRIUMPHANT ENTRY   378 20

ENTWINES
    AGAIN AND ENTWINES   562 3

ENUNCIATING
    BECAUSE HE IS ENUNCIATING A PRINCIPLE A LAW   708 14

ENVELOP
    FROM THE PRESENCE OF GOD AND ENVELOP US   698 9
    ENVELOP OUR DEN   748 6

ENVELOPE
    WHAT DO I CARE THOUGH FROM THE DAY'S WHITE ENVELOPE   772 22

ENVELOPED
    THAT HAS ENVELOPED ME   207 30
    EVER-BEATING DAWN-HEART ENVELOPED IN IRON AGAINST THE   305 18
    ENVELOPED IN ISOLATION   360 31
    ENVELOPED US   881 10

ENVELOPING
    ENVELOPING YOUR LATE-ENFRANCHISED PLAINS   308 32
    IN CIRCLES AND EVASIONS ENVELOPING ME   332 26
    ENVELOPING EVEN THE EDGES OF THE THOUGHT-WAVES   698 23
    ENVELOPING EVEN ME WHO HEAR NO MORE   698 24

ENVIED
    OF RIDING AND BEING ENVIED SUCH ENVY AS HAS NO END   175 9

ENVIOUS
    YOU WITH YOUR GRUDGING ENVIOUS FURTIVE RAGE   314 32
    AND DAY BY DAY OUT OF THE ENVIOUS BUD   *943 22

ENVY
    OF RIDING AND BEING ENVIED SUCH ENVY AS HAS NO END   175 9
    OF MAKING A TRIUMPH OF ENVY THE RICH AND SUCCESSFUL ONES   175 10
    YOU WOULD ENVY ME YOU WOULD THINK ME WONDERFUL   251 26
    AND A HALF-THREATENING ENVY   312 21
    WITHOUT ANY MORE ENVY   771 9

ENWOMBED
    WHO SWIMS ENWOMBED   335 27

'EN
    SCRAIGHTIN' MY-SEN AS WELL 'EN UNDID HER BLACK   *911 25

EPIDERMIS
    EPIDERMIS   432 14

EPILEPTICALLY
    EPILEPTICALLY RUINED   537 3

EPITHALAMION
    BAYING EPITHALAMION   306 19

EPOCH
    OUR EPOCH IS OVER   510 20
    ANOTHER EPOCH IN ANOTHER YEAR   746 3
    WHAT WE NEED IS A LONG LONG WAR-LESS EPOCH   833 22
    IT WILL TAKE AN EPOCH TWO THOUSAND YEARS AND MORE   833 29

EPOCHS
    BETWEEN THE EPOCHS   825 21
    BETWEEN THE EPOCHS   825 24

EQUAL
    EQUAL OPPORTUNITY   519 30
    EQUAL   547 9

EQUALITY
    EACH IMPERIOUSLY OVER-EQUAL TO EACH EQUALITY OVER-REACH+   300 8
    WICKED FIG-TREE EQUALITY PUZZLE WITH YOUR SELF-CONSCIOUS   300 16
    BUT NOT A TRACE OF FOUL EQUALITY   316 7
    BUT I WON'T BE PUT ON A CABBAGE-IDEALISTIC LEVEL OF EQU+   316 16
    DON'T DO IT FOR EQUALITY   517 9
    DO IT BECAUSE WE'VE GOT TOO MUCH EQUALITY   517 10
    ALL THIS TALK OF EQUALITY BETWEEN THE SEXES IS MERELY AN   620 1

EQUALLY
    IN SELF-ABSORPTION AND SELF-INTEREST THEY WERE EQUALLY   605 18

EQUALS
    AS EQUALS   316 19
    ARE MY EQUALS   316 22

EQUATOR
    EQUATOR   548 30

EQUILIBRIUM
    BALANCED IN GLORIOUS EQUILIBRIUM   251 17
    THE SWINGING BEAUTY OF EQUILIBRIUM   251 18
    THE GREEKS MADE EQUILIBRIUM THEIR GOAL EQUILIBRIUM IS H+   761 14

EQUIP
    PROVIDE FOR YOUR DEAD ONCE MORE EQUIP THEM   721 25

EQUIPOISE
    IF YOU KNEW HOW I SWERVE IN PEACE IN THE EQUIPOISE   251 22

ER
    EDITOR ER QUITE BUT ER BIOLOGICALLY HAVE YOU BEEN   582 9

ERA
    OUR ERA IS DYING   512 1
    OF OUR ERA HAS STRUCK AND IT CHIMES   512 17

ERASED
    FOR MEMORY TO BE ERASED   262 21
    ARE YOU WILLING TO BE SPONGED OUT ERASED CANCELLED   728 1

ER'D
    ER'D DO FOR TIM   77 0
    ER'D DO FOR TIM   *918 26

ERE
    FLESH OF MY HEART ERE DOWN REBUKED IT SLIPS   127 28
    AND LET ME LOVE YOU A LONG TIME ERE YOU GO   153 17
    PLANT OF YOUR BODY TO ME YOU LOOKED ERE SPRUNG   156 20
    OF RUSHES ERE THE ROMANS   171 11
    MEN ERE HE FALL   228 32
    ME TOO AT LAST ERE THOU GOEST CHILD DEAR TO MY EYE   750 3
    YET I HAVE LAIN IN HIS LOINS ERE HE BEGOT ME IN MOTHER +   801 14
    TO OPEN ERE THE THIEF HAVE DONE HIS WORK   878 29
    AND EVER ERE I COME YOU HAVE DEPARTED   880 13
    AND AH WITH ALL HIS BLOOD FOR ERE THE STAIN   885 4
    OF MY BREAKING HAD DIED UPON HIM ERE THE STAIN   885 5
    WHICH YIELDS THE DAY TO DEATH ERE YET THE LIGHT   885 7

ERECHTHEION
    ERECHTHEION MARBLES   312 3

ERECT
    AN ERECT SMALL GIRL LOOKING DOWN AT ME   105 15
    LIKE MEN WHO ARE DROWNED BUT FLOAT ERECT IN THE DEEP   146 10
    UPRAISED ON THE BED WITH FEET ERECT AS A BOW   155 19
    ERECT SCORCHED-PALLID OUT OF THE HAIR OF THE CEDAR   373   5
    ERECT WITH THE GOD-THRUST ENTERING HIM FROM BELOW   373   6
    ERECT ONE   373 21
    THAT LIVES ERECT THROUGH LONG NIGHTS PHYSICALLY   427 13
    STANDING THERE SO SLEEK AND ERECT AND EYEABLE   431 14
    WITH MASTS ERECT AND SPARS ALL SET AND SAILS SPREAD   542   2
    SITS AN EAGLE ERECT AND SCORCH-BREASTED   780 27
    ERECT WITH THE GOD-THRUST ENTERING FROM BELOW   781 11
    ERECT ONE   781 27
    OLD ONE ERECT ON A BUSH   782 28
    ERECT SCORCHED-PALLID OUT OF THE HAIR OF THE CEDAR   783   6
    RETURN WHERE ALL IN BEAUTY STAND ERECT   872   9
    RIBBED HELLISH FLOWERS ERECT WITH THEIR BLAZE OF DARKNE+   *956   4

ERECTED
    TO THE ROOT-RISING OF YOUR ERECTED TAIL   370 15

ERECTION
    AND ALL YOUR PONDEROUS ROOFED-IN ERECTION OF RIGHT AND   289 12
    EVERY SINGLE ERECTION OF HIS IS AN ERECTION OF MEAN SPI+   *949 15

'ERE
    AS THA NE'D TRUDGE UP 'ERE   79 18
    AN' 'ERE COMES THE CAT AS CAUGHT 'IM   81 16
    AN' COME IN 'ERE WI' ME   82 18
    BUT 'ARK THEE 'ERE THAT WIDDER WOMAN   84   3
    'ERE SHE'S A LIDY AREN'T YER OLD QUIZZ   434 24
    'ARK 'ERE LAD ATWEEN THEE AN' ME   490 28
    AN' 'ERE COMES THE CAT THAT CAUGHT 'IM   *923 16

ERINNYES
    THE CRIME FULL-EXPIATE THE ERINNYES SUNK   743 25

'ER'LL
    'ER'LL BE WANTIN' IT I 'EAR   79 20
    AS 'ER'LL BE WANTIN' MY WEDDIN'-DRESS   79 27
    AS 'ER'LL BE WANTIN' MY WEDDIN' DRESS   *921 23
    BUT WE MAUN MA'E THE BEST ON'T I'LL REAR THY CHILDT IF +   *925 18

ERMINE
    THAT HERE WE'RE SAFE FROM EVEN THE ERMINE MOTH'S   113 23
    THAT HERE WE'RE SAFE FROM EVEN THE ERMINE MOTH'S   *929 12

ERRAND
    UTTERLY GONE AWAY ON ANOTHER ERRAND   767 25

ERRANDS
    THEIR SEVERAL ERRANDS HERE AND THERE SHALL MAKE   872 19

ERST
    UPON THE FLOOR THAT ERST STOOD UP SO FRESH   87 29

'ER'S
    BUT 'ER'S OLD MOTHER 'ER'S TWENTY YEAR   77   5
    TILL 'ER'S TOUGH AS WHIT-LEATHER TO SLIVE   77 19
    'ER'S AS GOOD AS THEE   80 26
    'S LESS GRASPIN' IF 'ER'S POOR   84   4
    BUT 'ER'S OLD MOTHER 'ER'S TWENTY YEAR   *918 23
    TILL 'ER'S TOUGH AS WHIT-LEATHER TO SLIVE   *919   7
    AN' 'ER'S WANTIN IT I HEAR   *921 16

ERUPTION
    ALL MORE OR LESS IN ERUPTION   539   3
    IT'S NO GOOD THE WOMEN ARE IN ERUPTION   541   1

'ER
    'E SAYS TELL YOUR MOTHER AS 'ER MESTER'S   44 22
    AND WATCHED WHAT 'ER 'AD ON   61   4
    THA SHOULD HA' SEED 'ER SLIVE UP WHEN YER'D GONE   61   5
    THA SHOULD HA' SEED 'ER KNEEL AN' LOOK IN   61   6
    AT TH' SLOPPY GRAVE AN' 'ER LITTLE NECK SHONE   61   7
    THAT WHITE AN' 'ER CRIED THAT MUCH I'D LIKE TO BEGIN   61   8
    SCRAIGHTIN' MYSEN AS WELL 'ER UNDID 'ER BLACK   61   9
    AN' WARM FOR TH' SMELL COME WAFTIN' TO ME 'ER PUT 'ER F+   61 13
    THEN AFTER A BIT 'ER DROPPED 'EM DOWN THAT PLACE   61 15
    AS 'AS SLUDGED LIKE A HORSE ALL 'ER LIFE   77 18
    WITCH TEETH AN' 'ER BLACK HAWK-EYES AS I'VE   77 23
    'ER AS 'E LODGES WI'   78 10
    THEY SAY HE'S GOT 'ER WI' CHILDT BUT THERE   78 11
    'ER DOESNA WANT NO WEDDIN'-DRESS   79 21
    AN' IF 'ER CLAWKIN' EYES   80 14
    I COULD HA' KILLED 'ER   80 22
    COULD TER HA' KILLED 'ER   80 24
    TAKE 'ER I'STEAD O' ME   80 28
    THOUGH I SHONNA MARRY 'ER   80 30
    NOR 'ER NOR NUB'DY IT IS   80 31
    AN' 'ER MAUN TA'E 'ER LUCK   81   2
    I DAMN WELL SHANNA MARRY 'ER   81   9
    OF 'IM STOOPIN' TO 'ER YOU'D WONDER 'E COULD   81 19
    WI' A WOMAN AN' NAME 'ER A PRICE   82 10
    AN' GIVE 'ER THE MONEY THERE IS   82 14
    FOR I WON'T BE BEHOLDEN TO SUCH AS 'ER   82 15
    I WISH I COULD WESH 'ER OFF'N THEE   82 .25
    I'M SORRY FOR THEE I'M SORRY F'R 'ER   83 22
    AN' 'ER AS WELL   83 27
    WHAT 'ER GEN 'ER GEN ME   84   5
    'ER GEN ME SUMMAT I SHANNA   84   7
    FROM YOU AN' FROM 'ER   84 16
    AN' I REALLY LIKE 'ER NEITHER   84 21
    MORE FROM 'ER THAN FROM YOU BUT EITHER   84 23
    WHAT BIT O' CUNT I HAD WI' 'ER   84 29
    AN' WI' 'ER SOMEHOW IT ISN'T RIGHT   85   3
    AS 'UD WINCE WHEN THAT TOUCHED 'ER CLOSE AN'   138 31
    WHILE TH' PARSON WAS PRAYIN' I WATCHES 'ER AN' SHE WOR +   *910   1

'ER
    AN' 'ER BODY FAIR SHOOK AGAIN   *910 13
    AN' SHE UNDID 'ER JACKET NECK AN' THEN   *910 15
    A LOT O' VIOLETS FELL OUT OF 'ER BOSOM ON 'IM DOWN THEER   *910 16
    THEN SHE RUMMAGED HER HAND IN 'ER BOSOM AN' KISSED THE +   *910 20
    AN' WATCHED WHAT 'ER 'AD ON   *911 20
    AT TH' SLOPPY WET GRAVE AN' 'ER LITTLE NECK SHONE   *911 23
    THAT WHITE AN' 'ER SHOOK THAT MUCH I'D LIKE TO BEGIN   *911 24
    O' TH' SMELL COME WAFTIN' TO ME 'ER PUT 'ER FACE   *911 29
    THEN AFTER A BIT 'ER DROPPED 'EM DOWN THAT PLACE   *911 31
    WITCH TEETH AN' 'ER BLACK HAWK-EYES AS I'VE   *919 11
    'ER DOESNA WANT NO WEDDIN'-DRESS   *921 17
    AN' IF 'ER CLAWKIN' TIGER'S EYES   *922 14
    I DAMN WELL SHANNA MARRY 'ER   *923   9
    WI' A WOMAN AN' PAY 'ER A PRICE   *924 14
    AN' GIVE 'ER WHAT MONEY THERE IS   *924 18
    I WISH THA COULD WESH 'ER OFF'N THEE   *925   1
    AN' THEN WI' THAT TWENTY POUND WE GI'E 'ER I S'D THINK +   *925 20
    SO VERY MUCH WORSER OFF THAN 'ER WOR BEFORE AN' NOW LOO+   *925 21

ESCAPE
    TO ESCAPE IN SLEEP THE TERROR OF THIS GREAT BIVALVE DAR+   88 14
    STRIVE TO ESCAPE   103 28
    TO MAKE NEW WORDS WITH OUR LIPS TO ESCAPE THE FOUL DREAM   175 22
    I WILL ESCAPE FROM THE HOLLOW ROOM THE BOX OF LIGHT   179 24
    IS NO ESCAPE   465   2
    AND WHEN WE ESCAPE LIKE SQUIRRELS FROM TURNING IN THE   482 16
    BEAUTY OF COURSE BEAUTY IS STILL A DELICIOUS ESCAPE   532   8
    THE MILLS OF GOD WILL GRIND THEM SMALL ANYHOW THERE IS +   614 18
    AND THERE'S NO ESCAPE FOR THE IRON GOES THROUGH THEIR   631 21
    AND RISK BLEEDING TO DEATH BUT PERHAPS ESCAPE INTO SOME   632   5
    DEATH IS NO ESCAPE AH NO ONLY A DOORWAY TO THE INEVITAB+   662 25
    IN DEATH THEY CANNOT ANY MORE ESCAPE   663   2
    WHEN AT LAST WE ESCAPE THE BARBED-WIRE ENCLOSURE   667 12
    THAT WE CAN NEVER ESCAPE NOT EVEN IN SLEEP   833 32
    AN ESCAPE FROM THEIR HORROW OF IMPRISONMENT IN OUR CIVI+   838   8
    THE MEN IN THE END ONLY HATE THEM BECAUSE THE ESCAPE WA+   838 10

ESCAPED
    SOFT GLIMMERS OF DESIRE ESCAPED FROM PRISON   113   4
    THAT I JUST ESCAPED THE HUNGER FOR THESE   263 30
    YOU THOUGHT YOUR DAUGHTER HAD ESCAPED   309   1
    I ESCAPED HIM   347 23
    AND KICK OUR HEELS LIKE JOLLY ESCAPED ASSES   517 16
    OH WHEN MAN ESCAPED FROM THE BARBED-WIRE ENTANGLEMENT   667   1

ESCAPES
    INTELLECT ARE ONLY ESCAPES   532 12

ESCAPING
    AND JESUS ON A MEEK ASS-COLT MARES MARY ESCAPING TO   380   2
    ESCAPING THE PETROL FUMES OF HUMAN CONVERSATION   646   6

ESPECIALLY
    ESPECIALLY THE YOUNG WOMEN I LOOK AT THEM   269 22
    ESPECIALLY IF BEING GIVEN A NEEDLE'S EYE OF EGRESS ELSE+   381   4
    ESPECIALLY DEMOCRATIC LIVE-BY-LOVE HUMANITY   395 19
    ESPECIALLY THE MALE OF THE SPECIES   430 16
    ESPECIALLY THE MALE OF THE SPECIES   431 12
    AND DIRT IF IT ISN'T SIN IS WORSE ESPECIALLY DIRT INSIDE   464   5
    LOVE OUT OF SEASON ESPECIALLY AT THE END OF THE SEASON   478 12
    ESPECIALLY ABOUT THEMSELVES AND THEIR OWN FEELINGS   502   3
    WE WANT TO BE LOVED ESPECIALLY AUNTIE   572 23
    ESPECIALLY IF I SEE THEIR ALONENESS ALIVE IN THEM   602   5
    ESPECIALLY BIG ONES IS OBSCENE   622 20
    ESPECIALLY CLAPPER BELLS HARD TONGUES WAGGING IN HARD M+   623   2
    ONLY THE BEST MATTERS IN MAN ESPECIALLY   668   1
    FOR THE ANALYST IS TANGLED IN AN ESPECIALLY TANGLED BUN+   833 34
    AND ESPECIALLY AT NIGHTFALL   869   3

ESPOUSE
    AND LONG-HAIRED PEOPLE WHO PRETEND TO ESPOUSE   778   5

ESPRESSIONS
    SIFT MY LOOKS AND ESPRESSIONS   236 28

ESSAY
    AND ESSAY TO DISOWN OURSELVES AND THEN WHEN THE LIGHT   748 10
    OF MORNING IS BACK WE SHALL CHANGE AGAIN AND ESSAY   748 11

ESSENCE
    UNHOLY FEAR IN MY ESSENCE YOU WOULD PAUSE TO   131   4
    THE DISTILLED ESSENCE OF HELL   281 13
    NOR A DOSE OF CAPSICUM ESSENCE GIVING AN ORGASM   837   9

ESSENTIAL
    OF MY BODY AND LOOSE THE ESSENTIAL FLOOD   117 23
    THAT STRANGE ESSENTIAL COMMUNICATION OF LIFE   481   7
    THEY WOULD DISTIL THE ESSENTIAL OIL OUT OF EVERY   504   6
    THE ESSENTIAL OIL OF THEIR EXPERIENCE ENTERS   505   2
    NATURALLY WE DESTROY THE MOST ESSENTIAL SELF IN US   621   9
    WE HAVE LEARNED THAT ANOTHER MAN'S LIBERTY IS AS ESSENT+   833   1

ESSENTIALLY
    YOU ARE MIDDLE-CLASS AND ESSENTIALLY NON-EXISTENT   527 19

ESSENTIALS
    IN SOME ESSENTIALS   561   3

ESTABLISH
    THAT SOCIETY MUST ESTABLISH ITSELF UPON A DIFFERENT PRI+   487 19

ESTABLISHED
    THEY ARE ESTABLISHED ON THE MANY PILLARS OF THE PHALLUS   541 24

ESTABLISHING
    LIFE ESTABLISHING THE FIRST ETERNAL MATHEMATICAL TABLET   355 17

ESTATE
    AND WHEN TO MAN'S ESTATE I GROW   576 20
    AND SO TO MAN'S ESTATE HE GREW   576 24

EST SI BIEN CAMBREE ·
    MADAME EST SI BIEN CAMBREE   835 11

'E'S
    IF 'E'S NOT A MAN FOR MISCHANCE   . 45 8
    'E'S 'AD TWENTY ACCIDENTS IF 'E'S 'AD ONE   45 27
    AN' THESE IS THE WOMAN'S KIDS 'E'S SO FOND ON   81 15
    BUT I WANT YOU TO KNOW 'E'S NOT MARRYIN' YOU   82 5
    I WANT YOU TO KNOW 'E'S NON MARRYIN' YOU   *924 9

ETC
    I LOVE MY NATIVE LAND THE BEST ETC ETC   575 14
    ALL THE LOT OF THEM VICE MISSIONS ETC INSANELY UNHEALTHY   845 10

ETERNAL
    OF ETERNAL HEREAFTER   147 14
    THAT SAVES THE BLUE GRAIN OF ETERNAL FIRE   161 3
    HIDING AND COVERING IN THE ETERNAL SLEEP   195 28
    MY DEAR THE NIGHT IS SOFT AND ETERNAL NO DOUBT   211 11
    EACH OF US TO THE BALANCED ETERNAL ORBIT   236 18
    STICKILY GLISTENING WITH ETERNAL SHADOW   310 17
    IN THE SLOW DIGNITY OF YOUR ETERNAL PAUSE   354 9
    LIFE ESTABLISHING THE FIRST ETERNAL MATHEMATICAL TABLET   355 17
    UNDER ALL THE ETERNAL DOME OF MATHEMATICAL LAW   355 22
    THE LONE CLEAVAGE OF DIVISION UPRIGHT OF THE ETERNAL CR+   355 30
    THE MOMENT OF ETERNAL SILENCE   365 16
    ONLY THOSE ETERNAL FEMALES TO OVERLEAP AND SURPASS AND   382 33
    MYSELF SO LITTLE DODGING RATHER SCARED AGAINST THE ETER+   390 16
    STILL SHE WATCHES WITH ETERNAL COCKED WISTFULNESS   394 5
    OF ETERNAL SALT RAGE ANGRY IS OLD OCEAN WITHIN A MAN   454 11
    THAT SEX IS AN ETERNAL UPRIGHT DIVISION BEFORE WHICH WE   636 25
    THE ETERNAL DIVISION BETWEEN THE BASE AND THE BEAUTIFUL   637 3
    IN THE ETERNAL OPPOSITION   705 21
    FOURTH DIMENSION NOT IN YARDS AND MILES LIKE THE ETERNA+   761 16
    OF THIS ETERNAL LIFE   875 17
    AND DARKENING MY ETERNAL FAME   *929 5

ETERNALLY
    AS SHE MOVES ETERNALLY SLOWLY AWAY   363 7
    AND THAT'S WHAT MAKES IT ETERNALLY SPACIOUS AND UNSTUFFY   525 3
    GOD ONLY GOD IS ETERNALLY   759 16
    BUT LEAVES ALIGHT AND LOVELY ETERNALLY   *937 6

ETERNITY
    WHAT IF UNWITTING I SET THE DOOR OF ETERNITY WIDE   147 11
    TAKE THEN ETERNITY FOR WHAT IS THAT   158 13
    IN THE FIELDS OF ETERNITY   243 4
    SO I HOPE I SHALL SPEND ETERNITY   250 9
    AND LAUGH AT TIME AND LAUGH AT DULL ETERNITY   299 11
    DRAGGED OUT OF AN ETERNITY OF SILENT ISOLATION   362 27
    THE TORTOISE ETERNITY   365 25
    AS TIME HAS NOT DARED TO AVOUCH NOR ETERNITY BEEN ABLE +   370 31
    CAST YOUR LITTLE ANCHORS IN PORTS OF ETERNITY   542 13
    AND THERE IS NOTHING ELSE THROUGHOUT TIME AND ETERNITY   701 1
    AND YET OUT OF ETERNITY A THREAD   719 27
    HORIZONTAL ETERNITY FLUID OR NULL   827 16
    INTO ONE BUD ON THE STALK OF ETERNITY   *908 3
    AND I HOPE TO SPEND ETERNITY   *946 7

ETERNITY'S
    ARE LEFT ON ETERNITY'S LEVEL   243 14

ETHER
    RUNS A RAGE DRAWN IN FROM THE ETHER DIVINELY THROUGH HIM   381 21

ETHNOLOGY
    OF ETHNOLOGY   780 10

ETNA
    SO CONSTANTLY ROUND ETNA   301 7
    THE ETNA SNOW-WIND THROUGH THE LONG NIGHT   305 24
    AND FROM THE SICILIAN TOWNLETS SKIRTING ETNA   312 10
    ON THE DAY OF SICILIAN JULY WITH ETNA SMOKING   349 28

ETNA'S
    TO THE GREEN NIGHT-BAYING OF THE DOG-STAR ETNA'S SNOW-E+   306 11

ETON
    YOU LOOK LIKE THE TOPPINGEST TOPPING FIFTH-FORM ETON DO+   835 17

ETON-ADONIS
    AND YOUR FACE YOUR MOST MARVELLOUSLY ETON-ADONIS FACE   835 20

ETRURIA
    ETRUSCAN-DUSKY WAVERING MEN OF OLD ETRURIA   296 19
    ETRURIA   297 7
    LONG-NOSED MEN OF ETRURIA   297 15
    AS ROME DENIED ETRURIA   298 17

ETRUSCAN
    ETRUSCAN CYPRESSES   296 11
    ETRUSCAN SYLLABLES   296 28
    ETRUSCAN CYPRESSES   297 5
    THE SMILE THE SUBTLE ETRUSCAN SMILE STILL LURKING   297 22
    ETRUSCAN CYPRESSES   297 24
    NAY LEONARDO ONLY BUNGLED THE PURE ETRUSCAN SMILE   297 26
    EVIL-YCLEPT ETRUSCAN   297 29
    ETRUSCAN CYPRESSES   298 14

ETRUSCAN-DUSKY
    ETRUSCAN-DUSKY WAVERING MEN OF OLD ETRURIA   296 19

ETRUSCANS
    IS IT THE SECRET OF THE LONG-NOSED ETRUSCANS   296 14
    THE LONG-NOSED SENSITIVE-FOOTED SUBTLY-SMILING ETRUSCANS   296 15

EUNUCHS
    HYPOCRITES AND EUNUCHS   658 23
    EUNUCHS AND HYPOCRITES   658 24

EUROPE
    THIS MAY BE A WITHERING TREE THIS EUROPE   291 7
    THE EAST A DEAD LETTER AND EUROPE MORIBUND IS THAT SO   371 32

EUROPE'S
    AND EUROPE'S TAIL-SPIN ROLLS STILL UNROLLED   814 8

EVA
    FORGOTTEN IN THE GRASS EVA FEARFUL AND FLEET   864 16

EVACUATION-LUST
    MERE EVACUATION-LUST   466 8

EVADER
    EVADER   55 12
    EVADER   56 25

EVANESCENT
    YOU YOUR SOUL LIKE A LADY-SMOCK LOST EVANESCENT   90 17
    HOW EVANESCENT VARIEGATED ELDER SHE HESITATES ON THE GR+   646 25

EVANGELIST
    OH THAT MIND-SOARING EAGLE OF AN EVANGELIST   328 19

EVAPORATE
    AND VANQUISHED EVAPORATE AWAY   53 30

EVAPORATED
    HAS EVAPORATED FROM YOU LIKE STEAM FROM GLASS   871 6

EVASION
    IT IS A SNEAKING EVASION OF THE RESPONSIBILITY   621 13

EVASIONS
    IN CIRCLES AND EVASIONS ENVELOPING ME   332 26

EVASIVE
    EVASIVE   286 26
    OR WAS THEIR WAY ONLY EVASIVE AND DIFFERENT DARK LIKE   297 16

EVE
    EVE AND I   37 25
    I LEARNED IT ALL FROM MY EVE   38 18
    ME EVERY EVE WITH A LONG   108 27
    THE EVE THAT IS TO BE   240 12
    AND EVE APPROACHING OVER THE GROUND   262 7
    INVISIBLE THE HANDS OF EVE   263 10
    WHEN EVE ONCE KNEW IN HER MIND THAT SHE WAS NAKED   264 7
    EVE IN HER HAPPY MOMENTS   314 6
    WITH EVE AND THE AMAZON THE LIZARD AND THE FRAIL   633 3
    BURN THAT HE SEES EVE RUNNING FROM THE LIKES OF HIM I   633 28
    EVE IN THE AFTERWARD   768 25
    EVE OF THE AFTERWARDS   769 1
    EVE SWINGING HER DUSKY LIMBS DISCONSOLATE   863 21
    EVE ALONE UNSATISFIED AMONG THE ORANGE AND GUAVA TREES   864 1
    EVE PUSHING THE FESTOONED VANILLA TREMBLING ASIDE   864 7
    EVE WITH HER RESISTLESS VIRGIN-BUDDED BREAST   864 13
    EVE RUNNING WITH SWIFT LIMBS QUICKENED BY DREAD   864 19
    EVE WITH A HEART OF RESENTMENT IS QUICKLY SPED   864 21
    STRONG WITH EYES OF DEFIANCE EVE WALKS WITH SORROWS   864 23
    NOR EVE FOR YOUR HEAVY ANGUISH OF EMBRACE   876 17
    EVE AND ME   *892 13
    I HAVE LEARNED IT ALL FROM MY EVE   *893 1

EVENING
    WHICH WEAVES ITS WAY THROUGH THE EVENING WIND   42 3
    INTO THE YELLOW EVENING GLOW   42 19
    WITH WHITE PLUMES BLINKING UNDER THE EVENING GR KY   66 14
    BUT STILL TO ME ALL EVENING LONG YOU WERE COLD   98 26
    LAST EVENING AND SHE WHO WAS SOFTLY IN BLOOM   141 7
    A TWISTED THORN-TREE STILL IN THE EVENING STANDS   167 9
    BY THE ISAR IN THE EVENING   216 21
    OF THEIR PALE-GREEN GLACIER WATER FILLED THE EVENING   216 25
    AND EVENING HAS TAKEN ALL THE BEES FROM THE THYME   224 26
    AGAINST THE HARD AND PALE BLUE EVENING SKY   225 1
    HIS EVENING IS A FLAME OF WINE   228 17
    IN THE LONG DARK NIGHTS OF THE EVENING STAR AND SIRIUS   305 23
    SOMETHING MUST BE REASSURING TO THE ALMOND IN THE EVENI+   305 31
    BUT WHILE FLOWERS CLUB THEIR PETALS AT EVENING   321 22
    AND AT EVENING I MUST LEAVE OFF MY WINGS OF THE SPIRIT   321 27
    CURVETTING BITS OF TIN IN THE EVENING LIGHT   335 24
    AT EVENING SITTING IN THIS TERRACE   340 17
    AND NOW AT EVENING AS HE FLICKERS OVER THE RIVER   347 16
    THE DAWN ROOKS CALL AT EVENING WHEN THE NIGHTINGALE SIN+   368 11
    AND WHITE PEOPLE IN EVENING DRESS BUZZING AND CROWDING   387 23
    THE EVENING SULKS ALONG THE SHORE THE REDDENING SUN   625 10
    IN COLD BLOOD I CANNOT FEEL GODDESSES IN THE SUMMER EVE+   655 18
    AND WHEN IN THE SUMMER EVENING   655 26
    AGAIN AND AGAIN SOME GOD OF EVENING LEANS OUT OF IT   656 2
    FOR A MOMENT AT EVENING TIRED AS HE STEPPED OFF THE TRA+   672 7
    FOR A MOMENT PURE IN THE YELLOW EVENING LIGHT HE WAS HY+   672 11
    TO THE HONEYSUCKLE AT EVENING NOW   684 6
    WHO HAD WADED TO THE PALE GREEN SEA OF EVENING OUT OF A+   693 5
    NOW TURNED AND CAME SLOWLY BACK WITH HER BACK TO THE EV+   693 7
    THE EVENING SHADOW HAS SUNK   758 3
    BITTER TO ME IS THIS EVENING HOUR   758 8
    EACH EVENING BITTER AGAIN   758 9

EVENING
  EVENING   771 15
  SAVE FOR THE MORNING AND EVENING STARS UPON WHICH THEY +   799 27
  FROM THE TULIPS COLOURED WITH CHALK AND THE DULL GRASS'+   867 4
  TOGETHER WE TRODE THE EVENING WHERE THE SUN   884 23
  THAT EVENING EVERMORE HANGS RED FOR ME   885 2
  BY THE ISAR IN THE EVENING   *942 7
  OF THEIR PALE-GREEN GLACIER-WATER FILLED THE EVENING   *942 11

EVENING-GREEN
  HURT AT THE CHALK-COLOURED TULIPS AND THE EVENING-GREEN   153 12

EVENINGS
  BY ITS SHAPE LIKE THRUSHES IN CLEAR EVENINGS   101 16
  TO THE OLD SUNDAY EVENINGS AT HOME WITH WINTER OUTSIDE   148 12
  THAT PUT TO SEA ON CERTAIN EVENINGS   542 6
  IN A PUB PARLOUR IN LITERARY LONDON ON CERTAIN EVENINGS   542 10
  TO THE OLD SUNDAY EVENINGS WHEN DARKNESS WANDERED OUTSI+   940 11

EVENING STAR
  THE MORNING STAR AND THE EVENING STAR SHINE TOGETHER   800 13
  BUT THE MORNING STAR AND THE EVENING STAR   812 21

EVENING'S
  INTO THE EVENING'S ANXIOUS BREAST   42 7
  TO-MORROW SWIMMING IN EVENING'S VAGUE DIM VAPOUR   72 16

EVER-BEATING
  EVER-BEATING DAWN-HEART ENVELOPED IN IRON AGAINST THE   305 18

EVER-CHANGING
  PASSES THE EVER-CHANGING JOY OF HIS ACTIVE BODY   868 4

EVERLASTING
  EVERLASTING LAMENT IN EVERLASTING DESIRE   378 30
  TOWARDS THE TAIL OF THE EVERLASTING PROCESSION   389 1
  AND PASSIVE WITH EVERLASTING PATIENCE   390 8
  IN HOSTS TOWARDS THE EVERLASTING NIGHT   745 9
  BEFORE THE EVERLASTING WITNESSES   779 28
  YE EVERLASTING DOORS   818 7

EVERMORE
  STANDS WATCHING EVERMORE   200 16
  THAT EVENING EVERMORE HANGS RED FOR ME   885 2

EVERYBODY
  AS IT IS TO EVERYBODY   236 16
  DON'T YOU LOVE EVERYBODY   395 22
  JUST EVERYBODY   395 23
  LOVING EVERYBODY   396 11
  EVERYBODY SO DEAR AND YOURSELF SO ULTRA-BELOVED   398 26
  AND DOESN'T EVERYBODY LOATHE YOU THEN   400 12
  THE TROUBLE IS EVERYBODY THINKS THEY'RE JUST AS SUPERIOR   435 10
  SO EVERYBODY MAKES AN ASSERTION OF HIMSELF   496 22
  STAMPEDING OVER EVERYBODY   502 9
  AS THEY TRY TO SCREW EVERYBODY ELSE DOWN WITH THEIR WILL   502 12
  NOWADAYS EVERYBODY WANTS TO BE YOUNG   502 13
  OR THEY BEAR EVERYBODY A GRIM AND GRISLY GRUDGE   502 19
  BUT WHEN EVERYBODY GOES ROUND WITH SOUL HALF-BARED OR Q+   608 16
  AND EVERYBODY   762 25
  AND HURT HURT OURSELVES AND EVERYBODY   833 20
  WE VIOLATE OURSELVES EVERY MOMENT AND VIOLATE EVERYBODY+   839 6

EVERYDAY
  FOR EVERYDAY USE GIVE ME SOMEBODY WHIMSICAL WITH NOT   496 3

EVERYONE
  AND EVERYONE LISTENED AND LOVED IT THE   492 9
  WETTING AFTER EVERYONE THAT PASSES   493 28
  AND FORCED TO WATCH EVERYONE THAT COMES NEAR YOU LEST   522 17
  SUPERIOR TO EVERYONE ELSE SO DON'T START   576 13
  BUT EVERYONE OF THEM DIRTYISH   792 32
  MEANWHILE WE BITE OURSELVES AND EVERYONE NEAR US   833 30

EVERYTHING
  EVERYTHING MISS ILL-AT-EASE   96 4
  EVERYTHING TEAR-TREMBLING STARS OF AUTUMN   107 7
  THA WANTS IT AND EVERYTHING ELSE IS IN VAIN   139 19
  ITSELF AMONG EVERYTHING ELSE HERE HUNGRILY STEALING   141 18
  AND EVERYTHING SHUT UP AND GONE TO SLEEP   203 12
  EVERYTHING STARTS FROM US   204 26
  OBLITERATING EVERYTHING   205 8
  HOW EVERYTHING THAT WILL BE WILL NOT BE OF ME   247 15
  BALANCES EVERYTHING THROWN   251 5
  SINGLE AND PERFECTLY DISTINCT FROM EVERYTHING ELSE   254 25
  EVERYTHING WAS TAINTED WITH MYSELF   256 24
  WHEN EVERYTHING WAS ME I KNEW IT ALL ALREADY I ANTICIPA+   257 11
  FOR WHEN IT IS QUITE QUITE NOTHING THEN IT IS EVERYTHING   258 25
  WHERE EVERYTHING HAPPENS INVISIBLE FLOWERING AND FERTIL+   283 20
  AND EVERYTHING ELSE TO THEIR DISGUSTING LEVEL   317 31
  BEYOND EVERYTHING EXCEPT ITSELF   322 6
  TURNING HIS BACK ON EVERYTHING   375 4
  WITH EVERYTHING   398 7
  EVERYTHING NEW AND MACHINE-MADE SUCKS LIFE OUT OF US   448 16
  LET EVERYTHING GO AS THE WAVE SMASHES US   514 2
  SO EVERYTHING IS INSANE   516 2
  BECAUSE YOU'VE ALWAYS GOT TO PAY FOR EVERYTHING   517 24
  WHAT EVERYTHING MEANS   564 28
  BRITISH PUBLIC HAS EVERYTHING OBJECTIONABLE BEEN   582 13
  EVERYTHING THAT LIVES HAS ITS OWN PROPER PRIDE   621 15
  SENSIBILITIES HATE EVERYTHING THAT'S WELL   633 6
  EVERYTHING HAS BEEN SEEN TO DEATH   660 27
  EVERYTHING THAT HAS BEAUTY HAS A BODY AND IS A BODY   691 6
  EVERYTHING THAT HAS BEING HAS BEING IN THE FLESH   691 7
  AND EVERYTHING IS GONE THE BODY IS GONE   719 20
  AT THE CORE OF EVERYTHING   724 14
  OF EVERYTHING I'VE KNOWN EVEN DREAMILY   738 12
  EVERYTHING FROM ME   749 6

EVERYTHING
  CLOSE FRIEND IN EVERYTHING IS OUR LORD MY BOY   749 23
  TAKES EVERYTHING FROM YOU TOMORROW   752 19
  AND GIVES ME EVERYTHING   752 20
  THEY'VE SOLD EVERYTHING BUT EVERYTHING   762 24
  EVERYTHING IN THE WORLD OF CULTURE AND SUPERIORITY   763 10
  THAN EVERYTHING ELSE   764 2
  EVERYTHING EVERYTHING   826 18
  HEALTH IS EVERYTHING HEALTH IS ALL   826 21
  HEALTH IS EVERYTHING HEALTH IS ALL   827 29
  EVERYTHING GREAT AND MYSTERIOUS IN ONE SWELLING AND SHA+   *909 15
  AND LISTEN OH EVERYTHING LISTEN FOR WORDS   *914 14
  AND I GIVE YOU EVERYTHING THAT YOU WANT ME TO   *945 19
  THAT EVERYTHING TIES ITSELF UP INTO COMPLICATED LITTLE +   *947 8

EVERYWHERE
  YOU ARE HERE YOU ARE HERE WE HAVE FOUND YOU EVERYWHERE   34 16
  THE HIDDEN BODIES MATING EVERYWHERE   126 21
  I WISH IT WOULD BE COMPLETELY DARK EVERYWHERE   205 20
  EVERYWHERE DOWN IN THE GRASS WHERE DARKNESS WAS RAVELLED   206 18
  EVERYWHERE   251 31
  AND I JUT AGAINST YOU IF I TRY TO MOVE FOR YOU ARE EVER+   289 7
  AND SPY-GOVERNMENT EVERYWHERE   536 17
  AND GOD ABROAD AND ALIGHT ON US EVERYWHERE   742 30
  EVERYWHERE MEN AND WOMEN ALIGHT WITH GOD   742 31
  WONDERS SHINES OUT OF EVERYWHERE   802 28
  THE ANGELS HAVE EVERYWHERE FOUGHT AND LOST   823 6

EVE'S
  OF EDEN EVEN WAS EVE'S FRUIT TO HER IT BELONGED AND SHE+   277 6
  IT TO THE MAN EVEN THE APPLES OF KNOWLEDGE ARE EVE'S FR+   277 7

EVIDENT
  IT IS EVIDENT YOU WERE RIGHT   168 1
  SOUNDS STILL UNFROZEN AND THE TRAIL IS STILL EVIDENT   401 3

EVIDENTLY
  EVIDENTLY HE IS ALL THAT   323 30

EVIL
  WITH THIS YEAR'S NEWNESS AND IS THAT EVIL   127 20
  ALL GOOD EVIL BOTH   239 20
  BACK BEYOND GOOD AND EVIL   243 17
  FOR AS TO THE EVIL   297 30
  EVIL WHAT IS EVIL   298 15
  YOUR EVIL LITTLE AURA PROWLING AND CASTING NUMBNESS ON   332 19
  THE ROOT OF OUR PRESENT EVIL IS THAT WE BUY AND SELL   482 28
  TRIUMPH OVER EVIL   519 4
  WORSE THAN THE EVIL EYE   538 14
  AWAY THE EVIL STARINGS AND THE BREATH   581 7
  WHEN THE EVIL ANGLER HAS PLAYED THEM LONG ENOUGH   586 17
  WITH UNINTELLIGENT AND EVIL DESTRUCTION   677 26
  AND WORSTED BY THE EVIL WORLD-SOUL OF TODAY   709 2
  LIKE SAYING SNOW IS BLACK OR DESIRE IS EVIL   709 34
  BUT EVIL IS A THIRD THING   710 23
  IS EVIL   710 27
  BUT EVIL EVIL IS ANOTHER THING IN ANOTHER PLACE   711 11
  EVIL HAS NO HOME   711 12
  ONLY EVIL HAS NO HOME   711 13
  BUT EVIL   711 21
  WHERE THE GREY TWILIGHT OF EVIL SETS IN   711 25
  THAT IS THEY SIT AND ARE EVIL IN EVIL   712 1
  GREY EVIL WHICH HAS NO PATH AND SHOWS NEITHER LIGHT NOR   712 2
  AND THE WHEEL STARTS THE PRINCIPLE OF ALL EVIL   712 7
  THE WHEEL IS THE FIRST PRINCIPLE OF EVIL   712 9
  THERE AND THERE ALONE LIES THE PIVOT OF PURE EVIL   712 11
  THEN WE SEE EVIL PURE EVIL   712 20
  OH THERE IS EVIL THERE IS AN EVIL WORLD-SOUL   712 23
  WHICH HAS BROUGHT TO PASS THE FEARFUL THING CALLED EVIL   712 25
  EVERY WHEEL ON ITS HUB HAS A SOUL EVIL   713 2
  IT IS PART OF THE EVIL WORLD-SOUL SPINNING   713 3
  IS EVIL EVIL PART OF THE EVIL WORLD-SOUL   713 6
  INTO EVIL NEUTRALITY INTO MECHANISM   713 8
  THE ROBOT IS THE UNIT OF EVIL   713 9
  A CENTRE OF THE EVIL WORLD   714 21
  THEN STRIFE IS EVIL BECAUSE IT IS NOT STRIFE   714 29
  KILLING IS NOT EVIL   715 5
  BUT MURDER IS ALWAYS EVIL   715 8
  ARE EVIL EVIL   715 13
  REFINEMENTS OF EVIL   715 18
  THE EVIL WILL IN MANY EVIL MEN   716 1
  MAKES AN EVIL WORLD-SOUL WHICH PURPOSES   716 2
  WHEELS ARE EVIL   716 4
  AND THE WILL TO MAKE MONEY IS EVIL   716 6
  ALL FORMS OF ABSTRACTION ARE EVIL   716 7
  FINANCE IS A GREAT EVIL ABSTRACTION   716 8
  SCIENCE HAS NOW BECOME AN EVIL ABSTRACTION   716 9
  EDUCATION IS AN EVIL ABSTRACTION   716 10
  ARE ALL EVIL ABSTRACTIONS FROM LIFE   716 12
  AND POLITICS NOW ARE AN EVIL ABSTRACTION FROM LIFE   716 13
  EVIL IS UPON US AND HAS GOT HOLD OF US   716 14
  AGAINST EVIL   716 17

EVILLY
  EVILLY   715 4

EVIL-YCLEPT
  EVIL-YCLEPT ETRUSCAN   297 29

EVOKES
  IS THE GORGEOUSNESS THAT EVOKES MY MOST PUZZLED ADMIRAT+   369 7

EVOLUTION
  A CYCLE OF EVOLUTION IS FINISHED   510 21
  AND THIS I HOLD IS THE TRUE HISTORY OF EVOLUTION   761 13

EVOLUTIONARY
    AND IN THESE AWFUL PAUSES THE EVOLUTIONARY CHANGE TAKES   510 10

EWE
    OPENING GREAT WINGS IN THE FACE OF THE SHEEP-FACED EWE   414 25

EXACT
    WHICH IS VERY ODD BEING THE EXACT REVERSE OF THEIR FATH+   829 14

EXACTLY
    EXACTLY   384 11
    EXACTLY SHE SAID DON JUAN WAS ANOTHER OF THEM IN LOVE   447 2
    MILD FORMS OF COCAINE THEY'RE NOT LIFE EXACTLY   532 13
    I DECLARE I AM A SUPERIOR PERSON YES EXACTLY AND HERE I   546 16

EXAGGERATE
    THE CATASTROPHE OF YOUR EXAGGERATE LOVE   290 9

EXALT
    EXALT THE BOWL   96 25
    YOU DON'T NEED ONE SINGLE SOCIAL INFERIOR TO EXALT YOU   526 26

EXALTATION
    YOU EXALTATION   332 5
    IS IN HER EXALTATION AND CAN LOOK DOWN ON THE SUN   688 11

EXAMPLE
    ONE IS A MAN FOR EXAMPLE AND ONE IS A BIRD   320 2

EXAMS
    BITTER SCIENCE THE EXAMS ARE NEAR   41 13

EXCEEDING
    TRUST THE MILLS OF GOD THOUGH THEY GRIND EXCEEDING SMALL   441 14
    ROLLS ROUND AND ROUND GRINDING EXCEEDING SMALL   614 20
    BEING GROUND EXCEEDING SMALL   642 4

EXCELLENT
    EXCELLENT FARM-MACHINERY   778 30

EXCELSIOR
    UP LIKE A BLOOMIN' LITTLE EXCELSIOR   552 19

EXCEPT
    EXCEPT HER KISS BETRAYS ME THIS THIS ONLY   127 25
    LISTEN EXCEPT THOSE WHO STRIVE WITH THEIR DEAD   233 3
    AND HOW I AM NOT AT ALL EXCEPT A FLAME THAT MOUNTS OFF   245 10
    WHAT CAN I SAY MORE EXCEPT THAT I KNOW WHY IT IS TO SUR+   266 6
    EXCEPT RIGIDITY   289 6
    NAKED EXCEPT FOR FANCIFUL LONG SHOES   296 20
    SANS ANY DISTINCTION AT ALL EXCEPT LOUTISH COMMONNESS   313 3
    BEYOND EVERYTHING EXCEPT ITSELF   322 6
    EXCEPT THAT YOU MAKE SLOW AGELESS PROGRESS   352 31
    EXCEPT THAT PAPA AND MAMA ARE OLD ACQUAINTANCES OF   357 21
    THOUGH WHAT SHE DOES EXCEPT LAY FOUR EGGS AT RANDOM IN   358 26
    EXCEPT SCORCH-PALE-BREASTED   373 27
    EXCEPT OF COURSE FOR SECONDARY MOTIVES   485 18
    ANYHOW THEY NEVER WILL EXCEPT FOR SECONDARY MOTIVES   485 22
    OR EXCEPT YOU CHANGE   485 23
    NOBODY CAN BE WISE EXCEPT ON RARE OCCASIONS LIKE GETTING   495 24
    EXCEPT ADMIT IT AND LEAVE IT TO THE MOON   510 6
    EXCEPT TO BE LEFT IN THE LAST RESORT ALONE QUITE ALONE   602 24
    CAN'T LIVE ANY MORE EXCEPT FOR A SPELL WHEN THE LIVING   639 4
    EXCEPT TRUTH   661 12
    EXCEPT   767 2
    I ASK FOR NOTHING EXCEPT TO SLIP   812 25
    THE VASTNESS IS EMPTY EXCEPT THAT THERE PLY   823 20
    ALL EXCEPT   826 20
    SO IT NEVER MOVED ON ANY MORE EXCEPT MENTALLY AND IN ME+   841 14

EXCESS
    FANS OUT YOUR PETALS FOR EXCESS OF FLAME   219 3
    EXULTING WITH SECRET WARM EXCESS   272 11
    AH THE DEWLAP SWINGS PENDULOUS WITH EXCESS   326 17

EXCESSES
    FOR DIVINE EXCESSES   96 10

EXCESSIVELY
    THEY CARED SO EXCESSIVELY THEMSELVES   508 18

EXCHANGE
    ON THE EXCHANGE   312 24
    THEY EXCHANGE NO WORD NO SPASM NOT EVEN ANGER   337 18
    AND BINDERS IN EXCHANGE   779 10
    GRANTED THERE IS AN EXCHANGE OF GENUINE FEELING   845 5

EXCITATIONS
    WE HAVE ONLY CEREBRAL EXCITATIONS   472 10

EXCITED
    OF EXCITED FREEDOM   532 10

EXCITEMENT
    AND CURRENTS OF EXCITEMENT IN OUR LIMBS   707 22

EXCITES
    THE TOUCH OF SUN EXCITES YOU   353 1

EXCLUDE
    IN THE HOME-PLACE SHY IS IT SHE SHOULD EXCLUDE   48 25

EXCLUSIVE
    FOR VIRGINS ARE NOT EXCLUSIVE OF VIRGINS   412 28
    AGAINST THE SILVERY ADAMANT WALLS OF LIFE'S EXCLUSIVE C+   722 3
    AGAINST THE SILVERY ADAMANT WALLS OF THIS OUR EXCLUSIVE+ *958 3

EXCREMENTA
    AUTUMNAL EXCREMENTA   280 17

EXCREMENT-EATERS
    GODDESSES OF LOVE GODDESSES OF DIRT EXCREMENT-EATERS OR+   671 18

EXCRETIONS
    ARE EXCRETIONS OF THE WATER AND FIRE IN PLANTS   295 10

EXCRUCIATING
    MUST BE EXCRUCIATING UNLESS YOU STIFFEN INTO METAL WHEN   288 6
    IN THE EXCRUCIATING TORMENT OF HOPELESSNESS HELPLESSNESS   627 24

EXCUSE
    THERE'S NO EXCUSE   491 10
    EXCUSE ME BUT ARE YOU A SUPERIOR PERSON   546 5

EXECRABLE
    A PRIESTESS EXECRABLE TAKEN IN VAIN   151 21

EXECRATED
    A PRIESTESS EXECRATED FULL OF STAIN   874 1

EXECUTION
    AND WHEN THE EXECUTION IS PERFORMED   528 18

EXEMPT
    THE DAMNED BELLS CEASE AND WE ARE EXEMPT   54 28

EXERCISE
    EXERCISE   521 18
    THOUGHT IS NOT A TRICK OR AN EXERCISE OR A SET OF DODGES   673 14

EXHALATION
    THE SUN IS FOREVER THIRSTY THIRSTING FOR THE BRIGHTEST +   368 7

EXHALATIONS
    SNOWDROPS STRAIGHT DEATH-VEINED EXHALATIONS OF WHITE AND   271 6

EXHALES
    AS SHE GENTLY EXHALES TO THE SUN   166 21

EXHAUST
    LUBRICATING OIL EXHAUST GAS   703 20

EXHAUSTED
    THEN TO FALL BACK EXHAUSTED INTO THE UNCONSCIOUS MOLTEN+ *909 28

EXHAUSTING
    AND EXHAUSTING PENETRATING THE LAVA-CRATER OF A TINY   539 7

EXHAUSTIVE
    DOWNWARDS EXHAUSTIVE   701 24

EXHAUSTS
    A THRILL RATHER EASILY EXHAUSTS ITSELF TAKE EVEN THE WAR   532 5

EXHAUST-SMELL
    AND THE EXHAUST-SMELL OF PEOPLE   646 7

EXHIBITIONIST
    AND I HAD TO GIVE HIM CREDIT FOR HIS RATHER EXHIBITIONI+   533 5

EXILE
    THEY WANDER AND ARE EXILED THEY LIVE IN EXILE THROUGH   304 26
    AND THE ALMOND-TREE IN EXILE IN THE IRON AGE   305 11
    EXILE AGAINST THE AGES   305 19
    LIKE A KING IN EXILE UNCROWNED IN THE UNDERWORLD   351 25
    GONE DEAD OR WANDERING IN EXILE WITH THEIR FEATHERS   599 18
    FLEEING IN EXILE TO ENGLAND AT THE END OF THE FIGHT   859 6

EXILED
    THEY WANDER AND ARE EXILED THEY LIVE IN EXILE THROUGH   304 26

EXILES
    LIKE SAD PROCESSIONS OF EXILES YOU COULD HAVE SEEN THEM+   866 3

EXIST
    YOU DON'T KNOW THAT I EXIST AND I DON'T KNOW THAT YOU   333 10
    EXIST   333 11
    DO YOU EXIST AND CAN A MAN TOUCH YOUR HAND   430 2
    PERSONALITIES EXIST APART   471 10
    OF COURSE IT WOULD CEASE TO EXIST   479 14
    I EXIST AS AN ORGANISM   510 3
    THEY SHOULDN'T EXIST   526 24
    WE DON'T EXIST UNLESS WE ARE DEEPLY AND SENSUALLY IN TO+   613 6
    AND I ALMOST CEASE TO EXIST WEIGHED DOWN TO EXTINCTION   629 20
    IS THAT ALL THEY EXIST FOR   765 17
    COME TO PASS THAT DOES NOT YET EXIST SAVE AS A SUBTLE   775 21
    SHALL NOT EXIST FOR THEM   836 23

EXISTED
    EXISTS NO MORE NOR EVER TRULY EXISTED   453 17

EXISTENCE
    CRUEL SELF THE FIGHT IS NOT FOR EXISTENCE THE FIGHT IS +   93 14
    OUR EXISTENCE WE WAIT AND ARE STILL DENIED   166 10
    THE BUBBLE HEMMING THIS EMPTY EXISTENCE WITH LIGHTS   193 22
    AND THAT WILL BE PURE EXISTENCE REAL LIBERTY   266 33
    WANDERING IN THE SLOW TRIUMPH OF HIS OWN EXISTENCE   358 18
    EXISTENCE   394 9
    KILL MONEY PUT MONEY OUT OF EXISTENCE   487 14
    I HAVE PASSED FROM EXISTENCE I FEEL NOTHING ANY MORE   509 8
    OF EXISTENCE   523 4
    EXISTENCE   523 6
    AND OBVIOUSLY IT IS THE CULMINATING POINT OF HIS EXISTE+   523 12
    IMAGINE WHAT IT MUST HAVE BEEN TO HAVE EXISTENCE   529 22
    THE TREE OF HUMAN EXISTENCE NEEDS BADLY PRUNING   677 28

EXISTENCE
    DESTROY IT SHED ITS UNCLEAN BLOOD KILL IT PUT IT OUT OF+   679   4
    CAME INTO EXISTENCE AS LIGHT   682   6
    CAME INTO EXISTENCE AS COLD SHADOW   682   7
    THAT CORPORAL EXISTENCE IS A KIND OF DEATH   689 15
    THE LONG MEAN MARGINAL STRETCHES OF OUR EXISTENCE   722 21
    EXISTENCE   722 26
    OF MARGINAL EXISTENCE   723 25
    TO FIND HIMSELF ON THE CROWDED ARID MARGINS OF EXISTENCE *957 14
    THE LONG MARGINAL STRETCHES OF EXISTENCE CROWDED WITH L+ *957 23
    AGAINST THE SILVERY ADAMANT WALLS OF THIS OUR EXCLUSIVE+ *958   3
    OVER THE ADAMANT WALLS OF THIS OUR BY-NO-MEANS IMPREGNA+ *958   7
    TOUCHES THE MARGINS OF OUR LIFE'S EXISTENCE   *958 28
    THAT FRINGE WITH SHADOW ALL THIS WORLD'S EXISTENCE   *959   2

EXISTENT
    BUT NOT THE JAGGLING AND TWISTING OF ALREADY EXISTENT I+   673   8

EXISTS
    EXISTS NO MORE NOR EVER TRULY EXISTED   453 17
    ONLY THAT EXISTS WHICH EXISTS IN MY OWN CONSCIOUSNESS   474 17
    ONLY THAT EXISTS WHICH EXISTS DYNAMICALLY AND UNMENTALI+   474 19
    THEY SAY THAT REALITY EXISTS ONLY IN THE SPIRIT   689 15
    EXISTS AND MEANS JUST WHAT IT MEANS   837   4
    THE VIVIFIER EXISTS AND THEREFORE WE KNOW IT   840   9
    THE VIVIFIER EXISTS BUT FOR ME IS NEITHER MAN-LIKE NOR +   840 25

EXIT
    TO BRUISE THEMSELVES AN EXIT FROM THEMSELVES   716 21
    TO ONE'S OWN SELF AND FIND AN EXIT   716 23
    A BRUISE OR BREAK OF EXIT FOR HIS LIFE   717 13
    ALREADY OUR SOULS ARE OOZING THROUGH THE EXIT   718   4
    TO BRUISE THEMSELVES AN EXIT FROM THEMSELVES   *956 27
    A BRUISE OR BREAK OF EXIT FOR HIS LIFE   *957   4

EXONERATED
    WITH LAUGHTER AND CLEAR THE EXONERATED EYES SINCE PAIN   94 20
    FOR LAUGHTER AND GLAD THE EXONERATED EYES FOR I   *897   8

EXPAND
    EVERY DAY BY THE FENCE TO LOOK UP AT THE FLOWERS THAT E+   58 14

EXPANDS
    THE NERVE-BARE PLACE NOW A LITTLE SILENCE EXPANDS   167 14
    THE POOR SHUT DANDELIONS WHOM SMALL WARMTH EXPANDS   *896 19

EXPANSE
    A WASTE EXPANSE OF NOTHING LIKE WIDE FORESHORES WHERE N+   509 12

EXPECT
    I EXPECT YER KNOW WHO I AM MRS NAYLOR   81 21
    HOW DO YOU EXPECT THEM EVER TO DESIRE YOU   485 21
    I EXPECT THE DODO LOOKED LIKE A CLOD   523 28
    AND AT THE SAME TIME EXPECT TO GO ON CALMLY EATING GOOD   531   6
    THEY SAY APRES MOI LE DELUGE AND CALMLY EXPECT   531   8
    WHY SHOULD OUR LATTER-DAY SINNERS EXPECT SUCH A LONG   531 16
    YOU MUSTN'T EXPECT IT ALSO TO WAIT FOR YOUR CONVENIENCE   531 21
    AND YOU STAND THERE AND EXPECT ME TO TREAT YOU LIKE AN   547   8
    AND THERE YOU STAND WITH NOTHING AND EXPECT ME TO HAND   547 12
    YOU MUSTN'T EXPECT MY DEAR TO GET AWAY WITH IT   548 21
    AND NONE OF US MUST EXPECT MORALITY OF EACH OTHER   608   3
    I EXPECT YOU KNOW WHO I AM MRS NAYLOR   *923 21

EXPECTANCY
    DAISIES THAT WAKEN ALL MISTAKEN WHITE-SPREAD IN EXPECTA+   71   3
    DAISIES THAT WAKEN ALL MISTAKEN WHITE-SPREAD IN EXPECTA+ *917 22

EXPECTANT
    THE EXPECTANT ONE AND THEREIN TO INSTIL   127 13

EXPECTATION
    WHAT SUDDEN EXPECTATION OPENS YOU   126 29

EXPECTED
    THE ANGEL OF CHILDHOOD KISSED ME AND WENT I EXPECTED   48   5

EXPECTING
    IF YOU ARE EXPECTING A SECOND ADVENT IN THE SHAPE OF A   531 19

EXPENSE
    BECAUSE OF THE BEASTLY EXPENSE   518   5
    IS PLAYED AT THEIR EXPENSE   560 12
    HIS MIND DEVELOPED AT THE EXPENSE OF HIS MALE SELF   841 20

EXPERIENCE
    AT THE BACK OF MY LIFE'S EXPERIENCE WHERE DREAMS FROM   52 26
    THE BRANCHES INVISIBLE SEED OF EXPERIENCE BLOWS   89 30
    THAT PERFECT BRIGHT EXPERIENCE NEVER FALLS   193 10
    OF A DAY'S EXPERIENCE SLEEP DOES SLOWLY DRAW   195   2
    AND I THOUGHT YOU WANTED LIFE AND EXPERIENCE DEAR YOUNG   463   5
    SATISFACTORY EXPERIENCE FROM IT CAN'T YOU SEE IT   463 15
    OR THE EXPERIENCE AMOUNTS TO NOTHING   466   7
    SELF-FORGETFUL AND GEMMED WITH EXPERIENCE   478 16
    AND MY LEAVES ARE GREEN WITH THE BREATH OF HUMAN EXPERI+   499 11
    TO BE FULL OF THE PEACE THAT COMES OF EXPERIENCE   503 15
    EXPERIENCE   504   7
    NUTTING GATHERING NUTS OF RIPE EXPERIENCE   504 12
    THE ESSENTIAL OIL OF THEIR EXPERIENCE ENTERS   505   2
    SILKY WITH OIL OF DISTILLED EXPERIENCE   505   8
    SAFE FROM ALL EXPERIENCE   543   6
    AND THE NEXT DEEPEST SENSUAL EXPERIENCE   653   7
    SATISFACTORY SENSUAL EXPERIENCE   653 12
    THE PROFOUND SENSUAL EXPERIENCE OF TRUTH YEA THIS IS   653 13
    VAST RANGES OF EXPERIENCE LIKE THE HUMMING OF UNSEEN HA+   666 25
    THOUGHT IS PONDERING OVER EXPERIENCE AND COMING TO CONC+   673 13
    AFTER THE PAINFUL PAINFUL EXPERIENCE OF DYING   677   5
    EXPERIENCE   690 16
    THEY CALL ALL EXPERIENCE OF THE SENSES MYSTIC WHEN THE +   707 26

EXPERIENCE
    HAVE AN EXPERIENCE OF BLISS   708 23
    OF THE HONEY OF EXPERIENCE   820   3
    KILLS ENTIRELY THE TRUE EXPERIENCE OF SEX   843 18
    HAVE NO EXPERIENCE OF SEX AT ALL IT IS ALMOST NOTHING T+   843 20
    THE SKIRT OF THE SPIRIT'S EXPERIENCE HAS MELTED AWAY   *959 28

EXPERIENCES
    I SAY WONDERFUL ARE THE HELLISH EXPERIENCES   280 24
    IN THE WHITE SHIRT OF THE MIND'S EXPERIENCES   *957   9

EXPERIMENTAL
    EXPERIMENTAL   463 10

EXPERT
    NOT GOOD ENOUGH TO BE LOVED BY THIS EXPERT   *948 20

EXPIATE
    AND I HAVE SOMETHING TO EXPIATE   351 29
    LORD WHAT WE HAVE DONE WE HEREBY EXPIATE   743   6
    WE EXPIATE IN OUR BODIES' RENTS AND RAGS   743   7
    WE EXPIATE IT THUS THE UNKNOWABLE CRIME   743 14

EXPIATING
    EXPIATING THEIR SINS   627 23

EXPIATION
    OUR BODIES TO THE EXPIATION LORD   743 16

EXPIRATION
    OF EXPIRATION TURNED INTO THE WORLD AGAIN   784 15

EXPIRE
    AND SUFFER UNHEEDING ONLY FORBIDDEN TO EXPIRE   161   5

EXPLAIN
    I MUST HOLD MY FACE TO THE WIND AND LET IT EXPLAIN   180 32

EXPLICIT
    UPON ME MY OWN REFLECTION EXPLICIT GIST   141 19
    ISSUE OF THE EXPLICIT ROSE   285   8
    THE EXPLICIT   285 13

EXPLODE
    AND BUMP ON ONE ANOTHER AND EXPLODE INTO MORE MIST   437 34
    EXPLODE   642 15

EXPLODED
    EXPLODED THE HEART   629   9

EXPLODES
    SO IT EXPLODES AND YOU SEE THROUGH THE FISSURE THE SCAR+   283 28
    THE SUBSTANCE OF SHADOW THAT BURSTS AND EXPLODES   788 13

EXPLODING
    ABOVE THAT CRASH-GULF OF EXPLODING WHIPS   347 14

EXPLOITS
    AND IN PRIVATE BOASTS HIS EXPLOITS EVEN LOUDER IF YOU A+   432 30

EXPLORE
    YOU HAD THE POWER TO EXPLORE ME   111 13
    UNSEEN MY HANDS EXPLORE THE SILENCE DRAWING THE BARK   147   2
    THAT WE KNOW NOTHING OF THAT WE DARE NOT EXPLORE   606 22
    YEA I WAS FINE ENOUGH TO EXPLORE YOU   *927   6
    I WAS DILIGENT TO EXPLORE YOU   *928   6

EXPLORER
    LURE THE UNOCEANED EXPLORER   53   8
    UNOCEANED EXPLORER   *905 21

EXPLOSION
    AN EXPLOSION OF GREEN LIGHT   206 17
    SLOWLY REVOLVING TOWARDS UNEXPLODED EXPLOSION   381 18

EXPLOSIONS
    EXPLOSIONS HAVE WHIRLED   748 22

EXPLOSIVE
    AS FRICTIONAL AS PERILOUS EXPLOSIVE AS BRIMSTONE   301 31

EXPLOSIVES
    SO GUNS AND STRONG EXPLOSIVES   715 12

EXPOSE
    EACH ARC-LAMP GOLDEN DOES EXPOSE   104 26

EXPOSED
    NAKED EXPOSED ON THE BUSH   107 12
    AT THE SAME TIME STAND EXPOSED   108   1
    AND HAVING EXPOSED THE PINK PLACE OF HER NAKEDNESS   386   1

EXPOSURE
    LIKE A WOUND THE EXPOSURE OF HER SECRET ON THE OPEN DAY   283 32

EXPRESSED
    ANYTHING THAT EXPRESSED LIFE   837 17

EXPRESSES
    INSTEAD OF THIS MESS WHICH EXPRESSES THE IMPUDENT HUMAN   837 18

EXPRESSION
    AND ALL THE DIFFERENCES GIVEN EXPRESSION   611 20
    EXPRESSION OF SEX-HATE   620   2

EXPRESSIONS
  EXPRESSIONS   197 29

EXPRESSON
  WOULD BLUR NO WHISPER SPOIL NO EXPRESSON   250 27

EXQUISITE
  EMERGING WHITE AND EXQUISITE AND I IN AMAZE   67 9
  LIKE A FINE AN EXQUISITE CHISEL A WEDGE-BLADE INSERTED   250 20
  EXQUISITE HIGH ABOVE   252 6
  BRIGHT GLANCING EXQUISITE CORN OF MANY A STUBBORN   263 27
  COME SWEEP AWAY THESE EXQUISITE GHASTLY FIRST-FLOWERS   271 3
  JETS OF EXQUISITE FINALITY   271 10
  EVER MORE EXQUISITE DISTILLED IN SEPARATION   281 11
  THE EXQUISITE ODOUR OF LEAVE-TAKING   281 14
  EXQUISITE SPLENDOUR   305 28
  AND ALL THE EASTERN EXQUISITE ROYAL PLANTS   313 30
  THE EXQUISITE AND AGELESS ARISTOCRACY   314 14
  THE EXQUISITE ASSERTION OF NEW DELICATE LIFE   314 19
  SOFTLY FLUTTERING THE SENSES IN THE EXQUISITE ORGASM OF   481 24
  IN THE CURVE OF THINE EXQUISITE FORM THE JOY OF THE   *915 28

EXTANT
  I WOULD NOT EVEN ASK TO LEAVE A FOSSIL CLAW EXTANT   430 7
  AND THE MONEY-MUCK-WORMS THE EXTANT POWERS   456 20
  AND THEN TURN ROUND AND EMBRACE THE EXTANT BODY OF LIFE   482 4

EXTENSIVE
  THAT A NEW CHICK SHOULD CHIP THE EXTENSIVE SHELL   329 28

EXTINCT
  EXTINCT ONE YELLOW-FLUFFY SPARK   119 22
  O THE GOLDEN SPARKLES LAID EXTINCT   120 6
  MUST HAVE SUNK AND BECOME EXTINCT   193 15
  STILL IN FULL FLIGHT EXTINCT SHALL I THEN TURN   195 23
  RED ANGRY MEN ARE A RACE EXTINCT ALAS   317 12
  AND THE EXTINCT GIANT ELK TOO BIG IN ANTLERS   529 18
  AGAINST ME YET THEY CANNOT MAKE EXTINCT   745 35
  EXTINCT ONE YELLOW BLOODY SPARK   *932 31

EXTINCTION
  SHEER HARD EXTINCTION   266 3
  ANYHOW THE TOLSTOYAN LOT SIMPLY ASKED FOR EXTINCTION   533 24
  AND I ALMOST CEASE TO EXIST WEIGHED DOWN TO EXTINCTION   629 20
  NOW LIVING WOMEN AND MEN ARE THREATENED WITH EXTINCTION   640 15
  AND THE FALL TO EXTINCTION WHICH CAN NEVER COME   701 3
  AND GUTTER TO EXTINCTION LIKE A TAPER ON A FORGOTTEN AL+   859 4
  TO EXTINCTION RUSHING   862 25

EXTINGUISH
  THE WHOLE OF THE DAY TO EXTINGUISH THE SHADOW I LIFT ON+   133 20

EXTINGUISHES
  EXTINGUISHES THERE MY RISEN RESURRECTED LIFE   261 15

EXTINGUISHMENT
  OF LIVING AND WAVER IN SWEET EXTINGUISHMENT   879 31

EXTRA
  ROSES ARE ONLY ONCE-WILD ROSES THAT WERE GIVEN AN EXTRA+   831 2

EXTRACT
  EXTRACT AND EXTRICATE YOURSELF   642 7

EXTRACTING
  FISH-BLOOD SLOWLY RUNNING NEXT TO THE FLOOD EXTRACTING   336 31

EXTRAVAGANCE
  WITH THE EXTRAVAGANCE OF THE FROGS   206 32

EXTRAVAGANT
  TO THE RECKLESS EXTRAVAGANT TURMOIL OF LIVING THE STRIFE   *895 13

EXTREMITY
  OF THE MALE TORTOISE AT EXTREMITY   366 26

EXTRICATE
  EXTRACT AND EXTRICATE YOURSELF   642 7

EXTRUDED
  POOR OBSCURE FRUITS EXTRUDED OUT OF LIGHT   160 10
  LONG NECK AND LONG VULNERABLE LIMBS EXTRUDED SPREAD-EAG+   365 1

EXUBERANCE
  AND THE FROGS IN THE POOL BEYOND THRILLED WITH EXUBERAN+   206 29
  EXUBERANCE   272 10

EXUBERANT
  CAME UPON YOU PRANCING ROUND THE CORNER IN EXUBERANT   395 29

EXUDES
  TILL THE DROP OF RIPENESS EXUDES   283 25
  THAT SHE EXUDES LIKE PEARLY WHITE POISON GAS   619 21

EXULT
  THEN I LAUGHED IN THE DARK OF MY HEART I DID EXULT   125 25
  THEN I LAUGHED IN THE DARK OF MY HEART I DID EXULT   *936 24

EXULTANCE
  OF SNEAKING EXULTANCE   500 6

EXULTANT
  ABOVE THEM EXULTANT THE PEEWITS ARE SWEEPING   33 3
  ABOVE THEM EXULTANT THE PEEWITS ARE SWEEPING   *891 3

EXULTATION
  I HAVE DONE A QUIVER OF EXULTATION GOES THROUGH ME LIKE   209 26

EXULTING
  EXULTING WITH SECRET WARM EXCESS   272 11

EXULTS
  AND EXULTS IN ITS BITTER USAGE OF US ALL   746 12

EYE
  PATENT AND OPEN BENEATH MY EYE   59 27
  OF THE NIGHTLY HEAVENS OVERHEAD LIKE AN IMMENSE OPEN EYE   97 14
  THREADS AND THRILLS LIKE ORE THAT IS WEALTH TO THE EYE   146 31
  OF YOUR EYE BUNNY   241 7
  YOU JETTED OFF YOUR EYE AT ME   241 16
  IN THE INWARDNESS OF YOUR YOU THAT EYE WILL NEVER SEE   283 22
  AND A BULL'S LARGE SOMBRE GLANCING EYE   325 28
  AND SEEN HIS HORROR-TILTED EYE   339 7
  HIS RED-GOLD WATER-PRECIOUS MIRROR-FLAT BRIGHT EYE   339 8
  YOUR BRIGHT DARK LITTLE EYE   352 20
  YOUR EYE OF A DARK DISTURBED NIGHT   352 21
  AND THE FINE BRILLIANCE OF YOUR SO TINY EYE   353 22
  YOUR EYE IS VERY DARK VERY BRIGHT   359 10
  HER BRIGHT EYE SEES BUT NOT ME NOT ANYTHING   359 16
  HER LACONIC EYE HAS AN EARTHY MATERIALISTIC LOOK   359 33
  HIS BLACK SAD-LIDDED EYE SEES BUT BEHOLDS NOT   362 4
  WHY DO YOU ARCH YOUR NAKED-SET EYE WITH A MORE-THAN-COM+   369 16
  YOU BRITTLE WILL-TENSE BIRD WITH A FOOLISH EYE   370 35
  AND THE EYE OVERWEENING INTO MADNESS   371 17
  ONLY THE INNER EYE OF YOUR SCORCHED BROAD BREAST   373 24
  ESPECIALLY IF BEING GIVEN A NEEDLE'S EYE OF EGRESS ELSE+   381 6
  AND HIS SLITTED EYES SEEKING THE NEEDLE'S EYE   382 4
  SHUFFLE SHUFFLE AND HIS LITTLE WICKED EYE HAS SEEN YOU +   387 10
  AND A ME-ALMIGHTY EYE   414 16
  TO PEE IN THE EYE OF A POLICE-MAN   434 16
  NOR GUSTY JOVE WITH HIS EYE ON IMMORTAL TARTS   437 5
  OR THE ROUND WILD VIVID EYE OF A WILD-GOOSE STARING   438 31
  FOR THEN NOBODY WOULD HAVE THEIR EYE ON HIM   483 8
  IF JESUS HAD KEPT A SHARP EYE ON SATAN   483 16
  DO IT JUST TO SPIT IN THEIR EYE   517 6
  HAVE A STERN EYE ON LIFE   528 15
  WORSE THAN THE EVIL EYE   538 14
  AND BLINDED HIM IN HIS ONE BIG EYE   543 27
  IS BLINDED BRUTES OF CYCLOPS WITH OUR CYCLOPEAN EYE PUT   544 4
  HE WANTS HIS ONE GREAT WONDERING EYE THE EYE OF THE   544 9
  YOU NEED YOUR OWN GREAT WONDERING EYE THAT FLASHES WITH   544 22
  OVER THEIR MUTILATED CYCLOPEAN EYE   544 30
  OH HE KNOWS ALL ABOUT IT HE CASTS A YELLOW EYE   633 26
  TO SEE THE GLEAM OF THE GODS THERE REFLECTED IN THE HUM+   649 22
  LIKE THE EYE OF A VIOLET   658 15
  AND THE EYE CANNOT BEHOLD HIM   692 8
  AND THE EYE CANNOT BEHOLD HIM   692 19
  CHILD DEAR TO MY EYE GOD'S BLESSING IS ON THY SERVICE   749 21
  ME TOO AT LAST ERE THOU GOEST CHILD DEAR TO MY EYE   750 3
  YOU ONLY STARE AT THE SUN WITH THE ONE BROAD EYE OF YOUR   781 29
  AND SENT THE EAGLE TO KEEP AN EYE ON HIM   783 5
  INTO THE EYE OF THE FATHER   786 26
  AND FAR AT THE CENTRE WITH ONE UNBLINKING EYE THE DRAGO+   790 11
  THE ONE EYE OF OUR CYCLOPAEAN INSTINCT PUT OUT   833 18
  LAUGHS LIKE AN EYE AT ME AND I   887 14
  MET MY EYE   *925 4
  WITHOUT DELIVERING ONCE MY EYE   *930 17
  ALONG HER FOOT-SEARCHED WAY HER SORROW-CLOSED EYE   *937 26
  AND ONCE HE WAS GAY AND HEARTY WITH HIS EYE ON THE IMMO+   *946 17

EYEABLE
  STANDING THERE SO SLEEK AND ERECT AND EYEABLE   431 14

EYEBROW
  OVER THE LEFT EYEBROW   278 20

EYEING
  EYEING ME SIDEWAYS AND CUNNINGLY CONSCIOUS THAT I AM   333 2

EYELIDS
  AND SKYWARDS HIS FACE IS IMMOBILE EYELIDS ASLANT   66 11
  WITH SORROWFUL FINGERS STROKED HER EYELIDS SHUT   881 2

EYES
  THE LITTLE RED HEIFER TONIGHT I LOOKED IN HER EYES   38 6
  THE LIFE THAT LOOKS THROUGH MY EYES   38 30
  WITHOUT EYES WITHOUT HANDS   39 20
  SHE GLANCES QUICK HER STARTLED EYES   42 24
  TURNS BACK HER LIQUID ANGUISHED EYES   43 6
  YET CALM AND KINDLY ARE HIS EYES   43 14
  HIS STRONG TEETH IN A SMILE AND FLASHES HIS EYES   43 20
  HIS BRIGHT DARK EYES COME OVER ME LIKE A HOOD   43 34
  MISCHIEF HAS COME IN HER DAWNING EYES   46 9
  IN HER EYES AS A YOUNG BEE STUMBLETH   46 16
  WHITE AND GAUNT WITH WISTFUL EYES THAT HOVER   47 11
  I MUST LOOK AWAY FROM HIM HER FADED EYES   47 21
  FOR THE LIPS AND THE EYES OF GOD ARE BEHIND A VEIL   48 10
  AS THEIR EYES GLANCE AT ME FOR THE GRAIN   52 2
  EVEN THAN YOUR EYES   55 15
  STARTLED UPON YOUR EYES NOW SO WIDE WITH HEREAFTER   58 22
  POINTING MY EYES IN WRETCHED DEFIANCE WHERE LOVE HIDES +   63 25
  BUT WHEN I DRAW THE SCANTY CLOAK OF SILENCE OVER MY EYES   64 14
  UPON US DARK EYES AS HERE BENEATH THE BUSBIES GLITTERIN+   66 25
  AND SO IT IS EBB-TIME THEY TURN THE EYES BENEATH THE BU+   67 1
  THEN GAVE THEE THY DARK EYES O MAN THAT ALL   69 20
  NOW AT LAST THE INK AND DUDGEON PASSES FROM OUR FERVENT+   70 5
  AT THEIR EYES   71 14
  GIRLS WITH THEIR LARGE EYES WIDE WITH TRAGEDY   71 21
  BUT WHEN I MEET THE WEARY EYES   72 1
  THE REDDENED ACHING EYES OF THE BAR-MAN WITH THIN ARMS   72 2
  HOW CAN I ANSWER THE CHALLENGE OF SO MANY EYES   76 5
  AWFULLY MUST I CALL BACK A HUNDRED EYES A VOICE   76 7
  I HAVE STARTLED A HUNDRED EYES AND NOW I MUST LOOK   76 12

EYES
    THA CAN STARE AT ME WI' THY FIERCE BLUE EYES   79 11
    AN' IF 'ER CLAWKIN' EYES   80 14
    I DUNNO WHEER 'IS EYES WAS A GRET   81 17
    AND WE ARE CRUSHED BETWEEN THE COVERS WE CLOSE OUR EYES+   88 12
    OUR EYES   88 22
    AND THOUGH IT BE LOVE'S WET BLUE EYES THAT CRY   89 32
    HOVERING ABOUT THE JUDGMENT THAT STOOD IN MY EYES   94 17
    WITH LAUGHTER AND CLEAR THE EXONERATED EYES SINCE PAIN   94 20
    HER CHEEKS ARE VERY SMOOTH HER EYES ARE CLOSED   101 9
    OF MY EYES I SEE YOU BEAUTIFUL AND DEAR   118 13
    CLOSE YOUR EYES MY LOVE LET ME MAKE YOU BLIND   118 20
    AND ALGEBRA IN THE EYES OF DESIROUS MEN   118 23
    I WOULD KISS YOU OVER THE EYES TILL I KISSED YOU BLIND   118 26
    THE WAKING SMILE OF HER EYES   121 22
    LEST HER BRIGHT EYES LIKE SPARROWS SHOULD FLY IN   122 29
    OVER MY EYES AND I WAS BLIND   123 19
    TILL SHE TOOK HER EYES AWAY   123 33
    SHE SPOKE AND I CLOSED MY EYES   124 18
    LIKE A SUDDEN CHUCKLING OF MUSIC I BADE HER EYES   125 26
    MEET MINE I OPENED HER HELPLESS EYES TO CONSULT   125 27
    DEFEAT IN SUCH A BATTLE IN THE DARK OF HER EYES   125 29
    HER TAWNY EYES ARE ONYX OF THOUGHTLESSNESS   127 21
    I DO FORGET YOUR EYES THAT SEARCHING THROUGH   129 9
    MY EYES FROM DUTEOUS WORK MALINGERING   129 14
    A SOULLESS NECKAR WITH WINKING SEAS IN HIS EYES   130 19
    AND ALL THE MANIFOLD BLUE AMAZING EYES   136 14
    INVISIBLE BLINDING MY FACE AND MY EYES WHAT IF IN   147 5
    AND PALE HER IVORY FACE HER EYES WOULD FAIL   156 2
    THE SECRET OF THE MOON WITHIN YOUR EYES   156 21
    OUR DAUNTED EYES   166 7
    OPENS MY EYES TILL THE ROOTS OF MY VISION SEEM TORN   173 4
    THEIR EYES AND LOOK AT THE GRAVE ON THE HILL IN WONDER   176 16
    STRANDS OF MY EYES AND MY LIDS AND MY HANDS AND MY FEET+   180 5
    PASS THE MEN WHOSE EYES ARE SHUT LIKE ANEMONES IN A DAR+   180 20
    THE NIGHT YOU CLOSED YOUR EYES FOR EVER AGAINST ME   193 16
    AND JOSEPH SHADING HIS EYES WITH HIS HAND   200 15
    OVER HER STARTLED EYES   201 2
    HIS DARK EYES FULL OF PAIN   202 2
    BUT LOOKED INTO HER EYES   202 10
    YOU LOOKED INTO MY EYES AND SAID BUT THIS IS JOY   207 3
    BUT THE SHADOW OF LYING WAS IN YOUR EYES   207 5
    YET HOW I HAVE LEARNED TO KNOW THAT LOOK IN YOUR EYES   207 15
    MAKING HIDEOUS YOUR EYES   207 20
    YOUR EYES TAKE ALL OF ME IN AS A COMMUNICATION   210 12
    YOUR EYES WHEN YOU LOOK AT ME   215 19
    MY EYES FROM THE SHADOWS DARK   216 3
    SHE OPENED HER EYES AND GREEN   216 16
    DRAWN ON HIS MOUTH BROKEN AT LAST BY HIS PANGS   225 8
    AND CHRIST I HAVE MET HIS ACCUSING EYES AGAIN   225 22
    THE BROWN EYES BLACK WITH MISERY AND HATE THAT LOOK   225 23
    HOW YOU SIT IN THE THRONE OF MY EYES   227 30
    THE SUN IS IN MY EYES I MUST GET UP   230 11
    THE OTHER SHE TOO HAS STRANGE GREEN EYES   261 1
    WHOSE DOGES WERE OLD AND HAD ANCIENT EYES   278 11
    BEFORE EYES SAW TOO MUCH   285 32
    SOBERNESS SOBRIETY WITH HEAVY EYES PROPPED OPEN   287 4
    CLOSE THE EYES AND GO   287 9
    DARK ABORIGINAL EYES   292 28
    BEHOLD MY EYES TURN TAWNY YELLOW   301 22
    EYES OF YELLOW GOLDEN SAND   301 30
    PAST MY EYES   302 6
    WHEN SHE LIFTED HER MOP FROM HER EYES AND SCREWED IT IN   310 2
    EYES REVEALED   310 6
    AT THEIR DEFENCELESS EYES   310 8
    HIS EYES   324 14
    WATER-EAGER EYES   336 8
    WITH THEIR GOLD RED EYES AND GREEN-PURE GLEAM AND UNDER+   339 26
    WITH STICKING-OUT BEAD-BERRY EYES BLACK   345 29
    AND LOOK WITH LACONIC BLACK EYES   353 21
    WITH IRON BETWEEN YOUR TWO EYES   373 17
    YOU NEVER LOOK AT THE SUN WITH YOUR TWO EYES   373 23
    HIS BIG REGRETFUL EYES   377 24
    HENCE HIS BEAUTIFUL EYES   378 21
    WITH THE HALF-VEILED BEAUTIFUL EYES AND THE PENSIVE FACE   379 4
    YELLOW EYES INCOMPREHENSIBLE WITH THIN SLITS   380 28
    AND NERVES URGING FORWARD TO THE WALL YOU'D HAVE EYES   381 4
    AND STORM-LIGHTNING-SLITTED EYES   381 12
    AND HIS SLITTED EYES SEEKING THE NEEDLE'S EYE   382 4
    WHILE HIS SLITTED EYES SQUINT BACK TO THE ROOTS OF HIS +   386 22
    WHITES OF THEIR EYES   388 23
    AND LUSTROUS GREAT TROPICAL EYES UNVEILED NOW GLEAMING   389 13
    APPROACHING UNDER THAT SMALL PAVILION AND TROPICAL EYES   389 22
    WENT UP IN WAVELETS TO HIM FROM THE BREASTS AND EYES   389 29
    WITH THE STRANGE DARK LAUGH IN THEIR EYES GLANCING UP   389 33
    EYES THE UNBELIEVER   390 10
    SHOWING A GLINT OF TEETH AND GLANCING TROPICAL EYES ARO+   391 14
    HER FULL ANTIPODAL EYES SO DARK   393 11
    HOW FULL HER EYES ARE LIKE THE FULL FATHOMLESS SHINING +   394 6
    WISTFULLY WATCHING WITH WONDERFUL LIQUID EYES   394 20
    AND BLACK EYES BULGING BRIGHT IN A DUST-MASK   397 17
    COCKING YOUR EYES AT ME AS YOU COME ALONGSIDE TO SEE IF   397 23
    AND DIDN'T YOU TURN YOUR EYES UP AT ME THEN   400 9
    LOOK UP AT ME WITH MISGIVING IN YOUR BULGING EYES   400 25
    AND FEAR IN THE SMOKY WHITES OF YOUR EYES YOU NIGGER   400 26
    BEAUTIFUL DEAD EYES   402 7
    WRAPPED TO THE EYES THE SHEET BOUND CLOSE ON HIS BROWS   403 10
    AND THE COFFIN-LIFE SLIT WHERE THE INDIAN'S EYES ARE   403 30
    MAKE BIG EYES LITTLE PONY   409 26
    WOMEN WITH THE BEAUTIFUL EYES OF THE OLD DAYS   410 11
    WOMEN WITH EYES THAT WERE GENTLE IN OLDEN BELIEF IN LOVE   410 23
    HAVE AEONS OF WEARINESS ROUND THEIR EYES   425 20
    WITH THEIR THIN DARK HANDS AND THEIR WIDE DARK EYES AND   451 3
    OPEN YOUR HALF-DEAD EYES   456 14
    HAS OPENED HIS EYES AFRESH   459 26
    WIDE EYES AND WONDERING SPIRIT NOT   461 7
    WELL DAMN MY EYES I SAID TO MYSELF   489 17
    WELL DAMN MY LITTLE EYES   489 18

EYES
    HOVERING TO PECK OUT THE EYES OF THE STILL-LIVING CREAT+   500 17
    AND WOULD YOU PECK OUT HIS EYES IF HE DID   540 10
    WITH OUR SHARP LITTLE EYES AND OUR HIGH-POWER MACHINES   543 20
    WITH THEIR BULGING POLICEMAN'S-LAMP EYES   544 21
    ALL EYES SOUGHT THE SAME OLD SPOT   578 2
    NOT BY TIME BUT BY UNCLEAN BREATH AND EYES   580 24
    THAT ANCIENT EYES HAVE LEFT ON YOU WHERE OBSCENE EYES   581 3
    IN THE EYES OF THOSE WHO LOVED ME   601 14
    SUDDENLY HER YELLOW-BROWN EYES LOOKED WITH A FLARE INTO   618 1
    ONLY HERE AND THERE A PAIR OF EYES HAUNTED LOOKS OUT AS+   625 25
    UNLESS GOGGLING EYES TO GOGGLE AT THE FILM   630 29
    IF HE SHOW IT THE EYES AND THE BREATH OF THE CROWD   634 16
    EYES   634 20
    SONS OF MEN WITH THE WONDERING EYES OF LIFE   642 18
    SOME MEN LOOK STRAIGHT INTO THE EYES OF THE GODS   649 9
    WHO LOOK INTO THE EYES OF THE GODS   649 15
    AND WORSHIP IS THE JOY OF THE GLEAM FROM THE EYES OF TH+   649 16
    THOSE THAT LOOK INTO THE EYES OF THE GODS AND THESE ARE+   649 20
    AND THOSE THAT LOOK INTO THE EYES OF THE FEW OTHER MEN   649 21
    AND THE FEW LOOK INTO THE EYES OF THE GODS AND SERVE TH+   650 4
    THE FEW MUST LOOK INTO THE EYES OF THE GODS AND OBEY TH+   650 8
    IN THE EYES OF THE GODS   650 9
    AND THE MANY MUST OBEY THE FEW THAT LOOK INTO THE EYES +   650 10
    WHO HAS LOOKED INTO THE EYES OF THE GODS   650 16
    I SUDDENLY SAW DEEP INTO THE EYES OF GOD   650 22
    AND YOU LOOK IN HER EYES AND SEE IT IS A LIE   654 11
    WITH EYES LIKE THE INTERIORS OF STUFFY ROOMS FURNISHED   656 24
    I LIFT UP MINE EYES UNTO THE HILLS   660 20
    OF THE UNKNOWN AIR AND EYES SO SOFT   667 8
    AND LIFTED HIS FACE UP WITH BLUE EYES LOOKING AT THE EL+   672 9
    AND DREAMING WITH STRANGE WHALE EYES WIDE OPEN IN THE W+   694 31
    AND KEEN EYES THEY WILL HOVER THEY WILL COME BETWEEN YOU   706 19
    I CAN SEE HIS RAGING BLACK EYES BLAZE AT ME   733 3
    WITH SAVAGE BLACK EYES IS SULKY AND ALL THE TIME   734 18
    HIS EYES MEET MINE AS HE TAKES THE JUG OF WATER   734 27
    HIS EYES AND HE SULKED HE HAD ANOTHER LOVER   735 2
    WE LOOSE OUR GRIP AND WE UNSTRAIN OUR EYES   736 23
    BUT LET US FREE OUR EYES AND LOOK BEYOND   737 4
    TO THE TRENCHES I SEE AGAIN A FACE WITH BLUE EYES   742 6
    OUR EYES DARKEN AND IMPOTENCE HURTS   746 14
    YOU WILL KNOW BY HIS EYES   754 8
    INTO MY EYES AND NOSTRILS   760 11
    WHERE LIFE LOOKS ME IN THE EYES   768 19
    WITH SINGED HOT EYES AND RELENTLESSNESS   769 5
    WHOM THE LEOPARD LOOKS IN THE EYES   769 26
    LOOK INTO EACH OTHER'S EYES WITH KNOWLEDGE   770 30
    WITH IRON BETWEEN YOUR TWO EYES   781 23
    WITH TEARLESS EYES   783 9
    JUST TURN YOUR EYES THIS WAY MEXICANOS   790 20
    EYES   792 11
    DANCES BEFORE THE EYES   794 18
    YOU DO NOTHING BUT SQUAT ON YOUR HAMS AND STARE WITH VA+   795 2
    THERE ARE DEAD THAT SIT UNDER THE TREES WATCHING WITH A+   795 26
    ALL MEN COVER THEIR EYES   811 9
    ASK IN THE SPACE OF THEIR EYES   816 10
    NOW SHUT YOUR EYES   816 24
    A NEW THING COMES TO PASS EYES CLOSE   834 2
    IF TWILIGHT CAME IN THE EYES OF WOMEN   840 4
    THAT IMPRESS ME LIKE THE THOUGHT-DRENCHED EYES   854 26
    THE FIERCE BLACK EYES ARE CLOSED THEY WILL OPEN NO MORE   859 17
    EYES WHERE HIS HOT IMPRISONED SOUL HAS KEPT   859 19
    WITH YOUR TIRED EYES JEANNETTE WE SUFFER THE SAME DON'T+   859 31
    AND ROUND EYES AFIRE   861 24
    HER EYES GLOW AS SHE   862 7
    STRONG WITH EYES OF DEFIANCE EVE WALKS WITH SORROWS   864 23
    SHE TURNED AND KISSED HIM AND HIS EYES WERE THE SOUL OF+   865 8
    THE INRUSH THE CLATTER THE STAMPING EYES LAUGHING WIDE +   865 25
    CHILD EYES SO CLEAR   866 30
    THE GOLD-BROWN FLOWERS OF HER EYES UNFOLD   868 26
    SHE MAY COVER HER EYES YET THE AIMLESS BREEZE OF MY WOR+   868 29
    MY MOTHER HAD BLUE EYES   869 5
    BEAR THE THOUGHT OF MY MOTHER'S PAIN-DARKENED BLUE EYES   869 14
    AH BUT MY MOTHER HAD BLUE EYES   870 17
    EYES   871 23
    I DARE NOT LOOK AT HIS EYES   871 28
    BECAUSE WHEN YOUR EYES LOOK UP AT ME THEY STARTLE   874 27
    OF YOUR EYES DRAWS OPEN MY SHELTERING FLIMSY DOORS   875 13
    YEA I WOULD SHUT MY EYES I WOULD CLOSE MY WINDOWS   875 26
    EVEN WHILE IN HIS INNERMOST EYES THERE BURN   876 26
    AND ALL THE WONDER LOST FROM OUT HIS EYES   877 11
    AND SMILING CURIOUSLY WITH WATCHFUL EYES   878 13
    AND CURIOUS SMILING EYES   878 18
    MY EYES BEING DOWNCAST   880 17
    AND LOOKING IN HER EYES   880 27
    THEN LOOKED AGAIN WITHIN HER EYES   881 3
    THAT IS HER SMALL EAR AGAINST MY EYES   882 24
    LIFTING HIS HAUNTED EYES TO ME I AM WANTING IN SONG   884 11
    STREAMED REDNESS DOWN THE AIR SHOT RED ON HIS EYES   884 24
    A SHADOW WAS DEEP IN THEIR EYES   885 13
    I LOOKED IN HER EYES THE GLOOM   885 16
    AND AS I LAY AND LOOKED IN YOUR EYES   886 13
    MY LITTLE RED HEIFER GO AND LOOK AT HER EYES   *892 22
    AND THE LIFE THAT IS POLARISED IN MY EYES   *893 13
    THAT QUIVERS BETWEEN MY EYES AND MOUTH   *893 14
    LEAVING MY EYES HALF EMPTY AND CLAMOROUS   *893 16
    AND THE RELENTLESS NODALITY OF MY EYES REASSERTS ITSELF   *893 29
    TILL THE BURSTEN FLOOD OF LIFE EBBS BACK TO MY EYES   *893 30
    EYES LOOK AT ME SO   *894 2
    DO WATCH YOUR EYES   *894 8
    HOVERING TO PLUCK AT THE JUDGMENT WHICH STOOD IN MY EYES   *897 5
    FOR LAUGHTER AND GLAD THE EXONERATED EYES FOR I   *897 8
    HOW CAN I ANSWER THE CHALLENGE OF SO MANY EYES   *897 32
    AWFULLY MUST I CALL BACK THOSE HUNDRED EYES A VOICE   *898 2
    I HAVE STARTLED A HUNDRED EYES AND I MUST LOOK   *898 6
    AND MY EYES MEET HIS VERY QUIETLY   *898 27
    AS THEIR EYES GLANCE AT ME FOR THE GRAIN   *899 15
    HOW CAN I ANSWER THE CHALLENGE OF SO MANY EYES   *901 9

EYES

AWFULLY MUST I CALL BACK THOSE HUNDRED EYES A VOICE   *901 11
I HAVE STARTLED A HUNDRED EYES AND I MUST LOOK   *901 15
AND MY EYES MEET HIS VERY QUIETLY   *902 11
AS THEIR EYES GLANCE AT ME FOR THE GRAIN   *902 27
BEATS THE ACTIVE ECSTASY SUDDENLY LIFTING MY EYES   *906 21
EYES WHERE I CAN WATCH THE SWIM OF OLD DREAMS REFLECTED+   *907 11
VISIBLE UNDER THE CHANGING EYES   *907 16
IN THE SUDDEN LIFTING MY EYES IT IS CLEARER   *908 18
ALLURING MY EYES FOR I AM I NOT ALSO DREAM-STUFF   *909 3
EYES WHERE I CAN WATCH THE SWIM OF OLD DREAMS REFLECTED+   *909 7
VISIBLE THERE IN THE CHANGE OF EYES AND THE MOBILE FEAT+   *909 12
THEN GAVE THEE THY DARK EYES O MAN THAT ALL   *916 3
NOW AT LAST THE CLOSED CALYX OPENS FROM OUR TIRED EYES   *916 13
OUR EYES   *918 4
THA CAN STARE AT ME WI' THY FIERCE BLUE EYES   *921 7
AN' IF 'ER CLAWKIN' TIGER'S EYES   *922 14
I DUNNO WHERE HIS EYES WAS A GRET   *923 17
YI' THA'RT A MAN THA'RT A FINE BIG MAN BUT NIVER A BABY+   *925 24
CLOSE YOUR EYES MY LOVE LET ME MAKE YOU BLIND   *931 30
I'LL KISS YOU OVER THE EYES TILL I KISS YOU BLIND   *932 4
YOU'VE DISCOVERED SO MANY BITS WITH YOUR CLEVER EYES   *932 7
LEST HER BRIGHT EYES LIKE SPARROWS SHOULD FLY IN   *934 5
OVER MY EYES AND I WAS BLIND   *934 25
WAS I TILL SHE TOOK HER EYES AWAY   *935 5
SHE SPOKE AND I CLOSED MY EYES   *935 18
LIKE A SUDDEN CHUCKLING OF MUSIC I BADE HER EYES   *936 25
TO MINE I OPENED HER HELPLESS EYES TO CONSULT   *936 26
DEFEAT IN SUCH A BATTLE IN THE DARK OF HER EYES   *936 28
THEIR EYES TO YOUR BRIGHT PLACE AND THEN IN WONDER   *941 3
GOLD GOLD DEEP GOLD HER GLOWING EYES UNFOLD   *941 26
SO SHE CLOSES HER EYES BUT THE AIMLESS BREEZE OF THE WO+   *942 1
I SEE THE WOMAN'S SOUL STEAL IN HER EYES   *943 19

EYES'

MOVED WITH SLOW FEET AND HER EYES' FLAME STEADILY BURNED   156 10
I WILL CATCH IN MY EYES' QUICK NET   180 8
WITHIN HIS EYES' SINCEREST PUPILS THERE   876 36
FOR MYSELF IN MY OWN EYES' LAUGHTER BURNS   *891 31

'E

HOW 'ARD 'E KNOCKS   44 15
SHOUT AN' AX WHAT 'E WANTS   44 18
'E SAYS IS IT ARTHUR HOLLIDAY'S   44 20
'E SAYS TELL YOUR MOTHER AS 'ER MESTER'S   44 22
WHAT OH MY BIRD 'E NEVER SAYS THAT   44 34
WHEER'S 'E HURT THIS TIME LAD   45 9
IT'S A SHAME AS 'E SHOULD BE KNOCKED ABOUT   45 25
LAD NIVER STEPPED TILL 'E GOT IN WITH YOUR LOT   60 1
O' WARMTH AS 'E GOT DOWN THEER TH' REST WOR STONE COLD   61 18
'ER AS 'E LODGES WI'   78 10
OH BUT 'E DROPS 'IS FLAG WHEN 'E SEES ME   79 9
'E UP AN' FIRED 'IS PISTOL   81 7
AN' THEN AWAY 'E RAN   81 8
OF 'IM STOOPIN' TO 'ER YOU'D WONDER 'E COULD   81 19
YIS I KNOWED 'E WOR COURTIN' THEE   81 26
'E ISN'T GOIN' TER MARRY YER   81 31
THOUGH I'LL SEE AS 'E PAYS YOU AN' DOES WHAT'S RIGHT   82 7
HE IS AN' ALL YOU BET 'E IS   434 21
THA KNOWS 'E 'D A WINSOME WAY WI 'IM AN' SHE   *910 24
LIKE BETTER NOR ALL YOUR GOOD AN' 'E WAS ONE   *911 14
OH BUT HE DROPS HIS FLAG WHEN 'E SEES ME   *921 5
YIS I KNOWED 'E WOR COURTIN' THEE   *923 26
FOR 'E ISN'T GOIN' TO MARRY YOU   *924 3
THOUGH I'LL SEE AS 'E PAYS YOU AN' COMES TO THE SCRATCH   *924 11

FACE

OVER MY FACE AND MY HEAD UNTIL   35 24
HIS COMING WITH HIS HAND HE TURNS MY FACE TO HIM   43 26
DO SHUT THY FACE   45 4
I MUST FOLD MY HANDS AND TURN MY FACE TO THE FIRE   47 2
HIS FACE TO LOOK AT ME   51 14
AT HER TATTERED SILENCE AS SHE CROUCHES AND COVERS HER +   54 22
DO YOU SET YOUR FACE AGAINST THE DAUGHTER   55 4
WITH A HARD FACE WHITE-ENAMELLED   56 21
FACE FREED OF THE WAVERING BLAZE   59 8
AN' WARM FOR TH' SMELL COME WAFTIN' TO ME 'ER PUT 'ER F+   61 13
WHEN THE LIGHTNING FLEW ACROSS HER FACE   62 8
HER FACE LAY PALE AGAINST MY BREAST   62 14
POINTING MY EYES IN WRETCHED DEFIANCE WHERE LOVE HIDES +   63 25
AND SKYWARDS HIS FACE IS IMMOBILE EYELIDS ASLANT   66 11
OUT OF EACH FACE STRANGE DARK BEAMS THAT DISQUIET   76 1
AS STOUT AS THE TRUTH MY SIRS AN' 'IS FACE   79 6
YI AN' 'IS FACE GOES WHITE OH YES   79 10
FOR WHENEVER I LOOK THEE I' TH' FACE I S'LL SEE   82 23
HER FACE TOO   82 24
AN' WE'LL BE MARRIED AT TH' REGISTRAR NOW LIFT THY FACE   83 4
LIFT THY FACE AN' LOOK AT ME MAN CANNA TER LOOK AT ME   83 5
SOME DEWDROP MAYBE SPLASHED MY FACE DOWN HERE   87 4
YOUR FACE IN THE MARIGOLD BUNCH TO TOUCH AND CONTRAST Y+   90 10
YOU WITH YOUR FACE ALL RICH LIKE THE SHEEN ON A DOVE   90 18
THE LAST YEAR'S FIRE IS GONE AND YOUR FACE IS ASH   91 4
THAT SETTLED UPON MY FACE AND HANDS TILL IT SEEMED   99 4
TO THE FACE THAT GAZES OUTWARDS WATCHING FOR NIGHT TO W+   103 .2
HER FACE AND FORWARD LEANS TO CATCH THE SIGHT   105 27
OF A LOVER'S FACE   105 28
WITH DULL FACE LEANING TO FACE   106 14
IS YOUR FACE THAT FILLS ME WITH SHAME   112 12
ONLY PROBLEMS WRIT ON THE FACE OF THINGS   118 22
ONCE HIS FACE WAS OPEN LIKE THE SKY   119 24
AND STILL MY BLIND FACE   120 30
TO RAISE MY FACE I DID NOT DARE LOOK UP   122 28
SHE TURNED HER FLUSHED FACE I ME FOR THE GLINT   125 7
SHE HID HER FACE SHE MURMURED BETWEEN HER LIPS   125 19
AND YOU MY LASS WITH YOUR RICH WARM FACE AGLOW   126 28
I SEE YOUR BLANCHED FACE AT MY BREAST AND HIDE   129 13

ON THY FACE AS THA GOT MORE WHITE AN' WAN   138 5
COMES ENDLESSLY KISSING MY FACE AND MY HANDS   144 2
THEIR FACE IN THEIR FLANK SO THESE   144 21
WITH A FACE LIKE A CHICKWEED FLOWER   145 9
INVISIBLE BLINDING MY FACE AND MY EYES WHAT IF IN   147 5
THE FACE OF THE YOUNGEST ROSE   150 16
AND OVER MY FACE THE STRAY FIRE SLIPS   151 8
BUT NEVER THE MOTION HAS A HUMAN FACE   153 7
AND PALE HER IVORY FACE HER EYES WOULD FAIL   156 2
PURE LOOK OF YOUR LAST DEAD FACE WHENCE NOW IS GONE   157 17
AND NOW AT LAST I KISS YOUR PERFECT FACE   157 21
THROUGH THE SHADOWY FACE   161 10
A HAND IS OVER MY FACE   162 17
BETWEEN THE FINGERS THAT COVER MY FACE   162 22
ACROSS MY FACE   165 8
SOMETHING I WANT TO TOUCH I MUST HOLD MY FACE TO THE RA+   180 31
I MUST HOLD MY FACE TO THE WIND AND LET IT EXPLAIN   180 32
WITH HER FACE UPTURNED TO MINE   198 2
WITH HER FACE UPTURNED TO MINE   199 10
HER FACE IS BENT IN THE BITTER STEAM   202 27
SURELY ABOUT HIS SUNBURNT FACE IS SOMETHING   225 17
SHADING HIS FACE IN HIS BLACK FELT HAT   228 6
WITH PALE SHUT FACE NOR EITHER HEARS NOR FEELS   232 27
AND WHEN I LIFT MY FACE IT IS A FLAME THAT GOES UP   233 22
YOU ARE LOVELY YOUR FACE IS SOFT   240 16
WE LAY MOUTH TO MOUTH WITH YOUR FACE   248 25
WITH MY FACE DOWN BURIED BETWEEN HER BREASTS   250 10
MY FACE MAY NOT PLEASE YOU NOR MY STATURE YET IF YOU   251 9
AND THE YOUNG BULL IN THE FIELD WITH HIS WRINKLED SAD F+   255 33
I COULD PUT MY FACE AT LAST BETWEEN HER BREASTS   265 4
ON MY FACE   268 22
AND THE SEA LIKE A BLADE AT THEIR FACE   310 9
AND MAN'S DEFENCELESS BARE FACE   310 27
FACE DOWNWARDS   321 33
DROPPING BACK WITH A SLAP ON THE FACE OF THE FLOOD   337 4
YOUR FACE BABY TORTOISE   353 9
OPENING HER RATHER PRETTY WEDGE OF AN IRON PRISTINE FACE   359 2
HIS WIMPLE HIS BLUNT-PROWED FACE   360 1
PARTING HIS STEEL-TRAP FACE SO SUDDENLY AND SEIZING HER   360 20
AND CLOSING HIS STEEL-TRAP FACE   360 24
HIS STEEL-TRAP STOIC AGELESS HANDSOME FACE   360 25
OPENING ITS CLENCHED FACE FROM HIS OUTSTRETCHED NECK   365 9
WITH THE HALF-VEILED BEAUTIFUL EYES AND THE PENSIVE FACE   379 4
A WOODEN BLANK ON HER FACE   384 24
AND REACHED HER BLACK-STRIPED FACE UP LIKE A SNAKE FAR +   386 24
THERE WAS THE FAINTEST TWIST OF MOCKERY IN EVERY FACE   391 16
AND LIFTING HER BEAUTIFUL SLENDER FACE OH SO MUCH MORE   393 6
LIFTING HER FACE TO NIBBLE AT A ROUND WHITE PEPPERMINT   393 8
HER SENSITIVE LONG PURE-BRED FACE   393 10
LITTLE FACE COMES OUT AS FROM A WINDOW   393 31
ALL YOUR WRINKLED MISERERE CHINESE BLACK LITTLE FACE   396 3
ALL THAT DUST OUT OF YOUR WRINKLED FACE   397 31
BLACKBERRY FACE   398 1
WRINKLED OLD AUNTY'S FACE   400 19
LIFT UP HER FACE   402 2
HER ROUND BRIGHT FACE BRIGHT AS FROST   402 2
AND STRIPES IN THE BRILLIANT FROST OF HER FACE SHARP FI+   402 4
DARK KEEN FINE RAYS IN THE BRILLIANT FROST OF HER FACE   402 6
A BLACK MEMBRANE OVER THE FACE   408 16
OPENING GREAT WINGS IN THE FACE OF THE SHEEP-FACED EWE   414 25
AND LIFT HIS FACE AND SET HIS BREAST   428 18
LET HIM COME HOME TO A BIT OF MORAL DIFFICULTY LET LIFE+   431 8
BRUSH OVER MY FACE AS HE GOES   438 12
WITH SUN IN HIS FACE SO THAT A WOMAN CANNOT BUT OPEN   526 4
MEANING SOUR MAKE YOU PULL A FACE AFTER   530 19
OFF THE FACE OF THE EARTH   533 28
THE FILM FACE OF RUDOLF VALENTINO   538 2
THAT THE FACE IS NOT ONLY   562 20
THEY NIBBLE THE FACE OF THE EARTH TO A DESERT   606 20
AND DEMOS SERVES LIFE AS IT GLEAMS ON THE FACE OF THE F+   650 2
NOT A BOSS BUT THE GLEAM OF LIFE ON THE FACE OF A MAN   650 15
HARDLY EVER NOW HAS A HUMAN FACE   656 12
EVEN FROM THE FACE OF THE CHILDREN NOW   656 15
AND LIFTED HIS FACE UP WITH BLUE EYES LOOKING AT THE EL+   672 9
THOUGHT IS GAZING ON TO THE FACE OF LIFE AND READING WH+   673 12
HIS FACE IS LIKE THE RED LION   684 15
SHE LEANS FORWARD HER SMOOTH PALE FACE   731 10
AND ALL THE TIME HIS HANDSOME SWARTHY RED FACE   734 17
HAVE LENT YOU VOICE NOR SPOKEN OF THE FACE   737 21
AND LET THE DARK BE SOUNDLESS WITHOUT FACE   738 3
TO THE TRENCHES I SEE AGAIN A FACE WITH BLUE EYES   742 6
A BLANCHED FACE FIXED AND AGONIZED   742 7
ANOTHER TRIUMPH ON THE FACE OF EARTH   746 4
SHE WEPT BITTERLY HIDING HER FACE IN HER KERCHIEF I SAI+   749 16
YOU NOW AS YOU TURN YOUR FACE TOWARDS THE SKY   750 14
OVER THE FACE OF THE DARK   771 25
WITH YOUR FACE YOU FACE HIM WITH A ROCK   781 31
THE WEAPON OF YOUR FACE   781 33
OH YES YOU FACE THE SUN   782 1
EAGLE WITH EGYPTIAN DARKNESS JUTTING IN FRONT OF YOUR F+   782 27
MY FACE   786 11
AND PUT LIGHT ON YOUR FACE   787 24
GUADALUPE WHOSE FACE IS OVAL   798 8
DO NOT TELL ME MY FACE IS SHINING   802 18
AND THE FOUNTAIN COVERS YOUR FACE FOREVER   809 10
AND YOUR FACE YOUR MOST MARVELLOUSLY ETON-ADONIS FACE   835 20
NO MORE AND HE LAY AT HOME UNUTTERABLE DESPAIR IN HIS F+   859 16
THAT THE TIME-THREADS SPUN ACROSS MY FACE   860 13
HE HAD A SHOVEL AND A BRUSH ON HIS SHOULDER HIS FACE WA+   866 13
AND TERRIBLY STRANGE ARE HIS TEARS THAT ARE WETTING MY +   871 27
ARE YOU LETTING ME GO AND HIDING YOUR FACE TO THE GROUND   871 32
SIEGMUND DEAR WHAT ARE YOU DOING LYING WITH YOUR FACE O+   871 33
LYING RIGID AND SILENT WITH YOUR FACE ON THE SHORT SEA +   871 34
SIEGMUND LIFT UP YOUR FACE AGAIN OFF THE TURF   871 36
AND OVER MY FACE YOUR STRAY FIRE SLIPS   873 18
AND HANDS AND FACE AND BREAST WITH THAT HOT CLOAK   879 10
I RAISE MY FACE SO IT SHALL WREATHE ME   883 13

FACE
  SHY OF YOUR FACE STILL BEND TO WOO   887 15
  AND LIFTS HIS FACE AND LOOKS AT ME   *898 26
  AND LIFTS HIS FACE AND LOOKS AT ME   *902 10
  I COULDNA' SEE HER FACE BUT HER LITTLE NECK SHONE   *910 11
  O' TH' SMELL COME WAFTIN' TO ME 'ER PUT 'ER FACE   *911 29
  WHEN THE LIGHTNING FLEW ACROSS HER FACE   *912 15
  HER FACE LAY THERE BEFORE MY BREAST   *912 20
  ON EACH FACE FOR US TO SCAN   *915 16
  AS STOUT AS THE TRUTH MY SIRS AN' 'IS FACE   *921 2
  YES AN' 'IS FACE GOES WHITE OH YES   *921 6
  FOR WHENEVER I LOOK THEE I' TH' FACE I S'LL SEE   *924 27
  HER FACE TOO   *924 28
  FACE WAS THE FINEST THING THAT IVER   *925 3
  AN' WE'LL BE MARRIED AT TH' REGISTRAR NOW LIFT THY FACE   *925 8
  LIFT THY FACE AN' LOOK AT ME MAN UP AN' LOOK AT ME   *925 9
  HE WATERS OUR FACE WITH TEARS OUR YOUNG FRUITS FILLS WI+   *926 29
  A MUTE NEARLY BEAUTIFUL THING IS THY FACE   *927 28
  IS YOUR FACE THAT FILLS ME WITH SHAME   *929 2
  YOUR FACE TOWARD MY AGONY   *930 19
  ONLY A MEAN ARITHMETIC ON THE FACE OF THINGS   *931 32
  AH AND MY HAIR IS HANGING WET AND BITTER ON MY FACE   *933 31
  TO RAISE MY FACE I DID NOT DARE LOOK UP   *934 4
  SHE TURNED HER FLUSHED FACE TOWARDS ME FOR THE GLINT   *935 23
  SHE HID HER FACE SHE MURMURED BETWEEN HER LIPS   *936 18
  MET AND HER FACE AND MY FACE WERE ROSES   *942 18
  MY FACE BETWEEN HER BREASTS   *946 2
  WITH MY FACE DOWN-BURIED BETWEEN HER BREASTS   *946 8
  BRUSH OVER MY FACE AS HE GOES TO TREAD OUR WEIRD WOMEN   *947 20
  AH IF YOU WANT TO LIVE IN PEACE ON THE FACE OF THE EARTH   *961 5

FACED
  AND WE FACED OUR FIRST MISERIES   248 19
  LET HIM MEET A NEW EMOTION LET HIM BE FACED WITH ANOTHER   431 2
  MY FATHER HAS FACED ALL WEATHERS BUT IT'S BEEN A LIFE   503 30

FACE-REVEALED
  WHEN THEY CAME OUT FACE-REVEALED UNDER HEAVEN FROM   310 11

FACES
  NOW AT LAST WE LIFT OUR FACES AND OUR FACES COME AFLOWER   70 3
  OUR FACES FLOWER FOR A LITTLE HOUR PALE AND UNCERTAIN A+   71 1
  THE RED-GOLD SPOOLS OF THEIR HANDS AND THEIR FACES SWIN+   72 8
  BUT THE FACES OF THE BOYS IN THE BROODING YELLOW LIGHT   75 25
  TO SEE THE CLASS'S LIFTED AND BENDED FACES   90 5
  THE SHROUDED MOTHER OF A NEW IDEA MEN HIDE THEIR FACES   91 26
  OF YOUR SEVERAL FACES I HAD NEVER SEEN   100 21
  THE SPIDERS WITH WHITE FACES THAT SCUTTLE ON THE FLOOR +   112 28
  FACES OF PEOPLE BLOWING ACROSS MY GAZE   116 9
  TWO NAKED FACES ARE SEEN   144 26
  OVER THE PALLOR OF ONLY TWO FACES   145 4
  OVER TWO SHADOWLESS SHAMELESS FACES   146 1
  OF WALKING OVER THE FACES OF MEN LIKE COBBLE-STONES   175 8
  THE FACES OF ALL THE WOMEN AS THEY GO PAST   180 9
  AWAY THEIR PURPLE FACES AND THEIR GOLD   224 25
  AND BLACK-SCARVED FACES OF WOMEN FOLK WISTFULLY   232 22
  OF FEAR AND OF FRIGHTENED FACES   242 21
  ON THE FACES THAT DRIFT BELOW   252 16
  ON THE FACES THAT DRIFT AND BLOW   252 17
  GHOST-FLUX OF FACES THAT HIE   252 23
  ONLY TO BE WILL BE SUCH DELIGHT WE COVER OUR FACES WHEN+   267 32
  LEST OUR FACES BETRAY US TO SOME UNTIMELY FIEND   267 34
  WHAT IS IT THAT FROM THEIR FACES FRESH AS SPRING   270 4
  SUCH FAIR FRESH ALERT FIRST-FLOWER FACES   270 5
  WHAT IS IT THAT FROM THE FACES OF THE FAIR YOUNG WOMEN   270 12
  ABOUT OUR BEWILDERED FACES   271 28
  THEN WHY SHOULD I FEAR THEIR PALE FACES   288 18
  TO ME ALL FACES ARE DARK   288 21
  FAR-OFF KINGS PAINTED THEIR FACES VERMILION AND WERE AL+   303 22
  PELASGIC FACES UNCOVERED   311 16
  AND THEIR FACES ARE DARK AND FAT AND IMPORTANT   388 21
  AND THEN THE DEVIL COMES INTO THEIR FACES   390 3
  FACES DARK AS BLACK RICE GROWING   391 13
  O FACES UPTURNED TO THE GLARE O TROPICAL WONDER WONDER   391 20
  MONKEYS WITH A BLAND GRIN ON OUR FACES   450 17
  AND SEES STRANGE LOOKS ON THE FACES OF MEN   459 27
  LO I SEE FEAR IN THE TWISTED FACES   460 27
  SO THAT'S WHY SO MANY YOUNG MEN HAVE LONG FACES   530 21
  AND HID THEIR FACES FOR VERY SHAME   579 14
  THOUGHT HE MEANT THE FACES OF THE POLICE-COURT OFFICIALS   579 19
  THEN WHEN I SEE THE IRON HOOKED IN THEIR FACES   586 1
  THEIR POOR THEIR FEARFUL FACES   586 2
  CUT THE IRON HOOK OUT OF THEIR FACES THAT MAKES THEM SO   586 4
  WHEN I SEE THE IRON HOOKED INTO THEIR FACES   632 16
  THEIR POOR THEIR FEARFUL FACES   632 17
  TAKE THE IRON HOOK OUT OF THEIR FACES THAT MAKES THEM SO   632 19
  IN THEIR FACES AND MOTION NEVER MECHANICAL IN THEIR LIM+   635 31
  THE GODS ARE THERE BECAUSE OF THE GLEAM ON THE FACES OF+   649 11
  BY THE TRANSMITTED GLEAM FROM THE FACES OF VIVIDER MEN   649 14
  HOLBEIN AND TITIAN AND TINTORET COULD NEVER PAINT FACES+   656 20
  BECAUSE THOSE FACES WERE WINDOWS TO THE STRANGE HORIZON+   656 21
  WHEREAS FACES NOW ARE ONLY HUMAN GRIMACES   656 23
  BECAUSE ALL THE FACES CONTAIN SETS OF EMOTIONAL AND   657 2
  YOU SEE THEM IN GLIMPSES IN THE FACES AND FORMS OF PEOP+   671 23
  OH AND THEIR FACES SCARLET LIKE THE DOLPHIN'S BLOOD   689 5
  AND BEATING THEIR GREAT WINGS IN OUR PANTING FACES   707 5
  AND THEIR GROOMED AND MUSHROOM-LIKE FACES   765 12
  WITH FACES IN SHADOW BUT SMILING   770 11
  AND SEES WHAT HE SEES IN THE FACES OF MEN   771 5
  THE WOMEN WITH LIGHT ON THEIR FACES   771 12
  THE MEN WITH THEIR FACES IN SHADE   771 13
  SO HE BLEW DOWN ON THEM TO BLOW HIS BREATH IN THEIR FAC+   790 24
  AND THE STARS ARE READY WITH STONES TO THROW IN THE FAC+   792 13
  WHO ARE THESE STRANGE FACES IN MEXICO   793 10
  THEIR FACES ARE UGLY YET THEY MAKE WONDERFUL THINGS   794 7
  AND I QUETZALCOATL THE EAGLE OF THE AIR AM BRUSHING YOU+   802 1
  THE HAIR OF NIGHT IS DARK OVER OUR FACES   809 1
  TEARS WRINKLE OUR FACES LIKE RAIN IN THE HOLLY   814 24

FACES
  AND ALL THEIR FACES LIKE BRIGHT FLOWERS AWAKE   872 21
  BUT THE FACES OF THE BOYS IN THE BROODING YELLOW LIGHT   *897 24
  BUT THE FACES OF THE BOYS IN THE BROODING YELLOW LIGHT   *901 1
  NOW AT LAST WE LIFT OUR FACES AND OUR FACES COME AFLOWER   *916 11
  OUR FACES FLOWER FOR A LITTLE HOUR PALE AND UNCERTAIN A+   *917 21
  THE SHROUDED MOTHER OF A NEW IDEA MEN HIDE THEIR FACES   *926 19
  WITH THE LUSTY SOULS OF MY BOYS YET THEY HIDE THEIR FAC+   *926 23
  A CUNNING ALGEBRA .IN THE FACES OF MEN   *932 1
  WORN HER AWAY TO THE QUICK SO SHE FAINTLY FACES   *937 25

FACE'S
  FROM OUT YOUR FACE'S FAIR FORGETFUL CONTOURS   875 2

FACE-TO-FACE
  FIND AN ENEMY EGOIST AND CLASH THE CYMBALS IN FACE-TO-F+   383 17
  AND FEARLESS FACE-TO-FACE AWARENESS OF NOW-NAKED LIFE   667 4

FACE-WEAPON
  THAT DARK FACE-WEAPON TO TEMPER IT WELL   373 34

FACING
  AND RANGE THEMSELVES LIKE GREAT FIERCE SERAPHIM FACING +   695 3
  EAGLE SOUTH-WESTWARD FACING   781 6

FACT
  OUR HEAVEN AS A MATTER OF FACT   265 16
  FACT ON HER MIND   284 11
  SHE GOT THE FACT ON HER MIND AND QUICKLY SEWED FIG-LEAV+   284 12
  AS A MATTER OF FACT WE ARE BETTER THAN WE KNOW   519 10
  WHEN AS A MATTER OF FACT THE THOUGHT OF THIS ENDLESS   519 15
  AS A MATTER OF FACT WHEN THE TINKER LOOKS SO HAPPY   520 23
  AS A MATTER OF FACT THE ONLY CREATURES THAT SEEM TO SUR+   523 21
  AND CAN'T GET USED TO THE FACT   529 2
  I SUPPOSE AS A MATTER OF FACT IT'S GETTING A LITTLE DIF+   532 3
  LIES ARE NOT A QUESTION OF FALSE FACT   654 1
  EVEN THE FACT OF BIRTH EVEN LITTLE CHILDREN   656 19
  AS A MATTER OF FACT WE KNOW NOTHING   676 27
  THE KNOWLEDGE IS WITHIN ME WITHOUT BEING A MATTER OF FA+   677 3
  NONE AT ALL MIND YOU PROGRESS IS A FACT   774 8
  IN FACT A LITTLE BAWDY IS NECESSARY IN EVERY LIFE   844 30
  IN FACT A LITTLE WHORING IS NECESSARY IN EVERY LIFE   845 2
  AS A MATTER OF FACT   *948 28
  IN FACT A LITTLE BAWDY IS NECESSARY IN EVERY LIFE   *952 11
  IN FACT A LITTLE WHORING IS NECESSARY IN EVERY LIFE   *952 14
  IN FACT IT MAY BE THAT A LITTLE SODOMY IS NECESSARY TO +   *952 18
  IN FACT QUITE A LOT OF CHASTITY IS NECESSARY IN LIFE TO+   *952 21
  WHEREAS PURITANISM IS BENT ON SUPPRESSING THE FACT   *953 4
  AND SUPPRESSION OF SUCH FACT LEADS AS WE KNOW DIRECT TO+   *953 5

FACTORIES
  THE FACTORIES ON THE SURREY SIDE   146 28
  THEY SOLD PLATO TO THE SAUSAGE FACTORIES OF UNIVERSITIES   762 26
  FACTORIES   763 5
  FACTORIES AND THE AUTOMOBILES   794 22

FACTORY
  OF THE FACTORY WORLD   586 12
  OH OVER THE FACTORY CITIES THERE SEEMS TO HOVER A DOOM   586 13
  OF THE FACTORY WORLD   632 27
  THEY WILL HEAR FAR FAR AWAY THE LAST FACTORY HOOTER   *954 10

FACTORY-HAND
  SLEEP SLEEP SLEEP CORPSE-BODY FACTORY-HAND SLEEP   584 17
  I KNOW THE UNLIVING FACTORY-HAND LIVING-DEAD MILLIONS   629 26

FADE
  THE HOUSES FADE IN A MELT OF MIST   142 17
  WHERE FLOWERS SPROUT IN THE ACRID HUMUS AND FADE INTO H+   321 11
  LOVE IS LIKE A FLOWER IT MUST FLOWER AND FADE   472 24
  IF IT DOESN'T FADE IT IS NOT A FLOWER   472 25
  AND LOVE LIKE A FLOWER WILL FADE WILL CHANGE INTO SOMET+   476 3
  O FLOWERS THEY FADE BECAUSE THEY ARE MOVING SWIFTLY A   476 6
  FADE AND YET FLOURISH   826 11

FADED
  I MUST LOOK AWAY FROM HIM FOR MY FADED EYES   47 21
  ALL THE FLOWERS ARE FADED FROM THE ASPHALT ISLE IN THE +   71 10
  SINCE THE BELOVED FADED MOTHER THAT SET US ALIGHT   132 17
  FOLK-FLOWERS HAVE FADED MEN HAVE GROWN COLD   814 16
  AND THE FLUSH FADED AND IT CAME DARK I SLEPT STILL IGNO+   860 7
  THE BREATH OF MY DREAM IS FADED FROM OFF THE MIRROR   871 10
  SINCE THE BELOVED FADED MOON THAT SET US ALIGHT   *938 9
  THAT STOOD CLOSE TO THE WALL AND THE FRONT'S FADED SILK+   *940 3

FADES
  THE HOPELESS WINTRY TWILIGHT FADES   142 21
  FROM THE SKY THE LOW TIRED MOON FADES OUT   163 21

FADING
  AND HOVER LIKE A PRESENTIMENT FADING FAINT   53 29
  FIGHT DON'T YOU FEEL YOU'RE FADING   456 10
  WARM OF ME FADING TO WHITE   766 24
  THE STAR THAT WAS FALLING WAS FADING WAS DYING   786 14
  WHOOING AND COOING AND FADING AWAY WITH WONDERFUL   830 24

FADING-OFF
  UNDER THE COLOURED FADING-OFF OF THE SKY   884 32

FAERY
  SOMETHING FAERY AND FINE THE SHUTTLES SLIDING   72 7
  YOUR WESTERN BRUTAL FAERY QUALITY   291 25

FAFNIR
  YOU ARE FOR THAT MOMENT ONE OF THE GODS JESUS OR FAFNIR+   674 4

FAIL
    THE LOSS OF MYSELF TILL DEATH COMES WHO CANNOT FAIL   48   8
    O' TH' P'LICE FORCE WITHOUT FAIL   78 14
    AND PALE HER IVORY FACE HER EYES WOULD FAIL   156   2
    AND WHEN WE FAIL TO TRANSMIT LIFE LIFE FAILS TO FLOW   449   2
    YET YOU FAIL TO FIND THE WOMAN WHEN THERE ARE SO MANY   485 13
    OF THOSE THAT WILL WITHOUT FAIL COME BACK AGAIN   688 14
    WILL SHIRK OR FAIL IN POINT OF HONOUR   775 13
    ONLY KNOW THAT DOING IT YOU FAIL IN POINT OF HONOUR   780 20
    O' TH' P'LICE FORCE WITHOUT FAIL   *920   6
    AS THE MACHINES FAIL AND FINISH   *954   7

FAILED
    HER FORTH FROM THE DARK MY STRENGTH HAS FAILED   106   1
    SO I FAILED TO GIVE YOU THE LAST   111 26
    SINCE THE FIRE HAS FAILED IN ME   112   8
    DESIRE HAS FAILED DESIRE HAS FAILED   507 20
    AND DESIRE HAS FAILED   508   3
    AND I FAILED ENTIRELY TO SEE WHAT HE MEANT   603   6
    FOR HIS MISSION HAD CRUELLY FAILED WHILE HIS PASSIONATE+   859 11
    AND I FAILED IN MY COWARDICE TO GIVE THEE THE LAST   *927 14
    AND MY COURAGE FAILED TO GIVE YOU THE LAST   *928 14
    SINCE THE FIRE HAS FAILED IN ME   *928 28
    AND WHAT I HAVE FAILED IN WHAT I HAVE WRONGED   *946   4

FAILS
    AND WHEN WE FAIL TO TRANSMIT LIFE LIFE FAILS TO FLOW   449   2
    BUT UTTERLY FAILS TO RECOGNISE ANY MORE THE GREY RAT-HO+   640   5

FAILURE
    DARKNESS OF FAILURE WAS IN THEM WITHOUT AVAIL   156   4
    DARK IN INDOMITABLE FAILURE SHE WHO HAD LOST   156   5
    THE NIGHT WAS A FAILURE   204   1
    SUCCESS IS INSANE AND FAILURE IS INSANE   516   3
    IT HAS ALWAYS BEEN A FAILURE   602 18
    SUCCESS FAILURE LOVE CHASTITY DEBAUCHERY MONEY OR SOVIE+   839 19
    THEY ARE TOLLING HIS FAILURE AFTER ALL THESE YEARS TO T+   859   9

FAIN
    OLD QUESTION WITHOUT ANSWER STRANGE AND FAIN   69 27
    POISON IN HIS MOUTH FOR THE SUN IN HIM WOULD FAIN RISE + 348 10

FAINT
    AND HOVER LIKE A PRESENTIMENT FADING FAINT   53 29
    DROP THEIR LEAVES WITH A FAINT SHARP HISS OF CONTEMPT   54 25
    A FAINT SICKENING SCENT OF IRISES   90   1
    YOUR OWN DARK MOUTH WITH THE BRIDAL FAINT LADY-SMOCKS   90 11
    STILL YOU TREMBLE FAINT REPROACH   95 25
    OF FAINT NIGHT-BREATHS DID GO   165   7
    IN FRONT OF THE SOMBRE MOUNTAINS A FAINT LOST RIBBON OF   208 23
    THE FAINT FINE SEETHE IN THE AIR   216   6
    HARDLY A GREENISH LILY WATERY FAINT   286   4
    BESIDE THE INFINITESIMAL FAINT SMEAR OF YOU   334 17
    FIRST FAINT SCREAM   364   1
    THE INEXPRESSIBLE FAINT YELL   365 19
    STRANGE FAINT COITION YELL   366 25
    BUT BRITANNIA TURNED PALE AND BEGAN TO FAINT   577   7
    LONDON'S LILY-LIKE POLICEMEN FAINT   680 17
    WITH WEARINESS FAINT AS FLUFF   757 17
    I WAS FAINT WITH SURPRISE   886 15
    THEY WILL HEAR THE FAINT RENDING OF THE ASPHALT ROADS   *954   8

FAINT-BLOODEDNESS
    FOR I AM SICK OF THEM THEIR FAINT-BLOODEDNESS   271 15

FAINTED
    WHEREIN WE FAINTED LIKE A SMOKE OR DEW   90 30

FAINTEST
    THERE WAS THE FAINTEST TWIST OF MOCKERY IN EVERY FACE   391 16

FAINT-FASHIONED
    FAINT-FASHIONED WONDER WHEREIN LOST WE SPIN   875   4

FAINTLY
    WORN HER AWAY TO THE QUICK SO SHE FAINTLY FARES   131 26
    LIKE A GLOWING BRAZIER FAINTLY BLUE OF FLAME   151 25
    LIKE A GLOWING BRAZIER FAINTLY BLUE OF FLAME   874   4
    WORN HER AWAY TO THE QUICK SO SHE FAINTLY FACES   *937 25

FAIR
    WITH FAIR FLAKES LIGHTING DOWN ON IT BEYOND THE TOWN   76 18
    IS SMOOTH AND FAIR   101   8
    IT WAS SO FAIR THE BRIGHT   165   2
    OF THE IMPENDING BEE THEY WERE FAIR ENOUGH SIGHTS   243 29
    SUCH FAIR FRESH ALERT FIRST-FLOWER FACES   270   5
    WHAT IS IT THAT FROM THE FACES OF THE FAIR YOUNG WOMEN   270 12
    FOR MEN TO SHOOT AT PENNY-A-TIME IN A BOOTH AT A FAIR   272 17
    ONCE GOD WAS ALL NEGROID AS NOW HE IS FAIR   286 16
    AND SIT BESIDE THE STEEL-STRAIGHT ARMS OF YOUR FAIR WOM+ 291   5
    SHE WAS BOUGHT AT GIARDINI FAIR ON THE SANDS FOR SIX HU+ 385   7
    MEN THAT SEEM HARMLESS WOMEN WITH FAIR WORDS   807 26
    FALSE FAIR ONES CANNOT SLIP THROUGH   810   5
    WE WANT TO BE FAIR   829   8
    EVEN IN THE MOST IMMORAL SETS THERE IS STILL THIS DESIR+ 829 20
    SUCH PEARLED ZONES OF FAIR STERILITY   855   1
    SWEET FRAGRANCE OF LOVE AND FEED ME WITH KISSES FAIR   874   7
    FROM OUT YOUR FACE'S FAIR FORGETFUL CONTOURS   875   2
    THE BONNY FLOATING ARK OF THIS FAIR WORLD   876 10
    WITH FAIR FLAKES SETTLING DOWN ON IT BEYOND THE TOWN   *898 12
    WITH FAIR FLAKES SETTLING DOWN ON IT BEYOND THE TOWN   *901 21
    WHILE TH' PARSON WAS PRAYIN' I WATCHES 'ER AN' SHE WOR + *910   1
    AN' 'ER BODY FAIR SHOOK AGAIN   *910 13
    ON THE AIR FOR OUR NOURISHMENT WHO FROM THESE WEAVE FAI+ *938 24

FAIRLY
    MY MIND IF FAIRLY NIMBLE AND IS NOT BLANK   501 18
    JUST BE NICE YOU KNOW OH FAIRLY NICE   660 16
    BUT I'VE HAD SUCH A JOB MY CRUTCHES I FAIRLY DRAGGED TH+ 865 22

FAIRNESS
    WHERE WE CAN LEARN TO FULFIL OUR NEW KNOWLEDGE OF MATER+ 833 23

FAIRY-WIND
    FOR A FAIRY-WIND TO WAKE THEM FROM THEIR SLOTH   *943 13

FAITH
    NAY I PERSIST AND VERY FAITH SHALL KEEP   154 12
    AS FOR OUR FAITH IT WAS THERE   172 11
    SO THAT THE FAITH IN HIS HEART SMILES AGAIN   306   1
    FAITH   306   3
    AND PEOPLE WHO TALK ABOUT FAITH   626   4
    AS IF THERE WAS SAFETY IN NUMBERS EVEN FOR FAITH   626   6
    IN THE FRAGILE SHIP OF COURAGE THE ARK OF FAITH   719   3
    TELL HIM PRAYER IS STRONGER THAN IRON FAITH   754 11
    SCANDALS MAY DESTROY EVERY MAN'S FAITH IN MAN   775   6
    OUR DRAUGHT OF FAITH THAT SENT US ON ANEW   *941 12

FAITHFUL
    TO BE FAITHLESS AND FAITHFUL TOGETHER   199 31
    AND BECOMES THE FAITHFUL SHEEP-DOG OF THE SHEPHERD THIN+ 325   8
    IS MY OWN AS EVER AND FAITHFUL   768   8
    THE OLD COUNTRIES HAVE A PAST TO BE FAITHFUL TO   775 14
    TO BE FAITHFUL TO A TRADITION   775 19
    BUT TO BE FAITHFUL TO SOMETHING THAT HAS NOT YET   775 20
    THAT IS A DIFFICULT THING TO BE FAITHFUL TO   775 27

FAITHFULNESS
    ONE FAITHFULNESS MORE   561 27

FAITHLESS
    TO BE FAITHLESS AND FAITHFUL TOGETHER   199 31

FAKE
    IT'S NOT LIKE THAT YOU KNOW YOU FAKE IT   490   7

FAKED
    AND FAKED LOVE HAS ROTTED OUR MARROW   654   9

FALCON
    LIKE A FALCON 'TIS GOD HAS TAKEN THE VICTIM   239   5
    PEACE COMES FROM BEHIND THE SUN WITH THE PEREGRINE FALC+ 496 15

FALL
    LIKE DROWSY CREATURES THE HOUSES FALL ASLEEP   48 19
    OF BEES THAT VIBRATE WITH REVOLT WHO FALL TO EARTH   73 18
    MY LOVE WHERE IT IS WANTED YET WAIT AWHILE MY FALL   94   7
    THE LOW WORD DON'T I LET THE FLOWER FALL   125 20
    THEN LETS HER BLACK HAIR LOOSE THE DARKNESS FALL   128 33
    TO FALL LIKE A BREATH WITHIN THE BREATHING WIND   134 26
    FLOWERS OF THE BLEEDING-HEART FALL TO THE THROB   137   5
    I WOULD GIVE MY SOUL FOR THE HOMESTEAD TO FALL WITH ME + 160   3
    FALL ALL THE FRUITS MOST BITTERLY INTO EARTH   160 15
    IS LOST SINCE WE FALL APART   163   6
    THAT FALL FOR EVER KNOWING NONE   164 15
    THE HOURS HAVE CEASED TO FALL AND A STAR COMMANDS   167 17
    FALL ON MY SHALLOW BREAST   194   5
    WOULD FALL AND DARKNESS WOULD COME HURLING HEAVILY DOWN 205 10
    ROSES ARE READY TO FALL RELUCTANT AND LOTH   217 30
    OR THE RIPE ROSE-FRUITS OF THE LUSCIOUS FALL   219 10
    MEN ERE HE FALL   228 32
    IT IS GOOD I CAN MURDER AND MURDER AND SEE THEM FALL   257 30
    AND STRANGE WAYS WHERE I FALL INTO OBLIVION OF UTTERMOST 261   6
    FALL BLACK AND WET   268 15
    PILLARS OF WHITE BRONZE STANDING RIGID LEST THE SKIES F+ 287 16
    WHEN THE SKIES ARE GOING TO FALL FALL THEY WILL   287 20
    TO ME MEN'S FOOTFALLS FALL WITH A DULL SOFT RUMBLE   288 28
    THEY FALL BACK FROM THEE   322 11
    THEY FALL BACK AND LIKE A DRIPPING OF QUICKSILVER TAKIN+ 322 12
    SEEMING TO STUMBLE TO FALL IN AIR   345 15
    FALL SINK LURCH AND ROUND AND ROUND   345 20
    THE ASS WAS THE FIRST OF ALL ANIMALS TO FALL FINALLY IN+ 378 16
    AND OLD THINGS WILL FALL DOWN   482 25
    MY DEARS IF YOU WANT THE SKIES TO FALL   541 23
    AND IDEAS ARE HARD LIKE ACORNS READY TO FALL   608 23
    AS HE BITES AT THE STEMS OF LEAVES IN AUTUMN TO MAKE TH+ 609   3
    AND FALL INTO SHARP SELF-CENTRED SELF-ASSERTION SHARP O+ 616   6
    THEY FALL VICTIM AT ONCE TO THE VENGEANCE OF THE UNFORG+ 616   7
    IF I TRY LOVING THEM I FALL INTO THEIR ROBOT JIG-JIG-JIG 645   7
    AND I FALL ASLEEP WITH THE GODS THE GODS   652 15
    OR THE WHOLE TREE MAY FALL ROTTEN   677 29
    IT IS A FEARFUL THING TO FALL INTO THE HANDS OF THE LIV+ 699 12
    BUT IT IS A MUCH MORE FEARFUL THING TO FALL OUT OF THEM 699 13
    DID LUCIFER FALL THROUGH KNOWLEDGE   699 14
    IT IS NOT EASY TO FALL OUT OF THE HANDS OF THE LIVING G+ 700 17
    MAN CAN BREAK AWAY AND FALL FROM THE HANDS OF GOD   700 23
    IN THE LONG LONG FALL REVOLVING UPON HIMSELF   700 26
    AND THE FALL TO EXTINCTION WHICH CAN NEVER COME   701   3
    ONLY MAN CAN FALL FROM GOD   701 10
    THEN I WILL FALL AND PLANT THE PATHS TO HELL   710 15
    THE GRIM FROST IS AT HAND WHEN THE APPLES WILL FALL   717   3
    I FALL IN SICKNESS AND IN MISERY   727 18
    TO THE NEXT FARM PULLS UP WHERE THE ELDER FLOWERS FALL   732   4
    IN PUTRID AUTUMN ISSUING THROUGH THE FALL   745 22
    THE SKIES FALL   748 27
    STRANGER SOFT ARE THE TEARS THAT FALL   758 15
    TEARS NOW FALL ON WHITE SAND   767   4
    PEEPING THEY WILL LOSE THEIR SIGHT AND LINGERING THEY W+ 799 12
    AND WOMEN FALL FOR THESE LITTLE-BOY MINDS THEY FEEL QUI+ 841 24
    THE HOURS HAVE CEASED TO FALL AND A STAR COMMANDS   *896 22
    THEN TO FALL BACK EXHAUSTED INTO THE UNCONSCIOUS MOLTEN+ *909 28
    THE PLANE-LEAVES FALL THROUGH THE LAMP-LIGHT LIKE TIRED+ *917   9
    THE LOW WORD DON'T I LET THE FLOWER FALL   *936 19

FALL
    THEY WILL HEAR A SILENCE FALL   *954 6
    THEY FALL UPON THE NEW OUTCOMING SOULS WITH RAGE   *958 5

FALLEN
    IN THE TAPPING HASTE OF A FALLEN LEAF   68 21
    MY FALLEN STAR AMONG THE LEAVES MY DEAR   86 24
    THE TRAIN IN RUNNING ACROSS THE WEALD HAS FALLEN INTO A+   88 1
    SOFT SHE LAY AS A SHED FLOWER FALLEN NOR HEARD   155 26
    ARE FALLEN AND THEIR MAUVE-RED PETALS ON THE CLOTH   217 28
    HAS FALLEN DEAD UPON THE NAILS AND HANGS   225 6
    CUNNINGLY BLOWING ON THE FALLEN SPARKS ODDS AND ENDS OF+   271 31
    WINTER-ROTTEN AND FALLEN   273 34
    THE YEAR IS FALLEN OVER-RIPE   284 1
    THE YEAR OF OUR WOMEN IS FALLEN OVER-RIPE   284 3
    THE YEAR OF OUR WOMEN IS FALLEN OVER-RIPE   284 6
    WHEN YOUR WORLD IS IN RUINS UNDER YOUR FALLEN SKIES   289 20
    AND IS FALLEN   322 4
    AND THE COTTON-WOOD LEAVES ARE FALLEN AS GOOD AS FALLEN   403 15
    LIKE A WHITE CHRISTUS FALLEN TO DUST FROM A CROSS   403 22
    BUT WINDS OF HEAVEN ARE MILLS OF GOD TO THE FALLEN LEAV+   615 5
    AND THE THICK FALLEN CROWDS CRACKLE AND CRUMBLE UNDER T+   615 10
    BUT PEOPLE WHO ARE FALLEN FROM THE ORGANIC CONNECTION W+   615 17
    ONCE IT HAS FALLEN OFF   617 2
    IN THE MEN WHO HAVE NEVER FALLEN IN LIFE   648 15
    UNLESS THEY HAVE FALLEN AND BECOME ROBOTS   649 2
    AH THE FALLEN STILLNESS OF GOD AUTUMNUS AND IT IS ONLY +   651 18
    FROM THE HILLS WHERE SNOW MUST HAVE FALLEN THE WIND IS +   696 16
    WHEN I HAVE FALLEN OUT OF YOUR HANDS THE HANDS OF THE L+   699 20
    WHEN THE SELF HAS FALLEN FROM THE HANDS OF GOD   699 23
    EVEN OF THE SOUL FALLEN FROM THE HANDS OF GOD   699 27
    OF THOSE THAT HAVE FALLEN FROM GOD   701 9
    FROM THE FALLEN SELF   716 24
    ALREADY OUR BODIES ARE FALLEN BRUISED BADLY BRUISED   718 3
    FOLDED AS YET AND ALL THE FALLEN LEAVES   745 33
    BUT ALAS THIS IS NOT WHAT I CAME FOR I HAVE FALLEN SHORT   751 8
    THE RAIN OF BLOOD IS FALLEN IS GONE INTO THE EARTH   811 15
    IN THE TAPPING HASTE OF A FALLEN LEAF   *915 5
    ALL THE LEAVES ARE FALLEN AND THE STARLIGHT SHINES THRO+   *917 28
    AND ALL THE FLOWERS ARE FALLEN IN DISGUST   *939 16
    ARE FALLEN AND THEIR MAUVE-RED PETALS ON THE CLOTH   *943 11

FALLING
    FALLING ROUND US NO LONGER DAPPLE   37 27
    THEY ARE RIGHT YET CLAMOROUSLY FALLING   54 4
    MAY-BLOSSOM AND BLUE BIRD'S-EYE FLOWERS FALLING   65 15
    FALLING   65 16
    LIFTING AND FALLING LONG GASPS THROUGH THE SLUICES LIKE+   97 26
    LOW FROM THE ROOF AND THE WET DUST FALLING SOFTLY FROM +   112 26
    AND FALLING WAVES IN HIS ARMS AND THE LOST SOUL'S KISS   130 20
    AND NOW THAT THE SKIES ARE FALLING THE WORLD IS SPOUTIN+   160 1
    AND SCARLET BERRIES FALLING FROM THE BUSH   160 6
    FROM THE CREST OF A FALLING BREAKER   200 23
    THE DARKNESS FALLING THE DARKNESS RISING WITH MUFFLED   205 6
    AT LAST AS YOU STOOD YOUR WHITE GOWN FALLING FROM YOUR   207 1
    LIKE WET AND FALLING ROSES AND I LISTEN   217 21
    A DISARRAY OF FALLING STARS COMING TO NOUGHT   236 23
    IN FALLING SEEDS OF RAIN   268 20
    FALLING I HEAR AGAIN   268 23
    FALLING AS RAIN   269 13
    COMES OUT OF YOUR FALLING THROUGH THE STAGES OF DECAY   280 7
    SEE IF YOUR SKIES AREN'T FALLING   289 16
    AND FALLING BACK   341 14
    PLUNGING FALLING OUT OF THE WEB   345 4
    THAT HE LOST ANY OF HIS BRIGHTNESS IN FALLING   614 14
    AND SINKS DOWN WITH A SWIFT RUSTLE AND A STRANGE FALLING   651 15
    HE LOST ANY OF HIS BRIGHTNESS IN THE FALLING   697 25
    SAVE ME O GOD FROM FALLING INTO THE UNGODLY KNOWLEDGE   699 16
    OF SELF-AWARENESS NOW APART FROM GOD FALLING   701 21
    THE FRIZZLING FALLING FIRE THAT CANNOT GO OUT DROPPING +   701 27
    KNOWING ITSELF KNOWING ITSELF APART FROM GOD FALLING   701 32
    NOW IT IS AUTUMN AND THE FALLING FRUIT   716 16
    THE APPLES FALLING LIKE GREAT DROPS OF DEW   716 20
    I FEEL THE PAIN OF FALLING LEAVES AND STEMS THAT BREAK +   727 7
    RAIN AND A FALLING WORLD   748 19
    FROM FALLING IRON AND HORRIBLE SHELL'S REPORT   751 11
    INTO THE DEAD SEA FALLING   766 21
    AS ONE DYING WITH THE CHARRED RAGS FALLING AWAY   769 13
    I ROSE AGAIN TO SEE A STAR FALLING AND FEEL A BREATH ON   786 10
    THE STAR THAT WAS FALLING WAS FADING WAS DYING   786 14
    A FALLING STAR WAS RUNNING LIKE A WHITE DOG OVER A PLAIN   791 1
    FALLING ROUND US NO LONGER DAPPLE   *892 15
    I SING OF AUTUMN AND THE FALLING FRUIT   *956 24
    THE APPLES FALLING LIKE GREAT DROPS OF DEW   *956 26

FALLOW
    WITH TOO MUCH TINCTURE OF ME INSTEAD OF THE DARK'S DEEP+   92 29
    BUT FORM THE ASH-SCARRED FALLOW   315 33
    LIKE GRAINS OF MUSIC CROSSING THE FERTILE FALLOW   868 23
    THEN DOWN THE BREEZE LIGHT WAFTING O'ER THE FALLOW   *941 23

FALLS
    FALLS ON ME AS I LIE IN DEEP GRASS   49 22
    FALLS AGAIN AND AGAIN ON MY HEART WITH A HEAVY REPROACH   63 3
    WITH A HORSE INSISTENT REQUEST THAT FALLS   64 25
    THE SEED OF LIFE INCARNATE THAT FALLS AND WAKES   89 10
    IN HER VOICE AND A WEAK TEAR FALLS   106 2
    OF CRYSTAL HEAVEN FALLS ONE FULL BLACK DROP   147 26
    THAT FALLS ON YOUR LAP OF MOULD   162 11
    AS THE TRAIN FALLS LEAGUE AFTER LEAGUE   162 15
    WHICH THEN IS IT THAT FALLS FROM ITS PLACE   162 23
    THAT FALLS LIKE A METEORITE   162 26
    THAT FALLS FROM REALITY   163 2
    BEAT AFTER BEAT FALLS SOMBRE AND DULL   164 1
    A DARK BIRD FALLS FROM THE SUN   166 25
    ALWAYS KNEEL IN COURTSHIP TO THE SHELVES IN THE DOORWAY+   180 26
    THAT PERFECT BRIGHT EXPERIENCE NEVER FALLS   193 10
    LIGHTNING FALLS FROM HEAVEN   208 31

FALLS
    WHEN IT FALLS TO THE GROUND   235 6
    AS THE FIRELIGHT FALLS AND LEAPS   238 14
    LIKE A FLAME THAT FALLS OF A SUDDEN   246 26
    LIKE A BELL THAT IS CHIMING EACH STROKE AS A STROKE FAL+   251 12
    WHERE MY SOUL FALLS IN THE LAST THROES OF BOTTOMLESS CO+   322 3
    FROM HIS LEAP AT THE ZENITH IN HER SO IT FALLS JUST SHO+   382 23
    WHEN THE MOON FALLS ON A MAN'S BLOOD   453 13
    AND FALLS BACK DRAWING IN ITS BREATH WITH RAGE   467 14
    WHEN THE RIPE FRUIT FALLS   504 20
    ONCE DISILLUSION FALLS ON LIVING MEN AND THEY FEEL THE   639 19
    ONCE DISILLUSION FALLS ON LIVING MEN AND ILLUSION OF BR+   639 23
    AND BLOODY WATER FALLS UPON THE ROAD   734 8
    WHEN THE WATER OF MALINTZI FALLS   811 22
    AND FALLS WINGLESS BLOOD STREAMING THROUGH ITS YELLOW H+   855 25
    WINROW AFTER WINROW FALLS UNDER THIS FIRST STROKE OF NI+   858 10
    AT YOUR COTTAGE-END IT FALLS BACK AGAIN   885 29
    A RED FLOWER FALLS TO ITS DIM REFLECTION   887 18
    A RED FLOWER FALLS TO ITS RED REFLECTION   887 20

FALSE
    NEW THROB LIKE A STIRRING UNDER THE FALSE DAWN THAT PRE+   292 34
    FROM ALL THE FALSE FELICITY   469 25
    FROM AIRS AND FROM FALSE MODESTY   470 8
    ALREADY THE WHITENESS OF FALSE DAWN IS ON MY INNER OCEAN   513 13
    AND WHOEVER WALKS A MILE FULL OF FALSE SYMPATHY   653 1
    LIES ARE NOT A QUESTION OF FALSE FACT   654 1
    BUT OF FALSE FEELING AND PERVERTED JUSTICE   654 2
    FROM THE LIARS FROM THE THIEVES FROM THE FALSE AND TREA+   807 16
    FALSE FAIR ONES CANNOT SLIP THROUGH   810 5

FALSITY
    THROUGH THE DEAD WEED OF A LIFE-TIME'S FALSITY   *959 8

FALTER
    I HOLD HER STILL AND WAIT TILL THE BELL SHALL FALTER   859 1

FALTERING
    ONE NOTICES MEN HERE AND THERE GOING HESITATINGLY FALTE+   665 23
    AND THE LITTLE SHIP WINGS HOME FALTERING AND LAPSING   720 14
    WITH THIS APPEARANCE OF FALTERING   750 5
    WAKES FROM THE HUM FALTERING ABOUT A NOUN   *898 3
    WAKES FROM THE HUM FALTERING ABOUT A NOUN   *901 12

FALTERS
    FALTERS A STATEMENT ABOUT AN ABSTRACT NOUN   76 8
    AND FALTERS A FEW SHORT STEPS ACROSS THE LAKE   230 6

FAME
    AND DARKENING MY ETERNAL FAME   *929 5
    FAME   *950 15

FAMILY
    A WELL-TO-DO FAMILY   325 18
    THOUGH FAMILY FEELING THERE IS NONE NOT EVEN THE BEGINN+ 357 23
    WE'RE ALL IN IT ALL MY FAMILY   668 20
    AND THE ROOTS OF THE GREAT TREE OF FAMILY AND THE FORES+ *951 13

FAMOUS
    YET THE HUSBAND WAS MOST BRILLIANT AND FAMOUS   842 25

FAN
    DOES HE FAN GREAT WINGS ABOVE THE PRAIRIE LIKE A HOVERI+ 374 16
    WINDS OF HEAVEN FAN THE LEAVES OF THE TREE LIKE FLAMES + 615 4
    SHE FANNED HERSELF WITH A VIOLET FAN   617 19
    SISTERS THE SEARCHLIGHT'S SWINGING FAN   758 13

FANCIFUL
    NAKED EXCEPT FOR FANCIFUL LONG SHOES   296 20

FANCY
    THINKING THIS DOG SURE HAS TAKEN A FANCY TO ME   398 20
    DO WE REALLY WELL I NEVER FANCY NOW FANCY THAT   773 24
    DARTING HIS LIGHT PUNT WITH THE QUICK-SHIFTING FANCY OF+ 867 25

FANGED
    DARK GREEN GLOSSY FANGED LEAVES   383 31
    DARK GREEN GLOSSY FANGED LEAVES   387 2
    VERY HANDSOME AND SOME PURE YELLOW FANGED LEAVES   387 3

FANGS
    MY FINGERS TILL ITS HEAD LAY BACK ITS FANGS   125 14
    UGH HOW I LOVE ITS FANGS OF PERFECT RAGE   315 18
    HAVE LONG FANGS   405 14
    TO FEAR A FEW FANGS   405 17
    FANGS AND CLAWS AND TALONS AND BEAKS AND HAWK-EYES   409 29
    OR TEAR ME WITH THE FANGS OF DISAPPOINTMENT   604 11
    I BOUND THE BRIGHT FANGS OF THE SUN   786 23
    MY FINGERS TILL ITS HEAD GAPED BACK ITS FANGS   *936 13

FANNED
    IT WOULD BE NO WONDER IF GREAT WINGS LIKE FLAMES FANNED+ 326 12
    SHE FANNED HERSELF WITH A VIOLET FAN   617 19

FANNING
    LIFTS HIM FANNING IN THE HIGH EMPYREAN   782 23
    I AM FANNING YOUR BREASTS WITH MY BREATH   802 3

FANS
    FANS OUT YOUR PETALS FOR EXCESS OF FLAME   219 3
    ON FANS OF UNSUSPECTED TISSUE LIKE BATS   322 17
    FANS A FLAME   802 21

FANTASIES
    AND RUTHLESSLY STRANGLED OFF THE FANTASIES   141 28
    JUST FANTASIES OF SELF-IMPORTANCE   603 23

FANTASTIC
    BLACK BIRDS WHOSE SONGS ARE UNUTTERABLE SPINNING FANTAS+   *918 14

FARAGLIONI
    LIKE THE FULLNESS OF OCEAN ROUND MY FARAGLIONI   835 34

FARES
    WORN HER AWAY TO THE QUICK SO SHE FAINTLY FARES   131 26
    SHE FARES IN THE STARK IMMORTAL   199 13
    HOW SHE FARES AT HER END   748 16

FAREWELL
    SHE'S ONLY THE NEARER TO THE INEVITABLE FAREWELL   85 14
    IS THE FAREWELL SAID   102 2
    I AM DAZED WITH THE FAREWELL   108 11
    A KISS AND A SPASM OF FAREWELL A MOMENT'S ORGASM OF   280 27
    ORPHIC FAREWELL AND FAREWELL AND FAREWELL   281 27
    IN FAREWELL   695 30
    FAREWELL FAREWELL LOST SOUL   696 26
    AND IT IS TIME TO GO TO BID FAREWELL   716 22
    AND BID FAREWELL OF STATELY TRAVELLERS   740 20
    WHEN IN THE MORNING I ROSE TO DEPART MY LOVE CAME TO SA+   749 17
    FAREWELL FAREWELL DESPEDIDA   797 17
    FAREWELL LET ALL BE FORGOTTEN   798 25
    JESUS THE SON OF GOD BIDS YOU FAREWELL   798 29
    MARY THE MOTHER OF GOD BIDS YOU FAREWELL   798 30
    LIFT YOUR HAND SAY FAREWELL SAY WELCOME   803 14
    LIFT YOUR HAND SAY FAREWELL SAY WELCOME   803 19

FAREWELLS
    FROM HER FLUTTERED FAREWELLS AT THE APPROACH OF MY WELL+   865 14

FAR-GONE
    WATCH SILENT THE LOOMING OF THE HOARY FAR-GONE AGES   426 21

FARM
    SAUNTERS A MAN FROM THE FARM BELOW   42 20
    CLANGING AT THE FARM SUCH BEWILDERMENT   220 13
    TO THE NEXT FARM PULLS UP WHERE THE ELDER FLOWERS FALL   732 4
    IT GONE BY OUR FARM TO THE MOUNTAINS THAT STAND BACK BL+   732 7
    ON IF HE KNEW THAT I WAS AT THIS FARM   733 14

FARMER
    EVEN THE STUPIDEST FARMER GATHERS HIS HAY IN BLOOM IN   587 8

FARMERS
    ALL THE LITTLE BOYS WHOSE FATHERS WERE COLLIERS OR FARM+   774 1
    HE PREACHED TO THE STOLID FARMERS TILL AT LAST HE COULD+   859 15

FARM-IMPLEMENTS
    TO SUPPLY THEM WITH FARM-IMPLEMENTS   778 21

FARM-MACHINERY
    EXCELLENT FARM-MACHINERY   778 30

FAR-OFF
    AS WITH THOUGHTS THAT FLASH AND CRACKLE IN FAR-OFF MALI+   97 16
    FAR-OFF THE LILY-STATUES STAND WHITE-RANKED IN THE GARD+   159 13
    FAR-OFF KINGS PAINTED THEIR FACES VERMILION AND WERE AL+   303 22
    FAR-OFF MEDITERRANEAN MORNINGS   311 15
    TINY FROM UNDER THE VERY EDGE OF THE FARTHEST FAR-OFF   366 27
    STANDING WITHOUT FEET ON THE RIM OF THE FAR-OFF MESA   403 5
    FAR-OFF   435 21
    YOU'LL HAVE TO PRAY TO THE FAR-OFF GODS   472 5
    BUT IT IS FAR-OFF FOAM   687 8
    AND KISS OF THE FAR-OFF LINGERING LADY WHO LOOKS OVER T+   695 31
    FAR-OFF FAR-OFF IN THE HYACINTH AGES   814 4
    IN THE FAR-OFF LABOUR OF MEN IN THE FIELD   *915 2

FAR-OUT
    YET EVEN WASTE GREY FORESHORES AND SORRY FAR-OUT   509 17

FAR-REACHING
    A KEEN FAR-REACHING CURIOUS MIND CYNICAL WITH LITTLE-BO+   841 22

FARTHER
    FARTHER DOWN THE VALLEY THE CLUSTERED TOMBSTONES RECEDE   102 29
    AS FARTHER OFF THE SCYTHE OF NIGHT IS SWUNG   135 11
    ENTERED FARTHER   351 3
    BUT FARTHER OFF MUCH FARTHER   *946 20

FARTHEST
    WHILE NORTH OF THEM ALL AT THE FARTHEST ENDS STANDS ONE+   57 11
    TINY FROM UNDER THE VERY EDGE OF THE FARTHEST FAR-OFF   366 27
    OVER THE SEA OVER THE FARTHEST SEA   *959 3

FARVER
    WE AIN'T GOT NO FARVER ONLY A MOVVER AN' SHE 'AS TER GO   866 20

FASCINATING
    IN THE BIG MIRROR AT HIS OWN FASCINATING SHADOW   604 5

FASCINATION
    AT WHICH IN THE INTENSE STILL NOON I STARED WITH FASCIN+   351 17
    THE FASCINATION OF THE RESTLESS CREATOR THROUGH THE MES+ *906 23
    THE FASCINATION OF THE QUICK RESTLESS CREATOR MOVING TH+ *908 19
    OH THE GREAT MYSTERY AND FASCINATION OF THE UNSEEN SHAP+ *909 13

FASHION
    AND SWEAT OF LABOUR AND THE MEANEST FASHION   89 13
    TILL NAKED FOR HER IN THE FINEST FASHION   113 7

FAST
    I SAW HER STEP TO THE KERB AND FAST   122 3
    LOOKING EARNESTLY UNDER THE DARK UMBRELLAS HELD FAST   180 12
    COMING UP ON FIERCE LITTLE LEGS TEARING FAST TO CATCH U+ 397 15
    BUT SOMETIMES WE RUN AHEAD TOO FAST   543 16
    AND THE MACHINE HAS ENTANGLED THE BRAIN AND GOT IT FAST   629 7

FAST
    HAS THE IRON GOT THEM FAST   631 28
    AND FLY FAST AWAY   883 17
    INTO MUD THE SPACE FAST SHRINKS IN THE BUILDER'S HANDS   *896 11

FASTER
    AND THE WATER RUNS AND RUNS FASTER RUNS FASTER   34 4
    WHICH GET US AHEAD SO MUCH FASTER THAN OUR FEET COULD   543 21

FASTIDIOUS
    AND DANGLE IN A LAST FASTIDIOUS FINE DELIGHT   667 15

FASTNESS
    THINK OF IT FROM THE IRON FASTNESS   306 14

FAT
    NOR FRET THY FAT   83 21
    AND THEIR FACES ARE DARK AND FAT AND IMPORTANT   388 21
    THE REPULSIVE LIVING FAT DEAD   441 35
    THEIR GUTS WITH A CERTAIN FAT AND OFTEN   460 15
    THEIR GUTS WITH A CERTAIN FAT AND OFTEN   460 19
    YET LIVING ON THE FAT OF THE LAND   535 20
    AND WAS IMMENSELY FLATTERED WHEN ONE OF THE FAT LITTLE   618 18
    A MAGISTRATE AND SIX FAT SMALLER FRY   633 15
    SIX FAT SMALLER BOBBIES ARE THE INQUISITORS MINOR   633 16
    IF YOU POINT ME TO THAT FAT MONEY-SMELLING MAN IN A MOT+ 645 11
    THE FOOD OF THE NORTH TASTES TOO MUCH OF THE FAT   652 19
    FAT OF THE PIG   652 21
    NOT WITH THE FAT OF THE PIG   652 25
    OF FAT FROM   762 12
    THE SMOOTHED-FACED FAT-HAMMED FUNGUSSY FAT ONE   765 24

FATAL
    INSTEAD OF WHICH THE SILENT FATAL EMISSION FROM THAT PA+ 390 25

FATALLY
    WE HAVE BECOME FATALLY SELF-CONSCIOUS FATALLY SELF-IMPO+ 674 9

FATA MORGANA
    FOR THE MOON LIKE A FATA MORGANA WILL LEAN   748 1
    WE SHALL STRIP TO THE FATA MORGANA THEN   748 9

FAT-ARSED
    SUCH BLOOMIN' FAT-ARSED DOOL-OWLS   553 7

FATE
    THIS FATE OF MINE   59 32
    FORGETTING TILL FATE SHALL DELETE   146 26
    TAKE THEM AWAY FROM THEIR VENTURE BEFORE FATE WRESTS   147 16
    THE HOME OF MY FATHERS THE PLACE THAT IS MINE MY FATE A+ 159 29
    SURELY YOU TOOK YOUR FATE   167 23
    YOU HAVE SURELY ACHIEVED YOUR FATE   168 29
    WHEREIN WE CIRCLE ON OUR FATE   236 19
    IN ME OR A FLEA-BITTEN FATE   237 8
    GOGGLING OBSCENITIES IF THAT'S YOU AND YOUR FATE WHY TH+ 463 17
    TO ITS FEARFUL FATE   632 9
    LIKE SCREAMING BIRDS OF FATE   741 12

FATED
    THEY ARE CHOSEN AH THEY ARE FATED   228 25
    AND THE HUMAN SOUL IS FATED TO WIDE-EYED RESPONSIBILITY   347 2

FAT-EYED
    AND LOOK AT THE FAT-EYED LOT   556 22

FAT-FACED
    SMASH THEM UP THE SMOOTHED-FACED FAT-FACED PLAUSIBLES   765 29

FAT-HAMMED
    THE SMOOTHED-FACED FAT-HAMMED FUNGUSSY FAT ONE   765 24

FATHER
    AND THE THOUGHT OF THE LIPLESS VOICE OF THE FATHER SHAK+ 48 11
    IF MY FATHER CAN GET THEE A JOB ON T' BANK SAY THA'RT S+ 83 17
    MY FATHER SUDDENLY DIED IN THE HARVESTING CORN   173 1
    AND AT THE FOOT OF A GRAVE A FATHER STANDS   232 24
    I WAS A FATHER AND A BEGETTER OF CHILDREN   257 20
    LUKE THE BULL THE FATHER OF SUBSTANCE THE PROVIDENCE BU+ 327 16
    FATHER AND MOTHER   357 16
    AND DO YOU AWAIT US WATTLED FATHER WESTWARD   371 24
    OLD FATHER   380 20
    HAIRY HORRID GOD THE FATHER IN A WILLIAM BLAKE   385 20
    TOUCH ME CAREFULLY OLD FATHER   405 1
    I HAVE NO HOME OLD FATHER   405 5
    FATHER YOU ARE NOT ASKED   405 8
    I'M THE RED WOLF SAYS THE DARK OLD FATHER   405 31
    WHERE THE FATHER OF ALL THINGS SWIMS IN A MIST OF ATOMS   438 4
    SO YOU THINK SCIENTIFIC MAN YOU'LL BE FATHER OF YOUR OWN 438 18
    TO THE PROUD FATHER AND SHOWS ITS LITTLE WEBBED GREENISH 438 28
    AND WHEN THE FATHER SAYS THIS IS NONE OF MINE   439 4
    THEY FIND HE HAS SOLD THEM TO HIS FATHER   442 13
    MANSIONS OF MY FATHER   442 16
    MY FATHER WAS A WORKING MAN   490 9
    MY FATHER HAS FACED ALL WEATHERS BUT IT'S BEEN A LIFE   503 30
    THE FATHER EATS THE PEAR AND THE SON'S TEETH ARE SET ON+ 530 22
    I WANT MY SON TO BE SOMETHING BETTER THAN HIS FATHER WAS 773 26
    AND HIS FATHER WATCHING HIM   782 31
    THE OLD FATHER OF LIFE AT THE HEART OF THE WORLD LIFE-F+ 783 2
    INTO THE EYE OF THE FATHER   786 26
    NO MAN KNOWS MY FATHER AND I KNOW HIM NOT   799 15
    MY FATHER IS DEEP WITHIN THE DEEPS WHENCE HE SENT ME FO+ 799 16
    WHICH IS MY FATHER WHOM I KNOW NOT   799 24
    FROM THE PLACE WHICH I CALL MY FATHER   801 3
    THERE WILL ALWAYS BE A FATHER OF ALL THINGS IN SOME SHA+ 840 7
    BUT THE FATHER OF ALL THINGS IS HE WHO MAKES US EAGER   840 11
    HE HE'S IN PRISON MY FATHER YES SIR ONE AND SIX WITH MY+ 866 11
    THE WHITE DOG NIPPED THE MOTHER RAT THE FATHER RAT BESI+ *933 7
    AN' A MAN AN' A FATHER THA'LT HA'E TO BE   *944 15

FATHER
    AND RELIGION NOTHING WITHOUT THE FATHER OF ALL THINGS   *946 12
    AND THE FATHER WAS ONCE GREY-BEARDED AND FULMINATIVE   *946 14
    THE FATHER OF ALL THINGS SWIMS IN THE VAST DUSK OF ALL +   *947 17
    DON'T YOU THINK LITTLE MAN YOU'LL BE FATHER OF HUMAN BA+   *947 23

FATHER-BIRD
    ARE YOU THE FATHER-BIRD   782 32

FATHERHOOD
    NOR YET THAT PALE YOUNG MAN AFRAID OF FATHERHOOD   437 2
    AND ONCE HE WAS A YOUNG MAN PALE AND REFUSING FATHERHOOD   *946 15
    FATHERHOOD   *946 22

FATHERING
    FATHERING ENDLESS TEN-DOLLAR GOLDEN EGGS   414 12

FATHERLESS
    FATHERLESS MOTHERLESS BROTHERLESS SISTERLESS   357 24

FATHERLINESS
    BEING TOUCHED WITH LOVE AND DEVOID OF FATHERLINESS   357 15

FATHERLY
    HE IS NOT FATHERLY LIKE THE BULL MASSIVE PROVIDENCE OF +   382 8
    OR EVEN THE SLY GOLD SERPENT FATHERLY LIFTED HIS HEAD O+   437 18
    BEFORE THE GOLDEN FATHERLY SERPENT LIFTED HIS HEAD OFF +   *946 27

FATHER NEPTUNE
    FATHER NEPTUNE ONE DAY TO FREEDOM DID SAY   574 11
    SO FATHER NEPTUNE WALKED UP THE SHORE   574 19

FATHERS
    THE HOME OF MY FATHERS THE PLACE THAT IS MINE MY FATE A+   159 29
    ALL THE LITTLE BOYS WHOSE FATHERS WERE COLLIERS OR FARM+   774 1
    WHOSE FATHERS WERE SCHOOL-MASTERS OR BANK-CLERKS   774 4
    BE WELL IF THESE OLD FATHERS ABANDONED THEIR FOOLISH   777 30
    THAT THE OLD DARK FATHERS SHOULD NOT TRUST THESE ARTISTS   778 4
    WHICH IS VERY ODD BEING THE EXACT REVERSE OF THEIR FATH+   829 14

FATHER'S
    WHEN I WAS A CHILD I LOVED MY FATHER'S RIDING-WHIP   255 1

FATHERS'
    OUR FATHERS' AND GRANDFATHERS' IDEAL   831 13

FATHOM
    THE POOL FOR MY LIMBS TO FATHOM MY SOUL'S LAST SCHOOL   161 17
    IT WAS SOMETHING I NEVER COULD FATHOM   555 17
    THE DEEPS THAT LIFE CANNOT FATHOM   811 6

FATHOM-FLICKERING
    I CAN NO MORE DENY THE BAT-WINGS OF MY FATHOM-FLICKERIN+   323 2

FATHOMLESS
    INTO THE WOMAN'S FERTILE FATHOMLESS LAP   172 7
    BLESSED ARE THE PURE IN HEART AND THE FATHOMLESS IN BRI+   314 16
    INTO THE FATHOMLESS BOTTOMLESS PIT   322 2
    HOW FULL HER EYES ARE LIKE THE FULL FATHOMLESS SHINING +   394 6
    OUT OF FATHOMLESS SKIES AND SEAS   438 32
    IN THE CLASP AND THE SOFT WILD CLUTCH OF A SHE-WHALE'S +   694 19
    FATHOMLESS FATHOMLESS SELF-CONSCIOUSNESS WRIGGLING   701 22
    TO THE FATHOMLESS DEEPS AHEAD FAR FAR FROM THE GREY SHO+   723 24
    AMONG THE SPLENDOUR OF BLACK-BLUE TORCHES SHEDDING FATH+   *956 19
    FATHOMLESS DEEP AHEAD FAR FAR FROM THE GREY SHORES   *959 1

FATHOMLESSLY
    SO FATHOMLESSLY BLACK   454 6

FATIGUE
    CLAY-COLOURED WHO ROLL IN FATIGUE   162 14

FATNESS
    WITH SLEEKNESS AND FATNESS   826 15

FATTEN
    AND DEEP IN CENTRAL PARK I'LL FATTEN   815 15

FATTENING
    EVERY LORDLY TUPPENNY FOREIGNER FROM THE HOTELS FATTENI+   312 23

FATUITY
    YOU REALISE THE FATUITY OF SAVING UP AGAINST POSSIBLE L+   614 4

FAULT
    THAT YOUNG AN' A' THE FAULT OF DRINK   60 25
    ALL RIGHT ALL RIGHT IT'S MY FAULT BUT LET   61 1
    BUT THE REAL FAULT LIES IN THE EGO-BOUND CONDITION OF   475 24
    AS IF IT'S MY FAULT THAT THE OLD GIRL IS SEVENTY-SEVEN   502 22
    POLITICIANS MAY BE BAD INDUSTRIAL MAGNATES MAY BE AT FA+   775 5

FAULTLESSLY
    FAULTLESSLY NOW IT'S TOO LATE   167 24

FAVOURITE
    BUT THE WOMEN ARE MY FAVOURITE VESSELS OF WRATH   541 9
    BECAUSE FLAT-FOOT IS THE FAVOURITE OF THE WHITE LEGHORN+   761 17

FAWN
    LEAVING HER FAWN   222 4
    FAWN BEFORE THEM AND LOVE THEM AS IF THEY WERE THE ONES   399 14
    WHERE THE LONG FAWN FORESHORES LIE   746 21

FAWNINGS
    DAY WEARIES ME WITH ITS OSTENTATION AND FAWNINGS   193 19

FEAR
    OF FEAR   58 7
    PALE LOVE LOST IN A THAW OF FEAR   62 15
    MY FEAR IN ACCEPTING THE PORTENT THE TRAIN CAN NOW   88 27
    AND I ROSE IN FEAR NEEDING YOU FEARFULLY   99 6
    REMINISCENT OF SLINKING BEASTS MAKE ME FEAR   107 6
    THEIR FEAR THEIR SHAME THEIR JOY THAT UNDERLIES   125 28
    UNHOLY FEAR IN MY ESSENCE YOU WOULD PAUSE TO   131 4
    STARTLING A FEAR UNSPEAKABLE AS THE SHUDDERING WIND   140 17
    WHY DOES MY SOUL CONTRACT WITH UNNATURAL FEAR   140 21
    AND FEAR IS A PLASH OF WINGS   150 21
    NO SOUND FROM THE STRANGERS THE PLACE IS DARK AND FEAR   173 3
    STRONGER THAN FEAR OR DESTRUCTIVE MOTHER-LOVE IT STOOD   207 12
    FOR FEAR OF THE LACK IN DEATH   214 22
    I WALK IN FEAR OF YOU   215 16
    FEAR WAS ABROAD WE WHISPERED NO ONE KNOWS US   217 6
    DOES NOT MY FEAR COVER HER FEAR   222 21
    OF FEAR AND OF FRIGHTENED FACES   242 21
    THREE SIDES SET ON ME SPACE AND FEAR BUT THE FOURTH SIDE 249 10
    THE FEAR OF HUNGER IS MOLOCH BELIAL THE HORRIBLE GOD   263 6
    IT IS A FEARFUL THING TO BE DOMINATED BY THE FEAR OF HU+ 263 7
    THE FEAR OF THE WANT OF THESE THINGS SEEMS TO BE QUITE + 263 12
    WHEN A MAN IS RICH HE LOSES AT LAST THE HUNGER FEAR   265 2
    ON THE THRESHOLD OF SPRING I FEAR I SHALL DIE   273 29
    THEN WHY SHOULD I FEAR THEIR PALE FACES   288 18
    FEAR ALSO   336 12
    THEN GAY FEAR THAT TURNS THE TAIL SPRIGHTLY FROM A SHAD+ 336 18
    FOOD AND FEAR AND JOIE DE VIVRE   336 19
    JOIE DE VIVRE AND FEAR AND FOOD   336 22
    YET BLIND WITH FRENZY WITH CLUTTERED FEAR   343 15
    FEAR CRAVEN IN HIS TAIL   347 11
    AND FEAR IN THE SMOKY WHITES OF YOUR EYES YOU NIGGER   400 26
    MEN THE ONLY ANIMAL IN THE WORLD TO FEAR   401 6
    TO FEAR A FEW FANGS   405 17
    FROM FEAR   407 17
    SO HE LAUGHS FROM FEAR PURE FEAR IN THE GRIP OF THE SLE+ 407 22
    THEN CAME THE HUSH AGAIN LIKE A HUSH OF FEAR   444 23
    LO I SEE FEAR IN THE TWISTED FACES   460 27
    OF MEN THEY CLENCH FEAR IN THEIR FISTS   460 28
    I HAVE CONQUERED THE FEAR OF DEATH   460 30
    BUT THE FEAR OF LIFE IS STILL HERE I AM BRAVE   460 31
    YET I FEAR MY OWN BREATH   460 32
    NOW I MUST CONQUER THE FEAR OF LIFE   461 1
    AND IGNOBLE HASTE FOR FEAR OF BEING LATE   484 7
    AND THAT FEAR CAN BECOME A DELIRIUM   487 2
    IT IS FEAR OF MY MONEY-MAD FELLOW-MAN   487 3
    MEN ARE MADE MEAN BY FEAR AND A SYSTEM OF GRAB   520 28
    FEAR   522 11
    IT IS THE PENALTY OF FEAR AND MEANNESS BEING MEANER THAN 522 22
    OUT OF FEAR OF THE UNKNOWN ENEMY   529 19
    SO PERHAPS THEY TOO DIED OUT FROM FEAR   529 20
    SNAPPING OUT OF FEAR   535 18
    AND WHO DARE NOT DIE FOR FEAR THEY SHOULD BE NOTHING AT+ 613 4
    AND THEY FEAR THE COME-BACK   626 3
    TO FLOWER FREE OF FEAR   627 4
    HENCE THE RIDICULOUS WAY THEY RUSH IN WHERE ANGELS FEAR+ 665 20
    A THING OF FEAR   747 30
    LOVE ME AND PUT ME OUT OF FEAR   752 7
    FLUTTER OF FEAR IN THE NERVES   767 17
    AND I WOKE WONDERING WHO TOUCHED ME WITH SUCH FEAR AND + 860 10
    HER NAKED SOUL OF FEAR   880 30
    TAKE THE LANTERN AND WATCH THE SOW FOR FEAR SHE GRAB HE+ *892 24
    I COME AWAY FOR FEAR SHE SHOULD SEE   *910 22
    OF MY ARMS INERT WITH DREAD WILTED IN FEAR OF MY KISS   *912 18
    PALE LOVE LOST IN A SNOW OF FEAR   *912 21
    DO YOU FEAR I SHALL SWINDLE YOU   *932 11
    THEIR FEAR THEIR SHAME THEIR JOY THAT UNDERLIES   *936 27
    IT IS DEATH I FEAR SO MUCH IT IS NOT THE DEAD   *938 27
    THREE SIDES SET ON ME SPACE AND FEAR BUT THE FOURTH SID+ *945 22
    I NEED NOT GLANCE OVER MY SHOULDER IN FEAR OF THE TERRO+ *945 25
    I NEED NOT LOOK AFTER MY SOUL BEGUILE MY FEAR   *945 27
    DOOR ON THE LATCH AND SHUT MYSELF IN SHUT OUT FEAR   *945 29

FEARED
    SPEAK UP YOU NEDN'T BE FEARED   78 8
    SPEAK UP YOU NEDNA BE FEARED   *919 28

FEARFUL
    AND FEARFUL TO SALLY FORTH DOWN THE SKY'S LONG RANGE   132 20
    ALL FEARFUL LEST I FIND THE LAST WORDS BLEEDING   135 19
    AND FEARFUL YET OF BELIEVING   168 35
    CAN KNOW THE FEARFUL ANGUISH THAT THIS IS SO   173 12
    AH WITH A FEARFUL STRANGE DETECTION   262 16
    IT IS A FEARFUL THING TO BE DOMINATED BY THE FEAR OF HU+ 263 7
    SHE HAS NOT REALISED YET THAT FEARFUL THING THAT I AM T+ 266 25
    WHEN SHE KNOWS THE FEARFUL OTHER FLESH AH DARKNESS UNFA+ 267 11
    AND FEARFUL CONTIGUOUS AND CONCRETE   267 12
    O ACT OF FEARFUL TEMERITY   310 4
    IS HIDEOUS AND FEARFUL   475 7
    IS A FEARFUL THING TO BEHOLD   475 10
    AND NO WONDER FOR MONEY HAS A FEARFUL CRUEL POWER   486 16
    FEARFUL TO BEHOLD   502 18
    A FEARFUL THING IS THE MUTILATED SOCIAL CONSCIOUSNESS   516 1
    THEIR POOR THEIR FEARFUL FACES   586 2
    LIKE FEARFUL AND CORPSE-LIKE FISHES HOOKED AND BEING PL+ 586 9
    AND LEAVE THE FEARFUL LAOCOON OF HIS FELLOW-MAN ENTANGL+ 632 7
    TO ITS FEARFUL FATE   632 9
    THEIR POOR THEIR FEARFUL FACES   632 11
    LIKE FEARFUL AND CORPSE-LIKE FISHES HOOKED AND BEING PL+ 632 24
    IT IS A FEARFUL THING TO FALL INTO THE HANDS OF THE LIV+ 699 12
    BUT IT IS A MUCH MORE FEARFUL THING TO FALL OUT OF THEM 699 13
    WHICH HAS BROUGHT TO PASS THE FEARFUL THING CALLED EVIL 712 25
    FORGOTTEN IN THE GRASS EVA FEARFUL AND FLEET   864 16
    AND FEARFUL TO FILE FORTH NOW FOR THE FIRST TIME ALONE *938 12
    ALL FEARFUL LEST I FIND SOME NEXT WORD BLEEDING   *939 3

FEARFULLY
  AND I ROSE IN FEAR NEEDING YOU FEARFULLY   99   6

FEARING
  FEARING NOTHING LIFE-BLISSFUL AT THE CORE   307   2

FEARLESS
  AND THE CROSS SPROUTING ITS SUPERB AND FEARLESS FLOWERS   305 30
  MORE FEARLESS THAN IRON ALL THE TIME   306 24
  CLEAR AND FEARLESS EVEN IF TINY   526 12
  AND FEARLESS FACE-TO-FACE AWARENESS OF NOW-NAKED LIFE   667   4
  ANY CLEAR AND FEARLESS AND BEING GOD VERY GOD   691 21
  AND MY LOST WHITE FEARLESS BREAST   696   5

FEARS
  PITEOUS BROWN BALL OF QUIVERING FEARS   43 11
  TO FORGETFULNESS SOFT-SAILING WATERS WHERE FEARS   53 11
  I LOST AT LAST THE FIERCENESS THAT FEARS IT WILL STARVE   265   3
  PAIN YET THE LIGHT OF LAMPS AND CANDLES HAS NO FEARS FO+   331   4
  THEY ARE AFRAID WITH HORRIBLE AND OPPOSING FEARS   516 21
  INTO FORGETFULNESS SOFT SAILING WATERS WHERE FEARS   *906   3

FEAST
  FOR THE FEAST OF CORPUS CHRISTI   209 18
  AND IT WAS FOR A FEAST A FEAST OF MEAT FOR MEN AND MAIDS   679 13
  IS LIKE BISCUITS BAKED FOR A FEAST   758 20

FEASTS
  HOW TO WAIT FOR THE LONELIEST OF FEASTS   465 25

FEATHER
  FEATHER OVER FEATHER ON THE BREAST OF THE GREAT AND GOL+   409 16
  FEATHER THE NESTS OF ALL   413 15
  AND THE DREAM OF THE NIGHT RISES FROM ME LIKE A RED FEA+   806 30

FEATHER-ANKLES
  FEATHER-ANKLES   782 25

FEATHERED
  FOR I AM QUETZALCOATL THE FEATHERED SNAKE   801 27

FEATHER-GLOVED
  YOU FEATHER-GLOVED   373 18
  YOU FEATHER-GLOVED   781 24

FEATHERLESS
  FURROWS OUR FEATHERLESS WOMEN   436 16

FEATHER-LUSTROUS
  AND THOSE SOMBRE DEAD FEATHER-LUSTROUS AZTECS   371 33

FEATHERS
  WINGS AND FEATHERS ON THE CRYING MYSTERIOUS AGES PEEWIT+   34 26
  WITH HER WINGS AND HER FEATHERS TO DROWN   125   5
  FOR THE FIRE TO BURN IT UP FEATHERS AND ALL   329 32
  FEATHERS ARE SINGEING   330   7
  RUFFLING BLACK SHINING FEATHERS LIKE LIFTED MAIL   370 24
  EAGLE GLOVED IN FEATHERS   373   7
  IN SCORCHED WHITE FEATHERS   373   8
  IN BURNT DARK FEATHERS   373   9
  IN FEATHERS STILL FIRE-RUSTED   373 10
  I WISH THEY HAD GIVEN THE THREE FEATHERS TO ME   392   1
  TO STAND AND HOLD FEATHERS THREE FEATHERS ABOVE THE WOR+   392   4
  FEATHERS   409 15
  AND PLUCKING OUT OF HIS PLUMAGE A FEW LOOSE FEATHERS TO   413 14
  BUT THE FEATHERS WERE COMPARATIVELY A MERE FLEA-BITE   413 17
  SONG AND CHIRRUPING GAY FEATHERS FLUFF-SHADOWED   443 16
  WHOSE FEATHERS GLISTEN   505   7
  GONE DEAD OR WANDERING IN EXILE WITH THEIR FEATHERS   533 18
  OH YOU WHO MAKE MY FEATHERS BRISTLE WITH   762   1
  EAGLE GLOVED IN FEATHERS   781 12
  IN SCORCHED WHITE FEATHERS   781 14
  IN BURNT DARK FEATHERS   781 15
  IN FEATHERS STILL FIRE-RUSTED   781 16
  THEIR FEATHERS LIFELESS AND THE ROSE LIGHTS TURNING TO +   855 28
  I FEEL AS IF FEATHERS WERE LIFTED AND SHOOK   883   4
  ON MY BREAST WITH HER WINGS AND HER FEATHERS TO DROWN   *936   7

FEATHER-TIP
  AT EACH FEATHER-TIP   371 14

FEATHERY
  IN ITS OWN SPLENDOUR AND ITS OWN FEATHERY MALENESS   587 14

FEATURES
  UNDER THE MOBILE FEATURES   *907 17
  VISIBLE THERE IN THE CHANGE OF EYES AND THE MOBILE FEAT+   *909 12

FEBRUARY
  IN JANUARY AND IN FEBRUARY THE RE-BIRTH OF THE ALMOND T+   303   5

FECUND
  WOUNDING THEMSELVES AGAINST HER DENYING HER FECUND   91 28
  AND FECUND GLOBE OF DREAMS   127   9
  AND BE OUT IN THE BEWILDERING DARKNESS WHICH IS ALWAYS +   179 25
  AND IS FECUND WITH A NEW DAY OF NEW CREATURES DIFFERENT   429   7
  DARKLY FROM THE FECUND COSMOS FROM THE ANGRY RED SUN FR+   675 11
  THE HATE OF TERROR OR DENY THE FECUND SOUL HER EMBRACES   *926 25

FECUNDATES
  AND FECUNDATES THE ZENITH AND THE NADIR   506   8

FECUNDATING
  FECUNDATING HERD   326 31

FECUNDITY
  WITH WEBBED FECUNDITY PLUNGING THE SEED OF LIFE IN THE +   841   5

FED
  YOU HAVE FED ME WITH YOUR SWEETNESS NOW I AM SICK   234 23
  A WOMAN FED THAT HUNGER IN ME AT LAST   264 26
  WE ARE FED UP WITH COMBAT   519 18
  BUT ROSES IF THEY'RE FED TOO MUCH   534 25
  AND FED ON CONDITION THEY DANCE THIS DANCE OF CORPSES   631 15
  WHEN THE CATTLE ARE FED   756 11
  AND THE CHURCHES CRY PUSS PUSS COME AND BE FED   763   3
  THE LIGHT WHICH IS FED FROM TWO VESSELS   810 27

FEE
  OF EACH HEART'S ENTRANCE FEE   101 28

FEEBLE
  AUNT LIBBY'S REALLY A FEEBLE LOT   571 29

FEED
  THOUGH IT FEED NATIONS   263   4
  AND FEED THE YOUNG NEW FIELDS OF LIFE WITH ASH   315   5
  TO FEED THE BONNY BABY AND KEEP ITS TARA DRY   570 19
  AND THE FEED OF PAP THAT WE NURSES AND GUARDIAN ANGELS +   670 16
  FEED ON OUR WOUNDS LIKE BREAD RECEIVE OUR BLOOD   743   4
  AND LET THEM FEED FROM MY HAND   751   7
  AND FEED ON IT   843 12
  SWEET FRAGRANCE OF LOVE AND FEED ME WITH KISSES FAIR   874   7

FEEDING
  NOR FEEDING IN THE MARSHES   436   8
  AND CONFUSING YOU AND FEEDING ITSELF ON YOUR LIFE   642 21
  FOR THE FEEDING AND STRENGTHENING OF THE HANDSOMER FULL+   679 10
  HOGGING IT DOWN LIKE A PIG I CALL THE FEEDING OF CORPSES   708 11
  FEEDING ON PURE WHITE SUGAR   751   3

FEEDS
  WHICH THE SWEET BLOOD FEEDS   240   6

FEEL
  AND FEEL THE STREAM OF AWAKENING RIPPLE AND PASS   51 23
  TO FEEL THE LADS' LOOKS LIGHT ON ME   51 27
  TOUCH AFTER TOUCH I FEEL ON ME   52   1
  I FEEL THEM CLING AND CLEAVE TO ME   52   8
  DID YOU NEVER FEEL   56 29
  AND I LAUGHED TO FEEL IT PLUNGE AND BOUND   61 23
  AND I COULD FEEL HER FEET IN EITHER HAND   65   8
  BUT I SCARCELY FEEL YOUR LOSS   108 12
  I FEEL THE SILENCE WAITING   109 25
  I FEEL YOUR SILENCE TOUCH MY WORDS AS I TALK   110   3
  STRANGE BEAMS MUST TRAVEL STILL FOR I FEEL THAT I   115   3
  I LONGED TO FEEL MY HOT BLOOD BURN   123 29
  THEIR DUMB CONFESSION OF WHAT HER BLOOD MUST FEEL   128   9
  WEBBING OF STEEL ON YOUR FEET SO YOU SHALL FEEL   154 22
  I HAVE COME I FEEL THEM WHIMPER IN WELCOME AND MOURN   172 25
  I FEEL THICK WALLS OF STONE BEHIND THE ARRAS   173 26
  TO FEEL FRESH AIR IN OUR THROATS TO HAVE FRESH BREATH I+   175 21
  THERE IS SOMETHING I WANT TO FEEL IN MY RUNNING BLOOD   180 30
  I HOLD MYSELF UP AND FEEL A BIG WIND BLOWING   223   4
  FEEL THE SHAME-WOUNDS IN HIS HANDS PIERCE THROUGH MY OWN   226 10
  I FEEL NEW AND EAGER   244 23
  AND TO FEEL QUITE NEW   244 26
  HOW I LOVE ALL OF YOU DO YOU FEEL ME WRAP YOU   245   7
  THOSE SHOULDERS SO WARM AND SMOOTH I FEEL THAT I   245 18
  YOUR BREASTS YOUR KNEES AND FEET I FEEL THAT WE   245 23
  HOW SURE I FEEL HOW WARM AND STRONG AND HAPPY   247   4
  I FEEL LIKE A FIRM RICH HEALTHY ROOT   247 11
  THE JOY I FEEL   255   8
  GOD KNOWS WHAT I FEEL BUT IT IS JOY   255   9
  I TOUCH I FEEL THE UNKNOWN   259 21
  FLOWERS THAT COME FIRST FROM THE DARKNESS AND FEEL COLD+   270   9
  AS YOU SEE IT STANDING GROWING YOU FEEL AT ONCE IT IS S+   282 13
  DO YOU FEEL THE AIR FOR ELECTRIC INFLUENCES   301   3
  WAS IT HUMILITY TO FEEL SO HONOURED   350 15
  TO ROAM AND FEEL THE SLOW HEART BEAT   358 12
  THEY FEEL QUITE TENDER OVER YOU TILL YOU PLAY THE SAME   399 17
  AND FEEL ABSOLUTELY IT   414   4
  AND IN THE DARK UNSCIENTIFIC I FEEL THE DRUM-WINDS OF H+   438   9
  MODERN PEOPLE FEEL THEMSELVES AT A DISADVANTAGE   446   1
  THEN MORE THAN THAT HE MAKES A WOMAN FEEL HE IS SERVING   447 22
  ALL DAY LONG I FEEL THE TIDE ROCKING ROCKING   454 14
  FIGHT DON'T YOU FEEL YOU'RE FADING   456 10
  AND TREADS THE EARTH TO FEEL THE SOIL   459 23
  THEN HE CAN'T FEEL ANY MORE   474 26
  ALL I ASK OF A WOMAN IS THAT SHE SHALL FEEL GENTLY TOWA+   479   1
  TO FEEL A FINE FINE BREEZE BLOWING THROUGH THE NAVEL AND   481 21
  AND FEEL THE PEACELESSNESS OF THE MULTIMILLIONAIRE   498   3
  PEOPLE FEELING THINGS THEY INTEND TO FEEL THEY MEAN TO +   500 21
  THEY WILL FEEL   500 22
  FOR OF COURSE IF YOU REALLY FEEL SOMETHING   500 24
  YOU DON'T HAVE TO ASSERT THAT YOU FEEL IT   500 25
  SO IF YOU WANT EITHER OF US TO FEEL ANYTHING AT ALL   501 14
  AND FEEL NO MORE   508   2
  THEN SOMETIMES I FEEL DEFEATED AND THEN AGAIN I KNOW   508 22
  AND A MAN CAN NO LONGER FEEL HEROIC ABOUT BEING A HAMLET   508 26
  I HAVE PASSED FROM EXISTENCE I FEEL NOTHING ANY MORE   509   8
  I AM AWARE I FEEL NOTHING EVEN AT DAWN   509 24
  BUT I AM A LIAR I FEEL NO LOVELINESS IT IS A MENTAL REM+   509 27
  TILL WE ACTUALLY FEEL AS BLANK AS WE REALLY ARE   513 10
  AND THEY FEEL IT   518 10
  AND WE FEEL WE'VE GOT TO KEEP IT UP KEEP ON COMBATING   519 13
  WE FEEL THAT IF THE WHOLE COMBATIVE COMPETITIVE SYSTEM   519 19
  AND WE FEEL IS WORTH DOING   520   8
  MAKE YOU FEEL SAFE   522 16
  TO BE ALIVE YOU'VE GOT TO FEEL A GENEROUS FLOW   522 24
  AND THEY MAKE ME FEEL AS IF SPACE SHIFTED   524 21
  AND I FEEL ARISTOCRATIC NOBLE WHEN I FEEL A PULSE GO   525   7
  AND HOW DELICIOUS IT IS TO FEEL SUNSHINE UPON ONE   526   1

FEET
    PUT MY FEET UPON THE CRESCENT LIKE A LORD   684   9
    THAT WE SHOULD BE LOVELY IN THE FLESH WITH BRIGHT CRESC+   687 16
    WITH SLIM WAISTS OF WARRIORS AND THE LONG FEET   689   3
    AND SET ME AGAIN ON MOON-REMEMBERING FEET   696   6
    AND WATCHED FOR YOUR GLISTENING FEET DOWN THE GARDEN PA+   696 11
    IN THE FLAT RECURRENT BREAKERS OF MY TWO FEET   705   5
    TO THE WHITE-TREADING WAVES OF TWO SALT FEET   705 17
    FOOLING MY FEET DOES THE NIGHT-MOTH   731   3
    AS FREE AS THE RUNNING OF ANGEL'S FEET   746 18
    CURVING THEIR FEET AND DANCING AND FLUTTERING IN SPORT   751   4
    DOWN TO THE FEET   781 25
    THE FEET   782 20
    AND UP THE IRON FEET OF THE EAGLE IN THRILLS OF FIERY P+   782 22
    TO WITHDRAW HIS WARMTH FROM YOUR FEET SO YOUR FEET TURN+   797   3
    RUN UP THE FLAMES AND WITH FEET ON THE SPARKS   798 21
    HE SENDS THE SERPENT OF POWER UP MY FEET AND MY LOINS   799 20
    AND THE FEET OF MEN AND THE HANDS OF THE WOMEN KNOW ME   801 19
    THE SNAKE OF MY LEFT-HAND OUT OF THE DARKNESS IS KISSIN+   801 22
    WITHOUT FEET THE RED FLOORS   818 12
    AND CAN'T PUT ITS FEET TOGETHER   818 26
    IT COULDN'T PUT ITS FEET TOGETHER   818 30
    YET IT'S GOT TWO FEET   819   1
    THE FEET OF THE ARCH   819   9
    THE TWO FEET OF THE RAINBOW   819 13
    AND CAN'T PUT ITS FEET TOGETHER   820   6
    ALONG WHERE MY SLOW FEET NEVER TRODE   857 11
    DRIFTED WITH THE BLOOD OF THE FLOWERS ON HER FEET AND K+   864   5
    HAS BROUGHT DOWN A RIPE FRUIT HEAVILY TO HER FEET   864 14
    WE ALL MARCH OUT TO PRAYERS SOFT SLIPPERED FEET AND CLA+   866 13
    BY NATURE THAN BY BOOTS AND WET FEET OFTEN CARRY MERRY +   866 15
    HEAR RE-ECHO YOUR SLOW RELUCTANT FEET   880 16
    ABOUT HER FEET   880 21
    ABOUT HER FEET   880 26
    YOUR FEET AND TOUCHING YOUR ANKLES TRY   887 16
    WHEN THE WHITE FEET OF THE BABY BEAT ACROSS THE GRASS   *912 25
    WITH HER TWO BARE FEET ON MY HANDS   *913   9
    WHEN THE BARE FEET OF THE BABY BEAT ACROSS THE GRASS   *913 28
    THE LITTLE WHITE FEET NOD LIKE WHITE FLOWERS IN THE WIND   *913 29
    WITH HER LITTLE BARE FEET IN MY HANDS   *914   9
    ENDLESS WHISPER OF PASSING FEET   *917   6
    THEY SIGH JUST ONCE ROUND OUR FEET AND ARE STILL HEAVY +   *917 11
    OF HER FEET AS THEY LEPT FOR A SPACE THEN PAUSE TO PRESS   *934 10
    OVER THE FLOWERS AT MY FEET   *935 30
    PRESSING THE LITTLE POISED FEET OF THE MOTHER WHO SMILE+   *940   8
    BUT I'M SORRY FOR HIM ON HIS YOUNG FEET KNOWIN'   *944   7
    AND IN THE DARK I FEEL HIS COLD WEBBED FEET MUD BLACK   *947 19

FELICITY
    FROM ALL THE FALSE FELICITY   469 25

FELIPE
    FELIPE AND SAN CRISTOBAL   798   6

FELL
    LIKE FLOWERS I FELL TO BE CAUGHT   56 17
    AND MY ARMS FELL LOOSE AND I WAS DUMB   62 20
    AND NUTS FELL OUT OF THEIR HAIR   152 15
    THE PEACEFUL FLOOR WHEN FELL THE SWORD ON THEIR REST   155   8
    IT FELL FROM OUR HUSK IN A LITTLE HASTY SEED   172 13
    WHEN SNOW FELL ON THE APPLE-TREES   248 17
    HE FELL TO FROWNING AS HE LAY WITH HIS HEAD ON HIS PAWS   324 12
    TILL HE FELL IN A CORNER PALPITATING SPENT   345 27
    HE FELL AGAIN WITH A LITTLE THUD   346 26
    SOMEHOW ALAS HE FELL IN LOVE   378   9
    HE FELL INTO THE RUT OF LOVE   378 10
    THAT'S WHY THE NIGHT FELL IN FRUSTRATION   390 28
    HE FELL TO DUST AS THE TWILIGHT FELL   404 26
    FELL FROM THE HOOKS AND WERE DEAD   413   9
    ANGELS ARE BRIGHT STILL THOUGH THE BRIGHTEST FELL   614 12
    HE ONLY FELL OUT OF YOUR KEN YOU ORTHODOX ANGELS   614 15
    THE SPARK FELL AND KINDLED INSTANTLY ON MY BLOOD   618   4
    ANGELS ARE BRIGHT STILL THOUGH THE BRIGHTEST FELL   697 23
    WHEN SATAN FELL HE ONLY FELL   710   9
    SO SATAN ONLY FELL TO KEEP A BALANCE   710 12
    A MOMENT AS HE FELL AND GROVEL AND DIE   741 28
    HE WHISTLED TO IT LOUDLY TWICE TILL IT FELL TO HIS HAND   791   2
    IT FELL IN   791   8
    A LOT O' VIOLETS FELL OUT OF 'ER BOSOM ON 'IM DOWN THEER   *910 16

FELLER
    SHE'S A MARV'LOUS DELICIOUS HIGH-SPIRITED FELLER   583 17

FELLOW
    TO TOUCH ITS FELLOW ON EITHER SIDE   154   6
    AND SINGLE ME PERFECTED FROM MY FELLOW   218   8
    BUT MY DEAR FELLOW MY DEAR FELLOW   434 17
    NOR EVEN THE MUSICAL SUAVE YOUNG FELLOW   437   6
    AND WHAT A DANDY FELLOW THE RIGHT TOSS OF A CHIN FOR YOU   524 15
    AHEM THEY WENT THIS FELLOW   554 21
    DEATH OF MY FELLOW MEN   630   8
    AND LIVED TO LEARN THEY ARE NEITHER FELLOW NOR MEN   644   2
    THE GREED OF THIS INFAMOUS FELLOW LIVING FOR OUR SWEAT   750   8
    QUITE THE FRESH CLEAN MANLY FELLOW   830 13
    AND TRUE ENOUGH HE WAS INFINITELY THE MORE MANLY FELLOW   842 24

FELLOW-COUNTRYMEN
    WITH MY FELLOW-COUNTRYMEN OR ELSE I DON'T BELONG   579   6

FELLOW-MAN
    IT IS FEAR OF MY MONEY-MAD FELLOW-MAN   487   3
    NOR MY CHILDREN NOR MY COUNTRY NOR MY FELLOW-MAN   497 17
    AND IF STARK NAKED I APPROACH A FELLOW-MAN OR FELLOW-WO+   608   1
    AND LEAVE THE FEARFUL LAOCOON OF HIS FELLOW-MAN ENTANGL+   632   7

FELLOW-MEN
    FOR ME NO FELLOW-MEN   317   7
    TRIUMPH OVER THEIR FELLOW-MEN TRIUMPH OVER OBSTACLES   519   3
    OH LOOK AT MY FELLOW-MEN OH LOOK AT THEM   631   7
    THE MILLIONS MILLIONS OF MY FELLOW-MEN   631 30
    BETWEEN YOU AND THE ROBOT-HORDES MISNAMED YOUR FELLOW-M+   637 34
    A FEW ARE MY FELLOW-MEN   638   1
    THE MASS ARE NOT MY FELLOW-MEN   638   4
    OH I HAVE LOVED MY FELLOW-MEN   644   1

FELLOW-TRIBESMEN
    SINGING TO THE MEN BELOW THE FELLOW-TRIBESMEN   623 20

FELLOW-WOMAN
    AND IF STARK NAKED I APPROACH A FELLOW-MAN OR FELLOW-WO+   608   1

FELT
    I FELT THE LURCH AND HALT OF HER HEART   61 21
    AND I HEARD THE THUNDER AND FELT THE RAIN   62 19
    AND THE GENTLE LEAVES AND HAVE FELT WHERE THE ROOTS ARE+   92 10
    I FELT A BROWN BIRD HOVER   124 25
    I FELT THE BROWN BIRD COVER   124 33
    I HAVE SEEN IT FELT IT IN MY MOUTH MY THROAT MY CHEST MY   207 21
    AND FELT HER WATCHING   222 10
    SHADING HIS FACE IN HIS BLACK FELT HAT   228   6
    AND I FELT THAT WHICH WAS NOT I   259   8
    I WOULD COME IF I FELT MY HOUR HAD STRUCK   289 28
    WHEN THEY FELT THEIR FOREHEADS BARE NAKED TO HEAVEN THE+   310   5
    WHEN THEY FELT THE LIGHT OF HEAVEN BRANDISHING LIKE A K+   310   7
    AND FELT HIM BEAT IN MY HAND WITH HIS MUCOUS LEAPING   339   9
    I FELT SO HONOURED   350 16
    FEELINGS THAT NOBODY FELT   443 23
    EMOTIONS THAT NONE OF THEM FELT   443 25
    THEM FOR A MOMENT FELT   443 27
    KISSES THAT COULD NOT BE FELT   444   2
    WITHOUT EVER HAVING FELT SORRY FOR ITSELF   467   4
    AND FOUND OUT WHAT THEY REALLY FELT AND REALLY MEANT   504   4
    WOMEN FELT IT WAS NO LONGER ANY USE BEING A LINGER-LONG+   537 29
    WHEN OUR PARENTS FELT SPRY   562 26
    I HAVE FELT THE PULL OF DESIRE   602 11
    AND IN THAT THRILL HE FELT   605   7
    AND IN THAT THRILL SHE FELT   605 11
    YET FOREVER FELT IN THE SOUL   622 18
    IS DIFFERENT FROM THE LOVE I FELT LAST YEAR   662   2
    WHOSE POWER AND GLORY I HAVE OFTEN HEARD AND FELT   704 21
    I FELT THE LURCH AND HALT OF HER HEART   *912   1
    UNDER THE CARESSING LEAVES AND FELT WHERE THE ROOTS WER+   *926 10
    AGAIN AND I FELT A BROWN BIRD HOVER   *935 31
    HAVE FELT THE DAY DARKEN AND SHUDDER   *937 14

FEMALE
    THE FEMALE WHOSE VENOM CAN MORE THAN KILL CAN NUMB AND +   98   9
    HAVE I PROFANED SOME FEMALE MYSTERY ORGIES   141   3
    MALE AND FEMALE DARKNESSES   171 15
    MERE FEMALE ADJUNCT OF WHAT I WAS   264 22
    FOR FRUITS ARE ALL OF THEM FEMALE IN THEM LIES THE SEED+   277   1
    TO THE ARAB AND THE FIG HAS BEEN A CATCH-WORD FOR THE F+   277   4
    ROMANS IT IS FEMALE   282 16
    THAT'S HOW IT SHOULD BE THE FEMALE SHOULD ALWAYS BE SEC+   283   2
    FIG FRUIT OF THE FEMALE MYSTERY CONVERT AND INWARD   283 18
    FIRE AND WATER THEY CONTAIN THE PROPORTION OF MALE AND +   295   7
    FEMALE   364 29
    THE FEMALE SHIPS   380 27
    FORGET THE FEMALE HERD FOR A BIT   383 20
    WHAT DO I CARE FOR HER THE UGLY FEMALE STANDING UP THERE   384 25
    SHE TURNS HER HEAD AWAY WITH AN OBTUSE FEMALE SORT OF   385   1
    LITTLE BLACK FEMALE PUP SORT OF FRENCH BULL THEY SAY   395   1
    THE HUGE OLD FEMALE ON THE DRUM   426   4
    AND THE OTHER THE OLD ONE THE PALLID HOARY FEMALE   426   9
    HE FINDS A FEMALE THEY SHOW NO HASTE   465   9
    OF THE FEMALE FORM TECHNICALLY BEAUTIFUL ACTUALLY A WHI+   619 12
    FROM THE DRAGON OF THE MODERN FEMALE   619 27
    SHE IS THE FEMALE TUNNY-FISH ROUND AND HAPPY AMONG THE +   695 11

FEMALES
    AND ROWS AMONG THE FEMALES LIKE A SHIP PERTINACIOUSLY   380 18
    ONLY THOSE ETERNAL FEMALES TO OVERLEAP AND SURPASS AND   382 33
    IF ALL THOSE FEMALES WHO SO PASSIONATELY LOVED   538   1

FENCE
    ALONG THE FENCE PERPETUALLY SEEKING RELEASE   47 17
    EVERY DAY BY THE FENCE TO LOOK UP AT THE FLOWERS THAT E+   58 14
    A SQUIRREL COCKS HIS HEAD ON THE FENCE AND WONDERS   223 21
    FENCE   255 23
    OVER A FENCE   384 27
    THEY'VE SAT LONG ENOUGH ON THE FENCE   559 24
    OF SITTING THERE ON THE FENCE AND LETTING   560   3
    OF SITTING ON THE FENCE   560 10
    AND CAN'T SEE THROUGH THE FENCE   565   4
    AND KISS OF THE FAR-OFF LINGERING LADY WHO LOOKS OVER T+   695 31

FEND
    WHO LIFT SWART ARMS TO FEND ME OFF BUT I COME   86 18
    CRY OUT AND FEND HER OFF AS SHE SEEKS HER PROCREANT GRO+   91 27
    CRY OUT AND FEND HER OFF AS SHE SEEKS HER PROCREANT GRO+   *926 20

FERN
    AND THE FLOWER THAT PUTS ITS TONGUE OUT AND FERN THAT P+   89 27
    WITH FROZEN RIGGING SHE SAW HIM SHE DROOPED LIKE A FERN   155 22

FERNS
    OLDER THAN FLOWERS OLDER THAN FERNS OLDER THAN FORAMINI+   477 10
    THE UNROLLING OF FERNS WHITE TONGUES OF THE ACANTHUS LA+   623 27
    WHEN FROM A WORLD OF MOSSES AND OF FERNS   683   1
    THE UNROLLING OF FERNS WHILE TONGUES OF ACANTHUS LAPPIN+   *953 15

FERN-SCENTED
NAY WE FIND OURSELVES CROSSING THE FERN-SCENTED FRONTIE+ 286 24
OF THE LOST FERN-SCENTED WORLD   287 7

FERN-SEED
TAKE THE FERN-SEED ON OUR LIPS   287 8

FERRY
FLAT BROWN ROCKS TO WATCH THE FERRY IN THE SUN   386 24
AND YOU CROSS THE FERRY WITH THE NAKED PEOPLE GO UP THE 386 25

FERTILE
INTO THE WOMAN'S FERTILE FATHOMLESS LAP   172 7
LIKE GRAINS OF MUSIC CROSSING THE FERTILE FALLOW   868 23
INTO THE FERTILE DARKNESS AFTER DEATH   880 8

FERTILISATION
WHERE EVERYTHING HAPPENS INVISIBLE FLOWERING AND FERTIL+ 283 20

FERTILISE
TO FERTILISE THE ROOTS OF UNKNOWN MEN WHO ARE STILL TO + 614 24
AND FERTILISE THE WEEDS ON EVERY MEAD   634 5

FERTILISING
TILL THE SOUL OF THE STIFF-NECKED IS GROUND TO DUST TO + 616 14

FERTILIZED
AND PLANTED AND FERTILIZED HIM   742 14

FERVENT
NOW AT LAST THE INK AND DUDGEON PASSES FROM OUR FERVENT+ 70 5
YOUR FERVENT LIMBS WITH FLICKERS AND TENDRILS OF NEW   156 27

FERVOUR
FERVOUR WITHIN THE POOL OF HER TWILIGHT   125 34

FESCUE
COCK'S-FOOT FOX-TAIL FESCUE AND TOTTERING-GRASS   587 20

FESTOON
A FLOCCULENT DUST ON THE FLOOR OF THE WORLD THE FESTOON   98 13

FESTOONED
EVE PUSHING THE FESTOONED VANILLA TREMBLING ASIDE   864 7

FETCHED
I HAVE FETCHED THE TEARS UP OUT OF THE LITTLE WELLS   94 10
THE CRIMSON SHEAF OF THE WEST THE DEEP FETCHED SIGH   885 6
I HAVE FETCHED THE TEARS UP OUT OF THE LITTLE WELLS   *896 26

FETTERS
TOMORROW MARRIES TOMORROW FETTERS HIMSELF   877 5

FEVER
DRY FEVER IN HER POOL OF FULL TWILIGHT   *936 33

FEW
A FEW QUICK BEATS FROM A WOOD-PIGEON'S HEART AND WHEN I+ 38 14
SOME FEW DARK-CLEAVING THE DOORWAY SOULS THAT CLING AS + 75 10
A FEW TIMES ONLY AT THE BEGINNING   106 29
TO MY GAIETY A FEW LONG GREY HAIRS   107 2
THE HEART ALL CROWDED WITH SLAVES MOST WORKING SOME FEW+ 174 20
JUST A FEW OF THE ROSES WE GATHERED FROM THE ISAR   217 27
AND FALTERS A FEW SHORT STEPS ACROSS THE LAKE   230 6
IN SIGHTLESS BEAUTY AND THE FEW   262 5
PAY A FEW CENTS   387 18
AND A FEW VOMITING BOUTS   400 22
TO FEAR A FEW FANGS   405 17
THUS SAY A FEW WORDS TO EACH OTHER   405 20
AND PLUCKING OUT OF HIS PLUMAGE A FEW LOOSE FEATHERS TO 413 14
HANDING OUT A FEW LOOSE GOLDEN BREAST-FEATHERS AT MOULT+ 414 9
LEAVING A FEW BONES   414 24
WITH A FEW GOLD SPANGLES   444 25
AND DARTS A FEW GOLD RAYS   455 18
A FEW GOLD RAYS THICKENING DOWN TO RED   455 20
A FEW OF THE TOUCHES LIKE A LOW-BORN JAKE   489 15
I WOULD LIKE A FEW MEN TO BE AT PEACE WITH   499 20
NO WHEN IT COMES TO THRILLS THERE ARE REALLY VERY FEW 532 14
FOR THE REST NO I SHOULD SAY LIFE HELD VERY FEW   533 2
GIVE 'EM A FEW HARD POKES   560 20
ANOTHER LITTLE RUN FOR THEIR MONEY A FEW MORE TURNS OF + 586 18
HOW THEN ARE THE FEW MEN MEN OF THE WIND AND RAIN   637 29
A FEW ARE MY FELLOW-MEN   638 1
A FEW ONLY A FEW   638 2
ONLY THE FEW THE VERY FEW MATTER IN THE SIGHT OF GOD AND 638 13
THOSE THAT LOOK INTO THE EYES OF THE GODS AND THESE ARE+ 649 14
AND THOSE THAT LOOK INTO THE EYES OF THE FEW OTHER MEN 649 21
AND DEMOS SERVES LIFE AS IT GLEAMS ON THE FACE OF THE F+ 650 3
AND THE FEW LOOK INTO THE EYES OF THE GODS AND SERVE TH+ 650 4
THE FEW MUST LOOK INTO THE EYES OF THE GODS AND OBEY TH+ 650 8
AND THE MANY MUST OBEY THE FEW THAT LOOK INTO THE EYES + 650 10
MOON O MOON GREAT LADY OF THE HEAVENLY FEW   695 24
HE IS FAR TOO FEW TO CAUSE ANY APPREHENSION   777 10
RUNS INTO THE SHADOW WITH HER CAPTURE A FEW LITTLE BITE+ 864 17
AYE BUSY WITH A FEW HARD TASKS AND WRATH   875 31
WITH A FEW SWIFT PASSIONS WOULD I DRIFT AWAY   875 32
A FEW QUICK BEATS OF A WOODPIGEON'S HEART THEN RISE   *892 30
FEW   *910 21
WITH MULTITUDE OF WHITE ROSES AND JUST A FEW   *940 27
JUST A FEW OF THE ROSES WE GATHERED FROM THE ISAR   *943 10

FIBRE
YET NOW EVERY FIBRE OF ME CRIES IN PAIN   117 2
TILL YOU'VE RUINED A NATION'S FIBRE   537 15
YET EVERY FIBRE OF ME CRIES IN PAIN   *931 6

FIBRES
THE FIBRES OF THE HEART PARTING ONE AFTER THE OTHER   281 6

FIBRIL
AND THE SUN COMING IN THROUGH THE NARROWEST FIBRIL OF A+ 324 13

FICTION
A KIND OF FICTION   474 14
JUDGING FROM THE FICTION IT IS POSSIBLE TO READ I SHOUL+ 532 15

FIDDLE-BOW
SUBTLER THAN AN OLD SOFT-WORN FIDDLE-BOW   254 33

FIDELITY
AH HOW I ADMIRE YOUR FIDELITY   296 12
FIDELITY LOYALTY ATTACHMENT   399 19
FIDELITY AND LOVE ARE TWO DIFFERENT THINGS LIKE A FLOWER 476 1
THE SAPPHIRE OF FIDELITY   477 18

FIDGET
THEN IT BEGAN TO FIDGET SHIFTING FROM ONE LEG TO THE OT+ 413 12

FIELD
IN THE SILENT LABOURS OF MEN IN THE FIELD   68 18
THIS FIELD OF DELIGHT   124 17
LIKE ANY FIELD OF SNOW   165 5
FIELD AND AS VICTORS WE TRAVEL   243 15
AND THE YOUNG BULL IN THE FIELD WITH HIS WRINKLED SAD F+ 255 33
LIKE A FIELD OF FILTHY WEEDS   315 29
IN THE OPEN FIELD   382 31
AND THE CROWD LIKE A FIELD OF RICE IN THE DARK GAVE WAY 390 34
OH GOLDEN FIELD OF PEOPLE   627 11
LEAVING THEM SHADOW STRIPES BARRED ON A FIELD OF GREY 858 12
IN THE FAR-OFF LABOUR OF MEN IN THE FIELD   *915 2

FIELD-BEE
AS A FIELD-BEE BLACK AND AMBER   46 6

FIELDS
YESTERDAY THE FIELDS WERE ONLY GREY WITH SCATTERED SNOW 85 5
FORTH TO HER FIELDS THAT NOVEMBER   103 8
THE FIELDS OF AUTUMN   120 12
BEYOND THE WITHERING SNOW OF THE SHORN FIELDS   135 6
IN THE AUTUMN FIELDS THE STUBBLE   152 18
FIELDS OF DEATH   199 14
FIELDS BENEATH   199 16
IN THE FIELDS OF ETERNITY   243 4
IN HEAVEN'S FIELDS SET   268 18
AND FEED THE YOUNG NEW FIELDS OF LIFE WITH ASH   315 5
IN FRESH FIELDS   614 25
OH GOLDEN FIELDS OF PEOPLE   627 9
OF DANGER I FIND HER EVEN WORSE THAN THE FIELDS WHERE W+ 752 12
IN THE FIELDS WITH FOREIGN OVERSEERS   790 11
WE WORK WITH THEIR MACHINES WE WORK IN THEIR FIELDS 794 2
BEYOND THE WITHERING SNOW OF THE SHORN FIELDS   *939 6

FIEND
LEST OUR FACES BETRAY US TO SOME UNTIMELY FIEND   267 34
YOU POINTED FIEND   333 15
LIVES YOUR OWN LITTLE FIEND   563 24

FIENDISHLY
DOMINANT WOMEN ARE AS A RULE SO SUBTLY AND FIENDISHLY D+ 619 24

FIENDS
THAT EVER TURNED MEN INTO FIENDS   521 6

FIERCE
THA CAN STARE AT ME WI' THY FIERCE BLUE EYES   79 11
MY HEART WAS FIERCE TO MAKE HER LAUGHTER RISE   125 30
THE MOTHER IN YOU FIERCE AS A MURDERESS GLARING TO   207 6
WHERE FLAMES OF FIERCE LOVE TREMBLE   242 10
ON THE BODY OF FIERCE DESIRE   242 11
AND MY LIFE IS FIERCE AT ITS QUICK   246 15
I WHO AM SO FIERCE AND STRONG ENFOLDING YOU   246 23
AND SALVIA FIERCE TO CROW AND SHOUT FOR FIGHT   317 21
LIKE SOME FIERCE MAGNET BRINGING ITS POLES TOGETHER 370 18
BLOWS THE MAGNETIC CURRENT IN FIERCE BLASTS   370 23
SO FIERCE WHEN THE COYOTES HOWL BARKING LIKE A WHOLE 396 29
COMING UP ON FIERCE LITTLE LEGS TEARING FAST TO CATCH U+ 397 15
SETTING FIERCE AND UNDAUNTED WINTRY   455 22
AND IF IT FLUSHES AGAINST FIERCE ROCK   467 18
FOR THE FIERCE CURVE OF OUR LIVES IS MOVING AGAIN TO THE 478 1
AND FIERCE AS FIRE IS FIERCE   667 28
AND RANGE THEMSELVES LIKE GREAT FIERCE SERAPHIM FACING + 695 3
HE WAS A SOLDIER ONCE OUR FIERCE LITTLE BARON A POLE 859 5
THE FIERCE BLACK EYES ARE CLOSED THEY WILL OPEN NO MORE 859 17
THA CAN STARE AT ME WI' THY FIERCE BLUE EYES   *921 7
MY HEART WAS FIERCE TO MAKE HER HOMAGE RISE   *936 29

FIERCE-FACED
SILVERY-SIDED FISH-FANGED FIERCE-FACED WHISKERED MOTTLED 409 3

FIERCE-FOOT
FIERCE-FOOT   782 26

FIERCELY
THEN HE LAUGHED SEEING THE SUN DART FIERCELY AT HIM 790 1
GATHERS ITSELF FIERCELY TOGETHER   *893 22

FIERCENESS
BY VERY FIERCENESS INTO A QUIESCENCE   160 18
I LOST AT LAST THE FIERCENESS THAT FEARS IT WILL STARVE 265 3

FIERCER
   THE TOWN GROWS FIERCER WITH HEAT   746 8

FIERILY
   SONG FIERILY   108 28
   FIERILY PULSING UNABLE TO REFRAIN   194 25

FIERY
   THE VIVID AH THE FIERY SURPLUS OF LIFE   127 17
   OF FIERY COLDNESS TO BE GONE IN A LOST SOUL'S BLISS   130 23
   FROM THE RED ROSE-FLOWERS' FIERY TRANSIENCE   219 14
   THIS FIERY COAT   238 12
   BUT ALSO IT WAS A FIERY FORTRESS FROWNING SHAGGILY ON T+ 327 1
   BUT FISHES ARE VERY FIERY AND TAKE TO THE WATER TO COOL   331 1
   HIS POOR DARLING IS ALMOST FIERY   359 34
   DOES THE SUN IN NEW MEXICO SAIL LIKE A FIERY BIRD OF PR+ 374 12
   O RUDDY GOD IN OUR VEINS O FIERY GOD IN OUR GENITALS   440 12
   AND BE A BIT MORE FIERY AS INCAPABLE OF TELLING LIES   505 18
   WITH FIERY WEIGHT AND WILD LIFE AND COMING OUT   530 3
   AND UP THE IRON FEET OF THE EAGLE IN THRILLS OF FIERY P+ 782 22
   AND IS SILENT WITH A SENSE OF JUSTICE THE FIERY PRIMORD+ 844 26
   A FIERY SIGN OF THE CHAINED POWER THAT WASTED HIM TO TH+ 859 20
   FROM THE FIERY HAMMERING OF YOUR HEART I CAST   873 2
   THE FIERY MIXTURE OF THY LIFE SO I   879 11

FIERY-COLD
   IT IS THE SCENT OF THE FIERY-COLD DREGS OF CORRUPTION   270 20

FIFE
   BY NOISE OF SMALL BIRDS SINGING FIFE   *914 22

FIFTH
   YOU'RE A RANK OUTSIDER OF THE FIFTH REMOVE   576 15
   THE FIFTH GENERATION OF PURITANS WHEN IT ISN'T OBSCENEL+ 845 15
   THE FIFTH GENERATION OF PURITANS WHEN IT ISN'T DEBAUCHED *953 7

FIFTH-FORM
   YOU LOOK LIKE THE TOPPINGEST TOPPING FIFTH-FORM ETON BO+ 835 17

FIFTIES
   IN YOUR FIFTIES WITH A SHORT FROCK SHOWING YOUR FORE AN+ 835 10

FIFTY
   TWENTY POUND O' THY OWN THA HAST AN' FIFTY POUND HA'E I   83 1
   AS FOR THOSE OVER FIFTY EITHER THEY RUSH FORWARD   502 16
   BECAUSE OF THEIR OWN FIFTY OR SIXTY OR SEVENTY OR   502 20
   DINNERS FOR THE NEXT FIFTY YEARS   531 7
   GOOD DINNERS FOR FIFTY MORE LONG YEARS   531 15
   THOSE UNDER FIFTY AND MORE STILL THOSE UNDER FORTY   832 1
   A JOLLY GOOD SCREW WHEN THE DEAR LITTLE GIRLY-WIRLY'S O+ 834 21
   AT FIFTY YOU'RE NOT GOING TO BE THE APOLLO BELVEDERE DO+ 835 23
   THE LITTLE-BOY OF THIRTY OR FORTY OR FIFTY OR SIXTY   841 19
   TWENTY POUND O' THY OWN THA HAST AND FIFTY POUND HA'E I *925 5

FIG
   TO THE ARAB AND THE FIG HAS BEEN A CATCH-WORD FOR THE F+ 277 4
   FOR AGES I DON'T CARE A FIG FOR IT MEN SAY BUT WHY A FI+ 277 5
   THE PROPER WAY TO EAT A FIG IN SOCIETY   282 1
   THE FIG IS A VERY SECRETIVE FRUIT   282 12
   THE FIG THE HORSE-SHOE THE SQUASH-BLOSSOM   282 25
   FIG FRUIT OF THE FEMALE MYSTERY CONVERT AND INWARD   283 18
   AND THEN THE FIG HAS KEPT HER SECRET LONG ENOUGH   283 27
   AND THE FIG IS FINISHED THE YEAR IS OVER   283 29
   THAT'S HOW THE FIG DIES SHOWING HER CRIMSON THROUGH THE   283 30
   LIKE A PROSTITUTE THE BURSTEN FIG MAKING A SHOW OF HER + 283 33
   BUT NOW THEY STITCH TO ADORN THE BURSTEN FIG NOT TO COV+ 284 14
   WE ARE A RIPE FIG   284 22
   AND THE MOIST FIG   710 18

FIG-FRUIT
   FIG-FRUIT   282 18

FIGHT
   TAKE WRITHING FORMS OF ALL BEASTS THAT SWEAT AND THAT F+   73 15
   AND FIGHT   92 13
   WE ARE NOT LOVERS MY DARLING WE FIGHT AND WE DO NOT SPA+   92 16
   WHERE THE FIGHT THAT IS FIGHT FOR BEING IS FOUGHT THROU+   93 4
   CRUEL SELF THE FIGHT IS NOT FOR EXISTENCE THE FIGHT IS +   93 14
   WHAT'S BEYOND THEM AND FIGHT WITH ME IN DISCIPLINE'S LI+   93 18
   BLOOD SHED IN THE SILENT FIGHT   105 4
   THIS LAUGH IN THE FIGHT   124 15
   SO I DID NOT FIGHT YOU YOU WENT YOUR WAY INSTEAD   156 15
   FOR THE RIPPING OF ARRAS AND SMASHING OF WALLS AND THE + 174 15
   FOR THE FIGHT   228 26
   LET US FIGHT NO MORE   244 4
   WITH NOTHING TO FIGHT ANY MORE   245 1
   ALL THE LOT OF THEM AND LET THEM FIGHT IT OUT   316 6
   LET ME FIGHT THE WICKED OBSTREPEROUS WEEDS MYSELF AND P+ 316 11
   AND SALVIA FIERCE TO CROW AND SHOUT FOR FIGHT   317 21
   SOMETIMES HE TURNS WITH A START TO FIGHT TO CHALLENGE TO 381 8
   AND WE CAN'T FIGHT   382 7
   AND FIGHT TO BE BOSS OF THE WORLD   383 21
   FIGHT OLD SATAN WITH A SELFISH WILL FIGHT FOR YOUR SELF+ 383 22
   FIGHT TO BE THE DEVIL ON THE TIP OF THE PEAK   383 24
   THEN I AM WILLING TO FIGHT I WILL ROLL MY SLEEVES UP   430 11
   FIGHT DON'T YOU FEEL YOU'RE FADING   456 10
   FIGHT THEN POOR DUFFERS DEGRADING   456 12
   IT'S EITHER YOU FIGHT OR YOU DIE   458 1
   IT'S EITHER YOU FIGHT OR YOU DIE   458 4
   OR FIGHT AND MAKE THE SPLINTERS FLY   458 6
   FIGHT YOUR LITTLE FIGHT MY BOY   458 14
   FIGHT AND BE A MAN   458 15
   DO HOLD YOURSELF TOGETHER AND FIGHT   459 13
   I AM NOT SURE I WOULD ALWAYS FIGHT FOR MY LIFE   497 14
   I AM NOT SURE I WOULD ALWAYS FIGHT FOR MY WIFE   497 15
   THE ONLY THING MEN INVARIABLY FIGHT FOR   497 19
   IS THEIR MONEY BUT I DOUBT IF I'D FIGHT FOR MINE ANYHOW   497 20
   YET ONE THING I DO FIGHT FOR TOOTH AND NAIL ALL THE TIME 497 22

FIGHT
   THIS PRETTY PEACE WHERE EVERY MAN HAS TO FIGHT AND FIGHT 519 26
   WHY SHOULD WE HAVE TO FIGHT FOR A LIVING   520 1
   MEN FIGHT FOR LIBERTY AND WIN IT WITH HARD KNOCKS   535 23
   YES IT IS TRUE I FIGHT ALL THE TIME   606 14
   YET I AM NOT INTERESTED IN FIGHT IN STRIFE IN COMBAT   606 16
   OH NEVER FIGHT THE MACHINE   643 3
   AND FAR DOWN THE MUZZLE OF THE FIGHT   788 19
   AND THEY DART TO HER WOMB THEY FIGHT FOR THE CHANCE TO + 795 31
   FLEEING IN EXILE TO ENGLAND AT THE END OF THE FIGHT   859 6
   WITH GUSTO BEGIN AGAIN THE BRISK FIGHT   865 31
   OF JOY IN THE FIGHT   *930 4
   THIS LAUGH IN THE FIGHT   *935 14

FIGHTERS
   WOMEN WANT FIGHTERS FIGHTERS   457 25

FIGHTING
   SLEEP YET FIGHTING FIGHTING TO KEEP AWAKE   287 3
   AND THE FIGHTING COCK   457 26
   THE FIGHTING COCK THE FIGHTING COCK   457 28
   LIFE MIGHT NOT BE WORTH FIGHTING FOR   497 14
   A WIFE ISN'T ALWAYS WORTH FIGHTING FOR   497 16
   IT ALL DEPENDS WHETHER I FOUND THEM WORTH FIGHTING FOR   497 18
   FIGHTING FOR SOMETHING WORTH FIGHTING FOR   560 27

FIGHTINGS
   BUT LOVINGS AND HATINGS STRUGGLE AND FIGHTINGS   857 7

FIGHT'S
   THE FIGHT'S GOT TO GO IN SOME DIRECTION   538 17

FIG-LEAF
   THE FIG-LEAF THAT WAS NOT WOE IS ME   578 6
   AT THE SPOT WHERE THE FIG-LEAF JUST WAS NOT   578 13
   THE INNOCENT MEMBER THAT A FIG-LEAF WILL SCREEN   578 17
   WHERE A FIG-LEAF MIGHT HAVE BEEN AND WAS NOT   578 23
   WHERE A FIG-LEAF MIGHT HAVE BEEN BUT WAS NOT   579 4
   THERE'S NEVER A FIG-LEAF NEAR AT HAND   579 10
   A FIG-LEAF OR IF YOU CANNOT FIND IT   580 3

FIG-LEAVES
   SHE QUICKLY SEWED FIG-LEAVES AND SEWED THE SAME FOR THE+ 284 8
   SHE GOT THE FACT ON HER MIND AND QUICKLY SEWED FIG-LEAV+ 284 12

FIGMENT
   RUNNING AFTER A FIGMENT OF OURSELVES   543 17

FIGMENTS
   AND CARES NOT A STRAW FOR THE PUT-UP HUMAN FIGMENTS   481 16

FIGS
   THEY FORGET RIPE FIGS WON'T KEEP   284 24
   RIPE FIGS WON'T KEEP   284 25
   RIPE FIGS WON'T KEEP WON'T KEEP IN ANY CLIME   284 28
   AND BURSTEN FIGS WON'T KEEP   284 31
   THAT FIGS AREN'T FOUND IN THE LAND OF THE FREE   579 8

FIG-TREES
   FIG-TREES WEIRD FIG-TREES   298 19
   FIG-TREES DON'T GROW IN MY NATIVE LAND   579 9
   WITH VINES AND POPPIES AND FIG-TREES   710 16

FIG-TREE
   GREAT COMPLICATED NUDE FIG-TREE STEMLESS FLOWER-MESH   299 3
   FIG-TREE   300 6
   OH NAKED FIG-TREE   300 11
   WICKED FIG-TREE EQUALITY PUZZLE WITH YOUR SELF-CONSCIOUS 300 16
   EVEN THE WILFUL OBSTINATE GUMMY FIG-TREE   305 8

FIGURE
   THE GENTLE SOULS THAT FIGURE IN THE PAINT   580 22
   I SAW A DARK FIGURE APPROACHING A RAGGED SOLITARY CROW   866 17
   THE FIGURE OF SONG AFLUTTER IN A BLACK-WINGED REVELRY   *918 2

FIGURED
   ITS FIGURED PAGES AND SKY AND EARTH AND ALL BETWEEN ARE+   88 10

FIGURES
   EVER THE LONG BLACK FIGURES SWOOP BY THE BED   140 23
   FLUENT FIGURES OF MEN GO DOWN THE UPBORNE   174 7
   ALONG THE RAILWAY ACTIVE FIGURES OF MEN   174 9
   FLUENT ACTIVE FIGURES OF MEN PASS ALONG THE RAILWAY   *906 16
   FLUENT ACTIVE FIGURES OF MEN PASS ALONG THE RAILWAY AND+*908 11
   ALONG THE RAILWAY ACTIVE FIGURES OF MEN   *908 13

FILE
   AND FEARFUL TO FILE FORTH NOW FOR THE FIRST TIME ALONE *938 12

FILED
   AND HUNDREDS OF SOLDIERS ON HORSEBACK HAVE FILED BETWEEN 732 6

FILES
   DISASTROUSLY REMINISCENT OF HAMMERS AND FILES AND DOOR-+ 835 6

FILIGREE
   BUT THREADED WITH FILIGREE SILVER   101 5

FILING
   ENORMOUS SHADOW-PROCESSIONS FILING ON IN THE FLARE OF F+ 387 35

FILIUS MEUS
   FILIUS MEUS O REMORSELESS LOGIC   320 8
   FILIUS MEUS   320 17

FILL
NO LONGER HURT WHERE THE SILK SAILS FILL   53 12
FROM OFF MY MEASURE TO TOUCH YOU DEEP AND FILL   127 18
HAVING TASTED ALL THERE WAS TO TASTE AND HAVING SLEPT H+   324 11
TILL THEY MOUNT AND FILL AND ALL IS FULFILLED OF GOD'S +   698 20
RUSH IN AND FILL THE LIVING CAVITIES   784 11
AND FILL THEM STRONG WITH STRENGTH OF WINGS   799 19
TO FILL THEM UP A BRIMFUL MEASURE   868 18
TO FIND YOU AND FILL MY SOUL WITH YOU   887 17
LIFT UP YOUR MEASURE TO ME TO FILL   *931 10
TO FILL THEM UP THEIR BRIMMING MEASURES   *941 18

FILLED
ON HIS SLEEP THAT IS FILLED OF ME   60 2
OF EGYPT FILLED   96 9
OF THEIR PALE-GREEN GLACIER WATER FILLED THE EVENING   216 25
I SHALL NEVER CEASE TO BE FILLED WITH NEWNESS   248 14
WINGS AND MEN WHO SEE HIM WHEELING ARE FILLED WITH THE +   368 5
THAT PALE ONE FILLED WITH RENUNCIATION AND PAIN AND WHI+   439 22
I AM FILLED WITH HUMILIATION   484 8
YOU ARE EMPTY GOURD-SHELLS FILLED WITH DUST AND WIND   800 4
THE SUNBEAMS HAVE FILLED ME LIKE A HONEYCOMB   803 9
SO THEY BLOOMED OUT AND FILLED THEMSELVES WITH COLOURED+   831 3
HE IS NOT A PALE MAN FILLED WITH LOVE AND COMPASSION AN+   840 13
FILLED WITH REMORSEFUL TERROR TO THE MAN SHE SCORNED AN+   *891 30
OF THEIR PALE-GREEN GLACIER-WATER FILLED THE EVENING   *942 11

FILLET
IN A PURITAN FILLET A CHASTE WHITE SNARE   178 9

FILLING
THROUGH INVISIBLE PULSES SLOWLY FILLING THE NIGHT'S DAR+   97 28
GO MYRIAD SPARKS OF PEOPLE FILLING   110 19
I AM FILLING MY MOUTH WITH THE EARTH   259 31
FILLING THE HEART WITH PEACE   720 17
FILLING HIS SINGLE MEASURE WITH MUSIC FULL   877 27
FILLING MY STILL BREASTS WITH A FLUSH AND A FLAME   *893 17

FILLS
WITH DREAD AND FILLS MY HEART WITH THE TEARS OF DESIRE   48 12
UNDER TH' TANK AS FILLS TH' INGINES   79 3
IS YOUR FACE THAT FILLS ME WITH SHAME   112 12
AND FILLS THEM UP A POURING MEASURE   177 2
AND SUNSHINE FILLS ONE HIGH VALLEY BED   224 12
AND THE SAME FLAME THAT FILLS US WITH LIFE IT WILL DANC+   440 15
AND JUST FILLS YOU WITH HELL   565 30
NO LONGER SHAKE WHERE THE SILK SAIL FILLS   *906 4
UNDER THE TANK AS FILLS THE INGINES   *920 27
HE WATERS OUR FACE WITH TEARS OUR YOUNG FRUITS FILLS WI+   *926 29
THAT FILLS WITH GRIEF ALL THOSE THAT SEE   *927 29
IS YOUR FACE THAT FILLS ME WITH SHAME   *929 2

FILM
THE FILM OF THE BUBBLE NIGHT TO WHERE YOU ARE   194 2
THROUGH THE FILM I CAN ALMOST TOUCH YOU   194 3
WHILE YOU LISTEN IN WHILE YOU WATCH THE FILM WHILE YOU   441 20
WHEN I WENT TO THE FILM AND SAW ALL THE BLACK-AND-WHITE   443 22
THERE WAS NO GUSHING RESPONSE AS THERE IS AT THE FILM   445 30
ON THE FILM   446 5
WHILE THE MACHINE AMUSES US THE RADIO OR FILM OR   450 15
THE FILM FACE OF RUDOLF VALENTINO   538 2
STARE STARE STARE CORPSE-BODY AT THE FILM   584 14
UNLESS GOGGLING EYES TO GOGGLE AT THE FILM   630 29
IN THE HOT-BEDS OF THE BOARD-SCHOOLS AND THE FILM   644 7
JAZZ AND FILM AND WIRELESS   716 11

FILMS
LEAVING NASTY FILMS UPON YOU EVERY TIME   581 5

FILMY
FOR THE LUSCIOUS FILMY IMAGINATION LOATHES THE MALE   538 7

FILTERS
YOUR DEEP BEWILDERMENT FILTERS THROUGH   *894 3

FILTH
I FORCE MY CART THROUGH THE SODDEN FILTH THAT IS PRESSED   167 5
THAT YOU HAVE TO RUN OUT AT LAST AND EAT FILTH   398 27
GOBBLE UP FILTH YOU HORROR SWALLOW UTTER ABOMINATION   398 28
AND I HAVE TO CLEAN UP AFTER YOU FILTH WHICH EVEN BLIND   399 6
OF YOU MY BITCH TILL YOU GET SO FAR YOU EAT FILTH   400 17

FILTHY
OH MEN WITH THE AXE AND THE PICK-AXE BREAK THE WALLS OF+   175 26
THE DUST-HEAP OF MAN'S FILTHY WORLD ON FIRE   315 3
LIKE A FIELD OF FILTHY WEEDS   315 29
THAT IS YOUR TRICK YOUR BIT OF FILTHY MAGIC   332 21

FINAL
WHAT WILL BE IN THE FINAL LULL   164 3
INTOXICATION OF FINAL LONELINESS   281 30
AND FINAL HUMUS   318 2
AND NOW NO REALLY THE FINAL STRAW   491 21
AND IT'S FINAL   507 4
AT THE CORE OF SPACE THE FINAL KNELL   512 16
THAT INTERVENES BETWEEN THE FINAL SEA   722 7
THE KNOWING SMILE OF THE FINAL VIRGIN IN MAN   770 13
AND I WAIT FOR THE FINAL DAY WHEN THE DRAGON OF THUNDER+   797 7
AND THE OLD OLD FINAL LIFE-TRUTH   844 16
SHRIVELLING DOWN IN THE FINAL DOUR   *927 9
SHRIVELLING DOWN IN THE FINAL DOUR   *928 9
AND ROUND THE GREAT FINAL BEND OF UNBROKEN DARK   *959 27

FINALITY
JETS OF EXQUISITE FINALITY   271 10

FINALLY
FINALLY RIDGED WITH THE AUSTERE LINE OF THE DEAD   155 5
SHE HAS NOT CHOSEN ME FINALLY SHE SUSPENDS HER CHOICE   213 24
FINALLY   302 19
THE ASS WAS THE FIRST OF ALL ANIMALS TO FALL FINALLY IN+   378 16
AS IF NOW AT LAST HERE WAS THE ONE YOU FINALLY LOVED   398 17
FINALLY LOVED   398 18
THEN YOU WILL SETTLE THE HASH OF BUSINESS FINALLY   484 21
FINALLY OUR LITTLE LOT I DON'T WANT TO DIE BUT BY JINGO+   534 6
THAT ENGLISH ARTISTS MIGHT FINALLY LEARN   579 24
AH NO AH NO BEFORE WE FINALLY DIE   585 1
AND THE PERSON HAS BECOME FINALLY SELF-CENTRED   617 7
SOLVE THE INDIAN QUESTION FINALLY   780 1
FINALLY OUT OF THE HOST   823 5
AS THE MACHINE BREAKS FINALLY DOWN   *954 12

FINANCE
FINANCE IS A GREAT EVIL ABSTRACTION   716 8

FINANCIAL
WHY HAVE A FINANCIAL SYSTEM TO STRANGLE US ALL IN ITS   451 30
INDUSTRIAL AND FINANCIAL SYSTEMS MACHINES AND SOVIETS   452 10

FINANCIERS
AND EMPLOYERS ARE BOUGHT BY FINANCIERS AND FINANCIERS A+   483 4
WITH SATANICALLY INSPIRED FINANCIERS   483 15

FIND
AGAINST HIM DIE AND FIND DEATH GOOD   43 37
I COULD FIND NO TRACE   46 26
IT WILL FIND ME WATCHING AT THE MARRIAGE GATE   58 28
I LEANED IN THE DARKNESS TO FIND HER LIPS   62 6
TO FIND THE NEW HOUSES A CLUSTER OF LILIES GLITTERING   72 21
I SHOULD FIND FOR A REPRIMAND   107 1
THEN PERHAPS IN THE DARK YOU'D GET WHAT YOU WANT TO FIND   118 28
THINGS I WAS OUT TO FIND   123 23
WITHIN HER SPACIOUS SOUL TO FIND DELIGHT   125 35
ALL FEARFUL LEST I FIND THE LAST WORDS BLEEDING   135 19
SHE WON'T HARD TER FIND   138 34
AND CLIMB THE STAIRS TO FIND THE GROUP OF DOORS   140 9
RETURNING I FIND HER JUST THE SAME   150 24
I KNEW THAT SOME DAY SOON I SHOULD FIND YOU THUS   156 14
WHEN WE FIND THE PLACE WHERE THIS DEAD ROAD GOES   164 4
FIND OUT IF I'M SOUND OR BANKRUPT   237 3
FIND THE HESPERIDES   250 24
AND WHOSOEVER COMES AFTER WILL FIND ME IN THE NEW WORLD   260 22
AND IF WE SIP THE WINE WE FIND DREAMS COMING UPON US   286 22
NAY WE FIND OURSELVES CROSSING THE FERN-SCENTED FRONTIE+   286 24
YOU WHO NEVER FIND YOURSELF IN LOVE   290 10
FIND AN ENEMY EGOIST AND CLASH THE CYMBALS IN FACE-TO-F+   383 17
WHO NEVER IN ALL HER LIFE COULD FIND THE WAY HOME   412 7
FIND THE WAY NOW THAT YOU NEVER COULD FIND IN LIFE   412 12
AND ALLOW THE SOUL TO FIND ITS LEVEL   428 7
TOUCH HIM AND YOU'LL FIND HE'S ALL GONE INSIDE   431 19
THEY FIND HE HAS SOLD THEM TO HIS FATHER   442 13
WHO WILL FIND IT SO HARD TO MATE   459 4
WERE OUT TO FIND   463 11
FIND   464 4
YOU WILL FIND YOU HAVE A GREAT DESIRE TO DRINK LIFE DIR+   481 3
YET YOU FAIL TO FIND THE WOMAN WHEN THERE ARE SO MANY   485 13
BESIDES SHE'S HAD TWENTY LOVERS ONLY TO FIND SHE DIDN'T   539 16
JUST TO SUPPORT YOU AND FIND YOU MONEY   547 7
AND THEN YOU FIND THEY'RE NOT   549 26
I FIND I'D RATHER GET BACK TO EARTH   552 7
AN' IF YOU DID YOU'D FIND   552 28
AS FAR AS I CAN FIND   553 14
A FIG-LEAF OR IF YOU CANNOT FIND IT   580 3
LIFE WILL FIND A WAY   637 31
AND LIVED TO FIND OUT   644 10
NOT TO FIND SOMETHING   661 4
AND THE LOVELESS NEVER FIND LOVE   661 8
ONLY THE LOVING FIND LOVE   661 9
AND WE WILL FIND THE WAY TO IMMEDIATE CONTACT WITH LIFE   666 18
BECAUSE THEY DON'T KNOW WHAT THEY'LL FIND WHEN THEY DO +   667 21
TO FIND THE OTHER MANY ELEMENTS YOU MUST GO TO THE LABO+   706 6
TO ONE'S OWN SELF AND FIND AN EXIT   716 23
THAT CANNOT FIND THE WAY ACROSS THE SEA OF CHANGE   721 16
THERE IS NO PLACE FOR THE SOUL TO FIND HER OBLIVION   725 15
AND IF TONIGHT MY SOUL MAY FIND HER PEACE   726 22
LAST TWILIGHT OF THE GODS TO FIND AGAIN   737 8
OF DANGER I FIND HER EVEN WORSE THAN THE FIELDS WHERE W+   752 12
HOW CAN I FIND MY WAY TO THE RIVER   757 5
AMERICA WILL HAVE TO FIND HER OWN WAY INTO THE FUTURE   775 32
YOU SHALL FIND ME WHO AM NEITHER INCREASE   788 20
THEY SHALL FIND ME ONLY IN THE MORNING STAR   799 10
BUT ON WHAT THEY FIND DISTASTEFUL REPULSIVE OR ATTRACTI+   831 19
WHEN MORNING COMES I FIND ME A LOVE   858 5
STARTLED AND FULL OF AGONY TO FIND HE HAD BUT SLEPT   859 18
I RUN AWAKE TO THE HOUSE OF MY SOUL AND FIND IT EMPTY   871 9
SO GLAD TO FIND MYSELF AGAIN   882 12
TO FIND YOU AND FILL MY SOUL WITH YOU   887 17
MOUNTS UP TO MY HEART AND I FIND IT GOOD   *899 34
MOUNTS UP TO MY HEART AND I FIND IT GOOD   *903 13
I LEANED ME FORWARD TO FIND HER LIPS   *912 11
DID TER FIND HER GOOD   *922 20
IT IS ONLY I FIND IT HARD TO BEAR   *931 12
THEN PERHAPS IN THE DARK YOU'LL HAVE GOT WHAT YOU WANT + *932 6
THINGS I WAS OUT TO FIND   *934 29
ALL FEARFUL LEST I FIND SOME NEXT WORD BLEEDING   *939 3
WITH PRAYER I NEED ONLY COME HOME EACH NIGHT TO FIND TH+ *945 28
TO FIND HIMSELF ON THE CROWDED ARID MARGINS OF EXISTENCE *957 14

FINDING
OF THE STUFF OF THE NIGHT FINDING MYSELF ALL WRONGLY   133 7
THAT WHICH IS IN PART FINDING ITS WHOLE AGAIN THROUGHOUT   367 6
WE SHALL GO ON FINDING OUT ABOUT OURSELVES   832 24

FINDS
 HE FINDS A FEMALE THEY SHOW NO HASTE 465 9
 LIFE ALWAYS FINDS A WAY 637 32
 HE FEELS FOR HIS PURSE AND FINDS IT THERE AND SAYS 659 19
 WHICH GOES FURTHER AND FURTHER AND YET NEVER FINDS AN E+ 701 6
 FINDS ITSELF SHRINKING WINCING FROM THE COLD 717 8
 AND FINDS THAT THE SUBTLE DESTRUCTIVE CYNICISM IS ONLY + 842 2
 AND HOW HE FINDS THE DARKNESS THAT ENFOLDS HIM INTO UTT+ *961 13

FINE
 I KNOW NOT WHAT FINE WIRE IS ROUND MY THROAT 43 29
 THE CLINK OF THE SHUNTING ENGINES IS SHARP AND FINE 52 16
 SOMETHING FAERY AND FINE THE SHUTTLES SLIDING 72 7
 A FINE PROUD SPIKE OF PURPLE IRISES 90 3
 FINE TORTURE YOU DID DESERVE 111 27
 FINE THRILLS TO THE NEIGHBOUR STARS FINE HIDDEN BEAMS 127 7
 FOR SURELY THE FRAGILE FINE YOUNG THING HAD BEEN 132 3
 MY MISSAL BOOK OF FINE FLAMBOYANT HOURS 135 2
 MY MOUTH YOU MET BEFORE YOUR FINE RED MOUTH 156 22
 THE FAINT FINE SEETHE IN THE AIR 216 6
 FULL OF FINE WARMTH I ISSUE FORTH IN CLEAR 218 7
 TILL ALL YOUR BEING SMOKES WITH FINE DESIRE 219 4
 SHE PRICKED A FINE BLACK BLOTCH 222 7
 PUT BACK HER FINE LEVEL-BALANCED HEAD 222 15
 WITH THAT FINE DEMONIACAL SPARK 241 15
 A FINE WIND IS BLOWING THE NEW DIRECTION OF TIME 250 14
 BY THE FINE FINE WIND THAT TAKES ITS COURSE THROUGH THE 250 18
 LIKE A FINE AN EXQUISITE CHISEL A WEDGE-BLADE INSERTED 250 20
 LOOK YOU ARE CLEAN AND FINE AND SINGLED OUT 255 10
 I WANT THE FINE KINDLING WINE-SAP OF SPRING 271 17
 GOLD AND OF INCONCEIVABLY FINE QUINTESSENTIAL BRIGHTNESS 271 18
 KNOTTED IN HEAVEN UPON THE FINE LIGHT 307 9
 PURE BLOOD AND NOBLE BLOOD IN THE FINE AND ROSE-RED VEI+ 314 1
 BROWN NUT-BROWN FINE FUR 345 33
 AND THE FINE BRILLIANCE OF YOUR SO TINY EYE 353 22
 OF FINE LINEN 388 18
 AND STRIPES IN THE BRILLIANT FROST OF HER FACE SHARP FI+ 402 4
 DARK KEEN FINE RAYS IN THE BRILLIANT FROST OF HER FACE 402 6
 ISN'T HE HANDSOME ISN'T HE HEALTHY ISN'T HE A FINE 430 19
 TO FEEL A FINE FINE BREEZE BLOWING THROUGH THE NAVEL AND 481 21
 THE NOVEL IT SURE WAS MIGHTY FINE 489 11
 THOUGH THE HOUSE HAD A FINE INTERIOR 554 15
 AND SHE KENS IT FINE 573 16
 IN MY FINE PROSPERITY KICK THOSE IN THE DITCH 584 1
 FLOWERS OF GRASS FINE MEN 587 23
 AND DANGLE IN A LAST FASTIDIOUS FINE DELIGHT 667 15
 AND FINE AS FLOWERS ARE FINE 667 27
 I'VE BEEN UP TO LONDON TO SEE THE FINE QUEEN 670 2
 AND ENJOY MYSELF FINE 671 8
 AS A FINE GREY EGG OR A SLENDER ROD 752 16
 BRISTLING WITH ANIMATION OH PLEASE SIR HOW D'YOU LIKE T+ 865 21
 SLIPPED LIKE ANYTHING BUT DON'T YOU LIKE IT AIN'T IT FI+ 865 23
 HIS FULL FINE BODY BENDING AND URGING LIKE THE STRESS O+ 867 24
 OF MY OLD WHITE METAL OF MEANING YOU FINE 873 4
 FINE FOLIAGE OF LIVES THIS LIFE OF MINE *899 25
 TO FOLLOW MY LIFE ALOFT TO THE FINE WILD AIR OF LIFE AN+ *900 8
 FINE FOLIAGE OF LIVES THIS LIFE OF MINE *903 6
 TO FOLLOW MY LIFE ALOFT TO THE FINE WILD AIR OF LIFE AN+ *903 20
 THE CLINK OF THE SHUNTING ENGINES IS SHARP AND FINE *905 5
 YI' THA'RT A MAN THA'RT A FINE BIG MAN BUT NIVER A BABY+ *925 24
 YEA I WAS FINE ENOUGH TO EXPLORE YOU *927 6
 MY FINE CRAFTSMAN'S NERVE *927 12
 MY FINE CRAFTSMAN'S NERVE *928 12
 FINE TORTURE YOU DID DESERVE *928 15
 FOR SURELY THE FRAGILE FINE YOUNG THING HAD BEEN *937 30

FINE-FASHIONED
 HER ROUND FINE-FASHIONED HEAD WITH TWO DEAD EARS 402 3

FINELY
 FINELY DIVISIBLE 269 12
 GENTLY AND FINELY LINED THAN A RABBIT'S OR THAN A HARE'S 393 7
 IN MANY WAYS VERY FINELY BRED 400 15

FINER
 YOU HAVE WELDED YOUR THIN STEMS FINER 300 28
 THROUGHOUT THE AEONS AS THE LIZARD SWIRLS HIS TAIL FINE+ 683 7
 SHE'S A FINER INSTRUCTOR THAN YEARS *893 3

FINEST
 TILL NAKED FOR HER IN THE FINEST FASHION 113 7
 THE FINEST SPLINTER OF A SPARK 241 8
 IF YOU COPULATE WITH THE FINEST WOMAN ON EARTH 486 3
 FACE WAS THE FINEST THING THAT IVER *925 3

FINGER
 I ONLY KNOW I LET HIM FINGER THERE 43 30
 FOREVER OUT OF THE MIST THE CHURCH LIFTS UP A REPROACHF+ 63 24
 HOW WERT THOU SO STRANGE-SHAPEN WHAT WARM FINGER 69 13
 TEMPTINGLY IN MID-AIR BETWEEN A PLAYFUL THUMB AND FINGER 271 24
 SHE HAS NO QUALM WHEN SHE CATCHES MY FINGER IN HER STEEL 359 20
 SNAKE-LIKE SHE DRAWS AT MY FINGER WHILE I DRAG IN HORROR 359 26
 AND FINGER IT AND FORCE IT AND SHATTER THE RHYTHM IT KE+ 464 30
 FROM TRESPASSED CONTACTS FROM RED-HOT FINGER 601 10
 OF FINGER OR FIST OR SOFT-SKINNED STICKS UPON THE STRET+ 623 6
 LIFT NEVER A FINGER AGAINST THEM THAT THEY CAN SEE 643 5
 IF I CUT MY FINGER MY BLOOD IS HOT NOT COLD 655 22
 YOU WEAR ON YOUR FINGER SO GLADLY FOR GOD 752 18
 AND SO THOU WERT GOD-SHAPEN HIS FINGER *915 25

FINGERED
 YOU HAVE FINGERED ALL MY TREASURES 95 16
 OF BLOSSOM SHE FINGERED AND MY FINGERS ALL 125 22
 FINGERED BY THE MIND 469 16
 OF BLOSSOM SHE FINGERED AND MY POISED FINGERS ALL *936 21

FINGERING
 UNDER THE PALLID MOONLIGHT'S FINGERING 129 12
 O LEAVE ME CLEAN FROM MENTAL FINGERING 469 19
 AND SLOWLY FINGERING UP MY STEM AND FOLLOWING ALL TINILY *900 18
 AND SLOWLY FINGERING UP MY STEM AND FOLLOWING ALL TINILY *903 30

FINGER-NAILS
 WITH FINGER-NAILS OF SEPTIC CRITICISING 533 10

FINGERS
 SEE THE WOMAN'S TRINKLING FINGERS TEND HIM A COIN 36 6
 AND CARESSES ME WITH HIS FINGERS THAT STILL SMELL GRIM 43 27
 TOUCHES THE CLASP WITH TREMBLING FINGERS AND TRIES 64 16
 FEELING YOUR FINGERS GO 104 5
 CIGARETTE BETWEEN MY FINGERS 106 25
 COMES ON US LIFT YOUR FINGERS WHITE 117 12
 MY FINGERS TILL ITS HEAD LAY BACK ITS FANGS 125 14
 OF BLOSSOM SHE FINGERED AND MY FINGERS ALL 125 22
 AND OFTEN I SEE HER CLENCH HER FINGERS TIGHT 128 18
 ASLEEP MY FINGERS CREEP 143 10
 NOTHING TO MEET MY FINGERS BUT THE FLEECE OF NIGHT 147 4
 'TWAS I WHOSE FINGERS DID DRAW UP THE YOUNG 156 19
 A COLD HAND I PEEP BETWEEN THE FINGERS 162 18
 BETWEEN THE FINGERS THAT COVER MY FACE 162 22
 THEIR FINGERS IN SUNSET SHINE 168 14
 ALWAYS GLADDEN MY AMOROUS FINGERS WITH THE TOUCH OF THE+ 180 25
 THAT SHINE AS HER FINGERS STIR 200 20
 HE PUTS HIS SURF-WET FINGERS 201 1
 THAT MY FINGERS SHOULD TURN INTO THESE FLAMES 241 22
 THIS INTERMINGLING OF THE BLACK AND MONSTROUS FINGERS OF 242 2
 SAP THAT SMELLS STRANGE ON YOUR FINGERS THAT EVEN GOATS+ 283 12
 PUT THE FIRST CENTS INTO METALLIC FINGERS OF YOUR OFFIC+ 291 4
 NO FINGERS NO HANDS AND FEET NO LIPS 335 17
 AND DRINKING FROM CUPS THAT CAME OFF HIS FINGERS LIKE 451 26
 O YOU WITH MENTAL FINGERS O NEVER PUT YOUR HAND ON ME 468 24
 FROM HOT DIGGING-IN FINGERS OF LOVE 601 12
 AND ONE TRAPPED ONE'S FINGERS IN THEIR BRASSY POLISHED 644 13
 WITH A CIGARETTE BROWNING YOUR FINGERS 651 23
 CAN SLIP ENTIRELY THROUGH THE FINGERS OF THE HANDS OF G+ 701 14
 WHEN THEY POINT THEIR SLANTING FINGERS 731 7
 AND RUBS THE SILVER CLEAN WITH HIS THICK BROWN FINGERS 734 2
 JESUS HIS FINGERS ARE RED 734 11
 FINGERS ACROSS THE HARP 746 26
 SWIFTLY I WISH I MIGHT KISS HER FINGERS BUT FULL 752 11
 NIBBLED HIS FINGERS THE KNAVE 754 19
 AND BETWEEN OUR FINGERS ROSE A BLADE OF GREEN GRASS 806 27
 BUT THE FINGERS OF ALL TOUCH THE FINGERS OF ALL 811 29
 TINY FINGERS OUTSPREAD 861 21
 AND HER FINGERS MOVE IN THE RUTS OF MY EARS 863 3
 FROM OUT HIS FINGERS FROM THAT SUPPLE STRING 877 12
 WITH SORROWFUL FINGERS STROKED HER EYELIDS SHUT 881 2
 BUT SHE PUT HER FINGERS ON MY NECK UNDER MY COLLAR 882 30
 AND HER FINGERS WERE COOL 882 31
 COMES ON US YOU'LL LIFT YOUR FINGERS WHITE *931 16
 MY FINGERS TILL ITS HEAD GAPED BACK ITS FANGS *936 13
 OF BLOSSOM SHE FINGERED AND MY POISED FINGERS ALL *936 14
 HER FINGERS AS IF IT WOULD TWIST *937 10
 AND THE KEYS WITH LITTLE HOLLOWS THAT MY MOTHER'S FINGE+ *940 4
 FINGERS GLIDE *940 13
 AND DRINKING FROM THE CUPS THAT HAVE FLOWERED FROM HIS + *950 10

FINGER'S
 WHO SHOOK THY ROUNDNESS IN HIS FINGER'S CUP 69 9
 GOD SHOOK THY ROUNDNESS IN HIS FINGER'S CUP *915 21

FINISH
 WILL IT NEVER FINISH THE TWELVE 63 2
 BUT LET ME FINISH WHAT I HAVE BEGUN 154 18
 ARE WE AT LENGTH TO FINISH OUR REST OF DAYS 157 25
 YOU WOULD TAKE A STICK AND BREAK HIM NOW AND FINISH 350 6
 STRIKING US THE VIBRATIONS OF OUR FINISH 512 22
 LET US ONLY FINISH 826 9
 FINISH FINISH DIMINISH DIMINISH 826 10
 AS THE MACHINES FAIL AND FINISH *954 7

FINISHED
 IT IS FINISHED BETWEEN US HERE 102 14
 THA COME TER HA' FINISHED AN' DONE WI' ME 138 10
 NOT FINISHED HE HASN'T NO MATTER HOW 139 26
 OF FINISHED BRIDEGROOM SEEN HER RISE AND THROW 193 4
 IT IS FINISHED THE SPRING IS HERE 244 18
 WHY WAS NOT MY PEACH ROUND AND FINISHED LIKE A BILLIARD 279 21
 BUT IT WASN'T ROUND AND FINISHED LIKE A BILLIARD BALL 279 25
 TILL IT'S FINISHED AND YOU'RE OVER-RIPE AND YOU BURST T+ 283 23
 AND THE FIG IS FINISHED THE YEAR IS OVER 283 29
 HAVING SHED THEIR SOUND AND FINISHED ALL THEIR ECHOING 296 27
 HE SO FINISHED AND IMMUNE NOW BROKEN INTO DESIROUS 361 6
 WHY WERE WE NOT LEFT ROUNDED OFF AND FINISHED IN OURSEL+ 364 8
 IT IS OVER BEFORE IT IS FINISHED 382 25
 WE DODGED WHEN THE PERA-HERA WAS FINISHED UNDER THE 390 11
 ABSOLUTISM IS FINISHED IN THE HUMAN CONSCIOUSNESS TOO 473 14
 EVEN THE OLD EMOTIONS ARE FINISHED 510 16
 A CYCLE OF EVOLUTION IS FINISHED 510 21
 I SUDDENLY SAID I'VE FINISHED 556 15
 FINISHED FINISHED FINISHED 584 26
 IT IS FINISHED ITS RACE IS OVER 676 5
 ZIGZAGGING DOWN LIKE THE FIZZLE FROM A FINISHED ROCKET 701 26
 NOW LET IT ALL BE FINISHED LEAVE NO TRACE 737 23
 OH IT IS FINISHED I WOULD LIKE TO TAKE 738 9
 FINISHED OFF 777 21
 THEN OUR LIFE IS FINISHED OUR DAY IS OVER COMPLETELY 779 5
 IT IS FINISHED 779 8
 SO IT IS FINISHED 779 11
 COME THEN NOW IT IS FINISHED FOR ALL OF US 798 9
 IT IS FINISHED THE REST IS AFTERWARDS 816 21
 WE HAVE ONLY FINISHED 825 32
 O SO SMART AND SO MECHANICALLY FINISHED 845 23
 THE LAST ROW IS FINISHED THE JINGLING RAKE IS LIFTED 858 17

FINISHING
    FINISHING YOUR DREAMS FOR YOUR OWN SAKE ONLY   197 6

FINS
    A FLUSH AT THE FLAILS OF YOUR FINS DOWN THE WHORL OF YO+   335 9
    A SLIM YOUNG PIKE WITH SMART FINS   338 1
    I WISH I HAD FINS AND GILLS   837 15

FIRE
    HE STANDS THE COLUMN OF FIRE BY NIGHT   39 22
    TRAVELLER COLUMN OF FIRE   40 5
    OF SWEET FIRE SWEEPS ACROSS ME SO I DROWN   43 36
    I MUST FOLD MY HANDS AND TURN MY FACE TO THE FIRE   47 2
    CLOTTING TO ONE DEAD MASS IN THE SINKING FIRE   47 5
    WITH FIRE AS IT GUARDS THE WILD NORTH-COASTS RED-FIRE S+   57 13
    FIRE HORIZONTAL DECLINING AND EBBING THE TWILIT EBB OF +   67 6
    WARMIN' 'IS-SEN AT THE STOOL O' FIRE   79 2
    STRAY WHITEBEAM AND HER WHITE FIRE ALL UNLADENS   86 20
    FIRE ENTERS YOU LIKE FROST LIKE A CRUEL BLIGHT   87 17
    AND THE SAME FIRE THAT BOILS WITHIN THIS BALL   89 1
    OF A TRAIL OF OUR SMALL FIRE ON THE DARKENED SKY   89 15
    WHERE WE CAN SEE IT OUR FIRE TO THE INNERMOST FIRE   89 16
    A GRAIN OF THIS SAME FIRE WE CAN DESCRY   89 20
    INTO THE WOMB TO KINDLE AN UNKNOWN FIRE   89 35
    WITH FIRE ON YOUR CHEEKS AND YOUR BROW AND YOUR CHIN AS+   90 9
    THE LAST YEAR'S FIRE IS GONE AND YOUR FACE IS ASH   91 2
    BUT SOMETIMES THE OPENING PETALS ARE FIRE AND THE SCARL+   93 31
    THE FIRE ROSE UP IN THE BUSH AND BLAZED APACE   94 25
    YOU SENT ME A CLOVEN FIRE   108 17
    FIRE PASSED THROUGH YOUR FLESH   112 2
    SINCE THE FIRE HAS FAILED IN ME   112 8
    AND I WHAT SORT OF FIRE AM I AMONG   116 10
    BUT SINCE MY LIMBS GUSHED FULL OF FIRE   118 1
    OF MIDNIGHT AND SHAKE IT TO FIRE TILL THE FLAME OF THE   136 20
    OF YOUR HEART OF FIRE IN WHICH I LOOK   151 2
    AND OVER MY FACE THE STRAY FIRE SLIPS   151 8
    OF FIRE AND BEAUTY LOOSE NO MORE   151 11
    THAT STAYS WITH STEADY JOY OF ITS OWN FIRE   151 15
    YET WARM HERSELF AT THE FIRE THEN BLAME   151 35
    AWAITING THE FIRE   155 18
    TOUCHED YOU TO FIRE   158 6
    THAT SAVES THE BLUE GRAIN OF ETERNAL FIRE   161 3
    THAT CRUSHES ME TO AN UNSEEN ATOM OF FIRE   195 36
    THE INNERMOST FIRE OF MY OWN DIM SOUL OUT-SPINNING   218 22
    THE GREAT BREATH BLOWING A TINY SEED OF FIRE   219 2
    THE CORN-STALKS TIPPING WITH FIRE THE SPEARS   221 24
    FOR THE FIRE   228 22
    INTO THE FIRE   235 10
    I HAVE MADE THE FIRE UP BRIGHT   237 20
    AS IT CIRCULATES ROUND OUR FIRE   238 8
    IT SETS UP A STRANGE FIRE   241 10
    THIS FURNACE THIS DRAUGHT-MADDENED FIRE   241 18
    THAT HAS DRAWN THIS TERRIBLE DRAUGHT OF WHITE FIRE   241 29
    BETWEEN THE BICKERING FIRE   242 9
    YOU THE CORE OF THE FIRE CREPT INTO ME   245 25
    AND THE WOOD-ASH GATHERED IN THE FIRE   248 18
    OLD SCATTERED FIRE   271 32
    THE LAVA FIRE   293 26
    FIRE AND WATER THEY CONTAIN THE PROPORTION OF MALE AND +   295 7
    ARE EXCRETIONS OF THE WATER AND FIRE IN PLANTS   295 10
    SHOUTING FORTH FLAME TO SET THE WORLD ON FIRE   315 2
    THE DUST-HEAP OF MAN'S FILTHY WORLD ON FIRE   315 3
    AND GLUTTED SQUIRMING POPULOUSNESS ON FIRE   315 28
    ALL RUBBISH READY FOR FIRE   316 35
    CONSTRAINED TO POUR FORTH ALL HIS FIRE DOWN THE NARROW +   327 11
    FOR THE FIRE TO BURN IT UP FEATHERS AND ALL   329 32
    AND WATER WETLY ON FIRE IN THE GRATES OF YOUR GILLS   335 11
    SWEET FIRE OF DAY   346 5
    FOR WHEN FIRE IN ITS DOWNWARD PATH CHANCED TO MINGLE WI+   348 6
    OR MUST YOU GO THROUGH THE FIRE ONCE MORE TILL YOU'RE   372 1
    FLY SLOWLY AWAY WITH A RUST OF FIRE IN YOUR TAIL   374 30
    WAIT WAIT A BIT I'LL COME WHEN I'VE LIT THE FIRE   384 9
    FIRE   385 32
    SARDONIC SARDONYX ROCK OF COLD FIRE   386 6
    ENORMOUS SHADOW-PROCESSIONS FILING ON IN THE FLARE OF F+   387 35
    AS THEY APPROACH AND SALAAM UNDER THE DRIPPING FIRE OF   388 3
    HUGE MORE TASSELS SWINGING MORE DRIPPING FIRE OF NEW   388 27
    HIGH HIGH UP IN FLAKES SHIMMERING FLAKES OF BLUE FIRE   391 18
    O RIPPLING HARD FIRE OF COURAGE O FUSING OF HOT TRUST   440 13
    WHEN THE FIRE REACHES US O MY YOUNG MEN   440 14
    HIDING THEIR FIRE   465 22
    FIRE SHOULD BE FREE   487 9
    AND THE INDIVIDUAL MUST HAVE HIS HOUSE FOOD AND FIRE ALL   487 23
    FIRE AND RAIN AND AIR AND LIVE LOAM   505 13
    AS FIRE IS   505 19
    FIRE IS DEARER TO US THAN LOVE OR FOOD   505 25
    BUT OUR FIRE OUR ELEMENTAL FIRE   506 5
    WHO WAS LIKE A RED FIRE ON THE HEARTH   506 12
    SONS OF EARTH SONS OF FIRE SONS OF AIR AND WATER   635 3
    SONS OF THE WIND AND RAIN SONS OF THE FIRE AND ROCK   635 25
    AND THE SONS OF MEN WITH THE WIND AND THE FIRE OF LIFE   635 30
    MEN OF THE FIRE AND ROCK HOW ARE THEY GOING TO COME FOR+   637 28
    OH MEN LIVING MEN VIVID MEN OCEAN AND FIRE   639 1
    JUGFULL AFTER JUGFULL OF PURE WHITE LIQUID FIRE BRIGHT +   647 9
    THEIR HARDENED SOULS ARE WASHED WITH FIRE AND WASHED AN+   663 6
    AND FIERCE AS FIRE IS FIERCE   667 28
    SLEEPING ON THE HEARTH AND YAWNING BEFORE THE FIRE   700 7
    YAWNING AT HOME BEFORE THE FIRE OF LIFE   700 9
    THE FRIZZLING FALLING FIRE THAT CANNOT GO OUT DROPPING +   701 27
    BETWEEN THE TWO GREAT ONES FIRE AND THE WET   705 22
    OF FIRE AND THE WET EARTH AND THE WIDE AIR OF THE WORLD   706 5
    SO SALT IS THE BOUNDARY MARK BETWEEN FIRE THAT BURNS AN+   706 10
    THE TWO GREAT AND MOVING ONES FIRE AND THE YIELDING WET   706 12
    ARE MARKED OUT WITH THE BOUNDARY OF SALT BETWEEN FIRE A+   706 14
    ONE OF YOU KINDLE A FIRE TO CONSUME THEM WITHAL   750 24
    I AM INCLINED TO HEAP THY COALS OF FIRE ON MY OWN   760 15
    HAVING BEEN THROUGH THE FIRE   769 2
    HAVING BEEN THROUGH FIRE THROUGH MANY FIRES   769 3

FIRE
    TO BE CARRIED AT LAST FROM THE FIRE   769 12
    WHO HAVE BEEN THROUGH THE FIRE   770 3
    IN THE STONE AND IRON LEAPS IN FIRE   773 5
    THE FIRE   782 14
    THE HEART OF THE WORLD IS THE HEART OF THE EARTH WHERE +   782 16
    AS FIRE BUT SOFT AS SUNSHINE SOFT AS KISSES   784 16
    YOU WILL NEVER CATCH FIRE   784 22
    SOMEONE WILL COME TO THE PLACE OF FIRE   789 1
    I'LL SEND FIRE AND ASHES UPON THEM AND SMOTHER THEM ALL   792 5
    THE DEAD THAT HAVE MASTERED FIRE LIVE ON SALAMANDERS IN+   796 7
    WITH HIS MOUTH OF CARESSIVE FIRE   801 23
    WITH FIRE AND MY THROAT IS FULL   802 25
    I WATCH BY THE FIRE   804 17
    OF FIRE BENT BACK AGAIN   805 11
    HE IS WATCHING BY THE FIRE   805 25
    FIRE OF THE PASSION OF MEN   806 14
    AND YELLOW AS THE FIRE THAT CONSUMES   806 23
    RED IS THE BLOOD AND THE FIRE   808 25
    IS THE LIBERATING FIRE   810 16
    FIRE IN YOUR HEARTS OF MEN   811 25
    AND DEEPER STILL THE UNKNOWN FIRE UNKNOWN AND HEAVY HEA+   844 3
    LIES THE PONDEROUS FIRE OF NAKED LIFE   844 12
    AND DEEPER THAN THE BEDROCK OF PRIDE IS THE PRIMORDIAL +   844 20
    WHICH RESTS IN CONNECTION WITH THE FURTHER FOREVER UNKN+   844 22
    TO SEE HIM FLASH AND TREMBLE WITH THE FIRE OF HIS SOUL   859 8
    LOOKED WHERE THE RED FRUIT HUNG LIKE COALS OF FIRE   864 8
    OF YOUR HEART OF FIRE IN WHICH I LOOK   873 12
    AND OVER MY FACE YOUR STRAY FIRE SLIPS   873 18
    THAT STEADY STAYS WITH JOY OF ITS OWN FIRE   873 25
    OH DO NOT SEEK TO THRUST IN ME YOUR FIRE   873 27
    YET WARM HERSELF AT THE FIRE AND BLAME   874 13
    NOT TO REACH ONE TONGUE OF FIRE   874 19
    WE LEAP LIKE TWO CLASPED FLAMES FROM OFF THE FIRE   879 30
    LIKE A MURMUR OF FIRE   885 26
    TILL I ROUSE MY WILL LIKE A FIRE TO CONSUME   *895 28
    THE FIRE ROSE UP AND THE BUSH BLAZED FORTH GOD'S GRACE   *897 13
    TILL I ROUSE MY WILL LIKE A FIRE TO CONSUME   *904 17
    WARMIN' HIS-SEN AT THE STOOL O' FIRE   *920 26
    TILL THY FULL-FED FIRE OF CURIOSITY BORE YOU   *927 8
    TILL MY FIRE OF CREATION BORE YOU   *928 8
    SINCE THE FIRE HAS FAILED IN ME   *928 28
    YOU WATCH THE FIRE SPARKS SWIRL AND FLEE   *930 22
    TO THE FIRE AND RAIN WILL YOU TAKE THE FLOOD   *931 27
    THIRTEEN TIMES THE TEETH FLASHED IN A FIRE OF BLOOD   *933 1
    HER FIRE INFUSING ITS LIFELESSNESS   *937 17
    TORCHES' FIRE   *937 21
    THE CORN-STALKS TIPPING WITH FIRE THEIR SPEARS   *945 10
    AND GREATER HEAT INTO FIRE MORE HEAVY AND HOTTER THAN A+ *951 21
    CENTRAL PRIMORDIAL FIRE OF THE SOUL HEAVIER THAN IRON   *951 24
    BALANCE WITH THE OTHER THE VAST UNKNOWABLE FIRE   *951 30
    CENTRAL PRIMORDIAL FIRE OF THE SOUL HEAVIER THAN IRON   *952 1
    THE VASTER FIRE   *952 3
    CENTRAL PRIMORDIAL FIRE OF THE SOUL THAT LEANS AND YEAR+ *952 6

FIRE-BURNT
    WHERE THE FIRE-BURNT VIRGIN IN MAN AND THE VIRGIN IN FI+   770 27

FIRE-CORE
    SEEING I DEEP IN THE FIRE-CORE INVIOLATE   *930 11

FIRED
    'E UP AN' FIRED 'IS PISTOL   81 7
    HE UP AN' FIRED OFF HIS PISTOL   *923 7

FIRE-FLARE
    OF THE HUGEST OLDEST OF BEASTS IN THE NIGHT AND THE FIR+   388 11

FIREFLIES
    SOME FIREFLIES DRIFT THROUGH THE MIDDLE AIR   221 1
    AND THE DEAR DEAR FIREFLIES WAFTING IN BETWEEN   221 15
    AND THOSE BRIGHT FIREFLIES WAFTING IN BETWEEN   *945 1

FIREGLOW
    AND THIS FIREGLOW   238 3
    THIS FIREGLOW THE CORE   238 4
    THIS FIREGLOW IS A RED WOMB   239 22

FIRE-LAUGHING
    PERPETUAL FIRE-LAUGHING MOTION AMONG THE SLOW SHUFFLE   389 18

FIRELIGHT
    AND THE RED FIRELIGHT STEADILY REELING   41 8
    AND SIT BY FIRELIGHT   237 22
    AS THE FIRELIGHT FALLS AND LEAPS   238 14
    THAT LIVE BY NIGHT AND LAMPLIGHT AND FIRELIGHT DO THEM +   331 8

FIRE-MIST
    WHITE AND HALOED WITH FIRE-MIST DOWN IN THE TANGLED   206 11

FIRE-OPAL
    OF ME TO BE HER FIRE-OPAL   152 5

FIRE-RUSTED
    IN FEATHERS STILL FIRE-RUSTED   373 10
    IN FEATHERS STILL FIRE-RUSTED   781 16

FIRES
    AND WAVING FLAGS AND THE RAGGED FIRES   49 26
    BUT NOW I AM TRODDEN TO EARTH AND MY FIRES ARE LOW   94 1
    OF GREEN FIRES LIT ON THE SOIL OF EARTH THIS BLAZE   116 7
    THE SUN IS BLEEDING ITS FIRES UPON THE MIST   164 17
    AND THE LAST FIRES OF DISSOLUTION BURN IN THE BOSOM OF +   270 23
    HIS FIRES OF WRATH ARE BANKED DOWN   327 5
    THAT THE SUN IS MORE THAN BURNING MORE THAN THE BURNING+   331 6
    THE SUN LIVES IN HIS SHINING AND IS NOT LIKE FIRES THAT+   331 9
    SMALL SHARP RED FIRES IN THE NIGHT OF LEAVES   606 3
    AND KINDLING LITTLE FIRES UPON THE SHORES   688 15

FIRES
  FROM BURNING FIRES OF MANY SMOULDERING LIVES   744 24
  HAVING BEEN THROUGH FIRE THROUGH MANY FIRES   769 3
  WHERE NO PEOPLE ARE AND NO FIRES   769 18
  NO FIRES NO HEARTHS NO HOUSES   769 19
  STIRRING THE FIRES TO ACID OF BITTERNESS   795 25
  I AM GOING TO SPEAK TO THE DRAGON OF THE INNER FIRES   797 1
  NOT ALL FOR THEM SHALL THE FIRES OF MY LIFE BE HOT   *895 32
  NOT ALL FOR THEM SHALL THE FIRES OF MY LIFE BE HOT   *904 21

FIRE-SCATHED
  WHERE THE FIRE-BURNT VIRGIN IN MAN AND THE VIRGIN IN FI+   770 27

FIRE-SPOUTS
  SPINNING AND DANCING LIKE FLAMEY FIRE-SPOUTS IN THE DARK   440 10

FIRE'S
  TILL NIGHT WHEN BY THE FIRE'S RED STAIN   202 26

FIRE-THRESHING
  FIRE-THRESHING ANGUISH HAD BEEN FUSED AND CAST   *927 19
  FIRE-THRESHING ANGUISH WERE FUSED AND CAST   *928 19

FIRE-TONGS
  LIKE FIRE-TONGS A LIVE COAL   427 17

FIRE-WATERS
  AND DRINK FIRE-WATERS AND QUARREL AND STAB   795 3

FIREWORKS
  WAITING FOR THE FIREWORKS OF THE AFTER-SHOW   391 11

FIRING
  FOR IN THE FIRING ALL MY PORCELAIN   151 16
  A BIT OF SLAG STILL ADHERING AFTER YOUR FIRING IN THE F+   370 2
  FOR IN THE FIRING ALL MY PORCELAIN   873 28

FIRM
  OR FIRM AND SILKEN AS YOUNG PEONY FLOWERS   65 10
  BUT FIRM AT THE CENTRE   121 7
  WITH YOU THERE FIRM AT THE CORE OF ME   247 2
  I FEEL LIKE A FIRM RICH HEALTHY ROOT   247 11
  DUG FIRM IN MY BREAST AS YOU REACHED OUT RIGHT   886 8
  MY HEART IS FIRM AND SOLID IT NEEDS   888 9
  COOL AND FIRM AND SILKEN AS PINK YOUNG PEONY FLOWERS   *913 11
  FIRM AND SILKEN LIKE PINK YOUNG PEONY FLOWERS   *914 11

FIRMLY
  FIXING THE HOOK MORE TIGHTLY GETTING IT MORE FIRMLY IN   586 20

FIRMNESS
  WHO SUNK HIS HANDS IN FIRMNESS DOWN THY SIDES   69 10
  YOUR SIDES THIS FIRMNESS THIS HARD MOULD   255 12
  HE SUNK HIS HANDS IN FIRMNESS DOWN THY SIDES   *915 22

FIRS
  IS IT ME THE DARK FIRS MEAN   731 6

FIRST
  PRESSING ROUND AND LOW AT FIRST BUT SOON   50 4
  ON MY FIRST OF DAYS   59 4
  SHE SHINES THE FIRST WHITE LOVE OF MY YOUTH PASSIONLESS+   67 21
  THAT I COULD 'A' BIN FIRST WOMAN TER THEE AS THA'RT FIR+   83 13
  AND THEN YOU WILL REMEMBER FOR THE FIRST   91 17
  IN THE NIGHT WHERE WE FIRST HAVE BEING BEFORE WE RISE O+   92 15
  I DIED THE FIRST I IN THE AFTER-LIFE   156 17
  PERFECTING NOW OUR UNFINISHED FIRST EMBRACE   157 22
  HE'S THE STAR OF MY FIRST BELOVED   198 21
  THE FIRST   209 27
  FOR THE FIRST TIME NOW FOR THE FIRST TIME SEEN   216 18
  THE FIRST MAN OUT OF THE FOUR THAT'S MOWING   219 25
  AND WE FACED OUR FIRST MISERIES   248 19
  I AM THE FIRST COMER   259 22
  I AM THE FIRST COMER   259 25
  FLOWERS THAT COME FIRST FROM THE DARKNESS AND FEEL COLD+   270 9
  SAVE IT HAD FIRST APPROACHED HIM AND CAJOLED HIS SOUL   290 3
  AND ANSWER THE FIRST MACHINE-CUT QUESTION FROM THE LIPS+   291 2
  PUT THE FIRST CENTS INTO METALLIC FINGERS OF YOUR OFFIC+   291 4
  FLEA WHICH HOPS OVER SUCH AN OBSTRUCTION AT FIRST   292 5
  EMPEDOKLES SAYS TREES WERE THE FIRST LIVING CREATURES T+   295 4
  FOR THE FIRST TIME   310 11
  AND THE WORD WAS THE FIRST OFFSPRING OF THE ALMIGHTY JO+   329 11
  AND FOUND HIS FEET SO HE IS THE FIRST OF CREATURES TO S+   348 14
  THE FIRST DAY TO HEAVE YOUR FEET LITTLE BY LITTLE FROM +   352 3
  AND TAKE YOUR FIRST BITE AT SOME DIM BIT OF HERBAGE   352 14
  TO TAKE YOUR FIRST SOLITARY BITE   352 18
  OR IS IT JUST YOUR INDOMITABLE WILL AND PRIDE OF THE FI+   353 17
  LIFE ESTABLISHING THE FIRST ETERNAL MATHEMATICAL TABLET   355 17
  THE FIRST LITTLE MATHEMATICAL GENTLEMAN   355 20
  TORTOISE-WISE THE FIRST BELL SOUNDING   358 13
  FIRST FAINT SCREAM   364 1
  ALL TINY FAR AWAY REPTILE UNDER THE FIRST DAWN   364 21
  I REMEMBER WHEN I FIRST HEARD BULL-FROGS BREAK INTO SOU+   365 32
  I REMEMBER THE FIRST TIME OUT OF A BUSH IN THE DARKNESS+   366 1
  I REMEMBER MY FIRST TERROR HEARING THE HOWL OF WEIRD   366 8
  AND LISTENING INWARDLY TO THE FIRST BLEAT OF A LAMB   366 14
  THE FIRST WAIL OF AN INFANT   366 15
  AND THE FIRST TENOR SINGING OF THE PASSIONATE THROAT OF+   366 17
  THE FIRST ELEMENTS OF FOREIGN SPEECH   366 20
  THE WHEEL ON WHICH OUR SILENCE FIRST IS BROKEN   366 30
  THE ASS WAS THE FIRST OF ALL ANIMALS TO FALL FINALLY IN+   378 16
  JESUS RODE ON HIM THE FIRST BURDEN ON THE FIRST BEAST OF   379 25
  LENDING FIRST ONE EAR THEN ANOTHER   384 18
  FIRST GREAT BEASTS OF THE EARTH   392 10
  FIRST LIVE THING I'VE OWNED SINCE THE LOP-EARED RABBITS   395 7
  FIRST TIME I LOST YOU IN TAOS PLAZA   395 27
  VIRGINAL FIRST AND LAST   412 14
  TELL ME FIRST O TELL ME   428 23

FIRST
  THE SOUL'S FIRST PASSION IS FOR SHEER LIFE   482 1
  IT WAS 'IM AS MADE THE FIRST MISTAKE   493 5
  WITHOUT FIRST BEGETTING A NEW HOPE FOR THE CHILDREN TO   521 23
  TO MAKE SELF-PRESERVATION AND SELF-PROTECTION THE FIRST+   523 3
  IS ABOUT AS SCIENTIFIC AS MAKING SUICIDE THE FIRST LAW +   523 5
  IN THE FIRST PLACE I DON'T SCRAIGHT   540 20
  IT WAS YOU WHO GAVE HER HER FIRST KISS   550 21
  AT THE FIRST GO   557 24
  TELL ME FIRST WHAT I AM   606 11
  FIRST COMES THE DEATH THEN THE PURE ALONENESS WHICH IS +   611 12
  IF FIRST A MAN COULD HAVE HIS FULL REVENGE   628 11
  SOFTLY SUBTLY SECRETLY IN SOUL FIRST THEN IN SPIRIT THE+   642 22
  AND THE FIRST QUESTION TO ASK YOURSELF IS   661 14
  IT IS CREATION GOD LOOKS HIMSELF ON IT IN WONDER FOR TH+   690 11
  THE FOUR GREAT ONES THE FOUR ROOTS THE FIRST FOUR   706 4
  THE WHEEL IS THE FIRST PRINCIPLE OF EVIL   712 9
  CRAWLS THE FIRST LOAD INTO SIGHT AND NOW THERE ARE SOME   732 25
  HERE COMES THE FIRST OF THE WAGONS LIKE A GREY A DREARY   733 5
  WHY ARE YOU LAUGHING ASKED THE FIRST MAN OF QUETZALCOATL   791 13
  I HEAR THE VOICE OF MY FIRST MAN ASK ME WHY I AM LAUGHI+   791 14
  HEY FIRST MAN OF MY NAME HARK THERE   791 17
  THE FIRST THING I DID WHEN I SAW THEM WAS TO LAUGH AT T+   791 27
  TELL THEM SO FIRST MAN OF MY NAME   792 9
  FIRST AND LAST MAN IS ALONE   843 24
  WINROW AFTER WINROW FALLS UNDER THIS FIRST STROKE OF NI+   858 10
  WITH THE FIRST DAWN I ROSE TO LOOK IN THE GLASS   860 11
  HEAVY WITH DROPS OF THE FIRST CRUEL RAIN   863 15
  THAT I COULD HA' BEEN FIRST WOMAN TO THEE AS THOU'RT FI+   *925 17
  AND FEARFUL TO FILE FORTH NOW FOR THE FIRST TIME ALONE   *938 12
  SINGING LOVE'S FIRST SURPRISED GLADNESS ALONE IN THE GL+   *940 15
  THE FIRST MAN OUT O' THE FOUR THAT'S MOWIN'   *944 5
  THE FIRST EFFORT TO THINK   *946 28
  NOW FIRST CITIZEN OF NOTTINGHAM   *950 16
  FIRST AND LAST MAN IS ALONE   *951 3

FIRST-BORN
  AND IS THE SUN YOUR FIRST-BORN ONLY-BEGOTTEN   782 33

FIRST-FLOWERS
  COME SWEEP AWAY THESE EXQUISITE GHASTLY FIRST-FLOWERS   271 2

FIRST-FLOWER
  SUCH FAIR FRESH ALERT FIRST-FLOWER FACES   270 5
  THEY ARE THE ISSUE OF ACRID WINTER THESE FIRST-FLOWER Y+   270 15

FIRST-FROSTED
  DOWN THE WAY PERSEPHONE GOES JUST NOW IN FIRST-FROSTED +   *956 13

FIRSTLING
  O SPILL THE BLOOD NOT OF YOUR FIRSTLING LAMB WITHOUT SP+   678 22

FIR-TREE
  IN THE FIR-TREE OVERLOOKING THE MARSHES   216 23
  IN THE FIR-TREE OVERLOOKING THE MARSHES   *942 9

FIR-WORT
  AND FIR-WORT STINKING FOR THE CARRION WASP   510 5

FISH
  AT THE LITTLE FISH THREAD-THREADING THE WATERY NOOK   161 11
  AND THE FISH IN SHADOW-WAVED HERDS   172 2
  AND I MUST RESUME MY NAKEDNESS LIKE A FISH SINKING DOWN+   321 29
  LIKE A FISH SEEKING THE BOTTOM JESUS   321 31
  FISH OH FISH   334 20
  BUT OH FISH THAT ROCK IN WATER   335 14
  FISH IN THE WATERS UNDER THE EARTH   335 29
  TO BE A FISH   337 6
  TO BE A FISH   337 8
  AND SMALL FISH FLY LIKE SPLINTERS   338 20
  FISH ARE BEYOND ME   338 24
  FISH IN THE OUTERWARDS   338 30
  AND SUDDENLY PULLED A GOLD-AND-GREENISH LUCENT FISH FROM   339 2
  THIS IS BEYOND ME THIS FISH   339 13
  THIRST FOR FISH AS FOR MORE-THAN-WATER   340 8
  THE TRAPEZE MAN SLIM AND BEAUTIFUL AND LIKE A FISH IN T+   445 4
  THE TINY FISH ENJOY THEMSELVES   466 13
  FISH   586 22
  HARK THE STRANGE NOISE OF MILLIONS OF FISH IN PANIC   586 25
  IN PANIC IN REBELLION SLITHERING MILLIONS OF FISH   586 26
  DAWN IS NO LONGER IN THE HOUSE OF THE FISH   616 18
  PISCES OH FISH JESUS OF THE WATERY WAY   616 19
  APART FROM POPPIES AND THE FLYING FISH   691 23
  AS A VENDOR OF FRIED FISH ONCE MORE YELLOW   760 21
  HE THREW THE FISH IN THE BOAT   802 10

FISH-ALIVE
  FISH-ALIVE   338 13

FISH-BLOOD
  FISH-BLOOD SLOWLY RUNNING NEXT TO THE FLOOD EXTRACTING   336 31

FISH-DOTTED
  PLEASED TO BE OUT IN THE SAGE AND THE PINE FISH-DOTTED +   409 18

FISHERMAN
  BY SOME MALIGNANT FISHERMAN ON AN UNSEEN SAFE SHORE   586 10
  BY SOME MALIGNANT FISHERMAN ON AN UNSEEN SHORE   632 25

FISHERMEN
  THE SAME WITH THE FISHERMEN SITTING DARNING THEIR NETS   520 17

FISHES
  OF FISHES   161 22
  BUT FISHES ARE VERY FIERY AND TAKE TO THE WATER TO COOL   331 1
  FISHES   337 15
  AND WATCHING THE FISHES IN THE BREATHING WATERS   337 29
  THEY ARE BEYOND ME ARE FISHES   338 27

FISHES
  FISHES   339 25
  I DON'T KNOW FISHES   340 13
  AND GONE LIKE WEED LIKE WEED LIKE EGGS OF FISHES   428 27
  SPERM OF FISHES   429 4
  LIKE FEARFUL AND CORPSE-LIKE FISHES HOOKED AND BEING PL+   586 9
  WHERE HE DOES NOT CHOOSE TO LAND THEM YET HOOKED FISHES   586 11
  LIKE FEARFUL AND CORPSE-LIKE FISHES HOOKED AND BEING PL+   632 24
  WHERE HE DOES NOT CHOOSE TO LAND THEM YET HOOKED FISHES   632 26
  SMOOTH OCEAN WHERE THE FISHES REST ON EDGE   652 10
  MEN SLIMLY WENT LIKE FISHES AND DIDN'T CARE   688 22
  AND VENUS AMONG THE FISHES SKIPS AND IS A SHE-DOLPHIN   695 9
  WITH THE RINGS THAT THE FISHES HAVE MADE   867 21

FISH-FANGED
  SILVERY-SIDED FISH-FANGED FIERCE-FACED WHISKERED MOTTLED   409 3

FISH-FIRE
  FISH-FIRE   336 32

FISH-SILVERY
  KNOTS OF PINK FISH-SILVERY   307 4

FISH-VOICE
  ALMOST FISH-VOICE   336 16

FISSURE
  TO THE ARAB AND THE FIG HAS BEEN A CATCH-WORD FOR THE F+   277 4
  AND IF YOU DARE THE FISSURE   278 21
  DO YOU MEAN TO TELL ME YOU WILL SEE NO FISSURE   278 22
  ROSY TENDER GLITTERING WITHIN THE FISSURE   278 26
  DO YOU MEAN TO TELL ME THERE SHOULD BE NO FISSURE   278 27
  THE FISSURE THE YONI   282 19
  SO IT EXPLODES AND YOU SEE THROUGH THE FISSURE THE SCAR+   283 28
  HE REACHED DOWN FROM A FISSURE IN THE EARTH-WALL IN THE   349 8
  INTO THE BLACK HOLE THE EARTH-LIPPED FISSURE IN THE WAL+   351 16

FIST
  I WISH I COULD GRIP YOU LIKE THE FIST OF THE LORD   255 14
  OF FINGER OR FIST OR SOFT-SKINNED STICKS UPON THE STRET+   623 6

FISTS
  AND THRUST HER FISTS SUPPRESSED IN THE FOLDS OF HER SKI+   128 19
  OF NAKED LOVE CLENCHED IN HIS FISTS THE SHAME   226 7
  OF MEN THEY CLENCH FEAR IN THEIR FISTS   460 28

FIT
  FOR A PERMANENT FIT   84 32
  THEY SAY THE FIT SURVIVE   298 8
  THEY AREN'T EVEN FIT TO CURSE   553 8
  WE'RE NOT FIT FOR THE EARTH WE LIVE ON   553 29
  WE'RE NOT FIT FOR THE AIR WE BREATHE   553 30
  WHO COULD HOROSCOPE FIT FOR A QUEEN   845 18

FITLY
  KNOWING OUR DEAD ARE FITLY HOUSED IN DEATH   740 23

FITS
  IN HIS WILD FITS   *910 4

FITTING
  IT IS VERY FITTING THERE IS NAUGHT BESIDE   699 2
  FITTING AND READY FOR THE DEPARTING SOUL   718 26

FITTINGLY
  WHO VOICE THE DUMB NIGHT FITTINGLY   197 31

FITTINGS
  ALL THE FITTINGS AND ELABORATE FURNISHINGS   440 17
  AND ALL THE PEOPLE THAT GO WITH THE FITTINGS AND THE   440 18

FIVE
  THE FIVE OLD BELLS   54 1
  THE BALLS OF FIVE RED TOES   145 22
  FIVE VALLEYS GO FIVE PASSES LIKE GATES   224 9
  FIVE TIMES WIDE OPEN   307 12
  FIVE AND FIVE AGAIN AND FIVE AGAIN   355 7
  AND ON EITHER SIDE COUNT FIVE   355 31
  FOUR AND ONE MAKES FIVE WHICH IS THE CLUE TO ALL MATHEM+   356 1
  YOU'RE A CAGED MONKEY AGAIN IN FIVE MINUTES   486 5
  AND THE FIVE OTHERS THE TRAVELLERS   703 1
  THERE HE SITS IN THE SADDLE OF THIS THE FIVE   733 11

FIVE-FOLD
  THROUGH HIS FIVE-FOLD COMPLEX-NATURE   356 4
  FLOWERS OFF THEIR FIVE-FOLD STEM   451 27

FIVE-POINT
  AT LAST THE NARCISSUS LIFTED A TUFT OF FIVE-POINT STARS   683 2

FIVES
  FIVES AND TENS   355 23

FIVE THOUSAND
  IT SEEMS TO ME THAT FOR FIVE THOUSAND YEARS AT LEAST   519 1

FIXED
  FIXED IN THE DARKNESS GRAPPLING FOR THE DEEP SOIL'S CRO+   92 11
  BUT EVER FIXED AS YET   99 27
  FIXED WATER-EYES   335 12
  NEITHER MY DEAR I HAD HIM FIXED IT SAVES HIM FROM SO   581 12
  THEY HAD HIM FIXED   581 15
  WHO PETTED THEM AND HAD THEM FIXED   581 21
  FIXED ARRANGE YOU UNDERSTAND WHAT I MEAN   582 1C
  FIXED JIXED FIXED   659 18
  WHEREAS LETTERS ARE FIXED   661 18
  AS IF IT WERE COIN WITH A FIXED VALUE   662 5
  OLD PEOPLE FIXED IN A RANCID RESISTANCE   662 20

FIXED
  TO LIFE FIXED TO THE LETTER OF THE LAW   662 21
  LEAVE THE OLD ONES FIXED TO THEIR UGLY COGGED SELF-WILL   662 23
  BUT A MAN RE-BORN FROM THE RIGIDITY OF FIXED IDEAS   667 32
  FIXED UPON THE HUB OF THE EGO   713 29
  GOING YET NEVER WANDERING FIXED YET IN MOTION   713 30
  A BLANCHED FACE FIXED AND AGONIZED   742 7
  FIXED IN THE DARKNESS GRAPPLING FOR THE DEEP SOIL'S LIT+   *926 11

FIXEDLY
  FIXEDLY   386 2

FIXER
  OH MY JIXER MY FIXER   659 20

FIXERY
  ALL THE GREAT JIXERY UP IN THE FIXERY   659 8

FIXES
  FIXES ON IT   473 2

FIXING
  FIXING THE HOOK MORE TIGHTLY GETTING IT MORE FIRMLY IN   586 20

FIZZLE
  SO LONG AS IT DIDN'T ALL FIZZLE OUT IN TALK   507 12
  ZIGZAGGING DOWN LIKE THE FIZZLE FROM A FINISHED ROCKET   701 26

FLACCID
  AND THE FLAT FLACCID MOUNTAINS OF THE ELEPHANTS' STANDI+   390 13
  OUT OF THE FLACCID LIMBS   766 15

FLAG
  OH BUT 'E DROPS 'IS FLAG WHEN 'E SEES ME   79 9
  UNTIL HER PRIDE'S FLAG SMITTEN CLEAVED DOWN TO THE STAFF   125 18
  HE SAW IN A SHAFT OF LIGHT A LAMB ON A PINNACLE BALANCI+   324 16
  SINCE THE LAMB BETWITCHED HIM WITH THAT RED-STRUCK FLAG   327 3
  LET HIM CHARGE LIKE A MIGHTY CATAPULT ON THE RED-CROSS +   327 24
  OH BUT HE DROPS HIS FLAG WHEN 'E SEES ME   *921 5
  HER SOUL'S FLAG SANK AND HER PRIDE PUT OFF ITS CROWN   *936 17
  RED ONES A BLOODY-WHITE FLAG OVER YOU   *940 28

FLAGGED
  ALONG THE FLAGGED CLEAN PAVEMENT SUMMER-WHITE   36 2
  AGAIN FROM EARTH LIKE LILIES FLAGGED AND SERE   87 28

FLAGS
  AND WAVING FLAGS AND THE RAGGED FIRES   49 26
  LIKE FLAGS IN PALE BLOOD NEWLY WET   105 3

FLAGSTONES
  WASTRELS THAT SLEEP ON THE FLAGSTONES WITHOUT ANY HURT   145 33

FLAGS'
  ALL THE TREES ARE HANGING WITH DISHONOURED FLAGS' DISGR+   *933 29

FLAILS
  A FLUSH AT THE FLAILS OF YOUR FINS DOWN THE WHORL OF YO+   335 9

FLAKE
  HER FLAKE BY FLAKE AND SPREAD HER MEANING OUT   197 23

FLAKED
  FLAKED OUT AND COME UNPROMISED   306 35

FLAKES
  TO SHAKE FLAKES OF ITS SHADOW ABOUT   68 12
  IN FLAKES OF SHADOW DOWN WHILE THROUGH THE GAP   76 15
  WITH FAIR FLAKES LIGHTING DOWN ON IT BEYOND THE TOWN   76 18
  ODD FLAKES AS IF OF SNOW ODD BITS OF SNOW   304 13
  IN ROSE-HOT TIPS AND FLAKES OF ROSE-PALE SNOW   304 20
  HIGH HIGH UP IN FLAKES SHIMMERING FLAKES OF BLUE FIRE   391 18
  IN FLAKES OF SHADOW DOWN AND THROUGH THE GAP   *898 9
  WITH FAIR FLAKES SETTLING DOWN ON IT BEYOND THE TOWN   *898 12
  IN FLAKES OF SHADOW DOWN AND THROUGH THE GAP   *901 18
  WITH FAIR FLAKES SETTLING DOWN ON IT BEYOND THE TOWN   *901 21
  SHAKE FLAKES OF ITS MEANING ABOUT   *914 27

FLAKY
  INTO SUBSTANCE AND FLAKY WHITENESS   705 20

FLAMBEAUX
  AND AT LAST THE PERA-HERA PROCESSION FLAMBEAUX ALOFT IN   387 25
  HIGH HIGH FLAMBEAUX SMOKING OF THE EAST   388 29

FLAMBOYANT
  MY MISSAL BOOK OF FINE FLAMBOYANT HOURS   135 2
  THE BIG FLAMBOYANT RUSSIA   536 12

FLAME
  LITTLE JETS OF SUNLIGHT TEXTURE IMITATING FLAME   33 2
  YET FLAME OF THE LIVING GROUND   39 21
  WARM AS A FLAME IN THE CLOSE NIGHT AIR   61 29
  ON A SUBTLE RUSH OF COOL GREY FLAME   68 2
  AND KINDLE MY WILL TO A FLAME THAT SHALL CONSUME   74 20
  WHIRLING A FLAME   94 18
  YOU THROUGH THE FLAME   112 15
  IN MY FLAME OF LIVING THE INVISIBLE HEART OF THE ROSE   115 8
  WHAT MATTER THE STUFF I LICK UP IN MY DAILY FLAME   115 10
  POURED A HEAVY FLAME   118 3
  OF MIDNIGHT AND SHAKE IT TO FIRE TILL THE FLAME OF THE   136 20
  STILL SHE SAYS NAY LOOSE NO FLAME   150 26
  LIKE A GLOWING BRAZIER FAINTLY BLUE OF FLAME   151 25
  I WATCH HER WARD AWAY THE FLAME   151 34
  MOVED WITH SLOW FEET AND HER EYES' FLAME STEADILY BURNED   156 10
  LIKE A TONGUE OF DARKENED FLAME   169 28
  AND WHIRLING IN BLOSSOM OF FLAME AND BEING UPON ME   218 23
  FANS OUT YOUR PETALS FOR EXCESS OF FLAME   219 3

FLAME
HIS EVENING IS A FLAME OF WINE — 228 17
ITS FLAME OF LIFE NOW AND ALWAYS TILL THE END — 233 16
AND WHEN I LIFT MY FACE IT IS A FLAME THAT GOES UP — 233 22
YOU SHADOW AND FLAME — 239 7
UP WITH MYSELF AND MY WARMTH LIKE A FLAME ROUND THE — 245 8
AND HOW I AM NOT AT ALL EXCEPT A FLAME THAT MOUNTS OFF — 245 10
WHERE I TOUCH YOU I FLAME INTO BEING BUT IS IT ME OR — 245 12
ARE A BONFIRE OF ONENESS ME FLAME FLUNG LEAPING ROUND Y+ — 245 24
LIKE A FLAME ON A WICK — 246 3
HOW FULL AND BIG LIKE A ROBUST HAPPY FLAME — 246 13
LIKE A FLAME THAT FALLS OF A SUDDEN — 246 26
LIKE A SUNKEN FLAME THAT GRASPS FOR SUPPORT — 246 29
LIKE A FLAME BLOWN WHITER AND WHITER — 281 9
DARK FLAME — 297 11
SHOUTING FORTH FLAME TO SET THE WORLD ON FIRE — 315 2
TO LICK THE WORLD WITH FLAME THAT LICKS IT CLEAN — 315 26
INSTEAD OF FLAME AND FLAME-CLEAN ASH — 318 1
REVERSED FLAME — 322 22
SHALL GREAT WINGS FLAME FROM HIS SHOULDER SOCKETS — 326 6
HIS OWN BLACK BLOOD POURED OUT LIKE A SHEET OF FLAME OV+ — 326 30
THERE IS A SWAN-LIKE FLAME THAT CURLS ROUND THE CENTRE + — 440 2
AND FUSE IN A BROAD HARD FLAME OF MANY MEN IN A ONENESS — 440 8
O PILLARS OF FLAME BY NIGHT O MY YOUNG MEN — 440 9
AND THE SAME FLAME THAT FILLS US WITH LIFE IT WILL DANC+ — 440 15
FLAME OF FLESH FOREVER TRAVELLING — 460 6
LIKE THE FLAME OF A CANDLE SLOW AND QUICK — 460 7
FLAME DEVOURS THE WORLD — 511 9
FOR THERE ARE ALL SORTS OF FLAME — 511 11
BURNS THE SMALL FLAME OF ANGER GNAWING — 601 9
SHORT GASPS OF FLAME IN THE GREEN OF NIGHT WAY OFF — 606 1
AND BURN BLUE AND COLD LIKE THE FLAME IN A MINER'S LAMP — 619 5
IF THE ROBOT CAN RECOGNISE THE CLEAN FLAME OF LIFE — 648 14
SERVING WITH DELIGHT AND WITH REVERENCE THOSE MEN WHOSE+ — 648 20
O IF A FLAME IS IN YOU BE IT SO — 674 1
WHEN YOUR FLAME FLICKERS UP AND YOU FLICKER FORTH IN SH+ — 674 2
IS THE VERY INDIVIDUAL FLAME OF LIFE ITSELF — 679 25
YET A WOMAN CAN ADD HER FLAME TO A MAN'S — 680 3
OR A MAN CAN ADD HIS FLAME TO THE FLAME OF ANOTHER MAN — 680 4
I LIFT MY INEXTINGUISHABLE FLAME — 745 2
I LIFT MY LITTLE PURE AND LAMBENT FLAME — 745 10
OF FULL DESPAIR I LIFT MY TENDER FLAME — 745 13
THE PERFECT LAMBENT FLAME WHICH STILL GOES UP — 745 36
THE FLAME OF MY SOUL LIKE A TREMBLING STAR IS HUNG — 750 12
AND THE FLAME OF YOU SWEPT BACK IN A NEW BREATH OF LIFE — 784 26
AND PUTTING HIS STRENGTH IN YOUR HEELS AND ANKLES HIS F+ — 801 24
FANG A FLAME — 808 21
YELLOW IS THE FLAME — 808 26
OH YOU IN THE TENT OF THE CLOVEN FLAME — 812 11
WHO OPENS HIS FLAME LIKE A TENT-FLAP — 812 15
PITCH TENTS OF FLAME — 812 22
AND BE THERE IN THE HOUSE OF THE CLOVEN FLAME — 812 27
THEN LET THE FLAME WRAP ROUND US — 813 1
TORN WINGS OF FLAME ARE WAFTING DOWN THE SKY — 855 21
IS DEAD AT LAST THEN HIS POOR SUNK FLAME MUST FLICKER — 859 3
STILL TO SAY I WANT NO FLAME — 873 9
COMES LICKING IN FLAME THROUGH THE BARS OF YOUR LIPS — 873 17
LIKE A GLOWING BRAZIER FAINTLY BLUE OF FLAME — 874 4
THAT SHE SHOULD WARD AWAY THE FLAME — 874 12
TILL OFF THY MOUTH HAS LEAPT THE FLAME OF LIFE — 879 22
THY FLAME LEAP FREE WHAT IF I AM LEFT BEHIND — 879 25
AND WE WILL PASS TOGETHER LIKE ONE RED FLAME — 879 29
LITTLE JETS OF SUNLIGHT-TEXTURE IMITATING FLAME — *891 2
FILLING MY STILL BREASTS WITH A FLUSH AND A FLAME — *893 17
WHIRLING A FLAME — *897 6
WARM AS A FLAME IN THE CLOSE NIGHT AIR — *912 8
ON THE SUBTLE RUSH OF THE COOL GREY FLAME — *914 17
LIKE A CANDLE FLAME ON THIS BODY BUT I ENSHRINE — *930 6
IN MY FLAME OF LIVING A SHADOW WITHIN THE SHINE — *930 8
WHAT MATTER THE STUFF I LICK UP IN MY LIVING FLAME — *930 10

FLAME-BURNT
WE NEAR THE FLAME-BURNT PORCHES — 242 24

FLAME-CLEAN
INSTEAD OF FLAME AND FLAME-CLEAN ASH — 318 1

FLAME-FLUSHED
FLAME-FLUSHED ENRAGED SPLENDID SALVIA — 314 27

FLAME-GREEN
WILD PUFFING OF GREEN-FIRE TREES AND FLAME-GREEN BUSHES — 116 2

FLAMELETS
RED FLAMELETS HERE AND THERE REVEAL — 606 7

FLAME-LIGHT
SLOWLY SAILING IN GORGEOUS APPAREL THROUGH THE FLAME-LI+ — 387 30

FLAME-RAGE
AND FLAME-RAGE GOLDEN-THROATED — 313 23

FLAMES
OF THE BLOSSOM ARE ROSES TO LOOK AT BUT FLAMES WHEN THE+ — 93 32
OVER THE FORGES AND SMALL FLAMES PLY — 103 12
PALPITATING FLAMES OF LIFE — 115 14
YOUR REPTILE FLAMES OF LUST AH STORE — 151 12
THAT MY FINGERS SHOULD TURN INTO THESE FLAMES — 241 22
WHERE FLAMES OF FIERCE LOVE TREMBLE — 242 10
IT WOULD BE NO WONDER IF GREAT WINGS LIKE FLAMES FANNED+ — 326 12
THE NEST IS IN FLAMES — 330 6
AND THE SLOW COLD FLAMES — 511 15
PUFFING ITS LITTLE MALE STAMENS OUT INTO STERILE PETAL + — 535 6
WINDS OF HEAVEN FAN THE LEAVES OF THE TREE LIKE FLAMES + — 615 4
AND FLAMES OF KATABOLISTIC ENERGY ALTERNATE — 616 11
YOU FLUTTER IN A HOST OF FLAMES LIKE WINTER STARLINGS R+ — 784 1
WHERE FLAMES WHEEL IN LIKE BREATH — 784 10
RUN UP THE FLAMES AND WITH FEET ON THE SPARKS — 798 21

FLAMES
YOUR REPTILE FLAMES OF PASSION STORE — 873 22
WE LEAP LIKE TWO CLASPED FLAMES FROM OFF THE FIRE — 879 30
THAN WHO CAN SEPARATE TWO LITHE RICH FLAMES — 879 33
GIVE ME A FLOWER ON A TALL STEM AND THREE DARK FLAMES — *956 21

FLAMES'
THE FLAMES' STIFF SPEED — 242 15

FLAME-TALL
AMONG THE SINUOUS FLAME-TALL CYPRESSES — 296 17

FLAME-TIP
THERE IS A SPIRAL FLAME-TIP THAT CAN LICK OUR LITTLE AT+ — 440 5

FLAME-WILD
HE TAKES THE FLAME-WILD DROPS — 203 2

FLAMEY
SPINNING AND DANCING LIKE FLAMEY FIRE-SPOUTS IN THE DARK — 440 10
FLESH FLAMEY AND A LITTLE HEROIC EVEN IN A TUMBLING CLO+ — 445 28
AND TO SERVE THAT WHICH IS FLAMEY OR PURE AND WATERY OR — 637 10

FLAMILY
WHEN A WOMAN CAN ONLY LOVE FLAMILY THOSE OF HER OWN SEX — 619 19

FLAMING
ALOOF MY FLAMING HEART WILL NOT ALLOW — 122 22
DESOLATE AND DESPOILED AM I FOR THEIR FLAMING STORM — *897 11

FLAMIN'
I'LL CHUCK THE FLAMIN' LOT O' YOU — 81 11
OR I'LL CHUCK THE FLAMIN' LOT OF YOU — *923 11

FLAMY
LESS THAN THE WIND THAT RUNS TO THE FLAMY CALL — 116 13

FLANK
THEIR FACE IN THEIR FLANK SO THESE — 144 21
IT WAS THE FLANK OF MY WIFE — 260 1
IT WAS THE FLANK OF MY WIFE — 260 4
I TOUCHED HER FLANK AND KNEW I WAS CARRIED BY THE CURRE+ — 260 12

FLANNEL
SO I PICKED HIM UP IN A FLANNEL JACKET — 347 4

FLAP
WHOSE BLACK BOUGHS FLAP THE GROUND — 113 26
FLAP WHITE WINGS AND YELLOW PINIONS — 783 26
WHERE BLACK BOUGHS FLAP THE GROUND — *929 15

FLAPPING
IN THE FLAPPING OF RED-ROOF SMOKE AND THE SMALL — 68 22
WHAT THEN IF A SCARLET ROSE GOES FLAPPING — 150 22
WINGS DARK SKINNY AND FLAPPING THE AIR — 346 23
IN THE FLAPPING RED-ROOF SMOKE AND THE SMALL — *915 6

FLAPS
IN CURLS AND FLAPS BETWEEN WORLDS THAT PLOD — 823 26
FLAPS UP FROM THE PLAYGROUND AS A GREAT TRAIN STEAMS SO+ — *894 29

FLARE
ENORMOUS SHADOW-PROCESSIONS FILING ON IN THE FLARE OF F+ — 387 35
AND FLARE OF A TROPICAL ENERGY TIRELESS AFIRE IN THE DA+ — 389 16
SUDDENLY HER YELLOW-BROWN EYES LOOKED WITH A FLARE INTO — 618 1
AND HER PASSION COULD ONLY FLARE THROUGH THE MESHES — 619 2
FLARE BRIGHT TO WANDER AND DO NOTHING — 794 16

FLARING
AND I SAW HER FOR THE FLARING SPACE — 62 9
A SUDDEN FLARING BLAZE — 259 6
WARRIOR-LIKE DAWN-COCK'S-COMB FLARING FLOWER — 315 1
AND I SAW HER FOR THE FLARING SPACE — *912 16

FLASH
OH YOU WHO FLASH YOUR ARMS LIKE ROCKETS TO HEAVEN — 73 10
AND EVERY FLASH OF THOUGHT THAT WE AND OURS — 89 4
AS WITH THOUGHTS THAT FLASH AND CRACKLE IN FAR-OFF MALI+ — 97 16
ALL WITH A FLASH OF BLUE WHEN WILL SHE BE LEAVING — 129 28
WHEN I TELL YOU THE STARS FLASH SIGNALS EACH ONE — 130 25
HOLDING ALOFT THEIR UMBRELLAS THAT FLASH AND ARE BRIGHT — 146 19
DULL METEORITE FLASH ONLY INTO LIGHT — 195 21
AS THEY DART AND FLASH — 269 23
LIKE SHARP SLIM WAGTAILS THEY FLASH A LITTLE ASIDE — 269 26
FLASH OF A MOUNTAIN LION'S LONG SHOOT — 402 16
SEA-BEASTS IMMERSED LEAN SIDEWAYS AND FLASH BRIGHT — 455 25
ARE THOSE THAT GIVE THEMSELVES AWAY IN FLASH AND SPARKLE — 523 22
KEEP SUDDENLY SHOWING A WHITENESS A FLASH AND A FURL A + — 687 2
TO SEE HIM FLASH AND TREMBLE WITH THE FIRE OF HIS SOUL — 859 8

FLASHED
AND FLASHED UP THE HILL-SIDE — 222 3
IN THE WORLD WHERE THE HUMMING-BIRD FLASHED AHEAD OF — 372 15
THIRTEEN TIMES THE TEETH FLASHED IN A FIRE OF BLOOD — *933 1

FLASHES
WATCHING THE DOOR OPEN HE FLASHES BARE — 43 19
HIS STRONG TEETH IN A SMILE AND FLASHES HIS EYES — 43 20
MOVES IN SILVER-MOIST FLASHES IN MUSICAL TRIM — 147 20
AND THE LITTLE ELECTRIC FLASHES WENT WITH US IN THE GRA+ — 206 15
YOU NEED YOUR OWN GREAT WONDERING EYE THAT FLASHES WITH — 544 22
AND FLASHES ALL HERSELF AS SUN-BRIGHT — *943 8

FLASHING
GONE DOWN TO THE FLASHING SHORE — 200 14
STAND IN THEIR BLUENESS FLASHING WITH SNOW AND THE — 209 24
AND FLASHING KINGFISHERS THAT FLEW — 262 4
AND SO RAPIDLY AND SO FLASHING FLEEING BEFORE THE RAIN — 672 16

FLASHING
 BY HERMES AND APHRODITE FLASHING WHITE GLITTERING WORDS   702 10
 FLASHING OF DELICATE WRATH   735 23
 SEE ME THROUGH THE FLASHING OF WINGS   787 29
 FLASHING HIS BRIGHT BROWN ARMS AS HE LEANS ON THE POLE   867 28

FLASK
 FOR I AM FRAIL AS A FLASK OF GLASS   752 15

FLAT
 THA'S GOT IT FLAT   77 4
 SO THERE AN' I TELL THEE FLAT   80 2
 WITH WET FLAT LIGHTS WHAT I'VE DONE   143 23
 SHINE LIKE FLAT COIN WHICH JOVE IN THANKS   162 3
 LIKE A FLAT RED LILY WITH A MILLION PETALS   166 17
 FLAT BROWN ROCKS TO WATCH THE FERRY IN THE SUN   386 24
 AND THE FLAT FLACCID MOUNTAINS OF THE ELEPHANTS' STANDI+   390 13
 ON THE LONG FLAT SKIS OF HER LEGS   393 27
 IN FLAT ECSTASY SUPREMELY UNFELT   444 7
 THEY HAVE ONLY THEIR PERSONALITIES THAT ARE BEST SEEN F+   446 4
 FLAT PERSONALITIES IN TWO DIMENSIONS IMPONDERABLE AND   446 6
 AND PRISONERS' FLAT INEFFECTUAL PASTIME   518 13
 IN THE FLAT RECURRENT BREAKERS OF MY TWO FEET   705 13
 THESE WORDS THAT ARE ALL FLAT   792 27
 THA'S GOT IT FLAT   *918 22
 BLOWN FLAT INTO POINTS BY THE HEAVY WHITE DRAUGHT OF TH+   *956 5

FLAT-CHESTED
 FLAT-CHESTED CROP-HEADED CHEMICALISED WOMEN OF INDETERM+   522 2

FLAT-FOOT
 BECAUSE FLAT-FOOT IS THE FAVOURITE OF THE WHITE LEGHORN+   761 17

FLAT-IRON
 THEN YOU WILL HIT THE FLAT-IRON BUILDING AND FLATTEN IT+   484 19

FLATLY
 FLATLY ASSUMING THE SUN   50 24

FLATNESS
 FLATNESS   651 16

FLATTEN
 THEN YOU WILL HIT THE FLAT-IRON BUILDING AND FLATTEN IT+   484 19

FLATTENED
 THE THIN SYCAMORE IN THE PLAYGROUND IS SWINGING WITH FL+   92 2
 THE SWAN WILL LIFT UP AGAIN HIS FLATTENED SMITTEN HEAD   625 2
 DOWN FLATTENING INTO POINTS FLATTENED UNDER THE SWEEP O+   697 7
 THE THIN SYCAMORE IN THE PLAYGROUND IS SWINGING WITH FL+   *926 2

FLATTENING
 DOWN FLATTENING INTO POINTS FLATTENED UNDER THE SWEEP O+   697 7

FLATTENS
 BARES HIS LONG ASS'S TEETH FLATTENS HIS LONG ASS'S EARS   379 21

FLATTER
 HOW SHALL I FLATTER MYSELF THAT I CAN DO   223 10

FLATTERED
 AND WAS IMMENSELY FLATTERED WHEN ONE OF THE FAT LITTLE   618 18
 FROM THE DREAMS THAT THE DISTANCE FLATTERED   *908 12

FLAUNTS
 THE COMMON FLAUNTS BRAVELY BUT BELOW FROM THE RUSHES   33 10
 BLUSHES AND FLAUNTS IN THE SUNSHINE ABOVE   858 7
 THE COMMON FLAUNTS BRAVELY BUT BELOW FROM THE RUSHES   *891 11

FLAUTIST
 FLAUTIST OR JUST AN AMATEUR   453 2

FLAVOUR
 WHAT A RARE POWERFUL REMINISCENT FLAVOUR   280 6
 SOMETHING OF THE SAME FLAVOUR OF SYRACUSAN MUSCAT WINE   280 9

FLAWED
 FLAWED MY DELICATE COURAGE IN ITS STROKE   *927 13

FLAYED
 FLAYED RED IF THA COULD BUT SEE   78 24
 FLAYED RED IF THAT COULD BUT SEE   *920 16

FLEA
 FLEA WHICH HOPS OVER SUCH AN OBSTRUCTION AT FIRST   292 5
 OR A DOG WITH A HARROWING FLEA   489 24

FLEA-BITE
 BUT THE FEATHERS WERE COMPARATIVELY A MERE FLEA-BITE   413 17
 THE BIT OF LAND IN QUESTION IS A FLEA-BITE   779 13
 BITS OF RESERVED LAND IT WERE A FLEA-BITE   779 16

FLEA-BITTEN
 IN ME OR A FLEA-BITTEN FATE   237 8

FLEAS
 AND THE EARTH IS ALIVE AND READY TO SHAKE OFF HIS FLEAS   792 12

FLECK
 NO LONGER A LARGE FLECK MOVING IN THE SUNSHINE   870 14

FLED
 HAS SHE NOT FLED ON THE SAME WIND WITH ME   222 20
 BUT TIME HAS FLED OUR PARENTS ARE DEAD   490 21
 BUT THE BRITISH BOY HE TURNED AND FLED   577 20
 WHILE I FLED   604 23
 FOR A MOMENT SHE WAS IO IO WHO FLED FROM ZEUS OR THE DA+   672 17
 DOWN THE DARK BOUGH HAVE FLED   861 11

FLEDGE
 OUT OF THE DEEP SOFT FLEDGE OF SICILIAN WINTER-GREEN   300 22
 AND BRANDISHING AND STOOPING OVER EARTH'S WINTRY FLEDGE   301 15

FLEDGELING
 ASH FLUTTERS FLOCCULENT LIKE DOWN ON A BLUE WAN FLEDGEL+   330 8

FLEE
 DISCOVERY LIKE BIRDS THAT STEAL AND FLEE   51 30
 YOU WATCH THE RED SPARKS WHIRL AND FLEE   116 23
 PALE SHADOWS FLEE FROM US AS IF FROM THEIR FOES   163 18
 YET DID NOT FLEE   165 16
 PALE SHADOWS FLEE FROM US AS IF FROM THEIR FOES   857 18
 NOW SEE HER TURN TO FLEE   861 19
 AS BIRDS WHO ARE STEALING TURN AND FLEE   *899 13
 AS BIRDS WHO ARE STEALING TURN AND FLEE   *902 25
 YOU WATCH THE FIRE SPARKS SWIRL AND FLEE   *930 22

FLEECE
 UNDER THE FLEECE OF SHADOW AS IN BETWEEN   48 20
 NOTHING TO MEET MY FINGERS BUT THE FLEECE OF NIGHT   147 4
 YOUR YOUTHFUL SMOOTHNESS I FLEECED WHERE FLEECE WAS NONE   156 26
 AND WHEN I SEE THE HEAVY RED FLEECE   883 1

FLEECED
 YOUR YOUTHFUL SMOOTHNESS I FLEECED WHERE FLEECE WAS NONE   156 26
 YET ARE FLEECED WITH SOFT HAIR   827 20

FLEEING
 AND SO RAPIDLY AND SO FLASHING FLEEING BEFORE THE RAIN   672 16
 FLEEING IN EXILE TO ENGLAND AT THE END OF THE FIGHT   859 6

FLEES
 FLEES IN ITS AGITATION   242 14

FLEET
 FLEET HURRYING LIMBS   171 3
 FORGOTTEN IN THE GRASS EVA FEARFUL AND FLEET   864 16

FLEETING
 A PULSE THAT STILL WENT FLEETING   165 15
 I SPEAK ALOUD TO FLEETING HOSTS OF RED   745 25

FLEETS
 LITTLE FLEETS   542 5

FLESH
 AND THE SENSE OF HER CLINGING FLESH WAS SWEET   62 1
 TO HA' GONE AN' GIVEN HIS CLEAN YOUNG FLESH   77 31
 MEANS BUT TO YOU A BURDEN OF DEAD FLESH   87 26
 BEAT THROUGH THE FLESH   94 21
 AND THE FLESH OF THE STALK HOLDS UP FOR NOTHING A BLANK+   97 8
 AND MY HOLLOW FLESH STANDS UP IN THE NIGHT LIKE VANITY   97 10
 SO I WENT AND WASHED MY DEADENED FLESH IN THE SEA   99 12
 OF FLESH THAT STANDS DISMAYED ON THE BUSH   107 18
 A NEWLY-NAKED BERRY OF FLESH   108 3
 NO FLESH RESPONDED TO MY STROKE   111 25
 BUT OPAQUE AND NULL IN THE FLESH   111 29
 FIRE PASSED THROUGH YOUR FLESH   112 2
 WHAT MAN WILL STOOP IN YOUR FLESH TO PLOUGH   112 9
 THE SCENT OF HER FLESH   120 29
 THE CLOSED FLESH OF THE CLOVER   124 30
 FLESH OF MY HEART ERE DOWN REBUKED IT SLIPS   127 28
 IN MY FLESH AND MY BONE AND FORAGES INTO ME   128 16
 AND LEAVE MY FLESH DISCARDED LYING   134 8
 SITTING HUDDLED AGAINST THE CERULEAN ONE FLESH WITH THE+   142 11
 OF FLESH DOES CRACKLE AND SHIVER AND BREAK IN PAIN   151 17
 AND WHAT IS LIFE BUT THE SWELLING AND SHAPING THE DREAM+   176 6
 IN WHITE FLESH ROBED TO DRAPE ANOTHER DREAM   195 11
 SHALL I LESS THAN THE LEAST RED GRAIN OF FLESH   195 31
 MY FLESH IS WEARY WITH BOUNCE ON THEM AND   249 21
 WITH THE MAN IF YOU KNEW HOW MY FLESH ENJOYS   251 23
 IT WAS ALL ME I HAD DONE IT ALL IN MY OWN FLESH   257 9
 HERE IN THE FLESH   265 19
 WHEN SHE KNOWS THE FEARFUL OTHER FLESH AH DARKNESS UNFA+   267 11
 PIERCING THE FLESH TO BLOSSOM OF DEATH   273 17
 OF THRILLING RUIN IN THE FLESH OF PUNGENT PASSION OF RA+   273 19
 SOMEBODY'S POUND OF FLESH RENDERED UP   279 7
 IS JUST TO PUT YOUR MOUTH TO THE CRACK AND TAKE OUT THE+   282 9
 FLOWERILY NAKED IN FLESH AND GIVING OFF HUES OF LIFE   299 4
 COULD ONE AT NIGHT RUN UP AGAINST THE STANDING FLESH   428 2
 AND CATCH FLESH LIKE THE NIGHT IN ONE'S ARMS   428 5
 MARSHY FLESH   436 19
 FLESH FLAMEY AND A LITTLE HEROIC EVEN IN A TUMBLING CLO+   445 28
 IN THE BRIGHT WILD CIRCUS FLESH   446 18
 HAS RISEN IN THE FLESH   459 22
 THESE PEOPLE OF FLESH   460 2
 FLAME OF FLESH FOREVER TRAVELLING   460 6
 THEY ARE THEIR OWN FLESH I LAY   460 22
 LO I AM FLESH AND BLOOD THAT RACES   460 25
 WILL CLAMOUR FORTH FROM THE FLESH AND NEVER   461 19
 CONTACT OF CEREBRAL FLESH   469 18
 OTHER FLESH TO MY OWN   507 19
 THE RESURRECTION OF THE FLESH   513 4
 FOR OUR FLESH IS DEAD   513 5
 HAD HAD TO TAKE HIM FOR ONE NIGHT ONLY IN THE FLESH   538 3
 AND FLESH OF A MAN   538 6
 HELPED TO KILL HIM IN THE FLESH   538 12
 SURELY THEY ARE FLESH OF MY FLESH   585 23
 BRUISES ON MY INWARD FLESH   601 11
 COME PHYSICALLY NEARER BE FLESH TO MY FLESH   602 13
 TO TEACH THE RESURRECTION IN THE FLESH   609 18
 IN THE FLESH IS PART OF OUR CONSCIOUSNESS   621 4
 AND DAUBS THE SAND WITH ITS FLESH   628 6
 FOR MANKIND IS A SINGLE CORPUS WE ARE ALL ONE FLESH   631 24
 FOR OH THE POOR PEOPLE THAT ARE FLESH OF MY FLESH   632 14
 I THAT AM FLESH OF THEIR FLESH   632 15
 AN ENGINE OF FLESH USELESS UNLESS HE IS A TOOL   635 17

FLESH
     MACHINES OF IRON MUST BE TENDED BY HANDS OF FLESH   639   7
     TURN AWAY O TURN AWAY MAN OF FLESH   642   5
     THE PALE-GOLD FLESH OF PRIAPUS DROPPING ASLEEP   651 19
     OF THE FLESH   675 14
     THAT WE SHOULD BE LOVELY IN THE FLESH WITH BRIGHT CRESC+   687 16
     HIS URGE TAKES SHAPE IN FLESH AND LO   690 10
     EVERYTHING THAT HAS BEING HAS BEING IN THE FLESH   691   7
     OH IN THE WORLD OF THE FLESH OF MAN   712   5
     YOU ARE MISTAKEN THE VEIL OF THE FLESH IS RENT   742 18
     OUR FLESH THE BRIDE   742 26
     THIS FLESH THAT SMELLS   792 26
     THE CRISP FLESH   817 27
     LIKE SILK THEY ARE FLESH SHEER FLESH   827   3
     TILL A DREAM CAME TREMBLING THROUGH MY FLESH IN THE NIG+   860   9
     OF FLESH WOULD CRACK AND SHIVER WITH KEEN PAIN   873 29
     TWIN FLESH AND WHAT IS DEATH FOR ME WHAT IS IT   880   4
     MY FLESH IS READY LIKE TILLED LOAM   888   5
     HERE IN THE SUBTLE ROUNDED FLESH   *906 20
     MOVING VIBRATING ENDLESSLY IN THE ROUNDED FLESH   *906 24
     THE GREAT ACTIVITY SWELLING THROUGH THE ROUND FLESH PUL+ *907 14
     THE FLESH   *907 25
     THE WHOLE TEEMING FLESH OF MANKIND   *907 27
     THE GIGANTIC FLESH OF THE WORLD   *908   1
     HERE IN THE SUBTLE ROUNDED FLESH   *908 16
     OF MEN VIBRATING IN ECSTASY THROUGH THE ROUNDED FLESH   *908 21
     HERE IN THE SWELLING FLESH THE GREAT ACTIVITY WORKING   *909 11
     DREAM IN THE FLESH   *909 16
     FLESH OF THE WORLD   *909 24
     AND THE SENSE OF HER CLINGING FLESH WAS SWEET   *912   9
     TO HA'E GONE AN' GIVEN HIS YOUNG FLESH   *919 19
     BUT OPAQUE AND DULL IN THE FLESH   *927 17
     WOULD HAVE WITHERED THROUGH THY FLESH   *927 22
     BUT OPAQUE AND DULL IN THE FLESH   *928 17
     SUFFERING BURNT THROUGH YOUR FLESH   *928 22
     WHAT MAN WILL STOOP IN YOUR FLESH TO PLOUGH   *928 29
     THE CLOSED FLESH OF THE CLOVER   *935 36
     SENDING INTO ITS SLUMBERING FLESH   *937 16
     OF ALL US FLESH AND WE STAND IN OUR NAKEDNESS NESH   *938 11

FLESH-ANGUISH
     FLESH-ANGUISH THEN I SUFFERED A BALK   *927 10

FLESHED
     FLESHED ALL LIKE ME   38 24

FLESH-FRAGRANT
     STRANGELY HALF-SINISTERLY FLESH-FRAGRANT   280 20

FLESHLY
     PHYSICAL AND FLESHLY   468 19

FLESH-SCENT
     WITHIN THE FLESH-SCENT OF THIS WICKED TREE   299 13

FLEW
     HER BREATH FLEW WARM AGAINST MY NECK   61 28
     WHEN THE LIGHTNING FLEW ACROSS HER FACE   62   0
     OF HER FEET AS THEY FLEW FOR A SPACE THEN PAUSED TO PRE+   123   9
     CARESSES NEVER FLEW TO YOU LIKE BIRDS   158   9
     AND FLASHING KINGFISHERS THAT FLEW   262   4
     BUT HE ROSE AND FROM A TERROR WORSE THAN ME HE FLEW PAST   344   5
     SO THEY PECKED A SHRED OF MY LIFE AND FLEW OFF WITH A   500   4
     AT THE SIGHT OF EACH OTHER THE PAIR OF THEM FLEW   761   5
     HER BREATH FLEW WARM AGAINST MY NECK   *912   7
     WHEN THE LIGHTNING FLEW ACROSS HER FACE   *912 15

FLEXIBLE
     LIFE IS A THING YOU'VE GOT TO BE FLEXIBLE AND INTELLIGE+ *953   9

FLICK
     HERE FLICK THE RABBITS HERE PANTS THE GORSE HERE SAY TH+   34 11

FLICKED
     I FLICKED HIM ON   344   1

FLICKER
     PEOPLE FLICKER ROUND ME   115 15
     WHEN PEOPLE FLICKER DOWN THE PAVEMENT   115 25
     ME THAT I FLICKER IN THE BASKET   151 36
     TO FLICKER IN ME   169 29
     IN THE FLICKER OF A FLOWER   170   4
     THEY THREAD AND THRILL AND FLICKER EVER DOWNWARD   322 18
     FLICKER FLICKER-HEAVY   345 21
     LOST THEIR FLICKER   346 24
     AND GAY FLICKER OF JOYFUL LIFE   523 23
     AND ALL I WANT IS TO SEE THE SPARK FLICKER   524   5
     WHEN YOUR FLAME FLICKERS UP AND YOU FLICKER FORTH IN SH+   674   2
     NOW LET ME BE MYSELF AND FLICKER FORTH   674 16
     IS DEAD AT LAST THEN HIS POOR SUNK FLAME MUST FLICKER   859   3
     ME THAT I FLICKER IN THE BASKET   874 14

FLICKERED
     AND FLICKERED HIS TWO-FORKED TONGUE FROM HIS LIPS AND   349 23
     AND FLICKERED HIS TONGUE LIKE A FORKED NIGHT ON THE AIR+   350 25
     EVEN WHEN THE MIND HAS FLICKERED AWAKE   407 24
     THAT FLICKERED FORTH IN THE BEST HOURS OF LIFE   676 11

FLICKER-HEAVY
     FLICKER FLICKER-HEAVY   345 21

FLICKERING
     WHERE THE WOOD FUMES UP AND THE FLICKERING WATERY   116   4
     FLICKERING   207 13
     DUSKY SLIM MARROW-THOUGHT OF SLENDER FLICKERING MEN OF   297   6
     COMPELLED TO SEE THE DELICATE SKILL OF FLICKERING HUMAN   445 26
     FLICKERING GAY   445 32
     LIKE FLICKERING CANCERS   511 14

FLICKERING
     SOME MEN CAN SEE LIFE CLEAN AND FLICKERING ALL ROUND   649   7
     SHE WHO AT HER BEST HOURS WAS HERSELF WARM FLICKERING H+   676 16
     WHERE THE FLICKERING RIVER LOITERS   867   8
     ONLY THE BATS ARE FLICKERING ROUND AND ROUND AND KEEP   *918   1

FLICKERS
     YET THEIR DAUNTED LOOKING FLICKERS   109   5
     YOUR FERVENT LIMBS WITH FLICKERS AND TENDRILS OF NEW   156 21
     BECAUSE OF THE LITTLE LIGHTS AND FLICKERS AND INTERRUPT+   203 20
     THE FLICKERS COME AND GO   237 24
     AS THE DARKNESS FLICKERS AND DIPS   238 13
     AND NOW AT EVENING AS HE FLICKERS OVER THE RIVER   347 16
     WHEN YOUR FLAME FLICKERS UP AND YOU FLICKER FORTH IN SH+   674   2

FLICKER-SPLASHING
     FLICKER-SPLASHING ROUND MY ROOM   343 27

FLICKING
     SO TO DRIVE HIM OUT FLICKING WITH MY WHITE HANDKERCHIEF   343   5
     SHAKING ASUNDER AND FLICKING AT HIS RIBS   453 15
     AND UNDER THE FLICKING OF THE WHITE WHIP-LASH OF THE   453 23

FLIES
     WHOSE PLAINTIVE CRY IS HEARD AS SHE FLIES   42 29
     OF THE BEE BEFORE HE FLIES   46 12
     SPARK FLIES   47 25
     THE THOUGHTS OF THE SKIES THE EAGLE FLIES NEAREST TO TH+   368   2
     BIRD FLIES SO NEAR   368   3
     WHOSE VOICE FLIES ON AND ON CALLING LIKE A SWAN   623 17
     THERE ARE DEAD THAT ATTACK THE SUN LIKE SWARMS OF BLACK+   795 28
     FLIES LIKE A WILD THING ACROSS MY BODY   *893 15

FLIG
     THA ARENA VERY FLIG TER GO   138 16
     YOUR HAND WOULD NOT BE SO FLIG AND EASY   255 25

FLIGHT
     HAS FLUTTERED HER SPIRIT TO STUMBLING FLIGHT   46 15
     NOR PUT US TO FLIGHT   114   8
     ENJOYING THEIR GLANCING FLIGHT THOUGH LOVE IS DEAD   133 23
     THEIR FLIGHT   147   6
     STILL IN FULL FLIGHT EXTINCT SHALL I THEN TURN   195 23
     DRIFTING IN FLIGHT   253 10
     A TWITCH A TWITTER AN ELASTIC SHUDDER IN FLIGHT   341 11
     WITH A TWITCHY NERVOUS INTOLERABLE FLIGHT   342 22
     DIPPING WITH PETTY TRIUMPHANT FLIGHT AND TITTERING OVER   347 17
     OF THE PARABOLA OF CURVED FLIGHT   476 10
     FOR THE DARK FLIGHT DOWN OBLIVION   718 11
     BETWEEN WINGS OF THE ENDLESS FLIGHT   788 16
     AT THE DEPTHS OF THE PEACE AND THE FLIGHT   788 17
     A COOL OINTMENT OVER THE EARTH BLISTERED IN THE FLIGHT +   855 31
     WITH THE PAIN OF THIS FLIGHT   862 23
     THAT I PUT TO FLIGHT FROM OUT OF YOU   *894   5
     BLACK BIRDS WHOSE SONGS ARE UNUTTERABLE SPINNING FANTAS+ *918 14

FLIGHT-HEAVY
     AND HE LUNGED FLIGHT-HEAVY AWAY FROM ME SIDEWAYS A SOLID   340 13

FLIMSY
     IN THE DOWNWARD-DROPPING OF FLIMSY SHEAVES   68 19
     FLIMSY HUSK-BALL THROUGH WHOSE RIFTS THERE LOOKS   874 31
     OF YOUR EYES DRAWS OPEN MY SHELTERING FLIMSY DOORS   875 13
     IN THE DOWN-WARD DROOPING FLIMSY SHEAVES   *915   3

FLING
     SOMEWHERE THE WIND-FLOWERS FLING THEIR HEADS BACK   40 27
     AND FLING MYSELF AT THE DOORS OF SLEEP FOR REST   129 22
     TAKE MY WORDS AND FLING   236 25
     YET SEE HIM FLING HIMSELF ABROAD IN FRESH ABANDON   305   6
     AND FLING HIMSELF IN EFFORT AFTER EFFORT   428 21

FLINGING
     FLINGING HER SHAWL-FRINGE OVER THE RIVER   170 19
     WHY ARE THEY SO BURSTING FLINGING THEMSELVES ABOUT   537 23
     WHEN RED RAIN GOES FLINGING   861 15

FLINGS
     HE FLINGS THE RABBIT SOFT ON THE TABLE BOARD   43 22
     FLINGS OUT ITS VIVID BLACK NOTES   772 32

FLINT
     OF MY STEEL LOVELY WHITE FLINT OF DESIRE   118   5
     WITH A NEEDLE OF LONG RED FLINT HE STABS IN THE DARK   382 16

FLIP
     AND FLIP THEY GO WITH THE NOSE-DIVE OF SHEER DELIGHT   693 28

FLIPS
     WHEN A BIRD FLIPS HIS TAIL IN GETTING HIS BALANCE ON A +   496   6

FLIRT
     THE SUN-LIT FLIRT WHO ALL THE DAY   42 11

FLIT
     AND THE BRIGHT RIVERS FLIT   196 10

FLITTER
     OF THE NEW-BORN AND THEN THE OLD OWL THEN THE BATS THAT+   38 11
     THEY FLITTER   *892 27

FLITTERING
     AND A MOON-BLUE MOTH GOES FLITTERING BY   41 25

FLOAT
OF UNDERWATER FLOAT BRIGHT RIPPLES RUN 51 7
I WATCHED THEM FLOAT UP THE DARK CHIMNEY 107 4
THE GORGE OF THE GAPING FLOWER TILL THE BLOOD DID FLOAT 123 18
LIKE MEN WHO ARE DROWNED BUT FLOAT ERECT IN THE DEEP 146 10
FLOAT LIKE BOATS ON A RIVER WHILE OTHER 217 29
AND SOON THE OWL WINGED WITH STILLNESS WILL FLOAT OUT T+ 858 16
THE TWO IMMENSITIES WOULD FLOAT UNWILLING 875 29
OF UNDER-WATER FLOAT BRIGHT RIPPLES RUN *898 19
OF UNDER-WATER FLOAT BRIGHT RIPPLES RUN *902 3
THE GORGE OF THE GAPING FLOWER TILL THE BLOOD DID FLOAT *934 24
FLOAT LIKE BOATS ON A RIVER WAITING *943 12
AND SO KISS-BELADEN THAT IT SCARCE CAN FLOAT *943 17

FLOATED
RED FLOWERS THAT HAVE FLOATED AWAY 887 29

FLOATING
EVEN HER FLOATING HAIR SINKS HEAVILY 74 3
FLOATING UP FROM THE FORGOTTEN 106 24
HAVE RISEN FLOATING ON MY BLOOD THE RARE 113 3
AND LOOK YOU FLOATING JUST THEREBY 126 14
THE HEAVENS LIKE SPECKS OF DUST THAT ARE FLOATING ASUND+ 223 2
WITH STRANDS OF DOWN LIKE FLOATING ASH 728 10
FLOATING ABOVE MY SILVER SO THAT THE ADEPT 874 5
I SEE THE STRONG SOUND EARTH BETRAYED AS A FLOATING 874 30
THE BONNY FLOATING ARK OF THIS FAIR WORLD 876 10
LIKE FLOATING FROTH ON AN EBBING SHORE IN THE MOON *897 27
LIKE FLOATING FROTH ON AN EBBING SHORE IN THE MOON *901 4
EVEN HER FLOATING HAIR SINKS LIKE STORM-BRUISED YOUNG L+ *913 24

FLOATS
A QUICKENING MASCULINE GLEAM FLOATS IN TO ALL 127 2
AND WHAT IS THIS THAT FLOATS ON THE UNDERMIST 141 13
A CROW FLOATS PAST ON LEVEL WINGS 166 1
ADOWN THE PALE-GREEN GLACIER RIVER FLOATS 209 1
WILDLY FLOATS SWIRLS 425 17
TILL THE HEAD FLOATS TILTED LIKE A BOTTLE FORWARD TILTED 428 10
OVER THE SURFACE OF A SHADOW-COLOUR FLOATS 867 14

FLOCCULENT
A FLOCCULENT DUST ON THE FLOOR OF THE WORLD THE FESTOON 98 13
ASH FLUTTERS FLOCCULENT LIKE DOWN ON A BLUE WAN FLEDGEL+ 330 8
TO HOT AND FLOCCULENT ASH 728 8
IN THE FLOCCULENT ASH OF THE SAGE-GREY DESERT 780 24

FLOCK
RAMPING ROUND GUARDING THE FLOCK OF MANKIND 324 28
AND·INCREASING THE FLOCK AND PERHAPS GIVING A REAL NIP + 325 10
AND THEN THE GEESE SCUTTLED IN IN A LITTLE FLOCK 444 19
SAVE THE COLD GHOSTS THAT HOMELESS FLOCK ABOUT 736 8
FLOCK UNSEEN FROM MY LIPS TO HERS 868 32

FLOCKS
BLOWING LITTLE FLOCKS OF BIRDS 99 17

FLOOD
TO BE UNDER THE FLOOD 37 22
UPON MY MIND HIS LIPS MEET MINE AND A FLOOD 43 35
ON THE FLOOD THAT SOUNDLESS SWINGS 109 16
OF MY BODY AND LOOSE THE ESSENTIAL FLOOD 117 23
HE SITS LIKE A SHADE BY THE FLOOD ALONE 130 5
WHEN THE SLEEPER STIRS OR TURNS ON THE EBB OF THE FLOOD 145 27
DOWN IN THE FLOOD OF REMEMBRANCE I WEEP LIKE A CHILD FOR 148 18
THE FLOOD SO IT PASSES BEYOND 159 6
COMPARED TO THE FLOOD OF BLACK HEAT THAT ROLLS UPWARDS 302 5
WHO IS IT EJECTS HIS SPERM TO THE NAKED FLOOD 335 25
TO BREATHE FROM THE FLOOD AT THE GILLS 336 30
FISH-BLOOD SLOWLY RUNNING NEXT TO THE FLOOD EXTRACTING 336 31
DROPPING BACK WITH A SLAP ON THE FACE OF THE FLOOD 337 4
AND THE FLOOD STRIKES THE BELLY AND WE ARE GONE 425 18
FLOOD 428 9
WILL THE DARK FLOOD OF OUR DAY'S ANNIHILATION 428 24
TILL THEY TOUCH IN FLOOD 465 30
UNCONTAMINATED THE UNMENTAL FLOOD 471 13
A GATE TO THE FLOOD 563 2
AS HE'S ALWAYS BEEN SINCE THE FLOOD AND BEFORE 574 21
WHEN DANGER THREATENS ON THE SURFACE OF THE CEASELESS F+ 695 2
ALREADY THE FLOOD IS UPON US 718 8
HAS HER FOOTING WASHED AWAY AS THE DARK FLOOD RISES 718 13
AND OUR SOUL COWERS NAKED IN THE DARK RAIN OVER THE FLO+ 718 19
BLACKER UPON THE SOUNDLESS UNGURGLING FLOOD 719 12
THE FLOOD SUBSIDES AND THE BODY LIKE A WORN SEA-SHELL 720 12
ON THE PINK FLOOD 720 15
SILENTLY SWIMMING AND SLEEPING AND PRESSING THE FLOOD 841 4
STREWN ACROSS THE FLOOD 860 24
TO FOUNDER AT LAST WITHIN THE DREADFUL FLOOD 875 33
TILL THE BURSTEN FLOOD OF LIFE EBBS BACK TO MY EYES *893 30
TO THE FIRE AND RAIN WILL YOU TAKE THE FLOOD *931 27

FLOOD-DAWN
OF A FLOOD-DAWN 720 8

FLOODED
BUT MUD HAS FLOODED THE HOMES OF THESE WEARY LANDS 167 11

FLOODS
THE FLOODS 153 31
OF THE WORLD BEFORE THE FLOODS WHERE MAN WAS DARK AND 286 25
NIPPED UPON THE FROZEN FLOODS OF PHILOSOPHIC DESPAIR 542 21

FLOOD'S
THE FLOOD'S SLOW GAIT 146 9
UPON THE FLOOD'S BLACK WASTE 719 6

FLOOD-WINDS
SO NIGHT'S FLOOD-WINDS HAVE LIFTED MY LAST DESIRE FROM + 97 9

FLOOR
UPON THE FLOOR THAT ERST STOOD UP SO FRESH 87 29
A FLOCCULENT DUST ON THE FLOOR OF THE WORLD THE FESTOON 98 13
LIKE A LINTY RAW-COLD DUST DISTURBED FROM THE FLOOR 99 2
THE SPIDERS WITH WHITE FACES THAT SCUTTLE ON THE FLOOR + 112 28
BEYOND ME LIES ON THE LOW STILL FLOOR OF THE SKY 114 18
AND HER SHIFT IS LYING WHITE UPON THE FLOOR 120 2
LISTENING FOR THE SOUND OF HER FEET ACROSS THE FLOOR 121 16
I TELL YOU MY BLOOD RUNS OUT ON THE FLOOR OF THIS OAK 131 13
IN THE HOUSE OF LIFE THE FLOOR WAS RUFFLED WITH GOLD 141 6
THE WHITE RUGS ON THE FLOOR NOR THE SILENT BED 155 3
THE PEACEFUL FLOOR WHEN FELL THE SWORD ON THEIR REST 155 8
REFOLDING SHE SLIPPED TO THE FLOOR AS A GHOST-WHITE PEO+ 155 23
IN BLONDE AND WHITE ON THE FLOOR NOR EVEN TURNED 156 8
ON THE FLOOR WHERE NEVER MY NUMB FEET TRODE 163 11
SOON STREWS ITSELF ON THE FLOOR AND KEEP THE RADIANCE O+ 179 4
SLIPPED THROUGH MY ARMS ON THE THRESHING FLOOR 198 11
HEAVEN'S MUFFLED FLOOR 268 26
ON THE FLOOR OF HEAVEN 269 8
NEAR THE CURTAIN ON THE FLOOR 346 27
AND DIDN'T YOU CRINGE ON THE FLOOR LIKE ANY INKSPOT 400 10
TO DUST TO ASH ON THE TWILIT FLOOR OF THE DESERT 403 23
OR THEY ARE LIKE LEAVES RUSTLING THICK IN THE CROWDS ON+ 615 8
WITH GREY ON THE FLOOR OF THE DESERT 816 22
THE FLOOR 817 25
ON THE FLOOR 856 10

FLOOR-LIGHT
SING THROUGH AND EACH WITH A FLOOR-LIGHT RACING ALONG 144 9

FLOORS
WITHOUT FEET THE RED FLOORS 818 12

FLOP
OR FROGS THAT WHEN THEY LEAP COME FLOP AND FLOP TO THE 392 25

FLORENCE
WHEN THE TIRED FLOWER OF FLORENCE IS IN GLOOM BENEATH T+ 340 21
THEY HAVE GREEN TRAM IN FLORENCE NOW 845 22

FLORESCENCE
OUT OF CORROSION INTO NEW FLORESCENCE 160 20

FLOSS-GOLD
THEN UP COMES A GREY RAT A FLOSS-GOLD CHICKEN GRAPPLES *933 11

FLOSSIE
LIZZIE AND LUCY AND ME AND FLOSSIE 573 23
BUT FOR LIZZIE AND LUCY AND FLOSSIE AND ME 574 1
BUT ME AND LUCY AND FLOSSIE AND LIZZIE 574 3
AND LIZZIE AND ME AND FLOSSIE AND LUCY 574 8

FLOTILLA
WHITE DUCKS A QUACKING FLOTILLA OF CLOUD 126 13
O SMALL FLOTILLA OF SORRY SOULS 542 11

FLOTSAM
OF FLOTSAM UNTIL MY SOUL IS TIRED OR SATISFIED 180 7
THEIR DEBRIS IS FLOTSAM AND FLUNG ON THE COAST 823 8

FLOUNDERS
MEET HER AS SHE FLOUNDERS DOWN FROM THE CHICKEN-HOUSE A+ 761 20

FLOURISH
TO FLOURISH THERE AS PALE MOULD BLOOMS ON A CRUST 99 5
WILL FLOURISH ITS BRANCHES IN HEAVEN WHEN WE 172 16
FADE AND YET FLOURISH 826 11

FLOURISHETH
SEE HOW IT FLOURISHETH 172 9

FLOURISHING
GREEN DIM INVISIBLE FLOURISHING OF VINES 286 5
FLOURISHING FROM THE ROCK IN A MYSTERIOUS ARROGANCE 299 8

FLOW
IF UNDER YOUR SLIPPING WORDS THAT EASILY FLOW 122 10
TO HALT THE HEART DIVERT THE STREAMING FLOW 195 34
GREEN STREAMS THAT FLOW FROM THE INNERMOST CONTINENT OF 260 24
AND WHEN WE FAIL TO TRANSMIT LIFE LIFE FAILS TO FLOW 449 2
THAT IS PART OF THE MYSTERY OF SEX IT IS A FLOW ONWARDS 449 4
SEX ISN'T SIN IT'S A DELICATE FLOW BETWEEN WOMEN AND MEN 464 14
AND THE SIN IS TO DAMAGE THE FLOW FORCE IT OR DIRTY IT + 464 15
IT'S THE FLOW OF YOUR LIFE IT'S YOUR MOVING SELF AND YOU 464 18
INTO EACH OTHER AS TIDES FLOW 471 8
ALL FLOWS AND EVERY FLOW IS RELATED TO EVERY OTHER FLOW 476 27
IF ONCE FOR A SECOND THE UNIVERSE CEASED TO FLOW 479 13
ONLY MAN TRIES NOT TO FLOW 479 16
AND CHANGING IN A FLOW AS ALL PASSIONS CHANGE 482 9
TO BE ALIVE YOU'VE GOT TO FEEL A GENEROUS FLOW 522 24
FLOW THE HEART'S RIVERS OF FULNESS DESIRE AND DISTRESS 607 8
UPWARD FLOW OF FEELING 609 8
WITHDRAW WITHDRAW YOUR FLOW 639 12
THEY ARE OPEN TO THE RESTLESS SKIES AND STREAMS FLOW IN+ 675 10
DO THEY STOP THE FLOW 765 13
THERE IS SOMETHING STIRS IN ME FROM THE FLOW OF THEIR L+ *906 17

FLOWED
THAT IS DEAD THE MOTHER-LOVE LIKE LIGHT THAT FLOWED *938 14

FLOWER
A TINY MOON AS SMALL AND WHITE AS A SINGLE JASMINE FLOW+ 67 18
OUR FACES FLOWER FOR A LITTLE HOUR PALE AND UNCERTAIN A+ 71 1
HANGS NUMB AND HEAVY FROM A BENDING FLOWER 73 21
IN THE OPEN DEPTHS OF EACH FLOWER DARK RESTLESS DROPS 76 2

FLOWER
AND THE FLOWER THAT PUTS ITS TONGUE OUT AND FERN THAT P+   89 27
I HAVE PUSHED MY HANDS IN THE DARK SOIL UNDER THE FLOWE+   92   8
AT LAST INTO BLOSSOM OF BEING EACH ONE HIS OWN FLOWER O+   93 15
NOR BE THWARTED IN LIFE'S SLOW STRUGGLE TO UNFOLD THE F+   93 18
I THROW FROM OUT OF THE DARKNESS MYSELF LIKE A FLOWER I+   93 26
IS COMPLETE FOR THE MOMENT YET WAIT AND YOU'LL SEE THAT+   94   8
LIKE A FLOWER THAT THE FROST HAS HUGGED AND LET GO MY H+   95   1
AND NEVER A GIRL LIKE A CHESTNUT FLOWER   106 19
MINE WAS THE LOVE OF A GROWING FLOWER   111 11
A LOOK OF HATRED ON THE FLOWER THAT BURNS   113 11
SHE LAUGHED SHE REACHED HER HAND OUT TO THE FLOWER   123 13
THE GORGE OF THE GAPING FLOWER TILL THE BLOOD DID FLOAT   123 18
IN THE FLOWER'S THROAT AND THE FLOWER GAPED WIDE WITH W+   125 10
I PRESSED THE WRETCHED THROTTLED FLOWER BETWEEN   125 13
THE LOW WORD DON'T I LET THE FLOWER FALL   125 20
WITH A FACE LIKE A CHICKWEED FLOWER   145   9
SOFT SHE LAY AS A SHED FLOWER FALLEN NOR HEARD   155 26
SHE SOFTLY PASSED THE SORROWFUL FLOWER SHED   156   7
I WISH THE ELDER-TREES IN FLOWER COULD SUDDENLY HEAVE A+   159 23
DOWN THE LABYRINTH OF THE SINISTER FLOWER   166 23
FLOWER THE DAY HAS BEGUN   166 27
IN THE FLICKER OF A FLOWER   170   4
AND A TREMBLING FLOWER ENCLOSES   178 25
AND LEANING TO ME LIKE A FLOWER ON ITS STALK   178 29
FOR ME IT IS MORE THAN ENOUGH IF THE FLOWER UNCLOSE   219 20
ALMOST THE FLOWER IN THE BUD   239 17
LIKE A FLOWER IN BUD   240 17
I AM LIKE A SEED WITH A PERFECT FLOWER ENCLOSED   247   6
WHAT FLOWER MY LOVE   247   9
EVERY HUMAN BEING WILL THEN BE LIKE A FLOWER UNTRAMMELL+   267 30
AND BETRAYS ITS CANDOUR IN THE ROUND WHITE STRAWBERRY F+   272 28
COME NOW TO US YOUR ADHERENTS WHO CANNOT FLOWER FROM   273 10
FLOWER   278   7
FOUR-PETALLED FLOWER   282   4
THERE WAS A FLOWER THAT FLOWERED INWARD WOMB-WARD   282 27
HERE'S TO THE THORN IN FLOWER HERE IS TO UTTERANCE   283   8
HIBISCUS FLOWER   313 33
FLOWER   314 13
WARRIOR-LIKE DAWN-COCK'S-COMB FLARING FLOWER   315   1
I AM THEIR SUPERIOR SALUTING THE HIBISCUS FLOWER NOT TH+   316 23
AND I SALUTE HIBISCUS AND THE SALVIA FLOWER   317   1
WITH A HIBISCUS FLOWER BEHIND MY EAR   317 15
THAT THEY TAKE HIBISCUS AND THE SALVIA FLOWER   318   6
WHEN THE TIRED FLOWER OF FLORENCE IS IN GLOOM BENEATH T+   340 21
THAT FLOWER IN MERE MOVEMENT   446 10
LOVE IS LIKE A FLOWER IF IT MUST FLOWER AND FADE   472 24
IF IT DOESN'T FADE IT IS NOT A FLOWER   472 25
FIDELITY AND LOVE ARE TWO DIFFERENT THINGS LIKE A FLOWER   476   1
AND LOVE LIKE A FLOWER WILL FADE WILL CHANGE INTO SOMET+   476   3
AND A FLOWER IT TAKES A SUMMER   477   6
FLOWER   478 25
SHY FLOWER OF SEX   562 31
THE POMEGRANATES ARE IN FLOWER   605 21
THE POMEGRANATES ARE IN FLOWER   605 23
THE POMEGRANATES ARE IN FLOWER   606   2
AS A COLUMBINE FLOWER HAS OR EVEN A STARLING WALKING AN+   621 16
TO FLOWER FREE OF FEAR   627   4
AND WITHDRAWS ITSELF AND RECOGNISES A FLOWER OR THE   640   3
SOMETIMES I SEE HER LIKE A FLOWER NODDING HER WAY AND   645 22
INSTEAD OF A FLOWER THAT DIES AND OPENS A DIFFERENT BUD   662   6
AND MAN IS AN IRIDESCENT FOUNTAIN RISING UP TO FLOWER   675 15
LET ME GUIDE MYSELF WITH THE BLUE FORKED TORCH OF THIS +   697 14
WITH A HINT OF THE FROZEN BELLS OF THE SCYLLA FLOWER   708 29
AND IN THE MORNING WAKE LIKE A NEW-OPENED FLOWER   726 24
MY BODY GLAD AS THE BELL OF A FLOWER   742 32
OF DEATH A CYCLAMEN A CROCUS FLOWER   744   6
NOW LIKE A CYCLAMEN A CROCUS FLOWER   744 19
SO LIKE A CYCLAMEN A CROCUS FLOWER   745   1
NOW LIKE A CYCLAMEN A CROCUS FLOWER   745 21
JUST AS A CYCLAMEN OR CROCUS FLOWER   745 27
AS A FLOWER ABOVE CHARRED REMAINS   769 11
A RED FLOWER FALLS TO ITS DIM REFLECTION   887 18
A RED FLOWER FALLS TO ITS DIM REFLECTION   887 20
LIKE A FLOWER THAT THE FROST HAS HUGGED AND LET GO MY H+   *897 16
IN THE OPEN DEPTHS OF EACH FLOWER DARK RESTLESS DROPS   *897 29
IN THE OPEN DEPTHS OF EACH FLOWER DARK RESTLESS DROPS   *901   6
FLOWER   *913   4
HANGS NUMB AND HEAVY FROM THE BENDING FLOWER   *913 13
DRAWS DOWN THE BURDENED FLOWER   *913 21
OR AS TWO WHITE BUTTERFLIES SETTLE IN THE CUP OF ONE FL+   *914   4
OUR FACES FLOWER FOR A LITTLE HOUR PALE AND UNCERTAIN A+   *917 21
THE FLOWER OF FORGIVENESS IS PLUCKED FROM OFF THE OFFEN+   *926 26
MINE WAS THE LOVE OF THE SUN FOR A FLOWER   *927   4
MINE WAS THE LOVE OF THE SUN FOR A FLOWER   *928   4
SHE LAUGHED SHE REACHED HER HAND OUT DOWN TO THE FLOWER   *934 19
THE GORGE OF THE GAPING FLOWER TILL THE BLOOD DID FLOAT   *934 24
IN THE FLOWER'S THROAT AND THE FLOWER GAPED WIDE WITH W+   *935 26
I PRESSED THE WRETCHED THROTTLED FLOWER BETWEEN   *936 12
AND I KEPT THE CHOKED SNAKE FLOWER IN ITS PANGS   *936 15
THE LOW WORD DON'T I LET THE FLOWER FALL   *936 19
THE UNKNOWN FLOWER ISSUED MAGIC-WISE   *943 21
LET ME GUIDE MYSELF WITH THE BLUE FORKED TORCH OF A FLO+   *956 11
GIVE ME A FLOWER ON A TALL STEM AND THREE DARK FLAMES   *956 21

FLOWERBELL
AND HERS A FLOWERBELL SWINGING   742 33

FLOWERED
YOU MY LOVE THE FOREMOST IN A FLOWERED GOWN   58 20
WE WHO HAVE NEVER FLOWERED LIKE PATIENT CACTUSES   272 32
THERE WAS A FLOWER THAT FLOWERED INWARD WOMB-WARD   282 27
THAT HAS FLOWERED BEFORE   814   2
IT FLOWERED BEFORE MEN TOOK TO FLOWERING FOR WAGES   814   5
AND DRINKING FROM THE CUPS THAT HAVE FLOWERED FROM HIS +   *950 10

FLOWER-FOAMED
A NURSE IN WHITE AT THE DAWNING FLOWER-FOAMED PANE   155   1

FLOWERILY
FLOWERILY NAKED IN FLESH AND GIVING OFF HUES OF LIFE   299   4

FLOWERINESS
FLOWERS ACHIEVE THEIR OWN FLOWERINESS AND IT IS A MIRAC+   683 22

FLOWERING
BUT WHOEVER WOULD PLUCK APART MY FLOWERING WILL BURN TH+   93 29
OWN FLOWERING   257   2
THE FLOWERING ALL INWARD AND WOMB-FIBRILLED   282 23
ITS NAKEDNESS ALL WITHIN-WALLS ITS FLOWERING FOREVER UN+   283 15
WHERE EVERYTHING HAPPENS INVISIBLE FLOWERING AND FERTIL+   283 20
SAVE SOME SHOOTS SOME LOVELY FLOWERING SHOOTS   640 19
IT FLOWERED BEFORE MEN TOOK TO FLOWERING FOR WAGES   814   5
OF FLOWERING STRIFE   888   8
SWAY THE LIVE PEARLS THEIR FLOWERING PLEDGES   *941 20
UNDER THE SUMMERY FLOWERING OF THE ROSES OF LOVE   *951 12

FLOWERLESS
THERE WAS ANOTHER WORLD A DUSKY FLOWERLESS TENDRILLED W+   285 22

FLOWER-MESH
GREAT COMPLICATED NUDE FIG-TREE STEMLESS FLOWER-MESH   299   3

FLOWER-ROOTS
NO MORE STOCKINGS TO DARN FOR THE FLOWER-ROOTS DOWN   309   2

FLOWERS
BUT NOT EVEN THE SCENT OF INSOUCIANT FLOWERS   50 13
SHEDS ITS FLOWERS ON A RIVER   56 12
LIKE FLOWERS I FELL TO BE CAUGHT   56 17
SUCH A ONE IN THE NORTH IT FLOWERS ON THE STREET AND I +   58 13
EVERY DAY BY THE FENCE TO LOOK UP AT THE FLOWERS THAT E+   58 14
ON TH' YALLER CLAY WI' TH' WHITE FLOWERS TOP OF IT   60 13
THE LITTLE WHITE FEET NOD LIKE WHITE FLOWERS IN A WIND   64 30
OR FIRM AND SILKEN AS YOUNG PEONY FLOWERS   65 10
MAY-BLOSSOM AND BLUE BIRD'S-EYE FLOWERS FALLING   65 15
BY-PATHS WHERE THE WANTON-HEADED FLOWERS DOFF THEIR HOOD   65 30
WE HAVE SHUT THE DOORS BEHIND US AND THE VELVET FLOWERS+   70   1
ALL THE FLOWERS ARE FADED FROM THE ASPHALT ISLE IN THE +   71 10
FLOWERS OF ILLUSION WHO SHINE IN OUR GAUDS MAKE A PARAD+   71 17
LIKE HALF-BLOWN FLOWERS DIMLY SHAKING AT THE NIGHT   75 27
OF EARTH AND QUICKENS ALL HERSELF WITH FLOWERS   89   2
THE BUTTERCUP BOG-END WHERE THE FLOWERS ROSE UP   90 20
FOR FLOWERS ARE TENDER FOLK AND ROOTS CAN ONLY HIDE   93 30
THE FLOWERS OF ALL MY MUD SWIM INTO SIGHT   113   8
OVER THE FLOWERS AT MY FEET   124 24
US CREATURES PEOPLE AND FLOWERS UNDONE   127   3
AND DIAPERED ABOVE THE CHAUNTING FLOWERS   135 28
OF FLOWERS SURGE FROM BELOW TO THEIR LADDER-TOPS   136 13
FLOWERS OF THE BLEEDING-HEART FALL TO THE THROB   137   5
GLIMMERED AS FLOWERS THAT IN PERFUME AT TWILIGHT UNFOLD   141   8
LIKE FLOWERS OF INFERNAL MOLY   146 20
THE COLTSFOOT FLOWERS ALONG THE RAILWAY BANKS   162   2
WONDERING MOUNT AND PUT THE FLOWERS ASUNDER   176 17
SINCE THEN WITH FRITTER OF FLOWERS   193 18
HE GAVE HER NO CROWN OF FLOWERS   202 21
THAT COMES FROM THE FLOWERS OF PAIN   202 28
AND THE WHITE SHINING HOUSES AND THE GAY RED FLOWERS ON   205   2
THEY SHONE CLEAR LIKE FLOWERS UNDONE   216 17
AND I AS I STAND IN THE COLD AVERTED FLOWERS   226   9
OF THE SKY AND THE ALMOND FLOWERS   244   6
HOW HE BULLIES THE FLOWERS   244 11
HE CLOUTS THE TUFTS OF FLOWERS   244 14
SEE THE BIRD IN THE FLOWERS HE'S MAKING   244 27
SKIES TREES FLOWERS BIRDS WATER   256 25
WHEN I GATHERED FLOWERS I KNEW IT WAS MYSELF PLUCKING MY   257   1
THE PRESENCE OF THE FLOWERS THAT GREW   262   2
FLOWERS THAT COME FIRST FROM THE DARKNESS AND FEEL COLD+   270   9
FLOWERS SCENTLESS OR PUNGENT AMMONIACAL ALMOST   270 11
THEY ARE THE FLOWERS OF ICE-VIVID MORTIFICATION   270 24
FLOWERS OF THE PENUMBRA ISSUE OF CORRUPTION NOURISHED IN   271   8
I WISH THESE BRITTLE FROST-LOVELY FLOWERS OF PASSIONATE+   272   6
COME AND CAJOLE THE GAWKY COLT'S-FOOT FLOWERS   273   4
LIKE OTHER FLOWERS IN A REVELATION OF PETALS   283   4
AND THE CROSS SPROUTING ITS SUPERB AND FEARLESS FLOWERS   305 30
WHO GAVE US FLOWERS   307 17
JESUS THE GOD OF FLOWERS   307 23
FLOWERS CAME HELL-HOUNDS ON HER HEELS   308   6
ALL THE SPORT OF SUMMER AND SPRING AND FLOWERS SNAPPING   309 18
ALAS SALVIA AND HIBISCUS FLOWERS   313 10
SALVIA AND HIBISCUS FLOWERS   313 11
SALVIA AND HIBISCUS FLOWERS   313 13
SALVIA AND HIBISCUS FLOWERS   313 15
SALVIA AND HIBISCUS FLOWERS   313 18
WITH HIBISCUS FLOWERS IN THE BUTTONHOLES OF YOUR SUNDAY+   314 11
THE NATIVE ROYALTY OF RED HIBISCUS FLOWERS   314 18
AND IF IT BE NOT SO BRUTES TO PULL DOWN HIBISCUS FLOWERS   314 24
YOU LOOK WELL WITH YOUR SALVIA FLOWERS I MUST SAY   314 34
THAT I SALUTE THE RED HIBISCUS FLOWERS·   316 28
WHO HAVE PULLED DOWN THE SALVIA FLOWERS   317 29
AND ROSY DELICATE HIBISCUS FLOWERS   317 30
WHERE FLOWERS SPROUT IN THE ACRID HUMUS AND FADE INTO H+   321 11
BUT WHILE FLOWERS CLUB THEIR PETALS AT EVENING   321 22
I BELIEVE THERE WERE NO FLOWERS THEN   372 14
FLOWERS AND GOOSEBERRIES   451 16
FLOWERS OFF THEIR FIVE-FOLD STEM   451 27
THE MONEY-MUCK YOU SIMPLE FLOWERS   456 18
O FLOWERS THEY FADE BECAUSE THEY ARE MOVING SWIFTLY A   476   6
O FLOWERS THEY ARE ALL THE TIME TRAVELLING   476 12
EMBALMED FLOWERS ARE NOT FLOWERS IMMORTELLES ARE NOT   476 16
FLOWERS   476 17
FLOWERS ARE JUST A MOTION A SWIFT MOTION A COLOURED   476 18
AS FLOWERS ARE AND WE ARE ONLY SLOWER   476 25
FLOWERS AND SAPPHIRES AND US DIVERSELY STREAMING   476 28

FLOWERS
  FLOWERS   477 8
  OLDER THAN FLOWERS OLDER THAN FERNS OLDER THAN FORAMINI+   477 10
  FOR THE FLOWERS AND I'LL TELL YOU WHAT   578 1
  GRASS BLOSSOMS GRASS HAS FLOWERS FLOWERS OF GRASS   587 2
  OH WHEN THE GRASS FLOWERS THE GRASS   587 18
  FLOWERS OF GRASS FINE MEN   587 23
  ALL MOVING INTO FLOWERS   627 12
  AND THOUGH THE POMEGRANATE HAS RED FLOWERS OUTSIDE THE   630 1
  EVEN THE VERY FLOWERS IN THE SHOPS OR PARKS   634 18
  AND EVEN THE LOVELIEST FLOWERS YOU MUST GRAFT THEM ON A   640 23
  AND FINE AS FLOWERS ARE FINE   667 27
  I HAVE ALWAYS WANTED TO BE AS THE FLOWERS ARE   677 10
  AND IN DEATH I BELIEVE I SHALL BE AS THE FLOWERS ARE   677 12
  FLOWERS ACHIEVE THEIR OWN FLOWERINESS AND IT IS A MIRAC+   683 22
  AS THE FLOWERS DO   683 27
  AND LET ME COME PAST THE SILVER BELLS OF YOUR FLOWERS A+   696 2
  OF ANY SUCH FLOWERS   709 21
  TO THE SCARLET AND PURPLE FLOWERS AT THE DOORS OF HELL   711 20
  ODD WINTRY FLOWERS UPON THE WITHERED STEM YET NEW STRAN+   727 24
  FLOWERS   727 25
  TO THE NEXT FARM PULLS UP WHERE THE ELDER FLOWERS FALL   732 4
  FLOWERS NOW AS WE'RE CROSSING THE DREARY STAGES   814 6
  NOT FLOWERS NOR FRUIT   827 25
  EMOTIONS WHICH WOULD COME UP LIKE FLOWERS WERE THEY NOT+   833 27
  NEITHER BEASTS NOR FLOWERS ARE   836 8
  LOVE LIKE THE FLOWERS IS LIFE GROWING   844 1
  HISSES THROUGH THE FLOWERS THE TIMID NIGHT-AIRS BLOW   855 30
  PALE SLEEPY FLOWERS ARE TOSSED ABOUT   857 23
  DRIFTED WITH THE BLOOD OF THE FLOWERS ON HER FEET AND K+   864 3
  LIKE A BEE THAT PLAYS WITH THE REFLECTION OF FLOWERS   867 12
  THERE AMONG THE FLOWERS OF THE BOAT-ROOF   868 3
  THE GOLD-BROWN FLOWERS OF HER EYES UNFOLD   868 26
  EARTH-CLODS AND NIGHT TO FLOWERS THAT PRAISE AND BURN   872 4
  AND ALL THEIR FACES LIKE BRIGHT FLOWERS AWAKE   872 21
  SETTING THE FLOWERS ALONG THE MIDDAY MEAL   877 28
  THE WITHERING FLOWERS THAT DAYS AGO YOU BROUGHT ME   880 11
  THE FLOWERS AGAINST YOUR WINDOW PANE   886 1
  AS I LAY ON THE BED AND YOU SAT WITH THE FLOWERS ON YOU+   886 11
  RED FLOWERS THAT HAVE FLOATED AWAY   887 29
  BITTER AND PAINFUL FLOWERS   888 2
  WHAT IF THE GORSE FLOWERS SHRIVELLED AND KISSING WERE L+   *891 23
  WITHERED MY INSOLENT SOUL WOULD BE GONE LIKE FLOWERS TH+   *891 27
  LIKE FULL-BLOWN FLOWERS DIMLY SHAKING AT THE NIGHT   *897 26
  LIKE FULL-BLOWN FLOWERS DIMLY SHAKING AT THE NIGHT   *901 3
  ON TH' YALLER CLAY AN' TH' WHITE FLOWERS TOP OF IT   *910 28
  WHITE FLOWERS IN THE WIND BOB UP AND DOWN   *912 26
  COOL AND FIRM AND SILKEN AS PINK YOUNG PEONY FLOWERS   *913 11
  THE LITTLE WHITE FEET NOD LIKE WHITE FLOWERS IN THE WIND   *913 29
  FIRM AND SILKEN LIKE PINK YOUNG PEONY FLOWERS   *914 11
  WE HAVE SHUT THE DOORS BEHIND US AND THE VELVET FLOWERS+   *916 9
  I HAVE PUSHED MY HANDS IN THE DARK LOAM UNDER THE FLOWE+   *926 8
  OVER THE FLOWERS AT MY FEET   *935 30
  OF FLOWERS AND THE SWELTERING EARTH   *937 12
  AND ALL THE FLOWERS ARE FALLEN IN DISGUST   *939 16
  AND DIAPERED ABOVE THE CHAUNTING FLOWERS   *939 20
  SHOULD CLIMB THE HILL AND PUT THE FLOWERS ASUNDER   *941 4
  MY QUIVERING ANSWER AND KISSES LIKE FRAGRANCE OF FLOWERS   *942 3
  FLOWERS   *950 3
  DOWN THE BLUE DEPTHS OF MOUNTAIN GENTIAN FLOWERS   *955 19
  RIBBED HELLISH FLOWERS ERECT WITH THEIR BLAZE OF DARKNE+   *956 4

FLOWER-SERPENT
  AND I HELD THE CHOKED FLOWER-SERPENT IN ITS PANGS   125 16

FLOWER-SUMPTUOUS-BLOODED
  FLOWER-SUMPTUOUS-BLOODED   308 8

FLOWER'S
  DIM SELF THAT RISES SLOWLY TO LEAVES AND THE FLOWER'S G+   92 20
  IN THE FLOWER'S THROAT AND THE FLOWER GAPED WIDE WITH W+   125 10
  IN THE FLOWER'S THROAT AND THE FLOWER GAPED WIDE WITH W+ *935 26

FLOWERS'
  LEFT OF THEIR LIGHT AMONG THE MEAN FLOWERS' THRONG   855 16

FLOWER-VINE
  THROUGH THE FLOWER-VINE TRAILING SCREEN   179 11

FLOWERY
  ME YOUR SHADOW ON THE BOG-FLAME FLOWERY MAY-BLOBS   90 15
  FLOWERY MANTILLA OF LACE   105 30
  THE PAGEANT OF FLOWERY TREES ABOVE   106 7
  OR IT WOULD NOT BE FLOWERY   476 5
  CLEAR AND FLOWERY BLUE   530 4
  TO SOMETHING FLOWERY AND FULFILLED AND WITH A STRANGE S+ 677 16

FLOWING
  THE STEAM-FLAG FLOWING   110 14
  YET WE KNOW IT IS FLOWING AWAY   476 24
  THE WONDERFUL SLOW FLOWING OF THE SAPPHIRE   476 26
  AND FLOWING INVISIBLY GASPING   480 17
  ALL FLOWS AND EVEN THE OLD ARE RAPIDLY FLOWING AWAY   511 23
  AND THE YOUNG ARE FLOWING IN THE THROES OF A GREAT   511 24
  AND THE OLD UPWARD FLOWING OF OUR SAP THE PRESSURE OF O+ 609 7
  THE LIFE-CURRENT FLOWING   861 30
  THE AIR AND THE FLOWING SUNSHINE AND BRIGHT DUST   870 9
  FLOWING I KNOW NOT HOW YET SERIOUSLY   *907 8

FLOWN
  HAVE FLOWN AWAY   614 22
  AND THE WILD SWANS FLOWN AWAY SINGING THE SWAN-SONG OF + 624 2
  HELPLESS ANOTHER DAY HAS FLOWN TOO HIGH   855 24
  AND THE WILD SWANS FLOWN AWAY SINGING THE SWAN-SONG OF + *953 20

FLOWS
  IN A MEANER PAGEANT FLOWS   106 10
  THROUGH THE LOW WEST WINDOW A COLD LIGHT FLOWS   163 10
  THEY ARE SUBSTANCE ITSELF THAT FLOWS IN THICK   460 5
  THE WELLING OF PEACE WHEN IT RISES AND FLOWS   462 6
  THE SOFT BLOOD SOFTLY FLOWS TOGETHER   471 15
  ALL FLOWS AND EVERY FLOW IS RELATED TO EVERY OTHER FLOW 476 27
  THE UNIVERSE FLOWS IN INFINITE WILD STREAMS RELATED   479 9
  ALL FLOWS AND EVEN THE OLD ARE RAPIDLY FLOWING AWAY   511 23
  PEACE LIKE A RIVER FLOWS   770 24
  AND PEACE LIKE A RIVER FLOWS   770 31
  WHERE PEACE LIKE A RIVER FLOWS   771 16
  FROM THE LOW WEST WINDOWS THE COLD LIGHT FLOWS   857 10

FLUENT
  FLUENT FIGURES OF MEN GO DOWN THE UPBORNE   174 7
  AND MY DOCILE FLUENT ARMS   *893 23
  FLUENT ACTIVE FIGURES OF MEN PASS ALONG THE RAILWAY   *906 16
  FLUENT ACTIVE FIGURES OF MEN PASS ALONG THE RAILWAY AND+ *908 11

FLUFF
  RED MEN STILL STICK THEMSELVES OVER WITH BITS OF HIS FL+ 414 3
  OR FLUFF UP IN INDIGNANT FURY LIKE A CAT   528 24
  WITH WEARINESS FAINT AS FLUFF   757 17
  OR FLUFF UP IN INDIGNANT FURY LIKE A CAT   *950 27

FLUFFED
  OR FLUFFED UP RATHER ANGRY AS A CAT DOES   836 15

FLUFF-SHADOWED
  SONG AND CHIRRUPING GAY FEATHERS FLUFF-SHADOWED   443 17

FLUFFY
  MY PALE WET BUTTERFLY FLUFFY CHICKEN   863 6
  AND WHAT HAS BECOME OF THE FLUFFY YELLOW STARS   *933 24

FLUID
  BENEATH THIS POWERFUL TREE MY WHOLE SOUL'S FLUID   131 8
  THERE IS A MARVELLOUS RICH WORLD OF CONTACT AND SHEER F+ 667 3
  HORIZONTAL ETERNITY FLUID OR NULL   827 16

FLUIDITY
  THE GODS WHO ARE LIFE AND THE FLUIDITY OF LIVING CHANGE 662 22

FLUNG
  ARE A BONFIRE OF ONENESS ME FLAME FLUNG LEAPING ROUND Y+ 245 24
  STRETCHING OUT MY HAND MY HAND FLUNG LIKE A DROWNED   260 10
  THEIR DEBRIS IS FLOTSAM AND FLUNG ON THE COAST   823 8

FLUSH
  THE RED RANGE HEAVES AND COMPULSORY SWAYS AH SEE IN THE+ 66 17
  YOUR PALLOR INTO RADIANCE FLUSH YOUR COLD   86 12
  YOU FLUSH AND RIFE   127 19
  FOR THE FLUSH OF THE NIGHT WHEREAS NOW THE GLOOM   141 9
  A FLUSH AT THE FLAILS OF YOUR FINS DOWN THE WHORL OF YO+ 335 9
  A GREEN LIGHT ENTERS AGAINST STREAM FLUSH FROM THE WEST 340 25
  THE HUMAN WILL TO THE FLUSH OF THE VASTER IMPULSION OF + 617 14
  WAIT WAIT EVEN SO A FLUSH OF YELLOW   720 9
  AND STRANGELY O CHILLED WAN SOUL A FLUSH OF ROSE   720 10
  A FLUSH OF ROSE AND THE WHOLE THING STARTS AGAIN   720 11
  WAY DOWN THE COAST THEN COMES UP FLUSH   747 6
  AND THE FLUSH FADED AND IT CAME DARK I SLEPT STILL IGNO+ 860 7
  FILLING MY STILL BREASTS WITH A FLUSH AND A FLAME   *893 17
  THE FLUSH OF THE GREAT MYSTERY   *907 18
  BUT I WAS ROSY FOR HIM FOR HIM I DID FLUSH MELLOW   *933 25

FLUSHED
  FLUSHED WITH THE SONGS OF SEVEN LARKS SINGING AT ONCE G+ 34 14
  SHE TURNED HER FLUSHED FACE TO ME FOR THE GLINT   125 7
  FLUSHED AND GRAND AND NAKED AS FROM THE CHAMBER   193 3
  FLUSHED FRENZIED RELENTLESS ME   769 8
  SHE TURNED HER FLUSHED FACE TOWARDS ME FOR THE GLINT   *935 23

FLUSHES
  AND IF IT FLUSHES AGAINST FIERCE ROCK   467 18
  RISES AND FLUSHES INSIDIOUSLY   471 3

FLUSH-FALLEN
  FOR SUDDENLY FLUSH-FALLEN   107 9

FLUSHING
  ON THE MISTY WASTE LANDS AWAY FROM THE FLUSHING GREY   164 21
  FLUSHING THE AFTERNOON THEY ARE UNCOMFORTABLE   228 11
  AND REPEATS HIMSELF LIKE THE FLUSHING OF A W C   522 8
  AND REPEAT THEMSELVES LIKE THE FLUSHING OF A W C   837 22

FLUTTER
  THEN BACK IN A SWIFT BRIGHT FLUTTER TO WORK   51 28
  FLUTTER FOR A MOMENT OH THE BEAST IS QUICK AND KEEN   119 21
  WITH A FLUTTER OF HOPE AND A QUENCHING DOUBT   121 26
  AND DOWN ALL EAGLES BEGAN TO FLUTTER REELING FROM THEIR 413 5
  AND WHERE MY LITTLE LEAVES FLUTTER HIGHEST   499 8
  AND CAN'T EVEN FLUTTER   558 29
  FLUTTER OF FEAR IN THE NERVES   767 17
  SENT OUT THE SUN SO THAT SOMETHING SHOULD FLUTTER IN HE+ 783 4
  YOU FLUTTER IN A HOST OF FLAMES LIKE WINTER STARLINGS R+ 784 1
  TINY BLACK MOTHS FLUTTER OUT AT THE TOUCH OF THE FORK 858 13
  THEY SHOULD FLUTTER AND TURN HIS WAY AND SAVING THE FRE+ 877 30
  THEN BACK IN A SWIFT BRIGHT FLUTTER TO WORK   *899 12
  THEN BACK IN A SWIFT BRIGHT FLUTTER TO WORK   *902 24
  FOR A MOMENT THEN AWAY WITH A FLUTTER OF WINGS   *913 5
  FOR A MOMENT THEN AWAY WITH A FLUTTER OF WINGS   *914 5
  BUT THE NIGHT IS FULL OF THE FLUTTER OF INVISIBLE REVEL+ *918 10
  THEN FLUTTER FOR A MOMENT AND THE RAT'S LONG TEETH ARE + *932 30

FLUTTERED
  HAS FLUTTERED HER SPIRIT TO STUMBLING FLIGHT   46 15
  FROM HER FLUTTERED FAREWELLS AT THE APPROACH OF MY WELL+   865 14
  ON THE BREAST OF A ROBIN THAT IS FLUTTERED WITH PAIN   883   5
  TO THE CUCKOO BIRD AS SHE FLUTTERED ABOVE   *936 10

FLUTTERING
  IS WINSOME AS A ROBIN'S SONG SO FLUTTERING   65   2
  A FLUTTERING IN OF DOVES   179 12
  AND FLUTTERING AND BEING BIRDS   443 20
  FLUTTERING AND SOFTLY UNRAVELLING   460   8
  SOFTLY FLUTTERING THE SENSES IN THE EXQUISITE ORGASM OF 481 24
  PEOPLE ARE LIKE LEAVES FLUTTERING AND GAY ON THE BUSH O+ 615   7
  BUT WHEN I SEE THE LIFE-SPIRIT FLUTTERING AND STRUGGLIN+ 622   4
  WHEN I SEE THE FLUTTERING OF PURE LIFE IN THEM   622 10
  AND IN A STRANGE LEVEL FLUTTERING YOU GO OUT TO SEA-WAR+ 696 25
  CURVING THEIR FEET AND DANCING AND FLUTTERING IN SPORT   751   4
  DO YOU SEE THE GOLD SUN FLUTTERING BUOYANTLY IN HEAVEN   782 29
  AFTER THEM ISSUES A DARK-WINGED FLUTTERING SPRITE   858 15
  FORBIDDEN THINGS AND THOUGHTS COME FLUTTERING   *894 18

FLUTTERS
  A SPARROW FLUTTERS   244   7
  ASH FLUTTERS FLOCCULENT LIKE DOWN ON A BLUE WAN FLEDGEL+ 330   8
  AND FLUTTERS AT THE CORE OF THE ATOM   440   4
  AND GOLD-BRONZE FLUTTERS BENT THROUGH THE THICK UPPER A+ 647 12
  MOCK AS IT FLUTTERS BY   731   4
  HER KERCHIEF FLUTTERS RED   756 13

FLUX
  FLUX OF ANOTHER DAWN THE WIND THAT ALL NIGHT   154 28
  FLUX OF AUTUMN   281 22
  WHEN THE DIM FLUX OF UNFORMED LIFE   682   3
  AND BLOOD-BROWN FLUX OF LIVES THAT SWEEP THEIR WAY   745   8
  A FRAGILE STRANGER IN THE FLUX OF LIVES   745 18
  MY ALL INTO YOUR FLUX YOU MELTING POT   873   3

FLY
  THAT SPARK FLY UP AT US EVEN   49 14
  FLY LIKE A SPARK INTO THE WOMB OF PASSION   89   6
  AND SO FROM CUT THE SCREAMING BIRDS THAT FLY   89 22
  EVEN THERE I SEE A BLUE SPARK THAT WILL FLY   89 34
  THE LEAVES FLY OVER THE WINDOW AND UTTER A WORD AS THEY+ 103   1
  MY WORDS FLY OFF A FORGE   110   5
  CAN THIS SHOT ARROW OF TRAVEL FLY   116 15
  LEST HER BRIGHT EYES LIKE SPARROWS SHOULD FLY IN   122 29
  FOR MY HAND LIKE A SNAKE WATCHED HERS THAT COULD NOT FLY 125 24
  WHY I SHOULD THINK THAT FROM THE EARTH THERE FLY   127   6
  IF IT BE SO I FLY TO JOIN YOU   314 23
  AND SMALL FISH FLY LIKE SPLINTERS   338 20
  AND HAD HIM FLY LIKE A HALO ROUND MY HEAD   339   4
  LITTLE LUMPS THAT FLY IN AIR AND HAVE VOICES INDEFINITE+ 341 26
  BIRDS ARE THE LIFE OF THE SKIES AND WHEN THEY FLY THEY + 368   3
  FLY OFF BIG BIRD WITH A BIG BLACK BACK   374 29
  FLY SLOWLY AWAY WITH A RUST OF FIRE IN YOUR TAIL   374 30
  OR FIGHT AND MAKE THE SPLINTERS FLY   458   6
  IF YOU WANT TO MAKE HER AN OFFERING LET THE DOVES FLY F+ 678   9
  AND IN HER HANDS THE SPARKING NEEDLES FLY   752 10
  FLY THEN FLY   783 28
  BUT YOU FLY YOU SOAR YOU SWEEP AWAY   783 31
  YOU WILL NEVER FLY ON YELLOW KINDLED WINGS   784 23
  LIKE A FLY THAT WEAVES THROUGH THE SHADOWS   867 11
  BRISTLE AND FLY IN SHADOWS ACROSS THE WALLS   879   3
  AND FLY FAST AWAY   883 17
  WHEREIN THE TIMID WONDERS FLY   *894   9
  CAN THIS SHOT ARROW OF TRAVEL FLY   *930 14
  LEST HER BRIGHT EYES LIKE SPARROWS SHOULD FLY IN   *934   5
  AND MY HAND LIKE A SNAKE WATCHED HERS THAT COULD NOT FLY *936 23

FLYING
  THE ROCKS WHERE RAVENS FLYING TO WINDWARD MELT AS A WEL+ 57 15
  SOUTH WITH FLYING CURDS   99 21
  WHAT FOOD IS THIS FOR THE DARKLY FLYING   171 19
  FLYING NOT DOWN FROM HEAVEN BUT STORMING UP   304 17
  LOOK UP AND YOU SEE THINGS FLYING   341   7
  THE SWALLOWS ARE FLYING SO LATE   341 23
  FLYING MADLY   342 15
  FLYING ROUND THE ROOM IN INSANE CIRCLES   342 15
  FLYING SLOWER   345 14
  OR IS HE DRIVEN AGAINST HER WITH A BANG LIKE A BIRD FLY+ 363   8
  NOR FLYING NORTH DESOLATIVE ICEWARDS   436   6
  BELONGS TO THE BAMBOO THICKET AND THE DRAKE IN THE AIR + 623 12
  APART FROM POPPIES AND THE FLYING FISH   691 23

FLY-WHEEL
  THIS IS THE MASSIVE SOLID FLY-WHEEL WHICH SAVES MAN FRO+ 838 19

FOAL-FOOTS
  AND FOAL-FOOTS SPANGLING THE PATHS   152 11

FOALS
  CURIOUS LONG-LEGGED FOALS AND WIDE-EARED CALVES AND NAK+ 271 34

FOAM
  AND THE FOAM ON MY FEET   130 12
  AND BE LOST OUT OF SIGHT WITH YOU LIKE A MELTING FOAM   134 23
  ALL THESE PURE THINGS COME FOAM AND SPRAY OF THE SEA   136 17
  LIKE A SPURT OF WHITE FOAM RENT   200 22
  BATHING-SUIT FROM OUR MODERN SEA-SIDE FOAM   439 32
  IT IS A WONDER FOAM IS SO BEAUTIFUL   467 11
  WITH ALL HER GRACE OF FOAM   646 27
  WHEN THE LITTLE EGGY AMOEBA EMERGED OUT OF FOAM AND NOW+ 682 26
  BUT IT IS FAR-OFF FOAM   687   8
  WE GROPE AND FOAM AND LASH AROUND   833 19
  THE PEAR-BLOSSOM IS A FOUNTAIN OF FOAM   885 28
  IN SPRAYS AND SPURTS OF FOAM   885 30
  WITH A STEADY RUSH OF LIVING A FOAM   888   7

FOAM-CLOTS
  FOAM-CLOTS SHOWING BETWEEN   145   1

FOAM-FRINGE
  GREY FOAM-FRINGE OF ADVANCING GOD   *914 29

FOAM-MIST
  GREY FOAM-MIST OF ADVANCING TIME   68 14

FOAM'S
  TWIN-BUBBLING CHALLENGE AND MYSTERY IN THE FOAM'S   76   3
  TWIN BUBBLES SHADOW-FULL OF MYSTERY AND CHALLENGE IN TH+ *897 30
  TWIN BUBBLES SHADOW-FULL OF MYSTERY AND CHALLENGE IN TH+ *901   7

FOAMY
  THE FOAMY PAW OF THE POND   159 11
  ODYSSEUS CALLS THE COMMANDS AS HE STEERS PAST THOSE FOA+ 687 20
  AND BREAKS IN THE FOAMY HANDS WHOSE POWER ROLLS OUT   705 16
  NOR EVEN A LOVELY WOMAN FOAMY TO STING ME LIKE BRINE   840 23

FOE
  THE FOE CAN TAKE OUR GOODS OUR HOMES AND LAND   736 16
  AND PASS BEYOND WITH THE FOE AND THE HOMELESS GHOSTS   737   6
  CRYING POUR OUT THE BLOOD OF THE FOE   739 23
  LOVER YOU MAKE SUCH A HERO IN FRONT OF THE FOE   755   9

FOES
  PALE SHADOWS FLEE FROM US AS IF FROM THEIR FOES   163 18
  TO ALL MY FOES AND FRIENDS   492 24
  PALE SHADOWS FLEE FROM US AS IF FROM THEIR FOES   857 18

FOETID
  GOING UP IN A FOETID SMOKE TO GET RID OF THEM   258   4

FOG
  AS A CACHE SEXE I'D HAVE PUT A WHOLE FOG   580 12

FOIL
  FOIL THE SENSE   *914 15

FOILED
  THEY WERE FOILED THE MYRIAD WHISPERING DARK-FACED   391 25

FOLD
  I MUST FOLD MY HANDS AND TURN MY FACE TO THE FIRE   47   2
  THEN I LONGED FOR YOU WITH YOUR MANTLE OF LOVE TO FOLD   98 23
  TILL OLD DAYS DREW ME BACK INTO THEIR FOLD   98 28
  CLOSES HER ARMS THAT SHOULD FOLD ON ME IN SLEEP   128 30
  BITTER TO FOLD THE ISSUE AND MAKE NO SALLY   160 25
  FOLD ON FOLD UNTIL IT GLOWS AS   217 25
  FOLD HIM BE GOOD TO HIM CHERISH HIM   228 31
  OF HIS VOLUPTUOUS PLEASURE OF CHASING THE SHEEP TO THE + 325   9
  THE SUN OF IMMENSE DISTANCES THAT FOLD THEMSELVES TOGET+ 513 17
  WITH THEIR CATERPILLARS AND THE CARE WITH WHICH THEY FO+ 569   5
  FOLD UP ALL SOUNDS   698 13
  AND HOW HE ENTERS FOLD AFTER FOLD OF DEEPENING DARKNESS 724   3
  WHOSE WHORLS FOLD ROUND TO THE CORE OF SOUNDLESS SILENC+ 724   5
  BUT THE LIMBS OF MAN LONG TO FOLD AND CLOSE UPON THE LI+ 834   4
  TO FOLD IN A SHINING CONCAVE THE PALE NIGHT   882   3

FOLDED
  UNDER THE GLISTENING CHERRIES WITH FOLDED WINGS   36 23
  SUCH AS LIES ALONG THE FOLDED WINGS   46 11
  ALL THE BIRDS ARE FOLDED IN A SILENT BALL OF SLEEP   71   9
  FOLDED IN ITS LEGS AS IN A BED   112 21
  ONE BIRD ONE BLOT FOLDED AND STILL AT THE TOP   147 24
  WE ARE FOLDED TOGETHER MEN AND THE SNOWY GROUND   166 11
  WITH SUNKEN HEAD AND FORGOTTEN FOLDED HANDS   232 25
  IN THE NIGHT WHERE YOU'RE FOLDED UP   239 23
  WE TWO FOLDED SO SMALL TOGETHER   247 19
  FOLDED UPON ITSELF AND SECRET UNUTTERABLE   283 10
  FOLDED UPON ITSELF ENCLOSED LIKE ANY MOHAMMEDAN WOMAN   283 14
  FOLDED IN LIKE A DARK THOUGHT   296   3
  FOLDED AS YET AND ALL THE FALLEN LEAVES   745 33
  ALL THE BIRDS ARE FOLDED IN A SILENT BALL OF SLEEP   *917 27
  AND FOLDED IN THE DARK-RED UNSEEN   *957 10
  BUT SHADOWS FOLDED ON DEEPER SHADOWS   *959 18

FOLDING
  FOLDING BACK THEIR SOUNDLESS PETALLED EARS   311   9
  WHO IS LIKE A FUR FOLDING A FUR   383   2
  AND THEN THE SOFTNESS OF DEEP SHADOWS FOLDING FOLDING   727   9

FOLDINGS
  OR DEEPER LIKE THE FOLDINGS AND INVOLVINGS OF A WOMB   *959 21

FOLDS
  OH BUT THE WATER LOVES ME AND FOLDS ME   34 19
  TILL THE DISTANCE FOLDS OVER HIS OMINOUS TREAD   43   4
  AND THRUST HER FISTS SUPPRESSED IN THE FOLDS OF HER SKI+ 128 19
  BUT HE CATCHES THE FOLDS OF VULNERABLE LEATHERY SKIN   362   6
  ONLY HE SENSES THE VULNERABLE FOLDS OF SKIN   362 15
  HER FOLDS OF SKIN THAT WORK AND ROW   362 18
  IN WHOSE CLOSE FOLDS ABOVE YOU NEAR ABOVE   750 11
  RUNS ECSTATIC OVER THE PLIANT FOLDS RIPPLING DOWN TO MY+ *891 32
  OH BUT THE WATER LOVES ME AND FOLDS ME   *892   7

FOLIAGE
  IN THE DENSE FOLIAGE OF THE INNER GARDEN   278 12
  IN ITS OWN FOLIAGE   451   9
  ONLY FROM OUT THE FOLIAGE OF THE SECRET LOINS   606   6
  FOR HE IS HOSTILE TO ALL THE OLD LEAFY FOLIAGE OF OUR T+ 609   6
  FINE FOLIAGE OF LIVES THIS LIFE OF MINE   *899 25
  FINE FOLIAGE OF LIVES THIS LIFE OF MINE   *903   4

FOLK
AND FROM THE SWIRLING ANGRY FOLK THAT TRY   89 24
FOR FLOWERS ARE TENDER FOLK AND ROOTS CAN ONLY HIDE   93 30
TWO AND TWO ARE THE FOLK THAT WALK   106 11
NIGHT FOLK TUATHA DE DANAAN DARK GODS GOVERN HER SLEEP   213 25
AND BLACK-SCARVED FACES OF WOMEN FOLK WISTFULLY   232 22
AND THE VILLAGE FOLK OUTSIDE IN THE BURYING-GROUND   233 2
IT IS NOT LONG SINCE HERE AMONG ALL THESE FOLK   269 14
I IGNORE THOSE FOLK WHO LOOK OUT   375 28
COME PELTING TO ME NOW THE OTHER FOLK HAVE FOUND YOU   400 4
HE LEAVES ME GOES DOWN TO THE SOUTHRON FOLK   877 14

FOLK-FLOWERS
FOLK-FLOWERS HAVE FADED MEN HAVE GROWN COLD   814 16

FOLKS
OTHER FOLKS IN HELL   83 29
TO JOIN THE FOLKS ON HIGH   554 10

FOLK-SONG
WHICH ARE MEANT TO BE THE OLD FOLK-SONG STRAWBERRY FAIR   657 16

FOLK-STUFF
EFFLUENCE FROM SUFFERING FOLK-STUFF WHICH DEATH HAS LAI+   *938 23

FOLKS'
HIS WONDERFUL SPEECHES FULL OF OTHER FOLKS' WHORING   494 21

FOLLOW
I FOLLOW HER DOWN THE NIGHT BEGGING HER NOT TO DEPART   67 12
SHE MADE ME FOLLOW TO HER GARDEN WHERE   122 25
AND THE STILL MORE AWFUL NEED TO PERSIST TO FOLLOW FOLL+   363 12
FOLLOW THE TRAIL OF THE DEAD ACROSS GREAT SPACES FOR TH+   406 4
I MUST FOLLOW ALSO HER TREND   461 12
IT'S SO EASY TO FOLLOW SUIT   462 18
YOU STILL FEEL YOU MUST FOLLOW   564 20
THEN FOLLOW YOUR DEMON   564 23
AND THE LARK WILL FOLLOW TRILLING ANGERLESS AGAIN   625 6
AND WHY DO THE WOMEN FOLLOW US SATISFIED   743 3
FOLLOW ME NOW UP THE LADDERS OF SPARKS   798 11
FOLLOW HERE   798 16
THOSE THAT FOLLOW ME MUST CROSS THE MOUNTAINS OF THE SKY   799 8
BUT THOSE THAT WILL NOT FOLLOW MUST NOT PEEP   799 11
MIGHT FOLLOW SWIFT BEHIND THEE WHEN THOU LETS   879 12
MIGHT FOLLOW WARM AND GLAD WHO SIT HERE COLD   879 15
THAT HOLDS IT BACK MIGHT FOLLOW SOON TO THEE   879 17
TO FOLLOW MY LIFE ALOFT TO THE FINE WILD AIR OF LIFE AN+   *900 8
TO FOLLOW MY LIFE ALOFT TO THE FINE WILD AIR OF LIFE AN+   *903 20
SHE BADE ME FOLLOW TO HER GARDEN WHERE   *934 1

FOLLOWED
I FOLLOWED FOLLOWED THE SWING OF HER WHITE DRESS   123 2
THAT HAS FOLLOWED THE SUN FROM THE DAWN THROUGH THE EAST   404 14
I FOLLOWED FOLLOWED THE SWING OF HER WHITE DRESS   *934 8

FOLLOWING
LIMPING AND FOLLOWING RATHER AT MY SIDE   221 12
AND SO BEHOLD HIM FOLLOWING THE TAIL   361 13
AND THE SPARSE-HAIRED ELEPHANTS SLOWLY FOLLOWING   389 34
ONCE MORE FOLLOWING THE MASTER   798 23
AND SLOWLY FINGERING UP MY STEM AND FOLLOWING ALL TINILY   *900 18
AND SLOWLY FINGERING UP MY STEM AND FOLLOWING ALL TINILY   *903 30

FOLLOWS
SHE FOLLOWS HIS RESTLESS WANDERINGS   202 25
SO SHE FOLLOWS THE CRUEL JOURNEY   203 5
IT FOLLOWS YOU HATE ME TO ECSTASY   235 21
THE WRINKLED SMILE OF COMPLETENESS THAT FOLLOWS A LIFE   503 17

FOLLY
OF THE HOT-BORN INFANT BLESS THE FOLLY WHICH HAD   88 30
THE FOLLY OF THAT   565 21
THE WISDOM OF AGES DROOPS IT IS FOLLY   814 22

FOND
AN' THESE IS THE WOMAN'S KIDS 'E'S SO FOND ON   81 15
AN' THESE IS THE WOMAN'S KIDS HE'S SO FOND ON   *923 15
KISS ME THEN THERE NE'ER MIND IF I SCRAIGHT I WOR FOND + *925 28

FONDEST
AND SERVE THE BEST OF FOOD THE FONDEST WINE   723 11

FONDLING
LIVE THINGS CARESS ME AND ENTREAT MY FONDLING   876 33

FOOD
OF BATTLING FOR A LITTLE FOOD   105 6
WHAT FOOD IS THIS FOR THE DARKLY FLYING   171 19
FOOD UNTOWARDS   171 23
FOOD OF COURSE   336 7
FOOD AND FEAR AND JOIE DE VIVRE   336 19
JOIE DE VIVRE AND FEAR AND FOOD   336 22
WHEN FOOD IS GOING   358 32
SHE KNOWS WELL ENOUGH TO COME FOR FOOD   359 14
AND THE INDIVIDUAL MUST HAVE HIS HOUSE FOOD AND FIRE ALL   487 23
FIRE IS DEARER TO US THAN LOVE OR FOOD   505 25
AND ALL THE DAINTY FOOD   573 12
THE FOOD OF THE NORTH TASTES TOO MUCH OF THE FAT   652 19
AND ALL THE DAINTY FOOD   670 27
AND FURNISH IT WITH FOOD WITH LITTLE CAKES AND WINE   718 10
A LITTLE SHIP WITH OARS AND FOOD   718 24
WITH ITS STORE OF FOOD AND THE LITTLE COOLING PANS   719 4
SET FOOD FOR THEM AND ENCOURAGE THEM TO BUILD   722 13
AND SERVE THE BEST OF FOOD THE FONDEST WINE   723 11
SO THEY COULD HAVE MORE FOOD   778 22
OUR CORPUS WITH FOOD   826 13
NURSES DOCTORS PROPER FOOD HYGIENE SCHOOLS ALL THAT   832 5
LET ME BUILD A LITTLE SHIP WITH OARS AND FOOD   *958 20

FOOD-TABOO
WERE POLITICS BUT OTHERS SAY IT WAS A FOOD-TABOO OTHERS+   303 18

FOOL
WORK WORK YOU FOOL   41 5
WHY DO I WANDER AIMLESS AMONG THEM DESIROUS FOOL   180 23
ALAS WHAT A FOOL HE LOOKS IN THIS SCUFFLE   360 26
DOOMED TO MAKE AN INTOLERABLE FOOL OF HIMSELF   361 8
GET OUT YOU LITTLE SOFT FOOL   400 8
FOOL IN SPITE OF YOUR PRETTY WAYS AND QUAINT KNOW-ALL   400 18
WATCH HIM TURN INTO A MESS EITHER A FOOL OR A BULLY   431 7
IT DOESN'T MEAN HANDING IT OUT TO SOME MEAN FOOL OR   449 19
YOUR FOOL PRETENCE   565 2
IS LOST ENTIRELY YOU CANNOT FOOL US   824 5
YOU'RE A FOOL WOMAN I LOVE YOU AND YOU KNOW I DO   *945 17

FOOLED
SEX GETS DIRTIER AND DIRTIER THE MORE IT IS FOOLED WITH+ 464 3
LOOKING VERY FOOLED   532 31

FOOLING
FOOLING MY FEET DOES THE NIGHT-MOTH   731 3

FOOLISH
YOU BRITTLE WILL-TENSE BIRD WITH A FOOLISH EYE   370 35
BE WELL IF THESE OLD FATHERS ABANDONED THEIR FOOLISH   777 30

FOOLISHLY
HE SMILES FOOLISHLY AS IF HE WERE CAUGHT DOING WRONG   401 20
AND WE SMILE FOOLISHLY AS IF WE DIDN'T KNOW   401 21
HE TRAPPED HER THIS MORNING HE SAYS SMILING FOOLISHLY   401 26

FOOLS
AND SUFFER FOOLS THOUGH NOT GLADLY   499 13
POOR FOOLS   535 25
ROSE-LEAVES TO BEWILDER THE CLEVER FOOLS   634 29
BEING CONCEITED FOOLS   673 6
TELL THEM THEY ARE ALL FOOLS THAT I'M LAUGHING AT THEM   791 26
SUCH FOOLS   791 28
OH FOOLS MEXICANS AND PEONS   794 25
OH FOOLS MEXICANS AND PEONS WITH MUDDY HEARTS   794 32
OH DOGS AND FOOLS MEXICANS AND PEONS   795 5

FOOT
AND I AT THE FOOT OF HER CROSS DID SUFFER   103 21
AT THE FOOT OF EACH GLOWING THING   215 26
WHITE PEAKS OF SNOW AT THE FOOT OF THE SUNKEN CHRIST   225 30
AND AT THE FOOT OF A GRAVE A FATHER STANDS   232 24
AND AT THE FOOT OF A GRAVE A MOTHER KNEELS   232 26
FOOT IN THE MOUTH OF AN UP-STARTING SNAKE   365 31
WHERE IT DISAPPEARED AT THE FOOT OF THE CRUCIFIX   371 27
SPLENDIDLY PLANTING HIS FEET ONE ROCKY FOOT STRIKING THE 381 13
CHIEFTAINS THREE OF THEM ABREAST ON FOOT   388 16
BOWED AND LIFTED HER FOOT IN HER HAND SMILED SWUNG HER   444 28
GOES BEHIND ITS MOTHER ON BLITHE BARE FOOT   466 11
AND THE FOOT OF THE CROSS NO LONGER IS PLANTED IN THE P+ 616 21
THEY SET FOOT ON THIS LAND TO WHICH THEY HAVE THE RIGHT   739 13
AND STONES SHALL MAKE PLACE FOR THY FOOT BECOME EASY TO+ 750 1
GOES BEHIND HIS MOTHER WITH BARE BLITHE FOOT   757 10
IS ONE FOOT IN THE LAP OF A WOMAN   819 7
BECAUSE ONE FOOT IS THE HEART OF A MAN   820 8
WHEN HE LIFTS HIS FOOT I SEE THE PAD OF HIS SOAKED STOC+ 866 7

FOOTED
FOOTED CAUTIOUSLY OUT ON THE ROPE TURNED PRETTILY SPUN   444 26

FOOTFALLS
TO ME MEN'S FOOTFALLS FALL WITH A DULL SOFT RUMBLE   288 28

FOOT-FALLS
BUT NOT YOUR FOOT-FALLS PALE-FACES   288 31

FOOT-FIERCE
FOOT-FIERCE   373 20

FOOT-FLINT
YOU FOOT-FLINT   781 26

FOOTHILLS
PLEASED TO BE OUT IN THE SAGE AND THE PINE FISH-DOTTED + 409 18

FOOT-HILLS
TROT-TROT TO THE MOTTLED FOOT-HILLS CEDAR-MOTTLED AND P+ 409 1

FOOTHOLD
BODIES AND PRESENCES HERE AND NOW CREATURES WITH A FOOT+ 689 23

FOOTING
HAS HER FOOTING WASHED AWAY AS THE DARK FLOOD RISES   718 13

FOOT-SEARCHED
ALONG HER FOOT-SEARCHED WAY WITHOUT KNOWING WHY   131 27
ALONG HER FOOT-SEARCHED WAY HER SORROW-CLOSED EYE   *937 26

FOOTSTEP
IS A FOOTSTEP ONWARDS ONWARDS WE KNOW NOT WHITHER   713 13

FOOTSTEPPING
FOOTSTEPPING TAP OF MEN BENEATH   68 23
FOOTSTEPPING TAP OF MEN BENEATH   *915 7

FOOTSTEPS
YET HER DEEP FOOTSTEPS MARK THE SNOW AND GO   85 7
ONLY THE FOOTSTEPS FOOTSTEPS   703 26

FORAGES
   IN MY FLESH AND MY BONE AND FORAGES INTO ME   128 16

FORAMINIFERAE
   OLDER THAN FLOWERS OLDER THAN FERNS OLDER THAN FORAMINI+   477 10

FORBEARANCE
   IT IS NO GOOD DEAR GENTLENESS AND FORBEARANCE I ENDURED+   92 7
   IT IS NO GOOD DEAR MEEKNESS AND FORBEARANCE I ENDURED T+   *926 7

FORBIDDEN
   WE HAVE BIT NO FORBIDDEN APPLE   37 24
   AND SUFFER UNHEEDING ONLY FORBIDDEN TO EXPIRE   161 5
   FORBIDDEN LIQUOR   333 27
   WE HAVE BIT NO FORBIDDEN APPLE   *892 12
   FORBIDDEN THINGS AND THOUGHTS COME FLUTTERING   *894 18

FORCE
   AS ANY MAN I' TH' FORCE   77 30
   O' TH' P'LICE FORCE WITHOUT FAIL   78 14
   THEY'LL TURN THEE OUT O' TH' FORCE I DOUBT ME IF THEY D+   83 16
   I FORCE MY CART THROUGH THE SODDEN FILTH THAT IS PRESSED   167 5
   STRONG LIKE THE GREATEST FORCE OF WORLD-BALANCING   271 20
   AND THE SIN IS TO DAMAGE THE FLOW FORCE IT OR DIRTY IT +   464 15
   AND FINGER IT AND FORCE IT AND SHATTER THE RHYTHM IT KE+   464 30
   FOR IF CEREBRALLY WE FORCE OURSELVES INTO TOUCH   468 17
   AND THEY KEEP ON COMING WITH GREATER FORCE   512 21
   USUALLY WANT TO FORCE SOMEBODY TO AGREE WITH THEM   626 5
   THE POWER OF THE MELTING FUSING FORCE   *907 22
   THE POWER OF THE MELTING FUSING FORCE HEAT LIGHT ALL IN+   *909 14
   AS ANY MAN I' TH' FORCE   *919 18
   O' TH' P'LICE FORCE WITHOUT FAIL   *920 6

FORCED
   FORCED TO CRASH AGAINST HER   363 18
   THAT ARE BORN IN THEIR MINDS AND FORCED DOWN BY THE WILL   500 19
   AND FORCED TO DO A THOUSAND MEAN THINGS MEANER THAN   522 13
   AND FORCED TO CLUTCH ON TO POSSESSIONS IN THE HOPE THEY+   522 15
   AND FORCED TO WATCH EVERYONE THAT COMES NEAR YOU LEST   522 17
   I AM FORCED TO   606 15
   HE FORCED US TO LIVE A GREAT LIE OR TO DISOBEY   654 7

FORCES
   NOR CLACKS ACROSS THE FORCES FURROWING A GREAT GAY TRAIL   436 3
   WHERE THE FORCES TIE THEMSELVES UP INTO KNOTS OF ATOMS   437 29
   AND WHOEVER FORCES HIMSELF TO LOVE ANYBODY   653 3
   THOSE THAT HAVE MASTERED THE FORCES OF THE WORLD DIE IN+   796 14
   BUT WHAT CAN YOU DO IN A SYSTEM WHICH FORCES YOU TO GO +   831 9
   AND FORCES TIE THEMSELVES UP INTO KNOTS OF ATOMS THEN C+   *947 6

FORCING
   LIES IN FORCING YOURSELF OR SOMEBODY ELSE   836 18

FORCIN'
   FORCIN' US OUT OF THE UNAWAKE   493 7

FORE
   BRIGHT AND NAKED AFT AND FORE   574 20
   IN YOUR FIFTIES WITH A SHORT FROCK SHOWING YOUR FORE AN+   835 10

FORE-AND-AFT
   FULL FORE-AND-AFT IN GOOD GREY CREPE DE CHINE   835 28

FOREFATHERS'
   OF YOUR FOREFATHERS' MUCK-HEAP   456 19

FOREFEET
   HE STANDS WITH HIS FOREFEET ON THE DRUM   426 8

FOREGATHER
   WHERE WE FOREGATHER LIKE GYPSIES NONE KNOWING   812 23

FORE-GOD-LIKE
   DRIVEN AFTER AEONS OF PRISTINE FORE-GOD-LIKE SINGLENESS+   363 14

FOREHEAD
   BUT THE SHADE ON HER FOREHEAD ILL BECOMES   201 11
   NO SHADOW OF US ON THEIR SNOWY FOREHEAD OF DREAMS   223 24
   YOU WITH YOUR FOREHEAD NESTLING   224 3
   A LIVING FOREHEAD WITH ITS SLOW WHORL OF HAIR   325 27
   SEAL UP HIS FOREHEAD ONCE MORE TO A BASTION   327 22
   HIS LOW FOREHEAD HIS SKINNY NECK HIS LONG SCALED STRIVI+   360 2

FOREHEADS
   THEIR POOR IDEALIST FOREHEADS NAKED CAPITALS   287 18
   WHEN THEY FELT THEIR FOREHEADS BARE NAKED TO HEAVEN THE+   310 5

FOREIGN
   STRANGE TO ME LIKE A CAPTIVE IN A FOREIGN COUNTRY HAUNT+   47 9
   FOREIGN TO THEM   256 21
   THE FIRST ELEMENTS OF FOREIGN SPEECH   366 20
   THIS FOREIGN WOMAN OF THE WEALTHY NORTH   618 24
   SISTERS I AM SORRY FOR THIS FOREIGN MAN   758 11
   IN THE FIELDS WITH FOREIGN OVERSEERS   790 11
   FOR HIS MISSION HAD CRUELLY FAILED WHILE HIS PASSIONATE+   859 11

FOREIGNER
   EVERY LORDLY TUPPENNY FOREIGNER FROM THE HOTELS FATTENI+   312 23
   I AM COME BACK A FOREIGNER WONDERING AND SHRINKING FROM+   867 2

FOREIGNERS
   LORD OF THE TWO WAYS THESE ARE THE FOREIGNERS   793 13
   HOW NICE IF WE COULD TAKE ALL THESE THINGS AWAY FROM TH+   794 19

FOREMOST
   YOU MY LOVE THE FOREMOST IN A FLOWERED GOWN   58 20
   WHEN THOU RUNNEST THE RACE WITH THE FOREMOST GOD BLESS +   750 2

FORE-ORDAINING
   FOR THE ALMIGHTY EAGLE OF THE FORE-ORDAINING MIND   329 21

FORERUNNER
   AS IF IT WERE THE LEADER THE MAIN-STEM THE FORERUNNER   299 28

FORE-RUNNERS
   FORE-RUNNERS HAVE BARELY LANDED ON THE SHORE   607 4

FORE-RUNNER
   ROSE CYCLAMEN ECSTATIC FORE-RUNNER   311 21
   LITTLE ULYSSES FORE-RUNNER   353 29
   INVINCIBLE FORE-RUNNER   354 22
   FORE-RUNNER   360 32
   FORE-RUNNER   363 2

FORESEE
   TORTOISES ALWAYS FORESEE OBSTACLES   356 30

FORESHORES
   A WASTE EXPANSE OF NOTHING LIKE WIDE FORESHORES WHERE N+   509 12
   YET EVEN WASTE GREY FORESHORES AND SORRY FAR-OUT   509 17
   WHERE THE LONG FAWN FORESHORES LIE   746 21

FORESKINS
   COLLECTING FORESKINS   541 21

FOREST
   LIKE A FOREST DARKNESS LIKE A MARSH   171 10
   FOREST OF PILLARS THAT HOLD UP THE DOME OF HIGH IDEAL   287 28
   OF FOREST WITH THE HERD   465 16
   AND GET INTO THE FOREST AGAIN   482 18
   THINK HOW A PEACOCK IN A FOREST OF HIGH TREES   530 5
   INTO THE GLOOM-WOVEN FOREST WHERE THE BIRDS AND CICALAS+   864 5
   AND THE ROOTS OF THE GREAT TREE OF FAMILY AND THE FORES+   *951 13

FORESTALLING
   OH BOISTEROUS THE CUCKOO SHOUTS FORESTALLING   65 27

FORESTIERE
   AT EVERY FORESTIERE   312 22

FORESTS
   FORESTS CITIES BRIDGES   293 22

FORETHOUGHT
   COMING MY WAY WITHOUT FORETHOUGHT OR AFTERTHOUGHT   288 27

FOREVER
   FOREVER EVER BY MY SHOULDER PITIFUL LOVE WILL LINGER   63 22
   FOREVER OUT OF THE MIST THE CHURCH LIFTS UP A REPROACHF+   63 24
   ITS NAKEDNESS ALL WITHIN-WALLS ITS FLOWERING FOREVER UN+   283 15
   AND EVEN MY HEART LORD FOREVER AFTER ALL UPLIFTING   321 17
   MANY SUSPENDED TOGETHER FOREVER APART   337 20
   THE SUN IS FOREVER THIRSTY THIRSTING FOR THE BRIGHTEST +   368 7
   SNIFFING FOREVER AHEAD OF HIM AT THE REAR OF THE GOATS +   380 21
   HIS OWN UNTHREADED FOREVER   382 5
   AND DANCE AND DANCE FOREVER DANCE WITH BREATH HALF   389 11
   AND RIDE ON HORSEBACK ASLEEP FOREVER THROUGH THE DESERT   408 13
   AND LEAVE HIM FOREVER LISTENING FOR THE ANSWER   439 10
   FLAME OF FLESH FOREVER TRAVELLING   460 6
   AND THEREFORE THAT THOU ART FOREVER UNKNOWABLE   473 23
   BUT THE OTHER SIDE IS DARK FOREVER   473 27
   AND THY DARKNESS IS FOREVER INVISIBLE   474 3
   THE BLOOD KNOWS IN DARKNESS AND FOREVER DARK   474 5
   THAT IT SEEMS TO LAST FOREVER   476 23
   AN' BLAST 'EM FOREVER BUT THEY'D ONLY   550 11
   THAT A MAN IS FOREVER   563 3
   BUT ONCE AND FOREVER BARKS THE OLD DOG   580 13
   FOREVER NAMELESS   622 14
   FOREVER UNKNOWN   622 15
   FOREVER UNCONCEIVED   622 16
   YET FOREVER FELT IN THE SOUL   622 18
   MANKIND IS LOST AND LOST FOREVER   637 13
   DO NOW ONCE AND FOREVER RETIRE   681 10
   SEE GOD IS BORN HE IS BLUE HE IS DEEP BLUE HE IS FOREVE+   682 23
   THE CLEAVERS THAT CLEAVE US FOREVER APART FROM ONE ANOT+   707 17
   WHAT DO THEY WANT FOREVER THERE ON OUR THRESHOLD   740 17
   ME NOW IF I'VE LOST MY MESS-MATES LOST THEM FOREVER   757 7
   GOD IS FOREVER AND ONLY HE   759 17
   REMOVE THE INDIANS FOREVER FROM THE HANDS OF   780 3
   A SCORCHED BREAST SUN-TURNED FOREVER   781 2
   EAGLE IN THE SCORCH FOREVER   781 5
   ME FOREVER   801 13
   AND THE FOUNTAIN COVERS YOUR FACE FOREVER   809 13
   YOU WILL HAVE DEPARTED FOREVER FROM YOUR MISTAKE   809 14
   EACH MAN HIS OWN WAY FOREVER BUT TOWARDS   812 13
   FOREVER AND EVER AND NEVER COME TO THE END   832 25
   WHICH RESTS IN CONNECTION WITH THE FURTHER FOREVER UNKN+   844 22
   THE ROAD WINDS FOREVER AND WHICH OF US KNOWS   858 2
   BUT LAYING FOREVER OUR EFFORT AT MUSIC BY   884 2

FOR EVER
   I LOVE FOR EVER THERE IT SEEMS   151 5
   YOU SLEEP STRETCHED OUT FOR EVER EVER GIVING   194 21
   THAT WILL LAST FOR EVER   203 16
   THEY WOULD HAVE IT I HAVE LEFT HER FOR EVER   212 18
   PERHAPS WE ARE PARTED FOR EVER   212 23
   FOR EVER ONE EVEN MIGHT THINK THAT THEY LOVE US   223 27
   ARE JOINED TOGETHER FOR EVER AS IS BEST   231 4
   GREEN AND ILLUMINED AND TRAVELLING FOR EVER   260 27
   AND ARE YOU GOING TO GO ON FOR EVER   414 32
   BUT TO ABOLISH THE WORKING CLASSES FOR EVER   453 11
   SO IT IS SO IT WILL BE FOR EVER AND EVER   461 17

FOR EVER
    NOW AGAIN AND NOW FOR EVER BREAKS THE GREAT ILLUSION   635 1
    MAKE IT CEASE TO BE A POLITICAL QUESTION FOR EVER   780 2
    I LOVE FOR EVER AND IT SEEMS   873 15
    MY GOD TO THINK IT IS GONE FOR EVER   886 19
    TO THINK THAT YOU ARE GONE FOR EVER   886 20
    AM I FOR EVER MAKING LOVE TO YOU   886 25

FORFEND
    GOD FORFEND   152 25

FORGE
    MY WORDS FLY OFF A FORGE   110 5
    AND OFF THE FORGE OF THE WORLD   110 17
    IF SO LET US FORGE AHEAD STRAIGHT ON   164 13

FORGES
    OVER THE FORGES AND SMALL FLAMES PLY   103 12

FORGET
    YOU PROMISED TO SEND ME SOME VIOLETS DID YOU FORGET   58 8
    FORGET EACH OTHER AND THE BRUISE OF OUR BODIES' CLASH   91 6
    I FORGET MY BEREAVEMENT   115 16
    I FORGET MY BEREAVEMENT   115 26
    I DO FORGET THE SOUNDING OF YOUR VOICE   129 8
    I DO FORGET YOUR EYES THAT SEARCHING THROUGH   129 9
    OH LET US HERE FORGET LET US TAKE THE SHEER   132 23
    THE TOUCH WAS ON THE QUICK I WANT TO FORGET   143 25
    SLEEP TO MAKE US FORGET BUT HE UNDERSTANDS   167 19
    TILL AT LENGTH THEY INDUCE ME TO SLEEP AND TO FORGET   180 36
    AND WILL NOT FORGET   199 18
    I FORGET YOU HAVE FORGOTTEN YOU   233 18
    GROWS DIMMER WE BOTH FORGET   240 14
    IT IS GORGEOUS TO LIVE AND FORGET   244 25
    I SHALL NEVER FORGET THE MANIACAL HORROR OF IT ALL IN T+   257 10
    AND THEY WON'T LET US FORGET IT   284 16
    THEY FORGET RIPE FIGS WON'T KEEP   284 24
    THE HORSE BEING NOTHING BUT A NAG WILL FORGET   379 30
    FORGET THE FEMALE HERD FOR A BIT   383 20
    WITH DIRT THEY COULDN'T FORGET   491 20
    YET NOT SUFFICIENTLY CONSCIOUS TO BE ABLE TO FORGET OUR+   496 20
    IT WILL ONLY MAKE THEM FORGET   610 15
    TO BE ABLE TO FORGET IS TO BE ABLE TO YIELD   725 20
    TO FORGET   749 2
    FORGET ALL   749 3
    STRICTLY DON'T FORGET IT HE IS A SAVAGE WHO HAS FOR   776 24
    TO FORGET   817 10
    AND FORGET   870 2
    I PAUSE AND FORGET   870 4
    I FORGET THE TOWEL AND MY WET LIMBS   870 5
    WILL LEAVE YOU FOR I MUST FORGET MYSELF   876 8
    THEN OH I DO FORGET ALL MY   *894 11

FORGETFUL
    FROM OUT YOUR FACE'S FAIR FORGETFUL CONTOURS   875 2

FORGETFULNESS
    TO FORGETFULNESS SOFT-SAILING WATERS WHERE FEARS   53 11
    I START FROM THE DROOP OF FORGETFULNESS AS THE SOUND OF+   858 21
    INTO FORGETFULNESS SOFT SAILING WATERS WHERE FEARS   *906 3

FORGET-ME-NOTS
    AND THE PALE STARS OF FORGET-ME-NOTS HAVE CLIMBED TO TH+   854 2

FORGETS
    BUT THE ASS NEVER FORGETS   379 29
    BUT THE ASS IS A PRIMAL CREATURE AND NEVER FORGETS   379 33

FORGETTING
    FORGETTING TILL FATE SHALL DELETE   146 26
    FORGETTING THE PLACE FROM WHICH I CAME   151 33
    FAR ONE TO SLEEP AND A FORGETTING AND OFTEN THE DEAD LO+   406 5
    AND IF THERE WERE NOT AN ABSOLUTE UTTER FORGETTING   724 20
    FOR GOD IS DEEPER FORGETTING FAR THAN SLEEP   726 15
    IS CENTRES HERE AND THERE OF SILENCE AND FORGETTING   726 18
    TO THE POOL OF PEACE AND FORGETTING IN HEAVEN   798 27
    WILL WAKE AT LAST FROM THE CLEAN FORGETTING   809 16

FORGIVE
    DARK RUDDY PILLAR FORGIVE ME I   40 9
    WE CRY IN THE WILDERNESS FORGIVE ME I   40 13
    SO DO FORGIVE ME I SPRINKLE MY HAIR   492 29

FORGIVEN
    AND HAVEN'T FORGIVEN ME YET   491 18

FORGIVENESS
    THE FLOWER OF FORGIVENESS IS PLUCKED FROM OFF THE OFFEN+   *926 26

FORGOT
    HAVE ALMOST ALL FORGOT   379 32
    IT SNOWED AND HIS HELMET WAS LOST HE FORGOT ME HE DID N+   732 17
    THEN TURNED AWAY AND FORGOT   836 16

FORGOTTEN
    FLOATING UP FROM THE FORGOTTEN   106 24
    FORGOTTEN   146 25
    YET I'VE FORGOTTEN IN PLAYING THIS GAME   151 31
    HAS SLEPT UNNOTICED ON A FORGOTTEN HILL   176 27
    REMEMBERED AND FORGOTTEN   199 7
    AND SOMETHING IN ME HAS FORGOTTEN   199 21
    WITH SUNKEN HEAD AND FORGOTTEN FOLDED HANDS   232 25
    I FORGET YOU HAVE FORGOTTEN YOU   233 18
    I HAVE FORGOTTEN YOU   233 25
    NO DOUBT YOU HAVE FORGOTTEN THE POMEGRANATE-TREES IN   278 6
    BUT IT'S SO LONG AGO THE ANCIENT BUSHMAN HAS FORGOTTEN   286 17
    ABOUT A FORGOTTEN BUSINESS   296 23
    WARM STILL WITH THE LIFE OF FORGOTTEN MEN WHO MADE THEM   448 7

FORGOTTEN
    FORGOTTEN   462 22
    THE YOUNG TRAM-CONDUCTOR IN A BLUE UNIFORM TO HIMSELF F+   672 8
    FAR AND FORGOTTEN IS THE VILLA OF VENUS THE GLOWING   695 25
    FAREWELL LET ALL BE FORGOTTEN   798 25
    WAXES THEM OVER TILL ALL IS FORGOTTEN   825 1
    FORGOTTEN LIKE LAST YEAR'S LINNET SONG   855 14
    AND GUTTER TO EXTINCTION LIKE A TAPER ON A FORGOTTEN AL+   859 4
    FORGOTTEN IN THE GRASS EVA FEARFUL AND FLEET   864 16
    THOUGH THEY CLING FORGOTTEN THE MOST PART NOT COMPANION+ *900 14
    THOUGH THEY CLING FORGOTTEN THE MOST PART NOT COMPANIONS *903 26
    WE HAVE FORGOTTEN THE SUNNY APPLES OF DAY THAT WE CRAVE+ *917 15

FORK
    AN' A FORK AN' A SPOON 'E'LL WANT AN' WHAT ELSE   46 1
    TINY BLACK MOTHS FLUTTER OUT AT THE TOUCH OF THE FORK   858 13

FORKED
    AND FLICKERED HIS TONGUE LIKE A FORKED NIGHT ON THE AIR+   350 25
    LET ME GUIDE MYSELF WITH THE BLUE FORKED TORCH OF THIS +   697 14
    LET ME GUIDE MYSELF WITH THE BLUE FORKED TORCH OF A FLO+ *956 11

FORLORN
    LIKE A SNAKE WE THRESH ON THE LONG FORLORN   163 19
    BUT NOT ALONE NOR FORLORN   770 6
    FORLORN ENJOYMENTS FORLORNER SORROW   825 5
    AND SAVE FOR ME THE ROAD IS FORLORN   857 19

FORLORNER
    FORLORN ENJOYMENTS FORLORNER SORROW   825 5

FORM
    IN THE CURVES OF THY FORM THE TRACE OF THE UNKNOWN   69 16
    I AM ADRIFT AS A MOONBEAM AND WITHOUT FORM   86 10
    FORM AFTER FORM IN THE STREETS   108 23
    I ADAM FORM THE VEINS OF ME   240 11
    AND BROUGHT YOU TO THE VERY QUICK OF YOUR FORM   254 32
    BUT FORM THE ASH-SCARRED FALLOW   315 33
    FORM OF HOMOSEXUALITY SHE SAID   447 7
    AS IF SWAYING WERE ITS FORM OF STILLNESS   467 17
    IT IS A FORM OF WAR EVEN SELF-ASSERTION AND BEING WISE +   495 21
    FORM OF MACHINE CIVILISATION WILL MELT AWAY   611 15
    OF THE FEMALE FORM TECHNICALLY BEAUTIFUL ACTUALLY A WHI+   619 12
    I REFUSE TO DESCRIBE THE GODS BECAUSE THEY HAVE NO FORM+   651 8
    IS BRITISH HYPOCRISY A FORM OF SOFTENING OF THE BRAIN   659 22
    THAT THE IDEA OF THE FORM PRECEDES THE FORM SUBSTANTIAL   689 17
    LET ME THINK ABOUT IT LET ME FORM AN IDEA   690 13
    FAR BEYOND THE PRESENT SOCIAL FORM   829 23
    WITH HER SUAVE FORM DUSTY WITH SPICES HONEY SWEET STRAY+   864 4
    OVER HER STREWN WHITE LAUGHING FORM   868 16
    OF FORM OR MOVEMENT OR OF HARMONY   872 12
    IN THE CURVE OF THINE EXQUISITE FORM THE JOY OF THE   *915 28

FORMED
    LO THERE IS A CREATURE FORMED HOW STRANGE   690 12

FORMLESS
    STRIVE WITH THE FORMLESS THINGS AND GENTLY TOUCH   872 6

FORMS
    TAKE WRITHING FORMS OF ALL BEASTS THAT SWEAT AND THAT F+   73 15
    THE DARKNESS STEALS THE FORMS OF ALL THE QUEENS   135 21
    THE FORMS OF THE GODS LIKE HORSES AND OXEN LIKE OXEN AN+   376 3
    FORMS   428 30
    SLOWLY A GEM FORMS IN THE ANCIENT ONCE-MORE-MOLTEN   477 13
    MILD FORMS OF COCAINE THEY'RE NOT LIFE EXACTLY   532 13
    WHY THEN TRUST IT IT FORMS   561 26
    YOU SEE THEM IN GLIMPSES IN THE FACES AND FORMS OF PEOP+   671 23
    ALL FORMS OF ABSTRACTION ARE EVIL   716 7
    FORMS OF CIVILISATION   776 10
    THE DARKNESS STEALS THE FORMS OF ALL THE QUEENS   *938 25
    THE DARKNESS STEALS THE FORMS OF ALL THE QUEENS   *939 21

FORMULATE
    FORMULATE IT   541 16

FORNICATE
    I BOOZE AND FORNICATE AND USE FOUL LANGUAGE AND DESPISE   432 18
    AND IN THE BODY WE CAN ONLY MENTALLY FORNICATE   472 8

FORSAKE
    STILL I WILL LEAVE YOU STILL FORSAKE YOU TOO   875 22

FORSAKEN
    THE CHILDREN HAVE FORSAKEN THEIR PLAY   41 28
    THE STARS WATERS TROUBLED FORSAKEN   49 10
    YOUNG BIRDS FORSAKEN AND LEFT IN A NEST OF MUD   145 24

FORTHCOMING
    AND IN A GREAT AND SACRED FORTHCOMING STEPS FORTH STEPS   306 6

FORTHWITH
    CONSIDER MISS WILKS OR DEPART FORTHWITH   584 2

FORTIES
    IF I WERE YOU AS I PASSED THE FORTIES   835 31

FORTIFIED
    BEHIND I AM FORTIFIED I AM GLAD AT MY WORK   *945 26

FORTIFY
    ALL MOTHERS WHO FORTIFY THEMSELVES IN MOTHERHOOD DEVAST+   208 18
    TO GATHER AND FORTIFY THEMSELVES IN EVERY CLASS IN EVER+   666 3

FORTRESS
    NAY ONCE IT WAS ALSO A FORTRESS WALL AND THE WEIGHT OF +   326 25
    BUT ALSO IT WAS A FIERY FORTRESS FROWNING SHAGGILY ON T+   327 1
    HIS FORTRESS IS DISMANTLED   327 4

FORTUNATELY
    FORTUNATELY THOUGH SOME SUPERIOR PERSONS ARE STILL SUPE+   548 10

FORTUNE
    AS TO WHETHER YOU'VE FOUND A FORTUNE   237 7
    HE FEELS MUCH GAYER THAN IF SOMEBODY HAD LEFT HIM A FOR+   496 7

FORTY
    YOU FORTY LADIES IN THE HAREM BOWER   758 6
    THOSE UNDER FIFTY AND MORE STILL THOSE UNDER FORTY   832 1
    THE LITTLE-BOY OF THIRTY OR FORTY OR FIFTY OR SIXTY   841 19

FORTY-FIVE
    A WIDOW O' FORTY-FIVE   77 13
    A WIDOW O' FORTY-FIVE   77 17
    A WIDOW O' FORTY-FIVE   77 21
    AFORE I CAN TA'E THEE I'VE GOT A WIDDER O' FORTY-FIVE T+   83 8
    AND IF THEY'RE OVER FORTY-FIVE HURL GREAT STONES INTO T+   541 4
    A WIDOW O' FORTY-FIVE   *919 1
    A WIDOW O' FORTY-FIVE   *919 5
    A WIDOW O' FORTY-FIVE   *919 9
    BEFORE I CAN TA'E THEE I'VE GOT A WIDOW OF FORTY-FIVE T+   *925 12

FORTY-THREE
    THAT IS THE MEN OF MY AGE AND I AM FORTY-THREE   828 15

FORWARD
    DRIFTS DIMLY FORWARD EASILY HIDDEN   68 6
    HER FACE AND FORWARD LEANS TO CATCH THE SIGHT   105 27
    SOME STREET-ENDS THRUST FORWARD THEIR STACK   164 20
    AND MOUTH REACHING FORWARD TO KISS YOU   220 11
    HERE AMONG ALL THIS SILENCE CROUCHING FORWARD   225 19
    YOU DID NOT STRETCH FORWARD TO CARESS HER   255 29
    AND I RAN FORWARD TO FRIGHTEN HIM FORTH   344 4
    YOU DRAW YOUR HEAD FORWARD SLOWLY FROM YOUR LITTLE   352 25
    AND SET FORWARD SLOW-DRAGGING ON YOUR FOUR-PINNED TOES   352 27
    ROWING SLOWLY FORWARD   352 28
    TO ROW FORWARD AND REACH HIMSELF TALL ON SPINY TOES   950 1
    AND NERVES URGING FORWARD TO THE WALL YOU'D HAVE EYES   381 4
    AND STARTING FORWARD IN THE DUSK WITH YOUR LITTLE BLACK   396 31
    TILL THE HEAD FLOATS TILTED LIKE A BOTTLE FORWARD TILTED   428 10
    IF YOU'VE GOT THE GOODS COME FORWARD BOY AND LET'S SEE   483 20
    AS FOR THOSE OVER FIFTY EITHER THEY RUSH FORWARD   502 16
    FORWARD AND SAID   525 23
    SHE LEANS FORWARD HER SMOOTH PALE FACE   731 10
    BACKWARD AND FORWARD FROM WALL TO WALL   746 11
    GO FORWARD SUN DO NOT TORMENT US   750 4
    SO LEANING FORWARD ON HIS CLOUD HE SAID TO HIMSELF   790 17
    I LIFT MY BREAST AND LEAN FORWARD   883 10
    I LEANED ME FORWARD TO FIND HER LIPS   *912 13
    DRIFTS DIMLY FORWARD EASILY HIDDEN   *914 21

FORWARDS
    FORWARDS AS HE RUBS THE WOUND   734 7

FOSSIL
    I WOULD NOT EVEN ASK TO LEAVE A FOSSIL CLAW EXTANT   430 7

FOSTERED
    WHERE ALL THE PARTHENON MARBLES STILL FOSTERED THE ROOT+   311 28

FOUGHT
    WHERE THE FIGHT THAT IS FIGHT FOR BEING IS FOUGHT THROU+   93 4
    IF MEN ONLY FOUGHT OUTWARDS INTO THE WORLD   538 15
    THE ANGELS HAVE SOMEWHERE FOUGHT AND LOST   823 1
    FOUGHT AND LOST   823 2
    THE ANGELS HAVE EVERYWHERE FOUGHT AND LOST   823 6
    FOUGHT AND LOST   823 7
    THE BATTLE THAT THE ANGELS FOUGHT   824 4
    AS IF ROSES FOUGHT WITH ROSES   *943 9

FOUL
    LET US BREATHE FRESH AIR AND WAKE FROM FOUL DREAMS IN W+   175 19
    TO MAKE NEW WORDS WITH OUR LIPS TO ESCAPE THE FOUL DREAM   175 22
    OF REAL DAYLIGHT UPON US RELEASED FROM THE FOUL DREAM'S+   175 30
    BREAK OUT OF THIS FOUL HAS-BEEN   177 24
    THOUSANDS AND THOUSANDS OF GAPING HIDEOUS FOUL DEAD   258 8
    AND SET THE STINKING RUBBISH-HEAP OF THIS FOUL WORLD   315 23
    BUT NOT A TRACE OF FOUL EQUALITY   316 7
    NOR SOUND OF STILL MORE FOUL HUMAN PERFECTION   316 8
    I BOOZE AND FORNICATE AND USE FOUL LANGUAGE AND DESPISE   432 18
    FOUL   519 27
    OF THE FOUL ONES FROM MY PICTURES OH PURIFY   581 8
    LIKE A GREY DOG WHOSE MOUTH IS FOUL WITH RABIES   807 5

FOULED
    AH MY NICE PICTURES THEY ARE FOULED THEY ARE DIRTIED   580 23

FOUND
    YOU ARE HERE YOU ARE HERE WE HAVE FOUND YOU EVERYWHERE   34 16
    HAVING FOUND WHAT HE WANTED HAVING GOT WHAT WAS   51 19
    FOR A GREY RAT FOUND THE GOLD THIRTEEN   119 19
    THROAT WAS FOUND   120 17
    MY HEART WAS FOUND   121 8
    WHO WAS SEEKING ME AND HAD FOUND ME AT LAST TO FREE   180 16
    WE FOUND THE DARK WILD ROSES   217 1
    AS TO WHETHER YOU'VE FOUND A FORTUNE   237 7
    I HAVE FOUND THE OTHER WORLD   259 27
    I HAVE FOUND A PLACE OF LONELINESS   261 17
    THEN I FOUND MYSELF IN A WONDERLAND   261 26
    TO LET ME KNOW THAT I WAS FOUND   262 9
    SHE FOUND THE SOURCE OF MY SUBJECTION   262 17
    HE FOUND THE LAMB BEYOND HIM ON THE INACCESSIBLE PINNAC+ 324 20

FOUND
    AND FOUND HIS FEET SO HE IS THE FIRST OF CREATURES TO S+   348 14
    HAVING FOUND   366 37
    AND FOUND YOU AFTER ENDLESS CHASING   395 28
    COME PELTING TO ME NOW THE OTHER FOLK HAVE FOUND YOU   400 4
    OH YES YOU'RE FOUND OUT I HEARD THEM KICK YOU OUT OF   400 6
    AND ABOVE AND ABOVE THE TREES I FOUND HER LAIR   402 11
    WHAT WAS LOST IS FOUND   461 21
    IT ALL DEPENDS WHETHER I FOUND THEM WORTH FIGHTING FOR   497 18
    AND FOUND OUT WHAT THEY REALLY FELT AND REALLY MEANT   504 4
    SEEK ALL THE WORLD ROUND THERE'S NONE CAN BE FOUND   574 17
    THAT FIGS AREN'T FOUND IN THE LAND OF THE FREE   579 8
    AND FOR THE MOMENT SHE WAS ISIS GLEAMING HAVING FOUND H+ 672 24
    GOD IS THE GREAT URGE THAT HAS NOT YET FOUND A BODY   691 15
    AND ANXIOUSLY LIKE A BOY AFRAID TO BE FOUND OUT   734 4
    AND FOUND GREY DOVES IN THE FOUNTAIN COURT   751 2
    AND THE JACKAL FOUND HIS GRAVE   754 18
    SURELY HE SAID THIS IS A CURIOUS PEOPLE I HAVE FOUND   790 16
    HERE HAVE I FOUND AN ANSWER FOR MY HOLLOW YEARNING   *907 10
    FOR THE GREY RAT FOUND THE GOLD THIRTEEN   *932 28
    SO WE FOUND THE DEAD CLATCH SIDE BY SIDE   *933 5
    THIS FOUND REFRAIN   *935 13
    WE FOUND OUR WARM WILD ROSES   *942 13

FOUNDATION
    OUT AND IS THE FOUNDATION OF THE WORLD   348 16

FOUNDER
    TO FOUNDER AT LAST WITHIN THE DREADFUL FLOOD   875 33

FOUNT
    FOR THE JOY LIKE A FOUNT UNDONE   888 12

FOUNTAIN
    A CLOUD COMES UP LIKE THE SURGE OF A FOUNTAIN   50 3
    I WOULD BE A GOOD FOUNTAIN A GOOD WELL-HEAD   250 26
    TO PLAY WITH THE GLOBE OF EARTH LIKE A BALL ON A FOUNTA+ 272 19
    AND MAN IS AN IRIDESCENT FOUNTAIN RISING UP TO FLOWER   675 15
    AND FOUND GREY DOVES IN THE FOUNTAIN COURT   751 2
    IN THE FOUNTAIN YOU WILL LIE DOWN   809 10
    IF YOU REACH THE FOUNTAIN AND LIE DOWN   809 12
    AND THE FOUNTAIN COVERS YOUR FACE FORFVER   809 13
    SO THEY LEAP UP LIKE A FOUNTAIN   819 16
    THE PEAR-BLOSSOM IS A FOUNTAIN OF FOAM   885 28

FOUNTAINS
    JETS OF SPARKS IN FOUNTAINS OF BLUE COME LEAPING   136 6
    YOUR FOUNTAINS AS HEAVEN DRINKS FROM OUT THEIR COURSE   153 30
    FOUNTAINS OF DIRT   160 2
    UNLOCKS THE FOUNTAINS OF PEACE AGAIN   461 24
    THE FOUNTAINS OF PEACE THE FOUNTAINS OF PEACE   461 25
    OVER THE FOUNTAINS AND THE ORANGE-TREES   758 2
    WHERE THE BREATH AND THE FOUNTAINS COMMINGLE   811 4

FOUR
    I WILL SIFT THE SURF THAT EDGES THE NIGHT WITH MY NET T+   180 4
    THERE ARE FOUR MEN MOWING DOWN BY THE ISAR   219 21
    I CAN HEAR THE SWISH OF THE SCYTHE-STROKES FOUR   219 22
    THE FIRST MAN OUT OF THE FOUR THAT'S MOWING   219 25
    FOUR LABOURERS PASS WITH THEIR SCYTHES   220 16
    A GUN AND A BUNCHED-UP DEER ITS FOUR LITTLE FEET   220 18
    IS TO SPLIT IT IN FOUR HOLDING IT BY THE STUMP   282 2
    OH PUT THEM BACK PUT THEM BACK IN THE FOUR CORNERS OF T+ 319 1
    THE NIGHT LIVES FOUR LIVES AND MAN THAT SLEEPS THROUGH + 319 4
    SLEEPS FOUR SLEEPS THE SLEEP OF THE LION THE SLEEP ON T+ 319 5
    AND IT IS DAY THEN FROM THE FOUR QUARTERS THE FOUR WIND+ 319 7
    FOUR GREAT BEASTS THE FOUR NATURES THE FOUR WINDS THE F+ 319 9
    FOUR AND A KEYSTONE   355 10
    FOUR AND A KEYSTONE   355 12
    FOUR PIN-POINT TOES AND A PROBLEMATICAL THUMB-PIECE   356 6
    FOUR ROWING LIMBS AND ONE WEDGE-BALANCING HEAD   356 7
    FOUR AND ONE MAKES FIVE WHICH IS THE CLUE TO ALL MATHEM+ 356 8
    THOUGH WHAT SHE DOES EXCEPT LAY FOUR EGGS AT RANDOM IN   358 26
    SO HALTS THE LITTLE BLACK BITCH ON FOUR SPREAD PAWS IN + 375 10
    KISSES OF FOUR GREAT LORDS BEAUTIFUL AS THEY HELD ME TO+ 695 29
    TO OUR SENSES THE ELEMENTS ARE FOUR   706 1
    THE FOUR GREAT ONES THE FOUR ROOTS THE FIRST FOUR   706 4
    BUT THE FOUR WE HAVE ALWAYS WITH US THEY ARE OUR WORLD   706 8
    IN THE BOX AND FOUR HOT HORSES GOING DREARILY   733 7
    LIKE ANY OTHER WORD OF FOUR LETTERS   837 5
    THERE'S FOUR MEN MOWING DOWN BY THE RIVER   *944 1
    I CAN HEAR THE SOUND OF THE SCYTHE STROKES FOUR   *944 2
    THE FIRST MAN OUT O' THE FOUR THAT'S MOWIN'   *944 5

FOURFOLD
    LESS THAN A YEAR THE FOURFOLD FEET HAD PRESSED   155 7

FOUR-PETALLED
    FOUR-PETALLED FLOWER   282 4

FOUR-PINNED
    AND SET FORWARD SLOW-DRAGGING ON YOUR FOUR-PINNED TOES   352 27

FOURS
    THREES AND FOURS AND TWELVES   355 24

FOUR-SEPALLED
    WHICH IS JUST LIKE A FOUR-SEPALLED CALYX   282 6

FOURTEEN
    AND A BOY AS HE REACHES THE AGE OF FOURTEEN WHEN HE SHO+ 843 2

FOURTH
    THREE SIDES SET ON ME SPACE AND FEAR BUT THE FOURTH SIDE 249 10
    THREE SIDES SET ON ME CHAOS AND BOUNCE BUT THE FOURTH   249 21
    BECAUSE WE ARE THE THIRD AND FOURTH GENERATIONS   627 22
    AND WE ARE THE GELDED THIRD AND FOURTH GENERATION   627 28
    TIME BUT DIFFERENT DIRECTIONS IN CREATION WITHIN THE FO+ 760 25

FOURTH
   ACROSS THE FOURTH DIMENSION   760 28
   FOURTH DIMENSION NOT IN YARDS AND MILES LIKE THE ETERNA+   761 16
   THREE SIDES SET ON ME SPACE AND FEAR BUT THE FOURTH SID+   *945 22

FOWL
   APPROVAL GOGGLE-EYED FOWL   170 24

FOWLS
   FOWLS OF THE AFTERWARDS   171 20
   SWINE WASH IN MIRE AND BARNYARD FOWLS IN DUST   376 8

FOX
   LIKE THE KINGDOM OF THE FOX IN THE DARK   704 22
   AS WILD WHITE FOX GLOVES DROOPING WITH FULNESS   874 26

FOXES
   AS FOXES STOATS AND WOLVES AND PRAIRIE DOGS   392 21
   THERE ARE FOXES IN THE COVER OF HIS BEARD   *953 29

FOXGLOVE
   IS DIGNIFIED IN THE FOXGLOVE LIKE A RED INDIAN BRAVE   272 29

FOXGLOVES
   AS THE TALL FOXGLOVES AND THE MULLEINS AND MALLOWS   709 18

FOX-TAIL
   COCK'S-FOOT FOX-TAIL FESCUE AND TOTTERING-GRASS   587 20

FRAGILE
   FOR SURELY THE FRAGILE FINE YOUNG THING HAD BEEN   132 3
   A TINY FRAGILE HALF-ANIMATE BEAN   352 8
   AND GIVING THAT FRAGILE YELL THAT SCREAM   365 10
   AND LIFE DEPARTS LAUNCH OUT THE FRAGILE SOUL   719 2
   IN THE FRAGILE SHIP OF COURAGE THE ARK OF FAITH   719 3
   A FRAGILE STRANGER IN THE FLUX OF LIVES   745 18
   RUNG OF THEIR LIFE-LADDERS' FRAGILE HEIGHTS   854 3
   THE CAMPIONS DRIFT IN FRAGILE ROSY MIST   854 11
   AND IN MY FRAGILE AWKWARD BOAT BETWEEN   875 28
   FOR SURELY THE FRAGILE FINE YOUNG THING HAD BEEN   *937 30

FRAGILE-TENDER
   FRAGILE-TENDER FRAGILE-TENDER LIFE-BODY   306 23

FRAGMENT
   THAT PALE FRAGMENT OF A PRINCE UP THERE WHOSE MOTTO IS   388 5
   HE IS ROYALTY PALE AND DEJECTED FRAGMENT UP ALOFT   388 13

FRAGMENTARINESS
   FRAGMENTARINESS   361 7

FRAGMENTS
   AND AS THE DOG WITH ITS NOSTRILS TRACKING OUT THE FRAGM+   406 1

FRAGRANCE
   BRINGS A FRESH FRAGRANCE OF HEAVEN TO OUR SENSES   467 10
   FRAGRANCE OF ROSES IN A STALE STINK OF LIES   634 26
   BROTHER I LIKE YOUR FRAGRANCE   759 1
   SWEET FRAGRANCE OF LOVE AND FEED ME WITH KISSES FAIR   874 7
   MY QUIVERING ANSWER AND KISSES LIKE FRAGRANCE OF FLOWERS   *942 3

FRAGRANT
   FRAGRANT LIKE YELLOWING LEAVES AND DIM WITH THE SOFT   503 24
   AND NOW HANGS LIKE THE FRAGRANT CLOSE OF THE MEASURE   868 15
   LINEN WITHIN MY OWN OLD FRAGRANT CHEST   877 31
   OH I TORE THEM UP THOUGH THE WISTFUL LEAVES WERE FRAGRA+   *926 15

FRAIL
   FRAIL AND SAD WITH GREY BOWED HEAD   64 4
   FRAIL AS A SCAR UPON THE PALE BLUE SKY   131 24
   PUT GREAVES UPON YOUR THIGHS AND KNEES AND FRAIL   154 21
   WITH YELLOW FRAIL SEA-POPPIES   200 19
   LOOK AT THE MANY-CICATRISED FRAIL VINE NONE MORE SCARRED   305 4
   AND FRAIL   305 5
   GENTLE NURTURED FRAIL AND SPLENDID   313 32
   OF A FRAIL CORPUS   332 14
   AND BITING THE FRAIL GRASS ARROGANTLY   358 20
   TIME AFTER TIME THAT FRAIL TORN SCREAM   365 23
   DELICATE FRAIL CRESCENT OF THE GENTLE OUTLINE OF WHITE   371 13
   FRAIL DANGERS   630 15
   WITH EVE AND THE AMAZON THE LIZARD AND THE FRAIL   633 3
   BUT IF HE PRODUCES SOMETHING BEAUTIFUL WITH THE FRAIL   634 13
   BUT TO THE FRAIL WHO KNOW BEST   658 9
   AND THE FRAIL SOUL STEPS OUT INTO HER HOUSE AGAIN   720 16
   BREATHING ON HIS SMALL FRAIL SAIL AND HELPING HIM ON   723 23
   A FRAIL WHITE GLEAM OF RESURRECTION   744 12
   FOR I AM FRAIL AS A FLASK OF GLASS   752 15
   A NAKED NIGHTLY THING TOO FRAIL AND WISE FOR THE STRESS   771 23
   AND DAMAGE ONCE MORE THE FRAIL QUICK OF THE FUTURE   780 21
   SMASH IT IN LIKE A FRAIL VESSEL   869 23
   WHERE THIS FRAIL SHADOWY HUSK OF A DAY IS LOST   875 15
   FRAIL AS A SCAR UPON THE PALE BLUE SKY   *937 23

FRAILER
   FRAILER THAN THEY   772 3

FRAIL-FILIGREED
   FRAIL-FILIGREED AMONG THE REST   314 3

FRAILITY
   I WEAR FRAILITY AS A CROWN   772 8

FRAIL-NAKED
   FRAIL-NAKED UTTERLY UNCOVERED   306 10

FRAILTY
   ONLY YOUR ACCURSED HAIRY FRAILTY   334 6

FRAME
   THE SPIRIT FROM EACH LEAF'S FRAME   68 4
   HITHER AND THITHER ACROSS THE HIGH CRYSTALLINE FRAME   72 9
   OH LABOURERS OH SHUTTLES ACROSS THE BLUE FRAME OF MORNI+   73 8
   THROUGH THE BLACK FRAME   204 5
   I THINK I COULD ALTER THE FRAME OF THINGS IN MY AGONY   213 18
   IS THE FRAME OF THINGS TOO HEAVY   558 19
   IS A NEW FRAME OF SOCIETY   833 13
   TO ALTER THE PRESENT FRAME OF CIVILISATION   838 3
   THE FRAME OF THINGS HAS GROWN SO HEAVY IT'S JUST TOO HE+   842 29
   THE SPIRIT FROM EACH LEAF'S FRAME   *914 19

FRANCE
   OVER THERE IS RUSSIA AUSTRIA SWITZERLAND FRANCE IN A   213 1
   WHAT IS ENGLAND OR FRANCE FAR OFF   213 5
   NOW IF THE LILIES OF FRANCE LICK SOLOMON IN ALL HIS GLO+   413 27

FRANCIS
   JOAQUIN FRANCIS AND ANTHONY   798 13

FRANKINCENSE
   YOU LIKE FRANKINCENSE INTO SCENT   114 4
   THAT CHURN THE FRANKINCENSE AND OOZE THE MYRRH   298 5
   AROMATIC AS FRANKINCENSE   301 26
   YOU LIKE FRANKINCENSE INTO SCENT   *929 21

FRANTIC
   HER FRANTIC EFFORT THROTTLING   43 10
   THE TRAIN BEATS FRANTIC IN HASTE AND STRUGGLES AWAY   88 23
   THE FRANTIC THROB OF THE TRAIN   862 18

FRAUD
   A DAMN FRAUD UNDERLINED   553 4
   THE UPPER CLASSES ARE JUST A FRAUD   555 7
   THEY WERE JUST A BLOODY COLLECTIVE FRAUD   556 7

FRAY
   OF TROUSERS FRAY   145 20
   THEY SLIPPED INTO THE FRAY   560 8

FRAYED
   AND CAME BACK TINGLING CLEAN BUT WORN AND FRAYED   99 13

FREE
   THE CONFINES GAZING OUT BEYOND WHERE THE WINDS GO FREE   47 10
   YOUR BRIGHTNESS DIMS WHEN I DRAW TOO NEAR AND MY FREE   87 16
   THE BRIEF MATERIAL CONTROL OF THE HOUR LEAVE THEM FREE +   93 8
   AND ONLY IN HARMONY WITH OTHERS THE SINGLE SOUL CAN BE +   93 10
   THE NEWS THAT SHE IS FREE   99 26
   FREE OF ALL HEARTS MY DARLING   101 27
   NOW WHO WILL BURN YOU FREE   112 6
   OF HELL TO WAKE AND BE FREE   177 22
   WHO WAS SEEKING ME AND HAD FOUND ME AT LAST TO FREE   180 16
   SEA ONLY YOU ARE FREE SOPHISTICATED   197 18
   GRIEF MAKES US FREE   199 30
   I COULD NOT BE FREE   204 6
   NOT FREE MYSELF FROM THE PAST THOSE OTHERS   204 7
   IT DID NOT MAKE ME FREE   255 18
   HER HANDS SLID IN AND SET ME FREE   262 15
   THAT ONE IS FREE   267 4
   THEN WE SHALL BE FREE FREER THAN ANGELS AH PERFECT   267 23
   TO THE FREE CALM UPPER AIR   343 2
   WHILE SHE PULLS HERSELF FREE AND ROWS HER DULL MOUND   362 10
   NOW YOU ARE FREE OF THE TOILS OF A WOULD-BE-PERFECT LOVE   411 16
   GAY AND AMUSING TOGETHER AND FREE   470 7
   BREAD SHOULD BE FREE   487 7
   FIRE SHOULD BE FREE   487 9
   FREE   487 24
   MEN ARE NOT BAD WHEN THEY ARE FREE   488 1
   IF MEN WERE FREE FROM THE TERROR OF EARNING A LIVING   488 4
   WHY ISN'T ANYTHING FREE WHY IS IT ALWAYS PAY PAY PAY   518 3
   WE WANT A NEW WORLD OF WILD PEACE WHERE LIVING IS FREE   519 22
   WE CALL FREE COMPETITION AND INDIVIDUAL ENTERPRISE AND   519 29
   LIVING SHOULD BE AS FREE TO A MAN AS TO A BIRD   520 2
   BUT IT MUST BE FREE WORK NOT DONE JUST FOR MONEY BUT FOR   520 20
   ONE FREE CHEERFUL ACTIVITY STIMULATES ANOTHER   520 26
   WE MUST CHANGE THE SYSTEM AND MAKE LIVING FREE TO ALL   522 29
   I AM A DEMOCRAT IN SO FAR AS I LOVE THE FREE SUN IN MEN   526 7
   AND YOU FEEL MORE FREE   557 18
   HOW SHE SET US FREE   557 26
   WITH GIDDY FREEDOM IN THE LAND OF THE FREE   575 10
   THAT FIGS AREN'T FOUND IN THE LAND OF THE FREE   579 8
   THE HUMAN WILL IS FREE ULTIMATELY TO CHOOSE ONE OF TWO +   617 12
   TO FLOWER FREE OF FEAR   627 4
   TO SET ALL MEN FREE   636 17
   FOR A MOMENT FREE FROM ALL CONCEIT OF YOURSELF AND ALL +   674 3
   FREE MOTION OF LIFE   678 16
   BUT LET US FREE OUR EYES AND LOOK BEYOND   737 4
   AS FREE AS THE RUNNING OF ANGEL'S FEET   746 18
   SET FREE AGAIN   747 20
   BUT FOR THESE CHILDREN I SHOULD BE FREE   832 9
   FREE WHAT FOR NOBODY KNOWS BUT FREE   832 10
   THY FLAME LEAP FREE WHAT IF I AM LEFT BEHIND   879 25
   ME UP CARESS AND CLOTHE WITH FREE   *899 24
   ME UP CARESS AND CLOTHE WITH FREE   *903 3
   SWEET WISDOM OF GRACE NOW WHO WILL FREE   *927 24
   NOW WHO WILL BURN YOU FREE   *928 26

FREED
   FACE FREED OF THE WAVERING BLAZE   59 8

FREEDOM
    NEVER TO KNOW THE GLAD FREEDOM OF OBEDIENCE SINCE LONG   48   3
    IT IS NOT FREEDOM   236   22
    THAT WE ARE ALL DETACHED MOVING IN FREEDOM MORE THAN THE   267   26
    FREEDOM   345   18
    THIS IS CALLED UNIVERSAL FREEDOM   521   19
    OF EXCITED FREEDOM   532   10
    FOR FREEDOM AND THE FUN OF LIVING   560   31
    FATHER NEPTUNE ONE DAY TO FREEDOM DID SAY   574   17
    SAID FREEDOM WHY THAT'S MY OWN ISLAND   574   14
    OF FREEDOM SHRIEKING TILL HER THROAT WAS SORE   574   23
    WITH GIDDY FREEDOM IN THE LAND OF THE FREE   575   10
    ABSOLUTE FREEDOM ABSOLVED FROM THE GREAT NECESSITIES OF+   712   19

FREEDOM'S
    BUT I CAME AT FREEDOM'S INVITATION   575   5

FREEING
    THE FREEING ONESELF   620   19

FREELY
    I COULD CRY WITH JOY AND QUITE FREELY THERE IS NOBODY TO   256   12
    WHICH IS WHY THE YOUNG WHO COPULATE SO FREELY   843   19

FREEMAN
    DIVISION INTO SLAVE AND FREEMAN   636   14

FREER
    THEN WE SHALL BE FREE FREER THAN ANGELS AH PERFECT   267   23

FREES
    WHEN A MAN FREES HIS OWN SELF INTO HIS WORK   *949   24

FRENCH
    LITTLE BLACK FEMALE PUP SORT OF FRENCH BULL THEY SAY   395   1
    AMERICANS AND FRENCH AND GERMANS AND SO ON   660   4

FRENCHMAN
    AN OLD FRENCHMAN UTTERED THE TRUISM   641   17

FRENZIED
    AND DRIVING THEM AROUND IN FRENZIED ENERGY   502   8
    FLUSHED FRENZIED RELENTLESS ME   769   8

FRENZIES
    AND A MILLION FRENZIES OF TORTURED JEALOUSY   475   20

FRENZY
    AND AN IMPURE FRENZY   342   24
    YET BLIND WITH FRENZY WITH CLUTTERED FEAR   343   15
    A FRENZY OF TORTURED POSSESSION   475   19

FRESCO
    MY WORLD IS A PAINTED FRESCO WHERE COLOURED SHAPES   *906   11
    MY WORLD IS A PAINTED FRESCO WHERE COLOURED SHAPES   *908   5

FRESH
    AN' 'IM AS NICE AN' FRESH   11   29
    UPON THE FLOOR THAT ERST STOOD UP SO FRESH   87   29
    THE TEARS ARE DRY AND THE CHEEK'S YOUNG FRUITS ARE FRESH   94   19
    AN' FRESH AN' MORE NICER FOR MARRYIN' WI'   138   12
    BEATS THE NEW FRESH AIR OF LIFE THEY COME FOR STRIFE   174   14
    LET US BREATHE FRESH AIR AND WAKE FROM FOUL DREAMS IN W+   175   19
    TO FEEL FRESH AIR IN OUR THROATS TO HAVE FRESH BREATH I+   175   21
    FRESH QUIVERING KEEP THE SUNNY-SWIFT MARCH-DAYS WAITING   179   5
    WHAT IS IT THAT FROM THEIR FACES FRESH AS SPRING   270   4
    SUCH FAIR FRESH ALERT FIRST-FLOWER FACES   270   5
    YET SEE HIM FLING HIMSELF ABROAD IN FRESH ABANDON   305   6
    THE CRUMBLING DAMP FRESH LAND LIFE HORIZONTAL AND CEASE!   321   18
    DOESN'T HE LOOK THE FRESH CLEAN ENGLISHMAN OUTSIDE   430   21
    CONTENT IS THE WOMAN WITH FRESH LIFE RIPPLING IN TO HER   449   14
    A LITTLE FRESH AIR IN THE MONEY STY   459   17
    BRINGS A FRESH FRAGRANCE OF HEAVEN TO OUR SENSES   467   10
    SO THAT WHEN WE ARE RE-BORN WE CAN BE BORN INTO A FRESH   512   29
    THOSE THAT ARE FRESH AND ALIVE ARE THE SAME IN EVERY   612   10
    IN FRESH FIELDS   614   26
    AND LET MANKIND MAKE NEW BLOOD FRESH AND BRIGHT   679   7
    AS YOU WOULD A FRESH SWEET LOCUST-POD   752   14
    THE DARK ONES ARE CURIOUSLY PURPLISH LIKE FRESH   827   4
    FRESH CLEAN WELL-GROOMED ENGLISHMAN   830   9
    HE HAS FRESH CLEAN WELL-GROOMED EMOTIONS   830   11
    QUITE THE FRESH CLEAN MANLY FELLOW   830   13
    PULL IT DOWN AND PREPARE FOR A NEW FRESH HOUSE OF LIFE   838   12
    THEY SHOULD FLUTTER AND TURN HIS WAY AND SAVING THE FRE+   877   30
    THE TEARS ARE DRY THE CHEEKS' YOUNG FRUITS ARE FRESH   *897   7
    IN THE FRESH OF THE MORNING IT IS TO BE   *899   5
    IN THE FRESH OF THE MORNING IT IS TO BE   *902   17
    AN' 'IM AS NICE AN' FRESH   *919   17

FRESH-DROPPED
    AND FRESH-DROPPED DUNG   398   29

FRESHEN
    AND FRESHEN THE PUTRID LITTLE SPACE IN WHICH WE ARE CRI+   515   4

FRESHENING
    FRESHENING LIMBS   795   19

FRESHLY
    WITH THE RIPPLING FRESHLY CHANGE   460   12

FRET
    NOR FRET THY FAT   83   21
    WOULD TAKE AWAY THE SICKENING FRET   747   13
    HEY WITH THIS ENDLESS LABOUR AND LITTLE-SOULED FRET   859   26
    ALL THESE GLITTERING SEA-BIRDS WHEEL AND FRET   860   20
    AND AH MY BITTER BREASTS THAT SULK AND FRET   *933   32

FRETTED
    OUT OF THE DARKNESS FRETTED SOMETIMES IN ITS SLEEPING   136   5
    TO THE THING AND RATHER FRETTED AND HIS THICK BLACK HAIR   734   21
    OF LIFE UNBORN AND IS FRETTED   772   33
    LIFE IS DARK AND RIPPLING BUT FRETTED   773   1

FRETTING
    OF FRETTING OR OF GLADNESS SHOWS THE JETTING   89   14

FRICTION
    FRICTION   648   13
    FULL OF FRICTION FULL OF GRINDING FULL OF DANGER TO THE+   675   27
    BUT ON AND ON ON AND ON TILL THE FRICTION WEARS THEM OUT   676   1

FRICTIONAL
    AS FRICTIONAL AS PERILOUS EXPLOSIVE AS BRIMSTONE   301   31

FRIED
    AS A VENDOR OF FRIED FISH ONCE MORE YELLOW   760   21

FRIEND
    PUTS THE HARD HANDS OF MY FRIEND TO SLEEP   41   9
    AND YOU WANT TO ENLARGE YOURSELF WITH THIS FRIEND OF MI+   235   28
    SUCH A FRIEND AS HE IS   235   29
    HE SPOKE THIS WORD STOP DON'T BEAT IT FOR IT IS THE SOU+   376   6
    I READ A NOVEL BY A FRIEND OF MINE   489   9
    THE LOVE I FEEL FOR MY FRIEND THIS YEAR   662   1
    CLOSE FRIEND IN EVERYTHING IS OUR LORD MY BOY   749   23
    JOIN ME TO MY WELL-BELOVED FRIEND   754   22
    AND SAY BE WELCOME DEAREST FRIEND   754   25

FRIENDLINESS
    UNDER THE GREEN GRASSY UNISON OF ALL OUR FRIENDLINESS   *951   11

FRIENDS
    YOUR ASHES EVEN MY FRIENDS   315   8
    MOST OF MY FRIENDS WERE DEEPLY HURT   491   17
    TO ALL MY FOES AND FRIENDS   492   24
    NOT FRIENDS NECESSARILY THEY TALK SO MUCH   499   21
    HOW YOU REMIND ME OF MY LONDON FRIENDS   542   3

FRIENDSHIP
    THEN THE PRIVATE INTIMACY OF FRIENDSHIP WILL BE REAL AN+   608   14
    THEN FRIENDSHIP IS IMPOSSIBLE   608   18
    SINCE YOU REFUSE MY FRIENDSHIP   611   2

FRIENDS'
    MY LORD A MAN'S FRIENDS' IDEAS OF HIM   489   25

FRIGATES
    FRIGATES BARKS AND PINNACES YAWLS   542   7

FRIGHT
    WE SHALL SHIVER WITH COLD AND FRIGHT   482   19
    OF WAITING AND THE ROOM STANDS STILL WITH FRIGHT   878   35

FRIGHTEN
    AND I RAN FORWARD TO FRIGHTEN HIM FORTH   344   4

FRIGHTENED
    WAVE FRIGHTENED WHO COMES A LABOURER ALAS   41   4
    YOU ARE FRIGHTENED WITH JOY MY HEART LIKE A FRIGHTENED   47   33
    AN' LIE FRIGHTENED TER DEATH UNDER THEE   138   33
    COME YOU ARE COLD THE NIGHT HAS FRIGHTENED YOU   212   1
    OF FEAR AND OF FRIGHTENED FACES   242   21
    UPON THE FRIGHTENED AIR   315   17
    YOU ARE ALMOST TOO LARGE I AM ALMOST FRIGHTENED   359   29
    AND SMALLER MORE FRIGHTENED ELEPHANTS   389   4
    FRIGHTENED OF THE BARE EARTH AND THE TEMPORARY CANVAS   444   12
    AND THE PEOPLE APPLAUDED WITH HOLLOW FRIGHTENED   445   8
    YET THE STRANGE ALMOST FRIGHTENED SHOUT OF DELIGHT THAT   446   14
    BUT HE'S FRIGHTENED TO KNOW IT   446   30
    HE MIGHT POSSIBLY LIKE MEN IF HE WEREN'T TOO FRIGHTENED   447   13
    HE WAS FRIGHTENED TO LOOK ROUND   483   11
    IT IS THAT THAT I AM FRIGHTENED OF   487   1
    NOW IT'S A COUNTRY OF FRIGHTENED OLD MONGRELS   535   17
    DON'T GET TOO FRIGHTENED   564   5
    I FRIGHTENED A LITTLE MOUSE   670   4
    AND IN THE BRUISED BODY THE FRIGHTENED SOUL   717   7
    FRIGHTENED ME WITH THE STEADFASTNESS OF THEIR LOOKING   884   33
    FRIGHTENED AND ALONE THE SOUL SLIPS OUT OF THE HOUSE   *957   12

FRIGHTENING
    WITH A HUNGER MORE FRIGHTENING MORE PROFOUND   264   11
    IS NOT SO FRIGHTENING AS THAT CLEAN SMOOTH   290   27

FRIGHTENS
    LIKE A MAN IN A BOAT ON VERY CLEAR DEEP WATER SPACE FRI+   222   24
    LOOSED ONE MOMENT THE DARKNESS FRIGHTENS ME   225   28
    FRIGHTENS ME FRIGHTENS ME HE IS NOT MY SIEGMUND AT ALL   871   24

FRIGHTFUL
    NAY BUT HOW TORTURED IS THE FRIGHTFUL SEED   160   21

FRIGHTFULLY
    HE'S INSTINCTIVELY FRIGHTFULLY CLEVER   447   16
    HE'S MOST FRIGHTFULLY SKILFUL IN HIS LOVE-MAKING   *948   11

FRINGE
    THAT FRINGE WITH SHADOW ALL THIS WORLD'S EXISTENCE   *959   2

FRINGES
    THEY DWELL IN THE OUTSKIRT FRINGES OF NOWHERE   711   24
    SINCE I EMBARKED ON YOUR DARK BLUE FRINGES   *954   28

FRISK
    LAMBS FRISK AMONG THE DAISIES OF HIS BRAIN   624   9

FRISKINESS
    AND THE LAMBS WILL BITE OFF THE HEADS OF THE DAISIES FO+   625   7

FRISSON
    AND ONE INTENSE AND BACKWARD-CURVING FRISSON   370 16

FRISSON-SHAKEN
    AND KNOWN IT SUBTLER THAN FRISSON-SHAKEN NERVES   383   8

FRIT
    THA WERT FRIT O' SUMMAT   138   9
    YI BUT THA'RT FRIT O' SUMMAT   138 13

FRITTER
    SINCE THEN WITH FRITTER OF FLOWERS   193 18

FRIZZLING
    THE FRIZZLING FALLING FIRE THAT CANNOT GO OUT DROPPING +   701 27

FRO
    AND FRO   33 20
    YOUR VIOLENT HEART BEATS TO AND FRO   122 12
    BUT WHO ARE YOU TWITTERING TO AND FRO   131 17
    MOURNFULLY TO AND FRO TO AND FRO THE TREES ARE WAVING   136 22
    TO AND FRO IN OUR MISGIVINGS   166   5
    JOSTLING TO AND FRO   198   8
    THE SENSITIVE DELICACY OF YOUR SEX IN ITS EBBING TO AND+   464 25
    AND FRO   *891 22

FROCK
    NO LAMP-FRINGED FROCK   170 28
    SHE'S A HOLY TERROR SHE TAKES YOUR BEST FROCK   572   2
    IN YOUR FIFTIES WITH A SHORT FROCK SHOWING YOUR FORE AN+   835 10

FROG
    HOPS LIKE A FROG BEFORE ME   110 26
    I HEARD THE SCREAM OF A FROG WHICH WAS CAUGHT WITH HIS   365 30
    AND THE EGO WILL HAVE TO BURST LIKE THE SWOLLEN FROG   472 12

FROGS
    AND THE FROGS IN THE POOL BEYOND THRILLED WITH EXUBERAN+   206 29
    WITH THE EXTRAVAGANCE OF THE FROGS   206 32
    THE FROGS HELPED ALSO WHIRRING AWAY   207 14
    NEVERTHELESS ONCE THE FROGS THE GLOBE-FLOWERS OF BAVARIA   208   4
    FROGS WERE SINGING AND OVER THE RIVER CLOSES   217   4
    OR FROGS THAT WHEN THEY LEAP COME FLOP AND FLOP TO THE   392 25
    SO MUCH DENSER THAN COLD-BLOODED FROGS   393   3
    SUCH LUMPS SUCH FROGS WITH STONES IN THEIR BELLIES   791 29
    TELL THEM THEY ARE LIKE FROGS WITH STONES IN THEIR BELL+   791 30
    OF THOSE ILL-SMELLING TRIBES OF MEN THESE FROGS THAT CA+   792 23
    FROGS WERE SINGING AND OVER THE RIVER CLOSES   *942 15

FRONT
    AS I STAND ON THIS HILL WITH THE WHITENING CAVE OF THE +   97 11
    IN FRONT OF ME YES UP THE DARKNESS GOES THE GUSH OF THE+   97 18
    IN FRONT OF THE TERRIBLE RAGE THE DEATH   165 17
    IN FRONT OF THE SOMBRE MOUNTAINS A FAINT LOST RIBBON OF   208 23
    HE WAS BORN IN FRONT OF MY SUNRISE   339 20
    THEN CLOSE THE WEDGE OF YOUR LITTLE MOUNTAIN FRONT   353   8
    WHY DO YOU FRONT THE SUN SO OBSTINATELY   374   1
    IN FRONT OF A TOWERING GRIMACING WHITE IMAGE OF   387 31
    AND HOOING AND COOING AND SIDLING THROUGH THE FRONT TEE+   433 22
    ONLY IS MAN AGONISED IN FRONT OF THE NECESSITY TO BE SO+   529 14
    LOVER YOU MAKE SUCH A HERO IN FRONT OF THE FOE   755   9
    EAGLE WITH EGYPTIAN DARKNESS JUTTING IN FRONT OF YOUR F+   782 27
    OR THIS IS MY SISTER AT HOME IN THE OLD FRONT ROOM   *940 14

FRONTAL
    YET IF YOU HAD WHORLED HORNS OF BRONZE IN A FRONTAL DARK   381   1
    ELEPHANT ADVANCING HIS FRONTAL BONE HIS TRUNK CURLED   387   7
    AND THE HUGE FRONTAL OF THREE GREAT ELEPHANTS STEPPING   387 28

FRONTIERS
    NAY WE FIND OURSELVES CROSSING THE FERN-SCENTED FRONTIE+   286 24
    AND WE MUST CROSS THE FRONTIERS THOUGH WE WILL NOT   287   6

FRONT'S
    THAT STOOD CLOSE TO THE WALL AND THE FRONT'S FADED SILK+   *940   3

FRONT-TEETH
    BUT IT HAS FRONT-TEETH   830 30

FROST
    FIRE ENTERS YOU LIKE FROST LIKE A CRUEL BLIGHT   87 17
    LIKE A FLOWER THAT THE FROST HAS HUGGED AND LET GO MY H+   95   1
    THE FROST HAS SETTLED DOWN UPON THE TREES   141 27
    HER ROUND BRIGHT FACE BRIGHT AS FROST   402   2
    AND STRIPES IN THE BRILLIANT FROST OF HER FACE SHARP FI+   402   4
    DARK KEEN FINE RAYS IN THE BRILLIANT FROST OF HER FACE   402   6
    THE GRIM FROST IS AT HAND WHEN THE APPLES WILL FALL   717   3
    LIKE A FLOWER THAT THE FROST HAS HUGGED AND LET GO MY H+   *897 16

FROST-COLD
    A NEW INTOXICATION OF LONELINESS AMONG DECAYING FROST-C+   281   2

FROSTED
    EVEN WHERE PERSEPHONE GOES JUST NOW FROM THE FROSTED SE+   697 16

FROST-FACE
    AND HER BRIGHT STRIPED FROST-FACE WILL NEVER WATCH ANY   402 17
    YET WHAT A GAP IN THE WORLD THE MISSING WHITE FROST-FACE   402 32

FROST-FILIGREED
    FROST-FILIGREED   310 22

FROST-LOVELY
    I WISH THESE BRITTLE FROST-LOVELY FLOWERS OF PASSIONATE+   272   6

FROSTY
    SOBS STRUGGLING INTO HER FROSTY SIGH   85 12

FROTH
    LIKE HALF-SEEN FROTH ON AN EBBING SHORE IN THE MOON   75 28
    LIKE FLOATING FROTH ON AN EBBING SHORE IN THE MOON   *897 27
    LIKE FLOATING FROTH ON AN EBBING SHORE IN THE MOON   *901   4

FROWN
    IN MY SOUL FROM UNDER THE SUDDEN FROWN OF HIS BROW   47 26
    FROWN   633 24

FROWNING
    HE FELL TO FROWNING AS HE LAY WITH HIS HEAD ON HIS PAWS   324 12
    BUT ALSO IT WAS A FIERY FORTRESS FROWNING SHAGGILY ON T+   327   1

FROWNS
    HE FROWNS AS IF HE WERE WORRIED AS IF THE PLACE   734 19

FROZEN
    THAT RIDES THE ROOM LIKE A FROZEN BERG ITS CREST   155   4
    WITH FROZEN RIGGING SHE SAW HIM SHE DROOPED LIKE A FERN   155 22
    I IN THESE GOODLY FROZEN   199 15
    SOMETHING FROZEN IN THE SILENCE THAT DARE NOT BE   225 27
    AND BREATHING THE FROZEN MEMORY OF HIS WRONG   226   4
    STILL IN HIS NOSTRILS THE FROZEN BREATH OF DESPAIR   226   5
    THE HEART IS FROZEN THE SPIRIT DEAD   456   2
    A SMALL BIRD WILL DROP FROZEN DEAD FROM A BOUGH   467   3
    NIPPED UPON THE FROZEN FLOODS OF PHILOSOPHIC DESPAIR   542 21
    WITH A HINT OF THE FROZEN BELLS OF THE SCYLLA FLOWER   708 29
    THERE ARE DEAD THAT CLUSTER IN THE FROZEN NORTH SHUDDER+   795 21
    FOR WATCHING I AM FROZEN AS IN ICE   879 18
    CLEAVES FROZEN TO THE WALLS OF MY COLD BREAST   879 20

FRUIT
    OFFERS ME HER SCARLET FRUIT I WILL SEE   37   3
    THE ROOM IS THE HOLLOW RIND OF A FRUIT A GOURD   112 19
    THE MERE FRUIT OF YOUR WOMB   235   4
    WHAT IS THE FRUIT OF YOUR WOMB THEN YOU MOTHER YOU QUEEN   235   5
    THE SAME THAT DANGLES THE GLOBE-SHAPED PLEIADS OF FRUIT   271 23
    OF EDEN EVEN WAS EVE'S FRUIT TO HER IT BELONGED AND SHE+   277   6
    IT TO THE MAN EVEN THE APPLES OF KNOWLEDGE ARE EVE'S FR+   277   7
    EVERY FRUIT HAS ITS SECRET   282 11
    THE FIG IS A VERY SECRETIVE FRUIT   282 12
    NOW THERE IS A FRUIT LIKE A RIPE WOMB   282 28
    FIG FRUIT OF THE FEMALE MYSTERY CONVERT AND INWARD   283 18
    MEDITERRANEAN FRUIT WITH YOUR COVERT NAKEDNESS   283 19
    BAD INSIDE LIKE FRUIT   462 20
    WHEN THE RIPE FRUIT FALLS   504 20
    NOW IT IS AUTUMN AND THE FALLING FRUIT   716 18
    HIE HIE FRUIT TOPPLES   817   1
    NOT FLOWERS NOR FRUIT   827 25
    IN THE AUTUMN I'LL LOOK FOR IMMORTAL FRUIT   855   9
    IN THE GARNERING AUTUMN A GLOW OF IMMORTAL FRUIT   855 17
    SALLIES OF SWINGING FRUIT   861   5
    LOOKED WHERE THE RED FRUIT HUNG LIKE COALS OF FIRE   864   8
    TO PULL DOWN THE BOUGH THE LEAVES BROKE AND THE FRUIT S+   864 10
    HAS BROUGHT DOWN A RIPE FRUIT HEAVILY TO HER FEET   864 14
    HER FRUIT IS UNRIPE AND HER SOFT MOUTH IS BITTER AND RO+   864 18
    PRESSES HER HAND TO HER BOSOM WHERE THE FRUIT HAS LAIN   864 20
    ROUNDED AND SWELLING TOWARDS THE FRUIT OF A DREAM   *908   4
    SWELLING MANKIND LIKE ONE BUD TO BRING FORTH THE FRUIT +   *909 20
    I SING OF AUTUMN AND THE FALLING FRUIT   *956 24

FRUITED
    I WATCHED THE TEARS ON THE FRUITED CHEEKS OF THE BOYS   *897   2

FRUITFUL
    HUNGRY AND DISCONTENT IN THE FRUITFUL SHADE   864   2

FRUITING
    AND FRUITING   283 21

FRUITLESS
    YOU ARE SINGLE YOU ARE FRUITLESS PHOSPHORESCENT COLD AND   197 12

FRUITS
    THE TEARS ARE DRY AND THE CHEEK'S YOUNG FRUITS ARE FRESH   94 19
    POOR OBSCURE FRUITS EXTRUDED OUT OF LIGHT   160 10
    FALL ALL THE FRUITS MOST BITTERLY INTO EARTH   160 15
    WHITE SANDS AND FRUITS UNKNOWN AND PERFUMES THAT NEVER   261   2
    FOR FRUITS ARE ALL OF THEM FEMALE IN THEM LIES THE SEED+   277   1
    SO MANY FRUITS COME FROM ROSES   285   1
    ARE PARTS OF THE EARTH JUST AS EMBRYOS ARE PARTS OF THE+   295   9
    SECRET FRUITS   300 17
    IS SOUR BITTER FRUITS CANKERED BY LIES   504 14
    TREES RAISED FROM SEED HAVE WILD AND BITTER FRUITS   640 21
    AND THE RED FRUITS GLITTER   861   3
    THE TEARS ARE DRY THE CHEEKS' YOUNG FRUITS ARE FRESH   *897   7
    HE WATERS OUR FACE WITH TEARS OUR YOUNG FRUITS FILLS WI+   *926 29
    OF LEAVES LIKE YELLOW FRUITS SHOW PLAIN   *932 23
    ALL THE FRUITS ARE SULKING IN THE WET   *933 30
    MEN USED TO PUT THEM FORTH SENSITIVELY LIKE BOUGHS LEAV+   *950   2

FRUSTRATE
    THEIR BELLS SOUNDING FRUSTRATE AND SINISTER   391   4

FRUSTRATING
    IN FRUSTRATING HER JUST INWARDLY FRUSTRATING HER   618 23

FRUSTRATION
    THAT'S WHY THE NIGHT FELL IN FRUSTRATION   390 28
    WITH FRUSTRATION HOW BEAUTIFUL   467 15
    AND WITH HIDEOUS SHRIEKS OF STEELY RAGE AND FRUSTRATION   676 3
    AND THEY SEND ARROWS OF ANGER BULLETS AND BOMBS OF FRUS+   *958 6

FRY
    A MAGISTRATE AND SIX FAT SMALLER FRY   633 15
    TO THE LESSER FRY IN THE HIERARCHY   681 4

F'R
    F'R A BIT   45 30
    F'R I TELL YER I H'ARENA MARRYIN' NONE   81 3
    I'M SORRY FOR THEE I'M SORRY F'R 'ER   83 22
    I'M SORRY F'R US A'   83 23

FUCHSIA
    AS THE FUCHSIA DOES DANGLING HER RECKLESS DROP   667 16

FUCUS-DARK
    DOWN BETWEEN THE STEEP SLOPES OF DARKNESS FUCUS-DARK SE+   321 35

FUEL
    MY LAST DEAR FUEL OF LIFE TO HEAP ON MY SOUL   74 19
    SO THROUGH THESE DAYS WHILE BURN ON THE FUEL OF LIFE   115 9
    THE LAST DEAR FUEL AND HEAP IT ON MY SOUL   *895 27
    THE LAST DEAR FUEL AND HEAP IT ON MY SOUL   *904 16
    AND THROUGH THESE YEARS WHILE I BURN ON THE FUEL OF LIFE   *930 9

FUGITIVE
    WHICH OPENS EARTH AND HEAVEN TO LOVE'S FUGITIVE GLOWING   854 14
    WHICH TREADS OUT THE GLOW OF FUGITIVE ORANGE LIGHT   858 11

FULFIL
    IN ONE FULFIL   97 5
    TO LIVE THEIR OWN LIFE FULFIL THEIR OWN ENDS   779 24
    OR WILL YOU FULFIL IT   783 16
    WHERE WE CAN LEARN TO FULFIL OUR NEW KNOWLEDGE OF MATER+   833 23

FULFILL
    SHE WATCHED MY HAND TO SEE WHAT IT WOULD FULFILL   125 12

FULFILLED
    FULFILLED AND ALONE   198 18
    AT STARTING OTHER LIFE FULFILLED MY OWN   218 14
    FULFILLED OF THE SLOW PASSION OF PITCHING THROUGH IMMEM+   354 12
    WHEN FULFILLED PEOPLE DIE   505 1
    TO SOMETHING FLOWERY AND FULFILLED AND WITH A STRANGE S+   677 16
    TILL THEY MOUNT AND FILL AND ALL IS FULFILLED OF GOD'S +   698 20

FULFILMEMT
    REAL FULFILMEMT WILL DO   265 14

FULFILMENT
    YOU ARE THE WISH AND I THE FULFILMENT   203 23
    THAT MY OWN FULFILMENT IS UP AGAINST ME   215 7
    THE CHARGE OF FULFILMENT   215 10
    FULFILMENT   265 11
    BUT ONLY FULFILMENT WILL DO   265 13
    BUT ACTUAL FULFILMENT   265 18
    FOR THE MAIN ALREADY IS FULFILMENT   265 30
    AND WRINKLED RIPE FULFILMENT   503 16
    IS THE FULFILMENT OF NOTHINGNESS   511 2
    LIKE GLITTERING SEED UPON THEM FOR FULFILMENT   743 5
    AND SUPERFICIAL ATTENTION AND CARE AND FULFILMENT OF DU+   832 16

FULL
    SILENCE FULL OF SUMMONS   40 2
    THE GLOW OF THY FULL DESIRE   40 7
    FROM THE FULL RESOURCE OF SOME PURPLE DOME   50 10
    IS FULL OF DREAMS MY LOVE THE BOYS ARE ALL STILL   52 14
    THERE LIES THE WORLD MY DARLING FULL OF WONDER AND WIST+   52 20
    OF THE BOOKS THAT LIE OUT ON THE DESKS A FULL THREESCORE   74 13
    ME FULL LENGTH IN THE COWSLIPS MUTTERING YOU LOVE   90 16
    FULL ANGUISH PERHAPS HAD BEEN CAST   111 31
    BUT SINCE MY LIMBS GUSHED FULL OF FIRE   118 1
    FULL OF DISAPPOINTMENT AND OF RAIN   119 12
    O THE GREY GARNER THAT IS FULL OF HALF-GROWN APPLES   120 5
    STRANGLED MY HEART SWELLED UP SO FULL   123 15
    THERE'S A MOON FULL BLOW   137 23
    OF CRYSTAL HEAVEN FALLS ONE FULL BLACK DROP   147 26
    LIKE A SOFT FULL DROP OF DARKNESS IT SEEMS TO SWAY   148 1
    FULL MID-BETWEEN THE CHAMPAIGN OF YOUR BREAST   154 8
    THE TIME IS NOW THE WINE-CUP FULL AND FULL   177 9
    TILL MY HANDS ARE FULL OF THE CHILLNESS AND TOUCH OF LE+   180 35
    SOONER THAN OUR FULL CONSUMMATION HERE   193 12
    FOR WHEN AT NIGHT FROM OUT THE FULL SURCHARGE   195 1
    STILL IN FULL FLIGHT EXTINCT SHALL I THEN TURN   195 23
    NOT LIKE THE EARTH THE SPOUSE ALL FULL OF INCREASE   197 10
    HIS DARK EYES FULL OF PAIN   202 2
    I SEE YOU AH IN FULL   210 14
    IN THE WINDOW FULL OF SUNLIGHT   217 23
    FULL OF FINE WARMTH I ISSUE FORTH IN CLEAR   218 7
    FULL IN MY OWN AND THE TORMENT STARTS AGAIN   225 24
    AGAIN THE LOVE SO FULL   229 13
    HOW FULL AND BIG LIKE A ROBUST HAPPY FLAME   246 13
    BUT NOW I AM FULL AND STRONG AND CERTAIN   247 1
    AND MY STILL HEART FULL OF SECURITY   250 11
    AND MY STILL HANDS FULL OF HER BREASTS   250 12
    FULL OF SWEET STILLNESS   261 20
    THE FULL MOON SANK IN STATE   261 23
    WE SHALL KNOW IN FULL   268 12
    NUDE WITH THE DIM LIGHT OF FULL HEALTHY LIFE   298 26
    WINGS FULL OF STARS THEY RULE THE NIGHT AND MAN THAT WA+   319 3
    SUDDEN DEMONIC DAUNTLESSNESS FULL ABREAST   371 10
    AND FULL OF MALICE PREPENSE AND OVERWEENING DETERMINED   382 12
    HER FULL ANTIPODAL EYES SO DARK   393 11
    HOW FULL HER EYES ARE LIKE THE FULL FATHOMLESS SHINING +   394 6

FULL
    ENGLAND SEEMS FULL OF GRAVES TO ME   410 1
    FULL OF GRAVES   410 2
    THE FULL DOOM OF LOVING AND NOT BEING ABLE TO TAKE BACK   410 16
    OVERWEENING MEN FULL OF POWER OF LIFE COMMANDING A   414 19
    FULL OF SEETHING WORMY HOLLOW FEELINGS   431 22
    AS FULL OF WET AS A WATERING-CAN   434 15
    BUT WHEN OUR EAGERNESS LEAVES US WE ARE GODLESS AND FULL   439 19
    IT WAS FULL OF UNEASY PEOPLE   444 11
    GROW FULL OF DESIRE   465 20
    FOR THE FULL REPAST   465 26
    THE MOSQUITO KNOWS FULL WELL SMALL AS HE IS   466 18
    HIS WONDERFUL SPEECHES FULL OF OTHER FOLKS' WHORING   494 21
    AND FULL OF WINE   498 23
    ELDERLY DISCONTENTED WOMEN ARE SO FULL OF THEMSELVES   502 4
    TO BE FULL OF THE PEACE THAT COMES OF EXPERIENCE   503 15
    FULL OF INORDINATE ACTIVITIES   510 27
    TILL AT LAST IT'S A FULL FULL ROSE AND HAS NO MALE DUST+   535 7
    LET'S HAVE NO FULL STOPS LET'S JUST MANAGE WITH COMMAS   550 28
    IF FIRST A MAN COULD HAVE HIS FULL REVENGE   628 11
    YET LOOKING IN A GREAT FULL LIME-TREE OF SUMMER   650 21
    AND WHOEVER WALKS A MILE FULL OF FALSE SYMPATHY   653 1
    THREE BAGS FULL   669 22
    FULL OF FRICTION FULL OF GRINDING FULL OF DANGER TO THE+   675 27
    WITH THE FULL THIGHS SLOWLY LIFTING OF THE WADER WADING+   693 10
    THE EARTH'S LONG CONICAL SHADOW IS FULL OF SOULS   721 15
    FOR WHEN WE KNOW IN FULL WE HAVE LEFT OFF   725 23
    OF FULL DESPAIR I LIFT MY TENDER FLAME   745 13
    SWIFTLY I WISH I MIGHT KISS HER FINGERS BUT FULL   752 11
    IT'S A FULL MOON   755 17
    OH THE MOIST FULL WATER-JAR   759 5
    WITH FIRE AND MY THROAT IS FULL   802 25
    LET US IN FULL KNOW   818 21
    STRETCHING THEIR BIG FULL LIMBS TO SEEK   827 13
    FULL INSIDE OF WEIRD BROWN SLUSHY CRAB-MEAT   830 20
    FULL FORE-AND-AFT IN GOOD GREY CREPE DE CHINE   835 28
    STARTLED AND FULL OF AGONY TO FIND HE HAD BUT SLEPT   859 18
    ITS COOL WEIGHT LAY FULL ON HER BOSOM NOW IT ROLLS TO R+   864 15
    THE MOUTH OF THE MAN IS FULL OF THE TASTE OF PAIN   864 22
    SHONE SWEETLY THROUGH YELLOW SILK A MAN FULL IN THE LIG+   865 2
    HIS FULL FINE BODY BENDING AND URGING LIKE THE STRESS O+   867 24
    THREADING THE ROUND JOY OF HIS WHITE-FLANNELLED HIPS FU+   867 30
    HIS FULL ROUND HIPS SUPPORTING HIM ABOVE HER   868 9
    A PRIESTESS EXECRATED FULL OF STAIN   874 1
    FILLING HIS SINGLE MEASURE WITH MUSIC FULL   877 27
    FOR THE FULL MOON SHONE BUT WHETHER   881 32
    OF THE BOOKS THAT LIE OUT ON THE DESKS A FULL THREE SCO+   *895 21
    OF THE BOOKS THAT LIE OUT ON THE DESKS A FULL THREE SCO+   *904 10
    IS FULL OF DREAMS MY LOVE THE BOYS ARE ALL STILL   *905 3
    THERE LIES THE WORLD MY DARLING FULL OF WONDER AND WIST+   *905 9
    THE STREET THAT IS FULL OF THE RUSTLING SOUND OF A SHELL   *917 2
    BUT THE NIGHT IS FULL OF THE FLUTTER OF INVISIBLE REVEL+   *918 10
    FULL OF DISAPPOINTMENT AND OF RAIN   *932 21
    STRANGLED MY HEART SWELLED UP SO FULL   *934 21
    DRY FEVER IN HER POOL OF FULL TWILIGHT   *936 33
    TO STREW ROUND OUR WAY TO DIMINISH EACH FULL STAR'S GLI+   *938 6
    THE FULL THROATED WOMAN HAS CHOSEN A WINNING LIVING SONG   *940 9
    IN THE WINDOW FULL OF SUNLIGHT   *943 6
    AND MY STILL HEART FULL OF SECURITY   *946 9
    AND MY STILL HANDS FULL OF HER BREASTS   *946 10

FULL-BLOWN
    SWAY LIKE FULL-BLOWN YELLOW   217 17
    LIKE FULL-BLOWN FLOWERS DIMLY SHAKING AT THE NIGHT   *897 26
    LIKE FULL-BLOWN FLOWERS DIMLY SHAKING AT THE NIGHT   *901 3
    AND RIVER-LAMPS LIKE FULL-BLOWN ROSES   *916 21
    SWING LIKE FULL-BLOWN YELLOW   *942 26

FULLER
    FOR THE FEEDING AND STRENGTHENING OF THE HANDSOMER FULL+   679 10

FULL-EXPIATE
    THE CRIME FULL-EXPIATE THE ERINNYES SUNK   743 25

FULL-FED
    AND SUNBURNT AND WATER-WASHED FULL-FED AND SLEEK   827 11
    FULL-FED IN STALL   827 33
    WITH FULL-FED MEAT   828 7
    TILL THY FULL-FED FIRE OF CURIOSITY BORE YOU   *927 8

FULLNESS
    LIKE THE FULLNESS OF OCEAN ROUND MY FARAGLIONI   835 34

FULL-SAPPY
    THROWN LUSTILY OFF FROM OUR FULL-SAPPY HIGH   127 8

FULL-UNFOLDED
    THINK TO STAND THERE IN FULL-UNFOLDED NUDITY SMILING   306 17

FULLY
    THE ONLY REASON FOR LIVING IS BEING FULLY ALIVE   522 9
    AND YOU CAN'T BE FULLY ALIVE IF YOU ARE CRUSHED BY SECR+ 522 10
    A MAN CAN'T FULLY LIVE UNLESS HE DIES AND CEASES TO CARE 613 1

FULMINATIVE
    AND THE FATHER WAS ONCE GREY-BEARDED AND FULMINATIVE   *946 14

FULNESS
    FLOW THE HEART'S RIVERS OF FULNESS DESIRE AND DISTRESS   607 8
    IT IS THE MOMENT OF FULNESS   803 10
    SO THEY BLOOMED OUT AND FILLED THEMSELVES WITH COLOURED+ 831 3
    AS WILD WHITE FOX GLOVES DROOPING WITH FULNESS   874 26

FUMBLING
    FUMBLING A BEAST IN AIR   343 10

FUME
    OF GREYNESS MINGLED WITH A FUME OF GOLD   135 14
    IN THE FUME OF COCOA-NUT OIL IN THE SWEATING TROPICAL N+   387 36
    WAS FUME AS I TROD   404 27
    IS IT ILLUSION OR DOES THE PALLOR FUME   720 1
    OF BLUENESS MINGLED WITH A FUME OF GOLD   *939 14

FUMED
    OR THEY BOILED AND THEY FUMED IN FURY THEY SNEERED   578 9

FUMES
    WHERE THE WOOD FUMES UP AND THE FLICKERING WATERY   116 4
    ESCAPING THE PETROL FUMES OF HUMAN CONVERSATION   646 6
    FUMES   703 19
    AS OVER SOME DENSE MARSH THE FUMES   703 21
    THICKEN MIASMA THE FUMES OF THE AUTOMOBILE   703 22
    THROUGH THE MIRE OF FUMES   704 9
    THAT FUMES A LITTLE WITH PALLOR UPON THE DARK   719 30

FUMING
    ON HIGH TO THE FUMING SKY OF NIGHT   105 2
    WHAT DOES SHE WANT VOLCANIC VENUS AS SHE GOES FUMING   539 10

FUN
    TER ME IT'S NO FUN   84 28
    IF IT'S NEVER ANY FUN   450 22
    THEIR LITTLE LIVES ARE FUN TO THEM   466 16
    IF YOU MAKE A REVOLUTION MAKE IT FOR FUN   517 1
    DO IT FOR FUN   517 4
    AND IT WOULD BE FUN TO UPSET THE APPLE-CART   517 11
    WORK CAN BE FUN AND MEN CAN ENJOY IT THEN IT'S NOT   517 20
    LET'S HAVE IT SO LET'S MAKE A REVOLUTION FOR FUN   517 22
    NOTHING IS REALLY ANY FUN TODAY   517 23
    NO FUN   517 26
    A MAN CAN'T GET ANY FUN OUT OF WIFE SWEETHEART OR TART   518 4
    FUN   520 21
    AND HAVE A LITTLE FUN   560 26
    FOR FREEDOM AND THE FUN OF LIVING   560 31
    YOU'VE TOLD THEM THAT LIFE ISN'T REALLY MUCH FUN   583 6
    WHEN SHE READS THAT HER LIFE ISN'T REALLY MUCH FUN   583 11
    WHAT FUN STRONGER THAN MINE   605 13

FUNCTION
    I QUAILED AT MY APPOINTED FUNCTION TURNED POLTROON   194 29
    AS LITTLE SOCIAL ANTS PERHAPS WE FUNCTION ALL RIGHT   544 11

FUNERAL
    FUNERAL   496 2
    WALKS TO THE FUNERAL OF THE WHOLE HUMAN RACE   653 2
    BUT NEVER THE GHOST OF A GLIMPSE OF ANAXAGORAS' FUNERAL+   708 30
    THE DEAD ARE BURNING IN THE FUNERAL WIND   744 9
    BLACK FOR THE FUNERAL WOW WALY AND WORROW   815 3
    SHARPLY BEATS OUT A THRICE-TOLD FUNERAL KNELL   858 24

FUNGOID
    AND AN AMOUNT OF FUNGOID AND PARASITIC GROWTH   677 23
    SLOW SLOW FUNGOID CLAMMILY DECAY   784 28

FUNGUS
    AND LIKE A FUNGUS LIVING ON THE REMAINS OF BYGONE LIFE   431 15
    ARE THEY JUST THE DEADENING FUNGUS   765 20

FUNGUSSY
    THE SMOOTHED-FACED FAT-HAMMED FUNGUSSY FAT ONE   765 24

FUNNIEST
    BUT THE FUNNIEST THING THAT COULD BE   489 12

FUNNY
    LIKE A FUNNY TRIMMING TO THE MIDDLE OF HER BELLY THIN   393 19
    SO FUNNY   397 6
    A BIT AWKWARD AND WITH A FUNNY SQUAWK IN HIS VOICE   413 21
    THEN DOUBLED AND BACK WITH A FUNNY UP-FLUTTER OF WINGS   444 21
    AND IT'S FUNNY MY DEAR YOUNG MEN THAT YOU IN YOUR   462 29
    SUCH A FUNNY PUP IN ME   489 28
    IS EKKE SIR CLIFFORD IT'S REALLY FUNNY   669 1
    HOLALA MEXICANOS IT IS FUNNY   791 15
    WE'LL SEE THE JOKE AND HOW FUNNY IS SORROW   815 5
    THE FUNNY THING ABOUT A GENTLEMAN   830 3

FUR
    OF THE RABBIT'S FUR GOD I AM CAUGHT IN A SNARE   43 28
    OR RATHER 'TIS I AM NOTHING HERE IN THE FUR OF THE HEAT+   98 2
    I IN THE FUR OF THE WORLD ALONE BUT THIS HELEN CLOSE BY   98 6
    IN THE WINDOW HIS BODY BLACK FUR AND THE SOUND OF   243 24
    BROWN NUT-BROWN FINE FUR   345 33
    WHO IS LIKE A FUR FOLDING A FUR   383 2
    FUR ALL BRISTLING LIKE PLUSH   396 32
    ON TO THE FUR OF THE WOLF-PELT THAT STREWS THE PLAIN   409 20
    OUT OF THE WINTER'S SILKY FUR   814 13

FURL
    KEEP SUDDENLY SHOWING A WHITENESS A FLASH AND A FURL A +   687 2

FURLED
    BIRD WHO WAS WEARY TO HAVE FURLED   124 8
    ARE FURLED   175 20
    BIRD WHO WAS WEARY TO HAVE FURLED   *935 8

FURLS
    FOR THE SOUND OF THE SEA AS IT FURLS AND UNFURLS   747 21

FURNACE
    THIS FURNACE THIS DRAUGHT-MADDENED FIRE   241 18
    LIKE A FURNACE DRIPPING A MOLTEN DRIP   326 19
    FURNACE   344 19
    A BIT OF SLAG STILL ADHERING AFTER YOUR FIRING IN THE F+   370 2
    THAT ARE VIRGINS AT LAST FROM THE FURNACE WITH VIRGIN   771 6

FURNACE
    AH COIN ME SPEECH OF YOUR HEART'S GOLD FURNACE HEAT   872 27

FURNACE-CRACKS
    FROM THE FURNACE-CRACKS OF HIS SHOULDER-SOCKETS   326 13

FURNACE-DOORS
    THE OPEN FURNACE-DOORS OF HIS NOSTRILS   326 22

FURNACE-GATE
    THE MEN COME IN BY THE FURNACE-GATE OF THE WEST   771 10

FURNISH
    AND FURNISH IT WITH FOOD WITH LITTLE CAKES AND WINE   718 10

FURNISHED
    WITH EYES LIKE THE INTERIORS OF STUFFY ROOMS FURNISHED   656 24

FURNISHING
    SOME ONLY LIVE FOR THEIR EMOTIONAL FURNISHING   657 8

FURNISHINGS
    ALL THE FITTINGS AND ELABORATE FURNISHINGS   440 17
    FURNISHINGS   440 19

FURNITURE
    ALL AS WE S'LL WANT FOR FURNITURE WHEN THA LEAVES THIS +   83 3
    NEW HOUSES NEW FURNITURE NEW STREETS NEW CLOTHES NEW   448 14
    MENTAL FURNITURE   657 3
    SOME WOMEN LIVE FOR THE IDIOTIC FURNITURE OF THEIR HOUS+   657 6
    SOME MEN LIVE FOR THE CONCEITED FURNITURE OF THEIR MINDS   657 7
    AND IT ALL AMOUNTS TO THE SAME THING FURNITURE   657 9
    UGLY OLD FURNITURE UGLY OLD BOOKS UGLY OLD BUILDINGS UG+   678 14
    MONEY MACHINES FURNITURE   833 15
    ALL AS WE SHALL WANT FOR FURNITURE WHEN THA LEAVES THIS+ *925 7

FURRED
    COME AND SOFTEN THE WILLOW BUDS TILL THEY ARE PUFFED AN+   273 2

FURROWING
    NOR CLACKS ACROSS THE FORCES FURROWING A GREAT GAY TRAIL   436 3

FURROWS
    FURROWS OUR FEATHERLESS WOMEN   436 16

FURRY
    AND BROWN FURRY BODY   345 32
    HIS BIG FURRY HEAD   377 23

FURTHER
    I'M FURTHER OWER TH' TOP   78 32
    SO I PUT MY HAND OUT FURTHER A LITTLE FURTHER   259 7
    AND KINDLES IT FURTHER AT THE CORE OF UTTER MYSTERY   261 16
    A NEW GASP OF FURTHER ISOLATION   281 1
    BUT ONLY LOSE YOURSELF FURTHER DECOMPOSING   290 11
    AND BREAK FURTHER AND FURTHER DOWN   290 16
    STONE THAT CAN SINK NO FURTHER   383 12
    FURTHER STILL BEFORE THE CURLED HORNS OF THE RAM STEPPED   437 14
    MEANS ANYTHING FURTHER AND PHYSICAL   470 12
    AND FURTHER THE SUN WITHIN THE ATOM   513 19
    FURTHER THRILLING POSSIBILITIES   533 3
    THE WORLD IS MOVING MOVING STILL TOWARDS FURTHER DEMOCR+   611 6
    GOING A BIT FURTHER THAN HIS POCKET WHAT   659 16
    ON A DAY OF SPLENDOUR FOR THE FURTHER SPLENDOUR OF BEIN+   679 14
    WHICH GOES FURTHER AND FURTHER AND YET NEVER FINDS AN E+   701 6
    SO IT WRIGGLES ITS WAY EVEN FURTHER DOWN FURTHER DOWN   701 30
    THEIR LIMIT THEIR THUS FAR AND NO FURTHER   709 24
    YOU ABSTAIN FROM FURTHER INTERFERENCE   779 32
    WHICH RESTS IN CONNECTION WITH THE FURTHER FOREVER UNKN+   844 22
    FURTHER INTO ANOTHER RANK BEYOND   877 15
    AND FURTHER STILL 'NEATH THE SUNSET GATHER   887 28
    I'M FURTHER OWER TH' TOP   *920 24
    AS FURTHER OFF THE SCYTHE OF NIGHT IS SWUNG   *939 12
    AND FURTHER STILL BEFORE THE CURLED HORNS OF THE RAM ST+ *946 25

FURTHERMORE
    FURTHERMORE THE WHITE BIG-MEN SAID TO THE OLD INDIANS   778 17

FURTHEST
    PROUD BEYOND INKLING OR FURTHEST CONCEPTION OF PRIDE   258 31
    TO WHERE THE FURTHEST AND THE LONGEST SEA   *958 27

FURTIVE
    THE VOICE OF THE FURTIVE TRIUMPHANT ENGINE AS IT RUSHES+   58 4
    IN THE BLACK WET NIGHT AS THE FURTIVE RAIN SLINKS DOWN   143 2
    YOU WITH YOUR GRUDGING ENVIOUS FURTIVE RAGE   314 32
    AND SMILES AT MY FURTIVE SHADOW   731 11

FURTIVELY
    HOW COULD I LOOK WHEN I WAS MAD I LOOKED SIDEWAYS FURTI+   264 35
    THE PSALMS AND FURTIVELY FROM AMONG THE TEXTS   *894 17

FURY
    OR FLUFF UP IN INDIGNANT FURY LIKE A CAT   528 24
    OR THEY BOILED AND THEY FUMED IN FURY THEY SNEERED   578 9
    AND STRIKE WITH A BLINDNESS OF FURY AGAINST ME CAN I CA+ *926 24
    OR FLUFF UP IN INDIGNANT FURY LIKE A CAT   *950 27

FUSE
    NOT QUITE FUSE FROM THE DROSS   370 10
    AND FUSE IN A BROAD HARD FLAME OF MANY MEN IN A ONENESS   440 8
    YOU MUST FUSE MIND AND WIT WITH ALL THE SENSES   653 9
    FUSE TO IGNITE   788 12

FUSED
   THE MIND FUSED DOWN LIKE A BEAD   242 13
   IS THERE A RUBY OF FUSED BEING MINE AND YOURS AN INWARD   478 7
   THEY CAN'T THEY'RE SIMPLY FUSED   553 18
   FIRE-THRESHING ANGUISH HAD BEEN FUSED AND CAST   *927 19
   FIRE-THRESHING ANGUISH WERE FUSED AND CAST   *928 19

FUSING
   AND WATCH MY DEAD DAYS FUSING TOGETHER IN DROSS   47 3
   GREEN LANTERN OF PURE LIGHT A LITTLE INTENSE FUSING TRI+   206 10
   FUSING CLOSER AND CLOSER WITH LOVE   249 7
   O RIPPLING HARD FIRE OF COURAGE O FUSING OF HOT TRUST   440 13
   IN YOU IS TREMBLING AND FUSING   *907 2
   THE POWER OF THE MELTING FUSING FORCE   *907 23
   IN YOU IS TREMBLING AND FUSING   *908 23
   THE POWER OF THE MELTING FUSING FORCE HEAT LIGHT ALL IN+   *909 14

FUSION
   FUSION   440 6

FUSS
   WAS SUCH A MAN FOR FUSS   45 18
   WILL BE PASSING AWAY WE SHALL CEASE TO FUSS   471 18

FUTURE
   THE DIFFICULT GLEBE OF THE FUTURE   102 11
   NOR TOWARDS THE FUTURE   215 2
   FOR THE FUTURE HOW SURE THE FUTURE IS WITHIN ME   247 5
   INTO WHICH THE CREATIVE FUTURE SHALL BLOW STRANGE UNKNO+   428 29
   THAT DRIFTS UPON TIME AND CHAOS TILL SOME UNKNOWN FUTURE   429 5
   THAT FUTURE NOTTINGHAM LADS WOULD BE   489 1
   FUTURE   521 21
   THE FUTURE OF RELIGION IS IN THE MYSTERY OF TOUCH   611 10
   IF YOU WANT TO GET A GLIMPSE OF FUTURE POSSIBILITIES   612 8
   THE ILLUSION OF MANKIND THE ILLUSION OF A HOPEFUL FUTURE   639 21
   WHAT THE AMERICA OF THE FUTURE WILL BE WE DON'T KNOW   774 25
   WHAT WE KNOW IS THAT THE FUTURE AMERICA   774 26
   WE CAN'T KNOW WHAT THE FUTURE OF AMERICA WILL BE   775 1
   BUT THE GERM OF THAT FUTURE IS INSIDE THE AMERICAN PEOP+   775 2
   AND YET THERE IS A SPECK A GERM OF AMERICAN FUTURE   775 7
   AMERICAN FUTURE   775 11
   AMERICA STILL HAS ONLY AN UNREVEALED FUTURE   775 15
   TO AN UNBORN FUTURE THAN TO AN ACCOMPLISHED PAST   775 17
   AMERICA WILL HAVE TO FIND HER OWN WAY INTO THE FUTURE   775 32
   AND DAMAGE ONCE MORE THE FRAIL QUICK OF THE FUTURE   780 21
   WILL DREAM INTO THE FUTURE DID HE GUESS   878 10

F-
   LIKE B- AND F- AND SH-   491 16
   WAS WORDS LIKE SH- AND F-   491 22

GABBLING
   INTO GABBLING CONFUSION WITHOUT RESTING   54 5

GABRIEL
   ORTHODOX MICHAEL AND THAT WHISPERING GABRIEL   614 7
   MICHAEL AND GABRIEL ALL OF THEM SLAIN   823 13

GAD-FLIES
   THE OLIVE-LEAVES LIGHT AS GAD-FLIES   226 21

GADFLY
   ME LIKE A GADFLY INTO THE DUSK WITHOUT MY KNOWING   223 5

GAIETY
   TO MY GAIETY A FEW LONG GREY HAIRS   107 2
   YOUNG GAIETY   357 28
   OF GAIETY TOO OFTEN PAY ME THUS   872 24

GAILY
   SO SO GAILY A GENERAL CANTERS ACROSS THE SPACE   66 13
   AND MEN WOULD WORK GAILY   488 6
   SO THAT WE COULD ALL GET ALONG GAILY   518 24
   AND THERE ARE THE BRIGHT DOORS WHERE SOULS GO GAILY IN   711 3
   AND IN HER LEFT HAND GAILY   756 12
   THE BATS DEPRAVED ARE DROPPING GAILY FROM OFF THE TREE   *918 13

GAIT
   THE FLOOD'S SLOW GAIT   146 9
   I SAY HE CAN GO BACK THE SAME GAIT   405 24
   SHAKING THE HEATH-BELLS DOWN WITH HER PETULANT GAIT   863 23

GALL
   A NET ON THE UNDERSOIL THAT LIES PASSIVE AND QUICKENED +   94 4

GALLANT
   STIFF GALLANT IRASCIBLE CROOK-LEGGED REPTILE   363 19
   ALL HIS SOUL IN HIS GALLANT MEMBER   378 13

GALLANTRY
   GRIM GRUESOME GALLANTRY TO WHICH HE IS DOOMED   362 26

GALLING
   HOW IT DOGS ME WHAT A GALLING SHADOW   741 2

GALLIVANT
   PASSES THE GALLIVANT BEAM OF THE TRAMS   145 5

GALLOP
   LOOMING GALLOP OF THE BEASTS   390 36
   HOME AT A GALLOP   397 13

GALLOPED
   SWIFTNESS GALLOPED UPHILL IN THE NIGHT GOING BACK TO   390 30

GALLOPS
   THE WATER WE CAN AT THE GATES FOR THE HORSES HE GALLOPS   732 3

GAMBOLLING
   THE MOBILITY THE PANTHER'S GAMBOLLING   157 18

GAME
   AND LAUGHING WITH LABOUR LIVING THEIR WORK LIKE A GAME   72 11
   AT JUST THE SAME OLD DELICATE GAME   150 25
   SINGS ITSELF OVER AND SO THE GAME   151 23
   YET I'VE FORGOTTEN IN PLAYING THIS GAME   151 31
   ME THAT I INTERRUPT HER GAME   152 3
   PLAYING YOUR GREAT GAME AROUND THE WORLD ALONE   197 7
   YOU DEATH IN THE GAME   239 9
   BUT I KNOW YOUR GAME NOW STREAKY SORCERER   332 24
   AND SEE WHO WINS IN THIS SLY GAME OF BLUFF   333 8
   OH YES I KNOW YOUR LITTLE GAME   396 26
   ALL YOUR GAME LITTLE BODY DUST-SMOOTH LIKE A LITTLE PIG   397 26
   PLENTY OF GAME OLD SPIRIT IN YOU BIBBLES   397 28
   PLENTY OF GAME OLD SPUNK LITTLE BITCH   397 29
   I KNOW YOUR GAME   398 22
   ALL THE CREATURES SEEMED TO ENJOY THE GAME   445 22
   LIKE AN ABSORBING GAME   450 20
   OF THE GAME OF LIFE   452 8
   SUCCESS IS A PLAYED-OUT GAME SUCCESS SUCCESS   518 14
   THEY OUGHT AT LAST TO SEE THROUGH THE GAME   559 23
   IS A BLANK AT THE GAME   564 32
   HAVE A GAME OF TENNIS GO OUT IN THE CAR DO SOME SHOPPIN+   651 21
   I DESPISE THAT SELF-IMPORTANT GAME   673 9
   HAIL AND BE DAMNED TO THEE WINNING THE GAME   824 17
   I LEAVE YOU WHILE I PLAY MY GAME OF LIVING   875 37
   I PLAY MY RECKLESS GAME TO WIN MY POINT   876 1
   I GO TO PLAY MY GAME OF LIFE WITHIN   876 9
   SO MUCH SO RARE A GAME SO QUICK A HEART-BEATING   876 15

GANDER
   GOOSEY GOOSEY GANDER   669 12

GANG
   A GANG OF LABOURERS ON THE PILED WET TIMBER   72 4

GANGS
   STROLLING IN GANGS AND STARING ALONG THE CORSO   312 19

GANG-STARE
   WITH THE GANG-STARE   312 20

GAOL
   TO GAOL TO BE HID FROM THE LIGHT OF DAY   579 16
   POLICEMEN AND ARRESTED THEM AND HAULED THEM OFF TO GAOL   632 33

GAOL-BIRD
   AND A WAGE-EARNER IS A SORT OF GAOL-BIRD   521 8
   A GAOLER INSTEAD OF A GAOL-BIRD   521 10

GAOLER
   A GAOLER INSTEAD OF A GAOL-BIRD   521 10

GAP
   IN FLAKES OF SHADOW DOWN WHILE THROUGH THE GAP   76 15
   THE GAP IN MY LIFE'S CONSTELLATION   115 17
   THIS CONFLAGRATION OF SPRING THE GAP IN IT ALL   116 11
   SO STILL IN THE GAP   223 17
   THE GAP OF YOUR SHIRT WHY COVER IT UP   254 10
   YET WHAT A GAP IN THE WORLD THE MISSING WHITE FROST-FACE   402 32
   IN ALL HONESTY A WORD IS NEITHER A GAP IN THE CONSCIOUS+   837 8
   IN FLAKES OF SHADOW DOWN AND THROUGH THE GAP   *898 9
   IN FLAKES OF SHADOW DOWN AND THROUGH THE GAP   *901 18

GAPE
   SLOWLY TO GAPE THROUGH THE WATERS   336 26
   TO GAPE AND OUR HOUSE IS GOING TO WRACK   462 14

GAPED
   IN THE FLOWER'S THROAT AND THE FLOWER GAPED WIDE WITH W+   125 10
   IN THE FLOWER'S THROAT AND THE FLOWER GAPED WIDE WITH W+   *935 26
   MY FINGERS TILL ITS HEAD GAPED BACK ITS FANGS   *936 13

GAPES
   MY CHEST GAPES OPEN SOMETIMES   869 1

GAPING
   THE GORGE OF THE GAPING FLOWER TILL THE BLOOD DID FLOAT   123 18
   THOUSANDS AND THOUSANDS OF GAPING HIDEOUS FOUL DEAD   258 8
   GAPING PINCERS   353 6
   TAKING BREAD IN HER CURVED GAPING TOOTHLESS MOUTH   359 19
   THE GORGE OF THE GAPING FLOWER TILL THE BLOOD DID FLOAT   *934 24

GARBAGE
   SEEKING THE OFFAL AND GARBAGE OF LIFE IN THE INVISIBLE +   796 6
   CREEPING FOR THE GARBAGE OF LIFE AND BITING WITH VENOMO+   796 13

GARDEN
   INTO OUR SOOTY GARDEN HE DRAGS AND BEATS   47 16
   BEHIND THE BLACK SYCAMORE AT THE END OF THE GARDEN   62 26
   SHE MADE ME FOLLOW TO HER GARDEN WHERE   122 25
   THE BLIND TO HIDE THE GARDEN WHERE THE MOON   129 16
   FAR-OFF THE LILY-STATUES STAND WHITE-RANKED IN THE GARD+   159 19
   GARDEN WHICH GOD HAS HOARDED   243 11
   IN THE DENSE FOLIAGE OF THE INNER GARDEN   278 12
   IN THE GARDEN RAYING OUT   306 29
   OVER THE GARDEN EARTH   354 15
   SCATTERED IN THE GARDEN   357 19
   THINK OF IT IN A GARDEN OF INERT CLODS   358 8
   IN A GARDEN OF PEBBLES AND INSECTS   358 11

GARDEN
  THE GARDEN ONCE A YEAR   358 27
  THE BROKEN GREEK TOMB IN THE GARDEN   384 5
  QUEER IT IS SUDDENLY IN THE GARDEN   385 15
  BENEATH ENGLAND'S GARDEN STONES   492 14
  THE WILD ROSE IN A SHELTERED GARDEN   535 1
  AS THE GREEN GRASS GLOWS UPWARDS STRANGERS IN THE GARDEN   647 7
  IN THE GREEN GARDEN DARKENED THE SHADOW OF COMING RAIN   672 12
  AND WATCHED FOR YOUR GLISTENING FEET DOWN THE GARDEN PA+   696 11
  BUTTERFLY THE WIND BLOWS SEA-WARD STRONG BEYOND THE GAR+   696 12
  HERE IN THE GARDEN WITH RED GERANIUMS IT IS WARM IT IS +   696 18
  THE GREY NURSE ENTERED A ROSE GARDEN   753 8
  APPEAL FROM THE GARDEN   758 1
  SHE BADE ME FOLLOW TO HER GARDEN WHERE   *934 1

GARDENER
  ON THE GARDENER WHOSE SHIRT'S BLOWN BACK   633 27

GARMENT
  ABOUT YOU AS A GARMENT EASILY   122 11

GARMENTLESS
  YOU GLISTENING GARMENTLESS BEAUTY   695 14
  CROWNLESS AND JEWELLESS AND GARMENTLESS   695 17
  INTO YOUR HOUSE GARMENTLESS LADY OF THE LAST GREAT GIFT   696 3

GARMENTS
  MY PAIN LIKE GARMENTS   134 7
  GARMENTS GONE   171 8
  IN THEIR RAG GARMENTS SCUTTLING THROUGH THE STREETS   530 16
  MY GARMENTS OFF BUT ALL EVEN MEMORY   738 10

GARNER
  O THE GREY GARNER THAT IS FULL OF HALF-GROWN APPLES   120 5

GARNERING
  IN THE GARNERING AUTUMN A GLOW OF IMMORTAL FRUIT   855 17

GAS
  LIKE A POISON GAS   291 14
  THAT SHE EXUDES LIKE PEARLY WHITE POISON GAS   619 21
  USING ALL LIFE ONLY AS POWER AS AN ENGINE USES STEAM OR+   635 11
  AND GOD THE HOLY GHOST IS GAS THAT KEEPS IT ALL GOING   641 5
  AND THE HUMAN SPIRIT IS SO MUCH GAS TO KEEP IT ALL GOING   641 8
  IS THE PYRE OF BLAZING GAS   702 24
  LUBRICATING OIL EXHAUST GAS   703 20

GASES
  ARE POISON GASES AND AIR-BOMBS   715 17

GASP
  SLIPS AWAY SO I GASP IN SURPRISE   38 33
  AND A GASP OF RELIEF BUT THE SOUL IS STILL COMPRESSED   167 15
  A NEW GASP OF FURTHER ISOLATION   281 1

GASPED
  IN THAT MOST AWFUL STILLNESS THAT ONLY GASPED AND HUMMED   372 7

GASPING
  UNFINISHED FOR EVER BUT GASPING FOR MONEY AS THEY DREAM+   175 5
  AND FLOWING INVISIBLY GASPING   480 17
  BY A SLOW GASPING PUMP THAT HAS AWFUL INTERVALS   878 34

GASPS
  LIFTING AND FALLING LONG GASPS THROUGH THE SLUICES LIKE+   97 26
  SHORT GASPS OF FLAME IN THE GREEN OF NIGHT WAY OFF   606 1

GAS-TAR
  YET THE LANGUAGE SO LOVELY LIKE THE DYES FROM GAS-TAR   494 26

GASTHAUS
  AT THE DOOR OF THE GASTHAUS DOWN THE ROAD GREAT   732 21

GASTHAUS GREEN HAT
  MARIA OF THE GASTHAUS GREEN HAT WOLFRATSHAUSEN   734 33

GATE
  IT WILL FIND ME WATCHING AT THE MARRIAGE GATE   58 28
  TO LEAP DOWN AT OUR GATE   100 8
  NOR ONE NARROW GATE FOR THE MOON TO GO   103 7
  AT THE GATE THE NETS HUNG BALKING   152 16
  THROUGH THE STRAIT GATE OF PASSION   242 8
  WE APPROACH THE GATE   242 19
  FOR HER WATCHERS TO SHUT THE GATE   261 25
  THAT MY HEART WHICH LIKE A LARK AT HEAVEN'S GATE SINGIN+   322 30
  A GATE TO THE FLOOD   563 2
  LEANS LISTENING ON THE GATE IN ALL RESPECT   688 20
  BUT A NAKED MAN A STRANGER LEANED ON THE GATE   692 10
  NOW I AM AT YOUR GATE YOU BEAUTY YOU LADY OF ALL NAKEDN+   695 22
  NOW LADY OF THE MOON NOW OPEN THE GATE OF YOUR SILVERY +   696 1
  FOR NOW WE ARE PASSING THROUGH THE GATE STILLY   699 3
  ARE DUCKING THEIR HEADS IN THE WATER TUBS AT THE GATE   732 19
  DOWN TO THE GATE AND STAND AND WAIT   734 25
  FOR A WORD HE IS COMING TOWARDS THE GATE   734 26
  FOR THE WORD NOW LET US GO THROUGH THE GATE   757 19
  THE WOMEN BY THE GATE OF THE EAST   771 11
  THEY STRUGGLE AT THE GATE YOU HAVE OPENED   795 32
  SHINES AT THE GATE   811 2
  ONCE OUTSIDE THE GATE OF THE WALLED SILVERY LIFE OF DAYS   *957 27
  ONCE OUTSIDE THE GATE   *957 32

GATES
  THEY HAVE TAKEN THE GATES FROM THE HINGES   40 21
  IN STUPOR PERSIST AT THE GATES OF LIFE OBSTINATE DARK M+   75 12
  FIVE VALLEYS GO FIVE PASSES LIKE GATES   224 5
  GATES OF THE LONG-DISCARDED   243 10
  IN THE SACRED SILENCE OF GATES   699 4
  LIFT UP YOUR HEADS O YE GATES   699 9

GATES
  IN ALL THE CITIES WITH LION GATES   704 2
  THE WATER WE CAN AT THE GATES FOR THE HORSES HE GALLOPS   732 3
  THEN LEAD THEM TO THE GATES OF THE UNKNOWN   740 19
  SOMEONE WILL ENTER BETWEEN THE GATES   788 26
  O YE GATES EVEN LIFT THEM UP   818 6
  LIFT UP YOUR HEADS O YE GATES   818 10

GATHER
  WE COULD GATHER UP THE DRY HAY FROM   35 13
  I WANTED TO GATHER THEM ONE BY ONE   227 15
  CAN I GATHER THE MOUNTAIN-TIPS   227 18
  NOW I GATHER YOU UP   239 10
  THAT IS A GRAND OLD LUST OF HIS TO GATHER THE GREAT   381 23
  GATHER HIS WILL AND HIS ENERGY TOGETHER   428 20
  TO GATHER AND FORTIFY THEMSELVES IN EVERY CLASS IN EVER+   666 3
  AND BULL-WHALES GATHER THEIR WOMEN AND WHALE-CALVES IN +   695 1
  AND I'D GATHER MY HAIR   836 1
  AND GATHER MY BURNING BEAUTIFUL DREAMS FOR HER SHARE   874 8
  AND FURTHER STILL 'NEATH THE SUNSET GATHER   887 28
  MYSELF AND GATHER THE WATERS BENEATH ME AND LOSE   *894 22

GATHERED
  WHERE IT GATHERED TOWARDS THE PLAIT ON THAT VERY LAST D+   114 23
  THE BEGGAR HAD GATHERED AT NIGHT   202 18
  JUST A FEW OF THE ROSES WE GATHERED FROM THE ISAR   217 27
  AND THE WOOD-ASH GATHERED IN THE FIRE   248 18
  WHEN I GATHERED FLOWERS I KNEW IT WAS MYSELF PLUCKING MY   257 1
  BEFORE THE GLACIERS WERE GATHERED UP IN A BUNCH OUT OF +   285 19
  THE SOCIALISTS HAVE GATHERED UPON US TO LOOK AT US   312 11
  SLOW INFIRM DEATH HAS AT LAST GATHERED UP THE WASTE   859 21
  JUST A FEW OF THE ROSES WE GATHERED FROM THE ISAR   *943 10

GATHERING
  NUTTING GATHERING NUTS OF RIPE EXPERIENCE   504 12
  GATHERING THE SOFT RIPPLES BELOW MY BREASTS   *893 18
  ARE GATHERING TO A WEDDING IN THE WINTER DARK   *955 21

GATHERS
  EVEN THE STUPIDEST FARMER GATHERS HIS HAY IN BLOOM IN   587 8
  GATHERS ITSELF FIERCELY TOGETHER   *893 22

GAUDS
  FLOWERS OF ILLUSION WHO SHINE IN OUR GAUDS MAKE A PARAD+   71 17

GAUNT
  WHITE AND GAUNT WITH WISTFUL EYES THAT HOVER   47 11
  GAUNT GAUNT THEY CROWD THE GREY MUD-BEACHES OF SHADOW   722 6
  THE POOR GAUNT DEAD THAT CANNOT DIE   722 9
  GAUNT AND HORRIBLE   *958 10
  PITY THE POOR GAUNT DEAD THAT CANNOT DIE   *958 14

GAVE
  THEN GAVE THEE THY DARK EYES O MAN THAT ALL   69 20
  HURT AS I GAVE THEM YOU PUT ME AWAY   87 11
  TO CONSCIOUSNESS YOU GAVE ME THE DOUR   111 16
  SHE GAVE ON THE OPEN HEATHER   202 13
  HE GAVE HER NO CROWN OF FLOWERS   202 21
  GAVE ME SWEET LYMPH AGAINST THE SALT-BURNS   208 6
  WHO GAVE US FLOWERS   307 17
  AS HE GAVE HIMSELF FORTH   326 32
  AND THE CROWD LIKE A FIELD OF RICE IN THE DARK GAVE WAY   390 34
  AND GAVE YOU A COUPLE OF NUTS   549 10
  IT WAS YOU WHO GAVE HER HER FIRST KISS   550 21
  THIS IS WHAT YOU GAVE HIM LEAVE TO DO   629 4
  AND GAVE A BOARD-SCHOOL EDUCATION NEWSPAPERS AND THE   630 24
  WHO BEGGED OF YOU AND GAVE YOU HOMAGE   696 10
  THE BIRD GAVE A CLUCK THE COW GAVE A COO   761 4
  HOW GAVE THESE PALEFACES YELLOWFACES CROSSED THE WATERS+   794 30
  FOR IT GAVE THE SMART   *897 18
  THEN GAVE THEE THY DARK EYES O MAN THAT ALL   *916 3

GAWKY
  COME AND CAJOLE THE GAWKY COLT'S-FOOT FLOWERS   273 4
  SO LONG AS YOU LEAD THE GAWKY CHOIR   680 21

GAY
  AND STOLEN KISSES SHALLOW AND GAY   42 13
  ON THE SHORES OF THIS CEASELESS OCEAN GAY BIRDS OF THE   71 18
  DIM SELF THAT RISES SLOWLY TO LEAVES AND THE FLOWER'S G+   92 20
  AND THE WHITE SHINING HOUSES AND THE GAY RED FLOWERS ON   205 2
  THEN GAY FEAR THAT TURNS THE TAIL SPRIGHTLY FROM A SHAD+   336 18
  NOR CLACKS ACROSS THE FORCES FURROWING A GREAT GAY TRAIL   436 3
  SONG AND CHIRRUPING GAY FEATHERS FLUFF-SHADOWED   443 17
  HORSES GAY HORSES SWIRLING ROUND AND PLAITING   445 19
  FLICKERING GAY   445 32
  AND THEY GRUDGE THE CIRCUS PEOPLE THE SWOOPING GAY   446 8
  IN MENTAL CONTACT GAY AND SAD   469 2
  GAY AND AMUSING TOGETHER AND FREE   470 7
  WHY CAN'T PEOPLE BE GAY LIKE THAT   496 9
  AND GAY FLICKER OF JOYFUL LIFE   523 23
  AND THE WHITE SNOW GLISTENED THE WHITE WORLD WAS GAY   550 29
  HAS A GAY LITTLE GLINT   562 22
  FEELING ANYTHING BUT GAY   569 20
  PEOPLE ARE LIKE LEAVES FLUTTERING AND GAY ON THE BUSH O+   615 7
  ROBOT VOICES ROBOT EVEN THE GAY UMBRELLAS   651 3
  SHE IS THE GAY DELIGHTED PORPOISE SPORTING WITH LOVE AN+   695 10
  NOR YET THE GAY LORD RIBBLESDALE   835 24
  THERE WAS A GAY BIRD NAMED CHRISTINE   845 17
  STILL GAY AND LAUGHING IN MY OWN VAIN STRENGTH   875 30
  BEYOND THE GAY PINK BLOSSOM   886 23
  AND ONCE HE WAS GAY AND HEARTY WITH HIS EYE ON THE IMMO+   *946 17

GAYER
  HE FEELS MUCH GAYER THAN IF SOMEBODY HAD LEFT HIM A FOR+   496 7

GAZE
  WITH ME AS UNDER MY GAZE   59   6
  FACES OF PEOPLE BLOWING ACROSS MY GAZE   116   9
  TO GAZE ANY MORE AT THE CHRIST WHOM THE MOUNTAIN SNOWS   225 11
  SHORN LIKE THE SHORN LAMB TO EVERY ICY GAZE   836   4

GAZED
  AND GAZED AND GLOATED WITHOUT RHYME   578   4

GAZELLE
  THE GAZELLE CALF O MY CHILDREN   466   9

GAZELLE-CALF
  THE GAZELLE-CALF OH MY CHILDREN   757   8

GAZES
  TO THE FACE THAT GAZES OUTWARDS WATCHING FOR NIGHT TO W+   103   2

GAZING
  THE CONFINES GAZING OUT BEYOND WHERE THE WINDS GO FREE   47 10
  THOUGHT IS GAZING ON TO THE FACE OF LIFE AND READING WH+   673 12

GEAR
  OF ALL THIS GEAR   169   8

GEESE
  AND BABIES OF WOMEN WILL COME OUT YOUNG WILD GEESE   438 23
  THE GEESE THAT SAVED ROME AND WILL LOSE LONDON   438 25
  AND THEN THE GEESE SCUTTLED IN IN A LITTLE FLOCK   444 19
  SHAKEN THE MARSHES TILL THE GEESE HAVE GONE   624   1
  TILL GEESE CAN SWIM IN YOUR POOLS   754 14
  AND WILD GEESE O MY HEART   *947 25
  AND THE GEESE THAT SAVED ROME WILL LOSE LONDON   *947 26
  SHAKEN THE MARSHES TILL THE GEESE HAVE GONE   *953 19

GEL
  MY GEL OWT'LL DO FOR A MAN I' TH' DARK   77   3
  AN' OFF TO A GEL AS WOR YOUNGER THAN ME   138 11
  MY GEL OWT'LL DO FOR A MAN I' THE DARK   *918 21

GELDED
  AND WE ARE THE GELDED THIRD AND FOURTH GENERATION   627 28

GELDINGS
  AND MEN BEING MOSTLY GELDINGS AND KNACKER-BONED HACKS   379 31

GEM
  AND A GEM   476   2
  BUT A GEM IS DIFFERENT IT LASTS SO MUCH LONGER THAN WE +   476 21
  SLOWLY A GEM FORMS IN THE ANCIENT ONCE-MORE-MOLTEN   477 13
  THE GEM OF MUTUAL PEACE EMERGING FROM THE WILD CHAOS   477 19
  IS THERE A GEM WHICH CAME INTO BEING BETWEEN US   478   5

GEMMED
  SELF-FORGETFUL AND GEMMED WITH EXPERIENCE   478 16

GEMS
  HARDENED THEY ARE LIKE GEMS IN TIME-LONG PRUDERY   127 22
  BREAKS LIGHT INTO GEMS AND DEAD BREASTS WHITER   168 17
  IN THE DAYS CALLED CHAOS WHICH LEFT US ROCKS AND GEMS   529 25

GEN
  WHAT 'ER GEN 'ER GEN ME   84   5
  'ER GEN ME SUMMAT I SHANNA   84   7

GENERAL
  SO SO GAILY A GENERAL CANTERS ACROSS THE SPACE   66 13
  SO HALF LIES ON THE SKY FOR A GENERAL SIGN   114 25

GENERATION
  WOMEN OF THE OLDER GENERATION WHO KNOW   410 15
  THE WORST OF THE YOUNGER GENERATION THOSE LATTER-DAY   531   1
  AND WE ARE THE GELDED THIRD AND FOURTH GENERATION   627 28
  GENERATION   829   5
  THE FIFTH GENERATION OF PURITANS WHEN IT ISN'T OBSCENEL+   845 15
  THE CREATION OF A NEW-PATTERNED DREAM DREAM OF A GENERA+   *907   3
  THE CREATION OF A NEW-PATTERNED DREAM DREAM OF A GENERA+   *908 24
  THE FIFTH GENERATION OF PURITANS WHEN IT ISN'T DEBAUCHED   *953   7

GENERATIONS
  FOR SO MUCH I THANK THE GOOD GENERATIONS OF MANKIND   263 14
  IN WHICH TO PICKLE THE YOUNGER GENERATIONS   495   7
  BECAUSE WE ARE THE THIRD AND FOURTH GENERATIONS   627 22
  THE GOOD THING ABOUT THE YOUNGER GENERATIONS   828 14
  AS THE ELDER GENERATIONS ARE APT TO DO   828 21
  I SPEAK OF THE YOUNGER GENERATIONS   833   6

GENEROSITY
  A DELIBERATE GENEROSITY NON-ORIENTAL   292 14
  GENEROSITY   522 27

GENEROUS
  AND CROWNS KINGLY GENEROUS TILTING CROWNS   278 19
  MASS OF A GENEROUS BREAST   370   7
  WITH A SOFT ONE WARMTH AND A GENEROUS   471   6
  TO BE ALIVE YOU'VE GOT TO FEEL A GENEROUS FLOW   522 24
  O SACRIFICE NOT THAT WHICH IS NOBLE AND GENEROUS AND SP+   679   1
  AND BECOMES AT LAST HELEN OR NINON ANY LOVELY AND GENER+   691 18
  FOR ALL THAT LIFE WILL ONLY BE GOOD AGAIN WHEN THERE IS+   838   1
  THE QUICK KINDLING SPARK OF A GENEROUS TRUST   855   8

GENEROUSLY
  HE SLEEPS AS EVER GENEROUSLY UNLOCKED   878   1

GENITALS
  O RUDDY GOD IN OUR VEINS O FIERY GOD IN OUR GENITALS   440 12
  WITHIN THE GENITALS OF LIVING SPACE   513 18
  GENITALS BRAINS AND SOULS   631 22
  BUT MY GOD THEY SNEAK-THIEFED HIS VERY GENITALS AWAY FR+   659 15
  IT HAS NEITHER HEART NOR BOWELS NOR GENITALS   830 28
  THAT WE HAVE BLOOD AND BOWELS AND LIVELY GENITALS   *953   3

GENT
  ABAHT IT YES I'M A GENT AN' LIZ   434 23

GENTEEL
  GENTEEL DEPRECATION   830 25

GENTIAN
  TELL ME IS THE GENTIAN SAVAGE AT THE TOP OF ITS COARSE +   684   2
  I WANT YOU TO BE AS SAVAGE AS THE GENTIAN AND THE DAFFO+   684   4
  REACH ME A GENTIAN GIVE ME A TORCH   697 13
  DOWN THE BLUE DEPTHS OF MOUNTAIN GENTIAN FLOWERS   *955 19
  REACH ME A GENTIAN GIVE ME A TORCH   *956 10

GENTIANS
  NOT EVERY MAN HAS GENTIANS IN HIS HOUSE   697   1
  BAVARIAN GENTIANS BIG AND DARK ONLY DARK   697   3
  OH BAVARIAN GENTIANS TALL ONES   *954 18
  BAVARIAN GENTIANS   *954 24
  DARK GENTIANS   *954 27
  OF GENTIANS HERE IN THE SUNNY ROOM   *955   3
  OF DARK-BLUE GENTIANS TO PLUTO   *955 14
  OF GENTIANS HERE IN THE SUNNY ROOM   *955 24
  NOT EVERY MAN HAS GENTIANS IN HIS HOUSE   *955 25
  BAVARIAN GENTIANS TALL AND DARK BUT DARK   *956   1

GENTLE
  THE CHURCH DRAWS NEARER UPON US GENTLE AND GREAT   48 17
  I DO NOT LIKE TO HEAR THE GENTLE GRIEVING   65 19
  AND THE GENTLE LEAVES AND HAVE FELT WHERE THE ROOTS ARE+   92 10
  THAT I AM THE HART AND YOU ARE THE GENTLE HIND   118 31
  GENTLE NURTURED FRAIL AND SPLENDID   313 32
  DELICATE FRAIL CRESCENT OF THE GENTLE OUTLINE OF WHITE   371 13
  HE IS QUITE GENTLE AND DARK-FACED   401 22
  WOMEN WHO WERE GENTLE   410   7
  WOMEN WITH EYES THAT WERE GENTLE IN OLDEN BELIEF IN LOVE   410 23
  HE CAN BE SO GENTLE SO GENTLE   447 17
  GENTLE WOMAN GONE MAD   475 22
  WOMEN MIGHT BE DEVOTED AND GENTLE   538 16
  THE GENTLE SOULS THAT FIGURE IN THE PAINT   580 22
  GENTLE AND REFINED   644   9
  FULL OF FRICTION FULL OF GRINDING FULL OF DANGER TO THE+   675 27
  AND THE GENTLE TROTTING OF THE LITTER-BEARERS   703 28
  BE CAREFUL THEN AND BE GENTLE ABOUT DEATH   721   8
  ON THE HORSE'S BELLY HURT HIM FOR HE WAS RATHER GENTLE   734 20
  AND MAKES A POINT OF BEING VERY GENTLE VERY TENDER   *948 12
  AND HE IS VERY GENTLE AND TENDER   *948 14

GENTLE-KNEED
  THE GENTLE-KNEED WOMEN   410 32

GENTLEMAN
  LIKE A GENTLEMAN IN A LONG-SKIRTED COAT   354 20
  THE FIRST LITTLE MATHEMATICAL GENTLEMAN   355 20
  LITTLE GENTLEMAN   363 20
  SO SPOKE THE BRITISH GENTLEMAN   433 14
  I WISH I WAS A GENTLEMAN   434 14
  IS A GENTLEMAN IF HE THINKS HIMSELF SO   434 20
  ALL THE HINGLISH IS GENTLEMAN AN' LIDIES   434 27
  WHO IS SURE HE IS A GENTLEMAN   446 20
  THIS MODERATELY YOUNG GENTLEMAN   446 22
  BECAUSE WE ENGLISH DO APPRECIATE A REAL GENTLEMAN OR A   548 15
  OH AUNTIE ISN'T HE A BEAUTY AND IS HE A GENTLEMAN OR   581 10
  WHEN HE'S A GENTLEMAN   830   2
  THE FUNNY THING ABOUT A GENTLEMAN   830   3
  AND BY GENTLEMAN I MEAN THAT UBIQUITOUS ENGLISHMAN   830   4
  WHO CONSIDERS HIMSELF A GENTLEMAN   830   5
  THIS NOBLE GENTLEMAN   *948   1

GENTLEMEN
  ONE OF NATURE'S GENTLEMEN   *947 28

GENTLENESS
  IT IS NO GOOD DEAR GENTLENESS AND FORBEARANCE I ENDURED+   92   7
  WITH GENTLENESS CAME I WITH MY HEART 'TWIXT MY HANDS LI+   92 22
  WOMEN I'VE LOVED FOR GENTLENESS   412 10
  YOU WHOM I LOVED FOR GENTLENESS   412 17
  EVEN NOW THE THOUGHT OF IT BEWILDERS ME SUCH GENTLENESS   447 19

GENTLY
  PUSHED GENTLY AWAY AND HIDDEN IN THE THICK OF HER HAIR   114 22
  AND THE SOUND OF HER GENTLY RUSTLING IN HEAVEN LIKE A   134 18
  AS SHE GENTLY EXHALES TO THE SUN   166 21
  WHERE DEAD MEN'S LIVES GLOW GENTLY AND IRON HURTS   173 22
  GENTLY AND FINELY LINED THAN A RABBIT'S OR THAN A HARE'S   393   7
  BUT IT BREATHES GENTLY AND LANGUISHINGLY IN THE BACK OF+   434   3
  BURY A MAN GENTLY IF HE HAS LAIN DOWN AND DIED   442   1
  ALL I ASK OF A WOMAN IS THAT SHE SHALL FEEL GENTLY TOWA+   479   1
  OH TOUCH THE HARP TOUCH THE HARP GENTLY MY DEARS   576   4
  AH MY NICE PICTURES LET ME SPONGE YOU VERY GENTLY   581   1
  GENTLY ISSUING FROM THE MASSED GREEN   854 22
  STRIVE WITH THE FORMLESS THINGS AND GENTLY TOUCH   872   6

GENTRY
  WHY SHOULD THE DELUGE WAIT WHILE THESE YOUNG GENTRY GO   531 13
  AND ALL THE SACRED GENTRY   557   1

GENTS
  YOUNG GENTS YOU'VE GOT NO OPTION   458   2
  PLAYING WITH MUCK AND I THOUGHT YOU YOUNG GENTS   463   9

GENUINE
  OF GENUINE PLEASURE   565   13
  EVEN THOUGH THEY GROW ON GENUINE ENGLISH MOULD   569   4
  GRANTED THERE IS AN EXCHANGE OF GENUINE FEELING   845   5

GEOMETRY
  AND GOD LIKE GEOMETRY   118   24
  AND GOD LIKE GEOMETRY   *932   2

GEORGELETS
  PETERLETS GEORGELETS HAMLETS   457   18

GEORGE WASHINGTON'S GRANDPAPA
  GEORGE WASHINGTON'S GRANDPAPA   681   25

GERANIUM
  IMAGINE THAT ANY MIND EVER THOUGHT A RED GERANIUM   690   14
  AS IF THE REDNESS OF A RED GERANIUM COULD BE ANYTHING B+   690   15
  GERANIUM   690   20
  HEY-PRESTO SCARLET GERANIUM   690   31
  THAT BLOSSOMED AT LAST RED GERANIUM AND MIGNONETTE   691   5

GERANIUMS
  WHEN GERANIUMS WERE NOT AND MIGNONETTE NEITHER   690   22
  HERE IN THE GARDEN WITH RED GERANIUMS IT IS WARM IT IS +   696   18

GERM
  THE ROUND EARTH ROLLS LIKE A GERM IN THE SKY   126   8
  AS HE PLANTS HIS NEW GERM IN US WHAT IS THERE TO SHUN   127   5
  MATE MY HUNGRY SOUL WITH A GERM OF ITS WOMB   179   27
  NEW PHASE IN THE GERM OF YOU   240   7
  IS A GERM LYING IN THE HEARTS OF AMERICANS   774   27
  BUT A GERM IN THE HEARTS OF MEN AND WOMEN AMERICANS   774   31
  BUT THE GERM OF THAT FUTURE IS INSIDE THE AMERICAN PEOP+   775   2
  AND YET THERE IS A SPECK A GERM OF AMERICAN FUTURE   775   7
  STRUGGLING GERM IN INDIVIDUAL HEARTS   775   22
  BUT A SUBTLE STRUGGLING LITTLE GERM STRUGGLING HALF-UNR+   775   25

GERMANS
  AMERICANS AND FRENCH AND GERMANS AND SO ON   660   4

GERMANY
  IF I GO ON WALKING THROUGH THE WHOLE BREADTH OF GERMANY   212   24

GERMINATION
  BURST IT WITH GERMINATION WITH WORLD ANEW   273   9

GERMS
  LIKE SPERM OF WHALES LIKE GERMS OF THE GREAT DEAD PAST   428   28
  TURN THE POLES THE GERMS THE ENGLISH THE ITALIANS   777   1

GESTE
  THE STRANGE UNACCUSTOMED GESTE OF YOUR DEMONISH NEW WOR+   292   15

GESTICULATE
  ROYALLY GESTICULATE   286   6

GESTURE
  SEND SUDDENLY OUT AND EVERY GESTURE DOES   89   5
  BECAUSE IT WILL STILL BE A GESTURE OF THE OLD WORLD I AM   256   18
  GESTURE   476   19

GESTURES
  THEIR WEB WHO SHADOW THE SUN'S GREAT GESTURES AND   197   28

GETHSEMANE
  MY OWN GETHSEMANE   103   22
  GETHSEMANE   305   26
  AND THE GETHSEMANE BLOOD AT THE IRON PORES UNFOLDS UNFO+   306   4

GETS
  A LOWER ME GETS UP AND GREETS ME   39   10
  WHAT A TRAIPSE IT IS IF A MAN GETS HURT   46   3
  AND THE SEA GETS HOLD OF US   455   2
  AND SEX ALAS GETS DIRTIER AND DIRTIER WORKED FROM THE   464   1
  SEX GETS DIRTIER AND DIRTIER THE MORE IT IS FOOLED WITH+   464   3
  WHEN ALAS IT'S ONLY PART OF OUR CLEVER LITTLE SELF THAT+   543   23
  WHO GETS INTO THE CAR   565   29
  AS THE BOURGEOIS GETS SECRETLY MORE COWARDLY KNOWING HE+   663   20
  THE BOLSHEVIST GETS OPENLY MORE IMPUDENT ALSO KNOWING H+   663   22
  AND WHOEVER GETS IT IT'LL BE A DEAD BABY   664   15
  IT GETS BIGGER AND BIGGER   670   9
  AND THE JOB OF CHANGING ITS DIAPERS GETS BIGGER AND BIG+   670   12
  AND THE SOUND OF ITS HOWLING GETS BIGGER AND BIGGER AND+   670   14
  GETS BIGGER AND BIGGER AND BIGGER AND BIGGER AND BIGGER+   670   18
  GETS BITTEN AND MUST DIE   805   7

GETTING
  OF HAVING AND GETTING AND OWNING THE STRUGGLE WHICH WRE+   175   23
  GETTING TIRED   344   10
  NOBODY CAN BE WISE EXCEPT ON RARE OCCASIONS LIKE GETTING   495   24
  WHEN A BIRD FLIPS HIS TAIL IN GETTING HIS BALANCE ON A +   496   6
  GETTING THE BETTER OF OTHER PEOPLE WHO CARES   518   18
  GETTING THE BETTER OF THEM WHICH BETTER WHAT BETTER   518   19
  INSTEAD OF GETTING ON AND NOT BEING ABLE TO GET OFF AGA+   518   25
  I SUPPOSE AS A MATTER OF FACT IT'S GETTING A LITTLE DIF+   532   3
  PROVES IT QUITE THANK YOU SO MUCH WE'RE GETTING ON SIMP+   546   20
  MAYBE THEY'RE GETTING TIRED   560   9
  WE'RE GETTING TO BE BIG LADS NOW AN' SOON   573   19
  FIXING THE HOOK MORE TIGHTLY GETTING IT MORE FIRMLY IN   586   20
  HIS LIVING AND GETTING ON   837   26

GETTIN'
  AND THEN WHEN YOU'RE GETTIN' NICELY ON   493   9

GHASTLY
  THEIR GHASTLY GLOW   142   28
  OH COME AND WAKE US UP FROM THE GHASTLY DREAM OF TO-DAY   174   25
  THE GHASTLY DREAM OF LABOUR AND THE STENCH OF STEEL AND+   175   1
  AND GIVING OFF DREADFUL EFFLUVIA IN A GHASTLY EFFORT OF+   175   4
  THE GHASTLY DREAM OF RICHES OF MASSES OF MONEY TO SPEND   175   7
  COME SWEEP AWAY THESE EXQUISITE GHASTLY FIRST-FLOWERS   271   3
  DON'T MAKE IT IN GHASTLY SERIOUSNESS   517   2
  HOW GHASTLY IT WOULD BE TO STRIKE A MATCH AND MAKE A LI+   724   16
  EVEN WHILE WE ADMIT THE GHASTLY IMPORTANCE OF MONEY   831   15
  THEY SEEM TO FEEL THE CHILDREN A GHASTLY LIMITATION   832   8
  WE CAN UNCOIL THE GHASTLY SNAKE-TANGLE OF OUR UNCONSCIO+   833   26
  IN THE PULPIT WHERE SHRIVELLED AND GHASTLY IN UNINTELLI+   859   14

GHOST
  GHOST BEYOND GHOST OF BLOSSOM SHOWS   104   27
  WAVES LIKE A GHOST ALONG   108   24
  TO THE LEFT THIS GHOST LIKE A CANDLE SWEALING   141   16
  OF THE LUMINOUS GHOST   165   28
  WHAT GHOST OF US BOTH DO YOU THINK HE SAW   227   11
  UP YOUR GHOST   283   24
  GIVING UP THE GHOST   365   10
  OR SCREAMING IN PENTECOST RECEIVING THE GHOST   365   14
  BUT NEVER THE GHOST OF A GLIMPSE OF ANAXAGORAS' FUNERAL+   708   30
  AND GIVE UP THE GHOST INCONTINENT   760   19
  THE GOOD GHOST OF ME GOES DOWN THE DISTANCE   812   9
  THE GHOST OF EACH THROUGH THE LEAVES OF SHADOW   812   19

GHOST-FLUX
  GHOST-FLUX OF FACES THAT HIE   252   23

GHOSTLY
  I'LL WHISPER THE GHOSTLY TRUTH TO YOU   227   27
  AND THE GHOSTLY CREAMY COLOURED LITTLE TREES OF LEAVES   646   23
  SEEKING THEIR OLD HAUNTS WITH COLD GHOSTLY RAGE   722   27

GHOSTS
  IS PEOPLED WITH SHADOWS AND WAILING AND LAST GHOSTS LUR+   54   31
  LIKE GHOSTS ON THE GLOWING OF THE EMBER   103   13
  LIKE CANDID GHOSTS   108   22
  GLIMMERS WITH SUBTLE GHOSTS   109   2
  IS OUT OF BOUNDS AND ONLY THE OLD GHOSTS KNOW   172   24
  THE GHOSTS AND I WE MOURN TOGETHER AND SHRINK   173   6
  YOU STAND BEFORE ME LIKE GHOSTS LIKE A DARKNESS UPRIGHT   211   8
  MAGNIFICENT GHOSTS OF THE DARKNESS CARRY OFF HER DECISI+   213   26
  IN THE DISTANCE LIKE HOAR-FROST LIKE SILVERY GHOSTS COM+   306   26
  WE ARE GHOSTS WE ARE SEED   510   23
  AND GRAPES AND GHOULS AND GHOSTS AND GREEN MOONLIGHT   667   6
  OF GHOSTS THAT THRONG ABOUT OUR MUFFLED HEARTS   736   3
  ONLY BEHOLD THE GHOSTS THE GHOSTS OF THE SLAIN   736   4
  OF THEIR PATIENT WAITING UPON US THE THRONG OF THE GHOS+   736   6
  SAVE THE COLD GHOSTS THAT HOMELESS FLOCK ABOUT   736   8
  LET US RECEIVE OUR GHOSTS AND GIVE THEM PLACE   736   13
  LEAVE US TO TAKE OUR GHOSTS INTO OUR HEARTS   736   19
  FOR NOW THE HOSTS OF HOMELESS GHOSTS DO THRONG   737   1
  AND PASS BEYOND WITH THE FOE AND THE HOMELESS GHOSTS   737   6
  THEIR GHOSTS ARE ANGRY UNAPPEASED   739   6
  SO MANY GHOSTS AMONG US   739   7
  BETWEEN ME AND THEE SO MANY GHOSTS OF THE SLAIN   739   9
  INVISIBLE TROOPING HOME THE UNASSUAGED GHOSTS   739   11
  MULTITUDINOUS ENDLESS THE GHOSTS COMING HOME AGAIN   739   15
  SEEKING TO APPEASE WITH BLOOD THE INSISTENT GHOSTS   739   24
  OUT OF BLOOD RISE UP NEW GHOSTS   739   25
  GHOSTS AGAINST US   739   28
  VICTORIOUS GREY GRISLY GHOSTS IN OUR STREETS   740   2
  GREY UNAPPEASED GHOSTS SEATED IN THE MUSIC-HALLS   740   3
  WHAT DO THEY WANT THE GHOSTS WHAT IS IT   740   7
  SINCE FROM BLOOD POURED OUT RISE ONLY GHOSTS AGAIN   740   10

GHOST-WHITE
  REFOLDING SHE SLIPPED TO THE FLOOR AS A GHOST-WHITE PEO+   155   23

GHOUL
  GHOUL ON WINGS   332   27
  THAT UNNATURAL BARREL BODY THAT LONG GHOUL NOSE   338   8

GHOULISH
  TO CATCH SIGHT OF HER STANDING LIKE SOME HUGE GHOULISH   385   16

GHOULS
  AND GRAPES AND GHOULS AND GHOSTS AND GREEN MOONLIGHT   667   6

GIANT
  AND THE EXTINCT GIANT ELK TOO BIG IN ANTLERS   529   18

GIARDINI
  SHE WAS BOUGHT AT GIARDINI FAIR ON THE SANDS FOR SIX HU+   385   7

GIBBER
  YOU SIT IN THE BOUGHS AND GIBBER   549   17
  THEY ALL GIBBER AND GIBBER AND CHATTER   549   19

GIBBOUS
  A GIBBOUS MOON HANGS OUT OF THE TWILIGHT   113   17

GIBE
  LIKE ME AND LIKE A GIBE AT ME   601   20
  FROM THE GIBE OF IMAGE-MAKING LOVE   601   23

GIDDY
  ABOUT TO THE GIDDY TOP   552   22
  WITH GIDDY FREEDOM IN THE LAND OF THE FREE   575   10

GIE
'E'LL GIE THEE SOCKS   44 17

GI'E
AN' GI'E HER THEE BACK AGAIN   *922 28
AN' THEN WI' THAT TWENTY POUND WE GI'E 'ER I S'D THINK +   *925 20

GIFT
YOU LEFT ME A GIFT   108 13
SO THE GIFT   143 13
IF ONLY I AM SENSITIVE SUBTLE OH DELICATE A WINGED GIFT   250 16
AS A GIFT OF GLADNESS SEEING THE GLAMOUR OF LIFE GO UP   680 5
NOW I MUST ENTER YOUR MANSION AND BEG YOUR GIFT   695 23
INTO YOUR HOUSE GARMENTLESS LADY OF THE LAST GREAT GIFT   696 3

GIFTS
THE GIFTS OF THE GREAT   495 4
SO CULTURED EVEN BRINGING LITTLE GIFTS   500 3
AND SIX HAVE GIVEN ME GIFTS AND KISSED ME GOD-SPEED   695 28

GIGANTIC
THE GIGANTIC FLESH OF THE WORLD   *908 1

GIGGLED
AND THEY BLUSHED THEY GIGGLED THEY SNIGGERED THEY   578 7

GIGGLING
FROM THE ENTANGLEMENT OF THE GIGGLING MACHINE   642 25

GILLS
AND WATER WETLY ON FIRE IN THE GRATES OF YOUR GILLS   335 11
TO BREATHE FROM THE FLOOD AT THE GILLS   336 30
GILLS   586 16
I WISH I HAD FINS AND GILLS   837 15

GINGERLY
SHUFFLES GINGERLY ROUND   426 5

GIRDERS
THE GIRDERS   511 18

GIRDLING
GIRDLING WITH JEWELS THE MEANNESS OF COMMON THINGS   855 2

GIRL
IN THE HAIR OF AN EASTERN GIRL   36 20
AGAINST THE HAYSTACK A GIRL STANDS LAUGHING AT ME   37 1
ON THE GREEN WOOD'S EDGE A SHY GIRL HOVERS   41 1
LIGHTS THE SOFT HAIR OF A GIRL AS SHE READS   41 7
FOR THE MAN TO HEED LEST THE GIRL SHALL WEEP   41 11
MY LOVE LOOKS LIKE A GIRL TONIGHT   101 1
AN ERECT SMALL GIRL LOOKING DOWN AT ME   105 15
AND NEVER A GIRL LIKE A CHESTNUT FLOWER   106 19
ME MIGHT A YOUNG GIRL BE HEAPED WITH SUCH SHADOW OF   132 6
WHILE THE HARD GIRL HARDENS NOTHING IS SAID   228 7
CERES KISS YOUR GIRL YOU THINK YOU'VE GOT HER BACK   309 25
DON'T LIVE UP TO THE DEAR LITTLE GIRL WHO COSTS   458 22
AS IF IT'S MY FAULT THAT THE OLD GIRL IS SEVENTY-SEVEN   502 22
AND A GIRL SHOULD SAY   503 26
OH THE INNOCENT GIRL   564 25
THAN THE BLANK-IT-OUT GIRL   565 28
LOOKED AT THE LOVELY AND SELF-ABSORBED GIRL   605 2
THE LOVELY AND SELF-ABSORBED GIRL   605 4
AND A GIRL RAN SWIFTLY LAUGHING BREATHLESS TAKING IN HE+   672 13
SHE SAID TO ME STAY THREE HOURS TO COMFORT ME SUCH IS A+   749 14
HOLD UP JEANNETTE WHY POOR OLD GIRL ARE YOU SAD   859 29
AND NO MORE THAN THE BARON DID EH NO OLD GIRL AND NOT S+   859 32
OVER A GIRL WHO HAS STREWN HERSELF IN A HAMMOCK   868 6

GIRLS
WHO PLAY AROUND US COUNTRY GIRLS CLAPPING THEIR HANDS   58 19
GIRLS WITH THEIR LARGE EYES WIDE WITH TRAGEDY   71 21
AND FROM THE MEN THAT DANCE AND THE GIRLS THAT LAUGH   89 26
SMALL-BOSOMED GIRLS OF THE SPRING OF LOVE   179 17
TO EARN THEIR LIVINGS NOR YET GIRLS SWEET JOYS   459 3
AND I SUPPOSE MOST GIRLS ARE A BIT TARTY TODAY   530 20
SO BE A NICE UNCLE BE GOOD TO US GIRLS   574 5
WHEN MEN AND WOMEN WHEN LADS AND GIRLS ARE NOT THINKING   672 1
DRAW NEARER REDDEN AND LAUGH LIKE YOUNG GIRLS KISSED   854 12

GIRL'S
LIKE A GIRL'S TWINKLING MERRIMENT AT NIGHT WHEN THE SEA+   860 16

GIRLY-WIRLY'S
A JOLLY GOOD SCREW WHEN THE DEAR LITTLE GIRLY-WIRLY'S 0+   834 21

GIRLY-WIRLY
MY DEAR LITTLE GIRLY-WIRLY   834 14
WHAT ABOUT GIRLY-WIRLY AT HER AGE   834 19
TO THE EFFULGENT LANDSCAPE OF OUR IMMORTAL GIRLY-WIRLY   835 4
OH MY DEAR LITTLE GIRLY-WIRLY   835 9
DEAR LITTLE GIRLY-WIRLY   835 13

GIRTH
ROUND THEM FOR GIRTH   196 11

GIRTS
STRESS OF COMPULSION REMAINS AND A BAND THAT GIRTS   746 16

GIST
UPON ME MY OWN REFLECTION EXPLICIT GIST   141 19

GIUNTINA
LITTLE GIUNTINA   668 8

GIVE-AND-TAKE
LIKE SLITS IN AN AUTOMATIC-MACHINE YOU COLUMNS OF GIVE-+   288 25

GIVEN
TO HA' GONE AN' GIVEN HIS CLEAN YOUNG FLESH   77 31
IN A NEW NIGHT-SPASM OF BIRTH AND GIVEN US THIS NEW RED+   88 20
DREAMING YOUR YIELDED MOUTH IS GIVEN TO MINE   129 24
BUT YOU ARE GIVEN BACK AGAIN TO ME   157 9
AND ALL YOUR BEING IS GIVEN TO ME SO NONE   157 19
IN EVERY BUSH IS GIVEN YOU BACK AND WE   157 24
TO BEAR BUT RETALIATE NOTHING GIVEN TO SAVE   160 27
SHE HAS GIVEN THE CHILD TO JOSEPH   200 13
ONE TO BE QUENCHED TO BE GIVEN UP TO BE GONE IN THE DARK   212 8
WHERE 'TWAS GIVEN US TO REPOSE US   242 30
A WOMAN HAS GIVEN ME STRENGTH AND AFFLUENCE   262 25
THAT THEY WERE GIVEN WHEN I NEEDED THEM   263 31
AND KNOW THAT THEY WERE GIVEN FOR EVER   265 5
HERE TO US GIVEN   269 11
AND GIVEN AND PERFECT   307 14
ESPECIALLY IF BEING GIVEN A NEEDLE'S EYE OF EGRESS ELSE+   381 6
I WISH THEY HAD GIVEN THE THREE FEATHERS TO ME   392 1
GIVE AND IT SHALL BE GIVEN UNTO YOU   449 16
I AM SICK BECAUSE I HAVE GIVEN MYSELF AWAY   500 1
I HAVE GIVEN MYSELF TO THE PEOPLE WHEN THEY CAME   500 2
O GOD TO US MAY STRENGTH BE GIVEN   554 3
AND GIVEN YOU THIS JIG-JIG-JIG   585 16
THIS IS WHAT THEY'VE GIVEN YOU   585 20
AND ALL THE DIFFERENCES GIVEN EXPRESSION   611 20
AND SIX HAVE GIVEN ME GIFTS AND KISSED ME GOD-SPEED   695 28
WHEN THE PLANETS HAVE GIVEN SEVEN NODS   702 6
I AM GIVEN UP   725 2
THEY SHOULD NEVER HAVE GIVEN YOU NAMES AND NEVER NEVER   737 20
ROSES ARE ONLY ONCE-WILD ROSES THAT WERE GIVEN AN EXTRA+ 831 2
TO HA'E GONE AN' GIVEN HIS WHITE YOUNG FLESH   *919 19
AND WHAT OF GOOD I HAVE GIVEN THE DAY MY PEACE ATTESTS   *946 3

GIVES
WORLD WITHIN WORLDS A WOMB THAT GIVES AND TAKES   89 8
GIVES US ALL FORTH THAT WE MAY GIVE AGAIN   89 9
LABURNUM GIVES BACK TO LIGHT   104 32
AND GIVES ME PEACE YOU CANNOT SEE   252 9
I TRAMPLE ON THE SNOWDROPS IT GIVES ME PLEASURE TO TREA+ 271 12
GIVES THEM   277 9
HE CAUSALLY GIVES BIRTH TO ANOTHER YOUNG BUD FROM HIS   300 1
CAN PIERCE FOR THAT IS WHERE WILL GIVES OUT LIKE A SINK+ 383 11
ON THE CONTRARY HE MERELY GIVES HIMSELF AWAY   433 1
BUT THE PLUCKY LITTLE SPORT IT GIVES TO LIFE   443 16
I DIED AND DEATH IS NEUTER IT SPEAKS NOT IT GIVES   461 11
AND THE PURE INTELLECT GIVES ONE A LAST MASTURBATING SE+ 532 9
AND ALL YOUR BEST THINGS AND JUST GIVES THEM AWAY   572 3
AND NOW THAT THE MOON WHO GIVES MEN GLISTENING BODIES   688 10
IRON GIVES THE DEADLY WOUND   712 6
AND THE WILL THE LIVING DYNAMO GIVES THE MOTION AND THE+ 712 14
THAT GIVES ME PEACE   741 15
AND GIVES ME EVERYTHING   752 20
HUITZILOPOCHTLI GIVES THE BLACK BLADE OF DEATH   809 4

GIVING
NOW TO THE DEAD YOU ARE GIVING   168 32
AND GIVING OFF DREADFUL EFFLUVIA IN A GHASTLY EFFORT OF+ 175 4
YOU SLEEP STRETCHED OUT FOR EVER EVER GIVING   194 21
FLOWERILY NAKED IN FLESH AND GIVING OFF HUES OF LIFE   299 4
AND INCREASING THE FLOCK AND PERHAPS GIVING A REAL NIP+ 325 10
AND GIVING THAT FRAGILE YELL THAT SCREAM   365 10
GIVING UP THE GHOST   365 13
BUT GIVING LIFE IS NOT SO EASY   449 18
AND GIVING YOU A COLD IN YOUR INSIDE   506 24
HE IS GIVING HIMSELF AWAY IN EVERY SENSE OF THE WORD   523 11
COURSE YOU UNDERSTAND WHAT I MEAN SO WOULD YOU MIND GIV+ 546 9
AS IF IT WAS GIVING OFF POISON VAPOUR   583 13
GIVING A MESSAGE TO THE MAN   693 15
GIVING OFF DARKNESS BLUE DARKNESS AS DEMETER'S PALE LAM+ 697 10
TAKING AND GIVING   825 31
NOR A DOSE OF CAPSICUM ESSENCE GIVING AN ORGASM   837 9
GIVING OFF DARKNESS BLUE DARKNESS UPON DEMETER'S YELLOW+ *956 8

GIZZARD
OR A GIZZARD LIKE A TURKEY   837 16

GLACIER
ADOWN THE PALE-GREEN GLACIER RIVER FLOATS   209 1
OF THEIR PALE-GREEN GLACIER WATER FILLED THE EVENING   216 25

GLACIERS
BEFORE THE GLACIERS WERE GATHERED UP IN A BUNCH OUT OF + 285 19

GLACIER-WATER
OF THEIR PALE-GREEN GLACIER-WATER FILLED THE EVENING   *942 11

GLAD
ME GLAD   34 15
NEVER TO KNOW THE GLAD FREEDOM OF OBEDIENCE SINCE LONG   48 3
AND THEN HE TURNS AGAIN WITH A LITTLE GLAD   51 17
FROM THAT BIT OF A WENCH'S BOSOM 'E'D BE GLAD OF IT   61 19
I AM GLAD TO GO BACK TO WHERE I CAME FROM   72 3
LIKE A PORTENT BUT LORD I AM GLAD SO GLAD I DROWN   88 26
NOT PASS THE RED MOON RISEN AND I AM GLAD   88 28
GLAD AS THE MAGI WHEN THEY SAW THE BROW   88 29
HOW GLAD I SHOULD HAVE BEEN   100 15
THE LARK SINGS LOUD AND GLAD   110 9
AND GLAD ARE THE EAGER DEAD TO RECEIVE YOU THERE   168 9
HOW GLAD I SHOULD BE   180 18
THE LAND OF HER GLAD SURMISE   201 4
NOW EVERY TALL GLAD TREE   215 22
IN GLAD SURPRISE   227 32
AND YOUR BLITHE GLAD MIEN   234 18
YET I AM GLAD   248 5
I AM SO GLAD THERE IS ALWAYS YOU BEYOND BY SCOPE   248 6

GLAD
BE ROUGH AND HAIRY I'M GLAD THEY'RE LIKE THAT	254	12
I AM VERY GLAD AND ALL ALONE IN THE WORLD	256	7
ALL ALONE AND VERY GLAD IN A NEW WORLD	256	8
THEN I SHALL BE GLAD I SHALL NOT BE CONFUSED WITH HER	267	17
I SHALL BE SO GLAD WHEN IT COMES DOWN	288	13
HOW GLAD I WAS HE HAD COME LIKE A GUEST IN QUIET TO DRI+	350	9
CROOK THE KNEE AND BE GLAD	392	13
GLAD TO EMERGE AND LOOK BACK	409	13
BE GLAD	411	31
AND MY HEART IS GLAD TO HAVE THEM AT LAST	412	22
WHY SHOULD A MAN PRETEND TO BE GLAD ABOUT	499	14
GOD HOW GLAD I AM TO HEAR THE SHELLS	741	9
MY BODY GLAD AS THE BELL OF A FLOWER	742	32
DOWN THE GLAD STREETS PINCHED WAIFS IN ILL-ASSORTED CLO+	866	5
GO WINGING GLAD THE YELLOW MOTES	868	24
MIGHT FOLLOW WARM AND GLAD WHO SIT HERE COLD	879	15
HER SOUL TO ME,AND SHE WAS VERY GLAD	881	13
SO GLAD TO HAVE BEEN LOST	882	11
SO GLAD TO FIND MYSELF AGAIN	882	12
GLAD	*892	3
OWNING MY SUPPLE BODY A RARE GLAD THING SUPREMELY GOOD	*892	11
FOR LAUGHTER AND GLAD THE EXONERATED EYES FOR I	*897	8
WITH GLEE HE TURNS WITH A LITTLE GLAD	*899	1
WITH GLEE HE TURNS WITH A LITTLE GLAD	*902	13
BEHIND I AM FORTIFIED I AM GLAD AT MY WORK	*945	26

GLADDEN
ALWAYS GLADDEN MY AMOROUS FINGERS WITH THE TOUCH OF THE+	180	25

GLADDER
GLADDER NOR OF THY LILIES IF THA MAUN BE TOLD	61	20

GLADE
AND THEY MEET IN THE GLADE BETWEEN MORNING AND	771	14

GLADLY
WOULD SO GLADLY LIE	40	14
CHILL DUSK FOR YOU AND GLADLY GLEAMING	91	21
AND GLADLY I'D OFFERED MY BREAST TO THE TREAD OF HER	123	6
AND SUFFER FOOLS THOUGH NOT GLADLY	499	13
YOU WEAR ON YOUR FINGER SO GLADLY FOR GOD	752	18
WOULD GLADLY HAVE OFFERED MY BREAST FOR HER TREAD TO TRY	*934	12

GLADNESS
DEATH IN WHOSE SERVICE IS NOTHING OF GLADNESS TAKES ME	48	9
OF FRETTING OR OF GLADNESS SHOWS THE JETTING	89	14
AS A GIFT OF GLADNESS SEEING THE GLAMOUR OF LIFE GO UP	680	5
WITH GLADNESS	887	3
WITH GLADNESS REEL	888	16
IS IN ME A TREMBLING GLADNESS	*907	20
SINGING LOVE'S FIRST SURPRISED GLADNESS ALONE IN THE GL+	*940	15

GLAMOROUS
ALONG THE GLAMOROUS BIRCH-TREE AVENUE	206	5
BOTH BREASTS DIM AND MYSTERIOUS WITH THE GLAMOROUS KIND+	693	12

GLAMOUR
WITH THE GREAT BLACK PIANO APPASSIONATO THE GLAMOUR	148	16
SPINNING A GLAMOUR ROUND MONEY AND CLERGYMEN	456	24
AS A GIFT OF GLADNESS SEEING THE GLAMOUR OF LIFE GO UP	680	5
GLAMOUR	*940	24

GLANCE
BLADE OF HIS GLANCE THAT ASKS ME TO APPLAUD	43	25
AS THEIR EYES GLANCE AT ME,FOR THE GRAIN	52	2
THEN I SAW HIM TURN TO GLANCE AGAIN SURREPTITIOUSLY	604	4
HOLA HOLA MEXICANOS GLANCE AWAY A MOMENT TOWARDS ME	790	19
AS THEIR EYES GLANCE AT ME FOR THE GRAIN	*899	15
AS THEIR EYES GLANCE AT ME FOR THE GRAIN	*902	27
I NEED NOT GLANCE OVER MY SHOULDER IN FEAR OF THE TERRO+	*945	25

GLANCED
THEY TURNED NOT AT ALL THEY GLANCED NOT ONE HIS WAY	790	21
SHE GLANCED AT ME TIMIDLY	869	11

GLANCES
SHE GLANCES QUICK HER STARTLED EYES	42	24
HIS THROAT TO SING GLANCES DOWN	771	4

GLANCING
THE WILD YOUNG HEIFER GLANCING DISTRAUGHT	64	7
ENJOYING THEIR GLANCING FLIGHT THOUGH LOVE IS DEAD	133	23
BRIGHT GLANCING EXQUISITE CORN OF MANY A STUBBORN	263	27
GLANCING	292	30
AND A BULL'S LARGE SOMBRE GLANCING EYE	325	28
WITH THE STRANGE DARK LAUGH IN THEIR EYES GLANCING UP	389	33
SHOWING A GLINT OF TEETH AND GLANCING TROPICAL EYES ARO+	391	14
WHAT THOUGH THE CLOUDS GO GLANCING DOWN	772	4

GLARE
DAZZLE OF MAY-BLOBS WHERE THE MARIGOLD GLARE OVERCAST Y+	90	8
AS THE ROCKETS WENT UP AND THE GLARE PASSED OVER COUNTL+	391	12
O FACES UPTURNED TO THE GLARE O TROPICAL WONDER WONDER	391	20
HOW THOU CASTEST UP A SICKLY GLARE	760	7

GLARES
LINGERS BEHIND AS THE YELLOW SUN GLARES AND IS GONE BEY+	467	6

GLARING
THE MOTHER IN YOU FIERCE AS A MURDERESS GLARING TO	207	6

GLASS
WHERE THE GLASS IS DOMED ON THE SILENT AIR	52	19
OF GLASS PALACE ALOFT THERE AMONG MISTY INDEFINITE THIN+	52	24
OR LIKE TWO BUTTERFLIES THAT SETTLE ON A GLASS	65	3
MEANING OR A MESSAGE OVER THE WINDOW GLASS	103	3
SILVER-PINK PEACH VENETIAN GREEN GLASS OF MEDLARS AND S+	283	5

GLASS
WHEN WE GET OUT OF THE GLASS BOTTLES OF OUR OWN EGO	482	15
WHAT A PITY WHEN A MAN LOOKS AT HIMSELF IN A GLASS	528	22
SAIL LITTLE SHIPS IN YOUR GLASS BOTTLES	543	4
EVEN THE SHAKING WHITE POPLAR WILL DAZZLE LIKE SPLINTER+	624	18
FOR I AM FRAIL AS A FLASK OF GLASS	752	15
AND SEE YOURSELF AS IN A GLASS DARKLY	834	18
AND KNOW HIMSELF IN THE GLASS	836	10
WHEN HE LOOKS AT HIMSELF IN THE GLASS	836	12
WITH THE FIRST DAWN I ROSE TO LOOK IN THE GLASS	860	11
HAS EVAPORATED FROM YOU LIKE STEAM FROM GLASS	871	6
WHERE THE GLASS IS DOMED BY THE BLUE SOFT DAY	*905	8
WHAT A PITY WHEN A MAN LOOKS AT HIMSELF IN THE GLASS	*950	25

GLASSY
OH SAFER THAN ANYTHING ELSE IN A WELL-CORKED GLASSY EGO	543	2

GLAZED
AND GLAZED YOU OVER WITH A SHEEN OF GOLD	90	21

GLEAM
IN THE LUSTROUS GLEAM OF THE WATER THERE	126	17
A QUICKENING MASCULINE GLEAM FLOATS IN TO ALL	127	2
AND GLEAM AS OF SUNSHINE CROSSING THE LOW BLACK HEAP	144	25
THERE CAME A CLOVEN GLEAM	169	27
ONE ANOTHER IN WONDER OF WAKING LET US WAKE TO THE GLEAM	175	29
WITH THE HALF-SECRET GLEAM OF A PASSION-FLOWER HANGING	299	1
WITH THEIR GOLD RED EYES AND GREEN-PURE GLEAM AND UNDER+	339	26
THIS WET WHITE GLEAM	453	19
THE GODS ARE THERE BECAUSE OF THE GLEAM ON THE FACES OF+	649	11
BY THE TRANSMITTED GLEAM FROM THE FACES OF VIVIDER MEN	649	14
AND WORSHIP IS THE JOY OF THE GLEAM FROM THE EYES OF TH+	649	16
EVEN THE DENIAL THAT THERE IS ANY GLEAM	649	18
TO SEE THE GLEAM OF THE GODS THERE REFLECTED IN THE HUM+	649	22
THE ROBOTS THOSE WHO DENY THE GLEAM	649	26
NOT A BOSS BUT THE GLEAM OF LIFE ON THE FACE OF A MAN	650	15
THE BAFFLING LIGHT OR THE STRANGE STILL GLEAM OF THE GO+	656	13
INSTEAD OF WHICH THE MINORITIES THAT STILL SEE THE GLEA+	666	5
I SEE HIM MORE LIKE THE RUBY A GLEAM FROM WITHIN	697	28
A FRAIL WHITE GLEAM OF RESURRECTION	744	12
A TENDER GLEAM OF IMMORTALITY	746	1
DOWN THE RIVER IN THE GLEAM OF THE SUN	867	32

GLEAMED
A LIGHT LIKE MELLOW MOONLIGHT GLEAMED ON THIS WATER	864	29
IN THE DEEP CART-RUTS GLEAMED THROUGH THE BLUE OF THE D+	864	30
AND HYMNS GLEAMED ON OUR WARM LIPS AS WE WATCHED MOTHER+	*940	12

GLEAMING
CHILL DUSK FOR YOU AND GLADLY GLEAMING	91	21
GLEAMING LIKE METAL WITH RUNNING SWEAT AS THEY SUDDENLY	389	1
AND LUSTROUS GREAT TROPICAL EYES UNVEILED NOW GLEAMING	389	13
A NAKED GLEAMING DARK LAUGH LIKE A SECRET OUT IN THE DA+	389	15
AND FOR THE MOMENT SHE WAS ISIS GLEAMING HAVING FOUND H+	672	24
WITH THE DARK AND GLEAMING BEAUTY OF THE MESSAGELESS GO+	674	26
GLEAMING HER HOUR IN LIFE AS SHE NOW GLEAMS IN DEATH	676	14
FOR THE SUN AND THE MOON ARE ALIVE AND WATCHING WITH GL+	792	10

GLEAMS
THERE ARE NO GLEAMS ON THE RIVER	170	25
ALL THE WORLD GLEAMS WITH THE LILIES OF DEATH THE UNCON+	273	12
LEAPS UP TO THE SUMMIT OF THE STEM GLEAMS TURNS OVER	476	8
AND GLEAMS ON THE WORLD WITH THE WARM DARK VISION OF	544	24
AND DEMOS SERVES LIFE AS IT GLEAMS ON THE FACE OF THE F+	650	3
GLEAMING HER HOUR IN LIFE AS SHE NOW GLEAMS IN DEATH	676	14
THAT IS MY HOME WHERE THE LAMP GLEAMS AFAR	857	27

GLEANING
TINKLED THE MUSIC OF GLEANING	152	19

GLEBE
THE DIFFICULT GLEBE OF THE FUTURE	102	11
GLEBE IN THE UPTURNED DARKNESS	263	28

GLEE
CHATTERING THOUGH NOT WITH GLEE	552	10
THEN HE TURNS AGAIN TO HIS WORK WITH GLEE	*898	28
WITH GLEE HE TURNS WITH A LITTLE GLAD	*899	1
THEN HE TURNS AGAIN TO HIS WORK WITH GLEE	*902	12
WITH GLEE HE TURNS WITH A LITTLE GLAD	*902	13

GLIDE
THE EDGE OF THE BLUE AND THE SUN STANDS UP TO SEE US GL+	132	28
AND LONG SNAKES QUICKLY GLIDE INTO THE DARK HOLE IN THE+	321	24
FINGERS GLIDE	*940	13

GLIDED
AND A MIRACLE AS SHE GLIDED DELICATELY AWAY WITH SUCH	255	31

GLIDES
DO YOU HEAR MY ROLLS ROYCE PURR AS IT GLIDES AWAY	664	3

GLIMMER
THE GLIMMER OF THE LIMES SUN-HEAVY SLEEPING	35	26
O THE GREEN GLIMMER OF APPLES IN THE ORCHARD	119	7
NOW LAMPS LIKE YELLOW ECHOES GLIMMER AMONG	135	9
THEY GLIMMER WITH TISSUE OF GOLD AND GOLDEN THREADS ON	388	19
AND THE GLIMMER OF THE PRESENCE OF THE GODS WAS LIKE LI+	651	5
THE DEAD OF THE WATER-LORDS ROCK AND GLIMMER IN THE SEAS	796	8
OF SUNSET BUT MERGING UNNOTICED INTO THE ROSY GLIMMER	860	5
OH THE GREEN GLIMMER OF APPLES IN THE ORCHARD	*932	16

GLIMMERED
GLIMMERED AS FLOWERS THAT IN PERFUME AT TWILIGHT UNFOLD	141	8

GLIMMERING
  GLIMMERING STILL   97   1
  AS IF SHE WOULD SLIP THE GOLD AND GLIMMERING   106   5
  WAS SAVOUR OF ICE AND OF ROSES AND GLIMMERING   217   5
  AND THE GLIMMERING DREAMLETS OF THE MORNING ARE PALLID +   854   7
  HIS BLUE SHIRT GLIMMERING ON THE WATER AMONG THE SHADOW+   867 29
  WAS SCENT OF ROSES AND GLIMMERING   *942 16

GLIMMERS
  GLIMMERS LITTER OF DAY   41 30
  GLIMMERS WITH SUBTLE GHOSTS   109   2
  SOFT GLIMMERS OF DESIRE ESCAPED FROM PRISON   113   4
  GLIMMERS OUR   170   7

GLIMPSE
  IF YOU WANT TO GET A GLIMPSE OF FUTURE POSSIBILITIES   612   8
  UNLESS THERE'S THE GLIMPSE OF A GOD IN HIM   671 10
  UNLESS SHE'S A GLIMPSE OF A GODDESS OF SOME SORT   671 12
  BUT NEVER THE GHOST OF A GLIMPSE OF ANAXAGORAS' FUNERAL+   708 30
  AND STRIVING TO CATCH A GLIMPSE OF THE SHAPE OF THE COM+   *909 25

GLIMPSED
  GLIMPSED NOW AND THEN   292 17

GLIMPSES
  YOU SEE THEM IN GLIMPSES IN THE FACES AND FORMS OF PEOP+   671 23
  GLIMPSES   671 24
  YOU MAY SEE GLIMPSES OF THE GODS IN THEM   672   6

GLINT
  AND A GLINT OF COLOURED IRIS BRINGS   46 10
  SHE TURNED HER FLUSHED FACE TO ME FOR THE GLINT   125   7
  SHOWING A GLINT OF TEETH AND GLANCING TROPICAL EYES ARO+   391 14
  GLINT   478   8
  HAS A GAY LITTLE GLINT   562 22
  SHE TURNED HER FLUSHED FACE TOWARDS ME FOR THE GLINT   *935 23

GLINTING
  A GLINTING WEB QUICK HID IN THE GLOOM OF THE BROOK   161   7

GLISTEN
  AND THE KINGCUPS' GLISTEN THAT SHALL LONG OUTLAST YOU   90 12
  THEM NONE OF THE GLISTEN   170   9
  GLISTEN AS SILVER THEY CRUMPLE UP   217 20
  THE VEINS OF LIVING SPACE AND ADDS A GLISTEN   505   3
  WHOSE FEATHERS GLISTEN   505   7
  THEY GLISTEN AND SHAKE   615 15
  THAT SPANGLED GLISTEN IS GONE THAT AT-ONENESS WITHOUT A+   656 16
  GLISTEN   827   2
  PLUMS THE BLOND ONES ARE GOLD WITH LESS GLISTEN   827   5
  SEE THE MORNING SUN ON THE SHAKEN IRIS GLISTEN   *892 31
  WOODSTACKS BESIDE THE RAILWAY GLISTEN AND GLOW   *894 26
  GLISTEN AS SILVER THEY CRUMPLE UP   *943   3

GLISTENED
  SAW WHERE MORNING SUN ON THE SHAKEN IRIS GLISTENED   38 16
  AND THE WHITE SNOW GLISTENED THE WHITE WORLD WAS GAY   550 29

GLISTENING
  UNDER THE GLISTENING CHERRIES WITH FOLDED WINGS   36 23
  SO NOW YOU'RE A GLISTENING TOADSTOOL SHINING HERE   86 21
  THIS WONDER STOOD GLISTENING   165 18
  GLISTENING WITH ALL THE MOMENT AND ALL YOUR BEAUTY   210   4
  GLISTENING WHITE ON THE SHOULDERS   217 13
  GLISTENING IN STEADFAST STILLNESS LIKE TRANSCENDENT   225   3
  STICKILY GLISTENING WITH ETERNAL SHADOW   310 17
  AND GLISTENING ADHESIVE MUZZLE   325 29
  AND NOW THAT THE MOON WHO GIVES MEN GLISTENING BODIES   688 10
  HOW GLISTENING RED THEY ARE   689 13
  AND IS AN ARCHITECTURE OF GLISTENING ATOMS   692   3
  YOU GLISTENING GARMENTLESS BEAUTY   695 14
  AND WATCHED FOR YOUR GLISTENING FEET DOWN THE GARDEN PA+   696 11
  SO QUEENLY SHAKING HER GLISTENING BEAMS   702 26
  INTO A GLISTENING ROSARY   735 19
  GLISTENING WHITE ON THE SHOULDERS   *942 23

GLISTENING-FEATHERED
  GREAT AND GLISTENING-FEATHERED LEGS OF THE HAWK OF HORUS   409   7

GLITTER
  GLITTER AND SPILL   94 15
  TO NOUGHT DIMINISHING EACH STAR'S GLITTER   132 14
  INSCRUTABLE SMALL LIGHTS GLITTER IN ROWS   163 26
  IN A GLITTER OF ECSTASY   200   8
  HOW I KNOW THAT GLITTER OF SALT DRY STERILE SHARP CORRO+   207 17
  DARK SKY OF NIGHT A WANDERING GLITTER A SWARM   221 26
  THE DAWN COMES UP WITH A GLITTER AND A BLUENESS AND I S+   509 25
  WILL SWEEP ROUND AND UP TO GREET THE SUN WITH A SILKY G+   625   4
  BELOW THE PIT-LIGHTS GLITTER IN ROWS   857 26
  AND THE RED FRUITS GLITTER   861   3
  THE GLITTER OF THE BUCKLE OF YOUR SHOE   887 13
  DARK GLITTER OF LIFE AMID A SKY. THAT TEEMS   *895   7
  GLITTER AND SPILL   *897   3
  TO STREW ROUND OUR WAY TO DIMINISH EACH FULL STAR'S GLI+   *938   6
  DARK SKY OF NIGHT THE WANDERING GLITTER THE SWARM   *945 12

GLITTERING
  CROWDS OF GLITTERING KING-CUPS SURGE TO CHALLENGE THE B+   33 11
  ARE GLITTERING PATHS   35   3
  UPON US DARK EYES AS HERE BENEATH THE BUSBIES GLITTERIN+   66 25
  TO FIND THE NEW HOUSES A CLUSTER OF LILIES GLITTERING   72 21
  I WISH A WILD SEA-FELLOW WOULD COME DOWN THE GLITTERING   130 17
  THE MYRIAD GLITTERING CHIMNEY-TIPS   166 20
  WHERE AN ARCHWAY TORN AND GLITTERING   201 23
  SEE GLITTERING ON THE MILK-BLUE MORNING LAKE   230   8
  GLITTERING AT ME ON THE UNUTTERABLE DARKNESS   241   6
  ROSY TENDER GLITTERING WITHIN THE FISSURE   278 26
  NO GLITTERING COMPACT DROPS OF DAWN   278 28

GLITTERING
  AND OPEN IT SO THAT IT IS A GLITTERING ROSY MOIST HONIE+   282   3
  THOSE THAT GO GLITTERING ABROAD   523 24
  AND THRILL WITH GLITTERING RAYS   526   6
  BY HERMES AND APHRODITE FLASHING WHITE GLITTERING WORDS   702 10
  LIKE GLITTERING SEED UPON THEM FOR FULFILMENT   743   5
  ALL THESE GLITTERING SEA-BIRDS WHEEL AND FRET   860 20
  CROWDS OF GLITTERING KING-CUPS SURGE TO CHALLENGE THE B+   *891 12
  LIKE A GLITTERING OF SHADOWS WITHIN THE MORNING AIR   *895   6
  AND GUARDED BY A GLITTERING TEAR   *912 22

GLITTERS
  GLITTERS IN SALTY TRIUMPH   455   9

GLITTERY
  THE GREAT DARK GLITTERY WINDOW   193 21

GLOAMING
  OPEN THE CORE OF GLOAMING TASTE   114 15

GLOATED
  AND GAZED AND GLOATED WITHOUT RHYME   578   4
  OR GLOATED OR PEEPED AT THE SIMPLE SPOT   579   3

GLOBE
  BEAST CROUCHED ACROSS THE GLOBE READY IF NEED BE TO POU+   97 21
  I ON THE BUSH OF THE GLOBE   107 13
  HERE ON THE BUSH OF THE GLOBE   108   2
  AND FECUND GLOBE OF DREAMS   127   9
  THE GLOBE OF THE DAY OVER-RIPE   253 24
  TO TOSS THE GLOBE OF EARTH LIKE A BALL ON A WATER-JET   272 14
  TO PLAY WITH THE GLOBE OF EARTH LIKE A BALL ON A FOUNTA+   272 19
  COME QUICKLY AND STIR THE ROTTEN GLOBE OF THE WORLD FROM   273   7
  OR THE STOUT SWART BEETLE ROLLED THE GLOBE OF DUNG IN W+   437 16
  PEOPLE ARE LIKE LEAVES FLUTTERING AND GAY ON THE BUSH O+   615   7

GLOBED
  LOOK HOW BLACK HOW BLUE-BLACK HOW GLOBED IN EGYPTIAN   286   8

GLOBE-FLOWERS
  THE LOVELY PALE-GOLD BUBBLES OF THE GLOBE-FLOWERS   205 24
  NEVERTHELESS ONCE THE FROGS THE GLOBE-FLOWERS OF BAVARIA   208   4

GLOBES
  WITH LONG PINS LEANING OUT THEIR PORCELAIN GLOBES WREAT+   856 13

GLOBE-SHAPED
  THE SAME THAT DANGLES THE GLOBE-SHAPED PLEIADS OF FRUIT   271 23

GLOBULE
  THIS ROLLING DROPPING HEAVY GLOBULE   279 12

GLOBULES
  LIKE GLOBULES OF NIGHT ABOUT TO GO PLASH   427   8
  AND EMERGE AS SQUEAKY GLOBULES WITH NO BODIES TO SPEAK +   501   2

GLOIRE DE DIJON
  GLOIRE DE DIJON ROSES   217 18
  GLOIRE DE DIJON ROSES   *942 27

GLOOM
  AND THE BOYS AND THE ROOM IN A COLOURLESS GLOOM   51   6
  SET LIKE ROCKS BESIDE A SEA OF GLOOM   56 14
  DO THEY WIPE AWAY THE GLOOM THE GULF THROWS UP   90 24
  THE HEADS OF THE BOYS MOVE DIMLY THROUGH A YELLOW GLOOM+   92   4
  FOR THE FLUSH OF THE NIGHT WHEREAS NOW THE GLOOM   141   9
  GLOOM   149   2
  OUT OF THE SLEEP FROM THE GLOOM OF MOTION SOUNDLESSLY   149   9
  A GLINTING WEB QUICK HID IN THE GLOOM OF THE BROOK   161   7
  A DARK BOAT THROUGH THE GLOOM AND WHITHER   209   2
  WHEN THE TIRED FLOWER OF FLORENCE IS IN GLOOM BENEATH T+   340 21
  GLOOM   349   9
  WE GO ON INTO THE GLOOM OF LOBO   402 10
  HONKING IN THE GLOOM THE HONK OF PROCREATION FROM SUCH   437 25
  PLUTO'S GLOOM   697   5
  OF THE ARMS PLUTONIC AND PIERCED WITH THE PASSION OF DE+   697 20
  MY SPIRIT DARKENS AND GOES OUT AND SOFT STRANGE GLOOM   727   2
  GREATER GLOOM THAN FOR MANY YEARS   778 36
  AND TREMBLING SOMEWHERE DEEP IN THEIR SUNKIST GLOOM   868 27
  I LOOKED IN HER EYES THE GLOOM   885 16
  AND THE BOYS AND THE ROOM IN A COLOURLESS GLOOM   *898 18
  AND THE BOYS AND THE ROOM IN A COLOURLESS GLOOM   *902   2
  THE HEADS OF MY BOYS MOVE DIMLY THROUGH THE YELLOW GLOO+   *926   4
  WITHIN THE SPACIOUS GLOOM OF MYSTERY   *936 34
  OF DEATH COMMINGLES IN GOD'S MIGHTY GLOOM   *938 16
  SINGING LOVE'S FIRST SURPRISED GLADNESS ALONE IN THE GL+ *940 15
  WHILE TREMBLING SOMEWHERE IN THEIR WONDROUS GLOOM   *941 27
  WITH YOUR GLOOM AND YOUR DOUBT THAT YOU LOVE ME   *944 26
  HONKED IN THE GLOOM THE HONK OF PROCREATION FROM SUCH T+ *947   3
  MAKE A DARK-BLUE GLOOM   *954 19
  YOUR DARK BLUE GLOOM IS SO NOBLE   *954 25
  IN THE DARK BLUE GLOOM   *955   7
  DOWN THE THICKENING THICKENING GLOOM   *955 13
  WHAT A DARK-BLUE GLOOM   *955 23
  PLUTO'S GLOOM   *956   3
  A GLOOM INVISIBLE ENFOLDED IN THE DEEPER DARK   *956 16

GLOOM-WOVEN
  INTO THE GLOOM-WOVEN FOREST WHERE THE BIRDS AND CICALAS+   864   5

GLORIFIED
  GLORIFIED   321 21
  THAN THE WINGS OF THE MORNING AND THEE THOU GLORIFIED   323   4

GLORIOUS
BALANCED IN GLORIOUS EQUILIBRIUM   251 17
ARE MORE GLORIOUS   562 6
AND HE IS SUPPOSED TO BE MIGHTLY AND GLORIOUS   691 14
GREAT LADY GREAT GLORIOUS LADY   695 15
HAD BEEN WOVEN INTO A GLORIOUS MESH LIKE A BRIDAL LACE   860 14

GLORY
HOURS THAT WERE ONCE ALL GLORY AND ALL QUEENS   135 24
MELLOW AS THE GLORY ROSES   217 26
ALL STANDING IN CLOUDS OF GLORY   303 6
NOW IF THE LILIES OF FRANCE LICK SOLOMON IN ALL HIS GLO+   413 27
GLORY IS OF THE SUN TOO AND THE SUN OF SUNS   496 10
A TIGER IS STRIPED AND GOLDEN FOR HIS OWN GLORY   523 13
YOU A SIMILAR GLORY SINCE YOU'D RISEN   555 23
AND EMOTIONS AND DESIRES AND STRENGTH GLORY OR HONOUR   691 11
THE POWER AND THE GLORY   704 12
MY KINGDOM MY POWER AND MY GLORY   704 17
HAVE THEIR KINGDOM THEIR POWER AND THEIR GLORY   704 19
WHOSE POWER AND GLORY I HAVE OFTEN HEARD AND FELT   704 21
YAPPING IN HIS POWER AND HIS GLORY   704 23
LIKE THE POWER AND THE GLORY OF THE GOOSE IN THE MIST   704 25
MY KINGDOM MY POWER AND MY GLORY   704 29
TO START THE GLORY OF ANOTHER YEAR   746 2
I TELL YOU THE DAY SHOULD NOT TURN INTO GLORY   799 25
THAT THE KING OF GLORY MAY COME IN   818 8
WHO IS THIS KING OF GLORY   818 9
HOURS THAT WERE ONCE ALL GLORY AND ALL QUEENS   *939 24

GLOSS
ALL THE BRONZE GLOSS OF ALL HIS MYRIAD PETALS   371 11

GLOSSY
YOU GLOSSY DARK WIND   369 2
SEEMS LIKE THE BLACK AND GLOSSY SEEDS OF COUNTLESS CENT+   369 11
DARK GREEN GLOSSY FANGED LEAVES   383 31
DARK GREEN GLOSSY FANGED LEAVES   387 2

GLOVE
OF MIRTH THEN THE DRIPPING OF TEARS ON YOUR GLOVE   179 19
LIKE A GLOVE A BLACK GLOVE THROWN UP AT THE LIGHT   341 13
AND TURN THE POOR SILK GLOVE INTO A LUSTY SOW'S EAR   538 22

GLOVED
EAGLE GLOVED IN FEATHERS   373 7
EAGLE GLOVED IN FEATHERS   781 12

GLOVES
CHAMOIS GLOVES   433 10
PULLING ON HIS CHAMOIS GLOVES   433 15
ONLY IF YOU INSIST ON PULLING ON THOSE CHAMOIS GLOVES   433 19
AND THE POOR WILLY WET-LEGS THE SOFT SILK GLOVES   538 23
AND BESIDE IT ON THE TABLE HER GLOVES AND MY WILTED WIL+   856 15
AS WILD WHITE FOX GLOVES DROOPING WITH FULNESS   874 26

GLOW
IS WARM WITH A RUDDY GLOW   37 15
THE GLOW OF THY FULL DESIRE   40 7
INTO THE YELLOW EVENING GLOW   42 19
FROM OUT OF THE LOINS OF NIGHT TO GLOW IN OUR WAY   88 25
THEIR GHASTLY GLOW   142 28
GLOW AND ENACT THE DRAMAS AND DREAMS   151 4
ME THAT I GLOW NOT WITH CONTENT   152 1
WHERE DEAD MEN'S LIVES GLOW GENTLY AND IRON HURTS   173 22
YOU GLOW AT LAST LIKE THE MOUNTAIN TOPS WHEN THEY CATCH   209 29
UNTIL THEY GLOW   237 26
AS MUCH GLOW AS YOU SEE   561 22
WHEN YOU LIFT YOUR HANDS IN COURAGE AND BRAVERY ITS GLO+   800 10
IN THE GARNERING AUTUMN A GLOW OF IMMORTAL FRUIT   855 17
WHICH TREADS OUT THE GLOW OF FUGITIVE ORANGE LIGHT   858 11
HER EYES GLOW AS SHE   862 7
A WOMAN CAME INTO THE GLOW FROM OUT OF THE SHADOWY LIGHT   865 4
THE GLOW OF RED IN A GREY-GREEN SHADOW OF TREES   867 10
HIS RUDDY ARMS GLOW ACROSS HER   868 8
THE STEADY GLOW FOR OH THE CHARM   873 11
GLOW AND ENACT THE DRAMAS AND DREAMS   873 14
ME THAT I GLOW NOT STILL IN CONTENT   874 15
GLOW LIKE BLOSSOMS ASTART   887 2
WOODSTACKS BESIDE THE RAILWAY GLISTEN AND GLOW   *894 26

GLOWED
WHEN ONLY THERE GLOWED ON THE DARK OF THE SKY   103 16

GLOWING
LIKE GHOSTS ON THE GLOWING OF THE EMBER   103 13
LIKE A GLOWING BRAZIER FAINTLY BLUE OF FLAME   151 25
AT THE FOOT OF EACH GLOWING THING   215 26
GLOWING   340 22
ON GLOWING   448 4
GLOWING AFTER THE DAY'S RESTLESS DRAUGHTS   506 13
FOR THE THING THAT IS DONE WITHOUT THE GLOWING AS OF GOD   689 10
FAR AND FORGOTTEN IS THE VILLA OF VENUS THE GLOWING   695 25
COMING LIKE THE RUBY IN THE INVISIBLE DARK GLOWING   697 30
I HAVE A DARKNESS INTACT WITHIN ME GLOWING SECURE   772 10
AND THE GLOWING THRONE OF THE ABSOLUTE ONE   823 14
WHICH OPENS EARTH AND HEAVEN TO LOVE'S FUGITIVE GLOWING   854 14
LOVE-LIGHT IS GLOWING THOUGH THE GUELDER-ROSE IS TOO CH+   854 17
AND DEEP IN THE GLOWING WINE-FILLED CHALICES   868 19
LIKE A GLOWING BRAZIER FAINTLY BLUE OF FLAME   874 4
AS WE CROSSED THE MOW-FIELDS DOWN THE GLOWING HILL   884 28
GOLD GOLD DEEP GOLD HER GLOWING EYES UNFOLD   *941 26

GLOWS
OF THE AFTERNOON GLOWS STILL THE OLD ROMANCE OF DAVID A+   53 3
GOLDEN SHADOW GLOWS AS   217 15
FOLD ON FOLD UNTIL IT GLOWS AS   217 25
THAT GLOWS WITH JUST   561 21
AS THE GREEN GRASS GLOWS UPWARDS STRANGERS IN THE GARDEN   647 7

GLOWS
OF THE AFTERNOON GLOWS ONLY THE OLD ROMANCE OF DAVID AN+   *905 18
GOLDEN SHADOW GLOWS AND HER BREASTS   *942 25

GLOW-WORMS
THE GLOW-WORMS   208 5
AND LAMPS LIKE VENTUROUS GLOW-WORMS STEAL *AMONG   *939 9

GLOW-WORM'S
OF THE LONG LUSH UNDER-GRASS A GLOW-WORM'S SUDDEN   206 9

GLUM
A GLUM OLD OTCHEL WI' LONG   77 22
TO SEE THEM SO GLUM AND SO LUMPISH   791 16

GLUT
THE MIND WILL HAVE TO GLUT ITSELF   472 11

GLUTTED
AND BURN IT DOWN THE GLUTTED STUFFY WORLD   315 4
AND GLUTTED SQUIRMING POPULOUSNESS ON FIRE   315 28

GNASH
THAT GNASH THE AIR   315 19
THEY GNASH WHEN IT CLOSES AND HATE THE ONE THAT GOT IN +   795 33
THEY MOAN AND BEAT THEY GNASH THEY RAGE   *958 4

GNASHING
MORDANT CORROSION GNASHING AND CHAMPING HARD   160 23

GNAW
WAITING FOR THE RATS OF THE DARK TO COME AND GNAW YOUR +   800 24
NO RAT OF THE DARK DARED GNAW YOU   800 31

GNAWING
GNAWS JUST THE SAME GNAWING THE SUBSTANCE OUT OF LIFE   432 12
BUT HE INSISTS ON GNAWING A LITTLE HOLE IN THE SOCIAL   432 13
BURNS THE SMALL FLAME OF ANGER GNAWING   601 9
GNAWING   646 17
AND THE MUSIC OF MEN IS LIKE A MOUSE GNAWING   656 10
GNAWING IN A WOODEN TRAP TRAPPED IN   656 11
ALAS BUT THE ROPE IS GNAWING   751 17
DO YOU HEAR THE RATS OF THE DARKNESS GNAWING AT YOUR IN+   800 25

GNAWS
RESPECTABLY UNSEEN AND CHEERFULLY GNAWS AWAY AT THE   432 7
GNAWS JUST THE SAME GNAWING THE SUBSTANCE OUT OF LIFE   432 12

GOAL
FOR THE DARK GOAL   39 30
AS IT SILENTLY SWEEPS TO ITS SOMEWHERE ITS GOAL   68 15
THE GOAL OF A MARE   379 16
TOWARDS MY GOAL   684 13
I CAME HITHER NOR WHAT IS MY GOAL   757 4
THE GREEKS MADE EQUILIBRIUM THEIR GOAL EQUILIBRIUM IS H+   761 14
GOAL TO TRAVEL TOWARDS YET IT'S SOMETHING TO ATTAIN YOU+   761 15
AS HE SILENTLY SWEEPS TO HIS SOMEWHERE HIS GOAL   *914 30
QUIETUS IS THE GOAL OF THE LONG JOURNEY   *957 6
SHALL TAKE THEM ABOARD TOWARDS THE GREAT GOAL OF OBLIVI+ *958 13
ON THE LONGEST JOURNEY TOWARDS THE GREATEST GOAL   *959 16
AS THE SOUL AT LAST SLIPS PERFECT INTO THE GOAL THE CORE *959 31

GOAT
OF THE OPPOSITE ENEMY GOAT   381 27
THE GOAT IS AN EGOIST AWARE OF HIMSELF DEVILISH AWARE OF   382 10
OUR OLD GOAT WE TIE UP AT NIGHT IN THE SHED AT THE BACK+   384 4

GOATS
SAP THAT SMELLS STRANGE ON YOUR FINGERS THAT EVEN GOATS+   283 12
SNIFFING FOREVER AHEAD OF HIM AT THE REAR OF THE GOATS +   380 21
RAGE OF THE SULLEN-STAGNATING ATMOSPHERE OF GOATS   381 24
THUS HAMMERING THE METTLE OF GOATS INTO PROOF AND SMITI+   381 28
THE GODHEAD OF GOATS FROM THE SHOCK   381 30
IN THE BUSINESS OF BEATING THE METTLE OF GOATS TO A GOD+   381 33
GOATS GO PAST THE BACK OF THE HOUSE LIKE DRY LEAVES IN +   383 27
RAISING DUSK AND ACRIDITY OF GOATS AND BLEATING   384 3

GOATY
WHILE SHE WITH HER GOATY MOUTH STANDS SMILING THE WHILE   382 18
SHE SMILING WITH GOATY MUNCH-MOUTH MONA LISA ARRANGES   382 26

GOB
ISN'T EVEN AS GOOD AS A GOB   545 27

GOBBLE
GOBBLE UP FILTH YOU HORROR SWALLOW UTTER ABOMINATION   398 28

GOD
ALL THAT IS RIGHT ALL THAT IS GOOD ALL THAT IS GOD TAKE+   34 27
OF THE RABBIT'S FUR GOD I AM CAUGHT IN A SNARE   43 28
FOR THE LIPS AND THE EYES OF GOD ARE BEHIND A VEIL   48 10
THEN I SHALL KNOW WHICH IMAGE OF GOD   59 9
WHAT WAS MY QUESTION MY GOD MUST I BREAK THIS   76 9
GOD STEPPING THROUGH OUR LOINS IN ONE BRIGHT STRIDE   87 25
AND YES THANK GOD IT STILL IS POSSIBLE   90 28
LIKE VAPOUR DEW OR POISON NOW THANK GOD   91 1
THEN GOD LEFT THE PLACE   94 27
OH GOD IF I HAD NOT TO LEAVE YOU   102 17
I WONDER IF GOD ALLOWS   104 9
TO GOD TO REMOVE YOU   117 3
AND GOD LIKE GEOMETRY   118 24
DREAMING GOD KNOWS OF WHAT FOR TO ME SHE'S THE   129 2
GOD HOW SHE STARTS   143 14
GOD FORFEND   152 25
OF KISSES OH HELP ME GOD HERE AT THE SOURCE   153 28
GOD BOWS HIS HEAD AND GRANTS ME THIS SUPREME   157 16
YOUR YOUNG HUSHED LOOK THAT THEN SAW GOD ABLAZE   157 23
WOULD GOD THEY WERE SHATTERED QUICKLY THE CATTLE WOULD   159 21

GOD
AH GOD LIFE LAW SO MANY NAMES YOU KEEP   194 18
IF SO THE VAST THE GOD THE SLEEP THAT STILL GROWS RICHER   195 17
POLTROON AND BEG THE SILENT OUTSPREAD GOD   195 24
OH MY GOD HOW IT ACHES   212 19
OH GOD TO BE MUTILATED   213 19
GOD THAT I HAVE NO CHOICE   215 6
AND GOD THAT SHE IS NECESSARY   215 11
ARE YOU AFRAID OF GOD   231 21
I'M NOT AFRAID OF GOD   231 23
AND CALL TO GOD WHERE ART THOU   231 29
LET GOD COME FORTH TO JUSTIFY   232 3
GOD WILL KEEP   232 14
NOW I OFFER HER UP TO THE ANCIENT INEXORABLE GOD   238 23
LIKE A FALCON 'TIS GOD HAS TAKEN THE VICTIM   239 5
GARDEN WHICH GOD HAS HOARDED   243 11
ONLY GOD COULD HAVE BROUGHT IT TO ITS SHAPE   254 27
GOD KNOWS WHAT I FEEL BUT IT IS JOY   255 9
NOW I SAY TO HER NO TOOL NO INSTRUMENT NO GOD   255 19
I WAS THE GOD AND THE CREATION AT ONCE   257 14
AND GOD OF HORROR I WAS KISSING ALSO MYSELF   257 19
GOD BUT IT IS GOOD TO HAVE DIED AND BEEN TRODDEN OUT   258 18
MY GOD BUT I CAN ONLY SAY   259 20
THE FEAR OF HUNGER IS MOLOCH BELIAL THE HORRIBLE GOD   263 6
ONCE GOD WAS ALL NEGROID AS NOW HE IS FAIR   286 16
HEAVEN THE WHITE GOD   307 18
JESUS THE GOD OF FLOWERS   307 23
DIS THE DARK THE JEALOUS GOD THE HUSBAND   308 7
WHAT GOD DID THEY CONSULT   313 26
GOD MAY STAY IN MID-HEAVEN THE SON OF MAN HAS CLIMBED TO   323 14
SUCH AS MOSES HAD AND GOD   326 4
AND THE WORD WAS GOD   328 13
AND THE WORD WAS WITH GOD   328 14
OF GOD   328 28
BORN BEFORE GOD WAS LOVE   337 11
I DIDN'T KNOW HIS GOD   338 14
I DIDN'T KNOW HIS GOD   338 15
AND TO THE ONE GOD   338 17
BEYOND MY RANGE GODS BEYOND MY GOD   338 26
HIS GOD STANDS OUTSIDE MY GOD   339 14
LET THE GOD THAT CREATED HIM BE RESPONSIBLE FOR HIS DEA+   346 10
LET THE GOD WHO IS MAKER OF BATS WATCH WITH THEM IN   346 13
I ADMIT A GOD IN EVERY CREVICE   346 15
NOR THE GOD OF BATS WHILE THE SUN SHINES   346 17
AND LOOKED AROUND LIKE A GOD UNSEEING INTO THE AIR   350 28
AND THEN YOU SEE THE GOD THAT HE IS IN A CLOUD OF BLACK   381 10
GOD IN BLACK CLOUD WITH CURVING HORNS OF BRONZE   383 16
HAIRY HORRID GOD THE FATHER IN A WILLIAM BLAKE   385 20
WHERE'S YOUR GOD YOU WHITE ONE   404 24
WHERE'S YOUR WHITE GOD   404 25
BUT NOT GOD GREY-BEARDED AND DICTATORIAL   437 1
WHEN THE ONE MAN MADE A MONOPOLY OF IT   439 13
THE WEEPING MOTHER OF GOD INCONSOLABLE OVER HER SON   439 29
O RUDDY GOD IN OUR VEINS O FIERY GOD IN OUR GENITALS   440 12
PRETENDING THESE ARE THE MILLS OF GOD   441 9
THE MILLS OF INDUSTRY ARE NOT THE MILLS OF GOD   441 11
AND THE MILLS OF GOD GRIND OTHERWISE WITH THE WINDS OF   441 12
TRUST THE MILLS OF GOD THOUGH THEY GRIND EXCEEDING SMALL   441 14
GOD OF JUSTICE TO SAVE THEMSELVES   442 7
O GOD OF JUSTICE SEND NO MORE SAVIOURS   442 10
GOD OF JUSTICE WHEN WILT THOU TEACH THEM TO SAVE THEMSE+   443 9
STAND THEY AND GOD HOW THEY STINK   457 2
O GOD DELIVER ME   469 28
WHAT THE OLD PEOPLE CALL IMMEDIATE CONTACT WITH GOD   481 6
HIS GOD   482 13
WHICH IS GOD IN THE ATOM   513 20
THERE GOD IS   516 8
SO THEY CAN STILL RECOGNISE GOD   516 10
MY GOD IT TAKES SOME BEATING   547 18
GOD LET ME DOWN TO EARTH AGAIN   552 13
THOUGH YOU KNOWS IF YOU'RE ANY BETTER   553 29
O GOD TO US MAY STRENGTH BE GIVEN   554 3
MY GOD LET ME GET AWAY   556 16
GOD MAKE ME OF IT WORTHY   576 18
THE MILLS OF GOD WILL GRIND THEM SMALL ANYHOW THERE IS +   614 18
OH THEY ARE GRIST FOR THE MILLS OF GOD THEIR BONES GROU+   614 23
BUT WINDS OF HEAVEN ARE MILLS OF GOD TO THE FALLEN LEAV+   615 5
THEY FALL VICTIM AT ONCE TO THE VENGEANCE OF THE UNFORG+   616 7
NO ONE NOT EVEN GOD CAN PUT BACK A LEAF ON TO A TREE   617 1
AND NO ONE NOT GOD NOR CHRIST NOR ANY OTHER   617 3
GOD IS SUPREME   618 10
THERE IS NO SINNING AGAINST GOD WHAT DOES GOD CARE ABOU+   621 1
YET BELLS CALL THE CHRISTIANS IN   623 1
AND BRING US TO GOD   623 4
AND THE DAWN CRY FROM A MINARET GOD IS GREAT   623 15
MEN ARE NOT ALIKE IN THE SIGHT OF GOD   638 7
MEN ARE ANYTHING BUT ALIKE IN THE SIGHT OF GOD   638 9
IN THE SIGHT OF GOD AND THE UNKNOWN GODS   638 10
ONLY THE FEW THE VERY FEW MATTER IN THE SIGHT OF GOD AND   638 13
GOD CANNOT DO WITHOUT ME   641 18
CERTAINLY THE GOD IN THE MACHINE CANNOT   641 19
OH GREAT GOD OF THE MACHINE   643 26
I SUDDENLY SAW DEEP INTO THE EYES OF GOD   650 22
AH THE GODS THE SWAYING BODY OF GOD   651 17
AH THE FALLEN STILLNESS OF GOD AUTUMNS AND IT IS ONLY +   651 18
AGAIN AND AGAIN SOME GOD OF EVENING LEANS OUT OF IT   656 2
BUT MY GOD THEY SNEAK-THIEFED HIS VERY GENITALS AWAY FR+   659 15
AND SOON EVEN GOD WON'T BE BIG ENOUGH TO HANDLE THAT IN+   670 20
UNLESS THERE'S THE GLIMPSE OF A GOD IN HIM   671 10
AND EVERY GOD THAT HUMANITY HAS EVER KNOWN IS STILL A G+   671 14
WAS A GOD IN GODLINESS PURE AS CHRIST BEAUTIFUL   674 24
TERRIBLE AND STRANGE THE GOD LIES ON THE BED WISTFUL CO+   676 9
WHEN THE MAN WAS HIMSELF SO A GOD IN HIS SINGLENESS   676 12
THERE WAS NO GOD IN IT   681 13
BEHOLD GOD IS BORN   682 9
OH GOD IS BORN   682 16
LO GOD IS BORN   682 21
SEE GOD IS BORN HE IS BLUE HE IS DEEP BLUE HE IS FOREVE+   682 23

GOD
GOD IS BORN GOD IS BORN BRIGHT YELLOW AND DUCTILE HE IS+   682 25
ACH ACH NOW INDEED GOD IS BORN HE TWINKLES WITHIN   682 28
GOD IS BORN GOD IS BORN PERFUMED AND DANGLING AND WITH +   683 5
THE UNIVERSE TREMBLES GOD IS BORN GOD IS HERE   683 10
BEHOLD NOW VERY GOD IS BORN   683 13
GOD HIMSELF IS BORN   683 14
AND SO WE SEE GOD IS NOT   683 15
THERE IS NO END TO THE BIRTH OF GOD   683 18
FOR THE THING THAT IS DONE WITHOUT THE GLOWING AS OF GOD   689 10
EVEN THE MIND OF GOD CAN ONLY IMAGINE   689 21
GOD IS A GREAT URGE WONDERFUL MYSTERIOUS MAGNIFICENT   690 8
IT IS CREATION GOD LOOKS HIMSELF ON IT IN WONDER FOR TH+   690 11
WE KNOW THAT EVEN GOD COULD NOT IMAGINE THE REDNESS OF +   690 19
AND EVEN WHEN THEY WERE EVEN GOD WOULD HAVE TO HAVE A N+   690 23
GOD SIGHING AND YEARNING WITH TREMENDOUS CREATIVE YEARN+   691 2
AND GOD   691 9
FOR GOD EVEN THE RAREST GOD IS SUPPOSED TO LOVE US   691 12
GOD IS THE GREAT URGE THAT HAS NOT YET FOUND A BODY   691 15
AND BECOMES AT LAST A CLOVE CARNATION LO THAT IS GOD   691 17
AT HER BEST AND HER MOST BEAUTIFUL BEING GOD MADE MANIF+   691 20
ANY CLEAR AND FEARLESS AND BEING GOD VERY GOD   691 21
THERE IS NO GOD   691 22
THE LOVELY THINGS ARE GOD THAT HAS COME TO PASS LIKE JE+   692 7
GOD IS OLDER THAN THE SUN AND MOON   692 16
ENTERED ME I SMILED TO MYSELF SAYING HE IS GOD   692 16
GOD IS OLDER THAN THE SUN AND MOON   692 18
PONDERING FOR HE WAS A GREEK THAT GOD IS ONE AND ALL AL+   692 23
LO GOD IS ONE GOD BUT HERE IN THE TWILIGHT   693 18
WHERE GOD IS ALSO LOVE BUT WITHOUT WORDS   695 6
FROM THE PRESENCE OF GOD AND ENVELOP US   698 9
LO THE LAUGH OF GOD   698 14
LO THE LAST OF THE SEVEN GREAT LAUGHS OF GOD   698 16
THE SILENCE OF THE LAST OF THE SEVEN GREAT LAUGHS OF GOD   698 29
IT IS A FEARFUL THING TO FALL INTO THE HANDS OF THE LIV+   699 12
SAVE ME O GOD FROM FALLING INTO THE UNGODLY KNOWLEDGE   699 16
OF MYSELF AS I AM WITHOUT GOD   699 17
LET ME NEVER KNOW O GOD   699 18
WHEN I HAVE FALLEN OUT OF YOUR HANDS THE HANDS OF THE L+   699 20
WHEN THE SELF HAS FALLEN FROM THE HANDS OF GOD   699 23
EVEN OF THE SOUL FALLEN FROM THE HANDS OF GOD   699 27
SAVE ME FROM THAT O GOD   699 28
LET ME NEVER KNOW MYSELF APART FROM THE LIVING GOD   699 29
ALL THAT MATTERS IS TO BE AT ONE WITH THE LIVING GOD   700 1
FEELING THE PRESENCE OF THE LIVING GOD   700 10
IT IS NOT EASY TO FALL OUT OF THE HANDS OF THE LIVING G+ 700 17
EVEN THROUGH THE GREATEST BLASPHEMIES THE HANDS OF THE + 700 20
MAN CAN BREAK AWAY AND FALL FROM THE HANDS OF GOD   700 23
OF THOSE THAT HAVE FALLEN FROM GOD   701 9
ONLY MAN CAN FALL FROM GOD   701 10
CAN SLIP ENTIRELY THROUGH THE FINGERS OF THE HANDS OF G+ 701 14
OF SELF-AWARENESS NOW APART FROM GOD FALLING   701 21
KNOWING ITSELF KNOWING ITSELF APART FROM GOD FALLING   701 32
ARE YOU SO LOFTY O MY GOD   710 25
AH YES THE SLEEP OF GOD   725 9
TO GOD WHO DWELLS IN DEEP OBLIVION   725 21
ONLY IN SHEER OBLIVION ARE WE WITH GOD   725 22
MAY SINK INTO GOD AT LAST HAVING PASSED THE VEILS   726 11
BUT ANYONE WHO SHALL ASCRIBE ATTRIBUTES TO GOD OR   726 12
FOR GOD IS DEEPER FORGETTING FAR THAN SLEEP   726 15
THEN I HAVE BEEN DIPPED AGAIN IN GOD AND NEW-CREATED   726 25
WITH GOD WE ARE CLOSE TOGETHER NOW THE MOON'S IN SHADOW 727 5
I AM IN THE HANDS OF THE UNKNOWN GOD   727 28
OF WHAT WAS GOD BE GONE BE UTTERLY GONE   738 5
GOD HOW GLAD I AM TO HEAR THE SHELLS   741 9
MY GOD WHAT AGONY THEY ARE TO ME   741 18
MY GOD THAT THEY SHOULD ALWAYS BE WITH ME   741 21
NAY NOW AT LAST THANK GOD FOR THE JEOPARDY   741 22
AND GOD IS GOOD YES GOD IS VERY GOOD   741 26
AND GOD IS GOOD FOR I WANTED HIM TO DIE   742 1
AND GOD REVEALED THROUGH THE SWEAT AND THE HEAT OF LOVE 742 29
AND GOD ABROAD AND ALIGHT ON US EVERYWHERE   742 30
EVERYWHERE MEN AND WOMEN ALIGHT WITH GOD   742 31
WE TAKE THE BRIDE O GOD AND OUR SEED OF LIFE   743 12
WE GIVE HATE HER DUES O GOD WE YIELD HER UP   743 15
WHEN THOU RUNNEST THE RACE WITH THE FOREMOST GOD BLESS + 750 2
I HAVE COME TO THE HOUSE OF GOD   751 1
HAST THOU DETERMINED TO STRANGLE ME O GOD   751 14
YOU WEAR ON YOUR FINGER SO GLADLY FOR GOD   752 18
WE PRAY FOR THEE MARY DELIGHTFUL THAT GOD MAY BLESS THEE 753 2
SPEAK SOOTHINGLY FOR US TO GOD AND WHEN IN DISTRESS WE   753 4
LORD GOD ABOVE WOULD IT COST ME DEAR   759 16
GOD ONLY GOD IS ETERNALLY   759 16
GOD IS FOREVER AND ONLY HE   759 17
THEY ARE DEAD SO GOD AS BETWEEN YOU YOU SEE   759 19
GOD WHAT SHALL I DO IN THE WHITE DAYS   766 25
GOD OH MAKE IT STOP   767 5
OF SHARING THE NIGHT WITH GOD OF MINGLING UP AGAIN   772 25
BEFORE GOD YOU MUST BE CAREFUL   776 16
CONSUMMATUM EST OH GOD AND ON GOOD FRIDAY   779 7
YET YOU ARE HERE LIKE GOD UPON THE HEARTH   784 3
YOU ARE NOT WORTH A GOD   795 9
WHAT IS GOD WE SHALL NEVER KNOW   799 1
FROM HEAVEN PAST THE SLEEPING SONS OF GOD   801 5
IF GOD LOOKS LET HIM SEE   818 14
ARE ALL UNPEOPLED OF GOD   823 24
GOD THAT I SHOULD HAVE TO REPUDIATE HIM   871 37
OH MY GOD WHAT A BITTER SHAME   873 6
BUT OH MY GOD WHAT A BITTER SHAME   874 2
OH MY GOD WHAT A BITTER SHAME   874 10
MY GOD TO THINK IT IS GONE FOR EVER   886 19
THEN GOD LEFT THE PLACE   *897 15
MY QUESTION MY GOD I MUST BREAK FROM THIS HOARSE SILENCE *898 4
MY QUESTION MY GOD I MUST BREAK FROM THIS HOARSE SILENCE *901 13
GREY FOAM-FRINGE OF ADVANCING GOD   *914 29
SINCE GOD SWEEPS ONWARD DIM AND VAST   *915 13
GOD SHOOK THY ROUNDNESS IN HIS FINGER'S CUP   *915 21
GOD LONELY PUT DOWN HIS MOUTH IN A KISS OF CREATION   *916 5

GOD
  SO MUCH MORE ROOM FOR RIOT THE GREAT GOD SPARETH NOT   *926 28
  WARPING THE PERFECT IMAGE OF GOD   *929 4
  NOW TO GOD TO REMOVE YOU   *931 7
  AND GOD LIKE GEOMETRY   *932 2
  NOW STOP CARPING AT ME BUT GOD HOW I HATE YOU   *932 10
  AND ONCE AGAIN A SUAVE YOUNG GOD   *946 18

GOD-DAMN
  IN THE GOD-DAMN BOURGEOISIE   490 16

GODDESS
  UNLESS SHE'S A GLIMPSE OF A GODDESS OF SOME SORT   671 12
  AND THE WOMAN WAS HERSELF NEVER TO BE DUPLICATED A GODD+   676 13
  THEREFORE A GODDESS   676 17

GODDESSES
  NO ANGELS HERE FOR ME NO GODDESSES   234 19
  IN COLD BLOOD I CANNOT FEEL GODDESSES IN THE SUMMER EVE+   655 18
  I FEEL GODDESSES TRAFFICKING MYSTERIOUSLY THROUGH THE A+   655 27
  GODDESSES OF LOVE GODDESSES OF DIRT EXCREMENT-EATERS OR+   671 18

GOD-GIVEN
  THAT COULD ONLY BE GOD-GIVEN AND MURMURED   693 17

GODHEAD
  THEY DRAW THEIR SAP FROM THE GODHEAD NOT FROM ME BUT TH+   93 20
  THE GODHEAD OF GOATS FROM THE SHOCK   361 30
  IN THE BUSINESS OF BEATING THE METTLE OF GOATS TO A GOD+   381 33
  COMMUNION WITH THE GODHEAD THEY USED TO SAY IN THE   481 17
  WITH THE GODHEAD OF ENERGY THAT CANNOT TELL LIES   481 26
  THEY KNEW THE USEFUL GODHEAD OF PROVIDENCE   609 24
  OF ANY GODHEAD LEAVE US IN THE DARK   738 2

GODHEAD IN MAN
  OF GODHEAD IN MAN DESPISED CARELESSLY THROWN OVER   859 22

GOD HERMES
  AND STILL THIS IS THE GOD HERMES SITTING BY MY HEARTH   692 21

GOD-JOY
  THEE A GOD-JOY DIMINISHED   *927 30

GOD-KNOWS-WHAT
  AND HERE AM I PAYING INCOME TAX AND GOD-KNOWS-WHAT   547 5

GODLESS
  HE WORE US OUT SO NOW WE ARE GODLESS AND UNBELIEVING   439 14
  BUT WHEN OUR EAGERNESS LEAVES US WE ARE GODLESS AND FULL   439 19
  INTO HIMSELF ALONE DOWN THE GODLESS PLUNGE OF THE ABYSS   700 24

GODLINESS
  OH WONDERFUL MACHINE YOU ARE MAN'S IDEA OF GODLINESS   643 15
  WAS A GOD IN GODLINESS PURE AS CHRIST BEAUTIFUL   674 24

GOD-LOST
  A GOD-LOST CREATURE TURNING UPON HIMSELF   700 25

GODLY
  OH YOU GODLY AND SMOOTH MACHINE SPINNING ON IN YOUR   643 19
  FOR A MOMENT GODLY LIKE BAAL OR KRISHNA OR ADONIS OR BA+   675 16
  GODLY AND LOVELY COMES APHRODITE OUT OF THE SEA   693 19
  OF WHAT WAS GODLY LEAVE US QUITE ALONE   738 7

GOD OF LIFE
  TO BE A CREATURE IN THE HOUSE OF THE GOD OF LIFE   700 2

GODS
  THE PORTION TO THE GODS IS SPILLED   177 7
  NIGHT FOLK TUATHA DE DANAAN DARK GODS GOVERN HER SLEEP   213 25
  OH GODS OF THE LIVING DARKNESS POWERS OF NIGHT   213 29
  WHAT IS THAT REMINDS US OF WHITE GODS   280 18
  GODS NUDE AS BLANCHED NUT-KERNELS   280 19
  WHEN THE VINE WAS ROSE GODS WERE DARK-SKINNED   286 14
  FAR-OFF KINGS PAINTED THEIR FACES VERMILION AND WERE AL+   303 22
  OTHER GODS   338 25
  AWAY FROM AMONG GODS AND MEN HE DID NOT SEE THAT HE WAS+   348 2
  THE FORMS OF THE GODS LIKE HORSES AND OXEN LIKE OXEN AN+   376 3
  BEING ROYAL OF THE GODS   392 8
  OF INDIAN GODS   407 9
  GIVE US GODS OH GIVE THEM US   436 27
  GIVE US GODS   436 28
  GIVE US GODS   437 8
  GIVE US GODS BEFORE THESE   437 20
  THOU SHALT HAVE OTHER GODS BEFORE THESE   437 21
  BUT GIVE US GODS   438 2
  GODS DO YOU ASK FOR GODS   438 16
  THERE HAVE BEEN SO MANY GODS   439 11
  WE HAVE WORN OUT THE GODS AND THEY US   439 21
  YOU'LL HAVE TO PRAY TO THE FAR-OFF GODS   472 5
  TO MY DARK HEART GODS ARE   474 10
  GODS AND LOVE ALIKE ARE BUT AN IDEA   474 13
  TILL YOU PRAY TO THE RIGHT GODS FOR THE THUNDER-BOLT IN+   484 16
  BUT REMEMBER THE UNDAUNTED GODS   559 2
  THE INVISIBLE GODS HAVE NO MORAL TRUCK WITH US   607 32
  SONS OF THE LIVING ELEMENTS SONS OF THE UNTHINKING GODS   635 4
  SONS OF THE ELEMENTS AND THE UNSPEAKING GODS   635 24
  THE GODS THAT MADE US ARE GREATER THAN OUR CONSCIOUSNESS   636 29
  THAT WHICH IS ELEMENTAL AND OF THE SUBSTANTIAL GODS IN +   637 12
  IN THE SIGHT OF GOD AND THE UNKNOWN GODS   638 10
  THE LIVING SUBSTANTIAL GODS   638 14
  MEN WANTED TO BE LIKE GODS   640 25
  SEEM TO SMILE YE GODS   644 20
  SOME MEN LOOK STRAIGHT INTO THE EYES OF THE GODS   649 9
  AND SOME MEN CAN SEE NO GODS THEY ONLY KNOW   649 10
  THE GODS ARE THERE BECAUSE OF THE GLEAM ON THE FACES OF+   649 11
  WHO LOOK INTO THE EYES OF THE GODS   649 15
  AND WORSHIP IS THE JOY OF THE GLEAM FROM THE EYES OF TH+   649 16

GODS
  THOSE THAT LOOK INTO THE EYES OF THE GODS AND THESE ARE+   649 20
  TO SEE THE GLEAM OF THE GODS THERE REFLECTED IN THE HUM+   649 22
  AND THE FEW LOOK INTO THE EYES OF THE GODS AND SERVE TH+   650 4
  GODS   650 5
  THE FEW MUST LOOK INTO THE EYES OF THE GODS AND OBEY TH+   650 8
  IN THE EYES OF THE GODS   650 9
  AND THE MANY MUST OBEY THE FEW THAT LOOK INTO THE EYES +   650 10
  AND THE STREAM IS TOWARDS THE GODS NOT BACKWARDS TOWARD+   650 11
  WHO HAS LOOKED INTO THE EYES OF THE GODS   650 16
  WHAT ARE THE GODS THEN WHAT ARE THE GODS   650 19
  THE GODS ARE NAMELESS AND IMAGELESS   650 20
  AND THE GLIMMER OF THE PRESENCE OF THE GODS WAS LIKE LI+   651 5
  I REFUSE TO NAME THE GODS BECAUSE THEY HAVE NO NAME   651 7
  I REFUSE TO DESCRIBE THE GODS BECAUSE THEY HAVE NO FORM+   651 8
  BUT ALL THE TIME I SEE THE GODS   651 12
  AH THE GODS THE SWAYING BODY OF GOD   651 17
  THERE ARE NO GODS AND YOU CAN PLEASE YOURSELF   651 20
  THERE ARE NO GODS AND YOU CAN PLEASE YOURSELF   652 1
  AND I FALL ASLEEP WITH THE GODS   652 15
  YOU MAY SMELL THE BREATH OF THE GODS IN THE COMMON ROSES   655 7
  AND FEEL THE SPLENDOUR OF THE GODS GO THROUGH YOU EVEN +   655 8
  THE BAFFLING LIGHT OR THE STRANGE STILL GLEAM OF THE GO+   656 13
  AND UNDENIABLE NEW GODS SHARE THEIR LIFE WITH US WHEN WE   662 12
  WHOM THE GODS LOVE DIE YOUNG   662 14
  HOW THE GODS MUST HATE MOST OF THE OLD OLD MEN TODAY   662 15
  BECAUSE THE GODS DON'T WANT THEM   662 17
  THE GODS WHO ARE LIFE AND THE FLUIDITY OF LIVING CHANGE   662 22
  THERE'S ALL SORTS OF GODS ALL SORTS AND EVERY SORT   671 13
  ALL THE GODS AND YOU SEE THEM ALL IF YOU LOOK ALIVE AND+   671 20
  YOU MAY SEE GLIMPSES OF THE GODS IN THEM   672 6
  WHEN PEOPLE POSE AS GODS THEY ARE CRYSTAL PALACE STATUES   673 2
  WHEN MEN THINK THEY ARE LIKE GODS   673 4
  THE GODS ARE ALL THINGS AND SO ARE WE   673 16
  THE GODS ARE ONLY OURSELVES AS WE ARE IN OUR   673 17
  YOU ARE FOR THAT MOMENT ONE OF THE GODS JESUS OR FAFNIR+   674 4
  AND MAKES US COWARDS INSTEAD OF GODS   674 7
  NOW LET ME BE MYSELF IN THE BEING ONE OF THE GODS   674 17
  WITH THE DARK AND GLEAMING BEAUTY OF THE MESSAGELESS GO+   674 26
  SACRIFICE THAT TO THE BRIGHT GODS AND SATISFY THE DESTR+   678 17
  IT WAS TO THE GODS WHO MAKE US SPLENDID   679 12
  AND ROLL WITH MASSIVE STRONG DESIRE LIKE GODS   694 12
  LAST TWILIGHT OF THE GODS TO FIND AGAIN   737 8
  THE WILD GODS SEND VITALITY THEY PUT THE LIGHTNING INTO+   843 5

GOD-SHAPEN
  AND SO THOU WERT GOD-SHAPEN HIS FINGER   *915 25

GODS OF TIRYNS
  AND THE MINOAN GODS AND THE GODS OF TIRYNS   688 17

GOD-SPEED
  AND SIX HAVE GIVEN ME GIFTS AND KISSED ME GOD-SPEED   695 28

GOD'S
  AND TAKE WITHIN THE WINE THE GOD'S GREAT OATH   177 17
  ISN'T IT GOD'S OWN IMAGE TRAMPING HIS THIRTY MILES A DAY   430 22
  FOR GOD'S SAKE LET US BE MEN   450 12
  TILL THEY MOUNT AND FILL AND ALL IS FULFILLED OF GOD'S +   698 20
  CHILD DEAR TO MY EYE GOD'S BLESSING IS ON THY SERVICE   749 21
  BE NEAR US AND GOD'S WILL BE DONE   753 7
  FOR GOD'S SAKE LET US STOP OH YOU WHO STAND BEHIND US   756 1
  WITH BEAUTY SHINE AND BOW IN GOD'S GREAT WAKE   872 22
  THE FIRE ROSE UP AND THE BUSH BLAZED FORTH GOD'S GRACE   *897 13
  IN A BACKWARD RIPPLE GOD'S PROGRESS REVEAL   *915 10
  OF DEATH COMMINGLES IN GOD'S MIGHTY GLOOM   *938 16

GOD THE FATHER
  GOD THE FATHER IS A DYNAMO   641 3

GOD THE HOLY GHOST
  AND GOD THE HOLY GHOST IS GAS THAT KEEPS IT ALL GOING   641 5

GOD THE SON
  AND GOD THE SON A TALKING RADIO   641 4

GOD-THOUGHT
  IT TRUELY A GOD-THOUGHT DIMINISHED   *927 31

GOD-THRUST
  ERECT WITH THE GOD-THRUST ENTERING HIM FROM BELOW   373 6
  THE GOD-THRUST ENTERING YOU STEADILY FROM BELOW   373 22
  ERECT WITH THE GOD-THRUST ENTERING FROM BELOW   781 11
  WITH THE GOD-THRUST THRUSTING YOU SILENT FROM BELOW   781 28
  THE GOD-THRUST THRUSTING YOU SILENT AND DARK FROM BENEA+   782 9
  SOLDIER-ERECT FROM THE GOD-THRUST EAGLE   783 8

GOEST
  ME TOO AT LAST ERE THOU GOEST CHILD DEAR TO MY EYE   750 3

GOETH
  WHENCE COMETH WHITHER GOETH STILL THE SAME   69 26

GOETHE
  WHEN GOETHE BECOMES AN APOLLO HE BECOMES A PLASTER CAST   673 1

GOGGLE
  UNLESS GOGGLING EYES TO GOGGLE AT THE FILM   630 29

GOGGLE-EYED
  APPROVAL GOGGLE-EYED FOWL   170 24

GOGGLING
  NO GOGGLING CLOCK   170 26
  GOGGLING OBSCENITIES IF THAT'S YOU AND YOUR FATE WHY TH+   463 17
  UNLESS GOGGLING EYES TO GOGGLE AT THE FILM   630 29

GOINGS
  OF BROODING AND DELIGHTING IN THE SECRET OF LIFE'S GOIN+   197 17

GOIN'
  OH ARE YOU GOIN' TO UNDERWOOD   78 5
  I'M SCRAIGHTIN' MY-SEN BUT ARENA GOIN'   78 27
  'E ISN'T GOIN' TER MARRY YER   81 31
  AN' T' SHORT DAYS GOIN' UNKNOWN TER THEE   137 29
  GOIN' UP AN' BEIN' REFINED   553 2
  OH ARE YOU GOIN' TO UNDERWOOD   *919 25
  I'M SCREETIN' MY-SEN BUT ARE-NA GOIN'   *920 19
  FOR 'E ISN'T GOIN' TO MARRY YOU   *924 3

GOLD
  AH YOU STACK OF WHITE LILIES ALL WHITE AND GOLD   86 9
  SAVE IN A BROKEN PATTERN AMID PURPLE AND GOLD AND SABLE   90 6
  AND GLAZED YOU OVER WITH A SHEEN OF GOLD   90 21
  ARE NOT GOLD   101 4
  AS IF SHE WOULD SLIP THE GOLD AND GLIMMERING   106 5
  FOR A GREY RAT FOUND THE GOLD THIRTEEN   119 19
  AND SKIES OF GOLD AND LADIES IN BRIGHT TISSUE   135 4
  OF GREYNESS MINGLED WITH A FUME OF GOLD   135 14
  OF QUEENS IN HYACINTH AND SKIES OF GOLD   135 26
  IN THE HOUSE OF LIFE THE FLOOR WAS RUFFLED WITH GOLD   141 6
  AND GREAT GOLD MIDGES   146 32
  TO THIS SPRING OF COSMIC GOLD   162 10
  TO WHERE THE SUNSET HUNG ITS WAN GOLD CLOTHS   205 27
  AWAY THEIR PURPLE FACES AND THEIR GOLD   224 25
  I WANT TO GO THERE'S A GOLD ROAD BLAZES BEFORE   230 12
  THE PRIESTS IN GOLD AND BLACK THE VILLAGERS   232 19
  THE GREAT GOLD APPLES OF NIGHT   252 13
  GOLD WITH AN INNERMOST SPECK   253 1
  THE GOLD OF THEIR STRANGE PERSISTENCE   253 12
  GOLD AND OF INCONCEIVABLY FINE QUINTESSENTIAL BRIGHTNESS   271 18
  THEN BLOW THEM OVER WITH GOLD   273 3
  SMALL INTERSPERSED WITH JEWELS OF WHITE GOLD   314 2
  OR DRAGON-MOUTHED SALVIA WITH GOLD THROAT OF WRATH   314 26
  THE MOLTEN GOLD OF ITS INTOLERABLE RAGE   315 20
  AND THROAT OF BRIMSTONE-MOLTEN ANGRY GOLD   317 11
  WITH THEIR GOLD RED EYES AND GREEN-PURE GLEAM AND UNDER+   339 26
  FOR IN SICILY THE BLACK BLACK SNAKES ARE INNOCENT THE G+   350 3
  THEY GLIMMER WITH TISSUE OF GOLD AND GOLDEN THREADS ON   388 19
  GOLD EGG OF ALL THINGS   437 13
  OR EVEN THE SLY GOLD SERPENT FATHERLY LIFTED HIS HEAD O+   437 18
  WITH A FEW GOLD SPANGLES   444 25
  GOLD GOES OUT INTO A GREEN SHADOW   455 6
  AND DARTS A FEW GOLD RAYS   455 18
  A FEW GOLD RAYS THICKENING DOWN TO RED   455 20
  MY SUN AND THE GREAT GOLD SUN   455 29
  THERE IS A BAND OF DULL GOLD IN THE WEST AND SAY WHAT Y+   656 1
  WHEN GOLD LAY SHINING THREADING THE COOLED-OFF ROCK   682 24
  AND ON THE TREES HANG THE APPLES OF GOLD   770 22
  EVEN IF THERE WERE OIL COPPER GOLD UPON THESE   779 18
  OR OIL OR COPPER OR GOLD A CAUSE FOR POLITICAL ACTION   779 19
  DO YOU SEE THE GOLD SUN FLUTTERING BUOYANTLY IN HEAVEN   782 29
  THE GOLD SUN SHINES IN HEAVEN ONLY BECAUSE HE'S ALLOWED   783 1
  THEY WANT GOLD THEY WANT SILVER FROM THE MOUNTAINS   793 18
  AND BANK-NOTES ARE POETRY PURER THAN GOLD   814 10
  AND TWO POTS OF GOLD   819 3
  FROM THE BROW A GOLD   819 21
  IF THERE ARE POTS OF GOLD   820 1
  THEY ARE GOLD THEY ARE BROWN THEY ARE PURPLISH THEY   827 1
  PLUMS THE BLOND ONES ARE GOLD WITH LESS GLISTEN   827 5
  AS IT COMES OVER THE MILK-BLUE SEA HINTING AT GOLD AND +   840 5
  INSOLENT GOLD   861 10
  AH COIN ME SPEECH OF YOUR HEART'S GOLD FURNACE HEAT   872 27
  FAR OFF IN GOLD THE WILLOWS QUIVER   887 27
  INTO ROLLICKING SUNS AND THEIR LOST GOLD ROTS COMPRESSED   *896 20
  FOR THE GREY RAT FOUND THE GOLD THIRTEEN   *932 28
  OF BLUENESS MINGLED WITH A FUME OF GOLD   *939 14
  OF QUEENS IN HYACINTH 'NEATH SKIES OF GOLD   *939 18
  GOLD GOLD DEEP GOLD HER GLOWING EYES UNFOLD   *941 26

GOLD-AND-GREENISH
  AND SUDDENLY PULLED A GOLD-AND-GREENISH LUCENT FISH FROM   339 2

GOLD-AND-GREEN
  AND THE GOLD-AND-GREEN PURE LACQUER-MUCUS COMES OFF IN   339 15

GOLD-BARRED
  OF JOHN'S GREAT GOLD-BARRED EAGLE   328 9

GOLD-BRONZE
  AND GOLD-BRONZE FLUTTERS BENT THROUGH THE THICK UPPER A+   647 12

GOLD-BROWN
  THE GOLD-BROWN FLOWERS OF HER EYES UNFOLD   868 26

GOLDEN
  GRASPING IN THE GOLDEN LIGHT   42 2
  DIVESTING HERSELF OF HER GOLDEN SHIFT AND SO   67 8
  LEAN ABOUT US SCATTERING THEIR POLLEN GRAINS OF GOLDEN +   70 2
  OF GOLDEN DUST OUT WITH STAR AFTER STAR   70 18
  EACH ARC-LAMP GOLDEN DOES EXPOSE   104 26
  DRIPPING WITH ALL THE GOLDEN LEES   104 31
  O THE GOLDEN SPARKLES LAID EXTINCT   120 6
  YES SAY IT FOR SURE FROM THE GOLDEN SUN   127 1
  LAMPS IS RAYED WITH GOLDEN BANDS   144 4
  THE MOON WAS A GOLDEN PETAL BETWEEN   216 15
  GOLDEN SHADOW GLOWS AS   217 15
  CONCENTRATES HER GOLDEN SHADOW   217 24
  THEY ARE LAYING THE GOLDEN RACING-TRACK OF THE SUN   230 9
  THE POWER OF THE RISING GOLDEN ALL-CREATIVE SAP COULD T+   272 22
  EYES OF YELLOW GOLDEN SAND   301 30
  THE GOLDEN HORNS OF POWER   326 2
  THE POOR OLD GOLDEN EAGLE OF THE WORD-FLEDGED SPIRIT   329 30
  THEY GLIMMER WITH TISSUE OF GOLD AND GOLDEN THREADS ON   388 19
  BEHOLD ME TROTTING AT EASE BETWIXT THE SLOPES OF THE GO+   409 6

GOLDEN
  THE GOLDEN HAWK OF HORUS   409 8
  FEATHER OVER FEATHER ON THE BREAST OF THE GREAT AND GOL+   409 16
  HANDING OUT A FEW LOOSE GOLDEN BREAST-FEATHERS AT MOULT+   414 9
  FATHERING ENDLESS TEN-DOLLAR GOLDEN EGGS   414 12
  OR ARE YOU THE GOOSE THAT LAYS THE GOLDEN EGG   414 30
  LAYING THAT GOLDEN EGG   414 33
  THAT ADDLED GOLDEN EGG   414 34
  DON'T EARN GOLDEN OPINIONS OPINIONS GOLDEN   458 26
  A TIGER IS STRIPED AND GOLDEN FOR HIS OWN GLORY   523 13
  OH GOLDEN FIELDS OF PEOPLE   627 9
  OH GOLDEN FIELD OF PEOPLE   627 11
  AND BEHIND ME NOW IN THE GULFS OF SPACE LIES THE GOLDEN+   695 26
  AND ONE WARM KIND KISS OF THE LION WITH GOLDEN PAWS   695 33
  OH BROTHER AND I AM THE GOLDEN RING   752 17
  DOWN THE GOLDEN SLOPES TO SUNSET   769 30
  HUITZILOPOCHTLI THE GOLDEN   810 1
  HUITZILOPOCHTLI GOLDEN   810 15
  SWAYS THE GOLDEN PEARL OF PLEASURE   868 20
  AROUND ITS GOLDEN STOPPED NOTES   868 22
  FOR THE GOLDEN MOON COMMUNES   883 24
  LIKE IVORY AND GOLDEN MARBLE TWO BLACK CROWS HOLD   *894 27
  LEAN ABOUT US SCATTERING THEIR POLLEN PUFFS OF GOLDEN L+   *916 10
  THE GOLDEN GRAINED NIGHT AFLOWER ACROSS THE SKY   *916 17
  STREAM GOLDEN SMOKE   *916 20
  SHAKE DOWN THEIR GOLDEN LITTER THAT DISCLOSES   *916 22
  WITH GOLDEN CHICKS OF CLOUD AND A SKY OF RUNNING LAUGHT+   *933 15
  THEN THE DAYS RAN ROUND ME IN A GOLDEN BROOD   *933 17
  OH WHERE-OUT NOW HAS WANDERED THE GOLDEN HEN OF SUNSHINE   *933 21
  AND DEEP IN THE GOLDEN WINE OF THEIR CHALICES   *941 10
  PASS LIKE A TUNE THE SALLOW'S GOLDEN NOTES   *941 24
  GOLDEN SHADOW GLOWS AND HER BREASTS   *942 25
  SHE STIRS HER GOLDEN SHADOW   *943 7
  AND BEYOND THE EAGLE ROSE AND THE PHOENIX PARENT SOARIN+   *946 23
  BEFORE THE GOLDEN FATHERLY SERPENT LIFTED HIS HEAD OFF +   *946 27

GOLDEN-LIGHTED
  GOLDEN-LIGHTED TALL   146 12

GOLDEN-MOUTHED
  GOLDEN-MOUTHED OCCASIONALLY   236 10

GOLDEN-SPANIEL
  110 GOLDEN-SPANIEL SWEET ALERT NARCISSUS   309 7

GOLDEN-STOPPED
  ABOUT IT GOLDEN-STOPPED NOTES   *941 22

GOLDEN-THROATED
  AND FLAME-RAGE GOLDEN-THROATED   313 23
  THE ANGER-REDDENED GOLDEN-THROATED SALVIA   315 15

GOLD-FILMED
  DO YOU MEAN IT IS WRONG THE GOLD-FILMED SKIN INTEGUMENT   278 29

GOLD-GREY
  AND BEAUTIFULLY LAID IN BLACK ON A GOLD-GREY SKY   146 29

GOLD-MINES
  WHITE MEN MAKE GOLD-MINES AND THE MOUNTAINS UNMAKE   407 13

GOLD-TOOTHED
  O CEASE TO LABOUR FOR THE GOLD-TOOTHED DEAD   441 30

GOLLIWOG
  IN SECRET GREAT GOLLIWOG   492 22

GONG
  AND THE ACCUMULATED SPLASHING OF A GONG   623 9

GOOD
  ALL THAT IS RIGHT ALL THAT IS GOOD ALL THAT IS GOD TAKE+   34 27
  AGAINST HIM DIE AND FIND DEATH GOOD   43 37
  UNFOLDS FROM THE SKY FOR YOUR GOOD   56 9
  LOVE WILL YET AGAIN RETURN TO HER AND MAKE ALL GOOD   65 22
  A DECENT SHORT REGRET FOR THAT WHICH ONCE WAS VERY GOOD   66 4
  I AM SICK AND WHAT ON EARTH IS THE GOOD OF IT ALL   74 16
  WHAT GOOD TO THEM OR ME I CANNOT SEE   74 17
  HE WED HE'D HA'E SUMMAT GOOD   77 28
  I HOPE IT DID THEE GOOD   80 20
  'ER'S AS GOOD AS THEE   80 26
  LET ME GO WHAT'S GOOD O' TALKIN'   84 25
  AN' 'S NOT GOOD ENOUGH IT ISN'T   84 31
  IT IS NO GOOD DEAR GENTLENESS AND FORBEARANCE I ENDURED+   92 7
  AND IT WAS NO GOOD   111 22
  GOOD IT WOULD LET THE ACHE COME THROUGH   122 30
  BETROTHED YOUNG LADY WHO LOVES ME AND TAKES GOOD   129 4
  OF HER MAIDENLY VIRTUE AND OF MY GOOD NAME   129 6
  YEA WHAT GOOD BEGINNINGS   152 22
  BUT OH IT IS NOT ENOUGH IT IS ALL NO GOOD   180 29
  FOLD HIM BE GOOD TO HIM CHERISH HIM   228 31
  IT IS ALL NO GOOD   229 27
  MAKE A GOOD INVESTIGATION   237 9
  ALL GOOD EVIL BOTH   239 20
  BACK BEYOND GOOD AND EVIL   243 17
  I WOULD BE A GOOD FOUNTAIN A GOOD WELL-HEAD   250 26
  WHY SHOULDN'T YOUR LEGS AND YOUR GOOD STRONG THIGHS   254 11
  I BURIED MY BELOVED IT WAS GOOD I BURIED MYSELF AND WAS   257 28
  VERY GOOD VERY GOOD EVERY HAND RAISED TO MURDER   257 28
  VERY GOOD VERY GOOD I AM A MURDERER   257 29
  IT IS GOOD I CAN MURDER AND MURDER AND SEE THEM FALL   257 30
  GOD BUT IT IS GOOD TO HAVE DIED AND BEEN TRODDEN OUT   258 18
  FOR SO MUCH I THANK THE GOOD GENERATIONS OF MANKIND   263 14
  HERE AGAIN MAN HAS BEEN GOOD IN HIS LEGACY TO US IN THE+   263 18
  SO FAR SO GOOD   264 6
  WISE GOOD PROVISION THAT MAKES THE HEART SWELL WITH LOVE   264 7
  WHAT THEN GOOD LORD CRY THE WOMEN   284 20
  ARE OUR WORDS NO GOOD   296 7

GOOD

BOW DEEP FOR IT'S GOOD AS A DRAUGHT OF COOL WATER TO BOW	391	30
AND THE COTTON-WOOD LEAVES ARE FALLEN AS GOOD AS FALLEN	403	15
NO GOOD	407	12
NO GOOD	408	7
NO GOOD	408	14
IF LIFE GOES INTO THE PUDDING GOOD IS THE PUDDING	449	12
GOOD IS THE STOOL	449	13
GOOD HUSBANDS MAKE UNHAPPY WIVES	456	5
BUT THE UNHAPPINESS OF A WIFE WITH A GOOD HUSBAND	456	7
NO GOOD ASKING THE REASON WHY	458	3
DON'T BE A GOOD LITTLE GOOD LITTLE BOY	458	16
BEING AS GOOD AS YOU CAN	458	17
BY GOOD SIR JESSE BOOT	488	14
THAT MILDEWED PUP GOOD DOGGIE	491	26
HE DID HIS BEST THE GOOD OLD DOG	492	7
A GOOD KICK AT HIS DIRTY OLD HOLE	494	12
MY SHABBY LITTLE DEFEAT WOULD DO NEITHER ME ANY GOOD	508	23
YET WHEN THE TIME HAS COME TO BE NOTHING HOW GOOD IT IS	509	10
PAUSES THAT ARE AS GOOD AS DEATH EMPTY AND DEAD AS DEATH	510	8
AND AT THE SAME TIME EXPECT TO GO ON CALMLY EATING GOOD	531	6
GOOD DINNERS FOR FIFTY MORE LONG YEARS	531	15
THE WONDERFUL THOUGHTFUL WOMEN WHO MAKE SUCH GOOD	539	23
IT'S NO GOOD THE WOMEN ARE IN ERUPTION	541	1
AND THOSE THAT HAVE BEEN GOOD SO FAR	541	2
FOR SPECTACLES AND BULGING CLEVER ANT-EYES ARE NO GOOD +	544	7
ISN'T EVEN AS GOOD AS A GOB	545	27
THEY TOOK AWAY YOUR GOOD OLD STONES	549	9
AND IT WORRIED ME A GOOD DEAL	555	28
SO RESPONSIBLE AND GOOD	557	2
HOW GOOD WE WERE	557	20
AND IT'S NO GOOD WAILING FOR LOVE	559	7
AND IT'S NO GOOD MOONING FOR SLOPPY EASE	559	9
THEIR GOOD YOUTH GO TO WASTE	560	4
OF THE GOODY GOOD	562	11
NOT JUST A GOOD TURD	564	10
IF IT'S GOOD IF IT'S GOING TO BE A GOOD LITTLE MAN	570	26
IF IT'S GOOD	571	3
TO THE CHAR WHO'S AS GOOD AS YOU ARE ANY DAY	572	4
THEN WHY SHOULD WE BE GOOD	573	10
SO BE A NICE UNCLE BE GOOD TO US GIRLS	574	5
MR GLADSTONE WAS A VERY GOOD MAN	582	1
EDITOR GOOD MORNING DON'T TROUBLE TO CALL AGAIN WE	582	19
A MISS IS AS GOOD AS A MILE	603	13
SO I SAID GOOD MORNING AND LEFT HIM	620	9
THEN WHY SHOULD I BE GOOD	670	25
WHAT'S THE GOOD OF A MAN	671	9
AND WHAT'S THE GOOD OF A WOMAN	671	11
GOOD HEALTHY NATURAL FEELINGS INSTINCTS PASSIONS OR DES+	678	3
BE GOOD TO ME LADY GREAT LADY OF THE NEAREST	695	20
BE GOOD TO ME NOW AS I BEG YOU AS YOU'VE ALWAYS BEEN GO+	696	9
ALL OF WHICH THINGS I CAN SURELY TASTE IN A GOOD APPLE	708	1
NOTHING IN LIFE IS QUITE SO GOOD AS THIS	725	5
IN SLEEP AND SINK IN GOOD OBLIVION	726	23
AND GOD IS GOOD YES GOD IS VERY GOOD	741	26
AND GOD IS GOOD FOR I WANTED HIM TO DIE	742	1
DO YOU LIFT YOUR LIPS TO KISS ME GOOD NIGHT MY LOVE	750	16
OH YOU WHO MAKE ME FEEL SO GOOD WHEN	761	28
AND THE AIR THAT BLOWS GOOD BREATH IN THE NOSTRILS OF P+	792	14
WHAT ARE YOU GOOD FOR BUT TO BE SLAVES AND ROT AWAY	795	8
THE GOOD GHOST OF ME GOES DOWN THE DISTANCE	812	9
MIND AND SPIRIT BAD AND GOOD	824	14
BAD AND THE GOOD	826	19
THEY'D BE GOOD TO EAT	828	9
THE GOOD THING ABOUT THE YOUNGER GENERATIONS	828	14
IT'S NO GOOD MY DEAR	834	13
AT HER AGE WHY I'LL BE EARNING A JOLLY GOOD SCREW	834	20
A JOLLY GOOD SCREW WHEN THE DEAR LITTLE GIRLY-WIRLY'S O+	834	21
FULL FORE-AND-AFT IN GOOD GREY CREPE DE CHINE	835	28
THEY ARE EITHER IMMORALLY GOOD THE WORD DOES NOT AND	836	22
FOR ALL THAT LIFE WILL ONLY BE GOOD AGAIN WHEN THERE IS+	838	1
IN THEM DID ME GOOD	885	17
OWNING MY SUPPLE BODY A RARE GLAD THING SUPREMELY GOOD	*892	11
MOUNTS UP TO MY HEART AND I FIND IT GOOD	*899	34
MOUNTS UP TO MY HEART AND I FIND IT GOOD	*903	13
NO GOOD I WARRANT THIS TROUBLE IS SUCH AS SHE	*910	7
LIKE BETTER NOR ALL YOUR GOOD AN' 'E WAS ONE	*911	14
HE WED HE'D HA'E SUMMAT GOOD	*919	16
DID TER FIND HER GOOD	*922	20
IT IS NO GOOD DEAR MEEKNESS AND FORBEARANCE I ENDURED T+	*926	7
AND WHAT OF GOOD I HAVE GIVEN THE DAY MY PEACE ATTESTS	*946	3
FOR ME IT'S NOT GOOD ENOUGH	*947	14
NOT GOOD ENOUGH TO BE LOVED BY THIS EXPERT	*948	20

GOOD-BYE

THEN I'LL SAY GOOD-BYE TO THEE TIMOTHY	80	27
I'LL TA'E THY WORD GOOD-BYE LIZ	80	29
I'LL SAY GOOD-BYE LIZ TO YER	85	1
SO GOOD-BYE AN' LET'S LET BE	85	4
I KISS YOU GOOD-BYE MY DARLING	102	7
I KISS YOU GOOD-BYE MY DEAREST	102	13
THA COME TER SAY GOOD-BYE TER ME	138	8
TER SAY GOOD-BYE AN' A'	139	7
THA COME TER SAY GOOD-BYE TER ME	139	28
I'LL ONLY SAY GOOD-BYE TO THEE TIMOTHY	*922	27
I'LL TA'E THY WORD GOOD-BYE LIZ	*922	29

GOOD FRIDAY

GOOD FRIDAY CHRIST CRUCIFIED	777	23
ON GOOD FRIDAY THE BIG WHITE MEN OF THE INDIAN BUREAU	777	24
SO THE SPEECH IN THE PUEBLO ON GOOD FRIDAY	778	31
CONSUMMATUM EST OH GOD AND ON GOOD FRIDAY	779	7

GOOD-HEARTED

HIM TO PIECES THE GOOD-HEARTED SPANIELS	494	4

GOODLY

I IN THESE GOODLY FROZEN	199	15
AND ALSO TO ENSURE A GOODLY INCREASE IN THE WORLD	325	22

GOODNESS

GOODNESS KNOWS IF THEY'LL BE ABLE	45	15
WERE OPEN TO ME IN THE WISDOM AND GOODNESS OF MAN	264	5

GOODS

IF YOU'VE GOT THE GOODS COME FORWARD BOY AND LET'S SEE	483	20
THEY WERE CUNNING ABOUT THE GOODS	556	10
THE FOE CAN TAKE OUR GOODS OUR HOMES AND LAND	736	16

GOOD-UN

THA'RT A GOOD-UN AT SUCKIN'-IN YET TIMMY	79	25
THA'RT A GOOD-UN AT SUCKIN-IN YET TIMMY	*921	21

GOOD-WILL

IS NOT TO ADD OUR LOVE TOGETHER OR OUR GOOD-WILL	506	2

GOODY

OF THE GOODY GOOD	562	11

GOODY-GOOD

SO OUR GOODY-GOOD MEN BETRAY US	537	7

GOO-GOO

AND A GOO-GOO SORT OF VOICE-BOX	830	31

GOOSE

I REMEMBER HEARING A WILD GOOSE OUT OF THE THROAT OF NI+	365	34
OR ARE YOU THE GOOSE THAT LAYS THE GOLDEN EGG	414	30
SWEEPS THE HIGH GOOSE ABOVE THE MISTS	437	24
LIKE A WILD SWAN OR A GOOSE WHOSE HONK GOES THROUGH MY	438	7
WHICH IS DEATH TO THE GOOSE	704	24
LIKE THE POWER AND THE GLORY OF THE GOOSE IN THE MIST	704	25
GOOSE	841	2
THE NEXT DAY IS THE DAY OF THE GOOSE THE WILD SWAN'S DAY	841	9
SWAM THE STILL SWAN SWEPT THE WIDE GOOSE ABOVE THE MISTS	*947	2
LIKE A WILD SWAN OR A GOOSE WHOSE HONK GOES THROUGH MY +	*947	18

GOOSEBERRIES

FLOWERS AND GOOSEBERRIES	451	16

GOOSEY

GOOSEY GOOSEY GANDER	669	12

GORGE

THE GORGE OF THE GAPING FLOWER TILL THE BLOOD DID FLOAT	123	18
THE GORGE OF THE GAPING FLOWER TILL THE BLOOD DID FLOAT	*934	24

GORGED

AND DRINKS HIMSELF LIKE A SOAKED GORGED CREATURE DULL	877	9

GORGEOUS

I CAN SMELL THE BOG-END GORGEOUS IN ITS BREATHLESS	90	7
HOW GORGEOUS THAT SHOCK OF RED LILIES AND LARKSPUR CLEA+	129	27
IT IS GORGEOUS TO LIVE AND FORGET	244	25
SEE HOW GORGEOUS THE WORLD IS	245	3
SLOWLY SAILING IN GORGEOUS APPAREL THROUGH THE FLAME-LI+	387	30

GORGEOUSNESS

YOUR SORT OF GORGEOUSNESS	369	3
IS THE GORGEOUSNESS THAT EVOKES MY MOST PUZZLED ADMIRAT+	369	7

GORGING

SUCH GORGING	334	2

GORGON'S

HAS HE SEEN THE GORGON'S HEAD AND TURNED TO STONE	379	7

GORING

SUCH SUBURBAN AMBITION SO MESSILY GORING	494	23

GORPING

UNHOOKED HIS GORPING WATER-HONEY MOUTH	339	6

GORSE

HERE FLICK THE RABBITS HERE PANTS THE GORSE HERE SAY TH+	34	11
THE QUICK SPARKS ON THE GORSE BUSHES ARE LEAPING ·	*891	1
WHAT IF THE GORSE FLOWERS SHRIVELLED AND KISSING WERE L+	*891	23

GORSE-BUSHES

THE QUICK SPARKS ON THE GORSE-BUSHES ARE LEAPING	33	1

GORSE-FLOWERS

WHAT IF THE GORSE-FLOWERS SHRIVELLED AND I WERE GONE	33	21

GOSSAMER

BLIND WITH THE GOSSAMER OF PREVALENT DEATH	737	3

GOSSAMER'S

IS SEEN IN THE GOSSAMER'S RIME	68	16

GOTTEN

ME GOTTEN A CHILDT TER THY LANDLADY	80	3
THA'S GOTTEN THY ANSWER PAT	80	4
LAD THOU HAST GOTTEN A CHILD IN ME	220	6
PEOPLE IN THEIR THIRTIES AND THE OLDER ONES HAVE GOTTEN	462	19
ME GOTTEN A CHILDT TO THY LANDLADY	*922	3
THA'S GOTTEN THY ANSWER PAT	*922	4
LAD THA'S GOTTEN A CHILDT IN ME	*944	14

GOURD

THE ROOM IS THE HOLLOW RIND OF A FRUIT A GOURD	112	19
SO IT WILL LEAVE YOU AND YOU WILL HAND LIKE A GOURD ON +	800	22

GOURDS
   SEE YOU BE NOT RAT-GNAWED GOURDS   800 35

GOURD-SHELLS
   YOU ARE EMPTY GOURD-SHELLS FILLED WITH DUST AND WIND   800 4

GOUT
   GOUT UPON GOUT   131 14

GOVERN
   NIGHT FOLK TUATHA DE DANAAN DARK GODS GOVERN HER SLEEP   213 25

GOVERNING
   WORK RECREATION GOVERNING ANARCHY   256 28

GOVERNMENT
   WE'VE GOT A CHANGE OF GOVERNMENT   571 15
   AND IN RETURN THE GOVERNMENT WOULD SUPPLY THEM WITH   778 29

GOWN
   YOU MY LOVE THE FOREMOST IN A FLOWERED GOWN   58 20
   WHITE STAND NAKED OF GOWN   106 6
   AND HER BOSOM COUCHED IN THE CONFINES OF HER GOWN   123 9
   GOWN   143 9
   A TALL WOMAN WITH HER LONG WHITE GOWN AFLOW   155 13
   AT LAST AS YOU STOOD YOUR WHITE GOWN FALLING FROM YOUR   207 1
   NOR BY ANY DISTINCTIVE GOWN   312 15
   AND I SAW HER BOSOM COUCH IN THE NEST OF HER GOWN   *934 15

GRAB
   MEN ARE MADE MEAN BY FEAR AND A SYSTEM OF GRAB   520 28
   FOR OUR SOCIETY IS BASED ON GRAB AND DEVIL TAKE THE HIN+   829 24
   TO GRANDFATHERS AND GRANDMOTHERS IT WAS GRAB   829 27
   BUT OF COURSE THIS MEANS SMASHING THE PRESENT SYSTEM OF+   837 27
   TAKE THE LANTERN AND WATCH THE SOW FOR FEAR SHE GRAB HE+   *892 24

GRABBING
   LAST NIGHT WHEN I WENT WITH THE LANTERN THE SOW WAS GRA+   38 8
   AND IMPUDENT NETTLES GRABBING THE UNDER-EARTH   317 19

GRACE
   SEX IS A STATE OF GRACE   472 1
   SEX IS A STATE OF GRACE   485 7
   A CERTAIN PEACE A CERTAIN GRACE   499 2
   AND GRACE IF I DON'T LOSE IT FROM THE SAME PLACE   499 5
   THAT A MAN OR A WOMAN IN A STATE OF GRACE   570 25
   WITH ALL HER GRACE OF FOAM   646 27
   THE SECRET OF THE NOISELESS UTTER GRACE   744 27
   DRESSED IN THE GRACE OF IMMORTALITY   745 17
   THOUGH YOU MOVE WITH A QUIET GRACE LIKE A CLOUD   874 23
   THE FIRE ROSE UP AND THE BUSH BLAZED FORTH GOD'S GRACE   *897 11
   SWEET WISDOM OF GRACE NOW WHO WILL FREE   *927 24
   WITH A QUIVERING SWEET WISDOM OF GRACE BUT NOW   *928 24

GRACEFULLY
   GRACEFULLY SIGHING THROUGH THE WHITE   105 29

GRACES
   IT'S YOUR WIFE WI' HER AIRS AN' GRACES   493 20

GRACIOUS
   ALL THESE GRACIOUS LADIES   556 25

GRACIOUSLY
   GRACIOUSLY BOWING DOWN   556 26

GRADUALLY
   CHANGE FROM BEING SINGLE AND BECOME GRADUALLY DOUBLE   534 26
   THEN GRADUALLY I APPROXIMATE TO THE DOG   645 3

GRAFT
   TO GRAFT ON ANOTHER TREE   640 20
   AND EVEN THE LOVELIEST FLOWERS YOU MUST GRAFT THEM ON A   640 23

GRAFTING
   THEY NEED GRAFTING   640 22

GRAIL
   LIKE A LOVING-CUP LIKE A GRAIL BUT THEY SPILT IT TRIUMP+   92 23
   MY GRAIL A BROWN BOWL TWINED   123 24
   OF THE WITHERED TREE IN THE GRAIL   147 25
   MY GRAIL WHOSE BOWL WAS TWINED   *934 30

GRAIN
   AS THEIR EYES GLANCE AT ME FOR THE GRAIN   52 2
   OF THE TIME WHEN THE GRAIN STRUGGLES DOWN IN THE DARK   63 19
   OH BUT THE RAIN CREEPS DOWN TO WET THE GRAIN   63 27
   THE LITTLE GRAIN DRAWS THE EARTH TO HIDE   64 10
   A GRAIN OF THIS SAME FIRE WE CAN DESCRY   89 20
   SUMPTUOUS CENTRAL GRAIN   124 12
   THAT SAVES THE BLUE GRAIN OF ETERNAL FIRE   161 3
   SHALL I LESS THAN THE LEAST RED GRAIN OF FLESH   195 31
   OUT ALL THE GRAIN   268 28
   AND ROCKS IT TONS OF GRAIN ON THE RIPENING WIND   271 22
   THE INDIVIDUAL CARRIES HIS OWN GRAIN OF INSANITY AROUND+   486 9
   THE TINY GRAIN OF SOMETHING THAT NO WAVE CAN WASH AWAY   514 4
   HAY-SEED AND TINY GRAIN OF GRASS GRAMINIFERAE   587 4
   AS THEIR EYES GLANCE AT ME FOR THE GRAIN   *899 15
   AS THEIR EYES GLANCE AT ME FOR THE GRAIN   *902 27
   SUMPTUOUS CENTRAL GRAIN   *935 11

GRAINED
   THE GOLDEN GRAINED NIGHT AFLOWER ACROSS THE SKY   *916 17

GRAINS
   LEAN ABOUT US SCATTERING THEIR POLLEN GRAINS OF GOLDEN +   70 2
   NUMEROUS AND WHISPERING THIN GRAINS OF RICE IN A   391 6
   COUNT THE RED GRAINS OF THE HUITZILOPOCHTLI   811 24
   LIKE GRAINS OF MUSIC CROSSING THE FERTILE FALLOW   868 23

GRAMINIFERAE
   HAY-SEED AND TINY GRAIN OF GRASS GRAMINIFERAE   587 4

GRAMOPHONE
   THE DEAD GIVE SHIPS AND ENGINES CINEMA RADIO AND GRAMOP+   441 17
   GRAMOPHONE   450 16

GRAND
   FLUSHED AND GRAND AND NAKED AS FROM THE CHAMBER   193 3
   THAT IS A GRAND OLD LUST OF HIS TO GATHER THE GREAT   381 23
   BUILT IT MOST GRAND AND CAKEILY   488 11
   IN GRAND AND CAKEY STYLE   488 22
   WITH ITS ROOTS IT HAS A GRAND GRIP ON ITS DAILY BREAD   498 21
   AND EVEN THE GRAND HORSE OF PHYSICAL ENERGY   658 17
   IN GRAND CHORALE TO YOUR MONTHLY KICK-UP   681 8

GRANDCHILDREN
   AND THEIR GRANDCHILDREN ARE ONCE MORE SLAVES   535 26

GRANDFATHERS
   TO GRANDFATHERS AND GRANDMOTHERS IT WAS GRAB   829 27

GRANDFATHERS'
   OUR FATHERS' AND GRANDFATHERS' IDEAL   831 13

GRAND INQUISITOR
   BUT THE GRAND INQUISITOR IS A STALE MAGISTRATE   633 18

GRANDLY
   LIVING ON YOUR INCOME IS STROLLING GRANDLY OUTSIDE THE   521 11

GRANDMOTHERS
   DULLER THAN YOUR GRANDMOTHERS BUT LEAVE THAT ASIDE   464 11
   TO GRANDFATHERS AND GRANDMOTHERS IT WAS GRAB   829 27

GRANT
   TO GRANT IT YOU   472 6
   THEY WERE ONLY TOO EAGER TO GRANT   555 22

GRANTED
   GRANTED THERE IS AN EXCHANGE OF GENUINE FEELING   845 5
   GRANTED THERE IS A PROPER GIVE AND TAKE   *952 17

GRANTS
   GOD BOWS HIS HEAD AND GRANTS ME THIS SUPREME   157 16
   AND WHEN THIS CASH-CHEMIST UNIVERSITY GRANTS DEGREES LI+   *950 22

GRAPE
   WHAT IS IT IN THE GRAPE TURNING RAISIN   280 14
   SO THAT THE RAMBLING SKY-DROPPED GRAPE CAN ADD ITS SAVO+   281 25
   DROPPING AMONG HIS LEAVES HANGS THE DARK GRAPE   286 10
   THE GRAPE IS SWART THE AVENUES DUSKY AND TENDRILLED SUD+   286 32

GRAPES
   THE SICK GRAPES ON THE CHAIR BY THE BED LIE PRONE AT TH+   112 16
   AND GRAPES AND GHOULS AND GHOSTS AND GREEN MOONLIGHT   667 6
   SO THAT LOST SOULS MAY EAT GRAPES   710 17

GRAPE-VINES
   WITH GRAPE-VINES UP THE MAST AND DOLPHINS LEAPING   688 5

GRAPPLES
   THEN UP COMES A GREY RAT A FLOSS-GOLD CHICKEN GRAPPLES   *933 11

GRAPPLING
   WHO GRAPPLING DOWN WITH WORK OR HATE OR PASSION   73 14
   FIXED IN THE DARKNESS GRAPPLING FOR THE DEEP SOIL'S CRO+   92 11
   FIXED IN THE DARKNESS GRAPPLING FOR THE DEEP SOIL'S LIT+   *926 11

GRASP
   AND DREW THE CIRCLE OF HIS GRASP O MAN   69 11
   NEVER GRASP   335 7
   WHICH ELSE WERE A SILENT GRASP THAT HELD THE SKIES   773 9
   PRESSING TO GRASP MY HEART   869 21
   AND DREW THE CIRCLE OF HIS GRASP O MAN   *915 23

GRASPED
   HOLLOWED THIS GROOVE IN YOUR SIDES GRASPED YOU UNDER THE   254 30

GRASPING
   GRASPING IN THE GOLDEN LIGHT   42 2
   REACHING OUT AND GRASPING BY AN INSTINCT MORE DELICATE +   285 28
   THAT IS ALWAYS GRASPING ME   869 18

GRASPIN'
   'S LESS GRASPIN' IF 'ER'S POOR   84 4

GRASPS
   AND SOMETIMES HOW SHE GRASPS HER ARMS WITH HER   128 20
   LIKE A SUNKEN FLAME THAT GRASPS FOR SUPPORT   246 29

GRASS
   FROM OUT OF THE HAZEL-SCREEN ON TO THE GRASS   41 2
   UP THE WARM GRASS WHERE THE SUNBEAMS START   46 8
   FALLS ON ME AS I LIE IN DEEP GRASS   49 22
   I HEAR IT THROUGH THE GRASS   50 16
   THE GRASS   57 26
   WHEN THE WHITE FEET OF THE BABY BEAT ACROSS THE GRASS   64 29
   AND THE SIGHT OF THEIR WHITE PLAYING IN THE GRASS   65 1
   THE GRASS DEEP DOWN WITH THE ROYAL BURDEN OF HER   123 5
   HERE LAMPS ARE WHITE LIKE SNOWDROPS IN THE GRASS   136 1
   THE STARLING SHAKING ITS HEAD AS IT WALKS IN THE GRASS   137 11

GRASS
  OVER NOCTURNAL GRASS   146 21
  THE AIR IS DARK WITH NORTH AND WITH SULPHUR THE GRASS IS   148 24
  THE DAISIES IN THE GRASS ARE BENDING   150   4
  THE YOUNG GRASS TWINKLES IN THE WIND AND THE SOUND   152 28
  OF THIS MARCHING ALONG WITH THE INVISIBLE GRASS   164   7
  AND DARK GRASS UNDER MY FEET   194 10
  LIKE GRASS IN A BROOK   194 12
  DARKEN THE SHINING GRASS   196 13
  BUBBLES RAVELLED IN THE DARK GREEN GRASS   204 17
  THE DANDELION SEEDS STAY HALF-SUBMERGED IN THE GRASS   204 21
  AND THE LITTLE ELECTRIC FLASHES WENT WITH US IN THE GRA+   206 15
  EVERYWHERE DOWN IN THE GRASS WHERE DARKNESS WAS RAVELLED   206 18
  GREEN GRASS SHINING AND LITTLE WHITE HOUSES   224 13
  WHITELY CONFRONT I WAIT ON THE GRASS AM LAMED   225 12
  I STAND ASIDE ON THE GRASS TO LET THEM GO   225 21
  HIBISCUS AND MERE GRASS   316   2
  AND RABBITS MAKE PILLS AMONG THE SHORT GRASS   321 23
  AND BITING THE FRAIL GRASS ARROGANTLY   358 20
  THE STAND UPON THE GRASS BELOW AND OPPOSITE   387 24
  SOFT GRASS RUNS UPON A PATH THAT IS PATHLESS TO MEN SO +   406   3
  LOVE IS LIKE THE GRASS BUT THE HEART IS DEEP WILD ROCK   477 22
  BELOW THE GRASS AND TREES   480   4
  AS WELL AS THE GRASS   565   9
  LEAVES OF GRASS WHAT ABOUT LEAVES OF GRASS   587   1
  GRASS BLOSSOMS GRASS HAS FLOWERS FLOWERS OF GRASS   587   2
  DUSTY POLLEN OF GRASS TALL GRASS IN ITS MIDSUMMER MALEN+   587   3
  HAY-SEED AND TINY GRAIN OF GRASS GRAMINIFERAE   587   4
  GRASS IN BLOSSOM BLOSSOMING GRASS RISEN TO ITS HEIGHT A+   587 12
  THE GRASS THE GRASS   587 15
  LEAVES OF GRASS WHAT ARE LEAVES OF GRASS WHEN AT ITS BE+   587 16
  GRASS BLOSSOMS   587 17
  OH WHEN THE GRASS FLOWERS THE GRASS   587 18
  FLOWERS OF GRASS FINE MEN   587 23
  OF THE GRASS IN BLOSSOM   587 25
  HOW EVANESCENT VARIEGATED ELDER SHE HESITATES ON THE GR+   646 25
  AS THE GREEN GRASS GLOWS UPWARDS STRANGERS IN THE GARDEN   647   7
  WITH A BLADE OF GRASS BETWEEN MY TEETH   804 14
  THE GRASS FEELS WITH HIS ROOTS FOR THE OTHER SUN   804 21
  WITH A BLADE OF GREEN GRASS BETWEEN HIS TEETH   805 22
  GRASS FEELS DOWNWARDS WITH HIS ROOTS   806   3
  AND BETWEEN OUR FINGERS ROSE A BLADE OF GREEN GRASS   806 27
  IS MALINTZI'S BLADE OF GRASS   810 20
  OF THE DYING GRASS WITH A THRICE-TOLD TALE OF DEATH   858 27
  FORGOTTEN IN THE GRASS EVA FEARFUL AND FLEET   864 16
  CLINGING TO THE RADIATORS LIKE NUMBED BEES TO THE DRENC+   866   1
  THE YOUNG GRASS TWINKLED IN THE WIND AND THE SOUND   866 24
  I SAID THIS IS GRASS THAT TWINKLES IN THE DARK   882 15
  AND ALL THE SORREL SPEARS IN THE LUSH LONG GRASS   884 25
  LOW-ROUNDED ON THE MOURNFUL GRASS THEY HAVE BITTEN DOWN+   *891   7
  I PICK MY WAY OVER THREADBARE GRASS WHICH IS PRESSED   *896 10
  WHEN THE WHITE FEET OF THE BABY BEAT ACROSS THE GRASS   *912 25
  THE SIGHT OF THEIR WHITE PLAY AMONG THE GRASS   *913   1
  WHEN THE BARE FEET OF THE BABY BEAT ACROSS THE GRASS   *913 28
  AND THE SIGHT OF THEIR WHITE PLAY AMONG THE GRASS   *914   2
  IS HEARD IN THE GRASS OF THE SOD   *914 31
  DOWN IN THE GRASS   *917 10
  THE GRASS DEEP DOWN WITH HER ROYAL BURDEN AND I   *934 11
  THE LAMPS ARE WHITE LIKE SNOWDROPS IN THE GRASS   *938 29
  HIS SCYTHE STONE AN' OVER THE GRASS TO ME   *944 11
  WHICH CLOTHES OUR NAKEDNESS LIKE GRASS THE PLAINS AND T+   *951   8

GRASSES
  OF DUSTY GRASSES LIKE THE STARS THAT DAWN   864 31

GRASS-FLOWERS
  WHILE HIGHER THE DARTING GRASS-FLOWERS PASS   49 24

GRASSHOPPER
  AND THE CRITICAL GRASSHOPPER   507 21

GRASS-LEAVES
  AND NOW THE LONGEST GRASS-LEAVES HARDLY EMERGE   85   6

GRASSY
  UNDER THE GREEN GRASSY UNISON OF ALL OUR FRIENDLINESS   *951 11

GRASS'
  FROM THE TULIPS COLOURED WITH CHALK AND THE DULL GRASS'+   867   4

GRATE
  OF THE MIRROR TOWARDS THE DUSTY GRATE AS IF FEELING   141 14

GRATEFUL
  I SEE RIGHT WELL HOW I OUGHT TO BE GRATEFUL   234 11
  AND THEN IF IT'S WORTH IT BE GRATEFUL   237 11

GRATES
  AND WATER WETLY ON FIRE IN THE GRATES OF YOUR GILLS   335 11

GRATING
  AND THERE IS NO GRATING OF PEOPLE WITH THEIR PRESENCE   646 16

GRAVE
  WOULD THE DARKNESS LOOK LIKE A GRAVE   49 19
  ASIDE O' T' GRAVE AN' TH' COFFIN SET   60 12
  AT TH' SLOPPY GRAVE AN' 'ER LITTLE NECK SHONE   61   7
  THEY BURIED HER HALF IN THE GRAVE WHEN THEY LAID HER AW+   114 21
  HALF SUBSTANCELESS AND WITHOUT GRAVE WORTH   118 17
  I SHALL PUT ROSES ON ROSES AND COVER YOUR GRAVE   176 11
  THEIR EYES AND LOOK AT THE GRAVE ON THE HILL IN WONDER   176 16
  THAT BEAUTY IS A THING BEYOND THE GRAVE   193   9
  AND AT THE FOOT OF A GRAVE A FATHER STANDS   232 24
  AND AT THE FOOT OF A GRAVE A MOTHER KNEELS   232 26
  THOSE VILLAGERS ISOLATED AT THE GRAVE   233   5
  THE NAKED CANDLES BURN ON EVERY GRAVE   233   9
  ON YOUR GRAVE IN ENGLAND THE WEEDS GROW   233 10
  AND THAT IS NOT YOUR GRAVE IN ENGLAND   233 12

GRAVE
  THE WORLD IS YOUR GRAVE   233 13
  AND MY NAKED BODY STANDING ON YOUR GRAVE   233 14
  BUT MY FEET ARE ON YOUR GRAVE PLANTED   233 21
  I AM A NAKED CANDLE BURNING ON YOUR GRAVE   233 26
  ARE YOU THE GRAVE OF OUR DAY   289 26
  BUT WHO NEVER RISE RESURRECTED FROM THIS GRAVE OF   290 18
  WAS THE SEED OF THE BODY AND FROM THE GRAVE IT COULD GR+   303 10
  ENGLAND SEEMS LIKE ONE GRAVE TO ME   410 26
  REMEMBERING I TOLD THEM TO DIE TO SINK INTO THE GRAVE IN   410 30
  NOW THAT THE GRAVE IS MADE OF MOTHER AND WIFE   411 27
  NOW THAT THE GRAVE IS MADE AND LIDDED OVER WITH TURF   411 28
  LO ON THE OTHER SIDE THE GRAVE   460 29
  NOW ALL THE HOSTS ARE MARCHING TO THE GRAVE   743 29
  ALL BITTER AND CORRODING TO THE GRAVE   744 25
  OF RESURRECTION FROM THE ENDLESS GRAVE   745   4
  AND THE JACKAL FOUND HIS GRAVE   754 18
  ASIDE O' TH' GRAVE WHILE TH' COFFIN WOR LYIN' YET   *910 27
  AT TH' SLOPPY WET GRAVE AN' 'ER LITTLE NECK SHONE   *911 23
  I WOULD PUT ROSES ON ROSES AND COVER YOUR GRAVE   *940 26

GRAVE-EYED
  THE DARK THE GRAVE-EYED MISTRESS WHO THUS DARED   155 28

GRAVEL
  WHERE A STREAM CAME DOWN TO THE GRAVEL OF THE SEA AND S+   693   2
  WHO HAD SPREAD WHITE WASHING ON THE GRAVEL BANKED ABOVE+   693   3

GRAVES
  ENGLAND SEEMS FULL OF GRAVES TO ME   410   1
  FULL OF GRAVES   410   2
  ENGLAND SEEMS COVERED WITH GRAVES TO ME   410   5
  WOMEN'S GRAVES   410   6
  NOW THAT THE GRAVES ARE MADE AND COVERED   410 18
  GRAVES OF WOMEN   410 20
  COME AWAY FROM THE PLACE OF GRAVES COME WEST   411   2

GRAVE-STONE
  TO ROLL THE GRAVE-STONE OFF THEIR SOULS FROM THE CAVE O+   793   7

GRAVITY
  IS IT SO THAT YOU SHALL LIFT YOUR CENTRE OF GRAVITY UPW+   332   6

GRAY
  THEIR FEATHERS LIFELESS AND THE ROSE LIGHTS TURNING TO +   855 28
  NOT THIS GRAY BOOK BUT THE RED AND BLOODY SCENES   *938 30
  AND GRAY NOW NIGHT IS HERE NOR WILL   *938 31
  AND SO I SIT AND TURN THE BOOK OF GRAY   *939   1

GREAT BRITISH PUBLIC
  YOU'LL GIVE THE GREAT BRITISH PUBLIC A NERVOUS SHOCK   669 11

GREATER
  BUT I AM GREATER THAN HE   347 22
  SUCKING HIS LIFE OUT OF THE DEAD LEAVES OF GREATER LIFE+   431 16
  GO DEEPER THAN LOVE FOR THE SOUL HAS GREATER DEPTHS   477 21
  AND THEY KEEP ON COMING WITH GREATER FORCE   512 21
  I KNOW NO GREATER DELIGHT THAN THE SHEER DELIGHT OF BEI+   610 19
  THE GODS THAT MADE US ARE GREATER THAN OUR CONSCIOUSNESS   636 29
  IN HIS OWN AND GREATER BEING   700 15
  YET THROUGH THE TEARS STEALS A SENSE OF PEACE AND GREAT+   768   1
  GREATER GLOOM THAN FOR MANY YEARS   778 36
  AND GREATER HEAT INTO FIRE MORE HEAVY AND HOTTER THAN A+   *951 21

GREATEST
  STRONG LIKE THE GREATEST FORCE OF WORLD-BALANCING   271 20
  TO BE ALONE IS ONE OF LIFE'S GREATEST DELIGHTS THINKING+   610   3
  GREATEST OF LADIES   695 16
  TILL THEY MOUNT AND FILL AND ALL IS FULFILLED OF GOD'S +   698 20
  EVEN THROUGH THE GREATEST BLASPHEMIES THE HANDS OF THE +   700 20
  FOR PERHAPS THE GREATEST OF ALL ILLUSIONS   703 14
  AND THE GREATEST OF TEACHERS WILL TELL YOU   726   3
  AT THE SAME TIME THEY TAKE THE GREATEST POSSIBLE CARE O+   832   4
  THE GREATEST POSSIBLE CARE   832   6
  ON THE LONGEST JOURNEY TOWARDS THE GREATEST GOAL   *959 16

GREAT GOD
  THERE IS NO GREAT GOD IN THE INNERMOST   823 16

GREAT ONE
  LO THE GREAT ONE ANSWERS TRACK HIM DOWN   808   7

GREAVES
  PUT GREAVES UPON YOUR THIGHS AND KNEES AND FRAIL   154 21

GRECIAN
  BACK IN A GRECIAN KNOT OR A JUG HANDLE OR A CHIGNON   836   2

GREECE
  GREECE AND THE WORLD'S MORNING   311 27

GREED
  MONEY HYPOCRISY GREED MACHINES   457 11
  THE GREED OF THIS INFAMOUS FELLOW FOR OUR SWEAT   750   8
  IT IS SICK OF GREED   831   6
  PAST THE STRANGE WHIRLPOOLS OF REMEMBERED GREED   *959   7

GREEDILY
  OR GREEDILY SNUFFING BEHIND THE COWS   325 32

GREEDY
  I WAS GREEDY I WAS MAD FOR THE UNKNOWN   259 13
  THAT THE SUN SHOULD BE GREEDY FOR IT   374 24
  THEY ARE ONLY GREEDY FOR YOUR LIFE   441 29
  THEY ARE SO GREEDY YET SO HELPLESS IF NOT WORKED FOR   441 31
  EVEN WITH THE INDUSTRIAL MASSES AND THE GREEDY MIDDLE   631 25
  THEN AT ONCE THE IMPULSE OF THE GREEDY CLASSES AND MASS+   640   8
  O SHED THE UNCLEAN MEAN COWARDLY GREEDY EGOISTIC DEGENE+   679   5

GREEDY
    MOSTLY THEY ARE THE GREEDY ONES   793 16
    WONDERFUL ARE THE MACHINES OF THE GREEDY ONES   793 27
    WE HAVE LEARNED I THINK NOT TO BE GREEDY   833 3

GREEDY-MOUTHED
    TO PROTECT THEMSELVES AND THEIR GREEDY-MOUTHED GREEDY-M+   458 20

GREEK
    IN SYRACUSE ROCK LEFT BARE BY THE VICIOUSNESS OF GREEK   278 4
    THE BROKEN GREEK TOMB IN THE GARDEN   384 5
    THE GREEK BEAUTIFUL ONES THE PHOENICIAN UGLY ONES THE A+   671 16
    PONDERING FOR HE WAS A GREEK THAT GOD IS ONE AND ALL AL+   692 23

GREEKS
    THE GREEKS MADE EQUILIBRIUM THEIR GOAL EQUILIBRIUM IS H+   761 14

GREEN
    THE HILL-BROW AND LIE QUITE STILL TILL THE GREEN   35 14
    ON THE GREEN WOOD'S EDGE A SHY GIRL HOVERS   41 1
    OF THE SORREL'S CRESSET A GREEN BRAVE TOWN   49 27
    THIS SPRING AS IT COMES BURSTS UP IN BONFIRES GREEN   116 1
    OF GREEN FIRES LIT ON THE SOIL OF EARTH THIS BLAZE   116 7
    O THE GREEN GLIMMER OF APPLES IN THE ORCHARD   119 7
    NOTHING NOW WILL RIPEN THE BRIGHT GREEN APPLES   119 11
    A DARKER GREEN   148 25
    BUBBLES RAVELLED IN THE DARK GREEN GRASS   204 17
    GREEN LANTERN OF PURE LIGHT A LITTLE INTENSE FUSING TRI+   206 10
    AN EXPLOSION OF GREEN LIGHT   206 17
    AND DOWN BELOW IN THE GREEN WHEAT THE LABOURERS   208 26
    STAND LIKE DARK STUMPS STILL IN THE GREEN WHEAT   208 27
    GO BY WITH THEIR LOADS OF GREEN AND SILVER BIRCH-TREES   209 17
    THE SKY WAS GREEN WINE HELD UP IN THE SUN   216 14
    SHE OPENED HER EYES AND GREEN   216 16
    ITSELF MORE SHEER AND NAKED OUT OF THE GREEN   218 11
    ALL THE DARK-FEATHERED HELMETS LIKE LITTLE GREEN   221 17
    GREEN GRASS SHINING AND LITTLE WHITE HOUSES   224 13
    GREEN STAR SIRIUS   229 5
    SO GREEN   229 20
    GREEN STREAMS THAT FLOW FROM THE INNERMOST CONTINENT OF   260 24
    GREEN AND ILLUMINED AND TRAVELLING FOR EVER   260 27
    THE OTHER SHE TOO HAS STRANGE GREEN EYES   261 1
    ABHORRENT GREEN SLIPPERY CITY   278 10
    POMEGRANATES LIKE BRIGHT GREEN STONE   278 13
    OH CROWN OF SPIKED GREEN METAL   278 15
    SILVER-PINK PEACH VENETIAN GREEN GLASS OF MEDLARS AND S+   283 5
    IN A GREEN MUDDY WEB-FOOT UNUTTERLY SONGLESS WORLD   286 1
    GREEN DIM INVISIBLE FLOURISHING OF VINES   286 5
    OF UNEATABLE SOFT GREEN   301 17
    TO THE GREEN NIGHT-BAYING OF THE DOG-STAR ETNA'S SNOW-E+   306 11
    ON A GREEN HILL   306 27
    A GREEN LIGHT ENTERS AGAINST STREAM FLUSH FROM THE WEST   340 25
    DARK GREEN GLOSSY FANGED LEAVES   383 31
    AT SEASONS SHE CURLS BACK HER TAIL LIKE A GREEN LEAF IN+   385 31
    DARK GREEN GLOSSY FANGED LEAVES   387 2
    AND NEAR ACROSS AT THE OPPOSITE STEEP OF SNOW GREEN TRE+   402 25
    GOLD GOES OUT INTO A GREEN SHADOW   455 6
    AND ITS PLUMES LOOK LIKE GREEN CUPS HELD UP TO THE SUN +   498 22
    AND MY LEAVES ARE GREEN WITH THE BREATH OF HUMAN EXPERI+   499 11
    IT MAKES YOU TURN GREEN   551 16
    OH AREN'T THEY GREEN OH HAVEN'T WE HAVEN'T WE SPENT   569 11
    SHORT GASPS OF FLAME IN THE GREEN OF NIGHT WAY OFF   606 1
    HOW EVANESCENT VARIEGATED ELDER SHE HESITATES ON THE GR+   646 25
    AS THE GREEN GRASS GLOWS UPWARDS STRANGERS IN THE GARDEN   647 7
    AND GRAPES AND GHOULS AND GHOSTS AND GREEN MOONLIGHT   667 6
    IN THE GREEN GARDEN DARKENED THE SHADOW OF COMING RAIN   672 12
    TO THINK OUT IN THE ABSTRACT WHEN ALL WAS TWILIT GREEN +   690 29
    THAT DARK GREEN MESS   691 3
    WHO HAD WADED TO THE PALE GREEN SEA OF EVENING OUT OF A+   693 5
    THE WHEAT ON BOTH SIDES OF THE ROAD STANDS GREEN   732 5
    TILL THEY CHANCED TO MEET IN THE LORD'S GREEN ZOO   761 3
    WITH A BLADE OF GREEN GRASS BETWEEN HIS TEETH   805 22
    AND BETWEEN OUR FINGERS ROSE A BLADE OF GREEN GRASS   806 27
    MALINTZI OF THE GREEN DRESS WILL OPEN THE DOOR   809 10
    AND ONE GREEN LEAF SPRANG AMONG THE BLACK   809 20
    THE GREEN LEAF OF MALINTZI   809 21
    GREEN HUITZILOPOCHTLI   810 19
    LIKE THE GREEN CANDLES OF MALINTZI   811 13
    THEY HAVE GREEN TRAM IN FLORENCE NOW   845 22
    AND PUT A DIRTY GREEN LARGE CABAGE   845 25
    IN THOSE UGLY GREEN LARGE CARS   846 3
    GENTLY ISSUING FROM THE MASSED GREEN   854 22
    CHAPLETS OF CREAM AND DISTANT GREEN   854 25
    GREEN   867 5
    OH THE GREEN GLIMMER OF APPLES IN THE ORCHARD   *932 16
    NOTHING NOW WILL RIPEN THE BRIGHT GREEN APPLES   *932 20
    ALL THEIR DARK-FEATHERED HELMETS LIKE LITTLE GREEN   *945 3
    UNDER THE GREEN GRASSY UNISON OF ALL OUR FRIENDLINESS   *951 11

GREENEST
    THE OLD DOG'S GREENEST BONES   492 12

GREEN-FIRE
    WILD PUFFING OF GREEN-FIRE TREES AND FLAME-GREEN BUSHES   116 2

GREEN-FLY
    THE GREEN-FLY ON THE STEMS   655 9

GREENISH
    HARDLY A GREENISH LILY WATERY FAINT   286 4
    TO THE PROUD FATHER AND SHOWS ITS LITTLE WEBBED GREENISH   438 28

GREENNESS
    MAKING A GREENNESS   811 23

GREEN-PURE
    WITH THEIR GOLD RED EYES AND GREEN-PURE GLEAM AND UNDER+   339 26

GREENS
    WHITE IVORY WHITE AMONG THE RAMBLING GREENS   646 24

GREET
    GREET THE CLOUD   52 23
    TO QUICKEN MY HOPE AS I HASTENED TO GREET   121 21
    MAY I GREET   569 22
    THUS TO GREET   570 4
    WILL SWEEP ROUND AND UP TO GREET THE SUN WITH A SILKY G+   625 4
    GREET HIM FROM ME   754 2
    RECOGNITIONS AND GREETINGS OF HALF-ACQUAINT THINGS AS I+   *905 11

GREETING
    YOUR GREETING NOW   122 24
    UP WITH THEM AND GREAT IS THE PAIN OF GREETING AND DEAD+   406 7

GREETINGS
    RECOGNITIONS AND GREETINGS OF HALF-ACQUAINT THINGS AS I   52 22
    RECOGNITIONS AND GREETINGS OF HALF-ACQUAINT THINGS AS I+   *905 11

GREETS
    A LOWER ME GETS UP AND GREETS ME   39 10
    THE STAR ABOVE THE HOUSE-TOPS GREETS   108 26

GRESS
    T' SNOW IS WITHERIN' OFF'N TH' GRESS   137 18
    T' SNOW IS WITHERIN' OFF'N TH' GRESS   137 20

GRET
    I DUNNO WHEER 'IS EYES WAS A GRET   81 17
    I DUNNO WHERE HIS EYES WAS A GRET   *923 17

GREW
    OF STARS GREW SILENTLY   35 20
    COMPRESSED IT TILL ITS BEAM GREW WONDROUS DARK   69 19
    THE PRESENCE OF THE FLOWERS THAT GREW   262 2
    AND SO TO MAN'S ESTATE HE GREW   576 24
    AND GREW UP AND BECAME IN THE WONDER OF CREATION JESUS   689 29
    PROBABLY AS SHE GREW OLDER SHE ATE HER RIVALS   836 6
    COMPRESSED IT TILL ITS BEAM GREW WONDROUS DARK   *916 2

GREY
    IN SHADOW COVERING US UP WITH HER GREY   48 18
    THE CLOUDS ARE PUSHING IN GREY RELUCTANCE SLOWLY NORTHW+   57 10
    FRAIL AND SAD WITH GREY BOWED HEAD   64 4
    WITH WHITE PLUMES BLINKING UNDER THE EVENING GREY SKY   66 14
    ON A SUBTLE RUSH OF COOL GREY FLAME   68 2
    THE GREY PLASM-LIMPID PELLUCID ADVANCE   68 9
    GREY FOAM-MIST OF ADVANCING TIME   68 14
    YESTERDAY THE FIELDS WERE ONLY GREY WITH SCATTERED SNOW   85 5
    THE SEA AND THE SKY WENT GREY AS IF THERE HAD SUNK   98 12
    DEADENED ME THROUGH TILL THE GREY DOWNS DULLED TO SLEEP   98 22
    OF THE UNSWEPT SEA A GREY PALE LIGHT LIKE MUST   99 3
    WINDING ABOUT THEIR DIMNESS THE MIST'S GREY CEREMENTS A+   102 30
    WHY DOES THE THIN GREY STRAND   106 32
    TO MY GAIETY A FEW LONG GREY HAIRS   107 2
    BUT A GREY CAVE WITH GREAT GREY SPIDER-CLOTHS HANGING   112 25
    FOR A GREY RAT FOUND THE GOLD THIRTEEN   119 19
    THAT GREY ONE LIKE A SHADOW LIKE A RAT A THIEF A RAIN+   120 3
    O THE GREY GARNER THAT IS FULL OF HALF-GROWN APPLES   120 5
    BETWEEN THE OLD GREY WALLS I DID NOT DARE   122 27
    AND SO I SIT AND SCAN THE BOOK OF GREY   135 17
    AND GREY NOW NIGHT IS HERE NOR WILL   136 3
    OPEN AND A GREAT GREY DAWN SWIRLS OVER MY FEET BEFORE   147 9
    THAT HUDDLES IN GREY HEAPS COILING AND HOLDING BACK   164 18
    LIKE CLIFFS ABUTTING IN SHADOW A DEAD GREY SEA   164 19
    ON THE MISTY WASTE LANDS AWAY FROM THE FLUSHING GREY   164 21
    AND PILED THEM UP IN A DULL GREY HEAP IN THE WEST   167 2
    AND PILED THEM UP IN A DULL GREY HEAP IN THE WEST   167 12
    THE WANING MOON LOOKS UPWARD THIS GREY NIGHT   172 18
    FOR THE HOUSE IS SHUT AND SEALED AND THE BREATH OF THE+   174 27
    ARRIVING GREY FROM THE DARKNESS ABOVE SUDDENLY INTO THE+   179 22
    GREY DAYS AND WAN DREE DAWNINGS   193 17
    THEN JOSEPH GREY WITH WAITING   202 1
    NOT SLEEP WHICH IS GREY WITH DREAMS   205 12
    AND THEN IN A STRANGE GREY HOUR   248 24
    GREY LAVENDER SENSITIVE STEEL CURVING THINLY AND BRITTLY   300 30
    THIS GREY MONOTONOUS SOUL IN THE WATER   338 11
    GREY BIRD IN THE AIR ON THE BOUGH OF THE LEANING   385 17
    MONKEYS RODE RATHER GREY AND WIZENED   444 15
    THE ELEPHANTS HUGE AND GREY LOOMED THEIR CURVED BULK   445 10
    WITH GREY REPENTANT ASH   492 30
    YET EVEN WASTE GREY FORESHORES AND SONNY FAN OUT   509 17
    BUT WHEN I SEE THESE GREY SUCCESSFUL MEN   526 13
    A STRANGE GREY DISTANCE SEPARATES   607 1
    BUT UTTERLY FAILS TO RECOGNISE ANY MORE THE GREY RAT-HO+   640 5
    NOT LIKE GREY DANTE COLOUR-BLIND   711 19
    THE GREY VULTURE THE GREY HYAENA CORPSE-EATERS   711 23
    WHERE THE GREY TWILIGHT OF EVIL SETS IN   711 25
    SIT IN THE GREY MIST OF MOVEMENT WHICH MOVES NOT   711 28
    GREY EVIL WHICH HAS NO PATH AND SHOWS NEITHER LIGHT NOR   712 2
    THE KIND OF HELL THAT IS REAL GREY AND AWFUL   714 1
    THE KIND OF HELL GREY DANTE NEVER SAW   714 3
    A GREY VOID THING THAT GOES WITHOUT WANDERING   714 19
    TO REDUCE THE WORLD TO GREY ASH   716 3
    DRIFTING BENEATH THE DEATHLY ASHY GREY   720 7
    GAUNT GAUNT THEY CROWD THE GREY MUD-BEACHES OF SHADOW   722 6
    THE GREY GREY REACHES OF EARTH'S SHADOW   722 20
    TO THE FATHOMLESS DEEPS AHEAD FAR FAR FROM THE GREY SHO+   723 24
    HERE COMES THE FIRST OF THE WAGONS A GREY A DREARY   733 5
    LET US RISE UP AND GO FROM OUT THIS GREY   737 1
    GREY STERN ANGRY UNSATISFIED   739 26
    VICTORIOUS GREY GRISLY GHOSTS IN OUR STREETS   740 2
    GREY UNAPPEASED GHOSTS SEATED IN THE MUSIC-HALLS   740 3
    AND FOUND GREY DOVES IN THE FOUNTAIN COURT   751 2

GREY
    AS A FINE GREY EGG OR A SLENDER ROD   752 16
    THE GREY NURSE ENTERED A ROSE GARDEN   753 8
    IN THE DREAM OF THE NIGHT I SEE THE GREY DOGS PROWLING   807 2
    LIKE A GREY DOG WHOSE MOUTH IS FOUL WITH RABIES   807 5
    IN THE NIGHT I SEE THE GREY DOGS CREEPING OUT OF THE SL+   807 11
    BUT WHOSE DREAMS ARE DOGS GREY DOGS WITH YELLOW MOUTHS   807 15
    I SEE THE GREY DOGS CREEPING OUT WHERE MY DEER ARE BROW+   807 18
    THEN I TAKE MY KNIFE AND THROW IT UPON THE GREY DOG   807 20
    THE HOUSE OF THE GREY DOG   807 22
    YOU KNOW NOT HOW MANY ARE HOUSES OF GREY DOGS   807 25
    MAYBE THEY KENNEL THE GREY DOG   807 27
    THE GREY DOG CREEPS AMONG YOU   807 29
    THE GREY DOG IS CHEWING YOUR ENTRAILS   807 31
    THE GREY DOG CAUGHT ME AT THE CROSS-ROADS   808 2
    THE GREY DOG LEAPT AT MY ENTRAILS   808 5
    YOU TRACK THE GREY DOG HOME   808 10
    BUT THE GREY DOG BELONGS TO THE ASH OF THE WORLD   808 20
    DEAD ARE THE GREY DOGS   808 22
    BUT THE GREY DOGS ARE AMONG THE ASHES   809 2
    LIKE A MUD FROM WINTER DISGUISED IN GREY   815 8
    WITH GREY ON THE FLOOR OF THE DESERT   816 22
    FULL FORE-AND-AFT IN GOOD GREY CREPE DE CHINE   835 28
    PALE DREAMY CHAPLETS A GREY NUN-SISTER SETS   854 23
    LEAVING THEM SHADOW STRIPES BARRED ON A FIELD OF GREY   858 12
    NO DO NOT TOUCH ME LEAVE ME ON THE GREY SEA-TURF   870 23
    ON THE SUBTLE RUSH OF THE COOL GREY FLAME   *914 17
    THE GREY PHOSPHORESCENT PELLUCID ADVANCE   *914 24
    GREY FOAM-FRINGE OF ADVANCING GOD   *914 29
    FOR THE GREY RAT FOUND THE GOLD THIRTEEN   *932 28
    PLENISHING THE GREY RAT'S NEST   *933 6
    THEN UP COMES A GREY RAT A FLOSS-GOLD CHICKEN GRAPPLES   *933 11
    THE MARGINS THE GREY BEACHES OF SHADOW   *957 15
    THRUST OUT ON TO THE GREY GREY BEACHES OF SHADOW   *957 22
    ONCE OUTSIDE UPON THE GREY MARSH BEACHES WHERE LOST SOU+   *957 28
    AND CROWD THERE ON THE GREY MUD BEACHES OF THE MARGINS   *958 9
    FATHOMLESS DEEP AHEAD FAR FAR FROM THE GREY SHORES   *959 1

GREY-BEARDED
    BUT NOT GOD GREY-BEARDED AND DICTATORIAL   437 1
    AND THE FATHER WAS ONCE GREY-BEARDED AND FULMINATIVE   *946 14

GREY-BLACK
    GREY-BLACK ROCK   294 5

GREY-BLUE
    AND THE BALSAM-PINES THAT ARE BLUE WITH THE GREY-BLUE B+   647 2

GREY-DOGS
    NO GREY-DOGS COWARDS PASS HIM   810 3

GREY-DROPPING
    DEADENS THIS DAY'S GREY-DROPPING ARRAS-FOLD   141 12

GREY-GREEN
    BETWEEN THE CLIFFS OF THE TREES ON THE GREY-GREEN PARK   66 6
    GREY-GREEN   523 15
    THE GLOW OF RED IN A GREY-GREEN SHADOW OF TREES   867 10

GREYHOUND
    LONG PENSIVE SLIM-MUZZLED GREYHOUND BUDS   310 29
    LIKE DELICATE VERY-YOUNG GREYHOUND BITCHES   311 6
    GREYHOUND BITCHES   311 10

GREYING
    SHE SO LONELY GREYING NOW   63 14
    THE GREYING NERVE   766 14

GREYNESS
    OF GREYNESS MINGLED WITH A FUME OF GOLD   135 14
    WHICH WISHES TO BLASPHEME THE WORLD INTO GREYNESS   713 7

GREY-STRIPED
    AND GREY-STRIPED SUIT A YOUNG CUB OF A PIKE   338 2

GREY-WINGED
    TO THE HUSHED GREY-WINGED MINISTRANTS THE BATS OF NIGHT+   *916 12
    AND DRUNK WITH THE DEATH OF THE SOOTHING GREY-WINGED CR+   *918 11

GRIEF
    YOU WHO ARE TWISTED IN GRIEF LIKE CRUMPLING BEECH-LEAVES   73 16
    PAIN OR LOVE OR GRIEF   169 19
    AND GRIEF ARE BUT THE SAME LAST WONDER SLEEP   196 2
    GRIEF GRIEF I SUPPOSE AND SUFFICIENT   199 29
    GRIEF MAKES US FREE   199 30
    THEN GRIEF AND PAIN GO TOO WITHDRAWING   509 3
    HAD MADE AND PLAYED FOR ME HE SAID IN GRIEF   884 10
    THAT FILLS WITH GRIEF ALL THOSE THAT SEE   *927 29

GRIEFS
    MY GRIEFS AND ON NEW YORK NEWSPAPERS BATTEN   815 16

GRIEVE
    HAVE I CEASED TO GRIEVE THAT I WAS NOT GREAT ENOUGH   157 7
    OR LOVE OR REJOICE OR EVEN GRIEVE ANY MORE   474 27
    WHY SHOULD I GRIEVE THAT MY MOTHER IS NO LONGER CLOTTED   870 12
    WHY SHOULD IT GRIEVE ME   870 16

GRIEVES
    BECAUSE NO ONE GRIEVES OVER HER DEPARTURE   63 21

GRIEVING
    I DO NOT LIKE TO HEAR THE GENTLE GRIEVING   65 19
    GRIEVING   65 20
    AND GRIEVING WITH PUPPY-LIKE BLIND CRYING   544 29

GRIM
    AND CARESSES ME WITH HIS FINGERS THAT STILL SMELL GRIM   43 27
    IN THE GRIM UNDERTOW NAKED THE TREES CONFRONT   142 3
    IS TO LISTEN AND HEAR THE GRIM   159 15
    AND WITH A GRIM REPTILE DETERMINATION   360 14
    BUT WITH MORE THAN BOVINE GRIM EARTH-DANK PERSISTENCE   361 16
    GRIM GRUESOME GALLANTRY TO WHICH HE IS DOOMED   362 26
    THIS GRIM NECESSITY FROM WITHIN   363 5
    OR THEY BEAR EVERYBODY A GRIM AND GRISLY GRUDGE   502 19
    THE GRIM FROST IS AT HAND WHEN THE APPLES WILL FALL   717 3
    THE PEOPLE IN IT ARE GRIM   846 1
    AND PEOPLE ARE SAD AND GRIM   846 10

GRIMACE
    BENT IF WE DID BUT KNOW IT ON A WEARY AND BITTER GRIMACE   54 23

GRIMACES
    WHEREAS FACES NOW ARE ONLY HUMAN GRIMACES   656 23

GRIMACING
    IN FRONT OF A TOWERING GRIMACING WHITE IMAGE OF   387 31

GRIME
    A DANK SICKENING SCENT CAME UP FROM THE GRIME   98 16

GRIMLY
    LIKE IRON STICKING GRIMLY OUT OF EARTH   300 19
    AND HANGING GRIMLY ON   360 22
    AND STRANGE AND GRIMLY DRAGS AT HER   362 23

GRIN
    HOW IS IT I GRIN THEN AND CHUCKLE   199 27
    AND PANTING WITH THAT SPLIT GRIN   397 25
    WHILE HE STANDS ASIDE WATCHING WITH A SUPERIOR LITTLE G+   447 30
    MONKEYS WITH A BLAND GRIN ON OUR FACES   450 17

GRIND
    MILLS GRIND ON AND ON   441 7
    AND THE MILLS OF GOD GRIND OTHERWISE WITH THE WINDS OF   441 12
    TRUST THE MILLS OF GOD THOUGH THEY GRIND EXCEEDING SMALL   441 14
    THE MILLS OF GOD WILL GRIND THEM SMALL ANYHOW THERE IS +   614 18
    FEEL THE WINDS OF CHANGE GRIND THEM DOWN   615 19
    THEN LET THE MILLSTONES GRIND FOR THEY CANNOT STOP   642 9
    GRINDING SO LET THEM GRIND   642 10
    LET THEM GRIND ON ONE ANOTHER UPPER-CLASS ROBOT   642 12
    THEY MOVE IN A GREAT GRIND OF HATE SLOWLY BUT INEVITABLY   648 1
    THE GREAT GRIND OF UNWILLINGNESS THE SLOW UNDERGRIND OF+   648 10
    OF NERVES THAT GRIND AND A SOUL THAT STINGS   747 14

GRINDING
    ROLLS ROUND AND ROUND GRINDING EXCEEDING SMALL   614 20
    GRINDING THEM SMALL TO HUMUS ON EARTH'S NETHER MILL-STO+   615 6
    GRINDING SO LET THEM GRIND   642 10
    HE IS CAPABLE OF AN ENDLESS GRINDING NIHILISTIC HATE   648 3
    FULL OF FRICTION FULL OF GRINDING FULL OF DANGER TO THE+   675 27

GRINDS
    THAT GRINDS LIFE VERY SMALL   641 23

GRINNING
    AND GRINNING IN THEIR SLEEP   342 4
    CHINESE-DRAGON-WRINKLED WITH A PINK MOUTH GRINNING   397 18
    FROM THE GRINNING AND INSATIABLE ROBOTS   639 13

GRIP
    AND LOVE WOULD ONLY WEAKEN THEIR UNDER-EARTH GRIP MAKE +   92 27
    I WISH I COULD GRIP YOU LIKE THE FIST OF THE LORD   255 14
    SO HE LAUGHS FROM FEAR PURE FEAR IN THE GRIP OF THE SLE+   407 22
    WITH ITS ROOTS IT HAS A GRAND GRIP ON ITS DAILY BREAD   498 21
    WE HAVE MORE ENERGY AND OUR GRIP ON LIFE IS HARDER   503 6
    WE LOOSE OUR GRIP AND WE UNSTRAIN OUR EYES   736 23

GRIPPING
    REACHING AND GRIPPING TENSE MORE REACHING ANGUISH IN   365 5
    AND FEEL HIM GRIPPING MY WRIST AS IF HE WOULD BREAK IT   733 4

GRISLY
    OR THEY BEAR EVERYBODY A GRIM AND GRISLY GRUDGE   502 19
    VICTORIOUS GREY GRISLY GHOSTS IN OUR STREETS   740 2

GRIST
    OH THEY ARE GRIST FOR THE MILLS OF GOD THEIR BONES GROU+   614 23
    WITHOUT GRIST   642 11

GRITTING
    GRITTING AGAINST THE GREAT ADVERSITY   485 5

GROAN
    FOR WHAT DOES HE ACHE AND GROAN   326 23
    AND JUST LOVES TO HEAR YOU SOB AND GROAN   572 8
    GROAN THEN GROAN   702 22
    GROAN THEN GROAN   703 6
    GROAN THEN FOR EVEN THE MAIDEN EARTH   703 7
    OH GROAN   703 9
    IN THE CENTRE OF YOUR BEING GROAN NOT   703 12
    IN THE CENTRE OF YOUR BEING GROAN NOT DO NOT GROAN   703 13

GROANS
    GROAN WITH MIGHTY GROANS   703 10

GROOM
    BRIDE TO YOUR GROOM   56 3
    CRY OUT AND FEND HER OFF AS SHE SEEKS HER PROCREANT GRO+   91 27
    THE LOST BRIDE AND HER GROOM   697 22
    CRY OUT AND FEND HER OFF AS SHE SEEKS HER PROCREANT GRO+   *926 20

GROOMED
NICELY GROOMED LIKE A MUSHROOM 431 13
AND THEIR GROOMED AND MUSHROOM-LIKE FACES 765 12

GROOVE
HOLLOWED THIS GROOVE IN YOUR SIDES GRASPED YOU UNDER THE 254 30
WHY THE GROOVE 279 17
WITH A PINCH OF SNOW IN THE GROOVE OF YOUR SILLY SNUB N+ 375 17

GROOVED
AND THEIR NAKED BREASTS THE GROOVED LOINS 389 8

GROPE
ONLY I GROPE AMONG YOU PALE-FACES CARYATIDS AS AMONG A 287 27
AND WE STILL BLEED AND WE GROPE AND ROAR 544 6
WE GROPE AND FOAM AND LASH AROUND 833 19
IN HER BARBAROUS SOUL TO GROPE WITH ECSTASY *936 35

GROPED
AS HER HAND GROPED OVER ITS NAKEDNESS *937 15

GROSS
LIKE GROSS SUCCESSFUL SLAVES MECHANICALLY WADDLING 526 15
SAID GROSS COARSE HIDEOUS AND I LIKE A SILLY 579 18

GROUND
YET FLAME OF THE LIVING GROUND 39 21
AN' OUR TED'S COFFIN SET ON TH' GROUND 60 21
AND SUDDENLY AS IF THE GROUND MOVED 66 15
WHOSE BLACK BOUGHS FLAP THE GROUND 113 26
DRINK IT UP IN THE GROUND 117 30
AS ALL THE GROUND 120 25
SHE SITS ON THE RECREATION GROUND 152 26
AND SO AGAIN ON THE RECREATION GROUND 153 9
STUBBLE UPON THE GROUND 165 3
WE ARE FOLDED TOGETHER MEN AND THE SNOWY GROUND 166 11
AND LOOKS DOWN ON THE GROUND TO SEE 215 24
WHEN IT FALLS TO THE GROUND 235 6
AND EVE APPROACHING OVER THE GROUND 262 7
AND THE LAST FIRES OF DISSOLUTION BURN IN THE BOSOM OF + 270 23
DOWN ON THE DAMP UNCEASING GROUND WHERE MY FEET BELONG 321 16
DART AND TWIST STILL HE MUST GO WITH HIS BELLY ON THE G+ 348 12
GROUND WITH A SUDDEN ROCK-HAMMER ANNOUNCEMENT 381 14
THE GROUND 384 2
LIKE STAGS ON ROCKY GROUND OR PAWING HORSES OR SPRINGY 392 16
SUDDENLY THE GROUND GOES FROM UNDER HER FEET AND SHE 447 27
THAT HAVE GROUND YOU SO SMALL 457 12
BUST IN AND HOLD THE GROUND 560 32
OH THEY ARE GRIST FOR THE MILLS OF GOD THEIR BONES GROU+ 614 23
TILL THE SOUL OF THE STIFF-NECKED IS GROUND TO DUST TO + 616 14
BEING GROUND EXCEEDING SMALL 642 4
AND DEMOCRACY IS GROUND INTO DUST 648 11
TO BREAK AGAINST THE GROUND 705 12
NOW LIKE A STRANGE LIGHT BREAKING FROM THE GROUND 744 10
ON THEIR OWN GROUND 779 23
I HAVE SAT IN THE RECREATION GROUND 866 22
NOW TO THE RECREATION GROUND 867 1
AS A WHITE ROSE STREWS THE GROUND 868 7
ARE YOU LETTING ME GO AND HIDING YOUR FACE TO THE GROUND 871 32
AS YOU SIT ON THE TRESTLE I ON THE GROUND 887 12
BESIDE THE OPEN GROUND *911 7
WHERE BLACK BOUGHS FLAP THE GROUND *929 15

GROUP
THEN A GROUP OF TOADSTOOLS WAITING THE MOON'S WHITE TAP+ 72 19
AND CLIMB THE STAIRS TO FIND THE GROUP OF DOORS 140 9
THE MEN THAT LOUNGE IN A GROUP ON THE WHARF 228 16
MEN SHOULD GROUP THEMSELVES INTO A NEW ORDER 525 10

GROUPS
SOLEMN IN GROUPS 196 9

GROVEL
IT HAS GOT US DOWN WE GROVEL BEFORE IT IN STRANGE TERROR 486 15
A MOMENT AS HE FELL AND GROVEL AND DIE 741 28
TO TWIST AND GROVEL AND BECOME A HEAP OF DIRT 742 2

GROVES
WHO MADE SO LITTLE NOISE OUTSIDE THE CYPRESS GROVES 296 16

GROW
ON YOUR GRAVE IN ENGLAND THE WEEDS GROW 233 10
EMPEDOKLES SAYS TREES WERE THE FIRST LIVING CREATURES T+ 295 4
GROW RISING UP OWING TO THE HEAT WHICH IS IN THE EARTH + 295 8
WAS THE SEED OF THE BODY AND FROM THE GRAVE IT COULD GR+ 303 10
DARK GROW THE SPRUCE-TREES BLUE IS THE BALSAM WATER 401 2
NOW THAT IN ENGLAND PANSIES AND SUCH-LIKE GROW ON THE 410 19
GROW FULL OF DESIRE 465 20
IT MUST BE WONDERFUL TO LIVE AND GROW OLD 503 27
GROW UP TO 521 24
PERHAPS IF WE STARTED RIGHT ALL THE CHILDREN COULD GROW+ 527 4
WHY AS THEY GROW OLDER DO THEY SUFFER FROM BLOOD-PRESSU+ 537 24
EVEN THOUGH THEY GROW ON GENUINE ENGLISH MOULD 569 4
AND WHEN TO MAN'S ESTATE I GROW 576 20
FIG-TREES DON'T GROW IN MY NATIVE LAND 579 9
TILL THEY GROW HOT AND BURST AS EVEN STONE CAN 642 14
THIS SEA WILL NEVER DIE NEITHER WILL IT EVER GROW OLD 688 1
TO GROW UP TRUE HUNDRED-PER-CENT AMERICAN 778 2
THEY SEEMED TO GROW DARKER AS SHE CAME TO THE EDGE OF D+ 869 6

GROWING
MINE WAS THE LOVE OF A GROWING FLOWER 111 11
OF GROWING THESE SMOKE-PUFFS THAT PUFF IN WILD GYRATION 116 8
WE LOOK OVER THE GROWING WHEAT WHERE THE JADE-GREEN 209 20
ACTUALLY GROWING 278 16
AS YOU SEE IT STANDING GROWING YOU FEEL AT ONCE IT IS S+ 282 13
THEY SAW TINY ROSE CYCLAMENS BETWEEN THEIR TOES GROWING 310 14
FACES DARK AS BLACK RICE GROWING 391 13

GROWING
AND THE BUB-EAGLE THAT LIBERTY HAD HATCHED WAS GROWING A 413 18
OR THE SPLENDID GROWING OF AN ASH-TREE 610 22
BE ALONE AND FEEL THE TREES SILENTLY GROWING 646 9
OF GROWING LIFE 675 28
THOUGH THEIR SHOULD HAVE BEEN GROWING HEAVY FOR CENTURI+ 778 37
LOVE LIKE THE FLOWERS IS LIFE GROWING 844 1

GROWN
THAT DAY IS HALF GROWN OVER IT NEED NOT ABASH 91 4
AND CITIES MIGHT BE AS ONCE THEY WERE BOWERS GROWN OUT 451 18
FOR DESIRE HAS DIED IN ME SILENCE HAS GROWN 507 17
HAS THE SHELL GROWN TOO HEAVY FOR THE TORTOISE 558 17
FOLK-FLOWERS HAVE FADED MEN HAVE GROWN COLD 814 16
IT HAS GROWN UP OFTEN A BIG AND OFTEN INTERESTING-LOOKI+ 841 16
THE FRAME OF THINGS HAS GROWN SO HEAVY IT'S JUST TOO HE+ 842 29
AND DO I NOT SEEK TO MATE MY GROWN DESIROUS SOUL *926 22

GROWS
WHERE ASH ON THE DYING COALS GROWS SWIFTLY LIKE HEAVY 47 6
HE GROWS DISTINCT AND I SEE HIS HOT 59 7
IF SO THE VAST THE GOD THE SLEEP THAT STILL GROWS RICHER 195 17
GROWS DIMMER WE BOTH FORGET 240 14
THAT GROWS OUT OF ROCK AND PLUMES FORTH PLUMES FORTH 498 19
SHE GROWS AND THROWS 565 19
THE TOWN GROWS FIERCER WITH HEAT 746 8
BETWEEN THE DOWNS GROWS HAZY WITH SUNSHINE 886 27

GROWSE
AN' CLUB-MONEY I WON'T GROWSE 45 33

GROWTH
AND AN AMOUNT OF FUNGOID AND PARASITIC GROWTH 677 23

GRUDGE
AS IF YOU OWED HIM AN OLD OLD GRUDGE GREAT SUN OR AN OLD 374 3
AND THEY GRUDGE THE CIRCUS PEOPLE THE SWOOPING GAY 446 8
AND THEY GRUDGE THEM THE IMMEDIATE PHYSICAL UNDERSTANDI+ 446 11
AND THEY GRUDGE THEM THEIR CIRCUS-LIFE ALTOGETHER 446 13
OR THEY BEAR EVERYBODY A GRIM AND GRISLY GRUDGE 502 19
AND IT SEEMS TO ME THAT THE YOUNG ONES THOUGH THEY GRUD+ 829 1

GRUDGING
YOU WITH YOUR GRUDGING ENVIOUS FURTIVE RAGE 314 32

GRUESOME
GRIM GRUESOME GALLANTRY TO WHICH HE IS DOOMED 362 26

GRUNT
SO ENDING ON A GRUNT OF AGONISED RELIEF 377 16
THESE PIGS THAT CAN'T GRUNT 792 25

GUADALUPE
GUADALUPE WHOSE FACE IS OVAL 798 8

GUARD
WHENCE COMETH THIS THAT THOU MUST GUARD FROM THEFT 69 25
OUTCASTS KEEP GUARD 146 24
WILL SET A GUARD OF HONOUR AT EACH DOOR 153 21
GUARD MY SHEEP CAME THE SILVERY VOICE FROM THE PINNACLE 324 23
CHANGING GUARD 341 20
O THE STALE OLD DOGS WHO PRETEND TO GUARD 493 25
AND GUARD THE LAST TREASURE OF THE SOUL OUR SANITY 514 12

GUARDED
AND GUARDED BY A GLITTERING TEAR *912 22

GUARDIAN
AND THE FEED OF PAP THAT WE NURSES AND GUARDIAN ANGELS + 670 16

GUARDING
GUARDING THE PATH HIS HAND RELAXED AT HIS THIGH 66 10
RAMPING ROUND GUARDING THE FLOCK OF MANKIND 324 28

GUARDS
WITH FIRE AS IT GUARDS THE WILD NORTH-COASTS RED-FIRE S+ 57 13
RESTS A STILL LINE OF SOLDIERS RED MOTIONLESS RANGE OF + 66 7
WOMAN'S BUT THE APPLES OF LIFE THE DRAGON GUARDS AND NO+ 277 8
GUARDS LIFE FROM DEATH AND DEATH FROM LIFE 810 2

GUAVA
EVE ALONE UNSATISFIED AMONG THE ORANGE AND GUAVA TREES 864 1

GUDGEON
GUDGEON 33 23

GUELDER
THE GUELDER ROSE-BUSH IS HUNG WITH CORONETS 854 21

GUELDER-ROSE
LOVE-LIGHT IS GLOWING THOUGH THE GUELDER-ROSE IS TOO CH+ 854 17

GUESS
THA WON'T STARE ME OUT I GUESS 79 12
AN' 'APPEN YOU'D GUESS THEN WHAT I'VE COME FOR 81 23
WILL DREAM INTO THE FUTURE DID HE GUESS 878 10
BUT THA DOESNA STARE ME OUT I GUESS *921 8
'AN 'APPEN YOU MIGHT GUESS WHAT I'VE COME FOR *923 23

GUEST
WITH WOUNDS BETWEEN THEM AND SUFFERING LIKE A GUEST 155 10
HOW GLAD I WAS HE HAD COME LIKE A GUEST IN QUIET TO DRI+ 350 9
GUEST OF THE HOST 812 28
TO HIS GUEST CHAMBER KNOWING EACH SINEW AND VEIN 877 37

GUIDE
    GUIDE   148 14
    OH THE GREAT ADVENTURE OF DEATH WHERE THOMAS COOK CANNO+   677 8
    LET ME GUIDE MYSELF WITH THE BLUE FORKED TORCH OF THIS +   697 14
    LET ME GUIDE MYSELF WITH THE BLUE FORKED TORCH OF A FLO+   *956 11

GUILLOTINE
    THEN I AM MORE THAN RADICAL I WANT TO WORK A GUILLOTINE   526 16

GUILT
    MESHED AND TANGLED TOO MUCH IN THE SKEIN OF GUILT   884 14

GUILTY
    I WATCHED THE TEARS ON THE GUILTY CHEEKS OF THE BOYS   94 14

GULF
    THE GULF THAT CAME BETWEEN US AND DREW US IN   90 23
    DO THEY WIPE AWAY THE GLOOM THE GULF THROWS UP   90 24
    THE HEALING DAYS SHALL CLOSE THE DARK GULF UP   90 29
    AND THE GULF THAT CAME BETWEEN YOU WOMAN AND ME MAN   91 3
    DRIFTS OVER THE GULF THAT BARS   144 12
    BEHOLD THE GULF IMPASSABLE   635 27
    ONLY OH MAN STARE STARE INTO THE GULF   637 33
    THE SOFT GULF BE WISE   818 4

GULFS
    AND BEHIND ME NOW IN THE GULFS OF SPACE LIES THE GOLDEN+   695 26
    THE PATH BETWEEN GULFS OF THE DARK AND THE STEEPS OF   788 9

GULPING
    AND DESIROUS BELLY GULPING   336 11
    AND GULPING AT MORE THAN SHE CAN SWALLOW AND WORKING   359 5
    GULPING UP SCIENCE'S SMART ARMADA   824 11

GUMMY
    EVEN THE WILFUL OBSTINATE GUMMY FIG-TREE   305 8

GUMS
    SOFTLY DRANK THROUGH HIS STRAIGHT GUMS INTO HIS SLACK L+   349 16
    SOFT RED TONGUE AND HARD THIN GUMS   353 7
    OVERLAPPING GUMS   359 21
    NOT BLEEDING AWAY TO LEAVE ME WITH WHITENED GUMS   768 10

GUN
    A GUN AND A BUNCHED-UP DEER ITS FOUR LITTLE FEET   220 18
    THEY HAVE A GUN   401 9
    WE HAVE NO GUN   401 10

GUNS
    NO SOUND OF GUNS NOR OVERHEAD NO RUSHED   165 31
    SO GUNS AND STRONG EXPLOSIVES   715 12
    ARE THE GUNS AND THE STEEL THE BRIDEGROOM   742 25
    SISTERS THE GUNS ARE SPEAKING LET ALL   758 17
    HE WHO HOUSELS THE DEAD OF THE GUNS   797 2

GURGLES
    NIGHTINGALE'S PIERCING CRIES AND GURGLES STARTLED THE   366 2

GURGLING
    VOICES GURGLING LIKE WATER   425 12

GUSH
    IN FRONT OF ME YES UP THE DARKNESS GOES THE GUSH OF THE+   97 18
    THAT DREW THIS RED GUSH IN ME   241 26
    OH YES THE GUSH OF SPRING IS STRONG ENOUGH   272 13
    THE GUSH OF SPRING IS STRONG ENOUGH   272 18
    DREADFUL GUSH   628 17
    HE STRIKES THE GUSH OF PASSION EASILY   877 7

GUSHED
    BUT SINCE MY LIMBS GUSHED FULL OF FIRE   118 1

GUSHES
    HIS BENT COURSE MILDLY HERE WAKES AGAIN LEAPS LAUGHS AN+   33 14
    GUSHES   *891 16

GUSHING
    THERE WAS NO GUSHING RESPONSE AS THERE IS AT THE FILM   445 30
    AND PUTS HIS MOUTH DOWN TO THE GUSHING STREAM   877 8

GUSTO
    WITH GUSTO BEGIN AGAIN THE BRISK FIGHT   865 31

GUSTY
    NOR GUSTY JOVE WITH HIS EYE ON IMMORTAL TARTS   437 5

GUTS
    THEIR GUTS WITH A CERTAIN FAT AND OFTEN   460 15
    THEIR GUTS WITH A CERTAIN FAT AND OFTEN   460 19
    THE GUTS AND THE STONES AND THE WOMB ROTS THEM DOWN   463 21
    OF ENGLAND WITH THE GUTS TO TURN ROUND ON HIM AIMING   '494 11
    THEY SQUEEZED OUT MOST OF YOUR GUTS   549 8
    COMES REALLY OUT OF THEIR GUTS LAD   549 21
    AND KIN WITH MISS JUPSON WHOSE GUTS ARE NARROW   583 28
    AND IRRITATION SEETHES SECRETLY THROUGH THEIR GUTS AS T+   616 9

GUTTA-PERCHA
    GUTTA-PERCHA   625 20

GUTTER
    OUTSIDER SPRUNG UP FROM SOME HORRIBLE GUTTER   576 9
    AND GUTTER TO EXTINCTION LIKE A TAPER ON A FORGOTTEN AL+   859 4

GUTTERING
    WHO STAND ALONE IN DESPAIR LIKE A GUTTERING LIGHT   73 13

GUVNOR
    ALL RIGHT GUVNOR WHAT ABAHT IT   547 16

GYPSIES
    WHERE WE FOREGATHER LIKE GYPSIES NONE KNOWING   812 23

GYRATION
    OF GROWING THESE SMOKE-PUFFS THAT PUFF IN WILD GYRATION   116 8

HA
    HA SINCE YOU LOVE ME   235 19
    HA I WAS A BLAZE LEAPING UP   259 11

HABITATS
    OLD HAUNTS OLD HABITATS OLD HEARTHS   722 28

HACKED
    LIKE DRAWN BLADES NEVER SHEATHED HACKED AND GONE BLACK   304 28

HACKS
    AND MEN BEING MOSTLY GELDINGS AND KNACKER-BONED HACKS   379 31

HADES
    OH PERSEPHONE PERSEPHONE BRING BACK TO ME FROM HADES TH+   303 13
    FROM HADES   307 21
    THROUGH THE DARK HADES AT THE ROOTS OF THE TREE   617 10
    TO HADES   *955 10

HADNA
    I WISH THA HADNA DONE IT TIM   82 ,21
    I WISH THA HADNA DONE IT TIM   *924 25

HADN'T
    BUT TILL THEN TILL THAT APPLE OF KNOWLEDGE SHE HADN'T H+   284 10

HA'E
    AS SOME SHOULD HA'E HARDLY A SMITE O' TROUBLE   45 23
    HE WED HE'D HA'E SUMMAT GOOD   77 28
    THA'S NO 'CASIONS TER HA'E ME ON   79 29
    BUT THA'LL HA'E TER PROMISE TER BE TRUE TER ME   82 27
    TWENTY POUND O' THY OWN THA HAST AN' FIFTY POUND HA'E I   83 1
    GO THEN THALT' HA'E NO PEACE TILL TER'S HAD   140 3
    LADDIE A MAN THOU'LT HA'E TO BE   220 7
    EH MEN DOESNA HA'E BOSOMS 'APPEN NOT ON'Y THA KNOWS   540 16
    HE WED HE'D HA'E SUMMAT GOOD   *919 16
    TO HA'E GONE AN' GIVEN HIS WHITE YOUNG FLESH   *919 19
    THA'S NO OCCASIONS TER HA'E ME ON   *921 25
    TO THINK I SHOULD HA'E TO HAFFLE AN' CAFFLE   *924 13
    TWENTY POUND O' THY OWN THA HAST AND FIFTY POUND HA'E I   *925 5
    SORRY I AM FOR THIS BUSINESS AN' SORRY IF I HA'E DRIVEN+   *925 10
    AN' A MAN AN' A FATHER THA'LT HA'E TO BE   *944 15

HAFFLE
    TO THINK I SHOULD HA'E TO HAFFLE AN' CAFFLE   *924 13

HAG
    ROUND-SHOULDERED HAG MY SIRS TO THINK   81 18
    I KNOW THAT POVERTY IS A HARD OLD HAG   498 13
    ROUND-SHOULDERED HAG MY SIRS TO THINK   *923 18

HA-HA
    AND WHAT A SENSE OF TRUE HUMOUR THEY'VE GOT HA-HA   583 21

HAIL
    KEEP SUDDENLY SHOWING A WHITENESS A FLASH AND A FURL A +   687 2
    HAIL AND BE DAMNED TO THEE EMPTY MOST EMPTILY   824 9
    HAIL AND BE DAMNED TO THEE WINNING THE GAME   824 17

HAILED
    IN A LOW SHOCKING PERFUME TO KNOW WHO HAS HAILED   105 33

HAILING
    I LEFT OFF HAILING HIM   338 9
    OR LIKE A LIFTED HAND HAILING AT HER WRONG END   385 33

HAIR
    IN THE HAIR OF AN EASTERN GIRL   36 20
    LIGHTS THE SOFT HAIR OF A GIRL AS SHE READS   41 7
    THERE'S A SCENT OF CLOVER CREPT THROUGH MY HAIR   50 9
    MY BABY HER BROWN HAIR BRUSHED WITH WET TEARS   73 23
    EVEN HER FLOATING HAIR SINKS HEAVILY   74 3
    OVER MY HAIR AND TRACING MY BROWS   104 7
    PUSHED GENTLY AWAY AND HIDDEN IN THE THICK OF HER HAIR   114 22
    REVOLVE THROUGH HER HAIR   120 11
    THEN LETS HER BLACK HAIR LOOSE THE DARKNESS FALL   128 33
    AND SITS IN HER OWN DARK NIGHT OF HER BITTER HAIR   129 1
    AND NUTS FELL OUT OF THEIR HAIR   152 15
    THE STRANGER'S HAIR WAS SHORN LIKE A LAD'S DARK POLL   156 1
    EVEN DEAD HE STILL IS MORTAL AND HIS HAIR   158 19
    LONDON WITH HAIR   171 9
    COIFFING UP YOUR AUBURN HAIR   178 8
    TO CREEP THROUGH YOUR LOOSENED HAIR TILL HE REACHES   178 32
    HER HAIR FOR WOMANHOOD AND PLAY AWHILE WITH HER THEN   179 8
    CHEEKS AND HAIR A MOMENT SAYING IS IT YOU   180 11
    A WOMAN BINDS HER HAIR   200 18
    I DISTINGUISH THE SCENT OF YOUR HAIR SO NOW THE LIMBER   208 30
    YOUR HAIR FOR THE BLISS-DRENCHED REVEL   243 19
    BEHOLD MY HAIR TWISTING AND GOING BLACK   301 21
    AT HER ANKLES AND CATCHING HER BY THE HAIR   309 19
    WHEN HE PUSHED HIS BUSH OF BLACK HAIR OFF HIS BROW   310 1
    THE SHAGGY UNDERGROWTH OF THEIR OWN HAIR   310 12
    PUT HIBISCUS IN HER HAIR   314 7
    A LIVING FOREHEAD WITH ITS SLOW WHORL OF HAIR   325 27
    BUT IT MIGHT AS WELL HAVE BEEN HAIR ON A SPIDER THING   345 34
    ERECT SCORCHED-PALLID OUT OF THE HAIR OF THE CEDAR   373 5
    HAIR   381 11

HAIR
WITH HAIR ON THEM ARE BEING IDLE   386 30
LIKE YELLOW HAIR OF A TIGRESS BRINDLED WITH PINES   408 26
SO DO FORGIVE ME I SPRINKLE MY HAIR   492 29
AND WOMEN EVEN CUT THEIR SHIMMERY HAIR   530 8
WHY DID THEY CUT OFF THEIR LONG HAIR   537 26
EVEN THE OLD PRIEST IN HIS LONG BLACK ROBE AND SILVERY +   618 16
THEY HAD LONG HAIR LIKE SAMSON   688 23
MEN SINGING SONGS AND WOMEN BRUSHING THEIR HAIR IN THE +   691 24
OH LOVELY LOVELY WITH THE DARK HAIR PILED UP AS SHE WEN+   693 8
AND PUT SCARLET BUDS IN THEIR HAIR ON THE WAY TO HELL   710 19
HIS HELMET OFF AND WIPES HIS HAIR TRYING   733 21
SWARTHY AND STRONG WITH HIS DAMP THICK HAIR   733 24
TO THE THING AND RATHER FRETTED AND HIS THICK BLACK HAIR   734 21
EAGLE SCORCHED-PALLID OUT OF THE HAIR OF THE CEDAR   781 10
ERECT SCORCHED-PALLID OUT OF THE HAIR OF THE CEDAR   783 6
IS COMBING HER DARK HAIR   787 13
OF HIS HAIR SAY THE SAME TO THE WOMEN   791 25
BLUE DAYLIGHT SINKS IN MY HAIR   802 26
THE HAIR OF NIGHT IS DARK OVER OUR FACES   809 1
YET ARE FLEECED WITH SOFT HAIR   827 20
WITH HAIR THAT WAS BOBBED SO EARLY   834 15
AND I'D GATHER MY HAIR   836 1
SUCH ON THE VIRGIN HAIR OF DEAD SIXTEEN   854 24
AND FALLS WINGLESS BLOOD STREAMING THROUGH ITS YELLOW H+   855 25
THROUGH WIND-SNATCHED HAIR   861 18
AND SCATTERED WITH HER HAIR CLOUDS OF PALE MIMOSA SANDS   863 27
WHOSE EDGE OF HAIR CURVES THICKLY TO THE RED   878 21
LIKE A TRESS OF BLACK HAIR   883 14
AND I OPEN MY LIPS TO TAKE A STRAND OF KEEN HAIR   883 15
YOUR HAIR PEEP OUT ON THE LANE   866 3
WHITE WHEN THE WIND SHIFTED HER HAIR THAT WAS SOFT AN' +   *910 12
MY BABY HER BROWN HAIR BRUSHED WITH WET TEARS   *913 15
EVEN HER FLOATING HAIR SINKS LIKE STORM-BRUISED YOUNG L+   *913 24
SUNSHINE OF HIS HAIR I USED TO KISS   *933 28
AH AND MY HAIR IS HANGING WET AND BITTER ON MY FACE   *933 31

HAIRS
TO MY GAIETY A FEW LONG GREY HAIRS   107 2

HAIR'S
HER HAIR'S LIVE CURL   862 14

HAIRY
AND A HAIRY BIG BEE HUNG OVER THE PRIMULAS   243 23
BE ROUGH AND HAIRY I'M GLAD THEY'RE LIKE THAT   254 12
ONLY YOUR ACCURSED HAIRY FRAILTY   554 6
HAIRY HORRID GOD THE FATHER IN A WILLIAM BLAKE   385 20
HANGING HAIRY PIGS' TAILS   390 12
OF WOLF ALL HAIRY AND LEVEL A WOLF'S WILD PELT   408 29
AS UNDER THE HAIRY BELLY OF A GREAT BLACK BEAR   409 12

HAIRY-SHAGGY
ALL HER GREAT HAIRY-SHAGGY BELLY OPEN AGAINST THE MORNI+   385 30

HALF
AND ONE SIDE SHADOW HALF IN SIGHT   50 25
BUT SHE'S WAITING I KNOW IMPATIENT AND COLD HALF   85 11
THAT DAY IS HALF GROWN OVER IT NEED NOT ABASH   91 4
THEY PASS IN A HALF EMBRACE   106 12
THE MOON IS BROKEN IN TWAIN AND HALF A MOON   114 17
THE OTHER HALF OF THE BROKEN COIN OF TROTH   114 19
THEY BURIED HER HALF IN THE GRAVE WHEN THEY LAID HER AW+   114 21
SO HALF LIES ON THE SKY FOR A GENERAL SIGN   114 25
AND HALF LIES THERE IN THE DARK WHERE THE DEAD ALL LIE   115 1
IN WHICH I HALF LOVE YOU   116 31
HALF SUBSTANCELESS AND WITHOUT GRAVE WORTH   118 17
THOUGHTFUL AND HALF AFRAID   178 19
AND I WHO AM HALF IN LOVE WITH YOU   292 20
SLOUCHING ALONG AWAY BELOW HALF OUT OF SIGHT   338 13
RESTING YOUR HEAD HALF OUT OF YOUR WIMPLE   354 8
TORN WITH A SHRIEK HALF MUSIC HALF HORROR   364 26
WHILE LIFE WAS A HEAVE OF MATTER HALF INANIMATE   372 10
THAT IS HALF INSATIABLE DESIRE AND HALF UNQUENCHABLE   378 25
THE ARABS WERE ONLY HALF RIGHT THOUGH THEY HINTED THE   378 28
AND DANCE AND DANCE FOREVER DANCE WITH BREATH HALF   389 11
STOPS AGAIN HALF TURNS INQUISITIVE TO LOOK BACK   393 29
THEY MAKE IT UP HALF WAY   549 22
HALF BELIEVING 'EM TILL ONE DAY   556 14
SAID THE LOVELY YOUNG LADY HALF WISTFUL HALF MENACING   604 7
MADE HER HALF MADONNA HALF ASTARTE   617 22
IS HALF OPEN   702 16
THEN WHEN THE DOOR IS HALF OPEN   702 18
LEAVING MY EYES HALF EMPTY AND CLAMOROUS   *893 16

HALF-ACQUAINT
RECOGNITIONS AND GREETINGS OF HALF-ACQUAINT THINGS AS I   52 22
RECOGNITIONS AND GREETINGS OF HALF-ACQUAINT THINGS AS I+   *905 11

HALF-A-DOZEN
IN THE SHAPE OF HALF-A-DOZEN STOUT   632 32

HALF-AFRAID
WHILE THE WISPY MODERN CHILDREN HALF-AFRAID   426 20

HALF-ALIVE
YOU HALF-ALIVE YOUNG   456 15

HALF-ANIMATE
A TINY FRAGILE HALF-ANIMATE BEAN   352 8

HALF-BARED
BUT WHEN EVERYBODY GOES ROUND WITH SOUL HALF-BARED OR Q+   608 16

HALF-BITTER
SPEAK IN HALF-BITTER SCENT YOUR DREAM OF ME   880 12

HALF-BLOWN
LIKE HALF-BLOWN FLOWERS DIMLY SHAKING AT THE NIGHT   75 27

HALF-BUILT
IN A LITTLE HALF-BUILT STREET WHERE RED AND WHITE VILLAS   864 25

HALF-CAJOLED
MY SOUL IS HALF-CAJOLED HALF-CAJOLED   291 26

HALF-DARK
THAT IS ALWAYS HALF-DARK   298 27

HALF-DEAD
OPEN YOUR HALF-DEAD EYES   456 14

HALF-DEMON
DO THEY STAND UNDER THE DAWN HALF-GODLY HALF-DEMON   371 36

HALF-DEVILISH
THE HOT DARK BLOOD OF ITSELF A-LAUGHING WET HALF-DEVILI+   389 20

HALF-FOLDED
HER ROOM WHERE THE NIGHT STILL HANGS LIKE A HALF-FOLDED+   129 29

HALF-GODLY
DO THEY STAND UNDER THE DAWN HALF-GODLY HALF-DEMON   371 36

HALF-GROWN
O THE GREY GARNER THAT IS FULL OF HALF-GROWN APPLES   120 5

HALF-HIDDEN
AND THE HALF-HIDDEN PRIVATE PARTS JUST A LITTLE BRASS T+   625 22

HALF-HIDING
HALF-HIDING THE PAVEMENT-RUN   50 26

HALF-LIE
AS A HALF-LIE CAUSES THE IMMEDIATE CONTRADICTION OF THE+   664 11

HALF-MOON
WHEN SHALL I SEE THE HALF-MOON SINK AGAIN   62 25
AM LIT BENEATH MY HEART WITH A HALF-MOON WEIRD AND BLUE   115 4

HALF-OBSCURE
IT IS RAINING DOWN THE HALF-OBSCURE ROAD   220 15

HALF-SECRET
WITH THE HALF-SECRET GLEAM OF A PASSION-FLOWER HANGING   299 1

HALF-SEEN
LIKE HALF-SEEN FROTH ON AN EBBING SHORE IN THE MOON   75 28

HALF-SHUT
FROM THE TWILIGHT LIKE HALF-SHUT LILIES   227 19

HALF-SINISTERLY
STRANGELY HALF-SINISTERLY FLESH-FRAGRANT   280 20

HALF-SMILING
GOING WITH INSIDIOUS HALF-SMILING QUIETNESS   296 21

HALF-SUBMERGED
THE DANDELION SEEDS STAY HALF-SUBMERGED IN THE GRASS   204 21

HALF-THREATENING
AND A HALF-THREATENING ENVY   312 21

HALF-TRUTH
AS EVERY HALF-TRUTH AT LENGTH PRODUCES THE CONTRADICTION   663 10
IN THE OPPOSITE HALF-TRUTH   663 12

HALF-UNREALISED
BUT A SUBTLE STRUGGLING LITTLE GERM STRUGGLING HALF-UNR+   775 25

HALF-VEILED
WITH THE HALF-VEILED BEAUTIFUL EYES AND THE PENSIVE FACE   379 4

HALF-VISIBLE
BETWEEN THE HALF-VISIBLE HORDES   *958 26

HALF-WAY
HALF-WAY DOWN ITS HEAVING SIDES   144 5
AND IS HALF-WAY OVER THE LAKE   223 11
POISON IN HIS MOUTH FOR THE SUN IN HIM WOULD FAIN RISE +   348 10
HALF-WAY ROUND THE CIRCLE NOW   764 11

HALF-WITTED
AND THEY STARED AND THEY STARED THE HALF-WITTED LOT   578 12

HALF-YAWNING
HALF-YAWNING AT THE OPEN INEXPERIENCED   311 7

HALL
INTO THE TWILIGHT'S EMPTY HALL   42 31
LIKE A THING UNWARRANTABLE CROSS THE HALL   140 8
LADS IN THEIR WARM LIGHT SLIPPERS BOUND DOWN THE HALL T+   865 28

HALLOWED
HALLOWED BE THY NAME THEN   704 13

HALLS
ELSEWHERE HALLS OF HIGH DISGRACES   95 31
THE HALLS OF MY MIND COMPELLING MY LIFE TO CONFORM   173 20
I HAVE LIVED DELIGHTED IN THE HALLS OF THE PAST   173 21
BLACK LAMPS FROM THE HALLS OF DIS BURNING DARK BLUE   697 9

HALLS
    AND ITS HALLS OF THE GREAT DARK BELOW   711   2
    SURE OF OUR DEAD IN THE PROUD HALLS OF DEATH   740 27
    I VENTURE FROM THE HALLS OF SHADOWY DEATH   744 11
    AMBASSADOR FROM HALLS OF NOISELESS DEATH   745 15
    THE HALLS OF MY LIFE AND COMPELS MY SOUL TO CONFORM   *906 14
    THE HALLS OF MY LIFE COMPELLING MY SOUL TO CONFORM   *908   8
    BLACK LAMPS FROM THE HALLS OF DIS SMOKING DARK BLUE   *956   7

HALLUCINATIONS
    TO SHUT HALLUCINATIONS OUT   124 19
    TO SHUT HALLUCINATIONS OUT   *935 19

HALO
    AND HAD HIM FLY LIKE A HALO ROUND MY HEAD   339   4
    SEEMED TO THINK THEY'D GOT LIKE A HALO   555 19
    OR HALO OR PRESTIGE WENT   556   6
    THEY WERE THE HALO THE ELOQUENCE NOW IS NONE   855 15

HALOED
    WHITE AND HALOED WITH FIRE-MIST DOWN IN THE TANGLED   206 11

HALT
    I FELT THE LURCH AND HALT OF HER HEART   61 21
    TO HALT THE HEART DIVERT THE STREAMING FLOW   195 34
    TILL THEY HALT AT A CLIFF ON THE EDGE OF THE LAND   201 15
    I FELT THE LURCH AND HALT OF HER HEART   *912   1

HALTER
    THE YOUTH WALKS UP TO THE WHITE HORSE TO PUT ITS HALTER+   683 19

HALTS
    SO HALTS THE LITTLE BLACK BITCH ON FOUR SPREAD PAWS IN +   375 10

HAMLET
    AND HAMLET HOW BORING HOW BORING TO LIVE WITH   494 19
    OF LEAR AND MACBETH AND HAMLET AND TIMON   508 17
    AND A MAN CAN NO LONGER FEEL HEROIC ABOUT BEING A HAMLET   508 26

HAMLETS
    PETERLETS GEORGELETS HAMLETS   457 18

HAMMER
    WITH AXE IN HAND AND THE HAMMER AND THE PICK-AXE OVER-A+   174 16
    AND HE-GOAT IS ANVIL TO HE-GOAT AND HAMMER TO HE-GOAT   381 32

HAMMERED
    WAS HAMMERED OUT   168 22

HAMMER-HEADS
    THE RIGHT WHALES THE SPERM-WHALES THE HAMMER-HEADS THE +   694   5

HAMMERING
    THUS HAMMERING THE METTLE OF GOATS INTO PROOF AND SMITI+   381 28
    FROM THE FIERY HAMMERING OF YOUR HEART I CAST   873   2

HAMMERS
    DISASTROUSLY REMINISCENT OF HAMMERS AND FILES AND DOOR-+   835   6
    ALL DAY THE CLINK OF THE HAMMERS HAS OPPRESSED   *896 18

HAMMOCK
    OVER A GIRL WHO HAS STREWN HERSELF IN A HAMMOCK   868   6

HAMPER
    AND PAST LIVES HAMPER ME CLOG AND EMBARRASS   173 28

HAMS
    TRIPPING ABOUT WITH THEIR LADYLIKE HAMS   765 11
    DID THEY DO IT BY SQUATTING ON THEIR HAMS   795   1
    YOU DO NOTHING BUT SQUAT ON YOUR HAMS AND STARE WITH VA+   795   2
    I'D HANG MY HAMS WITH PUCKERED PETTICOATS SWAYING   835 32

HAN
    IF I HAN WHAT'S THAT TER THEE   81 30
    AN' IF I HAN WHAT'S THAT TO THEE   *924   2

HAND
    HER HAND GO STEALING   35 23
    I HEAR HIS HAND ON THE LATCH AND RISE FROM MY CHAIR   43 18
    OF HIS HAND AGAINST MY BOSOM AND OH THE BROAD   43 24
    HIS COMING WITH HIS HAND HE TURNS MY FACE TO HIM   43 26
    FROM ME FROM THE HAND OF MY LOVE WHICH CREEPS UP   47 18
    AND I COULD FEEL HER FEET IN EITHER HAND   65   8
    GUARDING THE PATH HIS HAND RELAXED AT HIS THIGH   66 10
    CLEAN OF THE COLD AND THE MUST WITH MY HAND ON THE LATCH   99   9
    AND I LINGERED ON THE THRESHOLD WITH MY HAND   121 14
    I HAD STOOD WITH MY HAND UPLIFTED   122   5
    SHE LAUGHED SHE REACHED HER HAND OUT TO THE FLOWER   123 13
    HER LARGE BROWN HAND STRETCHED OVER   123 20
    SHE MOVED HER HAND AND AGAIN   124 32
    CAN THEY MAKE THEM YAWN I PUT MY HAND TO THE DINT   125   9
    SHE WATCHED MY HAND TO SEE WHAT IT WOULD FULFILL   125 12
    POISED AT HER LIKE A WEAPON MY HAND WAS WHITE AND KEEN   125 15
    BUT HELD MY HAND AFLOAT TOWARDS THE SLIPS   125 21
    FOR MY HAND LIKE A SNAKE WATCHED HERS THAT COULD NOT FLY   125 24
    HUNGRY FOR LOVE YET IF I LAY MY HAND IN HER BREAST   128   2
    HOW CARESSINGLY SHE LAYS HER HAND ON MY KNEE   128 14
    HAS SOME HAND BALANCED MORE LEAVES IN THE DEPTHS OF THE   142   5
    SOME MONEY HER HAND SLIPS OUT OF THE BREAST OF HER   143   8
    AND LOOKS AT ME AND LOOKS IN THE PALM OF HER HAND   143 15
    A HAND IS OVER MY FACE   162 17
    A COLD HAND I PEEP BETWEEN THE FINGERS   162 18
    AS IF IT RIPPLED FROM OUT OF US HAND IN HAND   170 12
    CAST OUT BY THE HAND THAT SCATTERS   171 22
    WITH AXE IN HAND AND THE HAMMER AND THE PICK-AXE OVER-A+   174 16
    HOLD MY HAND TO CATCH THE RAINDROPS THAT SLANT INTO SIG+   179 21
    AND JOSEPH SHADING HIS EYES WITH HIS HAND   200 15
    THEN YOU PUT YOUR HAND IN MINE AGAIN KISSED ME AND WE   206 13

HAND
    AND MY HAND WITHERED IN YOUR HAND   206 22
    YOUR HAND WOULD NOT BE SO FLIG AND EASY   255 25
    WAR CAME AND EVERY HAND RAISED TO MURDER   257 27
    VERY GOOD VERY GOOD EVERY HAND RAISED TO MURDER   257 28
    I PUT OUT MY HAND IN THE NIGHT ONE NIGHT AND MY HAND   259   2
    SO I PUT MY HAND OUT FURTHER A LITTLE FURTHER   259   7
    NOW HERE WAS I NEW-AWAKENED WITH MY HAND STRETCHING   259 16
    I TOUCHED WITH MY HAND I CLUTCHED WITH MY HAND   260   2
    STRETCHING OUT MY HAND MY HAND FLUNG LIKE A DROWNED   260 10
    MAN'S HAND ON A ROCK   260 11
    WHEN SHE HAS PUT HER HAND ON MY SECRET DARKEST SOURCES +   267   6
    I ON THE OTHER HAND   320 14
    AND FELT HIM BEAT IN MY HAND WITH HIS MUCOUS LEAPING   339   9
    MY HAND   339 16
    AND HE HARDLY STIRRED IN MY HAND MUFFLED UP   347   8
    SHE SNAPS THE SOFT BREAD FROM MY HAND IN GREAT MOUTHFULS   359   1
    OR LIKE A LIFTED HAND HAILING AT HER WRONG END   385 33
    THAT LITTLE LIFTED BARE HAND   386 16
    DO YOU EXIST AND CAN A MAN TOUCH YOUR HAND   430   2
    IF I COULD SEE YOUR HAND AND IT WERE THUMBS DOWN   430   4
    I WISH YOU'D SHOW YOUR HAND   430 14
    BOWED AND LIFTED HER FOOT IN HER HAND SMILED SWUNG HER   444 28
    O YOU WITH MENTAL FINGERS O NEVER PUT YOUR HAND ON ME   468 24
    IF YOU CAN ONLY SIT WITH A MIRROR IN YOUR HAND AN AGEING   478 20
    AND KINDLY HAND ME THE CIGARETTES   540 27
    AND THERE YOU STAND WITH NOTHING AND EXPECT ME TO HAND   547 13
    HOLD MY HAND AUNTIE AUNTIE   572 17
    AUNTIE HOLD MY HAND   572 18
    HOLD MY HAND AND LOVE ME AUNTIE   572 21
    HOLD MY HAND AUNTIE AUNTIE   573   5
    AUNTIE HOLD MY HAND   573   6
    THERE'S NEVER A FIG-LEAF NEAR AT HAND   579 15
    THEY SAVED YOU FROM SQUALID COTTAGES AND POVERTY OF HAND   630 17
    FROM THE ROBOT CONTACT ON EVERY HAND   645 24
    YET YOU CAN'T LAY YOUR HAND ON IT   692   5
    SO IN THE CANE-BRAKE HE CLASPED HIS HAND IN DELIGHT   693 16
    THE GRIM FROST IS AT HAND WHEN THE APPLES WILL FALL   717   3
    HE COMES TO THE SIDE OF THE ROAD AND WASHES HIS HAND   734 13
    AND LET THEM FEED FROM MY HAND   751   7
    AND IN HER LEFT HAND GAILY   756 12
    AND GIVE ME A HAND   763 26
    HE PUT UP HIS HAND AND HELD BACK THE SUN WITH HIS SHADOW   790   2
    HE WHISTLED TO IT LOUDLY TWICE TILL IT FELL TO HIS HAND   791   2
    IN HIS HAND IT LAY AND WENT DARK   791   3
    SO HE TOSSED IT AWHILE IN HIS HAND AND PLAYED WITH IT   791   6
    SO IT WILL LEAVE YOU AND YOU WILL HAND LIKE A GOURD ON +   800 22
    AND THE STAR IS THE LAMP IN THE HAND OF THE UNKNOWN MOV+   801 11
    DAY IS AT HAND   803 13
    LIFT YOUR HAND SAY FAREWELL SAY WELCOME   803 14
    LIFT YOUR HAND SAY FAREWELL SAY WELCOME   803 19
    BUT I TOUCHED THE HAND OF QUETZALCOATL   806 26
    I TOUCHED THE HAND OF QUETZALCOATL   806 28
    BUT HUITZILOPOCHTLI TOUCHED THE HAND OF QUETZALCOATL   809 19
    AND NESTING HIS CHIN IN HIS HAND   842 18
    THE WILD GODS SEND VITALITY THEY PUT THE LIGHTNING INTO+   843   5
    PRESSES HER HAND TO HER BOSOM WHERE THE FRUIT HAS LAIN   864 20
    WHAT IS THE HEAVY HOT HAND   869 17
    I THINK IT IS THE HAND OF SORROW   869 20
    MINT ME BEAUTIFUL MEDALS AND HAND THEM ME HOT   873   1
    THIS ONE NIGHT YET HE LIETH HERE TO HAND   877 21
    MY HAND IS HEAVY AND HELPLESS SINCE WIELDING THE LASH   *897 19
    THEN SHE RUMMAGED HER HAND IN 'ER BOSOM AN' KISSED THE +   *910 20
    THEN LIKE CHICKENS MOUNTED IN MY HAND   *953 18
    SHE LAUGHED SHE REACHED HER HAND OUT DOWN TO THE FLOWER   *934 19
    HER LARGE BROWN HAND LOOMED OVER   *934 26
    CAN MAKE THEM YAWN I STRETCHED MY HAND TO THE DINT   *935 25
    SHE WATCHED MY HAND AND THE SKIES BEGAN TO THRILL   *935 28
    SHE SWOOPED HER HAND AND THE ROVER   *936   1
    POISED AT HER LIKE A WEAPON MY HAND WAS WHITE AND KEEN   *936 14
    BUT HELD MY HAND AFLOAT STILL TOWARDS THE SLIPS   *936 20
    AND MY HAND LIKE A SNAKE WATCHED HERS THAT COULD NOT FLY   *936 23
    AS HER HAND GROPED OVER ITS NAKEDNESS   *937 15

HANDCUFFS
    WITH HANDCUFFS AND TOOK HIM TO THE POLICE-STATION   575   3

HANDED
    I HANDED HER THE MIRROR AND SAID   604 14
    SO I HANDED HER THE MIRROR   604 19

HANDFUL
    WHO TOOK A HANDFUL OF LIGHT AND ROLLED A BALL   69 18
    HE TOOK A HANDFUL OF LIGHT AND ROLLED A BALL   *916   1

HANDFULS
    RABBITS HANDFULS OF BROWN EARTH LIE   33   5
    RABBITS HANDFULS OF BROWN EARTH LIE   *891   6

HANDGRASP
    IT FEELS AS IF HIS HANDGRASP WEARING YOU   254 28

HANDING
    HANDING OUT A FEW LOOSE GOLDEN BREAST-FEATHERS AT MOULT+   414   9
    IT DOESN'T MEAN HANDING IT OUT TO SOME MEAN FOOL OR   449 19
    AND DO YOU THINK IT'S MY BUSINESS TO BE HANDING OUT MON+   547 22

HANDKERCHIEF
    SO TO DRIVE HIM OUT FLICKING WITH MY WHITE HANDKERCHIEF   343   5
    WORSE EVEN THAN THE HIDEOUS TERROR OF ME WITH MY HANDKE+   344 23
    BUT HIS HANDKERCHIEF IS WHITE WITH A BROAD BLUE BORDER   733 28

HANDLE
    I LOVED TO HANDLE IT IT SEEMED LIKE A NEAR PART OF HIM   255   3
    AND SOON EVEN GOD WON'T BE BIG ENOUGH TO HANDLE THAT IN+   670 20
    BACK IN A GRECIAN KNOT OR A JUG HANDLE OR A CHIGNON   836   2

HANDLED
  HANDLED ALL MY TOOLS AND MEASURES   95 18
  THINGS MADE BY IRON AND HANDLED BY STEEL   448 8

HANDS
  WITHOUT EYES WITHOUT HANDS   39 20
  QUICKENS THE UNCLASPING HANDS OF HAZEL   40 26
  PUTS THE HARD HANDS OF MY FRIEND TO SLEEP   41 9
  WHAT LARGE DARK HANDS ARE THOSE AT THE WINDOW   42 1
  AH SOON IN HIS LARGE HARD HANDS SHE DIES   43 12
  I MUST FOLD MY HANDS AND TURN MY FACE TO THE FIRE   47 2
  I HAVE OPENED THE WINDOWS TO WARM MY HANDS ON THE SILL   52 12
  WHO PLAY AROUND US COUNTRY GIRLS CLAPPING THEIR HANDS   58 19
  YOU WITH LOOSE HANDS OF ABANDONMENT HANGING DOWN   58 23
  WHO SUNK HIS HANDS IN FIRMNESS DOWN THY SIDES   69 10
  THE RED-GOLD SPOOLS OF THEIR HANDS AND THEIR FACES SWIN+   72 8
  I HAVE PUSHED MY HANDS IN THE DARK SOIL UNDER THE FLOWE+   92 8
  WITH GENTLENESS CAME I WITH MY HEART 'TWIXT MY HANDS LI+   92 22
  BUT WHOEVER WOULD PLUCK APART MY FLOWERING WILL BURN TH+   93 29
  THAT SETTLED UPON MY FACE AND HANDS TILL IT SEEMED   99 4
  AND I DO NOT CARE THOUGH THE LARGE HANDS OF REVENGE   126 1
  THOUGH HER HANDS ARE STILL THE WOMAN HER LARGE STRONG   128 5
  HANDS   128 6
  FOR NEVER HER HANDS COME NIGH ME BUT THEY LIFT   128 10
  BIG HANDS AS IF SURELY HER ARMS DID HURT   128 22
  PRESSING HER SPREAD HANDS OVER HER BREASTS AS SHE   128 24
  SHE MAKES HER HANDS TAKE MY PART THE PART OF THE MAN   128 27
  AH AND SHE PUTS HER HANDS UPON THE WALL   128 31
  PRESSES THEM THERE AND KISSES HER BIG DARK HANDS   128 32
  ABOUT HER FROM HER MAIDEN-FOLDED HANDS   128 34
  BUT OH THE PALMS OF HIS TWO BLACK HANDS ARE RED   135 22
  COMES ENDLESSLY KISSING MY FACE AND MY HANDS   144 2
  UNSEEN MY HANDS EXPLORE THE SILENCE DRAWING THE BARK   147 2
  MY HANDS SHOULD TOUCH THE DOOR   147 7
  CATCH MY HANDS MY DARLING BETWEEN YOUR BREASTS   147 15
  CAN WARM HER HANDS AND INVITE HER SOUL   151 27
  INTO OOZE AND THE SOMBRE DIRT SPOUTS UP AT MY HANDS   167 6
  I IMAGINE DEAD HANDS ARE BRIGHTER   168 13
  THEY HAVE NO HANDS THEY HAVE NO BODIES ALL   174 1
  OF OPEN HANDS   179 15
  STRANDS OF MY EYES AND MY LIDS AND MY HANDS AND MY FEET+   180 5
  I WILL TRAIL MY HANDS AGAIN THROUGH THE DRENCHED COLD L+   180 34
  TILL MY HANDS ARE FULL OF THE CHILLNESS AND TOUCH OF LE+   180 35
  DOES MY SLOW HEART REBEL DO MY DEAD HANDS   195 6
  WHAT EFFECT I CAN HAVE MY HANDS WAVE UNDER   223 2
  FEEL THE SHAME-WOUNDS IN HIS HANDS PIERCE THROUGH MY OWN   226 10
  CAN I CATCH LIKE A MOTH BETWEEN MY HANDS   227 23
  AND HIS HANDS ARE AWKWARD AND WANT TO HIDE   228 3
  WITH SUNKEN HEAD AND FORGOTTEN FOLDED HANDS   232 25
  AND MY STILL HANDS FULL OF HER BREASTS   250 12
  SO SHE LAID HER HANDS AND PRESSED THEM DOWN MY SIDES   254 22
  WHAT A TOOL IN THE HANDS OF THE LORD   254 26
  INVISIBLE THE HANDS OF EVE   262 10
  HER HANDS SLID IN AND SET ME FREE   262 15
  AT THE SAME TIME IT OPENS THE TINY HANDS OF THE HAZEL   272 20
  POMEGRANATES TO WARM YOUR HANDS AT   278 18
  WRETCHES UTTER WRETCHES KEEP YOUR HANDS FROM BEANS SAITH   303 15
  NO FINGERS NO HANDS NO FEET NO LIPS   326 17
  YES AND IF OXEN OR LIONS HAD HANDS AND COULD PAINT WITH   376 1
  THEIR HANDS AND PRODUCE WORKS OF ART AS MEN DO HORSES W+   376 2
  HANDS TO EAT THE ACANTHUS OR BITE AT THE ALMOND BUDS   385 10
  PALE DISPIRITED PRINCE WITH HIS CHIN ON HIS HANDS HIS   388 7
  HER LITTLE LOOSE HANDS AND DROOPING VICTORIAN SHOULDERS   393 14
  AND CLAWS NOT MADE TO SHAKE HANDS WITH   414 15
  OF HANDS AND LIPS AND MURMURINGS   436 22
  THE DEAD IN THEIR NASTY DEAD HANDS   440 26
  THINGS MEN HAVE MADE WITH WAKENED HANDS AND PUT SOFT   448 1
  WITH THEIR THIN DARK HANDS AND THEIR WIDE DARK EYES AND   451 3
  AND A REAL TREMOR IF HE HANDS OUT A TEN-POUND NOTE   486 13
  AND YOU CLAPPED YOUR HANDS AND SAID SAY IT AGAIN   550 26
  DANGLING OUR USELESS HANDS   572 26
  SHOOK HANDS WITH HIM   618 20
  THEIR DOOM AT THE HANDS OF MR MEADE   634 2
  MACHINES OF IRON MUST BE TENDED BY HANDS OF FLESH   639 7
  THE HANDS OF LIFE   641 21
  AND DEPARTING INVIOLATE NOTHING CAN LAY HANDS ON HER   676 15
  THEN EVERY MOLECULE OF CREATION JUMPED AND CLAPPED ITS +   683 4
  IT IS A FEARFUL THING TO FALL INTO THE HANDS OF THE LIV+   699 12
  WHEN I HAVE FALLEN OUT OF YOUR HANDS THE HANDS OF THE L+   699 20
  WHEN THE SELF HAS FALLEN FROM THE HANDS OF GOD   699 23
  EVEN OF THE SOUL FALLING FROM THE HANDS OF GOD   699 27
  IT IS NOT EASY TO FALL OUT OF THE HANDS OF THE LIVING G+   700 17
  EVEN THROUGH THE GREATEST BLASPHEMIES THE HANDS OF THE +   700 20
  MAN CAN BREAK AWAY AND FALL FROM THE HANDS OF GOD   700 23
  CAN SLIP ENTIRELY THROUGH THE FINGERS OF THE HANDS OF G+   701 14
  ABROAD IN MY HANDS LIKE WAVES AMONG THE ROCKS OF SUBSTA+   705 6
  AND BREAKS IN THE FOAMY HANDS WHOSE POWER ROLLS OUT   705 16
  AND HANDS LIKE SALT   707 12
  I AM IN THE HANDS OF THE UNKNOWN GOD   727 28
  WE LET THE WEAPONS SLIP FROM OUT OUR HANDS   736 22
  HOW I WOULD LIKE TO CUT OFF MY HANDS   741 3
  BUT SHALL I TOUCH HANDS WITH DEATH IN KILLING THAT OTHER   743 17
  OUR HANDS OUR BREASTS REBEL AGAINST US   746 13
  AND IN HER HANDS THE SPARKING NEEDLES FLY   752 10
  THE DESTINY OF AMERICA IS IN THEIR HANDS   774 23
  REMOVE THE INDIANS FOREVER FROM THE HANDS OF   780 3
  BUT IF YOU CANNOT KEEP POLITICAL DOMINEERING HANDS   780 14
  WHEN YOU LIFT YOUR HANDS IN COURAGE AND BRAVERY ITS GLO+   800 10
  AND THE FEET OF MEN AND THE HANDS OF THE WOMEN KNOW ME   801 19
  ONE THING IS CERTAIN WE'VE GOT TO TAKE HANDS OFF LOVE   834 7
  NOW THE TREES WITH INTERLOCKED HANDS AND ARMS UPLIFTED +   854 4
  HANDS   863 26
  HANDS   865 30
  IN SHAPELINESS WITH HAPPY LINKED HANDS   872 14
  AND HANDS AND FACE AND BREAST WITH THAT HOT CLOAK   879 10
  INTO MUD THE SPACE FAST SHRINKS IN THE BUILDER'S HANDS   *896 11
  I HAVE OPENED THE WINDOW TO WARM MY HANDS ON THE SILL   *905 1
  WITH HER TWO BARE FEET ON MY HANDS   *913 9

HANDS
  WITH HER LITTLE BARE FEET IN MY HANDS   *914 9
  HE SUNK HIS HANDS IN FIRMNESS DOWN THY SIDES   *915 22
  I HAVE PUSHED MY HANDS IN THE DARK LOAM UNDER THE FLOWE+   *926 8
  AND I DO NOT CARE THOUGH THE LARGE HANDS OF REVENGE   *937 1
  BUT OH THE PALMS OF HER TWO BLACK HANDS ARE RED   *938 26
  BUT OH THE PALMS OF HIS BLACK HANDS ARE RED   *939 22
  SHE WILL START WHEN SHE SEES ME AND BLUSHING SPREAD OUT+   *940 16
  AND MY STILL HANDS FULL OF HER BREASTS   *946 10
  WHEN MEN WOVE WITH THEIR HANDS AND THEIR SOUL'S ATTENTI+   *949 26
  AND IT MADE THEM HAPPY AND THE WOVEN CLOTH OF THEIR HAN+   *949 29
  AND BUILD IT LOVINGLY AND PUT IT BETWEEN THE HANDS OF Y+   *957 26
  AND PUT IT BETWEEN THE HANDS OF THE TREMBLING SOUL   *958 23
  WITH DIM CALM THOUGHTS AND QUIET HANDS   *960 28

HANDSOME
  HIS STEEL-TRAP STOIC AGELESS HANDSOME FACE   360 25
  VERY HANDSOME AND SOME PURE YELLOW FANGED LEAVES   387 3
  ISN'T HE HANDSOME ISN'T HE HEALTHY ISN'T HE A FINE   430 19
  BUT YOU SEE SAID THE HANDSOME YOUNG MAN WITH THE   433 9
  HER HANDSOME THIGHS DOWN DOWN TILL SHE SLEPT HER   444 31
  THE HANDSOME AND SELF-ABSORBED YOUNG MAN   605 1
  LOOKED BACK AT THE HANDSOME AND SELF-ABSORBED YOUNG MAN   605 5
  OH THE HANDSOME BLUEY-BROWN BODIES THEY MIGHT JUST AS W+   625 19
  AND ALL THE TIME HIS HANDSOME SWARTHY RED FACE   734 17
  VERY HANDSOME UPPERS   774 13

HANDSOMER
  FOR THE FEEDING AND STRENGTHENING OF THE HANDSOMER FULL+   679 10

HANG
  HANG STRINGS OF CRIMSON CHERRIES AS IF HAD BLED   36 21
  HANG FROM THE STREET'S LONG BOUGH   252 14
  DON'T HANG MUCH WEIGHT ON   297 33
  CREATURES THAT HANG THEMSELVES UP LIKE AN OLD RAG TO SL+   342 1
  NO HE MUST NOT SQUAT NOR HANG OBSCENE IN MY ROOM   346 3
  I SHOT MY MAN I SAW HIM CRUMBLE AND HANG   741 27
  MY CASHMERE SHAWL I'LL HANG FOR A CANOPY   754 24
  AND ON THE TREES HANG THE APPLES OF GOLD   770 22
  I'D HANG MY HAMS WITH PUCKERED PETTICOATS SWAYING   835 32
  HANG HIGH SUSPENDED WITHOUTEN RESPITE   *929 8

HANGING
  SOMEWHERE THE LAMP HANGING LOW FROM THE CEILING   41 6
  YOU WITH LOOSE HANDS OF ABANDONMENT HANGING DOWN   58 23
  HER SOFT WHITE LEGS HANGING HEAVILY OVER MY ARM   73 25
  BUT A GREY CAVE WITH GREAT GREY SPIDER-CLOTHS HANGING   112 25
  HANGING RED AT THE RIVER AND SIMMERING   217 3
  WHY HANGING WITH SUCH INORDINATE WEIGHT   279 15
  WITH THE HALF-SECRET GLEAM OF A PASSION-FLOWER HANGING   299 1
  HANGING UPSIDE DOWN LIKE ROWS OF DISGUSTING OLD RAGS   342 3
  AND HAVING THE BREAD HANGING OVER HER CHIN   359 7
  AND HANGING GRIMLY ON   360 22
  THE OVER-DRIP OF A GREAT PASSION HANGING IN THE BALANCE   370 8
  HANGING HAIRY PIGS' TAILS   390 12
  WITH A THIN YOUNG YELLOW LITTLE PAW HANGING OUT AND   393 17
  LEAVING THE TRAIL OF A DIFFERENT PAW HANGING OUT   394 4
  BEYOND EVEN THAT EAGLE THAT PHOENIX HANGING OVER THE   437 12
  TILL YOU ARE AS EMPTY AS RAT-GNAWED POMEGRANATES HANGIN+ 800 26
  HANGING FROM THE SHOULDERS OF THE RAINBOW   820 4
  HEAVY HANGING CLUSTERS OF CRIMSON RED   855 18
  PINIONED LIKE SWEEPING SCYTHES NOW IDLY HANGING AT REST   855 22
  PEAR-BLOSSOM HANGING AND ONE SMALL KNEE   886 7
  HER SOFT WHITE LEGS HANGING HEAVILY OVER MY ARM   *913 17
  ALL THE TREES ARE HANGING WITH DISHONOURED FLAGS' DISGR+ *933 29
  AH AND MY HAIR IS HANGING WET AND BITTER ON MY FACE   *933 31
  HANGING RED AT THE RIVER AND SIMMERING   *942 14

HANGS
  HANGS NUMB AND HEAVY FROM A BENDING FLOWER   73 21
  WITH AFTER-PAIN MY SLEEPING BABY HANGS UPON MY LIFE   73 27
  LIKE A BURDEN SHE HANGS ON ME   73 28
  NOW WET WITH TEARS AND PAIN HANGS HEAVILY   74 2
  A GIBBOUS MOON HANGS OUT OF THE TWILIGHT   113 17
  HER ROOM WHERE THE NIGHT STILL HANGS LIKE A HALF-FOLDED+ 129 29
  HANGS IN THE AIR   147 22
  STILL HANGS THE HAWK WITH THE WHOLE SKY MOVING   150 1
  HAS FALLEN DEAD UPON THE NAILS AND HANGS   225 6
  DROPPING AMONG HIS LEAVES HANGS THE DARK GRAPE   286 10
  IN THE AVENUES WHERE THE BAT HANGS SLEEPING UPSIDE-DOWN 322 33
  BUT SHE HANGS ON AND MY SHOUT AND MY SHRINKING ARE   359 22
  AND NOW HANGS LIKE THE FRAGRANT CLOSE OF THE MEASURE   868 15
  THAT EVENING EVERMORE HANGS RED FOR ME   885 2
  HANGS NUMB AND HEAVY FROM THE BENDING FLOWER   *913 13
  MY SLEEPING BABY HANGS UPON MY LIFE   *913 19
  THE MOON LIKE A REDDENING LANTERN HANGS LOW ACROSS THE + *917 13
  A BIG BUD OF MOON HANGS OUT OF THE TWILIGHT   *929 6

HANKERIN'
  AN' HANKERIN' FOR ME BUT GO   139 34

HA'PENNY
  AND A BOARD-SCHOOL BRAIN STUFFED UP WITH THE HA'PENNY   630 30
  OH CARCASS WITH A BOARD-SCHOOL MIND AND A HA'PENNY NEWS+ 631 3

HAPPEN
  OR IF IT HAPPEN TO SHOW AT HER POINTED HEAVY TAIL   361 20
  BUT THINGS WILL HAPPEN TO US   482 20
  AND REFUSED TO LET SO MANY THINGS HAPPEN BEHIND HIS BACK 483 17
  THE INDUSTRIAL MASSES AH WHAT WILL HAPPEN WHAT WILL   586 21
  HAPPEN   586 24

HAPPENED
  AND IF BY A MIRACLE A WOMAN HAPPENED TO COME ALONG   507 8
  AND THAT'S WHAT'S HAPPENED TO THE ENGLISH ROSE   534 27
  WHAT HAS HAPPENED IN THE WORLD   539 1
  HE COULD NEVER HAVE THOUGHT IT BEFORE IT HAPPENED   690 4
  OH HOW THIS NIGHT HAS HAPPENED PERFECTLY   754 26

HAPPENED
OH SIEGMUND SIEGMUND WHAT HAS HAPPENED TO YOU   870 22

HAPPENING
OH DEAR WHAT'S HAPPENING   846 2
OH DEAR WHAT'S HAPPENING TO TUSCANS   846 12

HAPPENS
WHERE EVERYTHING HAPPENS INVISIBLE FLOWERING AND FERTIL+   283 20

HAPPILY
SO YOU TO MINE I IMAGINE YES HAPPILY   234 7

HAPPINESS
HIS HAPPINESS WHILST HE IN DISPLEASURE RETREATS   47 20
LIKE A BOILING POT THE POND CRACKLED WITH HAPPINESS   206 30
PERHAPS ONLY HAPPINESS   247 22
PERHAPS ONLY HAPPINESS WILL COME FORTH FROM US   247 23
OLD SORROW AND NEW HAPPINESS   247 24
IN CHINA THE BAT IS SYMBOL OF HAPPINESS   342 6
THEY HATE HAPPINESS IN OTHERS   500 14
AND ALL THIS HAPPINESS IN THE SEA IN THE SALT   695 5
THEIR WANDERING HAPPINESS AND THE WIND WASTED IN LIBERT+   *892 5
AND DAY BY DAY MY HAPPINESS VIBRATES   *943 24

HAPPY
UNDER THE ALMOND-TREE THE HAPPY LANDS   58 16
AND TRODDEN THAT THE HAPPY SUMMER YIELDS   135 8
AND HAPPY AS RAIN IN SUMMER WHY SHOULD IT BE SO   141 25
DEFENDING THE MEMORY OF LEAVES AND THE HAPPY ROUND NEST   167 10
I THANK YOU I DO YOU HAPPY CREATURES YOU DEARS   221 20
HOW HAPPY WE'LL BE SEE HIM   244 13
HE'S GOT IN HIS NEST WE'LL BE HAPPY   244 31
HOW FULL AND BIG LIKE A ROBUST HAPPY FLAME   246 13
HOW SURE I FEEL HOW WARM AND STRONG AND HAPPY   247 4
NO MATTER I AM SO HAPPY   247 10
HOW HAPPY I AM HOW MY HEART IN THE WIND RINGS TRUE   251 11
EVE IN HER HAPPY MOMENTS   314 6
OF HAPPY ENERGY   436 4
THEY WERE HAPPY THEY ENJOYED IT   445 21
THEY WERE NOT REALLY HAPPY   445 29
AND HAPPY AS A WAGTAIL BY A POOL   520 16
HAPPY AS PERHAPS KINGS USED TO BE BUT CERTAINLY AREN'T   520 18
AS A MATTER OF FACT WHEN THE TINKER LOOKS SO HAPPY   520 23
THEN THEY'D BE HAPPY FOR WE ARE ALL SO MUCH BETTER THAN   520 31
WHY ARE THEY NEVER HAPPY TO BE STILL   537 25
WERE HAPPY WEREN'T WE   557 29
SO HAPPY AS OUR LITTLE ISLAND   574 18
HAPPY   583 8
AS HAPPY AS HAPPY OH SO HAPPY YOU SAPPY   583 9
AND EASY TO SWALLOW ALWAYS TELL THEM THEY'RE HAPPY   583 19
O SLAY NOT THE BEST BRIGHT PROUD LIFE THAT IS IN YOU TH+   678 24
IN THE BOUNCING OF THESE SMALL AND HAPPY WHALES   693 30
MOST HAPPY HAPPY SHE   695 8
SHE IS THE FEMALE TUNNY-FISH ROUND AND HAPPY AMONG THE +   695 11
AND DENSE WITH HAPPY BLOOD DARK RAINBOW BLISS IN THE SEA   695 12
IN SHAPELINESS WITH HAPPY LINKED HANDS   872 14
HAPPY AM I A NAKED SPRIG   888 13
HOW I ADORE YOU YOU HAPPY THINGS YOU DEARS   *945 6
ALL DAY LONG I AM BUSY AND HAPPY AT MY WORK   *945 24
AND IT MADE THEM HAPPY AND THE WOVEN CLOTH OF THEIR HAN+   *949 29
HOW DEEP HOW DEEP HOW HAPPY   *954 29

HARBOURS
ALL THE CREATURES THAT CANNOT DIE WHILE ONE HEART HARBO+   *954 5

HARD
PUTS THE HARD HANDS OF MY FRIEND TO SLEEP   41 9
AH SOON IN HIS LARGE HARD HANDS SHE DIES   43 12
HOW CAN YOU LIE SO RELENTLESS HARD   55 2
WITH A HARD FACE WHITE-ENAMELLED   56 21
OF SHAPES BY A HARD WIND RIDDEN   68 8
YOU HOLD YOURSELF ALL HARD AS IF MY KISSES   87 10
TWO HARD CRUDE PAWS IN HUNGER ON THE LONELY   127 27
SHE WORN'T HARD TER FIND   138 34
MORDANT CORROSION GNASHING AND CHAMPING HARD   160 23
ONLY LED HER THROUGH HARSH HARD PLACES   202 23
AGAINST THE HARD AND PALE BLUE EVENING SKY   225 1
THE BREATH OF THE BULLOCK STAINS THE HARD CHILL AIR   225 13
WHILE THE HARD GIRL HARDENS NOTHING IS SAID   228 7
AND SHE WITH HER WOMEN HOT AND HARD   228 19
HOW IT IMPRESSES ME HOW HARD AND COMPRESSED   249 14
IF ONLY I AM KEEN AND HARD LIKE THE SHEER TIP OF A WEDGE   250 21
YOUR SIDES THIS FIRMNESS THIS HARD MOULD   255 12
SILENCE HARD TO UNDERSTAND   261 28
AH THAT WAS TORMENT HARD ENOUGH   264 23
SHEER HARD EXTINCTION   266 3
AND HARD WITH THE INTENTION TO KEEP THEM   279 9
SOFT RED TONGUE AND HARD THIN GUMS   353 7
YOU ARE SO HARD TO WAKE   353 15
SELF-EXPOSURE HARD HUMILIATION NEED TO ADD HIMSELF ON TO   362 31
AND FUSE IN A BROAD HARD FLAME OF MANY MEN IN A ONENESS   440 8
O RIPPLING HARD FIRE OF COURAGE O FUSING OF HOT TRUST   440 13
WHO WILL FIND IT SO HARD TO MATE   459 4
LAUGH AND LAUGH HARD   460 16
LAUGH AND LAUGH HARD   460 20
AND LOOSEN THE BRICK AND THE HARD CEMENT   462 11
THAT IS THE CRYSTAL OF PEACE THE SLOW HARD JEWEL OF TRU+   477 17
I KNOW THAT POVERTY IS A HARD OLD HAG   498 13
BUT IT IS HARD TO BE TOLERANT WITH THE SMARTIES   499 16
MEN FIGHT FOR LIBERTY AND WIN IT WITH HARD KNOCKS   535 23
AND WANT TO BE COLD AND DEVILISH HARD   537 17
GIVE 'EM A FEW HARD POKES   560 20
AND IDEAS ARE HARD LIKE ACORNS READY TO FALL   608 23
THAT HARD CLAPPER STRIKING IN A HARD MOUTH   622 21
ESPECIALLY CLAPPER BELLS HARD TONGUES WAGGING IN HARD M+   623 2
HARD HARD ON THE EARTH THE MACHINES ARE ROLLING   624 3
FOR IT IS HARD TO DIE IT IS DIFFICULT TO GO THROUGH   721 9

HARD
MY SOUL HAS HAD A LONG HARD DAY   725 11
AH IT IS VERY HARD TO CHANGE AND BE DIFFERENT   727 32
AYE BUSY WITH A FEW HARD TASKS AND WRATH   875 31
HE DRAWS A DEEP HARD BREATH FROM SPACE TO SPACE   878 23
THE OLD HARD STEM OF MY LIFE   *899 27
THE OLD HARD STEM OF MY LIFE   *903 6
THA MUST 'A' BEEN HARD TO WEAN   *921 20
IT IS ONLY I FIND IT HARD TO BEAR   *931 12
HARD HARD ON THE EARTH THE MACHINES ARE ROLLING   *953 21

HARD-BALANCED
AH YES BEING MALE IS NOT MY HEAD HARD-BALANCED   222 17

HARD-BOILED
OR THAT HARD-BOILED YOUNG WOMAN BESIDE HIM   645 12
O YOU HARD-BOILED CONSERVATIVES AND YOU SOFT-BOILED LIB+   664 12

HARDEN
NOURISH HER TRAIN HER HARDEN HER   228 29

HARDENED
HARDENED THEY ARE LIKE GEMS IN TIME-LONG PRUDERY   127 22
I KNOW FROM HER HARDENED LIPS THAT STILL HER HEART IS   128 1
THEIR HARDENED SOULS ARE WASHED WITH FIRE AND WASHED AN+   663 6
HARDENED THEMSELVES   663 8
THICK ALMOST THUNDROUS ON THE HARDENED EARTH   717 4
HARDENED THE EARTH SHAKING THE LARK'S NEST TILL THE EGG+   *953 18

HARDENING
AS I SEE IT HARDENING   112 13
AS I SEE IT HARDENING   *929 3

HARDENS
WHILE THE HARD GIRL HARDENS NOTHING IS SAID   228 7

HARDER
THE SHARPER MORE HORRID THE PRESSURE THE HARDER   161 1
WE HAVE MORE ENERGY AND OUR GRIP ON LIFE IS HARDER   503 6
HARDER YET   817 16

HARD-FACED
ONLY WE HARD-FACED CREATURES GO ROUND AND ROUND AND KEEP   71 11

HARDLY
AS SOME SHOULD HA'E HARDLY A SMITE O' TROUBLE   45 23
HARDLY A MURMUR COMES FROM THE SLEEPING BROOD   48 23
WHERE THAT LUMBERING BEE WHO CAN HARDLY BEAR   50 11
OF OUR EARLY LOVE THAT HARDLY HAS OPENED YET   58 11
AND NOW THE LONGEST GRASS-LEAVES HARDLY EMERGE   85 6
OPPRESSES ME SO I CAN HARDLY BEAR   116 26
THERE'S HARDLY OWT LEFT O' THEE GET UP AN' GO   138 18
HARDLY A GREENISH LILY WATERY FAINT   286 4
AND HE HARDLY STIRRED IN MY HAND MUFFLED UP   347 8
WATCHING AND HARDLY SEEING THE TRUNK-CURL APPROACH AND   388 9
SUCH A WAGGLE OF LOVE YOU CAN HARDLY DISTINGUISH ONE   399 22
HARDLY LOOSES EVEN A LAST BREATH OF PERFUME   646 22
HARDLY EVER NOW HAS A HUMAN FACE   656 12
THE GREEKS MADE EQUILIBRIUM THEIR GOAL EQUILIBRIUM IS H+   761 14
AND HARDLY DISTURBING WAVERING SHIMMER   860 4
IN BATTLE OF HEATED WORDS HARDLY STILLED BY MY REITERAT+   865 32

HARE
THE STAR-LIT RUSH OF A HARE   152 17
THE HARE SUDDENLY GOES UPHILL   311 18

HAREBELLS
BEFORE THE LAST-MOWN HAREBELLS ARE DEAD   35 7

HAREM
YOU FORTY LADIES IN THE HAREM BOWER   758 6
RESPONSE FROM THE HAREM   758 10

H'ARENA
F'R I TELL YER I H'ARENA MARRYIN' NONE   81 3

HARES
IN LITTLE BUNCHES LIKE BUNCHES OF WILD HARES   311 23

HARE'S
GENTLY AND FINELY LINED THAN A RABBIT'S OR THAN A HARE'S   393 7

HARK
IT'S NOT A BEGGAR MOTHER HARK   44 14
HARK AT THE RIVER IT PANTS AS IT HURRIES THROUGH   212 2
WHAT IS IT HARK   216 5
HARK HARK   312 4
HARK HARK   312 25
HARK HARK   313 16
HARK IN THE DUSK   425 11
AND HARK TO HIS HOLLOA   564 24
HARK THE STRANGE NOISE OF MILLIONS OF FISH IN PANIC   586 25
HARK HARK STEP ASIDE SILENTLY AND SWIFTLY   642 19
SO NOW THEY COME BACK HARK   689 1
HARK THE LOW AND SHATTERING LAUGHTER OF BEARDED MEN   689 2
AND LORD BUT HARK AT THE PIGEONS WHAT ARE THEY CHATTERI+   751 12
AND HARK TO THE WORDS OF THEIR HEART'S DESIRE   789 3
HEY FIRST MAN OF MY NAME HARK THERE   791 17
HARK HOW THEY THRESH   817 24
HARK HER QUICK OH   861 16

HARLOTS
NO MORE NARCISSUS PERFUME LILY HARLOTS THE BLADES OF SE+   273 16

HARM
TO LICK ME UP AND DO ME HARM   150 27
IT IS SOMEBODY WANTS TO DO US HARM   250 30
THE INDIAN DOES NO HARM   777 9

HARMLESS
MEN THAT SEEM HARMLESS WOMEN WITH FAIR WORDS   807 26

HARMONY
LEARN THEY MUST TO OBEY FOR ALL HARMONY IS DISCIPLINE   93 9
AND ONLY IN HARMONY WITH OTHERS THE SINGLE SOUL CAN BE +   93 10
SHEER HARMONY   235 33
YOU WOULD WEEP TO BE LAPSING ON SUCH HARMONY   251 28
AND RUINS OUR COMPLEX HARMONY   529 10
OF FORM OR MOVEMENT OR OF HARMONY   872 12

HARNESSED
DON'T BE HARNESSED TO THEM   441 16

HARP
OH TOUCH THE HARP TOUCH THE HARP GENTLY MY DEARS   576 4
FINGERS ACROSS THE HARP   746 26
HIS BODY THAT DOES SHAKE LIKE THE WIRE OF A HARP   877 13

HARPIST
LIKE A HARPIST THAT STRIKES HIS DEFT   746 25
AS A HARPIST RUNNING ALONG THE STRINGS   747 12

HARPS
VAST RANGES OF EXPERIENCE LIKE THE HUMMING OF UNSEEN HA+   666 25

HARROWING
THIS AWKWARD HARROWING PURSUIT   363 4
OR A DOG WITH A HARROWING FLEA   489 24

HARRY
CALL ME HARRY IF YOU WILL   404 8
CALL ME OLD HARRY SAYS HE   404 9

HARRYLETS
TOMLETS DICKLETS HARRYLETS WHINEY   457 19

HARSH
KILLING THE BLUE DUSK WITH HARSH SCENT UNNERVING   91 14
THE HARSH COLD WIND OF MY WORDS DROVE ON AND STILL   94 13
ONLY LED HER THROUGH HARSH HARD PLACES   202 23
FROM SPACE TO LONGER SPACE LIFTS A HARSH BREATH   878 24
AND STILL THE LONG HARSH BREATH SINKS HOARSELY OUT   878 27
THAT LIFT UP HIGH THEN DROP HIS STRANGE HARSH BREAST   879 1
THE HARSH COLD WRATH OF MY WORDS DROVE ON AND STILL   *897 1

HARSHLY
SUCH RESOLUTE SHAPES SO HARSHLY SET   53 24

HARSH-SURFACED
YOU ARE PAINFUL HARSH-SURFACED PILLARS THAT GIVE OFF NO+   289 5

HART
THAT I AM THE HART AND YOU ARE THE GENTLE HIND   118 31

HARVEST
HAVE RISEN RED ON MY NIGHT AS A HARVEST MOON   126 4
THE HARVEST THE SPENT ACTION TO ITSELF   195 3
MAN'S SWEETEST HARVEST OF THE CENTURIES SWEET PRINTED   263 25
THIS IS THE SAME THAT PICKS UP THE HARVEST OF WHEAT   271 21
SHALL HAVE RISEN RED ON MY NIGHT AS A HARVEST MOON   *937 4

HARVESTED
HARVESTED   269 2

HARVESTING
MY FATHER SUDDENLY DIED IN THE HARVESTING CORN   173 1

HAS-BEEN
NO HAS-BEEN NO HEREAFTER ONLY THE PERFECTED   169 24
BREAK OUT OF THIS FOUL HAS-BEEN   177 24

HASH
THEN YOU WILL SETTLE THE HASH OF BUSINESS FINALLY   484 21

HASNA
HASNA TER SENT ME WHOAM WHEN I   80 6
HASNA TER SENT ME WHOAM WHEN I   *922 6

HASN'T
NOT FINISHED HE HASN'T NO MATTER HOW   139 26
AND WONDERS IF A PARROT HASN'T MORE TO IT   842 11

HAST
WHO ART THOU WHAT HAST   39 17
LIFE COMES TO THEE ON WHICH THOU HAST NO CLAIM   69 28
TWENTY POUND O' THY OWN THA HAST AN' FIFTY POUND HA'E I   83 1
LAD THOU HAST GOTTEN A CHILD IN ME   220 6
FOR THOU HAST MADE HIM A LITTLE LOWER THAN THE ANGELS   548 33
HAST THOU DETERMINED TO STRANGLE ME O GOD   751 14
AS THA ALLERS HAST BUT LET ME TELL THEE   *922 5
TWENTY POUND O' THY OWN THA HAST AND FIFTY POUND HA'E I   *925 5
AS SULKY AN' ORMIN' AS THINE HAST OWT TO SAY OTHERWISE   *925 25

HASTE
AN' T' PARSON MAKIN' HASTE AN' A' T' BLACK   60 15
IN THE TAPPING HASTE OF A FALLEN LEAF   68 21
THE TRAIN BEATS FRANTIC IN HASTE AND STRUGGLES AWAY   88 23
'TIS THE SUN THAT ASKS THE QUESTION IN A LOVELY HASTE F+   119 29
WHAT A LOVELY HASTE FOR WISDOM IS IN MEN   119 31
SHE CLUNG TO THE DOOR IN HER HASTE TO ENTER   122 6
IN AN IMPURE HASTE   343 9
ROUND AND ROUND AND DITHERING WITH TIREDNESS AND HASTE   343 25

HASTE
GREAT HASTE AND STRAIGHT ALMOST BIRD STRAIGHT ABOVE THE   347 12
IN UNDIGNIFIED HASTE   351 14
OH YES SHE CAN MAKE HASTE WHEN SHE LIKES   358 33
BETWEEN THEIR LEGS IN HASTE TO GET AWAY   391 3
HE FINDS A FEMALE THEY SHOW NO HASTE   465 9
AND IGNOBLE HASTE FOR FEAR OF BEING LATE   484 7
THEIR HASTE   484 9
AN' PARSON MAKIN' HASTE AN' A' THE BLACK   *911 1
IN THE TAPPING HASTE OF A FALLEN LEAF   *915 5

HASTEN
HOW HASTEN AND WHAT WILL CONSOLE   757 6
THOUGH I SHALL HASTEN AFTER WHEN I SEE   879 24

HASTENED
TO QUICKEN MY HOPE AS I HASTENED TO GREET   121 21
SHE HASTENED TOWARDS THE ROOM DID SHE KNOW   155 15

HASTENING
WHERE HASTENING CREATURES PASS INTENT   50 27
LIFE IN THY MOUTH AND DIM BREATH'S HASTENING HISS   69 24
A HASTENING CAR SWEPT SHAMEFUL PAST   122 1
WHERE THRONGS OF ANGELS HASTENING UPON   872 18
QUICKENS THE HASTENING WHITE-HOT METAL   *907 22

HASTILY
A SILVER WIND IS HASTILY WIPING   150 15
HASTILY I SHOOK HIM OUT OF THE WINDOW   347 9

HASTY
IT FELL FROM OUR HUSK IN A LITTLE HASTY SEED   172 13
SUDDENLY HASTY RECKLESS ON HIGH TOES   354 6

HAT
SHADING HIS FACE IN HIS BLACK FELT HAT   228 6
TAKE OFF YOUR CLOAK AND YOUR HAT   237 17
I'LL HOLD YOUR HAT   560 16
CAME TO THE COUNTER WITH HIS HAT OFF HUMBLE AT THE SHRI+ 618 17
A HAT QUAINTLY CURIOUSLY WOVEN LUXURIOUS WITH BIG ROSES   856 12

HATCH
MAN SHOULD HATCH   437 17
BEFORE THE STOUT SWART BEETLE HAD A BALL OF DUNG TO ROL+ *940 26

HATCHED
AND HATCHED ANOTHER EAGLE   413 2
AND THE BUB-EAGLE THAT LIBERTY HAD HATCHED WAS GROWING A 413 18

HATE
WHO GRAPPLING DOWN WITH WORK OR HATE OR PASSION   73 14
THEM AGAIN ON A QUARRY OF KNOWLEDGE THEY HATE TO HUNT   74 10
HOW WE HATE ONE ANOTHER TO-NIGHT HATE SHE AND I   98 7
NOW STOP CARPING AT ME DO YOU WANT ME TO HATE YOU   119 1
THE BROWN EYES BLACK WITH MISERY AND HATE THAT LOOK   225 23
ONE MOMENT THE HATE LEAPS AT ME STANDING THERE   225 25
AND IN HIS BELLY THE SMOULDERING HATE OF ME   226 8
OF HATE HAS HURT US SO   229 14
OF THIS HATE   229 19
NOW THE HATE IS GONE   229 26
NOW THE HATE IS GONE   230 1
THINK YOU YOU DO NOT HATE ME   235 18
IT FOLLOWS YOU HATE ME TO ECSTASY   235 21
BUT WOULD NOT YOUR HATE REACH EVEN MORE MADLY THAN YOUR   236 3
YOUR IMPASSIONED UNFINISHED HATE   236 5
BURNED CLEAN BY REMORSELESS HATE   242 17
PASSING ON AND ON THE HATE   249 6
WE SHALL LOVE WE SHALL HATE   268 5
I HATE THE WAY YOU LURCH OFF SIDEWAYS INTO THE AIR   333 5
YET THE MOMENT I HATE HER SHE TRIPS MILD AND SMUG LIKE A 385 12
HOW YOU HATE BEING BRUSHED WITH THE BOOT-BRUSH TO BRUSH   397 30
HOW YOU HATE BEING MADE TO LOOK UNDIGNIFIED MA'AM   397 33
HOW YOU HATE BEING LAUGHED AT MISS SUPERB   397 34
THAT MOMENT I BEGIN TO HATE HER   472 18
THE YOUNG ONES COPULATE HATE IT AND WANT TO CRY   485 6
THEY HATE LIFE THEY ONLY LIKE CARRION   500 12
THEY HATE HAPPINESS IN OTHERS   500 14
DON'T DO IT BECAUSE YOU HATE PEOPLE   517 5
HOW THEY HATE THE WOMEN'S EFFORTS TO TURN THEM   538 24
BUT IT WAS NOT ENOUGH HE LOOKED AT ME ALMOST WITH HATE   603 5
LIKE SNAKES OF HATE AGAINST THE MAN IN THE MACHINE   624 17
THE MIDDLE CLASSES HATE IT   626 19
THEY HATE IT THEY HATE IT   626 20
THE MIDDLE CLASSES HATE IT   626 21
WE HATE THE VICTORIANS SO MUCH   627 21
SENSIBILITIES HATE EVERYTHING THAT'S WELL   633 6
AND THEIR LAST REFINEMENT BLUFF A HATE DISGUISED   644 12
HE IS CAPABLE OF AN ENDLESS GRINDING NIHILISTIC HATE   648 3
THEY MOVE IN A GREAT GRIND OF HATE SLOWLY BUT INEVITABLY 648 7
THE GREAT GRIND OF UNWILLINGNESS THE SLOW UNDERGRIND OF+ 648 10
HOW THE GODS MUST HATE MOST OF THE OLD OLD MEN TODAY   662 15
A RAINBOW OF LOVE AND HATE   714 12
HOW I HATE MYSELF THIS BODY WHICH IS ME   741 1
FOR I HATE THIS BODY WHICH IS SO DEAR TO ME   741 16
FOR I DOTE ON THEM WITH TENDERNESS AND I HATE THEM   741 19
I HATE THEM BITTERLY   741 20
WHY SHOULD WE HATE THEN WITH THIS HATE INCARNATE   742 35
WE GIVE UP O LORD OUR BODIES TO DEADLY HATE   743 11
WE GIVE HATE HER DUES O GOD WE YIELD HER UP   743 15
AND HOWLING WITH HATE   795 23
THEY GNASH WHEN IT CLOSES AND HATE THE ONE THAT GOT IN + 795 33
ALL YOU WHO HATE APPLES   816 25
IS HOW THEY HATE THEIR CHILDREN   831 21
THEY INSTINCTIVELY HATE THEIR OWN CHILDREN   832 2
AND THEY HATE THEM   832 7
I BEGIN TO HATE HER   834 9
IN THE SAME WAY IF I SWORE TO HATE A WOMAN ALL MY LIFE + 834 10
THE MEN IN THE END ONLY HATE THEM BECAUSE THE ESCAPE WA+ 838 10

HATE

THEM AGAIN ON A QUARRY OF KNOWLEDGE THEY HATE TO HUNT	*895 18
IT ALL FOR THEM I SHOULD HATE THEM	*896 4
THEM AGAIN ON A QUARRY OF KNOWLEDGE THEY HATE TO HUNT	*904 7
IT ALL FOR THEM I SHOULD HATE THEM	*904 25
THE HATE OF TERROR OR DENY THE FECUND SOUL HER EMBRACES	*926 25
NOW STOP CARPING AT ME BUT GOD HOW I HATE YOU	*932 10

HATED

ALMOST I HATED HER SACRIFICED	62 21
HATED MYSELF AND THE PLACE AND THE ICED	62 22
I SHOULD HAVE HATED YOU HELEN	117 33
BUT DO NOT TOUCH HIM FOR HE HATED YOU	158 25
WHO HATED YOU AND KEPT LOOKING ROUND AT YOU AND CURSING	395 33
HOW THEY'D HAVE HATED HIM	538 4
HATED HIM JUST BECAUSE HE WAS A MAN	538 5
HOW YOU HATED HER	557 13
THOUGH YOU HATED HER	557 23

HATEFUL

IT IS YOUR HATEFUL LITTLE TRUMP	333 14
IT IS YOUR SMALL HIGH HATEFUL BUGLE IN MY EAR	333 17

HATES

YI THA CAN GO THA HATES ME NOW	139 24

HATH

DRAWS TOWARDS THE DOWNARD SLOPE SOME SORROW HATH	131 25
LOOK HE HATH MOVEMENT UPWARD HE SPIRALS	682 18
DRAWS TOWARDS THE DOWNWARD SLOPE SOME SICKNESS HATH	*937 24

HATING

BUT HE HAS GONE MOTIONLESS HATING ME	226 1

HATINGS

BUT LOVINGS AND HATINGS STRUGGLE AND FIGHTINGS	857 7

HATRED

A LOOK OF HATRED ON THE FLOWER THAT BURNS	113 11
WHICH SHAKES MY SUDDEN BLOOD TO HATRED OF YOU	333 16
I'VE HAD MOMENTS OF HATRED OF YOU SINCE	396 10
WITH THIN SCREAMING HATRED	500 15
SHE HAS A SECRET ALMOST ECSTASIED HATRED OF MALENESS IN+	619 20

HATS

AND HATS COCKED UP AND DOWN	312 17
OF MEN IN BOWLER HATS HURRYING	484 4
MEN ARE UNSEEN BENEATH THE SHADING HATS	606 5

HATTER

EKED OUT BY HIS TAILOR AND HIS HATTER	*947 30

HAUL

I CAN HAUL THEM AND URGE THEM NO MORE	74 11
I CAN HAUL THEM AND URGE THEM NO MORE	*895 19
I CAN HAUL THEM AND URGE THEM NO MORE	*904 8

HAULED

POLICEMEN AND ARRESTED THEM AND HAULED THEM OFF TO GAOL	632 33

HAUNCHES

ARE NOT MY HAUNCHES LIGHT	222 19
HAUNCHES	390 14
HER BELLY HER BIG HAUNCHES	393 21
BEING DEAD YOU SHALL ROVE LIKE DOGS WITH THE BROKEN HAU+	796 5

HAUNT

AND CAN BUT HAUNT IN DISEMBODIED RAGE	723 2

HAUNTED

TO SAVE ME FROM THIS HAUNTED ROAD	104 22
ALONG THIS HAUNTED ROAD	106 16
HAUNTED BLUE BUSH	394 19
ONLY HERE AND THERE A PAIR OF EYES HAUNTED LOOKS OUT AS+	625 25
LIFTING HIS HAUNTED EYES TO ME I AM WANTING IN SONG	884 11

HAUNTING

STRANGE TO ME LIKE A CAPTIVE IN A FOREIGN COUNTRY HAUNT+	47 9
AND QUAILING HERE IN THE SUNSHINE BETRAYED FROM HAUNTING	133 3

HAUNTS

SEEKING THEIR OLD HAUNTS WITH COLD GHOSTLY RAGE	722 27
OLD HAUNTS OLD HABITATS OLD HEARTHS	722 28
WHO HAUNTS ME WITH HER LIES	854 28

HAVEN

SURE ON A HAVEN OF PEACE BETWEEN THE MOUNDS OF HER	249 29

HAVEN'T

AND HAVEN'T FORGIVEN ME YET	491 18
SURE THEY HAVEN'T GOT THEM	501 13
IF YOU HAVEN'T SMOKED THEM ALL	540 28
I DON'T KNOW WHAT YOU WANT BUT I CERTAINLY HAVEN'T GOT	541 11
THEY HAVEN'T THE SPUNK OF A BATTLE-TWIG	553 11
YOU HAVEN'T GOT MUCH TO LOSE	560 22
OH AREN'T THEY GREEN OH HAVEN'T WE HAVEN'T WE SPENT	569 11
HAVEN'T I TOLD YOU TO TAKE THE PITH	583 2

HAVIN'

I'M NOT HAVIN' YOUR ORTS AN' SLARTS	*924 7

HAVOC

COME SPRING MAKE HAVOC OF THEM	271 11
PERHAPS EVEN NOW YOU ARE SUFFERING FROM THE HAVOC THEY +	723 17

HAWK

A HAWK IS IN THE SKY HIS WINGS	149 27
STILL HANGS THE HAWK WITH THE WHOLE SKY MOVING	150 1
THE HAWK HAS DROPPED THE WIND IS SPENDING	150 5
THE HAWK HIS WINDSWEPT WAY IS WENDING	150 10
THE HAWK IS GONE A ROSE IS TAPPING	150 18
GREAT AND GLISTENING-FEATHERED LEGS OF THE HAWK OF HORUS	409 7
THE GOLDEN HAWK OF HORUS	409 8
HAWK AS I SAY OF HORUS	409 11
AND THE SMALL HAWK HIGH UP TURNS ROUND ON THE SLOW PIVO+	496 14
AND SOON THE OWL WINGED WITH STILLNESS WILL FLOAT OUT T+	858 16

HAWK-BEAK

TO LIFT THE UPPER HAWK-BEAK FROM THE LOWER BASE	352 12

HAWK-EYES

WITCH TEETH AN' 'ER BLACK HAWK-EYES AS I'VE	77 23
FANGS AND CLAWS AND TALONS AND BEAKS AND HAWK-EYES	409 29
WITCH TEETH AN' 'ER BLACK HAWK-EYES AS I'VE	*919 11

HAWTHORN

OF HAWTHORN AND OF LILAC TREES	104 29
AND SHOWS THE RED OF HAWTHORN SET	105 1

HAY

WE COULD GATHER UP THE DRY HAY FROM	35 13
ON THE HAY WITH MY HEAD ON HER KNEE	35 17
FROM THY HAY COMES THE CLAMOUR OF CHILDREN'S MIRTH	41 22
STILL PLAYING IN THE HAY	48 16
EVEN THE STUPIDEST FARMER GATHERS HIS HAY IN BLOOM IN	587 8
THE SHADOWS OF THE ASH-TREES STRIDE ACROSS THE HAY	858 9

HAY-SEED

HAY-SEED AND TINY GRAIN OF GRASS GRAMINIFERAE	587 4

HAYSTACK

AGAINST THE HAYSTACK A GIRL STANDS LAUGHING AT ME	37 1

HAYSTACKS

IS IT ONLY THAT THE GREAT WET HAYSTACKS MARS	*933 22

HAZE

SLOWLY THE MOON IS RISING OUT OF THE RUDDY HAZE	67 7
TO BE LOST IN THE HAZE OF THE SKY I WOULD LIKE TO COME	134 22

HAZEL

QUICKENS THE UNCLASPING HANDS OF HAZEL	40 26
AT THE SAME TIME IT OPENS THE TINY HANDS OF THE HAZEL	272 20

HAZEL-NUTS

AND LIKE HAZEL-NUTS IN AUTUMM AT LAST	504 8

HAZELS

AND SEE WHERE THE BUDDING HAZELS ARE THINNED	126 9

HAZEL-SCREEN

FROM OUT OF THE HAZEL-SCREEN ON TO THE GRASS	41 2

HAZEL-WOODS

WOULD BE AS IN THE HAZEL-WOODS OF SEPTEMBER	504 11

HAZY

BETWEEN THE DOWNS GROWS HAZY WITH SUNSHINE	886 27

HA'

THA SHOULD HA' SEED 'ER SLIVE UP WHEN YER'D GONE	61 5
THA SHOULD HA' SEED 'ER KNEEL AN' LOOK IN	61 6
TO HA' 'TICED A LAD O' TWENTY-FIVE	77 15
TO HA' GONE AN' GIVEN HIS CLEAN YOUNG FLESH	77 31
YI THA MUST HA' BIN 'ARD TER WEAN	79 24
I COULD HA' KILLED 'ER	80 22
COULD TER HA' KILLED 'ER	80 24
LET'S A' HA' DONE	84 26
THA COME TER HA' FINISHED AN' DONE WI' ME	138 10
THA SHOULD HA' SEED HER SLIVE UP WHEN WE'D GONE	*911 21
THA SHOULD HA' SEED HER KNEEL AN' LOOK IN	*911 22
TO HA' 'TICED A LAD O' TWENTY-FIVE	*919 3
I SHOULD LIKE TO HA' KILLED HER	*922 22
THAT I COULD HA' BEEN FIRST WOMAN TO THEE AS THOU'RT FI+	*925 17

HEAD

ON THE HAY WITH MY HEAD ON HER KNEE	35 17
OVER MY FACE AND MY HEAD UNTIL	35 24
ALL HEAD	41 19
HER SMALL HEAD MAKING WARM DISPLAY	42 26
WITH A SUNK UNCONSCIOUS HEAD	58 31
FRAIL AND SAD WITH GREY BOWED HEAD	64 4
SIT NODDIN' THY HEAD AT ME	78 22
LIKE A FLOWER THAT THE FROST HAS HUGGED AND LET GO MY H+	95 1
YOUR HEAD THROUGH BEING LONELY	104 20
MY FINGERS TILL ITS HEAD LAY BACK ITS FANGS	125 14
THE STARLING SHAKING ITS HEAD AS IT WALKS IN THE GRASS	137 11
ITS HEAD AS IT WALKED I CAN NEVER CALL HIM TO ME	137 15
LIKE THE PROW OF A BOAT HIS HEAD LAID BACK LIKE THE STE+	155 20
HER HEAD ASIDE BUT STRAIGHT TOWARDS THE BED	156 9
GOD BOWS HIS HEAD AND GRANTS ME THIS SUPREME	157 16
HIS HEAD AS PROUD AS A DEER THAT LOOKS	220 2
WITH HIS HEAD HELD HIGH-SERENE AGAINST THE SKY	221 11
PUT BACK HER FINE LEVEL-BALANCED HEAD	222 15
AH YES BEING MALE IS NOT MY HEAD HARD-BALANCED	222 17
A SQUIRREL COCKS HIS HEAD ON THE FENCE AND WONDERS	223 21
WHEN SOME ONE PASSES HE DROPS HIS HEAD	228 5
HER PROUD HEAD HELD IN ITS BLACK SILK SCARF	228 14
WITH SUNKEN HEAD AND FORGOTTEN FOLDED HANDS	232 25
PUT ASHES ON YOUR HEAD PUT SACKCLOTH ON	234 21
CREEP RIGHT UP WITH YOUR ROUND HEAD PUSHED IN MY BREAST	245 6
THAT ROUND HEAD PUSHED IN MY CHEST LIKE A NUT IN ITS	245 14
I SPREAD OVER YOU HOW LOVELY YOUR ROUND HEAD YOUR	245 21

HEAD

NOR THE ADDER WE SAW ASLEEP WITH HER HEAD ON HER SHOULD+   255 26
WHEN SHE LIFTED HER HEAD IN DELICATE STARTLED WONDER   255 28
AND MY HEAD AT LEAST IS THICK ENOUGH TO STAND IT THE   289 17
LIKE THE SNAKES ON MEDUSA'S HEAD   300 10
HE FELL TO FROWNING AS HE LAY WITH HIS HEAD ON HIS PAWS   324 12
THE BULL OF THE PROLETARIAT HAS GOT HIS HEAD DOWN   327 30
YOU TURN YOUR HEAD TOWARDS YOUR TAIL AND SMILE   332 11
WITH HIS HEAD UP STEERING LIKE A BIRD   337 26
AND HAD HIM FLY LIKE A HALO ROUND MY HEAD   339 4
HE LIFTED HIS HEAD FROM HIS DRINKING AS CATTLE DO   349 21
AND LIFTED HIS HEAD DREAMILY AS ONE WHO HAS DRUNKEN   350 24
AND SLOWLY TURNED HIS HEAD   350 29
AND AS HE PUT HIS HEAD INTO THAT DREADFUL HOLE   351 1
YOU DRAW YOUR HEAD FORWARD SLOWLY FROM YOUR LITTLE   352 25
HEAD IN ITS WIMPLE   353 11
RESTING YOUR HEAD HALF OUT OF YOUR WIMPLE   354 8
FOUR ROWING LIMBS AND ONE WEDGE-BALANCING HEAD   356 7
WHY DO YOU HAVE WATTLES AND A NAKED WATTLED HEAD   369 15
UNTIL YOUR VEILED HEAD ALMOST TOUCHES BACKWARD   370 14
BURNING PALE POSITIVE POLE OF YOUR WATTLED HEAD   370 19
THE BLUE JAY WITH A CREST ON HIS HEAD   375 1
HIS BIG FURRY HEAD   377 23
AND HIS HEAD GONE HEAVY WITH THE KNOWLEDGE OF DESIRE   378 14
HENCE HIS PONDEROUS HEAD BROODING OVER DESIRE AND DOWNF+ 378 22
SEE HIM STANDING WITH HIS HEAD DOWN NEAR THE PORTA CAPP+ 379 1
HAS HE SEEN THE GORGON'S HEAD AND TURNED TO STONE   379 7
AND SUDDENLY LOWERING HIS HEAD THE WHORLS OF BONE AND   381 16
AND BRING IT HURTLING TO A HEAD WITH CRASH OF HORNS AGA+ 381 25
KNOW ME TURNS HER HEAD AND IGNORES ME VULGARLY WITH   384 23
SHE TURNS HER HEAD AWAY WITH AN OBTUSE FEMALE SORT OF   385 1
HEAD   385 29
INSTEAD OF WHICH YOU SIT THERE AND ROLL YOUR HEAD LIKE A 398 9
HER ROUND FINE-FASHIONED HEAD WITH TWO DEAD EARS   402 3
TILL THE HEAD FLOATS TILTED LIKE A BOTTLE FORWARD TILTED 428 10
AND POKING HIS HEAD OUT AND WAVING HIMSELF   432 15
OR EVEN THE SLY GOLD SERPENT FATHERLY LIFTED HIS HEAD O+ 437 18
WITHOUT LOSING ITS HEAD   505 22
THEN I WISH LIKE TIBERIUS THE MULTITUDE HAD ONLY ONE HE+ 526 21
NIHIL WILL COME ALONG AND HIT YOU ON THE HEAD   531 12
WHICH ARE VERY LIKE TO HIT YOU ON THE HEAD AS YOU SIT   541 5
HITTING OURSELVES AGAINST UNSEEN ROCK CRASHING OUR HEAD   544 13
FROM THE TOP OF HER HEAD   565 25
I SEE YOU'RE OFF YOUR HEAD   570 3
FOR THE TRIDENT WAS LEVELLED AT HIS HEAD   577 21
AND SHE WOULD HAVE BROKEN IT OVER MY HEAD   604 20
THE SWAN WILL LIFT UP AGAIN HIS FLATTENED SMITTEN HEAD   626 7
WITH HEAD AGAINST THE SHAFT AND TAKES   733 20
HE DRINKS AND DRINKS THEN TURNS AWAY HIS HEAD   734 29
OH MY BALD HEAD   760 1
OH YOU WHO BEND YOUR HEAD DOWN AND   762 8
TO LEAN OVER MY HEAD AND MY NECK AND MY BREAST   799 18
OVER MY HEAD MY NOISELESS EAGLE   802 20
LEANS OVER TO READ HIS WORK AND HER DARK HEAD DIPS   865 5
SCATTER OVER THE WHITENESS ONE BOY ALONE IN THE CLASSRO+ 865 20
HIS ROUND BROWN HEAD BENDS LIKE A BEE ABOVE A BLOSSOM   868 5
WITH HEAD THROWN BACK AND PARTLY OPENED MOUTH   878 20
AND I LIFTED MY HEAD   882 6
AND I LIFT MY HEAD UPON THE TROUBLED TANGLED WORLD AND + *900 1
AND I LIFT MY HEAD UPON THE TROUBLED TANGLED WORLD AND + *903 14
SIT NODDIN' THY HEAD AT ME   *920 14
MY FINGERS TILL ITS HEAD GAPED BACK ITS FANGS   *936 15
HIS HEAD AS PROUD AS A DEER THAT LOOKS   *944 10
WITH MY HEAD HELD HIGH-SERENE AGAINST THE SKY   *944 24
BEFORE THE GOLDEN FATHERLY SERPENT LIFTED HIS HEAD OFF + *946 27

HEADLONG
I HAVE DROPPED AT LAST HEADLONG INTO NOUGHT PLUNGING UP+ 266 2
AND FALLS WINGLESS BLOOD STREAMING THROUGH ITS YELLOW H+ 855 25

HEAD-POWER
HEAD-POWER   326 5

HEAD-QUARTERS
PLEASE MAKE ALL REQUESTS TO HEAD-QUARTERS   604 16

HEADS
SOMEWHERE THE WIND-FLOWERS FLING THEIR HEADS BACK   40 27
AS THEY WRITE THEIR ROUND HEADS BUSILY BOWED   51 12
WHY SHOULD WE BEAT OUR HEADS AGAINST THE WALL   75 5
THE HEADS OF THE BOYS MOVE DIMLY THROUGH A YELLOW GLOOM+ 92 4
PACKED IN A LINE WITH THEIR HEADS AGAINST THE WALL   144 16
SO HIGH AND MIGHTY LOOK HOW THE HEADS ARE BORNE   221 7
THE ROUND DARK HEADS OF MEN CROWD SILENTLY   232 21
HELL REARING ITS HUSBAND-SPLENDID SERPENT HEADS   308 20
EAGLES WITH TWO HEADS EAGLES WITH ONE PRESENTLY EAGLES   413 7
IN A LONG LINE THEIR HEADS LAID OVER EACH OTHER'S NECKS 445 20
AND THE LAMBS WILL BITE OFF THE HEADS OF THE DAISIES FO+ 625 7
LIFT UP YOUR HEADS O YE GATES   699 9
ARE DUCKING THEIR HEADS IN THE WATER TUBS AT THE GATE   732 19
AND JERKED BACK THEIR BRIDLES PUSHING THEIR HEADS APART 735 9
LIFT UP YOUR HEADS   818 5
LIFT UP YOUR HEADS O YE GATES   818 10
HEADS THAT THINK NOT   827 22
WITH DIM LIGHT SHOWING THE HEADS OF THE SILVER NAILS   876 14
AS THEY WRITE THEIR ROUND HEADS BUSILY BOWED   *898 24
AS THEY WRITE THEIR ROUND HEADS BUSILY BOWED   *902 8
THE SMALL BIRDS THAT LIFTED THEIR HEADS WHEN MORNING LO+ *918 3
THE HEADS OF MY BOYS MOVE DIMLY THROUGH THE YELLOW GLOO+ *926 4
SO HIGH AND MIGHTY LOOK HOW ITS HEADS ARE BORNE   *944 20

HEADS OR TAILS
TO SETTLE THE QUESTION HEADS OR TAILS HAS CAUGHT   54 10

HEAD-STONE
BY A HEAD-STONE   *909 30

HEAD-STUN
BY A HEAD-STUN SOBBIN' AN' SOBBIN' AGAIN   *911 4

HEAL
TO HEAL THE SUFFERING OR TO MAKE REQUITE   100 26
HEAL ME FOR BODY AND SOUL I AM NOT WELL   759 15

HEALED
SOOTHED RESTORED AND HEALED   646 14
A HEALED WHOLE MAN O MOON   696 7
AND HEALED FROM ALL THIS ACHE OF BEING   724 30
SO HE TOO MAY BE HEALED BE SOOTHED TO PEACE   736 27

HEALING
YOU ASK ME DO THE HEALING DAYS CLOSE UP   90 22
THE HEALING DAYS SHALL CLOSE THE DARK GULF UP   90 29
SOOTHING AND RESTORING AND HEALING   646 13
SLEEPS IN THE HEALING WATERS   787 9

HEALS
THE HOT SUN WAXES AND HEALS   824 29

HEALTH
THEY CALL IT HEALTH IT LOOKS LIKE NULLITY   625 24
HEALTH IS EVERYTHING HEALTH IS ALL   826 21
TO HAVE HEALTH WEALTH HEALTH WEALTH HEALTH   826 24
HEALTH IS EVERYTHING HEALTH IS ALL   827 29

HEALTHY
I FEEL LIKE A FIRM RICH HEALTHY ROOT   247 11
NUDE WITH THE DIM LIGHT OF FULL HEALTHY LIFE   298 26
ISN'T HE HANDSOME ISN'T HE HEALTHY ISN'T HE A FINE   430 19
FOR OUR HONEST AND HEALTHY ENGLISH TONGUE   576 1
GOOD HEALTHY NATURAL FEELINGS INSTINCTS PASSIONS OR DES+ 678 3
ALL OF THEM HEALTHY MORE OR LESS WEALTHY   826 27
THEY ARE ALL HEALTHY HEALTHY HEALTHY   826 29
THEY ARE SO HEALTHY SUFFICIENTLY WEALTHY   827 10
THEY ARE ALL HEALTHY   827 30
TO BE ALWAYS HEALTHY   827 32
ALL OF THEM HEALTHY   828 2
HE'S LIKE A BONNY ROSY SEA-CRAB WITH HEALTHY CLAWS   830 19
TO KEEP IT SANE AND HEALTHY   *952 12
AND A LITTLE WHORING CAN BE SANE AND HEALTHY   *952 13

HEAP
MY LAST DEAR FUEL OF LIFE TO HEAP ON MY SOUL   74 19
AND GLEAM AS OF SUNSHINE CROSSING THE LOW BLACK HEAP   144 25
TOSSED ON THE LOW BLACK RUFFLED HEAP   145 13
STARK ON THE HEAP   146 2
AND PILED THEM UP IN A DULL GREY HEAP IN THE WEST   167 2
AND PILED THEM UP IN A DULL GREY HEAP IN THE WEST   167 12
THE RICH AND THE POOR ALIKE DREAMING AND WRITHING ALL I+ 175 15
WHEN SHE IS SLAIN AGAINST ME AND LIES IN A HEAP LIKE ON+ 267 13
FOR IF A MAN HAS NO LIFE IN HIS WORK HE IS MOSTLY A HEAP 450 10
TO TWIST AND GROVEL AND BECOME A HEAP OF DIRT   742 2
THE HOSTS AWAY TO DEATH WHERE HEAP ON HEAP   744 8
I AM INCLINED TO HEAP THY COALS OF FIRE ON MY OWN   760 15
THE LAST DEAR FUEL AND HEAP IT ON MY SOUL   *895 27
FOR MYSELF A HEAP OF ASHES OF WEARINESS TILL SLEEP   *896 1
THERE LIES THE DULL RED HEAP OF THEIR SAND IN THE WEST *896 7
THERE LIES A DULL RED HEAP OF HIS SAND IN THE WEST   *896 17
THE LAST DEAR FUEL AND HEAP IT ON MY SOUL   *904 16
FOR MYSELF A HEAP OF ASHES OF WEARINESS TILL SLEEP   *904 22

HEAPED
IN HOLLOW BLOCKS AND CUBES DEFORMED AND HEAPED   53 25
THE DEAD MOON HEAPED WITHIN THE NEW MOON'S ARMS   132 2
ME MIGHT A YOUNG GIRL BE HEAPED WITH SUCH SHADOW OF   132 6
AND UNDERNEATH A BLUE-GREY TWILIGHT HEAPED   135 5
ONE HEAPED MOUND   145 28
TILL PETALS HEAPED BETWEEN THE WINDOW-SHAFTS   154 31
THE DEAD MOON HEAPED WITHIN THE YOUNG MOON'S ARMS   *937 29
ME LEST YOU MY SISTER SHOULD GO HEAPED WITH SUCH SHADOW+ *937 33
UNDER THE BLUE-GREY TWILIGHT HEAPED   *939 5

HEAPS
THAT HUDDLES IN GREY HEAPS COILING AND HOLDING BACK   164 18
SMASHED ALL OOZING WITH BLOOD AND BURNED IN HEAPS   258 3
THE MURDERED BODIES OF YOUTHS AND MEN IN HEAPS   258 5
AND HEAPS AND HEAPS AND HORRIBLE REEKING HEAPS   258 6
HAVE HEAPS OF MONEY   440 27
MEN SHOULD REFUSE TO BE HEAPS OF WAGE-EARNING DUNG   450 6
AND CRIMSON AND THE BLOOD-BROWN HEAPS OF SLAIN   745 26

HEAR
IN A LAUGH AS THEY HEAR   34 10
IN CONFIRMATION I HEAR SEVENFOLD LARK-SONGS PEALING   34 29
REMOTE ALTHOUGH I HEAR THE BEGGAR'S COUGH   36 5
I HEAR HIS HAND ON THE LATCH AND RISE FROM MY CHAIR   43 18
I HEAR IT THROUGH THE GRASS   50 16
A SUDDEN CAR GOES SWEEPING PAST AND I STRAIN MY SOUL TO+ 58 3
TO HEAR ON ITS MOCKING TRIUMPHANCE UNWITTING THE AFTER-+ 58 6
AS I HEAR THE SHARP CLEAN TROT OF A PONY DOWN THE ROAD 63 9
I DO NOT LIKE TO HEAR THE GENTLE GRIEVING   65 19
YOUR BOW FOR BROKEN IT IS AND HURTING TO HEAR   85 22
WHEN I HEAR YOU JINGLING THROUGH   95 8
DO YOU NOT HEAR EACH MORSEL THRILL   127 11
BIRD I HEAR   134 19
YES MY LOVE I HEAR   136 26
THE ROSES LEAN DOWN WHEN THEY HEAR IT THE TENDER MILD 137 4
IS TO LISTEN AND HEAR THE GRIM   159 15
THE SPLINTERED STREETS HEAR NOISES   159 17
AND THE PLACE IS NO LONGER OURS WATCHING I HEAR   173 2
HE SAID DO YOU HEAR THEM WHISPERING   201 27
I CAN HEAR THE SWISH OF THE SCYTHE-STROKES FOUR   219 22

HEAR
  I CAN HEAR THE ISAR MOAN   220 23
  BEHIND ME ON THE LAKE I HEAR THE STEAMER DRUMMING   231 5
  IF YOU HEAR A RUSTLE   231 12
  BECAUSE WHEN YOU HEAR ME   235 22
  DEATH DO YOU HEAR IN MY ARMS I AM BRINGING   238 20
  FALLING I HEAR AGAIN   268 23
  SHOW ME I TREMBLE SO MUCH TO HEAR IT THAT EVEN NOW   273 28
  DO YOU HEAR THE CHEMICAL ACCENTS OF THE SUN   301 9
  AND HEAR HIM BELLOW AFTER MANY YEARS THE BULL THAT SERV+   327 8
  THEN I KNEW THEY WERE DEJECTED HAVING COME TO HEAR THE   390 19
  WHEN YOU HEAR IT LANGUISHING   433 21
  TILL NOW THE VERY WORD IS NAUSEATING WE CAN'T HEAR IT A+   519 5
  YOU HEAR THE STERTOROUS SELF-RIGHTEOUS HEAVY   528 19
  AND THEY THOUGHT YOU COULDN'T HEAR THEM   554 25
  SHOULD HEAR ALL THE ROUGH WORDS   565 6
  AND JUST LOVES TO HEAR YOU SOB AND GROAN   572 8
  WHEN I HEAR MAN SPOUTING ABOUT HUMILITY TODAY   621 22
  HEAR   623 22
  YOU WHO DON'T HEAR THE SEA'S UNEASINESS   643 12
  WHEN I HEAR SOMEBODY COMPLAIN OF BEING LONELY   646 1
  YOU HEAR A WOMAN SAY I LOVE MY HUSBAND DEARLY   654 10
  AND YOU WILL HEAR WHAT LIARS THEY ARE   654 14
  DOST THA HEAR MY HORSE'S FEET AS HE CANTERS AWAY   664 1
  DO YOU HEAR MY ROLLS ROYCE PURR AS IT GLIDES AWAY   664 3
  HOLD THE STARS STILL LEST WE HEAR THE HEAVENS DIMLY RIN+   698 11
  ENVELOPING EVEN ME WHO HEAR NO MORE   698 24
  SOME YOU MAY SING THROUGH AND ALL MEN HEAR   711 8
  AT LAST I HEAR A RATTLE AND THERE AWAY   732 24
  GOD HOW GLAD I AM TO HEAR THE SHELLS   741 9
  INTO THE UTTER DARK THEY CANNOT HEAR   744 31
  OF LIVES I SPEAK TO ALL WHO CANNOT HEAR   745 23
  ALONG THE COAST TO HEAR THE HUSH   747 3
  TO HEAR THE LONG WAVES STRIKE THE COAST   747 11
  BUT WHAT IF MY LOVE SHOULD CHANCE TO HEAR   752 2
  WHEN YOU HEAR THEM HUMMING   755 18
  HEAR A VOICE SAYING I KNOW YOU NOT   789 7
  I HEAR THE VOICE OF MY FIRST MAN ASK ME WHY I AM LAUGHI+   791 14
  DO YOU HEAR THE RATS OF THE DARKNESS GNAWING AT YOUR IN+   800 25
  IF YOU HEAR A MAN CALLED BRILLIANT YOU MAY BE PRETTY SU+   841 18
  HEAR RE-ECHO YOUR SLOW RELUCTANT FEET   880 16
  WI' LITTLE SOBS AS YOU SCARCE COULD HEAR   *910 14
  AN' 'ER'S WANTIN IT I HEAR   *921 16
  I CAN HEAR THE SOUND OF THE SCYTHE STROKES FOUR   *944 2
  THEY WILL HEAR A SILENCE FALL   *954 6
  THEY WILL HEAR THE FAINT RENDING OF THE ASPHALT ROADS   *954 8
  THEY WILL HEAR FAR FAR AWAY THE LAST FACTORY HOOTER   *954 10

HEARD
  WITH SNARLING RED JAWS AND I HEARD THE CRIES   38 10
  WHOSE PLAINTIVE CRY IS HEARD AS SHE FLIES   42 29
  I CRIED BUT NO ONE HEARD ME   46 23
  AND I HEARD THE THUNDER AND FELT THE RAIN   62 19
  IS HEARD IN THE WINDLESS WHISPER OF LEAVES   68 17
  I HEARD YOU IN YOUR SLEEP SPEAK STRANGELY TO ME   99 10
  TO SHOW THE PLACE WHENCE THE SCREAM WAS HEARD   150 13
  SOFT SHE LAY AS A SHED FLOWER FALLEN NOR HEARD   155 26
  HEARD I HAVE BEEN TO PATMOS   202 3
  WHEN I HEARD THE CANNON OF THE WAR I LISTENED WITH MY   257 5
  I HEARD A WOMAN CALL YOU THE WINGED VICTORY   332 9
  FOR THE DESTRUCTION OF THE UNIVERSE FOR IF HIS PRAYER W+   348 3
  NO ONE EVER HEARD YOU COMPLAIN   352 24
  I HEARD A WOMAN PITYING HER PITYING THE MERE TORTUE   361 31
  YET I'VE HEARD HIM CRY   363 27
  I HEARD THE SCREAM OF A FROG WHICH WAS CAUGHT WITH HIS   365 30
  I REMEMBER WHEN I FIRST HEARD BULL-FROGS BREAK INTO SOU+   365 32
  I RECOGNISED WHEN I HEARD ITS VOICE   376 7
  OH YES YOU'RE FOUND OUT I HEARD THEM KICK YOU OUT OF   400 6
  AND HEARD THE AUDIENCE SIGHING AND SOBBING WITH ALL THE   443 24
  I HEARD THE CAMEL'S BACK GO CRACK   491 23
  THE ONLY PEOPLE I EVER HEARD TALK ABOUT MY LADY POVERTY   498 9
  THAT YOU'VE OFTEN HEARD   551 10
  UP I ROSE MY LADS AN' I HEARD YER   552 17
  BUT OF COURSE I ALWAYS HEARD THEM   554 29
  LET YOUR DEMON BE HEARD   564 12
  IN WHICH IS HEARD THE CRASHING SPLINTER OF MACHINES   640 11
  I HEARD A LITTLE CHICKEN CHIRP   680 8
  ARE HEARD SOFTLY LAUGHING AND CHATTING AS EVER   688 18
  WHOSE POWER AND GLORY I HAVE OFTEN HEARD AND FELT   704 21
  I HEARD THE STAR SINGING LIKE A DYING BIRD   786 15
  SO HE LAUGHED AND ONE HEARD HIM LAUGHING   791 12
  I HEARD HER SAY TO HER BRILLIANT YOUNG HUSBAND   842 12
  PLEASE SIR I WAS SWEEPING SNOW AN' I NEVER HEARD THE BE+   866 9
  NEVER A SOUND WAS HEARD   887 23
  IS HEARD IN THE GRASS OF THE SOD   *914 31
  IS HEARD IN THE WINDLESS WHISPER OF LEAVES   *915 1
  I HEARD THY CRIES OF PAIN AND THEY BROKE   *927 11

HEARING
  HEARING MY MERE LIPS SHOUT   124 21
  HEARING MAN APPROACH   321 25
  I REMEMBER HEARING A WILD GOOSE OUT OF THE THROAT OF NI+   365 34
  I REMEMBER MY FIRST TERROR HEARING THE HOWL OF WEIRD   366 8
  HEARING HER TALK THAT IS   655 2
  HEARING MY MERE LIPS SHOUT   *935 21

HEARIN'
  'ARK THA'RT FOR HEARIN' SUMMAT   137 26
  AREN'T TER HEARIN' SUMMAT   138 7

HEARS
  MY SPIRIT HEARS   169 13
  WITH PALE SHUT FACE NOR EITHER HEARS NOR FEELS   232 27
  ON THE MOUNTAIN HEARS HIM   761 22

HEARSE
  IN THE HEARSE OF NIGHT YOU SEE THEIR TARNISHED COFFINS   703 3

HEART
  A FEW QUICK BEATS FROM A WOOD-PIGEON'S HEART AND WHEN I+   38 14
  LOVE HAS CREPT OUT OF HER SEALED HEART   46 5
  AS HE BLENCHES AND TURNS AWAY AND MY HEART STANDS STILL   47 27
  YOU ARE FRIGHTENED WITH JOY MY HEART LIKE A FRIGHTENED   47 33
  WITH DREAD AND FILLS MY HEART WITH THE TEARS OF DESIRE   48 12
  AND MY HEART REBELS WITH ANGUISH AS NIGHT DRAWS NIGHER   48 13
  TO BREAK MY HEART   55 11
  AS THE HEART BENEATH DID WIELD   55 29
  MY HEART IS TRAMMELLED   56 24
  TEARS AND SWORDS TO MY HEART ARROWS NO ARMOUR WILL TURN+   57 23
  I FELT THE LURCH AND HALT OF HER HEART   61 21
  NEXT TO MY BREAST WHERE MY OWN HEART WAS BEATING   61 22
  FALLS AGAIN AND AGAIN ON MY HEART WITH A HEAVY REPROACH   63 3
  OF THE MOURNFUL CONSTANT HEART THAT WHILE SHE'S WEAVING   65 25
  BUT THE BLOOD HAS SUSPENDED ITS TIMBRE THE HEART FROM O+   67 3
  I LOVED BUT THERE SHE GOES AND HER BEAUTY HURTS MY HEART·   67 11
  PATIENCE LITTLE HEART   91 7
  PATIENCE LITTLE HEART I SHALL BE SWEET   91 23
  WITH GENTLENESS CAME I WITH MY HEART 'TWIXT MY HANDS LI+   92 22
  IS HEAVY AND MY HEART BEATS SLOWLY LABORIOUSLY   95 2
  IF I COULD HAVE PUT YOU IN MY HEART   100 13
  AM LIT BENEATH MY HEART WITH A HALF-MOON WEIRD AND BLUE   115 4
  IN MY FLAME OF LIVING THE INVISIBLE HEART OF THE ROSE   115 8
  THAT WOULD POUR TO YOU FROM MY HEART   117 24
  BUT MY HEART AT THE CENTRE   120 22
  MY HEART WAS FOUND   121 8
  HOLLOW RE-ECHOED MY HEART   121 17
  YOUR VIOLENT HEART BEATS TO AND FRO   122 12
  ALOOF MY FLAMING HEART WILL NOT ALLOW   122 22
  STRANGLED MY HEART SWELLED UP SO FULL   123 15
  AND EMPTIED MY HEART OF LOVE   124 2
  SO I HELD MY HEART ALOFT   124 3
  OVER MY HEART AND SWEET   124 26
  ITS SHADOW LAY ON MY HEART   124 27
  AND BURROWING IN ITS HEART   124 31
  MY HEART AND THEN   124 34
  THE BIRD CAME DOWN ON MY HEART   124 35
  THE NEST IN A HEART OF LOVE   125 6
  THEN I LAUGHED IN THE DARK OF MY HEART I DID EXULT   125 25
  MY HEART WAS FIERCE TO MAKE HER LAUGHTER RISE   125 30
  AND MY HEART LEAPED UP IN LONGING TO PLUNGE ITS STARK   125 33
  FLESH OF MY HEART ERE DOWN REBUKED IT SLIPS   127 28
  I KNOW FROM HER HARDENED LIPS THAT STILL HER HEART IS   128 1
  WOULD CRUSH THEIR MOUNDS ON HER HEART TO KILL IN THERE   128 25
  BUT MY HEART STANDS STILL AS A NEW STRONG DREAD ALARMS   132 5
  BETRAYS ME BACK TILL THE HEART OF ME WEEPS TO BELONG   148 11
  BUT OH MY HEART WHAT BIRDS ARE PIPING   150 14
  AND OH MY HEART CEASE APPREHENDING   150 17
  OF YOUR HEART OF FIRE IN WHICH I LOOK   151 2
  THAT WILL HAVE THE OIL OF ILLUSION OH HEART   151 10
  ON THE SLOW BUBBLING OF YOUR RHYTHMIC HEART   154 11
  KNOWLEDGE I SET YOUR HEART TO ITS STRONGER BEAT   156 28
  HIS MIND UNTIL IT BURNT HIS HEART AWAY   158 2
  THE HEART   161 2
  IT CURVES IN A RUSH TO THE HEART OF THE VAST   166 26
  I WHOSE HEART IS·TORN WITH PARTING   169 10
  AFTER MANY DAYS MY HEART YEARNS   171 25
  AND SO MY HEART BEGINS TO CRY AND CALL   174 3
  THE HEART ALL CROWDED WITH SLAVES MOST WORKING SOME FEW+   174 20
  THE HEART OF THE LIVE WORLD PULSES AND THE BLOOD OF THE+   176 4
  YOUR HEART OF DESTINY   178 33
  THE CONSTELLATIONS YOUR GREAT HEART THE SUN   194 24
  DOES MY SLOW HEART REBEL DO MY DEAD HANDS   195 6
  TO HALT THE HEART DIVERT THE STREAMING FLOW   195 34
  HER HEART IS A SWINGING CRADLE   201 9
  FOR YOU WERE STRAINING WITH A WILD HEART BACK BACK AGAIN   206 23
  HAVE GONE OUT OF MY HEART   208 2
  NEVERTHELESS THE CURSE AGAINST YOU IS STILL IN MY HEART   208 15
  I THINK I COULD BREAK THE SYSTEM WITH MY HEART   213 19
  TO WAKE WITH A TIGHTENED HEART   210 10
  WITH A PALE DEAD CHRIST ON THE CRUCIFIX OF HIS HEART   226 3
  AND HEART LIKE A CROSS THAT BEARS DEAD AGONY   226 6
  MY HEART IS BITTER   232 2
  AND MY STILL HEART FULL OF SECURITY   250 11
  HOW HAPPY I AM HOW MY HEART IN THE WIND RINGS TRUE   251 11
  DISSOLVED WITH THE MYSTERY OF THE INNERMOST HEART OF THE   260 28
  I THANK MANKIND WITH PASSIONATE HEART   263 29
  WISE GOOD PROVISION THAT MAKES THE HEART SWELL WITH LOVE   264 7
  FOR WHAT KIND OF ICE-ROTTEN HOT-ACHING HEART MUST THEY +   270 27
  INCIPIENT PURPLING TOWARDS SUMMER IN THE WORLD OF THE H+   273 25
  FOR MY PART I PREFER MY HEART TO BE BROKEN   279 1
  THE FIBRES OF THE HEART PARTING ONE AFTER THE OTHER   281 6
  DEEP PULSING OF A STRANGE HEART   292 33
  MY HEART WILL KNOW NO PEACE   293 16
  BUT LET US TAKE HEART   304 4
  NAY WHAT A HEART OF DELICATE SUPER-FAITH   304 22
  THE HEART OF BLOSSOM   305 2
  THE UNQUENCHABLE HEART OF BLOSSOM   305 3
  FROM THE SNOW-REMEMBERING HEART   305 21
  SO THAT THE FAITH IN HIS HEART SMILES AGAIN   306 1
  RED YOUR HEART IS   306 22
  BLESSED ARE THE PURE IN HEART AND THE FATHOMLESS IN BRI+   314 16
  HOW MY HEART BEATS   320 19
  I AM MAN AND THEREFORE MY HEART BEATS AND THROWS THE DA+   320 21
  AS I AM IF MY HEART IN UPLIFTING CEASED TO BEAT TO TOSS+   320 27
  BEFORE MY HEART STOPS BEATING AND I BECOME WHAT I AM NOT   321 9
  AND EVEN MY HEART LORD FOREVER AFTER ALL UPLIFTING   321 17
  BAT-WINGED HEART OF MAN   322 21
  THAT MY HEART WHICH LIKE A LARK AT HEAVEN'S GATE SINGIN+   322 30
  KNOWING THE THUNDER OF HIS HEART   326 9
  AND I SAID TO MY HEART LOOK LOOK AT HIM   337 25
  I SAID TO MY HEART WHO ARE THESE   337 31
  AND MY HEART COULDN'T OWN THEM   337 32
  AND I SAID TO MY HEART THERE ARE LIMITS   338 21

HEART
TO YOU MY HEART   338 22
AND MY HEART ACCUSED ITSELF   339 11
TO ROAM AND FEEL THE SLOW HEART BEAT   358 12
WHEN YOU PICK THE RED SMOKY HEART FROM A RABBIT OR A   374 5
OVER THE HEART OF THE WEST THE TAOS DESERT   403 1
NO LONGER OR CARRY THE BURDEN OF A MAN ON YOUR HEART   411 12
IN MY HEART   412 3
AND MY HEART IS GLAD TO HAVE THEM AT LAST   412 22
HEART OF LIFE   432 8
O MY HEART   438 24
BUT HORRIBLE AS IF YOUR HEART WOULD WRENCH OUT   447 29
AND ONLY THE HEART   455 8
THE HEART IS FROZEN THE SPIRIT DEAD   456 2
DO YOU WANT WARM HEART AND WHAT   461 4
AT THE CORE OF YOUR HEART THE OTHER CREATURE   466 2
AND PERSONAL INTIMACY HAS NO HEART   471 11
TO MY DARK HEART GODS ARE   474 10
IN MY DARK HEART LOVE IS AND IS NOT   474 11
OF TWO HUMAN HEARTS TWO ANCIENT ROCKS A MAN'S HEART   477 15
LOVE IS LIKE THE GRASS BUT THE HEART IS DEEP WILD ROCK   477 22
GO DOWN TO YOUR DEEP OLD HEART WOMAN AND LOSE SIGHT OF   477 24
OUT OF SIGHT IN THE DEEP DARK LIFTING HEART   478 3
BUT SAY IN THE DARK WILD METAL OF YOUR HEART   478 4
HAVE YOU NO DEEP OLD HEART OF WILD WOMANHOOD   478 15
WITH THE HEART OF THE MAN YOU SUPPOSED TO HAVE LOVED   478 18
WHEN MY HEART FEELS KINDLY TOWARDS HER   479 3
WHO WARMED THE COCKLES OF MY HEART   507 9
HEART   507 11
HAS COME DOWN ON THE HEART IN A BURDEN OF LOCUSTS   507 22
AND THE HEART IS NUMB   508 4
THE HEART   509 2
FROM THE HEART AND LEAVING STRANGE COLD STRETCHES OF SA+   509 4
SO A MAN NO LONGER KNOWS HIS OWN HEART   509 5
I AM HERE YET MY HEART IS BARE AND UTTERLY EMPTY   509 7
AND SOMEWHERE IT HAS A WILD HEART   525 4
FROM THE WILD HEART OF SPACE THAT I CALL THE SUN OF SUNS   525 9
YET WHEN IT SPEAKS FROM HEART TO HEART   575 19
THIS BUSINESS OF SPEAKING FROM HEART TO HEART   575 25
HAVE THE WELFARE OF THE BRITISH PUBLIC AT HEART   582 20
THERE IS THE OTHER UNIVERSE OF THE HEART OF MAN   606 21
OF THE HEART OF MAN   607 3
THE HEART OF MAN IN SO FAR AS IT IS BUDDING IS BUDDING +   612 4
THE LARK NESTS IN HIS HEART   624 5
EXPLODED THE HEART   629 9
AND TOUCHES ME OVER THE HEART   652 7
SO THAT MY HEART BEATS SOOTHED SOOTHED SOOTHED AND AT P+   652 8
MAKES THE HEART SUDDENLY QUIVER WITH LOVE   653 17
TO SAVE THE STREAKED PANSY OF THE HEART FROM   658 11
BUT A TINY CORE OF STILLNESS IN THE HEART   658 14
A DEEP CALM IN THE HEART   700 12
AND SEPARATE HEART FROM HEART AND CUT AWAY ALL CARESSES   707 18
OF A STRONG HEART AT PEACE   717 19
FILLING THE HEART WITH PEACE   720 17
SWINGS THE HEART RENEWED WITH PEACE   720 18
OH FROM OUT OF YOUR HEART   721 24
WITHIN YOUR WALLS WITHIN YOUR VERY HEART   723 15
MY WRISTS SEEM BROKEN AND MY HEART SEEMS DEAD   727 19
TO MAKE SPORT OF ME WHEN THE DAYS OF MY HEART   731 16
TO START MY HEART AFRESH GIVE ME THE SOFT SMALL STRESS   738 31
THE HEART HEART THAT HAS BEAT   746 17
TO SING IN THE SHELL OF MY HEART THE LULL AND INCREASE   747 22
TO MY SILENCED HEART   748 21
EVEN NO PAIN OF HEART   749 14
THE STRINGS OF MY HEART   751 18
HOW CAN MY HEART KEEP BEATING IN THIS PALLOR OF WHITISH   766 28
HEART THERE IS NO WORD TO SAY   767 1
IN THE HEART OF EVERY INTELLIGENT AMERICAN WHETHER   775 8
FROM THE FIRE THAT BOILS IN THE MOLTEN HEART OF THE WOR+   782 15
THE HEART OF THE WORLD IS THE HEART OF THE EARTH WHERE +   782 16
THE OLD FATHER OF LIFE AT THE HEART OF THE WORLD LIFE-F+   783 2
WILL YOU STRIKE AT THE HEART OF THE SUN WITH YOUR BLOOD+   783 17
WILL YOU STRIKE THE SUN'S HEART OUT AGAIN   783 19
DRUMS FOR THE BEATING HEART   804 2
THE HEART CEASES NOT   804 3
TO HIS HOUSE IN THE HEART OF A TRAITOR   808 11
FROM THE HEART A RED RAY   819 20
BECAUSE ONE FOOT IS THE HEART OF A MAN   820 8
AND THE OTHER IS THE HEART OF A WOMAN   820 9
IT HAS NEITHER HEART NOR BOWELS NOR GENITALS   830 28
YOU LOOK SO LIKE BABY IT WRINGS MY HEART   842 15
MY HEART HAS A WARMTH LIKE THIS SEA WHERE THE DAWN   860 17
SETS MY HEART ALSO THROBBING WITH PAIN   862 22
THAT STINGS DOWN TO MY HEART   863 20
EVE WITH A HEART OF RESENTMENT IS QUICKLY SPED   864 21
DEEP INTO THE HEART OF THE LIGHT THE CENTRE OF A STAR   865 6
THERE IN THE HEART OF A STAR SET FAR OFF IN THE NIGHT   865 7
PRESSING TO GRASP MY HEART   869 21
I THINK SOMETIMES IT WILL CRUSH MY HEART INWARD   869 22
SIEGMUND THE STRONG BEATING OF YOUR HEART HURTS ME   870 19
SIEGMUND WITH YOUR ARMS AND YOUR HEART YOU ARE CHOKING +   870 20
AND NOW WITH THE KNOCKING OF HIS HEART AGAINST MY SOUL   871 8
OH WITH HIS HEART   871 21
HOW HE HURTS ME WITH HIS HEART AND HIS THROAT SO NEAR T+   871 22
HIS COAT AND HIS ARMS AND HIS LABOURING HEART ARE STRAN+   871 25
FROM THE FIERY HAMMERING OF YOUR HEART I CAST   873 2
OF YOUR HEART OF FIRE IN WHICH I LOOK   873 12
THAT MUST HAVE THE OIL OF ILLUSION OH HEART   873 20
MY LIMBS ARE NUMB AND HEAVY AND MY HEART   879 19
OR WHETHER MY HEART WAS ITS NEST   881 26
CAUGHT WHEN MY HEART WOULD LEAP IN A NET OF LIVES   884 15
FROM OUT OF MY HEART AND LOINS CHOKED AND SHACKLED   884 17
MY HEART IS FIRM AND SOLID IT NEEDS   888 9
A FEW QUICK BEATS OF A WOODPIGEON'S HEART THEN RISE   *892 30
LIKE A FLOWER THAT THE FROST HAS HUGGED AND LET GO MY H+   *897 16
MOUNTS UP TO MY HEART AND I FIND IT GOOD   *899 34
AND WHEN MY HEART IS CHILL WITH LONELINESS   *900 25
MOUNTS UP TO MY HEART AND I FIND IT GOOD   *903 13

HEART
AND WHEN MY HEART IS CHILL WITH LONELINESS   *904 1
I FELT THE LURCH AND HALT OF HER HEART   *912 1
NEXT MY BREAST WHERE MY OWN HEART WAS BEATING   *912 2
OF ME TO HEART   *931 28
TO THE VERY HEART   *931 29
STRANGLED MY HEART SWELLED UP SO FULL   *934 21
MY HEART RE-ECHOED IN SURPRISE   *935 20
OVER MY HEART LIKE HEAT   *935 32
ITS SHADOW LAY ON MY HEART   *935 33
AND DIP IN THE HEART   *935 37
BIRD ABOVE MY HEART   *936 2
AND AH I HELD MY HEART ALOFT   *936 9
THEN I LAUGHED IN THE DARK OF MY HEART I DID EXULT   *936 24
MY HEART WAS FIERCE TO MAKE HER HOMAGE RISE   *936 29
AND MY HEART LEAPED UP IN LONGING TO PLUNGE ITS STARK   *936 32
MY HEART DISTURBED IN ITS DREAM SLOW-STEPPING ALARMS   *937 32
AND SURELY THE HEART THAT IS IN ME MUST BELONG   *940 10
MY HEART TO SEE YOU SETTLING AND TRYING TO CLIMB   *945 9
AND MY STILL HEART FULL OF SECURITY   *946 9
AND WILD GEESE O MY HEART   *947 25
THE LARK NESTS IN HIS HEART   *953 25
ALL THE CREATURES THAT CANNOT DIE WHILE ONE HEART HARBO+   *954 5

HEART-ACHING
HEART-ACHING   198 24

HEARTBEAT
HEARTBEAT BOUND   121 10

HEART-BEATING
SO MUCH SO RARE A GAME SO QUICK A HEART-BEATING   876 15

HEART-BEAT'S
YOU HURT MY HEART-BEAT'S PRIVACY   116 28

HEART-BEAT
WATCH THE STIR WHICH IS RHYTHMIC AND MOVES THEM ALL AS +   *909 9

HEART-BURSTING
AND TO LEAP IN ONE LAST HEART-BURSTING LEAP LIKE A MALE+   379 15

HEARTENS
UP DIMLY FROM THEIR STRIVING IT HEARTENS MY STRIFE   *900 24
UP DIMLY FROM THEIR STRIVING IT HEARTENS MY STRIFE   *903 36

HEARTH
THE WALLS OF THE HOUSE AND NETTLES PUFF OUT FROM THE HE+   159 25
AT THE HEARTH   234 2
AND YOUR SHOES AND DRAW UP AT MY HEARTH   237 18
THE WINE IS WARM IN THE HEARTH   237 23
ROUND A WHITE HEARTH OF DESERT   407 2
ROUND THE ASH-WHITE HEARTH OF THE DESERT   408 20
WHO WAS LIKE A RED FIRE ON THE HEARTH   506 12
HE CAME IN SLOWLY AND SAT DOWN BY THE HEARTH   692 13
AND STILL THIS IS THE GOD HERMES SITTING BY MY HEARTH   692 21
SLEEPING ON THE HEARTH AND YAWNING BEFORE THE FIRE   700 7
SLEEPING ON THE HEARTH OF THE LIVING WORLD   700 8
AND LEANING TOWARDS THE OLD HEARTH   704 5
BECAUSE YOU ARE EVER THERE ON THE HEARTH   783 29
YET YOU ARE HERE LIKE GOD UPON THE HEARTH   784 3
REACH ACROSS THE HEARTH   813 6

HEARTH-RUG
DOWN ON MY HEARTH-RUG OF DESERT SAGE OF THE MESA   408 27

HEARTHS
OLD HAUNTS OLD HABITATS OLD HEARTHS   722 28
NO FIRES NO HEARTHS NO HOUSES   769 19

HEARTHSTONE
BUT NOW IT IS A BURNING HEARTHSTONE ONLY   326 27

HEART-HUNGRY
PREACHING IN SAD-MOVING SILENCE A HEART-HUNGRY PURITY   855 3

HEARTS
FREE OF ALL HEARTS MY DARLING   101 27
RED HEARTS OF MEN   374 8
BY THE LIFE IN THE HEARTS OF MEN   374 33
FOR THE SYMPATHY IN THEIR VAST SHY HEARTS   465 11
SO SLOWLY THE GREAT HOT ELEPHANT HEARTS   465 19
OF TWO HUMAN HEARTS TWO ANCIENT ROCKS A MAN'S HEART   477 15
WHILE THEIR HEARTS BECOME ABSOLUTELY EMPTY   502 10
IF WE LOOKED IN OUR HEARTS WE SHOULD SEE   519 7
NOTHINGNESS PALE NOTHINGNESS IN THEIR HEARTS   569 6
BUT THROUGH SOME HEARTS THEY WILL NEVER ROLL   624 4
ARE THEIR HEARTS THE HUB OF THE WHEEL   631 29
HEAVILY STEPPING WEARY ON OUR HEARTS   704 10
AND HOTNESS AND THE MORE CRUSTED BRINE IN OUR HEARTS   707 23
FOR YOUR DEAD YOUR UNSEEN DEAD AND WITH YOUR HEARTS   723 12
WAFTING WITH WARM LOVE FROM STILL-LIVING HEARTS   723 22
OF GHOSTS THAT THRONG ABOUT OUR MUFFLED HEARTS   736 3
OUR SERRIED HEARTS DRIFTING WITHOUT A PLACE   736 9
OPEN THE RANKS AND LET THEM IN OUR HEARTS   736 14
LEAVE US TO TAKE OUR GHOSTS INTO OUR HEARTS   736 19
THE BLOOD FROM OUR HEARTS OH YOU WHO STAND BEHIND US   756 7
OF THE HILLS AND THE HEARTS WITHIN US DITHER   757 16
THE LIVING AMERICA IS IN THE HEARTS OF AMERICANS   774 24
IS A GERM LYING IN THE HEARTS OF AMERICANS   774 27
BUT A GERM IN THE HEARTS OF MEN AND WOMEN AMERICANS   774 31
IN THEIR HEARTS   775 3
STRUGGLING GERM IN INDIVIDUAL HEARTS   775 22
IN INDIVIDUAL HEARTS AND NOWHERE ELSE   775 26
HE SAW THE HEARTS OF THEM ALL THAT WERE BLACK AND HEAVY+   790 14
OH FOOLS MEXICANS AND PEONS WITH MUDDY HEARTS   794 32
FIRE IN YOUR HEARTS OH MEN   811 25
OH HEARTS LEAP HIGH   820 14

HEARTS
    ALAS TOSSED BACK IN MY HEARTS SWIRL   862 16
    A ROSE-BUSH UNTO YOU IN ALL THEIR HEARTS   *941 14
    BUT THROUGH SOME HEARTS THEY WILL NEVER ROLL   *953 22
    AH NO IN THE HEARTS OF SOME MEN THERE STILL IS SANCTUARY   *953 23
    IN SOME HEARTS STILL THE SANCTUARIES OF WILD LIFE   *954 2

HEART-SPUN
    TO COVER MY MOUTH'S RAILLERY TILL I'M BOUND IN HER SHAM+   *940 17

HEART'S
    AT MY HEART'S DELIGHT   42 4
    OF EACH HEART'S ENTRANCE FEE   101 28
    MY HEART'S RED MEASURE IN HER CUP   123 28
    BECAUSE OF MY HEART'S   143 20
    HEART'S BLOOD   157 32
    YOUR HEART'S QUICK CORE   561 25
    FLOW THE HEART'S RIVERS OF FULNESS DESIRE AND DISTRESS   607 8
    SOFT AS A KIND HEART'S KINDNESS TREMULOUS   784 17
    AND HARK TO THE WORDS OF THEIR HEART'S DESIRE   789 3
    AH COIN ME SPEECH OF YOUR HEART'S GOLD FURNACE HEAT   872 27
    MY HEART'S RED MEASURE IN THE CUP   *934 34

HEART-THROB
    HEART-THROB SLOW HEART-THROB PERSISTENT FOR THE NEXT   365 27

HEARTY
    AND ONCE HE WAS GAY AND HEARTY WITH HIS EYE ON THE IMMO+   *946 17

HEAT
    AND THE SWEET CONSTANT BALANCED HEAT   263 15
    GROW RISING UP OWING TO THE HEAT WHICH IS IN THE EARTH +   295 8
    SUN OF BLACK VOID HEAT   301 19
    ROCK WAVES OF DARK HEAT   302 1
    WAVES OF DARK HEAT ROCK SWAY UPWARDS   302 2
    COMPARED TO THE FLOOD OF BLACK HEAT THAT ROLLS UPWARDS   302 5
    ON A HOT HOT DAY AND I IN PYJAMAS FOR THE HEAT   349 2
    I REMEMBER THE HEIFER IN HER HEAT BLORTING AND BLORTING   366 6
    THEN THE MILL-STONES BURST WITH THE INTERNAL HEAT OF TH+   648 12
    AND GOD REVEALED THROUGH THE SWEAT AND THE HEAT OF LOVE   742 29
    THE TOWN GROWS FIERCER WITH HEAT   746 8
    MY BROTHER DIED IN THE HEAT   754 17
    OUR OVERWEENING DAYS STRIVE TOO FAR TILL THE HEAT AND T+   856 1
    THERE FOR THE HEAT OF IT CAUSES A SMART   863 19
    AH COIN ME SPEECH OF YOUR HEART'S GOLD FURNACE HEAT   872 27
    AS THE SUBTLE HEAT   *907 21
    THE POWER OF THE MELTING FUSING FORCE HEAT LIGHT ALL IN+   *909 14
    OVER MY HEART LIKE HEAT   *935 32
    MY ANXIETY IN A HEAT OF LOVE   *936 8
    AND THE ROCK GOES DOWN DOWN DEEPER FROM COLD INTO HEAT   *951 20
    AND GREATER HEAT INTO FIRE MORE HEAVY AND HOTTER THAN A+   *951 21

HEATED
    IN BATTLE OF HEATED WORDS HARDLY STILLED BY MY REITERAT+   865 32

HEATH-BELLS
    SHAKING THE HEATH-BELLS DOWN WITH HER PETULANT GAIT   863 23

HEATHEN
    HEATHEN DANCES AND CEREMONIES AND TILLED THEIR   777 31

HEATHER
    OR RATHER 'TIS I AM NOTHING HERE IN THE FUR OF THE HEAT+   98 2
    SHE GAVE ON THE OPEN HEATHER   202 13

HEAVE
    I WISH THE ELDER-TREES IN FLOWER COULD SUDDENLY HEAVE A+   159 23
    I AM HERE MYSELF AS THOUGH THIS HEAVE OF EFFORT   218 13
    AND HEAVE IT OFF AMONG THE STARS INTO THE INVISIBLE   272 24
    THE FIRST DAY TO HEAVE YOUR FEET LITTLE BY LITTLE FROM +   352 3
    WHILE LIFE WAS A HEAVE OF MATTER HALF INANIMATE   372 10
    LET THE SEA HEAVE NO MORE IN SOUND   698 10
    THEY LIE ON THE SHORE AND HEAVE   827 7

HEAVED
    WITHIN THE IMMENSE AND TOILSOME LIFE-TIME HEAVED   195 29
    SO WHILE THE OTHER ONE HEAVED HER SIDES   492 5

HEAVEN
    THANK HEAVEN FOR A PEACEFUL HOUSE   45 31
    STARS ARE NOT SAFE IN HEAVEN   49 15
    SHALL SEE AN IMAGE OF HEAVEN OR OF EARTH   59 15
    OH YOU WHO FLASH YOUR ARMS LIKE ROCKETS TO HEAVEN   73 10
    AND NAKEDLY NOTHING 'TWIXT WORLD AND HEAVEN TWO CREATUR+   98 4
    AND THE SOUND OF HER GENTLY RUSTLING IN HEAVEN LIKE A   134 18
    OF CRYSTAL HEAVEN FALLS ONE FULL BLACK DROP   147 26
    YOUR FOUNTAINS AS HEAVEN DRINKS FROM OUT THEIR COURSE   153 30
    WILL SOUND IN HEAVEN BEFORE IT IS UNDONE   154 17
    WILL FLOURISH ITS BRANCHES IN HEAVEN WHEN WE   172 16
    OF LAMBENT HEAVEN A PLEDGING-CUP   177 10
    BY HEAVEN AND EARTH AND HELLISH STREAM   177 18
    PLUNDERED FROM HEAVEN   196 15
    PLUNDER FROM HEAVEN   196 17
    DIVIDING EARTH AND HEAVEN   200 7
    LIGHTNING FALLS FROM HEAVEN   208 31
    DAY AND MAKE MAGIC IN HEAVEN   209 30
    IS HEAVEN OF OUR OWN SHEER WITH REPUDIATION   210 18
    IN HEAVEN NOW THAT THE DARKNESS   226 15
    UPRIGHT TOWARDS HEAVEN IS BURNING OFF TO YOU   233 15
    OUR HEAVEN AS A MATTER OF FACT   265 16
    IMMORTALITY THE HEAVEN IS ONLY A PROJECTION OF THIS STR+   265 17
    THE SEED OF HEAVEN   268 21
    ON THE FLOOR OF HEAVEN   269 8
    HEAVEN KNOWS HOW IT CAME TO PASS   279 6
    OPENLY PLEDGING HEAVEN   283 7
    TO THE ENTABLATURE OF CLOUDED HEAVEN   287 19
    HEAVEN   287 29
    SEE IF I DON'T MOVE UNDER A DARK AND NUDE VAST HEAVEN   289 19

HEAVEN
    ITS CAGE-RIBS IN THE SOCIAL HEAVEN BENEFICENT   290 23
    AND WATCH IT PUTTING FORTH EACH TIME TO HEAVEN   299 24
    EACH TIME STRAIGHT TO HEAVEN   299 25
    FLYING NOT DOWN FROM HEAVEN BUT STORMING UP   304 17
    IN HEAVEN IN BLUE BLUE HEAVEN   307 5
    KNOTTED IN HEAVEN UPON THE FINE LIGHT   307 9
    HEAVEN THE WHITE GOD   307 18
    WHEN THEY FELT THEIR FOREHEADS BARE NAKED TO HEAVEN THE+   310 5
    WHEN THEY FELT THE LIGHT OF HEAVEN BRANDISHING LIKE A K+   310 7
    WHEN THEY CAME OUT FACE-REVEALED UNDER HEAVEN FROM   310 11
    AND ENJOYING THE SENSATION OF HEAVEN AND RIGHTEOUSNESS +   324 32
    NOW THAT IT IS A WEAPON OF HEAVEN   325 2
    OF HEAVEN   329 5
    TOES AND THE DOME OF HIS HOUSE IS HIS HEAVEN THEREFORE +   348 15
    DARK AS YOU ARE ON YOUR DARK SIDE EAGLE OF HEAVEN   374 31
    EVEN THE SUN IN HEAVEN CAN BE CURBED AND CHASTENED AT L+   374 32
    A MIRACLE IN HEAVEN   391 21
    HE SAYS NO YOU MUST GO TO HEAVEN AND EAT THE MOST   442 18
    BETWEEN HEEDLESS EARTH AND HEAVEN   443 14
    IT WAS LIKE BEING IN HEAVEN WHICH I AM SURE HAS A WHITE   444 3
    DOWN THE ABANDONED HEAVEN   455 13
    BRINGS A FRESH FRAGRANCE OF HEAVEN TO OUR SENSES   467 10
    AND A SUN IN HEAVEN   513 15
    THE SKY-BLUE WALLS OF OUR UNVENTILATED HEAVEN   515 5
    AND SAYS HE'S IN HEAVEN   515 10
    WE CLIMBED THE STEEP ASCENT TO HEAVEN   554 1
    WINDS OF HEAVEN FAN THE LEAVES OF THE TREE LIKE FLAMES +   615 4
    BUT WINDS OF HEAVEN ARE MILLS OF GOD TO THE FALLEN LEAV+   615 5
    IT IS THEIR HEAVEN AND THEIR DOOM   643 7
    TURNING THE BLUE WHEELS OF YOUR OWN HEAVEN   643 21
    THEY ARE AFRAID OF CLIMBING DOWN FROM THIS IDIOTIC TIN+   667 19
    WHILE NOTHING COMES FROM THE OPEN HEAVEN FROM EARTH FRO+   675 20
    GREAT HEAVEN OF WHALES IN THE WATERS OLD HIERARCHIES   694 28
    FOR THE SUN IS DEAD AND ALL THAT IS IN HEAVEN   702 23
    AND HELL AND HEAVEN ARE THE SCALES OF THE BALANCE OF LI+   710 21
    EVEN AS HEAVEN IS THE HOME OF SOULS LOST IN LIGHT   711 16
    THEY WANDER THEIR STRANGE AND DIFFERENT WAYS IN HEAVEN   713 22
    AH HEAVEN SEND   748 13
    THOU OUR MAIDEN THOU WHO DWELLEST IN HEAVEN   753 1
    THOU DOOR INTO HEAVEN SISTER   753 13
    IN HEAVEN HAS BEGUN   758 14
    THUNDERS IN HEAVEN TILL THE BRAVE WORLDS REEL   773 8
    DO YOU SEE THE GOLD SUN FLUTTERING BUOYANTLY IN HEAVEN   782 29
    THE GOLD SUN SHINES IN HEAVEN ONLY BECAUSE HE'S ALLOWED   783 1
    SENT OUT THE SUN SO THAT SOMETHING SHOULD FLUTTER IN HE+   783 4
    TO THE POOL OF PEACE AND FORGETTING IN HEAVEN   798 27
    FROM HEAVEN PAST THE SLEEPING SONS OF GOD   801 5
    WHICH OPENS EARTH AND HEAVEN TO LOVE'S FUGITIVE GLOWING   854 14
    SHALL SING OF HEAVEN ACHIEVED WHERE EVERY BRIGHT   872 15
    AND THAT WHITE SCUD OF HEAVEN   882 17

HEAVENLY
    AND HEAVENLY   444 8
    HEAVENLY MANSION AND LAST   695 21
    MOON O MOON GREAT LADY OF THE HEAVENLY FEW   695 24

HEAVENLY HOST
    THE ANGELS ARE GONE ALL THE HEAVENLY HOST   823 18

HEAVENS
    THE HEAVENS ARE NOT SHAKEN YOU SAY LOVE   49 11
    ACROSS THE HEAVENS WHEN THE STORM LEAPS HIGHER   89 23
    OF THE NIGHTLY HEAVENS OVERHEAD LIKE AN IMMENSE OPEN EYE   97 14
    AND ALL THE HEAVENS ARE WANDERING IN DISARRAY   115 21
    TOO HEAVILY BURDENED TO MOUNT THE HEAVENS SO   132 4
    RAIN FROM THE SHOWERY HEAVENS AND BRIGHT BLUE CROPS   136 12
    SLOPES ROUND THE HEAVENS IN ONE SMOOTH CURVE   172 19
    THROATS TO THE HEAVENS INCLINE   177 16
    THE NAKED LIGHTNINGS IN THE HEAVENS DITHER   209 4
    I COULD CONVULSE THE HEAVENS WITH MY HORROR   213 11
    THE HEAVENS LIKE SPECKS OF DUST THAT ARE FLOATING ASUND+   223 3
    OH AND I WISH THE HIGH AND SUPER-GOTHIC HEAVENS WOULD   287 22
    THE HEAVENS ABOVE THAT WE YEARN TO AND ASPIRE TO   287 24
    YOUR PARTICULAR HEAVENS   289 14
    HEAVENS WHERE THEY BELONG THE APOCALYPTIC BEASTS FOR WI+   319 2
    LIFE HAS ITS CHANGES BUT WHEN THE HEAVENS ARE EMPTY EMP+   319 8
    THE HEAVENS ARE THE NETHER MILL-STONE AND OUR HEAVY EAR+   614 19
    THE WHOLE GREAT HEAVENS HAVE SHIFTED OVER AND SLOWLY PU+   616 23
    AND THEN THE HEAVENS CACKLE WITH UNCOUTH SOUNDS   647 16
    HOLD THE STARS STILL LEST WE HEAR THE HEAVENS DIMLY RIN+   698 11
    OH DO NOT TELL ME THE HEAVENS AS WELL ARE A WHEEL   713 11
    BUT ONWARDS ONWARDS FOR THE HEAVENS ARE WANDERING   713 19
    TOO HEAVILY BURDENED TO MOUNT THE HEAVENS SO   *937 31

HEAVEN'S
    ACROSS THE SPACE ON THE CAT IN HEAVEN'S HOSTILE EMINENCE   97 22
    SOUNDLESSLY MOVING IN HEAVEN'S OTHER DIRECTION   161 23
    OUT OF THE HELL-QUEEN'S CUP THE HEAVEN'S PALE WINE   177 13
    IN HEAVEN'S FIELDS SET   268 18
    HEAVEN'S MUFFLED FLOOR   268 26
    FROM HEAVEN'S WOLFISH WANDERING ELECTRICITY THAT PROWLS   301 6
    THAT MY HEART WHICH LIKE A LARK AT HEAVEN'S GATE SINGIN+   322 30

HEAVES
    LIFT MY ARMS THE HILL BURSTS AND HEAVES UNDER THEIR SPU+   33 9
    THE RED RANGE HEAVES IN SLOW MAGNETIC REPLY   66 16
    THE RED RANGE HEAVES AND COMPULSORY SWAYS AH SEE IN THE+   66 17
    MOVE MY ARMS THE HILL BURSTS AND HEAVES UNDER THEIR SPU+   *891 10

HEAVIER
    HEAVIER THAN MINE YET LIKE LEVERETS CAUGHT IN STEEL   128 7
    HEAVIER   345 7
    THE HOT WILD CORE OF THE EARTH HEAVIER THAN WE CAN EVEN   480 8
    PIVOTAL CORE OF THE SOUL HEAVIER THAN IRON   480 10
    HEAVIER AND HOTTER THAN ANYTHING KNOWN   480 12
    A WEIGHT COMES OVER ME HEAVIER THAN LEADEN LININGS OF   629 18
    CENTRAL PRIMORDIAL FIRE OF THE SOUL HEAVIER THAN IRON   *951 24

HEAVIER
  SO PONDEROUSLY CENTRAL HEAVIER AND HOTTER THAN ANYTHING+   *951 25
  CENTRAL PRIMORDIAL FIRE OF THE SOUL HEAVIER THAN IRON   *952 1

HEAVILY
  HER SOFT WHITE LEGS HANGING HEAVILY OVER MY ARM   73 25
  NOW WET WITH TEARS AND PAIN HANGS HEAVILY   74 2
  EVEN HER FLOATING HAIR SINKS HEAVILY   74 3
  TOO HEAVILY BURDENED TO MOUNT THE HEAVENS SO   132 4
  WOULD FALL AND DARKNESS WOULD COME HURLING HEAVILY DOWN   205 10
  INSIDE ME AND OUT HEAVILY DARK   205 21
  THE DEAD TREAD HEAVILY THROUGH THE MUDDY AIR   704 8
  HEAVILY STEPPING WEARY ON OUR HEARTS   704 10
  HE SHOUTED RAN HEAVILY AFTER THEM   735 8
  AND THE OLD DARK-FACED MEN CAME OUT HEAVILY WITH A   778 35
  HAS BROUGHT DOWN A RIPE FRUIT HEAVILY TO HER FEET   864 14
  HER SOFT WHITE LEGS HANGING HEAVILY OVER MY ARM   *913 17
  TOO HEAVILY BURDENED TO MOUNT THE HEAVENS SO   *937 31

HEAVINESS
  ARE A HEAVINESS AND A WEARINESS   74 6
  BROKEN IN HEAVINESS   345 5
  SPINNING WITH THE HEAVINESS OF BALANCE   480 16
  GET RID OF THEIR HEAVINESS   792 1
  ARE A HEAVINESS AND A WEARINESS   *913 27
  HEAVY WITH THE HEAVINESS OF BALANCE   *951 29

HEAVING
  HEAVING AND PILING A ROUND WHITE DOME   50 5
  AND LIKE A LAUGHTER LEADS ME ONWARD HEAVING   66 1
  HEAVING   66 2
  HALF-WAY DOWN ITS HEAVING SIDES   144 5
  WITH VIOLENT ACHINGS HEAVING TO BURST THE SLEEP THAT IS+   149 23
  TO WHERE A MAN IN A HEAVING BOAT   201 19
  HERE I AM ALL MYSELF NO ROSE-BUSH HEAVING   218 9
  BLOOD OF A HEAVING WOMAN WHO HOLDS ME   *892 10

HEAVY
  THE HUM OF HIS HEAVY STAGGERING WINGS   46 18
  WHERE ASH ON THE DYING COALS GROWS SWIFTLY LIKE HEAVY   47 6
  FALLS AGAIN AND AGAIN ON MY HEART WITH A HEAVY REPROACH   63 3
  HANGS NUMB AND HEAVY FROM A BENDING FLOWER   73 21
  HEAVY TO REAR EVEN HEAVY TO UPREAR   67 27
  IS HEAVY AND MY HEART BEATS SLOWLY LABORIOUSLY   95 2
  POURED A HEAVY FLAME   118 3
  LIKE HEAVY BIRDS AT REST THERE SOFTLY STIRRED   123 10
  LIKE HEAVY BIRDS FROM THE MORNING STUBBLE TO SETTLE   128 11
  AND A HEAVY WOMAN SLEEPING STILL KEEPING   145 10
  ARE HEAVY WITH DEW   178 2
  PLAITING A HEAVY AUBURN BRAID   178 20
  WITH A HEAVY CHILD AT HER BREAST   200 2
  BUT HEAVY SEALING DARKNESS SILENCE ALL IMMOVABLE   205 14
  HEAVY AS A STONE PASSIVE   240 29
  THIS ROLLING DROPPING HEAVY GLOBULE   279 12
  WHY SO VELVETY WHY SO VOLUPTUOUS HEAVY   279 14
  IT IS LIKE THE AGONISED PERVERSENESS OF A CHILD HEAVY W+   287 2
  SOBERNESS SOBRIETY WITH HEAVY EYES PROPPED OPEN   287 4
  EVEN WINGS HEAVY   345 22
  OR IF IT HAPPEN TO SHOW AT HER POINTED HEAVY TAIL   361 20
  AND YOU GREAT BIRD SUN-STARER HEAVY BLACK BEAK   374 34
  AND HIS HEAD GONE HEAVY WITH THE KNOWLEDGE OF DESIRE   378 14
  HEAVY WITH A RANCID CARGO THROUGH THE LESSER SHIPS   380 19
  WHO CAN UNSEAT HER LIKE A LIQUID DROP THAT IS HEAVY AND   392 28
  EARTH'S DEEP HEAVY CENTRE   394 26
  HEAVY AND SWAYING LIKE A WHALE RECOVERING   428 12
  BUT THEY BUBBLE UNDER THE HEAVY WALL   461 27
  THEY BUBBLE UNDER THE HEAVY WALL   462 1
  YOU HEAR THE STERTOROUS SELF-RIGHTEOUS HEAVY   528 19
  HAS THE SHELL GROWN TOO HEAVY FOR THE TORTOISE   558 17
  IS THE FRAME OF THINGS TOO HEAVY   558 19
  THE HEAVENS ARE THE NETHER MILL-STONE AND OUR HEAVY EAR+   614 19
  THE UPPER DARKNESS IS HEAVY AS THE LOWER   719 22
  AND HE WINGS HIS HEAVY THIGH   733 15
  AND AGAIN ROLLING IN HIS HEAVY HIGH BOOTS   734 12
  WAS WET WITH SWEAT AND HIS MOVEMENTS STRONG AND HEAVY   734 22
  HE LOOKED AT ME AND HIS HEAVY BROWS CAME OVER   735 1
  SWUNG STRONG AND HEAVY TO SADDLE AGAIN   735 13
  DESTROY AT LAST THE HEAVY BOOKS OF STONE   737 25
  RAINS HEAVY TO ME   748 29
  A SLOW HEAVY PATTER OF LESSENING VIBRATION   767 20
  THOUGH THEIR SHOULD HAVE BEEN GROWING HEAVY FOR CENTURI+   778 37
  HE SAW THE HEARTS OF THEM ALL THAT WERE BLACK AND HEAVY+   790 14
  MY SOUL IS HEAVY WITH SUNSHINE AND STEEPED WITH STRENGTH   803 8
  BUT BY THE HEAVY DRIFT OF HIS UNPERVERTED INSTINCTS   838 17
  THE FRAME OF THINGS HAS GROWN SO HEAVY IT'S JUST TOO HE+   842 29
  AND DEEPER STILL THE UNKNOWN FIRE UNKNOWN AND HEAVY HEA+   844 3
  HEAVY NODDING CLUSTERS OF CRIMSON RED   855 10
  HEAVY HANGING CLUSTERS OF CRIMSON RED   855 18
  HEAVY WITH DROPS OF THE FIRST CRUEL RAIN   863 15
  SNOW AND THE SILENCE OF SNOW HEAVY ON THE ROUSING DAY   865 11
  WHAT IS THE HEAVY HOT HAND   869 7
  THAT CARRIES A HEAVY RICH LIQUOR   869 24
  ALWAYS BEFORE YOU GO THE HEAVY BLUE   875 24
  NOR EVE FOR YOUR HEAVY ANGUISH OF EMBRACE   876 17
  MY LIMBS ARE NUMB AND HEAVY AND MY HEART   879 19
  THE HEAVY PURPLE PERFUMED BUNCH   880 24
  AND WHEN I SEE THE HEAVY RED FLEECE   883 1
  RED ON MY MEMORY HEAVY WITH OUR OWN BLOOD   885 3
  IS HEAVY IS CLOGGED AND HEAVY WITH WASTED ASH   *897 17
  MY HAND IS HEAVY AND HELPLESS SINCE WIELDING THE LASH   *897 19
  HANGS NUMB AND HEAVY FROM THE BENDING FLOWER   *913 13
  THEY SIGH JUST ONCE ROUND OUR FEET AND ARE STILL HEAVY +   *917 11
  WILL YOU LOOSE THE HEAVY WEARY BUD   *931 26
  LIKE A HEAVY BIRD DISTURBED AND HER SHOULDERS STIRRED   *934 16
  AND GREATER HEAT INTO FIRE MORE HEAVY AND HOTTER THAN A+   *951 21
  HEAVY WITH THE HEAVINESS OF BALANCE   *951 29
  BLOWN FLAT INTO POINTS BY THE HEAVY WHITE DRAUGHT OF TH+   *956 5

HEAVY-BOTTOMED
  MUSHROOM-FACED HEAVY-BOTTOMED   765 18

HEAVY-BREASTED
  ONE DAY A HEAVY-BREASTED JUNE-HOT WOMAN   91 8

HEAVY-FOLDED
  SHAKEN SOFTLY FROM THE HEAVY-FOLDED SKIRTS OF NIGHT   858 14

HEAVY-INTENSE
  PLEASURE SO HEAVY-INTENSE IT HURT TOO MUCH   875 20

HEAVY-PETALLED
  AND OPEN IT SO THAT IT IS A GLITTERING ROSY MOIST HONIE+   282 3

HEDGE
  WHITE ONES AND BLUE ONES FROM UNDER THE ORCHARD HEDGE   58 9
  WE REST AT THE HEDGE MY HORSE AND I WHERE THE SCENT   858 18
  UNDER THE BEECHEN HEDGE   886 24

HEDGEROW
  SHOWED ME SOME OTHER LOVERS STEALING DOWN THE OTHER HED+   882 21

HE'D
  HE WED HE'D HA'E SUMMAT GOOD   77 28
  FOR I WOULD HAVE HAD TO KILL HIM IF HE'D BITTEN ME THE   347 6
  OR THAN IF HE'D JUST BUILT HIMSELF A NEST WITH A BATHRO+   496 8
  HE'D JUST LAUGH   528 13
  HE WED HE'D HA'E SUMMAT GOOD   *919 16

HEE
  HEE HEE EHEE EHOW EHAW OH OH OH-H-H   379 19
  HEE HEE EHEE EHOW-OW-OW-AW-AW-AW   380 4

HEED
  FOR THE MAN TO HEED LEST THE GIRL SHALL WEEP   41 11
  IS DELIVERED OUT AND PAYS NO HEED THOUGH WE MOAN   132 18

HEEDLESS
  BETWEEN HEEDLESS EARTH AND HEAVEN   443 14

HEEDLESSNESS
  IN HEEDLESSNESS   443 15

HEEL
  LEST HER HEEL OF ACHILLES SHOULD BE REVEALED   577 14
  HE WATERS THE HORSES DOES HE WASH HIS HEEL   733 33
  AND LOOKS AROUND AGAIN AT HIS HEEL THE BRIGHT SPUR   734 14
  THE SNAKE HAS KISSED MY HEEL   802 23

HEELS
  LIKE A CRINGING DOG AT HIS HEELS OFFEND HIM NOW   47 22
  FLOWERS CAME HELL-HOUNDS ON HER HEELS   308 6
  AND KICK OUR HEELS LIKE JOLLY ESCAPED ASSES   517 16
  I TOOK TO MY HEELS AND RAN   604 8
  AND PUTTING HIS STRENGTH IN YOUR HEELS AND ANKLES HIS F+ 801 24

HEFTY
  LEFT IN THE HEFTY BODIES   537 5

HE-GOAT
  AND HE-GOAT IS ANVIL TO HE-GOAT AND HAMMER TO HE-GOAT   381 32
  BUT HE-GOAT   383 13

HEIFER
  THE LITTLE RED HEIFER TONIGHT I LOOKED IN HER EYES   38 6
  THE WILD YOUNG HEIFER GLANCING DISTRAUGHT   64 7
  I REMEMBER THE HEIFER IN HER HEAT BLORTING AND BLORTING   366 6
  MY LITTLE RED HEIFER GO AND LOOK AT HER EYES   *892 22

HEIFERS
  CHEW ALSO YOUNG HEIFERS YOUR JUICIER CUDS   814 21

HEIGHT
  THE NEW MOON IN COOL HEIGHT ABOVE THE BLUSHES   467 9
  UP THERE AT THAT HEIGHT IN THE DIABLERETS   550 30
  GRASS IN BLOSSOM BLOSSOMING GRASS RISEN TO ITS HEIGHT A+ 587 12

HEIGHTS
  TO WALK THE LONELY DUSKY HEIGHTS   63 31
  RUNG OF THEIR LIFE-LADDERS' FRAGILE HEIGHTS   854 3

HEIRLOOM
  AND DAMP OLD WEB OF MISERY'S HEIRLOOM   141 11

HELD
  A TEAR WHICH I HAD HOPED THAT EVEN HELL HELD NOT AGAIN + 67 17
  SO I HELD MY HEART ALOFT   124 3
  AND I HELD THE CHOKED FLOWER-SERPENT IN ITS PANGS   125 16
  BUT HELD MY HAND AFLOAT TOWARDS THE SLIPS   125 21
  LOOKING EARNESTLY UNDER THE DARK UMBRELLAS HELD FAST   180 12
  HE HELD IN DELIGHT   202 20
  HELD STILL BENEATH THE SUNSHINE   204 18
  THE SKY WAS GREEN WINE HELD UP IN THE SUN   216 14
  WITH HIS HEAD HELD HIGH-SERENE AGAINST THE SKY   221 11
  HER PROUD HEAD HELD IN ITS BLACK SILK SCARF   228 14
  YOU ARE HELD BACK BY MY BEING IN THE SAME WORLD WITH YOU 235 31
  THAT ARE HELD IN STORE   238 6
  IN LONDON I SHOULD HAVE HELD MYSELF   269 15
  WAS MOIST AND COLD THE SUN IN HIM DARTED UNEASY HELD DO+ 348 8
  ALL HELD IN LEASH   459 28
  AND ITS PLUMES LOOK LIKE GREEN CUPS HELD UP TO THE SUN + 498 22
  FOR THE REST NO I SHOULD SAY LIFE HELD VERY FEW   533 2
  AND THAT HELD HER SPELLBOUND FOR TWO SECONDS   604 22
  THEN ALL THE ELECTRONS HELD THEIR BREATH   682 27
  KISSES OF FOUR GREAT LORDS BEAUTIFUL AS THEY HELD ME TO+ 695 29
  AND WE WALKED DARK SO HE HELD HIS ARM CLOSE ROUND ME   732 15
  WHICH ELSE WERE A SILENT GRASP THAT HELD THE SKIES   773 9

HELD
  HELD A MEETING BEHIND CLOSED DOORS   777 27
  AND HELD HIM WHILE JESUS PASSED   786 24
  HE PUT UP HIS HAND AND HELD BACK THE SUN WITH HIS SHADOW   790 2
  LOW NAKED CEILING OF THE NIGHT-SKY HELD   876 12
  AND AH I HELD MY HEART ALOFT   *936 9
  BUT HELD MY HAND AFLOAT STILL TOWARDS THE SLIPS   *936 20
  WITH MY HEAD HELD HIGH-SERENE AGAINST THE SKY   *944 24

HELEN
  YOU HELEN WHO SEE THE STARS   86 1
  HELEN YOU LET MY KISSES STEAM   86 5
  AND THIS HELEN BESIDE ME I AM BLANK BEING NOTHING I BEA+   97 12
  I IN THE FUR OF THE WORLD ALONE BUT THIS HELEN CLOSE BY   98 6
  SO HELEN WHEN ANOTHER NIGHT   117 11
  HELEN HAD I KNOWN YESTERDAY   117 25
  I SHOULD HAVE HATED YOU HELEN   117 33
  I CANNOT BUT CLEAVE TO YOU HELEN   118 9
  AND BECOMES AT LAST HELEN OR NINON ANY LOVELY AND GENER+   691 18

HELIOS
  BY THE GREAT SEVEN BY HELIOS THE BRIGHTEST   702 8

HELIOTROPE
  YOU CAN'T IMAGINE THE HOLY GHOST SNIFFING AT CHERRY-PIE+   690 25

HELL
  A TEAR WHICH I HAD HOPED THAT EVEN HELL HELD NOT AGAIN +   67 17
  OTHER FOLKS IN HELL   83 29
  WHAT IS THERE GONE AGAINST ME WHY AM I IN HELL   141 26
  OF HELL TO WAKE AND BE FREE   177 22
  NIGHT OR DEATH OR HELL   258 13
  GOING DOWN THE STRANGE LANES OF HELL MORE AND MORE   281 4
  THE DISTILLED ESSENCE OF HELL   281 13
  ORPHEUS AND THE WINDING LEAF-CLOGGED SILENT LANES OF HE+   281 16
  UP OUT OF HELL   307 20
  HELL RISEN IN PURSUIT OF HER ROYAL SUMPTUOUS   308 15
  HELL OPENING   308 18
  HELL REARING ITS HUSBAND-SPLENDID SERPENT HEADS   308 20
  IN HELL   309 3
  HELL IS UP   309 13
  HELL ON EARTH AND DIS WITHIN THE DEPTHS   309 14
  AND JUST FILLS YOU WITH HELL   565 30
  RENASCENCE ALL SENT TO HELL   633 4
  WHICH TURNS ON AND ON THE SAME AND IS HELL ON EARTH   662 24
  THEN I WILL FALL AND PLANT THE PATHS TO HELL   710 15
  AND PUT SCARLET BUDS IN THEIR HAIR ON THE WAY TO HELL   710 19
  AND HELL AND HEAVEN ARE THE SCALES OF THE BALANCE OF LI+   710 21
  NOT EVEN THE HOME OF DEMONIACAL HELL   711 14
  HELL IS THE HOME OF SOULS LOST IN DARKNESS   711 15
  TO THE SCARLET AND PURPLE FLOWERS AT THE DOORS OF HELL   711 20
  THE KIND OF HELL THAT IS REAL GREY AND AWFUL   714 1
  THE KIND OF HELL GREY DANTE NEVER SAW   714 3
  AND A DRAUGHT OF THEE IS STRENGTH TO A SOUL IN HELL   759 13
  THEN GO TO HELL   773 11
  GO TO HELL   773 13
  OF YOU MANGY HOUND GO TO HELL   774 18
  OR IN HELL OVERHEATS THEM   828 12
  BURNING LIKE DIVES IN HELL TO HER   874 20
  HITHER HAS TAKEN AWAY TO THAT HELL   887 7

HELLEBORE
  SCYLLAS AND YELLOW-HAIRED HELLEBORE JONQUILS DIM ANEMON+   270 7

HELL-GLAMOROUS
  HELL-GLAMOROUS AND PURPLE HUSBAND-TYRANNY   308 31

HELL-HOUNDS
  FLOWERS CAME HELL-HOUNDS ON HER HEELS   308 6

HELLISH
  BY HEAVEN AND EARTH AND HELLISH STREAM   177 18
  I SAY WONDERFUL ARE THE HELLISH EXPERIENCES   280 24
  RIBBED HELLISH FLOWERS ERECT WITH THEIR BLAZE OF DARKNE+   *956 4

HELLISHLY
  ARE MUCH MORE HELLISHLY PEACELESS THAN A LITTLE STRAIGH+   497 7

HELLO
  WITH HELLO BOY WHAT ABOUT SIN   493 12
  I SAY TO MYSELF HELLO I'M NOT WELL MY VITALITY IS LOW   498 8

HELL-PURPLE
  HELL-PURPLE TO GET AT HER   308 21

HELL-QUEEN'S
  OUT OF THE HELL-QUEEN'S CUP THE HEAVEN'S PALE WINE   177 13

HELL-QUEEN
  HUSBAND-SNARED HELL-QUEEN   309 21

HELLS
  LITTLE HELLS OF COLOUR CAVES OF DARKNESS   308 14

HELL'S
  HELL'S HUSBAND-BLOSSOMS   308 25

HE'LL
  OH AY HE'LL COME AN TELL THEE HIS-SEN   76 25
  CAN BE KEPT DOWN BUT HE'LL BURST LIKE A POLYP INTO   305 9
  IF HE EARNS HIS LIFE HE'LL BE LOVELY   443 11
  HENCEFORTH HE'LL KEEP CLEAR OF HER TOASTING-FORK   577 22
  A NICE ONE I LIKE IT HE'LL THINK IT'S A TALL ORDER   733 29
  OH AY HE'LL BE COMIN' TO TELL THEE HIS-SEN   *918 17

HELMET
  TA'E OFF THY P'LICEMAN'S HELMET   82 19
  IN THE STILLNESS HE TOOK OFF HIS HELMET TO KISS ME   732 16
  IT SNOWED AND HIS HELMET WAS LOST HE FORGOT ME HE DID N+   732 17
  HIS HELMET OFF AND WIPES HIS HAIR TRYING   733 21
  TA'E OFF THY P'LICE-MAN'S HELMET   *924 23

HELMETS
  ALL THE DARK-FEATHERED HELMETS LIKE LITTLE GREEN   221 17
  HELMETS AS HIS HE LOST IN THE WOOD THAT NIGHT   732 12
  ALL THEIR DARK-FEATHERED HELMETS LIKE LITTLE GREEN   *945 3

HELP
  OF KISSES OH HELP ME GOD HERE AT THE SOURCE   153 28
  BUT IT DOES NOT ALTER ME NOR HELP ME   205 17
  NEITHER LIFE NOR DEATH COULD HELP   214 30
  WITHOUT A SERVANT'S HELP SO HE BE NOT STRICKEN IN YEARS   277 11
  THEY SAY YOU CAN'T HELP IT   333 20
  DON'T HELP THEM   440 22
  AND THEY CAN'T HELP WANTING TO SPITE IT ON THEM   502 25
  I CANNOT HELP BUT BE ALONE   507 16
  HE CAN'T HELP BEING A SLAVE A WAGE-SLAVE   524 11
  ONE CANNOT NOW HELP THINKING   536 6
  POOR THINGS BUT WE CAN'T HELP THAT CAN WE   548 27
  TIME CAN HELP   620 16
  HELP HELP THEY WANT TO BURN MY PICTURES   633 7
  HELP HELP I AM CALLING IN ENGLISH   633 12
  HELP OH HELP THEY WANT TO BURN MY PICTURES   634 6
  AND HELP THEM TO BUILD THEIR LITTLE SHIP OF DEATH   721 19
  TO HELP HIM LIFT THE WELTERING DARKNESS TURN   872 3

HELPED
  THE FROGS HELPED ALSO WHIRRING AWAY   207 14
  FOR AFTER ALL HE HELPED TO SMASH A LOT OF OLD ROMAN LIES   497 3
  HELPED TO KILL HIM IN THE FLESH   538 12
  HELPED TO BRING   *910 8

HELPING
  FOR HELPING WITH LADY C   550 20
  BREATHING ON HIS SMALL FRAIL SAIL AND HELPING HIM ON   723 23

HELPLESS
  LIKE SOFT HOT ASHES ON MY HELPLESS CLAY   87 13
  I MUST GO BUT MY SOUL LIES HELPLESS   102 23
  MEET MINE I OPENED HER HELPLESS EYES TO CONSULT   125 27
  UPON THEM AND MOVING THEM HELPLESS MECHANIC THEIR WILL   149 15
  DELIVERED HELPLESS AND AMAZED   262 19
  THEN THE DUMB ACHING BITTER HELPLESS NEED   263 20
  THEY ARE SO GREEDY YET SO HELPLESS IF NOT WORKED FOR   441 31
  LEAVING THIS NAKED PALLID HELPLESS VULNERABLE REMAINS   767 26
  HELPLESS ANOTHER DAY HAS FLOWN TOO HIGH   855 24
  AGAINST MY HELPLESS SIGHT   862 21
  MY HAND IS HEAVY AND HELPLESS SINCE WIELDING THE LASH   *897 19
  TO MINE I OPENED HER HELPLESS EYES TO CONSULT   *936 26

HELPLESSLY
  AM HELPLESSLY BOUND   40 10
  HELPLESSLY   60 8

HELPLESSNESS
  IN THE EXCRUCIATING TORMENT OF HOPELESSNESS HELPLESSNESS   627 24

HELPMATE
  WITHOUT PLAYMATE OR HELPMATE HAVING NO ONE TO CHERISH   197 8

HEMISPHERE
  IN THE NORTHERN HEMISPHERE   392 14

HEMMING
  THE BUBBLE HEMMING THIS EMPTY EXISTENCE WITH LIGHTS   193 22

HEN
  O THE WET WALK OF MY BROWN HEN THROUGH THE STACKYARD   119 9
  ALL ROUND THE YEAR IT IS CLUCK MY BROWN HEN   119 15
  WHAT IS PEEPING FROM YOUR SKIRTS O MOTHER HEN   119 28
  THE HEN WILL NESTLE OVER HER CHICKENS   268 4
  OH THE WET WALK OF MY BROWN HEN THROUGH THE STACKYARD   *932 18
  ALL ROUND THE YARD IT IS CLUCK MY BROWN HEN   *932 24
  OH WHERE-OUT NOW HAS WANDERED THE GOLDEN HEN OF SUNSHINE   *933 21
  MY SIGHT BUT THEN WHO HAS STOLE THE BRIGHT WHITE HEN OF+   *933 23

HENCE
  HENCE HE BECAME A CURLY SHEEP-DOG WITH DANGEROUS PROPEN+   324 26
  AND HENCE SIX TIMES MORE SOLITARY   354 11
  HENCE JESUS RODE HIM IN THE TRIUMPHANT ENTRY   378 20
  HENCE HIS BEAUTIFUL EYES   378 21
  HENCE HIS PONDEROUS HEAD BROODING OVER DESIRE AND DOWNF+   378 22
  HENCE HE UNCOVERS HIS BIG ASS-TEETH AND HOWLS IN THAT A+   378 24
  HENCE THE BLACK CROSS ON HIS SHOULDERS   378 27
  AND HENCE IS A MESS   479 19
  HENCE THE RIDICULOUS WAY THEY RUSH IN WHERE ANGELS FEAR+   665 20
  STRENGTHEN PREPARE THEM FOR THE JOURNEY HENCE   740 18
  THE SUN IS GONE FROM MID-HEAVEN THE SOLDIERS ARE GONE F+   757 1

HENCEFORTH
  EITHER OF US ANY MORE HENCEFORTH WE CAN   91 5
  YET WAIT AWHILE FOR HENCEFORTH I WILL LOVE WHEN A BLOSS+   94 5
  AND HENCEFORTH I WILL NEVER USE   492 27
  HENCEFORTH HE'LL KEEP CLEAR OF HER TOASTING-FORK   577 22
  UNCHALLENGED INTACT UNABRIDGED HENCEFORTH A HOST   743 27
  BUT I WAS AFRAID HENCEFORTH   881 14

HENNA
  IN JAPANESE HENNA OR WHATEVER IT IS CHEAP AT THE PRICE   835 8

HIBISCUS-BREASTED
HIBISCUS-BREASTED ... 314 22

HIBISCUS-TREE
WHAT ROT TO SEE THE CABBAGE AND HIBISCUS-TREE ... 316 18

HICCUP
ALMOST AS EMPTY AS BELCHING OR HICCUP ... 681 7

HID
THAT THE BLACK NIGHT HID HER FROM ME BLOTTED OUT EVERY ... 62 4
I SAW HER HID IN THE SHADOW ... 122 2
SHE HID HER FACE SHE MURMURED BETWEEN HER LIPS ... 125 19
A GLINTING WEB QUICK HID IN THE GLOOM OF THE BROOK ... 161 7
BRITANNIA HID BEHIND HER SHIELD ... 577 13
AND HID THEIR FACES FOR VERY SHAME ... 579 14
TO GAOL TO BE HID FROM THE LIGHT OF DAY ... 579 16
THAT THE BLACK NIGHT HID HER FROM ME BLOTTED OUT EVERY + ... *912 12
SHE HID HER FACE SHE MURMURED BETWEEN HER LIPS ... *936 18

HIDDEN
IS HIDDEN IN THEIRS THEIR THRILLS ARE MINE ... 52 11
ASKS TO BE HIDDEN AND WISHES NOTHING TO TELL ... 64 13
DRIFTS DIMLY FORWARD EASILY HIDDEN ... 68 6
INTO THE HIDDEN ... 108 7
PUSHED GENTLY AWAY AND HIDDEN IN THE THICK OF HER HAIR ... 114 22
WHAT THEN IS THERE HIDDEN IN THE SKIRTS OF ALL THE BLOS+ ... 119 27
THE HIDDEN BODIES MATING EVERYWHERE ... 126 21
FINE THRILLS TO THE NEIGHBOUR STARS FINE HIDDEN BEAMS ... 127 7
HIDDEN HE WON'T COME FORTH ... 232 15
AND A HIDDEN VOICE LIKE WATER CLUCKING ... 427 3
IT IS A PERVERTED INSTINCT A HIDDEN THOUGHT ... 487 15
HIDDEN BLUE WITH THE BLUENESS OF ONE MORE DAY ... 815 9
WHILE THE SOFT CARESS OF HER HIDDEN LAUGHTER ... 868 10
DRIFTS DIMLY FORWARD EASILY HIDDEN ... *914 21
ON THE LONGEST JOURNEY OVER THE HIDDEN SEA ... *960 20

HIDE
HIDE YOUR QUAINTLY SCARLET BLUSHES ... 43 2
THE LITTLE GRAIN DRAWS DOWN THE EARTH TO HIDE ... 64 10
SO HERE I HIDE IN THE SHALIMAR ... 70 14
WHICH LIES ON THE KNEES OF THE NIGHT-TIME RUDDY AND MAK+ ... 88 21
THE SHROUDED MOTHER OF A NEW IDEA MEN HIDE THEIR FACES ... 91 26
FOR FLOWERS ARE TENDER FOLK AND ROOTS CAN ONLY HIDE ... 93 30
I SEE YOUR BLANCHED FACE AT MY BREAST AND HIDE ... 129 13
THE BLIND TO HIDE THE GARDEN WHERE THE MOON ... 129 16
WE DO NOT LOOK AT EACH OTHER WE HIDE ... 166 6
BUT WORN OUT THEY HIDE NO MORE THE WALLS THEY STAND BEF+ ... 174 22
AND HIS HANDS ARE AWKWARD AND WANT TO HIDE ... 228 3
IN THE NORTH TO HIDE WHERE THE TURTLES SING ... 580 6
LET HIM HIDE IT AWAY SO IT CAN GO ON BLOSSOMING ... 634 15
AND HIDE IN YOUR OWN WILD THEBAID ... 642 8
THE SHROUDED MOTHER OF A NEW IDEA MEN HIDE THEIR FACES ... *926 19
WITH THE LUSTY SOULS OF MY BOYS YET THEY HIDE THEIR FAC+ ... *926 23
MUST HIDE MY MOTHER'S PIANO LITTLE AND BROWN WITH THE B+ ... *940 2

HIDEOUS
MAKING HIDEOUS YOUR EYES ... 207 20
I MUST BE RECIPROCATING YOUR VACUOUS HIDEOUS PASSION ... 241 27
THOUSANDS AND THOUSANDS OF GAPING HIDEOUS FOUL DEAD ... 258 8
LIKE IRON IMPLEMENTS TWISTED HIDEOUS OUT OF THE EARTH ... 300 21
WORSE EVEN THAN THE HIDEOUS TERROR OF ME WITH MY HANDKE+ ... 344 23
IS HIDEOUS AND FEARFUL ... 475 7
SO HIDEOUS AND CORPSE-LIKE UTTERLY SUNLESS ... 526 14
SAID GROSS COARSE HIDEOUS AND I LIKE A SILLY ... 579 18
THE GREEK BEAUTIFUL ONES THE PHOENICIAN UGLY ONES THE A+ ... 671 16
AND WITH HIDEOUS SHRIEKS OF STEELY RAGE AND FRUSTRATION ... 676 3
NO COBRA NOR HYAENA NOR SCORPION NOR HIDEOUS WHITE ANT ... 701 13

HIDEOUSLY
WIERD RIGGING IN A STORM SHRIEKS HIDEOUSLY ... 36 12
AND SO HIDEOUSLY DANGEROUS TO BE AT THE MERCY ... 839 13

HIDES
POINTING MY EYES IN WRETCHED DEFIANCE WHERE LOVE HIDES + ... 63 25
REVEALED WHERE IT HIDES ... 144 6
AND IT IS HE WHO HIDES ... 231 30

HIDING
HIDING AND COVERING IN THE ETERNAL SLEEP ... 195 28
IF HE IS HIDING IN THE COVER ... 231 25
HIDING THEIR FIRE ... 465 22
IS NEITHER HIDING HIMSELF NOR PRESERVING HIMSELF NOR PR+ ... 523 9
SHE WEPT BITTERLY HIDING HER FACE IN HER KERCHIEF I SAI+ ... 749 16
ARE YOU LETTING ME GO AND HIDING YOUR FACE TO THE GROUND ... 871 32

HIE
GHOST-FLUX OF FACES THAT HIE ... 252 23
WITH A HIE HOP BELOW ... 564 18
HIE HIE FRUIT TOPPLES ... 817 1
LIKE SEALS IN SUNNY SUMMER THEY HIE ... 825 15
LIKE SEALS THAT HIE ... 826 2

HIERARCHIES
GREAT HEAVEN OF WHALES IN THE WATERS OLD HIERARCHIES ... 694 28

HIERARCHY
TO THE LESSER FRY IN THE HIERARCHY ... 681 4

HIGH
THAT SOMEBODY HAS SPUN SO HIGH ... 54 9
THE COOL HIGH MOON AT THEIR EASE WHILE THE DRONING CHUR+ ... 54 30
LIKE THE SOUGH OF A WIND THAT IS CAUGHT UP HIGH IN THE + ... 58 1
HIGH AND SMALLER GOES THE MOON SHE IS SMALL AND VERY FA+ ... 67 13
DRIVEN SO HIGH ... 71 8
HITHER AND THITHER ACROSS THE HIGH CRYSTALLINE FRAME ... 72 9
ELSEWHERE HALLS OF HIGH DISGRACES ... 95 31
AND DRINK MOST HIGH ... 96 28

HIGH
ON HIGH TO THE FUMING SKY OF NIGHT ... 105 2
THROWN LUSTILY OFF FROM OUR FULL-SAPPY HIGH ... 127 8
SUDDEN OUTSIDE THE HIGH WINDOW ONE CROW ... 147 21
SWORN TO A HIGH AND SPLENDID PURPOSELESSNESS ... 197 16
A BLOTCH OF PALLOR STIRS BENEATH THE HIGH ... 210 19
SO HIGH AND MIGHTY LOOK HOW THE HEADS ARE BORNE ... 221 7
AND SUNSHINE FILLS ONE HIGH VALLEY BED ... 224 12
THEN AMONG THE AVERTED PANSIES BENEATH THE HIGH ... 225 29
EXQUISITE HIGH ABOVE ... 252 6
OH AND I WISH THE HIGH AND SUPER-GOTHIC HEAVENS WOULD ... 287 22
FOREST OF PILLARS THAT HOLD UP THE DOME OF HIGH IDEAL ... 287 28
SEE IF I DON'T BRING YOU DOWN AND ALL YOUR HIGH OPINION ... 289 11
HIGH OVER THE MILD EFFULGENCE OF THE DOVE ... 328 7
LIKE A KING EAGLE BIRD OF THE MOST HIGH SWEEPING THE RO+ ... 329 4
WHAT DO YOU STAND ON SUCH HIGH LEGS FOR ... 332 3
IT IS YOUR SMALL HIGH HATFUL BUGLE IN MY EAR ... 333 17
AND CLEAVE IN A HIGH CORNER FOR A SECOND LIKE A CLOT AL+ ... 345 23
SUDDENLY HASTY RECKLESS ON HIGH TOES ... 354 6
NOT THE EAGLE SCREAMS WHEN THE SUN IS HIGH THE PEACOCK + ... 368 10
HIGH HIGH FLAMBEAUX SMOKING OF THE EAST ... 388 29
HIGH HIGH UP IN FLAKES SHIMMERING FLAKES OF BLUE FIRE ... 391 18
AND I I SIT ON THIS HIGH AMERICAN DESERT ... 410 27
THAT EVERY MAN WHETHER HIGH OR LOW ... 434 19
SWEEPS THE HIGH GOOSE ABOVE THE MISTS ... 437 24
WILL THE SINGING OF SWANS HIGH UP HIGH UP INVISIBLE ... 439 8
HIGH AND CLAWING WITH RAGE AT THE CLIFFS OF THE SOUL ... 454 9
AND THE SMALL HAWK HIGH UP TURNS ROUND ON THE SLOW PIVO+ ... 496 14
AS THE VULTURE THAT SCREAMS HIGH UP ALMOST INAUDIBLE ... 500 16
THEY HAVE HIGH BLOOD-PRESSURE AND ALMOST BURST ... 502 5
THINK HOW A PEACOCK IN A FOREST OF HIGH TREES ... 530 5
THEY LIE HIGH AND DRY ... 542 22
HIGH AND DRY ... 542 23
ROSE VERY HIGH FOR ME ... 551 26
BUT STILL I ROSE QUITE HIGH IN THE WORLD ... 552 3
TO JOIN THE FOLKS ON HIGH ... 554 10
BESIDE THE HIGH ROAD PAST THE DEATHLY DUST ... 605 24
AND THE CALLING OF THE OLD RED INDIAN HIGH ON THE PUEBL+ ... 623 16
IN ALL THE HIGH PLACES AND THEY ARE MASTERS OF INDUSTRY ... 637 19
BECAUSE THE LORD ALMIGHTY ROSE A BIT TOO HIGH ... 710 10
THE MOON IS HIGH I AM LITTLE ... 731 9
AND AGAIN ROLLING IN HIS HEAVY HIGH BOOTS ... 734 12
THE HIGH VIRGIN VALLEY ... 768 26
TO A VIRGIN VALLEY HIGH-UP ... 769 17
LIFTS HIM FANNING IN THE HIGH EMPYREAN ... 782 23
WHEAT FROM THE HIGH LANDS AND MAIZE ... 793 21
BACK AGAIN NOW ON HIGH ... 798 24
HIGH ... 820 13
THAT BASK AND WAKE OH HIGH AND DRY ... 824 19
HIGH AND DRY ... 824 20
HELPLESS ANOTHER DAY HAS FLOWN TOO HIGH ... 855 24
UP IN THE HIGH ... 860 25
THAT LIFT UP HIGH THEN DROP HIS STRANGE HARSH BREAST ... 879 1
MY TOP OF LIFE THAT BUDS ON HIGH ... *899 29
AMID THE HIGH WIND'S ENTERPRISE ... *899 30
MY TOP OF LIFE THAT BUDS ON HIGH ... *903 8
AMID THE HIGH WIND'S ENTERPRISE ... *903 9
WHILE THE STREET LAMP CENSERS SWINGING HIGH ... *916 19
WHEN THE TIDE WAS HIGH ... *917 5
DRIVEN SO HIGH ... *917 26
HANG HIGH SUSPENDED WITHOUTEN RESPITE ... *929 8
SO HIGH AND MIGHTY LOOK HOW ITS HEADS ARE BORNE ... *944 20

HIGH-BRED
AND AREN'T YOUR FEELINGS VIOLATED YOU HIGH-BRED LITTLE + ... 400 13

HIGHER
WHILE HIGHER THE DARTING GRASS-FLOWERS PASS ... 49 24
ACROSS THE HEAVENS WHEN THE STORM LEAPS HIGHER ... 89 23
SWIFTER AND HIGHER AND BRIGHTER OR THE YIELDING AND THE+ ... 680 6
A LITTLE HIGHER ... 720 2
TO A HIGHER PLACE THAT IS VIRGIN ... 769 16
TO PULL DOWN THE BOUGH THE LEAVES BROKE AND THE FRUIT S+ ... 864 10

HIGHEST
TO STAND ON THE HIGHEST PEAK ... 382 13
AND WHERE MY LITTLE LEAVES FLUTTER HIGHEST ... 499 8

HIGHLY
THE JOY I BOUGHT WAS NOT TOO HIGHLY PRICED ... 225 32
IT SHOWS AGAIN HOW HIGHLY DEVELOPED THE SOCIAL CONSCIEN+ ... 829 16
HOW HIGHLY AWARE WE ARE OF ONE ANOTHER SOCIALLY ... 829 17
YOU HIGHLY EVERY BLOOD-RED ROSE DISPLAY ... *941 7

HIGH-POWER
WITH OUR SHARP LITTLE EYES AND OUR HIGH-POWER MACHINES ... 543 20

HIGHROAD
MESSAGES OF TRUE-LOVE DOWN THE DUST OF THE HIGHROAD ... 65 18

HIGH-SERENE
WITH HIS HEAD HELD HIGH-SERENE AGAINST THE SKY ... 221 11
WITH MY HEAD HELD HIGH-SERENE AGAINST THE SKY ... *944 24

HIGH-SOARING
PROUD INTELLECT HIGH-SOARING MIND ... 329 3

HIGH-SPIRITED
SHE'S A MARV'LOUS DELICIOUS HIGH-SPIRITED FELLER ... 583 17

HILL
LIFT MY ARMS THE HILL BURSTS AND HEAVES UNDER THEIR SPU+ ... 33 9
THE HILL IS STEEP ON THE SNOW MY STEPS ARE SLOW ... 85 15
AS I STAND ON THIS HILL WITH THE WHITENING CAVE OF THE + ... 97 11
THEIR EYES AND LOOK AT THE GRAVE ON THE HILL IN WONDER ... 176 16
HAS SLEPT UNNOTICED ON A FORGOTTEN HILL ... 176 27
IT GOES OVER ME LIKE A SHADOW OVER A HILL ... 205 16
TILL THE HILL BURSTS ... 293 17

HILL (CONT.)

HILL
ON A GREEN HILL   306 27
AND UP THE HILL LIKE A RIVER IF YOU WATCH   383 29
THINKING HE WAS A LITTLE HILL AND SHE MURMURED SUCH   540 2
AND GOES SLOWLY DOWN THE HILL   687 14
PAUSES NEAR THE CREST OF THE HILL CLIMBING SLOWLY LIKE +   687 17
THE SUN HAS CLIMBED THE HILL THE DAY IS ON THE DOWNWARD+   803 5
WHAT LIES OVER THE NEXT DARK HILL   858 3
STRAYED DOWN THE HILL CRUSHING THE SILKEN MOSS   863 22
AS WE CROSSED THE MOW-FIELDS DOWN THE GLOWING HILL   884 28
MOVE MY ARMS THE HILL BURSTS AND HEAVES UNDER THEIR SPU+   *891 10
SHOULD CLIMB THE HILL AND PUT THE FLOWERS ASUNDER   *941 4

HILL-BROW
THE HILL-BROW AND LIE QUITE STILL TILL THE GREEN   35 14
LIGHT WENT OVER THE HILL-BROW SWIFTLY WITH THEIR TAILS   391 2

HILL-CREST
THEY MOUNT TO THE LAST HILL-CREST   200 4

HILL O' BEANS
AND THEN IF YOU AMOUNT TO A HILL O' BEANS   457 9

HILLS
OF THE DARK-GREEN HILLS NEW CALVES IN SHED PEEWITS TURN+   57 27
AND LITTERED LETTERING OF TREES AND HILLS AND HOUSES CL+   88 6
SPARKLE BENEATH LUMINOUS HILLS   162 7
YOU WOULD AMONG THE LAUGHING HILLS   178 5
YOU FROM THOSE STARTLED HILLS   178 16
BROWN HILLS SURROUNDING   340 23
I LIFT UP MINE EYES UNTO THE HILLS   660 20
CEASE TO LIFT UP ITS HILLS   688 3
FROM THE HILLS WHERE SNOW MUST HAVE FALLEN THE WIND IS +   696 16
OF THE HILLS AND THE HEARTS WITHIN US DITHER   757 16
ME AS A DARK BLUE WATER BETWEEN THE HILLS   874 28
WHICH CLOTHES OUR NAKEDNESS LIKE GRASS THE PLAINS AND T+   *951 8

HILLSIDE
AWAY ON THE HILLSIDE WAKES A STAR   857 25

HILL-SIDE
AND FLASHED UP THE HILL-SIDE   222 3
ALONE ON A HILL-SIDE IN THE NORTH HUMMING IN THE WIND   610 23

HILL'S
ON TOWARDS THE PINES AT THE HILL'S WHITE VERGE   85 8

HIND
THAT I AM THE HART AND YOU ARE THE GENTLE HIND   118 31
A POOR ROAN THING ITS HIND LEG TWITCHES   734 6

HINDER
WHO HINDER ME MAMMON GREAT SON OF A BITCH   584 8

HINDMOST
FOR OUR SOCIETY IS BASED ON GRAB AND DEVIL TAKE THE HIN+   829 24
AND DEVIL TAKE THE HINDMOST   829 28
DEVIL TAKE THE HINDMOST   837 28

HINDQUARTERS
HIS DIMINISHED DROOPING HINDQUARTERS   377 25

HINDU
A YARD OF INDIA MUSLIN IS ALIVE WITH HINDU LIFE   448 21

HINDUS
WHEN THE HINDUS WEAVE THIN WOOL INTO LONG-LONG LENGTHS   451 1

HINGES
THEY HAVE TAKEN THE GATES FROM THE HINGES   40 21

HINGLISH
ALL THE HINGLISH IS GENTLEMAN AN' LIDIES   434 27

HINT
NOT EVEN A HINT   562 20
WITH A HINT OF THE FROZEN BELLS OF THE SCYLLA FLOWER   708 29
HYAENAS ONLY HINT AT IT   712 26
SLEEP IS A HINT OF LOVELY OBLIVION   724 28

HINTED
LIVING WHERE LIFE WAS NEVER YET DREAMED OF NOR HINTED AT   258 32
THE ARABS WERE ONLY HALF RIGHT THOUGH THEY HINTED THE   378 28

HINTERLAND
AND WE WE ARE MOSTLY UNEXPLORED HINTERLAND   606 30

HINTING
AS IT COMES OVER THE MILK-BLUE SEA HINTING AT GOLD AND +   840 5

HIPS
LIKE A VOLCANO MY HIPS ARE MOVING   802 24
FROM THE HIPS A VIOLET   819 22
THREADING THE ROUND JOY OF HIS WHITE-FLANNELLED HIPS FU+   867 30
HIS FULL ROUND HIPS SUPPORTING HIM ABOVE HER   868 9

HIRED
AS IF SHE WERE A WORM OR A HIRED WHORE WHO BORED HIM   *948 17

HIS'N
DUNNA THEE TELL ME IT'S HIS'N MOTHER   76 23
DUNNA THEE TELL ME IT'S HIS'N MOTHER   *918 15

HISS
DROP THEIR LEAVES WITH A FAINT SHARP HISS OF CONTEMPT   54 25
LIFE IN THY MOUTH AND DIM BREATH'S HASTENING HISS   69 24
ACROSS THE HISS OF WONDERS AS THE ROCKET BURST   391 17
COME WITH A HISS OF WINGS   436 23

HISS
THEN DISAPPEARING BACK WITH A HISS   454 10
AND RESOUNDING AFTER WITH A LONG HISS OF INSISTENCE   622 22

HISSELF
THROW HISSELF IN THAT SINK   *923 20

HIS-SEN
OH AY HE'LL COME AN TELL THEE HIS-SEN   76 25
OH AY HE'LL BE COMIN' TO TELL THEE HIS-SEN   *918 17
WARMIN' HIS-SEN AT THE STOOL O' FIRE   *920 26

HISSES
NAY NEVER I PUT YOU AWAY YET EACH KISS HISSES   87 12
FROM THE PINE-TREE THAT TOWERS AND HISSES LIKE A PILLAR+   375 5
HISSES THROUGH THE FLOWERS THE TIMID NIGHT-AIRS BLOW   855 30

HISTORIANS
ANTHROPOLOGISTS HISTORIANS AND MEN OF LETTERS   780 8

HISTORIES
WHAT PLACE HAVE YOU IN MY HISTORIES   131 22

HISTORY
THE HISTORY OF THE COSMOS   682 1
IS THE HISTORY OF THE STRUGGLE OF BECOMING   682 2
AND THIS I HOLD IS THE TRUE HISTORY OF EVOLUTION   761 13

HIT
HIT HIM AND KILL HIM AND THROW HIM AWAY   346 7
I THINK IT DID NOT HIT HIM   351 12
THEN YOU WILL HIT THE FLAT-IRON BUILDING AND FLATTEN IT+   484 19
NIHIL WILL COME ALONG AND HIT YOU ON THE HEAD   531 12
WHICH ARE VERY LIKE TO HIT YOU ON THE HEAD AS YOU SIT   541 5
HE'S RESIGNED AND WHEN YOU HIT HIM   559 19
HE LETS YOU HIT HIM TWICE   559 20
THE SPOT I SHOULD HIT ON WOULD BE LITTLE BRITAIN   574 13

HITCH
MAKE ME RICH QUICKLY WITH NEVER A HITCH   584 6

HITHER
HITHER AND THITHER ACROSS THE HIGH CRYSTALLINE FRAME   72 9
NIGHT-LIGHTS HITHER AND THITHER SHED   142 27
MACHINES HAVE TRIUMPHED ROLLED US HITHER AND THITHER   623 30
MADLY WE RUSH HITHER AND THITHER   739 21
I CAME HITHER NOR WHAT IS MY GOAL   757 4
AH MASTER MASTER YOU WHO HAVE BROUGHT US HITHER   757 14
HITHER AND THITHER   867 17
HITHER HAS TAKEN AWAY TO THAT HELL   887 7
I WAIT FOR THE BABY TO WANDER HITHER TO ME   *913 6
I LONG FOR THE BABY TO WANDER HITHER TO ME   *914 6
MACHINES HAVE TRIUMPHED ROLLED US HITHER AND THITHER   *953 17

HIT-HIT
WITH A HIT-HIT HERE AND A HIT-HIT THERE   459 14

HITTING
TWITCHES AND EBBS HITTING WASHING INWARDLY SILVERILY   453 20
HITTING OURSELVES AGAINST UNSEEN ROCK CRASHING OUR HEAD   544 15
METAL HITTING ON METAL TO ENFORCE OUR ATTENTION   623 3

HO
HO GOLDEN-SPANIEL SWEET ALERT NARCISSUS   309 7
HO DO YOU THINK WE'LL GET ON   404 18
HO ALL MY SAINTS AND MY VIRGINS   798 17

HOAR
OH AGE THAT IS HOAR AS ANEMONE BUDS   814 19

HOARDED
GARDEN WHICH GOD HAS HOARDED   243 11

HOAR-FROST-LIKE
HOAR-FROST-LIKE AND MYSTERIOUS   306 28

HOAR-FROST
THE HOAR-FROST CRUMBLES IN THE SUN   100 1
IN THE DISTANCE LIKE HOAR-FROST LIKE SILVERY GHOSTS COM+   306 26

HOARSE
HAVE PRESSED IMMEASURABLE SPACES OF HOARSE SILENCE   75 21
HOARSE   76 10
ALONE WITHIN THE DIM AND HOARSE SILENCE   76 21
WITH A LOUD HOARSE SIGH   109 20
THEY DWELT IN A HUGE HOARSE SEA-CAVE   201 21
LIFE'S VOICE EVEN WHEN SHE'S HOARSE   491 8
HAVE PRESSED THE IMMEASURABLE SPACES OF HOARSE SILENCE   *897 21
MY QUESTION MY GOD I MUST BREAK FROM THIS HOARSE SILENCE   *898 4
WRAPPED UP IN THE SKY'S DIM SPACE OF HOARSE SILENCE   *898 15
HAVE PRESSED IMMEASURABLE SPACES OF HOARSE SILENCE   *900 29
MY QUESTION MY GOD I MUST BREAK FROM THIS HOARSE SILENCE   *901 13
WRAPPED UP IN THE SKY'S DIM SPACE OF HOARSE SILENCE   *901 24

HOARSELY
AND STILL THE LONG HARSH BREATH SINKS HOARSELY OUT   878 27
HOARSELY WHISPERING US HOW   *917 3

HOARSENESS
CLEAR UPON THE LONG-DRAWN HOARSENESS OF A TRAIN ACROSS +   63 11

HOARY
AND THE OTHER THE OLD ONE THE PALLID HOARY FEMALE   426 9
WATCH SILENT THE LOOMING OF THE HOARY FAR-GONE AGES   426 21

HOBBY
    WHOM SOME RECALCITRANT OLD MAID WILL ADOPT AS A HOBBY   665 15

HOG
    THE ONLY WAY TO EAT AN APPLE IS TO HOG IT DOWN LIKE A P+   708 7

HOGGING
    HOGGING IT DOWN LIKE A PIG I CALL THE FEEDING OF CORPSES   708 11

HOIST
    TO HOIST THE NEXT WHITE PLANK THEIR MOVEMENT SEEMS   *895 5

HOLA HOLA MEXICANOS
    HOLA HOLA MEXICANOS GLANCE AWAY A MOMENT TOWARDS ME   790 19

HOLALA
    HOLALA WHAT A PRETTY PEOPLE   790 26
    HOLALA HE SAID MEXICANOS   791 10

HOLALA MEXICANOS
    HOLALA MEXICANOS IT IS FUNNY   791 15

HOLA MEXICANOS HOLALA
    HOLA MEXICANOS HOLALA   790 22

HOLBEIN
    HOLBEIN AND TITIAN AND TINTORET COULD NEVER PAINT FACES+   656 20

HOLD
    YOU HOLD YOURSELF ALL HARD AS IF MY KISSES   87 10
    EACH ONE FOR ITS HOLD ON THE CONCRETE DARKNESS I KNOW T+   92 14
    THEIR HOLD ON REALITY ENFEEBLE THEIR RISING SHOOTS   92 28
    COLD THAT HAD SUNK TO MY SOUL AND THERE KEPT HOLD   98 25
    AND HOLD THEM IN THRALL   110 4
    BUT THAT YOU HOLD ME STILL SO KINDLY COLD   122 21
    WHEN I HOLD THEM MY SPENT SOUL UNDERSTANDS   128 8
    LET US NOT HOLD HER SHADOW BACK FROM THE DARK   132 22
    HOLD MY OWN IN THE MIDST OF THEM DARKLING DEFY   133 19
    LOOSING HOLD IN THE WIND'S INSISTENT PUSH   160 1
    WITHIN ITS QUICK COMMITTED TO HOLD AND WAIT   161 4
    SWEET-SCENTED TO HOLD IN THE THROAT   165 10
    NOW MORTALS ALL TAKE HOLD   177 8
    HOLD MY HAND TO CATCH THE RAINDROPS THAT SLANT INTO SIG+   179 21
    SOMETHING I WANT TO TOUCH I MUST HOLD MY FACE TO THE RA+   180 31
    I MUST HOLD MY FACE TO THE WIND AND LET IT EXPLAIN   180 32
    WE HOLD THEM PROUD AND BLITHE   204 23
    MY FEET HAVE NO HOLD YOU TAKE THE SKY FROM ABOVE ME   211 10
    I HOLD THE NIGHT IN HORROR   212 15
    I HOLD MYSELF UP AND FEEL A BIG WIND BLOWING   223 4
    TO HOLD TO YOUR LIPS   227 20
    HOLD HIM YOUR LIGHT   228 28
    BUT OF WHAT ACCOUNT DO I HOLD THEM   269 21
    FOREST OF PILLARS THAT HOLD UP THE DOME OF HIGH IDEAL   287 28
    INTENT TO HOLD THE CANDLE OF THE SUN UPON ITS SOCKET-TIP   299 29
    TO HOLD THE ONE AND ONLY LIGHTED CANDLE OF THE SUN IN H+   299 34
    AND HOLD THE LIGHTED CANDLE OF THE SUN   300 1
    TO STAND AND HOLD FEATHERS THREE FEATHERS ABOVE THE WOR+   392 4
    MUST WE HOLD ON HOLD ON   429 14
    MUST WE HOLD ON   429 28
    AND THE SEA GETS HOLD OF US   455 2
    DO HOLD YOURSELF TOGETHER AND FIGHT   459 13
    YET KEEP STILL AND HOLD   514 3
    NATURALLY TAKE HOLD OF THE TOWN   537 12
    I'LL HOLD YOUR HAT   560 16
    BUST IN AND HOLD THE GROUND   560 32
    HOLD MY HAND AUNTIE AUNTIE   572 17
    AUNTIE HOLD MY HAND   572 18
    HOLD MY HAND AND LOVE ME AUNTIE   572 21
    HOLD MY HAND AUNTIE AUNTIE   573 5
    AUNTIE HOLD MY HAND   573 6
    NOW THEN PRIME MINISTER HOLD ON A BIT   573 25
    HOLD THE STARS STILL LEST WE HEAR THE HEAVENS DIMLY RIN+   698 11
    EVIL IS UPON US AND HAS GOT HOLD OF US   716 14
    AND THIS I HOLD IS THE TRUE HISTORY OF EVOLUTION   761 11
    HOLD BACK THE DRAGON OF THE SUN   786 20
    HOLD BACK THE WILD HOT SUN   789 13
    THAT I MAY HOLD THEM LIKE MEMORIES IN MY ARMS WHEN I GO+   789 20
    AND HOLD MYRIAD THREADS FROM THEIR CLAWS   793 26
    THE LAST TWO THINGS WE CAN STILL HOLD DEARLY   826 25
    SO THE ONLY THING TO DO IS TO KEEP STILL TO HOLD STILL +   839 1
    NOW THE TREES WITH INTERLOCKED HANDS AND ARMS UPLIFTED +   854 4
    A THRILL THROUGH THE LISTENING TREES AND HOLD THE BREATH   858 26
    I HOLD HER STILL AND WAIT TILL THE BELL SHALL FALTER   859 1
    HOLD UP JEANNETTE WHY POOR OLD GIRL ARE YOU SAD   859 29
    OUT OF MY HOLD   861 12
    A LITTLE WILD BUBBLE IS LOOSENING HOLD   868 28
    DO NOT HOLD ME SIEGMUND   870 18
    BLUE DARKNESSES OF WONDER THAT HOLD ALL   876 27
    LIKE IVORY AND GOLDEN MARBLE TWO BLACK CROWS HOLD   *894 27
    A LITTLE WILD BUBBLE IS LOOSING HOLD   *941 28

HOLDING
    AND THE WHITE DOG DANCES AND QUIVERS I AM HOLDING HIS C+   34 5
    HOLDING HER THUS COULD I CARE   62 3
    HOLDING ALOFT THEIR UMBRELLAS THAT FLASH AND ARE BRIGHT   146 19
    THAT HUDDLES IN GREY HEAPS COILING AND HOLDING BACK   164 18
    AND JOSEPH HOLDING THE BRIDLE   200 3
    I WALK UP TO MY NECK IN MIST HOLDING MY MOUTH UP   212 13
    IS TO SPLIT IT IN FOUR HOLDING IT BY THE STUMP   282 2
    TO KEEP ON HOLDING UP THIS IDEAL CIVILISATION   288 8
    WHEN THEY'RE HOLDING OUT THE THUNDERBOLT   559 10
    HOLDING THEIR BREATH NAKED AND DARKLY ALONE   711 5
    HOLDING DOWN MY LEAPING ARMS   883 11
    HOLDING HER THUS DID I CARE   *912 11

HOLDS
    NO LONGER SHADOW AND IT HOLDS ME   34 22
    AND THE FLESH OF THE STALK HOLDS UP FOR NOTHING A BLANK+   97 8
    THE WILL THAT HOLDS HIM THERE   150 3
    WITH HIS BACK TO THE SUN HOLDS OUT   200 10
    THAT HOLDS THE PERFECT CHILD   201 10
    I THE MAN WHO ENFOLDS YOU AND HOLDS YOU CLOSE   246 4
    DROWNS ME AND SWEEPS ME AWAY AND HOLDS ME DOWN   261 13
    WHAT IS IT THAT CLOTS ME HOLDS ME TOGETHER OUT OF THESE   870 10
    THAT HOLDS IT BACK MIGHT FOLLOW SOON TO THEE   879 17
    BLOOD OF A HEAVING WOMAN WHO HOLDS ME   *892 10

HOLE
    GONE BACK TO HIS HOLE   231 14
    AND LONG SNAKES QUICKLY GLIDE INTO THE DARK HOLE IN THE+   321 24
    AND AS HE PUT HIS HEAD INTO THAT DREADFUL HOLE   351 1
    INTO THAT HORRID BLACK HOLE   351 5
    INTO THE BLACK HOLE THE EARTH-LIPPED FISSURE IN THE WAL+   351 16
    A HOLE IN THE BLOOD-ORANGE BRILLIANT ROCKS THAT STICK U+   402 12
    BUT HE INSISTS ON GNAWING A LITTLE HOLE IN THE SOCIAL   432 13
    KNOCKED A LITTLE HOLE IN THE HOLY PRISON   459 18
    A GOOD KICK AT HIS DIRTY OLD HOLE   494 12
    HOLE HOLE HOLE   545 4
    HE'S A HOLE HOLE HOLE   545 9
    A MAN'S A HOLE HOLE HOLE   545 14
    WON'T STOP A HOLE HOLE HOLE   545 22
    WOULD STOP A HOLE TO KEEP THE WIND AWAY   545 25
    HE'S JUST A HOLE   546 2
    AND DIE LIKE A DOG IN A HOLE 'TIS STRANGE WHAT A SHODDY   755 8

HOLING
    A DARK MEMBRANE OVER THE WILL HOLING A MAN DOWN   407 23

HOLLOA
    AND HARK TO HIS HOLLOA   564 24

HOLLOW
    IN HOLLOW BLOCKS AND CUBES DEFORMED AND HEAPED   53 25
    AND MY HOLLOW FLESH STANDS UP IN THE NIGHT LIKE VANITY   97 10
    THE ROOM IS THE HOLLOW RIND OF A FRUIT A GOURD   112 19
    HOLLOW RANG THE HOUSE WHEN I KNOCKED AT THE DOOR   121 13
    HOLLOW RE-ECHOED MY HEART   121 17
    ROLL HOLLOW IN THE INTERIM   159 18
    I WILL ESCAPE FROM THE HOLLOW ROOM THE BOX OF LIGHT   179 24
    STILL IN THE VAST HOLLOW   193 23
    COME MAKING THE CHAFFINCH NESTS HOLLOW AND COSY   273 1
    NAY TONGUES ARE DEAD AND WORDS ARE HOLLOW AS HOLLOW   296 25
    MOANING BOOING ROARING HOLLOW   327 10
    OR WHETHER THE WATERS WILT IN THE HOLLOW PLACES   334 23
    THEIR RHYTHMS ON LONG-DRAWN HOLLOW SINISTER DRUMS   371 5
    THROUGH THE PALM-TREES AND PAST HOLLOW PADDY-FIELDS WHE+   386 27
    JUST LIKE AN OLD MUSHROOM ALL WORMY INSIDE AND HOLLOW   431 20
    FULL OF SEETHING WORMY HOLLOW FEELINGS   431 22
    AND THE PEOPLE APPLAUDED WITH HOLLOW FRIGHTENED   445 8
    WITH MOANS AND HOLLOW BIBBLINGS   492 6
    INTO HOLLOW SPACE   506 7
    NOW THE OLD ONES RING HOLLOW   564 22
    MAKING POOLS IN NEW HOLLOW PLACES   768 15
    FAR IN THE HOLLOW OF SPACE   787 22
    HE SAT WITHIN THE HOLLOW OF A CLOUD AND SAW THE MEN THA+   790 10
    TILL YOU ARE AS EMPTY AS RAT-GNAWED POMEGRANATES HANGIN+   800 26
    IT SEEMS TO COME OUT OF SOME HOLLOW RIND OF A MAN   830 33
    HERE HAVE I FOUND AN ANSWER FOR MY HOLLOW YEARNING   *907 10

HOLLOWED
    HAD POLISHED YOU AND HOLLOWED YOU   254 29
    HOLLOWED THIS GROOVE IN YOUR SIDES GRASPED YOU UNDER THE 254 30

HOLLOWS
    SENDS SUMMONS IN THE OLD HOLLOWS OF THE SUN   623 8
    AND THE KEYS WITH LITTLE HOLLOWS THAT MY MOTHER'S FINGE+ *940 4

HOLLY
    TEARS WRINKLE OUR FACES LIKE RAIN IN THE HOLLY   814 24

HOLY
    AND CITY STARS SO DIM AND HOLY   121 31
    YOU WOMEN MOST HOLY YOU MOTHER YOU BEING BEYOND   235 13
    OR LOVE THE EFFULGENCE OF THEIR HOLY LIGHT   288 19
    BUST UP THE HOLY APPLE-PIE   458 7
    KNOCKED A LITTLE HOLE IN THE HOLY PRISON   459 18
    THAT LITTLE COD'S THE HOLY WORST   493 23
    AND THE HOLY CAN'T-HELP-IT TOUCH   537 14
    TO THEIR LEVELS MY HOLY AUNT   555 24
    STUFF IS JUST HOLY SKUNK   556 20
    SHE'S A HOLY TERROR SHE TAKES YOUR BEST FROCK   572 2
    COME HOLY SILENCE COME   698 6
    COME HOLY SILENCE REACH REACH   698 8
    OF HOLY SILENCE   698 28
    AH THE HOLY SILENCE IT IS MEET   699 1
    SISTER OH HOLY SISTER   753 12

HOLY GHOST
    SO WORRIED BY THE HOLY GHOST   536 21
    THE SIN AGAINST THE HOLY GHOST   620 23
    BUT THERE IS SINNING AGAINST THE HOLY GHOST SINCE THE H+   621 2
    THE HOLY GHOST IS THE DEEPEST PART OF OUR OWN CONSCIOUS+   621 5
    NOWADAYS TO TALK OF HUMILITY IS A SIN AGAINST THE HOLY +   621 12
    YOU CAN'T IMAGINE THE HOLY GHOST SNIFFING AT CHERRY-PIE+   690 25
    TO THE HOLY GHOST   812 10
    IN THE TENT OF THE HOLY GHOST   812 26

HOLY MARY
    TOMORROW JESUS AND HOLY MARY   797 19

HOLY MOSES
   FROM THEIR PEDESTALS HOLY MOSES   556 27

HOLY OF HOLIES
   HOLY OF HOLIES OF SHEER OBLIVION   726   9

HOMAGE
   SHYLY AND IN HOMAGE LINGER FOR AN INVITATION   256   5
   AND DOWN BELOW HUGE HOMAGE OF SHADOWY BEASTS BARE-FOOT   388 14
   AND STEPPING IN HOMAGE STUBBORN TO THAT NERVOUS PALE   388 24
   AS IF THE HOMAGE OF THE KINDLED BLOOD OF THE EAST   389 28
   HOMAGE IN LUST IN RAGE   390   7
   BRINGS HIM TO HIS KNEES IN HOMAGE AND PURE PASSION OF S+   648 17
   WHO BEGGED OF YOU AND GAVE YOU HOMAGE   696 10
   MY HEART WAS FIERCE TO MAKE HER HOMAGE RISE   *936 29

HOME
   OUR EDEN OUR HOME   38   2
   AND I KNEW THAT HOME THIS VALLEY WAS WIDER THAN PARADISE   38 17
   'TIS THE WOUND OF LOVE GOES HOME   42   8
   HOW LOVELY IT IS TO BE AT HOME   50   6
   HOME COME HOME THE LIGHTNING HAS MADE IT TOO PLAIN   62 24
   SPEAK YOU MY HOME WHAT IS IT I DON'T DO WELL   63   7
   AH HOME SUDDENLY I LOVE YOU   63   8
   OVERHEAD AT HOME AND HAD NOT ONE STAR   103   6
   BUT I AM ALONE AND WAVERING HOME   106 15
   TO THE OLD SUNDAY EVENINGS AT HOME WITH WINTER OUTSIDE   148 12
   SINCE THIS IS THE LAST NIGHT I KEEP YOU HOME   153 13
   YET SOON TOO SOON SHE HAD HIM HOME AGAIN   155   9
   AT HOME   159 20
   THE HOME OF MY FATHERS THE PLACE THAT IS MINE MY FATE A+   159 29
   NOW I AM GOING HOME   198 17
   AT HOME WE LEANED IN THE BEDROOM WINDOW   206 27
   GONE UNDER THE ARCHWAY HOME HE CAN JOIN   228 15
   COME TO ME LIKE A WOMAN COMING HOME   231   1
   TO EDEN HOME   243 16
   BETWEEN HER BREASTS IS MY HOME BETWEEN HER BREASTS   249   6
   BETWEEN HER BREASTS IS MY HOME BETWEEN HER BREASTS   249 26
   WHEN IT HAS STRUCK HOME TO HER LIKE A DEATH THIS IS HIM   267   8
   NO SIN IS IT TO DRINK AS MUCH AS A MAN CAN TAKE AND GET+   277 10
   HE WILL NEVER QUITE STRIKE HOME ON THE TARGET-QUICK FOR   382 20
   HOME AT A GALLOP   397 13
   HOME   404 16
   THIN RED WOLF GO HOME   405   4
   I HAVE NO HOME OLD FATHER   405   5
   THAT HAD NO HOME   411 23
   I WANTED THE VIRGIN YOU TO BE HOME AT LAST   412   2
   WHERE THE VIRGIN IN WOMAN COMES HOME TO A MAN   412   5
   WHO NEVER IN ALL HER LIFE COULD FIND THE WAY HOME   412   7
   NOW COME WEST COME HOME   412   9
   COME HOME TO ME   412 18
   COME HOME TO ME MY LOVE MY LOVES MY MANY LOVES   412 26
   LET HIM COME HOME TO A BIT OF MORAL DIFFICULTY LET LIFE+   431   4
   NOR A DEAR LITTLE HOME WITH ITS COST ITS COST   459   5
   AND BE WHIMSICALLY AT HOME IN OURSELVES   496 21
   HE THOUGHT THEM SO HE SENT THEM HOME   577   8
   AT HOME AT HOME IN THE HOUSE OF THE LIVING   700   6
   YAWNING AT HOME BEFORE THE FIRE OF LIFE   700   9
   EVIL HAS NO HOME   711 12
   ONLY EVIL HAS NO HOME   711 13
   NOT EVEN THE HOME OF DEMONIACAL HELL   711 14
   HELL IS THE HOME OF SOULS LOST IN DARKNESS   711 15
   EVEN AS HEAVEN IS THE HOME OF SOULS LOST IN LIGHT   711 16
   THERE ARE SOULS THAT ARE AT HOME IN BOTH HOMES   711 18
   AND HAS NO HOME NO HOME ANYWHERE   712   4
   AND THE LITTLE SHIP WINGS HOME FALTERING AND LAPSING   720 14
   TO THE SWEET HOME OF PURE OBLIVION   721 21
   WHEN I COME HOME PROMISE ME   735 25
   INVISIBLE TROOPING HOME THE UNASSUAGED GHOSTS   739 11
   MULTITUDINOUS ENDLESS THE GHOSTS COMING HOME AGAIN   739 19
   MUST WE OPEN THE DOORS AND ADMIT THEM RECEIVE THEM HOME   740 13
   THEN WE SHALL TURN US HOME AGAIN TO LIFE   740 22
   HOME AT LAST IN THE OPEN AGAIN AND UNHOUSELED   770   8
   I AM COMING HOME   786 17
   HOMEWARDS LET ME COME HOME   786 22
   I AM COMING HOME   789 10
   LET ME COME HOME   789 15
   YOU TRACK THE GREY DOG HOME   808 10
   THAT IS MY HOME WHERE THE LAMP GLEAMS AFAR   857 27
   NO MORE AND HE LAY AT HOME UNUTTERABLE DESPAIR IN HIS F+   859 16
   COME ON TURN HOME OLD LASS ARE WE WASTED TOO   859 25
   AS I CAME HOME IN THE DUSK DESPOILED BY SCHOOL A MERE B+   864 27
   THE BOYS FROM THE HOME BLUE AND INANIMATE   866   2
   COMING HOME OVER THE WASTE-LANDS WIDE AND LONELY WITH S+   866 16
   MY EDEN MY HOME   *892 19
   AND SAY THAT THIS HOME THIS VALLEY IS WIDER THAN PARADI+   *892 32
   OR THIS IS MY SISTER AT HOME IN THE OLD FRONT ROOM   *940 14
   BETWEEN HER BREASTS IS MY HOME BETWEEN HER BREASTS   *945 21
   WITH PRAYER I NEED ONLY COME HOME EACH NIGHT TO FIND TH+   *945 28
   I NEED ONLY COME HOME EACH NIGHT AND LAY   *946   1

HOMELESS
   I STILL AM NOT HOMELESS HERE I'VE A TENT BY DAY   133 24
   AND I'M A PALE-FACE LIKE A HOMELESS DOG   404 13
   AND LEFT ME HOMELESS HERE IN THE DARK AT YOUR DOOR   404 17
   THE HOMELESS VIRGIN   412   6
   BEHOLD THEM HOMELESS AND HOUSELESS WITHOUT COMPLAINT   736   5
   SAVE THE COLD GHOSTS THAT HOMELESS FLOCK ABOUT   736   8
   FOR NOW THE HOSTS OF HOMELESS GHOSTS DO THRONG   737   1
   AND PASS BEYOND WITH THE FOE AND THE HOMELESS GHOSTS   737   6
   SMOKELESS HOUSELESS HOMELESS   768 28
   NOR HOMELESS   770   7

HOMELY
   POOR HOMELY WORDS I MUST GIVE YOU BACK   492 19

HOME-PLACE
   IN THE HOME-PLACE SHY IS IT SHE SHOULD EXCLUDE   48 25

HOMER
   HOMER WAS WRONG IN SAYING WOULD THAT STRIFE MIGHT PASS   348   1

HOMES
   BUT MUD HAS FLOODED THE HOMES OF THESE WEARY LANDS   167 11
   THERE ARE SOULS THAT ARE AT HOME IN BOTH HOMES   711 18
   THE FOE CAN TAKE OUR GOODS OUR HOMES AND LAND   736 16
   THEY HAVE HOMES IN DEATH   796 15

HOMESTEAD
   I WOULD GIVE MY SOUL FOR THE HOMESTEAD TO FALL WITH ME +   160   3
   FOR EVER AND NEVER ENTER THE HOMESTEAD ANY MORE   173   8
   AS SHE GOES ABOUT THE HOMESTEAD   756   8

HOMEWARDS
   HOMEWARDS LET ME COME HOME   786 22

HOMICIDAL
   WHICH IN THE END IS ALWAYS HOMICIDAL   514 27

HOMOGENEOUS
   THERE IS HOWEVER THE VAST THIRD HOMOGENEOUS AMORPHOUS   649 24

HOMOSEXUAL
   IT IS FOR MEN HE'S AN INSTINCTIVE HOMOSEXUAL   *948 30

HOMOSEXUALITY
   FORM OF HOMOSEXUALITY SHE SAID   447   7

HOMUNCULUS
   HOMUNCULUS STIRS FROM HIS ROOTS AND STRIVES UNTIL   39 11

HONEST
   YOUR HONEST MAN   432 19
   LET'S BE HONEST AT LAST ABOUT SEX OR SHOW AT LEAST THAT+   464 12
   MILLIONS OF SIMILAR HONEST PENCE   488 19
   FOR OUR HONEST AND HEALTHY ENGLISH TONGUE   576   1
   AND PERFECTLY HONEST   659 10
   AND PERFECTLY HONEST TO PRETEND TO BE UNBEGOTTEN   659 12
   OH HE'S AN HONEST MAN ANYHOW   659 21

HONESTLY
   BUT I HONESTLY DON'T KNOW WHAT HE MEANS   611   3
   ALL WE CAN HONESTLY IMAGINE IN THE BEGINNING   681 26

HONESTY
   WHILE AS TO HONESTY OH LOOK WHERE THE MONEY LIES   432 33
   HONESTY   533   6
   IN ALL HONESTY A WORD IS NEITHER A GAP IN THE CONSCIOUS+   837   8

HONEY
   NO NOR EVEN MILK AND HONEY   263 11
   MY PICTURES EAGER AS THE HONEY BEE   577 25
   THOSE THAT PUT HONEY ON OUR LIPS AND THOSE THAT PUT SALT   709 28
   OF THE HONEY OF EXPERIENCE   820   3
   WITH HER SUAVE FORM DUSTY WITH SPICES HONEY SWEET STRAY+   864   4

HONEY-BODIED
   OH HONEY-BODIED BEAUTIFUL ONE   306 20
   SOUNDLESS BLISS-FULL WIDE-RAYED HONEY-BODIED   307   6

HONEYCOMB
   THE SUNBEAMS HAVE FILLED ME LIKE A HONEYCOMB   803   9

HONEY-DROP
   AND YIELD HER HONEY-DROP TO HER LOVER   42 18

HONEY-STILL
   AND ALMOND HONEY-STILL   316   4

HONEYSUCKLE
   TO THE HONEYSUCKLE AT EVENING NOW   684   6

HONEY-TRIUMPH
   INTO BLOSSOM INTO PRIDE INTO HONEY-TRIUMPH INTO MOST   305 27

HONEY-WHITE
   HONEY-WHITE FIGS OF THE NORTH BLACK FIGS WITH SCARLET I+   284 26

HONIED
   AND OPEN IT SO THAT IT IS A GLITTERING ROSY MOIST HONIE+   282   3

HONK
   HONKING IN THE GLOOM THE HONK OF PROCREATION FROM SUCH   437 25
   LIKE A WILD SWAN OR A GOOSE WHOSE HONK GOES THROUGH MY   438   7
   OF ONE WHO WILL SETTLE ON ICEBERGS AND HONK ACROSS THE   439   2
   HONKED IN THE GLOOM THE HONK OF PROCREATION FROM SUCH T+   *947   3
   LIKE A WILD SWAN OR A GOOSE WHOSE HONK GOES THROUGH MY +   *947 18

HONKED
   HONKED IN THE GLOOM THE HONK OF PROCREATION FROM SUCH T+   *947   3

HONKING
   NOR HONKING HORN-LIKE INTO THE TWILIGHT   436   9
   HONKING IN THE GLOOM THE HONK OF PROCREATION FROM SUCH   437 25
   HONKING OVER THE LAKE   704 26
   AND HONKING WITH A HORN-LIKE ANNUNCIATION OF LIFE FROM +   841   6

HONOUR
   WILL SET A GUARD OF HONOUR AT EACH DOOR   153 21
   AND EMOTIONS AND DESIRES AND STRENGTH GLORY OR HONOUR   691 11
   SPEAK WITH THEM AND GIVE THEM PEACE AND DO THEM HONOUR   723 13
   AND GIVE THEM PLACE AND HONOUR AND SERVICE MEET   740 15
   SOOTHE THEM WITH SERVICE AND HONOUR AND SILENCE MEET   740 17
   IT IS THEIR RESPONSIBILITY THEIR POINT OF HONOUR   775   4

HONOUR
WILL SHIRK OR FAIL IN POINT OF HONOUR   775 13
YET IT IS A POINT OF HONOUR   775 28
IT IS A POINT OF HONOUR   776 1
ON YOUR HONOUR AMERICANS WHAT ARE YOU DOING   777 16
THIS IS GOING BEYOND THE BOUNDS OF PRESENT HONOUR   779 20
ONLY KNOW THAT DOING IT YOU FAIL IN POINT OF HONOUR   780 20

HONOURABLE
THOU HONOURABLE BIRD   328 2

HONOURED
WAS IT HUMILITY TO FEEL SO HONOURED   350 15
I FELT SO HONOURED   350 16
BUT EVEN SO HONOURED STILL MORE   350 20

HOOD
HIS BRIGHT DARK EYES COME OVER ME LIKE A HOOD   43 34
PITEOUS LOVE COMES PEERING UNDER THE HOOD   64 15
BY-PATHS WHERE THE WANTON-HEADED FLOWERS DOFF THEIR HOOD 65 30

HOODS
THE KEEPER HOODS THE VAST KNEE THE CREATURE SALAAMS   387 16

HOOING
AND HOOING AND COOING AND SIDLING THROUGH THE FRONT TEE+ 433 22

HOOK
CUT THE IRON HOOK OUT OF THEIR FACES THAT MAKES THEM SO 586 4
AH THE INDUSTRIAL MASSES WITH THE IRON HOOK THROUGH THE+ 586 15
FIXING THE HOOK MORE TIGHTLY GETTING IT MORE FIRMLY IN   586 20
TAKE THE IRON HOOK OUT OF THEIR FACES THAT MAKES THEM SO 632 19

HOOKED
THEN WHEN I SEE THE IRON HOOKED IN THEIR FACES   586 1
LIKE FEARFUL AND CORPSE-LIKE FISHES HOOKED AND BEING PL+ 586 9
WHERE HE DOES NOT CHOOSE TO LAND THEM YET HOOKED FISHES 586 11
WHEN I SEE THE IRON HOOKED INTO THEIR FACES   632 16
LIKE FEARFUL AND CORPSE-LIKE FISHES HOOKED AND BEING PL+ 632 24
WHERE HE DOES NOT CHOOSE TO LAND THEM YET HOOKED FISHES 632 26

HOOKS
DECEMBER'S BARE IRON HOOKS STICKING OUT OF EARTH   304 8
FELL FROM THE HOOKS AND WERE DEAD   413 9
CALM WITH THE CALM OF SCIMITARS AND BRILLIANT REAPING H+ 609 11

HOOPS
AND DOGS JUMPED THROUGH HOOPS AND TURNED SOMERSAULTS   444 18

HOOT
AND THE WORLD IT DIDN'T GIVE A HOOT   577 1

HOOTER
IN AND OUT WHEN THE HOOTER HOOTS WHITE-FACED WITH A   628 16
THEY WILL HEAR FAR FAR AWAY THE LAST FACTORY HOOTER   *954 10

HOOTING
WHO IS IT THE OWL IS HOOTING   731 5

HOOTS
IN AND OUT WHEN THE HOOTER HOOTS WHITE-FACED WITH A   628 16

HOP
WITH A HIE HOP BELOW   564 18
TELL THEM THEY ARE LIKE FROGS WITH STONES IN THEIR BELL+ 791 30

HOPE
I HOPE IT DID THEE GOOD   80 20
AND HAVE NOT ANY LONGER ANY HOPE   100 25
UNSATISFIED IS THERE NO HOPE   119 5
TO QUICKEN MY HOPE AS I HASTENED TO GREET   121 21
WITH A FLUTTER OF HOPE AND A QUENCHING DOUBT   121 26
OVER THE WASTE WHERE NO HOPE IS SEEN   179 14
SHE IS BREWING HOPE FROM DESPAIR   203 8
SO I HOPE I SHALL SPEND ETERNITY   250 9
YOUNG MEN HAVING NO REAL JOY IN LIFE AND NO HOPE IN THE 521 20
WITHOUT FIRST BEGETTING A NEW HOPE FOR THE CHILDREN TO   521 23
AND FORCED TO CLUTCH ON TO POSSESSIONS IN THE HOPE THEY+ 522 15
BECAUSE THEIR HOPE IS PINNED DOWN BY THE SYSTEM   558 28
THAT'S WHAT WE HOPE WE HOPE SHE'LL BE   571 23
OH I DO HOPE AUNT MAUD WILL MANAGE ALL RIGHT   572 9
I KNOW THERE IS NO HOPE FOR US DEATH WAITS IT IS USELES+ 632 12
AND HOPE BLEEDS RIGHT AWAY   639 24
LET'S HOPE THERE'LL BE MORE SENSE IN TAIL-TUFTS   665 4
SAW MY LAST HOPE START   748 24
SEE NO HOPE OF ALTERING   750 7
I AM LOSING HOPE   751 19
IN THE HOPE OF RESURRECTING OR RATHER RE-INCARNATING   760 20
I BEAR THE HOPE   772 24
LIFE LOVERS WHO COULD HOPE FOR NO RANK AMONG THE PALLID+ 855 20
ALL HOPE OF MY ATTAINMENT THENCE SERENE   877 16
AND I HOPE TO SPEND ETERNITY   *946 7

HOPED
A TEAR WHICH I HAD HOPED THAT EVEN HELL HELD NOT AGAIN + 67 17
HE HAD HOPED TO DIE IN THE PULPIT TO CONQUER IN DEATH   859 10

HOPEFUL
THE ILLUSION OF MANKIND THE ILLUSION OF A HOPEFUL FUTURE 639 21

HOPELESS
THE HOPELESS WINTRY TWILIGHT FADES   142 21
NOW ON WITH THE HOPELESS JOURNEY   202 5
OH WHEN THE WORLD IS HOPELESS   631 9
IS IT HOPELESS HOPELESS HOPELESS   631 27
AND THE HOPELESS INFERIOR HE IS THE MACHINE INCARNATE   635 16
AND SILVERY CITY OF THE NOW HOPELESS BODY   721 12

HOPELESSLY
NOW I AM CAUGHT YOU ARE HOPELESSLY LOST O SELF   47 32

HOPELESSNESS
IN THE EXCRUCIATING TORMENT OF HOPELESSNESS HELPLESSNESS 627 24

HOPES
AND DIM HOPES CROWDED ME WARM WITH COMPANIONSHIP   98 29
HOPES   *926 14

HOPPING
AND TO BE LIMITED BY A MERE WORD IS TO BE LESS THAN A H+ 292 4
AND ALL THE UNSPEAKABLE CHARM OF BIRDS HOPPING   443 19
INSIPID UNSALTED RABBITY ENDLESSLY HOPPING   606 19

HOPS
HOPS LIKE A FROG BEFORE ME   110 26
FLEA WHICH HOPS OVER SUCH AN OBSTRUCTION AT FIRST   292 5

HORDES
AND THEN THE HORDES OF THE SPAWN OF THE MACHINE   635 6
THE HORDES OF THE EGO-CENTRIC THE ROBOTS   635 7
THE INFERIORS THE INFERIORS THERE THEY ARE IN HORDES   637 8
BETWEEN THE HALF-VISIBLE HORDES   *958 26

HORIZON
AH MY DARLING WHEN OVER THE PURPLE HORIZON SHALL LOOM   91 25
BACK FROM THE STRAIGHT HORIZON THAT ENDS ALL ONE SEES   168 6
HORIZON OF LIFE   366 28
OR ELSE RUSH HORIZONTAL TO CHARGE AT THE SKY'S HORIZON   392 18
LITTLE ISLANDS OUT AT SEA ON THE HORIZON   687 1
AT THE BACK OF MY LIFE'S HORIZON WHERE THE DREAMS FROM + *905 15
AH MY DARLING WHEN OVER THE PURPLE HORIZON SHALL LOOM   *926 18

HORIZONS
BECAUSE THOSE FACES WERE WINDOWS TO THE STRANGE HORIZON+ 656 21
THE HORIZONS OF LOVE AND STRIFE   788 23

HORIZON'S
FAR OFF SO FAR LIKE A MADNESS UNDER THE HORIZON'S DAWNI+ 364 3

HORIZONTAL
FIRE HORIZONTAL DECLINING AND EBBING THE TWILIT EBB OF + 67 6
WHAT IS THE HORIZONTAL ROLLING OF WATER   302 4
WHERE THE ADDER DARTS HORIZONTAL   321 15
THE CRUMBLING DAMP FRESH LAND LIFE HORIZONTAL AND CEASE+ 321 18
THE DARK BAR HORIZONTAL   355 33
OF HORIZONTAL PERSISTENCE   360 17
OR ELSE RUSH HORIZONTAL TO CHARGE AT THE SKY'S HORIZON   392 18
THE HORIZONTAL DIVISION OF MANKIND   636 8
OF THE HORIZONTAL DIVISION OF MANKIND   637 2
A HORIZONTAL THREAD   719 29
HORIZONTAL ETERNITY FLUID OR NULL   827 16
HORIZONTAL AND MEANINGLESS DESIRABLY DULL   827 18

HORN
OF HORN   381 17
COME BLOW UP YOUR HORN   659 6

HORNBEAM
AS THE HORNBEAM PUSHES UP HIS SPROUTS   *954 9

HORN-LIKE
NOR HONKING HORN-LIKE INTO THE TWILIGHT   436 9
AND HONKING WITH A HORN-LIKE ANNUNCIATION OF LIFE FROM + 841 6

HORNS
HORNS   326 1
THE GOLDEN HORNS OF POWER   326 2
HIS HORNS TURN AWAY FROM THE ENEMY   327 6
LET HIM REMEMBER HIS HORNS THEN   327 21
YET IF YOU HAD WHORLED HORNS OF BRONZE IN A FRONTAL DARK 381 1
TOWARDS A SHOCK AND A CRASH AND A SMITING OF HORNS AHEAD 381 22
AND BRING IT HURTLING TO A HEAD WITH CRASH OF HORNS AGA+ 381 25
THE HORNS   381 26
GOD IN BLACK CLOUD WITH CURVING HORNS OF BRONZE   383 16
FURTHER STILL BEFORE THE CURLED HORNS OF THE RAM STEPPED 437 14
AND FURTHER STILL BEFORE THE CURLED HORNS OF THE RAM ST+ *946 25
DEER CRASH THEIR HORNS IN THE MOUNTAINS OF HIS BREAST   *953 28

HOROSCOPE
WHO COULD HOROSCOPE FIT FOR A QUEEN   845 18

HORRIBLE
AND AM SWEPT AWAY IN THE HORRIBLE DAWN AM GONE   147 12
THE PILLAR OF SALT THE WHIRLING HORRIBLE COLUMN OF SALT+ 207 28
NAY I'M TOO SLEEPY AH YOU ARE HORRIBLE   211 7
AND HEAPS AND HEAPS AND HORRIBLE REEKING HEAPS   258 6
THE FEAR OF HUNGER IS MOLOCH BELIAL THE HORRIBLE GOD   263 6
YOUR HORRIBLE SKELETON AUREOLED IDEAL   292 7
BUT HORRIBLE AS IF YOUR HEART WOULD WRENCH OUT   447 29
THEY ARE AFRAID WITH HORRIBLE AND OPPOSING FEARS   516 21
WITH ALL OUR HORRIBLE COUSINS   572 12
OUTSIDER SPRUNG UP FROM SOME HORRIBLE GUTTER   576 9
AND EACH TIME IT CAME OUT THE SAME A HORRIBLE SEXLESS L+ 619 10
DRAW IT AWAY DRAW IT AWAY FOR THESE HORRIBLE MACHINE-PE+ 639 3
FROM FALLING IRON AND HORRIBLE SHELL'S REPORT   751 11
GAUNT AND HORRIBLE   *958 10

HORRID
THE SHARPER MORE HORRID THE PRESSURE THE HARDER   161 1
OF HORRID SORROW   207 16
INTO THAT HORRID BLACK HOLE   351 5
HAIRY HORRID GOD THE FATHER IN A WILLIAM BLAKE   385 20
LIFE IS FOR KISSING AND FOR HORRID STRIFE   709 25
LIFE IS FOR KISSING AND FOR HORRID STRIFE   710 1
NOR YET THE STRIVING AND THE HORRID STRIFE   710 8

HORRIFIC
AND LAID THE DESERT HORRIFIC OF SILENCE AND SNOW ON THE+   75 16
SUN OF THE TORRID MID-DAY'S HORRIFIC DARKNESS   301 20
THIS HORRIFIC CRUCIFIXION   636 21

HORROR
THERE WAS A HORROR   204 9
I HOLD THE NIGHT IN HORROR   212 15
I COULD CONVULSE THE HEAVENS WITH MY HORROR   213 17
I SHALL NEVER FORGET THE MANIACAL HORROR OF IT ALL IN T+   257 10
IT WAS A MANIACAL HORROR IN THE END   257 17
AND GOD OF HORROR I WAS KISSING ALSO MYSELF   257 19
AND OH OH HORROR I WAS BEGETTING AND CONCEIVING IN MY   257 21
AND I A MANY-FINGERED HORROR OF DAYLIGHT TO HIM   339 23
WAS THE HORROR OF WHITE DAYLIGHT IN THE WINDOW   344 25
A SORT OF HORROR A SORT OF PROTEST AGAINST HIS WITHDRAW+   351 4
SNAKE-LIKE SHE DRAWS AT MY FINGER WHILE I DRAG IN HORROR   359 26
TORN WITH A SHRIEK HALF MUSIC HALF HORROR   364 26
GOBBLE UP FILTH YOU HORROR SWALLOW UTTER ABOMINATION   398 28
AT LAST IN SHEER HORROR OF NOT BEING ABLE TO LEAVE OFF   701 31

HORRORS
DESTROY SHE MOANED THESE HORRORS IN PAINT   577 8
HORRORS   666 7

HORROR-STRUCK
THE MUTILATED HORROR-STRUCK YOUTHS A MULTITUDE   258 1

HORROR-TILTED
AND SEEN HIS HORROR-TILTED EYE   339 7

HORROW
AN ESCAPE FROM THEIR HORROW OF IMPRISONMENT IN OUR CIVI+   838 8

HORSE
WITH A HORSE INSISTENT REQUEST THAT FALLS   64 25
COLOSSAL IN NEARNESS A BLUE POLICE SITS STILL ON HIS HO+   66 9
AS 'AS SLUDGED LIKE A HORSE ALL 'ER LIFE   77 18
I REMEMBER THE SCREAM OF A TERRIFIED INJURED HORSE THE   366 10
THE HORSE BEING NOTHING BUT A NAG WILL FORGET   379 30
PELTING BEHIND ON THE DUSTY TRAIL WHEN THE HORSE SETS O+   397 12
I'M I ON THE HORSE   397 24
AS THE HORSE WAS AN IMPROVEMENT ON THE ICHTHYOSAURUS   429 27
I WOULD CALL ATTILA ON HIS LITTLE HORSE   497 10
SO THAT I WOULD CALL ATTILA ON HIS LITTLE HORSE   497 11
AND EVEN THE GRAND HORSE OF PHYSICAL ENERGY   660 17
THE YOUTH WALKS UP TO THE WHITE HORSE TO PUT ITS HALTER+   683 19
AND THE HORSE LOOKS AT HIM IN SILENCE   683 20
AND HE GOES AND WASHES THE BELLY OF THE HORSE   734 5
AND BENDS AGAIN AND LOOKS AT THE BELLY OF THE HORSE   734 15
WE REST AT THE HEDGE MY HORSE AND I WHERE THE SCENT   858 18
STARTLING MY HORSE WHO STIRS AND WOULD TURN HER ABOUT   858 28
AS HAS SLUDGED LIKE A HORSE ALL HER LIFE   *919 6

HORSEBACK
AND RIDE ON HORSEBACK ASLEEP FOREVER THROUGH THE DESERT   408 11
AND HUNDREDS OF SOLDIERS ON HORSEBACK HAVE FILED BETWEEN   732 6

HORSE-CHESTNUT
AS A JEWEL-BROWN HORSE-CHESTNUT NEWLY ISSUED   73 5
THE ENORMOUS CLIFF OF HORSE-CHESTNUT TREES   105 13

HORSE-HOOFED
FOR A MOMENT HE WAS THE CENTAUR THE WISE YET HORSE-HOOF+   672 28

HORSES
THE HORSES ARE UNTACKLED THE CHATTERING MACHINE   35 11
THE PINK YOUNG HORSES SHOW ONE SIDE BRIGHT   50 23
THEIR HANDS AND PRODUCE WORKS OF ART AS MEN DO HORSES W+   976 2
THE FORMS OF THE GODS LIKE HORSES AND OXEN LIKE OXEN AN+   376 3
LIKE STAGS ON ROCKY GROUND OR PAWING HORSES OR SPRINGY   392 16
AND THE SMELL OF HORSES AND OTHER BEASTS   444 13
HORSES GAY HORSES SWIRLING ROUND AND PLAITING   445 19
THE WATER WE CAN AT THE GATES FOR THE HORSES HE GALLOPS   732 3
IN THE BOX AND FOUR HOT HORSES GOING DREARILY   733 7
HAVE POURED FOR THE HORSES A DARK-BLUE STAGGERING   733 18
HE WATERS THE HORSES DOES HE WASH HIS HEEL   733 33
SUDDENLY HIS HORSES BEGAN TO START   735 7
HE STAYED WITH THE HORSES SULKILY   735 11
AND CALLED TO HIS HORSES AND HIS STRONG BLUE BODY   735 14

HORSE-SHOE
THE FIG THE HORSE-SHOE THE SQUASH-BLOSSOM   282 25

HORSE'S
DOST THA HEAR MY HORSE'S FEET AS HE CANTERS AWAY   664 1
ON THE HORSE'S BELLY HURT HIM FOR HE WAS RATHER GENTLE   734 20

HORUS
GREAT AND GLISTENING-FEATHERED LEGS OF THE HAWK OF HORUS   409 7
THE GOLDEN HAWK OF HORUS   409 8
HAWK AS I SAY OF HORUS   409 17

HOSPITALITY
THAT HE SHOULD SEEK MY HOSPITALITY   350 21

HOST
NOW CLAIMED THE HOST   156 6
AND THE PRESENT HOST   165 26
HOST ON THE SHORES OF THE LAKE LIKE THICK WILD RICE BY   391 9
UNCHALLENGED INTACT UNABRIDGED HENCEFORTH A HOST   743 27
FOR I KNOW THE HOST   772 28
YOU FLUTTER IN A HOST OF FLAMES LIKE WINTER STARLINGS R+   784 1
GUEST OF THE HOST   812 28
FINALLY OUT OF THE HOST   823 5

HOSTAGE
OF PURE AND LAMBENT HOSTAGE FROM THE DEAD   745 14

HOSTILE
ACROSS THE SPACE ON THE CAT IN HEAVEN'S HOSTILE EMINENCE   97 22
AND NAKEDLY NOTHING 'TWIXT WORLD AND HEAVEN TWO CREATUR+   98 4
SOMETIMES THE SUN TURNS HOSTILE TO MEN   608 20
THEN THE SUN TURNS HOSTILE TO US   609 1
FOR HE IS HOSTILE TO ALL THE OLD LEAFY FOLIAGE OF OUR T+   609 6
IN MYRIADS UNDER THE HOT AND HOSTILE SUN   628 7
FOR THE SUN IS HOSTILE NOW   684 14

HOSTS
BUT THE HOSTS OF MEN WITH ONE VOICE DENY   40 19
OF THE BREATHING HOSTS   108 19
FOR THE HOUSE IS SHUT AND SEALED AND THE BREATH OF THE +   174 27
SEE IF I AM NOT LORD OF THE DARK AND MOVING HOSTS   289 22
FOR NOW THE HOSTS OF HOMELESS GHOSTS DO THRONG   737 1
NOW ALL THE HOSTS ARE MARCHING TO THE GRAVE   743 29
THE HOSTS ARE LEAPING FROM THE EDGE OF LIFE   743 30
THE HOSTS AWAY TO DEATH WHERE HEAP ON HEAP   744 8
IN HOSTS TOWARDS THE EVERLASTING NIGHT   745 9
UNQUENCHABLE OF WIND OR HOSTS OF DEATH   745 11
I SPEAK ALOUD TO FLEETING HOSTS OF RED   745 25
BUT YOU WHAT HAVE YOU MASTERED AMONG THE DRAGON HOSTS O+   796 16

HOT
HE GROWS DISTINCT AND I SEE HIS HOT   59 7
REPEATING WITH TIGHTENED ARMS AND THE HOT BLOOD'S BLIND+   61 26
LIKE SOFT HOT ASHES ON MY HELPLESS CLAY   87 13
I LONGED TO FEEL MY HOT BLOOD BURN   123 29
AND SHE WITH HER WOMEN HOT AND HARD   228 19
LIE ON ME WITH A HOT PLUMB LIVE WEIGHT   240 28
YET HOT WAITING   240 30
WHAT IS THE HOT PLUMB WEIGHT OF YOUR DESIRE ON ME   241 3
YOU HAVE A HOT UNTHINKABLE DESIRE OF ME BUNNY   241 4
HOT IN THE THROAT   315 21
WITH CAVERNOUS NOSTRILS WHERE THE WINDS RUN HOT   325 30
ON A HOT HOT DAY AND I IN PYJAMAS FOR THE HEAT   349 2
AND HOT RED OVER YOU   369 21
HE IS NOT FATHERLY LIKE THE BULL MASSIVE PROVIDENCE OF +   382 8
AND SCARLET HOT EMBERS OF TORCHES KNOCKED OUT OF THE   388 30
IN THE LONG HOT NIGHT MORE DANCERS FROM INSIGNIFICANT   389 2
THE HOT DARK BLOOD OF ITSELF A-LAUGHING WET HALF-DEVILI+   389 20
O RIPPLING HARD FIRE OF COURAGE O FUSING OF HOT TRUST   440 13
SO SLOWLY THE GREAT HOT ELEPHANT HEARTS   465 19
THE HOT WILD CORE OF THE EARTH HEAVIER THAN WE CAN EVEN   480 8
HOT HURRYING YET IT BURNS IF YOU TOUCH IT   505 26
LOOK AT THAT ONE THERE THAT'S PRETTY HOT   578 11
FROM HOT DIGGING-IN FINGERS OF LOVE   601 12
IN MYRIADS UNDER THE HOT AND HOSTILE SUN   628 7
AND OLEANDER IS HOT WITH PERFUME UNDER THE AFTERNOON SUN   630 3
TILL THEY GROW HOT AND BURST AS EVEN STONE CAN   642 14
IF I CUT MY FINGER MY BLOOD IS HOT NOT COLD   655 22
ALL THE WHALES IN THE WIDER DEEPS HOT ARE THEY AS THEY +   694 3
THERE THEY BLOW THERE THEY BLOW HOT WILD WHITE BREATH O+   694 6
TO HOT AND FLOCCULENT ASH   728 8
IN THE BOX AND FOUR HOT HORSES GOING DREARILY   733 7
GOES BEHIND HIS MOTHER WHERE THE SAND IS HOT   757 9
WITH SINGED HOT EYES AND RELENTLESSNESS   769 5
THE COLD AND THE HOT   788 4
HOLD BACK THE WILD HOT SUN   789 13
COFFEE FROM THE BUSHES IN THE HOT LANDS EVEN THE JUICY +   793 22
SO THAT STRENGTH WELLS UP IN ME LIKE WATER IN HOT SPRIN+   799 21
THE HOT SUN WAXES AND HEALS   824 29
EYES WHERE HIS HOT IMPRISONED SOUL HAS KEPT   859 19
THERE PRESS YOUR HOT RED CHEEK AGAINST MINE   863 17
WHAT IS THE HEAVY HOT HAND   869 17
MINT ME BEAUTIFUL MEDALS AND HAND THEM ME HOT   873 1
AND HANDS AND FACE AND BREAST WITH THAT HOT CLOAK   879 10
WITHERED MY INSOLENT SOUL WOULD BE GONE LIKE FLOWERS TH+   *891 27
NOT ALL FOR THEM SHALL THE FIRES OF MY LIFE BE HOT   *895 32
NOT ALL FOR THEM SHALL THE FIRES OF MY LIFE BE HOT   *904 21
REPEATING WITH TIGHTENED ARMS AND THE HOT BLOOD'S BLIND+   *912 6
SWELL DOWN HER RICH HOT WRIST   *937 8
AND PALE HOT SKIES HAVE DARKENED AND GONE COLD   *939 15

HOT-ACHE
IT SMELLS OF BURNING SNOW OF HOT-ACHE   270 18

HOT-ACHING
FOR WHAT KIND OF ICE-ROTTEN HOT-ACHING HEART MUST THEY +   270 27

HOT-BEDS
IN THE HOT-BEDS OF THE BOARD-SCHOOLS AND THE FILM   644 7

HOT-BORN
OF THE HOT-BORN INFANT BLESS THE FOLLY WHICH HAD   88 30

HOTEL
WHEN I WAS WAITING AND NOT THINKING SITTING AT A TABLE +   672 18

HOTELS
EVERY LORDLY TUPPENNY FOREIGNER FROM THE HOTELS FATTENI+   312 23
THE SAME I SAY TO THE PROFITEERS FROM THE HOTELS THE MO+   316 24

HOTNESS
I THOUGHT I COULD PLUNGE IN YOUR LIVING HOTNESS AND BE   99 8
AND HOTNESS AND THEN MORE CRUSTED BRINE IN OUR HEARTS   707 23

HOTTER
HEAVIER AND HOTTER THAN ANYTHING KNOWN   480 12
AND GREATER HEAT INTO FIRE MORE HEAVY AND HOTTER THAN A+   *951 21
SO PONDEROUSLY CENTRAL HEAVIER AND HOTTER THAN ANYTHING+   *951 25

HOTTEST
    THE HOTTEST BLOOD OF ALL AND THE WILDEST THE MOST URGENT   694   2

HOUND
    LIKE A TOOTHLESS HOUND PURSUING HIM WITH MY WILL   47 23
    OF YOU MANGY HOUND GO TO HELL   774 18

HOUNDS
    MY PACK OF UNRULY HOUNDS I CANNOT START   74   9
    MY PACK OF UNRULY HOUNDS I CANNOT START   *895 17
    MY PACK OF UNRULY HOUNDS I CANNOT START   *904   6

HOUR
    FOR THIS LITTLE HOUR   51 25
    TO THE NIGHT THAT TAKES US WILLING LIBERATES US TO THE +   70   4
    OUR FACES FLOWER FOR A LITTLE HOUR PALE AND UNCERTAIN A+   71   1
    THE BRIEF MATERIAL CONTROL OF THE HOUR LEAVE THEM FREE +   93   8
    SO I LAY ON YOUR BREAST FOR AN OBSCURE HOUR   104   4
    I SHALL GET NO ANSWER IN ANY HOUR   106 21
    AT SUCH AN HOUR TO LAY HER CLAIM ABOVE   155 29
    THEREFORE EVEN IN THE HOUR OF MY DEEPEST PASSIONATE MALE 208   8
    THE LISTLESS BEAUTY OF THE HOUR   248 16
    AND THEN IN A STRANGE GREY HOUR   248 24
    GIVE US OUR TURN GIVE US A CHANCE LET OUR HOUR STRIKE   273 21
    I WOULD COME IF I FELT MY HOUR HAD STRUCK   289 28
    THE HOUR STRIKES   323   9
    YOUR HOUR HAS STRUCK   473 12
    ARE SEA-BED STILL THROUGH THEIR HOUR OF BARE DENUDING   509 19
    WHICH THEY COULD COMB BY THE HOUR IN LUXURIOUS QUIET   537 27
    GLEAMING HER HOUR IN LIFE AS SHE NOW GLEAMS IN DEATH   676 14
    BITTER TO ME IS THIS EVENING HOUR   758   8
    IN THE SAME WAY CHASTITY IN ITS HOUR IS SWEET AND WHOLE+ 845 11
    OUR FACES FLOWER FOR A LITTLE HOUR PALE AND UNCERTAIN A+ *917 21
    CHASTITY IN ITS HOUR IS SWEET AND WHOLESOME   *952 23
    SO THAT WHEN THE HOUR COMES AND THE LAST DOOR CLOSES BE+*958 24

HOURS
    MAKES PAUSE THE HOURS   50 14
    COOL AS SYRINGA BUDS IN MORNING HOURS.   65   9
    MY MISSAL BOOK OF FINE FLAMBOYANT HOURS   135   2
    NAY TAKE THIS WEARY BOOK OF HOURS AWAY   135 20
    HOURS THAT WERE ONCE ALL GLORY AND ALL QUEENS   135 24
    AND I REMEMBER STILL THE SUNNY HOURS   135 25
    AND ALL HOURS LONG THE TOWN   159   1
    THE HOURS HAVE TUMBLED THEIR LEADEN MONOTONOUS SANDS   167   1
    TO-MORROW WILL POUR THEM ALL BACK THE DULL HOURS I DETE+ 167   4
    THE HOURS HAVE TUMBLED THEIR LEADEN MONOTONOUS SANDS   167   8
    THE HOURS HAVE CEASED TO FALL AND A STAR COMMANDS   167 17
    TO-MORROW WILL POUR THEM ALL BACK THE DULL HOURS I DETE+ 167 20
    THE SILENT DRIFTING HOURS   249   1
    THROUGH THE HOURS PERSISTENT AND IRREPRESSIBLE   366   7
    THAT FLICKERED FORTH IN THE BEST HOURS OF LIFE   676 11
    SHE WHO AT HER BEST HOURS WAS HERSELF WARM FLICKERING H+ 676 16
    SHE SAID TO ME STAY THREE HOURS TO COMFORT ME SUCH IS A+ 749 19
    NO LONGER THEY SWEEP THE HOURS AS THE SCYTHE OF THE MOW+ 855 29
    I HAVE TRAVELLED IN RUSSIA TWO HOURS OR MORE   866 26
    THE HOURS HAVE TUMBLED THEIR LUSTRELESS TARNISHED SANDS *896   6
    FOR TOMORROW WILL POUR THEM ALL BACK THE SCHOOL HOURS I+*896   9
    THE HOURS HAVE TUMBLED THEIR LUSTRELESS TARNISHED SANDS *896 13
    THE HOURS HAVE CEASED TO FALL AND A STAR COMMANDS   *896 22
    TOMORROW WILL POUR THEM ALL BACK THE DULL HOURS I DETEST*896 25
    ALL THE SLOW SCHOOL HOURS ROUND THE IRREGULAR HUM OF TH+*897 20
    ALL THE SLOW SCHOOL HOURS ROUND THE IRREGULAR HUM OF TH+*900 28
    THE HOURS PECKED PLEASURE FROM ME AND THE SUN DELIGHTED+*933 19
    BUT I REMEMBER STILL THE SUNNY HOURS   *939 17
    HOURS THAT WERE ONCE ALL GLORY AND ALL QUEENS   *939 24

HOUR'S
    OF THIS HOUR'S IGNOMINY AND SWEAT   747 19

HOUSE
    OUTSIDE THE HOUSE AN ASH-TREE HUNG ITS TERRIBLE WHIPS   36   9
    WITHIN THE HOUSE TWO VOICES AROSE A SLENDER LASH   36 13
    WITH SWEAT I'LL ENTER A HOUSE FOR THY SAKE   44   8
    THANK HEAVEN FOR A PEACEFUL HOUSE   45 31
    ALL THE LONG YEARS OF SITTING IN MY HUSBAND'S HOUSE   47 30
    AS SLOWLY THE HOUSE OF DAY IS CLOSING ITS EASTERN SHUTT+ 102 28
    HOLLOW RANG THE HOUSE WHEN I KNOCKED AT THE DOOR   121 13
    RIGID SLEEPS THE HOUSE IN DARKNESS I ALONE   140   7
    IN THE HOUSE OF LIFE THE FLOOR WAS RUFFLED WITH GOLD   141   6
    ROUND THE HOUSE WERE LILACS AND STRAWBERRIES   152 10
    THE WALLS OF THE HOUSE AND NETTLES PUFF OUT FROM THE HE+ 159 25
    OF THIS SELF-SAME DARKNESS YET THE SHADOWY HOUSE BELOW   172 23
    OH COME AND BREAK THIS PRISON THIS HOUSE OF YESTERDAY   174 17
    INTERIOR A HOUSE OF DREAMS WHERE THE DREAMERS WRITHE AN+ 174 24
    FOR THE HOUSE IS SHUT AND SEALED AND THE BREATH OF THE + 174 27
    THE HOUSE IS SILENT IT IS LATE AT NIGHT I AM ALONE   220 21
    IN HIS HOUSE AWHILE   234   6
    GO DOWN THE ROAD OUTSIDE THE HOUSE   235 23
    HERE IN MY OWN HOUSE   235 27
    THE HOUSE   267 14
    THE HOUSE SWAYS   288 12
    TOES AND THE DOME OF HIS HOUSE IS HIS HEAVEN THEREFORE + 348 15
    YOUR LITTLE ROUND HOUSE IN THE MIDST OF CHAOS   354 14
    GOATS GO PAST THE BACK OF THE HOUSE LIKE DRY LEAVES IN + 383 27
    AND THEN YOU RUN IN TO VOMIT IT IN MY HOUSE   399   4
    THE RANCH HOUSE   400   7
    BURN THE HOUSE DOWN   440 16
    AND DWELLING IN HIS OWN BOWERY HOUSE LIKE A BEAVER'S   451 24
    OF THIS HOUSE OF LIFE THAT ENCLOSES US ALL   461 28
    THAT WAS ONCE A HOUSE AND IS NOW A PRISON   462   2
    OF THE PRISON HOUSE THAT ENCLOSES US ALL   462   8
    TO GAPE AND OUR HOUSE IS GOING TO WRACK   462 14
    AND THE INDIVIDUAL MUST HAVE HIS HOUSE FOOD AND FIRE ALL 487 23
    AND SINGES US AND BURNS THE HOUSE DOWN   506 10
    WE LIVE IN A VAST HOUSE   510 26
    AND THE HOUSE COMES DOWN WITH A SUBSIDING   511 19
    THOUGH THE HOUSE HAD A FINE INTERIOR   554 15

HOUSE
    AUNTIE MAUD HAS COME TO KEEP HOUSE   571 17
    DAWN IS NO LONGER IN THE HOUSE OF THE FISH   616 18
    WHEN I SAW HER STRAYING A LITTLE DAZED THROUGH HER UNTI+ 618 21
    WILL ROCK IN THE SHOCK OF THE MAD MACHINE AND THE HOUSE+ 624 29
    I SHALL TELL HER THE HOUSE IS MINE   671   6
    AND BEHIND ME NOW IN THE GULFS OF SPACE LIES THE GOLDEN- 695 26
    NOW LADY OF THE MOON NOW OPEN THE GATE OF YOUR SILVERY + 696   1
    INTO YOUR HOUSE GARMENTLESS LADY OF THE LAST GREAT GIFT 696   3
    LADY LADY OF THE LAST HOUSE DOWN THE LONG LONG STREET O+ 696   8
    WILL YOU GO WITH YOU GO FROM MY WARM HOUSE   696 21
    NOT EVERY MAN HAS GENTIANS IN HIS HOUSE   697   1
    TO BE A CREATURE IN THE HOUSE OF THE GOD OF LIFE   700   2
    AND AT ONE WITH THE MASTER OF THE HOUSE WITH THE MISTRE+ 700   5
    AT HOME AT HOME IN THE HOUSE OF THE LIVING   700   6
    IN THE HOUSE OF LIFE   700 16
    AND THE FRAIL SOUL STEPS OUT INTO HER HOUSE AGAIN   720 16
    WOULD YOU PEEP IN THE EMPTY HOUSE LIKE A PILFERER   742 17
    I HAVE COME TO THE HOUSE OF GOD   751   1
    WHERE NO HOUSE IS NEEDED   769 23
    THE HOUSE OF THE GREY DOG   807 22
    KILL HIM IN HIS UNCLEAN HOUSE   808   8
    TO HIS HOUSE IN THE HEART OF A TRAITOR   808 11
    AND BE THERE IN THE HOUSE OF THE CLOVEN FLAME   812 27
    PULL IT DOWN AND PREPARE FOR A NEW FRESH HOUSE OF LIFE   838 12
    I RUN AWAKE TO THE HOUSE OF MY SOUL AND FIND IT EMPTY   871   9
    AND THE HOUSE IS EMPTY AND I AM ALONE   871 12
    HERE IN THIS HOUSE WHERE I HAVE SERVED SO LONG   877 22
    OF THIS OLD HOUSE WHOSE STRANGERS I NOW ENTERTAIN   877 38
    OF THE CREEPER ON THE BREAST OF THE HOUSE OPPOSITE   883   2
    AND DWELLING IN HIS OWN BOWERY HOUSE LIKE A BIRD IN A B+*950   9
    NOT EVERY MAN HAS GENTIANS IN HIS HOUSE   *955 25
    FRIGHTENED AND ALONE THE SOUL SLIPS OUT OF THE HOUSE   *957 12

HOUSEBOATS
    TO KEEP THE REFLECTED VARIETY OF THE HOUSEBOATS   867   9

HOUSE-BOAT
    IN ONE SWIFT BOUND TO THE HOUSE-BOAT   868   2

HOUSED
    KNOWING OUR DEAD ARE FITLY HOUSED IN DEATH   740 23

HOUSE-INHABITING
    POOR LITTLE EARTHY HOUSE-INHABITING OSIRIS   361 10

HOUSEKEEPER
    MAUDIE IS NOUGHT BUT THE HOUSEKEEPER   573 15
    AUNTIE IS ONLY MY HOUSEKEEPER   671   3

HOUSEKEEPING
    IN YOUR CLOSE HOUSEKEEPING ROLE   95 11

HOUSELESS
    AND ALL THE MYRIAD HOUSELESS SEEDS   160   7
    BEHOLD THEM HOMELESS AND HOUSELESS WITHOUT COMPLAINT   736   5
    WE COVER THE HOUSELESS DEAD SO THEY SLEEP IN PEACE   736 25
    WHERE THE WORLD IS VIRGIN AND HOUSELESS   768 16
    SMOKELESS HOUSELESS HOMELESS   768 28
    WALKING SLOWLY WESTWARDS HOUSELESS   770   4

HOUSELS
    HE WHO HOUSELS THE DEAD OF THE GUNS   797   2

HOUSE-ROOF
    OVER HER HOUSE-ROOF   365   2

HOUSES
    LIKE DROWSY CREATURES THE HOUSES FALL ASLEEP   48 19
    THE NEW RED HOUSES SPRING LIKE PLANTS   50 19
    O STIFFLY SHAPEN HOUSES THAT CHANGE NOT   53 20
    CROUCHING AS LITTLE HOUSES CROUCH UNDER THE MIST WHEN I+ 63 23
    TO FIND THE NEW HOUSES A CLUSTER OF LILIES GLITTERING   72 21
    AND LITTERED LETTERING OF TREES AND HILLS AND HOUSES CL+ 88   6
    OVER THE WET DARK ROCKS THE HOUSES AND OVER   112 27
    STANDS RUBBLE OF STUNTED HOUSES ALL IS REAPED   135   7
    THE HOUSES FADE IN A MELT OF MIST   142 17
    AND THE WHITE SHINING HOUSES AND THE GAY RED FLOWERS ON 205   2
    GREEN GRASS SHINING AND LITTLE WHITE HOUSES   224 13
    PEOPLE HOUSES STREETS VEHICLES MACHINES   256 26
    NEW HOUSES NEW FURNITURE NEW STREETS NEW CLOTHES NEW   448 14
    AS WITH CLOTH SO WITH HOUSES SHIPS SHOES WAGONS OR CUPS 451 10
    AND STREETS AND HOUSES AND EVEN SEAS   480   5
    AND ENGINES WILL RUSH AT THE SOLID HOUSES THE EDIFICE O+624 28
    SOME WOMEN LIVE FOR THE IDIOTIC FURNITURE OF THEIR HOUS+657   6
    NO FIRES NO HEARTHS NO HOUSES   769 19
    AND IN THE BIGGEST HOUSES THEY KEEP THEIR MACHINES THAT+793 24
    AND SHALL PASS THE HOUSES OF THE STARS BY NIGHT   799   9
    YOU KNOW NOT HOW MANY ARE HOUSES OF GREY DOGS   807 25
    AND IN THE UNFINISHED HOUSES THE RING OF THE JOINER'S T+865 16
    A RUBBLE OF STUNTED HOUSES STANDS UNREAPED   *939   7
    AND AS WITH CLOTH SO WITH ALL THINGS HOUSES SHOES WAGON+*950 1

HOUSE-TOPS
    THE STAR ABOVE THE HOUSE-TOPS GREETS   108 26

HOUSEY
    AND SO HE STRAINS BENEATH HER HOUSEY WALLS   362 20

HOVEL
    BENEATH THE EARTH-SOILED HOVEL IN WHICH SHE MOVES   362 19

HOVEL-WALL
    MALE TORTOISE CLEAVING BEHIND THE HOVEL-WALL OF THAT DE+364 28

HOVER
AND WHEN ABOVE HER HIS MOTH-WINGS HOVER	42 16
WHITE AND GAUNT WITH WISTFUL EYES THAT HOVER	47 11
AND HOVER LIKE A PRESENTIMENT FADING FAINT	53 29
YOU LOVE ME WHILE I HOVER TENDERLY	87 19
I SEE MYSELF AS THE WINDS THAT HOVER	118 16
ARE THE EARTH I HOVER OVER	118 19
AGAIN I SAW A BROWN BIRD HOVER	124 23
I FELT A BROWN BIRD HOVER	124 25
SAVE AS THE TRAM-CARS HOVER	144 23
IN THE SHADOW OF THE CART-SHED MUST WE HOVER ON THE BRI+	173 7
OH OVER THE FACTORY CITIES THERE SEEMS TO HOVER A DOOM	586 13
AND KEEN EYES THEY WILL HOVER THEY WILL COME BETWEEN YOU	706 19
AND THEN I SAW A BROWN BIRD HOVER	*935 29
AGAIN AND I FELT A BROWN BIRD HOVER	*935 31

HOVERER
| THE HOVERER BETWEEN | 812 14 |

HOVERING
HOVERING ABOUT THE JUDGMENT THAT STOOD IN MY EYES	94 17
LIKE A BE-AUREOLED BLEACHED SKELETON HOVERING	290 22
HOVERING	374 14
DOES HE FAN GREAT WINGS ABOVE THE PRAIRIE LIKE A HOVERI+	374 16
HOVERING TO PECK OUT THE EYES OF THE STILL-LIVING CREAT+	500 17
BECAUSE NOW THE SUNDERERS ARE HOVERING AROUND	707 2
THAT IS MY SPIRIT HOVERING CLOSE ABOVE	750 13
HOVERING OVER IT	882 2
HOVERING TO PLUCK AT THE JUDGMENT WHICH STOOD IN MY EYES	*897 5

HOVERIN'
| HOVERIN' LOOKIN' POOR AN' PLAIN | 60 18 |

HOVERS
| ON THE GREEN WOOD'S EDGE A SHY GIRL HOVERS | 41 1 |
| THAT MY HEART WHICH LIKE A LARK AT HEAVEN'S GATE SINGIN+ | 322 30 |

HOWEVER
RELENTLESS HOWEVER OFTEN	55 17
YET I CANNOT MOVE HOWEVER MUCH	117 16
STILL WAITING FOR YOU HOWEVER OLD YOU ARE AND I AM	248 11
HE SAYS HOWEVER HE IS STAR-ROAD	405 23
THERE IS HOWEVER THE VAST THIRD HOMOGENEOUS AMORPHOUS	649 24
THE MYSTERY I STRIVE TOWARD HOWEVER	876 28
HOWEVER	*948 7
PURITY HOWEVER IS NEVER SANE AND NEVER WHOLESOME	*953 1

HOWL
I REMEMBER MY FIRST TERROR HEARING THE HOWL OF WEIRD	366 8
SO FIERCE WHEN THE COYOTES HOWL BARKING LIKE A WHOLE	396 29
WE CAN BUT HOWL THE LUGUBRIOUS HOWL OF IDIOTS	514 22
THE HOWL OF THE UTTERLY LOST	514 23
IS LASHING HIS TAIL IN HIS SLEEP THE WINDS HOWL THE COL+	795 14

HOWLING
AND YET AS HIS BRASS-RESONANT HOWLING YELL RESOUNDS	377 20
HOWLING THEIR NOWHERENESS	514 24
SOMETHING IS LEFT BEHIND LOST AND HOWLING AND WE KNOW IT	543 25
AND THE SOUND OF ITS HOWLING GETS BIGGER AND BIGGER AND+	670 14
AND HOWLING WITH HATE	795 23

HOWLS
HENCE HE UNCOVERS HIS BIG ASS-TEETH AND HOWLS IN THAT A+	378 24
AND HOWLS HIS PANDEMONIUM ON THE INDIGNANT AIR	379 23
LIFTS UP HIS VOICE AND HOWLS TO THE WALLS OF THE PUEBLO	405 11

HOWSOEVER
| HOWSOEVER THEY PASS BY | 270 3 |

HUB
ARE THEIR HEARTS THE HUB OF THE WHEEL	631 29
WHEN THE MIND MAKES A WHEEL WHICH TURNS ON THE HUB OF T+	712 13
EVERY WHEEL ON ITS HUB HAS A SOUL EVIL	713 2
IT STAYS ON ITS HUB	713 26
FIXED UPON THE HUB OF THE EGO	713 29
AND THOU SHALT BEGIN TO SPIN ROUND ON THE HUB OF THE	714 17

HUDDLED
HUDDLED AWAY IN THE DARK	119 20
SITTING HUDDLED AGAINST THE CERULEAN ONE FLESH WITH THE+	142 11
HAVE HUDDLED RAGS OR LIMBS ON THE NAKED SLEEP	144 22
I CAN ALWAYS LINGER OVER THE HUDDLED BOOKS ON THE STALLS	180 24
ALL MY PRETTY PICTURES HUDDLED IN THE DARK AWAITING	634 1
ENCIRCLING THEIR HUDDLED MONSTERS OF LOVE	695 4
HUDDLED AWAY IN THE DARK	*932 29

HUDDLES
| THAT HUDDLES IN GREY HEAPS COILING AND HOLDING BACK | 164 18 |

HUDDLIN'
| HUDDLIN' UP I' T' RAIN | 60 16 |
| HUDDLIN' CLOSE TOGETHER A CAUSE O' TH' RAIN | *911 2 |

HUE
| THE LEAF'S BROWN HUE | 178 4 |

HUES
| FLOWERILY NAKED IN FLESH AND GIVING OFF HUES OF LIFE | 299 4 |

HUGE
DIM TREES SO HUGE AND TALL	68 24
IN THE PLAYGROUND A SHAGGY SNOWBALL STANDS HUGE AND STI+	76 17
THEY DWELT IN A HUGE HOARSE SEA-CAVE	201 21
SHONE LIKE A HUGE SEA-SPARK	201 24
WHAT A HUGE VAST INANIMATE IT IS THAT YOU MUST ROW	353 25
HERS HUGE HIS SMALL	361 23
SHE HUGE HE SMALL	361 28
TO CATCH SIGHT OF HER STANDING LIKE SOME HUGE GHOULISH	385 16

HUGE
AND THERE OF COURSE YOU MEET A HUGE AND MUD-GREY	387 6
AND THE HUGE FRONTAL OF THREE GREAT ELEPHANTS STEPPING	387 28
AND DOWN BELOW HUGE HOMAGE OF SHADOWY BEASTS BARE-FOOT	388 14
HUGE MORE TASSELS SWINGING MORE DRIPPING FIRE OF NEW	388 27
SITTING UP THERE RABBIT-WISE BUT HUGE PLUMB-WEIGHTED	393 5
THE SUN AS HE WAITS A MOMENT HUGE AND LIQUID	403 4
THE HUGE OLD FEMALE ON THE DRUM	426 4
THE ELEPHANTS HUGE AND GREY LOOMED THEIR CURVED BULK	445 10
THE ELEPHANT THE HUGE OLD BEAST	465 7
SO THAT IT RUSHES UP IN A HUGE BLAZE LIKE A PHALLUS	506 6
AND HYGIENIC BABIES IN HUGE HULKS OF COFFIN-LIKE PERAMB+	522 5
OH IF THE HUGE TREE DIES	640 18
HUGE HUGE ROLL THE PEALS OF THE THUNDROUS LAUGH	698 18
HUGE HUGER HUGER AND HUGER PEALING	698 19
HOW NICE IN THE GREAT CITIES WHERE ALL THINGS RUSH AND +	794 15
THE ROUGH SNOWBALL IN THE PLAYGROUND STANDS HUGE AND ST+	*898 11
THE ROUGH SNOWBALL IN THE PLAYGROUND STANDS HUGE AND ST+	*901 20
THESE TREES SO HUGE AND TALL	*915 8

HUGER
| HUGE HUGER HUGER AND HUGER PEALING | 698 19 |

HUGEST
| OF THE HUGEST OLDEST OF BEASTS IN THE NIGHT AND THE FIR+ | 388 11 |

HUGGED
SITS INDIFFERENT HUGGED IN HER RAGS	54 18
LIKE A FLOWER THAT THE FROST HAS HUGGED AND LET GO MY H+	95 1
LIKE A FLOWER THAT THE FROST HAS HUGGED AND LET GO MY H+	*897 16

HUICHILOBOS
| HUICHILOBOS | 371 7 |

HUITZILOPOCHTLI
BUT PERHAPS ASHTAROTH PERHAPS SIVA PERHAPS HUITZILOPOCH+	674 25
I AM HUITZILOPOCHTLI	804 4
THE RED HUITZILOPOCHTLI	804 5
I AM HUITZILOPOCHTLI	804 7
I AM HUITZILOPOCHTLI	804 10
I AM HUITZILOPOCHTLI	804 13
I AM HUITZILOPOCHTLI SITTING IN THE DARK	804 15
HE IS HUITZILOPOCHTLI	805 12
THE RED HUITZILOPOCHTLI	805 13
HE IS HUITZILOPOCHTLI	805 15
HE IS HUITZILOPOCHTLI	805 18
HE IS HUITZILOPOCHTLI	805 21
HE IS HUITZILOPOCHTLI SITTING IN THE DARK	805 23
HE IS HUITZILOPOCHTLI SLEEPING OR WAKING	806 11
HUITZILOPOCHTLI LEAPING AND QUAKING	806 13
I AM HUITZILOPOCHTLI	806 21
THEN CALL ON HUITZILOPOCHTLI	808 1
HUITZILOPOCHTLI CALL HIM OFF	808 6
CRYING HUITZILOPOCHTLI IS THIS WELL DONE	808 14
RED IS HUITZILOPOCHTLI'S BLOOD	808 19
HUITZILOPOCHTLI GIVES THE BLACK BLADE OF DEATH	809 4
BUT HUITZILOPOCHTLI TOUCHED THE HAND OF QUETZALCOATL	809 19
RED HUITZILOPOCHTLI	809 23
HUITZILOPOCHTLI THE GOLDEN	810 1
INTO BLUE DAY PAST HUITZILOPOCHTLI	810 10
RED HUITZILOPOCHTLI	810 11
BLACK HUITZILOPOCHTLI	810 13
HUITZILOPOCHTLI GOLDEN	810 15
WHITE HUITZILOPOCHTLI	810 17
GREEN HUITZILOPOCHTLI	810 19
HUITZILOPOCHTLI HAS THROWN HIS BLACK MANTLE	811 18
COUNT THE RED GRAINS OF THE HUITZILOPOCHTLI	811 24

HULKS
| AND HYGIENIC BABIES IN HUGE HULKS OF COFFIN-LIKE PERAMB+ | 522 5 |

HULLABALOO
| INTO TANTRUMS AND STARTED THEIR HULLABALOO | 761 6 |

HUM
THE HUM OF HIS HEAVY STAGGERING WINGS	46 18
ALL THE LONG SCHOOL-HOURS ROUND THE IRREGULAR HUM OF TH+	75 20
OF THE MAN-LIFE NORTH IMPRISONED SHUT IN THE HUM OF THE	149 5
THE HUM OF THE BEES IN THE PEAR-TREE BLOOM	885 14
THE HUM AND WHISPER OF THE CLASS LIKE A LITTLE WIND	*894 15
ALL THE SLOW SCHOOL HOURS ROUND THE IRREGULAR HUM OF TH+	*897 20
WAKES FROM THE HUM FALTERING ABOUT A NOUN	*898 3
ALL THE SLOW SCHOOL HOURS ROUND THE IRREGULAR HUM OF TH+	*900 28
WAKES FROM THE HUM FALTERING ABOUT A NOUN	*901 12

HUMAN
TO THIS HUMAN BLIGHT	146 16
BUT NEVER THE MOTION HAS A HUMAN FACE	153 7
YOUR HUMAN SELF IMMORTAL TAKE THE WATERY TRACK	161 28
IN A MOTION HUMAN INHUMAN TWO AND ONE	252 15
EVERY HUMAN BEING WILL THEN BE LIKE A FLOWER UNTRAMMELL+	267 30
AND ALL THESE HUMAN PILLARS OF LOFTINESS GOING STIFF ME+	288 1
THE HUMAN PILLARS	288 10
OF THE IRON CLICK OF YOUR HUMAN CONTACT	291 10
WHAT WE CALL HUMAN	291 29
WHAT WE CALL HUMAN AND WHAT WE DON'T CALL HUMAN	292 2
SUCH AN AROMA OF LOST HUMAN LIFE	298 7
THICK SMOOTH-FLESHED SILVER DULL ONLY AS HUMAN LIMBS ARE	298 23
NOR SOUND OF STILL MORE FOUL HUMAN PERFECTION	316 8
AND THE HUMAN SOUL IS FATED TO WIDE-EYED RESPONSIBILITY	347 2
I DESPISED MYSELF AND THE VOICES OF MY ACCURSED HUMAN	351 20
THE MORE THAN HUMAN DENSE INSISTENCE OF WILL	371 29
BUT YOU LOVE LYING WARM BETWEEN WARM HUMAN THIGHS	396 19
HUMAN FROM ANOTHER	399 23
THAT WILL BLOSSOM FORTH THE WHOLE OF HUMAN NATURE	429 13
AND GO AHEAD WITH WHAT IS HUMAN NATURE	429 15
AND MAKE A NEW JOB OF THE HUMAN WORLD	429 16
AND LEAVE IT TO SOME NATURE THAT IS MORE THAN HUMAN	429 19

HUMAN
    COMPELLED TO SEE THE DELICATE SKILL OF FLICKERING HUMAN   445 26
    ABSOLUTISM IS FINISHED IN THE HUMAN CONSCIOUSNESS TOO   473 14
    OF TWO HUMAN HEARTS TWO ANCIENT ROCKS A MAN'S HEART   477 15
    NOT BOTTLED IN HUMAN BOTTLES   481 8
    WITH THE HUMAN TAINT   481 12
    AND CARES NOT A STRAW FOR THE PUT-UP HUMAN FIGMENTS   481 16
    AND MY LEAVES ARE GREEN WITH THE BREATH OF HUMAN EXPERI+   499 11
    CRUSHING OUT THE NATURAL HUMAN LIFE   508 21
    AND REFUSING THE PETTIFOGGING PROMPTINGS OF HUMAN   525 18
    BUT OH OUR HUMAN LIVES THE LUNGING BLIND CYCLOPS WE ARE   544 12
    TOO HUMAN TOO LONG   564 2
    SUCH A HUMAN BIRD   564 8
    CAN PUT BACK A HUMAN LIFE INTO CONNECTION WITH THE LIVI+   617 4
    THE HUMAN WILL IS FREE ULTIMATELY TO CHOOSE ONE OF TWO +   617 12
    THE HUMAN WILL TO THE FLUSH OF THE VASTER IMPULSION OF +   617 14
    I WANT TO SHOW ALWAYS THE HUMAN TENDER REVERENCE   622 5
    I FEEL ABSOLUTE REVERENCE TO NOBODY AND TO NOTHING HUMAN   622 6
    OF HUMAN ONENESS   635 2
    CHRIST THE HUMAN CONSCIOUSNESS   636 15
    AND THE HUMAN SPIRIT IS SO MUCH GAS TO KEEP IT ALL GOING   641 8
    AND BETWEEN THEM THE LAST LIVING HUMAN BEINGS   642 3
    ESCAPING THE PETROL FUMES OF HUMAN CONVERSATION   646 6
    TO SEE THE GLEAM OF THE GODS THERE REFLECTED IN THE HUM+   649 22
    MAN IS ONLY PERFECTLY HUMAN   650 31
    WALKS TO THE FUNERAL OF THE WHOLE HUMAN RACE   653 2
    HARDLY EVER NOW HAS A HUMAN FACE   656 12
    WHEREAS FACES NOW ARE ONLY HUMAN GRIMACES   656 23
    AND THE BOLSHEVIST ASSERTS THAT BY HUMAN RIGHT NO MAN S+   663 14
    THE TREE OF HUMAN EXISTENCE NEEDS BADLY PRUNING   677 28
    ONLY THE HUMAN BEING ABSOLVED FROM KISSING AND STRIFE   713 27
    JUSTICE HUMAN DECENCY IN MATERIAL THINGS   833 24
    ANOTHER HUMAN BEING   834 5
    WHEREAS TO THE ORDINARY MORAL HUMAN BEING THE WORD   837 3
    INSTEAD OF THIS MESS WHICH EXPRESSES THE IMPUDENT HUMAN   837 18
    DON'T YOU THINK LITTLE MAN YOU'LL BE FATHER OF HUMAN BA+   *947 23
    IN FACT IT MAY BE THAT A LITTLE SODOMY IS NECESSARY TO +   *952 18

HUMANITY
    HAVE OWNING HUMANITY   395 18
    ESPECIALLY DEMOCRATIC LIVE-BY-LOVE HUMANITY   395 19
    ALL HUMANITY IS JAM TO YOU   398 25
    HOW DISGUSTING HOW INFINITELY SORDID THIS HUMANITY IS   628 4
    WHEN HE LOOKS BEYOND HUMANITY   650 18
    AND EVERY GOD THAT HUMANITY HAS EVER KNOWN IS STILL A G+   671 14
    HUMANITY NEEDS PRUNING   677 20
    THE TREE OF HUMANITY NEEDS PRUNING BADLY   677 24
    HUMANITY   679 2

HUMANLY
    WE ARE HUMANLY OUT OF TOUCH   468 15

HUMANS
    SPARE A MILLION OR TWO OF HUMANS   402 30
    IS THE TIME COME FOR HUMANS   429 22
    HUMANS   429 26
    THE HUMANS LIE   824 21

HUMAN-TAINTED
    BUT EVEN THAT IS HUMAN-TAINTED NOW   481 19

HUMBLE
    TOO MUCH OF THE HUMBLE WILLY WET-LEG   537 13
    CAME TO THE COUNTER WITH HIS HAT OFF HUMBLE AT THE SHRI+   618 17
    THEY ARE HUMBLE WITH A CREEPING HUMILITY BEING PARASITE+   621 20
    TO BE HUMBLE BEFORE OTHER MEN IS DEGRADING I AM HUMBLE +   622 1
    AND I WANT NO MAN TO BE HUMBLE BEFORE ME   622 3
    AND WOMEN FALL FOR THESE LITTLE-BOY MINDS THEY FEEL QUI+   841 24
    SHE BOWS QUITE HUMBLE SUCH A SUBTLE DESTROYING MIND MUS+   841 28

HUMBLED
    BEFORE SHE HUMBLED HERSELF AND KNOCKED HER KNEES WITH   314 8

HUMILIATING
    HUMILIATING   484 11
    AND NAKED EMBRACE AN ANTI-CLIMAX HUMILIATING AND RIDICU+   608 19

HUMILIATION
    HUMILIATION DEEP TO ME THAT ALL MY BEST   87 23
    SELF-EXPOSURE HARD HUMILIATION NEED TO ADD HIMSELF ON TO   362 31
    AND HUMILIATION   378 15
    HUMILIATION   378 26
    I AM FILLED WITH HUMILIATION   484 8
    THIS I CALL A SHOCKING HUMILIATION   645 5

HUMILITY
    IN THE PRIDE OF HUMILITY   201 14
    WAS IT HUMILITY TO FEEL SO HONOURED   350 15
    NOWADAYS TO TALK OF HUMILITY IS A SIN AGAINST THE HOLY +   621 12
    THEY ARE HUMBLE WITH A CREEPING HUMILITY BEING PARASITE+   621 20
    WHEN I HEAR MAN SPOUTING ABOUT HUMILITY TODAY   621 22

HUMMED
    IN THAT MOST AWFUL STILLNESS THAT ONLY GASPED AND HUMMED   372 7

HUMMING
    ALONE ON A HILL-SIDE IN THE NORTH HUMMING IN THE WIND   610 23
    VAST RANGES OF EXPERIENCE LIKE THE HUMMING OF UNSEEN HA+   666 25
    WHEN YOU HEAR THEM HUMMING   755 18

HUMMING-BIRDS
    HUMMING-BIRDS RACED DOWN THE AVENUES   372 8

HUMMING-BIRD
    IN THE WORLD WHERE THE HUMMING-BIRD FLASHED AHEAD OF   372 15
    HUMMING-BIRD   523 17

HUMOUR
    AND WHAT A SENSE OF TRUE HUMOUR THEY'VE GOT HA-HA   583 21

HUMS
    DOWN WHERE THE LIVE WEB HUMS   *893 10

HUMUS
    AND FINAL HUMUS   318 3
    WHERE FLOWERS SPROUT IN THE ACRID HUMUS AND FADE INTO H+   321 11
    GRINDING THEM SMALL TO HUMUS ON EARTH'S NETHER MILL-STO+   615 6

HUNDRED
    AWFULLY MUST I CALL BACK A HUNDRED EYES A VOICE   76 7
    I HAVE STARTLED A HUNDRED EYES AND NOW I MUST LOOK   76 12
    AWFULLY MUST I CALL BACK THOSE HUNDRED EYES A VOICE   *898 2
    I HAVE STARTLED A HUNDRED EYES AND I MUST LOOK   *898 6
    AWFULLY MUST I CALL BACK THOSE HUNDRED EYES A VOICE   *901 11
    I HAVE STARTLED A HUNDRED EYES AND I MUST LOOK   *901 15

HUNDRED-PER-CENT AMERICAN
    TO GROW UP TRUE HUNDRED-PER-CENT AMERICAN   778 2
    PREVENT HIS BECOMING A HUNDRED-PER-CENT AMERICAN   778 8
    IF HE WERE A HUNDRED-PER-CENT AMERICAN CITIZEN   778 13

HUNDRED-PER-CENT
    A HUNDRED-PER-CENT THING   775 24
    BE CAREFUL HOW YOU TURN HIM INTO A HUNDRED-PER-CENT   776 19
    TURN THEM INTO HUNDRED-PER-CENT AMERICANS   777 3
    AS HUNDRED-PER-CENT AMERICANS WELL-EDUCATED   780 18

HUNDREDS
    STRUT LIKE PEG-TOPS WOUND AROUND WITH HUNDREDS OF YARDS   388 17
    AND HUNDREDS OF SOLDIERS ON HORSEBACK HAVE FILED BETWEEN   732 6
    HUNDREDS OF VIOLET-HEADS IN A SHOWER   880 19

HUNG
    OUTSIDE THE HOUSE AN ASH-TREE HUNG ITS TERRIBLE WHIPS   36 9
    CHERRIES HUNG ROUND HER EARS   37 2
    WHERE THE SWALLOW HAS HUNG HER MARRIAGE BED   42 22
    TO THE CUCKOO THAT HUNG LIKE A DOVE   124 4
    AT THE GATE THE NETS HUNG BALKING   152 16
    TO WHERE THE SUNSET HUNG ITS WAN GOLD CLOTHS   205 27
    AND A HAIRY BIG BEE HUNG OVER THE PRIMULAS   243 23
    HUNG ALL THE TIME DID WE BUT KNOW IT THE ALL-KNOWING SH+   328 8
    THE FLAME OF MY SOUL LIKE A TREMBLING STAR IS HUNG   750 12
    THE GUELDER ROSE-BUSH IS HUNG WITH CORONETS   854 21
    LOOKED WHERE THE RED FRUIT HUNG LIKE COALS OF FIRE   864 8
    OF THE WIND HUNG ROUND THE KNOTTED BUDS LIKE A CANOPY   866 25

HUNGARIAN
    A WOMAN IS SINGING ME A WILD HUNGARIAN AIR   *940 19

HUNGER
    TWO HARD CRUDE PAWS IN HUNGER ON THE LONELY   127 27
    HUNGER IS THE VERY SATAN   263 5
    THE FEAR OF HUNGER IS MOLOCH BELIAL THE HORRIBLE GOD   263 6
    IT IS A FEARFUL THING TO BE DOMINATED BY THE FEAR OF HU+   263 7
    OF THE SUAVE SENSITIVE BODY THE HUNGER FOR THIS   263 16
    THE GREAT AND DOMINANT HUNGER OF THE MIND   263 24
    THAT I JUST ESCAPED THE HUNGER FOR THESE   263 30
    BUT THEN CAME ANOTHER HUNGER   264 8
    WITH A HUNGER MORE FRIGHTENING MORE PROFOUND   264 11
    THE HUNGER FOR THE WOMAN ALAS   264 14
    YET THERE IT IS THE HUNGER WHICH COMES UPON US   264 18
    A WOMAN FED THAT HUNGER IN ME AT LAST   264 26
    A MAN IS SO TERRIFIED OF STRONG HUNGER   264 32
    WHEN A MAN IS RICH HE LOSES AT LAST THE HUNGER FEAR   265 2
    SO ANOTHER HUNGER WAS SUPPLIED   265 20
    THIS ACHE FOR BEING IS THE ULTIMATE HUNGER   265 26

HUNGRILY
    ITSELF AMONG EVERYTHING ELSE HERE HUNGRILY STEALING   141 18

HUNGRY
    HUNGRY FOR LOVE YET IF I LAY MY HAND IN HER BREAST   128 2
    MATE MY HUNGRY SOUL WITH A GERM OF ITS WOMB   179 27
    WE TAKE NO HUNGRY STRAY FROM THE PALE-FACE   405 7
    HUNGRY AND DISCONTENT IN THE FRUITFUL SHADE   864 2

HUNT
    THEM AGAIN ON A QUARRY OF KNOWLEDGE THEY HATE TO HUNT   74 10
    AND MOVE ON YOUR SLOW SOLITARY HUNT   352 19
    AND HUNT THEM DOWN   706 7
    THEM AGAIN ON A QUARRY OF KNOWLEDGE THEY HATE TO HUNT   *895 18
    THEM AGAIN ON A QUARRY OF KNOWLEDGE THEY HATE TO HUNT   *904 7

HUNTS
    THYSELF SLIP OUT THE LEASH AND HUNTS THY WAY   879 13

HUNTSMAN
    DEJECTEDLY A HUNTSMAN GOES BY WITH HIS LOAD   220 17

HUNTSMAN'S
    WE CLIMBED THE HUNTSMAN'S LADDER AND SAT SWINGING   216 22
    WE CLIMBED THE HUNTSMAN'S LADDER AND SAT SWINGING   *942 8

HURL
    AND IF THEY'RE OVER FORTY-FIVE HURL GREAT STONES INTO T+ 541 4

HURLED
    LIKE A THUNDERBOLT HURLED   163 4
    HIS MOUSTACHE WITH AN ELBOW LIFTED AND HURLED   814 29

HURLING
    WOULD FALL AND DARKNESS WOULD COME HURLING HEAVILY DOWN 205 10

HURRIES
ME ITS LIFE AS IT HURRIES IN SECRET   180 33
HARK AT THE RIVER IT PANTS AS IT HURRIES THROUGH   212 2
SHE HURRIES UP STRIDING REARED ON LONG UNCANNY LEGS   358 31

HURRY
SLIPPING INTO ITS BED OF DEAD LEAVES YOU HURRY INTO YOUR   254 16
THE WORLD IS ENDING LET'S HURRY TO BORROW   815 2

HURRYING
ARE HURRYING AND STRIDENTLY CALLING   54 2
HURRYING CREATURES RUN   166 22
FLEET HURRYING LIMBS   171 3
OF MEN IN BOWLER HATS HURRYING   484 4
HURRYING HURRYING LEGS GOING QUICK QUICK QUICK   484 6
HOT HURRYING YET IT BURNS IF YOU TOUCH IT   505 26
IGNORING OUR MOTOR-CAR BLACK AND ALWAYS HURRYING   780 25
HURRYING   780 26

HURT
GOT HURT I' TH' PIT   44 23
WHEER'S 'E HURT THIS TIME LAD   45 9
WHAT A TRAIPSE IT IS IF A MAN GETS HURT   46 3
NO LONGER HURT WHERE THE SILK SAILS FILL   53 12
IS IT BECAUSE I HURT YOU WITH PAIN MY DEAR   87 2
HURT AS I GAVE THEM YOU PUT ME AWAY   87 11
YOU HURT MY HEART-BEAT'S PRIVACY   116 28
BIG HANDS AS IF SURELY HER ARMS DID HURT   128 22
WASTRELS THAT SLEEP ON THE FLAGSTONES WITHOUT ANY HURT   145 33
HURT AT THE CHALK-COLOURED TULIPS AND THE EVENING-GREEN   153 12
WITH ME BOTH IN ONE HURT   160 4
I HAVE STEPPED ACROSS MY PEOPLE AND HURT THEM IN SPITE   209 10
OF HATE HAS HURT US SO   229 14
FEELING TRAMMELLED AND HURT   255 17
THAT LIVE BY NIGHT AND LAMPLIGHT AND FIRELIGHT DO THEM +   331 8
YOUR SENSITIVE LOVE-PRIDE BEING ALL HURT   400 29
THEY WON'T HURT YOU   409 28
MOST OF MY FRIENDS WERE DEEPLY HURT   491 17
WITH ALL THE HURT TO THEIR INSTINCTIVE AND EMOTIONAL SE+   544 28
AND ANYHOW THEY CAN'T DO ANY HURT   634 12
ON THE HORSE'S BELLY HURT HIM FOR HE WAS RATHER GENTLE   734 20
I MUST PRESERVE MY LIFE FROM HURT   741 6
I DO NOT DIE I AM NOT EVEN HURT   741 24
SOME ONE STOPPED ME AND SAID YOUR LOVER IS HURT   750 18
WE WOULDN'T HURT YOU FOR THE WORLD SAYS THE PARASITE   765 23
AND HURT HURT OURSELVES AND EVERYBODY   833 14
YOU SOUND SO DREADFUL SO CRUELLY HURT MY DEAR   871 18
PLEASURE SO HEAVY-INTENSE IT HURT TOO MUCH   875 20
AND I WAS HURT   880 31
WHOM I HAD HURT   881 5

HURTING
YOUR BOW FOR BROKEN IT IS AND HURTING TO HEAR   85 22
YOU HAVE STEPPED ACROSS YOUR PEOPLE CARELESSLY HURTING   209 8
IT SLIPS OVER IT AS SHADOWS DO WITHOUT HURTING ITSELF   467 19

HURTLING
AND BRING IT HURTLING TO A HEAD WITH CRASH OF HORNS AGA+   381 25
HURTLING LIKE A BLACK BALL THROUGH THE SNOW   397 8

HURTS
I LOVED BUT THERE SHE GOES AND HER BEAUTY HURTS MY HEART   67 11
WHAT HURTS FROM WHAT AMUSES   131 6
WHERE DEAD MEN'S LIVES GLOW GENTLY AND IRON HURTS   173 22
THE SHINING OF LAMPS BECAUSE WITH HIS RAYS HE HURTS THE+   331 1
OUR EYES DARKEN AND IMPOTENCE HURTS   746 14
AND SHAME THAT HURTS MOST   747 15
IN YOUR SLEEP YOU TWIST YOUR SOUL HURTS YOU   807 30
SIEGMUND THE STRONG BEATING OF YOUR HEART HURTS ME   870 19
HOW HE HURTS ME WITH HIS HEART AND HIS THROAT SO NEAR T+   871 22

HUSBAND
SO SHE TURNED AND SAID TO HER HUSBAND   202 11
TO THE MAN WHO IS HER HUSBAND ALL THE REST   231 2
DIS THE DARK THE JEALOUS GOD THE HUSBAND   308 7
AND PUT UP WITH HER HUSBAND   358 28
NOW YOU ARE HUSBANDLESS INDEED NO MORE HUSBAND TO   411 7
BUT THE UNHAPPINESS OF A WIFE WITH A GOOD HUSBAND   456 7
THAN THE UNHAPPINESS OF A WIFE WITH A BAD HUSBAND   456 9
I REALISED THE SECRET JOY HER YOUNG SPANISH HUSBAND HAD   618 22
AND DEVOTED HERSELF TO HER HUSBAND   619 8
YOU HEAR A WOMAN SAY I LOVE MY HUSBAND DEARLY   654 10
I HEARD HER SAY TO HER BRILLIANT YOUNG HUSBAND   842 12
AND THE BRILLIANT YOUNG HUSBAND MADE A LITTLE MOVE POUT+   842 16
YET THE HUSBAND WAS MOST BRILLIANT AND FAMOUS   842 25
AND THE WOOD LIKE A MANLY HUSBAND SPREADS SOFTNESS AND +   854 9

HUSBAND-BLOSSOMS
HELL'S HUSBAND-BLOSSOMS   308 25

HUSBANDLESS
NOW YOU ARE HUSBANDLESS INDEED NO MORE HUSBAND TO   411 7

HUSBANDLY
TO BE HUSBANDLY AND GIVE PERPENDICULAR TO THE LANDSCAPE   835 3

HUSBANDS
GOOD HUSBANDS MAKE UNHAPPY WIVES   456 5
SO DO BAD HUSBANDS JUST AS OFTEN   456 6

HUSBAND-SNARED
HUSBAND-SNARED HELL-QUEEN   309 21

HUSBAND-SPLENDID
HELL REARING ITS HUSBAND-SPLENDID SERPENT HEADS   308 20

HUSBAND-STRATEGY
AND POMP OF HUSBAND-STRATEGY ON EARTH   309 24

HUSBAND'S
ALL THE LONG YEARS OF SITTING IN MY HUSBAND'S HOUSE   47 30

HUSBAND-TILTH
THE BIT OF HUSBAND-TILTH SHE IS   309 26

HUSBAND-TYRANNY
HELL-GLAMOROUS AND PURPLE HUSBAND-TYRANNY   308 31

HUSH
HUSH NOW HUSH WHERE AM I BIURET   40 30
HUSH WE TRY   88 13
IT STANDS SO STILL IN THE HUSH COMPOSED OF TREES AND IN+   159 27
BUT HUSH I AM NOT REGRETTING   227 25
HUSH THEN   231 8
HUSH MY LOVE THEN HUSH   410 13
HUSH AND DIE MY DEAR   410 14
THEN CAME THE HUSH AGAIN LIKE A HUSH OF FEAR   444 23
WILL NO ONE SAY HUSH TO THEE   540 7
THEN THERE WAS A HUSH OF SUSPENSE AT THE CORE OF EVERY +   683 12
IN THE GREAT HUSH OF GOING FROM THIS INTO THAT   699 6
BUT OTHERS THE DARK DOORS OH HUSH HUSH   711 9
ALONG THE COAST TO HEAR THE HUSH   747 3
HUSH THEN NEVER A WORD   887 19

HUSHABY
HUSHABY BABY ON A TREE TOP   669 7

HUSHED
ALL THE BYGONE HUSHED YEARS   53 9
YOUR YOUNG HUSHED LOOK THAT THEN SAW GOD ABLAZE   157 23
BECAUSE OF THE SILENT SNOW WE ARE ALL HUSHED   165 29
NOW THEN THAT ALL THEIR YEARNING IS HUSHED AND COVERED   410 24
I STEAL ACROSS THE HUSHED CORRIDOR   877 36
OVER THE BYGONE HUSHED YEARS   *906 1
WAKE OF THE HUSHED TUMULT NOW SPENT AND GONE   *906 8
TO THE HUSHED GREY-WINGED MINISTRANTS THE BATS OF NIGHT+   *916 12

HUSK
RIPE LITTLE STARS COME ROLLING FROM THEIR HUSK   135 12
ROLLS OUT OF THE HUSK OF DEATH   172 6
IT FELL FROM OUR HUSK IN A LITTLE HASTY SEED   172 13
LIKE A SHED WHITE HUSK ON THE TORRID SKY   747 29
THE SUN HAS CREPT LIKE A SCARLET BEETLE IN THE HUSK   757 15
AS THEY DRINK THROUGH THEIR HUSK   824 24
HUSK   864 28
WHERE THIS FRAIL SHADOWY HUSK OF A DAY IS LOST   875 15
AND SILENCE ISSUES SLOWLY FROM THE HUSK   *939 11

HUSK-BALL
FLIMSY HUSK-BALL THROUGH WHOSE RIFTS THERE LOOKS   874 31

HUSKY
YOU THIRST FOR COOLNESS WITH A HUSKY THIRST   91 16

HUTCH
OF REAL DAYLIGHT UPON US RELEASED FROM THE FOUL DREAM'S+   175 30
I KNOW THE SWEET RED HUTCH OF HIS MOUTH WHERE WARM   876 32

HUTCHED
HUTCHED UP FOR WARMTH THE MUDDY RIMS   145 19

HUTS
AT HER CITIES OF STONE AND HER HUTS OF STRAW   790 8

HYACINTH
OF QUEENS IN HYACINTH AND SKIES OF GOLD   135 26
FAR-OFF FAR-OFF IN THE HYACINTH AGES   814 4
OF QUEENS IN HYACINTH 'NEATH SKIES OF GOLD   *939 18

HYACINTHS
LIKE LAVENDER CROCUSES SNOWDROPS LIKE ROMAN HYACINTHS   270 6

HYACINTHUS
FOR A MOMENT PURE IN THE YELLOW EVENING LIGHT HE WAS HY+   672 11

HYAENA
OR A HYAENA EATING CORPSES   621 24
NO COBRA NOR HYAENA NOR SCORPION NOR HIDEOUS WHITE ANT   701 13
THE GREY VULTURE THE GREY HYAENA CORPSE-EATERS   711 23

HYAENAS
AND THE BASE THINGS LIKE HYAENAS OR BED-BUGS HAVE LEAST+   621 18
HYAENAS ONLY HINT AT IT   712 26

HYDROCEPHALOUS
WAS A GREAT BIG HYDROCEPHALOUS WATER-IN-THE-BRAIN INFANT   670 22

HYDROGEN
WATER IS H2O HYDROGEN TWO PARTS OXYGEN ONE   515 11

HYENA
NOT THIS HYENA TAME PEACE WHERE NO MAN DARE TELL ANOTHER   519 23

HYGIENE
NURSES DOCTORS PROPER FOOD HYGIENE SCHOOLS ALL THAT   832 5

HYGIENIC
AND HYGIENIC BABIES IN HUGE HULKS OF COFFIN-LIKE PERAMB+   522 5

HYMN
THE MOVING HYMN   96 22
IN THE CHOIR THE BOYS ARE SINGING THE HYMN   147 18

HYMNS
    AND HYMNS IN THE COSY PARLOUR THE TINKLING PIANO OUR   148 13
    AND HYMNS GLEAMED ON OUR WARM LIPS AS WE WATCHED MOTHER+   *940 12

HYPERTROPHY
    HYPERTROPHY OF THE MIND ATROPHY OF THE SENSES   841 21

HYPOCRISY
    MONEY HYPOCRISY GREED MACHINES   457 11
    GIVE GREAT HYPOCRISY THE LIE   458 10
    AND AFTER ALL LYING AND BASE HYPOCRISY AND TREACHERY   497 6
    IS BRITISH HYPOCRISY A FORM OF SOFTENING OF THE BRAIN   659 22

HYPOCRITE
    TOO DIRTY A HYPOCRITE TO ADMIT HIS OWN NATURE   *949 3

HYPOCRITES
    HYPOCRITES AND EUNUCHS   658 23
    EUNUCHS AND HYPOCRITES   658 24

HYSTERICAL
    SOMETHING WHICH SETS THE BLACK POPLARS ASHAKE WITH HYST+ 102 26
    TO SUPPORT HER THE HYSTERICAL CAMEL   492 8

HYSTERICS
    SUCH SILLY HYSTERICS   581 25

H2O
    WATER IS H2O HYDROGEN TWO PARTS OXYGEN ONE   515 11

IACCOS
    IS THERE SOME GREAT IACCOS OF THESE SLOPES   141 1

ICE
    ARE BUBBLES OF ICE KISS ME YOU KNOW HOW IT RESTS   212 7
    WAS SAVOUR OF ICE AND OF ROSES AND GLIMMERING   217 5
    THE ICE   273 11
    TO THE SNOW OF THE SANGRE DE CRISTO MOUNTAINS THE ICE OF 402 23
    TO THE SLEEP OF ICE   436 7
    WHICH GOES THROUGH ALL THE STAGES OF STEAM AND STREAM A+ 505 21
    CHATTERING AMONG THE ICE   795 22
    THERE ARE DRAGONS OF SUN AND ICE DRAGONS OF THE MOON AN+ 796 18
    FOR WATCHING I AM FROZEN AS IN ICE   879 18

ICE-AGE
    IS YOUR CONTINENT COLD FROM THE ICE-AGE STILL THAT THE + 374 21

ICEBERGS
    OF ONE WHO WILL SETTLE ON ICEBERGS AND HONK ACROSS THE   439 2
    CAUGHT BETWEEN GREAT ICEBERGS OF DOUBT   542 18
    ON AND ON AND DIVE BENEATH THE ICEBERGS   694 4

ICE-CORRUPT
    THAW-COLD ICE-CORRUPT BLOSSOMS   270 25

ICED
    HATED MYSELF AND THE PLACE AND THE ICED   62 22

ICE-ROTTEN
    FOR WHAT KIND OF ICE-ROTTEN HOT-ACHING HEART MUST THEY + 270 27

ICE-VIVID
    THEY ARE THE FLOWERS OF ICE-VIVID MORTIFICATION   270 24

ICEWARDS
    NOR FLYING NORTH DESOLATIVE ICEWARDS   436 6

ICHABOD
    ICHABOD ICHABOD LO AND BEHOLD   814 18

ICH DIEN
    ICH DIEN   388 6
    WHOSE MOTTO IS ICH DIEN   389 27
    IF THEY KNEW THAT HIS MOTTO WAS ICH DIEN   389 35
    ICH DIEN   390 27
    MOTTO IS ICH DIEN   391 33

ICHTHYOSAURUS
    AS THE HORSE WAS AN IMPROVEMENT ON THE ICHTHYOSAURUS   429 27
    AND I DON'T SUPPOSE THE ICHTHYOSAURUS SPARKLED LIKE THE 523 16

ICONOCLAST
    THOU TO DO WITH ME THOU LUSTROUS ONE ICONOCLAST   39 18

ICY
    AND MELTED IN AN ICY TEAR   62 16
    WILL THERE BE A WHISTLE OF WINGS IN THE AIR AND AN ICY   439 6
    SHORN LIKE THE SHORN LAMB TO EVERY ICY GAZE   836 4
    SPEAKING OF PERVERTS HE TAKES ON AN AMUSED BUT ICY   *948 4

ICY-FLESHED
    SLOW-BLOODED ICY-FLESHED PORTENTOUS   271 16

IDEA
    THE SHROUDED MOTHER OF A NEW IDEA MEN HIDE THEIR FACES   91 26
    YOU'VE NO IDEA WHEN MEN ARE IN LOVE WITH THEMSELVES   447 8
    GODS AND LOVE ALIKE ARE BUT AN IDEA   474 13
    YOU'D BETTER ABANDON ALL IDEA OF FEELINGS ALTOGETHER   501 15
    BUT NOT A DEMOCRACY OF IDEA OR IDEAL NOR OF PROPERTY NO+ 611 7
    ALL OF THEM WHO WIND THEIR ENERGY ROUND THE IDEA OF THE+ 616 4
    OH WONDERFUL MACHINE YOU ARE MAN'S IDEA OF GODLINESS   643 15
    SELF-SACRIFICE AFTER ALL IS A WRONG AND MISTAKEN IDEA   678 1
    THE OLD IDEA OF SACRIFICE WAS THIS   679 8
    THAT THE IDEA OF THE FORM PRECEDES THE FORM SUBSTANTIAL 689 17
    LET ME THINK ABOUT IT LET ME FORM AN IDEA   690 13
    THE SHROUDED MOTHER OF A NEW IDEA MEN HIDE THEIR FACES *926 19

IDEAL
    FOREST OF PILLARS THAT HOLD UP THE DOME OF HIGH IDEAL   287 28
    TO KEEP ON HOLDING UP THIS IDEAL CIVILISATION   288 5
    EVEN THE WINGED SKELETON OF YOUR BLEACHED IDEAL   290 26
    THE WINDING-SHEET OF YOUR SELF-LESS IDEAL LOVE   291 12
    YOUR HORRIBLE SKELETON AUREOLED IDEAL   292 7
    THESE PRECIOUS AND IDEAL ONES   316 34
    OF THE ALL-SEEING ALL-FORE-ORDAINING IDEAL   329 18
    SINCE WE MADE AN IDEAL OF IT   472 15
    BUT NOT A DEMOCRACY OF IDEA OR IDEAL NOR OF PROPERTY NO+ 611 7
    OUR FATHERS' AND GRANDFATHERS' IDEAL   831 13

IDEALISM
    YOUR MORE-THAN-EUROPEAN IDEALISM   290 21

IDEALIST
    THEIR POOR IDEALIST FOREHEADS NAKED CAPITALS   287 18

IDEALISTIC
    SAY IN THE DEEP SOCKETS OF YOUR IDEALISTIC SKULL   292 27

IDEALLY
    DOES NOT A SUPREME INTELLECT IDEALLY PROCREATE THE UNIV+ 328 26

IDEALS
    NEITHER TO PERSONS NOR THINGS NOR IDEAS IDEALS NOR RELI+ 622 7
    BEFORE PLATO TOLD THE GREAT LIE OF IDEALS   688 21

IDEAS
    MY LORD A MAN'S FRIENDS' IDEAS OF HIM   489 25
    LOST BETWEEN GREAT WAVES OF ULTIMATE IDEAS   542 30
    AND IDEAS ARE HARD LIKE ACORNS READY TO FALL   608 23
    NEITHER TO PERSONS NOR THINGS NOR IDEAS IDEALS NOR RELI+ 622 7
    OF HIS OWN IDEAS AND HIS OWN MECHANICAL DEVICES   667 2
    BUT A MAN RE-BORN FROM THE RIGIDITY OF FIXED IDEAS   667 32
    BUT NOT THE JAGGLING AND TWISTING OF ALREADY EXISTENT I+ 673 8
    OPINIONS IDEAS AND SO FORTH   830 12

IDENTITY
    BELIEVE IN THE ONE IDENTITY DON'T YOU   395 25

IDIOCY
    IN ALL ITS IDIOCY   837 20
    BUT BAWDY ON THE BRAIN IS LEWD AND NAUSEOUS A SORT OF I+ *952 19

IDIOT
    AS I RUSHED LIKE AN IDIOT ROUND THE CORNER AFTER YOU   396 8
    THE IDIOT WITH HIS CHIN ALL WET   463 16
    AND OUR SOCIETY IS ONLY PART CONSCIOUS LIKE AN IDIOT   515 2
    MODERN LIFE IS A TALE TOLD BY AN IDIOT   522 1
    THE GREAT SOCIAL IDIOT IT MUST BE CONFESSED   522 6
    IS IDIOT SO YOU'VE GOT TO CHOOSE   845 16
    IS IDIOT   *953 8

IDIOTIC
    SOME WOMEN LIVE FOR THE IDIOTIC FURNITURE OF THEIR HOUS+ 657 6
    THEY ARE AFRAID OF CLIMBING DOWN FROM THIS IDIOTIC TIN-+ 667 19

IDIOTS
    BUT IF OBSCENE VILLAGE IDIOTS YOU WANT TO BE THEN BE IT 463 13
    WE CAN BUT HOWL THE LUGUBRIOUS HOWL OF IDIOTS   514 22
    I THINK IDIOTS TELL DULL STUPID DISGUSTING TALES   837 21

IDLE
    WITH HAIR ON THEM ARE BEING IDLE   386 30
    IDLE WE STAND BY THE KERB-EDGE AUNTIE   572 25

IDLY
    PINIONED LIKE SWEEPING SCYTHES NOW IDLY HANGING AT REST 855 22

IDOLS
    MY IVORY AND IDOLS SPLIT IN TWAIN   873 30

I'D
    ME SO DISTINCTLY FROM SLEEPING THE SLEEP I'D LOVE BEST   48 26
    I'D AS MUCH AS I COULD DO TO THINK   60 23
    THAT WHITE AN' 'ER CRIED THAT MUCH I'D LIKE TO BEGIN   61 8
    AFTER I'D KISSED THEE AT NIGHT LIZZIE   80 9
    AND GLADLY I'D OFFERED MY BREAST TO THE TREAD OF HER   123 6
    SURELY AH NOT IN WORDS ALONE I'D SPILL   127 16
    I'D LIE FOR EVER DRINKING AND DRAWING IN   153 29
    I'D NEVER HAVE LET YOU APPROPRIATE ME HAD I KNOWN   395 16
    I'D SAY IT WAS JUST A BIRD   453 3
    I'D LOADED THE CAMEL'S BACK BEFORE   491 19
    IS THEIR MONEY BUT I DOUBT IF I'D FIGHT FOR MINE ANYHOW 497 20
    I'D REJOICE OVER THE WOMAN AND THE WARMED COCKLES OF MY 507 10
    I'D BETRAY THE MIDDLE CLASSES   534 15
    I FIND I'D RATHER GET BACK TO EARTH   552 7
    AND I'D LET MYSELF BE SWINDLED   556 13
    AS A CACHE SEXE I'D HAVE PUT A WHOLE FOG   580 12
    I'D HANG MY HAMS WITH PUCKERED PETTICOATS SWAYING   835 32
    AND I'D GATHER MY HAIR   836 1
    THAT WHITE AN' 'ER SHOOK THAT MUCH I'D LIKE TO BEGIN   *911 24
    AN' IF IT'S NOT TRUE I'D BACK MY LIFE   *920 7
    I'D HAVE TORN THEM UP HAD THEY BORNE AWAY THE PATIENT B+ *926 13
    AND SO I'D RAISE   *941 13
    DO YOU THINK I'D HAVE A CREATURE LIKE YOU AT MY SIDE   *944 25

IGNITE
    FUSE TO IGNITE.   788 12

IGNOBLE
    WHEN I SEE THE IGNOBLE PROCESSION   484 1
    AND IGNOBLE HASTE FOR FEAR OF BEING LATE   484 7
    AND THE IGNOBLE PRAYERS OF THE PANIC-STRICKEN WHOM DARK+ 856 5

IGNOMINIOUSLY
  AND HE MUST STRUGGLE AFTER RECONSTRUCTION IGNOMINIOUSLY   361 12

IGNOMINY
  OF MULTITUDINOUS IGNOMINY   628 18
  WOULD WASH AWAY THIS IGNOMINY   747 9
  OF THIS HOUR'S IGNOMINY AND SWEAT   747 19

IGNORANT
  AND THE FLUSH FADED AND IT CAME DARK I SLEPT STILL IGNO+ 860 7

IGNORE
  OF THE DAY BUT IT'S NOTHING TO DO WITH THE BOYS SO LET + 93 27
  I IGNORE THOSE FOLK WHO LOOK OUT   375 28
  NOT QUITE TO IGNORE   563 15
  CAN YOU STILL IGNORE IT   781 8
  CAN YOU IGNORE OUR PASSING IN THIS MACHINE   781 9

IGNORES
  KNOW ME TURNS HER HEAD AND IGNORES ME VULGARLY WITH   384 23

IGNORING
  IGNORING ME   384 31
  IGNORING OUR MOTOR-CAR BLACK AND ALWAYS HURRYING   780 25

ILL
  AH BUT I AM ILL AND IT IS STILL RAINING COLDLY RAINING   112 29
  BUT THE SHADE ON HER FOREHEAD ILL BECOMES   201 11
  WHEN I WISH I WAS RICH THEN I KNOW I AM ILL   498 5
  THAT I AM ILL   620 12

ILL-ASSORTED
  DOWN THE GLAD STREETS PINCHED WAIFS IN ILL-ASSORTED CLO+ 866 5

ILL-FOUNDED
  AND MY DREAM IS ILL-FOUNDED   117 10

ILL-SMELLING
  OF THOSE ILL-SMELLING TRIBES OF MEN THESE FROGS THAT CA+ 792 23

ILLUMINED
  IN A LOVELY ILLUMINED MESH   111 32
  GREEN AND ILLUMINED AND TRAVELLING FOR EVER   260 27
  IN A LOVELY ILLUMINED MESH   *927 20
  IN A LOVELY ILLUMINED MESH   *928 20

ILLUSION
  FLOWERS OF ILLUSION WHO SHINE IN OUR GAUDS MAKE A PARAD+ 71 17
  THAT WILL HAVE THE OIL OF ILLUSION OH HEART   151 10
  THE ARRAS IS ALL ILLUSION OH COME AND TEAR IT AWAY   174 18
  I CAN STILL HAVE THE ILLUSION THAT THERE IS ROOM ENOUGH 602 8
  NOW AGAIN AND NOW FOR EVER BREAKS THE GREAT ILLUSION   635 1
  ILLUSION EBB AWAY   639 20
  THE ILLUSION OF MANKIND THE ILLUSION OF A HOPEFUL FUTURE 639 21
  ONCE DISILLUSION FALLS ON LIVING MEN AND ILLUSION OF BR+ 639 23
  IS THIS ILLUSION OF THE DEATH OF THE UNDYING   703 15
  IS IT ILLUSION OR DOES THE PALLOR FUME   720 1
  THAT MUST HAVE THE OIL OF ILLUSION OH HEART   879 20

ILLUSIONS
  FOR PERHAPS THE GREATEST OF ALL ILLUSIONS   703 14

ILLUSORY
  THE SHORES OF THIS INNERMOST OCEAN ALIVE AND ILLUSORY   71 12
  OR IS IT THE ILLUSORY WORLD   163 1

ILLYSSUS
  ILLYSSUS   161 20

I'LL
  I'LL WET MY BROW FOR THEE   44 7
  WITH SWEAT I'LL ENTER A HOUSE FOR THY SAKE   44 8
  I'LL SAY YOUR BOND OF UGLINESS IS VAIN   72 23
  I'LL TALK THEN   78 20
  THEN I'LL SAY GOOD-BYE TO THEE TIMOTHY   80 27
  I'LL TA'E THY WORD GOOD-BYE LIZ   80 29
  I'LL CHUCK THE FLAMIN' LOT O' YOU   81 11
  THOUGH I'LL SEE AS 'E PAYS YOU AN' DOES WHAT'S RIGHT   82 7
  I'LL SAY GOOD-BYE LIZ TO YER   85 1
  AY LAD I'LL TELL THEE THY MIND   138 28
  I'LL WHISPER THE GHOSTLY TRUTH TO YOU   227 27
  WAIT WAIT A BIT I'LL COME WHEN I'VE LIT THE FIRE   384 9
  AND I'LL PROTECT YOU   400 32
  I SWEAR I'LL PULL OFF MY KNICKERS RIGHT IN THE RUE DE L+ 433 13
  I'LL HOLD YOUR HAT   560 16
  FOR THE FLOWERS AND I'LL TELL YOU WHAT   578 1
  BUT I'LL NEVER REACH THE LONG SWEET SHORE   747 25
  MY CASHMERE SHAWL I'LL HANG FOR A CANOPY   754 24
  OR I'LL SMOTHER THEM ALL   792 3
  I'LL SHAKE THE EARTH AND SWALLOW THEM UP WITH THEIR CIT+ 792 4
  I'LL SEND FIRE AND ASHES UPON THEM AND SMOTHER THEM ALL 792 5
  I'LL TURN THEIR BLOOD LIKE SOUR MILK ROTTEN WITH THUNDER 792 6
  AND DEEP IN CENTRAL PARK I'LL FATTEN   815 15
  AT HER AGE WHY I'LL BE EARNING A JOLLY GOOD SCREW   834 20
  IN THE AUTUMN I'LL LOOK FOR IMMORTAL FRUIT   855 9
  I'LL WORK AND I'LL WIVE   857 8
  AND I'LL LIE IN HER LAP WHERE THE WORLD'S WILD ROSE   858 6
  I'LL TALK THEN   *920 12
  I'LL ONLY SAY GOOD-BYE TO THEE TIMOTHY   *922 27
  I'LL TA'E THY WORD GOOD-BYE LIZ   *922 29
  OR I'LL CHUCK THE FLAMIN' LOT OF YOU   *923 11
  THOUGH I'LL SEE AS 'E PAYS YOU AN' COMES TO THE SCRATCH *924 11
  BUT WE MAUN MA'E THE BEST ON'T I'LL REAR THY CHILDT IF +*925 18
  I'LL KISS YOU OVER THE EYES TILL I KISS YOU BLIND   *932 4

IL SIGNORE
  AND I AM IL SIGNORE AND THEY LOVE ME HERE   630 4

IMAGE
  THEN I SHALL KNOW WHICH IMAGE OF GOD   59 9
  SHALL SEE AN IMAGE OF HEAVEN OR OF EARTH   59 15
  BODIES IN THE IMAGE OF THEIR SEVERAL KINDS   376 4
  IN FRONT OF A TOWERING GRIMACING WHITE IMAGE OF   387 31
  ISN'T IT GOD'S OWN IMAGE TRAMPING HIS THIRTY MILES A DAY 430 22
  I HAVE SEEN AT LAST THE IMAGE OF HIM THEY LOVED   601 15
  WARPING THE PERFECT IMAGE OF GOD   *929 4

IMAGELESS
  THE GODS ARE NAMELESS AND IMAGELESS   650 20

IMAGE-MAKING
  FROM THE GIBE OF IMAGE-MAKING LOVE   601 23

IMAGES
  AH BUT THE SIMPLE ASK FOR IMAGES   651 10
  QUETZALCOATL MY BROTHER HE CALLED SEND ME MY IMAGES   789 17
  AND THE IMAGES OF MY MOTHER AND THE IMAGES OF MY SAINTS 789 18
  SEND JESUS HIS IMAGES BACK MARY AND THE SAINTS AND ALL 791 20

IMAGINABLE
  STORMS AND CUMULUS CLOUDS OF ALL IMAGINABLE BLOSSOM   271 27

IMAGINARY
  HE SAYS THE SOONER WILL YOU EAT IMAGINARY CAKE IN THE   442 15

IMAGINATION
  IMAGINATION   385 21
  FOR THE LUSCIOUS FILMY IMAGINATION LOATHES THE MALE   538 7

IMAGINE
  I IMAGINE DEAD HANDS ARE BRIGHTER   168 13
  SO YOU TO MINE I IMAGINE YES HAPPILY   234 7
  I CAN IMAGINE IN SOME OTHERWORLD   372 5
  DON'T IMAGINE IT   438 20
  BUT DON'T IMAGINE YOU'LL GET   463 14
  IMAGINE   480 9
  IMAGINE WHAT IT MUST HAVE BEEN TO HAVE EXISTENCE   529 22
  ALL WE CAN HONESTLY IMAGINE IN THE BEGINNING   681 26
  EVEN THE MIND OF GOD CAN ONLY IMAGINE   689 21
  IMAGINE THAT ANY MIND EVER THOUGHT A RED GERANIUM   690 14
  WE KNOW THAT EVEN GOD COULD NOT IMAGINE THE REDNESS OF +690 19
  YOU CAN'T IMAGINE THE HOLY GHOST SNIFFING AT CHERRY-PIE+690 25
  BUT IMAGINE AMONG THE MUD AND THE MASTODONS   691 1
  AT FIFTY YOU'RE NOT GOING TO BE THE APOLLO BELVEDERE DO+835 23

IMAGINED
  WERE RICH PEOPLE OR PEOPLE WHO IMAGINED THEMSELVES RICH 498 10
  AS IF ANY MIND COULD HAVE IMAGINED A LOBSTER   689 19

IMAGININGS
  MY OWN IMAGININGS   292 22

IMBECILE
  WITH YOUR IMBECILE BIT OF A TAIL IN A LOVE-FLUTTER   396 14
  IMBECILE STRUGGLE OF COMBAT   519 16
  HE JIGS ALONG IN THE IMBECILE CRUELTY OF THE MACHINE   645 15

IMBECILITY
  THAT SPRAWLS ACROSS THE EARTH IN IRON IMBECILITY   642 26

IMBIBES
  THE BUSY BUSY BOURGEOIS IMBIBES HIS LITTLE SHARE   432 25

IMITATE
  IMITATE THE MAGNIFICENT TREES   69 6
  IMITATE THE MAGNIFICENT TREES   *915 18

IMITATING
  LITTLE JETS OF SUNLIGHT TEXTURE IMITATING FLAME   33 4
  LITTLE JETS OF SUNLIGHT-TEXTURE IMITATING FLAME   *891 2

IMITATION
  AND THEN OUR ENGLISH IMITATION INTELLIGENTSIA   533 22

IMMACULATELY
  IMMACULATELY CONCEIVED   659 2

IMMANENCE
  WHICH BURNT JUST NOW WITH MARVELLOUS IMMANENCE   219 16

IMMATURE
  LITTLE DANGLE OF AN IMMATURE PAW AND ONE THIN EAR   393 20

IMMEASURABLE
  HAVE PRESSED IMMEASURABLE SPACES OF HOARSE SILENCE   75 21
  AND I IN IMMEASURABLE NIGHT LOOKED ON FROM AFAR AFAR   865 10
  HAVE PRESSED THE IMMEASURABLE SPACES OF HOARSE SILENCE *897 21
  HAVE PRESSED IMMEASURABLE SPACES OF HOARSE SILENCE   *900 29

IMMEDIATE
  AND THEY GRUDGE THEM THE IMMEDIATE PHYSICAL UNDERSTANDI+446 11
  WHAT THE OLD PEOPLE CALL IMMEDIATE CONTACT WITH GOD   481 6
  AS A HALF-LIE CAUSES THE IMMEDIATE CONTRADICTION OF THE+664 11
  AND WE WILL FIND THE WAY TO IMMEDIATE CONTACT WITH LIFE 666 18

IMMEDIATELY
  I BEAT MY WAY TO BE LOST IMMEDIATELY   223 9
  AND IMMEDIATELY I REGRETTED IT   351 18
  AND IMMEDIATELY SHE SEES ME SHE BLINKS STARES DOESN'T 384 22
  I IMMEDIATELY WANT TO GO AND DO SOMETHING JOLLY TOO   520 25
  MUNDANE EGG AT VARIOUS POINTS THEY STEPPED OUT AND IMME+760 23
  WHY SHOULD AMERICANS IMMEDIATELY ACQUIESCE   775 31

IMMEMORIAL
    FULFILLED OF THE SLOW PASSION OF PITCHING THROUGH IMMEM+   354 12
    TO SLEEP AT LAST IN IMMEMORIAL LOVE   736 21

IMMENSE
    OF THE NIGHTLY HEAVENS OVERHEAD LIKE AN IMMENSE OPEN EYE   97 14
    AS THE BREATH WHICH UPWARDS FROM THE NOSTRILS OF AN IMM+   97 20
    THE NIGHT IS IMMENSE AND AWFUL YET TO ME IT IS NOTHING +   98 1
    THE SUN IMMENSE AND ROSY   193 14
    WITHIN THE IMMENSE AND TOILSOME LIFE-TIME HEAVED   195 29
    THE SPACE OF THE WORLD IS IMMENSE BEFORE ME AND AROUND +   222 22
    IMMENSE ABOVE THE CABIN   375 7
    AND BEYOND THAT THE IMMENSE SUN BEHIND THE SUN   513 16
    THE SUN OF IMMENSE DISTANCES THAT FOLD THEMSELVES TOGET+   513 17

IMMENSELY
    AND WAS IMMENSELY FLATTERED WHEN ONE OF THE FAT LITTLE   618 18

IMMENSITIES
    THE TWO IMMENSITIES WOULD FLOAT UNWILLING   875 29

IMMENSITY
    REACH FROM IMMENSITY   159 12
    ANYTHING IN SUCH IMMENSITY I AM TOO   223 11
    BEWILDERED AMID THE MOVING IMMENSITY   875 16

IMMERSED
    SEA-BEASTS IMMERSED LEAN SIDEWAYS AND FLASH BRIGHT   453 25

IMMINENT
    SINCE I MUST SERVE AND STRUGGLE WITH THE IMMINENT   234 31
    OUT OF THE IMMINENT NIGHT   286 23
    LOUD PEACE PROPAGANDA MAKES WAR SEEM IMMINENT   495 20

IMMOBILE
    AND SKYWARDS HIS FACE IS IMMOBILE EYELIDS ASLANT   66 11

IMMORAL
    IT IS ONLY IMMORAL   528 5
    MAN IS IMMORAL BECAUSE HE HAS GOT A MIND   529 1
    THEY DON'T MIND BEING DEPRAVED IMMORAL OR ANYTHING OF T+   829 12
    EVEN IN THE MOST IMMORAL SETS THERE IS STILL THIS DESIR+   829 20
    AND TO THE YOUNG THIS IS REALLY IMMORAL AND DISTASTEFUL   829 25
    MAN ALONE IS IMMORAL   836 7
    IS THAT THEY ARE INVARIABLY IMMORAL PERSONS   836 21
    AFTER ALL IT IS IMMORAL FOR A WORD TO MEAN LESS THAN IT+   837 6

IMMORALITY
    AND WITHOUT MORALS AND WITHOUT IMMORALITY   607 31
    THE REAL IMMORALITY AS FAR AS I CAN SEE IT   836 17

IMMORALLY
    THEY ARE EITHER IMMORALLY GOOD THE WORD DOES NOT AND   836 22
    OR ELSE THEY ARE IMMORALLY NASTY AND THE WORD LOOMS   837 1

IMMORTAL
    YOUR HUMAN SELF IMMORTAL TAKE THE WATERY TRACK   161 28
    SHE FARES IN THE STARK IMMORTAL   199 13
    NOR GUSTY JOVE WITH HIS EYE ON IMMORTAL TARTS   437 5
    FOR THEIR OWN IMMORTAL ENDS   492 26
    TO THE ATOM TO THE BODY OF IMMORTAL CHAOS   505 4
    IMMORTAL CAESAR DEAD AND TURNED TO CLAY   545 24
    IMMORTAL BIRD   728 12
    TO THE EFFULGENT LANDSCAPE OF OUR IMMORTAL GIRLY-WIRLY   835 4
    IN THE AUTUMN I'LL LOOK FOR IMMORTAL FRUIT   855 9
    IN THE GARNERING AUTUMN A GLOW OF IMMORTAL FRUIT   855 17
    AND ONCE HE WAS GAY AND HEARTY WITH HIS EYE ON THE IMMO+   *946 17

IMMORTALITY
    AT LAST YOU CAN THROW IMMORTALITY OFF AND I SEE YOU   210 3
    IMMORTALITY THE HEAVEN IS ONLY A PROJECTION OF THIS STR+   265 17
    IT IS THE ABYSS OF THE IMMORTALITY   701 8
    OF IMMORTALITY INTO THE WORLD   745 3
    DRESSED IN THE GRACE OF IMMORTALITY   745 17
    OF IMMORTALITY TO KINDLE UP   745 31
    A TENDER GLEAM OF IMMORTALITY   746 1

IMMORTELLE
    IT'S EITHER AN ARTIFICIAL RAG BLOSSOM OR AN IMMORTELLE +   472 26
    SHE IS A MADE-UP LIE A DYED IMMORTELLE   478 28

IMMORTELLES
    EMBALMED FLOWERS ARE NOT FLOWERS IMMORTELLES ARE NOT   476 16

IMMOVABLE
    BUT HEAVY SEALING DARKNESS SILENCE ALL IMMOVABLE   205 14

IMMUNE
    THE IMMUNE THE ANIMATE   360 30
    HE SO FINISHED AND IMMUNE NOW BROKEN INTO DESIROUS   361 6
    SPREAD YOUR SMALL SAILS IMMUNE LITTLE SHIPS   543 10
    CONCEIT OF BEING IMMUNE   709 32

IMMUNITY
    ONENESS AND POISED IMMUNITY   710 4

IMPASSABLE
    BEHOLD THE GULF IMPASSABLE   635 27

IMPASSIONED
    YOUR IMPASSIONED UNFINISHED HATE   236 5

IMPATIENCE
    NEW FEET ON THE EARTH BEATING WITH IMPATIENCE   272 3

IMPATIENT
    BUT SHE'S WAITING I KNOW IMPATIENT AND COLD HALF   85 11

IMPEDIMENT
    ANYTHING THAT BELONGS TO US AND IS UGLY AND AN IMPEDIME+   678 15

IMPEDIMENTS
    OR ALL THE UGLY OLD POSSESSIONS THAT MAKE UP THE IMPEDI+   678 13

IMPELLING
    IMPELLING SHAPING THE COMING DREAM   *907 15

IMPENDING
    OF THE IMPENDING BEE THEY WERE FAIR ENOUGH SIGHTS   243 29

IMPERATIVE
    AND IS SILENT WITH A SENSE OF JUSTICE THE FIERY PRIMORD+   844 26

IMPERIOUSLY
    EACH IMPERIOUSLY OVER-EQUAL TO EACH EQUALITY OVER-REACH+   300 8

IMPERISHABLE
    ON ONE OLD SLIM IMPERISHABLE THOUGHT WHILE YOU REMAIN   297 4

IMPERTINENT
    SO LONG WILL THEY LIFT THEIR IMPERTINENT VOICES   681 5

IMPERTURBABLE
    AND SOME OF AFRICA'S IMPERTURBABLE SANG-FROID   296 22

IMPERVIOUS
    OPENING YOUR IMPERVIOUS MOUTH   353 4

IMPETUOUS
    STIRRED BY AN IMPETUOUS WIND SOME WAYS'LL   40 28

IMPINGES
    BUT TO DEFLOWER THEE THY TOWER IMPINGES   40 23

IMPLACABLE
    IMPLACABLE WINTER'S LONG CROSS-QUESTIONING BRUNT   142 4
    AND IS IMPLACABLE   645 16

IMPLEMENTS
    LIKE IRON IMPLEMENTS TWISTED HIDEOUS OUT OF THE EARTH   300 21
    IMPLEMENTS   301 14

IMPLICATED
    SINCE ALREADY I AM IMPLICATED WITH YOU   242 6

IMPLICITLY
    IMPLICITLY   234 30

IMPONDERABLE
    YOUR OWN IMPONDERABLE WEIGHTLESSNESS   334 7
    FLAT PERSONALITIES IN TWO DIMENSIONS IMPONDERABLE AND   446 6

IMPORTANCE
    I AM SO WEARY OF PALE-FACE IMPORTANCE   288 16
    THE ITEMS ARE OF SMALL IMPORTANCE   443 6
    THE NEW MOON OF NO IMPORTANCE   467 5
    IN ALL MATTERS OF EMOTIONAL IMPORTANCE   604 17
    EVEN WHILE WE ADMIT THE GHASTLY IMPORTANCE OF MONEY   831 15

IMPORTANT
    AND THEIR FACES ARE DARK AND FAT AND IMPORTANT   388 21
    BUT THAT WHICH IS SECONDARY IS ONLY IMPORTANT   668 3
    THAT IS THE IMPORTANT POINT REALLY DISTASTEFUL   829 26

IMPOSSIBLE
    PUTTING IN ALL THE IMPOSSIBLE WORDS   491 15
    AND UNDER A COMPETITIVE SYSTEM THAT IS IMPOSSIBLE REALLY   522 25
    THEN FRIENDSHIP IS IMPOSSIBLE   608 18

IMPOTENCE
    OUR EYES DARKEN AND IMPOTENCE HURTS   746 14

IMPREGNABLE
    THEIR CASTLE IS IMPREGNABLE THEIR CAVE   325 16
    WE MUST MAKE AN ISLE IMPREGNABLE   716 16
    THROUGH BREACHES IN THE WALLS OF THIS OUR BY-NO-MEANS I+   722 25
    OVER THE ADAMANT WALLS OF THIS OUR BY-NO-MEANS IMPREGNA+   *958 7

IMPREGNATE
    AND WISH I COULD PASS IMPREGNATE INTO THE PLACE   173 14

IMPRESS
    THAT IMPRESS ME LIKE THE THOUGHT-DRENCHED EYES   854 26

IMPRESSES
    HOW IT IMPRESSES ME HOW HARD AND COMPRESSED   249 14

IMPRISONED
    OF THE MAN-LIFE NORTH IMPRISONED SHUT IN THE HUM OF THE   149 5
    MOANS AND BOOMS THE SOUL OF A PEOPLE IMPRISONED ASLEEP   149 11
    EYES WHERE HIS HOT IMPRISONED SOUL HAS KEPT   859 19

IMPRISONMENT
    AN ESCAPE FROM THEIR HORROW OF IMPRISONMENT IN OUR CIVI+   838 8

IMPROPER
    AND IMPROPER DERISIVE EARS   345 30

IMPROVEMENT
    AS THE HORSE WAS AN IMPROVEMENT ON THE ICHTHYOSAURUS   429 27

IMPROVEMENT (CONT.)

IMPROVEMENT
TO BRING FORTH CREATURES THAT ARE AN **IMPROVEMENT** ON   429 25

IMPUDENCE
IN HIS IMPUDENCE   244 15
BOURGEOIS COWARDICE PRODUCES BOLSHEVIST IMPUDENCE   663 18
AND BETWEEN THE COWARDICE AND IMPUDENCE OF THIS PAIR WH+   663 24

IMPUDENT
AND IMPUDENT NETTLES GRABBING THE UNDER-EARTH   317 19
THE BOLSHEVIST GETS OPENLY MORE IMPUDENT ALSO KNOWING H+   663 22
INSTEAD OF THIS MESS WHICH EXPRESSES THE IMPUDENT HUMAN   837 18

IMPULSE
QUIVERING AWAKE WITH ONE IMPULSE AND ONE WILL   39 8
PURE IMPULSE TO MAKE SOMETHING TO PUT SOMETHING FORTH   520 11
IMPULSE   639 15
THEN AT ONCE THE IMPULSE OF THE GREEDY CLASSES AND MASS+   640 8
AND A CHAOS OF IMPULSE SUPERVENES   640 10
QUIVERING AWAKE WITH ONE IMPULSE OF DESIRE   *893 21
IMPULSE OF LIFE   *909 22

IMPULSION
THE HUMAN WILL TO THE FLUSH OF THE VASTER IMPULSION OF +   617 14

IMPULSIVE
AND AS IF THE ATOM WERE AN IMPULSIVE THING   524 24

IMPURE
WALLED IN WALLED IN THE WHOLE WORLD IS A VAST IMPURE   174 23
WE ASPHYXIATE IN A SLEEP OF DREAMS REBREATHING THE IMPU+   174 26
AND AN IMPURE FRENZY   342 24
IN AN IMPURE HASTE   343 9
IMPURE EVEN IN WEARINESS   346 22
IMPURE ONE   347 7

I'M
SAY I'M BUSY   44 13
LIKE THIS I'M SURE IT IS   45 26
AND YET I'M SUPPOSED TO CARE WITH ALL MY MIGHT   74 30
I'M OFF UP TH' LINE TO UNDERWOOD   78 3
WELL I'M BELIEVIN' NO TALE MISSIS   78 17
I'M SEEIN' FOR MY-SEN   78 18
I'M SCRAIGHTIN' MY-SEN BUT ARENA GOIN'   78 27
I'M FURTHER OWER TH' TOP   78 32
I'M TAKIN' 'OME A WEDDIN'-DRESS   79 15
I'M NOT 'AVIN' YOUR ORTS AN' SLARTS   82 3
TO DO SUCH A THING THOUGH IT'S A POOR TALE IT IS THAT+   83 7
AY I'M SORRY I'M SORRY   83 18
AY I'M SORRY THA NEDNA WORRY   83 20
I'M SORRY FOR THEE I'M SORRY F'R 'ER   83 22
I'M SORRY F'R US A'   83 23
I'M SORRY FOR TH' TROUBLE AY   84 9
I'M NOT THAT'S A'   84 12
LAD BUT I'M TELLIN' THEE SUMMAT   137 24
YI BUT I'M TELLIN' THEE SUMMAT   137 31
NOW LAD I'M AXIN' THEE SUMMAT   138 2
A GO AT T'OTHER FOR I'M A BAD   140 4
COME NO I'M A THING OF LIFE I GIVE   211 5
NAY I'M TOO SLEEPY AH YOU ARE HORRIBLE   211 7
NO NO I DANCE IN THE SUN I'M A THING OF LIFE   211 16
YEA THOUGH I'M SORRY FOR THEE   220 8
I'M NOT AFRAID OF GOD   231 23
FIND OUT IF I'M SOUND OR BANKRUPT   237 3
BE ROUGH AND HAIRY I'M GLAD THEY'RE LIKE THAT   254 12
COME ON YOU CRAPA I'M NOT YOUR SERVANT   384 33
I'M ON THE HORSE   397 24
STANDS SAYING SEE I'M INVISIBLE   403 11
AND I'M A PALE-FACE LIKE A HOMELESS DOG   404 13
I'M GOING TO SIT DOWN ON MY TAIL RIGHT HERE   405 29
I'M THE RED WOLF SAYS THE DARK OLD FATHER   405 31
ABAHT IT YES I'M A GENT AN' LIZ   434 23
OF COURSE I'M A LIDY WHAT D'YER THINK   434 25
I'M AMERICAN FROM NEW/ORLEANS   435 2
BUT I'M NOT HAVING ANY DODGING GOING ON BEHIND MY   483 23
I'M ABOUT AS MUCH LIKE A PERSIAN CAT   489 23
BUT I'M ALWAYS LONGING FOR SOMEONE TO SAY   490 27
I SAY TO MYSELF HELLO I'M NOT WELL MY VITALITY IS LOW   498 8
I LOVE NOBODY I'M GOING TO LOVE NOBODY   507 2
I'M NOT GOING TO TELL ANY LIES ABOUT IT   507 3
AND THE TCHEKOV LOT I'M TOO WEAK AND LOVABLE TO LIVE   534 1
OH I'M SURE YOU'LL UNDERSTAND WE'RE MAKING A CENSUS OF+   546 7
THAT SAYS I'M FOR YOU   561 6
I FEEL I'M GOING TO BE NAUGHTY AUNTIE   572 19
PERHAPS I'M GOING TO BE NAUGHTY AUNTIE   573 7
OH I'M A BRITISH BOY SIR   576 16
FOR I'M A BRITISH BOY SIR   576 22
I'M YOUR BRITISH BOY AND I DID BUT TRY   577 10
APPLICANT I'M AFRAID I DON'T   582 11
APPLICANT I DON'T THINK SO SIR I'M AFRAID NOT   582 18
AND WHEN I WANT TO I'M GOING TO   618 12
AND I'M GOING TO DO WHAT I JOLLY WELL PLEASE   671 7
I FEEL I'M COMING NEAR   764 12
TELL THEM THEY ARE ALL FOOLS THAT I'M LAUGHING AT THEM   791 26
I'M OFF UP TH' LINE TO UNDERWOOD   *919 23
WELL I'M BELIEVIN' NO TALE MISSIS   *920 9
I'M SEEIN' FOR MY-SEN   *920 10
I'M SCREETIN' MY-SEN BUT ARE-NA GOIN'   *920 19
I'M FURTHER OWER TH' TOP   *920 24
I'M TAKIN' 'OME A WEDDIN' DRESS   *921 11
I'M NOT HAVIN' YOUR ORTS AN' SLARTS   *924 7
TO SUCH A THING BUT IT'S A POOR TALE THAT I'M BOUND TO+   *925 11
AND I'M A KALEIDOSCOPE   *932 8
TO COVER MY MOUTH'S RAILLERY TILL I'M BOUND IN HER SHAM+   *940 17
BUT I'M SORRY FOR HIM ON HIS YOUNG FEET KNOWIN'   *944 7
MY YOUNG SLIM LAD AN' I'M SORRY FOR THEE   *944 16
I'M A RELIGIOUS SOUL   *947 15

'IM
AN' THEY TA'EIN' 'IM I' TH' AMBULANCE   45 6
IF ANYTHING AILED 'IM AT ANY RATE   45 19
I SHAN'T 'AVE 'IM TO NUSS   45 20

'IM
AX 'IM THY-SEN WENCH A WIDDER'S LODGER   77 11
AN' 'IM TO 'AVE BEEN TOOK IN   77 16
AN' 'IM AS NICE AN' FRESH   77 29
THOUGH IF IT'S TRUE THEY'LL TURN 'IM OUT   78 13
AN' THERE'S THE DARK-BLUE TIE I BOUGHT 'IM   81 14
AN' 'ERE COMES THE CAT AS CAUGHT 'IM   81 16
OF 'IM STOOPIN' TO 'ER YOU'D WONDER 'E COULD   81 19
AN' YET YER'VE BIN CARRYIN' ON WI' 'IM   81 27
AY AN' 'IM WI' ME   81 28
THA WANTS 'IM THY-SEN I SEE   81 32
THA WANTS 'IM THY-SEN TOO BAD   82 6
OUT OF 'IM INTO A WOMAN AS CAN   138 25
DRAW IT OUT OF 'IM DID TER KNOW IT   138 26
IT WAS 'IM AS MADE THE FIRST MISTAKE   493 5
I COULD THINK O' NOWT BUT OUR TED AN' 'IM TAKEN   *910 3
A LOT O' VIOLETS FELL OUT OF 'ER BOSOM ON 'IM DOWN THEE+   *910 16
THA KNOWS 'E 'D A WINSOME WAY WI 'IM AN' SHE   *910 24
YI AN' 'IM THAT YOUNG   *911 9
AH KNOW THA LIKED 'IM BETT'R NOR ME BUT LET   *911 17
AN' 'IM TO HAVE BEEN TOOK IN   *919 4
AN' 'IM AS NICE AN' FRESH   *919 17
AN' THAT'S THE DARK BLUE TIE I BOUGHT 'IM   *923 14
AN' 'ERE COMES THE CAT THAT CAUGHT 'IM   *923 16
AY AN' 'IM WI' ME   *923 28
THA WANTS 'IM THY-SEN TOO BAD   *924 10

INACCESSIBLE
HE FOUND THE LAMB BEYOND HIM ON THE INACCESSIBLE PINNAC+   324 20

INANIMATE
THE VAST INANIMATE   353 21
WHAT A HUGE VAST INANIMATE IT IS THAT YOU MUST ROW   353 25
INANIMATE UNIVERSE   354 2
WHILE LIFE WAS A HEAVE OF MATTER HALF INANIMATE   372 10
THE BOYS FROM THE HOME BLUE AND INANIMATE   866 2

INAUDIBLE
YET ALL THE WHILE COMES THE DRONING INAUDIBLE OUT OF THE   149 17
TO SPEAK ENDLESS INAUDIBLE WAVELETS INTO THE WAVE   336 29
AS THE VULTURE THAT SCREAMS HIGH UP ALMOST INAUDIBLE   500 16

INAUDIBLY
INVISIBLY INAUDIBLY   166 4

IN-BETWEENS
WE CHILDREN WERE THE IN-BETWEENS   490 17
BUT STILL WE ARE IN-BETWEENS WE TREAD   490 23

INBREATHING
IT MUST HAVE BEEN YOUR INBREATHING   241 25

INCALCULABLE
WHAT AN INCALCULABLE INERTIA   353 27

INCANDESCENCE
AT LAST TO CALM INCANDESCENCE   242 16

INCANDESCENT
WHITE PETALS INCANDESCENT SO THAT YOU   86 13
MY STACK OF LILIES ONCE WHITE INCANDESCENT   86 23

INCANTATION
YOU AMID THE BOG-END'S YELLOW INCANTATION   90 13

INCAPABLE
AND OF THIS THE MIND IS INCAPABLE   474 8
AND BE A BIT MORE FIERY AS INCAPABLE OF TELLING LIES   505 18
IS A ROBOT AND INCAPABLE OF LOVE   648 2

INCARNATE
THE SEED OF LIFE INCARNATE THAT FALLS AND WAKES   89 10
THIS IS THE MACHINE INCARNATE   635 13
AND THE ROBOT IS THE MACHINE INCARNATE   635 14
AND THE SLAVE IS THE MACHINE INCARNATE   635 15
AND THE HOPELESS INFERIOR HE IS THE MACHINE INCARNATE   635 16
WHY SHOULD WE HATE THEN WITH THIS HATE INCARNATE   742 35

INCARNATION
BUT URGES TOWARDS INCARNATION WITH THE GREAT CREATIVE U+   691 16

INCENSE
SPRINKLING INCENSE AND SALT OF WORDS   151 28
DARK INCENSE DID I FEEL HER OFFER UP   881 12

INCENSE-BOWL
OH MY WIFE'S BRASS INCENSE-BOWL   760 12

INCENSE-SMOKE
OF INCENSE-SMOKE THAT RISES LIKE BIRDS   151 30

INCIPIENT
INCIPIENT PURPLING TOWARDS SUMMER IN THE WORLD OF THE H+   273 25
OF INCIPIENT ENERGETIC LIFE   480 25
AND WHORING ON THE BRAIN AS BAD AS SYPHILIS INCIPIENT I+   *952 20

INCISION
WHY THE SUGGESTION OF INCISION   279 20

INCLINATION
THE SOUL OF MAN ALSO LEANS IN THE UNCONSCIOUS INCLINATI+   480 22
LEANING IN THE MASSIVE UNCONSCIOUS INCLINATION WE CALL +   *952 4

INCLINE
THROATS TO THE HEAVENS INCLINE   177 16

INCLINED
    I AM INCLINED TO HEAP THY COALS OF FIRE ON MY OWN   760 15

INCLUDING
    IT'S CALLED THE BRITISH PUBLIC INCLUDING YOU AND I   570 15

INCOGNISANT
    INCOGNISANT   357 8

INCOME
    LIVING ON YOUR INCOME IS STROLLING GRANDLY OUTSIDE THE   521 11
    WHAT IS MAN WITHOUT AN INCOME   545 1
    WHAT IS MAN WITHOUT AN INCOME   545 6
    AND HERE AM I PAYING INCOME TAX AND GOD-KNOWS-WHAT   547 5

INCOMING
    BUT BLEW BACK AS IF AN INCOMING WIND BLEW HIM IN AGAIN   343 17

INCOMPREHENSIBLE
    YELLOW EYES INCOMPREHENSIBLE WITH THIN SLITS   380 28
    IS THE INCOMPREHENSIBLE PLASM OF LIFE OF CREATION   681 27
INCOMPREHENSIBLY
    ONLY THE ELECTRON BEHAVES AND MISBEHAVES INCOMPREHENS+   *947 5
INCONCEIVABLY
    GOLD AND OF INCONCEIVABLY FINE QUINTESSENTIAL BRIGHTNESS   271 18

INCONSISTENT
    SUBSTANCE OF MY INCONSISTENT BREATH   118 8

INCONSOLABLE
    THE WEEPING MOTHER OF GOD INCONSOLABLE OVER HER SON   439 29
    INCONSOLABLE YOUTH DEAD-BEAT   457 22

INCONTINENT
    AND GIVE UP THE GHOST INCONTINENT   760 19

INCREASE
    MY OLD INCREASE   159 30
    NOT LIKE THE EARTH THE SPOUSE ALL FULL OF INCREASE   197 10
    AND ALSO TO ENSURE A GOODLY INCREASE IN THE WORLD   325 22
    WELL SOFTLY UP FOR A NEW INCREASE   461 26
    TO SING IN THE SHELL OF MY HEART THE LULL AND INCREASE   747 22
    YOU SHALL FIND ME WHO AM NEITHER INCREASE   788 20

INCREASING
    AND INCREASING THE FLOCK AND PERHAPS GIVING A REAL NIP +   325 10
    AND INCREASING DELIRIUM   343 26
    WHEN YEAR BY YEAR YEAR IN YEAR OUT IN MILLIONS IN INCRE+   631 17

INCULCATE
    TO INCULCATE THE NEW CONCEPTION OF THE RISEN MAN   609 21

INCURABLY
    AND LIKE TO BECOME INCURABLY DISEASED INSIDE   535 22

INCURRING
    AVOIDING EACH OTHER YET INCURRING ECLIPSES   823 28

INDECENCY
    HOW CAN THEY COMMIT THE INDECENCY OF BEGETTING CHILDREN   521 22

INDECENT
    LIKE SOME MALICIOUS INDECENT LITTLE BOY   447 31
    ARREST HIM HE'S INDECENT HE'S OBSCENE WHAT'S MORE   574 24
    AND CHIRRUP THEIR ALMOST INDECENT NOISES   681 6

INDEED
    KNIGHTS INDEED MUCH KNIGHT I KNOW WILL RIDE   221 10
    NOW YOU ARE HUSBANDLESS INDEED NO MORE HUSBAND TO   411 7
    ACH ACH NOW INDEED GOD IS BORN HE TWINKLES WITHIN   682 28
    WHAT WE NEED INDEED   833 12

INDEFINITE
    OF GLASS PALACE ALOFT THERE AMONG MISTY INDEFINITE THIN+   52 24
    LITTLE LUMPS THAT FLY IN AIR AND HAVE VOICES INDEFINITE+   341 26
    OF BLUE PALACE ALOFT THERE AMONG THE MISTY INDEFINITE D+   *905 13

INDENTED
    WHY SO INDENTED   279 16

INDEPENDENT
    A MAN NEEDS TO BE INDEPENDENT AT HIS WORK SO THAT HE CA+   *949 22

INDETERMINATE
    FLAT-CHESTED CROP-HEADED CHEMICALISED WOMEN OF INDETERM+   522 2
    AND WIMBLY-WAMBLY YOUNG MEN OF SEX STILL MORE INDETERMI+   522 4

INDEX
    THE MIND'S INDEX   562 29

INDIA
    A YARD OF INDIA MUSLIN IS ALIVE WITH HINDU LIFE   448 21

INDIAN
    IS DIGNIFIED IN THE FOXGLOVE LIKE A RED INDIAN BRAVE   272 29
    LIKE A RED INDIAN DARKLY UNFINISHED AND ALOOF   369 10
    TAKE UP THE PRIMORDIAL INDIAN OBSTINACY   371 28
    AND THE INDIAN IN A WHITE SHEET   403 9
    THE INDIAN SMILE   404 4
    OF INDIAN GODS   407 9
    BUT THE INDIAN NEVER CAME   777 5
    THE INDIAN DOES NO HARM   777 9
    THE INDIAN QUESTION HAS WORSE LUCK BECOME A POLITICAL   777 13
    THE INDIAN SHOULD NEVER HAVE BEEN MADE A CASUS BELLI   777 17
    YET THE CLASH HAS BEEN STARTED THE INDIAN IS ABOUT TO BE   777 20
    THE PUEBLO SUMMONED THE OLD INDIAN MEN AND   777 26
    THAT IT WOULD BE FAR FAR BETTER FOR THE INDIAN YOUTH   778 1
    PEOPLE WANT TO KEEP THE INDIAN BACK WANT TO   778 7

INDIAN
    LONG-HAIRED PEOPLE PAINTING THE INDIAN AND WRITING   778 10
    ABOUT THE INDIAN MAKE THEIR LIVING OFF HIM   778 11
    SOLVE THE INDIAN QUESTION FINALLY   780 1
    OH SINISTER INDIAN EAGLE   783 22
    AN INDIAN WALKING WRAPT IN HIS WINDING SHEET   816 7

INDIAN BUREAU
    ON GOOD FRIDAY THE BIG WHITE MEN OF THE INDIAN BUREAU   777 24
    EITHER MAKE THE INDIAN BUREAU INTO A PERMANENT OFFICE   780 5

INDIANS
    WHOM THE INDIANS ASPIRE TO   374 19
    INDIANS DANCE AND RUN AND STAMP   407 11
    THE INDIANS LAUGH IN THEIR SLEEP   407 16
    THE INDIANS THOUGHT THE WHITE MAN WOULD AWAKE THEM   408 8
    FURTHERMORE THE WHITE BIG-MEN SAID TO THE OLD INDIANS   778 17
    THAT THE INDIANS COMPLAINED OF BEING POOR   778 18
    THAT THE INDIANS WANTED THE WHITE MAN'S GOVERNMENT   778 20
    TO GIVE THE INDIANS ONE SINGLE THING NOT ONE CENT   778 25
    THE INDIANS OF THE PUEBLOS HAVE LAND   778 26
    TO DRAW A LINE AROUND THE INDIANS BEYOND WHICH LINE   779 31
    REMOVE THE INDIANS FOREVER FROM THE HANDS OF   780 3
    OFF THE INDIANS   780 15

INDIAN'S
    AND THE COFFIN-LIFE SLIT WHERE THE INDIAN'S EYES ARE   403 30

INDIA-RUBBER
    AND THE REDDENED LIMBS RED INDIA-RUBBER TUBING INFLATED   625 21
    LIKE INDIA-RUBBER AND ASBESTOS   765 15

INDICATION
    OUTWARD AND VISIBLE INDICATION OF THE PLAN WITHIN   356 11

INDICATOR
    AND THE DIM NOTCH OF BLACK MAIDENHAIR LIKE AN INDICATOR   693 14

INDIFFERENCE
    OF UNSWERVING INDIFFERENCE TO ME   55 9
    THEIR DROSS OF INDIFFERENCE AND TAKE THE TOLL   74 21
    OUT OF INDIFFERENCE I LOVE YOU   210 6
    THEIR DROSS OF INDIFFERENCE AND BURN THE SCROLL   *895 29
    THEIR DROSS OF INDIFFERENCE AND BURN THE SCROLL   *904 18

INDIFFERENT
    SITS INDIFFERENT HUGGED IN HER RAGS   54 18
    INDIFFERENT HERE OF MYSELF SINCE I AM GONE   157 12
    FOR I AM QUITE INDIFFERENT   237 5

INDIGESTIBLE
    INDIGESTIBLE TO MISS PONSONBY   583 25

INDIGNANT
    AND HOWLS HIS PANDEMONIUM ON THE INDIGNANT AIR   379 23
    OR FLUFF UP IN INDIGNANT FURY LIKE A CAT   528 24
    OR FLUFF UP IN INDIGNANT FURY LIKE A CAT   *950 27

INDIGNATION
    THAT LAUGH AT THE LORD'S INDIGNATION   284 19
    THREW THEMSELVES ON HIM IN INDIGNATION   575 2

INDISCRIMINATE
    I THOUGHT IT WAS WOMAN INDISCRIMINATE WOMAN   264 21
    WITH INDISCRIMINATE LOVE BIBBLES   396 6
    INDISCRIMINATE   396 20
    AND YOU LOVE TO MAKE SOMEBODY LOVE YOU INDISCRIMINATE   396 21
    INDISCRIMINATE   396 25
    INDISCRIMINATE   399 32

INDISCRIMINATING
    INDISCRIMINATING ANIMAL   396 2

INDISTINCT
    THE SHORN MOON TREMBLING INDISTINCT ON HER PATH   131 23
    THE SHORN MOON TREMBLING INDISTINCT ON HER PATH   *937 22

INDIVIDUAL
    DOES NO ONE REALISE THAT LOVE SHOULD BE INTENSE INDIVID+ 291 15
    THIS INTENSE INDIVIDUAL IN SHADOW   338 12
    THE COMPLEX MANIFOLD INVOLVEDNESS OF AN INDIVIDUAL   356 12
    THE INDIVIDUAL CARRIES HIS OWN GRAIN OF INSANITY AROUND+ 486 9
    AND THE INDIVIDUAL MUST HAVE HIS HOUSE FOOD AND FIRE ALL 487 23
    WE LOSE THAT WHICH KEEPS US INDIVIDUAL   514 15
    WE CALL FREE COMPETITION AND INDIVIDUAL ENTERPRISE AND   519 29
    IS THE VERY INDIVIDUAL FLAME OF LIFE ITSELF   679 25
    HE IS POLITICIAN OR MAGNATE OR MERE INDIVIDUAL   775 9
    STRUGGLING GERM IN INDIVIDUAL HEARTS   775 22
    IN INDIVIDUAL HEARTS AND NOWHERE ELSE   775 26

INDIVIDUALLY
    THIS IS WHY I TUG AT THEM INDIVIDUALLY WITH MY ARM ROUND 288 8

INDIVIDUALS
    INDIVIDUALS MUST GO MAD   475 26
    SINCE POOR INDIVIDUALS THAT WE ARE   514 13
    AH IN THE PAST TOWARDS RARE INDIVIDUALS   602 10

INDOMITABLE
    UPON YOU WRAPPED IN INDOMITABLE ME   154 26
    DARK IN INDOMITABLE FAILURE SHE WHO HAD LOST   156 5
    SO-INDOMITABLE   352 23
    OR IS IT JUST YOUR INDOMITABLE WILL AND PRIDE OF THE FI+ 353 17

INDOORS
PELTING INDOORS   400   3
INDOORS WE CALLED EACH OTHER YOU   490 19

INDRAWN
WHICH QUIVERS INDRAWN AS YOU CLENCH YOUR SPINE   370 13

INDUCE
TILL AT LENGTH THEY INDUCE ME TO SLEEP AND TO FORGET   180 36

INDUSTRIAL
LURKING AMONG THE DEEPS OF YOUR INDUSTRIAL THICKET   293   8
WHY HAVE THE INDUSTRIAL SYSTEM   452   1
INDUSTRIAL AND FINANCIAL SYSTEMS MACHINES AND SOVIETS   452 10
AH THE INDUSTRIAL MASSES WITH THE IRON HOOK THROUGH THE+   586 15
THE INDUSTRIAL MASSES AH WHAT WILL HAPPEN WHAT WILL   586 23
ONCE MEN TOUCH ONE ANOTHER THEN THE MODERN INDUSTRIAL   611 14
AFTER OUR INDUSTRIAL CIVILISATION HAS BROKEN AND THE CI+   612   1
OH WHEN I THINK OF THE INDUSTRIAL MILLIONS WHEN I SEE   629 16
AND ENSHROUDED IN THE VAST CORPSE OF THE INDUSTRIAL MIL+   629 30
INTO THE INDUSTRIAL DANCE OF THE LIVING DEATH THE JIGGI+   631 13
THEY DANCE DANCE DANCE THIS DRY INDUSTRIAL JIG OF THE   631 19
EVEN WITH THE INDUSTRIAL MASSES AND THE GREEDY MIDDLE   631 25
POLITICIANS MAY BE BAD INDUSTRIAL MAGNATES MAY BE AT FA+   775   5

INDUSTRIALISTS
THE GREAT INDUSTRIALISTS KNOW IT   635 19

INDUSTRY
THE MILLS OF INDUSTRY ARE NOT THE MILLS OF GOD   441 11
WHY HAVE INDUSTRY   451 32
AND MONEY AND INDUSTRY   534 16
IN ALL THE HIGH PLACES AND THEY ARE MASTERS OF INDUSTRY   637 19

INEFFABLE
IN TEDIUM AND MOUTH RELAXED AS IF SMILING INEFFABLE TED+   66 12

INEFFECTUAL
AND PRISONERS' FLAT INEFFECTUAL PASTIME   518 13
OF OLD INEFFECTUAL LIVES LINGER BLURRED AND WARM   *906 12
OF OLD INEFFECTUAL LIVES LINGER BLURRED AND WARM   *908   6

INEFFICACIOUS
THE DAY SHALL MOCK ME INEFFICACIOUS WHAT THEN   771 30

INERT
FROM A ROOF INERT WITH DEATH WEEPING NOT THIS NOT   62 11
THINK OF IT IN A GARDEN OF INERT CLODS   358   8
SULKY IN SPIRIT AND INERT   795   7
BUT LO YOU INERT ONES I WILL SET THE DRAGONS UPON YOU   796 25
OF MY ARMS INERT WITH DREAD WILTED IN FEAR OF MY KISS   *912 18

INERTIA
AND SLOWLY PITCHING ITSELF AGAINST THE INERTIA   353 19
WHAT AN INCALCULABLE INERTIA   353 27
SUN AND INERTIA ON THE BELLY ON THE BACK   827 14

INEVITABLE
SHE'S ONLY THE NEARER TO THE INEVITABLE FAREWELL   85 14
DEATH IS NO ESCAPE AH NO ONLY A DOORWAY TO THE INEVITAB+   662 25
DON'T YOU SEE HOW YOU MAKE BOLSHEVISM INEVITABLE   664 13
THROUGH AN INEVITABLE IRREPARABLE LEAK   767 13
BUT AS INEVITABLE   784 30

INEVITABLY
INEVITABLY LOOK UP   389 24
THEY MOVE IN A GREAT GRIND OF HATE SLOWLY BUT INEVITABLY   648   7
THE BOURGEOIS PRODUCES THE BOLSHEVIST INEVITABLY   663   9
ONLY MORE INEVITABLY THE BOLSHEVIST   664   9

INEXHAUSTIBLE
TO SHOW HOW INEXHAUSTIBLE IT IS   709   7

INEXORABLE
INEXORABLE LOVE GOES LAGGING   64   6
NOW I OFFER HER UP TO THE ANCIENT INEXORABLE GOD   238 23

INEXPERIENCED
HALF-YAWNING AT THE OPEN INEXPERIENCED   311   7

INEXPRESSIBLE
THE INEXPRESSIBLE FAINT YELL   365 19

INEXTINGUISHABLE
I LIFT MY INEXTINGUISHABLE FLAME   745   2

IN EXTREMIS
TORTOISE IN EXTREMIS   364   6

INFAMOUS
THE GREED OF THIS INFAMOUS FELLOW FOR OUR SWEAT   750   8

INFAMY
IT IS AN INFAMY   255 21

INFANT
OF THE HOT-BORN INFANT BLESS THE FOLLY WHICH HAD   88 30
THE FIRST WAIL OF AN INFANT   366 15
INFANT   438 27
AND SOON EVEN GOD WON'T BE BIG ENOUGH TO HANDLE THAT IN+   670 20
WAS A GREAT BIG HYDROCEPHALOUS WATER-IN-THE-BRAIN INFANT   670 22

INFERIOR
AND SEND MANKIND TO ITS INFERIOR BLAZES   316 29
MANKIND'S INFERIOR BLAZES   316 30
AND THESE ALONG WITH IT ALL THE INFERIOR LOT   316 31
YOU DON'T NEED ONE SINGLE SOCIAL INFERIOR TO EXALT YOU   526 26
AND IF THEY HAD NO UPPER CLASSES EITHER TO BE INFERIOR +   527 23

INFERIOR
YOU'RE MY INFERIOR THAT'S WHAT YOU ARE YOU'RE MY INFERI+   547 21
TO A LOT OF INFERIOR SWIPE   547 23
THE SUPERIOR PERSONS SOMEWHAT INFERIOR   547 30
WHEN REALLY YOU ARE SLIGHTLY INFERIOR   548 19
O I WAS BORN LOW AND INFERIOR   554   5
AND THE HOPELESS INFERIOR HE IS THE MACHINE INCARNATE   635 16

INFERIORITY
WITHOUT ANY DIVISION INTO INFERIORITY AND SUPERIORITY   636   4

INFERIORS
ALL MY INFERIORS ARE VERY SUPERIOR   548   7
THE INFERIORS   637   7
THE INFERIORS THE INFERIORS THERE THEY ARE IN HORDES   637   8
LESS THAN REAL MEN INFERIORS INFERIORS   637 26

INFERNAL
LIKE FLOWERS OF INFERNAL MOLY   146 20
INFERNAL DIS   307 22

INFINITE
WITH SUCH INFINITE PATIENCE   272 21
I AM SO TIRED OF THE LIMITATIONS OF THEIR INFINITE   288 14
OF INFINITE STALENESS   478 29
THE UNIVERSE FLOWS IN INFINITE WILD STREAMS RELATED   479   9
AND BUDDING TOWARDS INFINITE VARIETY VARIEGATION   612   5
AND WHERE THERE IS INFINITE VARIETY THERE IS NO INTERES+   612   6

INFINITELY
SO MUCH THERE IS OUTSIDE ME SO INFINITELY   223   7
HOW INFINITELY DEAR TO ME   469 13
HOW DISGUSTING HOW INFINITELY SORDID THIS HUMANITY IS   628   4
AND BORN HIM A SON OR SO WHO AT THE AGE OF SEVEN IS SO +   842   7
AND TRUE ENOUGH HE WAS INFINITELY THE MORE MANLY FELLOW   842 24

INFINITESIMAL
BESIDE THE INFINITESIMAL FAINT SMEAR OF YOU   334 17
BLACK PIPER ON AN INFINITESIMAL PIPE   341 25

INFINITIES
THEN WEIGH AND OUT TO THE INFINITIES   542 14

INFINITY
AND MAKE A JOKE OF STALE INFINITY   299 12

INFIRM
SLOW INFIRM DEATH HAS AT LAST GATHERED UP THE WASTE   859 21

INFLAMED
INFLAMED WITH BINDING UP THE SHEAVES OF THE DEAD   135 23
INFLAMED WITH BINDING UP THE SHEAVES OF DEAD   *939 23

INFLATED
INTO RUBBER-LIKE DEADNESS DUNLOP INFLATED UNCONCERN   625 18
AND THE REDDENED LIMBS RED INDIA-RUBBER TUBING INFLATED   625 21

INFLUENCES
DO YOU FEEL THE AIR FOR ELECTRIC INFLUENCES   301   3

INFORM
THAT DOES INFORM THIS VARIOUS DREAM OF LIVING   194 20

INFUSES
AND INFUSES   131   3

INFUSING
HER FIRE INFUSING ITS LIFELESSNESS   *937 17

INGINES
UNDER TH' TANK AS FILLS TH' INGINES   79   3
UNDER THE TANK AS FILLS THE INGINES   *920 27

INHERITANCE
AND US FROM THE DREARY INHERITANCE OF ROMAN STUPIDITY   479 27

INHERITING
INHERITING A SORT OF CONFINEMENT   518 11

INHUMAN
OUR BEACHED VESSEL DARKENED RENCONTRE INHUMAN AND CLOSE+   66 27
IN A MOTION HUMAN INHUMAN TWO AND ONE   252 10
AND HAVE A COOL SENSE OF TRUTH INHUMAN TRUTH AT LAST   481 23

INHUMANITY
THE EGO REVEALED IN ALL ITS MONSTROUS INHUMANITY   475 11

INITIALS
AND HOW RIGHT HE WAS AND I SIGNED MY INITIALS   579 20

INITIATED
THE PINING TO BE INITIATED   263 21

INJURED
I WOULD DIE RATHER THAN HAVE IT INJURED WITH ONE SCAR   255 13
I REMEMBER THE SCREAM OF A TERRIFIED INJURED HORSE THE   366 10
FOR I HAVE INJURED YOU   735 21

INJURY
I DID YOU AN INJURY   735 24

INK
NOW AT LAST THE INK AND DUDGEON PASSES FROM OUR FERVENT+   70   5
INK   386 18

INKLING
  PROUD BEYOND INKLING OR FURTHEST CONCEPTION OF PRIDE   258 31
  NOT EVEN AN INKLING   562 16

INKSPOT
  AND DIDN'T YOU CRINGE ON THE FLOOR LIKE ANY INKSPOT   400 10

INNER
  THE INNER DARK OF THE MYSTERY   114 11
  NOT THIS INNER NIGHT   114 14
  THE WALLS ARE THICK AND THE INNER ROOMS ARE SUCH THEY D+   174 19
  BOWED DOWN WITH HIS INNER MAGNIFICENCE   272 12
  IN THE DENSE FOLIAGE OF THE INNER GARDEN   278 12
  ONLY THE INNER EYE OF YOUR SCORCHED BROAD BREAST   373 24
  ALREADY THE WHITENESS OF FALSE DAWN IS ON MY INNER OCEAN   513 13
  TO DROWN THEIR INNER CACOPHONY AND OURS   656 7
  AND OUT OF THE INWARD ROARING OF THE INNER RED OCEAN OF+   694 16
  I AM GOING TO SPEAK TO THE DRAGON OF THE INNER FIRES   797 1
  NOT THE INNER NIGHT   *930 2

INNERLY
  I HAVE BEEN SO INNERLY PROUD AND SO LONG ALONE   214 1

INNERMOST
  THE SHORES OF THIS INNERMOST OCEAN ALIVE AND ILLUSORY   71 12
  WHERE WE CAN SEE IT OUR FIRE TO THE INNERMOST FIRE   89 16
  THE INNERMOST FIRE OF MY OWN DIM SOUL OUT-SPINNING   218 22
  GOLD WITH AN INNERMOST SPECK   253 1
  GREEN STREAMS THAT FLOW FROM THE INNERMOST CONTINENT OF   260 24
  DISSOLVED WITH THE MYSTERY OF THE INNERMOST HEART OF THE   260 28
  INSIDE MY INNERMOST HEART   412 4
  TO THAT DIFFICULT INNERMOST PLACE IN A MAN   412 8
  WITH SEVEN VEILS AND AN INNERMOST   726 8
  A GATE TO THE INNERMOST PLACE   811 3
  THERE IS NO GREAT GOD IN THE INNERMOST   823 16
  THERE IS EVEN NO INNERMOST   823 17
  EVEN WHILE IN HIS INNERMOST EYES THERE BURN   876 26
  THE LOOP-HOLES OF THAT INNERMOST NIGHT OF HIM   876 35
  OH THE TERROR OF LIFTING THE INNERMOST I OUT OF THE SWE+ *909 21

INNINGS
  HAVE WE HAD OUR INNINGS   152 24

INNOCENCE
  AND WINSOME CHILD OF INNOCENCE NOR   230 26
  AND RUIN OF HER INNOCENCE UPON   880 29

INNOCENT
  WALK INNOCENT IN THE DAFFODILS   178 7
  AS FOR INNOCENT JESUS   328 17
  THE INNOCENT   333 22
  FOR IN SICILY THE BLACK BLACK SNAKES ARE INNOCENT THE G+   350 3
  OH THE INNOCENT GIRL   564 25
  OH THE INNOCENT MAID   565 23
  IS MORE INNOCENT FAR   565 27
  THE INNOCENT MEMBER THAT A FIG-LEAF WILL SCREEN   578 17
  THOUGH THE PURPLE DREAMS OF THE INNOCENT SPRING HAVE GO+   854 6
  YOUR LOVE WAS INNOCENT AND THOROUGH   *927 3

INNUMERABLE
  AT LAST AT LAST BEYOND INNUMERABLE SEAS   *961 14

INORDINATE
  WHY HANGING WITH SUCH INORDINATE WEIGHT   279 15
  FULL OF INORDINATE ACTIVITIES   510 27

INORDINATELY
  AND INORDINATELY THERE O STOIC   358 17

IN PURIS NATURALIBUS
  IN PURIS NATURALIBUS DON'T YOU SEE   578 26

INQUIRINGLY
  AND LOOKS UP INQUIRINGLY INTO THE PILLAR OF CLOUD   375 12

INQUISITION
  WE'VE GOT THE INQUISITION BACK   634 7

INQUISITIVE
  WELL YOU ANXIOUS INQUISITIVE LOVER   95 14
  STOPS AGAIN HALF TURNS INQUISITIVE TO LOOK BACK   393 29

INQUISITORS
  SIX FAT SMALLER BOBBIES ARE THE INQUISITORS MINOR   633 16

INRUSH
  THE INRUSH THE CLATTER THE STAMPING EYES LAUGHING WIDE +   865 25

INRUSHING
  A STRONG INRUSHING WIND   343 18

INSANE
  FLYING ROUND THE ROOM IN INSANE CIRCLES   342 15
  IN INSANE CIRCLES   342 16
  BLUNDERING MORE INSANE AND LEAPING IN THROBS TO CLUTCH +   343 20
  SO EVERYTHING IS INSANE   516 2
  SUCCESS IS INSANE AND FAILURE IS INSANE   516 3
  CHASTITY IS INSANE AND DEBAUCHERY IS INSANE   516 4
  MONEY IS INSANE AND POVERTY IS INSANE   516 5
  THE PURITAN IS INSANE   516 11
  AND THE PROFLIGATE IS INSANE   516 12
  THE WEALTHY ARE INSANE   516 14
  AND THE POVERTY-STRICKEN ARE INSANE   516 15
  IN THE END WE GO INSANE   522 21
  WILL AT LAST SEND YOU INSANE   655 17
  INSANE   838 20
  AT THE MOMENT WE TEND TO RUN INSANE THE MIND HAVING BRO+   838 21
  IT IS SO SHAMEFUL TO BE INSANE   839 12

INSANE
  ALL INSANE   839 21

INSANELY
  ALL THE LOT OF THEM VICE MISSIONS ETC INSANELY UNHEALTHY   845 10

INSANITIES
  TODAY LIFE IS A CHOICE OF INSANITIES   839 18
  IT IS A STRING OF INSANITIES   839 20

INSANITY
  THE SAME INSANITY OF SPACE   214 19
  THE INDIVIDUAL CARRIES HIS OWN GRAIN OF INSANITY AROUND+   486 9
  IS SOCIAL INSANITY   514 26
  FOR AT PRESENT IN THE WHIRRING INSANITY OF THE MENTAL C+   839 5
  OF COLLECTIVE INSANITY   839 14
  IS A STRAIGHT WAY TO RAVING INSANITY   845 14
  AND WHORING ON THE BRAIN AS BAD AS SYPHILIS INCIPIENT I+ *952 20

INSATIABLE
  THAT IS HALF INSATIABLE DESIRE AND HALF UNQUENCHABLE   378 25
  SHE WATCHES WITH INSATIABLE WISTFULNESS   394 10
  FROM THE GRINNING AND INSATIABLE ROBOTS   639 13

INSCRUTABLE
  INSCRUTABLE SMALL LIGHTS GLITTER IN ROWS   163 26

INSECT
  LIKE AN INSECT IN THE GRASS   50 7
  ALONE SMALL INSECT   352 15
  IT GOES RIGHT THROUGH HIM THE SPROTTLING INSECT   356 2

INSECT-LIKE
  PALE AND MEAN AND INSECT-LIKE SCUTTLING ALONG   526 18

INSECTS
  HERE FLICK THE RABBITS HERE PANTS THE GORSE HERE SAY TH+   34 11
  IN A GARDEN OF PEBBLES AND INSECTS   358 11
  WHERE NOTHING BITES BUT INSECTS AND SNAKES AND THE SUN   394 14

INSENSATE
  COLD INSENSATE   56 30

INSENSIBLE
  ACROSS THE INSENSIBLE VOID TILL SHE STOOPS TO SEE   153 3

INSENSITIVE
  THE VIBRATION OF THE MOTOR-CAR HAS BRUISED THEIR INSENS+   625 17

INSERTED
  LIKE A FINE AN EXQUISITE CHISEL A WEDGE-BLADE INSERTED   250 20

INSIDE
  INSIDE ME AND OUT HEAVILY DARK   205 21
  HONEY-WHITE FIGS OF THE NORTH BLACK FIGS WITH SCARLET I+   284 26
  WITH SUCH A KNOT INSIDE HIM   377 29
  AND TIED IN A KNOT INSIDE DEAD-LOCKED BETWEEN TWO DESIR+   379 12
  INSIDE MY INNERMOST HEART   412 4
  TOUCH HIM AND YOU'LL FIND HE'S ALL GONE INSIDE   431 19
  JUST LIKE AN OLD MUSHROOM ALL WORMY INSIDE AND HOLLOW   431 20
  THE CONFORMING WORM STAYS JUST INSIDE THE SKIN   432 6
  MAKING IT ALL ROTTEN INSIDE   432 9
  TO THE HERD INSIDE THE PEN   458 29
  BAD INSIDE LIKE FRUIT   462 20
  ROTTEN INSIDE THEY ARE AND SEETHING   462 23
  IS A SEWER INSIDE IT POLLUTES O IT POLLUTES   463 20
  AND DIRT IF IT ISN'T SIN IS WORSE ESPECIALLY DIRT INSIDE   464 5
  IF YOU'RE DIRTY INSIDE YOU GO ROTTEN AND ONCE ROTTEN WOE   464 6
  AND GIVING YOU A COLD IN YOUR INSIDE   506 24
  AND THE END OF ALL THINGS IS INSIDE US   510 19
  THE OPTIMIST BUILDS HIMSELF SAFE INSIDE A CELL   515 7
  AND PAINTS THE INSIDE WALLS SKY-BLUE   515 8
  AND LIKE TO BECOME INCURABLY DISEASED INSIDE   535 22
  SAFE INSIDE THEIR BOTTLES   542 28
  SAFE INSIDE THEIR BOTTLES   542 32
  SOMEWHERE INSIDE YOU   563 23
  BUT OF WHICH HE HAD A BIT INSIDE HIM   714 4
  BUT THE GERM OF THAT FUTURE IS INSIDE THE AMERICAN PEOP+   775 2
  TO MAKE THEMSELVES CLEAN INSIDE AND OUT   793 6
  WAITING FOR THE RATS OF THE DARK TO COME AND GNAW YOUR +   800 24
  DO YOU HEAR THE RATS OF THE DARKNESS GNAWING AT YOUR IN+   800 25
  SO THAT HE DOESN'T SEEM TO HAVE ANY INSIDE TO HIM   830 7
  FULL INSIDE OF WEIRD BROWN SLUSHY CRAB-MEAT   830 20
  FOR THE ANALYST IS TANGLED IN AN ESPECIALLY TANGLED BUN+   833 34
  AND SINCE WOMEN ARE INSIDE THE PRISON JUST AS MUCH AS M+   838 9

INSIDIOUS
  IN SPITE OF MYSELF THE INSIDIOUS MASTERY OF SONG   148 10
  GOING WITH INSIDIOUS HALF-SMILING QUIETNESS   296 21

INSIDIOUSLY
  RISES AND FLUSHES INSIDIOUSLY   471 3
  SLOWLY INSIDIOUSLY INTO NEW PLACES   768 12

INSIGNIFICANT
  IN THE LONG HOT NIGHT MORE DANCERS FROM INSIGNIFICANT   389 2
  SWINGS ROUND THE STEMS OF THE MANY INSIGNIFICANT MUTE   855 19

INSINCERITY
  MAY I ASK YOU THEN WHERE INSINCERITY AND DISHONESTY BEG+   659 13

INSIPID
  INSIPID UNSALTED RABBITY ENDLESSLY HOPPING   606 19

INSIST
  ONLY IF YOU INSIST ON PULLING ON THOSE CHAMOIS GLOVES   433 19
  WE WOULDN'T INSIST ON IT FOR A MOMENT   434   9
  IF YOU INSIST ON IT I INSIST ON DEPARTURE   478 14

INSISTED
  THEY HAVE ALWAYS INSISTED ON LOVE   602 19

INSISTENCE
  AS YOU DRAW YOURSELF UPON YOURSELF IN INSISTENCE   370 29
  THE MORE THAN HUMAN DENSE INSISTENCE OF WILL   371 29
  AND RESOUNDING AFTER WITH A LONG HISS OF INSISTENCE   622 22
  AND THE INSISTENCE OF THE SUN   707 30

INSISTENT
  WITH A HORSE INSISTENT REQUEST THAT FALLS   64 25
  LOOSING HOLD IN THE WIND'S INSISTENT PUSH   160   8
  NOT A WEARY INSISTENT   561 30
  SEEKING TO APPEASE WITH BLOOD THE INSISTENT GHOSTS   739 24

INSISTING
  INSISTING PROTESTING   54   3
  INSISTING UPON YOUR MOTHERHOOD DEVASTATING   207   9
  I AM SO TIRED OF VIOLENT WOMEN LASHING OUT AND INSISTING   479   7

INSISTS
  BUT HE INSISTS ON GNAWING A LITTLE HOLE IN THE SOCIAL   432 13
  ASK BUT THE LEAGUE INSISTS THANK YOU SO MUCH NO SIGN HE+   546 14

INSOLENT
  AS AN INSOLENT MISTRESS TELLING MY PULSE'S BEAT   230 27
  NO WHEELS MIGHT RUN NO INSOLENT CHARIOTS   703 25
  INSOLENT GOLD   861 10
  WITHERED MY INSOLENT SOUL WOULD BE GONE LIKE FLOWERS TH+   *891 27

INSOLUBLE
  SO OF COURSE THE NATION IS SWOLLEN WITH INSOLUBLE PROBL+   535 21

INSOUCIANT
  BUT NOT EVEN THE SCENT OF INSOUCIANT FLOWERS   50 13

INSPIRED
  WHY BURNS YOUR CHEEK AGAINST ME HOW HAVE I INSPIRED   85 19
  WITH SATANICALLY INSPIRED FINANCIERS   483 15

INSTALL
  NOT TO INSTALL THE WORKING CLASSES   453 10

INSTANCES
  TWO PRIMARY INSTANCES   263 19

INSTANT
  AT A WAVERING INSTANT THE SWALLOWS GIVE WAY TO BATS   341 18
  NOT ONE INSTANT CLEAVE CLING LIKE A BLOT WITH HIS BREAS+   343 29
  NOT AN INSTANT   343 32
  EACH ONE APART AND INSTANT   371 12
  OH DON'T FOR AN INSTANT EVER DREAM   576   6
  TO BE REVOLVED AND IN ONE INSTANT CHANGED   784 25

INSTANTLY
  AND INSTANTLY ROSE A GREAT UPROAR   574 22
  THE SPARK FELL AND KINDLED INSTANTLY ON MY BLOOD   618   4
  INSTANTLY FEEL A PANG OF COMPUNCTION   834 11

INSTANT'S
  AND IN ONE INSTANT'S PAUSE ARE REVOLVED ROUND AND CHANG+   784 12

INSTEAD
  WITH TOO MUCH TINCTURE OF ME INSTEAD OF THE DARK'S DEEP+   92 29
  SO I DID NOT FIGHT YOU YOU WENT YOUR WAY INSTEAD   156 15
  INSTEAD   171   1
  INSTEAD OF FLAME AND FLAME-CLEAN ASH   318   1
  INSTEAD OF WHICH SHE STRANGELY REARS ON HER PERCH IN THE   385 23
  INSTEAD OF WHICH THE SILENT FATAL EMISSION FROM THAT PA+   390 25
  INSTEAD OF WHICH YOU SIT THERE AND ROLL YOUR HEAD LIKE A   398   9
  INSTEAD I LOOK OUT   402 21
  AND INSTEAD THE WHITE MEN SCRAMBLE ASLEEP IN THE   408   9
  INSTEAD OF MERELY THE SMELL OF MAN   444 14
  BUT INSTEAD   453 18
  TILL YOU ASK FOR LIGHTNING INSTEAD OF LOVE   484 15
  TILL YOU PRAY TO THE RIGHT GODS FOR THE THUNDER-BOLT IN+   484 16
  AND BE A BIT ELEMENTAL INSTEAD   505 11
  INSTEAD OF GETTING ON AND NOT BEING ABLE TO GET OFF AGA+   518 25
  A GAOLER INSTEAD OF A GAOL-BIRD   521 10
  INSTEAD OF KILLING THE PASSIONS AND THE INSTINCTS AND   529   7
  INSTEAD OF LEAVING IT TO LENIN   536 11
  ONLY INSTEAD OF CHANGING THINGS THAT MIGHT BE CHANGED   538 20
  INSTEAD OF AUNT GWENDOLINE   571 18
  SO MY PICTURES ARE IN PRISON INSTEAD OF IN THE ZOO   580 14
  INSTEAD OF A FLOWER THAT DIES AND OPENS A DIFFERENT BUD   662   6
  INSTEAD OF WHICH THE MINORITIES THAT STILL SEE THE GLEA+   666   5
  AND MAKES US COWARDS INSTEAD OF GODS   674   7
  HE KNOWS ME BUT DOES NOT SPEAK INSTEAD   734 28
  LAND BETTER INSTEAD OF WASTING TIME   777 32
  ONLY COLD INSTEAD OF QUICK   784 31
  INSTEAD OF THIS MESS WHICH EXPRESSES THE IMPUDENT HUMAN   837 18
  IF WE RALLY AT ALL TODAY INSTEAD OF KEEPING   839   8

INSTIL
  THE EXPECTANT ONE AND THEREIN TO INSTIL   127 13

INSTINCT
  REACHING OUT AND GRASPING BY AN INSTINCT MORE DELICATE +   285 28
  BY INSTINCT HE'S A SODOMIST   446 29
  IT IS A PERVERTED INSTINCT A HIDDEN THOUGHT   487 15
  AND OUR DEEP INSTINCT   527 11
  INSTINCT IN THE CAVERN   544 23
  SACRIFICE THAT TO THE BRIGHT GODS AND SATISFY THE DESTR+   678 17

INSTINCT
  ALMOST AN INSTINCT   829 21
  THE ONE EYE OF OUR CYCLOPAEAN INSTINCT PUT OUT   833 18

INSTINCTIVE
  BUT ALSO HE IS INSTINCTIVE INTUITIVE AND IN TOUCH   473 18
  WITH ALL THE HURT TO THEIR INSTINCTIVE AND EMOTIONAL SE+   544 28
  INSTINCTIVE CONTEMPT   612 13
  IT IS FOR MEN HE'S AN INSTINCTIVE HOMOSEXUAL   *948 30

INSTINCTIVELY
  HE'S INSTINCTIVELY FRIGHTFULLY CLEVER   447 16
  IN TOUCH BY INTUITION INSTINCTIVELY   474   6
  THEY INSTINCTIVELY HATE THEIR OWN CHILDREN   832   2

INSTINCTS
  THE DEEP INSTINCTS WHEN LEFT ALONE ARE QUITE MORAL   529   3
  INSTEAD OF KILLING THE PASSIONS AND THE INSTINCTS AND   529   7
  INSTINCTS AND INTUITIONS   630 23
  YOUR INSTINCTS GONE YOUR INTUITION GONE YOUR PASSIONS   631   1
  GOOD HEALTHY NATURAL FEELINGS INSTINCTS PASSIONS OR DES+   678   3
  AGAINST ALL YOUR DEEPER INSTINCTS AND YOUR INTUITION   836 19
  BUT BY THE HEAVY DRIFT OF HIS UNPERVERTED INSTINCTS   838 17
  DEEP INSTINCTS   838 22
  SO THAT IN THE LONG PAUSE THE INSTINCTS CAN REASSERT TH+   839   3
  BUT HE'S FAR TOO GREAT A COWARD EVER TO ADMIT HIS INSTI+   *948 32

INSTITUTE
  OR TRANSFER THE CONTROL TO THE AMERICAN INSTITUTE   780   9

INSTITUTIONS
  WE SHALL LAUGH THE INSTITUTIONS WILL CURL UP LIKE BURNT   482 26
  NOR INSTITUTIONS   622   8

INSTRUCTOR
  SHE'S A FINER INSTRUCTOR THAN YEARS   *893   3

INSTRUCTRESS
  SHE'S A QUICKER INSTRUCTRESS THAN YEARS   38 20

INSTRUMENT
  SUCH AN INSTRUMENT A SPADE LIKE A SPEAR OR AN OAR   254 20
  SHE SAID TO ME WHAT AN INSTRUMENT YOUR BODY   254 24
  NOW I SAY TO HER NO TOOL NO INSTRUMENT NO GOD   255 19

INSULT
  I WOULDN'T INSULT YOU WITH THE SUGGESTION   541 18

INSULTS
  OF SEVERAL INSULTS OF BLOTTED PAGES AND SCRAWL   74 14
  OF THEIR INSULTS IN PUNISHMENT I WILL NOT   74 22
  OF SEVERAL INSULTS OF BLOTTED PAGES AND SCRAWL   *895 22
  OF THEIR INSULTS IN PUNISHMENT I WILL NOT   *895 30
  OF SEVERAL INSULTS OF BLOTTED PAGES AND SCRAWL   *904 11
  OF THEIR INSULTS IN PUNISHMENT I WILL NOT   *904 19

INSUPERABLE
  WITH SUCH INSUPERABLE SUBTLY-SMILING ASSURANCE   300 31

INSURANCE
  YOU ARE ONLY KNOWN TO US NOW AS THE BADGE OF AN INSURAN+   330   3
  WITH BANK ACCOUNTS AND INSURANCE POLICIES   442   4
  AND SOUNDER THAN ALL INSURANCE IS A SHINY MENTAL CONCEIT   543   3

INSURGENT
  IN ONE MOMENT ROUSES INSURGENT   39   6
  DAWNS MY INSURGENT DAY   176 29

INTACT
  WHO HAVE KEPT INTACT FOR YOU YOUR VIRGINITY   157 10
  AND YET THE ROOTS BELOW THE BLACKNESS ARE INTACT   709 22
  I WALK THE EARTH INTACT HEREAFTERWARDS   743 24
  UNCHALLENGED INTACT UNABRIDGED HENCEFORTH A HOST   743 27
  I HAVE A DARKNESS INTACT WITHIN ME GLOWING SECURE   772 10

INTANGIBLE
  DIVIDED IN THE MYSTIC TANGIBLE AND INTANGIBLE DIFFERENCE   636   6
  AND IN THE GREAT STRUGGLE OF INTANGIBLE CHAOS   682 12

INTEGRAL
  YOU INTEGRAL TO ME EACH DOOR EACH MYSTIC PORT   154 13

INTEGRITY
  YOUR PRISTINE ISOLATE INTEGRITY LOST AEONS AGO   290 13
  SEX WHICH BREAKS UP OUR INTEGRITY OUR SINGLE INVIOLABIL+   366 31

INTEGUMENT
  DO YOU MEAN IT IS WRONG THE GOLD-FILMED SKIN INTEGUMENT   278 29

INTELLECT
  DOES NOT A SUPREME INTELLECT IDEALLY PROCREATE THE UNIV+   328 26
  PROUD INTELLECT HIGH-SOARING MIND   329   3
  AND THE PURE INTELLECT GIVES ONE A LAST MASTURBATING SE+   532   9
  INTELLECT ARE ONLY ESCAPES   532 12

INTELLECTUAL
  CHICK OF THE INTELLECTUAL EAGLE   329 13
  HE IS CEREBRAL INTELLECTUAL MENTAL SPIRITUAL   473 17
  QUITE COLD-BLOODED INTELLECTUAL MURDER WITH A SUFFICIENT   532 21
  AND THE INTELLECTUAL ASSES   534 17
  MECHANICAL AND INTELLECTUAL   635 29

INTELLECTUALS
  AS ONE OF OUR BRIGHTEST YOUNG INTELLECTUALS SAID TO ME   531 22
  SO ONE OF THE BRIGHTEST YOUNG INTELLECTUALS PUT IT TO ME   533   4
  EVEN OUR BRILLIANTEST YOUNG INTELLECTUALS   544 26

INTELLIGENCE
DEMAND ON HIS INTELLIGENCE   431 9
INTELLIGENCE   631 4

INTELLIGENT
IN THE HEART OF EVERY INTELLIGENT AMERICAN WHETHER   775 8
THERE IS I BELIEVE SCARCELY ONE INTELLIGENT AMERICAN WHO   775 12
LIFE IS A THING YOU'VE GOT TO BE FLEXIBLE AND INTELLIGE+   *953 9

INTELLIGENTLY
BUT PRUNING SEVERELY INTELLIGENTLY AND RUTHLESSLY PRUNI+   677 27

INTELLIGENTSIA
AND THEN OUR ENGLISH IMITATION INTELLIGENTSIA   533 22
THE YOUNGER INTELLIGENTSIA SO TO SPEAK   829 6

INTEND
PEOPLE FEELING THINGS THEY INTEND TO FEEL THEY MEAN TO +   500 21

INTENDING
STRANGE WHITE SIGNALS SEEM INTENDING   150 12

INTENSE
YOUR LOVE WAS INTENSE AND THOROUGH   111 10
THE SPARK INTENSE WITHIN IT ALL WITHOUT   160 22
GREEN LANTERN OF PURE LIGHT A LITTLE INTENSE FUSING TRI+   206 10
DOES NO ONE REALISE THAT LOVE SHOULD BE INTENSE INDIVID+   291 15
THIS INTENSE INDIVIDUAL IN SHADOW   338 12
AT WHICH IN THE INTENSE STILL NOON I STARED WITH FASCIN+   351 17
AND ONE INTENSE AND BACKWARD-CURVING FRISSON   370 16
THE LONG TIP REACHES STRONG INTENSE LIKE THE MAELSTROM-+   694 17
CRISPED WITH INTENSE DESIRE   861 22

INTENSELY
SHE WATCHED SHE WENT OF A SUDDEN INTENSELY STILL   125 11
INTENSELY ALONE   281 5
THEY WILL STILL SQUEAK INTENSELY ABOUT THEIR FEELINGS   501 4
SHE WATCHED SHE WENT OF A SUDDEN INTENSELY STILL   *935 27

INTENT
WHERE HASTENING CREATURES PASS INTENT   50 27
AND REMEMBER THE SMALL LAD LYING INTENT TO LOOK   161 9
INTENT TO HOLD THE CANDLE OF THE SUN UPON ITS SOCKET-TIP   299 29

INTENTION
AND HARD WITH THE INTENTION TO KEEP THEM   279 9

INTERCHANGE
YOU INTERCHANGE   239 8

INTERCOURSE
THAT CASTS ITS SPERM UPON THE WATERS AND KNOWS NO INTER+   616 25

INTEREST
THOROUGHLY I AM UNABLE TO FEEL ANY INTEREST IN   602 27
AND WHERE THERE IS INFINITE VARIETY THERE IS NO INTERES+   612 6
SIN DOESN'T INTEREST ME   618 8

INTERESTED
THE YOUNG AREN'T VITALLY INTERESTED IN IT ANY MORE   518 16
YOU ARE SO INTERESTED IN YOURSELF   602 25
I AM INTERESTED IN THE PROBLEM OF REALITY   604 2
YET I AM NOT INTERESTED IN FIGHT IN STRIFE IN COMBAT   606 16
AND NOBODY BUT THEMSELVES IS INTERESTED   618 15
IS TO CEASE TO BE INTERESTED IN IT TO BE SO INTERESTED +   665 7
IT IS ALL A QUESTION OF BEING PROFOUNDLY INTERESTED IN +   665 16
AND I AM NOT INTERESTED TO KNOW ABOUT MYSELF ANY MORE   674 13

INTERESTING
AND SO INTERESTING   528 27
YOUR INTERESTING SELF   602 28

INTERESTING-LOOKING
IT HAS GROWN UP OFTEN A BIG AND OFTEN INTERESTING-LOOKI+   841 16

INTERESTS
CONTENDING INTERESTS   777 19

INTERFERE
HE WILL INTERFERE WITH ME LESS   664 7

INTERFERENCE
YOU ABSTAIN FROM FURTHER INTERFERENCE   779 32

INTERFERES
THE MOMENT THE MIND INTERFERES WITH LOVE OR THE WILL   473 1

INTERIM
ROLL HOLLOW IN THE INTERIM   159 18

INTERIOR
INTERIOR A HOUSE OF DREAMS WHERE THE DREAMERS WRITHE AN+   174 24
THE WHOLE WIDE WORLD IS INTERIOR NOW AND WERE ALL SHUT +   175 11
THOUGH THE HOUSE HAD A FINE INTERIOR   554 15
THE MYSTERY OF THE INTERIOR   607 6

INTERIORS
WITH EYES LIKE THE INTERIORS OF STUFFY ROOMS FURNISHED   656 24

INTERLOCKED
NOW THE TREES WITH INTERLOCKED HANDS AND ARMS UPLIFTED +   854 4

INTERMINGLING
THIS INTERMINGLING OF THE BLACK AND MONSTROUS FINGERS OF   242 2

INTERMITTENT
NOR SOUND ONLY INTERMITTENT MACHINERY WHIRRING   153 8

INTERNAL
THEN THE MILL-STONES BURST WITH THE INTERNAL HEAT OF TH+   648 12

INTERNATIONAL LABOUR
DON'T DO IT ANYHOW FOR INTERNATIONAL LABOUR   517 17

INTERNECINE
WHAT IS IT INTERNECINE THAT IS LOCKED   160 17

INTERPRETATION
THIS IS THE AUTHENTIC ARABIC INTERPRETATION OF THE BRAY+   377 17

INTERPRETIVE
WHEN SCIENCE STARTS TO BE INTERPRETIVE   523 1

INTERRUPT
ME THAT I INTERRUPT HER GAME   152 3
NOT TO INTERRUPT HER WHY SHOULD I   152 8
TO INTERRUPT   883 28

INTERRUPTIONS
BECAUSE OF THE LITTLE LIGHTS AND FLICKERS AND INTERRUPT+   203 20

INTERSPERSED
SMALL INTERSPERSED WITH JEWELS OF WHITE GOLD   314 2

INTERTWINED
ABOVE INTERTWINED PLASM   146 35

INTERVAL
WITH AN INTERVAL OF SPACE BETWEEN   228 2
AFTER EACH JERK THE LONGISH INTERVAL   365 24

INTERVALS
AND IN THE INTERVALS OF THEIR THRILLS I SUPPOSE   533 7
BY A SLOW GASPING PUMP THAT HAS AWFUL INTERVALS   878 34

INTERVENE
AND I CRY ALOUD IN THE MOMENTS THAT INTERVENE   100 23
THAT INTERVENE BETWEEN OUR TOWER AND THE SLINKING SEA O+   *957 24

INTERVENES
THAT INTERVENES BETWEEN THE FINAL SEA   722 7

INTERWEAVES
DIM SPRING THAT INTERWEAVES   126 20

INTESTINES
AND TAKE OUT MY INTESTINES TO TORTURE THEM   741 4

INTIMACY
I SUFFOCATE IN THIS INTIMACY   116 30
THAT THIS QUITE REAL INTIMACY   470 10
ALL THIS TALKING INTIMACY   470 14
TO PROCEED FROM MENTAL INTIMACY   470 18
AND PERSONAL INTIMACY HAS NO HEART   471 11
THEN THE PRIVATE INTIMACY OF FRIENDSHIP WILL BE REAL AN+   608 14

INTIMATE
ELDERLY DISCONTENTED WOMEN ASK FOR INTIMATE COMPANIONSH+   502 1
IN PROMISCUOUS INTIMATE APPEAL   608 17

INTOLERABLE
AN INTOLERABLE PRISON TO YOU   236 15
BRILLIANT INTOLERABLE LAVA   293 18
THE MOLTEN GOLD OF ITS INTOLERABLE RAGE   315 20
WITH A TWITCHY NERVOUS INTOLERABLE FLIGHT   342 22
DOOMED TO MAKE AN INTOLERABLE FOOL OF HIMSELF   361 8

INTONATION
THAT EVERY SYLLABLE EVERY ACCENT EVERY INTONATION AND E+   655 4

INTOXICATION
TO THE INTOXICATION   242 12
A NEW INTOXICATION OF LONELINESS AMONG DECAYING FROST-C+   281 2
INTOXICATION OF FINAL LONELINESS   281 30

INTRICATE
A PROGRESS DOWN THE INTRICATE ENTHRALLING   65 29

INTRINSIC
SOMEHOW SO SAD SO INTRINSIC SO SPIRITUAL YET SO CAUTIOU+   *932 13

INTRODUCED
AND YOU'VE INTRODUCED ANARCHY INTO YOUR COUNTRY   536 5

INTRUDE
DO I INTRUDE ON YOUR RITES NOCTURNAL   140 30

INTUITION
IN TOUCH BY INTUITION INSTINCTIVELY   474 6
AND CLEAR INTUITION IS MORE THAN MORAL   529 4
INTUITION   544 25
YOUR INSTINCTS GONE YOUR INTUITION GONE YOUR PASSIONS   631 1
AND WHERE WITH THE SLOW PATIENCE OF INTUITION   833 25
AGAINST ALL YOUR DEEPER INSTINCTS AND YOUR INTUITION   836 19
AND HIS INTUITION   838 18
AND OUR INTUITION CAN COME TO LIFE AND GIVE US DIRECTION   859 4

INTUITIONS
INSTINCTS AND INTUITIONS   630 23

INTUITIVE
  BUT ALSO HE IS INSTINCTIVE INTUITIVE AND IN TOUCH   473 18
  AND DISLOCATED THE INTUITIVE CONSCIENCE   838 23

INTURNED
  INTURNED   282 22

INVADES
  AS THE BODY CORRODES WHEN DEATH INVADES   142 23

INVARIABLY
  AND THEN INVARIABLY SHE CROUCHES HER REAR AND MAKES   385 3
  THE ONLY THING MEN INVARIABLY FIGHT FOR   497 19
  IS THAT THEY ARE INVARIABLY IMMORAL PERSONS   836 21

INVENTED
  AS EVER WAS INVENTED   493 22
  MAN INVENTED THE MACHINE   641 1
  AND NOW THE MACHINE HAS INVENTED MAN   641 2
  MAN INVENTED THE MACHINE   641 9
  SO NOW THE MACHINE HAS INVENTED MAN   641 10
  BUT THE MACHINE IT IS THAT HAS INVENTED THEM BOTH   641 12

INVENTION
  MY OWN INVENTION   257 4

INVERTED
  FOR HIS OWN DEFICIENCY MOST MAWKISH IN ITS INVERTED SEN+   842 4

INVESTED
  AND PEOPLE DARKLY INVESTED WITH PURPLE MOVE PALPABLE   148 26

INVESTIGATE
  GOING OUT TO INVESTIGATE   324 19

INVESTIGATION
  MAKE A GOOD INVESTIGATION   237 9

INVINCIBLE
  WHICH HAD SEEMED INVINCIBLE   353 20
  INVINCIBLE FORE-RUNNER   354 22
  THE SOFT WELLING OF BLOOD INVINCIBLE EVEN BEYOND BONE OR   383 4

INVIOLABILITY
  SEX WHICH BREAKS UP OUR INTEGRITY OUR SINGLE INVIOLABIL+   366 31

INVIOLABLE
  IT WOUNDS ME TO DEATH WITH MY OWN NOT-BEING DEFINITE IN+   266 16
  AND WRAPT INVIOLABLE IN SOFT CYPRESS-TREES   298 13

INVIOLATE
  SEEING THE CORE IS A SHADOW INVIOLATE   115 11
  IT STANDS SO STILL IN THE HUSH COMPOSED OF TREES AND IN+   159 27
  AND DEPARTING INVIOLATE NOTHING CAN LAY HANDS ON HER   676 15
  SEEING I DEEP IN THE FIRE-CORE INVIOLATE   *930 11

INVISIBILITY
  LOOK NOW EVEN NOW HOW IT KEEPS ITS POWER OF INVISIBILITY   286 7
  INVISIBILITY AND THE ANAESTHETIC POWER   332 22

INVISIBLE
  THE BRANCHES INVISIBLE SEED OF EXPERIENCE BLOWS   89 30
  TAKEN LIKE A SACRIFICE IN THE NIGHT INVISIBLE   90 26
  THROUGH INVISIBLE PULSES SLOWLY FILLING THE NIGHT'S DAR+   97 28
  IN MY FLAME OF LIVING THE INVISIBLE HEART OF THE ROSE   115 8
  AND OUT OF THE INVISIBLE STREAMS OF BRIGHT BLUE DROPS   136 11
  THE RIVER'S INVISIBLE TIDE   146 30
  INVISIBLE BLINDING MY FACE AND MY EYES WHAT IF IN   147 5
  AN INVISIBLE WOE UNSEALS   159 7
  OF THIS MARCHING ALONG WITH THE INVISIBLE GRASS   164 7
  DRINK THEN INVISIBLE HEROES DRINK   177 14
  DRIVEN BY INVISIBLE BLOWS   250 22
  INVISIBLE THE HANDS OF EVE   262 10
  MANNA INVISIBLE   269 9
  AND HEAVE IT OFF AMONG THE STARS INTO THE INVISIBLE   272 24
  WHERE EVERYTHING HAPPENS INVISIBLE FLOWERING AND FERTIL+   283 20
  OF WHICH WORLD THE VINE WAS THE INVISIBLE ROSE   285 30
  GREEN DIM INVISIBLE FLOURISHING OF VINES   286 5
  SEE HIM THERE THE SWART SO PALPABLY INVISIBLE   286 11
  TO ME MEN ARE PALPABLE INVISIBLE NEARNESSES IN THE DARK   289 1
  STANDS SAYING SEE I'M INVISIBLE   403 11
  THE INVISIBLE IN ITS SHROUD   403 13
  WILL THE SINGING OF SWANS HIGH UP HIGH UP INVISIBLE   439 8
  AND THY DARKNESS IS FOREVER INVISIBLE   474 3
  SINKS AND IS GONE LIKE A COMET CURVING INTO THE INVISIB+   476 11
  HE WOULD CERTAINLY BE MUCH MORE INVISIBLE IF HE WERE   523 14
  AROUND THEM AN INVISIBLE WALL   555 20
  NOR CUT THE INVISIBLE WIRES OF STEEL THAT PULL THEM   586 6
  THE INVISIBLE GODS HAVE NO MORAL TRUCK WITH US   607 32
  AND PIVOTS ON THE INVISIBLE   616 29
  NOR CUT THE INVISIBLE WIRES OF STEEL THAT PULL THEM   632 21
  AS UP AN INVISIBLE RAINBOW AN ARCH   696 23
  OR A DARKNESS INVISIBLE ENFOLDED IN THE DEEPER DARK   697 19
  COMING LIKE THE RUBY IN THE INVISIBLE DARK GLOWING   697 30
  INVISIBLE YET STRONG   739 8
  INVISIBLE TROOPING HOME THE UNASSUAGED GHOSTS   739 11
  SEEKING THE OFFAL AND GARBAGE OF LIFE IN THE INVISIBLE +   796 6
  BUT I AM THE INWARD STAR INVISIBLE   801 10
  BUT THE NIGHT IS FULL OF THE FLUTTER OF INVISIBLE REVEL+   *918 10
  A GLOOM INVISIBLE ENFOLDED IN THE DEEPER DARK   *956 16
  SLIPS OUT THE SOUL INVISIBLE ONE WRAPPED STILL   *957 8
  HE SHALL SLIP DOWN THE SHORES INVISIBLE   *958 25
  NOW IN THE TWILIGHT SIT BY THE INVISIBLE SEA   *960 12
  RIGGING ITS MAST WITH THE SILENT INVISIBLE SAIL   *961 1

INVISIBLY
  IS HE MOVING INVISIBLY DOES HIS STEEP   40 3
  INVISIBLY INAUDIBLY   166 4
  THAT STIRS WITH A STIR WHICH IS COSMIC AS EVER INVISIBLY   176 3
  AND FLOWING INVISIBLY GASPING   480 17

INVITATION
  SHYLY AND IN HOMAGE LINGER FOR AN INVITATION   256 5
  THROBS OF INVITATION   289 3
  BUT I CAME AT FREEDOM'S INVITATION   575 5

INVITE
  CAN WARM HER HANDS AND INVITE HER SOUL   151 27

INVOKE
  BUT I INVOKE THE SPIRITS OF THE LOST   298 9

INVOLVED
  INVOLVED   282 21
  THE INVOLVED VOLUPTUOUSNESS OF THE SOFT-FOOTED CAT   383 1
  I AM ONLY INVOLVED   606 17

INVOLVEDNESS
  THE COMPLEX MANIFOLD INVOLVEDNESS OF AN INDIVIDUAL   356 12

INVOLVINGS
  OR DEEPER LIKE THE FOLDINGS AND INVOLVINGS OF A WOMB   *959 21

INVULNERABLE
  AND SHIRT YOU NOW INVULNERABLE IN THE MAIL   154 19
  ENSHEATHED INVULNERABLE WITH ME WITH SEVEN   154 23

INWARD
  OF SHADOW EMERGING AS BLOOD EMERGES FROM INWARD SHADES +   66 20
  THE FLOWERING ALL INWARD AND WOMB-FIBRILLED   282 23
  THERE WAS A FLOWER THAT FLOWERED INWARD WOMB-WARD   282 27
  FIG FRUIT OF THE FEMALE MYSTERY CONVERT AND INWARD   283 18
  IS THERE A RUBY OF FUSED BEING MINE AND YOURS AN INWARD   478 7
  AND THAT IS MY BIT OF INWARD PEACE WHERE I AM AT ONE   497 23
  AND FROM HIS OWN LITTLE INWARD SUN   525 14
  BRUISES ON MY INWARD FLESH   601 11
  THE INWARD COCKY ASSERTIVENESS OF THE SPANIARD SEEMS TO+   518 9
  AND AGAINST THIS INWARD REVOLT OF THE NATIVE CREATURES +   624 20
  AND OUT OF THE INWARD ROARING OF THE INNER RED OCEAN OF+   694 16
  THE SOUL HAS PEACE INWARD AND LOVELY PEACE   724 26
  BUT I AM THE INWARD STAR INVISIBLE   801 10
  CAVES INWARD KNOWING THE OUTSIDE WORLD   843 4
  I THINK SOMETIMES IT WILL CRUSH MY HEART INWARD   869 22

INWARDLY
  AND LISTENING INWARDLY TO THE FIRST BLEAT OF A LAMB   366 14
  TWITCHES AND EBBS HITTING WASHING INWARDLY SILVERILY   453 20
  THAT BURN INWARDLY   511 13
  IN FRUSTRATING HER JUST INWARDLY FRUSTRATING HER   618 23

INWARDNESS
  IN THE INWARDNESS OF YOUR YOU THAT EYE WILL NEVER SEE   283 22
  SNOW AND INWARDNESS OF THE LOBO VALLEY   401 19

INWARDS
  BUT INTO THE INWARDS OF THE UNSEEN   784 6
  INWARDS I CAN SEE WHENCE THE THORNS WERE RENT   856 21

IN-WEAVING
  IN-WEAVING THE BRIGHT THREAD OF HIS JOY   867 27

IO
  FOR A MOMENT SHE WAS IO IO WHO FLED FROM ZEUS OR THE DA+   672 17

IRASCIBLE
  BECAUSE HE IS IRASCIBLE THIS MORNING AN IRASCIBLE TORTO+   357 14
  STIFF GALLANT IRASCIBLE CROOK-LEGGED REPTILE   363 19

IRE
  AND SELF-SAME DARKNESS CHAFED TO IRE   773 7

IRIDESCENCE
  THROUGH THE STIRRED IRIDESCENCE THAT SWIMS IN THE WARM   53 16
  THROUGH THE COLOURED IRIDESCENCE THAT SWIMS IN THE WARM   *906 7

IRIDESCENT
  AND MAN IS AN IRIDESCENT FOUNTAIN RISING UP TO FLOWER   675 15

IRIS
  SAW WHERE MORNING SUN ON THE SHAKEN IRIS GLISTENED   38 16
  AND A GLINT OF COLOURED IRIS BRINGS   46 10
  I SAW THE PAIN AMONG THE IRIS THERE   880 28
  SEE THE MORNING SUN ON THE SHAKEN IRIS GLISTEN   *892 31

IRISES
  A FAINT SICKENING SCENT OF IRISES   90 1
  A FINE PROUD SPIKE OF PURPLE IRISES   90 3

IRON
  SCOOPED THEM UP WITH SMALL IRON WORDS   94 11
  OF IRON KISSES KISSES LINKED LIKE STEEL   154 20
  ALL DAY HAS THE CLANK OF IRON ON IRON DISTRESSED   167 13
  WHERE DEAD MEN'S LIVES GLOW GENTLY AND IRON HURTS   173 22
  YOUR IRON MEN   291 3
  OF THE IRON CLICK OF YOUR HUMAN CONTACT   291 10
  LIKE IRON STICKING GRIMLY OUT OF EARTH   300 19
  LIKE IRON IMPLEMENTS TWISTED HIDEOUS OUT OF THE EARTH   300 21
  BLACK RUSTED IRON TRUNK   300 27
  WITH IRON BRANCHING BLACKLY RUSTED LIKE OLD TWISTED   301 13
  EVEN IRON CAN PUT FORTH   304 1
  EVEN IRON   304 2
  THIS IS THE IRON AGE   304 3
  SEEING IRON BREAK AND BUD   304 5

IRON
    SEEING RUSTY IRON PUFF WITH CLOUDS OF BLOSSOM   304 6
    DECEMBER'S BARE IRON HOOKS STICKING OUT OF EARTH   304 8
    UPON THE IRON AND UPON THE STEEL   304 12
    FROM OUT THE IRON AND FROM OUT THE STEEL   304 16
    ALONG THE IRON TO THE LIVING STEEL   304 19
    AND THE ALMOND-TREE IN EXILE IN THE IRON AGE   305 11
    BRISTLING NOW WITH THE IRON OF ALMOND-TREES   305 15
    IRON BUT UNFORGOTTEN   305 16
    IRON DAWN-HEARTED   305 17
    EVER-BEATING DAWN-HEART ENVELOPED IN IRON AGAINST THE   305 18
    AND THE GETHSEMANE BLOOD AT THE IRON PORES UNFOLDS UNFO+   306 4
    THINK OF IT FROM THE IRON FASTNESS   306 14
    COME FORTH FROM IRON   306 21
    MORE FEARLESS THAN IRON ALL THE TIME   306 24
    WITHIN IRON AND EARTH   307 3
    LIKE SOME IRON DOOR   352 11
    OPENING HER RATHER PRETTY WEDGE OF AN IRON PRISTINE FACE   359 2
    AT THE END OF SOME MYSTERIOUS RED-HOT IRON   363 16
    WITH IRON BETWEEN YOUR TWO EYES   373 17
    THINGS OF IRON ARE BEATEN ON THE ANVIL   381 31
    THAT STRONG ONE RULING THE UNIVERSE WITH A ROD OF IRON   439 25
    HAS SICKENED US THOROUGHLY WITH RODS OF IRON AND RULERS   439 26
    THINGS MADE BY IRON AND HANDLED BY STEEL   448 8
    IRON WASHES AWAY LIKE AN OLD BLOOD-STAIN   455 5
    PIVOTAL CORE OF THE SOUL HEAVIER THAN IRON   480 10
    THEN WHEN I SEE THE IRON HOOKED IN THEIR FACES   586 1
    CUT THE IRON HOOK OUT OF THEIR FACES THAT MAKES THEM SO   586 4
    AH THE INDUSTRIAL MASSES WITH THE IRON HOOK THROUGH THE+   586 15
    BUT OVER THE MIDDLE OF THE EARTH WILL BE THE SMOKY RUIN+   625 6
    AND NOW THE IRON HAS ENTERED INTO THE SOUL   629 6
    AND DEVOURED YOU WITH THE MACHINE THE VAST MAW OF IRON   630 16
    CORPSES ENTANGLED IN IRON   631 20
    AND THERE'S NO ESCAPE FOR THE IRON GOES THROUGH THEIR   631 21
    HAS THE IRON GOT THEM FAST   631 28
    IRON   632 2
    IN IRON   632 8
    WHEN I SEE THE IRON HOOKED INTO THEIR FACES   632 16
    TAKE THE IRON HOOK OUT OF THEIR FACES THAT MAKES THEM SO   632 19
    MACHINES OF IRON MUST BE TENDED BY HANDS OF FLESH   639 7
    THAT SPRAWLS ACROSS THE EARTH IN IRON IMBECILITY   642 26
    MADE OF CEMENT POURED INTO A MOULD AROUND IRON STICKS   673 3
    DOZING IN THE UNDER-DEEPS THEN REACHING OUT A SAVAGE AN+   689 20
    IRON GIVES THE DEADLY WOUND   712 6
    FROM FALLING IRON AND HORRIBLE SHELL'S REPORT   751 11
    TELL HIM PRAYER IS STRONGER THAN IRON FAITH   754 11
    IN THE STONE AND IRON LEAPS IN FIRE   773 5
    WITH IRON BETWEEN YOUR TWO EYES   781 23
    WITH A DAGGER OF DARK LIVE IRON   782 2
    AND UP THE IRON FEET OF THE EAGLE IN THRILLS OF FIERY P+   782 22
    AND WORK IRON ELBOWS UP AND DOWN   793 25
    AND THEIR WILLS ARE LIKE THEIR MACHINES OF IRON   794 8
    SCOOPED THEM UP WITH SMALL IRON WORDS   *896 27
    CENTRAL PRIMORDIAL FIRE OF THE SOUL HEAVIER THAN IRON   *951 24
    CENTRAL PRIMORDIAL FIRE OF THE SOUL HEAVIER THAN IRON   *952 1

IRON-BREAKING
    IRON-BREAKING   304 23

IRON-DARK
    ALMOND TRUNKS CURVING BLACKLY IRON-DARK CLIMBING THE   300 24

IRON-ENTANGLED
    OR MUST HE TRY TO AMPUTATE HIMSELF FROM THE IRON-ENTANG+   632 3

IRON-GREY
    DARLING I SEE YOUR IRON-GREY CHEVELURE   835 5

IRON-WROUGHT
    HERE IRON-WROUGHT   57 8

IRONY
    I SERVE I SERVE IN ALL THE WEARY IRONY OF HIS MIEN 'TIS+   391 34

IRREGULAR
    ALL THE LONG SCHOOL-HOURS ROUND THE IRREGULAR HUM OF TH+   75 20
    ALL THE SLOW SCHOOL HOURS ROUND THE IRREGULAR HUM OF TH+   *897 20
    ALL THE SLOW SCHOOL HOURS ROUND THE IRREGULAR HUM OF TH+   *900 28

IRREPARABLE
    THROUGH AN INEVITABLE IRREPARABLE LEAK   767 13

IRREPRESSIBLE
    THROUGH THE HOURS PERSISTENT AND IRREPRESSIBLE   366 7

IRREVOCABLE
    IS IT IRREVOCABLE CAN I REALLY NOT GO   173 9

IRRITATING
    I SAW AN ANGRY ITALIAN SEIZE AN IRRITATING LITTLE OFFIC+   674 20

IRRITATION
    AND IRRITATION SEETHES SECRETLY THROUGH THEIR GUTS AS T+   616 9

ISAR
    AND I WAS HERE IN THE UNDER-DUSK OF THE ISAR   206 26
    BY THE ISAR IN THE TWILIGHT   216 19
    BY THE ISAR IN THE EVENING   216 21
    BY THE ISAR IN THE TWILIGHT   217 1
    JUST A FEW OF THE ROSES WE GATHERED FROM THE ISAR   217 27
    THERE ARE FOUR MEN MOWING DOWN BY THE ISAR   219 21
    I CAN HEAR THE ISAR MOAN   220 23
    THE ISAR WHISPERS AGAIN IN THE VALLEY THE CHILDREN   732 18
    BY THE ISAR IN THE TWILIGHT   *942 5
    BY THE ISAR IN THE EVENING   *942 7
    BY THE ISAR IN THE TWILIGHT   *942 12
    JUST A FEW OF THE ROSES WE GATHERED FROM THE ISAR   *943 10

ISIS
    IT IS ISIS THE MYSTERY   196 5
    ISIS THE MYSTERY   196 23
    AND FOR THE MOMENT SHE WAS ISIS GLEAMING HAVING FOUND H+   672 24

ISLAND
    SAID FREEDOM WHY THAT'S MY OWN ISLAND   574 14
    ON WHAT A BRIGHT LITTLE ISLAND   574 15
    A RIGHT LITTLE TIGHT LITTLE ISLAND   574 16
    SO HAPPY AS OUR LITTLE ISLAND   574 18
    OH WHAT A BRIGHT LITTLE ISLAND   575 11
    A RIGHT LITTLE TIGHT LITTLE ISLAND   575 12

ISLAND-BOUND
    IS LOOKING RATHER SHABBY AND ISLAND-BOUND THESE DAYS   329 22

ISLANDS
    LITTLE ISLANDS OUT AT SEA ON THE HORIZON   687 1
    ODYSSEUS CALLS THE COMMANDS AS HE STEERS PAST THOSE FOA+   687 20
    HAVE NOT YET PASSED THE ISLANDS I MUST WATCH THEM STILL   687 23
    DO YOU SEE THE SEA BREAKING ITSELF TO BITS AGAINST THE +   705 1

ISLE
    ALL THE FLOWERS ARE FADED FROM THE ASPHALT ISLE IN THE +   71 10
    WE MUST MAKE AN ISLE IMPREGNABLE   716 16

ISLES
    AND THE ISLES AND HER MEN AND HER SCARS   202 16

ISLET
    ABOVE THE PALM-TREES OF THE ISLET IN THE LAKE   391 19

ISLETS
    AND OVER THE SUBMERGED ISLETS OF MY KNEES   705 9

ISOLATE
    YOUR PRISTINE ISOLATE INTEGRITY LOST AEONS AGO   290 13

ISOLATED
    I SEE MYSELF ISOLATED IN THE UNIVERSE AND WONDER   223 1
    THOSE VILLAGERS ISOLATED AT THE GRAVE   233 5
    ONE CLEAR BURNISHED ISOLATED BEING UNIQUE   267 20
    AND SHE ALSO PURE ISOLATED COMPLETE   267 21

ISOLATION
    A NEW GASP OF FURTHER ISOLATION   281 1
    EACH SOUL DEPARTING WITH ITS OWN ISOLATION   281 17
    YOUR BOUNDS OF ISOLATION   290 17
    ISOLATION IS HIS BIRTHRIGHT   357 32
    ENVELOPED IN ISOLATION   360 31
    ALAS THE SPEAR IS THROUGH THE SIDE OF HIS ISOLATION   361 1
    DRAGGED OUT OF AN ETERNITY OF SILENT ISOLATION   362 27

'IS-SEN
    WARMIN' 'IS-SEN AT THE STOOL O' FIRE   79 2

ISSUE
    BITTER TO FOLD THE ISSUE AND MAKE NO SALLY   160 25
    FULL OF FINE WARMTH I ISSUE FORTH IN CLEAR   218 7
    I AM YOUR ISSUE   246 12
    THEY ARE THE ISSUE OF ACRID WINTER THESE FIRST-FLOWER Y+   270 15
    FLOWERS OF THE PENUMBRA ISSUE OF CORRUPTION NOURISHED IN   271 8
    ISSUE OF THE EXPLICIT ROSE   285 8
    LET THERE BE NO ACCOMMODATION AT THIS ISSUE   608 7
    FROM EMBASSY IN DEATH I ISSUE FORTH   744 21
    WHENCE ISSUE UNBLEMISHED THE ATOMS WHICH SOFT BESTOWED   *938 17

ISSUED
    AS A JEWEL-BROWN HORSE-CHESTNUT NEWLY ISSUED   73 5
    TWICE YOU HAVE ISSUED ME   101 24
    ME WHO AM ISSUED AMAZED FROM THE DARKNESS STRIPPED   133 2
    NO SOONER ISSUED SIDEWAYS FROM THE THIGH OF HIS PREDECE+   299 32
    THE UNKNOWN FLOWER ISSUED MAGIC-WISE   *943 21

ISSUES
    THE WORLD WITHIN WORLDS IS A WOMB WHENCE ISSUES ALL   88 33
    WE FEEL HIM STRANGLING EVEN MORE THE ISSUES OF OUR SOUL   609 5
    AFTER THEM ISSUES A DARK-WINGED FLUTTERING SPRITE   858 15
    OF THE DARK SHAFT THAT ISSUES TO THE NIGHT   879 35
    AND SILENCE ISSUES SLOWLY FROM THE HUSK   *939 11

ISSUING
    THAT ISSUING OUT OF THE EAST HAS SIFTED   68 3
    ISSUING STRAIGHT OUT OF THE UNKNOWN   268 7
    IN PUTRID AUTUMN ISSUING THROUGH THE FALL   745 22
    ISSUING LIKE A GREAT CLOVEN CANDLE-FLAME   780 29
    GENTLY ISSUING FROM THE MASSED GREEN   854 22
    THAT ISSUING OUT OF THE MOON HAS SIFTED   *914 18

I'S
    I'S THINK IT'S NOBBUT A BEGGAR   44 12
    I' TH' SNOW BUT I'S WARRANT THEE   78 31
    I' TH' SNOW BUT I'S WARANT THEE BUNNY   *920 23

'IS
    'AVE I PUT 'IS CLEAN STOCKIN'S AN' SHIRT   45 14
    TO TAKE OFF 'IS PIT-DIRT   45 16
    ATWEEN A LAD AN' 'IS WIFE   77 20
    MY CONSTABLE WI' 'IS BUTTONED BREAST   79 5
    AS STOUT AS THE TRUTH MY SIRS AN' 'IS FACE   79 6
    YI AN' 'IS FACE GOES WHITE OH YES   79 10
    'E UP AN' FIRED 'IS PISTOL   81 7
    THERE'S 'IS COLLAR ROUND TH' CANDLESTICK   81 13
    I DUNNO WHEER 'IS EYES WAS A GRET   81 17
    MY CONSTABLE WI' 'IS BUTTONED BREAST   *921 1
    AS STOUT AS THE TRUTH MY SIRS AN' 'IS FACE   *921 2
    YES AN' 'IS FACE GOES WHITE OH YES   *921 6

ITALIAN
NOR WOVEN WITH ITALIAN ART   575 18
PONDERING YET EAGER THE BROAD AND THICK-SET ITALIAN WHO+   672 26
I SAW AN ANGRY ITALIAN SEIZE AN IRRITATING LITTLE OFFIC+   674 20

ITALIANS
SO MORBID AS THE ITALIANS SAY   280 5
THE ITALIANS VULGARLY SAY IT STANDS FOR THE FEMALE PART+   282 17
TURN THE POLES THE GERMS THE ENGLISH THE ITALIANS   777 1

ITALY
PROVENCE JAPAN AND ITALY REPOSE   58 17
TO YOU OUT OF ITALY   226 26
IT IS SAID A DISEASE HAS ATTACKED THE CYPRESS TREES OF +   295 1

ITCH
ITCH   175 6
THEY MUST GO ON SCRATCHING THE ECZEMA OF THEIR MENTAL I+   533 9

ITCHING
OF THE ITCHING MIND AND THE MENTAL SELF WITH ITS PRURIE+   465 5

ITEM
AND EACH ITEM WILL GET ITS RATION   443 4

ITEMS
YOU ARE ITEMS IN THE SOVIET STATE   443 3
THE ITEMS ARE OF SMALL IMPORTANCE   443 6

ITHYPHALLIC
NO NOT THE ITHYPHALLIC DEMONS   710 24

IT'LL
HOW LONG IT'LL BE AFORE THA'LT BE   139 32
AND WHOEVER GETS IT IT'LL BE A DEAD BABY   664 15

I'VE-LAID-AN-EGG
ECHO OF HER I'VE-LAID-AN-EGG CACKLE IS RICH AND RESONAN+   761 21

IVER
FACE WAS THE FINEST THING THAT IVER   *925 3

I'VE
FOR I'VE LOST MY PEACE   46 28
OF THE MAN I'VE ACCEPTED AS MINE   59 14
WITCH TEETH AN' 'ER BLACK HAWK-EYES AS I'VE   77 23
WHAT'S THAT AS 'APPEN I'VE 'EERED ON MISSIS   78 7
AN' 'APPEN YOU'D GUESS THEN WHAT I'VE COME FOR   81 23
SORRY I AM FOR THIS BUSINESS AN' SORRY IF EVER I'VE DRI+   83 6
AFORE I CAN TA'E THEE I'VE GOT A WIDDER O' FORTY-FIVE T+   83 8
DUNNAT THEE THINK BUT WHAT I'VE LOVED THEE I'VE LOVED T+   83 9
EVEN THOUGH I'VE 'AD   84 22
I STILL AM NOT HOMELESS HERE I'VE A TENT BY DAY   133 24
AN' I'VE LOVED THEE FOR IT   139 16
WITH WET FLAT LIGHTS WHAT I'VE DONE   143 23
YET I'VE FORGOTTEN IN PLAYING THIS GAME   151 31
SHE'S A SILVERY DOVE WORTH MORE THAN ALL I'VE GOT   238 22
THOUGH I'VE EATEN IT NOW   279 24
YET I'VE HEARD HIM CRY   363 27
WAIT WAIT A BIT I'LL COME WHEN I'VE LIT THE FIRE   384 9
FIRST LIVE THING I'VE OWNED SINCE THE LOP-EARED RABBITS   395 7
I'VE HAD MOMENTS OF HATRED OF YOU SINCE   396 10
WOMEN I'VE LOVED FOR GENTLENESS   412 10
I'VE NEVER GOT TO THE BOTTOM OF SUPERIORITY   435 19
I'VE CHUCKED HIM I'VE REPENTED   493 24
NOW I'VE MADE UP MY MIND   507 1
I'VE GOT TO PUT UP WITH IT   508 7
NEED TO KNOW ABOUT ANYBODY AND DO YOU KNOW I'VE NEVER B+   546 18
I SUDDENLY SAID I'VE FINISHED   556 16
I'VE NEVER SEEN HER BUT THEY SAY   572 1
YOU MUST ADMIT I'VE RISEN   626 15
I'VE RISEN I'VE RISEN   626 16
YOU MUST ADMIT I'VE RISEN   626 17
BECAUSE I'VE RISEN CLEAR   626 26
I'VE BEEN UP TO LONDON TO SEE THE FINE QUEEN   670 2
AND WHAT I'VE UNDERSTOOD AND THEN THE UTTER ACHE   738 11
OF EVERYTHING I'VE KNOWN EVEN DREAMILY   738 12
ME NOW IF I'VE LOST MY MESS-MATES LOST THEM FOREVER   757 7
I'VE LAID AN EGG   761 24
I'VE LAID AN EGG   761 26
BUT I'VE HAD SUCH A JOB MY CRUTCHES I FAIRLY DRAGGED TH+   865 22
WITCH TEETH AN' 'ER BLACK HAWK-EYES AS I'VE   *919 11
WHAT'S THAT AS 'APPEN I'VE 'EERED-ON MISSIS   *919 27
'AN 'APPEN YOU MIGHT GUESS WHAT I'VE COME FOR   *923 23
BEFORE I CAN TA'E THEE I'VE GOT A WIDOW OF FORTY-FIVE T+   *925 12
AN' ANSWER ME FOR I'VE SAID MY SAY AN' THERE'S NO MORE +   *925 22
FROM WHAT I'VE ARRANGED WI' THEE EH MAN WHAT A STUBBORN+   *925 26
I'VE REALISED IT IS ALL A TRICK ON HIS PART   *948 22

IVORY
MY IVORY AND MARBLE BLACK WITH STAIN   151 18
AND PALE HER IVORY FACE HER EYES WOULD FAIL   156 2
WHITE IVORY WHITE AMONG THE RAMBLING GREENS   646 24
OF MY WILTED WILD ROSES PINK AND IVORY WHITE   856 18
MY IVORY AND IDOLS SPLIT IN TWAIN   873 30
LIKE IVORY AND GOLDEN MARBLE TWO BLACK CROWS HOLD   *894 27

IV'RYBODY
TER LET IV'RYBODY SEE   78 28
TO LET IV'RYBODY SEE   *920 20

IXTACCIHUATL
IXTACCIHUATL   539 8

IXTHYS
IXTHYS   321 32

I'
GOT HURT I' TH' PIT   44 23
AN' THEY TA'EIN' 'IM I' TH' AMBULANCE   45 6
HUDDLIN' UP I' T' RAIN   60 16
AH STOPPED BEHIND ON T' PAD I' T' POURIN' WET   61 3
MY GEL OWT'LL DO FOR A MAN I' TH' DARK   77 3
AY AN' YALLER AS A CROWFLOWER AN' YET I' TH' DARK   77 7
AS ANY MAN I' TH' FORCE   77 30
I' TH' SNOW BUT I'S WARRANT THEE   78 31
FOR WHENEVER I LOOK THEE I' TH' FACE I S'LL SEE   82 23
AH'N PUT MY-SEN I' TH' WRONG LIZ   83 26
YER TOO MUCH I' TH' RIGHT FOR ME   85 2
THA'S BIN SNOWED UP I' THIS COTTAGE WI' ME   137 25
THA'S BIN SNOWED UP I' THIS COTTAGE WI' ME   137 27
AH STOPPED BEHIND ON T' PAD I' TH' DRIPPIN WET   *911 19
MY GEL OWT'LL DO FOR A MAN I' TH' DARK   *918 21
AY AN' YALLER AS A CROWFLOWER AN' YET I' THE DARK   *918 25
AS ANY MAN I' TH' FORCE   *919 18
I' TH' SNOW BUT I'S WARANT THEE BUNNY   *920 23
FOR WHENEVER I LOOK THEE I' TH' FACE I S'LL SEE   *924 27
AM SORRY FOR WHAT'S I' STORE   *944 4

JABBED
AND SHE JABBED HER BRITISH TRIDENT CLEAN   577 17

JABBING
PROBABLY HE WAS A JABBING TERRIFYING MONSTER   372 21

JACKAL
AND THE JACKAL FOUND HIS GRAVE   754 18

JACKASS
NOW HE'S A JACKASS A PACK-ASS A DONKEY SOMARO BURRO   379 9
FROM WHAT I'VE ARRANGED WI' THEE EH MAN WHAT A STUBBORN+   *925 26

JACKET
JACKET AT TH' BOSOM AN' TOOK OUT   61 10
SO I PICKED HIM UP IN A FLANNEL JACKET   347 4
A JACKET OF VELVET   388 20
AN' SHE UNDID 'ER JACKET NECK AN' THEN   *910 15
JACKET AT TH' BOSOM AN' TOOK FROM OUT OF IT   *911 26

JADE-GREEN
WE LOOK OVER THE GROWING WHEAT WHERE THE JADE-GREEN   209 20

JAGGLING
BUT NOT THE JAGGLING AND TWISTING OF ALREADY EXISTENT I+   673 8

JAGUAR-SPLASHED
JAGUAR-SPLASHED PUMA-YELLOW LEOPARD-LIVID SLOPES OF   409 24

JAKE
A FEW OF THE TOUCHES LIKE A LOW BORN JAKE   489 16

JAM
ALL HUMANITY IS JAM TO YOU   398 25
WHY SHOULDN'T WE STEAL THE JAM IN THE CUPBOARD   573 11
WHY SHOULDN'T I STEAL THE JAM IN THE CUPBOARD   670 26
JAM   763 7

JAMES
JAMES AND JOHN AND MARK   798 5

JAMMED
SHAKESPEARE THEY SOLD TO CROSSE AND BLACKWELLS TO BE JA+   763 6

JAMQUE VALE
JAMQUE VALE   281 15

JANE
SO OUT SHE CAME AND SHE SAID SHE WAS JANE   550 25
MAY I BE JANE   558 5
SO MAY I BE JANE   558 12

JANUARY
IN JANUARY AND IN FEBRUARY THE RE-BIRTH OF THE ALMOND T+   303 5
NEW BODY AGAIN LIKE ALMOND BLOSSOM IN JANUARY   303 11
IN LONG-NIGHTED JANUARY   305 22
CLIMBING THROUGH THE JANUARY SNOW INTO THE LOBO CANYON   401 1

JANUARY'S
AND JANUARY'S LOUD-SEEMING SUN   306 13

JAPAN
PROVENCE JAPAN AND ITALY REPOSE   58 17

JAPANESE
IN JAPANESE HENNA OR WHATEVER IT IS CHEAP AT THE PRICE   835 8

JAR
PERSISTS ALL MORNING HERE IN A JAR ON THE TABLE   90 2

JASMINE
A TINY MOON AS SMALL AND WHITE AS A SINGLE JASMINE FLOW+   67 18

JASPER
SO I DID HIS PENS AND THE JASPER SEAL ON HIS NECK   255 4

JAUNTY
AND THE YOUNG THE MODERN AND JAUNTY YOUNG   494 5

JAW
    LITTLE BLACK SNUB-NOSED BITCH WITH A SHOVED-OUT JAW   394 29
    UNDER JAW SHOVED OUT   397 19

JAWS
    WITH SNARLING RED JAWS AND I HEARD THE CRIES   38 10
    WITH RED SNARLING JAWS LET YOURSELF LISTEN TO THE CRIES   *892 25

JAZZ
    DO THEY JAZZ AND JUMP AND WRIGGLE   558 21
    JAZZ AND FILM AND WIRELESS   716 11

JAZZY
    OR TO ENDURE THE JAZZY PERSON   499 18

JEALOUS
    JEALOUS OF THE SMALLEST COVER   95 12
    DIS THE DARK THE JEALOUS GOD THE HUSBAND   308 7
    AND MOTHERHOOD IS JEALOUS   412 30

JEALOUSY
    BUT IN VIRGINITY JEALOUSY DOES NOT ENTER   412 31
    THE JEALOUSY OF AN EGO-BOUND WOMAN   475 6
    THE JEALOUSY OF AN EGO-BOUND WOMAN   475 9
    AND A MILLION FRENZIES OF TORTURED JEALOUSY   475 20

JEANNETTE
    WE MUST KEEP YOUR LAMP ALIGHT NEVERTHELESS JEANNETTE   859 27
    HOLD UP JEANNETTE WHY POOR OLD GIRL ARE YOU SAD   859 29
    WITH YOUR TIRED EYES JEANNETTE WE SUFFER THE SAME DON'T+   859 31

JEER
    AND THE SHADOW OF A JEER OF UNDERNEATH DISAPPOINTMENT   391 22

JEERING
    IT'S THE BLUE JAY JEERING AT US BIBS   375 21
    BUT A DIFFERENT SORT A COLD REBELLIOUS JEERING DEVIL   390 4
    IT IS THEIR THREAT THEIR LOUD JEERING THREAT   741 11

JEHOVAH
    JESUS BUDDHA JEHOVAH AND RA EGYPT AND BABYLON   671 19
    THERE ARE ENOUGH OF GREAT SOULS TO COMPLETE AN EFFICIEN+   859 23

JEOPARDY
    NAY NOW AT LAST THANK GOD FOR THE JEOPARDY   741 22

JERK
    JERK OF COITION AND AT ONCE   365 18
    AFTER EACH JERK THE LONGISH INTERVAL   365 24
    AND OUT OF THE LIPS OF PEOPLE JERK STRANGE MECHANICAL N+   629 10

JERKED
    AND JERKED BACK THEIR BRIDLES PUSHING THEIR HEADS APART   735 9

JERKING
    TILL SUDDENLY IN THE SPASM OF COITION TUPPING LIKE A JE+   365 7
    AN OBSTINATE OLD WITCH ALMOST JERKING THE ROPE FROM MY   385 9

JESSE
    THAT JESSE BY TURNING MANY   488 18

JESTS
    MAKES TITTERING JESTS AT THE BELLS' OBSCENITY   54 15
    ME OUT OF MY PROPER DUES WITH YOUR CHINKING JESTS   872 26

JESUS
    JESUS THE GOD OF FLOWERS   307 23
    THAT IS JESUS   320 5
    PUT ME DOWN AGAIN ON THE EARTH JESUS ON THE BROWN SOIL   321 10
    LIKE A FISH SEEKING THE BOTTOM JESUS   321 31
    AND TO ME UNDENIABLE JESUS   322 34
    AND THOU ART JESUS SON OF MAN   323 7
    AS FOR INNOCENT JESUS   328 17
    JESUS WAS CALLED THE FISH   340 15
    HENCE JESUS RODE HIM IN THE TRIUMPHANT ENTRY   378 20
    JESUS AND A PACK-SADDLE   378 23
    JESUS RODE ON HIM THE FIRST BURDEN ON THE FIRST BEAST OF   379 25
    AND JESUS ON A MEEK ASS-COLT MARES MARY ESCAPING TO   380 2
    AND JESUS NEVER LOOKED ROUND   483 9
    IF JESUS HAD KEPT A SHARP EYE ON SATAN   483 16
    LET ME SIN MY WAY TO JESUS SO THEY SINNED THEMSELVES   533 27
    SAFER THAN IN THE ARMS OF JESUS   543 1
    STAND UP BUT NOT FOR JESUS   560 13
    PISCES OH FISH JESUS OF THE WATERY WAY   616 19
    OH JESUS DIDN'T YOU SEE WHEN YOU TALKED OF SERVICE   629 1
    WHO THEN O JESUS IS MY NEIGHBOUR   645 10
    WHEN JESUS COMMANDED US TO LOVE OUR NEIGHBOUR   654 6
    JESUS BUDDHA JEHOVAH AND RA EGYPT AND BABYLON   671 19
    YOU ARE FOR THAT MOMENT ONE OF THE GODS JESUS OR FAFNIR+   674 4
    AND JESUS HIMSELF COULD NOT HAVE DENIED THAT AT THAT MO+   674 22
    RELIGION KNOWS THAT JESUS NEVER WAS JESUS   689 27
    AND GREW UP AND BECAME IN THE WONDER OF CREATION JESUS   689 29
    THE LOVELY THINGS ARE GOD THAT HAS COME TO PASS LIKE JE+   691 25
    JESUS HIS SPURS ARE RED WITH SHINING BLOOD   733 34
    JESUS HIS FINGERS ARE RED   734 11
    THE PRAISE OF JESUS IS MY SUCCESS   749 22
    JESUS YOU'VE NOT ONLY SOLD JESUS   762 15
    MY NAME IS JESUS I AM MARY'S SON   786 16
    AND HELD HIM WHILE JESUS PASSED   786 24
    MY NAME IS JESUS I AM MARY'S SON   789 9
    JESUS HAD GONE FAR UP THE DARK SLOPE WHEN HE LOOKED BACK   789 16
    SEND JESUS HIS IMAGES BACK MARY AND THE SAINTS AND ALL   791 20
    TOMORROW JESUS AND HOLY MARY   797 19
    JESUS THE SON OF GOD BIDS YOU FAREWELL   798 29
    MARY AND JESUS HAVE LET YOU AND GONE TO THE PLACE OF RE+   799 5
    WE HAVE LEARNED A LOT SINCE JESUS FROM JESUS AND ALL TH+   832 27

JESUS THE CRUCIFIED
    JESUS THE CRUCIFIED   787 8

JESUS UPLIFTED
    JESUS UPLIFTED   322 20

JESUS'
    JESUS' PALE AND LAMBENT DOVE COOING IN THE LOWER BOUGHS   329 8

JET
    FOR I THOUGHT YOU WERE WARM AS A SUDDEN JET OF BLOOD   99 7

JETS
    LITTLE JETS OF SUNLIGHT TEXTURE IMITATING FLAME   33 2
    JETS OF SPARKS IN FOUNTAINS OF BLUE COME LEAPING   136 6
    JETS OF EXQUISITE FINALITY   271 10
    LITTLE JETS OF SUNLIGHT-TEXTURE IMITATING FLAME   *891 2

JETSAM
    INTO THE NIGHT AND ARE LOST TO SADDEN WITH JETSAM THE D+   *918 8

JETTED
    YOU JETTED OFF YOUR EYE AT ME   241 16

JETTING
    OF FRETTING OR OF GLADNESS SHOWS THE JETTING   89 14

JEW
    STAND YOU FAR OFF AND TRIUMPH LIKE A JEW   158 28
    TO HIM WORSE THAN A BOLSHEVIST JEW OR AN UTTER   576 8

JEWEL
    THAT IS THE CRYSTAL OF PEACE THE SLOW HARD JEWEL OF TRU+   477 17

JEWEL-BROWN
    AS A JEWEL-BROWN HORSE-CHESTNUT NEWLY ISSUED   73 5

JEWELLESS
    CROWNLESS AND JEWELLESS AND GARMENTLESS   695 17

JEWELS
    UNDER THE LONG DARK BOUGHS LIKE JEWELS RED   36 19
    WITH JEWELS OF PASSION ONCE BROKEN THROUGH YOU AS A   168 15
    YOU WHO ROLL THE STARS LIKE JEWELS IN YOUR PALM   197 24
    SMALL INTERSPERSED WITH JEWELS OF WHITE GOLD   314 2
    GIRDLING WITH JEWELS THE MEANNESS OF COMMON THINGS   855 2

JEWISH
    THE JEWISH SEVEN-BRANCHED TALLOW-STINKING CANDLESTICK   299 20

JIG
    THEY DANCE DANCE DANCE THIS DRY INDUSTRIAL JIG OF THE   631 19

JIGGING
    INTO THE INDUSTRIAL DANCE OF THE LIVING DEATH THE JIGGI+   631 13

JIG-JIG-JIG
    AND GIVEN YOU THIS JIG-JIG-JIG   585 16
    IF I TRY LOVING THEM I FALL INTO THEIR ROBOT JIG-JIG-JIG   645 7

JIGS
    HE JIGS ALONG IN THE IMBECILE CRUELTY OF THE MACHINE   645 15

JIMLETS
    JIMLETS AND SELF-SORRY SAMLETS   457 20

JINGLING
    WHEN I HEAR YOU JINGLING THROUGH   95 8
    THE LAST ROW IS FINISHED THE JINGLING RAKE IS LIFTED   858 17

JINGO
    FINALLY OUR LITTLE LOT I DON'T WANT TO DIE BUT BY JINGO+   534 6

JIXED
    AND THE POOR MAN NEVER KNEW HE WAS JIXED   659 17
    FIXED JIXED FIXED   659 18

JIXER
    OH MY JIXER MY FIXER   659 20

JIXERY
    ALL THE GREAT JIXERY UP IN THE FIXERY   659 8
    THE JIXERY PERHAPS NEVER PICKED A MAN'S POCKET   659 14

JOAQUIN
    JOAQUIN FRANCIS AND ANTHONY   798 13

JOB
    IF MY FATHER CAN GET THEE A JOB ON T' BANK SAY THA'RT S+   83 17
    WHAT A JOB THEY'VE GOT TO KEEP IT UP   287 17
    AND MAKE A NEW JOB OF THE HUMAN WORLD   429 16
    OH QUITE BUT HE MUST WORK HE MUST HAVE A JOB OF SOME   452 18
    EARNING A SALARY IS A PRISON OVERSEER'S JOB   521 9
    HE SHIFTED HIS JOB ON TO THE PEASANTS   536 22
    BUT A MAN WITHOUT A JOB   545 26
    NOT ONE OF THE WHOLE JOB LOT   549 28
    A JOB YOU DON'T LIKE AND A SCANTY CHANCE   560 23
    AND THE JOB OF CHANGING ITS DIAPERS GETS BIGGER AND BIG+ 670 12
    BUT I'VE HAD SUCH A JOB MY CRUTCHES I FAIRLY DRAGGED TH+ 865 22
    AWFUL JOB   865 24

JOBS
    EMBODIED JOBS   452 6
    DOING ONE'S OWN LITTLE JOBS SEEING THE WORLD BEYOND   610 5

JOCK'S
IT OUGHT ALL TO BE JOCK'S AND MINE 573 14

JOHANNINE
AND THE WORD WAS THE FIRST OFFSPRING OF THE ALMIGHTY JO+ 329 11
YET PUT SALT ON THE TAIL OF THE JOHANNINE BIRD 329 14

JOHN
JOHN OH JOHN 328 1
JOHN KNEW THE WHOLE PROPOSITION 328 10
JOHN KNEW THE WHOLE PROPOSITION 328 16
THE SLY BIRD OF JOHN 329 2
JAMES AND JOHN AND MARK 798 5

JOHN BULL
THEN OUT OF NOWHERE RUSHED JOHN BULL 491 25

JOHNNIES
WE THINK WE'RE SUCH CLEVER LITTLE JOHNNIES 543 19

JOHN'S
OF JOHN'S GREAT GOLD-BARRED EAGLE 328 9
JOHN'S EAGLE 329 16
JOHN'S EAGLE 330 2

JOHN THOMAS
JOHN THOMAS BY NAME 493 2
THEN WHEN JOHN THOMAS DON'T WORRY YOU 493 19
AND YOU CRIED 'OORAY PLAY UP JOHN THOMAS 550 27
OF JOHN THOMAS ABOUT 562 15

JOIE DE VIVRE
FOOD AND FEAR AND JOIE DE VIVRE 336 19
JOIE DE VIVRE AND FEAR AND FOOD 336 22
AND TURNING THE DAY SUDDENLY INTO A BLACK TORNADO OF JO+ 397 4

JOIN
BEYOND A WORLD I NEVER WANT TO JOIN 36 8
GONE UNDER THE ARCHWAY HOME HE CAN JOIN 228 15
IF IT BE SO I FLY TO JOIN YOU 314 23
TO JOIN THE FOLKS ON HIGH 554 10
JOIN ME TO MY WELL-BELOVED FRIEND 754 22

JOINED
ARE JOINED TOGETHER FOR EVER AS IS BEST 231 4

JOINER
ANYHOW A CARPENTER AND JOINER 452 26
THAT HE MADE CHAIRS AND WAS A JOINER AND CARPENTER 452 30

JOINER'S
AND IN THE UNFINISHED HOUSES THE RING OF THE JOINER'S T+ 865 16

JOINT
SHAFT-GOLDEN WITH LIGHT AT THE JOINT OF THE SKY *930 15

JOIST
THIRTEEN LAY THE YELLOW CHICKS BENEATH THE JOIST OF WOOD *933 3

JOISTS
BEFORE THEY'VE EATEN THROUGH THE JOISTS AND 511 17

JOKE
AND MAKE A JOKE OF STALE INFINITY 299 12
THE AGE IS A JOKE AND SURELY TOMORROW 815 4
WE'LL SEE THE JOKE AND HOW FUNNY IS SORROW 815 5

JOLLY
AND KICK OUR HEELS LIKE JOLLY ESCAPED ASSES 517 16
I IMMEDIATELY WANT TO GO AND DO SOMETHING JOLLY TOO 520 25
AND HOW JOLLY IT WAS WITH US UP IN THE SNOW 551 1
STAND UP FOR JUSTICE AND A JOLLY LIFE 560 15
STAND UP FOR JOLLY JUSTICE 560 21
THE JOLLY LITTLE MEMBER 563 16
YOU ALL OF YOU KNOW WHERE YOU'D JOLLY WELL BE 574 2
AND I'M GOING TO DO WHAT I JOLLY WELL PLEASE 671 7
THE WISDOM OF AGES DROOPS AIN'T IT JOLLY 814 25
AT HER AGE WHY I'LL BE EARNING A JOLLY GOOD SCREW 834 20
A JOLLY GOOD SCREW WHEN THE DEAR LITTLE GIRLY-WIRLY'S O+ 834 21

JONQUILS
SCYLLAS AND YELLOW-HAIRED HELLEBORE JONQUILS DIM ANEMON+ 270 7
THE JONQUILS 271 13

JOSEPH
AND JOSEPH HOLDING THE BRIDLE 200 3
SHE HAS GIVEN THE CHILD TO JOSEPH 200 13
AND JOSEPH SHADING HIS EYES WITH HIS HAND 200 15
WHILE JOSEPH PITCHES THE SLEEP-TENT 201 17
THEN JOSEPH GREY WITH WAITING 202 1
TILL A BEGGAR SPOKE TO JOSEPH 202 9
AND SHE DREAMED OF HER CHILDREN AND JOSEPH 202 15

JOSEPH'S
RIDING AT JOSEPH'S SIDE 201 6
EGYPT JOSEPH'S CUDGEL 380 3

JOSTLED
AMONG CROWDS OF THINGS IN THE SUNSHINE JOSTLED AND RACK+ 133 8

JOSTLING
JOSTLING TO AND FRO 198 8
JOSTLING PEOPLE TOUCHING AND TALKING AND MAKING SMALL 249 18
THOUGH ALL THE CROWDED SUNLIGHT JOSTLING 771 19

JOURNEY
THE COURSE OF OUR JOURNEY HERE HERE WHERE WE PART 100 18
COME I WILL CONSECRATE YOU FOR THE JOURNEY 153 14
SO ON WITH THE SLOW MEAN JOURNEY 201 13
NOW ON WITH THE HOPELESS JOURNEY 202 5
SO SHE FOLLOWS THE CRUEL JOURNEY 203 5
FOLLOW THE TRAIL OF THE DEAD ACROSS GREAT SPACES FOR TH+ 406 4
LIFE'S TOILSOME JOURNEY THROUGH 576 19
AND THE LONG JOURNEY TOWARDS OBLIVION 716 19
THE LONGEST JOURNEY TO OBLIVION 717 22
OF DEATH TO CARRY THE SOUL ON THE LONGEST JOURNEY 718 23
FOR THE SOUL HAS A LONG LONG JOURNEY AFTER DEATH 721 20
AND THE PROPER STORE OF MEAL FOR THE LONGEST JOURNEY 721 23
THE JOURNEY STILL THEY MOAN AND BEAT 722 2
TO CONTINUE ON THE LONGEST JOURNEY 722 18
SING THEN THE SONG OF DEATH AND THE LONGEST JOURNEY 724 1
STRENGTHEN PREPARE THEM FOR THE JOURNEY HENCE 740 18
OF THIS JOURNEY 748 17
OF THE DAY THAT BATTLES ITS JOURNEY 771 24
THE DEAD ARE ON THEIR JOURNEY THE WAY IS DARK 810 21
THE DEAD HAVE GONE THE LONG JOURNEY 811 16
I AM TIRED OF THIS JOURNEY IT IS STUPID AND CHILL 858 1
WHAT A JOURNEY FOR MY SOUL *955 1
AND THE LONG JOURNEY TOWARDS OBLIVION *956 25
QUIETUS IS THE GOAL OF THE LONG JOURNEY *957 6
THE LONGEST JOURNEY TOWARDS OBLIVION *957 7
TO SET SOFTLY FORTH ON THE LONGEST JOURNEY THE LONGEST + *957 19
THE JOURNEY STILL THEY MOAN AND BEAT *958 2
ON THE LONGEST JOURNEY *959 4
TAKING THE LONGEST JOURNEY *959 11
ON THE LONGEST JOURNEY TOWARDS THE GREATEST GOAL *959 16
AT THE END OF THE LONGEST JOURNEY *960 4
OH NOTHING MATTERS BUT THE LONGEST JOURNEY *960 9
ON ITS LAST JOURNEY ON AND ON SO STILL *960 15
ON THE LONGEST JOURNEY OVER THE HIDDEN SEA *960 20
FOR THE LONGEST JOURNEY OVER THE LAST OF SEAS *961 7
SING THEN THE SONG OF DEATH AND THE LONGEST JOURNEY *961 11

JOURNEYS
THIRTEEN WERE THE SLITHERING SILENT JOURNEYS *933 2

JOURNEY'S
AND NEVER NEVER ARRIVING AT JOURNEY'S END AT THE REAR OF 380 26

JOVE
SHINE LIKE FLAT COIN WHICH JOVE IN THANKS 162 3
NOR GUSTY JOVE WITH HIS EYE ON IMMORTAL TARTS 437 5
AND A YOUNG MAN SHOULD THINK BY JOVE 503 29

JOWL-FACED
I DON'T YIELD TO YOU BIG JOWL-FACED EAGLE 374 25

JOY
WHO SNIFFS WITH JOY BEFORE HE DRINKS THE BLOOD 43 32
YOU ARE FRIGHTENED WITH JOY MY HEART LIKE A FRIGHTENED 47 33
FOR JOY OR FOR MISERY 60 10
FOR JOY OF THE NIGHT WHEN MASTERS ARE 70 12
TO START A BIRTH FROM JOY OF THE BEGETTING 89 7
AND PANGS OF BIRTH AND JOY OF THE BEGETTING 89 12
ROUND IN JOY 121 2
THEIR FEAR THEIR SHAME THEIR JOY THAT UNDERLIES 125 28
IF THE JOY THAT THEY ARE LIFTED TO AVENGE 126 3
WITH JOY AT TRAVELLING TO PLANT ITSELF WITHIN 127 12
I WOULD LAUGH WITH JOY 134 13
THAT STAYS WITH STEADY JOY OF ITS OWN FIRE 151 15
LIKE A RATTLE A CHILD SPINS ROUND FOR JOY THE NIGHT RAT+ 206 31
YOU LOOKED INTO MY EYES AND SAID BUT THIS IS JOY 207 3
STILL THE JOY WAS THERE ALSO YOU SPOKE TRULY 207 10
THE JOY WAS NOT TO BE DRIVEN OFF SO EASILY 207 11
THE JOY I BOUGHT WAS NOT TOO HIGHLY PRICED 225 32
SUCH A JOY TO ME 254 21
THE JOY I FEEL 255 8
GOD KNOWS WHAT I FEEL BUT IT IS JOY 255 9
I COULD CRY WITH JOY BECAUSE I AM IN THE NEW WORLD JUST 256 10
I COULD CRY WITH JOY AND QUITE FREELY THERE IS NOBODY TO 256 12
THEY WILL NEVER UNDERSTAND MY WEEPING FOR JOY TO BE 256 16
YOU WHO COMPLAIN YOU KNOW NO JOY IN YOUR LIVES 484 13
NEVER WILL YOU KNOW ANY JOY IN YOUR LIVES 484 14
YOUNG MEN HAVING NO REAL JOY IN LIFE AND NO HOPE IN THE 521 20
A JOY TO TELL IT YOU 576 17
A JOY TO TELL IT YOU 576 23
I REALISED THE SECRET JOY HER YOUNG SPANISH HUSBAND HAD 618 22
AND WORSHIP IS THE JOY OF THE GLEAM FROM THE EYES OF TH+ 649 16
THERE COMES AN AFTER-GLADNES A STRANGE JOY 677 6
CUTTING YOU OFF FROM YOUR JOY 706 21
NEW JOY TO GIVE MORE LIFE NEW BLISS TO LIVE 740 26
BUT WITHOUT DESIRE WITHOUT JOY WITHOUT RELEASE 843 16
IN-WEAVING THE BRIGHT THREAD OF HIS JOY 867 27
THREADING THE ROUND JOY OF HIS WHITE-FLANNELLED HIPS FU+ 867 30
PASSES THE EVER-CHANGING JOY OF HIS ACTIVE BODY 868 4
THAT STEADY STAYS WITH JOY OF ITS OWN FIRE 873 25
FOR THE JOY LIKE A FOUNT UNDONE 888 12
IN THE CURVE OF THINE EXQUISITE FORM THE JOY OF THE *915 28
OF JOY IN THE FIGHT *930 4
THEIR FEAR THEIR SHAME THEIR JOY THAT UNDERLIES *936 27
IF THE JOY WHICH THEY ARE LIFTED TO AVENGE *937 3
OF QUESTING BRILLIANT THINGS YOU JOY YOU TRUE *945 13
SPIRIT OF CARELESS JOY AH HOW I WARM *945 14
MY POOR AND PERISHED SOUL AT THE JOY OF YOU *945 15
SWIMS THE MALLARD DUCK AT DAWN IN THAT QUICK JOY *953 27
BLUE JOY OF MY SOUL *954 23

JOY-BLOSSOMS
MY JOY-BLOSSOMS SHAPING AM BIG 888 15

JOYFUL
    AND GAY FLICKER OF JOYFUL LIFE   523 23
    ROUND HIS BRIGHT JOYFUL BODY   868 12

JOY-IN-RESURRECTION
    TO ADD THE MYSTERY OF JOY-IN-RESURRECTION TO THE MASS   609 20

JOYS
    TO EARN THEIR LIVINGS NOR YET GIRLS SWEET JOYS   459 3

JUDAH
    THERE WAS A LION IN JUDAH   323 19

JUDAS
    IT BEGAN WITH JUDAS AND GOES ON IN THE WAGE-SYSTEM   483 1
    DOSTOEVSKY THE JUDAS   537 1
    TRAITORS OH LIARS YOU JUDAS LOT   762 14

JUDEAN LORD
    NOT IN STONE LIKE THE JUDEAN LORD OR BRONZE BUT IN LIFE+   355 18

JUDGE
    SET UP TO JUDGE BETWEEN LIFE AND DEATH   528 11

JUDGES
    THE TROUBLE ABOUT THOSE THAT SET UP TO BE MORAL JUDGES   836 20

JUDGING
    JUDGING FROM THE FICTION IT IS POSSIBLE TO READ I SHOUL+   532 15

JUDGMENT
    HOVERING ABOUT THE JUDGMENT THAT STOOD IN MY EYES   94 17
    BENEATH BARE JUDGMENT STARS   202 14
    HOVERING TO PLUCK AT THE JUDGMENT WHICH STOOD IN MY EYES   *897 5

JUG
    NOW I TAKE THE BIG STONE JUG OF WATER   734 24
    HIS EYES MEET MINE AS HE TAKES THE JUG OF WATER   734 27
    BACK IN A GRECIAN KNOT OR A JUG HANDLE OR A CHIGNON   836 2
    DRINKING THE CONFIDENT WATER FROM THE LITTLE JUG   *959 13

JUGFULL
    JUGFULL AFTER JUGFULL OF PURE WHITE LIQUID FIRE BRIGHT +   647 9

JUICIER
    CHEW ALSO YOUNG HEIFERS YOUR JUICIER CUDS   814 21

JUICY
    JUICY   574 10
    COFFEE FROM THE BUSHES IN THE HOT LANDS EVEN THE JUICY +   793 22

JUJUBEY
    A WORSE LOT O' JUJUBEY ASSES   553 15

JULY
    ON THE DAY OF SICILIAN JULY WITH ETNA SMOKING   349 28
    AH THE FALLEN STILLNESS OF GOD AUTUMNUS AND IT IS ONLY +   651 18

JUMP
    JUMP   292 6
    AND JUMPS STACCATO TO EARTH A SHARP DRY JUMP STILL   384 30
    DO THEY JAZZ AND JUMP AND WRIGGLE   558 21
    OF THOSE ILL-SMELLING TRIBES OF MEN THESE FROGS THAT CA+   792 23

JUMPED
    AND DOGS JUMPED THROUGH HOOPS AND TURNED SOMERSAULTS   444 18
    THEN EVERY MOLECULE OF CREATION JUMPED AND CLAPPED ITS +   683 4

JUMPS
    AND JUMPS STACCATO TO EARTH A SHARP DRY JUMP STILL   384 30

JUNE
    IT IS JUNE IT IS JUNE   605 20

JUNE-HOT
    ONE DAY A HEAVY-BREASTED JUNE-HOT WOMAN   91 8

JUNGLE
    SO THEN THERE SHONE WITHIN THE JUNGLE DARKNESS   206 8
    THE JUNGLE SINGING   388 36
    MEN-PEASANTS FROM JUNGLE VILLAGES DANCING AND RUNNING   389 5
    OF JUNGLE TORCH-MEN   389 30
    WHAT WOULD THEY DO THOSE JUNGLE MEN RUNNING WITH SWEAT   389 32
    THE JUNGLE VILLAGES   390 31

JUNIPER
    THEN WHEN I DUST YOU A BIT WITH A JUNIPER TWIG   399 12
    AND A JUNIPER SWITCH   400 23

JUSTICE
    GOD OF JUSTICE TO SAVE THEMSELVES   442 7
    O GOD OF JUSTICE SEND NO MORE SAVIOURS   442 10
    GOD OF JUSTICE WHEN WILT THOU TEACH THEM TO SAVE THEMSE+   443 9
    WITH THE THRUSTING EMBRACE OF NEW JUSTICE NEW JUSTICE   482 5
    THE PASSION OF JUSTICE BEING PROFOUND AND SUBTLE   482 8
    BUT THE PASSION OF JUSTICE IS A PRIMAL EMBRACE   482 10
    STAND UP FOR JUSTICE AND A JOLLY LIFE   560 15
    STAND UP STAND UP FOR JUSTICE   560 17
    STAND UP FOR JOLLY JUSTICE   560 21
    IF YOU WANT JUSTICE   562 8
    LET IT BE DEMON JUSTICE   562 9
    TO DEMON JUSTICE   563 10
    BETTER DO HIM JUSTICE   563 27
    I DON'T KNOW WHAT THEY'VE DONE POOR THINGS BUT JUSTICE +   632 30
    IS THE SENSE OF JUSTICE   653 8
    THE PROFOUND AND THRILLING VIBRATION OF JUSTICE SENSE O+   653 15
    JUSTICE   653 16
    BUT OF FALSE FEELING AND PERVERTED JUSTICE   654 2

JUSTICE
    JUSTICE HUMAN DECENCY IN MATERIAL THINGS   833 24
    WITH ITS STRANGE PRIMORDIAL CONSCIOUSNESS OF JUSTICE   844 13
    AND IS SILENT WITH A SENSE OF JUSTICE THE FIERY PRIMORD+   844 26
    AND POISED WITH A SENSE OF JUSTICE AS WORLDS ARE POISED   *952 9

JUSTIFY
    LET GOD COME FORTH TO JUSTIFY   232 3

JUT
    AND I JUT AGAINST YOU IF I TRY TO MOVE FOR YOU ARE EVER+   289 7

JUTTING
    EAGLE WITH EGYPTIAN DARKNESS JUTTING IN FRONT OF YOUR F+   782 27
    PAST THE JUTTING ROCKS OF SHADOW   *959 5

KALEIDOSCOPE
    AM I A KALEIDOSCOPE   119 2
    MANY VIVID SMALL STATES LIKE A KALEIDOSCOPE ALL COLOURS   611 19
    AND I'M A KALEIDOSCOPE   *932 8

KANGAROO
    BUT THE YELLOW ANTIPODAL KANGAROO WHEN SHE SITS UP   392 27
    DELICATE MOTHER KANGAROO   393 4
    DROP WHICH SHE LOVES SENSITIVE MOTHER KANGAROO   393 9

KAPUT
    THE DEATH OF NOTHINGNESS WORN-OUT MACHINES KAPUT   676 7

KATABOLISM
    SINKING IN THE ENDLESS UNDOING THE AWFUL KATABOLISM INT+   699 26

KATABOLISTIC
    AND FLAMES OF KATABOLISTIC ENERGY ALTERNATE   616 11

KEEN
    SINCE YOU ARE SO KEEN TO KNOW   96 3
    FLUTTER FOR A MOMENT OH THE BEAST IS QUICK AND KEEN   119 21
    POISED AT HER LIKE A WEAPON MY HAND WAS WHITE AND KEEN   125 15
    RISING TO DREAM IN ME A SMALL KEEN DREAM   196 3
    IF ONLY I AM KEEN AND HARD LIKE THE SHEER TIP OF A WEDGE   250 21
    DARK KEEN FINE RAYS IN THE BRILLIANT FROST OF HER FACE   402 6
    YES IF IT'S A KEEN MATCH RAPE IS RATHER THRILLING   532 19
    AND KEEN EYES THEY WILL HOVER THEY WILL COME BETWEEN YOU   706 19
    A KEEN FAR-REACHING CURIOUS MIND CYNICAL WITH LITTLE-BO+   841 22
    OF FLESH WOULD CRACK AND SHIVER WITH KEEN PAIN   873 29
    AND I OPEN MY LIPS TO TAKE A STRAND OF KEEN HAIR   883 15
    THEN FLUTTER FOR A MOMENT AND THE RAT'S LONG TEETH ARE +   *932 30
    POISED AT HER LIKE A WEAPON MY HAND WAS WHITE AND KEEN   *936 14

KEEP
    TALL AND DARK THE CHURCH MOVES ANXIOUS TO KEEP   48 21
    SO I SHALL KNOW WHAT I HAVE TO KEEP   59 19
    ONLY WE HARD-FACED CREATURES GO ROUND AND ROUND AND KEEP   71 11
    I SHALL KEEP MY STRENGTH FOR MYSELF THEY CAN KEEP   75 3
    COOL LONELY NIGHT HER BREASTS WILL KEEP THE NIGHT AT BAY   91 11
    AND IN THE ORIGINAL DARK THE ROOTS CANNOT KEEP CANNOT K+   92 17
    CHALLENGE ME I KEEP ASIDE   95 26
    OF THE TROTH WITH THE DEAD THAT WE ARE PLEDGED TO KEEP   114 26
    OUTCASTS KEEP GUARD   146 24
    SINCE THIS IS THE LAST NIGHT I KEEP YOU HOME   153 13
    NAY I PERSIST AND VERY FAITH SHALL KEEP   154 12
    TO CATCH AND KEEP ME WITH YOU THERE   178 10
    SOON STREWS ITSELF ON THE FLOOR AND KEEP THE RADIANCE O+   179 4
    FRESH QUIVERING KEEP THE SUNNY-SWIFT MARCH-DAYS WAITING   179 5
    AH GOD LIFE LAW SO MANY NAMES YOU KEEP   194 18
    SAVE YOU AND ME AND SLEEP ALL THE REST WILL KEEP   212 11
    GOD WILL KEEP   232 14
    HOW QUAVERINGLY I DEPEND ON YOU TO KEEP ME ALIVE   246 2
    AND HARD WITH THE INTENTION TO KEEP THEM   279 9
    THEY FORGET RIPE FIGS WON'T KEEP   284 24
    RIPE FIGS WON'T KEEP   284 25
    RIPE FIGS WON'T KEEP WON'T KEEP IN ANY CLIME   284 28
    AND BURSTEN FIGS WON'T KEEP   284 31
    SLEEP YET FIGHTING FIGHTING TO KEEP AWAKE   287 3
    WHAT A JOB THEY'VE GOT TO KEEP IT UP   287 17
    TO KEEP ON HOLDING UP THIS IDEAL CIVILISATION   288 5
    WRETCHES UTTER WRETCHES KEEP YOUR HANDS FROM BEANS SAITH   303 15
    AND KEEP YOU IN MILLIONS AT THE MILLS SIGHTLESS PALE SL+   441 8
    THAT HAVE GOT YOU IN KEEP   456 21
    KEEP OURSELVES SEPARATE PHYSICALLY   470 16
    LET US LEAVE IT ALONE PHYSICALLY KEEP APART   471 26
    WHILE THEY KEEP THEIR OWN WILD PURITY   484 23
    FOR USING WORDS THEY PRIVATELY KEEP   492 25
    AND THEY KEEP ON COMING WITH GREATER FORCE   512 21
    TO KEEP STILL AND LET THE WRECKAGE OF OURSELVES GO   514 1
    YET KEEP STILL AND HOLD   514 3
    KEEP QUIET AND WAIT   514 7
    AND THEN THE ONLY THING WE CAN DO IS TO KEEP QUITE STILL   514 11
    AND WE FEEL WE'VE GOT TO KEEP IT UP KEEP ON COMBATING   519 13
    YOU'VE GOT TO KEEP UP WITH YOURSELF   543 13
    AND YOU'VE GOT TO RUN TO KEEP UP WITH IT   543 15
    WOULD STOP A HOLE TO KEEP THE WIND AWAY   545 25
    KEEP HIS PATH WELL CLEANED   563 28
    TO FEED THE BONNY BABY AND KEEP ITS TARA DRY   570 19
    AUNTIE MAUD HAS COME TO KEEP HOUSE   571 17
    WE THOUGHT WE'D ELECT YOU TO KEEP YOU ALL BUSY   574 4
    HENCEFORTH HE'LL KEEP CLEAR OF HER TOASTING-FORK   577 22
    KEEP YOUR ALONENESS LEAVE ME MY ALONENESS   602 16
    YET I CAN'T BE ALONE I WANT SOMEBODY TO KEEP ME WARM   603 20
    SHE CAN KEEP HER SIN   618 6
    AND THE HUMAN SPIRIT IS SO MUCH GAS TO KEEP IT ALL GOING   641 8
    PEOPLE KEEP IT UP BECAUSE THEY DAREN'T STOP   657 20
    KEEP SUDDENLY SHOWING A WHITENESS A FLASH AND A FURL A +   687 2
    THE BURNING ARCHANGELS UNDER THE SEA KEEP PASSING BACK +   694 23
    KEEP PASSING ARCHANGELS OF BLISS   694 24

KEEP
SO SATAN ONLY FELL TO KEEP A BALANCE   710 12
THE MAN ANDREW KEEP HIM SAFE IN THE WAR   751 10
HOW CAN MY HEART KEEP BEATING IN THIS PALLOR OF WHITISH   766 28
PEOPLE WANT TO KEEP THE INDIAN BACK WANT TO   778 7
SO NATURALLY THEY WANT TO KEEP HIM BACK DOWN POOR   778 12
BUT IF YOU CANNOT KEEP POLITICAL DOMINEERING HANDS   780 14
AND SENT THE EAGLE TO KEEP AN EYE ON HIM   783 5
AND IN THE BIGGEST HOUSES THEY KEEP THEIR MACHINES THAT+   793 24
SO THE ONLY THING TO DO IS TO KEEP STILL TO HOLD STILL +   839 1
TO KEEP A SANE CORE TO LIFE   839 17
TO KEEP IT SANE AND WHOLESOME   844 31
TO KEEP IT SANE AND WHOLESOME   845 3
WE MUST KEEP YOUR LAMP ALIGHT NEVERTHELESS JEANNETTE   859 27
TO KEEP THE REFLECTED VARIETY OF THE HOUSEBOATS   867 9
SHALL HAVE RAKED THE EMBERS CLEAR I WILL KEEP   *896 2
THEY KEEP ME ASSURED AND WHEN MY SOUL FEELS LONELY   *900 20
THEY KEEP ME ASSURED AND WHEN MY SOUL FEELS LONELY   *903 32
SHALL HAVE RAKED THE EMBERS CLEAR I WILL KEEP   *904 23
TRYIN' TO KEEP OFF 'N HIM A BIT O' TH' WET   *910 29
KEEP THEN THE KISS FROM THE ADULTRESS' THEFT   *916 8
ONLY THE BATS ARE FLICKERING ROUND AND ROUND AND KEEP   *918 1
TO KEEP IT SANE AND HEALTHY   *952 12
TO KEEP IT SANE AND WHOLESOME   *952 15
IN FACT QUITE A LOT OF CHASTITY IS NECESSARY IN LIFE TO+   *952 24

KEEPER
LIKE A MAGNET'S KEEPER   121 11
THE KEEPER HOODS THE VAST KNEE THE CREATURE SALAAMS   387 16

KEEPING
BELOW THE LAWN IN SOFT BLUE SHADE IS KEEPING   35 28
TO SIGHT REVEALING A SECRET NUMBERLESS SECRET KEEPING   136 7
AND A HEAVY WOMAN SLEEPING STILL KEEPING   145 10
KEEPING ME   247 3
KEEPING TO EARTH   310 18
IF WE RALLY AT ALL TODAY INSTEAD OF KEEPING   839 8

KEEPS
UNLESS THE LITTLE STAR THAT KEEPS HER COMPANY   54 14
BEHIND YET KEEPS PACE   162 20
LOOK NOW EVEN NOW HOW IT KEEPS ITS POWER OF INVISIBILITY   286 7
AND FINGER IT AND FORCE IT AND SHATTER THE RHYTHM IT KE+   464 30
WE LOSE THAT WHICH KEEPS US INDIVIDUAL   514 15
AND GOD THE HOLY GHOST IS GAS THAT KEEPS IT ALL GOING   641 5
KEEPS ME PROUD IN SHAME PLEDGE OF THE NIGHT DARK-PURE   772 15
KEEPS DAY AND NIGHT APART   809 24
I ALONE AM LIVING THEN IT KEEPS   *900 22
I ALONE AM LIVING THEN IT KEEPS   *903 34

KEN
LIKE COMETS AND THEY COME INTO OUR KEN   476 13
HE ONLY FELL OUT OF YOUR KEN YOU ORTHODOX ANGELS   614 15
WITHIN KEN   787 32

KENNEL
MAYBE THEY KENNEL THE GREY DOG   807 27

KENNELS
A DAMN FOR THEIR DIRTY KENNELS   494 2

KENS
AND SHE KENS IT FINE   573 16

KEP
AN' ME AS 'AS KEP MY-SEN   *919 13

KEPT
OF THE WORDS I KEPT REPEATING   61 25
COLD THAT HAD SUNK TO MY SOUL AND THERE KEPT HOLD   98 25
RESTARTS ITSELF WHEREIN I AM KEPT   151 24
WHO HAVE KEPT INTACT FOR YOU YOUR VIRGINITY   157 10
AND THEN THE FIG HAS KEPT HER SECRET LONG ENOUGH   283 27
WE HAVE KEPT OUR SECRET LONG ENOUGH   284 21
THAT HAS KEPT SO MANY SECRETS UP ITS SLEEVE   299 14
CAN BE KEPT DOWN BUT HE'LL BURST LIKE A POLYP INTO   305 9
WHO HATED YOU AND KEPT LOOKING ROUND AT YOU AND CURSING   395 33
IF JESUS HAD KEPT A SHARP EYE ON SATAN   483 16
THERE'S A LIST KEPT OF THE TRULY SUPERIOR   548 22
THEY ALL OF THEM ALWAYS KEPT UP THEIR SLEEVE   554 31
FOR THE ROBOT CLASSES AND MASSES ARE ONLY KEPT SANE   640 13
THAT THE BOYS MUST STAY AT SCHOOL NOT BE KEPT AWAY   777 33
MAN IS KEPT SANE NOT BY HIS MIND WHICH BY NATURE IS UNS+   838 16
EYES WHERE HIS HOT IMPRISONED SOUL HAS KEPT   859 19
THAT I WHO HAVE KNOWN HER A LITTLE AM KEPT   874 3
OF THE WORDS I KEPT REPEATING   *912 5
AND I KEPT THE CHOKED SNAKE FLOWER IN ITS PANGS   *936 15

KEP'
AN' ME AS 'AS KEP' MY-SEN   77 25

KERB
I SAW HER STEP TO THE KERB AND FAST   122 3

KERB-EDGE
IDLE WE STAND BY THE KERB-EDGE AUNTIE   572 25

KERCHIEF
SHE WEPT BITTERLY HIDING HER FACE IN HER KERCHIEF I SAI+   749 16
HER KERCHIEF FLUTTERS RED   756 13

KESTREL
RAMPING UP THROUGH THE AIR LIKE A KESTREL   324 30

KEY
THE KEY OF LIFE ON THE BODIES OF MEN   461 23
WITH HIS KEY TO THE TWO DARK DOORS   710 26

KEYS
I WILL GIVE YOU ALL MY KEYS   95 4
US ONLY ONE MOMENT HIS KEYS   104 10
BRINGING NIGHT ONCE MORE AND THE MAN WITH THE KEYS   758 4
AND THE KEYS WITH LITTLE HOLLOWS THAT MY MOTHER'S FINGE+   *940 4

KEYSTONE
FOUR AND A KEYSTONE   355 10
FOUR AND A KEYSTONE   355 12
THEN TWENTY-FOUR AND A TINY LITTLE KEYSTONE   355 13

KHAKI
THE DAUGHTER OF THE GREAT MAN ROLLS HER KHAKI WOOL   752 9

KHAKI-COLOURED
NO DOUBT HE WAS KHAKI-COLOURED WITH MUDDY PROTECTIVE   523 18

KICK
LIFT MY ARMS THE HILL BURSTS AND HEAVES UNDER THEIR SPU+   33 9
OH YES YOU'RE FOUND OUT I HEARD THEM KICK YOU OUT OF   400 6
AND A KICK OR TWO   400 21
WE SHOULD START AN' KICK THEIR -SES FOR 'EM   491 3
A GOOD KICK AT HIS DIRTY OLD HOLE   494 12
AND KICK OUR HEELS LIKE JOLLY ESCAPED ASSES   517 16
IN MY FINE PROSPERITY KICK THOSE IN THE DITCH   584 7
KICK THEM OVER THE TOADSTOOLS   765 28
MOVE MY ARMS THE HILL BURSTS AND HEAVES UNDER THEIR SPU+   *891 10

KICKED
KICKED OVER THE CLIFF   299 21
WHAT A PITY THEY CAN'T ALL BE KICKED OVER   431 27

KICKING
THE KICKING LITTLE BEETLE   355 28
AND SUBJECT REALLY TO THE DRAUGHT OF EVERY MOTOR-CAR OR+   617 17

KICKS
AND KICKS DUST OVER THE RED STAIN IN THE ROAD   734 16

KICK-UP
IN GRAND CHORALE TO YOUR MONTHLY KICK-UP   681 8

KID
EH THA'RT A MARD-ARSED KID   44 16

KIDS
AN' THESE IS THE WOMAN'S KIDS 'E'S SO FOND ON   81 15
YET SHE HAS SUCH ADORABLE SPURTY KIDS LIKE SPURTS OF BL+   386 17
AN' THESE IS THE WOMAN'S KIDS HE'S SO FOND ON   *923 15

KILL
THE FEMALE WHOSE VENOM CAN MORE THAN KILL CAN NUMB AND +   98 9
WOULD CRUSH THEIR MOUNDS ON HER HEART TO KILL IN THERE   128 25
A SHADOW OVER MY BREASTS THAT WILL KILL ME AT LAST   211 4
POWER TO KILL POWER TO CREATE   326 3
HIT HIM AND KILL HIM AND THROW HIM AWAY   346 7
FOR I WOULD HAVE HAD TO KILL HIM IF HE'D BITTEN ME THE   347 6
WAS IT COWARDICE THAT I DARED NOT KILL HIM   350 13
IF YOU WERE NOT AFRAID YOU WOULD KILL HIM   350 18
KILL MONEY PUT MONEY OUT OF EXISTENCE   487 14
AND BE PREPARED TO KILL YOU IF YOU SAY THEY'VE GOT NONE   501 5
HELPED TO KILL HIM IN THE FLESH   538 12
BUT KILL THE SCABBED AND UGLY LAMB THAT SPREADS CONTAGI+   678 23
UNHAPPY KILL IT THE UNLIVING THING   678 26
DESTROY IT SHED ITS UNCLEAN BLOOD KILL IT PUT IT OUT OF+   679 4
KILL OFF THE WORD THAT'S HAD SO MUCH TO SAY   737 26
BUT I KILL MY SHADOW'S SHADOW OF ME   741 25
SHALL I OFFER TO HIM MY BROTHERLY BODY TO KILL   743 19
AND KILL APHRODITE DON'T SPEAK DO NOT TALK   750 23
KILL HIM IN HIS UNCLEAN HOUSE   808 8
AND YOU KILL HIM THERE WITH ONE STROKE   808 13
THE CAGE WHICH DOES NOT KILL THE MECHANISM OF SEX   843 17

KILLED
NOR TH' CARRYIN' ON AS KILLED 'IM   60 28
I COULD HA' KILLED 'ER   80 22
COULD TER HA' KILLED 'ER   80 24
'TWAS YOU WHO KILLED HIM WHEN YOU BOTH CAROUSED   158 3
HE MUST BE KILLED   350 2
HAS SUCCESSFULLY KILLED ALL DESIRE IN US WHATSOEVER   439 33
YET WHO HAS KILLED IT   512 2
WHAT HAS KILLED MANKIND FOR THE BULK OF MANKIND IS DEAD   654 3
FOR MAN HAS KILLED THE SILENCE OF THE EARTH   725 17
I SHOULD LIKE TO HA' KILLED HER   *922 12
WOR IT THA'D LIKED TO 'A KILLED HER   *922 24

KILLERS
THE RIGHT WHALES THE SPERM-WHALES THE HAMMER-HEADS THE +   694 5

KILLING
KILLING THE BLUE DUSK WITH HARSH SCENT UNNERVING   91 14
BEFORE WE START KILLING ONE ANOTHER ABOUT IT   487 12
INSTEAD OF KILLING THE PASSIONS AND THE INSTINCTS AND   529 7
KILLING IS NOT EVIL   715 5
BUT SHALL I TOUCH HANDS WITH DEATH IN KILLING THAT OTHER   743 17

KILLS
YOU LOVE IT IT IS DARK IT KILLS ME I AM PUT OUT   211 12
KILLS SEX IN A MAN THE SIMPLICITY   485 2
KILLS US WE ARE SICK OF IT TO DIE   519 10
IT IS CONCEIT THAT KILLS US   674 6
KILLS ENTIRELY THE TRUE EXPERIENCE OF SEX   843 18

KILOSSA
   THOU WELL OF KILOSSA THY WELL-CHORDS ARE OF SILVER   759 12
   KILOSSA SWEET WELL OF MY STRENGTH THOU CORDED WITH SILK   759 14

KIN
   AND KIN WITH MISS JUPSON WHOSE GUTS ARE NARROW   583 28
   OF KIN   607 28

KIND
   KIND ON THE WEIGHT OF SUFFERING SMILES AGAIN   113 16
   IT IS A KIND OF DEATH WHICH IS NOT DEATH   266   8
   FOR WHAT KIND OF ICE-ROTTEN HOT-ACHING HEART MUST THEY +   270 27
   A KIND OF LAUGH   389 14
   DON'T EVER BE KIND TO THE SMILING TOOTH-MOUTHED DEAD   441 32
   DON'T EVER BE KIND TO THE DEAD   441 33
   A KIND OF FICTION   474 14
   KIND   475 15
   FEELING SO KIND TOWARDS YOU   557   3
   SUCH A DEAR KIND AUNTIE ISN'T SHE TO A LUCKY LITTLE   571 11
   HE USED TO GIVE KIND ADVICE TO THE PROSTITUTES ON PICCA+   582   2
   I KNOW YOU'LL BE VERY KIND TO ME   603   4
   AND THE TIME HAS COME TO CEASE TO BE KIND ANY MORE   640 16
   THAT CORPOREAL EXISTENCE IS A KIND OF DEATH   689 15
   AND ONE WARM KIND KISS OF THE LION WITH GOLDEN PAWS   695 33
   THE KIND OF HELL THAT IS REAL GREY AND AWFUL   714   1
   THE KIND OF HELL GREY DANTE NEVER SAW   714   3
   BE KIND OH BE KIND TO YOUR DEAD   721 17
   SOFT AS A KIND HEART'S KINDNESS TREMULOUS   784 17

KINDLE
   AND KINDLE MY WILL TO A FLAME THAT SHALL CONSUME   74 20
   INTO THE WOMB TO KINDLE AN UNKNOWN FIRE   89 35
   OF IMMORTALITY TO KINDLE UP   745 31
   ONE OF YOU KINDLE A FIRE TO CONSUME THEM WITHAL   750 24

KINDLED
   KINDLED TO ME   108 25
   OF SEED-SPECKS KINDLED LATELY AND SOFTLY BLOWN   218 16
   OR ARE WE KINDLED YOU AND I TO BE   219   5
   AS IF THE HOMAGE OF THE KINDLED BLOOD OF THE EAST   389 28
   KINDLED TOGETHERNESS SO WE GO   471   7
   THE SPARK FELL AND KINDLED INSTANTLY ON MY BLOOD   618   4
   WHEN MY BLOOD IS KINDLED   655 25
   YOU WILL NEVER FLY ON YELLOW KINDLED WINGS   784 23

KINDLES
   KINDLES THE DARKENING PYRE   108 20
   AND KINDLES IT FURTHER AT THE CORE OF UTTER MYSTERY   261 16

KINDLING
   I WANT THE FINE KINDLING WINE-SAP OF SPRING   271 17
   AND KINDLING SHAPELY LITTLE CONFLAGRATIONS   271 33
   IT MEANS KINDLING THE LIFE-QUALITY WHERE IT WAS NOT   449 21
   AND KINDLING LITTLE FIRES UPON THE SHORES   688 15
   THE QUICK KINDLING SPARK OF A GENEROUS TRUST   855   8

KINDLY
   YET CALM AND KINDLY ARE HIS EYES   43 14
   BUT THAT YOU HOLD ME STILL SO KINDLY COLD   122 21
   WHEN MY HEART FEELS KINDLY TOWARDS HER   479   3
   AND KINDLY HAND ME THE CIGARETTES   540 27

KINDNESS
   THERE IS A KINDNESS IN THE VERY RAIN   208   7
   BY THE KINDNESS OF LIVING WOMEN AND MEN   640 14
   BOTH BREASTS DIM AND MYSTERIOUS WITH THE GLAMOROUS KIND+   693 12
   SOFT AS A KIND HEART'S KINDNESS TREMULOUS   784 17
   OF THE KINDNESS OF THE COSMOS THAT WILL WAFT   *961   3

KINDRED
   IT IS VERY DARK OH KINDRED DEARER THAN BLOOD   765   1

KINDS
   BODIES IN THE IMAGE OF THEIR SEVERAL KINDS   376   4
   ALL KINDS OF THINGS TO ONE ANOTHER   470   5

KING
   AND CEASES TO BE A BLOOD-THIRSTY KING OF BEASTS   325   7
   LIKE A KING EAGLE BIRD OF THE MOST HIGH SWEEPING THE RO+   329   4
   FOR HE SEEMED TO ME AGAIN LIKE A KING   351 24
   LIKE A KING IN EXILE UNCROWNED IN THE UNDERWORLD   351 25
   NEVER A MOUNTAIN PEAK TO BE KING OF THE CASTLE   382 32
   LIKE THE KING AN' QUEEN THOUGH THEY'RE   434 28
   THAT THE KING OF GLORY MAY COME IN   818   8
   WHO IS THIS KING OF GLORY   818   9

KING-CUPS
   CROWDS OF GLITTERING KING-CUPS SURGE TO CHALLENGE THE B+   33 11
   CROWDS OF GLITTERING KING-CUPS SURGE TO CHALLENGE THE B+   *891 12

KINGCUPS'
   AND THE KINGCUPS' GLISTEN THAT SHALL LONG OUTLAST YOU   90 12

KINGDOM
   FOR THINE IS THE KINGDOM   704 11
   MY KINGDOM MY POWER AND MY GLORY   704 17
   HAVE THEIR KINGDOM THEIR POWER AND THEIR GLORY   704 19
   LIKE THE KINGDOM OF THE NIGHTINGALE AT TWILIGHT   704 20
   LIKE THE KINGDOM OF THE FOX IN THE DARK   704 22
   MY KINGDOM MY POWER AND MY GLORY   704 29

KINGFISHERS
   AND FLASHING KINGFISHERS THAT FLEW   262   4

KINGLY
   AND CROWNS KINGLY GENEROUS TILTING CROWNS   278 19

KINGS
   BUT BLOOD IS RED AND BLOOD IS LIFE RED WAS THE COLOUR O+   303 21
   FAR-OFF KINGS PAINTED THEIR FACES VERMILION AND WERE AL+   303 22
   WE ARE ALL KINGS AND QUEENS   435   4
   HAPPY AS PERHAPS KINGS USED TO BE BUT CERTAINLY AREN'T   520 18
   OH EAGLE OF KINGS AND EMPERORS   783 23

KING'S ENGLISH
   AND THEY TAUGHT YOU TO SPEAK KING'S ENGLISH   549 11

KISS
   I KISS IT IN DROUTH   55 18
   AND CLAIM HER UTTERLY IN A KISS   62   7
   WHO CROUCHING PUT HIS MOUTH DOWN IN A KISS   69 22
   NAY NEVER I PUT YOU AWAY YET EACH KISS HISSES   87 12
   I KISS YOU GOOD-BYE MY DARLING   102   7
   I KISS YOU GOOD-BYE MY DEAREST   102 13
   I WOULD KISS YOU OVER THE EYES TILL I KISSED YOU BLIND   118 26
   EXCEPT HER KISS BETRAYS ME THIS THIS ONLY   127 25
   AND FALLING WAVES IN HIS ARMS AND THE LOST SOUL'S KISS   130 20
   AH WUNNA KISS THEE THA TREMBLES SO   138 14
   I KISS YOUR MOUTH AH LOVE   153 24
   AND NOW AT LAST I KISS YOUR PERFECT FACE   157 21
   I KISS THE STONES I KISS THE MOSS ON THE WALL   173 13
   AND HER MOUTH UNCLOSED IN A LAST LONG KISS   198   3
   AND HER MOUTH UNCLOSED IN THE LAST LONG KISS   199 11
   STILL THE KISS WAS A TOUCH OF BITTERNESS ON MY MOUTH   206 20
   KISS ME HOW COLD YOU ARE YOUR LTTTLE BREASTS   212   6
   ARE BUBBLES OF ICE KISS ME YOU KNOW HOW IT RESTS   212   7
   AND MOUTH REACHING FORWARD TO KISS YOU   220 11
   A KISS AND A SPASM OF FAREWELL A MOMENT'S ORGASM OF   280 27
   CERES KISS YOUR GIRL YOU THINK YOU'VE GOT HER BACK   309 25
   IT WAS YOU WHO GAVE HER HER FIRST KISS   550 21
   THEN HE RECEIVES THE KISS OF RECONCILIATION   648 18
   THE WINDS OF THE AFTERWARDS KISS US INTO BLOSSOM OF MAN+   677 19
   AND KISS OF THE FAR-OFF LINGERING LADY WHO LOOKS OVER T+   695 31
   AND ONE WARM KIND KISS OF THE LION WITH GOLDEN PAWS   695 33
   THE ANGELS ARE STANDING BACK THE ANGELS OF THE KISS   707   6
   IN THE STILLNESS HE TOOK OFF HIS HELMET TO KISS ME   732 16
   AND THE VEIL OF THE TEMPLE RENT AT THE KISS ON KISS   742 28
   MY KISS TO WOUNDS   743   1
   DO YOU LIFT YOUR LIPS TO KISS ME GOOD NIGHT MY LOVE   750 16
   SWIFTLY I WISH I MIGHT KISS HER FINGERS BUT FULL   752 11
   HAS THE WARMTH OF A NIGHT KISS SPREAD THROUGH THEIR BLO+   860 22
   WITH A QUICK KISS CLIPS   862 12
   SIEGMUND DEAR KISS ME KISS ME   871 20
   AND CLAIM HER UTTERLY IN A KISS   *912 14
   OF MY ARMS INERT WITH DREAD WILTED IN FEAR OF MY KISS   *912 18
   GOD LONELY PUT DOWN HIS MOUTH IN A KISS OF CREATION   *916   5
   KEEP THEN THE KISS FROM THE ADULTRESS' THEFT   *916   8
   KISS ME THEN THERE NE'ER MIND IF I SCRAIGHT I WOR FOND +   *925 28
   KISS BUT THEN THE DUST FROM OFF MY LIPS   *929 26
   I'LL KISS YOU OVER THE EYES TILL I KISS YOU BLIND   *932   4
   RIPENESS WELLED THROUGH ME AT HIS KISS   *933 26
   SUNSHINE OF HIS HAIR I USED TO KISS   *933 28

KISS-BELADEN
   AND SO KISS-BELADEN THAT IT SCARCE CAN FLOAT   *943 17

KISSED
   SHE KISSED ME WARM ON THE MOUTH   37 13
   THE ANGEL OF CHILDHOOD KISSED ME AND WENT I EXPECTED   48   5
   AND KISSED THEE TO A PASSION OF LIFE AND LEFT   69 23
   OR LIKE A MIST THE MOON HAS KISSED FROM OFF A POOL IN T+   70 22
   AFTER I'D KISSED THEE AT NIGHT LIZZIE   80   9
   WE KISSED WE KISSED THOUGH WE SHOULD NOT   111 20
   I WOULD KISS YOU OVER THE EYES TILL I KISSED YOU BLIND   118 26
   THEN YOU PUT YOUR HAND IN MINE AGAIN KISSED ME AND WE   206 13
   I WAS A LOVER I KISSED THE WOMAN I LOVED   257 18
   AND SIX HAVE GIVEN ME GIFTS AND KISSED ME GOD-SPEED   695 28
   THE SNAKE HAS KISSED MY HEEL   802 23
   DRAW NEARER REDDEN AND LAUGH LIKE YOUNG GIRLS KISSED   854 12
   SHE KISSED THEIR COOLNESS LAST NIGHT BREATHED THEIR CLE+   856 19
   SHE TURNED AND KISSED HIM AND HIS EYES WERE THE SOUL OF+   865   8
   I KISSED HER ONCE AGAIN UPON THE MOUTH   881   1
   KISSED HER DELICIOUSLY   884   6
   THEN SHE RUMMAGED HER HAND IN 'ER BOSOM AN' KISSED THE +   *910 20
   HE KISSED THEE O MAN IN A PASSION OF LOVE AND LEFT   *916   6
   OR LIKE A MIST THE MOON HAS KISSED FROM OFF A POOL IN T+   *917 19

KISSES
   SIGNALLING THOSE TWO KISSES   37 17
   MY KISSES ARE SINKING SOON   37 21
   AND STOLEN KISSES SHALLOW AND GAY   42 13
   AND WE SWOON WITH KISSES SWOON TILL WE SEEM   70 16
   YOU SURELY SEEING I AM A BOWL OF KISSES   86   3
   HELEN YOU LET MY KISSES STEAM   86   5
   HOW CAN YOU FROM MY BOWL OF KISSES SHRINK   86   8
   YOU HOLD YOURSELF ALL HARD AS IF MY KISSES   87 10
   ONE BOWL OF KISSES   96   6
   MY BOWL OF KISSES   96 12
   AND TWICE AFTER WILD KISSES I SAW   103 24
   OF KISSES LONG SEEKING FOR A WIFE   105   7
   PRESSES THEM THERE AND KISSES HER BIG DARK HANDS   128 32
   AND KISSES PALE AND SIPPING THE TOLL   151 29
   OF KISSES OH HELP ME GOD HERE AT THE SOURCE   153 28
   I CLOSE YOUR EARS WITH KISSES   154   1
   NAY LET ME WORK A DELICATE CHAIN OF KISSES   154   4
   OF IRON KISSES KISSES LINKED LIKE STEEL   154 20
   MY MOUTH ON HERS IN KISSES AND SO SOFTLY   218 19
   WHAT YOUR THROAT IS BRUISED BRUISED WITH MY KISSES   230 14
   I WILL WARM YOUR LIMBS WITH KISSES   237 25
   COME NOT WITH KISSES   436 20
   AND CAUGHT THEM MOANING FROM CLOSE-UP KISSES BLACK-AND-+   444   1
   KISSES THAT COULD NOT BE FELT   444   2

KISSES
KISSES OF FOUR GREAT LORDS BEAUTIFUL AS THEY HELD ME TO+   695 29
LIKE NOW WHERE THE WHITE SUN KISSES THE SEA   709 9
KISSES OF THE SOFT-BALLED PAWS WHERE THE TALONS ARE   709 13
ABSOLUTE CONSCIOUSNESS ABSOLVED FROM STRIFE AND KISSES   712 17
A THING OF KISSES AND STRIFE   714 7
AS FIRE BUT SOFT AS SUNSHINE SOFT AS KISSES   784 16
HER QUIVERING ANSWERS AND KISSES LIKE THIEVING BIRDS   868 31
SWEET FRAGRANCE OF LOVE AND FEED ME WITH KISSES FAIR   874 7
BUT I THINK THE KISSES REACH   *893 9
AFTER THY KISSES LIZZIE AFTER   *922 9
MY QUIVERING ANSWER AND KISSES LIKE FRAGRANCE OF FLOWERS   *942 3
IN THE TWILIGHT OUR KISSES ACROSS THE ROSES   *942 17

KISSING
FLUSHED WITH THE SONGS OF SEVEN LARKS SINGING AT ONCE G+   34 14
LIKE MOONBEAMS KISSING YOU BUT THE BODY OF ME   87 20
COMES ENDLESSLY KISSING MY FACE AND MY HANDS   144 2
AND GOD OF HORROR I WAS KISSING ALSO MYSELF   257 19
LIFE IS FOR KISSING AND FOR HORRID STRIFE   709 25
LIFE IS FOR KISSING AND FOR HORRID STRIFE   710 1
THE KISSING AND COMMUNING CANNOT CEASE   710 7
ONLY THE HUMAN BEING ABSOLVED FROM KISSING AND STRIFE   713 27
THE SNAKE OF MY LEFT-HAND OUT OF THE DARKNESS IS KISSIN+   801 22
WHAT IF THE GORSE FLOWERS SHRIVELLED AND KISSING WERE L+ *891 23
RICH WITH THE SONGS OF SEVEN LARKS SINGING AT ONCE GOES+ *892 2

KISSIN'
AFTER KISSIN' AN' CUDDLIN' WI' ME THA COULD   80 18

KITCHEN
THINK THAT THE SAPPHIRE IS ONLY ALUMINA LIKE KITCHEN PA+   530 1

KITH
IF YOU STAY IN MY OFFICE YOU'VE GOT TO BE KITH   583 27

KITTENS
WHO CURL IN SLEEP LIKE KITTENS WHO MASS AS A SWARM   73 17

KNACKER-BONED
AND MEN BEING MOSTLY GELDINGS AND KNACKER-BONED HACKS   379 31

KNAVE
BUT OH WIND WHAT A KNAVE THOU ART   731 15
NIBBLED HIS FINGERS THE KNAVE   754 19

KNEADED
OF VICTORY KNEADED WITH SULPHUR   758 21

KNEADS
WHO IS IT THAT CLASPS AND KNEADS MY NAKED FEET TILL THE+   652 12

KNEE
ON THE HAY WITH MY HEAD ON HER KNEE   35 17
WITH TWO LITTLE BARE WHITE FEET UPON MY KNEE   65 7
HOW CARESSINGLY SHE LAYS HER HAND ON MY KNEE   128 14
THE KEEPER HOODS THE VAST KNEE THE CREATURE SALAAMS   387 16
CROOK THE KNEE AND BE GLAD   392 13
PEAR-BLOSSOM HANGING AND ONE SMALL KNEE   886 7
SO SHE MAY STAND ON MY KNEE   *913 8
SO THAT SHE CAN STAND ON MY KNEE   *914 8

KNEEL
THA SHOULD HA' SEED 'ER KNEEL AN' LOOK IN   61 6
ALWAYS KNEEL IN COURTSHIP TO THE SHELVES IN THE DOORWAY+ 180 26
YOU SHOULD 'A SEEN HER KNEEL AN' LOOK DOWN   *910 10
THA SHOULD HA' SEED HER KNEEL AN' LOOK IN   *911 22

KNEE-LIFTING
CLUMSY KNEE LIFTING SALAAM   388 10

KNEELS
AND AT THE FOOT OF A GRAVE A MOTHER KNEELS   232 26

KNEES
WHICH LIES ON THE KNEES OF THE NIGHT-TIME RUDDY AND MAK+   88 21
OF A WOMAN'S KNEES   145 26
AT A MOTHER'S KNEES THE TROUBLE   152 20
PUT GREAVES UPON YOUR THIGHS AND KNEES AND FRAIL   154 21
BETWEEN THE BITTER KNEES OF THE AFTER-NIGHT   160 12
MY KNEES AND LIE STILL   240 27
THIGHS AND KNEES   245 17
YOUR BREASTS YOUR KNEES AND FEET I FEEL THAT WE   245 23
BEFORE SHE HUMBLED HERSELF AND KNOCKED HER KNEES WITH   314 8
WASH OVER OUR KNEES AND SPLASH BETWEEN OUR THIGHS   425 4
WREATHE STRONG WEED ROUND THE KNEES AS THE DARKNESS   425 13
ON HER KNEES IN UTMOST CAUTION   426 11
WHEN HAVE YOU KNEES EVER NIPPED ME   427 16
THE KNEES   481 22
PRANCING THEIR KNEES UNDER THEIR TINY SKIRTS   537 20
BRINGS HIM TO HIS KNEES IN HOMAGE AND PURE PASSION OF S+ 648 17
AND OVER THE SUBMERGED ISLETS OF MY KNEES   705 9
WATERY-HEARTED WITH WISHY-WASHY KNEES   795 6
AND KNEES AND THIGHS AND LOINS AND THE BOWELS OF STRENG+ 801 20
KNEES AND YOUR LEGS AND YOUR LOINS HIS CIRCLE OF REST I+ 801 25
DRIFTED WITH THE BLOOD OF THE FLOWERS ON HER FEET AND K+ 864 3

KNELL
ITS KNELL HAS STRUCK   512 5
THE KNELL OF OUR BALD-HEADED CONSCIOUSNESS   512 10
WHO RANG THE KNELL   512 13
AT THE CORE OF SPACE THE FINAL KNELL   512 16
AND HIS GRAND-INQUISITORIAL KNELL   633 25
SHARPLY BEATS OUT A THRICE-TOLD FUNERAL KNELL   858 24

KNEW
AND I KNEW THAT HOME THIS VALLEY WAS WIDER THAN PARADISE   38 17
AS IF HE KNEW AUGHT   54 16
TILL I KNEW YOU NOT FROM A LITTLE WIND   104 8
EVEN YOU IF YOU KNEW   131 1
SOFTLY I KNEW IT WOULD COME TO THIS SHE SAID   156 13
I KNEW THAT SOME DAY SOON I SHOULD FIND YOU THUS   156 14
BETWEEN YOU BUT HIS TOUCH YOU NEVER KNEW   158 8
TO TOUCH HIM AND HE SAID SO AND YOU KNEW   158 26
AND I KNEW HER   222 16
THE THINGS YOU NEVER KNEW   227 14
KNEW   251 10
IF YOU KNEW HOW I SWERVE IN PEACE IN THE EQUIPOISE   251 22
WITH THE MAN IF YOU KNEW HOW MY FLESH ENJOYS   251 23
IT WAS ALL TAINTED WITH MYSELF I KNEW IT ALL TO START W+ 256 29
WHEN I GATHERED FLOWERS I KNEW IT WAS MYSELF PLUCKING MY 257 1
WHEN I WENT IN A TRAIN I KNEW IT WAS MYSELF TRAVELLING + 257 3
WHEN I SAW THE TORN DEAD I KNEW IT WAS MY OWN TORN DEAD 257 7
WHEN EVERYTHING WAS ME I KNEW IT ALL ALREADY I ANTICIPA+ 257 11
I TOUCHED HER FLANK AND KNEW I WAS CARRIED BY THE CURRE+ 260 12
I WAITED THEREFORE THEN I KNEW   262 1
WHEN EVE ONCE KNEW IN HER MIND THAT SHE WAS NAKED   284 7
JOHN KNEW THE WHOLE PROPOSITION   328 10
JOHN KNEW THE WHOLE PROPOSITION   328 16
OR LIFE KNEW LOVING   337 12
IF THEY KNEW THAT HIS MOTTO WAS ICH DIEN   369 35
THEN I KNEW THEY WERE DEJECTED HAVING COME TO HEAR THE   390 19
FROM THIS I LEARN THOUGH I KNEW IT BEFORE   489 5
I WISH I KNEW A WOMAN   506 11
AND HIS BRITISH BLOOD THE WORLD IT KNEW   576 25
BUT WHAT A PITY I NEVER KNEW   580 10
EVEN THE BISON KNEW IT   587 7
THEY KNEW THE USEFUL GODHEAD OF PROVIDENCE   609 24
AND THE POOR MAN NEVER KNEW HE WAS JIXED   659 17
THEY KNEW IT WAS NO USE KNOWING   688 26
ON IF HE KNEW THAT I WAS AT THIS FARM   733 14
WAITING AND I KNEW HE WANTED IT   742 8
BUT IN THE WEIGHT OF THEIR STUPEFACTION NONE OF THEM KN+ 790 25
I WISH I KNEW WHERE THIS PALE ROAD GOES   857 12
AND THEN I KNEW I HAD TAKEN MY MOUTH FROM HER THROAT   882 7
I KNEW THAT SHE WAS WAITING   885 18
I KNEW THAT SHE WAS BAITING   885 20
US A LITTLE WIFT AN' I KNEW THE SMELL   *910 19
I KNEW YOUR PAIN AND IT BROKE   *928 11
ONCE I KNEW A SUMMER THAT SPARKLED   *933 14
'TIS STRANGE WE NEVER KNEW   *941 9

KNICKERS
I SWEAR I'LL PULL OFF MY KNICKERS RIGHT IN THE RUE DE L+ 433 20

KNIFE
AT THE KNIFE OF A DRUID   131 10
WHEN THEY FELT THE LIGHT OF HEAVEN BRANDISHING LIKE A K+ 310 7
THEN I TAKE MY KNIFE AND THROW IT UPON THE GREY DOG   807 20

KNIFE-EDGED
OH WELL I SUPPOSE I SHALL HAVE SOME KNIFE-EDGED TERENCE+ 835 1

KNIFE-EDGE
AND THE SUDDEN DRIPPING OF THE KNIFE-EDGE CLEAVAGE OF T+ 707 13

KNIFE'S
BETWEEN YOU AND YOUR PURPOSE LIKE A KNIFE'S EDGE SHADOW 706 20

KNIGHT
KNIGHTS INDEED MUCH KNIGHT I KNOW WILL RIDE   221 10

KNIGHTS
DARK AND PROUD ON THE SKY LIKE A NUMBER OF KNIGHTS   221 8
KNIGHTS INDEED MUCH KNIGHT I KNOW WILL RIDE   221 10
OF THESE DARK KNIGHTS SHEDDING THEIR DELICATE SHEEN   221 19
PROUD KNIGHTS TO BATTLE SWEET HOW I WARM   221 28
DARK AND PROUD ON THE SKY LIKE A NUMBER OF KNIGHTS   *944 21

KNOB
A KNOB BEHIND   310 3

KNOCK
UPRAISED TO KNOCK AND KNOCK ONCE MORE   121 15
KNOCK KNOCK 'TIS NO MORE THAN A RED ROSE RAPPING   150 20
THE KNOCK OF THE BLOOD IN MY WRISTS   461 2
SOME ONE WILL KNOCK WHEN THE DOOR IS SHUT   789 5

KNOCKED
IT'S A SHAME AS 'E SHOULD BE KNOCKED ABOUT   45 25
HOLLOW RANG THE HOUSE WHEN I KNUCKLED AT THE DOOR   121 13
BEFORE SHE HUMBLED HERSELF AND KNOCKED HER KNEES WITH   314 8
AND SCARLET HOT EMBERS OF TORCHES KNOCKED OUT OF THE   388 30
KNOCKED A LITTLE HOLE IN THE HOLY PRISON   459 18
THE WIND THE RASCAL KNOCKED AT MY DOOR AND I SAID   731 13

KNOCKING
WITH A STRANGE NEW KNOCKING OF LIFE AT HER SIDE   64 8
WHAT IS THE KNOCKING   250 28
WHAT IS THE KNOCKING AT THE DOOR IN THE NIGHT   250 29
AND NOW WITH THE KNOCKING OF HIS HEART AGAINST MY SOUL   871 8

KNOCKIN'
SOMEBODY'S KNOCKIN' AT TH' DOOR   44 10

KNOCK-KNEED
HOW IS IT YOU HAVE TO BE LOOKED AFTER BY SOME KNOCK-KNE+ 643 23

KNOCKS
HOW 'ARD 'E KNOCKS   44 15
MEN FIGHT FOR LIBERTY AND WIN IT WITH HARD KNOCKS   535 23

KNOT
    WITH A KNOT OF LIFE THAT ONLY BLISS CAN UNRAVEL   160 14
    WITH SUCH A KNOT INSIDE HIM   377 29
    AND TIED IN A KNOT INSIDE DEAD-LOCKED BETWEEN TWO DESIR+   379 12
    KNOT IS UNTIED   384 29
    BACK IN A GRECIAN KNOT OR A JUG HANDLE OR A CHIGNON   836 2

KNOTS
    KNOTS OF PINK FISH-SILVERY   307 4
    WHERE THE FORCES TIE THEMSELVES UP INTO KNOTS OF ATOMS   437 29
    OF MISTINESS COMPLICATED INTO KNOTS AND CLOTS THAT BARGE   437 32
    AND FORCES TIE THEMSELVES UP INTO KNOTS OF ATOMS THEN C+   *947 6
    THAT EVERYTHING TIES ITSELF UP INTO COMPLICATED LITTLE +   *947 8

KNOTTED
    OF THE WIND IN THE KNOTTED BUDS MAKES A CANOPY   152 29
    SO SITTING UNDER THE KNOTTED CANOPY   153 1
    KNOTTED IN HEAVEN UPON THE FINE LIGHT   307 9
    OF THE WIND HUNG ROUND THE KNOTTED BUDS LIKE A CANOPY   866 25

KNOTTING
    KNOTTING THEMSELVES WITH WILD STRENGTH   *893 24

KNOW
    SO NOW I KNOW THE VALLEY   38 23
    I KNOW NOT WHAT FINE WIRE IS ROUND MY THROAT   43 29
    I ONLY KNOW I LET HIM FINGER THERE   43 30
    I DUNNA KNOW   45 10
    NEVER TO KNOW THE GLAD FREEDOM OF OBEDIENCE SINCE LONG   48 3
    I MUST SIT ALONE AND WAIT AND NEVER KNOW   48 7
    BENT IF WE DID BUT KNOW IT ON A WEARY AND BITTER GRIMACE   54 23
    YOU KNOW YOUR MOUTH   55 13
    THEN I SHALL KNOW WHICH IMAGE OF GOD   59 9
    SO I SHALL KNOW WHAT I HAVE TO KEEP   59 19
    I SHALL WEEP OH I SHALL WEEP I KNOW   60 9
    WHEN I KNOW THAT THERE MUST EVER BE DECEIVING   65 23
    SEE IN THE SKY BEFORE ME A WOMAN I DID NOT KNOW   67 10
    AN' WHEN I KNOW FOR SURE MISSIS   78 19
    IF YER MUN KNOW   79 16
    DOESN'T TER KNOW WHAT I MEAN TIMMY   79 23
    I EXPECT YER KNOW WHO I AM MRS NAYLOR   81 21
    BUT I WANT YOU TO KNOW 'E'S NOT MARRYIN' YOU   82 5
    BUT SHE'S WAITING I KNOW IMPATIENT AND COLD HALF   85 11
    WHY DOES SHE COME SO PROMPTLY WHEN SHE MUST KNOW   85 13
    DID I SHIVER NAY TRULY I DO NOT KNOW   87 3
    AND NOW I KNOW SO I MUST BE ASHAMED   87 18
    FOR NOW I KNOW   88 32
    EACH ONE FOR ITS HOLD ON THE CONCRETE DARKNESS I KNOW T+   92 14
    AND IN THE ORIGINAL DARK THE ROOTS CANNOT KEEP CANNOT K+   92 17
    I THOUGHT THAT LOVE WOULD DO ALL THINGS BUT NOW I KNOW +   93 1
    SINCE YOU ARE SO KEEN TO KNOW   96 3
    TOO FAR AWAY O LOVE I KNOW   104 21
    IN A LOW SHOCKING PERFUME TO KNOW WHO HAS HAILED   105 33
    AND DEATH I KNOW IS BETTER THAN NOT-TO-BE   126 6
    LIFT OF THE PULSING WIND AH SAY THAT YOU KNOW   126 32
    I KNOW FROM HER HARDENED LIPS THAT STILL HER HEART IS   128 1
    LET US RISE AND LEAVE HER NOW SHE WILL NEVER KNOW   132 26
    DO I NOT KNOW THE DARKNESS WITHIN THEM WHAT ARE THEY   133 14
    DOESN'T TER KNOW IT   138 21
    DRAW IT OUT OF 'IM DID TER KNOW IT   138 26
    KNOW   141 23
    I KNOW NOT MY SOUL IS IN STRIFE   143 24
    SHE HASTENED TOWARDS THE ROOM DID SHE KNOW   155 15
    WITHIN THE RAGE WE SHALL NOT KNOW TILL IT BURST   160 19
    TO KNOW   171 26
    WHEN WE DID NOT KNOW DID NOT CARE   172 12
    IS OUT OF BOUNDS AND ONLY THE OLD GHOSTS KNOW   172 24
    CAN KNOW THE FEARFUL ANGUISH THAT THIS IS SO   173 12
    I AM SHUT IN A PRISONER I KNOW NOT HOW   173 27
    AND AT LAST I KNOW MY LOVE FOR YOU IS HERE   203 17
    YET HOW I HAVE LEARNED TO KNOW THAT LOOK IN YOUR EYES   207 15
    HOW I KNOW THAT GLITTER OF SALT DRY STERILE SHARP CORRO+   207 17
    ARE BUBBLES OF ICE KISS ME YOU KNOW HOW IT RESTS   212 7
    KNIGHTS INDEED MUCH KNIGHT I KNOW WILL RIDE   221 10
    AND KNOW THE DEAD CHRIST WEIGHING ON MY BONE   226 12
    I KNOW YOU HERE IN THE DARKNESS   227 29
    AH YES I KNOW YOU WELL A SOJOURNER   234 1
    I KNOW RIGHT WELL THE MARRIAGE RING YOU WEAR   234 3
    WE NO LONGER KNOW   240 15
    NOTHING TO KNOW OR TO WEEP   254 2
    KNOW   256 12
    TO LET ME KNOW THAT I WAS FOUND   262 9
    THEN I SHALL KNOW THE ELYSIUM   262 22
    HAVE OPENED UP FOR US TO KNOW TO SATISFY   263 23
    AND KNOW THAT THEY WERE GIVEN FOR EVER   265 5
    WHAT REMAINS IN ME IS TO BE KNOWN AS I KNOW   265 31
    I KNOW HER NOW OR PERHAPS I KNOW MY OWN LIMITATION AGAI+   265 32
    I HAVE COME AS IT WERE NOT TO KNOW   266 4
    WHAT CAN I SAY MORE EXCEPT THAT I KNOW WHY IT IS TO SUR+   266 6
    WE SHALL KNOW IN FULL   268 12
    BUT WHEN YOU COME TO KNOW IT BETTER YOU AGREE WITH THE   282 15
    THE NEGRO MIGHT KNOW A LITTLE   286 13
    YOU DON'T KNOW YOURSELF   292 19
    MY HEART WILL KNOW NO PEACE   293 16
    FOR OH I KNOW IN THE DUST WHERE WE HAVE BURIED   298 1
    YET EVEN THIS IS NOT THE SECRET OF THE SECRET DO YOU KN+   303 8
    NO NO I KNOW NOTHING OF THAT   303 12
    HOW SHALL WE KNOW THEM WHEN WE SEE THEM   312 12
    HOW SHALL WE KNOW THEM NOW THEY'VE COME   312 13
    HOW DO WE KNOW THEM THAT THEY ARE THEY   313 4
    LET IT KNOW NOTHING   327 23
    HUNG ALL THE TIME DID WE BUT KNOW IT THE ALL-KNOWING SH+   328 8
    BUT I KNOW YOUR GAME NOW STREAKY SORCERER   332 24
    YOU DON'T KNOW THAT I EXIST AND I DON'T KNOW THAT YOU   333 10
    NEVER KNOW   335 6
    AHA THERE'S SOMEBODY IN THE KNOW   338 5
    I HAD MADE A MISTAKE I DIDN'T KNOW HIM   338 10
    I DIDN'T KNOW HIS GOD   338 14

KNOW
    I DIDN'T KNOW HIS GOD   338 15
    BUT NOT BEFORE I HAVE HAD TO KNOW   339 19
    AND DON'T KNOW   340 12
    YOU KNOW WHAT IT IS TO BE BORN ALONE   352 1
    GOES DEEPER IN THAN WE KNOW   354 24
    HE DOESN'T KNOW HE IS ALONE   357 31
    I DON'T KNOW   358 29
    SHE DOES NOT EVEN KNOW SHE IS NIPPING ME WITH HER CURVED   359 24
    DOES SHE KNOW   363 6
    YOU SHALL KNOW A BIRD BY HIS CRY AND GREAT BIRDS CRY LO+   368 9
    AND ARABS SHOULD KNOW   377 19
    I DON'T KNOW   380 8
    SHE IS SUCH AN ALERT LISTENER WITH HER EARS WIDE TO KNOW   384 15
    KNOW ME TURNS HER HEAD AND IGNORES ME VULGARLY WITH   384 23
    YOU KNOW WHICH SIDE YOUR BREAD IS BUTTERED   396 17
    OH YES I KNOW YOUR LITTLE GAME   396 26
    I KNOW YOUR GAME   398 22
    AND WE SMILE FOOLISHLY AS IF WE DIDN'T KNOW   401 21
    AND WE KNOW IT   408 3
    WOMEN OF THE OLDER GENERATION WHO KNOW   410 15
    NOW YOU NEED KNOW IN PART   411 11
    AND THEY KNOW IT   412 20
    YOU YOU DON'T KNOW ME   427 15
    CAN IT BE THAT YOU STILL DON'T KNOW   434 18
    AT THE BOTTOM THEY MUST KNOW WE ARE REALLY SUPERIOR   435 14
    DON'T YOU THINK REALLY THEY KNOW WE'RE THEIR   435 16
    AS YOU KNOW IT IS A COMPLETE LIE   441 24
    THEY KNOW THEY HAVE NO BODIES THAT COULD PLAY AMONG THE   446 2
    SHOWS THAT THE CHILDREN VAGUELY KNOW HOW CHEATED THEY   446 16
    I KNOW A NOBLE ENGLISHMAN   446 19
    YOU KNOW   446 25
    SAID RONALD YOU KNOW IS LIKE MOST ENGLISHMEN   446 28
    BUT HE'S FRIGHTENED TO KNOW   446 30
    YET I KNOW HE DOES IT DELIBERATELY AS CAUTIOUSLY AND   447 20
    I DON'T KNOW HE HAS LOTS OF LEISURE AND HE MAKES   452 22
    MORE THAN WE KNOW   454 20
    AND WE SHALL NOT KNOW WE SHALL NOT KNOW   462 9
    WHY DON'T YOU KNOW WHAT'S WHAT YOUNG PEOPLE SEEMS   464 9
    KNOW YOURSELF O KNOW YOURSELF THAT YOU ARE MORTAL AND   464 23
    KNOW   464 24
    O KNOW YOURSELF O KNOW YOUR SEX YOU MUST KNOW THERE   465 1
    YOU MUST KNOW SEX IN ORDER TO SAVE IT YOUR DEEPEST SELF   465 3
    SO THEY KNOW AT LAST   465 24
    UNDER A MOON THEY DO NOT KNOW   471 9
    AND THEN PERHAPS WE SHALL KNOW TRUE SEX IN OURSELVES   472 13
    THE MIND THAT NEEDS TO KNOW ALL THINGS   473 19
    MUST NEEDS AT LAST COME TO KNOW ITS OWN LIMITS   473 20
    KNOW THYSELF AND THAT THOU ART MORTAL   473 22
    YET WE KNOW IT IS FLOWING AWAY   476 24
    IN RHYTHMS TOO BIG AND TOO SMALL FOR US TO KNOW   479 10
    IS WE KNOW NOT WHAT   480 7
    SO THAT WE DON'T KNOW OURSELVES   482 21
    YOU WHO COMPLAIN YOU KNOW NO JOY IN YOUR LIVES   484 13
    NEVER WILL YOU KNOW ANY JOY IN YOUR LIVES   484 14
    AND THE BEST WON'T BREED THOUGH THEY DON'T KNOW WHY   484 27
    I KNOW A THING OR TWO ABOUT LOVE   490 3
    AND WHAT I KNOW IS THAT YOU MAKE IT   490 5
    IT'S NOT LIKE THAT YOU KNOW YOU FAKE IT   490 7
    WHEN I WISH I WAS RICH THEN I KNOW I AM ILL   498 5
    I KNOW THAT POVERTY IS A HARD OLD HAG   498 13
    I KNOW I AM NOBLE WITH THE NOBILITY OF THE SUN   499 1
    AND MAKES ME KNOW I AM NOT BLANK ANY LONGER   501 25
    THIS IS A PAUSE HOW LONG A PAUSE I KNOW NOT   508 9
    THEN SOMETIMES I FEEL DEFEATED AND THEN AGAIN I KNOW   508 22
    I KNOW I AM NOTHING   509 22
    AND WE KNOW HOW TO LIVE WORDLESS   510 25
    MADDEN US BUT WE DON'T KNOW WHAT TO DO   510 30
    ALL WE CAN KNOW AT THIS MOMENT   511 1
    POOR THINGS AND THEY KNOW IT   518 8
    AS A MATTER OF FACT WE ARE BETTER THAN WE KNOW   519 10
    THE YOUNG KNOW THESE THINGS QUITE WELL   520 29
    BUT WHAT DO YOU THRILL TO DO YOU KNOW   532 2
    DOESN'T TER KNOW   540 13
    I DON'T KNOW WHAT YOU WANT BUT I CERTAINLY HAVEN'T GOT   541 11
    IF YOU WANT TO KNOW YOURSELF   543 12
    SOMETHING IS LEFT BEHIND LOST AND HOWLING AND WE KNOW IT   543 25
    BUT WHAT WE ALSO ARE AND WE NEED TO KNOW IT   544 3
    REALLY PATRIOTIC PEOPLE THE RIGHT SORT OF PEOPLE YOU KN+   546 8
    PERSON THAT'S ALL WE NEED TO KNOW   546 11
    REALLY I DON'T KNOW WHAT YOU TAKE ME FOR   546 12
    YES I KNOW IT'S TOO BAD OF COURSE IT'S PERFECTLY SUPERF+   546 13
    NEED TO KNOW ABOUT ANYBODY AND DO YOU KNOW I'VE NEVER B+   546 18
    YOU'D HAVE MONEY AND YOU KNOW IT   546 25
    OR WE SHOULD NEVER KNOW WHEN WE WERE CROSSING THE   548 29
    AND NOW YOU KNOW   557 19
    YOU'VE HAD SOME YOU KNOW   564 14
    AND KNOW THAT SHE'S GOT   565 10
    IF YOU KNOW WHAT I MEAN   571 16
    THEY SAY THAT AUNTIE MAUD YOU KNOW   571 19
    BUT SO LONG AS WE KNOW THAT AUNTIE LOVES US   573 3
    YOU ALL OF YOU KNOW WHERE YOU'D JOLLY WELL BE   574 2
    MY BRITISH BLOOD THE WORLD SHALL KNOW   576 21
    WHEN YOU KNOW THAT THEY'VE GOT TO THINK THAT THEY'RE   583 7
    OH EVEN TO KNOW THE LAST WILD WINCING OF DESPAIR   585 6
    THEN I SCREAM IN MY SOUL FOR I KNOW I CANNOT   586 3
    I KNOW YOU WON'T PICK MY POCKET   603 3
    I KNOW YOU'LL BE VERY KIND TO ME   603 4
    THAT I MAY KNOW WHAT IS UNBECOMING TO ME   606 12
    THAT WE KNOW NOTHING OF THAT WE DARE NOT EXPLORE   606 22
    I NEVER KNOW WHAT PEOPLE MEAN WHEN THEY COMPLAIN OF   610 1
    I KNOW NO GREATER DELIGHT THAN THE SHEER DELIGHT OF BEI+   610 19
    BUT I HONESTLY DON'T KNOW WHAT HE MEANS   611 3
    ALL THAT WE KNOW IS NOTHING WE ARE MERELY CRAMMED WASTE+   613 8
    THE ONLY SALVATION IS TO REALISE THAT WE KNOW NOTHING A+   613 11
    BUT TELL ME TELL ME HOW DO YOU KNOW   614 13
    YET SHE SEEMED TO KNOW NOTHING ABOUT IT   619 7
    WHEREIN WE KNOW OURSELF FOR WHAT WE ARE   621 6

KNOW
AND KNOW OUR DEPENDENCE ON THE CREATIVE BEYOND 621 7
I KNOW HE IS EITHER A BED-BUG BATTENING ON SLEEPING PEO+ 621 23
BUT THE BLATANT BATHERS DON'T KNOW THEY KNOW NOTHING 625 16
THEREFORE I KNOW THE PEOPLE 627 1
THEN I KNOW 629 23
I KNOW THE UNLIVING FACTORY-HAND LIVING-DEAD MILLIONS 629 26
WHEN I AM IN A GREAT CITY I KNOW THAT I DESPAIR 632 11
I KNOW THERE IS NO HOPE FOR US DEATH WAITS IT IS USELES+ 632 12
I SCREAM IN MY SOUL FOR I KNOW I CANNOT 632 18
I DON'T KNOW WHAT THEY'VE DONE POOR THINGS BUT JUSTICE + 632 30
THE GREAT INDUSTRIALISTS KNOW IT 635 19
YOU WHO FEEL NOTHING WHO KNOW NOTHING WHO RUN ON 643 16
AND SOME MEN CAN SEE NO GODS THEY ONLY KNOW 649 10
AND YOU KNOW ALL THE WHILE 655 3
AND EVEN IN COLD BLOOD I KNOW THIS 655 23
BUT TO THE FRAIL WHO KNOW BEST 658 9
BUT THEY'RE NOT REALLY NICE YOU KNOW 660 6
BE NICE YOU KNOW JUST NICE 660 14
JUST BE NICE YOU KNOW OH FAIRLY NICE 660 16
THEY DARE NOT DIE BECAUSE THEY KNOW 663 1
TO KNOW THE MOON AS WE HAVE NEVER KNOWN 666 20
TO KNOW A MAN AS WE HAVE NEVER KNOWN 666 22
WE KNOW NOTHING OF WITHIN US 666 26
OF KNOW THYSELF KNOWING WE CAN NEVER KNOW 667 13
BECAUSE THEY DON'T KNOW WHAT THEY'LL FIND WHEN THEY DO + 667 21
I DON'T KNOW WHAT YOU MEAN 668 18
DON'T YOU KNOW THAT'S OBSCENE 669 17
UNDER THE GREAT COMMAND KNOW THYSELF AND THAT THOU ART + 674 8
NOW WE HAVE TO ADMIT WE CAN'T KNOW OURSELVES WE CAN ONL+ 674 11
AND I AM NOT INTERESTED TO KNOW ABOUT MYSELF ANY MORE 674 13
ABOUT YOU I KNOW NOTHING NOTHING 676 25
AS A MATTER OF FACT WE KNOW NOTHING 676 27
ALSO I KNOW SO MUCH ABOUT YOU 677 2
AND SO I KNOW 677 4
WE KNOW THAT EVEN GOD COULD NOT IMAGINE THE REDNESS OF + 690 19
WE KNOW IT COULDN'T BE DONE 690 32
BUT TELL ME TELL ME HOW DO YOU KNOW 697 24
LET ME NEVER KNOW O GOD 699 18
LET ME NEVER KNOW WHAT I AM OR SHOULD BE 699 19
LET ME NEVER KNOW MYSELF APART FROM THE LIVING GOD 699 29
BUT STILL I KNOW THAT LIFE IS FOR DELIGHT 709 3
AND PERHAPS IN UNKNOWN DEATH WE PERHAPS SHALL KNOW 710 3
IS A FOOTSTEP ONWARDS ONWARDS WE KNOW NOT WHITHER 713 13
ONWARDS WE KNOW NOT WHITHER 713 18
FOR LIFE IS A WANDERING WE KNOW NOT WHITHER BUT GOING 713 24
KNOW THYSELF AND THAT THOU ART MORTAL 714 5
BUT KNOW THYSELF DENYING THAT THOU ARE MORTAL 714 6
KNOW THYSELF IN DENIAL OF ALL THESE THINGS 714 16
O LET US TALK OF QUIET THAT WE KNOW 717 17
THAT WE CAN KNOW THE DEEP AND LOVELY QUIET 717 18
AND A CEASING TO KNOW A PERFECT CEASING TO KNOW 724 21
HOW TERRIBLE IT WOULD BE TO THINK AND KNOW TO HAVE CONS+ 724 24
FOR WHEN WE KNOW IN FULL WE HAVE LEFT OFF 725 23
WHERE WE MAY CEASE FROM KNOWING AND AS FAR AS WE KNOW 726 19
THEN I SHALL KNOW THAT I AM WALKING STILL 727 4
THEN I SHALL KNOW THAT MY LIFE IS MOVING STILL 727 14
THEN I MUST KNOW THAT STILL 727 27
TO COME AT LAST TO NOTHINGNESS AND KNOW 738 17
I WANT TO KNOW NO MORE I WANT TO SEE 738 25
I KNOW WHERE THEY ARE GOING ALL THE LIVES 744 13
OF NOISELESS DEATH I KNOW IT WELL 744 16
OH AS YOU STAND LOOKING UP DO YOU KNOW IT IS I 750 15
YOU WILL KNOW BY HIS EYES 754 8
ALAS MY LAND IS ENGLAND AND I KNOW NOT HOW NOR WHENCE 757 3
FOR I KNOW THE HOST 772 28
PROGRESS YOU KNOW WE BELIEVE IN PROGRESS 773 23
WHAT THE AMERICA OF THE FUTURE WILL BE WE DON'T KNOW 774 25
WHAT WE KNOW IS THAT THE FUTURE AMERICA 774 26
WE CAN'T KNOW WHAT THE FUTURE OF AMERICA WILL BE 775 1
ONLY KNOW THAT DOING IT YOU FAIL IN POINT OF HONOUR 780 20
HEAR A VOICE SAYING I KNOW YOU NOT 789 7
WHAT IS GOD WE SHALL NEVER KNOW 799 1
NO MAN KNOWS MY FATHER AND I KNOW HIM NOT 799 15
WHICH IS MY FATHER WHOM I KNOW NOT 799 24
ALL THINGS THAT LIFT IN THE LIFT OF LIVING BETWEEN EART+ 801 8
AND THE FEET OF MEN AND THE HANDS OF THE WOMEN KNOW ME 801 19
YOU KNOW NOT HOW MANY ARE HOUSES OF GREY DOGS 807 25
WHEN YOU SLEEP AND KNOW IT NOT 807 28
THE SOURCE AND THE END OF WHICH WE KNOW 811 7
OF LIFE AND TO KNOW 817 7
AND MAKE ME KNOW 817 11
LET US KNOW YOU AND ME 818 19
LET US IN FULL KNOW 818 21
AS YOU KNOW 819 2
AND THESE TWO AS YOU KNOW 820 10
BUT WHAT I WOULD LIKE TO KNOW 830 22
THE CHILDREN OF COURSE KNOW THAT THEY ARE CARED FOR 832 12
SOMETHING WE HAVE NOT BEEN AND THEREFORE CANNOT YET KNOW 832 23
AND KNOW HIMSELF IN THE GLASS 836 10
WE DON'T KNOW HOW LOVELY THE ELEMENTS ARE 839 23
THE VIVIFIER EXISTS AND THEREFORE WE KNOW IT 840 9
I ONLY WANT TO KNOW SOME THINGS TO KNOW ALL THINGS WOUL+ 840 19
SOMETHING THRILLS IN ME AND I KNOW 841 8
SAYING YOU KNOW I ALWAYS HAVE TO SAY THAT ARCHIE LOOKS + 842 20
I DID NOT KNOW LOVE HAD SETTLED DOWN ON ME 860 1
I DIDN'T KNOW IT WAS SO LATE NO SIR I 'AD TO BECAUSE 866 10
DO YOU KNOW WHY I COULD NOT 869 12
I KNOW I KNOW YOU ARE WINSOME SO BUT YOU CHEAT 872 25
I KNOW THE SWEET RED HUTCH OF HIS MOUTH WHERE WARM 876 32
AND WELL I KNOW TO OPEN SILENTLY 878 2
AND AH I KNOW THE SHADOWS THAT THE TREE 878 3
AND WELL I KNOW HE SLEEPS TO WAKE NO MORE 878 7
AH I KNOW HOW YOU HAVE SOUGHT ME 880 9
I DO NOT KNOW WHERE I HAD BEEN 881 18
I ONLY KNOW THAT LIKE A SOD 881 21
I DO NOT KNOW 881 27
I DO NOT KNOW 882 4

KNOW
MY MIND AND I KNOW *894 4
AND THOUGH I SCARCELY SEE THE BOYS OR KNOW THAT THEY AR+ *900 10
AND THOUGH I SCARCELY SEE THE BOYS OR KNOW THAT THEY AR+ *903 22
FLOWING I KNOW NOT HOW YET SERIOUSLY *907 8
AH KNOW THA LIKED 'IM BETT'R NOR ME BUT LET *911 17
AN' WHEN I KNOW FOR SURE MISSIS *920 11
IF THA MAUN KNOW *921 12
DOESN'T TER KNOW WHAT I MEAN TIM YI *921 19
I EXPECT YOU KNOW WHO I AM MRS NAYLOR *923 21
I WANT YOU TO KNOW 'E'S NON MARRYIN' YOU *924 9
BUT SURELY SURELY I KNOW THAT STILL *931 8
YOU'RE A FOOL WOMAN I LOVE YOU AND YOU KNOW I DO *945 17
I KNOW A NOBLE ENGLISHMAN *947 27
DON'T YOU KNOW *947 29
DON'T YOU KNOW *948 13
AND SUPPRESSION OF SUCH FACT LEADS AS WE KNOW DIRECT TO+ *953 5
OH I KNOW *955 11

KNOWABLE
YET SHE IS KNOWABLE 666 21
A MAN AS NEVER YET A MAN WAS KNOWABLE YET STILL SHALL BE 666 23

KNOW-ALL
FOOL IN SPITE OF YOUR PRETTY WAYS AND QUAINT KNOW-ALL 400 18

KNOWED
YER KNOWED AS I WAS COURTIN' TIM MERFIN 81 25
YIS I KNOWED 'E WOR COURTIN' THEE 81 26
AN' THA KNOWED IT AY YET THA COMES ACROSS 139 6
YOU KNOWED AS I WAS COURTIN' TIM MERFIN *923 25
YIS I KNOWED 'E WOR COURTIN' THEE *923 26

KNOWING
OR A DEEPER BRUISE OF KNOWING THAT STILL 100 11
ALONG HER FOOT-SEARCHED WAY WITHOUT KNOWING WHY 131 27
THAT FALL FOR EVER KNOWING NONE 164 15
THOUGH IT'S SORRY I AM ON HIS YOUNG FEET KNOWING 219 27
ME LIKE A GADFLY INTO THE DUSK WITHOUT MY KNOWING 223 5
AND YET A WOMAN KNOWING 239 19
WE MOVE WITHOUT KNOWING WE SLEEP AND WE TRAVEL ON 252 7
DIED AS IT WERE CEASED FROM KNOWING SURPASSED MYSELF 266 5
KNOWING THE THUNDER OF HIS HEART 326 9
NOT KNOWING EACH OTHER FROM BITS OF EARTH OR OLD TINS 357 20
AND I LOOK SHABBY YET MY ROOTS GO BEYOND MY KNOWING 499 6
THE PASSING-BELL OF OUR WAY OF KNOWING 512 9
AND NEVER KNOWING WHEN YOU'LL PROVOKE AN EARTHQUAKE 539 9
AND NEVER KNOWING WHAT WE ARE DOING ROARING BLIND WITH 544 18
UNLESS WE ARE IN TOUCH WITH THAT WHICH LAUGHS AT ALL OU+ 613 10
AS THE BOURGEOIS GETS SECRETLY MORE COWARDLY KNOWING HE+ 663 20
THE BOLSHEVIST GETS OPENLY MORE IMPUDENT ALSO KNOWING H+ 663 22
OF KNOW THYSELF KNOWING WE CAN NEVER KNOW 667 13
I ONLY ENTANGLE MYSELF IN THE KNOWING 674 14
THEY KNEW IT WAS NO USE KNOWING 688 26
KNOWING ITSELF KNOWING ITSELF APART FROM GOD FALLING 701 32
FOR THE DEAD VANITY OF KNOWING BETTER NOR THE BLANK 709 30
KNOWING 725 24
WHERE WE MAY CEASE FROM KNOWING AND AS FAR AS WE KNOW 726 19
KNOWING OUR DEAD ARE FITLY HOUSED IN DEATH 740 23
THE KNOWING SMILE OF THE FINAL VIRGIN IN MAN 770 13
WHERE WE FOREGATHER LIKE GYPSIES NONE KNOWING 812 23
NOR A WISE MAN KNOWING ALL THINGS 840 18
CAVES INWARD KNOWING THE OUTSIDE WORLD 843 4
TO HIS GUEST CHAMBER KNOWING EACH SINEW AND VEIN 877 37
KNOWING THEN I HAD TAKEN MY BOSOM FROM HER CRUSHED BREA+ 882 9

KNOWIN'
BUT I'M SORRY FOR HIM ON HIS YOUNG FEET KNOWIN' *944 7

KNOWLEDGE
THEM AGAIN ON A QUARRY OF KNOWLEDGE THEY HATE TO HUNT 74 10
MYSELF BUT A KNOWLEDGE OF ROOTS OF ROOTS IN THE DARK TH+ 94 3
KNOWLEDGE I SET YOUR HEART TO ITS STRONGER BEAT 156 28
NEW BEYOND KNOWLEDGE OF NEWNESS ALIVE BEYOND LIFE 258 30
WAKENED NOT TO THE OLD KNOWLEDGE 260 16
BUT TO A NEW EARTH A NEW I A NEW KNOWLEDGE A NEW WORLD 260 17
MYSTERY BEYOND KNOWLEDGE OR ENDURANCE SO SUMPTUOUS 260 30
TO HAVE ACCESS TO THE KNOWLEDGE THAT THE GREAT DEAD 263 22
IT TO THE MAN EVEN THE APPLES OF KNOWLEDGE ARE EVE'S FR+ 277 7
BUT TILL THEN TILL THAT APPLE OF KNOWLEDGE SHE HADN'T H+ 284 10
AND HIS HEAD GONE HEAVY WITH THE KNOWLEDGE OF DESIRE 378 14
INTO LOVE MARE-GOAL AND THE KNOWLEDGE OF LOVE 378 19
FOR A NEW DISPENSATION OF KNOWLEDGE 468 10
WITH KNOWLEDGE OF THINGS THAT SHALL NEVER BE ADMITTED 656 18
THE KNOWLEDGE IS WITHIN ME WITHOUT BEING A MATTER OF FA+ 677 3
DID LUCIFER FALL THROUGH KNOWLEDGE 699 14
SAVE ME O GOD FROM FALLING INTO THE UNGODLY KNOWLEDGE 699 16
THROUGH THE SLOW CORRUPTIVE LEVELS OF DISINTEGRATIVE KN+ 699 22
AND STILL THROUGH KNOWLEDGE AND WILL HE CAN BREAK AWAY 700 22
KNOWLEDGE OF THE SELF-APART-FROM-GOD 701 16
FOR THE KNOWLEDGE OF THE SELF-APART-FROM-GOD 701 17
THE END OF ALL KNOWLEDGE IS OBLIVION 726 4
IN A BREEZE OF KNOWLEDGE 742 34
LOOK INTO EACH OTHER'S EYES WITH KNOWLEDGE 770 30
I HAVE A KNOWLEDGE OF LOVELY NIGHT 772 16
WHERE WE CAN LEARN TO FULFIL OUR NEW KNOWLEDGE OF MATER+ 833 23
THEM AGAIN ON A QUARRY OF KNOWLEDGE THEY HATE TO HUNT *895 18
THEM AGAIN ON A QUARRY OF KNOWLEDGE THEY HATE TO HUNT *904 7
MUST HAVE ME ALL IN YOUR WILL AND YOUR KNOWLEDGE AND I *932 14
IN KNOWLEDGE MUST MATE YOU *932 15
AND EATING THE BRAVE BREAD OF A WHOLESOME KNOWLEDGE *959 14

KNOWLEDGELESS
ALL KNOWLEDGELESS 363 10

KNOWN
HELEN HAD I KNOWN YESTERDAY   117 25
HAD I KNOWN YESTERDAY YOU COULD TAKE   117 28
THINGS I HAVE KNOWN THAT SHALL HAVE NO NAME   151 32
SPREAD OUT AND KNOWN AT LAST AND WE ARE SURE   193 8
HAVING KNOWN THE WORLD SO LONG I HAVE NERVER CONFESSED   249 13
SO I HAVE KNOWN IT   264 28
WHAT REMAINS IN ME IS TO BE KNOWN EVEN AS I KNOW   265 31
MORE UTTERLY THAN WE WHO HAVE NEVER KNOWN   286 18
YOU ARE ONLY KNOWN TO US NOW AS THE BADGE OF AN INSURAN+   330 3
AND KNOWN IT SUBTLER THAN FRISSON-SHAKEN NERVES   383 8
I'D NEVER HAVE LET YOU APPROPRIATE ME HAD I KNOWN   395 16
OVER ALL IT HAS KNOWN THAT HAS GONE NOW   455 10
HEAVIER AND HOTTER THAN ANYTHING KNOWN   480 12
BETWEEN MAN AND ALL HIS KNOWN UNIVERSE   482 11
WITH THAT WHICH CAN BE TOUCHED BUT NOT KNOWN   613 7
TO KNOW THE MOON AS WE HAVE NEVER KNOWN   666 20
TO KNOW A MAN AS WE HAVE NEVER KNOWN   666 22
AND EVERY GOD THAT HUMANITY HAS EVER KNOWN IS STILL A G+   671 14
OF EVERYTHING I'VE KNOWN EVEN DREAMILY   738 12
LOVE MY LOVE NOW ALL IS KNOWN   752 6
LOOKS UP AND KNOWS AND IS KNOWN   771 2
AND BE KNOWN JUST SO   818 23
AND NEVER YET KNOWN TO NOD   823 29
THAT I WHO HAVE KNOWN HER A LITTLE AM KEPT   874 3
KNOWN   *900 15
SCARCELY KNOWN   *903 27
KNOWN   *951 22
SO PONDEROUSLY CENTRAL HEAVIER AND HOTTER THAN ANYTHING+   *951 25

KNOWS
AND HE KNOWS FROM THE DEPTHS HE QUITE   39 23
UNDERSTANDS AND KNOWS   39 26
GOODNESS KNOWS IF THEY'LL BE ABLE   45 15
SHE NEITHER KNOWS NOR CARES   54 19
SISTER THA KNOWS WHILE WE WAS ON TH' PLANKS   60 11
KNOWS BUT THE RETREAT OF THE BURNING SHOULDERS THE RED+   67 4
AN' THA'RT THAT RIGHT THA KNOWS 'TIS   83 28
WHY DOES SHE COME WHEN SHE KNOWS WHAT I HAVE TO TELL   85 16
INTO THE WOMB OF THE WORLDS THAT NOTHING KNOWS   89 31
DREAMING GOD KNOWS OF WHAT FOR TO ME SHE'S THE   129 2
GONE ONE KNOWS NOT WHITHER   134 10
AH WHO KNOWS HOW   137 12
THA WANTED TER LEAVE ME THAT BAD THA KNOWS   138 20
THA MIGHT AS WELL LISTEN THA KNOWS   139 9
IT'S TRUE THA KNOWS   139 14
SHE KNOWS THE WASTE ALL DRY BENEATH HER IN ONE PLACE   153 5
THE WIND IS UNCHANGING NOT ONE OF US KNOWS   164 2
FEAR WAS ABROAD WE WHISPERED NO ONE KNOWS US   217 6
WHO KNOWS ME NOT   238 24
GOD KNOWS WHAT I FEEL BUT IT IS JOY   255 9
WHEN SHE KNOWS THE FEARFUL OTHER FLESH AH DARKNESS UNFA+   267 11
HEAVEN KNOWS HOW IT CAME TO PASS   279 6
NOBODY KNOWS YOU   292 18
THAT KNOWS THE DEADLIEST POISON LIKE A SNAKE   304 10
THE LOVELINESS THAT KNOWS NOBLESSE OBLIGE   314 17
HE KNOWS FEAR   336 13
SHE KNOWS   359 13
THE CAT WHO LAPS BLOOD AND KNOWS   383 3
KNOWS THAT THE WATERS HAVE RISEN   462 4
NONE OF US KNOWS O NONE OF US KNOWS   462 5
THE MOSQUITO KNOWS FULL WELL SMALL AS HE IS   466 18
THE BLOOD KNOWS IN DARKNESS AND FOREVER DARK   474 5
THE BLOOD ALSO KNOWS RELIGIOUSLY   474 7
SO A MAN NO LONGER KNOWS HIS OWN HEART   509 5
AND NOBODY KNOWS WHAT THAT IS   515 13
BUT OF COURSE ONE KNOWS THAT BOTH BEAUTY AND PURE   532 11
EH MEN DOESNA HA'E BOSOMS 'APPEN NOT ON'Y THA KNOWS   540 16
THOUGH GOD KNOWS IF YOU'RE ANY BETTER   553 23
KNOWS PERFECTLY WELL   564 27
IF SHE NEVER KNOWS   565 17
WHEN SHE KNOWS WHAT'S WHAT   565 24
ONLY THE BEST MATTERS EVEN THE COW KNOWS IT   587 11
AND NO MAN KNOWS NO WOMAN KNOWS   607 5
THAT CASTS ITS SPERM UPON THE WATERS AND KNOWS NO INTER+   616 25
OH HE KNOWS ALL ABOUT IT HE CASTS A YELLOW EYE   633 26
MR FORD KNOWS IT   635 20
THE BRAIN OF THE MACHINE KNOWS THE LIMBS AND TRUNK OF   635 21
RELIGION KNOWS BETTER THAN PHILOSOPHY   689 26
RELIGION KNOWS THAT JESUS NEVER WAS JESUS   689 27
EVEN AN ARTIST KNOWS THAT HIS WORK WAS NEVER IN HIS MIND   690 3
BUT HE KNOWS NOTHING BEFOREHAND   690 9
EACH KNOWS THE OTHER IN STRUGGLE   714 23
WHO KNOWS WHO KNOWS HOW MUCH OUR MODERN WOE   723 4
MAN KNOWS NOTHING   726 1
TILL HE KNOWS HOW NOT-TO-KNOW   726 2
HE KNOWS ME BUT DOES NOT SPEAK INSTEAD   734 28
THEY RETURN RELENTLESSLY IN THE SILENCE ONE KNOWS THEIR+   739 14
AND KNOWS DEPARTING IN SILENCE   769 27
LOOKS UP AND KNOWS AND IS KNOWN   771 2
NO MAN KNOWS MY FATHER AND I KNOW HIM NOT   799 15
FREE WHAT FOR NOBODY KNOWS BUT FREE   832 10
THE ROAD WINDS FOREVER AND WHICH OF US KNOWS   858 2
FROM THE QUIET CHURCH-TOWER THAT KNOWS NO PRATTLE OF CH+   858 22
THA KNOWS 'E 'D A WINSOME WAY WI 'IM AN' SHE   *910 24
SISTER THA KNOWS WHILE WE WAS ON THE PLANKS   *910 26

KNOW THYSELF
OF KNOW THYSELF KNOWING WE CAN NEVER KNOW   667 13
KNOW THYSELF   832 21

KRISHNA
FOR A MOMENT GODLY LIKE BAAL OR KRISHNA OR ADONIS OR BA+   675 16

KRONOS
BY ARES AND KRONOS AND ZEUS   702 11

LABORATORY
AND MEN OFTEN SUCCUMB LIKE WHITE MICE IN A LABORATORY A+   619 22
TO FIND THE OTHER MANY ELEMENTS YOU MUST GO TO THE LABO+   706 6

LABORIOUSLY
IS HEAVY AND MY HEART BEATS SLOWLY LABORIOUSLY   95 2

LABOUR
AND LAUGHING WITH LABOUR LIVING THEIR WORK LIKE A GAME   72 11
AND SWEAT OF LABOUR AND THE MEANEST FASHION   89 13
THE GHASTLY DREAM OF LABOUR AND THE STENCH OF STEEL AND+   175 1
MONEY FROM OUT OF THE EARTH OR THE BEAST OR THE MAN AS +   175 24
SCORNING THE PANACEA EVEN OF LABOUR   197 15
AND RUNNING AWAY FROM THE SOUND OF A WOMAN IN LABOUR   366 12
O CEASE TO LABOUR FOR THE GOLD-TOOTHED DEAD   441 30
LABOUR IS THE ONE THING A MAN HAS HAD TOO MUCH OF   517 18
LET'S ABOLISH LABOUR LET'S HAVE DONE WITH LABOURING   517 19
LABOUR   517 21
HEY WITH THIS ENDLESS LABOUR AND LITTLE-SOULED FRET   859 26
IN THE FAR-OFF LABOUR OF MEN IN THE FIELD   *915 2

LABOURER
WAVE FRIGHTENED WHO COMES A LABOURER ALAS   41 4

LABOURERS
A GANG OF LABOURERS ON THE PILED WET TIMBER   72 4
OH LABOURERS OH SHUTTLES ACROSS THE BLUE FRAME OF MORNI+   73 8
AND DOWN BELOW IN THE GREEN WHEAT THE LABOURERS   208 26
FOUR LABOURERS PASS WITH THEIR SCYTHES   220 16

LABOURING
LET'S ABOLISH LABOUR LET'S HAVE DONE WITH LABOURING   517 19
SICKEN US AND WE ARE STUNNED BY THE RUSHINGS OF THE LAB+   856 2
HIS COAT AND HIS ARMS AND HIS LABOURING HEART ARE STRAN+   871 25
IS SWELLING WITH WIDESPREAD LABOURING CONCENTRATION   *908 2
OH THE MIRACLE OF THE WHOLE THE WIDESPREAD LABOURING CO+   *909 19
AND WATCHING THE GREAT THING LABOURING THROUGH THE WHOL+   *909 23
AS IT QUICKENS WITHIN THE LABOURING WHITE-HOT METAL   *909 26

LABOURS
NAY EVEN THE SLUMBEROUS EGG AS IT LABOURS UNDER THE SHE+   64 11
IN THE SILENT LABOURS OF MEN IN THE FIELD   68 18
THAT SLOWLY LABOURS IN A VAST TRAVAIL   195 33
WHO LABOURS ALL DAY IN THE SUN   758 12

LABURNUM
LABURNUM GIVES BACK TO LIGHT   104 32
OH AND SEE THE LABURNUM SHIMMERING   106 3

LABYRINTH
DOWN THE LABYRINTH OF THE SINISTER FLOWER   166 23

LACE
FLOWERY MANTILLA OF LACE   105 30
HAD BEEN WOVEN INTO A GLORIOUS MESH LIKE A BRIDAL LACE   860 14

LACERATE
WHEELING TO LACERATE AND RIP UP THIS MY BODY   741 13

LACERATING
THEIR SCENT IS LACERATING AND REPELLENT   270 17

LACK
FOR YOU ARE SULLEN-HEARTED STILL AND LACK   153 18
A POOL PUT OFF THE SOUL YOU'VE GOT OH LACK   161 27
LACK OF YOU   214 16
FOR FEAR OF THE LACK IN DEATH   214 22
LACK OF BREAD   263 10
AND LACK OF MEANING   510 29
DO YOU LACK VITALITY   558 16
PERHAPS WHAT'S WRONG IS SIMPLY LACK OF VITALITY   842 28

LACONIC
AND LOOK WITH LACONIC BLACK EYES   353 12
HER LACONIC EYE HAS AN EARTHY MATERIALISTIC LOOK   359 33

LACQUER-MUCUS
AND THE GOLD-AND-GREEN PURE LACQUER-MUCUS COMES OFF IN   339 15

LAD
LAD   34 18
WHEER'S 'E HURT THIS TIME LAD   45 9
LAD NEVER STEPPED TILL 'E GOT IN WITH YOUR LOT   60 31
TO HA' 'TICED A LAD O' TWENTY-FIVE   77 15
ATWEEN A LAD AN' 'IS WIFE   77 20
NO CAUSE FOR SURPRISE AT ALL MY LAD   80 17
THA'RT FOR DOIN' A LOT WI' T' LAD   82 8
FOR LETTIN' ME MARRY THE LAD AS I THOUGHT   82 11
OF YER'S TOO MUCH FOR THIS LAD   84 24
LAD SHOULD I TELL THEE SUMMAT   137 19
LAD BUT I'M TELLIN' THEE SUMMAT   137 24
NOW LAD I'M AXIN' THEE SUMMAT   138 2
SEVEN DAYS MY LAD OR NONE   138 6
AY LAD I'LL TELL THEE THY MIND   138 28
A WOMAN'S MAN THA ART MA LAD   140 1
SORT O' WOMAN FOR ANY LAD   140 5
AND REMEMBER THE SMALL LAD LYING INTENT TO LOOK   161 9
LAD THOU HAST GOTTEN A CHILD IN ME   220 6
LAD UP THERE   388 25
WHEN I WAS A LAD   395 8
LITTLE I THOUGHT WHEN I WAS A LAD   488 15
'ARK 'ERE LAD ATWEEN THEE AN' ME   490 28
AND THE LAD YOU USED TO BE   549 16

LAD
COMES REALLY OUT OF THEIR GUTS LAD   549 21
WHO'D EVER HAVE THOUGHT IT OF THAT LAD A   552 23
LOOK OUT MY LAD YOU'VE GOT 'EM ON YOUR TRACK   634 9
YOU LAD WILL YOU ASK THE BOSS   759 6
TO HA' 'TICED A LAD O' TWENTY-FIVE   *919 3
ATWEEN A LAD AN' 'IS WIFE   *919 8
NO CAUSE FOR SURPRISE AT ALL MY LAD   *922 17
THA'RT FOR DOIN' A LOT WI' TH' LAD   *924 12
FOR LETTIN' ME MARRY THE LAD AS I THOUGHT   *924 15
LAD THA'S GOTTEN A CHILDT IN ME   *944 14
MY YOUNG SLIM LAD AN' I'M SORRY FOR THEE   *944 16

LADDER
WE CLIMBED THE HUNTSMAN'S LADDER AND SAT SWINGING   216 22
UP HE GOES UP THE BLOOMIN' LADDER   552 21
WE CLIMBED THE HUNTSMAN'S LADDER AND SAT SWINGING   *942 8

LADDERS
FOLLOW ME NOW UP THE LADDERS OF SPARKS   798 11

LADDER-TOPS
OF FLOWERS SURGE FROM BELOW TO THEIR LADDER-TOPS   136 13

LADDIE
LADDIE A MAN THOU'LT HA'E TO BE   220 7

LADDIE-LASS
BUT MY DEAREST DEAREST LADDIE-LASS   835 21

LADEN
WISE WONDERFUL STRANDS OF WINDS THAT ARE LADEN WITH RARE *938 22

LADIES
LADIES   71 24
AND SKIES OF GOLD AND LADIES IN BRIGHT TISSUE   135 4
QUEENS LADIES ANGELS WOMEN RARE   234 25
DEAR LADIES NONE WHATSOEVER   541 14
ALL THESE GRACIOUS LADIES   556 25
GREATEST OF LADIES   695 16
YOU FORTY LADIES IN THE HAREM BOWER   758 6

LADS
SHOUTING LADS   75 9
THAT FUTURE NOTTINGHAM LADS WOULD BE   489 1
UP I ROSE MY LADS AN' I HEARD YER   552 17
NEVER YOU MIND MY LADS I LEFT YOU   552 25
WE'RE GETTING TO BE BIG LADS NOW AN' SOON   573 19
WHEN MEN AND WOMEN WHEN LADS AND GIRLS ARE NOT THINKING   672 1
LIKE A PICTURE BY THAULOW DARK CLUSTERS OF SHOUTING LADS   865 19
LADS IN THEIR WARM LIGHT SLIPPERS BOUND DOWN THE HALL T+   865 28
OF THEIR DANCING BLOOD LADS SUCKING THE COLD MOISTURE F+   865 29

LAD'S
THE STRANGER'S HAIR WAS SHORN LIKE A LAD'S DARK POLL   156 1

LADS'
TO FEEL THE LADS' LOOKS LIGHT ON ME   91 27
TO FEEL THE LADS' LOOKS LIGHT ON ME   *899 11
TO FEEL THE LADS' LOOKS LIGHT ON ME   *902 23

LADY
A LILAC THERE LIKE A LADY WHO BRAIDS   105 25
BETROTHED YOUNG LADY WHO LOVES ME AND TAKES GOOD   129 4
THE TIGHT-ROPE LADY PINK AND BLONDE AND NUDE-LOOKING   444 24
AND MACBETH AND HIS LADY WHO SHOULD HAVE BEEN CHORING   494 22
THEN SUDDENLY THE MASTODON ROSE WITH THE WONDERFUL LADY   540 5
REAL LADY   548 16
A LADY   581 11
SAID THE LOVELY YOUNG LADY HALF WISTFUL HALF MENACING   604 7
GREAT LADY GREAT GLORIOUS LADY   695 15
BE GOOD TO ME LADY GREAT LADY OF THE NEAREST   695 20
NOW I AM AT YOUR GATE YOU BEAUTY YOU LADY OF ALL NAKEDN+   695 22
MOON O MOON GREAT LADY OF THE HEAVENLY FEW   695 24
AND KISS OF THE FAR-OFF LINGERING LADY WHO LOOKS OVER T+   695 31
NOW LADY OF THE MOON NOW OPEN THE GATE OF YOUR SILVERY +   696 1
INTO YOUR HOUSE GARMENTLESS LADY OF THE LAST GREAT GIFT   696 3
LADY LADY OF THE LAST HOUSE DOWN THE LONG LONG STREET O+   696 8

LADY C
FOR HELPING WITH LADY C   550 20
AND WE TALKED AND WE ROARED AND YOU TYPED LADY C   550 32
OVER LADY C   557 12
WITH LADY C   557 22
WHEN WE PRINTED LADY C   668 7

LADY JANE
THAT LADY JANE   562 17

LADY JEAN
AND DEAR OLD LADY JEAN   668 17
WAIT DEAR LADY JEAN WAIT A MINUTE   668 23
AND YOU DEAR LADY JEAN ARE YOU CONNIE   669 2

LADYLIKE
TRIPPING ABOUT WITH THEIR LADYLIKE HAMS   765 11

LADY POVERTY
THE ONLY PEOPLE I EVER HEARD TALK ABOUT MY LADY POVERTY   498 9

LADY-SECRETARY
LIKE A SHOP-LADY OR A LADY-SECRETARY   548 20

LADY-SMOCKS
YOUR OWN DARK MOUTH WITH THE BRIDAL FAINT LADY-SMOCKS   90 11

LADY-SMOCK
YOU YOUR SOUL LIKE A LADY-SMOCK LOST EVANESCENT   90 17

LADY'S
IN THE LADY'S   669 15

LAGGING
INEXORABLE LOVE GOES LAGGING   64 6

LAGOON-WATER
LIKE LAGOON-WATER THAT HAS BEEN TOO MUCH SUNNED   708 4

LAID
MY LOVE THAT SPINNING COIN LAID STILL   59 21
ON HIS LIMBS IN SLEEP AT LAST LAID LOW   60 7
AND LAID AGAINST HER CHEEK   73 24
AND LAID THE DESERT HORRIFIC OF SILENCE AND SNOW ON THE+   75 16
AN' THA'S LAID AGAINST ME AN' MELTED   80 10
THEY BURIED HER HALF IN THE GRAVE WHEN THEY LAID HER AW+   114 21
O THE GOLDEN SPARKLES LAID EXTINCT   120 6
AND BEAUTIFULLY LAID IN BLACK ON A GOLD-GREY SKY   146 29
LIKE THE PROW OF A BOAT HIS HEAD LAID BACK LIKE THE STE+   155 20
SO SHE LAID HER HANDS AND PRESSED THEM DOWN MY SIDES   254 22
THE SECRET IS LAID BARE   284 4
WISE TORTOISE LAID HIS EARTHY PART AROUND HIM HE CAST I+   348 13
THIS IS YOUR MOTHER SHE LAID YOU WHEN YOU WERE AN EGG   357 2
ON THE YELLOW POINTED ASPEN-TREES LAID ONE ON ANOTHER L+   409 14
IN A LONG LINE THEIR HEADS LAID OVER EACH OTHER'S NECKS   445 20
IN TIMELESSNESS LAID BY IN NOISELESS DEATH   744 3
SHE'S LAID AN EGG   761 23
I'VE LAID AN EGG   761 24
I'VE LAID AN EGG   761 26
I BREATHED MY DREAMS UPON YOU I LAID MY MOUTH ON YOUR M+   871 1
THEN HE LAID DOWN THE BOW OF HIS VIOLIN   884 8
AND LAID LAUGHTERLESS ON HER CHEEK   *913 16
EFFLUENCE FROM SUFFERING FOLK-STUFF WHICH DEATH HAS LAI+   *938 23

LAIN
WE MIGHT HAVE LAIN   243 8
AT WHOSE SIDE I HAVE LAIN FOR OVER A THOUSAND NIGHTS   260 6
BURY A MAN GENTLY IF HE HAS LAIN DOWN AND DIED   442 1
WHO HAD LAIN HER SHIFT ON THE SHORE ON THE SHINGLE SLOPE   693 4
YET I HAVE LAIN IN HIS LOINS ERE HE BEGOT ME IN MOTHER +   801 14
PRESSES HER HAND TO HER BOSOM WHERE THE FRUIT HAS LAIN   864 20
THA'S LAIN RIGHT UP TO ME LIZZIE AN' MELTED   *922 10

LAIR
ON ITS LAIR   159 6
BROKE IN HER LAIR   171 12
THAT LONDON LAIR OF SUDDEN   171 14
THE SUN COMES IN THEIR LAIR THEY ARE WELL-OFF   325 17
AND ABOVE AND ABOVE THE TREES I FOUND HER LAIR   402 11

LAKE
HERE BY THE DARKENED LAKE   227 6
WITH THE MOUNTAIN SNOWS ACROSS THE LAKE   228 10
DRIBBLING OVER THE LAKE   229 6
AND IS HALF WAY OVER THE LAKE   229 11
AND FALTERS A FEW SHORT STEPS ACROSS THE LAKE   230 6
SEE GLITTERING ON THE MILK-BLUE MORNING LAKE   230 8
BEHIND ME ON THE LAKE I HEAR THE STEAMER DRUMMING   231 5
UNDER MINE LIKE A STAR ON THE LAKE   248 26
BUT SITTING IN A BOAT ON THE ZELLER LAKE   337 28
CRY LOUDLY BEYOND THE LAKE OF WATERS   365 35
HOST ON THE SHORES OF THE LAKE LIKE THICK WILD RICE BY   391 9
ABOVE THE PALM-TREES OF THE ISLET IN THE LAKE   391 19
HONKING OVER THE LAKE   704 26
THEN SUDDENLY HE SPIED THE OLD LAKE AND HE THREW IT IN   791 7
ALONG THE LAKE LIKE SEALS LIKE SEALS   824 18

LAKE-LIGHTS
WHEN I WOKE THE LAKE-LIGHTS WERE QUIVERING ON THE WALL   243 21

LAMB
HE SAW IN A SHAFT OF LIGHT A LAMB ON A PINNACLE BALANCI+   324 16
HE FOUND THE LAMB BEYOND HIM ON THE INACCESSIBLE PINNAC+   324 20
AND ALSO TO ENCOURAGE THE RED-CROSS LAMB   325 21
SINCE THE LAMB BEWITCHED HIM WITH THAT RED-STRUCK FLAG   327 3
AND LISTENING INWARDLY TO THE FIRST BLEAT OF A LAMB   366 14
WHO IS LOSING HER LAMB   414 26
O SPILL THE BLOOD NOT OF YOUR FIRSTLING LAMB WITHOUT SP+   678 22
BUT KILL THE SCABBED AND UGLY LAMB THAT SPREADS CONTAGI+   678 23
SHORN LIKE THE SHORN LAMB TO EVERY ICY GAZE   836 4
NOR EVEN LIKE AN ANIMAL BULL RAM OR LION OR LAMB   840 26

LAMBENT
OF LAMBENT HEAVEN A PLEDGING-CUP   177 10
OF BLISS TILL ALL HER LAMBENT BEAUTY SHAKES TOWARDS US   193 7
IT WOULD BE LAMBENT UNEASY   205 19
JESUS' PALE AND LAMBENT DOVE COOING IN THE LOWER BOUGHS   329 8
MY SOUL COMES LAMBENT FROM THE ENDLESS NIGHT   744 5
I LIFT MY LITTLE PURE AND LAMBENT FLAME   745 10
OF PURE AND LAMBENT HOSTAGE FROM THE DEAD   745 14
THE PERFECT LAMBENT FLAME WHICH STILL GOES UP   745 36

LAMB OF GOD
AH LAMB OF GOD   324 1

LAMBS
YOU TELL ME THE LAMBS HAVE COME THEY LIE LIKE DAISIES W+   57 25
LAMBS FRISK AMONG THE DAISIES OF HIS BRAIN   624 9
EVEN THE LAMBS WILL STRETCH FORTH THEIR NECKS LIKE SERP+   624 16
AND THE LAMBS WILL BITE OFF THE HEADS OF THE DAISIES FO+   625 7

LAME
  LAME   799 13

LAMED
  WHITELY CONFRONT I WAIT ON THE GRASS AM LAMED   225 12

LAMENT
  EVERLASTING LAMENT IN EVERLASTING DESIRE   378 30
  SHALL WE LAMENT FOR WHAT IS BEREFT US   *916 18

LAMP
  SOMEWHERE THE LAMP HANGING LOW FROM THE CEILING   41 6
  AND THEN YOU LAMP YOU LEMON-COLOURED BEAUTY   73 2
  IN THE DYING LAMP OF MY LOVE   121 27
  AWAY IN THE DISTANCE WAKES A LAMP   163 25
  NEVER A LAMP DISTRESS   261 22
  AND BURN BLUE AND COLD LIKE THE FLAME IN A MINER'S LAMP   619 5
  BURSTS LIKE AN ARC LAMP INTO LIGHT   773 2
  AND THE STAR IS THE LAMP IN THE HAND OF THE UNKNOWN MOV+ 801 11
  THAT IS MY HOME WHERE THE LAMP GLEAMS AFAR   857 27
  WE MUST KEEP YOUR LAMP ALIGHT NEVERTHELESS JEANNETTE   859 27
  AND I LOOKED IN A ROOM WHERE THE LAMP AS A MOON IN MIST   865 1
  THE LIGHTED LAMP INTO MY ROOM AT NIGHT   875 9
  WHILE THE STREET LAMP CENSERS SWINGING HIGH   *916 19

LAMP-FRINGED
  NO LAMP-FRINGED FROCK   170 28

LAMPLIGHT
  AGAINST THE WIND AND IF WHERE THE LAMPLIGHT BLEW   180 13
  THAT LIVE BY NIGHT AND LAMPLIGHT AND FIRELIGHT DO THEM + 331 8

LAMP-LIGHT
  THE PLANE-LEAVES FALL THROUGH THE LAMP-LIGHT LIKE TIRED+ *917 9

LAMP-LIKE
  HER WHITE HER LAMP-LIKE SHAPE   103 32

LAMP-LIT
  WHEN THE DAWN IS FAR BEHIND THE STAR THAT THE LAMP-LIT + *917 25

LAMPS
  BARE STEMS OF STREET LAMPS STIFFLY STAND   51 1
  OF LEAVES AND LAMPS AND THE CITY STREET MINGLED   111 6
  LAMPS IN A WASH OF RAIN   119 8
  THE LOW-HUNG LAMPS STRETCHED DOWN THE STREET   121 18
  NOW LAMPS LIKE YELLOW ECHOES GLIMMER AMONG   135 9
  HERE LAMPS ARE WHITE LIKE SNOWDROPS IN THE GRASS   136 1
  LAMPS IS RAYED WITH GOLDEN BANDS   144 4
  PAIN YET THE LIGHT OF LAMPS AND CANDLES HAS NO FEARS FO+ 331 4
  THE SHINING OF LAMPS BECAUSE WITH HIS RAYS HE HURTS THE+ 331 7
  BLACK LAMPS FROM THE HALLS OF DIS BURNING DARK BLUE   697 9
  GIVING OFF DARKNESS BLUE DARKNESS AS DEMETER'S PALE LAM+ 697 10
  LAMPS IN A WASH OF RAIN   *932 17
  THE LAMPS ARE WHITE LIKE SNOWDROPS IN THE GRASS   *938 29
  AND LAMPS LIKE VENTUROUS GLOW-WORMS STEAL AMONG   *939 9
  BLACK LAMPS FROM THE HALLS OF DIS SMOKING DARK BLUE   *956 7

LAMP-TOUCHED
  THE NIGHT WITH SILENCE CROSSING THE LAMP-TOUCHED TIDE   144 13

LANCE
  LANCE   57 16

LAND
  TO TESTIFY TO A BLIGHT ON THE LAND   51 3
  SCHOOL NOW IS THE ROCK IN THIS WEARY LAND THE WINTER BU+ 75 18
  LAND AS ONWARD THE LONG ROAD GOES   163 20
  OF THIS LAND WHEREON THE WRONG ROAD GOES   164 16
  AND ASKS IF SHE SEES THE LAND THE LAND   201 3
  THE LAND OF HER GLAD SURMISE   201 4
  TILL THEY HALT AT A CLIFF ON THE EDGE OF THE LAND   201 15
  AND LAND THAT BEATS WITH A PULSE   261 4
  THE CRUMBLING DAMP FRESH LAND LIFE HORIZONTAL AND CEASE+ 321 18
  TO BOW BEFORE ROYALTY IN THE LAND OF ELEPHANTS BOW DEEP 391 28
  FOR A NEW SIGNAL FROM LIFE IN THAT SILENT LOST LAND OF + 394 12
  WE WALK IN OUR SLEEP IN THIS LAND   407 26
  YET LIVING ON THE FAT OF THE LAND   535 20
  WORLD SHINE LIKE THE PROMISED LAND   554 8
  IS SETTLED ON THE LAND ROSES ARE SCARCE IN ENGLAND VERY 569 8
  IF EVER I LIVED UPON DRY LAND   574 12
  WITH GIDDY FREEDOM IN THE LAND OF THE FREE   575 10
  OF EVERY LAND OR EAST OR WEST   575 13
  I LOVE MY NATIVE LAND THE BEST ETC ETC   575 14
  THAT FIGS AREN'T FOUND IN THE LAND OF THE FREE   579 8
  FIG-TREES DON'T GROW IN MY NATIVE LAND   579 9
  WHERE HE DOES NOT CHOOSE TO LAND THEM YET HOOKED FISHES 586 11
  AH WHEN HE BEGINS TO DRAW THE LINE IN TIGHT TO LAND HIS 586 21
  WHERE HE DOES NOT CHOOSE TO LAND THEM YET HOOKED FISHES 632 26
  DON'T SPILL THE SALT FOR IT IS THE LAND MARK   706 15
  THE FOE CAN TAKE OUR GOODS OUR HOMES AND LAND   736 16
  THEY SET FOOT ON THIS LAND TO WHICH THEY HAVE THE RIGHT 739 13
  HAVE I NOTHING IN THIS DARK LAND   749 13
  ALAS MY LAND IS ENGLAND AND I KNOW NOT HOW NOR WHENCE   757 3
  LAND BETTER INSTEAD OF WASTING TIME   777 32
  THE INDIANS OF THE PUEBLOS HAVE LAND   778 26
  LET THEM LEASE THEIR LAND TO THE AMERICAN GOVERNMENT   778 27
  THE BIT OF LAND IN QUESTION IS A FLEA-BITE   779 13
  BITS OF RESERVED LAND IT WERE A FLEA-BITE   779 16
  TO MAKE THIS BIT OF LAND AND WATER-RIGHTS   779 18
  AND THITHER THEY RETURN FROM THE LAND OF MEN   799 4
  IN THE LAND OF THE LOST   816 15

LANDED
  AND LANDED THEM ALL ON TOAST   536 23
  FORE-RUNNERS HAVE BARELY LANDED ON THE SHORE   607 4

LANDLADY
  ME GOTTEN A CHILDT TER THY LANDLADY   80 3
  AN' IF MY LANDLADY SEED ME LIKE IT   80 13
  ME GOTTEN A CHILDT TO THY LANDLADY   *922 3
  AN' IF MY LANDLADY SEED ME LIKE IT   *922 13

LANDMARK
  IT IS THE WHITE STONE OF LIMITS THE TERM THE LANDMARK B+ 706 11
  AND CURSED BE HE THAT REMOVETH HIS NEIGHBOUR'S LANDMARK 706 16

LANDS
  UNDER THE ALMOND-TREE THE HAPPY LANDS   58 16
  ON THE MISTY WASTE LANDS AWAY FROM THE FLUSHING GREY   164 21
  I CARRY MY PATIENCE SULLENLY THROUGH THE WASTE LANDS   167 3
  BUT MUD HAS FLOODED THE HOMES OF THESE WEARY LANDS   167 11
  I CARRY MY PATIENCE SULLENLY THROUGH THE WASTE LANDS   167 16
  THE ALIEN TREES IN ALIEN LANDS AND YET   305 1
  SOME MEMORY OF FAR SUN-GENTLER LANDS   305 33
  THAT WE LEASE OUR LANDS AND GET REAPERS   779 9
  WHEAT FROM THE HIGH LANDS AND MAIZE   793 21
  COFFEE FROM THE BUSHES IN THE HOT LANDS EVEN THE JUICY + 793 22
  TAKE BACK OUR LANDS AND SILVER AND OIL TAKE THE TRAINS + 794 21
  I CARRY MY ANGER SULLENLY 'CROSS THESE WASTE LANDS   *896 21

LANDSCAPE
  THE OPEN BOOK OF LANDSCAPE NO MORE FOR THE COVERS OF DA+ 88 8
  LITTLE BLACK SPOT IN THE LANDSCAPE   397 10
  TO BE HUSBANDLY AND GIVE PERPENDICULAR TO THE LANDSCAPE 835 3
  TO THE EFFULGENT LANDSCAPE OF OUR IMMORTAL GIRLY-WIRLY 835 4

LANE
  TROPICAL LANE   366 26
  UP THE LANE   562 19
  SENDING THEM RIOTING AT DAWN DOWN THE LANE OF SCARLET P+ 860 23
  YOUR HAIR PEEP OUT ON THE LANE   886 3

LANES
  GOING DOWN THE STRANGE LANES OF HELL MORE AND MORE   281 4
  ORPHEUS AND THE WINDING LEAF-CLOGGED SILENT LANES OF HE+ 281 16
  SEEKING THE OFFAL AND GARBAGE OF LIFE IN THE INVISIBLE + 796 6

LANGUAGE
  I HAVE BEEN TAUGHT THE LANGUAGE OF UNDERSTANDING   264 2
  FOR WHICH THE LANGUAGE IS LOST   296 4
  I BOOZE AND FORNICATE AND USE FOUL LANGUAGE AND DESPISE 432 18
  THE PRETTY PRETTY BOURGEOIS PINKS HIS LANGUAGE JUST AS + 432 28
  IN LANGUAGE OF COMMON-SENSE   488 26
  IN SUCH LOVELY LANGUAGE   494 15
  YET THE LANGUAGE SO LOVELY LIKE THE DYES FROM GAS-TAR   494 26
  AND STILL SPEAK HIS NATIVE LANGUAGE THE BEST   575 23
  IS THE LANGUAGE DEAD AND EMPTY OF REPLY   633 13

LANGUAGES
  AND CROUCHING AND SPEAKING THE MUSIC OF LOST LANGUAGES 688 16

LANGUIDLY
  LANGUIDLY MONTH BY MONTH   766 8

LANGUISHING
  WHEN YOU HEAR IT LANGUISHING   433 21

LANGUISHINGLY
  BUT IT BREATHES GENTLY AND LANGUISHINGLY IN THE BACK OF+ 434 3

LANTERN
  LAST NIGHT WHEN I WENT WITH THE LANTERN THE SOW WAS GRA+ 38 8
  GREEN LANTERN OF PURE LIGHT A LITTLE INTENSE FUSING TRI+ 206 10
  A MAN WITH A LANTERN SWINGING   227 3
  TAKE THE LANTERN AND WATCH THE SOW FOR FEAR SHE GRAB HE+ *892 24
  THE MOON LIKE A REDDENING LANTERN HANGS LOW ACROSS THE + *917 13

LANTERNS
  TINY LIGHTHOUSES LITTLE SOULS OF LANTERNS COURAGE BURST+ 206 16
  YOUR LITTLE LANTERNS BEHIND YOU AH IT CHEERS   221 22
  YOUR LITTLE LANTERNS BEHIND YOU IT CHEERS   *945 8

LAOCOON
  AND LEAVE THE FEARFUL LAOCOON OF HIS FELLOW-MAN ENTANGL+ 632 7
  ENTANGLED IN THE LAOCOON COILS OF OUR CONCEIT   674 10

LAP
  THAT FALLS ON YOUR LAP OF MOULD   162 11
  INTO THE WOMAN'S FERTILE FATHOMLESS LAP   172 7
  SHADOWS IN THEIR LAP   223 14
  YOU LOVE TO LAP UP AFFECTION TO WALLOW IN IT   396 22
  TO LAP THEM ROUND WITH LOVE AND LAY THEM BY   736 20
  IS ONE FOOT IN THE LAP OF A WOMAN   819 7
  AND I'LL LIE IN HER LAP WHERE THE WORLD'S WILD ROSE   858 6

LAPPED
  LAPPED LIKE A BODY CLOSE UPON A SLEEP   195 27
  THE CAT HAS LAPPED   383 7
  CREEPING AMONG THE SLEEPING AND THE DREAMING WHO ARE LA+ 807 6
  LAPPED PRISONER IN THE CORDS OF LOVE I HAVE SPUN   884 16

LAPPING
  THE UNROLLING OF FERNS WHITE TONGUES OF THE ACANTHUS LA+ 623 27
  AND RIPPLES POISE AND RUN LAPPING ACROSS THE WATER   *912 27
  THEY POISE AND RUN LIKE RIPPLES LAPPING ACROSS THE WATER *914 1
  THE UNROLLING OF FERNS WHILE TONGUES OF ACANTHUS LAPPIN+ *953 15

LAPS
  LAPS LITTLE CREST AFTER CREST   194 8
  THE CAT WHO LAPS BLOOD AND KNOWS   383 3

LAPSE
LEAVE HER NO CHOICE MAKE HER LAPSE ME-WARD MAKE HER   213 28
IN THE LAPSE OF THE LOWEST OF TIDES   509 15
WITH THE DEEP OBLIVION OF EARTH'S LAPSE AND RENEWAL   727 16
OH LOVELY LAST LAST LAPSE OF DEATH INTO PURE OBLIVION   *960 3

LAPSED
AND REMAIN LAPSED ON EARTH   352 6
WHEN I AM GONE COMPLETELY LAPSED AND GONE   724 29

LAPSING
DRIFTS MY BOAT WISTFULLY LAPSING AFTER   53 18
YOU WOULD WEEP TO BE LAPSING ON SUCH HARMONY   251 28
ARE WE NOTHING ALREADY BUT THE LAPSING OF A GREAT DEAD 429 1
AND THE LITTLE SHIP WINGS HOME FALTERING AND LAPSING   720 14
DRIFTS MY BOAT WISTFULLY LAPSING AFTER   *906 9
AH PEACE AH LOVELY PEACE MOST LOVELY LAPSING   *960 1

LARCH
AND THE LARCH THAT IS ONLY A COLUMN IT GOES UP TOO TALL+ 647 1

LARD
THEMSELVES WITH OIL AND LARD   460 14
THEMSELVES WITH OIL AND LARD   460 18

LARGE
WHAT LARGE DARK HANDS ARE THOSE AT THE WINDOW   42 1
AH SOON IN HIS LARGE HARD HANDS SHE DIES   43 12
GIRLS WITH THEIR LARGE EYES WIDE WITH TRAGEDY   71 21
HER LARGE BROWN HAND STRETCHED OVER   123 20
AND I DO NOT CARE THOUGH THE LARGE HANDS OF REVENGE   126 1
THOUGH HER HANDS ARE STILL THE WOMAN HER LARGE STRONG   128 5
LARGE SHADOWS FROM THE OUTSIDE STREET-LAMP BLOWN   140 14
IT IS LARGE SO LARGE I COULD NOT SEE IT BEFORE   203 19
AND A BULL'S LARGE SOMBRE GLANCING EYE   325 28
SHE IS LARGE AND MATRONLY   358 22
YOU ARE ALMOST TOO LARGE I AM ALMOST FRIGHTENED   359 29
OR THE BURDEN OF MAN WRIT LARGE   411 13
IN THE W C WRIT LARGE   492 18
WHICH MANKIND AT LARGE HAS CHOSEN TO SANCTIFY   620 21
THEY ARE SO LARGE AND THEY CRADLE SO MUCH OF A MAN   700 18
FOR THE LORD TO COME FORTH AT LARGE ON THE SCENT OF BLO+ 742 19
THERE IS THE SPANGLED DRAGON OF THE STARS AT LARGE   796 20
AND PUT A DIRTY GREEN LARGE CABAGE   845 25
IN THOSE UGLY GREEN LARGE CARS   846 3
NO LONGER A LARGE FLECK MOVING IN THE SUNSHINE   870 14
HER LARGE BROWN HAND LOOMED OVER   *934 26
AND I DO NOT CARE THOUGH THE LARGE HANDS OF REVENGE   *937 1

LARGELY
BREATHE LARGELY THE LUMINOUS BREEZE   69 8
BREATHE LARGELY THE LUMINOUS BREEZE   *915 20

LARK
THE LARK SINGS LOUD AND GLAD   110 9
AND MOUNT LIKE A LARK BELOVED   322 28
THAT MY HEART WHICH LIKE A LARK AT HEAVEN'S GATE SINGIN+ 322 30
THE LARK NESTS IN HIS HEART   624 11
THE TRILLING LARK IN A WILD DESPAIR WILL TRILL DOWN ARR+ 624 14
AND THE LARK WILL FOLLOW TRILLING ANGERLESS AGAIN   625 6
WHERE THE LARK NESTS SAFELY   *953 24
THE LARK NESTS IN HIS HEART   *953 25

LARKS
FLUSHED WITH THE SONGS OF SEVEN LARKS SINGING AT ONCE G+ 34 14
RICH WITH THE SONGS OF SEVEN LARKS SINGING AT ONCE GOES+ *892 2

LARK-SONGS
IN CONFIRMATION I HEAR SEVENFOLD LARK-SONGS PEALING   34 29

LARKSPUR
HOW GORGEOUS THAT SHOCK OF RED LILIES AND LARKSPUR CLEA+ 129 27

LARK'S
SHAKING THE LARK'S NEST TILL THE EGGS HAVE BROKEN   623 31
HARDENED THE EARTH SHAKING THE LARK'S NEST TILL THE EGG+ *953 18

LARROPIN'
LARROPIN' NECK AN' CROP   78 30
LARROPIN' NECK AN' CROP   *920 22

LASH
AND AT NIGHT WHEN THE WIND ROSE THE LASH OF THE TREE   36 10
WITHIN THE HOUSE TWO VOICES AROSE A SLENDER LASH   36 13
THE PENITENTES LASH THEMSELVES TILL THEY RUN WITH BLOOD 408 4
WE GROPE AND FOAM AND LASH AROUND   833 19
MY HAND IS HEAVY AND HELPLESS SINCE WIELDING THE LASH   *897 19

LASHED
AND LASHED HIS TAIL SLOWLY SLOWLY   324 7
SO HE PASSED THE YELLOW LINE WHO LASHED LIKE A DRAGON I+ 790 3

LASHING
AND LASHING HIS TAIL ABOVE THE WORLD   324 31
I 'AM SO TIRED OF VIOLENT WOMEN LASHING OUT AND INSISTING 479 7
AND YOUR DEMON STARTS LASHING OUT   564 3
IN PEACE BEYOND THE LASHING OF THE SUN'S BRIGHT TAIL   786 2
IS LASHING HIS TAIL IN HIS SLEEP THE WINDS HOWL THE COL+ 795 14
HIM OF THE DISAPPOINTED DEAD HE IS LASHING AND TURNING + 796 31

LASS
DID T' 'APPEN TER NOTICE A BIT OF A LASS WAY BACK   60 17
ME TELL ABOUT THAT LASS WHEN YOU'D ALL GONE   61 2
AND YOU LASS WITH YOUR RICH WARM FACE AGLOW   126 28
ALONG WITH A RIPE SLACK COUNTRY LASS   198 7
THE BIG SOFT COUNTRY LASS   198 9
THE WARM SOFT COUNTRY LASS   198 13
BUT NOW MY LASS YOU'VE GOT NEMESIS ON YOUR TRACK   399 27

LASS
POOR LASS POOR BIT OF A WENCH   540 8
OH EVERY LASS   565 5
COME ON TURN HOME OLD LASS ARE WE WASTED TOO   859 25
DID TER NOTICE THAT LASS SISTER AS STOOD AWAY BACK   *909 29
DID T' 'APPEN TER NOTICE A BIT OF A LASS AWAY BACK   *911 3
ME TELL THEE ABOUT THIS LASS WHEN YOU HAD GONE   *911 18

LASSITUDE
WHO IN LASSITUDE LEAN AS YACHTS ON THE SEA-WIND LIE   73 11

LAST
IS STILL AT LAST IF SHE WOULD COME   35 12
LAST NIGHT WHEN I WENT WITH THE LANTERN THE SOW WAS GRA+ 38 8
WILL GIVE THEE WHAT I HAVE THIS LAST WEEK'S   44 2
LAST NIGHT A THIEF CAME TO ME   46 21
THIS IS THE LAST OF ALL THEN THIS IS THE LAST   47 1
THIS IS THE LAST IT WILL NOT BE ANY MORE   47 28
THIS LAST ONE TO CLAIM ME AND NOW MY SON O MY SON   48 6
IS PEOPLED WITH SHADOWS AND WAILING AND LAST GHOSTS LUR+ 54 31
YOU WANT AT LAST AH ME   55 10
ON HIS LIMBS IN SLEEP AT LAST LAID LOW   60 7
NOW AT LAST WE LIFT OUR FACES AND OUR FACES COME AFLOWER 70 3
NOW AT LAST THE INK AND DUDGEON PASSES FROM OUR FERVENT+ 70 5
ABOUT YOU ONLY LAST NIGHT YOU WERE   72 13
MY LAST DEAR FUEL OF LIFE TO HEAP ON MY SOUL   74 19
TO COME AT LAST TO THAT WHICH THEY REQUIRE   89 25
THE LAST YEAR'S FIRE IS GONE AND YOUR FACE IS ASH   91 2
AT LAST INTO BLOSSOM OF BEING EACH ONE HIS OWN FLOWER O+ 93 15
THE LAST SILK-FLOATING THOUGHT HAS GONE FROM THE DANDEL+ 97 7
SO NIGHT'S FLOOD-WINDS HAVE LIFTED MY LAST DESIRE FROM + 97 9
SHE LIES AT LAST THE DARLING IN THE SHAPE OF HER DREAM 101 14
IS THE LAST WORD NOW UTTERED   102 19
OR LAST NIGHT'S ECHOINGS   109 23
IN ITS LAST COMPLETENESS DRINKING   109 27
YOU YIELDED WE THREW THE LAST CAST   111 21
SO I FAILED TO GIVE YOU THE LAST   111 26
THE LAST DARK DELIGHT   114 16
WHERE IT GATHERED TOWARDS THE PLAIT ON THAT VERY LAST D+ 114 23
THE LAST CAR TRAILED THE NIGHT BEHIND   121 24
RUN TO THE SILENT DOOR WHERE LAST   122 4
SHALL GET MY THROAT AT LAST SHALL GET IT SOON   126 2
TO TOUCH THE SEA IN THE LAST SURPRISE   130 22
ALL FEARFUL LEST I FIND THE LAST WORDS BLEEDING   135 19
LIKE THEE CAN'T REST TILL HIS LAST SPUNK GOES   138 24
TILL A WOMAN HAS DRAWN THE LAST LAST DROP   139 11
THEIR BLOOD IN A WOMAN TO THE VERY LAST VEIN   139 17
LAST EVENING AND SHE WHO WAS SOFTLY IN BLOOM   141 7
I WAS LAST NIGHT WHEN MY SOUL RANG CLEAR AS A BELL   141 24
SINCE THIS IS THE LAST NIGHT I KEEP YOU HOME   153 13
PURE LOOK OF YOUR LAST DEAD FACE WHENCE NOW IS GONE   157 17
AND NOW AT LAST I KISS YOUR PERFECT FACE   157 21
THE POOL FOR MY LIMBS TO FATHOM MY SOUL'S LAST SCHOOL   161 17
DOWN THE ENDLESS SLOPE WHERE THE LAST ROAD GOES   164 12
YOUR LAST ALLEGIANCE   168 33
I WISH I COULD TAKE IT ALL IN A LAST EMBRACE   173 15
NO MORE AND MONEY STINKS NOT AND DEATH AT LAST   173 23
WHO WAS SEEKING ME AND HAD FOUND ME AT LAST TO FREE   180 16
SPREAD OUT AND KNOWN AT LAST AND WE ARE SURE   193 8
AND GRIEF ARE BUT THE SAME LAST WONDER SLEEP   196 2
AND HER MOUTH UNCLOSED IN A LAST LONG KISS   198 3
THIS LAST COMMISSION   198 26
AND HER MOUTH UNCLOSED IN THE LAST LONG KISS   199 11
THEY MOUNT TO THE LAST HILL-CREST   200 4
THAT WILL LAST FOR EVER   203 16
AND AT LAST I KNOW MY LOVE FOR YOU IS HERE   203 17
AT LAST AS YOU STOOD YOUR WHITE GOWN FALLING FROM YOUR 207 1
WE HAVE COME OUR WAYS AND MET AT LAST   209 13
YOU GLOW AT LAST LIKE THE MOUNTAIN TOPS WHEN THEY CATCH 209 29
AT LAST I CAN THROW AWAY WORLD WITHOUT END AND MEET YOU 210 1
AT LAST YOU CAN THROW IMMORTALITY OFF AND I SEE YOU   210 3
A SHADOW OVER MY BREASTS THAT WILL KILL ME AT LAST   211 4
I AM MYSELF AT LAST NOW I ACHIEVE   218 5
THIS THEN AT LAST IS THE DAWN AND THE BELL   220 12
WHITE AND LOOSE AT LAST WITH ALL THE PAIN   225 7
DRAWN ON HIS MOUTH EYES BROKEN AT LAST BY HIS PANGS   225 8
AND ASLEEP ON THE SNOW'S LAST SHADOW   226 19
OF YOUR LAST SOLUTION   235 16
NOW THEY ARE MINE TO-NIGHT AT LAST I SAY IT   238 16
I SACRIFICE ALL IN HER MY LAST OF THE WORLD   239 2
AT LAST TO CALM INCANDESCENCE   242 16
I AM NOR WILL I BE BOUNCED OUT OF IT SO AT LAST I TOUCH 250 2
IS BROKEN AT LAST AND DONE   253 16
IS SHATTERED AT LAST BENEATH THE STRIPE   253 25
TO SETTLE AT LAST IN THE DARK   253 31
WHERE I AM DISEMBARKED AT LAST   256 9
AT LAST CAME DEATH SUFFICIENCY OF DEATH   257 23
AND THAT AT LAST RELIEVED ME I DIED   257 24
AND TAINTS AND BLACKENS THE SKY TILL AT LAST IT IS DARK+ 258 12
A WOMAN FED THAT HUNGER IN ME AT LAST   264 26
THIS COMES RIGHT AT LAST   265 1
WHEN A MAN IS RICH HE LOSES AT LAST THE HUNGER FEAR   265 2
I LOST AT LAST THE FIERCENESS THAT FEARS IT WILL STARVE 265 3
I COULD PUT MY FACE AT LAST BETWEEN HER BREASTS   265 4
I HAVE DROPPED AT LAST HEADLONG INTO NOUGHT PLUNGING UP+ 266 2
I WANT HER TO TOUCH ME AT LAST AH ON THE ROOT AND QUICK 266 28
AND THE LAST FIRES OF DISSOLUTION BURN IN THE BOSOM OF + 270 23
HE LAUGHS LONGEST WHO LAUGHS LAST   297 25
CALLED THE ALMOND BONE IN THE BODY THE LAST BONE OF THE+ 303 9
AND RED AT THE CORE WITH THE LAST SORE-HEARTEDNESS   307 15
WHERE MY SOUL FALLS IN THE LAST THROES OF BOTTOMLESS CO+ 322 3
GOING BLIND AT LAST   325 25
MOULTING AND MOPING AND WAITING WILLING AT LAST   329 31
WHICH IS PERHAPS THE LAST ADMISSION THAT LIFE HAS TO WR+ 338 16
AT LAST HE SWERVED INTO THE WINDOW BAY   343 16
LETTING GO AT LAST AS SHE DRAGS AWAY   360 23
AND SO ON TILL THE LAST PLASM OF MY BODY WAS MELTED BACK 365 20
THIS LAST   366 24

LAST

EVEN THE SUN IN HEAVEN CAN BE CURBED AND CHASTENED AT L+   374 32
AND TO LEAP IN ONE LAST HEART-BURSTING LEAP LIKE A MALE+   379 15
AND AT LAST THE PERA-HERA PROCESSION FLAMBEAUX ALOFT IN   387 25
AS IF NOW AT LAST HERE WAS THE ONE YOU FINALLY LOVED   398 17
THAT YOU HAVE TO RUN OUT AT LAST AND EAT FILTH   398 27
SO YOU YOU GO OUT AT LAST AND EAT THE UNMENTIONABLE   399 2
SAYS LOOK AT A LAST LONG TIME THEN LOOK LOOK WELL   403 6
THE LAST STEP OUT OF THE EAST   404 28
IN THE LAST TWILIGHT   407 8
WHO UNDERSTOOD AT LAST WHAT IT WAS TO BE TOLD TO DIE   410 17
I WANTED THE VIRGIN YOU TO BE HOME AT LAST   412 2
VIRGINAL FIRST AND LAST   412 14
NOW AT THIS LAST MY LOVE MY MANY A LOVE   412 16
AND MY HEART IS GLAD TO HAVE THEM AT LAST   412 22
AT LAST FOR THE SAKE OF CLOTHING HIMSELF IN HIS OWN LEA+   451 21
LET'S BE HONEST AT LAST ABOUT SEX OR SHOW AT LEAST THAT+   464 12
AND THE GREAT BEASTS MATE IN SECRET AT LAST   465 21
SO THEY KNOW AT LAST   465 24
MUST NEEDS AT LAST COME TO KNOW ITS OWN LIMITS   473 20
THAT IT SEEMS TO LAST FOREVER   476 23
YOUR OWN SELF THAT HAS PASSED LIKE A LAST SUMMER'S   478 24
AND HAVE A COOL SENSE OF TRUTH INHUMAN TRUTH AT LAST   481 23
THAT WOULD RISE AT LAST AND BLOSSOM OUT   488 21
IS A LAST OFFSHOOT OF BOOTS   489 8
AND LIKE HAZEL-NUTS IN AUTUMN AT LAST   504 25
THE TRAGEDY IS OVER IT HAS CEASED TO BE TRAGIC THE LAST+   510 13
AND GUARD THE LAST TREASURE OF THE SOUL OUR SANITY   514 12
AND THE PURE INTELLECT GIVES ONE A LAST MASTURBATING SE+   532 9
TILL AT LAST IT'S A FULL FULL ROSE AND HAS NO MALE DUST+   535 7
THE LAST BIT OF SANITY   537 4
LIKE WAR-HORSES OR WAR-PONIES AT LAST   537 21
AND IF I COULD THE LAST PLACE I SHOULD CHOOSE   540 22
BUT WHEN AT LAST I GOT THERE   554 11
TILL AT LAST I SAW THE REASON   556 7
THOUGH LAST NIGHT I WAS MARY   558 8
AS TO THE LAST STRAW   558 25
THEY OUGHT AT LAST TO SEE THROUGH THE GAME   559 23
WILL GET TIRED AND SORE AT LAST   560 2
OH EVEN TO KNOW THE LAST WILD WINCING OF DESPAIR   585 6
AWARE AT LAST THAT OUR MANHOOD IS UTTERLY LOST   585 7
I HAVE SEEN AT LAST THE IMAGE OF HIM THEY LOVED   601 15
EXCEPT TO BE LEFT IN THE LAST RESORT ALONE QUITE ALONE   602 24
THAT THE YOUNG OF THEIR OWN SEX REVOLT AGAINST THEM AT +   619 25
AND AT LAST   624 10
AND BETWEEN THEM THE LAST LIVING HUMAN BEINGS   642 3
THAT THEIR LAST THOUGHT WAS MONEY   644 11
AND THEIR LAST REFINEMENT BLUFF A HATE DISGUISED   644 12
HARDLY LOOSES EVEN A LAST BREATH OF PERFUME   646 22
WILL AT LAST SEND YOU INSANE   655 17
IS DIFFERENT FROM THE LOVE I FELT LAST YEAR   662 2
WHEN AT LAST WE ESCAPE THE BARBED-WIRE ENCLOSURE   667 12
AND DANGLE IN A LAST FASTIDIOUS FINE DELIGHT   667 15
THE WORN-OUT MACHINE AT LAST BREAKS DOWN   676 4
AND BROKE AT LAST INTO LIGHT AND DARK   682 5
AT LAST THE NARCISSUS LIFTED A TUFT OF FIVE-POINT STARS   683 2
AND WHEN AT LAST MAN STOOD ON TWO LEGS AND WONDERED   683 11
THAT BLOSSOMED AT LAST RED GERANIUM AND MIGNONETTE   691 5
AND BECOMES AT LAST A CLOVE CARNATION LO THAT IS GOD   691 17
AND BECOMES AT LAST HELEN OR NINON ANY LOVELY AND GENER+   691 18
HEAVENLY MANSION AND LAST   695 21
INTO YOUR HOUSE GARMENTLESS LADY OF THE LAST GREAT GIFT   696 3
LADY LADY OF THE LAST HOUSE DOWN THE LONG LONG STREET O+   696 8
LO THE LAST OF THE SEVEN GREAT LAUGHS OF GOD   698 16
LO THE LAST OF THE SEVEN GREAT LAUGHS OF CREATION   698 17
TILL THEY MOUNT AND FILL AND ALL IS FULFILLED OF GOD'S +   698 20
THE SILENCE OF THE LAST OF THE SEVEN GREAT LAUGHS OF GOD   698 29
FOR THE SILENCE OF THE LAST GREAT THUNDROUS LAUGH   699 10
IN THE ENDLESS WRITHE OF THE LAST THE LAST SELF-KNOWLED+   700 27
AT LAST IN SHEER HORROR OF NOT BEING ABLE TO LEAVE OFF   701 31
COWERING IN THE LAST BRANCHES OF THE TREE OF OUR LIFE   718 20
WHERE THE SOUL COMES AT LAST AND HAS UTTER PEACE   724 7
OBLIVION WHERE THE SOUL AT LAST IS LOST   724 9
MAY SINK INTO GOD AT LAST HAVING PASSED THE VEILS   726 11
TO WOLFRATSHAUSEN LAST WINTER'S END COMES THROUGH   732 10
AT LAST I HEAR A RATTLE AND THERE AWAY   732 24
ONE BY ONE THEY GO BY AT LAST   733 10
AND AWAY WENT THE LAST OF THE WAGONS   735 16
TO SLEEP AT LAST IN IMMEMORIAL LOVE   736 21
WE YIELD THE ENEMY HIS LAST DEMANDS   736 26
LAST TWILIGHT OF THE GODS TO FIND AGAIN   737 8
DESTROY AT LAST THE HEAVY BOOKS OF STONE   737 25
TO COME AT LAST TO NOTHINGNESS AND KNOW   738 17
NAY NOW AT LAST THANK GOD FOR THE JEOPARDY   741 22
SAW MY LAST HOPE START   748 24
ME TOO AT LAST ERE THOU GOEST CHILD DEAR TO MY EYE   750 2
LET US EAT THE LAST MEAL   756 2
BECAUSE IT WAS THE SUREST WAY OF MEETING YOU AT LAST   764 24
DEATH DEATH TAKE ME WITH YOU TO SPARE ME THIS LAST   767 27
AND TO EMERGE AT LAST   769 9
TO BE CARRIED AT LAST FROM THE FIRE   769 12
HOME AT LAST IN THE OPEN AGAIN AND UNHOUSELED   770 8
AT LAST AT LAST AFTER ALL   770 23
AT LAST AT LAST AFTER ALL   770 29
THAT ARE VIRGINS AT LAST FROM THE FURNACE WITH VIRGIN   771 6
HE IS THE LAST OF THE ORIGINALLY AMERICAN RACE   776 34
FOR I AM SWEET I AM THE LAST AND THE BEST THE POOL OF N+   796 24
THE LAST OF MY DAYS IS GONE   797 18
LOOK BACK THE LAST TIME MARY MOTHER   798 3
FOR THE LAST TIME THEY BLESS YOU AS THEY LEAVE YOU   798 31
WILL WAKE AT LAST FROM THE CLEAN FORGETTING   809 16
CURVED CUT THE LAST THREADS   816 20
LAST RED LIGHT DAPPLES   816 26
LAST TIME WE WERE BOTH   817 31
AT LAST SO ARE WE   818 10
THE LAST TWO THINGS WE CAN STILL HOLD DEARLY   826 25
AND THE DESTINY OF MANKIND DEPENDS AT LAST   831 17
DON'T LET ME LAST BEYOND YOUR THIRTIES   835 14

LAST

FIRST AND LAST MAN IS ALONE   843 24
AND THE PALE STARS OF FORGET-ME-NOTS HAVE CLIMBED TO TH+   854 2
FORGOTTEN LIKE LAST YEAR'S LINNET SONG   855 14
AND THE STREWN TAWDRY TRAPPINGS THAT LAST NIGHT'S POETR+   856 11
SHE KISSED THEIR COOLNESS LAST NIGHT BREATHED THEIR CLE+   856 19
THE LAST ROW IS FINISHED THE JINGLING RAKE IS LIFTED   858 17
IS DEAD AT LAST THEN HIS POOR SUNK FLAME MUST FLICKER   859 3
HE PREACHED TO THE STOLID FARMERS TILL AT LAST HE COULD+   859 15
SLOW INFIRM DEATH HAS AT LAST GATHERED UP THE WASTE   859 21
TO FOUNDER AT LAST WITHIN THE DREADFUL FLOOD   875 33
IN ALL THINGS TO THE LAST LIKE A RHAPSODY   877 26
TONIGHT THIS VERY LAST OF OUR NIGHTS WE   878 9
THE LAST DEAR FUEL AND HEAP IT ON MY SOUL   *895 27
THE LAST DEAR FUEL AND HEAP IT ON MY SOUL   *904 16
THEN SHE RUMMAGED HER HAND IN 'ER BOSOM AN' KISSED THE +   *910 20
NOW AT LAST WE LIFT OUR FACES AND OUR FACES COME AFLOWER   *916 11
NOW AT LAST THE CLOSED CALYX OPENS FROM OUR TIRED EYES   *916 13
AND I FAILED IN MY COWARDICE TO GIVE THEE THE LAST   *927 14
LIKE A PAINTED WINDOW THAT LAST SUFFERING   *927 21
AND MY COURAGE FAILED TO GIVE YOU THE LAST   *928 14
SHALL GET MY THROAT AT LAST SHALL GET IT SOON   *937 2
AT LAST AND FOR THE SAKE OF CLOTHING HIMSELF IN HIS OWN+   *950 7
FIRST AND LAST MAN IS ALONE   *951 3
AND AT LAST   *954 4
THEY WILL HEAR FAR FAR AWAY THE LAST FACTORY HOOTER   *954 10
SEND UP THE LAST WILD CRY OF DESPAIR   *954 11
AND THEN AT LAST   *954 12
WAITING WAITING TILL AT LAST THE ANCIENT BOATMAN WITH T+   *958 11
SO THAT WHEN THE HOUR COMES AND THE LAST DOOR CLOSES BE+   *958 20
AS THE SOUL AT LAST SLIPS PERFECT INTO THE GOAL THE CORE   *959 31
OH LOVELY LAST LAST LAPSE OF DEATH INTO PURE OBLIVION   *960 3
ON ITS LAST JOURNEY ON AND ON SO STILL   *960 15
SO BEAUTIFUL OVER THE LAST OF SEAS   *960 16
THE LAST DAY AND THE SETTING FORTH   *960 19
TO THE LAST WONDER OF OBLIVION   *960 21
OBLIVION THE LAST WONDER   *960 22
FOR THE LONGEST JOURNEY OVER THE LAST OF SEAS   *961 7
AT LAST AT LAST BEYOND INNUMERABLE SEAS   *961 14

LAST-FLOWERS
WHICH ARE RATHER LAST-FLOWERS   271 4

LAST-MOWN
BEFORE THE LAST-MOWN HAREBELLS ARE DEAD   35 7

LASTS
BUT A GEM IS DIFFERENT IT LASTS SO MUCH LONGER THAN WE +   476 21

LATCH
I HEAR HIS HAND ON THE LATCH AND RISE FROM MY CHAIR   43 18
CLEAN OF THE COLD AND THE MUST WITH MY HAND ON THE LATCH   99 9
AND STILL HIS LIFE SHAKES AT THE LATCH OF SLEEP   878 28
DOOR ON THE LATCH AND SHUT MYSELF IN SHUT OUT FEAR   *945 29

LATE
AH WHEN TO-MORROW THE DAWN COMES LATE   58 26
FAULTLESSLY NOW IT'S TOO LATE   167 24
FOR YOUR LATE BEE WHO BESEECHES   178 31
THE HOUSE IS SILENT IT IS LATE AT NIGHT I AM ALONE   220 21
EVEN AS LATE AS DANIELE MANIN   323 24
THE SWALLOWS ARE FLYING SO LATE   341 7
AND THAT POOR LATE MAKESHIFT APHRODITE EMERGING IN A   439 31
AND IGNOBLE HASTE FOR FEAR OF BEING LATE   484 7
IT'S A LITTLE LATE FOR THAT   560 14
IT NEEDS THOROUGHLY PRUNING NOT AS IN THE LATE WAR BLAS+   677 25
LATE BORN   860 19
SHUFFLING HIS RAGGED BOOTS THERE COMES ONE BOY LATE   866 6
I DIDN'T KNOW IT WAS SO LATE NO SIR I 'AD TO BECAUSE   866 10

LATE-ENFRANCHISED
ENVELOPING YOUR LATE-ENFRANCHISED PLAINS   308 32

LATELY
OF SEED-SPECKS KINDLED LATELY AND SOFTLY BLOWN   218 16
LATELY I SAW A SIGHT MOST QUAINT   680 16

LATENT
LIES LATENT IN THE SOULS OF THE YOUNG A LATENT DESIRE   829 10
THE LATENT DESIRE IN ALL DECENT MEN TODAY   837 23

LATER
IS LATER THAN THE BEANS-COD   303 20
BUT LATER IN THE SUN OF THE AFTERNOON   324 10
OR LATER REPUBLICANS SAY YOU ARE SAVED   442 23

LATTER-DAY
THE WORST OF THE YOUNGER GENERATION THOSE LATTER-DAY   531 1
WHY SHOULD OUR LATTER-DAY SINNERS EXPECT SUCH A LONG   531 16

LAUGH
IN A LAUGH AS THEY HEAR   34 10
A CAR AT THE END OF THE STREET GOES BY WITH A LAUGH   54 26
AND FROM THE MEN THAT DANCE AND THE GIRLS THAT LAUGH   89 26
HOW I SIT AND LAUGH AT YOU   95 10
THIS LAUGH IN THE FIGHT   124 15
OF MORDANT ANGUISH TILL SHE CEASED TO LAUGH   125 17
I WOULD LAUGH WITH JOY   134 13
WITH A LAUGH AND A MERRY WILDNESS THAT IT WAS SHE   180 15
AGAINST ME GOES OFF WITH A LAUGH   223 20
THAT LAUGH AT THE LORD'S INDIGNATION   284 19
AND LAUGH AT TIME AND LAUGH AT DULL ETERNITY   299 11
COMES A STRIDENT LAUGH AS WE APPROACH THIS LITTLE BLACK   375 8
A KIND OF LAUGH   389 14
A NAKED GLEAMING DARK LAUGH LIKE A SECRET OUT IN THE DA+   389 15
WITH THE STRANGE DARK LAUGH IN THEIR EYES GLANCING UP   389 33
THE INDIANS LAUGH IN THEIR SLEEP   407 16
YOU DON'T EVEN LAUGH ANY MORE YOU CAN'T   433 26

LAUGH

LAUGH AND LAUGH HARD	460	16
LAUGH AND LAUGH HARD	460	20
LET US TALK LET US LAUGH LET US TELL	470	4
WE SHALL LAUGH THE INSTITUTIONS WILL CURL UP LIKE BURNT	482	26
HE'D JUST LAUGH	528	13
TO LAUGH AND TO BE	557	27
AND LAUGH LET THEM PASS	565	7
LO THE LAUGH OF GOD	698	14
HUGE HUGE ROLL THE PEALS OF THE THUNDROUS LAUGH	698	18
LAUGH	698	21
FOR THE SILENCE OF THE LAST GREAT THUNDROUS LAUGH	699	10
THE FIRST THING I DID WHEN I SAW THEM WAS TO LAUGH AT T+	791	27
AND LAUGH WITH ME WHILE THE WOMAN RESTS	813	7
TO LAUGH WHEN WE'RE FEELING MELANCHOLY	814	23
DRAW NEARER REDDEN AND LAUGH LIKE YOUNG GIRLS KISSED	854	12
SEE HER LAUGH UP AT ME	861	17
THIS LAUGH IN THE FIGHT	*935	14
OF ANGUISH TILL SHE CEASED TO LAUGH TILL DOWN	*936	16

LAUGHED

AND I LAUGHED TO FEEL IT PLUNGE AND BOUND	61	23
SHE LAUGHED SHE REACHED HER HAND OUT TO THE FLOWER	123	13
OF A MOMENT SEE SHE LAUGHED IF YOU ALSO	125	8
THEN I LAUGHED IN THE DARK OF MY HEART I DID EXULT	125	25
HOW YOU HATE BEING LAUGHED AT MISS SUPERB	397	34
THEN HE LAUGHED SEEING THE SUN DART FIERCELY AT HIM	790	1
SO HE LAUGHED AND ONE HEARD HIM LAUGHING	791	12
THAT I HAVE LAUGHED MY WAY ACROSS WITH ZEST	875	34
AND I LAUGHED TO FEEL IT PLUNGE AND BOUND	*912	3
SHE LAUGHED SHE REACHED HER HAND OUT DOWN TO THE FLOWER	*934	19
OF A MOMENT SEE SHE LAUGHED IF YOU ALSO	*935	24
THEN I LAUGHED IN THE DARK OF MY HEART I DID EXULT	*936	24

LAUGHING

AGAINST THE HAYSTACK A GIRL STANDS LAUGHING AT ME	37	1
AND LAUGHING WITH LABOUR LIVING THEIR WORK LIKE A GAME	72	11
SO WITH A DOWNCAST MIEN AND LAUGHING VOICE	123	1
YOU WOULD AMONG THE LAUGHING HILLS	178	5
AND HAS BEEN LAUGHING THROUGH SO MANY AGES	299	15
IT'S THE BLUE JAY LAUGHING AT US	375	20
WITH SWEAT AND LAUGHING	389	6
LISTEN TO PEOPLE LAUGHING	654	13
AND A GIRL RAN SWIFTLY LAUGHING BREATHLESS TAKING IN HE+	672	10
ARE HEARD SOFTLY LAUGHING AND CHATTING AS EVER	688	18
LAUGHING IN HIS BLACK BEARD	689	8
SO HE LAUGHED AND ONE HEARD HIM LAUGHING	791	12
WHY ARE YOU LAUGHING ASKED THE FIRST MAN OF QUETZCOATL	791	13
I HEAR THE VOICE OF MY FIRST MAN ASK ME WHY I AM LAUGHI+	791	14
TELL THEM THEY ARE ALL FOOLS THAT I'M LAUGHING AT THEM	791	26
THE INRUSH THE CLATTER THE STAMPING EYES LAUGHING WIDE +	865	25
OVER HER STREWN WHITE LAUGHING FORM	868	16
STILL GAY AND LAUGHING IN MY OWN VAIN STRENGTH	875	30
EVER AGAIN AND LAUGHING LOOK AT ME	876	24
HIS RECKLESS RED MOUTH LAUGHING CRUELLY	876	25
THE WAVES RAN LAUGHING UP THE SHORE AT THE SWELL	*917	4
SO WITH A DOWNCAST MIEN AND LAUGHING VOICE	*934	7

LAUGHS

HIS BENT COURSE MILDLY HERE WAKES AGAIN LEAPS LAUGHS AN+	33	14
SHE LAUGHS AT ME ACROSS THE TABLE SAYING	218	1
HE LAUGHS LONGEST WHO LAUGHS LAST	297	25
SO HE LAUGHS FROM FEAR PURE FEAR IN THE GRIP OF THE SLE+	407	22
UNLESS WE ARE IN TOUCH WITH THAT WHICH LAUGHS AT ALL OU+	613	10
LO THE LAST OF THE SEVEN GREAT LAUGHS OF GOD	698	16
LO THE LAST OF THE SEVEN GREAT LAUGHS OF CREATION	698	17
THE SILENCE OF THE LAST OF THE SEVEN GREAT LAUGHS OF GOD	698	29
LAUGHS LIKE AN EYE AT ME AND I	887	14
ITS CURIOUS COURSE MILDLY HERE IT WAKES AGAIN LEAPS LAU+	*891	15
SHE LAUGHS AT ME ACROSS THE TABLE SAYING	*943	14

LAUGHTER

STRANGE THROBS BEYOND LAUGHTER AND TEARS	38	22
WITH THE OLD SWEET SOOTHING TEARS AND LAUGHTER THAT	53	5
THE SILENCE OF VANISHING TEARS AND THE ECHOES OF LAUGHT+	53	19
ALL YOUR UNBEARABLE TENDERNESS YOU WITH THE LAUGHTER	58	21
AND LIKE A LAUGHTER LEADS ME ONWARD HEAVING	66	1
WITH LAUGHTER AND CLEAR THE EXONERATED EYES SINCE PAIN	94	20
LAUGHTER	102	27
OPEN LIKE THE SKY LOOKING DOWN IN ALL ITS LAUGHTER	119	25
MY HEART WAS FIERCE TO MAKE HER LAUGHTER RISE	125	30
AND UNCOVERS HER LAUGHTER	133	27
WITH A BUBBLE OF LAUGHTER AND SHRILLY SHOUT	179	18
HARK THE LOW AND SHATTERING LAUGHTER OF BEARDED MEN	689	2
FOR WITH THE REDNESS OF LAUGHTER THE BATTLE IS WAGING I+	854	19
I HAVE A CHARM LIKE LAUGHTER THROUGH A VEIL	860	15
WHILE THE SOFT CARESS OF HER HIDDEN LAUGHTER	868	10
FOR MYSELF IN MY OWN EYES' LAUGHTER BURNS	*891	31
US ALL ONE IN LAUGHTER AND TEARS	*893	5
FOR LAUGHTER AND GLAD THE EXONERATED EYES FOR I	*897	8
WITH THE OLD SWEET SOOTHING TEARS AND LAUGHTER THAT SHA+	*905	19
THE MISTS OF RECEDING TEARS AND THE ECHO OF LAUGHTER	*906	10
WITH GOLDEN CHICKS OF CLOUD AND A SKY OF RUNNING LAUGHT+	*933	15

LAUGHTERLESS

AND LAID LAUGHTERLESS ON HER CHEEK	*913	16

LAUNCH

THEN A LAUNCH ABROAD OF SHRINKING DOVES	179	13
NO MORE CHILDREN TO LAUNCH IN A WORLD YOU MISTRUST	411	10
NOW LAUNCH THE SMALL SHIP NOW AS THE BODY DIES	719	1
AND LIFE DEPARTS LAUNCH OUT THE FRAGILE SOUL	719	2
HAVING NO BOAT TO LAUNCH UPON THE SHAKEN SOUNDLESS	*957	30

LAUNCHED

AND ALL MY DOVES ARE LAUNCHED ABROAD AND LOST	875	24

LAUNCHING

AND LAUNCHING THERE HIS LITTLE SHIP	*958	30

LAVA

IN LAVA	293	14
BRILLIANT INTOLERABLE LAVA	293	18
GONE AGAIN IN THE BRIGHT TRAIL OF LAVA	293	23
THE LAVA FIRE	293	26
WITHIN WHITE-HOT LAVA NEVER AT PEACE	294	2

LAVA-CRATER

AND EXHAUSTING PENETRATING THE LAVA-CRATER OF A TINY	539	7

LAVENDER

LIKE LAVENDER CROCUSES SNOWDROPS LIKE ROMAN HYACINTHS	270	6
GREY LAVENDER SENSITIVE STEEL CURVING THINLY AND BRITTLY	300	30

LAVES

FROM ME TO THE BOYS WHOSE BRIGHTENING SOULS IT LAVES	51	24

LAW

AH GOD LIFE LAW SO MANY NAMES YOU KEEP	194	18
UNDER ALL THE ETERNAL DOME OF MATHEMATICAL LAW	355	22
TO MAKE SELF-PRESERVATION AND SELF-PROTECTION THE FIRST+	523	3
IS ABOUT AS SCIENTIFIC AS MAKING SUICIDE THE FIRST LAW +	523	5
TO LIFE FIXED TO THE LETTER OF THE LAW	662	21
AND SACRIFICE IS THE LAW OF LIFE WHICH ENACTS	679	20
BECAUSE HE IS ENUNCIATING A PRINCIPLE A LAW	708	14

LAWN

BELOW THE LAWN IN SOFT BLUE SHADE IS KEEPING	35	28
A WET BIRD WALKS ON THE LAWN CALL TO THE BOY TO COME	137	7
ON THE LAWN	268	16

LAWRENCE

THE NUDITY OF A LAWRENCE NUDE	680	19

LAWS

HAVING NO LAWS BUT THE LAWS OF OUR OWN BEING	267	29
THE LIFE WITHOUT LAWS	825	22

LAY

AND I WOKE TO THE SOUND OF THE WOOD PIGEON AND LAY AND +	38	12
I LAY DUMB AND STARK	46	24
HER FACE LAY PALE AGAINST MY BREAST	62	14
SO I LAY ON YOUR BREAST FOR AN OBSCURE HOUR	104	4
ITS SHADOW LAY ON MY HEART	124	27
MY FINGERS TILL ITS HEAD LAY BACK ITS FANGS	125	14
HUNGRY FOR LOVE YET IF I LAY MY HAND IN HER BREAST	128	2
SOFT SHE LAY AS A SHED FLOWER FALLEN NOR HEARD	155	26
AT SUCH AN HOUR TO LAY HER CLAIM ABOVE	155	29
SHE LOOKED AT HIM AS HE LAY WITH BANDED CHEEK	156	11
COME TO ME HERE AND LAY YOUR BODY BY MINE	211	26
WE LAY MOUTH TO MOUTH WITH YOUR FACE	248	25
ONCE HE LAY IN THE MOUTH OF A CAVE	324	5
HE FELL TO FROWNING AS HE LAY WITH HIS HEAD ON HIS PAWS	324	12
AND THERE LAY	346	28
DARK BREATH OF THE EARTH THE SERPENT SLID FORTH LAY REV+	348	7
THOUGH WHAT SHE DOES EXCEPT LAY FOUR EGGS AT RANDOM IN	358	26
THEY ARE THEIR OWN FLESH I LAY	460	22
AND OF COURSE ONE HAS NO RIGHT TO LAY	492	15
AND DEPARTING INVIOLATE NOTHING CAN LAY HANDS ON HER	676	15
WHEN GOLD LAY SHINING THREADING THE COOLED-OFF ROCK	682	24
YET YOU CAN'T LAY YOUR HAND ON IT	692	5
OH THEY CAN LAY YOU WASTE THE ANGRY DEAD	723	16
AND LAY THEM DEEP IN LOVE LAY THEM TO SLEEP	736	15
TO LAP THEM ROUND WITH LOVE AND LAY THEM BY	736	20
THAT I AM NOW AH LAY ONE LITTLE TOUCH	738	30
OH BRING HIM TO ME I SAID OH LAY HIM BETWEEN	750	19
IN HIS HAND IT LAY AND WENT DARK	791	3
NO MORE AND HE LAY AT HOME UNUTTERABLE DESPAIR IN HIS F+	859	16
ITS COOL WEIGHT LAY FULL ON HER BOSOM NOW IT ROLLS TO R+	864	15
IN A MEADOW LOST I LAY	881	22
IT LAY ON ME AS ON WATER	881	33
AND I LAY CLOSE DOWN	882	22
AS I LAY ON THE BED AND YOU SAT WITH THE FLOWERS ON YOU+	886	11
AND AS I LAY AND LOOKED IN YOUR EYES	886	13
HER FACE LAY THERE BEFORE MY BREAST	*912	20
THIRTEEN LAY THE YELLOW CHICKS BENEATH THE JOIST OF WOOD	*933	3
ITS SHADOW LAY ON MY HEART	*935	33
I NEED ONLY COME HOME EACH NIGHT AND LAY	*946	1

LAYERS

IN THE DARK-BLUE DEPTHS UNDER LAYERS AND LAYERS OF	697	26

LAYING

THEY ARE LAYING THE GOLDEN RACING-TRACK OF THE SUN	230	9
LAYING BACK HER LONG EARS WITH UNWINKING BLISS	311	19
LAYING THAT GOLDEN EGG	414	33
SEEMED TO THINK I WAS LAYING IT SIEGE	555	16
BUT LAYING FOREVER OUR EFFORT AT MUSIC BY	884	22

LAYS

HOW CARESSINGLY SHE LAYS HER HAND ON MY KNEE	128	14
OR ARE YOU THE GOOSE THAT LAYS THE GOLDEN EGG	414	30
SHE LAYS AN EGG HE BRISTLES LIKE A DOUBLE WHITE POPPY A+	761	19

LAZY

THERE THE LAZY STREAMLET PUSHES	33	13
THERE THE LAZY STREAMLET PUSHES	*891	14

LEAD
   AND I AM WRAPPED IN THE LEAD OF A COFFIN-LINING THE LIV+   630 7
   SO LONG AS YOU LEAD THE GAWKY CHOIR   680 21
   LEAD ME THEN LEAD THE WAY   697 12
   THEN LEAD THEM TO THE GATES OF THE UNKNOWN   740 19
   GREAT THIGHS THAT LEAD NOWHERE   827 19
   SO I LEAD THEM UP SO DO THEY TWINE   *899 23
   SO I LEAD THEM UP SO DO THEY TWINE   *903 2

LEADEN
   THE HOURS HAVE TUMBLED THEIR LEADEN MONOTONOUS SANDS   167 1
   THE HOURS HAVE TUMBLED THEIR LEADEN MONOTONOUS SANDS   167 8
   A WEIGHT COMES OVER ME HEAVIER THAN LEADEN LININGS OF   629 18

LEADER
   AS IF IT WERE THE LEADER THE MAIN-STEM THE FORERUNNER   299 28
   SOME WONDERFUL LEADER   564 21

LEADING
   THE WAY THAT I HAVE GONE AND NOW AM LEADING THEY ARE DE+   *900 19
   THE WAY THAT I HAVE GONE AND NOW AM LEADING THEY ARE DE+   *903 31

LEADS
   AND LIKE A LAUGHTER LEADS ME ONWARD HEAVING   66 1
   I THE GREAT VEIN THAT LEADS   240 4
   AN' THEN HE LEADS YOU BY THE NOSE   493 13
   AND SUPPRESSION OF SUCH FACT LEADS AS WE KNOW DIRECT TO+   *953 5

LEAF
   IN THE TAPPING HASTE OF A FALLEN LEAF   68 21
   AND LEAF FOR ITS PASSAGE A SHADOW CAST   69 3
   A YELLOW LEAF FROM THE DARKNESS   110 25
   TO DIE AND THE QUICK LEAF TORE ME   111 4
   AT SEASONS SHE CURLS BACK HER TAIL LIKE A GREEN LEAF IN+   385 31
   DEFIANT CURLING THE LEAF OF HER TAIL AS IF SHE WERE CUR+   386 13
   WEB OF LIVING LEAF   451 6
   OR REASON WHERE THE LEAF SHOULD BE   578 5
   NO ONE NOT EVEN GOD CAN PUT BACK A LEAF ON TO A TREE   617 1
   AND THE LIME-TREE LOVELY AND TALL EVERY LEAF SILENT   646 21
   AND ONE GREEN LEAF SPRANG AMONG THE BLACK   809 20
   THE GREEN LEAF OF MALINTZI   809 21
   LIKE A TREE IN NEW LEAF   811 14
   AND I TOOK HER EAR LIKE THE LEAF OF A WATER-FLOWER BETW+   882 27
   IN THE TAPPING HASTE OF A FALLEN LEAF   *915 5
   OR LEAF AND HIS PASSING SHADOW IS CAST   *915 15

LEAF-CLOGGED
   ORPHEUS AND THE WINDING LEAF-CLOGGED SILENT LANES OF HE+   281 16

LEAF-CLOTHS
   COME THEN UNDER THE TREES WHERE THE LEAF-CLOTHS   *929 10

LEAFLIKE
   AT LAST FOR THE SAKE OF CLOTHING HIMSELF IN HIS OWN LEA+   451 21

LEAF-LIKE
   AT LAST AND FOR THE SAKE OF CLOTHING HIMSELF IN HIS OWN+   *950 7

LEAF'S
   THE SPIRIT FROM EACH LEAF'S FRAME   68 4
   THE LEAF'S BROWN HUE   178 4
   THE SPIRIT FROM EACH LEAF'S FRAME   *914 19

LEAFY
   FOR HE IS HOSTILE TO ALL THE OLD LEAFY FOLIAGE OF OUR T+   609 6

LEAGUE
   AS THE TRAIN FALLS LEAGUE AFTER LEAGUE   162 15
   ASK BUT THE LEAGUE INSISTS THANK YOU SO MUCH NO SIGN HE+   546 14

LEAK
   WE LEAK LIKE A BARREL THAT IS SPRUNG BUT YET   750 6
   THROUGH AN INEVITABLE IRREPARABLE LEAK   767 13

LEAKING
   OR IS OUR SHATTERED ARGOSY OUR LEAKING ARK   429 9

LEAN
   LEAN ABOUT US SCATTERING THEIR POLLEN GRAINS OF GOLDEN +   70 2
   WHO IN LASSITUDE LEAN AS YACHTS ON THE SEA-WIND LIE   73 11
   THE ROSES LEAN DOWN WHEN THEY HEAR IT THE TENDER MILD   137 4
   WHILE SOMETHING STIRS QUICKLY IN HER BELLY AND A LEAN   393 30
   SEA-BEASTS IMMERSED LEAN SIDEWAYS AND FLASH BRIGHT   453 25
   FOR THE MOON LIKE A FATA MORGANA WILL LEAN   748 1
   I SHOULD LEAN AND WHISPER IN HIS EAR   752 5
   TO LEAN OVER MY HEAD AND MY NECK AND MY BREAST   799 18
   AND LEAN OVER   819 28
   LEAN TOGETHER AND LIFT WILD ARMS TO EMBRACE   883 9
   I LIFT MY BREAST AND LEAN FORWARD   883 10
   LEAN ABOUT US SCATTERING THEIR POLLEN PUFFS OF GOLDEN L+   *916 10

LEANED
   BUT IT LEANED YOU A NEW   56 5
   I LEANED IN THE DARKNESS TO FIND HER LIPS   62 6
   AT HOME WE LEANED IN THE BEDROOM WINDOW   206 27
   AND YOU LEANED YOUR CHEEK TO MINE   206 33
   BUT A NAKED MAN A STRANGER LEANED ON THE GATE   692 10
   THE ROSY PERIWINKLES THAT CLUSTERED AND LEANED ACROSS   863 24
   I LEANED ME FORWARD TO FIND HER LIPS   *912 13

LEANING
   LEANING IN YOUR ROOM LIKE TWO TIGER-LILIES CURVING   91 12
   BUT I SEE LEANING FROM THE SHADES   105 24
   WITH DULL FACE LEANING TO FACE   106 14
   PHANTOM TO PHANTOM LEANING STRANGE WOMEN WEEP   140 15
   AND LEANING TO ME LIKE A FLOWER ON ITS STALK   178 29
   GREY BIRD IN THE AIR ON THE BOUGH OF THE LEANING   385 17
   AND LEANING TOWARDS THE OLD HEARTH   704 5

LEANING
   SO LEANING FORWARD ON HIS CLOUD HE SAID TO HIMSELF   790 17
   WITH LONG PINS LEANING OUT THEIR PORCELAIN GLOBES WREAT+   856 13
   SO PONDEROUSLY CENTRAL YET LEANING ITS WEIGHT TOWARDS   *952 2
   LEANING IN THE MASSIVE UNCONSCIOUS INCLINATION WE CALL +   *952 4

LEANS
   LEANS AND LOOKS IN AT THE LOW-BUILT SHED   42 21
   LEANS ALL ALONE ABOVE MY WINDOW ON NIGHT'S WINTRY BOWER   67 19
   HER FACE AND FORWARD LEANS TO CATCH THE SIGHT   105 27
   OF MY PRESENCE THERE IN THE MIRROR THAT LEANS FROM THE   141 20
   LEANS   451 13
   THE EARTH LEANS ITS WEIGHT ON THE SUN AND THE SUN ON THE   480 19
   THE SOUL OF MAN ALSO LEANS IN THE UNCONSCIOUS INCLINATI+   480 22
   AGAIN AND AGAIN SOME GOD OF EVENING LEANS OUT OF IT   656 2
   A LITTLE MOON QUITE STILL LEANS AND SINGS TO HERSELF   656 8
   LEANS LISTENING ON THE GATE IN ALL RESPECT   688 20
   SHE LEANS FORWARD HER SMOOTH PALE FACE   731 10
   STRONG YOUNG MAN HE LEANS SIGHING   733 19
   LEANS OVER TO READ HIS WORK AND HER DARK HEAD DIPS   865 5
   FLASHING HIS BRIGHT BROWN ARMS AS HE LEANS ON THE POLE   867 28
   AS EARTH LEANS ON THE SUN   *952 5
   CENTRAL PRIMORDIAL FIRE OF THE SOUL THAT LEANS AND YEAR+   *952 6

LEAP
   TO LEAP DOWN AT OUR GATE   100 8
   OF THE LEAVES AS THOUGH THEY WOULD LEAP SHOULD I CALL   105 18
   BREAKS INTO DAZZLE OF LIVING AS DOLPHINS LEAP FROM THE +   136 19
   GONE IN ONE LEAP   146 4
   LEAP AND OH   365 8
   IN A LEAP AT THE SUN   379 14
   AND TO LEAP IN ONE LAST HEART-BURSTING LEAP LIKE A MALE+   379 15
   FROM HIS LEAP AT THE ZENITH IN HER SO IT FALLS JUST SHO+   382 23
   LIFE SEEMS TO LEAP AT THE AIR OR SKIM UNDER THE WIND   392 15
   OR FROGS THAT WHEN THEY LEAP COME FLOP AND FLOP TO THE   392 25
   LEAP THEN AND COME DOWN ON THE LINE THAT DRAWS TO THE   394 25
   LET THE MEREST SCALLYWAG COME TO THE DOOR AND YOU LEAP   398 15
   SO SHE WILL NEVER LEAP IN THAT WAY AGAIN WITH THE YELLOW   402 15
   THE DOLPHINS LEAP ROUND DIONYSOS' SHIP   693 25
   SO THEY LEAP UP LIKE A FOUNTAIN   819 16
   THAT LEAP   819 27
   SAVE THEY LEAP   820 12
   OH HEARTS LEAP HIGH   820 14
   THY FLAME LEAP FREE WHAT IF I AM LEFT BEHIND   879 25
   WE LEAP LIKE TWO CLASPED FLAMES FROM OFF THE FIRE   879 30
   THAT LEAP AND MEET TOGETHER AT THE MOUTH   879 34
   CAUGHT WHEN MY HEART WOULD LEAP IN A NET OF LIVES   884 15
   THAT THEY CLEAVE UNTO THAT THEY LEAP ALONG   *899 20
   THAT THEY CLEAVE UNTO THAT THEY LEAP ALONG   *902 32

LEAPED
   AND MY HEART LEAPED UP IN LONGING TO PLUNGE ITS STARK   125 33
   AND MY HEART LEAPED UP IN LONGING TO PLUNGE ITS STARK   *936 32

LEAPING
   THE QUICK SPARKS ON THE GORSE-BUSHES ARE LEAPING   33 1
   LEAPING LIKE SPRAY IN THE RETURN OF PASSION   89 17
   JETS OF SPARKS IN FOUNTAINS OF BLUE COME LEAPING   136 6
   ARE A BONFIRE OF ONENESS ME FLAME FLUNG LEAPING ROUND Y+   245 24
   HA I WAS A BLAZE LEAPING UP   259 11
   AND FELT HIM BEAT IN MY HAND WITH HIS MUCOUS LEAPING   339 9
   BLUNDERING MORE INSANE AND LEAPING IN THROBS TO CLUTCH +   343 20
   AND OVER-RODE HIS MARES AS IF HE WERE SAVAGELY LEAPING +   378 6
   RUSHING IN LIKE A LITTLE BLACK WHIRLWIND LEAPING STRAIG+   397 2
   WITH GRAPE-VINES UP THE MAST AND DOLPHINS LEAPING   688 5
   THE HOSTS ARE LEAPING FROM THE EDGE OF LIFE   743 30
   I AM THE LEAPING AND QUAKING   805 10
   HUITZILOPOCHTLI LEAPING AND QUAKING   806 13
   HOLDING DOWN MY LEAPING ARMS   883 11
   THE QUICK SPARKS ON THE GORSE BUSHES ARE LEAPING   *891 1

LEAPS
   HIS BENT COURSE MILDLY HERE WAKES AGAIN LEAPS LAUGHS AN+   33 14
   ACROSS THE HEAVENS WHEN THE STORM LEAPS HIGHER   89 23
   ONE MOMENT THE HATE LEAPS AT ME STANDING THERE   225 25
   AS THE FIRELIGHT FALLS AND LEAPS   238 14
   THEN SHE LEAPS THE ROCKS LIKE A QUICK ROCK   386 9
   GOES OFF IN SLOW SAD LEAPS   393 26
   AND THOUGH THE SUN LEAPS LIKE A THING UNLEASHED IN THE +   408 21
   LEAPS UP TO THE SUMMIT OF THE STEM GLEAMS TURNS OVER   476 8
   IN THE STONE AND IRON LEAPS IN FIRE   773 5
   HE LEAPS UP SHE LEAPS UP   819 17
   LEAPS   819 23
   ITS CURIOUS COURSE MILDLY HERE IT WAKES AGAIN LEAPS LAU+   *891 15

LEAPT
   YOU LEAPT ABOUT IN THE SLIPPERY ROCKS AND THREW   98 19
   THE GREY DOG LEAPT AT MY ENTRAILS   808 5
   TILL OFF THY MOUTH HAS LEAPT THE FLAME OF LIFE   879 22

LEAR
   LEAR THE OLD BUFFER YOU WONDER HIS DAUGHTERS   494 16
   OF LEAR AND MACBETH AND HAMLET AND TIMON   508 17

LEARN
   LEARN THEY MUST TO OBEY FOR ALL HARMONY IS DISCIPLINE   93 9
   LET THEM LIVE THE BOYS AND LEARN NOT TO TRESPASS I HAD +   93 11
   NOT TO TRESPASS ON THEM WITH LOVE THEY MUST LEARN NOT T+   93 12
   THEY ARE HERE TO LEARN BUT ONE LESSON THAT THEY SHALL N+   93 16
   AND LEARN TO SERVE   234 22
   BUT WE WILL LEARN TO SUBMIT   236 17
   WHICH WE MUST LEARN TO SATISFY WITH PURE REAL SATISFACT+   264 19
   YOU LEARN LOYALTY RATHER THAN LOVING   400 31
   DO LEARN TO DISCRIMINATE   459 12
   FROM THIS I LEARN THOUGH I KNEW IT BEFORE   489 5
   I AM TRYING NOW TO LEARN NEVER   500 8
   WHY DON'T WE LEARN TO TAME THE MIND   529 6
   THAT ENGLISH ARTISTS MIGHT FINALLY LEARN   579 24

LEARN
  HAVE YOU STILL TO LEARN THAT PITH   583 23
  MEN AND WOMEN SHOULD LEARN TENDERNESS TO EACH OTHER   620 3
  MUST LEARN THE SUPREME LESSON   636 24
  AND THEN RISEN WE MUST LEARN THE MOST CRUEL LESSON   637 1
  AND LIVED TO LEARN THEY ARE NEITHER FELLOW NOR MEN   644 2
  AH YES MEN MUST LEARN TO SERVE   650 12
  AH YES MEN MUST LEARN TO OBEY   650 14
  AT THE SAME TIME WE LEARN A LOT   832 26
  AND WHERE WE CAN BEGIN TO LEARN OUR GREAT EMOTIONAL LES+   833 16
  WHERE WE CAN LEARN TO FULFIL OUR NEW KNOWLEDGE OF MATER+   833 23
  IS TO LEARN TO CONTAIN HIMSELF   838 15
  TO LEARN TO CONTAIN OURSELVES   839 2
  WHY NOT STAY OUT AND LEARN TO CONTAIN ONESELF   839 22
  TRAVEL THINE AVOCATION HERE AND LEARN   872 2
  I DIDN'T LEARN IT FROM HER SPEECH   *893 6

LEARNED
  I LEARNED IT ALL FROM MY EVE   38 18
  YET HOW I HAVE LEARNED TO KNOW THAT LOOK IN YOUR EYES   207 15
  I HAVE LEARNED TO CURSE YOUR MOTHERHOOD   207 34
  THE YOUNG HAVE LEARNED SOME SENSE   559 22
  NO MAN UNLESS HE HAS DIED AND LEARNED TO BE ALONE   612 17
  WE HAVE LEARNED A LOT SINCE JESUS FROM JESUS AND ALL TH+   832 27
  WE HAVE LEARNED THAT ANOTHER MAN'S LIBERTY IS AS ESSENT+   833 1
  WE HAVE LEARNED I THINK NOT TO BE GREEDY   833 3
  THERE WE HAVE LEARNED NOTHING   833 10
  I HAVE LEARNED IT ALL FROM MY EVE   *893 1

LEARNING
  LEARNING OF THEIRS IT ALL GOES DOWN THE SAME ABYSS   74 26

LEARNT
  SAY WHAT WE LIKE OUR CIVILISATION HAS LEARNT A GREAT LE+   831 5
  WE HAVE LEARNT NOT TO HAVE SLAVES NOT TO WANT THEM   832 28

LEASE
  LET THEM LEASE THEIR LAND TO THE AMERICAN GOVERNMENT   778 27
  THAT WE LEASE OUR LANDS AND GET REAPERS   779 9

LEASH
  HOW LONG HAVE THEY TUGGED THE LEASH AND STRAINED APART   74 8
  ALL HELD IN LEASH   459 28
  THYSELF SLIP OUT THE LEASH AND HUNTS THY WAY   879 13
  WATCHING THY GREAT SOUL TUG WITHIN THE LEASH   879 16
  HOW LONG HAVE THEY TUGGED THE LEASH AND STRAINED APART   *896 16
  HOW LONG HAVE THEY TUGGED THE LEASH AND STRAINED APART   *904 5
  THY BODY FROM ITS TERRORS AWKWARD LEASH   *927 25

LEAST
  SHALL I LESS THAN THE LEAST RED GRAIN OF FLESH   195 31
  IN EACH OTHER AT LEAST   245 2
  LEAST   250 5
  AND MY HEAD AT LEAST IS THICK ENOUGH TO STAND IT THE   289 17
  AT LEAST AT VENICE   323 23
  OR AT LEAST WORTH TREASURY NOTES   458 27
  LET'S BE HONEST AT LAST ABOUT SEX OR SHOW AT LEAST THAT+   464 12
  BUT IN HIS CONSCIOUSNESS HE IS TWO FOLD AT LEAST   473 16
  IT SEEMS TO ME THAT FOR FIVE THOUSAND YEARS AT LEAST   519 1
  QUITE THRILLING I SHOULD SAY AT LEAST TO CONTEMPLATE   533 1
  MATTERING AT LEAST NOT TO ME   552 12
  AND SHE SHUTS YOU IN THE CELLAR FOR THE LEAST LITTLE TI+   572 7
  AND THE BASE THINGS LIKE HYAENAS OR BED-BUGS HAVE LEAST+   621 18
  THEN FOR A TIME AT LEAST THEY MUST DO WITHOUT   651 11
  I HAVE NO DESIRE IN THE LEAST TO BE SORROWED OVER OR CO+   840 22

LEATHERY
  BUT HE CATCHES THE FOLDS OF VULNERABLE LEATHERY SKIN   362 6

LEAVES
  BEYOND THE LEAVES THAT OVERHANG THE STREET   36 1
  AH ONLY THE LEAVES BUT IN THE WEST   42 5
  MY LIFE WITH OTHER LEAVES MY TIME   52 10
  DROP THEIR LEAVES WITH A FAINT SHARP HISS OF CONTEMPT   54 25
  THAT LEAVES THE BOUGHS   56 19
  BY BRIGHT LEAVES UTTERED ALOUD AND STRIFE   68 7
  IS HEARD IN THE WINDLESS WHISPER OF LEAVES   68 17
  THEN LEAVES THEE AND THOU CANST NOT BUT COMPLAIN   69 29
  ALL AS WE S'LL WANT FOR FURNITURE WHEN THA LEAVES THIS +   83 3
  LIGHTING THESE AUTUMN LEAVES LIKE A STAR DROPPED THROUGH   86 16
  MY FALLEN STAR AMONG THE LEAVES MY DEAR   86 24
  THE LEAVES AND DEAR YOU HAVE HAD YOUR WILL   87 9
  LEAVES   92 3
  AND THE GENTLE LEAVES AND HAVE FELT WHERE THE ROOTS ARE+   92 10
  DIM SELF THAT RISES SLOWLY TO LEAVES AND THE FLOWER'S G+   92 20
  THE LEAVES FLY OVER THE WINDOW AND UTTER A WORD AS THEY+   102 1
  OF THE LEAVES AS THOUGH THEY WOULD LEAP SHOULD I CALL   105 18
  OF LEAVES AND LAMPS AND THE CITY STREET MINGLED   111 6
  SCRAMBLE SEVEN TOADS ACROSS SILK OBSCURE LEAVES   126 18
  THE RAIN-BRUISED LEAVES ARE SUDDENLY SHAKEN AS A CHILD   136 24
  OF LEAVES THAT HAVE GONE UNNOTICED SWEPT LIKE OLD   141 29
  HAS SOME HAND BALANCED MORE LEAVES IN THE DEPTHS OF THE   142 5
  IT IS ONLY THE SPARROWS LIKE DEAD BLACK LEAVES ON THE   142 9
  RUSTLE OF LEAVES WASHES OUT THE RENDING   150 7
  LEAVES AN EMPTY BREAST   155 12
  DEFENDING THE MEMORY OF LEAVES AND THE HAPPY ROUND NEST   167 10
  ALWAYS GLADDEN MY AMOROUS FINGERS WITH THE TOUCH OF THE+   180 25
  I WILL TRAIL MY HANDS AGAIN THROUGH THE DRENCHED COLD L+   180 34
  TILL MY HANDS ARE FULL OF THE CHILLNESS AND TOUCH OF LE+   180 35
  LEAVES ME UNBURDENED TO BEGIN AGAIN   195 4
  SLIPPING INTO ITS BED OF DEAD LEAVES YOU HURRY INTO YOUR   254 16
  THE PLANE LEAVES   268 14
  LEAVES   281 3
  DROPPING AMONG HIS LEAVES HANGS THE DARK GRAPE   286 10
  AND NOW THE OLIVE LEAVES THOUSANDS OF FEET BELOW   293 25
  SLOW TOADS AND CYCLAMEN LEAVES   310 16
  CYCLAMEN LEAVES   310 19
  GOATS GO PAST THE BACK OF THE HOUSE LIKE DRY LEAVES IN +   383 27

LEAVES
  DARK GREEN GLOSSY FANGED LEAVES   383 31
  DARK GREEN GLOSSY FANGED LEAVES   387 2
  VERY HANDSOME AND SOME PURE YELLOW FANGED LEAVES   387 3
  NOW THAT THE SUN HAS GONE AND THE ASPEN LEAVES   403 14
  AND THE COTTON-WOOD LEAVES ARE FALLEN AS GOOD AS FALLEN   403 15
  AND THE ABSENCE OF COTTON-WOOD LEAVES OR OF ASPEN   404 1
  SWIM DEEPER DEEPER TILL IT LEAVES NO PEAK EMERGING   428 25
  SUCKING HIS LIFE OUT OF THE DEAD LEAVES OF GREATER LIFE+   431 16
  BUT WHEN OUR EAGERNESS LEAVES US WE ARE GODLESS AND FULL   439 19
  IT LEAVES ITS TRAIL   448 27
  WHILE A WAGE-SLAVE WORKS HE LEAVES LIFE ASIDE   450 3
  THEY ARE LIKE SLENDER TREES PUTTING FORTH LEAVES A LONG+   451 5
  LEAVES A RIND   463 22
  AN' LEAVES YOU NEVER A TRIMMIN'   493 16
  AND WHERE MY LITTLE LEAVES FLUTTER HIGHEST   499 8
  AND MY LEAVES ARE GREEN WITH THE BREATH OF HUMAN EXPERI+   499 11
  FRAGRANT LIKE YELLOWING LEAVES AND DIM WITH THE SOFT   503 24
  AND LEAVES MEN LIVING CLAY   524 9
  LEAVES OF GRASS WHAT ABOUT LEAVES OF GRASS   587 1
  LEAVES OF GRASS WHAT ARE LEAVES OF GRASS WHEN AT ITS BE+   587 16
  SMALL SHARP RED FIRES IN THE NIGHT OF LEAVES   606 3
  WHEN THOUGHTS ARE STIFF LIKE OLD LEAVES   608 22
  AS HE BITES AT THE STEMS OF LEAVES IN AUTUMN TO MAKE TH+   609 3
  THERE IS THE ORGANIC CONNECTION LIKE LEAVES THAT BELONG+   615 1
  AND THERE IS THE MECHANICAL CONNECTION LIKE LEAVES THAT+   615 2
  WINDS OF HEAVEN FAN THE LEAVES OF THE TREE LIKE FLAMES +   615 4
  BUT WINDS OF HEAVEN ARE MILLS OF GOD TO THE FALLEN LEAV+   615 5
  PEOPLE ARE LIKE LEAVES FLUTTERING AND GAY ON THE BUSH O+   615 7
  OR THEY ARE LIKE LEAVES RUSTLING THICK IN THE CROWDS ON+   615 8
  BUT THE LIVING LEAVES IN THE BREATH OF THE WIND ARE MOR+   615 14
  AND LEAVES OFF   623 11
  AND THE GHOSTLY CREAMY COLOURED LITTLE TREES OF LEAVES   646 23
  AND THE YOUNG COPPER BEECH ITS LEAVES RED-ROSY AT THE E+   647 4
  BECOME AWARE AS LEAVES ARE AWARE   667 26
  AND OUR STRENGTH LEAVES US   718 18
  AND WHAT THE SOUL TAKES WITH HIM AND WHAT HE LEAVES BEH+   724 2
  I FEEL THE PAIN OF FALLING LEAVES AND STEMS THAT BREAK +   727 7
  THAT WHIRL AND SWEEP LIKE ANXIOUS LEAVES AWAY   744 14
  BUT ON THEY GO LIKE LEAVES WITHIN A WIND   744 29
  FOLDED AS YET AND ALL THE FALLEN LEAVES   745 33
  THE WILLOW SHALL LIFT HER LEAVES TO SOOTHE THY DISTRESS   749 24
  THE GHOST OF EACH THROUGH THE LEAVES OF SHADOW   812 19
  LEAVES WHISPER AND TITTER   861 1
  TO PULL DOWN THE BOUGH THE LEAVES BROKE AND THE FRUIT S+   864 10
  BUT PRESSING HER SUPPLE BODY INTO THE COOL DARK LEAVES   864 11
  YEA AND HE LEAVES   877 3
  HE LEAVES ME GOES DOWN TO THE SOUTHRON FOLK   877 14
  IN TERRIBLE RHYTHM LIKE BLOWS THAT ARE STRUCK TILL THE +   879 2
  AND WHEN BLACK LEAVES STREAM OUT IN A TRAIL DOWN THE WI+   883 12
  EVEN HER FLOATING HAIR SINKS LIKE STORM-BRUISED YOUNG L+   *913 24
  IS HEARD IN THE WINDLESS WHISPER OF LEAVES   *915 1
  ALL THE LEAVES ARE FALLEN AND THE STARLIGHT SHINES THRO+   *917 28
  ALL AS WE SHALL WANT FOR FURNITURE WHEN THA LEAVES THIS+   *925 7
  LEAVES   *926 3
  UNDER THE CARESSING LEAVES AND FELT WHERE THE ROOTS WER+   *926 10
  FAR AND WIDE RUN THE EASY ROOTS THAT BEAR THE LEAVES OF+   *926 12
  OH I TORE THEM UP THOUGH THE WISTFUL LEAVES WERE FRAGRA+   *926 15
  AND I TWISTED THEM OVER THE BROKEN LEAVES INTO UNBREAKA+   *926 17
  OF LEAVES LIKE YELLOW FRUITS SHOW PLAIN   *932 23
  BUT LEAVES ALIGHT AND LOVELY ETERNALLY   *937 6
  THEY LIVED THEMSELVES FORTH LIKE A TREE PUTTING OUT WOV+   *949 28
  CAME FROM THEM LIVING LIKE LEAVES FROM THE TREE OF THEI+   *949 30
  AND CLOTHED THEM WITH LIVING LEAVES   *949 31
  MEN USED TO PUT THEM FORTH SENSITIVELY LIKE BOUGHS LEAV+   *950 2
  AND WHAT THE SOUL CARRIES WITH HIM AND WHAT HE LEAVES B+   *961 12

LEAVE-TAKING
  THE EXQUISITE ODOUR OF LEAVE-TAKING   281 14

LEAVING
  AND I LEAVING HER   63 15
  LOVE WHO HAD BORNE AND NOW WAS LEAVING ME   103 20
  IT SHUT BEHIND HER LEAVING THE STREET AGHAST   122 8
  ALL WITH A FLASH OF BLUE WHEN WILL SHE BE LEAVING   129 28
  LEAVING A BURN AND AN UGLY SMART   151 9
  LEAVING HER FAWN   222 4
  LEAVING A NERVOUS PEOPLE   374 28
  LEAVING THE TRAIL OF A DIFFERENT PAW HANGING OUT   394 4
  LEAVING A FEW BONES   414 24
  LEAVING IT TO THE VAST REVOLUTIONS OF CREATIVE CHAOS   429 24
  FROM THE HEART AND LEAVING STRANGE COLD STRETCHES OF SA+   509 4
  INSTEAD OF LEAVING IT TO LENIN   536 11
  FOR LEAVING THINGS OUT   562 13
  LEAVING NASTY FILMS UPON YOU EVERY TIME   581 5
  IS LEAVING A LONG THREAD OF DARK SMOKE   687 10
  LEAVING ME GOING AWAY FROM ME   766 11
  LEAVING THE RIVERBED   766 19
  LEAVING THIS CONGERIE BEHIND AND IN DANGER   767 24
  LEAVING THIS NAKED PALLID HELPLESS VULNERABLE REMAINS   767 26
  LEAVING THEM SHADOW STRIPES BARRED ON A FIELD OF GREY   858 12
  LEAVING A BURN AND A SMART   873 19
  LEAVING MY EYES HALF EMPTY AND CLAMOROUS   *893 16
  LEAVING ALL TO THE WOMAN MADONNA MIA POOR VIRGIN   *946 16
  LEAVING THEM CRUSHED WORMS   *949 13

LEAVINGS
  IS ONLY THE LEAVINGS OF A LIFE   727 21

LE BESTIE NON PARLANO POVERINE
  LE BESTIE NON PARLANO POVERINE   385 6

LECHERY
  FROM ALL THE WHITE SELF-CONSCIOUS LECHERY   469 21

LED
    ONLY LED HER THROUGH HARSH HARD PLACES   202 23
    NONE OF THE TROUBLE HE'S LED TO STALL   219 28
    FROM WHICH WE ARE LED TO ASSUME   329 26
    NONE O' THE TROUBLE HE'S LED TO STALL   *944 8

LEDGES
    HAS POISED ON EACH OF ITS LEDGES   105 14

LEEDS
    YET I AM A MILL-HAND IN LEEDS   630 5

LEERED
    LEERED   578 8
    THAT THEY STARED AND LEERED AT THE SINGLE SPOT   578 22

LEES
    DRIPPING WITH ALL THE GOLDEN LEES   104 31

LEFT-HAND
    AND A SOLDIER IN THE SADDLE OF THE LEFT-HAND DRAUGHT-HO+   733 8
    THE SNAKE OF MY LEFT-HAND OUT OF THE DARKNESS IS KISSIN+   801·22

LEG
    THEN IT BEGAN TO FIDGET SHIFTING FROM ONE LEG TO THE OT+   413 12
    A POOR ROAN THING ITS HIND LEG TWITCHES   734 6

LEGACY
    HERE AGAIN MAN HAS BEEN GOOD IN HIS LEGACY TO US IN THE+   263 18

LEGHORN
    BECAUSE FLAT-FOOT IS THE FAVOURITE OF THE WHITE LEGHORN+   761 17

LEGIONS
    IN YOUR PITILESS LEGIONS   168 36

LEGS
    HER SOFT WHITE LEGS HANGING HEAVILY OVER MY ARM   73 25
    FOLDED IN ITS LEGS AS IN A BED   112 21
    WHY SHOULDN'T YOUR LEGS AND YOUR GOOD STRONG THIGHS   254 11
    WHAT DO YOU STAND ON SUCH HIGH LEGS FOR   332 3
    QUEER WITH YOUR THIN WINGS AND YOUR STREAMING LEGS   332 15
    SHE HURRIES UP STRIDING REARED ON LONG UNCANNY LEGS   358 31
    LEGS   360 3
    WRINKLED PILLARS OF THEIR LEGS AS THEY WERE BEING   390 17
    BETWEEN THEIR LEGS IN HASTE TO GET AWAY   391 3
    ON THE LONG FLAT SKIS OF THEIR LEGS   393 27
    COMING UP ON FIERCE LITTLE LEGS TEARING FAST TO CATCH U+   397 15
    GREAT AND GLISTENING-FEATHERED LEGS OF THE HAWK OF HORUS   409 7
    HURRYING HURRYING LEGS GOING QUICK QUICK QUICK   484 6
    WITH BRIGHT LEGS AND UNCRINGING BUTTOCKS   525 21
    BECAUSE THEY ARE THE ARMS AND LEGS OF THE MACHINE   641 16
    AND WHEN AT LAST MAN STOOD ON TWO LEGS AND WONDERED   683 11
    MY LEGS MY BREAST MY BELLY   741 17
    KNEES AND YOUR LEGS AND YOUR LOINS HIS CIRCLE OF REST I+   801 25
    HER SOFT WHITE LEGS HANGING HEAVILY OVER MY ARM   *913 17

LEISURE
    I DON'T KNOW HE HAS LOTS OF LEISURE AND HE MAKES   452 22

LEISURED
    BECAUSE OBVIOUSLY HE'S NOT ONE OF THE LEISURED CLASSES   452 21

LEISURELY
    FOR THE TRAILING LEISURELY RAPTURE OF LIFE   68 5
    FOR THE TRAILING LEISURELY RAPTURE OF LIFE   *914 20

LEMON-COLOURED
    AND THEN YOU LAMP YOU LEMON-COLOURED BEAUTY   73 2

LENDING
    LENDING FIRST ONE EAR THEN ANOTHER   384 18

LENGTH
    ME FULL LENGTH IN THE COWSLIPS MUTTERING YOU LOVE   90 16
    THE LENGTH OF A SPARK   110 6
    ARE MET AT LENGTH TO FINISH OUR REST OF DAYS   157 25
    TILL AT LENGTH THEY INDUCE ME TO SLEEP AND TO FORGET   180 36
    TILL AT LENGTH THEY MATE   249 8
    THAT SWAYED THEIR LENGTH OF DARKNESS ALL AROUND   296 18
    WHY THIS LENGTH OF SHREDDED SHANK   332 4
    PROCEEDED TO DRAW HIS SLOW LENGTH CURVING ROUND   350 31
    AS EVERY HALF-TRUTH AT LENGTH PRODUCES THE CONTRADICTION   663 10
    SO WHEN I RUN AT LENGTH THITHER ACROSS   742 5
    THE PATH LIKE A SNAKE THAT IS GONE LIKE THE LENGTH OF A   788 11
    WAFTING LIKE SOLACE DOWN THEIR LENGTH OF DAYS   *941 16

LENGTHS
    WHEN THE HINDUS WEAVE THIN WOOL INTO LONG LONG LENGTHS   451 1

LENIN
    OR LENIN SAYS YOU ARE SAVED BUT YOU ARE SAVED WHOLESALE   443 1
    INSTEAD OF LEAVING IT TO LENIN   536 11

LENINISTS
    LENINISTS   313 6

LENT
    THE SEED IS ALL IN ALL THE BLOSSOM LENT   218 27
    TO DESTROY THE CHILL LENT LILIES   271 14
    HAVE LENT YOU VOICE NOR SPOKEN OF THE FACE   737 21

LEON
    LEON   401 19

LEONARDO
    NAY LEONARDO ONLY BUNGLED THE PURE ETRUSCAN SMILE   297 26

LEOPARD
    NO LEOPARD SCREECHED NO LION COUGHED NO DOG BARKED   394 17
    AND THE LEOPARD CANNOT CHANGE HIS SPOTS   413 28
    AS THE LEOPARD SMITES THE SMALL CALF WITH A SPANGLED PA+   683 9
    WHOM THE LEOPARD LOOKS IN THE EYES   769 26
    THE SMILE OF THE LEOPARD AND THE MEADOW-LARK   770 12
    WHERE THE LEOPARD PAUSING TO DRINK   771 1

LEOPARD-LIVID
    JAGUAR-SPLASHED PUMA-YELLOW LEOPARD-LIVID SLOPES OF   409 24

LEPT
    OF HER FEET AS THEY LEPT FOR A SPACE THEN PAUSE TO PRESS *934 10

LESBIAN
    EGO-BOUND WOMEN ARE OFTEN LESBIAN   475 12
    THE LESBIAN PASSION IS THE MOST APPALLING   475 18
    AND LOOK AT THE SODOMITICAL AND LESBIAN STUFF WEARING   532 6

LESS
    'S LESS GRASPIN' IF 'ER'S POOR   84 4
    LESS THAN THE WIND THAT RUNS TO THE FLAMY CALL   116 13
    MEANS EVEN LESS THAN HER MANY WORDS TO ME   127 24
    SHINE IN CONCEIT OF SUBSTANCE UPON ME WHO AM LESS THAN   133 12
    LESS THAN A YEAR THE FOURFOLD FEET HAD PRESSED   155 7
    SHALL I LESS THAN THE LEAST RED GRAIN OF FLESH   195 31
    SWARMS OF MANKIND IN THE WORLD AND WE WERE LESS LONELY   224 7
    IS MUCH LESS THAN THE BIT OF BLUE EGG   244 30
    AND TO BE LIMITED BY A MERE WORD IS TO BE LESS THAN A H+   292 4
    AND LESS THAN ALL THESE   366 23
    ALL MORE OR·LESS IN ERUPTION   539 3
    LESS THAN REAL MEN INFERIORS INFERIORS   637 26
    ALL MORE OR LESS ALIKE   657 4
    HE WILL INTERFERE WITH ME LESS   664 7
    THEY ARE USUALLY MUCH LESS THAN MEN   673 5
    ALL OF THEM HEALTHY MORE OR LESS WEALTHY   826 27
    PLUMS THE BLOND ONES ARE GOLD WITH LESS GLISTEN   827 5
    MORE OR LESS WEALTHY   828 3
    AFTER ALL IT IS IMMORAL FOR A WORD TO MEAN LESS THAN IT+   837 6
    TO WITHER ON THE BOSOM OF THE MERCIFUL SO MANY SEEDS TH+ *926 27

LESSENING
    A SLOW HEAVY PATTER OF LESSENING VIBRATION   767 20

LESSER
    HEAVY WITH A RANCID CARGO THROUGH THE LESSER SHIPS   380 19
    TO THE LESSER FRY IN THE HIERARCHY   681 4
    ME FOR ANOTHER LESSER SORRIER LOVE   877 4

LESSON
    THEY ARE HERE TO LEARN BUT ONE LESSON THAT THEY SHALL N+   93 16
    I WILL TEACH THEM THE BEGINNING OF THE LESSON AT THE RO+   93 24
    MUST LEARN THE SUPREME LESSON   636 24
    AND THEN RISEN WE MUST LEARN THE MOST CRUEL LESSON   637 1
    SAY WHAT WE LIKE OUR CIVILISATION HAS LEARNT A GREAT LE+   831 5
    MORAL LESSON   *950 29

LESSONS
    DOWN THE SOILED STREET WE HAVE PATTERED THE LESSONS   75 23
    AND WHERE WE CAN BEGIN TO LEARN OUR GREAT EMOTIONAL LES+   833 16
    AND ALL THE LESSONS LET SLIP BY   *894 13
    DOWN THE SOILED STREET WE HAVE PATTERED THE LESSONS CEA+ *897 23
    DOWN THE SOILED STREET WE HAVE PATTERED THE LESSONS   *900 31

LEST
    FOR THE MAN TO HEED LEST THE GIRL SHALL WEEP   41 11
    LEST HER BRIGHT EYES LIKE SPARROWS SHOULD FLY IN   122 29
    ALL FEARFUL LEST I FIND THE LAST WORDS BLEEDING   135 19
    LEST OUR FACES BETRAY US TO SOME UNTIMELY FIEND   267 34
    PILLARS OF WHITE BRONZE STANDING RIGID LEST THE SKIES F+ 287 16
    WELL COVERED LEST HE SHOULD BITE ME   347 5
    IN TERROR LEST YOU HAVE TO GO IN AND SINCE THE WORK-PRI+ 521 13
    AND FORCED TO WATCH EVERYONE THAT COMES NEAR YOU LEST   522 17
    LEST THE HEEL OF ACHILLES SHOULD BE REVEALED   577 14
    HOLD THE STARS STILL LEST WE HEAR THE HEAVENS DIMLY RIN+ 698 11
    LET US TURN BACK LEST WE SHOULD ALL BE LOST   737 12
    LEST HER BRIGHT EYES LIKE SPARROWS SHOULD FLY IN   *934 5
    ME LEST YOU MY SISTER SHOULD GO HEAPED WITH SUCH SHADOW+ *937 33
    ALL FEARFUL LEST I FIND SOME NEXT WORD BLEEDING   *939 3

LETS
    THEN LETS HER BLACK HAIR LOOSE THE DARKNESS FALL   128 33
    AS A PIGEON LETS ITSELF OFF FROM A CATHEDRAL DOME   134 21
    THERE'S A BREACH IN THE WALLS OF THE PAST LETS THE DAYL+ 174 6
    HE LETS YOU HIT HIM TWICE   559 20
    MIGHT FOLLOW SWIFT BEHIND THEE WHEN THOU LETS   879 12

LET'S
    LET'S A' HA' DONE   84 26
    SO GOOD-BYE AN' LET'S LET BE   85 4
    LET'S BE HONEST AT LAST ABOUT SEX OR SHOW AT LEAST THAT+ 464 12
    BUT AT THE SAME TIME DON'T LET'S THINK   470 9
    IF YOU'VE GOT THE GOODS COME FORWARD BOY AND LET'S SEE   483 20
    LET'S ABOLISH LABOUR LET'S HAVE DONE WITH LABOURING   517 19
    LET'S HAVE IT SO LET'S MAKE A REVOLUTION FOR FUN   517 22
    LET'S HAVE NO FULL STOPS LET'S JUST MANAGE WITH COMMAS   550 28
    WHY LET'S ALL OF US DO A BUNK   553 28
    LET'S HOPE THERE'LL BE MORE SENSE IN TAIL-TUFTS   665 4
    THE WORLD IS ENDING LET'S HURRY TO BORROW   815 2
    NOW LET'S EAT UP THE CORE   817 20
    COME ON LET'S TAKE OFF YOUR COLLAR AND DON'T REPROACH ME 859 30

LETTER
THE EAST A DEAD LETTER AND EUROPE MORIBUND IS THAT SO   371 32
AND WE LIVE BY THE LETTER OF TRUTH   661 19
TO LIFE FIXED TO THE LETTER OF THE LAW   662 21
HER LETTER SOMEHOW   748 14
HAS SHE SENT ME A LETTER   748 26

LETTERING
AND LITTERED LETTERING OF TREES AND HILLS AND HOUSES CL+   88 6

LETTERS
WHEREAS LETTERS ARE FIXED   661 18
ANTHROPOLOGISTS HISTORIANS AND MEN OF LETTERS   780 8
LIKE ANY OTHER WORD OF FOUR LETTERS   837 5

LETTING
WOULD WORSHIP THEE LETTING MY BUTTOCKS PRANCE   40 18
LETTING LIFE PASS   50 8
DREAMING AND LETTING THE BULLOCK TAKE ITS WILL   225 20
LETTING GO AT LAST AS SHE DRAGS AWAY   360 23
LETTING THE LIVING DEAD EAT YOU UP   449 20
OF SITTING THERE ON THE FENCE AND LETTING   560 3
ARE YOU LETTING ME GO AND HIDING YOUR FACE TO THE GROUND   871 32

LETTIN'
FOR LETTIN' ME MARRY THE LAD AS I THOUGHT   82 11
FOR LETTIN' ME MARRY THE LAD AS I THOUGHT   *924 15

LEVEL
IN LEVEL ROWS   50 20
ON THEIR LEVEL WAY   50 28
HOW NIGHT AFTER NIGHT SWEPT LEVEL AND LOW   103 5
A CROW FLOATS PAST ON LEVEL WINGS   166 1
ARE LEFT ON ETERNITY'S LEVEL   243 14
BUT I WON'T BE PUT ON A CABBAGE-IDEALISTIC LEVEL OF EQU+   316 16
AND EVERYTHING ELSE TO THEIR DISGUSTING LEVEL   317 31
SLOW WATERY ROTTING BACK TO LEVEL MUCK   318 2
OF WOLF ALL HAIRY AND LEVEL A WOLF'S WILD PELT   408 29
AND ALLOW THE SOUL TO FIND ITS LEVEL   428 7
AND REDUCE ME TO THE LEVEL OF A THING   620 8
INTO THAT WHICH IS BELOW THE LEVEL AND THAT WHICH IS   636 9
AND IN A STRANGE LEVEL FLUTTERING YOU GO OUT TO SEA-WAR+   696 25
YET REMAINING UNBROKEN THE LEVEL GREAT SEA   705 2

LEVEL-BALANCED
PUT BACK HER FINE LEVEL-BALANCED HEAD   222 15

LEVELLED
FOR THE TRIDENT WAS LEVELLED AT HIS HEAD   577 21

LEVELS
ACROSS THE RIVER LEVELS   206 6
STRANGE SHEER SLOPES AND WHITE LEVELS   261 9
TO THEIR LEVELS MY HOLY AUNT   555 24
THROUGH THE SLOW CORRUPTIVE LEVELS OF DISINTEGRATIVE KN+   699 22
DOWN TO THE LEVELS WHERE YOU HAVE STAYED   763 19

LEVERETS
HEAVIER THAN MINE YET LIKE LEVERETS CAUGHT IN STEEL   128 7

LEWD
AND SHE SAID DON'T DARE YOU WRETCH TO BE LEWD   577 15
BUT BAWDY ON THE BRAIN IS LEWD AND NAUSEOUS A SORT OF I+   *952 19

LIABILITY
LIABILITY COMPANY   550 4
LIKE A LIMITED LIABILITY COMPANY   550 5
THEY ARE ALL LIMITED LIABILITY   550 6

LIABLE
WHAT THEY'RE LIMITED TO OR LIABLE   550 7

LIAR
IF THERE ISN'T MY DEARLY-BELOVED LIAR   79 4
AND WHOEVER SAYS SHE ISN'T IS A LIAR   498 15
BUT I AM A LIAR I FEEL NO LOVELINESS IT IS A MENTAL REM+   509 27
HOW GREAT A LIAR AM I   661 15
MEANS A LIAR   708 6
IF THERE ISN'T MY DEARLY-BELOVED LIAR   *920 28

LIARS
AND YOU WILL HEAR WHAT LIARS THEY ARE   654 14
WE ARE ALL LIARS BECAUSE   661 16
TRAITORS OH LIARS YOU JUDAS LOT   762 14
YOU LIARS YOU DIRTY LOT   762 17
WHO ARE COWARDS WHO ARE LIARS WHO ARE TRAITORS WHO HAVE+   807 12
FROM THE LIARS FROM THE THIEVES FROM THE FALSE AND TREA+   807 16

LIBERALS
O YOU HARD-BOILED CONSERVATIVES AND YOU SOFT-BOILED LIB+   664 12

LIBERATES
TO THE NIGHT THAT TAKES US WILLING LIBERATES US TO THE +   70 4
AND YET HOW HIS SEPARATE BEING LIBERATES ME   252 3

LIBERATING
IS THE LIBERATING FIRE   810 16

LIBERTY
AND THAT WILL BE PURE EXISTENCE REAL LIBERTY   266 33
THE DOVE OF LIBERTY SAT ON AN EGG   413 1
AND THE BUB-EAGLE THAT LIBERTY HAD HATCHED WAS GROWING A   413 18
HIS MOTHER LIBERTY TRYING ALWAYS TO TEACH HIM TO COO   413 22
MEN FIGHT FOR LIBERTY AND WIN IT WITH HARD KNOCKS   535 23
WE HAVE LEARNED THAT ANOTHER MAN'S LIBERTY IS AS ESSENT+   833 1
THEIR WANDERING HAPPINESS AND THE WIND WASTED IN LIBERT+   *892 5

LIBIDINOUS
BLACK PROCREANT MALE OF THE SELFISH WILL AND LIBIDINOUS   383 14
ALONG WHICH RIDGE OF LIBIDINOUS MAGNETISM   386 12
LIBIDINOUS DESIRE RUNS BACK AND FORTH ASSERTING ITSELF +   386 15

LIBIDINOUSNESS
AND LEFT HIM ONLY HIS LIBIDINOUSNESS   382 2

LIBRARY
THINK OF ME HERE IN THE LIBRARY TRYING AND TRYING A SON+   57 21

LICE
AND LIVING LIKE LICE ON POOR MONEY   526 19
FOR MEN UPON THE BODY OF THE EARTH ARE LIKE LICE   793 1
AND MEN ARE THE LICE THAT CREEP ON IT   843 8
ALL PEOPLE LIKE LICE   843 10

LICHENS
TIMELESS AS BRANCHING LICHENS PALE AS MUST   135 15

LICK
WHAT MATTER THE STUFF I LICK UP IN MY DAILY FLAME   115 10
TO LICK ME UP AND DO ME HARM   150 27
TO LICK THE WORLD WITH FLAME THAT LICKS IT CLEAN   315 26
SEEMING TO LICK HIS LIPS   350 27
NOW IF THE LILIES OF FRANCE LICK SOLOMON IN ALL HIS GLO+   413 27
THERE IS A SPIRAL FLAME-TIP THAT CAN LICK OUR LITTLE AT+   440 5
I LICK THE CREAM OFF PROPERTY THAT'S WHAT IT SEEMS TO S+   664 4
AND LICK UP THY ASHES WITH A REPENTANT TONGUE   760 17
TO LICK ME UP BUT ONLY THE WARM   873 10
WHAT MATTER THE STUFF I LICK UP IN MY LIVING FLAME   *930 10

LICKING
COMES LICKING THROUGH THE BARS OF YOUR LIPS   151 7
THERE IS A NEW SWEETNESS IN HIS VOLUPTUOUSLY LICKING HI+   325 1
AND START PRANCING AND LICKING AND CUDDLING AGAIN   396 24
COMES LICKING IN FLAME THROUGH THE BARS OF YOUR LIPS   873 17

LICKIN'
AFTER LICKIN' AND SNUFFIN' AT ME THA COULD   *922 18

LICKS
TO LICK THE WORLD WITH FLAME THAT LICKS IT CLEAN   315 26
NOW THAT THE SUN LIKE A LION LICKS HIS PAWS   687 13

LID
A MOMENT THEN DARKNESS SHUT THE LID OF THE SACRED ARK   62 18
UNDER ITS SLOW LID TINY BABY TORTOISE   352 22

LIDDED
NOW THAT THE GRAVE IS MADE AND LIDDED OVER WITH TURF   411 28

LIDIES
YOU MIND WHO YER SAYIN' ISN'T LIDIES   434 26
ALL THE HINGLISH IS GENTLEMAN AN' LIDIES   434 27

LIDLESS
INTO THE LIDLESS SHADE   786 25

LIDS
STRANDS OF MY EYES AND MY LIDS AND MY HANDS AND MY FEET+   180 5

LIDY
'ERE SHE'S A LIDY AREN'T YER OLD QUIZZ   434 24
OF COURSE I'M A LIDY WHAT D'YER THINK   434 25

LIE
RABBITS HANDFULS OF BROWN EARTH LIE   33 5
THE HILL-BROW AND LIE QUITE STILL TILL THE GREEN   35 14
AND LIE DEAD STILL WHILE SHE   35 18
I SHOULD LIKE TO LIE STILL   35 21
THREE DEAD BIRDS LIE   36 24
WOULD SO GLADLY LIE   40 14
WASTES LIKE A LIE   41 27
STILL YOUR QUICK TAIL LIE STILL AS DEAD   43 3
FALLS ON ME AS I LIE IN DEEP GRASS   49 22
HOW CAN YOU LIE SO RELENTLESS HARD   55 2
YOU TELL ME THE LAMBS HAVE COME THEY LIE LIKE DAISIES W+   57 25
AND THEN HE WILL BE MINE HE WILL LIE   59 25
HE WILL LIE NEGLIGENT RESIGN   59 29
WHO IN LASSITUDE LEAN AS YACHTS ON THE SEA-WIND LIE   73 11
OF THE BOOKS THAT LIE OUT ON THE DESKS A FULL THREESCORE   74 13
EMBRACE OF DARKNESS LIE AROUND AND CRUSHED BETWEEN THEM+   88 4
LIE   88 15
AND EVEN IN THE WATERY SHELLS THAT LIE   89 18
THE PLAITS THAT LIE ALONG HER PILLOW   101 3
THE SICK GRAPES ON THE CHAIR BY THE BED LIE PRONE AT TH+   112 16
LIE DOWN AND OPEN TO ME   114 10
IS BURIED AWAY IN THE DARK WHERE THE DEAD ALL LIE   114 20
AND HALF LIES THERE IN THE DARK WHERE THE DEAD ALL LIE   115 1
THE WILD ANEMONES LIE   126 10
AN' LIE FRIGHTENED TER DEATH UNDER THEE   138 33
FOR A PLACE TO LIE DOWN AND STILL AS THEY STAND THEY SL+   146 7
I WILL NOT AGAIN REPROACH YOU LIE BACK   153 16
I'D LIE FOR EVER DRINKING AND DRAWING IN   153 29
THEY LIE SPILT ROUND THE CUP   216 4
WE LIE SIDE BY SIDE   229 15
MY KNEES AND LIE STILL   240 27
LIE ON ME WITH A HOT PLUMB LIVE WEIGHT   240 28
WOULD A WINGLESS LION LIE DOWN BEFORE THEE AS THIS WING+   324 2
EVEN SNAKES LIE TOGETHER   335 13
YOU LIE ONLY WITH THE WATERS   335 15
IT IS THE GREAT LIE OF THE DEAD   441 10
AS YOU KNOW IT IS A COMPLETE LIE   441 24
LISTENING IN TO THE LIE   441 26
GIVE GREAT HYPOCRISY THE LIE   458 10
SHE IS A MADE-UP LIE A DYED IMMORTELLE   478 28
UNCONTAMINATED BY EVEN THE BEGINNINGS OF A LIE   481 30

LIE
    SOMEHOW THEY ARE A LIE   505 24
    THEY LIE HIGH AND DRY   542 22
    HE FORCED US TO LIVE A GREAT LIE OR TO DISOBEY   654 7
    AND YOU LOOK IN HER EYES AND SEE IT IS A LIE   654 11
    CADENCE IS A LIE   655 5
    THE TRUTH OF YESTERDAY BECOMES A LIE TOMORROW   661 17
    IF IT WERE NOT SO IT WOULD BE A LIE   662 3
    MY CHILD I CANNOT TELL A LIE   681 23
    BEFORE PLATO TOLD THE GREAT LIE OF IDEALS   688 13
    AND ENORMOUS WHALES LIE DREAMING SUCKLING THEIR WHALE-T+   694 29
    I STUMBLE WHERE THE SHADOWS LIE   731 2
    WHERE THE LONG FAWN FORESHORES LIE   746 21
    ALREADY I SEE THE SHELLED MOON LIE   747 28
    IN THE FOUNTAIN YOU WILL LIE DOWN   809 11
    IF YOU REACH THE FOUNTAIN AND LIE DOWN   809 12
    DOWN APPLES LIE   817 2
    EAT AND LIE DOWN   818 1
    LIE DOWN BENEATH THE TREE   818 13
    THE HUMANS LIE   824 21
    THESE PEOPLE THAT LIE LIKE SEALS   824 30
    THEY LIE LIKE SEALS   825 9
    THEY LIE ON THE SHORE AND HEAVE   827 7
    CRAWL OUT OF THE WATER AND LIE ON THE BEACH   827 17
    THE SOFT CLUSTERED SHOULDER-FEATHERS IN ROSY CONFUSION +   855 23
    AND I'LL LIE IN HER LAP WHERE THE WORLD'S WILD ROSE   858 6
    AND HAVING WON I WILL LIE DOWN TO SLEEP   876 4
    RABBITS HANDFULS OF BROWN EARTH LIE   *891 6
    AND WAKE TO THE SOUND OF THE WOODPIGEONS AND LIE AND LI+   *892 28
    OF THE BOOKS THAT LIE OUT ON THE DESKS A FULL THREE SCO+   *895 21
    OF THE BOOKS THAT LIE OUT ON THE DESKS A FULL THREE SCO+   *904 10
    THAT LIE OUTSIDE THE SILVERY WALLS OF OUR BODY'S BUILDE+   *957 17

LIES
    THE BIRD LIES WARM AGAINST THE WALL   42 23
    SUCH AS LIES ALONG THE FOLDED WINGS   46 11
    THERE LIES THE WORLD MY DARLING FULL OF WONDER AND WIST+   52 20
    NOW SHUT IT LIES   55 16
    THE MOON LIES BACK AND REDDENS   64 20
    YOU ARE ALL THESE AND ON ME LIES THE DUTY   73 6
    IT'S SOMEBODY'S LIES   77 10
    WHICH LIES ON THE KNEES OF THE NIGHT-TIME RUDDY AND MAK+   88 21
    A NET ON THE UNDERSOIL THAT LIES PASSIVE AND QUICKENED +   94 4
    SHE LIES AT LAST THE DARLING IN THE SHAPE OF HER DREAM   101 14
    I MUST GO BUT MY SOUL LIES HELPLESS   102 23
    LIES ON THE DUST WATCHING WHERE THERE IS NOTHING TO SEE+   112 22
    BEYOND ME LIES ON THE LOW STILL FLOOR OF THE SKY   114 18
    SO HALF LIES ON THE SKY FOR A GENERAL SIGN   114 25
    AND HALF LIES THERE IN THE DARK WHERE THE DEAD ALL LIE   115 1
    UNKNOWN THAT LIES BEFORE US BEARING THE ARK OF THE COVE+   132 24
    ON THE THIN BARE SHINS OF A MAN WHO UNEASILY LIES   145 21
    MY LOVE LIES UNDERGROUND   198 1
    MY LOVE LIES UNDERGROUND   199 9
    A THICK MIST-SHEET LIES OVER THE BROKEN WHEAT   212 12
    A NIGHT LIES LOOKING UP   215 27
    FROM AUSTRIA THERE LIES THE WORLD AND HERE   231 6
    THAT LIES OUTSIDE THE MONSTROUS WOMB   262 23
    WHEN SHE IS SLAIN AGAINST ME AND LIES IN A HEAP LIKE ON+   267 13
    FOR FRUITS ARE ALL OF THEM FEMALE IN THEM LIES THE SEED+   277 1
    LION LIES   324 3
    WHO LIES WITH THE WATERS OF HIS SILENT PASSION WOMB-ELE+   335 20
    AND HE LIES LIKE A LOG AND SCREAMS AND HIS SCREAM IS SI+   407 20
    WHILE AS TO HONESTY OH LOOK WHERE THE MONEY LIES   432 33
    THE MYSTERY THAT LIES IN BEASTS   445 18
    BUT THE REAL FAULT LIES IN THE EGO-BOUND CONDITION OF   475 24
    WITH THE GODHEAD OF ENERGY THAT CANNOT TELL LIES   481 26
    ENTERING IN SHOCKS OF TRUTH UNFOLDED BY LIES   482 2
    HE SURE THINKS A LOT OF LIES   489 20
    FOR AFTER ALL HE HELPED TO SMASH A LOT OF OLD ROMAN LIES   497 3
    THE LIES THE TREACHERY THE SLIPPERY CULTURED SQUALOR OF+   497 4
    LIVED UNDAUNTED AND UNSOURED WITH ACCEPTED LIES   503 18
    IF PEOPLE LIVED WITHOUT ACCEPTING LIES   503 19
    IS THAT THEY ACCEPT LIES   504 2
    IF PEOPLE HAD COURAGE AND REFUSED LIES   504 3
    IS SOUR BITTER FRUITS CANKERED BY LIES   504 14
    AND BE A BIT MORE FIERY AS INCAPABLE OF TELLING LIES   505 18
    FOR WE'RE SURE TO BRING IN A LOT OF LIES   506 4
    I'M NOT GOING TO TELL ANY LIES ABOUT IT   507 3
    LOOKING DIRT ON THEM AND BREATHING ON THEM LIES   580 26
    WHILE THE POLE STAR LIES ASIDE LIKE AN OLD AXLE TAKEN F+   630 16
    FRAGRANCE OF ROSES IN A STALE STINK OF LIES   634 28
    AND THEREIN LIES THE DANGER OF ROBOT-DEMOCRACY AND ALL +   648 5
    LIES ARE NOT A QUESTION OF FALSE FACT   654 1
    IS LIES   654 4
    TERRIBLE AND STRANGE THE GOD LIES ON THE BED WISTFUL CO+   676 9
    THEN THE GREAT BULL LIES UP AGAINST HIS BRIDE   694 13
    AND BEHIND ME NOW IN THE GULFS OF SPACE LIES THE GOLDEN+   695 26
    THERE AND THERE ALONE LIES THE PIVOT OF PURE EVIL   712 11
    THAT LIES BETWEEN THE OLD SELF AND THE NEW   718 2
    ONLY THE WASTE NIGHT LIES IN STORE   747 27
    LIES A CHASM   763 22
    LIES LATENT IN THE SOULS OF THE YOUNG A LATENT DESIRE   829 10
    LIES IN FORCING YOURSELF OR SOMEBODY ELSE   836 18
    LIES THE LIVING ROCK OF A SINGLE CREATURE'S PRIDE   844 9
    LIES THE PONDEROUS FIRE OF NAKED LIFE   844 12
    BUT BELOW ALL ROOTS OF LOVE LIES THE BEDROCK OF NAKED P+   844 19
    WHO HAUNTS ME WITH HER LIES   854 28
    WHAT LIES OVER THE NEXT DARK HILL   858 3
    THERE LIES THE DULL RED HEAP OF THEIR SAND IN THE WEST   *896 7
    THERE LIES A DULL RED HEAP OF HIS SAND IN THE WEST   *896 17
    THERE LIES THE WORLD MY DARLING FULL OF WONDER AND WIST+   *905 9
    IT'S SOMEBODY'S LIES   *918 28

LIETH
    THIS ONE NIGHT YET HE LIETH HERE TO HAND   877 21

LIFE
    THE LIFE THAT LOOKS THROUGH MY EYES   38 30
    MY PULSE OF LIFE AND LET HIM NOSE LIKE A STOAT   43 31
    ALL MY LIFE I HAVE BORNE THE BURDEN OF MYSELF   47 29
    LETTING LIFE PASS   50 8
    MY LIFE WITH OTHER LEAVES MY TIME   52 10
    OF LIFE CAN YOU NEVER DISCARD   55 5
    BE WEALTH OF LIFE TO ME   59 24
    WITH A STRANGE NEW KNOCKING OF LIFE AT HER SIDE   64 8
    FOR THE TRAILING LEISURELY RAPTURE OF LIFE   68 5
    OF THE LUMINOUS PURPOSE OF LIFE SHINES OUT   68 10
    SINCE LIFE SWEEPS WHIRLING DIM AND VAST   69 1
    AND KISSED THEE TO A PASSION OF LIFE AND LEFT   69 23
    LIFE IN THY MOUTH AND DIM BREATH'S HASTENING HISS   69 24
    LIFE COMES TO THEE ON WHICH THOU HAST NO CLAIM   69 28
    WITH AFTER-PAIN MY SLEEPING BABY HANGS UPON MY LIFE   73 27
    MY LAST DEAR FUEL OF LIFE TO HEAP ON MY SOUL   74 19
    IN STUPOR PERSIST AT THE GATES OF LIFE OBSTINATE DARK M+   75 12
    AS 'AS SLUDGED LIKE A HORSE ALL 'ER LIFE   77 18
    AN' IF IT'S NOT TRUE YOU MAY BACK YOUR LIFE   78 15
    THE SEED OF LIFE INCARNATE THAT FALLS AND WAKES   89 10
    FOR ALL YOUR LIFE OF ASKING AND DESPAIR   100 27
    TO LIFE AND TO DEATH IN YOU   102 4
    AND THIS IS THE LIFE HEREAFTER   102 5
    LIFE WOULD HAVE BEEN SHOULD I HAVE SPENT   104 18
    OF LIFE WITH LOVE AND LOVE WITH LIFE   105 5
    ALL MY LIFE IN A RUSH   107 10
    WHIRLING IN THE DRAUGHT OF LIFE   110 18
    SO THROUGH THESE DAYS WHILE BURN ON THE FUEL OF LIFE   115 9
    PALPITATING FLAMES OF LIFE   115 14
    FROM THE DROWSE OF LIFE WAKE UP ANOTHER WILL   127 15
    THE VIVID AH THE FIERY SURPLUS OF LIFE   127 17
    MY LIFE RUNS OUT   131 12
    IN THE HOUSE OF LIFE THE FLOOR WAS RUFFLED WITH GOLD   141 6
    DOWN THE EMBANKMENT RUN FOR MY LIFE   143 18
    YOU ARE LOVELIER THAN LIFE ITSELF TILL DESIRE   151 6
    STIRRING WITH EARTH-COLOURED LIFE EVER TURNING AND STIR+   153 6
    MY LIFE AT YOUR FEET   156 30
    WHO FOR THE REST OF LIFE WALK OUT OF CARE   157 11
    WITH A KNOT OF LIFE THAT ONLY BLISS CAN UNRAVEL   160 14
    THE HALLS OF MY MIND COMPELLING MY LIFE TO CONFORM   173 20
    BEATS THE NEW FRESH AIR OF LIFE THEY COME FOR STRIFE   174 14
    FOR THE RIPPING OF ARRAS AND SMASHING OF WALLS AND THE +   174 14
    AND WHAT IS LIFE BUT THE SWELLING AND SHAPING THE DREAM+   176 6
    ME ITS LIFE AS IT HURRIES IN SECRET   180 33
    IN THIS ODD LIFE WILL TARNISH OR PASS AWAY   193 13
    AH GOD LIFE LAW SO MANY NAMES YOU KEEP   194 18
    WHEN TEARING THROUGH THE ANGUISH OF THIS LIFE   195 22
    THE WHOLE GREAT CONFLAGRATION OF ALL LIFE   195 26
    THAT ENDED HER LIFE AND MINE   198 4
    THAT ENDED HER LIFE AND MINE   199 12
    THE STREAM OF MY LIFE IN THE DARKNESS   199 19
    COME NO I'M A THING OF LIFE I GIVE   211 5
    NO NO I DANCE IN THE SUN I'M A THING OF LIFE   211 16
    THE SAME WANT LIFE OR DEATH   214 17
    NEITHER LIFE NOR DEATH COULD HELP   214 30
    AT STARTING OTHER LIFE FULFILLED MY OWN   218 14
    ANOTHER LIFE FROM OUR LIVES SO SHOULD SEND   218 21
    ANOTHER LIFE FROM MINE FOR IT SO LOOKS   218 25
    OF PERFECT LIFE AND IS OUR POSSIBLE SEED   219 7
    ITS FLAME OF LIFE NOW AND ALWAYS TILL THE END   233 16
    I AM BUSY ONLY AT MY LIFE   233 20
    IN US LIFE UNTO DEATH AGREEING   243 7
    AND MY LIFE IS FIERCE AT ITS QUICK   246 15
    LOOK FOR LIKE THE BREATH OF LIFE AS LONG AS I LIVE   248 10
    YOUR LIFE AND MINE MY LOVE   249 5
    NEW BEYOND KNOWLEDGE OF NEWNESS ALIVE BEYOND LIFE   258 30
    LIVING WHERE LIFE WAS NEVER YET DREAMED OF NOR HINTED AT   258 32
    STARVED FROM A LIFE OF DEVOURING ALWAYS MYSELF   259 15
    RISEN NOT TO THE OLD WORLD THE OLD CHANGELESS I THE OLD+   260 15
    SIGHTLESS AND STRONG OBLIVION IN UTTER LIFE TAKES POSSE+   261 10
    THE UNKNOWN STRONG CURRENT OF LIFE SUPREME   261 12
    EXTINGUISHES THERE MY RISEN RESURRECTED LIFE   261 15
    BETWEEN THE BODY OF LIFE AND ME   262 14
    COME LIFE SURGE THROUGH THIS MASS OF MORTIFICATION   271 2
    WOMAN'S BUT THE APPLES OF LIFE THE DRAGON GUARDS AND NO+   277 8
    WE HAVE BURIED SO MUCH OF THE DELICATE MAGIC OF LIFE   298 3
    SUCH AN AROMA OF LOST HUMAN LIFE   298 7
    TO BRING THEIR MEANING BACK INTO LIFE AGAIN   298 11
    THERE IS ONLY ONE EVIL TO DENY LIFE   298 16
    NUDE WITH THE DIM LIGHT OF FULL HEALTHY LIFE   298 26
    FLOWERILY NAKED IN FLESH AND GIVING OFF HUES OF LIFE   299 4
    OH PERSEPHONE PERSEPHONE BRING BACK TO ME FROM HADES TH+   303 13
    BUT BLOOD IS RED AND BLOOD IS LIFE RED WAS THE COLOUR O+   303 21
    OH GIVE ME THE TREE OF LIFE IN BLOSSOM   305 29
    THE EXQUISITE ASSERTION OF NEW DELICATE LIFE   314 19
    AND FEED THE YOUNG NEW FIELDS OF LIFE WITH ASH   315 5
    IN SIGN OF LIFE OF LOVELY DANGEROUS LIFE   317 16
    LIFE HAS ITS CHANGES BUT WHEN THE HEAVENS ARE EMPTY EMP+   319 8
    THE CRUMBLING DAMP FRESH LAND LIFE HORIZONTAL AND CEASE+   321 18
    YOUR LIFE A SLUICE OF SENSATION ALONG YOUR SIDES   335 8
    OR LIFE KNEW LOVING   337 12
    WHICH IS PERHAPS THE LAST ADMISSION THAT LIFE HAS TO WR+   338 16
    ONLY LIFE HAS A WAY OUT   347 1
    IN LIFE   347 3
    OF LIFE   351 28
    OR IS IT JUST YOUR INDOMITABLE WILL AND PRIDE OF THE FI+   353 17
    ALL LIFE CARRIED ON YOUR SHOULDER   354 21
    DEEPER INTO LIFE   354 25
    IT NEEDED PYTHAGORAS TO SEE LIFE PLAYING WITH COUNTERS +   355 14
    LIFE ESTABLISHING THE FIRST ETERNAL MATHEMATICAL TABLET   355 17
    PEDIMENT OF LIFE   356 21
    TO THE PRIMEVAL RUDIMENTS OF LIFE AND THE SECRET   365 21
    HORIZON OF LIFE   366 28
    BIRDS ARE THE LIFE OF THE SKIES AND WHEN THEY FLY THEY +   368 1
    SO HE BRINGS DOWN THE LIFE OF THE SUN AND THE POWER OF +   368 4
    A RAW AMERICAN WILL THAT HAS NEVER BEEN TEMPERED BY LIFE   370 34
    WHILE LIFE WAS A HEAVE OF MATTER HALF INANIMATE   372 10

LIFE
  BY THE LIFE IN THE HEARTS OF MEN   374 33
  HER LIP BEHIND HER AT ALL LIFE   386 14
  LIFE SEEMS TO LEAP AT THE AIR OR SKIM UNDER THE WIND   392 15
  FOR A NEW SIGNAL FROM LIFE IN THAT SILENT LOST LAND OF +   394 12
  SMALL LIFE   394 15
  WHO NEVER IN ALL HER LIFE COULD FIND THE WAY HOME   412 7
  FIND THE WAY NOW THAT YOU NEVER COULD FIND IN LIFE   412 12
  OVERWEENING MEN FULL OF POWER OF LIFE COMMANDING A   414 19
  LET HIM COME HOME TO A BIT OF MORAL DIFFICULTY LET LIFE+   431 4
  AND LIKE A FUNGUS LIVING ON THE REMAINS OF BYGONE LIFE   431 15
  SUCKING HIS LIFE OUT OF THE DEAD LEAVES OF GREATER LIFE+   431 16
  HEART OF LIFE   432 8
  GNAWS JUST THE SAME GNAWING THE SUBSTANCE OUT OF LIFE   432 12
  AND THE SAME FLAME THAT FILLS US WITH LIFE IT WILL DANC+   440 15
  LIFE FOR THE MILL-STONES   441 13
  AND THEY SAY NOW BEHOLD YOU ARE LIVING THE GREAT LIFE   441 19
  BEHOLD YOU ARE LIVING THE GREAT LIFE THE STUPENDOUS LIFE   441 23
  THEY ARE ONLY GREEDY FOR YOUR LIFE   441 29
  IF HE EARNS HIS LIFE HE'LL BE LOVELY   443 11
  BUT THE PLUCKY LITTLE SPORT IT GIVES TO LIFE   443 16
  LIFE INTO   448 2
  WARM STILL WITH THE LIFE OF FORGOTTEN MEN WHO MADE THEM   448 7
  ARE BORN DEAD THEY ARE SHROUDS THEY SOAK LIFE OUT OF US   448 9
  IN OUR LIFE   448 11
  EVERYTHING NEW AND MACHINE-MADE SUCKS LIFE OUT OF US   448 16
  LIVES BECAUSE OF THE LIFE PUT INTO IT   448 20
  A YARD OF INDIA MUSLIN IS ALIVE WITH HINDU LIFE   448 21
  AS WE LIVE WE ARE TRANSMITTERS OF LIFE   449 1
  AND WHEN WE FAIL TO TRANSMIT LIFE LIFE FAILS TO FLOW   449 4
  AND IF AS WE WORK WE CAN TRANSMIT LIFE INTO OUR WORK   449 6
  LIFE STILL MORE LIFE RUSHES INTO US TO COMPENSATE TO BE   449 7
  AND WE RIPPLE WITH LIFE THROUGH THE DAYS   449 9
  IF LIFE GOES INTO THE PUDDING GOOD IS THE PUDDING   449 12
  CONTENT IS THE WOMAN WITH FRESH LIFE RIPPLING IN TO HER   449 14
  IS STILL THE TRUTH ABOUT LIFE   449 17
  BUT GIVING LIFE IS NOT SO EASY   449 18
  ALL THAT WE HAVE WHILE WE LIVE IS LIFE   449 23
  AND IF YOU DON'T LIVE DURING YOUR LIFE YOU ARE A PIECE +   449 24
  AND WORK IS LIFE AND LIFE IS LIVED IN WORK   450 1
  WHILE A WAGE-SLAVE WORKS HE LEAVES LIFE ASIDE   450 3
  FOR IF A MAN HAS NO LIFE IN HIS WORK HE IS MOSTLY A HEAP   450 10
  TISSUED FROM HIS LIFE   451 23
  OF THE GAME OF LIFE   452 8
  AND THE SUGAR MELTS OUT OF LIFE   455 4
  EARNING YOUR LIVING WHILE YOUR LIFE IS LOST   459 7
  BUT THE FEAR OF LIFE IS STILL HERE I AM BRAVE   460 31
  NOW I MUST CONQUER THE FEAR OF LIFE   461 1
  THE KEY OF LIFE ON THE BODIES OF MEN   461 23
  OF THIS HOUSE OF LIFE THAT ENCLOSES US ALL   461 28
  AND I THOUGHT YOU WANTED LIFE AND EXPERIENCE DEAR YOUNG   463 5
  NEW LIFE FOR YOURSELVES AND YOUR WOMEN COMPLEMENTAL   463 12
  IT'S THE FLOW OF YOUR LIFE IT'S YOUR MOVING SELF AND YOU   464 18
  QUICK LITTLE SPLINTERS OF LIFE   466 15
  ALL MY LIFE   472 17
  LITTLE TORRENT OF LIFE   476 7
  OF INCIPIENT ENERGETIC LIFE   480 25
  YOU WILL FIND YOU HAVE A GREAT DESIRE TO DRINK LIFE DIR+   481 3
  THAT STRANGE ESSENTIAL COMMUNICATION OF LIFE   481 7
  LIFE FROM THE SOURCE UNADULTERATED   481 11
  THE SOUL'S FIRST PASSION IS FOR SHEER LIFE   482 1
  AND THEN TURN ROUND AND EMBRACE THE EXTANT BODY OF LIFE   482 4
  COOL UNLYING LIFE WILL RUSH IN   482 22
  BUT ON A RELIGION OF LIFE   483 28
  AN' LIFE SEEMS TO BEGIN   493 10
  TOO MUCH PURPOSE IN LIFE   496 4
  I AM NOT SURE I WOULD ALWAYS FIGHT FOR MY LIFE   497 13
  LIFE MIGHT NOT BE WORTH FIGHTING FOR   497 14
  SO THEY PECKED A SHRED OF MY LIFE AND FLEW OFF WITH A   500 4
  TO GIVE OF MY LIFE TO THE DEAD   500 9
  THEY HATE LIFE THEY ONLY LIKE CARRION   500 12
  WE HAVE MORE ENERGY AND OUR GRIP ON LIFE IS HARDER   503 6
  THE WRINKLED SMILE OF COMPLETENESS THAT FOLLOWS A LIFE   503 17
  MY FATHER HAS FACED ALL WEATHERS BUT IT'S BEEN A LIFE   503 30
  AND IT STIRS LIFE A SWAN   505 6
  CRUSHING OUT THE NATURAL HUMAN LIFE   508 21
  AH WHEN I HAVE SEEN MYSELF LEFT BY LIFE LEFT NOTHING   509 16
  LIFE HAS GONE AWAY BELOW MY LOW-WATER MARK   509 23
  IF ONLY WE COULD MAKE LIFE A BIT MORE JUST   518 23
  WORK IS THE CLUE TO A MAN'S LIFE   520 19
  YOUNG MEN HAVING NO REAL JOY IN LIFE AND NO HOPE IN THE   521 20
  MODERN LIFE IS A TALE TOLD BY AN IDIOT   522 1
  AND GAY FLICKER OF JOYFUL LIFE   523 23
  SET UP TO JUDGE BETWEEN LIFE AND DEATH   528 11
  HAVE A STERN EYE ON LIFE   528 15
  IN ALL CREATION ONLY MAN COWERS AND IS AFRAID OF LIFE   529 11
  IN THE WILD DAYS WHEN LIFE WAS SLIDING WHIRLWINDS BLUE-+   529 23
  WITH FIERY WEIGHT AND WILD LIFE AND COMING OUT   530 3
  HOW VIVIDLY THEY MAKE THEIR ASSERTION OF LIFE   530 14
  MILD FORMS OF COCAINE THEY'RE NOT LIFE EXACTLY   532 13
  FOR THE REST NO I WOULD SAY LIFE HELD VERY FEW   533 2
  SAFE ABOVE ALL FROM LIFE   543 7
  STAND UP FOR JUSTICE AND A JOLLY LIFE   560 15
  FOR A CHANCE OF LIFE ALL ROUND   560 30
  WITH YOUR LIFE AND AFFAIRS DON'T THRUST   561 16
  YOU'VE TOLD THEM THAT LIFE ISN'T REALLY MUCH FUN   583 6
  WHEN SHE READS THAT HER LIFE ISN'T REALLY MUCH FUN   583 11
  LIFE   585 15
  THIS LIFE WHICH IS NO-MAN'S-LIFE   585 18
  IN PLACE OF YOUR OWN LIFE   585 21
  IS LIFE STRIFE IS IT THE LONG COMBAT   606 13
  HE SAID TO ME YOUR LIFE WILL BE SO MUCH THE POORER   611 1
  THE BREATH OF LIFE   615 13
  THE BREATH OF LIFE AND THE SHARP WINDS OF CHANGE ARE TH+   615 16
  AND THE BREATH OF LIFE NEVER COMES TO NOURISH THEM   615 20
  AND SO THE LORD OF VENGEANCE PAYS BACK REPAYS LIFE   616 16
  CAN PUT BACK A HUMAN LIFE INTO CONNECTION WITH THE LIVI+   617 4
  CAN MELT THE DETACHED LIFE BACK   617 9

LIFE
  WHEN I SEE THE FLUTTERING OF PURE LIFE IN THEM   622 10
  AND ENGINES WILL RUSH AT THE SOLID HOUSES THE EDIFICE O+   624 28
  WHERE THEN IS LIFE   625 26
  BEAUTY OF LIFE   634 14
  USING ALL LIFE ONLY AS POWER AS AN ENGINE USES STEAM OR+   635 11
  AND THE SONS OF MEN WITH THE WIND AND THE FIRE OF LIFE   635 30
  LIFE WILL FIND A WAY   637 31
  DON'T GIVE ANY MORE LIFE TO THE MACHINES   639 2
  AND GIVE THEM LIFE   639 6
  VIVID LIFE   639 9
  OH MEN OF LIFE AND OF LIVING   639 11
  OH LIFE IS NOTHING IF NOT CHOICE   639 26
  THE HANDS OF LIFE   641 21
  THAT GRINDS LIFE VERY SMALL   641 23
  SONS OF MEN WITH THE WONDERING EYES OF LIFE   642 18
  AND CONFUSING YOU AND FEEDING ITSELF ON YOUR LIFE   642 21
  THEY CAN'T LIFE MEANS TOO MUCH TO THEM   647 23
  IF THE ROBOT CAN RECOGNISE THE CLEAN FLAME OF LIFE   648 14
  IN THE MEN WHO HAVE NEVER FALLEN IN LIFE   648 15
  THEN HE REPENTS AND HIS WILL BREAKS AND A GREAT LOVE OF+   648 16
  AND CEASES TO BE A ROBOT AND BECOMES A SERVANT OF LIFE   648 19
  OF LIFE UNDIMMED DELIGHTS HIM SO EVEN HE IS LIT UP   648 21
  ALL MEN WORSHIP THE WONDER OF LIFE   649 3
  SOME MEN CAN SEE LIFE CLEAN AND FLICKERING ALL ROUND   649 7
  DEMOCRACY IS DEMOS SERVING LIFE   650 2
  AND DEMOS SERVES LIFE AS IT GLEAMS ON THE FACE OF THE F+   650 3
  NOT FOR MONEY BUT FOR LIFE   650 13
  NOT A BOSS BUT THE GLEAM OF LIFE ON THE FACE OF A MAN   650 15
  AND UNDENIABLE NEW GODS SHARE THEIR LIFE WITH US WHEN WE   662 12
  TO LIFE FIXED TO THE LETTER OF THE LAW   662 21
  THE GODS WHO ARE LIFE AND THE FLUIDITY OF LIVING CHANGE   662 22
  AND THESE THE MINORITY OF MEN WHO CAN STILL SEE THE LIG+   665 25
  THOSE WHO ARE NEITHER BOURGEOIS NOR BOLSHEVIST BUT TRUE+   666 2
  INSTEAD OF WHICH THE MINORITIES THAT STILL SEE THE GLEA+   666 5
  AND OPEN OUR CONSCIOUSNESS TO THE DEEP MYSTERIOUS LIFE   666 13
  AND WE WILL FIND THE WAY TO IMMEDIATE CONTACT WITH LIFE   666 18
  AND FEARLESS FACE-TO-FACE AWARENESS OF NOW-NAKED LIFE   667 4
  THOUGHT IS THE WELLING UP OF UNKNOWN LIFE INTO CONSCIOU+   673 10
  THOUGHT IS GAZING ON TO THE FACE OF LIFE AND READING WH+   673 12
  AND ALL BUT SQUEEZE THE LIFE OUT OF HIM   674 21
  WHILE PEOPLE LIVE THE LIFE   675 9
  OF GROWING LIFE   675 28
  THAT FLICKERED FORTH IN THE BEST HOURS OF LIFE   676 11
  GLEAMING HER HOUR IN LIFE AS SHE NOW GLEAMS IN DEATH   676 14
  EAGERLY RAGGING OVER FROM THE ENTANGLEMENT OF LIFE   676 20
  ARE ALL THE OBSTRUCTIONS TO LIFE SELF-IMPORTANCE SELF-C+   678 11
  OR ALL THE UGLY OLD POSSESSIONS THAT MAKE UP THE IMPEDI+   678 13
  FREE MOTION OF LIFE   678 16
  DOES IT MEAN THAT LIFE WHICH HAS GONE UGLY AND UNLIVING+   678 20
  O SLAY NOT THE BEST BRIGHT PROUD LIFE THAT IS IN YOU TH+   678 24
  THAT BLOOD OF THE LOWER LIFE MUST BE SHED   679 9
  FOR THE FEEDING AND STRENGTHENING OF THE HANDSOMER FULL+   679 10
  INTO THE DANCE AND SPLENDOUR OF A BIGGER LIFE   679 17
  THERE IS ONLY LIFE AND ANTI-LIFE   679 19
  AND SACRIFICE IS THE LAW OF LIFE WHICH ENACTS   679 20
  IS THE VERY INDIVIDUAL FLAME OF LIFE ITSELF   679 26
  AS A GIFT OF GLADNESS SEEING THE GLAMOUR OF LIFE GO UP   680 5
  IS THE INCOMPREHENSIBLE PLASM OF LIFE OF CREATION   681 27
  WHEN THE DIM FLUX OF UNFORMED LIFE   682 3
  OF LOVELESS LIFE   693 23
  AS MOUNTAIN PRESSING ON MOUNTAIN IN THE ZEST OF LIFE   694 15
  THE BREATH OF LIFE IS IN THE SHARP WINDS OF CHANGE   698 1
  BUT IF YOU WANT TO BREATHE DEEP SUMPTUOUS LIFE   698 3
  YAWNING AT HOME BEFORE THE FIRE OF LIFE   700 9
  IN THE HOUSE OF LIFE   700 16
  FOR THEY ARE THE ELEMENTS OF LIFE OF POETRY AND OF PERC+   706 3
  AND LIFE IS FOR DELIGHT AND FOR BLISS   708 24
  BUT STILL I KNOW THAT LIFE IS FOR DELIGHT   709 3
  AND LIFE IS FOR DELIGHT AND BLISS   709 8
  LIFE IS FOR KISSING AND FOR HORRID STRIFE   709 25
  LIFE IS FOR THE ANGELS AND THE SUNDERERS   709 26
  LIFE IS FOR THE DAIMONS AND THE DEMONS   709 27
  BUT LIFE IS NOT   709 29
  LIFE IS FOR KISSING AND FOR HORRID STRIFE   710 1
  AND HELL AND HEAVEN ARE THE SCALES OF THE BALANCE OF LI+   710 21
  LIFE HAS ITS PLACE OF BLUE DAY ALOFT   711 1
  FOR LIFE IS A WANDERING WE KNOW NOT WHITHER BUT GOING   713 24
  ARE ALL EVIL ABSTRACTIONS FROM LIFE   716 12
  AND POLITICS NOW ARE AN EVIL ABSTRACTION FROM LIFE   716 13
  A BRUISE OR BREAK OF EXIT FOR HIS LIFE   717 13
  COWERING IN THE LAST BRANCHES OF THE TREE OF OUR LIFE   718 20
  AND LIFE DEPARTS LAUNCH OUT THE FRAGILE SOUL   719 2
  MAYBE LIFE IS STILL OUR PORTION   721 6
  OH PITY THE DEAD THAT WERE OUSTED OUT OF LIFE   722 4
  AND THE WHITE SHORES OF LIFE   722 8
  BUT MUST ROAM LIKE OUTCAST DOGS ON THE MARGINS OF LIFE   722 11
  BEWARE THE UNHAPPY DEAD THRUST OUT OF LIFE   722 16
  OLD PLACES OF SWEET LIFE FROM WHICH THEY ARE THRUST OUT   723 1
  THAT WERE THRUST OUT OF LIFE AND NOW COME BACK AT US   723 6
  FOR WITHOUT THE SONG OF DEATH THE SONG OF LIFE   723 27
  HOW TERRIBLE LIFE WOULD BE   724 23
  NOTHING IN LIFE IS QUITE SO GOOD AS THIS   725 5
  THEN I SHALL KNOW THAT MY LIFE IS MOVING STILL   727 14
  AND IF IN THE CHANGING PHASES OF MAN'S LIFE   727 17
  AND STRENGTH IS GONE AND MY LIFE   727 20
  IS ONLY THE LEAVINGS OF A LIFE   727 21
  SUCH AS MY LIFE HAS NOT BROUGHT FORTH BEFORE NEW BLOSSO+   727 26
  THEN WE SHALL TURN US HOME AGAIN TO LIFE   740 24
  AND WE SHALL HAVE NEW PEACE IN THIS OUR LIFE   740 25
  NEW JOY TO GIVE MORE LIFE NEW BLISS TO LIVE   740 26
  I MUST PRESERVE MY LIFE FROM HURT   741 6
  WE TAKE THE BRIDE O GOD AND OUR SEED OF LIFE   743 12
  THE HOSTS ARE LEAPING FROM THE EDGE OF LIFE   743 30
  SO LONG AS WE'RE HERE IN LIFE OUR SISTER WE COME   753 17
  THE VANITY OF LIFE   762 2
  THE WOMAN WEEPS HER CHANGE OF LIFE   766 7
  MY LIFE MY BROODY SELF   766 23

LIFE
I CANNOT EVEN REMEMBER MY LIFE THAT HAS BEEN 767 11
MY LIFE FROM THE ME THAT REMAINS 767 15
ALIVE AND YET DRAINED OF LIFE 767 16
RIVER OF MY LIFE 768 13
WHERE LIFE LOOKS ME IN THE EYES 768 19
THAT NOTHING NOT LIFE CAN STAIN 772 27
VIBRATES UNTOUCHED AND VIRILE IN LIFE UNUTTERABLE RICH 772 30
OF LIFE UNBORN AND IS FRETTED 772 33
LIFE IS DARK AND RIPPLING BUT FRETTED 773 1
THEN OUR LIFE IS FINISHED OUR DAY IS OVER COMPLETELY 779 5
TO LIVE THEIR OWN LIFE FULFIL THEIR OWN ENDS 779 24
THE OLD FATHER OF LIFE AT THE HEART OF THE WORLD LIFE-F+ 783 2
AND THE FLAME OF YOU SWEPT BACK IN A NEW BREATH OF LIFE 784 26
OF TOSSING AND ROLLING THE SUBSTANCE OF LIFE TO YOUR LI+ 792 21
HIS LIFE 795 29
SEEKING THE OFFAL AND GARBAGE OF LIFE IN THE INVISIBLE + 796 6
CREEPING FOR THE GARBAGE OF LIFE AND BITING WITH VENOMO+ 796 13
FOR I AM SWEET I AM THE LAST AND THE BEST THE POOL OF N+ 796 24
SO IT WILL LEAVE YOU AND YOU WILL HAND LIKE A GOURD ON + 800 22
GUARDS LIFE FROM DEATH AND DEATH FROM LIFE 810 2
THE DEEPS THAT LIFE CANNOT FATHOM 811 6
ONLY THAT IT IS AND ITS LIFE IS OUR LIFE AND OUR DEATH 811 8
AND MORE SPACE THAN IN LIFE 816 23
OF LIFE AND TO KNOW 817 7
AND TATTERED AND RED WITH THE LIFE THAT HAS BLED 823 4
THE LIFE WITHOUT LAWS 825 22
NEW LIFE BUBBLES IN WE BECOME SOMETHING ELSE 832 22
THE MOMENT I SWEAR TO LOVE A WOMAN ALL MY LIFE THAT VER+ 834 8
IN THE SAME WAY IF I SWORE TO HATE A WOMAN ALL MY LIFE + 834 10
I LOVE LIFE I LOVE LIFE SO DEARLY I COULD ALMOST DIE 837 10
ANYTHING THAT EXPRESSED LIFE 837 17
WHEREIN A MAN CAN LIVE HIS LIFE WITHOUT BEING A SLAVE T+ 837 25
FOR ALL THAT LIFE WILL ONLY BE GOOD AGAIN WHEN THERE IS+ 838 1
PULL IT DOWN AND PREPARE FOR A NEW FRESH HOUSE OF LIFE 838 12
AND OUR INTUITION CAN COME TO LIFE AND GIVE US DIRECTION 839 4
TO KEEP A SANE CORE TO LIFE 839 17
TODAY LIFE IS A CHOICE OF INSANITIES 839 18
WITH WEBBED FECUNDITY PLUNGING THE SEED OF LIFE IN THE + 841 5
LOVE LIKE THE FLOWERS IS LIFE GROWING 844 1
LIES THE PONDEROUS FIRE OF NAKED LIFE 844 12
LIKE THE LIVING LIFE ON THE EARTH 844 18
IN FACT A LITTLE BAWDY IS NECESSARY IN EVERY LIFE 844 30
IN FACT A LITTLE WHORING IS NECESSARY IN EVERY LIFE 845 2
LIFE LOVERS WHO COULD HOPE FOR NO RANK AMONG THE PALLID+ 855 20
THERE IS NO PASSION IN MY LIFE 856 22
RICHER THAN LIFE ITSELF TILL DESIRE 873 16
OF THIS ETERNAL LIFE 875 17
UPON THESE AWFUL WATERS OF LIFE AND DEATH 875 27
I GO TO PLAY MY GAME OF LIFE WITHIN 876 9
AND WHERE HE CAME TO LILT MY LIFE ALONG 877 23
AND STILL HIS LIFE SHAKES AT THE LATCH OF SLEEP 878 28
BEFORE THE LIFE SHALL CEASE TO URGE AND STRIDE 879 6
THE FIERY MIXTURE OF THY LIFE SO I 879 11
TILL OFF THY MOUTH HAS LEAPT THE FLAME OF LIFE 879 22
WERE WORSE THAN BEING LEFT ALONE IN LIFE 879 27
LIKE SEED FROM OUT THE RIPENED LOINS OF LIFE 880 6
HE OPENED THE VALVES OF LIFE AND HIS LIFE SIGHED OUT 885 9
LIFE TWISTING ITS CRAZED MACHINERY 887 5
TO CATCH AFIRE WITH LIFE 888 6
AND THE LIFE THAT IS POLARISED IN MY EYES *893 13
TILL THE BURSTEN FLOOD OF LIFE EBBS BACK TO MY EYES *893 30
MYSELF IN THE ROAR OF LIFE WHICH SHALL TAKE AND OBLITER+ *894 23
DARK GLITTER OF LIFE AMID A SKY THAT TEEMS *895 7
BUT THE NOISE OF LIFE *895 9
THE SURGE AND TIDE OF LIFE IN THE TURBULENT CLASS *895 10
NOT ALL FOR THEM SHALL THE FIRES OF MY LIFE BE HOT *895 32
FINE FOLIAGE OF LIVES THIS LIFE OF MINE *899 25
THE LOWEST STEM OF THIS LIFE OF MINE *899 26
THE OLD HARD STEM OF MY LIFE *899 27
MY TOP OF LIFE THAT BUDS ON HIGH *899 29
THEY ALL DO CLOTHE MY UNGROWING LIFE *899 31
WITH A RICH A THRILLED YOUNG CLASP OF LIFE *899 32
OF LIVING MY LIFE WERE DOUBLED I STILL HAVE THIS TO COM+ *900 3
TO FOLLOW MY LIFE ALOFT TO THE FINE WILD AIR OF LIFE AN+ *900 8
AS I AM WITH LIVING MY LIFE IN EARNESTNESS STILL PROGRE+ *900 12
OF ALL THE STRAYS OF LIFE THAT CLIMB MY LIFE *900 27
FINE FOLIAGE OF LIVES THIS LIFE OF MINE *903 4
THE LOWEST STEM OF THIS LIFE OF MINE *903 5
THE OLD HARD STEM OF MY LIFE *903 6
MY TOP OF LIFE THAT BUDS ON HIGH *903 8
THEY ALL DO CLOTHE MY UNGROWING LIFE *903 10
WITH A RICH A THRILLED YOUNG CLASP OF LIFE *903 11
OF LIVING MY LIFE WERE DOUBLED I STILL HAVE THIS TO COM+ *903 16
TO FOLLOW MY LIFE ALOFT TO THE FINE WILD AIR OF LIFE AN+ *903 20
AS I AM WITH LIVING MY LIFE IN EARNESTNESS STILL PROGRE+ *903 24
OF ALL THE STRAYS OF LIFE THAT CLIMB MY LIFE *904 3
NOT ALL FOR THEM SHALL THE FIRES OF MY LIFE BE HOT *904 21
THE HALLS OF MY LIFE AND COMPELS MY SOUL TO CONFORM *906 14
THE HALLS OF MY LIFE COMPELLING MY SOUL TO CONFORM *908 8
OH THE TERRIBLE ECSTASY OF THE CONSCIOUSNESS THAT I AM + *909 18
IMPULSE OF LIFE *909 22
THEN TO FALL BACK EXHAUSTED INTO THE UNCONSCIOUS MOLTEN+ *909 28
MY SLEEPING BABY HANGS UPON MY LIFE *913 19
FOR THE TRAILING LEISURELY RAPTURE OF LIFE *914 20
THE VIVID LIFE OF HIS LOVE IN THY MOUTH AND THY NOSTRILS *916 7
WHERE THE EBB OF LIFE SLIPS BY *917 8
AS HAS SLUDGED LIKE A HORSE ALL HER LIFE *919 6
AN' IF IT'S NOT TRUE I'D BACK MY LIFE *920 7
LOVED TO LIFE IN SUNSHINE *927 5
AND THROUGH THESE YEARS WHILE I BURN ON THE FUEL OF LIFE *930 9
WITH LIFE TILL THE EARTH AND THE SKY HAVE TUMBLED *937 18
LIFE IS NOTHING WITHOUT RELIGION *946 11
CAME FROM THEM LIVING LIKE LEAVES FROM THE TREE OF THEI+ *949 30
TISSUED FROM HIS LIFE *950 8
IT WOULD BE A NAKED LIFE WITHOUT LOVE *951 7
THAT CONVULSES AND TREMBLES AGAIN WITH THE SYMPATHY OF + *952 7
COILS AND RECOILS SENSITIVE TO LIFE AND CONSCIOUS OF TR+ *952 8

LIFE
IN FACT A LITTLE BAWDY IS NECESSARY IN EVERY LIFE *952 11
IN FACT A LITTLE WHORING IS NECESSARY IN EVERY LIFE *952 14
IN FACT IT MAY BE THAT A LITTLE SODOMY IS NECESSARY TO + *952 18
IN FACT QUITE A LOT OF CHASTITY IS NECESSARY IN LIFE TO+ *952 24
LIFE IS A THING YOU'VE GOT TO BE FLEXIBLE AND INTELLIGE+ *953 9
IN SOME HEARTS STILL THE SANCTUARIES OF WILD LIFE *954 2
A BRUISE OR BREAK OF EXIT FOR HIS LIFE *957 4
ONCE OUTSIDE THE GATE OF THE WALLED SILVERY LIFE OF DAYS *957 27
PITY OH PITY THE POOR DEAD THAT ARE ONLY OUSTED FROM LI+ *958 8
BUT MUST ROAM LIKE OUTCAST DOGS ON THE MARGINS OF LIFE *958 16
FOR WITHOUT THE SONG OF DEATH THE SONG OF LIFE *961 9

LIFE-BLISSFUL
FEARING NOTHING LIFE-BLISSFUL AT THE CORE 307 2

LIFE-BODY
FRAGILE-TENDER FRAGILE-TENDER LIFE-BODY 306 23

LIFE-CLOUDED
NOT IN STONE LIKE THE JUDEAN LORD OR BRONZE BUT IN LIFE+ 355 18

LIFE-CURRENT
THE LIFE-CURRENT FLOWING 861 30

LIFE-DEMAND
A NEW LIFE-DEMAND 431 10

LIFE-DIVINE
THE TREE BEING LIFE-DIVINE 307 1

LIFE-FIRE
THE OLD FATHER OF LIFE AT THE HEART OF THE WORLD LIFE-F+ 783 2
CONNECTION WITH STILL DEEPER STILL MORE TERRIBLE LIFE-F+ 844 15

LIFE-FLOW
IN THE SHEER COITION OF THE LIFE-FLOW STARK AND UNLYING 482 14
LOST THEIR LIFE-FLOW 610 10

LIFE-LADDERS'
RUNG OF THEIR LIFE-LADDERS' FRAGILE HEIGHTS 854 3

LIFELESS
AND MAKES US COLD MAKES US LIFELESS 448 17
AND EACH TIME IT CAME OUT THE SAME A HORRIBLE SEXLESS L+ 619 10
THEIR FEATHERS LIFELESS AND THE ROSE LIGHTS TURNING TO + 855 28

LIFELESSLY
MEN SHOULD REFUSE TO BE LIFELESSLY AT WORK 450 5

LIFELESSNESS
HER FIRE INFUSING ITS LIFELESSNESS *937 17

LIFE-LOVING
BUT OF THOSE LIFE-LOVING CARELESS OF THEIR RANK AMONG T+ 855 12

LIFE-LUSTRE
WITH THE LIFE-LUSTRE 298 25

LIFE-QUALITY
IT MEANS KINDLING THE LIFE-QUALITY WHERE IT WAS NOT 449 21

LIFE-SPIRIT
BUT WHEN I SEE THE LIFE-SPIRIT FLUTTERING AND STRUGGLIN+ 622 4

LIFE-STUFF
TILL THEY ARE SOFTENED BACK TO LIFE-STUFF AGAIN AGAINST+ 663 7

LIFE'S
AT THE BACK OF MY LIFE'S EXPERIENCE WHERE DREAMS FROM 52 26
OR MY LIFE'S REWARD 59 12
NOR BE THWARTED IN LIFE'S SLOW STRUGGLE TO UNFOLD THE F+ 93 18
THE GAP IN MY LIFE'S CONSTELLATION 115 17
OF BROODING AND DELIGHTING IN THE SECRET OF LIFE'S GOIN+ 197 17
OUT OF LIFE'S UNFATHOMABLE DAWN 364 2
LIFE'S VOICE EVEN WHEN SHE'S HOARSE 491 8
LIFE'S TOILSOME JOURNEY THROUGH 576 19
TO BE ALONE IS ONE OF LIFE'S GREATEST DELIGHTS THINKING+ 610 3
LONG DIFFICULT REPENTANCE REALISATION OF LIFE'S MISTAKE+ 620 18
AGAINST THE SILVERY ADAMANT WALLS OF LIFE'S EXCLUSIVE C+ 722 3
THE LOINS OF THIS OUR TISSUE OF TRAVAIL OUR LIFE'S 880 3
AT THE BACK OF MY LIFE'S HORIZON WHERE THE DREAMS FROM + *905 15
TOUCHES THE MARGINS OF OUR LIFE'S EXISTENCE *958 28

LIFE-THROB
LIFE-THROB 339 10

LIFE-TIME'S
THROUGH THE DEAD WEED OF A LIFE-TIME'S FALSITY *959 8
PULLING THE LONG OARS OF A LIFE-TIME'S COURAGE *959 12

LIFE-TIME
WITHIN THE IMMENSE AND TOILSOME LIFE-TIME HEAVED 195 29

LIFE-TRUTH
AND THE OLD OLD FINAL LIFE-TRUTH 844 16

LIFT
LIFT MY ARMS THE HILL BURSTS AND HEAVES UNDER THEIR SPU+ 33 9
NOW AT LAST WE LIFT OUR FACES AND OUR FACES COME AFLOWER 70 3
WHEN THEY LIFT THEIR TRUNKS AND SCREAM ALOUD 70 11
LIFT LOOKS OF SHOCKED AND MOMENTOUS EMOTION UP AT ME 71 22
AN' WE'LL BE MARRIED AT TH' REGISTRAR NOW LIFT THY FACE 83 4
LIFT THY FACE AN' LOOK AT ME MAN CANNA TER LOOK AT ME 83 5
WHO LIFT SWART ARMS TO FEND ME OFF BUT I COME 86 18
I LIFT TO YOU 96 11
COMES ON US LIFT YOUR FINGERS WHITE 117 12
IF I COULD LIFT MY NAKED SELF TO YOU 122 18

LIFT
LIFT OF THE PULSING WIND AH SAY THAT YOU KNOW — 126 32
FOR NEVER HER HANDS COME NIGH ME BUT THEY LIFT — 128 10
AND I DO LIFT MY ACHING ARMS TO YOU — 129 19
AND I DO LIFT MY ANGUISHED AVID BREAST — 129 20
THE WHOLE OF THE DAY TO EXTINGUISH THE SHADOW I LIFT ON+ — 133 20
FOR I AM TIRED MY DEAR AND IF I COULD LIFT MY FEET — 134 24
IN THE SUBTLE LIFT OF THE THIGHS AS THEY COME UNMARCHING — 174 13
AND DANCE BUT I CAN'T LIFT UP — 216 2
AND WHEN I LIFT MY FACE IT IS A FLAME THAT GOES UP — 233 22
COME AND LIFT US TOWARDS OUR CULMINATION WE MYRIADS — 272 31
COME AND LIFT US TO OUR END TO BLOSSOM BRING US TO OUR + — 272 33
WILT THOU LIFT ME UP SON OF MAN — 320 18
IS IT SO THAT YOU SHALL LIFT YOUR CENTRE OF GRAVITY UPW+ — 332 6
LIFT AND SWIM AND GO THEIR WAY — 337 30
TO LIFT THE UPPER HAWK-BEAK FROM THE LOWER BASE — 352 12
DO YOU LIFT IT TO THE SUN AS THE AZTEC PRIESTS USED TO + — 374 7
THEY LIFT THE LITTLE DOOR — 380 22
LIFT UP HER FACE — 402 1
AND LIFT HIS FACE AND SET HIS BREAST — 428 18
OF OBSCENITY AND LIFT YOUR NOSES WHERE THE VENT IS — 462 32
THE SWAN WILL LIFT UP AGAIN HIS FLATTENED SMITTEN HEAD — 625 2
LIFT NEVER A FINGER AGAINST THEM THAT THEY CAN SEE — 643 5
I LIFT UP MINE EYES UNTO THE HILLS — 660 20
SO LONG WILL THEY LIFT THEIR IMPERTINENT VOICES — 681 5
CEASE TO LIFT UP ITS HILLS — 688 3
LIFT UP YOUR HEADS O YE GATES — 699 9
I LIFT MY INEXTINGUISHABLE FLAME — 745 2
I LIFT MY LITTLE PURE AND LAMBENT FLAME — 745 10
OF FULL DESPAIR I LIFT MY TENDER FLAME — 745 13
THE WILLOW SHALL LIFT HER LEAVES TO SOOTHE THY DISTRESS — 749 24
DO YOU LIFT YOUR LIPS TO KISS ME GOOD NIGHT MY LOVE — 750 16
WHEN YOU LIFT YOUR HANDS IN COURAGE AND BRAVERY ITS GLO+ — 800 10
ALL THINGS THAT LIFT IN THE LIFT OF LIVING BETWEEN EART+ — 801 8
AND LIFT IT UP — 803 7
LIFT YOUR HAND SAY FAREWELL SAY WELCOME — 803 14
LIFT YOUR HAND SAY FAREWELL SAY WELCOME — 803 19
LIFT UP YOUR HEADS — 818 5
O YE GATES EVEN LIFT THEM UP — 818 6
LIFT UP YOUR HEADS O YE GATES — 818 10
SIEGMUND LIFT UP YOUR FACE AGAIN OFF THE TURF — 871 36
TO HELP HIM LIFT THE WELTERING DARKNESS TURN — 872 3
THAT LIFT UP HIGH THEN DROP HIS STRANGE HARSH BREAST — 879 1
LIFT AND RUFFLE IN THE WIND — 883 8
LEAN TOGETHER AND LIFT WILD ARMS TO EMBRACE — 883 9
I LIFT MY BREAST AND LEAN FORWARD — 883 10
AND I LIFT MY HEAD UPON THE TROUBLED TANGLED WORLD AND I — *900 1
AND I LIFT MY HEAD UPON THE TROUBLED TANGLED WORLD AND + — *903 14
NOW AT LAST WE LIFT OUR FACES AND OUR FACES COME AFLOWER — *916 11
AN' WE'LL BE MARRIED AT TH' REGISTRAR NOW LIFT THY FACE — *925 8
LIFT THY FACE AN' LOOK AT ME MAN UP AN' LOOK AT ME — *925 9
LIFT UP YOUR MEASURE TO ME TO FILL — *931 10
COMES ON US YOU'LL LIFT YOUR FINGERS WHITE — *931 16

LIFTED
THE TREES RISE TALLER AND TALLER LIFTED — 68 1
TO SEE THE CLASS'S LIFTED AND BENDED FACES — 90 5
SO NIGHT'S FLOOD-WINDS HAVE LIFTED MY LAST DESIRE FROM + — 97 9
IF THE JOY THAT THEY ARE LIFTED TO AVENGE — 126 3
OF THE WIND SHE IS LIFTED AND CARRIED AWAY AS IN A BALL+ — 153 2
WAITS WITH A LIFTED OAR — 201 20
AND THIS IS BEAUTY TO ME TO BE LIFTED AND GONE — 252 9
WHEN SHE LIFTED HER HEAD IN DELICATE STARTLED WONDER — 255 28
WHEN SHE LIFTED HER MOP FROM HER EYES AND SCREWED IT IN — 310 2
AND I IF I BE LIFTED UP WILL DRAW ALL MEN UNTO ME — 320 4
CANNOT BE LIFTED UP THE PARACLETE — 320 11
ALL THE TIME I AM LIFTED UP — 320 23
SO I WILL BE LIFTED UP SAVIOUR — 321 7
NAY SON OF MAN I HAVE BEEN LIFTED UP — 322 7
HE LIFTED HIS HEAD FROM HIS DRINKING AS CATTLE DO — 349 21
AND LIFTED HIS HEAD DREAMILY AS ONE WHO HAS DRUNKEN — 350 24
RUFFLING BLACK SHINING FEATHERS LIKE LIFTED MAIL — 370 24
OR LIKE A LIFTED HAND HAILING AT HER WRONG END — 385 33
THAT LITTLE LIFTED BARE HAND — 386 16
OR EVEN THE SLY GOLD SERPENT FATHERLY LIFTED HIS HEAD O+ — 437 18
BOWED AND LIFTED HER FOOT IN HER HAND SMILED SWUNG HER — 444 28
AND LIFTED HIS FACE UP WITH BLUE EYES LOOKING AT THE EL+ — 672 9
AT LAST THE NARCISSUS LIFTED A TUFT OF FIVE-POINT STARS — 683 2
AND LIFTED IN THE LONG SEEPING SWOON — 769 14
HIS MOUSTACHE WITH AN ELBOW LIFTED AND HURLED — 814 29
WELL-GROWN LIKE POTATOES ON A LIFTED ROOT — 827 21
WHERE THE ATTENTION WILL BE LIFTED OFF MATERIAL THINGS — 833 14
THE LAST ROW IS FINISHED THE JINGLING RAKE IS LIFTED — 858 17
OVERHEAD THE REDDEST SHE LIFTED HER LONG ARMS AND TRIED — 864 9
AND I LIFTED MY HEAD — 882 6
I FEEL AS IF FEATHERS WERE LIFTED AND SHOOK — 883 4
THE TREES RISE TALLER AND TALLER LIFTED — *914 16
THE SMALL BIRDS THAT LIFTED THEIR HEADS WHEN MORNING LO+ — *918 1
IF THE JOY WHICH THEY ARE LIFTED TO AVENGE — *937 3
BEFORE THE GOLDEN FATHERLY SERPENT LIFTED HIS HEAD OFF + — *946 27

LIFTING
LIFTING AND FALLING LONG GASPS THROUGH THE SLUICES LIKE+ — 97 26
THORN-BLOSSOM LIFTING IN WREATHS OF SMOKE BETWEEN — 116 3
AND LIFTING HER BEAUTIFUL SLENDER FACE OH SO MUCH MORE — 393 6
LIFTING HER FACE TO NIBBLE AT A ROUND WHITE PEPPERMINT — 393 8
LIFTING THE RABBIT-BLOOD OF THE MYRIADS UP INTO SOMETHI+ — 414 22
LIFTING A BANK-BOOK TO BLESS US — 456 25
OUT OF SIGHT IN THE DEEP DARK LIFTING HEART — 478 3
WITH THE FULL THIGHS SLOWLY LIFTING OF THE WADER WADING+ — 693 10
LIFTING YOUR VEINED WINGS LIFTING THEM BIG WHITE BUTTER+ — 696 14
AND IN WHOM THE DREAM SITS UP LIKE A RABBIT LIFTING LON+ — 807 8
LIFTING HIS HAUNTED EYES TO ME I AM WANTING IN SONG — 884 11
BEATS THE ACTIVE ECSTASY SUDDENLY LIFTING MY EYES — *906 21
IN THE SUDDEN LIFTING MY EYES IT IS CLEARER — *908 18
OH THE TERROR OF LIFTING THE INNERMOST I OUT OF THE SWE+ — *909 21

LIFTS
PLAYS WITH ME SWAYS ME LIFTS ME AND SINKS ME MURMURS OH — 34 20
FOREVER OUT OF THE MIST THE CHURCH LIFTS UP A REPROACHF+ — 63 24
AS HE SEES ME BRINGING THE DINNER HE LIFTS — 220 1
AS IT LIFTS ITS STRAIGHT WHITE THROAT — 255 24
THE PEACOCK LIFTS HIS RODS OF BRONZE — 371 1
LIFTS UP HIS VOICE AND HOWLS TO THE WALLS OF THE PUEBLO — 405 11
LIFTS US OFF OUR FEET — 425 14
LIFTS HIM FANNING IN THE HIGH EMPYREAN — 782 23
AS A BIRD THAT LIFTS ITS WINGS AND STANDS — 787 17
WHEN HE LIFTS HIS FOOT I SEE THE PAD OF HIS SOAKED STOC+ — 866 7
FROM SPACE TO LONGER SPACE LIFTS A HARSH BREATH — 878 24
PLAYS WITH ME SWAYS ME LIFTS ME AND SINKS ME AS THOUGH + — *892 8
AND LIFTS HIS FACE AND LOOKS AT ME — *898 26
AND LIFTS HIS FACE AND LOOKS AT ME — *902 10
AS HE SEES ME BRINGIN' THE DINNER HE LIFTS — *944 9

LIGHT
ROUND HIS BASE HIS DARK LIGHT ROLLS — 39 32
A SINGLE STAR IN A VEIL OF LIGHT — 41 29
GRASPING IN THE GOLDEN LIGHT — 42 2
TO FEEL THE LADS' LOOKS LIGHT ON ME — 51 27
AND WAITING WHILE LIGHT IS SHED — 58 29
SHALL WATCH THE DAWN LIGHT UP FOR ME — 59 31
AND AS I WATCH THE WAN LIGHT SHINE — 60 1
ON HIS LIPS WHERE THE LIGHT BREATHS COME AND GO — 60 5
THE LIGHT HAS GONE OUT FROM UNDER MY MOTHER'S DOOR — 63 12
WHO TOOK A HANDFUL OF LIGHT AND ROLLED A BALL — 69 18
LEAN ABOUT US SCATTERING THEIR POLLEN GRAINS OF GOLDEN + — 70 2
WHEN INTO THE NIGHT THE YELLOW LIGHT IS ROUSED LIKE DUST — 70 20
BELOW THE OCEAN OF SHIMMERING LIGHT YOU WILL BE — 72 18
WHO STAND ALONE IN DESPAIR LIKE A GUTTERING LIGHT — 73 13
SHE WHO HAS ALWAYS SEEMED SO LIGHT — 74 1
BUT THE FACES OF THE BOYS IN THE BROODING YELLOW LIGHT — 75 25
WENT THROUGH ME AS THE LIGHT WENT OUT — 80 15
OR SUBSTANCE SAVE I LIGHT ON YOU TO WARM — 86 11
LIKE A LITTLE LIGHT AT YOUR FEET — 91 22
IN THE NIGHT WHERE WE FIRST HAVE BEING BEFORE WE RISE O+ — 92 15
OF THE UNSWEPT SEA A GREY PALE LIGHT LIKE MUST — 99 3
LABURNUM GIVES BACK TO LIGHT — 104 32
OR THE WIND SHAKES A RAVEL OF LIGHT — 109 21
SO I AM CLOTHED ALL OVER WITH THE LIGHT — 113 5
SHAFT-GOLDEN WITH LIGHT SHEER INTO THE SKY — 116 16
AND STRIP ME NAKED TOUCH ME LIGHT — 117 13
LIGHT LIGHT ALL OVER — 117 14
OF HER SPIRIT WAVERED LIKE WATER THRILLED WITH LIGHT — 126 32
FEELING MYSELF UNDAWNING THE DAY'S LIGHT PLAYING UPON ME — 133 5
TWO PALE CLOTS SWEPT BY THE LIGHT OF THE CARS — 144 28
PASSES THE LIGHT OF THE TRAM AS IT RACES — 145 14
TRAVELS THE LIGHT AS IT TILTS IN ITS PACES — 146 3
THE MORNING LIGHT ON THEIR LIPS — 147 19
POOR OBSCURE FRUITS EXTRUDED OUT OF LIGHT — 160 10
THROUGH THE LOW WEST WINDOW A COLD LIGHT FLOWS — 163 10
WAS A GREAT LIGHT — 164 26
BREAKS LIGHT INTO GEMS AND DEAD BREASTS WHITER — 168 17
SWIFT TRAINS GO BY IN A RUSH OF LIGHT — 169 1
ALMOND AND APPLE AND PEAR DIFFUSE WITH LIGHT THAT VERY — 179 3
ARRIVING GREY FROM THE DARKNESS ABOVE SUDDENLY INTO THE+ — 179 23
I WILL ESCAPE FROM THE HOLLOW ROOM THE BOX OF LIGHT — 179 24
DULL METEORITE FLASH ONLY INTO LIGHT — 195 21
I WISH THAT WHATEVER PROPS UP THE WALLS OF LIGHT — 205 9
GREEN LANTERN OF PURE LIGHT A LITTLE INTENSE FUSING TRI+ — 206 10
AN EXPLOSION OF GREEN LIGHT — 206 17
ARE NOT MY HAUNCHES LIGHT — 222 19
THE BIG MOUNTAINS SIT STILL IN THE AFTERNOON LIGHT — 223 13
THE OLIVE-LEAVES LIGHT AS GAD-FLIES — 226 21
A LITTLE LIGHT — 227 4
HOLD HIM YOUR LIGHT — 228 28
LIKE A LIGHT THAT HAS NO SUSTENANCE — 246 8
DRIPPING THEIR LIGHT — 252 15
THE LIGHT — 283 17
OR LOVE THE EFFULGENCE OF THEIR HOLY LIGHT — 288 19
NUDE WITH THE DIM LIGHT OF FULL HEALTHY LIFE — 298 26
KNOTTED IN HEAVEN UPON THE FINE LIGHT — 307 9
WHEN THEY FELT THE LIGHT OF HEAVEN BRANDISHING LIKE A K+ — 310 7
HE SAW IN A SHAFT OF LIGHT A LAMB ON A PINNACLE BALANCI+ — 324 16
OF LIGHT — 324 21
TO THOSE THINGS THAT LOVE DARKNESS THE LIGHT OF DAY IS + — 331 3
PAIN YET THE LIGHT OF LAMPS AND CANDLES HAS NO FEARS FO+ — 331 4
CURVETTING BITS OF TIN IN THE EVENING LIGHT — 335 24
A GREEN LIGHT ENTERS AGAINST STREAM FLUSH FROM THE WEST — 340 25
WHERE LIGHT PUSHES THROUGH — 341 3
LIKE A GLOVE A BLACK GLOVE THROWN UP AT THE LIGHT — 341 13
IT WAS THE LIGHT OF DAY WHICH HE COULD NOT ENTER — 344 17
SO I SWITCHED ON THE ELECTRIC LIGHT THINKING NOW — 344 26
AND HE DID NOT MIND THE YELLOW ELECTRIC LIGHT — 344 30
YET NEVER ABLE TO PASS THE WHITENESS OF LIGHT INTO — 345 17
LIGHT WENT OVER THE HILL-BROW SWIFTLY WITH THEIR TAILS — 391 4
FOR THE STRONGEST LIGHT THROWS ALSO THE DARKEST SHADOW — 474 4
PUT OUT A LIGHT OF CONSCIOUSNESS AND LEFT A BLINDED BRU+ — 543 28
PLEASING BRITANNIA IS NO LIGHT WORK — 577 23
TO GAOL TO BE HID FROM THE LIGHT OF DAY — 579 16
AND OUR CONSCIOUSNESS IS A SPOT OF LIGHT IN A GREAT BUT — 636 31
THE BAFFLING LIGHT OR THE STRANGE STILL GLEAM OF THE GO+ — 656 13
AND THESE THE MINORITY OF MEN WHO CAN STILL SEE THE LIG+ — 665 25
FOR A MOMENT PURE IN THE YELLOW EVENING LIGHT HE WAS HY+ — 672 11
AND BECOMING LIGHT — 681 29
AND BROKE AT LAST INTO LIGHT AND DARK — 682 5
CAME INTO EXISTENCE AS LIGHT — 682 6
HE IS BRIGHT LIGHT — 682 10
AND THE SHOULDERS PALLID WITH LIGHT FROM THE SILENT SKY+ — 693 11
LIGHT — 697 11
TIP THE MORNING LIGHT ON EDGE AND SPILL IT WITH DELIGHT — 709 6
EVEN AS HEAVEN IS THE HOME OF SOULS LOST IN LIGHT — 711 16
GREY EVIL WHICH HAS NO PATH AND SHOWS NEITHER LIGHT NOR — 712 2
HOW GHASTLY IT WOULD BE TO STRIKE A MATCH AND MAKE A LI+ — 724 16
NOW LIKE A STRANGE LIGHT BREAKING FROM THE GROUND — 744 10
THE THICK RANK STREETS AND A STARK WHITE LIGHT — 748 5

LIGHT
```
    AND ESSAY TO DISOWN OURSELVES AND THEN WHEN THE LIGHT       748 10
    WITH SUFFUSED LIGHT                                         768 27
    THE WOMEN WITH LIGHT ON THEIR FACES                         771 12
    BURSTS LIKE AN ARC LAMP INTO LIGHT                          773  2
    AND BEFORE YOU PUT OUT THE OLD SAVAGE LIGHT FOR EVER        777  7
    AND PUT LIGHT ON YOUR FACE                                  787 24
    THE LIGHT                                                   788 10
    SEE THE LIGHT ON THE MAN THAT WAITS                         788 28
    LET THE DARKNESS LEAVE YOU LET THE LIGHT COME INTO YOU      803 16
    THE LIGHT WHICH IS FED FROM TWO VESSELS                     810 27
    LAST RED LIGHT DAPPLES                                      816 26
    OF DARKENING NIGHT AND THE QUIVERING LIGHT                  823  9
    THE LIGHT THAT REELS                                        824 25
    THE LIGHT                                                   854  5
    LEFT OF THEIR LIGHT AMONG THE MEAN FLOWERS' THRONG          855 16
    FROM THE LOW WEST WINDOWS THE COLD LIGHT FLOWS              857 10
    WHICH TREADS OUT THE GLOW OF FUGITIVE ORANGE LIGHT          858 11
    A LIGHT LIKE MELLOW MOONLIGHT GLEAMED ON THIS WATER         864 29
    SHONE SWEETLY THROUGH YELLOW SILK A MAN FULL IN THE LIG+    865  2
    A WOMAN CAME INTO THE GLOW FROM OUT OF THE SHADOWY LIGHT    865  4
    DEEP INTO THE HEART OF THE LIGHT THE CENTRE OF A STAR       865  6
    LADS IN THEIR WARM LIGHT SLIPPERS BOUND DOWN THE HALL T+    865 28
    DARTING HIS LIGHT PUNT WITH THE QUICK-SHIFTING FANCY OF+    867 25
    SOME SHAPELESS DARK TO THE LOVELY CURVE OF LIGHT            872  7
    WITH DIM LIGHT SHOWING THE HEADS OF THE SILVER NAILS        876 14
    AND THE BOUGHS OF THE LIME TREE SHAKE AND TOSS THE LIGHT    878  5
    WHICH YIELDS THE DAY TO DEATH ERE YET THE LIGHT             885  7
    WITH LIGHT AND LUXURIOUS BLUENESS                          *895  8
    BUT THE FACES OF THE BOYS IN THE BROODING YELLOW LIGHT     *897 24
    TO FEEL THE LADS' LOOKS LIGHT ON ME                        *899 11
    BUT THE FACES OF THE BOYS IN THE BROODING YELLOW LIGHT     *901  1
    TO FEEL THE LADS' LOOKS LIGHT ON ME                        *902 23
    ON THE UPLIFTED BLUE PALACE LIGHT POOLS STIR AND SHINE     *905  7
    THE POWER OF THE MELTING FUSING FORCE HEAT LIGHT ALL IN+   *909 14
    SHE WHO HAS ALWAYS SEEMED SO LIGHT                         *913 22
    HE TOOK A HANDFUL OF LIGHT AND ROLLED A BALL               *916  1
    LEAN ABOUT US SCATTERING THEIR POLLEN PUFFS OF GOLDEN L+   *916 10
    WHEN INTO THE NIGHT THE YELLOW LIGHT IS ROUSED LIKE DUS+   *917 17
    WENT THROUGH ME JUST AS THE LIGHT WENT OUT                 *922 15
    SHAFT-GOLDEN WITH LIGHT AT THE JOINT OF THE SKY            *930 15
    LIGHT LIGHT ALL OVER                                       *931 18
    THIS CLOT OF LIGHT                                         *935 15
    OF HER SPIRIT WAVERED LIKE WATER THREADED WITH LIGHT       *936 31
    THAT IS DEAD THE MOTHER-LOVE LIKE LIGHT THAT FLOWED        *938 14
    THEN DOWN THE BREEZE LIGHT WAFTING O'ER THE FALLOW         *941 23
```

LIGHT-BLOODED
```
    LIGHT-BLOODED BIRD                                          374  6
```

LIGHTED
```
    TO HOLD THE ONE AND ONLY LIGHTED CANDLE OF THE SUN IN H+    299 34
    AND HOLD THE LIGHTED CANDLE OF THE SUN                      300  4
    THE LIGHTED LAMP INTO MY ROOM AT NIGHT                      875  9
```

LIGHT-EYED
```
    AND THE BULL NOR WAKES FROM THE LIGHT-EYED EAGLE SLEEP      319 11
```

LIGHTHOUSE
```
    HE STANDS LIKE A LIGHTHOUSE NIGHT CHURNS                     39 31
```

LIGHTHOUSES
```
    TINY LIGHTHOUSES LITTLE SOULS OF LANTERNS COURAGE BURST+    206 16
```

LIGHTING
```
    WITH FAIR FLAKES LIGHTING DOWN ON IT BEYOND THE TOWN         76 18
    LIGHTING THESE AUTUMN LEAVES LIKE A STAR DROPPED THROUGH     86 16
```

LIGHTNING
```
    WHEN THE LIGHTNING FLEW ACROSS HER FACE                      62  8
    HOME COME HOME THE LIGHTNING HAS MADE IT TOO PLAIN           62 24
    SOUL'S NAKED LIGHTNING WHICH SHOULD SURE ATTEST              87 24
    OF YOUR SOFT WHITE BODY AS LIGHTNING                        117 31
    AS LIGHTNING COMES ALL WHITE AND TREMBLING                  195 12
    LIGHTNING FALLS FROM HEAVEN                                 208 31
    THE LIGHTNING AND THE RAINBOW APPEARING IN US UNBIDDEN +    268  8
    WRITHED LIKE LIGHTNING AND WAS GONE                         351 15
    AND LET THE LIGHTNING OUT OF YOUR SMOTHERED DUSK            383 19
    TILL YOU ASK FOR LIGHTNING INSTEAD OF LOVE                  484 15
    BUT SOMETIMES THEY GIVE IT AS LIGHTNING                     559  6
    IF THEY ONLY OFFER YOU LIGHTNING                            559  8
    YOU MIGHT AS WELL TAKE THE LIGHTNING                        559 12
    LIGHTNING                                                   707 14
    WITH THE WHITE TRIUMPHANCE OF LIGHTNING AND ELECTRIC DE+    707 19
    THE WILD GODS SEND VITALITY THEY PUT THE LIGHTNING INTO+    843  5
    WHEN THE LIGHTNING FLEW ACROSS HER FACE                    *912 15
```

LIGHTNING-CONDUCTOR
```
    AS FROM THE STEM OF HIS BRISTLING LIGHTNING-CONDUCTOR T+    381 19
```

LIGHTNING-FLAMED
```
    CLOSING UPON YOU IN THE LIGHTNING-FLAMED                     87 21
```

LIGHTNINGS
```
    THE NAKED LIGHTNINGS IN THE HEAVENS DITHER                  209  4
```

LIGHTS
```
    LIGHTS THE SOFT HAIR OF A GIRL AS SHE READS                  41  7
    ON THE GREAT BLUE PALACE AT SYDENHAM LIGHTS STIR AND SH+     52 18
    DESOLATE I AM AS A CHURCH WHOSE LIGHTS ARE PUT OUT          94 23
    IN FRONT OF ME YES UP THE DARKNESS GOES THE GUSH OF THE+     97 18
    OF LIGHTS EACH SOLITARY ROSE                                104 25
    THE TIRED LIGHTS DOWN THE STREET WENT OUT                   121 23
    WITH WET FLAT LIGHTS WHAT I'VE DONE                         143 23
    AND LIGHTS ON A WITHERED OAK-TREE'S TOP OF WOE              147 23
    INSCRUTABLE SMALL LIGHTS GLITTER IN ROWS                    163 26
    USED TO WEAR HER LIGHTS SPLENDIDLY                          170 18
    THE BUBBLE HEMMING THIS EMPTY EXISTENCE WITH LIGHTS         193 22
```

LIGHTS
```
    HIS ARMS SO SHE LIGHTS FROM HER PALFREY                     200 11
    BECAUSE OF THE LITTLE LIGHTS AND FLICKERS AND INTERRUPT+    203 20
    I DID NOT REMEMBER WHY SHOULD I THE RUNNING LIGHTS          243 27
    THAT NOTTINGHAM LIGHTS WOULD RISE AND SAY                   489  5
    WHERE THE MEADOW-LARK AS HE LIGHTS                          771  3
    THE OLD LIGHTS WON'T SHOW THE WAY                           775 33
    HOW NICE IN THE GREAT CITIES WHERE ALL THINGS RUSH AND +    794 15
    THEIR FEATHERS LIFELESS AND THE ROSE LIGHTS TURNING TO +    855 28
```

LIKED
```
    BUT MUST I CONFESS HOW I LIKED HIM                          350  8
    AN' COS I LIKED HIM BEST YI BETT'R NOR THEE                *911 15
    AH KNOW THA LIKED 'IM BETT'R NOR ME BUT LET                *911 17
    WOR IT THA'D LIKED TO 'A KILLED HER                        *922 24
```

LIKELY
```
    AS MAN IS LIKELY TO DO                                      529 21
    WHICH YOU'RE MUCH MORE LIKELY TO DO                         540 29
    AND ALWAYS LIKELY OH IF I COULD RIDE                       *944 23
```

LIKES
```
    THIS WOMAN WHO LIKES TO LOVE ME BUT SHE TURNS               113 10
    WEARY AN' SICK O' THE LIKES O' SHE                          139 33
    SHE LIKES TO EAT                                            358 30
    OH YES SHE CAN MAKE HASTE WHEN SHE LIKES                    358 33
    MY BODY LIKES ITS DINNER AND THE WARM SUN BUT OTHERWISE+    501 19
    BURN THAT HE SEES EVE RUNNING FROM THE LIKES OF HIM I       633 28
```

LIKEWISE
```
    DO THOU OH TRAVELLING APPRENTICE LIKEWISE                   872  5
```

LILAC
```
    OF HAWTHORN AND OF LILAC TREES                              104 29
    WHITE LILAC SHOWS DISCOLOURED NIGHT                         104 30
    A LILAC THERE LIKE A LADY WHO BRAIDS                        105 25
    AND ANOTHER LILAC IN PURPLE VEILED                          105 31
```

LILACS
```
    ROUND THE HOUSE WERE LILACS AND STRAWBERRIES                152 10
```

LILIES
```
    GLADDER NOR OF THY LILIES IF THA MAUN BE TOLD               61 20
    TO FIND THE NEW HOUSES A CLUSTER OF LILIES GLITTERING       72 21
    AH YOU STACK OF WHITE LILIES ALL WHITE AND GOLD             86  9
    ARE NOT A STACK OF WHITE LILIES NOW BUT A WHITE             86 14
    MY STACK OF LILIES ONCE WHITE INCANDESCENT                  86 23
    AGAIN FROM EARTH LIKE LILIES FLAGGED AND SERE               87 28
    HOW MANY TIMES LIKE LOTUS LILIES RISEN                     113  1
    HOW GORGEOUS THAT SHOCK OF RED LILIES AND LARKSPUR CLEA+   129 27
    FROM THE TWILIGHT LIKE HALF-SHUT LILIES                    227 19
    TO DESTROY THE CHILL LENT LILIES                           271 14
    ALL THE WORLD GLEAMS WITH THE LILIES OF DEATH THE UNCON+   273 12
    ENOUGH OF THE VIRGINS AND LILIES OF PASSIONATE SUFFOCAT+   273 14
    NOW IF THE LILIES OF FRANCE LICK SOLOMON IN ALL HIS GLO+   413 27
    AND THE GLIMMER OF THE PRESENCE OF THE GODS WAS LIKE LI+   651  5
```

LILLY
```
    THEY HAVE TAKEN OFF THE BEAUTIFUL RED LILLY                845 24
    THEY HAD RED LILLY AND PEOPLE SINGING SONGS               846  8
```

LILT
```
    THAT ROCKED IN A LILT ALONG I WATCHED THE POISE            123  3
    AND WHERE HE CAME TO LILT MY LIFE ALONG                    877 23
    BEING TOO MIRTHLESS TO MOVE THE LILT OF SINGING            884 13
    THAT ROCKED IN A LILT ALONG I WATCHED THE POISE           *934  9
```

LILY
```
    LIKE A FLAT RED LILY WITH A MILLION PETALS                 166 17
    NO MORE NARCISSUS PERFUME LILY HARLOTS THE BLADES OF SE+   273 16
    HARDLY A GREENISH LILY WATERY FAINT                        286  4
    AND MR MEAD THAT OLD OLD LILY                              579 17
    NOT FAR FROM THE LILY THE CONSIDERABLE LILY                587  5
    GODDESSES OF LOVE GODDESSES OF DIRT EXCREMENT-EATERS OR+   671 18
    AND CONSIDER THE LILY NOT THE PAWPAW NOR THE MANGO-FLESH   760 18
```

LILY-LIKE
```
    LONDON'S LILY-LIKE POLICEMEN FAINT                         680 17
```

LILY-LIVEREDLY
```
    DIE DIE LILY-LIVEREDLY DIE                                 458  5
```

LILY-STATUES
```
    FAR-OFF THE LILY-STATUES STAND WHITE-RANKED IN THE GARD+   159 19
```

LIMB
```
    SUDDENLY OR HER SKINNY LIMB                                362 22
```

LIMBER
```
    I DISTINGUISH THE SCENT OF YOUR HAIR SO NOW THE LIMBER     208 30
```

LIMBO
```
    AND RUDDY-ORANGE LIMBS STIRRING THE LIMBO                  667  7
```

LIMBS
```
    ON HIS LIMBS IN SLEEP AT LAST LAID LOW                      60  7
    ALONG THY LIMBS DELIGHTED AS A BRIDE'S                      69 12
    BUT SINCE MY LIMBS GUSHED FULL OF FIRE                     118  1
    FOR THE MOON ON MY BREAST AND THE AIR ON MY LIMBS          130 11
    HAVE HUDDLED RAGS OR LIMBS ON THE NAKED SLEEP              144 22
    ELOQUENT LIMBS                                             145 16
    SLEEP-SUAVE LIMBS OF A YOUTH WITH LONG SMOOTH THIGHS       145 18
    SOME LIMBS LIKE PARCELS AND TEAR                           145 26
    AS SHE STRODE HER LIMBS AMONGST IT ONCE MORE               155 14
    YOUR FERVENT LIMBS WITH FLICKERS AND TENDRILS OF NEW       156 21
    THE POOL FOR MY LIMBS TO FATHOM MY SOUL'S LAST SCHOOL      161 17
    FLEET HURRYING LIMBS                                       171  3
    EACH WITH A SECRET WHICH STIRS IN HIS LIMBS AS THEY MOVE   174 10
```

LIMBS
  LIKE THE AGONY OF LIMBS CUT OFF AND ACHING   213   9
  I WILL WARM YOUR LIMBS WITH KISSES   237 25
  THICK SMOOTH-FLESHED SILVER DULL ONLY AS HUMAN LIMBS ARE   298 23
  RATHER LIKE A BABY WORKING ITS LIMBS   352 30
  FOUR ROWING LIMBS AND ONE WEDGE-BALANCING HEAD   356   7
  LONG NECK AND LONG VULNERABLE LIMBS EXTRUDED SPREAD-EAG+   365   1
  SLIM LIMBS AND BREASTS   369 17
  BEASTS' LIMBS AND THE BREATH FROM THEIR FEET THAT THEY +   406   2
  WEIGHT OF LIMBS   446   9
  AND THE REDDENED LIMBS RED INDIA-RUBBER TUBING INFLATED   625 21
  THE BRAIN OF THE MACHINE KNOWS THE LIMBS AND TRUNK OF   635 21
  IN THEIR FACES AND MOTION NEVER MECHANICAL IN THEIR LIM+   635 31
  AND ALL WAS DREARY GREAT ROBOT LIMBS ROBOT BREASTS   651   2
  AND RUDDY-ORANGE LIMBS STIRRING THE LIMBO   667   7
  WHO WILL GIVE ME BACK MY LOST LIMBS   696   4
  AND CURRENTS OF EXCITEMENT IN OUR LIMBS   707 22
  WHY IF YOU SAW MY LIMBS HOW THEY SHINE ON MY BODY   755   6
  OUT OF THE FLACCID LIMBS   766 15
  FRESHENING LIMBS   795 19
  STRETCHING THEIR BIG FULL LIMBS TO SEEK   827 13
  BUT THE LIMBS OF MAN LONG TO FOLD AND CLOSE UPON THE LI+   834   4
  EVE SWINGING HER DUSKY LIMBS DISCONSOLATE   863 21
  EVE RUNNING WITH SWIFT LIMBS QUICKENED BY DREAD   864 19
  I FORGET THE TOWEL AND MY WET LIMBS   870   5
  MY LIMBS ARE NUMB AND HEAVY AND MY HEART   879 19
  THERE IS SOMETHING STIRS IN ME FROM THE FLOW OF THEIR L+   *906 17
  THEY HAVE A SECRET THAT STIRS IN THEIR LIMBS AS THEY MO+   *908 14
  ALONG THY LIMBS DELIGHTED THINE HIS BRIDE'S   *915 24

LIME
  AND THE BOUGHS OF THE LIME TREE SHAKE AND TOSS THE LIGHT   878   5

LIMES
  THE GLIMMER OF THE LIMES SUN-HEAVY SLEEPING   35 26
  BUT SLEEPS THE LONG WEEK OUT EMBOSOMED IN MURMURING LIM+   858 23

LIME-TREE
  LIQUID AS LIME-TREE BLOSSOM SOFT AS BRILLIANT WATER OR +   67 20
  AND THE LIME-TREE LOVELY AND TALL EVERY LEAF SILENT   646 21
  YET LOOKING IN A GREAT FULL LIME-TREE OF SUMMER   650 21

LIMIT
  THEIR LIMIT THEIR THUS FAR AND NO FURTHER   709 24

LIMITATION
  I KNOW HER NOW OR PERHAPS I KNOW MY OWN LIMITATION AGAI+   265 32
  LIMITATION   266 17
  THEY SEEM TO FEEL THE CHILDREN A GHASTLY LIMITATION   832   8

LIMITATIONS
  I AM SO TIRED OF THE LIMITATIONS OF THEIR INFINITE   288 14

LIMITED
  AND TO BE LIMITED BY A MERE WORD IS TO BE LESS THAN A H+   292   4
  ENCLOSED IN HIS OWN LIMITED MENTAL CONSCIOUSNESS   474 25
  LIKE MONKEYS OR ANGELS OR SOMETHING IN A LIMITED   550   3
  LIKE A LIMITED LIABILITY COMPANY   550   5
  THEY ARE ALL LIMITED LIABILITY   550   6
  WHAT THEY'RE LIMITED TO OR LIABLE   550   7

LIMITS
  AND I SAID TO MY HEART THERE ARE LIMITS   338 21
  MUST NEEDS AT LAST COME TO KNOW ITS OWN LIMITS   473 20
  IT IS THE WHITE STONE OF LIMITS THE TERM THE LANDMARK B+   706 11

LIMPID
  ITS LIMPID SAP TO CULMINATION HAS BROUGHT   218 10

LIMPING
  LIMPING AND FOLLOWING RATHER AT MY SIDE   221 12

LINCOLNSHIRE
  OF LINCOLNSHIRE   747 26

LINE
  RESTS A STILL LINE OF SOLDIERS RED MOTIONLESS RANGE OF +   66   7
  I'M OFF UP TH' LINE TO UNDERWOOD   78   3
  PACKED IN A LINE WITH THEIR HEADS AGAINST THE WALL   144 16
  FINALLY RIDGED WITH THE AUSTERE LINE OF THE DEAD   155   5
  TO DRAW HIS NET THROUGH THE SURF'S THIN LINE AT THE DAW+   180   2
  LUNGING IN THE AIR ON THE LINE   339   5
  LEAP THEN AND COME DOWN ON THE LINE THAT DRAWS TO THE   394 25
  IN A LONG LINE THEIR HEADS LAID OVER EACH OTHER'S NECKS   445 20
  WE MUST DRAW A LINE SOMEWHERE   548 28
  AH WHEN HE BEGINS TO DRAW THE LINE IN TIGHT TO LAND HIS   586 21
  IN RAPID ARMFULS FROM THE LINE TOSSING IT IN THE BASKET   672 15
  TO DRAW A LINE AROUND THE INDIANS BEYOND WHICH LINE   779 31
  DELICATE LINE OF NON-INTERFERENCE   780 12
  SO HE PASSED THE YELLOW LINE WHO LASHED LIKE A DRAGON I+   790   3
  AND HAVING PASSED THE YELLOW LINE HE SAW THE EARTH BENE+   790   4
  I'M OFF UP TH' LINE TO UNDERWOOD   *919 23

LINED
  GENTLY AND FINELY LINED THAN A RABBIT'S OR THAN A HARE'S   393   7

LINEN
  OF LINEN GO THE CHANTING CHORISTERS   232 15
  OF FINE LINEN   388 18
  LINEN WITHIN MY OWN OLD FRAGRANT CHEST   877 31

LINER
  AND AN OCEAN LINER GOING EAST LIKE A SMALL BEETLE WALKI+   687   9

LINES
  STREWS EACH SIDE THE LINES   162   4

LINGER
  FOREVER EVER BY MY SHOULDER PITIFUL LOVE WILL LINGER   63 22
  OF OLD SPENT LIVES LINGER BLURRED AND WARM   173 18
  I CAN ALWAYS LINGER OVER THE HUDDLED BOOKS ON THE STALLS   180 24
  I LINGER TO WATCH HER   217 10
  SHYLY AND IN HOMAGE LINGER FOR AN INVITATION   256   5
  LINGER FOR NOW THEY REALISE ALL THAT IS LOST THEN THE L+   406   6
  THEY LINGER IN THE SHADOW OF THE EARTH   721 14
  OF OLD INEFFECTUAL LIVES LINGER BLURRED AND WARM   *906 12
  OF OLD INEFFECTUAL LIVES LINGER BLURRED AND WARM   *908   6
  I LINGER TO WATCH HER   *942 20

LINGERED
  AND I LINGERED ON THE THRESHOLD WITH MY HAND   121 14

LINGERING
  AND THE LONG AGES AND THE LINGERING CHILL   353   2
  AND KISS OF THE FAR-OFF LINGERING LADY WHO LOOKS OVER T+   695 31
  THE DEAD THREADED THE AIR LINGERING   704   3
  LINGERING IN THE EARTH'S SHADOW   704   4
  PEEPING THEY WILL LOSE THEIR SIGHT AND LINGERING THEY W+   799 12

LINGER-LONGER-LUCY
  WOMEN FELT IT WAS NO LONGER ANY USE BEING A LINGER-LONG+   537 29

LINGERS
  TO WATCH THE WORLD THAT LINGERS   162 19
  LINGERS BEHIND AS THE YELLOW SUN GLARES AND IS GONE BEY+   467   6
  SHE LINGERS IN THE DOORWAYS   756 10
  THE AMERICAN INDIAN LINGERS HERE WARD OF THE   776   5
  HE LINGERS ON FROM AN OLD SAVAGE WORLD THAT STILL HAS   776   8

LININGS
  A WEIGHT COMES OVER ME HEAVIER THAN LEADEN LININGS OF   629 18

LINKED
  OF IRON KISSES KISSES LINKED LIKE STEEL   154 20
  IN SHAPELINESS WITH HAPPY LINKED HANDS   872 14

LINKING
  OF LINKING ELBOWS AND THEY TALK   106 13
  AND OVER THE BRIDGE OF THE WHALE'S STRONG PHALLUS LINKI+   694 21

LINKS
  DRAGGING THE LINKS OF MY SHORTENING CHAIN   50 17

LINNET
  FORGOTTEN LIKE LAST YEAR'S LINNET SONG   855 14
  IS LIKE A LITTLE LINNET SONG WINSOME   *913   2

LINTY
  LIKE A LINTY RAW-COLD DUST DISTURBED FROM THE FLOOR   99   2

LION
  SLEEPS FOUR SLEEPS THE SLEEP OF THE LION THE SLEEP ON T+   319   5
  SLEEP OF THE MAN AND THE EAGLE'S SLEEP AFTER WHICH THE +   319   6
  QUARTERS THEN SLEEP IS EMPTY TOO MAN SLEEPS NO MORE LIK+   319 10
  THERE WAS A LION IN JUDAH   323 19
  A LION WITH WINGS   323 22
  THE LION OF THE SPIRIT   323 31
  WOULD A WINGLESS LION LIE DOWN BEFORE THEE AS THIS WING+   324   2
  LION LIES   324   3
  THE LION OF THE SPIRIT   324   4
  SO THE LION OF THE SENSES THOUGHT IT WAS WORTH IT   324 25
  WHELPS PLAY BETWEEN THE PAWS OF THE LION   325 14
  THEN THE PROUD LION STALKS ABROAD ALONE   325 19
  NO LEOPARD SCREECHED NO LION COUGHED NO DOG BARKED   394 17
  LITTLE LION AND RUMBLING   396 30
  IT IS A MOUNTAIN LION   401 23
  AND A MOUNTAIN LION   402 28
  OF THAT SLIM YELLOW MOUNTAIN LION   402 33
  NOR THE BRITISH LION HIS APPETITE   413 29
  HIS FACE IS LIKE THE RED LION   684 15
  NOW THAT THE SUN LIKE A LION LICKS HIS PAWS   687 13
  LOOKING DOWN ON THE LION AS HE RETREATS   687 18
  AND ONE WARM KIND KISS OF THE LION WITH GOLDEN PAWS   695 33
  IN ALL THE CITIES WITH LION GATES   704   2
  NOR EVEN LIKE AN ANIMAL BULL RAM OR LION OR LAMB   840 26

LIONESS
  AND SOMEWHERE THERE IS A LIONESS   325 12
  A LONG LONG SLIM CAT YELLOW LIKE A LIONESS   401 24

LIONS
  YES AND IF OXEN OR LIONS HAD HANDS AND COULD PAINT WITH   376   1
  LIKE THE TWO LIONS WHO DEVOURED ONE ANOTHER AND LEFT TH+   665   2
  THAN THERE WAS IN THE LIONS   665   5
  ACQUIESCENCE OF WATCHFUL LIONS   770 17

LION'S
  FLASH OF A MOUNTAIN LION'S LONG SHOOT   402 16

LIP.
  NAKED ON THE STEEP SOFT LIP   33 18
  I WILL SET A SEAL UPON YOU FROM MY LIP   153 20
  HER LIP BEHIND HER AT ALL LIFE   386 14
  NAKED ON THE STEEP SOFT LIP   *891 20

LIPLESS
  AND THE THOUGHT OF THE LIPLESS VOICE OF THE FATHER SHAK+   48 11

LIPS
HAS POISED ABOVE HER LIPS IN PLAY   42 12
UPON MY MIND HIS LIPS MEET MINE AND A FLOOD   43 35
FOR THE LIPS AND THE EYES OF GOD ARE BEHIND A VEIL   48 10
ON HIS LIPS WHERE THE LIGHT BREATHS COME AND GO   60 5
I LEANED IN THE DARKNESS TO FIND HER LIPS   62 6
AND OPEN LIPS DISTRESSED   62 17
LIPS AND DARK   66 28
ROUNDED LIKE PEARLS FOR SLEEP AND THEN FROM BETWEEN SHU+   88 16
HEARING MY MERE LIPS SHOUT   124 21
SHE HID HER FACE SHE MURMURED BETWEEN HER LIPS   125 19
CONSOLATION THAT IN HER LIPS HER BLOOD AT CLIMAX CLIPS   127 26
I KNOW FROM HER HARDENED LIPS THAT STILL HER HEART IS   128 1
ON HIS LIPS I LONG TO BE SOULLESS I TINGLE   130 21
I WITH THE NIGHT ON MY LIPS I SIGH WITH THE SILENCE OF +   133 9
THE MORNING LIGHT ON THEIR LIPS   147 19
COMES LICKING THROUGH THE BARS OF YOUR LIPS   151 7
TO MAKE NEW WORDS WITH OUR LIPS TO ESCAPE THE FOUL DREAM   175 22
LIPS TO THE VESSELS NEVER SHRINK   177 15
TO HOLD TO YOUR LIPS   227 20
FROM YOUR FEET TO YOUR LIPS   238 15
AFTER YOU HAVE TAKEN OFF THE BLOSSOM WITH YOUR LIPS   282 7
BECOMES AN AFFIRMATION THROUGH MOIST SCARLET LIPS   284 18
TAKE THE FERN-SEED ON OUR LIPS   287 8
ALL LIPS ARE DUSKY AND VALVED   288 22
SAVE YOUR LIPS O PALE-FACES   288 23
WHICH ARE LIPS OF METAL   288 24
AND ANSWER THE FIRST MACHINE-CUT QUESTION FROM THE LIPS+   291 6
NO FINGERS NO HANDS AND FEET NO LIPS   335 17
AND FLICKERED HIS TWO-FORKED TONGUE FROM HIS LIPS AND   349 23
SEEMING TO LICK HIS LIPS   350 27
ON WILD DARK LIPS   366 21
TO PUT TO MY LIPS   427 14
OF HANDS AND LIPS AND MURMURINGS   436 22
AND OUT OF THE LIPS OF PEOPLE JERK STRANGE MECHANICAL N+   629 10
THOSE THAT PUT HONEY ON OUR LIPS AND THOSE THAT PUT SALT   709 28
AROUND MY SOUL AND SPIRIT AROUND MY LIPS   727 10
BETWEEN HIS THICK LIPS I WONDER WHERE   733 26
RED STROKE ACROSS MY LIPS   735 27
DO YOU LIFT YOUR LIPS TO KISS ME GOOD NIGHT MY LOVE   750 16
AND DELIVER OUR LIPS OF THEIR PRAISE AND THEIR BITTERNE+   753 18
OF TOSSING AND ROLLING THE SUBSTANCE OF LIFE TO YOUR LIPS   792 21
WHEN YOU SPEAK TRUE AND TRUE IT IS BRIGHT ON YOUR LIPS +   800 8
DREW HER LIPS OVER THE MOON-PALE PETALS SOFTLY BENT   856 20
HER WARM RED LIPS   862 10
LOOKED UP AND THE WORDS MOVED LIKE A SMILE FROM HIS LIPS   865 3
FLOCK UNSEEN FROM MY LIPS TO HERS   868 32
COMES LICKING IN FLAME THROUGH THE BARS OF YOUR LIPS   873 17
AND I TOOK HER EAR LIKE THE LEAF OF A WATER-FLOWER BETW+   882 27
AND I OPEN MY LIPS TO TAKE A STRAND OF KEEN HAIR   883 15
I LEANED ME FORWARD TO FIND HER LIPS   *912 13
AND LIPS APART WITH DUMB CRIES   *912 23
KISS BUT THEN THE DUST FROM OFF MY LIPS   *929 26
HEARING MY MERE LIPS SHOUT   *935 21
SHE HID HER FACE SHE MURMURED BETWEEN HER LIPS   *936 18
AND HYMNS GLEAMED ON OUR WARM LIPS AS WE WATCHED MOTHER+   *940 12
PASS UNSEEN FROM MY LIPS TO HERS   *942 4

LIP-STICK
IF YOU DON'T USE ROUGE AND A LIP-STICK IN PARIS   433 12

LIPS'
AS TO MY LIPS'   96 17

LIQUID
TURNS BACK HER LIQUID ANGUISHED EYES   43 6
LIQUID AS LIME-TREE BLOSSOM SOFT AS BRILLIANT WATER OR +   67 20
LIKE LIQUID TO THE DARK   390 35
WHO CAN UNSEAT HER LIKE A LIQUID DROP THAT IS HEAVY AND   392 28
WISTFULLY WATCHING WITH WONDERFUL LIQUID EYES   394 20
THE SUN AS HE WAITS A MOMENT HUGE AND LIQUID   403 4
JUGFULL AFTER JUGFULL OF PURE WHITE LIQUID FIRE BRIGHT +   647 9
AND AS THE ELECTRIC LIQUID POURS OUT SOMETIMES   647 13

LIQUOR
FORBIDDEN LIQUOR   333 27
THAT CARRIES A HEAVY RICH LIQUOR   869 24

LIQUORS
WHENCE HE DREW THE CURIOUS LIQUORS   202 19

LIRE
LIRE   385 8

LIST
UNSIGHTLY ITS WAY TO THE WARMTH THIS THING WITH A LIST   141 15
THERE'S A LIST KEPT OF THE TRULY SUPERIOR   548 22
AND IF YOU'RE NOT ON THE LIST WHY THERE YOU ARE MY DEAR   548 23
NOT ON THE LIST   548 26

LISTEN
LISTEN HER SHOON   37 9
AH LISTEN FOR SILENCE IS NOT LONELY   69 5
THEY'LL LISTEN TO HER TALE   78 16
THE PINE-TREES BEND TO LISTEN TO THE AUTUMN WIND AS IT +   102 25
I LISTEN TO THE STILLNESS OF YOU   110 1
THA MIGHT AS WELL LISTEN THA KNOWS   139 9
IS TO LISTEN AND HEAR THE GRIM   159 15
IN A MOUSE THAT PAUSES TO LISTEN   170 6
LIKE WET AND FALLING ROSES AND I LISTEN   217 21
LISTEN EXCEPT THOSE WHO STRIVE WITH THEIR DEAD   233 3
LISTEN I HAVE NO USE   234 13
LISTEN THE DARKNESS RINGS   238 7
LISTEN AGAIN   313 12
LISTEN PARACLETE   323 1
WHILE YOU LISTEN IN WHILE YOU WATCH THE FILM WHILE YOU   441 20
O CEASE TO LISTEN TO THE LIVING DEAD   441 28
AND LISTEN TO BODILESS NOISES   558 23

LISTEN
LISTEN LISTEN LISTEN CORPSE-BODY TO THE WIRELESS   564 15
THERE ARE OTHER WAYS OF SUMMONS CRYING LISTEN LISTEN CO+   623 23
FOR LISTEN THE EGO-CENTRIC SELF IS THE SAME AS THE MACH+   635 8
LISTEN TO PEOPLE LAUGHING   654 13
IF THEY WOULD LISTEN I COULD TELL THEM NOW   744 26
LISTEN FOR I WILL COMPLAIN   758 7
SIEGMUND SIEGMUND GET UP AND LOOK AT ME LISTEN   871 35
WITH RED SNARLING JAWS LET YOURSELF LISTEN TO THE CRIES   *892 25
AND WAKE TO THE SOUND OF THE WOODPIGEONS AND LIE AND LI+   *892 28
AND LISTEN OH EVERYTHING LISTEN FOR WORDS   *914 14
THEN LISTEN FOR SILENCE IS NOT LONELY   *915 17
THEY'LL LISTEN TO HER TALE   *920 8
LIKE WET AND SHAKEN ROSES AND I LISTEN   *943 4

LISTENED
AND I WOKE TO THE SOUND OF THE WOOD-PIGEON AND LAY AND +   38 12
AS SHE LISTENED IN SILENCE OUTSIDE THE SILENT DOOR   155 16
WHEN I HEARD THE CANNON OF THE WAR I LISTENED WITH MY   257 5
AND EVERYONE LISTENED AND LOVED IT THE   492 9

LISTENER
SHE IS SUCH AN ALERT LISTENER WITH HER EARS WIDE TO KNOW   384 15
SUCH A CANNY LISTENER FROM A DISTANCE LOOKING UPWARDS   384 17

LISTENERS
AND TRAMPLED ALL THE LISTENERS TO A SMUSH   540 6

LISTENING
LISTENING FOR THE SOUND OF HER FEET ACROSS THE FLOOR   121 16
I AM LISTFNING IS ANYTHING SAID   140 22
ARRESTED LISTENING   165 20
AND LISTENING INWARDLY TO THE FIRST BLEAT OF A LAMB   366 14
AND LEAVE HIM FOREVER LISTENING FOR THE ANSWER   439 10
LISTENING IN TO THE LIE   441 26
A LIZARD RAN OUT ON A ROCK AND LOOKED LISTENING   524 13
WHO GO BY WITHOUT PAUSING SOFT-FOOT WITHOUT LISTENING Y+   623 21
LEANS LISTENING ON THE GATE IN ALL RESPECT   688 20
A THRILL THROUGH THE LISTENING TREES AND HOLD THE BREATH   858 26

LISTLESS
THE LISTLESS BEAUTY OF THE HOUR   248 16
LET US TRIUMPH AND LET THE YOUNG BE LISTLESS   503 7

LISTLESSNESS
LISTLESSNESS   627 25

LIT
AM LIT BENEATH MY HEART WITH A HALF-MOON WEIRD AND BLUE   115 4
OF GREEN FIRES LIT ON THE SOIL OF EARTH THIS BLAZE   116 7
WAIT WAIT A BIT I'LL COME WHEN I'VE LIT THE FIRE   384 9
OF LIFE UNDIMMED DELIGHTS HIM SO EVEN HE IS LIT UP   648 21
I SAW SUDDENLY COMING TOWARDS ME LIT UP AND UPLIFTED WI+   672 20
ARE LIT WITH ME   801 21
FROM THE LIT ROOM OF LIVING   879 36
I SAW THE SKY WAS LIT   883 19

LITERARY
IN A PUB PARLOUR IN LITERARY LONDON ON CERTAIN EVENINGS   542 10
APPLICANT FOR POST AS LITERARY CRITIC HERE ARE MY   582 7

LITHE
THAN WHO CAN SEPARATE TWO LITHE RICH FLAMES   879 33

LITTER
LITTER   38 9
GLIMMERS LITTER OF DAY   41 30
IN A LITTER THROUGH THE ELM-TREE SHADE ARE SCRAWLING   65 17
RISING UP IN THE CLASS-ROOM LITTER MAKES ME UNABLE   90 4
STREWN STARS OF UNKNOWN PEOPLE AND LUMINOUS LITTER   132 12
TAKE THE LANTERN AND WATCH THE SOW FOR FEAR SHE GRAB HE+   *892 24
SHAKE DOWN THEIR GOLDEN LITTER THAT DISCLOSES   *916 22
STREWN STARS OF PALLID PEOPLE AND THROUGH LUMINOUS LITT+   *938 4

LITTER-BEARERS
AND THE GENTLE TROTTING OF THE LITTER-BEARERS   703 28

LITTERED
AND LITTERED LETTERING OF TREES AND HILLS AND HOUSES CL+   88 6
SPORT ON HER LITTERED PIANO AND MOCK AT THE SIGHT   856 17

LITTERING
LITTERING THE WAVES WITH HER OWN SUPERSCRIPTION   193 6

LITTLE-BOY
IS THE LITTLE-BOY BRILLIANT   841 12
THE LITTLE-BOY OF THIRTY OR FORTY OR FIFTY OR SIXTY   841 19
A KEEN FAR-REACHING CURIOUS MIND CYNICAL WITH LITTLE-BO+   841 22
AND WOMEN FALL FOR THESE LITTLE-BOY MINDS THEY FEEL QUI+   841 24
SO SHE MARRIES ONE OF THESE LITTLE-BOY BRILLIANTS   842 1
AND WHEN SHE HAS MOST UNSATISFACTORILY SHARED HIS LITTL+   842 5
WHY THE MODERN YOUNG WIFE OF THE LITTLE-BOY BRILLIANT B+   842 9

LITTLE-ONE
AND THE LIVE LITTLE-ONE TAKING IN ITS PAW AT THE DOOR O+   394 23

LITTLE-SOULED
HEY WITH THIS ENDLESS LABOUR AND LITTLE-SOULED FRET   859 26

LIT-UP
A LIT-UP SHAFT OF RAIN   714 8

LIVE
LET THEM LIVE THE BOYS AND LEARN NOT TO TRESPASS I HAD +   93 11
WILL LIVE   94 9
TO LIVE ALONE IS MY DOOM   106 22
THE HEART OF THE LIVE WORLD PULSES AND THE BLOOD OF THE+   176 4
YOU ARMFULS OF SUNSHINE AND YOU WON'T LET ME LIVE   211 6

LIVE
AND I DAREN'T LIVE   214 23
THE SHADOWS THAT LIVE IN THE SUN   215 21
LIE ON ME WITH A HOT PLUMB LIVE WEIGHT   240 28
IT IS GORGEOUS TO LIVE AND FORGET   244 25
LOOK FOR LIKE THE BREATH OF LIFE AS LONG AS I LIVE   248 10
PRAY TO LIVE THROUGH   273 37
THEY WANDER AND ARE EXILED THEY LIVE IN EXILE THROUGH   304 26
THAT LIVE BY NIGHT AND LAMPLIGHT AND FIRELIGHT DO THEM +   331 8
SUCKING LIVE BLOOD   333 31
AND THE LIVE LITTLE-ONE TAKING IN ITS PAW AT THE DOOR O+   394 23
FIRST LIVE THING I'VE OWNED SINCE THE LOP-EARED RABBITS   395 7
YOU RUN STRAIGHT AWAY TO LIVE WITH SOMEBODY ELSE   399 13
LIKE FIRE-TONGS A LIVE COAL   427 17
IF YOU LIVE ALONG WITH ALL THE OTHER PEOPLE   431 30
AND IF YOU LIVE WITH ALL THE OTHER PEOPLE   432 1
AND CURLING THEIR PRECIOUS LIVE TRUNKS LIKE AMMONITES   445 14
WHATEVER MAN MAKES AND MAKES IT LIVE   448 19
AS WE LIVE WE ARE TRANSMITTERS OF LIFE   449 1
ALL THAT WE HAVE WHILE WE LIVE IS LIFE   449 23
AND IF YOU DON'T LIVE DURING YOUR LIFE YOU ARE A PIECE +   449 24
AND PUT THEIR LIVE IN IT   450 9
DON'T LIVE UP TO THE DEAR LITTLE GIRL WHO COSTS   458 22
AND HAMLET HOW BORING HOW BORING TO LIVE WITH   494 19
IT MUST BE WONDERFUL TO LIVE AND GROW OLD   503 27
FIRE AND RAIN AND AIR AND LIVE LOAM   505 13
AND WE KNOW NOT HOW TO LIVE WORDLESS   510 25
WE LIVE IN A VAST HOUSE   510 26
THE WAGES OF VICIOUS COMPETITION IS THE WORLD WE LIVE IN   521 4
LIVE   522 20
FOR NO LIVE SUNNY MAN WOULD BE A CENSOR   528 12
AND THE TCHEKOV LOT I'M TOO WEAK AND LOVABLE TO LIVE   534 1
SO IF ANY OF YOU'S LIVE WIRES WITH WITS   553 19
WE'RE NOT FIT FOR THE EARTH WE LIVE ON   553 29
A MAN CAN'T FULLY LIVE UNLESS HE DIES AND CEASES TO CARE   613 1
AND LIVE IN THE ACCEPTANCE OF IT   636 27
CAN'T LIVE ANY MORE EXCEPT FOR A SPELL WHEN THE LIVING   639 4
MOST MEN EVEN UNFALLEN CAN ONLY LIVE   649 13
HE FORCED US TO LIVE A GREAT LIE OR TO DISOBEY   654 7
SOME WOMEN LIVE FOR THE IDIOTIC FURNITURE OF THEIR HOUS+   657 6
SOME MEN LIVE FOR THE CONCEITED FURNITURE OF THEIR MINDS   657 7
SOME ONLY LIVE FOR THEIR EMOTIONAL FURNISHING   657 8
AND WE LIVE BY THE LETTER OF TRUTH   661 19
WHILE PEOPLE LIVE THE LIFE   675 9
SO LET ME LIVE THAT I MAY DIE   676 19
VENUS WOULD RATHER HAVE LIVE DOVES THAN DEAD IF YOU WAN+   678 7
LOVE CANNOT LIVE BUT ONLY BARE SALT SPLINTERS   693 22
BUT WHY THEN SHOULD WE DIE WHILE WE CAN LIVE   710 5
AND WHILE WE LIVE   710 6
NEW JOY TO GIVE MORE LIFE NEW BLISS TO LIVE   740 26
BECAUSE THEY LIVE ON HIM ARTISTS AND   778 9
TO LIVE THEIR OWN LIFE FULFIL THEIR OWN ENDS   779 24
WITH A DAGGER OF DARK LIVE IRON   782 2
CHILD OF THE LIVING DEAD THE DEAD THAT LIVE AND ARE NOT+   796 1
THE DEAD THAT HAVE MASTERED FIRE LIVE ON SALAMANDERS IN+   796 7
FOR THE LIVING LIVE   811 27
I SHALL COME TO NEW YORK AND LIVE ON MANHATTAN   815 14
WHEREIN A MAN CAN LIVE HIS LIFE WITHOUT BEING A SLAVE T+   837 35
AND LIVE FROM ITS SECONDARY SWEAT   843 9
HER HAIR'S LIVE CURL   862 14
LIVE THINGS CARESS ME AND ENTREAT MY FONDLING   876 33
DOWN WHERE THE LIVE WEB HUMS   *893 10
OF A LIVE SAD WORK UNFINISHED   *927 27
SWAY THE LIVE PEARLS THEIR FLOWERING PLEDGES   *941 20
AH IF YOU WANT TO LIVE IN PEACE ON THE FACE OF THE EARTH   *961 5

LIVE-BY-LOVE
ESPECIALLY DEMOCRATIC LIVE-BY-LOVE HUMANITY   395 19

LIVED
I HAVE LIVED DELIGHTED IN THE HALLS OF THE PAST   173 21
AND WORK IS LIFE AND LIFE IS LIVED IN WORK   450 1
LIVED UNDAUNTED AND UNSOURED WITH ACCEPTED LIES   503 18
IF PEOPLE LIVED WITHOUT ACCEPTING LIES   503 19
IF EVER I LIVED UPON DRY LAND   574 12
BODILESS AS WE LIVED   584 20
AND LIVED TO LEARN THEY ARE NEITHER FELLOW NOR MEN   644 2
AND LIVED TO SEE THEM SPAWN INTO MACHINE-ROBOTS   644 6
AND LIVED TO FIND OUT   644 10
UTTERLY DEAD WHO LIVED BUT TO BANISH   855 7
THEY LIVED THEMSELVES FORTH LIKE A TREE PUTTING OUT WOV+ *949 28
FROM THEIR TREE OF LIFE AND VILLAGES WHOLE CITIES LIVED+ *950 4

LIVELY
LOVELESS AND SO LIVELY   337 10
BUT THE LIVING LEAVES IN THE BREATH OF THE WIND ARE MOR+   615 14
THAT WE HAVE BLOOD AND BOWELS AND LIVELY GENITALS   *953 3

LIVE-ROSY
LIVE-ROSY TORTOISE SHELL   355 19

LIVES
UP TO THEIR LIVES SO THEY TO ME   52 7
THE OLD LIVES CROWD   52 27
BLUE SHADOW WITHIN ME A PRESENCE WHICH LIVES CONTAINED   115 7
OF LIVES WHICH SORROWS LIKE MISCHIEVOUS DARK MICE CHAVEL 132 13
OF OLD SPENT LIVES LINGER BLURRED AND WARM   173 18
WHERE DEAD MEN'S LIVES GLOW GENTLY AND IRON HURTS   173 22
AND PAST LIVES HAMPER ME CLOG AND EMBARRASS   173 28
ANOTHER LIFE FROM OUR LIVES SO SHOULD SEND   218 21
THAT LIVES UPON THIS ROCK   299 10
THE NIGHT LIVES FOUR LIVES AND MAN THAT SLEEPS THROUGH + 319 4
THE SUN LIVES IN HIS SHINING AND IS NOT LIKE FIRES THAT+ 331 9
THAT LIVES ERECT THROUGH LONG NIGHTS PHYSICALLY   427 13
LIVES BECAUSE OF THE LIFE PUT INTO IT   448 30
HE LIVES AND IS A MAN   452 17
WITH MOUTH AND LOINS AND NEEDS HE LIVES   461 15
OF THE WALLS WITHIN WHICH OUR LIVES ARE SPENT   462 12

LIVES
THEIR LITTLE LIVES ARE FUN TO THEM   466 16
FOR THE FIERCE CURVE OF OUR LIVES IS MOVING AGAIN TO THE 478 1
YOU WHO COMPLAIN YOU KNOW NO JOY IN YOUR LIVES   484 13
NEVER WILL YOU KNOW ANY JOY IN YOUR LIVES   484 14
THOUGH MOST BIRDS HAVE TO PAY WITH THEIR LIVES WHERE MEN 520 3
BUT OH OUR HUMAN LIVES THE LUNGING BLIND CYCLOPS WE ARE   544 12
LIVES YOUR OWN LITTLE FIEND   563 24
EVERYTHING THAT LIVES HAS ITS OWN PROPER PRIDE   621 15
NEVER HAVING SEEN A MULBERRY BUSH IN OUR LIVES   658 4
AND ONE FOR THE LITTLE BOY THAT LIVES DOWN THE   669 24
IT WAS THE EATING UP OF LITTLE LIVES   679 15
OF BIGGER LIVES WITH DUE REVERENCE AND ACKNOWLEDGEMENT   679 22
ALSO THE LIVES THAT STILL HE MAY REQUIRE   736 17
I KNOW WHERE THEY ARE GOING ALL THE LIVES   744 13
FROM BURNING FIRES OF MANY SMOULDERING LIVES   744 24
AND BLOOD-BROWN FLUX OF LIVES THAT SWEEP THEIR WAY   745 8
A FRAGILE STRANGER IN THE FLUX OF LIVES   745 18
OF LIVES I SPEAK TO ALL WHO CANNOT HEAR   745 23
AND ALONE HE IS WHILE HE LIVES IN HIS DEEPEST SELF   843 26
BUT UNDERNEATH ARE THE DEEP ROCKS THE LIVING ROCK THAT + 844 2
CAUGHT WHEN MY HEART WOULD LEAP IN A NET OF LIVES   884 15
UP TO THEIR LIVES SO THEY TO ME   *899 21
FINE FOLIAGE OF LIVES THIS LIFE OF MINE   *899 25
I HAVE SUCH SWARMING SENSE OF LIVES AT THE BASE OF ME S+ *900 5
LIVES   *900 6
UP TO THEIR LIVES SO THEY TO ME   *902 33
FINE FOLIAGE OF LIVES THIS LIFE OF MINE   *903 2
I HAVE SUCH SWARMING SENSE OF LIVES AT THE BASE OF ME S+ *903 17
LIVES   *903 18
LIVES CROWD   *905 16
OF OLD INEFFECTUAL LIVES LINGER BLURRED AND WARM   *906 12
OF OLD INEFFECTUAL LIVES LINGER BLURRED AND WARM   *908 6
OF LIVES THAT SORROWS LIKE MISCHIEVOUS STRANGE MICE CHA+ *938 5
LIVES WHILE HE LIVES MOST OF HIS TIME ALONE   *951 5

LIVING
ARE THEY ASLEEP ARE THEY LIVING NOW SEE WHEN I   33 8
YET FLAME OF THE LIVING GROUND   39 21
OF LIVING HAS PASSED EBBING ON   53 15
AND LAUGHING WITH LABOUR LIVING THEIR WORK LIKE A GAME   72 11
I THOUGHT I COULD PLUNGE IN YOUR LIVING HOTNESS AND BE   99 8
IN MY FLAME OF LIVING THE INVISIBLE HEART OF THE ROSE   115 8
BREAKS INTO DAZZLE OF LIVING AS DOLPHINS LEAP FROM THE + 136 19
BUT WHAT OF US WHO ARE LIVING   168 34
WITH A TOUCH THE DEAD AND THE LIVING WHILE TIME COUNTS I 174 12
IN A TISSUE AS ALL THE MOLTEN CELLS IN THE LIVING MESH   176 8
THAT DOES INFORM THIS VARIOUS DREAM OF LIVING   194 20
AT THIS MY TASK OF LIVING THIS MY DREAM   195 9
OH GODS OF THE LIVING DARKNESS POWERS OF NIGHT   213 29
THE THING WITH MY BODY THAT WOULD GO ON LIVING   214 28
LIVING AS THE MOUNTAINS DO BECAUSE THEY ARE STRONG   226 2
LIVING WHERE LIFE WAS NEVER YET DREAMED OF NOR HINTED AT 258 32
LIVING   261 7
OH IF IT BE TRUE AND THE LIVING DARKNESS OF THE BLOOD O+ 273 31
IT WILL BE SPRING IN THE WORLD OF THE LIVING   274 4
EMPEDOKLES SAYS TREES WERE THE FIRST LIVING CREATURES T+ 295 4
ALONG THE IRON TO THE LIVING STEEL   304 19
BLOOM ALONG THE CORSO ON THE LIVING PERAMBULATING BUSH   313 24
OF YELLOW-RED OUTREACHING LIVING WRATH   317 9
A LIVING FOREHEAD WITH ITS SLOW WHORL OF HAIR   325 27
THE LIVING BACK   355 15
AT THE LIVING ROCK HE IS UP AGAINST   382 17
LINGER FOR NOW THEY REALISE ALL THAT IS LOST THEN THE L+ 406 6
AND LIKE A FUNGUS LIVING ON THE REMAINS OF BYGONE LIFE   431 15
AND THEY SAY NOW BEHOLD YOU ARE LIVING THE GREAT LIFE   441 19
BEHOLD YOU ARE LIVING THE GREAT LIFE THE STUPENDOUS LIFE 441 23
O CEASE TO LISTEN TO THE LIVING DEAD   441 28
THE REPULSIVE LIVING FAT DEAD   441 35
A MAN SHOULD NEVER EARN HIS LIVING   443 10
REALLY LIVING IN HER SERVICE AND SERVING HER   447 24
LETTING THE LIVING DEAD EAT YOU UP   449 20
HE IS LIVING NOT MERELY WORKING   450 26
WEB OF LIVING LEAF   451 6
EARNING YOUR LIVING WHILE YOUR LIFE IS LOST   459 7
I DOUBT IF ANY MAN LIVING HANDS OUT A POUND NOTE WITHOUT 486 11
WE MUST HAVE THE MODESTY OF SIMPLE LIVING   487 22
IF MEN WERE FREE FROM THE TERROR OF EARNING A LIVING   488 4
THE VEINS OF LIVING SPACE AND ADDS A GLISTEN   505 3
WITHIN THE GENITALS OF LIVING SPACE   513 18
WE WANT A NEW WORLD OF WILD PEACE WHERE LIVING IS FREE   519 22
TO GET A LIVING IN THE DASTARDLY MEAN COMBAT   519 28
WHY SHOULD WE HAVE TO FIGHT FOR A LIVING   520 1
LIVING SHOULD BE AS FREE TO A MAN AS TO A BIRD   520 2
LIVING ON YOUR INCOME IS STROLLING GRANDLY OUTSIDE THE   521 11
ALMOST EVERY SCRAP OF THE LIVING EARTH YOU STROLL UP AND 521 15
THE ONLY REASON FOR LIVING IS BEING FULLY ALIVE   522 9
WE MUST CHANGE THE SYSTEM AND MAKE LIVING FREE TO ALL   522 29
AND LEAVES MEN LIVING CLAY   524 9
AND LIVING LIKE LICE ON POOR MONEY   526 19
YET LIVING ON THE FAT OF THE LAND   535 20
FOR FREEDOM AND THE FUN OF LIVING   560 31
FROM YOUR OWN BODY SAVED YOU FROM LIVING YOUR OWN   585 14
LOST SOME LIVING CONNECTION WITH THE COSMOS OUT OF THEM+ 610 9
BUT THE LIVING LEAVES IN THE BREATH OF THE WIND ARE MOR+ 615 14
CAN PUT BACK A HUMAN LIFE INTO CONNECTION WITH THE LIVI+ 617 4
I WITH THEM AM LIVING DEAD MECHANICAL ENSLAVED AT THE   629 28
AND I AM WRAPPED IN THE LEAD OF A COFFIN-LINING THE LIV+ 630 7
INTO THE INDUSTRIAL DANCE OF THE LIVING DEATH THE JIGGI+ 631 13
SONS OF THE LIVING ELEMENTS SONS OF THE UNTHINKING GODS 635 4
LIVING DARKNESS   636 32
THE LIVING SUBSTANTIAL GODS   638 14
OH MEN LIVING MEN VIVID MEN OCEAN AND FIRE   639 1
CAN'T LIVE ANY MORE EXCEPT FOR A SPELL WHEN THE LIVING   639 4
OH MEN OF LIFE AND OF LIVING   639 11
ONCE DISILLUSION FALLS ON LIVING MEN AND THEY FEEL THE   639 19
ONCE DISILLUSION FALLS ON LIVING MEN AND ILLUSION OF BR+ 639 23
AND THEN WHEN THE SOUL OF LIVING MEN REPUDIATES THEM   640 7

LIVING
    BY THE KINDNESS OF LIVING WOMEN AND MEN   640 14
    NOW LIVING WOMEN AND MEN ARE THREATENED WITH EXTINCTION   640 15
    AND BETWEEN THEM THE LAST LIVING HUMAN BEINGS   642 3
    BE QUITE ALONE AND FEEL THE LIVING COSMOS SOFTLY ROCKING   646 12
    LIVING PEOPLE NEVER MAKE REVOLUTIONS   647 22
    THE GODS WHO ARE LIFE AND THE FLUIDITY OF LIVING CHANGE   662 22
    BUT WHEN LIVING PEOPLE DIE IN THE RIPENESS OF THEIR TIME   676 8
    SO UNHAMPERED IN THEIR LIVING AND DYING   677 11
    OF ENDLESS AND LIVING SILENCE   698 27
    IT IS A FEARFUL THING TO FALL INTO THE HANDS OF THE LIV+   699 12
    WHEN I HAVE FALLEN OUT OF YOUR HANDS THE HANDS OF THE L+   699 20
    LET ME NEVER KNOW MYSELF APART FROM THE LIVING GOD   699 29
    ALL THAT MATTERS IS TO BE AT ONE WITH THE LIVING GOD   700 1
    AT HOME AT HOME IN THE HOUSE OF THE LIVING   700 6
    SLEEPING ON THE HEARTH OF THE LIVING WORLD   700 8
    FEELING THE PRESENCE OF THE LIVING GOD   700 10
    IT IS NOT EASY TO FALL OUT OF THE HANDS OF THE LIVING G+   700 17
    EVEN THROUGH THE GREATEST BLASPHEMIES THE HANDS OF THE +   700 20
    AND THE WILL THE LIVING DYNAMO GIVES THE MOTION AND THE+   712 14
    THE LIVING AMERICA IS IN THE HEARTS OF AMERICANS   774 24
    ABOUT THE INDIAN MAKE THEIR LIVING OFF HIM   778 11
    THAT IS LIVING THROBS   782 17
    AND THROWS UP STRENGTH THAT IS LIVING STRENGTH AND REGA+   782 19
    RUSH IN AND FILL THE LIVING CAVITIES   784 11
    CHILD OF THE LIVING DEAD THE DEAD THAT LIVE AND ARE NOT+   796 1
    I AM THE LIVING QUETZALCOATL   800 33
    I AM THE LIVING QUETZALCOATL   801 1
    ALL THINGS THAT LIFT IN THE LIFT OF LIVING BETWEEN EART+   801 8
    LIVING ARE THE LORDS OF LIFE   808 23
    WHERE THE DEAD ARE LIVING AND THE LIVING ARE DEAD   811 5
    FOR THE LIVING LIVE   811 27
    YET WE ARE NOT LIVING   825 29
    BUT THE LIMBS OF MAN LONG TO FOLD AND CLOSE UPON THE LI+   834 4
    HIS LIVING AND GETTING ON   837 26
    BUT UNDERNEATH ARE THE DEEP ROCKS THE LIVING ROCK THAT +   844 2
    LIFS THE LIVING ROCK OF A SINGLE CREATURE'S PRIDE   844 9
    LIKE THE LIVING LIFE ON THE EARTH   844 18
    I LEAVE YOU WHILE I PLAY MY GAME OF LIVING   875 37
    OF LIVING AND WAVER IN SWEET EXTINGUISHMENT   879 31
    FROM THE LIT ROOM OF LIVING   879 36
    AS IF WITHDRAWN FROM LIVING WOUNDS RAN RED   884 26
    WITH A STEADY RUSH OF LIVING A FOAM   888 7
    LIVING BLOOD   *892 9
    TO THE RECKLESS EXTRAVAGANT TURMOIL OF LIVING THE STRIFE   *895 13
    OF LIVING MY LIFE WERE DOUBLED I STILL HAVE THIS TO COM+   *900 9
    AS I AM WITH LIVING MY LIFE IN EARNESTNESS STILL PROGRE+   *900 12
    I ALONE AM LIVING THEN IT KEEPS   *900 22
    OF LIVING MY LIFE WERE DOUBLED I STILL HAVE THIS TO COM+   *903 16
    AS I AM WITH LIVING MY LIFE IN EARNESTNESS STILL PROGRE+   *903 24
    I ALONE AM LIVING THEN IT KEEPS   *903 34
    OF LIVING HAS PASSED ON AND ON   *906 6
    IN MY FLAME OF LIVING A SHADOW WITHIN THE SHINE   *930 8
    WHAT MATTER THE STUFF I LICK UP IN MY LIVING FLAME   *930 10
    THE FULL THROATED WOMAN HAS CHOSEN A WINNING LIVING SONG   *940 9
    HE IS LIVING NOT MERELY WORKING   *949 25
    CAME FROM THEM LIVING LIKE LEAVES FROM THE TREE OF THEI+   *949 30
    AND CLOTHED THEM WITH LIVING LEAVES   *949 31
    AT THE MARRIAGE OF THE LIVING DARK   *956 23
    THE WOMB OF SILENCE IN THE LIVING NIGHT   *959 33

LIVING-DEAD
    I KNOW THE UNLIVING FACTORY-HAND LIVING-DEAD MILLIONS   629 26
    IS UNLIVING ME LIVING-DEAD ME   629 27

LIVINGS
    TO EARN THEIR LIVINGS NOR YET GIRLS SWEET JOYS   459 3

LIZ
    SAY NO MORE LIZ DUNNA THEE   80 25
    I'LL TA'E THY WORD GOOD-BYE LIZ   80 29
    I WON'T OR MY NAME'S NOT LIZ   82 16
    AH'N PUT MY-SEN I' TH' WRONG LIZ   83 26
    THA ART SO SURE THA'RT RIGHT LIZ   84 1
    I DON'T LIKE YER LIZ I WANT TER   84 19
    I'LL SAY GOOD-BYE LIZ TO YER   85 1
    ABAHT IT YES I'M A GENT AN' LIZ   434 23
    SAY NO MORE LIZ DUNNA THEE   *922 25
    I'LL TA'E THY WORD GOOD-BYE LIZ   *922 29

LIZARD
    A LIZARD RAN OUT ON A ROCK AND LOOKED LISTENING   524 13
    WITH EVE AND THE AMAZON THE LIZARD AND THE FRAIL   633 3
    THROUGHOUT THE AEONS AS THE LIZARD SWIRLS HIS TAIL FINE+   683 7

LIZARDS
    AS MOSSES AND LITTLE LIZARDS THEY SAY WERE ONCE BIG   372 20
    IF MEN WERE AS MUCH MEN AS LIZARDS ARE LIZARDS   524 17
    TO THINK AMONG THE MOSS AND MUD OF LIZARDS AND MASTODONS   690 28

LIZZIE
    LIZZIE WHAT'S DONE IS DONE   79 30
    AFTER I'D KISSED THEE AT NIGHT LIZZIE   80 9
    INTO ME MELTED RIGHT INTO ME LIZZIE   80 11
    LIZZIE AND LUCY AND ME AND FLOSSIE   573 23
    BUT FOR LIZZIE AND LUCY AND FLOSSIE AND ME   574 1
    BUT ME AND LUCY AND FLOSSIE AND LIZZIE   574 3
    AND LIZZIE AND ME AND FLOSSIE AND LUCY   574 8
    LIZZIE WHAT'S DONE IS DONE   *921 26
    LIZZIE I TELL THEE THAT   *922 2
    AFTER THY KISSES LIZZIE AFTER   *922 9
    THA'S LAIN RIGHT UP TO ME LIZZIE AN' MELTED   *922 10
    INTO ME MELTED INTO ME LIZZIE   *922 11

LIZZIE STAINWRIGHT
    WHO Y'ARE YIS YOU'RE LIZZIE STAINWRIGHT   81 22
    WHO YER ARE YIS YOU'RE LIZZIE STAINWRIGHT   *923 22

LLOYD GEORGE
    YOU WON'T EVEN BE LLOYD GEORGE   835 25

LO
    LO I AM FLESH AND BLOOD THAT RACES   460 25
    LO I SEE FEAR IN THE TWISTED FACES   460 27
    LO ON THE OTHER SIDE THE GRAVE   460 29
    LO THERE IS WOMAN AND HER WAY IS A STRANGE WAY   461 11
    LO I AM NOTHING   511 3
    LO AGAIN THE SHUDDER OR BLISS THROUGH ALL THE ATOMS   682 15
    LO GOD IS BORN   682 21
    LO THE LOVELIEST IS RED ALL OVER RIPPLING VERMILION   689 6
    HIS URGE TAKES SHAPE IN FLESH AND LO   690 10
    LO THERE IS A CREATURE FORMED HOW STRANGE   690 12
    AND BECOMES AT LAST A CLOVE CARNATION LO THAT IS GOD   691 17
    LO GOD IS ONE GOD BUT HERE IN THE TWILIGHT   693 18
    LO THE LAUGH OF GOD   698 14
    LO THE LAST OF THE SEVEN GREAT LAUGHS OF GOD   698 16
    LO THE LAST OF THE SEVEN GREAT LAUGHS OF CREATION   698 17
    LO WE ARE IN THE MIDST OF THE SUNDERERS   707 16
    THE BREATH SAID GO AND LO   786 12
    LO I AM ALWAYS HERE   787 21
    BUT LO I AM ALWAYS HERE   787 31
    LO THE UNIVERSE TANGLES ITS GREAT DRAGONS   795 10
    BUT LO YOU INERT ONES I WILL SET THE DRAGONS UPON YOU   796 25
    LO IN THE BACK STREETS OF THE AIR DEAD ONES ARE CRAWLIN+   796 29
    LO I RELEASE THE DRAGONS THE GREAT WHITE ONE OF THE NOR+   796 30
    LO I AM LORD OF THE WATCHES OF THE NIGHT   806 29
    AND LO IT STICKS BETWEEN THE RIBS OF A MAN   807 21
    LO THE GREAT ONE ANSWERS TRACK HIM DOWN   808 7
    ICHABOD ICHABOD LO AND BEHOLD   814 18

LOAD
    ON A NIGHT-SKY BENT WITH A LOAD   104 24
    TO MY ARMS WITH HER WELCOME LOAD   106 18
    DEJECTEDLY A HUNTSMAN GOES BY WITH HIS LOAD   220 17
    TO DRAW THE LOAD SO STILL AND SLOW IT MOVES   225 15
    CRAWLS THE FIRST LOAD INTO SIGHT AND NOW THERE ARE SOME   732 25

LOADED
    I'D LOADED THE CAMEL'S BACK BEFORE   491 19

LOADS
    GO BY WITH THEIR LOADS OF GREEN AND SILVER BIRCH-TREES   209 17
    WITH A BOSS PILING LOADS ON HIS BACK   379 10

LOAF
    THEY SAY CAN'T WE HAVE A LOAF OF COMMON BREAD   442 17

LOAM
    TREAD THEM OUT IN THE LOAM   159 22
    ON OUR PRIMAL LOAM   243 20
    FIRE AND RAIN AND AIR AND LIVE LOAM   505 13
    MY FLESH IS READY LIKE TILLED LOAM   888 5
    I HAVE PUSHED MY HANDS IN THE DARK LOAM UNDER THE FLOWE+   *926 8

LOATHE
    YEA BUT I LOATHE YOU THAT YOU SHOULD WITHHOLD   122 23
    DO YOU NOT LOATHE THE CONFINEMENT   236 13
    WITH A LOVELINESS I LOATHE   270 26
    AND DOESN'T EVERYBODY LOATHE YOU THEN   400 12
    WE LOATHE THE THOUGHT OF ANY SORT OF TRIUMPH   519 8
    AND THEY LOATHE ALL FEELING AS SUCH   537 16
    AND I LOATHE THE THOUGHT OF BEING A PILFERER   607 19

LOATHES
    FOR THE LUSCIOUS FILMY IMAGINATION LOATHES THE MALE   538 7

LOATHING
    WITH DEADLY LOATHING   538 9

LOAVES
    OR LOAVES   451 11

LOBBING
    LOBBING WILDLY THROUGH DEEP SNOW LIKE A RABBIT   397 7

LOBO
    SNOW AND INWARDNESS OF THE LOBO VALLEY   401 13
    WE GO ON INTO THE GLOOM OF LOBO   402 10
    ABOVE THE TREES OF THE LOBO DARK VALLEY-MOUTH   402 20

LOBO CANYON
    CLIMBING THROUGH THE JANUARY SNOW INTO THE LOBO CANYON   401 1

LOBS
    RABBIT LOBS   34 28

LOBSTER
    AS IF ANY MIND COULD HAVE IMAGINED A LOBSTER   689 19
    EVEN IF IT IS ONLY A LOBSTER ON TIP-TOE   689 25

LOBSTER'S
    SCALE-LAPPING LIKE A LOBSTER'S SECTIONS   355 3

LOCALISED
    AND CANNOT BE LOCALISED   627 20

LOCKED
    WHAT IS IT INTERNECINE THAT IS LOCKED   160 17
    THE SCALES ARE LOCKED IN AN ARCH LIKE A BRIDGE   355 2
    LOCKED UP IN A DUNGEON CELL   633 2

LOCKS
  THE ATOM LOCKS UP TWO ENERGIES   515 14

LOCUST-POD
  AS YOU WOULD A FRESH SWEET LOCUST-POD   752 14

LOCUSTS
  HAS COME DOWN ON THE HEART IN A BURDEN OF LOCUSTS   507 22

LODE
  TO THE LODE OF HER AGONY   99 28

LODGER
  AX 'IM THY-SEN WENCH A WIDDER'S LODGER   77 11
  AX HIM THY-SEN WENCH A WIDDER'S LODGER   *918 29

LODGES
  'ER AS 'E LODGES WI'   78 10
  HER AS HE LODGES WI'   *920 2

LOFTILY
  TALL AND LOFTILY SHADOWED BUT THE MOON   103 30
  OF THE MORNING THE ELMS ARE LOFTILY DIMMED AND TALL   164 22

LOFTINESS
  AND ALL THESE HUMAN PILLARS OF LOFTINESS GOING STIFF ME+   288 1

LOFTY
  WHERE LOFTY TREES ATHWART-STREAM CHANCE   68 11
  WHOSE LOFTY ROSES BREAK AND BLOW   104 23
  LOFTY SPIRIT   473 11
  ARE YOU SO LOFTY O MY GOD   710 13
  ARE YOU SO PURE AND LOFTY UP ALOFT   710 14
  WHERE THE LOFTY TREES ATHWART STREAM PERCHANCE   *914 26

LOG
  I PICKED UP A CLUMSY LOG   351 10
  ROUND A LOG OF WOOD   387 8
  AND HE LIES LIKE A LOG AND SCREAMS AND HIS SCREAM IS SI+   407 20

LOGIC
  FILIUS MEUS O REMORSELESS LOGIC   320 8

LOGOS
  THE LOGOS THE LOGOS   328 23

LOINS
  GOD STEPPING THROUGH OUR LOINS IN ONE BRIGHT STRIDE   87 25
  FROM OUT OF THE LOINS OF NIGHT TO GLOW IN OUR WAY   88 25
  THROUGH SUCH NARROW LOINS TOO NARROW   327 13
  NO LOINS OF DESIRE   335 20
  AND THEIR NAKED BREASTS THE GROOVED LOINS   389 8
  THRUSTS WARM THROUGH THE LOINS SO THE LITTLE ONE   425 16
  WHAT DO YOU WANT WILD LOINS AND WHAT   461 5
  WITH MOUTH AND LOINS AND NEEDS HE LIVES   461 15
  SUCH ADORATION PIERCES THE LOINS AND PERISHES THE MAN   538 11
  ONLY FROM OUT THE FOLIAGE OF THE SECRET LOINS   606 6
  AND THE WHITE SWAN SWIMS IN THE MARSHES OF HIS LOINS   624 6
  AND STEEL HAS TWISTED THE LOINS OF MAN ELECTRICITY HAS   629 8
  UNKNOWN WITHIN YOUR BREAST AND YOUR DEADENED LOINS   723 18
  HE SENDS THE SERPENT OF POWER UP MY FEET AND MY LOINS   799 25
  YET I HAVE LAIN IN HIS LOINS ERE HE BEGOT ME IN MOTHER +   801 14
  AND KNEES AND THIGHS AND LOINS AND THE BOWELS OF STRENG+   801 20
  KNEES AND YOUR LEGS AND YOUR LOINS HIS CIRCLE OF REST I+   801 25
  AND ONE IN THE LOINS OF A MAN   819 8
  THE LOINS OF THIS OUR TISSUE OF TRAVAIL OUR LIFE'S   880 3
  LIKE SEED FROM OUT THE RIPENED LOINS OF LIFE   880 6
  FROM OUT OF MY HEART AND LOINS CHOKED AND SHACKLED   884 17
  AND THROUGH THE REEDS OF HIS MARSHY LOINS   *953 26

LOINS'
  OF DESIRES IN THE LOINS' DARK TWISTS   461 4

LOITER
  AS THEY LOITER ALONG THE RIVER-BEDS   465 13

LOITERING
  PALE-FACE AUTHORITIES LOITERING TEPIDLY   316 27

LOITERS
  WHERE THE FLICKERING RIVER LOITERS   867 8

LONDON
  LONDON   170 17
  LONDON   171 5
  LONDON WITH HAIR   171 9
  THAT LONDON LAIR OF SUDDEN   171 14
  IN LONDON I SHOULD HAVE HELD MYSELF   269 15
  THE GEESE THAT SAVED ROME AND WILL LOSE LONDON   438 25
  HOW YOU REMIND ME OF MY LONDON FRIENDS   542 3
  IN A PUB PARLOUR IN LITERARY LONDON ON CERTAIN EVENINGS   542 10
  AH IN THAT PARLOUR OF THE LONDON PUB   542 16
  OF LONDON TOWN   551 8
  OH WHEN MERCURY CAME TO LONDON   581 14
  I'VE BEEN UP TO LONDON TO SEE THE FINE QUEEN   670 2
  IN LONDON NEW YORK PARIS   704 6
  AND THE GEESE THAT SAVED ROME WILL LOSE LONDON   *947 26

LONDON'S MERCURY
  OH LONDON'S MERCURY SUNDAY-SCHOOL SQUIRE   681 1

LONDON'S
  LONDON'S LILY-LIKE POLICEMEN FAINT   680 17

LONE
  IS HE CALLING THE LONE ONE IS HIS DEEP   40 1
  THE LONE CLEAVAGE OF DIVISION UPRIGHT OF THE ETERNAL CR+   355 30

LONELIER
  LONELIER THAN LYONESSE   261 18

LONELIEST
  HOW TO WAIT FOR THE LONELIEST OF FEASTS   465 25

LONELILY
  YOUR PRESENCE PEERING LONELILY THERE   116 25

LONELINESS
  RUNS SEEKING A LONELINESS   64 9
  THE LONELINESS DAUNTS THEM THEIR STIFF THROATS ACHE   228 12
  I HAVE FOUND A PLACE OF LONELINESS   261 17
  A NEW INTOXICATION OF LONELINESS AMONG DECAYING FROST-C+   281 2
  INTOXICATION OF FINAL LONELINESS   281 30
  AND THEIR PRE-WORLD LONELINESS   339 27
  LONELINESS   610 2
  PEOPLE WHO COMPLAIN OF LONELINESS MUST HAVE LOST SOMETH+   610 8
  AND WHEN MY HEART IS CHILL WITH LONELINESS   *900 25
  AND WHEN MY HEART IS CHILL WITH LONELINESS   *904 1

LONELY
  SHE SO LONELY GREYING NOW   63 14
  THE MOON WALKS HER LONELY WAY WITHOUT ANGUISH   63 20
  TO WALK THE LONELY DUSKY HEIGHTS   63 31
  AH LISTEN FOR SILENCE IS NOT LONELY   69 5
  COOL LONELY NIGHT HER BREASTS WILL KEEP THE NIGHT AT BAY   91 11
  YOUR HEAD THROUGH BEING LONELY   104 20
  SO I AM NOT LONELY NOR SAD   109 7
  TWO HARD CRUDE PAWS IN HUNGER ON THE LONELY   127 27
  ONE LONELY BELL ONE ONLY THE STORM-TOSSED AFTERNOON IS   137 1
  YOU FROM YOUR LONELY WALK   178 27
  THE SUN WARMS THE SEA LITTLE LONELY AND SAD SIFTING THE+   180 3
  RESTLESS AND LONELY SHAKEN BY YOUR OWN MOODS   197 2
  SWARMS OF MANKIND IN THE WORLD AND WE WERE LESS LONELY   224 7
  THE LONELY RAMBLER THE STOIC DIGNIFIED STALKER THROUGH   360 28
  LEFT LONELY IN THE NIGHT   403 26
  WHEN I HEAR SOMEBODY COMPLAIN OF BEING LONELY   646 1
  LIKE A LONELY STAR DROPPING THROUGH SPACE   862 24
  COMING HOME OVER THE WASTE-LANDS WIDE AND LONELY WITH S+   866 16
  HOW LONELY IN THE WIDE WORLD IS THIS PLAYGROUND   867 6
  HOW LONELY UNDER THE TREE UNNOTICED   867 7
  BACK FROM MY BEAUTIFUL LONELY BODY   *893 31
  THEY KEEP ME ASSURED AND WHEN MY SOUL FEELS LONELY   *900 20
  THEY KEEP ME ASSURED AND WHEN MY SOUL FEELS LONELY   *903 32
  THEN LISTEN FOR SILENCE IS NOT LONELY   *915 17
  GOD LONELY PUT DOWN HIS MOUTH IN A KISS OF CREATION   *916 5
  THE SIGHT OF YOU PEERING LONELY THERE   *930 24

LONESOME
  OR IN AMERICAN LONESOME   646 2

LONG-DISCARDED
  GATES OF THE LONG-DISCARDED   243 10

LONG-DRAWN
  CLEAR UPON THE LONG-DRAWN HOARSENESS OF A TRAIN ACROSS +   63 11
  THEIR RHYTHMS ON LONG-DRAWN HOLLOW SINISTER DRUMS   371 5
  THE LONG-DRAWN BRAY OF THE ASS   377 1

LONGED
  THEN I LONGED FOR YOU WITH YOUR MANTLE OF LOVE TO FOLD   98 23
  HOW I HAVE LONGED FOR THIS NIGHT IN THE TRAIN   117 1
  I LONGED TO TASTE I LONGED TO TURN   123 27
  I LONGED TO FEEL MY HOT BLOOD BURN   123 29
  WAS IT PERVERSITY THAT I LONGED TO TALK TO HIM   350 14
  HOW I HAVE LONGED FOR THIS NIGHT IN THE TRAIN   *931 5
  PULSED THICKLY AND I LONGED TO POUR   *934 33
  I LONGED TO POUR THE BURNING STORE   *935 1

LONGER
  NO LONGER SHADOW AND IT HOLDS ME   34 22
  FALLING ROUND US NO LONGER DAPPLE   37 27
  NO LONGER HURT WHERE THE SILK SAILS FILL   53 12
  DO YOU CARE NO LONGER HOW   56 23
  NO LONGER NOW CAN I ENDURE THE BRUNT   74 12
  AND HAVE NOT ANY LONGER ANY HOPE   100 25
  AND THE PLACE IS NO LONGER OURS WATCHING I HEAR   173 2
  WE NO LONGER KNOW   240 15
  IF IT CEASED I SHOULD BE NO LONGER MAN   320 26
  NO LONGER OR CARRY THE BURDEN OF A MAN ON YOUR HEART   411 12
  NO LONGER HE SWIMS CALMLY   436 2
  YOU ARE NO LONGER MEN THAT IS BOURGEOIS   443 2
  WHY SHOULD WE BE BELITTLED ANY LONGER   452 13
  HE IS NO LONGER MY CONCERN HE CEASES TO BE   468 10
  BUT A GEM IS DIFFERENT IT LASTS SO MUCH LONGER THAN WE +   476 21
  SO MUCH MUCH LONGER   476 22
  COME SATAN DON'T GO DODGING BEHIND MY BACK ANY LONGER   483 19
  AND MAKES ME KNOW I AM NOT BLANK ANY LONGER   501 25
  AND A MAN CAN NO LONGER FEEL HEROIC ABOUT BEING A HAMLET   508 26
  SO A MAN NO LONGER KNOWS HIS OWN HEART   509 5
  WOMEN FELT IT WAS NO LONGER ANY USE BEING A LINGER-LONG+   537 29
  DAWN IS NO LONGER IN THE HOUSE OF THE FISH   616 18
  AND THE FOOT OF THE CROSS NO LONGER IS PLANTED IN THE P+   616 21
  NO LONGER AT THE MERCY   627 13
  WHAT IS MAN THAT THOU ART NO LONGER MINDFUL OF HIM   629 12
  ARE THESE NO LONGER MEN THESE MILLIONS MILLIONS   629 14
  NO LONGER THEY SWEEP THE HOURS AS THE SCYTHE OF THE MOW+   855 29
  MY CHAFED CURBED BLOOD NO LONGER BROOKS   857 3
  SHE IS NO LONGER TWO DAYS OLD   863 11
  WHY SHOULD I GRIEVE THAT MY MOTHER IS NO LONGER CLOTTED   870 2
  NO LONGER A LARGE FLECK MOVING IN THE SUNSHINE   870 14
  FROM SPACE TO LONGER SPACE LIFTS A HARSH BREATH   878 24
  FALLING ROUND US NO LONGER DAPPLE   *892 15

LONGER
    NO LONGER SHAKE WHERE THE SILK SAIL FILLS   *906   4

LONGEST
    AND NOW THE LONGEST GRASS-LEAVES HARDLY EMERGE   85   6
    HE LAUGHS LONGEST WHO LAUGHS LAST   297 25
    THE LONGEST JOURNEY TO OBLIVION   717 22
    OF DEATH TO CARRY THE SOUL ON THE LONGEST JOURNEY   718 23
    AND THE PROPER STORE OF MEAL FOR THE LONGEST JOURNEY   721 23
    TO CONTINUE ON THE LONGEST JOURNEY   722 18
    SING THEN THE SONG OF DEATH AND THE LONGEST JOURNEY   724   1
    THE LONGEST JOURNEY TOWARDS OBLIVION   *957   7
    TO SET SOFTLY FORTH ON THE LONGEST JOURNEY THE LONGEST +   *957 19
    DEEPEST AND LONGEST OF SEAS   *957 31
    TO WHERE THE FURTHEST AND THE LONGEST SEA   *958 27
    ON THE LONGEST JOURNEY   *959   4
    TAKING THE LONGEST JOURNEY   *959 11
    ON THE LONGEST JOURNEY TOWARDS THE GREATEST GOAL   *959 16
    AT THE END OF THE LONGEST JOURNEY   *960   4
    OH NOTHING MATTERS BUT THE LONGEST JOURNEY   *960   9
    ON THE LONGEST JOURNEY OVER THE HIDDEN SEA   *960 20
    FOR THE LONGEST JOURNEY OVER THE LAST OF SEAS   *961   7
    SING THEN THE SONG OF DEATH AND THE LONGEST JOURNEY   *961 11

LONG-HAIRED
    AND LONG-HAIRED PEOPLE WHO PRETEND TO ESPOUSE   778   5
    THEIR CAUSE BECAUSE THEY THE ARTISTS AND LONG-HAIRED   778   6
    LONG-HAIRED PEOPLE PAINTING THE INDIAN AND WRITING   778 10

LONGING
    TIME WITH TRUE LONGING WHAT I WAS TO YOU   91 18
    AND MY HEART LEAPED UP IN LONGING TO PLUNGE ITS STARK   125 33
    NOT EVEN LONGING   213 10
    BUT I'M ALWAYS LONGING FOR SOMEONE TO SAY   490 27
    AND LONGING UTTERLY TO DIE   721   2
    AND STEALING INTO HIS SLEEP SHOULD SET HIM LONGING   877 33
    AND MY HEART LEAPED UP IN LONGING TO PLUNGE ITS STARK   *936 32

LONGISH
    AFTER EACH JERK THE LONGISH INTERVAL   365 24

LONG-LEGGED
    CURIOUS LONG-LEGGED FOALS AND WIDE-EARED CALVES AND NAK+   271 34

LONG-NIGHTED
    IN LONG-NIGHTED JANUARY   305 22
    SWEATING HIS DROPS OF BLOOD THROUGH THE LONG-NIGHTED   305 25

LONG-NOSED
    IS IT THE SECRET OF THE LONG-NOSED ETRUSCANS   296 14
    THE LONG-NOSED SENSITIVE-FOOTED SUBTLY-SMILING ETRUSCANS   296 15
    LONG-NOSED MEN OF ETRURIA   297 15

LONG-SKIRTED
    LIKE A GENTLEMAN IN A LONG-SKIRTED COAT   354 20

LONG-TRESSED
    SHIMMERS IN A STREAM OF BLUENESS AND LONG-TRESSED   530   6

LOOK
    WHAT IS THIS THING THAT I LOOK DOWN UPON   33 24
    I MUST LOOK AWAY FROM HIM FOR MY FADED EYES   47 21
    WOULD THE DARKNESS LOOK LIKE A GRAVE   49 19
    HIS FACE TO LOOK AT ME   51 14
    EVERY DAY BY THE FENCE TO LOOK UP AT THE FLOWERS THAT E+   58 14
    THA SHOULD HA' SEED 'ER KNEEL AN' LOOK IN   61   6
    I HAVE STARTLED A HUNDRED EYES AND NOW I MUST LOOK   76 12
    AN' LOOK AT ME   82 20
    FOR WHENEVER I LOOK THEE I' TH' FACE I S'LL SEE   82 23
    LIFT THY FACE AN' LOOK AT ME MAN CANNA TER LOOK AT ME   83   5
    BUT WE MAUN MA'E THE BEST ON'T SO NOW ROUSE UP AN' LOOK+   83 14
    LOOK UP AN' SAY THA'RT SORRY THA DID IT SAY THA'RT SORR+   83 15
    MY COMING WHY DO YOU LOOK AWAY FROM ME   85 18
    OF THE BLOSSOM ARE ROSES TO LOOK AT BUT FLAMES WHEN THE+   93 32
    A LOOK OF HATRED ON THE FLOWER THAT BURNS   113 11
    AND THE NIGHT LOOK THROUGH   116 24
    TO RAISE MY FACE I DID NOT DARE LOOK UP   122 28
    AND LOOK YOU FLOATING JUST THEREBY   126 14
    LOOK NOW THROUGH THE WOOD WHERE THE BEECH-GREEN   126 22
    I LOOK AT THE SWALING SUNSET   134   1
    AND LOOK   137   8
    NO LOOK AT THE WET STARLING   137 17
    AS 'UD MAKE THEE A WIFE AN' LOOK UP TER THEE   138 30
    A LOOK AS HE STANDS ON THE EDGE OF THIS NAKED STALL   144 19
    OF YOUR HEART OF FIRE IN WHICH I LOOK   151   2
    PURE LOOK OF YOUR LAST DEAD FACE WHENCE NOW IS GONE   157 17
    YOUR YOUNG HUSHED LOOK THAT THEN SAW GOD ABLAZE   157 23
    AND REMEMBER THE SMALL LAD LYING INTENT TO LOOK   161   9
    AS WE LOOK OR ARE WE   163   3
    WE DO NOT LOOK AT EACH OTHER WE HIDE   166   6
    LOOK IT HAS TAKEN ROOT   172   8
    THEIR EYES AND LOOK AT THE GRAVE ON THE HILL IN WONDER   176 16
    AT THE OPEN DOOR OF THE ROOM I STAND AND LOOK AT THE NI+   179 20
    I CAN LOOK THROUGH   194   1
    FOR LOOK   194 16
    NOR DO I GET ANY LOOK   198 27
    THE WAN WONDERING LOOK OF THE PALE SKY   203 10
    AND LOOK AT THE MOUNTAIN-WALLS   204 13
    YET HOW I HAVE LEARNED TO KNOW THAT LOOK IN YOUR EYES   207 15
    THAT YOU NEVER LOOK QUITE BACK NINE-TENTHS AH MORE   208 12
    YOU LOOK ROUND OVER YOUR SHOULDER   208 13
    WE LOOK OVER THE GROWING WHEAT WHERE THE JADE-GREEN   209 20
    WHAT SHOULD I LOOK FOR   214   6
    THINK I COULDN'T LOOK TOWARDS DEATH   215   1
    ONLY NOT LOOK   215   3
    YOUR EYES WHEN YOU LOOK AT ME   215 19
    I AM BEAUTIFUL I LOOK AT THE RUMPLED YOUNG ROSES   218   2
    LOOK AT THE LITTLE DARLINGS IN THE CORN   221   5

LOOK
    SO HIGH AND MIGHTY LOOK HOW THE HEADS ARE BORNE   221   7
    THE BROWN EYES BLACK WITH MISERY AND HATE THAT LOOK   225 23
    AT PEACE AND LOOK OUT OF THE WINDOWS   227 31
    THE BRAND IS UPON HIM LOOK YOU   228 23
    LOOK SHE'S A WONDERFUL DOVE WITHOUT BLEMISH OR SPOT   239   1
    WE LOOK BACK ON THE WITHERING ROSES   242 28
    LOOK FOR LIKE THE BREATH OF LIFE AS LONG AS I LIVE   248 10
    I SHALL ALWAYS WONDER OVER YOU AND LOOK FOR YOU   248 12
    YOU MAY LOOK AND SAY TO YOURSELVES I DO   251   7
    LOOK YOU ARE CLEAN AND FINE AND SINGLED OUT   255 10
    HOW COULD I LOOK WHEN I WAS MAD I LOOKED SIDEWAYS FURTI+   264 35
    WE SHALL NOT LOOK BEFORE AND AFTER   268 10
    ESPECIALLY THE YOUNG WOMEN I LOOK AT THEM   269 22
    WHEN THEY BREAK AND SHOW THE SEED THEN WE LOOK INTO THE+   277   2
    DO YOU PREFER TO LOOK ON THE PLAIN SIDE   278 23
    LOOK NOW EVEN NOW HOW IT KEEPS ITS POWER OF INVISIBILITY   286   7
    LOOK HOW BLACK HOW BLUE-BLACK HOW GLOBED IN EGYPTIAN   286   8
    LOOK AT THEM STANDING THERE IN AUTHORITY   287 11
    AND WHAT IS DAYLIGHT TO ME THAT I SHOULD LOOK SKYWARD   287 26
    LOOK AT THE MANY-CICATRISED FRAIL VINE NONE MORE SCARRED   305   4
    LOOK OUT PERSEPHONE   308 27
    THE SOCIALISTS HAVE GATHERED UPON US TO LOOK AT US   312 11
    YOU LOOK WELL WITH YOUR SALVIA FLOWERS I MUST SAY   314 34
    LOOK AT HIM WITH HIS PAW ON THE WORLD   325 23
    AND I SAID TO MY HEART LOOK LOOK AT HIM   337 25
    AND LOOK BEYOND AND SEE   338 29
    LOOK UP AND YOU SEE THINGS FLYING   340 27
    AND LOOK WITH LACONIC BLACK EYES   353 12
    DOES HE LOOK FOR A COMPANION   357 29
    HER LACONIC EYE HAS AN EARTHY MATERIALISTIC LOOK   359 33
    NOW LOOK AT HIM   360 33
    HE DOES NOT LOOK AT HER NOR SNIFF AT HER   362 13
    WE OUGHT TO LOOK THE OTHER WAY   363 22
    WE LOOK AT HIM THROUGH THE WRONG END OF THE LONG TELESC+   372 22
    YOU NEVER LOOK AT THE SUN WITH YOUR TWO EYES   373 23
    WHAT DO YOU LOOK AT ME FOR   375 18
    WHAT DO YOU LOOK AT ME FOR WITH SUCH MISGIVING   375 19
    I IGNORE THOSE FOLK WHO LOOK OUT   375 28
    YOU TRIED TO LOOK BACK TO IT AND COULDN'T   381   7
    LIKE THE DEVIL AND LOOK ON THE WORLD AS HIS OWN   382 14
    PRETENDING TO LOOK ROUND THE STALL   384 32
    AND IF YOU LOOK AT HER SHE LOOKS BACK WITH A COLD SARDO+   386   4
    DILATED LOOK UP   389 23
    INEVITABLY LOOK UP   389 24
    STOPS AGAIN HALF TURNS INQUISITIVE TO LOOK BACK   393 29
    AND A WRINKLED REPROACHFUL LOOK   394 30
    HOW YOU HATE BEING MADE TO LOOK UNDIGNIFIED MA'AM   397 33
    YOU LOOK AT ME FOR DISCRIMINATION DON'T YOU   400 24
    LOOK UP AT ME WITH MISGIVING IN YOUR BULGING EYES   400 25
    INSTEAD I LOOK OUT   402 21
    SAYS LOOK FOR A LAST LONG TIME THEN LOOK LOOK WELL   403   6
    FAR ONE TO SLEEP AND A FORGETTING AND OFTEN THE DEAD LO+   406   5
    GLAD TO EMERGE AND LOOK BACK   409 13
    AND THEN TO LOOK BACK TO THE ROUNDED SIDES OF THE SQUAT+   409 21
    TRYING TO LOOK LIKE A PELICAN   413 13
    DOESN'T HE LOOK THE FRESH CLEAN ENGLISHMAN OUTSIDE   430 21
    AND SAYING LOOK AT ME I AM NOT RESPECTABLE   432 16
    WHILE AS TO HONESTY OH LOOK WHERE THE MONEY LIES   432 33
    THE UNTURNED SAYS YOU LOOK IT   433   5
    LOOK THEN   438   3
    LET THE DEAD LOOK AFTER THE DEAD   440 23
    LOOK ROUND AND REALISE   456 16
    TO LOOK THE OTHER WAY   460 24
    ANY MORE THAN AUGUST CAN BE BULLIED TO LOOK LIKE MARCH   478 11
    MEN SELL THEMSELVES FOR A WAGE AND EMPLOYERS LOOK OUT   483   2
    HE WAS FRIGHTENED TO LOOK ROUND   483 11
    TILL YOU LOOK TO THE RIGHT MAN TO PUT YOU INTO TOUCH   484 18
    THEY LOOK AT YOU THEY SEE A CAGED MONKEY   485 20
    WHEN I LOOK AT THIS PINE-TREE NEAR THE SEA   498 18
    AND ITS PLUMES LOOK LIKE GREEN CUPS HELD UP TO THE SUN +   498 22
    AND I LOOK SHABBY YET MY ROOTS GO BEYOND MY KNOWING   499   6
    AND MAKE THE YOUNG LOOK AFTER US   503   4
    LOOK AT MY MOTHER HOW RICH AND STILL SHE IS   503 28
    BUT THEN YOU NEED ONLY LOOK AT THE MODERN PERAMBULATOR   521 25
    BUT HOW PALTRY MINGY AND DINGY AND SQUALID PEOPLE LOOK   530 15
    AND LOOK AT THE SODOMITICAL AND LESBIAN STUFF WEARING   532   6
    MY DEARS DON'T LOOK AT ME I AM MERELY TERRIFIED OF YOU   541 10
    NOW LOOK HERE   546 22
    OR IF YOU ONLY LOOK IT SO WONDERFULLY   548 14
    AND IF YOU ONLY LOOK SO DISTINGUISHED AND SUPERIOR   548 18
    AND LOOK AT THE FAT-EYED LOT   556 22
    DON'T LOOK FOR A SAVIOUR   564 13
    BUT LOOK AT THE CABBAGES OH COUNT THEM BY THE SCORE   569 10
    AND YOU WILL BE AGAIN THEREFORE WHY LOOK BLUE   577 12
    LOOK AT THAT ONE THERE THAT'S PRETTY HOT   578 11
    AND NOW LOOK HERE WHAT YOU'VE GONE AND DONE   583   5
    LOOK AT THE YOUNG MEN UNDER THIRTY   612   9
    AND LOOK ROUND AND RISE AND ON THE GREAT VAULTS OF HIS +   625   3
    EMBEDDED IN THEM I LOOK OUT ON THE SUNSHINE OF THE SOUTH   629 31
    OH LOOK AT MY FELLOW-MEN LOOK AT THEM   631   7
    LOOK OUT MY LAD YOU'VE GOT 'EM ON YOUR TRACK   634   9
    AND STILL I LOOK FOR THE MEN WHO WILL DARE TO BE   634 21
    SOME MEN LOOK STRAIGHT INTO THE EYES OF THE GODS   649   9
    WHO LOOK INTO THE EYES OF THE GODS   649 15
    THOSE THAT LOOK INTO THE EYES OF THE GODS AND THESE ARE+   649 20
    AND THOSE THAT LOOK INTO THE EYES OF THE FEW OTHER MEN   649 21
    AND THE FEW LOOK INTO THE EYES OF THE GODS AND SERVE TH+   650   4
    THE FEW MUST LOOK INTO THE EYES OF THE GODS AND OBEY TH+   650   8
    AND THE MANY MUST OBEY THE FEW THAT LOOK INTO THE EYES +   650 10
    AND YOU LOOK IN HER EYES AND SEE IT IS A LIE   654 11
    THERE IS NOTHING TO LOOK AT ANY MORE   660 26
    NOW I DON'T WANT TO LOOK AT THE WORLD ANY MORE   662   8
    DO OPEN THE BOOK AND LOOK   669   3
    ALL THE GODS AND YOU SEE THEM ALL IF YOU LOOK ALIVE AND+   671 20
    LOOK HE HATH MOVEMENT UPWARD HE SPIRALS   682 18
    IS IN HER EXALTATION AND CAN LOOK DOWN ON THE SUN   688 11
    BUT LET US FREE OUR EYES AND LOOK BEYOND   737   4

LOOK

LOOK IN THE SKY AT THE BRIGHT   755 12
LOOK AT THE SHAKING WHITE   755 14
LOOK INTO EACH OTHER'S EYES WITH KNOWLEDGE   770 30
DO YOU WANT TO LOOK LIKE A BANK-CLERK   773 16
DO YOU WANT TO LOOK LIKE A BANK-MANAGER   773 18
LOOK BACK THE LAST TIME MARY MOTHER   798 3
SAYING WITHOUT SPEECH LOOK YOU   802 29
AND STAND UP AND LOOK ABOUT HIM   809 17
TRUE MEN LOOK UP AT THE DAWN   810 8
WHEN I LOOK AT THE RAINBOW   819 6
JUST LOOK AT YOUR MAMMA   834 17
YOU LOOK LIKE THE TOPPINGEST TOPPING FIFTH-FORM ETON BO+   835 17
AND DO LOOK AT YOUR MAMMA   835 27
BECAUSE MAN POOR BEAST CAN LOOK AT HIMSELF   836 9
DARLING YOU LOOK SO LIKE BABY   842 14
YOU LOOK SO LIKE BABY IT WRINGS MY HEART   842 15
IN THE AUTUMN I'LL LOOK FOR IMMORTAL FRUIT   855 9
WITH THE FIRST DAWN I ROSE TO LOOK IN THE GLASS   860 11
LOOK BRIGHTLY ON A CONFUSION OF MUD AND SAND AND MORTAR   864 26
AND I COULD NOT BEAR HER LOOK UPON ME   869 7
I DARE NOT LOOK AT HIS EYES   871 28
SIEGMUND SIEGMUND GET UP AND LOOK AT ME LISTEN   871 35
OF YOUR HEART OF FIRE IN WHICH I LOOK   873 12
BECAUSE WHEN YOUR EYES LOOK UP AT ME THEY STARTLE   874 27
SO AS YOU LOOK UP AT ME   875 1
EVER AGAIN AND LAUGHING LOOK AT ME   876 24
HE WILL LOOK ROUND AND NOTE ME NOT NO MORE   877 17
MY LITTLE RED HEIFER GO AND LOOK AT HER EYES   *892 22
EYES LOOK AT ME SO   *894 2
I HAVE STARTLED A HUNDRED EYES AND I MUST LOOK   *898 6
I HAVE STARTLED A HUNDRED EYES AND I MUST LOOK   *901 15
YOU SHOULD 'A SEEN HER KNEEL AN' LOOK DOWN   *910 10
THA SHOULD HA' SEED HER KNEEL AN' LOOK IN   *911 22
AN' LOOK ME CLEAR   *924 24
FOR WHENEVER I LOOK THEE I' TH' FACE I S'LL SEE   *924 27
LIFT THY FACE AN' LOOK AT ME MAN UP AN' LOOK AT ME   *925 9
SO VERY MUCH WORSER OFF THAN 'ER WOR BEFORE AN' NOW LOO+ *925 21
AND THE NIGHT LOOK THROUGH   *930 23
TO RAISE MY FACE I DID NOT DARE LOOK UP   *934 4
LOOK AT THE LITTLE DARLINGS IN THE CORN   *944 18
SO HIGH AND MIGHTY LOOK HOW ITS HEADS ARE BORNE   *944 20
I NEED NOT LOOK AFTER MY SOUL BEGUILE MY FEAR   *945 27

LOOKED

THE LITTLE RED HEIFER TONIGHT I LOOKED IN HER EYES   38 6
WANTON SPARROWS THAT TWITTERED WHEN MORNING LOOKED IN   71 13
THEN SUDDENLY SHE LOOKED UP   123 31
IN SILENCE WHEN SHE LOOKED FOR ALL THE WHOLE   156 3
SHE LOOKED AT HIM AS HE LAY WITH BANDED CHEEK   156 11
PLANT OF YOUR BODY TO ME YOU LOOKED ERE SPRUNG   156 20
I WONDERED I LOOKED AROUND   165 1
AND LOOKED FAR DOWN THE DARK   201 22
BUT LOOKED INTO HER EYES   202 10
YOU LOOKED INTO MY EYES AND SAID BUT THIS IS JOY   207 3
I LOOKED AT HER   222 9
THOUGH SHE LOOKED RARELY BEAUTIFUL   255 30
CREATOR I LOOKED AT MY CREATION   257 15
CREATED I LOOKED AT MYSELF THE CREATOR   267 16
HOW COULD I LOOK WHEN I WAS MAD I LOOKED SIDEWAYS FURTI+   264 35
AND THERE A CLOT HE SQUATTED AND LOOKED AT ME   345 28
AND LOOKED AT ME VAGUELY AS DRINKING CATTLE DO   349 12
AND LOOKED AROUND LIKE A GOD UNSEEING INTO THE AIR   350 28
I LOOKED ROUND I PUT DOWN MY PITCHER   351 1
AND JESUS NEVER LOOKED ROUND   483 9
IF WE LOOKED IN OUR HEARTS WE SHOULD SEE   519 7
I EXPECT THE DODO LOOKED LIKE A CLOD   523 28
A LIZARD RAN OUT ON A ROCK AND LOOKED LISTENING   524 13
BUT IT WAS NOT ENOUGH HE LOOKED AT ME ALMOST WITH HATE   603 5
LOOKED AT THE LOVELY AND SELF-ABSORBED GIRL   605 2
LOOKED BACK AT THE HANDSOME AND SELF-ABSORBED YOUNG MAN   605 6
AND LOOKED SULKY UNDER HER THICK STRAIGHT BROWS   617 20
SUDDENLY HER YELLOW-BROWN EYES LOOKED WITH A FLARE INTO   618 1
ARE DEFLOWERED BY BEING LOOKED AT BY SO MANY UNCLEAN   634 19
HOW IS IT YOU HAVE TO BE LOOKED AFTER BY SOME KNOCK-KNE+   643 23
WHO HAS LOOKED INTO THE EYES OF THE GODS   650 16
I HAVE TRAVELLED AND LOOKED AT THE WORLD AND LOVED IT   662 7
FOR A MOMENT AS HE LOOKED AT ME THROUGH HIS SPECTACLES   672 25
HE LOOKED AT ME WITHOUT ANSWER BUT SUCH A LOVELINESS   692 15
HE LOOKED AT ME AND HIS HEAVY BROWS CAME OVER   735 1
HE LOOKED AWAY DOWN THE ROAD   735 6
JESUS HAD GONE FAR UP THE DARK SLOPE WHEN HE LOOKED BACK   789 16
WONDERING HE STEPPED NEARER AND LOOKED AT HER   790 6
AND TWO MEN LOOKED UP   791 9
IF A MAN LOOKED AT ME FOR ONE MOMENT AS THE SUN DOES   840 2
LOOKED WHERE THE RED FRUIT HUNG LIKE COALS OF FIRE   864 8
AND I LOOKED IN A ROOM WHERE THE LAMP AS A MOON IN MIST   865 1
LOOKED UP AND THE WORDS MOVED LIKE A SMILE FROM HIS LIPS   865 3
AND I IN IMMEASURABLE NIGHT LOOKED ON FROM AFAR AFAR   865 10
THEN LOOKED AGAIN WITHIN HER EYES   881 3
LOOKED UP AT THE NIGHT AND HE   884 5
AND I WAS SONGLESS AS HE WAS AND LOOKED AT HIM   884 20
I LOOKED IN HER EYES THE GLOOM   885 16
AND LOOKED AT ME   886 12
AND AS I LAY AND LOOKED IN YOUR EYES   886 13
THE SMALL BIRDS THAT LIFTED THEIR HEADS WHEN MORNING LO+ *918 3
THEN SUDDENLY SHE LOOKED UP   *935 3

LOOKING

I ON THE BANK ALL SUBSTANCE MY SHADOW ALL SHADOW LOOKIN+   34 2
ME LOOKING BACK   34 3
AN ERECT SMALL GIRL LOOKING DOWN AT ME   105 15
YET THEIR DAUNTED LOOKING FLICKERS   109 5
OPEN LIKE THE SKY LOOKING DOWN IN ALL ITS LAUGHTER   119 25
LOOKING EARNESTLY UNDER THE DARK UMBRELLAS HELD FAST   180 12
LOOKING DOWN   198 20
LOOKING BLEAK AHEAD SHE RODE   202 6
A NIGHT LIES LOOKING UP   215 27

LOOKING

SHE LOVED ME AND STOOD BEFORE ME LOOKING TO ME   264 34
WITH A BODY LIKE SPRAY DAWN-TENDER AND LOOKING ABOUT   306 30
IS LOOKING RATHER SHABBY AND ISLAND-BOUND THESE DAYS   329 22
LOOKING ROUND   353 18
SUCH A CANNY LISTENER FROM A DISTANCE LOOKING UPWARDS   384 17
THERE SHE IS PERCHED ON HER MANGER LOOKING OVER THE   384 19
STRAIGHT AS A BOARD ON THE BOUGH LOOKING DOWN LIKE SOME   365 19
WHO HATED YOU AND KEPT LOOKING ROUND AT YOU AND CURSING   395 33
BUT ONE OF HIS BELOVEDS LOOKING A LITTLE PEAKED   446 26
THEY'D BE WORTH LOOKING AT   524 18
WHEN A MAN COMES LOOKING DOWN UPON ONE   526 3
AND NEVER LOOKING UP   526 20
LOOKING VERY FOOLED   532 31
LIKE LUNATICS LOOKING THEY BUBBLED AND RAVED   579 2
LOOKING DIRT ON THEM AND BREATHING ON THEM LIES   580 26
AS A COLUMBINE FLOWER HAS OR EVEN A STARLING WALKING AN+   621 16
YET LOOKING IN A GREAT FULL LIME-TREE OF SUMMER   650 21
AND LIFTED HIS FACE UP WITH BLUE EYES LOOKING AT THE EL+   672 9
LOOKING DOWN ON THE LION AS HE RETREATS   687 18
OH AS YOU STAND LOOKING UP DO YOU KNOW IT IS I   750 15
WHY DO YOU GO ABOUT LOOKING FOR ME MOTHER   756 14
THEY'RE ALL LOOKING SUPERIOR   773 20
BEHIND THE SUN LOOKING THROUGH HIM AS A WINDOW   786 6
WHEN I SEE THIS SEA LOOKING SHODDY AND DEAD   815 10
LOOKING TIMIDLY UPON ME   869 15
AND LOOKING AT HER BOSOM   880 22
AND LOOKING IN HER EYES   880 27
YET LOOKING AGAIN AT THE NIGHT   882 13
FRIGHTENED ME WITH THE STEADFASTNESS OF THEIR LOOKING   884 33
ONE OF HIS BELOVEDS LOOKING RATHER A WRECK   *948 8

LOOKIN'

HOVERIN' LOOKIN' POOR AN' PLAIN   60 18
HOW SHOULD I BE LOOKIN' ROUND   60 19
HOW SHOULD I BE LOOKIN' ROUND   *911 5

LOOKS

HOW IT LOOKS BACK LIKE A WHITE DOG TO ITS MASTER   34 1
THE LIFE THAT LOOKS THROUGH MY EYES   38 30
LEANS AND LOOKS IN AT THE LOW-BUILT SHED   42 21
TO FEEL THE LADS' LOOKS LIGHT ON ME   51 27
LIFT LOOKS OF SHOCKED AND MOMENTOUS EMOTION UP AT ME   71 22
MY LOVE LOOKS LIKE A GIRL TONIGHT   101 1
SHE LOOKS LIKE A YOUNG MAIDEN SINCE HER BROW   101 7
AN' THA LOOKS AT ME AN' THA UNDERSTAN'S   139 23
AND LOOKS AT ME AND LOOKS IN THE PALM OF HER HAND   143 15
THE WANING MOON LOOKS UPWARD THIS GREY NIGHT   172 18
AND THE SUN LOOKS THROUGH   178 15
FROM OUT THE CLOUD OF SLEEP LOOKS ROUND ABOUT   195 13
AND LOOKS DOWN ON THE GROUND TO SEE   215 24
ANOTHER LIFE FROM MINE FOR SO IT LOOKS   218 25
HIS HEAD AS PROUD AS A DEER THAT LOOKS   220 2
SIFT MY LOOKS AND ESPRESSIONS   236 28
AS ONE STANDS ON A BANK AND LOOKS IN   338 31
TO OPEN YOUR TINY BEAK-MOUTH THAT LOOKS AS IF IT WOULD   352 9
HE WEARILY LOOKS THE OTHER WAY   357 5
AND SHE EVEN MORE WEARILY LOOKS ANOTHER WAY STILL   357 6
ALAS WHAT A FOOL HE LOOKS IN THIS SCUFFLE   360 26
LOOKS STRAIGHT AT THE SUN   373 25
AND LOOKS UP INQUIRINGLY INTO THE PILLAR OF CLOUD   375 12
AND IF YOU LOOK AT HER SHE LOOKS BACK WITH A COLD SARDO+   386 4
WRINKLED UNDERHUNG PHYSIOG THAT LOOKS AS IF IT HAD DONE   398 6
AND SEES STRANGE LOOKS ON THE FACES OF MEN   459 27
TRAGEDY LOOKS TO ME LIKE MAN   508 13
AS A MATTER OF FACT WHEN THE TINKER LOOKS SO HAPPY   520 23
WHAT A PITY WHEN A MAN LOOKS AT HIMSELF IN A GLASS   528 22
THEY CALL IT HEALTH IT LOOKS LIKE NULLITY   625 24
ONLY HERE AND THERE A PAIR OF EYES HAUNTED LOOKS OUT AS+   625 25
IF MAN ONLY LOOKS TO MAN AND NO-ONE SEES BEYOND   650 6
WHEN HE LOOKS BEYOND HUMANITY   650 18
THE WOMAN WHO LOOKS FOR ME IN THE WORLD   672 23
AND THE HORSE LOOKS AT HIM IN SILENCE   683 20
IT IS CREATION GOD LOOKS HIMSELF ON IT IN WONDER FOR TH+   690 11
AND KISS OF THE FAR-OFF LINGERING LADY WHO LOOKS OVER T+   695 31
AND LOOKS AROUND AGAIN AT HIS HEEL THE BRIGHT SPUR   734 14
AND BENDS AGAIN AND LOOKS AT THE BELLY OF THE HORSE   734 15
WHERE LIFE LOOKS ME IN THE EYES   768 19
WHOM THE LEOPARD LOOKS IN THE EYES   769 26
LOOKS UP AND KNOWS AND IS KNOWN   771 2
AND HE SAID SURELY THIS LOOKS VERY CURIOUS   790 9
IF GOD LOOKS LET HIM SEE   818 14
WHEN HE LOOKS AT HIMSELF IN THE GLASS   836 12
SAYING YOU KNOW I ALWAYS HAVE TO SAY THAT ARCHIE LOOKS +   842 20
I CAN NEVER EVEN THINK THAT IT'S BABY WHO LOOKS LIKE AR+   842 21
FLIMSY HUSK-BALL THROUGH WHOSE RIFTS THERE LOOKS   874 31
HER LOOKS HER BEARING TO ME   885 21
HER LOOKS WITH DESIRE   885 23
AND LIFTS HIS FACE AND LOOKS AT ME   *898 26
TO FEEL THE LADS' LOOKS LIGHT ON ME   *899 11
AND LIFTS HIS FACE AND LOOKS AT ME   *902 10
TO FEEL THE LADS' LOOKS LIGHT ON ME   *902 23
HIS HEAD AS PROUD AS A DEER THAT LOOKS   *944 10
AND LOOKS IT AND I PUT IT TO YOU   *950 18
WHAT A PITY WHEN A MAN LOOKS AT HIMSELF IN THE GLASS   *950 25

LOOM

AH MY DARLING WHEN OVER THE PURPLE HORIZON SHALL LOOM   91 25
MORE ELEPHANTS TONG TONG-TONG LOOM UP   388 26
AH MY DARLING WHEN OVER THE PURPLE HORIZON SHALL LOOM   *926 18

LOOMED

THE ELEPHANTS HUGE AND GREY LOOMED THEIR CURVED BULK   445 10
HER LARGE BROWN HAND LOOMED OVER   *934 26

LOOMING
  LOOMING GALLOP OF THE BEASTS   390 36
  WATCH SILENT THE LOOMING OF THE HOARY FAR-GONE AGES 426 21

LOOMS
  OR ELSE THEY ARE IMMORALLY NASTY AND THE WORD LOOMS 837 1

LOOP
  YET MISSING THE PURE LOOP 341 10
  LOOP BACK THE CURTAINS 343 3

LOOP-HOLES
  THE LOOP-HOLES OF THAT INNERMOST NIGHT OF HIM 876 35

LOOPING
  DARK AIR-LIFE LOOPING 341 9

LOOSE
  AND SWINGS ALL LOOSE FROM THE SWING OF HIS WALK 43 13
  YOU WITH LOOSE HANDS OF ABANDONMENT HANGING DOWN 58 23
  AND MY ARMS FELL LOOSE AND I WAS DUMB 62 20
  LOOSE 88 5
  OF MY BODY AND LOOSE THE ESSENTIAL FLOOD 117 23
  THEN LETS HER BLACK HAIR LOOSE THE DARKNESS FALL 128 33
  STILL SHE SAYS NAY LOOSE NO FLAME 150 26
  OF FIRE AND BEAUTY LOOSE NO MORE 151 11
  LIKE A LOOSE SHEAF OF WHEAT 198 10
  WHITE AND LOOSE AT LAST WITH ALL THE PAIN 225 7
  STEPPING WEE MITE IN HIS LOOSE TROUSERS 355 21
  TO TRAVEL TO BURROW INTO A LITTLE LOOSE EARTH AFRAID OF+ 358 2
  PERHAPS IT IS A SORT OF UNCANNY DECORATION A VEIL OF LO+ 369 25
  HER LITTLE LOOSE HANDS AND DROOPING VICTORIAN SHOULDERS 393 14
  AND PLUCKING OUT OF HIS PLUMAGE A FEW LOOSE FEATHERS TO 413 14
  HANDING OUT A FEW LOOSE GOLDEN BREAST-FEATHERS AT MOULT+ 414 9
  IS THE BEST THAT WE ARE BUT SPERM LOOSE SPERM LIKE THE 429 3
  WE LOOSE OUR GRIP AND WE UNSTRAIN OUR EYES 736 23
  OF LOVE AND BEAUTY LOOSE NO MORE 873 21
  YOU ALWAYS LOOSE ME ADRIFT 875 6
  WILL YOU LOOSE THE HEAVY WEARY BUD *931 26

LOOSE-ALL
  OH MASTER LET IT BE LOOSE-ALL IT IS ENOUGH 757 12

LOOSED
  LOOSED ONE MOMENT THE DARKNESS FRIGHTENS ME 225 28

LOOSEN
  AND LOOSEN THE BRICK AND THE HARD CEMENT 462 11
  TILL THE WALLS BEGIN TO LOOSEN AND CRACK 462 13
  LOOSEN THIS ROPE 751 16

LOOSENED
  TO CREEP THROUGH YOUR LOOSENED HAIR TILL HE REACHES 178 32

LOOSENING
  A LITTLE WILD BUBBLE IS LOOSENING HOLD 868 28

LOOSES
  HARDLY LOOSES EVEN A LAST BREATH OF PERFUME 646 22

LOOSING
  LOOSING HOLD IN THE WIND'S INSISTENT PUSH 160 8
  A LITTLE WILD BUBBLE IS LOOSING HOLD *941 28

LOOT
  OUT OF THE NOBLE LOOT 488 12
  SWAYING I SNATCH AND LOOT 861 7

LOP
  SO THAT I COULD LOP IT OFF 526 22

LOP-EARED
  FIRST LIVE THING I'VE OWNED SINCE THE LOP-EARED RABBITS 395 7

LOP-SIDED
  MAN IS LOP-SIDED ON THE SIDE OF THE ANGELS 505 16

LORD
  LIKE A PORTENT BUT LORD I AM GLAD SO GLAD I DROWN 88 26
  WHAT A TOOL IN THE HANDS OF THE LORD 254 26
  I WISH I COULD GRIP YOU LIKE THE FIST OF THE LORD 255 14
  'TIS LIKE THE UNUTTERABLE NAME OF THE DREAD LORD 264 16
  WHAT THEN GOOD LORD CRY THE WOMEN 284 20
  SEE IF I AM NOT LORD OF THE DARK AND MOVING HOSTS 289 22
  AND EVEN MY HEART LORD FOREVER AFTER ALL UPLIFTING 321 17
  I MUST BE PUT DOWN LORD IN THE AFTERNOON 321 26
  THE LORD WROTE IT ALL DOWN ON THE LITTLE SLATE 356 9
  WHAT VOICE OF THE LORD IS THAT FROM THE TREE OF SMOKE 375 15
  I NEVER DREAMED TILL NOW OF THE AWFUL TIME THE LORD MUST 395 17
  THE RISEN LORD THE RISEN LORD 459 21
  THE RISEN LORD THE RISEN LORD 459 25
  MY LORD A MAN'S FRIENDS' IDEAS OF HIM 489 25
  VENGEANCE IS MINE SAITH THE LORD 541 8
  DEAR LORD OF DELIGHT 558 4
  DEAR LORD OF RIGHT 558 10
  VENGEANCE IS MINE SAITH THE LORD I WILL REPAY 616 1
  IT IS THE VENGEANCE OF THE LORD LONG AND UNREMITTING 616 13
  AND SO THE LORD OF VENGEANCE PAYS BACK REPAYS LIFE 616 16
  NOW RISEN MAN AND RISEN LORD 636 22
  PUT MY FEET UPON THE CRESCENT LIKE A LORD 684 9
  FOR THE LORD TO COME FORTH AT LARGE ON THE SCENT OF BLO+ 742 19
  LORD WHAT WE HAVE DONE WE HEREBY EXPIATE 743 6
  WE GIVE UP O LORD OUR BODIES TO DEADLY HATE 743 11
  OUR BODIES TO THE EXPIATION LORD 743 16
  CLOSE FRIEND IN EVERYTHING IS OUR LORD MY BOY 749 23
  LORD CHERISH AND COMFORT 751 9
  AND LORD BUT HARK AT THE PIGEONS WHAT ARE THEY CHATTERI+ 751 12
  LORD GOD ABOVE WOULD IT COST ME DEAR 759 10

LORD
  YEA I AM ALWAYS HERE I AM LORD 787 27
  YEA LORD EVEN TRAINS AND CAMIONS AND AUTOMOBILES 794 11
  HE IS YOUR LORD 799 7
  BEYOND ME IS A LORD WHO IS TERRIBLE AND WONDERFUL AND D+ 801 12
  LO I AM LORD OF THE WATCHES OF THE NIGHT 806 29
  LORD TAKE HIS LOVE AWAY IT MAKES HIM WHINE *945 18
  LORD DEAR LORD DO YOU THINK HE EVER CAN SHINE *945 20

LORD ALMIGHTY
  BECAUSE THE LORD ALMIGHTY ROSE A BIT TOO HIGH 710 10

LORD GOD
  EVEN IF THE LORD GOD SHOUTED 818 28
  THAT THE LORD GOD RESTED THE WORLDS ON 819 10
  THE LORD GOD SAID SO 819 32

LORDLY
  EVERY LORDLY TUPPENNY FOREIGNER FROM THE HOTELS FATTENI+ 312 23
  CLIMB DOWN O LORDLY MIND 473 8

LORD OF HOSTS
  THE LORD OF HOSTS AND THE DEVIL 243 13

LORD OF THE MORNING STAR
  THE LORD OF THE MORNING STAR 787 15

LORD OF THE TWO WAYS
  LORD OF THE TWO WAYS THESE ARE THE FOREIGNERS 793 13
  I AM LORD OF THE TWO WAYS 800 39

LORD RIBBLESDALE
  NOR YET THE GAY LORD RIBBLESDALE 835 24

LORDS
  AND SO I MISSED MY CHANCE WITH ONE OF THE LORDS 351 27
  KISSES OF FOUR GREAT LORDS BEAUTIFUL AS THEY HELD ME TO+ 695 29
  IN EVERY WAY AND THE LORDS AMONG MEN 787 28
  THEY ARE LORDS OF THE DESOLATE WASTES OF SADNESS THEIR + *891 4

LORDS OF LIFE
  THAT WASHES THE LORDS OF LIFE 788 25
  THE LORDS OF LIFE ARE THE MASTERS OF DEATH 808 17
  THE LORDS OF LIFE ARE THE MASTERS OF DEATH 808 21
  LIVING ARE THE LORDS OF LIFE 808 23
  THE LORDS OF LIFE ARE THE MASTERS OF DEATH 809 3

LORDS OF THE WAY
  I MAKE YOU THE LORDS OF THE WAY 788 7

LORD'S
  THAT LAUGH AT THE LORD'S INDIGNATION 284 19
  TILL THEY CHANCED TO MEET IN THE LORD'S GREEN ZOO 761 3

LORE
  IN THE DEEP DUNG OF CASH AND LORE 469 7

LORNA DOONE
  IN A WISTFUL DREAM OF LORNA DOONE 52 15
  IN A WISHFUL DREAM OF LORNA DOONE *905 4

LOSE
  THAT YOU LOSE THE BRICK-STUFF OUT OF YOU 53 28
  AND LOSE THEM BOTH 110 12
  BUT ONLY LOSE YOURSELF FURTHER DECOMPOSING 290 11
  THE GEESE THAT SAVED ROME AND WILL LOSE LONDON 438 25
  BUT TO LOSE IT ALL FOR EVER 453 8
  GO DOWN TO YOUR DEEP OLD HEART WOMAN AND LOSE SIGHT OF 477 24
  AND LOSE SIGHT OF ME THE ME WHOM YOU TURBULENTLY LOVED 477 26
  LET US LOSE SIGHT OF OURSELVES AND BREAK THE MIRRORS 477 27
  AND GRACE IF I DON'T LOSE IT FROM THE SAME PLACE 499 5
  IF WE LOSE OUR SANITY 514 14
  WE LOSE THAT WHICH KEEPS US INDIVIDUAL 514 15
  BUT IF WE LOSE OUR SANITY 514 19
  AS IF THEY'D GOT SOMETHING TO LOSE 555 12
  YOU HAVEN'T GOT MUCH TO LOSE 560 22
  THE ONE THING EASIEST TO LOSE IS SAVINGS 614 5
  A SOUL TO LOSE 638 17
  THE AUTOMAT HAS NO SOUL TO LOSE 638 18
  YOU WERE ONLY SEEKING TO LOSE SOMETHING 661 3
  THEY SEE ME AND LOSE ME AGAIN 787 30
  PEEPING THEY WILL LOSE THEIR SIGHT AND LINGERING THEY W+ 799 12
  ASIDE TO LOSE MYSELF FOR VERY SMALLNESS I 876 7
  OF SEED TO LOSE MYSELF IN THE BODY OF THIS BLUE 876 19
  MYSELF AND GATHER THE WATERS BENEATH ME AND LOSE *894 22
  I MIGHT LOSE MY-SEN 922 30
  AND THE GEESE THAT SAVED ROME WILL LOSE LONDON *947 26

LOSES
  WHEN A MAN IS RICH HE LOSES AT LAST THE HUNGER FEAR 265 2

LOSING
  FROM EACH OTHER OR LOSING THE DOLOROUS 116 19
  WHO IS LOSING HER LAMB 414 26
  DRINK A LITTLE BLOOD AND LOSING ANOTHER ROYALTY UNTO 414 27
  WITHOUT LOSING ITS HEAD 505 22
  I AM LOSING HOPE 751 19
  THEY AREN'T AFRAID OF LOSING SOMETHING AS THE OLDER ONE+ 828 25
  AND LOSING MINGLE IN THE PROCREANT WOMB 876 20

LOSS
  THE LOSS OF MYSELF TILL DEATH COMES WHO CANNOT FAIL 48 8
  BUT I SCARCELY FEEL YOUR LOSS 108 12
  YOU REALISE THE FATUITY OF SAVING UP AGAINST POSSIBLE L+ 614 4
  NOT MERELY LOSS 768 5

LOST
SKY CEASED TO QUIVER AND LOST ITS ACTIVE SHEEN 55 15
FOR I'VE LOST MY PEACE 46 28
NOW I AM CAUGHT YOU ARE HOPELESSLY LOST O SELF 47 32
DISTORTED EVEN LOST 49 7
PALE LOVE LOST IN A THAW OF FEAR 62 15
IS LOST IN THIS SHADOWED SILENCE THE SKIES DISTIL 76 19
YOU YOUR SOUL LIKE A LADY-SMOCK LOST EVANESCENT 90 17
SINCE I LOST YOU I AM SILENCE-HAUNTED 109 13
LOST AND YET STILL CONNECTED AND BETWEEN THE TWO 115 2
AND FALLING WAVES IN HIS ARMS AND THE LOST SOUL'S KISS 130 20
OF FIERY COLDNESS TO BE GONE IN A LOST SOUL'S BLISS 130 23
SINCE I LOST YOU MY DARLING THE SKY HAS COME NEAR 134 14
TO BE LOST IN THE HAZE OF THE SKY I WOULD LIKE TO COME 134 22
AND BE LOST OUT OF SIGHT WITH YOU LIKE A MELTING FOAM 134 23
WHERE YOU ARE LOST WHAT REST MY LOVE WHAT REST 134 27
LOST ALL ITS MEANING 152 21
DARK IN INDOMITABLE FAILURE SHE WHO HAD LOST 156 5
LIKE A LOST TUNE 158 24
IS LOST SINCE WE FALL APART 163 6
SO YOU ARE LOST TO ME 171 17
FOR YOU ARE LOST TO ME 172 4
UNNOTICED AMONG THEM A STILL QUEEN LOST IN THE MAZE 176 24
IN FRONT OF THE SOMBRE MOUNTAINS A FAINT LOST RIBBON OF 208 23
AND THE RESTLESS RIVER WE ARE LOST AND GONE WITH ALL 211 22
I BEAT MY WAY TO BE LOST IMMEDIATELY 223 9
I LOST AT LAST THE FIERCENESS THAT FEARS IT WILL STARVE 265 3
OF THE LOST FERN-SCENTED WORLD 287 7
YOUR PRISTINE ISOLATE INTEGRITY LOST AEONS AGO 290 13
NOW EVEN THE SHADOW OF THE LOST SECRET IS VANISHING FRO+ 295 3
FOR WHICH THE LANGUAGE IS LOST 296 4
SUCH AN AROMA OF LOST HUMAN LIFE 298 7
BUT I INVOKE THE SPIRITS OF THE LOST 298 9
THOSE THAT HAVE NOT SURVIVED THE DARKLY LOST 298 10
LOST THEIR FLICKER 346 24
IS LOST 367 2
WHO HAS BEEN LOST SO MANY CENTURIES ON THE MARGINS OF 394 8
FOR A NEW SIGNAL FROM LIFE IN THAT SILENT LOST LAND OF + 394 12
FIRST TIME I LOST YOU IN TAOS PLAZA 395 27
THEN YOU'RE A LOST WHITE DOG OF A PALE-FACE 404 29
AND LOST HIM HERE 405 28
LINGER FOR NOW THEY REALISE ALL THAT IS LOST THEN THE L+ 406 6
SHALL WE BE LOST ALL OF US 428 26
EARNING YOUR LIVING WHILE YOUR LIFE IS LOST 459 7
WHAT WAS LOST IS FOUND 461 21
SO NOW I HAVE LOST TOO MUCH AND AM SICK 500 7
AND THE SEA IS LOST 509 14
OUR ACTIVITY HAS LOST ITS MEANING 510 22
THE HOWL OF THE UTTERLY LOST 514 23
LOST BETWEEN GREAT WAVES OF ULTIMATE IDEAS 542 30
SOMETHING IS LEFT BEHIND LOST AND HOWLING AND WE KNOW IT 543 25
YOU LEAVE A LOT YOU'VE LOST A LOT 549 3
AWARE AT LAST THAT OUR MANHOOD IS UTTERLY LOST 585 7
SO DARK SO DARK THE MIND IS LOST IN IT 586 14
AND WHICH WE HAVE LOST 609 27
PEOPLE WHO COMPLAIN OF LONELINESS MUST HAVE LOST SOMETH+ 610 8
LOST SOME LIVING CONNECTION WITH THE COSMOS OUT OF THEM+ 610 9
LOST THEIR LIFE-FLOW 610 10
THEN IF WE REALISE THAT WE NEVER WERE LOST WE REALISE W+ 613 15
FOR YOU CAN'T SAVE THAT WHICH WAS NEVER LOST 614 1
AND ONCE YOU REALISE THAT YOU NEVER WERE LOST 614 3
THAT HE LOST ANY OF HIS BRIGHTNESS IN FALLING 614 14
SO THAT ALL MAY BE LOST TOGETHER EN MASSE THE GREAT 620 25
MANKIND IS LOST AND LOST FOREVER 637 13
THEN ALL IS LOST THE ROBOT SUPERVENES 650 7
THERE IS NOTHING TO SAVE NOW ALL IS LOST 658 13
AND CROUCHING AND SPEAKING THE MUSIC OF LOST LANGUAGES 688 16
WHO WILL GIVE ME BACK MY LOST LIMBS 696 4
AND MY LOST WHITE FEARLESS BREAST 696 5
FAREWELL FAREWELL LOST SOUL 696 26
THE LOST BRIDE AND HER GROOM 697 22
HE LOST ANY OF HIS BRIGHTNESS IN THE FALLING 697 25
SO THAT LOST SOULS MAY EAT GRAPES 710 17
HELL IS THE HOME OF SOULS LOST IN DARKNESS 711 15
EVEN AS HEAVEN IS THE HOME OF SOULS LOST IN LIGHT 711 16
MEN MUST DEPART FROM IT OR ALL IS LOST 716 15
ARE CROWDED WITH LOST SOULS THE UNEASY DEAD 722 22
OBLIVION WHERE THE SOUL AT LAST IS LOST 724 9
HELMETS AS HIS HE LOST IN THE WOOD THAT NIGHT 732 12
IT SNOWED AND HIS HELMET WAS LOST HE FORGOT ME HE DID N+ 732 17
THE LOST HESPERIDES WHERE LOVE IS PURE 737 9
LET US TURN BACK LEST WE SHOULD ALL BE LOST 737 12
AND WAIT TILL THEY ARE LOST UPON OUR SIGHT 740 21
AM I LOST 749 8
ME NOW IF I'VE LOST MY MESS-MATES LOST THEM FOREVER 757 7
ALL MEN BE LOST IN SILENCE 811 11
WHAT HAVE WE LOST 816 11
WHAT HAVE WE LOST IN THE WEST 816 12
IN THE LAND OF THE LOST 816 15
NOTHING BUT TO MAKE LOST MUSIC 816 16
ROUND THE LOST MAN'S CAMP-FIRE 816 18
THE ANGELS HAVE SOMEWHERE FOUGHT AND LOST 823 1
FOUGHT AND LOST 823 2
THE ANGELS HAVE EVERYWHERE FOUGHT AND LOST 823 6
FOUGHT AND LOST 823 7
IS LOST ENTIRELY YOU CANNOT FOOL US 824 5
AND WE HAVE LOST OUR NATURAL SPONTANEITY 833 11
IN A DAY THEY ARE LOST IN THE NOTHINGNESS PURITY BRINGS 855 4
FAINT-FASHIONED WONDER WHEREIN LOST WE SPIN 875 4
WHERE THIS FRAIL SHADOWY HUSK OF A DAY IS LOST 875 15
AND ALL MY DOVES ARE LAUNCHED ABROAD AND LOST 875 24
AND ALL THE WONDER LOST FROM OUT HIS EYES 877 11
IN A MEADOW LOST I LAY 881 22
SO GLAD TO HAVE BEEN LOST 882 11
WHAT IF THE GORSE FLOWERS SHRIVELLED AND KISSING WERE L+ *891 23
INTO ROLLICKING SUNS AND THEIR LOST GOLD ROTS COMPRESSED *896 20
IS LOST IN THE SHADOWED SILENCE THE SKIES DISTIL *898 13
IS LOST IN THE SHADOWED SILENCE THE SKIES DISTIL *901 22

LOST
PALE LOVE LOST IN A SNOW OF FEAR *912 21
INTO THE NIGHT AND ARE LOST TO SADDEN WITH JETSAM THE D+ *918 8
THE LONG MARGINAL STRETCHES OF EXISTENCE CROWDED WITH L+ *957 23
ONCE OUTSIDE UPON THE GREY MARSH BEACHES WHERE LOST SOU+ *957 28

LOT
LAD NEVER STEPPED TILL 'E GOT IN WITH YOUR LOT 60 31
I'LL CHUCK THE FLAMIN' LOT O' YOU 81 11
THA'RT FOR DOIN' A LOT WI' T' LAD 82 8
PRIDE STRENGTH ALL THE LOT 239 3
OH SO RED AND SUCH A LOT OF THEM 278 8
ALL THE LOT OF THEM AND LET THEM FIGHT IT OUT 316 6
AND THESE ALONG WITH IT ALL THE INFERIOR LOT 316 31
LOT 444 10
DEATH NO NOT DEATH FOR YOUR LOT 461 8
HE SURE THINKS A LOT OF LIES 489 20
THEY'RE A' A B-D LOT O' -S 491 1
AFTER A LOT O' WOMEN 493 14
FOR AFTER ALL HE HELPED TO SMASH A LOT OF OLD ROMAN LIES 497 3
NOT TO SHED A LOT OF BLOOD OVER IT 497 21
FOR WE'RE SURE TO BRING IN A LOT OF LIES 506 4
PIERRES ALL THE TOLSTOYAN LOT 533 12
THE DOSTOEVSKY LOT 533 15
WILL THE PROUSTIAN LOT GO NEXT 533 21
ANYHOW THE TOLSTOYAN LOT SIMPLY ASKED FOR EXTINCTION 533 24
AND THE DOSTOEVSKY LOT WALLOWED IN THE THOUGHT 533 26
AND THE TCHEKOV LOT I'M TOO WEAK AND LOVABLE TO LIVE 534 1
NOW THE PROUSTIAN LOT DEAR DARLING DEATH LET ME WRIGGLE 534 3
FINALLY OUR LITTLE LOT I DON'T WANT TO DIE BUT BY JINGO+ 534 6
TO A LOT OF INFERIOR SWIPE 547 23
YOU LEAVE A LOT BEHIND YOU 549 2
YOU LEAVE A LOT YOU'VE LOST A LOT 549 3
NOT ONE OF THE WHOLE JOB LOT 549 28
A WORSE LOT O' JUJUBEY ASSES 553 15
THAN THE LOT I LEFT BEHIND 553 16
AND SLY WITH A LOT OF AFTER-THOUGHT 556 11
AND LOOK AT THE FAT-EYED LOT 556 22
THAT MAY YET GIVE A LOT 565 12
A LOT OF MONEY REARING THEM 569 12
SO WE'VE GOT A LOT OF NURSES OF NURSES OF NURSES 570 18
AUNT LIBBY'S REALLY A FEEBLE LOT 571 29
AND THEY STARED AND THEY STARED THE HALF-WITTED LOT 578 12
I HAVE NOTICED THAT PEOPLE WHO TALK A LOT ABOUT LOYALTY 626 1
AND QUITE A LOT OF PEOPLE ARE NOT 665 17
IT IS LIKE A VAST GREAT TREE WITH A VAST GREAT LOT OF S+ 677 21
TRAITORS OH LIARS YOU JUDAS LOT 762 14
YOU LIARS YOU DIRTY LOT 762 17
AT THE SAME TIME WE LEARN A LOT 832 26
WE HAVE LEARNED A LOT SINCE JESUS FROM JESUS AND ALL TH+ 832 27
ALL THE LOT OF THEM VICE MISSIONS ETC INSANELY UNHEALTHY 845 10
A LOT O' VIOLETS FELL OUT OF 'ER BOSOM ON 'IM DOWN THEER *910 16
OR I'LL CHUCK THE FLAMIN' LOT OF YOU *923 11
THA'RT FOR DOIN' A LOT WI' TH' LAD *924 12
IN FACT QUITE A LOT OF CHASTITY IS NECESSARY IN LIFE TO+ *952 24

LOTH
YET I AM NOT LOTH 110 10
ROSES ARE READY TO FALL RELUCTANT AND LOTH 217 30

LOTS
I DON'T KNOW HE HAS LOTS OF LEISURE AND HE MAKES 452 22

LOT'S
AH LOT'S WIFE LOT'S WIFE 207 27
LOT'S WIFE NOT WIFE BUT MOTHER 207 33

LOTUS
HOW MANY TIMES LIKE LOTUS LILIES RISEN 113 1
AND ALL THE LOTUS BUDS OF LOVE SINK OVER 113 14

LOTUS-LILIES
TILL ALL IS WELL TILL ALL IS UTTERLY WELL THE LOTUS-LIL+ 652 13

LOUD
WITH A LOUD HOARSE SIGH 109 20
THE LARK SINGS LOUD AND GLAD 110 9
THERE HE SITS THE LONG LOUD ONE 347 21
YOU SHALL KNOW A BIRD BY HIS CRY AND GREAT BIRDS CRY LO+ 368 9
THE LOUD LOVE OF PEACE MAKES ONE QUIVER MORE THAN ANY 495 16
LOUD PEACE PROPAGANDA MAKES WAR SEEM IMMINENT 495 20
TRAGEDY SEEMS TO ME A LOUD NOISE 508 11
IT IS THEIR THREAT THEIR LOUD JEERING THREAT 741 11
IT IS THE LOUD CRIES OF THESE BIRDS OF PAIN 741 14

LOUDER
AND IN PRIVATE BOASTS HIS EXPLOITS EVEN LOUDER IF YOU A+ 432 30
LOUDER THAN IS SEEMLY 508 12

LOUDLY
CRY LOUDLY BEYOND THE LAKE OF WATERS 365 35
HE WHISTLED TO IT LOUDLY TWICE TILL IT FELL TO HIS HAND 791 2

LOUD-SEEMING
AND JANUARY'S LOUD-SEEMING SUN 306 13

LOUNGE
THE MEN THAT LOUNGE IN A GROUP ON THE WHARF 228 16

LOUSY
WHAT LOUSY ARCHANGELS AND ANGELS YOU HAVE TO SURROUND 643 27

LOUT
STRETCHED OUT ON THE WAY AND A LOUT CASTS 144 18
LIKE A LOUT ON AN OBSCURE PAVEMENT 338 4
COWARDICE EVERY OLD LOUT 458 21
THINK YOU A LOWER-CLASS LOUT 550 12

LOUTISH
    SANS ANY DISTINCTION AT ALL EXCEPT LOUTISH COMMONNESS   313   3
    UPON THE BREASTS OF LOUTISH BOLSHEVISTS   317   2
    DAMNED LOUTISH BOLSHEVISTS   317   3

LOUTISHLY
    YET THERE THEY ARE YOUTHS LOUTISHLY   312 18

LOUTS
    BUT THESE THEMSELVES MUST BURN THESE LOUTS   315 13
    WHAT ROT TO SAY THE LOUTS ALONG THE CORSO   316 20

LOVABLE
    WHY DON'T PEOPLE LEAVE OFF BEING LOVABLE   505   9
    OR THINKING THEY ARE LOVABLE OR WANTING TO BE LOVABLE   505 10
    AND NONE OF THESE IS LOVABLE   505 14
    I AM SICK OF LOVABLE PEOPLE   505 23
    AND THE TCHEKOV LOT I'M TOO WEAK AND LOVABLE TO LIVE   534   1

LOVABLENESS
    AND UTTER LOVABLENESS YOU UGLY-MUG   398   4

LOVE
    'TIS THE WOUND OF LOVE GOES HOME   42   8
    LOVE HAS CREPT OUT OF HER SEALED HEART   46   5
    LOVE MAKES THE BURDEN OF HER VOICE   46 17
    FROM ME FROM THE HAND OF MY LOVE WHICH CREEPS UP   47 18
    ME SO DISTINCTLY FROM SLEEPING THE SLEEP I'D LOVE BEST   48 26
    SEE THE STARS LOVE   48 27
    STAR-SHADOWS SHINE LOVE   49   1
    ONLY MINE LOVE MINE   49   4
    THE HEAVENS ARE NOT SHAKEN YOU SAY LOVE   49 11
    WHAT OF ME THEN LOVE ME   49 16
    WHAT THEN LOVE IF SOON   49 17
    WOULD YOU SWOON LOVE SWOON   49 20
    IS FULL OF DREAMS MY LOVE THE BOYS ARE ALL STILL   52 14
    OF OUR EARLY LOVE THAT HARDLY HAS OPENED YET   58 11
    YOU MY LOVE THE FOREMOST IN A FLOWERED GOWN   58 20
    MY LOVE THAT SPINNING COIN LAID STILL   59 21
    PALE LOVE LOST IN A THAW OF FEAR   62 15
    AH HOME SUDDENLY I LOVE YOU   63   8
    THAT SHE SHOULD LOVE ME SO   63 13
    LOVE IS THE GREAT ASKER   63 17
    FOREVER EVER BY MY SHOULDER PITIFUL LOVE WILL LINGER   63 22
    POINTING MY EYES IN WRETCHED DEFIANCE WHERE LOVE HIDES +   63 25
    NO TEARS OF LOVE UNNERVING   64   1
    INEXORABLE LOVE GOES LAGGING   64   6
    PITEOUS LOVE COMES PEERING UNDER THE HOOD   64 15
    LOVE WILL YET AGAIN RETURN TO HER AND MAKE ALL GOOD   65 22
    SHE SHINES THE FIRST WHITE LOVE OF MY YOUTH PASSIONLESS+   67 21
    TALK ABOUT LOVE O' WOMEN   84 27
    YOU LOVE ME WHILE I HOVER TENDERLY   87 19
    TO THE OTHER LOVE TO RELINQUISH HIS DESIRE   89 33
    ME FULL LENGTH IN THE COWSLIPS MUTTERING YOU LOVE   90 16
    I CAME TO THE BOYS WITH LOVE DEAR AND ONLY THEY TURNED +   92 21
    AND LOVE WOULD ONLY WEAKEN THEIR UNDER-EARTH GRIP MAKE +   92 27
    I THOUGHT THAT LOVE WOULD DO ALL THINGS BUT NOW I KNOW +   93   1
    THERE ARE DEPTHS BELOW DEPTHS MY DARLING WHERE LOVE DOE+   93   2
    YOUNG YEARS AND THE OLD MUST NOT WIN NOT EVEN IF THEY L+   93   5
    NOT TO TRESPASS ON THEM WITH LOVE THEY MUST LEARN NOT T+   93 12
    YET WAIT AWHILE FOR HENCEFORTH I WILL LOVE WHEN A BLOSS+   94   5
    MY LOVE WHERE IT IS WANTED YET WAIT AWHILE MY FALL   94   7
    CRINGING PITY AND LOVE WHITE-HANDED CAME   94 16
    THEN I LONGED FOR YOU WITH YOUR MANTLE OF LOVE TO FOLD   98 23
    THAT MY LOVE CAN DAWN IN WARMTH AGAIN UNAFRAID   99 15
    SOME OF YOUR SELVES MY LOVE THAT SOME   100 20
    AND OH MY LOVE AS I ROCK FOR YOU TONIGHT   100 24
    MY LOVE LOOKS LIKE A GIRL TONIGHT   101   1
    MY LITTLE LOVE MY DARLING   101 17
    MY LITTLE LOVE MY DEAREST   101 23
    AND SO MY LOVE MY MOTHER   102   1
    LOVE WHO HAD BORNE AND NOW WAS LEAVING ME   103 20
    OF YOUR LOVE WE BOTH HAVE ENTERED THEN THE RIGHT   104 14
    TOO FAR AWAY O LOVE I KNOW   104 21
    OF LIFE WITH LOVE AND LOVE WITH LIFE   105   5
    TOO FAR AWAY YOU ARE MY LOVE   105   9
    AND DOWN BELOW ON THE PAVEMENT LOVE   106   9
    MY LOVE   109   9
    YOUR LOVE WAS INTENSE AND THOROUGH   111 10
    MINE WAS THE LOVE OF A GROWING FLOWER   111 11
    LOVE YOU ALTHOUGH I WOULD   111 19
    THIS WOMAN WHO LIKES TO LOVE ME BUT SHE TURNS   113 10
    AND ALL THE LOTUS BUDS OF LOVE SINK OVER   113 14
    ENDS LIKE A BROKEN LOVE THAT TURNS TO THE DARK OF SLEEP   114 28
    IN WHICH I HALF LOVE YOU   116 31
    CLOSE YOUR EYES MY LOVE LET ME MAKE YOU BLIND   118 20
    IN THE DYING LAMP OF MY LOVE   121 27
    AND EMPTIED MY HEART OF LOVE   124   2
    OF LOVE TAKES POSSESSION AND SETTLES HER DOWN   125   4
    THE NEST IN A HEART OF LOVE   125   6
    HUNGRY FOR LOVE YET IF I LAY MY HAND IN HER BREAST   128   2
    ENJOYING THEIR GLANCING FLIGHT THOUGH LOVE IS DEAD   133 23
    OF LOVE AND HEREAFTER   133 31
    WHERE YOU ARE LOST WHAT REST MY LOVE WHAT REST   134 27
    YES MY LOVE I HEAR   136 26
    I LOVE FOR EVER THERE IT SEEMS   151   5
    AND LET ME LOVE YOU A LONG TIME ERE YOU GO   153 17
    THE WILL TO LOVE ME BUT EVEN SO   153 19
    YOUR LOVE FOR ME   153 23
    I PLACE A GREAT AND BURNING SEAL OF LOVE   154   9
    THE OMINOUS ENTRY NOR SAW THE OTHER LOVE   155 27
    MY LOVE TILL YOU WENT SOUTH   156 24
    HOW DID YOU LOVE HIM YOU WHO ONLY ROUSED   158   1
    PAIN OR LOVE OR GRIEF   169 19
    SMALL-BOSOMED GIRLS OF THE SPRING OF LOVE   179 17
    MUST BE IN LOVE WITH ME   196   6
    MUST BE IN LOVE WITH ME   196 24
    NAKED OF WORSHIP OF LOVE OR OF ADORNMENT   197 14

LOVE
    MY LOVE LIES UNDERGROUND   198   1
    MY LOVE LIES UNDERGROUND   199   9
    AND AT LAST I KNOW MY LOVE FOR YOU IS HERE   203 17
    AND OUR LOVE WAS A CONFUSION   204   8
    ON OUR LOVE   204 24
    THEY STAND UPRIGHT ON OUR LOVE   204 25
    SHAMELESS AND CALLOUS I LOVE YOU   210   5
    OUT OF INDIFFERENCE I LOVE YOU   210   6
    I HOW CAN YOU TREAT ME SO AND LOVE ME   211   9
    YOU LOVE IT IT IS DARK IT KILLS ME I AM PUT OUT   211 12
    THE PINE-WOODS HOW I LOVE THEM SO IN THEIR MYSTERY OF   212   3
    BUT NEVER MIND MY LOVE NOTHING MATTERS SAVE SLEEP   212 10
    MOANING FOR ME TO LOVE HIM O DARLING RYE   221 13
    STARS COME LOW AND WANDERING HERE FOR LOVE   221 18
    FOR EVER ONE EVEN MIGHT THINK THAT THEY LOVE US   223 27
    OF NAKED LOVE CLENCHED IN HIS FISTS THE SHAME   226   7
    FOR WHAT IS LOVELINESS MY LOVE   226 27
    AGAIN THE LOVE SO FULL   229 13
    WHAT IF I LOVE YOU THIS MISERY   230 17
    AND BECAUSE YOU LOVE ME   235 17
    HA SINCE YOU LOVE ME   235 19
    LOVE   236   4
    WHAT IS CHAOS MY LOVE   236 21
    MY LOVE MY BLOSSOM A CHILD   239 16
    WHERE FLAMES OF FIERCE LOVE TREMBLE   242 10
    HOW I LOVE ALL OF YOU DO YOU FEEL ME WRAP YOU   245   7
    WHAT FLOWER MY LOVE   247   9
    YOUR LIFE AND MINE MY LOVE   249   5
    FUSING CLOSER AND CLOSER WITH LOVE   249   7
    WITHOUT PITY OR LOVE   252   2
    AND I LOVE YOU SO STRAIGHT AND CLEAN AND ALL OF A PIECE+ 254 18
    AND VALLEYS THAT DRAW CLOSE IN LOVE   261   5
    WISE GOOD PROVISION THAT MAKES THE HEART SWELL WITH LOVE 264   7
    WE SHALL LOVE WE SHALL HATE   268   5
    AND SEE ITS SECRETS SO IT IS THAT THE POMEGRANATE IS TH+ 277   3
    I LOVE YOU ROTTEN   280   1
    I LOVE TO SUCK YOU OUT FROM YOUR SKINS   280   3
    OR LOVE THE EFFULGENCE OF THEIR HOLY LIGHT   288 19
    THE CATASTROPHE OF YOUR EXAGGERATE LOVE   290   9
    YOU WHO NEVER FIND YOURSELF IN LOVE   290 10
    THE WINDING-SHEET OF YOUR SELF-LESS IDEAL LOVE   291 12
    BOUNDLESS LOVE   291 13
    DOES NO ONE REALISE THAT LOVE SHOULD BE INTENSE INDIVID+ 291 15
    THIS BOUNDLESS LOVE IS LIKE THE BAD SMELL   291 17
    AND I WHO AM HALF IN LOVE WITH YOU   292 20
    WHAT AM I IN LOVE WITH   292 21
    UGH HOW I LOVE ITS FANGS OF PERFECT RAGE   315 18
    THERE IS A NEW ECSTASY IN HIS ROAR OF DESIROUS LOVE   325   3
    TO THOSE THINGS THAT LOVE DARKNESS THE LIGHT OF DAY IS + 331   3
    WITHOUT LOVE   336 20
    ALL WITHOUT LOVE   336 23
    BORN BEFORE GOD WAS LOVE   337 11
    BEING TOUCHED WITH LOVE AND DEVOID OF FATHERLINESS   357 15
    IN THE RACE OF LOVE   361 26
    SOMEHOW ALAS HE FELL IN LOVE   378   8
    HE FELL INTO THE RUT OF LOVE   378 10
    THE ASS WAS THE FIRST OF ALL ANIMALS TO FALL FINALLY IN+ 378 16
    INTO LOVE MARE-GOAL AND THE KNOWLEDGE OF LOVE   378 19
    ALAS LOVE DID IT   379   8
    LOVE ON A SUBMISSIVE ASS   379 27
    AND AS FOR LOVE   382 15
    DON'T YOU LOVE EVERYBODY   395 22
    YOU LOVE 'EM ALL   395 24
    WHILE YOU PRANCED AND BOUNCED WITH LOVE OF HER YOU   396   1
    WITH INDISCRIMINATE LOVE BIBBLES   396   6
    BUT YOU LOVE LYING WARM BETWEEN WARM HUMAN THIGHS   396 19
    AND YOU LOVE TO MAKE SOMEBODY LOVE YOU INDISCRIMINATE   396 21
    YOU LOVE TO LAP UP AFFECTION TO WALLOW IN IT   396 22
    YOUR VERY DEAREST LOVE AT HIM   398 16
    I GET MY LOVE BACK   399   5
    MUCH IN LOVE   399 10
    FAWN BEFORE THEM AND LOVE THEM AS IF THEY WERE THE ONES   399 14
    YOU MUST ALWAYS BE A-WAGGLE WITH LOVE   399 21
    SUCH A WAGGLE OF LOVE YOU CAN HARDLY DISTINGUISH ONE   399 22
    YOU LOVE ONE AFTER ANOTHER ON ONE CONDITION THAT EACH   399 24
    YOU DON'T LOVE 'EM NOW   400   1
    BUT BRED IN CONCEIT THAT THE WORLD IS ALL FOR LOVE   400 16
    BELIEF IN LOVE AND SORROW OF SUCH BELIEF   410 12
    HUSH MY LOVE THEN HUSH   410 13
    WOMEN WITH EYES THAT WERE GENTLE IN OLDEN BELIEF IN LOVE 410 23
    AND WRESTLE WITH FOR THE PRIZE OF PERFECT LOVE   411   9
    NOW YOU ARE FREE OF THE TOILS OF A WOULD-BE-PERFECT LOVE 411 16
    COME BACK THEN MOTHER MY LOVE WHOM I TOLD TO DIE   411 21
    MY LOVE   411 25
    NOW AT THIS LAST MY LOVE MY MANY A LOVE   412 16
    THEY ARE MANY AND I LOVED THEM SHALL ALWAYS LOVE THEM   412 19
    COME HOME TO ME MY LOVE MY LOVES MY MANY LOVES   412 26
    LOVE   439 23
    EXACTLY SHE SAID DON JUAN WAS ANOTHER OF THEM IN LOVE   447   2
    BUT IF A MAN IS IN LOVE WITH HIMSELF ISN'T THAT THE MEA+ 447   6
    YOU'VE NO IDEA WHEN MEN ARE IN LOVE WITH THEMSELVES   447   8
    PRETENDING TO LOVE THEM   447 10
    SO HE VERY CLEVERLY TORTURES WOMEN WITH HIS SORT OF LOVE 447 15
    NO DON'T TALK TO ME ABOUT THE LOVE OF ENGLISHMEN   447 32
    SHOULD LOVE THE SEWER SCENT   462 31
    THE MODERN MIND CALLS LOVE   469 22
    WE'VE MADE A GREAT MESS OF LOVE   472 14
    THE MOMENT I SWEAR TO LOVE A WOMAN A CERTAIN WOMAN   472 16
    THE MOMENT I EVEN SAY TO A WOMAN I LOVE YOU   472 19
    MY LOVE DIES DOWN CONSIDERABLY   472 20
    THE MOMENT LOVE IS AN UNDERSTOOD THING BETWEEN US WE   472 21
    IT'S A COLD EGG IT ISN'T LOVE ANY MORE   472 23
    LOVE IS LIKE A FLOWER IT MUST FLOWER AND FADE   472 24
    THE MOMENT THE MIND INTERFERES WITH LOVE OR THE WILL   473   1
    IT IS NOT LOVE ANY MORE IT'S JUST A MESS   473   5
    AND WE'VE MADE A GREAT MESS OF LOVE MIND-PERVERTED WILL+ 473   6
    EGO-PERVERTED LOVE   473   7

LOVE
IN MY DARK HEART LOVE IS AND IS NOT   474 11
GODS AND LOVE ALIKE ARE BUT AN IDEA   474 13
OR LOVE OR REJOICE OR EVEN GRIEVE ANY MORE   474 27
IT IS SO MUCH STRONGER THAN HER LOVE COULD EVER BE   475 8
PERHAPS THE EGO-BOUND CAN ONLY LOVE THEIR OWN   475 14
IF THEY CAN LOVE AT ALL   475 16
FIDELITY AND LOVE ARE TWO DIFFERENT THINGS LIKE A FLOWER   476 1
AND LOVE LIKE A FLOWER WILL FADE WILL CHANGE INTO SOMET+   476 3
THAT IS THEIR LOVELINESS AND THAT IS LOVE   476 20
IN SUMMER AND LOVE BUT UNDERNEATH IS ROCK   477 9
AND WHEN THROUGHOUT ALL THE WILD ORGASMS OF LOVE   477 12
OF LOVE   477 20
LOVE IS LIKE THE GRASS BUT THE HEART IS DEEP WILD ROCK   477 22
FOR I CANNOT BE BULLIED BACK INTO THE APPEARANCES OF LO+   478 10
LOVE OUT OF SEASON ESPECIALLY AT THE END OF THE SEASON   478 12
IN LOVE WITH A SELF THAT NOW IS SHALLOW AND WITHERED   478 23
ON BEING LOVED WHEN THERE IS NO LOVE IN THEM   479 8
TILL YOU ASK FOR LIGHTNING INSTEAD OF LOVE   484 15
I KNOW A THING OR TWO ABOUT LOVE   490 3
PEOPLE ALWAYS MAKE WAR WHEN THEY SAY THEY LOVE PEACE   495 15
THE LOUD LOVE OF PEACE MAKES ONE QUIVER MORE THAN ANY   495 16
WHY SHOULD ONE LOVE PEACE IT IS SO OBVIOUSLY VILE TO MA+   495 18
WHEN ONE IS TIRED OF LOVE   503 23
FIRE IS DEARER TO US THAN LOVE OR FOOD   505 25
IS NOT TO ADD OUR LOVE TOGETHER OR OUR GOOD-WILL   506 2
WITH THE EFFORT OF TRYING TO LOVE PEOPLE   506 26
I LOVE NOBODY I'M GOING TO LOVE NOBODY   507 2
DO YOU REALLY LOVE ME   507 14
WHEN A MAN CAN LOVE NO MORE   508 1
IN LOVE WITH HIS OWN DEFEAT   508 14
WHICH IS ONLY A SLOPPY WAY OF BEING IN LOVE WITH YOURSE+   508 15
WHEN LOVE IS GONE AND DESIRE IS DEAD AND TRAGEDY HAS LE+   509 1
I AM A DEMOCRAT IN SO FAR AS I LOVE THE FREE SUN IN MEN   526 7
I LOVE THE SUN IN ANY MAN   526 10
AND YOUNG WASH-OUTS PRETENDING TO BE IN LOVE WITH DEATH   535 19
THOUGH THEY'RE ALWAYS ON ABOUT LOVE   550 16
AND SOMETIMES THEY GIVE IT AS LOVE   559 4
AH LOVE SWEET LOVE NOT SO EASY   559 5
AND IT'S NO GOOD WAILING FOR LOVE   559 7
AND STILL IN SPITE OF ALL THEY DO I LOVE THE ROSE OF EN+   569 1
HOLD MY HAND AND LOVE ME AUNTIE   572 21
LOVE YOUR LITTLE BOY   572 22
BUT WE DON'T MIND SO MUCH IF YOU LOVE US AND WE   572 27
IF MAUDIE DOESN'T LOVE US   573 9
I LOVE MY NATIVE LAND THE BEST ETC ETC   575 14
I LOVE MY NATIVE TONGUE THE BEST   575 16
FROM HOT DIGGING-IN FINGERS OF LOVE   601 12
FROM THE GIBE OF IMAGE-MAKING LOVE   601 23
THEY HAVE ALWAYS INSISTED ON LOVE   602 19
DON'T YOU CARE FOR MY LOVE SHE SAID BITTERLY   604 13
WHEN A WOMAN CAN ONLY LOVE FLAMILY THOSE OF HER OWN SEX   619 19
AND THE PEOPLE ALWAYS LOVE ME   626 11
THEY LOVE ME THEY LOVE ME   626 12
THE PEOPLE ALWAYS LOVE ME   626 13
BUT THE PEOPLE ALWAYS LOVE ME   626 23
THEY LOVE ME THEY LOVE ME   626 24
THE PEOPLE ALWAYS LOVE ME   626 25
AND I AM IL SIGNORE AND THEY LOVE ME HERE   630 4
I LOVE MY NEIGHBOUR   644 15
I WILL LOVE DOGS AS MYSELF   645 2
IS A ROBOT AND INCAPABLE OF LOVE   648 2
THEN HE REPENTS AND HIS WILL BREAKS AND A GREAT LOVE OF+   648 16
AND WHOEVER FORCES HIMSELF TO LOVE ANYBODY   653 3
MAKES THE HEART SUDDENLY QUIVER WITH LOVE   653 17
WHEN JESUS COMMANDED US TO LOVE OUR NEIGHBOUR   654 6
FOR WE CAN'T LOVE ANYBODY NEIGHBOUR OR NO NEIGHBOUR TO +   654 8
AND FAKED LOVE HAS ROTTED OUR MARROW   654 9
YOU HEAR A WOMAN SAY I LOVE MY HUSBAND DEARLY   654 10
WHEN MERCURY AND LOVE AND DEATH   658 16
THOSE THAT GO SEARCHING FOR LOVE   661 6
AND THE LOVELESS NEVER FIND LOVE   661 8
ONLY THE LOVING FIND LOVE   661 9
THE LOVE I FEEL FOR MY FRIEND THIS YEAR   662 1
IS DIFFERENT FROM THE LOVE I FELT LAST YEAR   662 2
YET WE REITERATE LOVE LOVE LOVE   662 4
WHOM THE GODS LOVE DIE YOUNG   662 14
IF AUNTIE DOESN'T LOVE ME   670 24
SO IF AUNTIE DOESN'T LOVE ME   671 5
GODDESSES OF LOVE GODDESSES OF DIRT EXCREMENT-EATERS OR+   671 18
THOUGHT I LOVED   673 7
FOR GOD EVEN THE RAREST GOD IS SUPPOSED TO LOVE US   691 12
LOVE CANNOT LIVE BUT ONLY BARE SALT SPLINTERS   693 22
AND THE SEA IS MAKING LOVE TO DIONYSOS   693 29
AND IN THE TROPICS TREMBLE THEY WITH LOVE   694 11
ENCIRCLING THEIR HUDDLED MONSTERS OF LOVE   695 4
WHERE GOD IS ALSO LOVE BUT WITHOUT WORDS   695 6
SHE IS THE GAY DELIGHTED PORPOISE SPORTING WITH LOVE AN+   695 10
A RAINBOW OF LOVE AND HATE   714 12
WAFTING WITH WARM LOVE FROM STILL-LIVING HEARTS   723 22
MY LOVE IS COME   731 14
WHAT MATTERS ANY MORE BUT ONLY LOVE   736 10
THERE'S ONLY LOVE THAT MATTERS ANY MORE   736 11
THERE'S ONLY LOVE THE REST IS ALL OUTSPENT   736 12
AND LAY THEM DEEP IN LOVE LAY THEM TO SLEEP   736 15
BUT LEAVE US STILL TO LOVE STILL LEAVE US LOVE   736 18
TO LAP THEM ROUND WITH LOVE AND LAY THEM BY   736 20
TO SLEEP AT LAST IN IMMEMORIAL LOVE   736 21
THE LOST HESPERIDES WHERE LOVE IS PURE   737 9
LET US GO BACK THE ONLY WAY IS LOVE   737 15
I HAD DREAMED OF LOVE OH LOVE I HAD DREAMED OF LOVE   742 27
AND GOD REVEALED THROUGH THE SWEAT AND THE HEAT OF LOVE   742 29
WHEN IN THE MORNING I ROSE TO DEPART MY LOVE CAME TO SA+   749 17
OVER YOUR TENT THE ONE TENT OF US ALL MY LOVE   750 10
DO YOU LIFT YOUR LIPS TO KISS ME GOOD NIGHT MY LOVE   750 16
AH MY LOVE MY DEAR   752 1
BUT WHAT IF MY LOVE SHOULD CHANCE TO HEAR   752 2
LOVE MY LOVE NOW ALL IS KNOWN   752 6

LOVE
LOVE ME AND PUT ME OUT OF FEAR   752 7
AND IF THIS NIGHT MY LOVE SHOULD COME TO ME   754 23
WHAT SORT OF TIMOROUS POTION OF LOVE HAVE YOU DRUNK   755 2
DEARER THAN LOVE   765 6
THROUGH THE AUTO-DA-FE OF LOVE   769 6
NO WILL TO LOVE   769 21
IN THE PLACE OF MY LOVE THAT WAS   772 12
THE HORIZONS OF LOVE AND STRIFE   788 23
DO YOU LOVE THEM THEN   794 5
WE LOVE THEM NOT AND NEVER   794 6
ONE THING IS CERTAIN WE'VE GOT TO TAKE HANDS OFF LOVE   834 7
THE MOMENT I SWEAR TO LOVE A WOMAN ALL MY LIFE THAT VER+   834 8
AMOUNTING ALMOST TO LOVE   834 12
I LOVE LIFE I LOVE LIFE SO DEARLY I COULD ALMOST DIE   837 10
AND LOVE AND SEX AND ALL THAT   838 6
BECAUSE THEY ONLY TRY TO MAKE WOMEN AND LOVE AND SEX   838 7
THEN THEY'D BE ABLE TO LOVE DESPAIR CAN'T LOVE IT CAN O+   838 13
SUCCESS FAILURE LOVE CHASTITY DEBAUCHERY MONEY OR SOVIE+   839 19
HE IS NOT A PALE MAN FILLED WITH LOVE AND COMPASSION AN+   840 13
LOVE NOR COMPASSION NOR PITY NOR DEARNESS NOR PAIN MAKE+   840 14
THERE IS LOVE AND IT IS A DEEP THING   843 22
BUT THERE ARE DEEPER THINGS THAN LOVE   843 23
LOVE LIKE THE FLOWERS IS LIFE GROWING   844 1
LOVE IS A THING OF TWONESS   844 5
AND UNDERNEATH THE GREAT TURBULENT EMOTIONS OF LOVE THE+   844 7
LOVE IS OF TWONESS AND IS LOVELY   844 17
BUT BELOW ALL ROOTS OF LOVE LIES THE BEDROCK OF NAKED P+   844 19
ALL THIS IS DEEPER THAN LOVE   844 27
DEEPER THAN LOVE   844 28
OH FOR A DELIRIUM OF LOVE OR OF STRIFE   856 24
WHEN MORNING COMES I FIND ME A LOVE   858 5
I DID NOT KNOW LOVE HAD SETTLED DOWN ON ME   860 1
AND THE FLUSH FADED AND IT CAME DARK I SLEPT STILL IGNO+   860 7
HAS STREWN MYRIAD TWINKLING POPPY-PETALS DOWN THE PATH +   860 18
I LOVE FOR EVER AND IT SEEMS   873 15
OF LOVE AND BEAUTY LOOSE NO MORE   873 21
AT LOVE SHOULD SPRINKLE ME DAILY WITH A RARE   874 6
SWEET FRAGRANCE OF LOVE AND FEED ME WITH KISSES FAIR   874 7
OF LOVE NOT TO DESIRE   874 18
HAVE CLOSED IN LOVE LIKE VERY DEATH FOR STRESS   875 19
ME FOR ANOTHER LESSER SORRIER LOVE   877 4
AND I SAID LOVE   882 28
THE MOON WAS IN LOVE AND SHE   884 4
YOU MUST MAKE MY SONGS FOR ME LOVE I HAVE NONE   884 12
LAPPED PRISONER IN THE CORDS OF LOVE I HAVE SPUN   884 16
AM I FOR EVER MAKING LOVE TO YOU   886 25
SIT AND MAKE LOVE TO EACH OTHER   887 11
FROM THIS LOVE OF OURS   888 4
IF MY VEINS AND MY BREASTS WITH LOVE EMBOSSED   *891 21
FILLED WITH REMORSEFUL TERROR TO THE MAN SHE SCORNED AN+ *891 30
IS FULL OF DREAMS MY LOVE THE BOYS ARE ALL STILL   *905 3
PALE LOVE LOST IN A SNOW OF FEAR   *912 21
HE KISSED THEE O MAN IN A PASSION OF LOVE AND LEFT   *916 6
THE VIVID LIFE OF HIS LOVE IN THY MOUTH AND THY NOSTRILS *916 7
DUNNAT THEE THINK BUT WHAT I LOVE THEE I LOVE THEE WELL *925 13
YOUR LOVE WAS INNOCENT AND THOROUGH   *927 3
MINE WAS THE LOVE OF THE SUN FOR THE FLOWER   *927 4
YOUR LOVE WAS DARK AND THOROUGH   *928 3
MINE WAS THE LOVE OF THE SUN FOR A FLOWER   *928 4
OH I WOULD NOT LOVE YOU   *931 4
BUT MY DEAR LOVE WHEN ANOTHER NIGHT   *931 15
CLOSE YOUR EYES MY LOVE LET ME MAKE YOU BLIND   *931 30
MY ANXIETY IN A HEAT OF LOVE   *936 8
STILL PLIES THE LOVE OF OUR MOTHER FOR US STRAINING OUR+ *938 21
WITH YOUR GLOOM AND YOUR DOUBT THAT YOU LOVE ME   *944 26
STARS COME LOW AND WANDERING HERE FOR LOVE   *945 4
YOU'RE A FOOL WOMAN I LOVE YOU AND YOU KNOW I DO   *945 17
LORD TAKE HIS LOVE AWAY IT MAKES HIM WHINE   *945 18
O LOVE IS A DEEP THING   *951 1
BUT THERE ARE DEEPER THINGS THAN LOVE   *951 2
IT WOULD BE A NAKED LIFE WITHOUT LOVE   *951 7
UNDER THE SUMMERY FLOWERING OF THE ROSES OF LOVE   *951 12

LOVE-ADEPT
SO THAT THE DELICATE LOVE-ADEPT   151 26

LOVE-AFFAIRS
AND MOST LOVE-AFFAIRS JUST SNEAK-THIEF POCKET-PICKING   607 22

LOVE-BIRD
YOU LITTLE BLACK LOVE-BIRD   395 21
YOU LOVE-BIRD   398 33

LOVE-BITCH
AND AREN'T YOUR FEELINGS VIOLATED YOU HIGH-BRED LITTLE * 400 13

LOVED
YOU THAT I LOVED YOU WONDERFUL   56 33
I LOVED BUT THERE SHE GOES AND HER BEAUTY HURTS MY HEART 67 11
DUNNAT THEE THINK BUT WHAT I'VE LOVED THEE I'VE LOVED T+ 83 9
AN' I'VE LOVED THEE FOR IT   139 16
HE NEVER LOVED YOU NEVER WITH DESIRE   158 5
WHEN I WAS A CHILD I LOVED MY FATHER'S RIDING-WHIP   255 1
I LOVED TO HANDLE IT IT SEEMED LIKE A NEAR PART OF HIM 255 3
I WAS A LOVER I KISSED THE WOMAN I LOVED   257 18
SHE LOVED ME AND STOOD BEFORE ME LOOKING TO ME   264 34
AIMING AGAIN AT BEING LOVED   398 14
AS IF NOW AT LAST HERE WAS THE ONE YOU FINALLY LOVED   398 17
FINALLY LOVED   398 18
YOU HAD REALLY LOVED ALL ALONG   399 15
YOU LOVED 'EM ALL SO MUCH BEFORE DIDN'T YOU LOVED 'EM   399 31
WOMEN I LOVED AND CHERISHED LIKE MY MOTHER   410 3
AND WHO LOVED ME   410 8
AND WHOM I LOVED   410 9
WOMEN WHOM I LOVED AND TOLD TO DIE   411 4
WOMEN I'VE LOVED FOR GENTLENESS   412 10
YOU WHOM I LOVED FOR GENTLENESS   412 17

LOVED
  THEY ARE MANY AND I LOVED THEM SHALL ALWAYS LOVE THEM   412 19
  AND LOSE SIGHT OF ME THE ME WHOM YOU TURBULENTLY LOVED   477 26
  WITH THE HEART OF THE MAN YOU SUPPOSED TO HAVE LOVED   478 18
  ON BEING LOVED WHEN THERE IS NO LOVE IN THEM   479 8
  AND EVERYONE LISTENED AND LOVED IT THE   492 9
  IF ALL THOSE FEMALES WHO SO PASSIONATELY LOVED   538 1
  WE WANT TO BE LOVED ESPECIALLY AUNTIE   572 23
  IN THE EYES OF THOSE WHO LOVED ME   601 14
  I HAVE SEEN AT LAST THE IMAGE OF HIM THEY LOVED   601 15
  OH I HAVE LOVED MY FELLOW-MEN   644 1
  OH I HAVE LOVED THE WORKING CLASS   644 4
  OH HOW I LOVED THE THOUGHT OF THOUGHTFUL PEOPLE   644 8
  I HAVE TRAVELLED AND LOOKED AT THE WORLD AND LOVED IT   662 7
  WHERE WHITE MAID ARE THE MEN YOU HAVE LOVED   759 18
  I ALWAYS LOVED HER   869 16
  LOVED TO LIFE IN SUNSHINE   *927 5
  NOT GOOD ENOUGH TO BE LOVED BY THIS EXPERT   *948 20

LOVE-FIRE
  LOVE-FIRE IS DRIFTING THOUGH THE BUGLE IS PRIM AND DEMU+   854 16

LOVE-FLUTTER
  WITH YOUR IMBECILE BIT OF A TAIL IN A LOVE-FLUTTER   396 14

LOVELESS
  YOU YOU ARE ALL UNLOVING LOVELESS YOU   197 1
  LOVELESS AND SO LIVELY   337 10
  AND THE LOVELESS NEVER FIND LOVE   661 8
  THEY SAY THE SEA IS LOVELESS THAT IN THE SEA   693 21
  OF LOVELESS LIFE   693 23

LOVELESSNESS
  ONLY MAKE MANIFEST THEIR OWN LOVELESSNESS   661 7

LOVELIER
  YOU ARE LOVELIER THAN LIFE ITSELF TILL DESIRE   151 6
  LOVELIER THAN PARADISE   261 19
  BUT WHAT IS LOVELIER THAN TO BE ALONE   646 5
  AND NOTHING IN THE WORLD IS LOVELIER THAN SLEEP   725 3

LOVELIEST
  AND EVEN THE LOVELIEST FLOWERS YOU MUST GRAFT THEM ON A   640 23
  LO THE LOVELIEST IS RED ALL OVER RIPPLING VERMILION   689 6
  THE DARKNESS IS LOVELIEST WHERE I COULD SEAR   *929 20

LOVE-LIGHT
  LOVE-LIGHT IS GLOWING THOUGH THE GUELDER-ROSE IS TOO CH+   854 17

LOVELINESS
  FOR WHAT IS LOVELINESS MY LOVE   226 27
  WITH A LOVELINESS I LOATHE   270 26
  THE LOVELINESS THAT KNOWS NOBLESSE OBLIGE   314 17
  THAT IS THEIR LOVELINESS AND THAT IS LOVE   476 20
  BUT I AM A LIAR I FEEL NO LOVELINESS IT IS A MENTAL REM+   509 27
  HE LOOKED AT ME WITHOUT ANSWER BUT SUCH A LOVELINESS   692 15

LOVELY
  HOW LOVELY IT IS TO BE AT HOME   50 6
  ALL THE LOVELY MACROCOSM   56 1
  IN A LOVELY ILLUMINED MESH   111 32
  OF MY STEEL LOVELY WHITE FLINT OF DESIRE   118 5
  'TIS THE SUN THAT ASKS THE QUESTION IN A LOVELY HASTE F+   119 29
  WHAT A LOVELY HASTE FOR WISDOM IS IN MEN   119 31
  THE LOVELY PALE-GOLD BUBBLES OF THE GLOBE-FLOWERS   205 24
  HOW LOVELY IS THE SELF THIS DAY DISCLOSES   218 4
  ALL THE THINGS THAT ARE LOVELY   227 13
  I SEE YOU ALL THE TIME YOU BIRD-BLITHE LOVELY   254 9
  YOU ARE LOVELY YOUR FACE IS SOFT   240 16
  BUT HOW LOVELY TO BE YOU CREEP CLOSER IN THAT I AM MORE   245 20
  I SPREAD OVER YOU HOW LOVELY YOUR ROUND HEAD YOUR   245 21
  IF ONLY MOST LOVELY OF ALL IS YIELD MYSELF AND AM BORRO+   250 17
  IT IS SO LOVELY DAWN-KALEIDOSCOPIC WITHIN THE CRACK   279 2
  WHY THE LOVELY BIVALVE ROUNDNESSES   279 18
  OMINOUS AND LOVELY   288 29
  IN SIGN OF LIFE OF LOVELY DANGEROUS LIFE   317 16
  UNFOLDING ALL HER COILED AND LOVELY SELF   317 23
  IF HE EARNS HIS LIFE HE'LL BE LOVELY   443 11
  AND THEN SUDDENLY WHEN SHE'S FEELING ALL LOVELY ABOUT IT   447 26
  AND FOR THIS REASON SOME OLD THINGS ARE LOVELY   448 6
  IN SUCH LOVELY LANGUAGE   494 15
  YET THE LANGUAGE SO LOVELY LIKE THE DYES FROM GAS-TAR   494 26
  IT OUGHT TO BE LOVELY TO BE OLD   503 14
  HOW LOVELY   509 26
  WOULD BE LOVELY IF THEY ROSE FROM THE MAN HIMSELF SPONT+   520 10
  SAID THE LOVELY YOUNG LADY HALF WISTFUL HALF MENACING   604 7
  LOOKED AT THE LOVELY AND SELF-ABSORBED GIRL   605 2
  THE LOVELY AND SELF-ABSORBED GIRL   605 4
  SAVE SOME SHOOTS SOME LOVELY FLOWERING SHOOTS   640 19
  AND THE LIME-TREE LOVELY AND TALL EVERY LEAF SILENT   646 21
  THAT MAKES THE AIR SO STILL AND LOVELY TO ME   652 5
  THAT WE SHOULD BE LOVELY IN THE FLESH WITH BRIGHT CRESC+   689 30
  WITH A BODY AND WITH NEEDS AND A LOVELY SPIRIT   689 30
  AND BECOMES AT LAST HELEN OR NINON ANY LOVELY AND GENER+   691 18
  THE LOVELY THINGS ARE GOD THAT HAS COME TO PASS LIKE JE+   691 25
  OH LOVELY LOVELY WITH THE DARK HAIR PILED UP AS SHE WEN+   693 8
  GODLY AND LOVELY COMES APHRODITE OUT OF THE SEA   693 19
  OF SILENCE LOVELY SILENCE   698 26
  WITH A LOVELY BLOOM OF WHITENESS UPON WHITE   708 21
  THAT WE CAN KNOW THE DEEP AND LOVELY QUIET   717 18
  EMERGES STRANGE AND LOVELY   720 13
  THE SOUL HAS PEACE INWARD AND LOVELY PEACE   724 26
  SLEEP IS A HINT OF LOVELY OBLIVION   724 28
  AND STILL AMONG IT ALL SNATCHES OF LOVELY OBLIVION AND +   727 22
  A LOVELY SHADOW OF DEATH   772 11
  I HAVE A KNOWLEDGE OF LOVELY NIGHT   772 16
  IS WHERE DOES IT COME FROM THIS LOVELY ENGLISH VOICE   830 23
  THE LOVELY ENGLISH VOICE   830 32

LOVELY
  WE DON'T KNOW HOW LOVELY THE ELEMENTS ARE   839 23
  THE SUN IS SO LOVELY   840 1
  OH LOVELY WOMEN   840 6
  NOR EVEN A LOVELY WOMAN FOAMY TO STING ME LIKE BRINE   840 23
  LOVE IS OF TWONESS AND IS LOVELY   844 17
  NOT ON THE STEMS OF VIRGINITY LOVELY AND MUTE   855 11
  SOME SHAPELESS DARK TO THE LOVELY CURVE OF LIGHT   872 7
  IN A LOVELY ILLUMINED MESH   *927 20
  IN A LOVELY ILLUMINED MESH   *928 20
  BUT LEAVES ALIGHT AND LOVELY ETERNALLY   *937 6
  AH PEACE AH LOVELY PEACE MOST LOVELY LAPSING   *960 1
  OH LOVELY LAST LAST LAPSE OF DEATH INTO PURE OBLIVION   *960 3

LOVE-MAKING
  LOVE-MAKING   198 22
  SO DELICATE IN HIS LOVE-MAKING   447 18
  OF DELIBERATE LOVE-MAKING   469 24
  HE'S MOST FRIGHTFULLY SKILFUL IN HIS LOVE-MAKING   *948 11

LOVE-PRIDE
  YOUR SENSITIVE LOVE-PRIDE BEING ALL HURT   400 29

LOVER
  CALLING LOW TO HER LOVER   42 10
  AND YIELD HER HONEY-DROP TO HER LOVER   42 18
  STRANGE HE IS MY SON FOR WHOM I HAVE WAITED LIKE A LOVER   47 8
  HER WOES HER LOVER WOOS AND SINGS WITHIN ANOTHER WOOD   65 26
  WELL YOU ANXIOUS INQUISITIVE LOVER   95 14
  TO DIE UNOPENED WHEN THIS MOON-FACED LOVER   113 15
  I WOULD BE YOUR LOVER   117 17
  ONCE I HAD A LOVER BRIGHT LIKE RUNNING WATER   119 23
  I WAS A LOVER I KISSED THE WOMAN I LOVED   257 18
  TO HAVE THE ELEMENT UNDER ONE LIKE A LOVER   337 1
  POSING ON AND ON AS A LOVER   478 22
  SHE SAYS SHE WANTS A LOVER BUT DON'T YOU BELIEVE HER   539 13
  HIS EYES AND HE SULKED HE HAD ANOTHER LOVER   735 2
  AND I THE LOVER AM CONSUMMATE   742 12
  SOME ONE STOPPED ME AND SAID YOUR LOVER IS HURT   750 18
  LOVER YOU MAKE SUCH A HERO IN FRONT OF THE FOE   755 9
  FOR YOU MY LOVER   *931 21
  ONCE I HAD A LOVER BRIGHT LIKE RUNNING WATER   *933 13
  A WOMAN TAUNTS HER LOVER   *944 17
  AND IS HIMSELF NORMAL A LOVER OF WOMEN   *949 6

LOVERS
  WE ARE NOT LOVERS MY DARLING WE FIGHT AND WE DO NOT SPA+   92 16
  BEAUTIFUL CANDID LOVERS   243 1
  LOVERS   539 15
  BESIDES SHE'S HAD TWENTY LOVERS ONLY TO FIND SHE DIDN'T   539 16
  LIFE LOVERS WHO COULD HOPE FOR NO RANK AMONG THE PALLID+   855 20
  SHOWED ME SOME OTHER LOVERS STEALING DOWN THE OTHER HED+   882 21

LOVER'S
  OF A LOVER'S FACE   105 28

LOVES
  OH BUT THE WATER LOVES ME AND FOLDS ME   34 19
  BETROTHED YOUNG LADY WHO LOVES ME AND TAKES GOOD   129 4
  AN' A WOMAN LIKE ME LOVES THEE FOR IT   139 20
  A COME AND GO OF MARCH-DAY LOVES   179 10
  DROP WHICH SHE LOVES SENSITIVE MOTHER KANGAROO   393 9
  ONE LOVES YOU MOST   399 25
  COME HOME TO ME MY LOVE MY LOVES MY MANY LOVES   412 26
  WHO LOVES HER LITTLE MAN   571 10
  AND JUST LOVES TO HEAR YOU SOB AND GROAN   572 8
  BUT SO LONG AS WE KNOW THAT AUNTIE LOVES US   573 3
  QUETZALCOATL LOVES THE SHADE OF TREES   802 14
  OH BUT THE WATER LOVES ME AND FOLDS ME   *892 7
  SHE LOVES ME AND I BLOW A LITTLE BOAT   *943 15

LOVE-SONG
  THERE'S A LOVE-SONG FOR YOU AH IF ONLY   224 5

LOVE'S
  AND THOUGH IT BE LOVE'S WET BLUE EYES THAT CRY   89 32
  LOVE'S LONG MOILED MADDENED AUTO-DA-FE   769 7
  WHICH OPENS EARTH AND HEAVEN TO LOVE'S FUGITIVE GLOWING   854 14
  EVER TO SUFFER LOVE'S WILD ATTACK   854 18
  SINGING LOVE'S FIRST SURPRISED GLADNESS ALONE IN THE GL+   *940 15

LOVE-TRICKS
  YOU MISERABLE LITTLE BITCH OF LOVE-TRICKS   398 21

LOVING
  THE PAIN OF LOVING YOU   215 14
  THE PAIN OF LOVING YOU   216 11
  OF OUR LOVING   231 19
  YOU WHO NEVER RECOVER FROM OUT OF THE ORGASM OF LOVING   290 12
  YOU WHO IN LOVING BREAK DOWN   290 15
  OR LIFE KNEW LOVING   337 12
  LOVING EVERYBODY   396 11
  YOU LEARN LOYALTY RATHER THAN LOVING   400 31
  THE FULL DOOM OF LOVING AND NOT BEING ABLE TO TAKE BACK   410 16
  WITHOUT HAVING TO MAKE THE POLITE EFFORT OF LOVING HER   506 17
  AND OF COURSE THRILLING IS LIKE LOVING YOU HAVE NO CHOI+   531 28
  IF I TRY LOVING THEM I FALL INTO THEIR ROBOT JIG-JIG-JIG   645 7
  ONLY THE LOVING FIND LOVE   661 9
  LOVING HER TENDERLY   881 4

LOVING-CUP
  LIKE A LOVING-CUP LIKE A GRAIL BUT THEY SPILT IT TRIUMP+   92 23

LOVINGLY
  LIKE DEPARTING MARINERS LOVINGLY   721 26
  AND BUILD IT LOVINGLY AND PUT IT BETWEEN THE HANDS OF Y+   *957 26

LOVINGS
    BUT LOVINGS AND HATINGS STRUGGLE AND FIGHTINGS   857 7

LOVIN'
    WAS TH' LITTLE LOVIN' SORT AS 'AS NOWT TER SCREEN 'EM   *910 25

LOW
    SOMEWHERE THE LAMP HANGING LOW FROM THE CEILING   41 6
    CALLING LOW TO HER LOVER   42 10
    SHE WOOS THE MOTH WITH HER SWEET LOW WORD   42 15
    AND CROUCHES LOW THEN WITH WILD SPRING   43 7
    PRESSING ROUND AND LOW AT FIRST BUT SOON   50 4
    ON HIS LIMBS IN SLEEP AT LAST LAID LOW   60 7
    AND ALL THE LITTLE ROOFS OF THE VILLAGE BOW LOW PITIFUL+   63 5
    BUT NOW I AM TRODDEN TO EARTH AND MY FIRES ARE LOW   94 1
    HOW NIGHT AFTER NIGHT SWEPT LEVEL AND LOW   103 5
    IN A LOW SHOCKING PERFUME TO KNOW WHO HAS HAILED   105 33
    LOW FROM THE ROOF AND THE WET DUST FALLING SOFTLY FROM +   112 26
    BEYOND ME LIES ON THE LOW STILL FLOOR OF THE SKY   114 18
    THE LOW WORD DON'T I LET THE FLOWER FALL   125 20
    AND GLEAM AS OF SUNSHINE CROSSING THE LOW BLACK HEAP   144 25
    THE LONG LOW TIDAL-HEAP   145 2
    TOSSED ON THE LOW BLACK RUFFLED HEAP   145 13
    THROUGH THE LOW WEST WINDOW A COLD LIGHT FLOWS   163 10
    FROM THE SKY THE LOW TIRED MOON FADES OUT   163 21
    STARS COME LOW AND WANDERING HERE FOR LOVE   221 18
    AND SINKS LOW   246 9
    LOW DOWN   310 25
    HIS LOW FOREHEAD HIS SKINNY NECK HIS LONG SCALED STRIVI+   360 2
    BUT WATCH A TURKEY PRANCING LOW ON EARTH   371 3
    AN EAGLE AT THE TOP OF A LOW CEDAR-BUSH   373 1
    VERY VERY LOW TO THE ROYAL   391 31
    THAT EVERY MAN WHETHER HIGH OR LOW   434 19
    WHEN A LOW BULL-MONGREL STARTS DECLAIMING   494 9
    I SAY TO MYSELF HELLO I'M NOT WELL MY VITALITY IS LOW   498 8
    O I WAS BORN LOW AND INFERIOR   554 5
    HARK THE LOW AND SHATTERING LAUGHTER OF BEARDED MEN   689 2
    SO SWEET LIKE A SWOON OR MORE LIKE THE DROWSE OF A LOW +   727 11
    ALONG THE NERVES A LOW THROBBING   767 19
    AND THE SINGING IS LOW AND SENSITIVE   768 17
    ON A LOW CEDAR-BUSH   780 23
    THEY ARE REALLY LOW CLASS PEOPLE OUT ON THE MAKE   831 8
    FROM THE LOW WEST WINDOWS THE COLD LIGHT FLOWS   857 10
    IN THE SKY THE LOW TIRED MOON GOES OUT   857 21
    ACROSS THE RIVER BENDING LOW   868 1
    CARRIES A DIM LOW GONG THAT SLIPS   868 20
    LOW NAKED CEILING OF THE NIGHT-SKY HELD   876 12
    THE MOON LIKE A REDDENING LANTERN HANGS LOW ACROSS THE +   *917 13
    THE LOW WORD DON'T I LET THE FLOWER FALL   *936 19
    STARS COME LOW AND WANDERING HERE FOR LOVE   *945 4

LOW-BORN
    A FEW OF THE TOUCHES LIKE A LOW-BORN JAKE   489 15

LOW-BUILT
    LEANS AND LOOKS IN AT THE LOW-BUILT SHED   42 21

LOW-DROPPING
    BENEATH THE LOW-DROPPING BACK-BOARD OF HER SHELL   361 21

LOWED
    WHERE NO BULL ROARED NO COW EVER LOWED NO STAG CRIED   394 16

LOWER
    A LOWER ME GETS UP AND GREETS ME   39 10
    DROP A LITTLE LOWER WITHOUTEN RESPITE   113 19
    JESUS' PALE AND LAMBENT DOVE COOING IN THE LOWER BOUGHS   329 8
    TO LIFT THE UPPER HAWK-BEAK FROM THE LOWER BASE   352 12
    AT THE BASE OF THE LOWER BRAIN   455 16
    A LITTLE LOWER THAN THE ANGELS   528 26
    FOR THOU HAST MADE HIM A LITTLE LOWER THAN THE ANGELS   548 33
    THE LOWER MILLSTONE OF THE ROBOT-MASSES   642 2
    THAT BLOOD OF THE LOWER LIFE MUST BE SHED   679 9
    THE UPPER DARKNESS IS HEAVY AS THE LOWER   719 22
    SLOWLY THE WINGS OF DAY ARE EDDYING LOWER   855 27

LOWER CLASSES
    TILL THERE WON'T BE ANY LOWER CLASSES LEFT   774 7
    THE LOWER CLASSES SHALL BE MADE UPPER   774 9

LOWER-CLASS
    THINK YOU A LOWER-CLASS LOUT   550 12
    WEIGHT UPON LOWER-CLASS ROBOT WEIGHT   642 13

LOWERED
    LOWERED TO PAIN   767 21

LOWERING
    AND SUDDENLY LOWERING HIS HEAD THE WHORLS OF BONE AND   381 16

LOWEST
    IN THE LAPSE OF THE LOWEST OF TIDES   509 15
    THE LOWEST STEM OF THIS LIFE OF MINE   *899 26
    THE LOWEST STEM OF THIS LIFE OF MINE   *903 5

LOW-HUNG
    THE LOW-HUNG LAMPS STRETCHED DOWN THE STREET   121 18

LOWLY
    THE DARK VAN DRUMMED DOWN THE DISTANCE LOWLY   121 30

LOW-ROUNDED
    LOW-ROUNDED ON THE MOURNFUL TURF THEY HAVE BITTEN DOWN +   33 6
    LOW-ROUNDED ON THE MOURNFUL GRASS THEY HAVE BITTEN DOWN+   *891 7

LOW-WATER
    LIFE HAS GONE AWAY BELOW MY LOW-WATER MARK   509 23

LOYALTY
    FIDELITY LOYALTY ATTACHMENT   399 19
    YOU LEARN LOYALTY RATHER THAN LOVING   400 31
    I HAVE NOTICED THAT PEOPLE WHO TALK A LOT ABOUT LOYALTY   626 1

LTTTLE
    KISS ME HOW COLD YOU ARE YOUR LTTTLE BREASTS   212 6
    LTTTLE ULYSSES FORE-RUNNER   353 29
    ON HE GOES THE LTTTLE ONE   356 19

LUBRICATING
    LUBRICATING OIL EXHAUST GAS   703 20

LUCENT
    AND SUDDENLY PULLED A GOLD-AND-GREENISH LUCENT FISH FROM   339 2

LUCIFER
    LUCIFER   675 17
    DID LUCIFER FALL THROUGH KNOWLEDGE   699 14

LUCIFER'S
    IT IS LUCIFER'S TURN THE TURN OF THE SON OF THE MORNING   614 9

LUCK
    T' CHILDT MAUN TA'E ITS LUCK IT MUN   81 1
    AN' 'ER MAUN TA'E 'ER LUCK   81 2
    ALONG WITH THE OTHERS WHAT LUCK   669 6
    THE INDIAN QUESTION HAS WORSE LUCK BECOME A POLITICAL   777 13
    THE CHILDT MAUN TA'E ITS LUCK IT MAUN   *923 1
    AN' SHE MAUN TA'E HER LUCK   *923 2

LUCKILY
    LUCKILY FOR US   372 24

LUCKY
    OH ISN'T IT A LUCKY LITTLE MAN   571 7
    SUCH A DEAR KIND AUNTIE ISN'T SHE TO A LUCKY LITTLE   571 11
    FOR OH THE BRITISH PUBLIC IS A LUCKY LITTLE MAN   571 14

LUCRATIVE
    IN THE ODOUR OF LUCRATIVE SANCTITY   457 1

LUCY
    LIZZIE AND LUCY AND ME AND FLOSSIE   573 23
    BUT FOR LIZZIE AND LUCY AND FLOSSIE AND ME   574 1
    BUT ME AND LUCY AND FLOSSIE AND LIZZIE   574 3
    AND LIZZIE AND ME AND FLOSSIE AND LUCY   574 8

LUGGAGE
    LIKE LUGGAGE OF SOME DEPARTED TRAVELLER   134 9

LUGUBRIOUS
    WE CAN BUT HOWL THE LUGUBRIOUS HOWL OF IDIOTS   514 22

LUKE
    LUKE THE BULL THE FATHER OF SUBSTANCE THE PROVIDENCE BU+   327 16

LULL
    WHAT WILL BE IN THE FINAL LULL   164 3
    TO SING IN THE SHELL OF MY HEART THE LULL AND INCREASE   747 22

LULLABY
    SWINGING TO MY LULLABY   *913 18

LUMBER
    AND SEEING MY CAST-OFF BODY LYING LIKE LUMBER   134 12

LUMBERING
    WHERE THAT LUMBERING BEE WHO CAN HARDLY BEAR   50 11

LUMINOUS
    OF THE LUMINOUS PURPOSE OF LIFE SHINES OUT   68 10
    BREATHE LARGELY THE LUMINOUS BREEZE   69 8
    THE LUMINOUS MIST WHICH THE POOR THINGS WIST WAS DAWN   71 5
    STREWN STARS OF UNKNOWN PEOPLE AND LUMINOUS LITTER   132 12
    SPARKLE BENEATH LUMINOUS HILLS   162 7
    OF THE LUMINOUS GHOST   165 28
    IN PELTS OF WOLVES ALL HER LUMINOUS   171 7
    AND DEVIL-DANCERS LUMINOUS WITH SWEAT DANCING ON TO THE   388 33
    OF THE LUMINOUS PURPOSE OF GOD SHINES OUT   *914 25
    BREATHE LARGELY THE LUMINOUS BREEZE   *915 20
    THE LUMINOUS MIST WHICH THE POOR THINGS WIST WAS DAWN A+   *917 23
    STREWN STARS OF PALLID PEOPLE AND THROUGH LUMINOUS LITT+   *920 4

LUMP
    THE LUMP OF WOOD CAREFULLY   387 15

LUMPISH
    TO SEE THEM SO GLUM AND SO LUMPISH   791 16

LUMPISHNESS
    THEIR LUMPISHNESS   792 2

LUMPS
    LITTLE LUMPS THAT FLY IN AIR AND HAVE VOICES INDEFINITE+   341 26
    SUCH LUMPS SUCH FROGS WITH STONES IN THEIR BELLIES   791 29

LUNACY
    BUT CHASTITY ON THE BRAIN IS ANOTHER VICE IT ENDS IN LU+   *952 26

LUNATICS
    LIKE LUNATICS LOOKING THEY BUBBLED AND RAVED   579 2

LUNGE
    AND A' NEURASTHENIC LUNGE   342 23

LUNGED
    AND HE LUNGED FLIGHT-HEAVY AWAY FROM ME SIDEWAYS A SGHE+   346 19

LUNGING
    LUNGING IN THE AIR ON THE LINE   339 5
    AND STUMBLING LUNGING AND TOUCHING THE WALLS THE BELL-w+   343 11
    LUNGING BLINDLY   345 6
    BUT OH OUR HUMAN LIVES THE LUNGING BLIND CYCLOPS WE ARE   544 12

LUNGS
    AND BREATHE DESPAIR THAT TURNS MY LUNGS TO STONE   226 11

LURCH
    IS PEOPLED WITH SHADOWS AND WAILING AND LAST GHOSTS LUR+   54 31
    I FELT THE LURCH AND HALT OF HER HEART   61 21
    I HATE THE WAY YOU LURCH OFF SIDEWAYS INTO THE AIR   333 5
    FALL SINK LURCH AND ROUND AND ROUND   345 20
    THEY MAKE TRAINS CHUFF MOTOR-CARS TITTER SHIPS LURCH   441 6
    I FELT THE LURCH AND HALT OF HER HEART   *912 1

LURE
    LURE THE UNOCEANED EXPLORER   53 8
    OF THE SHIP OF THE SOUL OVER SEAS WHERE DREAMED DREAMS +   *905 20

LURID
    LUSCIOUSLY LURID TO THEM   837 2

LURK
    I NEED NOT GLANCE OVER MY SHOULDER IN FEAR OF THE TERRO+   *945 25

LURKING
    DEMONISH LURKING AMONG THE UNDERGROWTH   293 2
    LURKING AMONG THE DEEPS OF YOUR INDUSTRIAL THICKET   293 8
    THE SMILE THE SUBTLE ETRUSCAN SMILE STILL LURKING   297 22
    THEN THE LITTLE CUNNING PIG-DEVIL OF THE ELEPHANT'S LUR+   390 9
    PAST THE LURKING OCTOPUS ARMS OF AGONISED MEMORY   *959 6

LUSCIOUS
    OR THE RIPE ROSE-FRUITS OF THE LUSCIOUS FALL   219 10
    FOR THE LUSCIOUS FILMY IMAGINATION LOATHES THE MALE   538 7

LUSCIOUSLY
    LUSCIOUSLY LURID TO THEM   837 2

LUSH
    PROWLING ABOUT THE LUSH   107 20
    OF THE LONG LUSH UNDER-GRASS A GLOW-WORM'S SUDDEN   206 9
    AND ALL THE SORREL SPEARS IN THE LUSH LONG GRASS   884 25

LUST
    YOUR REPTILE FLAMES OF LUST AH STORE   151 12
    WE WRITHE AND LUST IN BOTH   177 20
    IN YOUR STRANGE LUST   242 7
    THAT IS A GRAND OLD LUST OF HIS TO GATHER THE GREAT   381 23
    HOMAGE IN LUST IN RAGE   390 7
    WITH LUST CRUSHES OUT THE SPARK   524 8
    I REALISED WHAT A LUST THERE WAS IN HIM TO WREAK HIS SO+   620 6

LUSTILY
    THROWN LUSTILY OFF FROM OUR FULL-SAPPY HIGH   127 8
    ROCKED ON THE WAVE AND SUNG LUSTILY   575 8

LUSTRELESS
    THE HOURS HAVE TUMBLED THEIR LUSTRELESS TARNISHED SANDS   *896 6
    THE HOURS HAVE TUMBLED THEIR LUSTRELESS TARNISHED SANDS   *896 13

LUSTROUS
    THOU TO DO WITH ME THOU LUSTROUS ONE ICONOCLAST   39 18
    IN THE LUSTROUS GLEAM OF THE WATER THERE   126 17
    DARK AND LUSTROUS   369 4
    AND LUSTROUS GREAT TROPICAL EYES UNVEILED NOW GLEAMING   389 13
    AND NOON IS SUDDENLY DARK IS LUSTROUS IS SILENT AND DARK   606 4

LUSTROUSLY
    LUSTROUSLY SURE UNKNOWN   39 27

LUSTS
    TO QUENCH THEIR OVER-SULPHUREOUS LUSTS   340 10

LUSTY
    AND TURN THE POOR SILK GLOVE INTO A LUSTY SOW'S EAR   538 22
    SUNBEAMS LUSTY AND CLEAN FROM THE BATH OF NIGHT   856 16
    WITH THE LUSTY SOULS OF MY BOYS YET THEY HIDE THEIR FAC+   *926 23

LUXURIOUS
    WHICH THEY COULD COMB BY THE HOUR IN LUXURIOUS QUIET   537 27
    A HAT QUAINTLY CURIOUSLY WOVEN LUXURIOUS WITH BIG ROSES   856 12
    WITH LIGHT AND LUXURIOUS BLUENESS   *895 8

LYING
    AND HER SHIFT IS LYING WHITE UPON THE FLOOR   120 2
    AND LEAVE MY FLESH DISCARDED LYING   134 8
    AND SEEING MY CAST-OFF BODY LYING LIKE LUMBER   134 12
    TO TOUCH HIM WHILE HE STILL IS LYING THERE   158 21
    AND REMEMBER THE SMALL LAD LYING INTENT TO LOOK   161 9
    AH YOU YOU EAR OF CORN STRAIGHT LYING   171 18
    BUT THE SHADOW OF LYING WAS IN YOUR EYES   207 5
    BUT YOU LOVE LYING WARM BETWEEN WARM HUMAN THIGHS   396 19
    AND AFTER ALL LYING AND BASE HYPOCRISY AND TREACHERY   497 6
    THE NASTY LYING PRETENCE OF SEEMING TO FEEL WHAT WE DON+   654 5
    IS A GERM LYING IN THE HEARTS OF AMERICANS   774 27
    AND HE SAW MEXICO LYING LIKE A DARK WOMAN WITH WHITE BR+   790 5
    EVER AGAIN LYING PRONE LYING SLACK   827 12
    SIEGMUND DEAR WHAT ARE YOU DOING LYING WITH YOUR FACE O+   871 33
    LYING RIGID AND SILENT WITH YOUR FACE ON THE SHORT SEA +   871 34

LYIN'
    ASIDE O' TH' GRAVE WHILE TH' COFFIN WOR LYIN' YET   *910 27

LYMPH
    GAVE ME SWEET LYMPH AGAINST THE SALT-BURNS   208 6
    AND OIL ME WITH THE LYMPH OF SILVERY TREES   652 23
    OIL ME WITH THE LYMPH OF TREES   652 24

LYONESSE
    LONELIER THAN LYONESSE   261 18

LYRE
    SO LONG AS YOU TUNE YOUR TURN-TURN LYRE   681 2

MA
    A WOMAN'S MAN THA ART MA LAD   140 1

MA'AM
    AND EVEN NOW BIBBLES LITTLE MA'AM IT'S YOU WHO   395 11
    HOW YOU HATE BEING MADE TO LOOK UNDIGNIFIED MA'AM   397 33

MABLETHORPE
    WAS AT MABLETHORPE   746 20

MACBETH
    AND MACBETH AND HIS LADY WHO SHOULD HAVE BEEN CHORING   494 22
    OF LEAR AND MACBETH AND HAMLET AND TIMON   508 17

MACHINE
    THE HORSES ARE UNTACKLED THE CHATTERING MACHINE   35 11
    OF THE STRONG MACHINE THAT RUNS MESMERIC BOOMING THE   149 13
    MACHINE AMERICAN   290 29
    WHILE THE MACHINE AMUSES US THE RADIO OR FILM OR   450 15
    PARTS OF THE MACHINE   452 4
    FORM OF MACHINE CIVILISATION WILL MELT AWAY   611 15
    THEY TALK OF THE TRIUMPH OF THE MACHINE   623 24
    BUT THE MACHINE WILL NEVER TRIUMPH   623 25
    LIKE SNAKES OF HATE AGAINST THE MAN IN THE MACHINE   624 17
    MECHANICAL MAN IN TRIUMPH SEATED UPON THE SEAT OF HIS M+   624 21
    SO MECHANICAL MAN IN TRIUMPH SEATED UPON THE SEAT OF HI+   624 24
    WILL ROCK IN THE SHOCK OF THE MAD MACHINE AND THE HOUSE+   624 29
    THE TRIUMPH OF THE MACHINE   625 9
    AND THE MACHINE HAS ENTANGLED THE BRAIN AND GOT IT FAST   629 7
    MACHINE   629 29
    AND DEVOURED YOU WITH THE MACHINE THE VAST MAW OF IRON   630 16
    MACHINE   631 12
    AND ROSE-BRIARS TO STRANGLE THE MACHINE   634 30
    AND THEN THE HORDES OF THE SPAWN OF THE MACHINE   635 6
    FOR LISTEN THE EGO-CENTRIC SELF IS THE SAME AS THE MACH+   635 8
    THIS IS THE MACHINE INCARNATE   635 13
    AND THE ROBOT IS THE MACHINE INCARNATE   635 14
    AND THE SLAVE IS THE MACHINE INCARNATE   635 15
    AND THE HOPELESS INFERIOR HE IS THE MACHINE INCARNATE   635 16
    THE BRAIN OF THE MACHINE KNOWS THE LIMBS AND TRUNK OF   635 21
    THE MACHINE   635 22
    IT IS MERELY A MACHINE BREAKS DOWN   638 22
    MAN INVENTED THE MACHINE   641 1
    AND NOW THE MACHINE HAS INVENTED MAN   641 2
    MAN INVENTED THE MACHINE   641 9
    SO NOW THE MACHINE HAS INVENTED MAN   641 10
    BUT THE MACHINE IT IS THAT HAS INVENTED THEM BOTH   641 12
    BECAUSE THEY ARE THE BRAINS OF THE MACHINE   641 14
    BECAUSE THEY ARE THE ARMS AND LEGS OF THE MACHINE   641 16
    CERTAINLY THE GOD IN THE MACHINE CANNOT   641 19
    THE MACHINE HAS GOT YOU IS TURNING YOU ROUND AND ROUND   642 20
    FROM THE ENTANGLEMENT OF THE GIGGLING MACHINE   642 25
    THE MACHINE WILL RUN ON AND ON AND ON   643 1
    OH NEVER FIGHT THE MACHINE   643 3
    OH WONDERFUL MACHINE SO SELF-SUFFICIENT SO SUFFICIENT U+   643 8
    OH WONDERFUL MACHINE YOU ARE MAN'S IDEA OF GODLINESS   643 15
    OH YOU GODLY AND SMOOTH MACHINE SPINNING ON IN YOUR   643 19
    ALMIGHTY MACHINE   643 22
    OH GREAT GOD OF THE MACHINE   643 26
    HE JIGS ALONG IN THE IMBECILE CRUELTY OF THE MACHINE   645 15
    THE MACHINE SHALL BE ABOLISHED FROM THE EARTH AGAIN   666 15
    AND THE MACHINE BEGINS TO WOBBLE   676 2
    THE WORN-OUT MACHINE AT LAST BREAKS DOWN   676 4
    DO NOT THINK THAT A MACHINE IS WITHOUT A SOUL   713 1
    A MACHINE THAT IN ITSELF IS NOTHING   714 20
    CAN YOU IGNORE OUR PASSING IN THIS MACHINE   781 9
    THEY TALK OF THE TRIUMPH OF THE MACHINE   *953 12
    BUT THE MACHINE WILL NEVER TRIUMPH   *953 13
    AH NO THE MACHINE WILL NEVER TRIUMPH   *954 1
    AS THE MACHINE BREAKS FINALLY DOWN   *954 12

MACHINE-CUT
    AND ANSWER THE FIRST MACHINE-CUT QUESTION FROM THE LIPS+   291 2

MACHINE-DRAWING
    MACHINE-DRAWING MORE NULL THAN DEATH   619 13

MACHINE-MADE
    EVERYTHING NEW AND MACHINE-MADE SUCKS LIFE OUT OF US   448 16

MACHINE-PEOPLE
    DRAW IT AWAY DRAW IT AWAY FOR THESE HORRIBLE MACHINE-PE+   639 3
    THREADING HIS WAY AMONG THE ROBOT MACHINE-PEOPLE   645 20

MACHINE-ROBOTS
    BUT MACHINE-ROBOTS   644 3
    AND LIVED TO SEE THEM SPAWN INTO MACHINE-ROBOTS   644 6

MACHINERY
  AND MASCULINE MACHINERY   95 19
  NOR SOUND ONLY INTERMITTENT MACHINERY WHIRRING   153 8
  LIFE TWISTING ITS CRAZED MACHINERY   887 5

MACHINES
  PEOPLE HOUSES STREETS VEHICLES MACHINES   256 26
  OF ALL YOUR MACHINES   292 26
  SAY IN THE SOUND OF ALL YOUR MACHINES   292 31
  OF MANY-STEMMED MACHINES AND CHIMNEYS THAT SMOKE LIKE   293 3
  NOT MONKEYS MINDING MACHINES   450 13
  AND SO IT WILL BE AGAIN MEN WILL SMASH THE MACHINES   451 20
  HE WILL CANCEL THE MACHINES WE HAVE GOT   451 28
  WHY HAVE MACHINES THAT WE ONLY HAVE TO SERVE   452 2
  INDUSTRIAL AND FINANCIAL SYSTEMS MACHINES AND SOVIETS   452 10
  MONEY HYPOCRISY GREED MACHINES   457 11
  LIKE MACHINES AND YOU CAN'T WONDER MUCH   537 18
  WITH OUR SHARP LITTLE EYES AND OUR HIGH-POWER MACHINES   543 20
  AND RUSH ABOUT IN MACHINES   558 22
  TICK-TICK-TICKING OF MACHINES   585 17
  MACHINES HAVE TRIUMPHED ROLLED US HITHER AND THITHER   623 30
  HARD HARD ON THE EARTH THE MACHINES ARE ROLLING   624 3
  THE MACHINES WILL TURN TO RUN INTO ONE ANOTHER   624 26
  THE SMALL ONES EGO-BOUND LITTLE MACHINES RUNNING IN AN   637 5
  DON'T GIVE ANY MORE LIFE TO THE MACHINES   639 2
  MACHINES OF IRON MUST BE TENDED BY HANDS OF FLESH   639 7
  IN WHICH IS HEARD THE CRASHING SPLINTER OF MACHINES   640 11
  SO THEY BECAME LIKE MACHINES   640 26
  DRIVES THEM ON AND ON LIKE MACHINES   675 24
  ON AND ON WITH THE TRIUMPHANT SENSE OF POWER LIKE MACHI+   675 25
  THE DEATH OF NOTHINGNESS WORN-OUT MACHINES KAPUT   676 7
  AND MEN THAT SIT IN MACHINES   711 26
  AND IN HIS MACHINES   712 22
  BUT IT IS THE SOUL OF MAN ONLY AND HIS MACHINES   712 24
  AND MACHINES ARE EVIL   716 5
  AND IN THE BIGGEST HOUSES THEY KEEP THEIR MACHINES THAT+   793 24
  WONDERFUL ARE THE MACHINES OF THE GREEDY ONES   793 27
  WE WORK WITH THEIR MACHINES WE WORK IN THEIR FIELDS   794 2
  AND THEIR WILLS ARE LIKE THEIR MACHINES OF IRON   794 8
  WHO ARE YOU TO BE MASTERS OF MACHINES WHICH YOU CANNOT +   794 26
  THOSE THAT CAN MAKE ARE MASTERS OF THESE MACHINES   794 28
  THE DEAD OF THE STEEL MACHINES GO UP IN MOTION AWAY   796 9
  MONEY MACHINES FURNITURE   833 15
  IT WILL BE SO AGAIN FOR MAN WILL SMASH ALL HIS MACHINES+   *950 6
  HE WILL CANCEL AGAIN THESE MACHINES WE HAVE GOT   *950 11
  MACHINES HAVE TRIUMPHED ROLLED US HITHER AND THITHER   *953 17
  HARD HARD ON THE EARTH THE MACHINES ARE ROLLING   *953 21
  AS THE MACHINES FAIL AND FINISH   *954 7

MACHINE-SPAWN
  BETWEEN MACHINE-SPAWN MYRIADS   635 28

MACHINE-UPRISEN
  INTO MACHINE-UPRISEN PERFECT MAN   290 25

MACROCOSM
  ALL THE LOVELY MACROCOSM   56 1

MACULA
  THE RED MACULA   302 21

MACULATE
  MACULATE   302 20

MAD
  WAS A'MOST BURSTIN' MAD O' MY-SEN   80 7
  I WAS GREEDY I WAS MAD FOR THE UNKNOWN   259 13
  I CANNOT TELL YOU THE MAD ASTOUNDED RAPTURE OF ITS DISC+   260 20
  I SHALL BE MAD WITH DELIGHT BEFORE I HAVE DONE   260 21
  A MAD MAN IN RAPTURE   260 23
  HOW COULD I LOOK WHEN I WAS MAD I LOOKED SIDEWAYS FURTI+   264 35
  BEING MAD WITH VORACIOUS DESIRE   264 36
  AND SHOOT ONE ANOTHER AMAZED AND MAD WITH SOMNAMBULISM   408 12
  GENTLE WOMAN GONE MAD   475 22
  INDIVIDUALS MUST GO MAD   475 26
  AND OF COURSE IF THE MULTITUDE IS MAD   486 8
  OR SEE OURSELVES AS WE ARE AND GO MAD   585 2
  WILL BE DRIVEN MAD FROM HIMSELF AND SIGHTLESS AND ON TH+   624 25
  WILL ROCK IN THE SHOCK OF THE MAD MACHINE AND THE HOUSE+   624 29
  WE ARE DRIVEN MAD   739 20
  TILL WE ARE MAD WITH TERROR SEEING THE SLAIN   740 1
  OUR SOUL NOTHING BUT THE MAD MONOTONOUS   746 15
  WAS A'MOST BURSTIN' MAD O' MY-SEN   *922 7

MADAME
  MADAME EST SI BIEN CAMBREE   835 11

MADAME CERES
  YOU MADAME CERES MIND YOURSELF THE ENEMY IS UPON   308 28

MADAME TUSSAUDS
  NAPOLEON THEY SOLD TO MADAME TUSSAUDS AND TO THE ARTIFI+   763 4

MADDEN
  MADDEN US BUT WE DON'T KNOW WHAT TO DO   510 30

MADDENED
  LOVE'S LONG MOILED MADDENED AUTO-DA-FE   769 7

MADE-UP
  SHE IS A MADE-UP LIE A DYED IMMORTELLE   478 28

MADLY
  BUT WOULD NOT YOUR HATE REACH EVEN MORE MADLY THAN YOUR   236 3
  FLYING MADLY   341 23
  MADLY WE RUSH HITHER AND THITHER   739 21

MADNESS
  AND THROWING HIMSELF UPON IT THROW OFF THE MADNESS OF H+   327 26
  FAR OFF SO FAR LIKE A MADNESS UNDER THE HORIZON'S DAWNI+   364 3
  AND THE EYE OVERWEENING INTO MADNESS   371 17
  MONEY IS OUR MADNESS OUR VAST COLLECTIVE MADNESS   486 7

MADONNA
  MADE HER HALF MADONNA HALF ASTARTE   617 22

MADONNA MIA
  SHELVING SUBSTANCE ON TO THE WOMAN MADONNA MIA   437 3
  LEAVING ALL TO THE WOMAN MADONNA MIA POOR VIRGIN   *946 16

MAELSTROM-TIP
  THE LONG TIP REACHES STRONG INTENSE LIKE THE MAELSTROM-+   694 17

MA'E
  BUT WE MAUN MA'E THE BEST ON'T SO NOW ROUSE UP AN' LOOK+   83 14
  BUT WE MAUN MA'E THE BEST ON'T I'LL REAR THY CHILDT IF +   *925 18

MAGENTA
  THE PRIESTS TO WEAR ROSE-COLOUR OR MAGENTA IN THE STREE+   609 17

MAGI
  GLAD AS THE MAGI WHEN THEY SAW THE BROW   88 29

MAGIC
  DAY AND MAKE MAGIC IN HEAVEN   209 30
  WE HAVE BURIED SO MUCH OF THE DELICATE MAGIC OF LIFE   298 3
  THAT IS YOUR TRICK YOUR BIT OF FILTHY MAGIC   332 21

MAGICAL
  SEE HOW IT RISES WITH MAGICAL ROSY SAP   172 10

MAGIC-WISE
  THE UNKNOWN FLOWER ISSUED MAGIC-WISE   *943 21

MAGISTRATE
  AT THE WHIM OF SIX POLICEMEN AND A MAGISTRATE WHOSE STA+   633 5
  A MAGISTRATE AND SIX FAT SMALLER FRY   633 15
  BUT THE GRAND INQUISITOR IS A STALE MAGISTRATE   633 18

MAGISTRATES
  WITH A SET OF CANKERED MAGISTRATES AND BUSY-BUSY BOBBIES   634 8

MAGNATE
  HE IS POLITICIAN OR MAGNATE OR MERE INDIVIDUAL   775 9

MAGNATES
  POLITICIANS MAY BE BAD INDUSTRIAL MAGNATES MAY BE AT FA+   775 5

MAGNET
  LIKE SOME FIERCE MAGNET BRINGING ITS POLES TOGETHER   370 18

MAGNETIC
  THE RED RANGE HEAVES IN SLOW MAGNETIC REPLY   66 16
  SENDING OUT MAGNETIC VIBRATIONS OF WARNING PITCH-DARK   289 2
  LIKE SOME STRANGE MAGNETIC APPARATUS   301 4
  BLOWS THE MAGNETIC CURRENT IN FIERCE BLASTS   370 23
  SETTLE UPON US MAGNETIC SO WE WAX AND BLOOM   *938 18

MAGNETISM
  A MAGNETISM IN THE WATER BETWEEN THEM ONLY   337 23
  ALONG WHICH RIDGE OF LIBIDINOUS MAGNETISM   386 12

MAGNET'S
  LIKE A MAGNET'S KEEPER   121 11

MAGNIFICENCE
  BOWED DOWN WITH HIS INNER MAGNIFICENCE   272 12
  MAGNIFICENCE   530 7
  OF HIS OWN MAGNIFICENCE   697 29

MAGNIFICENT
  IMITATE THE MAGNIFICENT TREES   69 6
  MAGNIFICENT GHOSTS OF THE DARKNESS CARRY OFF HER DECISI+   213 26
  GOD IS A GREAT URGE WONDERFUL MYSTERIOUS MAGNIFICENT   690 8
  IMITATE THE MAGNIFICENT TREES   *915 18

MAGNOLIA-LIKE
  NEVER MAGNOLIA-LIKE UNFURLED   103 31

MAHOMET
  MAHOMET NEVER WENT TO ANY MOUNTAIN   290 2

MAID
  AND COILING IT ROUND THE WISE BROWS OF A MAID   178 21
  THE MAN AND THE MAID GO SIDE BY SIDE   228 1
  AND SO YOU ARE A MAID   239 13
  OH THE INNOCENT MAID   565 23
  IS SUMMED UP IN A NICE NARROW-GUTTED OLD MAID   584 4
  WHOM SOME RECALCITRANT OLD MAID WILL ADOPT AS A HOBBY   665 15
  WHERE WHITE MAID ARE THE MEN YOU HAVE LOVED   759 18

MAIDEN
  SHE LOOKS LIKE A YOUNG MAIDEN SINCE HER BROW   101 7
  HOW ARE WE GOING TO APPEASE HER MAIDEN AND MOTHER   539 19
  IN HER MAIDEN TEENS   564 26
  GROAN THEN FOR EVEN THE MAIDEN EARTH   703 7
  THOU OUR MAIDEN THOU WHO DWELLEST IN HEAVEN   753 1

MAIDEN-FOLDED
  ABOUT HER FROM HER MAIDEN-FOLDED HANDS   128 34

MAIDENHAIR
  AND THE DIM NOTCH OF BLACK MAIDENHAIR LIKE AN INDICATOR   693 14

MAIDENLY
  OF HER MAIDENLY VIRTUE AND OF MY GOOD NAME   129 6

MAIDS
  WHITE LITTLE SHEAVES OF NIGHTGOWNED MAIDS   105 22
  AND IT WAS FOR A FEAST A FEAST OF MEAT FOR MEN AND MAIDS   679 13

MAIL
  AND SHIRT YOU NOW INVULNERABLE IN THE MAIL   154 19
  RUFFLING BLACK SHINING FEATHERS LIKE LIFTED MAIL   370 24

MAIMED
  BUT WE ARE MAIMED CRIPPLED CONTORTED AND SICK   833 8

MAIN
  FOR THE MAIN ALREADY IS FULFILMENT   265 30

MAIN-STEM
  AS IF IT WERE THE LEADER THE MAIN-STEM THE FORERUNNER   299 28

MAIZE
  WHEAT FROM THE HIGH LANDS AND MAIZE   793 21

MAJOR
  IT IS THE MAJOR PART OF BEING THIS HAVING SURPASSED ONE+   266 20

MAKER
  LET THE GOD WHO IS MAKER OF BATS WATCH WITH THEM IN   346 13
  THERE YOU ARE THEN HE'S A CABINET MAKER   452 24

MAKESHIFT
  AND THAT POOR LATE MAKESHIFT APHRODITE EMERGING IN A   439 31

MAKE-UP
  IF IT IS PERFECTLY SINCERE TO DENY YOUR OWN MAKE-UP   659 11

MAKIN'
  AN' T' PARSON MAKIN' HASTE AN' A' T' BLACK   60 15
  ARE YOU MAKIN' BRINSLEY WAY   78 2
  AN' PARSON MAKIN' HASTE AN' A' THE BLACK   *911 1
  ARE YOU MAKIN' BRINSLEY WAY   *919 22

MALADY
  OF HER SOFT-FOOT MALADY   106 30

MALE
  OF A MALE THONG BOOMING AND BRUISING UNTIL IT HAD   36 15
  MALE AND FEMALE DARKNESSES   171 15
  THEREFORE EVEN IN THE HOUR OF MY DEEPEST PASSIONATE MALE   208 8
  AH YES BEING MALE IS NOT MY HEAD HARD-BALANCED   222 17
  AND IT SEEMS MALE   282 14
  FIRE AND WATER THEY CONTAIN THE PROPORTION OF MALE AND +   295 7
  BEAN WAS ONE OF THE OLDEST SYMBOLS OF THE MALE ORGAN FO+   303 19
  THE MALE SOUL'S MEMBRANE   364 25
  MALE TORTOISE CLEAVING BEHIND THE HOVEL-WALL OF THAT DE+   364 28
  OF THE MALE TORTOISE AT EXTREMITY   366 26
  TO OVERLEAP LIKE A MALE ALL MARES AS OBSTACLES   379 13
  AND TO LEAP IN ONE LAST HEART-BURSTING LEAP LIKE A MALE+   379 15
  BLACK PROCREANT MALE OF THE SELFISH WILL AND LIBIDINOUS   383 14
  ESPECIALLY THE MALE OF THE SPECIES   430 16
  ESPECIALLY THE MALE OF THE SPECIES   431 12
  DOWN THE SINK OF THE MALE CONCEIT   457 24
  SOFTLY BLOWS OUT ITS THIN LITTLE MALE STAMENS   535 3
  PUFFING ITS LITTLE MALE STAMENS OUT INTO STERILE PETAL +   535 6
  TILL AT LAST IT'S A FULL FULL ROSE AND HAS NO MALE DUST+   535 7
  FOR THE LUSCIOUS FILMY IMAGINATION LOATHES THE MALE   538 7
  HIS MIND DEVELOPED AT THE EXPENSE OF HIS MALE SELF   841 20
  SO THE POOR MALE HAS SUCCUMBED UNDER IT   843 1

MALEDICTION
  MALEDICTION   208 9

MALENESS
  AND THEIR TRUE MALENESS IS GONE   535 12
  DUSTY POLLEN OF GRASS TALL GRASS IN ITS MIDSUMMER MALEN+   587 3
  IN ITS OWN SPLENDOUR AND ITS OWN FEATHERY MALENESS   587 14
  SHE HAS A SECRET ALMOST ECSTASIED HATRED OF MALENESS IN+   619 20

MALES
  SHE IS THE FEMALE TUNNY-FISH ROUND AND HAPPY AMONG THE +   695 11

MALICE
  AND FULL OF MALICE PREPENSE AND OVERWEENING DETERMINED   382 12
  OF MAQUILLAGE AND POSE AND MALICE TO SHAME THE BRUTES   463 23
  TO MAKE AN END OF THE MALICE OF THIS OVERSEER   759 11

MALICIOUS
  LIKE SOME MALICIOUS INDECENT LITTLE BOY   447 31

MALIGNANCY
  AS WITH THOUGHTS THAT FLASH AND CRACKLE IN FAR-OFF MALI+   97 16

MALIGNANT
  BY SOME MALIGNANT FISHERMAN ON AN UNSEEN SAFE SHORE   586 10
  BY SOME MALIGNANT FISHERMAN ON AN UNSEEN SHORE   632 25
  MALIGNANT MALIGNANT FOR WE WILL NOT SUCCOUR THEM   723 7

MALINGERING
  MY EYES FROM DUTEOUS WORK MALINGERING   129 14

MALINTZI
  MALINTZI OF THE GREEN DRESS WILL OPEN THE DOOR   809 10
  THE GREEN LEAF OF MALINTZI   809 21
  LIKE THE GREEN CANDLES OF MALINTZI   811 13
  WHEN THE WATER OF MALINTZI FALLS   811 22

MALINTZI'S
  IS MALINTZI'S BLADE OF GRASS   810 20

MALLARD
  SWIMS THE MALLARD DUCK AT DAWN IN THAT QUICK JOY   *953 27

MALLOW-FLOWER
  AND POMEGRANATE BLOOM AND SCARLET MALLOW-FLOWER   313 29

MALLOWS
  AS THE TALL FOXGLOVES AND THE MULLEINS AND MALLOWS   709 18

MALNUTRITION
  YOU ARE LIKE TO DIE OF MALNUTRITION OF THE SENSES   655 15

MAMA
  EXCEPT THAT PAPA AND MAMA ARE OLD ACQUAINTANCES OF   357 21

MAMMA
  JUST LOOK AT YOUR MAMMA   834 17
  AND DO LOOK AT YOUR MAMMA   835 27

MAMMON
  WHO HINDER ME MAMMON GREAT SON OF A BITCH   584 8

MAMMOTH
  THOUGH MAYBE THE MAMMOTH GOT TOO BIG IN TUSK AND TEETH   529 17

MAN
  FOR THE MAN TO HEED LEST THE GIRL SHALL WEEP   41 11
  SAUNTERS A MAN FROM THE FARM BELOW   42 20
  I THE MAN WITH THE RED SCARF   44 1
  IF 'E'S NOT A MAN FOR MISCHANCE   45 8
  WAS SUCH A MAN FOR FUSS   45 18
  WHAT A TRAIPSE IT IS IF A MAN GETS HURT   46 3
  AH STERN COLD MAN   55 1
  MY MAN IS MADE TOWARD   59 10
  OF THE MAN I'VE ACCEPTED AS MINE   59 14
  CREATING THE CHANNELLED VEIN OF MAN   69 2
  AND DREW THE CIRCLE OF HIS GRASP O MAN   69 11
  THEN GAVE THEE THY DARK EYES O MAN THAT ALL   69 20
  MY GEL OWT'LL DO FOR A MAN I' TH' DARK   77 3
  AS ANY MAN I' TH' FORCE   77 30
  WHY YOUR YOUNG MAN AN' WIDOW NAYLOR   78 9
  THAT'S SPOKEN LIKE A MAN TIMMY   81 5
  THAT'S SPOKEN LIKE A MAN   81 6
  LIFT THY FACE AN' LOOK AT ME MAN CANNA TER LOOK AT ME   83 5
  THAT I COULD 'A' BIN FIRST WOMAN TER THEE AS THA'RT FIR+   83 13
  AND THE GULF THAT CAME BETWEEN YOU WOMAN AND ME MAN   91 3
  I AM A MAN TO PLOUGH   102 10
  LIKE A MAN WHO HAS DIED   107 28
  WHAT MAN WILL STOOP IN YOUR FLESH TO PLOUGH   112 9
  SHE MAKES HER HANDS TAKE MY PART THE PART OF THE MAN   128 27
  FOR SURELY THIS EARNEST MAN HAS NONE   130 13
  FEELING THE SHADOWS LIKE A BLIND MAN READING   135 18
  THA COULD LET THY VERY SOUL OUT A MAN   138 23
  A WOMAN'S MAN THA ART MA LAD   140 1
  A LITTLE BEARDED MAN PEAKED IN SLEEPING   145 8
  ON THE THIN BARE SHINS OF A MAN WHO UNEASILY LIES   145 21
  BUT DO NOT TOUCH THIS MAN WHO NEVER YET   158 15
  THAT MAN HAS A COURSE TO GO   168 2
  AGAINST US SWORD THAT NO MAN WILL   168 24
  MONEY FROM OUT OF THE EARTH OR THE BEAST OR THE MAN AS +   175 24
  I WILL GO OUT TO THE NIGHT AS A MAN GOES DOWN TO THE SH+   180 1
  WHILE A NAKED MAN COMES SWIFTLY   200 21
  TO WHERE A MAN IN A HEAVING BOAT   201 19
  AND THE MAN AND THE CHILD OF NO MORE ACCOUNT   202 7
  THE FIRST MAN OUT OF THE FOUR THAT'S MOWING   219 25
  LADDIE A MAN THOU'LT HA'E TO BE   220 7
  LIKE A MAN IN A BOAT ON VERY CLEAR DEEP WATER SPACE FRI+   222 24
  A MAN WITH A LANTERN SWINGING   227 3
  THE MAN AND THE MAID GO SIDE BY SIDE   228 1
  TO THE MAN WHO IS HER HUSBAND ALL THE REST   231 2
  OF THE MAN IN ME   240 21
  I THE MAN WHO ENFOLDS YOU AND HOLDS YOU CLOSE   246 4
  A MAN BALANCES BONE UNTO BONE   251 4
  WITH THE MAN IF YOU KNEW HOW MY FLESH ENJOYS   251 23
  THE BODY OF A MAN   254 19
  A MAD MAN IN RAPTURE   260 23
  HERE AGAIN MAN HAS BEEN GOOD IN HIS LEGACY TO US IN THE+   263 18
  BECAUSE I AM THE SON OF MAN   263 32
  WERE OPEN TO ME IN THE WISDOM AND GOODNESS OF MAN   264 5
  A MAN IS SO TERRIFIED OF STRONG HUNGER   264 32
  WHEN A MAN IS RICH HE LOSES AT LAST THE HUNGER FEAR   265 2
  EVERY MAN HIMSELF AND THEREFORE A SURPASSING SINGLENESS+   268 1
  IF I PASS THEM CLOSE OR ANY MAN   269 25
  OF MAN   273 26
  OH IF IT BE TRUE AND THE LIVING DARKNESS OF THE BLOOD O+   273 31
  OF MAN   274 2
  IT TO THE MAN EVEN THE APPLES OF KNOWLEDGE ARE EVE'S FR+   277 7
  NO SIN IS IT TO DRINK AS MUCH AS A MAN CAN TAKE AND GET+   277 10
  IT WOULD HAVE BEEN IF MAN HAD MADE IT   279 23
  SHE QUICKLY SEWED FIG-LEAVES AND SEWED THE SAME FOR THE+   284 8
  OF THE WORLD BEFORE THE FLOODS WHERE MAN WAS DARK AND   286 25
  INTO MACHINE-UPRISEN PERFECT MAN   290 25
  AT MAN AND HIS UNCOMFORTABLENESSES   299 16
  OF A DEAD MAN   303 14
  WINGS FULL OF STARS THEY RULE THE NIGHT AND MAN THAT WA+   319 3
  THE NIGHT LIVES FOUR LIVES AND MAN THAT SLEEPS THROUGH +   319 4
  SLEEP OF THE MAN AND THE EAGLE'S SLEEP AFTER WHICH THE +   319 6
  QUARTERS THEN SLEEP IS EMPTY TOO MAN SLEEPS NO MORE LIK+   319 10
  ONE IS A MAN FOR EXAMPLE AND ONE IS A BIRD   320 2
  I MATTHEW AM A MAN   320 3
  BUT THEN JESUS WAS NOT QUITE A MAN   320 6
  HE WAS THE SON OF MAN   320 7
  I MATTHEW BEING A MAN   320 10
  I AM MAN   320 20
  IF IT CEASED I SHOULD BE NO LONGER MAN   320 26

MAN

I AM MATTHEW THE MAN	321	5
MATTHEW I AM THE MAN	321	19
HEARING MAN APPROACH	321	25
BAT-WINGED HEART OF MAN	322	21
I AM MATTHEW THE MAN	323	5
WHICH IS MY WAY BEING MAN	323	13
BUT I MATTHEW BEING A MAN	323	16
HE SERVES THE SON OF MAN	327	7
THE SON OF MAN	327	9
MAN OR MOSQUITO	333	9
AND VOICES IN ME SAID IF YOU WERE A MAN	350	5
LITTLE OLD MAN	360	18
POOR ASS LIKE MAN ALWAYS IN RUT	378	11
AND THE SLIM NAKED MAN SLIPS DOWN AND THE BEAST DEPOSITS	387	11
WHITE MAN YOU ARE SALUTED	387	17
LIKE A MAN WHEN HE SLEEPS AND HIS SLEEP IS OVER AND HE	407	18
A DARK MEMBRANE OVER THE WILL HOLING A MAN DOWN	407	23
THE INDIANS THOUGHT THE WHITE MAN WOULD AWAKE THEM	408	8
NO LONGER OR CARRY THE BURDEN OF A MAN ON YOUR HEART	411	12
OR THE BURDEN OF MAN WRIT LARGE	411	13
NOW YOU ARE DISEMBURDENED OF MAN AND A MAN	411	14
WHERE THE VIRGIN IN WOMAN COMES HOME TO A MAN	412	5
TO THAT DIFFICULT INNERMOST PLACE IN A MAN	412	8
SHALL A MAN BRACE HIMSELF UP	428	17
OF A SWAMPED CIVILISATION AND START A NEW WORLD OF MAN	429	12
DO YOU EXIST AND CAN A MAN TOUCH YOUR HAND	430	2
YOUR HONEST MAN	432	19
BUT YOU SEE SAID THE HANDSOME YOUNG MAN WITH THE	433	9
THAT EVERY MAN WHETHER HIGH OR LOW	434	19
NOR YET THAT PALE YOUNG MAN AFRAID OF FATHERHOOD	437	2
MAN SHOULD HATCH	437	17
SO YOU THINK SCIENTIFIC MAN YOU'LL BE FATHER OF YOUR OWN	438	18
BURY A MAN GENTLY IF HE HAS LAIN DOWN AND DIED	442	1
A MAN SHOULD NEVER EARN HIS LIVING	443	10
INSTEAD OF MERELY THE SMELL OF MAN	444	14
THE TRAPEZE MAN SLIM AND BEAUTIFUL AND LIKE A FISH IN T+	445	4
BUT IF A MAN IS IN LOVE WITH HIMSELF ISN'T THAT THE MEA+	447	6
AS NO MAN EVER SERVED BEFORE	447	25
WHATEVER MAN MAKES AND MAKES IT LIVE	448	19
EVEN IF IT IS A WOMAN MAKING AN APPLE DUMPLING OR A MAN	449	10
CONTENT IS THE MAN	449	15
FOR IF A MAN HAS NO LIFE IN HIS WORK HE IS MOSTLY A HEAP	450	10
WHEN A MAN GOES OUT INTO HIS WORK	450	24
A MAN OF COURSE	452	15
HE LIVES AND IS A MAN	452	17
AND I SAY HE IS JUST A MAN	453	4
OF ETERNAL SALT RAGE ANGRY IS OLD OCEAN WITHIN A MAN	454	11
TOWARDS WOMAN OR MAN BIRD BEAST OR CREATURE OR THING	454	13
FIGHT AND BE A MAN	458	15
NO ANSWER MAN RISES AGAIN	461	14
AGAIN MAN AMONG MAN	461	16
A MAN IS MANY THINGS HE IS NOT ONLY A MIND	473	15
MAN IS AN ALTERNATING CONSCIOUSNESS	474	15
MAN IS AN ALTERNATING CONSCIOUSNESS	474	16
MAN BECOMES EGO-BOUND	474	24
AND MAN AND WOMAN ARE LIKE THE EARTH THAT BRINGS FORTH	477	7
OLDER THAN PLASM ALTOGETHER IS THE SOUL OF A MAN UNDERN+	477	11
WITH THE HEART OF THE MAN YOU SUPPOSED TO HAVE LOVED	478	18
SINCE MAN IS JUST MIDDLING AND HIS COMPREHENSION JUST	479	11
ONLY MAN TRIES NOT TO FLOW	479	16
THE SOUL OF MAN ALSO LEANS IN THE UNCONSCIOUS INCLINATI+	480	22
BETWEEN MAN AND ALL HIS KNOWN UNIVERSE	482	11
AND THE PASSION OF TRUTH IS THE EMBRACE BETWEEN MAN AND	482	12
TILL YOU LOOK TO THE RIGHT MAN TO PUT YOU INTO TOUCH	484	18
KILLS SEX IN A MAN THE SIMPLICITY	485	2
MOURNFUL YOUNG MAN IN YOUR TWENTIES	485	10
I DOUBT IF ANY MAN LIVING HANDS OUT A POUND NOTE WITHOUT	486	11
MY FATHER WAS A WORKING MAN	490	9
IF A MAN GOES WHO DOESN'T GIVE	494	1
THERE'S NOT A YOUNG MAN IN THE WHOLE	494	10
A MAN OF PEACE	497	2
A MAN OF PEACE	497	12
SAINT FRANCIS HIMSELF WAS A RICH AND SPOILED YOUNG MAN	498	11
DEEP BEYOND THE WORLD OF MAN	499	7
WHY SHOULD A MAN PRETEND TO BE GLAD ABOUT	499	14
AND A YOUNG MAN SHOULD THINK BY JOVE	503	29
AND STILL A MAN CAN BE	504	16
SINCE MAN IS MADE UP OF THE ELEMENTS	505	12
MAN IS LOP-SIDED ON THE SIDE OF THE ANGELS	505	16
IF THERE'S A MAN HERE AND THERE OR A WOMAN	507	5
WHEN A MAN CAN LOVE NO MORE	508	1
TRAGEDY LOOKS TO ME LIKE MAN	508	13
AND A MAN CAN NO LONGER FEEL HEROIC ABOUT BEING A HAMLET	508	26
SO A MAN NO LONGER KNOWS HIS OWN HEART	509	5
LABOUR IS THE ONE THING A MAN HAS HAD TOO MUCH OF	517	19
A MAN CAN'T GET ANY FUN OUT OF WIFE SWEETHEART OR TART	518	4
NOT THIS HYENA TAME PEACE WHERE NO MAN DARE TELL ANOTHER	519	23
AND YET EVERY MAN IS DRIVEN INTO ROBBING EVERY OTHER MAN	519	25
THIS PRETTY PEACE WHERE EVERY MAN HAS TO FIGHT AND FIGHT	519	26
LIVING SHOULD BE AS FREE TO A MAN AS TO A BIRD	520	2
WOULD BE LOVELY IF THEY ROSE FROM THE MAN HIMSELF SPONT+	520	10
ALL I CARE ABOUT IN A MAN	524	1
BECAUSE WHEN THE SPARK IS CRUSHED IN A MAN	524	10
WHEN A MAN COMES LOOKING DOWN UPON ONE	526	3
I LOVE THE SUN IN ANY MAN	526	10
FOR NO LIVE SUNNY MAN WOULD BE A CENSOR	528	12
WHAT A PITY WHEN A MAN LOOKS AT HIMSELF IN A GLASS	528	22
MAN IS IMMORAL BECAUSE HE HAS GOT A MIND	529	1
IN ALL CREATION ONLY MAN COWERS AND IS AFRAID OF LIFE	529	11
ONLY MAN IS TERRIFIED OF HIS OWN POSSIBLE SPLENDOUR AND	529	12
ONLY IS MAN AGONISED IN FRONT OF THE NECESSITY TO BE SO+	529	14
AS MAN IS LIKELY TO DO	529	21
TILL MAN DESTROYS THEM	530	13
THE STUFF OF A MAN	534	20
HATED HIM JUST BECAUSE HE WAS A MAN	538	5
AND FLESH OF A MAN	538	6
ALL THE WOMEN WHO ADORED THE SHADOW OF THE MAN ON	538	10
SUCH ADORATION PIERCES THE LOINS AND PERISHES THE MAN	538	13
THEY WANT TO CHANGE THE MAN HIMSELF	538	21
COMPANIONS TO A MAN	539	24
WILL NEVER A MAN SAY COME MY PIGEON	540	9
WHAT IS MAN WITHOUT AN INCOME	545	1
WHAT IS MAN WITHOUT AN INCOME	545	6
BUT A MAN WITHOUT A JOB	545	26
IF YOU WERE A MAN AND UP TO MY MARK YOU'D HAVE MONEY	547	19
WHAT IS MAN THAT THOU ART MINDFUL OF HIM	548	31
THERE ISN'T A MAN AMONG 'EM	550	1
THAT A MAN IS FOREVER	563	3
TO A DECENT MAN	565	14
YET ONCE MORE I MET A MAN AND I HAD TO STAY	569	21
EAT YOUR PAP LITTLE MAN LIKE A MAN	570	20
DRINK ITS MINKY-WINKY THEN LIKE A MAN	570	21
TAKE ITS DUMMY GO TO BYE-BYE LIKE A MAN LITTLE MAN	570	24
IF IT'S GOOD IF IT'S GOING TO BE A GOOD LITTLE MAN	570	26
IN A MOTOR IN A PAP-PAP PAP-PAP MOTOR LITTLE MAN	571	6
OH ISN'T IT A LUCKY LITTLE MAN	571	7
WHO LOVES HER LITTLE MAN	571	10
MAN	571	12
FOR OH THE BRITISH PUBLIC IS A LUCKY LITTLE MAN	571	14
OH A MAN MAY TRAVEL BOTH EAST AND WEST	575	22
THAT A MAN OR A WOMAN IN A STATE OF GRACE	578	25
MR GLADSTONE WAS A VERY GOOD MAN	582	1
A MAN WROTE TO ME WE MISSED IT YOU AND I	603	9
THE ONLY QUESTION TO ASK TODAY ABOUT MAN OR WOMAN	603	15
A YOUNG MAN SAID TO ME	604	1
THE HANDSOME AND SELF-ABSORBED YOUNG MAN	605	1
LOOKED BACK AT THE HANDSOME AND SELF-ABSORBED YOUNG MAN	605	5
A MAN A WOMAN THERE	606	8
I DARE DO ALL THAT MAY BECOME A MAN	606	9
BUT TELL ME OH TELL ME WHAT IS BECOMING TO A MAN	606	10
THERE IS THE OTHER UNIVERSE OF THE HEART OF MAN	606	21
OF THE HEART OF MAN	607	3
AND NO MAN KNOWS NO WOMAN KNOWS	607	5
WHEN I AM CLOTHED I AM A MORAL MAN	607	9
SO I WISH NO MAN TO PICK MY POCKET	607	13
AND I WILL PICK THE POCKET OF NO MAN	607	14
THE HEART OF MAN IN SO FAR AS IT IS BUDDING IS BUDDING +	612	4
NO MAN UNLESS HE HAS DIED AND LEARNED TO BE ALONE	612	17
A MAN CAN'T FULLY LIVE UNLESS HE DIES AND CEASES TO CARE	613	1
THE PRESENCE OF A MAN MADE HER RECOIL	619	4
SHE HAS A SECRET ALMOST ECSTASIED HATRED OF MALENESS IN+	619	20
WHEN I HEAR MAN SPOUTING ABOUT HUMILITY TODAY	621	22
NO MAN	622	2
BUT WHEN I SEE THE LIFE-SPIRIT FLUTTERING AND STRUGGLIN+	622	4
OUT OF THE THOUSANDS AND THOUSANDS OF CENTURIES OF MAN	623	26
LIKE SNAKES OF HATE AGAINST THE MAN IN THE MACHINE	624	17
MECHANICAL MAN IN TRIUMPH SEATED UPON THE SEAT OF HIS M+	624	21
DEPTHS OF A MAN	624	23
SO MECHANICAL MAN IN TRIUMPH SEATED UPON THE SEAT OF HI+	624	24
IF FIRST A MAN COULD HAVE HIS FULL REVENGE	628	11
MEWED AND MANGLED IN THE MILLS OF MAN	628	23
WHAT IS THIS AWFUL ASPECT OF MAN	628	25
AND STEEL HAS TWISTED THE LOINS OF MAN ELECTRICITY HAS	629	8
WHAT IS MAN THAT THOU ART NO LONGER MINDFUL OF HIM	629	12
WHAT IS A MAN TO DO	631	10
THEN WHAT IS A SINGLE MAN TO DO	631	23
THEN MUST A SINGLE MAN DIE WITH THEM IN THE CLUTCH OF	632	1
TODAY IF A MAN DOES SOMETHING PRETENTIOUS AND DELIBERATE	634	10
THAT WHICH IS TRULY MAN AND THAT WHICH IS ROBOT	636	11
NOW RISEN MAN AND RISEN LORD	636	22
THAT WHICH IS ELEMENTAL AND OF THE SUBSTANTIAL GODS IN +	637	12
ONLY OH MAN STARE STARE INTO THE GULF	637	33
YOU TELL ME EVERY MAN HAS A SOUL TO SAVE	638	15
I TELL YOU NOT ONE MAN IN A THOUSAND HAS EVEN	638	16
MAN INVENTED THE MACHINE	641	1
AND NOW THE MACHINE HAS INVENTED MAN	641	2
MAN INVENTED THE MACHINE	641	9
SO NOW THE MACHINE HAS INVENTED MAN	641	10
TURN AWAY O TURN AWAY MAN OF FLESH	642	5
IF YOU POINT ME TO THAT FAT MONEY-SMELLING MAN IN A MOT+	645	11
MY NEIGHBOUR IS NOT THE MAN IN THE STREET AND NEVER WAS	645	14
THIS IS THE ELECTRICITY THAT MAN IS SUPPOSED TO HAVE MA+	647	18
IT IS CURIOUS TOO THAT THOUGH THE MODERN MAN IN THE STR+	648	1
IF MAN ONLY GOES TO MAN AND NO-ONE SEES BEYOND	650	6
AND THE STREAM IS TOWARDS THE GODS NOT BACKWARDS TOWARD+	650	11
NOT A BOSS BUT THE GLEAM OF LIFE ON THE FACE OF A MAN	650	15
MAN IS ONLY PERFECTLY HUMAN	650	17
THE MAN WHO IS MOWING THE TALL WHITE CORN	651	13
I TELL YOU IT IS NO MAN IT IS NO MAN FOR I AM ALONE	652	14
AND THE POOR MAN NEVER KNEW HE WAS JIXED	659	17
OH HE'S AN HONEST MAN ANYHOW	659	21
AND THE BOLSHEVIST ASSERTS THAT BY HUMAN RIGHT NO MAN S+	663	14
IF YOU ARE A MAN AND BELIEVE IN THE DESTINY OF MANKIND	666	10
TO KNOW A MAN AS WE HAVE NEVER KNOWN	666	22
A MAN AS NEVER YET A MAN WAS KNOWABLE YET STILL SHALL BE	666	23
OH WHEN MAN ESCAPED FROM THE BARBED-WIRE ENTANGLEMENT	667	1
AND STILL A MAN	667	31
BUT A MAN RE-BORN FROM THE RIGIDITY OF FIXED IDEAS	667	32
ONLY THE BEST MATTERS IN MAN ESPECIALLY	668	1
WHAT'S THE GOOD OF A MAN	671	9
THOUGHT IS A MAN IN HIS WHOLENESS WHOLLY ATTENDING	673	15
MAN IS NOT QUITE A MAN	674	18
ANGRY MAN	674	23
POOR LITTLE MAN POOR LITTLE MAN	675	2
AND MAN IS AN IRIDESCENT FOUNTAIN RISING UP TO FLOWER	675	15
WHEN THE MAN WAS HIMSELF SO A GOD IN HIS SINGLENESS	676	12
SELF-SACRIFICE IS PERHAPS THE VILEST DEED A MAN CAN DO	679	23
OR A MAN CAN ADD HIS FLAME TO THE FLAME OF ANOTHER MAN	680	4
AND WHEN AT LAST MAN STOOD ON TWO LEGS AND WONDERED	683	11
BUT A NAKED MAN A STRANGER LEANED ON THE GATE	692	12
THE MAN OF TYRE WENT DOWN TO THE SEA	692	22
GIVING A MESSAGE TO THE MAN	693	15
A HEALED WHOLE MAN O MOON	696	7
NOT EVERY MAN HAS GENTIANS IN HIS HOUSE	697	1

MAN

THEY ARE SO LARGE AND THEY CRADLE SO MUCH OF A MAN   700 18
IT IS A LONG TIME BEFORE A MAN CAN GET HIMSELF AWAY   700 19
MAN CAN BREAK AWAY AND FALL FROM THE HANDS OF GOD   700 23
ONLY MAN CAN FALL FROM GOD   701 10
ONLY MAN   701 11
AND I A NAKED MAN CALLING   704 27
OH IN THE WORLD OF THE FLESH OF MAN   712 5
BUT IN THE WORLD OF THE SOUL OF MAN   712 10
ONLY IN THE SOUL OF MAN WHEN IT PIVOTS UPON THE EGO   712 12
AND WE SEE IT ONLY IN MAN   712 21
BUT IT IS THE SOUL OF MAN ONLY AND HIS MACHINES   712 24
AND EVERY MAN WHO HAS BECOME A DETACHED AND SELF-ACTIVA+   713 4
A MAN MAY BE MY ENEMY TO THE DEATH   715 6
AND CAN A MAN HIS OWN QUIETUS MAKE   717 10
WITH DAGGERS BODKINS BULLETS MAN CAN MAKE   717 12
FOR MAN HAS KILLED THE SILENCE OF THE EARTH   725 17
MAN KNOWS NOTHING   726 1
TO SEND ME FORTH ON A NEW MORNING A NEW MAN   727 30
I THINK PERHAPS THE MAN THAT CAME   732 9
STRONG YOUNG MAN HE LEANS SIGHING   733 19
TO TAKE IT OFF THIS CLOTHING OF A MAN   738 13
I SHOT MY MAN I SAW HIM CRUMBLE AND HANG   741 27
BE BRIDEGROOM OR BEST MAN AS THE CASE TURNS OUT   743 20
THE MAN ANDREW KEEP HIM SAFE IN THE WAR   751 10
THE DAUGHTER OF THE GREAT MAN ROLLS HER KHAKI WOOL   752 9
IF YOU MEET MY YOUNG MAN   754 1
AH YOUNG MAN   755 1
BRINGING NIGHT ONCE MORE AND THE MAN WITH THE KEYS   758 4
SISTERS I AM SORRY FOR THIS FOREIGN MAN   758 11
YOU'VE SOLD EVERY MAN THERE WAS TO BE SOLD   762 16
YOU'VE SOLD EVERY GREAT MAN THAT EVER APPEARED   762 18
THE KNOWING SMILE OF THE FINAL VIRGIN IN MAN   770 13
WHERE THE FIRE-BURNT VIRGIN IN MAN AND THE VIRGIN IN FI+   770 27
OH BUT A MAN WANTS TO GET ON IN THE WORLD   773 21
SCANDALS MAY DESTROY EVERY MAN'S FAITH IN MAN   775 6
SEE THE LIGHT ON THE MAN THAT WAITS   788 28
WHY ARE YOU LAUGHING ASKED THE FIRST MAN OF QUETZALCOATL   791 13
I HEAR THE VOICE OF MY FIRST MAN ASK ME WHY I AM LAUGHI+   791 14
HEY FIRST MAN OF MY NAME HARK THERE   791 17
ON THE SEVENTH DAY LET EVERY MAN WASH HIMSELF AND PUT O+   791 22
TELL THEM SO FIRST MAN OF MY NAME   792 9
NO MAN KNOWS MY FATHER AND I KNOW HIM NOT   799 15
FOR MAN IS THE MORNING STAR   800 14
BUT HAVE YOU SEEN A DEAD MAN HOW HIS STAR HAS GONE OUT +   800 18
SO THE STAR WILL GO OUT OF YOU EVEN AS A WOMAN WILL LEA+   800 19
CALL ME A MAN   803 4
MAN IN THE TWILIGHT   803 17
MAN IN THE TWILIGHT   803 20
MAN THAT IS MAN IS MORE THAN A MAN   806 15
NO MAN IS MAN TILL HE IS MORE THAN A MAN   806 16
AND LO IT STICKS BETWEEN THE RIBS OF A MAN   807 21
AND THE MAN THAT IS MORE THAN A MAN IN YOU   809 15
READY AGAIN FOR THE BUSINESS OF BEING A MAN   809 18
EACH MAN HIS OWN WAY FOREVER BUT TOWARDS   812 13
A MAN CANNOT TREAD LIKE A WOMAN   812 17
NOR A WOMAN STEP OUT LIKE A MAN   812 18
AND A MAN WHEN HE ISN'T BOUGHT FEELS SOLD   814 12
WHY 'TWAS ONLY YESTERDAY EVERY MAN TWIRLED   814 28
AND ONE IN THE LOINS OF A MAN   819 8
BECAUSE ONE FOOT IS THE HEART OF A MAN   820 8
WHEN IS A MAN NOT A MAN   830 1
IT SEEMS TO COME OUT OF SOME HOLLOW RIND OF A MAN   830 33
BUT THE LIMBS OF MAN LONG TO FOLD AND CLOSE UPON THE LI+   834 4
MAN ALONE IS IMMORAL   836 7
BECAUSE MAN POOR BEAST CAN LOOK AT HIMSELF   836 9
OF CHAGRIN AT BEING A MAN   837 11
WHEREIN A MAN CAN LIVE HIS LIFE WITHOUT BEING A SLAVE T+   837 25
THE ONLY THING FOR A MAN TO DO NOW OR A WOMAN   838 14
MAN IS KEPT SANE NOT BY HIS MIND WHICH BY NATURE IS UNS+   838 16
THIS IS THE MASSIVE SOLID FLY-WHEEL WHICH SAVES MAN FRO+   838 19
IF A MAN LOOKED AT MAN FOR ONE MOMENT AS THE SUN DOES   840 2
HE IS NOT A PALE MAN FILLED WITH LOVE AND COMPASSION AN+   840 13
NOR IS HE A STRONG MAN RULING THE EARTH   840 16
NOR A WISE MAN KNOWING ALL THINGS   840 19
IT HAS GROWN UP OFTEN A BIG AND OFTEN INTERESTING-LOOKI+   841 16
IF YOU HEAR A MAN CALLED BRILLIANT YOU MAY BE PRETTY SU+   841 18
BETTER MAN OF THE TWO   842 8
THEN SHE TURNED TO THE OTHER MAN THERE WAS USUALLY ANOT+   842 19
MAN IS ONE OF THOSE BEASTS THAT WILL BREED IN A CAGE   843 14
FIRST AND LAST MAN IS ALONE   843 24
BUT UNDERNEATH ANY TWONESS MAN IS ALONE   844 6
THE MOUTH OF THE MAN IS FULL OF THE TASTE OF PAIN   864 22
SHONE SWEETLY THROUGH YELLOW SILK A MAN FULL IN THE LIG+   865 2
DARTS A MAN AT PLAY   867 13
A SWIFT DEXTEROUS MAN PLYING THE SLENDER POLE   867 22
THE MAN SPEAKS   874 22
FILLED WITH REMORSEFUL TERROR TO THE MAN SHE SCORNED AN+   *891 30
TO THE MAN WHO THRESHES AND SOWS THE SHEAVES   *899 9
TO THE MAN WHO THRESHES AND SOWS THE SHEAVES   *902 21
DOWN EVERY CHANNELLED VEIN OF MAN   *915 14
AND DREW THE CIRCLE OF HIS GRASP O MAN   *915 23
THEN GAVE THEE THY DARK EYES O MAN THAT ALL   *916 3
HE KISSED THEE O MAN IN A PASSION OF LOVE AND LEFT   *916 6
MY GEL OWT'LL DO FOR A MAN I' THE DARK   *918 21
AS ANY MAN I' THE FORCE   *919 18
WHY YOUR YOUNG MAN AN' WIDOW NAYLOR   *920 1
THAT'S SPOKEN LIKE A MAN TIMMY   *923 5
THAT'S SPOKEN LIKE A MAN   *923 6
LIFT THY FACE AN' LOOK AT ME MAN UP AN' LOOK AT ME   *925 9
THAT I COULD HA' BEEN FIRST WOMAN TO THEE AS THOU'RT FI+   *925 17
YI' THA'RT A MAN THA'RT A FINE BIG MAN BUT NIVER A BABY+   *925 24
FROM WHAT I'VE ARRANGED WI' THEE EH MAN WHAT A STUBBORN+   *925 26
WHAT MAN WILL STOOP IN YOUR FLESH TO PLOUGH   *928 29
FEELING THE SHADOWS LIKE A BLIND MAN READING   *939 2
THE FIRST MAN OUT O' THE FOUR THAT'S MOWIN'   *944 5
AN' A MAN AN' A FATHER THA'LT HA'E TO BE   *944 15
THE MAN ANSWERS AND SHE MOCKS   *945 16

MAN

AND ONCE HE WAS A YOUNG MAN PALE AND REFUSING FATHERHOOD *946 15
DON'T YOU THINK LITTLE MAN YOU'LL BE FATHER OF HUMAN BA+ *947 23
A MAN NEEDS TO BE INDEPENDENT AT HIS WORK SO THAT HE CA+ *949 22
WHEN A MAN FREES HIS OWN SELF INTO HIS WORK   *949 24
IT WILL BE SO AGAIN FOR MAN WILL SMASH ALL HIS MACHINES+ *950 6
WHAT A PITY WHEN A MAN LOOKS AT HIMSELF IN THE GLASS   *950 25
FIRST AND LAST MAN IS ALONE   *951 3
BUT UNDERNEATH MAN IS ALONE EACH ONE A ROCK TO HIMSELF   *951 10
AND EACH MAN A ROCK UNTO HIMSELF   *951 16
MAN   *951 19
AND THIS IS THE CORE OF A MAN   *951 23
OUT OF THE THOUSANDS AND THOUSANDS OF CENTURIES OF MAN   *953 14
NOT EVERY MAN HAS GENTIANS IN HIS HOUSE   *955 25
CAN MAN HIS OWN QUIETUS MAKE   *957 1
WITH DAGGERS BODKINS BULLETS MAN CAN MAKE   *957 3

MANA
CALLING TO THEE FOR MY MANA   704 28

MANAGE
LET'S HAVE NO FULL STOPS LET'S JUST MANAGE WITH COMMAS   550 28
OH I DO HOPE AUNT MAUD WILL MANAGE ALL RIGHT   572 9

MANAGER
A BETTER MANAGER FOR OH DEAR ME   571 24

MANGER
THERE SHE IS PERCHED ON HER MANGER LOOKING OVER THE   364 19

MANGLED
MEWED AND MANGLED IN THE MILLS OF MAN   628 23

MANGO
DEEPER THAN THE ROOTS OF THE MANGO TREE   805 1
DEEPER THAN THE ROOTS OF THE MANGO TREE   806 4

MANGO-FLESHED
A MANGO-FLESHED AURA NAUSEOUSLY STEAMING   760 9

MANGO-FLESH
AND CONSIDER THE LILY NOT THE PAWPAW NOR THE MANGO-FLESH   760 18

MANGY
OF YOU MANGY HOUND GO TO HELL   774 18

MANHATTAN
I SHALL COME TO NEW YORK AND LIVE ON MANHATTAN   815 14

MANHOOD
OF CHILDISH DAYS IS UPON ME MY MANHOOD IS CAST   148 17
'TWAS I WHO PLACED THE BLOOM OF MANHOOD ON   156 25
SHADOWS TO COVER OUR STRICKEN MANHOOD AND BLEST   167 18
THAT MY COMPLETION OF MANHOOD SHOULD BE THE BEGINNING   218 24
TERRESTRIAL MANHOOD   322 10
YOU YOUR MANHOOD AND MAKES YOU PAY   458 23
AWARE AT LAST THAT OUR MANHOOD IS UTTERLY LOST   585 7
THE WINDS OF THE AFTERWARDS KISS US INTO BLOSSOM OF MAN+   677 19
MEN DON'T ACHIEVE THEIR OWN MANHOOD ALAS OH ALAS ALAS   683 23
OF THE ANGER OF THE MANHOOD OF MEN   805 9
MEN IN THEIR MANHOOD WALK OUT   810 9

MANIACAL
I SHALL NEVER FORGET THE MANIACAL HORROR OF IT ALL IN T+   257 10
IT WAS A MANIACAL HORROR IN THE END   257 17

MANIFEST
ONLY MAKE MANIFEST THEIR OWN LOVELESSNESS   661 7
AT HER BEST AND HER MOST BEAUTIFUL BEING GOD MADE MANIF+   691 20

MANIFESTATION
MOMENTS OF PURE MANIFESTATION   673 18

MANIFOLD
AND ALL THE MANIFOLD BLUE AMAZING EYES   136 14
THE COMPLEX MANIFOLD INVOLVEDNESS OF AN INDIVIDUAL   356 12

MANKIND
MANKIND   75 17
SWARMS OF MANKIND IN THE WORLD AND WE WERE LESS LONELY   224 7
FOR SO MUCH I THANK THE GOOD GENERATIONS OF MANKIND   263 14
I THANK MANKIND WITH PASSIONATE HEART   263 29
NOT MANKIND FOR MANKIND WOULD HAVE PREVENTED ME   265 22
MANKIND   268 2
AND SEND MANKIND TO ITS INFERIOR BLAZES   316 29
RAMPING ROUND GUARDING THE FLOCK OF MANKIND   324 28
BUT IF IT IS THUMBS UP AND MANKIND MUST GO ON BEING MAN+   430 10
MANKIND   475 25
IT IS THE COLLECTIVE MONEY-MADNESS OF MANKIND   486 19
FOR MANKIND SAYS WITH ONE VOICE HOW MUCH IS HE WORTH   486 20
MANKIND AND MONEY   527 16
WHICH MANKIND AT LARGE HAS CHOSEN TO SANCTIFY   620 21
FOR MANKIND IS A SINGLE CORPUS WE ARE ALL ONE FLESH   631 24
BODY OF MANKIND   632 4
THE HORIZONTAL DIVISION OF MANKIND   636 8
OF THE HORIZONTAL DIVISION OF MANKIND   637 2
MANKIND IS LOST AND LOST FOREVER   637 13
THE ILLUSION OF MANKIND THE ILLUSION OF A HOPEFUL FUTURE   639 21
WHAT HAS KILLED MANKIND FOR THE BULK OF MANKIND IS DEAD   654 3
IF YOU ARE A MAN AND BELIEVE IN THE DESTINY OF MANKIND   666 10
IT IS A MISTAKE THAT MANKIND HAS MADE   666 16
AND LET MANKIND MAKE NEW BLOOD FRESH AND BRIGHT   679 7
ON THE DECAYING EFFORT OF MANKIND   765 21
AND THE DESTINY OF MANKIND DEPENDS AT LAST   831 17
THE WHOLE TEEMING FLESH OF MANKIND   *907 27
SWELLING MANKIND LIKE ONE BUD TO BRING FORTH THE FRUIT + *909 20

MANKIND'S
   MANKIND'S INFERIOR BLAZES   316 30

MAN-LIFE
   OF THE MAN-LIFE NORTH IMPRISONED SHUT IN THE HUM OF THE   149 5

MAN-LIKE
   THE VIVIFIER EXISTS BUT FOR ME IS NEITHER MAN-LIKE NOR +   840 25

MANLY
   PASSING WITH SPEARS AND PENNANTS AND MANLY SCORN   221 9
   OF MY MANLY BREAST   237 2
   OR YOUR MANLY BOSOM EITHER   540 24
   QUITE THE FRESH CLEAN MANLY FELLOW   830 13
   THIS MANLY VOICE   830 27
   AND TRUE ENOUGH HE WAS INFINITELY THE MORE MANLY FELLOW   842 24
   MANLY AND TACKLE THE OUTSIDE WORLD   843 3
   AND THE WOOD LIKE A MANLY HUSBAND SPREADS SOFTNESS AND +   854 9
   PASSING WITH SPEARS AND PENNANTS AND MANLY SCORN   *944 22

MANNA
   MANNA INVISIBLE   269 9

MANNERS
   AND TO HAVE MANNERS FOR ALL OCCASIONS   608 9

MANSION
   NIBBLED MANSION   451 25
   HEAVENLY MANSION AND LAST   695 21
   NOW I MUST ENTER YOUR MANSION AND BEG YOUR GIFT   695 23

MANSIONS
   OH THE SINGING MANSIONS   146 11
   MANSIONS OF MY FATHER   442 16

MAN'S
   BUT THA'LT COME AGAIN BECAUSE WHEN A MAN'S   139 25
   CHRIST ON THE CROSS HIS BEAUTIFUL YOUNG MAN'S BODY   225 5
   MAN'S HAND ON A ROCK   260 11
   MAN'S SWEETEST HARVEST OF THE CENTURIES SWEET PRINTED   263 25
   AND MAN'S DEFENCELESS BARE FACE   310 27
   THE DUST-HEAP OF MAN'S FILTHY WORLD ON FIRE   315 3
   MAN'S NEED   431 3
   WHEN THE MOON FALLS ON A MAN'S BLOOD   453 13
   OF TWO HUMAN HEARTS TWO ANCIENT ROCKS A MAN'S HEART   477 15
   MY LORD A MAN'S FRIENDS' IDEAS OF HIM   489 25
   WORK IS THE CLUE TO A MAN'S LIFE   520 19
   NOW THEN YOU LEAVE A MAN'S MISFORTUNES ALONE   545 11
   A MAN'S A HOLE HOLE HOLE   545 19
   AND WHEN TO MAN'S ESTATE I GROW   576 20
   AND SO TO MAN'S ESTATE HE GREW   576 24
   A MAN'S BUSINESS IS ONE OF HIS POCKETS HIS BANK   607 15
   THEY TOOK AWAY OH THEY TOOK AWAY YOUR MAN'S NATIVE   630 22
   OH WONDERFUL MACHINE YOU ARE MAN'S IDEA OF GODLINESS   643 15
   THE JIXERY PERHAPS NEVER PICKED A MAN'S POCKET   659 14
   WHICH IS THE MAN'S PURE SELF   679 26
   YET A WOMAN CAN ADD HER FLAME TO A MAN'S   680 3
   JUST MAN'S CONCEIT   691 21
   AND IF IN THE CHANGING PHASES OF MAN'S LIFE   727 17
   SCANDALS MAY DESTROY EVERY MAN'S FAITH IN MAN   775 6
   ROUND THE LOST MAN'S CAMP-FIRE   816 18
   WE HAVE LEARNED THAT ANOTHER MAN'S LIBERTY IS AS ESSENT+   833 1

MANTILLA
   HER WHITE MANTILLA ABOUT   105 26
   FLOWERY MANTILLA OF LACE   105 30
   BUT ONLY YOU HAVE THROWN THIS AMAZING MANTILLA OF   369 19
   AND THE POINT OF YOUR MANTILLA DROPS ACROSS YOUR NOSE   369 30
   THE WISP OF MODERN BLACK MANTILLA   617 21

MANTLE
   THEN I LONGED FOR YOU WITH YOUR MANTLE OF LOVE TO FOLD   98 23
   AGAIN IN HER BLUE BLUE MANTLE   201 5
   WRAPPED IN THE DARK-RED MANTLE OF WARM MEMORIES   723 19
   HUITZILOPOCHTLI HAS THROWN HIS BLACK MANTLE   811 18
   MANTLE OF THE BODY'S STILL MORTAL MEMORIES   *957 11
   WRAPPED IN THE DARK-RED MANTLE OF THE BODY'S MEMORIES   *958 31
   AND AT THE PENULTIMATE PORCHES THE DARK-RED MANTLE   *959 24

MANUFACTURING
   PUTTING THEM FORTH NOT MANUFACTURING THEM   451 17

MANURE
   WITH WHICH TO MANURE AFRESH THE ROOTS OF THE TREE OF LI+   616 15
   NAPOLEON THEY SOLD TO MADAME TUSSAUDS AND TO THE ARTIFI+   763 4

MANURE-GOOD
   TO BURN THE WORLD BACK TO MANURE-GOOD ASH   315 11

MANY-BRANCHING
   LET ME SIT DOWN BENEATH THE MANY-BRANCHING CANDELABRUM   299 9
   LET ME SIT DOWN BENEATH THIS MANY-BRANCHING CANDELABRUM   299 19
   OH MANY-BRANCHING CANDELABRUM OH STRANGE UP-STARTING   300 5

MANY-CICATRISED
   LOOK AT THE MANY-CICATRISED FRAIL VINE NONE MORE SCARRED   305 4

MANY-FINGERED
   AND I A MANY-FINGERED HORROR OF DAYLIGHT TO HIM   339 23

MANY-MOUTHED
   MOILED OVER WITH THE REARING OF HER MANY-MOUTHED YOUNG   197 11

MANY-NAMED
   AND MANY-NAMED MARIA   798 14

MANYNESS
   AND MAKES OUR BARE MANYNESS INTO A ONENESS   *951 9

MANY-STEMMED
   OF MANY-STEMMED MACHINES AND CHIMNEYS THAT SMOKE LIKE   293 3

MAQUILLAGE
   OF MAQUILLAGE AND POSE AND MALICE TO SHAME THE BRUTES   463 23

MARBLE
   MY IVORY AND MARBLE BLACK WITH STAIN   151 18
   LIKE IVORY AND GOLDEN MARBLE TWO BLACK CROWS HOLD   *894 27

MARBLES
   WHERE ALL THE PARTHENON MARBLES STILL FOSTERED THE ROOT+   311 28
   ERECHTHEION MARBLES   312 3

MARCH
   OF A MARCH   66 18
   PERHAPS WE SHALL MARCH TILL OUR TIRED TOES   164 10
   ANY MORE THAN AUGUST CAN BE BULLIED TO LOOK LIKE MARCH   478 11
   WE ALL MARCH OUT TO PRAYERS SOFT SLIPPERED FEET AND CLA+   866 13

MARCH-DAYS
   FRESH QUIVERING KEEP THE SUNNY-SWIFT MARCH-DAYS WAITING   179 5

MARCH-DAY
   A COME AND GO OF MARCH-DAY LOVES   179 10

MARCHES
   WHIRL IN THESE PERILOUS MARCHES   242 26

MARCHING
   OF THIS MARCHING ALONG WITH THE INVISIBLE GRASS   164 7
   NOW ALL THE HOSTS ARE MARCHING TO THE GRAVE   743 29

MARD-ARSED
   EH THA'RT A MARD-ARSED KID   44 16

MARE
   MARE OBSTACLE   378 18
   THE GOAL OF A MARE   379 16

MARE-GOAL
   INTO LOVE MARE-GOAL AND THE KNOWLEDGE OF LOVE   378 19

MARES
   ALL MARES ARE DEAD   377 3
   ALL MARES ARE DEAD   377 4
   AND OVER-RODE HIS MARES AS IF HE WERE SAVAGELY LEAPING +   378 6
   TO OVERLEAP LIKE A MALE ALL MARES AS OBSTACLES   379 13
   AND JESUS ON A MEEK ASS-COLT MARES MARY ESCAPING TO   380 2
   ALL MARES ARE DEAD   380 5

MARGIN
   AND ON THE MARGIN MEN SOFT-FOOTED AND PRISTINE   285 24

MARGINAL
   THE LONG MEAN MARGINAL STRETCHES OF OUR EXISTENCE   722 21
   OF MARGINAL EXISTENCE   723 5
   THE LONG MARGINAL STRETCHES OF EXISTENCE CROWDED WITH L+   *957 23

MARGINS
   WHO HAS BEEN LOST SO MANY CENTURIES ON THE MARGINS OF   394 8
   BUT MUST ROAM LIKE OUTCAST DOGS ON THE MARGINS OF LIFE   722 11
   TO FIND HIMSELF ON THE CROWDED ARID MARGINS OF EXISTENCE   *957 14
   THE MARGINS THE GREY BEACHES OF SHADOW   *957 15
   AND CROWD THERE ON THE GREY MUD BEACHES OF THE MARGINS   *958 9
   BUT MUST ROAM LIKE OUTCAST DOGS ON THE MARGINS OF LIFE   *958 16
   TOUCHES THE MARGINS OF OUR LIFE'S EXISTENCE   *958 28

MARIA
   MARIA OF THE GASTHAUS GREEN HAT WOLFRATSHAUSEN   734 33
   AND MANY-NAMED MARIA   798 14

MARIGOLD
   DAZZLE OF MAY-BLOBS WHERE THE MARIGOLD GLARE OVERCAST Y+   90 8
   YOUR FACE IN THE MARIGOLD BUNCH TO TOUCH AND CONTRAST Y+   90 10
   CLUCK MY MARIGOLD BIRD AND AGAIN   119 17
   AND HOW DELICIOUS TO OPEN LIKE A MARIGOLD   526 2
   LIKE A MARIGOLD TO THE SUN   526 5
   OH MY MARIGOLD ROBE   760 6
   CLUCK MY MARIGOLD BIRD AND AGAIN   *932 26

MARIGOLDS
   WHAT IF THE WATERS CEASED WHERE WERE THE MARIGOLDS THEN+   33 22
   WITHOUT THE PULSING WATERS WHERE WERE THE MARIGOLDS AND+   *891 24

MARINERS
   LIKE DEPARTING MARINERS LOVINGLY   721 26

MARK
   YET HER DEEP FOOTSTEPS MARK THE SNOW AND GO   85 7
   WHICH WHELPED AND WAS MARK   323 20
   THE MARK FAR ENOUGH   382 24
   LIFE HAS GONE AWAY BELOW MY LOW-WATER MARK   509 23
   IF YOU WERE A MAN AND UP TO MY MARK YOU'D HAVE MONEY   547 19
   AND CLEAN AS ARROWS THEY SPED AT THE MARK   688 24
   SO SALT IS THE BOUNDARY MARK BETWEEN FIRE THAT BURNS AN+   706 10
   DON'T SPILL THE SALT FOR IT IS THE LAND MARK   706 15
   JAMES AND JOHN AND MARK   798 5

MARKED
   SHE IS MARKED SHE IS SINGLED OUT   228 21
   ARE MARKED OUT WITH THE BOUNDARY OF SALT BETWEEN FIRE A+   706 14

MARKET-CROPS
    WITH THE MARKET-CROPS   203   4

MARLBOROUGH ROAD
    IN MARLBOROUGH ROAD AND IT IS NOW HIS TURN   633   19

MARRIAGE
    WHERE THE SWALLOW HAS HUNG HER MARRIAGE BED   42   22
    IT WILL FIND ME WATCHING AT THE MARRIAGE GATE   58   28
    THE DAYS PERCEIVE OUR MARRIAGE AND REJOICE   129   10
    I KNOW RIGHT WELL THE MARRIAGE RING YOU WEAR   234   3
    THE MARRIAGE OF PRIESTS   609   16
    IS MARRIAGE ONLY WITH DEATH   742   22
    AND THE MARRIAGE SHALL BE MY BROTHER'S IT MAY BE SO   743   23
    AT THE MARRIAGE OF THE LIVING DARK   *956   23

MARRIED
    AN' WE'LL BE MARRIED AT TH' REGISTRAR NOW LIFT THY FACE   83   4
    WHOM I MARRIED YEARS AGO   260   5
    MARRIED OR DYING   495   25
    MARRIED MAKE PERFECT BEAUTY NO DEFECT   872   11
    AN' WE'LL BE MARRIED AT TH' REGISTRAR NOW LIFT THY FACE   *925   8
    TO THE SIGHTLESS REALM WHERE DARKNESS IS MARRIED TO DARK   *956   14

MARRIES
    SO SHE MARRIES ONE OF THESE LITTLE-BOY BRILLIANTS   842   1
    TOMORROW MARRIES TOMORROW FETTERS HIMSELF   877   5

MARROW
    RIGHT INTO THE MARROW   354   26
    AND MARROW AND SUBSTANCE OUT OF ALL   583   3
    AND MARROW AND SUBSTANCE ARE SURE TO BE   583   24
    AND CAN'T PASS SUCH THINGS AS SUBSTANCE AND MARROW   583   29
    AND FAKED LOVE HAS ROTTED OUR MARROW   654   9

MARROW-THOUGHT
    DUSKY SLIM MARROW-THOUGHT OF SLENDER FLICKERING MEN OF   297   6

MARRY
    THOUGH I SHONNA MARRY 'ER   80   30
    I DAMN WELL SHANNA MARRY 'ER   81   9
    'E ISN'T GOIN' TER MARRY YER   81   31
    FOR LETTIN' ME MARRY THE LAD AS I THOUGHT   82   11
    TER MARRY WI' CABS AN' RICE   82   12
    AS FOR MARRYIN' I SHANNA MARRY   84   13
    THA THOUGHT THA WANTED TER MARRY AN' SEE   139   3
    NOW GO AN' MARRY THAT WENCH AN' SEE   139   31
    AN' THEN SOMEBODY HAS TER MARRY YOU   493   17
    WHEN I SAY HE OUGHT TO MARRY ME AND SMALL   733   30
    BUT I SHONNA MARRY HER   *922   30
    FOR I TELL YE I SHONNA MARRY HER   *923   3
    I DAMN WELL SHANNA MARRY 'ER   *923   9
    FOR 'E ISN'T GOIN' TO MARRY YOU   *924   3
    FOR LETTIN' ME MARRY THE LAD AS I THOUGHT   *924   13
    TO MARRY WI' CABS AN' RICE   *924   16

MARRYIN'
    F'R I TELL YER I H'ARENA MARRYIN' NONE   81   3
    BUT I WANT YOU TO KNOW 'E'S NOT MARRYIN' YOU   82   5
    AS FOR MARRYIN' I SHANNA MARRY   84   13
    AN' FRESH AN' MORE NICER FOR MARRYIN' WI'   138   12
    I WANT YOU TO KNOW 'E'S NON MARRYIN' YOU   *924   9

MARS
    SO DISTANT THEY CANNOT TOUCH ME WHOM NOW NOTHING MARS   97   17
    IS IT ONLY THAT THE GREAT WET HAYSTACKS MARS   *933   22

MARSALA
    OR VULGAR MARSALA   280   10
    THOUGH EVEN THE WORD MARSALA WILL SMACK OF PRECIOSITY   280   11
    AND SIPPED DOWN PERHAPS WITH A SIP OF MARSALA   281   24

MARSH
    LIKE A FOREST DARKNESS LIKE A MARSH   171   10
    HERE IN THIS SIMMERING MARSH   217   8
    SINGING BETWEEN THE SUN AND THE MARSH   623   18
    AS OVER DENSE MARSH THE FUMES   703   21
    ONCE OUTSIDE UPON THE GREY MARSH BEACHES WHERE LOST SOU+   *957   28

MARSHES
    IN THE FIR-TREE OVERLOOKING THE MARSHES   216   23
    AS I WENT THROUGH THE MARSHES   222   1
    NOR FEEDING IN THE MARSHES   436   8
    WHERE THE WATERS END IN MARSHES   437   22
    IS DEATH TO US ALL IN THE MARSHES OF PEACE   462   16
    SHAKEN THE MARSHES TILL THE GEESE HAVE GONE   624   1
    AND THE WHITE SWAN SWIMS IN THE MARSHES OF HIS LOINS   624   6
    WILL BE POWERLESS FOR NO ENGINE CAN REACH INTO THE MARS+   624   22
    AND HONKING WITH A HORN-LIKE ANNUNCIATION OF LIFE FROM +   841   6
    IN THE FIR-TREE OVERLOOKING THE MARSHES   *942   9
    UPON THE WATERS THAT ENDED IN MARSHES   *947   1
    SHAKEN THE MARSHES TILL THE GEESE HAVE GONE   *953   19

MARSH-FEET
    AND STAMPS HIS BLACK MARSH-FEET ON THEIR WHITE AND   436   18

MARSH-SOFT
    INTO THE MARSH-SOFT BELLY   436   26

MARSHY
    AND CREATURES WEBBED AND MARSHY   285   23
    MARSHY FLESH   436   19
    AND THROUGH THE REEDS OF HIS MARSHY LOINS   *953   26

MART
    SHE PUTS ME AWAY LIKE A SALESWOMAN WHOSE MART IS   128   3

MARTYRS
    OF SUCH MARTYRS WHILE MARXIAN TENETS   537   11

MARVEL
    MORE MARVEL THAN WOE   171   29
    AND SLOW MOUNTING MARVEL OF A LITTLE TREE   667   18

MARVELLOUS
    MARVELLOUS STUFF   34   21
    WHICH BURNT JUST NOW WITH MARVELLOUS IMMANENCE   219   16
    I HAVE CHOSEN AMONG THE BRIGHT AND MARVELLOUS BOOKS   264   3
    WITH MARVELLOUS NAKED ASSURANCE EACH SINGLE TWIG   299   26
    MARVELLOUS CAKE   442   19
    WITH A MARVELLOUS OUTFIT HOW DID ARCHIE SEE   489   27
    THERE IS A MARVELLOUS RICH WORLD OF CONTACT AND SHEER F+   667   3

MARVELLOUSLY
    AND YOUR FACE YOUR MOST MARVELLOUSLY ETON-ADONIS FACE   835   20

MARV'LOUS
    SHE'S A MARV'LOUS DELICIOUS HIGH-SPIRITED FELLER   583   17

MARXIAN
    OF SUCH MARTYRS WHILE MARXIAN TENETS   537   11

MARY
    AND JESUS ON A MEEK ASS-COLT MARES MARY ESCAPING TO   380   2
    THOUGH LAST NIGHT I WAS MARY   558   8
    FROM BEING MARY   558   14
    WE PRAY FOR THEE MARY DELIGHTFUL THAT GOD MAY BLESS THEE   753   2
    SEND JESUS HIS IMAGES BACK MARY AND THE SAINTS AND ALL   791   20
    MARY THE MOTHER OF GOD BIDS YOU FAREWELL   798   30
    MARY AND JESUS HAVE LET YOU AND GONE TO THE PLACE OF RE+   799   5

MARY MOTHER
    LOOK BACK THE LAST TIME MARY MOTHER   798   3

MARY'S SON
    MY NAME IS JESUS I AM MARY'S SON   786   16
    MY NAME IS JESUS I AM MARY'S SON   789   9

MASCULINE
    AND MASCULINE MACHINERY   95   19
    A QUICKENING MASCULINE GLEAM FLOATS IN TO ALL   127   2
    BUT MASCULINE AS THE SUN   764   6

MASKED-ONE
    MASKED-ONE   373   14
    MASKED-ONE   781   20

MASQUERADER
    YOU MASQUERADER   55   7
    OH MASQUERADER   56   20

MASS
    CLOTTING TO ONE DEAD MASS IN THE SINKING FIRE   47   5
    WHO CURL IN SLEEP LIKE KITTENS WHO MASS AS A SWARM   73   17
    COME LIFE SURGE THROUGH THIS MASS OF MORTIFICATION   271   2
    SICILY DECEMBER'S SICILY IN A MASS OF RAIN   301   12
    MASS OF A GENEROUS BREAST   370   7
    WOMAN GOING TO MASS   385   13
    BEYOND THE MASS   563   22
    TO ADD THE MYSTERY OF JOY-IN-RESURRECTION TO THE MASS   609   20
    MASS   631   26
    FROM THE ROBOT MASS OF RICH AND POOR MECHANICAL EGO-BOU+   637   29
    THE MASS ARE NOT   638   3
    NOT A MOB THING NOR A MASS THING NOR A CLASS THING NOR   775   23

MASSED
    GENTLY ISSUING FROM THE MASSED GREEN   854   22

MASSES
    THE GHASTLY DREAM OF RICHES OF MASSES OF MONEY TO SPEND   175   7
    THE MORALS OF THE MASSES   493   26
    WHAT HAVE THEY DONE TO YOU MEN OF THE MASSES   585   9
    AH THE INDUSTRIAL MASSES WITH THE IRON HOOK|THROUGH THE+   586   15
    THE INDUSTRIAL MASSES AH WHAT WILL HAPPEN WHAT WILL   586   23
    WHAT HAVE THEY DONE TO YOU MEN OF THE MASSES CREEPING   630   9
    THE MASSES OH WHAT HAS BEEN DONE TO THEM   631   8
    WHEN THE VAST MASSES OF MEN HAVE BEEN CAUGHT BY THE   631   11
    EVEN WITH THE INDUSTRIAL MASSES AND THE GREEDY MIDDLE   631   25
    FOR THESE MASSES AND CLASSES OF MEN   639   22
    OF CLASSES AND MASSES   640   6
    THEN AT ONCE THE IMPULSE OF THE GREEDY CLASSES AND MASS+   640   8
    FOR THE ROBOT CLASSES AND MASSES ARE ONLY KEPT SANE   640   13
    TO THE ROBOT CLASSES AND MASSES   640   17
    THERE ARE MASSES AND THERE ARE CLASSES   641   11
    AND THE MASSES ARE ALSO SUPERIOR   641   15
    NOR ITS MECHANISED ROBOTS ROBOT CLASSES AND MASSES   643   4

MASSIVE
    THE MASSIVE THUNDER OF HIS DEW-LAPPED CHEST   326   10
    THE URGE THE MASSIVE BURNING ACHE   326   20
    MASSIVE OLD ALTAR OF HIS OWN BURNT OFFERING   326   28
    MASSIVE BLACK BLOOD   327   15
    HE IS NOT FATHERLY LIKE THE BULL MASSIVE PROVIDENCE OF +   382   8
    AND SLEEP IN MASSIVE SILENCE AND WAKE   465   17
    THEIR MASSIVE BLOOD   465   28
    NOT EVEN THE MOST MASSIVE WAVE OF DESTINY   514   5
    AND ROLL WITH MASSIVE STRONG DESIRE LIKE GODS   694   12
    THIS IS THE MASSIVE SOLID FLY-WHEEL WHICH SAVES MAN FRO+   838   19
    LEANING IN THE MASSIVE UNCONSCIOUS INCLINATION WE CALL +   *952   4

MAST
    WITH GRAPE-VINES UP THE MAST AND DOLPHINS LEAPING   688   5
    RIGGING ITS MAST WITH THE SILENT INVISIBLE SAIL   *961   1

MASTER
    HOW IT LOOKS BACK LIKE A WHITE DOG TO ITS MASTER   34   1
    IF TER COULDNA BE MASTER AN' TH' WOMAN'S BOSS   139   4
    PROSERPINE'S MASTER   308   3
    BUT PUT ME DOWN AGAIN IN TIME MASTER   321   8
    ONE FOR THE MASTER AND ONE FOR THE DAME   669   23
    AND AT ONE WITH THE MASTER OF THE HOUSE WITH THE MISTRE+ 700   5
    AS OF THE MASTER SITTING AT THE BOARD   700   14
    OH MASTER LET IT BE LOOSE-ALL IT IS ENOUGH   757   12
    AH MASTER MASTER YOU WHO HAVE BROUGHT US HITHER   757   14
    WE ARE SO LET US HAVE DONE AH MASTER WE WAIT   757   18
    AFTER YOUR MASTER THE CRUCIFIED   798   19
    ONCE MORE FOLLOWING THE MASTER   798   23
    I AM THE WATCHER AND MASTER OF THE DREAM   807   1

MASTERED
    THIS IS THE ELECTRICITY THAT MAN IS SUPPOSED TO HAVE MA+ 647   18
    THE DEAD THAT HAVE MASTERED FIRE LIVE ON SALAMANDERS IN+ 796   7
    BUT THE DEAD OF THOSE WHO HAVE MASTERED NOTHING NOTHING+ 796   11
    THOSE THAT HAVE MASTERED THE FORCES OF THE WORLD DIE IN+ 796   14
    BUT YOU WHAT HAVE YOU MASTERED AMONG THE DRAGON HOSTS O+ 796   16

MASTERLESS
    CRAWL LIKE MASTERLESS DOGS IN THE BACK STREETS OF THE A+ 796   12

MASTER OF CASH SCIENCE
    IT WILL BE BACHELOR OF CASH ARTS MASTER OF CASH SCIENCE *950   23

MASTERS
    FOR JOY OF THE NIGHT WHEN MASTERS ARE   70   12
    EAGLE OF THE ROCKIES BIRD OF MEN THAT ARE MASTERS   414   21
    IN ALL THE HIGH PLACES AND THEY ARE MASTERS OF INDUSTRY 637   19
    WHO ARE YOU TO BE MASTERS OF MACHINES WHICH YOU CANNOT + 794   26
    THOSE THAT CAN MAKE ARE MASTERS OF THESE MACHINES   794   28
    AND THEN RUN LIKE SURLY DOGS AT THE BIDDING OF PALEFACE+ 795   4
    THE DEAD OF ELECTRIC MASTERS ARE ELECTRICITY ITSELF   796   10

MASTERS OF DEATH
    THE LORDS OF LIFE ARE THE MASTERS OF DEATH   808   17
    THE LORDS OF LIFE ARE THE MASTERS OF DEATH   808   21
    THE LORDS OF LIFE ARE THE MASTERS OF DEATH   809   3

MASTERY
    IN SPITE OF MYSELF THE INSIDIOUS MASTERY OF SONG   148   10
    AH MASTERY   308   24

MASTODON
    OR LIKE THE WOMAN WHO SAT DOWN ON A SLEEPING MASTODON   540   1
    THEN SUDDENLY THE MASTODON ROSE WITH THE WONDERFUL LADY 540   5

MASTODONS
    TO THINK AMONG THE MOSS AND MUD OF LIZARDS AND MASTODONS 690   28
    BUT IMAGINE AMONG THE MUD AND THE MASTODONS   691   1

MASTS
    WITH MASTS ERECT AND SPARS ALL SET AND SAILS SPREAD   542   2
    WHOSE MASTS HAVE PURPLE VINES   693   26

MASTURBATING
    AND THE PURE INTELLECT GIVES ONE A LAST MASTURBATING SE+ 532   9

MATCH
    YES IF IT'S A KEEN MATCH RAPE IS RATHER THRILLING   532   19
    HOW GHASTLY IT WOULD BE TO STRIKE A MATCH AND MAKE A LI+ 724   16
    SO IS A CANDLE EVEN AS A MATCH   724   19

MATCHED
    MATCHED   605   19

MATE
    AM I DOOMED IN A LONG COITION OF WORDS TO MATE YOU   119   4
    MATE MY HUNGRY SOUL WITH A GERM OF ITS WOMB   179   27
    TILL AT LENGTH THEY MATE   249   8
    WHO WILL FIND IT SO HARD TO MATE   459   4
    IS SLOW TO MATE   465   8
    AND THE GREAT BEASTS MATE IN SECRET AT LAST   465   21
    AND DO I NOT SEEK TO MATE MY GROWN DESIROUS SOUL   *926   22
    IN KNOWLEDGE MUST MATE YOU   *932   15

MATER
    NOR THE DEAR OLD MATER WHO SO PROUDLY BOASTS   458   24

MATERIAL
    THE BRIEF MATERIAL CONTROL OF THE HOUR LEAVE THEM FREE + 93   8
    AND OUT OF THE STRUGGLE WITH HIS MATERIAL IN THE SPELL + 690   6
    IS THAT THEY ARE NOT MEAN IN MATERIAL THINGS   828   17
    WHERE THE ATTENTION WILL BE LIFTED OFF MATERIAL THINGS 833   14
    WHERE WE CAN LEARN TO FULFIL OUR NEW KNOWLEDGE OF MATER+ 833   23
    JUSTICE HUMAN DECENCY IN MATERIAL THINGS   833   24

MATERIALISTIC
    HER LACONIC EYE HAS AN EARTHY MATERIALISTIC LOOK   359   33

MATERIAL-MECHANICAL
    AND WHEN I THINK OF THE GREAT TRAGEDY OF OUR MATERIAL-M+ 508   19

MATHEMATICAL
    LIFE ESTABLISHING THE FIRST ETERNAL MATHEMATICAL TABLET 355   17
    THE FIRST LITTLE MATHEMATICAL GENTLEMAN   355   20
    UNDER ALL THE ETERNAL DOME OF MATHEMATICAL LAW   355   22

MATHEMATICS
    FOUR AND ONE MAKES FIVE WHICH IS THE CLUE TO ALL MATHEM+ 356   8

MATING
    THE HIDDEN BODIES MATING EVERYWHERE   126   21

MATRIMONIAL
    ON THE VERY SLOPES OF THE MATRIMONIAL MOUNTAIN   541   6

MATRIX
    ME FROM THE MATRIX TO RELIEVE   262   12
    OUT OF THE SOFT MATRIX   870   8

MATRONLY
    SHE IS LARGE AND MATRONLY   358   22

MATTER
    WHAT DOES IT MATTER TO ME IF THEY CAN WRITE   74   27
    WHAT MATTER THE STUFF I LICK UP IN MY DAILY FLAME   115   10
    NOT FINISHED HE HASN'T NO MATTER HOW   139   26
    AND THE BODIES OF MEN AND WOMEN ARE MOLTEN MATTER OF DR+ 176   2
    SMALL AM I WHAT MATTER IF MINUTELY   223   8
    NO MATTER I AM SO HAPPY   247   10
    OUR HEAVEN AS A MATTER OF FACT   265   16
    FOR THAT MATTER   290   1
    WHAT DOES IT MATTER   292   1
    BUT THAT IS ANOTHER MATTER   321   4
    AND I AM NOT THAT OTHER ANGELIC MATTER   321   6
    WHILE LIFE WAS A HEAVE OF MATTER HALF INANIMATE   372   10
    AND ROWING ON UNARRIVED NO MATTER HOW OFTEN HE ENTER   380   23
    AS A MATTER OF FACT WE ARE BETTER THAN WE KNOW   519   10
    WHEN AS A MATTER OF FACT THE THOUGHT OF THIS ENDLESS   519   15
    AS A MATTER OF FACT WHEN THE TINKER LOOKS SO HAPPY   520   23
    AS A MATTER OF FACT THE ONLY CREATURES THAT SEEM TO SUR+ 523   21
    I SUPPOSE AS A MATTER OF FACT IT'S GETTING A LITTLE DIF+ 532   3
    WELL IT WON'T MATTER SO VERY MUCH EITHER   534   8
    NO NO MATTER HOW YOU MAY SHOVE   550   18
    NO MATTER OF WHAT SORT THE CABBAGE BE   569   14
    WHAT'S THE MATTER WITH THEM AREN'T THEY WOMEN AND   578   18
    DIE DIE DIE CORPSE-BODY DOESN'T MATTER   584   18
    MOST MEN DON'T MATTER AT ALL ANY MORE THAN ANTS MATTER 638   11
    ONLY THE FEW THE VERY FEW MATTER IN THE SIGHT OF GOD AND 638   13
    BUT IT DOESN'T REALLY MATTER WHAT YOU SAY TO THEM   660   11
    AS A MATTER OF FACT WE KNOW NOTHING   676   27
    THE KNOWLEDGE IS WITHIN ME WITHOUT BEING A MATTER OF FA+ 677   3
    ALL MATTER AND ALL SPIRIT STANDING UPRIGHT   872   13
    WHAT MATTER THE STUFF I LICK UP IN MY LIVING FLAME   *930   10
    AS A MATTER OF FACT   *948   28

MATTERING
    MATTERING AT LEAST NOT TO ME   552   12

MATTERS
    BUT NEVER MIND MY LOVE NOTHING MATTERS SAVE SLEEP   212   10
    OUR CONSUMMATION MATTERS OR DOES IT NOT   219   12
    SO LITTLE MATTERS   334   21
    THAT MATTERS SO VERY MUCH   531   25
    WHAT MATTERS IS WHAT WE THRILL TO   531   26
    ONLY THE BEST MATTERS EVEN THE COW KNOWS IT   587   11
    IN ALL MATTERS OF EMOTIONAL IMPORTANCE   604   12
    AND THAT WHICH IS CHOICE ALONE MATTERS   639   27
    ONLY THE BEST MATTERS IN MAN ESPECIALLY   668   1
    ALL THAT MATTERS IS TO BE AT ONE WITH THE LIVING GOD   700   1
    AND SAY WHAT MATTERS ANY MORE WHAT MATTERS   736   7
    WHAT MATTERS ANY MORE BUT ONLY LOVE   736   10
    THERE'S ONLY LOVE THAT MATTERS ANY MORE   736   11
    OH NOTHING MATTERS BUT THE LONGEST JOURNEY   *960   9

MATTHEW
    I MATTHEW AM A MAN   320   3
    I MATTHEW BEING A MAN   320   10
    I AM MATTHEW THE MAN   321   5
    MATTHEW I AM THE MAN   321   19
    I AM MATTHEW THE MAN   323   5
    BUT I MATTHEW BEING A MAN   323   16

MAUDIE
    IF MAUDIE DOESN'T LOVE US   573   9
    MAUDIE IS NOUGHT BUT THE HOUSEKEEPER   573   15
    SO IF MAUDIE DOESN'T SUIT US   573   17

MAUN
    GLADDER NOR OF THY LILIES IF THA MAUN BE TOLD   61   20
    T' CHILDT MAUN TA'E ITS LUCK IT MUN   81   1
    AN' 'ER MAUN TA'E 'ER LUCK   81   2
    BUT WE MAUN MA'E THE BEST ON'T SO NOW ROUSE UP AN' LOOK+ 81   14
    MAUN THA CLING TO THE WA' AS THA STAN'S   139   21
    AY AN' THA MAUN   139   22
    GO THEN SIN' THA MAUN   139   27
    IF THA MAUN KNOW   *921   12
    THE CHILDT MAUN TA'E ITS LUCK IT MAUN   *923   1
    AN' SHE MAUN TA'E HER LUCK   *923   2
    BUT WE MAUN MA'E THE BEST ON'T I'LL REAR THY CHILDT IF + *925   18

MAUVE-RED
    ARE FALLEN AND THEIR MAUVE-RED PETALS ON THE CLOTH   217   28
    ARE FALLEN AND THEIR MAUVE-RED PETALS ON THE CLOTH   *943   11

MAW
    AND DEVOURED YOU WITH THE MACHINE THE VAST MAW OF IRON   630   16

MAWKISH
    FOR HIS OWN DEFICIENCY MOST MAWKISH IN ITS INVERTED SEN+ 842   4

MAYBE
  SOME DEWDROP MAYBE SPLASHED MY FACE DOWN HERE   67 4
  MAYBE YES AND MAYBE NO   95 28
  MAYBE THERE ARE SECRET PLACES   95 29
  MAYBE YES AND MAYBE NO   96 1
  IN ELEPHANTS AND THE EAST ARE TWO DEVILS IN ALL MEN MAY+   390 5
  MAYBE A BLACK EAGLE WITH ITS WINGS OUT   403 25
  NICK OLD NICK MAYBE   404 11
  THOUGH MAYBE THE MAMMOTH GOT TOO BIG IN TUSK AND TEETH   529 17
  AH WELL AH WELL MAYBE   559 21
  MAYBE THEIR LITTLE BOTTOMS   560 1
  MAYBE A SENSE OF DESTINY   560 5
  MAYBE THEY'LL REALISE IT'S TIME   560 7
  MAYBE THEY'RE GETTING TIRED   560 9
  MAYBE LIFE IS STILL OUR PORTION   721 6
  MAYBE THEY KENNEL THE GREY DOG   807 27

MAY-BLOBS
  I AM HERE I AM HERE SCREAMS THE PEEWIT THE MAY-BLOBS BU+   34 9
  DAZZLE OF MAY-BLOBS WHERE THE MARIGOLD GLARE OVERCAST Y+   90 8
  ME YOUR SHADOW ON THE BOG-FLAME FLOWERY MAY-BLOBS   90 15

MAY-BLOSSOM
  MAY-BLOSSOM AND BLUE BIRD'S-EYE FLOWERS FALLING   65 15

MAZE
  UNNOTICED AMONG THEM A STILL QUEEN LOST IN THE MAZE   176 24

MAZY
  NOW SUDDENLY DISTRACTED INTO THIS MAZY SIDE-TRACK   363 3

M A
  BY BOOTS I AM M A   489 4

MEAD
  AND FERTILISE THE WEEDS ON EVERY MEAD   634 5

MEADOW
  YOU SITTING IN THE COWSLIPS OF THE MEADOW ABOVE   90 14
  AND SEE SO NEAR AT OUR FEET IN THE MEADOW   204 15
  LIKE A BOY IN A MEADOW PLAYING   782 30
  IN A MEADOW LOST I LAY   881 22
  AND LIKE A SOD IN A MEADOW   881 29
  SLOW CATTLE STIR ON THE STEEP MEADOW NEAR BY   886 28

MEADOW-LARK
  WHERE THE MEADOW-LARK WEARS HIS COLLAR OF SUBMISSION   768 21
  WHOM THE MEADOW-LARK SINGING SPEAKS TO   769 28
  THE SMILE OF THE LEOPARD AND THE MEADOW-LARK   770 12
  WHERE THE MEADOW-LARK AS HE LIGHTS   771 3

MEADOWS
  AND IN SICILY ON THE MEADOWS OF ENNA   308 10

MEADOW-SWEET
  MEDICINAL OF THE ELDER-FLOWERS WITH MEADOW-SWEET IS BLE+   858 19

MEAL
  CHEW CHEW CHEW CORPSE-BODY AT THE MEAL   584 12
  TILL THE SOUL OF THE STIFF-NECKED IS GROUND TO DUST TO +   616 14
  AND THE PROPER STORE OF MEAL FOR THE LONGEST JOURNEY   721 23
  LET US EAT THE LAST MEAL   756 2
  SETTING THE FLOWERS ALONG THE MIDDAY MEAL   877 28

ME-ALMIGHTY
  AND A ME-ALMIGHTY EYE   414 16

MEALY-MOUTHED
  AND AGREEING WITH ALL THE MEALY-MOUTHED MEALY-MOUTHED   458 18

MEAN
  AT REST IN THE BLUE AND WONDER AT WHAT THEY MEAN   58 15
  THA DOESNA MEAN TER SAY TER ME MOTHER   77 1
  WHY BUT WHAT DOST MEAN   79 22
  DOESN'T TER KNOW WHAT I MEAN TIMMY   79 23
  SO ON WITH THE SLOW MEAN JOURNEY   201 13
  WHAT WOULD IT MEAN THIS   214 10
  DO YOU MEAN TO TELL ME YOU WILL SEE NO FISSURE   278 22
  DO YOU MEAN TO TELL ME THERE SHOULD BE NO FISSURE   278 27
  DO YOU MEAN IT IS WRONG THE GOLD-FILMED SKIN INTEGUMENT   278 29
  I SAY UNTARNISHED BUT I MEAN OPAQUE   298 22
  I THOUGHT HOW PALTRY HOW VULGAR WHAT A MEAN ACT   351 19
  I MEAN PEOPLE LIKE YOU AND ME   435 8
  IT DOESN'T MEAN HANDING IT OUT TO SOME MEAN FOOL OR   449 19
  SO MEAN AND SELF-CONSCIOUS BLOWING AND SNORING   494 20
  PEOPLE FEELING THINGS THEY INTEND TO FEEL THEY MEAN TO +   500 21
  BY WHICH THEY MEAN MORE TALK TALK TALK   502 2
  TO GET A LIVING IN THE DASTARDLY MEAN COMBAT   519 28
  WHY SHOULD WE BRACE OURSELVES UP WITH MEAN EMULATION   520 5
  MEN ARE NOT REALLY MEAN   520 27
  MEN ARE MADE MEAN BY FEAR AND A SYSTEM OF GRAB   520 28
  AND FORCED TO DO A THOUSAND MEAN THINGS MEANER THAN   522 13
  PALE AND MEAN AND INSECT-LIKE SCUTTLING ALONG   526 18
  WHILE PEOPLE MINCE MEAN WORDS THROUGH THEIR TEETH   530 11
  WHAT I MEAN   540 17
  COURSE YOU UNDERSTAND WHAT I MEAN SO WOULD YOU MIND GIV+   546 9
  DO YOU MEAN TO SAY WHAT ABOUT IT   547 17
  IT WAS ONLY AFFECTED AND MEAN   554 14
  I MEAN THEY WERE NEVER ENTIRELY   554 17
  IF YOU KNOW WHAT I MEAN   571 16
  MEAN   577 19
  FIXED ARRANGE YOU UNDERSTAND WHAT I MEAN   582 10
  WE WERE MEANT TO MEAN A GREAT DEAL TO ONE ANOTHER   603 10
  I NEVER KNOW WHAT PEOPLE MEAN WHEN THEY COMPLAIN OF   610 1
  I REALLY WONDER AND WONDER WHAT THEY MEAN   646 3
  DO THEY MEAN THEY ARE A GREAT DEAL ALONE   646 4
  I DON'T KNOW WHAT YOU MEAN   668 18
  WHAT DOES IT MEAN   678 19

MEAN
  DOES IT MEAN THAT LIFE WHICH HAS GONE UGLY AND UNLIVING+   678 20
  BUT THAT WHICH IS MEAN AND BASE AND SQUALID AND DEGENER+   679 3
  O SHED THE UNCLEAN MEAN COWARDLY GREEDY EGOISTIC DEGENE+   679 5
  THE LONG MEAN MARGINAL STRETCHES OF OUR EXISTENCE   722 21
  IS IT ME THE DARK FIRS MEAN   731 6
  WHAT DOES IT MEAN THEY SAY   779 1
  MEAN   807 17
  IS THAT THEY ARE NOT MEAN IN MATERIAL THINGS   828 17
  AND BY GENTLEMAN I MEAN THAT UBIQUITOUS ENGLISHMAN   830 4
  AFTER ALL IT IS IMMORAL FOR A WORD TO MEAN LESS THAN IT+   837 6
  OR TO MEAN MORE THAN IT MEANS   837 7
  LEFT OF THEIR LIGHT AMONG THE MEAN FLOWERS' THRONG   855 16
  THA DOESNA MEAN TO SAY TO ME MOTHER   *918 19
  WHAT BUT WHAT DOST MEAN   *921 18
  DOESN'T TER KNOW WHAT I MEAN TIM YI   *921 19
  ONLY A MEAN ARITHMETIC ON THE FACE OF THINGS   *931 32
  IF THE MEAN DEVIL HAS ANY SEX-FEELING AT ALL   *948 29
  EVERY SINGLE ERECTION OF HIS IS AN ERECTION OF MEAN SPI+   *949 15

ME-AND-THEE
  OF TALK AND THOUGHT AND ME-AND-THEE   470 11
  AND ON THE ME-AND-THEE AND WHAT WE MEANT TO EACH   602 21

MEANER
  IN A MEANER PAGEANT FLOWS   106 10
  AND FORCED TO DO A THOUSAND MEAN THINGS MEANER THAN   522 13
  IT IS THE PENALTY OF FEAR AND MEANNESS BEING MEANER THAN   522 22

MEANEST
  AND SWEAT OF LABOUR AND THE MEANEST FASHION   89 13
  BUT IF A MAN IS IN LOVE WITH HIMSELF ISN'T THAT THE MEA+   447 6

MEANING
  MEANING OR A MESSAGE OVER THE WINDOW GLASS   103 3
  THE MEANING OUT OF THEM   147 17
  LOST ALL ITS MEANING   152 21
  HER FLAKE BY FLAKE AND SPREAD HER MEANING OUT   197 23
  BOUNCE OFF AGAIN MEANING NOTHING ASSERTIONS ASSERTIONS   249 24
  WITHOUT MEANING OR REASON WHY   252 25
  TO BRING THEIR MEANING BACK INTO LIFE AGAIN   298 11
  OUR ACTIVITY HAS LOST ITS MEANING   510 22
  AND LACK OF MEANING   510 29
  MEANING SOUR MAKE YOU PULL A FACE AFTER   530 19
  AND UNCLOTHED THE WORD HAS NO MEANING FOR ME   607 10
  NO MEANING IN THE SKY THE MEANING HAS VANISHED FROM THE   871 14
  OF MY OLD WHITE METAL OF MEANING YOU FINE   873 4
  SHAKE FLAKES OF ITS MEANING ABOUT   *914 27

MEANINGLESS
  OF A MEANINGLESS MONOTONY IS PALLING   65 13
  TELLS DULL MEANINGLESS DISGUSTING TALES   522 7
  THE MIDDLE CLASSES ARE MORE MEANINGLESS   528 3
  HORIZONTAL AND MEANINGLESS DESIRABLY DULL   827 18

MEANNESS
  IT IS THE PENALTY OF FEAR AND MEANNESS BEING MEANER THAN   522 22
  THEIR SUPERIORITY WAS MEANNESS   556 9
  GIRDLING WITH JEWELS THE MEANNESS OF COMMON THINGS   855 2

MEANS
  MEANS BUT TO YOU A BURDEN OF DEAD FLESH   87 26
  MEANS EVEN LESS THAN HER MANY WORDS TO ME   127 24
  THAT MEANS   266 19
  BIRDS HAVE THEIR VOICES EACH MEANS A DIFFERENT THING   368 12
  IT MEANS KINDLING THE LIFE-QUALITY WHERE IT WAS NOT   449 21
  MEANS ANYTHING FURTHER AND PHYSICAL   470 12
  I DON'T WANT TO BE POOR IT MEANS I AM PINCHED   498 16
  AND THE NEW WORD MEANS NOTHING TO US   513 7
  SANITY MEANS THE WHOLENESS OF THE CONSCIOUSNESS   515 1
  WHAT EVERYTHING MEANS   564 28
  BUT I HONESTLY DON'T KNOW WHAT HE MEANS   611 3
  THEY CAN'T LIFE MEANS TOO MUCH TO THEM   647 23
  WHEN THEY ARE PURE WHICH MEANS WHEN THEY ARE QUITE CLEA+   672 2
  MEANS A LIAR   708 6
  IT MEANS PASSING THROUGH THE WATERS OF OBLIVION   727 33
  THERE IS NO MEANS OF REALLY DECEIVING A CHILD   832 14
  EXISTS AND MEANS JUST WHAT IT MEANS   837 4
  AFTER ALL IT IS IMMORAL FOR A WORD TO MEAN LESS THAN IT+   837 6
  OR TO MEAN MORE THAN IT MEANS   837 7
  BUT OF COURSE THIS MEANS SMASHING THE PRESENT SYSTEM OF+   837 27

MEANT
  ALL THAT THE WORLDLY DAY HAS MEANT   41 26
  WHATEVER HE MEANT   293 12
  AND THERE A REAL PINCH BUT ALWAYS WELL MEANT   325 11
  AND THAT HE MEANT IT   389 36
  AND FOUND OUT WHAT THEY REALLY FELT AND REALLY MEANT   504 4
  THAT WAS WHAT THEIR AHEM MEANT   556 8
  THOUGHT HE MEANT THE FACES OF THE POLICE-COURT OFFICIALS   579 19
  TO CONFIRM WHAT HE SAID BUT ALAS HE MEANT   579 21
  AND ON THE ME-AND-THEE AND WHAT WE MEANT TO EACH   602 21
  AND I FAILED ENTIRELY TO SEE WHAT HE MEANT   603 6
  WE WERE MEANT TO MEAN A GREAT DEAL TO ONE ANOTHER   603 10
  WHICH ARE MEANT TO BE THE OLD FOLK-SONG STRAWBERRY FAIR   657 16

MEANWHILE
  MEANWHILE ALAS   317 6
  MEANWHILE IF WE MUST LET US THINK ABOUT IT AND TALK   471 21
  MEANWHILE WE BITE OURSELVES AND EVERYONE NEAR US   833 30

MEASURE
  MY HEART'S RED MEASURE IN HER CUP   123 28
  FROM OFF MY MEASURE TO TOUCH YOU DEEP AND FILL   127 18
  AND FILLS THEM UP A POURING MEASURE   177 2
  THINKING I AM NOT THE MEASURE OF CREATION   339 12
  AND PEOPLE ARE NOT MY MEASURE   527 3
  AS SOON AS YOU LET PEOPLE BE YOUR MEASURE   527 18

MEASURE
  IT AWAY AND YOU MEASURE   565 20
  LADS IN THEIR WARM LIGHT SLIPPERS BOUND DOWN THE HALL T+   865 28
  AND NOW HANGS LIKE THE FRAGRANT CLOSE OF THE MEASURE   868 15
  TO FILL THEM UP A BRIMFUL MEASURE   868 18
  FILLING HIS SINGLE MEASURE WITH MUSIC FULL   877 27
  LIFT UP YOUR MEASURE TO ME TO FILL   *931 10
  MY HEART'S RED MEASURE IN THE CUP   *934 34

MEASURED
  BY HER MEASURED BREATHS I LIKE TO SEE SAID SHE   123 11
  REFUSING TO SIT STILL AND BE MEASURED   524 23

MEASURES
  HANDLED ALL MY TOOLS AND MEASURES   95 18
  THEY HAVE ONLY TWO MEASURES   527 15
  TO FILL THEM UP THEIR BRIMMING MEASURES   *941 18

MEAT
  AND WHITE MEAT   339 29
  WHICH IS JUST A STONE TO ANYONE ASKING FOR MEAT   414 31
  AND IT WAS FOR A FEAST A FEAST OF MEAT FOR MEN AND MAIDS   679 13
  WITH FULL-FED MEAT   828 7

MECHANIC
  UPON THEM AND MOVING THEM HELPLESS MECHANIC THEIR WILL   149 15

MECHANICAL
  MECHANICAL   56 31
  AND MECHANICAL AMERICA MONTEZUMA STILL   298 18
  REPEATS HIMSELF OVER AND OVER IN MECHANICAL MONOTONY OF   479 17
  IN THIS WORLD OF MECHANICAL SELF-ASSERTION   511 5
  AND THERE IS THE MECHANICAL CONNECTION LIKE LEAVES THAT+   615 2
  MECHANICAL MAN IN TRIUMPH SEATED UPON THE SEAT OF HIS M+   624 21
  SO MECHANICAL MAN IN TRIUMPH SEATED UPON THE SEAT OF HI+   624 24
  AND OUT OF THE LIPS OF PEOPLE JERK STRANGE MECHANICAL N+   629 10
  I WITH THEM AM LIVING DEAD MECHANICAL ENSLAVED AT THE   629 28
  MECHANICAL AND INTELLECTUAL   635 29
  IN THEIR FACES AND MOTION NEVER MECHANICAL IN THEIR LIM+   635 31
  MECHANICAL ROBOT   637 24
  FROM THE ROBOT MASS OF RICH AND POOR MECHANICAL EGO-BOU+   637 29
  YOU CAN'T EVEN COUNT ON THE MECHANICAL IMPULSE FOR   639 16
  UNTIL THEY COLLAPSE INTO EGOISM THE MECHANICAL SELF-CEN+   649 4
  GIVE WAY ALL THE TIME BEFORE THE MECHANICAL RUSHING OF +   665 26
  SUBMIT ABJECTLY TO THE BLIND MECHANICAL TRAFFIC-STREAMS+   666 6
  ABOUT PROPERTY AND MONEY AND MECHANICAL DEVICES   666 12
  OF HIS OWN IDEAS AND HIS OWN MECHANICAL DEVICES   667 2
  RESURRECTED FROM THE DEATH OF MECHANICAL MOTION AND EMO+   667 33
  ONLY THE MECHANICAL POWER OF SELF-DIRECTED ENERGY   675 23
  AND ALL SO VERY MECHANICAL   846 11

MECHANICALLY
  LIKE GROSS SUCCESSFUL SLAVES MECHANICALLY WADDLING   526 15
  O SO SMART AND SO MECHANICALLY FINISHED   845 23

MECHANISED
  AND YET AS WE DIE WHY SHOULD NOT OUR VAST MECHANISED   512 27
  NOR ITS MECHANISED ROBOTS ROBOT CLASSES AND MASSES   843 4

MECHANISM
  YOUR WEIRD BRIGHT MOTOR-PRODUCTIVE MECHANISM   292 8
  I AM NOT A MECHANISM AN ASSEMBLY OF VARIOUS SECTIONS   620 10
  AND IT IS NOT BECAUSE THE MECHANISM IS WORKING WRONGLY   620 11
  INTO EVIL NEUTRALITY INTO MECHANISM   713 8
  THE CAGE WHICH DOES NOT KILL THE MECHANISM OF SEX   843 17

MEDALS
  MINT ME BEAUTIFUL MEDALS AND HAND THEM ME HOT   873 1

MEDDLING
  ABSOLUTE SELF-AWARENESS ABSOLVED FROM THE MEDDLING OF C+   712 18

MEDICINAL
  MEDICINAL OF THE ELDER-FLOWERS WITH MEADOW-SWEET IS BLE+   858 19

MEDITERRANEAN
  MEDITERRANEAN FRUIT WITH YOUR COVERT NAKEDNESS   283 19
  HAVE YOU NOT SEEN IN THE WILD WINTER SUN OF THE SOUTHER+   303 4
  MEDITERRANEAN SAVAGES   310 10
  AH MEDITERRANEAN MORNING WHEN OUR WORLD BEGAN   311 14
  FAR-OFF MEDITERRANEAN MORNINGS   311 15
  AND UP THE PALLID SEA-BLENCHED MEDITERRANEAN STONE-SLOP+   311 20

MEDLAR
  IN THE MEDLAR IN THE SORB-APPLE   280 15

MEDLARS
  SORB-APPLES MEDLARS WITH DEAD CROWNS   280 23
  SO IN THE STRANGE RETORTS OF MEDLARS AND SORB-APPLES   281 12
  MEDLARS SORB-APPLES   281 20
  SILVER-PINK PEACH VENETIAN GREEN GLASS OF MEDLARS AND S+   283 5

MEDUSA'S
  LIKE THE SNAKES ON MEDUSA'S HEAD   300 10

MEEK
  AND JESUS ON A MEEK ASS-COLT MARES MARY ESCAPING TO   380 2

MEEKNESS
  IT IS NO GOOD DEAR MEEKNESS AND FORBEARANCE I ENDURED T+   *926 7

MESSAGE
  ON THE SEA WITH NO MESSAGE IN IT AND THE BODY SUBMERGED   428 11

MEET
  UPON MY MIND HIS LIPS MEET MINE AND A FLOOD   43 35
  WHERE HER ARMS AND MY NECK'S THICK PULSE COULD MEET   62 2
  TO MEET   71 4
  BUT WHEN I MEET THE WEARY EYES   72 1
  MEET MINE I OPENED HER HELPLESS EYES TO CONSULT   125 27
  NOTHING TO MEET MY FINGERS BUT THE FLEECE OF NIGHT   147 4
  AT LAST I CAN THROW AWAY WORLD WITHOUT END AND MEET YOU   210 1
  AS THEY CROSS AND PART AND MEET   253 13
  AND THERE OF COURSE YOU MEET A HUGE AND MUD-GREY   387 6
  SERVE ME I AM MEET TO BE SERVED   392 7
  THEN WE ALL ADVANCE TO MEET   401 11
  LET HIM MEET A NEW EMOTION LET HIM BE FACED WITH ANOTHER   431 2
  BUT THE CREATURE THERE THAT HAS COME TO MEET YOU   466 5
  WHEN WE MEET   569 18
  AH THE HOLY SILENCE IT IS MEET   699 1
  HIS EYES MEET MINE AS HE TAKES THE JUG OF WATER   734 27
  AND GIVE THEM PLACE AND HONOUR AND SERVICE MEET   740 15
  SOOTHE THEM WITH SERVICE AND HONOUR AND SILENCE MEET   740 17
  IN OUR SHEAF OF SELF-GATHERED WOUNDS WE GO TO MEET   743 8
  IF YOU MEET MY YOUNG MAN   754 1
  TILL THEY CHANCED TO MEET IN THE LORD'S GREEN ZOO   761 3
  MEET HER AS SHE FLOUNDERS DOWN FROM THE CHICKEN-HOUSE A+   761 20
  IS A SURE WAY TO MEET   764 14
  WITH MEN OF THE AFTERWARDS WALKING TO MEET US FROM   770 9
  AND THEY MEET IN THE GLADE BETWEEN MORNING AND   771 14
  AND MEET THERE   812 4
  MEET ME YOU I LIKE MOST   812 12
  NEVER MEET   820 11
  AND THEREFORE SINCE THE PEOPLE I MEET OF THE YOUNGER   829 4
  THAT LEAP AND MEET TOGETHER AT THE MOUTH   879 34
  AND IT MUST BE SO, EVER WE MUST NOT MEET   880 14
  AND MY EYES MEET HIS VERY QUIETLY   *898 27
  AND MY EYES MEET HIS VERY QUIETLY   *902 11
  WHERE HER ARMS AND MY NECK'S BLOOD-SURGE COULD MEET   *912 10
  DAISIES THAT WAKEN ALL MISTAKEN WHITE-SPREAD IN EXPECTA+   *917 22

MEETING
  ENCROACHING TOWARDS A CRISIS A MEETING A SPASM AND THRO+   66 22
  A MEETING PLACE FOR SUN AND RAIN   504 17
  BECAUSE IT WAS THE SUREST WAY OF MEETING YOU AT LAST   764 24
  HELD A MEETING BEHIND CLOSED DOORS   777 27

MELANCHOLY
  TO LAUGH WHEN WE'RE FEELING MELANCHOLY   814 23

MELLOW
  SOMEWHERE THE LONG MELLOW NOTE OF THE BLACKBIRD   40 25
  OVER THE NEARNESS OF NORWOOD HILL THROUGH THE MELLOW   53 1
  THE MELLOW SUNLIGHT STOOD AS IN A CUP   122 26
  WHILE DOWN HER SIDES THE MELLOW   217 14
  MELLOW AS THE GLORY ROSES   217 26
  MY VERY SELF I WITH THE WONDER MELLOW   218 6
  A LIGHT LIKE MELLOW MOONLIGHT GLEAMED ON THIS WATER   864 29
  OVER THE NEARNESS OF NORWOOD HILL THROUGH THE MELLOW VE+   *905 17
  BUT I WAS ROSY FOR HIM FOR HIM I DID FLUSH MELLOW   *933 25
  THE MELLOW SUNLIGHT STOOD AS IN A CUP   *934 2
  WHILE DOWN HER SIDES THE MELLOW   *942 24

MELODIOUS
  AND USING HIS MOST MELODIOUS WOULD-BE-OXFORD VOICE   433 16

MELODY
  SHAPE SHINES ALONE LIKE A MELODY AND WHERE   872 16

MELT
  THE ROCKS WHERE RAVENS FLYING TO WINDWARD MELT AS A WEL+   57 15
  THE HOUSES FADE IN A MELT OF MIST   142 17
  LIKE SICKENING TOADSTOOLS AND LEFT TO MELT BACK SWIFTLY   491 28
  FORM OF MACHINE CIVILISATION WILL MELT AWAY   611 15
  CAN MELT THE DETACHED LIFE BACK   617 9
  THEY'LL MELT MERCILESSLY BACK INTO SLIME   828 13

MELTED
  AND MELTED IN AN ICY TEAR   62 16
  AN' THA'S LAID AGAINST ME AN' MELTED   80 10
  INTO ME MELTED RIGHT INTO ME LIZZIE   80 11
  AND SO ON TILL THE LAST PLASM OF MY BODY WAS MELTED BACK   365 20
  YOU HAVE MELTED IN THE CRYSTALLINE DISTANCE   696 27
  THA'S LAIN RIGHT UP TO ME LIZZIE AN' MELTED   *922 10
  INTO ME MELTED INTO ME LIZZIE   *922 11
  THE SKIRT OF THE SPIRIT'S EXPERIENCE HAS MELTED AWAY   *959 28

MELTING
  AND BE LOST OUT OF SIGHT WITH YOU LIKE A MELTING FOAM   136 23
  ODD CRUMBS OF MELTING SNOW   304 14
  MY ALL INTO YOUR FLUX YOU MELTING POT   873 3
  THE POWER OF THE MELTING FUSING FORCE   *907 23
  THE POWER OF THE MELTING FUSING FORCE HEAT LIGHT ALL IN+   *909 14

MELTS
  MELTS IN THE AIR WHILE TWO BLACK BIRDS   100 3
  AND THE SUGAR MELTS OUT OF LIFE   455 4

MEMBER
  ALL HIS SOUL IN HIS GALLANT MEMBER   378 13
  O I AM A MEMBER OF THE BOURGEOISIE   490 25
  THE JOLLY LITTLE MEMBER   563 16
  A MEMBER OF THE BRITISH PUBLIC DON'T YOU SEE   570 6
  THE INNOCENT MEMBER THAT A FIG-LEAF WILL SCREEN   578 17
  IF I WAS A MEMBER OF THE CHURCH OF ROME   609 14

MEMBRANE
  BURST THE NIGHT'S MEMBRANE OF TRANQUIL STARS   302 18
  THE SILKEN SHRIEK OF THE SOUL'S TORN MEMBRANE   364 24
  THE MALE SOUL'S MEMBRANE   364 25
  A DARK MEMBRANE OVER THE WILL HOLING A MAN DOWN   407 23
  A MEMBRANE OF SLEEP LIKE A BLACK BLANKET   407 25

MEMBRANE
  TO TEAR THE MEMBRANE OF THIS SLEEP   408   6
  A BLACK MEMBRANE OVER THE FACE   408 16
  OF FINGER OR FIST OR SOFT-SKINNED STICKS UPON THE STRET+   623   6

MEMBRANED
  MEMBRANED BLOOD-VEINED WINGS   322 16

ME MER MERRRRRRR
  ME MER MERRRRRRR   384 12

MEMORIES
  AND MEMORIES CLUSTERED ME CLOSE AND SLEEP WAS CAJOLED   98 30
  OF ROCK DISTILLING OUR MEMORIES   223 18
  LIKE MEMORIES   302 10
  MEMORIES NORTHERN MEMORIES   302 11
  WRAPPED IN THE DARK-RED MANTLE OF WARM MEMORIES   723 19
  TILL ALL MY MEMORIES DROWN   754 16
  THAT I MAY HOLD THEM LIKE MEMORIES IN MY ARMS WHEN I GO+   789 20
  MANTLE OF THE BODY'S STILL MORTAL MEMORIES   *957 11
  WRAPPED IN THE DARK-RED MANTLE OF THE BODY'S MEMORIES   *958 31
  OF THE BODY'S MEMORIES SLIPS AND IS ABSORBED   *959 25

MEMORY
  IN AFTER YEARS IN MEMORY TO YOU   91 24
  OF MEMORY UNROLLS AGAIN TO ME   100 17
  TAKE WHAT YOU'VE GOT YOUR MEMORY OF WORDS   158   7
  DEFENDING THE MEMORY OF LEAVES AND THE HAPPY ROUND NEST   167 10
  THE WORLD IS A PAINTED MEMORY WHERE COLOURED SHAPES   173 17
  AND BREATHING THE FROZEN MEMORY OF HIS WRONG   226   4
  FOR MEMORY TO BE ERASED   262 21
  SOME MEMORY OF FAR SUN-GENTLER LANDS   305 33
  AWAY FROM MEMORY   454   3
  MY GARMENTS OFF BUT ALL EVEN MEMORY   738 10
  RED ON MY MEMORY HEAVY WITH OUR OWN BLOOD   885   3
  DEFENDING THE MEMORY OF BIRDS THAT USED TO NEST   *896 15
  A ROSE OF MEMORY WITH A SCENT OF PRAISE   *941 15
  PAST THE LURKING OCTOPUS ARMS OF AGONISED MEMORY   *959   6

MEN
  AND BEHAVES LIKE THE REST OF MEN   38 32
  BUT THE HOSTS OF MEN WITH ONE VOICE DENY   40 19
  YOU WERE MANY MEN IN ONE   57   1
  IN THE SILENT LABOURS OF MEN IN THE FIELD   68 18
  FOOTSTEPPING TAP OF MEN BENEATH   68 23
  WITHIN THE WOMB NEW SHAPES AND THEN NEW MEN   89 11
  AND FROM THE MEN THAT DANCE AND THE GIRLS THAT LAUGH   89 26
  THE SHROUDED MOTHER OF A NEW IDEA MEN HIDE THEIR FACES   91 26
  DOWN THE NOISE OF MEN   109 28
  AND ALGEBRA IN THE EYES OF DESIROUS MEN   118 23
  WHAT A LOVELY HASTE FOR WISDOM IS IN MEN   119 31
  THA'RT ONE O' TH' MEN AS HAS GOT TO DRAIN   139 15
  LIKE MEN WHO ARE DROWNED BUT FLOAT ERECT IN THE DEEP   146 10
  WE ARE FOLDED TOGETHER MEN AND THE SNOWY GROUND   166 11
  VOICES OF MEN   169 14
  PRESENCE OF MEN   169 25
  IS ONLY SAD MEN TAKING OFF THEIR SHIRTS   173 24
  THESE SHAPES THAT NOW ARE DREAMS AND ONCE WERE MEN   174   2
  FLUENT FIGURES OF MEN GO DOWN THE UPBORNE   174   7
  ALONG THE RAILWAY ACTIVE FIGURES OF MEN   174   9
  OF WALKING OVER THE FACES OF MEN LIKE COBBLE-STONES   175   8
  OH COME OH MEN ALONG THE RAILWAY OH COME AS MEN   175 16
  OH MEN WITH THE AXE AND THE PICK-AXE BREAK THE WALLS OF+   175 26
  AND THE BODIES OF MEN AND WOMEN ARE MOLTEN MATTER OF DR+   176   2
  LET NOW ALL MORTAL MEN TAKE UP   177 11
  PASS THE MEN WHOSE EYES ARE SHUT LIKE ANEMONES IN A DAR+   180 20
  WAYS OF MEN   199   4
  AND THE ISLES AND HER MEN AND HER SCARS   202 16
  THERE ARE FOUR MEN MOWING DOWN BY THE ISAR   219 21
  THE MEN THAT LOUNGE IN A GROUP ON THE WHARF   228 16
  AMONG THE EAGER CORDIAL MEN   228 18
  CHAMPION HER ALL YOU WOMEN MEN MENFOLK   228 27
  MEN ERE HE FALL   228 32
  THIS MEN IS YOURS   229   2
  THE ROUND DARK HEADS OF MEN CROWD SILENTLY   232 21
  IS IT MORE THAN THE APPLES OF SODOM YOU SCORN SO THE MEN   235   7
  STONES WOMEN AND MEN   249 25
  MEN ARE THE SHYEST CREATURES THEY NEVER WILL COME   254 14
  THE MURDERED BODIES OF YOUTHS AND MEN IN HEAPS   258   5
  THAT ARE YOUTHS AND MEN AND ME   258   9
  AFTER THAT THERE WILL ONLY REMAIN THAT ALL MEN DETACH T+   267 24
  MEN THAT ARE SLAIN   269   6
  PROBABLY THEY THINK ALL MEN ADORE THEM   270   2
  FOR MEN TO SHOOT AT PENNY-A-TIME IN A BOOTH AT A FAIR   272 17
  IF THE VIOLETS ARE COMING OUT FROM UNDER THE RACK OF MEN   273 33
  FOR AGES I DON'T CARE A FIG FOR IT MEN SAY BUT WHY A FI+   277   5
  AND ON THE MARGIN MEN SOFT-FOOTED AND PRISTINE   285 24
  TO ME MEN ARE PALPABLE INVISIBLE NEARNESSES IN THE DARK   289   1
  YOUR IRON MEN   291   3
  ETRUSCAN-DUSKY WAVERING MEN OF OLD ETRURIA   296 19
  DUSKY SLIM MARROW-THOUGHT OF SLENDER FLICKERING MEN OF   297   6
  LONG-NOSED MEN OF ETRURIA   297 15
  SUNBLACK MEN   301 28
  RED ANGRY MEN ARE A RACE EXTINCT ALAS   317 12
  AND PASSIONATE DISQUALITY OF MEN   317 17
  AND I IF I BE LIFTED UP WILL DRAW ALL MEN UNTO ME   320   4
  TO DRAW ALL MEN UNTO ME   320 12
  SEEING I AM ON A PAR WITH ALL MEN   320 13
  AM DRAWN TO THE UPLIFTED AS ALL MEN ARE DRAWN   320 15
  DRAWING ALL MEN UNTO THEE BUT BOUND TO RELEASE THEM WHEN   323   8
  AWAY FROM AMONG GODS AND MEN HE DID NOT SEE THAT HE WAS+   348   2
  WINGS AND MEN WHO SEE HIM WHEELING ARE FILLED WITH THE +   368   5
  RED HEARTS OF MEN   374   8
  BY THE LIFE IN THE HEARTS OF MEN   374 33
  THEIR HANDS AND PRODUCE WORKS OF ART AS MEN DO HORSES W+   376   2
  AND MEN BEING MOSTLY GELDINGS AND KNACKER-BONED HACKS   379 31
  YOU GO DOWN SHADE TO THE RIVER WHERE NAKED MEN SIT ON   386 23
  NAKED MEN ARE THRESHING RICE   386 28

MEN
  NAKED DARK MEN BENEATH   387 27
  SOCKETS AMONG BARE FEET OF ELEPHANTS AND MEN ON THE   388 31
  TOM-TOMS WEIRD MUSIC OF THE DEVIL VOICES OF MEN FROM   388 35
  NAKED DARK MEN WITH ORNAMENTS ON ON THEIR NAKED ARMS   369   7
  MEN ALL MOTION   389 21
  WHAT WOULD THEY DO THOSE JUNGLE MEN RUNNING WITH SWEAT   389 32
  IN ELEPHANTS AND THE EAST ARE TWO DEVILS IN ALL MEN MAY+   390   5
  MEN   401   4
  SOFT GRASS RUNS UPON A PATH THAT IS PATHLESS TO MEN SO +   406   3
  WHITE MEN MAKE GOLD-MINES AND THE MOUNTAINS UNMAKE   407 13
  AND INSTEAD THE WHITE MEN SCRAMBLE ASLEEP IN THE   408   9
  RED MEN STILL STICK THEMSELVES OVER WITH BITS OF HIS FL+   414   3
  OVERWEENING MEN FULL OF POWER OF LIFE COMMANDING A   414 19
  EAGLE OF THE ROCKIES BIRD OF MEN THAT ARE MASTERS   414 21
  AND WE MEN ARE PUT OUT   436 14
  WE ARE SO TIRED OF MEN   436 29
  YET O MY YOUNG MEN THERE IS A VIVIFIER   439 15
  AND STRONG MEN   439 27
  YET O MY YOUNG MEN THERE IS A VIVIFIER   440   1
  AND FUSE IN A BROAD HARD FLAME OF MANY MEN IN A ONENESS   440   8
  O PILLARS OF FLAME BY NIGHT O MY YOUNG MEN   440   9
  WHEN THE FIRE REACHES US O MY YOUNG MEN   440 14
  BUT AS FOR THE MILLS OF MEN   441 15
  YOU ARE NO LONGER MEN THAT IS BOURGEOIS   443   2
  YOU'VE NO IDEA WHEN MEN ARE IN LOVE WITH THEMSELVES   447   8
  HE MIGHT POSSIBLY LIKE MEN IF HE WEREN'T TOO FRIGHTENED   447 13
  THINGS MEN HAVE MADE WITH WAKENED HANDS AND PUT SOFT   448   1
  WARM WITH THE LIFE OF FORGOTTEN MEN WHO MADE THEM   448   3
  MEN SHOULD REFUSE TO BE LIFELESSLY AT WORK   450   5
  MEN SHOULD REFUSE TO BE HEAPS OF WAGE-EARNING DUNG   450   6
  MEN SHOULD REFUSE TO WORK AT ALL AS WAGE-SLAVES   450   7
  MEN SHOULD DEMAND TO WORK FOR THEMSELVES OF THEMSELVES   450   8
  FOR GOD'S SAKE LET US BE MEN   450 12
  MEN MIGHT PUT THEM FORTH AS A SNAIL ITS SHELL AS A BIRD+   451 12
  AND SO IT WILL BE AGAIN MEN WILL SMASH THE MACHINES   451 20
  WHY HAVE WORKING CLASSES AT ALL AS IF MEN WERE ONLY   452   5
  WHY NOT HAVE MEN AS MEN AND THE WORK AS MERELY PART   452   7
  AND HAVE A WORLD OF MEN   453 12
  RISE THEN MY YOUNG MEN RISE AT THEM   457   3
  MUSHY PATHETIC YOUNG MEN   457 14
  FROM ALL SORTS OF MEN DON'T BE BEHOLDEN   458 28
  AND SEES STRANGE LOOKS ON THE FACES OF MEN   459 27
  THEY WOULD NOT BE MEN AND THEY MUST BE MEN   460 21
  OF MEN THEY CLENCH FEAR IN THEIR FISTS   460 28
  AND STILL THE GREAT NEEDS OF MEN   461 18
  THE KEY OF LIFE ON THE BODIES OF MEN   461 23
  BEWARE O MY DEAR YOUNG MEN OF GOING ROTTEN   462 17
  AND IT'S FUNNY MY DEAR YOUNG MEN THAT YOU IN YOUR   462 29
  FOR OBSCENITY AFTER ALL MY DEAR YOUNG MEN   463   1
  MEN   463   6
  SEX ISN'T SIN IT'S A DELICATE FLOW BETWEEN WOMEN AND MEN   464 14
  MEN AND WOMEN LET US BE   470   6
  SLOWLY UP IN THE BLOOD OF MEN   470 26
  BETWEEN MEN AND MEN MEN AND WOMEN AND EARTH AND   482   6
  MEN SELL THEMSELVES FOR A WAGE AND EMPLOYERS LOOK OUT   483   2
  AND MEN AND THE BREAD OF MEN   483 13
  OF MEN IN BOWLER HATS HURRYING   484   4
  NEVER MY YOUNG MEN   484 12
  ALL MEN ARE IN CAPTIVITY   484 25
  AMONG MEN   486 17
  MEN ARE NOT BAD WHEN THEY ARE FREE   488   1
  PRISON MAKES MEN BAD AND THE MONEY COMPULSION MAKES   488   2
  MEN BAD   488   3
  IF MEN WERE FREE FROM THE TERROR OF EARNING A LIVING   488   4
  AND MEN WOULD WORK GAILY   488   6
  WHERE SMART MEN WOULD DISPENSE   488 24
  CARRY THE SALT OF THE EARTH THE WISDOM OF WISE MEN   495   2
  THE ONLY THING MEN INVARIABLY FIGHT FOR   497 19
  I WOULD LIKE A FEW MEN TO BE AT PEACE WITH   499 20
  BUT MEN TO BE AT PEACE WITH   499 25
  WHEN MEN ARE MADE IN BOTTLES   501   1
  I WISH MEN WOULD GET BACK THEIR BALANCE AMONG THE ELEME+   505 17
  WORK CAN BE FUN AND MEN CAN ENJOY IT THEN IT'S NOT   517 20
  MEN HAVE BEEN WANTING TO TRIUMPH TRIUMPH TRIUMPH   519   2
  THOUGH MOST BIRDS HAVE TO PAY WITH THEIR LIVES WHERE MEN   520   3
  THE EFFORTS OF MEN LIKE THE EFFORTS OF BIRDS IN SPRING   520   9
  MEN ARE NOT REALLY MEAN   520 27
  MEN ARE MADE MEAN BY FEAR AND A SYSTEM OF GRAB   520 28
  THAT EVER TURNED MEN INTO FIENDS   521   6
  YOUNG MEN HAVING NO REAL JOY IN LIFE AND NO HOPE IN THE   521 20
  AND WIMBLY-WAMBLY YOUNG MEN OF SEX STILL MORE INDETERMI+   522   4
  MEN   522 30
  OR WE MUST SEE MEN DIE AND THEN DIE OURSELVES   522 31
  AND LEAVES MEN LIVING CLAY   524   9
  IF MEN WERE AS MUCH MEN AS LIZARDS ARE LIZARDS   524 17
  MEN SHOULD GROUP THEMSELVES INTO A NEW ORDER   525 10
  WE BELONG NEITHER TO MEN NOR OUR CHILDREN NOR   525 25
  I AM A DEMOCRAT IN SO FAR AS I LOVE THE FREE SUN IN MEN   526   7
  BUT WHEN I SEE THESE GREY SUCCESSFUL MEN   526 13
  AND WHEN I SEE WORKING MEN   526 17
  CENSORS ARE DEAD MEN   528 10
  BUT CENSORS BEING DEAD MEN   528 14
  BREATHING OF THE DEAD MEN   528 20
  IT REALLY MAKES US MEN   529   5
  SO THAT'S WHY SO MANY YOUNG MEN HAVE LONG FACES   530 21
  ENGLAND WAS ALWAYS A COUNTRY OF MEN   535 15
  MEN FIGHT FOR LIBERTY AND WIN IT WITH HARD KNOCKS   535 23
  SO OUR GOODY-GOOD MEN BETRAY US   537   7
  I SUPPOSE WHEN THE MEN ALL STARTED BEING WILLY WET-LEGS   537 28
  IF MEN ONLY FOUGHT OUTWARDS INTO THE WORLD   538 15
  BUT WHEN MEN TURN WILLY WET-LEGS   538 18
  THE MEN STOOD AROUND LIKE CROCUSES AGAPE IN THE SUN   540   4
  EH MEN DOESNA HA'E BOSOMS 'APPEN NOT ON'Y THA KNOWS   540 16
  UP THERE BUT NOT ANY MEN   552 16
  ALAS MY POOR YOUNG MEN   558 15
  FOR POOR YOUNG WRETCHED MEN   558 20
  MEN   578 19

MEN
  MEN AGAIN   585   5
  WHAT HAVE THEY DONE TO YOU MEN OF THE MASSES   585   9
  FLOWERS OF GRASS FINE MEN   587   23
  MEN ARE UNSEEN BENEATH THE SHADING HATS   606   5
  SOMETIMES THE SUN TURNS HOSTILE TO MEN   608   20
  BUT A DEMOCRACY OF MEN A DEMOCRACY OF TOUCH   611   9
  ONCE MEN TOUCH ONE ANOTHER THEN THE MODERN INDUSTRIAL   611   14
  LOOK AT THE YOUNG MEN UNDER THIRTY   612   9
  TO SWAY THE EARTH OF MEN   614   10
  TO FERTILISE THE ROOTS OF UNKNOWN MEN WHO ARE STILL TO +   614   24
  AND MEN OFTEN SUCCUMB LIKE WHITE MICE IN A LABORATORY A+   619   22
  AND TURN ONCE MORE TO MEN TO SAVE THEM PERSEUS ST GEORGE   619   26
  MEN AND WOMEN SHOULD LEARN TENDERNESS TO EACH OTHER   620   3
  TO BE HUMBLE BEFORE OTHER MEN IS DEGRADING I AM HUMBLE +   622   1
  SINGING TO THE MEN BELOW THE FELLOW-TRIBESMEN   623   20
  ARE THESE NO LONGER MEN THESE MILLIONS MILLIONS   629   14
  THAT WITH SO MANY DEAD MEN IN MILLS   629   24
  DEATH OF MY FELLOW MEN   630   8
  WHEN THE VAST MASSES OF MEN HAVE BEEN CAUGHT BY THE   631   11
  AND STILL I LOOK FOR THE MEN WHO WILL DARE TO BE   634   21
  MEN WHO ARE WILD ROSES OF ENGLAND   634   24
  OF OTHER MEN   635   18
  BUT OH MEN MEN STILL UNMECHANISED   635   23
  AND THE SONS OF MEN WITH THE WIND AND THE FIRE OF LIFE   635   30
  MEN ON THIS SIDE WOMEN ON THAT SIDE   636   3
  TO SET ALL MEN FREE   636   17
  TO MAKE ALL MEN NOBLE   635   18
  UNLESS MEN SWIFTLY DIVIDE AGAIN AND THE BASE ARE THRUST   637   14
  LESS THAN REAL MEN INFERIORS INFERIORS   637   26
  HOW THEN ARE THE FEW MEN MEN OF THE WIND AND RAIN   637   27
  MEN OF THE FIRE AND ROCK HOW ARE THEY GOING TO COME FOR+   637   28
  MEN ARE NOT ALIKE IN THE SIGHT OF GOD   638   7
  MEN ARE ANYTHING BUT ALIKE IN THE SIGHT OF GOD   638   9
  MOST MEN DON'T MATTER AT ALL ANY MORE THAN ANTS MATTER   638   11
  TO MEN   638   12
  WHEN MOST MEN DIE TODAY   638   20
  OH MEN LIVING MEN VIVID MEN OCEAN AND FIRE   639   1
  AND ROBOTS MUST HAVE ENCOURAGEMENT FROM MEN OF THE   639   8
  OH MEN OF LIFE AND OF LIVING   639   11
  ONCE DISILLUSION FALLS ON LIVING MEN AND THEY FEEL THE   639   19
  FOR THESE MASSES AND CLASSES OF MEN   639   22
  ONCE DISILLUSION FALLS ON LIVING MEN AND ILLUSION OF BR+ 639   23
  AND THEN WHEN THE SOUL OF LIVING MEN REPUDIATES THEM   640   7
  BY THE KINDNESS OF LIVING WOMEN AND MEN   640   14
  NOW LIVING WOMEN AND MEN ARE THREATENED WITH EXTINCTION   640   15
  MEN WANTED TO BE LIKE GODS   640   25
  AND MEN HAVE PERFORCE TO BE LITTLE DYNAMOS   641   6
  SONS OF MEN FROM THE WOMBS OF WISTFUL WOMEN   642   16
  SONS OF MEN WITH THE WONDERING EYES OF LIFE   642   18
  O STEP ASIDE WITH DECISION SONS OF MEN WITH DECISION   642   29
  AND LIVED TO LEARN THEY ARE NEITHER FELLOW NOR MEN   644   2
  MEN IN THE STREET   648   6
  IN THE MEN WHO HAVE NEVER FALLEN IN LIFE   648   15
  SERVING WITH DELIGHT AND WITH REVERENCE THOSE MEN WHOSE+ 648   20
  ALL MEN ARE WORSHIPPERS   649   1
  ALL MEN WORSHIP THE WONDER OF LIFE   649   3
  BUT EVEN IN PRISTINE MEN THERE IS THE DIFFERENCE   649   6
  SOME MEN CAN SEE LIFE CLEAN AND FLICKERING ALL ROUND   649   7
  SOME MEN LOOK STRAIGHT INTO THE EYES OF THE GODS   649   9
  AND SOME MEN CAN SEE NO GODS THEY ONLY KNOW   649   10
  MEN WHO SEE   649   12
  BY THE TRANSMITTED GLEAM FROM THE FACES OF VIVIDER MEN   649   14
  THERE ARE TWO CLASSES OF MEN   649   19
  AND THOSE THAT LOOK INTO THE EYES OF THE FEW OTHER MEN   649   21
  AH YES MEN MUST LEARN TO SERVE   650   12
  AH YES MEN MUST LEARN TO OBEY   650   14
  BUT IT IS ONLY UNHAPPY MEN MAKING A NOISE   656   6
  AND THE MUSIC OF MEN IS LIKE A MOUSE GNAWING   656   10
  SOME MEN LIVE FOR THE CONCEITED FURNITURE OF THEIR MINDS 657   7
  HOW THE GODS MUST HATE MOST OF THE OLD OLD MEN TODAY   662   15
  THE RANCID OLD MEN THAT DON'T DIE   662   16
  OLD MEN OLD OBSTINATE MEN AND WOMEN   663   4
  ONE NOTICES MEN HERE AND THERE GOING HESITATINGLY FALTE+ 665   23
  AND THESE THE MINORITY OF MEN WHO CAN STILL SEE THE LIG+ 665   25
  NOW ABOVE ALL IS THE TIME FOR THE MINORITIES OF MEN   666   1
  AND ME AND YOU MINORITIES OF MEN AND WOMEN   667   5
  WHEN MEN AND WOMEN WHEN LADS AND GIRLS ARE NOT THINKING 672   1
  WHEN MEN THINK THEY ARE LIKE GODS   673   4
  THEY ARE USUALLY MUCH LESS THAN MEN   673   5
  MEN PREVENT ONE ANOTHER FROM BEING MEN   677   17
  AND IT WAS FOR A FEAST A FEAST OF MEAT FOR MEN AND MAIDS 679   13
  ON A DAY OF SPLENDOUR FOR THE FURTHER SPLENDOUR OF BEIN+ 679   14
  MEN DON'T ACHIEVE THEIR OWN MANHOOD ALAS OH ALAS ALAS   683   23
  ALL I WANT OF YOU MEN AND WOMEN   683   24
  IT IS AEGEAN SHIPS AND MEN WITH ARCHAIC POINTED BEARDS   687   6
  AND NOW THAT THE MOON WHO GIVES MEN GLISTENING BODIES   688   10
  SLIM NAKED MEN FROM CNOSSOS SMILING THE ARCHAIC SMILE   688   13
  MEN SLIMLY WENT LIKE FISHES AND DIDN'T CARE   688   22
  HARK THE LOW AND SHATTERING LAUGHTER OF BEARDED MEN   689   2
  MEN SINGING AND WOMEN BRUSHING THEIR HAIR IN THE +   691   24
  BE GOOD TO ME NOW AS I BEG YOU AS YOU'VE ALWAYS BEEN GO+ 696   9
  SOME YOU MAY SING THROUGH AND ALL MEN HEAR   711   8
  AND MEN THAT SIT IN MACHINES   711   26
  THEY LET DEATH UPON UNSEEN MEN   715   14
  NOW SOME MEN MUST GET UP AND DEPART   715   19
  THE EVIL WILL IN MANY EVIL MEN   716   1
  MEN MUST DEPART FROM IT OR ALL IS LOST   716   15
  EVERYWHERE MEN AND WOMEN ALIGHT WITH GOD   742   31
  AND NOT LIKE MEN   748   8
  IT SMELLS STRANGE LIKE THE SHOUTING OF MEN   759   2
  WHERE WHITE MAID ARE THE MEN YOU HAVE LOVED   759   18
  MEN DUMB IN THE DUSK   763   28
  BUT MEN   763   29
  MEN IN THE DUSK   764   4
  OH MEN DUMB IN THE DARKNESS   765   3
  OH MEN DEARER THAN SUCCESS TO ME   765   4
  MEN DEARER TO ME THAN PEACE   765   5

MEN
  SHE SEES MEN WALKING TOWARDS HER UNDER THE TREES   770   1
  WITH MEN OF THE AFTERWARDS WALKING TO MEET US FROM   770   9
  AND SEES WHAT HE SEES IN THE FACES OF MEN   771   5
  THE MEN COME IN BY THE FURNACE-GATE OF THE WEST   771   10
  THE MEN WITH THEIR FACES IN SHADE   771   13
  BUT A GERM IN THE HEARTS OF MEN AND WOMEN AMERICANS   774   31
  ON GOOD FRIDAY THE BIG WHITE MEN OF THE INDIAN BUREAU   777   24
  AND THE BIG WHITE MEN FROM WASHINGTON DROVE OUT TO   777   25
  THE PUEBLO SUMMONED THE OLD INDIAN MEN AND   777   26
  THEN THE BIG MEN OF THE WHITE AMERICANS   777   28
  WITH THE WHITE MEN HIS BROTHERS   778   16
  THE WHITE MEN DROVE AWAY   778   34
  AND THE OLD DARK-FACED MEN CAME OUT HEAVILY WITH A   778   35
  AND CONTROLLED BY MEN OF SCIENCE COMPETENT   780   7
  ANTHROPOLOGISTS HISTORIANS AND MEN OF LETTERS   780   8
  IN EVERY WAY AND THE LORDS AMONG MEN   787   28
  HE SAT WITHIN THE HOLLOW OF A CLOUD AND SAW THE MEN THA+ 790 10
  HE SAW THE MEN THAT WERE BLIND REELING WITH AGUARDIENTE 790 12
  AND TWO MEN LOOKED UP   791   9
  ARE ABOUT TO DANCE THE WAR DANCE ROUND YOU MEN   792   18
  OF THOSE ILL-SMELLING TRIBES OF MEN THESE FROGS THAT CA+ 792 23
  THESE WHITE MEN AND RED MEN AND YELLOW MEN AND BROWN MEN 792 29
  AND BLACK MEN   792   30
  FOR MEN UPON THE BODY OF THE EARTH ARE LIKE LICE   793   1
  SO TELL THE MEN I AM COMING TO   793   5
  TO PREPARE TO BE MEN   793   8
  AND THITHER THEY RETURN FROM THE LAND OF MEN   799   4
  WHEN YOU TURN TO YOUR WIVES AS BRAVE MEN TURN TO THEIR + 800 12
  I TELL YOU YOU ARE NOT MEN ALONE   800   16
  IF YOU WERE MEN WITH THE MORNING STAR   800   29
  AND YOU ARE MEN WHO SHOULD BE MEN OF THE MORNING STAR 800   34
  AND THE FEET OF MEN AND THE HANDS OF THE WOMEN KNOW ME 801 18
  I WAIT BEHIND MEN   804   18
  OF THE ANGER OF THE MANHOOD OF MEN   805   9
  WAITING BEHIND MEN   805   26
  OH MEN TAKE CARE TAKE CARE   806   7
  SERPENT IN THE BELLIES OF MEN   806   12
  FIRE OF THE PASSION OF MEN   806   14
  IN THE NIGHT I SEE THE GREY DOGS CREEPING OUT OF THE SL+ 807 11
  OF THE MEN AND THE WOMEN WHO WALK AMONG YOU   807   24
  MEN THAT SEEM HARMLESS WOMEN WITH FAIR WORDS   807   26
  BRAVE MEN HAVE PEACE AT NIGHTFALL   810   7
  TRUE MEN LOOK UP AT THE DAWN   810   8
  MEN IN THEIR MANHOOD WALK OUT   810   9
  ALL MEN COVER THEIR EYES   811   9
  ALL MEN BE LOST IN SILENCE   811   11
  FIRE IN YOUR HEARTS OH MEN   811   25
  BE THERE ALONG WITH ME OH MEN   813   5
  IT FLOWERED BEFORE MEN TOOK TO FLOWERING FOR WAGES   814   5
  FOLK-FLOWERS HAVE FADED MEN HAVE GROWN COLD   814   16
  THAT IS THE MEN OF MY AGE AND I AM FORTY-THREE   828   15
  THE MEN OLDER THAN ME   828   22
  NOT ON WHAT MEN THINK   831   18
  WHEN I SEE WHAT A MESS MEN HAVE MADE OF THE WORLD   837   12
  WHEN I SEE WHAT MESSES MEN HAVE MADE OF THEMSELVES   837   13
  THE LATENT DESIRE IN ALL DECENT MEN TODAY   837   23
  DETERMINED EFFORT AMONG MEN   838   2
  IT IS TIME MEN TOOK THEIR THOUGHTS OFF WOMEN   838   5
  AND SINCE WOMEN ARE INSIDE THE PRISON JUST AS MUCH AS M+ 838 9
  THE MEN IN THE END ONLY HATE THEM BECAUSE THE ESCAPE WA+ 838 10
  THE THING FOR MEN TO DO IS TO START TO PULL DOWN MONEY 838 11
  I COULD ACCEPT MEN   840   3
  THE FRAME OF THINGS HAS GROWN SO HEAVY IT'S JUST TOO HE+ 842 29
  AND MEN ARE LICE THAT CREEP ON IT   843   8
  AS IF FOR HIM ALONE OF ALL OUR MEN   877   29
  THE MEN UPLIFTED ON THE NEW WHITE WOODSTACK STAND   *895   1
  FLUENT ACTIVE FIGURES OF MEN PASS ALONG THE RAILWAY   *906   16
  THE FASCINATION OF THE RESTLESS CREATOR THROUGH THE MES+ *906 23
  FLUENT ACTIVE FIGURES OF MEN PASS ALONG THE RAILWAY AND+ *908 11
  ALONG THE RAILWAY ACTIVE FIGURES OF MEN   *908   13
  OF MEN VIBRATING IN ECSTASY THROUGH THE ROUNDED FLESH *908 21
  IN THE FAR-OFF LABOUR OF MEN IN THE FIELD   *915   2
  FOOTSTEPPING TAP OF MEN BENEATH   *915   7
  THE SHROUDED MOTHER OF A NEW IDEA MEN HIDE THEIR FACES *926 19
  A CUNNING ALGEBRA IN THE FACES OF MEN   *932   1
  THERE'S FOUR MEN MOWING DOWN BY THE RIVER   *944   1
  IT IS FOR MEN HE'S AN INSTINCTIVE HOMOSEXUAL   *948   30
  WHEN MEN WOVE WITH THEIR HANDS AND THEIR SOUL'S ATTENTI+ *949 26
  MEN USED TO PUT THEM FORTH SENSITIVELY LIKE BOUGHS LEAV+ *950 2
  BOWERS OF MEN   *950   5
  AH NO IN THE HEARTS OF SOME MEN THERE STILL IS SANCTUARY *953 23

MENACE
  YOUR STUFF ALL GONE YOUR MENACE ALMOST RASED   53   23
  THEY DEMAND AS THEY STAND IN MENACE OVER AGAINST US   740   0

MENACING
  SAID THE LOVELY YOUNG LADY HALF WISTFUL HALF MENACING 604   7

MENAGERIE
  WOULD STOCK A MENAGERIE   469   26

MENDED
  AND CAN'T BE MENDED   638   23

MENDING
  MENDING AND TINNING THE PANS OF ALL THE VILLAGE   520   15

MENFOLK
  CHAMPION HER ALL YOU WOMEN MEN MENFOLK   228   27

MEN-PEASANTS
  MEN-PEASANTS FROM JUNGLE VILLAGES DANCING AND RUNNING 389   5

MEN'S
WHERE DEAD MEN'S LIVES GLOW GENTLY AND IRON HURTS   173 22
TO ME MEN'S FOOTFALLS FALL WITH A DULL SOFT RUMBLE   288 28

MENTAL
IS ONLY MENTAL DIRT   463 2
ALL THIS OBSCENITY IS JUST MENTAL MENTAL MENTAL   463 7
OF THE ITCHING MIND AND THE MENTAL SELF WITH ITS PRURIE+ 465 5
O YOU WITH MENTAL FINGERS O NEVER PUT YOUR HAND ON ME   468 24
O YOU WITH MENTAL BODIES STAY A LITTLE DISTANCE FROM ME   468 25
IN MENTAL CONTACT GAY AND SAD   469 2
O LEAVE ME CLEAN FROM MENTAL FINGERING   469 19
FROM ALL THE MENTAL POETRY   469 23
TO PROCEED FROM MENTAL INTIMACY   470 18
DAY OF THE MENTAL WELTER AND BLETHER   471 17
HE IS CEREBRAL INTELLECTUAL MENTAL SPIRITUAL   473 17
ENCLOSED IN HIS OWN LIMITED MENTAL CONSCIOUSNESS   474 27
OR THE MENTAL EFFORT OF MAKING HER ACQUAINTANCE   506 18
BUT I AM A LIAR I FEEL NO LOVELINESS IT IS A MENTAL REM+ 509 27
POOR MENTAL WORM   529 16
THEY MUST GO ON SCRATCHING THE ECZEMA OF THEIR MENTAL I+ 533 9
AND SOUNDER THAN ALL INSURANCE IS A SHINY MENTAL CONCEIT 543 3
MENTAL FURNITURE   657 3
I CALL IT MENTAL CONCEIT AND MYSTIFICATION   708 18
FOR AT PRESENT IN THE WHIRRING INSANITY OF THE MENTAL C+ 839 5

MENTALITY
WRIGGLE AND WAG AND SLAVER AND GET THE MENTALITY OF A D+ 645 4

MENTALLY
AND IN THE BODY WE CAN ONLY MENTALLY FORNICATE   472 8
SO IT NEVER MOVED ON ANY MORE EXCEPT MENTALLY AND IN ME+ 841 14

MERCIFUL
A MOMENT AND SHE WAS TAKEN AGAIN IN THE MERCIFUL DARK   *912 24
TO WITHER ON THE BOSOM OF THE MERCIFUL SO MANY SEEDS TH+ *926 27

MERCILESS
THEN MERCILESS AND RUTHLESS   203 1

MERCILESSLY
THEY'LL MELT MERCILESSLY BACK INTO SLIME   828 13

MERCURY
OH WHEN MERCURY CAME TO LONDON   581 14
WHEN MERCURY AND LOVE AND DEATH   658 16

MERCY
NO LONGER AT THE MERCY   627 13
THE MERCY THE MERCY   627 14
HE IS SO ABSOLUTELY AT YOUR MERCY   776 33
AND SO HIDEOUSLY DANGEROUS TO BE AT THE MERCY   839 13

MERE
HEARING MY MERE LIPS SHOUT   124 21
THE MERE FRUIT OF YOUR WOMB   235 4
MERE FEMALE ADJUNCT OF WHAT I WAS   264 22
AND TO BE LIMITED BY A MERE WORD IS TO BE LESS THAN A H+ 292 4
HIBISCUS AND MERE GRASS   316 2
A MERE OBSTACLE   356 28
BUT THE FEATHERS WERE COMPARATIVELY A MERE FLEA-BITE   413 17
THAT FLOWER IN MERE MOVEMENT   446 10
MERE EVACUATION-LUST   466 8
EITHER IN ANGER OR TENDERNESS OR DESIRE OR SADNESS OR W+ 672 4
ON AND ON AND THEIR TRIUMPH IN MERE MOTION   675 26
HE IS POLITICIAN OR MAGNATE OR MERE INDIVIDUAL   775 9
SO IT NEVER MOVED ON ANY MORE EXCEPT MENTALLY AND IN ME+ 841 14
AS I CAME HOME IN THE DUSK DESPOILED BY SCHOOL A MERE B+ 864 27
HEARING MY MERE LIPS SHOUT   *935 21

MERELY
NOT THAT YOU'RE MERELY A SOFTY OH DEAR ME NO   396 16
ON THE CONTRARY HE MERELY GIVES HIMSELF AWAY   433 1
INSTEAD OF MERELY THE SMELL OF MAN   444 14
HE IS LIVING NOT MERELY WORKING   450 26
WHY NOT HAVE MEN AS MEN AND THE WORK AS MERELY PART   452 7
NOT MERELY THE PERSONAL UPSTART   466 4
IS MERELY RIDICULOUS   478 13
MY DEARS DON'T LOOK AT ME I AM MERELY TERRIFIED OF YOU   541 10
ALL THAT WE KNOW IS NOTHING WE ARE MERELY CRAMMED WASTE+ 613 8
ALL THIS TALK OF EQUALITY BETWEEN THE SEXES IS MERELY AN 620 1
BUT BRAINY ROBOT OR AESTHETIC ROBOT OR MERELY MUSCULAR + 637 23
IT IS MERELY A MACHINE BREAKS DOWN   638 22
YOU TO WHOM THE SUN IS MERELY SOMETHING THAT MAKES THE   643 13
THEY'LL MERELY DESTROY ALL PROPERTY AND A GREAT MANY PE+ 665 1
IF IT IS MERELY VENUS OR HERMES YOU ARE THINKING OF   678 6
NOT MERELY LOSS   768 5
MONEY IS MERELY   826 22
HE IS LIVING NOT MERELY WORKING   *949 25

MEREST
TO LEAVE BUT ONLY THE MEREST POSSIBLE TAINT   53 31
LET THE MEREST SCALLYWAG COME TO THE DOOR AND YOU LEAP   398 15

MERE TORTUE
I HEARD A WOMAN PITYING HER PITYING THE MERE TORTUE   361 31

MERGE
BUT YOU YOU SNOUT-FACE YOU REJECT NOTHING YOU MERGE SO   399 9

MERGING
NOT IN MIXING MERGING NOT IN SIMILARITY   267 5
AND MERGING ONESELF   337 5
OF SUNSET BUT MERGING UNNOTICED INTO THE ROSY GLIMMER   860 5

MERINGUE
AND THEN WATCH HIM GO SOGGY LIKE A WET MERINGUE   431 6

MERR ERERRR ERE
MERR ERERRR ERE   384 14

MERR ERR ERR ME
MERR ERR ERR ME   384 8

MERRILY
CLINGING MERRILY   860 28

MERRIMENT
LIKE A GIRL'S TWINKLING MERRIMENT AT NIGHT WHEN THE SEA+ 860 16

MERRR
MERRR   384 10

MERRY
WITH A LAUGH AND A MERRY WILDNESS THAT IT WAS SHE   180 15
BY NATURE THAN BY BOOTS AND WET FEET OFTEN CARRY MERRY + 866 15

MESA
STANDING WITHOUT FEET ON THE RIM OF THE FAR-OFF MESA   403 5
DOWN ON MY HEARTH-RUG OF DESERT SAGE OF THE MESA   408 27

MESH
LIKE THE SOUGH OF A WIND THAT IS CAUGHT UP HIGH IN THE +   58 1
IN A LOVELY ILLUMINED MESH   111 32
IN A TISSUE AS ALL THE MOLTEN CELLS IN THE LIVING MESH   176 8
IN THE PHYSICAL MESH   460 4
HAD BEEN WOVEN INTO A GLORIOUS MESH LIKE A BRIDAL LACE   860 14
AM CAUGHT IN THE MESH   *897 9
THE FASCINATION OF THE RESTLESS CREATOR THROUGH THE MES+ *906 23
MESH   *908 20
IN A LOVELY ILLUMINED MESH   *927 20
IN A LOVELY ILLUMINED MESH   *928 20

MESHED
MESHED AND TANGLED TOO MUCH IN THE SKEIN OF GUILT   884 14

MESHES
AND HER PASSION COULD ONLY FLARE THROUGH THE MESHES   619 2

MESMERIC
OF THE STRONG MACHINE THAT RUNS MESMERIC BOOMING THE   149 13

MESS
AN' OWER A' THE THAW AN' MESS   137 22
WATCH HIM TURN INTO A MESS EITHER A FOOL OR A BULLY   431 7
WE'VE MADE A GREAT MESS OF LOVE   472 14
IT IS NOT LOVE ANY MORE IT'S JUST A MESS   473 5
AND WE'VE MADE A GREAT MESS OF LOVE MIND-PERVERTED WILL+ 473 6
AND HENCE IS A MESS   479 19
THAT DARK GREEN MESS   691 3
WHEN I SEE WHAT A MESS MEN HAVE MADE OF THE WORLD   837 12
INSTEAD OF THIS MESS WHICH EXPRESSES THE IMPUDENT HUMAN   837 18
AND MAKE THE CONSIDERABLE MESS THAT ISN'T EVEN WORTH TH+ *947 12

MESSAGE
MEANING OR A MESSAGE OVER THE WINDOW GLASS   103 3
GIVING A MESSAGE TO THE MAN   693 15

MESSAGELESS
WITH THE DARK AND GLEAMING BEAUTY OF THE MESSAGELESS GO+ 674 26

MESSAGES
MESSAGES OF TRUE-LOVE DOWN THE DUST OF THE HIGHROAD   65 18
DO YOU TAKE IN MESSAGES IN SOME STRANGE CODE   301 5

MESSED-UP
WHEN I SEE THE MESSED-UP CHEMICALISED WOMEN   837 14

MESSENGER
IN AUTUMN LIKE TO A MESSENGER COME BACK   744 20

MESSES
WHEN I SEE WHAT MESSES MEN HAVE MADE OF THEMSELVES   837 13

MESSILY
SUCH SUBURBAN AMBITION SO MESSILY GORING   494 23

MESS-MAKERS
OR TO PUT UP WITH THE CLEVER MESS-MAKERS   499 17

MESS-MATES
ME NOW IF I'VE LOST MY MESS-MATES LOST THEM FOREVER   757 7

MESSY
TO PHYSICAL IS JUST MESSY   470 19

MESTER'S
'E SAYS TELL YOUR MOTHER AS 'ER MESTER'S   44 22
YOUR MESTER'S 'AD A ACCIDENT   45 5

MET
WITH SWOLLEN VEINS THAT MET IN THE WRIST   123 25
MY MOUTH YOU MET BEFORE YOUR FINE RED MOUTH   156 22
ARE MET AT LENGTH TO FINISH OUR REST OF DAYS   157 25
WE HAVE COME OUR WAYS AND MET AT LAST   209 13
WHILE RIVER MET WITH RIVER AND THE RINGING   216 24
AND CHRIST I HAVE MET HIS ACCUSING EYES AGAIN   225 22
I NEVER MET A SINGLE   555 9
I MET HIM IN THE STREET   569 15
YET ONCE MORE I MET A MAN AND I HAD TO STAY   569 21
MET MY EYE   *925 4
WITH SWOLLEN VEINS THAT MET IN THE WRIST   *934 31
WHILE RIVER MET WITH RIVER AND THE RINGING   *942 10

MET
  MET AND HER FACE AND MY FACE WERE ROSES   *942 18

METAL
  ON HIS MINTED METAL SHINE   59 16
  OH CROWN OF SPIKED GREEN METAL   278 15
  MUST BE EXCRUCIATING UNLESS YOU STIFFEN INTO METAL WHEN   288 6
  WHICH ARE LIPS OF METAL   288 24
  THEY ARE A CLICKETING OF BITS OF DISJOINTED METAL   288 32
  HE RUNS IN THE SNOW LIKE A BIT OF BLUE METAL   375 3
  METAL OF BONE   383 5
  GLEAMING LIKE METAL WITH RUNNING SWEAT AS THEY SUDDENLY   389 9
  BUT SAY IN THE DARK WILD METAL OF YOUR HEART   478 4
  METAL HITTING ON METAL TO ENFORCE OUR ATTENTION   623 3
  WITH METAL THORNS BEWARE   634 25
  METAL FOR RESISTANCE   804 1
  OF MY OLD WHITE METAL OF MEANING YOU FINE   873 4
  MOLTEN METAL OF DREAMS   *907 12
  QUICKENS THE HASTENING WHITE-HOT METAL   *907 22
  MOLTEN METAL OF DREAMS   *909 8
  AS IT QUICKENS WITHIN THE LABOURING WHITE-HOT METAL   *909 26

METAL-COLD
  COLD METAL-COLD   57 6

METALLIC
  METALLIC OBDURATE   56 27
  PUT THE FIRST CENTS INTO METALLIC FINGERS OF YOUR OFFIC+   291 4
  YOU ACID-BLUE METALLIC BIRD   375 29

METALLIC-STUNNED
  AND ALL THESE HUMAN PILLARS OF LOFTINESS GOING STIFF ME+   288 1

METEORITE
  THAT FALLS LIKE A METEORITE   162 26
  DULL METEORITE FLASH ONLY INTO LIGHT   195 21

METTLE
  UNEASILY IN THEIR SLEEP DISTURBING MY METTLE   128 13
  THUS HAMMERING THE METTLE OF GOATS INTO PROOF AND SMITI+   381 28
  IN THE BUSINESS OF BEATING THE METTLE OF GOATS TO A GOD+   381 33

ME-WARD
  LEAVE HER NO CHOICE MAKE HER LAPSE ME-WARD MAKE HER   213 28

MEWED
  MEWED AND MANGLED IN THE MILLS OF MAN   628 23

MEXICAN
  AFTER THE BLACK-GREEN SKIRTS OF A YELLOW-GREEN OLD MEXI+   395 31
  ME OR THE MEXICAN WHO COMES TO CHOP WOOD   398 23
  THEY GIVE US PESOS MADE OF MEXICAN SILVER   794 3

MEXICANOS
  JUST TURN YOUR EYES THIS WAY MEXICANOS   790 20
  HOLALA HE SAID MEXICANOS   791 10

MEXICANS
  TWO MEXICANS STRANGERS EMERGING OUT OF THE DARK AND   401 12
  PALEFACES YELLOWFACES BLACKFACES THESE ARE NO MEXICANS   793 11
  AND YOU MEXICANS AND PEONS WHAT DO YOU DO   794 1
  OH FOOLS MEXICANS AND PEONS   794 25
  OH FOOLS MEXICANS AND PEONS WITH MUDDY HEARTS   794 32
  OH DOGS AND FOOLS MEXICANS AND PEONS   795 5
  MEXICANS LIKE PEOPLE WHO HAVE DIED   816 9

MEXICO
  IN PYRAMID MEXICO DURING SACRIFICE   371 8
  LITTLE BLACK DOG IN NEW MEXICO   394 28
  WHITE BREAST-TIPS OF MY MEXICO   787 6
  AND HE SAW MEXICO LYING LIKE A DARK WOMAN WITH WHITE BR+   790 5
  WHO ARE THESE STRANGE FACES IN MEXICO   793 10
  FROM MEXICO TO THE POOL OF HEAVEN   798 2
  IN MEXICO   798 26

MIASMA
  THICKEN MIASMA THE FUMES OF THE AUTOMOBILE   703 22

MICE
  OF LIVES WHICH SORROWS LIKE MISCHIEVOUS DARK MICE CHAVEL   132 13
  ONLY MICE AND MOLES AND RATS AND BADGERS AND BEAVERS   392 22
  AND THOSE OVER-PROLIFIC WHITE MICE AND ADOLPH AND REX   395 9
  EVEN MICE PLAY QUITE BEAUTIFULLY AT SHADOWS   523 26
  AND MEN OFTEN SUCCUMB LIKE WHITE MICE IN A LABORATORY A+   619 22
  THERE ARE NO MICE IN OUR ROYAL PALACES OMIT IT   670 6
  THEY BUILD UPON AS MICE ARE SLAVES   *899 8
  THEY BUILD UPON AS MICE ARE SLAVES   *902 20
  OF LIVES THAT SORROWS LIKE MISCHIEVOUS STRANGE MICE CHA+   *938 5

MICHAEL
  ORTHODOX MICHAEL AND THAT WHISPERING GABRIEL   614 7
  MICHAEL AND GABRIEL ALL OF THEM SLAIN   823 13

MICHAELMAS
  IN SOFT SEPTEMBER AT SLOW SAD MICHAELMAS   697 2
  IN SOFT SEPTEMBER AT SLOW SAD MICHAELMAS   *955 26

MID-AIR
  TEMPTINGLY IN MID-AIR BETWEEN A PLAYFUL THUMB AND FINGER   271 24
  CLUTCHES IN MID-AIR   447 28

MID-BETWEEN
  FULL MID-BETWEEN THE CHAMPAIGN OF YOUR BREAST   154 8

MIDDAY
  SETTING THE FLOWERS ALONG THE MIDDAY MEAL   877 28

MID-DAY'S
  SUN OF THE TORRID MID-DAY'S HORRIFIC DARKNESS   301 20

MIDDLE
  SOME FIREFLIES DRIFT THROUGH THE MIDDLE AIR   221 1
  OF SOMETHING GONE WRONG IN THE MIDDLE   291 18
  LIKE A FUNNY TRIMMING TO THE MIDDLE OF HER BELLY THIN   393 19
  OUT OF THE SOUL'S MIDDLE TO THE MIDDLE-MOST SUN WAY-OFF   480 26
  IN THE MIDDLE OF VOLUTED SPACE   512 4
  AND IN THE MIDDLE OF EVERY ATOM WHICH IS THE SAME THING   512 6
  BUT OVER THE MIDDLE OF THE EARTH WILL BE THE SMOKY RUIN+   625 8
  EVEN WITH THE INDUSTRIAL MASSES AND THE GREEDY MIDDLE   631 25
  AT THE MIDDLE OF THE EARTH THIS EARTH   783 3
  AND FROM MIDDLE EARTH   806 20
  MIDDLE   844 21
  HOW DIFFERENT IN THE MIDDLE OF SNOWS THE GREAT SCHOOL R+   865 18

MIDDLE CLASSES
  THE MIDDLE CLASSES   527 13
  BECAUSE IF THE MIDDLE CLASSES HAD NO POORER PEOPLE TO BE   527 20
  THE MIDDLE CLASSES ARE MORE MEANINGLESS   528 3
  I'D BETRAY THE MIDDLE CLASSES   534 15
  WHEN YOU CLIMB UP TO THE MIDDLE CLASSES   549 1
  THE MIDDLE CLASSES HATE IT   626 19
  THE MIDDLE CLASSES HATE IT   626 21
  ANOTHER CURIOUS THING ABOUT THE ENGLISH MIDDLE CLASSES   831 20

MIDDLE-CLASS
  YOU ARE MIDDLE-CLASS AND ESSENTIALLY NON-EXISTENT   527 19
  MIDDLE-CLASS PERSON WHOSE   555 10
  OF MIDDLE-CLASS MOWING-MACHINES AND   627 15
  THE MIDDLE-CLASS MONEY-POWER   627 16

MIDDLE-MOST
  OUT OF THE SOUL'S MIDDLE TO THE MIDDLE-MOST SUN WAY-OFF   480 26

MIDDLENESS
  FOR THEIR MIDDLENESS IS ONLY AN UNREALITY SEPARATING TWO   527 26

MIDDLING
  SINCE MAN IS JUST MIDDLING AND HIS COMPREHENSION JUST   479 11
  MIDDLING   479 12

MIDDLINGNESS
  NOTHING THAT TRANSCENDS THE BOURGEOIS MIDDLINGNESS   528 2

MIDGE
  FAR OFF OH MIDGE AFTER MIDGE   144 11

MIDGES
  AND GREAT GOLD MIDGES   146 32

MID-HEAVEN
  TO THEE I ROSE LIKE A ROCKET ENDING IN MID-HEAVEN   322 8
  GOD MAY STAY IN MID-HEAVEN THE SUN OF MAN HAS CLIMBED TO   323 14
  THE SUN IS GONE FROM MID-HEAVEN THE SOLDIERS ARE GONE F+   757 1
  THEY TOUCH IN MID-HEAVEN LIKE AN ACROBAT   820 15

MIDLANDS
  I SAW THE MIDLANDS   120 10

MID-MORNING
  WHEN I WENT INTO MY ROOM AT MID-MORNING   342 8
  WHEN I WENT INTO MY ROOM AT MID-MORNING   342 12
  AT MID-MORNING   342 19

MIDMOST
  BUT MIDMOST SHINES AS THE MORNING STAR MIDMOST SHINES   799 22

MID-NAVEL
  SEEM BELLY-PLUMBED TO THE EARTH'S MID-NAVEL   392 24

MIDNIGHT
  WHY IS IT THE LONG SLOW STROKE OF THE MIDNIGHT BELL   63 1
  OF MIDNIGHT AND SHAKE IT TO FIRE TILL THE FLAME OF THE   136 20
  TALL BLACK BACCHAE OF MIDNIGHT WHY THEN WHY   140 28
  WOOD AT MIDNIGHT   366 5
  BUT THE BEST IS THE PERA-HERA AT MIDNIGHT UNDER THE   387 19
  THE MIDNIGHT SHADOW SINKING DOWN HAS SLUNG   750 9

MID-OCEAN
  ONLY MID-OCEAN   454 17
  THAT WAIT ON WHALES IN MID-OCEAN SUSPENDED IN THE WAVES+   694 26

MIDST
  MIDST OF THE DOWNS   70 23
  HOW DIFFERENT IN THE MIDST OF SNOW THE GREAT SCHOOL RIS+   75 7
  HOLD MY OWN IN THE MIDST OF THEM DARKLING DEFY   133 19
  IN THE MIDST OF THE SPHERES   253 23
  YOUR LITTLE ROUND HOUSE IN THE MIDST OF CHAOS   354 14
  LO WE ARE IN THE MIDST OF THE SUNDERERS   707 16
  OR LIKE A MIST THE MOON HAS KISSED FROM OFF A POOL IN T+   *917 19

MIDSUMMER
  DUSTY POLLEN OF GRASS TALL GRASS IN ITS MIDSUMMER MALEN+   587 3

MIEN
  SO WITH A DOWNCAST MIEN AND LAUGHING VOICE   123 1
  AND YOUR BLITHE GLAD MIEN   234 18
  I SERVE I SERVE IN ALL THE WEARY IRONY OF HIS MIEN 'TIS+   391 34
  SO WITH A DOWNCAST MIEN AND LAUGHING VOICE   *934 7

MIGHTN'T
'APPEN I MIGHTN'T 'APPEN I MIGHT   81 24
MIGHTN'T WE TRY   404 23
'APPEN I MIGHTN'T 'APPEN I MIGHT   *923 24

MIGHTY
FOR A MOMENT THE MIGHTY DIRECTION SNATCH   68 27
SO HIGH AND MIGHTY LOOK HOW THE HEADS ARE BORNE   221 7
AND THE ROAR OF BLACK BULL'S BLOOD IN THE MIGHTY PASSAG+ 326 15
LET HIM CHARGE LIKE A MIGHTY CATAPULT ON THE RED-CROSS + 327 24
THE DEAD ARE IN MYRIADS THEY SEEM MIGHTY   441 5
THE NOVEL IT SURE WAS MIGHTY FINE   489 11
OR THE MOST HIGH DURING THE COAL AGE CUDGELLING HIS MIG+ 690 26
EVEN IF HE HAD ANY BRAINS STRAINING HIS MIGHTY MIND   690 27
AND HE IS SUPPOSED TO BE **MIGHTY** ' AND GLORIOUS   691 14
GROAN WITH MIGHTY GROANS   703 10
OF DEATH COMMINGLES IN GOD'S MIGHTY GLOOM   *938 16
SO HIGH AND MIGHTY LOOK HOW ITS HEADS ARE BORNE   *944 20

MIGNONETTE
NOR THE SMELL OF MIGNONETTE   690 21
WHEN GERANIUMS WERE NOT AND MIGNONETTE NEITHER   690 22
TO SMELL AT THE MIGNONETTE   690 24
THAT BLOSSOMED AT LAST RED GERANIUM AND MIGNONETTE   691 5

MILD
THE ROSES LEAN DOWN WHEN THEY HEAR IT THE TENDER MILD 137 4
A MOTHER MILD   201 12
HIGH OVER THE MILD EFFULGENCE OF THE DOVE   328 2
YET THE MOMENT I HATE HER SHE TRIPS MILD AND SMUG LIKE A 385 12
MILD FORMS OF COCAINE THEY'RE NOT LIFE EXACTLY   532 13

MILDEWED
THAT MILDEWED PUP GOOD DOGGIE   491 26

MILDLY
HIS BENT COURSE MILDLY HERE WAKES AGAIN LEAPS LAUGHS AN+ 33 14
ITS CURIOUS COURSE MILDLY HERE IT WAKES AGAIN LEAPS LAU+ *891 15

MILE
A MISS IS AS GOOD AS A MILE   603 13
AND WHOEVER WALKS A MILE FULL OF FALSE SYMPATHY   653 1
AND HIS SINGING SOUND AS THEY ALWAYS DO AT THE BEGINNIN+ 865 17

MILES
ISN'T IT GOD'S OWN IMAGE TRAMPING HIS THIRTY MILES A DAY 430 22
FOURTH DIMENSION NOT IN YARDS AND MILES LIKE THE ETERNA+ 761 16

MILK
NO NOR EVEN MILK AND HONEY   263 11
AND MILKY-SAPPED SAP THAT CURDLES MILK AND MAKES RICOTTA 283 11
SEE THE MILK OF NORTHERN SPUME   301 24
I'LL TURN THEIR BLOOD LIKE SOUR MILK ROTTEN WITH THUNDER 792 6
LIKE MILK WITH ELECTRIC VENOM   797 11
AS HE DID SIP THE BITTER MILK OF SLEEP   878 14

MILK-BLUE
SEE GLITTERING ON THE MILK-BLUE MORNING LAKE   230 8
AS IT COMES OVER THE MILK-BLUE SEA HINTING AT GOLD AND + 840 5

MILKY
A GREAT BULL BELLOWED THROUGH SPACE CALLING TO THE MILK+ *946 21

MILKY-SAPPED
AND MILKY-SAPPED SAP THAT CURDLES MILK AND MAKES RICOTTA 283 11

MILKY-WAY
THE STREET'S LONG OUTSTRETCHED MILKY-WAY   115 24

MILL
AM I NOT BLIND AT THE ROUND-TURNING MILL   288 17
MODERN SOCIETY IS A MILL   641 22
POOR DREAM-HEAVY SLAVES AT THE MILL WHAT WE HAVE TO DO + 859 28

MILL-HAND
YET I AM A MILL-HAND IN LEEDS   630 5

MILLING
AND THE THICK FALLEN CROWDS CRACKLE AND CRUMBLE UNDER T+ 615 10

MILLION
LIKE A FLAT RED LILY WITH A MILLION PETALS   166 17
SPARE A MILLION OR TWO OF HUMANS   402 30
AND A MILLION FRENZIES OF TORTURED JEALOUSY   475 20

MILLIONS
YOU HAVE CAJOLED THE SOULS OF MILLIONS OF US   290 4
AND KEEP YOU IN MILLIONS AT THE MILLS SIGHTLESS PALE SL+ 441 8
MILLIONS OF SIMILAR HONEST PENCE   488 19
AND SENDS OFF MILLIONS OF SPARKS OF NEW ATOMS   506 9
MILLIONS FOR THERE'S MILLIONS OF 'EM   552 15
HARK THE STRANGE NOISE OF MILLIONS OF FISH IN PANIC   586 25
IN PANIC IN REBELLION SLITHERING MILLIONS OF FISH   566 26
THEY ARE MILLIONS TO MY ONE   628 20
THEY ARE MILLIONS TO MY ONE BUT OH   628 21
WHAT HAVE THEY DONE TO YOU WHITE-FACED MILLIONS   628 22
ARE THESE NO LONGER MEN THESE MILLIONS MILLIONS   629 14
OH WHEN I THINK OF THE INDUSTRIAL MILLIONS WHEN I SEE 629 16
I KNOW THE UNLIVING FACTORY-HAND LIVING-DEAD MILLIONS 629 26
AND ENSHROUDED IN THE VAST CORPSE OF THE INDUSTRIAL MIL+ 629 30
WHEN YEAR BY YEAR YEAR IN YEAR OUT IN MILLIONS IN INCRE+ 631 17
MILLIONS   631 18
THE MILLIONS MILLIONS OF MY FELLOW-MEN   631 30
AND RULERS OF MILLIONS OF ROBOTS BEING ROBOTS THEMSELVES 637 20
IN MILLIONS UNABLE TO DEPART   *957 29

MILLS
MILLS GRIND ON AND ON   441 7
AND KEEP YOU IN MILLIONS AT THE MILLS SIGHTLESS PALE SL+ 441 8
PRETENDING THESE ARE THE MILLS OF GOD   441 9
THE MILLS OF INDUSTRY ARE NOT THE MILLS OF GOD   441 11
AND THE MILLS OF GOD GRIND OTHERWISE WITH THE WINDS OF 441 12
TRUST THE MILLS OF GOD THOUGH THEY GRIND EXCEEDING SMALL 441 14
BUT AS FOR THE MILLS OF MEN   441 15
THE MILLS OF GOD WILL GRIND THEM SMALL ANYHOW THERE IS + 614 18
OH THEY ARE GRIST FOR THE MILLS OF GOD THEIR BONES GROU+ 614 23
BUT WINDS OF HEAVEN ARE MILLS OF GOD TO THE FALLEN LEAV+ 615 5
THE DARK SATANIC MILLS OF BLAKE   628 13
MEWED AND MANGLED IN THE MILLS OF MAN   628 23
THAT WITH SO MANY DEAD MEN IN MILLS   629 24

MILLSTONE
THE UPPER MILLSTONE OF THE ROBOT-CLASSES   642 1
THE LOWER MILLSTONE OF THE ROBOT-MASSES   642 2

MILLSTONES
SLIP OUT O SLIP OUT FROM BETWEEN THE MILLSTONES   642 6
THEN LET THE MILLSTONES GRIND FOR THEY CANNOT STOP   642 9

MILL-STONES
LIFE FOR THE MILL-STONES   441 13
THEN THE MILL-STONES BURST WITH THE INTERNAL HEAT OF TH+ 648 12

MILL-STONE
THE HEAVENS ARE THE NETHER MILL-STONE AND OUR HEAVY EAR+ 614 19
GRINDING THEM SMALL TO HUMUS ON EARTH'S NETHER MILL-STO+ 615 6

MIMOSA
AND SCATTERED WITH HER HAIR CLOUDS OF PALE MIMOSA SANDS 863 27

MINARET
AND THE DAWN CRY FROM A MINARET GOD IS GREAT   623 15

MINCE
WHILE PEOPLE MINCE MEAN WORDS THROUGH THEIR TEETH   530 11
OH MINCE YOUR WORDS AND MINCE THEM WELL   576 10

MIND
UPON MY MIND HIS LIPS MEET MINE AND A FLOOD   43 35
MUFFLING MY MIND AS SNOW MUFFLES THE SOUNDS THAT PASS 75 22
THE SOLUTION THAT EVER IS MUCH TOO DEEP FOR THE MIND 118 29
THE WINDOWS OF MY MIND   123 21
AY LAD I'LL TELL THEE THY MIND   138 28
ALOUD SUDDENLY ON MY MIND   140 16
HIS MIND UNTIL IT BURNT HIS HEART AWAY   158 2
THE HALLS OF MY MIND COMPELLING MY LIFE TO CONFORM   173 20
BUT NEVER MIND MY LOVE NOTHING MATTERS SAVE SLEEP   212 10
I DON'T MIND THIS CONTINENT STRETCHING THE SEA FAR AWAY 213 7
THE MIND FUSED DOWN LIKE A BEAD   242 13
IT WOULD BE SO BITTER NEVER MIND   244 17
THE GREAT AND DOMINANT HUNGER OF THE MIND   263 24
THAN STOMACH OR THROAT OR EVEN THE MIND   264 12
WHEN EVE ONCE KNEW IN HER MIND THAT SHE WAS NAKED   284 7
FACT ON HER MIND   284 11
SHE GOT THE FACT ON HER MIND AND QUICKLY SEWED FIG-LEAV+ 284 12
THEY HAVE THEIR NAKEDNESS MORE THAN EVER ON THEIR MIND 284 15
YOU MADAME CERES MIND YOURSELF THE ENEMY IS UPON   308 28
IS THERE NOT A GREAT MIND PRE-ORDAINING   328 25
PROUD INTELLECT HIGH-SOARING MIND   329 3
MIND   329 12
FOR THE ALMIGHTY EAGLE OF THE FORE-ORDAINING MIND   329 21
MY MIND   332 20
AND HE DID NOT MIND THE YELLOW ELECTRIC LIGHT   344 30
YOU THINK YOU'D BETTER MIND YOUR P'S AND Q'S FOR A BIT 400 28
EVEN WHEN THE MIND HAS FLICKERED AWAKE   407 24
THOUGH THE MIND IS AWAKE   408 18
SO BETTER MAKE UP YOUR MIND AMERICAN EAGLE   414 5
YOU MIND WHO YER SAYIN' ISN'T LIDIES   434 26
THE DIRTY MIND LIKE A URINAL AGAIN   463 3
IT'S THE VILLAGE-IDIOT MIND   463 8
THE BODY OF ITSELF IS CLEAN BUT THE CAGED MIND   463 19
NOR IS IT DIRTY NOT UNTIL THE DIRTY MIND POKES IN   463 25
MIND   464 2
AND DON'T WITH THE NASTY PRYING MIND DRAG IT OUT FROM 464 28
OF THE ITCHING MIND AND THE MENTAL SELF WITH ITS PRURIE+ 465 5
O YOU CREATURES OF MIND DON'T TOUCH ME   468 23
FINGERED BY THE MIND   469 16
THE MODERN MIND CALLS LOVE   469 22
TOUCH COMES WHEN THE WHITE MIND SLEEPS   470 23
FOR WHILE WE HAVE SEX IN THE MIND WE TRULY HAVE NONE IN 471 27
THE MIND WILL HAVE TO GLUT ITSELF   472 11
THE MOMENT THE MIND INTERFERES WITH LOVE OR THE WILL 473 1
CLIMB DOWN O LORDLY MIND   473 8
O EAGLE OF THE MIND ALAS YOU ARE MORE LIKE A BUZZARD 473 9
COME DOWN NOW FROM YOUR PRE-EMINENCE O MIND O   473 10
A MAN IS MANY THINGS HE IS NOT ONLY A MIND   473 15
THE MIND THAT NEEDS TO KNOW ALL THINGS   473 19
THE MIND CAN NEVER REACH THEE   473 24
AND THE WHITE MIND SHINES ON ONE SIDE OF THEE   473 26
AND OF THIS THE MIND IS INCAPABLE   474 1
THE MIND IS NON-RELIGIOUS   474 9
BUT TO MY WHITE MIND   474 12
MAKE UP YOUR MIND ABOUT IT   487 18
I DON'T MIND TELLING YOU   490 2
MY MIND IF FAIRLY NIMBLE AND IS NOT BLANK   501 18
NOW I'VE MADE UP MY MIND   507 1
ALWAYS CHANGING ITS MIND   524 25
MAN IS IMMORAL BECAUSE HE HAS GOT A MIND   529 1
WHY DON'T WE LEARN TO TAME THE MIND   529 6
IT IS THE MIND WHICH IS UNCOUTH AND OVERWEENING   529 9
COURSE YOU UNDERSTAND WHAT I MEAN SO WOULD YOU MIND GIV+ 546 9
THAT YOU DON'T MIND THE THING   551 23
NEVER YOU MIND MY LADS I LEFT YOU   552 25
YOU DON'T MIND A BIT   557 16

MIND
  BUT WE DON'T MIND SO MUCH IF YOU LOVE US AND WE   572 27
  SO DARK SO DARK THE MIND IS LOST IN IT   586 14
  OUR PALE MIND STILL FROM THE PULSING CONTINENT   607 2
  THE MIND IS TOUCHLESS SO IS THE WILL SO IS THE SPIRIT   611 11
  OH CARCASS WITH A BOARD-SCHOOL MIND AND A HA'PENNY NEWS+   631 3
  YOU MUST FUSE MIND AND WIT WITH ALL THE SENSES   653 9
  REMEMBER THE STATE OF MIND OF THE BRITISH PUBLIC   669 27
  AS IF ANY MIND COULD HAVE IMAGINED HIM A LOBSTER   689 19
  EVEN THE MIND OF GOD CAN ONLY IMAGINE   689 21
  BUT IT IS A GREAT STRANGE URGE IT IS NOT A MIND   690 2
  EVEN AN ARTIST KNOWS THAT HIS WORK WAS NEVER IN HIS MIND   690 3
  HIS WORK TOOK PLACE IT CAME TO PASS IT STOOD UP AND SAL+   690 7
  IMAGINE THAT ANY MIND EVER THOUGHT A RED GERANIUM   690 14
  EVEN IF HE HAD ANY BRAINS STRAINING HIS MIGHTY MIND   690 27
  NAY NOR EVEN YOUR MIND   692 6
  WHEN THE MIND MAKES A WHEEL WHICH TURNS ON THE HUB OF T+   712 13
  NONE AT ALL MIND YOU PROGRESS IS A FACT   774 8
  NOW MAKE UP YOUR MIND ABOUT HIM HE IS NOT AS WE ARE   776 7
  MIND AND SPIRIT BAD AND GOOD   824 14
  THEY DON'T EVEN MIND DOING THINGS FOR YOU IN REASON   828 24
  THEY DON'T MIND BEING DEPRAVED IMMORAL OR ANYTHING OF T+   829 12
  BUT THEY DO MIND BEING UNJUST UNFAIR   829 13
  MIND THE BANANA-SKIN   829 30
  MAN IS KEPT SANE NOT BY HIS MIND WHICH BY NATURE IS UNS+   838 16
  AT THE MOMENT WE TEND TO RUN INSANE THE MIND HAVING BRO+   858 21
  HIS MIND DEVELOPED AT THE EXPENSE OF HIS MALE SELF   841 20
  HYPERTROPHY OF THE MIND ATROPHY OF THE SENSES   841 21
  A KEEN FAR-REACHING CURIOUS MIND CYNICAL WITH LITTLE-BO+   841 22
  SHE BOWS QUITE HUMBLE SUCH A SUBTLE DESTROYING MIND MUS+   841 28
  MY MIND AND I KNOW   *894 4
  MUFFLING MY MIND AS SNOW MUFFLES THE SOUNDS THAT PASS   *897 22
  MUFFLING MY MIND AS SNOW MUFFLES THE SOUNDS THAT PASS   *900 30
  KISS ME THEN THERE NE'ER MIND IF I SCRAIGHT I WOR FOND +   *925 28
  THAT YOU SHAKE AND SHAKE AND YET IT WON'T COME TO YOUR +   *932 9
  THE WINDOWS OF MY MIND   *934 27

MINDFUL
  WHAT IS MAN THAT THOU ART MINDFUL OF HIM   548 31
  WHAT IS MAN THAT THOU ART NO LONGER MINDFUL OF HIM   629 12

MINDING
  NOT MONKEYS MINDING MACHINES   450 13

MIND-MISCHIEVOUS
  IN THIS MIND-MISCHIEVOUS AGE   470 3

MIND-PERVERTED
  AND WE'VE MADE A GREAT MESS OF LOVE MIND-PERVERTED WILL+   473 6

MINDS
  THE DEAD IN THEIR SEETHING MINDS   441 1
  THAT ARE BORN IN THEIR MINDS AND FORCED DOWN BY THE WILL   500 19
  SOME MEN LIVE FOR THE CONCEITED FURNITURE OF THEIR MINDS   657 7
  MINDS   840 8
  AND WOMEN FALL FOR THESE LITTLE-BOY MINDS THEY FEEL QUI+   841 24

MIND-SOARING
  OH THAT MIND-SOARING EAGLE OF AN EVANGELIST   328 19

MIND'S
  AT PRESENT SEX IS THE MIND'S PREOCCUPATION   472 7
  THE MIND'S INDEX   562 29
  IN THE WHITE SHIRT OF THE MIND'S EXPERIENCES   *957 9

MINER'S
  AND BURN BLUE AND COLD LIKE THE FLAME IN A MINER'S LAMP   619 5

MINGLE
  FOR WHEN FIRE IN ITS DOWNWARD PATH CHANCED TO MINGLE WI+   348 6
  AND LET US IF YOU WILL TALK AND MINGLE   469 1
  AND LOSING MINGLE IN THE PROCREANT WOMB   876 20

MINGLED
  OF LEAVES AND LAMPS AND THE CITY STREET MINGLED   111 6
  OF GREYNESS MINGLED WITH A FUME OF GOLD   135 14
  MINGLED WITH THE BREATH OF DESTRUCTION   698 2
  OF BLUENESS MINGLED WITH A FUME OF GOLD   *939 14

MINGLING
  MINGLING   290 19
  AND A MINGLING OF WALLET-CARRYING WOMEN   484 5
  OF SHARING THE NIGHT WITH GOD OF MINGLING UP AGAIN   772 25

MINGY
  BUT HOW PALTRY MINGY AND DINGY AND SQUALID PEOPLE LOOK   530 15

MINING
  OF DAY TROLLS AT THE CAVE OF RINGING CERULEAN MINING   72 10

MINISTRANTS
  TO THE HUSHED GREY-WINGED MINISTRANTS THE BATS OF NIGHT+   *916 12

MINKY
  DROP OF WHISKEY IN ITS MINKY WELL IT SHALL YET IT SHALL   570 25
  TO HAVE WHISKEY IN ITS MINKY   571 8

MINKY-WINKY
  DRINK ITS MINKY-WINKY THEN LIKE A MAN   570 21

MINNOWS
  WHERE THE MINNOWS TRACE   161 6

MINOAN
  CROSS LIKE CLOCK-WORK THE MINOAN DISTANCE   688 8

MINOAN GODS
  AND THE MINOAN GODS AND THE GODS OF TIRYNS   688 17

MINOR
  SIX FAT SMALLER BOBBIES ARE THE INQUISITORS MINOR   633 16

MINORITIES
  NOW ABOVE ALL IS THE TIME FOR THE MINORITIES OF MEN   666 1
  INSTEAD OF WHICH THE MINORITIES THAT STILL SEE THE GLEA+   666 5

MINORITY
  AND THESE THE MINORITY OF MEN WHO CAN STILL SEE THE LIG+   665 25
  DURING MY MINORITY   671 4

MINOS
  IN MINOS IN MYCENAE   704 1

MINT
  TOO MUCH YOU MINT ME THAT CHEATING COUNTERFEIT   872 23
  MINT ME BEAUTIFUL MEDALS AND HAND THEM ME HOT   873 1

MINTED
  ON HIS MINTED METAL SHINE   59 16

MINUTE
  FOR A MINUTE   427 18
  WAIT DEAR LADY JEAN WAIT A MINUTE   668 23
  MINUTE BY MINUTE EBBS   766 9
  THE MINUTE SPARKING OF DARKNESS WHICH   772 29
  IN SHOWERS OF MINUTE RUDDY DROPS FROM THEIR BLADES   884 29

MINUTELY
  SMALL AM I WHAT MATTER IF MINUTELY   223 8

MINUTES
  YOU'RE A CAGED MONKEY AGAIN IN FIVE MINUTES   486 5

MINUTIAE
  WRITHING DEEPER AND DEEPER IN ALL THE MINUTIAE OF SELF-+   701 23

MIRACLE
  AND A MIRACLE AS SHE GLIDED DELICATELY AWAY WITH SUCH   255 31
  A MIRACLE IN HEAVEN   391 21
  AND IF BY A MIRACLE A WOMAN HAPPENED TO COME ALONG   507 8
  FLOWERS ACHIEVE THEIR OWN FLOWERINESS AND IT IS A MIRAC+   683 22
  OH THE MIRACLE OF THE WHOLE THE WIDESPREAD LABOURING CO+   *909 19

MIRE
  SWINE WASH IN MIRE AND BARNYARD FOWLS IN DUST   376 8
  THROUGH THE MIRE OF FUMES   704 9

MIRROR
  OF THE MIRROR TOWARDS THE DUSTY GRATE AS IF FEELING   141 14
  OF MY PRESENCE THERE IN THE MIRROR THAT LEANS FROM THE   141 20
  YOU WOULD DRAW YOUR MIRROR TOWARDS YOU YOU WOULD WISH   251 14
  IF YOU CAN ONLY SIT WITH A MIRROR IN YOUR HAND AN AGEING   478 20
  IN THE BIG MIRROR AT HIS OWN FASCINATING SHADOW   604 5
  I HANDED HER THE MIRROR AND SAID   604 14
  SO I HANDED HER THE MIRROR   604 19
  THE BREATH OF MY DREAM IS FADED FROM OFF THE MIRROR   871 10

MIRROR-EYE
  AND THE RED-GOLD MIRROR-EYE STARES AND DIES   339 17

MIRROR-FLAT
  HIS RED-GOLD WATER-PRECIOUS MIRROR-FLAT BRIGHT EYE   339 8

MIRRORS
  LET US LOSE SIGHT OF OURSELVES AND BREAK THE MIRRORS   477 27

MIRTH
  FROM THE HAY COMES THE CLAMOUR OF CHILDREN'S MIRTH   41 22
  OF MIRTH THEN THE DRIPPING OF TEARS ON YOUR GLOVE   179 19

MIRTHLESS
  BEING TOO MIRTHLESS TO MOVE THE LILT OF SINGING   884 13

MISBEHAVES
  WHERE THE ELECTRON BEHAVES AND MISBEHAVES AS IT WILL   437 28
  ONLY THE ELECTRON BEHAVES AND MISBEHAVES INCOMPREHENSIB+   *947 5

MISCHANCE
  IF 'E'S NOT A MAN FOR MISCHANCE   45 8

MISCHIEF
  MISCHIEF HAS COME IN HER DAWNING EYES   46 9

MISCHIEVOUS
  OF LIVES WHICH SORROWS LIKE MISCHIEVOUS DARK MICE CHAVEL   152 13
  OF LIVES THAT SORROWS LIKE MISCHIEVOUS STRANGE MICE CHA+   *938 5

MISERABLE
  YOU MISERABLE LITTLE BITCH OF LOVE-TRICKS   398 21

MISERERE
  ALL YOUR WRINKLED MISERERE CHINESE BLACK LITTLE FACE   396 3

MISERIES
  AND WE FACED OUR FIRST MISERIES   248 19

MISERY
  FOR JOY OR FOR MISERY   60 10
  WITH MISERY NO MORE PROUD   155 31
  THE BROWN EYES BLACK WITH MISERY AND HATE THAT LOOK   225 23
  WHAT IF I LOVE YOU THIS MISERY   230 17
  I FALL IN SICKNESS AND IN MISERY   727 18

MISERY'S
    AND DAMP OLD WEB OF MISERY'S HEIRLOOM   141 11

MISFORTUNES
    NOW THEN YOU LEAVE A MAN'S MISFORTUNES ALONE   545 11

MISGIVING
    SO UTTERLY WITHOUT MISGIVING   337 7
    WITH A TINGE OF MISGIVING   375 13
    WHAT DO YOU LOOK AT ME FOR WITH SUCH MISGIVING   375 19
    LOOK UP AT ME WITH MISGIVING IN YOUR BULGING EYES   400 25

MISGIVINGS
    TO AND FRO IN OUR MISGIVINGS   166 5

MISNAMED
    BETWEEN YOU AND THE ROBOT-HORDES MISNAMED YOUR FELLOW-M+   637 34

MISPRISION
    OF YOUR DISSATISFACTION AND MISPRISION   230 18

MISS
    WHAT PAIN TO WAKE AND MISS YOU   220 9
    HOW YOU HATE BEING LAUGHED AT MISS SUPERB   397 34
    AND NEVER MISS THEM   402 31
    A MISS IS AS GOOD AS A MILE   603 13
    IT SNOWED AND HIS HELMET WAS LOST HE FORGOT ME HE DID N+   732 17
    I WOULD NOT MISS IT FOR YOUR ACHE OF WONDER   876 16

MISSAL
    MY MISSAL BOOK OF FINE FLAMBOYANT HOURS   135 2
    NAY TAKE MY PAINTED MISSAL BOOK AWAY   *939 4

MISSED
    PALE-BLURRED WITH TWO ROUND BLACK DROPS AS IF IT MISSED   141 17
    AND SO I MISSED MY CHANCE WITH ONE OF THE LORDS   351 27
    A MAN WROTE TO ME WE MISSED IT YOU AND I   603 9
    BUT WE MISSED IT   603 11

MISSES
    LIKE BEADS THEY GO AROUND AND NOT ONE MISSES   154 5

MISS HARRISON
    THINK OF THE EFFECT ON MISS HARRISON   583 10

MISS ILL-AT-EASE
    EVERYTHING MISS ILL-AT-EASE   96 4

MISSING
    YET MISSING THE PURE LOOP   341 10
    YET WHAT A GAP IN THE WORLD THE MISSING WHITE FROST-FACE   402 32
    OR IS SOMETHING MISSING OR WHAT'S WRONG WITH THEM   578 20

MISSION
    AND SODOMY ON THE BRAIN BECOMES A MISSION   845 9
    FOR HIS MISSION HAD CRUELLY FAILED WHILE HIS PASSIONATE+   859 11
    AND SODOMY ON THE BRAIN IS A SORT OF MISSION AND WHAT I+   *952 21

MISSIONS
    ALL THE LOT OF THEM VICE MISSIONS ETC INSANELY UNHEALTHY   845 10

MISSIS
    WHAT'S THAT AS 'APPEN I'VE 'EERED ON MISSIS   78 7
    WELL I'M BELIEVIN' NO TALE MISSIS   78 17
    AN' WHEN I KNOW FOR SURE MISSIS   78 19
    WHAT'S THAT AS 'APPEN I'VE 'EERED-ON MISSIS   *919 27
    WELL I'M BELIEVIN' NO TALE MISSIS   *920 9
    AN' WHEN I KNOW FOR SURE MISSIS   *920 11

MISS JUPSON
    AND KIN WITH MISS JUPSON WHOSE GUTS ARE NARROW   583 28

MISS PONSONBY
    INDIGESTIBLE TO MISS PONSONBY   563 25

MISS STAINWRIGHT
    YOU'RE STOUT TO BRAVE THIS SNOW MISS STAINWRIGHT   78 1
    YOU'RE STOUT TO BRAVE THIS SNOW MISS STAINWRIGHT   *919 21

MISS WILKS
    CONSIDER MISS WILKS OR DEPART FORTHWITH   584 2

MIST
    THE MOON-MIST IS OVER THE VILLAGE OUT OF THE MIST SPEAK+   63 4
    CROUCHING AS LITTLE HOUSES CROUCH UNDER THE MIST WHEN I+   63 23
    FOREVER OUT OF THE MIST THE CHURCH LIFTS UP A REPROACHF+   63 24
    OR LIKE A MIST THE MOON HAS KISSED FROM OFF A POOL IN T+   70 22
    THE LUMINOUS MIST WHICH THE POOR THINGS WIST WAS DAWN   71 5
    AN' MIST IS SUCKIN' AT TH' SPOTS O' SNOW   137 21
    THE HOUSES FADE IN A MELT OF MIST   142 17
    THE SUN IS BLEEDING ITS FIRES UPON THE MIST   164 17
    BEFORE THE MIST DISCLOSES   178 3
    WHEN THE BLUE MIST UNCLOSES   178 14
    I WALK UP TO MY NECK IN MIST HOLDING MY MOUTH UP   212 13
    AND BUMP ON ONE ANOTHER AND EXPLODE INTO MORE MIST   437 34
    MIST OF ENERGY MOST SCIENTIFIC   438 1
    WHERE THE FATHER OF ALL THINGS SWIMS IN A MIST OF ATOMS   438 4
    A WREATH OF MIST WITH NOTHING BEHIND IT   580 4
    A WREATH OF MIST IS THE USUAL THING   580 5
    A WREATH OF ENGLISH MIST WOULD DO   580 11
    LIKE THE POWER AND THE GLORY OF THE GOOSE IN THE MIST   704 25
    SIT IN THE GREY MIST OF MOVEMENT WHICH MOVES NOT   711 28
    THEY COME BACK OVER THE WHITE SEA IN THE MIST   739 10
    THE CAMPIONS DRIFT IN FRAGILE ROSY MIST   854 11
    AND I LOOKED IN A ROOM WHERE THE LAMP AS A MOON IN MIST   865 1
    AND NOW THE MIST OF MY DREAMS HAS DRIED FROM YOU   871 5
    AND MOONY-DAISIES UNDERNEATH THE MIST   884 30
    THE MIST IS A CUP OF WINE AND THE NEW AND OLD   *894 25

MIST
    STREAMING BACK WHERE THE MIST DISTILS   *906 2
    OR LIKE A MIST THE MOON HAS KISSED FROM OFF A POOL IN T+   *917 19
    THE LUMINOUS MIST WHICH THE POOR THINGS WIST WAS DAWN A+   *917 23

MISTAKE
    BUT YOU MISTAKE IT IS NOT FROM THE SKY   304 15
    I HAD MADE A MISTAKE I DIDN'T KNOW HIM   338 10
    IT WAS 'IM AS MADE THE FIRST MISTAKE   493 5
    LONG DIFFICULT REPENTANCE REALISATION OF LIFE'S MISTAKE+   620 18
    FROM THE ENDLESS REPETITION OF THE MISTAKE   620 20
    IT IS A MISTAKE THAT MANKIND HAS MADE   666 16
    GO BRAVELY ACROSS THE BORDER ADMITTING YOUR MISTAKE   809 7
    YOU WILL HAVE DEPARTED FOREVER FROM YOUR MISTAKE   809 14

MISTAKEN
    DAISIES THAT WAKEN ALL MISTAKEN WHITE-SPREAD IN EXPECTA+   71 3
    SELF-SACRIFICE AFTER ALL IS A WRONG AND MISTAKEN IDEA   678 1
    YOU ARE MISTAKEN THE VEIL OF THE FLESH IS RENT   742 18
    DAISIES THAT WAKEN ALL MISTAKEN WHITE-SPREAD IN EXPECTA+   *917 22

MISTAKES
    NEVER MAKE UP FOR SOME MISTAKES   406 9

MISTER
    MISTER   603 14

MISTINESS
    OF MISTINESS COMPLICATED INTO KNOTS AND CLOTS THAT BARGE   437 32

MISTLETOE
    AS MISTLETOE BERRIES BURNING IN A BLACK TREE   86 2
    ABOVE ME SPRINGS THE BLOOD-BORN MISTLETOE   131 15
    UNDER THE MISTLETOE   198 6

MISTOOK
    MISTOOK FOR ME   601 17

MISTRESS
    THE DARK THE GRAVE-EYED MISTRESS WHO THUS DARED   155 28
    THE SHADOW ALWAYS OFFER MYSELF TO ONE MISTRESS WHO ALWA+   180 27
    AS AN INSOLENT MISTRESS TELLING MY PULSE'S BEAT   230 27
    O MISTRESS MISTRESS   359 8
    REPTILE MISTRESS   359 9
    REPTILE MISTRESS   359 18
    MISTRESS REPTILE MISTRESS   359 28
    NOW THAT THE WIFE AND MOTHER AND MISTRESS IS BURIED IN   412 23
    AND AT ONE WITH THE MASTER OF THE HOUSE WITH THE MISTRE+   700 5

MISTRESSES
    WHAT OF THE MISTRESSES   196 18

MISTRUST
    NO MORE CHILDREN TO LAUNCH IN A WORLD YOU MISTRUST   411 10
    IN SPACES WIDE WITH MISTRUST   823 22

MISTRUSTED
    MISTRUSTED ALL ALONG   77 24
    MISTRUSTED ALL ALONG   *919 12

MISTRUSTFUL
    ALL MISTRUSTFUL OF THRUSTING ITS SHOOTS WHERE ONLY   *900 21
    ALL MISTRUSTFUL OF THRUSTING ITS SHOOTS WHERE ONLY   *903 33

MISTS
    STREAMING BACK WHERE THE MISTS DISTIL   53 10
    SWEEPS THE HIGH GOOSE ABOVE THE MISTS   437 24
    MISTS   437 27
    MISTS   437 31
    MISTS WREATHING MISTS   438 6
    THE MISTS OF RECEDING TEARS AND THE ECHO OF LAUGHTER   *906 10
    SWAM THE STILL SWAN SWEPT THE WIDE GOOSE ABOVE THE MISTS   *947 2

MIST-SHEET
    A THICK MIST-SHEET LIES OVER THE BROKEN WHEAT   212 12

MIST'S
    I CANNOT SEE HER SINCE THE MIST'S PALE SCARF   85 9
    WINDING ABOUT THEIR DIMNESS THE MIST'S GREY CEREMENTS A+   102 30

MISTY
    OF GLASS PALACE ALOFT THERE AMONG MISTY INDEFINITE THIN+   52 24
    ON THE MISTY WASTE LANDS AWAY FROM THE FLUSHING GREY   164 21
    FAR OFF UPON THE MISTY WATERS OF THE DEPTHS OF SPACE   841 3
    OF BLUE PALACE ALOFT THERE AMONG THE MISTY INDEFINITE D+   *905 13

MISUNDERSTOOD
    GOES CLOUDED HAVING MISUNDERSTOOD   37 19
    WE MISUNDERSTOOD   37 23

MITE
    STEPPING WEE MITE IN HIS LOOSE TROUSERS   355 21

MIXED
    SWEET DARK PURPLE AND WHITE ONES MIXED FOR A PLEDGE   58 10
    AND STUMBLING MIXED UP IN ONE ANOTHER   361 25
    YOU'RE AS MIXED AS THE WEATHER   564 9
    THAT ALL THINGS ARE MIXED AND THEREFORE THE PUREST WHIT+   708 15

MIXING
    NOT IN MIXING MERGING NOT IN SIMILARITY   267 5

MIXING-POT
    AND DREAMS AS SHE STIRS THE MIXING-POT   203 7

MIXTURE
  TILL THEN WE ARE CONFUSED A MIXTURE UNRESOLVED UNEXTRIC+   267   1
  NIGHT WERE DISTINGUISHED FROM THE SYMMETRY OF THEIR MIX+   295   6
  A MIXTURE OF YEA AND NAY   714 11
  THE FIERY MIXTURE OF THY LIFE SO I   879 11

MOAN
  AN' WHAT A MOAN 'E'LL MAKE THERE NIVER   45 17
  IS DELIVERED OUT AND PAYS NO HEED THOUGH WE MOAN   132 18
  MOAN SOFTLY WITH AUTUMNAL PARTURITION   160   9
  I CAN HEAR THE ISAR MOAN   220 23
  THE JOURNEY STILL THEY MOAN AND BEAT   722   2
  OH NOW THEY MOAN AND THRONG IN ANGER AND PRESS BACK   722 24
  IS DELIVERED FROM US HERSELF BORN AGAIN AMID THE MOAN   *938 10
  ONCE OUTSIDE UPON THE GREY MARSH BEACHES WHERE LOST SOU+   *957 28
  THE JOURNEY STILL THEY MOAN AND BEAT   *958   2
  THEY MOAN AND BEAT THEY GNASH THEY RAGE   *958   4

MOANED
  DESTROY SHE MOANED THESE HORRORS IN PAINT   577   8

MOANING
  THE MOANING OF SLEEP-BOUND BEINGS IN TRAVAIL THAT TOIL +   149 19
  MOANING FOR ME TO LOVE HIM O DARLING RYE   221 13
  MOANING BOOING ROARING HOLLOW   327 10
  AND CAUGHT THEM MOANING FROM CLOSE-UP KISSES BLACK-AND-+   444   1
  ARE ALSO POOR BLIND CYCLOPS MOANING   544 27

MOANS
  MOANS AND BOOMS THE SOUL OF A PEOPLE IMPRISONED ASLEEP   149 11
  WITH MOANS AND HOLLOW BIBBLINGS   492   6

MOB
  NOT A MOB THING NOR A MASS THING NOR A CLASS THING NOR   775 23

MOBILE
  UNDER THE MOBILE FEATURES   *907 17
  VISIBLE THERE IN THE CHANGE OF EYES AND THE MOBILE FEAT+   *909 12

MOBILITY
  THE MOBILITY THE PANTHER'S GAMBOLLING   157 18

MOCK
  CAN MOCK MY STRUGGLING   157 20
  SEA YOU SHADOW OF ALL THINGS NOW MOCK US TO DEATH WITH   197 32
  MOCK AS IT FLUTTERS BY   731   4
  ITS WAY ACROSS THE DARK SHOULD MOCK MY NAKEDNESS   771 20
  THE DAY SHALL MOCK ME INEFFICACIOUS WHAT THEN   771 30
  SPORT ON HER LITTERED PIANO AND MOCK AT THE SIGHT   856 17

MOCKERY
  OF MY MOCKERY MOCKS AT HIM OVER THE WAVES' BRIGHT   130   7
  OUT OF MOCKERY WE DANCE TOGETHER   210   7
  THERE WAS THE FAINTEST TWIST OF MOCKERY IN EVERY FACE   391 16

MOCKING
  TO HEAR ON ITS MOCKING TRIUMPHANCE UNWITTING THE AFTER-+   58   6

MOCKS
  OF MY MOCKERY MOCKS AT HIM OVER THE WAVES' BRIGHT   130   7
  THE MAN ANSWERS AND SHE MOCKS   *945 16

MODELS
  AS THE TURNIP MODELS HIS ROUND ROOT AS THE BUSH MAKES   451 15

MODERATELY
  THIS MODERATELY YOUNG GENTLEMAN   446 22

MODERN
  MODERN UNISSUED UNCANNY AMERICA   293   6
  WHILE THE WISPY MODERN CHILDREN HALF-AFRAID   426 20
  BATHING-SUIT FROM OUR MODERN SEA-SIDE FOAM   439 32
  WHEN MODERN PEOPLE SEE THE CARNAL BODY DAUNTLESS AND   445 31
  MODERN PEOPLE ARE DEPRESSED   445 35
  MODERN PEOPLE FEEL THEMSELVES AT A DISADVANTAGE   446   1
  THE MODERN MIND CALLS LOVE   469 22
  AND THE YOUNG THE MODERN AND JAUNTY YOUNG   494   5
  IT IS AS IF MODERN WOMEN HAD ALL GOT THEMSELVES ON THE +   502   6
  BUT THEN YOU NEED ONLY LOOK AT THE MODERN PERAMBULATOR   521 25
  MODERN LIFE IS A TALE TOLD BY AN IDIOT   522   1
  THE MODERN CIRCE-DOM   538 26
  ONCE MEN TOUCH ONE ANOTHER THEN THE MODERN INDUSTRIAL   611 14
  THE WISP OF MODERN BLACK MANTILLA   617 21
  FROM THE DRAGON OF THE MODERN FEMALE   619 27
  MODERN SOCIETY IS A MILL   641 22
  IT IS CURIOUS TOO THAT THOUGH THE MODERN MAN IN THE STR+   648   1
  WHO KNOWS WHO KNOWS HOW MUCH OUR MODERN WOE   723   4
  AND QUITE CLEVER BRILLIANT IS THE MODERN WORD   841 17
  THE MODERN YOUNG WOMAN THINKS IT WONDERFUL TO BE SO BRI+   841 26
  WHY THE MODERN YOUNG WIFE OF THE LITTLE-BOY BRILLIANT B+   842   9

MODEST
  AND TURNED MY MODEST PENNY   488 16

MODESTY
  FROM AIRS AND FROM FALSE MODESTY   470   8
  WE MUST HAVE THE MODESTY OF SIMPLE LIVING   487 22

MOHAMMEDAN
  FOLDED UPON ITSELF ENCLOSED LIKE ANY MOHAMMEDAN WOMAN   283 14

MOHAMMEDANS
  THE MOHAMMEDANS SAY THAT THE SOUND OF BELLS   622 19

MOILED
  MOILED OVER WITH THE REARING OF HER MANY-MOUTHED YOUNG   197 11
  LOVE'S LONG MOILED MADDENED AUTO-DA-FE   769   7

MOIST
  AND OPEN IT SO THAT IT IS A GLITTERING ROSY MOIST HONIE+   282   3
  THE WONDERFUL MOIST CONDUCTIVITY TOWARDS THE CENTRE   282 20
  BECOMES AN AFFIRMATION THROUGH MOIST SCARLET LIPS   284 18
  WAS MOIST AND COLD THE SUN IN HIM DARTED UNEASY HELD DO+   348   8
  MOIST EARTH NEVER COULD HE RISE ON HIS FEET AND THIS IS+   348   9
  AND MOVE ON FEET BUT MOIST EARTH WEIGHS HIM DOWN THOUGH+   348 11
  AND THE MOIST FIG   710 18
  OH THE MOIST FULL WATER-JAR   759   5
  THE ROOTS ARE MINE DOWN THE DARK MOIST PATH OF THE SNAKE   801 16

MOISTURE
  OF THEIR DANCING BLOOD LADS SUCKING THE COLD MOISTURE F+   865 29

MOISTURES
  DEEP IN THE MOISTURES OF PEACE   788 18

MOLECULE
  THEN EVERY MOLECULE OF CREATION JUMPED AND CLAPPED ITS +   683   4

MOLES
  ONLY MICE AND MOLES AND RATS AND BADGERS AND BEAVERS   392 22

MOLOCH
  MOLOCH   242   3
  THE FEAR OF HUNGER IS MOLOCH BELIAL THE HORRIBLE GOD   263   6
  IT IS SO DEEP A MOLOCH RUTHLESS AND STRONG   264 15
  A THREATENING TORTURING PHALLIC MOLOCH   264 25

MOLTEN
  FOR THE PROPER DREAM-STUFF IS MOLTEN AND MOVING MYSTERI+   176   1
  AND THE BODIES OF MEN AND WOMEN ARE MOLTEN MATTER OF DR+   176   2
  AND OUR BODIES MOLTEN DROPS OF DREAM-BLOOD THAT SWIRL A+   176   7
  IN A TISSUE AS ALL THE MOLTEN CELLS IN THE LIVING MESH   176   8
  THE MOLTEN GOLD OF ITS INTOLERABLE RAGE   315 20
  LIKE A FURNACE DRIPPING A MOLTEN DRIP   326 19
  MOLTEN YET DENSE AND PERMANENT   477 23
  WHEN SAPPHIRES COOLED OUT OF MOLTEN CHAOS   682 22
  FROM THE FIRE THAT BOILS IN THE MOLTEN HEART OF THE WOR+   782 15
  BUT THE DREAM-STUFF IS MOLTEN AND MOVING MYSTERIOUSLY   *907   5
  MOLTEN METAL OF DREAMS   *907 12
  BUT THE DREAM-STUFF IS MOLTEN AND MOVING MYSTERIOUSLY   *909   2
  MOLTEN METAL OF DREAMS   *909   8
  THEN TO FALL BACK EXHAUSTED INTO THE UNCONSCIOUS MOLTEN+   *909 28

MOLY
  LIKE FLOWERS OF INFERNAL MOLY   146 20

MOMENT
  A MOMENT AGO   37 12
  IN ONE MOMENT ROUSES INSURGENT   39   6
  A MOMENT THERE LIKE SNOW IN THE DARK   62 13
  A MOMENT THEN DARKNESS SHUT THE LID OF THE SACRED ARK   62 18
  CUP FOR A MOMENT SOFT LITTLE WING-BEATS UTTERING   63   4
  FOR A MOMENT THE MIGHTY DIRECTION SNATCH   68 27
  MOMENT DESTROYS YOU YOU ARE JUST DESTROYED   87 22
  IS COMPLETE FOR THE MOMENT YET WAIT AND YOU'LL SEE THAT+   94   8
  US ONLY ONE MOMENT HIS KEYS   104 10
  A MOMENT THEN IN WEARINESS SETTLE   109 15
  FLUTTER FOR A MOMENT OH THE BEAST IS QUICK AND KEEN   119 21
  OF A MOMENT SEE SHE LAUGHED IF YOU ALSO   125   8
  CHEEKS AND HAIR A MOMENT SAYING IS IT YOU   180 11
  ONE MOMENT SEES AND SWIFT ITS DREAM IS OVER   195 14
  GLISTENING WITH ALL THE MOMENT AND ALL YOUR BEAUTY   210   4
  ONE MOMENT THE HATE LEAPS AT ME STANDING THERE   225 25
  ONE MOMENT I SEE THE STILLNESS OF AGONY   225 26
  LOOSED ONE MOMENT THE DARKNESS FRIGHTENS ME   225 28
  THAT THEY ARE AT THIS MOMENT   241 24
  MUSED A MOMENT   349 24
  THE MOMENT OF ETERNAL SILENCE   365 16
  YET UNRELEASED AND AFTER THE MOMENT THE SUDDEN STARTLING   365 17
  YET THE MOMENT I HATE HER SHE TRIPS MILD AND SMUG LIKE A   385 12
  THE MOMENT I REALLY DETEST HER   385 14
  THE SUN AS HE WAITS A MOMENT HUGE AND LIQUID   403   4
  IN THEIR EFFORTS TO COME AWAKE FOR ONE MOMENT   408   5
  AT THIS MOMENT SCRAPING TARDY ARARAT   429 10
  WE WOULDN'T INSIST ON IT FOR A MOMENT   434   9
  THEM FOR A MOMENT FELT   443 27
  THE MOMENT I SWEAR TO LOVE A WOMAN A CERTAIN WOMAN   472 16
  THAT MOMENT I BEGIN TO HATE HER   472 18
  THE MOMENT I EVEN SAY TO A WOMAN I LOVE YOU   472 19
  THE MOMENT LOVE IS AN UNDERSTOOD THING BETWEEN US WE   472 21
  THE MOMENT THE MIND INTERFERES WITH LOVE OR THE WILL   473   1
  ALL WE CAN KNOW AT THIS MOMENT   511   1
  THEN THEN COMES THE GREAT MOMENT OF CHOICE   639 25
  IN THE MOMENT OF CHOICE THE SOUL ROLLS BACK   640   1
  AS IF IN ANOTHER MOMENT SHE WOULD DISAPPEAR   646 26
  FOR A MOMENT AT EVENING TIRED AS HE STEPPED OFF THE TRA+   672   7
  FOR A MOMENT PURE IN THE YELLOW EVENING LIGHT HE WAS HY+   672 11
  FOR A MOMENT SHE WAS IO IO WHO FLED FROM ZEUS OR THE DA+   672 17
  AND FOR THE MOMENT SHE WAS ISIS GLEAMING HAVING FOUND H+   672 24
  FOR A MOMENT AS HE LOOKED AT ME THROUGH HIS SPECTACLES   672 25
  FOR A MOMENT HE WAS THE CENTAUR THE WISE YET HORSE-HOOF+   672 28
  FOR A MOMENT FREE FROM ALL CONCEIT OF YOURSELF AND ALL +   674   3
  YOU ARE FOR THAT MOMENT ONE OF THE GODS JESUS OR FAFNIR+   674   4
  AND JESUS HIMSELF COULD NOT HAVE DENIED THAT AT THAT MO+   674 22
  FOR A MOMENT GODLY LIKE BAAL OR KRISHNA OR ADONIS OR BA+   675 16
  IN THE SUSPENSION OF WHOLENESS IN THE MOMENT OF DIVISIO+   699   7
  A MOMENT AS HE FELL AND GROVEL AND DIE   741 28
  AND AT THIS MOMENT THERE IS AN OBLIGATION   776   2
  NOW AT THIS MOMENT AY   788 27
  NOW AT THIS MOMENT AY   789   2
  AY IN A MOMENT AY   789   6
  HOLA HOLA MEXICANOS GLANCE AWAY A MOMENT TOWARDS ME   790 19

MOMENT
    IT IS THE MOMENT OF FULNESS   803 10
    THE MOMENT I SWEAR TO LOVE A WOMAN ALL MY LIFE THAT VER+   834   8
    AT THE MOMENT WE TEND TO RUN INSANE THE MIND HAVING BRO+   838 21
    WE VIOLATE OURSELVES EVERY MOMENT AND VIOLATE EVERYBODY+   839   6
    IF A MAN LOOKED AT ME FOR ONE MOMENT AS THE SUN DOES   840   2
    A MOMENT LIKE A WAVERING SPARK   *912 19
    A MOMENT AND SHE WAS TAKEN AGAIN IN THE MERCIFUL DARK   *912 24
    FOR A MOMENT THEN AWAY WITH A FLUTTER OF WINGS   *913   5
    FOR A MOMENT THEN AWAY WITH A FLUTTER OF WINGS   *914   5
    CEASE FOR A MOMENT IN REVERENCE   *914 13
    FOR A MOMENT HIS GREAT DIRECTION SCRATCH   *915 11
    THEN FLUTTER FOR A MOMENT AND THE RAT'S LONG TEETH ARE +   *932 30
    OF A MOMENT SEE SHE LAUGHED IF YOU ALSO   *935 24
    FOR ME AT THE MOMENT   *947 16

MOMENTOUS
    LIFT LOOKS OF SHOCKED AND MOMENTOUS EMOTION UP AT ME   71 22

MOMENTS
    AND I CRY ALOUD IN THE MOMENTS THAT INTERVENE   100 23
    EVE IN HER HAPPY MOMENTS   314   6
    I'VE HAD MOMENTS OF HATRED OF YOU SINCE   396 10
    MOMENTS OF PURE MANIFESTATION   673 18
    UNLESS HE HAS HIS PURE MOMENTS WHEN HE IS SURPASSING   674 19

MOMENT'S
    A KISS AND A SPASM OF FAREWELL A MOMENT'S ORGASM OF   280 27
    HIS SCREAM AND HIS MOMENT'S SUBSIDENCE   365 15
    I HAD A MOMENT'S PURE DETESTATION OF YOU   396   7
    THERE'S NO RELIEF ONLY A MOMENT'S SULLEN RESPITE   486   4

MONADS
    IN STUPOR PERSIST AT THE GATES OF LIFE OBSTINATE DARK M+   75 12

MONA LISA
    SHE SMILING WITH GOATY MUNCH-MOUTH MONA LISA ARRANGES   382 26

MONEY
    AN' GIVE 'ER THE MONEY THERE IS   82 14
    SOME MONEY HER HAND SLIPS OUT OF THE BREAST OF HER   143   8
    NO MORE AND MONEY STINKS NOT AND DEATH AT LAST   173 23
    UNFINISHED FOR EVER BUT GASPING FOR MONEY AS THEY DREAM+   175   5
    THE GHASTLY DREAM OF RICHES OF MASSES OF MONEY TO SPEND   175   7
    MONEY FROM OUT OF THE EARTH OR THE BEAST OR THE MAN AS +   175 24
    WHILE AS TO HONESTY OH LOOK WHERE THE MONEY LIES   432 33
    HAVE HEAPS OF MONEY   440 27
    WHY HAVE MONEY   451 29
    NOT TO GET THE MONEY   453   7
    MONEY MAKES EVEN NO SEDIMENT   455   7
    SPINNING A GLAMOUR ROUND MONEY AND CLERGYMEN   456 24
    MONEY HYPOCRISY GREED MACHINES   457 11
    OF MONEY DO IT OR DIE   458 12
    A LITTLE FRESH AIR IN THE MONEY STY   459 17
    AND WEARING OUR SEATS OUT SITTING ON MONEY   485 26
    MONEY IS OUR MADNESS OUR VAST COLLECTIVE MADNESS   486   7
    WE QUAIL MONEY MAKES US QUAIL   486 14
    AND NO WONDER FOR MONEY HAS A FEARFUL CRUEL POWER   486 16
    BUT IT IS NOT MONEY WE ARE SO TERRIFIED OF   486 18
    HAS HE NO MONEY THEN LET HIM EAT DIRT AND GO COLD   486 21
    AND IF I HAVE NO MONEY THEY WILL GIVE ME A LITTLE BREAD   486 22
    IF I HAVE NO MONEY   486 26
    WE MUST HAVE SOME MONEY   487   4
    WE MUST REGAIN OUR SANITY ABOUT MONEY   487 11
    KILL MONEY PUT MONEY OUT OF EXISTENCE   487 14
    PRISON MAKES MEN BAD AND THE MONEY COMPULSION MAKES   488   2
    IS THEIR MONEY BUT I DOUBT IF I'D FIGHT FOR MINE ANYHOW   497 20
    I HAVE A CERTAIN AMOUNT OF MONEY SO MY ANXIETIES ARE BL+   501 21
    MONEY IS INSANE AND POVERTY IS INSANE   516   5
    DON'T DO IT FOR THE MONEY   517   7
    DO IT AND BE DAMNED TO THE MONEY   517   8
    AND WHATEVER COSTS YOU MONEY MONEY MONEY IS REALLY   517 15
    WHY DON'T WE DO SOMETHING ABOUT THE MONEY SYSTEM   518   6
    BUT IT MUST BE FREE WORK NOT DONE JUST FOR MONEY BUT FOR   520 20
    AND BULLIED WITH THE THREAT GET MONEY OR EAT DIRT   522 12
    AND LIVING LIKE LICE ON POOR MONEY   526 19
    MANKIND AND MONEY   527 16
    THAN PAPER MONEY WHEN THE BANK IS BROKE   528   4
    FOR THEIR VERY PALTRY LITTLE BIT OF MONEY   531 18
    AND MONEY AND INDUSTRY   534 16
    YOU'D HAVE MONEY AND YOU KNOW IT   546 25
    HERE YOU ARE WITH NO MONEY   547   4
    JUST TO SUPPORT YOU AND FIND YOU MONEY   547   7
    YOU'D HAVE MONEY YOU'D HAVE IT ENOUGH TO SUPPORT YOURSE+   547 11
    IF YOU WERE A MAN AND UP TO MY MARK YOU'D HAVE MONEY   547 19
    AND DO YOU THINK IT'S MY BUSINESS TO BE HANDING OUT MON+   547 22
    A LOT OF MONEY REARING THEM   569 12
    YOU'VE GOT MONEY OF YOUR OWN   572   6
    ANOTHER LITTLE RUN FOR THEIR MONEY A FEW MORE TURNS OF +   586 18
    THE MONEY   630 13
    MONEY AND MOTOR-CARS   639 17
    THAT THEIR LAST THOUGHT WAS MONEY   644 11
    NOT FOR MONEY BUT FOR LIFE   650 13
    ABOUT PROPERTY AND MONEY AND MECHANICAL DEVICES   666 12
    MONEY SHALL CEASE TO BE AND PROPERTY SHALL CEASE TO PER+   666 17
    AND THE WILL TO MAKE MONEY IS EVIL   716   6
    WHICH THE SUPERIOR CLASSES ARE MAKING MONEY OUT OF   763 14
    THAN WOMAN OR TRIUMPH MONEY OR SUCCESS   764   3
    AND DEARLY DEARER THAN MONEY   765   2
    THESE MONEY VERMIN   792 28
    MONEY IS MERELY   826 22
    OR EVEN A LITTLE MONEY   828 20
    OF SUCCESS MONEY   831 14
    EVEN WHILE WE ADMIT THE GHASTLY IMPORTANCE OF MONEY   831 15
    MONEY MACHINES FURNITURE   833 14
    TO ABOLISH THE TYRANNY OF MONEY   838   4
    THE THING FOR MEN TO DO IS TO START TO PULL DOWN MONEY   838 11
    SUCCESS FAILURE LOVE CHASTITY DEBAUCHERY MONEY OR SOVIE+   839 19

MONEY
    MONEY IS THE VAST STINKING BEAST   843   7
    AN' GIVE 'ER WHAT MONEY THERE IS   *924 18
    VERY SUMPTUOUS WITH THE MONEY OF SIR JESSE BOOT OF CASH+   *950 14
    THE WHOLE THING HAS RISEN OUT OF THIS CASH-CHEMIST MONEY   *950 17

MONEY-BEAST
    CREEP ON THE VAST MONEY-BEAST   843 11

MONEY-BRUISE
    BLUE-ARSED WITH THE MONEY-BRUISE   485 25

MONEY-FAT-ONES
    THE SAME I SAY TO THE PROFITEERS FROM THE HOTELS THE MO+   316 24

MONEYLESSNESS
    A CERTAIN WARLESSNESS EVEN MONEYLESSNESS   612 15

MONEY-MADNESS
    IT IS THE COLLECTIVE MONEY-MADNESS OF MANKIND   486 19

MONEY-MAD
    IT IS FEAR OF MY MONEY-MAD FELLOW-MAN   487   3

MONEY-MUCK-WORMS
    AND THE MONEY-MUCK-WORMS THE EXTANT POWERS   456 20

MONEY-MUCK
    THE MONEY-MUCK YOU SIMPLE FLOWERS   456 18

MONEY-POWER
    THE MIDDLE-CLASS MONEY-POWER   627 16

MONEY-SLAVES
    WE NEED HAVE NO DEAD PEOPLE MONEY-SLAVES AND SOCIAL   527   7

MONEY-SLAVE
    A MONEY-SLAVE   524 12

MONEY-SMELLING
    IF YOU POINT ME TO THAT FAT MONEY-SMELLING MAN IN A MOT+   645 11

MONEY-WORMS
    OLD MONEY-WORMS YOUNG MONEY-WORMS   456 22

MONEY-WORM
    MONEY-WORM PROFESSORS   456 23

MONGRELS
    NOW IT'S A COUNTRY OF FRIGHTENED OLD MONGRELS   535 17
    THIS PAIR OF PROPERTY MONGRELS   663 26

MONKEY
    THEY LOOK AT YOU THEY SEE A CAGED MONKEY   485 20
    YOU'RE A CAGED MONKEY AGAIN IN FIVE MINUTES   486   5
    AS STRIPS YOU STARK AS A MONKEY NUT   493 15
    OH YOU'VE GOT TO BE LIKE A MONKEY   549 13

MONKEYS
    MONKEYS RODE RATHER GREY AND WIZENED   444 15
    NOT MONKEYS MINDING MACHINES   450 13
    MONKEYS WITH A BLAND GRIN ON OUR FACES   450 17
    THERE IS NO WAY OUT WE ARE ALL CAGED MONKEYS   485 24
    LIKE MONKEYS OR ANGELS OR SOMETHING IN A LIMITED   550   3

MONOLITH
    THOUGH HE IS ALL WISTFUL AND PATHETIC LIKE A MONOLITH   255 35

MONOLITHIC
    AND THE MONOLITHIC WATER-BUFFALOES LIKE OLD MUDDY STONES   386 29

MONOMANIA
    IS THE SHADOWY MONOMANIA OF SOME CYPRESSES   297 20

MONOPOLY
    WHEN THE ONE GOD MADE A MONOPOLY OF IT   439 13

MONOTONOUS
    A MONOTONOUS WEIRD OF DEPARTURE AWAY FROM ME   47 13
    THE HOURS HAVE TUMBLED THEIR LEADEN MONOTONOUS SANDS   167   1
    THE HOURS HAVE TUMBLED THEIR LEADEN MONOTONOUS SANDS   167   8
    THIS GREY MONOTONOUS SOUL IN THE WATER   338 11
    OUR SOUL NOTHING BUT THE MAD MONOTONOUS   746 15

MONOTONOUSLY
    MONOTONOUSLY   64 22

MONOTONY
    OF A MEANINGLESS MONOTONY IS PALLING   65 13
    REPEATS HIMSELF OVER AND OVER IN MECHANICAL MONOTONY OF   479 17

MONSIEUR
    MONSIEUR   332   2
    WHILE I I PITY MONSIEUR   361 32

MONSTER
    PROBABLY HE WAS A JABBING TERRIFYING MONSTER   372 21
    TRIUMPH THE ANCIENT PIG-TAILED MONSTER   426 14
    AND A MONSTER WHEN YOU'RE PINCHED FOR ACTUAL NECESSITIES   498 14

MONSTERS
    ENCIRCLING THEIR HUDDLED MONSTERS OF LOVE   695   4

MONSTROUS
    THIS INTERMINGLING OF THE BLACK AND MONSTROUS FINGERS OF   242   2
    THAT LIES OUTSIDE THE MONSTROUS WOMB   262 23
    THE EGO REVEALED IN ALL ITS MONSTROUS INHUMANITY   475 11
    INTO THE PASSIVE UNKNOWN MONSTROUS WOMB   880   7

MONTEZUMA
    AND MECHANICAL AMERICA MONTEZUMA STILL   298 18

MONTH
    SINCE THE MONTH OF CHILDHOOD IS OVER AND WE STAND ALONE 132 16
    AND IN A MONTH AGAIN IS AS IF SHE HAD NEVER HAD THEM   386 19
    IS DEAD TOO A DEAD ORB WHEELED ONCE A MONTH ROUND THE P+ 702 27
    LANGUIDLY MONTH BY MONTH   766 8
    SINCE THE MONTH OF CHILDHOOD IS OVER AND WE START AFRESH *938 8

MONTHLY
    IN GRAND CHORALE TO YOUR MONTHLY KICK-UP   681 8

MONTHS
    HIS OWN SONG-MEASURE MANY MONTHS AGO   877 24

MONUMENTAL
    DARKLY MONUMENTAL IN YOU   296 10
    MONUMENTAL TO A DEAD DEAD RACE   297 12

MOO
    MOO   761 11

MOODS
    RESTLESS AND LONELY SHAKEN BY YOUR OWN MOODS   197 2
    MOODS THOUGHTS DESIRES AND DEEDS THAT CHIME   460 11

MOON
    IS THAT THE MOON   37 5
    THE VERY MOON IN THE SOUTH   37 14
    THE MOON FROM FAR ABYSSES   37 16
    AND NOW THE MOON   37 18
    SURGES THE WHITE OF THE MOON   50 2
    THE SILVER MOON   54 8
    THE COOL HIGH MOON AT THEIR EASE WHILE THE DRONING CHUR+ 54 30
    THE WHITE MOON SHOW LIKE A BREAST REVEALED   55 26
    THE MOON WALKS HER LONELY WAY WITHOUT ANGUISH   63 20
    THE MOON SETS FORTH O' NIGHTS   63 30
    THE MOON LIES BACK AND REDDENS   64 20
    SLOWLY THE MOON IS RISING OUT OF THE RUDDY HAZE   67 7
    HIGH AND SMALLER GOES THE MOON SHE IS SMALL AND VERY FA+ 67 13
    A TINY MOON AS SMALL AND WHITE AS A SINGLE JASMINE FLOW+ 67 18
    OR LIKE A MIST THE MOON HAS KISSED FROM OFF A POOL IN T+ 70 22
    LIKE HALF-SEEN FROTH ON AN EBBING SHORE IN THE MOON   75 28
    AS IF FROM THE WOMB THE SLOW MOON RISES AS IF THE TWIN-+ 88 18
    NOT PASS THE RED MOON RISEN AND I AM GLAD   88 28
    WITH COLD LIKE THE SHELL OF THE MOON AND STRANGE IT SEE+ 99 14
    NOR ONE NARROW GATE FOR THE MOON TO GO   103 7
    THE RIM OF THE MOON DIVINELY RISE   103 25
    TALL AND LOFTILY SHADOWED BUT THE MOON   103 30
    YOU COULD HAVE UNLOCKED THE MOON ON THE NIGHT   104 12
    A GIBBOUS MOON HANGS OUT OF THE TWILIGHT   113 17
    THE MOON IS BROKEN IN TWAIN AND HALF A MOON   114 17
    AND LIKE A MOON UNSHOWING IT MUST STILL SHINE THERE   114 24
    HAVE RISEN RED ON MY NIGHT AS A HARVEST MOON   126 4
    THE BLIND TO HIDE THE GARDEN WHERE THE MOON   129 16
    AND THE SUAVE SEA CHUCKLES AND TURNS TO THE MOON   130 2
    AND THE MOON SIGNIFICANT SMILES AT THE CLIFFS AND THE 130 3
    DANCE TO THE SLIDING SEA AND THE MOON   130 10
    FOR THE MOON ON MY BREAST AND THE AIR ON MY LIMBS   130 11
    THE SHORN MOON TREMBLING INDISTINCT ON HER PATH   131 23
    THE DEAD MOON HEAPED WITHIN THE NEW MOON'S ARMS   132 2
    SINCE DEATH FROM THE MOTHER MOON HAS PARED US DOWN TO 132 8
    THE WHITE MOON GOING AMONG THEM LIKE A WHITE BIRD   134 16
    THERE'S A MOON FULL BLOW   137 23
    THE SECRET OF THE MOON WITHIN YOUR EYES   156 21
    FROM THE SKY THE LOW TIRED MOON FADES OUT   163 21
    THE WANING MOON LOOKS UPWARD THIS GREY NIGHT   172 18
    AND WHO HAS SEEN THE MOON WHO HAS NOT SEEN   193 1
    TO NOTHINGNESS AND TIME WILL DIM THE MOON   193 11
    YOU WHO TAKE THE MOON AS IN A SIEVE AND SIFT   197 22
    ACROSS THERE A DISCOLOURED MOON BURNS ITSELF OUT   212 14
    THE MOON WAS A GOLDEN PETAL BETWEEN   216 15
    THE FULL MOON SANK IN STATE   261 32
    COME UP AND BE CALLED A MOON   302 8
    WHEN THE MOON FALLS ON A MAN'S BLOOD   453 13
    MOON   453 24
    AND THE MOON MAKES AWAY WITH SO MUCH   454 19
    ONCE THE MOON COMES DOWN   455 1
    BUT THE MOON IS WENDING HER WAY ATTENDING   456 3
    THE NEW MOON OF NO IMPORTANCE   467 5
    THE NEW MOON IN COOL HEIGHT ABOVE THE BLUSHES   467 9
    UNDER A MOON THEY DO NOT KNOW   471 9
    THOU ART LIKE THE MOON   473 25
    AND THE DARK MOON DRAWS THE TIDES ALSO   473 28
    IT IS THE MOON THAT TURNS THE TIDES   509 20
    EXCEPT ADMIT IT AND LEAVE IT TO THE MOON   510 6
    THEN ONLY UNDER THE MOON COOL AND UNCONCERNED   609 10
    IT MAKES ME REALISE THE DELICIOUS PLEASURE OF THE MOON 610 20
    YOU WHO HAVE NO FEELING OF THE MOON AS SHE CHANGES HER 643 10
    A LITTLE MOON QUITE STILL LEANS AND SINGS TO HERSELF   656 8
    TO KNOW THE MOON AS WE HAVE NEVER KNOWN   666 20
    MOON   675 12
    SUN AND MOON   675 21
    GIVE ME THE MOON AT MY FEET   684 8
    NOW THAT THE MOON WHO REMEMBERS AND ONLY CARES   687 15
    AND NOW THAT THE MOON WHO GIVES MEN GLISTENING BODIES 688 10
    GOD IS OLDER THAN THE SUN AND MOON   692 7
    GOD IS OLDER THAN THE SUN AND MOON   692 18
    MOON O MOON GREAT LADY OF THE HEAVENLY FEW   695 24
    NOW LADY OF THE MOON NOW OPEN THE GATE OF YOUR SILVERY + 696 1
    A HEALED WHOLE MAN O MOON   696 7
    WHEN THE MOON FROM OUT OF THE DARKNESS   702 13
    AND THE MOON THAT WENT   702 25
    FROM OFF THE SHEER WHITE SNOW OR THE POISED MOON   708 27
    ABSOLUTE ABSOLVED FROM THE SUN AND THE EARTH AND THE MO+ 712 16
    THE MOON AND THE EARTH THE SUN SATURN AND BETELGEUSE   713 20
    AND IF AS WEEKS GO ROUND IN THE DARK OF THE MOON   727 1

MOON
    WITH THE WHITE OF THE MOON BETWEEN   731 8
    THE MOON IS HIGH I AM LITTLE   731 9
    ALREADY I SEE THE SHELLED MOON LIE   747 28
    FOR THE MOON LIKE A FATA MORGANA WILL LEAN   748 1
    THE MOON IS NOT ANY WARMER THE SUN NO   754 5
    MOON ALL ABLAZE   755 13
    IT'S A FULL MOON   755 17
    SALLY GO ROUND THE MOON   755 23
    MY MOTHER THE MOON IS DARK   786 18
    MY MOTHER THE MOON IS DARK   789 11
    FOR THE SUN AND THE MOON ARE ALIVE AND WATCHING WITH GL+ 792 10
    THE STARS AND THE EARTH AND THE SUN AND THE MOON AND TH+ 792 17
    THIS IS WHAT STARS AND SUN AND EARTH AND MOON AND WINDS+ 793 3
    THERE ARE DRAGONS OF SUN AND ICE DRAGONS OF THE MOON AN+ 796 18
    THE NEW MOON SETS AT SUNDOWN   816 5
    WATCH THE NEW MOON   816 19
    IN THE SKY THE LOW TIRED MOON GOES OUT   857 21
    AND I LOOKED IN A ROOM WHERE THE LAMP AS A MOON IN MIST 865 1
    ALONG WITH THE MOON   881 31
    FOR THE FULL MOON SHONE BUT WHETHER   881 32
    IS A TRACK OF CLOUDS ACROSS THE MOON   882 18
    AND THE MOON STOOD OPPOSITE   883 22
    FOR THE GOLDEN MOON COMMUNES   883 24
    OF THE MOON AND THE NIGHT   884 3
    THE MOON WAS IN LOVE AND SHE   884 4
    LIKE FLOATING FROTH ON AN EBBING SHORE IN THE MOON   *897 27
    LIKE FLOATING FROTH ON AN EBBING SHORE IN THE MOON   *901 4
    THAT ISSUING OUT OF THE MOON HAS SIFTED   *914 18
    THE MOON LIKE A REDDENING LANTERN HANGS LOW ACROSS THE + *917 13
    THE MOON OF SLEEP IS ALIGHT   *917 16
    OR LIKE A MIST THE MOON HAS KISSED FROM OFF A POOL IN T+ *917 19
    A BIG BUD OF MOON HANGS OUT OF THE TWILIGHT   *929 6
    SHALL HAVE RISEN RED ON MY NIGHT AS A HARVEST MOON   *937 4
    THE SHORN MOON TREMBLING INDISTINCT ON HER PATH   *937 22
    THE DEAD MOON HEAPED WITHIN THE YOUNG MOON'S ARMS   *937 29
    SINCE DEATH FROM THE MOTHER MOON HAS PARED CLOSE TO THE+ *938 1
    SINCE THE BELOVED FADED MOON THAT SET US ALIGHT   *938 9
    LET US SEEK TO WIN HER BACK UNTO US THE MOON   *938 13

MOONBEAM
    I AM ADRIFT AS A MOONBEAM AND WITHOUT FORM   86 10

MOONBEAMS
    LIKE MOONBEAMS KISSING YOU BUT THE BODY OF ME   87 20

MOON-BLUE
    AND A MOON-BLUE MOTH GOES FLITTERING BY   41 25

MOON-FACED
    TO DIE UNOPENED WHEN THIS MOON-FACED LOVER   113 15

MOONING
    AND IT'S NO GOOD MOONING FOR SLOPPY EASE   559 9

MOONLIGHT
    BE ALONE AND SEE THE MOONLIGHT OUTSIDE WHITE AND BUSY 646 10
    AND GRAPES AND GHOULS AND GHOSTS AND GREEN MOONLIGHT 667 6
    O LET MY ANKLES BE BATHED IN MOONLIGHT THAT I   684 10
    A LIGHT LIKE MELLOW MOONLIGHT GLEAMED ON THIS WATER   864 29

MOONLIGHT'S
    UNDER THE PALLID MOONLIGHT'S FINGERING   129 12

MOON-LIKE
    THAT MOON-LIKE SWORD THE ASCENDANT DEAD UNSHEATHE   168 23

MOON-LIT
    OF MOON-LIT DANCERS   689 4

MOON-MIST
    THE MOON-MIST IS OVER THE VILLAGE OUT OF THE MIST SPEAK+ 63 4

MOON-PALE
    DREW HER LIPS OVER THE MOON-PALE PETALS SOFTLY BENT 856 20

MOON-REMEMBERING
    AND SET ME AGAIN ON MOON-REMEMBERING FEET   696 6

MOONRISE
    CALL IT MOONRISE   302 14

MOON-RISE
    IN A NEW NIGHT-SPASM OF BIRTH AND GIVEN US THIS NEW RED+ 88 20

MOONS
    AND CAST US FORTH LIKE THIN SHORN MOONS TO TRAVEL   132 10
    THAT CARRIES MOONS ALONG AND SPARE THE STRESS   195 35
    AND CAST US FORTH LIKE SHORN THIN MOONS TO TRAVEL   *938 2

MOONSHINE
    MY SIGHT BUT THEN WHO HAS STOLE THE BRIGHT WHITE HEN OF+ *933 23

MOON-SHOD
    SURE AND MOON-SHOD COOL AND BRIGHT-FOOTED   684 12

MOON'S
    THEN A GROUP OF TOADSTOOLS WAITING THE MOON'S WHITE TAP+ 72 19
    THE DEAD MOON HEAPED WITHIN THE NEW MOON'S ARMS   132 2
    THE MOON'S AS SHE FEELS FOR THE TIDES   285 29
    WITH GOD WE ARE CLOSE TOGETHER NOW THE MOON'S IN SHADOW 727 5
    UNDER THE MOON'S SHARP SCIMITAR'S   735 22
    THE DEAD MOON HEAPED WITHIN THE YOUNG MOON'S ARMS   *937 29

MOON-TIDES
    MOVES AS THE MOON-TIDES NEAR MORE NEAR   465 29

MOONY-DAISIES
    AND MOONY-DAISIES UNDERNEATH THE MIST   884 30

MOORED
    MOORED BUT NO   229 16

MOP
    WHEN SHE LIFTED HER MOP FROM HER EYES AND SCREWED IT IN   310 2

MOPE
    WON'T BREED THEY MOPE THEY DIE   484 24

MOPING
    MOULTING AND MOPING AND WAITING WILLING AT LAST   329 31
    ARE OPEN FOR THEM THEY ARE MOPING OR THEY BREAK WITH LI+   *918 7

MORAL
    LET HIM COME HOME TO A BIT OF MORAL DIFFICULTY LET LIFE+   431 4
    THE DEEP INSTINCTS WHEN LEFT ALONE ARE QUITE MORAL   529 3
    AND CLEAR INTUITION IS MORE THAN MORAL   529 4
    WHEN I AM CLOTHED I AM A MORAL MAN   607 9
    THE INVISIBLE GODS HAVE NO MORAL TRUCK WITH US   607 32
    THEY TELL ME THAT THESE BRITISH MORAL BIRDS   659 7
    THE TROUBLE ABOUT THOSE THAT SET UP TO BE MORAL JUDGES   836 20
    WHEREAS TO THE ORDINARY MORAL HUMAN BEING THE WORD   837 3
    MORAL LESSON   *950 29

MORALITY
    THEREFORE NO MORALITY OF POCKETS   607 25
    AND NONE OF US MUST EXPECT MORALITY OF EACH OTHER   608 3

MORALS
    THE MORALS OF THE MASSES   493 26
    AND WITHOUT MORALS AND WITHOUT IMMORALITY   607 31

MORBID
    SO MORBID AS THE ITALIANS SAY   280 5

MORBIDITY
    WINESKINS OF BROWN MORBIDITY   280 16

MORDANT
    OF MORDANT ANGUISH TILL SHE CEASED TO LAUGH   125 17
    MORDANT CORROSION GNASHING AND CHAMPING HARD   160 23

MOREOVER
    BUT MOREOVER   292 10

MORE-THAN-COMPREHENSIBLE
    WHY DO YOU ARCH YOUR NAKED-SET EYE WITH A MORE-THAN-COM+   369 16

MORE-THAN-EUROPEAN
    YOUR MORE-THAN-EUROPEAN IDEALISM   290 21

MORE-THAN-LOVELESSNESS
    AND MORE-THAN-LOVELESSNESS   339 28

MORE-THAN-WATER
    THIRST FOR FISH AS FOR MORE-THAN-WATER   340 8

MORIBUND
    THE EAST A DEAD LETTER AND EUROPE MORIBUND IS THAT SO   371 32

MORN
    OF MORN AFTER MORN   249 2
    OF CLOUD THE MORN SKIES YIELD   *915 4

MORNING
    SAW WHERE MORNING SUN ON THE SHAKEN IRIS GLISTENED   38 16
    WHEN I AWOKE THIS MORNING   46 25
    IN THE RIPENING MORNING TO SIT ALONE WITH THE CLASS   51 22
    THIS MORNING SWEET IT IS   51 26
    THE MORNING BREAKS LIKE A POMEGRANATE   58 24
    COOL AS SYRINGA BUDS IN MORNING HOURS   65 9
    WANTON SPARROWS THAT TWITTERED WHEN MORNING LOOKED IN   71 13
    SEEM TO BE MAKING OUT OF THE BLUE OF THE MORNING   72 6
    AND WHEN I WAKE IN THE MORNING AFTER RAIN   72 20
    OH LABOURERS OH SHUTTLES ACROSS THE BLUE FRAME OF MORNI+   73 8
    PERSISTS ALL MORNING HERE IN A JAR ON THE TABLE   90 2
    IT SEEMED THAT I AND THE MORNING WORLD   124 6
    LIKE HEAVY BIRDS FROM THE MORNING STUBBLE TO SETTLE   128 11
    AND MORNING SINGING WHERE THE WOODS ARE SCROLLED   135 27
    THE MORNING LIGHT ON THEIR LIPS   147 19
    MORNING STRONG   149 22
    OF THE MORNING THE ELMS ARE LOFTILY DIMMED AND TALL   164 22
    NOW IN THE MORNING   204 11
    MORNING   209 25
    BREEZE OF THE MORNING THROUGH A NARROW WHITE BIRCH   209 28
    WHEN SHE RISES IN THE MORNING   217 9
    SEE GLITTERING ON THE MILK-BLUE MORNING LAKE   230 8
    AH MEDITERRANEAN MORNING WHEN OUR WORLD BEGAN   311 14
    GREECE AND THE WORLD'S MORNING   311 27
    SUNDAY MORNING   312 9
    ALONG THE CORSO ALL THIS SUNDAY MORNING   314 29
    AND I TAKE THE WINGS OF THE MORNING TO THEE CRUCIFIED   321 20
    MORNING COMES AND I SHAKE THE DEWS OF NIGHT FROM THE WI+   322 26
    THAN THE WINGS OF THE MORNING AND THEE THOU GLORIFIED   323 4
    I HAVE MOUNTED UP ON THE WINGS OF THE MORNING AND I HAVE   323 11
    AND I WILL GIVE THEE THE WINGS OF THE MORNING   324 24
    BECAUSE HE IS IRASCIBLE THIS MORNING AN IRASCIBLE TORTO+   357 14
    FROM THE WARM BLOOD IN THE DARK-CREATION MORNING   358 14
    ALL HER GREAT HAIRY-SHAGGY BELLY OPEN AGAINST THE MORNI+   385 30
    AND IN THE MORNING WHEN THE BEDROOM DOOR IS OPENED   397 1
    HE TRAPPED HER THIS MORNING HE SAYS SMILING FOOLISHLY   401 26
    AT SIX IN THE MORNING THEY TURNED HIM DOWN   490 11

MORNING
    EDITOR GOOD MORNING DON'T TROUBLE TO CALL AGAIN WE   582 19
    SO I SAID GOOD MORNING AND LEFT HIM   620 9
    IN THE SUMMER MORNING   655 10
    IT IS SHIPS OF CNOSSOS COMING OUT OF THE MORNING END OF+   687 5
    TIP THE MORNING LIGHT ON EDGE AND SPILL IT WITH DELIGHT   709 6
    AND IN THE MORNING WAKE LIKE A NEW-OPENED FLOWER   726 24
    TO SEND ME FORTH ON A NEW MORNING A NEW MAN   727 30
    THIS MORNING   732 8
    OF MORNING IS BACK WE SHALL CHANGE AGAIN AND ESSAY   748 11
    WHEN IN THE MORNING I ROSE TO DEPART MY LOVE CAME TO SA+   749 17
    AND THEY MEET IN THE GLADE BETWEEN MORNING AND   771 14
    SAVE FOR THE MORNING AND EVENING STARS UPON WHICH THEY +   799 27
    BETWEEN THE MORNING AND THE AFTERNOON STAND I HERE WITH+   803 6
    AND THE TOP OF THE MORNING   803 11
    AND THE GLIMMERING DREAMLETS OF THE MORNING ARE PALLID +   854 7
    IN THE WHITE MORNING WHERE IS THE ENCHANTED ROOM OF THE+   856 7
    WHEN MORNING COMES I FIND ME A LOVE   858 5
    SIEGMUND ONLY THIS MORNING YOU WERE SHINING FOR ME   870 24
    YOU WERE ALL THE MORNING TO ME ALL THE SEA AND THE MORN+   870 25
    MORNING   871 15
    SEE THE MORNING SUN ON THE SHAKEN IRIS GLISTEN   *892 31
    LIKE A GLITTERING OF SHADOWS WITHIN THE MORNING AIR   *895 6
    COMES OVER THE SOFTNESS AND SILENCE OF MORNING I PASS   *895 11
    IN THE FRESH OF THE MORNING IT IS TO BE   *899 5
    IN THE FRESH OF THE MORNING IT IS TO BE   *902 17
    THE SMALL BIRDS THAT LIFTED THEIR HEADS WHEN MORNING LO+   *918 3
    AND OUT INTO MORNING   *930 16
    THEN UP WITH WRATH THE RED-EYED MORNING QUICKENS   *933 12
    AND MORNING SINGING WHERE THE WOODS WERE SCROLLED   *939 19
    WHEN SHE RISES IN THE MORNING   *942 19

MORNING-BRIGHT
    MORNING-BRIGHT TO THEE   322 31

MORNINGS
    FAR-OFF MEDITERRANEAN MORNINGS   311 15

MORNING SMILE
    THE MORNING SMILE SURE THAT IT WILL AFFORD HER   583 15

MORNING-STAR
    MORNING-STAR   640 4

MORNING STAR
    THE MORNING STAR   614 11
    THERE ARE DEAD THAT SLEEP IN THE WAVES OF THE MORNING S+   795 18
    MORNING STAR   796 22
    THEY COME FROM BEYOND THE MORNING STAR   799 3
    THEY SHALL FIND ME ONLY IN THE MORNING STAR   799 10
    BUT MIDMOST SHINES AS THE MORNING STAR MIDMOST SHINES   799 22
    THE MORNING STAR AND THE EVENING STAR SHINE TOGETHER   800 13
    FOR MAN IS THE MORNING STAR   800 14
    IF YOU WERE MEN WITH THE MORNING STAR   800 29
    BUT I AM QUETZALCOATL OF THE MORNING STAR   800 32
    AND YOU ARE MEN WHO SHOULD BE MEN OF THE MORNING STAR   800 34
    OF THE MORNING STAR   800 38
    DETERMINE TO GO ON AND ON TILL YOU ENTER THE MORNING ST+   809 8
    THERE IS ONLY THE MORNING STAR   810 22
    IN THE MORNING STAR   811 30
    LET US SEPARATELY GO TO THE MORNING STAR   812 3
    BUT THE MORNING STAR AND THE EVENING STAR   812 21

MORNING'S
    ALL MY MORNING'S PLEASURE IN THE SUN-FLECK-SCATTERED WO+   65 14

MORPHINE
    UNLESS THERE WERE A MORPHINE OR A DRUG   214 24

MORROW
    IN VAIN TRYING TO WAKE THE MORROW   371 23

MORSEL
    DO YOU NOT HEAR EACH MORSEL THRILL   127 11
    IN EVERY SHAKEN MORSEL   170 10

MORSELS
    FOR HE HAS DRUNK THE MORSELS WHITE OF SLEEP   878 11

MORT
    NOW IT IS DONE THE MORT   154 16

MORTAL
    IS NOT FOR YOU AND HE IS MORTAL STILL   158 17
    EVEN DEAD HE STILL IS MORTAL AND HIS HAIR   158 19
    LET NOW ALL MORTAL MEN TAKE UP   177 11
    KNOW YOURSELF O KNOW YOURSELF THAT YOU ARE MORTAL AND   464 23
    AND THE MORTAL RESERVE OF YOUR SEX AS IT STAYS IN YOUR   464 26
    KNOW THYSELF AND THAT THOU ART MORTAL   473 22
    AND FOR EVERY BLOOMIN' MORTAL THING   493 3
    UNDER THE GREAT COMMAND KNOW THYSELF AND THAT THOU ART +   674 8
    KNOW THYSELF AND THAT THOU ART MORTAL   714 5
    BUT KNOW THYSELF DENYING THAT THOU ARE MORTAL   714 6
    MANTLE OF THE BODY'S STILL MORTAL MEMORIES   *957 11

MORTALITY
    TOOK PLEASURE IN TOUCHING YOU MORTALITY   158 16

MORTALS
    NOW MORTALS ALL TAKE HOLD   177 8

MORTAR
    LOOK BRIGHTLY ON A CONFUSION OF MUD AND SAND AND MORTAR   864 26

MORTIFICATION
    THEY ARE THE FLOWERS OF ICE-VIVID MORTIFICATION   270 24
    COME LIFE SURGE THROUGH THIS MASS OF MORTIFICATION   271 2
    MORTIFICATION   271 9

MORTIFIED
    O' THY SPUNK AN' THA'RT EMPTY AN' MORTIFIED   139 12
    WHEN DESTRUCTION SOAKS THROUGH THE MORTIFIED DECOMPOSING 270 21

MOSES
    SUCH AS MOSES HAD AND GOD   326 4

MOSQUITO
    MAN OR MOSQUITO   333 9
    AM I NOT MOSQUITO ENOUGH TO OUT-MOSQUITO YOU   334 15
    THE MOSQUITO KNOWS FULL WELL SMALL AS HE IS   466 18

MOSQUITOES
    THE MOSQUITOES ARE BITING TO-NIGHT   302 9

MOSS
    MOSS   47 7
    I KISS THE STONES I KISS THE MOSS ON THE WALL   173 13
    TO THINK AMONG THE MOSS AND MUD OF LIZARDS AND MASTODONS 690 28
    STRAYED DOWN THE HILL CRUSHING THE SILKEN MOSS   863 22

MOSSES
    AS MOSSES AND LITTLE LIZARDS THEY SAY WERE ONCE BIG   372 20
    WHEN FROM A WORLD OF MOSSES AND OF FERNS   683 1
    OVER THE WITHERED MOSSES AND RED EARTH   880 20

MOST HIGH
    OR THE MOST HIGH DURING THE COAL AGE CUDGELLING HIS MIG+ 690 26

MOSTLY
    BUT MOSTLY DO YOU NOT DETEST MY BRAY   236 11
    AND MEN BEING MOSTLY GELDINGS AND KNACKER-BONED HACKS   379 31
    FOR IF A MAN HAS NO LIFE IN HIS WORK HE IS MOSTLY A HEAP 450 10
    AND WE WE ARE MOSTLY UNEXPLORED HINTERLAND   636 30
    MOSTLY THEY ARE THE GREEDY ONES   793 16

MOTE
    HAVE SAID THAT I THIS MOTE IN THE BODY OF SLEEP   195 18

MOTES
    GO WINGING GLAD THE YELLOW MOTES   060 24

MOTH
    AND A MOON-BLUE MOTH GOES FLITTERING BY   41 25
    SHE WOOS THE MOTH WITH HER SWEET LOW WORD   42 15
    LIKE A MOTH ON A STONE   226 20
    CAN I CATCH LIKE A MOTH BETWEEN MY HANDS   227 23
    ABOUT MOTH AND RUST   561 11

MOTHER
    MOTHER COME DOWN AN' SEE   44 11
    IT'S NOT A BEGGAR MOTHER HARK   44 14
    'E SAYS TELL YOUR MOTHER AS 'ER MEETEN'S   44 22
    DUNNA THEE TELL ME IT'S HIS'N MOTHER   76 23
    THA DOESNA MEAN TER SAY TER ME MOTHER   77 1
    BUT 'ER'S OLD MOTHER 'ER'S TWENTY YEAR   77 5
    THA NIVER BELIEVES IT DOES TER MOTHER   77 9
    THE SHROUDED MOTHER OF A NEW IDEA MEN HIDE THEIR FACES   91 26
    ONCE FROM YOUR WOMB SWEET MOTHER   101 25
    AND SO MY LOVE MY MOTHER   102 1
    WHEN I CARRIED MY MOTHER DOWNSTAIRS   106 28
    WHAT IS PEEPING FROM YOUR SKIRTS O MOTHER HEN   119 28
    SINCE DEATH FROM THE MOTHER MOON HAS PARED US DOWN TO   132 8
    SINCE THE BELOVED FADED MOTHER THAT SET US ALIGHT   132 17
    AND PRESSING THE SMALL POISED FEET OF A MOTHER WHO SMIL+ 148 8
    A MOTHER MILD   201 12
    THE MOTHER IN YOU FIERCE AS A MURDERESS GLARING TO   207 6
    LOT'S WIFE NOT WIFE BUT MOTHER   207 33
    AND AT THE FOOT OF A GRAVE A MOTHER KNEELS   232 26
    WHAT IS THE FRUIT OF YOUR WOMB THEN YOU MOTHER YOU QUEEN 235 5
    YOU WOMEN MOST HOLY YOU MOTHER YOU BEING BEYOND   235 13
    HIS MOTHER DEPOSITED HIM ON THE SOIL AS IF HE WERE NO M+ 356 24
    THIS IS YOUR MOTHER SHE LAID YOU WHEN YOU WERE AN EGG   357 2
    FATHER AND MOTHER   357 16
    AND MY MOTHER SINGING TO HERSELF   366 16
    DELICATE MOTHER KANGAROO   393 4
    DROP WHICH SHE LOVES SENSITIVE MOTHER KANGAROO   393 9
    WOMEN I LOVED AND CHERISHED LIKE MY MOTHER   410 3
    COME BACK MOTHER MY LOVE WHOM I TOLD TO DIE   411 21
    NOW THAT THE GRAVE IS MADE OF MOTHER AND WIFE   411 27
    NOW THAT THE WIFE AND MOTHER AND MISTRESS IS BURIED IN   412 23
    HIS MOTHER LIBERTY TRYING ALWAYS TO TEACH HIM TO COO   413 22
    THE WEEPING MOTHER OF GOD INCONSOLABLE OVER HER SON   439 29
    GOES BEHIND ITS MOTHER ACROSS THE DESERT   466 10
    GOES BEHIND ITS MOTHER ON BLITHE BARE FOOT   466 11
    MY MOTHER WAS A SUPERIOR SOUL   490 13
    LOOK AT MY MOTHER HOW RICH AND STILL SHE IS   503 28
    HOW ARE WE GOING TO APPEASE HER MAIDEN AND MOTHER   539 19
    IN MOTHER ENGLISH OR YOU'RE IN THE CART   575 26
    NO MOTHER WEEPS FOR ME   751 21
    COME IN MY MOTHER SAYS   755 11
    WHY DO YOU GO ABOUT LOOKING FOR ME MOTHER   756 14
    GOES BEHIND HIS MOTHER WHERE THE SAND IS HOT   757 9
    GOES BEHIND HIS MOTHER WITH BARE BLITHE FOOT   757 10
    MY MOTHER THE MOON IS DARK   786 18
    MY MOTHER THE MOON IS DARK   789 11
    AND THE IMAGES OF MY MOTHER AND THE IMAGES OF MY SAINTS 789 18
    YET I HAVE LAIN IN HIS LOINS ERE HE BEGOT ME IN MOTHER + 801 14
    ITS MOTHER DID SOMETHING TO IT AT ABOUT THE AGE OF TWEL+ 841 13
    MY MOTHER HAD BLUE EYES   869 5
    WHY SHOULD I GRIEVE THAT MY MOTHER IS NO LONGER CLOTTED 870 12
    AH BUT MY MOTHER HAD BLUE EYES   870 17
    DUNNA THEE TELL ME IT'S HIS'N MOTHER   *918 15

MOTHER
    THA DOESNA MEAN TO SAY TO ME MOTHER   *918 19
    BUT 'ER'S OLD MOTHER 'ER'S TWENTY YEAR   *918 23
    THA NIVER BELIEVES IT MOTHER DOES TER   *918 27
    THE SHROUDED MOTHER OF A NEW IDEA MEN HIDE THEIR FACES *926 19
    THE WHITE DOG NIPPED THE MOTHER RAT THE FATHER RAT BESI+ *933 7
    SINCE DEATH FROM THE MOTHER MOON HAS PARED CLOSE TO THE+ *938 1
    STILL PLIES THE LOVE OF OUR MOTHER FOR US STRAINING OUR+ *938 21
    PRESSING THE LITTLE POISED FEET OF THE MOTHER WHO SMILE+ *940 8

MOTHERHOOD
    INSISTING UPON YOUR MOTHERHOOD DEVASTATING   207 9
    I HAVE LEARNED TO CURSE YOUR MOTHERHOOD   207 34
    I HAVE CURSED MOTHERHOOD BECAUSE OF YOU   207 36
    ACCURSED BASE MOTHERHOOD   207 37
    ALL MOTHERS WHO FORTIFY THEMSELVES IN MOTHERHOOD DEVAST+ 208 18
    AND MOTHERHOOD IS JEALOUS   412 30

MOTHERLESS
    FATHERLESS MOTHERLESS BROTHERLESS SISTERLESS   357 24

MOTHER-LOVE
    AND THAT MOTHER-LOVE LIKE A DEMON DREW YOU FROM ME   206 2
    STRONGER THAN FEAR OR DESTRUCTIVE MOTHER-LOVE IT STOOD 207 12
    THAT IS DEAD THE MOTHER-LOVE LIKE LIGHT THAT FLOWED   *938 14

MOTHER OF GOD
    THAT HE'S STOLEN FROM THE MOTHER OF GOD   797 16
    MARY THE MOTHER OF GOD BIDS YOU FAREWELL   798 30

MOTHERS
    THE CURSE AGAINST ALL MOTHERS   208 17
    ALL MOTHERS WHO FORTIFY THEMSELVES IN MOTHERHOOD DEVAST+ 208 18
    COME BACK THEN YOU WHO WERE WIVES AND MOTHERS   411 18
    MOTHERS   829 15

MOTHERS-IN-LAW
    POOR MOTHERS-IN-LAW   309 28

MOTHER'S
    THE LIGHT HAS GONE OUT FROM UNDER MY MOTHER'S DOOR   63 12
    AT A MOTHER'S KNEES THE TROUBLE   152 20
    BEAR THE THOUGHT OF MY MOTHER'S PAIN-DARKENED BLUE EYES 069 14
    MUST HIDE MY MOTHER'S PIANO LITTLE AND BROWN WITH THE B+ *940 2
    AND THE KEYS WITH LITTLE HOLLOWS THAT MY MOTHER'S FINGE+ *940 4
    AND HYMNS IN GAMED IN OUR WARM LINE AS WE WATCHED MOTHER+ *940 12
    AND THE GREAT BLACK PIANO IS CLAMOURING AS MY MOTHER'S + *940 21
    AND MY MOTHER'S TUNES ARE DEVOURED OF THIS MUSIC'S RAVA+ *940 23

MOTHS
    NOT EVEN THE MOTHS CAN ALIGHT   114 6
    TINY BLACK MOTHS FLUTTER OUT AT THE TOUCH OF THE FORK   858 13
    NOT EVEN THE WHITE MOTHS WRITE   *929 23

MOTH'S
    THAT HERE WE'RE SAFE FROM EVEN THE ERMINE MOTH'S   113 23
    THAT HERE WE'RE SAFE FROM EVEN THE ERMINE MOTH'S   *929 12

MOTH-WINGS
    AND WHEN ABOVE HER HIS MOTH-WINGS HOVER   42 16

MOTION
    AS IT SPINS TO SLEEP ON ITS MOTION DRUGGED DENSE IN THE 149 7
    OUT OF THE SLEEP FROM THE GLOOM OF MOTION SOUNDLESSLY   149 9
    BUT NEVER THE MOTION HAS A HUMAN FACE   153 7
    ENDLESSLY IN ONE MOTION DEPART   163 7
    ALL OVER THE DIM CORN'S MOTION AGAINST THE BLUE   221 25
    IN A MOTION HUMAN INHUMAN TWO AND ONE   252 10
    WORKING IN MOTION   288 33
    THAT MOTIONLESS DEADLY MOTION   338 7
    PERPETUAL FIRE-LAUGHING MOTION AMONG THE SLOW SHUFFLE   389 18
    MEN ALL MOTION   389 21
    FLOWERS ARE JUST A MOTION A SWIFT MOTION A COLOURED   476 18
    IN THEIR FACES AND MOTION NEVER MECHANICAL IN THEIR LIM+ 635 31
    RESURRECTED FROM THE DEATH OF MECHANICAL MOTION AND EMO+ 667 33
    ON AND ON AND THEIR TRIUMPH IN MERE MOTION   675 26
    FREE MOTION OF LIFE   678 16
    AND THE WILL THE LIVING DYNAMO GIVES THE MOTION AND THE+ 712 14
    GOING YET NEVER WANDERING FIXED YET IN MOTION   713 30
    THE DEAD OF THE STEEL MACHINES GO UP IN MOTION AWAY   796 9
    ALL OVER THE CORN'S DIM MOTION AGAINST THE BLUE   *945 11

MOTIONLESS
    RESTS A STILL LINE OF SOLDIERS RED MOTIONLESS RANGE OF + 66 7
    BUT HE HAS GONE MOTIONLESS HATING ME   226 1
    SO NINE-TENTHS ASLEEP MOTIONLESS BORED AND STATICALLY A+ 324 15
    THAT MOTIONLESS DEADLY MOTION   338 7
    MOTIONLESS LIKE A BIT OF ROCK   379 6
    MOTIONLESS STANDING IN SNOW LIKE A CHRISTMAS TOY   402 26
    WITH DARK-WRAPPED ROCKY MOUNTAINS MOTIONLESS SQUATTING 410 28

MOTIONS
    POWERS TO REPEAT ITS OWN EGOCENTRIC MOTIONS   635 12

MOTIVE
    FOR ROSINESS ONLY WITHOUT AN ULTERIOR MOTIVE   219 19
    COOL MOTIVE   532 22

MOTIVES
    EXCEPT OF COURSE FOR SECONDARY MOTIVES   485 18
    ANYHOW THEY NEVER WILL EXCEPT FOR SECONDARY MOTIVES   485 22

MOTOR
    IN A MOTOR IN A PAP-PAP PAP-PAP MOTOR LITTLE MAN   571 6

MOTOR-CARS
    THEY MAKE TRAINS CHUFF MOTOR-CARS TITTER SHIPS LURCH   441 6
    MONEY AND MOTOR-CARS   639 17

MOTOR-CAR
    THAN RIDE IN THE MOTOR-CAR OF A MULTIMILLIONAIRE   498 2
    AND SUBJECT REALLY TO THE DRAUGHT OF EVERY MOTOR-CAR OR+ 617 17
    THE VIBRATION OF THE MOTOR-CAR HAS BRUISED THEIR INSENS+ 625 17
    IF YOU POINT ME TO THAT FAT MONEY-SMELLING MAN IN A MOT+ 645 11
    IGNORING OUR MOTOR-CAR BLACK AND ALWAYS HURRYING   780 25

MOTOR-DRIVEN
    AT THE TRASHY MOTOR-DRIVEN TRANSIT OF DIRTY DAY   453 27

MOTOR-POWER
    AND MOTOR-POWER   436 30

MOTOR-PRODUCTIVE
    YOUR WEIRD BRIGHT MOTOR-PRODUCTIVE MECHANISM   292 8

MOTTLED
    TROT-TROT TO THE MOTTLED FOOT-HILLS CEDAR-MOTTLED AND P+ 409 1
    SILVERY-SIDED FISH-FANGED FIERCE-FACED WHISKERED MOTTLED 409 3

MOTTO
    THAT PALE FRAGMENT OF A PRINCE UP THERE WHOSE MOTTO IS   388 5
    WHOSE MOTTO IS ICH DIEN   389 27
    IF THEY KNEW THAT HIS MOTTO WAS ICH DIEN   389 35
    MOTTO IS ICH DIEN   391 33

MOULD
    TO FLOURISH THERE AS PALE MOULD BLOOMS ON A CRUST   99 5
    OF EVERY DIRTY MUST-BESPRINKLED MOULD   141 10
    THAT FALLS ON YOUR LAP OF MOULD   162 11
    ALL ALL PERSEPHONE'S PALE CUPS OF MOULD   177 5
    YOUR SIDES THIS FIRMNESS THIS HARD MOULD   255 12
    EVEN THOUGH THEY GROW ON GENUINE ENGLISH MOULD   569 4
    MADE OF CEMENT POURED INTO A MOULD AROUND IRON STICKS   673 3
    NOTHING REMAINS NOW BUT MOULD UNTO MOULD   814 17
    TOMORROW COMES STEALTHILY OUT OF THE MOULD   815 7

MOULDED
    REFUSED TO BE MOULDED IN ARROWS OF ENGLISH WORDS   859 12

MOULDER
    MOULDER   69 17
    MOULDER   *915 29

MOULT
    AND LET IT MOULT THERE AMONG THE STONES OF THE BITTER S+ 329 20

MOULTING
    MOULTING AND RATHER NAKED ABOUT THE RUMP AND DOWN IN THE 329 23
    MOULTING AND MOPING AND WAITING WILLING AT LAST   329 31
    HANDING OUT A FEW LOOSE GOLDEN BREAST-FEATHERS AT MOULT+ 414 9

MOUND
    ONE HEAPED MOUND   145 28
    HE VEERS ROUND THE SLOW GREAT MOUND OF HER   356 29
    AS HER EARTHEN MOUND MOVES ON   362 5
    WHILE SHE PULLS HERSELF FREE AND ROWS HER DULL MOUND   362 10

MOUNDS
    WOULD CRUSH THEIR MOUNDS ON HER HEART TO KILL IN THERE   128 25
    SURE ON A HAVEN OF PEACE BETWEEN THE MOUNDS OF HER   249 29

MOUNT
    TOO HEAVILY BURDENED TO MOUNT TWE HEAVENS SO   132 4
    WONDERING MOUNT AND PUT THE FLOWERS ASUNDER   176 17
    THEY MOUNT TO THE LAST HILL-CREST   200 4
    AND MOUNT LIKE A LARK BELOVED   322 28
    TILL THEY MOUNT AND FILL AND ALL IS FULFILLED OF GOD'S + 698 20
    PAST THE MOUNT OF THE SUN   787 4
    TOO HEAVILY BURDENED TO MOUNT THE HEAVENS SO   *937 31

MOUNTAIN
    OVER THE TREE'S EDGE AS OVER A MOUNTAIN   50 1
    YOU GLOW AT LAST LIKE THE MOUNTAIN TOPS WHEN THEY CATCH 209 29
    AND SLOWLY DOWN THE MOUNTAIN ROAD BELATED   225 9
    TO GAZE ANY MORE AT THE CHRIST WHOM THE MOUNTAIN SNOWS   225 11
    WITH THE MOUNTAIN SNOWS ACROSS THE LAKE   228 10
    ON A MOUNTAIN CROFT   240 18
    MAHOMET NEVER WENT TO ANY MOUNTAIN   290 2
    WALKING LIKE A ROYAL SNAKE DOWN THE MOUNTAIN   293 10
    THEN CLOSE THE WEDGE OF YOUR LITTLE MOUNTAIN FRONT   353 8
    NEVER A MOUNTAIN PEAK TO BE KING OF THE CASTLE   382 32
    THE MYSTERY OF THE DARK MOUNTAIN OF BLOOD REEKING IN   390 6
    IT IS A MOUNTAIN LION   401 23
    FLASH OF A MOUNTAIN LION'S LONG SHOOT   402 16
    AND A MOUNTAIN LION·   402 28
    OF THAT SLIM YELLOW MOUNTAIN LION   402 33
    ON THE VERY SLOPES OF THE MATRIMONIAL MOUNTAIN   541 6
    AS MOUNTAIN PRESSING ON MOUNTAIN IN THE ZEST OF LIFE   694 11
    ON THE MOUNTAIN HEARS HIM   761 22
    DOWN THE BLUE DEPTHS OF MOUNTAIN GENTIAN FLOWERS   *955 19

MOUNTAINOUS
    SERVE VAST MOUNTAINOUS BLOOD IN SUBMISSION AND SPLENDOUR 390 23

MOUNTAINS
    WHERE ALL THE MOUNTAINS SIT   196 8
    THE MOUNTAINS ARE BALANCED   204 20
    AND THE BLUISH MOUNTAINS BEYOND WOULD BE CRUSHED OUT   205 4
    IN FRONT OF THE SOMBRE MOUNTAINS A FAINT LOST RIBBON OF 208 23
    OVER AND BEYOND TO WHERE THE MANY MOUNTAINS   209 23
    THE BIG MOUNTAINS SIT STILL IN THE AFTERNOON LIGHT   223 13
    THE MOUNTAINS HAVE   223 23
    OUT OF THIS OUBLIETTE BETWEEN THE MOUNTAINS   224 8

MOUNTAINS
    LIVING AS THE MOUNTAINS DO BECAUSE THEY ARE STRONG   226 2
    THE MOUNTAINS MAKE   227 8
    THEN THE MOUNTAINS LIKE CHARIOT CARS   248 21
    MOUNTAINS OF CARRARA   340 19
    AND THE FLAT FLACCID MOUNTAINS OF THE ELEPHANTS' STANDI+ 390 13
    THE MOUNTAINS OF PICORIS   402 24
    MOUNTAINS BLANKET-WRAPPED   407 1
    THE MOUNTAINS NEVER GET UP AND WALK ABOUT   407 5
    WHITE MEN MAKE GOLD-MINES AND THE MOUNTAINS UNMAKE   407 13
    MOUNTAINS   408 10
    MOUNTAINS BLANKET-WRAPPED   408 19
    IT GONE BY OUR FARM TO THE MOUNTAINS THAT STAND BACK BL+ 732 7
    THEY WANT GOLD THEY WANT SILVER FROM THE MOUNTAINS   793 18
    THOSE THAT FOLLOW ME MUST CROSS THE MOUNTAINS OF THE SKY 799 8
    DEER CRASH THEIR HORNS IN THE MOUNTAINS OF HIS BREAST   *953 28

MOUNTAIN'S
    THE MOUNTAIN'S NEW-DROPPED SUMMER SNOW IS CLEAR   225 2

MOUNTAIN-TIPS
    CAN I GATHER THE MOUNTAIN-TIPS   227 18

MOUNTAIN-TOP
    THE YELLOW SUN STEPS OVER THE MOUNTAIN-TOP   230 5

MOUNTAIN-WALLS
    AND LOOK AT THE MOUNTAIN-WALLS   204 13

MOUNTED
    I HAVE MOUNTED UP ON THE WINGS OF THE MORNING AND I HAVE 323 11
    MOUNTED AND TENSE SPREAD-EAGLE OUT-REACHING OUT OF THE   364 30
    THEN LIKE CHICKENS MOUNTED IN MY HAND   *933 18

MOUNTING
    A BALE-FIRE MOUNTING MOUNTING UP IN ME   241 12
    AND SLOW MOUNTING MARVEL OF A LITTLE TREE   667 18

MOUNTS
    WHICH MOUNTS UP MY ARMS   241 19
    AND HOW I AM NOT AT ALL EXCEPT A FLAME THAT MOUNTS OFF   245 10
    AND WHEN THE BILLY GOAT MOUNTS HER   386 20
    MOUNTS UP TO MY HEART AND I FIND IT GOOD   *899 34
    MOUNTS UP TO MY HEART AND I FIND IT GOOD   *903 13

MOURN
    TO MOURN   63 26
    I HAVE COME I FEEL THEM WHIMPER IN WELCOME AND MOURN   172 25
    THE GHOSTS AND I WE MOURN TOGETHER AND SHRINK   173 6

MOURNFUL
    LOW-ROUNDED ON THE MOURNFUL TURF THEY HAVE BITTEN DOWN + 33 6
    OF THE MOURNFUL CONSTANT HEART THAT WHILE SHE'S WEAVING   65 25
    OF THE MOURNFUL TILL PEOPLE WAFT   108 21
    MOURNFUL YOUNG MAN IN YOUR TWENTIES   485 10
    LOW-ROUNDED ON THE MOURNFUL GRASS THEY HAVE BITTEN DOWN+*891 7

MOURNFULLY
    MOURNFULLY TO AND FRO TO AND FRO THE TREES ARE WAVING   136 22

MOURNFULNESS
    WHO THINK THE ONLY WAY OUT OF YOUR MOURNFULNESS IS   485 11

MOUSE
    MOUSE   47 34
    IN A MOUSE THAT PAUSES TO LISTEN   170 6
    AND THE MUSIC OF MEN IS LIKE A MOUSE GNAWING   656 10
    I FRIGHTENED A LITTLE MOUSE   670 4
    MY WEE MOUSE   863 2

MOUSTACHE
    HIS MOUSTACHE WITH AN ELBOW LIFTED AND HURLED   814 29

MOUTH
    SHE KISSED ME WARM ON THE MOUTH   37 13
    AND QUIVERS IN WORDS THROUGH MY MOUTH   38 31
    AND DOWN HIS MOUTH COMES TO MY MOUTH AND DOWN   43 33
    YOU KNOW YOUR MOUTH   55 13
    WHAT IS THIS MOUTH OF STONE   55 22
    IN TEDIUM AND MOUTH RELAXED AS IF SMILING INEFFABLE TED+ 66 12
    CURVED THY MOUTH FOR THEE AND WHAT STRONG SHOULDER   69 14
    WHO CROUCHING PUT HIS MOUTH DOWN IN A KISS   69 22
    LIFE IN THY MOUTH AND DIM BREATH'S HASTENING HISS   69 24
    TURN THY MOUTH ON A WOMAN LIKE THAT   80 19
    SUCH ANGER AS SETS YOUR MOUTH UNWONTEDLY   85 20
    SHOULD PUT YOUR MOUTH TO MINE AND DRINK OF ME   86 4
    YOUR OWN DARK MOUTH WITH THE BRIDAL FAINT LADY-SMOCKS   90 11
    AND HER DEAD MOUTH SINGS   101 15
    MY MOUTH ON HER PULSING   120 18
    DREAMING YOUR YIELDED MOUTH IS GIVEN TO MINE   129 24
    I KISS YOUR MOUTH AH LOVE   153 24
    MY MOUTH YOU MET BEFORE YOUR FINE RED MOUTH   156 22
    AND HER MOUTH UNCLOSED IN A LAST LONG KISS   198 3
    AND HER MOUTH UNCLOSED IN THE LAST LONG KISS   199 11
    STILL THE KISS WAS A TOUCH OF BITTERNESS ON MY MOUTH   206 20
    I HAVE SEEN IT FELT IT IN MY MOUTH MY THROAT MY CHEST MY 207 21
    I WALK UP TO MY NECK IN MIST HOLDING MY MOUTH UP   212 13
    MY MOUTH ON HERS IN KISSES AND SO SOFTLY   218 19
    AND MOUTH REACHING FORWARD TO KISS YOU   220 11
    DRAWN ON HIS MOUTH EYES BROKEN AT LAST BY HIS PANGS   225 8
    WE LAY MOUTH TO MOUTH WITH YOUR FACE   248 25
    I AM FILLING MY MOUTH WITH THE EARTH   259 31
    HOW CAN ONE SPEAK WHERE THERE IS A DUMBNESS ON ONE'S MO+ 266 10
    IS JUST TO PUT YOUR MOUTH TO THE CRACK AND TAKE OUT THE+ 282 9
    OUT OF HIS OWN MOUTH   320 9
    ONCE HE LAY IN THE MOUTH OF A CAVE   324 5
    UNHOOKED HIS GORPING WATER-HONEY MOUTH   339 6
    POISON IN HIS MOUTH FOR THE SUN IN HIM WOULD FAIN RISE + 348 10

MOUTH
  HE SIPPED WITH HIS STRAIGHT MOUTH   349 15
  OPENING YOUR IMPERVIOUS MOUTH   353   4
  INTO AN ENORMOUSLY SIDE-BEAKED MOUTH   359   3
  TAKING BREAD IN HER CURVED GAPING TOOTHLESS MOUTH   359 19
  FROM HIS PINK CLEFT OLD-MAN'S MOUTH   365 12
  FOOT IN THE MOUTH OF AN UP-STARTING SNAKE   365 31
  WHILE SHE WITH HER GOATY MOUTH STANDS SMILING THE WHILE   382 18
  CHINESE-DRAGON-WRINKLED WITH A PINK MOUTH GRINNING   397 18
  WITH AN OLIVE-SPRIG IN HIS MOUTH   413 31
  WITH MOUTH AND LOINS AND NEEDS HE LIVES   461 15
  THAT HARD CLAPPER STRIKING IN A HARD MOUTH   622 21
  TO MOUTH   630 18
  THE SECRET IN THE BLIND MOUTH OF THE WORM   744 28
  I SPEAK WITH A VAIN MOUTH   745 29
  AND HIS MOUTH WIPED CLEAN OF THE BITTERNESS OF REPROACH   770 19
  WITH HIS MOUTH OF CARESSIVE FIRE   801 23
  LIKE A GREY DOG WHOSE MOUTH IS FOUL WITH RABIES   807   5
  COOL ON MY MOUTH   861   4
  AND THE LITTLE MOUTH RED   861 23
  HER FRUIT IS UNRIPE AND HER SOFT MOUTH IS BITTER AND RO+   864 18
  THE MOUTH OF THE MAN IS FULL OF THE TASTE OF PAIN   864 22
  I BREATHED MY DREAMS UPON YOU I LAID MY MOUTH ON YOUR M+   871   1
  AH WITH HIS BLESSING BRIGHT ON THY MOUTH AND THY BROW   872   1
  HIS RECKLESS RED MOUTH LAUGHING CRUELLY   876 25
  I KNOW THE SWEET RED HUTCH OF HIS MOUTH WHERE WARM   876 32
  AND PUTS HIS MOUTH DOWN TO THE GUSHING STREAM   877   8
  IN RECKLESSNESS HE DRANK WITH A BITTER MOUTH   878 17
  WITH HEAD THROWN BACK AND PARTLY OPENED MOUTH   878 20
  TILL OFF THY MOUTH HAS LEAPT THE FLAME OF LIFE   879 22
  THAT LEAP AND MEET TOGETHER AT THE MOUTH   879 34
  I KISSED HER ONCE AGAIN UPON THE MOUTH   881   1
  AND THEN I KNEW I HAD TAKEN MY MOUTH FROM HER THROAT   882   7
  AND I WENT BACK WITH MY MOUTH TO HER MOUTH   882 10
  THAT QUIVERS BETWEEN MY EYES AND MOUTH   *893 14
  CURVED THY MOUTH FOR THEE AND HIS STRONG SHOULDER   *915 26
  GOD LONELY PUT DOWN HIS MOUTH IN A KISS OF CREATION   *916   5
  THE VIVID LIFE OF HIS LOVE IN THY MOUTH AND THY NOSTRILS   *916   7
  TURN THY MOUTH ON A WOMAN LIKE HER   *922 19
  THEY WOULD SAY SEEING EACH MOUTH OF WHITE ROSE PRAISE   *941   6

MOUTHFUL
  CHAMPING IT TOSSING A MOUTHFUL   397   9

MOUTHFULS
  SHE SNAPS THE SOFT BREAD FROM MY HAND IN GREAT MOUTHFULS   399   1

MOUTH-GATE
  MOUTH-GATE OPEN   336   9

MOUTH-HAIR
  MOUTH-HAIR OF SOLDIERS PASSING ABOVE US OVER THE WRECK +   66 29

MOUTHS
  SOFT SHAFTS SUNBREATHING MOUTHS   301 29
  THE SUN BUT ALL CREATURES OF THE SUN MUST DIP THEIR MOU+   368   6
  A VAPOUR OF ROTTENNESS OUT OF THEIR MOUTHS LIKE SEWER-S+   462 27
  ESPECIALLY CLAPPER BELLS HARD TONGUES WAGGING IN HARD M+   615   2
  WHO PUT SALT IN OUR MOUTHS   707 21
  CREEPING FOR THE GARBAGE OF LIFE AND BITING WITH VENOMO+   796 13
  BUT WHOSE DREAMS ARE DOGS GREY DOGS WITH YELLOW MOUTHS   807 15

MOUTH'S
  YEA AND HER MOUTH'S PRUDENT AND CRUDE CARESS   127 23
  AH WHERE HIS MOUTH'S RED SUMMER AND WHERE IS NOW THE YE+   *933 27
  TO COVER MY MOUTH'S RAILLERY TILL I'M BOUND IN HER SHAM+   *940 17

MOVE
  WHEN I MOVE THE OARS SEE   49   5
  THE HEADS OF THE BOYS MOVE DIMLY THROUGH A YELLOW GLOOM+   92   4
  I MOVE AMONG A TOWNFOLK CLAD   109 10
  THEIR WORDS AS THEY MOVE   109 12
  YET I CANNOT MOVE HOWEVER MUCH   117 16
  PUT FORTH TO HER SHE DID NOT MOVE NOR I   125 23
  SEVEN TOADS THAT MOVE IN THE DUSK TO SHARE   126 19
  AND PEOPLE DARKLY INVESTED WITH PURPLE MOVE PALPABLE   148 26
  TO SHOW WHERE THE SHIPS AT SEA MOVE OUT OF SIGHT   172 21
  EACH WITH A SECRET WHICH STIRS IN HIS LIMBS AS THEY MOVE   174 10
  OF A ROSE-TREE MOVE TO ROSES AND THORNS AND A DELICATE +   176   9
  ALL THINGS ON THE MOVE GOING THEIR OWN LITTLE WAYS AND +   249 17
  WE MOVE WITHOUT KNOWING WE SLEEP AND WE TRAVEL ON   252   7
  IT IS EASIER TO STAND STOCK RIGID THAN TO MOVE   288   7
  AND I JUT AGAINST YOU IF I TRY TO MOVE FOR YOU ARE EVER+   289   7
  SEE IF I DON'T MOVE UNDER A DARK AND NUDE VAST HEAVEN   289 19
  THEY MOVE IN OTHER CIRCLES   339 30
  AND MOVE ON FEET BUT MOIST EARTH WEIGHS HIM DOWN THOUGH+   341 23
  AND MOVE ON YOUR SLOW SOLITARY HUNT   352 19
  TO MOVE AND TO BE QUITE SURE THAT HE IS MOVING   358   5
  ARE CAST IN BLACK AND WHITE AND MOVE   444   6
  AN' YOU COULD NO MORE GET 'EM A MOVE ON   550 17
  BECAUSE THEIR SPIRIT CAN'T MOVE   558 27
  THEY MOVE IN A GREAT GRIND OF HATE SLOWLY BUT INEVITABLY   648   7
  MOVE IN THE UNDER   762   9
  AND THE BRILLIANT YOUNG HUSBAND MADE A LITTLE MOVE POUT+   842 16
  AND HER FINGERS MOVE IN THE RUTS OF MY EARS   863   3
  THOUGH YOU MOVE WITH A QUIET GRACE LIKE A CLOUD   874 23
  BEING TOO MIRTHLESS TO MOVE THE LILT OF SINGING   884 13
  MOVE MY ARMS THE HILL BURSTS AND HEAVES UNDER THEIR SPU+   *891 10
  MOVE   *906 18
  THEY HAVE A SECRET THAT STIRS IN THEIR LIMBS AS THEY MO+   *908 14
  THE HEADS OF MY BOYS MOVE DIMLY THROUGH THE YELLOW GLOO+   *926   4
  PUT FORTH TOWARD HER SHE DID NOT MOVE NOR I   *936 22

MOVED
  AND SUDDENLY AS IF THE GROUND MOVED   66 15
  SHE MOVED HER HAND AND AGAIN   124 32
  MOVED WITH SLOW FEET AND HER EYES' FLAME STEADILY BURNED   156 10
  SHE MOVED ROUND TO WATCH   222   6

MOVED
  SO IT NEVER MOVED ON ANY MORE EXCEPT MENTALLY AND IN ME+   841 14
  LOOKED UP AND THE WORDS MOVED LIKE A SMILE FROM HIS LIPS   865   3

MOVEMENT
  SWING TO MY WALKING MOVEMENT WEAK   73 26
  COURSED ROUND BY RHYTHMIC MOVEMENT OF ALL TIME   194 23
  EVERY MOVEMENT WILL BE DIRECT   267 31
  THAT FLOWER IN MERE MOVEMENT   446 10
  THE WORLD IS WAITING FOR A NEW GREAT MOVEMENT OF   522 26
  THE GREAT MOVEMENT OF CENTRALISING INTO ONENESS WILL ST+   611 17
  LOOK HE HATH MOVEMENT UPWARD HE SPIRALS   682 18
  SIT IN THE GREY MIST OF MOVEMENT WHICH MOVES NOT   711 28
  BACK AND FORTH IN A BLIND MOVEMENT   825 19
  OF FORM OR MOVEMENT OR OF HARMONY   872 12
  MOVEMENT OF MULTITUDES SURPASSING RHYTHM   872 20
  TO HOIST THE NEXT WHITE PLANK THEIR MOVEMENT SEEMS   *895   5

MOVEMENTS
  PERVADES MY MOVEMENTS AND MY THOUGHTS AND WORDS   727   3
  WAS WET WITH SWEAT AND HIS MOVEMENTS STRONG AND HEAVY   734 22

MOVES
  MOVES ON TO THE SEA   38 28
  TALL AND DARK THE CHURCH MOVES ANXIOUS TO KEEP   48 21
  AS THE AIR MOVES IN   112 18
  MOVES IN SILVER-MOIST FLASHES IN MUSICAL TRIM   147 20
  TO DRAW THE LOAD SO STILL AND SLOW IT MOVES   225 15
  MOVES AT HER EASE AGAIN   228 20
  AS HER EARTHEN MOUND MOVES ON   362   5
  BENEATH THE EARTH-SOILED HOVEL IN WHICH SHE MOVES   362 19
  AS SHE MOVES ETERNALLY SLOWLY AWAY   363   7
  AS WHEN A GREAT SHIP MOVES TO ANCHOR   445 16
  IT MOVES IT RIPPLES AND ALL THE TIME   460   9
  MOVES AS THE MOON-TIDES NEAR MORE NEAR   465 29
  THAT'S WHY IT MOVES ABOUT   525   2
  YOUR SELF MOVES ON AND IS NOT TODAY WHAT IT WAS YESTERD+   543 14
  SIT IN THE GREY MIST OF MOVEMENT WHICH MOVES NOT   711 28
  MOVES AS IT CAN   812 20
  WATCH THE STIR WHICH IS RHYTHMIC AND MOVES THEM ALL AS +   *909   9
  MOVES THE BLOOD   *909 10

MOVING
  IS HE MOVING INVISIBLY DOES HIS STEEP   40   3
  THE MOVING HYMN   96 22
  URGING THEM AND MOVING THEM HELPLESS MECHANIC THEIR WILL   149 15
  STILL HANGS THE HAWK WITH THE WHOLE SKY MOVING   150   1
  SOUNDLESSLY MOVING IN HEAVEN'S OTHER DIRECTION   161 23
  UNDINE TOWARDS THE WATERS MOVING BACK   161 25
  AS IF MOVING IN AIR TOWARDS US TALL ANGELS   164 23
  FOR THE PROPER DREAM-STUFF IS MOLTEN AND MOVING MYSTERI+   176   1
  MOVING ALONG IN THE MYSTERIOUS EBB OF THE NIGHT   180 19
  OVERHEAD IT WILL BE A SQUIRREL MOVING   231 17
  HOW THE STARS ARE MOVING IN SURETY   252   5
  THAT WE ARE ALL DETACHED MOVING IN FREEDOM MORE THAN THE   267 26
  SEE IF I AM NOT LORD OF THE DARK AND MOVING HOSTS   289 22
  AND YOU ARE SLOWLY MOVING PIONEER YOU ALONE   354   3
  TO MOVE AND TO BE QUITE SURE THAT HE IS MOVING   358   5
  MOVING AND BEING HIMSELF   358 15
  NOW THAT IN ENGLAND IS SILENCE WHERE BEFORE WAS A MOVING   410 21
  AND MOVING ALWAYS WITH A SOFT SLOW PRECISION   445 15
  COMPELLED TO ADMIRE THE BRIGHT RHYTHMS OF MOVING BODIES   445 25
  IT'S THE FLOW OF YOUR LIFE IT'S YOUR MOVING SELF AND YOU   464 18
  O FLOWERS THEY FADE BECAUSE THEY ARE MOVING SWIFTLY A   476   6
  FOR THE FIERCE CURVE OF OUR LIVES IS MOVING AGAIN TO THE   478   1
  IT IS VERY UNNERVING MOVING IN A WORLD OF SMOULDERING   539   4
  SWEEPING THE CURVE OF SPACE AND MOVING THE SILENCE   609 12
  THE WORLD IS MOVING MOVING STILL TOWARDS FURTHER DEMOCR+   611   6
  ALL MOVING INTO FLOWERS   627 12
  ALL THE GODS AND YOU SEE THEM ALL IF YOU LOOK ALIVE AND+   671 20
  AND ALIVE AND MOVING TOMORROW MANY TOMORROWS AS YESTERD+   671 21
  THE TWO GREAT AND MOVING ONES FIRE AND THE YIELDING WET   706 12
  THEN I SHALL KNOW THAT MY LIFE IS MOVING STILL   727 14
  LIKE A VOLCANO MY HIPS ARE MOVING   802 24
  NO LONGER A LARGE FLECK MOVING IN THE SUNSHINE   870 14
  BEWILDERED AMID THE MOVING IMMENSITY   875 16
  MOVING VIBRATING ENDLESSLY IN THE ROUNDED FLESH   *906 24
  BUT THE DREAM-STUFF IS MOLTEN AND MOVING MYSTERIOUSLY   *907   5
  THE FASCINATION OF THE QUICK RESTLESS CREATOR MOVING TH+   *908 19
  BUT THE DREAM-STUFF IS MOLTEN AND MOVING MYSTERIOUSLY   *909   2

MOVVER
  TILL HE SAW ME BUT PLEASE SIR MY MOVVER SAID I COULD AN'   866 19
  WE AIN'T GOT NO FARVER ONLY A MOVVER AN' SHE 'AS TER GO   866 20

MOW
  THEY MOW AND THEY PLASH IN THE WATER   827   6

MOWER
  NO LONGER THEY SWEEP THE HOURS AS THE SCYTHE OF THE MOW+   855 29
  OF THE LONG SCYTHE THE STOOPING MOWER WIELDS   *939   8

MOW-FIELDS
  AS WE CROSSED THE MOW-FIELDS DOWN THE GLOWING HILL   884 28

MOWIE
  AND THROUGH TO THE MOWIE ONLY THE DEAD IN THEIR BEDS   173 11

MOWING
  THERE ARE FOUR MEN MOWING DOWN BY THE ISAR   219 21
  THE FIRST MAN OUT OF THE FOUR THAT'S MOWING   219 25
  THE MAN WHO IS MOWING THE TALL WHITE CORN   651 13
  THERE'S FOUR MEN MOWING DOWN BY THE RIVER   *944   1

MOWING-MACHINES
    OF MIDDLE-CLASS MOWING-MACHINES AND   627 15

MOWIN'
    THE FIRST MAN OUT O' THE FOUR THAT'S MOWIN'   *944 5

MR FORD
    MR FORD KNOWS IT   635 20

MR GLADSTONE
    MR GLADSTONE WAS A VERY GOOD MAN   582 1

MR GOD
    ALL THAT STORY OF MR GOD SWITCHING ON DAY   681 19

MR LAWRENCE
    NO MR LAWRENCE IT'S NOT LIKE THAT   490 1

MR MEADE
    THEIR DOOM AT THE HANDS OF MR MEADE   634 2

MR MEAD
    AND MR MEAD THAT OLD OLD LILY   579 17
    OR MR MEAD WILL BE AFTER YOU   580 9

MRS JUSTICE ENNIS
    BOUGHT SECOND-HAND FROM MRS JUSTICE ENNIS   760 13

MR SMITH
    MR SMITH MR SMITH   583 1
    MR SMITH MR SMITH   583 22
    MR SMITH MR SMITH   583 26
    MR SMITH MR SMITH   584 1

MRS NAYLOR
    I EXPECT YER KNOW WHO I AM MRS NAYLOR   81 21
    I EXPECT YOU KNOW WHO I AM MRS NAYLOR   *923 21

MR SQUIRE
    DEARLY-BELOVED MR SQUIRE   680 20
    SO NOW WE BEG YOU MR SQUIRE   681 9

MR WATTS
    HAVE ALL BY MR WATTS AND THE VICTORIANS BEEN CAREFULLY   658 18

MUCK
    SLOW WATERY ROTTING BACK TO LEVEL MUCK   318 2
    THE MUCK FROM WHICH YOU'VE SPRUNG   456 17
    PLAYING WITH MUCK AND I THOUGHT YOU YOUNG GENTS   463 9
    BENEATH THE WEIGHT OF MUCK   491 24

MUCK-HEAP
    OF YOUR FOREFATHERS' MUCK-HEAP   456 19

MUCOUS
    AND FELT HIM BEAT IN MY HAND WITH HIS MUCOUS LEAPING   339 9

MUD
    THE FLOWERS OF ALL MY MUD SWIM INTO SIGHT   113 8
    YOUNG BIRDS FORSAKEN AND LEFT IN A NEST OF MUD   145 24
    BUT MUD HAS FLOODED THE HOMES OF THESE WEARY LANDS   167 11
    SPUMED WITH MUD   310 23
    EMOTIONS TO MUD   544 17
    IN ITS MUD AND ITS TALK SLOWLY SWIRLED   551 6
    BEING TRAMPLED TO MUD   658 12
    TO THINK AMONG THE MOSS AND MUD OF LIZARDS AND MASTODONS   690 28
    BUT IMAGINE AMONG THE MUD AND THE MASTODONS   691 1
    LIKE A MUD FROM WINTER DISGUISED IN GREY   815 8
    AND YOU STIR UP THE MOST AMAZING MUD   830 15
    LOOK BRIGHTLY ON A CONFUSION OF MUD AND SAND AND MORTAR   864 26
    INTO MUD THE SPACE FAST SHRINKS IN THE BUILDER'S HANDS   *896 11
    AND IN THE DARK I FEEL HIS COLD WEBBED FEET MUD BLACK   *947 19
    AND CROWD THERE ON THE GREY MUD BEACHES OF THE MARGINS   *958 9

MUD-BEACHES
    GAUNT GAUNT THEY CROWD THE GREY MUD-BEACHES OF SHADOW   722 6

MUD-BLACK
    AND THE DRIP OF HIS COLD WEBBED FEET MUD-BLACK   •   438 11

MUDDY
    HUTCHED UP FOR WARMTH THE MUDDY RIMS   145 19
    IN A GREEN MUDDY WEB-FOOT UNUTTERLY SONGLESS WORLD   286 1
    AND THE MONOLITHIC WATER-BUFFALOES LIKE OLD MUDDY STONES   386 29
    NO DOUBT HE WAS KHAKI-COLOURED WITH MUDDY PROTECTIVE   523 18
    TO THINK OUT IN THE ABSTRACT WHEN ALL WAS TWILIT GREEN +   690 29
    THE DEAD TREAD HEAVILY THROUGH THE MUDDY AIR   704 8
    OH FOOLS MEXICANS AND PEONS WITH MUDDY HEARTS   794 32

MUD-GREY
    AND THERE OF COURSE YOU MEET A HUGE AND MUD-GREY   387 6

MUD-HOVEL
    OF THAT MUD-HOVEL OF HIS SLOWLY RAMBLING SPOUSE   361 14

MUD-WEED
    THE MUD-WEED OPENING TWO PALE SHADOWLESS STARS   145 3

MUFFLED
    THE DARKNESS FALLING THE DARKNESS RISING WITH MUFFLED   205 6
    HEAVEN'S MUFFLED FLOOR   268 26
    AND HE HARDLY STIRRED IN MY HAND MUFFLED UP   347 8
    OF GHOSTS THAT THRONG ABOUT OUR MUFFLED HEARTS   736 3

MUFFLES
    MUFFLING MY MIND AS SNOW MUFFLES THE SOUNDS THAT PASS   75 22
    MUFFLING MY MIND AS SNOW MUFFLES THE SOUNDS THAT PASS   *897 22
    MUFFLING MY MIND AS SNOW MUFFLES THE SOUNDS THAT PASS   *900 30

MUFFLING
    MUFFLING MY MIND AS SNOW MUFFLES THE SOUNDS THAT PASS   75 22
    MUFFLING MY MIND AS SNOW MUFFLES THE SOUNDS THAT PASS   *897 22
    MUFFLING MY MIND AS SNOW MUFFLES THE SOUNDS THAT PASS   *900 30

MULBERRY
    SO HERE WE GO ROUND THE MULBERRY BUSH   658 1
    MULBERRY BUSH MULBERRY BUSH   658 2
    HERE WE GO ROUND THE MULBERRY BUSH   658 3
    NEVER HAVING SEEN A MULBERRY BUSH IN OUR LIVES   658 4

MULE-DRAWING
    RELEASE ME FROM THIS MULE-DRAWING   751 15

MULLEINS
    AS THE TALL FOXGLOVES AND THE MULLEINS AND MALLOWS   709 18

MULTIFORM
    AH NO YOU MULTIFORM   56 32
    AND ROT LIKE A BEAN-POD WHAT ARE YOU OH MULTIFORM   73 19

MULTIMILLIONAIRE
    THAN RIDE IN THE MOTOR-CAR OF A MULTIMILLIONAIRE   498 2
    AND FEEL THE PEACELESSNESS OF THE MULTIMILLIONAIRE   498 3

MULTIPLICITY
    STRONGER THAN MULTIPLICITY OF BONE ON BONE   383 9

MULTIPLY
    AS ABRAHAM WHOSE SEED SHALL MULTIPLY   126 16

MULTITUDE
    WITH MULTITUDE OF WHITE ROSES AND SINCE YOU WERE BRAVE   176 12
    THE MUTILATED HORROR-STRUCK YOUTHS A MULTITUDE   258 1
    AHEAD OF THE MULTITUDE   440 11
    AND OF COURSE IF THE MULTITUDE IS MAD   486 8
    THEN I WISH LIKE TIBERIUS THE MULTITUDE HAD ONLY ONE HE+   526 21
    WITH MULTITUDE OF WHITE ROSES AND JUST A FEW   *940 27

MULTITUDES
    THE MULTITUDES ARE LIKE DROPPINGS OF BIRDS LIKE DUNG OF+   614 21
    ONLY ATTEND TO THE NOISELESS MULTITUDES   736 2
    THE MULTITUDES SEE ME NOT   788 1
    MOVEMENT OF MULTITUDES SURPASSING RHYTHM   872 20

MULTITUDINOUS
    OF MULTITUDINOUS IGNOMINY   628 18
    MULTITUDINOUS ENDLESS THE GHOSTS COMING HOME AGAIN   739 15
    THE MULTITUDINOUS PEOPLE UNFUSED   746 6

MUMBLE
    FOR HER TO MUMBLE AND HIM TO CRACK   492 21

MUN
    IF YER MUN KNOW   79 16
    T' CHILDT MAUN TA'E ITS LUCK IT MUN   81 1
    IS MINE I MUN CLAIM HIM ONCE FOR ALL   *944 6

MUNCHEN
    DRAWING NEAR THEY COVER THE MUNCHEN ROAD   732 26

MUNCH-MOUTH
    SHE SMILING WITH GOATY MUNCH-MOUTH MONA LISA ARRANGES   382 26

MUNDANE EGG
    OF THE MUNDANE EGG   329 29
    MUNDANE EGG AT VARIOUS POINTS THEY STEPPED OUT AND IMME+   760 23

MURDER
    WAR CAME AND EVERY HAND RAISED TO MURDER   257 27
    VERY GOOD VERY GOOD EVERY HAND RAISED TO MURDER   257 28
    IT IS GOOD I CAN MURDER AND MURDER AND SEE THEM FALL   257 30
    MURDER SUICIDE RAPE   531 4
    AND THEN PERHAPS MURDER THAT IS TO SAY   532 20
    QUITE COLD-BLOODED INTELLECTUAL MURDER WITH A SUFFICIENT   532 21
    IT WAS MURDER   715 2
    EACH SIDE TRYING TO MURDER THE OTHER SIDE   715 3
    BUT MURDER IS ALWAYS EVIL   •   715 8
    IN SHEER MURDER   715 15
    SURELY NOT SO FOR HOW COULD MURDER EVEN SELF-MURDER   717 15

MURDERED
    THE MURDERED BODIES OF YOUTHS AND MEN IN HEAPS   258 5

MURDERER
    VERY GOOD VERY GOOD I AM A MURDERER   257 29
    AND A COMPLETE ABSENCE OF CONSEQUENCE TO THE MURDERER   532 23
    BEGETS A MURDERER IN HIS OWN BODY   653 4
    A THIEF A MURDERER OF DREAMS   808 12

MURDERESS
    THE MOTHER IN YOU FIERCE AS A MURDERESS GLARING TO   207 6

MURDEROUS
    AND MOST MURDEROUS OF ALL DEVICES   715 16

MURMUR
    HARDLY A MURMUR COMES FROM THE SLEEPING BROOD   48 23
    LIKE A MURMUR OF FIRE   885 26

MURMURED
  SHE HID HER FACE SHE MURMURED BETWEEN HER LIPS   125 19
  THINKING HE WAS A LITTLE HILL AND SHE MURMURED SUCH   540 2
  THAT COULD ONLY BE GOD-GIVEN AND MURMURED   693 17
  SHE HID HER FACE SHE MURMURED BETWEEN HER LIPS   *936 18

MURMURING
  BUT SLEEPS THE LONG WEEK OUT EMBOSOMED IN MURMURING LIM+   858 23

MURMURINGS
  OF HANDS AND LIPS AND MURMURINGS   436 22

MURMURS
  PLAYS WITH ME SWAYS ME LIFTS ME AND SINKS ME MURMURS OH   34 20

MUSCAT
  SOMETHING OF THE SAME FLAVOUR OF SYRACUSAN MUSCAT WINE   280 9

MUSCULAR
  AND IN ADDITION THE GREAT MUSCULAR PYTHON-STRETCH OF HER   393 22
  BUT BRAINY ROBOT OR AESTHETIC ROBOT OR MERELY MUSCULAR +   637 23

MUSE
  THAT SUCH TRIVIAL PEOPLE SHOULD MUSE AND THUNDER   494 14

MUSED
  MUSED A MOMENT   349 24

MUSHROOM
  NICELY GROOMED LIKE A MUSHROOM   431 13
  JUST LIKE AN OLD MUSHROOM ALL WORMY INSIDE AND HOLLOW   431 20

MUSHROOM-FACED
  MUSHROOM-FACED HEAVY-BOTTOMED   765 18

MUSHROOM-LIKE
  AND THEIR GROOMED AND MUSHROOM-LIKE FACES   765 12

MUSHY
  MUSHY PATHETIC YOUNG MEN   457 14
  MUSHY AND TREACHEROUS TINY   457 17

MUSIC
  LIKE SAVAGE MUSIC STRIKING FAR OFF AND THERE   52 17
  MUSIC SCREAMS AS ELEPHANTS SCREAM   70 10
  NOW HERE I SIT WHILE YOU BREAK THE MUSIC BENEATH   05 21
  CEASE THEN FROM MUSIC DOES ANGUISH OF ABSENCE BEQUEATH   85 23
  LIKE A SUDDEN CHUCKLING OF MUSIC I BADE HER EYES   125 26
  TINKLED THE MUSIC OF GLEANING   152 19
  BUT IT WILL BE LIKE MUSIC SHEER UTTERANCE   268 6
  TORN WITH A SHRIEK HALF MUSIC HALF HORROR   364 26
  TO MUSIC AND QUEER CHANTING   387 34
  TOM-TOMS WEIRD MUSIC OF THE DEVIL VOICES OF MEN FROM   388 35
  AND THE MUSIC OF MEN IS LIKE A MOUSE GNAWING   656 10
  AND CROUCHING AND SPEAKING THE MUSIC OF LOST LANGUAGES   688 16
  NOTHING BUT TO MAKE LOST MUSIC   816 16
  THE BREEZE WAKES UP A MUSIC IN THE SALLOW   868 21
  FILLING HIS SINGLE MEASURE WITH MUSIC FULL   877 27
  AND TURNING ROUND IN PAIN FROM THE MUSIC HE   884 9
  WHO ACHE WITH AN ANGUISH OF MUSIC TO MAKE FOR YOU   884 19
  BUT LAYING FOREVER OUR EFFORT AT MUSIC BY   884 22
  LIKE SAVAGE MUSIC STRIKING FAR OFF AND AWAY   *905 6
  THE MUSIC OF MUSIC IS STILLNESS YOU BIRDS   *914 12
  LIKE A SUDDEN CHUCKLING OF MUSIC I BADE HER EYES   *936 25
  THE BREEZE WAKES UP A MUSIC IN THE SALLOW   *941 21
  COMES OVER TO ME WITH A COVERT MUSIC THAT STIRS   *942 2

MUSICAL
  MOVES IN SILVER-MOIST FLASHES IN MUSICAL TRIM   147 20
  OR SUN-BRIGHT APOLLO HIM SO MUSICAL   307 25
  NOR EVEN THE MUSICAL SUAVE YOUNG FELLOW   437 6

MUSIC-HALLS
  GREY UNAPPEASED GHOSTS SEATED IN THE MUSIC-HALLS   740 3

MUSIC-LESS
  BY MY OWN BONDS OF BLOOD AND MUSIC-LESS   864 18

MUSIC'S
  AND MY MOTHER'S TUNES ARE DEVOURED OF THIS MUSIC'S RAVA+   *940 23

MUSLIN
  A YARD OF INDIA MUSLIN IS ALIVE WITH HINDU LIFE   448 21

MUSTARD
  THE CHILD LIKE MUSTARD SEED   172 5

MUST-BESPRINKLED
  OF EVERY DIRTY MUST-BESPRINKLED MOULD   141 10

MUSTN'T
  YOU MUSTN'T EXPECT IT ALSO TO WAIT FOR YOUR CONVENIENCE   531 21
  YOU MUSTN'T EXPECT MY DEAR TO GET AWAY WITH IT   548 21

MUTABLE
  THIS MUTABLE WITCH   124 13
  THIS MUTABLE WITCH   *935 12

MUTE
  A MUTE NEARLY BEAUTIFUL THING   112 11
  WITHOUT MYSTERY MUTE   827 26
  NOT ON THE STEMS OF VIRGINITY LOVELY AND MUTE   855 11
  SWINGS ROUND THE STEMS OF THE MANY INSIGNIFICANT MUTE   855 19
  A MUTE NEARLY BEAUTIFUL THING IS THY FACE   *927 28
  A MUTE NEARLY BEAUTIFUL THING   *929 1

MUTILATED
  OH GOD TO BE MUTILATED   213 13
  THE MUTILATED HORROR-STRUCK YOUTHS A MULTITUDE   258 1
  TODAY THE SOCIAL CONSCIOUSNESS IS MUTILATED   516 1
  A FEARFUL THING IS THE MUTILATED SOCIAL CONSCIOUSNESS   516 6
  OVER THEIR MUTILATED CYCLOPEAN EYE   544 30

MUTTER
  YOU IN A MUTTER   395 34

MUTTERING
  ME FULL LENGTH IN THE COWSLIPS MUTTERING YOU LOVE   90 16
  FROM THE SURF HAS ARISEN THE BOYS ARE MUTTERING   *894 16

MUTTERS
  THE PINE-TREES BEND TO LISTEN TO THE AUTUMN WIND AS IT +   102 25

MUTUAL
  THE GEM OF MUTUAL PEACE EMERGING FROM THE WILD CHAOS   477 19
  IS THERE A SAPPHIRE OF MUTUAL TRUST A BLUE SPARK   478 6
  WE MUST HAVE THE COURAGE OF MUTUAL TRUST   487 21

MUZZLE
  AND GLISTENING ADHESIVE MUZZLE   325 29
  AND FAR DOWN THE MUZZLE OF THE FIGHT   788 19

MUZZLES
  BENDING THEIR ROSY MUZZLES PENSIVE DOWN   311 11
  MUZZLES TOGETHER EAR-APRICK   311 24
  NO TENDER MUZZLES   335 18

MYCENAE
  IN MINOS IN MYCENAE   704 1

MY-EYE
  IT WAS ALL MY-EYE TO ME   555 4

MYRIAD
  GO MYRIAD SPARKS OF PEOPLE FILLING   110 19
  AN UNCHARTED WAY AMONG THE MYRIAD THICK   132 11
  AND ALL THE MYRIAD HOUSELESS SEEDS   160 7
  THE MYRIAD GLITTERING CHIMNEY-TIPS   166 20
  AFIRE AT A MYRIAD SCARLET POINTS   315 24
  BLOOD FROM SIDE TO SIDE CAUSING MY MYRIAD SECRET STREAMS   320 28
  ALL THE BRONZE GLOSS OF ALL HIS MYRIAD PETALS   371 11
  THEY WERE FOILED THE MYRIAD WHISPERING DARK-FACED   391 25
  AND YOU OH SEE THE MYRIAD DOVES THAT WALK   750 21
  MYRIAD MYRIAD DEAD TWIGS OF PALLID AND CHAFING PEOPLE   784 21
  AND HOLD MYRIAD THREADS FROM THEIR CLAWS   793 26
  HAS STREWN MYRIAD TWINKLING POPPY-PETALS DOWN THE PATH +   860 18
  OUR CHARTERED WAY AMONG THE MYRIAD THICK   *938 3

MYRIADS
  THE WRITHING OF MYRIADS OF WORKMEN ALL DREAMING THEY AR+   175 2
  MYRIADS OF DANDELION PAPPUS   204 16
  COME AND LIFT US TOWARDS OUR CULMINATION WE MYRIADS   272 31
  LIFTING THE RABBIT-BLOOD OF THE MYRIADS UP INTO SOMETHI+   414 22
  THE DEAD ARE IN MYRIADS THEY SEEM MIGHTY   441 5
  IN MYRIADS UNDER THE HOT AND HOSTILE SUN   628 7
  BETWEEN MACHINE-SPAWN MYRIADS   635 28
  MYRIADS   637 30

MYRIAD-WISE
  OUT MYRIAD-WISE   253 27

MYRRH
  THAT CHURN THE FRANKINCENSE AND OOZE THE MYRRH   298 5

MYSEN
  SCRAIGHTIN' MYSEN AS WELL 'ER UNDID 'ER BLACK   61 9
  BUT I THOWT TER MYSEN AS THAT WOR TH' ONLY BIT   61 17

MY-SEN
  AN' ME AS 'AS KEP' MY-SEN   77 25
  I'M SEEIN' FOR MY-SEN   78 18
  I'M SCRAIGHTIN' MY-SEN BUT ARENA GOIN'   78 27
  WAS A'MOST BURSTIN' MAD O' MY-SEN   80 7
  AH'N PUT MY-SEN I' TH' WRONG LIZ   83 26
  SCRAIGHTIN' MY-SEN AS WELL 'EN UNDID HER BLACK   *911 25
  AN' ME AS 'AS KEP MY-SEN   *919 13
  I'M SEEIN' FOR MY-SEN   *920 10
  I'M SCREETIN' MY-SEN BUT ARE-NA GOIN'   *920 19
  WAS A'MOST BURSTIN' MAD O' MY-SEN   *922 7
  I MIGHT LOSE MY-SEN   *922 26

MYSHKINS
  AND THE ALYOSHAS AND DMITRIS AND MYSHKINS AND STAVROGINS   533 14

MYSTERIES
  WHAT HAVE YOU TO DO WITH THE MYSTERIES   131 20
  COME BACK TO BED LET US SLEEP ON OUR MYSTERIES   211 25

MYSTERIOUS
  WINGS AND FEATHERS ON THE CRYING MYSTERIOUS AGES PEEWIT+   34 26
  MOVING ALONG IN THE MYSTERIOUS EBB OF THE NIGHT   180 19
  I WISH THESE BRITTLE FROST-LOVELY FLOWERS OF PASSIONATE+   272 6
  FLOURISHING FROM THE ROCK IN A MYSTERIOUS ARROGANCE   299 8
  HOAR-FROST-LIKE AND MYSTERIOUS   306 28
  THE MYSTERIOUS BULL TORE HIM AT ADOLESCENCE INTO PIECES   361 11
  AT THE END OF SOME MYSTERIOUS RED-HOT IRON   363 16
  SOME MYSTERIOUS SORT OF PRESTIGE   555 14
  THAT MYSTERIOUS PRESTIGE WHICH THEY ALL   555 18
  AND OPEN OUR CONSCIOUSNESS TO THE DEEP MYSTERIOUS LIFE   666 13
  GOD IS A GREAT URGE WONDERFUL MYSTERIOUS MAGNIFICENT   690 8
  BOTH BREASTS DIM AND MYSTERIOUS WITH THE GLAMOROUS KIND+   693 12
  THE GREAT MYSTERIOUS ONE IS SWELLING AND SHAPING THE DR+   *907 24
  EVERYTHING GREAT AND MYSTERIOUS IN ONE SWELLING AND SHA+   *909 15

MYSTERIOUSLY
    OF DARKNESS ABUNDANT WHICH SHAKEN MYSTERIOUSLY   136 18
    FOR THE PROPER DREAM-STUFF IS MOLTEN AND MOVING MYSTERI+ 176 1
    TRAFFICKING MYSTERIOUSLY THROUGH THE AIR   655 19
    I FEEL GODDESSES TRAFFICKING MYSTERIOUSLY THROUGH THE A+ 655 27
    BUT THE DREAM-STUFF IS MOLTEN AND MOVING MYSTERIOUSLY   *907 5
    BUT THE DREAM-STUFF IS MOLTEN AND MOVING MYSTERIOUSLY   *909 2

MYSTERY
    TWIN-BUBBLING CHALLENGE AND MYSTERY IN THE FOAM'S   76 3
    LIKE A MYSTERY   96 32
    THE MYSTERY   97 6
    ON OUR MYSTERY NOUGHT CAN DESCRY US   114 7
    THE INNER DARK OF THE MYSTERY   114 11
    HAVE I PROFANED SOME FEMALE MYSTERY ORGIES   141 3
    MY VEIL OF SENSITIVE MYSTERY RENT IN TWAIN   151 19
    LIKE A DARK ROSE A MYSTERY OF REST   154 10
    TO HAVE THE MYSTERY BUT NOT GO FORTH   160 26
    IT IS ISIS THE MYSTERY   196 5
    ISIS THE MYSTERY   196 23
    THE PINE-WOODS HOW I LOVE THEM SO IN THEIR MYSTERY OF   212 3
    WATCH AT THE BANNER OF DEATH AND THE MYSTERY   232 23
    ARE PROPPED ON END THERE WHERE THE MYSTERY STARTS   233 8
    MYSTERY   234 32
    DISSOLVED WITH THE MYSTERY OF THE INNERMOST HEART OF THE 260 28
    MYSTERY BEYOND KNOWLEDGE OR ENDURANCE SO SUMPTUOUS   260 30
    TO THE SOURCES OF MYSTERY IN THE DEPTHS   261 14
    AND KINDLES IT FURTHER AT THE CORE OF UTTER MYSTERY   261 16
    AND DRENCHED WITH MYSTERY   280 22
    FIG FRUIT OF THE FEMALE MYSTERY CONVERT AND INWARD   283 18
    THE MYSTERY OF THE DARK MOUNTAIN OF BLOOD REEKING IN   390 6
    BASED ON THE MYSTERY OF PRIDE   414 18
    THE MYSTERY THAT LIES IN BEASTS   445 18
    THAT IS PART OF THE MYSTERY OF SEX IT IS A FLOW ONWARDS 449 4
    THE MYSTERY OF THE INTERIOR   607 6
    TO ADD THE MYSTERY OF JOY-IN-RESURRECTION TO THE MASS   609 20
    THE FUTURE OF RELIGION IS IN THE MYSTERY OF TOUCH   611 10
    THE MYSTERY OF CREATION IS THE DIVINE URGE OF CREATION   690 1
    WITHOUT MYSTERY MUTE   827 26
    THE MYSTERY I STRIVE TOWARD HOWEVER   876 28
    TWIN BUBBLES SHADOW-FULL OF MYSTERY AND CHALLENGE IN TH+ *897 30
    TWIN BUBBLES SHADOW-FULL OF MYSTERY AND CHALLENGE IN TH+ *901 7
    THE FLUSH OF THE GREAT MYSTERY   *907 7
    OH THE GREAT MYSTERY AND FASCINATION OF THE UNSEEN SHAP+ *909 13
    WITHIN THE SPACIOUS GLOOM OF MYSTERY   *936 34

MYSTIC
    YOU INTEGRAL TO ME EACH DOOR EACH MYSTIC PORT   154 13
    CHAIN OF MY MYSTIC WILL WRAPPED PERFECTLY   154 25
    WE THE MYSTIC NOW   268 13
    DIVIDED IN THE MYSTIC TANGIBLE AND INTANGIBLE DIFFERENCE 636 6
    TO WIPE AWAY THE MYSTIC BARRIERS OF SEX   636 19
    THEY CALL ALL EXPERIENCE OF THE SENSES MYSTIC WHEN THE + 707 26
    SO AN APPLE BECOMES MYSTIC WHEN I TASTE IT IN   707 28
    IF I SAY I TASTE THESE THINGS IN AN APPLE I AM CALLED M+ 708 5
    OF SOME PRE-RAPHAELITE MYSTIC QUEEN   854 27

MYSTICISM
    IT IS MORE UNSCIENTIFIC EVEN THAN MYSTICISM   523 2

MYSTIFICATION
    I CALL IT MENTAL CONCEIT AND MYSTIFICATION   708 18

NADA
    NICHTS AND NIENTE RIEN AND NADA   824 8

NADIR
    AND FECUNDATES THE ZENITH AND THE NADIR   506 8
    THERE MUST BE A NADIR SOMEWHERE   547 27
    IT IS A NADIR   764 16

NAG
    THE HORSE BEING NOTHING BUT A NAG WILL FORGET   379 30

NAIF
    THE DARK NAIF PRIDE   844 10

NAIL
    YET ONE THING I DO FIGHT FOR TOOTH AND NAIL ALL THE TIME 497 22

NAILS
    HAS FALLEN DEAD UPON THE NAILS AND HANGS   225 6
    WITH DIM LIGHT SHOWING THE HEADS OF THE SILVER NAILS 876 14

NAIL-STUDDED
    NAIL-STUDDED THAT SHAKE BENEATH HER SHELL   362 7

NAIVETE
    OF RUSSIA THROUGH THE NEW GREAT NAIVETE OF RUSSIA HER W+ 866 29

NAKED
    NAKED ON THE STEEP SOFT LIP   33 18
    WE SOUGHT YOU SUBSTANTIAL YOU TOUCHSTONE OF CARESSES YO+ 34 17
    SOUL'S NAKED LIGHTNING WHICH SHOULD SURE ATTEST   87 24
    WHITE STAND NAKED OF GOWN   106 6
    NAKED EXPOSED ON THE BUSH   107 12
    ABROAD I IN THIS NAKED BERRY   107 17
    TILL NAKED FOR HER IN THE FINEST FASHION   113 7
    AND STRIP ME NAKED TOUCH ME LIGHT   117 13
    IF I COULD LIFT MY NAKED SELF TO YOU   122 18
    THE TREES DOWN THE BOULEVARD STAND NAKED IN THOUGHT   142 1
    IN THE GRIM UNDERTOW NAKED THE TREES CONFRONT   142 3
    A LOOK AS HE STANDS ON THE EDGE OF THIS NAKED STALL   144 19
    HAVE HUDDLED RAGS OR LIMBS ON THE NAKED SLEEP   144 22
    TWO NAKED FACES ARE SEEN   144 26
    FOR RUIN ON THE NAKED SMALL REDOUBT   160 24

NAKED
    FLUSHED AND GRAND AND NAKED AS FROM THE CHAMBER   193 3
    NAKED OF WORSHIP OF LOVE OR OF ADORNMENT   197 14
    WHILE A NAKED MAN COMES SWIFTLY   200 21
    YOU ARE NEAR TO ME AND YOUR NAKED FEET IN THEIR SANDALS 208 28
    AND THROUGH THE SCENT OF THE BALCONY'S NAKED TIMBER   208 29
    THE NAKED LIGHTNINGS IN THE HEAVENS DITHER   209 4
    UNSHEATHED AND NAKED AND NARROW AND WHITE   210 2
    ITSELF MORE SHEER AND NAKED OUT OF THE GREEN   218 11
    OF NAKED LOVE CLENCHED IN HIS FISTS THE SHAME   226 7
    THE NAKED CANDLES BURN ON EVERY GRAVE   233 9
    BUT I AM YOUR NAKED CANDLE BURNING   233 11
    AND MY NAKED BODY STANDING ON YOUR GRAVE   233 14
    I AM A NAKED CANDLE BURNING ON YOUR GRAVE   233 26
    HERE IN MY ARMS MY NAKED SACRIFICE   238 19
    CURIOUS LONG-LEGGED FOALS AND WIDE-EARED CALVES AND NAK+ 271 34
    WHEN EVE ONCE KNEW IN HER MIND THAT SHE WAS NAKED   284 7
    SHE'D BEEN NAKED ALL HER DAYS BEFORE   284 9
    AND ALL IN NAKED COMMUNION COMMUNICATING AS NOW OUR   286 28
    THEIR POOR IDEALIST FOREHEADS NAKED CAPITALS   287 18
    NAKED EXCEPT FOR FANCIFUL LONG SHOES   296 20
    FLOWERILY NAKED IN FLESH AND GIVING OFF HUES OF LIFE 299 4
    WITH MARVELLOUS NAKED ASSURANCE EACH SINGLE TWIG   299 26
    OH NAKED FIG-TREE   300 11
    A NAKED TREE OF BLOSSOM LIKE A BRIDEGROOM BATHING IN DEW 306 8
    SUDDENLY TO DARE TO COME OUT NAKED IN PERFECTION OF   306 15
    WHEN THEY FELT THEIR FOREHEADS BARE NAKED TO HEAVEN THE+ 310 5
    MOULTING AND RATHER NAKED ABOUT THE RUMP AND DOWN IN THE 329 23
    YOU AND THE NAKED ELEMENT   335 22
    WHO IS IT EJECTS HIS SPERM TO THE NAKED FLOOD   335 25
    WHY DO YOU HAVE WATTLES AND A NAKED WATTLED HEAD   369 15
    YOU GO DOWN SHADE TO THE RIVER WHERE NAKED MEN SIT ON 366 23
    AND YOU CROSS THE FERRY WITH THE NAKED PEOPLE GO UP THE 386 25
    NAKED MEN ARE THRESHING RICE   386 28
    AND THE SLIM NAKED MAN SLIPS DOWN AND THE BEAST DEPOSITS 387 14
    NAKED DARK MEN BENEATH   387 27
    NAKED DARK MEN WITH ORNAMENTS ON ON THEIR NAKED ARMS 389 7
    AND THEIR NAKED BREASTS THE GROOVED LOINS   389 8
    A NAKED GLEAMING DARK LAUGH LIKE A SECRET OUT IN THE DA+ 389 15
    THE NEW NAKED LITTLE REPUBLICS COME INTO THE WORLD   413 16
    BRIGHT AND NAKED AFT AND FORE   574 20
    ONLY WHEN I AM STRIPPED STARK NAKED I AM ALONE   607 30
    AND IF STARK NAKED I APPROACH A FELLOW-MAN OR FELLOW-WO+ 608 1
    THEY MUST BE NAKED TOO   608 2
    IT IS ABSURD FOR ME TO DISPLAY MY NAKED SOUL AT THE TEA+ 608 11
    AND OUR NAKED CONTACT WILL BE RARE AND VIVID AND TREMEN+ 608 18
    AND NAKED EMBRACE AN ANTI-CLIMAX HUMILIATING AND RIDICU+ 608 19
    WHO IS IT THAT CLASPS AND KNEADS MY NAKED FEET TILL THE+ 652 12
    SLIM NAKED MEN FROM CNOSSOS SMILING THE ARCHAIC SMILE 688 13
    BUT A NAKED MAN A STRANGER LEANED ON THE GATE   692 10
    BECAUSE NAKED YOU ARE MORE WONDERFUL THAN ANYTHING WE C+ 695 18
    AND I A NAKED MAN CALLING   704 27
    HOLDING THEIR BREATH NAKED AND DARKLY ALONE   711 5
    AND OUR SOUL COWERS NAKED IN THE DARK RAIN OVER THE FLO+ 718 19
    LEAVING THIS NAKED HELPLESS VULNERABLE REMAINS   767 26
    A NAKED NIGHTLY THING TOO FRAIL AND WISE FOR THE STRESS 771 23
    NAKED I COME FROM OUT OF THE DEEP   801 2
    NAKED HAVE I TRAVELLED THE LONG WAY ROUND   801 4
    THE NAKED ONE CLIMBED IN   802 12
    NAKED AND WHITE NOT QUITE NOT QUITE   824 22
    NAKED PRESENTABLE   828 4
    LIES THE PONDEROUS FIRE OF NAKED LIFE   844 12
    BUT BELOW ALL ROOTS OF LOVE LIES THE BEDROCK OF NAKED P+ 844 19
    THE NAKED SKY   874 32
    LOW NAKED CEILING OF THE NIGHT-SKY HELD   876 12
    HER NAKED SOUL OF FEAR   880 30
    AS YOU CRAWLED NAKED OVER ME   886 5
    AND YOU CLIMBED BACK NAKED OVER ME   886 10
    HAPPY AM I A NAKED SPRIG   888 13
    NAKED ON THE STEEP SOFT LIP   *891 20
    AND STRIP ME NAKED TOUCH ME ALIGHT   *931 17
    SINCE DEATH HAS DELIVERED NAKED AND THIN AND WHITE   *938 7
    IT WOULD BE A NAKED LIFE WITHOUT LOVE   *951 7

NAKED-FOOTED
    AND YET THE SOUL CONTINUING NAKED-FOOTED EVER MORE VIVI+ 281 7

NAKEDLY
    AND NAKEDLY NOTHING 'TWIXT WORLD AND HEAVEN TWO CREATUR+ 98 4
    NAKEDLY TO BE ALONE UNSEEN   601 4

NAKEDNESS
    DEFENCELESS NAKEDNESS   207 24
    YOUR BREASTS YOUR NAKEDNESS   238 11
    ITS NAKEDNESS ALL WITHIN-WALLS ITS FLOWERING FOREVER UN+ 283 15
    MEDITERRANEAN FRUIT WITH YOUR COVERT NAKEDNESS   283 19
    THEY HAVE THEIR NAKEDNESS MORE THAN EVER ON THEIR MIND 284 15
    AND I MUST RESUME MY NAKEDNESS LIKE A FISH SINKING DOWN+ 321 29
    AND HAVING EXPOSED THE PINK PLACE OF HER NAKEDNESS   386 1
    TO PRESERVE MY NAKEDNESS   601 22
    BUT STILL MY NAKEDNESS IS CLOTHED WITH RESPONSIBILITY 607 26
    NOW I AM AT YOUR GATE YOU BEAUTY YOU LADY OF ALL NAKEDN+ 695 22
    BY TOUCH AND A NEW NAKEDNESS   738 24
    SHE REJOICES IN HER NEW NAKEDNESS   768 23
    ITS WAY ACROSS THE DARK SHOULD MOCK MY NAKEDNESS   771 20
    AS HER HAND GROPED OVER ITS NAKEDNESS   *937 15
    OF ALL US FLESH AND WE STAND IN OUR NAKEDNESS NESH   *938 11
    WHICH CLOTHES OUR NAKEDNESS LIKE GRASS THE PLAINS AND T+ *951 8

NAKED-SET
    WHY DO YOU ARCH YOUR NAKED-SET EYE WITH A MORE-THAN-COM+ 369 16

NAME
    WI' A WOMAN AN' NAME 'ER A PRICE   82 10
    YOU HAVE NO NAME   118 6
    OF HER MAIDENLY VIRTUE AND OF MY GOOD NAME   129 6
    THINGS I HAVE KNOWN THAT SHALL HAVE NO NAME   151 32
    BUT A NAME SHE MIGHT TAKE   213 6

NAME
'TIS LIKE THE UNUTTERABLE NAME OF THE DREAD LORD   264 16
JOHN THOMAS BY NAME   493 2
YET THE NAME IS TABOO   551 24
HIS CREDIT HIS NAME HIS WIFE EVEN MAY BE JUST ANOTHER   607 17
I REFUSE TO NAME THE GODS BECAUSE THEY HAVE NO NAME   651 7
MY NAME IS THOMAS THOMAS EARP   680 9
AND MY NAME IS THOMAS THOMAS EARP   680 15
I SAID TO HIM AND WHAT IS YOUR NAME   692 14
HALLOWED BE THY NAME THEN   704 13
MY NAME IS JESUS I AM MARY'S SON   786 16
MY NAME IS JESUS I AM MARY'S SON   789 9
HEY FIRST MAN OF MY NAME HARK THERE   791 17
TELL THEM SO FIRST MAN OF MY NAME   792 9
NULLUS NOTHINGNESS WHAT'S IN A NAME   824 16
PALS WORSE N'R ONY NAME AS YOU COULD CALL   *911 12
AND MAKE THE CONSIDERABLE MESS THAT ISN'T EVEN WORTH TH+   *947 12

NAMED
THERE WAS A GAY BIRD NAMED CHRISTINE   845 17

NAMELESS
FOREVER NAMELESS   622 14
THE GODS ARE NAMELESS AND IMAGELESS   650 20
THOU WHO ART NAMELESS   704 14
OH THEN BE NAMELESS AND BE NEVER SEEN   737 16

NAMES
AH GOD LIFE LAW SO MANY NAMES YOU KEEP   194 18
I CALL HIM NO NAMES   405 22
THEY SHOULD NEVER HAVE GIVEN YOU NAMES AND NEVER NEVER   737 20

NAME'S
I WON'T OR MY NAME'S NOT LIZ   82 16

NAPE
I CAN JUST SEE THE NAPE OF HER WHITE LITTLE NECK   863 5
AND THE WHITE NAPE OF HER NECK WAS THE BEAUTY OF THE ST+   865 9

NAPOLEON
OR NAPOLEON SAYS SINCE I HAVE SAVED YOU FROM THE CIDEVA+   442 20
NAPOLEON THEY SOLD TO MADAME TUSSAUDS AND TO THE ARTIFI+   763 4

NARCISSUS
NARCISSUS   161 18
NO MORE NARCISSUS PERFUME LILY HARLOTS THE BLADES OF TH+   273 16
HO GOLDEN-SPANIEL SWEET ALERT NARCISSUS   309 7
AT LAST THE NARCISSUS LIFTED A TUFT OF FIVE-POINT STARS   683 2

NARCOTIC
NARCOTIC OF WEARINESS   *917 12

NARCOTICS
HAVE EATEN THE NARCOTICS OF NIGHT   *917 14

NARROW
NOR ONE NARROW GATE FOR THE MOON TO GO   103 7
BREEZE OF THE MORNING THROUGH A NARROW WHITE BIRCH   209 28
UNSHEATHED AND NAKED AND NARROW AND WHITE   210 2
CONSTRAINED TO POUR FORTH ALL HIS FIRE DOWN THE NARROW +   327 11
THROUGH SUCH NARROW LOINS TOO NARROW   327 13
ON A NARROW BEAT ABOUT THE SAME AS A PRISONER TAKING HIS   521 17
NOT THE NARROW LITTLE   561 4
AND KIN WITH MISS JUPSON WHOSE GUTS ARE NARROW   583 28

NARROWEST
AND THE SUN COMING IN THROUGH THE NARROWEST FIBRIL OF A+   324 13

NARROW-GUTTED
AND AN ARISTOCRAT IN SO FAR AS I DETEST NARROW-GUTTED   526 8
SOME NARROW-GUTTED SUPERIORITY   555 1
IS SUMMED UP IN A NICE NARROW-GUTTED OLD MAID   584 4

NARROWS
IS ME IN THE NARROWS OF MY WRISTS   460 26
THOUGH IT NARROWS NOW   763 23

NASCENT
NASCENT AMERICAN   293 1
YOUR NASCENT DEMON PEOPLE   293 7
AND FOR THE SAKE OF THIS NASCENT UNBORN AS-YET-UNKNOWAB+   775 10

NASTY
OH THESE ARE ABSTRACTIONS TO YOUR NASTY LITTLE BELLY   399 20
RATHER NASTY   431 23
THE DEAD IN THEIR NASTY DEAD HANDS   440 26
AND DON'T WITH THE NASTY PRYING MIND DRAG IT OUT FROM   464 28
AND REALLY A NASTY VIOLATION   470 20
OF COURSE IF YOU MAKE NAUGHTINESS NASTY   491 5
SPICILY NASTY OF COURSE   491 6
OF ALL THOSE NASTY POLICE-EYES LIKE SNAIL-TRACKS SMEARI+   580 21
LEAVING NASTY FILMS UPON YOU EVERY TIME   581 5
THE NASTY LYING PRETENCE OF SEEMING TO FEEL WHAT WE DON+   654 5
OR ELSE THEY ARE IMMORALLY NASTY AND THE WORD LOOMS   837 1

NATION
SO OF COURSE THE NATION IS SWOLLEN WITH INSOLUBLE PROBL+   535 21
POLICEMEN AND THE BRITISH NATION   575 1
OR WHAT IS IT THAT MY NATION IS SUFFERING FROM   659 23
TO THIS GREAT NATION   779 14
TO THIS GREAT NATION   779 17
AND THE ROOTS OF THE GREAT TREE OF FAMILY AND THE FORES+   *951 13

NATIONS
NATIONS ARMIES WAR PEACE-TALKING   256 27
THOUGH IT FEED NATIONS   263 4
NATIONS BESIDE THE SEA ARE OLD   814 15

NATION'S
TILL YOU'VE RUINED A NATION'S FIBRE   537 15
IN THE NATION'S POCKET   545 10
IN THE NATION'S POCKET   545 20
DOWN WHICH THE NATION'S RESOURCES ROLL   546 3

NATIVE
THE NATIVE ROYALTY OF RED HIBISCUS FLOWERS   314 18
I LOVE MY NATIVE LAND THE BEST ETC ETC   575 14
I LOVE MY NATIVE TONGUE THE BEST   575 16
AND STILL SPEAK HIS NATIVE LANGUAGE THE BEST   575 23
FIG-TREES DON'T GROW IN MY NATIVE LAND   579 9
AND AGAINST THIS INWARD REVOLT OF THE NATIVE CREATURES +   624 20
THEY TOOK AWAY OH THEY TOOK AWAY YOUR MAN'S NATIVE   630 22
PRIDE PRISTINE AND DEEPER THAN CONSCIOUSNESS THE NATIVE+   *951 18

NATURAL
I SEE IT HAS A NATURAL ABUNDANCE   498 20
I WANT TO BE LIKE THAT TO HAVE A NATURAL ABUNDANCE   498 24
CRUSHING OUT THE NATURAL HUMAN LIFE   508 21
NATURAL PRIDE   587 13
GOOD HEALTHY NATURAL FEELINGS INSTINCTS PASSIONS OR DES+   678 3
AND WE HAVE LOST OUR NATURAL SPONTANEITY   833 11
IS FOR SOME MORE NATURAL MORE DECENT SOCIAL ARRANGEMENT   837 24

NATURALLY
NATURALLY TAKE HOLD OF THE TOWN   537 12
NATURALLY WE DESTROY THE MOST ESSENTIAL SELF IN US   621 9
OF COURSE NATURALLY   660 10
SO NATURALLY THEY WANT TO KEEP HIM BACK DOWN POOR   778 12

NATURE
NATURE   292 16
IT WAS ASKING TOO MUCH OF HIS NATURE   344 22
NATURE REJECTS   399 7
IT'S NOT HIS NATURE   414 1
THAT WILL BLOSSOM FORTH THE WHOLE OF HUMAN NATURE   429 13
AND GO AHEAD WITH WHAT IS HUMAN NATURE   429 15
AND LEAVE IT TO SOME NATURE THAT IS MORE THAN HUMAN   429 19
TO BE TRUE TO THE NATURE OF IT ITS RESERVE ITS SENSITIV+   464 20
YOUR NATURE   522 14
ARE ALWAYS THEMSELVES BY NATURE DISLOYAL   626 2
NATURE RESPONDS SO BEAUTIFULLY   831 1
MAN IS KEPT SANE NOT BY HIS MIND WHICH BY NATURE IS UNS+   838 16
BY NATURE THAN BY BOOTS AND WET FEET OFTEN CARRY MERRY +   866 15
TOO DIRTY A HYPOCRITE TO ADMIT HIS OWN NATURE   *949 3
BALKING HIS OWN NATURE   *949 11

NATURES
FOUR GREAT BEASTS THE FOUR NATURES THE FOUR WINDS THE F+   319 9
OUR NATURES ARE   522 23

NATURE'S
HE WAS ONE OF NATURE'S PHENOMENA NO DOUBT   328 18
ONE OF NATURE'S GENTLEMEN   *947 28

NAUGHT
SERENELY SMILING AT NAUGHT   54 13
IS IT ALL NAUGHT   57 5
IT IS VERY FITTING THERE IS NAUGHT BESIDE   699 2

NAUGHTINESS
OF COURSE IF YOU MAKE NAUGHTINESS NASTY   491 5
BUT IF YOU GO AND MAKE NAUGHTINESS NICE   491 9

NAUGHTY
THEY SAY I WROTE A NAUGHTY BOOK   491 13
I FEEL I'M GOING TO BE NAUGHTY AUNTIE   572 19
PERHAPS I'M GOING TO BE NAUGHTY AUNTIE   573 7
FOR PRINTING THOSE NAUGHTY WORDS   668 13

NAUSEATING
TILL NOW THE VERY WORD IS NAUSEATING WE CAN'T HEAR IT A+   519 5

NAUSEOUS
TO BREAK THIS SICK AND NAUSEOUS DREAM   177 19
BUT BAWDY ON THE BRAIN IS LEWD AND NAUSEOUS A SORT OF I+   *952 19

NAUSEOUSLY
A MANGO-FLESHED AURA NAUSEOUSLY STEAMING   760 9

NAVAJO
AND A NAVAJO WOMAN WEAVING HER RUG IN THE PATTERN OF   448 22

NAVEL
TO FEEL A FINE FINE BREEZE BLOWING THROUGH THE NAVEL AND   481 21

NAVVIES
IT IS WELL FOR YOU FOR ME THE NAVVIES WORK IN THE ROAD +   57 29

NAXOS
NAXOS THOUSANDS OF FEET BELOW THE OLIVE-ROOTS   293 24

NAY
NAY EVEN THE SLUMBEROUS EGG AS IT LABOURS UNDER THE SHE+   64 11
NAY ROBIN RED-BREAST THA NEDNA   78 21
NAY YO' BLESSED PEE-WHIPS   78 25
DID I SHIVER NAY TRULY I DO NOT KNOW   87 3
NAY DEAR BE STILL   87 7
NAY NEVER I PUT YOU AWAY YET EACH KISS HISSES   87 12
NAY BUT SHE SLEEPS LIKE A BRIDE AND DREAMS HER DREAMS   101 12
NAY THOUGH THE POLE-STAR   115 19
NAY TAKE THIS WEARY BOOK OF HOURS AWAY   135 20
DOST WANT ME TER WANT THEE AGAIN NAY THOUGH   138 17
STILL SHE SAYS NAY LOOSE NO FLAME   150 26
RATHER I HAD YOU WOULD NOT GO NAY COME   153 15
NAY LET ME WORK A DELICATE CHAIN OF KISSES   154 4
NAY I PERSIST AND VERY FAITH SHALL KEEP   154 12

NAY
  NAY BUT HOW TORTURED IS THE FRIGHTFUL SEED   160 21
  NAY I'M TOO SLEEPY AH YOU ARE HORRIBLE   211 7
  NAY WE FIND OURSELVES CROSSING THE FERN-SCENTED FRONTIE+   286 24
  NAY TONGUES ARE DEAD AND WORDS ARE HOLLOW AS HOLLOW   296 25
  NAY LEONARDO ONLY BUNGLED THE PURE ETRUSCAN SMILE   297 26
  NAY WHAT A HEART OF DELICATE SUPER-FAITH   304 22
  NAY SON OF MAN I HAVE BEEN LIFTED UP   322 7
  NAY ONCE IT WAS ALSO A FORTRESS WALL AND THE WEIGHT OF +   326 25
  NAY   346 8
  NAY TINY SHELL-BIRD   353 24
  NAY ON THE VERY CONTRARY   470 13
  ALL I CAN SAY THEN IS NAY NAY NAY NAY NAY   644 22
  NAY NOR EVEN YOUR MIND   692 6
  A MIXTURE OF YEA AND NAY   714 11
  NAY   733 1
  NAY NOW AT LAST THANK GOD FOR THE JEOPARDY   741 22
  NAY I SAW NOWT BUT TH' COFFIN AN' TH' YELLER CLAY AN' +   *909 31
  NAY ROBIN RED-BREAST THA NEDNA   *920 13
  NAY YOU BLESSED PEE-WHIPS   *920 17
  NAY TAKE MY PAINTED MISSAL BOOK AWAY   *939 4

NEAPOLITANS
  CATS AND THE NEAPOLITANS   340 6

NEAR
  FAR AND NEAR   34 12
  NO-ONE NEAR THE BED   37 8
  BITTER SCIENCE THE EXAMS ARE NEAR   41 13
  NOT TOO NEAR AND NOT TOO FAR   70 8
  BUT BARBED ALOOFNESS WHEN I WOULD DRAW NEAR   85 24
  YOUR BRIGHTNESS DIMS WHEN I DRAW TOO NEAR AND MY FREE   87 16
  SINCE I LOST YOU MY DARLING THE SKY HAS COME NEAR   134 14
  AND I AM OF IT THE SMALL SHARP STARS ARE QUITE NEAR   134 15
  IN THE SPELLBOUND NORTH CONVULSIVE NOW WITH A DREAM NEAR   149 21
  AND SEE SO NEAR AT OUR FEET IN THE MEADOW   204 15
  IT IS ENOUGH YOU ARE NEAR   204 19
  YOU ARE NEAR TO ME AND YOUR NAKED FEET IN THEIR SANDALS   208 28
  WE NEAR THE FLAME-BURNT PORCHES   242 24
  HAVING YOU NEAR ME   248 15
  I LOVED TO HANDLE IT IT SEEMED LIKE A NEAR PART OF HIM   255 3
  THEY DRAW NEAR TO TASTE IT AS IF SAYING NOW WHAT IS THI+   331 5
  NEAR THE CEILING AS IF IN A WEB   345 2
  NEAR THE CURTAIN ON THE FLOOR   346 27
  BIRD FLIES SO NEAR   368 3
  SEE HIM STANDING WITH HIS HEAD DOWN NEAR THE PORTA CAPP+   379 1
  AND NEAR ACROSS AT THE OPPOSITE STEEP OF SNOW GREEN TRE+   402 25
  MOVES AS THE MOON-TIDES NEAR MORE NEAR   465 29
  THEN IF HE COMES NEAR ME   468 5
  WHEN I LOOK AT THIS PINE-TREE NEAR THE SEA   498 18
  SO THAT ONE COULD DRAW NEAR HER   506 14
  I WISH PEOPLE WHEN YOU SIT NEAR THEM   506 20
  AND FORCED TO WATCH EVERYONE THAT COMES NEAR YOU LEST   522 17
  THERE'S NEVER A FIG-LEAF NEAR AT HAND   579 10
  YET I DON'T WANT THEM TO COME NEAR   602 6
  TOWARDS THOSE NEAR AND DEAR TO ME MY VERY NEXT   607 27
  THERE ARE OTHER WAYS OF SUMMONS CRYING LISTEN LISTEN CO+   623 23
  PAUSES NEAR THE CREST OF THE HILL CLIMBING SLOWLY LIKE +   687 17
  OH NOW AS NOVEMBER DRAWS NEAR   722 19
  DRAWING NEAR THEY COVER THE MUNCHEN ROAD   732 26
  IN WHOSE CLOSE FOLDS ABOVE YOU NEAR ABOVE   750 11
  BE NEAR US AND GOD'S WILL BE DONE   753 7
  I FEEL I'M COMING NEAR   764 12
  ARE YOU NEAR   764 17
  ARE YOU NEAR   764 21
  ARE YOU NEAR HAVE YOU TRAVELLED YOUR PORTION   764 30
  MEANWHILE WE BITE OURSELVES AND EVERYONE NEAR US   833 30
  HOW HE HURTS ME WITH HIS HEART AND HIS THROAT SO NEAR T+   871 22
  ROOFED WITH A DAY'S NEAR CEILING AND A DARK   876 11
  SLOW CATTLE STIR ON THE STEEP MEADOW NEAR BY   886 28

NEARER
  THE CHURCH DRAWS NEARER UPON US GENTLE AND GREAT   48 17
  SHE'S ONLY THE NEARER TO THE INEVITABLE FAREWELL   85 14
  CAME NEARER TO SEARCH THROUGH THE STREETS   121 32
  THEY COME NO NEARER AND STILL WE TRAMP   163 27
  CAN I GO NO NEARER NEVER TOWARDS THE DOOR   173 5
  OUT OF THE DISTANCE NEARER COMING TO PROVE   174 11
  NOW IN NOVEMBER NEARER COMES THE SUN   455 12
  AS THE DARK CLOSES ROUND HIM HE DRAWS NEARER   455 14
  OH COME COME NEARER COME INTO TOUCH   602 12
  COME PHYSICALLY NEARER BE FLESH TO MY FLESH   602 13
  WONDERING HE STEPPED NEARER AND LOOKED AT HER   790 6
  DRAW NEARER REDDEN AND LAUGH LIKE YOUNG GIRLS KISSED   854 12
  OUT OF THE DISTANCE NEARER   *906 19
  OUT OF THE DISTANCE NEARER COMMANDING MY DREAMY WORLD   *908 15
  WAFT NEARER TO THEM THE BARK OF DELIVERY   *958 18

NEAREST
  THE THOUGHTS OF THE SKIES THE EAGLE FLIES NEAREST TO TH+   368 2
  BE GOOD TO ME LADY GREAT LADY OF THE NEAREST   695 20

NEARLY
  A MUTE NEARLY BEAUTIFUL THING   112 11
  AND FOR MYSELF I CAN SAY ALMOST ALMOST OH VERY NEARLY   265 27
  HERE THEY ARE NEARLY   826 26
  IN A BOAT ON A ROUGH SEA WHEN WE WERE ALL NEARLY SEA-SI+   842 13
  A MUTE NEARLY BEAUTIFUL THING IS THY FACE   *927 28
  A MUTE NEARLY BEAUTIFUL THING   *929 1

NEARNESS
  OVER THE NEARNESS OF NORWOOD HILL THROUGH THE MELLOW   53 1
  COLOSSAL IN NEARNESS A BLUE POLICE SITS STILL ON HIS HO+   66 9
  THE ANGEL OF JUDGMENT HAS DEPARTED AGAIN TO THE NEARNESS   94 22
  OVER THE NEARNESS OF NORWOOD HILL THROUGH THE MELLOW VE+   *905 17

NEARNESSES
  TO ME MEN ARE PALPABLE INVISIBLE NEARNESSES IN THE DARK   289 1

NEAT
  THEIR SKINS ALL NEAT   828 6

'NEATH
  THE OTHER VOICE IN A SILENCE OF BLOOD 'NEATH THE NOISE   36 17
  AND FURTHER STILL 'NEATH THE SUNSET GATHER   887 28
  OF QUEENS IN HYACINTH 'NEATH SKIES OF GOLD   *939 18

NEATLY
  PLAYING AMONG THE ELEMENTS NEATLY BEYOND COMPETITION   445 33
  SO LONG AS THE THING IS DONE NEATLY AND THE WORLD IS LE+   532 30

NECESSARILY
  NOT FRIENDS NECESSARILY THEY TALK SO MUCH   499 21

NECESSARY
  AND GOD THAT SHE IS NECESSARY   215 11
  NECESSARY AND I HAVE NO CHOICE   215 12
  WOULDN'T THINK IT NECESSARY TO MAKE CONVERSATION   506 21
  IN FACT A LITTLE BAWDY IS NECESSARY IN EVERY LIFE   844 30
  IN FACT A LITTLE WHORING IS NECESSARY IN EVERY LIFE   845 2
  IN FACT A LITTLE BAWDY IS NECESSARY IN EVERY LIFE   *952 11
  IN FACT A LITTLE WHORING IS NECESSARY IN EVERY LIFE   *952 14
  IN FACT IT MAY BE THAT A LITTLE SODOMY IS NECESSARY TO +   *952 18
  IN FACT QUITE A LOT OF CHASTITY IS NECESSARY IN LIFE TO+   *952 24

NECESSITIES
  AND A MONSTER WHEN YOU'RE PINCHED FOR ACTUAL NECESSITIES   498 14
  ABSOLUTE FREEDOM ABSOLVED FROM THE GREAT NECESSITIES OF+   712 19

NECESSITY
  THIS GRIM NECESSITY FROM WITHIN   363 5
  ONLY IS MAN AGONISED IN FRONT OF THE NECESSITY TO BE SO+   529 14

NECK
  AT TH' SLOPPY GRAVE AN' 'ER LITTLE NECK SHONE   61 7
  HER BREATH FLEW WARM AGAINST MY NECK   61 28
  LARROPIN' NECK AN' CROP   78 30
  AND SEAL YOUR NOSTRILS AND ROUND YOUR NECK YOU'LL   154 2
  I WALK UP TO MY NECK IN MIST HOLDING MY MOUTH UP   212 13
  SO I DID HIS PENS AND THE JASPER SEAL ON HIS NECK   255 4
  AND REACH YOUR SKINNY LITTLE NECK   352 13
  HIS LOW FOREHEAD HIS SKINNY NECK HIS LONG SCALED STRIVI+   360 2
  LONG NECK AND LONG VULNERABLE LIMBS EXTRUDED SPREAD-EAG+   365 1
  OPENING ITS CLENCHED FACE FROM HIS OUTSTRETCHED NECK   365 9
  STRAIGHTENS HIS DONKEY NECK   379 22
  NECK   434 4
  BLOWING DOWN YOUR NECK AND YOUR EARS   506 23
  SHE BITES HIM IN THE NECK AND PASSES ON   539 22
  TO LEAN OVER MY HEAD AND MY NECK AND MY BREAST   799 18
  ANYTHING RATHER THAN THAT CERTAIN BACK OF A NECK   836 3
  SEE HOW SHE SNUGGLES AGAINST MY NECK   863 1
  I CAN JUST SEE THE NAPE OF HER WHITE LITTLE NECK   863 5
  AND THE WHITE NAPE OF HER NECK WAS THE BEAUTY OF THE ST+   865 9
  BUT SHE PUT HER FINGERS ON MY NECK UNDER MY COLLAR   882 30
  I COULDNA' SEE HER FACE BUT HER LITTLE NECK SHONE   *910 11
  AN' SHE UNDID 'ER JACKET NECK AN' THEN   *910 15
  AT TH' SLOPPY WET GRAVE AN' 'ER LITTLE NECK SHONE   *911 23
  HER BREATH FLEW WARM AGAINST MY NECK   *912 7
  LARROPIN' NECK AN' CROP   *920 22

NECKAR
  A SOULLESS NECKAR WITH WINKING SEAS IN HIS EYES   130 19

NECKS
  IN A LONG LINE THEIR HEADS LAID OVER EACH OTHER'S NECKS   445 20
  EVEN THE LAMBS WILL STRETCH FORTH THEIR NECKS LIKE SERP+   624 16

NECK'S
  WHERE HER ARMS AND MY NECK'S THICK PULSE COULD MEET   62 2
  WHERE HER ARMS AND MY NECK'S BLOOD-SURGE COULD MEET   *912 10

NEDNA
  NAY ROBIN RED-BREAST THA NEDNA   78 21
  YO' NEDNA SCRAIGHT AT ME   78 26
  AY I'M SORRY THA NEDNA WORRY   83 20
  SPEAK UP YOU NEDNA BE FEARED   *919 28
  NAY ROBIN RED-BREAST THA NEDNA   *920 13
  YOU NEDNA SCREET AT ME   *920 18

NEDN'T
  SPEAK UP YOU NEDN'T BE FEARED   78 8
  YER NEDN'T 'AVE SWORE   81 12
  YOU NEDN'T HAVE SWORE   *923 12

NE'D
  AS THA NE'D TRUDGE UP 'ERE   -79 18
  AS THA NE'D TRUDGE UP HERE   *921 14

NEED
  THAT DAY IS HALF GROWN OVER IT NEED NOT ABASH   91 4
  BEAST CROUCHED ACROSS THE GLOBE READY IF NEED BE TO POU+   97 21
  THA'D NEED A WOMAN DIFFERENT FROM ME   139 5
  ONE SHADOW AND WE NEED NOT DISSEMBLE   170 14
  SAY IS IT ALL WE NEED   172 14
  DRIFTS OVER THE TOWN IN ITS NEED   253 29
  THEN THE DUMB ACHING BITTER HELPLESS NEED   263 20
  FOR WHAT KIND OF ICE-ROTTEN HOT-ACHING HEART MUST THEY +   270 27
  YOU NEED NOT CLEAR THE WORLD LIKE A CABBAGE PATCH FOR ME   316 9
  SELF-EXPOSURE HARD HUMILIATION NEED TO ADD HIMSELF ON TO   362 31
  AND THE STILL MORE AWFUL NEED TO PERSIST TO FOLLOW FOLL+   363 12
  DOES THE SUN NEED STEAM OF BLOOD DO YOU THINK   374 9
  NOW YOU NEED KNOW IN PART   411 11
  MAN'S NEED   431 3
  GREAT IS MY NEED TO BE CHASTE   469 6

NEED
  GREAT IS MY NEED TO BE UNTOUCHED   469   8
  THAT MY BODY NEED NOT ME   469 15
  SINCE THE NEED IS ON US   471 14
  BUT THEN YOU NEED ONLY LOOK AT THE MODERN PERAMBULATOR   521 25
  YOU DON'T NEED ONE SINGLE SOCIAL INFERIOR TO EXALT YOU   526 26
  WE NEED HAVE NO DEAD PEOPLE MONEY-SLAVES AND SOCIAL   527   7
  WHEN IT NEED STRUGGLE NO MORE   535   2
  BUT WHAT WE ALSO ARE AND WE NEED TO KNOW IT   544   3
  YOU NEED YOUR OWN GREAT WONDERING EYE THAT FLASHES WITH   544 22
  PERSON THAT'S ALL WE NEED TO KNOW   546 11
  NEED TO KNOW ABOUT ANYBODY AND DO YOU KNOW I'VE NEVER B+   546 18
  THEY NEED GRAFTING   640 22
  O BUILD YOUR SHIP OF DEATH FOR YOU WILL NEED IT   717   2
  FOR YOU WILL NEED IT   720 21
  WHAT WE NEED INDEED   833 12
  WHAT WE NEED IS A LONG LONG WAR-LESS EPOCH   833 22
  I NEED NOT GLANCE OVER MY SHOULDER IN FEAR OF THE TERRO+   *945 25
  I NEED NOT LOOK AFTER MY SOUL BEGUILE MY FEAR   *945 27
  WITH PRAYER I NEED ONLY COME HOME EACH NIGHT TO FIND TH+   *945 28
  I NEED ONLY COME HOME EACH NIGHT AND LAY   *946   1
  BUILD THEN YOUR SHIP OF DEATH FOR YOU WILL NEED IT   *956 29
  OH BUILD YOUR SHIP OF DEATH FOR YOU WILL NEED IT   *960 11

NEEDED
  THAT THEY WERE GIVEN WHEN I NEEDED THEM   263 31
  IT NEEDED PYTHAGORAS TO SEE LIFE PLAYING WITH COUNTERS +   355 14
  TO THE RUSSIA THAT NEEDED HIM MOST   536 19
  WHERE NO HOUSE IS NEEDED   769 23

NEEDING
  NEEDING   47 19
  AND I ROSE IN FEAR NEEDING YOU FEARFULLY   99   6

NEEDLE
  LIKE A NEEDLE STEADFASTLY   99 24
  WITH A NEEDLE OF LONG RED FLINT HE STABS IN THE DARK   382 16

NEEDLES
  AND IN HER HANDS THE SPARKING NEEDLES FLY   752 10
  AND DART HIS ELECTRIC NEEDLES INTO YOUR BONES AND CURDL+   797 10

NEEDLE'S
  ESPECIALLY IF BEING GIVEN A NEEDLE'S EYE OF EGRESS ELSE+   381   6
  AND HIS SLITTED EYES SEEKING THE NEEDLE'S EYE   382   4

NEEDN'T
  IF SUCH THINGS WERE NICE AND WE NEEDN'T THINK TWICE   491 11
  THEN WE SHAN'T HAVE WAR AND WE NEEDN'T TALK ABOUT PEACE   496   5
  THEY NEEDN'T BOTHER MOST OF THEM WILL NEVER GET DOWN AT+   667 22

NEEDS
  WITH MOUTH AND LOINS AND NEEDS HE LIVES   461 15
  AND STILL THE GREAT NEEDS OF MEN   461 18
  THE MIND THAT NEEDS TO KNOW ALL THINGS   473 19
  MUST NEEDS AT LAST COME TO KNOW ITS OWN LIMITS   473 20
  AND NEEDS TO BE RAISED FROM SEED   535 14
  HUMANITY NEEDS PRUNING   677 20
  THE TREE OF HUMANITY NEEDS PRUNING BADLY   677 24
  IT NEEDED THOROUGHLY PRUNING NOT AS IN THE LATE WAR BLAS+   677 25
  THE TREE OF HUMAN EXISTENCE NEEDS BADLY PRUNING   677 28
  WITH A BODY AND WITH NEEDS AND A LOVELY SPIRIT   689 30
  EACH NEEDS A LITTLE SHIP A LITTLE SHIP   721 22
  MY HEART IS FIRM AND SOLID IT NEEDS   888   9
  A MAN NEEDS TO BE INDEPENDENT AT HIS WORK SO THAT HE CA+   *949 22

NE'ER
  KISS ME THEN THERE NE'ER MIND IF I SCRAIGHT I WOR FOND +   *925 28

NEGLECTED
  THE OLD DRAGON WILL DWINDLE DOWN TO THE SIZE OF A STRAY+   665 14

NEGLIGENT
  HE WILL LIE NEGLIGENT RESIGN   59 29

NEGRO
  THE NEGRO MIGHT KNOW A LITTLE   286 13
  WITH A SHOCK AS AGAINST THE BLACKNESS OF A NEGRO   428   4

NEGROES
  AMONG THE NEGROES   780 17

NEGROID
  ONCE GOD WAS ALL NEGROID AS NOW HE IS FAIR   286 16
  NEGROID   301 23

NEIGHBOUR
  THE SUN FROM THEIR NEIGHBOUR EITHER NOR BE SMOTHERED IN+   93 22
  FINE THRILLS TO THE NEIGHBOUR STARS FINE HIDDEN BEAMS   127   7
  I LOVE MY NEIGHBOUR   644 15
  WHO THEN O JESUS IS MY NEIGHBOUR   645 10
  MY NEIGHBOUR IS NOT THE MAN IN THE STREET AND NEVER WAS   645 14
  MY NEIGHBOUR O MY NEIGHBOUR   645 17
  O MY NEIGHBOUR   645 21
  HOW CAN THAT BE MY NEIGHBOUR   645 25
  WHEN JESUS COMMANDED US TO LOVE OUR NEIGHBOUR   654   6
  FOR WE CAN'T LOVE ANYBODY NEIGHBOUR OR NO NEIGHBOUR TO +   654   8

NEIGHBOURS
  ARE THESE THINGS MY NEIGHBOURS   644 17
  AM I TOLD THAT THESE THINGS ARE MY NEIGHBOURS   644 21
  SUPPOSING I SAY DOGS ARE MY NEIGHBOURS   645   1
  THE SAME WITH MY ROBOT NEIGHBOURS   645   6

NEIGHBOUR'S
  AND CURSED BE HE THAT REMOVETH HIS NEIGHBOUR'S LANDMARK   706 16

NEITHER
  MY SHADOW IS NEITHER HERE NOR THERE BUT I I AM ROYALLY +   34   8
  SHE NEITHER KNOWS NOR CARES   54 19
  LET THAT BE 'APPEN IT WORNA TH' DRINK NEITHER   60. 27
  NEITHER ON YER   84 14
  AN' I REALLY LIKE 'ER NEITHER   84 21
  NEITHER LIFE NOR DEATH COULD HELP   214 30
  HIM NEITHER   307 26
  NEITHER CAN A YOUNG COCK-EAGLE SIT SIMPERING   413 30
  BUT NEITHER DO I WANT TO BE RICH   498 17
  NEITHER OF US HAVE   501 10
  MY SHABBY LITTLE DEFEAT WOULD DO NEITHER ME ANY GOOD   508 23
  IS NEITHER HIDING HIMSELF NOR PRESERVING HIMSELF NOR PR+   523   9
  WE BELONG NEITHER TO MEN NOR OUR CHILDREN NOR   525 25
  NEITHER MY DEAR I HAD HIM FIXED IT SAVES HIM FROM SO   581 12
  BECAUSE YOU SEE HE IS NEITHER MY DEAR   581 18
  NEITHER TO PERSONS NOR THINGS NOR IDEAS NOR RELI+   622   7
  AND LIVED TO LEARN THEY ARE NEITHER FELLOW NOR MEN   644   2
  THOSE WHO ARE NEITHER BOURGEOIS NOR BOLSHEVIST BUT TRUE+   666   2
  AND I CAN NEITHER PAINT NOR WRITE   680 10
  THIS SEA WILL NEVER DIE NEITHER WILL IT EVER GROW OLD   688   1
  WHEN GERANIUMS WERE NOT AND MIGNONETTE NEITHER   690 22
  NEITHER CAN IT REACH THE DEPTH   701 28
  GREY EVIL WHICH HAS NO PATH AND SHOWS NEITHER LIGHT NOR   712   2
  YOU SHALL FIND ME WHO AM NEITHER INCREASE   788 20
  THAT ARE NEITHER WHITE NOR RED NOR YELLOW NOR BROWN NOR+   792 31
  IT HAS NEITHER HEART NOR BOWELS NOR GENITALS   830 28
  NEITHER BEASTS NOR FLOWERS ARE   836   8
  IN ALL HONESTY A WORD IS NEITHER A GAP IN THE CONSCIOUS+   837   8
  THE VIVIFIER EXISTS BUT FOR ME IS NEITHER MAN-LIKE NOR +   840 25
  NEITHER STRAIGHT NOR CROOKED NEITHER HERE NOR THERE   *959 17

NEMESIS
  BUT NOW MY LASS YOU'VE GOT NEMESIS ON YOUR TRACK   399 27
  THE NEMESIS THAT AWAITS OUR CIVILISATION   514 25

NENUPHARS
  LIKE NENUPHARS   48 30

NEPTUNE
  THINKING OLD NEPTUNE WAS OFF ON A SPREE   575   9

NERVE
  MY CRAFTSMAN'S NERVE   111 24
  THE GREYING NERVE   766 14
  MY FINE CRAFTSMAN'S NERVE   *927 12
  MY FINE CRAFTSMAN'S NERVE   *928 12

NERVE-BARE
  THE NERVE-BARE PLACE NOW A LITTLE SILENCE EXPANDS   167 14

NERVELESS
  ARE NERVELESS JUST NOW   409 30

NERVER
  HAVING KNOWN THE WORLD SO LONG I HAVE NERVER CONFESSED   249 13

NERVES
  THAT YOU THROW OFF STRAIGHT ON THE TINDER OF MY NERVES   241   9
  AND NERVES URGING FORWARD TO THE WALL YOU'D HAVE EYES   381   4
  AND KNOWN IT SUBTLER THAN FRISSON-SHAKEN NERVES   383   8
  NERVES TIRED OUT   388   8
  NERVES DIDN'T TIGHTEN AGAINST ME   555 11
  AS THEIR NERVES ARE STRETCHED TILL THEY TWANGLE AND SNAP   616   8
  OF NERVES THAT GRIND AND A SOUL THAT STINGS   747 14
  FLUTTER OF FEAR IN THE NERVES   767 17
  ALONG THE NERVES A LOW THROBBING   767 19

NERVOUS
  WITH A TWITCHY NERVOUS INTOLERABLE FLIGHT   342 22
  LEAVING A NERVOUS PEOPLE   374 28
  AND STEPPING IN HOMAGE STUBBORN TO THAT NERVOUS PALE   388 24
  THEY WERE BOTH NERVOUS WRECKS BECAUSE   605 17
  YOU'LL GIVE THE GREAT BRITISH PUBLIC A NERVOUS SHOCK   669 11

NERVOUSLY
  THEY CHEERED BUT NERVOUSLY   445   3

NESH
  THOUGH HIS FEET ARE STILL NESH   459 24
  TOO NESH   817 32
  OF ALL US FLESH AND WE STAND IN OUR NAKEDNESS NESH   *938 11

NEST
  AS ON A NEST THE ROVER   125   1
  THE NEST IN A HEART OF LOVE   125   6
  YOUNG BIRDS FORSAKEN AND LEFT IN A NEST OF MUD   145 24
  DEFENDING THE MEMORY OF LEAVES AND THE HAPPY ROUND NEST   167 10
  HE'S GOT IN HIS NEST WE'LL BE HAPPY   244 31
  THE NEST IS IN FLAMES   330   6
  ITS BREAST AGAINST ITS NEST TO MAKE IT ROUND   451 14
  OR THAN IF HE'D JUST BUILT HIMSELF A NEST WITH A BATHRO+   496   8
  SHAKING THE LARK'S NEST TILL THE EGGS HAVE BROKEN   623 31
  THEN THE SMALL STIRRING OF A NEW SMALL BUB IN THE NEST   728   9
  AND BUILDING MY NEST OF PEACE IN YOUR BONES   802   4
  OR WHETHER MY HEART WAS ITS NEST   881 26
  DEFENDING THE MEMORY OF BIRDS THAT USED TO NEST   *896 15
  PLENISHING THE GREY RAT'S NEST   *933   6
  AND I SAW HER BOSOM COUCH IN THE NEST OF HER GOWN   *934 15
  HARDENED THE EARTH SHAKING THE LARK'S NEST TILL THE EGG+   *953 18

NESTING
    NOR IS HE NESTING PASSIVE UPON THE ATOMS   436   5
    AND NESTING HIS CHIN IN HIS HAND   842 18

NESTLE
    THE HEN WILL NESTLE OVER HER CHICKENS   268   4

NESTLED
    WE MIGHT HAVE NESTLED LIKE PLOVERS   243   3

NESTLING
    YOU WITH YOUR FOREHEAD NESTLING   224   3

NESTS
    COME MAKING THE CHAFFINCH NESTS HOLLOW AND COSY   273   1
    FEATHER THE NESTS OF ALL   413 15
    THE LARK NESTS IN HIS HEART   624   5
    WHERE THE LARK NESTS SAFELY   *953 24
    THE LARK NESTS IN HIS HEART   *953 25

NEST'S
    HER OUT OF THE NEST'S WARM BUSY BALL   42 28

NET
    IN THE NET OF THE NIGHT'S BALLOON   54 11
    THE CLASS OVER THEM ALL THE DARK NET OF MY DISCIPLINE W+   92   6
    A NET ON THE UNDERSOIL THAT LIES PASSIVE AND QUICKENED +   94   4
    TO DRAW HIS NET THROUGH THE SURF'S THIN LINE AT THE DAW+   180   2
    I WILL SIFT THE SURF THAT EDGES THE NIGHT WITH MY NET T+   180   4
    I WILL CATCH IN MY EYES' QUICK NET   180   8
    THE SUBSTANCE TANGLED IN THE NET   747 18
    CAUGHT WHEN MY HEART WOULD LEAP IN A NET OF LIVES   884 15
    THE CLASS OVER THEM ALL THE DARK NET OF MY DISCIPLINE W+ *926   6

NETHER
    THE HEAVENS ARE THE NETHER MILL-STONE AND OUR HEAVY EAR+   614 19
    GRINDING THEM SMALL TO HUMUS ON EARTH'S NETHER MILL-STO+   615   6

NETS
    AT THE GATE THE NETS HUNG BALKING   152 16
    THE SAME WITH THE FISHERMEN SITTING DARNING THEIR NETS   520 17
    THEY ARE LIKE CATS WITH UNCLEAN CLAWS TANGLED UP IN NETS 675   6
    UNDER THE SPIDER-WEB NETS   797   8

NETTLES
    THE WALLS OF THE HOUSE AND NETTLES PUFF OUT FROM THE HE+ 159 25
    NETTLES AND A ROSE SPROUT   316   1
    LEAVE ME MY NETTLES   316 10
    AND IMPUDENT NETTLES GRABBING THE UNDER-EARTH   317 19
    THE STINGING NETTLES ON MY WRISTS WOKE ME   881 16
    I AWOKE WITH THE YOUNG NETTLES ON MY WRISTS   882   5
    THEN THE STINGING NETTLES ON MY WRISTS   882 20
    PERHAPS THE TINY YOUNG NETTLES HAVE STUNG HER EARS   882 26

NEURASTHENIC
    AND A NEURASTHENIC LUNGE   342 23

NEUTER
    I DIED AND DEATH IS NEUTER IT SPEAKS NOT IT GIVES   461 13

NEUTRALITY
    INTO EVIL NEUTRALITY INTO MECHANISM   713   8

NEVERTHELESS
    NEVERTHELESS ONCE THE FROGS THE GLOBE-FLOWERS OF BAVARIA 208   4
    NEVERTHELESS THE CURSE AGAINST YOU IS STILL IN MY HEART   208 15
    WE MUST KEEP YOUR LAMP ALIGHT NEVERTHELESS JEANNETTE   859 27

NEVER-WARM
    THIS NEVER-WARM   57   3

NEW
    VEGETABLE NEW IN RENOWN   49 28
    THE NEW RED HOUSES SPRING LIKE PLANTS   50 19
    BUT IT LEANED YOU A NEW   56   5
    OF THE DARK-GREEN HILLS NEW CALVES IN SHED PEEWITS TURN+   57 27
    WITH A STRANGE NEW KNOCKING OF LIFE AT HER SIDE   64   8
    TO FIND THE NEW HOUSES A CLUSTER OF LILIES GLITTERING   72 21
    THIS NEW RED ROCK IN A WASTE OF WHITE RISES AGAINST THE+   75 13
    CLEAN AN' NEW AN' NICE SO'S WHEN   77 27
    IN A NEW NIGHT-SPASM OF BIRTH AND GIVEN US THIS NEW RED+   88 20
    WITHIN THE WOMB NEW SHAPES AND THEN NEW MEN   89 11
    THE SHROUDED MOTHER OF A NEW IDEA MEN HIDE THEIR FACES   91 26
    IN CLEAN NEW AWARENESS BUT NOW   112   4
    THAT A NEW NIGHT POURING DOWN SHALL SWILL   117   5
    COME ANOTHER NIGHT COME A NEW NIGHT SAY   117 20
    AS HE PLANTS HIS NEW GERM IN US WHAT IS THERE TO SHUN   127   5
    NEWNESS NEW SHAPE TO WIN   127 14
    THE DEAD MOON HEAPED WITHIN THE NEW MOON'S ARMS   132   2
    BUT MY HEART STANDS STILL AS A NEW STRONG DREAD ALARMS   132   5
    NEW SPARKS OF WONDER OPENING IN SURPRISE   136 16
    YOUR FERVENT LIMBS WITH FLICKERS AND TENDRILS OF NEW   156 27
    OUT OF CORROSION INTO NEW FLORESCENCE   160 20
    BEATS THE NEW FRESH AIR OF LIFE THEY COME FOR STRIFE   174 14
    TO MAKE NEW WORDS WITH OUR LIPS TO ESCAPE THE FOUL DREAM 175 22
    TO CROWN THE TRIUMPH OF THIS NEW DESCENT   218 28
    THE NEW YOUNG YEAR COMES IN   229 10
    AGAIN MY DARLING BUT NEW   239 14
    NEW PHASE IN THE GERM OF YOU   240   7
    NEW SUNNY STREAMS OF BLOOD   240   8
    I FEEL NEW AND EAGER   244 23
    AND TO FEEL QUITE NEW   244 26
    OLD SORROW AND NEW HAPPINESS   247 24
    A FINE WIND IS BLOWING THE NEW DIRECTION OF TIME   250 14
    ALL ALONE AND VERY GLAD IN A NEW WORLD   256   8
    I COULD CRY WITH JOY BECAUSE I AM IN THE NEW WORLD JUST   256 10
    NEW BEYOND KNOWLEDGE OF NEWNESS ALIVE BEYOND LIFE   258 30
    MYSELF THE SAME AS BEFORE YET UNACCOUNTABLY NEW   258 34

NEW
    THE UNKNOWN THE NEW WORLD   259 33
    OVER TO THE NEW WORLD AND WAS CLIMBING OUT ON THE SHORE   260 14
    BUT TO A NEW EARTH A NEW I A NEW KNOWLEDGE A NEW WORLD   260 17
    AH NO I CANNOT TELL YOU WHAT IT IS THE NEW WORLD   260 19
    AND WHOSOEVER COMES AFTER WILL FIND ME IN THE NEW WORLD   260 22
    THE NEW WORLD   260 25
    OUT OF THE WELL-HEADS OF THE NEW WORLD   260 31
    NEW FEET ON THE EARTH BEATING WITH IMPATIENCE   272   3
    STIRRING OF NEW SEASONS   274   6
    AND THERE A NEW PARTNER A NEW PARTING A NEW UNFUSING   280 30
    A NEW GASP OF FURTHER ISOLATION   281   1
    A NEW INTOXICATION OF LONELINESS AMONG DECAYING FROST-C+ 281   2
    IN A NEW PROUD SINGLENESS AMERICA   290 20
    NEW THROB LIKE A STIRRING UNDER THE FALSE DAWN THAT PRE+ 292 34
    NEW BODY AGAIN LIKE ALMOND BLOSSOM IN JANUARY   303 11
    AND BREATHING SOFT UNWILLING TO WAKE TO THE NEW DAY   311 12
    THE EXQUISITE ASSERTION OF NEW DELICATE LIFE   314 19
    AND FEED THE YOUNG NEW FIELDS OF LIFE WITH ASH   315   5
    AND THEN TO SEE THE NEW REAL SOULS SPROUT UP   315 31
    NEW WILD SOULS   315 34
    THERE IS A NEW SWEETNESS IN HIS VOLUPTUOUSLY LICKING HI+ 325   1
    THERE IS A NEW ECSTASY IN HIS ROAR OF DESIROUS LOVE   325   3
    THAT A NEW CHICK SHOULD CHIP THE EXTENSIVE SHELL   329 28
    SO THAT A NEW CONCEPTION OF THE BEGINNING AND END   329 33
    NEW DAY WITH THEM   371 31
    HUGE MORE TASSELS SWINGING MORE DRIPPING FIRE OF NEW   388 27
    FOR A NEW SIGNAL FROM LIFE IN THAT SILENT LOST LAND OF + 394 12
    LITTLE BLACK DOG IN NEW MEXICO   394 28
    AND THEN TURN TAIL TO THE NEXT COMER FOR A NEW DOLLOP   396 23
    AND WAIT FOR HIM TO COME BACK WITH A NEW STORY   405 30
    THE NEW NAKED LITTLE REPUBLICS COME INTO THE WORLD   413 16
    THE NEW PROUD REPUBLIC   414 17
    AND IS FECUND WITH A NEW DAY OF NEW CREATURES DIFFERENT   429   7
    OF A SWAMPED CIVILISATION AND START A NEW WORLD OF MAN   429 12
    AND MAKE A NEW JOB OF THE HUMAN WORLD   429 16
    LET HIM MEET A NEW EMOTION LET HIM BE FACED WITH ANOTHER 431   2
    HIM WITH A NEW DEMAND ON HIS UNDERSTANDING   431   5
    JUST WATCH THE DISPLAY OF HIM CONFRONTED WITH A NEW   431   8
    A NEW LIFE-DEMAND   431 10
    NEW HOUSES NEW FURNITURE NEW STREETS NEW CLOTHES NEW   448 14
    EVERYTHING NEW AND MACHINE-MADE SUCKS LIFE OUT OF US   448 16
    WELL SOFTLY UP FOR A NEW INCREASE   461 26
    NEW LIFE FOR YOURSELVES AND YOUR WOMEN COMPLEMENTAL   463 12
    THE NEW MOON OF NO IMPORTANCE   467   5
    THE NEW MOON IN COOL HEIGHT ABOVE THE BLUSHES   467   9
    WITH THE THRUSTING EMBRACE OF NEW JUSTICE NEW JUSTICE   482   5
    WE SHALL STAMP OUR FEET WITH NEW POWER   482 24
    THEY'VE BUILT A NEW UNIVERSITY   488   9
    FOR A NEW DISPENSATION OF KNOWLEDGE   488 10
    AND SENDS OFF MILLIONS OF SPARKS OF NEW ATOMS   506   9
    FOR THE NEW WORD IS RESURRECTION   512 31
    SHALL I TELL YOU AGAIN THE NEW WORD   513   1
    THE NEW WORD OF THE UNBORN DAY   513   2
    AND THE NEW WORD MEANS NOTHING TO US   513   7
    WE WANT A NEW WORLD OF WILD PEACE WHERE LIVING IS FREE   519 22
    WITHOUT FIRST BEGETTING A NEW HOPE FOR THE CHILDREN TO   521 23
    THE WORLD IS WAITING FOR A NEW GREAT MOVEMENT OF   522 26
    MEN SHOULD GROUP THEMSELVES INTO A NEW ORDER   525 10
    PONDERING THIS NEW TRUTH OF THE SENSATIONAL YOUNG I SAID 532   1
    NEW BROOMS SWEEP CLEAN   536   1
    STAND UP FOR A NEW ARRANGEMENT   560 29
    TO INCULCATE THE NEW CONCEPTION OF THE RISEN MAN   609 21
    BUT THE PRESENCE OF OTHER PEOPLE WILL NOT GIVE THEM NEW   610 13
    FORTH NEW ROOTS   610 17
    NEW DAY   625   5
    NEW STOCK   640 24
    COMES A NEW STRENGTH   662 11
    AND UNDENIABLE NEW GODS SHARE THEIR LIFE WITH US WHEN WE 662 12
    INTO SOMETHING NEW AND STRANGE   667 25
    TO THE BREATH THAT IS OF NEW BEAUTY UNFOLDING IN DEATH   676 23
    AND LET MANKIND MAKE NEW BLOOD FRESH AND BRIGHT   679   7
    THAT LIES BETWEEN THE OLD SELF AND THE NEW   718   2
    WAKING AND WAKING NEW   725   7
    ODD WINTRY FLOWERS UPON THE WITHERED STEM YET NEW STRAN+ 727 24
    SUCH AS MY LIFE HAS NOT BROUGHT FORTH BEFORE NEW BLOSSO+ 727 26
    TO SEND ME FORTH ON A NEW MORNING A NEW MAN   727 30
    THEN THE SMALL STIRRING OF A NEW SMALL BUB IN THE NEST   728   9
    BY TOUCH AND A NEW NAKEDNESS   738 24
    OUT OF BLOOD RISE UP NEW GHOSTS   739 25
    THE MORE WE SLAY AND ARE SLAIN THE MORE WE RAISE UP NEW   739 27
    AND WE SHALL HAVE NEW PEACE IN THIS OUR LIFE   740 25
    NEW JOY TO GIVE MORE LIFE NEW BLISS TO LIVE   740 26
    AND WHATEVER NEW COMES ALONG WILL BE SUCCESSFULLY SOLD   763 12
    SLOWLY INSIDIOUSLY INTO NEW PLACES   768 12
    WANDERING INTO NEW VALLEYS   768 14
    MAKING POOLS IN NEW HOLLOW PLACES   768 15
    SHE REJOICES IN HER NEW NAKEDNESS   768 23
    THEN DRIVEN BACK IN A NEW SILENT RUSH   784 14
    AND THE FLAME OF YOU SWEPT BACK IN A NEW BREATH OF LIFE+ 784 26
    FOR I AM SWEET I AM THE LAST AND THE BEST THE POOL OF N+ 796 24
    LIKE A TREE IN NEW LEAF   811 14
    THE NEW MOON SETS AT SUNDOWN   816   5
    WATCH THE NEW MOON   816 19
    NEW LIFE BUBBLES IN WE BECOME SOMETHING ELSE   832 22
    IS A NEW FRAME OF SOCIETY   833 13
    WHERE WE CAN LEARN TO FULFIL OUR NEW KNOWLEDGE OF MATER+ 833 23
    A NEW THING COMES TO PASS EYES CLOSE   834   2
    PULL IT DOWN AND PREPARE FOR A NEW FRESH HOUSE OF LIFE   838 12
    TO TOUCH IT THAT NEW THING   861 25
    YET IN THE LITTLE NEW ROAD THE YOUNG WIFE TURNS AWAY   865 13
    OF RUSSIA THROUGH THE NEW GREAT NAIVETE OF RUSSIA HER W+ 866 29
    CRUCIBLE WHERE NEW BLOSSOMS OF SHAPE ARE BEGOT   873   5
    TAKE THE LANTERN AND WATCH THE SOW FOR FEAR SHE GRAB HE+ *892 24
    THE MIST IS A CUP OF WINE AND THE NEW AND OLD   *894 26
    THE MEN UPLIFTED ON THE NEW WHITE WOODSTACK STAND   *895   1
    CLEAN AN' NEW AN' NICE SO'S WHEN   *919 15
    THE SHROUDED MOTHER OF A NEW IDEA MEN HIDE THEIR FACES   *926 19

NEW
  THEY HAVE BUILT A NEW AND CAKEY UNIVERSITY   *950 13
  THEY FALL UPON THE NEW OUTCOMING SOULS WITH RAGE   *958 5

NEW-AWAKENED
  NOW HERE WAS I NEW-AWAKENED WITH MY HAND STRETCHING   259 16
  RISING NEW-AWAKENED FROM THE TOMB   260 3

NEW-BORN
  OF THE NEW-BORN AND THEN THE OLD OWL THEN THE BATS THAT+   38 11
  WORSE THAN THE CRY OF THE NEW-BORN   364 13
  WON'T IT BE STRANGE WHEN THE NURSE BRINGS THE NEW-BORN   438 26
  OF THE NEW-BORN AND THE UNBORN AND THE OLD OWL AND THE +   *892 26

NEWCOMER
  THOU NEWCOMER TO THE ANGELS   753 15

NEW-CREATED
  THEN I HAVE BEEN DIPPED AGAIN IN GOD AND NEW-CREATED   726 25

NEW-DROPPED
  THE MOUNTAIN'S NEW-DROPPED SUMMER SNOW IS CLEAR   225 2

NEW ENGLAND
  YOUR NEW ENGLAND UNCANNINESS   291 24

NEWLY
  AS A JEWEL-BROWN HORSE-CHESTNUT NEWLY ISSUED   73 5
  LIKE FLAGS IN PALE BLOOD NEWLY WET   105 3

NEWLY-NAKED
  LIKE A NEWLY-NAKED BERRY SHRINK   107 14
  A NEWLY-NAKED BERRY OF FLESH   108 3

NEW MEXICO
  DOES THE SUN IN NEW MEXICO SAIL LIKE A FIERY BIRD OF PR+   374 12

NEWNESS
  NEWNESS NEW SHAPE TO WIN   127 14
  WITH THIS YEAR'S NEWNESS AND IS THAT EVIL   127 20
  ONLY THAT ONE NEWNESS   247 25
  I SHALL NEVER CEASE TO BE FILLED WITH NEWNESS   248 14
  NEW BEYOND KNOWLEDGE OF NEWNESS ALIVE BEYOND LIFE   258 30

NEW-OPENED
  AND IN THE MORNING WAKE LIKE A NEW-OPENED FLOWER   726 24

NEW ORLEANS
  I'M AMERICAN FROM NEW ORLEANS   435 2

NEW-PATTERNED
  THE CREATION OF A NEW-PATTERNED DREAM DREAM OF A GENERA+   *907 3
  THE CREATION OF A NEW-PATTERNED DREAM DREAM OF A GENERA+   *908 24

NEW-RISEN
  I NEW-RISEN RESURRECTED STARVED FROM THE TOMB   259 14

NEWS
  THE NEWS THAT SHE IS FREE   99 26
  I TEAR BUT NEWS OF SORROW AND PAIN   772 23

NEWSPAPER
  NEWSPAPER SHEETS ENCLOSE   145 25
  TALK TALK TALK CORPSE-BODY NEWSPAPER TALK   584 16
  OH CARCASS WITH A BOARD-SCHOOL MIND AND A HA'PENNY NEWS+   631 3

NEWSPAPERS
  AND GAVE A BOARD-SCHOOL EDUCATION NEWSPAPERS AND THE   630 24
  MY GRIEFS AND ON NEW YORK NEWSPAPERS BATTEN   815 16

NEW WORLD
  THE STRANGE UNACCUSTOMED GESTE OF YOUR DEMONISH NEW WOR+   292 15

NEW YORK
  IN LONDON NEW YORK PARIS   704 6
  I SHALL COME TO NEW YORK AND LIVE ON MANHATTAN   815 14
  MY GRIEFS AND ON NEW YORK NEWSPAPERS BATTEN   815 16

NEXT
  NEXT TO MY BREAST WHERE MY OWN HEART WAS BEATING   61 22
  THEN ALONG THE DAMP ROAD ALONE TILL THE NEXT TURNING   280 29
  FISH-BLOOD SLOWLY RUNNING NEXT TO THE FLOOD EXTRACTING   336 31
  HEART-THROB SLOW HEART-THROB PERSISTENT FOR THE NEXT   365 27
  ARE YOU THE BIRD OF THE NEXT DAWN   371 19
  AND THEN TURN TAIL TO THE NEXT COMER FOR A NEW DOLLOP   396 29
  AND THE SOUL'S NEXT PASSION IS TO REFLECT   482 3
  DINNERS FOR THE NEXT FIFTY YEARS   531 7
  WILL THE PROUSTIAN LOT GO NEXT   533 16
  TOWARDS THOSE NEAR AND DEAR TO ME MY VERY NEXT   607 27
  AND THE NEXT DEEPEST SENSUAL EXPERIENCE   653 7
  TO THE NEXT FARM PULLS UP WHERE THE ELDER FLOWERS FALL   732 4
  AND I AM ONLY NEXT TO NOTHINGNESS   738 22
  UPON THE WINCINGNESS OF NEXT TO NOTHINGNESS   738 29
  YOU SIT NEXT TO ME ON THE PERCH   761 29
  WHAT NEXT   783 24
  THE NEXT DAY IS THE DAY OF THE GOOSE THE WILD SWAN'S DAY   841 9
  WHAT LIES OVER THE NEXT DARK HILL   858 3
  TO HOIST THE NEXT WHITE PLANK THEIR MOVEMENT SEEMS   *895 5
  NEXT MY BREAST WHERE MY OWN HEART WAS BEATING   *912 2
  ALL FEARFUL LEST I FIND SOME NEXT WORD BLEEDING   *939 3
  AND GOING BLANDLY ON TO HIS NEXT SPITE   *949 14

NIBBLE
  LIFTING HER FACE TO NIBBLE AT A ROUND WHITE PEPPERMINT   393 8
  THEY NIBBLE THE FACE OF THE EARTH TO A DESERT   606 20

NIBBLED
  NIBBLED MANSION   451 25
  NIBBLED HIS FINGERS THE KNAVE   754 19

NICE
  CLEAN AN' NEW AN' NICE SO'S WHEN   77 27
  AN' 'IM AS NICE AN' FRESH   77 29
  FOR THIS NICE OLD SHAME AN' DISGRACE   79 8
  YET YOU'RE SO NICE   396 27
  AND ARE JUST LIKE THEM AND CONFORM AND ARE NICE   431 31
  HOW NICE IT IS TO BE SUPERIOR   435 5
  TOO NICE TOO BEAUTIFUL   490 6
  BUT IF YOU GO AND MAKE NAUGHTINESS NICE   491 9
  IF SUCH THINGS WERE NICE AND WE NEEDN'T THINK TWICE   491 11
  SO BE A NICE UNCLE BE GOOD TO US GIRLS   574 5
  AH MY NICE PICTURES THEY ARE FOULED THEY ARE DIRTIED   580 25
  AH MY NICE PICTURES LET ME SPONGE YOU VERY GENTLY   581 1
  IS SUMMED UP IN A NICE NARROW-GUTTED OLD MAID   584 4
  THE ENGLISH ARE SO NICE   659 24
  SO AWFULLY NICE   659 25
  AND WHAT'S MORE THEY'RE VERY NICE ABOUT BEING NICE   660 1
  ABOUT YOUR BEING NICE AS WELL   660 2
  IF YOU'RE NOT NICE THEY SOON MAKE YOU FEEL IT   660 3
  BUT THEY'RE NOT REALLY NICE YOU KNOW   660 6
  THEY'RE NOT NICE IN OUR SENSE OF THE WORD ARE THEY NOW   660 7
  WE MUST BE NICE TO THEM OF COURSE   660 9
  BE NICE YOU KNOW JUST NICE   660 14
  JUST BE NICE YOU KNOW OH FAIRLY NICE   660 16
  NOT TOO NICE OF COURSE THEY TAKE ADVANTAGE   660 17
  BUT NICE ENOUGH JUST NICE ENOUGH   660 18
  TO LET THEM FEEL THEY'RE NOT QUITE AS NICE AS THEY MIGH+   660 19
  A NICE ONE I LIKE IT HE'LL THINK IT'S A TALL ORDER   733 29
  HOW NICE SAYS THE PEON TO GO RUSHING IN A TRAIN   794 13
  HOW NICE TO GET IN THE CAMION AND FOR TWENTY CENTAVOS T+   794 14
  HOW NICE IN THE GREAT CITIES WHERE ALL THINGS RUSH AND +   794 15
  HOW NICE TO SIT IN THE CINE WHERE THE PICTURE OF ALL TH+   794 17
  HOW NICE IF WE COULD TAKE ALL THESE THINGS AWAY FROM TH+   794 19
  HOW NICE   794 24
  HE HAS A VERY NICE APPLE-OF-SODOM RIND   830 8
  CLEAN AN' NEW AN' NICE SO'S WHEN   *919 15
  AN' 'IM AS NICE AN' FRESH   *919 17
  FOR THIS NICE OLD SHAME AND DISGRACE   *921 4
  VERY NICE ON YOU SIR   *922 32

NICELY
  NICELY GROOMED LIKE A MUSHROOM   431 13
  AND THEN WHEN YOU'RE GETTIN' NICELY ON   490 9

NICER
  AN' FRESH AN' MORE NICER FOR MARRYIN' WI'   138 12
  IT WOULD BE SO MUCH NICER IF HE JUST BARKED AT HIMSELF   836 14

NICEST
  THEY ARE THE NICEST PEOPLE IN THE WORLD   659 26

NICHTS
  NICHTS AND NIENTE RIEN AND NADA   824 8

NICK
  NICK OLD NICK MAYBE   404 11

NICOLAS
  OR THE ABBREVIATION OF NICOLAS   404 10

NIENTE RIEN
  NICHTS AND NIENTE RIEN AND NADA   824 8

NIGGER
  AND FEAR IN THE SMOKY WHITES OF YOUR EYES YOU NIGGER   400 26

NIGH
  FOR NEVER HER HANDS COME NIGH ME BUT THEY LIFT   128 10
  THE CATTLE RUN ANXIOUS IN QUEST AS THE TIME DRAWS NIGH   749 25

NIGHER
  AND MY HEART REBELS WITH ANGUISH AS NIGHT DRAWS NIGHER   48 13

NIGHT
  TO COOL IN THE NIGHT IF SHE CAME TO ME NOW   35 10
  AND AT NIGHT WHEN THE WIND ROSE THE LASH OF THE TREE   36 10
  YET THE SPLASHES OF DAY AND NIGHT   37 26
  AND THE PALLOR OF NIGHT DOES NOT TALLY   38 4
  LAST NIGHT WHEN I WENT WITH THE LANTERN THE SOW WAS GRA+   38 8
  HE STANDS THE COLUMN OF FIRE BY NIGHT   39 22
  HE STANDS LIKE A LIGHTHOUSE NIGHT CHURNS   39 31
  LAST NIGHT A THIEF CAME TO ME   46 21
  AND MY HEART REBELS WITH ANGUISH AS NIGHT DRAWS NIGHER   48 13
  WHILE PATIENT NIGHT   54 17
  WARM AS A FLAME IN THE CLOSE NIGHT AIR   61 29
  THAT THE BLACK NIGHT HID HER FROM ME BLOTTED OUT EVERY   62 4
  NIGHT   66 21
  I FOLLOW HER DOWN THE NIGHT BEGGING HER NOT TO DEPART   67 12
  WE HAVE SHUT THE DOORS BEHIND US AND THE VELVET FLOWERS+   70 1
  TO THE NIGHT THAT TAKES US WILLING LIBERATES US TO THE +   70 4
  FOR JOY OF THE NIGHT WHEN MASTERS ARE   70 12
  WHEN INTO THE NIGHT THE YELLOW LIGHT IS ROUSED LIKE DUST   70 20
  ABOUT YOU ONLY LAST NIGHT YOU WERE   72 13
  THEN BRILLIANT EARTH FROM THE BURR OF NIGHT IN BEAUTY   73 4
  LIKE HALF-BLOWN FLOWERS DIMLY SHAKING AT THE NIGHT   75 27
  AFTER I'D KISSED THEE AT NIGHT LIZZIE   80 9
  FROM OUT OF THE LOINS OF NIGHT TO GLOW IN OUR WAY   88 25
  TAKEN LIKE A SACRIFICE IN THE NIGHT INVISIBLE   90 26
  COOL LONELY NIGHT HER BREASTS WILL KEEP THE NIGHT AT BAY   91 11
  IN THE NIGHT WHERE WE FIRST HAVE BEING BEFORE WE RISE O+   92 15
  AND MY HOLLOW FLESH STANDS UP IN THE NIGHT LIKE VANITY   97 10
  THE NIGHT IS IMMENSE AND AWFUL YET TO ME IT IS NOTHING +   98 1
  TO THE FACE THAT GAZES OUTWARDS WATCHING FOR NIGHT TO W+   103 2
  HOW NIGHT AFTER NIGHT SWEPT LEVEL AND LOW   103 5

NIGHT

YOU COULD HAVE UNLOCKED THE MOON ON THE NIGHT 104 12
NIGHT BLENCHED WITH A THOUSAND SNOWS 104 28
WHITE LILAC SHOWS DISCOLOURED NIGHT 104 30
ON HIGH TO THE FUMING SKY OF NIGHT 105 2
AND THE SNORE OF THE NIGHT IN MY EAR 107 8
AND ACRID NIGHT OF AUTUMN 107 21
FOR THE NIGHT WITH A GREAT BREATH TAKEN 107 25
WITH WORDS BUT THE NIGHT SHOWS THROUGH 109 11
THE NIGHT WITH STRIFE 110 20
THIS RARE ANCIENT NIGHT FOR IN HERE 114 1
NOT THIS INNER NIGHT 114 14
I WONDER CAN THE NIGHT GO BY 116 14
AND THE NIGHT LOOK THROUGH 116 24
TO SHARE THE NIGHT WITH YOU 116 27
HOW I HAVE LONGED FOR THIS NIGHT IN THE TRAIN 117 1
THAT A NEW NIGHT POURING DOWN SHALL SWILL 117 5
SO HELEN WHEN ANOTHER NIGHT 117 11
NIGHT AFTER NIGHT WITH A BLEMISH OF DAY 117 18
COME ANOTHER NIGHT COME A NEW NIGHT SAY 117 20
THE LAST CAR TRAILED THE NIGHT BEHIND 121 24
THIS CLOT OF NIGHT 124 16
HAVE RISEN RED ON MY NIGHT AS A HARVEST MOON 126 4
AND SITS IN HER OWN DARK NIGHT OF HER BITTER HAIR 129 1
AND I DO TOSS THROUGH THE TROUBLED NIGHT FOR YOU 129 23
HER ROOM WHERE THE NIGHT STILL HANGS LIKE A HALF-FOLDFD+ 129 29
OF THE NIGHT IN HIS SOUL AND NONE OF THE TUNE 130 14
THE NIGHT IS WONDERFUL 130 28
THE SOUNDLESS NIGHT WHEREON OUR DAYS ARE SHIPPED 133 4
OF THE STUFF OF THE NIGHT FINDING MYSELF ALL WRONGLY 133 7
I WITH THE NIGHT ON MY LIPS I SIGH WITH THE SILENCE OF + 133 9
AS FARTHER OFF THE SCYTHE OF NIGHT IS SWUNG 135 11
AND GREY NOW NIGHT IS HERE NOR WILL 136 3
FOR THE FLUSH OF THE NIGHT WHEREAS NOW THE GLOOM 141 9
I WAS LAST NIGHT WHEN MY SOUL RANG CLEAR AS A BELL 141 24
IN THE BLACK WET NIGHT AS THE FURTIVE RAIN SLINKS DOWN 143 2
THE NIGHT RAIN DRIPPING UNSEEN 144 1
THE NIGHT WITH SILENCE CROSSING THE LAMP-TOUCHED TIDE 144 13
TRAMS THAT PASS BLOWN RUDDILY DOWN THE NIGHT 146 13
NOTHING TO MEET MY FINGERS BUT THE FLEECE OF NIGHT 147 4
SINCE THIS IS THE LAST NIGHT I KEEP YOU HOME 153 13
FLUX OF ANOTHER DAWN THE WIND THAT ALL NIGHT 154 28
THE NIGHT THROUGH 158 12
THE NIGHT UPRISEN STOOD 164 27
WHITE-BODIED AND WARM THE NIGHT WAS 165 9
WHITE AND ALIGHT THE NIGHT WAS 165 11
THE WHOLE WHITE NIGHT 165 22
THE NIGHT TURNS SLOWLY ROUND 169 1
THE WANING MOON LOOKS UPWARD THIS GREY NIGHT 172 18
AT THE OPEN DOOR OF THE ROOM I STAND AND LOOK AT THE NI+ 179 20
I WILL GO OUT TO THE NIGHT AS A MAN GOES DOWN TO THE SH+ 180 1
I WILL SIFT THE SURF THAT EDGES THE NIGHT WITH MY NET T+ 180 4
MOVING ALONG IN THE MYSTERIOUS EBB OF THE NIGHT 180 19
THE NIGHT YOU CLOSED YOUR EYES FOR EVER AGAINST ME 193 16
THE FILM OF THE BUBBLE NIGHT TO WHERE YOU ARE 194 2
FOR WHEN AT NIGHT FROM OUT THE FULL SURCHARGE 195 1
AT NIGHT I SAY WHEN I AM GONE IN SLEEP 195 5
WHO VOICE THE DUMB NIGHT FITTINGLY 197 31
THE BEGGAR HAD GATHERED AT NIGHT 202 18
TILL NIGHT WHEN BY THE FIRE'S RED STAIN 202 26
YOU ARE THE NIGHT AND I THE DAY 203 24
THE NIGHT WAS A FAILURE 204 1
LIKE A RATTLE A CHILD SPINS ROUND FOR JOY THE NIGHT RAT+ 206 31
MY DEAR THE NIGHT IS SOFT AND ETERNAL NO DOUBT 211 11
YOUR OWN SMALL NIGHT GOES WITH YOU WHY TREAT IT SO 211 14
COME YOU ARE COLD THE NIGHT HAS FRIGHTENED YOU 212 1
TO BE BLOWN OUT TO LET NIGHT DOWSE THE SPARK 212 9
I HOLD THE NIGHT IN HORROR 212 15
NIGHT FOLK TUATHA DE DANAAN DARK GODS GOVERN HER SLEEP 213 25
OH GODS OF THE LIVING DARKNESS POWERS OF NIGHT 213 29
YOU STAND AND THE NIGHT COMES THROUGH 215 18
A NIGHT LIES LOOKING UP 215 27
FOR WHICH I WANTED THE NIGHT TO RETREAT 220 20
THE HOUSE IS SILENT IT IS LATE AT NIGHT I AM ALONE 220 21
DARK SKY OF NIGHT A WANDERING GLITTER A SWARM 221 26
THE GREAT BLACK NIGHT SCOOPED OUT 238 2
IN THE NIGHT WHERE YOU'RE FOLDED UP 239 23
FROM THE NIGHT TO THE SOURCE OF YOU 240 5
AND NIGHT DRIFTING UP TO THE NIGHT 249 3
WHAT IS THE KNOCKING AT THE DOOR IN THE NIGHT 250 29
THE GREAT GOLD APPLES OF NIGHT 252 13
THE RIPENESS OF THESE APPLES OF NIGHT 252 20
BENEATH THE NIGHT 253 3
NIGHT OR DEATH OR HELL 258 13
I PUT OUT MY HAND IN THE NIGHT ONE NIGHT AND MY HAND 259 2
OUT OF THE IMMINENT NIGHT 286 23
NIGHT WERE DISTINGUISHED FROM THE SYMMETRY OF THEIR MIX+ 295 6
SUBSIDING INTO THIS NIGHT 302 13
THE ETNA SNOW-WIND THROUGH THE LONG NIGHT 305 24
WINGS FULL OF STARS THEY RULE THE NIGHT AND MAN THAT WA+ 319 3
THE NIGHT LIVES FOUR LIVES AND MAN THAT SLEEPS THROUGH + 319 4
DARK REVERSION OF NIGHT 321 30
MORNING COMES AND I SHAKE THE DEWS OF NIGHT FROM THE WI+ 322 26
THAT LIVE BY NIGHT AND LAMPLIGHT AND FIRELIGHT DO THEM + 331 8
BETWEEN THE DAY AND NIGHT 340 28
AND FLICKERED HIS TONGUE LIKE A FORKED NIGHT ON THE AIR+ 350 25
YOUR EYE OF A DARK DISTURBED NIGHT — 352 21
NIGHT 358 3
I REMEMBER HEARING A WILD GOOSE OUT OF THE THROAT OF NI+ 365 34
OUR OLD GOAT WE TIE UP AT NIGHT IN THE SHED AT THE BACK+ 384 4
THE TROPICAL NIGHT OF BLAZING COCOA-NUT 387 26
IN THE FUME OF COCOA-NUT OIL IN THE SWEATING TROPICAL N+ 387 36
OF THE HUGEST OLDEST OF BEASTS IN THE NIGHT AND THE FIR+ 388 11
AND TRUNK-LIPPED IN THE NIGHT 388 15
IN THE LONG HOT NIGHT MORE DANCERS FROM INSIGNIFICANT 389 2
THAT'S WHY THE NIGHT FELL IN FRUSTRATION 390 28
SWIFTNESS GALLOPED UPHILL IN THE NIGHT GOING BACK TO 390 30
TEMPLE OF BLOOD IN THE NIGHT SWIFT-STRIKING 390 33

NIGHT

RICE-FIELD AT NIGHT 391 7
IN THE NIGHT 391 15
AND IT'S NIGHT 403 17
LEFT LONELY IN THE NIGHT 403 26
OUR DAY IS OVER NIGHT COMES UP 425 1
NIGHT COMES UP 425 10
LIKE GLOBULES OF NIGHT ABOUT TO GO PLASH 427 8
COULD ONE AT NIGHT RUN UP AGAINST THE STANDING FLESH 428 2
AND CATCH FLESH LIKE THE NIGHT IN ONE'S ARMS 428 5
O PILLARS OF FLAME BY NIGHT O MY YOUNG MEN 440 9
THAT HAS LEFT SCUM ON THE SEA EVEN IN THE NIGHT 453 28
THE DAY IS ENDING THE NIGHT DESCENDING 456 1
AND A COMFORTABLE FEELING AT NIGHT 459 15
BUT THOU ART ALSO LIKE THE NIGHT 474 2
HAD HAD TO TAKE HIM FOR ONE NIGHT ONLY IN THE FLESH 538 3
YOUR PRAYERS AT NIGHT 558 2
THOUGH LAST NIGHT I WAS MARY 558 8
SHORT GASPS OF FLAME IN THE GREEN OF NIGHT WAY OFF 606 1
SMALL SHARP RED FIRES IN THE NIGHT OF LEAVES 606 3
NOW IT IS ALMOST NIGHT FROM THE BRONZEY SOFT SKY 647 8
THERE IS A BAND PLAYING IN THE EARLY NIGHT 656 5
THROUGH THE NIGHT 656 9
IN THE HEARSE OF NIGHT YOU SEE THEIR TARNISHED COFFINS 703 3
HOW BIG AND WHITE THE NIGHT IS 731 1
HELMETS AS HIS HE LOST IN THE WOOD THAT NIGHT 732 12
AND THEN WITHIN THE NIGHT WHERE NOTHING IS 738 21
MY SOUL COMES LAMENT FROM THE ENDLESS NIGHT 744 5
TO HAVE NO REST SAVE IN THE UTTER NIGHT 744 15
IN HOSTS TOWARDS THE EVERLASTING NIGHT 745 9
ONLY THE WASTE NIGHT LIES IN STORE 747 27
TO DISOWN THE NIGHT 748 12
DO YOU LIFT YOUR LIPS TO KISS ME GOOD NIGHT MY LOVE 750 16
CRY FOR THEE OUT OF THE NIGHT WHEREIN WE ARE PRONE 753 5
AND IF THIS NIGHT MY LOVE SHOULD COME TO ME 754 23
OH HOW THIS NIGHT HAS HAPPENED PERFECTLY 754 26
NOW WILL YOU PLAY ALL NIGHT 755 10
BRINGING NIGHT ONCE MORE AND THE MAN WITH THE KEYS 758 4
AT NIGHT TEMPORARILY OF COURSE 761 30
ONLY TO WRECK ON THE SHORES OF NIGHT AGAIN 771 26
KEEPS ME PROUD IN SHAME PLEDGE OF THE NIGHT DARK-PURE 772 13
I HAVE A KNOWLEDGE OF LOVELY NIGHT 772 16
OF SHARING THE NIGHT WITH GOD OF MINGLING UP AGAIN 772 25
A BLADE ON THE WHEEL THEN THE SLUMBERING NIGHT 773 4
STOOD BETWEEN THE DAY AND THE NIGHT 787 16
THE TREMORS OF NIGHT AND THE DAY 788 6
AND SHALL PASS THE HOUSES OF THE STARS BY NIGHT 799 9
BETWEEN NIGHT AND DAY MY SOUL-STAR IN ONE 799 23
AND THE NIGHT SHOULD NOT TURN DEEP 799 26
NIGHT TURNS UPON ME AND DAY WHO AM THE STAR BETWEEN 800 1
YOU BELONG TO THE NIGHT 803 23
IN THE STILLNESS OF MY NIGHT 804 19
WITH HIS REDNESS STAINING THE BODY OF THE NIGHT 805 24
IN THE STILLNESS OF HIS NIGHT 806 1
LO I AM LORD OF THE WATCHES OF THE NIGHT 806 29
AND THE DREAM OF THE NIGHT RISES FROM ME LIKE A RED FEA+ 806 30
IN THE DREAM OF THE NIGHT I SEE THE GREY DOGS PROWLING 807 2
IN THE NIGHT THE SOUL OF A COWARD CREEPS OUT OF HIM 807 4
WITH NIGHT 807 9
IN THE NIGHT I SEE THE GREY DOGS CREEPING OUT OF THE SL+ 807 11
THE HAIR OF NIGHT IS DARK OVER OUR FACES 809 1
KEEPS DAY AND NIGHT APART 809 24
BEYOND THE UNSPOKEN PASSION OF NIGHT 810 26
OF DARKENING NIGHT AND THE QUIVERING LIGHT 823 9
NOW THAT THE NIGHT IS HERE 834 1
OF THEIR VAIN UP-STRIVING AND NIGHT REMAINS FOR REGRET 856 4
IN THE WHITE MORNING WHERE IS THE ENCHANTED ROOM OF THE+ 856 7
SUNBEAMS LUSTY AND CLEAN FROM THE BATH OF NIGHT 856 16
SHE KISSED THEIR COOLNESS LAST NIGHT BREATHED THEIR CLE+ 856 19
WITH SHUTTERS OF CLOUDED NIGHT WILL CLOSE 857 14
WEARILY THROUGH THE OAKS THE NIGHT WIND BLOWS 857 22
WINROW AFTER WINROW FALLS UNDER THIS FIRST STROKE OF NI+ 858 10
SHAKEN SOFTLY FROM THE HEAVY-FOLDED SKIRTS OF NIGHT 858 14
TILL A DREAM CAME TREMBLING THROUGH MY FLESH IN THE NIG+ 860 9
AND I STARTED WITH PLEASURE FOR IN THE NIGHT IT HAD COM+ 860 12
LIKE A GIRL'S TWINKLING MERRIMENT AT NIGHT WHEN THE SEA+ 860 16
HAS THE WARMTH OF A NIGHT KISS SPREAD THROUGH THEIR BLO+ 860 22
AS WE DROP THROUGH THE NIGHT 862 19
THE NIGHT A BIG BLACK STAIN 862 20
THROUGH EVER ONWARD NIGHT PUSHING 862 29
THERE IN THE HEART OF A STAR SET FAR OFF IN THE NIGHT 865 7
AND I IN IMMEASURABLE NIGHT LOOKED ON FROM AFAR AFAR 865 10
EARTH-CLODS AND NIGHT TO FLOWERS THAT PRAISE AND BURN 872 4
THE LIGHTED LAMP INTO MY ROOM AT NIGHT 875 9
THE LOOP-HOLES OF THAT INNERMOST NIGHT OF HIM 876 35
THIS ONE NIGHT YET HE LIETH HERE TO HAND 877 21
SHAKES O'ER HIS WALLS WHEN THE WIND DISTURBS THE NIGHT 878 4
OF THE DARK SHAFT THAT ISSUES TO THE NIGHT 879 35
TO FOLD IN A SHINING CONCAVE THE PALE NIGHT 882 3
YET LOOKING AGAIN AT THE NIGHT 882 13
OF THE MOON AND THE NIGHT 884 3
LOOKED UP AT THE NIGHT AND HE 884 5
YET THE SPLASHES OF DAY AND NIGHT *892 14
AND THE PALLOR OF NIGHT DOES NOT TALLY *892 20
LIKE FULL-BLOWN FLOWERS DIMLY SHAKING AT THE NIGHT *897 26
LIKE FULL-BLOWN FLOWERS DIMLY SHAKING AT THE NIGHT *901 3
WARM AS A FLAME IN THE CLOSE NIGHT AIR *912 8
THAT THE BLACK NIGHT HID HER FROM ME BLOTTED OUT EVERY + *912 12
WE HAVE SHUT THE DOORS BEHIND US AND THE VELVET FLOWERS+ *916 9
TO THE HUSHED GREY-WINGED MINISTRANTS THE BATS OF NIGHT+ *916 12
THE GOLDEN GRAINED NIGHT AFLOWER ACROSS THE SKY *916 17
HAVE EATEN THE NARCOTICS OF NIGHT *917 14
WHEN INTO THE NIGHT THE YELLOW LIGHT IS ROUSED LIKE DUS+ *917 17
INTO THE NIGHT AND ARE LOST TO SADDEN WITH JETSAM THE D+ *918 8
BUT THE NIGHT IS FULL OF THE FLUTTER OF INVISIBLE REVEL+ *918 10
OF NIGHT *918 12
THIS RARE RICH NIGHT FOR IN HERE *929 18
NOT THE INNER NIGHT *930 2

NIGHT
    I WONDER CAN THE NIGHT GO BY   *930 13
    AND THE NIGHT LOOK THROUGH   *930 23
    HOW I HAVE LONGED FOR THIS NIGHT IN THE TRAIN   *931 5
    COME ON US ANOTHER NIGHT YOU WILL   *931 9
    BUT MY DEAR LOVE WHEN ANOTHER NIGHT   *931 15
    FOR NIGHT AFTER NIGHT WITH A BLEMISH OF DAY   *931 22
    COME ANOTHER NIGHT COME TOMORROW SAY   *931 24
    THIS BROWN CORE OF NIGHT   *935 16
    SHALL HAVE RISEN RED ON MY NIGHT AS A HARVEST MOON   *937 4
    AND GRAY NOW NIGHT IS HERE NOR WILL   *938 31
    AS FURTHER OFF THE SCYTHE OF NIGHT IS SWUNG   *939 12
    DARK SKY OF NIGHT THE WANDERING GLITTER THE SWARM   *945 12
    WITH PRAYER I NEED ONLY COME HOME EACH NIGHT TO FIND TH+   *945 28
    I NEED ONLY COME HOME EACH NIGHT AND LAY   *946 1
    THE WOMB OF SILENCE IN THE LIVING NIGHT   *959 33

NIGHT-AIRS
    HISSES THROUGH THE FLOWERS THE TIMID NIGHT-AIRS BLOW   855 30

NIGHT-BAYING
    TO THE GREEN NIGHT-BAYING OF THE DOG-STAR ETNA'S SNOW-E+   306 11

NIGHT-BREATHS
    OF FAINT NIGHT-BREATHS DID GO   165 7

NIGHTFALL
    ALONG THE ROAD AFTER NIGHTFALL   206 4
    BRAVE MEN HAVE PEACE AT NIGHTFALL   810 7
    THE NIGHTFALL I   817 4
    AND ESPECIALLY AT NIGHTFALL   869 3
    WHEN THE SKY'S BLUE DARKENS AT NIGHTFALL   869 8

NIGHTGOWNED
    WHITE LITTLE SHEAVES OF NIGHTGOWNED MAIDS   105 22

NIGHTINGALE
    THE DAWN ROOKS CALL AT EVENING WHEN THE NIGHTINGALE SIN+   368 11
    A NIGHTINGALE SINGING AT THE TOP OF HIS VOICE   523 8
    AND THINK HOW THE NIGHTINGALE WHO IS SO SHY   530 9
    LIKE THE KINGDOM OF THE NIGHTINGALE AT TWILIGHT   704 20
    SINGING DARKER THAN THE NIGHTINGALE ON ON TO THE SOLSTI+   727 12

NIGHTINGALE'S
    NIGHTINGALE'S PIERCING CRIES AND GURGLES STARTLED THE   366 2

NIGHT-LIGHTS
    NIGHT-LIGHTS HITHER AND THITHER SHED   142 27

NIGHTLY
    OF THE NIGHTLY HEAVENS OVERHEAD LIKE AN IMMENSE OPEN EYE   97 14
    THAT PASSES THE NIGHTLY ROAD ABOVE   105 11
    A NAKED NIGHTLY THING TOO FRAIL AND WISE FOR THE STRESS   771 23

NIGHTMARE
    FROM THIS NIGHTMARE WE WRITHE IN   177 23

NIGHT-MOTH
    FOOLING MY FEET DOES THE NIGHT-MOTH   731 3

NIGHTS
    THE MOON SETS FORTH O' NIGHTS   63 30
    STILL YOU LEFT ME THE NIGHTS   193 20
    AT WHOSE SIDE I HAVE LAIN FOR OVER A THOUSAND NIGHTS   260 6
    IN THE LONG DARK NIGHTS OF THE EVENING STAR AND SIRIUS +   305 23
    STAR AND THE SNOW-WIND AND THE LONG LONG NIGHTS   305 32
    THAT LIVES ERECT THROUGH LONG NIGHTS PHYSICALLY   427 13
    THOUGH WE HAVE CLOSED TOGETHER THROUGH THE NIGHTS   875 21
    TONIGHT THIS VERY LAST OF OUR NIGHTS WE   878 9

NIGHT-SKY
    ON A NIGHT-SKY BENT WITH A LOAD   104 24
    LOW NAKED CEILING OF THE NIGHT-SKY HELD   876 12

NIGHT-SPASM
    IN A NEW NIGHT-SPASM OF BIRTH AND GIVEN US THIS NEW RED+   88 20

NIGHT-STOCK
    THE NIGHT-STOCK OOZES SCENT   41 24

NIGHT'S
    IN THE NET OF THE NIGHT'S BALLOON   54 11
    LEANS ALL ALONE ABOVE MY WINDOW ON NIGHT'S WINTRY BOWER   67 19
    WASTEFUL INTO THE NIGHT'S BLACK NOSTRILS DRINK   86 6
    ME UP I PRAY OH YOU WHO ARE NIGHT'S BACCHANTE   86 7
    SO NIGHT'S FLOOD-WINDS HAVE LIFTED MY LAST DESIRE FROM +   97 9
    ALL ROUND ME ABOVE AND BELOW THE NIGHT'S TWIN CONSCIOUS+   97 23
    THROUGH INVISIBLE PULSES SLOWLY FILLING THE NIGHT'S DAR+   97 28
    OR LAST NIGHT'S ECHOINGS   109 23
    THE NIGHT'S SLOW CARE   142 10
    BURST THE NIGHT'S MEMBRANE OF TRANQUIL STARS   302 18
    AND THE STREWN TAWDRY TRAPPINGS THAT LAST NIGHT'S POETR+   856 11

NIGHT-TIME
    WHICH LIES ON THE KNEES OF THE NIGHT-TIME RUDDY AND MAK+   88 21
    YOU ARE A SEED IN THE NIGHT-TIME   102 9
    DOWN THE NIGHT-TIME OUT OF SIGHT   252 18

NIGHT-WIND
    THROUGH THE POPLARS THE NIGHT-WIND BLOWS   163 22

NIHIL
    NIHIL WILL COME ALONG AND HIT YOU ON THE HEAD   531 12

NIHILISTIC
    HE IS CAPABLE OF AN ENDLESS GRINDING NIHILISTIC HATE   648 3

NILE
    NILE   439 3

NILLY
    THEN WILLY NILLY   39 9

NIMBLE
    HER NIMBLE SHADOW TROTTING   222 13
    MY MIND IF FAIRLY NIMBLE AND IS NOT BLANK   501 18

NINE
    OF THE SEA-BLOWN WEEK OF NINE   702 4

NINE-TENTHS
    THAT YOU NEVER LOOK QUITE BACK NINE-TENTHS AH MORE   208 12
    SO NINE-TENTHS ASLEEP MOTIONLESS BORED AND STATICALLY A+   324 15

NINON
    AND BECOMES AT LAST HELEN OR NINON ANY LOVELY AND GENER+   691 18

NIP
    AND INCREASING THE FLOCK AND PERHAPS GIVING A REAL NIP +   325 10

NIPPED
    WHEN HAVE YOU KNEES EVER NIPPED ME   427 16
    NIPPED UPON THE FROZEN FLOODS OF PHILOSOPHIC DESPAIR   542 21
    THE WHITE DOG NIPPED THE MOTHER RAT THE FATHER RAT BESI+   *933 7

NIPPING
    SHE DOES NOT EVEN KNOW SHE IS NIPPING ME WITH HER CURVED   359 24
    NIPPING HER ANKLES   360 10

NIPPLE
    WITH A NIPPLE CENTRE OF RED   886 18

NIPPLE-THRUST
    YOUR BODY WITH THEIR NIPPLE-THRUST UNTIL   91 15

NIRVANA
    OWN NIRVANA   643 20

NIVER
    AN' WHAT A MOAN 'E'LL MAKE THERE NIVER   45 17
    THA NIVER BELIEVES IT DOES TER MOTHER   77 9
    AN' 'DEED AN' I WISH AS THIS TALE O' THINE WOR NIVER MY+   83 10
    THA NIVER BELIEVES IT MOTHER DOES TER   *918 27
    BUT 'DEED AN' I WISH AS THIS TALE O' THINE WOR NIVER MY+   *925 14
    YI' THA'RT A MAN THA'RT A FINE BIG MAN BUT NIVER A BABY+   *925 24

NIXIE
    THE WOMAN YOU ARE SHOULD BE NIXIE THERE IS A POOL   161 13

NOAH'S FLOOD
    OR ELSE BEFORE THEY HAD BEEN LET DOWN AGAIN IN NOAH'S F+   285 21

NOBBUT
    I'S THINK IT'S NOBBUT A BEGGAR   44 12

NOBILITY
    I KNOW I AM NOBLE WITH THE NOBILITY OF THE SUN   499 1
    YOU DRAW YOUR NOBILITY DIRECT FROM THE SUN   526 27
    OF THE RUSSIAN NOBILITY   537 6
    IS A PATENT OF NOBILITY   775 35

NOBLE
    THAT NOBLE BLOOD HAS BROUGHT US DOWN THE AGES   313 31
    PURE BLOOD AND NOBLE BLOOD IN THE FINE AND ROSE-RED VEI+   314 1
    I KNOW A NOBLE ENGLISHMAN   446 19
    OUT OF THE NOBLE LOOT   488 12
    I KNOW I AM NOBLE WITH THE NOBILITY OF THE SUN   499 1
    AND I FEEL ARISTOCRATIC NOBLE WHEN I FEEL A PULSE GO   525 7
    TO MAKE ALL MEN NOBLE   636 18
    O SACRIFICE NOT THAT WHICH IS NOBLE AND GENEROUS AND SP+   679 1
    I KNOW A NOBLE ENGLISHMAN   *947 27
    THIS NOBLE GENTLEMAN   *948 1
    AFTER AN AFFAIR WITH THIS NOBLE ENGLISHMAN   *948 9
    UNDER HIS NOBLE BOOT-SOLE   *948 27
    YOUR DARK-BLUE GLOOM IS SO NOBLE   *954 25

NOBLESSE
    SUBMIT TO IT AND LET YOUR AMERICAN NOBLESSE COMPEL YOU   779 30

NOBLESSE OBLIGE
    THE LOVELINESS THAT KNOWS NOBLESSE OBLIGE   314 17
    THEN NOBLESSE OBLIGE   775 37
    NOBLESSE OBLIGE   776 17
    AND NOBLESSE OBLIGE   776 36

NOBODY
    I COULD CRY WITH JOY AND QUITE FREELY THERE IS NOBODY TO   256 12
    NOBODY KNOWS YOU   292 18
    FEELINGS THAT NOBODY FELT   443 23
    THAT NOBODY EATS AND NOBODY WANTS SO IT ROTS BUT IS NOT   462 21
    FOR THEN NOBODY WOULD HAVE THEIR EYE ON HIM   483 8
    NOBODY CAN BE WISE EXCEPT ON RARE OCCASIONS LIKE GETTING   495 24
    I LOVE NOBODY I'M GOING TO LOVE NOBODY   507 2
    NOTHING AND NOBODY IN THE WHOLE VAST REALM OF SPACE   514 20
    AND NOBODY KNOWS WHAT THAT IS   515 13
    AND YOU'VE NOBODY TO REMIND YOU   549 4
    AND NOBODY BUT THEMSELVES IS INTERESTED   618 15
    NOBODY ELSE DID   619 17
    I FEEL ABSOLUTE REVERENCE TO NOBODY AND TO NOTHING HUMAN   622 6
    IN A ROBOT-DEMOCRACY NOBODY IS WILLING TO SERVE   648 8
    LET NOBODY BE ABOUT SLIP IN GO ALL UNSEEN   711 10
    SINCE NOBODY SEES IT   774 11

NOBODY
  BUT IF NOBODY EATS THEM   828 10
  FREE WHAT FOR NOBODY KNOWS BUT FREE   832 10
  I SHONNA FOR NOBODY IT IS   *922 31

NOCTURNAL
  DO I INTRUDE ON YOUR RITES NOCTURNAL   140 30
  OVER NOCTURNAL GRASS   146 21

NOD
  THE LITTLE WHITE FEET NOD LIKE WHITE FLOWERS IN A WIND   64 30
  AND NEVER YET KNOWN TO NOD   823 29
  THE LITTLE WHITE FEET NOD LIKE WHITE FLOWERS IN THE WIND   *913 29

NODALITY
  AND THE RELENTLESS NODALITY OF MY EYES REASSERTS ITSELF   *893 29

NODDING
  NODDING TO THE GREAT ONE   525 15
  AND LET THE NODDING TEMPESTS OF VERBOSITY   543 8
  SOMETIMES I SEE HER LIKE A FLOWER NODDING HER WAY AND   645 22
  HEAVY NODDING CLUSTERS OF CRIMSON RED   855 10

NODDIN'
  SIT NODDIN' THY HEAD AT ME   78 22
  SIT NODDIN' THY HEAD AT ME   *920 14

NODS
  WHEN THE PLANETS HAVE GIVEN SEVEN NODS   702 6

NOEL
  THIS IS NOEL FOR ME   240 19

NOISE
  THE OTHER VOICE IN A SILENCE OF BLOOD 'NEATH THE NOISE   36 17
  THE NOISE DISTRESSES HER EARS AND TEARS   54 21
  DOWN THE NOISE OF MEN   109 28
  NOR BLENCH IT WITH NOISE   110 22
  PAST WITH THE NOISE OF A BREEZE   144 24
  THAT NO NOISE CAN TRANSGRESS   261 21
  WHO MADE SO LITTLE NOISE OUTSIDE THE CYPRESS GROVES   296 16
  IN THE NOISE OF THE TOM-TOMS AND SINGERS   387 37
  TRAGEDY SEEMS TO ME A LOUD NOISE   508 11
  AND THE NOISE AND THE STENCH AND THE DREARINESS   510 28
  HARK THE STRANGE NOISE OF MILLIONS OF FISH IN PANIC   586 25
  BUT IT IS ONLY UNHAPPY MEN MAKING A NOISE   656 6
  THERE HAS BEEN SO MUCH NOISE   739 1
  HE SHAKES THE TID-BIT FOR HER WITH A MOST WOOING NOISE +   761 18
  FROM THE NOISE OF CHILDREN PLAYING AROUND   867 3
  BUT THE NOISE OF LIFE   *895 9
  BY NOISE OF SMALL BIRDS SINGING FIFE   *914 22

NOISELESS
  NOISELESS THEIR WONDER NOISELESS BLEW   262 3
  ONLY ATTEND TO THE NOISELESS MULTITUDES   736 5
  IN TIMELESSNESS LAID BY IN NOISELESS DEATH   744 3
  OF NOISELESS DEATH I KNOW IT WELL   744 16
  THE SECRET OF THE NOISELESS UTTER GRACE   744 27
  AMBASSADOR FROM HALLS OF NOISELESS DEATH   745 15
  OVER MY HEAD HIS NOISELESS EAGLE   802 20
  WITHIN THE NOISELESS   811 12

NOISELESSLY
  NOISELESSLY   166 2

NOISES
  THE SPLINTERED STREETS HEAR NOISES   159 17
  AND LISTEN TO BODILESS NOISES   558 23
  AND OUT OF THE LIPS OF PEOPLE JERK STRANGE MECHANICAL N+   629 10
  AND CHIRRUP THEIR ALMOST INDECENT NOISES   681 6

NOISY
  THEN THE NOISY DIRTY DAY-WORLD   453 16
  OF NOISY BIRDS BE YOU CHIDDEN   *914 23

NOLI ME TANGERE
  AND NOLI ME TANGERE   378 3
  NOLI ME TANGERE TOUCH ME NOT   468 22
  NOLI ME TANGERE   469 10

NO-MAN'S-LAND
  OH A NO-MAN'S-LIFE IN A NO-MAN'S-LAND   585 19

NO-MAN'S-LIFE
  THIS LIFE WHICH IS NO-MAN'S-LIFE   585 18
  OH A NO-MAN'S-LIFE IN A NO-MAN'S-LAND   585 19

NON
  I WANT YOU TO KNOW 'E'S NON MARRYIN' YOU   *924 9

NON COGITO ERGO SUM
  NON COGITO ERGO SUM   474 21

NON-COMBATIVE
  NON-COMBATIVE   768 18

NON-DESCRIPTS
  LITTLE NON-DESCRIPTS WERE WE   490 18

NONE
  F'R I TELL YER I H'ARENA MARRYIN' NONE   81 3
  FOR SURELY THIS EARNEST MAN HAS NONE   130 13
  OF THE NIGHT IN HIS SOUL AND NONE OF THE TUNE   130 14
  SEVEN DAYS MY LAD OR NONE   138 6
  YOUR YOUTHFUL SMOOTHNESS I FLEECED WHERE FLEECE WAS NONE   156 26
  AND ALL YOUR BEING IS GIVEN TO ME SO NONE   157 19
  THAT FALL FOR EVER KNOWING NONE   164 15
  THEM NONE OF THE GLISTEN   170 9

NONE
  NONE OF THE TROUBLE HE'S LED TO STALL   219 28
  ENCOMPASSED AND MANY REDUCED TO NONE   252 11
  LOOK AT THE MANY-CICATRISED FRAIL VINE NONE MORE SCARRED   305 4
  NONE IN RAGS AND NONE IN TAGS   312 7
  NONE   335 21
  AND A BABY MAKES NONE   352 32
  THOUGH FAMILY FEELING THERE IS NONE NOT EVEN THE BEGINN+   357 23
  WITH NONE   413 8
  AND WHEN THE FATHER SAYS THIS IS NONE OF MINE   439 4
  THAT NOW THERE ARE NONE   439 12
  EMOTIONS THEY NONE OF THEM FELT   443 25
  AND SAW THEM CUDDLING WITH RISING PASSIONS THEY NONE OF   443 26
  NONE OF US KNOWS O NONE OF US KNOWS   462 5
  FOR WHILE WE HAVE SEX IN THE MIND WE TRULY HAVE NONE IN   471 27
  AND BE PREPARED TO KILL YOU IF YOU SAY THEY'VE GOT NONE   501 5
  AND NONE OF THESE IS LOVABLE   505 14
  DEAR LADIES NONE WHATSOEVER   541 14
  YOU'LL NONE OF YOU RISE IN THE WORLD LIKE I DID   552 27
  IF YOU'VE NONE OF YOU GOT MORE SPUNK   553 26
  SCARCE THERE ARE NONE ANY MORE   569 9
  SEEK ALL THE WORLD ROUND THERE'S NONE CAN BE FOUND   574 17
  AND NONE OF US MUST EXPECT MORALITY OF EACH OTHER   608 3
  THEY HAVE NO SONG IN THEIR SOULS NONE IN THEIR SPIRITS   657 13
  NONE IN THEIR LITTLE THROATS OR CLASS-ROOM BODIES   657 14
  NONE AT ALL MIND YOU PROGRESS IS A FACT   774 8
  BUT IN THE WEIGHT OF THEIR STUPEFACTION NONE OF THEM KN+   790 26
  WHERE WE FOREGATHER LIKE GYPSIES NONE KNOWING   812 23
  THEY WERE THE HALO THE ELOQUENCE NOW IS NONE   855 15
  FOR NONE GO WHITHER THIS LONG ROAD GOES   857 20
  YOU MUST MAKE MY SONGS FOR ME LOVE I HAVE NONE   884 12
  NONE O' THE TROUBLE HE'S LED TO STALL   *944 8

NONENTITY
  I AM A NONENTITY   509 9
  NONENTITY IS OUR PORTION   621 11

NON-EUROPEAN
  A SET STOIC ENDURANCE NON-EUROPEAN   292 12

NON-EXISTENCE
  OF NON-EXISTENCE TO FAR OBLIVION   722 15

NON-EXISTENT
  YOU ARE MIDDLE-CLASS AND ESSENTIALLY NON-EXISTENT   527 19

NON-INTERFERENCE
  DELICATE LINE OF NON-INTERFERENCE   780 12

NON-LIFE
  THE NON-LIFE   353 14

NON-ORIENTAL
  A DELIBERATE GENEROSITY NON-ORIENTAL   292 14

NON-RELIGIOUS
  THE MIND IS NON-RELIGIOUS   474 9

NONSENSE
  NONSENSE   307 19
  BUT WHAT NONSENSE IT IS   689 18
  AND NONSENSE FOR PURE SNOW IS WHITE TO US   708 19

NOOK
  AT THE LITTLE FISH THREAD-THREADING THE WATERY NOOK   161 11

NOON
  THEN THE SWEEPING SUNSHINE OF NOON   248 20
  AT WHICH IN THE INTENSE STILL NOON I STARED WITH FASCIN+   351 17
  AND NOON IS SUDDENLY DARK IS LUSTROUS IS SILENT AND DARK   606 4
  ALONG THE TABLE AT NOON OR WHEN YOU BRING   875 8
  THROUGH THE WHOLE BLUE SKY AND THE NOON   *937 11

NO-ONE
  NO-ONE IN THE ROOM   37 7
  NO-ONE NEAR THE BED   37 8
  IF MAN ONLY LOOKS TO MAN AND NO-ONE SEES BEYOND   650 6

NO-PROPERTY
  AND BETWEEN THE TWO BLADES OF THIS PAIR OF SHEARS PROPE+   663 16

NORMAL
  IS VERY NORMAL AS BECOMES AN ENGLISHMAN   446 23
  HAD NORMAL PUDENDA LIKE YOU AND ME   578 27
  SO THEY ACCEPT COVERED DISLIKE AS THE NORMAL FEELING BE+   832 15
  AS NORMAL ACTIVITY   832 17
  IS NOTHING IF NOT NORMAL   *948 2
  SO HE CLEVERLY PLAYS THE NORMAL THE DON JUAN   *948 25
  AND IS HIMSELF NORMAL A LOVER OF WOMEN   *949 6

NORTH
  LIKE A BIRD FROM THE FAR NORTH BLOWN WITH A BROKEN WING   47 15
  WHILE NORTH OF THEM ALL AT THE FARTHEST ENDS STANDS ONE+   57 11
  SUCH A ONE IN THE NORTH IT FLOWERS ON THE STREET AND I +   58 13
  THE WIND COMES FROM THE NORTH   99 16
  OF STEAM FROM THE DARKENING NORTH   99 22
  HOW TOWARDS THE NORTH A RED BLOTCH ON THE SKY   103 10
  THE AIR IS DARK WITH NORTH AND WITH SULPHUR THE GRASS IS   148 24
  THAT WRAPS THE NORTH IN STUPOR AND PURPLE TRAVELS THE D+   149 3
  OF THE MAN-LIFE NORTH IMPRISONED SHUT IN THE HUM OF THE   149 5
  IN THE SPELLBOUND NORTH CONVULSIVE NOW WITH A DREAM NEAR   149 21
  FROM THE NORTH   160 29
  HONEY-WHITE FIGS OF THE NORTH BLACK FIGS WITH SCARLET I+   284 26
  NOR FLYING NORTH DESOLATIVE ICEWARDS   436 6
  IN THE NORTH TO HIDE WHERE THE TURTLES SING   580 6
  ALONE ON A HILL-SIDE IN THE NORTH HUMMING IN THE WIND   610 23
  THIS FOREIGN WOMAN OF THE WEALTHY NORTH   618 24
  THE FOOD OF THE NORTH TASTES TOO MUCH OF THE FAT   652 19

NORTH
  NORTH   795 13
  THERE ARE DEAD THAT CLUSTER IN THE FROZEN NORTH SHUDDER+   795 21
  LO I RELEASE THE DRAGONS THE GREAT WHITE ONE OF THE NOR+   796 30

NORTH-COASTS
  WITH FIRE AS IT GUARDS THE WILD NORTH-COASTS RED-FIRE S+   57 13

NORTHERN
  LIKE A THIN WHITE BIRD BLOWN OUT OF THE NORTHERN SEAS   47 14
  OR THERE IN THE WOODS OF THE TWILIGHT WITH NORTHERN WIN+   57 19
  SEE THE MILK OF NORTHERN SPUME   301 24
  MEMORIES NORTHERN MEMORIES   302 11
  IN THE NORTHERN HEMISPHERE   392 14

NORTH SEA
  I COME TO THE NORTH SEA OR THE BALTIC   212 25

NORTHWARD
  THE CLOUDS ARE PUSHING IN GREY RELUCTANCE SLOWLY NORTHW+   57 10

NORWOOD HILL
  OVER THE NEARNESS OF NORWOOD HILL THROUGH THE MELLOW   53 1
  OVER THE NEARNESS OF NORWOOD HILL THROUGH THE MELLOW VE+   *905 17

NOSE
  MY PULSE OF LIFE AND LET HIM NOSE LIKE A STOAT   43 31
  SO HE PUT HIS PAW TO HIS NOSE AND PONDERED   324 22
  THAT UNNATURAL BARREL BODY THAT LONG GHOUL NOSE   338 8
  NO NOT EVEN SNIFF AT HER HIS NOSE IS BLANK   362 14
  AND THE POINT OF YOUR MANTILLA DROPS ACROSS YOUR NOSE   369 30
  WITH A PINCH OF SNOW IN THE GROOVE OF YOUR SILLY SNUB N+   375 17
  TIED BY THE NOSE AT THE PORTA CAPPUCCINI   379 11
  SEE HIS BLACK NOSE SNUBBED BACK PRESSED OVER LIKE A WHA+   380 13
  AND HE SMELLS SO RANK AND HIS NOSE GOES BACK   382 29
  BUT SHE PUTS HER NOSE DOWN SHREWDLY ENOUGH WHEN THE   384 28
  WITH A ROMAN NOSE   414 14
  THE BREATH THAT RUSHES THROUGH MY NOSE THE STRIFE   461 3
  AN' THEN HE LEADS YOU BY THE NOSE   493 13
  AND EVEN WHEN THEY WERE EVEN GOD WOULD HAVE TO HAVE A N+   690 23

NOSE-DIVE
  AND FLIP THEY GO WITH THE NOSE-DIVE OF SHEER DELIGHT   693 28

NOSE-RED
  AS I WENT DOWN THE STREET IN MY NOSE-RED PELERINE   750 17

NOSES
  OF OBSCENITY AND LIFT YOUR NOSES WHERE THE VENT IS   462 32

NOSTRILS
  WASTEFUL INTO THE NIGHT'S BLACK NOSTRILS DRINK   86 6
  AS THE BREATH WHICH UPWARDS FROM THE NOSTRILS OF AN IMM+   97 20
  AND STILL IN MY NOSTRILS   120 28
  AND SEAL YOUR NOSTRILS AND ROUND YOUR NECK YOU'LL   154 2
  STILL IN HIS NOSTRILS THE FROZEN BREATH OF DESPAIR   226 5
  WITH CAVERNOUS NOSTRILS WHERE THE WINDS RUN HOT   325 30
  THE OPEN FURNACE-DOORS OF HIS NOSTRILS   338 11
  AS IF HIS NOSTRILS WERE GOING TO CURVE BACK TO THE ROOT+   380 15
  HIS NOSTRILS TURNING BACK TO SNIFF AT EVEN HIMSELF   382 3
  AND AS THE DOG WITH ITS NOSTRILS TRACKING OUT THE FRAGM+   406 1
  INTO MY EYES AND NOSTRILS   760 11
  AND THE AIR THAT BLOWS GOOD BREATH IN THE NOSTRILS OF P+   792 14
  THE VIVID LIFE OF HIS LOVE IN THY MOUTH AND THY NOSTRILS   *916 7

NOT-BEING
  IT WOUNDS ME TO DEATH WITH MY OWN NOT-BEING DEFINITE IN+   266 16
  SKIRTING THE POLES OF BEING AND OF NOT-BEING   542 15
  AND ALL THINGS AND NOTHING AND BEING AND NOT-BEING   667 10

NOTCH
  AND THE DIM NOTCH OF BLACK MAIDENHAIR LIKE AN INDICATOR   693 14

NOTE
  SOMEWHERE THE LONG MELLOW NOTE OF THE BLACKBIRD   40 25
  AND A REAL TREMOR IF HE HANDS OUT A TEN-POUND NOTE   486 13
  HE WILL LOOK ROUND AND NOTE ME NOT NO MORE   877 17
  THAN HE WILL NOTE THE OTHER ORDINARY WOMEN   877 18

NOTED
  TUNES HER VOICE MANY NOTED   862 8

NOTES
  OR AT LEAST WORTH TREASURY NOTES   458 27
  FLINGS OUT ITS VIVID BLACK NOTES   772 32
  THAT MADE SHADOWS AND SHIMMERING RIPPLES THE SOFT NOTES+   868 14
  AROUND ITS GOLDEN STOPPED NOTES   868 22
  ABOUT IT GOLDEN-STOPPED NOTES   *941 22
  PASS LIKE A TUNE THE SALLOW'S GOLDEN NOTES   *941 24

NOTHING
  DEATH IN WHOSE SERVICE IS NOTHING OF GLADNESS TAKES ME   48 9
  AND HAVE NOTHING TO SAY   50 30
  AND ASKING NOTHING PATIENTLY STEALS BACK AGAIN   63 29
  ASKS TO BE HIDDEN AND WISHES NOTHING TO TELL   64 13
  IT'S NOTHING TO DO WI' ME   78 12
  INTO THE WOMB OF THE WORLDS THAT NOTHING KNOWS   89 31
  OF THE DAY BUT IT'S NOTHING TO DO WITH THE BOYS SO LET +   93 27
  AND THE FLESH OF THE STALK HOLDS UP FOR NOTHING A BLANK+   97 8
  AND THIS HELEN BESIDE ME I AM BLANK BEING NOTHING I BEA+   97 12
  SO DISTANT THEY CANNOT TOUCH ME WHOM NOW NOTHING MARS   97 17
  THE NIGHT IS IMMENSE AND AWFUL YET TO ME IT IS NOTHING +   98 1
  OR RATHER 'TIS I AM NOTHING HERE IN THE FUR OF THE HEAT+   98 2
  AND NAKEDLY NOTHING 'TWIXT WORLD AND HEAVEN TWO CREATUR+   98 4
  LIES ON THE DUST WATCHING WHERE THERE IS NOTHING TO SEE+   112 22
  NOTHING NOW WILL RIPEN THE BRIGHT GREEN APPLES   119 11
  NOTHING TO MEET MY FINGERS BUT THE FLEECE OF NIGHT   147 4
  TO BEAR BUT RETALIATE NOTHING GIVEN TO SAVE   160 27

NOTHING
  WHITE EARTH AND RUINS OURSELVES AND NOTHING BESIDE   166 8
  BUT I AM MYSELF I HAVE NOTHING TO DO WITH THESE   211 24
  BUT NEVER MIND MY LOVE NOTHING MATTERS SAVE SLEEP   212 10
  WHILE THE HARD GIRL HARDENS NOTHING IS SAID   228 7
  THERE IS NOTHING TO WONDER OR CAVIL AT   228 8
  THERE IS NOTHING LEFT   230 2
  WITH NOTHING TO FIGHT ANY MORE   245 1
  HOW SUDDENLY I SHALL GO DOWN INTO NOTHING   246 25
  BOUNCE OFF AGAIN MEANING NOTHING ASSERTIONS ASSERTIONS   249 24
  NOTHING OF ME THAT YOU SEE IS MY OWN   251 3
  NOTHING TO KNOW OR TO WEEP   254 2
  IS THERE NOTHING IN ME TO MAKE YOU HESITATE   256 1
  ABSOLUTELY TO NOTHING   258 21
  NOTHING   258 22
  NOTHING   258 24
  CORTES PISARRO COLUMBUS CABOT THEY ARE NOTHING   259 23
  NOTHING   259 24
  YOU ARE PAINFUL HARSH-SURFACED PILLARS THAT GIVE OFF NO+ 289 5
  NO NO I KNOW NOTHING OF THAT   303 12
  FEARING NOTHING LIFE-BLISSFUL AT THE CORE   307 2
  LET IT KNOW NOTHING   327 23
  NOTHING MORE   336 4
  YET NOTHING ON EARTH WILL GIVE HIM COURAGE TO PASS THE   346 4
  NOTHING   357 10
  NOTHING TO HER   359 23
  THE HORSE BEING NOTHING BUT A NAG WILL FORGET   379 30
  WHERE NOTHING BITES BUT INSECTS AND SNAKES AND THE SUN   394 14
  REJECT NOTHING SINGS WALT WHITMAN   399 1
  BUT YOU YOU SNOUT-FACE YOU REJECT NOTHING YOU MERGE SO   399 9
  I DIDN'T TELL YOU TO DIE FOR NOTHING   412 1
  ARE WE NOTHING ALREADY BUT THE LAPSING OF A GREAT DEAD   429 1
  WHILE WE ARE EAGER WE THINK NOTHING OF IT   439 17
  AND WE WE GET IT ALL FROM THEM FOR NOTHING   443 21
  SEXLESS PEOPLE TRANSMIT NOTHING   449 5
  OR THE EXPERIENCE AMOUNTS TO NOTHING   466 7
  AND THEREFORE NOTHING TO HAVE FEELINGS WITH   501 3
  AND NOTHING NOW REACHES OUT TO DRAW   507 18
  I HAVE PASSED FROM EXISTENCE I FEEL NOTHING ANY MORE   509 8
  YET WHEN THE TIME HAS COME TO BE NOTHING HOW GOOD IT IS   509 10
  TO BE NOTHING   509 11
  AH WHEN I HAVE SEEN MYSELF LEFT BY LIFE LEFT NOTHING   509 16
  THE BEACHES CAN DO NOTHING ABOUT IT   509 21
  I KNOW I AM NOTHING   509 22
  I AM AWARE I FEEL NOTHING EVEN AT DAWN   509 24
  BUT I CAN DO NOTHING ABOUT IT   510 5
  LO I AM NOTHING   511 3
  AND THE NEW WORD MEANS NOTHING TO US   513 7
  NOTHING AND NOBODY IN THE WHOLE VAST REALM OF SPACE   514 20
  NOTHING IS REALLY ANY FUN TODAY   517 23
  THEY'D BECOME NOTHING   527 25
  NOTHING THAT TRANSCENDS THE BOURGEOIS MIDDLINGNESS   528 2
  AND THERE YOU STAND WITH NOTHING AND EXPECT ME TO HAND   547 13
  THE WHOLE OF THE TIME AND NOTHING   552 11
  THAT WAS NOTHING TO ME THOUGH THEY ALWAYS   555 15
  A WREATH OF MIST WITH NOTHING BEHIND IT   580 4
  THAT WE KNOW NOTHING OF THAT WE DARE NOT EXPLORE   606 22
  OFFER ME NOTHING BUT THAT WHICH YOU ARE STARK AND   608 5
  AND WHO DARE NOT DIE FOR FEAR THEY SHOULD BE NOTHING AT+ 613 4
  PROBABLY ARE NOTHING AT ALL   613 5
  ALL THAT WE KNOW IS NOTHING WE ARE MERELY CRAMMED WASTE+ 613 8
  THE ONLY SALVATION IS TO REALISE THAT WE KNOW NOTHING A+ 613 11
  AND THERE IS NOTHING TO SAVE   613 12
  AND NOTHING TO DO   613 13
  YET SHE SEEMED TO KNOW NOTHING ABOUT IT   619 7
  I FEEL ABSOLUTE REVERENCE TO NOBODY AND TO NOTHING HUMAN 622 6
  BUT THE BLATANT BATHERS DON'T KNOW THEY KNOW NOTHING   625 16
  TO WORK WITH AND NOTHING ELSE   630 28
  OH LIFE IS NOTHING IF NOT CHOICE   639 26
  SOFTLY SUBTLY SECRETLY SAYING NOTHING   642 27
  YOU WHO FEEL NOTHING WHO KNOW NOTHING WHO RUN ON   643 16
  PEOPLE GO ON TALKING WHEN THEY HAVE NOTHING TO SAY   657 18
  THERE IS NOTHING TO SAVE NOW ALL IS LOST   658 13
  THERE IS NOTHING TO LOOK AT ANY MORE   660 26
  SEARCH FOR NOTHING ANY MORE NOTHING   661 11
  THERE SEEMS NOTHING THERE   662 9
  WE KNOW NOTHING OF WITHIN US   666 26
  AND ALL THINGS AND NOTHING AND BEING AND NOT-BEING   667 10
  WHILE NOTHING COMES FROM THE OPEN HEAVEN FROM EARTH FRO+ 675 20
  TO THEM NOTHING NOTHING   675 22
  AND DEPARTING INVIOLATE NOTHING CAN LAY HANDS ON HER   676 15
  ABOUT YOU I KNOW NOTHING NOTHING   676 25
  AS A MATTER OF FACT WE KNOW NOTHING   676 27
  THERE WAS NOTHING TO SAY   681 17
  FOR THEY WERE NOT NOTHING   688 28
  BUT HE KNOWS NOTHING BEFOREHAND   690 9
  AND SEE NOTHING   698 5
  AND THERE IS NOTHING ELSE THROUGHOUT TIME AND ETERNITY   701 1
  AND TASTE NOTHING   708 8
  A MACHINE THAT IN ITSELF IS NOTHING   714 20
  AND NOTHING WILL STAY THE DEATH-FLOOD RISING WITHIN US   718 15
  SHE IS NOT SEEN FOR THERE IS NOTHING TO SEE HER BY   719 16
  AND NOTHING IN THE WORLD IS LOVELIER THAN SLEEP   725 3
  NOTHING IN LIFE IS QUITE SO GOOD AS THIS   725 5
  MAN KNOWS NOTHING   726 1
  MADE NOTHING   728 2
  YOUR NOTHING AND MY NOTHINGNESS TOUCH ME   737 19
  REVEAL US NOTHING ROLL THE SCRIPTS AWAY   737 24
  AND SHOW US NOTHING LEAVE US QUITE ALONE   737 27
  NOTHING AND NOTHING ANY MORE AND SO   738 18
  AND THEN WITHIN THE NIGHT WHERE NOTHING IS   738 21
  OUR SOUL NOTHING BUT THE MAD MONOTONOUS   746 15
  NOTHING AGAIN   748 30
  HAVE I NOTHING IN THIS DARK LAND   749 13
  SAYING NOTHING NO MORE TO BE SAID   771 17
  THAT NOTHING CAN STALE OR PROFANE   772 15
  THAT NOTHING NOT LIFE CAN STAIN   772 27
  FLARE BRIGHT TO WANDER AND DO NOTHING   794 16

NOTHING

YOU DO NOTHING BUT SQUAT ON YOUR HAMS AND STARE WITH VA+	795	2
BUT THE DEAD OF THOSE WHO HAVE MASTERED NOTHING NOTHING+	796	11
WITH NOTHING BUT RIND	800	23
THERE IS NOTHING MORE TO ASK FOR	802	8
I ASK FOR NOTHING EXCEPT TO SLIP	812	25
NOTHING REMAINS NOW BUT MOULD UNTO MOULD	814	17
NOTHING BUT TO MAKE LOST MUSIC	816	16
WITH NOTHING BUT DESIRE BETWEEN THEM	819	12
THEREFORE NOTHING AND THEREFORE NOUGHT	824	3
NULLUS NULLUS NOTHING AND NOUGHT	824	7
NOTHING TO SELL IN THEE NOUGHT TO BE BOUGHT	824	10
THERE IS NOTHING BETWEEN	825	4
THERE IS NOTHING BETWEEN	825	7
NOW IS NOTHING	825	8
WHEN NOTHING IS SAID	825	25
AND NOTHING IS DONE	025	26
THERE WE HAVE LEARNED NOTHING	833	10
HAVE NO EXPERIENCE OF SEX AT ALL IT IS ALMOST NOTHING T+	843	20
IT'S NOTHING TO DO WI' ME	*920	4
NOTHING NOW WILL RIPEN THE BRIGHT GREEN APPLES	*932	20
LIFE IS NOTHING WITHOUT RELIGION	*946	11
AND RELIGION NOTHING WITHOUT THE FATHER OF ALL THINGS	*946	12
AND NOTHING ELSE BUT THIS	*947	7
IS NOTHING IF NOT NORMAL	*948	2
AN ABSOLUTE NOTHING	*948	18
OH NOTHING MATTERS BUT THE LONGEST JOURNEY	*960	9

NOTHINGNESS

ON NOTHINGNESS PARDON ME	40	24
TO NUMBNESS AND NOTHINGNESS I DEAD SHE REFUSING TO DIE	98	8
TO NOTHINGNESS AND TIME WILL DIM THE MOON	193	11
A NOTHINGNESS	332	17
INTO SALTY NOTHINGNESS	455	11
IS THE FULFILMENT OF NOTHINGNESS	511	2
NOTHINGNESS PALE NOTHINGNESS IN THEIR HEARTS	569	6
THE DEATH OF NOTHINGNESS WORN-OUT MACHINES KAPUT	676	7
THEIR OWN NOTHINGNESS	688	27
YOUR NOTHING AND MY NOTHINGNESS TOUCH ME	737	19
TO COME AT LAST TO NOTHINGNESS AND KNOW	738	17
AND I AM ONLY NEXT TO NOTHINGNESS	738	22
UPON THE WINCINGNESS OF NEXT TO NOTHINGNESS	738	29
SIPPING TO NOTHINGNESS EVEN THOUGHT	824	12
NULLUS NOTHINGNESS WHAT'S IN A NAME	824	16
IN A DAY THEY ARE LOST IN THE NOTHINGNESS PURITY BRINGS	855	4

NOTHIN'

IT 'ASN'T NOTHIN' TO DO WITH ME	82	1

NOTICE

DID T' 'APPEN TER NOTICE A BIT OF A LASS WAY BACK	60	17
AND LET ME NOTICE IT BEHAVE ITSELF	299	23
DID TER NOTICE THAT LASS SISTER AS STOOD AWAY BACK	*909	29
DID T' 'APPEN TER NOTICE A BIT OF A LASS AWAY BACK	*911	3

NOTICED

I HAVE NOTICED THAT PEOPLE WHO TALK A LOT ABOUT LOYALTY	626	1

NOTICES

ONE NOTICES MEN HERE AND THERE GOING HESITATINGLY FALTE+	665	23

NOTION

NOTION	635	10

NOT-LOOKING

IN NOT-LOOKING AND IN NOT-SEEING	662	10

NOT-ME

SHE IS ALL NOT-ME ULTIMATELY	266	12

NOT-SEEING

IN NOT-LOOKING AND IN NOT-SEEING	662	10

NOTTINGHAM

TER NOTTINGHAM EH DEAR O' ME	45	7
IN NOTTINGHAM THAT DISMAL TOWN	488	11
THAT FUTURE NOTTINGHAM LADS WOULD BE	489	1
THAT NOTTINGHAM LIGHTS WOULD RISE AND SAY	489	3
IN NOTTINGHAM WHERE I WENT TO SCHOOL AND COLLEGE	*950	12
NOW FIRST CITIZEN OF NOTTINGHAM	*950	16

NOT-TO-BE

AND DEATH I KNOW IS BETTER THAN NOT-TO-BE	126	6
NOT-TO-BE	212	4

NOT-TO-KNOW

TILL HE KNOWS HOW NOT-TO-KNOW	726	2

NOTWITHSTANDING

BUT STEADILY SURELY AND NOTWITHSTANDING	209	12

NOUGHT

SAY IT WOR NOUGHT	84	8
ON OUR MYSTERY NOUGHT CAN DESCRY US	114	7
TO NOUGHT DIMINISHING EACH STAR'S GLITTER	132	14
ADD YOURSELF UP AND YOUR SEED TO THE NOUGHT	235	15
A DISARRAY OF FALLING STARS COMING TO NOUGHT	236	23
AND I AM DEAD AND TRODDEN TO NOUGHT IN THE SMOKE-SODDEN	258	14
DEAD AND TRODDEN TO NOUGHT IN THE SOUR BLACK EARTH	258	16
OF THE TOMB DEAD AND TRODDEN TO NOUGHT TRODDEN TO NOUGHT	258	17
TRODDEN TO NOUGHT IN SOUR DEAD EARTH	258	19
QUITE TO NOUGHT	258	20
I HAVE DROPPED AT LAST HEADLONG INTO NOUGHT PLUNGING UP+	266	2
MAUDIE IS NOUGHT BUT THE HOUSEKEEPER	573	15
THEREFORE NOTHING AND THEREFORE NOUGHT	824	3
NULLUS NULLUS NOTHING AND NOUGHT	824	7
NOTHING TO SELL IN THEE NOUGHT TO BE BOUGHT	824	10

NOUN

FALTERS A STATEMENT ABOUT AN ABSTRACT NOUN	76	8
WAKES FROM THE HUM FALTERING ABOUT A NOUN	*898	3
WAKES FROM THE HUM FALTERING ABOUT A NOUN	*901	12

NOURISH

NOURISH HER TRAIN HER HARDEN HER	228	29
NOURISH ME AND ENDUE ME I AM ONLY OF YOU	246	11
AND THE BREATH OF LIFE NEVER COMES TO NOURISH THEM	615	20
PASS OUT AND YET NOURISH	826	12

NOURISHED

FLOWERS OF THE PENUMBRA ISSUE OF CORRUPTION NOURISHED IN	271	8

NOURISHMENT

ON THE AIR FOR OUR NOURISHMENT WHO FROM THESE WEAVE FAI+	*938	24

NOVEL

I READ A NOVEL BY A FRIEND OF MINE	489	9
THE NOVEL IT SURE WAS MIGHTY FINE	489	11

NOVEMBER

FORTH TO HER FIELDS THAT NOVEMBER	103	8
NOW IN NOVEMBER NEARER COMES THE SUN	455	12
OH NOW AS NOVEMBER DRAWS NEAR	722	19
OH ON THIS DAY FOR THE DEAD NOW NOVEMBER IS HERE	723	8

NOWADAYS

FOR EVERY BLOOMING BIRD IS AN OXFORD CUCKOO NOWADAYS	434	1
NOWADAYS EVERYBODY WANTS TO BE YOUNG	502	13
ONLY THIRD-RATE SWABS ARE PUSHING TO GET ON NOWADAYS	518	17
BUT APPEARANCES ARE DECEPTIVE NOWADAYS AREN'T THEY	548	17
NOWADAYS TO TALK OF HUMILITY IS A SIN AGAINST THE HOLY +	621	12

NOWHERE

OUT OF NOWHERE HE ROSE	39	28
OH AND SUDDENLY FROM OUT OF NOWHERE WHIRLS THE PEAR-BLO+	271	25
THEN OUT OF NOWHERE RUSHED JOHN BULL	491	25
PEOPLE GO ON WALKING WHEN THEY HAVE NOWHERE TO GO	657	19
WHEN THE LITTLE EGGY AMOEBA EMERGED OUT OF FOAM AND NOW+	682	26
THEY DWELL IN THE OUTSKIRT FRINGES OF NOWHERE	711	24
THERE IS NO PORT THERE IS NOWHERE TO GO	719	10
NOWHERE	719	19
THERE AND NOWHERE ELSE	774	28
IN INDIVIDUAL HEARTS AND NOWHERE ELSE	775	26
THEY COME OUT OF NOWHERE	793	14
YOU SHALL HAVE NOWHERE TO DIE INTO	796	28
GREAT THIGHS THAT LEAD NOWHERE	827	19
ANYWHERE NOWHERE THE DEAD ROAD GOES	858	4

NOWHERENESS

HOWLING THEIR NOWHERENESS	514	24

NOW-NAKED

AND FEARLESS FACE-TO-FACE AWARENESS OF NOW-NAKED LIFE	667	4

NOWT

AN' I RECKON IT'S NOWT BUT RIGHT	491	2
IT WAS NOWT BUT A DIRTY SELL THAT'S ALL	553	3
NO THERE'S NOWT IN THE UPPER CLASSES	553	13
NAY I SAW NOWT BUT TH' COFFIN AN' TH' YELLER CLAY AN' '+	*909	31
I COULD THINK O' NOWT BUT OUR TED AN' 'IM TAKEN	*910	3
WAS TH' LITTLE LOVIN' SORT AS 'AS NOWT TER SCREEN 'EM	*910	25

N'R

PALS WORSE N'R ONY NAME AS YOU COULD CALL	*911	12

NUB'DY

NOR 'ER NOR NUB'DY IT IS	80	31

NUDE

GODS NUDE AS BLANCHED NUT-KERNELS	280	19
SEE IF I DON'T MOVE UNDER A DARK AND NUDE VAST HEAVEN	289	19
NUDE WITH THE DIM LIGHT OF FULL HEALTHY LIFE	298	26
GREAT COMPLICATED NUDE FIG-TREE STEMLESS FLOWER-MESH	299	3
LIKE A NUDE LIKE A ROCK-LIVING SWEET-FLESHED SEA-ANEMONE	299	7
IF MY PICTURES ARE NUDE SO ONCE WERE YOU	577	11
I NEVER WAS NOR WILL BE NUDE	577	16
WHEN THEY PAINTED A NUDE TO PUT A CACHE SEXE ON	580	1
AND MADE HIM PAINT HER NUDE TIME AFTER TIME	619	9
THE NUDITY OF A LAWRENCE NUDE	680	19

NUDE-LOOKING

THE TIGHT-ROPE LADY PINK AND BLONDE AND NUDE-LOOKING	444	24

NUDGES

SO I AM JUST GOING TO GO ON BEING A BLANK TILL SOMETHIN+	501	23

NUDITY

THINK TO STAND THERE IN FULL-UNFOLDED NUDITY SMILING	306	17
THE NUDITY OF A LAWRENCE NUDE	680	19

NUISANCE

NOR PALS THEY'RE SUCH A NUISANCE	499	24

NULL

IN VOID AND NULL PROFUSION HOW IS THIS	53	26
BUT NEVER THIS NULL	57	2
BUT OPAQUE AND NULL IN THE FLESH	111	29
AND I AM NULL	510	2
MACHINE-DRAWING MORE NULL THAN DEATH	619	13
HORIZONTAL ETERNITY FLUID OR NULL	827	16

NULLIFY

NULLIFY	98	10

NULLITY
  INTO NULLITY   166 12
  EVEN ITS OWN NULLITY BEYOND A CERTAIN POINT   473 21
  THEY WOULD THEMSELVES AT ONCE COLLAPSE INTO NULLITY   527 22
  THEY CALL IT HEALTH IT LOOKS LIKE NULLITY   625 24
  WAGE OF NULLITY   630 21

NULLUS
  AND A NULLUS   510 4
  NULLUS NOTHINGNESS WHAT'S IN A NAME   824 16

NULLUS NULLUS
  NULLUS NULLUS NOTHING AND NOUGHT   824 7

NUMB
  HANGS NUMB AND HEAVY FROM A BENDING FLOWER   73 21
  THE FEMALE WHOSE VENOM CAN MORE THAN KILL CAN NUMB AND +   98 9
  AND I WAS NUMB WITH A BITTER DEATHLY ACHE   98 27
  ON THE FLOOR WHERE NEVER MY NUMB FEET TRODE   163 11
  AND THE HEART IS NUMB   508 4
  STILL YEARNING BUT WITHERED AND NUMB   862 2
  MY LIMBS ARE NUMB AND HEAVY AND MY HEART   879 19
  HANGS NUMB AND HEAVY FROM THE BENDING FLOWER   *913 13

NUMBED
  CLINGING TO THE RADIATORS LIKE NUMBED BEES TO THE DRENC+   866 1

NUMBER
  DARK AND PROUD ON THE SKY LIKE A NUMBER OF KNIGHTS   221 8
  DARK AND PROUD ON THE SKY LIKE A NUMBER OF KNIGHTS   *944 21

NUMBERLESS
  TO SIGHT REVEALING A SECRET NUMBERLESS SECRET KEEPING   136 7

NUMBERS
  THERE ARE GREAT NUMBERS OF QUITE SUPERIOR PERSONS WHO A+   548 25
  AS IF THERE WAS SAFETY IN NUMBERS EVEN FOR FAITH   626 6

NUMBNESS
  TO NUMBNESS AND NOTHINGNESS I DEAD SHE REFUSING TO DIE   98 8
  YOUR EVIL LITTLE AURA PROWLING AND CASTING NUMBNESS ON   332 19

NUMEROUS
  NUMEROUS AND WHISPERING THIN GRAINS OF RICE IN A   391 6

NUN-SISTER
  PALE DREAMY CHAPLETS A GREY NUN-SISTER SETS   854 23

NUPTIALS
  ON THE NUPTIALS   *956 20

NURSE
  A NURSE IN WHITE AT THE DAWNING FLOWER-FOAMED PANE   155 1
  WON'T IT BE STRANGE WHEN THE NURSE BRINGS THE NEW-BORN   438 26
  THE GREY NURSE ENTERED A ROSE GARDEN   753 8

NURSED
  AT WHICH I WAS NURSED   159 26

NURSES
  SO WE'VE GOT A LOT OF NURSES OF NURSES OF NURSES   570 18
  AND THE FEED OF PAP THAT WE NURSES AND GUARDIAN ANGELS +   670 16
  NURSES DOCTORS PROPER FOOD HYGIENE SCHOOLS ALL THAT   832 5

NURTURED
  GENTLE NURTURED FRAIL AND SPLENDID   313 32

NUSS
  I SHAN'T 'AVE 'IM TO NUSS   45 20

NUT
  THAT ROUND HEAD PUSHED IN MY CHEST LIKE A NUT IN ITS   245 14
  AS STRIPS YOU STARK AS A MONKEY NUT   493 15

NUT-BROWN
  BROWN NUT-BROWN FINE FUR   345 33

NUT-KERNELS
  GODS NUDE AS BLANCHED NUT-KERNELS   280 19

NUTS
  AND NUTS FELL OUT OF THEIR HAIR   152 15
  NUTTING GATHERING NUTS OF RIPE EXPERIENCE   504 12
  AND GAVE YOU A COUPLE OF NUTS   549 10

NUTTING
  NUTTING GATHERING NUTS OF RIPE EXPERIENCE   504 12

NYMPHOLEPHT
  A NYMPHOLEPHT   293 10

'N
  TRYIN' TO KEEP OFF 'N HIM A BIT O' TH' WET   *910 29

OAK
  I TELL YOU MY BLOOD RUNS OUT ON THE FLOOR OF THIS OAK   131 13
  BENEATH THE OAK   131 18
  UNDER AN OAK WHOSE YELLOW BUDS DOT THE PALE BLUE SKY   152 27
  UNDER AN OAK TREE WHOSE YELLOW BUDS DOTTED THE PALE BLU+   866 23
  SENTRY UPON THE DEAD OAK WHILE ANOTHER BELOW   *894 28

OAKS
  WEARILY THROUGH THE OAKS THE NIGHT WIND BLOWS   857 22

OAK'S
  THE COOL OF AN OAK'S UNCHEQUERED SHADE   49 21

OAK-TREE'S
  AND LIGHTS ON A WITHERED OAK-TREE'S TOP OF WOE   147 23

OAR
  WAITS WITH A LIFTED OAR   201 20
  SUCH AN INSTRUMENT A SPADE LIKE A SPEAR OR AN OAR   254 20

OARS
  WHEN I MOVE THE OARS SEE   49 5
  A LITTLE SHIP WITH OARS AND FOOD   718 24
  INTO THE DISTANCE WITH RECEDING OARS   722 10
  THE LITTLE SLENDER SOUL SITS SWIFTLY DOWN AND TAKES THE+ 723 20
  INTO THE DISTANCE WITH RECEDING OARS   *958 15
  LET ME BUILD A LITTLE SHIP WITH OARS AND FOOD   *958 20
  THE LITTLE SLENDER SOUL SITS SWIFTLY DOWN AND TAKES THE+ *958 32
  PULLING THE LONG OARS OF A LIFE-TIME'S COURAGE   *959 12
  THE OARS HAVE GONE FROM THE BOAT AND THE LITTLE DISHES   *959 29

OATH
  AND TAKE WITHIN THE WINE THE GOD'S GREAT OATH   177 17

OBDURATE
  METALLIC OBDURATE   56 27

OBEDIENCE
  NEVER TO KNOW THE GLAD FREEDOM OF OBEDIENCE SINCE LONG   48 3
  TEEMING OBEDIENCE   414 20

OBEY
  LEARN THEY MUST TO OBEY FOR ALL HARMONY IS DISCIPLINE   93 9
  THE FEW MUST LOOK INTO THE EYES OF THE GODS AND OBEY TH+ 650 8
  AND THE MANY MUST OBEY THE FEW THAT LOOK INTO THE EYES + 650 10
  AH YES MEN MUST LEARN TO OBEY   650 14

OBJECTIONABLE
  BRITISH PUBLIC HAS EVERYTHING OBJECTIONABLE BEEN   582 13

OBLIGATION
  CARRIES ITS OWN PATENT AND ITS OWN OBLIGATION   774 21
  AND AT THE MOMENT THERE IS AN OBLIGATION   776 2
  IT IS THE OBLIGATION OF THE CITIZENS OF THIS COUNTRY TO+ 776 3
  THE WHITE MAN'S GOVERNMENT WAS UNDER NO OBLIGATION   778 24

OBLITERATE
  MYSELF IN THE ROAR OF LIFE WHICH SHALL TAKE AND OBLITER+ *894 23

OBLITERATING
  OBLITERATING EVERYTHING   205 8

OBLITERATION
  AND ACCEPT OBLITERATION   430 6

OBLIVION
  BUT THE BLOOD HAS SUSPENDED ITS TIMBRE THE HEART FROM O+ 67 3
  A STRICKEN WIFE SO SUNK IN OBLIVION BOWED   155 30
  PERHAPS WE SHALL COME TO OBLIVION   164 9
  YET RISING FROM THE TOMB FROM THE BLACK OBLIVION   260 9
  AND STRANGE WAYS WHERE I FALL INTO OBLIVION OF UTTERMOST 261 6
  SIGHTLESS AND STRONG OBLIVION IN UTTER LIFE TAKES POSSE+ 261 10
  FOR A SECOND ENSPASMED IN OBLIVION   333 29
  AND THE LONG JOURNEY TOWARDS OBLIVION   716 19
  THE LONGEST JOURNEY TO OBLIVION   717 22
  FOR THE DARK FLIGHT DOWN OBLIVION   718 11
  IT IS THE END IT IS OBLIVION   719 26
  OUT OF OBLIVION   720 5
  EVEN OF OBLIVION   720 19
  FOR THE VOYAGE OF OBLIVION AWAITS YOU   720 22
  TO DARK OBLIVION   721 5
  AFTER THE BITTER PASSAGE OF OBLIVION   721 7
  TO THE SWEET HOME OF PURE OBLIVION   721 21
  OF NON-EXISTENCE TO FAR OBLIVION   722 15
  OBLIVION   724 6
  OBLIVION WHERE THE SOUL AT LAST IS LOST   724 9
  OF SILENCE AND SHEER OBLIVION   724 13
  UPON A CORE OF PURE OBLIVION   724 18
  BUT DIPPED ONCE DIPPED IN DARK OBLIVION   724 25
  SLEEP IS A HINT OF LOVELY OBLIVION   724 28
  DARK DREAMLESS SLEEP IN DEEP OBLIVION   725 4
  SHE IS SEEKING HER OBLIVION   725 13
  THERE IS NO PLACE FOR THE SOUL TO FIND HER OBLIVION   725 15
  TO GOD WHO DWELLS IN DEEP OBLIVION   725 21
  ONLY IN SHEER OBLIVION ARE WE WITH GOD   725 22
  THE END OF ALL KNOWLEDGE IS OBLIVION   726 4
  SWEET DARK OBLIVION WHEN I CEASE   726 5
  COME LET US BUILD A TEMPLE TO OBLIVION   726 7
  HOLY OF HOLIES OF SHEER OBLIVION   726 9
  AND THERE OBLIVION DWELLS AND THE SILENT SOUL   726 10
  OBLIVION   726 13
  IN THE SWEET WHOLENESS OF OBLIVION   726 21
  IN SLEEP AND SINK IN GOOD OBLIVION   726 23
  WITH THE DEEP OBLIVION OF EARTH'S LAPSE AND RENEWAL   727 16
  AND STILL AMONG IT ALL SNATCHES OF LOVELY OBLIVION AND + 727 22
  HE IS BREAKING ME DOWN TO HIS OWN OBLIVION   727 29
  IT MEANS PASSING THROUGH THE WATERS OF OBLIVION   727 33
  DIPPED INTO OBLIVION   728 4
  OF SHEER OBLIVION   745 20
  AND THE LONG JOURNEY TOWARDS OBLIVION   *956 25
  THE LONGEST JOURNEY TOWARDS OBLIVION   *957 7
  SHALL TAKE THEM ABOARD TOWARDS THE GREAT GOAL OF OBLIVI+ *958 13
  AND DEEPER TO A CORE OF SHEER OBLIVION   *959 19
  MOST DARK OBLIVION   *959 23
  OF SHEER OBLIVION AND OF UTTER PEACE   *959 32
  OH LOVELY LAST LAST LAPSE OF DEATH INTO PURE OBLIVION *960 3
  TO THE LAST WONDER OF OBLIVION   *960 21
  OBLIVION THE LAST WONDER   *960 22

OBLIVION
   INTO PURE OBLIVION   *960 26

OBLIVIOUS
   AND THE AIRY PRIMULAS OBLIVIOUS   243 28
   AND RAVISHED ALL THE PEACEFUL OBLIVIOUS PLACES   725 18

OBSCENE
   NO HE MUST NOT SQUAT NOR HANG OBSCENE IN MY ROOM   346 3
   BUT IF OBSCENE VILLAGE IDIOTS YOU WANT TO BE THEN BE IT   463 13
   ARREST HIM HE'S INDECENT HE'S OBSCENE WHAT'S MORE   574 24
   THAT ANCIENT EYES HAVE LEFT ON YOU WHERE OBSCENE EYES   581 3
   ESPECIALLY BIG ONES IS OBSCENE   622 20
   IS OBSCENE   622 23
   DON'T YOU KNOW THAT'S OBSCENE   669 17
   OBSCENE EGO   714 18
   BUT THE REST WERE OBSCURE OR OBSCENE   845 21

OBSCENELY
   OBSCENELY ECSTASIED   333 30
   THE VULTURE IS BALD SO IS THE CONDOR OBSCENELY   369 18
   THE FIFTH GENERATION OF PURITANS WHEN IT ISN'T OBSCENEL+   845 15

OBSCENITIES
   WITH SMALL OBSCENITIES   462 24
   GOGGLING OBSCENITIES IF THAT'S YOU AND YOUR FATE WHY TH+   463 17

OBSCENITY
   MAKES TITTERING JESTS AT THE BELLS' OBSCENITY   54 15
   SUCH OBSCENITY OF TRESPASS   334 3
   OF OBSCENITY AND LIFT YOUR NOSES WHERE THE VENT IS   462 32
   FOR OBSCENITY AFTER ALL MY DEAR YOUNG MEN   463 1
   ALL THIS OBSCENITY IS JUST MENTAL MENTAL MENTAL   463 7
   BAWDY ON THE BRAIN BECOMES OBSCENITY VICIOUS   845 7

OBSCURE
   SO I LAY ON YOUR BREAST FOR AN OBSCURE HOUR   104 4
   SCRAMBLE SEVEN TOADS ACROSS SILK OBSCURE LEAVES   126 18
   POOR OBSCURE FRUITS EXTRUDED OUT OF LIGHT   160 10
   LIKE A LOUT ON AN OBSCURE PAVEMENT   338 4
   AGAINST THE CURRENT OF OBSCURE ARNO   340 26
   IN AN OBSCURE CORNER   343 31
   IT WAS AS IF THE GREAT BULKS OF ELEPHANTS IN THE OBSCURE   391 1
   BUT THE REST WERE OBSCURE OR OBSCENE   845 21

OBSCURES
   OBSCURES THE DARK WOOD AND THE DULL ORANGE SKY   85 10

OBSERVANCES
   PECULIAR CUSTOMS AND OBSERVANCES   776 29
   CUSTOMS AND OBSERVANCES   776 31

OBSESSION
   ONENESS MAKES WAR AND THE OBSESSION OF ONENESS   612 7

OBSOLETE
   WE SHALL DO AS WE LIKE SIN IS OBSOLETE THE YOUNG ASSERT   463 26
   SIN IS OBSOLETE SIN IS OBSOLETE BUT NOT SO DIRT   463 27
   SO THEY GO ON SINNING THOUGH SIN IS OBSOLETE   618 14
   THE GREAT COMMAND WILL NEVER BE OBSOLETE   832 20

OBSTACLE
   A MERE OBSTACLE   356 28
   OBSTACLE TO SET HIS TEETH IN THE SUN   378 7
   MARE OBSTACLE   378 18

OBSTACLE-LEAPING
   FROM OBSTACLE-LEAPING PRIDE   378 17

OBSTACLES
   TORTOISES ALWAYS FORESEE OBSTACLES   356 30
   TO OVERLEAP LIKE A MALE ALL MARES AS OBSTACLES   379 13
   TRIUMPH OVER THEIR FELLOW-MEN TRIUMPH OVER OBSTACLES   519 3

OBSTINACY
   OBSTINACY   360 16
   TAKE UP THE PRIMORDIAL INDIAN OBSTINACY   371 28
   THE RETRIBUTION FOR THEIR OBSTINACY   663 3

OBSTINATE
   IN STUPOR PERSIST AT THE GATES OF LIFE OBSTINATE DARK M+   75 12
   EVEN THE WILFUL OBSTINATE GUMMY FIG-TREE   305 18
   AN OBSTINATE OLD WITCH ALMOST JERKING THE ROPE FROM MY   385 9
   OLD MEN OLD OBSTINATE MEN AND WOMEN   663 4

OBSTINATELY
   WHY DO YOU FRONT THE SUN SO OBSTINATELY   374 1

OBSTREPEROUS
   LET ME FIGHT THE WICKED OBSTREPEROUS WEEDS MYSELF AND P+   316 11

OBSTRUCT
   DO THEY OBSTRUCT   765 10

OBSTRUCTION
   FLEA WHICH HOPS OVER SUCH AN OBSTRUCTION AT FIRST   292 5

OBSTRUCTIONS
   ARE ALL THE OBSTRUCTIONS TO LIFE SELF-IMPORTANCE SELF-C+   678 11

OBTUSE
   SHE TURNS HER HEAD AWAY WITH AN OBTUSE FEMALE SORT OF   385 1

OBVIOUS
   THAT'S OBVIOUS   377 31
   WHY ISN'T IT OBVIOUS   547 3

OBVIOUSLY
   BECAUSE OBVIOUSLY HE'S NOT ONE OF THE LEISURED CLASSES   452 21
   WHY SHOULD ONE LOVE PEACE IT IS SO OBVIOUSLY VILE TO MA+   495 18
   AND OBVIOUSLY IT IS THE CULMINATING POINT OF HIS EXISTE+   523 12

OCCASIONALLY
   GOLDEN-MOUTHED OCCASIONALLY   236 10
   BUT ALL WAS SILENT SAVE FOR PARROTS OCCASIONALLY IN THE   394 18
   WHICH MAY OCCASIONALLY BE A PRELIMINARY TO THE PEACE TH+   497 9
   OCCASIONALLY I SEE HIM SILENT A LITTLE WONDERING   645 18

OCCASIONS
   NOBODY CAN BE WISE EXCEPT ON RARE OCCASIONS LIKE GETTING   495 24
   AND TO HAVE MANNERS FOR ALL OCCASIONS   608 9
   THA'S NO OCCASIONS TER HA'E ME ON   *921 25

OCCUPATION
   EARNING A WAGE IS A PRISON OCCUPATION   521 7

OCCUPIED
   WHEN YOU ARE ONLY OCCUPIED YOU ARE AN EMPTY SHELL   *949 21

OCCUPIES
   UNLESS IT PRE-OCCUPIES YOU AS WELL AS OCCUPIES YOU   *949 20

OCEAN
   THE SHORES OF THIS INNERMOST OCEAN ALIVE AND ILLUSORY   71 12
   ON THE SHORES OF THIS CEASELESS OCEAN GAY BIRDS OF THE   71 18
   BELOW THE OCEAN OF SHIMMERING LIGHT YOU WILL BE   72 18
   ON HIS SOUL THAT IS DARK OCEAN WITHIN HIM   453 22
   THERE IS OCEAN IN ME   454 4
   OF ETERNAL SALT RAGE ANGRY IS OLD OCEAN WITHIN A MAN   454 11
   DOWN TO THE OCEAN OF THE AFTERWARDS WHERE IT REMAINS   495 5
   ALREADY THE WHITENESS OF FALSE DAWN IS ON MY INNER OCEAN   513 13
   OH MEN LIVING MEN VIVID MEN OCEAN AND FIRE   639 1
   SMOOTH OCEAN WHERE THE FISHES REST ON EDGE   652 10
   AND AN OCEAN LINER GOING EAST LIKE A SMALL BEETLE WALKI+   687 9
   AND OUT OF THE INWARD ROARING OF THE INNER RED OCEAN OF+   694 16
   AND IS MY BODY OCEAN OCEAN   705 14
   ALREADY THE DARK AND ENDLESS OCEAN OF THE END   718 6
   LIKE THE FULLNESS OF OCEAN ROUND MY FARAGLIONI   835 34

O'CLOCK
   SAY TEN O'CLOCK   342 9
   LET IT CROW THEN LIKE ONE O'CLOCK   457 30

OCTOBER
   ALREADY IT IS OCTOBER AND THE WIND BLOWS STRONG TO THE +   696 15

OCTOPUS
   RATHER LIKE AN OCTOPUS BUT STRANGE AND SWEET-MYRIAD-LIM+   299 5
   OCTOPUS   299 6
   OCTOPUS ARMS   451 31
   PAST THE LURKING OCTOPUS ARMS OF AGONISED MEMORY   *959 6

ODD
   OF EASY SAILING ODD RED WICKS SERVE   172 20
   IN THIS ODD LIFE WILL TARNISH OR PASS AWAY   193 13
   ODD FLAKES AS IF OF SNOW ODD BITS OF SNOW   304 13
   ODD CRUMBS OF MELTING SNOW   304 14
   BUT IN THE ODD PATTERN LIKE SNAKE-MARKS ON THE SAND   448 26
   ODD WINTRY FLOWERS UPON THE WITHERED STEM YET NEW STRAN+   727 24
   IT IS ODD AGAIN ABOUT THE YOUNG   829 11
   WHICH IS VERY ODD BEING THE EXACT REVERSE OF THEIR FATH+   829 14

ODDS
   CUNNINGLY BLOWING ON THE FALLEN SPARKS ODDS AND ENDS OF+   271 31
   THE ODDS ARE EVEN AND HE WILL HAVE IT SO   743 21
   WHAT ARE THE ODDS TO ME   751 23

ODOUR
   THE EXQUISITE ODOUR OF LEAVE-TAKING   281 14
   IN THE ODOUR OF LUCRATIVE SANCTITY   457 1
   TO RISE AN ODOUR OF PURPLE VIOLETS CRUSHED   881 7

ODOURS
   AND I IN THE STEALTHY BRINDLED ODOURS   107 19

ODYSSEUS
   AH CLEVER ODYSSEUS WHO OUTWITTED THE CYCLOP   543 26
   ODYSSEUS CALLS THE COMMANDS AS HE STEERS PAST THOSE FOA+   687 20

ODYSSEUS'
   THE DAWN IS NOT OFF THE SEA AND ODYSSEUS' SHIPS   687 22

OENOCHOE
   BAKED AMPHORAS CRATERS CANTHARUS OENOCHOE AND   305 13

O'ER
   THEY HAVE TRIUMPHED AGAIN O'ER THE AGES THEIR SCREAMING+   33 4
   SHAKES O'ER HIS WALLS WHEN THE WIND DISTURBS THE NIGHT   878 4
   THEN DOWN THE BREEZE LIGHT WAFTING O'ER THE FALLOW   *941 23

OFFAL
   SEEKING THE OFFAL AND GARBAGE OF LIFE IN THE INVISIBLE +   796 6

OFFEND
   LIKE A CRINGING DOG AT HIS HEELS OFFEND HIM NOW   47 22

OFFENDER'S
   THE FLOWER OF FORGIVENESS IS PLUCKED FROM OFF THE OFFEN+   *926 26

OFFER
   AND THEN I OFFER ALL MYSELF UNTO   113 9
   THE SHADOW ALWAYS OFFER MYSELF TO ONE MISTRESS WHO ALWA+   180 27
   NOW I OFFER HER UP TO THE ANCIENT INEXORABLE GOD   238 23
   IS HE NOT OVER-FULL OF OFFERING A VAST VAST OFFER OF HI+   327 18
   HE SNAPS WHEN I OFFER HIM HIS OFFSPRING   357 12

OFFER

AS IT IS ALL THAT THE OLD CAN OFFER	504	13
IF THEY ONLY OFFER YOU LIGHTNING	559	8
OFFER ME NOTHING BUT THAT WHICH YOU ARE STARK AND	608	5
SHALL I OFFER TO HIM MY BROTHERLY BODY TO KILL	743	19
DARK INCENSE DID I FEEL HER OFFER UP	881	12

OFFERED

THREE TIMES HAVE I OFFERED MYSELF THREE TIMES REJECTED	48	1
OF SLOVENLY WORK THAT THEY HAVE OFFERED ME	74	15
AND GLADLY I'D OFFERED MY BREAST TO THE TREAD OF HER	123	6
OF EDEN EVEN WAS EVE'S FRUIT TO HER IT BELONGED AND SHE+	277	6
OF SLOVENLY WORK THAT THEY HAVE OFFERED ME	*895	23
OF SLOVENLY WORK THAT THEY HAVE OFFERED ME	*904	12
WOULD GLADLY HAVE OFFERED MY BREAST FOR HER TREAD TO TRY	*934	12

OFFERING

COMMUNION OFFERING A BETTER THING	104	3
IT IS MY OFFERING TO YOU EVERY DAY IS ALL SOULS' DAY	233	17
MY OFFERING BOUGHT AT A GREAT PRICE	238	21
MASSIVE OLD ALTAR OF HIS OWN BURNT OFFERING	326	28
IT WAS ALWAYS AN ALTAR OF BURNT OFFERING	326	29
IS HE NOT OVER-FULL OF OFFERING A VAST VAST OFFER OF HI+	327	18
AN OFFERING	678	8
IF YOU WANT TO MAKE HER AN OFFERING LET THE DOVES FLY F+	678	9

OFFERS

OFFERS ME HER SCARLET FRUIT I WILL SEE	37	3

OFFICE

CAN BE PUT OUT OF OFFICE AS SACRIFICE BRINGER	374	35
IF YOU STAIN IN MY OFFICE YOU'VE GOT TO BE KITH	583	27
HAVE HAD THEIR TERM OF OFFICE THEY MUST GO	614	8
EITHER MAKE THE INDIAN BUREAU INTO A PERMANENT OFFICE	780	5

OFFICERS

PUT THE FIRST CENTS INTO METALLIC FINGERS OF YOUR OFFIC+	291	4
AS THEY GO FROM SCHOOL SOME OF THE OFFICERS RALLY	732	20

OFFICIAL

START A SYSTEM OF OFFICIAL SPYING	536	4
AND SO THE OFFICIAL ARCHANGELS	614	6
I SAW AN ANGRY ITALIAN SEIZE AN IRRITATING LITTLE OFFIC+	674	20

OFFICIALS

THOUGHT HE MEANT THE FACES OF THE POLICE-COURT OFFICIALS	579	19

OFF'N

I WISH I COULD WESH 'ER OFF'N THEE	82	25
T' SNOW IS WITHERIN' OFF'N TH' GRESS	137	18
T' SNOW IS WITHERIN' OFF'N TH' GRESS	137	20
I WISH THA COULD WESH 'ER OFF'N THEE	*925	1

OFFSHOOT

IS A LAST OFFSHOOT OF BOOTS	489	8

OFFSPRING

AND THE WORD WAS THE FIRST OFFSPRING OF THE ALMIGHTY JO+	329	11
HE SNAPS WHEN I OFFER HIM HIS OFFSPRING	357	12

OFTEN

RELENTLESS HOWEVER OFTEN	55	17
AND OFTEN I SEE HER CLENCH HER FINGERS TIGHT	128	18
THAT HE USED SO OFTEN	255	2
AND ROWING ON UNARRIVED NO MATTER HOW OFTEN HE ENTER	380	23
FAR ONE TO SLEEP AND A FORGETTING AND OFTEN THE DEAD LO+	406	5
THEY HAVE BEEN SAVED SO OFTEN	442	8
SO DO BAD HUSBANDS JUST AS OFTEN	456	6
THEIR GUTS WITH A CERTAIN FAT AND OFTEN	460	15
THEIR GUTS WITH A CERTAIN FAT AND OFTEN	460	19
EGO-BOUND WOMEN ARE OFTEN LESBIAN	475	12
AND I MUST SAY I AM OFTEN WORSTED	497	25
BUT THEY OFTEN RAISE SUCH A DUST IN THE SWEEPING	536	2
THAT YOU'VE OFTEN HEARD	551	10
THAT YOU'VE OFTEN SEEN	551	14
THAT YOU OFTEN DO	551	18
AND MEN OFTEN SUCCUMB LIKE WHITE MICE IN A LABORATORY A+	619	22
WHOSE POWER AND GLORY I HAVE OFTEN HEARD AND FELT	704	21
IT HAS GROWN INTO A BIG AND OFTEN INTERESTING-LOOKI+	841	16
BY NATURE THAN BY BOOTS AND WET FEET OFTEN CARRY MERRY +	866	15
OF GAIETY TOO OFTEN PAY ME THUS	872	24

OH-H-H

HEE HEE EHEE EHOW EHAW OH OH OH-H-H	379	19

OHO

OHO THERE	309	11

OIL

THAT WILL HAVE THE OIL OF ILLUSION OH HEART	151	10
THE GHASTLY DREAM OF LABOUR AND THE STENCH OF STEEL AND+	175	1
BEING BURNED WITH OIL AND CONSUMED IN CORRUPT THICK	258	10
IN THE FUME OF COCOA-NUT OIL IN THE SWEATING TROPICAL N+	387	36
THEMSELVES WITH OIL AND LARD	460	14
THEMSELVES WITH OIL AND LARD	460	18
THEY WOULD DISTIL THE ESSENTIAL OIL OUT OF EVERY	504	6
THE ESSENTIAL OIL OF THEIR EXPERIENCE ENTERS	505	2
SILKY WITH OIL OF DISTILLED EXPERIENCE	505	8
AND OIL ME WITH THE LYMPH OF SILVERY TREES	652	23
OIL ME WITH THE LYMPH OF TREES	652	24
LUBRICATING OIL EXHAUST GAS	703	20
EVEN IF THERE WERE OIL COPPER GOLD UPON THESE	779	15
OR OIL OR COPPER OR GOLD A CAUSE FOR POLITICAL ACTION	779	19
WASH YOURSELF AND RUB OIL IN YOUR SKIN	791	21
ON THE SEVENTH DAY LET EVERY MAN WASH HIMSELF AND PUT O+	791	22
AND OIL MUCH OIL FROM THE COAST	793	19
TAKE BACK OUR LANDS AND SILVER AND OIL TAKE THE TRAINS +	794	21
FROM THE BLACK OIL AND THE WHITE	811	1

OIL

THAT MUST HAVE THE OIL OF ILLUSION OH HEART	873	20

OINTMENT

A COOL OINTMENT OVER THE EARTH BLISTERED IN THE FLIGHT +	855	31

OKLAHOMA INDIANS

AS THE OKLAHOMA INDIANS HAVE DONE	778	28

OLD

INTO A DEEP POND AN OLD SHEEP-DIP	33	15
OF THE NEW-BORN AND THEN THE OLD OWL THEN THE BATS THAT+	38	11
WANES THE OLD PALIMPSEST	41	23
THE OLD LIVES CROWD	52	27
OF THE AFTERNOON GLOWS STILL THE OLD ROMANCE OF DAVID A+	53	3
WITH THE OLD SWEET SOOTHING TEARS AND LAUGHTER THAT	53	5
THE FIVE OLD BELLS	54	1
WHY THE OLD CHURCH BELLOWS AND BRAGS	54	20
THE WISE OLD TREES	54	24
OLD QUESTION WITHOUT ANSWER STRANGE AND FAIN	69	27
BUT 'ER'S OLD MOTHER 'ER'S TWENTY YEAR	77	5
A GLUM OLD OTCHEL WI' LONG	77	22
FOR THIS NICE OLD SHAME AN' DISGRACE	79	8
YOUNG YEARS AND THE OLD MUST NOT WIN NOT EVEN IF THEY L+	93	5
TILL OLD DAYS DREW ME BACK INTO THEIR FOLD	98	28
BUT SHE IS OLD	101	2
BETWEEN THE OLD GREY WALLS I DID NOT DARE	122	27
OF THE WATERS WITHIN HIM ONLY THE WORLD'S OLD WISDOM	130	15
AND DAMP OLD WEB OF MISERY'S HEIRLOOM	141	11
OF LEAVES THAT HAVE GONE UNNOTICED SWEPT LIKE OLD	141	29
TO THE OLD SUNDAY EVENINGS AT HOME WITH WINTER OUTSIDE	148	12
AT JUST THE SAME OLD DELICATE GAME	150	25
WITH THE OLD SWEET THINGS OF OUR YOUTH AND NEVER YET	157	6
ALL BOUNDS THE GREAT OLD CITY	159	9
MY OLD INCREASE	159	30
THAT GOES WHEREVER THIS OLD ROAD GOES	164	8
IS OUT OF BOUNDS AND ONLY THE OLD GHOSTS KNOW	172	24
OF OLD SPENT LIVES LINGER BLURRED AND WARM	173	18
THE OLD DREAMS ARE BEAUTIFUL BELOVED SOFT-TONED AND SURE	174	21
OF THE OLD BAVARIAN GASTHAUS	206	28
IT BURNS WITHIN ME LIKE A DEEP OLD BURN	208	21
FOR THE ABOMINATION OF OUR OLD RIGHTEOUSNESS	232	8
WE ARE NOT OUR OLD SELVES ANY MORE	244	22
OLD SORROW AND NEW HAPPINESS	247	24
STILL WAITING FOR YOU HOWEVER OLD YOU ARE AND I AM	248	11
SUBTLER THAN AN OLD SOFT-WORN FIDDLE-BOW	254	23
BECAUSE IT WILL STILL BE A GESTURE OF THE OLD WORLD I AM	256	18
RISEN NOT TO THE OLD WORLD THE OLD CHANGELESS I THE OLD+	260	15
WAKENED NOT TO THE OLD KNOWLEDGE	260	16
OLD SCATTERED FIRE	271	32
WHOSE DOGES WERE OLD AND HAD ANCIENT EYES	278	11
ETRUSCAN-DUSKY WAVERING MEN OF OLD ETRURIA	296	19
ON ONE OLD THOUGHT	297	3
ON ONE OLD SLIM IMPERISHABLE THOUGHT WHILE YOU REMAIN	297	4
WITH IRON BRANCHING BLACKLY RUSTED LIKE OLD TWISTED	301	13
MASSIVE OLD ALTAR OF HIS OWN BURNT OFFERING	326	28
THAT THE OLD BIRD IS WEARY AND ALMOST WILLING	329	27
THE POOR OLD GOLDEN EAGLE OF THE WORD-FLEDGED SPIRIT	329	30
CREATURES THAT HANG THEMSELVES UP LIKE AN OLD RAG TO SL+	342	1
HANGING UPSIDE DOWN LIKE ROWS OF DISGUSTING OLD RAGS	342	3
AND NOW HE SCUFFLES TINILY PAST HER AS IF SHE WERE AN O+	356	26
NOT KNOWING EACH OTHER FROM BITS OF EARTH OR OLD TINS	357	20
EXCEPT THAT PAPA AND MAMA ARE OLD ACQUAINTANCES OF	357	21
LITTLE OLD MAN	360	18
AS IF YOU OWED HIM AN OLD OLD GRUDGE GREAT SUN OR AN OLD	374	3
OLD ALLEGIANCE	374	4
OLD EAGLE	374-11	
OLD FATHER	380	20
THAT IS A GRAND OLD LUST OF HIS TO GATHER THE GREAT	381	23
FIGHT OLD SATAN WITH A SELFISH WILL FIGHT FOR YOUR SELF+	383	22
OUR OLD GOAT WE TIE UP AT NIGHT IN THE SHED AT THE BACK+	384	4
WITH HER LONG TANGLED SIDES LIKE AN OLD RUG THROWN	384	26
AN OBSTINATE OLD WITCH ALMOST JERKING THE ROPE FROM MY	385	9
AND THE MONOLITHIC WATER-BUFFALOES LIKE OLD MUDDY STONES	386	29
AFTER THE BLACK-GREEN SKIRTS OF A YELLOW-GREEN OLD MEXI+	395	31
PLENTY OF GAME OLD SPIRIT IN YOU BIBBLES	397	28
PLENTY OF GAME OLD SPUNK LITTLE BITCH	397	29
WRINKLED OLD AUNTY'S FACE	400	19
COME TALL OLD DEMONS SMILING	404	3
I AM VERY WELL OLD DEMON	404	6
CALL ME OLD HARRY SAYS HE	404	9
NICK OLD NICK MAYBE	404	11
WELL YOU'RE A DARK OLD DEMON	404	12
OLD DEMON YOU AND I	404	19
TOUCH ME CAREFULLY OLD FATHER	405	1
I HAVE NO HOME OLD FATHER	405	5
THAT DARK OLD DEMON AND I	405	19
I'M THE RED WOLF SAYS THE DARK OLD FATHER	405	31
WOMEN WITH THE BEAUTIFUL EYES OF THE OLD DAYS	410	11
THE HUGE OLD FEMALE ON THE DRUM	426	4
AND THE OTHER THE OLD ONE THE PALLID HOARY FEMALE	426	9
JUST LIKE AN OLD MUSHROOM ALL WORMY INSIDE AND HOLLOW	431	20
'ERE SHE'S A LIDY AREN'T YER OLD QUIZZ	434	24
AND FOR THIS REASON SOME OLD THINGS ARE LOVELY	448	6
TILL AFTER A LONG TIME WHEN THEY ARE OLD AND HAVE STEEP+	448	10
OF ETERNAL SALT RAGE ANGRY IS OLD OCEAN WITHIN A MAN	454	11
IRON WASHES AWAY LIKE AN OLD BLOOD-STAIN	455	5
BACK TO THE OLD YEAR'S SUN ACROSS THE SEA	455	19
OLD MONEY-WORMS YOUNG MONEY-WORMS	456	22
COWARDICE EVERY OLD LOUT	458	21
NOR THE DEAR OLD MATER WHO SO PROUDLY BOASTS	458	24
THE ELEPHANT THE HUGE OLD BEAST	465	7
IN THE OLD DAYS WHEN SAPPHIRES WERE BREATHED UPON AND	477	1
GO DOWN TO YOUR DEEP OLD HEART WOMAN AND LOSE SIGHT OF	477	24
HAVE YOU NO DEEP OLD HEART OF WILD WOMANHOOD	478	15
WHAT THE OLD PEOPLE CALL IMMEDIATE CONTACT WITH GOD	481	6
AND OLD THINGS WILL FALL DOWN	482	25
HE COULDN'T BITE 'EM HE WAS MUCH TOO OLD	492	3

OLD
HE DID HIS BEST THE GOOD OLD DOG	492	7
THE OLD DOG'S GREENEST BONES	492	12
O THE STALE OLD DOGS WHO PRETEND TO GUARD	493	25
A GOOD KICK AT HIS DIRTY OLD HOLE	494	12
LEAR THE OLD BUFFER YOU WONDER HIS DAUGHTERS	494	16
THE OLD CHOUGH THE OLD CHUFFER	494	18
OLD DUNCAN WITH DAGGERS	494	24
TO GET A REFRESHING DRINK OUT OF OLD WISDOM	495	13
OLD TRUTH OLD TEACHING OF ANY SORT	495	14
FOR AFTER ALL HE HELPED TO SMASH A LOT OF OLD ROMAN LIES	497	3
I KNOW THAT POVERTY IS A HARD OLD HAG	498	13
SO MUCH SO THAT EVEN THE YOUNG ARE OLD WITH THE	502	14
AS IF IT'S MY FAULT THAT THE OLD GIRL IS SEVENTY-SEVEN	502	22
THE OLD ONES WANT TO BE YOUNG AND THEY AREN'T YOUNG	502	23
THE OLD ONES SAY TO THEMSELVES WE ARE NOT GOING TO BE O+	503	1
TILL THEY ARE OLD WE ARE STRONGER·THAN THE YOUNG	503	5
IT OUGHT TO BE LOVELY TO BE OLD	503	14
IN THEIR OLD AGE	503	21
SOOTHING OLD PEOPLE SHOULD BE LIKE APPLES	503	22
IT MUST BE WONDERFUL TO LIVE AND GROW OLD	503	27
AND THE YOUNG AMONG THE OLD	504	10
AS IT IS ALL THAT THE OLD CAN OFFER	504	13
EVEN THE OLD EMOTIONS ARE FINISHED	510	16
THE ONE THING THE OLD WILL NEVER UNDERSTAND	511	21
ALL FLOWS AND EVEN THE OLD ARE RAPIDLY FLOWING AWAY	511	23
IT IS SUCH AN OLD WORD	513	8
OUR POOR OLD DADDIES GOT ON	518	21
THE TOUGH OLD ENGLAND THAT MADE US	534	13
THE OLD ENGLAND THAT DOESN'T UPBRAID ME	534	21
NOW IT'S A COUNTRY OF FRIGHTENED OLD MONGRELS	535	17
THEY TOOK AWAY YOUR GOOD OLD STONES	549	9
NOW THE OLD ONES RING HOLLOW	564	22
WE'LL SHOW THESE OLD UNCLES WHO'S GOING TO BE BOSSY	573	24
THINKING OLD NEPTUNE WAS OFF ON A SPREE	575	9
ALL EYES SOUGHT THE SAME OLD SPOT	578	2
AND MR MEAD THAT OLD OLD LILY	579	17
BUT ONCE AND FOREVER BARKS THE OLD DOG	580	13
CALLED HIM OLD DADDY DO NOTHING	582	4
IS SUMMED UP IN A NICE NARROW-GUTTED OLD MAID	584	4
WHEN THOUGHTS ARE STIFF LIKE OLD LEAVES	608	22
FOR HE IS HOSTILE TO ALL THE OLD LEAFY FOLIAGE OF OUR T+	609	6
AND THE OLD UPWARD FLOWING OF OUR SAP THE PRESSURE OF O+	609	7
FOR OLD VALUES AND OLD PEOPLE	612	14
WHILE THE POLE STAR LIES ASIDE LIKE AN OLD AXLE TAKEN F+	616	30
EVEN THE OLD PRIEST IN HIS LONG BLACK ROBE AND SILVERY +	618	16
SENDS SUMMONS IN THE OLD HOLLOWS OF THE SUN	623	8
AND THE CALLING OF THE OLD RED INDIAN HIGH ON THE PUEBL+	623	16
AN OLD FRENCHMAN UTTERED THE TRUISM	641	17
WHICH ARE MEANT TO BE THE OLD FOLK-SONG STRAWBERRY FAIR	657	16
HOW THE GODS MUST HATE MOST OF·THE OLD OLD MEN TODAY	662	15
THE RANCID OLD MEN THAT DON'T DIE	662	16
OLD PEOPLE FIXED IN A RANCID RESISTANCE	662	20
LEAVE THE OLD ONES FIXED TO THEIR UGLY COGGED SELF-WILL	662	23
THAT'S WHY THE DOGGED RESISTANT OLD ONES DARE NOT DIE	662	26
OLD MEN OLD OBSTINATE MEN AND WOMEN	663	4
THE OLD DRAGON WILL DWINDLE DOWN TO THE SIZE OF A STRAY+	665	14
WHOM SOME RECALCITRANT OLD MAID WILL ADOPT AS A HOBBY	665	15
AND DEAR OLD LADY JEAN	668	17
OR ALL THE UGLY OLD POSSESSIONS THAT MAKE UP THE IMPEDI+	678	13
UGLY OLD FURNITURE UGLY OLD BOOKS UGLY OLD BUILDINGS UG+	678	14
THE OLD IDEA OF SACRIFICE WAS THIS	679	8
O WHEN THE OLD WORLD SACRIFICED A RAM	679	11
THIS SEA WILL NEVER DIE NEITHER WILL IT EVER GROW OLD	688	1
GREAT HEAVEN OF WHALES IN THE WATERS OLD HIERARCHIES	694	25
THE ANCIENT RIVER WEEK THE OLD ONE	702	20
AND LEANING TOWARDS THE OLD HEARTH	704	5
THAT LIES BETWEEN THE OLD AND THE NEW	718	2
SEEKING THEIR OLD HAUNTS WITH COLD GHOSTLY RAGE	722	27
OLD HAUNTS OLD HABITATS OLD HEARTHS	722	28
OLD PLACES OF SWEET LIFE FROM WHICH THEY ARE THRUST OUT	723	1
LET HIS OLD CART	751	24
THE OLD COUNTRIES HAVE A PAST TO BE FAITHFUL TO	775	14
THE OLD LIGHTS WON'T SHOW THE WAY	775	33
HE LINGERS ON FROM AN OLD SAVAGE WORLD THAT STILL HAS	776	8
AND BEFORE YOU PUT OUT THE OLD SAVAGE LIGHT FOR EVER	777	7
THE PUEBLO SUMMONED THE OLD INDIAN MEN AND	777	26
TOLD THE OLD AMERICAN ABORIGINES THAT IT WOULD	777	29
BE WELL IF THESE OLD FATHERS ABANDONED THEIR FOOLISH	777	30
THAT THE OLD DARK FATHERS SHOULD NOT TRUST THESE ARTISTS	778	4
FURTHERMORE THE WHITE BIG-MEN SAID TO THE OLD INDIANS	778	17
AND THE OLD DARK-FACED MEN CAME OUT HEAVILY WITH A	778	35
CAN YOU LEAVE THE REMNANTS OF THE OLD RACE	779	22
OLD ONE ERECT ON A BUSH	782	28
THE OLD FATHER OF LIFE AT THE HEART OF THE WORLD LIFE-F+	783	2
THEN SUDDENLY HE SPIED THE OLD LAKE AND HE THREW IT IN	791	7
TODAY WHEN THE SUN IS COMPUTED OLD	814	7
NATIONS BESIDE THE SEA ARE OLD	814	15
OH CHEW OLD COWS AT YOUR ANCIENT CUDS	814	20
AND THE OLD OLD FINAL LIFE-TRUTH	844	16
OLD THINGS THRICE SAID	857	4
WHY SHOULD I CARE WHERE THE OLD ROAD GOES	858	8
COME ON TURN HOME OLD LASS ARE WE WASTED TOO	859	26
HOLD UP JEANNETTE WHY POOR OLD GIRL ARE YOU SAD	859	29
AND NO MORE THAN THE BARON DID EH NO OLD GIRL AND NOT S+	859	32
SHE IS NO LONGER TWO DAYS OLD	863	11
OF MY OLD WHITE METAL OF MEANING YOU FINE	873	4
LINEN WITHIN MY OWN OLD FRAGRANT CHEST	877	31
OF THIS OLD HOUSE WHOSE STRANGERS I NOW ENTERTAIN	877	38
INTO A DEEP POND AN OLD SHEEP-DIP	*891	17
OF THE NEW-BORN AND THE UNBORN AND THE OLD OWL AND THE +	*892	26
THE MIST IS A CUP OF WINE AND THE NEW AND OLD	*894	25
THE OLD HARD STEM OF MY LIFE	899	27
THE OLD HARD STEM OF MY LIFE	*903	6
OF THE AFTERNOON GLOWS ONLY THE OLD ROMANCE OF DAVID AN+	*905	18
WITH THE OLD SWEET SOOTHING TEARS AND LAUGHTER THAT SHA+	*905	19
OF OLD INEFFECTUAL LIVES LINGER BLURRED AND WARM	*906	12
THE OLD DREAMS ARE BELOVED BEAUTIFUL SOFT-TONED AND SURE	*907	4

OLD
EYES WHERE I CAN WATCH THE SWIM OF OLD DREAMS REFLECTED+	*907	11
OF OLD INEFFECTUAL LIVES LINGER BLURRED AND WARM	*908	6
THE OLD DREAMS ARE BEAUTIFUL BELOVED SOFT-TONED AND SURE	*909	1
EYES WHERE I CAN WATCH THE SWIM OF OLD DREAMS REFLECTED+	*909	7
BUT 'ER'S OLD MOTHER 'ER'S TWENTY YEAR	*918	23
A TOUGH OLD OTCHEL WI' LONG	*919	10
FOR THIS NICE OLD SHAME AND DISGRACE	*921	4
BETWEEN THE OLD RED WALLS I DID NOT DARE	*934	3
TO THE OLD SUNDAY EVENINGS WHEN DARKNESS WANDERED OUTSI+	*940	11
OR THIS IS MY SISTER AT HOME IN THE OLD FRONT ROOM	*940	14

OLDEN
WOMEN WITH EYES THAT WERE GENTLE IN OLDEN BELIEF IN LOVE	410	23

OLDER
OLDER NOR HIM	77	6
WOMEN OF THE OLDER GENERATION WHO KNOW	410	15
TO THE WOMAN RATHER OLDER THAN HIMSELF	433	11
PEOPLE IN THEIR THIRTIES AND THE OLDER ONES HAVE GOTTEN	462	19
OLDER THAN FLOWERS OLDER THAN FERNS OLDER THAN FORAMINI+	477	10
OLDER THAN PLASM ALTOGETHER IS THE SOUL OF A MAN UNDERN+	477	11
WHY AS THEY GROW OLDER DO THEY SUFFER FROM BLOOD-PRESSU+	537	24
GOD IS OLDER THAN THE SUN AND MOON	692	7
GOD IS OLDER THAN THE SUN AND MOON	692	18
THE MEN OLDER THAN ME	828	22
THEY AREN'T AFRAID OF LOSING SOMETHING AS THE OLDER ONE+	828	25
PROBABLY AS SHE GREW OLDER SHE ATE HER RIVALS	836	6
OLDER NOR HIM	*918	24

OLDEST
BEAN WAS ONE OF THE OLDEST SYMBOLS OF THE MALE ORGAN FO+	303	19
ROSE OF THE OLDEST RACES OF PRINCESSES POLYNESIAN	314	4
OF THE HUGEST OLDEST OF BEASTS IN THE NIGHT AND THE FIR+	388	11
OLDEST THEY ARE AND THE WISEST OF BEASTS	465	23

OLD-MAN'S
FROM HIS PINK CLEFT OLD-MAN'S MOUTH	365	12

'OLD
I BET I AM YOU CAN 'OLD YER PHIZ	434	22

OLEANDER
AND OLEANDER IS HOT WITH PERFUME UNDER THE AFTERNOON SUN	630	3

OLIVE
AND NOW THE OLIVE LEAVES THOUSANDS OF FEET BELOW	293	25
TAKE ME SOUTH AGAIN TO THE OLIVE TREES	652	22

OLIVE-LEAVES
THE OLIVE-LEAVES LIGHT AS GAD-FLIES	226	21

OLIVE-ROOTS
NAXOS THOUSANDS OF FEET BELOW THE OLIVE-ROOTS	293	24

OLIVE-SPRIG
WITH AN OLIVE-SPRIG IN HIS MOUTH	413	31

OLIVE-TREES
UNDER THE OLIVE-TREES	227	12

'OME
I'M TAKIN' 'OME A WEDDIN'-DRESS	79	15
I'M TAKIN' 'OME A WEDDIN' DRESS	*921	11

OMINOUS
TILL THE DISTANCE FOLDS OVER HIS OMINOUS TREAD	43	4
THE OMINOUS ENTRY NOR SAW THE OTHER LOVE	155	27
OMINOUS AND LOVELY	288	29

OMINOUSLY
NOW BEGIN TO STEAM OMINOUSLY	541	3

OMINOUSNESS
AND DREAD AND THE DARK ROLLING OMINOUSNESS OF DOOM	708	25

OMISSION
FOR THE SINS OF OMISSION	562	12

OMIT
YOU'D BETTER OMIT THAT TOO COMMUNISTIC	669	26
THERE ARE NO MICE IN OUR ROYAL PALACES OMIT IT	670	6

OMITTED
THINGS OMITTED	563	6

OMNES VOS OMNES SERVITE
OMNES VOS OMNES SERVITE	392	6

OMNIPIP
YOU OMNIPIP	396	15

ONCE
FLUSHED WITH THE SONGS OF SEVEN LARKS SINGING AT ONCE G+	34	14
WITH DARK SLEEP THAT ONCE COVERED THE CEILING	38	5
ONCE YOU COULD SEE	55	25
WAS WOMAN ONCE TO YOU	56	2
A DECENT SHORT REGRET FOR THAT WHICH ONCE WAS VERY GOOD	66	4
MY STACK OF LILIES ONCE WHITE INCANDESCENT	86	23
YOU UPON THE DRY DEAD BEECH-LEAVES ONCE MORE ONLY ONCE	90	25
ONCE FROM YOUR WOMB SWEET MOTHER	101	25
ONCE FROM YOUR SOUL TO BE	101	26
ONCE I HAD A LOVER BRIGHT LIKE RUNNING WATER	119	23
ONCE HIS FACE WAS OPEN LIKE THE SKY	119	24
UPRAISED TO KNOCK AND KNOCK ONCE MORE	121	15
LONG HAVE I WAITED NEVER ONCE CONFESSED	122	13
HOURS THAT WERE ONCE ALL GLORY AND ALL QUEENS	135	24
AS SHE STRODE HER LIMBS AMONGST IT ONCE MORE	155	14

ONCE
    WITH JEWELS OF PASSION ONCE BROKEN THROUGH YOU AS A   168 15
    TO HAVE WON ONCE MORE   168 31
    THESE SHAPES THAT NOW ARE DREAMS AND ONCE WERE MEN   174 2
    NEVERTHELESS ONCE THE FROGS THE GLOBE-FLOWERS OF BAVARIA   208 4
    IS MINE I CLAIM HIM ONCE AND FOR ALL   219 26
    I WAS THE GOD AND THE CREATION AT ONCE   257 14
    AS YOU SEE IT STANDING GROWING YOU FEEL AT ONCE IT IS S+   282 13
    WHEN EVE ONCE KNEW IN HER MIND THAT SHE WAS NAKED   284 7
    ONCE GOD WAS ALL NEGROID AS NOW HE IS FAIR   286 16
    WHICH AT ONCE SETS OFF TO BE THE ONE AND ONLY   300 3
    ONCE HE LAY IN THE MOUTH OF A CAVE   324 5
    NAY ONCE IT WAS ALSO A FORTRESS WALL AND THE WEIGHT OF +   326 25
    SEAL UP HIS FOREHEAD ONCE MORE TO A BASTION   327 22
    ONCE A BIG PIKE RUSH   338 19
    THE GARDEN ONCE A YEAR   358 27
    JERK OF COITION AND AT ONCE   365 18
    OR MUST YOU GO THROUGH THE FIRE ONCE MORE TILL YOU'RE   372 1
    AS MOSSES AND LITTLE LIZARDS THEY SAY WERE ONCE BIG   372 20
    STARING TWO WAYS AT ONCE TO RIGHT AND LEFT   373 13
    ONCE THEY SAY HE WAS PASSING BY WHEN A DOG WAS BEING BE+   376 5
    AND CITIES MIGHT BE AS ONCE THEY WERE BOWERS GROWN OUT   451 18
    ONCE THE MOON COMES DOWN   455 1
    THAT WAS ONCE A HOUSE AND IS NOW A PRISON   462 2
    IF YOU'RE DIRTY INSIDE YOU GO ROTTEN AND ONCE ROTTEN WOE   464 6
    IF ONCE FOR A SECOND THE UNIVERSE CEASED TO FLOW   479 13
    THEY WOULD THEMSELVES AT ONCE COLLAPSE INTO NULLITY   527 22
    AND THEIR GRANDCHILDREN ARE ONCE MORE SLAVES   535 26
    AN EARL ONCE ASKED ME DOWN TO STAY   551 27
    AND A DUCHESS ONCE CAME TO TEA   551 28
    ONCE AND FOR ALL HAVE DONE WITH IT   556 11
    FOR ONCE AND FEEL IT GO THROUGH YOU   559 13
    YET ONCE MORE I MET A MAN AND I HAD TO STAY   569 21
    IF MY PICTURES ARE NUDE SO ONCE WERE YOU   577 11
    BUT ONCE AND FOREVER BARKS THE OLD DOG   580 13
    FOR THE BRITISH PUBLIC ONCE MORE BE IT SAID   584 3
    ONCE MEN TOUCH ONE ANOTHER THEN THE MODERN INDUSTRIAL   611 14
    AND ONCE YOU REALISE THAT YOU NEVER WERE LOST   614 3
    THEY FALL VICTIM AT ONCE TO THE VENGEANCE OF THE UNFORG+   616 7
    ONCE IT HAS FALLEN OFF   617 2
    ONCE THE CONNECTION HAS BEEN BROKEN   617 6
    INTO THE CIRCULATING SAP ONCE MORE OF THE TREE OF LIFE   617 11
    AND TURN ONCE MORE TO MEN TO SAVE THEM PERSEUS ST GEORGE   619 26
    AND ONCE DONE THERE IS NO REMEDY NO SALVATION FOR THIS   621 10
    ONCE DISILLUSION FALLS ON LIVING MEN AND THEY FEEL THE   639 19
    ONCE DISILLUSION FALLS ON LIVING MEN AND ILLUSION OF BR+   639 23
    THEN AT ONCE THE IMPULSE OF THE GREEDY CLASSES AND MASS+   640 8
    STOP THAT AT ONCE   669 10
    DO NOW ONCE AND FOREVER RETIRE   681 10
    IS DEAD TOO A DEAD ORB WHEELED ONCE A MONTH ROUND THE P+   702 27
    PROVIDE FOR YOUR DEAD ONCE MORE EQUIP THEM   721 25
    BUT DIPPED ONCE DIPPED IN DARK OBLIVION   724 25
    BRINGING NIGHT ONCE MORE AND THE MAN WITH THE KEYS   758 4
    AS A VENDOR OF FRIED FISH ONCE MORE YELLOW   760 21
    WHERE ONCE THE BLOOD SANG   767 3
    THIS BLOOD THAT WAS ONCE MY OWN   768 7
    AND DAMAGE ONCE MORE THE FRAIL QUICK OF THE FUTURE   780 21
    STARING TWO WAYS AT ONCE TO RIGHT AND LEFT   781 19
    ONCE MORE FOLLOWING THE MASTER   798 23
    WHO PARDONS ONCE AND NO MORE   809 22
    LONG AGO ONCE BEFORE   817 17
    WHICH SHOWS ONCE MORE THAT OUR SOCIAL CONSCIENCE IS DEV+   829 22
    ONCE THEY'VE GOT THEM   832 3
    HE WAS A SOLDIER ONCE OUR FIERCE LITTLE BARON A POLE   859 5
    AND ONCE AGAIN AS MANY A TIME BEFORE   877 35
    I KISSED HER ONCE AGAIN UPON THE MOUTH   881 1
    RICH WITH THE SONGS OF SEVEN LARKS SINGING AT ONCE GOES+   *892 2
    WITH THE DARK SLEEP THAT ONCE COVERED THE CEILING   *892 2
    THEY SIGH JUST ONCE ROUND OUR FEET AND ARE STILL HEAVY +   *917 11
    WITHOUT DELIVERING ONCE MY EYE   *930 17
    FROM SIGHT OF ME WITHOUT ONCE YOUR TURNING   *930 18
    ONCE I HAD A LOVER BRIGHT LIKE RUNNING WATER   *933 13
    ONCE I KNEW A SUMMER THAT SPARKLED   *933 14
    HOURS THAT WERE ONCE ALL GLORY AND ALL QUEENS   *939 24
    IS MINE I MUN CLAIM HIM ONCE FOR ALL   *944 6
    AND THE FATHER WAS ONCE GREY-BEARDED AND FULMINATIVE   *946 14
    AND ONCE HE WAS A YOUNG MAN PALE AND REFUSING FATHERHOOD   *946 15
    AND ONCE HE WAS GAY AND HEARTY WITH HIS EYE ON THE IMMO+   *946 17
    AND ONCE AGAIN A SUAVE YOUNG GOD   *946 18
    OF THE ARMS OF PLUTO AS HE RAVISHES HER ONCE AGAIN   *956 17
    AND PIERCES HER ONCE MORE WITH HIS PASSION OF THE UTTER+   *956 18
    ONCE OUTSIDE THE GATE OF THE WALLED SILVERY LIFE OF DAYS   *957 27
    ONCE OUTSIDE UPON THE GREY MARSH BEACHES WHERE LOST SOU+   *957 28
    ONCE OUTSIDE THE GATE   *957 32

ONCE-MORE-MOLTEN
    SLOWLY A GEM FORMS IN THE ANCIENT ONCE-MORE-MOLTEN   477 13

ONCE-MORE-VINDICATED
    AND HIS BLOOD RIPPLES WITH THAT UNTELLABLE DELIGHT OF O+   306 2

ONCE-WILD
    ROSES ARE ONLY ONCE-WILD ROSES THAT WERE GIVEN AN EXTRA+   831 2

ONCOMING
    SPURTS FROM THE TERROR OF HIS ONCOMING   43 8

ONE
    IN ONE MOMENT ROUSES INSURGENT   39 6
    QUIVERING AWAKE WITH ONE IMPULSE AND ONE WILL   39 8
    THOU TO DO WITH ME THOU LUSTROUS ONE ICONOCLAST   39 18
    IS HE CALLING THE LONE ONE IS HIS DEEP   40 1
    THOU DARK ONE THOU PROUD CURVED BEAUTY I   40 17
    BUT THE HOSTS OF MEN WITH ONE VOICE DENY   40 19
    IN ONE BLUE STOOP FROM OUT THE SKIES   43 30
    'E'S 'AD TWENTY ACCIDENTS IF 'E'S 'AD ONE   45 27
    THERE'S ONE THING WE S'LL 'AVE A PEACEFUL 'OUSE   45 29
    I CRIED BUT NO ONE HEARD ME   46 23

ONE
    CLOTTING TO ONE DEAD MASS IN THE SINKING FIRE   47 5
    THIS LAST ONE TO CLAIM ME AND NOW MY SON O MY SON   48 6
    THE PINK YOUNG HORSES SHOW ONE SIDE BRIGHT   50 23
    AND ONE SIDE SHADOW HALF IN SIGHT   50 25
    AND ONE AFTER ANOTHER ROUSES   51 13
    EACH ONE DARTING AWAY WITH HIS   51 29
    YOU WERE MANY MEN IN ONE   57 1
    WHILE NORTH OF THEM ALL AT THE FARTHEST ENDS STANDS ONE+   57 11
    SUCH A ONE IN THE NORTH IT FLOWERS ON THE STREET AND I +   58 13
    BECAUSE NO ONE GRIEVES OVER HER DEPARTURE   63 21
    BETWEEN THE SCHOOLS SWEEPS ONE BLACK ROOK   76 16
    GOD STEPPING THROUGH OUR LOINS IN ONE BRIGHT STRIDE   87 25
    SO EVEN IT BEATS LIKE SILENCE AND SKY AND EARTH IN ONE +   88 3
    ONE   88 11
    ONE DAY A HEAVY-BREASTED JUNE-HOT WOMAN   91 8
    EACH ONE FOR ITS HOLD ON THE CONCRETE DARKNESS I KNOW T+   92 14
    AT LAST INTO BLOSSOM OF BEING EACH ONE HIS OWN FLOWER O+   93 15
    THEY ARE HERE TO LEARN BUT ONE LESSON THAT THEY SHALL N+   93 16
    ONE BOWL OF KISSES   96 6
    IN ONE FULFIL   97 5
    HOW WE HATE ONE ANOTHER TO-NIGHT HATE SHE AND I   98 7
    OVERHEAD AT HOME AND HAD NOT ONE STAR   103 6
    NOR ONE NARROW GATE FOR THE MOON TO GO   103 7
    US ONLY ONE MOMENT HIS KEYS   104 10
    ON THE BREAST OF MY COAT AND ONE BY ONE   107 3
    WE ARE ONE SMOOTH-ROUNDED   117 7
    EXTINCT ONE YELLOW-FLUFFY SPARK   119 22
    THAT A GREY ONE LIKE A SHADOW LIKE A RAT A THIEF A RAIN+   120 3
    AND STILL ONE PULSE   120 32
    THIS ONE REFRAIN   124 14
    THE EXPECTANT ONE AND THEREIN TO INSTIL   127 13
    WHEN I TELL YOU THE STARS FLASH SIGNALS EACH ONE   130 25
    GONE ONE KNOWS NOT WHITHER   134 10
    ONE LONELY BELL ONE ONLY THE STORM-TOSSED AFTERNOON IS   137 1
    THA'RT ONE O' TH' MEN AS HAS GOT TO DRAIN   139 15
    SITTING HUDDLED AGAINST THE CERULEAN ONE FLESH WITH THE+   142 11
    ONE HEAPED MOUND   145 28
    GONE IN ONE LEAP   146 4
    ONE FROM THE WARD   146 27
    SUDDEN OUTSIDE THE HIGH WINDOW ONE CROW   147 21
    ONE BIRD ONE BLOT FOLDED AND STILL AT THE TOP   147 24
    OF CRYSTAL HEAVEN FALLS ONE FULL BLACK DROP   147 26
    BE ALL YOURSELF ONE BONNY BURNING COAL   151 14
    SHE KNOWS THE WASTE ALL DRY BENEATH HER IN ONE PLACE   153 5
    LIKE BEADS THEY GO AROUND AND NOT ONE MISSES   154 5
    WHO FOR ONE STRANGE YEAR WAS AS A BRIDE TO YOU YOU SET +   157 4
    WALK NOW AS ONE   157 14
    WITH ME BOTH IN ONE HURT   160 4
    ONE OR ANOTHER   163 5
    ENDLESSLY IN ONE MOTION DEPART   163 7
    THE WIND IS UNCHANGING NOT ONE OF US KNOWS   164 2
    BACK FROM THE STRAIGHT HORIZON THAT ENDS ALL ONE SEES   168 6
    IN ONE WORLD WITH ME   170 3
    ONE SHADOW AND WE NEED NOT DISSEMBLE   170 14
    SLOPES ROUND THE HEAVENS IN ONE SMOOTH CURVE   172 19
    THE RICH AND THE POOR ALIKE DREAMING AND WRITHING ALL I+   175 15
    ONE ANOTHER IN WONDER OF WAKING LET US WAKE TO THE GLEAM   175 29
    ONE BRIGHT RED RAY   176 13
    IN A LITTLE THRONG AT YOUR DOOR AND ADMIT THE ONE WHO IS   179 6
    THE SHADOW ALWAYS OFFER MYSELF TO ONE MISTRESS WHO ALWA+   180 27
    ONE MOMENT SEES AND SWIFT ITS DREAM IS OVER   195 14
    IN ONE RICH DRIP IT SINKS TO ANOTHER SLEEP   195 15
    AND SLEEP THEREBY IS ONE MORE CREAM ENRICHENED   195 16
    TO ALTER MY ONE SPECK OF DOOM WHEN ROUND ME BURNS   195 25
    WITHOUT PLAYMATE OR HELPMATE HAVING NO ONE TO CHERISH   197 8
    NO ONE TO COMFORT AND REFUSING ANY COMFORTER   197 9
    ONE TO BE QUENCHED TO BE GIVEN UP TO BE GONE IN THE DARK   212 8
    FEAR WAS ABROAD WE WHISPERED NO ONE KNOWS US   217 6
    ONE ROSE OF WONDERMENT UPON THE TREE   219 6
    FOR EVER ONE EVEN MIGHT THINK THAT THEY LOVE US   223 27
    AND SUNSHINE FILLS ONE HIGH VALLEY BED   224 12
    ONE MOMENT THE HATE LEAPS AT ME STANDING THERE   225 25
    ONE MOMENT I SEE THE STILLNESS OF AGONY   225 26
    LOOSED ONE MOMENT THE DARKNESS FRIGHTENS ME   225 28
    I WANTED TO GATHER THEM ONE BY ONE   227 15
    WHEN SOME ONE PASSES HE DROPS HIS HEAD   228 5
    IN ONE BLOSSOM BLOWING   239 21
    COME MY LITTLE ONE CLOSER UP AGAINST ME   245 5
    AND OH MY LITTLE ONE YOU WHOM I ENFOLD   246 1
    CHERISH ME MY TINY ONE CHERISH ME WHO ENFOLD YOU   246 10
    MY LITTLE ONE MY BIG ONE   246 17
    MY PIGEON MY LITTLE ONE SO WARM   246 20
    MY LITTLE ONE MY BIG ONE   246 22
    MY LITTLE ONE MY BIG ONE   247 14
    ONLY THAT ONE NEWNESS   247 25
    IN A MOTION HUMAN INHUMAN TWO AND ONE   252 10
    I WOULD DIE RATHER THAN HAVE IT INJURED WITH ONE SCAR   255 13
    ONE ON ANOTHER AND THEN IN CLUSTERS TOGETHER   258 2
    I PUT OUT MY HAND IN THE NIGHT ONE NIGHT AND MY HAND   259 2
    HAS NOT SO MUCH OF STRENGTH AS THE BODY OF ONE WOMAN   263 2
    WHAT MANY WOMEN CANNOT GIVE ONE WOMAN CAN   264 27
    AND FOR THIS I HAVE TO THANK ONE WOMAN   265 21
    BUT ONE WOMAN   265 23
    HOW CAN ONE SPEAK WHERE THERE IS A DUMBNESS ON ONE'S MO+   266 10
    IT IS THAT THAT ONE COMES TO   266 13
    SHE THINKS WE ARE ALL OF ONE PIECE   266 26
    ONE FROM THE OTHER   267 2
    THAT ONE IS FREE   267 4
    WHEN SHE IS SLAIN AGAINST ME AND LIES IN A HEAP LIKE ON+   267 13
    ONE CLEAR BURNISHED ISOLATED BEING UNIQUE   267 20
    THE FIBRES OF THE HEART PARTING ONE AFTER THE OTHER   281 6
    IN ONE BITE   282 10
    AND BUT ONE ORIFICE   282 24
    ONE SMALL WAY OF ACCESS ONLY AND THIS CLOSE-CURTAINED F+   283 16
    DOES NO ONE REALISE THAT LOVE SHOULD BE INTENSE INDIVID+   291 15
    ON ONE OLD THOUGHT   297 3
    ON ONE OLD SLIM IMPERISHABLE THOUGHT WHILE YOU REMAIN   297 4

ONE
THERE IS ONLY ONE EVIL TO DENY LIFE   298 16
EACH ONE SETTING OFF STRAIGHT TO THE SKY   299 27
TO HOLD THE ONE AND ONLY LIGHTED CANDLE OF THE SUN IN H+   299 34
WHICH AT ONCE SETS OFF TO BE THE ONE AND ONLY   300 3
STILL NO DOUBT EVERY ONE OF YOU CAN BE THE SUN-SOCKET AS   300 12
BEAN WAS ONE OF THE OLDEST SYMBOLS OF THE MALE ORGAN FO+   303 19
OUT IN ONE STRIDE   306 7
OH HONEY-BODIED BEAUTIFUL ONE   306 20
THE DARK ONE   308 2
ONE IS A MAN FOR EXAMPLE AND ONE IS A BIRD   320 2
HE WAS ONE OF NATURE'S PHENOMENA NO DOUBT   328 18
ARE YOU ONE TOO MANY FOR ME   334 13
ALL ONE TO YOU   334 24
ONE TOUCH   335 16
TO HAVE THE ELEMENT UNDER ONE LIKE A LOVER   337 1
NOT ONE TOUCH   337 19
EACH ONE ALONE WITH THE WATERS UPON ONE WAVE WITH THE   337 21
HE'S A RARE ONE BUT HE BELONGS   337 27
AND TO THE ONE GOD   338 23
AS ONE STANDS ON A BANK AND LOOKS IN   338 31
THINGS OF ONE ELEMENT   340 3
NOT ONE INSTANT CLEAVE CLING LIKE A BLOT WITH HIS BREAS+   343 29
AND CLUTCHING CLUTCHING FOR ONE SECOND'S PAUSE   345 8
ALWAYS AS IF FOR ONE DROP OF REST   345 9
ONE LITTLE DROP   345 10
IMPURE ONE   347 7
THERE HE SITS THE LONG LOUD ONE   347 21
AND LIFTED HIS HEAD DREAMILY AS ONE WHO HAS DRUNKEN   350 24
AND SO I MISSED MY CHANCE WITH ONE OF THE LORDS   351 27
SLOW ONE   352 17
NO ONE EVER HEARD YOU COMPLAIN   352 24
WITH YOUR TAIL TUCKED A LITTLE ON ONE SIDE   354 19
FOUR ROWING LIMBS AND ONE WEDGE-BALANCING HEAD   356 7
FOUR AND ONE MAKES FIVE WHICH IS THE CLUE TO ALL MATHEM+   356 8
THIS SLOW ONE   356 18
ON HE GOES THE LITTLE ONE   356 19
AND STUMBLING MIXED UP IN ONE ANOTHER   361 25
AND ONE INTENSE AND BACKWARD-CURVING FRISSON   370 16
AND FROM THE DARKNESS OF THAT OPPOSITE ONE   370 20
EACH ONE APART AND INSTANT   371 12
ERECT ONE   373 21
THERE'S ONE LEFT   377 12
ONE   377 14
AND TO LEAP IN ONE LAST HEART-BURSTING LEAP LIKE A MALE+   379 15
ONE OF US OR THE PAIR OF US   380 7
SPLENDIDLY PLANTING HIS FEET ONE ROCKY FOOT STRIKING THE   381 13
LENDING FIRST ONE EAR THEN ANOTHER   384 18
LITTLE DANGLE OF AN IMMATURE PAW AND ONE THIN EAR   393 20
BELIEVE IN THE ONE IDENTITY DON'T YOU   395 25
AS IF NOW AT LAST HERE WAS THE ONE YOU FINALLY LOVED   398 17
SUCH A WAGGLE OF LOVE YOU CAN HARDLY DISTINGUISH ONE   399 22
YOU LOVE ONE AFTER ANOTHER ON ONE CONDITION THAT EACH   399 24
ONE LOVES YOU MOST   399 25
WHERE'S YOUR DOG YOU WHITE ONE   404 24
FAR ONE TO SLEEP AND A FORGETTING AND OFTEN THE DEAD LO+   406 5
IN THEIR EFFORTS TO COME AWAKE FROM ONE MOMENT   408 5
AND SHOOT ONE ANOTHER AMAZED AND MAD WITH SOMNAMBULISM   408 12
ON THE YELLOW POINTED ASPEN-TREES LAID ONE ON ANOTHER L+   409 14
ENGLAND SEEMS LIKE ONE GRAVE TO ME   410 26
EAGLES WITH TWO HEADS EAGLES WITH ONE PRESENTLY EAGLES   413 7
THEN IT BEGAN TO FIDGET SHIFTING FROM ONE LEG TO THE OT+   413 12
THRUSTS WARM THROUGH THE LOINS SO THE LITTLE ONE   425 16
AND THE OTHER THE OLD ONE THE PALLID HOARY FEMALE   426 9
COULD ONE AT NIGHT RUN UP AGAINST THE STANDING FLESH   428 2
THE OTHER SAYS HAVE ONE WITH ME   433 3
BECAUSE REALLY IT'S NO USE PRETENDING ONE IS SUPERIOR   435 4
ISN'T ONE   435 7
AND BUMP ON ONE ANOTHER AND EXPLODE INTO MORE MIST   437 34
OF ONE WHO WILL SETTLE ON ICEBERGS AND HONK ACROSS THE   439 2
WHEN THE ONE GOD MADE A MONOPOLY OF IT   439 13
THAT PALE ONE FILLED WITH RENUNCIATION AND PAIN AND WHI+   439 22
THAT STRONG ONE RULING THE UNIVERSE WITH A ROD OF IRON   439 25
LEAVE THEM TO ONE ANOTHER   440 24
BUT ONE OF HIS BELOVEDS LOOKING A LITTLE PEAKED   446 26
BECAUSE OBVIOUSLY HE'S NOT ONE OF THE LEISURED CLASSES   452 21
HAVE YOU GOT ONE LITTLE BLIGHTERS   457 29
LET IT CROW THEN LIKE ONE O'CLOCK   457 30
AND NEVER A ONE AMONG US ALL   462 3
ALL KINDS OF THINGS TO ONE ANOTHER   470 5
WITH A SOFT ONE WARMTH AND A GENEROUS   471 6
AND THE WHITE MIND SHINES ON ONE SIDE OF THEE   473 26
ULTIMATELY WE ARE ALL BUSY BUYING AND SELLING ONE ANOTH+   482 29
FOR MANKIND SAYS WITH ONE VOICE HOW MUCH IS HE WORTH   486 20
BEFORE WE START KILLING ONE ANOTHER ABOUT IT   487 1
IT'S ONE THING OR THE OTHER   487 13
FROM THE ONE WE'VE GOT NOW   487 20
IN WHICH ONE OF THE CHARACTERS WAS ME   489 10
SO WHILE THE OTHER ONE HEAVED HER SIDES   492 5
BUT STILL ONE HAS NO RIGHT TO TAKE   492 11
AND OF COURSE ONE HAS NO RIGHT TO LAY   492 15
THE LOUD LOVE OF PEACE MAKES ONE QUIVER MORE THAN ANY   495 16
WHY SHOULD ONE LOVE PEACE IT IS SO OBVIOUSLY VILE TO MA+   495 18
YET ONE THING I DO FIGHT FOR TOOTH AND NAIL ALL THE TIME   497 22
AND THAT IS MY BIT OF INWARD PEACE WHERE I AM AT ONE   497 23
ONE CAN BE TOLERANT WITH A BORE   499 12
ONE CAN'T STAND PEACELESS PEOPLE ANY MORE   499 19
WHEN ONE IS TIRED OF LOVE   503 23
SO THAT ONE COULD DRAW NEAR HER   506 14
THE ONE THING THE OLD WILL NEVER UNDERSTAND   511 21
WATER IS H2O HYDROGEN TWO PARTS OXYGEN ONE   515 11
ONE MIGHT TALK OF THE SANITY OF THE ATOM   515 16
LABOUR IS THE ONE THING A MAN HAS HAD TOO MUCH OF   517 18
WHY SHOULD WE COMPETE WITH ONE ANOTHER   520 22
ONE FREE CHEERFUL ACTIVITY STIMULATES ANOTHER   520 26
WITHOUT A BIT OF COMMON TRUST IN ONE ANOTHER WE CAN'T   522 19
EACH ONE TURNING HIS BREAST STRAIGHT TO THE SUN OF SUNS   525 12
NODDING TO THE GREAT ONE   525 15
AND RECEIVING FROM THE GREAT ONE   525 16
AND HOW DELICIOUS IT IS TO FEEL SUNSHINE UPON ONE   526 1
WHEN A MAN COMES LOOKING DOWN UPON ONE   526 3
THEN I WISH LIKE TIBERIUS THE MULTITUDE HAD ONLY ONE HE+   526 21
YOU DON'T NEED ONE SINGLE SOCIAL INFERIOR TO EXALT YOU   526 26
AS ONE OF OUR BRIGHTEST YOUNG INTELLECTUALS SAID TO ME   531 22
AND THE PURE INTELLECT GIVES ONE A LAST MASTURBATING SE+   532 9
BUT OF COURSE ONE KNOWS THAT BOTH BEAUTY AND PURE   532 11
SO ONE OF THE BRIGHTEST YOUNG INTELLECTUALS PUT IT TO ME   533 4
I WAS ONE OF THE LITTLE BLIGHTERS   534 11
ONE CANNOT NOW HELP THINKING   536 6
HAD HAD TO TAKE HIM FOR ONE NIGHT ONLY IN THE FLESH   538 3
WILL NO ONE SAY HUSH TO THEE   540 7
AND BLINDED HIM IN HIS ONE BIG EYE   543 27
HE WANTS HIS ONE GREAT WONDERING EYE THE EYE OF THE   544 9
OF THE ANCIENT CAVE SMASHING INTO ONE ANOTHER   544 15
ONE MUST COME DOWN TO TERRA FIRMA SOMEWHERE   548 5
OR MUST ONE SIMPLY SAY   548 6
NOT ONE OF THE WHOLE JOB LOT   549 28
NOT ONE THEY ALL SEEMED TO ME   550 2
WITH SUCH PEOPLE ONE HAS TO BE CAREFUL   554 23
THAT I COULDN'T FEEL ONE OF THEM   556 2
HALF BELIEVING 'EM TILL ONE DAY   556 14
WILL RISE IN THEM ONE DAY   560 6
ONE ANOTHER AGAIN   561 2
IN ONE ANOTHER   561 13
ONE FAITHFULNESS MORE   561 27
AUNT GWEN WAS A POOR ONE BUT AUNT MAUD YOU SEE   571 25
OH AUNT LOUIE'S THE ONE I DREAD   572 16
FATHER NEPTUNE ONE DAY TO FREEDOM DID SAY   574 11
LOOK AT THAT ONE THERE THAT'S PRETTY HOT   578 11
WHEN YOU WANT ONE SO I DID WITHOUT   579 11
GIVE US BACK OUR BODIES FOR ONE DAY   585 8
WE WERE MEANT TO MEAN A GREAT DEAL TO ONE ANOTHER   603 10
SO THEY SIMPLY ADORED ONE ANOTHER   605 15
A MAN'S BUSINESS IS ONE OF HIS POCKETS HIS BANK   607 15
TO BE ALONE IS ONE OF LIFE'S GREATEST DELIGHTS THINKING+   610 3
ONCE MEN TOUCH ONE ANOTHER THEN THE MODERN INDUSTRIAL   611 14
THE ONE THING EASIEST TO LOSE IS SAVINGS   614 5
NO ONE NOT EVEN GOD CAN PUT BACK A LEAF ON TO A TREE   617 1
AND NO ONE NOT GOD NOR CHRIST NOR ANY OTHER   617 3
THE HUMAN WILL IS FREE ULTIMATELY TO CHOOSE ONE OF TWO +   617 18
AND WAS IMMENSELY FLATTERED WHEN ONE OF THE FAT LITTLE   618 18
AND SHE WAS SO PLEASED WITH IT SHE THOUGHT ONE DAY IT W+   619 14
AND TO LEAVE ONE ANOTHER ALONE   620 4
FOR ONE SAD CENTURY   623 29
THE MACHINES WILL TURN TO RUN INTO ONE ANOTHER   624 26
THEY ARE MILLIONS TO MY ONE   628 20
THEY ARE MILLIONS TO MY ONE BUT OH   628 21
FOR MANKIND IS A SINGLE CORPUS WE ARE ALL ONE FLESH   631 24
I TELL YOU NOT ONE MAN IN A THOUSAND HAS EVEN   638 16
SO IT CAN'T HAVE ONE TO SAVE   638 19
LET THEM GRIND ON ONE ANOTHER UPPER-CLASS ROBOT   642 12
AND ONE TRAPPED ONE'S FINGERS IN THEIR BRASSY POLISHED   644 13
IN THE THUNDER AIR ALL STRANGERS TO ONE ANOTHER   647 6
THAT'S WHY ONE DOESN'T HAVE TO TAKE THEM SERIOUSLY   660 8
BUT IN CHOOSING THE BOURGEOIS ONE BRINGS TO PASS   664 8
LIKE THE TWO LIONS WHO DEVOURED ONE ANOTHER AND LEFT TH+   665 2
ONE NOTICES MEN HERE AND THERE GOING HESITATINGLY FALTE+   665 23
AND WITH ONE ANOTHER   666 19
ONE FOR THE MASTER AND ONE FOR THE DAME   669 23
AND ONE FOR THE LITTLE BOY THAT LIVES DOWN THE   669 24
YOU ARE FOR THAT MOMENT ONE OF THE GODS JESUS OR FAFNIR+   674 4
NOW LET ME BE MYSELF IN THE BEING ONE OF THE GODS   674 17
MEN PREVENT ONE ANOTHER FROM BEING MEN   677 17
PONDERING FOR HE WAS A GREEK THAT GOD IS ONE AND ALL AL+   692 23
LO GOD IS ONE GOD BUT HERE IN THE TWILIGHT   693 18
AND ONE WARM KIND KISS OF THE LION WITH GOLDEN PAWS   695 33
ALL THAT MATTERS IS TO BE AT ONE WITH THE LIVING GOD   700 1
AND AT ONE WITH THE MASTER OF THE HOUSE WITH THE MISTRE+   700 5
THE ANCIENT RIVER WEEK THE OLD ONE   702 20
THE CLEAVERS THAT CLEAVE US FOREVER APART FROM ONE ANOT+   707 17
BUT WHEN STRIFE IS A THING OF ONE   714 26
BEING AN ACT OF ONE   715 9
DARKNESS OF MEN WITH DARKNESS UP AND DOWN   719 13
ONE BY ONE THEY GO BY AT LAST   733 10
A NICE ONE I LIKE IT HE'LL THINK IT'S A TALL ORDER   733 29
THAT I AM NOW AH LAY ONE LITTLE TOUCH   738 30
OF JUST ONE TOUCH EVEN SO DO I ASK TOO MUCH   738 32
THEY RETURN RELENTLESSLY IN THE SILENCE ONE KNOWS THEIR+   739 14
FOR ONE YEAR'S SPACE ATTEND ON OUR ANGRY DEAD   740 16
OVER YOUR TENT THE ONE TENT OF US ALL MY LOVE   750 10
SOME ONE STOPPED ME AND SAID YOUR LOVER IS HURT   750 18
ONE OF YOU KINDLE A FIRE TO CONSUME THEM WITHAL   750 24
PERHAPS ONE COULD STEP ACROSS   763 24
THE SMOOTHED-FACED FAT-HAMMED FUNGUSSY FAT ONE   765 24
AS ONE DYING WITH THE CHARRED RAGS FALLING AWAY   769 13
THERE IS I BELIEVE SCARCELY ONE INTELLIGENT AMERICAN WHO 775 12
HE IS THE ONE THING THAT IS ABORIGINALLY AMERICAN   776 21
TO GIVE THE INDIANS ONE SINGLE THING NOT ONE CENT   778 25
DO ANYTHING BUT DO SOMETHING TO DRAW THIS ONE   780 11
ERECT ONE   781 27
YOU ONLY STARE AT THE SUN WITH THE ONE BROAD EYE OF YOUR 781 29
OLD ONE ERECT ON A BUSH   782 28
INTO THE VERITY OF THE ONLY ONE   784 7
AND IN ONE INSTANT'S PAUSE ARE REVOLVED ROUND AND CHANG+ 784 12
TO BE REVOLVED AND IN ONE INSTANT CHANGED   784 25
SOME ONE WILL KNOCK WHEN THE DOOR IS SHUT   789 5
THEY TURNED NOT AT ALL THEY GLANCED NOT ONE HIS WAY   790 21
SO HE LAUGHED AND ONE HEARD HIM LAUGHING   791 12
THEY ARE SAYING TO ONE ANOTHER LET US MAKE AN END   792 22
ARE DISCUSSING WITH ONE ANOTHER THEY ARE MAKING READY T+ 793 4
THEY GNASH WHEN IT CLOSES AND HATE THE ONE THAT GOT IN + 795 33
AND FAR AT THE CENTRE WITH ONE UNBLINKING EYE THE DRAGO+ 796 21
LO I RELEASE THE DRAGONS THE GREAT WHITE ONE OF THE NOR+ 796 30
EVERY ONE   798 12
BETWEEN NIGHT AND DAY MY SOUL-STAR IN ONE   799 23

ONE
THE NAKED ONE CLIMBED IN   802 12
AND YOU KILL HIM THERE WITH ONE STROKE   808 13
AND ONE GREEN LEAF SPRANG AMONG THE BLACK   809 20
PAST HIM FROM THE ONE TO THE OTHER   810 6
SHOWS ONE BUD MORE   814 3
AND BANK-TELLERS TELL THE ONE TALE THAT IS TOLD   814 9
HIDDEN BLUE WITH THE BLUENESS OF ONE MORE DAY   815 9
WHICH IS BLUE WITH THE BLUENESS OF ONE MORE DAY   815 18
ONE ANOTHER   818 20
ONE ANOTHER   818 22
ONE THING THAT IS BOW-LEGGED   818 25
IS ONE FOOT IN THE LAP OF A WOMAN   819 7
AND ONE IN THE LOINS OF A MAN   819 8
BUT THE ONE THING THAT IS BOW-LEGGED   820 5
BECAUSE ONE FOOT IS THE HEART OF A MAN   820 8
IT WAS WON BY THE ONE ALMIGHTY NULLUS   824 6
AND THEN ONE STEALS   825 11
CALLING ANOTHER ONE   825 13
HOW HIGHLY AWARE WE ARE OF ONE ANOTHER SOCIALLY   829 17
HOW DECENT IS OUR DESIRE TOWARDS ONE ANOTHER SOCIALLY   829 18
THEY MAY EVEN ONE DAY DISCOVER SIMPLE AFFECTION AS A GR+   832 18
THE ONE EYE OF OUR CYCLOPAEAN INSTINCT PUT OUT   833 18
STRANGLING ON ONE ANOTHER LIKE SNAKES   833 28
ONE THING IS CERTAIN WE'VE GOT TO TAKE HANDS OFF LOVE   834 7
IF A MAN LOOKED AT ME FOR ONE MOMENT AS THE SUN DOES   840 2
SO SHE MARRIES ONE OF THESE LITTLE-BOY BRILLIANTS   842 1
MAN IS ONE OF THOSE BEASTS THAT WILL BREED IN A CAGE   843 14
ABOUT ONE OR TWO   845 20
THE ONE THAT WENT TO VINGONE   846 7
SCATTER OVER THE WHITENESS ONE BOY ALONE IN THE CLASSRO+   865 20
SHUFFLING HIS RAGGED BOOTS THERE COMES ONE BOY LATE   866 6
HE HE'S IN PRISON MY FATHER YES SIR ONE AND SIX WITH MY+   866 11
IN ONE SWIFT BOUND TO THE HOUSE-BOAT   868 2
BE ALL YOURSELF ONE BONNY BURNING COAL   873 24
NOT TO REACH ONE TONGUE OF FIRE   874 19
NOT TO UTTER ONE CRY TO HER   874 21
ALOFT BY ONE GREAT BENDING RAFTER DUSTY   876 13
THIS ONE NIGHT YET HE LIETH HERE TO HAND   877 21
AND WE WILL PASS TOGETHER LIKE ONE RED FLAME   879 29
PEAR-BLOSSOM HANGING AND ONE SMALL KNEE   886 7
AND TWO ARF ONE IN SWEET CONNECTION   887 22
US ALL ONE IN LAUGHTER AND TEARS   *893 5
QUIVERING AWAKE WITH ONE IMPULSE OF DESIRE   *893 21
ONE BROKEN THORN-TREE STILL IN THE TWILIGHT STANDS   *896 14
BETWEEN THE RUDDY SCHOOLS SWEEPS ONE BLACK ROOK   *898 10
AND ONE AFTER ANOTHER ROUSES   *898 25
BETWEEN THE RUDDY SCHOOLS SWEEPS ONE BLACK ROOK   *901 19
AND ONE AFTER ANOTHER ROUSES   *902 9
THE GREAT MYSTERIOUS ONE IS SWELLING AND SHAPING THE DR+ *907 24
INTO ONE BUD ON THE STALK OF ETERNITY   *908 3
THE POWER OF THE MELTING FUSING FORCE HEAT LIGHT ALL IN+ *909 14
EVERYTHING GREAT AND MYSTERIOUS IN ONE SWELLING AND SHA+ *909 15
SWELLING MANKIND LIKE ONE BUD TO BRING FORTH THE FRUIT + *909 20
LIKE BETTER NOR ALL YOUR GOOD AN' 'E WAS ONE   *911 14
IS LIKE WHEN TWO WHITE BUTTERFLIES SETTLE IN THE ARMS O+ *913 3
OR AS TWO WHITE BUTTERFLIES SETTLE IN THE CUP OF ONE FL+ *914 4
EXTINCT ONE YELLOW BLOODY SPARK   *932 31
AND BUMP ON ONE ANOTHER AND COME UNTIED   *947 10
ONE OF NATURE'S GENTLEMEN   *947 28
ONE OF HIS BELOVEDS LOOKING RATHER A WRECK   *948 8
BUT UNDERNEATH MAN IS ALONE EACH ONE A ROCK TO HIMSELF   *951 10
FOR ONE SAD CENTURY   *953 16
ALL THE CREATURES THAT CANNOT DIE WHILE ONE HEART HARBO+ *954 5
SLIPS OUT THE SOUL INVISIBLE ONE WRAPPED STILL   *957 8

ONENESS
ARE A BONFIRE OF ONENESS ME FLAME FLUNG LEAPING ROUND Y+   245 24
OF THE WIND AND ITS ONENESS VEERS   253 26
YOU WASH IN ONENESS   335 4
ONENESS   363 15
AND FUSE IN A BROAD HARD FLAME OF MANY MEN IN A ONENESS   440 8
THE ONLY ONENESS IS THE ONENESS OF SANITY   515 23
THE GREAT MOVEMENT OF CENTRALISING INTO ONENESS WILL ST+   611 17
ONENESS MAKES WAR AND THE OBSESSION OF ONENESS   612 7
OF HUMAN ONENESS   635 2
ONENESS AND POISED IMMUNITY   710 4
AND MAKES OUR BARE MANYNESS INTO A ONENESS   *951 9

ONES
WHITE ONES AND BLUE ONES FROM UNDER THE ORCHARD HEDGE   58 9
SWEET DARK PURPLE AND WHITE ONES MIXED FOR A PLEDGE   58 10
OF MAKING A TRIUMPH OF ENVY THE RICH AND SUCCESSFUL ONES   175 10
AND RELEASE US POOR ONES AND RICH ONES LET US BREATHE A+   175 28
TWO WHITE ONES SHARP VINDICATED   210 18
STUMBLING-BLOCKS PAINFUL ONES   288 4
THESE PRECIOUS AND IDEAL ONES   316 34
AND ROUND THE EDGES TWENTY-FIVE LITTLE ONES   355 8
FAWN BEFORE THEM AND LOVE THEM AS IF THEY WERE THE ONES   399 14
PEOPLE IN THEIR THIRTIES AND THE OLDER ONES HAVE GOTTEN   462 19
THE YOUNG ONES COPULATE HATE IT AND WANT TO CRY   485 6
THE OLD ONES WANT TO BE YOUNG AND THEY AREN'T YOUNG   502 23
THE OLD ONES SAY TO THEMSELVES WE ARE NOT GOING TO BE O+   503 1
SLOW CREEPING COLD ONES   511 12
NOW THE OLD ONES RING HOLLOW   564 22
OF THE FOUL ONES FROM MY PICTURES OH PURIFY   581 8
ONES THE SELF-RIGHTEOUS SELF-ABSORBED   616 3
FOR THE DEFECTION OF THE SELF-CENTRED ONES   616 17
ESPECIALLY BIG ONES IS OBSCENE   622 20
THE SMALL ONES EGO-BOUND LITTLE MACHINES RUNNING IN AN   637 5
LEAVE THE OLD ONES FIXED TO THEIR UGLY COGGED SELF-WILL   662 23
THAT'S WHY THE DOGGED RESISTANT OLD ONES DARE NOT DIE   662 26
STONE-BLIND ONES   665 27
THE AFRICAN QUEER ONES AND SCANDINAVIAN QUEER ONES   671 15
THE GREEK BEAUTIFUL ONES THE PHOENICIAN UGLY ONES THE A+   671 16
ONES   671 17
THE SEVEN GREAT ONES WHO MUST ALL SAY YES   702 12
BETWEEN THE TWO GREAT ONES FIRE AND THE WET   705 22

ONES
THE FOUR GREAT ONES THE FOUR ROOTS THE FIRST FOUR   706 4
THE TWO GREAT AND MOVING ONES FIRE AND THE YIELDING WET   706 12
AND THE WATCHERS THE DIVIDERS THOSE SWIFT ONES WITH DAR+   706 17
TO THE SUNDERERS TO THE SWIFT ONES   707 8
THE ONES WITH THE SHARP BLACK WINGS   707 9
THE DIVIDERS THE THUNDERERS THE SWIFT ONES BLIND WITH S+   707 20
MOSTLY THEY ARE THE GREEDY ONES   793 16
WONDERFUL ARE THE MACHINES OF THE GREEDY ONES   793 27
THEY ARE THE CLEVER ONES   794 4
BUT LO YOU INERT ONES I WILL SET THE DRAGONS UPON YOU   796 25
LO IN THE BACK STREETS OF THE AIR DEAD ONES ARE CRAWLIN+   796 29
FALSE FAIR ONES CANNOT SLIP THROUGH   810 5
THE DARK ONES ARE CURIOUSLY PURPLISH LIKE FRESH   827 4
PLUMS THE BLOND ONES ARE GOLD WITH LESS GLISTEN   827 5
AND THE YOUNGER ONES   828 16
THEY AREN'T AFRAID OF LOSING SOMETHING AS THE OLDER ONE+   828 25
AND IT SEEMS TO ME THAT THE YOUNG ONES THOUGH THEY GRUD+   829 1
THEY WAS WILD ONES WHITE AND BLUE I COULD TELL   *910 17
RED ONES A BLOODY-WHITE FLAG OVER YOU   *940 28
OH BAVARIAN GENTIANS TALL ONES   *954 18
AND ALL THE DARK GREAT ONES OF THE UNDERWORLD   *955 17

ONESELF
IT IS THE MAJOR PART OF BEING THIS HAVING SURPASSED ONE+   266 20
AND MERGING ONESELF   337 5
AND FEELING ONESELF UNINTERRUPTED IN THE ROOTED CONNECT+   610 6
INTO THE UNKNOWN AND TAKE ROOTS BY ONESELF   610 18
THE FREEING ONESELF   620 19
WHY NOT STAY OUT AND LEARN TO CONTAIN ONESELF   839 22

ONE'S
HOW CAN ONE SPEAK WHERE THERE IS A DUMBNESS ON ONE'S MO+   266 10
BATS AND AN UNEASY CREEPING IN ONE'S SCALP   341 21
AND CATCH FLESH LIKE THE NIGHT IN ONE'S ARMS   428 5
IS TO BE ALONE TO POSSESS ONE'S SOUL IN SILENCE   601 3
TO BE ALONE IS ONE OF LIFE'S GREATEST DELIGHTS THINKING+   610 3
AND ONE TRAPPED ONE'S FINGERS IN THEIR BRASSY POLISHED   644 13
TO ONE'S OWN SELF AND FIND AN EXIT   716 23

ONLY-BEGOTTEN
AND IS THE SUN YOUR FIRST-BORN ONLY-BEGOTTEN   782 33

ONRUSH
DRUM AND THE TURKEY ONRUSH   371 9
AND DISDAIN AND BLANKNESS AND ONRUSH AND PRISE OPEN THE   371 30

ON'T
BUT WE MAUN MA'E THE BEST ON'T SO NOW ROUSE UP AN' LOOK+   83 14
BUT WE MAUN MA'E THE BEST ON'T I'LL REAR THY CHILDT IF + *925 18

ONWARD
AND LIKE A LAUGHTER LEADS ME ONWARD HEAVING   66 1
BEFORE ONWARD THE STRANGE ROAD GOES   163 12
LAND AS ONWARD THE LONG ROAD GOES   163 20
ONWARD WHEREVER THE STRANGE ROAD GOES   163 28
THROUGH EVER ONWARD NIGHT PUSHING   862 29
SINCE GOD SWEEPS ONWARD DIM AND VAST   *915 13

ONWARDS
ONWARDS WHERE SHE CANNOT GO   132 25
THAT IS PART OF THE MYSTERY OF SEX IT IS A FLOW ONWARDS   449 4
IS A FOOTSTEP ONWARDS ONWARDS WE KNOW NOT WHITHER   713 13
BUT A STEP ONWARDS IN UNTRAVELLED SPACE   713 15
ONWARDS WE KNOW NOT WHITHER   713 18
BUT ONWARDS ONWARDS FOR THE HEAVENS ARE WANDERING   713 19

ONY
PALS WORSE N'R ONY NAME AS YOU COULD CALL   *911 12

ONYX
HER TAWNY EYES ARE ONYX OF THOUGHTLESSNESS   127 21

ON'Y
THEY ON'Y TOWD ME IT WOR BAD   45 11
EH MEN DOESNA HA'E BOSOMS 'APPEN NOT ON'Y THA KNOWS   540 16

OORAY
I ROSE UP IN THE WORLD OORAY   551 25

'OORAY
AND YOU CRIED 'OORAY PLAY UP JOHN THOMAS   550 27

OOZE
INTO OOZE AND THE SOMBRE DIRT SPOUTS UP AT MY HANDS   167 6
THAT CHURN THE FRANKINCENSE AND OOZE THE MYRRH   298 5

OOZES
THE NIGHT-STOCK OOZES SCENT   41 24
OOZES AWAY FROM ME AS A SACRIFICE STEAM   131 9

OOZING
SMASHED ALL OOZING WITH BLOOD AND BURNED IN HEAPS   258 3
ALREADY OUR SOULS ARE OOZING THROUGH THE EXIT   718 4

OOZY
ALIVE WITHIN THE OOZY UNDER-MIRE   89 19

OPAQUE
BUT OPAQUE AND NULL IN THE FLESH   111 29
I SAY UNTARNISHED BUT I MEAN OPAQUE   298 22
BUT OPAQUE AND DULL IN THE FLESH   *927 17
BUT OPAQUE AND DULL IN THE FLESH   *928 17

OPEN
    AND READY TO OPEN IN BROWN SURPRISE   43 15
    WATCHING THE DOOR OPEN HE FLASHES BARE   43 19
    PATENT AND OPEN BENEATH MY EYE   59 27
    AND OPEN LIPS DISTRESSED   62 17
    CREEP UP THE WALL TO ME AND IN AT MY OPEN WINDOW   62 28
    IN THE OPEN DEPTHS OF EACH FLOWER DARK RESTLESS DROPS   76 2
    THE OPEN BOOK OF LANDSCAPE NO MORE FOR THE COVERS OF DA+   88 8
    OF THE NIGHTLY HEAVENS OVERHEAD LIKE AN IMMENSE OPEN EYE   97 14
    LIE DOWN AND OPEN TO ME   114 10
    OPEN THE CORE OF GLOAMING TASTE   114 15
    WILL YOU OPEN THE AMOROUS ACHING BUD   117 22
    ONCE HIS FACE WAS OPEN LIKE THE SKY   119 24
    OPEN LIKE THE SKY LOOKING DOWN IN ALL ITS LAUGHTER   119 25
    ENJOYS THE OPEN BLOSSOMS AS THEY STRAW   129 17
    OPEN AND A GREAT GREY DAWN SWIRLS OVER MY FEET BEFORE   147 9
    WE ARE OUT ON THE OPEN ROAD   163 9
    THROUGH THE OPEN YARD-WAY CAN I NOT GO PAST THE SHEDS   173 10
    OF OPEN HANDS   179 15
    AT THE OPEN DOOR OF THE ROOM I STAND AND LOOK AT THE NI+   179 20
    WHY DON'T THEY OPEN WITH VISION AND SPEAK TO ME WHAT HA+   180 21
    THE STARS THAT OPEN AND SHUT   194 4
    SHE GAVE ON THE OPEN HEATHER   202 13
    ALONE ON THE OPEN ROAD AGAIN   228 9
    AH YES YOUR OPEN ARMS AH YES AH YES   230 20
    AH THROUGH THE OPEN DOOR   244 1
    WERE OPEN TO ME IN THE WISDOM AND GOODNESS OF MAN   264 5
    FOR ALL THAT THE SETTING SUNS ARE OPEN   278 24
    THE END CRACKS OPEN WITH THE BEGINNING   278 25
    AND OPEN IT SO THAT IT IS A GLITTERING ROSY MOIST HONIE+   282 3
    LIKE A WOUND THE EXPOSURE OF HER SECRET ON THE OPEN DAY   283 32
    SOBERNESS SOBRIETY WITH HEAVY EYES PROPPED OPEN   287 4
    SHALL I COME TO YOU THE OPEN TOMB OF MY RACE   289 27
    OPEN   307 10
    FIVE TIMES WIDE OPEN   307 12
    SIX TIMES WIDE OPEN   307 13
    HALF-YAWNING AT THE OPEN INEXPERIENCED   311 7
    THE OPEN FURNACE-DOORS OF HIS NOSTRILS   326 22
    MOUTH-GATE OPEN   336 9
    TO OPEN YOUR TINY BEAK-MOUTH THAT LOOKS AS IF IT WOULD   352 9
    NEVER OPEN   352 10
    AND DISDAIN AND BLANKNESS AND ONRUSH AND PRISE OPEN THE   371 30
    IN THE OPEN FIELD   382 31
    ALL HER GREAT HAIRY-SHAGGY BELLY OPEN AGAINST THE MORNI+   385 30
    OUT INTO THE OPEN WHERE THE PATH RUNS ON THE TOP OF A   387 4
    THEY GO OUT TOWARDS THE OPEN   402 9
    OPEN YOUR HALF-DEAD EYES   456 14
    IF WE DO NOT RAPIDLY OPEN ALL THE DOORS OF CONSCIOUSNESS   515 3
    AND HOW DELICIOUS TO OPEN LIKE A MARIGOLD   526 2
    WITH SUN IN HIS FACE SO THAT A WOMAN CANNOT BUT OPEN   526 4
    IS A LITTLE TOO OPEN FOR ME   554 22
    AND OPEN OUR CONSCIOUSNESS TO THE DEEP MYSTERIOUS LIFE   666 13
    DID YOU EVER OPEN THE BOOK   668 25
    DO OPEN THE BOOK AND LOOK   669 3
    THEY ARE OPEN TO THE RESTLESS SKIES AND STREAMS FLOW IN+   675 10
    WHILE NOTHING COMES FROM THE OPEN HEAVEN FROM EARTH FRO+   675 20
    AND DREAMING WITH STRANGE WHALE EYES WIDE OPEN IN THE W+   694 31
    NOW LADY OF THE MOON NOW OPEN THE GATE OF YOUR SILVERY +   696 1
    IS HALF OPEN   702 16
    THEN WHEN THE DOOR IS HALF OPEN   702 18
    OPEN THE RANKS AND LET THEM IN OUR HEARTS   736 16
    MUST WE OPEN THE DOORS AND ADMIT THEM RECEIVE THEM HOME   740 13
    HOME AT LAST IN THE OPEN AGAIN AND UNHOUSELED   770 8
    MALINTZI OF THE GREEN DRESS WILL OPEN THE DOOR   809 10
    THE FIERCE BLACK EYES ARE CLOSED THEY WILL OPEN NO MORE   859 17
    MY CHEST GAPES OPEN SOMETIMES   869 1
    TEARS OPEN   869 10
    OF YOUR EYES DRAWS OPEN MY SHELTERING FLIMSY DOORS   875 14
    SO TINY WHEN YOU OPEN SKY-DOORS ON ME   876 2
    AND WELL I KNOW TO OPEN SILENTLY   878 2
    TO OPEN ERE THE THIEF HAVE DONE HIS WORK   878 29
    AND I OPEN MY LIPS TO TAKE A STRAND OF KEEN HAIR   883 15
    TO OPEN MY BLOSSOM-FULL BREAST FROM ITS DREARY BANDS   *896 24
    IN THE OPEN DEPTHS OF EACH FLOWER DARK RESTLESS DROPS   *897 29
    IN THE OPEN DEPTHS OF EACH FLOWER DARK RESTLESS DROPS   *901 6
    BESIDE THE OPEN GROUND   *911 7
    ARE OPEN FOR THEM THEY ARE MOPING OR THEY BREAK WITH LI+   *918 7
    INTO DARKNESS OPEN AND EAGER FOR THE THRUST OF THE   *937 20
    AND THE DOOR IS OPEN   *955 5
    AND THE WAY IS OPEN   *955 9

OPEN-COUNTENANCED
    THE OPEN-COUNTENANCED SKYWARD-SMILING ROSE   285 9

OPENED
    HAS OPENED THE WINGS OF THE WILD YOUNG SPRITE   46 14
    I HAVE OPENED THE WINDOWS TO WARM MY HANDS ON THE SILL   52 12
    OF OUR EARLY LOVE THAT HARDLY HAS OPENED YET   58 11
    MEET MINE I OPENED HER HELPLESS EYES TO CONSULT   125 27
    AND OPENED UNDER HIS THRALL   127 4
    THE TOWN HAS OPENED TO THE SUN   166 16
    SHE OPENED HER EYES AND GREEN   216 16
    HAVE OPENED UP FOR US TO KNOW TO SATISFY   263 23
    BUT OPENED AROUND HER PURPLE ANEMONES   308 12
    AND IN THE MORNING WHEN THE BEDROOM DOOR IS OPENED   397 1
    HAS OPENED HIS EYES AFRESH   459 26
    AND WHEN THE DOORS WERE OPENED   778 33
    THEY STRUGGLE AT THE GATE YOU HAVE OPENED   795 32
    WITH HEAD THROWN BACK AND PARTLY OPENED MOUTH   878 21
    HE OPENED THE VALVES OF LIFE AND HIS LIFE SIGHED OUT   885 9
    I HAVE OPENED THE WINDOW TO WARM MY HANDS ON THE SILL   *905 1
    TO MINE I OPENED HER HELPLESS EYES TO CONSULT   *936 26

OPEN-HEARTED
    OPEN-HEARTED CYLIX   305 14

OPENING
    BUT SOMETIMES THE OPENING PETALS ARE FIRE AND THE SCARL+   93 31
    NEW SPARKS OF WONDER OPENING IN SURPRISE   136 16
    THE MUD-WEED OPENING TWO PALE SHADOWLESS STARS   145 3
    HELL OPENING   308 18
    OPENING YOUR IMPERVIOUS MOUTH   353 4
    OPENING HER RATHER PRETTY WEDGE OF AN IRON PRISTINE FACE   359 2
    OPENING ITS CLENCHED FACE FROM HIS OUTSTRETCHED NECK   365 9
    OPENING GREAT WINGS IN THE FACE OF THE SHEEP-FACED EWE   414 25
    HAS COME LIKE A THREAD LIKE A DOOR JUST OPENING   702 14
    OPENING TILL THE ROUND WHITE DOORWAY OF DELIGHT   702 15

OPENLY
    OPENLY PLEDGING HEAVEN   283 7
    THE BOLSHEVIST GETS OPENLY MORE IMPUDENT ALSO KNOWING H+   663 22

OPENS
    WHAT SUDDEN EXPECTATION OPENS YOU   126 29
    BUT WHEN THE APPLE-BLOSSOM OPENS WIDE   129 11
    OPENS MY EYES TILL THE ROOTS OF MY VISION SEEM TORN   173 4
    AT THE SAME TIME IT OPENS THE TINY HANDS OF THE HAZEL   272 20
    INSTEAD OF A FLOWER THAT DIES AND OPENS A DIFFERENT BUD   662 6
    THE DOOR EVEN WHEN IT OPENS   721 10
    WHO OPENS HIS FLAME LIKE A TENT-FLAP   812 15
    WHICH OPENS EARTH AND HEAVEN TO LOVE'S FUGITIVE GLOWING   854 14
    AND MY OWN BREAST OPENS IN QUICK RESPONSE   883 6
    NOW AT LAST THE CLOSED CALYX OPENS FROM OUR TIRED EYES   *916 13

OPERATION
    EDITOR BY SURGICAL OPERATION DID YOUR PARENTS HAVE YOU   582 16

'OPE
    I DO 'OPE AS IT'S NOT VERY BAD   45 21

OPINE
    FOR YOUR WRATH AND YES I OPINE   168 18

OPINION
    SEE IF I DON'T BRING YOU DOWN AND ALL YOUR HIGH OPINION   289 11
    PA HAS SUCH A POOR OPINION OF HIMSELF   773 28

OPINIONS
    DON'T EARN GOLDEN OPINIONS OPINIONS GOLDEN   458 26
    OPINIONS IDEAS AND SO FORTH   830 12

OPPORTUNITY
    SCUFFING BESIDE HER BENDING DOWN CATCHING HIS OPPORTUNI+   360 19
    EQUAL OPPORTUNITY   519 30

OPPOSING
    THEY ARE AFRAID WITH HORRIBLE AND OPPOSING FEARS   516 21

OPPOSITE
    AND FROM THE DARKNESS OF THAT OPPOSITE ONE   370 20
    OF THE OPPOSITE ENEMY GOAT   381 27
    THE STAND UPON THE GRASS BELOW AND OPPOSITE   387 24
    AND NEAR ACROSS AT THE OPPOSITE STEEP OF SNOW GREEN TRE+   402 25
    IN THE OPPOSITE HALF-TRUTH   663 12
    OPPOSITE WAYS ROUND THE CIRCLE   764 13
    I WENT THE OPPOSITE WAY ROUND THE CIRCLE   764 23
    OF THE CREEPER ON THE BREAST OF THE HOUSE OPPOSITE   883 2
    AND THE MOON STOOD OPPOSITE   883 22
    WITH THE DARKNESS OPPOSITE   883 25

OPPOSITES
    ALL THINGS WOULD PASS AWAY FOR IN THE TENSION OF OPPOSI+   348 4

OPPOSITION
    IN THE ETERNAL OPPOSITION   705 21

OPPRESSED
    ALL DAY THE CLINK OF THE HAMMERS HAS OPPRESSED   *896 18

OPPRESSES
    OPPRESSES ME SO I CAN HARDLY BEAR   116 26
    OPPRESSES ME I CAN SCARCELY BEAR   *930 25

OPTIMIST
    THE OPTIMIST BUILDS HIMSELF SAFE INSIDE A CELL   515 7

OPTIMISTS
    BECAUSE THEY WERE SUCH BASE AND SORDID OPTIMISTS   627 26

OPTION
    YOUNG GENTS YOU'VE GOT NO OPTION   458 2
    YOU'VE GOT NO OPTION   458 8
    YOU'VE GOT NO OPTION   458 13

ORANGE
    OBSCURES THE DARK WOOD AND THE DULL ORANGE SKY   85 10
    COCK-CRESTED CROWING YOUR ORANGE SCARLET LIKE A TOCSIN   314 28
    RUDDY ROSY AND ORANGE   766 27
    WHICH TREADS OUT THE GLOW OF FUGITIVE ORANGE LIGHT   858 11
    EVE ALONE UNSATISFIED AMONG THE ORANGE AND GUAVA TREES   864 1

ORANGE-TREES
    OVER THE FOUNTAINS AND THE ORANGE-TREES   758 2

ORATOR
    LIKE SPATTERING SHOUTS OF AN ORATOR ENDLESSLY DROPPING   54 6

ORB
    IS THE ORB OF DAY   253 17
    IS DEAD TOO A DEAD ORB WHEELED ONCE A MONTH ROUND THE P+   702 27

ORBIT
    ON ITS PROWLING ORBIT   120 26
    SINCE YOU ARE CONFINED IN THE ORBIT OF ME   236 12
    IS NOT EVEN THE BEAUTY AND PEACE OF AN ORBIT   236 14
    EACH OF US TO THE BALANCED ETERNAL ORBIT   236 18

ORCHARD
    YOU SHOULD BE OUT BY THE ORCHARD WHERE VIOLETS SECRETLY+   57 17
    WHITE ONES AND BLUE ONES FROM UNDER THE ORCHARD HEDGE   58 9
    O THE GREEN GLIMMER OF APPLES IN THE ORCHARD   119 7
    ON THE LITTLE BANK BELOW THE ORCHARD   886 22
    OH THE GREEN GLIMMER OF APPLES IN THE ORCHARD   *932 16

ORCHID-LIKE
    TO BRING BACK THE RARE AND ORCHID-LIKE   297 28

ORDER
    YOU MUST KNOW SEX IN ORDER TO SAVE IT YOUR DEEPEST SELF   465 3
    MEN SHOULD GROUP THEMSELVES INTO A NEW ORDER   525 10
    AND SHE'LL AVOID IT SHE'LL GO AND ORDER   583 14
    ORDER YOU DESTROY THE WHOLE VILE PACK   633 29
    FOR WE CAN'T LOVE ANYBODY NEIGHBOUR OR NO NEIGHBOUR TO +   654 8
    A NICE ONE I LIKE IT HE'LL THINK IT'S A TALL ORDER   733 29

ORDINARY
    THE SIGHT OF AN ORDINARY TOM WOULDN'T SEND THEM INTO   581 24
    WHEREAS TO THE ORDINARY MORAL HUMAN BEING THE WORD   837 3
    THAN HE WILL NOTE THE OTHER ORDINARY WOMEN   877 18

ORE
    THREADS AND THRILLS LIKE ORE THAT IS WEALTH TO THE EYE   146 31

ORGAN
    BEAN WAS ONE OF THE OLDEST SYMBOLS OF THE MALE ORGAN FO+   303 19

ORGANIC
    THERE IS THE ORGANIC CONNECTION LIKE LEAVES THAT BELONG+   615 1
    BUT PEOPLE WHO ARE FALLEN FROM THE ORGANIC CONNECTION W+   615 17

ORGANISING
    WONDERMENT ORGANISING ITSELF HERALDING ITSELF WITH THE +   274 5

ORGANISM
    I EXIST AS AN ORGANISM   510 3

ORGASM
    A KISS AND A SPASM OF FAREWELL A MOMENT'S ORGASM OF   280 27
    YOU WHO NEVER RECOVER FROM OUT OF THE ORGASM OF LOVING   290 12
    ORGASM AFTER ORGASM AFTER ORGASM   382 28
    SOFTLY FLUTTERING THE SENSES IN THE EXQUISITE ORGASM OF   481 24
    NOR A DOSE OF CAPSICUM ESSENCE GIVING AN ORGASM   837 9

ORGASMS
    DURING THE WILD ORGASMS OF CHAOS   477 3
    AND WHEN THROUGHOUT ALL THE WILD ORGASMS OF LOVE   477 12

ORGIES
    HAVE I PROFANED SOME FEMALE MYSTERY ORGIES   141 3

ORIENTATES
    AUDILE TACTILE SENSITIVENESS AS OF A TENDRIL WHICH ORIE+   285 26

ORIENT LINE
    OF THE P AND O AND THE ORIENT LINE AND ALL THE OTHER ST+   688 7

ORIFICE
    AND BUT ONE ORIFICE   282 24

ORIFICES
    THAT BLOWS UPON IT THROUGH THE ORIFICES   717 9

ORIGINAL
    AND IN THE ORIGINAL DARK THE ROOTS CANNOT KEEP CANNOT K+   92 17
    ORIGINAL WOLF-WRAPPED   171 6

ORIGINALLY
    HE IS THE LAST OF THE ORIGINALLY AMERICAN RACE   776 34

ORION
    I SEE THE GREAT ORION STANDING   198 19

ORMIN'
    AS SULKY AN' ORMIN' AS THINE HAST OWT TO SAY OTHERWISE   *925 25

ORNAMENTS
    NAKED DARK MEN WITH ORNAMENTS ON ON THEIR NAKED ARMS   389 7

ORPHEUS
    ORPHEUS AND THE WINDING LEAF-CLOGGED SILENT LANES OF HE+   281 16

ORPHIC
    ORPHIC DELICATE   280 25
    ORPHIC FAREWELL AND FAREWELL AND FAREWELL   281 27

ORTHODOX
    ORTHODOX MICHAEL AND THAT WHISPERING GABRIEL   614 7
    HE ONLY FELL OUT OF YOUR KEN YOU ORTHODOX ANGELS   614 15

ORTS
    I'M NOT 'AVIN' YOUR ORTS AN' SLARTS   82 3
    JUST ORTS AND SLARTS BERRIES THAT SMOULDER IN THE BUSH   219 15
    I'M NOT HAVIN' YOUR ORTS AN' SLARTS   *924 7

OSIRIS
    POOR LITTLE EARTHY HOUSE-INHABITING OSIRIS   361 10
    AND FOR THE MOMENT SHE WAS ISIS GLEAMING HAVING FOUND H+   672 24

OSIRIS-CRY
    THE SAME CRY FROM THE TORTOISE AS FROM CHRIST THE OSIRI+   367 3

OSTENTATION
    DAY WEARIES ME WITH ITS OSTENTATION AND FAWNINGS   193 19
    PERHAPS IT IS YOUR ASSERTION IN ALL THIS OSTENTATION OF+   369 27

OTCHEL
    A GLUM OLD OTCHEL WI' LONG   77 22
    A TOUGH OLD OTCHEL WI' LONG   *919 10

OTHERS
    AN' OTHERS 'AS REAMS   45 24
    AND ONLY IN HARMONY WITH OTHERS THE SINGLE SOUL CAN BE +   93 10
    NOT FREE MYSELF FROM THE PAST THOSE OTHERS   204 7
    WERE POLITICS BUT OTHERS SAY IT WAS A FOOD-TABOO OTHERS+   303 18
    THEY HATE HAPPINESS IN OTHERS   500 14
    ALONG WITH THE OTHERS WHAT LUCK   669 6
    AND THE FIVE OTHERS THE TRAVELLERS   703 1
    BUT OTHERS THE DARK DOORS OH HUSH HUSH   711 9

OTHER'S
    HOW AWFULLY DISTINCT AND FAR OFF FROM EACH OTHER'S BEING   248 3
    IN A LONG LINE THEIR HEADS LAID OVER EACH OTHER'S NECKS   445 20
    TEARING EACH OTHER'S FEELINGS TRAMPLING EACH OTHER'S TE+   544 16
    LOOK INTO EACH OTHER'S EYES WITH KNOWLEDGE   770 30

OTHERWISE
    AND THE MILLS OF GOD GRIND OTHERWISE WITH THE WINDS OF   441 12
    MY BODY LIKES ITS DINNER AND THE WARM SUN BUT OTHERWISE+   501 19
    IT MUST BE SO OTHERWISE   581 23
    AS SULKY AN' ORMIN' AS THINE HAST OWT TO SAY OTHERWISE   *925 25

OTHERWORLD
    DOWN THE TENDRILLED AVENUES OF WINE AND THE OTHERWORLD   287 10
    I CAN IMAGINE IN SOME OTHERWORLD   372 5

OTTER
    DID YOU EVER SEE AN OTTER   409 2

OTTER'S
    PAST THE OTTER'S WHISKERS   409 19

OUBLIETTE
    OUT OF THIS OUBLIETTE BETWEEN THE MOUNTAINS   224 8
    WHY DO I CRAWL ABOUT THIS POT THIS OUBLIETTE   224 17

OUGHT
    I OUGHT TO BE PROUD THAT SHE SHOULD ASK IT   152 4
    WHERE WE OUGHT TO BE   161 14
    AS THEY OUGHT TO HAVE THEY RISE ABOVE US   223 25
    I SEE RIGHT WELL HOW I OUGHT TO BE GRATEFUL   234 11
    THERE WAS SOMETHING I OUGHT TO REMEMBER AND YET   243 26
    WE OUGHT TO LOOK THE OTHER WAY   363 22
    THAT IT ALWAYS HAS TO BEGIN WITH AND BY WHICH YOU OUGHT   464 21
    THE FEELINGS PEOPLE OUGHT TO HAVE THEY NEVER HAVE   501 11
    IT OUGHT TO BE LOVELY TO BE OLD   503 14
    WHAT WE OUGHT TO DO   506 1
    THEY OUGHT AT LAST TO SEE THROUGH THE GAME   559 23
    IT OUGHT ALL TO BE JOCK'S AND MINE   573 14
    WHEN I SAY HE OUGHT TO MARRY ME AND SMALL   733 30

OUGHTER
    IF SHE DIDN'T SHE OUGHTER   564 29

OURS
    AND EVERY FLASH OF THOUGHT THAT WE AND OURS   89 4
    AND THE PLACE IS NO LONGER OURS WATCHING I HEAR   173 2
    OURS IS THE UNIVERSE OF THE UNFOLDED ROSE   205 12
    TO DROWN THEIR INNER CACOPHONY AND OURS   656 7
    OF OURS   667 20
    FROM THIS LOVE OF OURS   888 4
    OURS EVEN NOW   *917 1

OURSELF
    WHEREIN WE KNOW OURSELF FOR WHAT WE ARE   621 6

OURSELVES
    WHITE EARTH AND RUINS OURSELVES AND NOTHING BESIDE   166 8
    NAY WE FIND OURSELVES CROSSING THE FERN-SCENTED FRONTIE+   286 24
    WHY WERE WE NOT LEFT ROUNDED OFF AND FINISHED IN OURSEL+   364 8
    FOR IF CEREBRALLY WE FORCE OURSELVES INTO TOUCH   468 17
    WE VIOLATE OURSELVES   468 20
    KEEP OURSELVES SEPARATE PHYSICALLY   470 16
    AND THEN PERHAPS WE SHALL KNOW TRUE SEX IN OURSELVES   472 13
    LET US LOSE SIGHT OF OURSELVES AND BREAK THE MIRRORS   477 27
    SO THAT WE DON'T KNOW OURSELVES   482 21
    FOR WE'RE ALL SELF-CONSCIOUSLY AWARE OF OURSELVES   496 19
    YET NOT SUFFICIENTLY CONSCIOUS TO BE ABLE TO FORGET OUR+   496 20
    AND BE WHIMSICALLY AT HOME IN OURSELVES   496 21
    ONLY EGOISTICALLY WE ASSERT OURSELVES   513 6
    IS TO CONTAIN OURSELVES   513 24
    TO KEEP STILL AND LET THE WRECKAGE OF OURSELVES GO   514 1
    WE CALL SANITY IN OURSELVES   515 22
    WHY SHOULD WE BRACE OURSELVES UP WITH MEAN EMULATION   520 5
    IF WE BRACE OURSELVES UP IT SHOULD BE FOR SOMETHING WE   520 6
    OR WE MUST SEE MEN DIE AND THEN DIE OURSELVES   522 31
    EVEN OURSELVES   525 26
    RUNNING AFTER A FIGMENT OF OURSELVES   543 17
    HITTING OURSELVES AGAINST UNSEEN ROCK CRASHING OUR HEAD   544 13
    OR SEE OURSELVES AS WE ARE AND GO MAD   585 2
    THE GODS ARE ONLY OURSELVES AS WE ARE IN OUR   673 17
    NOW WE HAVE TO ADMIT WE CAN'T KNOW OURSELVES WE CAN ONL+   674 11
    ABOUT OURSELVES   674 12
    AND ESSAY TO DISOWN OURSELVES AND THEN WHEN THE LIGHT   748 10
    WE SHALL GO ON FINDING OUT ABOUT OURSELVES   832 24
    NOT TO WANT TO BULLY THOSE WEAKER THAN OURSELVES   833 5
    AND HURT HURT OURSELVES AND EVERYBODY   833 20

OURSELVES
    MEANWHILE WE BITE OURSELVES AND EVERYONE NEAR US   833 30
    TO LEARN TO CONTAIN OURSELVES   839 2
    WE VIOLATE OURSELVES EVERY MOMENT AND VIOLATE EVERYBODY+   839 6
    LET US CONTAIN OURSELVES   839 15
    WHEN WE HAVE TRUSTED OURSELVES ENTIRELY   *960 23

'OUSE
    THERE'S ONE THING WE S'LL 'AVE A PEACEFUL 'OUSE   45 29

OUSTED
    OH PITY THE DEAD THAT WERE OUSTED OUT OF LIFE   722 4
    PITY OH PITY THE POOR DEAD THAT ARE ONLY OUSTED FROM LI+   *958 8

OUTCAST
    BUT MUST ROAM LIKE OUTCAST DOGS ON THE MARGINS OF LIFE   722 11
    BUT MUST ROAM LIKE OUTCAST DOGS ON THE MARGINS OF LIFE   *958 16

OUTCASTS
    SLEEP IN A ROW THE OUTCASTS   144 15
    OUTCASTS KEEP GUARD   146 24

OUTCOMING
    THEY FALL UPON THE NEW OUTCOMING SOULS WITH RAGE   *958 5

OUTER
    ON THE OUTER PAVEMENT SLOWLY   146 17
    UPON THE OUTER AIR   784 10
    THE SUN IS IN THE OUTER PORCH CRY TO HIM THANKS OH THAN+   803 21

OUTERWARDS
    FISH IN THE OUTERWARDS   338 30

OUTFIT
    WITH A MARVELLOUS OUTFIT HOW DID ARCHIE SEE   489 27

OUTFLUNG
    AT LAST INTO BLOSSOM OF BEING EACH ONE HIS OWN FLOWER O+   93 15

OUTGOINGS
    GREAT SEALS UPON YOUR OUTGOINGS AND WOVEN   154 24
    DARKEST OUTGOINGS   267 7

OUT-LANDER
    OH OUT-LANDER WEARY SOUL   757 2

OUTLAST
    AND THE KINGCUPS' GLISTEN THAT SHALL LONG OUTLAST YOU   90 12

OUTLINE
    ENTERING SHE SAW HIM IN OUTLINE RAISED ON A PYRE   155 17
    DELICATE FRAIL CRESCENT OF THE GENTLE OUTLINE OF WHITE   371 13

OUT-MOSQUITO
    AM I NOT MOSQUITO ENOUGH TO OUT-MOSQUITO YOU   334 15

OUTRAGE
    IN VIRGIN OUTRAGE AS THEY VIEWED   680 18

OUTREACH
    THE UPRIGHT IS TEMPORAL IS EFFORT OUTREACH   827 15

OUTREACHING
    OF YELLOW-RED OUTREACHING LIVING WRATH   317 9

OUT-REACHING
    MOUNTED AND TENSE SPREAD-EAGLE OUT-REACHING OUT OF THE   364 30

OUTRIGHT
    BLOSSOMED OUTRIGHT   165 24

OUTSIDE
    OUTSIDE THE HOUSE AN ASH-TREE HUNG ITS TERRIBLE WHIPS   36 9
    HAS DRAWN MY SPIRIT OUTSIDE   107 26
    AND IF THE DAY OUTSIDE WERE MINE WHAT IS THE DAY   112 24
    LARGE SHADOWS FROM THE OUTSIDE STREET-LAMP BLOWN   140 14
    SUDDEN OUTSIDE THE HIGH WINDOW ONE CROW   147 21
    TO THE OLD SUNDAY EVENINGS AT HOME WITH WINTER OUTSIDE   148 12
    AS SHE LISTENED IN SILENCE OUTSIDE THE SILENT DOOR   155 16
    SO MUCH THERE IS OUTSIDE ME SO INFINITELY   223 7
    AND THE VILLAGE FOLK OUTSIDE IN THE BURYING-GROUND   233 2
    GO DOWN THE ROAD OUTSIDE THE HOUSE   235 23
    OUTSIDE THE DOOR   245 4
    THAT LIES OUTSIDE THE MONSTROUS WOMB   262 23
    WHEN SHE IS SLAIN AGAINST ME AND LIES IN A HEAP LIKE ON+   267 13
    WHO MADE SO LITTLE NOISE OUTSIDE THE CYPRESS GROVES   296 16
    HIS GOD STANDS OUTSIDE MY GOD   339 14
    THE OUTSIDE WILL SEEM BROWN   344 27
    THE OUTSIDE DID NOT SEEM BROWN   344 29
    DOESN'T HE LOOK THE FRESH CLEAN ENGLISHMAN OUTSIDE   430 21
    OUTSIDE IT WAS THA AND THEE   490 20
    LIVING ON YOUR INCOME IS STROLLING GRANDLY OUTSIDE THE   521 11
    OUTSIDE ALL CLASS   563 18
    AND THOUGH THE POMEGRANATE HAS RED FLOWERS OUTSIDE THE   630 1
    BE ALONE AND SEE THE MOONLIGHT OUTSIDE WHITE AND BUSY   646 10
    AND SOON IT WILL RISE ON THE WORLD ON THE OUTSIDE WORLD   718 16
    AND SO WHEN THE OUTSIDE WORLD CALLS UPON AMERICA TO ACT+   775 29
    MANLY AND TACKLE THE OUTSIDE WORLD   843 3
    CAVES INWARD KNOWING THE OUTSIDE WORLD   843 4
    FOR THE SUN IS POURING LIKE YELLOW WINE OUTSIDE   *894 24
    TO THE OLD SUNDAY EVENINGS WHEN DARKNESS WANDERED OUTSI+   *940 11
    THAT LIE OUTSIDE THE SILVERY WALLS OF OUR BODY'S BUILDE+   *957 17
    ONCE OUTSIDE THE GATE OF THE WALLED SILVERY LIFE OF DAYS   *957 27
    ONCE OUTSIDE UPON THE GREY MARSH BEACHES WHERE LOST SOU+   *957 28
    ONCE OUTSIDE THE GATE   *957 32

OUTSIDER
    OUTSIDER SPRUNG UP FROM SOME HORRIBLE GUTTER   576 9
    YOU'RE A RANK OUTSIDER OF THE FIFTH REMOVE   576 15

OUTSIDERS
    OUTSIDERS   340 1
    THOUGH YOU BLOODY OUTSIDERS HAD BETTER NOT TRY IT ON   618 13

OUTSKIRT
    THEY DWELL IN THE OUTSKIRT FRINGES OF NOWHERE   711 24

OUTSPENT
    THERE'S ONLY LOVE THE REST IS ALL OUTSPENT   736 12

OUT-SPINNING
    THE INNERMOST FIRE OF MY OWN DIM SOUL OUT-SPINNING   218 22

OUTSPREAD
    POLTROON AND BEG THE SILENT OUTSPREAD GOD   195 24
    TINY FINGERS OUTSPREAD   861 21

OUTSTARTS
    HE OUTSTARTS ME   339 22

OUTSTRETCHED
    THE STREET'S LONG OUTSTRETCHED MILKY-WAY   115 24
    SINCE YOU VAST OUTSTRETCHED WORDLESS SLEEP   194 26
    OPENING ITS CLENCHED FACE FROM HIS OUTSTRETCHED NECK   365 9

OUTWAITING
    WONDER OUTWAITING PAIN   504 18

OUTWARD
    THIS TRAIN BEATS ANXIOUSLY OUTWARD BOUND   169 4
    OUTWARD AND VISIBLE INDICATION OF THE PLAN WITHIN   356 11

OUTWARDS
    TO THE FACE THAT GAZES OUTWARDS WATCHING FOR NIGHT TO W+   103 2
    IF MEN ONLY FOUGHT OUTWARDS INTO THE WORLD   538 15

OUTWITTED
    AH CLEVER ODYSSEUS WHO OUTWITTED THE CYCLOP   543 26

OVAL
    GUADALUPE WHOSE FACE IS OVAL   798 8

OVER-ARCHING
    WITH AXE IN HAND AND THE HAMMER AND THE PICK-AXE OVER-A+   174 16

OVERCAME
    OVERCAME ME NOW HIS BACK WAS TURNED   351 8

OVERCAST
    DAZZLE OF MAY-BLOBS WHERE THE MARIGOLD GLARE OVERCAST Y+   90 8

OVER-CHARGED
    IS HE NOT OVER-CHARGED BY THE DAMMED-UP PRESSURE OF HIS+   327 14

OVER-DRIP
    THE OVER-DRIP OF A GREAT PASSION HANGING IN THE BALANCE   370 8

OVER-EQUAL
    EACH IMPERIOUSLY OVER-EQUAL TO EACH EQUALITY OVER-REACH+   300 8

OVER-FILLED
    ARE ON THE BOARD ARE OVER-FILLED   177 6

OVERFLOW
    TILL THE SECRET WATERS OVERFLOW   462 10

OVER-FULL
    IS HE NOT OVER-FULL OF OFFERING A VAST VAST OFFER OF HI+   327 18

OVERGROWN
    DARK OVERGROWN WITH WILLOWS COOL WITH THE BROOK EBBING +   33 16
    DARK OVERGROWN WITH WILLOWS COOL WITH THE BROOK EBBING +   *891 18

OVERHANG
    BEYOND THE LEAVES THAT OVERHANG THE STREET   36 1

OVERHANGS
    OVERHANGS THE STREET WHERE THE BULLOCK-WAGONS SLOWLY   209 16

OVERHEAD
    OF THE NIGHTLY HEAVENS OVERHEAD LIKE AN IMMENSE OPEN EYE   97 14
    OVERHEAD AT HOME AND HAD NOT ONE STAR   103 6
    WATCHING US OVERHEAD   113 20
    NO SOUND OF GUNS NOR OVERHEAD NO RUSHED   165 31
    OVERHEAD IT WILL BE A SQUIRREL MOVING   231 17
    AS THE BATS SWOOP OVERHEAD   341 22
    SUBTLY TO THE TWIGS OVERHEAD FAR UP VAST BEAST   385 27
    AND THIS SUN CEASE SHINING OVERHEAD   815 11
    OVERHEAD THE REDDEST SHE LIFTED HER LONG ARMS AND TRIED   864 9
    WATCHING US OVERHEAD   *929 9

OVERHEATS
    OR IN HELL OVERHEATS THEM   828 12

OVERLAPPING
    OVERLAPPING GUMS   359 21

OVERLEAP
    TO OVERLEAP LIKE A MALE ALL MARES AS OBSTACLES   379 13
    ONLY THOSE ETERNAL FEMALES TO OVERLEAP AND SURPASS AND   382 33

OVERLOOK
   AND WHY SHOULD YOU OVERLOOK THEM IN ME   256 3

OVERLOOKED
   OVERLOOKED   411 20
   THE OVERLOOKED VIRGIN   411 24
   YOU OVERLOOKED HER TOO   411 26
   COME DELICATE OVERLOOKED VIRGIN COME BACK TO ME   411 29

OVERLOOKING
   IN THE FIR-TREE OVERLOOKING THE MARSHES   216 23
   OVERLOOKING THE WORLD FOR HIS OWN   383 25
   IN THE FIR-TREE OVERLOOKING THE MARSHES   *942 9

OVER-PROLIFIC
   AND THOSE OVER-PROLIFIC WHITE MICE AND ADOLPH AND REX   395 9

OVER-REACHING
   EACH IMPERIOUSLY OVER-EQUAL TO EACH EQUALITY OVER-REACH+   300 8

OVER-RIPE
   THE GLOBE OF THE DAY OVER-RIPE   253 24
   TILL IT'S FINISHED AND YOU'RE OVER-RIPE AND YOU BURST T+   283 23
   THE YEAR IS FALLEN OVER-RIPE   284 1
   THE YEAR OF OUR WOMEN IS FALLEN OVER-RIPE   284 3
   THE YEAR OF OUR WOMEN IS FALLEN OVER-RIPE   284 6

OVER-RODE
   AND OVER-RODE HIS MARES AS IF HE WERE SAVAGELY LEAPING +   378 6

OVERSEER
   TO MAKE AN END OF THE MALICE OF THIS OVERSEER   759 11

OVERSEERS
   IN THE FIELDS WITH FOREIGN OVERSEERS   790 11

OVERSEER'S
   EARNING A SALARY IS A PRISON OVERSEER'S JOB   521 9

OVERSET
   OVERSET IN DISDAIN   823 15

OVERSHADOWS
   WHICH OVERSHADOWS THE OTHER   609 26

OVER-SULPHUREOUS
   TO QUENCH THEIR OVER-SULPHUREOUS LUSTS   340 10

OVERTAKE
   CAN I NOT OVERTAKE YOU   334 12

OVERWEENING
   AND THE EYE OVERWEENING INTO MADNESS   371 17
   AND FULL OF MALICE PREPENSE AND OVERWEENING DETERMINED   382 12
   OVERWEENING MEN FULL OF POWER OF LIFE COMMANDING A   414 19
   IT IS THE MIND WHICH IS UNCOUTH AND OVERWEENING   529 9
   WHEN THE DAYTIME CONSCIOUSNESS HAS GOT OVERWEENING   608 21
   OUR OVERWEENING DAYS STRIVE TOO FAR TILL THE HEAT AND I+   858 1

OVERWHELMED
   BUT THEY LET THEMSELVES BE OVERWHELMED BY THOSE THAT ARE   665 18

OVERWHELMINGLY
   RARE ALMOST AS BEAMS YET OVERWHELMINGLY POTENT   271 19

OWED
   AS IF YOU OWED HIM AN OLD OLD GRUDGE GREAT SUN OR AN OLD   374 3

OWER
   I'M FURTHER OWER TH' TOP   78 32
   AN' OWER A' THE THAW AN' MESS   137 22
   I'M FURTHER OWER TH' TOP   *920 24

OWING
   GROW RISING UP OWING TO THE HEAT WHICH IS IN THE EARTH +   295 8

OWL
   OF THE NEW-BORN AND THEN THE OLD OWL THEN THE BATS THAT+   38 11
   A TWO-EYED CLOCK LIKE AN OWL   170 22
   SOMETHING LIKE AN OWL WHOOING   366 13
   THE OWL   496 16
   WHO IS IT THE OWL IS HOOTING   731 5
   AND SOON THE OWL WINGED WITH STILLNESS WILL FLOAT OUT T+   858 16
   OF THE NEW-BORN AND THE UNBORN AND THE OLD OWL AND THE +   *892 26

OWNED
   FIRST LIVE THING I'VE OWNED SINCE THE LOP-EARED RABBITS   395 7

OWNING
   OF HAVING AND GETTING AND OWNING THE STRUGGLE WHICH WRE+   175 23
   HAVE OWNING HUMANITY   395 18
   OWNING MY SUPPLE BODY A RARE GLAD THING SUPREMELY GOOD   *892 11

OWNS
   THE BOURGEOIS ASSERTS THAT HE OWNS HIS PROPERTY BY DIVI+   663 13

OWT
   OWT BAD AN' IT'S HIS   45 28
   THERE'S HARDLY OWT LEFT O' THEE GET UP AN' GO   138 18
   ME WATCHIN' DOST THINK THERE WAS OWT BETWEEN 'EM   *910 23
   AS SULKY AN' ORMIN' AS THINE HAST OWT TO SAY OTHERWISE   *925 25

OWT'LL
   MY GEL OWT'LL DO FOR A MAN I' TH' DARK   77 3
   MY GEL OWT'LL DO FOR A MAN I' THE DARK   *918 21

'OW
   NAY I SAW NOWT BUT TH' COFFIN AN' TH' YELLER CLAY AN' '+   *909 31

OXEN
   SO THERE'S AN OXEN WAGON   227 1
   YES AND IF OXEN OR LIONS HAD HANDS AND COULD PAINT WITH   376 1
   THE FORMS OF THE GODS LIKE HORSES AND OXEN LIKE OXEN AN+   376 3

OXFORD
   THE OXFORD VOICE   433 23
   THE WOULD-BE OXFORD VOICE   433 25
   FOR EVERY BLOOMING BIRD IS AN OXFORD CUCKOO NOWADAYS   434 1

OXYDISED
   OXYDISED SKY-BLUE   369 20

OXYGEN
   WATER IS H2O HYDROGEN TWO PARTS OXYGEN ONE   515 11

OYSTER
   OYSTER   396 34

O'
   COME OUT O' TH' WAY AN' LET ME SEE   45 1
   TER NOTTINGHAM EH DEAR O' ME   45 7
   OUT O' MY WAY CHILDT DEAR O' ME WHEER   45 13
   AS SOME SHOULD HA'E HARDLY A SMITE O' TROUBLE   45 23
   ASIDE O' T' GRAVE AN' TH' COFFIN SET   60 12
   WAITIN' TER BE BURIED OUT O' TH' WET   60 14
   OVER A DOUBLE 'ANDFUL O' VIOLETS A' IN A PACK   61 11
   AN' I COME AWAY ACAUSE O' TH' TEEMIN' RAIN   61 16
   O' WARMTH AS 'E GOT DOWN THEER TH' REST WOR STONE COLD   61 18
   THE MOON SETS FORTH O' NIGHTS   63 30
   A WIDOW O' FORTY-FIVE   77 13
   TO HA' 'TICED A LAD O' TWENTY-FIVE   77 15
   O' TH' P'LICE FORCE WITHOUT FAIL   78 14
   WARMIN' 'IS-SEN AT THE STOOL O' FIRE   79 2
   IN A' THIS DEPTH O' SNOW   79 14
   WAS A'MOST BURSTIN' MAD O' MY-SEN   80 7
   TAKE 'ER I'STEAD O' ME   80 28
   I'LL CHUCK THE FLAMIN' LOT O' YOU   81 11
   TWENTY POUND O' THY OWN THA HAST AN' FIFTY POUND HA'E I   83 1
   AFORE I CAN TA'E THEE I'VE GOT A WIDDER O' FORTY-FIVE T+   83 8
   AN' 'DEED AN' I WISH AS THIS TALE O' THINE WOR NIVER MY+   83 10
   DEED AN' I WISH I C'D 'A' STOOD AT TH' ALTAR WI' THEE A+   83 11
   THEY'LL TURN THEE OUT O' TI' FORCE I DOWOT ME IF THEY D+   83 16
   BUT WHAT O' THAT   83 19
   LET ME GO WHAT'S GOOD O' TALKIN'   84 25
   TALK ABOUT LOVE O' WOMEN   84 27
   WHAT BIT O' CUNT I HAD WI' 'ER   84 29
   AN' MIST IS SUCKIN' AT TH' SPOTS O' SNOW   137 21
   THA WERT FRIT O' SUMMAT   138 9
   YI BUT THA'RT FRIT O' SUMMAT   138 13
   THERE'S HARDLY OWT LEFT O' THEE GET UP AN' GO   138 18
   OR DEAR O' ME SAY SUMMAT   138 19
   THA THOUGHT THA WANTED TER BE RID O' ME   139 1
   O' THY SPUNK AN' THA'RT EMPTY AN' MORTIFIED   139 12
   THA'RT ONE O' TH' MEN AS HAS GOT TO DRAIN   139 16
   WEARY AN' SICK O' THE LIKES O' SHE   139 33
   BUT IT'S MY SORT O' WOMAN   140 2
   SORT O' WOMAN FOR ANY LAD   140 5
   WELL THINK O' THAT NOW THINK O' THAT   489 21
   THEY'RE A' A B-D LOT O' -S   491 1
   AFTER A LOT O' WOMEN   493 14
   A WORSE LOT O' JUJUBEY ASSES   553 15
   I COULD THINK O' NOWT BUT OUR TED AN' 'IM TAKEN   *910 3
   A LOT O' VIOLETS FELL OUT O' 'ER BOSOM ON 'IM DOWN THEER   *910 16
   ASIDE O' TH' GRAVE WHILE TH' COFFIN WOR LYIN' YET   *910 27
   TRYIN' TO KEEP OFF 'N HIM A BIT O' TH' WET   *910 29
   HUDDLIN' CLOSE TOGETHER A CAUSE O' TH' RAIN   *911 2
   LET BE THAT THERE'S SOME O' TH' BAD AS WE   *911 13
   O' TH' SMELL COME WAFTIN' TO ME 'ER PUT 'ER FACE   *911 29
   AN' I COME AWAY BECAUSE O' THE TEEMIN' RAIN   *911 32
   TO HA' 'TICED A LAD O' TWENTY-FIVE   *919 3
   A WIDOW O' FORTY-FIVE   *919 5
   O' TH' P'LICE FORCE WITHOUT FAIL   *920 6
   WARMIN' HIS-SEN AT THE STOOL O' FIRE   *920 26
   IN A' THIS DEPTH O' SNOW   *921 10
   WAS A'MOST BURSTIN' MAD O' MY-SEN   *922 7
   TWENTY POUND O' THY OWN THA HAST AND FIFTY POUND HA'E I   *925 5
   BUT 'DEED AN' I WISH AS THIS TALE O' THINE WOR NIVER MY+   *925 14
   O' THEE   *925 16
   KISS ME THEN THERE NE'ER MIND IF I SCRAIGHT I WOR FOND +   *925 28
   THE FIRST MAN OUT O' THE FOUR THAT'S MOWIN'   *944 5
   NONE O' THE TROUBLE HE'S LED TO STALL   *944 8
   SHOULDER-DEEP OUT O' TH' CORN AND WIPES   *944 11

PA
   PA HAS SUCH A POOR OPINION OF HIMSELF   773 28

PACE
   BEHIND YET KEEPS PACE   162 20
   THAT SOFTLY PACE   268 25
   IN HER UNGAINLY PACE   362 17

PACES
   TRAVELS THE LIGHT AS IT TILTS IN ITS PACES   146 3
   THE BLUE JAY PACES ROUND THE CABIN VERY BUSY PICKING UP   375 23
   TO PUT HIM THROUGH 'IS PACES   493 18

PACIFIED
   AND DEPART PEACEFUL PACIFIED AND THANKLESS   350 11

PACK
OVER A DOUBLE 'ANDFUL O' VIOLETS A' IN A PACK   61 11
MY PACK OF UNRULY HOUNDS I CANNOT START   74   9
SHE'S GOT TO PACK AND GO   573 18
ORDER YOU DESTROY THE WHOLE VILE PACK   633 29
MY PACK OF UNRULY HOUNDS I CANNOT START   *895 17
MY PACK OF UNRULY HOUNDS I CANNOT START   *904   6
OVER A DOUBLE 'ANDFUL OF VIOLETS ALL IN A PACK   *911 27

PACK-ASS
NOW HE'S A JACKASS A PACK-ASS A DONKEY SOMARO BURRO   379   9

PACKED
PACKED IN A LINE WITH THEIR HEADS AGAINST THE WALL   144 16

PACK-SADDLE
JESUS AND A PACK-SADDLE   378 23

PAD
AH STOPPED BEHIND ON T' PAD I' T' POURIN' WET   61   3
WHEN HE LIFTS HIS FOOT I SEE THE PAD OF HIS SOAKED STOC+   866   7
AH STOPPED BEHIND ON T' PAD I' TH' DRIPPIN WET   *911 19

PADDLES
THEIR SPLAY FEET RAMBLING AND ROWING LIKE PADDLES   361 24

PADDY-FIELDS
THROUGH THE PALM-TREES AND PAST HOLLOW PADDY-FIELDS WHE+   386 27
DYKE BETWEEN PADDY-FIELDS   387   5

PADS
MOST OF HIS TIME THE TIGER PADS AND SLOUCHES IN A BURNI+   496 13
BUT I'VE HAD SUCH A JOB MY CRUTCHES I FAIRLY DRAGGED TH+   865 22

PAEAN
AWAY WITH A PAEAN OF DERISION   334 10
A PAEAN   364 17

PAGAN
PAGAN ROSY-MUZZLED VIOLETS   311 31

PAGEANT
THE PAGEANT OF FLOWERY TREES ABOVE   106   7
IN A MEANER PAGEANT FLOWS   106 10

PAGES
OF SEVERAL INSULTS OF BLOTTED PAGES AND SCRAWL   74 14
ITS FIGURED PAGES AND SKY AND EARTH AND ALL BETWEEN ARE+   88 10
OF SEVERAL INSULTS OF BLOTTED PAGES AND SCRAWL   *895 22
OF SEVERAL INSULTS OF BLOTTED PAGES AND SCRAWL   *904 11

PAGODA
IN A SMALL PAGODA ON THE TEMPLE SIDE   387 22

PAIL
HE SPLASHES WATER FROM THE PAIL UPON THEM   734   1

PAILS
THEY ARE PAILS   820   2

PAIN
BECOMES PAIN   40   8
NOW WET WITH TEARS AND PAIN HANGS HEAVILY   74   2
IS IT WITH PAIN MY DEAR THAT YOU SHUDDER SO   87   1
IS IT BECAUSE I HURT YOU WITH PAIN MY DEAR   87   2
WITH LAUGHTER AND CLEAR THE EXONERATED EYES SINCE PAIN   94 20
AND SLOWLY ALL THE BLOSSOM SHUTS IN PAIN   113 13
YET NOW EVERY FIBRE OF ME CRIES IN PAIN   117   2
THE PAIN THAT IS HER SIMPLE ACHE FOR ME   128 26
AND I DO WEEP FOR VERY PAIN OF YOU   129 21
MY PAIN LIKE GARMENTS   134   7
OF FLESH DOES CRACKLE AND SHIVER AND BREAK IN PAIN   151 17
THAT WILL NOT GO NOW SUDDENLY GOING THE PAIN   155 11
THEY ANOINT THEIR BROWS WITH YOUR PAIN AS A PERFECT   168 19
PAIN OR LOVE OR GRIEF   169 19
MUST IN MY TRANSIENCY PASS ALL THROUGH PAIN   195 19
MUST BE A DREAM OF ALL THROUGH PAIN   195 20
WHEN PAIN AND ALL   196   1
HIS DARK EYES FULL OF PAIN   202   2
THAT COMES FROM THE FLOWERS OF PAIN   202 28
ALL THE TROUBLES AND ANXIETIES AND PAIN   203 13
I WOULD BEAR THE PAIN   214 25
THE PAIN OF LOVING YOU   215 14
THE PAIN OF LOVING YOU   216 11
WHAT PAIN TO WAKE AND MISS YOU   220   9
CLEAN PAIN SENDING ON US A CHILL DOWN HERE   225   4
WHITE AND LOOSE AT LAST WITH ALL THE PAIN   225   7
AGAINST OUR PAIN   243 12
IN THE SHEAVES OF PAIN   269   3
OF ALL THE PAIN   269 10
PAIN YET THE LIGHT OF LAMPS AND CANDLES HAS NO FEARS FO+   331   4
UP WITH THEM AND GREAT IS THE PAIN OF GREETING AND DEAD+   406   7
THAT PALE ONE FILLED WITH RENUNCIATION AND PAIN AND WHI+   439 22
HAS WORN US WEARY OF RENUNCIATION AND PAIN AND EVEN PAIN   439 24
WONDER OUTWAITING PAIN   504 18
THEN GRIEF AND PAIN GO TOO WITHDRAWING   509   3
PAIN AND DISMAY   544 19
THROUGH PERIL TOIL AND PAIN   554   2
ARE LONG SLOW VIBRATIONS OF PAIN   627 18
I HAVE BEEN DEFEATED AND DRAGGED DOWN BY PAIN   709   1
I FEEL THE PAIN OF FALLING LEAVES AND STEMS THAT BREAK +   727   7
IT IS THE LOUD CRIES OF THESE BIRDS OF PAIN   741 14
EVEN NO PAIN OF HEART   749 14
LOWERED TO PAIN   767 21
I TEAR BUT NEWS OF SORROW AND PAIN   772 23
HE IS NOT A PALE MAN FILLED WITH LOVE AND COMPASSION AN+   840 13
LOVE NOR COMPASSION NOR PITY NOR DEARNESS NOR PAIN MAKE+   840 14
SETS MY HEART ALSO THROBBING WITH PAIN   862 22

PAIN
WITH THE PAIN OF THIS FLIGHT   862 23
TEARS FOR HER PAIN   863 16
THE MOUTH OF THE MAN IS FULL OF THE TASTE OF PAIN   864 22
AFTER ALL THIS TIME OF PATIENCE AND PAIN   873   7
OF FLESH WOULD CRACK AND SHIVER WITH KEEN PAIN   873 29
I SAW THE PAIN AMONG THE IRIS THERE   880 28
ON THE BREAST OF A ROBIN THAT IS FLUTTERED WITH PAIN   883   5
AND ITS BEAT OF PAIN IS DISTRIBUTED ON THE WIND   883   7
AND TURNING ROUND IN PAIN FROM THE MUSIC HE   884   9
THROUGH A PAIN OF RISING TEARS AND DID NOT REPLY   884 21
PAIN   *900   2
PAIN   *903 15
I HEARD THY CRIES OF PAIN AND THEY BROKE   *927 11
I KNEW YOUR PAIN AND IT BROKE   *928 11
BUT DRAW THE TURGID PAIN   *929 27
YET EVERY FIBRE OF ME CRIES IN PAIN   *931   6
OH TEARS ON THE WINDOW PAIN   *932 19

PAIN-DARKENED
BEAR THE THOUGHT OF MY MOTHER'S PAIN-DARKENED BLUE EYES   869 14

PAINED
OF HER SOUL'S PAINED PERFUME   881   9

PAINFUL
TO PUT HER EARS TO THE PAINFUL SOB OF MY BLOOD   64 17
STUMBLING-BLOCKS PAINFUL ONES   288   4
YOU ARE PAINFUL HARSH-SURFACED PILLARS THAT GIVE OFF NO+   289   5
AFTER THE PAINFUL PAINFUL EXPERIENCE OF DYING   677   5
AND DIE THE DEATH THE LONG AND PAINFUL DEATH   718   1
BITTER AND PAINFUL FLOWERS   888   2

PAINFULLY
IT IS PAINFULLY UNTRUE   266 27
THE THING TO DO IS IN SOLITUDE SLOWLY AND PAINFULLY PUT   610 16

PAIN GRILLE
WAIT WAIT DON'T BRING THE COFFEE YET NOR THE PAIN GRILLE   687 21

PAINS
TROUBLES ANXIETIES AND PAINS   203 21

PAINT
YES AND IF OXEN OR LIONS HAD HANDS AND COULD PAINT WITH   376   1
THEIR HANDS AND PRODUCE WORKS OF ART AS MEN DO HORSES W+   376   2
DESTROY SHE MOANED THESE HORRORS IN PAINT   577   8
THE GENTLE SOULS THAT FIGURE IN THE PAINT   580 22
AND MADE HIM PAINT HER NUDE TIME AFTER TIME   619   9
HOLBEIN AND TITIAN AND TINTORET COULD NEVER PAINT FACES+   656 20
AND I CAN NEITHER PAINT NOR WRITE   680 10
ALL PEOPLE THAT CAN WRITE OR PAINT   680 12

PAINTED
LIKE A PAINTED WINDOW THE BEST   112   1
THE WORLD IS A PAINTED MEMORY WHERE COLOURED SHAPES   173 17
WHERE THE CANDLES BURN IN THE DAYLIGHT AND THE PAINTED   233   6
FAR-OFF KINGS PAINTED THEIR FACES VERMILION AND WERE AL+   303 22
HE PAINTED SOME PICTURES REAL BEAUTIES   577   4
WHEN THEY PAINTED A NUDE TO PUT A CACHE SEXE ON   580   1
MY WORLD IS A PAINTED FRESCO WHERE COLOURED SHAPES   *906 11
MY WORLD IS A PAINTED FRESCO WHERE COLOURED SHAPES   *908   5
LIKE A PAINTED WINDOW THAT LAST SUFFERING   *927 21
LIKE A PAINTED WINDOW THE BEST   *928 21
NAY TAKE MY PAINTED MISSAL BOOK AWAY   *939   4

PAINTING
AND PAINTING THE WOOD-WORK RED   572 14
LONG-HAIRED PEOPLE PAINTING THE INDIAN AND WRITING   778 10

PAINTS
AND PAINTS THE INSIDE WALLS SKY-BLUE   515   8

PAIR
ON TWO WINGS LIKE A PAIR OF COMPASSES   329   7
THE PAIR OF THEM ALIKE IN THAT   378 12
ONE OF US OR THE PAIR OF US   380   7
MIGHT HAVE BEEN SAVED IF A PAIR   536 13
ONLY HERE AND THERE A PAIR OF EYES HAUNTED LOOKS OUT AS+   625 25
AND BETWEEN THE TWO BLADES OF THIS PAIR OF SHEARS PROPE+   663 16
AND BETWEEN THE COWARDICE AND IMPUDENCE OF THIS PAIR WH+   663 24
THIS PAIR OF PROPERTY MONGRELS   663 26
AT THE SIGHT OF EACH OTHER THE PAIR OF THEM FLEW   761   5

PALACE
ON THE GREAT BLUE PALACE AT SYDENHAM LIGHTS STIR AND SH+   52 18
OF GLASS PALACE ALOFT THERE AMONG MISTY INDEFINITE THIN+   52 24
ON THE UPLIFTED BLUE PALACE LIGHT POOLS STIR AND SHINE   *905   7
OF BLUE PALACE ALOFT THERE AMONG THE MISTY INDEFINITE D+   *905 13

PALE
HER FACE LAY PALE AGAINST MY BREAST   62 14
PALE LOVE LOST IN A THAW OF FEAR   62 15
OUR FACES FLOWER FOR A LITTLE HOUR PALE AND UNCERTAIN A+   71   1
I CANNOT SEE HER SINCE THE MIST'S PALE SCARF   85   9
OF THE UNSWEPT SEA A GREY PALE LIGHT LIKE MUST   99   3
TO FLOURISH THERE AS PALE MOULD BLOOMS ON A CRUST   99   5
LIKE FLAGS IN PALE BLOOD NEWLY WET   105   3
FRAIL AS A SCAR UPON THE PALE BLUE SKY   131 24
I CEASE I TURN PALE   133 28
I CEASE I TURN PALE   133 33
TIMELESS AS BRANCHING LICHENS PALE AS MUST   135 15
TWO PALE CLOTS SWEPT BY THE LIGHT OF THE CARS   144 28
THE MUD-WEED OPENING TWO PALE SHADOWLESS STARS   145   3
AND KISSES PALE AND SIPPING THE TOLL   151 29
UNDER AN OAK WHOSE YELLOW BUDS DOT THE PALE BLUE SKY   152 27
AND PALE HER IVORY FACE HER EYES WOULD FAIL   156   2
PALE SHADOWS FLEE FROM US AS IF FROM THEIR FOES   163 18

PALE
```
  PALE SLEEPY PHANTOMS ARE TOSSED ABOUT                               163 23
  A PALE STROKE SMOTE                                                 165 12
  ALL ALL PERSEPHONE'S PALE CUPS OF MOULD                             177  5
  OUT OF THE HELL-QUEEN'S CUP THE HEAVEN'S PALE WINE                  177 13
  SWEAR IN THE PALE WINE POURED FROM THE CUPS OF THE QUEEN            177 21
  THE WAN WONDERING LOOK OF THE PALE SKY                              203 10
  WITH THE PALE DAWN SEETHING AT THE WINDOW                           204  4
  THE PALE BUBBLES                                                    205 23
  AGAINST THE HARD AND PALE BLUE EVENING SKY                          225  1
  WITH A PALE DEAD CHRIST ON THE CRUCIFIX OF HIS HEART                226  3
  WITH PALE SHUT FACE NOR EITHER HEARS NOR FEELS                      232 27
  OUR PALE DAY IS SINKING INTO TWILIGHT                               286 21
  THEN WHY SHOULD I FEAR THEIR PALE FACES                             288 18
  THE SAME I SAY TO THE PALE AND ELEGANT PERSONS                      316 26
  JESUS' PALE AND LAMBENT DOVE COOING IN THE LOWER BOUGHS             329  8
  I STAND AT THE PALE OF MY BEING                                     338 28
  BURNING PALE POSITIVE POLE OF YOUR WATTLED HEAD                     370 19
  WITH A PALE LITTLE WISP OF A PRINCE OF WALES DIFFIDENT +            387 21
  THAT PALE FRAGMENT OF A PRINCE UP THERE WHOSE MOTTO IS              388  5
  PALE DISPIRITED PRINCE WITH HIS CHIN ON HIS HANDS HIS               388  7
  HE IS ROYALTY PALE AND DEJECTED FRAGMENT UP ALOFT                   388 13
  AND STEPPING IN HOMAGE STUBBORN TO THAT NERVOUS PALE                388 24
  INSTEAD OF WHICH THE SILENT FATAL EMISSION FROM THAT PA+            390 25
  AND THEN HER GREAT WEIGHT BELOW THE WAIST HER VAST PALE             393 15
  NOR YET THAT PALE YOUNG MAN AFRAID OF FATHERHOOD                    437  2
  THAT PALE ONE FILLED WITH RENUNCIATION AND PAIN AND WHI+            439 22
  AND KEEP YOU IN MILLIONS AT THE MILLS SIGHTLESS PALE SL+            441  8
  PALE AND MEAN AND INSECT-LIKE SCUTTLING ALONG                       526 18
  NOTHINGNESS PALE NOTHINGNESS IN THEIR HEARTS                        569  6
  BUT BRITANNIA TURNED PALE AND BEGAN TO FAINT                        577  7
  OUR PALE MIND STILL FROM THE PULSING CONTINENT                      607  2
  WHO HAD WADED TO THE PALE GREEN SEA OF EVENING OUT OF A+            693  5
  GIVING OFF DARKNESS BLUE DARKNESS AS DEMETER'S PALE LAM+            697 10
  SHE LEANS FORWARD HER SMOOTH PALE FACE                              731 10
  MAKING US PALE AND BLOODLESS WITHOUT RESISTANCE                     740  6
  HE IS NOT A PALE MAN FILLED WITH LOVE AND COMPASSION AN+            840 13
  AND THE PALE STARS OF FORGET-ME-NOTS HAVE CLIMBED TO TH+            854  4
  PALE DREAMY CHAPLETS A GREY NUN-SISTER SETS                         854 23
  I WISH I KNEW WHERE THIS PALE ROAD GOES                             857 12
  PALE SHADOWS FLEE FROM US AS IF FROM THEIR FOES                     857 18
  PALE SLEEPY FLOWERS ARE TOSSED ABOUT                                857 23
  LIKE A GIRL'S TWINKLING MERRIMENT AT NIGHT WHEN THE SEA+            860 16
  MY PALE WET BUTTERFLY FLUFFY CHICKEN                                863  6
  AND SCATTERED WITH HER HAIR CLOUDS OF PALE MIMOSA SANDS             863 23
  UNDER AN OAK TREE WHOSE YELLOW BUDS DOTTED THE PALE BLU+            866 23
  TO FOLD IN A SHINING CONCAVE THE PALE NIGHT                         882  3
  PALE LOVE LOST IN A SNOW OF FEAR                                   *912 21
  OUR FACES FLOWER FOR A LITTLE HOUR PALE AND UNCERTAIN A+           *917 21
  INTO THE NIGHT AND ARE LOST TO SADDEN WITH JETSAM THE D+          *918  8
  WITH THEIR LITTLE PALE SIGNS ON THE WALL TO TRY US               *929 24
  FRAIL AS A SCAR UPON THE PALE BLUE SKY                            *937 23
  AND PALE HOT SKIES HAVE DARKENED AND GONE COLD                   *939 15
  AND ONCE HE WAS A YOUNG MAN PALE AND REFUSING FATHERHOOD         *946 15
```

PALE-BLURRED
```
  PALE-BLURRED WITH TWO ROUND BLACK DROPS AS IF IT MISSED            141 17
```

PALE-BREASTED
```
  PALE-BREASTED THROSTLES AND A BLACKBIRD ROBBERLINGS                 36 25
```

PALEFACE
```
  AND THEN RUN LIKE SURLY DOGS AT THE BIDDING OF PALEFACE+           795  4
```

PALEFACES
```
  PALEFACES YELLOWFACES BLACKFACES THESE ARE NO MEXICANS             793 11
  HOW GAVE THESE PALEFACES YELLOWFACES CROSSED THE WATERS+           794 30
```

PALE-FACES
```
  THE PALE-FACES                                                     287 12
  ONLY I GROPE AMONG YOU PALE-FACES CARYATIDS AS AMONG A             287 27
  SAVE YOUR LIPS O PALE-FACES                                        288 23
  BUT NOT YOUR FOOT-FALLS PALE-FACES                                 288 31
  BUT YOU PALE-FACES                                                 289  4
  CARYATIDS PALE-FACES                                               289 21
```

PALE-FACE
```
  PALE-FACE AUTHORITY                                                287 14
  I AM SO WEARY OF PALE-FACE IMPORTANCE                              288 16
  PALE-FACE AUTHORITIES LOITERING TEPIDLY                            316 27
  SAYING HOW DO YOU DO YOU PALE-FACE                                 404  5
  AND I'M A PALE-FACE LIKE A HOMELESS DOG                            404 13
  YOU AND I YOU PALE-FACE                                            404 20
  PALE-FACE YOU AND I                                                404 21
  THEN YOU'RE A LOST WHITE DOG OF A PALE-FACE                        404 29
  THIN RED WOLF OF A PALE-FACE                                       405  3
  WE TAKE NO HUNGRY STRAY FROM THE PALE-FACE                         405  7
```

PALE-GOLD
```
  THEIR PALE-GOLD PETALS BACK WITH STEADY WILL                       91 13
  THE LOVELY PALE-GOLD BUBBLES OF THE GLOBE-FLOWERS                  205 24
  THE PALE-GOLD FLESH OF PRIAPUS DROPPING ASLEEP                     651 19
```

PALE-GREEN
```
  ADOWN THE PALE-GREEN GLACIER RIVER FLOATS                          209  1
  OF THEIR PALE-GREEN GLACIER WATER FILLED THE EVENING               216 25
  OF THEIR PALE-GREEN GLACIER-WATER FILLED THE EVENING             *942 11
```

PALE-OXYDISED
```
  COOLING TO A POWDERY PALE-OXYDISED SKY-BLUE                        369 14
```

PALE-PASSIONATE
```
  THE STREET PALE-PASSIONATE GOES                                    106  8
```

PALFREY
```
  UPON HER PLODDING PALFREY                                          200  1
  HIS ARMS SO SHE LIGHTS FROM HER PALFREY                            200 11
  THAN THE EARTH THE PALFREY TRODE                                   202  8
  NO CHILD AND NO PALFREY SLOW                                       202 22
```

PALIMPSEST
```
  WANES THE OLD PALIMPSEST                                            41 23
```

PALISH
```
  NOT EVEN PALISH SMOKE LIKE THE REST OF THE THRONG                  116 12
```

PALL
```
  STOOPS LIKE A PALL                                                 146 15
```

PALLID
```
  UNDER THE PALLID MOONLIGHT'S FINGERING                             129 12
  AND UP THE PALLID SEA-BLENCHED MEDITERRANEAN STONE-SLOP+           311 20
  AND THE OTHER THE OLD ONE THE PALLID HOARY FEMALE                  426  9
  AND THE SHOULDERS PALLID WITH LIGHT FROM THE SILENT SKY+           693 11
  LEAVING THIS NAKED PALLID HELPLESS VULNERABLE REMAINS              767 26
  MYRIAD MYRIAD DEAD TWIGS OF PALLID AND CHAFING PEOPLE              784 21
  PALLID POOR THING YET I                                            817 13
  AND THE GLIMMERING DREAMLETS OF THE MORNING ARE PALLID +           854  7
  LIFE LOVERS WHO COULD HOPE FOR NO RANK AMONG THE PALLID+           855 20
  STREWN STARS OF PALLID PEOPLE AND THROUGH LUMINOUS LITT+          *938  4
```

PALLING
```
  OF A MEANINGLESS MONOTONY IS PALLING                               65 13
```

PALLOR
```
  AND THE PALLOR OF NIGHT DOES NOT TALLY                              38  4
  AND SWALLOWS DIP INTO THE PALLOR OF THE WEST                       41 21
  TREMBLING BLUE IN HER PALLOR A TEAR THAT SURELY I HAVE +           67 16
  YOUR PALLOR INTO RADIANCE FLUSH YOUR COLD                          86 12
  OVER THE PALLOR OF ONLY TWO FACES                                 145  4
  OVER THE PALLOR OF ONLY TWO PLACES                                145 12
  A BLOTCH OF PALLOR STIRS BENEATH THE HIGH                          210 19
  THAT FUMES A LITTLE WITH PALLOR UPON THE DARK                      719 30
  IS IT ILLUSION OR DOES THE PALLOR FUME                             720  1
  HOW CAN MY HEART KEEP BEATING IN THIS PALLOR OF WHITISH            766 28
  AND THE PALLOR OF NIGHT DOES NOT TALLY                           *892 20
```

PALM
```
  AND LOOKS AT ME AND LOOKS IN THE PALM OF HER HAND                 143 15
  YOU WHO ROLL THE STARS LIKE JEWELS IN YOUR PALM                   197 24
```

PALMS
```
  BUT OH THE PALMS OF HIS TWO BLACK HANDS ARE RED                   135 22
  YOUR PALMS                                                        800 11
  BUT OH THE PALMS OF HER TWO BLACK HANDS ARE RED                  *938 26
  BUT OH THE PALMS OF HIS BLACK HANDS ARE RED                      *939 22
```

PALM'S
```
  THUMB-MOUND INTO THE PALM'S DEEP POUCHES                          143 12
```

PALM-TREES
```
  THROUGH THE PALM-TREES AND PAST HOLLOW PADDY-FIELDS WHE+          386 27
  ABOVE THE PALM-TREES OF THE ISLET IN THE LAKE                     391 19
```

PALPABLE
```
  AND PEOPLE DARKLY INVESTED WITH PURPLE MOVE PALPABLE              148 26
  THE PLACE IS PALPABLE ME FOR HERE I WAS BORN                      172 22
  TO ME MEN ARE PALPABLE INVISIBLE NEARNESSES IN THE DARK           289  1
```

PALPABLY
```
  SEE HIM THERE THE SWART SO PALPABLY INVISIBLE                     286 11
```

PALPITANT
```
  ALTERNATELY PALPITANT                                            667 11
```

PALPITATING
```
  PALPITATING DOWN THE STAIR                                         37 10
  PALPITATING FLAMES OF LIFE                                        115 14
  TILL HE FELL IN A CORNER PALPITATING SPENT                       345 27
```

PALS
```
  NOR PALS THEY'RE SUCH A NUISANCE                                 499 24
  PALS WORSE N'R ONY NAME AS YOU COULD CALL                       *911 12
```

PALTRY
```
  I THOUGHT HOW PALTRY HOW VULGAR WHAT A MEAN ACT                  351 19
  BUT HOW PALTRY MINGY AND DINGY AND SQUALID PEOPLE LOOK           530 15
  FOR THEIR VERY PALTRY LITTLE BIT OF MONEY                        531 18
```

PAMELIE
```
  ME AND EKKERHART AND SOMERS AND PAMELIE                          668 21
```

PAN
```
  EVEN IF IT WAS ONLY A TIN PAN                                    520 12
```

PANACEA
```
  SCORNING THE PANACEA EVEN OF LABOUR                              197 15
```

PANDEMONIUM
```
  AND HOWLS HIS PANDEMONIUM ON THE INDIGNANT AIR                   379 23
```

PANDER
```
  AND PANDER TO THEM                                               666  9
```

PANDERING
```
  IT IS PANDERING TO CORPSES                                       441 34
```

P AND O
```
  OF THE P AND O AND THE ORIENT LINE AND ALL THE OTHER ST+         688  7
```

PANE
THE TASSEL OF THE BLIND SWINGS CONSTANTLY TAPPING THE P+   112 17
A NURSE IN WHITE AT THE DAWNING FLOWER-FOAMED PANE   155 1
OF THE STREET-LAMP THROUGH THE UNBLINDED WINDOW PANE   878 6
THE FLOWERS AGAINST YOUR WINDOW PANE   886 1
IT IS STORMY AND RAIN-DROPS CLING LIKE SILVER BEES TO T+   *926 1

PANES
IT IS STORMY AND RAINDROPS CLING LIKE SILVER BEES TO TH+   92 1

PANG
A PANG   486 12
INSTANTLY FEEL A PANG OF COMPUNCTION   834 11

PANGS
AND PANGS OF BIRTH AND JOY OF THE BEGETTING   89 12
AND I HELD THE CHOKED FLOWER-SERPENT IN ITS PANGS   125 16
DRAWN ON HIS MOUTH EYES BROKEN AT LAST BY HIS PANGS   225 8
AND I KEPT THE CHOKED SNAKE FLOWER IN ITS PANGS   *936 15

PANIC
AND DASH IN PANIC THROUGH THE BRAKE   465 15
HARK THE STRANGE NOISE OF MILLIONS OF FISH IN PANIC   586 25
IN PANIC IN REBELLION SLITHERING MILLIONS OF FISH   586 26

PANIC-STRICKEN
AND THE IGNOBLE PRAYERS OF THE PANIC-STRICKEN WHOM DARK+   856 5

PANS
MENDING AND TINNING THE PANS OF ALL THE VILLAGE   520 15
THINK THAT THE SAPPHIRE IS ONLY ALUMINA LIKE KITCHEN PA+   530 1
WITH ITS STORE OF FOOD AND THE LITTLE COOLING PANS   719 4

PANSIES
THE LITTLE PANSIES BY THE ROAD HAVE TURNED   224 24
THEN AMONG THE AVERTED PANSIES BENEATH THE HIGH   225 29
NOW THAT IN ENGLAND PANSIES AND SUCH-LIKE GROW ON THE   410 19

PANSY
TO SAVE THE STREAKED PANSY OF THE HEART FROM   658 11
I SHALL BLOSSOM LIKE A DARK PANSY AND BE DELIGHTED   677 13

PANTHER
AND PLAYS WITH THE WAVELETS LIKE A PANTHER PLAYING WITH+   709 10

PANTHER'S
THE MOBILITY THE PANTHER'S GAMBOLLING   157 18

PANTING
AND PANTING WITH THAT SPLIT GRIN   397 25
AND BEATING THEIR GREAT WINGS IN OUR PANTING FACES   707 5
DEEP PANTING BREATHS LIKE GREAT BEASTS READY FOR   827 8

PANTS
HERE FLICK THE RABBITS HERE PANTS THE GORSE HERE SAY TH+   34 11
HARK AT THE RIVER IT PANTS AS IT HURRIES THROUGH   212 2

PAP
EAT YOUR PAP LITTLE MAN LIKE A MAN   570 20
AND THE FEED OF PAP THAT WE NURSES AND GUARDIAN ANGELS +   670 16

PAPA
AS FOR PAPA   357 11
EXCEPT THAT PAPA AND MAMA ARE OLD ACQUAINTANCES OF   357 21

PAPER
PAPER   482 27
THAN PAPER MONEY WHEN THE BANK IS BROKE   528 4
SHE'LL TAKE OFF HER SPECS AND SHE'LL PUT DOWN THE PAPER   583 12

PAP-PAP
IN A MOTOR IN A PAP-PAP PAP-PAP MOTOR LITTLE MAN   571 6

PAPPUS
MYRIADS OF DANDELION PAPPUS   204 16

PAPPY
YOU MUST CHOP UP EACH ARTICLE MAKE IT PAPPY   583 18

PAR
SEEING I AM ON A PAR WITH ALL MEN   320 13

PARABOLA
UP IN A PARABOLA   300 31
A CIRCLE SWOOP AND A QUICK PARABOLA UNDER THE BRIDGE   341 1
BACK ON A STRANGE PARABOLA THEN ROUND ROUND DIZZY IN   344 13
OF THE PARABOLA OF CURVED FLIGHT   476 10

PARACLETE
CANNOT BE LIFTED UP THE PARACLETE   320 11
LISTEN PARACLETE   323 1

PARADISAL
PARADISAL THROUGH THE LONG AFTERNOON   768 29
IN TONES OF THE AFTERWARDS PARADISAL   769 29

PARADISE
AND I KNEW THAT HOME THIS VALLEY WAS WIDER THAN PARADISE   38 17
FLOWERS OF ILLUSION WHO SHINE IN OUR GAUDS MAKE A PARAD+   71 17
LOVELIER THAN PARADISE   261 19
BACK INTO PARADISE   770 15
AND SAY THAT THIS HOME THIS VALLEY IS WIDER THAN PARADI+ *892 32

PARALYSIS
AND OUR SCREAM IS SOUNDLESS IN THE PARALYSIS OF SLEEP   408 2

PARAMOUR
WHY AM I BRIDEGROOM OF WAR WAR'S PARAMOUR   742 36

PARASITE
WE WOULDN'T HURT YOU FOR THE WORLD SAYS THE PARASITE   765 23

PARASITES
THEY ARE HUMBLE WITH A CREEPING HUMILITY BEING PARASITE+   621 20

PARASITIC
AND AN AMOUNT OF FUNGOID AND PARASITIC GROWTH   677 23

PARASOL
PARASOL   444 29
WHEN SHE ROSE TILTING HER PARASOL AND SMILED AT THE   445 1

PARCEL
AS IF IT WERE PART AND PARCEL   170 13

PARCELS
SOME LIMBS LIKE PARCELS AND TEAR   145 26

PARCH
OF PASSION PARCH IT UP DESTROY REMOVE   153 26

PARCHED
TILL MY PARCHED VISION COOLS   754 15

PARDON
ON NOTHINGNESS PARDON ME   40 24
I BEG YOUR PARDON   546 6

PARDONS
WHO PARDONS ONCE AND NO MORE   809 22

PARED
SINCE DEATH FROM THE MOTHER MOON HAS PARED US DOWN TO   132 8
SINCE DEATH FROM THE MOTHER MOON HAS PARED CLOSE TO THE+ *938 1

PARENT
AND BEYOND THE EAGLE ROSE AND THE PHOENIX PARENT SOARIN+ *946 23

PARENTHOOD
A CLUTCH OF ATTACHMENT LIKE PARENTHOOD   *899 33
A CLUTCH OF ATTACHMENT LIKE PARENTHOOD   *903 12

PARENTS
BUT TIME HAS FLED OUR PARENTS ARE DEAD   490 21
IS PUT BY ITS PARENTS INTO ITS COFFIN   521 27
WHEN OUR PARENTS FELT SPRY   562 26
EDITOR BY SURGICAL OPERATION DID YOUR PARENTS HAVE YOU   582 16

PARIS
IF YOU DON'T USE ROUGE AND A LIP-STICK IN PARIS   433 12
IN LONDON NEW YORK PARIS   704 6

PARK
BETWEEN THE CLIFFS OF THE TREES ON THE GREY-GREEN PARK   66 6
IS DEAD TOO A DEAD ORB WHEELED ONCE A MONTH ROUND THE P+ 702 27

PARKS
EVEN THE VERY FLOWERS IN THE SHOPS OR PARKS   634 18

PARLOUR
AND HYMNS IN THE COSY PARLOUR THE TINKLING PIANO OUR   148 13
IN A PUB PARLOUR IN LITERARY LONDON ON CERTAIN EVENINGS   542 10
AH IN THAT PARLOUR OF THE LONDON PUB   542 16

PARROT
AND WONDERS IF A PARROT HASN'T MORE TO IT   842 11

PARROTS
BUT ALL WAS SILENT SAVE FOR PARROTS OCCASIONALLY IN THE   394 18

PARSON
AN' T' PARSON MAKIN' HASTE AN' A' T' BLACK   60 15
WHILE T' PARSON WAS PRAYIN' I WATCHES 'ER AN' SHE WOR + *910 1
AN' PARSON MAKIN' HASTE AN' A' THE BLACK   *911 1

PART
HOW CAN YOU SHAME TO ACT THIS PART   55 8
THE COURSE OF OUR JOURNEY HERE HERE WHERE WE PART   100 18
THE BRIM EACH CAREFUL PART   125 3
SHE MAKES HER HANDS TAKE MY PART THE PART OF THE MAN   128 27
AS IF IT WERE PART AND PARCEL   170 13
AS THEY CROSS AND PART AND MEET   253 13
I LOVED TO HANDLE IT IT SEEMED LIKE A NEAR PART OF HIM   255 3
IT IS THE MAJOR PART OF BEING THIS HAVING SURPASSED ONE+ 266 20
SHE HAS NO PART IN IT NO PART WHATEVER   267 9
FOR MY PART I PREFER MY HEART TO BE BROKEN   279 1
THE ITALIANS VULGARLY SAY IT STANDS FOR THE FEMALE PART+ 282 17
WISE TORTOISE LAID HIS EARTHY PART AROUND HIM HE CAST I+ 348 13
BUT SUDDENLY THAT PART OF HIM THAT WAS LEFT BEHIND CONV+ 351 13
THAT WHICH IS IN PART FINDING ITS WHOLE AGAIN THROUGHOUT 367 6
NOW YOU NEED KNOW IN PART   411 11
THAT IS PART OF THE MYSTERY OF SEX IT IS A FLOW ONWARDS   449 4
WHY NOT HAVE MEN AS MEN AND THE WORK AS MERELY PART   452 7
AND OUR SOCIETY IS ONLY PART CONSCIOUS LIKE AN IDIOT   515 2
WHEN ALAS IT'S ONLY PART OF OUR CLEVER LITTLE SELF THAT+ 543 23
IN THE FLESH IS PART OF OUR CONSCIOUSNESS   621 4
THE HOLY GHOST IS THE DEEPEST PART OF OUR OWN CONSCIOUS+ 621 5
IT IS PART OF THE EVIL WORLD-SOUL SPINNING   713 3
IS EVIL EVIL PART OF THE EVIL WORLD-SOUL   713 6
DO NOT ASK ME ALMIGHTY GOD TO PART FROM HER AGAIN   749 20
NO WOMAN TAKES MY PART   751 20
STRUCK DOWN DO THOU PART US THE DARKNESS THAT WE SEE TH+ 753 6
THE MOST PART LONG AGO ENTERED THE ROMAN CATHOLIC   776 25
BUT COME BEFORE WE PART   812 2

PART
    THOUGH THEY CLING FORGOTTEN THE MOST PART NOT COMPANION+   *900 14
    THOUGH THEY CLING FORGOTTEN THE MOST PART NOT COMPANIONS   *903 26
    I'VE REALISED IT IS ALL A TRICK ON HIS PART   *948 22

PARTAKE
    AT SEASONS TO PREPARE THEMSELVES TO PARTAKE   777 34

PARTED
    PERHAPS WE ARE PARTED FOR EVER   212 23

PARTHENON
    WHERE ALL THE PARTHENON MARBLES STILL FOSTERED THE ROOT+ 311 28

PARTIAL
    AND DOOMED TO PARTIALITY PARTIAL BEING   362 28

PARTIALITY
    AND DOOMED TO PARTIALITY PARTIAL BEING   362 28

PARTICUALR
    TOWARDS THE END OF HER PARTICUALR AFFAIR WITH HIM   446 27

PARTICULAR
    YOUR PARTICULAR HEAVENS   289 14

PARTIES
    BETWEEN CONFLICTING POLITICAL PARTIES AND   777 18

PARTING
    I WHOSE HEART IS TORN WITH PARTING   169 10
    AND THERE A NEW PARTNER A NEW PARTING A NEW UNFUSING   280 30
    THE FIBRES OF THE HEART PARTING ONE AFTER THE OTHER   281 6
    PARTING HIS STEEL-TRAP FACE SO SUDDENLY AND SEIZING HER 360 20
    UP WITH THEM AND GREAT IS THE PAIN OF GREETING AND DEAD+ 406 7

PARTLY
    WITH HEAD THROWN BACK AND PARTLY OPENED MOUTH   878 20

PARTNER
    AND THERE A NEW PARTNER A NEW PARTING A NEW UNFUSING   280 30

PARTRIDGES
    AFTER PARTRIDGES OR A LITTLE RUBBER BALL   430 23

PARTS
    AND HE SIGHS WITH RELIEF WHEN SHE PARTS FROM HIM   228 13
    ARE PARTS OF THE EARTH JUST AS EMBRYOS ARE PARTS OF THE+ 295 9
    PARTS OF THE MACHINE   452 4
    WATER IS H2O HYDROGEN TWO PARTS OXYGEN ONE   515 11
    AND THE HALF-HIDDEN PRIVATE PARTS JUST A LITTLE BRASS T+ 625 22
    THAT WE'VE HAD ENOUGH THE BRAIN IS STRETCHED TILL IT PA+ 756 5

PARTURITION
    MOAN SOFTLY WITH AUTUMNAL PARTURITION   160 9

PARTY
    I DANCE AT THE CHRISTMAS PARTY   198 5

PASS
    WHILE HIGHER THE DARTING GRASS-FLOWERS PASS   49 24
    LETTING LIFE PASS   50 8
    WHERE HASTENING CREATURES PASS INTENT   50 27
    AND FEEL THE STREAM OF AWAKENING RIPPLE AND PASS   51 23
    IT IS WELL FOR YOU FOR ME THE NAVVIES WORK IN THE ROAD + 57 29
    THEY POISE AND RUN LIKE PUFFS OF WIND THAT PASS   64 31
    MUFFLING MY MIND AS SNOW MUFFLES THE SOUNDS THAT PASS   75 22
    NOT PASS THE RED MOON RISEN AND I AM GLAD   88 28
    THE LEAVES FLY OVER THE WINDOW AND UTTER A WORD AS THEY+ 103 1
    THEY PASS IN A HALF EMBRACE   108 12
    ANOTHER TORN RED SUNSET COME TO PASS   136 4
    NEVER HE IS NOT WHATEVER SHALL COME TO PASS   137 16
    TRAMS THAT PASS BLOWN RUDDILY DOWN THE NIGHT   146 13
    THEATRE PEOPLE PASS   146 18
    FOR SOMETHING MUST COME SINCE WE PASS AND PASS   164 5
    AND WISH I COULD PASS IMPREGNATE INTO THE PLACE   173 14
    PASS THE MEN WHOSE EYES ARE SHUT LIKE ANEMONES IN A DAR+ 180 20
    IN THIS ODD LIFE WILL TARNISH OR PASS AWAY   193 13
    MUST IN MY TRANSIENCY PASS ALL THROUGH PAIN   195 19
    AND MANY PEOPLE PASS   196 14
    MANY BRIGHT PEOPLE PASS   196 16
    FOUR LABOURERS PASS WITH THEIR SCYTHES   220 16
    AND PASS OUT OF SIGHT   253 14
    IF I PASS THEM CLOSE OR ANY MAN   269 25
    HOWSOEVER THEY PASS BY   270 3
    HEAVEN KNOWS HOW IT CAME TO PASS   279 6
    YET NEVER ABLE TO PASS THE WHITENESS OF LIGHT INTO   345 17
    YET NOTHING ON EARTH WILL GIVE HIM COURAGE TO PASS THE 346 4
    HOMER WAS WRONG IN SAYING WOULD THAT STRIFE MIGHT PASS 348 1
    ALL THINGS WOULD PASS AWAY FOR IN THE TENSION OF OPPOSI+ 348 4
    UPON THE WORLD TO BRING A CHANGE TO PASS   428 22
    IT TOOK AEONS TO MAKE A SAPPHIRE AEONS FOR IT TO PASS A+ 477 5
    WHEN THINGS GET VERY BAD THEY PASS BEYOND TRAGEDY   514 10
    AND LAUGH LET THEM PASS   565 7
    AND CAN'T PASS SUCH THINGS AS SUBSTANCE AND MARROW   583 29
    BUT IN CHOOSING THE BOURGEOIS ONE BRINGS TO PASS   664 8
    HIS WORK TOOK PLACE IT CAME TO PASS IT STOOD UP AND SAL+ 690 7
    THE LOVELY THINGS ARE GOD THAT HAS COME TO PASS LIKE JE+ 691 25
    AND THERE ARE THE DARK DOORS WHERE SOULS PASS SILENTLY 711 4
    WHICH HAS BROUGHT TO PASS THE FEARFUL THING CALLED EVIL 712 25
    AND PASS BEYOND WITH THE FOE AND THE HOMELESS GHOSTS   737 6
    NOT EVEN DREAM NOT EVEN PASS AWAY   738 19
    COME TO PASS THAT DOES NOT YET EXIST SAVE AS A SUBTLE   775 21
    BIND HIM WITH SHADOW WHILE I PASS   786 21
    BIND HIM WITH SHADOW WHILE I PASS   789 14
    CONQUER SAYS THE MORNING STAR PASS THE DRAGONS AND PASS+ 796 23
    AND SHALL PASS THE HOUSES OF THE STARS BY NIGHT   799 9
    NO GREY-DOGS COWARDS PASS HIM   810 3

PASS
    PASS OUT AND YET NOURISH   826 12
    A NEW THING COMES TO PASS EYES CLOSE   834 2
    AND I STARTED WITH PLEASURE FOR IN THE NIGHT IT HAD COM+ 860 12
    PASS   866 4
    WHO PASS ALONG THE STREET   877 19
    AND WE WILL PASS TOGETHER LIKE ONE RED FLAME   879 29
    COMES OVER THE SOFTNESS AND SILENCE OF MORNING I PASS *895 11
    MUFFLING MY MIND AS SNOW MUFFLES THE SOUNDS THAT PASS *897 22
    MUFFLING MY MIND AS SNOW MUFFLES THE SOUNDS THAT PASS *900 30
    FLUENT ACTIVE FIGURES OF MEN PASS ALONG THE RAILWAY   *906 16
    FLUENT ACTIVE FIGURES OF MEN PASS ALONG THE RAILWAY AND+ *908 11
    ANOTHER TORN RED SUNSET COME TO PASS   *938 32
    PASS LIKE A TUNE THE SALLOW'S GOLDEN NOTES   *941 24
    PASS UNSEEN FROM MY LIPS TO HERS   *942 4

PASSAGE
    AND LEAF FOR ITS PASSAGE A SHADOW CAST   69 3
    AFTER THE BITTER PASSAGE OF OBLIVION   721 7

PASSAGES
    AND THE ROAR OF BLACK BULL'S BLOOD IN THE MIGHTY PASSAG+ 326 15

PASSED
    OF LIVING HAS PASSED EBBING ON   53 15
    HE HAS PASSED US BY BUT IS IT   100 9
    FIRE PASSED THROUGH YOUR FLESH   112 2
    SHE SOFTLY PASSED THE SORROWFUL FLOWER SHED   156 7
    YOU HAVE PASSED FROM OUT OF SIGHT   168 4
    APPROACHED AND PASSED BY   242 23
    WHEN SHE PASSES AWAY AS I HAVE PASSED AWAY   267 15
    AS THE ROCKETS WENT UP AND THE GLARE PASSED OVER COUNTL+ 391 12
    YOUR OWN SELF THAT HAS PASSED LIKE A LAST SUMMER'S   478 24
    I HAVE PASSED FROM EXISTENCE I FEEL NOTHING ANY MORE   509 8
    HAVE NOT YET PASSED THE ISLANDS I MUST WATCH THEM STILL 687 23
    MAY SINK INTO GOD AT LAST HAVING PASSED THE VEILS   726 11
    AND HELD HIM WHILE JESUS PASSED   786 24
    SO HE PASSED THE YELLOW LINE WHO LASHED LIKE A DRAGON I+ 790 3
    AND HAVING PASSED THE YELLOW LINE HE SAW THE EARTH BENE+ 790 4
    IF I WERE YOU AS I PASSED THE FORTIES   835 31
    THE UNCLOUDED SEAS OF BLUEBELLS HAVE EBBED AND PASSED 854 1
    UP THROUGH THE VEIL AS WE PASSED   884 34
    PASSED INTO MY BLOOD   885 27
    OF LIVING HAS PASSED ON AND ON   *906 6

PASSENGERS
    FULL OF FRICTION FULL OF GRINDING FULL OF DANGER TO THE+ 675 27

PASSER-BY
    TREAD OF EVERY PASSER-BY   617 18

PASSES
    PASSES THE WORLD WITH SHADOWS AT THEIR FEET   36 3
    NOW AT LAST THE INK AND DUDGEON PASSES FROM OUR FERVENT+ 70 5
    THAT PASSES THE NIGHTLY ROAD ABOVE   105 11
    PASSES THE GALLIVANT BEAM OF THE TRAMS   145 5
    PASSES THE LIGHT OF THE TRAM AS IT RACES   145 14
    THE FLOOD SO IT PASSES BEYOND   159 8
    FIVE VALLEYS GO FIVE PASSES LIKE GATES   224 9
    HE SAYS NOT A WORD BUT PASSES   227 9
    WHEN SOME ONE PASSES HE DROPS HIS HEAD   228 5
    WHEN SHE PASSES AWAY AS I HAVE PASSED AWAY   267 15
    WETTING AFTER EVERYONE THAT PASSES   493 28
    PASSES UNDERSTANDING   497 10
    SHE BITES HIM IN THE NECK AND PASSES ON   539 22
    PASSES THE EVER-CHANGING JOY OF HIS ACTIVE BODY   868 4

PASSING
    AND PASSING FEET ARE CHATTER AND CLAPPING OF THOSE   58 18
    MOUTH-HAIR OF SOLDIERS PASSING ABOVE US OVER THE WRECK + 66 29
    WITH PEOPLE PASSING UNDERNEATH   121 19
    SO PEOPLE PASSING UNDER   176 14
    SO THAT HE SEEMS A STRANGER IN HIS PASSING   197 30
    PASSING ACROSS THE SHADOW INTO THE SUNLIGHT   210 9
    PASSING WITH SPEARS AND PENNANTS AND MANLY SCORN   221 9
    PASSING ON AND ON THE HATE   249 6
    SHADOWS THE PASSING WILD-BEAST THREW   262 6
    ONCE THEY SAY HE WAS PASSING BY WHEN A DOG WAS BEING BE+ 376 5
    WILL BE PASSING AWAY WE SHALL CEASE TO FUSS   471 18
    THE ARTICLES PASSING BENEATH YOUR SCRAWL   583 4
    I LIKE TO SEE THEM PASSING AND PASSING   602 3
    EAGERLY PASSING OVER FROM THE ENTANGLEMENT OF LIFE   676 20
    THE BURNING ARCHANGELS UNDER THE SEA KEEP PASSING BACK + 694 23
    KEEP PASSING ARCHANGELS OF BLISS   694 24
    FOR NOW WE ARE PASSING THROUGH THE GATE STILLY   699 3
    IN THE SILENCE OF PASSING THROUGH DOORS   699 5
    IT MEANS PASSING THROUGH THE WATERS OF OBLIVION   727 33
    AS HE IS PASSING UNBEKNOWN   752 3
    CAN YOU IGNORE OUR PASSING IN THIS MACHINE   781 9
    OR LEAF AND HIS PASSING SHADOW IS CAST   *915 15
    ENDLESS WHISPER OF PASSING FEET   *917 6
    SO PEOPLE PASSING UNDER   *941 1
    PASSING WITH SPEARS AND PENNANTS AND MANLY SCORN   *944 22

PASSING-BELL
    THE PASSING-BELL OF OUR WAY OF KNOWING   512 9

PASSION
    AND KISSED THEE TO A PASSION OF LIFE AND LEFT   69 23
    WHO GRAPPLING DOWN WITH WORK OR HATE OR PASSION   73 14
    FLY LIKE A SPARK INTO THE WOMB OF PASSION   89 6
    LEAPING LIKE SPRAY IN THE RETURN OF PASSION   89 17
    THE PASSION SLIPS   96 19
    RARE PASSION AND NEVER AGAIN   104 15
    AND SENSITIVE BUD-LIKE BLOSSOMING OF PASSION   113 6
    AND PASSION UNBEARABLE SEETHES IN THE DARKNESS LIKE MUST 129 30
    YOUR PASSION IN THE BASKET OF YOUR SOUL   151 13
    OF PASSION PARCH IT UP DESTROY REMOVE   153 26

PASSION
    WITH JEWELS OF PASSION ONCE BROKEN THROUGH YOU AS A   168 15
    SINCE YOU HAVE A PASSION FOR ME   236 6
    DOES NOT THAT PASSION STAND IN YOUR WAY LIKE A BALAAM'S+   236 8
    I MUST BE RECIPROCATING YOUR VACUOUS HIDEOUS PASSION   241 27
    THROUGH THE STRAIT GATE OF PASSION   242 8
    OF THRILLING RUIN IN THE FLESH OF PUNGENT PASSION OF RA+   273 19
    WHO LIES WITH THE WATERS OF HIS SILENT PASSION WOMB-ELE+   335 28
    FULFILLED OF THE SLOW PASSION OF PITCHING THROUGH IMMEM+   354 12
    THE OVER-DRIP OF A GREAT PASSION HANGING IN THE BALANCE   370 8
    ONLY YOURS WOULD BE A RAW UNSMELTED PASSION THAT WILL   370 9
    THE LESBIAN PASSION IS THE MOST APPALLING   475 18
    THE SOUL'S FIRST PASSION IS FOR SHEER LIFE   482 1
    AND THE SOUL'S NEXT PASSION IS TO REFLECT   482 3
    THE PASSION OF JUSTICE BEING PROFOUND AND SUBTLE   482 8
    BUT THE PASSION OF JUSTICE IS A PRIMAL EMBRACE   482 10
    AND THE PASSION OF TRUTH IS THE EMBRACE BETWEEN MAN AND   482 12
    AND PASSION WILL MAKE OUR BODIES TAUT WITH POWER   482 23
    AND HER PASSION COULD ONLY FLARE THROUGH THE MESHES   619 2
    BRINGS HIM TO HIS KNEES IN HOMAGE AND PURE PASSION OF S+   648 17
    OF THE ARMS PLUTONIC AND PIERCED WITH THE PASSION OF DE+   697 20
    AND THAT IS PASSION AND COMMUNION   715 7
    FIRE OF THE PASSION OF MEN   806 14
    BEYOND THE UNSPOKEN PASSION OF NIGHT   810 26
    THERE IS NO PASSION IN MY LIFE   856 22
    YOUR REPTILE FLAMES OF PASSION STORE   873 22
    HE STRIKES THE GUSH OF PASSION EASILY   *877 7
    HE KISSED THEE O MAN IN A PASSION OF LOVE AND LEFT   *916 6
    AND PIERCES HER ONCE MORE WITH HIS PASSION OF THE UTTER+   *956 18

PASSIONATE
    THEREFORE EVEN IN THE HOUR OF MY DEEPEST PASSIONATE MALE   208 8
    I THANK MANKIND WITH PASSIONATE HEART   263 29
    I WISH THESE BRITTLE FROST-LOVELY FLOWERS OF PASSIONATE+   272 6
    ENOUGH OF THE VIRGINS AND LILIES OF PASSIONATE SUFFOCAT+   273 14
    AND PASSIONATE DISQUALITY OF MEN   317 17
    DIVIDED INTO PASSIONATE DUALITY   361 5
    AND THE FIRST TENOR SINGING OF THE PASSIONATE THROAT OF+   366 17
    FOR HIS MISSION HAD CRUELLY FAILED WHILE HIS PASSIONATE+   859 11
    SO MY SOUL LIKE A PASSIONATE WOMAN TURNS   *891 29
    INTO URGENT PASSIONATE WAVES   *893 19

PASSIONATELY
    IF ALL THOSE FEMALES WHO SO PASSIONATELY LOVED   538 1

PASSION-FLOWERS
    LIKE PASSION-FLOWERS   298 29

PASSION-FLOWER
    AND SUAVE LIKE PASSION-FLOWER PETALS   298 28
    WITH THE HALF-SECRET GLEAM OF A PASSION-FLOWER HANGING   299 1

PASSIONLESS
    SHE SHINES THE FIRST WHITE LOVE OF MY YOUTH PASSIONLESS+   67 21

PASSIONS
    THRESHING YOUR OWN PASSIONS WITH NO WOMAN FOR THE   197 4
    AND SAW THEM CUDDLING WITH RISING PASSIONS THEY NONE OF   443 26
    AND OF ALL PASSIONS   475 17
    AND CHANGING IN A FLOW AS ALL PASSIONS CHANGE   482 9
    INSTEAD OF KILLING THE PASSIONS AND THE INSTINCTS AND   529 7
    YOUR INSTINCTS GONE YOUR INTUITION GONE YOUR PASSIONS   631 1
    GOOD HEALTHY NATURAL FEELINGS INSTINCTS PASSIONS OR DES+   678 3
    WITH A FEW SWIFT PASSIONS WOULD I DRIFT AWAY   875 32

PASSIVE
    A NET ON THE UNDERSOIL THAT LIES PASSIVE AND QUICKENED +   94 4
    BEAUTIFUL PASSIVE AND STRONG AS THE BREATH   118 14
    HEAVY AS A STONE PASSIVE   240 29
    AND PASSIVE WITH EVERLASTING PATIENCE   390 8
    NOR IS HE NESTING PASSIVE UPON THE ATOMS   436 5
    INTO THE PASSIVE UNKNOWN MONSTROUS WOMB   880 7

PAST
    GOES TREMBLING PAST ME UP THE COLLEGE WALL   35 27
    SHAPE AFTER SHAPE AND SCENE AFTER SCENE OF MY PAST   47 4
    A SUDDEN CAR GOES SWEEPING PAST AND I STRAIN MY SOUL TO+   58 3
    THE VOICE OF THE FURTIVE TRIUMPHANT ENGINE AS IT RUSHES+   58 4
    SWEEP PAST THE WINDOW AGAIN   100 4
    A HASTENING CAR SWEPT SHAMEFUL PAST   122 1
    PAST WITH THE NOISE OF A BREEZE   144 24
    THE PAST   148 19
    PAST HIM ONLY A WING-BEAT PROVING   150 2
    A CROW FLOATS PAST ON LEVEL WINGS   161 1
    SLOW TRAINS STEAL PAST   169 3
    THROUGH THE OPEN YARD-WAY CAN I NOT GO PAST THE SHEDS   173 10
    AN ENDLESS TAPESTRY THE PAST HAS WOVEN DRAPES   173 19
    I HAVE LIVED DELIGHTED IN THE HALLS OF THE PAST   173 21
    AND PAST LIVES HAMPER ME CLOG AND EMBARRASS   173 28
    THERE'S A BREACH IN THE WALLS OF THE PAST LETS THE DAYL+   174 6
    THE FACES OF ALL THE WOMEN AS THEY GO PAST   180 9
    NOT FREE MYSELF FROM THE PAST THOSE OTHERS   204 7
    OF THE PAST   206 25
    FOR THE ABOMINATION OF OUR PAST RIGHTEOUSNESS   232 13
    PAST MY EYES   302 6
    WHERE THE SLOW TOADS SAT BROODING ON THE PAST   310 15
    BUT HE ROSE AND FROM A TERROR WORSE THAN ME HE FLEW PAST   344 5
    AND NOW HE SCUFFLES TINILY PAST HER AS IF SHE WERE AN O+   356 26
    GOATS GO PAST THE BACK OF THE HOUSE LIKE DRY LEAVES IN +   383 27
    THROUGH THE PALM-TREES AND PAST HOLLOW PADDY-FIELDS WHE+   386 27
    PAST THE OTTER'S WHISKERS   409 19
    LIKE SPERM OF WHALES LIKE GERMS OF THE GREAT DEAD PAST   428 28
    PAST   429 2
    WHAT EVEN THE WILD WITCHCRAFT OF THE PAST WAS SEEKING   481 9
    PAST   481 18
    THEY STREAM PAST STREAM PAST GOING TO WORK   585 25
    AH IN THE PAST TOWARDS RARE INDIVIDUALS   602 10
    I USED TO SAY THIS IN THE PAST BUT NOW NO MORE   602 17

PAST
    BESIDE THE HIGH ROAD PAST THE DEATHLY DUST   605 24
    BELONGS TO THE BAMBOO THICKET AND THE DRAKE IN THE AIR + 623 12
    ODYSSEUS CALLS THE COMMANDS AS HE STEERS PAST THOSE FOA+ 687 20
    AND LET ME COME PAST THE SILVER BELLS OF YOUR FLOWERS A+ 696 2
    PAST VENUS AND URANUS AND THE SIGNS   713 23
    AND TWENTIETH WAGON AND HE WILL NOT DRIVE PAST   733 12
    PAST SALUTING SWORDS OF THE ANGELS   770 16
    THE OLD COUNTRIES HAVE A PAST TO BE FAITHFUL TO   775 14
    TO AN UNBORN FUTURE THAN TO AN ACCOMPLISHED PAST   775 17
    PAST THE MOUNT OF THE SUN   787 4
    FROM HEAVEN PAST THE SLEEPING SONS OF GOD   801 5
    THE DARK IS DIVIDING THE SUN IS COMING PAST THE WALL   803 12
    PAST HIM FROM THE ONE TO THE OTHER   810 6
    INTO BLUE DAY PAST HUITZILOPOCHTLI   810 10
    PAST AND WE'RE BRUSHING   862 27
    AT THE BACK OF MY LIFE'S HORIZON WHERE THE DREAMS FROM + *905 15
    AN ENDLESS TAPESTRY THE PAST HAS WOVEN DRAPES   *906 13
    AN ENDLESS TAPESTRY THE PAST HAS WOVEN DRAPES   *908 7
    THE PICTURE OF THE PAST IS SHAKEN AND SCATTERED   *908 10
    PAST THE JUTTING ROCKS OF SHADOW   *959 5
    PAST THE LURKING OCTOPUS ARMS OF AGONISED MEMORY   *959 6
    PAST THE STRANGE WHIRLPOOLS OF REMEMBERED GREED   *959 7

PASTIME
    AND PRISONERS' FLAT INEFFECTUAL PASTIME   518 13

PASTURE
    AND SHEEP ON THE PASTURE   120 14
    WHERE BEASTS DROP THEIR UNLICKED YOUNG AND PASTURE AND + 321 13

PASTY
    PASTY LITTLE SNOT   552 24

PAT
    THA'S GOTTEN THY ANSWER PAT   80 4
    THA'S GOTTEN THY ANSWER PAT   *922 4

PATCH
    NOT THIS VAST ROTTING CABBAGE PATCH WE CALL THE WORLD   315 32
    YOU NEED NOT CLEAR THE WORLD LIKE A CABBAGE PATCH FOR ME 316 9

PATE
    BALD AND PRICKLY PATE   760 16

PATENT
    PATENT AND OPEN BENEATH MY EYE   59 27
    CARRIES ITS OWN PATENT AND ITS OWN OBLIGATION   774 21
    IS A PATENT OF NOBILITY   775 35

PATH
    GUARDING THE PATH HIS HAND RELAXED AT HIS THIGH   66 10
    THE SHORN MOON TREMBLING INDISTINCT ON HER PATH   131 23
    AND ALL ALONG THE PATH TO THE CEMETERY   232 20
    FOR WHEN FIRE IN ITS DOWNWARD PATH CHANCED TO MINGLE WI+ 348 6
    OUT INTO THE OPEN WHERE THE PATH RUNS ON THE TOP OF A   387 4
    PATH IN THE DARK   388 32
    SOFT GRASS RUNS UPON A PATH THAT IS PATHLESS TO MEN SO + 406 2
    KEEP HIS PATH WELL CLEANED   563 28
    AND WATCHED FOR YOUR GLISTENING FEET DOWN THE GARDEN PA+ 696 11
    GREY EVIL WHICH HAS NO PATH AND SHOWS NEITHER LIGHT NOR   712 2
    THE PATH BETWEEN GULFS OF THE DARK AND THE STEEPS OF   788 9
    THE PATH LIKE A SNAKE THAT IS GONE LIKE THE LENGTH OF A   788 11
    THE ROOTS ARE MINE DOWN THE DARK MOIST PATH OF THE SNAKE 801 16
    HAS STREWN MYRIAD TWINKLING POPPY-PETALS DOWN THE PATH + 860 18
    THE SHORN MOON TREMBLING INDISTINCT ON HER PATH   *937 22
    DOWN THE DARK BLUE PATH   *955 22

PATHETIC
    THOUGH HE IS ALL WISTFUL AND PATHETIC LIKE A MONOLITH   255 35
    MUSHY PATHETIC YOUNG MEN   457 14

PATHLESS
    SOFT GRASS RUNS UPON A PATH THAT IS PATHLESS TO MEN SO + 406 3

PATHOS
    WITH THE PATHOS OF THOSE WHO CAN SEE BUT WHOSE SIGHT IS+ 665 24

PATHS
    ARE GLITTERING PATHS   35 3
    AND FOAL-FOOTS SPANGLING THE PATHS   152 11
    THEN I WILL FALL AND PLANT THE PATHS TO HELL   710 15
    AND THE BRANCHES ARE MINE IN THE PATHS OF THE SKY AND T+ 801 17

PATHWAY
    YET NO PATHWAY WORN   249 4

PATIENCE
    PATIENCE LITTLE HEART   91 7
    PATIENCE LITTLE HEART I SHALL BE SWEET   91 23
    I CARRY MY PATIENCE SULLENLY THROUGH THE WASTE LANDS   167 3
    I CARRY MY PATIENCE SULLENLY THROUGH THE WASTE LANDS   167 16
    WITH SUCH INFINITE PATIENCE   272 21
    AND PASSIVE WITH EVERLASTING PATIENCE   390 8
    AND PATIENCE AND A CERTAIN DIFFICULT REPENTANCE   620 17
    AND WHERE WITH THE SLOW PATIENCE OF INTUITION   833 25
    AFTER ALL THIS TIME OF PATIENCE AND PAIN   873 7

PATIENT
    WHILE PATIENT NIGHT   54 17
    YOU GREAT YOU PATIENT EFFORT AND YOU SLEEP   194 19
    WE WHO HAVE NEVER FLOWERED LIKE PATIENT CACTUSES   272 32
    OF THEIR PATIENT WAITING UPON US THE THRONG OF THE GHOS+ 736 6
    I'D HAVE TORN THEM UP HAD THEY BORNE AWAY THE PATIENT B+ *926 13

PATIENTLY
  AND ASKING NOTHING PATIENTLY STEALS BACK AGAIN   63 29
  PATIENTLY TO DIVIDE AND SELF-DIVIDE   64 12
  PATIENTLY ROUND AND ROUND IN ELLIPSES   823 27

PATMOS
  HEARD I HAVE BEEN TO PATMOS   202 3
  MAKE IT ROOST ON BIRD-SPATTERED ROCKY PATMOS   329 19
  RATHER DIRTY ON DUNG-WHITENED PATMOS   329 25

PATRIOTIC
  REALLY PATRIOTIC PEOPLE THE RIGHT SORT OF PEOPLE YOU KN+   546 8

PATTER
  AT DUSK THEY PATTER BACK LIKE A BOUGH BEING DRAGGED ON   384 1
  A SLOW HEAVY PATTER OF LESSENING VIBRATION   767 20

PATTERED
  DOWN THE SOILED STREET WE HAVE PATTERED THE LESSONS   75 23
  DOWN THE SOILED STREET WE HAVE PATTERED THE LESSONS CEA+   *897 23
  DOWN THE SOILED STREET WE HAVE PATTERED THE LESSONS   *900 31

PATTERING
  LIKE PATTERING RIPPLES GO BY   109 18

PATTERN
  SAVE IN A BROKEN PATTERN AMID PURPLE AND GOLD AND SABLE   90 6
  AND A NAVAJO WOMAN WEAVING HER RUG IN THE PATTERN OF   448 22
  MUST RUN THE PATTERN OUT IN A LITTLE BREAK AT THE END   448 24
  BUT IN THE ODD PATTERN LIKE SNAKE-MARKS ON THE SAND   448 26
  FOR AM I NOT ALSO DREAM-STUFF DIFFUSING MYSELF IN THE P+   *907 7
  AM I NOT QUICKENING DIFFUSING MYSELF IN THE PATTERN SHA+   *909 4

PATTERNS
  AND I WATCH TO SEE THE CREATOR THE POWER THAT PATTERNS +   *908 25

PAUSE
  MAKES PAUSE THE HOURS   50 14
  UNHOLY FEAR IN MY ESSENCE YOU WOULD PAUSE TO   131 4
  AND CLUTCHING CLUTCHING FOR ONE SECOND'S PAUSE   345 8
  MAKE YOU PAUSE TO YAWN   353 3
  IN THE SLOW DIGNITY OF YOUR ETERNAL PAUSE   354 9
  THIS IS A PAUSE HOW LONG A PAUSE I KNOW NOT   508 9
  THE TRAGEDY IS OVER IT HAS CEASED TO BE TRAGIC THE LAST+   510 1
  PAUSE BRETHREN PAUSE   510 15
  AND IN ONE INSTANT'S PAUSE ARE REVOLVED ROUND AND CHANG+   784 12
  THEY ARE MAKING THE PAUSE   825 20
  SO THAT IN THE LONG PAUSE THE INSTINCTS CAN REASSERT TH+   839 3
  AS I PAUSE AT THE SIDE OF THE BATH   870 1
  I PAUSE AND FORGET   870 4
  OF HER FEET AS THEY LEPT FOR A SPACE THEN PAUSE TO PRESS   *934 10

PAUSED
  OF HER FEET AS THEY FLEW FOR A SPACE THEN PAUSED TO PRE+   123 4

PAUSES
  IN A MOUSE THAT PAUSES TO LISTEN   170 6
  SO HE PAUSES AND IS BEHOLDEN AND STRAIGHTWAY IS GONE   603 8
  THERE ARE SAID TO BE CREATIVE PAUSES   510 7
  PAUSES THAT ARE AS GOOD AS DEATH EMPTY AND DEAD AS DEATH   510 8
  AND IN THESE AWFUL PAUSES THE EVOLUTIONARY CHANGE TAKES   510 10
  PAUSES NEAR THE CREST OF THE HILL CLIMBING SLOWLY LIKE +   687 17

PAUSING
  PAUSING TO SIGH   242 27
  WHO GO BY WITHOUT PAUSING SOFT-FOOT WITHOUT LISTENING Y+   623 21
  WHERE THE LEOPARD PAUSING TO DRINK   771 1

PAVEMENT
  ALONG THE FLAGGED CLEAN PAVEMENT SUMMER-WHITE   36 2
  AND DOWN BELOW ON THE PAVEMENT LOVE   106 9
  WHEN ALONG THE PAVEMENT   115 13
  WHEN PEOPLE FLICKER DOWN THE PAVEMENT   115 25
  ON THE OUTER PAVEMENT SLOWLY   146 17
  LIKE A LOUT ON AN OBSCURE PAVEMENT   338 4

PAVEMENT-ROSES
  AND THE CYPRIAN'S PAVEMENT-ROSES ARE GONE AND NOW   71 15

PAVEMENT-RUN
  HALF-HIDING THE PAVEMENT-RUN   50 26

PAVILION
  APPROACHING UNDER THAT SMALL PAVILION AND TROPICAL EYES   389 22
  THAT I HAD BEEN HE IN THE PAVILION AS IN A PEPPER-BOX A+   392 2

PAW
  THE FOAMY PAW OF THE POND   159 11
  ON ITS PAW   324 17
  SO HE PUT HIS PAW TO HIS NOSE AND PONDERED   324 22
  THERE IS A NEW SWEETNESS IN HIS VOLUPTUOUSLY LICKING HI+   325 1
  LOOK AT HIM WITH HIS PAW ON THE WORLD   325 23
  WITH A THIN YOUNG YELLOW LITTLE PAW HANGING OUT AND   393 16
  LITTLE DANGLE OF AN IMMATURE PAW AND ONE THIN EAR   393 20
  LEAVING THE TRAIL OF A DIFFERENT PAW HANGING OUT   394 4
  AND THE LIVE LITTLE-ONE TAKING IN ITS PAW AT THE DOOR O+   394 23
  AS THE LEOPARD SMITES THE SMALL CALF WITH A SPANGLED PA+   683 9

PAWING
  LIKE STAGS ON ROCKY GROUND OR PAWING HORSES OR SPRINGY   392 16

PAWPAW
  A PAWPAW EFFULGENCE   760 10
  AND CONSIDER THE LILY NOT THE PAWPAW NOR THE MANGO-FLESH   760 18

PAWS
  TWO HARD CRUDE PAWS IN HUNGER ON THE LONELY   127 27
  HE FELL TO FROWNING AS HE LAY WITH HIS HEAD ON HIS PAWS   324 12
  WHELPS PLAY BETWEEN THE PAWS OF THE LION   325 14
  SO HALTS THE LITTLE BLACK BITCH ON FOUR SPREAD PAWS IN +   375 10
  AND STRANGELY PAWS THE AIR DELICATE   385 25
  NOW THAT THE SUN LIKE A LION LICKS HIS PAWS   687 13
  AND ONE WARM KIND KISS OF THE LION WITH GOLDEN PAWS   695 33
  CUFFING THEM WITH SOFT PAWS   709 11
  KISSES OF THE SOFT-BALLED PAWS WHERE THE TALONS ARE   709 13

PAY
  WELL NOW YER'VE GOT TER PAY FOR IT   81 29
  THINE SHALL GO TER PAY THE WOMAN AN' WI' MY BIT WE'LL B+   83 2
  AFORE I CAN TA'E THEE I'VE GOT A WIDDER O' FORTY-FIVE T+   83 8
  PAY A FEW CENTS   387 18
  YOU YOUR MANHOOD AND MAKES YOU PAY   458 23
  THAT YOU HAVE TO PAY   459 6
  BECAUSE YOU'VE ALWAYS GOT TO PAY FOR EVERYTHING   517 24
  TO PAY FOR THEM   517 28
  OR ELSE POOR THINGS THEY'RE HAVING TO PAY FOR THEMSELVES   518 1
  WHY ISN'T ANYTHING FREE WHY IS IT ALWAYS PAY PAY PAY   518 3
  THOUGH MOST BIRDS HAVE TO PAY WITH THEIR LIVES WHERE MEN   520 3
  DOESN'T PAY   545 15
  AND THEN ALL OUR DAYS IN A PLUNGE OF DEATH PAY THE DEBT   856 3
  OF GAIETY TOO OFTEN PAY ME THUS   872 24
  WELL NOW YOU'VE GOT TO PAY FOR IT   *924 1
  WI' A WOMAN AN' PAY 'ER A PRICE   *924 14
  THINE SHALL GO TO PAY THE WOMAN AN' WI' MY BIT WE'LL BUY   *925 6
  BEFORE I CAN TA'E THEE I'VE GOT A WIDOW OF FORTY-FIVE T+   *925 12

PAYING
  AND HERE AM I PAYING INCOME TAX AND GOD-KNOWS-WHAT   547 5

PAYS
  THOUGH I'LL SEE AS 'E PAYS YOU AN' DOES WHAT'S RIGHT   82 7
  IS DELIVERED OUT AND PAYS NO HEED THOUGH WE MOAN   132 18
  AND SO THE LORD OF VENGEANCE PAYS BACK REPAYS LIFE   616 16
  THOUGH I'LL SEE AS 'E PAYS YOU AN' COMES TO THE SCRATCH   *924 11

PEACE
  EH THERE'S NO PEACE   45 2
  FOR I'VE LOST MY PEACE   46 28
  LET THEM THITHER TO PEACE   88 31
  GO THEN THALT' HA'E NO PEACE TILL TER'S HAD   140 3
  PEACE   159 28
  WHERE IS THERE PEACE FOR ME   196 22
  AT PEACE AND LOOK OUT OF THE WINDOWS   227 31
  IS NOT EVEN THE BEAUTY AND PEACE OF AN ORBIT   236 14
  SURE ON A HAVEN OF PEACE BETWEEN THE MOUNDS OF HER   249 29
  HAS FOR ME A DOOR INTO PEACE WARM DAWN IN THE EAST   250 6
  IF YOU KNEW HOW I SWERVE IN PEACE IN THE EQUIPOISE   251 22
  AND GIVES ME PEACE YOU CANNOT SEE   252 4
  THERE WAS PEACE AND RICHNESS   265 10
  PEACE IS WRITTEN ON THE DOORSTEP   293 13
  PEACE BLACK PEACE CONGEALED   293 13
  MY HEART WILL KNOW NO PEACE   293 16
  PEACE CONGEALED IN BLACK LAVA ON THE DOORSTEP   294 1
  WITHIN WHITE-HOT LAVA NEVER AT PEACE   294 2
  CALL IT PEACE   294 6
  UNLOCKS THE FOUNTAINS OF PEACE AGAIN   461 24
  THE FOUNTAINS OF PEACE THE FOUNTAINS OF PEACE   461 25
  THE WELLING OF PEACE WHEN IT RISES AND FLOWS   462 6
  IS DEATH TO US ALL IN THE MARSHES OF PEACE   462 16
  THAT IS THE CRYSTAL OF PEACE THE SLOW HARD JEWEL OF TRU+   477 17
  THE GEM OF MUTUAL PEACE EMERGING FROM THE WILD CHAOS   477 19
  PEOPLE ALWAYS MAKE WAR WHEN THEY SAY THEY LOVE PEACE   495 15
  THE LOUD LOVE OF PEACE MAKES ONE QUIVER MORE THAN ANY   495 16
  WHY SHOULD ONE LOVE PEACE IT IS SO OBVIOUSLY VILE TO MA+   495 18
  LOUD PEACE PROPAGANDA MAKES WAR SEEM IMMINENT   495 20
  THEN WE SHAN'T HAVE WAR AND WE NEEDN'T TALK ABOUT PEACE   496 5
  RUN TINY RIVERS OF PEACE   496 12
  MOST OF HIS TIME THE TIGER PADS AND SLOUCHES IN A BURNI+   496 13
  AND THE SMALL HAWK HIGH UP TURNS ROUND ON THE SLOW PIVO+   496 14
  PEACE COMES FROM BEHIND THE SUN WITH THE PEREGRINE FALC+   496 15
  A MAN OF PEACE   497 2
  WHICH MAY OCCASIONALLY BE A PRELIMINARY TO THE PEACE TH+   497 9
  A MAN OF PEACE   497 12
  AND THAT IS MY BIT OF INWARD PEACE WHERE I AM AT ONE   497 23
  I WOULD RATHER SIT STILL IN A STATE OF PEACE ON A STONE   498 1
  A CERTAIN PEACE A CERTAIN GRACE   499 2
  PEACE I HAVE FROM THE CORE OF THE ATOM FROM THE CORE OF+   499 4
  I WOULD LIKE A FEW MEN TO BE AT PEACE WITH   499 20
  BUT MEN TO BE AT PEACE WITH   499 25
  TO BE FULL OF THE PEACE THAT COMES OF EXPERIENCE   503 15
  WE WANT A NEW WORLD OF WILD PEACE WHERE LIVING IS FREE   519 22
  NOT THIS HYENA TAME PEACE WHERE NO MAN DARE TELL ANOTHER   519 23
  THIS PRETTY PEACE WHERE EVERY MAN HAS TO FIGHT AND FIGHT   519 26
  WE HAVE PEACE   609 13
  SO THAT MY HEART BEATS SOOTHED SOOTHED SOOTHED AND AT P+   652 8
  AT PEACE IN PEACE   700 4
  A CREATURE OF BEAUTIFUL PEACE LIKE A RIVER   714 14
  OF A STRONG HEART AT PEACE   717 19
  FILLING THE HEART WITH PEACE   720 17
  SWINGS THE HEART RENEWED WITH PEACE   720 18
  SPEAK WITH THEM AND GIVE THEM PEACE AND DO THEM HONOUR   723 13
  WHERE THE SOUL COMES AT LAST AND HAS UTTER PEACE   724 7
  IN UTTER PEACE   724 10
  THE SOUL HAS PEACE INWARD AND LOVELY PEACE   724 26
  AND AFTER DARKNESS OF HER PEACE   725 16
  AND IF TONIGHT MY SOUL MAY FIND HER PEACE   726 22
  WE COVER THE HOUSELESS DEAD SO THEY SLEEP IN PEACE   736 25
  SO HE TOO MAY BE HEALED BE SOOTHED TO PEACE   736 27
  AND WE SHALL HAVE NEW PEACE IN THIS OUR LIFE   740 25
  THAT GIVES ME PEACE   741 15
  FOR A RHYTHM TO COMPEL ME BACK FOR PEACE   747 23
  MEN DEARER TO ME THAN PEACE   765 5
  YET THROUGH THE TEARS STEALS A SENSE OF PEACE AND GREAT+   768 1

PEACE
  PEACE LIKE A RIVER FLOWS   770 24
  AND PEACE LIKE A RIVER FLOWS   770 31
  WHERE PEACE LIKE A RIVER FLOWS   771 16
  IN PEACE BEYOND THE LASHING OF THE SUN'S BRIGHT TAIL   786 2
  AT THE DEPTHS OF THE PEACE AND THE FLIGHT   788 17
  DEEP IN THE MOISTURES OF PEACE   788 18
  TO THE POOL OF PEACE AND FORGETTING IN HEAVEN   798 27
  AND BUILDING MY NEST OF PEACE IN YOUR BONES   802 4
  BRAVE MEN HAVE PEACE AT NIGHTFALL   810 7
  AND WHAT OF GOOD I HAVE GIVEN THE DAY MY PEACE ATTESTS   *946 3
  OF SHEER OBLIVION AND OF UTTER PEACE   *959 32
  AH PEACE AH LOVELY PEACE MOST LOVELY LAPSING   *960 1
  OF THIS MY SOUL INTO THE PLASM OF PEACE   *960 2
  PEACE COMPLETE PEACE   *960 5
  OF PEACE AND BUILD YOUR LITTLE SHIP   *960 13
  AH IF YOU WANT TO LIVE IN PEACE ON THE FACE OF THE EARTH   *961 5
  AND HOW HE FINDS THE DARKNESS THAT ENFOLDS HIM INTO UTT+   *961 13

PEACEFUL
  THERE'S ONE THING WE S'LL 'AVE A PEACEFUL 'OUSE   45 29
  THANK HEAVEN FOR A PEACEFUL HOUSE   45 31
  THE PEACEFUL FLOOR WHEN FELL THE SWORD ON THEIR REST   155 5
  AND DEPART PEACEFUL PACIFIED AND THANKLESS   350 11
  AND RAVISHED ALL THE PEACEFUL OBLIVIOUS PLACES   725 18
  WHY ARE YOU SO ANXIOUS LEAVE ME PEACEFUL WITH MY DEAD   756 17

PEACEFULLY
  WHERE YOU'VE SAT PEACEFULLY ALL THESE YEARS   541 7
  OH THINK OF IT IN THE TWILIGHT PEACEFULLY   *960 18

PEACELESS
  ARE MUCH MORE HELLISHLY PEACELESS THAN A LITTLE STRAIGH+   497 7
  ONE CAN'T STAND PEACELESS PEOPLE ANY MORE   499 19
  WHEN PEOPLE ARE DEAD AND PEACELESS   500 11
  WHEN PEOPLE ARE DEAD AND PEACELESS   500 13

PEACELESSNESS
  AND FEEL THE PEACELESSNESS OF THE MULTIMILLIONAIRE   498 3

PEACE-TALKING
  NATIONS ARMIES WAR PEACE-TALKING   256 27

PEACH
  HERE TAKE ALL THAT'S LEFT OF MY PEACH   279 4
  I AM THINKING OF COURSE OF THE PEACH BEFORE I ATE IT   279 13
  WHY WAS NOT MY PEACH ROUND AND FINISHED LIKE A BILLIARD   279 21
  HERE YOU CAN HAVE MY PEACH STONE   279 28
  SILVER-PINK PEACH VENETIAN GREEN GLASS OF MEDLARS AND S+   283 5

PEACH-BLOOM
  WHY FROM SILVERY PEACH-BLOOM   279 10

PEACHES
  ADMIT THAT APPLES AND STRAWBERRIES AND PEACHES AND PEAR+   285 5
  OR THE BUTTER OR THE APPLES OR PEACHES FROM THE BASKET   828 19

PEACOCK
  NOT THE EAGLE SCREAMS WHEN THE SUN IS HIGH THE PEACOCK +   368 10
  WHEREAS THE PEACOCK HAS A DIADEM   369 23
  THE PEACOCK LIFTS HIS RODS OF BRONZE   371 1
  HAS THE PEACOCK HAD HIS DAY DOES HE CALL IN VAIN SCREEC+   371 20
  THINK HOW A PEACOCK IN A FOREST OF HIGH TREES   530 5
  AS THE PEACOCK TURNS TO THE SUN AND COULD NOT BE MORE S+   683 8

PEACOCKS
  TWO STREAMING PEACOCKS GONE IN A CLOUD   70 17

PEAK
  AGAINST ME AND BRIGHT PEAK SHINING TO PEAK   224 4
  TO STAND ON THE HIGHEST PEAK   382 13
  NEVER A MOUNTAIN PEAK TO BE KING OF THE CASTLE   382 32
  FIGHT TO BE THE DEVIL ON THE TIP OF THE PEAK   383 24
  SWIM DEEPER DEEPER TILL IT LEAVES NO PEAK EMERGING   428 25

PEAKED
  A LITTLE BEARDED MAN PEAKED IN SLEEPING   145 8
  PEAKED AND A BIT DISMAYED   394 1
  BUT ONE OF HIS BELOVEDS LOOKING A LITTLE PEAKED   446 26

PEAKS
  WHITE PEAKS OF SNOW AT THE FOOT OF THE SUNKEN CHRIST   225 30

PEALING
  IN CONFIRMATION I HEAR SEVENFOLD LARK-SONGS PEALING   34 29
  HUGE HUGER HUGER AND HUGER PEALING   698 19

PEALS
  HUGE HUGE ROLL THE PEALS OF THE THUNDROUS LAUGH   698 18

PEAR
  A WHIRL LIKE SNOW FROM THE PLUM-TREES AND THE PEAR   154 30
  ALMOND AND APPLE AND PEAR DIFFUSE WITH LIGHT THAT VERY   179 3
  THE FATHER EATS THE PEAR AND THE SON'S TEETH ARE SET ON+   530 22
  THAT YEAR WHEN THE PEAR WAS OUT MY DELIGHT   886 4

PEAR-BLOOM
  OH AND SUDDENLY FROM OUT OF NOWHERE WHIRLS THE PEAR-BLO+   271 25

PEAR-BLOSSOM
  THE PEAR-BLOSSOM IS A FOUNTAIN OF FOAM   885 28
  PEAR-BLOSSOM HANGING AND ONE SMALL KNEE   886 7
  I AM TERRIFIED OF THE PEAR-BLOSSOM   886 16

PEARL
  SWAYS THE GOLDEN PEARL OF PLEASURE   868 20
  GONE GONE AND THE BOAT DISSOLVES LIKE PEARL   *959 30

PEARLED
  SUCH PEARLED ZONES OF FAIR STERILITY   855 1

PEARLS
  ROUNDED LIKE PEARLS FOR SLEEP AND THEN FROM BETWEEN SHU+   88 16
  PEARLS ITSELF INTO TENDERNESS OF BUD   306 5
  SWAY THE LIVE PEARLS THEIR FLOWERING PLEDGES   *941 20

PEARLY
  YOU UNDINE-CLEAR AND PEARLY SOULLESSLY COOL   161 15
  THAT SHE EXUDES LIKE PEARLY WHITE POISON GAS   619 21

PEARS
  ADMIT THAT APPLES AND STRAWBERRIES AND PEACHES AND PEAR+   285 5

PEAR-TREE
  THE HUM OF THE BEES IN THE PEAR-TREE BLOOM   885 14
  AND THE BUSTLE OF BEES IN THE PEAR-TREE BLOOM   885 24
  TO THE WINDOW AND THE WHITE PEAR-TREE   886 9

PEASANT
  EAT ME UP DEAR PEASANT SO THE PEASANT ATE HIM   533 25

PEASANTS
  HE SHIFTED HIS JOB ON TO THE PEASANTS   536 22
  THE PEASANTS ARE BENDING CUTTING THE BEARDED WHEAT   605 22

PEAS-COD
  BEAN WAS ONE OF THE OLDEST SYMBOLS OF THE MALE ORGAN FO+ 303 19

PEBBLE
  ROW ON THEN SMALL PEBBLE   357 26

PEBBLES
  AND ALL RAMBLING AIMLESS LIKE LITTLE PERAMBULATING PEBB+ 357 18
  IN A GARDEN OF PEBBLES AND INSECTS   358 11

PECK
  HOVERING TO PECK OUT THE EYES OF THE STILL-LIVING CREAT+ 500 17
  AND WOULD YOU PECK OUT HIS EYES IF HE DID   540 11

PECKED
  SO THEY PECKED A SHRED OF MY LIFE AND FLEW OFF WITH A   500 4
  THE HOURS PECKED PLEASURE FROM ME AND THE SUN DELIGHTED+ *933 19

PECULIAR
  HE IS A SAVAGE WITH HIS OWN PECULIAR CONSCIOUSNESS HIS + 776 28
  PECULIAR CUSTOMS AND OBSERVANCES   776 29

PEDESTALS
  FROM THEIR PEDESTALS HOLY MOSES   556 27

PEDIMENT
  THIS LITTLE DOME THIS PEDIMENT   356 16
  PEDIMENT OF LIFE   356 21

PEE
  TO PEE IN THE EYE OF A POLICE-MAN   434 16

PEEP
  AND THEY PEEP AT ME OVER THE EDGES   105 17
  A COLD HAND I PEEP BETWEEN THE FINGERS   162 18
  ALWAYS THERE AS I PEEP   162 21
  WOULD YOU PEEP IN THE EMPTY HOUSE LIKE A PILFERER   742 17
  BUT THOSE THAT WILL NOT FOLLOW MUST NOT PEEP   799 11
  ARE A POPPY-SHOW PEEP WHILE YOU COMB   886 2
  YOUR HAIR PEEP OUT ON THE LANE   886 3
  THEY WILL PEEP FORTH   *954 16

PEEPED
  OR GLOATED OR PEEPED AT THE SIMPLE SPOT   579 3

PEEPING
  WHAT IS PEEPING FROM YOUR SKIRTS O MOTHER HEN   119 28
  PEEPING THEY WILL LOSE THEIR SIGHT AND LINGERING THEY W+ 799 12

PEER
  PEER ANXIOUSLY FORTH AS IF FOR A BOAT TO CARRY THEM OUT+   71 26

PEERING
  PITEOUS LOVE COMES PEERING UNDER THE HOOD   64 15
  YOUR PRESENCE PEERING LONELILY THERE   116 25
  BETWEEN YOUR THIGHS FAR FAR FROM YOUR PEERING SIGHT   119 6
  AND WHAT ARE YOU WOMAN PEERING THROUGH THE RENTS   742 15
  THE SIGHT OF YOU PEERING LONELY THERE   *930 24

PEERLESS
  OF A PEERLESS SOUL   314 15

PEEVISH
  PEEVISH AND SEASICK   842 17

PEE-WHIPS
  NAY YO' BLESSED PEE-WHIPS   78 25
  NAY YOU BLESSED PEE-WHIPS   *920 17

PEEWIT
  I AM HERE I AM HERE SCREAMS THE PEEWIT THE MAY-BLOBS BU+   34 9
  AND THAT A PEEWIT CALLED   881 23

PEEWITS
  ABOVE THEM EXULTANT THE PEEWITS ARE SWEEPING   33 3
  WINGS AND FEATHERS ON THE CRYING MYSTERIOUS AGES PEEWIT+   34 26
  OF THE DARK-GREEN HILLS NEW CALVES IN SHED PEEWITS TURN+   57 27
  ABOVE THEM EXULTANT THE PEEWITS ARE SWEEPING   *891 3

PEG-TOPS
  STRUT LIKE PEG-TOPS WOUND AROUND WITH HUNDREDS OF YARDS 388 17

PELASGIC
  PELASGIC FACES UNCOVERED 311 16

PELERINE
  AS I WENT DOWN THE STREET IN MY NOSE-RED PELERINE 750 17

PELF
  PELF 93 23

PELICAN
  TRYING TO LOOK LIKE A PELICAN 413 13
  OR A PELICAN 414 8

PELLUCID
  THE GREY PLASM-LIMPID PELLUCID ADVANCE 68 9
  THE GREY PHOSPHORESCENT PELLUCID ADVANCE *914 24

PELT
  AN ASH-GREY PELT 408 28

PELTING
  PELTING BEHIND ON THE DUSTY TRAIL WHEN THE HORSE SETS O+ 397 12
  PELTING INDOORS 400 3
  COME PELTING TO ME NOW THE OTHER FOLK HAVE FOUND YOU 400 4

PELTS
  IN PELTS OF WOLVES ALL HER LUMINOUS 171 7

PEN
  TO THE HERD INSIDE THE PEN 458 29

PENALTY
  IT IS THE PENALTY OF FEAR AND MEANNESS BEING MEANER THAN 522 22

PENCE
  MILLIONS OF SIMILAR HONEST PENCE 488 19

PENDULOUS
  AH THE DEWLAP SWINGS PENDULOUS WITH EXCESS 326 17

PENDULUM
  WHICH SLIPS DOWN LIKE A PENDULUM TO BALANCE THE THROBBI+ 370 6

PENETRATE
  BE PENETRATE LIKE THE TREE 114 12

PENETRATED
  PENETRATED MY BLOOD 885 15

PENETRATING
  AND EXHAUSTING PENETRATING THE LAVA-CRATER OF A TINY 539 7

PENIS
  I TELL YOU THE PENIS WON'T DO IT 539 21
  NO MY POOR LITTLE PENIS WOULD BE OF NO USE TO YOU 541 13

PENITENTES
  THE PENITENTES LASH THEMSELVES TILL THEY RUN WITH BLOOD 408 4

PENNANTS
  PASSING WITH SPEARS AND PENNANTS AND MANLY SCORN 221 9
  PASSING WITH SPEARS AND PENNANTS AND MANLY SCORN *944 22

PENNY
  AND TURNED MY MODEST PENNY 488 16

PENNY-A-TIME
  FOR MEN TO SHOOT AT PENNY-A-TIME IN A BOOTH AT A FAIR 272 17

PENS
  SO I DID HIS PENS AND THE JASPER SEAL ON HIS NECK 255 4

PENSIVE
  LONG PENSIVE SLIM-MUZZLED GREYHOUND BUDS 310 29
  BENDING THEIR ROSY MUZZLES PENSIVE DOWN 311 11
  WITH THE HALF-VEILED BEAUTIFUL EYES AND THE PENSIVE FACE 379 4

PENTECOST
  OR SCREAMING IN PENTECOST RECEIVING THE GHOST 365 14

PENULTIMATE
  AND AT THE PENULTIMATE PORCHES THE DARK-RED MANTLE *959 24

PENUMBRA
  FLOWERS OF THE PENUMBRA ISSUE OF CORRUPTION NOURISHED IN 271 8

PEON
  HOW NICE SAYS THE PEON TO GO RUSHING IN A TRAIN 794 13

PEONS
  AND YOU MEXICANS AND PEONS WHAT DO YOU DO 794 1
  OH FOOLS MEXICANS AND PEONS 794 25
  OH FOOLS MEXICANS AND PEONS WITH MUDDY HEARTS 794 32
  OH DOGS AND FOOLS MEXICANS AND PEONS 795 5

PEONY
  OR FIRM AND SILKEN AS YOUNG PEONY FLOWERS 65 10
  REFOLDING SHE SLIPPED TO THE FLOOR AS A GHOST-WHITE PEO+ 155 23
  AZALEA AND CAMELLIA SINGLE PEONY 313 28
  COOL AND FIRM AND SILKEN AS PINK YOUNG PEONY FLOWERS *913 11
  FIRM AND SILKEN LIKE PINK YOUNG PEONY FLOWERS *914 11

PEOPLE
  WHERE PEOPLE ARE CROWDED LIKE THISTLES 101 21
  OF THE MOURNFUL TILL PEOPLE WAFT 108 21
  WHETHER THE PEOPLE IN THE STREET 109 17
  GO MYRIAD SPARKS OF PEOPLE FILLING 110 19
  PEOPLE FLICKER ROUND ME 115 15
  YET WHEN PLEIADS OF PEOPLE ARE 115 22
  WHEN PEOPLE FLICKER DOWN THE PAVEMENT 115 25
  FACES OF PEOPLE BLOWING ACROSS MY GAZE 116 9
  WITH PEOPLE PASSING UNDERNEATH 121 19
  US CREATURES PEOPLE AND FLOWERS UNDONE 127 3
  STREWN STARS OF UNKNOWN PEOPLE AND LUMINOUS LITTER 132 12
  THEATRE PEOPLE PASS 146 18
  AND PEOPLE DARKLY INVESTED WITH PURPLE MOVE PALPABLE 148 26
  MOANS AND BOOMS THE SOUL OF A PEOPLE IMPRISONED ASLEEP 149 11
  BEYOND AND NO PEOPLE 162 8
  SO PEOPLE PASSING UNDER 176 14
  AND MANY PEOPLE PASS 196 14
  MANY BRIGHT PEOPLE PASS 196 16
  YOU HAVE STEPPED ACROSS YOUR PEOPLE CARELESSLY HURTING 209 8
  I HAVE STEPPED ACROSS MY PEOPLE AND HURT THEM IN SPITE 209 10
  NO HOW CRUEL YOU ARE YOU PEOPLE THE SUNSHINE 211 18
  WITH SHADOWS WITH YOURS I PEOPLE THE SUNSHINE 211 19
  JOSTLING PEOPLE TOUCHING AND TALKING AND MAKING SMALL 249 16
  AND WHOSOEVER THE UNKNOWN PEOPLE OF THIS UNKNOWN 256 14
  PEOPLE HOUSES STREETS VEHICLES MACHINES 256 26
  YOUR NASCENT DEMON PEOPLE 293 7
  LEAVING A NERVOUS PEOPLE 374 28
  AND YOU CROSS THE FERRY WITH THE NAKED PEOPLE GO UP THE 386 25
  AND WHITE PEOPLE IN EVENING DRESS BUZZING AND CROWDING 387 23
  AND ALL THE DARK-FACED COTTON-WRAPPED PEOPLE MORE 391 5
  ALL THE DARK-FACED COTTON-WRAPPED PEOPLE A COUNTLESS 391 8
  COTTON-WRAPPED PEOPLE 391 26
  IF YOU LIVE ALONG WITH ALL THE OTHER PEOPLE 431 30
  AND IF YOU LIVE WITH ALL THE OTHER PEOPLE 432 1
  THEY'LL TAKE YOU FOR A WOMAN OF THE PEOPLE 433 13
  I MEAN PEOPLE LIKE YOU AND ME 435 8
  THAT'S WHAT'S SO BORING PEOPLE ARE SO BORING 435 12
  AND ALL THE PEOPLE THAT GO WITH THE FITTINGS AND THE 440 18
  WHEN WILT THOU TEACH THE PEOPLE 442 6
  OF THE PEOPLE 442 11
  WHEN A SAVIOUR HAS SAVED A PEOPLE 442 12
  AND SO IT GOES ON WITH THE SAVING OF THE PEOPLE 443 8
  UPON WHICH SHADOWS OF PEOPLE PURE PERSONALITIES 444 5
  IT WAS FULL OF UNEASY PEOPLE 444 11
  CAUTIOUS PEOPLE 445 2
  AND THE PEOPLE APPLAUDED WITH HOLLOW FRIGHTENED 445 8
  THE PEOPLE WATCHED AND WONDERED AND SEEMED TO RESENT 445 17
  IN THE CIRCUS WITH THEIR CIRCUS PEOPLE 445 23
  WHEN MODERN PEOPLE SEE THE CARNAL BODY DAUNTLESS AND 445 31
  MODERN PEOPLE ARE DEPRESSED 445 35
  MODERN PEOPLE FEEL THEMSELVES AT A DISADVANTAGE 446 1
  AND THEY GRUDGE THE CIRCUS PEOPLE THE SWOOPING GAY 446 8
  SEXLESS PEOPLE TRANSMIT NOTHING 449 5
  FROM THE BUSY BODIES OF PEOPLE 451 19
  THESE PEOPLE OF FLESH 460 1
  PEOPLE IN THEIR THIRTIES AND THE OLDER ONES HAVE GOTTEN 462 19
  WHY DON'T YOU KNOW WHAT'S WHAT YOUNG PEOPLE SEEMS 464 9
  WHAT THE OLD PEOPLE CALL IMMEDIATE CONTACT WITH GOD 481 6
  THAT SUCH TRIVIAL PEOPLE SHOULD MUSE AND THUNDER 494 14
  HOW DROLL HOW SMALL SHAKESPEARE'S PEOPLE ARE 494 25
  PEOPLE ALWAYS MAKE WAR WHEN THEY SAY THEY LOVE PEACE 495 15
  OTHER PEOPLE 495 22
  LET PEOPLE BE WISE FOR THEMSELVES AND ANYHOW 495 23
  WHY CAN'T PEOPLE BE GAY LIKE THAT 496 9
  THE ONLY PEOPLE I EVER HEARD TALK ABOUT MY LADY POVERTY 498 9
  WERE RICH PEOPLE OR PEOPLE WHO IMAGINED THEMSELVES RICH 498 10
  BEING BORN AMONG THE WORKING PEOPLE 498 12
  THERE ARE NO PEOPLE NOR EVER WILL BE 499 9
  ONE CAN'T STAND PEACELESS PEOPLE ANY MORE 499 19
  I HAVE GIVEN MYSELF TO THE PEOPLE WHEN THEY CAME 500 2
  WHEN PEOPLE ARE DEAD AND PEACELESS 500 11
  WHEN PEOPLE ARE DEAD AND PEACELESS 500 13
  PEOPLE FEELING THINGS THEY INTEND TO FEEL THEY MEAN TO + 500 21
  THE FEELINGS PEOPLE OUGHT TO HAVE THEY NEVER HAVE 501 11
  IF PEOPLE SAY THEY'VE GOT FEELINGS YOU MAY BE PRETTY 501 12
  IF PEOPLE LIVED WITHOUT ACCEPTING LIES 503 19
  SOOTHING OLD PEOPLE SHOULD BE LIKE APPLES 503 22
  WHAT MAKES PEOPLE UNSATISFIED 504 1
  IF PEOPLE HAD COURAGE AND REFUSED LIES 504 3
  WHEN FULFILLED PEOPLE DIE 505 1
  WHY DON'T PEOPLE LEAVE OFF BEING LOVABLE 505 9
  I AM SICK OF LOVABLE PEOPLE 505 23
  I WISH PEOPLE WHEN YOU SIT NEAR THEM 506 20
  WITH THE EFFORT OF TRYING TO LOVE PEOPLE 506 26
  DON'T DO IT BECAUSE YOU HATE PEOPLE 517 5
  GETTING THE BETTER OF OTHER PEOPLE WHO CARES 518 18
  I FEEL THAT WHEN PEOPLE HAVE GONE UTTERLY SUNLESS 526 23
  LET OTHER PEOPLE BE WHAT THEY MAY 526 28
  AND PEOPLE ARE NOT MY MEASURE 527 3
  WE NEED HAVE NO DEAD PEOPLE MONEY-SLAVES AND SOCIAL 527 7
  AS SOON AS YOU LET PEOPLE BE YOUR MEASURE 527 18
  BECAUSE IF THE MIDDLE CLASSES HAD NO POORER PEOPLE TO BE 527 20
  IN OTHER PEOPLE 528 9
  WHILE PEOPLE MINCE MEAN WORDS THROUGH THEIR TEETH 530 11
  BUT HOW PALTRY MINGY AND DINGY AND SQUALID PEOPLE LOOK 530 15
  AND A SICKLY PEOPLE WILL SLAY US 537 9
  REALLY PATRIOTIC PEOPLE THE RIGHT SORT OF PEOPLE YOU KN+ 546 8
  DENIED A SIGNATURE WE ENGLISH ARE A SOLID PEOPLE AFTER + 546 19
  THERE MUST BE A BED-ROCK SOMEWHERE OF PEOPLE WHO ARE 548 3
  WHO ARE VERY SUPERIOR PEOPLE 548 34

PEOPLE
    THE PEOPLE WERE NEVER IN   554 16
    WITH SUCH PEOPLE ONE HAS TO BE CAREFUL   554 23
    THIRTEEN THOUSAND PEOPLE CAME TO SEE   577 24
    OF ALL THE SORDID PEOPLE THAT HAVE STARED AT THEM UNCLE+   580 25
    WHAT HAVE THEY DONE TO YOU THE SAVIOURS OF THE PEOPLE   585 11
    AH THE PEOPLE THE PEOPLE   585 22
    I LIKE PEOPLE QUITE WELL   602   1
    MOST PEOPLE TODAY ARE CHIMAERA   603 21
    THERE ARE TOO MANY PEOPLE ON EARTH   606 18
    OF DRESSED-UP PEOPLE   607 23
    I NEVER KNOW WHAT PEOPLE MEAN WHEN THEY COMPLAIN OF   610   1
    PEOPLE WHO COMPLAIN OF LONELINESS MUST HAVE LOST SOMETH+   610   8
    BUT THE PRESENCE OF OTHER PEOPLE WILL NOT GIVE THEM NEW   610 13
    FOR OLD VALUES AND OLD PEOPLE   612 14
    PEOPLE WHO CARE WHO CARE WHO CARE   613   3
    WHY SEEK TO ALTER PEOPLE WHY NOT LEAVE THEM ALONE   614 17
    PEOPLE ARE LIKE LEAVES FLUTTERING AND GAY ON THE BUSH O+   615   7
    BUT PEOPLE WHO ARE FALLEN FROM THE ORGANIC CONNECTION W+   615 17
    AND THE STIFF-NECKED PEOPLE AND THE SELF-WILLED PEOPLE +   616   2
    I KNOW HE IS EITHER A BED-BUG BATTENING ON SLEEPING PEO+   621 23
    SEA-BATHING CITY PEOPLE   625 12
    I HAVE NOTICED THAT PEOPLE WHO TALK A LOT ABOUT LOYALTY   626   1
    AND PEOPLE WHO TALK ABOUT FAITH   626   4
    OH I AM OF THE PEOPLE   626   7
    OH I AM OF THE PEOPLE   626   9
    AND THE PEOPLE ALWAYS LOVE ME   626 11
    THE PEOPLE ALWAYS LOVE ME   626 13
    BUT THE PEOPLE ALWAYS LOVE ME   626 23
    THE PEOPLE ALWAYS LOVE ME   626 25
    THEREFORE I KNOW THE PEOPLE   627   1
    THE PEOPLE THE PEOPLE   627   2
    OH GOLDEN FIELDS OF PEOPLE   627   9
    OF PEOPLE OF PEOPLE   627 10
    OH GOLDEN FIELD OF PEOPLE   627 11
    AND OUT OF THE LIPS OF PEOPLE JERK STRANGE MECHANICAL N+   629 10
    WHAT HAVE THEY DONE TO YOU THE SAVIOURS OF THE PEOPLE OH   630 11
    FOR OH THE POOR PEOPLE THAT ARE FLESH OF MY FLESH   632 14
    OH HOW I LOVED THE THOUGHT OF THOUGHTFUL PEOPLE   644   8
    AND THE EXHAUST-SMELL OF PEOPLE   646   7
    AND THERE IS NO GRATING OF PEOPLE WITH THEIR PRESENCE   646 16
    LIVING PEOPLE NEVER MAKE REVOLUTIONS   647 22
    PEOPLE WERE BATHING AND POSTURING THEMSELVES ON THE BEA+   651   1
    LISTEN TO PEOPLE LAUGHING   654 13
    PEOPLE GO ON SINGING WHEN THEY HAVE NO SONG IN THEM   657 17
    PEOPLE GO ON TALKING WHEN THEY HAVE NOTHING TO SAY   657 18
    PEOPLE GO ON WALKING WHEN THEY HAVE NOWHERE TO GO   657 19
    PEOPLE KEEP IT UP BECAUSE THEY DAREN'T STOP   657 20
    THEY ARE THE NICEST PEOPLE IN THE WORLD   659 26
    OLD PEOPLE FIXED IN A RANCID RESISTANCE   662 20
    THEY'LL MERELY DESTROY ALL PROPERTY AND A GREAT MANY PE+   665   1
    AND QUITE A LOT OF PEOPLE ARE NOT   665 17
    YOU SEE THEM IN GLIMPSES IN THE FACES AND FORMS OF PEOP+   671 23
    WHEN PEOPLE POSE AS GODS THEY ARE CRYSTAL PALACE STATUES   673   2
    WHILE PEOPLE LIVE THE LIFE   675   9
    BUT WHEN PEOPLE ARE ONLY SELF-CONSCIOUS AND SELF-WILLED   675 18
    SO SELF-WILLED SELF-CENTRED SELF-CONSCIOUS PEOPLE DIE   676   6
    BUT WHEN LIVING PEOPLE DIE IN THE RIPENESS OF THEIR TIME   676   8
    I ONLY CAN SET OTHER PEOPLE RIGHT   680 11
    ALL PEOPLE THAT CAN WRITE OR PAINT   680 12
    OF PEOPLE   703 27
    THE MULTITUDINOUS PEOPLE UNFUSED   746   6
    WHERE NO PEOPLE ARE AND NO FIRES   769 18
    AMERICANS ARE THE PEOPLE OF AMERICA   774 22
    BUT THE GERM OF THAT FUTURE IS INSIDE THE AMERICAN PEOP+   775   2
    AND LONG-HAIRED PEOPLE WHO PRETEND TO ESPOUSE   778   5
    PEOPLE WANT TO KEEP THE INDIAN BACK WANT TO   778   7
    LONG-HAIRED PEOPLE PAINTING THE INDIAN AND WRITING   778 10
    OH WITHERED CRACKLING TWIGS OF BRUSHWOOD PEOPLE   784 20
    MYRIAD MYRIAD DEAD TWIGS OF PALLID AND CHAFING PEOPLE   784 21
    SURELY HE SAID THIS IS A CURIOUS PEOPLE I HAVE FOUND   790 16
    HOLALA WHAT A PRETTY PEOPLE   790 26
    AND THE AIR THAT BLOWS GOOD BREATH IN THE NOSTRILS OF P+   792 14
    THERE ARE PEOPLE THERE BEYOND THE ROCKIES   816   1
    AS THERE ARE PEOPLE HERE ON THIS SIDE   816   2
    BUT THE PEOPLE THERE BEYOND THE ROCKIES   816   3
    MEXICANS LIKE PEOPLE WHO HAVE DIED   816   9
    THESE PEOPLE THAT LIE LIKE SEALS   824 30
    AND THEREFORE SINCE THE PEOPLE I MEET OF THE YOUNGER   829   4
    IT IS SICK OF PEOPLE OUT ON THE MAKE   831   7
    THEY ARE REALLY LOW CLASS PEOPLE OUT ON THE MAKE   831   8
    SO THEY ACCEPT COVERED DISLIKE AS THE NORMAL FEELING BE+   832 15
    WHY TROUBLE ABOUT PEOPLE   839 24
    ALL PEOPLE LIKE LICE   843 10
    THE PEOPLE IN IT ARE GRIM   846   1
    THEY HAD RED LILLY AND PEOPLE SINGING SONGS   846   8
    AND PEOPLE ARE SAD AND GRIM   846 10
    STREWN STARS OF PALLID PEOPLE AND THROUGH LUMINOUS LITT+   *938   4
    SO PEOPLE PASSING UNDER   *941   1

PEOPLED
    IS PEOPLED WITH SHADOWS AND WAILING AND LAST GHOSTS LUR+   54 31

PEOPLE'S
    ALL THIS PHILANTHROPY AND BENEVOLENCE ON OTHER PEOPLE'S   291 19
    I AM SICK OF PEOPLE'S CEREBRAL EMOTIONS   500 18

PEPPER-BOX
    THAT I HAD BEEN HE IN THE PAVILION AS IN A PEPPER-BOX A+   392   2

PEPPERMINT
    LIFTING HER FACE TO NIBBLE AT A ROUND WHITE PEPPERMINT   393   8
    THERE SHE SHAN'T HAVE ANY MORE PEPPERMINT DROPS   393 24

PERA-HERA
    BUT THE BEST IS THE PERA-HERA AT MIDNIGHT UNDER THE   387 19
    AND AT LAST THE PERA-HERA PROCESSION FLAMBEAUX ALOFT IN   387 25
    WE DODGED WHEN THE PERA-HERA WAS FINISHED UNDER THE   390 11

PERAMBULATING
    BLOOM ALONG THE CORSO ON THE LIVING PERAMBULATING BUSH   313 24
    AND ALL RAMBLING AIMLESS LIKE LITTLE PERAMBULATING PEBB+   357 18
    THEY ARE ALL PERAMBULATING EGGS   603 18

PERAMBULATOR
    BUT THEN YOU NEED ONLY LOOK AT THE MODERN PERAMBULATOR   521 25
    AND ITS PERAMBULATOR HAS TO GET BIGGER AND BIGGER   670 10

PERAMBULATORS
    AND HYGIENIC BABIES IN HUGE HULKS OF COFFIN-LIKE PERAMB+   522   5

PER BACCO
    AND NEVER ANOTHER PER BACCO IS SAID   815 13

PERCEIVE
    THE DAYS PERCEIVE OUR MARRIAGE AND REJOICE   129 10
    BUT YE THAT PERCEIVE ME BETWEEN   788   5

PERCEPTION
    FOR THEY ARE THE ELEMENTS OF LIFE OF POETRY AND OF PERC+   706   3

PERCH
    PERCH   142 12
    INSTEAD OF WHICH SHE STRANGELY REARS ON HER PERCH IN THE   385 23
    YOU SIT NEXT TO ME ON THE PERCH   761 29

PERCHANCE
    WHERE THE LOFTY TREES ATHWART STREAM PERCHANCE   *914 26

PERCHED
    THERE SHE IS PERCHED ON HER MANGER LOOKING OVER THE   384 19

PERCHES
    PERCHES   413   6

PERDITION
    ON THE WAY TO DARK PERDITION   710 20

PEREGRINE
    PEACE COMES FROM BEHIND THE SUN WITH THE PEREGRINE FALC+   496 15

PERFECT
    OF PERFECT THINGS   101 13
    ALONE ON THE PERFECT SILENCE   110 23
    MY OWN TO HER PERFECT   121   9
    OF DARKNESS WHEREON SHE SLEEPS ON HER PERFECT BED   133 25
    IN PERFECT CHRISM   154 15
    AND NOW AT LAST I KISS YOUR PERFECT FACE   157 21
    THEY ANOINT THEIR BROWS WITH YOUR PAIN AS A PERFECT   168 19
    AND THE PERFECT DEAD ARE ELATE   168 30
    THAT PERFECT BRIGHT EXPERIENCE NEVER FALLS   193 10
    THAT HOLDS THE PERFECT CHILD   201 10
    WHAT ELSE IT IS PERFECT ENOUGH   203 25
    OF PERFECT LIFE AND IS OUR POSSIBLE SEED   219   7
    IT IS FAR MORE PERFECT NOW   227 26
    I AM LIKE A SEED WITH A PERFECT FLOWER ENCLOSED   247   6
    THEN WE SHALL BE FREER THAN ANGELS AH PERFECT   267 23
    THE SONO IO OF PERFECT DRUNKENNESS   281 29
    INTO MACHINE-UPRISEN PERFECT MAN   290 25
    AND GIVEN AND PERFECT   307 14
    UGH HOW I LOVE ITS FANGS OF PERFECT RAGE   315 18
    AND WRESTLE WITH FOR THE PRIZE OF PERFECT LOVE   411   9
    AS THE LEOPARD SMITES THE SMALL CALF WITH A SPANGLED PA+   683   9
    AND A CEASING TO KNOW A PERFECT CEASING TO KNOW   724 21
    THE PERFECT LAMBENT FLAME WHICH STILL GOES UP   745 36
    MARRIED MAKE PERFECT BEAUTY NO DEFECT   872 11
    WARPING THE PERFECT IMAGE OF GOD   *929   4
    AS THE SOUL AT LAST SLIPS PERFECT INTO THE GOAL THE CORE   *959 31

PERFECTED
    NO HAS-BEEN NO HEREAFTER ONLY THE PERFECTED   169 24
    AND SINGLE ME PERFECTED FROM MY FELLOW   218   8

PERFECTING
    PERFECTING NOW OUR UNFINISHED FIRST EMBRACE   157 22

PERFECTION
    SUDDENLY TO DARE TO COME OUT NAKED IN PERFECTION OF   306 15
    NOR SOUND OF STILL MORE FOUL HUMAN PERFECTION   316   8
    UNBLEMISHED BELIEF IN YOUR OWN PERFECTION   398   3

PERFECTLY
    CHAIN OF MY MYSTIC WILL WRAPPED PERFECTLY   154 25
    IT IS PERFECTLY COMPLETE   203 26
    SINGLE AND PERFECTLY DISTINCT FROM EVERYTHING ELSE   254 25
    AS HE CERTAINLY BEGAN SO PERFECTLY ALONE   364 10
    I'M PERFECTLY WILLING TO STRIKE A DECENT BARGAIN   483 22
    WITH PERFECTLY AWFUL THINGS IN IT   491 14
    YES I KNOW IT'S TOO BAD OF COURSE IT'S PERFECTLY SUPERF+   546 13
    KNOWS PERFECTLY WELL   564 27
    MAN IS ONLY PERFECTLY HUMAN   650 17
    ARE PERFECTLY SINCERE   659   9
    IF IT IS PERFECTLY SINCERE TO DENY YOUR OWN MAKE-UP   659 11
    AND PERFECTLY HONEST TO PRETEND TO BE UNBEGOTTEN   659 12
    OH HOW THIS NIGHT HAS HAPPENED PERFECTLY   754 26

PERFORCE
    AND MEN HAVE PERFORCE TO BE LITTLE DYNAMOS   641   6

PERFORM
CERTAIN WAYS PERFORM CERTAIN SACRIFICES   775 30

PERFORMED
AND WHEN THE EXECUTION IS PERFORMED   528 18

PERFORMING
PERFORMING OUR ANTICS   544 2

PERFUME
TO MY BLOSSOM IN PERFUME AND SEED-DUST AND ONLY THEN I +   94 6
IN A LOW SHOCKING PERFUME TO KNOW WHO HAS HAILED   105 33
GLIMMERED AS FLOWERS THAT IN PERFUME AT TWILIGHT UNFOLD   141 8
PERFUME OF CORRUPTION   273 15
AND OLEANDER IS HOT WITH PERFUME UNDER THE AFTERNOON SUN   630 3
HARDLY LOOSES EVEN A LAST BREATH OF PERFUME   646 22
TO SOMETHING FLOWERY AND FULFILLED AND WITH A STRANGE S+   677 16
OF HER SOUL'S PAINED PERFUME   881 9
AND OUT OF THE CHAMBERED WEARINESS WANDERS A PERFUME AB+   *916 14

PERFUMED
AND THE TINY VINE-FLOWER ROSE OF ALL ROSES PERFUMED   286 27
GOD IS BORN GOD IS BORN PERFUMED AND DANGLING AND WITH +   683 5
THE HEAVY PURPLE PERFUMED BUNCH   880 24

PERFUMES
WHITE SANDS AND FRUITS UNKNOWN AND PERFUMES THAT NEVER   261 2

PERIL
THROUGH PERIL TOIL AND PAIN   554 2

PERILOUS
WHIRL IN THESE PERILOUS MARCHES   242 26
AS FRICTIONAL AS PERILOUS EXPLOSIVE AS BRIMSTONE   301 31
AND BONES AND TWIGS AND A PERILOUS ASCENT   402 14
SAIL ON OVER PERILOUS SEAS OF THOUGHT   542 12

PERISH
OR PERISH THERE IS NOT ALTERNATIVE   264 20
NEVER PERISH   265 7
AND PERISH ON ME AS I HAVE PERISHED ON HER   266 30
IS READY TO BLOW BAD BREATH UPON THEM TO PERISH THEM ALL   792 16

PERISHED
MY POOR MY PERISHED SOUL WITH THE SIGHT OF YOU   221 29
THIS HAVING TOUCHED THE EDGE OF THE BEYOND AND PERISHED+   266 21
NOT PERISHED   266 22
AND PERISH ON ME AS I HAVE PERISHED ON HER   266 30
AS SHADOWS FROM THE AGES GONE AND PERISHED   426 18
MY POOR AND PERISHED SOUL AT THE JOY OF YOU   *945 15

PERISHES
SUCH ADORATION PIERCES THE LOINS AND PERISHES THE MAN   538 13

PERIWINKLES
THE ROSY PERIWINKLES THAT CLUSTERED AND LEANED ACROSS   863 24

PERMANENT
FOR A PERMANENT FIT   84 32
MOLTEN YET DENSE AND PERMANENT   477 23
FIRST COMES THE DEATH THEN THE PURE ALONENESS WHICH IS +   611 12
EITHER MAKE THE INDIAN BUREAU INTO A PERMANENT OFFICE   780 5

PERMIT
PERMIT OF NO BEYOND AH YOU WHOSE DREAMS   194 27

PERNICIOUS
BUT GET ANY OF THEM ON THE BRAIN AND THEY BECOME PERNIC+   845 6

PERPENDICULAR
WAVER PERPENDICULAR   302 3
TO BE HUSBANDLY AND GIVE PERPENDICULAR TO THE LANDSCAPE   835 3

PERPETRATED
PERPETRATED UPON THE OTHER   715 10

PERPETUAL
PERPETUAL FIRE-LAUGHING MOTION AMONG THE SLOW SHUFFLE   389 18
IT'S BAD TASTE TO BE WISE ALL THE TIME LIKE BEING A PER+   496 1

PERPETUALLY
ALONG THE FENCE PERPETUALLY SEEKING RELEASE   47 17

PERPLEX
MONEY SHALL CEASE TO BE AND PROPERTY SHALL CEASE TO PER+   666 17

PERSEPHONE
OH PERSEPHONE PERSEPHONE BRING BACK TO ME FROM HADES TH+   303 13
LOOK OUT PERSEPHONE   308 27
RUN PERSEPHONE HE IS AFTER YOU ALREADY   309 15
POOR PERSEPHONE AND HER RIGHTS FOR WOMEN   309 20
PERSEPHONE   309 27
EVEN WHERE PERSEPHONE GOES JUST NOW FROM THE FROSTED SE+   697 16
AND PERSEPHONE HERSELF IS BUT A VOICE   697 18
AND LIKE PERSEPHONE OR ATTIS   711 17
PERSEPHONE HAS JUST GONE BACK   *955 12
DOWN THE WAY PERSEPHONE GOES JUST NOW IN FIRST-FROSTED +   *956 13
AND PERSEPHONE HERSELF IS BUT A VOICE AS A BRIDE   *956 15

PERSEPHONE'S
ALL ALL PERSEPHONE'S PALE CUPS OF MOULD   177 5

PERSEUS
AND TURN ONCE MORE TO MEN TO SAVE THEM PERSEUS ST GEORGE   619 26

PERSIAN
I'M ABOUT AS MUCH LIKE A PERSIAN CAT   489 23

PERSIST
IN STUPOR PERSIST AT THE GATES OF LIFE OBSTINATE DARK M+   75 12
NAY I PERSIST AND VERY FAITH SHALL KEEP   154 12
AND THE STILL MORE AWFUL NEED TO PERSIST TO FOLLOW FOLL+   363 12

PERSISTENCE
TILL HE CHAFES AT MY CROUCHING PERSISTENCE AND A SHARP   47 24
THE GOLD OF THEIR STRANGE PERSISTENCE   253 12
OF HORIZONTAL PERSISTENCE   360 17
BUT WITH MORE THAN BOVINE GRIM EARTH-DANK PERSISTENCE   361 16
AND HE HAS A REPTILE'S AWFUL PERSISTENCE   361 30
AGE-LONG REPTILIAN PERSISTENCE   365 26

PERSISTENCY
ONLY AGELESSLY SILENT WITH A REPTILE'S AWFUL PERSISTENCY   362 25

PERSISTENT
SHE CREEPS PERSISTENT DOWN THE SKY'S LONG STAIRS   131 28
HEART-THROB SLOW HEART-THROB PERSISTENT FOR THE NEXT   365 27
THROUGH THE HOURS PERSISTENT AND IRREPRESSIBLE   366 7

PERSISTS
PERSISTS ALL MORNING HERE IN A JAR ON THE TABLE   90 2

PERSON
OR TO ENDURE THE JAZZY PERSON   499 18
EXCUSE ME BUT ARE YOU A SUPERIOR PERSON   546 5
PERSON THAT'S ALL WE NEED TO KNOW   546 11
I DECLARE I AM A SUPERIOR PERSON YES EXACTLY AND HERE I   546 16
MIDDLE-CLASS PERSON WHOSE   555 10
PLEASE ADDRESS THESE QUESTIONS TO THE PROPER PERSON   604 15
AND THE PERSON HAS BECOME FINALLY SELF-CENTRED   617 7

PERSONAL
NOT MERELY THE PERSONAL UPSTART   466 4
AND PERSONAL INTIMACY HAS NO HEART   471 11
FROM THE SOURCE NOT OUT OF BOTTLES AND BOTTLED PERSONAL   481 4

PERSONALITIES
UPON WHICH SHADOWS OF PEOPLE PURE PERSONALITIES   444 5
THEY HAVE ONLY THEIR PERSONALITIES THAT ARE BEST SEEN F+   446 4
FLAT PERSONALITIES IN TWO DIMENSIONS IMPONDERABLE AND   446 6
PERSONALITIES EXIST APART   471 10

PERSONALITY
AND DISPLAYING NO PERSONALITY   445 34
OVER THE CONSCIOUS PERSONALITY   471 4
OR THE PERSONALITY ASSUMES IT AS AN ATTRIBUTE OR THE EGO   473 3
PERSONALITY   481 2
TAINTED WITH THE EGO AND THE PERSONALITY   481 20
CAGES OF OUR PERSONALITY   482 17
PERSONALITY   561 31

PERSONS
THE SAME I SAY TO THE PALE AND ELEGANT PERSONS   316 26
POSSESSIVE PERSONS   526 9
THE SUPERIOR PERSONS SOMEWHAT INFERIOR   547 30
FORTUNATELY THOUGH SOME SUPERIOR PERSONS ARE STILL SUPE+   548 10
TO THE QUITE SUPERIOR PERSONS WHO ARE NOT SO SUPERIOR AS   548 11
THERE ARE GREAT NUMBERS OF QUITE SUPERIOR PERSONS WHO A+   548 25
NEITHER TO PERSONS NOR THINGS NOR IDEAS IDEALS NOR RELI+   622 7
IS THAT THEY ARE INVARIABLY IMMORAL PERSONS   836 21

PERSUADES
PERSUADES ME TO STAY SINCE STAY I MAY   815 21

PERSUASIVE
BUT WITH THE WALKING AND TALKING AND CONVENTIONALLY PER+   442 2

PERTINACIOUSLY
AND ROWS AMONG THE FEMALES LIKE A SHIP PERTINACIOUSLY   380 18

PERVADES
PERVADES MY MOVEMENTS AND MY THOUGHTS AND WORDS   727 3

PERVERSENESS
IT IS LIKE THE AGONISED PERVERSENESS OF A CHILD HEAVY W+   287 2

PERVERSION
BUT CHASTITY ON THE BRAIN IS A VICE A PERVERSION   845 12

PERVERSITY
WAS IT PERVERSITY THAT I LONGED TO TALK TO HIM   350 14
AND SO WITH BITTER PERVERSITY   485 4
IS THAT THEY CALMLY ASSERT WE ONLY THRILL TO PERVERSITY   531 3

PERVERTED
IT IS A PERVERTED INSTINCT A HIDDEN THOUGHT   487 15
BUT OF FALSE FEELING AND PERVERTED JUSTICE   654 2

PERVERTS
SPEAKING OF PERVERTS HE TAKES ON AN AMUSED BUT ICY   *948 4

PESOS
THEY GIVE US PESOS MADE OF MEXICAN SILVER   794 3

PESTERED
HOW MUCH MORE IS HE PESTERED AND TORMENTED SAY I   361 34

PESTERS
HE PESTERS HER AND TORMENTS HER SAID THE WOMAN   361 33

PESTILENCE
  THEY WILL BLEED ROTTEN BLOOD IN PESTILENCE   792   7

PETAL
  THE MOON WAS A GOLDEN PETAL BETWEEN   216 15
  PUFFING ITS LITTLE MALE STAMENS OUT INTO STERILE PETAL +   535   6

PETALLED
  FOLDING BACK THEIR SOUNDLESS PETALLED EARS   311   9

PETALS
  WHITE PETALS INCANDESCENT SO THAT YOU   86 13
  THEIR PALE-GOLD PETALS BACK WITH STEADY WILL   91 13
  BUT SOMETIMES THE OPENING PETALS ARE FIRE AND THE SCARL+   93 31
  TILL PETALS HEAPED BETWEEN THE WINDOW-SHAFTS   154 31
  LIKE A FLAT RED LILY WITH A MILLION PETALS   166 17
  FOR THE SLUICING OF THEIR RAIN-DISHEVELLED PETALS   217 22
  ARE FALLEN AND THEIR MAUVE-RED PETALS ON THE CLOTH   217 28
  FANS OUT YOUR PETALS FOR EXCESS OF FLAME   219   3
  LIKE OTHER FLOWERS IN A REVELATION OF PETALS   283   4
  BEFORE PETALS SPREAD BEFORE COLOUR MADE ITS DISTURBANCE   285 31
  AND SUAVE LIKE PASSION-FLOWER PETALS   298 28
  ROSE-RED PRINCESS HIBISCUS ROLLING HER POINTED CHINESE +   313 27
  BUT WHILE FLOWERS CLUB THEIR PETALS AT EVENING   321 22
  ALL THE BRONZE GLOSS OF ALL HIS MYRIAD PETALS   371 11
  INTO BROAD SWEET PETALS   535   4
  DREW HER LIPS OVER THE MOON-PALE PETALS SOFTLY BENT   856 20
  SENDING THEM RIOTING AT DAWN DOWN THE LANE OF SCARLET P+   860 23
  FOR THE RUSTLING OF THEIR WHITE UNFOLDING PETALS   *943   5
  ARE FALLEN AND THEIR MAUVE-RED PETALS ON THE CLOTH   *943 11

PETERLETS
  PETERLETS GEORGELETS HAMLETS   457 18

PETROL
  ESCAPING THE PETROL FUMES OF HUMAN CONVERSATION   646   6
  THE WEATHER IN TOWN IS ALWAYS BENZINE OR ELSE PETROL   703 18

PETS
  MY LITTLE CRITICS DEAR SAFE LITTLE PETS   581 26

PETTED
  WHO PETTED THEM AND HAD THEM FIXED   581 21

PETTICOATS
  I'D HANG MY HAMS WITH PUCKERED PETTICOATS SWAYING   835 32

PETTIFOGGING
  AND REFUSING THE PETTIFOGGING PROMPTINGS OF HUMAN   525 18

PETTINESS
  A PETTINESS   351 30

PETTY
  DIPPING WITH PETTY TRIUMPHANT FLIGHT AND TITTERING OVER   347 17

PETULANT
  WHERE WHEELING AND SCREAMING THE PETULANT PLOVERS   41   3
  SHAKING THE HEATH-BELLS DOWN WITH HER PETULANT GAIT   863 23

PHALLIC
  A THREATENING TORTURING PHALLIC MOLOCH   264 25

PHALLUS
  SO THAT IT RUSHES UP IN A HUGE BLAZE LIKE A PHALLUS   506   6
  THEY ARE ESTABLISHED ON THE MANY PILLARS OF THE PHALLUS   541 24
  AND OVER THE BRIDGE OF THE WHALE'S STRONG PHALLUS LINKI+   694 21
  NOT EVEN THE DOUBLE PHALLUS OF THE DEVIL HIMSELF   710 25

PHANTASMAL
  BLACK AND PHANTASMAL   141   4

PHANTOM
  TO STEADY MY BRAIN IN THIS PHANTOM SHOW   105 10
  PHANTOM TO PHANTOM LEANING STRANGE WOMEN WEEP   140 15
  STAND UPON ME WEIGHTLESS YOU PHANTOM   332   8
  INTO THAT TRANSLUCENT PHANTOM SHRED   332 13

PHANTOMS
  PALE SLEEPY PHANTOMS ARE TOSSED ABOUT   163 23

PHASE
  NEW PHASE IN THE GERM OF YOU   240   7

PHASES
  AND IF IN THE CHANGING PHASES OF MAN'S LIFE   727 17

PHENOMENA
  HE WAS ONE OF NATURE'S PHENOMENA NO DOUBT   328 18

PHILANTHROPY
  ALL THIS PHILANTHROPY AND BENEVOLENCE ON OTHER PEOPLE'S   291 19

PHILOSOPHIC
  NIPPED UPON THE FROZEN FLOODS OF PHILOSOPHIC DESPAIR   542 21

PHILOSOPHY
  RELIGION KNOWS BETTER THAN PHILOSOPHY   689 26

PHIZ
  I BET I AM YOU CAN 'OLD YER PHIZ   434 22

PHLEGM
  CAUTIOUSLY SWALLOWING THEIR PHLEGM   554 28

PHLOX
  WHEN WILL THE SCENT OF THE DIM WHITE PHLOX   62 27

PHOENICIAN
  THE GREEK BEAUTIFUL ONES THE PHOENICIAN UGLY ONES THE A+   671 16

PHOENIX
  AH PHOENIX PHOENIX   330   1
  PHOENIX PHOENIX   330   5
  BEYOND EVEN THAT EAGLE THAT PHOENIX HANGING OVER THE   437 12
  THE PHOENIX RENEWS HER YOUTH   728   6
  AND BEYOND THE EAGLE ROSE AND THE PHOENIX PARENT SOARIN+   *946 23

PHOSPHORESCENT
  AMONG THE CRUMPLED BEECH-LEAVES PHOSPHORESCENT   86 22
  YOU ARE SINGLE YOU ARE FRUITLESS PHOSPHORESCENT COLD AND   197 12
  HAVE PHOSPHORESCENT TEEMING WHITE WORDS   441   2
  THE GREY PHOSPHORESCENT PELLUCID ADVANCE   *914 24

PHYSICAL
  AND THEY GRUDGE THEM THE IMMEDIATE PHYSICAL UNDERSTANDI+   446 11
  IN THE PHYSICAL MESH   460   4
  PHYSICAL AND FLESHLY   468 19
  MEANS ANYTHING FURTHER AND PHYSICAL   470 12
  TO PHYSICAL IS JUST MESSY   470 19

PHYSICAL ENERGY
  AND EVEN THE GRAND HORSE OF PHYSICAL ENERGY   658 17

PHYSICALLY
  THAT LIVES ERECT THROUGH LONG NIGHTS PHYSICALLY   427 13
  KEEP OURSELVES SEPARATE PHYSICALLY   470 16
  LET US LEAVE IT ALONE PHYSICALLY KEEP APART   471 26
  COME PHYSICALLY NEARER BE FLESH TO MY FLESH   602 13

PHYSIOG
  WRINKLED UNDERHUNG PHYSIOG THAT LOOKS AS IF IT HAD DONE   398   6

PIANO
  A CHILD SITTING UNDER THE PIANO IN THE BOOM OF THE TING+   148   6
  AND HYMNS IN THE COSY PARLOUR THE TINKLING PIANO OUR   148 13
  WITH THE GREAT BLACK PIANO APPASSIONATO THE GLAMOUR   148 16
  SPORT ON HER LITTERED PIANO AND MOCK AT THE SIGHT   856 17
  MUST HIDE MY MOTHER'S PIANO LITTLE AND BROWN WITH THE B+   *940   2
  A CHILD SITTING UNDER THE PIANO IN THE BOOM OF THE SHAK+   *940   7
  AND THE GREAT BLACK PIANO IS CLAMOURING AS MY MOTHER'S +   *940 21

PIANO'S
  SOMEWHERE BENEATH THAT PIANO'S SUPERB SLEEK BLACK   *940   1

PICCADILLY
  HE USED TO GIVE KIND ADVICE TO THE PROSTITUTES ON PICCA+   582   2
  AND THE PROSTITUTES ON PICCADILLY OR IN THE CIRCUS   582   3

PICK
  WHEN YOU PICK THE RED SMOKY HEART FROM A RABBIT OR A   374   5
  I KNOW YOU WON'T PICK MY POCKET   603   3
  SO I WISH NO MAN TO PICK MY POCKET   607 13
  AND I WILL PICK THE POCKET OF NO MAN   607 14
  I PICK MY WAY OVER THREADBARE GRASS WHICH IS PRESSED   *896 10

PICK-AXE
  WITH AXE IN HAND AND THE HAMMER AND THE PICK-AXE OVER-A+   174 16
  OH MEN WITH THE AXE AND THE PICK-AXE BREAK THE WALLS OF+   175 26

PICKED
  SO I PICKED HIM UP IN A FLANNEL JACKET   347   4
  I PICKED UP A CLUMSY LOG   351 10
  THE JIXERY PERHAPS NEVER PICKED A MAN'S POCKET   659 14

PICKING
  THE BLUE JAY PACES ROUND THE CABIN VERY BUSY PICKING UP   375 23

PICKLE
  IN WHICH TO PICKLE THE YOUNGER GENERATIONS   495   7

PICKLING
  WHO WOULD BE SO MUCH BETTER WITHOUT PICKLING   495   8

PICK-POCKET
  A PICK-POCKET   607 20

PICKS
  THIS IS THE SAME THAT PICKS UP THE HARVEST OF WHEAT   271 21
  PICKS UP ITS SEEDS OR LITTLE SNAILS   443 13

PICORIS
  THE MOUNTAINS OF PICORIS   402 24

PICTURE
  IN EVERY PICTURE EVERY TIME   578   3
  THE UPSHOT WAS MY PICTURE MUST BURN   579 23
  HOW NICE TO SIT IN THE CINE WHERE THE PICTURE OF ALL TH+   794 17
  LIKE A PICTURE BY THAULOW DARK CLUSTERS OF SHOUTING LADS   865 19
  THE PICTURE OF THE PAST IS SHAKEN AND SCATTERED   *908 10

PICTURE-DUSK
  SQUARE PICTURE-DUSK THE WINDOW OF DARK SKY   210 20

PICTURE-MIST
  AND BREATHED ON YOU THE PICTURE-MIST OF MY DREAMS   871   2

PICTURES
  HE PAINTED SOME PICTURES REAL BEAUTIES   577   4
  IF MY PICTURES ARE NUDE SO ONCE WERE YOU   577 11
  THROUGH THE POOR BOY'S PICTURES YOU SEE WHAT I   577 18
  MY PICTURES EAGER AS THE HONEY BEE   577 25
  MY PICTURES AND ON THE PROCEEDINGS WENT   579 22

PICTURES
    SO MY PICTURES ARE IN PRISON INSTEAD OF IN THE ZOO   580 14
    WITH MY THIRTEEN SORRY PICTURES THAT HAVE JUST BEEN RES+   580 17
    AH MY NICE PICTURES THEY ARE FOULED THEY ARE DIRTIED   580 23
    AH MY NICE PICTURES LET ME SPONGE YOU VERY GENTLY   581 1
    OF THE FOUL ONES FROM MY PICTURES OH PURIFY   581 8
    O MY THIRTEEN PICTURES ARE IN PRISON   632 28
    HELP HELP THEY WANT TO BURN MY PICTURES   633 7
    PICTURES   633 10
    AN UNHOLY INQUISITION HAS ARRESTED ALL MY PICTURES   633 14
    WHERE MY DARLING PICTURES PRISONERS AWAIT HIS DEADLY   633 23
    ALL MY PRETTY PICTURES HUDDLED IN THE DARK AWAITING   634 1
    BUT THE DAY THEY BURN MY PICTURES THEY BURN THE ROSE OF   634 3
    HELP OH HELP THEY WANT TO BURN MY PICTURES   634 6

PIEBALD
    ON CURLY PLUMP PIEBALD PONIES   444 16
    AND SOME OF THEM ARE BRILLIANTLY PIEBALD   523 27

PIECE
    AND I LOVE YOU SO STRAIGHT AND CLEAN AND ALL OF A PIECE+   254 18
    SHE THINKS WE ARE ALL OF ONE PIECE   266 26
    AND IF YOU DON'T LIVE DURING YOUR LIFE YOU ARE A PIECE +   449 24
    AND STANDS THERE A PIECE OF DUNG   450 4

PIECEMEAL
    PIECEMEAL THE BODY DIES AND THE TIMID SOUL   718 12
    WE ARE DYING WE ARE DYING PIECEMEAL OUR BODIES ARE DYING   718 17

PIECES
    THE MYSTERIOUS BULL TORE HIM AT ADOLESCENCE INTO PIECES   361 11
    HIM TO PIECES THE GOOD-HEARTED SPANIELS   494 4
    AND THE WORLD IS GOING TO PIECES BETWEEN THEM   516 16

PIE-JAW
    SO SHUT UP PIE-JAW BLETHER   564 11

PIERCE
    FEEL THE SHAME-WOUNDS IN HIS HANDS PIERCE THROUGH MY OWN   226 10
    CAN PIERCE FOR THAT IS WHERE WILL GIVES OUT LIKE A SINK+   383 11

PIERCED
    WHO HAD I BUT PIERCED WITH THE THORNED   111 30
    I BELIEVE HE PIERCED THE SLOW VEGETABLE VEINS WITH HIS +   372 17
    OF THE ARMS PLUTONIC AND PIERCED WITH THE PASSION OF DE+   697 20
    WHO IF I BUT PIERCED WITH THE THORNED   *927 18
    WHO HAD I BUT PIERCED WITH THE THORNED   *928 18

PIERCES
    SUCH ADORATION PIERCES THE LOINS AND PERISHES THE MAN   538 13
    AND PIERCES HER ONCE MORE WITH HIS PASSION OF THE UTTER+   *956 18

PIERCING
    PIERCING THE BLUE WITH THEIR CROCKETED SPIRES   49 25
    PIERCING THE FLESH TO BLOSSOM OF DEATH   273 17
    NIGHTINGALE'S PIERCING CRIES AND GURGLES STARTLED THE   366 2

PIERRES
    PIERRES ALL THE TOLSTOYAN LOT   533 12

PIG
    ALL YOUR GAME LITTLE BODY DUST-SMOOTH LIKE A LITTLE PIG   397 26
    AND HIM FROM STICKING HIMSELF LIKE A PIG   479 26
    OF THE PIG   652 20
    FAT OF THE PIG   652 21
    NOT WITH THE FAT OF THE PIG   652 25
    THE ONLY WAY TO EAT AN APPLE IS TO HOG IT DOWN LIKE A P+   708 7
    HOGGING IT DOWN LIKE A PIG I CALL THE FEEDING OF CORPSES   708 11

PIG-DEVIL
    THEN THE LITTLE CUNNING PIG-DEVIL OF THE ELEPHANT'S LUR+   390 9

PIGEON
    AS A PIGEON LETS ITSELF OFF FROM A CATHEDRAL DOME   134 21
    MY PIGEON MY LITTLE ONE SO WARM   246 20
    WILL NEVER A MAN SAY COME MY PIGEON   540 9

PIGEONS
    LIKE THE PIGEONS AND THE OTHER LITTLE BIRDS   668 16
    AND LORD BUT HARK AT THE PIGEONS WHAT ARE THEY CHATTERI+   751 12

PIGGY-WIGGIES
    AND LEAVE THE CRITICAL PIGGY-WIGGIES   681 11

PIGS
    LIKE BULLS OR BISONS OR WILD PIGS   392 19
    THESE PIGS THAT CAN'T GRUNT   792 25

PIGS'
    HANGING HAIRY PIGS' TAILS   390 12

PIG-TAILED
    TRIUMPH THE ANCIENT PIG-TAILED MONSTER   426 14

PIKE
    AS THE PIKE COMES   336 17
    A SLIM YOUNG PIKE WITH SMART FINS   338 1
    AND GREY-STRIPED SUIT A YOUNG CUB OF A PIKE   338 2
    ONCE A BIG PIKE RUSH   338 19

PILE
    NOT TO WANT TO PILE UP POSSESSIONS   833 4

PILED
    A GANG OF LABOURERS ON THE PILED WET TIMBER   72 4
    AND PILED THEM UP IN A DULL GREY HEAP IN THE WEST   167 2
    AND PILED THEM UP IN A DULL GREY HEAP IN THE WEST   167 12
    OH LOVELY LOVELY WITH THE DARK HAIR PILED UP AS SHE WEN+   693 8

PILFERER
    ENDANGERED BY THE PILFERER ON HIS QUEST   128 4
    AND I LOATHE THE THOUGHT OF BEING A PILFERER   607 19
    WOULD YOU PEEP IN THE EMPTY HOUSE LIKE A PILFERER   742 17

PILFERERS
    NOT FOR THE THIEVES TO ENTER THE PILFERERS   742 20

PILING
    HEAVING AND PILING A ROUND WHITE DOME   50 5
    WITH A BOSS PILING LOADS ON HIS BACK   379 10

PILLAR
    DARK RUDDY PILLAR FORGIVE ME I   40 9
    THE PILLAR OF SALT THE WHIRLING HORRIBLE COLUMN OF SALT+   207 28
    YOU PILLAR OF SALT ACCURSED   207 35
    FROM THE PINE-TREE THAT TOWERS AND HISSES LIKE A PILLAR+   375 5
    AND LOOKS UP INQUIRINGLY INTO THE PILLAR OF CLOUD   375 12
    SO THAT WITHIN A PILLAR OF PURPLE SMOKE   881 11

PILLARS
    PILLARS OF WHITE BRONZE STANDING RIGID LEST THE SKIES F+   287 16
    FOREST OF PILLARS THAT HOLD UP THE DOME OF HIGH IDEAL   287 28
    AND ALL THESE HUMAN PILLARS OF LOFTINESS GOING STIFF ME+   288 1
    THE HUMAN PILLARS   288 10
    YOU ARE PAINFUL HARSH-SURFACED PILLARS THAT GIVE OFF NO+   289 5
    VICIOUS YOU SUPPLE BROODING SOFTLY-SWAYING PILLARS OF   297 10
    WRINKLED PILLARS OF THEIR LEGS AS THEY WERE BEING   390 17
    O PILLARS OF FLAME BY NIGHT O MY YOUNG MEN   440 9
    THEY ARE ESTABLISHED ON THE MANY PILLARS OF THE PHALLUS   541 24

PILLOW
    THE PLAITS THAT LIE ALONG HER PILLOW   101 3
    AN ARROW ON THE BED AT THE PILLOW   397 3

PILLS
    AND RABBITS MAKE PILLS AMONG THE SHORT GRASS   321 23

PINCE-NEZ
    OH HE HAS PUT HIS PINCE-NEZ ON AND STOUTLY HAS STEPPED   633 20

PINCERS
    GAPING PINCERS   353 6

PINCH
    AND THERE A REAL PINCH BUT ALWAYS WELL MEANT   325 11
    WITH A PINCH OF SNOW IN THE GROOVE OF YOUR SILLY SNUB N+   375 17

PINCHED
    AND A MONSTER WHEN YOU'RE PINCHED FOR ACTUAL NECESSITIES   498 14
    I DON'T WANT TO BE POOR IT MEANS I AM PINCHED   498 16
    DOWN THE GLAD STREETS PINCHED WAIFS IN ILL-ASSORTED CLO+   866 5

PINE
    PLEASED TO BE OUT IN THE SAGE AND THE PINE FISH-DOTTED +   409 18

PINES
    ON TOWARDS THE PINES AT THE HILL'S WHITE VERGE   85 8
    RIFT OF THE RIVER EERILY BETWEEN THE PINES UNDER A   220 25
    LIKE YELLOW HAIR OF A TIGRESS BRINDLED WITH PINES   408 26
    BUT UNDER THE PINES   409 10

PINE-TREES
    THE PINE-TREES BEND TO LISTEN TO THE AUTUMN WIND AS IT +   102 25
    PINE-TREES   293 4

PINE-TREE
    FROM THE PINE-TREE THAT TOWERS AND HISSES LIKE A PILLAR+   375 5
    WHEN I LOOK AT THIS PINE-TREE NEAR THE SEA   498 18
    ECHO OF HER I'VE-LAID-AN-EGG CACKLE IS RICH AND RESONAN+   761 21

PINE-WOODS
    GOES BETWEEN THE PINE-WOODS   209 22
    THE PINE-WOODS HOW I LOVE THEM SO IN THEIR MYSTERY OF   212 3

PINE-WOOD
    IF I COME TO A PINE-WOOD I CAN'T SAY   224 21

PINING
    THE PINING TO BE INITIATED   263 21
    ARE YOU PINING TO BE SUPERIOR   773 10
    AREN'T YOU PINING TO BE CLASSY SUPERIOR UPPER   774 17

PINIONED
    PINIONED LIKE SWEEPING SCYTHES NOW IDLY HANGING AT REST   855 22

PINIONS
    AND DOWN THE SHAFTS OF HIS SPLENDID PINIONS   496 11
    AND THE DRUMMING OF PINIONS OF THUNDER   707 11
    FLAP WHITE WINGS AND YELLOW PINIONS   783 26

PINK
    THE PINK YOUNG HORSES SHOW ONE SIDE BRIGHT   50 23
    AMONG THE PINK AND BLUE   244 5
    KNOTS OF PINK FISH-SILVERY   307 4
    FROM HIS PINK CLEFT OLD-MAN'S MOUTH   365 12
    AND HAVING EXPOSED THE PINK PLACE OF HER NAKEDNESS   386 1
    CHINESE-DRAGON-WRINKLED WITH A PINK MOUTH GRINNING   397 18
    THE PRETTY PRETTY BOURGEOIS PINKS HIS LANGUAGE JUST AS +   432 28
    THE TIGHT-ROPE LADY PINK AND BLONDE AND NUDE-LOOKING   444 24
    AND SAT UP TAKING STRANGE POSTURES SHOWING THE PINK SOL+   445 12
    ON THE PINK FLOOD   720 15
    SOME TURNING PINK SOME TURNING PURPLE DUSK   824 25
    OF MY WILTED WILD ROSES PINK AND IVORY WHITE   856 18
    BEYOND THE GAY PINK BLOSSOM   886 23
    COOL AND FIRM AND SILKEN AS PINK YOUNG PEONY FLOWERS   *913 11
    FIRM AND SILKEN LIKE PINK YOUNG PEONY FLOWERS   *914 11

PINKER
   IF NOT PINKER   432 29

PINKS
   THE PRETTY PRETTY BOURGEOIS PINKS HIS LANGUAGE JUST AS +   432 28

PIN-MONEY
   JUST VOTE US SOME PIN-MONEY TO ENCOURAGE OUR   574 6

PINNACES
   FRIGATES BARKS AND PINNACES YAWLS   542 7

PINNACLE
   HE SAW IN A SHAFT OF LIGHT A LAMB ON A PINNACLE BALANCI+   324 16
   HE FOUND THE LAMB BEYOND HIM ON THE INACCESSIBLE PINNAC+   324 20
   GUARD MY SHEEP CAME THE SILVERY VOICE FROM THE PINNACLE   324 23
   THE WHIRLIGIG OF DOZENS AND THE PINNACLE OF SEVEN   355 26

PINNED
   BECAUSE THEIR HOPE IS PINNED DOWN BY THE SYSTEM   558 28

PINO
   O PINO   668 5

PINON
   TROT-TROT TO THE MOTTLED FOOT-HILLS CEDAR-MOTTLED AND P+   409 1

PIN-POINT
   FOUR PIN-POINT TOES AND A PROBLEMATICAL THUMB-PIECE   356 6

PINS
   WITH LONG PINS LEANING OUT THEIR PORCELAIN GLOBES WREAT+   856 13

PIONEER
   AND YOU ARE SLOWLY MOVING PIONEER YOU ALONE   354 3

PIPE
   BLACK PIPER ON AN INFINITESIMAL PIPE   341 25
   OF CRITICAL CHERUBS THAT CHIRRUP AND PIPE   680 22

PIPER
   BLACK PIPER ON AN INFINITESIMAL PIPE   341 25

PIPING
   BUT OH MY HEART WHAT BIRDS ARE PIPING   150 14

PIPISTRELLO
   PIPISTRELLO   341 24
   I BELIEVE HE CHIRPS PIPISTRELLO SEEING ME HERE ON THIS   347 19

PIPPINS
   THEY WOULD RIPEN LIKE APPLES AND BE SCENTED LIKE PIPPINS   503 20

PIPS
   AND WE THE TWO RIPE PIPS   238 5
   OH BIBBLES OH PIPS OH PIPSEY   395 20
   YELLING PIPS PIPS BIBBLES   396 9
   POOR PIPS   397 27

PIPSEY
   OH BIBBLES OH PIPS OH PIPSEY   395 20
   THAT'S YOU PIPSEY   396 13

PISA
   WHEN THE SUN FROM THE WEST BEYOND PISA BEYOND THE   340 18

PISARRO
   CORTES PISARRO COLUMBUS CABOT THEY ARE NOTHING   259 23

PISCES
   PISCES OH FISH JESUS OF THE WATERY WAY   616 19
   THE CROSS THE VIRGIN PISCES THE SACRED FISH   616 24

PISGAH
   PRAY NOT TO DIE ON THIS PISGAH BLOSSOMING WITH VIOLETS   273 36

PISTOL
   'E UP AN' FIRED 'IS PISTOL   81 7
   HE UP AN' FIRED OFF HIS PISTOL   *923 7

PISTON-MECHANICAL-BEGOTTEN
   NOT PISTON-MECHANICAL-BEGOTTEN   642 17

PIT
   GOT HURT I' TH' PIT   44 23
   TREAD OVER THE EDGE OF THE PIT AND WE'RE GONE   164 11
   INTO THE FATHOMLESS BOTTOMLESS PIT   322 2
   SHUDDERING A STRANGE WAY DOWN THE BOTTOMLESS PIT   322 23
   FROM THE PIT OF YOUR STOMACH   399 8
   TO THE PIT OF ANNIHILATION   468 8

PITCH
   HE IS PITCH DARK AND COLD   682 11
   PITCH TENTS OF FLAME   812 22

PITCH-DARK
   SENDING OUT MAGNETIC VIBRATIONS OF WARNING PITCH-DARK   289 2

PITCHED
   WHEN I WENT TO THE CIRCUS THAT HAD PITCHED ON THE WASTE   444 9

PITCHER
   I CAME DOWN THE STEPS WITH MY PITCHER   349 5
   I LOOKED ROUND I PUT DOWN MY PITCHER   351 9

PITCHES
   WHILE JOSEPH PITCHES THE SLEEP-TENT   201 17

PITCHING
   AND SLOWLY PITCHING ITSELF AGAINST THE INERTIA   353 19
   FULFILLED OF THE SLOW PASSION OF PITCHING THROUGH IMMEM+   354 12

PIT-DIRT
   TO TAKE OFF 'IS PIT-DIRT   45 16

PITEOUS
   PITEOUS BROWN BALL OF QUIVERING FEARS   43 11
   PITEOUS LOVE COMES PEERING UNDER THE HOOD   64 15

PIT-FALLS
   PIT-FALLS   308 16

PITH
   HAVEN'T I TOLD YOU TO TAKE THE PITH   583 2
   HAVE YOU STILL TO LEARN THAT PITH   583 23

PITIEST
   OR THE SON OF MAN THAT THOU PITIEST HIM   548 32
   AND THE SON OF MAN THAT THOU PITIEST HIM NOT   629 13

PITIFUL
   AND ALL THE LITTLE ROOFS OF THE VILLAGE BOW LOW PITIFUL+   63 5
   FOREVER EVER BY MY SHOULDER PITIFUL LOVE WILL LINGER   63 22

PITILESS
   IN YOUR PITILESS LEGIONS   168 36

PIT-LIGHTS
   BELOW THE PIT-LIGHTS GLITTER IN ROWS   857 26

PITY
   CRINGING PITY AND LOVE WHITE-HANDED CAME   94 16
   WITHOUT PITY OR LOVE   252 2
   WHILE I I PITY MONSIEUR   361 32
   WHAT A PITY THEY CAN'T ALL BE KICKED OVER   431 27
   OF PITY   484 17
   WHAT A PITY WHEN A MAN LOOKS AT HIMSELF IN A GLASS   528 22
   WHAT A PITY HE SEES HIMSELF SO WONDERFUL   528 25
   OH WHAT A PITY OH DON'T YOU AGREE   579 7
   BUT WHAT A PITY I NEVER KNEW   580 10
   OH THEN PITY HIM PITY HIM THAT PLUNGE   699 15
   OH PITY THE DEAD THAT ARE DEAD BUT CANNOT TAKE   722 1
   OH PITY THE DEAD THAT WERE OUSTED OUT OF LIFE   722 4
   FOR PITY OF THEE   758 16
   LOVE NOR COMPASSION NOR PITY NOR DEARNESS NOR PAIN MAKE+   840 14
   CRINGING PITY AND MY SELF WHITE-HANDED CAME   *897 4
   FAR AND WIDE RUN THE EASY ROOTS THAT BEAR THE LEAVES OF+   *926 12
   WHAT A PITY WHEN A MAN LOOKS AT HIMSELF IN THE GLASS   *950 25
   WHAT A PITY HE TAKES HIMSELF SERIOUSLY AND DRAWS A   *950 28
   OH PITY THE DEAD THAT ARE DEAD BUT CANNOT TAKE   *958 1
   PITY OH PITY THE POOR DEAD THAT ARE ONLY OUSTED FROM LI+   *958 8
   PITY THE POOR GAUNT DEAD THAT CANNOT DIE   *958 14

PITYING
   I HEARD A WOMAN PITYING HER PITYING THE MERE TORTUE   361 31

PIVOT
   WAS STILL AS A PIVOT   120 24
   THERE WHERE THE PIVOT IS THE AXIS   169 7
   THE PIVOT AGAIN   169 17
   THERE AT THE PIVOT   169 22
   AND THE SMALL HAWK HIGH UP TURNS ROUND ON THE SLOW PIVO+   496 14
   THERE AND THERE ALONE LIES THE PIVOT OF PURE EVIL   712 11

PIVOTAL
   PIVOTAL CORE OF THE SOUL HEAVIER THAN IRON   480 10
   WHOSE WHORLS FOLD ROUND TO THE CORE OF SOUNDLESS SILENC+   724 5

PIVOTED
   BUT THE VERY SUN HIMSELF IS PIVOTED   724 17

PIVOTS
   THAT SHINES SOMEWHERE IN THE ATOM SOMEWHERE PIVOTS THE   481 14
   AND PIVOTS ON THE INVISIBLE   616 29
   ONLY IN THE SOUL OF MAN WHEN IT PIVOTS UPON THE EGO   712 12

PLACE
   THEN AFTER A BIT 'ER DROPPED 'EM DOWN THAT PLACE   61 15
   HATED MYSELF AND THE PLACE AND THE ICED   62 22
   ALL AS WE S'LL WANT FOR FURNITURE WHEN THA LEAVES THIS +   83 3
   THEN GOD LEFT THE PLACE   94 27
   THE PLACE WHERE A STAR USED TO BE   115 18
   OF THIS ANCIENT PLACE OF MY ANCIENT CURSE   131 21
   WHAT PLACE HAVE YOU IN MY HISTORIES   131 22
   FOR A PLACE TO LIE DOWN AND STILL AS THEY STAND THEY SL+   146 7
   TO SHOW THE PLACE WHENCE THE SCREAM WAS HEARD   150 13
   FORGETTING THE PLACE FROM WHICH I CAME   151 33
   SHE KNOWS THE WASTE ALL DRY BENEATH HER IN ONE PLACE   153 5
   I PLACE A GREAT AND BURNING SEAL OF LOVE   154 9
   THE HOME OF MY FATHERS THE PLACE THAT IS MINE MY FATE A+   159 29
   WHEN I THINK OF THE PLACE   161 8
   WHICH THEN IS IT THAT FALLS FROM ITS PLACE   162 23
   WHEN WE FIND THE PLACE WHERE THIS DEAD ROAD GOES   164 4
   THE NERVE-BARE PLACE NOW A LITTLE SILENCE EXPANDS   167 14
   THE PLACE IS PALPABLE ME FOR HERE I WAS BORN   172 22
   AND THE PLACE IS NO LONGER OURS WATCHING I HEAR   173 2
   NO SOUND FROM THE STRANGERS THE PLACE IS DARK AND FEAR   173 3
   AND WISH I COULD PASS IMPREGNATE INTO THE PLACE   173 14
   I HAVE FOUND A PLACE OF LONELINESS   261 17
   THEM IN THEIR PLACE   316 12
   SEVERELY IN THEIR PLACE   316 13
   AND HAVING EXPOSED THE PINK PLACE OF HER NAKEDNESS   386 1
   SNIFFS ROUND YOUR PLACE   405 10

PLACE
    COME AWAY FROM THE PLACE OF GRAVES COME WEST   411   2
    TO THAT DIFFICULT INNERMOST PLACE IN A MAN   412   8
    IN A CAGE IT CAN'T TAKE PLACE   485   8
    AND GRACE IF I DON'T LOSE IT FROM THE SAME PLACE   499   5
    A MEETING PLACE FOR SUN AND RAIN   504 17
    PLACE   510 11
    IN THE FIRST PLACE I DON'T SCRAIGHT   540 20
    AND IF I COULD THE LAST PLACE I SHOULD CHOOSE   540 22
    IN PLACE OF YOUR OWN LIFE   585 21
    AND THE FOOT OF THE CROSS NO LONGER IS PLANTED IN THE P+   616 21
    IN PLACE OF SPEECH   629 11
    UNPOPULAR PLACE   632   6
    HIS WORK TOOK PLACE IT CAME TO PASS IT STOOD UP AND SAL+   690   7
    AND AS IF SENSUAL EXPERIENCE COULD TAKE PLACE BEFORE TH+   690 17
    LIFE HAS ITS PLACE OF BLUE DAY ALOFT   711   1
    BUT EVIL EVIL IS ANOTHER THING IN ANOTHER PLACE   711 11
    SET A PLACE FOR THE DEAD WITH A CUSHION AND SOFT SEAT   723   9
    THERE IS NO PLACE FOR THE SOUL TO FIND HER OBLIVION   725 15
    THIS PLACE TODAY THESE SOLDIERS WEAR THE SAME   732 11
    HE FROWNS AS IF HE WERE WORRIED AS IF THE PLACE   734 19
    OUR SERRIED HEARTS DRIFTING WITHOUT A PLACE   736   9
    LET US RECEIVE OUR GHOSTS AND GIVE THEM PLACE   736 13
    AND GIVE THEM PLACE AND HONOUR AND SERVICE MEET   740 15
    AND STONES SHALL MAKE PLACE FOR THY FOOT BECOME EASY TO+   750   1
    TO A HIGHER PLACE THAT IS VIRGIN   769 16
    IN THE PLACE OF MY LOVE THAT WAS   772 12
    IN THE PLACE OF THE WEST   786   1
    IS THE PLACE THERE THE WATERS RISE   786   7
    BUT I I AM ALWAYS IN PLACE   787 26
    SOMEONE WILL COME TO THE PLACE OF FIRE   789   1
    GET A PLACE READY FOR ME   791 19
    MARY AND JESUS HAVE LET YOU AND GONE TO THE PLACE OF RE+   799   5
    FROM THE PLACE WHICH I CALL MY FATHER   801   3
    A GATE TO THE INNERMOST PLACE   811   3
    SUNDAY AFTER SUNDAY THEY CARRIED HIM TREMBLING TO HIS P+   859 13
    THEN GOD LEFT THE PLACE   *897 15
    GOING INTO MY PLACE   *907   9
    THEN AFTER A BIT 'ER DROPPED 'EM DOWN THAT PLACE   *911 31
    ALL AS WE SHALL WANT FOR FURNITURE WHEN THA LEAVES THIS+   *925   7
    THEIR EYES TO YOUR BRIGHT PLACE AND THEN IN WONDER   *941   3

PLACED
    SOME DIM LITTLE EFFORTS PLACED IN THE THREADS OF THE   142   7
    'TWAS I WHO PLACED THE BLOOM OF MANHOOD ON   156 25

PLACES
    MAYBE THERE ARE SECRET PLACES   95 29
    WITH REDDISH PLACES THAT STILL RESIST   142 19
    SHOWS IN ONLY TWO SAD PLACES   145   6
    OVER THE PALLOR OF ONLY TWO PLACES   145 12
    ONLY LED HER THROUGH HARSH HARD PLACES   202 23
    OR WHETHER THE WATERS WILT IN THE HOLLOW PLACES   334 23
    THEN FAR BEYOND THE RUIN IN THE FAR IN THE ULTIMATE REM+   625   1
    IN ALL THE HIGH PLACES AND THEY ARE MASTERS OF INDUSTRY   637 19
    OLD PLACES OF SWEET LIFE FROM WHICH THEY ARE THRUST OUT   723   1
    AND RAVISHED ALL THE PEACEFUL OBLIVIOUS PLACES   725 18
    SLOWLY INSIDIOUSLY INTO NEW PLACES   768 12
    MAKING POOLS IN NEW HOLLOW PLACES   768 15

PLAIN
    AND PLAIN AT THE SIDE OF ME   59 22
    HOVERIN' LOOKIN' POOR AN' PLAIN   60 18
    HOME COME HOME THE LIGHTNING HAS MADE IT TOO PLAIN   62 24
    DO YOU PREFER TO LOOK ON THE PLAIN SIDE   278 23
    ON TO THE FUR OF THE WOLF-PELT THAT STREWS THE PLAIN   409 20
    WHEN I HAD TO TELL MYSELF PLAIN   555   6
    OF SPEAKING PLAIN ENGLISH TO AN ENGLISHMAN YOU'LL SEEM   576   7
    A FALLING STAR WAS RUNNING LIKE A WHITE DOG OVER A PLAIN   791   1
    OF LEAVES LIKE YELLOW FRUITS SHOW PLAIN   *932 23

PLAINLY
    FOR I HAVE TOLD YOU PLAINLY HOW IT IS   170 16

PLAINS
    ENVELOPING YOUR LATE-ENFRANCHISED PLAINS   308 32
    WHICH CLOTHES OUR NAKEDNESS LIKE GRASS THE PLAINS AND T+   *951   8

PLAINTIVE
    WHOSE PLAINTIVE CRY IS HEARD AS SHE FLIES   42 29
    WITH A PLAINTIVE UNALTERABLE VOICE THAT DEADENS   64 23

PLAIT
    WHERE IT GATHERED TOWARDS THE PLAIT ON THAT VERY LAST D+   114 23

PLAITING
    PLAITING A HEAVY AUBURN BRAID   178 20
    PLAITING   179   7
    HORSES GAY HORSES SWIRLING ROUND AND PLAITING   445 19

PLAITS
    THE PLAITS THAT LIE ALONG HER PILLOW   101   3

PLAN
    OUTWARD AND VISIBLE INDICATION OF THE PLAN WITHIN   356 11

PLANE
    THE PLANE LEAVES   268 14

PLANE-LEAVES
    THE PLANE-LEAVES FALL THROUGH THE LAMP-LIGHT LIKE TIRED+   *917   9

PLANETS
    WHEN THE PLANETS HAVE GIVEN SEVEN NODS   702   6
    IF I STRING THE PLANETS AND THE BEADY STARS   735 18

PLANK
    AN' ME STANDIN' THERE ON TH' PLANK   60 20
    TO HOIST THE NEXT WHITE PLANK THEIR MOVEMENT SEEMS   *895   5
    AN' ME STANDIN' ON THE PLANK   *911   6

PLANKS
    SISTER THA KNOWS WHILE WE WAS ON TH' PLANKS   60 11
    SISTER THA KNOWS WHILE WE WAS ON THE PLANKS   *910 26

PLANT
    NOW I AM BROKEN DOWN LIKE A PLANT IN WINTER AND ALL   94   2
    WITH JOY AT TRAVELLING TO PLANT ITSELF WITHIN   127 12
    PLANT OF YOUR BODY TO ME YOU LOOKED ERE SPRUNG   156 20
    AS A PLANT BECOMES POT-BOUND   474 23
    UNLESS HE IS A STURDY PLANT   475   1
    LIKE A PLANT WHOSE ROOTS ARE CUT   610 11
    THEN I WILL FALL AND PLANT THE PATHS TO HELL   710 15

PLANTED
    PLANTED THEE UPRIGHT ART PROUD TO SEE   69 15
    BUT MY FEET ARE ON YOUR GRAVE PLANTED   233 21
    AND THE FOOT OF THE CROSS NO LONGER IS PLANTED IN THE P+   616 21
    AND PLANTED AND FERTILIZED HIM   742 14
    PLANTED THEE UPRIGHT ART NOT PROUD TO SEE   *915 27

PLANTING
    SPLENDIDLY PLANTING HIS FEET ONE ROCKY FOOT STRIKING THE   381 13
    IN TOUCHING HIM AND PLANTING HER ROUND FEET   426 19

PLANTS
    THE NEW RED HOUSES SPRING LIKE PLANTS   50 19
    AS HE PLANTS HIS NEW GERM IN US WHAT IS THERE TO SHUN   127   5
    ARE EXCRETIONS OF THE WATER AND FIRE IN PLANTS   295 10
    AND ALL THE EASTERN EXQUISITE ROYAL PLANTS   313 30
    AND THEY ARE CRYING LIKE PLANTS WHOSE ROOTS ARE CUT   610 12

PLASH
    SLOWLY BEGIN TO PLASH   149 28
    AND FEAR IS A PLASH OF WINGS   150 21
    LIKE GLOBULES OF NIGHT ABOUT TO GO PLASH   427   8
    THEY MOW AND THEY PLASH IN THE WATER   827   6

PLASM
    ABOVE INTERTWINED PLASM   146 35
    OR DID IT SOUND ON THE PLASM DIRECT   364 12
    AND SO ON TILL THE LAST PLASM OF MY BODY WAS MELTED BACK   365 20
    OLDER THAN PLASM ALTOGETHER IS THE SOUL OF A MAN UNDERN+   477 11
    IS THE INCOMPREHENSIBLE PLASM OF LIFE OF CREATION   681 27
    OF THIS MY SOUL INTO THE PLASM OF PEACE   *960   2

PLASM-LIMPID
    THE GREY PLASM-LIMPID PELLUCID ADVANCE   68   9

PLASTER
    WHEN GOETHE BECOMES AN APOLLO HE BECOMES A PLASTER CAST   673   1

PLATE
    AND PUT A PLATE AND PUT A WINE-GLASS OUT   723 10

PLATFORM
    PLATFORM   169 12

PLATO
    BEFORE PLATO TOLD THE GREAT LIE OF IDEALS   688 21
    THEY SOLD PLATO TO THE SAUSAGE FACTORIES OF UNIVERSITIES   762 26

PLATOON
    THE SANDY DESERT BENEATH HER THE DREARY PLATOON   153   4

PLATO-SAUSAGE
    WHERE NOW THEY DEAL OUT SLICES OF PLATO-SAUSAGE TO THE +   762 27

PLAUSIBLE
    SO PLAUSIBLE OH SO PLAUSIBLE   765 22

PLAUSIBLES
    SMASH THEM UP THE SMOOTHED-FACED FAT-FACED PLAUSIBLES   765 29

PLAY
    THE CHILDREN HAVE FORSAKEN THEIR PLAY   41 28
    HAS POISED ABOVE HER LIPS IN PLAY   42 12
    WHO PLAY AROUND US COUNTRY GIRLS CLAPPING THEIR HANDS   58 19
    THE HEART ALL CROWDED WITH SLAVES MOST WORKING SOME FEW+   174 20
    WHO WAS SCARED IN HER PLAY   178 22
    HER HAIR FOR WOMANHOOD AND PLAY AWHILE WITH HER THEN   179   8
    TO PLAY WITH THE GLOBE OF EARTH LIKE A BALL ON A FOUNTA+   272 19
    WHELPS PLAY BETWEEN THE PAWS OF THE LION   325 14
    COME THEN LET US PLAY AT UNAWARES   333   7
    THEY FEEL QUITE TENDER OVER YOU TILL YOU PLAY THE SAME   399 17
    THEY KNOW THEY HAVE NO BODIES THAT COULD PLAY AMONG THE   446   2
    SEX ISN'T SOMETHING YOU'VE GOT TO PLAY WITH SEX IS YOU   464 17
    CUT OUT TO PLAY A SUPERIOR ROLE   490 15
    EVEN MICE PLAY QUITE BEAUTIFULLY AT SHADOWS   523 26
    IF IT'S SERIOUS OR IF IT'S PLAY   549 24
    AND YOU CRIED 'OORAY PLAY UP JOHN THOMAS   550 27
    NOW WILL YOU PLAY ALL NIGHT   755 10
    AND PLAY WITH THEM ALL THE TIME   794 23
    DARTS A MAN AT PLAY   867 13
    HIS BODY PULSING WITH PLAY   867 23
    THREADING THE ROUND JOY OF HIS WHITE-FLANNELLED HIPS FU+   867 30
    I LEAVE YOU WHILE I PLAY MY GAME OF LIVING   875 37
    I PLAY MY RECKLESS GAME TO WIN MY POINT   876   1
    I GO TO PLAY MY GAME OF LIFE WITHIN   876   9
    THE SIGHT OF THEIR WHITE PLAY AMONG THE GRASS   *913   1
    AND THE SIGHT OF THEIR WHITE PLAY AMONG THE GRASS   *914   2

PLAYED
    IS PLAYED AT THEIR EXPENSE   560 12
    LIKE FEARFUL AND CORPSE-LIKE FISHES HOOKED AND BEING PL+   586 9
    WHEN THE EVIL ANGLER HAS PLAYED THEM LONG ENOUGH   586 17
    LIKE FEARFUL AND CORPSE-LIKE FISHES HOOKED AND BEING PL+   632 24
    SO HE TOSSED IT AWHILE IN HIS HAND AND PLAYED WITH IT   791 6
    PLAYS ROUND HIM AS COLOUR-RIPPLES PLAYED   868 11
    HAD MADE AND PLAYED FOR ME HE SAID IN GRIEF   884 10

PLAYED-OUT
    SUCCESS IS A PLAYED-OUT GAME SUCCESS SUCCESS   518 14

PLAYFUL
    TEMPTINGLY IN MID-AIR BETWEEN A PLAYFUL THUMB AND FINGER   271 24

PLAYGROUND
    IN THE PLAYGROUND A SHAGGY SNOWBALL STANDS HUGE AND STI+   76 17
    THE THIN SYCAMORE IN THE PLAYGROUND IS SWINGING WITH FL+   92 2
    HOW LONELY IN THE WIDE WORLD IS THIS PLAYGROUND   867 6
    FLAPS UP FROM THE PLAYGROUND AS A GREAT TRAIN STEAMS SO+   *894 29
    THE ROUGH SNOWBALL IN THE PLAYGROUND STANDS HUGE AND ST+   *898 11
    THE ROUGH SNOWBALL IN THE PLAYGROUND STANDS HUGE AND ST+   *901 20
    THE THIN SYCAMORE IN THE PLAYGROUND IS SWINGING WITH FL+   *926 2

PLAYING
    STILL PLAYING IN THE HAY   48 16
    AND THE SIGHT OF THEIR WHITE PLAYING IN THE GRASS   65 1
    FEELING MYSELF UNDAWNING THE DAY'S LIGHT PLAYING UPON ME   133 5
    YET I'VE FORGOTTEN IN PLAYING THIS GAME   151 31
    SUFFERING AT SIGHT OF THE CHILDREN PLAYING AROUND   153 11
    PLAYING YOUR GREAT GAME AROUND THE WORLD ALONE   197 7
    IT NEEDED PYTHAGORAS TO SEE LIFE PLAYING WITH COUNTERS +   355 14
    PLAYING AMONG THE ELEMENTS NEATLY BEYOND COMPETITION   445 33
    PLAYING WITH MUCK AND I THOUGHT YOU YOUNG GENTS   463 9
    THERE IS A BAND PLAYING IN THE EARLY NIGHT   656 5
    AND PLAYS WITH THE WAVELETS LIKE A PANTHER PLAYING WITH+   709 10
    LIKE A BOY IN A MEADOW PLAYING   782 30
    FROM THE NOISE OF CHILDREN PLAYING AROUND   867 3
    PLAYING WITH THE EDDIES   867 16
    PLAYING WITH THE SOFT-SLIPPING WATER   867 19
    PLAYING WITH THE SHADOW COLOURS AND THE WAVING REFLECTE+   867 20

PLAYMATE
    WITHOUT PLAYMATE OR HELPMATE HAVING NO ONE TO CHERISH   197 8

PLAYS
    PLAYS WITH ME SWAYS ME LIFTS ME AND SINKS ME MURMURS OH   34 20
    AND PLAYS WITH THE WAVELETS LIKE A PANTHER PLAYING WITH+   709 10
    LIKE A BEE THAT PLAYS WITH THE REFLECTION OF FLOWERS   867 12
    PLAYS ROUND HIM AS COLOUR-RIPPLES PLAYED   868 11
    PLAYS WITH ME SWAYS ME LIFTS ME AND SINKS ME AS THOUGH +   *892 8
    SO HE CLEVERLY PLAYS THE NORMAL THE DON JUAN   *948 25

PLAZA
    FIRST TIME I LOST YOU IN TAOS PLAZA   395 27

PLEASE
    YOU SHALL ENTER AS YOU PLEASE   95 6
    AS YOU PLEASE SHALL GO AGAIN   95 7
    YOU MAY HAVE IT AS YOU PLEASE   96 2
    PLEASE YOURSELF HOW YOU HAVE IT   236 24
    MY FACE MAY NOT PLEASE YOU NOR MY STATURE YET IF YOU   251 9
    ME YOUR WORD AND SIGNING HERE PLEASE THAT YOU ARE A SUP+   546 10
    PLEASE AND THERE I COUNTERSIGN THAT'S RIGHT YES THAT'S +   546 15
    PLEASE ADDRESS THESE QUESTIONS TO THE PROPER PERSON   604 15
    PLEASE MAKE ALL REQUESTS TO HEAD-QUARTERS   604 16
    PLEASE APPROACH THE SUPREME AUTHORITY DIRECT   604 18
    THERE ARE NO GODS AND YOU CAN PLEASE YOURSELF   651 20
    THERE ARE NO GODS AND YOU CAN PLEASE YOURSELF   652 1
    GO AND PLEASE YOURSELF   652 2
    AND I'M GOING TO DO WHAT I JOLLY WELL PLEASE   671 7
    HE CONSIDERS HIMSELF SUCH IF YOU PLEASE   830 6
    BRISTLING WITH ANIMATION OH PLEASE SIR HOW D'YOU LIKE T+   865 21
    PLEASE SIR I WAS SWEEPING SNOW AN' I NEVER HEARD THE BE+   866 9
    TILL HE SAW ME BUT PLEASE SIR MY MOVVER SAID I COULD AN'   866 19

PLEASED
    ARE YOU PLEASED WITH WHAT'S IN STORE   95 15
    PLEASED TO BE OUT IN THE SAGE AND THE PINE FISH-DOTTED +   409 18
    AND SHE WAS SO PLEASED WITH IT SHE THOUGHT ONE DAY IT W+   619 14

PLEASES
    WHICH PLEASES ME   71 31

PLEASING
    PLEASING BRITANNIA IS NO LIGHT WORK   577 23

PLEASURE
    ALL MY MORNING'S PLEASURE IN THE SUN-FLECK-SCATTERED WO+   65 14
    TOOK PLEASURE IN TOUCHING YOU MORTALITY   158 16
    I TRAMPLE ON THE SNOWDROPS IT GIVES ME PLEASURE TO TREA+   271 12
    OF HIS VOLUPTUOUS PLEASURE OF CHASING THE SHEEP TO THE +   325 9
    OF GENUINE PLEASURE   565 13
    IT MAKES ME REALISE THE DELICIOUS PLEASURE OF THE MOON   610 20
    I SAW SUDDENLY COMING TOWARDS ME LIT UP AND UPLIFTED WI+   672 20
    AND I STARTED WITH PLEASURE FOR IN THE NIGHT IT HAD COM+   860 12
    PLEASURE   865 26
    SWAYS THE GOLDEN PEARL OF PLEASURE   868 20
    PLEASURE SO HEAVY-INTENSE IT HURT TOO MUCH   875 20
    THE HOURS PECKED PLEASURE FROM ME AND THE SUN DELIGHTED+   *933 19

PLEDGE
    SWEET DARK PURPLE AND WHITE ONES MIXED FOR A PLEDGE   58 10
    KEEPS ME PROUD IN SHAME PLEDGE OF THE NIGHT DARK-PURE   772 13

PLEDGED
    OF THE TROTH WITH THE DEAD THAT WE ARE PLEDGED TO KEEP   114 26

PLEDGES
    SWAY THE LIVE PEARLS THEIR FLOWERING PLEDGES   *941 20

PLEDGING
    OPENLY PLEDGING HEAVEN   283 7

PLEDGING-CUP
    OF LAMBENT HEAVEN A PLEDGING-CUP   177 10

PLEIADS
    YET WHEN PLEIADS OF PEOPLE ARE   115 22
    THE SAME THAT DANGLES THE GLOBE-SHAPED PLEIADS OF FRUIT   271 23

PLENISHING
    PLENISHING THE GREY RAT'S NEST   *933 6

PLENTY
    PLENTY OF GAME OLD SPIRIT IN YOU BIBBLES   397 28
    PLENTY OF GAME OLD SPUNK LITTLE BITCH   397 29
    PLENTY OF CONCEIT IN YOU   398 2

PLIANT
    RUNS ECSTATIC OVER THE PLIANT FOLDS RIPPLING DOWN TO MY+   *891 32

P'LICE-MAN'S
    TA'E OFF THY P'LICE-MAN'S HELMET   *924 23

P'LICEMAN'S
    TA'E OFF THY P'LICEMAN'S HELMET   82 19

P'LICE
    O' TH' P'LICE FORCE WITHOUT FAIL   78 14
    O' TH' P'LICE FORCE WITHOUT FAIL   *920 6

PLIES
    STILL PLIES THE LOVE OF OUR MOTHER FOR US STRAINING OUR+   *938 21

PLIGHT
    SORRY PLIGHT   363 21

PLOD
    PLOD PLOD   426 1
    IN CURLS AND FLAPS BETWEEN WORLDS THAT PLOD   823 26

PLODDING
    UPON HER PLODDING PALFREY   200 1

PLOT
    THE FLOWER OF FORGIVENESS IS PLUCKED FROM OFF THE OFFEN+   *926 26

PLOTTED
    PLOTTED OUT   356 14

PLOUGH
    THE PLOUGH   57 28
    I AM A MAN TO PLOUGH   102 10
    WHAT MAN WILL STOOP IN YOUR FLESH TO PLOUGH   112 9
    WHAT MAN WILL STOOP IN YOUR FLESH TO PLOUGH   *928 29

PLOVERS
    WHERE WHEELING AND SCREAMING THE PETULANT PLOVERS   41 3
    WE MIGHT HAVE NESTLED LIKE PLOVERS   243 3

PLUCK
    BUT WHOEVER WOULD PLUCK APART MY FLOWERING WILL BURN TH+   93 29
    WILL YOU PLUCK IT APART   117 21
    HOVERING TO PLUCK AT THE JUDGMENT WHICH STOOD IN MY EYES *897 5
    WILL YOU PLUCK IT APART   *931 25

PLUCKED
    PLUCKED   533 19
    THE FLOWER OF FORGIVENESS IS PLUCKED FROM OFF THE OFFEN+   *926 26

PLUCKING
    WHEN I GATHERED FLOWERS I KNEW IT WAS MYSELF PLUCKING MY   257 1
    AND PLUCKING OUT OF HIS PLUMAGE A FEW LOOSE FEATHERS TO   413 14

PLUCKY
    BUT THE PLUCKY LITTLE SPORT IT GIVES TO LIFE   443 16

PLUMAGE
    AND PLUCKING OUT OF HIS PLUMAGE A FEW LOOSE FEATHERS TO   413 14

PLUMB
    LIE ON ME WITH A HOT PLUMB LIVE WEIGHT   240 28
    WHAT IS THE HOT PLUMB WEIGHT OF YOUR DESIRE ON ME   241 3

PLUMB-WEIGHTED
    SITTING UP THERE RABBIT-WISE BUT HUGE PLUMB-WEIGHTED   393 5

PLUME
    AND PLUME FORTH AND BE SPLENDID   498 25

PLUMES
    WITH WHITE PLUMES BLINKING UNDER THE EVENING GREY SKY   66 14
    THAT GROWS OUT OF ROCK AND PLUMES FORTH PLUMES FORTH   498 19
    AND ITS PLUMES LOOK LIKE GREEN CUPS HELD UP TO THE SUN +   498 22
    SEE THEM WAVE SEE THEM WAVE PLUMES   587 21

PLUMP
    ON CURLY PLUMP PIEBALD PONIES   444 16

PLUMS
    PLUMS THE BLOND ONES ARE GOLD WITH LESS GLISTEN   827 5

PLUM-TREES
    A WHIRL LIKE SNOW FROM THE PLUM-TREES AND THE PEAR   154 30

PLUNDER
    PLUNDER FROM HEAVEN ·   196 17

PLUNDERED
    PLUNDERED FROM HEAVEN   196 15

PLUNGE
    AND I LAUGHED TO FEEL IT PLUNGE AND BOUND   61 23
    I THOUGHT I COULD PLUNGE IN YOUR LIVING HOTNESS AND BE   99 8
    AND MY HEART LEAPED UP IN LONGING TO PLUNGE ITS STARK   125 33
    HE COULD NOT PLUNGE INTO THE DAYLIGHT THAT STREAMED AT + 344 20
    LIKE A POOL INTO WHICH WE PLUNGE OR DO NOT PLUNGE   652 18
    OH THEN PITY HIM PITY HIM THAT PLUNGE   699 15
    INTO HIMSELF ALONE DOWN THE GODLESS PLUNGE OF THE ABYSS 700 24
    AND THE TURNING DOWN PLUNGE OF WRITHING OF SELF-KNOWLED+ 701 5
    OF THE UNFINISHED PLUNGE   701 20
    AND THEN ALL OUR DAYS IN A PLUNGE OF DEATH PAY THE DEBT 856 3
    AND I LAUGHED TO FEEL IT PLUNGE AND BOUND   *912 3
    AND MY HEART LEAPED UP IN LONGING TO PLUNGE ITS STARK   *936 32

PLUNGES
    THE THICK SNOW IS CRUMPLED ON THE ROOF IT PLUNGES DOWN   76 6
    WHERE TISSUE PLUNGES INTO BRONZE WITH WIDE WILD CIRCLES+ 623 10
    THE THICK SNOW IS CRUMPLED ON THE ROOF IT PLUNGES DOWN *898 1
    THE THICK SNOW IS CRUMPLED ON THE ROOF IT PLUNGES DOWN *901 10

PLUNGING
    PLUNGING AS I HAVE DONE OVER OVER THE BRINK   266 1
    I HAVE DROPPED AT LAST HEADLONG INTO NOUGHT PLUNGING UP+ 266 2
    PLUNGING FALLING OUT OF THE WEB   345 4
    WITH WEBBED FECUNDITY PLUNGING THE SEED OF LIFE IN THE + 841 5

PLUSH
    FUR ALL BRISTLING LIKE PLUSH   396 32

PLUTO
    SAY IT AND IT IS PLUTO   307 29
    OF DARK-BLUE GENTIANS TO PLUTO   *955 14
    OF THE ARMS OF PLUTO AS HE RAVISHES HER ONCE AGAIN   *956 17

PLUTONIC
    OF THE ARMS PLUTONIC AND PIERCED WITH THE PASSION OF DE+ 697 20

PLUTO'S
    PLUTO'S GLOOM   697 5
    PLUTO'S GLOOM   *956 3
    TORCH-FLOWERS OF THE BLUE-SMOKING DARKNESS PLUTO'S DARK+*956 6

PLY
    IN THE WOMANLY VALLEY AND PLY   40 15
    OVER THE FORGES AND SMALL FLAMES PLY   103 12
    OVER THE BLUE OF THE DUCK POND PLY   126 12
    AND THE LONG WAVES RUSH AND PLY   746 23
    THE VASTNESS IS EMPTY EXCEPT THAT THERE PLY   823 20

PLYING
    A SWIFT DEXTEROUS MAN PLYING THE SLENDER POLE   867 22

POCKET
    IN THE NATION'S POCKET   545 10
    IN THE NATION'S POCKET   545 20
    I KNOW YOU WON'T PICK MY POCKET   603 3
    SO I WISH NO MAN TO PICK MY POCKET   607 13
    AND I WILL PICK THE POCKET OF NO MAN   607 14
    THE JIXERY PERHAPS NEVER PICKED A MAN'S POCKET   659 14
    GOING A BIT FURTHER THAN HIS POCKET WHAT   659 16

POCKETED
    WHAT HAVE THEY SAVED YOU FROM WHILE THEY POCKETED   630 12

POCKET-HANDKERCHIEF
    EVEN IF IT'S ONLY IN THE WHITENESS OF A WASHED POCKET-H+449 22

POCKET-PICKING
    AND MOST LOVE-AFFAIRS JUST SNEAK-THIEF POCKET-PICKING   607 22

POCKETS
    WHEN I PUT ON MY COAT MY COAT HAS POCKETS   607 11
    AND IN THE POCKETS ARE THINGS I REQUIRE   607 12
    A MAN'S BUSINESS IS ONE OF HIS POCKETS HIS BANK   607 15
    OF HIS POCKETS   607 18
    WHEN I STAND IN MY SHIRT I HAVE NO POCKETS   607 24
    THEREFORE NO MORALITY OF POCKETS   607 25

POEM
    AND HIS POEM WOULD BE   761 27
    WHEN HE SWUNG LIKE THE RHYTHM OF A POEM OVER THE RIVER 868 13

POETRY
    FROM ALL THE MENTAL POETRY   469 23
    FOR THEY ARE THE ELEMENTS OF LIFE OF POETRY AND OF PERC+706 3
    AND BANK-NOTES ARE POETRY PURER THAN GOLD   814 10
    AND THE STREWN TAWDRY TRAPPINGS THAT LAST NIGHT'S POETR+856 11

POINT
    WHAT IS THE POINT OF THIS TEACHING OF MINE AND OF THIS   74 25
    WHAT IS THE POINT TO US BOTH IT IS ALL MY AUNT   74 29
    AND THE POINT OF YOUR MANTILLA DROPS ACROSS YOUR NOSE   369 30
    THERE IS NO POINT IN WORK   450 18
    EVEN ITS OWN NULLITY BEYOND A CERTAIN POINT   473 21
    AND OBVIOUSLY IT IS THE CULMINATING POINT OF HIS EXISTE+523 12
    IF YOU POINT ME TO THAT FAT MONEY-SMELLING MAN IN A MOT+645 11

POINT
    WHEN AT A CERTAIN POINT A DROP OF WATER BEGAN TO DRIP D+ 682 13
    WHEN THEY POINT THEIR SLANTING FINGERS   731 7
    IT IS THEIR RESPONSIBILITY THEIR POINT OF HONOUR   775 4
    WILL SHIRK OR FAIL IN POINT OF HONOUR   775 13
    YET IT IS A POINT OF HONOUR   775 28
    IT IS A POINT OF HONOUR   776 1
    ONLY KNOW THAT DOING IT YOU FAIL IN POINT OF HONOUR   780 20
    I DO NOT POINT YOU TO MY ROAD NOR YET   812 5
    THAT IS THE IMPORTANT POINT REALLY DISTASTEFUL   829 26
    I PLAY MY RECKLESS GAME TO WIN MY POINT   876 1
    AND MAKES A POINT OF BEING VERY GENTLE VERY TENDER   *948 12
    THERE IS NO POINT IN WORK   *949 19

POINTED
    STEPPING LIKE BIRDS WITH THEIR BRIGHT AND POINTED FEET   71 25
    ROSE-RED PRINCESS HIBISCUS ROLLING HER POINTED CHINESE +313 27
    YOU POINTED FIEND   333 15
    OR IF IT HAPPEN TO SHOW AT HER POINTED HEAVY TAIL   361 20
    ON THE YELLOW POINTED ASPEN-TREES LAID ONE ON ANOTHER L+409 14
    IT IS AEGEAN SHIPS AND MEN WITH ARCHAIC POINTED BEARDS 687 6

POINTING
    POINTING MY EYES IN WRETCHED DEFIANCE WHERE LOVE HIDES + 63 25

POINTLESS
    BECOMES POINTLESS AND SILLY   723 28
    BECOMES POINTLESS AND SILLY   *961 10

POINTS
    AFIRE AT A MYRIAD SCARLET POINTS   315 24
    DOWN FLATTENING INTO POINTS FLATTENED UNDER THE SWEEP O+697 7
    MUNDANE EGG AT VARIOUS POINTS THEY STEPPED OUT AND IMME+760 23
    BLOWN FLAT INTO POINTS BY THE HEAVY WHITE DRAUGHT OF TH+*956 5

POISE
    THEY POISE AND RUN LIKE PUFFS OF WIND THAT PASS   64 31
    THAT ROCKED IN A LILT ALONG I WATCHED THE POISE   123 3
    AND RIPPLES POISE AND RUN LAPPING ACROSS THE WATER   *912 27
    THEY POISE AND RUN LIKE RIPPLES LAPPING ACROSS THE WATER*914 1
    THAT ROCKED IN A LILT ALONG I WATCHED THE POISE   *934 9

POISED
    HAS POISED ABOVE HER LIPS IN PLAY   42 12
    HAS POISED ON EACH OF ITS LEDGES   105 14
    POISED AT HER LIKE A WEAPON MY HAND WAS WHITE AND KEEN 125 15
    AND PRESSING THE SMALL POISED FEET OF A MOTHER WHO SMIL+148 8
    TO ANOTHER BALANCE TRIPPED ROUND POISED AND SLOWLY SANK 444 30
    FROM OFF THE SHEER WHITE SNOW OR THE POISED MOON   708 27
    ONENESS AND POISED IMMUNITY   710 4
    POISED AT HER LIKE A WEAPON MY HAND WAS WHITE AND KEEN *936 14
    OF BLOSSOM SHE FINGERED AND MY POISED FINGERS ALL   *936 21
    PRESSING THE LITTLE POISED FEET OF THE MOTHER WHO SMILE+*940 8
    AND POISED WITH A SENSE OF JUSTICE AS WORLDS ARE POISED *952 9

POISON
    LIKE VAPOUR DEW OR POISON NOW THANK GOD   91 1
    LIKE A POISON GAS   291 14
    THAT KNOWS THE DEADLIEST POISON LIKE A SNAKE   304 10
    POISON IN HIS MOUTH FOR THE SUN IN HIM WOULD FAIN RISE +348 10
    IF HIS PRESENCE AND HIS BREATH ARE POISON TO ME   468 4
    AS IF IT WAS GIVING OFF POISON VAPOUR   583 13
    THAT SHE EXUDES LIKE PEARLY WHITE POISON GAS   619 21
    ARE POISON GASES AND AIR-BOMBS   715 17

POISONED
    AS THEY DREAM CORRUPTED DREAMS ALL POISONED WITH CARE   174 28

POISONING
    POISONING ME   498 4

POISONOUS
    THE AIR IS ALL CLOSE AND POISONOUS IT HAS DRUGGED OUR S+175 12

POKE
    JUST AS HE SNAPS WHEN I POKE A BIT OF STICK AT HIM   357 13
    HOW THOU DOST POKE UP AMONG THE SPOKES OF MY   760 4
    BUT POKE HIM A LITTLE   830 14

POKES
    NOR IS IT DIRTY NOT UNTIL THE DIRTY MIND POKES IN   463 25
    GIVE 'EM A FEW HARD POKES   560 20

POKING
    AND POKING HIS HEAD OUT AND WAVING HIMSELF   432 15

POLARISED
    AND THE LIFE THAT IS POLARISED IN MY EYES   *893 13

POLE
    BURNING PALE POSITIVE POLE OF YOUR WATTLED HEAD   370 19
    OVER WOULD MAKE A POLE   488 20
    EVEN THE POLE ITSELF HAS DEPARTED NOW FROM THE POLE STAR616 28
    HE WAS A SOLDIER ONCE OUR FIERCE LITTLE BARON A POLE   859 5
    A SWIFT DEXTEROUS MAN PLYING THE SLENDER POLE   867 22
    FLASHING HIS BRIGHT BROWN ARMS AS HE LEANS ON THE POLE 867 28

POLES
    LIKE SOME FIERCE MAGNET BRINGING ITS POLES TOGETHER   370 18
    SKIRTING THE POLES OF BEING AND OF NOT-BEING   542 15
    TURN THE POLES THE GERMS THE ENGLISH THE ITALIANS   777 1

POLE-STAR
    NAY THOUGH THE POLE-STAR   115 19

POLE STAR
EVEN THE POLE ITSELF HAS DEPARTED NOW FROM THE POLE STAR   616 28
WHILE THE POLE STAR LIES ASIDE LIKE AN OLD AXLE TAKEN F+   616 30

POLICE
COLOSSAL IN NEARNESS A BLUE POLICE SITS STILL ON HIS HO+   66 9

POLICE-COURT
THOUGHT HE MEANT THE FACES OF THE POLICE-COURT OFFICIALS   579 19

POLICE-EYES
OF ALL THOSE NASTY POLICE-EYES LIKE SNAIL-TRACKS SMEARI+   580 21

POLICEMAN
THE POLICEMAN ON HIS BEAT   570 7

POLICEMAN'S-LAMP
WITH THEIR BULGING POLICEMAN'S-LAMP EYES   544 21

POLICE-MAN
TO PEE IN THE EYE OF A POLICE-MAN   434 16

POLICEMEN
BOULEVARDS TRAM-CARS POLICEMEN   286 35
POLICEMEN AND THE BRITISH NATION   575 1
VIRGINAL PURE POLICEMEN CAME   579 13
POLICEMEN AND ARRESTED THEM AND HAULED THEM OFF TO GAOL   632 33
AT THE WHIM OF SIX POLICEMEN AND A MAGISTRATE WHOSE STA+   633 5
LONDON'S LILY-LIKE POLICEMEN FAINT   680 17

POLICE-STATION
WITH HANDCUFFS AND TOOK HIM TO THE POLICE-STATION   575 3
TO THE POLICE-STATION CELL   633 22

POLICIES
WITH BANK ACCOUNTS AND INSURANCE POLICIES   442 4

POLICY
SURELY IT IS BAD POLICY   333 19

POLISHED
HAD POLISHED YOU AND HOLLOWED YOU   254 29
AND ONE TRAPPED ONE'S FINGERS IN THEIR BRASSY POLISHED   644 13
FROM THE HILLS WHERE SNOW MUST HAVE FALLEN THE WIND IS +   696 16

POLITE
WITHOUT HAVING TO MAKE THE POLITE EFFORT OF LOVING HER   506 17

POLITIC
SUCCESSFULLY CASTRATING THE BODY POLITIC   627 27

POLITICAL
THE INDIAN QUESTION HAS WORSE LUCK BECOME A POLITICAL   777 13
BETWEEN CONFLICTING POLITICAL PARTIES AND   777 18
OR OIL OR COPPER OR GOLD A CAUSE FOR POLITICAL ACTION   779 19
MAKE IT CEASE TO BE A POLITICAL QUESTION FOR EVER   780 2
BUT IF YOU CANNOT KEEP POLITICAL DOMINEERING HANDS   780 14

POLITICIAN
HE IS POLITICIAN OR MAGNATE OR MERE INDIVIDUAL   775 9

POLITICIANS
POLITICIANS MAY BE BAD INDUSTRIAL MAGNATES MAY BE AT FA+   775 5
THE POLITICIANS   780 4

POLITICS
WERE POLITICS BUT OTHERS SAY IT WAS A FOOD-TABOO OTHERS+   303 18
AND POLITICS NOW ARE AN EVIL ABSTRACTION FROM LIFE   716 13

POLL
THE STRANGER'S HAIR WAS SHORN LIKE A LAD'S DARK POLL   156 1

POLLEN
OF POLLEN NOW HAS GONE AWAY   42 14
LEAN ABOUT US SCATTERING THEIR POLLEN GRAINS OF GOLDEN +   70 2
DUSTY POLLEN OF GRASS TALL GRASS IN ITS MIDSUMMER MALEN+   587 3
LEAN ABOUT US SCATTERING THEIR POLLEN PUFFS OF GOLDEN L+   *916 10

POLLUTES
IS A SEWER INSIDE IT POLLUTES O IT POLLUTES   463 20

POLTROON
I QUAILED AT MY APPOINTED FUNCTION TURNED POLTROON   194 29
NEVER LET IT BE SAID I WAS POLTROON   195 8
POLTROON AND BEG THE SILENT OUTSPREAD GOD   195 24

POLYNESIAN
ROSE OF THE OLDEST RACES OF PRINCESSES POLYNESIAN   314 4

POLYP
CAN BE KEPT DOWN BUT HE'LL BURST LIKE A POLYP INTO   305 9

POMEGRANATE
THE MORNING BREAKS LIKE A POMEGRANATE   58 24
AND SEE ITS SECRETS SO IT IS THAT THE POMEGRANATE IS TH+   277 3
AND POMEGRANATE BLOOM AND SCARLET MALLOW-FLOWER   313 29
AND THOUGH THE POMEGRANATE HAS RED FLOWERS OUTSIDE THE   630 1

POMEGRANATES
POMEGRANATES LIKE BRIGHT GREEN STONE   278 13
POMEGRANATES TO WARM YOUR HANDS AT   278 18
THE POMEGRANATES ARE IN FLOWER   605 21
THE POMEGRANATES ARE IN FLOWER   605 23
THE POMEGRANATES ARE IN FLOWER   606 2
TILL YOU ARE AS EMPTY AS RAT-GNAWED POMEGRANATES HANGIN+   800 26

POMEGRANATE-TREES
NO DOUBT YOU HAVE FORGOTTEN THE POMEGRANATE-TREES IN   278 6

POMP
AND POMP OF HUSBAND-STRATEGY ON EARTH   309 24

POMPOMS
MY THE BLOOMIN' POMPOMS   557 5

POND
INTO A DEEP POND AN OLD SHEEP-DIP   33 15
LIKE A WIND-SHADOW RUNNING ON A POND SO SHE COULD STAND   65 6
POND   148 21
THE FOAMY PAW OF THE POND   159 11
LIKE A BOILING POT THE POND CRACKLED WITH HAPPINESS   206 30
LIKE A STAR LIKE A POND   788 24
INTO A DEEP POND AN OLD SHEEP-DIP   *891 17

PONDER
TO PONDER VERY QUIETLY   51 15
WE CAN BUT TOUCH AND WONDER AND PONDER AND MAKE OUR EFF+   667 14

PONDERED
SO HE PUT HIS PAW TO HIS NOSE AND PONDERED   324 22

PONDERING
PONDERING THIS NEW TRUTH OF THE SENSATIONAL YOUNG I SAID   532 1
PONDERING YET EAGER THE BROAD AND THICK-SET ITALIAN WHO+   672 26
THOUGHT IS PONDERING OVER EXPERIENCE AND COMING TO CONC+   673 13
PONDERING FOR HE WAS A GREEK THAT GOD IS ONE AND ALL AL+   692 23

PONDEROUS
AND ALL YOUR PONDEROUS ROOFED-IN ERECTION OF RIGHT AND   289 12
THE PONDEROUS PREPONDERATE   354 1
THE PONDEROUS SOMBRE SOUND OF THE GREAT DRUM OF   371 6
HENCE HIS PONDEROUS HEAD BROODING OVER DESIRE AND DOWNF+   378 22
LIES THE PONDEROUS FIRE OF NAKED LIFE   844 12

PONDEROUSLY
TO ME THE EARTH ROLLS PONDEROUSLY SUPERBLY   288 26
THAT'S WHY AS THE ELEPHANTS PONDEROUSLY WITH UNSEEMING   390 29
SO PONDEROUSLY CENTRAL   480 11
SO PONDEROUSLY CENTRAL HEAVIER AND HOTTER THAN ANYTHING+ *951 25
SO PONDEROUSLY CENTRAL YET LEANING ITS WEIGHT TOWARDS   *952 2

PONIES
TWO BROWN PONIES TROTTING SLOWLY   121 28
AND THE PONIES ARE IN CORRAL   403 16
ON CURLY PLUMP PIEBALD PONIES   444 16

PONTE VECCHIO
WHEN UNDER THE ARCHES OF THE PONTE VECCHIO   340 24
BY THE PONTE VECCHIO   341 19

PONY
AS I HEAR THE SHARP CLEAN TROT OF A PONY DOWN THE ROAD   63 9
WHEN I TROT MY LITTLE PONY THROUGH THE ASPEN-TREES OF T+   409 4
MAKE BIG EYES LITTLE PONY   409 26

POOL
ON THE COMFORTED POOL LIKE BLOOM   56 18
OR LIKE A MIST THE MOON HAS KISSED FROM OFF A POOL IN T+   70 22
FERVOUR WITHIN THE POOL OF HER TWILIGHT   125 34
THE WOMAN YOU ARE SHOULD BE NIXIE THERE IS A POOL   161 13
THE POOL FOR MY LIMBS TO FATHOM MY SOUL'S LAST SCHOOL   161 17
A POOL PUT OFF THE SOUL YOU'VE GOT OH LACK   161 27
PASS THE MEN WHOSE EYES ARE SHUT LIKE ANEMONES IN A DAR+   180 20
LIKE STARS ON A POOL   194 6
AND THE FROGS IN THE POOL BEYOND THRILLED WITH EXUBERAN+   206 29
BEFORE THE SHOPS LIKE WAGTAILS ON THE EDGE OF A POOL   269 24
BUT HE MADE A POOL OF DRIBBLINGS   492 4
AND HAPPY AS A WAGTAIL BY A POOL   520 16
LIKE A POOL INTO WHICH WE PLUNGE OR DO NOT PLUNGE   652 18
AND A WOMAN WHO HAS BEEN WASHING CLOTHES IN THE POOL OF+   693 1
FOR I AM SWEET I AM THE LAST AND THE BEST THE POOL OF N+   796 24
TO THE POOL OF PEACE AND FORGETTING IN HEAVEN   798 27
OR LIKE A MIST THE MOON HAS KISSED FROM OFF A POOL IN T+ *917 19
DRY FEVER IN HER POOL OF FULL TWILIGHT   *936 33

POOL OF HEAVEN
FROM MEXICO TO THE POOL OF HEAVEN   798 2

POOLS
TILL GEESE CAN SWIM IN YOUR POOLS   754 14
MAKING POOLS IN NEW HOLLOW PLACES   768 15
ON THE UPLIFTED BLUE PALACE LIGHT POOLS STIR AND SHINE   *905 7

POOR
THE POOR WATERS SPILL   49 9
HOVERIN' LOOKIN' POOR AN' PLAIN   60 18
THE LUMINOUS MIST WHICH THE POOR THINGS WIST WAS DAWN   71 5
TO DO SUCH A THING THOUGH IT'S A POOR TALE IT IS THAT I+   83 7
'S LESS GRASPIN' IF 'ER'S POOR   84 4
POOR OBSCURE FRUITS EXTRUDED OUT OF LIGHT   160 10
THE RICH MEN WHOSE POOR ALIKE DREAMING AND WRITHING ALL I+ 175 15
AND RELEASE US POOR ONES AND RICH ONES LET US BREATHE A+   175 28
MY POOR MY PERISHED SOUL WITH THE SIGHT OF YOU   221 29
OR A POOR THING AT BEST   237 4
THEIR POOR IDEALIST FOREHEADS NAKED CAPITALS   287 18
POOR PERSEPHONE AND HER RIGHTS FOR WOMEN   309 20
POOR MOTHERS-IN-LAW   309 28
THE POOR OLD GOLDEN EAGLE OF THE WORD-FLEDGED SPIRIT   329 30
HIS POOR DARLING IS ALMOST FIERY   359 34
POOR DARLING BITING AT HER FEET   360 7
POOR LITTLE EARTHY HOUSE-INHABITING OSIRIS   361 10
POOR ASS LIKE MAN ALWAYS IN RUT   378 11
BUT BAH HOW CAN HE POOR DOMESTICATED BEAST   383 26
POOR PIPS   397 27

POOR
    AND THAT POOR LATE MAKESHIFT APHRODITE EMERGING IN A   439 31
    FIGHT THEN POOR DUFFERS DEGRADING   456 12
    POOR HOMELY WORDS I MUST GIVE YOU BACK   492 19
    I DON'T WANT TO BE POOR IT MEANS I AM PINCHED   498 16
    ON TO THEIR POOR DERANGED BODIES   500 20
    SINCE POOR INDIVIDUALS THAT WE ARE   514 13
    OR ELSE POOR THINGS THEY'RE HAVING TO PAY FOR THEMSELVES   518 1
    POOR THINGS AND THEY KNOW IT   518 8
    OUR POOR OLD DADDIES GOT ON   518 21
    AND LIVING LIKE LICE ON POOR MONEY   526 19
    POOR MENTAL WORM   529 16
    POOR FOOLS   535 25
    AND TURN THE POOR SILK GLOVE INTO A LUSTY SOW'S EAR   538 22
    AND THE POOR WILLY WET-LEGS THE SOFT SILK GLOVES   538 23
    POOR LASS POOR BIT OF A WENCH   540 8
    NO MY POOR LITTLE PENIS WOULD BE OF NO USE TO YOU   541 13
    ARE ALSO POOR BLIND CYCLOPS MOANING   544 27
    POOR THINGS BUT WE CAN'T HELP THAT CAN WE   548 27
    ALAS MY POOR YOUNG MEN   558 15
    FOR POOR YOUNG WRETCHED MEN   558 20
    IF POOR LITTLE BLEEDER   564 19
    AUNT GWEN WAS A POOR ONE BUT AUNT MAUD YOU SEE   571 25
    WAS BROUGHT UP POOR SO SHE'LL HAVE TO BE   571 26
    THROUGH THE POOR BOY'S PICTURES YOU SEE WHAT I   577 18
    THEIR POOR THEIR FEARFUL FACES   586 2
    FOR OH THE POOR PEOPLE THAT ARE FLESH OF MY FLESH   632 14
    THEIR POOR THEIR FEARFUL FACES   632 17
    I DON'T KNOW WHAT THEY'VE DONE POOR THINGS BUT JUSTICE +   632 30
    FROM THE ROBOT MASS OF RICH AND POOR MECHANICAL EGO-BOU+   637 29
    AND THE POOR MAN NEVER KNEW HE WAS JIXED   659 17
    POOR LITTLE MAN POOR LITTLE MAN   675 2
    POOR WOMAN POOR WOMAN   675 4
    AND THE POOR DEAD WHEN THEY HAVE LEFT THE WALLED   721 11
    THE POOR GAUNT DEAD THAT CANNOT DIE   722 9
    A POOR ROAN THING ITS HIND LEG TWITCHES   734 6
    PA HAS SUCH A POOR OPINION OF HIMSELF   773 28
    SO NATURALLY THEY WANT TO KEEP HIM BACK DOWN POOR   778 12
    THAT THE INDIANS COMPLAINED OF BEING POOR   778 18
    NOT YOU POOR BOOBS   794 29
    PALLID POOR THING YET I   817 13
    BECAUSE MAN POOR BEAST CAN LOOK AT HIMSELF   836 9
    SO THE POOR MALE HAS SUCCUMBED UNDER IT   843 1
    IS DEAD AT LAST THEN HIS POOR SUNK FLAME MUST FLICKER   859 3
    POOR DREAM-HEAVY SLAVES AT THE MILL WHAT WE HAVE TO DO +   859 28
    HOLD UP JEANNETTE WHY POOR OLD GIRL ARE YOU SAD   859 29
    POOR SIEGMUND TAKE THE SOBS FROM OUT OF YOUR VOICE   871 17
    THE POOR SHUT DANDELIONS WHOM SMALL WARMTH EXPANDS   *896 19
    POOR THING   *910 6
    THE LUMINOUS MIST WHICH THE POOR THINGS WIST WAS DAWN A+   *917 23
    TO SUCH A THING BUT IT'S A POOR TALE THAT I'M BOUND TO +   *925 11
    MY POOR AND PERISHED SOUL AT THE JOY OF YOU   *945 15
    LEAVING ALL TO THE WOMAN MADONNA MIA POOR VIRGIN   *946 16
    SO THE POOR THING IS LEFT FEELING AN UTTER WORM   *948 19
    PITY OH PITY THE POOR DEAD THAT ARE ONLY OUSTED FROM LI+   *958 8
    PITY THE POOR GAUNT DEAD THAT CANNOT DIE   *958 14

POORER
    BECAUSE IF THE MIDDLE CLASSES HAD NO POORER PEOPLE TO BE   527 20
    HE SAID TO ME YOUR LIFE WILL BE SO MUCH THE POORER   611 1

POORLY
    POORLY   211 15

POPLAR
    EVEN THE SHAKING WHITE POPLAR WILL DAZZLE LIKE SPLINTER+   624 18

POPLARS
    SOMETHING WHICH SETS THE BLACK POPLARS ASHAKE WITH HYST+   102 26
    IN ANOTHER COUNTRY BLACK POPLARS SHAKE THEMSELVES OVER A   148 20
    THROUGH THE POPLARS THE NIGHT-WIND BLOWS   163 22

POPPIES
    OVER THE POPPIES SENT   200 24
    THERE WERE NO POPPIES OR CARNATIONS   286 3
    APART FROM POPPIES AND THE FLYING FISH   691 23
    WITH VINES AND POPPIES AND FIG-TREES   710 16

POPPY
    LIKE A POPPY IN ITS CUP   239 12
    SHE LAYS AN EGG HE BRISTLES LIKE A DOUBLE WHITE POPPY A+   761 19
    SENDING THEM RIOTING AT DAWN DOWN THE LANE OF SCARLET P+   860 23

POPPY-GLOSSY
    AND POPPY-GLOSSY   369 6

POPPY-PETALS
    HAS STREWN MYRIAD TWINKLING POPPY-PETALS DOWN THE PATH +   860 18

POPPY-SHOW
    ARE A POPPY-SHOW PEEP WHILE YOU COMB   886 2

POPULOUSNESS
    AND GLUTTED SQUIRMING POPULOUSNESS ON FIRE   315 28

PORCELAIN
    FOR IN THE FIRING ALL MY PORCELAIN   151 16
    WITH LONG PINS LEANING OUT THEIR PORCELAIN GLOBES WREAT+   856 13
    FOR IN THE FIRING ALL MY PORCELAIN   873·28

PORCH
    MY SHAME LIKE SHOES IN THE PORCH   134 6
    THE SUN IS IN THE OUTER PORCH CRY TO HIM THANKS OH THAN+   803 21

PORCHES
    WE NEAR THE FLAME-BURNT PORCHES   242 24
    AND AT THE PENULTIMATE PORCHES THE DARK-RED MANTLE   *959 24

PORES
    AND THE GETHSEMANE BLOOD AT THE IRON PORES UNFOLDS UNFO+   306 4

PORPOISE
    SHE IS THE GAY DELIGHTED PORPOISE SPORTING WITH LOVE AN+   695 10

PORT
    YOU INTEGRAL TO ME EACH DOOR EACH MYSTIC PORT   154 13
    NOW LIKE A VESSEL IN PORT   168 7
    WHITE AND SLIPPERY AS ON THE BLACK WATER IN A PORT   453 14
    INTO PORT   672 22
    DARKLY FOR WE CANNOT STEER AND HAVE NO PORT   719 9
    THERE IS NO PORT THERE IS NOWHERE TO GO   719 10

PORTA CAPPUCCINI
    SEE HIM STANDING WITH HIS HEAD DOWN NEAR THE PORTA CAPP+   379 1
    TIED BY THE NOSE AT THE PORTA CAPPUCCINI   379 11

PORTENT
    LIKE A PORTENT BUT LORD I AM GLAD SO GLAD I DROWN   88 26
    MY FEAR IN ACCEPTING THE PORTENT THE TRAIN CAN NOW   88 27
    CAVERN AND THE PORTENT   544 10

PORTENTOUS
    SLOW-BLOODED ICY-FLESHED PORTENTOUS   271 16

PORTENTOUSNESS
    COME THAW DOWN THEIR COOL PORTENTOUSNESS DISSOLVE THEM   271 5

PORTION
    THE PORTION TO THE GODS IS SPILLED   177 7
    IF DESPAIR IS OUR PORTION   237 13
    NONENTITY IS OUR PORTION   621 11
    MAYBE LIFE IS STILL OUR PORTION   721 6
    ARE YOU NEAR HAVE YOU TRAVELLED YOUR PORTION   764 30

PORTRAITS
    PORTRAITS ARE NOW SUPREMELY UNINTERESTING   657 1

PORTS
    CAST YOUR LITTLE ANCHORS IN PORTS OF ETERNITY   542 13

POSE
    OF MAQUILLAGE AND POSE AND MALICE TO SHAME THE BRUTES   463 23
    WHEN PEOPLE POSE AS GODS THEY ARE CRYSTAL PALACE STATUES   673 2

POSIES
    DIFFERENT YES SHALL THE POSIES BE   888 3

POSING
    POSING ON AND ON AS A LOVER   478 22

POSITIVE
    BURNING PALE POSITIVE POLE OF YOUR WATTLED HEAD   370 19

POSSESS
    IS TO BE ALONE TO POSSESS ONE'S SOUL IN SILENCE   601 3
    THAT POSSESS THE WHOLE BODY   627 19
    AND POSSESS THEM   794 20

POSSESSED
    A STRANGE ACHE POSSESSED HIM AND HE ENTERED THE STRUGGLE   690 5
    AND ALL THINGS ARE POSSESSED BY SILENCE AND THEY CAN BR+   *898 14
    AND ALL THINGS ARE POSSESSED BY SILENCE AND THEY CAN BR+   *901 23

POSSESSION
    OF LOVE TAKES POSSESSION AND SETTLES HER DOWN   125 4
    AND BREAK THE WALLS OF POSSESSION OF ALL THE WIDE WORLD   175 17
    SIGHTLESS AND STRONG OBLIVION IN UTTER LIFE TAKES POSSE+   261 10
    TAKES POSSESSION OF IT   473 4
    A FRENZY OF TORTURED POSSESSION   475 19

POSSESSIONS
    AND FORCED TO CLUTCH ON TO POSSESSIONS IN THE HOPE THEY+   522 15
    OR ALL THE UGLY OLD POSSESSIONS THAT MAKE UP THE IMPEDI+   678 13
    NOT TO WANT TO PILE UP POSSESSIONS   833 4

POSSESSIVE
    POSSESSIVE POSSESSIVE POSSESSIVE   475 21
    WITH POSSESSIVE VINDICTIVENESS   475 23
    POSSESSIVE PERSONS   526 9

POSSIBILITIES
    FURTHER THRILLING POSSIBILITIES   533 3
    IF YOU WANT TO GET A GLIMPSE OF FUTURE POSSIBILITIES   612 8

POSSIBLE
    TO LEAVE BUT ONLY THE MEREST POSSIBLE TAINT   53 31
    AND YES THANK GOD IT STILL IS POSSIBLE   90 28
    OF PERFECT LIFE AND IS OUR POSSIBLE SEED   219 7
    OR IS IT EVEN POSSIBLE WE MUST DO BOTH   429 30
    ONLY MAN IS TERRIFIED OF HIS OWN POSSIBLE SPLENDOUR AND   529 12
    JUDGING FROM THE FICTION IT IS POSSIBLE TO READ I SHOUL+   532 15
    YOU REALISE THE FATUITY OF SAVING UP AGAINST POSSIBLE L+   614 4
    AT THE SAME TIME THEY TAKE THE GREATEST POSSIBLE CARE O+   832 4
    THE GREATEST POSSIBLE CARE   832 6

POSSIBLY
    HE MIGHT POSSIBLY LIKE MEN IF HE WEREN'T TOO FRIGHTENED   447 13
    AND YOU CAN'T POSSIBLY DO WITHOUT THEM   643 29

POST
    APPLICANT FOR POST AS LITERARY CRITIC HERE ARE MY   582   7

POST ME NIHIL
    POST ME NIHIL BUT PERHAPS MY DEARS   531 11

POSTURES
    AND SAT UP TAKING STRANGE POSTURES SHOWING THE PINK SOL+   445 12

POSTURING
    PEOPLE WERE BATHING AND POSTURING THEMSELVES ON THE BEA+   651   1

POSY
    TAKES ALL BUT THE TALLEST POSY   226 16

POT
    LIKE A BOILING POT THE POND CRACKLED WITH HAPPINESS   206 30
    WHY DO I CRAWL ABOUT THIS POT THIS OUBLIETTE   224 17
    IN THE POT OF HIS OWN CONCEIT   474 30
    THEN HE CAN BURST THE POT   475   2
    MY ALL INTO YOUR FLUX YOU MELTING POT   873   3

POTATOES
    WELL-GROWN LIKE POTATOES ON A LIFTED ROOT   827 27

POT-BOUND
    AS A PLANT BECOMES POT-BOUND   474 23
    POT-BOUND   474 29

POTENT
    RARE ALMOST AS BEAMS YET OVERWHELMINGLY POTENT   271 19

POTION
    WHAT SORT OF TIMOROUS POTION OF LOVE HAVE YOU DRUNK   755   2

POTS
    AND TWO POTS OF GOLD   819   3
    IF THERE ARE POTS OF GOLD   820   1

POUCH
    OH BROTHER PUT ME IN YOUR POUCH   752 13

POUCHES
    THUMB-MOUND INTO THE PALM'S DEEP POUCHES   143 12

POUNCE
    BEAST CROUCHED ACROSS THE GLOBE READY IF NEED BE TO POU+   97 21

POUND
    TWENTY POUND O' THY OWN THA HAST AN' FIFTY POUND HA'E I   83   1
    SOMEBODY'S POUND OF FLESH RENDERED UP   279   7
    I DOUBT IF ANY MAN LIVING HANDS OUT A POUND NOTE WITHOUT   486 11
    TWENTY POUND O' THY OWN THA HAST AND FIFTY POUND HA'E I   *925   5
    AN' THEN WI' THAT TWENTY POUND WE GI'E 'ER I S'D THINK + *925 20

POUNDS
    AT TWO POUNDS A WEEK   643 25

POUR
    TO BREAK AND POUR HER OUT ITS PRECIOUS DEW   113 12
    THAT WOULD POUR TO YOU FROM MY HEART   117 24
    TO-MORROW WILL POUR THEM ALL BACK THE DULL HOURS I DETE+   167   4
    TO-MORROW WILL POUR THEM ALL BACK THE DULL HOURS I DETE+   167 20
    CONSTRAINED TO POUR FORTH ALL HIS FIRE DOWN THE NARROW +   327 11
    CRYING POUR OUT THE BLOOD OF THE FOE   739 23
    THAT POUR CASCADE-LIKE DOWN THE BLACKENING WIND   745 19
    RAIN POUR DOWN POUR DOWN   754 13
    FOR TOMORROW WILL POUR THEM ALL BACK THE SCHOOL HOURS I+ *896   9
    TOMORROW WILL POUR THEM ALL BACK THE DULL HOURS I DETEST *896 25
    PULSED THICKLY AND I LONGED TO POUR   *934 33
    I LONGED TO POUR THE BURNING STORE   *935   1

POURED
    POURED A HEAVY FLAME   118   3
    SWEAR IN THE PALE WINE POURED FROM THE CUPS OF THE QUEEN   177 21
    HIS OWN BLACK BLOOD POURED OUT LIKE A SHEET OF FLAME OV+   326 30
    WHICH MUST BE POURED THROUGH SO SMALL A VENT   327 19
    MADE OF CEMENT POURED INTO A MOULD AROUND IRON STICKS   673   3
    HAVE POURED FOR THE HORSES A DARK-BLUE STAGGERING   733 18
    SINCE FROM BLOOD POURED OUT RISE ONLY GHOSTS AGAIN   740 10

POURING
    THAT A NEW NIGHT POURING DOWN SHALL SWILL   117   5
    AND FILLS THEM UP A POURING MEASURE   177   2
    POURING COMFORT AND CONDOLING   457 23
    POURING INTO THE VEINS FROM THE DIRECT CONTACT WITH THE   481 28
    POURING OUT HIS BREATH   684   7
    POURING SEA WATER OVER HERSELF   693   6
    FOR THE SUN IS POURING LIKE YELLOW WINE OUTSIDE   *894 24

POURIN'
    AH STOPPED BEHIND ON T' PAD I' T' POURIN' WET   61   3

POURS
    POURS   97 27
    AND AS THE ELECTRIC LIQUID POURS OUT SOMETIMES   647 13

POUTING
    AND THE BRILLIANT YOUNG HUSBAND MADE A LITTLE MOVE POUT+   842 16

POVERTY
    I KNOW THAT POVERTY IS A HARD OLD HAG   498 13
    MONEY IS INSANE AND POVERTY IS INSANE   516   5
    THEY SAVED YOU FROM SQUALID COTTAGES AND POVERTY OF HAND   630 17

POVERTY-STRICKEN
    AND THE POVERTY-STRICKEN ARE INSANE   516 15
    AND THE POVERTY-STRICKEN ARE AFRAID   516 20

POWDERY
    PUT SACKCLOTH ON BE CROWNED WITH POWDERY ASH   234 27
    COOLING TO A POWDERY PALE-OXYDISED SKY-BLUE   369 14

POWER
    IN MY POWER UTTERLY   59 18
    YOU HAD THE POWER TO EXPLORE ME   111 13
    CLOSING ITS CRIMSON THROAT MY OWN THROAT IN HER POWER   123 14
    THE POWER OF THE RISING GOLDEN ALL-CREATIVE SAP COULD T+   272 22
    LOOK NOW EVEN NOW HOW IT KEEPS ITS POWER OF INVISIBILITY   286   7
    THE GOLDEN HORNS OF POWER   326   2
    POWER TO KILL POWER TO CREATE   326   3
    INVISIBILITY AND THE ANAESTHETIC POWER   332 22
    SO HE BRINGS DOWN THE LIFE OF THE SUN AND THE POWER OF +   368   4
    OVERWEENING MEN FULL OF POWER OF LIFE COMMANDING A   414 19
    AND SWINGING IN A STRANGE UNISON OF POWER   478 17
    AND PASSION WILL MAKE OUR BODIES TAUT WITH POWER   482 23
    WE SHALL STAMP OUR FEET WITH NEW POWER   482 24
    AND NO WONDER FOR MONEY HAS A FEARFUL CRUEL POWER   486 16
    USING ALL LIFE ONLY AS POWER AS AN ENGINE USES STEAM OR+   635 11
    ONLY THE MECHANICAL POWER OF SELF-DIRECTED ENERGY   675 23
    ON AND ON WITH THE TRIUMPHANT SENSE OF POWER LIKE MACHI+   675 25
    THE POWER AND THE GLORY   704 12
    MY KINGDOM MY POWER AND MY GLORY   704 17
    HAVE THEIR KINGDOM THEIR POWER AND THEIR GLORY   704 19
    WHOSE POWER AND GLORY I HAVE OFTEN HEARD AND FELT   704 21
    YAPPING IN HIS POWER AND HIS GLORY   704 23
    LIKE THE POWER AND THE GLORY OF THE GOOSE IN THE MIST   704 25
    MY KINGDOM MY POWER AND MY GLORY   704 29
    WITH POWER SEA-POWER   705 10
    WHOSE POWER RUNS UP TO THE SHORES ALONG MY ARMS   705 15
    AND BREAKS IN THE FOAMY HANDS WHOSE POWER ROLLS OUT   705 16
    BECAUSE HE IS SO ABSOLUTELY IN YOUR POWER THAT   776 15
    AND UP THE IRON FEET OF THE EAGLE IN THRILLS OF FIERY P+   782 22
    HE SENDS THE SERPENT OF POWER UP MY FEET AND MY LOINS   799 20
    TILL THE POWER IS IN HIM   806 17
    THE POWER IS IN ME FROM BEHIND THE SUN   806 19
    A FIERY SIGN OF THE CHAINED POWER THAT WASTED HIM TO TH+   859 20
    THE POWER OF THE MELTING FUSING FORCE   *907 23
    AND I WATCH TO SEE THE CREATOR THE POWER THAT PATTERNS + *908 25
    THE POWER OF THE MELTING FUSING FORCE HEAT LIGHT ALL IN+ *909 14
    CLOSING ITS CRIMSON THROAT MY OWN THROAT IN HER POWER   *934 20

POWERFUL
    BENEATH THIS POWERFUL TREE MY WHOLE SOUL'S FLUID   131   8
    BURNING OF POWERFUL SALT BURNING EATING THROUGH MY   207 23
    WHAT A RARE POWERFUL REMINISCENT FLAVOUR   280   6
    BRILLIANT AS A POWERFUL BURNING-GLASS   293 19

POWERLESS
    WILL BE POWERLESS FOR NO ENGINE CAN REACH INTO THE MARS+   624 22

POWERS
    OH GODS OF THE LIVING DARKNESS POWERS OF NIGHT   213 29
    AND THE MONEY-MUCK-WORMS THE EXTANT POWERS   456 20
    POWERS TO REPEAT ITS OWN EGOCENTRIC MOTIONS   635 12

PRACTICALLY
    OR PRACTICALLY STARVE   831 11

PRACTICES
    IN THESE USELESS PRACTICES OF CEREMONIAL   777 35

PRAIRIE
    DOES HE FAN GREAT WINGS ABOVE THE PRAIRIE LIKE A HOVERI+   374 16
    AS FOXES STOATS AND WOLVES AND PRAIRIE DOGS   392 21

PRAIRIES
    AND THROUGH THE WIDE PRAIRIES OF HIS BREAST A YOUNG BUL+   624   7

PRAISE
    TO SEE WHOSE PRAISE   176 18
    LET THEM PRAISE DESIRE WHO WILL   265 12
    THE PRAISE OF JESUS IS MY SUCCESS   749 22
    AND DELIVER OUR LIPS OF THEIR PRAISE AND THEIR BITTERNE+   753 18
    EARTH-CLODS AND NIGHT TO FLOWERS THAT PRAISE AND BURN   872   4
    THEY WOULD SAY SEEING EACH MOUTH OF WHITE ROSE PRAISE   *941   6
    A ROSE OF MEMORY WITH A SCENT OF PRAISE   *941 15

PRANCE
    WOULD WORSHIP THEE LETTING MY BUTTOCKS PRANCE   40 18
    CIRCLE WHILE I PRANCE IN THE UPPER   762 10

PRANCED
    WHILE YOU PRANCED AND BOUNCED WITH LOVE OF HER YOU   396   1

PRANCING
    BUT WATCH A TURKEY PRANCING LOW ON EARTH   371   3
    CAME UPON YOU PRANCING ROUND THE CORNER IN EXUBERANT   395 29
    AND START PRANCING AND LICKING AND CUDDLING AGAIN   396 24
    PRANCING THEIR KNEES UNDER THEIR TINY SKIRTS   537 20

PRATTLE
    FROM THE QUIET CHURCH-TOWER THAT KNOWS NO PRATTLE OF CH+   858 22

PRAY
    ME UP I PRAY OH YOU WHO ARE NIGHT'S BACCHANTE   86   7
    PRAY NOT TO DIE ON THIS PISGAH BLOSSOMING WITH VIOLETS   273 36
    PRAY TO LIVE THROUGH   273 37
    YOU'LL HAVE TO PRAY TO THE FAR-OFF GODS   472   5
    TILL YOU PRAY TO THE RIGHT GODS FOR THE THUNDER-BOLT IN+   484 16
    YOU MUST SOMETIMES PRAY   558   3
    WE PRAY FOR THEE MARY DELIGHTFUL THAT GOD MAY BLESS THEE   753   2

PRAYED
  HER APRON WAS BROWN WITH BLOOD SHE PRAYED   753 10

PRAYER
  A PRAYER   345 24
  FOR THE DESTRUCTION OF THE UNIVERSE FOR IF HIS PRAYER W+   348 3
  AND ROSES WONDERED AT HER PRAYER   753 11
  TELL HIM PRAYER IS STRONGER THAN IRON FAITH   754 11
  WITH PRAYER I NEED ONLY COME HOME EACH NIGHT TO FIND TH+   *945 28

PRAYERS
  YOUR PRAYERS AT NIGHT   558 2
  I HAVE MANY PRAYERS TO SAY   735 17
  'TWILL NOT BE TOO MANY PRAYERS TO SAY   735 20
  AND THE IGNOBLE PRAYERS OF THE PANIC-STRICKEN WHOM DARK+   856 5
  WE ALL MARCH OUT TO PRAYERS SOFT SLIPPERED FEET AND CLA+   866 13

PRAYING
  AWAY FROM AMONG GODS AND MEN HE DID NOT SEE THAT HE WAS+   348 2

PRAYIN'
  WHILE TH' PARSON WAS PRAYIN' I WATCHES 'ER AN' SHE WOR +   *910 1

PREACH
  HE PREACHED TO THE STOLID FARMERS TILL AT LAST HE COULD+   859 15

PREACHED
  HE PREACHED TO THE STOLID FARMERS TILL AT LAST HE COULD+   859 15

PREACHING
  PREACHING IN SAD-MOVING SILENCE A HEART-HUNGRY PURITY   855 3

PRECEDES
  NEW THROB LIKE A STIRRING UNDER THE FALSE DAWN THAT PRE+   292 34
  THAT THE IDEA OF THE FORM PRECEDES THE FORM SUBSTANTIAL   689 17

PRECIOSITY
  THOUGH EVEN THE WORD MARSALA WILL SMACK OF PRECIOSITY   280 11

PRECIOUS
  TO BREAK AND POUR HER OUT ITS PRECIOUS DEW   113 12
  FROM THE WOMB OF YOUR PRECIOUS DESIRE   235 12
  THESE PRECIOUS AND IDEAL ONES   316 34
  AND CURLING THEIR PRECIOUS LIVE TRUNKS LIKE AMMONITES   445 14
  THEN THE PRIVATE INTIMACY OF FRIENDSHIP WILL BE REAL AN+   808 14

PRECISION
  AND MOVING ALWAYS WITH A SOFT SLOW PRECISION   445 15

PREDECESSOR
  NO SOONER ISSUED SIDEWAYS FROM THE THIGH OF HIS PREDECE+   299 32

PRE-EMINENCE
  COME DOWN NOW FROM YOUR PRE-EMINENCE O MIND O   473 10

PREFER
  DO YOU PREFER TO LOOK ON THE PLAIN SIDE   278 23
  FOR MY PART I PREFER MY HEART TO BE BROKEN   279 1
  MAKES US PREFER TO BE WOMANLESS RATHER THAN BE WEPT OVER   439 30

PREFERS
  WHEN SHE PREFERS TO HAVE THEM LEFT   492 17

PREGNANT
  UP FROM THE BOUNDING EARTH STRANGE PREGNANT STREAMS IN +   675 13

PREHENSILE
  PREHENSILE   286 33

PRELIMINARY
  WHICH MAY OCCASIONALLY BE A PRELIMINARY TO THE PEACE TH+   497 9

PREOCCUPATION
  AT PRESENT SEX IS THE MIND'S PREOCCUPATION   472 7

PRE-OCCUPIES
  UNLESS IT PRE-OCCUPIES YOU AS WELL AS OCCUPIES YOU   *949 20

PRE-ORDAINING
  IS THERE NOT A GREAT MIND PRE-ORDAINING   328 25

PREPARATIONS
  FOR CEREMONIES AND CEREMONIAL PREPARATIONS   779 4

PREPARE
  WHY DON'T THEY PREPARE TO ACT ON THEM   520 30
  AND PREPARE FOR STORMS   559 15
  STRENGTHEN PREPARE THEM FOR THE JOURNEY HENCE   740 18
  AT SEASONS TO PREPARE THEMSELVES TO PARTAKE   777 34
  TO PREPARE TO BE MEN   793 8
  OR ELSE PREPARE FOR THE OTHER THINGS   793 9
  PREPARE FOR DOOM   795 16
  PULL IT DOWN AND PREPARE FOR A NEW FRESH HOUSE OF LIFE   838 12

PREPARED
  YOU ARE MY PROPERTY BE PREPARED TO DIE FOR ME AND TO   442 21
  THEREFORE BE PREPARED TO TACKLE THE CAGE   486 6
  AND BE PREPARED TO KILL YOU IF YOU SAY THEY'VE GOT NONE   501 5

PREPENSE
  AND FULL OF MALICE PREPENSE AND OVERWEENING DETERMINED   382 12

PREPONDERANTLY
  THOUGH SOME APPLES TASTE PREPONDERANTLY OF WATER WET AN+   708 2

PREPONDERATE
  THE PONDEROUS PREPONDERATE   354 1

PRE-RAPHAELITE
  OF SOME PRE-RAPHAELITE MYSTIC QUEEN   854 27

PRESENCE
  BLUE SHADOW WITHIN ME A PRESENCE WHICH LIVES CONTAINED   115 7
  YOUR PRESENCE PEERING LONELILY THERE   116 25
  OF MY PRESENCE THERE IN THE MIRROR THAT LEANS FROM THE   141 20
  IN THE PRESENCE OF THESE   145 32
  PRESENCE OF MEN   169 25
  THE PRESENCE OF THE FLOWERS THAT GREW   262 2
  RINGING THE SOUNDLESS BELL OF HIS PRESENCE IN CHAOS   358 19
  IF HIS PRESENCE AND HIS BREATH ARE POISON TO ME   468 4
  BUT THE PRESENCE OF OTHER PEOPLE WILL NOT GIVE THEM NEW   610 13
  THE PRESENCE OF A MAN MADE HER RECOIL   619 4
  AND THERE IS NO GRATING OF PEOPLE WITH THEIR PRESENCE   646 16
  AND THE GLIMMER OF THE PRESENCE OF THE GODS WAS LIKE LI+   651 5
  AND THEN IN THE ROOM WHOSE IS THE PRESENCE   652 4
  FROM THE PRESENCE OF GOD AND ENVELOP US   698 9
  FEELING THE PRESENCE OF THE LIVING GOD   700 10
  A PRESENCE   700 13
  OF ELSE BEWARE THEIR ANGRY PRESENCE NOW   723 14
  THOU SILVER BEAM IN THE PRESENCE   753 14
  A DARKNESS WITHIN ME A PRESENCE WHICH SLEEPS CONTAINED   *930 7

PRESENCES
  SOUND OF ARTILLERY AEROPLANES PRESENCES   169 15
  BODIES AND PRESENCES HERE AND NOW CREATURES WITH A FOOT+   689 23

PRESENT
  AND THE PRESENT HOST   165 26
  DREAMY NOT YET PRESENT   310 30
  SHALL I MAKE YOU A PRESENT OF HIM   430 18
  AT PRESENT SEX IS THE MIND'S PREOCCUPATION   472 7
  THE ROOT OF OUR PRESENT EVIL IS THAT WE BUY AND SELL   482 28
  AT PRESENT I AM A BLANK AND I ADMIT IT   501 16
  BUT IT IS A THIRD THING PRESENT WHICH MAKES IT AN ATOM   515 15
  THIS IS GOING BEYOND THE BOUNDS OF PRESENT HONOUR   779 20
  FAR BEYOND THE PRESENT SOCIAL FORM   829 23
  BUT OF COURSE THIS MEANS SMASHING THE PRESENT SYSTEM OF+   837 27
  TO ALTER THE PRESENT FRAME OF CIVILISATION   838 3
  FOR AT PRESENT IN THE WHIRRING INSANITY OF THE MENTAL C+   839 5

PRESENTABLE
  PRESENTABLE EMINENTLY PRESENTABLE   430 17
  NAKED PRESENTABLE   828 4

PRESENTIMENT
  AND HOVER LIKE A PRESENTIMENT FADING FAINT   53 29

PRESENTLY
  EAGLES WITH TWO HEADS EAGLES WITH ONE PRESENTLY EAGLES   413 7

PRESERVE
  TO PRESERVE MY NAKEDNESS   601 22
  I MUST PRESERVE MY LIFE FROM HURT   741 6

PRESERVING
  IS NEITHER HIDING HIMSELF NOR PRESERVING HIMSELF NOR PR+   523 9

PRESS
  OF HER FEET AS THEY FLEW FOR A SPACE THEN PAUSED TO PRE+   123 4
  PRESS   630 31
  AND THE FEED OF PAP THAT WE NURSES AND GUARDIAN ANGELS +   670 16
  IN THE WEEKLY PRESS THEIR SELF-SATISFIED SWIPE   680 23
  OH NOW THEY MOAN AND THRONG IN ANGER AND PRESS BACK   722 24
  THEY WATCH US THEY PRESS ON US   739 16
  THEY PRESS THEIR CLAIM UPON US   739 17
  AND STONES SHALL MAKE PLACE FOR THY FOOT BECOME EASY TO+   750 1
  THERE PRESS YOUR HOT RED CHEEK AGAINST MINE   863 17
  OF HER FEET AS THEY LEPT FOR A SPACE THEN PAUSE TO PRESS   *934 10

PRESSED
  HAVE PRESSED IMMEASURABLE SPACES OF HOARSE SILENCE   75 21
  WERE PRESSED CUP-SHAPE TO TAKE THIS REIVER   124 7
  I PRESSED THE WRETCHED THROTTLED FLOWER BETWEEN   125 13
  LESS THAN A YEAR THE FOURFOLD FEET HAD PRESSED   155 7
  I FORCE MY CART THROUGH THE SODDEN FILTH THAT IS PRESSED   167 5
  SO SHE LAID HER HANDS AND PRESSED THEM DOWN MY SIDES   254 22
  BEING PRESSED UP AGAINST THE OTHER   267 16
  SEE HIS BLACK NOSE SNUBBED BACK PRESSED OVER LIKE A WHA+   380 13
  I PICK MY WAY OVER THREADBARE GRASS WHICH IS PRESSED   *896 10
  HAVE PRESSED THE IMMEASURABLE SPACES OF HOARSE SILENCE   *897 21
  HAVE PRESSED IMMEASURABLE SPACES OF HOARSE SILENCE   *900 29
  WERE PRESSED CUP-SHAPE TO TAKE THIS REIVER   *935 7
  I PRESSED THE WRETCHED THROTTLED FLOWER BETWEEN   *936 12

PRESSES
  THE RABBIT PRESSES BACK HER EARS   43 5
  PRESSES THEM THERE AND KISSES HER BIG DARK HANDS   128 24
  PRESSES HER HAND TO HER BOSOM WHERE THE FRUIT HAS LAIN   864 20

PRESSING
  PRESSING ROUND AND LOW AT FIRST BUT SOON   50 4
  PRESSING HER SPREAD HANDS OVER HER BREASTS AS SHE   128 24
  AND PRESSING THE SMALL POISED FEET OF A MOTHER WHO SMIL+   148 8
  AS MOUNTAIN PRESSING ON MOUNTAIN IN THE ZEST OF LIFE   694 15
  SILENTLY SWIMMING AND SLEEPING AND PRESSING THE FLOOD   841 4
  BUT PRESSING HER SUPPLE BODY INTO THE COOL DARK LEAVES   864 11
  PRESSING TO GRASP MY HEART   869 21
  PRESSING THE LITTLE POISED FEET OF THE MOTHER WHO SMILE+   *940 8

PRESSURE
    THE SHARPER MORE HORRID THE PRESSURE THE HARDER   161 1
    IS HE NOT OVER-CHARGED BY THE DAMMED-UP PRESSURE OF HIS+   327 14
    AND THE OLD UPWARD FLOWING OF OUR SAP THE PRESSURE OF O+   609 7

PRESTIGE
    SOME MYSTERIOUS SORT OF PRESTIGE   555 14
    THAT MYSTERIOUS PRESTIGE WHICH THEY ALL   555 18
    OR HALO OR PRESTIGE WENT   556 6

PRETENCE
    YOUR FOOL PRETENCE   565 2
    THE NASTY LYING PRETENCE OF SEEMING TO FEEL WHAT WE DON+   654 5

PRETEND
    O THE STALE OLD DOGS WHO PRETEND TO GUARD   493 25
    WHY SHOULD A MAN PRETEND TO BE GLAD ABOUT   499 14
    TO PRETEND THAT YOUR DAUGHTER   564 31
    IF YOU DON'T THEN DON'T PRETEND YOU DO   655 12
    AND PERFECTLY HONEST TO PRETEND TO BE UNBEGOTTEN   659 12
    AND LONG-HAIRED PEOPLE WHO PRETEND TO ESPOUSE   778 5

PRETENDING
    PRETENDING TO AVOID US YET ALL THE TIME   269 27
    PRETENDING TO LOOK ROUND THE STALL   384 32
    BECAUSE REALLY IT'S NO USE PRETENDING ONE IS SUPERIOR   435 6
    PRETENDING THESE ARE THE MILLS OF GOD   441 9
    PRETENDING TO LOVE THEM   447 10
    AND YOUNG WASH-OUTS PRETENDING TO BE IN LOVE WITH DEATH   535 19

PRETENSIONS
    I AM SO SICK OF THE PRETENSIONS OF THE SPIRIT   288 15

PRETENTIOUS
    TODAY IF A MAN DOES SOMETHING PRETENTIOUS AND DELIBERATE   634 10

PRETTILY
    FOOTED CAUTIOUSLY OUT ON THE ROPE TURNED PRETTILY SPUN   444 26

PRETTY
    OPENING HER RATHER PRETTY WEDGE OF AN IRON PRISTINE FACE   359 2
    FOOL IN SPITE OF YOUR PRETTY WAYS AND QUAINT KNOW-ALL   400 18
    THE PRETTY PRETTY BOURGEOIS PINKS HIS LANGUAGE JUST AS +   432 28
    IF PEOPLE SAY THEY'VE GOT FEELINGS YOU MAY BE PRETTY   501 12
    THIS PRETTY PEACE WHERE EVERY MAN HAS TO FIGHT AND FIGHT   519 26
    THAT A PRETTY BOTTOM   562 21
    WE GET A PRETTY THIN TIME   573 2
    LOOK AT THAT ONE THERE THAT'S PRETTY HOT   578 11
    O MY BOCCACCIO O HOW GOES YOUR PRETTY TALE   633 1
    THEY WANT TO MAKE AN ACT OF FAITH AND BURN MY PRETTY   633 9
    ALL MY PRETTY PICTURES HUDDLED IN THE DARK AWAITING   634 1
    HOLALA WHAT A PRETTY PEOPLE   790 26
    IF YOU HEAR A MAN CALLED BRILLIANT YOU MAY BE PRETTY SU+   841 18
    AND PRETTY   *926 16

PREVALENCE
    HE SHOWS AN AMUSED SUPERIOR CONTEMPT AT THE PREVALENCE +   *949 4

PREVALENT
    BLIND WITH THE GOSSAMER OF PREVALENT DEATH   737 3
    THIS SERRIED ECSTASY OF PREVALENT DEATH   737 5

PREVENT
    IS THAT YOU CAN'T PREVENT CHANGE   511 22
    MEN PREVENT ONE ANOTHER FROM BEING MEN   677 17
    DO THEY PREVENT THE TOUCH   765 14
    DO THEY PREVENT THE CURRENT   765 16
    PREVENT HIS BECOMING A HUNDRED-PER-CENT AMERICAN   778 8

PREVENTED
    NOT MANKIND FOR MANKIND WOULD HAVE PREVENTED ME   265 22

PREVIOUS
    AND ALL THAT PREVIOUS WHILE SHE WAS I SHE WAS I   260 7

PRE-WORLD
    AND THEIR PRE-WORLD LONELINESS   339 27

PREY
    DOES THE SUN IN NEW MEXICO SAIL LIKE A FIERY BIRD OF PR+   374 12
    HE'S A BEAST OF PREY   466 19

PRIAPUS
    THE PALE-GOLD FLESH OF PRIAPUS DROPPING ASLEEP   651 19
    YOU ARE FOR THAT MOMENT ONE OF THE GODS JESUS OR FAFNIR+   674 4

PRICE
    WI' A WOMAN AN' NAME 'ER A PRICE   82 10
    MY OFFERING BOUGHT AT A GREAT PRICE   238 21
    WHAT PRICE HIS BREAD UPON THE WATERS   335 30
    CAN'T STAND HIM AT ANY PRICE   559 18
    IN JAPANESE HENNA OR WHATEVER IT IS CHEAP AT THE PRICE   835 8
    AT ANY PRICE   835 15
    SO THE ONLY THING TO DO IS TO KEEP STILL TO HOLD STILL +   839 1
    WI' A WOMAN AN' PAY 'ER A PRICE   *924 14

PRICED
    THE JOY I BOUGHT WAS NOT TOO HIGHLY PRICED   225 32

PRICK
    THAT PRICK THEIR EARS LIKE A RABBIT OR BROWSE IN THE DA+   807 14

PRICKED
    SHE PRICKED A FINE BLACK BLOTCH   222 7
    WITH HIS EARS PRICKED AND HIS BODY WINCING   645 19

PRICKING
    WAKING PRICKING THEIR EARS   311 5

PRICKLY
    BALD AND PRICKLY PATE   760 16

PRIDE
    IN THE PRIDE OF HUMILITY   201 14
    HOW I ADORE YOU FOR YOUR SIMPLE PRIDE   221 14
    PRIDE STRENGTH ALL THE LOT   239 3
    PROUD BEYOND INKLING OR FURTHEST CONCEPTION OF PRIDE   258 31
    INTO BLOSSOM INTO PRIDE INTO HONEY-TRIUMPH INTO MOST   305 27
    OR IS IT JUST YOUR INDOMITABLE WILL AND PRIDE OF THE FI+   353 17
    FROM OBSTACLE-LEAPING PRIDE   378 17
    BASED ON THE MYSTERY OF PRIDE   414 18
    TO BE TRUE TO THE NATURE OF IT ITS RESERVE ITS SENSITIV+   464 20
    NATURAL PRIDE   587 13
    EVERYTHING THAT LIVES HAS ITS OWN PROPER PRIDE   621 15
    AND THE BASE THINGS LIKE HYAENAS OR BED-BUGS HAVE LEAST+   621 18
    LIES THE LIVING ROCK OF A SINGLE CREATURE'S PRIDE   844 9
    THE DARK NAIF PRIDE   844 10
    AND DEEPER EVEN THAN THE BEDROCK OF PRIDE   844 11
    BUT BELOW ALL ROOTS OF LOVE LIES THE BEDROCK OF NAKED P+   844 19
    AND DEEPER THAN THE BEDROCK OF PRIDE IS THE PRIMORDIAL +   844 20
    HER SOUL'S FLAG SANK AND HER PRIDE PUT OFF ITS CROWN   *936 17
    HOW I ADORE YOU FOR YOUR SIMPLE PRIDE   *944 28
    BED-ROCKED IN HIS OWN PRIMORDIAL PRIDE   *951 17
    PRIDE PRISTINE AND DEEPER THAN CONSCIOUSNESS THE NATIVE+   *951 18

PRIDE'S
    YOUR CURT PRIDE'S BAN   55 6
    UNTIL HER PRIDE'S FLAG SMITTEN CLEAVED DOWN TO THE STAFF   125 18

PRIEST
    AND ARE YOU HIS PRIEST BIG EAGLE   374 18
    EVEN THE OLD PRIEST IN HIS LONG BLACK ROBE AND SILVERY +   618 16
    WHEN A BLACK PRIEST BLOWS ON A CONCH   623 14

PRIESTESS
    A PRIESTESS EXECRABLE TAKEN IN VAIN   151 21
    A PRIESTESS EXECRATED FULL OF STAIN   874 1

PRIESTS
    THE PRIESTS IN GOLD AND BLACK THE VILLAGERS   232 19
    DO YOU LIFT IT TO THE SUN AS THE AZTEC PRIESTS USED TO +   374 7
    THE MARRIAGE OF PRIESTS   609 16
    THE PRIESTS TO WEAR ROSE-COLOUR OR MAGENTA IN THE STREE+   609 17

PRIM
    LOVE-FIRE IS DRIFTING THOUGH THE BUGLE IS PRIM AND DEMU+   854 16

PRIMAL
    ON OUR PRIMAL LOAM   243 20
    BUT THE ASS IS A PRIMAL CREATURE AND NEVER FORGETS   379 33
    BUT THE PASSION OF JUSTICE IS A PRIMAL EMBRACE   482 10

PRIMARY
    TWO PRIMARY INSTANCES   263 19

PRIME MINISTER
    NOW THEN PRIME MINISTER HOLD ON A BIT   573 25

PRIMEVAL
    TO THE PRIMEVAL RUDIMENTS OF LIFE AND THE SECRET   365 21

PRIMEVAL-DUMB
    PRIMEVAL-DUMB FAR BACK   372 6

PRIMORDIAL
    TAKE UP THE PRIMORDIAL INDIAN OBSTINACY   371 28
    WITH ITS STRANGE PRIMORDIAL CONSCIOUSNESS OF JUSTICE   844 13
    AND ITS PRIMORDIAL CONSCIOUSNESS OF CONNECTION   844 14
    AND DEEPER THAN THE BEDROCK OF PRIDE IS THE PRIMORDIAL +   844 20
    AND TREMBLES WITH A SENSE OF TRUTH PRIMORDIAL CONSCIOUS+   844 25
    AND IS SILENT WITH A SENSE OF JUSTICE THE FIERY PRIMORD+   844 26
    BED-ROCKED IN HIS OWN PRIMORDIAL PRIDE   *951 17
    CENTRAL PRIMORDIAL FIRE OF THE SOUL HEAVIER THAN IRON   *951 24
    CENTRAL PRIMORDIAL FIRE OF THE SOUL HEAVIER THAN IRON   *952 1
    CENTRAL PRIMORDIAL FIRE OF THE SOUL THAT LEANS AND YEAR+   *952 6

PRIMROSE
    COMES OUT IN THE HESITATING TREMOR OF THE PRIMROSE   272 27

PRIMULAS
    AND A HAIRY BIG BEE HUNG OVER THE PRIMULAS   243 23
    AND THE AIRY PRIMULAS OBLIVIOUS   243 28

PRINCE
    LIKE ANY PRINCE SUCH STORES OF THE WORLD'S SUPPLY   264 4
    THAT PALE FRAGMENT OF A PRINCE UP THERE WHOSE MOTTO IS   388 5
    PALE DISPIRITED PRINCE WITH HIS CHIN ON HIS HANDS HIS   388 7
    ENDLESS UNDER THE PRINCE   388 37
    TO THE PRINCE   389 25
    A PRINCE HAS COME BACK TO YOU   392 11

PRINCE OF WALES
    WITH A PALE LITTLE WISP OF A PRINCE OF WALES DIFFIDENT +   387 21

PRINCESS
    WITH A WANTON PRINCESS SLENDER AND PROUD   70 15
    CURLED UP IN THE SUNSHINE LIKE A PRINCESS   255 27
    ROSE-RED PRINCESS HIBISCUS ROLLING HER POINTED CHINESE +   313 27

PRINCESSES
    ROSE OF THE OLDEST RACES OF PRINCESSES POLYNESIAN   314 4

PRINCIPLE
    THAT SOCIETY MUST ESTABLISH ITSELF UPON A DIFFERENT PRI+   487 19
    BECAUSE HE IS ENUNCIATING A PRINCIPLE A LAW   708 14
    AND THE WHEEL STARTS THE PRINCIPLE OF ALL EVIL   712 7
    THE WHEEL IS THE FIRST PRINCIPLE OF EVIL   712 9

PRINT
    IF YOU SEE IT IN PRINT   551 12

PRINTED
    MAN'S SWEETEST HARVEST OF THE CENTURIES SWEET PRINTED   263 25
    WHEN WE PRINTED LADY C   668 7

PRINTING
    FOR PRINTING THOSE NAUGHTY WORDS   668 13

PRISE
    AND DISDAIN AND BLANKNESS AND ONRUSH AND PRISE OPEN THE   371 30

PRISM
    PRISM   168 16

PRISON
    SOFT GLIMMERS OF DESIRE ESCAPED FROM PRISON   113 4
    OH COME AND BREAK THIS PRISON THIS HOUSE OF YESTERDAY   174 17
    AN INTOLERABLE PRISON TO YOU   236 15
    WHICH IS MY PRISON   287 30
    KNOCKED A LITTLE HOLE IN THE HOLY PRISON   459 18
    THAT WAS ONCE A HOUSE AND IS NOW A PRISON   462 2
    OF THE PRISON HOUSE THAT ENCLOSES US ALL   462 8
    PRISON MAKES MEN BAD AND THE MONEY COMPULSION MAKES   488 2
    EARNING A WAGE IS A PRISON OCCUPATION   521 7
    EARNING A SALARY IS A PRISON OVERSEER'S JOB   521 9
    PRISON   521 12
    SO MY PICTURES ARE IN PRISON INSTEAD OF IN THE ZOO   580 14
    O MY THIRTEEN PICTURES ARE IN PRISON   632 28
    AND SINCE WOMEN ARE INSIDE THE PRISON JUST AS MUCH AS M+   838 9
    HE HE'S IN PRISON MY FATHER YES SIR ONE AND SIX WITH MY+   866 11

PRISONER
    I AM SHUT IN A PRISONER I KNOW NOT HOW   173 27
    ON A NARROW BEAT ABOUT THE SAME AS A PRISONER TAKING HIS   521 17
    LAPPED PRISONER IN THE CORDS OF LOVE I HAVE SPUN   884 16

PRISONERS
    THE YOUNG TODAY ARE BORN PRISONERS   518 7
    WHERE MY DARLING PICTURES PRISONERS AWAIT HIS DEADLY   633 23

PRISONERS'
    WORK AND PRISONERS' ROUTINE   518 12
    AND PRISONERS' FLAT INEFFECTUAL PASTIME   518 13

PRISON-LIKE
    IN THE COMMON PRISON-LIKE DRESS   109 4

PRISTINE
    AND ON THE MARGIN MEN SOFT-FOOTED AND PRISTINE   285 24
    YOUR PRISTINE ISOLATE INTEGRITY LOST AEONS AGO   290 13
    OPENING HER RATHER PRETTY WEDGE OF AN IRON PRISTINE FACE   359 2
    DRIVEN AFTER AEONS OF PRISTINE FORE-GOD-LIKE SINGLENESS+   363 14
    BUT EVEN IN PRISTINE MEN THERE IS THE DIFFERENCE   649 6
    PRIDE PRISTINE AND DEEPER THAN CONSCIOUSNESS THE NATIVE+   *951 18

PRIVACY
    YOU HURT MY HEART-BEAT'S PRIVACY   116 28
    BROKE INTO THE PRIVACY   884 2

PRIVATE
    AND IN PRIVATE BOASTS HIS EXPLOITS EVEN LOUDER IF YOU A+   432 30
    AWAY IN SOME PRIVATE CUPBOARD   554 19
    THEN THE PRIVATE INTIMACY OF FRIENDSHIP WILL BE REAL AN+   608 14
    AND THE HALF-HIDDEN PRIVATE PARTS JUST A LITTLE BRASS T+   625 22

PRIVATELY
    FOR USING WORDS THEY PRIVATELY KEEP   492 25
    PRIVATELY COUGHING AHEM   554 26

PRIZE
    AND WRESTLE WITH FOR THE PRIZE OF PERFECT LOVE   411 9

PROBABLY
    PROBABLY THEY THINK ALL MEN ADORE THEM   270 2
    PROBABLY HE WAS BIG   372 19
    PROBABLY HE WAS A JABBING TERRIFYING MONSTER   372 21
    PROBABLY ARE NOTHING AT ALL   613 6
    LET HIM SHOW IT TO THE CROWD PROBABLY THEY WILL APPLAUD   634 11
    PROBABLY AS SHE GREW OLDER SHE ATE HER RIVALS   836 6

PROBE
    FOR THE STARS TO PROBE   108 4

PROBLEM
    I AM INTERESTED IN THE PROBLEM OF REALITY   604 2
    THAT THE PROPERTY PROBLEM SOLVES ITSELF BY THE WAY   665 9

PROBLEMATICAL
    FOUR PIN-POINT TOES AND A PROBLEMATICAL THUMB-PIECE   356 6

PROBLEMS
    ONLY PROBLEMS WRIT ON THE FACE OF THINGS   118 22
    SO OF COURSE THE NATION IS SWOLLEN WITH INSOLUBLE PROBL+   535 21

PROCEED
    TO PROCEED FROM MENTAL INTIMACY   470 18

PROCEEDED
    PROCEEDED TO DRAW HIS SLOW LENGTH CURVING ROUND   350 31

PROCEEDINGS
    MY PICTURES AND ON THE PROCEEDINGS WENT   579 22

PROCESS
    THE PROCESS WILL AMOUNT TO THE SAME IN THE END   317 35
    DEATH ALONE THROUGH THE LONG PROCESS OF DISINTEGRATION   617 8

PROCESSION
    AND AT LAST THE PERA-HERA PROCESSION FLAMBEAUX ALOFT IN   387 25
    TOWARDS THE TAIL OF THE EVERLASTING PROCESSION   389 1
    WHEN I SEE THE IGNOBLE PROCESSION   484 1

PROCESSIONS
    LIKE SAD PROCESSIONS OF EXILES YOU COULD HAVE SEEN THEM+   866 3

PROCLAIM
    THEY HAVE TRIUMPHED AGAIN O'ER THE AGES THEIR SCREAMING+   33 4
    PROCLAIM   *891 5

PROCREANT
    CRY OUT AND FEND HER OFF AS SHE SEEKS HER PROCREANT GRO+   91 27
    BLACK PROCREANT MALE OF THE SELFISH WILL AND LIBIDINOUS   383 14
    AND LOSING MINGLE IN THE PROCREANT WOMB   876 20
    CRY OUT AND FEND HER OFF AS SHE SEEKS HER PROCREANT GRO+   *926 20

PROCREATE
    DOES NOT A SUPREME INTELLECT IDEALLY PROCREATE THE UNIV+   328 26

PROCREATION
    OF PROCREATION   327 12
    HONKING IN THE GLOOM THE HONK OF PROCREATION FROM SUCH   437 25
    HONKED IN THE GLOOM THE HONK OF PROCREATION FROM SUCH T+   *947 3
    BUT CAN IT BE THAT ALSO IT IS PROCREATION   *960 6

PRODUCE
    THEIR HANDS AND PRODUCE WORKS OF ART AS MEN DO HORSES W+   376 2
    TRUE YOU CAN'T PRODUCE THE BEST WITHOUT ATTENDING TO TH+   668 2

PRODUCED
    WHEREVER IS IT PRODUCED   830 26
    ANOTHER TYPE THAT ENGLAND HAS PRODUCED   841 10

PRODUCES
    BUT IF HE PRODUCES SOMETHING BEAUTIFUL WITH THE FRAIL   634 13
    THE BOURGEOIS PRODUCES THE BOLSHEVIST INEVITABLY   663 9
    AS EVERY HALF-TRUTH AT LENGTH PRODUCES THE CONTRADICTION   663 10
    BOURGEOIS COWARDICE PRODUCES BOLSHEVIST IMPUDENCE   663 18

PROFANE
    TONIGHT PROFANE   558 6
    THAT NOTHING CAN STALE OR PROFANE   772 15

PROFANED
    HAVE I PROFANED SOME FEMALE MYSTERY ORGIES   141 3

PROFESSIONAL
    PERHAPS WOULD YOU SAY A THRUSH WAS A PROFESSIONAL   453 1

PROFESSOR OF QUINTESSENTIAL CASH
    PROFESSOR OF QUINTESSENTIAL CASH   *950 24

PROFESSORS
    MONEY-WORM PROFESSORS   456 23
    CLERGYMEN PROFESSORS BANK-DIRECTORS AND STOCK-BROKERS   774 6

PROFITEERS
    THE SAME I SAY TO THE PROFITEERS FROM THE HOTELS THE MO+   316 24
    PROFITEERS HERE BEING CALLED DOG-FISH STINKING DOG-FISH+   316 25

PROFITS
    NOT BASED ON WAGES NOR PROFITS NOR ANY SORT OF BUYING A+   483 26

PROFLIGATE
    AND THE PROFLIGATE IS INSANE   516 12
    AND THE PROFLIGATE IS AFRAID   516 18
    THE FIFTH GENERATION OF PURITANS WHEN IT ISN'T OBSCENEL+   845 15

PROFOUND
    WITH A HUNGER MORE FRIGHTENING MORE PROFOUND   264 11
    THE PASSION OF JUSTICE BEING PROFOUND AND SUBTLE   482 8
    WHELMED IN PROFUNDITIES OF PROFOUND CONVERSATION   542 29
    THE PROFOUND SENSUAL EXPERIENCE OF TRUTH YEA THIS IS   653 13
    THE PROFOUND AND THRILLING VIBRATION OF JUSTICE SENSE O+   653 15

PROFOUNDEST
    THE PROFOUNDEST OF ALL SENSUALITIES   653 5

PROFOUNDLY
    IT IS ALL A QUESTION OF BEING PROFOUNDLY INTERESTED IN +   665 16

PROFUNDITIES
    WHELMED IN PROFUNDITIES OF PROFOUND CONVERSATION   542 29

PROFUSION
    IN VOID AND NULL PROFUSION HOW IS THIS   53 26

PROGRESS
    A PROGRESS DOWN THE INTRICATE ENTHRALLING   65 29
    EXCEPT THAT YOU MAKE SLOW AGELESS PROGRESS   352 31
    THERE HAS BEEN GREAT PROGRESS   548 8
    PROGRESS YOU KNOW WE BELIEVE IN PROGRESS   773 23
    PROGRESS   773 25
    NONE AT ALL MIND YOU PROGRESS IS A FACT   774 8
    IN A BACKWARD RIPPLE GOD'S PROGRESS REVEAL   *915 10

PROGRESSION
    PROGRESSION   854 15

PROGRESSIVELY
    AS I AM WITH LIVING MY LIFE IN EARNESTNESS STILL PROGRE+   *900 12
    AS I AM WITH LIVING MY LIFE IN EARNESTNESS STILL PROGRE+   *903 24

PROJECTILE
    LIKE A TRUNDLING PROJECTILE SWIFTLY WHIRLING UP   397 22

PROJECTION
    IMMORTALITY THE HEAVEN IS ONLY A PROJECTION OF THIS STR+   265 17

PROLETARIAT
    THE BULL OF THE PROLETARIAT HAS GOT HIS HEAD DOWN   327 30

PROLIFIC
    PROLIFIC I AM A BLOSSOMING TWIG   888 17

PROLIXITY
    PROLIXITY   305 10

PROMISCUOUS
    IN PROMISCUOUS INTIMATE APPEAL   608 17

PROMISE
    BUT THA'LL HA'E TER PROMISE TER BE TRUE TER ME   82 27
    WHEN I COME HOME PROMISE ME   735 25
    PROMISE YOU WILL NOT WATCH THE SCAR'S   735 26

PROMISED
    YOU PROMISED TO SEND ME SOME VIOLETS DID YOU FORGET   58 8
    WORLD SHINE LIKE THE PROMISED LAND   554 8

PROMPTINGS
    HIS STRENGTH AND HIS PROMPTINGS   525 17
    AND REFUSING THE PETTIFOGGING PROMPTINGS OF HUMAN   525 18

PROMPTLY
    WHY DOES SHE COME SO PROMPTLY WHEN SHE MUST KNOW   85 13

PRONE
    THE SICK GRAPES ON THE CHAIR BY THE BED LIE PRONE AT TH+   112 16
    CRY FOR THEE OUT OF THE NIGHT WHEREIN WE ARE PRONE   753 5
    EVER AGAIN LYING PRONE LYING SLACK   827 12

PROOF
    THUS HAMMERING THE METTLE OF GOATS INTO PROOF AND SMITI+   381 28

PROPAGANDA
    LOUD PEACE PROPAGANDA MAKES WAR SEEM IMMINENT   495 20

PROPAGATES
    IT PROPAGATES NO MORE   535 9

PROPAGATING
    IS NEITHER HIDING HIMSELF NOR PRESERVING HIMSELF NOR PR+   523 9

PROPELLED
    STEERED AND PROPELLED BY THAT STEEL-STRONG SNAKE OF A T+   393 28

PROPENSITIES
    HENCE HE BECAME A CURLY SHEEP-DOG WITH DANGEROUS PROPEN+   324 26

PROPER
    FOR THE PROPER DREAM-STUFF IS MOLTEN AND MOVING MYSTERI+   176 1
    THE PROPER WAY TO EAT A FIG IN SOCIETY   282 1
    THE PROPER UNCTION ABOUT IT   555 27
    PLEASE ADDRESS THESE QUESTIONS TO THE PROPER PERSON   604 15
    A WAITING FOR THE PROPER TOUCH NOT FOR ANY WORD OR DEED   612 16
    EVERYTHING THAT LIVES HAS ITS OWN PROPER PRIDE   621 15
    AND THE PROPER STORE OF MEAL FOR THE LONGEST JOURNEY   721 23
    NURSES DOCTORS PROPER FOOD HYGIENE SCHOOLS ALL THAT   832 5
    ME OUT OF MY PROPER DUES WITH YOUR CHINKING JESTS   872 26
    GRANTED THERE IS A PROPER GIVE AND TAKE   *952 17

PROPERLY
    IF WE ARE PROPERLY CLOTHED AND DISCIPLINED IN THE DININ+   608 12

PROPERTY
    YOU ARE MY PROPERTY BE PREPARED TO DIE FOR ME AND TO   442 21
    BUT NOT A DEMOCRACY OF IDEA OR IDEAL NOR OF PROPERTY NO+   611 7
    THE BOURGEOIS ASSERTS THAT HE OWNS HIS PROPERTY BY DIVI+   663 13
    PROPERTY   663 15
    AND BETWEEN THE TWO BLADES OF THIS PAIR OF SHEARS PROPE+   663 16
    THIS PAIR OF PROPERTY MONGRELS   663 26
    PROPERTY PROPERTY PROPERTY THAT'S WHAT THEY SEEM TO SAY   664 2
    I LICK THE CREAM OFF PROPERTY THAT'S WHAT IT SEEMS TO S+   664 4
    PROPERTY IS NOW SOLOMON'S BABY   664 14
    A CORPSE EVEN OF PROPERTY   664 16
    IN SETTLING THE PROPERTY QUESTION BETWEEN THEM   664 17
    THEY'LL MERELY DESTROY ALL PROPERTY AND A GREAT MANY PE+   665 1
    THE ONLY WAY TO SETTLE THE PROPERTY QUESTION   665 6
    THAT THE PROPERTY PROBLEM SOLVES ITSELF BY THE WAY   665 9
    THE MORE YOU TACKLE THE PROPERTY DRAGON   665 10
    IT IS ALL A QUESTION OF BEING PROFOUNDLY INTERESTED IN +   665 16
    ABOUT PROPERTY AND MONEY AND MECHANICAL DEVICES   666 12
    MONEY SHALL CEASE TO BE AND PROPERTY SHALL CEASE TO PER+   666 17

PROPORTION
    AND SEE WHAT PROPORTION THERE IS   236 29
    FIRE AND WATER THEY CONTAIN THE PROPORTION OF MALE AND +   295 7

PROPOSITION
    JOHN KNEW THE WHOLE PROPOSITION   328 10
    JOHN KNEW THE WHOLE PROPOSITION   328 16

PROPPED
    ARE PROPPED ON END THERE WHERE THE MYSTERY STARTS   233 8
    SOBERNESS SOBRIETY WITH HEAVY EYES PROPPED OPEN   287 4

PROPS
    I WISH THAT WHATEVER PROPS UP THE WALLS OF LIGHT   205 9

PROSERPINE'S
    PROSERPINE'S MASTER   308 3

PROSPERITY
    IN MY FINE PROSPERITY KICK THOSE IN THE DITCH   584 7

PROSPERITY-GANDER
    OR A SORT OF PROSPERITY-GANDER   414 11

PROSTITUTE
    LIKE A PROSTITUTE THE BURSTEN FIG MAKING A SHOW OF HER +   283 33

PROSTITUTED
    OR PROSTITUTED BY THE DREE   469 17

PROSTITUTES
    HE USED TO GIVE KIND ADVICE TO THE PROSTITUTES ON PICCA+   582 2
    AND THE PROSTITUTES ON PICCADILLY OR IN THE CIRCUS   582 3

PROTECT
    AND I'LL PROTECT YOU   400 32
    TO PROTECT THEMSELVES AND THEIR GREEDY-MOUTHED GREEDY-M+   458 20

PROTECTING
    IF THAT IS SO THEN I BELIEVE A LITTLE IN PROVIDENCE PRO+   333 21
    WELL HE'S THERE PROTECTING ME   570 8

PROTECTIVE
    NO DOUBT HE WAS KHAKI-COLOURED WITH MUDDY PROTECTIVE   523 18

PROTEST
    A SORT OF HORROR A SORT OF PROTEST AGAINST HIS WITHDRAW+   351 4
    BUT WHY SHOULD THE WORM THAT HAS TURNED PROTEST SO   432 20

PROTESTANT CHURCHES
    THE PROTESTANT CHURCHES HAVE HAD THEIR DAY   609 22

PROTESTING
    INSISTING PROTESTING   54 3

PROUD
    THOU DARK ONE THOU PROUD CURVED BEAUTY I   40 17
    WHERE THE TREES RISE LIKE CLIFFS PROUD AND BLUE-TINTED +   66 5
    PLANTED THEE UPRIGHT ART PROUD TO SEE   69 15
    WITH A WANTON PRINCESS SLENDER AND PROUD   70 15
    DEED AN' I WISH I C'D 'A' STOOD AT TH' ALTAR WI' THEE A+   83 11
    A FINE PROUD SPIKE OF PURPLE IRISES   90 3
    THE BLUE-GLEAMED DRAKE STEMS PROUD   126 15
    I OUGHT TO BE PROUD THAT SHE SHOULD ASK IT   152 4
    WITH MISERY NO MORE PROUD   155 31
    WE HOLD THEM PROUD AND BLITHE   204 23
    I HAVE BEEN SO INNERLY PROUD AND SO LONG ALONE   214 1
    HIS HEAD AS PROUD AS A DEER THAT LOOKS   220 2
    DARK AND PROUD ON THE SKY LIKE A NUMBER OF KNIGHTS   221 8
    PROUD KNIGHTS TO BATTLE SWEET HOW I WARM   221 28
    HER PROUD HEAD HELD IN ITS BLACK SILK SCARF   228 14
    PROUD BEYOND INKLING OR FURTHEST CONCEPTION OF PRIDE   258 31
    IN A NEW PROUD SINGLENESS AMERICA   290 20
    THEN THE PROUD LION STALKS ABROAD ALONE   325 19
    PROUD INTELLECT HIGH-SOARING MIND   329 3
    THE NEW PROUD REPUBLIC   414 17
    TO THE PROUD FATHER AND SHOWS ITS LITTLE WEBBED GREENISH   438 28
    RATHER PROUD OF BEING A BIT OF A DON JUAN   446 24
    AND PROUD OF MY DESCENT   626 10
    O SLAY NOT THE BEST BRIGHT PROUD LIFE THAT IS IN YOU TH+   678 24
    SURE OF OUR DEAD IN THE PROUD HALLS OF DEATH   740 27
    IS DEATH SO PROUD   749 4
    KEEPS ME PROUD IN SHAME PLEDGE OF THE NIGHT DARK-PURE   772 13
    PLANTED THEE UPRIGHT ART NOT PROUD TO SEE   *915 27
    DEED AN' I WISH AS I COULD STOOD AT THE ALTAR WI' THEE +   *925 15
    HIS HEAD AS PROUD AS A DEER THAT LOOKS   *944 10
    DARK AND PROUD ON THE SKY LIKE A NUMBER OF KNIGHTS   *944 21

PROUDER
    AND SO MUCH PROUDER SO DISDAINFUL OF RELUCTANCES   306 25
    PROUDER THAN THE BLACK PRINCE   587 22

PROUDLY
    NOR THE DEAR OLD MATER WHO SO PROUDLY BOASTS   458 24

PROUSTIAN
    WILL THE PROUSTIAN LOT GO NEXT   533 21
    NOW THE PROUSTIAN LOT DEAR DARLING DEATH LET ME WRIGGLE   534 3

PROVE
    OUT OF THE DISTANCE NEARER COMING TO PROVE   174 11
    IS APT TO PROVE A GREAT DEAL TOO STRONG   576 2
    BEING CRUDE AND STRAIGHTFORWARD YOU'LL ONLY PROVE   576 14

PROVENCE
    PROVENCE JAPAN AND ITALY REPOSE   58 17

PROVES
    PROVES IT QUITE THANK YOU SO MUCH WE'RE GETTING ON SIMP+   546 20

PROVIDE
    PROVIDE FOR YOUR DEAD ONCE MORE EQUIP THEM   721 25

PROVIDENCE
    IF THAT IS SO THEN I BELIEVE A LITTLE IN PROVIDENCE PRO+   333 21
    HE IS NOT FATHERLY LIKE THE BULL MASSIVE PROVIDENCE OF +   382 8
    AS BENJAMIN FRANKLIN APPROPRIATED PROVIDENCE TO HIS   395 13
    THEY KNEW THE USEFUL GODHEAD OF PROVIDENCE   609 24

PROVIDENCE BULL
    LUKE THE BULL THE FATHER OF SUBSTANCE THE PROVIDENCE BU+   327 16

PROVING
    PAST HIM ONLY A WING-BEAT PROVING   150 2

PROVISION
    WISE GOOD PROVISION THAT MAKES THE HEART SWELL WITH LOVE   264 7

PROVOCATIVE
    PROVOCATIVE   337 3

PROVOKE
    AND NEVER KNOWING WHEN YOU'LL PROVOKE AN EARTHQUAKE   539 9

PROW
    LIKE THE PROW OF A BOAT HIS HEAD LAID BACK LIKE THE STE+   155 20

PROWL
    QUEER HOW YOU STALK AND PROWL THE AIR   332 25

PROWLING
    DISCLOSED BUT 'TIS I WHO AM PROWLING   107 15
    PROWLING ABOUT THE LUSH   107 20
    RANK AND TREACHEROUS PROWLING   107 23
    ON ITS PROWLING ORBIT   120 26
    YOUR EVIL LITTLE AURA PROWLING AND CASTING NUMBNESS ON   332 19
    IN THE DREAM OF THE NIGHT I SEE THE GREY DOGS PROWLING   807 2
    PROWLING TO DEVOUR THE DREAM   807 3

PROWLS
    FROM HEAVEN'S WOLFISH WANDERING ELECTRICITY THAT PROWLS   301 6

PROXIMITY
    IN TORTURE OF YOUR PROXIMITY   *931 3

PRUDENT
    YEA AND HER MOUTH'S PRUDENT AND CRUDE CARESS   127 23

PRUDERY
    HARDENED THEY ARE LIKE GEMS IN TIME-LONG PRUDERY   127 22

PRUNING
    HUMANITY NEEDS PRUNING   677 20
    THE TREE OF HUMANITY NEEDS PRUNING BADLY   677 24
    IT NEEDS THOROUGHLY PRUNING NOT AS IN THE LATE WAR BLAS+   677 25
    BUT PRUNING SEVERELY INTELLIGENTLY AND RUTHLESSLY PRUNI+   677 27
    THE TREE OF HUMAN EXISTENCE NEEDS BADLY PRUNING   677 28

PRURIENCY
    OF THE ITCHING MIND AND THE MENTAL SELF WITH ITS PRURIE+   465 5

PRYING
    AND DON'T WITH THE NASTY PRYING MIND DRAG IT OUT FROM   464 28

PSALMS
    THE PSALMS AND FURTIVELY FROM AMONG THE TEXTS   *894 17

PSYCHE
    THROUGH HIS CROSS-WISE CLOVEN PSYCHE   356 3

P'S
    YOU THINK YOU'D BETTER MIND YOUR P'S AND Q'S FOR A BIT   400 28

PTERODACTYL
    I WOULD BE WILLING TO GIVE WAY LIKE THE PTERODACTYL   430 5

PUB
    IN A PUB PARLOUR IN LITERARY LONDON ON CERTAIN EVENINGS   542 10
    AH IN THAT PARLOUR OF THE LONDON PUB   542 16

PUBLIC
    DRUDGE TO THE PUBLIC   391 36
    IT'S CALLED THE BRITISH PUBLIC THE PUBLIC THE PUBLIC   570 14
    FOR OH THE BRITISH PUBLIC THE PUBLIC THE PUBLIC   571 13
    AND THE ROCK OF AGES OF HIS PUBLIC SCHOOL   *947 31

PUBLISHING
    BY PUBLISHING SUCH A BOOK   668 19

PUCKERED
    I'D HANG MY HAMS WITH PUCKERED PETTICOATS SWAYING   835 32

PUDDING
    IF LIFE GOES INTO THE PUDDING GOOD IS THE PUDDING   449 12

PUDENDA
    HAD NORMAL PUDENDA LIKE YOU AND ME   578 27

PUEBLO
    LIFTS UP HIS VOICE AND HOWLS TO THE WALLS OF THE PUEBLO   405 11
    THE DOGS OF THE DARK PUEBLO   405 13
    AND THE CALLING OF THE OLD RED INDIAN HIGH ON THE PUEBL+   623 16
    THE PUEBLO SUMMONED THE OLD INDIAN MEN AND   777 26
    SO THE SPEECH IN THE PUEBLO ON GOOD FRIDAY   778 31

PUEBLO RIVER
    ACROSS THE PUEBLO RIVER   405 18

PUEBLOS
    THE INDIANS OF THE PUEBLOS HAVE LAND   778 26

PUERILITY
    NOR PUERILITY OF CONTRADICTIONS   709 33

PUFF
    OF GROWING THESE SMOKE-PUFFS THAT PUFF IN WILD GYRATION   116 8
    THE WALLS OF THE HOUSE AND NETTLES PUFF OUT FROM THE HE+   159 25
    SEEING RUSTY IRON PUFF WITH CLOUDS OF BLOSSOM   304 6

PUFF-BALL
    DUST AS THE PUFF-BALL DOES AND BIRDS THAT CHAFF   89 28

PUFFED
    COME AND SOFTEN THE WILLOW BUDS TILL THEY ARE PUFFED AN+   273 2

PUFFING
    WILD PUFFING OF GREEN-FIRE TREES AND FLAME-GREEN BUSHES   116 2
    PUFFING ITS LITTLE MALE STAMENS OUT INTO STERILE PETAL +   535 6

PUFFS
    THEY POISE AND RUN LIKE PUFFS OF WIND THAT PASS   64 31
    AND THE FLOWER THAT PUTS ITS TONGUE OUT AND FERN THAT P+   89 27
    LEAN ABOUT US SCATTERING THEIR POLLEN PUFFS OF GOLDEN L+ *916 10

PULL
    CHOKE ME IN MY OWN CRIMSON I WATCHED HER PULL   123 17
    THE DRINK AND A LONG STRONG PULL   177 12
    AND IF IT BE NOT SO BRUTES TO PULL DOWN HIBISCUS FLOWERS 314 24
    IF THEY PULL ALL THE WORLD DOWN   317 34
    I SWEAR I'LL PULL OFF MY KNICKERS RIGHT IN THE RUE DE L+ 433 20
    MEANING SOUR MAKE YOU PULL A FACE AFTER   530 19
    NOR CUT THE INVISIBLE WIRES OF STEEL THAT PULL THEM   586 6
    I HAVE FELT THE PULL OF DESIRE   602 11
    NOR CUT THE INVISIBLE WIRES OF STEEL THAT PULL THEM   632 21
    ARE COMING BEHIND AND WE MUST PULL OUT ALL   732 2
    PULL   817 22
    THE THING FOR MEN TO DO IS TO START TO PULL DOWN MONEY   838 11
    PULL IT DOWN AND PREPARE FOR A NEW FRESH HOUSE OF LIFE   838 12
    TO PULL DOWN THE BOUGH THE LEAVES BROKE AND THE FRUIT S+ 864 10
    AND CHOKE ME IN MY OWN CRIMSON I WATCHED HER PULL   *934 23
    A BROWN BEE PULL APART   *935 35

PULLED
    WHO HAVE PULLED DOWN THE SALVIA FLOWERS   917 29
    AND SUDDENLY PULLED A GOLD-AND-GREENISH LUCENT FISH FROM 339 2

PULLETS
    TO THE PULLETS UP ABOVE   550 14

PULLING
    A BROWN BEE PULLING APART   124 29
    PULLING ON HIS CHAMOIS GLOVES   433 15
    ONLY IF YOU INSIST ON PULLING ON THOSE CHAMOIS GLOVES   433 19
    WHISTLING AND SEETHING AND PULLING THE ANGLER DOWN INTO   586 27
    PULLING THE LONG OARS OF A LIFE-TIME'S COURAGE   *959 12

PULLS
    WHILE SHE PULLS HERSELF FREE AND ROWS HER DULL MOUND   362 10
    TO THE NEXT FARM PULLS UP WHERE THE ELDER FLOWERS FALL   732 4
    HE PULLS UP FOR OUR WATER WOULD HE DRIVE   733 13

PULPIT
    HE HAD HOPED TO DIE IN THE PULPIT TO CONQUER IN DEATH   859 10
    IN THE PULPIT WHERE SHRIVELLED AND GHASTLY IN UNINTELLI+ 859 14

PULSE
    SHE HAS QUICKENED MY PULSE TO RECEIVE   38 21
    MY PULSE OF LIFE AND LET HIM NOSE LIKE A STOAT   43 31
    WHERE HER ARMS AND MY NECK'S THICK PULSE COULD MEET   62 2
    AND STILL ONE PULSE   120 32
    THE PULSE THROUGH THE WHOLE BLAND BEING   165 13
    A PULSE THAT STILL WENT FLEETING   165 15
    AND LAND THAT BEATS WITH A PULSE   261 4
    AND I FEEL ARISTOCRATIC NOBLE WHEN I FEEL A PULSE GO   525 7
    AND I CAN SEE THE PULSE WITHIN HIS THROAT   878 25

PULSED
    PULSED THICKLY AND I LONGED TO POUR   *934 33

PULSES
    THROUGH INVISIBLE PULSES SLOWLY FILLING THE NIGHT'S DAR+ 97 28
    THE HEART OF THE LIVE WORLD PULSES AND THE BLOOD OF THE+ 176 4
    THAT SENDS PULSES EVEN THROUGH ME   525 5

PULSE'S
    AS AN INSOLENT MISTRESS TELLING MY PULSE'S BEAT   230 27

PULSING
    MY MOUTH ON HER PULSING   120 18
    LIFT OF THE PULSING WIND AH SAY THAT YOU KNOW   126 32
    FIERILY PULSING UNABLE TO REFRAIN   194 25
    DEEP PULSING OF A STRANGE HEART   292 33
    OUR PALE MIND STILL FROM THE PULSING CONTINENT   607 2
    HIS BODY PULSING WITH PLAY   867 23
    WITHOUT THE PULSING WATERS WHERE WERE THE MARIGOLDS AND+ *891 24
    THE GREAT ACTIVITY SWELLING THROUGH THE ROUND FLESH PUL+ *907 14

PUMA-YELLOW
    JAGUAR-SPLASHED PUMA-YELLOW LEOPARD-LIVID SLOPES OF   409 24

PUMP
    BY A SLOW GASPING PUMP THAT HAS AWFUL INTERVALS   878 34

PUNCHING
   STAND UP AND DO SOME PUNCHING   560 19

PUNGENT
   FLOWERS SCENTLESS OR PUNGENT AMMONIACAL ALMOST   270 11
   COMES LIKE A PUNGENT SCENT A VIBRATION BENEATH   270 13
   OF THRILLING RUIN IN THE FLESH OF PUNGENT PASSION OF RA+   273 19

PUNISHMENT
   OF THEIR INSULTS IN PUNISHMENT I WILL NOT   74 22
   OF THEIR INSULTS IN PUNISHMENT I WILL NOT   *895 30
   OF THEIR INSULTS IN PUNISHMENT I WILL NOT   *904 19

PUNT
   HIS LITTLE PUNT AN AUTUMN-BROWN BEECH-LEAF   867 15
   DARTING HIS LIGHT PUNT WITH THE QUICK-SHIFTING FANCY OF+   867 25

PUNY
   WITH THEIR PUNY YOUTH   503 8

PUP
   LITTLE BLACK FEMALE PUP SORT OF FRENCH BULL THEY SAY   395 1
   SUCH A FUNNY PUP IN ME   489 28
   THAT MILDEWED PUP GOOD DOGGIE   491 26

PUPIL
   LIKE A CAT'S DISTENDED PUPIL THAT SPARKLES WITH LITTLE +   97 15

PUPILS
   WITHIN HIS EYES' SINCEREST PUPILS THERE   876 36

PUPPY-LIKE
   AND GRIEVING WITH PUPPY-LIKE BLIND CRYING   544 29

PURE
   ALL THESE PURE THINGS COME FOAM AND SPRAY OF THE SEA   136 17
   PURE LOOK OF YOUR LAST DEAD FACE WHENCE NOW IS GONE   157 17
   PURE RELIEF   169 21
   GREEN LANTERN OF PURE LIGHT A LITTLE INTENSE FUSING TRI+   206 10
   I AM PURE LIKE BONE   230 3
   DO YOU THINK IT IS PURE WORSHIP   235 25
   WHICH WE MUST LEARN TO SATISFY WITH PURE REAL SATISFACT+   264 19
   AND THAT WILL BE PURE EXISTENCE REAL LIBERTY   266 33
   IT IS IN PURE UNUTTERABLE RESOLVEDNESS DISTINCTION OF B+   267 3
   AND SHE ALSO PURE ISOLATED COMPLETE   267 21
   CONDITIONED ONLY BY OUR OWN PURE SINGLE BEING   267 28
   NAY LEONARDO ONLY BUNGLED THE PURE ETRUSCAN SMILE   297 26
   PURE BLOOD AND NOBLE BLOOD IN THE FINE AND ROSE-RED VEI+   314 1
   BLESSED ARE THE PURE IN HEART AND THE FATHOMLESS IN BRI+   314 16
   AND THE GOLD-AND-GREEN PURE LACQUER-MUCUS COMES OFF IN   339 15
   YET MISSING THE PURE LOOP   341 10
   SMELTED PURE   372 2
   VERY HANDSOME AND SOME PURE YELLOW FANGED LEAVES   387 3
   YOU'RE NOT PURE   395 3
   I HAD A MOMENT'S PURE DETESTATION OF YOU   396 7
   SO HE LAUGHS FROM FEAR PURE FEAR IN THE GRIP OF THE SLE+   407 22
   UPON WHICH SHADOWS OF PEOPLE PURE PERSONALITIES   444 5
   IN PURE BRILLIANCE OF ANGER SEA-IMMERSED ANGER   453 26
   THE COOL COOL TRUTH OF PURE VITALITY   481 27
   PURE IMPULSE TO MAKE SOMETHING TO PUT SOMETHING FORTH   520 11
   AND THE PURE INTELLECT GIVES ONE A LAST MASTURBATING SE+   532 9
   BUT OF COURSE ONE KNOWS THAT BOTH BEAUTY AND PURE   532 11
   VIRGINAL PURE POLICEMEN CAME   579 13
   SUGGEST THAT THEY'RE SPICY YET HOW PURE THEY ARE   583 20
   FIRST COMES THE DEATH THEN THE PURE ALONENESS WHICH IS +   611 12
   WHEN I SEE THE FLUTTERING OF PURE LIFE IN THEM   622 10
   AND TO SERVE THAT WHICH IS FLAMEY OR PURE AND WATERY OR   637 10
   JUGFULL AFTER JUGFULL OF PURE WHITE LIQUID FIRE BRIGHT +   647 9
   BRINGS HIM TO HIS KNEES IN HOMAGE AND PURE PASSION OF S+   648 17
   SO THAT ALL OUR DADDIES WERE QUITE BRITISH PURE   658 20
   WHEN THEY ARE PURE WHICH MEANS WHEN THEY ARE QUITE CLEA+   672 2
   FOR A MOMENT PURE IN THE YELLOW EVENING LIGHT HE WAS HY+   672 11
   MOMENTS OF PURE MANIFESTATION   673 18
   UNLESS HE HAS HIS PURE MOMENTS WHEN HE IS SURPASSING   674 19
   WAS A GOD IN GODLINESS PURE AS CHRIST BEAUTIFUL   674 24
   WHICH IS THE MAN'S PURE SELF   679 26
   THAT PURE BEING IS BODILESS   689 16
   AND NONSENSE FOR PURE SNOW IS WHITE TO US   708 19
   ARE YOU SO PURE AND LOFTY UP ALOFT   710 14
   THERE AND THERE ALONE LIES THE PIVOT OF PURE EVIL   712 11
   THEN WE SEE EVIL PURE EVIL   712 20
   TO THE SWEET HOME OF PURE OBLIVION   721 21
   UPON A CORE OF PURE OBLIVION   724 18
   WE LET OUR SOULS BE PURE AND VULNERABLE   736 24
   THE LOST HESPERIDES WHERE LOVE IS PURE   737 9
   I LIFT MY LITTLE PURE AND LAMBENT FLAME   745 10
   OF PURE AND LAMBENT HOSTAGE FROM THE DEAD   745 14
   YET IS UPLIFTED IN ME THE PURE BEAM   745 30
   FEEDING ON PURE WHITE SUGAR   751 3
   LOVE-LIGHT IS GLOWING THOUGH THE GUELDER-ROSE IS TOO CH+   854 17
   DRIFT ON DRIFT ON MY SOUL TOWARDS THE MOST PURE   *959 22
   OH LOVELY LAST LAST LAPSE OF DEATH INTO PURE OBLIVION   *960 3
   INTO PURE OBLIVION   *960 26

PURE-BRED
   HER SENSITIVE LONG PURE-BRED FACE   393 10

PURELY
   SCREENS US PURELY AND WE CAN SLIP THROUGH   699 11

PURER
   AND BANK-NOTES ARE POETRY PURER THAN GOLD   814 10

PUREST
   THAT ALL THINGS ARE MIXED AND THEREFORE THE PUREST WHIT+   708 15

PURIFIER
   IS THE PURIFIER   810 12

PURIFY
   OF THE FOUL ONES FROM MY PICTURES OH PURIFY   581 8

PURISIMA
   PURISIMA REFUGIO AND SOLEDAD   798 15

PURITAN
   IN A PURITAN FILLET A CHASTE WHITE SNARE   178 9
   THE PURITAN IS INSANE   516 11
   THE PURITAN IS AFRAID   516 17

PURITANISM
   WHEREAS PURITANISM IS BENT ON SUPPRESSING THE FACT   *953 4

PURITANS
   THE FIFTH GENERATION OF PURITANS WHEN IT ISN'T OBSCENEL+   845 15
   THE FIFTH GENERATION OF PURITANS WHEN IT ISN'T DEBAUCHED   *953 7

PURITY
   WHILE THEY KEEP THEIR OWN WILD PURITY   484 23
   WHEN YOUR FLAME FLICKERS UP AND YOU FLICKER FORTH IN SH+   674 2
   BEYOND US NOW BEYOND DEPARTING WITH THAT PURITY   676 10
   PREACHING IN SAD-MOVING SILENCE A HEART-HUNGRY PURITY   855 3
   IN A DAY THEY ARE LOST IN THE NOTHINGNESS PURITY BRINGS   855 4
   ELOQUENT PURITY VOICELESS IN THE DUST   855 6
   PURITY HOWEVER IS NEVER SANE AND NEVER WHOLESOME   *953 1

PURPLE
   THE SAME VALLEY WITH PURPLE AND WHITE   37 28
   FROM THE FULL RESOURCE OF SOME PURPLE DOME   50 10
   SWEET DARK PURPLE AND WHITE ONES MIXED FOR A PLEDGE   58 10
   A FINE PROUD SPIKE OF PURPLE IRISES   90 3
   SAVE IN A BROKEN PATTERN AMID PURPLE AND GOLD AND SABLE   90 6
   AH MY DARLING WHEN OVER THE PURPLE HORIZON SHALL LOOM   91 25
   AND ANOTHER LILAC IN PURPLE VEILED   105 31
   AND PEOPLE DARKLY INVESTED WITH PURPLE MOVE PALPABLE   148 26
   THAT WRAPS THE NORTH IN STUPOR AND PURPLE TRAVELS THE D+   162 6
   IN PURPLE ELMS DAFFODILS   162 6
   AWAY THEIR PURPLE FACES AND THEIR GOLD   224 25
   STILL IN THE PURPLE DISTANCE   253 11
   PURPLE CROCUSES   271 7
   PURPLE SLIT   283 31
   BUT OPENED AROUND HER PURPLE ANEMONES   308 12
   HELL-GLAMOROUS AND PURPLE HUSBAND-TYRANNY   308 31
   OF PURPLE AFTER SO MUCH PUTTING FORTH   667 17
   WHOSE MASTS HAVE PURPLE VINES   693 26
   AND UP THEY COME WITH THE PURPLE DARK OF RAINBOWS   693 27
   TO THE SCARLET AND PURPLE FLOWERS AT THE DOORS OF HELL   711 20
   IN THE PURPLE VEIL   742 16
   SOME TURNING PINK SOME TURNING PURPLE DUSK   824 23
   THOUGH THE PURPLE DREAMS OF THE INNOCENT SPRING HAVE GO+   854 6
   THE HEAVY PURPLE PERFUMED BUNCH   880 24
   TO RISE AN ODOUR OF PURPLE VIOLETS CRUSHED   881 7
   AND BROKEN BY MY WEIGHT AND THE PURPLE STEAM   881 8
   SO THAT WITHIN A PILLAR OF PURPLE SMOKE   881 11
   THE SAME EDEN WITH PURPLE AND WHITE   *892 16
   AH MY DARLING WHEN OVER THE PURPLE HORIZON SHALL LOOM   *926 18

PURPLED
   PURPLED STEEL   149 6

PURPLING
   INCIPIENT PURPLING TOWARDS SUMMER IN THE WORLD OF THE H+   273 25
   IS PURPLING WITH VIOLETS   273 32

PURPLISH
   THEY ARE GOLD THEY ARE BROWN THEY ARE PURPLISH THEY   827 1
   THE DARK ONES ARE CURIOUSLY PURPLISH LIKE FRESH   827 4

PURPOSE
   OF THE LUMINOUS PURPOSE OF LIFE SHINES OUT   68 10
   THE SEED IS PURPOSE BLOSSOM ACCIDENT   218 26
   TOO MUCH PURPOSE IN LIFE   496 4
   AND SERVED THEIR GREAT PURPOSE   609 23
   BETWEEN YOU AND YOUR PURPOSE LIKE A KNIFE'S EDGE SHADOW   706 20

PURPOSELESS
   OF ROSES UNCHIDDEN AND PURPOSELESS A ROSE   219 18

PURPOSELESSNESS
   SWORN TO A HIGH AND SPLENDID PURPOSELESSNESS   197 16

PURPOSE OF GOD
   OF THE LUMINOUS PURPOSE OF GOD SHINES OUT   *914 25

PURPOSES
   PURPOSES   395 14
   TURNED ON FOR DIFFERENT PURPOSES   625 23
   MAKES AN EVIL WORLD-SOUL WHICH PURPOSES   716 2

PURR
   DO YOU HEAR MY ROLLS ROYCE PURR AS IT GLIDES AWAY   664 3

PURRS
   THE SHE-MATE PURRS   325 15

PURSE
   HE FEELS FOR HIS PURSE AND FINDS IT THERE AND SAYS   659 19

PURSUED
   PURSUED BY NO SIGH OF BEREAVEMENT   63 33

PURSUING
LIKE A TOOTHLESS HOUND PURSUING HIM WITH MY WILL   47 23

PURSUIT
HELL RISEN IN PURSUIT OF HER ROYAL SUMPTUOUS   308 15
THIS AWKWARD HARROWING PURSUIT   363 4

PURSUITS
BENT ON MY PURSUITS   63 16

PURVEYORS
THE PURVEYORS OF EDUCATION   762 22

PUSH
WHAT IF I SUDDENLY STUMBLE AND PUSH THE DOOR   147 8
LOOSING HOLD IN THE WIND'S INSISTENT PUSH   160 8
THE VENETIAN SHUTTERS I PUSH WIDE   343 1

PUSHED
I HAVE PUSHED MY HANDS IN THE DARK SOIL UNDER THE FLOWE+ 92 8
PUSHED GENTLY AWAY AND HIDDEN IN THE THICK OF HER HAIR 114 22
WAVING SLOWLY BEFORE ME PUSHED INTO THE DARK   147 1
CREEP RIGHT UP WITH YOUR ROUND HEAD PUSHED IN MY BREAST 245 6
THAT ROUND HEAD PUSHED IN MY CHEST LIKE A NUT IN ITS   245 14
WHEN HE PUSHED HIS BUSH OF BLACK HAIR OFF HIS BROW   310 1
THE WHOLE GREAT HEAVENS HAVE SHIFTED OVER AND SLOWLY PU+ 616 23
PUSHED THEM ALL ASIDE DISCARDED THEM MAKE WAY NOW FOR S+ 616 26
PUSHED UP ON END AND THE BREATH SIGHING   733 25
I HAVE PUSHED MY HANDS IN THE DARK LOAM UNDER THE FLOWE+ *926 8
OR IS PUSHED OUT   *957 13
IT IS EASY TO BE PUSHED OUT OF THE SILVERY CITY OF THE + *957 20

PUSHES
THERE THE LAZY STREAMLET PUSHES   33 13
WHERE LIGHT PUSHES THROUGH   341 3
THERE THE LAZY STREAMLET PUSHES   *891 14
AS THE HORNBEAM PUSHES UP HIS SPROUTS   *954 9

PUSHING
THE CLOUDS ARE PUSHING IN GREY RELUCTANCE SLOWLY NORTHW+ 57 10
LIKE A BIG SHIP PUSHING HER BOWSPRIT OVER THE LITTLE SH+ 380 24
ONLY THIRD-RATE SWABS ARE PUSHING TO GET ON NOWADAYS   518 17
AND JERKED BACK THEIR BRIDLES PUSHING THEIR HEADS APART 735 9
THROUGH EVER ONWARD NIGHT PUSHING   862 29
EVE PUSHING THE FESTOONED VANILLA TREMBLING ACIDE   864 7

PUSS PUSS
AND THE CHURCHES CRY PUSS PUSS COME AND BE FED   763 3

PUSSY-CAT
PUSSY-CAT PUSSY-CAT WHERE HAVE YOU BEEN   670 1
PUSSY-CAT PUSSY-CAT WHAT DID YOU THERE   670 3

PUSSYFOOT
SOON IN THE PUSSYFOOT WEST   280 12

PUTRESCENT
OF PUTRESCENT WISDOM AND SAPIENCE THAT SUBTLY STINKS   441 3
ARE AN AMAZING PUTRESCENT SLUSH   830 18

PUTRID
AND FRESHEN THE PUTRID LITTLE SPACE IN WHICH WE ARE CRI+ 515 4
IN PUTRID AUTUMN ISSUING THROUGH THE FALL   745 22

PUTS
PUTS THE HARD HANDS OF MY FRIEND TO SLEEP   41 9
AND THE FLOWER THAT PUTS ITS TONGUE OUT AND FERN THAT P+ 89 27
SHE PUTS ME AWAY LIKE A SALESWOMAN WHOSE MART IS   120 3
AH AND SHE PUTS HER HANDS UPON THE WALL   128 31
HE PUTS HIS SURF-WET FINGERS   201 1
BUT SHE PUTS HER NOSE DOWN SHREWDLY ENOUGH WHEN THE   384 28
SO I CAN'T SEE WHERE THE WORM THAT HAS TURNED PUTS ANYT+ 432 34
THAT PUTS SALT ON THE TAILS   562 10
THAT PUTS FORTH ITS OWN ARISTOCRACY   627 7
ANSWERS THE QUESTION AS HE PUTS IT IN HIS STRIDE   816 8
AND PUTS HIS MOUTH DOWN TO THE GUSHING STREAM   877 8

PUTTING
AND WATCH IT PUTTING FORTH EACH TIME TO HEAVEN   299 24
AND CYCLAMENS PUTTING THEIR EARS BACK   310 28
THEY ARE LIKE SLENDER TREES PUTTING FORTH LEAVES A LONG+ 451 5
PUTTING THEM FORTH NOT MANUFACTURING THEM   451 12
PUTTING IN ALL THE IMPOSSIBLE WORDS   491 15
OF PUTTING US IN THE WORLD   493 6
AND BUSY PUTTING OUT THE SUN   528 8
OF PURPLE AFTER SO MUCH PUTTING FORTH   667 17
AND PUTTING HIS STRENGTH IN YOUR HEELS AND ANKLES HIS F+ 801 24
THEY LIVED THEMSELVES FORTH LIKE A TREE PUTTING OUT WOV+ *949 28
PUTTING ITS TIMBERS TOGETHER IN THE DUSK   *960 29

PUT-UP
AND CARES NOT A STRAW FOR THE PUT-UP HUMAN FIGMENTS   481 16

PUZZLE
WICKED FIG-TREE EQUALITY PUZZLE WITH YOUR SELF-CONSCIOUS 300 16

PUZZLED
IS THE GORGEOUSNESS THAT EVOKES MY MOST PUZZLED ADMIRAT+ 369 7
AND YOU'RE PUZZLED   400 27

PUZZLE-FACE
CHINESE PUZZLE-FACE   398 5

PYJAMAS
ON A HOT HOT DAY AND I IN PYJAMAS FOR THE HEAT   349 2

PYRAMID
IN PYRAMID MEXICO DURING SACRIFICE   371 8

PYRE
KINDLES THE DARKENING PYRE   108 20
ENTERING SHE SAW HIM IN OUTLINE RAISED ON A PYRE   155 17
IS THE PYRE OF BLAZING GAS   702 24

PYTHAGORAS
IT NEEDED PYTHAGORAS TO SEE LIFE PLAYING WITH COUNTERS + 355 14

PYTHON-STRETCH
AND IN ADDITION THE GREAT MUSCULAR PYTHON-STRETCH OF HER 393 22

Q'S
YOU THINK YOU'D BETTER MIND YOUR P'S AND Q'S FOR A BIT 400 28

QUACKING
WHITE DUCKS A QUACKING FLOTILLA OF CLOUD   126 13

QUAFF
BUT EVEN THOU SON OF MAN CANST NOT QUAFF OUT THE DREGS + 322 9

QUAIL
WE QUAIL MONEY MAKES US QUAIL   486 14

QUAILED
I QUAILED AT MY APPOINTED FUNCTION TURNED POLTROON   194 29
YOUR BODY QUAILED AT MY STROKE   *928 13

QUAILING
AND QUAILING HERE IN THE SUNSHINE BETRAYED FROM HAUNTING 133 3

QUAILS
THE PLANE-LEAVES FALL THROUGH THE LAMP-LIGHT LIKE TIRED+ *917 9

QUAINT
FOOL IN SPITE OF YOUR PRETTY WAYS AND QUAINT KNOW-ALL 400 18
LATELY I SAW A SIGHT MOST QUAINT   680 16

QUAINTLY
HIDE YOUR QUAINTLY SCARLET BLUSHES   43 2
A HAT QUAINTLY CURIOUSLY WOVEN LUXURIOUS WITH BIG ROSES 656 12

QUAKING
I AM THE LEAPING AND QUAKING   805 10
HUITZILOPOCHTLI LEAPING AND QUAKING   806 13

QUALITY
YOUR WESTERN BRUTAL FAERY QUALITY   291 25

QUALM
THAN OFF HE STARTS WITHOUT A QUALM   299 33
SHE HAS NO QUALM WHEN SHE CATCHES MY FINGER IN HER STEEL 359 20

QUANDARY
YES IT'S A QUANDARY   379 24

QUANTUM
I LIKE RELATIVITY AND QUANTUM THEORIES   524 19

QUANTUMS
ELECTRONS AND ENERGIES QUANTUMS AND RELATIVITIES   438 5

QUARK
COO COO COO COO-ARK COO-ARK QUARK QUARK   413 24
WHETHER YOU'RE A SUCKING DOVE ROO COO OOO QUARK   414 6

QUARREL
AND DRINK FIRE-WATERS AND QUARREL AND STAB   795 3

QUARRY
THEM AGAIN ON A QUARRY OF KNOWLEDGE THEY HATE TO HUNT   74 10
THEM AGAIN ON A QUARRY OF KNOWLEDGE THEY HATE TO HUNT *895 18
THEM AGAIN ON A QUARRY OF KNOWLEDGE THEY HATE TO HUNT *904 7

QUARTERS
AND IT IS DAY THEN FROM THE FOUR QUARTERS THE FOUR WIND+ 319 7
QUARTERS THEN SLEEP IS EMPTY TOO MAN SLEEPS NO MORE LIK+ 319 10
WHEN IN THE STREETS OF THE WORKING QUARTERS   585 24
QUARTERS   643 11

QUARTZ
LIKE QUARTZ CRYSTALS   224 14

QUASH
BUT BE CAREFUL HOW YOU UTTERLY QUASH THEM   776 32

QUAVERINGLY
HOW QUAVERINGLY I DEPEND ON YOU TO KEEP ME ALIVE   246 2

QUEEN
UNNOTICED AMONG THEM A STILL QUEEN LOST IN THE MAZE   176 24
A QUEEN THEY'LL SAY   176 26
SWEAR IN THE PALE WINE POURED FROM THE CUPS OF THE QUEEN 177 21
NOR ANY QUEEN   234 20
WHAT IS THE FRUIT OF YOUR WOMB THEN YOU MOTHER YOU QUEEN 235 5
LIKE THE KING AN' QUEEN THOUGH THEY'RE   434 28
I'VE BEEN UP TO LONDON TO SEE THE FINE QUEEN   670 2
PAUSES NEAR THE CREST OF THE HILL CLIMBING SLOWLY LIKE + 687 17
WHO COULD HOROSCOPE FIT FOR A QUEEN   845 18
OF SOME PRE-RAPHAELITE MYSTIC QUEEN   854 27

QUEENLY
    SO QUEENLY SHAKING HER GLISTENING BEAMS   702 26

QUEENS
    THE DARKNESS STEALS THE FORMS OF ALL THE QUEENS   135 21
    HOURS THAT WERE ONCE ALL GLORY AND ALL QUEENS   135 24
    OF QUEENS IN HYACINTH AND SKIES OF GOLD   135 26
    QUEENS LADIES ANGELS WOMEN RARE   234 25
    WE ARE ALL KINGS AND QUEENS   435 4
    THE DARKNESS STEALS THE FORMS OF ALL THE QUEENS   *938 25
    OF QUEENS IN HYACINTH 'NEATH SKIES OF GOLD   *939 18
    THE DARKNESS STEALS THE FORMS OF ALL THE QUEENS   *939 21
    HOURS THAT WERE ONCE ALL GLORY AND ALL QUEENS   *939 24

QUEER
    QUEER WITH YOUR THIN WINGS AND YOUR STREAMING LEGS   332 15
    QUEER HOW YOU STALK AND PROWL THE AIR   332 25
    QUEER WHAT A BIG STAIN MY SUCKED BLOOD MAKES   334 16
    QUEER WHAT A DIM DARK SMUDGE YOU HAVE DISAPPEARED   334 18
    THIS QUEER DROSS SHAWL OF BLUE AND VERMILION   369 22
    QUEER IT IS SUDDENLY IN THE GARDEN   385 15
    TO MUSIC AND QUEER CHANTING   387 34
    THE AFRICAN QUEER ONES AND SCANDINAVIAN QUEER ONES   671 15

QUELLE JOIE DE VIVRE
    QUELLE JOIE DE VIVRE   336 24

QUENCH
    TO QUENCH THEIR OVER-SULPHUREOUS LUSTS   340 10

QUENCHED
    ONE TO BE QUENCHED TO BE GIVEN UP TO BE GONE IN THE DARK   212 8

QUENCHING
    WITH A FLUTTER OF HOPE AND A QUENCHING DOUBT   121 26

QUEST
    ENDANGERED BY THE PILFERER ON HIS QUEST   128 4
    THE CATTLE RUN ANXIOUS IN QUEST AS THE TIME DRAWS NIGH   749 25
    WHERE THE BLUE CRABS RUSTLED IN QUEST OF HER AIMLESS WI+   864 6

QUESTING
    OF QUESTING BRILLIANT SOULS GOING OUT WITH THEIR TRUE   221 27
    OF QUESTING BRILLIANT THINGS YOU JOY YOU TRUE   *945 13

QUESTION
    TO SETTLE THE QUESTION HEADS OR TAILS HAS CAUGHT   54 10
    OLD QUESTION WITHOUT ANSWER STRANGE AND FAIN   69 27
    WHAT WAS MY QUESTION MY GOD MUST I BREAK THIS   76 9
    'TIS THE SUN THAT ASKS THE QUESTION IN A LOVELY HASTE F+   119 29
    SWORD THAT SEVERS THE QUESTION FROM US WHO BREATHE   168 26
    QUESTION OR DIMINUTION   235 14
    TO BE OR NOT TO BE IS STILL THE QUESTION   265 25
    AND ANSWER THE FIRST MACHINE-CUT QUESTION FROM THE LIPS+   291 2
    IF IT IS A QUESTION OF HIM OR ME   468 1
    THE ONLY QUESTION TO ASK TODAY ABOUT MAN OR WOMAN   603 15
    LIES ARE NOT A QUESTION OF FALSE FACT   654 1
    AND THE FIRST QUESTION TO ASK YOURSELF IS   661 14
    IN SETTLING THE PROPERTY QUESTION BETWEEN THEM   664 17
    THE ONLY WAY TO SETTLE THE PROPERTY QUESTION   665 6
    IT IS ALL A QUESTION OF BEING PROFOUNDLY INTERESTED IN +   665 16
    FOR THE SHELLS THAT THE QUESTION IS NOW NO MORE BEFORE +   741 23
    THE INDIAN QUESTION HAS WORSE LUCK BECOME A POLITICAL   777 13
    QUESTION   777 14
    THE BIT OF LAND IN QUESTION IS A FLEA-BITE   779 13
    SOLVE THE INDIAN QUESTION FINALLY   780 1
    MAKE IT CEASE TO BE A POLITICAL QUESTION FOR EVER   780 2
    ANSWERS THE QUESTION AS HE PUTS IT IN HIS STRIDE   816 8
    MY QUESTION MY GOD I MUST BREAK FROM THIS HOARSE SILENCE *898 4
    MY QUESTION MY GOD I MUST BREAK FROM THIS HOARSE SILENCE *901 13

QUESTIONING
    BEFORE SHE COULD SET THE CLAWS OF HER SELF-CONSCIOUS QU+   604 9

QUESTIONS
    AND MY QUESTIONS BLOW   168 5
    PLEASE ADDRESS THESE QUESTIONS TO THE PROPER PERSON   604 15

QUE TIENE AMIGO
    QUE TIENE AMIGO   401 18

QUETZALCOATL
    SLEPT I QUETZALCOATL   786 4
    OH BROTHER QUETZALCOATL   786 19
    SAYING TO HERSELF QUETZALCOATL   787 14
    BROTHER QUETZALCOATL   789 12
    QUETZALCOATL MY BROTHER HE CALLED SEND ME MY IMAGES   789 17
    AND QUETZALCOATL CALLED BACK I WILL DO IT   789 21
    WHY ARE YOU LAUGHING ASKED THE FIRST MAN OF QUETZALCOATL   791 12
    AND QUETZALCOATL HAS COME HE IS HERE   799 6
    BUT I AM QUETZALCOATL OF THE MORNING STAR   800 32
    I AM THE LIVING QUETZALCOATL   800 33
    I AM QUETZALCOATL OF THE EAGLE AND THE SNAKE   800 36
    I AM THE LIVING QUETZALCOATL   801 1
    FOR I AM QUETZALCOATL THE FEATHERED SNAKE   801 27
    AND I QUETZALCOATL THE EAGLE OF THE AIR AM BRUSHING YOU+   802 1
    QUETZALCOATL HAS COME   802 7
    QUETZALCOATL HAS COME   802 9
    QUETZALCOATL HAS COME   802 13
    QUETZALCOATL LOVES THE SHADE OF TREES   802 14
    QUETZALCOATL IS AMONG THE TREES   802 17
    QUETZALCOATL HAS COME   802 19
    AH QUETZALCOATL   803 1
    BUT I TOUCHED THE HAND OF QUETZALCOATL   806 26
    I TOUCHED THE HAND OF QUETZALCOATL   806 28
    BLUE IS THE BREATH OF QUETZALCOATL   808 18
    QUETZALCOATL WILL SHOW YOU THE WAY   809 9
    BUT HUITZILOPOCHTLI TOUCHED THE HAND OF QUETZALCOATL   809 19

QUETZALCOATL
    WHEN THE BLUE WIND OF QUETZALCOATL   811 20

QUETZALCOATL OF THE TWO WAYS
    I AM QUETZALCOATL OF THE TWO WAYS   802 5

QUIBBLE
    ALL RIGHT YOU ALWAYS DID QUIBBLE   453 5

QUICK
    THE QUICK SPARKS ON THE GORSE-BUSHES ARE LEAPING   33 1
    QUICK   33 7
    A FEW QUICK BEATS FROM A WOOD-PIGEON'S HEART AND WHEN I+   38 14
    SHE GLANCES QUICK HER STARTLED EYES   42 24
    STILL YOUR QUICK TAIL LIF STILL AS DEAD   43 3
    TO DIE AND THE QUICK LEAF TORE ME   111 4
    FLUTTER FOR A MOMENT OH THE BEAST IS QUICK AND KEEN   119 21
    WORN HER AWAY TO THE QUICK SO SHE FAINTLY FARES   131 26
    THE QUICK   132 9
    THE TOUCH WAS ON THE QUICK I WANT TO FORGET   143 25
    WITHIN ITS QUICK COMMITTED TO HOLD AND WAIT   161 4
    A GLINTING WEB QUICK HID IN THE GLOOM OF THE BROOK   161 7
    I WILL CATCH IN MY EYES' QUICK NET   180 8
    THE VERY QUICK OF MY BEING   246 6
    AND MY LIFE IS FIERCE AT ITS QUICK   246 15
    AND BROUGHT YOU TO THE VERY QUICK OF YOUR FORM   254 32
    I WANT HER TO TOUCH ME AT LAST AH ON THE ROOT AND QUICK 266 28
    A CIRCLE SWOOP AND A QUICK PARABOLA UNDER THE BRIDGE   341 1
    HER QUICK   382 21
    THEN SHE LEAPS THE ROCKS LIKE A QUICK ROCK   386 9
    SO QUICK LIKE A LITTLE BLACK DRAGON   396 28
    AT THE QUICK   435 23
    LIKE THE FLAME OF A CANDLE SLOW AND QUICK   460 7
    QUICK LITTLE SPLINTERS OF LIFE   466 15
    HURRYING HURRYING LEGS GOING QUICK QUICK QUICK   484 6
    YOUR HEART'S QUICK CORE   561 25
    THE DEAD TRIUMPHANT AND THE QUICK CAST DOWN   740 4
    AND DAMAGE ONCE MORE THE FRAIL QUICK OF THE FUTURE   780 21
    ONLY COLD INSTEAD OF QUICK   784 31
    THE QUICK KINDLING SPARK OF A GENEROUS TRUST   855 8
    HARK HER QUICK OH   861 16
    WITH A QUICK KISS CLIPS   862 12
    SO MUCH SO RARE A GAME SO QUICK A HEART-BEATING   876 15
    AND MY OWN BREAST OPENS IN QUICK RESPONSE   883 6
    THE QUICK SPARKS ON THE GORSE BUSHES ARE LEAPING   *891 1
    QUICK   *891 8
    A FEW QUICK BEATS OF A WOODPIGEON'S HEART THEN RISE   *892 30
    INTO QUICK RESPONSE   *906 22
    THE FASCINATION OF THE QUICK RESTLESS CREATOR MOVING TH+ *908 19
    WORN HER AWAY TO THE QUICK SO SHE FAINTLY FACES   *937 25
    SINCE DEATH FROM THE MOTHER MOON HAS PARED CLOSE TO THE+ *938 1
    SWIMS THE MALLARD DUCK AT DAWN IN THAT QUICK JOY   *953 27

QUICKEN
    TO QUICKEN MY HOPE AS I HASTENED TO GREET   121 21
    TO QUICKEN THE SPHERES SPRING-VIRGIN AGAIN IN THE SKY   127 10

QUICKENED
    SHE HAS QUICKENED MY PULSE TO RECEIVE   38 21
    A NET ON THE UNDERSOIL THAT LIES PASSIVE AND QUICKENED + 94 4
    EVE RUNNING WITH SWIFT LIMBS QUICKENED BY DREAD   864 19

QUICKENING
    A QUICKENING MASCULINE GLEAM FLASHES IN TO ALL   127 2
    AM I NOT QUICKENING DIFFUSING MYSELF IN THE PATTERN SHA+ *909 4

QUICKENS
    QUICKENS THE UNCLASPING HANDS OF HAZEL   40 26
    OF EARTH AND QUICKENS ALL HERSELF WITH FLOWERS   89 2
    QUICKENS THE HASTENING WHITE-HOT METAL   *907 22
    AS IT QUICKENS WITHIN THE LABOURING WHITE-HOT METAL   *909 26
    THEN UP WITH WRATH THE RED-EYED MORNING QUICKENS   *933 12

QUICKER
    SHE'S A QUICKER INSTRUCTRESS THAN YEARS   38 20

QUICKLY
    ENTERED AND QUICKLY CAST   122 7
    WOULD GOD THEY WERE SHATTERED QUICKLY THE CATTLE WOULD 159 21
    IF I TURN QUICKLY I AM TERRIFIED FEELING SPACE SURROUND+ 222 23
    AH COME COME QUICKLY SPRING   272 30
    COME QUICKLY AND VINDICATE US   273 5
    COME QUICKLY AND STIR THE ROTTEN GLOBE OF THE WORLD FROM 273 7
    SHE QUICKLY SEWED FIG-LEAVES AND SEWED THE SAME FOR THE+ 284 8
    SHE GOT THE FACT ON HER MIND AND QUICKLY SEWED FIG-LEAV+ 284 12
    AND LONG SNAKES QUICKLY GLIDE INTO THE DARK HOLE IN THE+ 321 24
    WHILE SOMETHING STIRS QUICKLY IN HER BELLY AND A LEAN   393 30
    ONLY TO DISAPPEAR AGAIN QUICKLY AWAY FROM THE SIGHT OF 394 2
    MAKE ME RICH QUICKLY WITH NEVER A HITCH   584 6
    EVE WITH A HEART OF RESENTMENT IS QUICKLY SPED   864 21

QUICK-SHIFTING
    DARTING HIS LIGHT PUNT WITH THE QUICK-SHIFTING FANCY OF+ 867 25

QUICKSILVER
    THEY FALL BACK AND LIKE A DRIPPING OF QUICKSILVER TAKIN+ 322 12

QUIESCENCE
    BY VERY FIERCENESS INTO A QUIESCENCE   160 18

QUIESCENT
    THE DAISY-FROTH QUIESCENT SOFTLY IN THRALL   35 29

QUIET
    BREATHED QUIET ABOVE ME AND THE CROP   35 19
    HOW GLAD I WAS HE HAD COME LIKE A GUEST IN QUIET TO DRI+ 350 1
    SO BIG AND QUIET AND REMOTE HAVING WATCHED SO MANY   393 12
    KEEP QUIET AND WAIT   514 7

QUIET
WHICH THEY COULD COMB BY THE HOUR IN LUXURIOUS QUIET   537 27
O LET US TALK OF QUIET THAT WE KNOW   717 17
THAT WE CAN KNOW THE DEEP AND LOVELY QUIET   717 18
FROM THE QUIET CHURCH-TOWER THAT KNOWS NO PRATTLE OF CH+   858 22
THOUGH YOU MOVE WITH A QUIET GRACE LIKE A CLOUD   874 23
WITH DIM CALM THOUGHTS AND QUIET HANDS   *960 28

QUIETLY
TO PONDER VERY QUIETLY   51 15
IS QUIETLY TWINKLIN'   562 18
AND MY EYES MEET HIS VERY QUIETLY   *898 27
AND MY EYES MEET HIS VERY QUIETLY   *902 11
QUIETLY THROUGH THE YEARS I HAVE CREPT BACK TO SEE   *940 6

QUIETNESS
GOING WITH INSIDIOUS HALF-SMILING QUIETNESS   296 21

QUIETUS
AND CAN A MAN HIS OWN QUIETUS MAKE   717 10
BUT IS THAT A QUIETUS O TELL ME IS IT QUIETUS   717 13
EVER A QUIETUS MAKE   717 16
HOW CAN WE THIS OUR OWN QUIETUS MAKE   717 20
CAN MAN HIS OWN QUIETUS MAKE   *957 1
BUT IS THAT A QUIETUS OH TELL ME IS IT QUIETUS   *957 5
QUIETUS IS THE GOAL OF THE LONG JOURNEY   *957 6

QUINCE-BLOSSOM
UPON US AND APPLE- AND ALMOND- AND APRICOT- AND QUINCE-+   271 26

QUINTESSENTIAL
GOLD AND OF INCONCEIVABLY FINE QUINTESSENTIAL BRIGHTNESS   271 18

QUIVER
SKY CEASED TO QUIVER AND LOST ITS ACTIVE SHEEN   35 15
WITH FEELINGS THAT CHANGE AND QUIVER   38 25
I HAVE DONE A QUIVER OF EXULTATION GOES THROUGH ME LIKE   209 26
THE LOUD LOVE OF PEACE MAKES ONE QUIVER MORE THAN ANY   495 16
MAKES THE HEART SUDDENLY QUIVER WITH LOVE   653 17
FAR OFF IN GOLD THE WILLOWS QUIVER   887 27

QUIVERING
ON THE TURF I STAND WATCHING MY OWN WHITE SHADOW QUIVER+   33 19
QUIVERING AWAKE WITH ONE IMPULSE AND ONE WILL   39 8
PITEOUS BROWN BALL OF QUIVERING FEARS   43 11
SETS QUIVERING WITH WISDOM THE COMMON THINGS   46 19
FRESH QUIVERING KEEP THE SUNNY-SWIFT MARCH-DAYS WAITING   179 5
WHEN I WOKE THE LAKE-LIGHTS WERE QUIVERING ON THE WALL   243 21
OF DARKENING NIGHT AND THE QUIVERING LIGHT   823 9
HER QUIVERING ANSWERS AND KISSES LIKE THIEVING BIRDS   868 31
OF THE BANK I STAND WATCHING MY OWN WHITE SHADOW QUIVER+   *891 21
QUIVERING AWAKE WITH ONE IMPULSE OF DESIRE   *893 21
UNDROSSED IT AND BLESSED IT WITH A QUIVERING   *927 23
WITH A QUIVERING SWEET WISDOM OF GRACE BUT NOW   *928 24
MY QUIVERING ANSWER AND KISSES LIKE FRAGRANCE OF FLOWERS   *942 3

QUIVERS
AND THE WHITE DOG DANCES AND QUIVERS I AM HOLDING HIS C+   34 5
AND QUIVERS IN WORDS THROUGH MY MOUTH   38 31
NOR DEATH WHICH QUIVERS WITH BIRTH   205 13
WHICH QUIVERS INDRAWN AS YOU CLENCH YOUR SPINE   370 13
AND THERE BEYOND THE SUNSET QUIVERS   816 6
THAT QUIVERS BETWEEN MY EYES AND MOUTH   *893 14

QUIZZ
'ERE SHE'S A LIDY AREN'T YER OLD QUIZZ   434 24

QUOS VULT PERDERE DEUS
IS IT THE QUOS VULT PERDERE DEUS BUSINESS   533 23

RA
JESUS BUDDHA JEHOVAH AND RA EGYPT AND BABYLON   671 19

RABBIT
RABBIT LOBS   34 28
THE RABBIT PRESSES BACK HER EARS   43 5
HE FLINGS THE RABBIT SOFT ON THE TABLE BOARD   43 22
IT'S ONLY A RABBIT   231 13
I REMEMBER THE SCREAM OF A RABBIT AS I WENT THROUGH A   366 4
WHEN YOU PICK THE RED SMOKY HEART FROM A RABBIT OR A   374 5
LOBBING WILDLY THROUGH DEEP SNOW LIKE A RABBIT   397 7
AND IN WHOM THE DREAM SITS UP LIKE A RABBIT LIFTING LON+   807 8
THAT PRICK THEIR EARS LIKE A RABBIT OR BROWSE IN THE DA+   807 14

RABBIT-BLOOD
LIFTING THE RABBIT-BLOOD OF THE MYRIADS UP INTO SOMETHI+   414 22

RABBITS
RABBITS HANDFULS OF BROWN EARTH LIE   33 5
HERE FLICK THE RABBITS HERE PANTS THE GORSE HERE SAY TH+   34 11
AND RABBITS MAKE PILLS AMONG THE SHORT GRASS   321 23
SCUT-TAILED RABBITS   392 17
FIRST LIVE THING I'VE OWNED SINCE THE LOP-EARED. RABBITS   395 7
RABBITS HANDFULS OF BROWN EARTH LIE   *891 6

RABBIT'S
OF THE RABBIT'S FUR GOD I AM CAUGHT IN A SNARE   43 28
GENTLY AND FINELY LINED THAN A RABBIT'S OR THAN A HARE'S   393 7

RABBIT-WISE
SITTING UP THERE RABBIT-WISE BUT HUGE PLUMB-WEIGHTED   393 5

RABBITY
INSIPID UNSALTED RABBITY ENDLESSLY HOPPING   606 19

RABIES
LIKE A GREY DOG WHOSE MOUTH IS FOUL WITH RABIES   807 5

RACE
SHALL I COME TO YOU THE OPEN TOMB OF MY RACE   289 27
DEAD WITH A DEAD RACE AND A DEAD SPEECH AND YET   296 9
MONUMENTAL TO A DEAD DEAD RACE   297 12
RED ANGRY MEN ARE A RACE EXTINCT ALAS   317 12
IN THE RACE OF LOVE   361 26
AND WHITE TEETH SHOWING IN YOUR DRAGON-GRIN AS YOU RACE   397 20
DOWNWARD THEY RACE IN DECLINE   455 28
FOR WE ENGLISH ARE REALLY A RACE APART   576 12
WALKS TO THE FUNERAL OF THE WHOLE HUMAN RACE   653 2
THE RACE IS NOT TO THE SWIFT   658 5
IN EVERY RACE   666 4
IT IS FINISHED ITS RACE IS OVER   676 5
ANOTHER RACE ANOTHER SPEECH AMONG   746 5
WHEN THOU RUNNEST THE RACE WITH THE FOREMOST GOD BLESS +   750 2
HE IS THE LAST OF THE ORIGINALLY AMERICAN RACE   776 34
CAN YOU LEAVE THE REMNANTS OF THE OLD RACE   779 22
TOWNS CONSTELLATIONS RACE   862 26

RACED
HUMMING-BIRDS RACED DOWN THE AVENUES   372 8

RACES
PASSES THE LIGHT OF THE TRAM AS IT RACES   145 14
THE SILENCED RACES AND ALL THEIR ABOMINATIONS   298 2
TREES SUFFER LIKE RACES DOWN THE LONG AGES   304 25
ROSE OF THE OLDEST RACES OF PRINCESSES POLYNESIAN   314 4
LO I AM FLESH AND BLOOD THAT RACES   460 25
AS THE WIND RACES SOUTH   861 12
TO THE VAST OF SPACE WHERE BRIGHTNESS RACES THE BLUE   875 14

RACING
SING THROUGH AND EACH WITH A FLOOR-LIGHT RACING ALONG   144 9
AND DARKNESS RUNS THE RACING WHEEL   773 6

RACING-TRACK
THEY ARE LAYING THE GOLDEN RACING-TRACK OF THE SUN   230 9

RACK
IF THE VIOLETS ARE COMING OUT FROM UNDER THE RACK OF MEN   273 33

RACKED
AMONG CROWDS OF THINGS IN THE SUNSHINE JOSTLED AND RACK+   133 8

RADIANCE
YOUR PALLOR INTO RADIANCE FLUSH YOUR COLD   86 12
SOON STREWS ITSELF ON THE FLOOR AND KEEP THE RADIANCE O+   179 4
THE RADIANCE OF THE UNSEEN SHAPER   *907 19

RADIANT-TISSUED
TO SEE YOU ALL SORDID OR RADIANT-TISSUED   73 7

RADIATORS
CLINGING TO THE RADIATORS LIKE NUMBED BEES TO THE DRENC+   866 1

RADICAL
THEN I AM MORE THAN RADICAL I WANT TO WORK A GUILLOTINE   526 16

RADIO
THE DEAD GIVE SHIPS AND ENGINES CINEMA RADIO AND GRAMOP+   441 17
WHILE THE MACHINE AMUSES US THE RADIO OR FILM OR   450 15
AND GOD THE SON A TALKING RADIO   641 4

RADIOS
AND LITTLE TALKING RADIOS   641 7

RAFTER
ALOFT BY ONE GREAT BENDING RAFTER DUSTY   876 13

RAG
CREATURES THAT HANG THEMSELVES UP LIKE AN OLD RAG TO SL+   342 1
IT'S EITHER AN ARTIFICIAL RAG BLOSSOM OR AN IMMORTELLE +   472 26
IN THEIR RAG GARMENTS SCUTTLING THROUGH THE STREETS   530 16

RAGE
WHISTLING SHE-DELIRIOUS RAGE AND THE DREADFUL SOUND   36 14
RAIN THAT BURNT ON MY RAGE SAYING COME   62 23
WITHIN THE RAGE WE SHALL NOT KNOW TILL IT BURST   160 19
IN FRONT OF THE TERRIBLE RAGE THE DEATH   165 17
YOU WITH YOUR GRUDGING ENVIOUS FURTIVE RAGE   314 32
WITH ITS LONG ANTENNAE OF RAGE PUT OUT   315 16
UGH HOW I LOVE ITS FANGS OF PERFECT RAGE   315 18
THE MOLTEN GOLD OF ITS INTOLERABLE RAGE   315 20
SALVIA STILL IN A RAGE   316 3
RUNS A RAGE DRAWN IN FROM THE ETHER DIVINELY THROUGH HIM   381 21
RAGE OF THE SULLEN-STAGNATING ATMOSPHERE OF GOATS   381 24
HOMAGE IN LUST IN RAGE   390 7
HIGH AND CLAWING WITH RAGE AT THE CLIFFS OF THE SOUL   454 9
OF ETERNAL SALT RAGE ANGRY IS OLD OCEAN WITHIN A MAN   454 11
AND FALLS BACK DRAWING IN ITS BREATH WITH RAGE   467 14
NOW A VOLCANO OF RAGE   539 20
THE SWAN WILL BEAT THE WATERS IN RAGE WHITE RAGE OF AN +   624 15
AND WITH HIDEOUS SHRIEKS OF STEELY RAGE AND FRUSTRATION   676 3
SEEKING THEIR OLD HAUNTS WITH COLD GHOSTLY RAGE   722 27
AND CAN BUT HAUNT IN DISEMBODIED RAGE   723 2
OR STORMS OF TEARS OR RAGE OR BLACKENING RAIN   745 12
WHICH YOU'VE THROWN UPON HIM SHALL SUDDENLY SHAKE WITH +   797 9
THEY MOAN AND BEAT THEY GNASH THEY RAGE   *958 4
THEY FALL UPON THE NEW OUTCOMING SOULS WITH RAGE   *958 5

RAGGED
    AND WAVING FLAGS AND THE RAGGED FIRES   49 26
    SHUFFLING HIS RAGGED BOOTS THERE COMES ONE BOY LATE   866 6
    I SAW A DARK FIGURE APPROACHING A RAGGED SOLITARY CROW   866 17
    REVEALING THE SKY THROUGH THE RAGGED EARTH AND SUDDEN   874 29

RAGING
    I CAN SEE HIS RAGING BLACK EYES BLAZE AT ME   733 3

RAGS
    SITS INDIFFERENT HUGGED IN HER RAGS   54 18
    HAVE HUDDLED RAGS OR LIMBS ON THE NAKED SLEEP   144 22
    NONE IN RAGS AND NONE IN TAGS   312 7
    NOT BY THEIR RAGS AND NOT BY THEIR TAGS   312 14
    SANS RAGS SANS TAGS   313 1
    HANGING UPSIDE DOWN LIKE ROWS OF DISGUSTING OLD RAGS   342 3
    WE EXPIATE IN OUR BODIES' RENTS AND RAGS   743 7
    AS ONE DYING WITH THE CHARRED RAGS FALLING AWAY   769 13

RAIL
    ALMOND-TREE BENEATH THE TERRACE RAIL   300 26

RAILLERY
    TO COVER MY MOUTH'S RAILLERY TILL I'M BOUND IN HER SHAM+   *940 17

RAILROAD
    NOW SITHEE THEER AT TH' RAILROAD CROSSIN'   *920 25

RAILWAY
    THAT SHINES BLOOD-RED BESIDE THE RAILWAY SIDING   72 5
    THE COLTSFOOT FLOWERS ALONG THE RAILWAY BANKS   162 2
    TRACK OF THE RAILWAY ALIVE AND WITH SOMETHING TO DO   174 8
    ALONG THE RAILWAY ACTIVE FIGURES OF MEN   174 9
    OH COME OH MEN ALONG THE RAILWAY OH COME AS MEN   175 16
    WOODSTACKS BESIDE THE RAILWAY GLISTEN AND GLOW   *894 26
    FLUENT ACTIVE FIGURES OF MEN PASS ALONG THE RAILWAY   *906 16
    FLUENT ACTIVE FIGURES OF MEN PASS ALONG THE RAILWAY AND+   *908 11
    ALONG THE RAILWAY ACTIVE FIGURES OF MEN   *908 13

RAILWAYS
    AT HER TRAINS AT HER RAILWAYS AND HER AUTOMOBILES   790 7

RAIN
    HUDDLIN' UP I' T' RAIN   60 16
    AN' I COME AWAY ACAUSE O' TH' TEEMIN' RAIN   61 16
    AND I HEARD THE THUNDER AND FELT THE RAIN   62 19
    RAIN THAT BURNT ON MY RAGE SAYING COME   62 23
    THE SUN AND THE RAIN DO NOT ASK THE SECRET   63 18
    OH BUT THE RAIN CREEPS DOWN TO WET THE GRAIN   63 27
    SMOULDERING WITH DARKENED BUSBIES BENEATH THE BAYONETS'+   66 8
    LIQUID AS LIME-TREE BLOSSOM SOFT AS BRILLIANT WATER OR +   67 20
    AND WHEN I WAKE IN THE MORNING AFTER RAIN   72 20
    LAMPS IN A WASH OF RAIN   119 8
    FULL OF DISAPPOINTMENT AND OF RAIN   119 12
    THE RAIN   133 13
    RAIN FROM THE SHOWERY HEAVENS AND BRIGHT BLUE CROPS   136 12
    AND HAPPY AS RAIN IN SUMMER WHY SHOULD IT BE SO   141 25
    IN THE BLACK WET NIGHT AS THE FURTIVE RAIN SLINKS DOWN   143 2
    THE NIGHT RAIN DRIPPING UNSEEN   144 1
    SOMETHING I WANT TO TOUCH I MUST HOLD MY FACE TO THE RA+   180 31
    THERE IS A KINDNESS IN THE VERY RAIN   208 7
    IN FALLING SEEDS OF RAIN   268 20
    FALLING AS RAIN   269 13
    WET ALMOND-TREES IN THE RAIN   300 18
    BLACK ALMOND TRUNKS IN THE RAIN   300 20
    WHAT ARE YOU DOING IN THE DECEMBER RAIN   301 1
    SICILY DECEMBER'S SICILY IN A MASS OF RAIN   301 12
    THERE IS RAIN IN ME   454 1
    A MEETING PLACE FOR SUN AND RAIN   504 17
    FIRE AND RAIN AND AIR AND LIVE LOAM   505 13
    SONS OF THE WIND AND RAIN SONS OF THE FIRE AND ROCK   635 25
    HOW THEN ARE THE FEW MEN MEN OF THE WIND AND RAIN   637 27
    AND THE RAIN WON'T COME THE RAIN REFUSES TO COME   647 17
    IN THE GREEN GARDEN DARKENED THE SHADOW OF COMING RAIN   672 12
    AND SO RAPIDLY AND SO FLASHING FLEEING BEFORE THE RAIN   672 16
    MADE OF THE DRIZZLING RAIN   692 2
    A LIT-UP SHAFT OF RAIN   714 8
    AND OUR SOUL COWERS NAKED IN THE DARK RAIN OVER THE FLO+   718 19
    OR STORMS OF TEARS OR RAGE OR BLACKENING RAIN   745 12
    RAIN AND A FALLING WORLD   748 19
    RAIN POUR DOWN POUR DOWN   754 13
    THIS IS WHAT STARS AND SUN AND EARTH AND MOON AND WINDS+   793 3
    THE RAIN OF BLOOD IS FALLEN IS GONE INTO THE EARTH   811 15
    TEARS WRINKLE OUR FACES LIKE RAIN IN THE HOLLY   814 24
    WHEN RED RAIN GOES FLINGING   861 15
    HEAVY WITH DROPS OF THE FIRST CRUEL RAIN   863 15
    HUDDLIN' CLOSE TOGETHER A CAUSE O' TH' RAIN   *911 2
    AN' I COME AWAY BECAUSE O' THE TEEMIN' RAIN   *911 32
    TO THE FIRE AND RAIN WILL YOU TAKE THE FLOOD   *931 27
    LAMPS IN A WASH OF RAIN   *932 17
    FULL OF DISAPPOINTMENT AND OF RAIN   *932 21

RAINBOW
    YOU FEET OF THE RAINBOW BALANCING THE SKY   73 9
    THE RAINBOW ARCHING OVER IN THE SKIES   136 15
    RAINBOW   208 24
    THE LIGHTNING AND THE RAINBOW APPEARING IN US UNBIDDEN +   268 8
    EVEN THE RAINBOW HAS A BODY   692 1
    AND DENSE WITH HAPPY BLOOD DARK RAINBOW BLISS IN THE SEA   695 12
    AS UP AN INVISIBLE RAINBOW AN ARCH   696 23
    A RAINBOW OF LOVE AND HATE   714 12
    IS THE RAINBOW   818 27
    WHEN I LOOK AT THE RAINBOW   819 6
    THE TWO FEET OF THE RAINBOW   819 13
    OF THE RAINBOW   819 30
    HANGING FROM THE SHOULDERS OF THE RAINBOW   820 4
    IS THE RAINBOW   820 7
    AND MAKE A RAINBOW   820 16

RAINBOWS
    AND UP THEY COME WITH THE PURPLE DARK OF RAINBOWS   693 27

RAIN-BRUISED
    THE RAIN-BRUISED LEAVES ARE SUDDENLY SHAKEN AS A CHILD   136 24

RAIN-DISHEVELLED
    FOR THE SLUICING OF THEIR RAIN-DISHEVELLED PETALS   217 22

RAINDROPS
    IT IS STORMY AND RAINDROPS CLING LIKE SILVER BEES TO TH+   92 1
    HOLD MY HAND TO CATCH THE RAINDROPS THAT SLANT INTO SIG+   179 21
    SLOWLY THE RAINDROPS OF APPRECIATION   495 2

RAIN-DROPS
    IT IS STORMY AND RAIN-DROPS CLING LIKE SILVER BEES TO T+   *926 1
    RATTLE THE RAIN-DROPS RUIN THE APPLES   *933 9

RAINING
    AH BUT I AM ILL AND IT IS STILL RAINING COLDLY RAINING   112 29
    IT IS RAINING DOWN THE HALF-OBSCURE ROAD   220 15

RAINS
    RAINS HEAVY TO ME   748 29
    FOR SUN AND STARS AND EARTH AND THE VERY RAINS ARE WEARY   792 20
    THERE ARE DEAD THAT WEEP IN BITTER RAINS   795 20
    AND SPUE OUT CORROSIONS INTO YOUR STREAMS ON YOUR RAINS   797 6

RAIN-SKIES
    OF CLOUD THE RAIN-SKIES YIELD   68 20

RAIN-STORM
    THAT A GREY ONE LIKE A SHADOW LIKE A RAT A THIEF A RAIN+   120 3

RAIN-WATER
    AS RAIN-WATER   667 30

RAIN-WET
    CLUCK AND THE RAIN-WET WINGS   119 16
    CLUCK AND THE RAIN-WET WINGS   *932 25

RAINY
    BACK TO THIS RAINY SWILL   111 5
    ITS RAINY SWILL ABOUT US SHE ANSWERED ME   180 14

RAISE
    CAUTIOUSLY I SHALL RAISE   59 2
    TO RAISE MY FACE I DID NOT DARE LOOK UP   122 28
    THE ASH-TREES OF THE VALLEY-ROAD WILL RAISE   176 15
    BUT THEY OFTEN RAISE SUCH A DUST IN THE SWEEPING   536 2
    THE MORE WE SLAY AND ARE SLAIN THE MORE WE RAISE UP NEW   739 27
    I RAISE MY FACE SO IT SHALL WREATHE ME   883 13
    DARKNESS TO RAISE THE STRICKEN DIGNITY AND REST   *896 23
    TO RAISE MY FACE I DID NOT DARE LOOK UP   *934 4
    THE ASH-TREES OF THE VALLEY ROAD SHOULD RAISE   *941 2
    AND SO I'D RAISE   *941 13

RAISED
    WHAT CONJURER'S CLOTH WAS THROWN ACROSS YOU AND RAISED   53 21
    ENTERING SHE SAW HIM IN OUTLINE RAISED ON A PYRE   155 17
    WAR CAME AND EVERY HAND RAISED TO MURDER   257 27
    VERY GOOD VERY GOOD EVERY HAND RAISED TO MURDER   257 28
    AND NEEDS TO BE RAISED FROM SEED   535 14
    TREES RAISED FROM SEED HAVE WILD AND BITTER FRUITS   640 21
    HOW SHALL WE NOW APPEASE WHOM WE HAVE RAISED UP   740 9
    AND I RAISED MY BREAST   882 8

RAISIN
    WHAT IS IT IN THE GRAPE TURNING RAISIN   280 14

RAISING
    RAISING DUSK AND ACRIDITY OF GOATS AND BLEATING   384 3

RAKE
    THE LAST ROW IS FINISHED THE JINGLING RAKE IS LIFTED   858 17

RAKED
    SHALL HAVE RAKED THE EMBERS CLEAR I WILL KEEP   *896 2
    SHALL HAVE RAKED THE EMBERS CLEAR I WILL KEEP   *904 23

RALLY
    AS THEY GO FROM SCHOOL SOME OF THE OFFICERS RALLY   732 20
    IF WE RALLY AT ALL TODAY INSTEAD OF KEEPING   839 8
    LET US RALLY FOR OUR OWN SANITY   839 10
    AND RALLY TOGETHER   839 16

RAM
    FURTHER STILL BEFORE THE CURLED HORNS OF THE RAM STEPPED   437 14
    O WHEN THE OLD WORLD SACRIFICED A RAM   679 11
    NOR EVEN LIKE AN ANIMAL BULL RAM OR LION OR LAMB   840 26
    AND FURTHER STILL BEFORE THE CURLED HORNS OF THE RAM ST+   *946 25

RAMBLER
    THE LONELY RAMBLER THE STOIC DIGNIFIED STALKER THROUGH   360 28

RAMBLING
    SO THAT THE RAMBLING SKY-DROPPED GRAPE CAN ADD ITS SAVO+   281 25
    AND ALL RAMBLING AIMLESS LIKE LITTLE PERAMBULATING PEBB+   357 18
    OF THAT MUD-HOVEL OF HIS SLOWLY RAMBLING SPOUSE   361 14
    THEIR SPLAY FEET RAMBLING AND ROWING LIKE PADDLES   361 24
    WHITE IVORY WHITE AMONG THE RAMBLING GREENS   646 24

RAMPING
    RAMPING ROUND GUARDING THE FLOCK OF MANKIND   324 28
    RAMPING UP THROUGH THE AIR LIKE A KESTREL   324 30

RAN
AN' THEN AWAY 'E RAN   81   8
AND I RAN FORWARD TO FRIGHTEN HIM FORTH   344   4
A LIZARD RAN OUT ON A ROCK AND LOOKED LISTENING   524   13
AND THEY RAN ME IN TO TEACH ME WHY   570   11
I TOOK TO MY HEELS AND RAN   604   8
AND A GIRL RAN SWIFTLY LAUGHING BREATHLESS TAKING IN HE+   672   13
HE SHOUTED RAN HEAVILY AFTER THEM   735   8
AS IF WITHDRAWN FROM LIVING WOUNDS RAN RED   884   26
THE WAVES RAN LAUGHING UP THE SHORE AT THE SWELL   *917   4
AN' THEN AWAY HE RAN   *923   8
THEN THE DAYS RAN ROUND ME IN A GOLDEN BROOD   *933   17

RANCH
THE RANCH HOUSE   400   7

RANCH-DOGS
NOW YOU'VE COME SEX-ALIVE AND THE GREAT RANCH-DOGS ARE   399   28

RANCID
HEAVY WITH A RANCID CARGO THROUGH THE LESSER SHIPS   380   19
THE RANCID OLD MEN THAT DON'T DIE   662   16
OLD PEOPLE FIXED IN A RANCID RESISTANCE   662   20

RANDOM
AT RANDOM DESOLATE TWIGS   51   2
THOUGH WHAT SHE DOES EXCEPT LAY FOUR EGGS AT RANDOM IN   358   26

RANG
ME WORDS THAT RANG WITH A BRASSY SHALLOW CHIME   98   20
HOLLOW RANG THE HOUSE WHEN I KNOCKED AT THE DOOR   121   13
I WAS LAST NIGHT WHEN MY SOUL RANG CLEAR AS A BELL   141   24
WHO RANG THE KNELL   512   13
OR WHETHER IT RANG IN THE AIR   881   25

RANGE
THAT RANGE   52   25
RESTS A STILL LINE OF SOLDIERS RED MOTIONLESS RANGE OF +   66   7
THE RED RANGE HEAVES IN SLOW MAGNETIC REPLY   66   16
THE RED RANGE HEAVES AND COMPULSORY SWAYS AH SEE IN THE+   66   17
AND FEARFUL TO SALLY FORTH DOWN THE SKY'S LONG RANGE   132   20
BEYOND MY RANGE GODS BEYOND MY GOD   338   26
IS JUST BEYOND RANGE OF THE ARROW HE SHOOTS   382   22
AND RANGE THEMSELVES LIKE GREAT FIERCE SERAPHIM FACING +   695   3
RANGE   *905   14

RANGES
VAST RANGES OF EXPERIENCE LIKE THE HUMMING OF UNSEEN HA+   666   25

RANK
RANK AND TREACHEROUS PROWLING   107   23
AND HE SMELLS SO RANK AND HIS NOSE GOES BACK   382   29
YOU'RE A RANK OUTSIDER OF THE FIFTH REMOVE   576   15
THE THICK RANK STREETS AND A STARK WHITE LIGHT   748   5
BUT OF THOSE LIFE-LOVING CARELESS OF THEIR RANK AMONG T+   855   12
LIFE LOVERS WHO COULD HOPE FOR NO RANK AMONG THE PALLID+   855   20
FURTHER INTO ANOTHER RANK BEYOND   877   15
AND RANK AND DRIPPED WITH BLOOD AND DRIPPED AGAIN   884   27

RANKED
WERE RANKED TO BLUE BATTLE AND YOU AND I   248   22

RANKLES
AND IT RANKLES THEY ACHE WHEN THEY SEE THE YOUNG   502   24

RANKS
OPEN THE RANKS AND LET THEM IN OUR HEARTS   736   14

RAP
YOU DON'T CARE A RAP FOR ANYBODY   396   18

RAPE
FROM THE RAPE   465   4
MURDER SUICIDE RAPE   531   4
RAPE WAS RATHER THRILLING   532   16
YES IF IT'S A KEEN MATCH RAPE IS RATHER THRILLING   532   19

RAPED
OR BEING RAPED EITHER WAY SO LONG AS IT WAS CONSCIOUSLY   532   17

RAPID
IN RAPID ARMFULS FROM THE LINE TOSSING IT IN THE BASKET   672   15

RAPIDLY
ALL FLOWS AND EVEN THE OLD ARE RAPIDLY FLOWING AWAY   511   23
IF WE DO NOT RAPIDLY OPEN ALL THE DOORS OF CONSCIOUSNESS   515   3
AND SO RAPIDLY AND SO FLASHING FLEEING BEFORE THE RAIN   672   16

RAPPING
THE ROSES WITH THE WEST WIND RAPPING   149   29
KNOCK KNOCK 'TIS NO MORE THAN A RED ROSE RAPPING   150   20

RAPTURE
FOR THE TRAILING LEISURELY RAPTURE OF LIFE   68   5
THAT SPEAK NO WORD OF THEIR RAPTURE BUT ONLY   69   7
YOU HAVE HAD YOUR LITTLE RAPTURE   95   21
I CANNOT TELL YOU THE MAD ASTOUNDED RAPTURE OF ITS DISC+   260   20
A MAD MAN IN RAPTURE   260   23
FOR THE TRAILING LEISURELY RAPTURE OF LIFE   *914   20
THAT SPEAK NO WORD OF THEIR RAPTURE BUT ONLY   *915   19

RARE
SHE SLEEPS A RARE   101   10
RARE PASSION AND NEVER AGAIN   104   15
HAVE RISEN FLOATING ON MY BLOOD THE RARE   113   3
THIS RARE ANCIENT NIGHT FOR IN HERE   114   1
FOR SO RARE A VISIT   234   14
QUEENS LADIES ANGELS WOMEN RARE   234   25

RARE
A RARE TO-DO   244   28
RARE ALMOST AS BEAMS YET OVERWHELMINGLY POTENT   271   19
OF THRILLING RUIN IN THE FLESH OF PUNGENT PASSION OF RA+   273   19
WHAT A RARE POWERFUL REMINISCENT FLAVOUR   280   6
TO BRING BACK THE RARE AND ORCHID-LIKE   297   28
HE'S A RARE ONE BUT HE BELONGS   337   27
NOBODY CAN BE WISE EXCEPT ON RARE OCCASIONS LIKE GETTING   495   24
AH IN THE PAST TOWARDS RARE INDIVIDUALS   602   10
AND OUR NAKED CONTACT WILL BE RARE AND VIVID AND TREMEN+   608   15
BUT STILL MORE BRAVE AND STILL MORE RARE   634   26
AT LOVE SHOULD SPRINKLE ME DAILY WITH A RARE   874   6
SO MUCH SO RARE A GAME SO QUICK A HEART-BEATING   876   15
OWNING MY SUPPLE BODY A RARE GLAD THING SUPREMELY GOOD   *892   11
RARE BIRDS THAT NO   *894   6
THIS RARE RICH NIGHT FOR IN HERE   *929   18
WISE WONDERFUL STRANDS OF WINDS THAT ARE LADEN WITH RARE   *938   22

RARELY
THOUGH SHE LOOKED RARELY BEAUTIFUL   255   30

RARER
THAT BEARS ALOFT TOWARD RARER SKIES   *899   28
THAT BEARS ALOFT TOWARDS RARER SKIES   *903   7

RAREST
FOR GOD EVEN THE RAREST GOD IS SUPPOSED TO LOVE US   691   12

RASCAL
THE WIND THE RASCAL KNOCKED AT MY DOOR AND I SAID   731   13

RASED
YOUR STUFF ALL GONE YOUR MENACE ALMOST RASED   53   23

RASH
YES BE RASH   817   28

RAT
FOR A GREY RAT FOUND THE GOLD THIRTEEN   119   19
THAT A GREY ONE LIKE A SHADOW LIKE A RAT A THIEF A RAIN+   120   3
NO RAT OF THE DARK DARED GNAW YOU   800   31
FOR THE GREY RAT FOUND THE GOLD THIRTEEN   *932   28
THE WHITE DOG NIPPED THE MOTHER RAT THE FATHER RAT BESI+   *933   7
THEN UP COMES A GREY RAT A FLOSS-GOLD CHICKEN GRAPPLES   *933   11

RAT-BAIRNIES
AND RESTLESS WERE THE WHIMPERING RAT-BAIRNIES   *933   4

RATE
IF ANYTHING AILED 'IM AT ANY RATE   45   19

RAT-GNAWED
TILL YOU ARE AS EMPTY AS RAT-GNAWED POMEGRANATES HANGIN+   800   26
SEE YOU BE NOT RAT-GNAWED GOURDS   800   35

RAT-HORDES
BUT UTTERLY FAILS TO RECOGNISE ANY MORE THE GREY RAT-HO+   640   5

RATIFICATION
IT IS OUR RATIFICATION   265   15

RATIO
IN DIRECT RATIO   663   19

RATION
AND EACH ITEM WILL GET ITS RATION   443   4

RATS
ONLY MICE AND MOLES AND RATS AND BADGERS AND BEAVERS   392   22
WAITING FOR THE RATS OF THE DARK TO COME AND GNAW YOUR +   800   24
DO YOU HEAR THE RATS OF THE DARKNESS GNAWING AT YOUR IN+   800   25

RAT'S
THEN FLUTTER FOR A MOMENT AND THE RAT'S LONG TEETH ARE +   *932   30
PLENISHING THE GREY RAT'S NEST   *933   6

RATTLE
LIKE A RATTLE A CHILD SPINS ROUND FOR JOY THE NIGHT RAT+   206   31
MY ROOM A CRASH-BOX OVER THAT GREAT STONE RATTLE   342   10
RATTLE RATTLE RATTLE   584   24
AT LAST I HEAR A RATTLE AND THERE AWAY   732   24
RATTLE THE RAIN-DROPS RUIN THE APPLES   *933   9

RATTLED
LIKE A RATTLE A CHILD SPINS ROUND FOR JOY THE NIGHT RAT+   206   31
BUT OFF SHE WENT BEING REALLY RATTLED   669   4

RATTLES
AND THE CHAOS THAT BOUNCES AND RATTLES LIKE SHRAPNEL AT   250   4

RATTLING
THEIR ROBOT CACHINNATION COMES RATTLING OUT OF MY THROAT   645   8

RAVAGING
AND MY MOTHER'S TUNES ARE DEVOURED OF THIS MUSIC'S RAVA+   *940   23

RAVED
LIKE LUNATICS LOOKING THEY BUBBLED AND RAVED   579   2

RAVEL
AN' WHITE AN' BLUE IN A RAVEL LIKE A CLOUT   61   12
OR THE WIND SHAKES A RAVEL OF LIGHT   109   21

RAVELLED
BUBBLES RAVELLED IN THE DARK GREEN GRASS   204   17
EVERYWHERE DOWN IN THE GRASS WHERE DARKNESS WAS RAVELLED   206   18
RAVELLED BLUE AND WHITE WARM FOR A BIT   *911   28

RAVENING
    VERY DEEP AND RAVENING   264   9
    EVEN THEN IN THE DARK I WAS TORTURED RAVENING UNFREE   264 30

RAVENNA
    SNEAKING COURT OF RAVENNA   497   5

RAVENS
    THE ROCKS WHERE RAVENS FLYING TO WINDWARD MELT AS A WEL+   57 15

RAVING
    IS A STRAIGHT WAY TO RAVING INSANITY   845 14
    AND SUPPRESSION OF SUCH FACT LEADS AS WE KNOW DIRECT TO+   *953   5

RAVISHED
    AND RAVISHED ALL THE PEACEFUL OBLIVIOUS PLACES   725 18

RAVISHES
    CREEPS UPON HER THEN AND RAVISHES HER STORE   120   4
    OF THE ARMS OF PLUTO AS HE RAVISHES HER ONCE AGAIN   *956 17

RAW
    FEELING THE RAW COLD DUN ME AND ALL THE TIME   98 18
    AND ALL DAY LONG THAT RAW AND ANCIENT COLD   98 21
    AND STRIVE TO DETACH HERSELF FROM THE RAW   103 26
    PERHAPS IT IS YOUR ASSERTION IN ALL THIS OSTENTATION OF+   369 27
    ONLY YOURS WOULD BE A RAW UNSMELTED PASSION THAT WILL   370   9
    A RAW AMERICAN WILL THAT HAS NEVER BEEN TEMPERED BY LIFE   370 34
    RAW EARTH   475   5
    THE BITTER AND SWEET RAW AND THE ROTTEN   825   2

RAW-COLD
    LIKE A LINTY RAW-COLD DUST DISTURBED FROM THE FLOOR   99   2

RAY
    ONE BRIGHT RED RAY   176 13
    FROM THE HEART A RED RAY   819 20

RAYED
    LAMPS IS RAYED WITH GOLDEN BANDS   144   4

RAYING
    IN THE GARDEN RAYING OUT   306 29

RAYS
    THE SHINING OF LAMPS BECAUSE WITH HIS RAYS HE HURTS THE+   331   7
    DARK RAYS   402   5
    DARK KEEN FINE RAYS IN THE BRILLIANT FROST OF HER FACE   402   6
    AND DARTS A FEW GOLD RAYS   455 18
    A FEW GOLD RAYS THICKENING DOWN TO RED   455 20
    AND THRILL WITH GLITTERING RAYS   526   6
    SEARCHLIGHT RAYS   755 15
    NOR RUN ASLANT HIS RAYS   806   9
    BRINDLED WITH RAYS   819 25

REACH
    AS TENDRILS REACH OUT YEARNINGLY   52   4
    OUT OF MY REACH MY DARLING   108   6
    REACH FROM IMMENSITY   159 12
    REACH INTO DEATH AFTER ME   236   2
    BUT WOULD NOT YOUR HATE REACH EVEN MORE MADLY THAN YOUR   236   3
    AND REACH YOUR SKINNY LITTLE NECK   352 13
    TO ROW FORWARD AND REACH HIMSELF TALL ON SPINY TOES   358   1
    THE MIND CAN NEVER REACH THEE   473 24
    WILL BE POWERLESS FOR NO ENGINE CAN REACH INTO THE MARS+   624 22
    REACH ME A GENTIAN GIVE ME A TORCH   697 13
    COME HOLY SILENCE REACH REACH   698   8
    WHICH HE CAN NEVER REACH TILL HE TOUCH THE BOTTOM OF TH+   700 28
    NEITHER CAN IT REACH THE DEPTH   701 28
    BUT I'LL NEVER REACH THE LONG SWEET SHORE   747 25
    REACH OVER THEN REACH OVER   763   5
    BUT REACH OVER REACH OVER   763 25
    REACH OVER THEN REACH OVER   764   8
    REACH OUT REACH OUT TOWARDS ME   764 20
    REACH OUT REACH OUT SAY NOT A WORD   764 31
    SILENT REACH OUT LET US TOUCH   764 32
    REACH OUT REACH OUT IN THIS DARK   765   8
    IF YOU REACH THE FOUNTAIN AND LIE DOWN   809 12
    REACH ACROSS THE HEARTH   813   6
    NOT TO REACH ONE TONGUE OF FIRE   874 19
    BUT I THINK THE KISSES REACH   *893   9
    REACH ME A GENTIAN GIVE ME A TORCH   *956 10

REACHED
    SHE LAUGHED SHE REACHED HER HAND OUT TO THE FLOWER   123 13
    HE REACHED DOWN FROM A FISSURE IN THE EARTH-WALL IN THE   349   8
    DUG FIRM IN MY BREAST AS YOU REACHED OUT RIGHT   886   8
    AS TENDRILS REACHED OUT YEARNINGLY   *899 18
    AS TENDRILS REACHED OUT YEARNINGLY   *902 30
    SHE LAUGHED SHE REACHED HER HAND OUT DOWN TO THE FLOWER   *934 19

REACHES
    TO CREEP THROUGH YOUR LOOSENED HAIR TILL HE REACHES   178 32
    REACHES OUT   285 27
    AND REACHES HER BLACK-STRIPED FACE UP LIKE A SNAKE FAR +   385 26
    WHEN THE FIRE REACHES US O MY YOUNG MEN   440 14
    AND NOTHING NOW REACHES OUT TO DRAW   507 18
    TILL IT REACHES US AND ITS VIBRATIONS SHATTER US   512 19
    THE LONG TIP REACHES STRONG INTENSE LIKE THE MAELSTROM-+   694 17
    THE GREY GREY REACHES OF EARTH'S SHADOW   722 20
    THE VAST GREAT REACHES BETWEEN THE SUNS   823 23
    AND A BOY AS HE REACHES THE AGE OF FOURTEEN WHEN HE SHO+   843   2

REACHING
    REACHING DOWNWARDS   74   4
    AND MOUTH REACHING FORWARD TO KISS YOU   220 11
    REACHING OUT IN ANGUISH YET UNABLE QUITE TO TOUCH THEM   233   4
    REACHING OUT AND GRASPING BY AN INSTINCT MORE DELICATE +   285 28

REACHING
    REACHING AND GRIPPING TENSE MORE REACHING ANGUISH IN   365   5
    DOZING IN THE UNDER-DEEPS THEN REACHING OUT A SAVAGE AN+   689 20
    STRETCHING REACHING   861 26
    CLUSTERING UPON ME REACHING UP AS EACH AFTER THE OTHER +   *900   7
    CLUSTERING UPON ME REACHING UP AS EACH AFTER THE OTHER +   *903 19
    REACHING DOWNWARDS   *913 25

READ
    HAVING READ MY THOUGHTS AGAINST YOU   333   6
    WHILE YOU READ ABOUT THE AIR-SHIP CROSSING THE WILD ATL+   441 22
    I READ A NOVEL BY A FRIEND OF MINE   489   9
    WHEN I READ SHAKESPEARE I AM STRUCK WITH WONDER   494 13
    JUDGING FROM THE FICTION IT IS POSSIBLE TO READ I SHOUL+   532 15
    THOUGHT IS GAZING ON TO THE FACE OF LIFE AND READING WH+   673 12
    LEANS OVER TO READ HIS WORK AND HER DARK HEAD DIPS   865   5

READINESS
    THEN BUILD YOUR SHIP OF DEATH IN READINESS   *961   6

READING
    FEELING THE SHADOWS LIKE A BLIND MAN READING   135 18
    THOUGHT IS GAZING ON TO THE FACE OF LIFE AND READING WH+   673 12
    FEELING THE SHADOWS LIKE A BLIND MAN READING   *939   2

READINGS
    NO READINGS AND WRITINGS   857   5

READS
    LIGHTS THE SOFT HAIR OF A GIRL AS SHE READS   41   7
    WHEN SHE READS THAT HER LIFE ISN'T REALLY MUCH FUN   583 11

READY
    AND READY TO OPEN IN BROWN SURPRISE   43 15
    BEAST CROUCHED ACROSS THE GLOBE READY IF NEED BE TO POU+   97 21
    ROSES ARE READY TO FALL RELUCTANT AND LOTH   217 30
    ALL RUBBISH READY FOR FIRE   316 35
    AND ANNOUNCING BATTLE READY   327   2
    READY   449   8
    AND IDEAS ARE HARD LIKE ACORNS READY TO FALL   608 23
    FITTING AND READY FOR THE DEPARTING SOUL   718 26
    GET A PLACE READY FOR ME   791 19
    AND THE EARTH IS ALIVE AND READY TO SHAKE OFF HIS FLEAS   792 12
    IS READY TO BLOW BAD BREATH UPON THEM TO PERISH THEM ALL   792 16
    ARE DISCUSSING WITH ONE ANOTHER THEY ARE MAKING READY T+   793   4
    READY AGAIN FOR THE BUSINESS OF BEING A MAN   809 18
    DEEP PANTING BREATHS LIKE GREAT BEASTS READY FOR   827   8
    MY FLESH IS READY LIKE TILLED LOAM   888   5
    DAINTY AND READY FOR THE DEPARTING SOUL   *958 22

READY-MADE
    CORPSE-ANATOMIES WITH READY-MADE SENSATIONS   584 21

REAL
    OF REAL DAYLIGHT UPON US RELEASED FROM THE FOUL DREAM'S+   175 30
    HAVE A REAL STOCK-TAKING   237   1
    AND TOUCHING THE UNKNOWN THE REAL UNKNOWN THE UNKNOWN   259 18
    WHICH WE MUST LEARN TO SATISFY WITH PURE REAL SATISFACT+   264 19
    REAL FULFILMEMT WILL DO   265 14
    AND THAT WILL BE PURE EXISTENCE REAL LIBERTY   266 33
    THE REAL   292 35
    AND THEN TO SEE THE NEW REAL SOULS SPROUT UP   315 31
    AND INCREASING THE FLOCK AND PERHAPS GIVING A REAL NIP +   325 10
    AND THERE A REAL PINCH BUT ALWAYS WELL MEANT   325 11
    REAL LIVING DUST-PIG EARS ALMOST BLOWN AWAY   397 16
    AND OUT TO THE DIM OF THE DESERT LIKE A DREAM NEVER REAL   402 22
    THAT THIS QUITE REAL INTIMACY   470 10
    IS ONLY REAL AND RIGHT IF WE   470 15
    BUT THE REAL FAULT LIES IN THE EGO-BOUND CONDITION OF   475 24
    AND A REAL TREMOR IF HE HANDS OUT A TEN-POUND NOTE   486 13
    BUT THE REST WAS A REAL SURPRISE   489 16
    YOUNG MEN HAVING NO REAL JOY IN LIFE AND NO HOPE IN THE   521 20
    BECAUSE WE ENGLISH DO APPRECIATE A REAL GENTLEMAN OR A   548 15
    REAL LADY   548 16
    HE PAINTED SOME PICTURES REAL BEAUTIES   577   4
    THEN THE PRIVATE INTIMACY OF FRIENDSHIP WILL BE REAL AN+   608 14
    LESS THAN REAL MEN INFERIORS INFERIORS   637 26
    THAT IS REAL   708   9
    THE KIND OF HELL THAT IS REAL GREY AND AWFUL   714   1
    THE REAL IMMORALITY AS FAR AS I CAN SEE IT   836 17
    AND MY SOUL'S DESIRE AND MADE YOU REAL   871   3

REALISATION
    LONG DIFFICULT REPENTANCE REALISATION OF LIFE'S MISTAKE+   620 18

REALISE
    DOES NO ONE REALISE THAT LOVE SHOULD BE INTENSE INDIVID+   291 15
    LINGER FOR NOW THEY REALISE ALL THAT IS LOST THEN THE L+   406   6
    LOOK ROUND AND REALISE   456 16
    WHY DON'T YOU REALISE   485 15
    MAYBE THEY'LL REALISE IT'S TIME   560   7
    IT MAKES ME REALISE THE DELICIOUS PLEASURE OF THE MOON   610 20
    THE ONLY SALVATION IS TO REALISE THAT WE KNOW NOTHING A+   613 11
    THEN IF WE REALISE THAT WE NEVER WERE LOST WE REALISE W+   613 15
    AND ONCE YOU REALISE THAT YOU NEVER WERE LOST   614   3
    YOU REALISE THE FATUITY OF SAVING UP AGAINST POSSIBLE L+   614   4
    YOU WILL REALISE THERE WAS NEVER ANYTHING TO SEEK FOR   661   2
    TOO GREAT A BOOR TO REALISE HIS TRUE FEELINGS   *949   1

REALISED
    SHE HAS NOT REALISED YET THAT FEARFUL THING THAT I AM T+   266 25
    I ALSO REALISED   344 16
    I REALISED THE SECRET JOY HER YOUNG SPANISH HUSBAND HAD   618 22
    I REALISED WHAT A LUST THERE WAS IN HIM TO WREAK HIS SO+   620   6
    I'VE REALISED IT IS ALL A TRICK ON HIS PART   *948 22

REALITIES
  REALITIES   527 27

REALITY
  THEIR HOLD ON REALITY ENFEEBLE THEIR RISING SHOOTS   92 28
  THAT FALLS FROM REALITY   163 2
  I AM INTERESTED IN THE PROBLEM OF REALITY   604 2
  THEY SAY THAT REALITY EXISTS ONLY IN THE SPIRIT   689 14
  THAT THEY CALL SCIENCE AND REALITY   708 17

REALIZE
  AND SUDDENLY REALIZE IN THEM AS IN ME   218 3
  REALIZE   776 23

REALM
  NOTHING AND NOBODY IN THE WHOLE VAST REALM OF SPACE   514 20
  TO THE SIGHTLESS REALM WHERE DARKNESS IS AWAKE UPON THE+   697 17
  TO THE SIGHTLESS REALM WHERE DARKNESS IS MARRIED TO DARK   *956 14

REALMS
  THERE ARE VAST REALMS OF CONSCIOUSNESS STILL UNDREAMED +   666 24

REAMS
  AN' OTHERS 'AS REAMS   45 24

REAPED
  STANDS RUBBLE OF STUNTED HOUSES ALL IS REAPED   135 7

REAPERS
  THAT WE LEASE OUR LANDS AND GET REAPERS   779 9

REAPING
  CALM WITH THE CALM OF SCIMITARS AND BRILLIANT REAPING H+   609 11

REAR
  SNIFFING FOREVER AHEAD OF HIM AT THE REAR OF THE GOATS +   380 21
  AND NEVER NEVER ARRIVING AT JOURNEY'S END AT THE REAR OF   380 26
  AND THEN INVARIABLY SHE CROUCHES HER REAR AND MAKES   385 3
  BUT WE MAUN MA'E THE BEST ON'T I'LL REAR THY CHILDT IF +   *925 18

REARED
  BUT I WHOM THE YEARS HAD REARED TO BE YOUR BRIDE   157 1
  SHE HURRIES UP STRIDING REARED ON LONG UNCANNY LEGS   358 31
  OTHER WOMEN HAVE REARED IN ME   888 1

REARING
  MOILED OVER WITH THE REARING OF HER MANY-MOUTHED YOUNG   197 11
  HELL REARING ITS HUSBAND-SPLENDID SERPENT HEADS   308 20
  REARING   454 8
  A LOT OF MONEY REARING THEM   569 12

REARS
  INSTEAD OF WHICH SHE STRANGELY REARS ON HER PERCH IN THE   385 23

REASON
  MY SENSE AND REASON   121 5
  WITHOUT MEANING OR REASON WHY   252 25
  AND FOR THIS REASON SOME OLD THINGS ARE LOVELY   440 6
  NO GOOD ASKING THE REASON WHY   458 3
  THE ONLY REASON FOR LIVING IS BEING FULLY ALIVE   522 9
  TILL AT LAST I SAW THE REASON   556 3
  OR REASON WHERE THE LEAF SHOULD BE   578 5
  WORLDS WITHOUT END WITHOUT REASON WHY   823 21
  WITHOUT REASON WHY   826 4
  THEY DON'T EVEN MIND DOING THINGS FOR YOU IN REASON   828 24

REASSERT
  SO THAT IN THE LONG PAUSE THE INSTINCTS CAN REASSERT TH+   839 3

REASSERTS
  AND THE RELENTLESS NODALITY OF MY EYES REASSERTS ITSELF   *893 29

REASSURANCE
  LIKE A GREAT REASSURANCE   700 11

REASSURING
  SOMETHING MUST BE REASSURING TO THE ALMOND IN THE EVENI+   305 31

REBEL
  DOES MY SLOW HEART REBEL DO MY DEAD HANDS   195 6
  OUR HANDS OUR BREASTS REBEL AGAINST US   746 13

REBELLION
  IN PANIC IN REBELLION SLITHERING MILLIONS OF FISH   586 26

REBELLIOUS
  BUT A DIFFERENT SORT A COLD REBELLIOUS JEERING DEVIL   390 4

REBELS
  AND MY HEART REBELS WITH ANGUISH AS NIGHT DRAWS NIGHER   48 13
  OF REBELS LIKE ANNA AND VRONSKY   536 14

RE-BIRTH
  IN JANUARY AND IN FEBRUARY THE RE-BIRTH OF THE ALMOND T+   303 5

RE-BORN
  SO THAT WHEN WE ARE RE-BORN WE CAN BE BORN INTO A FRESH   512 29
  BUT A MAN RE-BORN FROM THE RIGIDITY OF FIXED IDEAS   667 32

REBREATHING
  WE ASPHYXIATE IN A SLEEP OF DREAMS REBREATHING THE IMPU+   174 26

REBUKED
  FLESH OF MY HEART ERE DOWN REBUKED IT SLIPS   127 28

RECALCITRANT
  WHOM SOME RECALCITRANT OLD MAID WILL ADOPT AS A HOBBY   665 15

RECALL
  ENTICING WILL RECALL WHEN I   *894 7

RECEDE
  FARTHER DOWN THE VALLEY THE CLUSTERED TOMBSTONES RECEDE   102 29

RECEDING
  AND WHO NOW DRAWS SLOWLY AWAY COLD THE WISTFUL GODDESS +   676 18
  INTO THE DISTANCE WITH RECEDING OARS   722 10
  SEEPING SEEPING RECEDING   767 14
  THE MISTS OF RECEDING TEARS AND THE ECHO OF LAUGHTER   *906 10
  INTO THE DISTANCE WITH RECEDING OARS   *958 15

RECEIVE
  SHE HAS QUICKENED MY PULSE TO RECEIVE   38 21
  AS WE WERE WEARY TO RECEIVE HER   124 10
  AND GLAD ARE THE EAGER DEAD TO RECEIVE YOU THERE   168 9
  LET US RECEIVE OUR GHOSTS AND GIVE THEM PLACE   736 13
  MUST WE OPEN THE DOORS AND ADMIT THEM RECEIVE THEM HOME   740 13
  FEED ON OUR WOUNDS LIKE BREAD RECEIVE OUR BLOOD   743 4
  HER WINGS AS WE WERE WEARY TO RECEIVE HER   *935 9

RECEIVES
  RECEIVES   180 28
  THEN HE RECEIVES THE KISS OF RECONCILIATION   648 18

RECEIVING
  OR SCREAMING IN PENTECOST RECEIVING THE GHOST   365 14
  AND RECEIVING FROM THE GREAT ONE   525 16

RECESSES
  BLUE RECESSES   96 14

RECIPROCATING
  I MUST BE RECIPROCATING YOUR VACUOUS HIDEOUS PASSION   241 27

RECKLESS
  SUDDENLY HASTY RECKLESS ON HIGH TOES   354 6
  AS THE FUCHSIA DOES DANGLING HER RECKLESS DROP   667 16
  I PLAY MY RECKLESS GAME TO WIN MY POINT   876 1
  HIS RECKLESS RED MOUTH LAUGHING CRUFILY   876 25
  RECKLESS ABOUT THE BITTERNESS OF THE DRAUGHT   878 12
  TO THE RECKLESS EXTRAVAGANT TURMOIL OF LIVING THE STRIFE   *895 13

RECKLESSLY
  DISCREETLY YET RECKLESSLY CALLS   105 32

RECKLESSNESS
  IN RECKLESSNESS HE DRANK WITH A BITTER MOUTH   878 17

RECKON
  FOR ME TO RECKON FOR SURELY HE WILL   59 23
  MY BREAST'S AS RED AS THINE I RECKON   78 23
  AN' I RECKON IT'S NOWT BUT RIGHT   491 2
  MY BREAST'S AS RED AS THINE I RECKON   *920 15

RECKONING
  WHAT IS THE RECKONING   140 27
  HE CAN ADD THE RECKONING UP   199 1

RECOGNISE
  FOR I HAD TO RECOGNISE   489 14
  AND THE SANE CAN STILL RECOGNISE SANITY   516 9
  SO THEY CAN STILL RECOGNISE GOD   516 10
  BUT UTTERLY FAILS TO RECOGNISE ANY MORE THE GREY RAT-HO+   640 5
  IF THE ROBOT CAN RECOGNISE THE CLEAN FLAME OF LIFE   648 14

RECOGNISED
  I RECOGNISED WHEN I HEARD ITS VOICE   376 7
  BE RECOGNISED AS GREAT   619 15

RECOGNISES
  AND WITHDRAWS ITSELF AND RECOGNISES A FLOWER OR THE   640 3

RECOGNITION
  WITH RECOGNITION AND I   108 9

RECOGNITIONS
  RECOGNITIONS AND GREETINGS OF HALF-ACQUAINT THINGS AS I   52 22
  RECOGNITIONS AND GREETINGS OF HALF-ACQUAINT THINGS AS I+   *905 11

RECOGNIZE
  I DON'T RECOGNIZE MY TUSCANS   846 5

RECOIL
  AND THERE WILL BE A VIVID RECOIL INTO SEPARATENESS   611 18
  THE PRESENCE OF A MAN MADE HER RECOIL   619 4

RECOILED
  OF WEED THAT BLACKENED THE SHORE SO THAT I RECOILED   98 17
  YOU RECOILED AWAY FROM ME   204 10

RECOILS
  COILS AND RECOILS SENSITIVE TO LIFE AND CONSCIOUS OF TR+   *952 8

RECOLLECTION
  BROKE THE BOUNDS AND BEYOND DIM RECOLLECTION   161 21

RECONCILED
  AND THE SERPENTS WANDER THEIR OWN WAYS RECONCILED   771 8

RECONCILIATION
    THEN HE RECEIVES THE KISS OF RECONCILIATION   648 18
    IS THERE NO RECONCILIATION   742 21

RECONSTRUCTION
    AND HE MUST STRUGGLE AFTER RECONSTRUCTION IGNOMINIOUSLY   361 12

RECOVER
    YOU WHO NEVER RECOVER FROM OUT OF THE ORGASM OF LOVING   290 12

RECOVERING
    HEAVY AND SWAYING LIKE A WHALE RECOVERING   428 12
    LIKE A WHALE RECOVERING ITS VELOCITY AND STRENGTH   428 14

RECREATION
    SHE SITS ON THE RECREATION GROUND   152 26
    AND SO AGAIN ON THE RECREATION GROUND   153 9
    WORK RECREATION GOVERNING ANARCHY   256 28
    I HAVE SAT IN THE RECREATION GROUND   866 22
    NOW TO THE RECREATION GROUND   867 1

RECUMBENT
    RECUMBENT ROARS AS IT FEELS   159 10

RECURRENT
    IN THE FLAT RECURRENT BREAKERS OF MY TWO FEET   705 13

RED
    WHILE THAT VETCH-CLUMP STILL BURNS RED   35 8
    UNDER THE LONG DARK BOUGHS LIKE JEWELS RED   36 19
    STAINED WITH RED DYE   36 26
    AT THE WINDOW SO BIG AND RED   37 6
    THE LITTLE RED HEIFER TONIGHT I LOOKED IN HER EYES   38 6
    WITH SNARLING RED JAWS AND I HEARD THE CRIES   38 10
    AND THE RED FIRELIGHT STEADILY REELING   41 8
    OF RED UPON THE THROAT HER TERRORS SWAY   42 27
    I THE MAN WITH THE RED SCARF   44 1
    THE NEW RED HOUSES SPRING LIKE PLANTS   50 19
    IN A SHINING CRACK OF RED   58 25
    RESTS A STILL LINE OF SOLDIERS RED MOTIONLESS RANGE OF +   66 7
    THE RED RANGE HEAVES IN SLOW MAGNETIC REPLY   66 16
    THE RED RANGE HEAVES AND COMPULSORY SWAYS AH SEE IN THE+   66 17
    THE WAVE OF SOLDIERS THE COMING WAVE THE THROBBING RED +   66 23
    HOW DIFFERENT IN THE MIDST OF SNOW THE GREAT SCHOOL RIS+   75 7
    A RED ROCK SILENT AND SHADOWLESS CLUNG ROUND WITH CLUST+   75 8
    THIS NEW RED ROCK IN A WASTE OF WHITE RISES AGAINST THE+   75 13
    MY BREAST'S AS RED AS THINE I RECKON   78 23
    FLAYED RED IF THA COULD BUT SEE   78 24
    THE DARKNESS RED   88 17
    IN A NEW NIGHT-SPASM OF BIRTH AND GIVEN US THIS NEW RED+   88 20
    NOT PASS THE RED MOON RISEN AND I AM GLAD   88 28
    ALONG THE VACANT ROAD A RED   100 5
    HOW TOWARDS THE NORTH A RED BLOTCH ON THE SKY   103 10
    THE RED REFLECTION OF HER AGONY   103 17
    AND SHOWS THE RED OF HAWTHORN SET   105 1
    YOU WATCH THE RED SPARKS WHIRL AND FLEE   116 23
    MY HEART'S RED MEASURE IN HER CUP   123 28
    HAVE RISEN RED ON MY NIGHT AS A HARVEST MOON   126 4
    HOW GORGEOUS THAT SHOCK OF RED LILIES AND LARKSPUR CLEA+   129 27
    THROUGH THE RED DOORS BEYOND THE BLACK-PURPLE BAR   134 3
    THROUGH THE RED DOORS WHERE I COULD PUT OFF   134 5
    BUT OH THE PALMS OF HIS TWO BLACK HANDS ARE RED   135 22
    ANOTHER TORN RED SUNSET COME TO PASS   136 4
    THE BALLS OF FIVE RED TOES   145 22
    AS RED AND DIRTY BARE   145 23
    OF RED GOES DOWN THE BILLOWING AIR   149 31
    A RED ROSE GOES ON THE WIND ASCENDING   150 9
    KNOCK KNOCK 'TIS NO MORE THAN A RED ROSE RAPPING   150 20
    MY MOUTH YOU MET BEFORE YOUR FINE RED MOUTH   156 22
    LIKE A FLAT RED LILY WITH A MILLION PETALS   166 17
    OF EASY SAILING ODD RED WICKS SERVE   172 20
    ONE BRIGHT RED RAY   176 13
    IS BLAZONED HERE SO WHITE AND SO BLOODILY RED   176 19
    SHALL I LESS THAN THE LEAST RED GRAIN OF FLESH   195 10
    TILL NIGHT WHEN BY THE FIRE'S RED STAIN   202 26
    AND THE WHITE SHINING HOUSES AND THE GAY RED FLOWERS ON   205 2
    HANGING RED AT THE RIVER AND SIMMERING   217 3
    FROM THE RED ROSE-FLOWERS' FIERY TRANSIENCE   219 14
    LITTLE RED CRANBERRIES CHEEK TO CHEEK   224 1
    THIS FIREGLOW IS A RED WOMB   239 22
    THAT DREW THIS RED GUSH IN ME   241 26
    IS DIGNIFIED IN THE FOXGLOVE LIKE A RED INDIAN BRAVE   272 29
    OH SO RED AND SUCH A LOT OF THEM   278 8
    COME UP THOU RED THING   302 7
    THIS RED ANATHEMA   302 15
    RISE THOU RED THING   302 16
    THE RED MACULA   302 21
    BUT BLOOD IS RED AND BLOOD IS LIFE RED WAS THE COLOUR O+   303 21
    RED YOUR HEART IS   306 22
    RED AT THE CORE   307 7
    RED AT THE CORE   307 8
    AND RED AT THE CORE WITH THE LAST SORE-HEARTEDNESS   307 15
    THE NATIVE ROYALTY OF RED HIBISCUS FLOWERS   314 18
    IS YOUR WRATH RED AS SALVIAS   314 30
    THAT I SALUTE THE RED HIBISCUS FLOWERS   316 28
    RED ANGRY MEN ARE A RACE EXTINCT ALAS   317 12
    BLOOD RED BLOOD   333 25
    WITH THEIR GOLD RED EYES AND GREEN-PURE GLEAM AND UNDER+   339 26
    SOFT RED TONGUE AND HARD THIN GUMS   353 7
    LIKE A RED INDIAN DARKLY UNFINISHED AND ALOOF   369 10
    AND HOT RED OVER YOU   369 21
    TOSSES THE CRAPE OF RED ACROSS YOUR BROW AND DOWN YOUR   370 27
    IN ALL THE SINISTER SPLENDOUR OF THEIR RED BLOOD-SACRIF+   371 35
    WHEN YOU PICK THE RED SMOKY HEART FROM A RABBIT OR A   374 5
    RED HEARTS OF MEN   374 8
    WITH A NEEDLE OF LONG RED FLINT HE STABS IN THE DARK   382 16
    A RED WOLF STANDS ON THE SHADOW'S DARK RED RIM   403 20
    MY BEARD IS RED   405 2

RED
    THIN RED WOLF OF A PALE-FACE   405 3
    THIN RED WOLF GO HOME   405 4
    HAS THE RED WOLF TROTTED EAST AND EAST AND EAST   405 15
    AND WOLF HE CALLS ME AND RED   405 21
    I'M THE RED WOLF SAYS THE DARK OLD FATHER   405 31
    RED MEN STILL STICK THEMSELVES OVER WITH BITS OF HIS FL+   414 3
    A FEW GOLD RAYS THICKENING DOWN TO RED   455 20
    WHO WAS LIKE A RED FIRE ON THE HEARTH   506 12
    IN THE RED STILLNESS OF THE DUSK   506 15
    WILL BE BRIGHT RED WITH BLOOD   515 6
    AND DAMASKED RED AND WHITE   534 24
    AND PAINTING THE WOOD-WORK RED   572 14
    SMALL SHARP RED FIRES IN THE NIGHT OF LEAVES   606 3
    RED FLAMELETS HERE AND THERE REVEAL   606 7
    AND THE REDDENED LIMBS RED INDIA-RUBBER TUBING INFLATED   625 21
    AND THOUGH THE POMEGRANATE HAS RED FLOWERS OUTSIDE THE   630 1
    DARKLY FROM THE FECUND COSMOS FROM THE ANGRY RED SUN FR+   675 11
    HIS FACE IS LIKE THE RED LION   684 15
    LO THE LOVELIEST IS RED ALL OVER RIPPLING VERMILION   689 6
    HOW GLISTENING RED THEY ARE   689 13
    IMAGINE THAT ANY MIND EVER THOUGHT A RED GERANIUM   690 14
    AS IF THE REDNESS OF A RED GERANIUM COULD BE ANYTHING B+   690 15
    WE KNOW THAT EVEN GOD COULD NOT IMAGINE THE REDNESS OF +   690 19
    THAT BLOSSOMED AT LAST RED GERANIUM AND MIGNONETTE   691 5
    AND OUT OF THE INWARD ROARING OF THE INNER RED OCEAN OF+   694 16
    HERE IN THE GARDEN WITH RED GERANIUMS IT IS WARM IT IS +   696 18
    JESUS HIS SPURS ARE RED WITH SHINING BLOOD   733 34
    JESUS HIS FINGERS ARE RED   734 11
    AND KICKS DUST OVER THE RED STAIN IN THE ROAD   734 16
    AND ALL THE TIME HIS HANDSOME SWARTHY RED FACE   734 17
    RED STROKE ACROSS MY LIPS   735 27
    AMID THE AUTUMN RUSHING RED ABOUT   744 22
    AGAINST THE SCARLET AND AGAINST THE RED   745 7
    I SPEAK ALOUD TO FLEETING HOSTS OF RED   745 25
    HER KERCHIEF FLUTTERS RED   756 13
    FROM A RED BREAST   783 27
    THESE WHITE MEN AND RED MEN AND YELLOW MEN AND BROWN MEN   792 29
    THAT ARE NEITHER WHITE NOR RED NOR YELLOW NOR BROWN NOR+   792 31
    THE RED HUITZILOPOCHTLI   804 5
    THE RED HUITZILOPOCHTLI   805 13
    AND RED AS BLOOD   806 25
    AND THE DREAM OF THE NIGHT RISES FROM ME LIKE A RED FEA+   806 30
    RED IS HUITZILOPOCHTLI'S BLOOD   808 19
    RED IS THE BLOOD AND THE FIRE   808 25
    RED HUITZILOPOCHTLI   809 23
    RED HUITZILOPOCHTLI   810 11
    COUNT THE RED GRAINS OF THE HUITZILOPOCHTLI   811 24
    LAST RED LIGHT DAPPLES   816 26
    WITHOUT FEET THE RED FLOORS   818 12
    FROM THE HEART A RED RAY   819 20
    AND TATTERED AND RED WITH THE LIFE THAT HAS BLED   823 4
    THEY HAVE TAKEN OFF THE BEAUTIFUL RED LILLY   845 24
    THEY HAD RED LILLY AND PEOPLE SINGING SONGS   846 8
    HEAVY NODDING CLUSTERS OF CRIMSON RED   855 10
    HEAVY HANGING CLUSTERS OF CRIMSON RED   855 18
    AND THE RED FRUITS GLITTER   861 3
    SCARLET AND CHERRY RED   861 9
    WHEN RED RAIN GOES FLINGING   861 15
    AND THE LITTLE MOUTH RED   861 23
    HER WARM RED LIPS   862 10
    THERE PRESS YOUR HOT RED CHEEK AGAINST MINE   863 17
    LOOKED WHERE THE RED FRUIT HUNG LIKE COALS OF FIRE   864 8
    IN A LITTLE HALF-BUILT STREET WHERE RED AND WHITE VILLAS 864 25
    HOW DIFFERENT IN THE MIDDLE OF SNOWS THE GREAT SCHOOL R+   865 18
    THE GLOW OF RED IN A GREY-GREEN SHADOW OF TREES   867 10
    HIS RECKLESS RED MOUTH LAUGHING CRUELLY   876 25
    I KNOW THE SWEET RED HUTCH OF HIS MOUTH WHERE WARM   876 32
    WHOSE EDGE OF HAIR CURVES THICKLY TO THE RED   878 21
    THE STREAM AND CLOAK ME OVER WITH THY RED   879 9
    AND WE WILL PASS TOGETHER LIKE ONE RED FLAME   879 29
    I SAW ON THE RED EARTH   880 18
    OVER THE WITHERED MOSSES AND RED EARTH   880 20
    AND WHEN I SEE THE HEAVY RED FLEECE   883 1
    STREAMED REDNESS DOWN THE AIR SHOT RED ON HIS EYES   884 24
    AS IF WITHDRAWN FROM LIVING WOUNDS RAN RED   884 26
    THAT EVENING EVERMORE HANGS RED FOR ME   885 2
    RED ON MY MEMORY HEAVY WITH OUR OWN BLOOD   885 3
    WITH A NIPPLE CENTRE OF RED   886 18
    A RED FLOWER FALLS TO ITS DIM REFLECTION   887 18
    A RED FLOWER FALLS TO ITS RED REFLECTION   887 20
    RED FLOWERS THAT HAVE FLOATED AWAY   887 29
    MY LITTLE RED HEIFER GO AND LOOK AT HER EYES   *892 22
    WITH RED SNARLING JAWS LET YOURSELF LISTEN TO THE CRIES *892 25
    THERE LIES THE DULL RED HEAP OF THEIR SAND IN THE WEST *896 7
    THERE LIES A DULL RED HEAP OF HIS SAND IN THE WEST   *896 17
    MY BREAST'S AS RED AS THINE I RECKON   *920 15
    FLAYED RED IF THAT COULD BUT SEE   *920 16
    AH WHERE HIS MOUTH'S RED SUMMER AND WHERE IS NOW THE YE+ *933 27
    BETWEEN THE OLD RED WALLS I DID NOT DARE   *934 3
    MY HEART'S RED MEASURE IN THE CUP   *934 34
    SHALL HAVE RISEN RED ON MY NIGHT AS A HARVEST MOON   *937 4
    BUT OH THE PALMS OF HER TWO BLACK HANDS ARE RED   *938 26
    NOT THIS GRAY BOOK BUT THE RED AND BLOODY SCENES   *938 28
    ANOTHER TORN RED SUNSET COME TO PASS   *938 32
    BUT OH THE PALMS OF HIS BLACK HANDS ARE RED   *939 22
    RED ONES A BLOODY-WHITE FLAG OVER YOU   *940 28
    HANGING RED AT THE RIVER AND SIMMERING   *942 14

RED-BREAST
    NAY ROBIN RED-BREAST THA NEDNA   78 21
    NAY ROBIN RED-BREAST THA NEDNA   *920 13

RED-CROSS
    AND ALSO TO ENCOURAGE THE RED-CROSS LAMB   325 21
    LET HIM CHARGE LIKE A MIGHTY CATAPULT ON THE RED-CROSS + 327 24

RED-DAWN-WOLF
    I AM COME I AM HERE THE RED-DAWN-WOLF   405   9
    ALL RIGHT THE RED-DAWN-WOLF I AM   405 32

RED-DECKED
    IS THIS HOW YOU'LL HAVE IT RED-DECKED SOCIALISTS   314 21

REDDEN
    DRAW NEARER REDDEN AND LAUGH LIKE YOUNG GIRLS KISSED   854 12

REDDENED
    THE REDDENED ACHING EYES OF THE BAR-MAN WITH THIN ARMS   72   2
    AND THE REDDENED LIMBS RED INDIA-RUBBER TUBING INFLATED   625 21

REDDENING
    THE EVENING SULKS ALONG THE SHORE THE REDDENING SUN   625 10
    THE MOON LIKE A REDDENING LANTERN HANGS LOW ACROSS THE +   *917 13

REDDENS
    THE MOON LIES BACK AND REDDENS   64   20
    REDDENS STILL MORE ON THE BLATANT BODIES OF THESE ALL-B+   625 11

REDDER
    REDDER THAN DEATH MORE CLAMOROUS   264 13

REDDEST
    OVERHEAD THE REDDEST SHE LIFTED HER LONG ARMS AND TRIED   864   9

REDDISH
    OF REDDISH HERBAGE THAT BRISTLES AND SLANTS   50   21
    WITH REDDISH PLACES THAT STILL RESIST   142 19

RED-EYED
    THEN UP WITH WRATH THE RED-EYED MORNING QUICKENS   *933 12

RED-FIBRED
    FROM THE RED-FIBRED BOUGH OF THE CEDAR FROM THE CEDAR-R+   782 11

RED-FIRE
    WITH FIRE AS IT GUARDS THE WILD NORTH-COASTS RED-FIRE S+   57   13

RED-GOLD
    THE RED-GOLD SPOOLS OF THEIR HANDS AND THEIR FACES SWIN+   72   8
    HIS RED-GOLD WATER-PRECIOUS MIRROR-FLAT BRIGHT EYF   339   8
    AND THE RED-GOLD MIRROR-EYE STARES AND DIES   339 17

RED-HOT
    AT THE END OF SOME MYSTERIOUS RED-HOT IRON   363 16
    YOUR WATTLES ARE THE COLOUR OF STEEL-SLAG WHICH HAS BEE+   369 12
    FROM TRESPASSED CONTACTS FROM RED-HOT FINGER   601 10

RED INDIAN
    AND THE CALLING OF THE OLD RED INDIAN HIGH ON THE PUEBL+   623 16

RED-LETTER
    AND THERE ARE MY RED-LETTER THANKSGIVINGS   265 24

REDNESS
    I SEE A REDNESS SUDDENLY COME   42   6
    AS IF THE REDNESS OF A RED GERANIUM COULD BE ANYTHING B+   690 15
    WE KNOW THAT EVEN GOD COULD NOT IMAGINE THE REDNESS OF +   690 19
    TRANSMUTED THE DARK REDNESS TAKEN OUT   784 13
    WITH MY REDNESS STAINING THE BODY OF THE DARK   804 16
    WITH HIS REDNESS STAINING THE BODY OF THE NIGHT   805 24
    FOR WITH THE REDNESS OF LAUGHTER THE BATTLE IS WAGING I+   854 19
    STREAMED REDNESS DOWN THE AIR SHOT RED ON HIS EYES   884 24

REDOUBT
    FOR RUIN ON THE NAKED SMALL REDOUBT   160 24

RED-ROOF
    IN THE FLAPPING OF RED-ROOF SMOKE AND THE SMALL   68   22
    IN THE FLAPPING RED-ROOF SMOKE AND THE SMALL   *915   6

RED-ROSY
    AND THE YOUNG COPPER BEECH ITS LEAVES RED-ROSY AT THE E+   647   4

RED-STRUCK
    SINCE THE LAMB BETWITCHED HIM WITH THAT RED-STRUCK FLAG   327   3

RED-SWIFT
    KNOWS BUT THE RETREAT OF THE BURNING SHOULDERS THE RED-+   67   4

RED-THORN
    MY BOOK OF TURRETS AND OF RED-THORN BOWERS   135   3

REDUCE
    AND REDUCE ME TO THE LEVEL OF A THING   620   8
    TO REDUCE THE WORLD TO GREY ASH   716   3

REDUCED
    ENCOMPASSED AND MANY REDUCED TO NONE   252 11
    TILL IT IS ALMOST ENOUGH TILL I AM REDUCED PERHAPS   258   7

RE-ECHOED
    HOLLOW RE-ECHOED MY HEART   121 17
    MY HEART RE-ECHOED IN SURPRISE   *935 20

RE-ECHO
    HEAR RE-ECHO YOUR SLOW RELUCTANT FEET   880 16

REEDS
    AND THROUGH THE REEDS OF HIS MARSHY LOINS   *953 26

REEKING
    AND HEAPS AND HEAPS AND HORRIBLE REEKING HEAPS   258   6
    THE MYSTERY OF THE DARK MOUNTAIN OF BLOOD REEKING IN   390   6
    REEKING DUNG-MOUTH   398 32

REEL
    ME TILL I REEL WITH DISSEMINATED CONSCIOUSNESS   107 27
    REEL   586 19
    AND THROUGH THE SALT THEY REEL WITH DRUNK DELIGHT   694 10
    THUNDERS IN HEAVEN TILL THE BRAVE WORLDS REEL   773   8
    WITH GLADNESS REEL   888 16

REELING
    AND THE RED FIRELIGHT STEADILY REELING   41   8
    AND DOWN ALL EAGLES BEGAN TO FLUTTER REELING FROM THEIR   413   5
    REELING WITH CONNECTION   480 15
    REELING IN THE BLACK END OF ALL BELIEFS   542 24
    HE SAW THE MEN THAT WERE BLIND REELING WITH AGUARDIENTE   790 12
    REELING WITH CONNECTION   *951 28

REELROAD
    NOW SITHEE THEER AT TH' REELROAD CROSSIN'   79   1

REELS
    THE LIGHT THAT REELS   824 25

REEVE
    UPON ME TRAVELLING TO REEVE   262 11

REEVES
    HER BREASTS UPLIFTED IN ENDEAVER SHE TOUCHES SHE REEVES   864 12

REFERENCE
    THEY HAVE UTTERLY NO REFERENCE TO THE SUN   527 17

REFINED
    WHEN THEY TOOK YOU AND REFINED YOU   549   6
    WHEN THEY TOOK YOU AND REFINED YOU   549   7
    GOIN' UP AN' BEIN' REFINED   553   2
    GENTLE AND REFINED   644   9
    VERY REFINED UPPERS   774 14

REFINEMENT
    AND THEIR LAST REFINEMENT BLUFF A HATE DISGUISED   644 12

REFINEMENTS
    REFINEMENTS OF EVIL   715 18

REFLECT
    AND THE SOUL'S NEXT PASSION IS TO REFLECT   482   3

REFLECTED
    TO SEE THE GLEAM OF THE GODS THERE REFLECTED IN THE HUM+   649 22
    TO KEEP THE REFLECTED VARIETY OF THE HOUSEBOATS   867   9
    PLAYING WITH THE SHADOW COLOURS AND THE WAVING REFLECTE+   867 20
    EYES WHERE I CAN WATCH THE SWIM OF OLD DREAMS REFLECTED+   *907 11
    EYES WHERE I CAN WATCH THE SWIM OF OLD DREAMS REFLECTED+   *909   7

REFLECTING
    REFLECTING THE SCORCH OF THE SUN FROM HIS BREAST   373   3

REFLECTION
    THE RED REFLECTION OF HER AGONY   103 17
    UPON ME MY OWN REFLECTION EXPLICIT GIST   141 19
    VENTURED SO LONG AGO IN THE DEEPS OF REFLECTION   161 19
    BUT SHE CAUGHT SIGHT OF HER OWN REFLECTION   604 21
    LIKE A BEE THAT PLAYS WITH THE REFLECTION OF FLOWERS   867 12
    A RED FLOWER FALLS TO ITS DIM REFLECTION   887 18
    A RED FLOWER FALLS TO ITS RED REFLECTION   887 20

REFOLDING
    REFOLDING SHE SLIPPED TO THE FLOOR AS A GHOST-WHITE PEO+   155 23

REFORM
    I SHOULD ADVOCATE REFORM   609 15

REFRAIN
    THIS ONE REFRAIN   124 14
    SO THE REFRAIN   151 22
    FIERILY PULSING UNABLE TO REFRAIN   194 25
    TONIGHT AND REFRAIN   558 13
    AND SCARCELY CAN REFRAIN   772 17
    THIS FOUND REFRAIN   *935 13

REFRESHED
    CHILD OF THE LIVING DEAD THE DEAD THAT LIVE AND ARE NOT+   796   1
    AND BEING DEAD YOU SHALL NOT BE REFRESHED   796   3

REFRESHING
    TO GET A REFRESHING DRINK OUT OF OLD WISDOM   495 13

REFRESHMENT
    INTO THE WOMB OF REFRESHMENT   786 27

REFUGIO
    PURISIMA REFUGIO AND SOLEDAD   798 15

REFUSE
    MEN SHOULD REFUSE TO BE LIFELESSLY AT WORK   450   5
    MEN SHOULD REFUSE TO BE HEAPS OF WAGE-EARNING DUNG   450   6
    MEN SHOULD REFUSE TO WORK AT ALL AS WAGE-SLAVES   450   7
    SINCE YOU REFUSE MY FRIENDSHIP   611   2
    I CAN'T SEE THAT I REFUSE ANYTHING   611   4
    I SHALL HAVE TO REFUSE ENTIRELY TO ACCEPT EITHER OF THEM   645 13
    I REFUSE TO NAME THE GODS BECAUSE THEY HAVE NO NAME   651   7
    I REFUSE TO DESCRIBE THE GODS BECAUSE THEY HAVE NO FORM+   651   8

REFUSED
AND REFUSED TO LET SO MANY THINGS HAPPEN BEHIND HIS BACK   483 17
IF PEOPLE HAD COURAGE AND REFUSED LIES   504 3
REFUSED TO BE MOULDED IN ARROWS OF ENGLISH WORDS   859 12

REFUSES
AND THE RAIN WON'T COME THE RAIN REFUSES TO COME   647 17

REFUSING
TO NUMBNESS AND NOTHINGNESS I DEAD SHE REFUSING TO DIE   98 8
NO ONE TO COMFORT AND REFUSING ANY COMFORTER   197 9
ALWAYS REFUSING TO GO OUT INTO THE AIR   343 13
REFUSING TO SIT STILL AND BE MEASURED   524 23
AND REFUSING THE PETTIFOGGING PROMPTINGS OF HUMAN   525 18
AND ONCE HE WAS A YOUNG MAN PALE AND REFUSING FATHERHOOD *946 15

REGAIN
WE MUST REGAIN OUR SANITY ABOUT MONEY   487 11

REGAL
AND THROWS UP STRENGTH THAT IS LIVING STRENGTH AND REGA+   782 19

REGISTRAR
BUT WE'LL GO UNBEKNOWN TER TH' REGISTRAR   82 13
AN' WE'LL BE MARRIED AT TH' REGISTRAR NOW LIFT THY FACE   83 4
BUT WE'LL GO UNBEKNOWN TO THE REGISTRAR   *924 17
AN' WE'LL BE MARRIED AT TH' REGISTRAR NOW LIFT THY FACE   *925 8

REGRET
A DECENT SHORT REGRET FOR THAT WHICH ONCE WAS VERY GOOD   66 4
OF THEIR VAIN UP-STRIVING AND NIGHT REMAINS FOR REGRET   856 4

REGRETFUL
HIS BIG REGRETFUL EYES   377 24

REGRETS
HE REGRETS SOMETHING THAT HE REMEMBERS   377 30

REGRETTED
AND IMMEDIATELY I REGRETTED IT   351 18

REGRETTING
BUT HUSH I AM NOT REGRETTING   227 25

RE-INCARNATING
IN THE HOPE OF RESURRECTING OR RATHER RE-INCARNATING   760 20

REITERATE
YET WE REITERATE LOVE LOVE LOVE   662 4

REITERATED
IN BATTLE OF HEATED WORDS HARDLY STILLED BY MY REITERAT+   865 32

REIVER
WERE PRESSED CUP-SHAPE TO TAKE THIS REIVER   124 7
WERE PRESSED CUP-SHAPE TO TAKE THIS REIVER   *935 7

REIVING
LIKE A REIVING CUCKOO SHE SETTLED DOWN   *936 6

REJECT
REJECT ME NOT IF I SHOULD SAY TO YOU   129 7
REJECT NOTHING SINGS WALT WHITMAN   399 1
BUT YOU YOU SNOUT-FACE YOU REJECT NOTHING YOU MERGE SO   399 9

REJECTED
THREE TIMES HAVE I OFFERED MYSELF THREE TIMES REJECTED   48 1

REJECTS
NATURE REJECTS   399 7

REJOICE
THAT SHE SAYS AND HER WORDS REJOICE   46 20
THE DAYS PERCEIVE OUR MARRIAGE AND REJOICE   129 10
OR LOVE OR REJOICE OR EVEN GRIEVE ANY MORE   474 27
I'D REJOICE OVER THE WOMAN AND THE WARMED COCKLES OF MY   507 10

REJOICES
SHE REJOICES IN HER NEW NAKEDNESS   768 23

REJOICING
REJOICING IN WHAT IS TO COME   247 12

RELATED
ALL FLOWS AND EVERY FLOW IS RELATED TO EVERY OTHER FLOW   476 27
THE UNIVERSE FLOWS IN INFINITE WILD STREAMS RELATED   479 9

RELATION
AND THE RUIN OF ANY DECENT RELATION   470 21

RELATIVITIES
ELECTRONS AND ENERGIES QUANTUMS AND RELATIVITIES   438 5

RELATIVITY
I LIKE RELATIVITY AND QUANTUM THEORIES   524 19

RELAX
RELAX AND RELINQUISH   826 17

RELAXED
GUARDING THE PATH HIS HAND RELAXED AT HIS THIGH   66 10
IN TEDIUM AND MOUTH RELAXED AS IF SMILING INEFFABLE TED+   66 12

RELAXING
NOR ANY RELAXING WHERE   55 20

RELEASE
ALONG THE FENCE PERPETUALLY SEEKING RELEASE   47 17
AND RELEASE US POOR ONES AND RICH ONES LET US BREATHE A+   175 28
DRAWING ALL MEN UNTO THEE BUT BOUND TO RELEASE THEM WHEN   323 8
AND RUIN ABOVE US AND THE CRASH OF RELEASE   462 15
RELEASE ME FROM THIS MULE-DRAWING   751 15
LO I RELEASE THE DRAGONS THE GREAT WHITE ONE OF THE NOR+   796 30
BUT WITHOUT DESIRE WITHOUT JOY WITHOUT RELEASE   843 16
AND EITHER RELEASE ENERGY OR SWALLOW IT UP   *947 11

RELEASED
OF REAL DAYLIGHT UPON US RELEASED FROM THE FOUL DREAM'S+   175 30

RELENT
THREADING LIKE ANTS THAT CAN NEVER RELENT   50 29

RELENTLESS
HOW CAN YOU LIE SO RELENTLESS HARD   55 2
RELENTLESS HOWEVER OFTEN   55 17
ON AND ON WATCHED RELENTLESS BY ME ROUND AND ROUND IN   343 23
FLUSHED FRENZIED RELENTLESS ME   769 8
AND THE RELENTLESS NODALITY OF MY EYES REASSERTS ITSELF *893 29

RELENTLESSLY
THEY RETURN RELENTLESSLY IN THE SILENCE ONE KNOWS THEIR+   739 14

RELENTLESSNESS
WITH SINGED HOT EYES AND RELENTLESSNESS   769 5

RELIEF
RELIEF THAT STARTS IN MY BREAST   100 10
AND A GASP OF RELIEF BUT THE SOUL IS STILL COMPRESSED   167 15
PURE RELIEF   169 21
AND HE SIGHS WITH RELIEF WHEN SHE PARTS FROM HIM   228 13
A CURIOUS AGONY AND A RELIEF WHEN I TOUCH THAT WHICH IS+ 266 14
SO ENDING ON A GRUNT OF AGONISED RELIEF   377 16
THERE'S NO RELIEF ONLY A MOMENT'S SULLEN RESPITE   486 4
THE CENSORS BREATHING WITH RELIEF   528 21
A RELIEF LIKE DEATH   601 6

RELIEVE
ME FROM THE MATRIX TO RELIEVE   262 12
RELIEVE US NOW OF ALL REMEMBERANCE EVEN   738 6

RELIEVED
AND THAT AT LAST RELIEVED ME I DIED   257 24

RELIGION
WE CALL RELIGION   480 23
BUT ON A RELIGION OF LIFE   483 28
THE FUTURE OF RELIGION IS IN THE MYSTERY OF TOUCH   611 10
RELIGION KNOWS BETTER THAN PHILOSOPHY   689 26
RELIGION KNOWS THAT JESUS NEVER WAS JESUS   689 27
AND WHICH ROCKS WITH A SENSE OF CONNECTION RELIGION   844 24
LIFE IS NOTHING WITHOUT RELIGION   *946 11
AND RELIGION NOTHING WITHOUT THE FATHER OF ALL THINGS   *946 12
LEANING IN THE MASSIVE UNCONSCIOUS INCLINATION WE CALL + *952 4

RELIGIONS
NEITHER TO PERSONS NOR THINGS NOR IDEAS IDEALS NOR RELI+   622 7

RELIGIOUS
I'M A RELIGIOUS SOUL   *947 15

RELIGIOUSLY
THE BLOOD ALSO KNOWS RELIGIOUSLY   474 7

RELINQUISH
TO THE OTHER LOVE TO RELINQUISH HIS DESIRE   89 33
WHILE WE RELINQUISH   826 16
RELAX AND RELINQUISH   826 17

RELUCTANCE
THE CLOUDS ARE PUSHING IN GREY RELUCTANCE SLOWLY NORTHW+   57 10

RELUCTANCES
AND SO MUCH PROUDER SO DISDAINFUL OF RELUCTANCES   306 25

RELUCTANCY
IS THIS ARMOUR OF STIFF RELUCTANCY   117 9

RELUCTANT
ROSES ARE READY TO FALL RELUCTANT AND LOTH   217 30
HEAR RE-ECHO YOUR SLOW RELUCTANT FEET   880 16
I STAND RELUCTANT TO ENTER TO DREAM NO MORE BUT TO BOW   *894 21

RELUCTANTLY
RELUCTANTLY   *895 12

REMAIN
MY ALTARS SULLIED I BEREFT REMAIN   151 20
SOMETHING SHALL NOT ALWAYS REMAIN   265 29
AFTER THAT THERE WILL ONLY REMAIN THAT ALL MEN DETACH T+ 267 24
ON ONE OLD SLIM IMPERISHABLE THOUGHT WHILE YOU REMAIN   297 4
AND REMAIN LAPSED ON EARTH   352 6
AND SO WE MUST REMAIN   468 16
THAN TO REMAIN A DANCING SAVAGE   778 3
MY TEMPLES BROKEN THEN I SHOULD REMAIN   873 31

REMAINING
YET REMAINING UNBROKEN THE LEVEL GREAT SEA   705 2

REMAINS
YET SOMETHING REMAINS   265 28
WHAT REMAINS IN ME IS TO BE KNOWN EVEN AS I KNOW   265 31
AND LIKE A FUNGUS LIVING ON THE REMAINS OF BYGONE LIFE   431 15
DOWN TO THE OCEAN OF THE AFTERWARDS WHERE IT REMAINS   495 5
STRESS OF COMPULSION REMAINS AND A BAND THAT GIRTS   746 16

338

REMAINS
  MY LIFE FROM THE ME THAT REMAINS   767 15
  LEAVING THIS NAKED PALLID HELPLESS VULNERABLE REMAINS   767 26
  AS A FLOWER ABOVE CHARRED REMAINS   769 11
  NOTHING REMAINS NOW BUT MOULD UNTO MOULD   814 17
  OF THEIR VAIN UP-STRIVING AND NIGHT REMAINS FOR REGRET   856 4

REMARK
  TWITCHING REMARK   113 24
  BUT I AM A LIAR I FEEL NO LOVELINESS IT IS A MENTAL REM+   509 27
  SUSPICIOUS REMARK   *929 13

REMEDY
  AND ONCE DONE THERE IS NO REMEDY NO SALVATION FOR THIS   621 10

REMEMBER
  YOU ARE ALWAYS ASKING DO I REMEMBER REMEMBER   90 19
  AND THEN YOU WILL REMEMBER FOR THE FIRST   91 17
  AND YOU REMEMBER IN THE AFTERNOON   98 11
  DO YOU REMEMBER   103 4
  AND YOU REMEMBER   103 9
  AND I REMEMBER STILL THE SUNNY HOURS   135 25
  AND REMEMBER THE SMALL LAD LYING INTENT TO LOOK   161 9
  I TRY TO REMEMBER IT IS ALSO WELL BETWEEN US   208 10
  THERE WAS SOMETHING I OUGHT TO REMEMBER AND YET   243 26
  I DID NOT REMEMBER WHY SHOULD I THE RUNNING LIGHTS   243 27
  BUT REMEMBER SAVIOUR   322 29
  LET HIM REMEMBER HIS HORNS THEN   327 21
  I REMEMBER WHEN I WAS A BOY   365 29
  I REMEMBER WHEN I FIRST HEARD BULL-FROGS BREAK INTO SOU+   365 32
  I REMEMBER HEARING A WILD GOOSE OUT OF THE THROAT OF NI+   365 34
  I REMEMBER THE FIRST TIME OUT OF A BUSH IN THE DARKNESS+   366 1
  I REMEMBER THE SCREAM OF A RABBIT AS I WENT THROUGH A   366 4
  I REMEMBER THE HEIFER IN HER HEAT BLORTING AND BLORTING   366 6
  I REMEMBER MY FIRST TERROR HEARING THE HOWL OF WEIRD   366 8
  I REMEMBER THE SCREAM OF A TERRIFIED INJURED HORSE THE   366 10
  I REMEMBER YET   557 10
  BUT REMEMBER THE UNDAUNTED GODS   559 2
  ARSE PERHAPS YOU'LL REMEMBER   563 14
  REMEMBER WHO VOTED YOU INTO YOUR SEAT   573 26
  REMEMBER THE BRITISH PUBLIC   669 18
  REMEMBER THE STATE OF MIND OF THE BRITISH PUBLIC   669 27
  DO YOU REMEMBER ME   734 30
  I CANNOT EVEN REMEMBER MY LIFE THAT HAS BEEN   767 11
  BUT I REMEMBER STILL THE SUNNY HOURS   *939 17

REMEMBERANCE
  RELIEVE US NOW OF ALL REMEMBERANCE EVEN   738 6

REMEMBERED
  WHO HAS REMEMBERED HER AFTER MANY DAYS   176 21
  REMEMBERED AND FORGOTTEN   199 7
  PAST THE STRANGE WHIRLPOOLS OF REMEMBERED GREED   *959 7

REMEMBERING
  REMEMBERING I TOLD THEM TO DIE TO SINK INTO THE GRAVE IN   410 30

REMEMBERS
  SOMETHING IN ME REMEMBERS   199 17
  HE REGRETS SOMETHING THAT HE REMEMBERS   377 30
  NOW THAT THE MOON WHO REMEMBERS AND ONLY CARES   687 15

REMEMBRANCE
  DOWN IN THE FLOOD OF REMEMBRANCE I WEEP LIKE A CHILD FOR   148 18
  EVEN REMEMBRANCE SEEPS OUT   767 9

REMIND
  HOW YOU REMIND ME OF MY LONDON FRIENDS   542 3
  AND YOU'VE NOBODY TO REMIND YOU   549 4

REMINDS
  WHAT IS THAT REMINDS US OF WHITE GODS   280 18

REMINISCENCE
  YOU STARTLE ME WITH REMINISCENCE OF THE GREAT   875 3

REMINISCENT
  REMINISCENT OF SLINKING BEASTS MAKE ME FEAR   107 6
  WHAT A RARE POWERFUL REMINISCENT FLAVOUR   280 6
  DISASTROUSLY REMINISCENT OF HAMMERS AND FILES AND DOOR-+   835 6
  OR STILL MORE DISASTROUSLY REMINISCENT OF THAT-WILL-BE-+   835 7

REMISSION
  WITHOUT SHEDDING OF BLOOD THERE IS NO REMISSION OF SIN   678 18

REMNANT
  TO THAT TIRED REMNANT OF ROYALTY UP THERE   389 26

REMNANTS
  CAN YOU LEAVE THE REMNANTS OF THE OLD RACE   779 22

REMORSEFUL
  FILLED WITH REMORSEFUL TERROR TO THE MAN SHE SCORNED AN+   *891 30

REMORSELESS
  BURNED CLEAN BY REMORSELESS HATE   242 17
  FILIUS MEUS O REMORSELESS LOGIC   320 8

REMOTE
  REMOTE ALTHOUGH I HEAR THE BEGGAR'S COUGH   36 5
  SO BIG AND QUIET AND REMOTE HAVING WATCHED SO MANY   393 12
  THEN FAR BEYOND THE RUIN IN THE FAR IN THE ULTIMATE REM+   625 1

REMOVE
  TO GOD TO REMOVE YOU   117 3
  OF PASSION PARCH IT UP DESTROY REMOVE   153 26
  YOU'RE A RANK OUTSIDER OF THE FIFTH REMOVE   576 15
  REMOVE THE INDIANS FOREVER FROM THE HANDS OF   780 3

REMOVE
  AND WHO WILL REMOVE FROM ME THE DISGRACE   *927 26
  NOW TO GOD TO REMOVE YOU   *931 7

REMOVED
  REMOVED FROM YOU   582 14

REMOVETH
  AND CURSED BE HE THAT REMOVETH HIS NEIGHBOUR'S LANDMARK   706 16

RENASCENCE
  NOW AT THE DAY'S RENASCENCE   242 18
  RENASCENCE ALL SENT TO HELL   633 4

RENCONTRE
  OUR BEACHED VESSEL DARKENED RENCONTRE INHUMAN AND CLOSE+   66 27

RENDERED
  SOMEBODY'S POUND OF FLESH RENDERED UP   279 7

RENDING
  RUSTLE OF LEAVES WASHES OUT THE RENDING   150 7
  THEY WILL HEAR THE FAINT RENDING OF THE ASPHALT ROADS   *954 8

RENEWAL
  WITH THE DEEP OBLIVION OF EARTH'S LAPSE AND RENEWAL   727 16
  RENEWAL   727 23
  MARY AND JESUS HAVE LET YOU AND GONE TO THE PLACE OF RE+   799 5

RENEWED
  SWINGS THE HEART RENEWED WITH PEACE   720 18

RENEWING
  SHOWS THAT SHE IS RENEWING HER YOUTH LIKE THE EAGLE   728 11

RENEWS
  THE PHOENIX RENEWS HER YOUTH   728 6

RENOWN
  VEGETABLE NEW IN RENOWN   49 28
  I HAVE WON MY RENOWN   239 6

RENT
  MY VEIL OF SENSITIVE MYSTERY RENT IN TWAIN   151 19
  LIKE A SPURT OF WHITE FOAM RENT   200 22
  YOU ARE MISTAKEN THE VEIL OF THE FLESH IS RENT   742 18
  AND THE VEIL OF THE TEMPLE RENT AT THE KISS ON KISS   742 28
  INWARDS I CAN SEE WHENCE THE THORNS WERE RENT   856 21

RENTS
  AND WHAT ARE YOU WOMAN PEERING THROUGH THE RENTS   742 15
  WE EXPIATE IN OUR BODIES' RENTS AND RAGS   743 7

RENUNCIATION
  THAT PALE ONE FILLED WITH RENUNCIATION AND PAIN AND WHI+   439 22
  HAS WORN US WEARY OF RENUNCIATION AND LOVE AND EVEN PAIN   439 24

REPARATION
  REPARATION   122 16

REPAST
  FOR THE FULL REPAST   465 26

REPAY
  VENGEANCE IS MINE SAITH THE LORD I WILL REPAY   616 1

REPAYS
  AND SO THE LORD OF VENGEANCE PAYS BACK REPAYS LIFE   616 16

REPEAT
  POWERS TO REPEAT ITS OWN EGOCENTRIC MOTIONS   635 12
  AND REPEAT THEMSELVES LIKE THE FLUSHING OF A W C   837 22

REPEATED
  REPEATED   390 20

REPEATING
  OF THE WORDS I KEPT REPEATING   61 25
  REPEATING WITH TIGHTENED ARMS AND THE HOT BLOOD'S BLIND+   61 26
  OF THE WORDS I KEPT REPEATING   *912 5
  REPEATING WITH TIGHTENED ARMS AND THE HOT BLOOD'S BLIND+   *912 6

REPEATS
  REPEATS HIMSELF OVER AND OVER IN MECHANICAL MONOTONY OF   479 17
  AND REPEATS HIMSELF LIKE THE FLUSHING OF A W C   522 8

REPELLENT
  THEIR SCENT IS LACERATING AND REPELLENT   270 17

REPENT
  YOU'LL EVEN HAVE TO REPENT   472 3

REPENTANCE
  REPENTANCE   314 9
  AND PATIENCE AND A CERTAIN DIFFICULT REPENTANCE   620 17
  LONG DIFFICULT REPENTANCE REALISATION OF LIFE'S MISTAKE+   620 18

REPENTANT
  WITH GREY REPENTANT ASH   492 30
  AND LICK UP THY ASHES WITH A REPENTANT TONGUE   760 17

REPENTED
  I'VE CHUCKED HIM I'VE REPENTED   493 24

REPENTS
    THEN HE REPENTS AND HIS WILL BREAKS AND A GREAT LOVE OF+   648 16

REPETITION
    FROM THE ENDLESS REPETITION OF THE MISTAKE   620 20

REPLIED
    HE REPLIED TO THRILL TO ANYTHING   532 4

REPLY
    THE RED RANGE HEAVES IN SLOW MAGNETIC REPLY   66 16
    BREAK IN BY MAKING ANY REPLY   152 9
    AND I COULD ONLY REPLY   603 12
    IS THE LANGUAGE DEAD AND EMPTY OF REPLY   633 13
    THROUGH A PAIN OF RISING TEARS AND DID NOT REPLY   884 21

REPORT
    FROM FALLING IRON AND HORRIBLE SHELL'S REPORT   751 11

REPOSE
    PROVENCE JAPAN AND ITALY REPOSE   58 17
    WHERE 'TWAS GIVEN US TO REPOSE US   242 30

REPRIMAND
    I SHOULD FIND FOR A REPRIMAND   107 1

REPROACH
    FALLS AGAIN AND AGAIN ON MY HEART WITH A HEAVY REPROACH   63 3
    STILL YOU TREMBLE FAINT REPROACH   95 25
    I WILL NOT AGAIN REPROACH YOU LIE BACK   153 16
    THAT IS THE GREAT REPROACH WE HAVE AGAINST HIM   483 10
    AND HIS MOUTH WIPED CLEAN OF THE BITTERNESS OF REPROACH   770 19
    HE IS BASICALLY A SAVAGE IT IS A TERM OF REPROACH   776 11
    BUT ALSO IT IS NOT A TERM OF REPROACH   776 12
    COME ON LET'S TAKE OFF YOUR COLLAR AND DON'T REPROACH ME   859 30

REPROACHFUL
    FOREVER OUT OF THE MIST THE CHURCH LIFTS UP A REPROACHF+   63 24
    AND A WRINKLED REPROACHFUL LOOK   394 30

REPTILE
    YOUR REPTILE FLAMES OF LUST AH STORE   151 12
    REPTILE MISTRESS   359 9
    REPTILE MISTRESS   359 18
    MISTRESS REPTILE MISTRESS   359 28
    AND WITH A GRIM REPTILE DETERMINATION   360 14
    STIFF GALLANT IRASCIBLE CROOK-LEGGED REPTILE   363 19
    ALL TINY FAR AWAY REPTILE UNDER THE FIRST DAWN   364 21
    YOUR REPTILE FLAMES OF PASSION STORE   873 22

REPTILE'S
    AND HE HAS A REPTILE'S AWFUL PERSISTENCE   361 30
    ONLY AGELESSLY SILENT WITH A REPTILE'S AWFUL PERSISTENCY 362 25

REPTILIAN
    WAR-CRY TRIUMPH ACUTE-DELIGHT DEATH-SCREAM REPTILIAN   364 22
    AGE-LONG REPTILIAN PERSISTENCE   365 26
    IS THE BLOOD OF YOUR CONTINENT SOMEWHAT REPTILIAN STILL   374 23

REPUBLIC
    THE NEW PROUD REPUBLIC   414 17

REPUBLICANS
    OR LATER REPUBLICANS SAY YOU ARE SAVED   442 23

REPUBLICS
    THE NEW NAKED LITTLE REPUBLICS COME INTO THE WORLD   413 16

REPUDIATE
    I REPUDIATE THEM AS SUCH   638 5
    GOD THAT I SHOULD HAVE TO REPUDIATE HIM   871 37

REPUDIATES
    AND THEN WHEN THE SOUL OF LIVING MEN REPUDIATES THEM   640 7

REPUDIATION
    IS HEAVEN OF OUR OWN SHEER WITH REPUDIATION   210 18

REPUGNANT
    THEY ARE REALLY REPUGNANT TO HIM   *948 24

REPULSE
    OR IF ONLY YOU WOULD REPULSE ME A WOUND WOULD BE   122 19

REPULSION
    THAT STARTLES ME ALARMS ME STIRS UP A REPULSION   270 14

REPULSIVE
    AND SKINNY REPULSIVE   369 5
    THE REPULSIVE LIVING FAT DEAD   441 35
    BUT ON WHAT THEY FIND DISTASTEFUL REPULSIVE OR ATTRACTI+ 831 19

REQUEST
    WITH A HORSE INSISTENT REQUEST THAT FALLS   64 25

REQUESTS
    PLEASE MAKE ALL REQUESTS TO HEAD-QUARTERS   604 16

REQUIRE
    TO COME AT LAST TO THAT WHICH THEY REQUIRE   89 25
    AND IN THE POCKETS ARE THINGS I REQUIRE   607 12
    ALSO THE LIVES THAT STILL HE MAY REQUIRE   736 17

REQUIRING
    REQUIRING NO SHOES O MY CHILDREN   466 12
    SINCE THERE WAS NO CIRCUMSTANCE REQUIRING TRUST BETWEEN   603 7

REQUISITE
    REQUISITE   234 16

REQUITE
    TO HEAL THE SUFFERING OR TO MAKE REQUITE   100 26

REQUITTAL
    NOW MAKE REQUITTAL   563 7

RE-REMEMBRANCE
    FOR WE ARE ON THE BRINK OF RE-REMEMBRANCE   286 19

RESCUED
    WITH MY THIRTEEN SORRY PICTURES THAT HAVE JUST BEEN RES+ 580 17

RESENT
    THE PEOPLE WATCHED AND WONDERED AND SEEMED TO RESENT   445 17

RESENTMENT
    EVE WITH A HEART OF RESENTMENT IS QUICKLY SPED   864 21

RESERVE
    TO BE TRUE TO THE NATURE OF IT ITS RESERVE ITS SENSITIV+ 464 20
    AND THE MORTAL RESERVE OF YOUR SEX AS IT STAYS IN YOUR   464 26

RESERVED
    BITS OF RESERVED LAND IT WERE A FLEA-BITE   779 16

RESIDUUM
    BUT THE RESIDUUM OF THE ECSTASY   219 8

RESIGN
    HE WILL LIE NEGLIGENT RESIGN   59 29

RESIGNED
    RESIGNED   63 6
    HE'S RESIGNED AND WHEN YOU HIT HIM   559 19

RESIST
    WITH REDDISH PLACES THAT STILL RESIST   142 19

RESISTANCE
    OLD PEOPLE FIXED IN A RANCID RESISTANCE   662 20
    MAKING US PALE AND BLOODLESS WITHOUT RESISTANCE   740 6
    METAL FOR RESISTANCE   804 1

RESISTANCES
    AND BEATING DOWN RESISTANCES   714 28

RESISTANT
    THAT'S WHY THE DOGGED RESISTANT OLD ONES DARE NOT DIE   662 26

RESISTLESS
    EVE WITH HER RESISTLESS VIRGIN-BUDDED BREAST   864 13

RESOLUTE
    SUCH RESOLUTE SHAPES SO HARSHLY SET   53 24

RESOLVEDNESS
    IT IS IN PURE UNUTTERABLE RESOLVEDNESS DISTINCTION OF B+ 267 3

RESONANT
    SOUNDLESSLY DOWN ACROSS THE COUNTIES OUT OF THE RESONANT 149 1
    ECHO OF HER I'VE-LAID-AN-EGG CACKLE IS RICH AND RESONAN+ 761 21

RESORT
    EXCEPT TO BE LEFT IN THE LAST RESORT ALONE QUITE ALONE   602 24

RESOUNDING
    AND RESOUNDING AFTER WITH A LONG HISS OF INSISTENCE   622 22

RESOUNDS
    AND YET AS HIS BRASS-RESONANT HOWLING YELL RESOUNDS   377 20

RESOURCE
    FROM THE FULL RESOURCE OF SOME PURPLE DOME   50 10

RESOURCES
    DOWN WHICH THE NATION'S RESOURCES ROLL   546 3

RESPECT
    TO THESE THINGS I FEEL ONLY RESPECT AND A TINGE OF REVE+ 622 9
    LEANS LISTENING ON THE GATE IN ALL RESPECT   688 20

RESPECTABLE
    AND SAYING LOOK AT ME I AM NOT RESPECTABLE   432 16

RESPECTABLY
    RESPECTABLY UNSEEN AND CHEERFULLY GNAWS AWAY AT THE   432 7

RESPITE
    DROP A LITTLE LOWER WITHOUTEN RESPITE   113 19
    THERE'S NO RELIEF ONLY A MOMENT'S SULLEN RESPITE   486 4
    HANG HIGH SUSPENDED WITHOUTEN RESPITE   *929 8

RESPONDED
    NO FLESH RESPONDED TO MY STROKE   111 25

RESPONDS
    NATURE RESPONDS SO BEAUTIFULLY   831 1

RESPONSE
    THERE WAS NO GUSHING RESPONSE AS THERE IS AT THE FILM   445 30
    RESPONSE FROM THE HAREM   758 10
    AND MY OWN BREAST OPENS IN QUICK RESPONSE   883 6
    INTO QUICK RESPONSE   *906 22

RESPONSIBILITY
  WITH THE WEIGHT OF THEIR RESPONSIBILITY   288 2
  AND THE HUMAN SOUL IS FATED TO WIDE-EYED RESPONSIBILITY   347 2
  BUT STILL MY NAKEDNESS IS CLOTHED WITH RESPONSIBILITY   607 26
  IT IS A SNEAKING EVASION OF THE RESPONSIBILITY   621 13
  IT IS THEIR RESPONSIBILITY THEIR POINT OF HONOUR   775 4
  OF RESPONSIBILITY   *936 5

RESPONSIBLE
  LET THE GOD THAT CREATED HIM BE RESPONSIBLE FOR HIS DEA+   346 10
  SO RESPONSIBLE AND GOOD   557 2

REST
  AND BEHAVES LIKE THE REST OF MEN   38 32
  FOR THE REST WHEN THOU ART WEDDED   44 6
  I WISH THE CHURCH HAD COVERED ME UP WITH THE REST   48 24
  AT REST IN THE BLUE AND WONDER AT WHAT THEY MEAN   58 15
  O' WARMTH AS 'E GOT DOWN THEER TH' REST WOR STONE COLD   61 18
  THE REST HAD DOORWAY TO THEE THROUGH THAT SPARK   69 21
  SHE HAS NO REST   100 12
  NOT EVEN PALISH SMOKE LIKE THE REST OF THE THRONG   116 12
  LIKE HEAVY BIRDS AT REST THERE SOFTLY STIRRED   123 10
  AND FLING MYSELF AT THE DOORS OF SLEEP FOR REST   129 22
  WHERE YOU ARE LOST WHAT REST MY LOVE WHAT REST   134 27
  LIKE THEE CAN'T REST TILL HIS LAST SPUNK GOES   138 24
  LIKE A DARK ROSE A MYSTERY OF REST   154 10
  STRETCHED OUT AT REST   155 6
  THE PEACEFUL FLOOR WHEN FELL THE SWORD ON THEIR REST   155 8
  WHO FOR THE REST OF LIFE WALK OUT OF CARE   157 11
  ARE MET AT LENGTH TO FINISH OUR REST OF DAYS   157 25
  HIS BODY DOWN IN WEIGHT TO REST IN YOU   158 11
  AS I MAKE MY WAY IN TWILIGHT NOW TO REST   167 7
  SAVE YOU AND ME AND SLEEP ALL THE REST WILL KEEP   212 11
  TO THE MAN WHO IS HER HUSBAND ALL THE REST   231 2
  LET US LEAVE THE REST IN THE DARK   237 21
  NOT SHOW LIKE THE REST   251 8
  ME FROM THE REST AH TERRIBLY   262 13
  FRAIL-FILIGREED AMONG THE REST   314 3
  REST   337 22
  I WOULD NOT LET HIM REST   343 28
  HE WAS HAVING A SILENT REST   344 32
  ALWAYS AS IF FOR ONE DROP OF REST   345 9
  BUT THE REST WAS A REAL SURPRISE   489 16
  FOR THE REST NO I SHOULD SAY LIFE HELD VERY FEW   533 2
  SMOOTH OCEAN WHERE THE FISHES REST ON EDGE   652 10
  THE REST THE UNDISCOVERABLE IS THE DEMI-URGE   691 20
  COMES TO REST   694 18
  THERE'S ONLY LOVE THE REST IS ALL OUTSPENT   736 12
  AND IT SANK TO REST FROM ME IN HIM   742 11
  TO HAVE NO REST SAVE IN THE UTTER NIGHT   744 15
  KNEES AND YOUR LEGS AND YOUR LOINS HIS CIRCLE OF REST I+   801 25
  AND I AM NOT WITH YOU TILL MY SERPENT HAS COILED HIS CI+   801 28
  IT IS FINISHED THE REST IS AFTERWARDS   816 21
  FOR THE REST DON'T BOTHER   818 24
  WE HAVE LEARNED A LOT SINCE JESUS FROM JESUS AND ALL TH+   832 27
  BUT THE REST WERE OBSCURE OR OBSCENE   845 21
  PINIONED LIKE SWEEPING SCYTHES NOW IDLY HANGING AT REST   855 22
  WE REST AT THE HEDGE MY HORSE AND I WHERE THE SCENT   858 10
  THE REST IS A CLOUD OF THISTLE DOWN   863 7
  ITS COOL WEIGHT LAY FULL ON HER BOSOM NOW IT ROLLS TO R+   864 15
  SHAKE AND SINK DOWN TO REST THEN SHAKE AGAIN   878 26
  I WAS EMBEDDED IN THE REST OF THINGS   881 30
  DARKNESS TO RAISE THE STRICKEN DIGNITY AND REST   *896 23
  AND THE BROWN DOG SETTLED THE REST   *933 8

RESTARTS
  RESTARTS ITSELF WHEREIN I AM KEPT   151 24

RE-START
  WHENCE THE RE-START   318 4

RESTED
  AND RESTED HIS THROAT UPON THE STONE BOTTOM   349 12
  THAT THE LORD GOD RESTED THE WORLDS ON   819 10

RESTING
  INTO GABBLING CONFUSION WITHOUT RESTING   54 5
  RESTING YOUR HEAD HALF OUT OF YOUR WIMPLE   354 8

RESTLESS
  IN THE OPEN DEPTHS OF EACH FLOWER DARK RESTLESS DROPS   76 2
  LONG HAS WAITED RESTLESS SUDDENLY WAFTS   154 29
  RESTLESS AND LONELY SHAKEN BY YOUR OWN MOODS   197 2
  SHE FOLLOWS HIS RESTLESS WANDERINGS   202 25
  AND THE RESTLESS RIVER WE ARE LOST AND GONE WITH ALL   211 22
  GLOWING AFTER THE DAY'S RESTLESS DRAUGHTS   506 13
  THEY ARE OPEN TO THE RESTLESS SKIES AND STREAMS FLOW IN+   675 10
  IN THE OPEN DEPTHS OF EACH FLOWER DARK RESTLESS DROPS   *897 29
  IN THE OPEN DEPTHS OF EACH FLOWER DARK RESTLESS DROPS   *901 6
  THE FASCINATION OF THE RESTLESS CREATOR THROUGH THE MES+   *906 23
  THE FASCINATION OF THE QUICK RESTLESS CREATOR MOVING TH+   *908 19
  THE WATERS' RESTLESS STROKE   *916 23
  AND RESTLESS WERE THE WHIMPERING RAT-BAIRNIES   *933 4
  THE CARES AND THE RESTLESS SMART   *936 4

RESTORED
  SOOTHED RESTORED AND HEALED   646 14

RESTORING
  SOOTHING AND RESTORING AND HEALING   646 13

RESTS
  RESTS A STILL LINE OF SOLDIERS RED MOTIONLESS RANGE OF +   66 7
  ARE BUBBLES OF ICE KISS ME YOU KNOW HOW IT RESTS   212 7
  RESTS   249 11
  SIDE RESTS   249 28
  AND LAUGH WITH ME WHILE THE WOMAN RESTS   813 7
  WHICH RESTS IN CONNECTION WITH THE FURTHER FOREVER UNKN+   844 22

RESTS
  THREE SIDES SET ON ME SPACE AND FEAR BUT THE FOURTH SID+   *945 22

RESULT
  BECAUSE I WAS THE AUTHOR AND THE RESULT   257 13
  THIS WOULD BE THE RESULT   629 2

RESUME
  AND I MUST RESUME MY NAKEDNESS LIKE A FISH SINKING DOWN+   321 29

RESUMED
  RONALD SHE RESUMED DOESN'T LIKE WOMEN JUST ACUTELY   447 11

RESURRECT
  I SHALL SLOWLY RESURRECT   513 12

RESURRECTED
  I NEW-RISEN RESURRECTED STARVED FROM THE TOMB   259 14
  EXTINGUISHES THERE MY RISEN RESURRECTED LIFE   261 15
  BUT WHO NEVER RISE RESURRECTED FROM THIS GRAVE OF   290 18
  RESURRECTED FROM THE DEATH OF MECHANICAL MOTION AND EMO+   667 33

RESURRECTING
  IN THE HOPE OF RESURRECTING OR RATHER RE-INCARNATING   760 20

RESURRECTION
  RISEN ACCOMPLISHING A RESURRECTION   258 28
  AND THEN YOUR SINGLE RESURRECTION   290 24
  AND LONG AGO THE ALMOND WAS THE SYMBOL OF RESURRECTION   303 1
  RESURRECTION   303 3
  EVEN OF CALVARY AND RESURRECTION   328 5
  FOR THE NEW WORD IS RESURRECTION   512 31
  IT IS RESURRECTION   513 3
  THE RESURRECTION OF THE FLESH   513 4
  FOR THE WORD IS RESURRECTION   514 8
  TO TEACH THE RESURRECTION IN THE FLESH   609 18
  THEN THE RESURRECTION INTO TOUCH   611 13
  A FRAIL WHITE GLEAM OF RESURRECTION   744 13
  OF RESURRECTION FROM THE ENDLESS GRAVE   745 4
  CALLS TO THE AUTUMN RESURRECTION   745 28

RETALIATE
  TO BEAR BUT RETALIATE NOTHING GIVEN TO SAVE   160 27

RETIRE
  DO NOW ONCE AND FOREVER RETIRE   601 10

RETORT
  LIKE A RETORT   372 28

RETORTS
  SO IN THE STRANGE RETORTS OF MEDLARS AND SORB-APPLES   281 12

RETREAT
  KNOWS BUT THE RETREAT OF THE BURNING SHOULDERS THE RED-+   67 4
  FIRE HORIZONTAL DECLINING AND EBBING THE TWILIT EBB OF +   67 6
  FOR WHICH I WANTED THE NIGHT TO RETREAT   220 20
  MY BROOD IN RETREAT   766 10

RETREATING
  WHICH SHE DRAGS APATHETIC AWAY THOUGH WITHOUT RETREATING   360 11

RETREATS
  HIS HAPPINESS WHILST HE IN DISPLEASURE RETREATS   47 20
  LOOKING DOWN ON THE LION AS HE RETREATS   687 18

RETRIBUTION
  THE RETRIBUTION FOR THEIR OBSTINACY   663 3

RETRIEVING
  A SIGH AMONG THE SHADOWS THUS RETRIEVING   66 3

RETRO ME SATANAS
  WHEN YOU SAID RETRO ME SATANAS   629 3

RETURN
  LOVE WILL YET AGAIN RETURN TO HER AND MAKE ALL GOOD   65 22
  LEAPING LIKE SPRAY IN THE RETURN OF PASSION   89 17
  WILL YOU RETURN AFTER MANY DAYS   171 27
  RETURN WE EVEN DISHEVEL   243 18
  THEY ARE DANCING THEY RETURN AS THEY WENT DANCING   689 9
  THEY RETURN RELENTLESSLY IN THE SILENCE ONE KNOWS THEIR+   739 14
  AND IN RETURN THE GOVERNMENT WOULD SUPPLY THEM WITH   778 29
  AND THITHER THEY RETURN FROM THE LAND OF MEN   799 4
  RETURN WHERE ALL IN BEAUTY STAND ERECT   872 9

RETURNED
  I HAVE BEEN AND I HAVE RETURNED   323 10

RETURNING
  RETURNING I FIND HER JUST THE SAME   150 24
  ENDLESSLY RETURNING ON THE UNEASY SEA   739 12
  OF SWEET RETURNING FROM THE SLEEP OF DEATH   745 5

RETURNS
  INTO DARKNESS AND DARKLY RETURNS   39 33
  AND RETURNS AGAIN BELOW   105 12
  HE WHO RETURNS AGAIN FROM OUT THE TOMB   745 16

REVEAL
  IN A BACKWARD RIPPLE THE WAVE-LENGTH REVEAL   68 26
  REVEAL THE UNIVERSAL TINT THAT DYES   197 27
  BIRDS ARE THE LIFE OF THE SKIES AND WHEN THEY FLY THEY +   368 1
  RED FLAMELETS HERE AND THERE REVEAL   606 7
  REVEAL US NOTHING ROLL THE SCRIPTS AWAY   737 24
  IN A BACKWARD RIPPLE GOD'S PROGRESS REVEAL   *915 10

REVEALED
    THE WHITE MOON SHOW LIKE A BREAST REVEALED   55 26
    REVEALED TO ME   59 26
    REVEALED WHERE IT HIDES   144 6
    EYES REVEALED   310 6
    DARK BREATH OF THE EARTH THE SERPENT SLID FORTH LAY REV+   348 7
    THE EGO REVEALED IN ALL ITS MONSTROUS INHUMANITY   475 11
    LEST HER HEEL OF ACHILLES SHOULD BE REVEALED   577 14
    AND GOD REVEALED THROUGH THE SWEAT AND THE HEAT OF LOVE   742 29

REVEALING
    WITH HER WHITENESS REVEALING MY SUNKEN WORLD   103 29
    TO SIGHT REVEALING A SECRET NUMBERLESS SECRET KEEPING   136 7
    REVEALING THE SKY THROUGH THE RAGGED EARTH AND SUDDEN   874 29

REVEL
    YOUR HAIR FOR THE BLISS-DRENCHED REVEL   243 19

REVELATION
    LIKE OTHER FLOWERS IN A REVELATION OF PETALS   283 4
    THE CANDID REVELATION   285 14

REVELRY
    THE FIGURE OF SONG AFLUTTER IN A BLACK-WINGED REVELRY   *918 2
    BUT THE NIGHT IS FULL OF THE FLUTTER OF INVISIBLE REVEL+ *918 10

REVENGE
    AND I DO NOT CARE THOUGH THE LARGE HANDS OF REVENGE   126 1
    IF FIRST A MAN COULD HAVE HIS FULL REVENGE   628 11
    SHOUTING REVENGE REVENGE   739 22
    AND I DO NOT CARE THOUGH THE LARGE HANDS OF REVENGE   *937 1

REVERBERATING
    DEEP AND REVERBERATING   326 11

REVERENCE
    I WANT TO SHOW ALWAYS THE HUMAN TENDER REVERENCE   622 5
    I FEEL ABSOLUTE REVERENCE TO NOBODY AND TO NOTHING HUMAN 622 6
    TO THESE THINGS I FEEL ONLY RESPECT AND A TINGE OF REVE+ 622 9
    I FEEL ABSOLUTE REVERENCE SAY NO MORE   622 13
    SERVING WITH DELIGHT AND WITH REVERENCE THOSE MEN WHOSE+ 648 20
    OF BIGGER LIVES WITH DUE REVERENCE AND ACKNOWLEDGEMENT   679 22
    CEASE FOR A MOMENT IN REVERENCE   *914 13

REVERENT
    SMITTEN WITH REVERENT SURPRISE   234 12

REVERENTLY
    AND IN THE SILENCE REVERENTLY WELCOME THEM   740 14

REVERIE
    IN ECSTATIC REVERIE   165 21

REVERSAL
    DREDGED DOWN TO THE ZENITH'S REVERSAL   323 12

REVERSE
    WHICH IS VERY ODD BEING THE EXACT REVERSE OF THEIR FATH+ 829 14

REVERSED
    REVERSED FLAME   322 22
    TO THE GREAT DEPTH OF ITS REVERSED ZENITH   322 24
    WILL YOU LIKE AN AZTEC SACRIFICE REVERSED   783 20

REVERSION
    DARK REVERSION OF NIGHT   321 30

REVIVE
    REVIVE ME WITH APPLES   817 9
    REVIVE WITH APPLES   817 14

REVOLT
    OF BEES THAT VIBRATE WITH REVOLT WHO FALL TO EARTH   73 18
    THAT THE YOUNG OF THEIR OWN SEX REVOLT AGAINST THEM AT + 619 25
    AND AGAINST THIS INWARD REVOLT OF THE NATIVE CREATURES + 624 20

REVOLUTION
    O START A REVOLUTION SOMEBODY   453 6
    O START A REVOLUTION SOMEBODY   453 9
    IF YOU MAKE A REVOLUTION MAKE IT FOR FUN   517 1
    LET'S HAVE IT SO LET'S MAKE A REVOLUTION FOR FUN   517 22
    FOR EVERY REVOLUTION OF THE EARTH AROUND THE SUN   713 12

REVOLUTIONS
    LEAVING IT TO THE VAST REVOLUTIONS OF CREATIVE CHAOS   429 24
    CURIOUSLY ENOUGH ACTUAL REVOLUTIONS ARE MADE BY ROBOTS   647 21
    LIVING PEOPLE NEVER MAKE REVOLUTIONS   647 22
    WRITHING AND TWISTING IN ALL THE REVOLUTIONS   701 19

REVOLVE
    REVOLVE THROUGH HER HAIR   120 11

REVOLVED
    AND IN ONE INSTANT'S PAUSE ARE REVOLVED ROUND AND CHANG+ 784 12
    TO BE REVOLVED AND IN ONE INSTANT CHANGED   784 25

REVOLVING
    SLOWLY REVOLVING TOWARDS UNEXPLODED EXPLOSION   381 18
    IN THE LONG LONG FALL REVOLVING UPON HIMSELF   700 26
    AND THE SYMBOL OF THE ROBOT IS THE WHEEL REVOLVING   713 10

REWARD
    OR MY LIFE'S REWARD   59 12

REX
    AND THOSE OVER-PROLIFIC WHITE MICE AND ADOLPH AND REX   395 9

RHAPSODY
    IN ALL THINGS TO THE LAST LIKE A RHAPSODY   877 26

RHODODENDRONS
    WHO CROWD IN CROWDS LIKE RHODODENDRONS IN BLOSSOM   73 12

RHYME
    AND GAZED AND GLOATED WITHOUT RHYME   578 4

RHYTHM
    RHYTHM STARTS AND MY SILENT AND SLUMBEROUS BELLY   39 5
    WITH A RHYTHM OF TAPPING COMING FEET   121 20
    AND FINGER IT AND FORCE IT AND SHATTER THE RHYTHM IT KE+ 464 30
    FOR OH TO FEEL THE RHYTHM SET   747 16
    FOR A RHYTHM TO COMPEL ME BACK FOR PEACE   747 23
    TO SHARE THE RHYTHM OF THE DEATHLESS WAVE   772 19
    WHEN HE SWUNG LIKE THE RHYTHM OF A POEM OVER THE RIVER   868 13
    MOVEMENT OF MULTITUDES SURPASSING RHYTHM   872 20
    IN TERRIBLE RHYTHM LIKE BLOWS THAT ARE STRUCK TILL THE + 879 2
    WATCH THE STIR WHOSE RHYTHM IS SECRET WHOSE SECRET IS S+ *907 13

RHYTHMIC
    LIKE A RHYTHMIC BREEZE   104 6
    ON THE SLOW BUBBLING OF YOUR RHYTHMIC HEART   154 11
    COURSED ROUND BY RHYTHMIC MOVEMENT OF ALL TIME   194 23
    WATCH THE STIR WHICH IS RHYTHMIC AND MOVES THEM ALL AS + *909 9

RHYTHMS
    THEIR RHYTHMS ON LONG-DRAWN HOLLOW SINISTER DRUMS   371 5
    COMPELLED TO ADMIRE THE BRIGHT RHYTHMS OF MOVING BODIES 445 25
    IN RHYTHMS TOO BIG AND TOO SMALL FOR US TO KNOW   479 10

RIBBED
    RIBBED AND TORCH-LIKE WITH THEIR BLAZE OF DARKNESS SPRE+ 697 6
    RIBBED HELLISH FLOWERS ERECT WITH THEIR BLAZE OF DARKNE+ *956 4

RIBBON
    IN FRONT OF THE SOMBRE MOUNTAINS A FAINT LOST RIBBON OF 208 23
    STRAGGLE OF A LONG THIN EAR LIKE RIBBON   393 18

RIBS
    SHAKING ASUNDER AND FLICKING AT HIS RIBS   453 15
    AGAINST HIS RIBS   453 21
    MY RIBS   455 24
    AND LO IT STICKS BETWEEN THE RIBS OF A MAN   807 21

RICE
    TER MARRY WI' CABS AN' RICE   82 12
    NAKED MEN ARE THRESHING RICE   386 28
    AND THE CROWD LIKE A FIELD OF RICE IN THE DARK GAVE WAY 390 34
    NUMEROUS AND WHISPERING THIN GRAINS OF RICE IN A   391 6
    HOST ON THE SHORES OF THE LAKE LIKE THICK WILD RICE BY   391 9
    FACES DARK AS BLACK RICE GROWING   391 13
    TO MARRY WI' CABS AN' RICE   *924 16

RICE-FIELD
    RICE-FIELD AT NIGHT   391 7

RICH
    YOU WITH YOUR FACE ALL RICH LIKE THE SHEEN ON A DOVE   90 18
    THIS BIRD THIS RICH   124 11
    AND YOU MY LASS WITH YOUR RICH WARM FACE AGLOW   126 28
    TO BE RICH   175 3
    OF MAKING A TRIUMPH OF ENVY THE RICH AND SUCCESSFUL ONES 175 10
    THE RICH AND THE POOR ALIKE DREAMING AND WRITHING ALL I+ 175 15
    AND RELEASE US POOR ONES AND RICH ONES LET US BREATHE A+ 175 28
    IN ONE RICH DRIP IT SINKS TO ANOTHER SLEEP   195 15
    I FEEL LIKE A FIRM RICH HEALTHY ROOT   247 11
    WHEN A MAN IS RICH HE LOSES AT LAST THE HUNGER FEAR   265 15
    LET THE DARKNESS TURN VIOLET WITH RICH DAWN   273 23
    WHEN I WISH I WAS RICH THEN I KNOW I AM ILL   498 5
    SO WHEN I CATCH MYSELF THINKING AH IF I WAS RICH   498 7
    WERE RICH PEOPLE OR PEOPLE WHO IMAGINED THEMSELVES RICH 498 10
    SAINT FRANCIS HIMSELF WAS A RICH AND SPOILED YOUNG MAN   498 11
    BUT NEITHER DO I WANT TO BE RICH   498 17
    LOOK AT MY MOTHER HOW RICH AND STILL SHE IS   503 28
    ALMIGHTY MAMMON MAKE ME RICH   584 5
    MAKE ME RICH QUICKLY WITH NEVER A HITCH   584 6
    FROM THE ROBOT MASS OF RICH AND POOR MECHANICAL EGO-BOU+ 637 29
    THERE IS A MARVELLOUS RICH WORLD OF CONTACT AND SHEER F+ 667 3
    ECHO OF HER I'VE-LAID-AN-EGG CACKLE IS RICH AND RESONAN+ 761 21
    VIBRATES UNTOUCHED AND VIRILE IN LIFE UNUTTERABLE RICH   772 30
    AS RICH AS ANYBODY ELSE ON THE SAME TERMS   778 15
    THAT CARRIES A HEAVY RICH LIQUOR   869 24
    THOUGH WHITE YOU ARE COOL-DROOPING AND RICH   874 25
    THAN WHO CAN SEPARATE TWO LITHE RICH FLAMES   879 33
    RICH WITH THE SONGS OF SEVEN LARKS SINGING AT ONCE GOES+ *892 2
    WITH A RICH A THRILLED YOUNG CLASP OF LIFE   *899 32
    WITH A RICH A THRILLED YOUNG CLASP OF LIFE   *903 11
    THIS RARE RICH NIGHT FOR IN HERE   *929 18
    THIS BIRD THIS RICH   *935 10
    SWELL DOWN HER RICH HOT WRIST   *937 8

RICHER
    IF SO THE VAST THE GOD THE SLEEP THAT STILL GROWS RICHER 195 17
    RICHER THAN LIFE ITSELF TILL DESIRE   873 16

RICHES
    YOU UNLADE YOUR RICHES INTO DEATH   168 8
    THE GHASTLY DREAM OF RICHES OF MASSES OF MONEY TO SPEND 175 7
    SHE STOOD BEFORE ME LIKE RICHES THAT WERE MINE   264 29

RICHLY
RUNS RICHLY FROM US   743 13

RICHNESS
THERE WAS PEACE AND RICHNESS   265 10

RICKSHAW
THE RICKSHAW BOYS BEGIN TO UNDERSTAND   390 2

RICOTTA
AND MILKY-SAPPED SAP THAT CURDLES MILK AND MAKES RICOTTA   283 11

RID
THA THOUGHT THA WANTED TER BE RID O' ME   139 1
GOING UP IN A FOETID SMOKE TO GET RID OF THEM   258 4
AND ALL ITS TALLOW RIGHTEOUSNESS GOT RID OF   299 22
GET RID OF THEIR HEAVINESS   792 1

RIDDEN
OF SHAPES BY A HARD WIND RIDDEN   68 8

RIDDLE
BECAUSE I COULD NOT ANSWER THE RIDDLE OF HER OWN SELF-I+   604 12

RIDE
KNIGHTS INDEED MUCH KNIGHT I KNOW WILL RIDE   221 10
AND RIDE ON HORSEBACK ASLEEP FOREVER THROUGH THE DESERT   408 11
THAN RIDE IN THE MOTOR-CAR OF A MULTIMILLIONAIRE   498 2
WHEREAS IF YOU RIDE AWAY AND BECOME DEEPLY CONCERNED IN+   665 12
AND ALWAYS LIKELY OH IF I COULD RIDE   *944 23

RIDES
THAT RIDES THE ROOM LIKE A FROZEN BERG ITS CREST   155 4

RIDGE
THEIR FEET IN A BROKEN RIDGE   144 17
AT THE END OF A BACK-BONE RIDGE LIKE A STRAIGHT SIERRA +   381 3
ALONG WHICH RIDGE OF LIBIDINOUS MAGNETISM   386 12

RIDGED
FINALLY RIDGED WITH THE AUSTERE LINE OF THE DEAD   155 5

RIDICULE
CA-A-A COMES THE SCRAPE OF RIDICULE OUT OF THE TREE   375 14

RIDICULOUS
IS MERELY RIDICULOUS   478 13
RIDICULOUS BIMMEL-BAMMEL   492 10
AND NAKED EMBRACE AN ANTI-CLIMAX HUMILIATING AND RIDICU+   608 19
HENCE THE RIDICULOUS WAY THEY RUSH IN WHERE ANGELS FEAR+   665 20
RIDICULOUS   840 20

RIDICULOUSLY
AND RIDICULOUSLY SMALL   359 32

RIDING
OF RIDING AND BEING ENVIED SUCH ENVY AS HAS NO END   175 9
RIDING AT JOSEPH'S SIDE   201 6
RIDING THE AIR AND CARRYING ALL THE TIME   221 21
THROUGH THE WAKENED AFTERNOON RIDING DOWN MY DREAMS   *906 15
RIDING THE AIR AND CARRYING ALL THE TIME   *945 7

RIDING-WHIP
WHEN I WAS A CHILD I LOVED MY FATHER'S RIDING-WHIP   255 1

RIFE
YOU FLUSH AND RIFE   127 19

RIFT
RIFT OF THE RIVER EERILY BETWEEN THE PINES UNDER A   220 25

RIFTS
FLIMSY HUSK-BALL THROUGH WHOSE RIFTS THERE LOOKS   874 31

RIGGED
ALL BEAUTIFULLY RIGGED AND BOTTLED UP   542 8

RIGGING
WIERD RIGGING IN A STORM SHRIEKS HIDEOUSLY   36 12
WITH FROZEN RIGGING SHE SAW HIM SHE DROOPED LIKE A FERN   155 22
RIGGING ITS MAST WITH THE SILENT INVISIBLE SAIL   *961 1

RIGHT
ALL THAT IS RIGHT ALL THAT IS GOOD ALL THAT IS GOD TAKE+   34 27
GOING LEFT AND RIGHT   36 4
I SH'D THINK 'E'LL GET RIGHT AGAIN   46 4
THEY ARE RIGHT YET CLAMOROUSLY FALLING   54 4
ALL RIGHT ALL RIGHT IT'S MY FAULT BUT LET   61 1
RIGHT IN 'EM AN' SCRAIGHTED A BIT AGAIN   61 14
INTO ME MELTED RIGHT INTO ME LIZZIE   80 11
THOUGH I'LL SEE AS 'E PAYS YOU AN' DOES WHAT'S RIGHT   82 7
AN' THA'RT THAT RIGHT THA KNOWS 'TIS   83 28
THA ART SO SURE THA'RT RIGHT LIZ   84 1
YER TOO MUCH I' TH' RIGHT FOR ME   85 2
AN' WI' 'ER SOMEHOW IT ISN'T RIGHT   85 3
AND PERHAPS THEY WERE RIGHT FOR THE YOUNG ARE BUSY DEEP+   92 25
OF YOUR LOVE WE BOTH HAVE ENTERED THEN THE RIGHT   104 14
FOR YOU TO SHAKE AND SHAKE AND IT WON'T COME RIGHT   119 3
IT IS EVIDENT YOU WERE RIGHT   168 1
STILL I HAD MY RIGHT TO BE THERE WITH HER   222 12
I AM BRUISED RIGHT THROUGH   230 16
BUT THIS TIME WE BEGIN TO DO RIGHT   232 11
I KNOW RIGHT WELL THE MARRIAGE RING YOU WEAR   234 3
I SEE RIGHT WELL HOW I OUGHT TO BE GRATEFUL   234 11
CREEP RIGHT UP WITH YOUR ROUND HEAD PUSHED IN MY BREAST   245 6
THIS COMES RIGHT AT LAST   265 1
HAD MORE RIGHT THAN I FOR WHO WAS I   269 19
AND ALL YOUR PONDEROUS ROOFED-IN ERECTION OF RIGHT AND   289 12

RIGHT
COME NOW SPEAKING OF RIGHTS WHAT RIGHT HAVE YOU TO THIS   314 12
RIGHT INTO THE MARROW   354 26
IT GOES RIGHT THROUGH HIM THE SPROTTLING INSECT   356 2
STARING TWO WAYS AT ONCE TO RIGHT AND LEFT   373 13
THE ARABS WERE ONLY HALF RIGHT THOUGH THEY HINTED THE   378 28
ALL RIGHT MY LITTLE BITCH   400 30
I'M GOING TO SIT DOWN ON MY TAIL RIGHT HERE   405 29
ALL RIGHT THE RED-DAWN-WOLF I AM   405 32
I SWEAR I'LL PULL OFF MY KNICKERS RIGHT IN THE RUE DE L+   433 20
ALL RIGHT THEN HE'S JUST AN AMATEUR   452 33
ALL RIGHT YOU ALWAYS DID QUIBBLE   453 5
IS ONLY REAL AND RIGHT IF WE   470 15
LEAVE SEX ALONE LEAVE SEX ALONE LET IT DIE RIGHT AWAY   471 19
LET IT DIE RIGHT AWAY TILL IT RISES OF ITSELF AGAIN   471 20
TILL YOU PRAY TO THE RIGHT GODS FOR THE THUNDER-BOLT IN+   484 16
TILL YOU LOOK TO THE RIGHT MAN TO PUT YOU INTO TOUCH   484 18
AN' I RECKON IT'S NOWT BUT RIGHT   491 2
THEN IT'S QUITE ALL RIGHT WE UNDERSTAND   491 7
BUT STILL ONE HAS NO RIGHT TO TAKE   492 11
AND OF COURSE ONE HAS NO RIGHT TO LAY   492 15
AND WHAT A DANDY FELLOW THE RIGHT TOSS OF A CHIN FOR YOU   524 15
PERHAPS IF WE STARTED RIGHT ALL THE CHILDREN COULD GROW+   527 4
AS LITTLE SOCIAL ANTS PERHAPS WE FUNCTION ALL RIGHT   544 11
REALLY PATRIOTIC PEOPLE THE RIGHT SORT OF PEOPLE YOU KN+   546 8
PLEASE AND THERE I COUNTERSIGN THAT'S RIGHT YES THAT'S +   546 15
ALL RIGHT GUVNOR WHAT ABAHT IT   547 16
RIGHT CH'ARE BOSS AN' WHAT ABAHT IT   547 25
DEAR LORD OF RIGHT   558 10
OH I DO HOPE AUNT MAUD WILL MANAGE ALL RIGHT   572 9
A RIGHT LITTLE TIGHT LITTLE ISLAND   574 16
A RIGHT LITTLE TIGHT LITTLE ISLAND   575 12
AND HOW RIGHT HE WAS AND I SIGNED MY INITIALS   579 20
AND HOPE BLEEDS RIGHT AWAY   639 24
BUT WHAT RIGHT HAS MY BLOOD TO BE COLD   655 20
THE BOURGEOIS ASSERTS THAT HE OWNS HIS PROPERTY BY DIVI+   663 13
AND THE BOLSHEVIST ASSERTS THAT BY HUMAN RIGHT NO MAN S+   663 14
I ONLY CAN SET OTHER PEOPLE RIGHT   680 11
THE RIGHT WHALES THE SPERM-WHALES THE HAMMER-HEADS THE +   694 5
IT WAS COLD AND HE PUT HIS CLOAK RIGHT ROUND ME   732 14
THEY SET FOOT ON THIS LAND TO WHICH THEY HAVE THE RIGHT   739 13
STARING TWO WAYS AT ONCE TO RIGHT AND LEFT   781 19
WITH THE BRIGHT WING ON THE RIGHT   787 18
CLEANIN' YES SIR A SHILLN BY MYSELF ALL RIGHT SIR   866 21
DUG FIRM IN MY BREAST AS YOU REACHED OUT RIGHT   886 8
RIGHT UNTIL 'EM AND SCRAIGHTED OUT AGAIN   *911 30
THA'S LAIN RIGHT UP TO ME LIZZIE AN' MELTED   *922 10
EVEN AT THE RIGHT TIMES SODOMY CAN BE SANE AND WHOLESOME   *952 16

RIGHTEOUSNESS
FOR THE ABOMINATION OF OUR OLD RIGHTEOUSNESS   232 8
FOR THE ABOMINATION OF OUR PAST RIGHTEOUSNESS   232 13
THE SUN OF THEIR RIGHTEOUSNESS   288 20
AND ALL ITS TALLOW RIGHTEOUSNESS GOT RID OF   299 22
AND ENJOYING THE SENSATION OF HEAVEN AND RIGHTEOUSNESS +   324 32

RIGHTS
POOR PERSEPHONE AND HER RIGHTS FOR WOMEN   309 20
COME NOW SPEAKING OF RIGHTS WHAT RIGHT HAVE YOU TO THIS   314 12

RIGID
OF THE SICK-ROOM RIGID WITH WILL   111 3
RIGID SLEEPS THE HOUSE IN DARKNESS I ALONE   140 7
PILLARS OF WHITE BRONZE STANDING RIGID LEST THE SKIES F+   287 16
IT IS EASIER TO STAND STOCK RIGID THAN TO MOVE   288 7
AND RIGID SUPPRESSION OF ALL BAWDY WHORING OR OTHER SUC+   845 13
LYING RIGID AND SILENT WITH YOUR FACE ON THE SHORT SEA +   871 34

RIGIDITY
EXCEPT RIGIDITY   289 6
BUT A MAN RE-BORN FROM THE RIGIDITY OF FIXED IDEAS   667 32

RIGMAROLE
ANSWER WITHOUT A RIGMAROLE   545 7

RIGOUR
OF RIGOUR THEY TASTE DELIGHTEDLY   52 3
OF RIGOUR THEY TASTE DELIGHTEDLY   *899 16
OF RIGOUR THEY TASTE DELIGHTEDLY   *902 28

RIM
BRIGHT CRIMSON RIM   96 18
THE RIM OF THE MOON DIVINELY RISE   103 25
RIM   364 4
STANDING WITHOUT FEET ON THE RIM OF THE FAR-OFF MESA   403 5
A RED WOLF STANDS ON THE SHADOW'S DARK RED RIM   403 20
OF SOMETHING COMING SHIPS A-SAIL FROM OVER THE RIM OF T+   687 3
ON THE RIM OF THE DESERT   816 17

RIME
IS SEEN IN THE GOSSAMER'S RIME   68 16

RIMS
HUTCHED UP FOR WARMTH THE MUDDY RIMS   145 19
BRAGGADOCCIOS AROUND THE BLUE RIMS OF THE WORLD   814 30
BUT THERE WITHIN THE BLUE-SKY RIMS THAT COPE   876 34

RIND
THE ROOM IS THE HOLLOW RIND OF A FRUIT A GOURD   112 19
LEAVES A RIND   463 22
WITH NOTHING BUT RIND   800 23
HE HAS A VERY NICE APPLE-OF-SODOM RIND   830 8
IT SEEMS TO COME OUT OF SOME HOLLOW RIND OF A MAN   830 33

RING
      TO BE CHOKED BACK THE WIRE RING   43   9
      TAKE THEM AND BUY THEE A SILVER RING   44   4
      WHEN WILL THE BELL RING AND END THIS WEARINESS   74   7
      WHY NOT LET IT RING   137   3
      I KNOW RIGHT WELL THE MARRIAGE RING YOU WEAR   234   3
      SEE IF THEY RING   236   27
      AROUND IN A RING   410   29
      AND ROUND THE RING THEY WENT TO THE SOUND OF THE WHIP   444   20
      NOW THE OLD ONES RING HOLLOW   564   22
      AND BULL-WHALES GATHER THEIR WOMEN AND WHALE-CALVES IN +   695   1
      HOLD THE STARS STILL LEST WE HEAR THE HEAVENS DIMLY RIN+   698   11
      OH BROTHER AND I AM THE GOLDEN RING   752   17
      AND IN THE UNFINISHED HOUSES THE RING OF THE JOINER'S T+   865   16
      WHEN WILL THE BELL RING AND END THIS WEARINESS   *895   15
      WHEN WILL THE BELL RING AND END THIS WEARINESS   *904   4

RINGING
      OF DAY TROLLS AT THE CAVE OF RINGING CERULEAN MINING   72   10
      WHILE RIVER MET WITH RIVER AND THE RINGING   216   24
      RINGING THE SOUNDLESS BELL OF HIS PRESENCE IN CHAOS   358   19
      SWIFT WIND OR SOUND RINGING ROCK   637   11
      WHILE RIVER MET WITH RIVER AND THE RINGING   *942   10

RINGS
      LISTEN THE DARKNESS RINGS   238   7
      HOW HAPPY I AM HOW MY HEART IN THE WIND RINGS TRUE   251   11
      IF YOU SEE MY RINGS HOW THEY SPARKLE WITHIN MY EARS   755   5
      WITH THE RINGS THAT THE FISHES HAVE MADE   867   21

RIOT
      WHISPERING RIOT   76   4
      WHISPERING RIOT   *897   31
      WHISPERING RIOT   *901   8
      SO MUCH MORE ROOM FOR RIOT THE GREAT GOD SPARETH NOT   *926   28

RIOTING
      SENDING THEM RIOTING AT DAWN DOWN THE LANE OF SCARLET P+   860   23

RIP
      WHEELING TO LACERATE AND RIP UP THIS MY BODY   741   13

RIPE
      RIPE LITTLE STARS COME ROLLING FROM THEIR HUSK   135   12
      ALONG WITH A RIPE SLACK COUNTRY LASS   198   7
      OR THE RIPE ROSE-FRUITS OF THE LUSCIOUS FALL   219   10
      AND WE THE TWO RIPE PIPS   238   5
      NOW THERE IS A FRUIT LIKE A RIPE WOMB   282   28
      WE ARE A RIPE FIG   284   22
      THEY FORGET RIPE FIGS WON'T KEEP   284   24
      RIPE FIGS WON'T KEEP   284   25
      RIPE FIGS WON'T KEEP WON'T KEEP IN ANY CLIME   284   28
      AND WRINKLED RIPE FULFILMENT   503   16
      NUTTING GATHERING NUTS OF RIPE EXPERIENCE   504   12
      WHEN THE RIPE FRUIT FALLS   504   20
      HAS BROUGHT DOWN A RIPE FRUIT HEAVILY TO HER FEET   864   14

RIPEN
      NOTHING NOW WILL RIPEN THE BRIGHT GREEN APPLES   119   11
      THEY WOULD RIPEN LIKE APPLES AND BE SCENTED LIKE PIPPINS   503   20
      NOTHING NOW WILL RIPEN THE BRIGHT GREEN APPLES   *932   20

RIPENED
      WHAT ARE WE BUT AS SEED RIPENED WITHIN   880   2
      LIKE SEED FROM OUT THE RIPENED LOINS OF LIFE   880   6

RIPENESS
      THE RIPENESS OF THESE APPLES OF NIGHT   252   20
      TILL THE DROP OF RIPENESS EXUDES   283   25
      BUT WHEN LIVING PEOPLE DIE IN THE RIPENESS OF THEIR TIME   676   8
      RIPENESS WELLED THROUGH ME AT HIS KISS   *933   26

RIPENING
      IN THE RIPENING MORNING TO SIT ALONE WITH THE CLASS   51   22
      ALL THE ROCKING WHEAT OF CANADA RIPENING NOW   263   1
      AND ROCKS IT TONS OF GRAIN ON THE RIPENING WIND   271   22
      THOUGH THE YEAR IS RIPENING LIKE A WOMAN WHO HAS CONCEI+   854   8

RIPPING
      FOR THE RIPPING OF ARRAS AND SMASHING OF WALLS AND THE +   174   15

RIPPLE
      AND FEEL THE STREAM OF AWAKENING RIPPLE AND PASS   51   23
      IN A BACKWARD RIPPLE THE WAVE-LENGTH REVEAL   68   26
      WHY THE RIPPLE DOWN THE SPHERE   279   19
      AND WE RIPPLE WITH LIFE THROUGH THE DAYS   449   9
      A RIPPLE IS LEFT   509   13
      IN A BACKWARD RIPPLE GOD'S PROGRESS REVEAL   *915   10

RIPPLED
      AS IF IT RIPPLED FROM OUT OF US HAND IN HAND   170   12

RIPPLE-MARKED
      YET WHEN I THINK OF THE WILD SWAN OR THE RIPPLE-MARKED +   841   1

RIPPLES
      RIPPLES BELOW THE BREAST AN URGENT   39   4
      OF UNDERWATER FLOAT BRIGHT RIPPLES RUN   51   7
      LIKE PATTERING RIPPLES GO BY   109   18
      OF RIPPLES ACROSS MY BREAST   194   9
      AND HIS BLOOD RIPPLES WITH THAT UNTELLABLE DELIGHT OF O+   306   2
      IT MOVES IT RIPPLES AND ALL THE TIME   460   9
      AS HE RIPPLES UPWARDS   689   7
      THAT MADE SHADOWS AND SHIMMERING RIPPLES THE SOFT NOTES+   868   14
      GATHERING THE SOFT RIPPLES BELOW MY BREASTS   *893   18
      OF UNDER-WATER FLOAT BRIGHT RIPPLES RUN   *898   19
      OF UNDER-WATER FLOAT BRIGHT RIPPLES RUN   *902   3
      AND RIPPLES POISE AND RUN LAPPING ACROSS THE WATER   *912   27

RIPPLES
      THEY POISE AND RUN LIKE RIPPLES LAPPING ACROSS THE WATER   *914   1

RIPPLING
      O RIPPLING HARD FIRE OF COURAGE O FUSING OF HOT TRUST   440   13
      CONTENT IS THE WOMAN WITH FRESH LIFE RIPPLING IN TO HER   449   14
      WITH THE RIPPLING FRESHLY CHANGE   460   12
      IN TERRIBLE RIPPLING CIRCLES BETWEEN THE STARS   512   18
      AND SUBTLE SILVERY TINKLING AND RIPPLING   667   29
      LO THE LOVELIEST IS RED ALL OVER RIPPLING VERMILION   689   6
      LIFE IS DARK AND RIPPLING BUT FRETTED   773   1
      RUNS ECSTATIC OVER THE PLIANT FOLDS RIPPLING DOWN TO MY+   *891   32

RISE
      RISE   38   15
      I HEAR HIS HAND ON THE LATCH AND RISE FROM MY CHAIR   43   18
      WHERE THE TREES RISE LIKE CLIFFS PROUD AND BLUE-TINTED +   66   5
      THE TREES RISE TALLER AND TALLER LIFTED   68   1
      IN THE NIGHT WHERE WE FIRST HAVE BEING BEFORE WE RISE O+   92   15
      THE RIM OF THE MOON DIVINELY RISE   103   25
      MY HEART WAS FIERCE TO MAKE HER LAUGHTER RISE   125   30
      LET US RISE AND LEAVE HER NOW SHE WILL NEVER KNOW   132   26
      HER RISE FROM OUT OF THE CHAMBER OF THE DEEP   193   2
      OF FINISHED BRIDEGROOM SEEN HER RISE AND THROW   193   4
      AS THEY OUGHT TO HAVE THEY RISE ABOVE US   223   25
      RISE UP AND GO I HAVE NO USE FOR YOU   234   17
      NO SUN WILL EVER RISE   253   21
      BUT WHO NEVER RISE RESURRECTED FROM THIS GRAVE OF   290   18
      RISE THOU RED THING   302   16
      CAN RISE FROM THE ASHES   329   34
      WHETHER THE WATERS RISE AND COVER THE EARTH   334   22
      TO SINK AND RISE AND GO TO SLEEP WITH THE WATERS   336   28
      MOIST EARTH NEVER COULD HE RISE ON HIS FEET AND THIS IS+   348   9
      POISON IN HIS MOUTH FOR THE SUN IN HIM WOULD FAIN RISE +   348   10
      FOR THE SUN TO RISE   371   21
      RISE THEN MY YOUNG MEN RISE AT THEM   457   3
      OR IF YOU CAN'T RISE JUST THINK   457   4
      THAT WOULD RISE AT LAST AND BLOSSOM OUT   488   21
      THAT NOTTINGHAM LIGHTS WOULD RISE AND SAY   489   3
      A SUN WILL RISE IN ME   513   11
      YOU'LL NONE OF YOU RISE IN THE WORLD LIKE I DID   552   27
      WILL RISE IN THEM ONE DAY   560   6
      AND LOOK ROUND AND RISE AND ON THE GREAT VAULTS OF HIS +   625   3
      THERMOMETER RISE   643   14
      AND SOON IT WILL RISE ON THE WORLD ON THE OUTSIDE WORLD   718   16
      LET US RISE UP AND GO FROM OUT THIS GREY   737   7
      OUT OF BLOOD RISE UP NEW GHOSTS   739   25
      SINCE FROM BLOOD POURED OUT RISE ONLY GHOSTS AGAIN   740   10
      DO THOU O VIRGIN AT DAY WHEN WE RISE FROM OUR SLEEPING   753   3
      WAITING FOR THE SUN TO RISE ON YOU   764   7
      DO YOU WANT TO RISE IN THE WORLD   773   12
      RISE DO YOU WANT TO RISE   773   14
      DEAR DEAR DEAR DEAR THEY'RE ALL ON THE RISE   773   19
      IS THE PLACE THERE THE WATERS RISE   786   7
      AND NO MORE ANEMONES RISE FROM THE DEAD   815   12
      TO RISE AN ODOUR OF PURPLE VIOLETS CRUSHED   881   7
      A FEW QUICK BEATS OF A WOODPIGEON'S HEART THEN RISE   *892   30
      THE TREES RISE TALLER AND TALLER LIFTED   *914   16
      MY HEART WAS FIERCE TO MAKE HER HOMAGE RISE   *936   29

RISEN
      RISEN UP HE BEATS ME   39   12
      NOT PASS THE RED MOON RISEN AND I AM GLAD   88   28
      HOW MANY TIMES LIKE LOTUS LILIES RISEN   113   1
      HAVE RISEN FLOATING ON MY BLOOD THE RARE   113   3
      HAVE RISEN RED ON MY NIGHT AS A HARVEST MOON   126   4
      RISEN ACCOMPLISHING A RESURRECTION   258   28
      RISEN NOT BORN AGAIN BUT RISEN BODY THE SAME AS BEFORE   258   29
      RISEN NOT TO THE OLD WORLD THE OLD CHANGELESS I THE OLD+   260   15
      EXTINGUISHES THERE MY RISEN RESURRECTED LIFE   261   15
      HELL RISEN IN PURSUIT OF HER ROYAL SUMPTUOUS   308   15
      RISEN FROM THE ROOTS   314   20
      THAT THE RISEN CHRIST SHOULD BE RISEN   459   20
      THE RISEN LORD THE RISEN LORD   459   21
      HAS RISEN IN THE FLESH   459   22
      THE RISEN LORD THE RISEN LORD   459   25
      IN THE TOMB AND WAS NOT I HAVE RISEN AGAIN   460   23
      KNOWS THAT THE WATERS HAVE RISEN   462   4
      WE'VE RISEN IN THE WORLD ALL THREE   490   22
      YOU A SIMILAR GLORY SINCE YOU'D RISEN   555   23
      GRASS IN BLOSSOM BLOSSOMING GRASS RISEN TO ITS HEIGHT A+   587   12
      YOU MUST ADMIT I'VE RISEN   626   15
      I'VE RISEN I'VE RISEN   626   16
      YOU MUST ADMIT I'VE RISEN   626   17
      BECAUSE I'VE RISEN CLEAR   626   26
      NOW RISEN MAN AND RISEN LORD   636   22
      RISEN FROM THE DEAD AFTER THIS CRUCIFIXION   636   23
      AND THEN RISEN WE MUST LEARN THE MOST CRUEL LESSON   637   1
      I WHO HAVE BEEN AND NOW AM RISEN AGAIN   744   18
      YOU FLUTTER IN A HOST OF FLAMES LIKE WINTER STARLINGS R+   784   1
      SHALL HAVE RISEN RED ON MY NIGHT AS A HARVEST MOON   *937   18
      THE WHOLE THING HAS RISEN OUT OF THIS CASH-CHEMIST MONEY *950   17

RISEN MAN
      TO INCULCATE THE NEW CONCEPTION OF THE RISEN MAN   609   21

RISES
      HOW DIFFERENT IN THE MIDST OF SNOW THE GREAT SCHOOL RIS+   75   7
      THIS NEW RED ROCK IN A WASTE OF WHITE RISES AGAINST THE+   75   13
      AS IF FROM THE WOMB THE SLOW MOON RISES AS IF THE TWIN-+   88   18
      DIM SELF THAT RISES SLOWLY TO LEAVES AND THE FLOWER'S G+   92   20
      OF INCENSE-SMOKE THAT RISES LIKE BIRDS   151   30
      NOW AS THE TIDE RISES   159   14
      SEE HOW IT RISES WITH MAGICAL ROSY SAP   172   10
      THIS ME WHICH RISES FROM THE DARK OF SLEEP   195   10
      WHEN SHE RISES IN THE MORNING   217   9
      YOU ARE AFRAID IF HE RISES TO HIS FEET   255   34
      NO ANSWER MAN RISES AGAIN   461   14

RISES
THE WELLING OF PEACE WHEN IT RISES AND FLOWS   462 6
RISES AND FLUSHES INSIDIOUSLY   471 3
LET IT DIE RIGHT AWAY TILL IT RISES OF ITSELF AGAIN   471 20
HAS HER FOOTING WASHED AWAY AS THE DARK FLOOD RISES   718 13
AND THE DREAM OF THE NIGHT RISES FROM ME LIKE A RED FEA+   806 30
HOW DIFFERENT IN THE MIDDLE OF SNOWS THE GREAT SCHOOL R+   865 18
WHEN SHE RISES IN THE MORNING   *942 19

RISING
SLOWLY THE MOON IS RISING OUT OF THE RUDDY HAZE   67 7
RISING UP IN THE CLASS-ROOM LITTER MAKES ME UNABLE   90 4
THEIR HOLD ON REALITY ENFEEBLE THEIR RISING SHOOTS   92 28
VESSEL OF DARKNESS TAKES THE RISING TIDE   132 30
AND ROOKS AND THE RISING SMOKE-WAVES SCATTER AND WHEEL   148 22
RISING TO DREAM IN ME A SMALL KEEN DREAM   196 3
THE DARKNESS FALLING THE DARKNESS RISING WITH MUFFLED   205 6
RISING NEW-AWAKENED FROM THE TOMB   260 3
YET RISING FROM THE TOMB FROM THE BLACK OBLIVION   260 9
THE POWER OF THE RISING GOLDEN ALL-CREATIVE SAP COULD T+   272 22
GROW RISING UP OWING TO THE HEAT WHICH IS IN THE EARTH +   295 8
AND SAW THEM CUDDLING WITH RISING PASSIONS THEY NONE OF   443 26
AND MAN IS AN IRIDESCENT FOUNTAIN RISING UP TO FLOWER   675 15
AND NOTHING WILL STAY THE DEATH-FLOOD RISING WITHIN US   718 15
THROUGH A PAIN OF RISING TEARS AND DID NOT REPLY   884 21

RISK
AND RISK BLEEDING TO DEATH BUT PERHAPS ESCAPE INTO SOME   632 5

RITES
DO I INTRUDE ON YOUR RITES NOCTURNAL   140 30

RIVALS
PROBABLY AS SHE GREW OLDER SHE ATE HER RIVALS   836 6

RIVE
HOW THEY RUSH OUT AND WANT TO RIVE   494 3

RIVER
LIKE ALL THE CLASH OF A RIVER   38 27
SHEDS ITS FLOWERS ON A RIVER   56 12
OVER THE DEAD-BLACK RIVER   109 22
BY THE RIVER   143 1
THE RIVER SLIPPING BETWEEN   144 3
FLINGING HER SHAWL-FRINGE OVER THE RIVER   170 19
THERE ARE NO GLEAMS ON THE RIVER   170 25
THE LITTLE RIVER TWITTERING IN THE TWILIGHT   203 9
ONLY THE TWILIGHT NOW AND THE SOFT SH OF THE RIVER   203 15
WENT ROLLING IN THE DUSK TOWARDS THE RIVER   205 26
ACROSS THE RIVER LEVELS   206 6
ADOWN THE PALE-GREEN GLACIER RIVER FLOATS   209 1
RIVER   209 21
AND THE RESTLESS RIVER WE ARE LOST AND GONE WITH ALL   211 22
HARK AT THE RIVER IT PANTS AS IT HURRIES THROUGH   212 2
BUT LET ME BE MYSELF NOT A RIVER OR A TREE   212 5
WHILE RIVER MET WITH RIVER AND THE RINGING   216 24
HANGING RED AT THE RIVER AND SIMMERING   217 3
FROGS WERE SINGING AND OVER THE RIVER CLOSES   217 4
FLOAT LIKE BOATS ON A RIVER WHILE OTHER   217 29
RIFT OF THE RIVER EERILY BETWEEN THE PINES UNDER A   220 25
AND NOW AT EVENING AS HE FLICKERS OVER THE RIVER   347 16
AND UP THE HILL LIKE A RIVER IF YOU WATCH   383 29
YOU GO DOWN SHADE TO THE RIVER WHERE NAKED MEN SIT ON   386 23
THE ANCIENT RIVER WEEK THE OLD ONE   702 20
A CREATURE OF BEAUTIFUL PEACE LIKE A RIVER   714 14
HOW CAN I FIND MY WAY TO THE RIVER   757 5
THE ROSY RIVER THAT SPRANG   766 17
MY ROSY RIVER MY BEST   766 22
RIVER OF MY LIFE   768 13
PEACE LIKE A RIVER FLOWS   770 24
AND PEACE LIKE A RIVER FLOWS   770 31
WHERE PEACE LIKE A RIVER FLOWS   771 16
WHERE THE FLICKERING RIVER LOITERS   867 31
UP THE RIVER UNDER THE TREES   867 31
DOWN THE RIVER IN THE GLEAM OF THE SUN   867 32
ACROSS THE RIVER BENDING LOW   868 1
WHEN HE SWUNG LIKE THE RHYTHM OF A POEM OVER THE RIVER   868 13
SOMETHING HAS GONE DOWN THE SILENT RIVER   887 24
SILVER SLOW GOES BY THE RIVER   887 26
THE MOON LIKE A REDDENING LANTERN HANGS LOW ACROSS THE + *917 13
WHILE RIVER MET WITH RIVER AND THE RINGING   *942 10
HANGING RED AT THE RIVER AND SIMMERING   *942 14
FROGS WERE SINGING AND OVER THE RIVER CLOSES   *942 15
FLOAT LIKE BOATS ON A RIVER WAITING   *943 12
THERE'S FOUR MEN MOWING DOWN BY THE RIVER   *944 1

RIVERBED
LEAVING THE RIVERBED   766 19

RIVER-BEDS
AS THEY LOITER ALONG THE RIVER-BEDS   465 13

RIVER-LAMPS
AND RIVER-LAMPS LIKE FULL-BLOWN ROSES   *916 21

RIVERS
AND THE BRIGHT RIVERS FLIT   196 10
CITYWARDS IN LITTLE RIVERS THAT SWELL TO A GREAT STREAM   484 3
RUN TINY RIVERS OF PEACE   496 12
FLOW THE HEART'S RIVERS OF FULNESS DESIRE AND DISTRESS   607 8

RIVER'S
THE RIVER'S INVISIBLE TIDE   146 30

ROAD
IT IS WELL FOR YOU FOR ME THE NAVVIES WORK IN THE ROAD +   57 29
AS I HEAR THE SHARP CLEAN TROT OF A PONY DOWN THE ROAD   63 9
ALONG THE VACANT ROAD A RED   100 5
TO SAVE ME FROM THIS HAUNTED ROAD   104 22
THAT PASSES THE NIGHTLY ROAD ABOVE   105 11
ALONG THIS HAUNTED ROAD   106 16
WE ARE OUT ON THE OPEN ROAD   163 9
BEFORE ONWARD THE STRANGE ROAD GOES   163 12
BUT WE'LL STILL BE TOGETHER THIS ROAD AND I   163 15
TOGETHER WHEREVER THE LONG ROAD GOES   163 16
LAND AS ONWARD THE LONG ROAD GOES   163 20
AS THE WIND ASKS WHITHER THE WAN ROAD GOES   163 24
ONWARD WHEREVER THE STRANGE ROAD GOES   163 28
WHEN WE FIND THE PLACE WHERE THIS DEAD ROAD GOES   164 4
THAT GOES WHEREVER THIS OLD ROAD GOES   164 8
OF THIS LAND WHEREON THE WRONG ROAD GOES   164 16
ALONG THE ROAD AFTER NIGHTFALL   206 4
I HERE IN THE UNDERMIST ON THE BAVARIAN ROAD   213 3
IT IS RAINING DOWN THE HALF-OBSCURE ROAD   220 15
THE LITTLE PANSIES BY THE ROAD HAVE TURNED   224 24
AND SLOWLY DOWN THE MOUNTAIN ROAD BELATED   225 9
ALONE ON THE OPEN ROAD AGAIN   228 9
THE STARS HAVE GONE SO FAR ON THEIR ROAD   229 7
I WANT TO GO THERE'S A GOLD ROAD BLAZES BEFORE   230 12
GO DOWN THE ROAD OUTSIDE THE HOUSE   235 23
THEN ALONG THE DAMP ROAD ALONE TILL THE NEXT TURNING   280 29
BESIDE THE HIGH ROAD PAST THE DEATHLY DUST   605 24
THE WHEAT ON BOTH SIDES OF THE ROAD STANDS GREEN   732 5
AT THE DOOR OF THE GASTHAUS DOWN THE ROAD GREAT   732 21
THREADS OF BLUE WIND FAR AND DOWN THE ROAD   732 22
DRAWING NEAR THEY COVER THE MUNCHEN ROAD   732 26
AND BLOODY WATER FALLS UPON THE ROAD   734 8
HE COMES TO THE SIDE OF THE ROAD AND WASHES HIS HAND   734 13
AND KICKS DUST OVER THE RED STAIN IN THE ROAD   734 16
HE LOOKED AWAY DOWN THE ROAD   735 6
AS I WENT DOWN THE ROAD OF SLEEP   808 3
AND CROSSED THE ROAD OF THE UNEASY   808 4
DOWN THE ROAD OF THE UNEASY   808 9
I DO NOT POINT YOU TO MY ROAD NOR YET   812 5
I AM OUT ALONE ON THE ROAD   857 9
I WISH I KNEW WHERE THIS PALE ROAD GOES   857 12
AND WE STILL BE TOGETHER THE ROAD AND I   857 15
TOGETHER WHEREVER THE DUMB ROAD GOES   857 16
AND SAVE FOR ME THE ROAD IS FORLORN   857 19
FOR NONE GO WHITHER THIS LONG ROAD GOES   857 20
AS THE WIND ASKS WHITHER THE DARK ROAD GOES   857 24
BUT IT'S THE OTHER WAY THAT MY DARK ROAD NOW GOES   857 28
THE ROAD WINDS FOREVER AND WHICH OF US KNOWS   858 2
ANYWHERE NOWHERE THE DEAD ROAD GOES   858 4
WHY SHOULD I CARE WHERE THE OLD ROAD GOES   858 8
YET IN THE LITTLE NEW ROAD THE YOUNG WIFE TURNS AWAY   865 13
THE ASH-TREES OF THE VALLEY ROAD SHOULD RAISE   *941 2

ROADS
WELL YOU CAN'T HAVE IT BOTH ROADS   379 18
AND THE COFFEE-PLANT STARTED COFFING THREE VERY DISTINC+   760 27
THEY WILL HEAR THE FAINT RENDING OF THE ASPHALT ROADS   *954 8

ROAM
AND NEVER A BLOSSOMING WOMAN WILL ROAM   106 17
TO ROAM AND FEEL THE SLOW HEART BEAT   358 12
BUT MUST ROAM LIKE OUTCAST DOGS ON THE MARGINS OF LIFE   722 11
BUT MUST ROAM LIKE OUTCAST DOGS ON THE MARGINS OF LIFE   *958 16

ROAMING
ROAMING OVER THE SODS   361 19
NOT ROAMING HERE DISCONSOLATE ANGRILY   740 24

ROAN
A POOR ROAN THING ITS HIND LEG TWITCHES   734 6

ROAR
DO YOU TELEPHONE THE ROAR OF THE WATERS OVER THE EARTH   301 10
THERE IS A NEW ECSTASY IN HIS ROAR OF DESIROUS LOVE   325 3
AND THE ROAR OF BLACK BULL'S BLOOD IN THE MIGHTY PASSAG+   326 15
LET HIM ROAR OUT CHALLENGE ON THE WORLD   327 25
SO WE ROAR UP LIKE BONFIRES OF VITALITY   440 7
AND WE STILL BLEED AND WE GROPE AND ROAR   544 6
MYSELF IN THE ROAR OF LIFE WHICH SHALL TAKE AND OBLITER+   *894 23

ROARED
WHERE NO BULL ROARED NO COW EVER LOWED NO STAG CRIED   394 16
AND WE TALKED AND WE ROARED AND YOU TYPED LADY C   550 32

ROARING
AND A TRAIN ROARING FORTH   99 19
A TRAIN GOES ROARING SOUTH   110 13
THE GREAT ROARING WEIGHT ABOVE   326 18
MOANING BOOING ROARING HOLLOW   327 10
AND NEVER KNOWING WHAT WE ARE DOING ROARING BLIND WITH   544 18
AND OUT OF THE INWARD ROARING OF THE INNER RED OCEAN OF+   694 16
ROARING AND DOING DAMAGE   833 21

ROARS
DOWN THE VALLEY ROARS A TOWNWARD TRAIN   50 15
ALL ROUND ME ABOVE AND BELOW THE NIGHT'S TWIN CONSCIOUS+   97 23
ROARS LIKE A BEAST IN A CAVE   159 2
RECUMBENT ROARS AS IT FEELS   159 10
THE THUNDER ROARS BUT STILL WE HAVE EACH OTHER   209 3
AND ROARS TO ANNOUNCE HIMSELF TO THE WOLVES   325 20

ROAST
THE ROAST VEAL I AM SHAKING IT FOR YOU   762 13

ROBBERLINGS
    PALE-BREASTED THROSTLES AND A BLACKBIRD ROBBERLINGS   36 25

ROBBIE BURNS
    SO LEAVE OFF TRYING TO PUT THE ROBBIE BURNS TOUCH   540 25

ROBBING
    AND YET EVERY MAN IS DRIVEN INTO ROBBING EVERY OTHER MAN   519 25

ROBE
    EVEN THE OLD PRIEST IN HIS LONG BLACK ROBE AND SILVERY +   618 16
    OH MY MARIGOLD ROBE   760 6

ROBED
    IN WHITE FLESH ROBED TO DRAPE ANOTHER DREAM   195 11

ROBIN
    NAY ROBIN RED-BREAST THA NEDNA   78 21
    AS BOLD AS A ROBIN IT'S MUCH HE CARES   79 7
    ON THE BREAST OF A ROBIN THAT IS FLUTTERED WITH PAIN   883 5
    WHAT DOES THE ROBIN SAY   887 25
    NAY ROBIN RED-BREAST THA NEDNA   *920 13
    AS BOLD AS A ROBIN IT'S MUCH HE CARES   *921 3

ROBINETTO
    AND THE HALF-HIDDEN PRIVATE PARTS JUST A LITTLE BRASS T+   625 22

ROBIN'S
    IS WINSOME AS A ROBIN'S SONG SO FLUTTERING   65 2
    IS LIKE A LITTLE ROBIN'S SONG WINSOME   *914 3

ROBOT
    AND THE ROBOT IS THE MACHINE INCARNATE   635 14
    THAT WHICH IS TRULY MAN AND THAT WHICH IS ROBOT   636 11
    BUT BRAINY ROBOT OR AESTHETIC ROBOT OR MERELY MUSCULAR +   637 23
    MECHANICAL ROBOT   637 24
    FROM THE ROBOT MASS OF RICH AND POOR MECHANICAL EGO-BOU+   637 29
    FOR THE ROBOT CLASSES AND MASSES ARE ONLY KEPT SANE   640 13
    TO THE ROBOT CLASSES AND MASSES   640 17
    LET THEM GRIND ON ONE ANOTHER UPPER-CLASS ROBOT   642 12
    WEIGHT UPON LOWER-CLASS ROBOT WEIGHT   642 13
    NOR ITS MECHANISED ROBOTS ROBOT CLASSES AND MASSES   643 4
    THE SAME WITH MY ROBOT NEIGHBOURS   645 6
    IF I TRY LOVING THEM I FALL INTO THEIR ROBOT JIG-JIG-JIG   645 7
    THEIR ROBOT CACHINNATION COMES RATTLING OUT OF MY THROAT   645 8
    THREADING HIS WAY AMONG THE ROBOT MACHINE-PEOPLE   645 20
    FROM THE ROBOT CONTACT ON EVERY HAND   645 24
    IS A ROBOT AND INCAPABLE OF LOVE   648 2
    IF THE ROBOT CAN RECOGNISE THE CLEAN FLAME OF LIFE   648 14
    AND CEASES TO BE A ROBOT AND BECOMES A SERVANT OF LIFE   648 19
    SYSTEM OF THE ROBOT   649 5
    AND THE ROBOT IS DENIAL OF THE SAME   649 17
    THEN ALL IS LOST THE ROBOT SUPERVENES   650 7
    AND ALL WAS DREARY GREAT ROBOT LIMBS ROBOT BREASTS   651 2
    ROBOT VOICES ROBOT EVEN THE GAY UMBRELLAS   651 3
    THE ROBOT IS THE UNIT OF EVIL   713 9
    AND THE SYMBOL OF THE ROBOT IS THE WHEEL REVOLVING   713 10

ROBOT-CLASSES
    WHICH RULES THE ROBOT-CLASSES AND THE ROBOT-MASSES NOW   639 18
    AWAY FROM THE ROBOT-CLASSES AND THE ROBOT-MASSES   640 2
    THE UPPER MILLSTONE OF THE ROBOT-CLASSES   642 1

ROBOT-DEMOCRACY
    AND THEREIN LIES THE DANGER OF ROBOT-DEMOCRACY AND ALL +   648 5
    IN A ROBOT-DEMOCRACY NOBODY IS WILLING TO SERVE   648 8

ROBOT-HORDES
    BETWEEN YOU AND THE ROBOT-HORDES MISNAMED YOUR FELLOW-M+   637 34

ROBOT-MASSES
    WHICH RULES THE ROBOT-CLASSES AND THE ROBOT-MASSES NOW   639 18
    AWAY FROM THE ROBOT-CLASSES AND THE ROBOT-MASSES   640 2
    THE LOWER MILLSTONE OF THE ROBOT-MASSES   642 2

ROBOTS
    THE HORDES OF THE EGO-CENTRIC THE ROBOTS   635 7
    FOR TODAY THE BASE THE ROBOTS SIT ON THE THRONES OF THE   637 17
    AND RULERS OF MILLIONS OF ROBOTS BEING ROBOTS THEMSELVES   637 20
    AND ROBOTS MUST HAVE ENCOURAGEMENT FROM MEN OF THE   639 8
    FROM THE GRINNING AND INSATIABLE ROBOTS   639 13
    NOR ITS MECHANISED ROBOTS ROBOT CLASSES AND MASSES   643 4
    CURIOUSLY ENOUGH ACTUAL REVOLUTIONS ARE MADE BY ROBOTS   647 21
    UNLESS THEY HAVE FALLEN AND BECOME ROBOTS   649 2
    THE ROBOTS THOSE WHO DENY THE GLEAM   649 26

ROBUST
    HOW FULL AND BIG LIKE A ROBUST HAPPY FLAME   246 13

ROCK
    TO THE ROCK OF VIRGINITY THY   40 11
    AND I WANT TO SMITE IN ANGER THE BARREN ROCK OF EACH WA+   57 30
    A RED ROCK SILENT AND SHADOWLESS CLUNG ROUND WITH CLUST+   75 8
    THIS NEW RED ROCK IN A WASTE OF WHITE RISES AGAINST THE+   75 13
    SCHOOL NOW IS THE ROCK IN THIS WEARY LAND THE WINTER BU+   75 18
    AND OH MY LOVE AS I ROCK FOR YOU TONIGHT   100 24
    OF ROCK DISTILLING OUR MEMORIES   223 18
    THE ROCK WILL SPLIT WE SHALL COME AT THE WONDER WE SHALL   250 23
    MAN'S HAND ON A ROCK   260 11
    IN SYRACUSE ROCK LEFT BARE BY THE VICIOUSNESS OF GREEK   278 14
    TO SET AGAIN INTO ROCK   294 4
    GREY-BLACK ROCK   294 5
    FROM THE ROCK   299 2
    FLOURISHING FROM THE ROCK IN A MYSTERIOUS ARROGANCE   299 8
    THAT LIVES UPON THIS ROCK   299 10
    ROCK WAVES OF DARK HEAT   302 1
    WAVES OF DARK HEAT ROCK SWAY UPWARDS   302 2
    BUT OH FISH THAT ROCK IN WATER   335 14

ROCK
    MOTIONLESS LIKE A BIT OF ROCK   379 6
    AT THE LIVING ROCK HE IS UP AGAINST   382 17
    SARDONIC SARDONYX ROCK OF COLD FIRE   386 6
    THEN SHE LEAPS THE ROCKS LIKE A QUICK ROCK   386 9
    HER BACKBONE SHARP AS A ROCK   386 10
    ROCK   402 19
    A WAVE BURSTS IN ANGER ON A ROCK BROKEN UP   467 12
    AND IF IT FLUSHES AGAINST FIERCE ROCK   467 18
    IN SUMMER AND LOVE BUT UNDERNEATH IS ROCK   477 9
    LOVE IS LIKE THE GRASS BUT THE HEART IS DEEP WILD ROCK   477 22
    IS ROCK AND BELOW THE ROCK THE ROCK   480 8
    THAT GROWS OUT OF ROCK AND PLUMES FORTH PLUMES FORTH   498 19
    A LIZARD RAN OUT ON A ROCK AND LOOKED LISTENING   524 13
    HITTING OURSELVES AGAINST UNSEEN ROCK CRASHING OUR HEAD   544 13
    WILL ROCK IN THE SHOCK OF THE MAD MACHINE AND THE HOUSE+   624 29
    SONS OF THE WIND AND RAIN SONS OF THE FIRE AND ROCK   635 25
    SWIFT WIND OR SOUND RINGING ROCK   637 11
    MEN OF THE FIRE AND ROCK HOW ARE THEY GOING TO COME FOR+   637 28
    WHEN THE WIND BLOWS THE CRADLE SHALL ROCK   669 8
    WHEN GOLD LAY SHINING THREADING THE COOLED-OFF ROCK   682 24
    AND A WOMAN WHO HAS BEEN WASHING CLOTHES IN THE POOL OF+   693 1
    AND THEY ROCK AND THEY ROCK THROUGH THE SENSUAL AGELESS+   694 8
    WITH YOUR FACE YOU FACE HIM WITH A ROCK   781 31
    FROM THE DARK EARTH OVER THE ROCK FROM THE DARK ROCK OV+   782 13
    YOU WHO CAME BEFORE ROCK WAS SMITTEN INTO WEEPING   783 10
    THE DEAD OF THE WATER-LORDS ROCK AND GLIMMER IN THE SEAS   796 8
    BUT UNDERNEATH ARE THE DEEP ROCKS THE LIVING ROCK THAT +   844 2
    LIES THE LIVING ROCK OF A SINGLE CREATURE'S PRIDE   844 9
    UPON A ROCK FROM WHENCE AH CHARLATAN   877 6
    BUT UNDERNEATH MAN IS ALONE EACH ONE A ROCK TO HIMSELF   *951 10
    IS ROCK   *951 15
    AND THE ROCK GOES DOWN DOWN DEEPER FROM COLD INTO HEAT   *951 20

ROCKED
    THAT ROCKED IN A LILT ALONG I WATCHED THE POISE   123 3
    ROCKED ON THE WAVE AND SUNG LUSTILY   575 8
    THAT ROCKED IN A LILT ALONG I WATCHED THE POISE   *934 9

ROCKET
    TO THEE I ROSE LIKE A ROCKET ENDING IN MID-HEAVEN   322 8
    ACROSS THE HISS OF WONDERS AS THE ROCKET BURST   391 17
    ZIGZAGGING DOWN LIKE THE FIZZLE FROM A FINISHED ROCKET   701 26
    OFF LIKE A ROCKET   762 4

ROCKET-CORUSCATION
    AS THE ROCKET-CORUSCATION DIED AND SHADOW WAS THE   391 23

ROCKETS
    OH YOU WHO FLASH YOUR ARMS LIKE ROCKETS TO HEAVEN   73 10
    AS THE ROCKETS WENT UP AND THE GLARE PASSED OVER COUNTL+ 391 12
    LIKE ROCKETS   819 18

ROCK-HAMMER
    GROUND WITH A SUDDEN ROCK-HAMMER ANNOUNCEMENT   381 14

ROCKIES
    OVER THE ROUNDED SIDES OF THE ROCKIES THE ASPENS OF   408 23
    ROCKIES   409 22
    EAGLE OF THE ROCKIES BIRD OF MEN THAT ARE MASTERS   414 21
    THERE ARE PEOPLE THERE BEYOND THE ROCKIES   816 1
    BUT THE PEOPLE THERE BEYOND THE ROCKIES   816 3

ROCKING
    SHOWING THE ROCKING DARKNESS NOW A-REEL   136 10
    ALL THE ROCKING WHEAT OF CANADA RIPENING NOW   263 1
    ALL DAY LONG I FEEL THE TIDE ROCKING ROCKING   454 14
    BE QUITE ALONE AND FEEL THE LIVING COSMOS SOFTLY ROCKING 646 12
    TO SINK UNCONSCIOUS IN THE ROCKING DARK   771 28
    ROCKING DOWN THE SHOALS BETWEEN THE TEA-CUPS   *943 16

ROCK-LIVING
    LIKE A NUDE LIKE A ROCK-LIVING SWEET-FLESHED SEA-ANEMONE 299 7

ROCK OF AGES
    AND THE ROCK OF AGES OF HIS PUBLIC SCHOOL   *947 31

ROCKS
    SET LIKE ROCKS BESIDE A SEA OF GLOOM   56 14
    THE ROCKS WHERE RAVENS FLYING TO WINDWARD MELT AS A WEL+   57 15
    YOU LEAPT ABOUT IN THE SLIPPERY ROCKS AND THREW   98 19
    OVER THE WET DARK ROCKS THE HOUSES AND OVER   112 27
    WHILE I DANCE A TARANTELLA ON THE ROCKS AND THE CROON   130 6
    ROCKS SEEM AND EARTH AND AIR UNEASY AND WATERS STILL   249 15
    AND ROCKS IT TONS OF GRAIN ON THE RIPENING WIND   271 22
    THEN SHE LEAPS THE ROCKS LIKE A QUICK ROCK   386 9
    FLAT BROWN ROCKS TO WATCH THE FERRY IN THE SUN   386 24
    A HOLE IN THE BLOOD-ORANGE BRILLIANT ROCKS THAT STICK U+ 402 12
    TIME WAS MUCH SLOWER WHEN THE ROCKS CAME FORTH   477 4
    ROCKS   477 14
    IN THE DAYS CALLED CHAOS WHICH LEFT US ROCKS AND GEMS   529 25
    ABROAD IN MY HANDS LIKE WAVES AMONG THE ROCKS OF SUBSTA+ 705 6
    IS LASHING HIS TAIL IN HIS SLEEP THE WINDS HOWL THE COL+ 795 14
    BUT UNDERNEATH ARE THE DEEP ROCKS THE LIVING ROCK THAT + 844 2
    AND WHICH ROCKS WITH A SENSE OF CONNECTION RELIGION   844 24
    PAST THE JUTTING ROCKS OF SHADOW   *959 5

ROCK-SALT
    CITIES DISSOLVE LIKE ROCK-SALT   455 3

ROCKY
    MAKE IT ROOST ON BIRD-SPATTERED ROCKY PATMOS   329 19
    SPLENDIDLY PLANTING HIS FEET ONE ROCKY FOOT STRIKING THE 381 13
    LIKE STAGS ON ROCKY GROUND OR PAWING HORSES OR SPRINGY 392 16

ROCKY MOUNTAINS
    WITH DARK-WRAPPED ROCKY MOUNTAINS MOTIONLESS SQUATTING   410 28
ROD
    AND I SHALL SEE MY SLEEPING ROD   59 11
    I HAVE WAITED WITH A LONG ROD   339 1
    THAT STRONG ONE RULING THE UNIVERSE WITH A ROD OF IRON   439 25
    AND LIFTED HIS FACE UP WITH BLUE EYES LOOKING AT THE EL+   672 9
    AS A FINE GREY EGG OR A SLENDER ROD   752 16
RODE
    LOOKING BLEAK AHEAD SHE RODE   202 6
    HENCE JESUS RODE HIM IN THE TRIUMPHANT ENTRY   378 20
    JESUS RODE ON HIM THE FIRST BURDEN ON THE FIRST BEAST OF   379 25
    MONKEYS RODE RATHER GREY AND WIZENED   444 15
RODS
    THE PEACOCK LIFTS HIS RODS OF BRONZE   371 1
    HAS SICKENED US THOROUGHLY WITH RODS OF IRON AND RULERS   439 26
ROLE
    IN YOUR CLOSE HOUSEKEEPING ROLE   95 11
    CUT OUT TO PLAY A SUPERIOR ROLE   490 15
ROLL
    ROUND CLOUDS ROLL IN THE ARMS OF THE WIND   126 7
    ROLL HOLLOW IN THE INTERIM   159 18
    CLAY-COLOURED WHO ROLL IN FATIGUE   162 14
    YOU WHO ROLL THE STARS LIKE JEWELS IN YOUR PALM   197 24
    THE BEES ROLL ROUND IN THE WILD-THYME WITH DELIGHT   223 15
    AS THE WATERS ROLL   335 1
    ROLL YOU   335 2
    INSTEAD OF WHICH YOU SIT THERE AND ROLL YOUR HEAD LIKE A   398 9
    THEN I AM WILLING TO FIGHT I WILL ROLL MY SLEEVES UP   430 11
    DOWN WHICH THE NATION'S RESOURCES ROLL   546 3
    BUT THROUGH SOME HEARTS THEY WILL NEVER ROLL   624 4
    AND ROLL WITH MASSIVE STRONG DESIRE LIKE GODS   694 12
    HUGE HUGE ROLL THE PEALS OF THE THUNDROUS LAUGH   698 18
    ROLL DOWN MY THIGHS   705 8
    REVEAL US NOTHING ROLL THE SCRIPTS AWAY   737 24
    TO ROLL THE GRAVE-STONE OFF THEIR SOULS FROM THE CAVE O+   793 7
    BEFORE THE STOUT SWART BEETLE HAD A BALL OF DUNG TO ROL+   *946 26
    BUT THROUGH SOME HEARTS THEY WILL NEVER ROLL   *953 22
ROLLED
    WHO TOOK A HANDFUL OF LIGHT AND ROLLED A BALL   69 18
    OR THE STOUT SWART BEETLE ROLLED THE GLOBE OF DUNG IN W+   437 16
    MACHINES HAVE TRIUMPHED ROLLED US HITHER AND THITHER   623 30
    HE TOOK A HANDFUL OF LIGHT AND ROLLED A BALL   *916 1
    MACHINES HAVE TRIUMPHED ROLLED US HITHER AND THITHER   *953 17
ROLLERS
    DO THE ROLLERS OF THE SEA   705 7
ROLLICKING
    INTO ROLLICKING SUNS AND THEIR LOST GOLD ROTS COMPRESSED   *896 20
ROLLING
    OH EARTH YOU ROTTEN APPLE ROLLING DOWNWARD   73 3
    RIPE LITTLE STARS COME ROLLING FROM THEIR HUSK   135 12
    WENT ROLLING IN THE DUSK TOWARDS THE RIVER   205 26
    THIS ROLLING DROPPING HEAVY GLOBULE   279 12
    WHAT IS THE HORIZONTAL ROLLING OF WATER   302 4
    ROSE-RED PRINCESS HIBISCUS ROLLING HER POINTED CHINESE +   313 27
    HARD HARD ON THE EARTH THE MACHINES ARE ROLLING   624 4
    AND DREAD AND THE DARK ROLLING OMINOUSNESS OF DOOM   708 25
    AND AGAIN ROLLING IN HIS HEAVY HIGH BOOTS   734 12
    OF TOSSING AND ROLLING THE SUBSTANCE OF LIFE TO YOUR LI+   792 21
    ROLLING BELOW   017 3
    HARD HARD ON THE EARTH THE MACHINES ARE ROLLING   *953 21
ROLLS
    CLOSE AND IT ROLLS ME ENFOLDS ME TOUCHES ME AS IF NEVER+   34 23
    ROUND HIS BASE HIS DARK LIGHT ROLLS   39 32
    THE ROUND EARTH ROLLS LIKE A GERM IN THE SKY   126 8
    AND ROLLS DOWN THE STEEP   162 24
    ROLLS OUT OF THE HUSK OF DEATH   172 6
    SMOKE THAT ROLLS   258 11
    TO ME THE EARTH ROLLS PONDEROUSLY SUPERBLY   288 26
    COMPARED TO THE FLOOD OF BLACK HEAT THAT ROLLS UPWARDS   302 5
    ROLLS ROUND AND ROUND GRINDING EXCEEDING SMALL   614 20
    IN THE MOMENT OF CHOICE THE SOUL ROLLS BACK   640 1
    AND BREAKS IN THE FOAMY HANDS WHOSE POWER ROLLS OUT   705 16
    THE DAUGHTER OF THE GREAT MAN ROLLS HER KHAKI WOOL   752 9
    AND EUROPE'S TAIL-SPIN ROLLS STILL UNROLLED   814 8
    ITS COOL WEIGHT LAY FULL ON HER BOSOM NOW IT ROLLS TO R+   864 15
ROLLS ROYCE
    DO YOU HEAR MY ROLLS ROYCE PURR AS IT GLIDES AWAY   664 3
ROMAN
    LIKE LAVENDER CROCUSES SNOWDROPS LIKE ROMAN HYACINTHS   270 6
    WE HAVE ONLY ROMAN WORD FOR IT   297 31
    WHICH I BEING A LITTLE WEARY OF ROMAN VIRTUE   297 32
    WITH A ROMAN NOSE   414 14
    AND US FROM THE DREARY INHERITANCE OF ROMAN STUPIDITY   479 27
    FOR AFTER ALL HE HELPED TO SMASH A LOT OF OLD ROMAN LIES   497 3
ROMAN CATHOLIC
    THE MOST PART LONG AGO ENTERED THE ROMAN CATHOLIC   776 25
ROMANCE
    OF THE AFTERNOON GLOWS STILL THE OLD ROMANCE OF DAVID A+   53 3
    OF THE AFTERNOON GLOWS ONLY THE OLD ROMANCE OF DAVID AN+   *905 18

ROMANS
    OF RUSHES ERE THE ROMANS   171 11
    ROMANS IT IS FEMALE   282 16
ROMANTIC
    ROMANTIC STORIES NOW NO MORE TO BE TOLD   141 30
ROME
    WHOM ROME CALLED VICIOUS   297 8
    AS ROME DENIED ETRURIA   298 17
    THE GEESE THAT SAVED ROME AND WILL LOSE LONDON   438 25
    IN ANCIENT ROME DOWN THE THRONGED STREETS   703 24
    AND THE GEESE THAT SAVED ROME WILL LOSE LONDON   *947 26
RONALD
    SAID RONALD YOU KNOW IS LIKE MOST ENGLISHMEN   446 28
    OH COME SAID I THAT DON JUAN OF A RONALD   447 1
    RONALD SHE RESUMED DOESN'T LIKE WOMEN JUST ACUTELY   447 11
    SAID RONALD YOU SEE IS QUITE A CLEVER SADIST   *948 10
ROO COO OOO
    WHETHER YOU'RE A SUCKING DOVE ROO COO OOO QUARK   414 6
ROOD
    ONLY I AND THE CLASS MUST WRANGLE THIS WORK IS A BITTER+   76 22
    EARNESTLY AND OH FOR ME THIS CLASS IS A BITTER ROOD   *898 16
    EARNESTLY AND OH FOR ME THIS CLASS IS A BITTER ROOD   *901 25
ROOF
    FROM A ROOF INERT WITH DEATH WEEPING NOT THIS NOT   62 11
    THE THICK SNOW IS CRUMPLED ON THE ROOF IT PLUNGES DOWN   76 6
    LOW FROM THE ROOF AND THE WET DUST FALLING SOFTLY FROM +   112 26
    ON THE ROOF OF THE WORLD   413 20
    AGAINST THE ROOF   544 14
    AND THE CALLING OF THE OLD RED INDIAN HIGH ON THE PUEBL+   623 16
    THE THICK SNOW IS CRUMPLED ON THE ROOF IT PLUNGES DOWN   *898 1
    THE THICK SNOW IS CRUMPLED ON THE ROOF IT PLUNGES DOWN   *901 10
ROOFED
    ROOFED WITH A DAY'S NEAR CEILING AND A DARK   876 11
ROOFED-IN
    AND ALL YOUR PONDEROUS ROOFED-IN ERECTION OF RIGHT AND   289 12
ROOFS
    AND ALL THE LITTLE ROOFS OF THE VILLAGE BOW LOW PITIFUL+   62 6
ROOK
    BETWEEN THE SCHOOLS SWEEPS ONE BLACK ROOK   76 16
    BETWEEN THE RUDDY SCHOOLS SWEEPS ONE BLACK ROOK   *898 10
    BETWEEN THE RUDDY SCHOOLS SWEEPS ONE BLACK ROOK   *901 19
ROOKS
    AND ROOKS AND THE RISING SMOKE-WAVES SCATTER AND WHEEL   148 22
    THE DAWN ROOKS CALL AT EVENING WHEN THE NIGHTINGALE SIN+   368 11
ROOM
    NO-ONE IN THE ROOM   27 7
    AND THE BOYS AND THE ROOM IN A COLOURLESS GLOOM   51 6
    LEANING IN YOUR ROOM LIKE TWO TIGER-LILIES CURVING   91 12
    WILL TIPTOE INTO MY ROOM   106 20
    THE ROOM IS THE HOLLOW RIND OF A FRUIT A GOURD   112 19
    HER ROOM WHERE THE NIGHT STILL HANGS LIKE A HALF-FOLDED+   129 24
    HOW HAVE I WANDERED HERE TO THIS VAULTED ROOM   141 5
    THAT RIDES THE ROOM LIKE A FROZEN BERG ITS CREST   155 4
    SHE HASTENED TOWARDS THE ROOM DID SHE KNOW   155 15
    CARRY INTO YOUR ROOM THE BLOSSOMING BOUGHS OF CHERRY   179 2
    AT THE OPEN DOOR OF THE ROOM I STAND AND LOOK AT THE NI+   179 20
    THE ROOM   179 23
    HERE IN THIS UPPER ROOM   209 14
    COMES WITH THE SIGHT OF THE ROOM I CANNOT TELL   220 14
    BECAUSE WHEN I SIT IN THE ROOM   235 26
    WHEN I WENT INTO MY ROOM AT MID-MORNING   342 8
    MY ROOM A CRASH-BOX OVER THAT GREAT STONE RATTLE   342 10
    WHEN I WENT INTO MY ROOM AT MID-MORNING   342 12
    FLYING ROUND THE ROOM IN INSANE CIRCLES   342 15
    OUT OUT OF MY ROOM   342 26
    NOW OUT OUT FROM MY ROOM   343 4
    ABOUT MY ROOM   343 12
    MY ROOM   343 24
    FLICKER-SPLASHING ROUND MY ROOM   343 27
    BACK INTO MY ROOM AND ROUND ROUND ROUND IN MY ROOM   344 7
    MY ROOM   344 14
    NOT IN MY ROOM   344 34
    NO HE MUST NOT SQUAT NOR HANG OBSCENE IN MY ROOM   346 3
    ROOM   346 12
    BUT NOT BATS IN MY ROOM   346 16
    AND ROUND AND ROUND AND ROUND MY ROOM A CLOT WITH   346 20
    AND I THINK IN THIS EMPTY WORLD THERE WAS ROOM FOR ME   402 27
    I CAN STILL HAVE THE ILLUSION THAT THERE IS ROOM ENOUGH   602 8
    AND THEN IN THE ROOM WHOSE IS THE PRESENCE   652 4
    IN THE WHITE MORNING WHERE IS THE ENCHANTED ROOM OF THE+   856 7
    AND I LOOKED IN A ROOM WHERE THE LAMP AS A MOON IN MIST   865 1
    WHEN SOFTLY I CALL AT HER DOOR AND ENTER THE ROOM   868 25
    THE LIGHTED LAMP INTO MY ROOM AT NIGHT   875 9
    OF WAITING AND THE ROOM STANDS STILL WITH FRIGHT   878 35
    FROM THE LIT ROOM OF LIVING   879 36
    AND THE BOYS AND THE ROOM IN A COLOURLESS GLOOM   *898 18
    AND THE BOYS AND THE ROOM IN A COLOURLESS GLOOM   *902 2
    SO MUCH MORE ROOM FOR RIOT THE GREAT GOD SPARETH NOT   *926 28
    OR THIS IS MY SISTER AT HOME IN THE OLD FRONT ROOM   *940 14
    WHEN SOFTLY I CALL AT HER DOOR AND ENTER THE ROOM   *941 25
    IN THE SUNNY ROOM   *954 20
    OF GENTIANS HERE IN THE SUNNY ROOM   *955 3
    OF GENTIANS HERE IN THE SUNNY ROOM   *955 24

ROOMS
THE WALLS ARE THICK AND THE INNER ROOMS ARE SUCH THEY D+ 174 19
WITH EYES LIKE THE INTERIORS OF STUFFY ROOMS FURNISHED 656 24

ROOM'S
I WANT MY OWN ROOM'S SHELTER BUT WHAT IS THIS 140 11

ROOST
MAKE IT ROOST ON BIRD-SPATTERED ROCKY PATMOS 329 19

ROOSTER
THE EAGLE THE DOVE AND THE BARNYARD ROOSTER DO THEY CALL 371 22

ROOT
LOOK IT HAS TAKEN ROOT 172 8
I FEEL LIKE A FIRM RICH HEALTHY ROOT 247 11
AND THIS TERROR IS THE ROOT OF ALL CRUELTY 264 33
I WANT HER TO TOUCH ME AT LAST AH ON THE ROOT AND QUICK 266 28
TO ROOT IN 270 28
AS IF HIS NOSTRILS WERE GOING TO CURVE BACK TO THE ROOT+ 380 15
AS THE TURNIP MODELS HIS ROUND ROOT AS THE BUSH MAKES 451 15
THE ROOT OF OUR PRESENT EVIL IS THAT WE BUY AND SELL 482 28
WELL-GROWN LIKE POTATOES ON A LIFTED ROOT 827 27

ROOTED
AND FEELING ONESELF UNINTERRUPTED IN THE ROOTED CONNECT+ 610 6
ROOTED CONNECTION 610 14

ROOT-RISING
TO THE ROOT-RISING OF YOUR ERECTED TAIL 370 15

ROOTS
HOMUNCULUS STIRS FROM HIS ROOTS AND STRIVES UNTIL 39 11
AND THE GENTLE LEAVES AND HAVE FELT WHERE THE ROOTS ARE+ 92 10
AND THERE IN THE DARK MY DARLING WHERE THE ROOTS ARE EN+ 92 12
AND IN THE ORIGINAL DARK THE ROOTS CANNOT KEEP CANNOT K+ 92 17
THE ROOTS 92 26
I WILL TEACH THEM THE BEGINNING OF THE LESSON AT THE RO+ 93 24
FOR FLOWERS ARE TENDER FOLK AND ROOTS CAN ONLY HIDE 93 30
MYSELF BUT A KNOWLEDGE OF ROOTS OF ROOTS IN THE DARK TH+ 94 3
OPENS MY EYES TILL THE ROOTS OF MY VISION SEEM TORN 173 4
WHERE ALL THE PARTHENON MARBLES STILL FOSTERED THE ROOT+ 311 28
RISEN FROM THE ROOTS 314 20
WHILE HIS SLITTED EYES SQUINT BACK TO THE ROOTS OF HIS + 386 22
AND GET HIS ROOTS IN EARTH AGAIN 475 4
THAT CULTURE HAS HER ROOTS 489 6
WITH ITS ROOTS IT HAS A GRAND GRIP ON ITS DAILY BREAD 498 21
AND I LOOK SHABBY YET MY ROOTS GO BEYOND MY KNOWING 499 6
YET MY ROOTS ARE IN A WOMAN TOO 499 10
LIKE A PLANT WHOSE ROOTS ARE CUT 610 11
AND THEY ARE CRYING LIKE PLANTS WHOSE ROOTS ARE CUT 610 12
FORTH NEW ROOTS 610 17
INTO THE UNKNOWN AND TAKE ROOTS BY ONESELF 610 18
TO FERTILISE THE ROOTS OF UNKNOWN MEN WHO ARE STILL TO + 614 24
WITH WHICH TO MANURE AFRESH THE ROOTS OF THE TREE OF LI+ 616 15
THROUGH THE DARK HADES AT THE ROOTS OF THE TREE 617 10
INTO SERVICE LIKE THE ROOTS OF TREES 637 16
THE FOUR GREAT ONES THE FOUR ROOTS THE FIRST FOUR 706 4
AND YET THE ROOTS BELOW THE BLACKNESS ARE INTACT 709 22
INTO THE ROOTS OF THE CEDAR INTO THE CEDAR-BOUGHS 782 21
THE ROOTS ARE MINE DOWN THE DARK MOIST PATH OF THE SNAKE 801 16
THE GRASS FEELS WITH HIS ROOTS FOR THE OTHER SUN 804 21
DEEPER THAN THE ROOTS OF THE MANGO TREE 805 1
GRASS FEELS DOWNWARDS WITH HIS ROOTS 806 3
DEEPER THAN THE ROOTS OF THE MANGO TREE 806 4
BUT BELOW ALL ROOTS OF LOVE LIES THE BEDROCK OF NAKED P+ 844 19
UNDER THE CARESSING LEAVES AND FELT WHERE THE ROOTS WER+ *926 10
FAR AND WIDE RUN THE EASY ROOTS THAT BEAR THE LEAVES OF+ *926 12
AND THE ROOTS OF THE GREAT TREE OF FAMILY AND THE FORES+ *951 13

ROPE
AN OBSTINATE OLD WITCH ALMOST JERKING THE ROPE FROM MY 385 9
FOOTED CAUTIOUSLY OUT ON THE ROPE TURNED PRETTILY SPUN 444 26
SPLENDID BODY ON THE ROPE 444 32
LOOSEN THIS ROPE 751 16
ALAS BUT THE ROPE IS GNAWING 751 17

ROPES
AND I TWISTED THEM OVER THE BROKEN LEAVES INTO UNBREAKA+ *926 17

ROSACEAE
THE BRAVE ADVENTUROUS ROSACEAE 283 9
ARE ALL ROSACEAE 285 7

ROSARY
INTO A GLISTENING ROSARY 735 19

ROSE
AND AT NIGHT WHEN THE WIND ROSE THE LASH OF THE TREE 36 10
OUT OF NOWHERE HE ROSE 39 28
THE BUTTERCUP BOG-END WHERE THE FLOWERS ROSE UP 90 20
THE FIRE ROSE UP IN THE BUSH AND BLAZED APACE 94 25
AND I ROSE IN FEAR NEEDING YOU FEARFULLY 99 6
OF LIGHTS EACH SOLITARY ROSE 104 25
IN MY FLAME OF LIVING THE INVISIBLE HEART OF THE ROSE 115 8
A RED ROSE GOES ON THE WIND ASCENDING 150 9
THE FACE OF THE YOUNGEST ROSE 150 16
THE HAWK IS GONE A ROSE IS TAPPING 150 18
KNOCK KNOCK 'TIS NO MORE THAN A RED ROSE RAPPING 150 20
WHAT THEN IF A SCARLET ROSE GOES FLAPPING 150 22
LIKE A DARK ROSE A MYSTERY OF REST 154 10
THE OTHER WOMAN ROSE AND SWIFTLY SAID 157 27
ONE ROSE OF WONDERMENT UPON THE TREE 219 6
HOW WILL YOU HAVE IT THE ROSE IS ALL IN ALL 219 9
BLOSSOM MY DARLING BLOSSOM BE A ROSE 219 17
OF ROSES UNCHIDDEN AND PURPOSELESS A ROSE 219 18
FROM THE ROSE OF ALL ROSES 285 2
FROM THE UNFOLDED ROSE 285 3

ROSE
ROSE OF ALL THE WORLD 285 4
ISSUE OF THE EXPLICIT ROSE 285 8
THE OPEN-COUNTENANCED SKYWARD-SMILING ROSE 285 9
OURS IS THE UNIVERSE OF THE UNFOLDED ROSE 285 12
BEFORE THE ROSE BEGAN TO SIMPER SUPREME 285 16
BEFORE THE ROSE OF ALL ROSES ROSE OF ALL THE WORLD WAS + 285 17
OF WHICH WORLD THE VINE WAS THE INVISIBLE ROSE 285 30
THE VINE WAS ROSE OF ALL ROSES 286 2
WHEN THE VINE WAS ROSE GODS WERE DARK-SKINNED 286 14
AND THE TINY VINE-FLOWER ROSE OF ALL ROSES PERFUMED 286 27
THE ROSE WOULD SMELL AS SWEET 292 5
THEY SAW TINY ROSE CYCLAMENS BETWEEN THEIR TOES GROWING 310 14
ROSE CYCLAMEN ECSTATIC FORE-RUNNER 311 21
ROSE OF THE OLDEST RACES OF PRINCESSES POLYNESIAN 314 4
NETTLES AND A ROSE SPROUT 316 1
TO THEE I ROSE LIKE A ROCKET ENDING IN MID-HEAVEN 322 8
BUT HE ROSE AND FROM A TERROR WORSE THAN ME HE FLEW PAST 344 5
WHEN SHE ROSE TILTING HER PARASOL AND SMILED AT THE 445 1
WOULD BE LOVELY IF THEY ROSE FROM THE MAN HIMSELF SPONT+ 520 10
OH THE ROSE OF ENGLAND IS A SINGLE ROSE 534 23
AND THAT'S WHAT'S HAPPENED TO THE ENGLISH ROSE 534 27
THE WILD ROSE IN A SHELTERED GARDEN 535 1
TILL AT LAST IT'S A FULL FULL ROSE AND HAS NO MALE DUST+ 535 7
OH THE ROSE OF ENGLAND IS A SINGLE ROSE 535 13
THEN SUDDENLY THE MASTODON ROSE WITH THE WONDERFUL LADY 540 5
I ROSE UP IN THE WORLD OORAY 551 25
ROSE VERY HIGH FOR ME 551 26
BUT STILL I ROSE QUITE HIGH IN THE WORLD 552 3
UP I ROSE MY LADS AN' I HEARD YER 552 17
AND STILL IN SPITE OF ALL THEY DO I LOVE THE ROSE OF EN+ 569 1
AND INSTANTLY ROSE A GREAT UPROAR 574 22
BUT THE DAY THEY BURN MY PICTURES THEY BURN THE ROSE OF 634 9
DEEPER DOWN THE CHANNEL THEN ROSE SHALLOWER SHALLOWER 693 9
BECAUSE THE LORD ALMIGHTY ROSE A BIT TOO HIGH 710 10
A ROSE TREE BRONZEY WITH THORNS 714 10
AND STRANGELY O CHILLED WAN SOUL A FLUSH OF ROSE 720 10
A FLUSH OF ROSE AND THE WHOLE THING STARTS AGAIN 720 11
WHEN IN THE MORNING I ROSE TO DEPART MY LOVE CAME TO SA+ 749 17
THE GREY NURSE ENTERED A ROSE GARDEN 753 8
I ROSE AGAIN TO SEE A STAR FALLING AND FEEL A BREATH ON 786 10
THE COCK ROSE AND CREW OVER THE WATERS 802 11
AND BETWEEN OUR FINGERS ROSE A BLADE OF GREEN GRASS 806 27
THEIR FEATHERS LIFELESS AND THE ROSE LIGHTS TURNING TO + 855 28
AND I'LL LIE IN HER LAP WHERE THE WORLD'S WILD ROSE 858 6
WITH THE FIRST DAWN I ROSE TO LOOK IN THE GLASS 860 11
AS A WHITE ROSE STREWS THE GROUND 868 7
FOR ME WHO AM COLD AS A CHRISTMAS ROSE 877 34
THE FIRE ROSE UP AND THE BUSH BLAZED FORTH GOD'S GRACE *897 13
THEY WOULD SAY SEEING EACH MOUTH OF WHITE ROSE PRAISE *941 6
YOU HIGHLY EVERY BLOOD-RED ROSE DISPLAY *941 7
A ROSE OF MEMORY WITH A SCENT OF PRAISE *941 15
NOW LIKE A ROSE COME TIP-TOE OUT OF BUD *943 18
AND BEYOND THE EAGLE ROSE AND THE PHOENIX PARENT SOARIN+ *946 23

ROSE-BRIARS
AND ROSE-BRIARS TO STRANGLE THE MACHINE 634 30

ROSE-BUSH
HERE I AM ALL MYSELF NO ROSE-BUSH HEAVING 218 9
BY ALL THE BLOOD OF THE ROSE-BUSH INTO BEING 218 17
THE GUELDER ROSE-BUSH IS HUNG WITH CORONETS 854 21
A ROSE-BUSH UNTO YOU IN ALL THEIR HEARTS *941 14

ROSE-COLOUR
THE PRIESTS TO WEAR ROSE-COLOUR OR MAGENTA IN THE STREE+ 609 17

ROSE-FLOWERS'
FROM THE RED ROSE-FLOWERS' FIERY TRANSIENCE 219 14

ROSE-FRUITS
OR THE RIPE ROSE-FRUITS OF THE LUSCIOUS FALL 219 10

ROSE-HOT
IN ROSE-HOT TIPS AND FLAKES OF ROSE-PALE SNOW 304 20

ROSE-LEAVES
ROSE-LEAVES THAT WHIRL IN COLOUR ROUND A CORE 218 15
ROSE-LEAVES TO BEWILDER THE CLEVER FOOLS 634 29

ROSE-PALE
IN ROSE-HOT TIPS AND FLAKES OF ROSE-PALE SNOW 304 20

ROSE-RED
ROSE-RED PRINCESS HIBISCUS ROLLING HER POINTED CHINESE + 313 27
PURE BLOOD AND NOBLE BLOOD IN THE FINE AND ROSE-RED VEI+ 314 1

ROSES
OF THE BLOSSOM ARE ROSES TO LOOK AT BUT FLAMES WHEN THE+ 93 32
WHOSE LOFTY ROSES BREAK AND BLOW 104 23
THE ROSES LEAN DOWN WHEN THEY HEAR IT THE TENDER MILD 137 4
MANY ROSES IN THE WIND 149 25
THE ROSES WITH THE WEST WIND RAPPING 149 29
ALL THE ROSES AND UNENDING 150 6
OF A ROSE-TREE MOVE TO ROSES AND THORNS AND A DELICATE + 176 9
I SHALL PUT ROSES ON ROSES AND COVER YOUR GRAVE 176 11
WITH MULTITUDE OF WHITE ROSES AND SINCE YOU WERE BRAVE 176 12
WHEN THE AUTUMN ROSES 178 1
WHEN THE AUTUMN ROSES 178 12
WHEN IN THE AUTUMN ROSES 178 23
WE FOUND THE DARK WILD ROSES 217 2
WAS SAVOUR OF ICE AND OF ROSES AND GLIMMERING 217 5
GLOIRE DE DIJON 217 18
LIKE WET AND FALLING ROSES AND I LISTEN 217 21
MELLOW AS THE GLORY ROSES 217 26
JUST A FEW OF THE ROSES WE GATHERED FROM THE ISAR 217 27
ROSES ARE READY TO FALL RELUCTANT AND LOTH 217 30
I AM BEAUTIFUL I LOOK AT THE RUMPLED YOUNG ROSES 218 2

ROSES
  IN STARK-CLEAR ROSES THAN I TO MYSELF AM BROUGHT   218 12
  OF ROSES UNCHIDDEN AND PURPOSELESS A ROSE   219 18
  WE LOOK BACK ON THE WITHERING ROSES   242 28
  SO MANY FRUITS COME FROM ROSES   285 1
  FROM THE ROSE OF ALL ROSES   285 2
  BEFORE THE ROSE OF ALL ROSES ROSE OF ALL THE WORLD WAS +   285 17
  THE VINE WAS ROSE OF ALL ROSES   286 2
  AND THE TINY VINE-FLOWER ROSE OF ALL ROSES PERFUMED   286 27
  BUT ROSES IF THEY'RE FED TOO MUCH   534 25
  THEY ARE ALL DOUBLE ROSES   535 11
  IS SETTLED ON THE LAND ROSES ARE SCARCE IN ENGLAND VERY   569 8
  ROSES OF ENGLAND   634 22
  WILD ROSES OF ENGLAND   634 23
  MEN WHO ARE WILD ROSES OF ENGLAND   634 24
  FRAGRANCE OF ROSES IN A STALE STINK OF LIES   634 28
  YOU MAY SMELL THE BREATH OF THE GODS IN THE COMMON ROSES   655 7
  AND ROSES WONDERED AT HER PRAYER   753 5
  ROSES ARE ONLY ONCE-WILD ROSES THAT WERE GIVEN AN EXTRA+   831 2
  A HAT QUAINTLY CURIOUSLY WOVEN LUXURIOUS WITH BIG ROSES   856 12
  ROSES   856 14
  AND BESIDE IT ON THE TABLE HER GLOVES AND MY WILTED WIL+   856 15
  OF MY WILTED WILD ROSES PINK AND IVORY WHITE   856 18
  AND RIVER-LAMPS LIKE FULL-BLOWN ROSES   *916 21
  I WOULD PUT ROSES ON ROSES AND COVER YOUR GRAVE   *940 26
  WITH MULTITUDE OF WHITE ROSES AND JUST A FEW   *940 27
  WE FOUND OUR WARM WILD ROSES   *942 13
  WAS SCENT OF ROSES AND GLIMMERING   *942 16
  IN THE TWILIGHT OUR KISSES ACROSS THE ROSES   *942 17
  MET AND HER FACE AND MY FACE WERE ROSES   *942 18
  GLOIRE DE DIJON ROSES   *942 27
  LIKE WET AND SHAKEN ROSES AND I LISTEN   *943 4
  AS IF ROSES FOUGHT WITH ROSES   *943 9
  JUST A FEW OF THE ROSES WE GATHERED FROM THE ISAR   *943 10
  UNDER THE SUMMERY FLOWERING OF THE ROSES OF LOVE   *951 12

ROSES'
  WHERE ROSES' SHADOWS DAPPLED HER   753 9

ROSE-TREE
  OF A ROSE-TREE MOVE TO ROSES AND THORNS AND A DELICATE +   176 9

ROSINESS
  FOR ROSINESS ONLY WITHOUT AN ULTERIOR MOTIVE   219 19
  THE COURAGE OF ROSINESS IN A CABBAGE WORLD   634 27

ROSY
  FROM THIS ROSY TERROR OF BIRTH THAT HAS SLID DOWN   88 24
  SEE HOW IT RISES WITH MAGICAL ROSY SAP   172 10
  THE SUN IMMENSE AND ROSY   193 14
  THE SNOW-TOPS SHINING ROSY   226 14
  ROSY TENDER GLITTERING WITHIN THE FISSURE   278 26
  AND OPEN IT SO THAT IT IS A GLITTERING ROSY MOIST HONIE+   282 3
  BENDING THEIR ROSY MUZZLES PENSIVE DOWN   311 11
  ROSY ROSY SCARLET   313 22
  AND ROSY DELICATE HIBISCUS FLOWERS   317 30
  THE ROSY RIVER THAT SPRANG   766 17
  MY ROSY RIVER MY BEST   766 22
  RUDDY ROSY AND ORANGE   766 27
  ROSY BEST OF THE BLOOD GONE OUT OF THE BODY   767 22
  HE'S LIKE A BONNY ROSY SEA-CRAB WITH HEALTHY CLAWS   830 19
  THE CAMPIONS DRIFT IN FRAGILE ROSY MIST   854 11
  ROSY WRACK   854 20
  THE SOFT CLUSTERED SHOULDER-FEATHERS IN ROSY CONFUSION +   855 23
  OF SUNSET BUT MERGING UNNOTICED INTO THE ROSY GLIMMER   860 5
  THE ROSY PERIWINKLES THAT CLUSTERED AND LEANED ACROSS   863 24
  BUT I WAS ROSY FOR HIM FOR HIM I DID FLUSH MELLOW   *933 25

ROSY-MUZZLED
  PAGAN ROSY-MUZZLED VIOLETS   311 31

ROSY-RED
  AND ROSY-RED HIBISCUS WINCINGLY   317 22

ROT
  AND ROT LIKE A BEAN-POD WHAT ARE YOU OH MULTIFORM   73 19
  WHAT ROT TO SEE THE CABBAGE AND HIBISCUS-TREE   316 18
  WHAT ROT TO SAY THE LOUTS ALONG THE CORSO   316 20
  THIS SUPERIOR ROT   556 24
  WHAT ARE YOU GOOD FOR BUT TO BE SLAVES AND ROT AWAY   795 8

ROTATE
  SLOWLY ROTATE TILL THEY TOUCH THE TREE   52 5
  SLOWLY ROTATE TILL THEY TOUCH THE TREE   *899 19
  SLOWLY ROTATE TILL THEY TOUCH THE TREE   *902 31

ROTS
  THAT NOBODY EATS AND NOBODY WANTS SO IT ROTS BUT IS NOT   462 21
  THE GUTS AND THE STONES AND THE WOMB ROTS THEM DOWN   463 21
  WHICH ROTS THE BRAIN THE BLOOD THE BONES THE STONES THE   487 16
  INTO ROLLICKING SUNS AND THEIR LOST GOLD ROTS COMPRESSED   *896 20

ROTTED
  AND FAKED LOVE HAS ROTTED OUR MARROW   654 9

ROTTEN
  OH EARTH YOU ROTTEN APPLE ROLLING DOWNWARD   73 3
  AND STILL BY THE ROTTEN ROW OF SHATTERED FEET   146 23
  COME QUICKLY AND STIR THE ROTTEN GLOBE OF THE WORLD FROM   273 7
  I LOVE YOU ROTTEN   280 1
  MAKING IT ALL ROTTEN INSIDE   432 9
  BEWARE O MY DEAR YOUNG MEN OF GOING ROTTEN   462 17
  ROTTEN INSIDE THEY ARE AND SEETHING   462 23
  IF YOU'RE DIRTY INSIDE YOU GO ROTTEN AND ONCE ROTTEN WOE   464 6
  OR THE WHOLE TREE MAY FALL ROTTEN   677 29
  I'LL TURN THEIR BLOOD LIKE SOUR MILK ROTTEN WITH THUNDER   792 6
  THEY WILL BLEED ROTTEN BLOOD IN PESTILENCE   792 7
  THE BITTER AND SWEET RAW AND THE ROTTEN   825 2

ROTTENNESS
  DELICIOUS ROTTENNESS   280 2
  AND ROTTENNESS SOON SETS IN   284 5
  A VAPOUR OF ROTTENNESS OUT OF THEIR MOUTHS LIKE SEWER-S+   462 27

ROTTING
  NOT THIS VAST ROTTING CABBAGE PATCH WE CALL THE WORLD   315 32
  SLOW WATERY ROTTING BACK TO LEVEL MUCK   318 2
  AND IN THEM IS ROTTING AWAY   534 14
  ROTTING WOOD   677 22

ROUGE
  IF YOU DON'T USE ROUGE AND A LIP-STICK IN PARIS   433 12

ROUGH
  BE ROUGH AND HAIRY I'M GLAD THEY'RE LIKE THAT   254 12
  HOW ROUGH THAT WOULD BE ON YOU DARLING   433 18
  SHOULD HEAR ALL THE ROUGH WORDS   565 6
  IN A BOAT ON A ROUGH SEA WHEN WE WERE ALL NEARLY SEA-SI+   842 13
  HER FRUIT IS UNRIPE AND HER SOFT MOUTH IS BITTER AND RO+   864 18
  THE ROUGH SNOWBALL IN THE PLAYGROUND STANDS HUGE AND ST+   *898 11
  THE ROUGH SNOWBALL IN THE PLAYGROUND STANDS HUGE AND ST+   *901 20

ROUGHER
  DIDN'T TREAT HIM ROUGHER   494 17

ROUND-BARRED
  THE UPSTART OF YOUR ROUND-BARRED SUN-ROUND TAIL   370 21

ROUNDED
  ROUNDED LIKE PEARLS FOR SLEEP AND THEN FROM BETWEEN SHU+   88 16
  WHY WERE WE NOT LEFT ROUNDED OFF AND FINISHED IN OURSEL+   364 8
  OVER THE ROUNDED SIDES OF THE ROCKIES THE ASPENS OR   408 23
  AND THEN TO LOOK BACK TO THE ROUNDED SIDES OF THE SQUAT+   409 21
  HERE IN THE SUBTLE ROUNDED FLESH   *906 20
  MOVING VIBRATING ENDLESSLY IN THE ROUNDED FLESH   *906 24
  ROUNDED AND SWELLING TOWARDS THE FRUIT OF A DREAM   *908 4
  HERE IN THE SUBTLE ROUNDED FLESH   *908 16
  OF MEN VIBRATING IN ECSTASY THROUGH THE ROUNDED FLESH   *908 21

ROUND-EYED
  TO ROUND-EYED US   380 29

ROUNDLY
  THEM DOWN ON THE COUNTER ROUNDLY   236 26

ROUNDNESS
  WHO SHOOK THY ROUNDNESS IN HIS FINGER'S CUP   69 9
  GOD SHOOK THY ROUNDNESS IN HIS FINGER'S CUP   *915 21

ROUNDNESSES
  WHY THE LOVELY BIVALVE ROUNDNESSES   279 18

ROUND-SHOULDERED
  ROUND-SHOULDERED HAG MY SIRS TO THINK   81 18
  ROUND-SHOULDERED HAG MY SIRS TO THINK   *923 18

ROUND-TURNING
  AM I NOT BLIND AT THE ROUND-TURNING MILL   288 17

ROUSE
  BUT WE MAUN MA'E THE BEST ON'T SO NOW ROUSE UP AN' LOOK+   83 14
  SLOWLY SLOWLY TO ROUSE   465 12
  TILL I ROUSE MY WILL LIKE A FIRE TO CONSUME   *895 28
  TILL I ROUSE MY WILL LIKE A FIRE TO CONSUME   *904 17

ROUSED
  WHEN INTO THE NIGHT THE YELLOW LIGHT IS ROUSED LIKE DUST   70 20
  HOW DID YOU LOVE HIM YOU WHO ONLY ROUSED   158 1
  WHEN INTO THE NIGHT THE YELLOW LIGHT IS ROUSED LIKE DUS+   *917 17

ROUSES
  IN ONE MOMENT ROUSES INSURGENT   39 6
  AND ONE AFTER ANOTHER ROUSES   51 13
  WHEN IT'S LEFT ALONE AS IT STIRS AND ROUSES AND SLEEPS   464 31
  RULING THE EARTH ROUSES NO EAGERNESS IN ME AT ALL   840 17
  AND ONE AFTER ANOTHER ROUSES   *898 25
  AND ONE AFTER ANOTHER ROUSES   *902 9

ROUSING
  SNOW AND THE SILENCE OF SNOW HEAVY ON THE ROUSING DAY   865 11

ROUT
  MY SOUL ALONG WITH THE ROUT   107 22
  PUT TO ROUT   168 25

ROUTINE
  WORK AND PRISONERS' ROUTINE   518 12

ROVE
  BEING DEAD YOU SHALL ROVE LIKE DOGS WITH THE BROKEN HAU+   796 5

ROVER
  AS ON A NEST THE ROVER   125 1
  SLOWLY INTO ANOTHER DAY SLOWLY THE ROVER   132 29
  SHE SWOOPED HER HAND AND THE ROVER   *936 1

ROW
  SLEEP IN A ROW THE OUTCASTS   144 15
  AND STILL BY THE ROTTEN ROW OF SHATTERED FEET   146 23
  I LIKE A ROW WITH THEM   316 15
  WHAT A HUGE VAST INANIMATE IT IS THAT YOU MUST ROW   353 25
  ROW ON THEN SMALL PEBBLE   357 26
  TO ROW FORWARD AND REACH HIMSELF TALL ON SPINY TOES   358 1
  HER FOLDS OF SKIN THAT WORK AND ROW   362 18
  THE LAST ROW IS FINISHED THE JINGLING RAKE IS LIFTED   858 17
  ROW LITTLE SOUL ROW ON   *959 15

ROWING
    ROWING SLOWLY FORWARD   352 28
    FOUR ROWING LIMBS AND ONE WEDGE-BALANCING HEAD   356 7
    THEIR SPLAY FEET RAMBLING AND ROWING LIKE PADDLES   361 24
    AND ROWING ON UNARRIVED NO MATTER HOW OFTEN HE ENTER   380 23

ROWS
    IN LEVEL ROWS   50 20
    INSCRUTABLE SMALL LIGHTS GLITTER IN ROWS   163 26
    HANGING UPSIDE DOWN LIKE ROWS OF DISGUSTING OLD RAGS   342 3
    WHILE SHE PULLS HERSELF FREE AND ROWS HER DULL MOUND   362 10
    AND ROWS AMONG THE FEMALES LIKE A SHIP PERTINACIOUSLY   380 18
    SITTIN' THERE IN ROWS ON YOUR SHELVES   553 24
    BELOW THE PIT-LIGHTS GLITTER IN ROWS   857 26

ROW'S
    AND THAT IS WHAT THE ROW'S ABOUT   579 12

ROYAL
    THE GRASS DEEP DOWN WITH THE ROYAL BURDEN OF HER   123 5
    WALKING LIKE A ROYAL SNAKE DOWN THE MOUNTAIN   293 20
    HELL RISEN IN PURSUIT OF HER ROYAL SUMPTUOUS   308 15
    AND ALL THE EASTERN EXQUISITE ROYAL PLANTS   313 30
    ROYAL SUMMONS DIENT IHR   390 21
    VERY VERY LOW TO THE ROYAL   391 31
    BEING ROYAL OF THE GODS   392 8
    THE GRASS DEEP DOWN WITH HER ROYAL BURDEN AND I   *934 11

ROYALLY
    MY SHADOW IS NEITHER HERE NOR THERE BUT I I AM ROYALLY +   34 8
    ROYALLY GESTICULATE   286 6

ROYAL PALACES
    THERE ARE NO MICE IN OUR ROYAL PALACES OMIT IT   670 6

ROYALTY
    THE NATIVE ROYALTY OF RED HIBISCUS FLOWERS   314 18
    HE IS ROYALTY PALE AND DEJECTED FRAGMENT UP ALOFT   388 13
    THEY ARE ROYALTY DARK-FACED ROYALTY SHOWING THE CONSCIO+   388 22
    TO THAT TIRED REMNANT OF ROYALTY UP THERE   389 26
    SERVE ROYALTY   390 24
    THEY HAD COME TO SEE ROYALTY   391 27
    TO BOW BEFORE ROYALTY IN THE LAND OF ELEPHANTS BOW DEEP   391 28
    DRINK A LITTLE BLOOD AND LOSING ANOTHER ROYALTY UNTO   414 27

RUB
    WASH YOURSELF AND RUB OIL IN YOUR SKIN   791 21

RUBBER
    AFTER PARTRIDGES OR A LITTLE RUBBER BALL   430 23
    COFFEE FROM THE BUSHES IN THE HOT LANDS EVEN THE JUICY +   793 22

RUBBER-LIKE
    INTO RUBBER-LIKE DEADNESS DUNLOP INFLATED UNCONCERN   625 18

RUBBISH
    ALL RUBBISH READY FOR FIRE   316 35
    THINK OF THE RUBBISH YOU'RE TRIFLING IN   457 7

RUBBISH-HEAP
    AND SET THE STINKING RUBBISH-HEAP OF THIS FOUL WORLD   315 23

RUBBLE
    STANDS RUBBLE OF STUNTED HOUSES ALL IS REAPED   135 7
    A RUBBLE OF STUNTED HOUSES STANDS UNREAPED   *939 7

RUBS
    AND RUBS THE SILVER CLEAN WITH HIS THICK BROWN FINGERS   734 2
    FORWARDS AS HE RUBS THE WOUND   734 7
    SOILING THE CLEAN WHITE DUST HE RUBS THE BELLY   734 9

RUBY
    IS THERE A RUBY OF FUSED BEING MINE AND YOURS AN INWARD   478 7
    I SEE HIM MORE LIKE THE RUBY A GLEAM FROM WITHIN   697 28
    COMING LIKE THE RUBY IN THE INVISIBLE DARK GLOWING   697 30

RUDDILY
    TRAMS THAT PASS BLOWN RUDDILY DOWN THE NIGHT   146 13

RUDDY
    IS WARM WITH A RUDDY GLOW   37 15
    DARK RUDDY PILLAR FORGIVE ME I   40 9
    SLOWLY THE MOON IS RISING OUT OF THE RUDDY HAZE   67 7
    WHICH LIES ON THE KNEES OF THE NIGHT-TIME RUDDY AND MAK+   88 21
    COULD I BUT SEAL ITS RUDDY SHINING SPRING   153 25
    LET THE DARKNESS BE WARMED WARMED THROUGH TO A RUDDY VI+   273 24
    O RUDDY GOD IN OUR VEINS O FIERY GOD IN OUR GENITALS   440 12
    RUDDY ROSY AND ORANGE   766 27
    HIS RUDDY ARMS GLOW ACROSS HER   868 8
    IN SHOWERS OF MINUTE RUDDY DROPS FROM THEIR BLADES   884 29
    BETWEEN THE RUDDY SCHOOLS SWEEPS ONE BLACK ROOK   *898 10
    BETWEEN THE RUDDY SCHOOLS SWEEPS ONE BLACK ROOK   *901 19

RUDDY-MUZZLED
    CYCLAMENS RUDDY-MUZZLED CYCLAMENS   311 22

RUDDY-ORANGE
    AND RUDDY-ORANGE LIMBS STIRRING THE LIMBO   667 7

RUDIMENT
    ON THIS SMALL BIRD THIS RUDIMENT   356 15

RUDIMENTS
    TO THE PRIMEVAL RUDIMENTS OF LIFE AND THE SECRET   365 21

RUDOLF VALENTINO
    THE FILM FACE OF RUDOLF VALENTINO   538 2

RUE DE LA PAIX
    I SWEAR I'LL PULL OFF MY KNICKERS RIGHT IN THE RUE DE L+   433 20

RUFFLE
    LIFT AND RUFFLE IN THE WIND   883 3

RUFFLED
    IN THE HOUSE OF LIFE THE FLOOR WAS RUFFLED WITH GOLD   141 6
    TOSSED ON THE LOW BLACK RUFFLED HEAP   145 13
    AS SHE THRUSTS THEM UPWARD UNDER THE RUFFLED SKIRT   145 30
    YOU RUFFLED BLACK BLOSSOM   369 1

RUFFLING
    WHO WITH A RUFFLING CAREFUL BREATH   46 13
    RUFFLING BLACK SHINING FEATHERS LIKE LIFTED MAIL   370 24

RUG
    WITH HER LONG TANGLED SIDES LIKE AN OLD RUG THROWN   384 26
    AND A NAVAJO WOMAN WEAVING HER RUG IN THE PATTERN OF   448 22

RUGS
    THE WHITE RUGS ON THE FLOOR NOR THE SILENT BED   155 3

RUIN
    DOWN THE BRIGHT-GREY RUIN OF THINGS   150 23
    FOR RUIN ON THE NAKED SMALL REDOUBT   160 24
    OF THRILLING RUIN IN THE FLESH OF PUNGENT PASSION OF RA+   273 19
    AND RUIN ABOVE US AND THE CRASH OF RELEASE   462 15
    AND THE RUIN OF ANY DECENT RELATION   470 21
    AND EFFORT IS THE RUIN OF ALL THINGS   613 14
    THEN FAR BEYOND THE RUIN IN THE FAR IN THE ULTIMATE REM+   625 1
    BUT OVER THE MIDDLE OF THE EARTH WILL BE THE SMOKY RUIN+   625 8
    AND RUIN OF HER INNOCENCE UPON   880 29
    RATTLE THE RAIN-DROPS RUIN THE APPLES   *933 9

RUINED
    EPILEPTICALLY RUINED   537 3
    TILL YOU'VE RUINED A NATION'S FIBRE   537 15

RUINS
    WHITE EARTH AND RUINS OURSELVES AND NOTHING BESIDE   166 8
    WHEN YOUR WORLD IS IN RUINS UNDER YOUR FALLEN SKIES   289 20
    AND RUINS OUR COMPLEX HARMONY   529 10

RULE
    IN THE RULE   149 12
    WINGS FULL OF STARS THEY RULE THE NIGHT AND MAN THAT WA+   319 3
    DOMINANT WOMEN ARE AS A RULE SO SUBTLY AND FIENDISHLY D+   619 24

RULERS
    HAS SICKENED US THOROUGHLY WITH RODS OF IRON AND RULERS   439 26
    AND RULERS OF MILLIONS OF ROBOTS BEING ROBOTS THEMSELVES 637 20

RULES
    WHICH RULES THE ROBOT-CLASSES AND THE ROBOT-MASSES NOW   639 18

RULING
    THAT STRONG ONE RULING THE UNIVERSE WITH A ROD OF IRON   439 25
    NOR IS HE A STRONG MAN RULING THE EARTH   840 16
    RULING THE EARTH ROUSES NO EAGERNESS IN ME AT ALL   840 17

RUM
    AY IT'S A RUM UN   140 6

RUMBLE
    TO ME MEN'S FOOTFALLS FALL WITH A DULL SOFT RUMBLE   288 28

RUMBLING
    LITTLE LION AND RUMBLING   396 30

RUMMAGED
    THEN SHE RUMMAGED HER HAND IN 'ER BOSOM AN' KISSED THE + *910 20

RUMP
    MOULTING AND RATHER NAKED ABOUT THE RUMP AND DOWN IN THE 329 23
    YOUR DEMON RUMP TWINKLING   564 17

RUMPLED
    I AM BEAUTIFUL I LOOK AT THE RUMPLED YOUNG ROSES   218 2

RUN
    STRING TO RUN ON   33 26
    OF UNDERWATER FLOAT BRIGHT RIPPLES RUN   51 7
    THEY POISE AND RUN LIKE PUFFS OF WIND THAT PASS   64 31
    RUN TO THE SILENT DOOR WHERE LAST   122 4
    WHILE T' CLOCKS 'AS A' RUN DOWN AN' STOPPED   137 28
    I TURN AND RUN   143 17
    HURRYING CREATURES RUN   166 22
    RUN PERSEPHONE HE IS AFTER YOU ALREADY   309 15
    IN THE LONG RUN IN SPITE OF THEMSELVES   317 5
    WITH CAVERNOUS NOSTRILS WHERE THE WINDS RUN HOT   325 30
    THAT YOU HAVE TO RUN OUT AT LAST AND EAT FILTH   398 27
    AND THEN YOU RUN IN TO VOMIT IT IN MY HOUSE   399 4
    YOU RUN STRAIGHT AWAY TO LIVE WITH SOMEBODY ELSE   399 13
    INDIANS DANCE AND RUN AND STAMP   407 11
    THE PENITENTES LASH THEMSELVES TILL THEY RUN WITH BLOOD   408 4
    COULD ONE AT NIGHT RUN UP AGAINST THE STANDING FLESH   428 2
    MUST RUN THE PATTERN OUT IN A LITTLE BREAK AT THE END   448 24
    AND RUN TOWARDS IT BENT   462 33
    RUN TINY RIVERS OF PEACE   496 12
    SMOOTH RUN   531 17
    AND YOU'VE GOT TO RUN TO KEEP UP WITH IT   543 15
    BUT SOMETIMES WE RUN AHEAD TOO FAST   543 16
    WE CAN RUN OUR OWN SHOW   573 20
    ANOTHER LITTLE RUN FOR THEIR MONEY A FEW MORE TURNS OF + 586 18

RUN
THE MACHINES WILL TURN TO RUN INTO ONE ANOTHER   624 26
ABOVE THE COMMON RUN   626 18
THE MACHINE WILL RUN ON AND ON AND ON   643 1
LET THEM RUN ON AND ON AND ON   643 6
YOU WHO FEEL NOTHING WHO KNOW NOTHING WHO RUN ON   643 16
IS DEAD WE RUN WHEELS ACROSS HER CORPSE   703 8
NO WHEELS MIGHT RUN NO INSOLENT CHARIOTS   703 25
SO WHEN I RUN AT LENGTH THITHER ACROSS   742 5
THE CATTLE RUN ANXIOUS IN QUEST AS THE TIME DRAWS NIGH   749 25
AND THEN RUN LIKE SURLY DOGS AT THE BIDDING OF PALEFACE+   795 4
RUN UP THE FLAMES AND WITH FEET ON THE SPARKS   798 21
NOR RUN ASLANT HIS RAYS   806 9
AT THE MOMENT WE TEND TO RUN INSANE THE MIND HAVING BRO+   838 21
I RUN AWAKE TO THE HOUSE OF MY SOUL AND FIND IT EMPTY   871 9
OF UNDER-WATER FLOAT BRIGHT RIPPLES RUN   *898 19
OF UNDER-WATER FLOAT BRIGHT RIPPLES RUN   *902 3
AND RIPPLES POISE AND RUN LAPPING ACROSS THE WATER   *912 27
THEY POISE AND RUN LIKE RIPPLES LAPPING ACROSS THE WATER   *914 1
FAR AND WIDE RUN THE EASY ROOTS THAT BEAR THE LEAVES OF+   *926 12

RUNG
RUNG OF THEIR LIFE-LADDERS' FRAGILE HEIGHTS   854 3

RUNNELS
DRIPPING OVER THE RUNNELS   94 12
DRIPPING OVER THE RUNNELS   *896 28

RUNNEST
WHEN THOU RUNNEST THE RACE WITH THE FOREMOST GOD BLESS +   750 2

RUNNING
WITH FIRE AS IT GUARDS THE WILD NORTH-COASTS RED-FIRE S+   57 13
LIKE A WIND-SHADOW RUNNING ON A POND SO SHE COULD STAND   65 6
THE TRAIN IN RUNNING ACROSS THE WEALD HAS FALLEN INTO A+   88 1
ONCE I HAD A LOVER BRIGHT LIKE RUNNING WATER   119 23
THERE IS SOMETHING I WANT TO FEEL IN MY RUNNING BLOOD   180 30
I DID NOT REMEMBER WHY SHOULD I THE RUNNING LIGHTS   243 27
FISH-BLOOD SLOWLY RUNNING NEXT TO THE FLOOD EXTRACTING   336 31
RUNNING BESIDE HER LIKE A DOG BITING HER EARTHY SPLAY   360 8
AND RUNNING AWAY FROM THE SOUND OF A WOMAN IN LABOUR   366 12
MEN-PEASANTS FROM JUNGLE VILLAGES DANCING AND RUNNING   389 5
GLEAMING LIKE METAL WITH RUNNING SWEAT AS THEY SUDDENLY   389 9
WHAT WOULD THEY DO THOSE JUNGLE MEN RUNNING WITH SWEAT   389 32
RUNNING DOWN RUNNING DOWN TRICKLING   454 2
RUNNING AFTER A FIGMENT OF OURSELVES   543 17
BURN THAT HE SEES EVE RUNNING FROM THE LIKES OF HIM I   633 28
THE EGO RUNNING IN ITS OWN COMPLEX AND DISCONNECTED   635 9
THE SMALL ONES EGO-BOUND LITTLE MACHINES RUNNING IN AN   637 5
AS FREE AS THE RUNNING OF ANGEL'S FEET   746 18
AS A HARPIST RUNNING ALONG THE STRINGS   747 12
A FALLING STAR WAS RUNNING LIKE A WHITE DOG OVER A PLAIN   791 1
THIS IS THE MASSIVE SOLID FLY-WHEEL WHICH SAVES MAN FRO+   838 19
EVE RUNNING WITH SWIFT LIMBS QUICKENED BY DREAD   864 19
ONCE I HAD A LOVER BRIGHT LIKE RUNNING WATER   *933 13
WITH GOLDEN CHICKS OF CLOUD AND A SKY OF RUNNING LAUGHT+   *933 15

RUNS
AND THE WATER RUNS AND RUNS FASTER RUNS FASTER   34 4
RUNS SEEKING A LONELINESS   64 9
LESS THAN THE WIND THAT RUNS TO THE FLAMY CALL   116 13
MY LIFE RUNS OUT   131 12
I TELL YOU MY BLOOD RUNS OUT ON THE FLOOR OF THIS OAK   131 13
RUNS INTO SPEED LIKE A DREAM THE BLUE OF THE STEEL   136 9
OF THE STRONG MACHINE THAT RUNS MESMERIC BOOMING THE   149 13
RUNS WASTE DOWN THEIR CHALICES   177 4
HE RUNS IN THE SNOW LIKE A BIT OF BLUE METAL   375 3
RUNS A RAGE DRAWN IN FROM THE ETHER DIVINELY THROUGH HIM   381 21
LIBIDINOUS DESIRE RUNS BACK AND FORTH ASSERTING ITSELF +   386 15
OUT INTO THE OPEN WHERE THE PATH RUNS ON THE TOP OF A   387 4
SOFT GRASS RUNS UPON A PATH THAT IS PATHLESS TO MEN SO +   406 3
THEY CANNOT DIE THEIR CORPSE STILL RUNS ON   675 19
THAT RUNS DOWN TO THE SHALLOWS OF MY WRISTS AND BREAKS   705 5
WHOSE POWER RUNS TO THE SHORES ALONG MY ARMS   705 15
RUNS RICHLY FROM US   743 19
AND DARKNESS RUNS THE RACING WHEEL   773 6
WHO RUNS ATHWART MY SERPENT-FLAME   805 6
UNINHABITED SPACE NOW RUNS   823 25
RUNS INTO THE SHADOW WITH HER CAPTURE A FEW LITTLE BITE+   864 17
RUNS ECSTATIC OVER THE PLIANT FOLDS RIPPLING DOWN TO MY+   *891 32

RUPEES
FOR FOR 3-1 2 RUPEES   760 14

RUPTURE
RUPTURE   280 28

RUPTURED
SHOWN RUPTURED   278 30

RUSH
ON A SUBTLE RUSH OF COOL GREY FLAME   68 2
THE SUBTLE STEADY RUSH OF THE WHOLE   68 13
ALL MY LIFE IN A RUSH   107 10
DO YOU RUSH TO ASSAIL ME   140 29
THE STAR-LIT RUSH OF A HARE   152 17
WHILE DAYS RUSH WAVE AFTER WAVE   159 5
IT CURVES IN A RUSH TO THE HEART OF THE VAST   166 26
SWIFT TRAINS GO BY IN A RUSH OF LIGHT   169 2
COME RUSH OF CREATION   271 1
IN A GREAT CHUTE AND RUSH OF DEBACLE DOWNWARDS   287 21
A RUSH THAT ALMOST SCREAMS   336 15
ONCE A BIG PIKE RUSH   338 19
IN A RUSH UP THE SHRIEKING DUCT OF HIS VERTEBRAL WAY   381 20
OR ELSE RUSH HORIZONTAL TO CHARGE AT THE SKY'S HORIZON   392 18
COOL UNLYING LIFE WILL RUSH IN   482 22
HOW THEY RUSH OUT AND WANT TO RIVE   494 3
AS FOR THOSE OVER FIFTY EITHER THEY RUSH FORWARD   502 16

RUSH
AND RUSH ABOUT IN MACHINES   558 22
AND ENGINES WILL RUSH AT THE SOLID HOUSES THE EDIFICE O+   624 28
HENCE THE RIDICULOUS WAY THEY RUSH IN WHERE ANGELS FEAR+   665 20
MADLY WE RUSH HITHER AND THITHER   739 21
AND THE LONG WAVES RUSH AND PLY   746 23
OH TO SEE THE LONG WAVES RUSH   747 1
RUSH IN AND FILL THE LIVING CAVITIES   784 11
THEN DRIVEN BACK IN A NEW SILENT RUSH   784 14
HOW NICE IN THE GREAT CITIES WHERE ALL THINGS RUSH AND +   794 15
WITH A STEADY RUSH OF LIVING A FOAM   888 7
ON THE SUBTLE RUSH OF THE COOL GREY FLAME   *914 17
THE SUBTLE STEADY RUSH OF THE WHOLE   *914 28

RUSHED
NO SOUND OF GUNS NOR OVERHEAD NO RUSHED   165 31
AS I RUSHED LIKE AN IDIOT ROUND THE CORNER AFTER YOU   396 8
WE WADE WE WADE WE STAGGER DARKNESS RUSHED   425 6
THEN OUT OF NOWHERE RUSHED JOHN BULL   491 25

RUSHES
THE COMMON FLAUNTS BRAVELY BUT BELOW FROM THE RUSHES   33 10
OH WATER-HEN BESIDE THE RUSHES   43 1
WHICH RUSHES UPWARD BLADE BEYOND BLADE   49 23
THE VOICE OF THE FURTIVE TRIUMPHANT ENGINE AS IT RUSHES+   58 4
RUSHES STAMPEDING DOWN   99 20
RUSHES   116 5
OF RUSHES ERE THE ROMANS   171 11
LIFE STILL MORE LIFE RUSHES INTO US TO COMPENSATE TO BE   449 7
THE BREATH THAT RUSHES THROUGH MY NOSE THE STRIFE   461 3
SO THAT IT RUSHES UP IN A HUGE BLAZE LIKE A PHALLUS   506 6
SHE LAYS AN EGG HE BRISTLES LIKE A DOUBLE WHITE POPPY A+   761 19
AMONG THE SHADOWS OF BLOSSOMS AND TREES AND RUSHES   867 26
THE COMMON FLAUNTS BRAVELY BUT BELOW FROM THE RUSHES   *891 11

RUSHING
THEY SEEM TO BE BECKONING RUSHING AWAY AND   140 24
SHUDDERING STORM WIND OR A WATER RUSHING THROUGH   -370 25
RUSHING IN LIKE A LITTLE BLACK WHIRLWIND LEAPING STRAIG+   397 2
AND THAT SENT THE BLOOD RUSHING TO THE SURFACE OF THE B+   502 7
GIVE WAY ALL THE TIME BEFORE THE MECHANICAL RUSHING OF +   665 26
AMID THE AUTUMN RUSHING RED ABOUT   744 22
I SEE DARK THINGS RUSHING ACROSS THE COUNTRY   794 10
HOW NICE SAYS THE PEON TO GO RUSHING IN A TRAIN   794 13
TO EXTINCTION RUSHING   862 25

RUSHINGS
SICKEN US AND WE ARE STUNNED BY THE RUSHINGS OF THE LAB+   856 2

RUSSIA
OVER THERE IS RUSSIA AUSTRIA SWITZERLAND FRANCE IN A   213 1
RUSSIA ACROSS HER CRISIS   536 10
THE BIG FLAMBOYANT RUSSIA   536 12
TO THE RUSSIA THAT NEEDED HIM MOST   536 19
THE CLUMSY BEWILDERED RUSSIA   536 20
I HAVE TRAVELLED IN RUSSIA TWO HOURS OR MORE   866 26
OF RUSSIA THROUGH THE NEW GREAT NAIVETE OF RUSSIA HER W+   866 29

RUSSIAN
OF THE RUSSIAN NOBILITY   537 6

RUSSIANS
THE RUSSIANS   777 2

RUST
FLY SLOWLY AWAY WITH A RUST OF FIRE IN YOUR TAIL   374 30
WITH BITS OF BRINDLE COMING THROUGH LIKE RUST TO SHOW   395 2
ABOUT MOTH AND RUST   561 11
SCARLET AND CRIMSON AND A RUST OF BLOOD   744 30

RUSTED
BLACK RUSTED IRON TRUNK   300 27
WITH IRON BRANCHING BLACKLY RUSTED LIKE OLD TWISTED   301 13
THERE IS NO WAY OUT THE CAGE HAS NO DOOR IT'S RUSTED   486 1

RUSTIES
ACROSS YOUR RUSTIES   563 12

RUSTLE
RUSTLE OF LEAVES WASHES OUT THE RENDING   150 7
IF YOU HEAR A RUSTLE   231 12
AND SINKS DOWN WITH A SWIFT RUSTLE AND A STRANGE FALLING   651 15

RUSTLED
WHERE THE BLUE CRABS RUSTLED IN QUEST OF HER AIMLESS WI+   864 6

RUSTLES
SILENCE THAT RUSTLES BEYOND THE STARS THERE   76 11
THAT RUSTLES BEYOND THE STARS TO ME THERE   *898 13
THAT RUSTLES BEYOND THE STARS TO ME THERE   *901 14

RUSTLING
AND THE SOUND OF HER GENTLY RUSTLING IN HEAVEN LIKE A   134 18
OR THEY ARE LIKE LEAVES RUSTLING THICK IN THE CROWDS ON+   615 8
OUR BRIDE AMONG THE RUSTLING CHORUS OF SHELLS   743 9
WE ARE LIKE TREES TALL AND RUSTLING   802 16
THE STREET THAT IS FULL OF THE RUSTLING SOUND OF A SHELL *917 2
FOR THE RUSTLING OF THEIR WHITE UNFOLDING PETALS   *943 5

RUSTY
SEEING RUSTY IRON PUFF WITH CLOUDS OF BLOSSOM   304 6
THE RUSTY SWORDS OF ALMOND-TREES   304 24
RUSTY TIN   356 27

RUT
HE FELL INTO THE RUT OF LOVE   378 10
POOR ASS LIKE MAN ALWAYS IN RUT   378 11

RUTHLESS
THEN MERCILESS AND RUTHLESS   203 1
IT IS SO DEEP A MOLOCH RUTHLESS AND STRONG   264 15

RUTHLESSLY
AND RUTHLESSLY STRANGLED OFF THE FANTASIES   141 28
BUT PRUNING SEVERELY INTELLIGENTLY AND RUTHLESSLY PRUNI+   677 27
BUT SOFTLY SOFTLY AND RUTHLESSLY   766 5

RUTS
AND HER FINGERS MOVE IN THE RUTS OF MY EARS   863 3

RYE
THE RYE IS TALLER THAN YOU WHO THINK YOURSELF   221 6
MOANING FOR ME TO LOVE HIM O DARLING RYE   221 13
THE RYE IS TALLER THAN YOU WHO THINK YOURSELF   *944 19
O DARLING RYE   *944 27

SABBATH
OF OUR SABBATH SUFFUSING OUR SACRED DAY   148 3

SABLE
SAVE IN A BROKEN PATTERN AMID PURPLE AND GOLD AND SABLE   90 6

SACKCLOTH
PUT ASHES ON YOUR HEAD PUT SACKCLOTH ON   234 21
PUT SACKCLOTH ON BE CROWNED WITH POWDERY ASH   234 27

SACK-WISE
AND ALL HER WEIGHT ALL HER BLOOD DRIPPING SACK-WISE DOWN   394 21

SACRED
A MOMENT THEN DARKNESS SHUT THE LID OF THE SACRED ARK   62 18
OF OUR SABBATH SUFFUSING OUR SACRED DAY   148 3
AND IN A GREAT AND SACRED FORTHCOMING STEPS FORTH STEPS   306 6
AND ALL THE SACRED GENTRY   557 1
IN THE SACRED SILENCE OF GATES   699 4

SACRED FISH
THE CROSS THE VIRGIN PISCES THE SACRED FISH   616 24

SACREDNESS
THERE IS A DOUBLE SACREDNESS OF DOORS   711 7

SACRIFICE
TAKEN LIKE A SACRIFICE IN THE NIGHT INVISIBLE   90 26
OOZES AWAY FROM ME AS A SACRIFICE STEAM   131 9
YOU'RE A DOVE I HAVE BOUGHT FOR SACRIFICE   238 17
HERE IN MY ARMS MY NAKED SACRIFICE   238 19
I SACRIFICE ALL IN HER MY LAST OF THE WORLD   239 2
IN PYRAMID MEXICO DURING SACRIFICE   371 8
CAN BE PUT OUT OF OFFICE AS SACRIFICE BRINGER   374 35
IT CANNOT BE ANYTHING BUT WRONG TO SACRIFICE   678 2
BUT WHAT WE MAY SACRIFICE IF WE CALL IT SACRIFICE FROM +   678 10
SACRIFICE THAT TO THE BRIGHT GODS AND SATISFY THE DESTR+   678 17
O SACRIFICE NOT THAT WHICH IS NOBLE AND GENEROUS AND SP+   679 1
THE OLD IDEA OF SACRIFICE WAS THIS   679 8
AND SACRIFICE IS THE LAW OF LIFE WHICH ENACTS   679 20
AND TO SACRIFICE THAT TO ANYTHING OR ANYBODY WHATSOEVER   680 1
WILL YOU LIKE AN AZTEC SACRIFICE REVERSED   783 20

SACRIFICED
ALMOST I HATED HER SACRIFICED   62 21
O WHEN THE OLD WORLD SACRIFICED A RAM   679 11

SACRIFICES
CERTAIN WAYS PERFORM CERTAIN SACRIFICES   775 30

SAD
FRAIL AND SAD WITH GREY BOWED HEAD   64 4
SO I AM NOT LONELY NOR SAD   109 7
SAD AS HE SITS ON THE WHITE SEA-STONE   130 1
SHOWS IN ONLY TWO SAD PLACES   145 6
TO THIS SAD END   152 23
IS ONLY SAD MEN TAKING OFF THEIR SHIRTS   173 24
THE SUN WARMS THE SEA LITTLE LONELY AND SAD SIFTING THE+   180 3
IN THE WIND'S SAD SOUGH   252 19
AND THE YOUNG BULL IN THE FIELD WITH HIS WRINKLED SAD F+   255 33
GOES OFF IN SLOW SAD LEAPS   393 26
IN MENTAL CONTACT GAY AND SAD   469 2
FOR ONE SAD CENTURY   623 29
IN SOFT SEPTEMBER AT SLOW SAD MICHAELMAS   697 2
SO SWEET LIKE A SWOON OR MORE LIKE THE DROWSE OF A LOW +   727 11
AND PEOPLE ARE SAD AND GRIM   846 10
HOLD UP JEANNETTE WHY POOR OLD GIRL ARE YOU SAD   859 29
LIKE SAD PROCESSIONS OF EXILES YOU COULD HAVE SEEN THEM+   866 3
OF RUSSIA THROUGH THE NEW GREAT NAIVETE OF RUSSIA HER W+   866 29
ON AND IS SAD   *892 6
OF A LIVE SAD WORK UNFINISHED   *927 27
SOMEHOW SO SAD SO INTRINSIC SO SPIRITUAL YET SO CAUTIOU+   *932 13
FOR ONE SAD CENTURY   *953 16
IN SOFT SEPTEMBER AT SLOW SAD MICHAELMAS   *955 26

SADDEN
INTO THE NIGHT AND ARE LOST TO SADDEN WITH JETSAM THE D+   *918 8

SADDEST
AND SO THERE CAME THE SADDEST DAY   555 5

SADDLE
AND A SOLDIER IN THE SADDLE OF THE LEFT-HAND DRAUGHT-HO+   733 8
THERE HE SITS IN THE SADDLE OF THIS THE FIVE   733 11
OUT OF THE SADDLE AND STAGGERING   733 16
SWUNG STRONG AND HEAVY TO SADDLE AGAIN   735 13

SADIST
SAID RONALD YOU SEE IS QUITE A CLEVER SADIST   *948 10

SAD-LIDDED
HIS BLACK SAD-LIDDED EYE SEES BUT BEHOLDS NOT   362 4

SADLY
I SADLY WENT MY WAY   569 19

SAD-MOVING
PREACHING IN SAD-MOVING SILENCE A HEART-HUNGRY PURITY   855 3

SADNESS
EITHER IN ANGER OR TENDERNESS OR DESIRE OR SADNESS OR W+   672 4
THEY ARE LORDS OF THE DESOLATE WASTES OF SADNESS THEIR +   *891 4

SAFE
STARS ARE NOT SAFE IN HEAVEN   49 15
THAT HERE WE'RE SAFE FROM EVEN THE ERMINE MOTH'S   113 23
THE OPTIMIST BUILDS HIMSELF SAFE INSIDE A CELL   515 7
MAKE YOU FEEL SAFE   522 16
SAFE INSIDE THEIR BOTTLES   542 28
SAFE INSIDE THEIR BOTTLES   542 32
SAFE FROM EVERY CONTACT   543 5
SAFE FROM ALL EXPERIENCE   543 6
SAFE ABOVE ALL FROM LIFE   543 7
MY LITTLE CRITICS DEAR SAFE LITTLE PETS   581 26
EDITOR STERNLY HAVE YOU BEEN MADE SAFE FOR THE GREAT   582 12
BY SOME MALIGNANT FISHERMAN ON AN UNSEEN SAFE SHORE   586 10
THE MAN ANDREW KEEP HIM SAFE IN THE WAR   751 10
WATCH THE STIR WHOSE RHYTHM IS SECRET WHOSE SECRET IS S+   *907 13
THAT HERE WE'RE SAFE FROM EVEN THE ERMINE MOTH'S   *929 12

SAFE-ISH
SEVEN IS STILL A SAFE-ISH AGE   842 27

SAFELY
WHERE THE LARK NESTS SAFELY   *953 24

SAFER
SAFER THAN IN THE ARMS OF JESUS   543 1
OH SAFER THAN ANYTHING ELSE IN A WELL-CORKED GLASSY EGO   543 2

SAFETY
AS IF THERE WAS SAFETY IN NUMBERS EVEN FOR FAITH   626 6

SAGE
DOWN ON MY HEARTH-RUG OF DESERT SAGE OF THE MESA   408 27
PLEASED TO BE OUT IN THE SAGE AND THE PINE FISH-DOTTED +   409 18

SAGE-ASH
ON THE SAGE-ASH DESERT   373 2

SAGE-GREY
DAY HAS GONE TO DUST ON THE SAGE-GREY DESERT   403 21
IN THE FLOCCULENT ASH OF THE SAGE-GREY DESERT   780 24

SAGGED
OF THE SKY SAGGED DUSTY AS SPIDER CLOTH   98 14

SAIL
SHAKES THE SAIL   53 6
A VOYAGE TO SAIL BEYOND THE CHARTED SEAS   168 3
HOW YOU SAIL LIKE A HERON OR A DULL CLOT OF AIR   332 16
DOES THE SUN IN NEW MEXICO SAIL LIKE A FIERY BIRD OF PR+   374 12
SAIL ON OVER PERILOUS SEAS OF THOUGHT   542 12
SAIL LITTLE SHIPS IN YOUR GLASS BOTTLES   543 4
UPON THE SEA OF DEATH WHERE WE STILL SAIL   719 8
BREATHING ON HIS SMALL FRAIL SAIL AND HELPING HIM ON   723 23
WITH THE OLD SWEET SOOTHING TEARS AND LAUGHTER THAT SHA+   *905 19
NO LONGER SHAKE WHERE THE SILK SAIL FILLS   *906 4
RIGGING ITS MAST WITH THE SILENT INVISIBLE SAIL   *961 1

SAILING
OF EASY SAILING ODD RED WICKS SERVE   172 20
SLOWLY SAILING IN GORGEOUS APPAREL THROUGH THE FLAME-LI+   387 30
AND LET THE SLIM BLACK SHIP OF DIONYSOS COME SAILING IN   688 4
INTO FORGETFULNESS SOFT SAILING WATERS WHERE FEARS   *906 3

SAILS
NO LONGER HURT WHERE THE SILK SAILS FILL   53 12
WITH MASTS ERECT AND SPARS ALL SET AND SAILS SPREAD   542 2
SPREAD YOUR SMALL SAILS IMMUNE LITTLE SHIPS   543 10
ADVANCING WITH THE SLOW-SWIFTNESS OF A SHIP BACKING HER+   672 21

SAINT FRANCIS
SAINT FRANCIS HIMSELF WAS A RICH AND SPOILED YOUNG MAN   498 11

SAINTS
AND THE IMAGES OF MY MOTHER AND THE IMAGES OF MY SAINTS   789 18
SEND JESUS HIS IMAGES BACK MARY AND THE SAINTS AND ALL   791 20
ALL MY SAINTS AND ANNA TERESA   798 7
HO ALL MY SAINTS AND MY VIRGINS   798 17

SAINTY-SAINTS
AND OUR SAINTY-SAINTS LET US DOWN   537 8

SAITH
WRETCHES UTTER WRETCHES KEEP YOUR HANDS FROM BEANS SAITH   303 15
VENGEANCE IS MINE SAITH THE LORD   541 8
VENGEANCE IS MINE SAITH THE LORD I WILL REPAY   616 1

SAKE
    WITH SWEAT I'LL ENTER A HOUSE FOR THY SAKE   44   8
    FINISHING YOUR DREAMS FOR YOUR OWN SAKE ONLY   197   6
    FOR GOD'S SAKE LET US BE MEN   450   12
    AT LAST FOR THE SAKE OF CLOTHING HIMSELF IN HIS OWN LEA+   451   21
    FOR GOD'S SAKE LET US STOP OH YOU WHO STAND BEHIND US   756   1
    AND FOR THE SAKE OF THIS NASCENT UNBORN AS-YET-UNKNOWAB+   775   10
    AT LAST AND FOR THE SAKE OF CLOTHING HIMSELF IN HIS OWN+   *950   7

SALAAM
    AS THEY APPROACH AND SALAAM UNDER THE DRIPPING FIRE OF   388   3
    CLUMSY KNEE-LIFTING SALAAM   388   10

SALAAMS
    THE KEEPER HOODS THE VAST KNEE THE CREATURE SALAAMS   387   16

SALAMANDERS
    THE DEAD THAT HAVE MASTERED FIRE LIVE ON SALAMANDERS IN+   796   7

SALARY
    EARNING A SALARY IS A PRISON OVERSEER'S JOB   521   9

SALESWOMAN
    SHE PUTS ME AWAY LIKE A SALESWOMAN WHOSE MART IS   128   3

SALLIES
    SALLIES OF SWINGING FRUIT   861   5

SALLOW
    THE BREEZE WAKES UP A MUSIC IN THE SALLOW   868   21
    THE BREEZE WAKES UP A MUSIC IN THE SALLOW   *941   21

SALLOW'S
    PASS LIKE A TUNE THE SALLOW'S GOLDEN NOTES   *941   24

SALLY
    AND FEARFUL TO SALLY FORTH DOWN THE SKY'S LONG RANGE   132   20
    BITTER TO FOLD THE ISSUE AND MAKE NO SALLY   160   25
    AFRAID OF THE WORLD BUT TO SALLY FORTH   550   23
    SALLY GO ROUND THE SUN   755   22
    SALLY GO ROUND THE MOON   755   23
    SALLY GO ROUND THE CHIMNEY-POTS   755   24

SALT
    SPRINKLING INCENSE AND SALT OF WORDS   151   28
    LIKE SALT BURNING IN   206   21
    HOW I KNOW THAT GLITTER OF SALT DRY STERILE SHARP CORRO+   207   17
    SALT   207   18
    BURNING OF POWERFUL SALT BURNING EATING THROUGH MY   207   23
    THE PILLAR OF SALT THE WHIRLING HORRIBLE COLUMN OF SALT+   207   28
    SNOW OF SALT WHITE BURNING EATING SALT   207   31
    YOU PILLAR OF SALT ACCURSED   207   35
    PUT SALT ON HIS TAIL   329   1
    YET PUT SALT ON THE TAIL OF THE JOHANNINE BIRD   329   14
    PUT SALT ON ITS TAIL   329   15
    OF ETERNAL SALT RAGE ANGRY IS OLD OCEAN WITHIN A MAN   454   11
    SLOWLY THE SALT OF THE EARTH BECOMES SALT OF THE SEA   495   1
    CARRY THE SALT OF THE EARTH THE WISDOM OF WISE MEN   495   3
    SLOWLY THE SALT OF THE EARTH BECOMES SALT OF THE SEA   495   9
    THAT PUTS SALT ON THE TAILS   562   10
    LOVE CANNOT LIVE BUT ONLY BARE SALT SPLINTERS   693   22
    AND THROUGH THE SALT THEY REEL WITH DRUNK DELIGHT   694   10
    AND ALL THIS HAPPINESS IS THE SEA IN THE SALT   695   5
    TO THE WHITE-TREADING WAVES OF TWO SALT FEET   705   17
    SALT IS SCORCHED WATER THAT THE SUN HAS SCORCHED   706   6
    SO SALT IS THE BOUNDARY MARK BETWEEN FIRE THAT BURNS AN+   706   10
    ARE MARKED OUT WITH THE BOUNDARY OF SALT BETWEEN FIRE A+   706   14
    DON'T SPILL THE SALT FOR IT IS THE LAND MARK   706   15
    AND HANDS LIKE SALT   707   12
    WHO PUT SALT IN OUR MOUTHS   707   21
    THOSE THAT PUT HONEY ON OUR LIPS AND THOSE THAT PUT SALT   709   28

SALT-BURNS
    GAVE ME SWEET LYMPH AGAINST THE SALT-BURNS   208   6

SALTY
    GLITTERS IN SALTY TRIUMPH   455   9
    INTO SALTY NOTHINGNESS   455   11
    DRAGONS OF SALTY WATERS DRAGONS OF THUNDER   796   19

SALUTE
    AND BUILT UP THE WAY I SALUTE THEE   40   22
    THAT I SALUTE THE RED HIBISCUS FLOWERS   316   28
    AND I SALUTE HIBISCUS AND THE SALVIA FLOWER   317   1

SALUTED
    WHITE MAN YOU ARE SALUTED   387   17
    HIS WORK TOOK PLACE IT CAME TO PASS IT STOOD UP AND SAL+   690   7

SALUTING
    I AM THEIR SUPERIOR SALUTING THE HIBISCUS FLOWER NOT TH+   316   23
    PAST SALUTING SWORDS OF THE ANGELS   770   16

SALVATION
    THE ONLY SALVATION IS TO REALISE THAT WE KNOW NOTHING A+   613   11
    AND ONCE DONE THERE IS NO REMEDY NO SALVATION FOR THIS   621   10

SALVIA
    ALAS SALVIA AND HIBISCUS FLOWERS   313   10
    SALVIA AND HIBISCUS FLOWERS   313   11
    SALVIA AND HIBISCUS FLOWERS   313   13
    SALVIA AND HIBISCUS FLOWERS   313   15
    SALVIA AND HIBISCUS FLOWERS   313   18
    OR SALVIA   314   25
    OR DRAGON-MOUTHED SALVIA WITH GOLD THROAT OF WRATH   314   26
    FLAME-FLUSHED ENRAGED SPLENDID SALVIA   314   27
    YOU LOOK WELL WITH YOUR SALVIA FLOWERS I MUST SAY   314   34
    WOULDN'T I STICK THE SALVIA IN MY COAT   315   12

SALVIA
    THE ANGER-REDDENED GOLDEN-THROATED SALVIA   315   15
    SALVIA STILL IN A RAGE   316   3
    AND I SALUTE HIBISCUS AND THE SALVIA FLOWER   317   1
    AND SALVIA FIERCE TO CROW AND SHOUT FOR FIGHT   317   21
    WHO HAVE PULLED DOWN THE SALVIA FLOWERS   317   29
    THAT THEY TAKE HIBISCUS AND THE SALVIA FLOWER   318   6

SALVIA-FACE
    A BOLSHEVIST A SALVIA-FACE   315   25

SALVIA-FRENZIED
    NO SALVIA-FRENZIED COMRADES ANTENNAE   317   8

SALVIAS
    PUT SALVIAS AND HIBISCUS   313   21
    IS YOUR WRATH RED AS SALVIAS   314   30

SALVIA-SAVAGE
    IF THERE WERE SALVIA-SAVAGE BOLSHEVISTS   315   10

SAME
    THE SAME VALLEY WITH PURPLE AND WHITE   37   28
    THOUGH IT'S ALL THE SAME WHEN WE ARE DEAD   41   17
    WHENCE COMETH WHITHER GOETH STILL THE SAME   69   26
    LEARNING OF THEIRS IT ALL GOES DOWN THE SAME ABYSS   74   26
    AND THE SAME FIRE THAT BOILS WITHIN THIS BALL   89   1
    A GRAIN OF THIS SAME FIRE WE CAN DESCRY   89   20
    AT THE SAME TIME STAND EXPOSED   108   1
    A DARKNESS THAT DREAMS MY DREAM FOR ME EVER THE SAME   115   12
    SAME   129   3
    RETURNING I FIND HER JUST THE SAME   150   24
    AT JUST THE SAME OLD DELICATE GAME   150   25
    TO HAVE YOU STILL THE SAME   170   2
    AND GRIEF ARE BUT THE SAME LAST WONDER SLEEP   196   2
    IT WOULD BE SIMPLY THE SAME   214   15
    THE SAME WANT LIFE OR DEATH   214   17
    THE SAME INSANITY OF SPACE   214   19
    HAS SHE NOT FLED ON THE SAME WIND WITH ME   222   20
    THE SAME AS BEFORE   231   11
    YOU ARE HELD BACK BY MY BEING IN THE SAME WORLD WITH YOU   235   31
    RISEN NOT BORN AGAIN BUT RISEN BODY THE SAME AS BEFORE   258   29
    MYSELF THE SAME AS BEFORE YET UNACCOUNTABLY NEW   258   34
    I WANT HER THOUGH TO TAKE THE SAME FROM ME   266   23
    NOW I SEE THEM JUST THE SAME AND WATCH THEM   269   20
    THIS IS THE SAME THAT PICKS UP THE HARVEST OF WHEAT   271   21
    THE SAME THAT DANGLES THE GLOBE-SHAPED PLEIADS OF FRUIT   271   23
    AT THE SAME TIME IT OPENS THE TINY HANDS OF THE HAZEL   272   20
    THE SAME SETS THE THROSTLE AT SUNSET ON A BOUGH   272   25
    SOMETHING OF THE SAME FLAVOUR OF SYRACUSAN MUSCAT WINE   280   9
    SHE QUICKLY SEWED FIG-LEAVES AND SEWED THE SAME FOR THE+   284   8
    THE SAME UNREMARKABLE SUNDAY SUIT   312   16
    THE SAME I SAY TO THE PROFITEERS FROM THE HOTELS THE MO+   316   24
    THE SAME I SAY TO THE PALE AND ELEGANT PERSONS   316   26
    THE PROCESS WILL AMOUNT TO THE SAME IN THE END   317   35
    THE SAME CRY FROM THE TORTOISE AS FROM CHRIST THE OSIRI+   367   3
    SAME AS BEFORE   391   24
    ALL THE SAME   398   24
    THEY FEEL QUITE TENDER OVER YOU TILL YOU PLAY THE SAME   399   17
    I SAY HE CAN GO BACK THE SAME GAIT   405   24
    GNAWS JUST THE SAME GNAWING THE SUBSTANCE OUT OF LIFE   432   12
    JUST THE SAME   432   24
    JUST THE SAME   432   26
    AND THE SAME FLAME THAT FILLS US WITH LIFE IT WILL DANC+   440   15
    BUT AT THE SAME TIME DON'T LET'S THINK   470   9
    I WOULD SAY THE SAME IF I WERE A CHAFFINCH OR TREE   499   3
    AND GRACE IF I DON'T LOSE IT FROM THE SAME PLACE   499   5
    AND IN THE MIDDLE OF EVERY ATOM WHICH IS THE SAME THING   512   6
    THE SAME WITH THE FISHERMEN SITTING DARNING THEIR NETS   520   17
    ON A NARROW BEAT ABOUT THE SAME AS A PRISONER TAKING HIS   521   17
    AND AMOUNTS TO VERY MUCH THE SAME THING   523   7
    AND AT THE SAME TIME EXPECT TO GO ON CALMLY EATING GOOD   531   6
    THEY MAKE IT UP AND IT'S ALWAYS THE SAME   549   23
    YOU THINK THEY'RE THE SAME AS YOU ARE   549   25
    AND EVERY TIME THE SAME   554   30
    ALL EYES SOUGHT THE SAME OLD SPOT   578   2
    AREN'T THEY MADE QUITE THE SAME THEN AS YOU AND I   578   15
    THOSE THAT ARE FRESH AND ALIVE ARE THE SAME IN EVERY   612   10
    THE BREATH OF LIFE AND THE SHARP WINDS OF CHANGE ARE TH+   615   16
    AND EACH TIME IT CAME OUT THE SAME A HORRIBLE SEXLESS L+   619   10
    WOMEN WOMEN THE SAME   635   5
    FOR LISTEN THE EGO-CENTRIC SELF IS THE SAME AS THE MACH+   635   8
    THE SAME   637   21
    IT IS ALL THE SAME   637   25
    THE SAME WITH MY ROBOT NEIGHBOURS   645   6
    AND THE ROBOT IS DENIAL OF THE SAME   649   17
    AND IT ALL AMOUNTS TO THE SAME THING FURNITURE   657   9
    WHICH TURNS ON AND ON THE SAME AND IS HELL ON EARTH   662   24
    THIS PLACE TODAY THESE SOLDIERS WEAR THE SAME   732   11
    AND THEIR UNIFORMS ARE THE SAME OF WHITE AND BLUE   732   13
    IT IS THE SAME THIS DEATH   742   4
    SOME SUGAR OF THE SAME WHITE SORT   751   6
    WOMEN THE SAME   771   7
    AS RICH AS ANYBODY ELSE ON THE SAME TERMS   778   15
    OF HIS HAIR SAY THE SAME TO THE WOMEN   791   25
    BUT THE STAR IS THE SAME FOR BOTH OF US   812   7
    THOU SIPS THEM UP AND 'TIS ALL THE SAME   824   15
    AT THE SAME TIME THEY TAKE THE GREATEST POSSIBLE CARE O+   832   4
    AT THE SAME TIME WE LEARN A LOT   832   26
    IN THE SAME WAY IF I SWORE TO HATE A WOMAN ALL MY LIFE +   834   10
    IN THE SAME WAY CHASTITY IN ITS HOUR IS SWEET AND WHOLE+   845   11
    WITH YOUR TIRED EYES JEANNETTE WE SUFFER THE SAME DON'T+   859   31
    STILL TO ANSWER ME JUST THE SAME   873   8
    AFTER ALL THIS TIME IT SHOULD BE THE SAME   874   11
    THE SAME EDEN WITH PURPLE AND WHITE   *892   16
    A DARKNESS THAT DREAMS MY DREAMS FOR ME EVER THE SAME   *930   12

SAMLETS
    JIMLETS AND SELF-SORRY SAMLETS   457 20

SAMSON
    I DO NOT YEARN NOR ASPIRE FOR I AM A BLIND SAMSON   287 25
    THEY ARE NOT STRONGER THAN I AM BLIND SAMSON   288 11
    I MUST SEE IF I CAN'T ABSORB THIS SAMSON OF SELF-ABSORP+   605 14
    THEY HAD LONG HAIR LIKE SAMSON   688 23

SAN CRISTOBAL
    FELIPE AND SAN CRISTOBAL   798 6

SANCTIFIED
    TODAY SOCIETY HAS SANCTIFIED   620 22

SANCTIFY
    WHICH MANKIND AT LARGE HAS CHOSEN TO SANCTIFY   620 21

SANCTITY
    SURE ON OUR SANCTITY   242 31
    IN THE ODOUR OF LUCRATIVE SANCTITY   457 1

SANCTUARIES
    IN SOME HEARTS STILL THE SANCTUARIES OF WILD LIFE   *954 2

SANCTUARY
    AH NO IN THE HEARTS OF SOME MEN THERE STILL IS SANCTUARY *953 23

SAND
    NO SAND IN MY DOUBTFUL SUGAR   236 30
    I AM COVERING MYSELF WITH THE SAND   259 30
    EYES OF YELLOW GOLDEN SAND   301 30
    BUT IN THE ODD PATTERN LIKE SNAKE-MARKS ON THE SAND   448 26
    FROM THE HEART AND LEAVING STRANGE COLD STRETCHES OF SA+   509 4
    AND DAUBS THE SAND WITH ITS FLESH   628 6
    GOES BEHIND HIS MOTHER WHERE THE SAND IS HOT   757 9
    TEARS NOW FALL ON WHITE SAND   767 4
    LOOK BRIGHTLY ON A CONFUSION OF MUD AND SAND AND MORTAR   864 26
    AND SMALL ON THE SAND SWILLS   883 26
    THERE LIES THE DULL RED HEAP OF THEIR SAND IN THE WEST   *896 7
    THERE LIES A DULL RED HEAP OF HIS SAND IN THE WEST   *896 17
    BAWDY CAN BE SAND AND WHOLESOME   *952 10

SANDALS
    YOU ARE NEAR TO ME AND YOUR NAKED FEET IN THEIR SANDALS   208 28
    SO I TOOK THE SANDALS OF THE SAVIOUR   787 2

SAND-HILLS
    AND FAR AWAY ON THE SAND-HILLS DEWBERRIES   152 12
    BEHIND THE SAND-HILLS   883 20

SANDS
    THE HOURS HAVE TUMBLED THEIR LEADEN MONOTONOUS SANDS   167 1
    THE HOURS HAVE TUMBLED THEIR LEADEN MONOTONOUS SANDS   167 8
    WHITE SANDS AND FRUITS UNKNOWN AND PERFUMES THAT NEVER   261 2
    SHE WAS BOUGHT AT GIARDINI FAIR ON THE SANDS FOR SIX HU+   385 7
    AND SCATTERED WITH HER HAIR CLOUDS OF PALE MIMOSA SANDS   863 27
    THE HOURS HAVE TUMBLED THEIR LUSTRELESS TARNISHED SANDS   *896 6
    THE HOURS HAVE TUMBLED THEIR LUSTRELESS TARNISHED SANDS   *896 13

SANDY
    THE SANDY DESERT BENEATH HER THE DREARY PLATOON   153 4

SANE
    AND THE SANE CAN STILL RECOGNISE SANITY   516 9
    FOR THE ROBOT CLASSES AND MASSES ARE ONLY KEPT SANE   640 13
    MAN IS KEPT SANE NOT BY HIS MIND WHICH BY NATURE IS UNS+   838 16
    TO KEEP A SANE CORE TO LIFE   839 17
    BAWDY CAN BE SANE AND WHOLESOME   844 29
    TO KEEP IT SANE AND WHOLESOME   844 31
    AND A LITTLE WHORING CAN BE SANE AND WHOLESOME   845 1
    TO KEEP IT SANE AND WHOLESOME   845 3
    EVEN SODOMY CAN BE SANE AND WHOLESOME   845 4
    TO KEEP IT SANE AND HEALTHY   *952 12
    AND A LITTLE WHORING CAN BE SANE AND HEALTHY   *952 13
    TO KEEP IT SANE AND WHOLESOME   *952 15
    EVEN AT THE RIGHT TIMES SODOMY CAN BE SANE AND WHOLESOME *952 16
    IN FACT QUITE A LOT OF CHASTITY IS NECESSARY IN LIFE TO+ *952 24
    PURITY HOWEVER IS NEVER SANE AND NEVER WHOLESOME   *953 1

SANG
    WHERE ONCE THE BLOOD SANG   767 3

SANG-FROID
    AND SOME OF AFRICA'S IMPERTURBABLE SANG-FROID   296 22

SANGRE DE CRISTO MOUNTAINS
    TO THE SNOW OF THE SANGRE DE CRISTO MOUNTAINS THE ICE OF 402 23

SANITY
    WE MUST REGAIN OUR SANITY ABOUT MONEY   ‡87 11
    AND GUARD THE LAST TREASURE OF THE SOUL OUR SANITY   514 12
    IF WE LOSE OUR SANITY   514 14
    BUT IF WE LOSE OUR SANITY   514 19
    SANITY MEANS THE WHOLENESS OF THE CONSCIOUSNESS   515 1
    ONE MIGHT TALK OF THE SANITY OF THE ATOM   515 16
    THE SANITY OF SPACE   515 17
    THE SANITY OF THE ELECTRON   515 18
    THE SANITY OF WATER   515 19
    WE CALL SANITY IN OURSELVES   515 22
    THE ONLY ONENESS IS THE ONENESS OF SANITY   515 23
    WHERE SANITY IS   516 7
    AND THE SANE CAN STILL RECOGNISE SANITY   516 9
    THE LAST BIT OF SANITY   537 4
    LET US RALLY FOR OUR OWN SANITY   839 10
    AND EVEN OUR COLLECTIVE SANITY   839 11
    SANITY   *953 6

SANK
    WAITIN' TO BE SANK   60 22
    THE FULL MOON SANK IN STATE   261 23
    TO ANOTHER BALANCE TRIPPED ROUND POISED AND SLOWLY SANK   444 30
    WHERE A STREAM CAME DOWN TO THE GRAVEL OF THE SEA AND S+   693 2
    AND IT SANK TO REST FROM ME IN HIM   742 11
    WHERE OUR TED 'UD SOON BE SANK   *911 8
    HER SOUL'S FLAG SANK AND HER PRIDE PUT OFF ITS CROWN   *936 17

SANS
    SANS RAGS SANS TAGS   313 1
    SANS BEARDS SANS BAGS   313 2
    SANS ANY DISTINCTION AT ALL EXCEPT LOUTISH COMMONNESS   313 3

SAP
    THEY DRAW THEIR SAP FROM THE GODHEAD NOT FROM ME BUT TH+   93 20
    SEE HOW IT RISES WITH MAGICAL ROSY SAP   172 10
    ITS LIMPID SAP TO CULMINATION HAS BROUGHT   218 10
    COME BUBBLING SURGING TIDE OF SAP   270 31
    THE POWER OF THE RISING GOLDEN ALL-CREATIVE SAP COULD T+   272 22
    AND MILKY-SAPPED SAP THAT CURDLES MILK AND MAKES RICOTTA   283 11
    SAP THAT SMELLS STRANGE ON YOUR FINGERS THAT EVEN GOATS+   283 12
    AND THE OLD UPWARD FLOWING OF OUR SAP THE PRESSURE OF O+   609 7
    INTO THE CIRCULATING SAP ONCE MORE OF THE TREE OF LIFE   617 11

SAPIENCE
    OF PUTRESCENT WISDOM AND SAPIENCE THAT SUBTLY STINKS   441 3

SAPPHIRE
    THE WONDERFUL SLOW FLOWING OF THE SAPPHIRE   476 26
    IT TOOK AEONS TO MAKE A SAPPHIRE AEONS FOR IT TO PASS A+   477 5
    THE SAPPHIRE OF FIDELITY   477 18
    IS THERE A SAPPHIRE OF MUTUAL TRUST A BLUE SPARK   478 6
    THINK THAT THE SAPPHIRE IS ONLY ALUMINA LIKE KITCHEN PA+   530 1

SAPPHIRES
    FLOWERS AND SAPPHIRES AND US DIVERSELY STREAMING   476 28
    IN THE OLD DAYS WHEN SAPPHIRES WERE BREATHED UPON AND   477 1
    WHEN SAPPHIRES COOLED OUT OF MOLTEN CHAOS   682 22

SAPPY
    AS HAPPY AS HAPPY OH SO HAPPY YOU SAPPY   583 9

SARDONIC
    AND IF YOU LOOK AT HER SHE LOOKS BACK WITH A COLD SARDO+   386 4
    SARDONIC SARDONYX ROCK OF COLD FIRE   386 6

SARDONIC-LOOKING
    A LITTLE SARDONIC-LOOKING AS IF DOMESTICITY HAD DRIVEN +   358 24

SARDONYX
    SARDONIC SARDONYX ROCK OF COLD FIRE   386 6

SAT
    WE CLIMBED THE HUNTSMAN'S LADDER AND SAT SWINGING   216 22
    WHERE NEVER WOMAN SAT   237 19
    WHERE THE SLOW TOADS SAT BROODING ON THE PAST   310 15
    THE DOVE OF LIBERTY SAT ON AN EGG   413 1
    AND SAT UP TAKING STRANGE POSTURES SHOWING THE PINK SOL+   445 12
    OR LIKE THE WOMAN WHO SAT DOWN ON A SLEEPING MASTODON   540 1
    WHERE YOU'VE SAT PEACEFULLY ALL THESE YEARS   541 7
    THEY'VE SAT LONG ENOUGH ON THE FENCE   559 24
    HE CAME IN SLOWLY AND SAT DOWN BY THE HEARTH   692 13
    HE SAT WITHIN THE HOLLOW OF A CLOUD AND SAW THE MEN THA+   790 10
    I HAVE SAT IN THE RECREATION GROUND   866 22
    AS I LAY ON THE BED AND YOU SAT WITH THE FLOWERS ON YOU+   886 11
    WE CLIMBED THE HUNTSMAN'S LADDER AND SAT SWINGING   *942 8

SATAN
    HUNGER IS THE VERY SATAN   263 5
    FIGHT OLD SATAN WITH A SELFISH WILL FIGHT FOR YOUR SELF+   383 22
    GET THOU BEHIND ME SATAN   483 6
    THAT WAS JUST WHAT SATAN WANTED TO DO   483 7
    AND SEE SATAN BARGAINING THE WORLD AWAY   483 12
    IF JESUS HAD KEPT A SHARP EYE ON SATAN   483 16
    COME SATAN DON'T GO DODGING BEHIND MY BACK ANY LONGER   483 19
    WHEN SATAN FELL HE ONLY FELL   710 9
    SO SATAN ONLY FELL TO KEEP A BALANCE   710 12

SATANIC
    THE DARK SATANIC MILLS OF BLAKE   628 13
    HOW MUCH DARKER AND MORE SATANIC THEY ARE NOW   628 14

SATANICALLY
    WITH SATANICALLY INSPIRED FINANCIERS   483 15

SATIATE
    ON HIM WHO IS SLEEPING SATIATE   58 30

SATISFACTION
    WHICH WE MUST LEARN TO SATISFY WITH PURE REAL SATISFACT+   264 19
    STILLNESS AND SATISFACTION OF AUTUMN   503 25
    BREATHLESS SOUNDS OF SATISFACTION CLAMOUR OF DELIGHT   865 27

SATISFACTORY
    SATISFACTORY EXPERIENCE FROM IT CAN'T YOU SEE IT   463 15
    SATISFACTORY SENSUAL EXPERIENCE   653 12

SATISFIED
    STILL YOU ARE NOT SATISFIED   95 24
    I TELL THEE THA WON'T BE SATISFIED   139 8
    I TELL THEE THA WON'T BE SATISFIED   139 10
    OF FLOTSAM UNTIL MY SOUL IS TIRED OR SATISFIED   180 7
    AND NOW EVEN THEY'RE NOT SATISFIED   640 27
    AND WHY DO THE WOMEN FOLLOW US SATISFIED   743 3

SATISFIES
  I HAD EATEN OF THE BREAD THAT SATISFIES   265 8
  ALONE SATISFIES US IN THE END   653 14

SATISFY
  HAVE OPENED UP FOR US TO KNOW TO SATISFY   263 23
  WHICH WE MUST LEARN TO SATISFY WITH PURE REAL SATISFACT+   264 19
  SACRIFICE THAT TO THE BRIGHT GODS AND SATISFY THE DESTR+   678 17

SATURN
  THE MOON AND THE EARTH THE SUN SATURN AND BETELGEUSE   713 20

SAUNTERING
  SAUNTERING DOWN THE LONG SLOPE FROM THE EAST   770 21

SAUNTERS
  SAUNTERS A MAN FROM THE FARM BELOW   42 20

SAUSAGE
  THEY SOLD PLATO TO THE SAUSAGE FACTORIES OF UNIVERSITIES   762 26

SAVAGE
  LIKE SAVAGE MUSIC STRIKING FAR OFF AND THERE   52 17
  TELL ME IS THE GENTIAN SAVAGE AT THE TOP OF ITS COARSE +   684 2
  I WANT YOU TO BE AS SAVAGE AS THE GENTIAN AND THE DAFFO+   684 4
  DOZING IN THE UNDER-DEEPS THEN REACHING OUT A SAVAGE AN+   689 20
  WITH SAVAGE BLACK EYES IS SULKY AND ALL THE TIME   734 18
  HE LINGERS ON FROM AN OLD SAVAGE WORLD THAT STILL HAS   776 8
  HE IS BASICALLY A SAVAGE IT IS A TERM OF REPROACH   776 11
  THE AMERICAN INDIAN IS BASICALLY A SAVAGE   776 13
  STRICTLY DON'T FORGET IT HE IS A SAVAGE WHO HAS FOR   776 24
  BUT STRICTLY HE IS A SAVAGE   776 27
  HE IS A SAVAGE WITH HIS OWN PECULIAR CONSCIOUSNESS HIS +   776 28
  DON'T SENTIMENTALIZE HIS SAVAGE CONSCIOUSNESS   776 30
  AND BEFORE YOU PUT OUT THE OLD SAVAGE LIGHT FOR EVER   777 7
  THAN TO REMAIN A DANCING SAVAGE   778 3
  LIKE SAVAGE MUSIC STRIKING FAR OFF AND AWAY   *905 6

SAVAGELY
  AND OVER-RODE HIS MARES AS IF HE WERE SAVAGELY LEAPING +   378 6

SAVAGES
  MEDITERRANEAN SAVAGES   310 10
  DRUMMING HIS VAULTED WINGS AS SAVAGES DRUM   371 4
  OH LEAVE OFF SAYING I WANT YOU TO BE SAVAGES   684 1

SAVE
  OR SUBSTANCE SAVE I LIGHT ON YOU TO WARM   86 11
  SAVE IN A BROKEN PATTERN AMID PURPLE AND GOLD AND SABLE   90 6
  TO SAVE ME FROM THIS HAUNTED ROAD   104 22
  SAVE AS THE TRAM-CARS HOVER   144 23
  TO BEAR BUT RETALIATE NOTHING GIVEN TO SAVE   160 27
  BUT NEVER MIND MY LOVE NOTHING MATTERS SAVE SLEEP   212 10
  SAVE YOU AND ME AND SLEEP ALL THE REST WILL KEEP   212 11
  SAVE YOU HAVE IT WITH ME   226 28
  SAVE YOUR LIPS O PALE-FACES   288 23
  SAVE IT HAD FIRST APPROACHED HIM AND CAJOLED HIS SOUL   290 3
  SAVE THAT HAVING COME WITH YOU SO FAR   363 23
  BUT ALL WAS SILENT SAVE FOR PARROTS OCCASIONALLY IN THE   394 18
  GOD OF JUSTICE TO SAVE THEMSELVES   442 7
  GOD OF JUSTICE WHEN WILT THOU TEACH THEM TO SAVE THEMSE+ 443 9
  YOU MUST KNOW SEX IN ORDER TO SAVE IT YOUR DEEPEST SELF   465 3
  TO SAVE US FROM EATING DIRT   487 5
  TO SAVE THEM FROM UNDESIRABLE ASSOCIATIONS   581 22
  AND THERE IS NOTHING TO SAVE   613 12
  FOR YOU CAN'T SAVE THAT WHICH WAS NEVER LOST   614 1
  AT THE WORST YOU CAN ONLY SAVE IT UP   614 2
  AND TURN ONCE MORE TO MEN TO SAVE THEM PERSEUS ST GEORGE 619 26
  YOU TELL ME EVERY MAN HAS A SOUL TO SAVE   638 15
  SO IT CAN'T HAVE ONE TO SAVE   638 19
  SAVE SOME SHOOTS SOME LOVELY FLOWERING SHOOTS   640 19
  TO SAVE THE STREAKED PANSY OF THE HEART FROM   658 11
  THERE IS NOTHING TO SAVE NOW ALL IS LOST   658 13
  SAVE ME O GOD FROM FALLING INTO THE UNGODLY KNOWLEDGE   699 16
  SAVE ME FROM THAT O GOD   699 28
  SAVE THE COLD GHOSTS THAT HOMELESS FLOCK ABOUT   736 8
  TO HAVE NO REST SAVE IN THE UTTER NIGHT   744 15
  COME TO PASS THAT DOES NOT YET EXIST SAVE AS A SUBTLE   775 21
  SAVE FOR THE MORNING AND EVENING STARS UPON WHICH THEY + 799 22
  SAVE THEY LEAP   820 12
  AND SAVE FOR ME THE ROAD IS FORLORN   857 19

SAVED
  THE GEESE THAT SAVED ROME AND WILL LOSE LONDON   438 25
  THEY HAVE BEEN SAVED SO OFTEN   442 8
  WHEN A SAVIOUR HAS SAVED A PEOPLE   442 12
  THEY SAY WE ARE SAVED BUT WE ARE STARVING   442 14
  OR NAPOLEON SAYS SINCE I HAVE SAVED YOU FROM THE CIDEVA+ 442 20
  OR LATER REPUBLICANS SAY YOU ARE SAVED   442 23
  OR LENIN SAYS YOU ARE SAVED BUT YOU ARE SAVED WHOLESALE   443 1
  THE STATE HAVING SAVED THEM ALL   443 7
  SHE MIGHT HAVE SAVED HERSELF THE ASP   479 25
  MIGHT HAVE BEEN SAVED IF A PAIR   536 13
  OH WHAT HAVE THEY SAVED YOU FROM   585 12
  ALAS THEY HAVE SAVED YOU FROM YOURSELF   585 13
  FROM YOUR OWN BODY SAVED YOU FROM LIVING YOUR OWN   585 14
  BE SAVED   613 16
  WHAT HAVE THEY SAVED YOU FROM WHILE THEY POCKETED   630 12
  ALAS THEY HAVE SAVED YOU FROM YOURSELF FROM YOUR OWN   630 14
  THEY SAVED YOU FROM SQUALID COTTAGES AND POVERTY OF HAND 630 17
  AND THE GEESE THAT SAVED ROME WILL LOSE LONDON   *947 26

SAVES
  THAT SAVES THE BLUE GRAIN OF ETERNAL FIRE   161 3
  SAVES YOU WAFTS YOU AWAY ON THE VERY DRAUGHT MY ANGER   334 12
  NEITHER MY DEAR I HAD HIM FIXED IT SAVES HIM FROM SO   581 12
  IT SAVES HIM FROM SO MANY UNDESIRABLE ASSOCIATIONS   581 16
  THIS IS THE MASSIVE SOLID FLY-WHEEL WHICH SAVES MAN FRO+ 838 19

SAVING
  AND SO IT GOES ON WITH THE SAVING OF THE PEOPLE   443 8
  YOU REALISE THE FATUITY OF SAVING UP AGAINST POSSIBLE L+ 614 4
  THEY SHOULD FLUTTER AND TURN HIS WAY AND SAVING THE FRE+ 877 30

SAVINGS
  THEREFORE YOU ARE OUR SAVINGS OUR CAPITAL   442 24
  THE ONE THING EASIEST TO LOSE IS SAVINGS   614 5

SAVIOUR
  SO I WILL BE LIFTED UP SAVIOUR   321 7
  BUT REMEMBER SAVIOUR   322 29
  WHEN A SAVIOUR HAS SAVED A PEOPLE   442 12
  DON'T LOOK FOR A SAVIOUR   564 13
  SO I TOOK THE SANDALS OF THE SAVIOUR   787 2

SAVIOURS
  O GOD OF JUSTICE SEND NO MORE SAVIOURS   442 10
  WHAT HAVE THEY DONE TO YOU THE SAVIOURS OF THE PEOPLE   585 11
  WHAT HAVE THEY DONE TO YOU THE SAVIOURS OF THE PEOPLE OH 630 11

SAVOUR
  WAS SAVOUR OF ICE AND OF ROSES AND GLIMMERING   217 5
  SO THAT THE RAMBLING SKY-DROPPED GRAPE CAN ADD ITS SAVO+ 281 25

SAW
  SAW WHERE MORNING SUN ON THE SHAKEN IRIS GLISTENED   38 16
  I SAW YOUR BROWS   56 13
  AND I SAW HER FOR THE FLARING SPACE   62 9
  GLAD AS THE MAGI WHEN THEY SAW THE BROW   88 29
  AND TWICE AFTER WILD KISSES I SAW   103 24
  I SAW THE MIDLANDS   120 10
  I SAW HER HID IN THE SHADOW   122 2
  I SAW HER STEP TO THE KERB AND FAST   122 3
  AGAIN I SAW A BROWN BIRD HOVER   124 23
  I THOUGHT I SAW ON THE CLOVER   124 28
  ENTERING SHE SAW HIM IN OUTLINE RAISED ON A PYRE   155 17
  WITH FROZEN RIGGING SHE SAW HIM SHE DROOPED LIKE A FERN   155 22
  THE OMINOUS ENTRY NOR SAW THE OTHER LOVE   155 27
  YOUR YOUNG HUSHED LOOK THAT THEN SAW GOD ABLAZE   157 23
  I SAW THE TRANSFIGURATION   165 25
  WHAT GHOST OF US BOTH DO YOU THINK HE SAW   227 11
  NOR THE ADDER WE SAW ASLEEP WITH HER HEAD ON HER SHOULD+ 255 26
  WHEN I SAW THE TORN DEAD I KNEW IT WAS MY OWN TORN DEAD   257 7
  I SAW HER STAND AND WAIT   261 24
  BEFORE EYES SAW TOO MUCH   285 32
  THEY SAW TINY ROSE CYCLAMENS BETWEEN THEIR TOES GROWING   310 14
  HE SAW IN A SHAFT OF LIGHT A LAMB ON A PINNACLE BALANCI+ 324 16
  I SAW A WATER-SERPENT SWIM ACROSS THE ANAPO   337 24
  I SAW DIMLY   338 18
  HIS ADOLESCENCE SAW HIM CRUCIFIED INTO SEX   361 2
  IT WAS ONLY I WHO SAW THE VIRGIN YOU   411 22
  WHEN I WENT TO THE FILM AND SAW ALL THE BLACK-AND-WHITE   443 22
  AND SAW THEM CUDDLING WITH RISING PASSIONS THEY NONE OF   443 26
  I NEVER SAW THEM HOW THEY MUST SOFTEN   460 13
  I NEVER SAW A WILD THING   467 1
  I SAW THE WHOLE SUPERIOR   554 7
  TILL AT LAST I SAW THE REASON   556 9
  THEN I SAW HIM TURN TO GLANCE AGAIN SURREPTITIOUSLY   604 4
  WHEN I SAW HER STRAYING A LITTLE DAZED THROUGH HER UNTI+ 618 21
  I SUDDENLY SAW DEEP INTO THE EYES OF GOD   650 22
  I SAW SUDDENLY COMING TOWARDS ME LIT UP AND UPLIFTED WI+ 672 20
  I SAW AN ANGRY ITALIAN SEIZE AN IRRITATING LITTLE OFFIC+ 674 20
  LATELY I SAW A SIGHT MOST QUAINT   680 16
  IT IS ENOUGH I SAW YOU VANISH INTO AIR   696 28
  THE KIND OF HELL GREY DANTE NEVER SAW   714 3
  I SHOT MY MAN I SAW HIM CRUMBLE AND HANG   741 27
  SAW MY LAST HOPE START   748 24
  WHAT IF HE TURNED AND SAW ME HERE   752 4
  WHY IF YOU SAW MY LIMBS HOW THEY SHINE ON MY BODY   755 6
  TILL I SAW BENEATH ME   787 5
  AND HAVING PASSED THE YELLOW LINE HE SAW THE EARTH BENE+ 790 4
  AND HE SAW MEXICO LYING LIKE A DARK WOMAN WITH WHITE BR+ 790 5
  HE SAT WITHIN THE HOLLOW OF A CLOUD AND SAW THE MEN THA+ 790 10
  HE SAW THE MEN THAT WERE BLIND REELING WITH AGUARDIENTE   790 12
  HE SAW THE WOMEN THAT WERE NOT CLEAN   790 13
  HE SAW THE HEARTS OF THEM ALL THAT WERE BLACK AND HEAVY+ 790 14
  THE FIRST THING I DID WHEN I SAW THEM WAS TO LAUGH AT T+ 791 27
  I SAW A DARK FIGURE APPROACHING A RAGGED SOLITARY CROW   866 17
  TILL HE SAW ME BUT PLEASE SIR MY MOVVER SAID I COULD AN' 866 19
  I SAW ON THE RED EARTH   880 18
  I SAW THE BROKEN VIOLETS   880 23
  I SAW THE PAIN AMONG THE IRIS THERE   880 28
  I SAW THE SKY WAS LIT   883 19
  NAY I SAW NOWT BUT TH' COFFIN AN' TH' YELLER CLAY AN' '+ *909 31
  AND I SAW HER FOR THE FLARING SPACE   *912 16
  AND I SAW HER BOSOM COUCH IN THE NEST OF HER GOWN   *934 15
  AND THEN I SAW A BROWN BIRD HOVER   *935 29
  I THOUGHT I SAW ON THE CLOVER   *935 34

SAYIN'
  YOU MIND WHO YER SAYIN' ISN'T LIDIES   434 26
  SAYIN' UP HE GOES   552 18

SAY'T
  IF THA CANNA SAY'T COME THEN AN' SCRAIGHT IT OUT ON MY   540 14

SCABBED
  BUT KILL THE SCABBED AND UGLY LAMB THAT SPREADS CONTAGI+ 678 23

SCALE
  IN THE SCALE YOU OTHER WOMEN   251 6

SCALED
  HIS LOW FOREHEAD HIS SKINNY NECK HIS LONG SCALED STRIVI+ 360 2

SCALE-LAPPING
    SCALE-LAPPING LIKE A LOBSTER'S SECTIONS   355 3

SCALES
    THE SCALES ARE LOCKED IN AN ARCH LIKE A BRIDGE   355 2
    AND HELL AND HEAVEN ARE THE SCALES OF THE BALANCE OF LI+   710 21

SCALLYWAG
    LET THE MEREST SCALLYWAG COME TO THE DOOR AND YOU LEAP   398 15
    AND EVEN THE DIRTIEST SCALLYWAG IS TAKEN IN   398 19

SCALP
    A YELL OF TRIUMPH AS YOU SNATCH MY SCALP   333 24
    BATS AND AN UNEASY CREEPING IN ONE'S SCALP   341 21

SCALY
    SCALY ANKLE   360 21

SCAN
    AND GONE BEFORE WE CAN SCAN   69 4
    AND SO I SIT AND SCAN THE BOOK OF GREY   135 17
    ON EACH FACE FOR US TO SCAN   *915 16

SCANDALS
    SCANDALS MAY DESTROY EVERY MAN'S FAITH IN MAN   775 6

SCANDINAVIAN
    THE AFRICAN QUEER ONES AND SCANDINAVIAN QUEER ONES   671 15

SCANTY
    BUT WHEN I DRAW THE SCANTY CLOAK OF SILENCE OVER MY EYES   64 14
    A JOB YOU DON'T LIKE AND A SCANTY CHANCE   560 23

SCAR
    FRAIL AS A SCAR UPON THE PALE BLUE SKY   131 24
    I WOULD DIE RATHER THAN HAVE IT INJURED WITH ONE SCAR   255 13
    AND HE HAS A CRUEL SCAR ON HIS SHELL   360 6
    FRAIL AS A SCAR UPON THE PALE BLUE SKY   *937 23

SCARCE
    IS SETTLED ON THE LAND ROSES ARE SCARCE IN ENGLAND VERY   569 8
    SCARCE THERE ARE NONE ANY MORE   569 9
    WI' LITTLE SOBS AS YOU SCARCE COULD HEAR   *910 14
    AND SO KISS-BELADEN THAT IT SCARCE CAN FLOAT   *943 17

SCARCELY
    BUT I SCARCELY FEEL YOUR LOSS   108 12
    DRAWS DOWN THE BLINDS WHOSE SHADOWS SCARCELY STAIN   155 2
    THE BAND IS ACROSS ITS BROW AND IT SCARCELY SEEMS   225 14
    AND SCARCELY CAN REFRAIN   772 17
    THERE IS I BELIEVE SCARCELY ONE INTELLIGENT AMERICAN WHO   775 12
    AND THOUGH I SCARCELY SEE THE BOYS OR KNOW THAT THEY AR+   *900 10
    THOUGH THEY CLING FORGOTTEN THE MOST PART NOT COMPANION+   *900 14
    AND THOUGH I SCARCELY SEE THE BOYS OR KNOW THAT THEY AR+   *903 22
    SCARCELY KNOWN   *903 27
    OPPRESSES ME I CAN SCARCELY BEAR   *930 25

SCARE
    TOSSED BACK IN A SCARE   120 15

SCARED
    WHO WAS SCARED IN HER PLAY   178 22
    MYSELF SO LITTLE DODGING RATHER SCARED AGAINST THE ETER+   390 16
    HOW SCARED THEY ALL ARE EVEN NOW   494 6

SCARF
    I THE MAN WITH THE RED SCARF   44 1
    I CANNOT SEE HER SINCE THE MIST'S PALE SCARF   85 9
    HER PROUD HEAD HELD IN ITS BLACK SILK SCARF   228 14

SCARLET
    OFFERS ME HER SCARLET FRUIT I WILL SEE   37 3
    HIDE YOUR QUAINTLY SCARLET BLUSHES   43 2
    IN SCARLET ALIVE WITH THE BIRDS' BRIGHT TWITTERING   72 22
    BUT SOMETIMES THE OPENING PETALS ARE FIRE AND THE SCARL+   93 31
    WHAT THEN IF A SCARLET ROSE GOES FLAPPING   150 22
    AND SCARLET BERRIES FALLING FROM THE BUSH   160 6
    ALL IN THEIR SCARLET CLOAKS AND SURPLICES   232 17
    SO IT EXPLODES AND YOU SEE THROUGH THE FISSURE THE SCAR+   283 28
    BECOMES AN AFFIRMATION THROUGH MOIST SCARLET LIPS   284 18
    HONEY-WHITE FIGS OF THE NORTH BLACK FIGS WITH SCARLET I+   284 26
    ROSY ROSY SCARLET   313 22
    AND POMEGRANATE BLOOM AND SCARLET MALLOW-FLOWER   313 29
    COCK-CRESTED CROWING YOUR ORANGE SCARLET LIKE A TOCSIN   314 28
    AFIRE AT A MYRIAD SCARLET POINTS   315 24
    AND SCARLET HOT EMBERS OF TORCHES KNOCKED OUT OF THE   388 30
    OH AND THEIR FACES SCARLET LIKE THE DOLPHIN'S BLOOD   689 5
    HEY-PRESTO SCARLET GERANIUM   690 31
    AND PUT SCARLET BUDS IN THEIR HAIR ON THE WAY TO HELL   710 19
    TO THE SCARLET AND PURPLE FLOWERS AT THE DOORS OF HELL   711 20
    SCARLET AND CRIMSON AND A RUST OF BLOOD   744 30
    AGAINST THE SCARLET AND AGAINST THE RED   745 7
    THE SUN HAS CREPT LIKE A SCARLET BEETLE IN THE HUSK   757 15
    SENDING THEM RIOTING AT DAWN DOWN THE LANE OF SCARLET P+   860 23
    SCARLET AND CHERRY RED   861 9

SCARRED
    LOOK AT THE MANY-CICATRISED FRAIL VINE NONE MORE SCARRED   305 4

SCARS
    AND THE ISLES AND HER MEN AND HER SCARS   202 16
    COUNTED OUR SCARS   248 23

SCAR'S
    PROMISE YOU WILL NOT WATCH THE SCAR'S   735 26

SCATTER
    AND ROOKS AND THE RISING SMOKE-WAVES SCATTER AND WHEEL   148 22
    SCATTER OVER THE WHITENESS ONE BOY ALONE IN THE CLASSRO+   865 20

SCATTERED
    YESTERDAY THE FIELDS WERE ONLY GREY WITH SCATTERED SNOW   85 5
    OLD SCATTERED FIRE   271 32
    SCATTERED IN THE GARDEN   357 19
    AND SCATTERED WITH HER HAIR CLOUDS OF PALE MIMOSA SANDS   863 27
    THE PICTURE OF THE PAST IS SHAKEN AND SCATTERED   *908 10

SCATTERING
    LEAN ABOUT US SCATTERING THEIR POLLEN GRAINS OF GOLDEN +   70 2
    LEAN ABOUT US SCATTERING THEIR POLLEN PUFFS OF GOLDEN L+   *916 10

SCATTERS
    CAST OUT BY THE HAND THAT SCATTERS   171 22

SCENE
    SHAPE AFTER SHAPE AND SCENE AFTER SCENE OF MY PAST   47 4
    THROUGH THE SCENE   148 27
    SHE ALIGHTS A STRANGER WONDERING UNUSED TO THE SCENE   153 10
    I AM COME BACK A FOREIGNER WONDERING AND SHRINKING FROM+   867 2

SCENES
    NOT THIS GRAY BOOK BUT THE RED AND BLOODY SCENES   *938 28

SCENT
    THE NIGHT-STOCK OOZES SCENT   41 24
    THERE'S A SCENT OF CLOVER CREPT THROUGH MY HAIR   50 9
    BUT NOT EVEN THE SCENT OF INSOUCIANT FLOWERS   50 13
    WHEN WILL THE SCENT OF THE DIM WHITE PHLOX   62 27
    A FAINT SICKENING SCENT OF IRISES   90 1
    ONLY THE DARKNESS AND THE SCENT OF YOU   90 27
    KILLING THE BLUE DUSK WITH HARSH SCENT UNNERVING   91 14
    A DANK SICKENING SCENT CAME UP FROM THE GRIME   98 16
    YOU LIKE FRANKINCENSE INTO SCENT   114 4
    THE SCENT OF HER FLESH   120 29
    AND THROUGH THE SCENT OF THE BALCONY'S NAKED TIMBER   208 29
    I DISTINGUISH THE SCENT OF YOUR HAIR SO NOW THE LIMBER   208 30
    AND ALL THE SCENT IS SHED AWAY BY THE COLD   224 27
    COMES LIKE A PUNGENT SCENT A VIBRATION BENEATH   270 13
    THEIR SCENT IS LACERATING AND REPELLENT   270 17
    IT IS THE SCENT OF THE FIERY-COLD DREGS OF CORRUPTION   270 20
    SHOULD LOVE THE SEWER SCENT   462 31
    FOR THE LORD TO COME FORTH AT LARGE ON THE SCENT OF BLO+   742 19
    BROTHER THE SCENT OF YOUR CLOTHING   758 19
    SHE KISSED THEIR COOLNESS LAST NIGHT BREATHED THEIR CLE+   856 19
    WE REST AT THE HEDGE MY HORSE AND I WHERE THE SCENT   858 18
    AND ALONG THE SCENT AND THE COOLNESS A DROWSE OF SLEEP +   858 20
    SPEAK IN HALF-BITTER SCENT YOUR DREAM OF ME   880 12
    CATCH THE SCENT AND THE COLOUR OF THE COMING DREAM   *909 27
    YOU LIKE FRANKINCENSE INTO SCENT   *929 21
    A ROSE OF MEMORY WITH A SCENT OF PRAISE   *941 15
    WAS SCENT OF ROSES AND GLIMMERING   *942 16

SCENTED
    THEY WOULD RIPEN LIKE APPLES AND BE SCENTED LIKE PIPPINS   503 20

SCENTLESS
    FLOWERS SCENTLESS OR PUNGENT AMMONIACAL ALMOST   270 11

SCENTS
    THE ACRID SCENTS OF AUTUMN   107 5
    AS WELL IN THE SCENTS THAT SLINK   107 16

SCHOOL
    HOW DIFFERENT IN THE MIDST OF SNOW THE GREAT SCHOOL RIS+   75 7
    SCHOOL NOW IS THE ROCK IN THIS WEARY LAND THE WINTER BU+   75 18
    THE POOL FOR MY LIMBS TO FATHOM MY SOUL'S LAST SCHOOL   161 17
    HAVING BEEN TO SCHOOL   328 15
    WHERE I WENT TO SCHOOL AND COLLEGE   488 8
    CLASS-CHILDREN ARE SINGING IN SCHOOL   657 11
    AS THEY GO FROM SCHOOL SOME OF THE OFFICERS RALLY   732 20
    THAT THE BOYS MUST STAY AT SCHOOL NOT BE KEPT AWAY   777 33
    THAT OUR BOYS MUST STAY AT SCHOOL TILL THEY ARE EIGHTEEN   779 2
    AS I CAME HOME IN THE DUSK DESPOILED BY SCHOOL A MERE B+   864 27
    SURELY I CANNOT JUST BE GOING TO SCHOOL   865 12
    HOW DIFFERENT IN THE MIDDLE OF SNOWS THE GREAT SCHOOL R+   865 18
    FOR TOMORROW WILL POUR THEM ALL BACK THE SCHOOL HOURS I+   *896 9
    ALL THE SLOW SCHOOL HOURS ROUND THE IRREGULAR HUM OF TH+   *897 20
    ALL THE SLOW SCHOOL HOURS ROUND THE IRREGULAR HUM OF TH+   *900 28
    AND THE ROCK OF AGES OF HIS PUBLIC SCHOOL   *947 31
    IN NOTTINGHAM WHERE I WENT TO SCHOOL AND COLLEGE   *950 12

SCHOOL-HOURS
    ALL THE LONG SCHOOL-HOURS ROUND THE IRREGULAR HUM OF TH+   75 20

SCHOOL-MASTERS
    WHOSE FATHERS WERE SCHOOL-MASTERS OR BANK-CLERKS   774 4

SCHOOLS
    BETWEEN THE SCHOOLS SWEEPS ONE BLACK ROOK   76 16
    NURSES DOCTORS PROPER FOOD HYGIENE SCHOOLS ALL THAT   832 5
    BETWEEN THE RUDDY SCHOOLS SWEEPS ONE BLACK ROOK   *898 10
    BETWEEN THE RUDDY SCHOOLS SWEEPS ONE BLACK ROOK   *901 19

SCHOOL-TEACHERS
    THEY ARE GOING TO BE SCHOOL-TEACHERS OR BANK-CLERKS   774 2

SCIENCE
    BITTER SCIENCE THE EXAMS ARE NEAR   41 13
    WHEN SCIENCE STARTS TO BE INTERPRETIVE   523 1
    SCIENCE ON ME   620 7
    THAT THEY CALL SCIENCE AND REALITY   708 17
    SCIENCE HAS NOW BECOME AN EVIL ABSTRACTION   716 9
    AND CONTROLLED BY MEN OF SCIENCE COMPETENT   780 7

SCIENCE'S
  GULPING UP SCIENCE'S SMART ARMADA   824 11

SCIENTIFIC
  MIST OF ENERGY MOST SCIENTIFIC   438 1
  SO YOU THINK SCIENTIFIC MAN YOU'LL BE FATHER OF YOUR OWN   438 18
  IS ABOUT AS SCIENTIFIC AS MAKING SUICIDE THE FIRST LAW +   523 5
  WHEN I WENT TO THE SCIENTIFIC DOCTOR   620 5

SCIENTISTS
  HE IS TAKEN BY THE SCIENTISTS VERY SERIOUSLY   708 13

SCIMITARS
  CALM WITH THE CALM OF SCIMITARS AND BRILLIANT REAPING H+   609 11

SCIMITAR'S
  UNDER THE MOON'S SHARP SCIMITAR'S   735 22

SCISSORS
  LIKE SUDDEN CURVED SCISSORS   359 4

SCOFF
  SHOULD SCOFF ME DISCOVERED   771 22

SCOLD
  PERHAPS THEY'D SCOLD HIM   668 12

SCOOPED
  SCOOPED THEM UP WITH SMALL IRON WORDS   94 11
  SCOOPED OUT AND BARE WHERE A SPIDER   112 20
  THE GREAT BLACK NIGHT SCOOPED OUT   238 2
  SCOOPED THEM UP WITH SMALL IRON WORDS   *896 27

SCOPE
  I AM AWAY BEYOND THE SCOPE OF THIS TURNING   169 6
  I AM SO GLAD THERE IS ALWAYS YOU BEYOND BY SCOPE   248 6

SCORCH
  REFLECTING THE SCORCH OF THE SUN FROM HIS BREAST   373 3
  EAGLE IN THE SCORCH FOREVER   781 5

SCORCH-BREASTED
  SITS AN EAGLE ERECT AND SCORCH-BREASTED   780 27

SCORCHED
  A SCORCHED BREAST   373 26
  A SCORCHED BREAST BREASTING THE SUN LIKE AN ANSWER   372 27
  IN SCORCHED WHITE FEATHERS   373 8
  ONLY THE INNER EYE OF YOUR SCORCHED BROAD BREAST   373 24
  AT YOUR SCORCHED BREAST   373 30
  SALT IS SCORCHED WATER THAT THE SUN HAS SCORCHED   705 19
  A SCORCHED BREAST SUN-TURNED FOREVER   781 2
  A SCORCHED BREAST BREASTING THE BLAZE   781 3
  IN SCORCHED WHITE FEATHERS   781 14

SCORCHED-PALLID
  ERECT SCORCHED-PALLID OUT OF THE HAIR OF THE CEDAR   373 5
  EAGLE SCORCHED-PALLID OUT OF THE HAIR OF THE CEDAR   701 10
  ERECT SCORCHED-PALLID OUT OF THE HAIR OF THE CEDAR   783 6

SCORCH-PALE-BREASTED
  EXCEPT SCORCH-PALE-BREASTED   373 27

SCORE
  BUT LOOK AT THE CABBAGES OH COUNT THEM BY THE SCORE   569 10
  OF THE BOOKS THAT LIE OUT ON THE DESKS A FULL THREE SCO+   *895 21
  OF THE BOOKS THAT LIE OUT ON THE DESKS A FULL THREE SCO+   *904 10

SCORN
  CASTING A SHADOW OF SCORN UPON ME FOR MY SHARE IN DEATH   133 17
  PASSING WITH SPEARS AND PENNANTS AND MANLY SCORN   221 9
  IS IT MORE THAN THE APPLES OF SODOM YOU SCORN SO THE MEN   235 7
  AND CAST ME SCORN   772 6
  PASSING WITH SPEARS AND PENNANTS AND MANLY SCORN   *944 22

SCORNED
  FILLED WITH REMORSEFUL TERROR TO THE MAN SHE SCORNED AN+   *891 30

SCORNING
  YOU ARE CELIBATE AND SINGLE SCORNING A COMRADE EVEN   197 3
  SCORNING THE PANACEA EVEN OF LABOUR   197 15

SCORPION
  NO COBRA NOR HYAENA NOR SCORPION NOR HIDEOUS WHITE ANT   701 13

SCRAIGHT
  YO' NEDNA SCRAIGHT AT ME   78 26
  IF THA CANNA SAY'T COME THEN AN' SCRAIGHT IT OUT ON MY   540 14
  COME THEN THA CAN SCRAIGHT IT OUT ON MY SHIRT-FRONT   540 18
  IN THE FIRST PLACE I DON'T SCRAIGHT   540 20
  AND IF I DID I CERTAINLY COULDN'T SCRAIGHT IT OUT   540 21
  KISS ME THEN THERE NE'ER MIND IF I SCRAIGHT I WOR FOND + *925 28

SCRAIGHTED
  RIGHT IN 'EM AN' SCRAIGHTED A BIT AGAIN   61 14
  RIGHT UNTIL 'EM AND SCRAIGHTED OUT AGAIN   *911 30

SCRAIGHTIN'
  AN' STOP THY SCRAIGHTIN' CHILDT   45 3
  SCRAIGHTIN' MYSEN AS WELL 'ER UNDID 'ER BLACK   61 9
  I'M SCRAIGHTIN' MY-SEN BUT ARENA GOIN'   78 27
  SCRAIGHTIN' MY-SEN AS WELL 'EN UNDID HER BLACK   *911 25

SCRAMBLE
  SCRAMBLE SEVEN TOADS ACROSS SILK OBSCURE LEAVES   126 18
  AND INSTEAD THE WHITE MEN SCRAMBLE ASLEEP IN THE   408 9
  TO SCRAMBLE BACK AGAIN   554 4

SCRAP
  ALMOST EVERY SCRAP OF THE LIVING EARTH YOU STROLL UP AND   521 15

SCRAPE
  CA-A-A COMES THE SCRAPE OF RIDICULE OUT OF THE TREE   375 14

SCRAPING
  AT THIS MOMENT SCRAPING TARDY ARARAT   429 10

SCRATCH
  FOR A MOMENT HIS GREAT DIRECTION SCRATCH   *915 11
  THOUGH I'LL SEE AS 'E PAYS YOU AN' COMES TO THE SCRATCH   *924 11

SCRATCHING
  THEY MUST GO ON SCRATCHING THE ECZEMA OF THEIR MENTAL I+   533 9

SCRAWL
  OF SEVERAL INSULTS OF BLOTTED PAGES AND SCRAWL   74 14
  THE ARTICLES PASSING BENEATH YOUR SCRAWL   583 4
  OF SEVERAL INSULTS OF BLOTTED PAGES AND SCRAWL   *895 22
  OF SEVERAL INSULTS OF BLOTTED PAGES AND SCRAWL   *904 11

SCRAWLING
  IN A LITTER THROUGH THE ELM-TREE SHADE ARE SCRAWLING   65 17

SCREAM
  MUSIC SCREAMS AS ELEPHANTS SCREAM   70 10
  WHEN THEY LIFT THEIR TRUNKS AND SCREAM ALOUD   70 11
  TO SHOW THE PLACE WHENCE THE SCREAM WAS HEARD   150 13
  FIRST FAINT SCREAM   364 1
  FAR FAR OFF FAR SCREAM   364 5
  A FAR WAS-IT-AUDIBLE SCREAM   364 11
  A SCREAM   364 14
  AND GIVING THAT FRAGILE YELL THAT SCREAM   365 10
  HIS SCREAM AND HIS MOMENT'S SUBSIDENCE   365 15
  TIME AFTER TIME THAT FRAIL TORN SCREAM   365 23
  I HEARD THE SCREAM OF A FROG WHICH WAS CAUGHT WITH HIS   365 30
  I REMEMBER THE SCREAM OF A RABBIT AS I WENT THROUGH A   366 4
  I REMEMBER THE SCREAM OF A TERRIFIED INJURED HORSE THE   366 10
  AND HE LIES LIKE A LOG AND SCREAMS AND HIS SCREAM IS SI+ 407 20
  WE SCREAM FOR SOMEONE TO WAKE US   408 1
  AND OUR SCREAM IS SOUNDLESS IN THE PARALYSIS OF SLEEP   408 2
  THEN I SCREAM IN MY SOUL FOR I KNOW I CANNOT   586 3
  I SCREAM IN MY SOUL FOR I KNOW I CANNOT   652 18

SCREAMING
  WHERE WHEELING AND SCREAMING THE PETULANT PLOVERS   41 3
  AND SO FROM OUT THE SCREAMING BIRDS THAT FLY   89 22
  OR SCREAMING IN PENTECOST RECEIVING THE GHOST   365 14
  WITH THIN SCREAMING HATRED   500 15
  LIKE SCREAMING BIRDS OF FATE   741 12

SCREAMINGS
  THEY HAVE TRIUMPHED AGAIN O'ER THE AGES THEIR SCREAMING+   33 4
  THEY ARE LORDS OF THE DESOLATE WASTES OF SADNESS THEIR + *891 4

SCREAMS
  I AM HERE I AM HERE SCREAMS THE PEEWIT THE MAY-BLOBS BU+   34 9
  MUSIC SCREAMS AS ELEPHANTS SCREAM   70 10
  A RUSH THAT ALMOST SCREAMS   336 15
  SO HE TUPS AND SCREAMS   365 22
  NOT THE EAGLE SCREAMS WHEN THE SUN IS HIGH THE PEACOCK   368 10
  AND HE LIES LIKE A LOG AND SCREAMS AND HIS SCREAM IS SI+ 407 20
  AS THE VULTURE THAT SCREAMS HIGH UP ALMOST INAUDIBLE   500 16

SCREECHED
  NO LEOPARD SCREECHED NO LION COUGHED NO DOG BARKED   394 17

SCREECHER
  HAS THE PEACOCK HAD HIS DAY DOES HE CALL IN VAIN SCREEC+ 371 20

SCREEN
  THROUGH THE FLOWER-VINE TRAILING SCREEN   179 11
  THE SCREEN   538 11
  THE INNOCENT MEMBER THAT A FIG-LEAF WILL SCREEN   578 17
  WAS TH' LITTLE LOVIN' SORT AS 'AS NOWT TER SCREEN 'EM   *910 25

SCREENS
  SCREENS US PURELY AND WE CAN SLIP THROUGH   699 11

SCREET
  YOU NEDNA SCREET AT ME   *920 18

SCREETIN'
  I'M SCREETIN' MY-SEN BUT ARE-NA GOIN'   *920 19

SCREW
  WHY HAVE A SOVIET THAT ONLY WANTS TO SCREW US ALL IN AS   452 3
  AS THEY TRY TO SCREW EVERYBODY ELSE DOWN WITH THEIR WILL 502 12
  AT HER AGE WHY I'LL BE EARNING A JOLLY GOOD SCREW   834 20
  A JOLLY GOOD SCREW WHEN THE DEAR LITTLE GIRLY-WIRLY'S O+ 834 21

SCREW-DRIVERS
  AND THEIR VOICES ARE LIKE SCREW-DRIVERS   502 11

SCREWED
  WHEN SHE LIFTED HER MOP FROM HER EYES AND SCREWED IT IN   310 2

SCRIPTS
  REVEAL US NOTHING ROLL THE SCRIPTS AWAY   737 24

SCROLL
  THEIR DROSS OF INDIFFERENCE AND BURN THE SCROLL   *895 29
  THEIR DROSS OF INDIFFERENCE AND BURN THE SCROLL   *904 18

SCROLLED
    AND MORNING SINGING WHERE THE WOODS ARE SCROLLED   135 27
    WHEN THE END OF THE WORLD WE ARE TOLD IS SCROLLED   814 11
    AND MORNING SINGING WHERE THE WOODS WERE SCROLLED   *939 19

SCUD
    AND THAT WHITE SCUD OF HEAVEN   882 17

SCUFFING
    SCUFFING BESIDE HER BENDING DOWN CATCHING HIS OPPORTUNI+ 360 19

SCUFFLE
    ALAS WHAT A FOOL HE LOOKS IN THIS SCUFFLE   360 26

SCUFFLES
    AND NOW HE SCUFFLES TINILY PAST HER AS IF SHE WERE AN O+ 356 26

SCUM
    THAT HAS LEFT SCUM ON THE SEA EVEN IN THE NIGHT   453 28

SCUT-TAILED
    SCUT-TAILED RABBITS   392 17

SCUTTLE
    THE SPIDERS WITH WHITE FACES THAT SCUTTLE ON THE FLOOR + 112 28

SCUTTLED
    AND THEN THE GEESE SCUTTLED IN IN A LITTLE FLOCK   444 19

SCUTTLING
    PALE AND MEAN AND INSECT-LIKE SCUTTLING ALONG   526 18
    IN THEIR RAG GARMENTS SCUTTLING THROUGH THE STREETS   530 16

SCYLLA
    WITH A HINT OF THE FROZEN BELLS OF THE SCYLLA FLOWER   708 29

SCYLLAS
    SCYLLAS AND YELLOW-HAIRED HELLEBORE JONQUILS DIM ANEMON+ 270 7

SCYTHE
    AS FARTHER OFF THE SCYTHE OF NIGHT IS SWUNG   135 11
    NO LONGER THEY SWEEP THE HOURS AS THE SCYTHE OF THE MOW+ 855 29
    OF THE LONG SCYTHE THE STOOPING MOWER WIELDS   *939 8
    AS FURTHER OFF THE SCYTHE OF NIGHT IS SWUNG   *939 12
    I CAN HEAR THE SOUND OF THE SCYTHE STROKES FOUR   *944 2
    HIS SCYTHE BLADE BRIGHT UNHOOKS   *944 12
    HIS SCYTHE STONE AN' OVER THE GRASS TO ME   *944 13

SCYTHE-BLADE
    HIS SCYTHE-BLADE BRIGHT UNHOOKS   220 4

SCYTHES
    FOUR LABOURERS PASS WITH THEIR SCYTHES   220 16
    PINIONED LIKE SWEEPING SCYTHES NOW IDLY HANGING AT REST 855 22

SCYTHE-STONE
    THE SCYTHE-STONE AND OVER THE STUBBLE TO ME   220 5

SCYTHE-STROKES
    I CAN HEAR THE SWISH OF THE SCYTHE-STROKES FOUR   219 22

S'D
    AN' THEN WI' THAT TWENTY POUND WE GI'E 'ER I S'D THINK + *925 20

SEA
    MOVES ON TO THE SEA   38 28
    SET LIKE ROCKS BESIDE A SEA OF GLOOM   56 14
    ALL THE FLOWERS ARE FADED FROM THE ASPHALT ISLE IN THE + 71 10
    TOWN-DARK SEA   71 19
    LIKE A WEEDED CITY IN SHADOW UNDER THE SEA   72 17
    THE SEA AND THE SKY WENT GREY AS IF THERE HAD SUNK   98 12
    AND COLDNESS CLOGGED THE SEA TILL IT CEASED TO CROON   98 15
    OF THE UNSWEPT SEA A GREY PALE LIGHT LIKE MUST   99 3
    SO I WENT AND WASHED MY DEADENED FLESH IN THE SEA   99 12
    AND THE SUAVE SEA CHUCKLES AND TURNS TO THE MOON   130 2
    DANCE TO THE SLIDING SEA AND THE MOON   130 10
    TO TOUCH THE SEA IN THE LAST SURPRISE   130 12
    THE EARTH AGAIN LIKE A SHIP STEAMS OUT OF THE DARK SEA + 132 27
    ALL THESE PURE THINGS COME FOAM AND SPRAY OF THE SEA   136 17
    BREAKS INTO DAZZLE OF LIVING AS DOLPHINS LEAP FROM THE + 155 21
    OF A SHIP THAT STANDS IN A SHADOWY SEA OF SNOW   155 21
    LIKE CLIFFS ABUTTING IN SHADOW A DEAD GREY SEA   164 19
    TO SHOW WHERE THE SHIPS AT SEA MOVE OUT OF SIGHT   172 21
    THE SUN WARMS THE SEA LITTLE LONELY AND SAD SIFTING THE+ 180 3
    SEA ONLY YOU ARE FREE SOPHISTICATED   197 18
    SEA YOU SHADOW OF ALL THINGS NOW MOCK US TO DEATH WITH 197 32
    SHE SEES THE BLADE OF THE SEA   200 6
    THE SEA IN THE STONES IS SINGING   200 17
    OVER A SULLEN SEA   201 16
    I DON'T MIND THIS CONTINENT STRETCHING THE SEA FAR AWAY 213 7
    TOWARDS THE SEA   293 21
    AND THE SEA LIKE A BLADE AT THEIR FACE   310 9
    THE SHAKING ASPECT OF THE SEA   310 26
    VALLEYS OF THE WATERS UNDER THE SEA   321 36
    AND LET IT MOULT THERE AMONG THE STONES OF THE BITTER S+ 329 20
    ON THE SEA WITH NO MESSAGE IN IT AND THE BODY SUBMERGED 428 11
    THAT HAS LEFT SCUM ON THE SEA EVEN IN THE NIGHT   453 28
    THE SEA DISSOLVES SO MUCH   454 18
    AND THE SEA GETS HOLD OF US   455 2
    BACK TO THE OLD YEAR'S SUN ACROSS THE SEA   455 19
    BUT SETTING SETTING BEHIND THE SOUNDING SEA BETWEEN   455 23
    THE WIDE SEA WINS AND THE DARK   455 25
    IN THE SEA   466 14
    IN THE SEA   466 17
    BETWEEN THE DEVIL AND THE DEEP COLD SEA   490 24
    SLOWLY THE SALT OF THE EARTH BECOMES SALT OF THE SEA   495 1
    SLOWLY THE SALT OF THE EARTH BECOMES SALT OF THE SEA   495 9
    WHEN I LOOK AT THIS PINE-TREE NEAR THE SEA   498 18

SEA
    AND THE SEA IS LOST   509 14
    AND EVEN THE SEA OF SEAS WILL HAVE TO GIVE UP ITS DEAD 514 9
    THAT PUT TO SEA ON CERTAIN EVENINGS   542 6
    THAT PUT TO SEA AND BOLDLY SINK ARMADAS   542 9
    AND ALL THE SEA-NYMPHS OUT AT SEA   575 7
    AND EVEN THE SEA IS SILENT IN THE SUN   605 25
    AND THE SEA IS ALIVE AND CAN SULK   625 14
    THINGS FROM THE SEA   647 3
    LITTLE ISLANDS OUT AT SEA ON THE HORIZON   687 1
    OF SOMETHING COMING SHIPS A-SAIL FROM OVER THE RIM OF T+ 687 3
    IT IS SHIPS OF CNOSSOS COMING OUT OF THE MORNING END OF+ 687 5
    NOW THE SEA IS THE ARGONAUTS' SEA AND IN THE DAWN   687 19
    THE DAWN IS NOT OFF THE SEA AND ODYSSEUS' SHIPS   687 22
    THIS SEA WILL NEVER DIE NEITHER WILL IT EVER GROW OLD 688 1
    THE MAN OF TYRE WENT DOWN TO THE SEA   692 22
    WHERE A STREAM CAME DOWN TO THE GRAVEL OF THE SEA AND S+ 693 2
    WHO HAD WADED TO THE PALE GREEN SEA OF EVENING OUT OF A+ 693 5
    POURING SEA WATER OVER HERSELF   693 6
    GODLY AND LOVELY COMES APHRODITE OUT OF THE SEA   693 19
    THEY SAY THE SEA IS LOVELESS THAT IN THE SEA   693 21
    BUT FROM THE SEA   693 24
    AND THE SEA IS MAKING LOVE TO DIONYSOS   693 29
    THEY SAY THE SEA IS COLD BUT THE SEA CONTAINS   694 1
    SEA   694 7
    IN THE BLUE DEEP BED OF THE SEA   694 14
    THE BURNING ARCHANGELS UNDER THE SEA KEEP PASSING BACK + 694 23
    SEA   694 27
    AND ALL THIS HAPPINESS IN THE SEA IN THE SALT   695 5
    SHE IS THE GAY DELIGHTED PORPOISE SPORTING WITH LOVE AN+ 695 10
    AND DENSE WITH HAPPY BLOOD DARK RAINBOW BLISS IN THE SEA 695 12
    ALREADY IT IS OCTOBER AND THE WIND BLOWS STRONG TO THE + 696 15
    LET THE SEA HEAVE NO MORE IN SOUND   698 10
    DO YOU SEE THE SEA BREAKING ITSELF TO BITS AGAINST THE + 705 1
    YET REMAINING UNBROKEN THE LEVEL GREAT SEA   705 2
    DO THE ROLLERS OF THE SEA   705 7
    I AM THE SEA I AM THE SEA   705 18
    AS NOW WHEN THE TINY WAVELETS OF THE SEA   709 5
    LIKE NOW WHERE THE WHITE SUN KISSES THE SEA   709 9
    UPON THE SEA OF DEATH WHERE WE STILL SAIL   719 8
    THAT CANNOT FIND THE WAY ACROSS THE SEA OF CHANGE   721 16
    THAT INTERVENES BETWEEN THE FINAL SEA   722 7
    THAT CANNOT EMBARK ON THE SLINKING SEA BEYOND   722 23
    THEY COME BACK OVER THE WHITE SEA IN THE MIST   739 10
    ENDLESSLY RETURNING ON THE UNEASY SEA   739 12
    THE COOL THE CLEANNESS OF THE SEA   747 7
    THE SEA ALL WET   747 8
    FOR THE SOUND OF THE SEA AS IT FURLS AND UNFURLS   747 21
    INTO THE DEAD SEA FALLING   766 21
    NATIONS BESIDE THE SEA ARE OLD   814 15
    THE SEA HAS ITS BUD-LIPS SMILINGLY CURLED   814 26
    WHEN I SEE THIS SEA LOOKING SHODDY AND DEAD   815 10
    TILL THEN I LIKE BETTER THIS SEA I MUST SAY   815 17
    AS IT COMES OVER THE MILK-BLUE SEA HINTING AT GOLD AND + 840 5
    IN A BOAT ON A ROUGH SEA WHEN WE WERE ALL NEARLY SEA-SI+ 842 13
    SLOW-BREATHING SEA   860 3
    LIKE A GIRL'S TWINKLING MERRIMENT AT NIGHT WHEN THE SEA+ 860 16
    MY HEART HAS A WARMTH LIKE THIS SEA WHERE THE DAWN   860 17
    YOU WERE ALL THE MORNING TO ME ALL THE SEA AND THE MORN+ 870 25
    LYING RIGID AND SILENT WITH YOUR FACE ON THE SHORT SEA 871 34
    AS BUOYANT AS A SEA-BIRD ON THE SEA   876 5
    THE SEA AFRAID   883 27
    NOW I AM ON THE STRAND OF A TURBULENT SEA   *894 19
    A TOSSING SEA OF TURBULENT STRIFE WHERE NOW   *894 20
    THAT INTERVENE BETWEEN OUR TOWER AND THE SLINKING SEA O+ *957 24
    TO WHERE THE FURTHEST AND THE LONGEST SEA   *958 27
    OVER THE SEA OVER THE FARTHEST SEA   *959 3
    NOW IN THE TWILIGHT SIT BY THE INVISIBLE SEA   *960 12
    ON THE LONGEST JOURNEY OVER THE HIDDEN SEA   *960 20

SEA-ANEMONE
    LIKE A NUDE LIKE A ROCK-LIVING SWEET-FLESHED SEA-ANEMONE 299 7

SEA-BATHING
    SEA-BATHING CITY PEOPLE   625 12

SEA-BEASTS
    SEA-BEASTS IMMERSED LEAN SIDEWAYS AND FLASH BRIGHT   453 25

SEA-BED
    ARE SEA-BED STILL THROUGH THEIR HOUR OF BARE DENUDING 509 19

SEA-BIRDS
    ALL THESE GLITTERING SEA-BIRDS WHEEL AND FRET   860 20

SEA-BIRD
    AS BUOYANT AS A SEA-BIRD ON THE SEA   876 5

SEA-BLENCHED
    AND UP THE PALLID SEA-BLENCHED MEDITERRANEAN STONE-SLOP+ 311 20

SEA-BLOWN
    OF THE SEA-BLOWN WEEK OF NINE   702 4

SEA-CAVE
    THEY DWELT IN A HUGE HOARSE SEA-CAVE   201 21

SEA-CRAB
    HE'S LIKE A BONNY ROSY SEA-CRAB WITH HEALTHY CLAWS   830 19

SEA-CURVED
    AND THE SOUND OF A BLAST THROUGH THE SEA-CURVED CORE OF+ 623 13

SEA-FELLOW
    I WISH A WILD SEA-FELLOW WOULD COME DOWN THE GLITTERING 130 17

SEA-FOWL
    THE MULTITUDES ARE LIKE DROPPINGS OF BIRDS LIKE DUNG OF+   614 21

SEA-GOD
    THE SEA-GOD SAID IN CONSTERNATION   575 4

SEA-GULL
    HE CAME LIKE A SEA-GULL SINKING WITH UPLIFTED WINGS DOW+   860 2

SEA-IMMERSED
    IN PURE BRILLIANCE OF ANGER SEA-IMMERSED ANGER   453 26

SEAL
    I WILL SET A SEAL UPON YOU FROM MY LIP   153 20
    SEAL UP EACH CHANNEL OUT OF WHICH MIGHT SLIP   153 22
    COULD I BUT SEAL ITS RUDDY SHINING SPRING   153 25
    AND SEAL YOUR NOSTRILS AND ROUND YOUR NECK YOU'LL   154 2
    I PLACE A GREAT AND BURNING SEAL OF LOVE   154 9
    OF EGRESS FROM YOU I WILL SEAL AND STEEP   154 14
    SO I DID HIS PENS AND THE JASPER SEAL ON HIS NECK   255 4
    SEAL UP HIS FOREHEAD ONCE MORE TO A BASTION   327 22

SEALED
    LOVE HAS CREPT OUT OF HER SEALED HEART   46 5
    FOR THE HOUSE IS SHUT AND SEALED AND THE BREATH OF THE +   174 27
    AND WE SHALL BE SEALED AND STOWED AWAY   748 7

SEALING
    BUT HEAVY SEALING DARKNESS SILENCE ALL IMMOVABLE   205 14

SEALS
    GREAT SEALS UPON YOUR OUTGOINGS AND WOVEN   154 24
    ALONG THE LAKE LIKE SEALS LIKE SEALS   824 18
    THESE PEOPLE THAT LIE LIKE SEALS   824 30
    THEY LIE LIKE SEALS   825 9
    LIKE SEALS IN SUNNY SUMMER THEY HIE   825 15
    LIKE SEALS THAT HIE   826 2

SEA-NYMPHS
    AND ALL THE SEA-NYMPHS OUT AT SEA   575 7

SEA-POPPIES
    WITH YELLOW FRAIL SEA-POPPIES   200 19

SEA-POWER
    WITH POWER SEA-POWER   705 10
    SEA-POWER   705 11

SEAR
    THE DARKNESS IS SECRET AND I COULD SEAR   114 3
    THE DARKNESS IS LOVELIEST WHERE I COULD SEAR   *929 20

SEARCH
    CAME NEARER TO SEARCH THROUGH THE STREETS   121 32
    WHEN YOU WENT FORTH SO VIGOROUSLY IN SEARCH   661 5
    SEARCH FOR NOTHING ANY MORE NOTHING   661 11

SEARCHING
    I DO FORGET YOUR EYES THAT SEARCHING THROUGH   129 9
    THOSE THAT GO SEARCHING FOR LOVE   661 6

SEARCHLIGHT
    SEARCHLIGHT RAYS   755 15

SEARCHLIGHT'S
    SISTERS THE SEARCHLIGHT'S SWINGING FAN   758 13

SEARED
    THEIR HARDENED SOULS ARE WASHED WITH FIRE AND WASHED AN+   663 6

SEAS
    LIKE A THIN WHITE BIRD BLOWN OUT OF THE NORTHERN SEAS   47 14
    OF THE SHIP OF THE SOUL OVER SEAS WHERE DREAMED DREAMS   53 7
    WITH THAT UNFELT BREEZE THAT EBBS OVER THE SEAS WHERE T+   53 13
    WITH FIRE AS IT GUARDS THE WILD NORTH-COASTS RED-FIRE S+   57 13
    A SOULLESS NECKAR WITH WINKING SEAS IN HIS EYES   130 19
    A VOYAGE TO SAIL BEYOND THE CHARTED SEAS   168 3
    CAN BLOW ACROSS THE DARK SEAS TO OUR USUAL WORLD   261 3
    UNSETTLED SEAS AND WINDS   285 20
    OUT OF FATHOMLESS SKIES AND SEAS   438 32
    AND STREETS AND HOUSES AND EVEN SEAS   480 5
    AND EVEN THE SEA OF SEAS WILL HAVE TO GIVE UP ITS DEAD   514 9
    SAIL ON OVER PERILOUS SEAS OF THOUGHT   542 12
    ON THE DEPTHS OF THE SEVEN SEAS   694 9
    MY BRIDE BETWEEN THE SEAS   707 12
    THE DEAD OF THE WATER-LORDS ROCK AND GLIMMER IN THE SEAS   796 8
    THE UNCLOUDED SEAS OF BLUEBELLS HAVE EBBED AND PASSED   854 1
    OF THE SHIP OF THE SOUL OVER SEAS WHERE DREAMED DREAMS + *905 20
    WITH THE UNFELT BREEZE THAT EBBS OVER THE SEAS WHEN THE+ *906 5
    DEEPEST AND LONGEST OF SEAS   *957 31
    ON THE MOST SOUNDLESS OF ALL SEAS   *959 10
    SO BEAUTIFUL OVER THE LAST OF SEAS   *960 16
    FOR THE LONGEST JOURNEY OVER THE LAST OF SEAS   *961 7
    AT LAST AT LAST BEYOND INNUMERABLE SEAS   *961 14

SEA-SHELL
    THE FLOOD SUBSIDES AND THE BODY LIKE A WORN SEA-SHELL   720 12

SEASICK
    PEEVISH AND SEASICK   842 17

SEA-SICK
    IN A BOAT ON A ROUGH SEA WHEN WE WERE ALL NEARLY SEA-SI+   842 13

SEA-SIDE
    BATHING-SUIT FROM OUR MODERN SEA-SIDE FOAM   439 32

SEASON
    LOVE OUT OF SEASON ESPECIALLY AT THE END OF THE SEASON   478 12
    NO A LONG SEASON I HAVE BEEN WITH DOSTOIEVSKY IN THE DA+   866 27

SEASONS
    STIRRING OF NEW SEASONS   274 6
    AT SEASONS SHE CURLS BACK HER TAIL LIKE A GREEN LEAF IN+   385 31
    AT SEASONS TO PREPARE THEMSELVES TO PARTAKE   777 34

SEA-SOUTHERN
    MADE OF SWEET UNTARNISHED SILVER IN THE SEA-SOUTHERN AIR   298 21

SEA-SPARK
    SHONE LIKE A HUGE SEA-SPARK   201 24

SEA-STONE
    SAD AS HE SITS ON THE WHITE SEA-STONE   130 1

SEA'S
    CAUGHT DUST FROM THE SEA'S LONG SWATHS   152 13
    THE SEA'S EDGE   467 7
    YOU WHO DON'T HEAR THE SEA'S UNEASINESS   643 12

SEAT
    ALONE ON A SEAT   143 4
    AS WE SIT IN THE SUNSHINE ON THE SEAT BY THE LITTLE SHR+   204 12
    REMEMBER WHO VOTED YOU INTO YOUR SEAT   573 26
    MECHANICAL MAN IN TRIUMPH SEATED UPON THE SEAT OF HIS M+   624 21
    SO MECHANICAL MAN IN TRIUMPH SEATED UPON THE SEAT OF HI+   624 24
    SET A PLACE FOR THE DEAD WITH A CUSHION AND SOFT SEAT   723 9

SEATED
    MECHANICAL MAN IN TRIUMPH SEATED UPON THE SEAT OF HIS M+   624 21
    SO MECHANICAL MAN IN TRIUMPH SEATED UPON THE SEAT OF HI+   624 24
    GREY UNAPPEASED GHOSTS SEATED IN THE MUSIC-HALLS   740 3

SEA-TOUCH
    AND SEA-TOUCH TIP OF A BEAK   436 24

SEATS
    AND WEARING OUR SEATS OUT SITTING ON MONEY   485 26

SEA-TURF
    NO DO NOT TOUCH ME LEAVE ME ON THE GREY SEA-TURF   870 23

SEA-WARD
    BUTTERFLY THE WIND BLOWS SEA-WARD STRONG BEYOND THE GAR+   696 12
    BUT THE WIND BLOWS STRONG TO SEA-WARD WHITE BUTTERFLY C+   696 19
    AND IN A STRANGE LEVEL FLUTTERING YOU GO OUT TO SEA-WAR+   696 25

SEA-WATER
    TO DISTIL SEA-WATER INTO SWEET   495 11

SEAWEED-FRINGED
    DOWN BETWEEN THE STEEP SLOPES OF DARKNESS FOCUS-DARK SE+   921 95

SEA-WEED
    SEA-WEED SWAYS AND SWAYS AND SWIRLS   467 16

SEA-WIND
    WHO IN LASSITUDE LEAN AS YACHTS ON THE SEA-WIND LIE   73 11

SECOND
    OF A SECOND LIKE SNOW THAT SLIPS   62 10
    FOR A SECOND ENSPASMED IN OBLIVION   333 29
    AND CLEAVE IN A HIGH CORNER FOR A SECOND LIKE A CLOT AI+   345 23
    AND I LIKE A SECOND COMER WAITING   349 20
    IF ONCE FOR A SECOND THE UNIVERSE CEASED TO FLOW   479 13
    IF YOU ARE EXPECTING A SECOND ADVENT IN THE SHAPE OF A   531 19
    OF A SECOND AFRAID OF THE CLIPS   *912 17

SECONDARY
    EXCEPT OF COURSE FOR SECONDARY MOTIVES   485 18
    ANYHOW THEY NEVER WILL EXCEPT FOR SECONDARY MOTIVES   485 22
    BUT THAT WHICH IS SECONDARY IS ONLY IMPORTANT   668 3
    AND LIVE FROM ITS SECONDARY SWEAT   843 9

SECOND-HAND
    BOUGHT SECOND-HAND FROM MRS JUSTICE ENNIS   760 13

SECONDS
    AND THAT HELD HER SPELLBOUND FOR TWO SECONDS   604 22

SECOND'S
    AND CLUTCHING CLUTCHING FOR ONE SECOND'S PAUSE   345 8

SECRET
    THE SUN AND THE RAIN DO NOT ASK THE SECRET   63 18
    MAYBE THERE ARE SECRET PLACES   95 29
    HERE IN THIS SWARTHY SECRET TENT   113 25
    THE DARKNESS IS SECRET AND I COULD SEAR   114 3
    TO SIGHT REVEALING A SECRET NUMBERLESS SECRET KEEPING   136 7
    THE SECRET OF THE MOON WITHIN YOUR EYES   156 21
    EACH WITH A SECRET WHICH STIRS IN HIS LIMBS AS THEY MOVE   174 10
    ME ITS LIFE AS IT HURRIES IN SECRET   180 33
    OF BROODING AND DELIGHTING IN THE SECRET OF LIFE'S GOIN+   197 17
    WHEN SHE HAS PUT HER HAND ON MY SECRET DARKEST SOURCES +   267 6
    EXULTING WITH SECRET WARM EXCESS   272 11
    EVERY FRUIT HAS ITS SECRET   282 11
    IT WAS ALWAYS A SECRET   283 1
    FOLDED UPON ITSELF AND SECRET UNUTTERABLE   283 10
    AND THEN THE FIG HAS KEPT HER SECRET LONG ENOUGH   283 27
    LIKE A WOUND THE EXPOSURE OF HER SECRET ON THE OPEN DAY   283 32
    LIKE A PROSTITUTE THE BURSTEN FIG MAKING A SHOW OF HER +   283 33
    THE SECRET IS LAID BARE   284 4

SECRET
    NOW THE SECRET   284 17
    WE HAVE KEPT OUR SECRET LONG ENOUGH   284 21
    NOW EVEN THE SHADOW OF THE LOST SECRET IS VANISHING FRO+   295 3
    IS THERE A GREAT SECRET   296 6
    THE UNDELIVERABLE SECRET   296 8
    IS IT THE SECRET OF THE LONG-NOSED ETRUSCANS   296 14
    SECRET FRUITS   300 17
    YET EVEN THIS IS NOT THE SECRET OF THE SECRET DO YOU KN+   303 8
    BLOOD FROM SIDE TO SIDE CAUSING MY MYRIAD SECRET STREAMS   320 28
    FROM OUT THE DARK DOOR OF THE SECRET EARTH   350 22
    AND THE DEEP SECRET ALL-PENETRATING TAIL CURVED BENEATH   365 3
    TO THE PRIMEVAL RUDIMENTS OF LIFE AND THE SECRET   365 21
    THE SOFT THE SECRET THE UNFATHOMABLE BLOOD   383 6
    A NAKED GLEAMING DARK LAUGH LIKE A SECRET OUT IN THE DA+   389 15
    IN SECRET UNDER THE SICKENING WALL   462 7
    TILL THE SECRET WATERS OVERFLOW   462 10
    AND THE GREAT BEASTS MATE IN SECRET AT LAST   465 21
    IN SECRET GREAT GOLLIWOG   492 22
    AND YOU CAN'T BE FULLY ALIVE IF YOU ARE CRUSHED BY SECR+   522 10
    ONLY FROM OUT THE FOLIAGE OF THE SECRET LOINS   606 6
    I REALISED THE SECRET JOY HER YOUNG SPANISH HUSBAND HAD   618 22
    SHE HAS A SECRET ALMOST ECSTASIED HATRED OF MALENESS IN+   619 20
    THE SECRET OF THE NOISELESS UTTER GRACE   744 27
    THE SECRET IN THE BLIND MOUTH OF THE WORM   744 28
    PUT SLEEP AS BLACK AS BEAUTY IN THE SECRET OF MY BELLY   803 2
    WATCH THE STIR WHOSE RHYTHM IS SECRET WHOSE SECRET IS S+   *907 13
    THEY HAVE A SECRET THAT STIRS IN THEIR LIMBS AS THEY MO+   *908 14
    HERE IN THIS SWARTHY SECRET TENT   *929 14

SECRETIVE
    THE FIG IS A VERY SECRETIVE FRUIT   282 12

SECRETLY
    YOU SHOULD BE OUT BY THE ORCHARD WHERE VIOLETS SECRETLY+   57 17
    AND IRRITATION SEETHES SECRETLY THROUGH THEIR GUTS AS T+   616 9
    SOFTLY SUBTLY SECRETLY IN SOUL FIRST THEN IN SPIRIT THE+   642 22
    SOFTLY SUBTLY SECRETLY SAYING NOTHING   642 27
    AS THE BOURGEOIS GETS SECRETLY MORE COWARDLY KNOWING HE+   663 20

SECRETS
    SECRETS THAT YOU MAY NOT BROACH   95 27
    AND SEE ITS SECRETS SO IT IS THAT THE POMEGRANATE IS TH+   277 3
    WRINKLED WITH SECRETS   279 8
    THAT HAS KEPT SO MANY SECRETS UP ITS SLEEVE   299 14

SECTIONS
    SCALE-LAPPING LIKE A LOBSTER'S SECTIONS   355 3
    THE SECTIONS OF THE BABY TORTOISE SHELL   355 9
    I AM NOT A MECHANISM AN ASSEMBLY OF VARIOUS SECTIONS   620 10

SECURE
    I HAVE A DARKNESS INTACT WITHIN ME GLOWING SECURE   772 10

SECURITY
    AND MY STILL HEART FULL OF SECURITY   250 11
    AND MY STILL HEART FULL OF SECURITY   *946 9

SEDIMENT
    MONEY MAKES EVEN NO SEDIMENT   455 7

SEDUCTIVELY
    AND OH SO SEDUCTIVELY SUPERIOR SO SEDUCTIVELY   434 5

SEE
    ARE THEY ASLEEP ARE THEY LIVING NOW SEE WHEN I   33 8
    SEE THE WOMAN'S TRINKLING FINGERS TEND HIM A COIN   36 6
    OFFERS ME HER SCARLET FRUIT I WILL SEE   37 3
    I SEE A REDNESS SUDDENLY COME   42 6
    MOTHER COME DOWN AN' SEE   44 11
    COME OUT O' TH' WAY AN' LET ME SEE   45 1
    SEE THE STARS LOVE   48 27
    WHEN I MOVE THE OARS SEE   49 5
    EVEN YOURS DO YOU SEE   49 8
    THERE DID YOU SEE   49 13
    AS SEEING HE DOES NOT SEE   51 16
    ONCE YOU COULD SEE   55 25
    COULD SEE THE SMALL STARS TREMBLE   55 28
    HE GROWS DISTINCT AND I SEE HIS HOT   59 7
    AND I SHALL SEE MY SLEEPING ROD   59 11
    SHALL SEE AN IMAGE OF HEAVEN OR OF EARTH   59 15
    OH AND I LONG TO SEE HIM SLEEP   59 17
    I LONG TO SEE   59 20
    WHEN SHALL I SEE THE HALF-MOON SINK AGAIN   62 25
    THE RED RANGE HEAVES AND COMPULSORY SWAYS AH SEE IN THE+   66 17
    SEE IN THE SKY BEFORE ME A WOMAN I DID NOT KNOW   67 10
    I SEE   67 15
    PLANTED THEE UPRIGHT ART PROUD TO SEE   69 15
    TO SEE YOU ALL SORDID OR RADIANT-TISSUED   73 7
    WHAT GOOD TO THEM OR ME I CANNOT SEE   74 17
    FLAYED RED IF THA COULD BUT SEE   78 24
    TER LET IV'RYBODY SEE   78 28
    THA WANTS 'IM THY-SEN I SEE   81 32
    THOUGH I'LL SEE AS 'E PAYS YOU AN' DOES WHAT'S RIGHT   82 7
    FOR WHENEVER I LOOK THEE I' TH' FACE I S'LL SEE   82 23
    THEY'LL TURN THEE OUT O' TH' FORCE I DOUBT ME IF THEY D+   83 16
    I CANNOT SEE HER SINCE THE MIST'S PALE SCARF   85 9
    YOU HELEN WHO SEE THE STARS   86 1
    WHERE WE CAN SEE IT OUR FIRE TO THE INNERMOST FIRE   89 16
    EVEN THERE I SEE A BLUE SPARK THAT WILL FLY   89 34
    TO SEE THE CLASS'S LIFTED AND BENDED FACES   90 5
    IS COMPLETE FOR THE MOMENT YET WAIT AND YOU'LL SEE THAT+   94 8
    YET ARE SHAPELY AND COMELY TO SEE   101 22
    WHITE-NIGHTGOWNED LITTLE CHITS I SEE   105 16
    BUT I SEE LEANING FROM THE SHADES   105 24
    OH AND SEE THE LABURNUM SHIMMERING   106 3
    I SEE EACH SHADOW START   108 8
    I SEE THE SILENCE EASILY SIP THEM   110 7

SEE
    I SEE THE STEALTHY SHADOW OF SILENCE   110 15
    AS I SEE IT HARDENING   112 13
    LIES ON THE DUST WATCHING WHERE THERE IS NOTHING TO SEE+   112 22
    DEPLOYED AROUND ME AND I SEE   115 23
    WHAT IS IT THEN THAT YOU CAN SEE   116 21
    OF MY EYES I SEE YOU BEAUTIFUL AND DEAR   118 13
    I SEE MYSELF AS THE WINDS THAT HOVER   118 16
    THEY HAVE TAUGHT YOU TO SEE   118 21
    DID YOU SEE THE WICKED SUN THAT WINKED   120 9
    I LIKE TO SEE SHE SAID AND SHE CROUCHED HER DOWN   123 7
    BY HER MEASURED BREATHS I LIKE TO SEE SAID SHE   123 11
    OF A MOMENT SEE SHE LAUGHED IF YOU ALSO   125 8
    SHE WATCHED MY HAND TO SEE WHAT IT WOULD FULFILL   125 12
    AND SEE WHERE THE BUDDING HAZELS ARE THINNED   126 9
    LIKE A STORM OF EMERALD SNOW NOW SEE   126 24
    AND OFTEN I SEE HER CLENCH HER FINGERS TIGHT   128 18
    I SEE YOUR BLANCHED FACE AT MY BREAST AND HIDE   129 13
    SOME SAY THEY SEE THOUGH I HAVE NEVER SEEN   132 1
    THE EDGE OF THE BLUE AND THE SUN STANDS UP TO SEE US GL+   132 28
    SHADOW WE SEE   136 21
    CALL TO HIM OUT OF THE SILENCE CALL HIM TO SEE   137 10
    HE CANNOT SEE IT I CAN NEVER SHOW IT HIM HOW IT SHOOK   137 13
    THA THOUGHT THA WANTED TER MARRY AN' SEE   139 3
    NOW GO AN' MARRY THAT WENCH AN' SEE   139 31
    TAKING ME BACK DOWN THE VISTA OF YEARS TILL I SEE   148 5
    ACROSS THE INSENSIBLE VOID TILL SHE STOOPS TO SEE   153 3
    SEE IN HIM YOUR SELF'S DREAM IN HIS SORE   157 31
    I SEE OUR SHADOW TREMBLE   170 11
    SEE HOW IT FLOURISHETH   172 9
    SEE HOW IT RISES WITH MAGICAL ROSY SAP   172 10
    TO SEE WHOSE PRAISE   176 18
    I SEE THE GREAT ORION STANDING   198 19
    HE SAID DO YOU SEE THE SPIRITS   201 25
    I CAN SEE IT ALL IT IS WHOLE LIKE THE TWILIGHT   203 18
    IT IS LARGE SO LARGE I COULD NOT SEE IT BEFORE   203 19
    AND SEE SO NEAR AT OUR FEET IN THE MEADOW   204 15
    AT LAST YOU CAN THROW IMMORTALITY OFF AND I SEE YOU   210 3
    I SEE YOU AH IN FULL   210 14
    AND IF I NEVER SEE HER AGAIN   213 15
    AH NEVER BEFORE DID I SEE   215 20
    AND LOOKS DOWN ON THE GROUND TO SEE   215 24
    CAN SEE THE WHITE   220 24
    MY SOUL TO SEE YOU SETTLING AND TRYING TO CLIMB   221 23
    I SEE MYSELF ISOLATED IN THE UNIVERSE AND WONDER   223 1
    ONE MOMENT I SEE THE STILLNESS OF AGONY   225 26
    WHAT DOES HE SEE MY DARLING   227 5
    SEE GLITTERING ON THE MILK-BLUE MORNING LAKE   230 8
    I SEE YOU ALL THE TIME YOU BIRD-BLITHE LOVELY   234 9
    I SEE RIGHT WELL HOW I OUGHT TO BE GRATEFUL   234 11
    SEE IF THEY RING   236 27
    AND SEE WHAT PROPORTION THERE IS   236 29
    IT IS REALLY SPRING SEE   244 9
    HOW HAPPY WE'LL BE SEE HIM   244 13
    SEE THE BIRD IN THE FLOWERS HE'S MAKING   244 27
    SEE HOW GORGEOUS THE WORLD IS   245 3
    NOTHING OF ME THAT YOU SEE IS MY OWN   251 3
    THERE'S THE BEAUTY YOU CANNOT SEE MYSELF AND HIM   251 16
    YOU SEE HE IS DIFFERENT HE IS DANGEROUS   252 1
    AND GIVES ME PEACE YOU CANNOT SEE   252 4
    IT IS GOOD I CAN MURDER AND MURDER AND SEE THEM FALL   257 30
    NOW I SEE THEM JUST THE SAME AND WATCH THEM   269 20
    AS YOU SEE A TINY CELLULOID BALL TOSSING ON A SQUIRT OF+   272 16
    AND SEE ITS SECRETS SO IT IS THAT THE POMEGRANATE IS TH+   277 3
    DO YOU MEAN TO TELL ME YOU WILL SEE NO FISSURE   278 22
    AS YOU SEE IT STANDING GROWING YOU FEEL AT ONCE IT IS S+   282 13
    IN THE INWARDNESS OF YOUR YOU THAT EYE WILL NEVER SEE   283 22
    SO IT EXPLODES AND YOU SEE THROUGH THE FISSURE THE SCAR+   283 28
    SEE HIM THERE THE SWART SO PALPABLY INVISIBLE   286 11
    SEE IF I DON'T BRING YOU DOWN AND ALL YOUR HIGH OPINION   289 11
    SEE IF YOUR SKIES AREN'T FALLING   289 16
    SEE IF I DON'T MOVE UNDER A DARK AND NUDE VAST HEAVEN   289 19
    SEE IF I AM NOT LORD OF THE DARK AND MOVING HOSTS   289 22
    YET MORE I SEE YOU DARKLY CONCENTRATE   297 1
    SEE THE MILK OF NORTHERN SPUME   301 24
    AH YES AH YES WOULD I MIGHT SEE IT AGAIN   303 7
    SEE IT COME FORTH IN BLOSSOM   305 20
    HOW SHALL WE KNOW THEM WHEN WE SEE THEM   312 12
    I LONG TO SEE ITS CHOCK-FULL CROWDEDNESS   315 27
    AND THEN TO SEE THE NEW REAL SOULS SPROUT UP   315 31
    WHAT ROT TO SEE THE CABBAGE AND HIBISCUS-TREE   316 18
    THEY DRAW NEAR TO TASTE IT AS IF SAYING NOW WHAT IS THI+   331 5
    AND SEE WHO WINS IN THIS SLY GAME OF BLUFF   333 8
    AND LOOK BEYOND AND SEE   338 29
    LOOK UP AND YOU SEE THINGS FLYING   340 27
    AWAY FROM AMONG GODS AND MEN HE DID NOT SEE THAT HE WAS+   348 2
    IT NEEDED PYTHAGORAS TO SEE LIFE PLAYING WITH COUNTERS +   355 14
    WINGS AND MEN WHO SEE HIM WHEELING ARE FILLED WITH THE +   368 5
    SEE HIM STANDING WITH HIS HEAD DOWN NEAR THE PORTA CAPP+   379 1
    SEE HIS BLACK NOSE SNUBBED BACK PRESSED OVER LIKE A WHA+   380 13
    AND THEN YOU SEE THE GOD THAT HE IS IN A CLOUD OF BLACK   381 10
    SEE ME SHE SAYS THAT'S ME   386 7
    THEY HAD COME TO SEE ROYALTY   391 27
    COCKING YOUR EYES AT ME AS YOU COME ALONGSIDE TO SEE IF   397 23
    STANDS SAYING SEE I'M INVISIBLE   403 11
    DID YOU EVER SEE AN OTTER   409 2
    IF I COULD SEE YOUR HAND AND IT WERE THUMBS DOWN   430 4
    SO I CAN'T SEE WHERE THE WORM THAT HAS TURNED PUTS ANYT+   432 34
    BUT YOU SEE SAID THE HANDSOME YOUNG MAN WITH THE   433 9
    COMPELLED TO SEE THE DELICATE SKILL OF FLICKERING HUMAN   445 26
    WHEN MODERN PEOPLE SEE THE CARNAL BODY DAUNTLESS AND   445 31
    LO I SEE FEAR IN THE TWISTED FACES   460 27
    SATISFACTORY EXPERIENCE FROM IT CAN'T YOU SEE IT   463 15
    AND SEE SATAN BARGAINING THE WORLD AWAY   483 12
    IF YOU'VE GOT THE GOODS COME FORWARD BOY AND LET'S SEE   483 20
    WHEN I SEE THE IGNOBLE PROCESSION   484 1
    THEY LOOK AT YOU THEY SEE A CAGED MONKEY   485 20
    WITH A MARVELLOUS OUTFIT HOW DID ARCHIE SEE   489 27

SEE

I SEE IT HAS A NATURAL ABUNDANCE	498	20
AND IT RANKLES THEY ACHE WHEN THEY SEE THE YOUNG	502	24
IT DOES EVEN IF WE DON'T SEE IT	511	10
AND SEE WHICH WAY THE APPLES WOULD GO A-ROLLING	517	12
IF WE LOOKED IN OUR HEARTS WE SHOULD SEE	519	7
I SEE THE TIN-MAN THE TINKER SITTING DAY AFTER DAY ON T+	520	13
TO SEE THAT A CHILD AS SOON AS IT IS BORN	521	26
OR WE MUST SEE MEN DIE AND THEN DIE OURSELVES	522	31
AND ALL I WANT IS TO SEE THE SPARK FLICKER	524	1
WHEN I SEE IT BETWEEN HIS BROWS	526	11
BUT WHEN I SEE THESE GREY SUCCESSFUL MEN	526	13
AND WHEN I SEE WORKING MEN	526	17
CAN'T YOU SEE IT	547	20
IF YOU SEE IT IN PRINT	551	12
WHERE I BELONG YOU SEE	552	8
THOUGH OF COURSE WE WON'T LET HIM SEE	554	24
AND THEY THOUGHT YOU COULDN'T SEE THEM	554	27
IF YOU WERE WILLING TO SEE IT	555	21
BUT NEVER NO NEVER COULD I SEE IT	555	25
YET NOW YOU SEE	557	15
YET NOW YOU CAN SEE	557	25
THEY OUGHT AT LAST TO SEE THROUGH THE GAME	559	23
AND WE SEE IT SHINING	561	12
AS MUCH GLOW AS YOU SEE	561	22
AND CAN'T SEE THROUGH THE FENCE	565	4
I SEE YOU'RE OFF YOUR HEAD	570	3
A MEMBER OF THE BRITISH PUBLIC DON'T YOU SEE	570	6
AUNT GWEN WAS A POOR ONE BUT AUNT MAUD YOU SEE	571	25
THROUGH THE POOR BOY'S PICTURES YOU SEE WHAT I	577	18
THIRTEEN THOUSAND PEOPLE CAME TO SEE	577	24
IN PURIS NATURALIBUS DON'T YOU SEE	578	26
BECAUSE YOU SEE HE IS NEITHER MY DEAR	581	18
OR SEE OURSELVES AS WE ARE AND GO MAD	585	2
THEN WHEN I SEE THE IRON HOOKED IN THEIR FACES	586	1
SEE THEM WAVE SEE THEM WAVE PLUMES	587	21
I LIKE TO SEE THEM PASSING AND PASSING	602	3
ESPECIALLY IF I SEE THEIR ALONENESS ALIVE IN THEM	602	5
AND I FAILED ENTIRELY TO SEE WHAT HE MEANT	603	6
I MUST SEE IF I CAN'T BREAK THROUGH IT	605	2
I MUST SEE IF I CAN'T ABSORB THIS SAMSON OF SELF-ABSORP+	605	14
I CAN'T SEE THAT I REFUSE ANYTHING	611	4
BUT WHEN I SEE THE LIFE-SPIRIT FLUTTERING AND STRUGGLIN+	622	4
WHEN I SEE THE FLUTTERING OF PURE LIFE IN THEM	622	10
OH JESUS DIDN'T YOU SEE WHEN YOU TALKED OF SERVICE	629	1
OH WHEN I THINK OF THE INDUSTRIAL MILLIONS WHEN I SEE	629	16
WHEN I SEE THE GREAT CITIES	632	10
WHEN I SEE THE IRON HOOKED INTO THEIR FACES	632	16
LIFT NEVER A FINGER AGAINST THEM THAT THEY CAN SEE	643	5
AND LIVED TO SEE THEM SPAWN INTO MACHINE-ROBOTS	644	6
OCCASIONALLY I SEE HIM SILENT A LITTLE WONDERING	645	18
SOMETIMES I SEE HER LIKE A FLOWER NODDING HER WAY AND	645	22
BE ALONE AND SEE THE MOONLIGHT OUTSIDE WHITE AND BUSY	646	10
AND THE LARCH THAT IS ONLY A COLUMN IT GOES UP TOO TALL+	647	1
SOME MEN CAN SEE LIFE CLEAN AND FLICKERING ALL ROUND	649	7
AND SOME CAN ONLY SEE WHAT THEY ARE SHOWN	649	8
AND SOME MEN CAN SEE NO GODS THEY ONLY KNOW	649	10
MEN WHO SEE	649	12
TO SEE THE GLEAM OF THE GODS THERE REFLECTED IN THE HUM+	649	22
BUT ALL THE TIME I SEE THE GODS	651	12
AND YOU LOOK IN HER EYES AND SEE IT IS A LIE	654	11
AND FEEL THE SPLENDOUR OF THE GODS GO THROUGH YOU EVEN +	655	8
AND CEASING TO SEE	660	24
CEASE TO SEE	662	13
DON'T YOU SEE HOW YOU MAKE BOLSHEVISM INEVITABLE	664	13
THEY CAN'T SEE IT	665	21
WITH THE PATHOS OF THOSE WHO CAN SEE BUT WHOSE SIGHT IS+	665	24
AND THESE THE MINORITY OF MEN WHO CAN STILL SEE THE LIG+	665	25
INSTEAD OF WHICH THE MINORITIES THAT STILL SEE THE GLEA+	666	5
I'VE BEEN UP TO LONDON TO SEE THE FINE QUEEN	670	2
TO SEE THE WAY THEY TREAT IT	670	23
ALL THE GODS AND YOU SEE THEM ALL IF YOU LOOK ALIVE AND+	671	20
WHERE DO YOU SEE THEM YOU SAY	671	22
YOU SEE THEM IN GLIMPSES IN THE FACES AND FORMS OF PEOP+	671	23
YOU MAY SEE GLIMPSES OF THE GODS IN THEM	672	6
SEE GOD IS BORN HE IS BLUE HE IS DEEP BLUE HE IS FOREVE+	682	23
AND SO WE SEE GOD IS NOT	683	15
AND ALSO WE SEE	683	17
I SEE DESCENDING FROM THE SHIPS AT DAWN	688	12
I SEE HIM MORE LIKE THE RUBY A GLEAM FROM WITHIN	697	28
AND SEE NOTHING	698	5
IN THE HEARSE OF NIGHT YOU SEE THEIR TARNISHED COFFINS	703	3
DO YOU SEE THE SEA BREAKING ITSELF TO BITS AGAINST THE +	705	1
THEN WE SEE EVIL PURE EVIL	712	20
AND WE SEE IT ONLY IN MAN	712	21
SHE IS NOT SEEN FOR THERE IS NOTHING TO SEE HER BY	719	16
I CAN SEE HIS RAGING BLACK EYES BLAZE AT ME	733	3
ME WANT TO CRY TO SEE HIM SO STRONG AND EASY	733	23
I WANT TO KNOW NO MORE I WANT TO SEE	738	25
TO THE TRENCHES I SEE AGAIN A FACE WITH BLUE EYES	742	6
OH TO SEE THE LONG WAVES RUSH	747	1
ALREADY I SEE THE SHELLED MOON LIE	747	28
SEE NO HOPE OF ALTERING	750	7
AND YOU OH SEE THE MYRIAD DOVES THAT WALK	750	21
STRUCK DOWN DO THOU PART US THE DARKNESS THAT WE SEE TH+	753	6
IF YOU SEE MY RINGS HOW THEY SPARKLE WITHIN MY EARS	755	3
THEY ARE DEAD SO GOD AS BETWEEN YOU YOU SEE	759	19
DO YOU SEE THE GOLD SUN FLUTTERING BUOYANTLY IN HEAVEN	782	29
I ROSE AGAIN TO SEE A STAR FALLING AND FEEL A BREATH ON	786	10
SEE ME THROUGH THE FLASHING OF WINGS	787	29
THEY SEE ME AND LOSE ME AGAIN	787	30
THE MULTITUDES SEE ME NOT	788	1
THEY SEE ONLY THE WAVING OF WINGS	788	2
SEE THE LIGHT ON THE MAN THAT WAITS	788	28
TO SEE THEM SO GLUM AND SO LUMPISH	791	16
I SEE DARK THINGS RUSHING ACROSS THE COUNTRY	794	10
SEE YOU BE NOT RAT-GNAWED GOURDS	800	35
IN THE DREAM OF THE NIGHT I SEE THE GREY DOGS PROWLING	807	2

SEE

IN THE NIGHT I SEE THE GREY DOGS CREEPING OUT OF THE SL+	807	11
I SEE THE GREY DOGS CREEPING OUT WHERE MY DEER ARE BROW+	807	18
WE'LL SEE THE JOKE AND HOW FUNNY IS SORROW	815	5
WHEN I SEE THIS SEA LOOKING SHODDY AND DEAD	815	10
IF GOD LOOKS LET HIM SEE	818	14
WHAT I SEE	819	5
AND SEE YOURSELF AS IN A GLASS DARKLY	834	18
DARLING I SEE YOUR IRON-GREY CHEVELURE	835	5
THE REAL IMMORALITY AS FAR AS I CAN SEE IT	836	17
WHEN I SEE WHAT A MESS MEN HAVE MADE OF THE WORLD	837	12
WHEN I SEE WHAT MESSES MEN HAVE MADE OF THEMSELVES	837	13
WHEN I SEE THE MESSED-UP CHEMICALISED WOMEN	837	14
AND WE STILL HAVE TO SEE WHAT BABY WILL BE LIKE AT THIR+	842	26
INWARDS I CAN SEE WHENCE THE THORNS WERE RENT	856	21
TO SEE HIM FLASH AND TREMBLE WITH THE FIRE OF HIS SOUL	859	8
SEE HER LAUGH UP AT ME	861	17
NOW SEE HER TURN TO FLEE	861	19
SEE HOW SHE SNUGGLES AGAINST MY NECK	863	1
I CAN JUST SEE THE NAPE OF HER WHITE LITTLE NECK	863	5
WHEN HE LIFTS HIS FOOT I SEE THE PAD OF HIS SOAKED STOC+	866	7
WHEN I SEE THE SKY'S BLUE DARKEN	869	4
AND WHERE HE STOOD I SEE MY OWN SHADOW STAND	871	11
THERE I CANNOT BEAR TO SEE THE SOBS IN YOUR THROAT	871	19
I SEE THE STRONG SOUND EARTH BETRAYED AS A FLOATING	874	30
FOR WHETHER I SEE YOU SET THE DAFFODILS	875	7
AND SHALL I SEE HIM NEVER NOR WILL HE TURN	876	23
AFTER TONIGHT FOR SEE I SAID TO HIM	878	8
AND I CAN SEE THE PULSE WITHIN HIS THROAT	878	25
THOUGH I SHALL HASTEN AFTER WHEN I SEE	879	24
AND EVER I SEE YOUR TRACES BROKEN-HEARTED	880	15
AND WHEN I SEE THE HEAVY RED FLEECE	883	1
AND WHEN I SEE THE TREES SWAY CLOSE	883	8
AND WHEN I SEE THE THICK WHITE BODY OF TRAIN-SMOKE BREAK	883	16
ARE THEY ASLEEP ARE THEY ALIVE NOW SEE WHEN I	*891	9
SEE THE MORNING SUN ON THE SHAKEN IRIS GLISTEN	*892	31
STILL IN THE SUN TO WATCH AND I CAN SEE	*895	2
AND THOUGH I SCARCELY SEE THE BOYS OR KNOW THAT THEY AR+	*900	10
AND THOUGH I SCARCELY SEE THE BOYS OR KNOW THAT THEY AR+	*903	22
AND I WATCH TO SEE THE CREATOR THE POWER THAT PATTERNS +	*908	25
WHEN YOU'D GONE I SLIPPED BACK TER SEE WHO SHE MIGHT BE	*910	5
I COULDNA' SEE HER FACE BUT HER LITTLE NECK SHONE	*910	11
I COME AWAY FOR FEAR SHE SHOULD SEE	*910	22
PLANTED THEE UPRIGHT ART NOT PROUD TO SEE	*915	27
FLAYED RED IF THAT COULD BUT SEE	*920	16
TO LET EVERYBODY SEE	*920	20
THOUGH I'LL SEE AS 'E PAYS YOU AN' COMES TO THE SCRATCH	*924	11
FOR WHENEVER I LOOK THEE I' TH' FACE I S'LL SEE	*924	27
THAT FILLS WITH GRIEF ALL THOSE THAT SEE	*927	29
AS I SEE IT HARDENING	*929	3
WHAT IS IT THEN THAT YOU CAN SEE	*930	20
THEY HAVE TAUGHT YOU TO SEE	*931	31
I LIKE TO SEE SHE SAID AND SHE CROUCHED HER DOWN	*934	13
STRONG AND SLOW I LIKE TO SEE SAID SHE	*934	17
OF A MOMENT SEE SHE LAUGHED IF YOU ALSO	*935	24
SOME SAY THEY SEE THOUGH I HAVE NEVER SEEN	*937	28
QUIETLY THROUGH THE YEARS I HAVE CREPT BACK TO SEE	*940	6
I SEE THE WOMAN'S SOUL STEAL IN HER EYES	*940	19
MY HEART TO SEE YOU SETTLING AND TRYING TO CLIMB	*945	9
SAID RONALD YOU SEE IS QUITE A CLEVER SADIST	*948	10

SEED

THA SHOULD HA' SEED 'ER SLIVE UP WHEN YER'D GONE	61	5
THA SHOULD HA' SEED 'ER KNEEL AN' LOOK IN	61	6
AN' IF MY LANDLADY SEED ME LIKE IT	80	13
THE SEED OF LIFE INCARNATE THAT FALLS AND WAKES	89	10
THE BRANCHES INVISIBLE SEED OF EXPERIENCE BLOWS	89	30
YOU ARE A SEED IN THE NIGHT-TIME	102	9
FOR SEED TO ENDOW	102	12
AS ABRAHAM WHOSE SEED SHALL MULTIPLY	126	16
NAY BUT HOW TORTURED IS THE FRIGHTFUL SEED	160	21
THE CHILD LIKE MUSTARD SEED	172	5
IT FELL FROM OUR HUSK IN A LITTLE HASTY SEED	172	13
THE SEED IS PURPOSE BLOSSOM ACCIDENT	218	26
THE SEED IS ALL IN ALL THE BLOSSOM LENT	218	27
THE GREAT BREATH BLOWING A TINY SEED OF FIRE	219	2
OF PERFECT LIFE AND IS OUR POSSIBLE SEED	219	7
TO ME IT SEEMS THE SEED IS JUST LEFT OVER	219	13
ADD YOURSELF UP AND YOUR SEED TO THE NOUGHT	235	15
I AM LIKE A SEED WITH A PERFECT FLOWER ENCLOSED	247	6
SEED AFTER DAY-SEED WENDS	253	19
SEED AFTER SEED AFTER SEED	253	28
WHERE THE SEED SINKS IN	254	3
THE SEED OF HEAVEN	260	21
FOR FRUITS ARE ALL OF THEM FEMALE IN THEM LIES THE SEED+	277	1
WHEN THEY BREAK AND SHOW THE SEED THEN WE LOOK INTO THE+	277	2
WAS THE SEED OF THE BODY AND FROM THE GRAVE IT COULD GR+	303	10
WE ARE GHOSTS WE ARE SEED	510	23
AND NEEDS TO BE RAISED FROM SEED	535	14
TREES RAISED FROM SEED HAVE WILD AND BITTER FRUITS	640	21
AND HE IS THE BRIDE I HAVE SOWN HIM WITH THE SEED	742	13
WHAT IS THE CRIME THAT MY SEED IS TURNED TO BLOOD	742	37
LIKE GLITTERING SEED UPON THEM FOR FULFILMENT	743	5
WE TAKE THE BRIDE O GOD AND OUR SEED OF LIFE	743	12
AND KNEES AND THIGHS AND LOINS AND THE BOWELS OF STRENG+	801	20
WITH WEBBED FECUNDITY PLUNGING THE SEED OF LIFE IN THE +	841	5
OF SEED TO LOSE MYSELF IN THE BODY OF THIS BLUE	876	19
WHAT ARE WE BUT AS SEED RIPENED WITHIN	880	2
LIKE SEED FROM OUT THE RIPENED LOINS OF LIFE	880	6
THA SHOULD HA' SEED HER SLIVE UP WHEN WE'D GONE	*911	21
THA SHOULD HA' SEED HER KNEEL AN' LOOK IN	*911	22
AN' IF MY LANDLADY SEED ME LIKE IT	*922	13

SEED-BALL

THE SEED-BALL OF THE SUN	253	15

SEED-DUST
TO MY BLOSSOM IN PERFUME AND SEED-DUST AND ONLY THEN I +   94   6

SEED-PODS
SEED-PODS   296 26

SEEDS
AND ALL THE MYRIAD HOUSELESS SEEDS   160   7
THE SPARK FROM STORMS OF CORROSION AS SEEDS   160 28
THE DANDELION SEEDS STAY HALF-SUBMERGED IN THE GRASS   204 21
IN FALLING SEEDS OF RAIN   268 20
SEEMS LIKE THE BLACK AND GLOSSY SEEDS OF COUNTLESS CENT+   369 11
PICKS UP ITS SEEDS OR LITTLE SNAILS   443 13
JUST BEFORE IT SEEDS   587 10
TO WITHER ON THE BOSOM OF THE MERCIFUL SO MANY SEEDS TH+ *926 27

SEED-SPECKS
OF SEED-SPECKS KINDLED LATELY AND SOFTLY BLOWN   218 16

SEEING
AS SEEING HE DOES NOT SEE   51 16
YOU SURELY SEEING I AM A BOWL OF KISSES   86   3
SEEING THE CORE IS A SHADOW INVIOLATE   115 11
AND SEEING MY CAST-OFF BODY LYING LIKE LUMBER   134 12
SEEING IRON BREAK AND BUD   304   5
SEEING RUSTY IRON PUFF WITH CLOUDS OF BLOSSOM   304   6
SEEING I AM ON A PAR WITH ALL MEN   320 13
I BELIEVE HE CHIRPS PIPISTRELLO SEEING ME HERE ON THIS   347 19
SIGHTFUL SIGHTLESS SEEING AND VISIONLESS   359 17
WATCHING AND HARDLY SEEING THE TRUNK-CURL APPROACH AND   388   9
DOING ONE'S OWN LITTLE JOBS SEEING THE WORLD BEYOND   610   5
AS A GIFT OF GLADNESS SEEING THE GLAMOUR OF LIFE GO UP   680   5
TILL WE ARE MAD WITH TERROR SEEING THE SLAIN   740   1
THEN HE LAUGHED SEEING THE SUN DART FIERCELY AT HIM   790   1
SEEING I DEEP IN THE FIRE-CORE INVIOLATE   *930 11
AND SEEING IT IS YOUR BIRTHDAY   *941   6
THEY WOULD SAY SEEING EACH MOUTH OF WHITE ROSE PRAISE   *941   6

SEEIN'
I'M SEEIN' FOR MY-SEN   78 18
I'M SEEIN' FOR MY-SEN   *920 10

SEEK
THAT HE SHOULD SEEK MY HOSPITALITY   350 21
DOOMED IN THE LONG CRUCIFIXION OF DESIRE TO SEEK HIS CO+ 361   3
TO SEEK THE WOMEN IN THE DARK OUR WOMEN OUR WEIRD   438 13
SEEK ALL THE WORLD ROUND THERE'S NONE CAN BE FOUND   574 17
WHY SEEK TO ALTER PEOPLE WHY NOT LEAVE THEM ALONE   614 17
YOU WILL REALISE THERE WAS NEVER ANYTHING TO SEEK FOR   661   2
AND THEY NEVER HAVE TO SEEK FOR IT   661 10
STRETCHING THEIR BIG FULL LIMBS TO SEEK   827 13
BUT DO NOT SEEK TO TAKE ME BY DESIRE   873 26
OH DO NOT SEEK TO THRUST IN ME YOUR FIRE   873 27
AND DO I NOT SEEK TO MATE MY GROWN DESIROUS SOUL   *926 22
LET US SEEK TO WIN HER BACK UNTO US THE MOON   *938 13

SEEKERS
OH SEEKERS WHEN YOU LEAVE OFF SEEKING   661   1

SEEKING
ALONG THE FENCE PERPETUALLY SEEKING RELEASE   47 17
RUNS SEEKING A LONELINESS   64   9
OF KISSES LONG SEEKING FOR A WIFE   105   7
WHO WAS SEEKING ME AND HAD FOUND ME AT LAST TO FREE   180 16
SEEKING WHERE TO ALIGHT   253   7
LIKE A FISH SEEKING THE BOTTOM JESUS   321 31
TORN TO BECOME WHOLE AGAIN AFTER LONG SEEKING FOR WHAT   367   1
AND HIS SLITTED EYES SEEKING THE NEEDLE'S EYE   382   4
WHAT EVEN THE WILD WITCHCRAFT OF THE PAST WAS SEEKING   481   9
OH SEEKERS WHEN YOU LEAVE OFF SEEKING   661   1
YOU WERE ONLY SEEKING TO LOSE SOMETHING   661   3
SEEKING THEIR OLD HAUNTS WITH COLD GHOSTLY RAGE   722 27
SHE IS SEEKING HER OBLIVION   725 13
SEEKING TO APPEASE WITH BLOOD THE INSISTENT GHOSTS   739 24
FROM SEEKING THE UTTER DROWNING   772 18
SEEKING THE OFFAL AND GARBAGE OF LIFE IN THE INVISIBLE + 796   6

SEEKS
CRY OUT AND FEND HER OFF AS SHE SEEKS HER PROCREANT GRO+   91 27
CRY OUT AND FEND HER OFF AS SHE SEEKS HER PROCREANT GRO+ *926 20

SEEM
AND CLASH AND YET SEEM TO TALLY   38 26
AND WE SWOON WITH KISSES SWOON TILL WE SEEM   70 16
SEEM TO BE MAKING OUT OF THE BLUE OF THE MORNING   72   6
THEY SEEM TO BE BECKONING RUSHING AWAY AND   140 24
STRANGE WHITE SIGNALS SEEM INTENDING   150 12
AND SO I SEEM   170   1
OPENS MY EYES TILL THE ROOTS OF MY VISION SEEM TORN   173   4
SO THAT THEY SEEM TO UTTER THEMSELVES ALOUD   197 25
ROCKS SEEM AND EARTH AND AIR UNEASY AND WATERS STILL   249 15
THE OUTSIDE WILL SEEM BROWN   344 27
THE OUTSIDE DID NOT SEEM BROWN   344 29
SEEM BELLY-PLUMBED TO THE EARTH'S MID-NAVEL   392 24
THE DEAD ARE IN MYRIADS THEY SEEM MIGHTY   441   5
LOUD PEACE PROPAGANDA MAKES WAR SEEM IMMINENT   495 20
AS A MATTER OF FACT THE ONLY CREATURES THAT SEEM TO SUR+ 523 21
AND YOU DON'T SEEM TO UNDERSTAND   572 20
AND YOU DON'T SEEM TO UNDERSTAND   573   8
OF SPEAKING PLAIN ENGLISH TO AN ENGLISHMAN YOU'LL SEEM   576   7
AND EAT AND CACHINNATE AND EVEN SEEM TO SMILE   644 19
SEEM TO SMILE YE GODS   644 20
PROPERTY PROPERTY PROPERTY THAT'S WHAT THEY SEEM TO SAY   664   2
MY WRISTS SEEM BROKEN AND MY HEART SEEMS DEAD   727 19
MEN THAT SEEM HARMLESS WOMEN WITH FAIR WORDS   807 26
SEEM ALWAYS TO BE ASKING ASKING SOMETHING   816   4
SO THAT HE DOESN'T SEEM TO HAVE ANY INSIDE TO HIM   830   7
THEY SEEM TO FEEL THE CHILDREN A GHASTLY LIMITATION   832   8

SEEMED
SHE WHO HAS ALWAYS SEEMED SO LIGHT   74   1
THAT SETTLED UPON MY FACE AND HANDS TILL IT SEEMED   99   4
IT SEEMED THAT I AND THE MORNING WORLD   124   6
I LOVED TO HANDLE IT IT SEEMED LIKE A NEAR PART OF HIM   255   3
SOMETHING SEEMED TO SURGE THROUGH ME WHEN I TOUCHED   255   5
SOMETHING SEEMED TO BLOW HIM BACK FROM THE WINDOW   344 11
FOR HE SEEMED TO ME AGAIN LIKE A KING   351 24
WHICH HAD SEEMED INVINCIBLE   353 20
THE PEOPLE WATCHED AND WONDERED AND SEEMED TO RESENT   445 17
ALL THE CREATURES SEEMED TO ENJOY THE GAME   445 22
NOT ONE THEY ALL SEEMED TO ME   550   2
SEEMED TO THINK I WAS LAYING IT SIEGE   555 16
SEEMED TO THINK THEY'D GOT LIKE A HALO   555 19
YET SHE SEEMED TO KNOW NOTHING ABOUT IT   619   7
THEY SEEMED TO GROW DARKER AS SHE CAME TO THE EDGE OF D+ 869   6
THEN UP FROM OUT HER VERY SOUL THERE SEEMED   881   6
SHE WHO HAS ALWAYS SEEMED SO LIGHT   *913 22
IT SEEMED THAT I AND THE WOVEN WORLD   *935   6

SEEMING
SEEMING TO STUMBLE TO FALL IN AIR   345 15
SEEMING TO LICK HIS LIPS   350 27
THE NASTY LYING PRETENCE OF SEEMING TO FEEL WHAT WE DON+ 654   5

SEEMLY
LOUDER THAN IS SEEMLY   508 12

SEEMS
EH WHAT A SHAME IT SEEMS   45 22
WITH COLD LIKE THE SHELL OF THE MOON AND STRANGE IT SEE+   99 14
LIKE A SOFT FULL DROP OF DARKNESS IT SEEMS TO SWAY   148   1
I LOVE FOR EVER THERE IT SEEMS   151   5
IT SEEMS TO ME   161 12
SEEMS TO DABBLE IN ME   194 11
SO THAT HE SEEMS A STRANGER IN HIS PASSING   197 30
TO ME IT SEEMS THE SEED IS JUST LEFT OVER   219 13
WHAT ABOUT SIN FOR IT SEEMS   223 22
THE BAND IS ACROSS ITS BROW AND IT SCARCELY SEEMS   225 14
THE FEAR OF THE WANT OF THESE THINGS SEEMS TO BE QUITE + 263 12
AND IT SEEMS MALE   282 14
HOW VIVID YOUR TRAVELLING SEEMS NOW IN THE TROUBLED SUN+ 354   4
SHE SEEMS EARTHILY APATHETIC   361 29
SEEMS LIKE THE BLACK AND GLOSSY SEEDS OF COUNTLESS CENT+ 369 11
LIFE SEEMS TO LEAP AT THE AIR OR SKIM UNDER THE WIND   392 15
ENGLAND SEEMS FULL OF GRAVES TO ME   410   1
ENGLAND SEEMS COVERED WITH GRAVES TO ME   410   5
ENGLAND SEEMS LIKE ONE GRAVE TO ME   410 26
WHY DON'T YOU KNOW WHAT'S WHAT YOUNG PEOPLE SEEMS   464   9
THAT IT SEEMS TO LAST FOREVER   476 23
AN' LIFE SEEMS TO BEGIN   493 10
TRAGEDY SEEMS TO ME A LOUD NOISE   508 11
IT SEEMS TO ME THAT FOR FIVE THOUSAND YEARS AT LEAST   519   1
OH OVER THE FACTORY CITIES THERE SEEMS TO HOVER A DOOM   586 13
THAT IS WHY BUSINESS SEEMS TO ME DESPICABLE   607 21
THE INWARD COCKY ASSERTIVENESS OF THE SPANIARD SEEMS TO+ 618   9
IT SEEMS TO ME THEY ARE SAYING   628   3
THERE SEEMS NOTHING THERE   662   9
I LICK THE CREAM OFF PROPERTY THAT'S WHAT IT SEEMS TO S+ 664   4
YET ITS BELLY-ACHE SEEMS TO GET BIGGER TOO   670 19
MY WRISTS SEEM BROKEN AND MY HEART SEEMS DEAD   727 19
WHICH SEEMS TO ME A GREAT ADVANCE   828 27
AND IT SEEMS TO ME THAT THE YOUNG ONES THOUGH THEY GRUD+ 829   1
IT SEEMS TO ME THAT SOME SORT OF DECENT SOCIALIZATION E+ 829   8
EVEN ITS BRAIN SEEMS UPSIDE DOWN   830 29
I LOVE FOR EVER AND IT SEEMS   873 15
TO HOIST THE NEXT WHITE PLANK THEIR MOVEMENT SEEMS   *895   5

SEEN
HERE THERE'S AN ALMOND-TREE YOU HAVE NEVER SEEN   58 12
TREMBLING BLUE IN HER PALLOR A TEAR THAT SURELY I HAVE + 67 16
IS SEEN IN THE GOSSAMER'S RIME   68 16
OF YOUR SEVERAL FACES I HAD NEVER SEEN   100 21
AND I HAVE SEEN HER STAND ALL UNAWARE   128 23
SOME SAY THEY SEE THOUGH I HAVE NEVER SEEN   132   1
TWO NAKED FACES ARE SEEN   144 26
BUT NOW I THINK I HAVE SEEN IT ALL AND NOW   173 25
OVER THE WASTE WHERE NO HOPE IS SEEN   179 14
AND WHO HAS SEEN THE MOON WHO HAS NOT SEEN   193   1
OF FINISHED BRIDEGROOM SEEN HER RISE AND THROW   193   4
I HAVE SEEN IT FELT IT IN MY MOUTH MY THROAT MY CHEST MY 207 21
FOR THE FIRST TIME NOW FOR THE FIRST TIME SEEN   216 18
SHE BRAVES IT OUT SINCE SHE MUST BE SEEN   228   4
HAVE YOU NOT SEEN IN THE WILD WINTER SUN OF THE SOUTHER+ 303 14
AND SEEN HIS HORROR-TILTED EYE   339   7
HAS HE SEEN THE GORGON'S HEAD AND TURNED TO STONE   379   7
SHUFFLE SHUFFLE AND HIS LITTLE WICKED EYE HAS SEEN YOU + 387 10
THEY HAVE ONLY THEIR PERSONALITIES THAT ARE BEST SEEN F+ 446   4
AND HE SAYS I NEVER HAVE SEEN THEM BEFORE   460   1
AH WHEN I HAVE SEEN MYSELF LEFT BY LIFE LEFT NOTHING   509 16
HAD STOOD UP FOR THEMSELVES AND SEEN   536   9
THAT YOU'VE OFTEN SEEN   551 14
I'VE NEVER SEEN HER BUT THEY SAY   572   1
THAT WE'VE NEVER SEEN COMING STAMPING AND SWEARING   572 13
CAN IT BE THEY'VE BEEN TRIMMED SO THEY'VE NEVER SEEN   578 16
I HAVE SEEN AT LAST THE IMAGE OF HIM THEY LOVED   601 15
NEVER HAVING SEEN A MULBERRY BUSH IN OUR LIVES   658   4
EVERYTHING HAS BEEN SEEN TO DEATH   660 27
SHE IS NOT SEEN FOR THERE IS NOTHING TO SEE HER BY   719 16
OH THEN BE NAMELESS AND BE NEVER SEEN   737 16
BUT HAVE YOU SEEN A DEAD MAN HOW HIS STAR HAS GONE OUT + 800 18
LIKE SAD PROCESSIONS OF EXILES YOU COULD HAVE SEEN THEM+ 866   3
YOU SHOULD 'A SEEN HER SLIVE UP WHEN WE'D GO   *910   9
YOU SHOULD 'A SEEN HER KNEEL AN' LOOK DOWN   *910 10
FOR I HAVE SEEN THE VEIN   *937   7
SOME SAY THEY SEE THOUGH I HAVE NEVER SEEN   *937 28

SEEPING
  SEEPING SEEPING RECEDING   767 14
  AND LIFTED IN THE LONG SEEPING SWOON   769 14

SEEPS
  TOUCH COMES SLOWLY IF EVER IT SEEPS   470 25
  EVEN REMEMBRANCE SEEPS OUT   767 9

SEES
  OH BUT 'E DROPS 'IS FLAG WHEN 'E SEES ME   79 9
  BACK FROM THE STRAIGHT HORIZON THAT ENDS ALL ONE SEES   168 6
  ONE MOMENT SEES AND SWIFT ITS DREAM IS OVER   195 14
  NOW HE SEES THIS AS WELL   198 25
  SHE SEES THE BLADE OF THE SEA   200 6
  AND ASKS IF SHE SEES THE LAND THE LAND   201 3
  AS HE SEES ME BRINGING THE DINNER HE LIFTS   220 1
  WHO THEN SEES THE TWO-WINGED   226 17
  STARING AT WHAT HE SEES   227 10
  YET SHE SEES ME NOT   359 15
  HER BRIGHT EYE SEES BUT NOT ME NOT ANYTHING   359 16
  HIS BLACK SAD-LIDDED EYE SEES BUT BEHOLDS NOT   362 4
  AND IMMEDIATELY SHE SEES ME SHE BLINKS STARES DOESN'T   384 22
  AND SEES STRANGE LOOKS ON THE FACES OF MEN   459 27
  THAT'S WHAT HE SEES IN ME   489 22
  WHAT A PITY HE SEES HIMSELF SO WONDERFUL   528 25
  BURN THAT HE SEES EVE RUNNING FROM THE LIKES OF HIM I   633 28
  IF MAN ONLY LOOKS TO MAN AND NO-ONE SEES BEYOND   650 6
  SHE SEES MEN WALKING TOWARDS HER UNDER THE TREES   770 1
  AND SEES WHAT HE SEES IN THE FACES OF MEN   771 5
  SINCE NOBODY SEES IT   774 11
  OH BUT HE DROPS HIS FLAG WHEN 'E SEES ME   *921 5
  SHE WILL START WHEN SHE SEES ME AND BLUSHING SPREAD OUT+   *940 16
  AS HE SEES ME BRINGIN' THE DINNER HE LIFTS   *944 9

SEETHE
  THE FAINT FINE SEETHE IN THE AIR   216 6

SEETHES
  OH YOU STIFF SHAPES SWIFT TRANSFORMATION SEETHES   72 12
  AND PASSION UNBEARABLE SEETHES IN THE DARKNESS LIKE MUST   129 30
  AND IRRITATION SEETHES SECRETLY THROUGH THEIR GUTS AS T+   616 9

SEETHING
  WITH THE PALE DAWN SEETHING AT THE WINDOW   204 4
  LIKE THE SEETHING SOUND IN A SHELL   216 7
  IT IS DEATH STILL SEETHING WHERE   218 8
  FULL OF SEETHING WORMY HOLLOW FEELINGS   431 22
  THE DEAD IN THEIR SEETHING MINDS   441 1
  ROTTEN INSIDE THEY ARE AND SEETHING   462 23
  SHE'S SEETHING LIKE A VOLCANO AND VOLCANOS DON'T WANT   539 14
  WHISTLING AND SEETHING AND PULLING THE ANGLER DOWN INTO   586 27
  AND SINKS SEETHING AND SINKING CORRUPT   699 24

SEIZE
  I SAW AN ANGRY ITALIAN SEIZE AN IRRITATING LITTLE OFFIC+   674 20

SEIZED
  HAS NEVER SEIZED ME AND TERRIFIED ME   263 17
  THEY'VE SEIZED AND CARRIED THEM AWAY   633 11

SEIZES
  SEIZES YOU AS YOU CLENCH YOURSELF TOGETHER   370 17

SEIZING
  PARTING HIS STEEL-TRAP FACE SO SUDDENLY AND SEIZING HER   360 20
  SUDDENLY SEIZING THE UGLY ANKLE AS SHE STRETCHES OUT TO   361 17

SELF
  NOW I AM CAUGHT YOU ARE HOPELESSLY LOST O SELF   47 32
  DIM SELF THAT RISES SLOWLY TO LEAVES AND THE FLOWER'S G+   92 20
  CRUEL SELF THE FIGHT IS NOT FOR EXISTENCE THE FIGHT IS +   93 14
  SELF   93 19
  IF I COULD LIFT MY NAKED SELF TO YOU   122 18
  YOUR HUMAN SELF IMMORTAL TAKE THE WATERY TRACK   161 28
  HOW LOVELY IS THE SELF THIS DAY DISCLOSES   218 4
  MY VERY SELF I WITH THE WONDER MELLOW   218 6
  AUTOMATON OF YOUR UPRISEN SELF   290 28
  UNFOLDING ALL HER COILED AND LOVELY SELF   317 23
  IT'S THE FLOW OF YOUR LIFE IT'S YOUR MOVING SELF AND YOU   464 18
  YOU MUST KNOW SEX IN ORDER TO SAVE IT YOUR DEEPEST SELF   465 3
  OF THE ITCHING MIND AND THE MENTAL SELF WITH ITS PRURIE+   465 5
  IN LOVE WITH A SELF THAT NOW IS SHALLOW AND WITHERED   478 23
  YOUR OWN SELF THAT HAS PASSED LIKE A LAST SUMMER'S   478 24
  IF ONLY SHE HAD GONE DOWN TO A DEEPER SELF IN HERSELF   479 22
  YOUR SELF MOVES ON AND IS NOT TODAY WHAT IT WAS YESTERD+   543 14
  WHEN ALAS IT'S ONLY PART OF OUR CLEVER LITTLE SELF THAT+   543 23
  YOUR INTERESTING SELF   602 28
  SELF   620 14
  NATURALLY WE DESTROY THE MOST ESSENTIAL SELF IN US   621 9
  FOR LISTEN THE EGO-CENTRIC SELF IS THE SAME AS THE MACH+   635 8
  ENCLOSED CIRCLE OF SELF   637 6
  BUT WHAT WE MAY SACRIFICE IF WE CALL IT SACRIFICE FROM +   678 10
  THE SELF THAT WE ARE AT ITS BEST IS ALL THAT WE ARE   679 24
  WHICH IS THE MAN'S PURE SELF   679 26
  WHEN THE SELF HAS FALLEN FROM THE HANDS OF GOD   699 23
  AND THE WHEEL OF THE CONSCIOUS SELF SPINS ON IN ABSOLUT+   712 15
  TO ONE'S OWN SELF AND FIND AN EXIT   716 23
  FROM THE FALLEN SELF   716 24
  THAT LIES BETWEEN THE OLD SELF AND THE NEW   718 2
  MY LIFE MY BROODY SELF   766 23
  HIS MIND DEVELOPED AT THE EXPENSE OF HIS MALE SELF   841 20
  AND ALONE HE IS WHILE HE LIVES IN HIS DEEPEST SELF   843 26
  CRINGING PITY AND MY SELF WHITE-HANDED CAME   *897 4
  TOO GREAT A SKUNK TO ABIDE BY HIS OWN SELF   *949 2
  OWN SELF INTO IT   *949 23
  WHEN A MAN FREES HIS OWN SELF INTO HIS WORK   *949 24
  AND IN HIS DEEPEST SELF NEVER CEASES TO BE ALONE   *951 6

SELF-ABSORBED
  THE HANDSOME AND SELF-ABSORBED YOUNG MAN   605 1
  LOOKED AT THE LOVELY AND SELF-ABSORBED GIRL   605 2
  THE LOVELY AND SELF-ABSORBED GIRL   605 4
  LOOKED BACK AT THE HANDSOME AND SELF-ABSORBED YOUNG MAN   605 5
  ONES THE SELF-RIGHTEOUS SELF-ABSORBED   616 3

SELF-ABSORPTION
  HER SELF-ABSORPTION IS EVEN AS STRONG AS MINE   605 8
  HIS SELF-ABSORPTION IS EVEN STRONGER THAN MINE   605 12
  I MUST SEE IF I CAN'T ABSORB THIS SAMSON OF SELF-ABSORP+   605 14
  IN SELF-ABSORPTION AND SELF-INTEREST THEY WERE EQUALLY   605 18

SELF-ACCOMPLISHMENT
  THE BURDEN OF SELF-ACCOMPLISHMENT   215 9

SELF-ACTIVATED
  AND EVERY MAN WHO HAS BECOME A DETACHED AND SELF-ACTIVA+   713 4

SELF-ANALYSIS
  AND THE TURNING DOWN PLUNGE OF WRITHING OF SELF-KNOWLED+   701 5

SELF-APART-FROM-GOD
  KNOWLEDGE OF THE SELF-APART-FROM-GOD   701 16
  FOR THE KNOWLEDGE OF THE SELF-APART-FROM-GOD   701 17

SELF-ASSERTION
  SELF-ASSERTION   284 30
  IT IS A FORM OF WAR EVEN SELF-ASSERTION AND BEING WISE +   495 21
  AND EVERY SELF-ASSERTION CLASHES ON EVERY OTHER   496 23
  IN SELF-ASSERTION   502 17
  IN THIS WORLD OF MECHANICAL SELF-ASSERTION   511 5
  AND FALL INTO SHARP SELF-CENTRED SELF-ASSERTION SHARP O+   616 6

SELF-AWARENESS
  OF SELF-AWARENESS NOW APART FROM GOD FALLING   701 21
  ABSOLUTE SELF-AWARENESS ABSOLVED FROM THE MEDDLING OF C+   712 18

SELF-CENTRED
  AND FALL INTO SHARP SELF-CENTRED SELF-ASSERTION SHARP O+   616 6
  FOR THE DEFECTION OF THE SELF-CENTRED ONES   616 17
  AND THE PERSON HAS BECOME FINALLY SELF-CENTRED   617 7
  OR ELSE TO SEVER THE CONNECTION TO BECOME SELF-CENTRED +   617 15
  UNTIL THEY COLLAPSE INTO EGOISM THE MECHANICAL SELF-CEN+   649 4
  SO SELF-WILLED SELF-CENTRED SELF-CONSCIOUS PEOPLE DIE   676 6

SELF-CONCEIT
  SHE WAS TANGLED UP IN HER OWN SELF-CONCEIT A WOMAN   619 1
  ARE ALL THE OBSTRUCTIONS TO LIFE SELF-IMPORTANCE SELF-C+   678 11

SELF-CONSCIOUSLY
  FOR WE'RE ALL SELF-CONSCIOUSLY AWARE OF OURSELVES   496 19

SELF-CONSCIOUSNESS
  AND SPHINXES OF SELF-CONSCIOUSNESS   603 25
  SELF-CONSCIOUSNESS   672 3
  FATHOMLESS FATHOMLESS SELF-CONSCIOUSNESS WRIGGLING   701 22

SELF-CONSCIOUS
  WICKED FIG-TREE EQUALITY PUZZLE WITH YOUR SELF-CONSCIOUS   300 16
  NOW THAT IT SOUNDS SELF-CONSCIOUS THROUGH THE UNLIMITED+   325 4
  THAT BEING HER WAY OF ANSWER IF I SPEAK TO HER SELF-CON+   385 5
  SELF-CONSCIOUS LITTLE BITCH   398 13
  FROM ALL THE WHITE SELF-CONSCIOUS LECHERY   469 21
  SO MEAN AND SELF-CONSCIOUS BLOWING AND SNORING   494 20
  BEFORE SHE COULD SET THE CLAWS OF HER SELF-CONSCIOUS QU+   604 9
  WE HAVE BECOME FATALLY SELF-CONSCIOUS FATALLY SELF-IMPO+   674 9
  BUT WHEN PEOPLE ARE ONLY SELF-CONSCIOUS AND SELF-WILLED   675 18
  SO SELF-WILLED SELF-CENTRED SELF-CONSCIOUS PEOPLE DIE   676 6

SELF-DIRECTED
  ONLY THE MECHANICAL POWER OF SELF-DIRECTED ENERGY   675 23

SELF-DIVIDE
  PATIENTLY TO DIVIDE AND SELF-DIVIDE   64 12

SELF-EFFACINGLY
  SELF-EFFACINGLY   434 6

SELF-EXPOSURE
  SELF-EXPOSURE HARD HUMILIATION NEED TO ADD HIMSELF ON TO   362 31

SELF-FORGETFUL
  SELF-FORGETFUL AND GEMMED WITH EXPERIENCE   478 16

SELF-GATHERED
  IN OUR SHEAF OF SELF-GATHERED WOUNDS WE GO TO MEET   743 8

SELF-IMPORTANCE
  JUST FANTASIES OF SELF-IMPORTANCE   603 23
  THEIR OWN SELF-IMPORTANCE   603 24
  BECAUSE I COULD NOT ANSWER THE RIDDLE OF HER OWN SELF-I+   604 12
  ARE ALL THE OBSTRUCTIONS TO LIFE SELF-IMPORTANCE SELF-C+   678 11

SELF-IMPORTANT
  AND THE STIFF-NECKED PEOPLE AND THE SELF-WILLED PEOPLE +   616 2
  I DESPISE THAT SELF-IMPORTANT GAME   673 9
  WE HAVE BECOME FATALLY SELF-CONSCIOUS FATALLY SELF-IMPO+   674 9

SELF-INTEREST
  IN SELF-ABSORPTION AND SELF-INTEREST THEY WERE EQUALLY   605 18

SELFISH
  BLACK PROCREANT MALE OF THE SELFISH WILL AND LIBIDINOUS   383 14
  FIGHT OLD SATAN WITH A SELFISH WILL FIGHT FOR YOUR SELF+   383 22

SELF-KNOWLEDGE
    IN THE ENDLESS WRITHE OF THE LAST THE LAST SELF-KNOWLED+   700 27
    AND THE TURNING DOWN PLUNGE OF WRITHING OF SELF-KNOWLED+   701   5
    INTO THE ABYSS OF SELF-KNOWLEDGE   701 15
    WRITHING DEEPER AND DEEPER IN ALL THE MINUTIAE OF SELF-+   701 23

SELF-LESS
    THE WINDING-SHEET OF YOUR SELF-LESS IDEAL LOVE   291 12

SELF-MOTIVED
    SELF-MOTIVED   617 16

SELF-MURDER
    SURELY NOT SO FOR HOW COULD MURDER EVEN SELF-MURDER   717 15

SELF-PRESERVATION
    TO MAKE SELF-PRESERVATION AND SELF-PROTECTION THE FIRST+   523   3

SELF-PROTECTION
    TO MAKE SELF-PRESERVATION AND SELF-PROTECTION THE FIRST+   523   3

SELF-RIGHTEOUS
    YOU HEAR THE STERTOROUS SELF-RIGHTEOUS HEAVY   528 19
    ONES THE SELF-RIGHTEOUS SELF-ABSORBED   616   3

SELF-SACRIFICE
    SELF-SACRIFICE AFTER ALL IS A WRONG AND MISTAKEN IDEA   678   1
    SELF-SACRIFICE IS PERHAPS THE VILEST DEED A MAN CAN DO   679 23

SELF-SAME
    OF THIS SELF-SAME DARKNESS YET THE SHADOWY HOUSE BELOW   172 23
    AND SELF-SAME DARKNESS CHAFED TO IRE   773   7

SELF-SATISFIED
    IN THE WEEKLY PRESS THEIR SELF-SATISFIED SWIPE   680 23

SELF-SORRY
    JIMLETS AND SELF-SORRY SAMLETS   457 20

SELF-SUFFICIENT
    OH WONDERFUL MACHINE SO SELF-SUFFICIENT SO SUFFICIENT U+   643   8

SELF'S
    SEE IN HIM YOUR SELF'S DREAM IN HIS SORE   157 31

SELF-THWARTED
    DON JUAN WAS NEVER ANYTHING BUT A SELF-THWARTED SODOMIST   *949 17

SELF-WILLED
    AND THE STIFF-NECKED PEOPLE AND THE SELF-WILLED PEOPLE +   616   2
    OR ELSE TO SEVER THE CONNECTION TO BECOME SELF-CENTRED +   617 15
    BUT WHEN PEOPLE ARE ONLY SELF-CONSCIOUS AND SELF-WILLED   675 18
    SO SELF-WILLED SELF-CENTRED SELF-CONSCIOUS PEOPLE DIE   676   6

SELF-WILL
    LEAVE THE OLD ONES FIXED TO THEIR UGLY COGGED SELF-WILL   662 23
    SELF-WILL   678 12

SELL
    TO THE TOWN AND TRIES TO SELL THEM   203   3
    THE ROOT OF OUR PRESENT EVIL IS THAT WE BUY AND SELL   482 28
    MEN SELL THEMSELVES FOR A WAGE AND EMPLOYERS LOOK OUT   483   2
    IT WAS NOWT BUT A DIRTY SELL THAT'S ALL   553   3
    NOTHING TO SELL IN THEE NOUGHT TO BE BOUGHT   824 10
    SOME OF MY STRENGTH FOR MYSELF FOR IF I SHOULD SELL   *896   3
    SOME OF MY STRENGTH FOR MYSELF FOR IF I SHOULD SELL   *904 24

SELLING
    ULTIMATELY WE ARE ALL BUSY BUYING AND SELLING ONE ANOTH+   482 29
    SELLING   483 27

SELVES
    SOME OF YOUR SELVES MY LOVE THAT SOME   100 20
    WE ARE NOT OUR OLD SELVES ANY MORE   244 22
    WITH ALL THE HURT TO THEIR INSTINCTIVE AND EMOTIONAL SE+   544 28
    WHEN IT COMES TO OUR EMOTIONAL SELVES   833   9

SEND
    YOU PROMISED TO SEND ME SOME VIOLETS DID YOU FORGET   58   8
    SEND SUDDENLY OUT AND EVERY GESTURE DOES   89   5
    ANOTHER LIFE FROM OUR LIVES SO SHOULD SEND   218 21
    AND SEND MANKIND TO ITS INFERIOR BLAZES   316 29
    THEY SEND AEROPLANES ACROSS THE SKY   441 18
    O GOD OF JUSTICE SEND NO MORE SAVIOURS   442 10
    AND SEND THIN DRAUGHTS OF WORDS   506 22
    THE SIGHT OF AN ORDINARY TOM WOULDN'T SEND THEM INTO   581 24
    WILL SEND UP THE WILD CRY OF DESPAIR   624 13
    WILL AT LAST SEND YOU INSANE   655 17
    TO SEND ME FORTH ON A NEW MORNING A NEW MAN   727 30
    AH HEAVEN SEND   748 13
    QUETZALCOATL MY BROTHER HE CALLED SEND ME MY IMAGES   789 17
    SEND ME THEM BY THE SWIFT WAY THE WAY OF THE SPARKS   789 19
    SEND JESUS HIS IMAGES BACK MARY AND THE SAINTS AND ALL   791 20
    I'LL SEND FIRE AND ASHES UPON THEM AND SMOTHER THEM ALL   792   5
    THE WILD GODS SEND VITALITY THEY PUT THE LIGHTNING INTO+   843   5
    SEND UP THE LAST WILD CRY OF DESPAIR   *954 11
    AND THEY SEND ARROWS OF ANGER BULLETS AND BOMBS OF FRUS+   *958   6

SENDING
    EASILY DOWN THE SKY THE DAISIES SENDING   150 11
    CLEAN PAIN SENDING ON US A CHILL DOWN HERE   225   4
    SENDING OUT MAGNETIC VIBRATIONS OF WARNING PITCH-DARK   289   2
    SENDING THEM RIOTING AT DAWN DOWN THE LANE OF SCARLET P+   860 23
    SENDING INTO ITS SLUMBERING FLESH   *937 16

SENDS
    AND SENDS OFF MILLIONS OF SPARKS OF NEW ATOMS   506   9
    THAT SENDS PULSES EVEN THROUGH ME   525   5
    NO MORE HE SENDS HIS DAUGHTER   541 20
    SENDS SUMMONS IN THE OLD HOLLOWS OF THE SUN   623   8
    HE SENDS THE EAGLE OF SILENCE DOWN ON WIDE WINGS   799 17
    HE SENDS THE SERPENT OF POWER UP MY FEET AND MY LOINS   799 20

SENSATION
    NO MORE NARCISSUS PERFUME LILY HARLOTS THE BLADES OF SE+   273 16
    AND ENJOYING THE SENSATION OF HEAVEN AND RIGHTEOUSNESS +   324 32
    YOUR LIFE A SLUICE OF SENSATION ALONG YOUR SIDES   335   8

SENSATIONAL
    PONDERING THIS NEW TRUTH OF THE SENSATIONAL YOUNG I SAID   532   1

SENSATIONS
    CORPSE-ANATOMIES WITH READY-MADE SENSATIONS   584 21
    CARRION-GREEDY IN ITS SENSATIONS   830 21

SENSE
    AND THE SENSE OF HER CLINGING FLESH WAS SWEET   62   1
    MY SENSE AND REASON   121   5
    ME IN ANY SENSE   266 15
    ALONE WITH NO SENSE OF BEING ALONE   354 10
    AND HAVE A COOL SENSE OF TRUTH INHUMAN TRUTH AT LAST   481 23
    HE IS GIVING HIMSELF AWAY IN EVERY SENSE OF THE WORD   523 11
    AND THE PURE INTELLECT GIVES ONE A LAST MASTURBATING SE+   532   9
    THE YOUNG HAVE LEARNED SOME SENSE   559 22
    MAYBE A SENSE OF DESTINY   560   5
    AND WHAT A SENSE OF TRUE HUMOUR THEY'VE GOT HA-HA   583 21
    IS THE SENSE OF TRUTH   653   6
    IS THE SENSE OF JUSTICE   653   8
    THE PROFOUND AND THRILLING VIBRATION OF JUSTICE SENSE O+   653 15
    THEY'RE NOT NICE IN OUR SENSE OF THE WORD ARE THEY NOW   660   7
    LET'S HOPE THERE'LL BE MORE SENSE IN TAIL-TUFTS   665   4
    ON AND ON WITH THE TRIUMPHANT SENSE OF POWER LIKE MACHI+   675 25
    YET THROUGH THE TEARS STEALS A SENSE OF PEACE AND GREAT+   768   1
    AND WHICH ROCKS WITH A SENSE OF CONNECTION RELIGION   844 24
    AND TREMBLES WITH A SENSE OF TRUTH PRIMORDIAL CONSCIOUS+   844 25
    AND IS SILENT WITH A SENSE OF JUSTICE THE FIERY PRIMORD+   844 26
    I HAVE SUCH SWARMING SENSE OF LIVES AT THE BASE OF ME S+   *900   5
    TO ME YET STILL BECAUSE OF THE SENSE OF THEIR CLOSENESS+   *900 16
    I HAVE SUCH SWARMING SENSE OF LIVES AT THE BASE OF ME S+   *903 17
    TO ME YET STILL BECAUSE OF THE SENSE OF THEIR CLOSENESS+   *903 28
    AND THE SENSE OF HER CLINGING FLESH WAS SWEET   *912   9
    FOIL THE SENSE   *914 15
    AND POISED WITH A SENSE OF JUSTICE AS WORLDS ARE POISED   *952   9

SENSE-CHANGE
    AND THOSE THAT DO DESCEND HAVE GOT TO SUFFER A SENSE-CH+   667 24

SENSELESS
    TILL ALL IS SOUNDLESS AND SENSELESS A TREMENDOUS BODY O+   698 22

SENSES
    SO THE LION OF THE SENSES THOUGHT IT WAS WORTH IT   324 25
    ONLY HE SENSES THE VULNERABLE FOLDS OF SKIN   362 15
    BRINGS A FRESH FRAGRANCE OF HEAVEN TO OUR SENSES   467 10
    SOFTLY FLUTTERING THE SENSES IN THE EXQUISITE ORGASM OF   481 24
    YOU MUST FUSE MIND AND WIT WITH ALL THE SENSES   653   9
    OF THE SENSES   655 14
    SENSES   690 18
    TO OUR SENSES THE ELEMENTS ARE FOUR   706   1
    THEY CALL ALL EXPERIENCE OF THE SENSES MYSTIC WHEN THE +   707 26
    BUT IF I EAT AN APPLE I LIKE TO EAT IT WITH ALL MY SENS+   708 10
    IN WHICH THE SOUL DELIGHTS AND THE SENSES   708 22
    HYPERTROPHY OF THE MIND ATROPHY OF THE SENSES   841 21
    WITH ALL YOUR SENSES ASHRINK   *931 14

SENSIBILITIES
    SENSIBILITIES HATE EVERYTHING THAT'S WELL   633   6

SENSIBLE
    YOU IF YOU WERE SENSIBLE   130 24

SENSITIVE
    AND SENSITIVE BUD-LIKE BLOSSOMING OF PASSION   113   6
    MY VEIL OF SENSITIVE MYSTERY RENT IN TWAIN   151 19
    IF ONLY I AM SENSITIVE SUBTLE OH DELICATE A WINGED GIFT   250 16
    OF THE SUAVE SENSITIVE BODY THE HUNGER FOR THIS   263 16
    STILL AND SENSITIVE AND ACTIVE   285 25
    LIKE STEEL LIKE SENSITIVE STEEL IN THE AIR   300 29
    GREY LAVENDER SENSITIVE STEEL CURVING THINLY AND BRITTLY   300 30
    DROP WHICH SHE LOVES SENSITIVE MOTHER KANGAROO   393   9
    HER SENSITIVE LONG PURE-BRED FACE   393 10
    FOR YOU'RE SENSITIVE   400 14
    YOUR SENSITIVE LOVE-PRIDE BEING ALL HURT   400 29
    SHE SKIMS HIM SENSITIVE   426 17
    TO BE TRUE TO THE NATURE OF IT ITS RESERVE ITS SENSITIV+   464 20
    THE SENSITIVE DELICACY OF YOUR SEX IN ITS EBBING TO AND+   464 25
    WE ENGLISH ARE SO SENSITIVE MUCH MORE THAN APPEARS   576   5
    AND THE SINGING IS LOW AND SENSITIVE   768 17
    COILS AND RECOILS SENSITIVE TO LIFE AND CONSCIOUS OF TR+   *952   8

SENSITIVE-FOOTED
    THE LONG-NOSED SENSITIVE-FOOTED SUBTLY-SMILING ETRUSCANS   296 15

SENSITIVELY
    SO SHE WISTFULLY SENSITIVELY SNIFFS THE AIR AND THEN TU+   393 25
    MEN USED TO PUT THEM FORTH SENSITIVELY LIKE BOUGHS LEAV+   *950   2

SENSITIVENESS
    AUDILE TACTILE SENSITIVENESS AS OF A TENDRIL WHICH ORIE+   285 26
    HAVE YOU A STRANGE ELECTRIC SENSITIVENESS IN YOUR STEEL+   301   2

SENSUAL
  AND THE NEXT DEEPEST SENSUAL EXPERIENCE   653   7
  SATISFACTORY SENSUAL EXPERIENCE   653 12
  THE PROFOUND SENSUAL EXPERIENCE OF TRUTH YEA THIS IS   653 13
  AND YOUR SENSUAL ATROPHY   655 16
  AS IF THE REDNESS OF A RED GERANIUM COULD BE ANYTHING B+   690 15
  AND AS IF SENSUAL EXPERIENCE COULD TAKE PLACE BEFORE TH+   690 17
  AND THEY ROCK AND THEY ROCK THROUGH THE SENSUAL AGELESS+   694   8

SENSUALITIES
  THE PROFOUNDEST OF ALL SENSUALITIES   653   5

SENSUALLY
  WE DON'T EXIST UNLESS WE ARE DEEPLY AND SENSUALLY IN TO+   613   6

SENT
  HASNA TER SENT ME WHOAM WHEN I   80   6
  YOU SENT ME A CLOVEN FIRE   108 17
  OVER THE POPPIES SENT   200 24
  AND THAT SENT THE BLOOD RUSHING TO THE SURFACE OF THE B+   502   7
  HE THOUGHT THEM SO HE SENT THEM HOME   577   5
  RENASCENCE ALL SENT TO HELL   633   4
  HAS SHE SENT ME A LETTER   748 26
  SENT OUT THE SUN SO THAT SOMETHING SHOULD FLUTTER IN HE+   783   4
  AND SENT THE EAGLE TO KEEP AN EYE ON HIM   783   5
  MY FATHER IS DEEP WITHIN THE DEEPS WHENCE HE SENT ME FO+   799 16
  HASNA TER SENT ME WHOAM WHEN I   *922   6
  OUR DRAUGHT OF FAITH THAT SENT US ON ANEW   *941 12

SENTENCE
  AWAITING THE SENTENCE OUT FROM THE WELKIN BROUGHT   142 16

SENTIMENTALISM
  FOR HIS OWN DEFICIENCY MOST MAWKISH IN ITS INVERTED SEN+   842   4

SENTIMENTALIZE
  DON'T SENTIMENTALIZE ABOUT HIM   776 22
  DON'T SENTIMENTALIZE HIS SAVAGE CONSCIOUSNESS   776 30

SENTRY
  SENTRY UPON THE DEAD OAK WHILE ANOTHER BELOW   *894 28

SEPARATE
  BEHIND SEPARATE DOORS   229   4
  AND YET HOW HIS SEPARATE BEING LIBERATES ME   252   3
  NOW TO THEIR SEPARATE ENDS   253 18
  A SEPARATE WAY   253 20
  SEPARATE BEING   266 32
  KEEP OURSELVES SEPARATE PHYSICALLY   470 16
  AND SEPARATE HEART FROM HEART AND CUT AWAY ALL CARESSES   707 18
  AND WHO CAN SEPARATE US ANY MORE   879 32
  THAN WHO CAN SEPARATE TWO LITHE RICH FLAMES   879 33

SEPARATELY
  LET US SEPARATELY GO TO THE MORNING STAR   812   3

SEPARATENESS
  AND THERE WILL BE A VIVID RECOIL INTO SEPARATENESS   611 18

SEPARATES
  A STRANGE GREY DISTANCE SEPARATES   607   1
  SEPARATES ITSELF ON THE BLACKNESS   719 28

SEPARATING
  FOR THEIR MIDDLENESS IS ONLY AN UNREALITY SEPARATING TWO   527 26

SEPARATION
  EVEN TO MYSELF HOW BITTER THE SEPARATION   122 14
  EVER MORE EXQUISITE DISTILLED IN SEPARATION   281 11

SEPTEMBER
  WOULD BE AS IN THE HAZEL-WOODS OF SEPTEMBER   504 11
  IN SOFT SEPTEMBER AT SLOW SAD MICHAELMAS   697   2
  EVEN WHERE PERSEPHONE GOES JUST NOW FROM THE FROSTED SE+   697 16
  IN SOFT SEPTEMBER AT SLOW SAD MICHAELMAS   *955 26
  DOWN THE WAY PERSEPHONE GOES JUST NOW IN FIRST-FROSTED +   *956 13

SEPTIC
  WITH FINGER-NAILS OF SEPTIC CRITICISING   533 10

SERAPHIM
  AND RANGE THEMSELVES LIKE GREAT FIERCE SERAPHIM FACING +   695   3

SERE
  AGAIN FROM EARTH LIKE LILIES FLAGGED AND SERE   87 28

SERENE
  ALL HOPE OF MY ATTAINMENT THENCE SERENE   877 16
  OF THIS DARK EARTH AND WANDERING ALL SERENE   ·*945   5

SERENELY
  SERENELY SMILING AT NAUGHT   54 13
  SERENELY WITH STEPS UNSWERVING   63 32

SERGEANT
  THE SERGEANT SAYS THAT EIGHT AND TWENTY WAGONS   732   1

SERIOUS
  IF IT'S SERIOUS OR IF IT'S PLAY   549 24

SERIOUSLY
  THAT'S WHY ONE DOESN'T HAVE TO TAKE THEM SERIOUSLY   660   8
  BUT YOU MUST NEVER TAKE THEM SERIOUSLY THEY WOULDN'T UN+   660 15
  HE IS TAKEN BY THE SCIENTISTS VERY SERIOUSLY   708 13
  HE TAKES HIMSELF SERIOUSLY   836 13
  FLOWING I KNOW NOT HOW YET SERIOUSLY   *907   8
  WHAT A PITY HE TAKES HIMSELF SERIOUSLY AND DRAWS A   *950 28

SERIOUSNESS
  DON'T MAKE IT IN GHASTLY SERIOUSNESS   517   2

SERPENT
  HELL REARING ITS HUSBAND-SPLENDID SERPENT HEADS   308 20
  DARK BREATH OF THE EARTH THE SERPENT SLID FORTH LAY REV+   348   7
  OR EVEN THE SLY GOLD SERPENT FATHERLY LIFTED HIS HEAD O+   437 18
  FOURTH DIMENSION NOT IN YARDS AND MILES LIKE THE ETERNA+   761 16
  HE SENDS THE SERPENT OF POWER UP MY FEET AND MY LOINS   799 20
  AND I AM NOT WITH YOU TILL MY SERPENT HAS COILED HIS CI+   801 28
  SERPENT IN THE BELLIES OF MEN   806 12
  BEFORE THE GOLDEN FATHERLY SERPENT LIFTED HIS HEAD OFF +   *946 27

SERPENT-FLAME
  WHO RUNS ATHWART MY SERPENT-FLAME   805   6

SERPENTS
  EVEN THE LAMBS WILL STRETCH FORTH THEIR NECKS LIKE SERP+   624 16
  AND THE SERPENTS WANDER THEIR OWN WAYS RECONCILED   771   8

SERPENTS'
  COLD VOICELESS AGE-AFTER-AGE BEHIND HIM SERPENTS' LONG   360 15

SERPENT-YELLOW
  IS THE YELLOW SERPENT-YELLOW SHINING OF MY SUN   805   3
  SHINES THE YELLOW SERPENT-YELLOW SHINING OF THE SUN   806   6

SERRATED
  AND SERRATED WINGS AGAINST THE SKY   341 12

SERRIED
  OUR SERRIED HEARTS DRIFTING WITHOUT A PLACE   736   9
  THIS SERRIED ECSTASY OF PREVALENT DEATH   737   5

SERVANT
  COME ON YOU CRAPA I'M NOT YOUR SERVANT   384 33
  AND CEASES TO BE A ROBOT AND BECOMES A SERVANT OF LIFE   648 19

SERVANT-MAID
  AND A SERVANT-MAID BRINGS ME MY TEA   490 26

SERVANT'S
  WITHOUT A SERVANT'S HELP SO HE BE NOT STRICKEN IN YEARS   277 11

SERVE
  OF EASY SAILING ODD RED WICKS SERVE   172 20
  AND LEARN TO SERVE   234 22
  AND SERVE NOW WOMAN SERVE AS A WOMAN SHOULD   234 29
  SINCE I MUST SERVE AND STRUGGLE WITH THE IMMINENT   234 31
  SERVE THEN I TELL YOU ADD YOUR STRENGTH TO MINE   235   1
  SERVE   390 22
  SERVE VAST MOUNTAINOUS BLOOD IN SUBMISSION AND SPLENDOUR   390 23
  SERVE ROYALTY   390 24
  I SERVE I SERVE IN ALL THE WEARY IRONY OF HIS MIEN 'TIS+   391 34
  WHO SERVE   391 35
  SERVE ME I AM MEET TO BE SERVED   392   7
  DON'T SERVE THEM   440 25
  WHY HAVE MACHINES THAT WE ONLY HAVE TO SERVE   452   2
  AND TO SERVE THAT WHICH IS FLAMEY OR PURE AND WATERY OR   637 10
  LET THEM SERVE   638   6
  IN A ROBOT-DEMOCRACY NOBODY IS WILLING TO SERVE   648   8
  AND THE FEW LOOK INTO THE EYES OF THE GODS AND SERVE TH+   650   4
  AH YES MEN MUST LEARN TO SERVE   650 12
  AND SERVE THE BEST OF FOOD THE FONDEST WINE   723 11

SERVED
  SERVE ME I AM MEET TO BE SERVED   392   7
  AS NO MAN EVER SERVED BEFORE   447 25
  AND SERVED THEIR GREAT PURPOSE   609 23
  HERE IN THIS HOUSE WHERE I HAVE SERVED SO LONG   877 22
  I SERVED HIM SO   877 25

SERVES
  HE SERVES THE SON OF MAN   327   7
  AND HEAR HIM BELLOW AFTER MANY YEARS THE BULL THAT SERV+   327   8
  AND DEMOS SERVES LIFE AS IT GLEAMS ON THE FACE OF THE F+   650   3

SERVICE
  DEATH IN WHOSE SERVICE IS NOTHING OF GLADNESS TAKES ME   48   9
  THEY ARE CHANTING NOW THE SERVICE OF ALL THE DEAD   233   1
  REALLY LIVING IN HER SERVICE AND SERVING HER   447 24
  OH JESUS DIDN'T YOU SEE WHEN YOU TALKED OF SERVICE   629   1
  INTO SERVICE LIKE THE ROOTS OF TREES   637 16
  BRINGS HIM TO HIS KNEES IN HOMAGE AND PURE PASSION OF S+   648 17
  DEMOCRACY IS SERVICE BUT NOT THE SERVICE OF DEMOS   650   1
  AND GIVE THEM PLACE AND HONOUR AND SERVICE MEET   740 15
  SOOTHE THEM WITH SERVICE AND HONOUR AND SILENCE MEET   740 17
  CHILD DEAR TO MY EYE GOD'S BLESSING IS ON THY SERVICE   749 21

SERVING
  THEN MORE THAN THAT HE MAKES A WOMAN FEEL HE IS SERVING   447 22
  REALLY LIVING IN HER SERVICE AND SERVING HER   447 24
  SERVING WITH DELIGHT AND WITH REVERENCE THOSE MEN WHOSE+   648 20
  DEMOCRACY IS DEMOS SERVING LIFE   650   2

SET
  SUCH RESOLUTE SHAPES SO HARSHLY SET   53 24
  DO YOU SET YOUR FACE AGAINST THE DAUGHTER   55   4
  SET LIKE ROCKS BESIDE A SEA OF GLOOM   56 14
  ASIDE O' T' GRAVE AN' TH' COFFIN SET   60 12
  AN' OUR TED'S COFFIN SET ON TH' GROUND   60 21
  WHITHER I TURN AND SET   99 23
  AND SHOWS THE RED OF HAWTHORN SET   105   1
  SINCE THE BELOVED FADED MOTHER THAT SET US ALIGHT   132 17
  WHAT IF UNWITTING I SET THE DOOR OF ETERNITY WIDE   147 11
  I WILL SET A SEAL UPON YOU FROM MY LIP   153 20
  WILL SET A GUARD OF HONOUR AT EACH DOOR   153 21
  WAS SET TO SONG AND NEVER YOUR SONG DENIES   156 23

SET

KNOWLEDGE I SET YOUR HEART TO ITS STRONGER BEAT   156 28
WHO FOR ONE STRANGE YEAR WAS AS A BRIDE TO YOU YOU SET +   157   4
DEATHWARD SET   199 20
STRANGE THAT THE URGENT WILL IN ME TO SET   218 18
THREE SIDES SET ON ME SPACE AND FEAR BUT THE FOURTH SIDE   249 10
THREE SIDES SET ON ME CHAOS AND BOUNCE BUT THE FOURTH   249 27
HER HANDS SLID IN AND SET ME FREE   262 15
IN HEAVEN'S FIELDS SET   268 18
A SET STOIC ENDURANCE NON-EUROPEAN   292 12
TO SET AGAIN INTO ROCK   294   4
NO BOUNDS BEING SET   306 34
SHOUTING FORTH FLAME TO SET THE WORLD ON FIRE   315   2
AND SET THE STINKING RUBBISH-HEAP OF THIS FOUL WORLD   315 23
AND SET FORWARD SLOW-DRAGGING ON YOUR FOUR-PINNED TOES   352 27
SET FORTH LITTLE TITAN UNDER YOUR BATTLE-SHIELD   353 33
OBSTACLE TO SET HIS TEETH IN THE SUN   378   7
AND LIFT HIS FACE AND SET HIS BREAST   428 18
SET UP TO JUDGE BETWEEN LIFE AND DEATH   528 11
THE FATHER EATS THE PEAR AND THE SON'S TEETH ARE SET ON+   530 22
WITH MASTS ERECT AND SPARS ALL SET AND SAILS SPREAD   542   2
HOW SHE SET US FREE   557 26
BEFORE SHE COULD SET THE CLAWS OF HER SELF-CONSCIOUS QU+   604   9
WITH A SET OF CANKERED MAGISTRATES AND BUSY-BUSY BOBBIES   634   8
TO SET ALL MEN FREE   636 17
THOUGHT IS NOT A TRICK OR AN EXERCISE OR A SET OF DODGES   673 14
I ONLY CAN SET OTHER PEOPLE RIGHT   680 11
AND SET ME AGAIN ON MOON-REMEMBERING FEET   696   6
IT IS SET UP AS A BOUNDARY AND BLOOD AND SWEAT   706 13
SET FOOD FOR THEM AND ENCOURAGE THEM TO BUILD   722 13
SET A PLACE FOR THE DEAD WITH A CUSHION AND SOFT SEAT   723   9
THEY SET FOOT ON THIS LAND TO WHICH THEY HAVE THE RIGHT   739 13
FOR OH TO FEEL THE RHYTHM SET   747 16
SET FREE AGAIN   747 20
HAS DEATH SET ME APART   749   9
SET OFF IN DIFFERENT DIRECTIONS NOT DIFFERENT DIRECTION+   760 24
BUT LO YOU INERT ONES I WILL SET THE DRAGONS UPON YOU   796 25
THE TROUBLE ABOUT THOSE THAT SET UP TO BE MORAL JUDGES   836 20
THERE IN THE HEART OF A STAR SET FAR OFF IN THE NIGHT   865   7
FOR WHETHER I SEE YOU SET THE DAFFODILS   875   7
SET DOWN THE TRAY BEFORE ME AS I WORK   875 11
FOR YOU SET WIDE THE DOORS OF MY VENTURESOME ARK   875 23
AND STEALING INTO HIS SLEEP SHOULD SET HIM LONGING   877 33
AND SET US AFFRIGHT   *929 25
SINCE THE BELOVED FADED MOON THAT SET US ALIGHT   *938   9
THREE SIDES SET ON ME SPACE AND FEAR BUT THE FOURTH SID+   *945 22
TO SET SOFTLY FORTH ON THE LONGEST JOURNEY THE LONGEST +   *957 19

SETS

SETS QUIVERING WITH WISDOM THE COMMON THINGS   46 19
THE MOON SETS FORTH O' NIGHTS   63 30
SUCH ANGER AS SETS YOUR MOUTH UNWONTEDLY   85 20
SOMETHING WHICH SETS THE BLACK POPLARS ASHAKE WITH HYST+   102 26
THE SUN SETS OUT THE AUTUMN CROCUSES   177   1
IT SETS UP A STRANGE FIRE   241 10
THE SAME SETS THE THROSTLE AT SUNSET ON A BOUGH   272 25
AND ROTTENNESS SOON SETS IN   284   5
THE SUN SETS IN YOU   289 25
WHICH AT ONCE SETS OFF TO BE THE ONE AND ONLY   300   3
SEX WHICH BREAKS US INTO VOICE SETS US CALLING ACROSS T+   366 34
PELTING BEHIND ON THE DUSTY TRAIL WHEN THE HORSE SETS O+   397 12
BECAUSE ALL THE FACES CONTAIN SETS OF EMOTIONAL AND   657   2
WHERE THE GREY TWILIGHT OF EVIL SETS IN   711 25
THE NEW MOON SETS AT SUNDOWN   816   5
EVEN IN THE MOST IMMORAL SETS THERE IS STILL THIS DESIR+   829 20
PALE DREAMY CHAPLETS A GREY NUN-SISTER SETS   854 23
SETS MY HEART ALSO THROBBING WITH PAIN   862 22
THE SUN SETS WIDE THE YELLOW CROCUSES   868 17
THE SUN SETS WIDE THE YELLOW CROCUSES   *941 17

SETTING

INTO THE SETTING SUN IF SHE CAME TO ME HERE   35   5
FOR ALL THAT THE SETTING SUNS ARE OPEN   278 24
EACH ONE SETTING OFF STRAIGHT TO THE SKY   299 27
SETTING SUPREME ANNUNCIATION TO THE WORLD   304 21
SETTING OFF SOMEWHERE APPARENTLY   356 22
AS THE SUN OF MY SOUL IS SETTING   455 21
SETTING FIERCE AND UNDAUNTED WINTRY   455 22
BUT SETTING SETTING BEHIND THE SOUNDING SEA BETWEEN   455 23
SINKS SINKS TO SETTING AND THE WINTER SOLSTICE   455 27
SETTING THE FLOWERS ALONG THE MIDDAY MEAL   877 28
THE LAST DAY AND THE SETTING FORTH   *960 19

SETTLE

TO SETTLE THE QUESTION HEADS OR TAILS HAS CAUGHT   54 10
OR LIKE TWO BUTTERFLIES THAT SETTLE ON A GLASS   65   3
A MOMENT THEN IN WEARINESS SETTLE   109 15
LIKE HEAVY BIRDS FROM THE MORNING STUBBLE TO SETTLE   128 11
TO SETTLE AT LAST IN THE DARK   253 31
SETTLE AND STAND ON LONG THIN SHANKS   333   1
OF ONE WHO WILL SETTLE ON ICEBERGS AND HONK ACROSS THE   439   2
THEN YOU WILL SETTLE THE HASH OF BUSINESS FINALLY   484 21
ABOUT LIKE A SWAN THAT CAN'T SETTLE   524 22
THE ONLY WAY TO SETTLE THE PROPERTY QUESTION   665   6
BUTTERFLY WHY DO YOU SETTLE ON MY SHOE AND SIP THE DIRT+   696 13
IS LIKE WHEN TWO WHITE BUTTERFLIES SETTLE IN THE ARMS O+   *913   3
OR AS TWO WHITE BUTTERFLIES SETTLE IN THE CUP OF ONE FL+   *914   4
SETTLE UPON US MAGNETIC SO WE WAX AND BLOOM   *938 18

SETTLED

THAT SETTLED UPON MY FACE AND HANDS TILL IT SEEMED   99   4
AND SHE SETTLED SOFT   124   5
THE FROST HAS SETTLED DOWN UPON THE TREES   141 27
IS SETTLED ON THE LAND ROSES ARE SCARCE IN ENGLAND VERY   569   8
I DID NOT KNOW LOVE HAD SETTLED DOWN ON ME   860   1
IT SETTLED SO SOFTLY I WAS ALL UNAWARE   860   6
AND THE BROWN DOG SETTLED THE REST   *933   8
LIKE A REIVING CUCKOO SHE SETTLED DOWN   *936   6

SETTLED

SO SHE SETTLED SOFT   *936 11

SETTLES

OF LOVE TAKES POSSESSION AND SETTLES HER DOWN   125   4

SETTLING

SHE SUNK INTO MY SIGHT LIKE A SETTLING BIRD   123   8
MY SOUL TO SEE YOU SETTLING AND TRYING TO CLIMB   221 23
IN SETTLING THE PROPERTY QUESTION BETWEEN THEM   664 17
WITH FAIR FLAKES SETTLING DOWN ON IT BEYOND THE TOWN   *898 12
WITH FAIR FLAKES SETTLING DOWN ON IT BEYOND THE TOWN   *901 21
SHE SUNK INTO MY SIGHT LIKE A SETTLING BIRD   *934 14
MY HEART TO SEE YOU SETTLING AND TRYING TO CLIMB   *945   9

SEVEN

FLUSHED WITH THE SONGS OF SEVEN LARKS SINGING AT ONCE G+   34 14
SCRAMBLE SEVEN TOADS ACROSS SILK OBSCURE LEAVES   126 18
SEVEN TOADS THAT MOVE IN THE DUSK TO SHARE   126 19
SEVEN DAYS MY LAD OR NONE   138   6
IT'S TA'EN THEE SEVEN DAYS TER SAY IT TER ME   139 30
ENSHEATHED INVULNERABLE WITH ME WITH SEVEN   154 23
WHAT THE BELOVED SEVEN   196 19
THE WHIRLIGIG OF DOZENS AND THE PINNACLE OF SEVEN   355 26
ON THE DEPTHS OF THE SEVEN SEAS   694   9
LO THE LAST OF THE SEVEN GREAT LAUGHS OF GOD   698 16
LO THE LAST OF THE SEVEN GREAT LAUGHS OF CREATION   698 17
THE SILENCE OF THE LAST OF THE SEVEN GREAT LAUGHS OF GOD 698 29
WHEN THE PLANETS HAVE GIVEN SEVEN NODS   702   6
IT SHALL BE IT SHALL BE ASSENTED SEVEN TIMES   702   7
BY THE GREAT SEVEN BY HELIOS THE BRIGHTEST   702   8
THE SEVEN GREAT ONES WHO MUST ALL SAY YES   702 12
WITH SEVEN VEILS AND AN INNERMOST   726   8
AND BORN HIM A SON OR SO WHO AT THE AGE OF SEVEN IS SO + 842   7
BABY WAS HER LITTLE BOY OF SEVEN   842 23
SEVEN IS STILL A SAFE-ISH AGE   842 27
RICH WITH THE SONGS OF SEVEN LARKS SINGING AT ONCE GOES+ *892   2

SEVEN-BRANCHED

THE JEWISH SEVEN-BRANCHED TALLOW-STINKING CANDLESTICK   299 20

SEVEN-DAY

YES YES IN THE SEVEN-DAY WEEK   702   2

SEVENFOLD

IN CONFIRMATION I HEAR SEVENFOLD LARK-SONGS PEALING   34 29

SEVENTH

ON THE SEVENTH DAY LET EVERY MAN WASH HIMSELF AND PUT O+ 791 22

SEVENTY

BECAUSE OF THEIR OWN FIFTY OR SIXTY OR SEVENTY OR   502 20

SEVENTY-NINE

THE BURDENED AGE SEVENTY-NINE THE VICAR   859   2

SEVENTY-SEVEN

AS IF IT'S MY FAULT THAT THE OLD GIRL IS SEVENTY-SEVEN   502 22

SEVER

OR ELSE TO SEVER THE CONNECTION TO BECOME SELF-CENTRED + 617 15

SEVERAL

OF SEVERAL INSULTS OF BLOTTED PAGES AND SCRAWL   74 14
OF YOUR SEVERAL FACES I HAD NEVER SEEN   100 21
BODIES IN THE IMAGE OF THEIR SEVERAL KINDS   376   4
BENEATH THE STEPS OF ST PAUL'S CATCH SEVERAL   750 22
THEIR SEVERAL ERRANDS HERE AND THERE SHALL MAKE   872 19
OF SEVERAL INSULTS OF BLOTTED PAGES AND SCRAWL   *895 22
OF SEVERAL INSULTS OF BLOTTED PAGES AND SCRAWL   *904 11

SEVERED

TO THE ALL AND SEVERED THE CONNECTION   262 18

SEVERELY

SEVERELY IN THEIR PLACE   316 13
BUT PRUNING SEVERELY INTELLIGENTLY AND RUTHLESSLY PRUNI+ 677 27

SEVERS

SWORD THAT SEVERS THE QUESTION FROM US WHO BREATHE   168 26

SEWED

SHE QUICKLY SEWED FIG-LEAVES AND SEWED THE SAME FOR THE+ 284   8
SHE GOT THE FACT ON HER MIND AND QUICKLY SEWED FIG-LEAV+ 284 12

SEWER

SHOULD LOVE THE SEWER SCENT   462 31
IS A SEWER INSIDE IT POLLUTES O IT POLLUTES   463 20

SEWER-STENCH

A VAPOUR OF ROTTENNESS OUT OF THEIR MOUTHS LIKE SEWER-S+ 462 27

SEWING

AND WOMEN HAVE BEEN SEWING EVER SINCE   284 13
SWALLOWS WITH SPOOLS OF DARK THREAD SEWING THE SHADOWS   340 29

SEX

HIS ADOLESCENCE SAW HIM CRUCIFIED INTO SEX   361   2
WHY WERE WE CRUCIFIED INTO SEX   364   7
SEX WHICH BREAKS UP OUR INTEGRITY OUR SINGLE INVIOLABIL+ 366 31
SEX WHICH BREAKS US INTO VOICE SETS US CALLING ACROSS T+ 366 34
THAT IS PART OF THE MYSTERY OF SEX IT IS A FLOW ONWARDS   449   4
SEX ISN'T SIN AH NO SEX ISN'T SIN   463 24
AND SEX ALAS GETS DIRTIER AND DIRTIER WORKED FROM THE   464   1
SEX GETS DIRTIER AND DIRTIER THE MORE I IS FOOLED WITH+ 464   3
SEX ISN'T SIN BUT DIRTY SEX IS WORSE SO THERE YOU ARE   464   8
LET'S BE HONEST AT LAST ABOUT SEX OR SHOW AT LEAST THAT+ 464 12
SEX ISN'T SIN IT'S A DELICATE FLOW BETWEEN WOMEN AND MEN 464 14

SEX
  SEX ISN'T SOMETHING YOU'VE GOT TO PLAY WITH SEX IS YOU   464 17
  THE SENSITIVE DELICACY OF YOUR SEX IN ITS EBBING TO AND+   464 25
  AND THE MORTAL RESERVE OF YOUR SEX AS IT STAYS IN YOUR   464 26
  O KNOW YOURSELF O KNOW YOUR SEX YOU MUST KNOW THERE   465 1
  YOU MUST KNOW SEX IN ORDER TO SAVE IT YOUR DEEPEST SELF   465 3
  IF YOU WANT TO HAVE SEX YOU'VE GOT TO TRUST   466 1
  LEAVE SEX ALONE LEAVE SEX ALONE LET IT DIE RIGHT AWAY   471 19
  FOR WHILE WE HAVE SEX IN THE MIND WE TRULY HAVE NONE IN   471 27
  SEX IS A STATE OF GRACE   472 1
  AT PRESENT SEX IS THE MIND'S PREOCCUPATION   472 7
  TO-DAY WE'VE GOT NO SEX   472 9
  AND THEN PERHAPS WE SHALL KNOW TRUE SEX IN OURSELVES   472 13
  KILLS SEX IN A MAN THE SIMPLICITY   485 2
  SEX IS A STATE OF GRACE   485 7
  SEX   522 3
  SHY FLOWER OF SEX   562 31
  WHEN A WOMAN CAN ONLY LOVE FLAMILY THOSE OF HER OWN SEX   619 19
  THAT THE YOUNG OF THEIR OWN SEX REVOLT AGAINST THEM AT +   619 25
  WITH THE UPRIGHT DIVISION INTO SEX   636 2
  ON THIS CROSS OF DIVISION DIVISION INTO SEX   636 13
  TO WIPE AWAY THE MYSTIC BARRIERS OF SEX   636 19
  THAT SEX IS AN ETERNAL UPRIGHT DIVISION BEFORE WHICH WE   636 25
  AND LOVE AND SEX AND ALL THAT   838 6
  BECAUSE THEY ONLY TRY TO MAKE WOMEN AND LOVE AND SEX   838 7
  SEX WON'T WORK IN CAPTIVITY   843 13
  THE CAGE WHICH DOES NOT KILL THE MECHANISM OF SEX   843 17
  KILLS ENTIRELY THE TRUE EXPERIENCE OF SEX   843 18
  HAVE NO EXPERIENCE OF SEX AT ALL IT IS ALMOST NOTHING T+ 843 20

SEX-ALIVE
  NOW YOU'VE COME SEX-ALIVE AND THE GREAT RANCH-DOGS ARE   399 28

SEXES
  ALL THIS TALK OF EQUALITY BETWEEN THE SEXES IS MERELY AN   620 1

SEX-FEELING
  IF THE MEAN DEVIL HAS ANY SEX-FEELING AT ALL   *948 29

SEX-HATE
  EXPRESSION OF SEX-HATE   620 2

SEXLESS
  SEXLESS PEOPLE TRANSMIT NOTHING   449 5
  AND EACH TIME IT CAME OUT THE SAME A HORRIBLE SEXLESS L+   619 10

SEXUAL
  BUT WATCH YOUR SEXUAL STEP OH DEAR MY DEAR   829 29

SH
  ONLY THE TWILIGHT NOW AND THE SOFT SH OF THE RIVER   203 15

SHABBY
  IS LOOKING RATHER SHABBY AND ISLAND-BOUND THESE DAYS   329 22
  SHABBY VIRGIN   437 4
  AND I LOOK SHABBY YET MY ROOTS GO BEYOND MY KNOWING   499 6
  MY SHABBY LITTLE DEFEAT WOULD DO NEITHER ME ANY GOOD   508 23

SHACKLED
  FROM OUT OF MY HEART AND LOINS CHOKED AND SHACKLED   884 17

SHADE
  BELOW THE LAWN IN SOFT BLUE SHADE IS KEEPING   35 28
  THE COOL OF AN OAK'S UNCHEQUERED SHADE   49 21
  IN A LITTER THROUGH THE ELM-TREE SHADE ARE SCRAWLING   65 17
  HE SITS LIKE A SHADE BY THE FLOOD ALONE   130 5
  THEN WILL SOMEBODY SQUARE THIS SHADE WITH THE BEING I   141 22
  WHO FOR YEARS WAS SUN FOR YOUR SHIVERING SHADE FOR YOUR   157 2
  BUT THE SHADE ON HER FOREHEAD ILL BECOMES   201 11
  IN THE DEEP STRANGE-SCENTED SHADE OF THE GREAT DARK CAR+ 349 4
  YOU GO DOWN SHADE TO THE RIVER WHERE NAKED MEN SIT ON   386 23
  THE MEN WITH THEIR FACES IN SHADE   771 11
  INTO THE LIDLESS SHADE   786 25
  QUETZALCOATL LOVES THE SHADE OF TREES   802 14
  HUNGRY AND DISCONTENT IN THE FRUITFUL SHADE   864 2

SHADES
  OF SHADOW EMERGING AS BLOOD EMERGES FROM INWARD SHADES +   66 20
  BUT I SEE LEANING FROM THE SHADES   105 24

SHADING
  AND JOSEPH SHADING HIS EYES WITH HIS HAND   200 15
  SHADING HIS FACE IN HIS BLACK FELT HAT   228 6
  MEN ARE UNSEEN BENEATH THE SHADING HATS   606 5

SHADOW
  ON THE TURF I STAND WATCHING MY OWN WHITE SHADOW QUIVER+   33 19
  WHITE ON THE WATER WIMPLES MY SHADOW STRAINS LIKE A DOG+   33 25
  I ON THE BANK ALL SUBSTANCE MY SHADOW ALL SHADOW LOOKIN+   34 2
  MY SHADOW IS NEITHER HERE NOR THERE BUT I I AM ROYALLY +   34 8
  NO LONGER SHADOW AND IT HOLDS ME   34 22
  I TREMBLE IN HIS SHADOW AS HE BURNS   39 29
  IN SHADOW COVERING US UP WITH HER GREY   48 18
  UNDER THE FLEECE OF SHADOW AS IN BETWEEN   48 20
  AND ONE SIDE SHADOW HALF IN SIGHT   50 25
  OF SHADOW EMERGING AS BLOOD EMERGES FROM INWARD SHADES +   66 20
  TO SHAKE FLAKES OF ITS SHADOW ABOUT   68 12
  AND LEAF FOR ITS PASSAGE A SHADOW CAST   69 3
  LIKE A WEEDED CITY IN SHADOW UNDER THE SEA   72 17
  IN FLAKES OF SHADOW DOWN WHILE THROUGH THE GAP   76 15
  ME YOUR SHADOW ON THE BOG-FLAME FLOWERY MAY-BLOBS   90 15
  I SEE EACH SHADOW START   108 7
  I SEE THE STEALTHY SHADOW OF SILENCE   110 15
  BLUE SHADOW WITHIN ME A PRESENCE WHICH LIVES CONTAINED   115 7
  SEEING THE CORE IS A SHADOW INVIOLATE   115 11
  THAT A GREY ONE LIKE A SHADOW LIKE A RAT A THIEF A RAIN+ 120 3
  I SAW HER HID IN THE SHADOW   122 2
  ITS SHADOW LAY ON MY HEART   124 27

SHADOW
  ME MIGHT A YOUNG GIRL BE HEAPED WITH SUCH SHADOW OF   132 6
  LET US NOT HOLD HER SHADOW BACK FROM THE DARK   132 22
  I WHO AM SUBSTANCE OF SHADOW I ALL COMPACT   133 6
  CASTING A SHADOW OF SCORN UPON ME FOR MY SHARE IN DEATH   133 17
  THE WHOLE OF THE DAY TO EXTINGUISH THE SHADOW I LIFT ON+ 133 20
  SHADOW WE SEE   136 21
  INTO THE WORLD OF SHADOW CARRIED DOWN   160 11
  LIKE CLIFFS ABUTTING IN SHADOW A DEAD GREY SEA   164 19
  I SEE OUR SHADOW TREMBLE   170 11
  ONE SHADOW AND WE NEED NOT DISSEMBLE   170 14
  IN THE SHADOW OF THE CART-SHED MUST WE HOVER ON THE BRI+ 173 7
  THE SHADOW ALWAYS OFFER MYSELF TO ONE MISTRESS WHO ALWA+ 180 27
  THEIR WEB WHO SHADOW THE SUN'S GREAT GESTURES AND   197 28
  SEA YOU SHADOW OF ALL THINGS NOW MOCK US TO DEATH WITH   197 32
  WALLS OF BLUE SHADOW   204 14
  IT GOES OVER ME LIKE A SHADOW OVER A HILL   205 16
  BUT THE SHADOW OF LYING WAS IN YOUR EYES   207 5
  OUT OF THE SUNSHINE INTO THE SHADOW   210 8
  PASSING ACROSS THE SHADOW INTO THE SUNLIGHT   210 9
  OUT OF SUNLIGHT TO SHADOW   210 10
  A SHADOW OVER MY BREASTS THAT WILL KILL ME AT LAST   211 4
  AND I WILL BE ALL THE SHADOW YOU THE SHINE   211 27
  THE SHADOW IT USED TO SHUN   215 25
  GOLDEN SHADOW GLOWS AS   217 15
  CONCENTRATES HER GOLDEN SHADOW   217 24
  HER NIMBLE SHADOW TROTTING   222 13
  NO SHADOW OF US ON THEIR SNOWY FOREHEAD OF DREAMS   223 24
  THREE OF THEM BLACK IN SHADOW TWO OF THEM BRIGHT   224 10
  AND ASLEEP ON THE SNOW'S LAST SHADOW   226 19
  HERE IN THE SLOPING SHADOW   227 7
  YOU SHADOW AND FLAME   239 7
  ALL OF SHADOW AND OF BLAND   261 27
  IF YOU CATCH A WHIFF OF VIOLETS FROM THE DARKNESS OF TH+ 274 1
  NOW EVEN THE SHADOW OF THE LOST SECRET IS VANISHING FRO+ 295 3
  STICKILY GLISTENING WITH ETERNAL SHADOW   310 17
  HUNG ALL THE TIME DID WE BUT KNOW IT THE ALL-KNOWING SH+ 328 8
  THEN GAY FEAR THAT TURNS THE TAIL SPRIGHTLY FROM A SHAD+ 336 18
  THIS INTENSE INDIVIDUAL IN SHADOW   338 12
  AND THROUGH THE SHADOW OF BREAD-FRUIT TREES WITH THEIR   383 30
  AND THROUGH THE SHADOW OF BREAD-FRUIT TREES WITH THEIR   387 1
  AND THE SHADOW OF A JEER OF UNDERNEATH DISAPPOINTMENT   391 22
  AS THE ROCKET-CORUSCATION DIED AND SHADOW WAS THE   391 23
  MORE OUT OF THE SHADOW OF THE CAVE IN THE BLOOD-ORANGE   402 18
  GOLD GOES OUT INTO A GREEN SHADOW   455 6
  FOR THE STRONGEST LIGHT THROWS ALSO THE DARKEST SHADOW   474 4
  ALL THE WOMEN WHO ADORED THE SHADOW OF THE MAN ON   590 10
  IN THE BIG MIRROR AT HIS OWN FASCINATING SHADOW   604 5
  IN THE GREEN GARDEN DARKENED THE SHADOW OF COMING RAIN   672 12
  CAME INTO EXISTENCE AS COLD SHADOW   682 7
  LINGERING IN THE EARTH'S SHADOW   704 4
  BETWEEN YOU AND YOUR PURPOSE LIKE A KNIFE'S EDGE SHADOW 706 20
  AND IN THE SHADOW OF THE SUN THE SNOW IS BLUE SO BLUE-A+ 708 28
  THEY LINGER IN THE SHADOW OF THE EARTH   721 14
  THE EARTH'S LONG CONICAL SHADOW IS FULL OF SOULS   721 15
  GAUNT GAUNT THEY CROWD THE GREY MUD-BEACHES OF SHADOW   722 6
  THE GREY GREY REACHES OF EARTH'S SHADOW   722 20
  SLEEP IS THE SHADOW OF DEATH BUT NOT ONLY THAT   724 27
  WITH GOD WE ARE CLOSE TOGETHER NOW THE MOON'S IN SHADOW 727 5
  AND THE SILENCE OF SHORT DAYS THE SILENCE OF THE YEAR T+ 727 13
  AND SMILES AT MY FURTIVE SHADOW   731 11
  TOWARDS THE DARKNESS AND THE SHADOW OF DEATH   737 11
  HOW IT DOGS ME WHAT A GALLING SHADOW   741 2
  BUT THEN THAT SHADOW'S SHADOW OF ME   741 7
  BUT I KILL MY SHADOW'S SHADOW AS I PASS   741 25
  THE MIDNIGHT SHADOW SINKING DOWN HAS SLUNG   750 9
  THE EVENING SHADOW HAS SUNK   758 5
  WITH FACES IN SHADOW BUT SMILING   770 11
  A LOVELY SHADOW OF DEATH   772 11
  BIND HIM WITH SHADOW WHILE I PASS   786 21
  THE SUBSTANCE OF SHADOW THAT BURSTS AND EXPLODES   788 13
  BIND HIM WITH SHADOW WHILE I PASS   789 14
  HE PUT UP HIS HAND AND HELD BACK THE SUN WITH HIS SHADOW 790 2
  LET HIM HAVE NO ANIMAL WALK ON HIS BODY NOR THROUGH THE+ 791 24
  THE GHOST OF EACH THROUGH THE LEAVES OF SHADOW   812 19
  LEAVING THEM SHADOW STRIPES BARRED ON A FIELD OF GREY   858 12
  RUNS INTO THE SHADOW WITH HER CAPTURE A FEW LITTLE BITE+ 864 17
  THE GLOW OF RED IN A GREY-GREEN SHADOW OF TREES   867 10
  PLAYING WITH THE SHADOW COLOURS AND THE WAVING REFLECTE+ 867 20
  HIS BLUE SHIRT GLIMMERING ON THE WATER AMONG THE SHADOW+ 867 29
  AND WHERE HE STOOD I SEE MY OWN SHADOW STAND   871 11
  A SHADOW WAS DEEP IN THEIR EYES   885 13
  THE SHADOW DANCES UP IN AFFECTION   887 21
  OF THE BANK I STAND WATCHING MY OWN WHITE SHADOW QUIVER+ *891 21
  IN FLAKES OF SHADOW DOWN AND THROUGH THE GAP   *898 9
  IN FLAKES OF SHADOW DOWN AND THROUGH THE GAP   *901 18
  OR LEAF AND HIS PASSING SHADOW IS CAST   *915 15
  IN MY FLAME OF LIVING A SHADOW WITHIN THE SHINE   *930 8
  ITS SHADOW LAY ON MY HEART   *935 33
  ME LEST YOU MY SISTER SHOULD GO HEAPED WITH SUCH SHADOW+ *937 33
  GOLDEN SHADOW GLOWS AND HER BREASTS   *942 25
  SHE STIRS HER GOLDEN SHADOW   *943 7
  THE MARGINS THE GREY BEACHES OF SHADOW   *957 15
  THRUST OUT ON TO THE GREY GREY BEACHES OF SHADOW   *957 22
  THAT FRINGE WITH SHADOW ALL THIS WORLD'S EXISTENCE   *959 2
  PAST THE JUTTING ROCKS OF SHADOW   *959 5
  INTO THE SHELL-LIKE WOMB-LIKE CONVOLUTED SHADOW   *959 26

SHADOW-COLOUR
  OVER THE SURFACE OF A SHADOW-COLOUR FLOATS   867 14

SHADOWED
  IS LOST IN THIS SHADOWED SILENCE THE SKIES DISTIL   76 19
  TALL AND LOFTILY SHADOWED BUT THE MOON   103 30
  IS LOST IN THE SHADOWED SILENCE THE SKIES DISTIL   *898 13
  IS LOST IN THE SHADOWED SILENCE THE SKIES DISTIL   *901 22

SHADOW-FULL
TWIN BUBBLES SHADOW-FULL OF MYSTERY AND CHALLENGE IN TH+   *897 30
TWIN BUBBLES SHADOW-FULL OF MYSTERY AND CHALLENGE IN TH+   *901   7

SHADOWING
YOUR SHADOWING   197 33

SHADOWLESS
A RED ROCK SILENT AND SHADOWLESS CLUNG ROUND WITH CLUST+   75   8
THE MUD-WEED OPENING TWO PALE SHADOWLESS STARS   145   3
OVER TWO SHADOWLESS SHAMELESS FACES   146   1

SHADOW-LIKE
WITH WHAT SHADOW-LIKE SLOW CAREFULNESS   426 16

SHADOW-PROCESSIONS
ENORMOUS SHADOW-PROCESSIONS FILING ON IN THE FLARE OF F+   387 35

SHADOWS
PASSES THE WORLD WITH SHADOWS AT THEIR FEET   36   3
HOW MANY SHADOWS IN YOUR SOUL   49   3
ITS SQUARE SHADOWS   50 22
IS PEOPLED WITH SHADOWS AND WAILING AND LAST GHOSTS LUR+   54 31
A SIGH AMONG THE SHADOWS THUS RETRIEVING   66   3
OF TONGUES SO THE SHADOWS TELL   108 14
FEELING THE SHADOWS LIKE A BLIND MAN READING   135 18
LARGE SHADOWS FROM THE OUTSIDE STREET-LAMP BLOWN   140 14
DRAWS DOWN THE BLINDS WHOSE SHADOWS SCARCELY STAIN   155   2
PALE SHADOWS FLEE FROM US AS IF FROM THEIR FOES   163 18
SHADOWS TO COVER OUR STRICKEN MANHOOD AND BLEST   167 18
SHADOWS YET IT DEPRIVES   170   8
WITH SHADOWS WITH YOURS I PEOPLE THE SUNSHINE   211 19
THE SHADOWS THAT LIVE IN THE SUN   215 21
MY EYES FROM THE SHADOWS DARK   216   3
SHADOWS IN THEIR LAP   223 14
SHADOWS THE PASSING WILD-BEAST THREW   262   6
SWALLOWS WITH SPOOLS OF DARK THREAD SEWING THE SHADOWS   340 29
ELEPHANTS AFTER ELEPHANTS CURL THEIR TRUNKS VAST SHADOWS 388   1
SHADOWS STEAL OUT OF THE EARTH   425   2
SHADOWS SHADOWS   425   3
AS SHADOWS FROM THE AGES GONE AND PERISHED   426 18
UPON WHICH SHADOWS OF PEOPLE PURE PERSONALITIES   444   5
IT SLIPS OVER IT AS SHADOWS DO WITHOUT HURTING ITSELF   467 19
EVEN MICE PLAY QUITE BEAUTIFULLY AT SHADOWS   523 26
AND THEN THE SOFTNESS OF DEEP SHADOWS FOLDING FOLDING   727   9
I STUMBLE WHERE THE SHADOWS LIE   731   2
WHERE ROSES' SHADOWS DAPPLED HER   753   9
PALE SHADOWS FLEE FROM US AS IF FROM THEIR FOES   857 18
THE SHADOWS OF THE ASH-TREES STRIDE ACROSS THE HAY   858   9
LIKE A FLY THAT WEAVES THROUGH THE SHADOWS   867 11
AMONG THE SHADOWS OF BLOSSOMS AND TREES AND RUSHES   867 26
THAT MADE SHADOWS AND SHIMMERING RIPPLES THE SOFT NOTES+ 868 14
AND AH I KNOW THE SHADOWS THAT THE TREE   878   3
BRISTLE AND FLY IN SHADOWS ACROSS THE WALLS   879   3
LIKE A GLITTERING OF SHADOWS WITHIN THE MORNING AIR   *895   6
FEELING THE SHADOWS LIKE A BLIND MAN READING   *939   2
SOFTLY IN THE SHADOWS A WOMAN IS SINGING TO ME   *940   5
BUT SHADOWS FOLDED ON DEEPER SHADOWS   *959 18

SHADOW-SHELL
LIKE THE CONVOLUTIONS OF SHADOW-SHELL   *959 20

SHADOW'S
A RED WOLF STANDS ON THE SHADOW'S DARK RED RIM   403 20
BUT THEN THAT SHADOW'S SHADOW OF ME   741   7
BUT I KILL MY SHADOW'S SHADOW OF ME   741 25

SHADOW-WAVED
AND THE FISH IN SHADOW-WAVED HERDS   172   2

SHADOW-WHITE
INTO THE SHADOW-WHITE CHAMBER SILTS THE WHITE   154 27

SHADOWY
THE SHADOWY STUBBLE OF THE UNDER-DUSK   135 10
OF A SHIP THAT STANDS IN A SHADOWY SEA OF SNOW   155 21
THROUGH THE SHADOWY FACE   161 10
OF THIS SELF-SAME DARKNESS YET THE SHADOWY HOUSE BELOW 172 23
IS THE SHADOWY MONOMANIA OF SOME CYPRESSES   297 20
CYPRESS SHADOWY   298   6
AND DOWN BELOW HUGE HOMAGE OF SHADOWY BEASTS BARE-FOOT 388 14
I VENTURE FROM THE HALLS OF SHADOWY DEATH   744 11
A WOMAN CAME INTO THE GLOW FROM OUT OF THE SHADOWY LIGHT 865   4
WHERE THIS FRAIL SHADOWY HUSK OF A DAY IS LOST   875 15
THE SHADOWY STUBBLE OF THE UNDER-DUSK   *939 10

SHADY
IN THE SHADY SMOKE   131 16

SHAFT
WHILE THE DRIVER ON THE SHAFT SITS CROUCHED IN DREAMS   225 16
HE SAW IN A SHAFT OF LIGHT A LAMB ON A PINNACLE BALANCI+ 324 16
A LIT-UP SHAFT OF RAIN   714   8
WITH HEAD AGAINST THE SHAFT AND TAKES   733 20
UP THE DARK SHAFT TO DEATH AND WHAT IF I   879 23
OF THE DARK SHAFT THAT ISSUES TO THE NIGHT   879 35

SHAFT-GOLDEN
SHAFT-GOLDEN WITH LIGHT SHEER INTO THE SKY   116 16
SHAFT-GOLDEN WITH LIGHT AT THE JOINT OF THE SKY   *930 15

SHAFTS
SOFT SHAFTS SUNBREATHING MOUTHS   301 29
AND DOWN THE SHAFTS OF HIS SPLENDID PINIONS   496 11

SHAGGILY
BUT ALSO IT WAS A FIERY FORTRESS FROWNING SHAGGILY ON T+ 327   1

SHAGGY
IN THE PLAYGROUND A SHAGGY SNOWBALL STANDS HUGE AND STI+ 76 17
THE SHAGGY UNDERGROWTH OF THEIR OWN HAIR   310 12
SHAGGY CLOUD   375   6

SHAKE
TO SHAKE FLAKES OF ITS SHADOW ABOUT   68 12
FOR YOU TO SHAKE AND SHAKE AND IT WON'T COME RIGHT   119   3
OF MIDNIGHT AND SHAKE IT TO FIRE TILL THE FLAME OF THE 136 20
IN ANOTHER COUNTRY BLACK POPLARS SHAKE THEMSELVES OVER A 148 20
MORNING COMES AND I SHAKE THE DEWS OF NIGHT FROM THE WI+ 322 26
NAIL-STUDDED THAT SHAKE BENEATH HER SHELL   362   7
AND CLAWS NOT MADE TO SHAKE HANDS WITH   414 15
THEY GLISTEN AND SHAKE   615 15
I'LL SHAKE THE EARTH AND SWALLOW THEM UP WITH THEIR CIT+ 792   4
AND THE EARTH IS ALIVE AND READY TO SHAKE OFF HIS FLEAS 792 12
WHICH YOU'VE THROWN UPON HIM SHALL SUDDENLY SHAKE WITH + 797   9
SHAKE THE BOUGH   817 15
STARTLING THE THICK-SPUN TWILIGHT THE BELLS SHAKE OUT   858 25
HIS BODY THAT DOES SHAKE LIKE THE WIRE OF A HARP   877 13
AND THE BOUGHS OF THE LIME TREE SHAKE AND TOSS THE LIGHT 878   5
SHAKE AND SINK DOWN TO REST THEN SHAKE AGAIN   878 26
NO LONGER SHAKE WHERE THE SILK SAIL FILLS   *906   4
SHAKE FLAKES OF ITS MEANING ABOUT   *914 27
SHAKE DOWN THEIR GOLDEN LITTER THAT DISCLOSES   *916 22
THAT YOU SHAKE AND SHAKE AND YET IT WON'T COME TO YOUR + *932   9

SHAKEN
SAW WHERE MORNING SUN ON THE SHAKEN IRIS GLISTENED   38 16
THE HEAVENS ARE NOT SHAKEN YOU SAY LOVE   49 11
SHAKEN ASTIR   57 20
OF DARKNESS ABUNDANT WHICH SHAKEN MYSTERIOUSLY   136 18
THE RAIN-BRUISED LEAVES ARE SUDDENLY SHAKEN AS A CHILD 136 24
IN EVERY SHAKEN MORSEL   170 10
RESTLESS AND LONELY SHAKEN BY YOUR OWN MOODS   197   2
SHAKEN THE MARSHES TILL THE GEESE HAVE GONE   624   1
SHAKEN SOFTLY FROM THE HEAVY-FOLDED SKIRTS OF NIGHT   858 14
THROUGH THAT WHITE STRAIT OF THY THICK SHAKEN THROAT   879   7
SEE THE MORNING SUN ON THE SHAKEN IRIS GLISTEN   *892 31
THE PICTURE OF THE PAST IS SHAKEN AND SCATTERED   *908 10
WHILE TH' PARSON WAS PRAYIN' I WATCHES 'ER AN' SHE WOR + *910   1
LIKE WET AND SHAKEN ROSES AND I LISTEN   *943   4
SHAKEN THE MARSHES TILL THE GEESE HAVE GONE   *953 19
HAVING NO BOAT TO LAUNCH UPON THE SHAKEN SOUNDLESS   *957 30

SHAKES
AND THE THOUGHT OF THE LIPLESS VOICE OF THE FATHER SHAK+ 48 11
SHAKES THE SAIL   53   6
AND CHITTER AND WIND THAT SHAKES AND CUFFS   89 29
OR THE WIND SHAKES A RAVEL OF LIGHT   109 21
ASLEEP STILL SHAKES IN THE CLUTCH OF A SOB   136 25
OF BLISS TILL ALL HER LAMBENT BEAUTY SHAKES TOWARDS US 193   7
THE WILD-FLOWER SHAKES ITS BELL   216   9
WHICH SHAKES MY SUDDEN BLOOD TO HATRED OF YOU   333 16
HE SHAKES THE TID-BIT FOR HER WITH A MOST WOOING NOISE + 761 18
SHAKES O'ER HIS WALLS WHEN THE WIND DISTURBS THE NIGHT 878   4
AND STILL HIS LIFE SHAKES AT THE LATCH OF SLEEP   878 28
WITH THE OLD SWEET SOOTHING TEARS AND LAUGHTER THAT SHA+ *905 19

SHAKESPEARE
WHEN I READ SHAKESPEARE I AM STRUCK WITH WONDER   494 13
SHAKESPEARE THEY SOLD TO CROSSE AND BLACKWELLS TO BE JA+ 763   6

SHAKESPEARE'S
HOW BORING HOW SMALL SHAKESPEARE'S PEOPLE ARE   494 25

SHAKING
LIKE HALF-BLOWN FLOWERS DIMLY SHAKING AT THE NIGHT   75 27
THE STARLING SHAKING ITS HEAD AS IT WALKS IN THE GRASS 137 11
THE SHAKING ASPECT OF THE SEA   310 26
SHAKING ASUNDER AND FLICKING AT HIS RIBS   453 15
SHAKING THE LARK'S NEST TILL THE EGGS HAVE BROKEN   623 31
EVEN THE SHAKING WHITE POPLAR WILL DAZZLE LIKE SPLINTER+ 624 18
SO QUEENLY SHAKING HER GLISTENING BEAMS   702 26
LOOK AT THE SHAKING WHITE   755 14
THE ROAST VEAL I AM SHAKING IT FOR YOU   762 13
SHAKING THE HEATH-BELLS DOWN WITH HER PETULANT GAIT   863 23
LIKE FULL-BLOWN FLOWERS DIMLY SHAKING AT THE NIGHT   *897 26
LIKE FULL-BLOWN FLOWERS DIMLY SHAKING AT THE NIGHT   *901   3
A CHILD SITTING UNDER THE PIANO IN THE BOOM OF THE SHAK+ *940   7
HARDENED THE EARTH SHAKING THE LARK'S NEST TILL THE EGG+ *953 18

SHALIMAR
SO HERE I HIDE IN THE SHALIMAR   70 14

SHALLOW
AND STOLEN KISSES SHALLOW AND GAY   42 13
AND LOVE WOULD ONLY WEAKEN THEIR UNDER-EARTH GRIP MAKE + 92 27
ME WORDS THAT RANG WITH A BRASSY SHALLOW CHIME   98 20
FALL ON MY SHALLOW BREAST   194   5
SHALLOW WINE-CUPS ON SHORT BULGING STEMS   283   6
IN LOVE WITH A SELF THAT NOW IS SHALLOW AND WITHERED 478 23

SHALLOWER
DEEPER DOWN THE CHANNEL THEN ROSE SHALLOWER SHALLOWER 693   9

SHALLOWS
THAT RUNS DOWN TO THE SHALLOWS OF MY WRISTS AND BREAKS 705   5

SHALLOW-SILVERY
FROM THAT SHALLOW-SILVERY WINE-GLASS ON A SHORT STEM 279 11

SHALT
THOU SHALT SHUT DOORS ON ME   44   9
THOU SHALT HAVE OTHER GODS BEFORE THESE   437 21
AND THOU SHALT BEGIN TO SPIN ROUND ON THE HUB OF THE   714 17

SHAM
WITH HIS SHAM CHRISTIANITY   537   2
THEY WERE JUST A BLOODY SHAM   556   4

SHAME
EH WHAT A SHAME IT SEEMS   45 22
IT'S A SHAME AS 'E SHOULD BE KNOCKED ABOUT   45 25
HOW CAN YOU SHAME TO ACT THIS PART   55   8
FOR THIS NICE OLD SHAME AN' DISGRACE   79   8
IS YOUR FACE THAT FILLS ME WITH SHAME   112 12
THEIR FEAR THEIR SHAME THEIR JOY THAT UNDERLIES   125 28
MY SHAME LIKE SHOES IN THE PORCH   134   6
OF NAKED LOVE CLENCHED IN HIS FISTS THE SHAME   226   7
OF MAQUILLAGE AND POSE AND MALICE TO SHAME THE BRUTES   463 23
IT'S A SILLY SHAME   564 30
AND HID THEIR FACES FOR VERY SHAME   579 14
AND SHAME THAT HURTS MOST   747 15
KEEPS ME PROUD IN SHAME PLEDGE OF THE NIGHT DARK-PURE   772 13
OH MY GOD WHAT A BITTER SHAME   873   6
BUT OH MY GOD WHAT A BITTER SHAME   874   2
OH MY GOD WHAT A BITTER SHAME   874 10
WHAT A BITTER SHAME THAT SHE SHOULD ASK IT   874 17
FOR THIS NICE OLD SHAME AND DISGRACE   *921   4
IT IS YOU WHO HAVE BORNE THE SHAME AND SORROW   *927   1
YOURS IS THE SHAME AND SORROW   *928   1
IS YOUR FACE THAT FILLS ME WITH SHAME   *929   2
THEIR FEAR THEIR SHAME THEIR JOY THAT UNDERLIES   *936 27

SHAMEFUL
A HASTENING CAR SWEPT SHAMEFUL PAST   122   1
ASHAMED AND SHAMEFUL AND VICIOUS   264 31
IT IS SO SHAMEFUL TO BE INSANE   839 12

SHAMEFULLY
WHEN I STAND IN THE DOORWAY SHAMEFULLY   735 28

SHAMELESS
OVER TWO SHADOWLESS SHAMELESS FACES   146   1
SHAMELESS AND CALLOUS I LOVE YOU   210   5
WHILE THEY CARRIED THE SHAMELESS THINGS AWAY   579 15

SHAME'S
TO COVER MY MOUTH'S RAILLERY TILL I'M BOUND IN HER SHAM+   *940 17

SHAME-WOUNDS
FEEL THE SHAME-WOUNDS IN HIS HANDS PIERCE THROUGH MY OWN   226 10

SHAMS
THE WHITE BARE BONE OF OUR SHAMS   145   7

SHANK
WHY THIS LENGTH OF SHREDDED SHANK   332   4

SHANKS
SETTLE AND STAND ON LONG THIN SHANKS   333   1

SHANNA
I DAMN WELL SHANNA MARRY 'ER   81   9
'ER GEN ME SUMMAT I SHANNA   84   7
AS FOR MARRYIN' I SHANNA MARRY   84 13
I DAMN WELL SHANNA MARRY 'ER   *923   9

SHAN'T
I SHAN'T 'AVE 'IM TO NUSS   45 20
THERE SHE SHAN'T HAVE ANY MORE PEPPERMINT DROPS   393 24
THEN WE SHAN'T HAVE WAR AND WE NEEDN'T TALK ABOUT PEACE   496   5

SHAPE
SHAPE AFTER SHAPE AND SCENE AFTER SCENE OF MY PAST   47   4
SHE LIES AT LAST THE DARLING IN THE SHAPE OF HER DREAM   101 14
BY ITS SHAPE LIKE THRUSHES IN CLEAR EVENINGS   101 16
HER WHITE HER LAMP-LIKE SHAPE   103 32
NEWNESS NEW SHAPE TO WIN   127 14
ONLY GOD COULD HAVE BROUGHT IT TO ITS SHAPE   254 27
IF YOU ARE EXPECTING A SECOND ADVENT IN THE SHAPE OF A   531 19
IN THE SHAPE OF HALF-A-DOZEN STOUT   632 32
SHAPE NOR SUBSTANCE   651   9
HIS URGE TAKES SHAPE IN FLESH AND LO   690 10
THERE WILL ALWAYS BE A FATHER OF ALL THINGS IN SOME SHA+   840   7
WHERE SHAPE ON SPIRIT IN SUPERB DEGREE   872 10
SHAPE SHINES ALONE LIKE A MELODY AND WHERE   872 16
SHAPE ANSWERS SHAPE IN CHORUS TO THE SIGHT   872 17
CRUCIBLE WHERE NEW BLOSSOMS OF SHAPE ARE BEGOT   873   5
AND STRIVING TO CATCH A GLIMPSE OF THE SHAPE OF THE COM+   *909 25

SHAPELESS
SOME SHAPELESS DARK TO THE LOVELY CURVE OF LIGHT   872   7

SHAPELINESS
THE SHAPELINESS THAT DECKS US HERE-BELOW   88 34
IN SHAPELINESS WITH HAPPY LINKED HANDS   872 14

SHAPELY
YET ARE SHAPELY AND COMELY TO SEE   101 22
YOU ARE SHAPELY YOU ARE ADORNED   111 28
AND KINDLING SHAPELY LITTLE CONFLAGRATIONS   271 33
THOU ART SHAPELY THOU ART ADORNED   *927 16
YOU ARE SHAPELY YOU ARE ADORNED   *928 16

SHAPEN
O STIFFLY SHAPEN HOUSES THAT CHANGE NOT   53 20
SHAPEN   *909   5

SHAPER
OH THE GREAT MYSTERY AND FASCINATION OF THE UNSEEN SHAP+   *909 13

SHAPES
SUCH RESOLUTE SHAPES SO HARSHLY SET   53 24
OF SHAPES BY A HARD WIND RIDDEN   68   8
OH YOU STIFF SHAPES SWIFT TRANSFORMATION SEETHES   72 12
WITHIN THE WOMB NEW SHAPES AND THEN NEW MEN   89 11
ALL SHAPES OF WONDER WITH SUSPENDED BREATH   165 19
THE WORLD IS A PAINTED MEMORY WHERE COLOURED SHAPES   173 11
THESE SHAPES THAT NOW ARE DREAMS AND ONCE WERE MEN   174   2
MY WORLD IS A PAINTED FRESCO WHERE COLOURED SHAPES   *906 11
MY WORLD IS A PAINTED FRESCO WHERE COLOURED SHAPES   *908   5
AS IT SWELLS AND SHAPES A BUD INTO BLOSSOM   *909 17

SHAPING
AND WHAT IS LIFE BUT THE SWELLING AND SHAPING THE DREAM+   176   6
MY JOY-BLOSSOMS SHAPING AM BIG   888 15
IMPELLING SHAPING THE COMING DREAM   *907 15
THE GREAT MYSTERIOUS ONE IS SWELLING AND SHAPING THE DR+   *907 24
IS SWELLING AND SHAPING A BUD INTO BLOSSOM   *907 26
AM I NOT QUICKENING MYSELF IN THE PATTERN SHA+   *909   4
EVERYTHING GREAT AND MYSTERIOUS IN ONE SWELLING AND SHA+   *909 15

SHARE
TO SHARE THE NIGHT WITH YOU   116 27
SEVEN TOADS THAT MOVE IN THE DUSK TO SHARE   126 19
CASTING A SHADOW OF SCORN UPON ME FOR MY SHARE IN DEATH   133 17
LET THEM DISENCUMBER YOUR BOUNTY LET THEM ALL SHARE   168 12
THE BUSY BUSY BOURGEOIS IMBIBES HIS LITTLE SHARE   432 25
AND UNDENIABLE NEW GODS SHARE THEIR LIFE WITH US WHEN WE   662 12
TO SHARE THE RHYTHM OF THE DEATHLESS WAVE   772 19
AND GATHER MY BURNING BEAUTIFUL DREAMS FOR HER SHARE   874   8
TO SHARE THE TRAIN WITH YOU   *930 26

SHARED
AND WHEN SHE HAS MOST UNSATISFACTORILY SHARED HIS LITTL+   842   5

SHARES
AND SHARES BEING WITH ME SILKILY   656   3

SHARING
OF SHARING THE NIGHT WITH GOD OF MINGLING UP AGAIN   772 25

SHARKS
PROFITEERS HERE BEING CALLED DOG-FISH STINKING DOG-FISH+   316 25

SHARP
TILL HE CHAFES AT MY CROUCHING PERSISTENCE AND A SHARP   47 24
THE CLINK OF THE SHUNTING ENGINES IS SHARP AND FINE   52 16
DROP THEIR LEAVES WITH A FAINT SHARP HISS OF CONTEMPT   54 25
AS I HEAR THE SHARP CLEAN TROT OF A PONY DOWN THE ROAD   63   9
SUCCEEDING SHARP LITTLE SOUNDS DROPPING INTO SILENCE   63 10
AND I AM OF IT THE SMALL SHARP STARS ARE QUITE NEAR   104 15
A SHARP SKY BRUSHES UPON   166 19
HOW I KNOW THAT GLITTER OF SALT DRY STERILE SHARP CORRO+   207 17
NOT TEARS BUT WHITE SHARP BRINE   207 19
I HAVE BEEN THRUST INTO WHITE SHARP CRYSTALS   207 25
TWO WHITE ONES SHARP VINDICATED   210 16
THE SHARP BEGETTING OR THE CHILD BEGOT   219 11
SHARP BREATHS TAKEN YEA AND I   219 23
LIKE SHARP SLIM WAGTAILS THEY FLASH A LITTLE ASIDE   269 26
AND JUMPS STACCATO TO EARTH A SHARP DRY JUMP STILL   384 30
HER BACKBONE SHARP AS A ROCK   386 10
AND STRIPES IN THE BRILLIANT FROST OF HER FACE SHARP FI+   402   4
IF JESUS HAD KEPT A SHARP EYE ON SATAN   483 16
WITH OUR SHARP LITTLE EYES AND OUR HIGH-POWER MACHINES   543 20
SMALL SHARP RED FIRES IN THE NIGHT OF LEAVES   606   3
THE BREATH OF LIFE AND THE SHARP WINDS OF CHANGE ARE TH+   615 16
AND FALL INTO SHARP SELF-CENTRED SELF-ASSERTION SHARP O+   616   6
THE BREATH OF LIFE IS IN THE SHARP WINDS OF CHANGE   698   1
AND THE WATCHERS THE DIVIDERS THOSE SWIFT ONES WITH DAR+   706 17
BUT ALSO THE SUNDERERS THE ANGELS WITH BLACK SHARP WING+   706 23
THE ONES WITH THE SHARP BLACK WINGS   707   9
UNDER THE MOON'S SHARP SCIMITAR'S   735 22
WITH SHARP DESIRE I AM NOT EAGER FOR SHARP DESIRE ANY M+   840 24
THE CLINK OF THE SHUNTING ENGINES IS SHARP AND FINE   *905   5
SHARP BREATHS SWISHING YEA BUT I   *944   3

SHARPEN
CACTUSES SHARPEN THEIR THORNS   806   2

SHARPENING
SHARPENING HIS TEETH ON THE WOLVES   324 29

SHARPENS
THE CACTUS SHARPENS HIS THORN   804 20

SHARPER
THE SHARPER MORE HORRID THE PRESSURE THE HARDER   161   1

SHARPLY
SHARPLY BEATS OUT A THRICE-TOLD FUNERAL KNELL   858 24

SHARP-RIMMED
FOR WHAT CAN ALL SHARP-RIMMED SUBSTANCE BUT CATCH   68 25
FOR WHAT CAN ALL THAT SHARP-RIMMED SUBSTANCE BUT CATCH   *915   9

SHATTER
AND FINGER IT AND FORCE IT AND SHATTER THE RHYTHM IT KE+   464 30
THEN YOU WILL SHATTER THE BANK   484 20
TILL IT REACHES US AND ITS VIBRATIONS SHATTER US   512 19

SHATTERED
  AND STILL BY THE ROTTEN ROW OF SHATTERED FEET   146 23
  WOULD GOD THEY WERE SHATTERED QUICKLY THE CATTLE WOULD   159 21
  IS SHATTERED AT LAST BENEATH THE STRIPE   253 25
  SHATTERED BOY UP THERE   390 26
  OR IS OUR SHATTERED ARGOSY OUR LEAKING ARK   429 9
  WERE BROKEN AGAINST HER THIGHS SHE SHATTERED THE HIBISC+   863 25
  WAS SHATTERED ALTOGETHER   880 25

SHATTERING
  THE SWINGING BLISS NO SHATTERING EVER DESTROYS   251 24
  HARK THE LOW AND SHATTERING LAUGHTER OF BEARDED MEN   689 2

SHAVES
  DELIBERATELY AS WHEN HE SHAVES HIMSELF   447 21

SHAWL
  BY THE SLIPPING SHAWL OF STARS   55 27
  THIS QUEER DROSS SHAWL OF BLUE AND VERMILION   369 22
  YOUR WATTLES DRIP DOWN LIKE A SHAWL TO YOUR BREAST   369 29
  MY CASHMERE SHAWL I'LL HANG FOR A CANOPY   754 24

SHAWL-FRINGE
  FLINGING HER SHAWL-FRINGE OVER THE RIVER   170 19

SH'D
  I SH'D THINK 'E'LL GET RIGHT AGAIN   46 4

SHEAF
  LIKE A LOOSE SHEAF OF WHEAT   198 10
  IN OUR SHEAF OF SELF-GATHERED WOUNDS WE GO TO MEET   743 8
  THE CRIMSON SHEAF OF THE WEST THE DEEP FETCHED SIGH   885 6

SHEARS
  AND BETWEEN THE TWO BLADES OF THIS PAIR OF SHEARS PROPE+   663 16

SHEATHE
  AND I THE SWIFT BRACTS THAT SHEATHE IT THOSE BREASTS TH+   245 16

SHEATHED
  LIKE DRAWN BLADES NEVER SHEATHED HACKED AND GONE BLACK   304 28

SHEAVES
  IN THE DOWNWARD-DROPPING OF FLIMSY SHEAVES   68 19
  WHITE LITTLE SHEAVES OF NIGHTGOWNED MAIDS   105 22
  INFLAMED WITH BINDING UP THE SHEAVES OF THE DEAD   135 23
  THE CLOUD SHEAVES   268 17
  IN THE SHEAVES OF PAIN   269 3
  THE SHEAVES OF DEAD   269 5
  TO THE MAN WHO THRESHES AND SOWS THE SHEAVES   *899 9
  TO THE MAN WHO THRESHES AND SOWS THE SHEAVES   *902 21
  IN THE DOWN-WARD DROOPING FLIMSY SHEAVES   *915 3
  INFLAMED WITH BINDING UP THE SHEAVES OF DEAD   *939 23

SHED
  THIS ACHE WAS SHED   35 25
  LEANS AND LOOKS IN AT THE LOW-BUILT SHED   42 21
  AND I SHED MY VERY SOUL DOWN INTO YOUR   56 15
  OF THE DARK-GREEN HILLS NEW CALVES IN SHED PEEWITS TURN+   57 21
  AND WAITING WHILE LIGHT IS SHED   58 29
  BLOOD SHED IN THE SILENT FIGHT   105 4
  NIGHT-LIGHTS HITHER AND THITHER SHED   142 27
  SOFT SHE LAY AS A SHED FLOWER FALLEN NOR HEARD   155 26
  SHE SOFTLY PASSED THE SORROWFUL FLOWER SHED   156 7
  AND ALL THE SCENT IS SHED AWAY BY THE COLD   224 27
  HAVING SHED THEIR SOUND AND FINISHED ALL THEIR ECHOING   296 27
  OUR OLD GOAT WE TIE UP AT NIGHT IN THE SHED AT THE BACK+   384 4
  NOT TO SHED A LOT OF BLOOD OVER IT   497 21
  DESTROY IT SHED ITS UNCLEAN BLOOD KILL IT PUT IT OUT OF+   679 4
  O SHED THE UNCLEAN MEAN COWARDLY GREEDY EGOISTIC DEGENE+   679 5
  THAT BLOOD OF THE LOWER LIFE MUST BE SHED   679 9
  AND AM AND WAS SHED IT ALL THOROUGHLY   738 16
  LIKE A SHED WHITE HUSK ON THE TORRID SKY   747 29
  I AND MY BETROTHED ARE TOGETHER IN THE SHED   756 15

SHEDDING
  SHEDDING YOU DOWN AS A TREE   56 11
  OF SHEDDING AWAY HAS LEFT ME   107 11
  OF THESE DARK KNIGHTS SHEDDING THEIR DELICATE SHEEN   221 19
  WITHOUT SHEDDING OF BLOOD THERE IS NO REMISSION OF SIN   678 18
  AMONG THE SPLENDOUR OF TORCHES OF DARKNESS SHEDDING DAR+   697 21
  AMONG THE SPLENDOUR OF BLACK-BLUE TORCHES SHEDDING FATH+   *956 19

SHE-DELIRIOUS
  WHISTLING SHE-DELIRIOUS RAGE AND THE DREADFUL SOUND   36 14

SHE-DOLPHIN
  AND VENUS AMONG THE FISHES SKIPS AND IS A SHE-DOLPHIN   695 9

SHE-DOVE
  OF THE SHE-DOVE IN THE BLOSSOM STILL BELIEVING   65 21

SHEDS
  SHEDS ITS FLOWERS ON A RIVER   56 12
  THROUGH THE OPEN YARD-WAY CAN I NOT GO PAST THE SHEDS   173 10

SHE'D
  SHE'D BEEN NAKED ALL HER DAYS BEFORE   284 9

SHEEN
  SKY CEASED TO QUIVER AND LOST ITS ACTIVE SHEEN   35 15
  YOU WITH YOUR FACE ALL RICH LIKE THE SHEEN ON A DOVE   90 18
  AND GLAZED YOU OVER WITH A SHEEN OF GOLD   90 21
  OF THESE DARK KNIGHTS SHEDDING THEIR DELICATE SHEEN   221 19

SHEEP
  AND SHEEP ON THE PASTURE   120 14
  GUARD MY SHEEP CAME THE SILVERY VOICE FROM THE PINNACLE   324 23
  OF HIS VOLUPTUOUS PLEASURE OF CHASING THE SHEEP TO THE +   325 9
  THAT SHE'S JUST A SHEEP   565 3
  BAA-BAA BLACK SHEEP   669 19

SHEEP-DIP
  INTO A DEEP POND AN OLD SHEEP-DIP   33 15
  INTO A DEEP POND AN OLD SHEEP-DIP   *891 17

SHEEP-DOG
  HENCE HE BECAME A CURLY SHEEP-DOG WITH DANGEROUS PROPEN+   324 26
  AND BECOMES THE FAITHFUL SHEEP-DOG OF THE SHEPHERD THIN+   325 8

SHEEP-FACED
  OPENING GREAT WINGS IN THE FACE OF THE SHEEP-FACED EWE   414 25

SHEER
  SHAFT-GOLDEN WITH LIGHT SHEER INTO THE SKY   116 16
  OH LET US HERE FORGET LET US TAKE THE SHEER   132 23
  IS HEAVEN OF OUR OWN SHEER WITH REPUDIATION   210 18
  ITSELF MORE SHEER AND NAKED OUT OF THE GREEN   218 11
  SHEER HARMONY   235 33
  IF ONLY I AM KEEN AND HARD LIKE THE SHEER TIP OF A WEDGE   250 21
  STRANGE SHEER SLOPES AND WHITE LEVELS   261 9
  SHEER HARD EXTINCTION   266 3
  BUT IT WILL BE LIKE MUSIC SHEER UTTERANCE   268 6
  SHEER WILL   386 11
  THE SOUL'S FIRST PASSION IS FOR SHEER LIFE   482 1
  IN THE SHEER COITION OF THE LIFE-FLOW STARK AND UNLYING   482 14
  I KNOW NO GREATER DELIGHT THAN THE SHEER DELIGHT OF BEI+   610 19
  AND THE FEW LOOK INTO THE EYES OF THE GODS AND SERVE TH+   650 4
  THERE IS A MARVELLOUS RICH WORLD OF CONTACT AND SHEER F+   667 3
  WHEN YOUR FLAME FLICKERS UP AND YOU FLICKER FORTH IN SH+   674 2
  AND FLIP THEY GO WITH THE NOSE-DIVE OF SHEER DELIGHT   693 28
  TILL THE WIND SLIDES YOU SHEER FROM THE ARCH-CREST   696 24
  AT LAST IN SHEER HORROR OF NOT BEING ABLE TO LEAVE OFF   701 31
  FROM OFF THE SHEER WHITE SNOW OR THE POISED MOON   708 27
  IN SHEER MURDER   715 15
  OF SILENCE AND SHEER OBLIVION   724 13
  AND A SILENT SHEER CESSATION OF ALL AWARENESS   724 22
  ONLY IN SHEER OBLIVION ARE WE WITH GOD   725 22
  HOLY OF HOLIES OF SHEER OBLIVION   726 9
  OF SHEER OBLIVION   745 20
  LIKE SILK THEY ARE FLESH SHEER FLESH   827 3
  OUT OF SHEER DESIRE TO BE SPLENDID AND MORE SPLENDID   831 4
  AND DEEPER TO A CORE OF SHEER OBLIVION   *959 19
  OF SHEER OBLIVION AND OF UTTER PEACE   *959 32

SHEET
  HIS OWN BLACK BLOOD POURED OUT LIKE A SHEET OF FLAME OV+   326 30
  AND THE INDIAN IN A WHITE SHEET   403 9
  WRAPPED TO THE EYES THE SHEET BOUND CLOSE ON HIS BROWS   403 10
  AN INDIAN WALKING WRAPT IN HIS WINDING SHEET   816 7

SHEET-LIGHTNING
  SHEET-LIGHTNING   366 11

SHEETS
  NEWSPAPER SHEETS ENCLOSE   145 25
  SHEETS   448 15

SHELL
  NAY EVEN THE SLUMBEROUS EGG AS IT LABOURS UNDER THE SHE+   64 11
  WITH COLD LIKE THE SHELL OF THE MOON AND STRANGE IT SEE+   99 14
  LIKE THE SEETHING SOUND IN A SHELL   216 7
  THAT A NEW CHICK SHOULD CHIP THE EXTENSIVE SHELL   329 28
  SHELL   352 4
  THE SECTIONS OF THE BABY TORTOISE SHELL   355 9
  LIVE-ROSY TORTOISE SHELL   355 19
  AND HE HAS A CRUEL SCAR ON HIS SHELL   360 6
  INTO HER SHELL   360 12
  BENEATH THE LOW-DROPPING BACK-BOARD OF HER SHELL   361 21
  NAIL-STUDDED THAT SHAKE BENEATH HER SHELL   362 7
  SHELL   364 31
  MEN MIGHT PUT THEM FORTH AS A SNAIL ITS SHELL AS A BIRD+   451 12
  SHELL OFF HIS EGO   475 3
  HAS THE SHELL GROWN TOO HEAVY FOR THE TORTOISE   558 17
  IS HAS SHE CHIPPED THE SHELL OF HER OWN EGO   603 16
  HAS HE CHIPPED THE SHELL OF HIS OWN EGO   603 17
  AND THE SOUND OF A BLAST THROUGH THE SEA-CURVED CORE OF+   623 13
  WHO AM EMBEDDED IN A SHELL OF SILENCE   698 25
  FOR THE COSMOS EVEN IN DEATH IS LIKE A DARK WHORLED SHE+   724 4
  TO SING IN THE SHELL OF MY HEART THE LULL AND INCREASE   747 22
  AND ON THE SURFACE SHELL OF HIM   830 10
  AND I AM DRIFTING LIKE A SHELL DISCARDED   875 25
  THE STREET THAT IS FULL OF THE RUSTLING SOUND OF A SHELL *917 2
  WHEN YOU ARE ONLY OCCUPIED YOU ARE AN EMPTY SHELL   *949 21

SHELL-BIRD
  NAY TINY SHELL-BIRD   353 24

SHELLED
  ALREADY I SEE THE SHELLED MOON LIE   747 28

SHELL-LIKE
  INTO THE SHELL-LIKE WOMB-LIKE CONVOLUTED SHADOW   *959 26

SHELLS
  AND EVEN IN THE WATERY SHELLS THAT LIE   89 18
  THEIR TWO SHELLS LIKE DOMED BOATS BUMPING   361 22
  GOD HOW GLAD I AM TO HEAR THE SHELLS   741 9
  FOR THE SHELLS THAT THE QUESTION IS NOW NO MORE BEFORE +   741 23
  OUR BRIDE AMONG THE RUSTLING CHORUS OF SHELLS   743 9

SHELL'S
    FROM FALLING IRON AND HORRIBLE SHELL'S REPORT   751 11

SHELL-TENDER
    AND THERE AGAIN ON HIS SHELL-TENDER EARTH-TOUCHING BELLY   355 29

SHE'LL
    SO PERHAPS SHE'LL BE MORE ON THE SPOT   571 22
    THAT'S WHAT WE HOPE WE HOPE SHE'LL BE   571 23
    WAS BROUGHT UP POOR SO SHE'LL HAVE TO BE   571 26
    SHE'LL TAKE OFF HER SPECS AND SHE'LL PUT DOWN THE PAPER   583 12
    AND SHE'LL AVOID IT SHE'LL GO AND ORDER   583 14

SHELTER
    WITH SHELTER NOW AND WITH BLANDISHMENT SINCE THE WINDS +   75 14
    I WANT MY OWN ROOM'S SHELTER BUT WHAT IS THIS   140 11
    SHELTER SHOULD BE FREE   487 8
    THAN TO SHELTER ANYBODY FROM THE COLD BLAST   540 30

SHELTERED
    THE WILD ROSE IN A SHELTERED GARDEN   535 1

SHELTERING
    OF YOUR EYES DRAWS OPEN MY SHELTERING FLIMSY DOORS   875 13

SHELVES
    ALWAYS KNEEL IN COURTSHIP TO THE SHELVES IN THE DOORWAY+   180 26
    SITTIN' THERE IN ROWS ON YOUR SHELVES   553 24

SHELVING
    SHELVING SUBSTANCE ON TO THE WOMAN MADONNA MIA   437 3

SHE-MATE
    THE SHE-MATE   325 13
    THE SHE-MATE PURRS   325 15

SHEPHERD
    AND BECOMES THE FAITHFUL SHEEP-DOG OF THE SHEPHERD THIN+   325 8

SHE'S
    SHE'S A QUICKER INSTRUCTRESS THAN YEARS   38 20
    OF THE MOURNFUL CONSTANT HEART THAT WHILE SHE'S WEAVING   65 25
    BUT SHE'S WAITING I KNOW IMPATIENT AND COLD HALF   85 11
    SHE'S ONLY THE NEARER TO THE INEVITABLE FAREWELL   85 14
    DREAMING GOD KNOWS OF WHAT FOR TO ME SHE'S THE   129 2
    SHE'S A SILVERY DOVE WORTH MORE THAN ALL I'VE GOT   238 22
    LOOK SHE'S A WONDERFUL DOVE WITHOUT BLEMISH OR SPOT   239 1
    'ERE SHE'S A LIDY AREN'T YER OLD QUIZZ   434 24
    AND THEN SUDDENLY WHEN SHE'S FEELING ALL LOVELY ABOUT IT   447 26
    LIFE'S VOICE EVEN WHEN SHE'S HOARSE   491 8
    SHE'S SEETHING LIKE A VOLCANO AND VOLCANOS DON'T WANT   539 14
    BESIDES SHE'S HAD TWENTY LOVERS ONLY TO FIND SHE DIDN'T   539 16
    THAT SHE'S JUST A SHEEP   565 3
    AND KNOW THAT SHE'S GOT   565 10
    IS RATHER COMMON SHE'S NOT   571 20
    MORE CAREFUL THOUGH IF SHE'S NOT   571 27
    SHE'S A HOLY TERROR SHE TAKES YOUR BEST FROCK   572 2
    SHE'S GOT TO PACK AND GO   573 18
    SHE'S A MARV'LOUS DELICIOUS HIGH-SPIRITED FELLER   583 17
    UNLESS SHE'S A GLIMPSE OF A GODDESS OF SOME SORT   671 12
    SHE'S LAID AN EGG   761 23
    SHE'S LAID AN EGG   761 25
    SHE'S A FINER INSTRUCTOR THAN YEARS   *893 3

SHE-WHALE'S
    IN THE CLASP AND THE SOFT WILD CLUTCH OF A SHE-WHALE'S +   694 19

SHIELD
    BRITANNIA HID BEHIND HER SHIELD   577 13

SHIFT
    DIVESTING HERSELF OF HER GOLDEN SHIFT AND SO   67 8
    AND HER SHIFT IS LYING WHITE UPON THE FLOOR   120 2
    UPON ME LIKE SLEEPING BIRDS LIKE BIRDS THAT SHIFT   128 12
    WHO HAD LAIN HER SHIFT ON THE SHORE ON THE SHINGLE SLOPE   693 4

SHIFTED
    SHIFTED ROUND   120 27
    AND THEY MAKE ME FEEL AS IF SPACE SHIFTED   524 21
    HE SHIFTED HIS JOB ON TO THE PEASANTS   536 22
    THE WHOLE GREAT HEAVENS HAVE SHIFTED OVER AND SLOWLY PU+   616 23
    WHITE WHEN THE WIND SHIFTED HER HAIR THAT WAS SOFT AN' +   *910 12

SHIFTING
    THEN IT BEGAN TO FIDGET SHIFTING FROM ONE LEG TO THE OT+   413 12

SHILLN
    CLEANIN' YES SIR A SHILLN BY MYSELF ALL RIGHT SIR   866 21

SHIMMER
    AND HARDLY DISTURBING WAVERING SHIMMER   860 4

SHIMMERING
    BELOW THE OCEAN OF SHIMMERING LIGHT YOU WILL BE   72 18
    OH AND SEE THE LABURNUM SHIMMERING   106 3
    HIGH HIGH UP IN FLAKES SHIMMERING FLAKES OF BLUE FIRE   391 18
    THAT MADE SHADOWS AND SHIMMERING RIPPLES THE SOFT NOTES+   868 14

SHIMMERS
    SHIMMERS IN A STREAM OF BLUENESS AND LONG-TRESSED   530 6

SHIMMERY
    AND WOMEN EVEN CUT THEIR SHIMMERY HAIR   530 8

SHINE
    STAR-SHADOWS SHINE LOVE   49 1
    ON THE GREAT BLUE PALACE AT SYDENHAM LIGHTS STIR AND SH+   52 18
    ON HIS MINTED METAL SHINE   59 16
    AND AS I WATCH THE WAN LIGHT SHINE   60 1
    FLOWERS OF ILLUSION WHO SHINE IN OUR GAUDS MAKE A PARAD+   71 17
    AND LIKE A MOON UNSHOWING IT MUST STILL SHINE THERE   114 24
    TURNING ITS BROKEN EDGE TO THE DARK ITS SHINE   114 27
    SHINE IN CONCEIT OF SUBSTANCE UPON ME WHO AM LESS THAN   133 12
    SHINE LIKE FLAT COIN WHICH JOVE IN THANKS   162 3
    THEIR FINGERS IN SUNSET SHINE   168 14
    THAT SHINE AS HER FINGERS STIR   200 20
    AND I WILL BE ALL THE SHADOW YOU THE SHINE   211 27
    WORLD SHINE LIKE THE PROMISED LAND   554 8
    WHY IF YOU SAW MY LIMBS HOW THEY SHINE ON MY BODY   755 6
    WHAT THOUGH THE CLOUDS SHOULD SHINE   772 1
    THE MORNING STAR AND THE EVENING STAR SHINE TOGETHER   800 13
    AND WILL SHINE IF I STAY OR I GO AWAY   815 20
    WITH BEAUTY SHINE AND BOW IN GOD'S GREAT WAKE   872 22
    ON THE UPLIFTED BLUE PALACE LIGHT POOLS STIR AND SHINE   *905 7
    HE CREATES WITH HIS SHINE   *928 5
    IN MY FLAME OF LIVING A SHADOW WITHIN THE SHINE   *930 8
    LORD DEAR LORD DO YOU THINK HE EVER CAN SHINE   *945 20

SHINES
    SHE SHINES THE FIRST WHITE LOVE OF MY YOUTH PASSIONLESS+   67 21
    OF THE LUMINOUS PURPOSE OF LIFE SHINES OUT   68 10
    THAT SHINES BLOOD-RED BESIDE THE RAILWAY SIDING   72 5
    THE SUN SHINES   162 1
    AM A SUNLIGHT UPON THEM THAT SHINES THEM INTO BEING   245 19
    NOR THE GOD OF BATS WHILE THE SUN SHINES   346 17
    AND THE WHITE MIND SHINES ON ONE SIDE OF THEE   473 26
    THAT SHINES SOMEWHERE IN THE ATOM SOMEWHERE PIVOTS THE   481 14
    BUT A SUN THAT SHINES   562 1
    AND GOES DARK BUT SHINES   562 2
    THE GOLD SUN SHINES IN HEAVEN ONLY BECAUSE HE'S ALLOWED   783 1
    BUT MIDMOST SHINES AS THE MORNING STAR MIDMOST SHINES   799 22
    WHEN YOU SLEEP IT SOFTLY SHINES   800 7
    WONDERS SHINES OUT OF EVERYWHERE   802 28
    SHINES THE YELLOW SERPENT-YELLOW SHINING OF THE SUN   806 6
    SHINES AT THE GATE   811 2
    SHAPE SHINES ALONE LIKE A MELODY AND WHERE   872 16
    OF THE LUMINOUS PURPOSE OF GOD SHINES OUT   *914 25
    ALL THE LEAVES ARE FALLEN AND THE STARLIGHT SHINES THRO+   *917 28

SHINGLE
    SHINGLE   130 18
    WHO HAD LAIN HER SHIFT ON THE SHORE ON THE SHINGLE SLOPE   693 4

SHINING
    IN A SHINING CRACK OF RED   58 25
    SO NOW YOU'RE A GLISTENING TOADSTOOL SHINING HERE   86 21
    COULD I BUT SEAL ITS RUDDY SHINING SPRING   153 25
    DARKEN THE SHINING GRASS   196 13
    AND THE WHITE SHINING HOUSES AND THE GAY RED FLOWERS ON   205 2
    SHINING AND TOUCHING   210 17
    AGAINST ME AND BRIGHT PEAK SHINING TO PEAK   224 4
    GREEN GRASS SHINING AND LITTLE WHITE HOUSES   224 13
    THE SNOW-TOPS SHINING ROSY   226 14
    THE SHINING OF LAMPS BECAUSE WITH HIS RAYS HE HURTS THE+   331 7
    RUFFLING BLACK SHINING FEATHERS LIKE LIFTED MAIL   370 24
    HOW FULL HER EYES ARE LIKE THE FULL FATHOMLESS SHINING +   394 6
    BUT SHINING UP BEYOND   554 6
    AND WE SEE IT SHINING   561 12
    WHEN GOLD LAY SHINING THREADING THE COOLED-OFF ROCK   682 24
    JESUS HIS SPURS ARE RED WITH SHINING BLOOD   733 34
    DO NOT TELL ME MY FACE IS SHINING   802 18
    IS THE YELLOW SERPENT-YELLOW SHINING OF MY SUN   805 3
    SHINES THE YELLOW SERPENT-YELLOW SHINING OF THE SUN   806 6
    AND THIS SUN CEASE SHINING OVERHEAD   815 11
    SIEGMUND ONLY THIS MORNING YOU WERE SHINING FOR ME   870 24
    TO FOLD IN A SHINING CONCAVE THE PALE NIGHT   882 3

SHINS
    ON THE THIN BARE SHINS OF A MAN WHO UNEASILY LIES   145 21
    SHOWING HER SHINS   835 29

SHINY
    AND SOUNDER THAN ALL INSURANCE IS A SHINY MENTAL CONCEIT   543 3

SHIP
    OF THE SHIP OF THE SOUL OVER SEAS WHERE DREAMED DREAMS   53 7
    THE EARTH AGAIN LIKE A SHIP STEAMS OUT OF THE DARK SEA +   132 27
    OF A SHIP THAT STANDS IN A SHADOWY SEA OF SNOW   155 21
    AND ROWS AMONG THE FEMALES LIKE A SHIP PERTINACIOUSLY   380 18
    LIKE A BIG SHIP PUSHING HER BOWSPRIT OVER THE LITTLE GIL+   390 24
    AS WHEN A GREAT SHIP MOVES TO ANCHOR   445 16
    O SHIP IN A BOTTLE   542 1
    ADVANCING WITH THE SLOW-SWIFTNESS OF A SHIP BACKING HER+   672 21
    AND LET THE SLIM BLACK SHIP OF DIONYSOS COME SAILING IN   688 4
    THE DOLPHINS LEAP ROUND DIONYSOS' SHIP   693 25
    HAVE YOU BUILT YOUR SHIP OF DEATH O HAVE YOU   717 1
    O BUILD YOUR SHIP OF DEATH FOR YOU WILL NEED IT   717 2
    BUILD THEN THE SHIP OF DEATH FOR YOU MUST TAKE   717 21
    OH BUILD YOUR SHIP OF DEATH YOUR LITTLE ARK   718 9
    IS NOW TO BE WILLING TO DIE AND TO BUILD THE SHIP   718 22
    A LITTLE SHIP WITH OARS AND FOOD   718 24
    NOW LAUNCH THE SMALL SHIP NOW AS THE BODY DIES   719 1
    IN THE FRAGILE SHIP OF COURAGE THE ARK OF FAITH   719 3
    AND THE LITTLE SHIP IS THERE YET SHE IS GONE   719 15
    BETWEEN THEM THE LITTLE SHIP   719 23
    WAIT WAIT THE LITTLE SHIP   720 6
    AND THE LITTLE SHIP WINGS HOME FALTERING AND LAPSING   720 14
    OH BUILD YOUR SHIP OF DEATH OH BUILD IT   720 20
    SO BUILD YOUR SHIP OF DEATH AND LET THE SOUL DRIFT   721 4
    AND HELP THEM TO BUILD THEIR LITTLE SHIP OF DEATH   721 19
    EACH NEEDS A LITTLE SHIP A LITTLE SHIP   721 22
    OF THE SHIP OF THE SOUL OVER SEAS WHERE DREAMED DREAMS +   *905 20

SHIP
HAVE YOU BUILT YOUR SHIP OF DEATH OH HAVE YOU *956 28
BUILD THEN YOUR SHIP OF DEATH FOR YOU WILL NEED IT *956 29
OH BUILD YOUR SHIP OF DEATH OH BUILD IT IN TIME *957 25
WHAT WILL YOU DO IF YOU HAVE NO SHIP OF THE SOUL *957 33
LET ME BUILD A LITTLE SHIP WITH OARS AND FOOD *958 20
AND LAUNCHING THERE HIS LITTLE SHIP *958 30
SLOW SLOW MY SOUL IN HIS LITTLE SHIP *959 9
OH BUILD YOUR SHIP OF DEATH *960 7
HAVE YOU BUILT YOUR SHIP OF DEATH OH HAVE YOU *960 10
OH BUILD YOUR SHIP OF DEATH FOR YOU WILL NEED IT *960 11
OF PEACE AND BUILD YOUR LITTLE SHIP *960 13
OH BUILD YOUR SHIP OF DEATH BE BUILDING IT NOW *960 27
THE LITTLE SHIP WITH ITS SOUL TO THE WONDER-GOAL *961 4
THEN BUILD YOUR SHIP OF DEATH IN READINESS *961 6

SHIPPED
THE SOUNDLESS NIGHT WHEREON OUR DAYS ARE SHIPPED 133 4

SHIPS
TO SHOW WHERE THE SHIPS AT SEA MOVE OUT OF SIGHT 172 21
HEAVY WITH A RANCID CARGO THROUGH THE LESSER SHIPS 380 19
LIKE A BIG SHIP PUSHING HER BOWSPRIT OVER THE LITTLE SH+ 380 24
THE FEMALE SHIPS 380 27
THEY MAKE TRAINS CHUFF MOTOR-CARS TITTER SHIPS LURCH 441 6
THE DEAD GIVE SHIPS AND ENGINES CINEMA RADIO AND GRAMOP+ 441 17
AS WITH CLOTH SO WITH HOUSES SHIPS SHOES WAGONS OR CUPS 451 10
O SHIPS IN BOTTLES 542 4
LITTLE SHIPS 542 20
LITTLE SHIPS 542 27
SPREAD YOUR SMALL SAILS IMMUNE LITTLE SHIPS 543 10
OF SOMETHING COMING SHIPS A-SAIL FROM OVER THE RIM OF T+ 687 3
AND EVERY TIME IT IS SHIPS IT IS SHIPS 687 4
IT IS SHIPS OF CNOSSOS COMING OUT OF THE MORNING END OF+ 687 5
IT IS AEGEAN SHIPS AND MEN WITH ARCHAIC POINTED BEARDS 687 6
THE DAWN IS NOT OFF THE SEA AND ODYSSEUS' SHIPS 687 22
WHAT DO I CARE IF THE SMOKING SHIPS 688 6
I SEE DESCENDING FROM THE SHIPS AT DAWN 688 12
OUT OF OUR LITTLE SHIPS OF DEATH *960 25

SHIP'S
SHRIEKED AND SLASHED THE WIND AS A SHIP'S 36 11

SHIRK
WILL SHIRK OR FAIL IN POINT OF HONOUR 775 13

SHIRT
'AVE I PUT 'IS CLEAN STOCKIN'S AN' SHIRT 45 14
AND SHIRT YOU NOW INVULNERABLE IN THE MAIL 154 19
THE GAP OF YOUR SHIRT WHY COVER IT UP 254 10
WHEN I STAND IN MY SHIRT I HAVE NO POCKETS 607 24
HIS BLUE SHIRT GLIMMERING ON THE WATER AMONG THE SHADOW+ 867 29
IN THE WHITE SHIRT OF THE MIND'S EXPERIENCES *957 9

SHIRT-FRONT
COME THEN THA CAN SCRAIGHT IT OUT ON MY SHIRT-FRONT 540 18
WOULD BE YOUR SHIRT-FRONT 540 23

SHIRTS
IS ONLY SAD MEN TAKING OFF THEIR SHIRTS 173 24

SHIRT'S
ON THE GARDENER WHOSE SHIRT'S BLOWN BACK 633 27

SHIVER
DID I SHIVER NAY TRULY I DO NOT KNOW 87 3
MAKE THE DAYBREAK SHIVER 109 24
OF FLESH DOES CRACKLE AND SHIVER AND BREAK IN PAIN 151 17
WE SHALL SHIVER WITH COLD AND FRIGHT 482 19
OF FLESH WOULD CRACK AND SHIVER WITH KEEN PAIN 873 29

SHIVERING
WHO FOR YEARS WAS SUN FOR YOUR SHIVERING SHADE FOR YOUR 157 2
LIKE SAD PROCESSIONS OF EXILES YOU COULD HAVE SEEN THEM+ 866 3

SHIVERS
IN UNDULATING SHIVERS BENEATH THE WIND 126 11

SHOAL
THE SUNSHINE SWAM IN A SHOAL ACROSS AND ACROSS 243 22
WHO HAD WADED TO THE PALE GREEN SEA OF EVENING OUT OF A+ 693 5

SHOALS
THEY DRIVE IN SHOALS 337 16
ROCKING DOWN THE SHOALS BETWEEN THE TEA-CUPS *943 16

SHOCK
HOW GORGEOUS THAT SHOCK OF RED LILIES AND LARKSPUR CLEA+ 129 27
TOWARDS A SHOCK AND A CRASH AND A SMITING OF HORNS AHEAD 381 22
THE GODHEAD OF GOATS FROM THE SHOCK 381 30
WITH A SHOCK AS AGAINST THE BLACKNESS OF A NEGRO 428 4
WILL ROCK IN THE SHOCK OF THE MAD MACHINE AND THE HOUSE+ 624 29
YOU'LL GIVE THE GREAT BRITISH PUBLIC A NERVOUS SHOCK 669 11

SHOCKED
LIFT LOOKS OF SHOCKED AND MOMENTOUS EMOTION UP AT ME 71 22

SHOCKING
IN A LOW SHOCKING PERFUME TO KNOW WHO HAS HAILED 105 33
THIS I CALL A SHOCKING HUMILIATION 645 5

SHOCKS
WITH UNKNOWN SHOCKS 436 17
ENTERING IN SHOCKS OF TRUTH UNFOULED BY LIES 482 2
SHOCKS YOU THROUGH AND THROUGH 551 20

SHODDY
AND DIE LIKE A DOG IN A HOLE 'TIS STRANGE WHAT A SHODDY 755 8
WHEN I SEE THIS SEA LOOKING SHODDY AND DEAD 815 10

SHOE
BUTTERFLY WHY DO YOU SETTLE ON MY SHOE AND SIP THE DIRT+ 696 13
MY SHOE 696 20
WE CAN DO WITHOUT THE SOLE OF THE SHOE 774 10
THE GLITTER OF THE BUCKLE OF YOUR SHOE 887 13

SHOES
MY SHAME LIKE SHOES IN THE PORCH 134 6
AND YOUR SHOES AND DRAW UP AT MY HEARTH 237 18
NAKED EXCEPT FOR FANCIFUL LONG SHOES 296 20
IN SUNDAY SUITS AND YELLOW SHOES 316 21
TO THE YOUTHS IN SUNDAY SUITS AND YELLOW SHOES 317 28
AS WITH CLOTH SO WITH HOUSES SHIPS SHOES WAGONS OR CUPS 451 10
REQUIRING NO SHOES O MY CHILDREN 466 12
TIE MY SPOTTED SHOES FOR DANCING 802 22
AND AS WITH CLOTH SO WITH ALL THINGS HOUSES SHOES WAGON+ *950 1

SHONE
YOU WHO DARKENED AND SHONE 56 34
AT TH' SLOPPY GRAVE AN' 'ER LITTLE NECK SHONE 61 7
HOW MANY TIMES HAS T' CANDLE-LIGHT SHONE 138 4
SHONE WHITE 165 4
SHONE LIKE A HUGE SEA-SPARK 201 24
SO THEN THERE SHONE WITHIN THE JUNGLE DARKNESS 206 8
THEY SHONE CLEAR LIKE FLOWERS UNDONE 216 17
THAT SHONE AND DARKENED THEY WERE ALL TOO CLEVER 737 22
IF THE STAR SHONE THEY DARE NOT THEY COULD NOT 800 28
IF THE STAR SHONE WITHIN YOU 800 30
SHONE SWEETLY THROUGH YELLOW SILK A MAN FULL IN THE LIG+ 865 2
FOR THE FULL MOON SHONE BUT WHETHER 881 32
HAVE SHONE FOR ME LIKE A CROWDED CONSTELLATION OF STARS *897 25
HAVE SHONE FOR ME LIKE A CROWDED CONSTELLATION OF STARS *901 2
I COULDNA' SEE HER FACE BUT HER LITTLE NECK SHONE *910 11
AT TH' SLOPPY WET GRAVE AN' 'ER LITTLE NECK SHONE *911 23

SHONNA
THOUGH I SHONNA MARRY 'ER 80 30
BUT I SHONNA MARRY HER *922 30
I SHONNA FOR NOBODY IT IS *922 31
FOR I TELL YE I SHONNA MARRY HER *923 3

SHOO
SHOO IT DOWN OUT OF THE EMPYREAN 329 17

SHOOK
WHO SHOOK THY ROUNDNESS IN HIS FINGER'S CUP 69 9
THE SNOW DESCENDS AS IF THE SLOW SKY SHOOK 76 14
TILL HER DARK DEEPS SHOOK WITH CONVULSIVE THRILLS AND T+ 125 31
HE CANNOT SEE IT I CAN NEVER SHOW IT HIM HOW IT SHOOK 137 13
HASTILY I SHOOK HIM OUT OF THE WINDOW 347 9
SHOOK HANDS WITH HIM 618 20
I FEEL AS IF FEATHERS WERE LIFTED AND SHOOK 883 4
THE SNOW DESCENDS AS IF THE DULL SKY SHOOK *898 8
THE SNOW DESCENDS AS IF THE DULL SKY SHOOK *901 17
AN' 'ER BODY FAIR SHOOK AGAIN *910 13
THAT WHITE AN' 'ER SHOOK THAT MUCH I'D LIKE TO BEGIN *911 24
GOD SHOOK THY ROUNDNESS IN HIS FINGER'S CUP *915 21
TILL HER DARK DEEPS SHOOK WITH CONVULSIVE THRILLS AND T+ *936 30

SHOON
LISTEN HER SHOON 37 9

SHOOT
FOR MEN TO SHOOT AT PENNY-A-TIME IN A BOOTH AT A FAIR 272 17
FLASH OF A MOUNTAIN LION'S LONG SHOOT 402 16
AND SHOOT ONE ANOTHER AMAZED AND MAD WITH SOMNAMBULISM 408 12

SHOOTS
THEIR HOLD ON REALITY ENFEEBLE THEIR RISING SHOOTS 92 28
IS JUST BEYOND RANGE OF THE ARROW HE SHOOTS 382 22
SAVE SOME SHOOTS SOME LOVELY FLOWERING SHOOTS 640 19
ALL MISTRUSTFUL OF THRUSTING ITS SHOOTS WHERE ONLY *900 21
ALL MISTRUSTFUL OF THRUSTING ITS SHOOTS WHERE ONLY *903 33

SHOP-LADY
LIKE A SHOP-LADY OR A LADY-SECRETARY 548 20

SHOPPING
HAVE A GAME OF TENNIS GO OUT IN THE CAR DO SOME SHOPPIN+ 651 21

SHOPS
BEFORE THE SHOPS LIKE WAGTAILS ON THE EDGE OF A POOL 269 24
EVEN THE VERY FLOWERS IN THE SHOPS OR PARKS 634 18

SHORE
LIKE HALF-SEEN FROTH ON AN EBBING SHORE IN THE MOON 75 28
OF WEED THAT BLACKENED THE SHORE SO THAT I RECOILED 98 17
I WILL GO OUT TO THE NIGHT AS A MAN GOES DOWN TO THE SH+ 180 1
GONE DOWN TO THE FLASHING SHORE 200 14
SHE GOES FAR DOWN TO THE SHORE 201 18
I AM THROWN UPON THE SHORE 259 29
OVER TO THE NEW WORLD AND WAS CLIMBING OUT ON THE SHORE 260 14
THOUGH IT STRIKES NO SHORE 454 15
SO FATHER NEPTUNE WALKED UP THE SHORE 574 19
BY SOME MALIGNANT FISHERMAN ON AN UNSEEN SAFE SHORE 586 10
FORE-RUNNERS HAVE BARELY LANDED ON THE SHORE 607 4
THE EVENING SULKS ALONG THE SHORE THE REDDENING SUN 625 10
BY SOME MALIGNANT FISHERMAN ON AN UNSEEN SHORE 632 25
WHO HAD LAIN HER SHIFT ON THE SHORE ON THE SHINGLE SLOPE 693 4
BUT I'LL NEVER REACH THE LONG SWEET SHORE 747 25
THEY LIE ON THE SHORE AND HEAVE 827 7
LIKE FLOATING FROTH ON AN EBBING SHORE IN THE MOON *897 27
LIKE FLOATING FROTH ON AN EBBING SHORE IN THE MOON *901 4
THE WAVES RAN LAUGHING UP THE SHORE AT THE SWELL *917 4

SHORES SHOWING

SHORES
AS I SIT ON THE SHORES OF THE CLASS ALONE 51 10
THE SHORES OF THIS INNERMOST OCEAN ALIVE AND ILLUSORY 71 12
ON THE SHORES OF THIS CEASELESS OCEAN GAY BIRDS OF THE 71 18
HOST ON THE SHORES OF THE LAKE LIKE THICK WILD RICE BY 391 9
AND KINDLING LITTLE FIRES UPON THE SHORES 688 15
WHOSE POWER RUNS TO THE SHORES ALONG MY ARMS 705 15
AND THE WHITE SHORES OF LIFE 722 8
TO THE FATHOMLESS DEEPS AHEAD FAR FAR FROM THE GREY SHO+ 723 24
ONLY TO WRECK ON THE SHORES OF NIGHT AGAIN 771 26
SHORES *918 9
HE SHALL SLIP DOWN THE SHORES INVISIBLE *958 25
FATHOMLESS DEEP AHEAD FAR FAR FROM THE GREY SHORES *959 1

SHOREWARDS
WITH THE FULL THIGHS SLOWLY LIFTING OF THE WADER WADING+ 693 10

SHORN
THE SHORN MOON TREMBLING INDISTINCT ON HER PATH 131 23
AND CAST US FORTH LIKE THIN SHORN MOONS TO TRAVEL 132 10
BEYOND THE WITHERING SNOW OF THE SHORN FIELDS 135 6
THE STRANGER'S HAIR WAS SHORN LIKE A LAD'S DARK POLL 156 1
SHORN LIKE THE SHORN LAMB TO EVERY ICY GAZE 836 4
THE SHORN MOON TREMBLING INDISTINCT ON HER PATH *937 22
AND CAST US FORTH LIKE SHORN THIN MOONS TO TRAVEL *938 2
BEYOND THE WITHERING SNOW OF THE SHORN FIELDS *939 6

SHORT
A DECENT SHORT REGRET FOR THAT WHICH ONCE WAS VERY GOOD 66 4
AN' T' SHORT DAYS GOIN' UNKNOWN TER THEE 137 29
SINCE I AM HERE FOR SO SHORT A SPELL 152 7
AND FALTERS A FEW SHORT STEPS ACROSS THE LAKE 230 6
FROM THAT SHALLOW-SILVERY WINE-GLASS ON A SHORT STEM 279 11
SHALLOW WINE-CUPS ON SHORT BULGING STEMS 283 6
AND RABBITS MAKE PILLS AMONG THE SHORT GRASS 321 23
FROM HIS LEAP AT THE ZENITH IN HER SO IT FALLS JUST SHO+ 382 23
MORE THAN THE CHASTE SHORT DASH 492 28
SHORT GASPS OF FLAME IN THE GREEN OF NIGHT WAY OFF 606 1
AND THE SILENCE OF SHORT DAYS THE SILENCE OF THE YEAR T+ 727 13
BUT ALAS THIS IS NOT WHAT I CAME FOR I HAVE FALLEN SHORT 751 8
OF HAVING SHORT CROPS 778 19
IN YOUR FIFTIES WITH A SHORT FROCK SHOWING YOUR FORE AN+ 835 10
AND DESTRUCTIVE IN SHORT BRILLIANT 841 23
LYING RIGID AND SILENT WITH YOUR FACE ON THE SHORT SEA + 871 34

SHORT-BREATH'D
INTO A DARING SHORT-BREATH'D CONFESSION 854 13

SHORTENING
DRAGGING THE LINKS OF MY SHORTENING CHAIN 50 17

SHOT
CAN THIS SHOT ARROW OF TRAVEL FLY 116 15
I SHOT MY MAN I SAW HIM CRUMBLE AND HANG 741 27
STREAMED REDNESS DOWN THE AIR SHOT RED ON HIS EYES 884 24
CAN THIS SHOT ARROW OF TRAVEL FLY *930 14

SHOULDER
FOREVER EVER BY MY SHOULDER PITIFUL LOVE WILL LINGER 63 22
CURVED THY MOUTH FOR THEE AND WHAT STRONG SHOULDER 69 14
YOU LOOK ROUND OVER YOUR SHOULDER 208 13
NOR THE ADDER WE SAW ASLEEP WITH HER HEAD ON HER SHOULD+ 255 26
SHALL GREAT WINGS FLAME FROM HIS SHOULDER SOCKETS 326 6
ALL ANIMATE CREATION ON YOUR SHOULDER 353 32
ALL LIFE CARRIED ON YOUR SHOULDER 354 21
TOUCH HIM ON THE SHOULDER 754 3
HE HAD A SHOVEL AND A BRUSH ON HIS SHOULDER HIS FACE WA+ 866 18
CURVED THY MOUTH FOR THEE AND HIS STRONG SHOULDER *915 26
I NEED NOT GLANCE OVER MY SHOULDER IN FEAR OF THE TERRO+ *945 25

SHOULDER-DEEP
SHOULDER-DEEP OUT OF THE CORN AND WIPES 220 3
SHOULDER-DEEP OUT O' TH' CORN AND WIPES *944 11

SHOULDER-FEATHERS
THE SOFT CLUSTERED SHOULDER-FEATHERS IN ROSY CONFUSION + 855 23

SHOULDERS
KNOWS BUT THE RETREAT OF THE BURNING SHOULDERS THE RED-+ 67 4
SHOULDERS 130 8
GLISTENING WHITE ON THE SHOULDERS 217 13
SHE DRIPS HERSELF WITH WATER AND HER SHOULDERS 217 19
YOUR SHOULDERS YOUR BRUISED THROAT 238 10
THOSE SHOULDERS SO WARM AND SMOOTH I FEEL THAT I 245 18
AND AS HE SLOWLY DREW UP SNAKE-EASING HIS SHOULDERS AND 351 2
HENCE THE BLACK CROSS ON HIS SHOULDERS 378 27
HER LITTLE LOOSE HANDS AND DROOPING VICTORIAN SHOULDERS 393 14
AND THE SHOULDERS PALLID WITH LIGHT FROM THE SILENT SKY+ 693 11
HANGING FROM THE SHOULDERS OF THE RAINBOW 820 4
LIKE A HEAVY BIRD DISTURBED AND HER SHOULDERS STIRRED *934 16
GLISTENING WHITE ON THE SHOULDERS *942 23
AND HER SHOULDERS *943 2

SHOULDER-SOCKETS
FROM THE FURNACE-CRACKS OF HIS SHOULDER-SOCKETS 326 13

SHOULDN'T
WHY SHOULDN'T YOUR LEGS AND YOUR GOOD STRONG THIGHS 254 11
WE SHOULDN'T BE WHERE WE ARE NOW 483 18
THEY SHOULDN'T EXIST 526 24
WHY SHOULDN'T WE STEAL THE JAM IN THE CUPBOARD 573 11
WHY SHOULDN'T I STEAL THE JAM IN THE CUPBOARD 670 26

SHOUT
SHOUT AN' AX WHAT 'E WANTS 44 18
HEARING MY MERE LIPS SHOUT 124 21
WITH A BUBBLE OF LAUGHTER AND SHRILLY SHOUT 179 18
AND SALVIA FIERCE TO CROW AND SHOUT FOR FIGHT 317 21

SHOUT
BUT SHE HANGS ON AND MY SHOUT AND MY SHRINKING ARE 359 22
A SHOUT 364 16
YET THE STRANGE ALMOST FRIGHTENED SHOUT OF DELIGHT THAT 446 14
WANT TO GET UP AN' SHOUT 550 10
HEARING MY MERE LIPS SHOUT *935 21

SHOUTED
AND THE CHILDREN SUDDENLY SHOUTED OUT 444 22
HE SHOUTED RAN HEAVILY AFTER THEM 735 8
EVEN IF THE LORD GOD SHOUTED 818 28

SHOUTING
SHOUTING LADS 75 9
SHOUTING FORTH FLAME TO SET THE WORLD ON FIRE 315 2
BLEEDING AND SHOUTING AND DYING 739 2
SHOUTING REVENGE REVENGE 739 22
IT SMELLS STRANGE LIKE THE SHOUTING OF MEN 759 2
WOMANLESS SHOUTING IN ANGER 759 3
WITH NO SHOUTING 766 3
LIKE A PICTURE BY THAULOW DARK CLUSTERS OF SHOUTING LADS 865 19

SHOUTS
LIKE SPATTERING SHOUTS OF AN ORATOR ENDLESSLY DROPPING 54 6
OH BOISTEROUS THE CUCKOO SHOUTS FORESTALLING 65 27
THE TURNED WORM SHOUTS I BRAVELY BOOZE 433 2

SHOVE
NO NO MATTER HOW YOU MAY SHOVE 550 18

SHOVED
UNDER JAW SHOVED OUT 397 19

SHOVED-OUT
LITTLE BLACK SNUB-NOSED BITCH WITH A SHOVED-OUT JAW 394 29

SHOVEL
HE HAD A SHOVEL AND A BRUSH ON HIS SHOULDER HIS FACE WA+ 866 18

SHOVES
CUCKOO COMES AND SHOVES OVER 125 2

SHOVING
CAME DOWN ON MY BREAST SHOVING OVER *936 3

SHOW
THE PINK YOUNG HORSES SHOW ONE SIDE BRIGHT 50 23
TO SHOW YOU THUS TRANSFIGURED CHANGED 53 22
THE WHITE MOON SHOW LIKE A BREAST REVEALED 55 26
TO STEADY MY BRAIN IN THIS PHANTOM SHOW 105 10
HE CANNOT SEE IT I CAN NEVER SHOW IT HIM HOW IT SHOOK 137 13
TO SHOW THE PLACE WHENCE THE SCREAM WAS HEARD 150 13
TO SHOW WHERE THE SHIPS AT SEA MOVE OUT OF SIGHT 172 21
NOT SHOW LIKE THE REST 251 8
SHOW ME I TREMBLE SO MUCH TO HEAR IT THAT EVEN NOW 273 28
SHOW ME THE VIOLETS THAT ARE OUT 273 30
WHEN THEY BREAK AND SHOW THE SEED THEN WE LOOK INTO THE+ 277 2
LIKE A PROSTITUTE THE BURSTEN FIG MAKING A SHOW OF HER + 283 33
OR IF IT HAPPEN TO SHOW AT HER POINTED HEAVY TAIL 361 20
WITH BITS OF BRINDLE COMING THROUGH LIKE RUST TO SHOW 395 2
AND SHOW A TINY BUNCH OF WHITE TEETH IN YOUR UNDERHUNG 398 11
AND SHOW VAST BELLIES TO THE CHILDREN 425 22
I WISH YOU'D SHOW YOUR HAND 430 14
LET'S BE HONEST AT LAST ABOUT SEX OR SHOW AT LEAST THAT+ 464 12
HE FINDS A FEMALE THEY SHOW NO HASTE 465 9
AND START IN TO SHOW 564 16
JUST TO SHOW HOW DANGEROUS THEY ARE 572 15
WE CAN RUN OUR OWN SHOW 573 20
WE'LL SHOW 'EM A THING OR TWO NEVER YOU DOUBT 573 22
WE'LL SHOW THESE OLD UNCLES WHO'S GOING TO BE BOSSY 573 24
I WANT TO SHOW ALWAYS THE HUMAN TENDER REVERENCE 622 5
LET HIM SHOW IT TO THE CROWD PROBABLY THEY WILL APPLAUD 634 11
IF HE SHOW IT THE EYES AND THE BREATH OF THE CROWD 634 16
TO SHOW HOW INEXHAUSTIBLE IT IS 709 7
AND SHOW US NOTHING LEAVE US QUITE ALONE 737 27
THE OLD LIGHTS WON'T SHOW THE WAY 775 33
QUETZALCOATL WILL SHOW YOU THE WAY 809 9
OF LEAVES LIKE YELLOW FRUITS SHOW PLAIN *932 23

SHOWED
SHOWED ME SOME OTHER LOVERS STEALING DOWN THE OTHER HED+ 882 21

SHOWER
HUNDREDS OF VIOLET-HEADS IN A SHOWER 880 19
AS A SILENT BEE AT THE END OF A SHOWER *913 20

SHOWERS
IN SHOWERS OF MINUTE RUDDY DROPS FROM THEIR BLADES 884 29

SHOWERY
RAIN FROM THE SHOWERY HEAVENS AND BRIGHT BLUE CROPS 136 12

SHOWING
SHOWING THE ROCKING DARKNESS NOW A-REEL 136 10
FOAM-CLOTS SHOWING BETWEEN 145 1
THAT'S HOW THE FIG DIES SHOWING HER CRIMSON THROUGH THE 283 30
THEY ARE ROYALTY DARK-FACED ROYALTY SHOWING THE CONSCIO+ 388 22
SHOWING A GLINT OF TEETH AND GLANCING TROPICAL EYES ARO+ 391 14
AND WHITE TEETH SHOWING IN YOUR DRAGON-GRIN AS YOU RACE 397 20
AND SAT UP TAKING STRANGE POSTURES SHOWING THE PINK SOL+ 445 12
KEEP SUDDENLY SHOWING A WHITENESS A FLASH AND A FURL A + 687 2
IN YOUR FIFTIES WITH A SHORT FROCK SHOWING YOUR FORE AN+ 835 10
SHOWING HER SHINS 835 29
WITH DIM LIGHT SHOWING THE HEADS OF THE SILVER NAILS 876 14

SHOWN`
  SHOWN RUPTURED   278 30
  AND SOME CAN ONLY SEE WHAT THEY ARE SHOWN   649 8
  AS THOU ART SHOWN AND HAVING DONE SO MUCH   872 8
  SHE HAS SHOWN ME THE STRANDS THAT WEAVE   *893 4

SHOWS
  BUT DAY SHOWS IT VIVID WITH FEELING   38 3
  AS IT SHOWS HIM SLEEPING A SLEEP HE GOT   59 5
  OF FRETTING OR OF GLADNESS SHOWS THE JETTING   89 14
  GHOST BEYOND GHOST OF BLOSSOM SHOWS   104 27
  WHITE LILAC SHOWS DISCOLOURED NIGHT   104 30
  AND SHOWS THE RED OF HAWTHORN SET   105 1
  WITH WORDS BUT THE NIGHT SHOWS THROUGH   109 11
  SHOWS IN ONLY TWO SAD PLACES   145 6
  THAT LITTLE BIT OF YOUR CHEST THAT SHOWS BETWEEN   254 9
  TO THE PROUD FATHER AND SHOWS ITS LITTLE WEBBED GREENISH 438 28
  SHOWS THAT THE CHILDREN VAGUELY KNOW HOW CHEATED THEY   446 16
  GREY EVIL WHICH HAS NO PATH AND SHOWS NEITHER LIGHT NOR   712 2
  SHOWS THAT SHE IS RENEWING HER YOUTH LIKE THE EAGLE   728 11
  SHOWS ONE BUD MORE   814 3
  IT SHOWS AGAIN HOW HIGHLY DEVELOPED THE SOCIAL CONSCIEN+ 829 16
  WHICH SHOWS ONCE MORE THAT OUR SOCIAL CONSCIENCE IS DEV+ 829 22
  BUT THE DAY SHOWS IT VIVID WITH FEELING   *892 19
  HE SHOWS AN AMUSED SUPERIOR CONTEMPT AT THE PREVALENCE + *949 4

SHRAPNEL
  AND THE CHAOS THAT BOUNCES AND RATTLES LIKE SHRAPNEL AT   250 4

SHRED
  INTO THAT TRANSLUCENT PHANTOM SHRED   332 13
  SO THEY PECKED A SHRED OF MY LIFE AND FLEW OFF WITH A   500 4
  NEVER NOT THE TINIEST SHRED   500 10
  AND YOUR SHRED OF A SKIRT   835 19

SHREDDED
  WHY THIS LENGTH OF SHREDDED SHANK   332 4

SHREWD
  DERIVED FROM SHREWD CASH-CHEMISTRY   488 13

SHREWDLY
  BUT SHE PUTS HER NOSE DOWN SHREWDLY ENOUGH WHEN THE   384 28

SHRIEK
  THE SILKEN SHRIEK OF THE SOUL'S TORN MEMBRANE   364 24
  TORN WITH A SHRIEK HALF MUSIC HALF HORROR   364 26
  DOES HE SHRIEK FOR BLOOD   374 15

SHRIEKED
  SHRIEKED AND SLASHED THE WIND AS A SHIP'S   36 11

SHRIEKING
  THE SHRIEKING CROSS   112 10
  IN A RUSH UP THE SHRIEKING DUCT OF HIS VERTEBRAL WAY   381 20
  OF FREEDOM SHRIEKING TILL HER THROAT WAS SORE   574 23
  THE SHRIEKING CROSS   *928 30

SHRIEKS
  WIERD RIGGING IN A STORM SHRIEKS HIDEOUSLY   36 12
  AND WITH HIDEOUS SHRIEKS OF STEELY RAGE AND FRUSTRATION   676 3

SHRILL
  MY WINDOWS OF DISCOVERY AND SHRILL SIN   122 30
  MY WINDOWS OF DISCOVERY AND SHRILL SIN   *934 6

SHRILLY
  WITH A BUBBLE OF LAUGHTER AND SHRILLY SHOUT   179 18

SHRINE
  AS WE SIT IN THE SUNSHINE ON THE SEAT BY THE LITTLE SHR+ 204 12
  CAME TO THE COUNTER WITH HIS HAT OFF HUMBLE AT THE SHRI+ 618 17

SHRINES
  TROOP OUT OF YOUR SHRINES   798 18

SHRINK
  HOW CAN YOU FROM MY BOWL OF KISSES SHRINK   86 8
  LIKE A NEWLY-NAKED BERRY SHRINK   107 14
  THE GHOSTS AND I WE MOURN TOGETHER AND SHRINK   173 6
  LIPS TO THE VESSELS NEVER SHRINK   177 15
  WHICH I SHRINK FROM   645 26
  BELLIES THAT SHRINK NOT   827 23

SHRINKING
  THEN A LAUNCH ABROAD OF SHRINKING DOVES   179 13
  BUT SHE HANGS ON AND MY SHOUT AND MY SHRINKING ARE   359 22
  SHRINKING   645 23
  FINDS ITSELF SHRINKING WINCING FROM THE COLD   717 8
  I AM COME BACK A FOREIGNER WONDERING AND SHRINKING FROM+ 867 2

SHRINKS
  INTO MUD THE SPACE FAST SHRINKS IN THE BUILDER'S HANDS   *896 11
  AS MY WILD SOUL SHRINKS AND THE SONGS ARE DRIVEN FROM M+ *896 12

SHRIVEL
  IT DOES NOT SHRIVEL LIKE BIG HERBAGE   746 9

SHRIVELLED
  WHAT IF THE GORSE-FLOWERS SHRIVELLED AND I WERE GONE   33 21
  IN THE PULPIT WHERE SHRIVELLED AND GHASTLY IN UNINTELLI+ 859 14
  WHAT IF THE GORSE FLOWERS SHRIVELLED AND KISSING WERE L+ *891 23

SHRIVELLING
  SHRIVELLING DOWN IN THE FINAL DOUR   *927 9
  SHRIVELLING DOWN IN THE FINAL DOUR   *928 9

SHROUD
  THROUGH THE SHROUD OF THE TOWN AS SLOW   142 26
  THE INVISIBLE IN ITS SHROUD   403 13

SHROUDED
  THE SHROUDED MOTHER OF A NEW IDEA MEN HIDE THEIR FACES   91 26
  THE SHROUDED MOTHER OF A NEW IDEA MEN HIDE THEIR FACES   *926 19

SHROUDS
  BUT SHROUDS   133 15
  ARE BORN DEAD THEY ARE SHROUDS THEY SOAK LIFE OUT OF US   448 9

SHUDDER
  IS IT WITH PAIN MY DEAR THAT YOU SHUDDER SO   87 1
  A TWITCH A TWITTER AN ELASTIC SHUDDER IN FLIGHT   341 11
  SHUDDER OF DRUMS   388 34
  LO AGAIN THE SHUDDER OR BLISS THROUGH ALL THE ATOMS   682 15
  AND THE SHUDDER OF ELECTRIC ANGER   707 10
  HAVE FELT THE DAY DARKEN AND SHUDDER   *937 14

SHUDDERING
  STARTLING A FEAR UNSPEAKABLE AS THE SHUDDERING WIND   140 17
  HAVE DONE HAVE DONE WITH THIS SHUDDERING DELICIOUS BUSI+ 273 18
  SHUDDERING A STRANGE WAY DOWN THE BOTTOMLESS PIT   322 23
  SHUDDERING STORM WIND OR A WATER RUSHING THROUGH   370 25
  AH BE STILL BE STILL AND STOP SHUDDERING   768 6
  THERE ARE DEAD THAT CLUSTER IN THE FROZEN NORTH SHUDDER+ 795 21

SHUFFLE
  SHUFFLE SHUFFLE AND HIS LITTLE WICKED EYE HAS SEEN YOU + 387 10
  PERPETUAL FIRE-LAUGHING MOTION AMONG THE SLOW SHUFFLE   389 18
  AND SHUFFLE OF BROKEN SODDENED BOOTS YET SINGING GOES R+ 866 14

SHUFFLES
  SHUFFLES GINGERLY ROUND   426 5

SHUFFLING
  SHUFFLING HIS RAGGED BOOTS THERE COMES ONE BOY LATE   866 6

SHUN
  AS HE PLANTS HIS NEW GERM IN US WHAT IS THERE TO SHUN   127 5
  WHAT IS IT THEY SHUN   166 24
  THE SHADOW IT USED TO SHUN   215 25

SHUNTING
  THE CLINK OF THE SHUNTING ENGINES IS SHARP AND FINE   52 16
  THE CLINK OF THE SHUNTING ENGINES IS SHARP AND FINE   *905 5

SHUT
  THOU SHALT SHUT DOORS ON ME   44 9
  DO SHUT THY FACE   45 4
  NOW SHUT IT LIES   55 16
  A MOMENT THEN DARKNESS SHUT THE LID OF THE SACRED ARK   62 18
  WE HAVE SHUT THE DOORS BEHIND US AND THE VELVET FLOWERS+ 70 1
  SHUT LIKE A DAISY BUD   77 26
  SHUT UPON   88 9
  ROUNDED LIKE PEARLS FOR SLEEP AND THEN FROM BETWEEN SHU+ 88 16
  WILL ENTER AND SHUT THE DOOR TO STAY   91 9
  IT SHUT BEHIND HER LEAVING THE STREET AGHAST   122 8
  TO SHUT HALLUCINATIONS OUT   124 19
  OF THE MAN-LIFE NORTH IMPRISONED SHUT IN THE HUM OF THE 149 5
  I AM SHUT IN A PRISONER I KNOW NOT HOW   173 27
  FOR THE HOUSE IS SHUT AND SEALED AND THE BREATH OF THE + 174 27
  THE WHOLE WIDE WORLD IS INTERIOR NOW AND WERE ALL SHUT + 175 11
  PASS THE MEN WHOSE EYES ARE SHUT LIKE ANEMONES IN A DAR+ 180 20
  THE STARS THAT OPEN AND SHUT   194 4
  AND EVERYTHING SHUT UP AND GONE TO SLEEP   203 12
  WITH PALE SHUT FACE NOR EITHER HEARS NOR FEELS   232 27
  FOR HER WATCHERS TO SHUT THE GATE   261 25
  AND SHUT WINGS   345 31
  SO SHUT UP PIE-JAW BLETHER   564 11
  THAT SHUT ME UP IN MY BUNK   758 5
  SOME ONE WILL KNOCK WHEN THE DOOR IS SHUT   789 5
  NOW SHUT YOUR EYES   816 24
  YEA I WOULD SHUT MY EYES I WOULD CLOSE MY WINDOWS   875 26
  WITH SORROWFUL FINGERS STROKED HER EYELIDS SHUT   881 2
  THE POOR SHUT DANDELIONS WHOM SMALL WARMTH EXPANDS   *896 19
  WE HAVE SHUT THE DOORS BEHIND US AND THE VELVET FLOWERS+ *916 9
  SHUT LIKE A DAISY BUD   *919 14
  TO SHUT HALLUCINATIONS OUT   *935 19
  DOOR ON THE LATCH AND SHUT MYSELF IN SHUT OUT FEAR   *945 29

SHUT-EYED
  IN SHUT-EYED TOUCH   834 6

SHUTS
  AND SLOWLY ALL THE BLOSSOM SHUTS IN PAIN   113 13
  AND SHE SHUTS YOU IN THE CELLAR FOR THE LEAST LITTLE TI+ 572 7

SHUTTERS
  AS SLOWLY THE HOUSE OF DAY IS CLOSING ITS EASTERN SHUTT+ 102 28
  WITH SHUTTERS OF SOMBRE CLOUD WILL CLOSE   163 14
  THE VENETIAN\ SHUTTERS I PUSH WIDE   343 1
  WITH SHUTTERS OF CLOUDED NIGHT WILL CLOSE   857 14

SHUTTLE
  LIKE A SHUTTLE THAT CARRIES THE WEFT   746 24
  LIKE THE WOOF THE SHUTTLE CARRIES   747 2

SHUTTLES
  SOMETHING FAERY AND FINE THE SHUTTLES SLIDING   72 7
  OH LABOURERS OH SHUTTLES ACROSS THE BLUE FRAME OF MORNI+ 73 8

SHUT-UP
  SHUT-UP COFFIN OF A THING WITH A SOLDIER WEARY   733 6

SHY
    ON THE GREEN WOOD'S EDGE A SHY GIRL HOVERS   41   1
    IN THE HOME-PLACE SHY IS IT SHE SHOULD EXCLUDE   48 25
    YOU ARE SHY YOU SILLY YOU SILLY SHY THING   254 13
    FOR THE SYMPATHY IN THEIR VAST SHY HEARTS   465 11
    AND THINK HOW THE NIGHTINGALE WHO IS SO SHY   530   9
    SHY FLOWER OF SEX   562 31
    BUT A WOMAN SHY AND ALONE WAS WASHING HERSELF UNDER A T+   651   4
    SHY OF YOUR FACE STILL BEND TO WOO   887 15

SHYEST
    MEN ARE THE SHYEST CREATURES THEY NEVER WILL COME   254 14

SHYLY
    SHYLY AND IN HOMAGE LINGER FOR AN INVITATION   256   5

SHYNESS
    FOR ALL HER SHYNESS BAITING   885 22

SH-
    LIKE B- AND F- AND SH-   491 16
    WAS WORDS LIKE SH- AND F-   491 22

SIBILANT
    IN WILD WHITE SIBILANT SPRAY   467 13

SICILIAN
    OUT OF THE DEEP SOFT FLEDGE OF SICILIAN WINTER-GREEN   300 22
    AND FROM THE SICILIAN TOWNLETS SKIRTING ETNA   312 10
    ALAS THE SUNDAY COATS OF SICILIAN BOLSHEVISTS   313 34
    SICILIAN BOLSHEVISTS   314 10
    ON THE DAY OF SICILIAN JULY WITH ETNA SMOKING   349 28
    IN THE SICILIAN TWILIGHT   377   2
    THROUGH THE SICILIAN TWILIGHT   377 21

SICILY
    SICILY DECEMBER'S SICILY IN A MASS OF RAIN   301 12
    AND IN SICILY ON THE MEADOWS OF ENNA   308 10
    FOR IN SICILY THE BLACK BLACK SNAKES ARE INNOCENT THE G+   350   3

SICK
    I AM SICK AND WHAT ON EARTH IS THE GOOD OF IT ALL   74 16
    THE SICK GRAPES ON THE CHAIR BY THE BED LIE PRONE AT TH+   112 16
    WEARY AN' SICK O' THE LIKES O' SHE   139 33
    TO BREAK THIS SICK AND NAUSEOUS DREAM   177 19
    YOU HAVE FED ME WITH YOUR SWEETNESS NOW I AM SICK   234 23
    I WAS SO SICK OF IT   256 23
    FOR I AM SICK OF THEM THEIR FAINT-BLOODEDNESS   271 15
    I AM SO SICK OF THE PRETENSIONS OF THE SPIRIT   288   5
    WOMEN ARE SICK OF CONSOLING   457 21
    I AM SICK BECAUSE I HAVE GIVEN MYSELF AWAY   500   1
    SO NOW I HAVE LOST TOO MUCH AND AM SICK   500   7
    I AM SICK OF PEOPLE'S CEREBRAL EMOTIONS   500 18
    I AM SICK OF LOVABLE PEOPLE   505 23
    WE ARE SICK OF IT   519   9
    KILLS US WE ARE SICK OF IT TO DIE   519 17
    IT IS SICK OF GREED   831   6
    IT IS SICK OF PEOPLE OUT ON THE MAKE   831   7
    BUT WE ARE MAIMED CRIPPLED CONTORTED AND SICK   833   8
    I AM QUITE SICK OF BOOKS   857   1
    I AM SICK AND TIRED MORE THAN ANY THRALL   *895 24
    I AM SICK AND TIRED MORE THAN ANY THRALL   *904 13

SICKEN
    SICKEN US AND WE ARE STUNNED BY THE RUSHINGS OF THE LAB+   856   2

SICKENED
    HAS SICKENED US THOROUGHLY WITH RODS OF IRON AND RULERS   439 26

SICKENING
    A FAINT SICKENING SCENT OF IRISES   90   1
    A DANK SICKENING SCENT CAME UP FROM THE GRIME   98 16
    MAKES SICKENING WHITE THE WHITE   252 22
    LIKE SICKENING TOADSTOOLS AND LEFT TO MELT BACK SWIFTLY   431 28
    IN SECRET UNDER THE SICKENING WALL   462   7
    THAT AWFUL AND SICKENING ENDLESS SINKING SINKING   699 21
    WOULD TAKE AWAY THE SICKENING FRET   747 13

SICKLE
    EAGLE WITH THE SICKLE DRIPPING DARKLY ABOVE   373   4
    SICKLE-OVERSWEPT SICKLE DRIPPING OVER AND ABOVE   373 11
    EAGLE WITH THE SICKLE DRIPPING DARKLY ABOVE   781   7
    SICKLE-OVERSWEPT SICKLE DRIPPING OVER AND ABOVE   781 17
    ALL SICKLE-OVERSWEPT SICKLE DRIPPING OVER AND ABOVE   783   7

SICKLE-MASKED
    SICKLE-MASKED   373 16
    SICKLE-MASKED   781 22

SICKLE-OVERSWEPT
    SICKLE-OVERSWEPT SICKLE DRIPPING OVER AND ABOVE   373 11
    SICKLE-OVERSWEPT SICKLE DRIPPING OVER AND ABOVE   781 17
    ALL SICKLE-OVERSWEPT SICKLE DRIPPING OVER AND ABOVE   783   7

SICKLY
    HAD BLASTED THE SICKLY AIR   536 15
    AND A SICKLY PEOPLE WILL SLAY US   537   9
    HOW THOU CASTEST UP A SICKLY GLARE   760   7

SICKNESS
    I FALL IN SICKNESS AND IN MISERY   727 18
    DRAWS TOWARDS THE DOWNWARD SLOPE SOME SICKNESS HATH   *937 24

SICK-ROOM
    OF THE SICK-ROOM RIGID WITH WILL   111   3

SIDE
    THE PINK YOUNG HORSES SHOW ONE SIDE BRIGHT   50 23
    AND ONE SIDE SHADOW HALF IN SIGHT   50 25
    AND PLAIN AT THE SIDE OF ME   59 22
    WHILE EVER AT MY SIDE   64   3
    WITH A STRANGE NEW KNOCKING OF LIFE AT HER SIDE   64   8
    AT ITS SIDE   144 10
    THE FACTORIES ON THE SURREY SIDE   146 28
    TO TOUCH ITS FELLOW ON EITHER SIDE   154   6
    STREWS EACH SIDE THE LINES   162   4
    RIDING AT JOSEPH'S SIDE   201   6
    LIMPING AND FOLLOWING RATHER AT MY SIDE   221 12
    THE MAN AND THE MAID GO SIDE BY SIDE   228   1
    WE LIE SIDE BY SIDE   229 15
    THREE SIDES SET ON ME SPACE AND FEAR BUT THE FOURTH SIDE   249 10
    SIDE RESTS   249 28
    AT WHOSE SIDE I HAVE LAIN FOR OVER A THOUSAND NIGHTS   260   6
    DO YOU PREFER TO LOOK ON THE PLAIN SIDE   278 23
    BLOOD FROM SIDE TO SIDE   320 22
    BLOOD FROM SIDE TO SIDE CAUSING MY MYRIAD SECRET STREAMS   320 28
    WITH YOUR TAIL TUCKED A LITTLE ON ONE SIDE   354 19
    AND ON EITHER SIDE COUNT FIVE   355 31
    ON EACH SIDE TWO ABOVE ON EACH SIDE TWO BELOW   355 32
    ALAS THE SPEAR IS THROUGH THE SIDE OF HIS ISOLATION   361   1
    DARK AS YOU ARE ON YOUR DARK SIDE EAGLE OF HEAVEN   374 31
    IN A SMALL PAGODA ON THE TEMPLE SIDE   387 22
    YOU KNOW WHICH SIDE YOUR BREAD IS BUTTERED   396 17
    LO ON THE OTHER SIDE THE GRAVE   460 29
    AND THE WHITE MIND SHINES ON ONE SIDE OF THEE   473 26
    BUT THE OTHER SIDE IS DARK FOREVER   473 27
    MAN IS LOP-SIDED ON THE SIDE OF THE ANGELS   505 16
    MEN ON THIS SIDE WOMEN ON THAT SIDE   636   3
    EACH SIDE TRYING TO MURDER THE OTHER SIDE   715   3
    HE COMES TO THE SIDE OF THE ROAD AND WASHES HIS HAND   734 13
    AS THERE ARE PEOPLE HERE ON THIS SIDE   816   2
    AS I PAUSE AT THE SIDE OF THE BATH   870   1
    SO WE FOUND THE DEAD CLATCH SIDE BY SIDE   *933   5
    DO YOU THINK I'D HAVE A CREATURE LIKE YOU AT MY SIDE   *944 25
    THREE SIDES SET ON ME SPACE AND FEAR BUT THE FOURTH SID+   *945 22

SIDE-BEAKED
    INTO AN ENORMOUSLY SIDE-BEAKED MOUTH   359   3

SIDES
    WHO SUNK HIS HANDS IN FIRMNESS DOWN THY SIDES   69 10
    HALF-WAY DOWN ITS HEAVING SIDES   144   5
    WHILE DOWN HER SIDES THE MELLOW   217 14
    THREE SIDES SET ON ME SPACE AND FEAR BUT THE FOURTH SIDE   249 10
    THREE SIDES SET ON ME CHAOS AND BOUNCE BUT THE FOURTH   249 27
    SO SHE LAID HER HANDS AND PRESSED THEM DOWN MY SIDES   254 22
    HOLLOWED THIS GROOVE IN YOUR SIDES GRASPED YOU UNDER THE   254 30
    YOUR SIDES THIS FIRMNESS THIS HARD MOULD   255 12
    YOUR LIFE A SLUICE OF SENSATION ALONG YOUR SIDES   335   8
    THEN CROSSWAYS DOWN HIS SIDES   355   5
    WITH HER LONG TANGLED SIDES LIKE AN OLD RUG THROWN   384 26
    OVER THE ROUNDED SIDES OF THE ROCKIES THE ASPENS OF   408 23
    AND THEN TO LOOK BACK TO THE ROUNDED SIDES OF THE SQUAT+   409 21
    SO WHILE THE OTHER ONE HEAVED HER SIDES   492   5
    WHO IS IT THAT SOFTLY TOUCHES THE SIDES OF MY BREAST   652   6
    THE WHEAT ON BOTH SIDES OF THE ROAD STANDS GREEN   732   5
    HE SUNK HIS HANDS IN FIRMNESS DOWN THY SIDES   *915 22
    WHILE DOWN HER SIDES THE MELLOW   *942 24
    THREE SIDES SET ON ME SPACE AND FEAR BUT THE FOURTH SID+   *945 22

SIDE-TRACK
    NOW SUDDENLY DISTRACTED INTO THIS MAZY SIDE-TRACK   363   3

SIDEWAYS
    HOW COULD I LOOK WHEN I WAS MAD I LOOKED SIDEWAYS FURTH   264 35
    NO SOONER ISSUED SIDEWAYS FROM THE THIGH OF HIS PREDECE+   299 32
    EYEING ME SIDEWAYS AND CUNNINGLY CONSCIOUS THAT I AM   333   2
    I HATE THE WAY YOU LURCH OFF SIDEWAYS INTO THE AIR   333   5
    AND HE LUNGED FLIGHT-HEAVY AWAY FROM ME SIDEWAYS A SGHE+   346 19
    SEA-BEASTS IMMERSED LEAN SIDEWAYS AND FLASH BRIGHT   453 25
    AND SIDEWAYS UTTERLY DARK SO THERE IS NO DIRECTION ANY +   719 14

SIDING
    THAT SHINES BLOOD-RED BESIDE THE RAILWAY SIDING   72   5

SIDLING
    AND HOOING AND COOING AND SIDLING THROUGH THE FRONT TEE+   433 22

SIEGE
    SEEMED TO THINK I WAS LAYING IT SIEGE   555 16

SIEGMUND
    DO NOT HOLD ME SIEGMUND   870 18
    SIEGMUND THE STRONG BEATING OF YOUR HEART HURTS ME   870 19
    SIEGMUND WITH YOUR ARMS AND YOUR HEART YOU ARE CHOKING +   870 20
    OH SIEGMUND SIEGMUND WHAT HAS HAPPENED TO YOU   870 22
    SIEGMUND ONLY THIS MORNING YOU WERE SHINING FOR ME   870 24
    AND WHAT WAS THE SOUND OF THE BIRDS AND THE WATER BUT S+   870 26
    ALWAYS SIEGMUND WHERE ARE YOU NOW   870 27
    I AM ALONE ALONE THERE IS NO MORE SIEGMUND FOR ME   871 13
    POOR SIEGMUND TAKE THE SOBS FROM OUT OF YOUR VOICE   871 17
    SIEGMUND DEAR KISS ME KISS ME   871 20
    FRIGHTENS ME FRIGHTENS ME HE IS NOT MY SIEGMUND AT ALL   871 24
    OH MY OTHER SIEGMUND   871 29
    THAT ARE DEAD YOU HAVE LEFT ME CRUELLY SIEGMUND   871 30
    SIEGMUND DEAR WHAT ARE YOU DOING LYING WITH YOUR FACE O+   871 33
    SIEGMUND SIEGMUND GET UP AND LOOK AT ME LISTEN   871 35
    SIEGMUND LIFT UP YOUR FACE AGAIN OFF THE TURF   871 36

SIERRA ROQUENA
    AT THE END OF A BACK-BONE RIDGE LIKE A STRAIGHT SIERRA +   381   3

SIEVE
  YOU WHO TAKE THE MOON AS IN A SIEVE AND SIFT   197 22

SIFT
  I WILL SIFT THE SURF THAT EDGES THE NIGHT WITH MY NET T+   180   4
  YOU WHO TAKE THE MOON AS IN A SIEVE AND SIFT   197 22
  SIFT MY LOOKS AND ESPRESSIONS   236 28

SIFTED
  THAT ISSUING OUT OF THE EAST HAS SIFTED   68   3
  THEY ALL SHOULD BE UNDERGROUND SIFTED WITH SOOT   827 28
  THAT ISSUING OUT OF THE MOON HAS SIFTED   *914 18

SIFTING
  THE SUN WARMS THE SEA LITTLE LONELY AND SAD SIFTING THE+   180   3
  STRANDS OF MY EYES AND MY LIDS AND MY HANDS AND MY FEET+   180   5

SIGH
  PURSUED BY NO SIGH OF BEREAVEMENT   63 33
  A SIGH AMONG THE SHADOWS THUS RETRIEVING   66   3
  SOBS STRUGGLING INTO HER FROSTY SIGH   85 12
  AND IT IS ALWAYS SO YOU SIGH AGAINST ME   87 15
  WITH A LOUD HOARSE SIGH   109 20
  I WITH THE NIGHT ON MY LIPS I SIGH WITH THE SILENCE OF +   133   9
  PAUSING TO SIGH   242 27
  OH THINK OF THEM AND WITH THE SOUL'S DEEP SIGH   722 12
  THE CRIMSON SHEAF OF THE WEST THE DEEP FETCHED SIGH   885   6
  THEY SIGH JUST ONCE ROUND OUR FEET AND ARE STILL HEAVY +   *917 11
  AND THINK OF THEM AND WITH THE SOUL'S DEEP SIGH   *958 17

SIGHED
  HE OPENED THE VALVES OF LIFE AND HIS LIFE SIGHED OUT   885   9

SIGHING
  GRACEFULLY SIGHING THROUGH THE WHITE   105 29
  AND HEARD THE AUDIENCE SIGHING AND SOBBING WITH ALL THE   443 24
  GOD SIGHING AND YEARNING WITH TREMENDOUS CREATIVE YEARN+   691   2
  STRONG YOUNG MAN HE LEANS SIGHING   733 19
  PUSHED UP ON END AND THE BREATH SIGHING   733 25
  INTO THE DARKNESS SIGHING ON DARK AND I   885 10

SIGHS
  OR WHETHER THE THEATRE SIGHS AND SIGHS   109 19
  AND HE SIGHS WITH RELIEF WHEN SHE PARTS FROM HIM   228 13

SIGHT
  IS GONE FROM SIGHT   41 31
  AND ONE SIDE SHADOW HALF IN SIGHT   50 25
  AND THE SIGHT OF THEIR WHITE PLAYING IN THE GRASS   65   1
  I THROW FROM OUT OF THE DARKNESS MYSELF LIKE A FLOWER I+   93 26
  HER FACE AND FORWARD LEANS TO CATCH THE SIGHT   105 27
  THE FLOWERS OF ALL MY MUD SWIM INTO SIGHT   113   8
  BETWEEN YOUR THIGHS FAR FAR FROM YOUR PEERING SIGHT   119   6
  SHE SUNK INTO MY SIGHT LIKE A SETTLING BIRD   123   8
  AND BE LOST OUT OF SIGHT WITH YOU LIKE A MELTING FOAM   134 23
  TO SIGHT REVEALING A SECRET NUMBERLESS SECRET KEEPING   136   7
  THE CITY CORRODES OUT OF SIGHT   142 22
  WETLY BOBBING AND DRIFTING AWAY ON OUR SIGHT   146 22
  SUFFERING AT SIGHT OF THE CHILDREN PLAYING AROUND   153 11
  YOU HAVE PASSED FROM OUT OF SIGHT   168   4
  TO SHOW WHERE THE SHIPS AT SEA MOVE OUT OF SIGHT   172 21
  HOLD MY HAND TO CATCH THE RAINDROPS THAT SLANT INTO SIG+   179 21
  IN SIGHT   180 22
  COMES WITH THE SIGHT OF THE ROOM I CANNOT TELL   220 14
  MY POOR MY PERISHED SOUL WITH THE SIGHT OF YOU   221 29
  COMES DARKLY INTO SIGHT   227   2
  DOWN THE NIGHT-TIME OUT OF SIGHT   252 18
  AND PASS OUT OF SIGHT   253 14
  SLOUCHING ALONG AWAY BELOW HALF OUT OF SIGHT   338   3
  TO CATCH SIGHT OF HER STANDING LIKE SOME HUGE GHOULISH   385 16
  ONLY TO DISAPPEAR AGAIN QUICKLY AWAY FROM THE SIGHT OF   394   2
  GO DOWN TO YOUR DEEP OLD HEART WOMAN AND LOSE SIGHT OF   477 24
  AND LOSE SIGHT OF ME THE ME WHOM YOU TURBULENTLY LOVED   477 26
  LET US LOSE SIGHT OF OURSELVES AND BREAK THE MIRRORS   477 27
  OUT OF SIGHT IN THE DEEP DARK LIFTING HEART   478   3
  BUT SWEET IN YOUR SIGHT   558   7
  THE SIGHT OF AN ORDINARY TOM WOULDN'T SEND THEM INTO   581 24
  BUT SHE CAUGHT SIGHT OF HER OWN REFLECTION   604 21
  MEN ARE NOT ALIKE IN THE SIGHT OF GOD   638   7
  MEN ARE ANYTHING BUT ALIKE IN THE SIGHT OF GOD   638   9
  IN THE SIGHT OF GOD AND THE UNKNOWN GODS   638 10
  ONLY THE FEW THE VERY FEW MATTER IN THE SIGHT OF GOD AND   638 13
  WITH THE PATHOS OF THOSE WHO CAN SEE BUT WHOSE SIGHT IS+   665 24
  LATELY I SAW A SIGHT MOST QUAINT   680 16
  CRAWLS THE FIRST LOAD INTO SIGHT AND NOW THERE ARE SOME   732 25
  AND WAIT TILL THEY ARE LOST UPON OUR SIGHT   740 21
  AT THE SIGHT OF EACH OTHER THE PAIR OF THEM FLEW   761   5
  THE DAWN STAR STOOD INTO SIGHT   787 20
  INTO SIGHT   788 14
  THE FIRST THING I DID WHEN I SAW THEM WAS TO LAUGH AT T+   791 27
  PEEPING THEY WILL LOSE THEIR SIGHT AND LINGERING THEY W+   799 12
  SPORT ON HER LITTERED PIANO AND MOCK AT THE SIGHT   856 17
  HE WAS A SOLDIER ALWAYS IN CHURCH IT WAS A SIGHT   859   7
  AGAINST MY HELPLESS SIGHT   862 21
  SHAPE ANSWERS SHAPE IN CHORUS TO THE SIGHT   872 17
  THE SIGHT OF THEIR WHITE PLAY AMONG THE GRASS'   *913   1
  AND THE SIGHT OF THEIR WHITE PLAY AMONG THE GRASS   *914   2
  FROM SIGHT OF ME WITHOUT ONCE YOUR TURNING   *930 18
  THE SIGHT OF YOU PEERING LONELY THERE   *930 24
  MY SIGHT BUT THEN WHO HAS STOLE THE BRIGHT WHITE HEN OF+ *933 23
  SHE SUNK INTO MY SIGHT LIKE A SETTLING BIRD   *934 14

SIGHTFUL
  SIGHTFUL SIGHTLESS SEEING AND VISIONLESS   359 17

SIGHTLESS
  DRIFT THEN FOR THE SIGHTLESS BIRDS   172   1
  SIGHTLESS AND STRONG OBLIVION IN UTTER LIFE TAKES POSSE+   261 10
  IN SIGHTLESS BEAUTY AND THE FEW   262   5
  SIGHTLESS AMONG ALL YOUR VISUALITY   289   9
  SIGHTFUL SIGHTLESS SEEING AND VISIONLESS   359 17
  AND KEEP YOU IN MILLIONS AT THE MILLS SIGHTLESS PALE SL+   441   8
  WILL BE DRIVEN MAD FROM HIMSELF AND SIGHTLESS AND ON TH+   624 25
  TO THE SIGHTLESS REALM WHERE DARKNESS IS AWAKE UPON THE+   697 17
  TO THE SIGHTLESS REALM WHERE DARKNESS IS MARRIED TO DARK *956 14

SIGHTS
  OF THE IMPENDING BEE THEY WERE FAIR ENOUGH SIGHTS   243 29

SIGN
  SO HALF LIES ON THE SKY FOR A GENERAL SIGN   114 25
  IN SIGN OF LIFE OF LOVELY DANGEROUS LIFE   317 16
  IN SIGN OF DAUNTLESS SILENT VIOLETS   317 18
  ASK BUT THE LEAGUE INSISTS THANK YOU SO MUCH NO SIGN HE+   546 14
  HERE IS MY SIGN   791 18
  A FIERY SIGN OF THE CHAINED POWER THAT WASTED HIM TO TH+   859 20

SIGNAL
  FOR A NEW SIGNAL FROM LIFE IN THAT SILENT LOST LAND OF +   394 12

SIGNALLING
  SIGNALLING THOSE TWO KISSES   37 17

SIGNALS
  WHEN I TELL YOU THE STARS FLASH SIGNALS EACH ONE   130 25
  STRANGE WHITE SIGNALS SEEM INTENDING   150 12

SIGNATURE
  DENIED A SIGNATURE WE ENGLISH ARE A SOLID PEOPLE AFTER +   546 19

SIGNED
  AND HOW RIGHT HE WAS AND I SIGNED MY INITIALS   579 20

SIGNIFICANT
  AND THE MOON SIGNIFICANT SMILES AT THE CLIFFS AND THE   130   3

SIGNING
  ME YOUR WORD AND SIGNING HERE PLEASE THAT YOU ARE A SUP+   546 10

SIGNS
  PAST VENUS AND URANUS AND THE SIGNS   713 23
  BRING ALL YOUR SIGNS   798 20
  WITH THEIR LITTLE PALE SIGNS ON THE WALL TO TRY US   *929 24

SILENCE
  THE OTHER VOICE IN A SILENCE OF BLOOD 'NEATH THE NOISE   36 17
  SILENCE FULL OF SUMMONS   40   2
  THE SILENCE OF VANISHING TEARS AND THE ECHOES OF LAUGHT+   53 19
  AT HER TATTERED SILENCE AS SHE CROUCHES AND COVERS HER +   54 22
  SUCCEEDING SHARP LITTLE SOUNDS DROPPING INTO SILENCE   63 10
  BUT WHEN I DRAW THE SCANTY CLOAK OF SILENCE OVER MY EYES   64 14
  AH LISTEN FOR SILENCE IS NOT LONELY   69   5
  AND LAID THE DESERT HORRIFIC OF SILENCE AND SNOW ON THE+   75 16
  HAVE PRESSED IMMEASURABLE SPACES OF HOARSE SILENCE   75 21
  SILENCE THAT RUSTLES BEYOND THE STARS THERE   76 11
  IS LOST IN THIS SHADOWED SILENCE THE SKIES DISTIL   76 19
  AND ALL THINGS ARE IN SILENCE THEY CAN BROOD   76 20
  ALONE WITHIN THE DIM AND HOARSE SILENCE   76 21
  SO EVEN IT BEATS LIKE SILENCE AND SKY AND EARTH IN ONE +   88   3
  LIFTING AND FALLING LONG GASPS THROUGH THE SLUICES LIKE+   97 26
  I FEEL THE SILENCE WAITING   109 25
  I FEEL YOUR SILENCE TOUCH MY WORDS AS I TALK   110   3
  I SEE THE SILENCE EASILY SIP THEM   110   7
  THAT SILENCE SHOULD TAKE THE SONG AND THE BIRD   110 11
  I SEE THE STEALTHY SHADOW OF SILENCE   110 15
  ALONE ON THE PERFECT SILENCE   110 23
  I WITH THE NIGHT ON MY LIPS I SIGH WITH THE SILENCE OF +   133   9
  CALL TO HIM OUT OF THE SILENCE CALL HIM TO SEE   137 10
  THE NIGHT WITH SILENCE CROSSING THE LAMP-TOUCHED TIDE   144 13
  UNSEEN MY HANDS EXPLORE THE SILENCE DRAWING THE BARK   147   2
  AS SHE LISTENED IN SILENCE OUTSIDE THE SILENT DOOR   155 16
  IN SILENCE WHEN SHE LOOKED FOR ALL THE WHOLE   156   3
  UNINTERRUPTED SILENCE SWINGS   166   3
  THERE IS SILENCE ONLY THE SILENCE NEVER A SOUND   166 13
  THE NERVE-BARE PLACE NOW A LITTLE SILENCE EXPANDS   167 14
  AND MORE THAN ALL THE DEAD-SURE SILENCE   169 16
  BUT HEAVY SEALING DARKNESS SILENCE ALL IMMOVABLE   205 14
  WE WENT IN SILENCE AND YOU STARING TO ENGLAND   206   7
  HERE AMONG ALL THIS SILENCE CROUCHING FORWARD   225 19
  SOMETHING FROZEN IN THE SILENCE THAT DARE NOT BE   225 27
  THE SILENCE OF THE MANY VILLAGERS   232 30
  SILENCE HARD TO UNDERSTAND   261 28
  SUCH SILENCE SUCH SUSPENDED TRANSPORT   334   1
  THE MOMENT OF ETERNAL SILENCE   365 16
  THE WHEEL ON WHICH OUR SILENCE FIRST IS BROKEN   366 30
  OUR DEEP SILENCE   366 32
  NOW THAT IN ENGLAND IS SILENCE WHERE BEFORE WAS A MOVING   410 21
  AND SILENCE IN MASSIVE SILENCE AND WAKE   465 11
  IN SILENCE FROM THE GREAT BOW-WOW   494   8
  FOR DESIRE HAS DIED IN ME SILENCE HAS GROWN   507 17
  IS TO BE ALONE TO POSSESS ONE'S SOUL IN SILENCE   601   3
  SWEEPING THE CURVE OF SPACE AND MOVING THE SILENCE   609 12
  AND THE HORSE LOOKS AT HIM IN SILENCE   683 20
  BREATHE ALL ALONE IN SILENCE IN THE DARK   698   4
  COME HOLY SILENCE COME   698   6
  COME HOLY SILENCE REACH REACH   698   8
  TILL ALL IS SOUNDLESS AND SENSELESS A TREMENDOUS BODY O+   698 22
  WHO AM EMBEDDED IN A SHELL OF SILENCE   698 25
  OF SILENCE LOVELY SILENCE   698 26
  OF ENDLESS AND LIVING SILENCE   698 27
  OF HOLY SILENCE   698 28
  THE SILENCE OF THE LAST OF THE SEVEN GREAT LAUGHS OF GOD   698 29
  AH THE HOLY SILENCE IT IS MEET   699   1

SILENCE
    IN THE SACRED SILENCE OF GATES   699   4
    IN THE SILENCE OF PASSING THROUGH DOORS   699   5
    FOR THE SILENCE OF THE LAST GREAT THUNDROUS LAUGH   699   10
    WHOSE WHORLS FOLD ROUND TO THE CORE OF SOUNDLESS SILENC+   724   5
    OF SILENCE AND SHEER OBLIVION   724   13
    FOR MAN HAS KILLED THE SILENCE OF THE EARTH   725   17
    IS CENTRES HERE AND THERE OF SILENCE AND FORGETTING   726   18
    AND THE SILENCE OF SHORT DAYS THE SILENCE OF THE YEAR T+   727   13
    WITHIN THE SILENCE VOID OF ECHOES EVEN   738   8
    THEY RETURN RELENTLESSLY IN THE SILENCE ONE KNOWS THEIR+   739   14
    AND IN THE SILENCE REVERENTLY WELCOME THEM   740   14
    SOOTHE THEM WITH SERVICE AND HONOUR AND SILENCE MEET   740   17
    AND A SILENCE THAT STIRRED   748   23
    AND KNOWS DEPARTING IN SILENCE   769   27
    HE SENDS THE EAGLE OF SILENCE DOWN ON WIDE WINGS   799   17
    ALL MEN BE LOST IN SILENCE   811   11
    AND THE WOOD LIKE A MANLY HUSBAND SPREADS SOFTNESS AND +   854   9
    PREACHING IN SAD-MOVING SILENCE A HEART-HUNGRY PURITY   855   3
    SNOW AND THE SILENCE OF SNOW HEAVY ON THE ROUSING DAY   865   11
    I WAITED AND MY SILENCE CHALLENGED HIM   878   16
    COMES OVER THE SOFTNESS AND SILENCE OF MORNING I PASS   *895   11
    HAVE PRESSED THE IMMEASURABLE SPACES OF HOARSE SILENCE   *897   21
    MY QUESTION MY GOD I MUST BREAK FROM THIS HOARSE SILENCE   *898   4
    IS LOST IN THE SHADOWED SILENCE THE SKIES DISTIL   *898   13
    AND ALL THINGS ARE POSSESSED BY SILENCE AND THEY CAN BR+   *898   14
    WRAPPED UP IN THE SKY'S DIM SPACE OF HOARSE SILENCE   *898   15
    HAVE PRESSED IMMEASURABLE SPACES OF HOARSE SILENCE   *900   29
    MY QUESTION MY GOD I MUST BREAK FROM THIS HOARSE SILENCE   *901   13
    IS LOST IN THE SHADOWED SILENCE THE SKIES DISTIL   *901   22
    AND ALL THINGS ARE POSSESSED BY SILENCE AND THEY CAN BR+   *901   23
    WRAPPED UP IN THE SKY'S DIM SPACE OF HOARSE SILENCE   *901   24
    THEN LISTEN FOR SILENCE IS NOT LONELY   *915   17
    AND SILENCE ISSUES SLOWLY FROM THE HUSK   *939   11
    THEY WILL HEAR A SILENCE FALL   *954   6
    THE WOMB OF SILENCE IN THE LIVING NIGHT   *959   33

SILENCE-BOUND
    TO ASSIST US DISASTROUSLY SILENCE-BOUND   166   15

SILENCED
    THEIR ABUNDANT SUMMERY WORDAGE SILENCED CAUGHT   142   2
    THE SILENCED RACES AND ALL THEIR ABOMINATIONS   298   2
    TO MY SILENCED HEART   748   21

SILENCE-HAUNTED
    SINCE I LOST YOU I AM SILENCE-HAUNTED   109   13

SILENCES
    ME THINGS AND THE SILENCES TOSS   108   15

SILENCING
    THE DEAD UNASSUAGED AND ANGRY SILENCING US   740   5

SILENT
    RHYTHM STARTS AND MY SILENT AND SLUMBEROUS BELLY   39   5
    WHERE THE GLASS IS DOMED ON THE SILENT AIR   52   19
    IN THE SILENT LABOURS OF MEN IN THE FIELD   68   18
    ALL THE BIRDS ARE FOLDED IN A SILENT BALL OF SLEEP   71   9
    A RED ROCK SILENT AND SHADOWLESS CLUNG ROUND WITH CLUST+   75   8
    BLOOD SHED IN THE SILENT FIGHT   105   4
    RUN TO THE SILENT DOOR WHERE LAST   122   4
    THE WHITE RUGS ON THE FLOOR NOR THE SILENT BED   155   3
    AS SHE LISTENED IN SILENCE OUTSIDE THE SILENT DOOR   155   16
    BECAUSE OF THE SILENT SNOW WE ARE ALL HUSHED   165   29
    POLTROON AND BEG THE SILENT OUTSPREAD GOD   195   24
    THE HOUSE IS SILENT IT IS LATE AT NIGHT I AM ALONE   220   21
    THE SILENT DRIFTING HOURS   249   1
    WHERE ALL IS SILENT QUITE   254   5
    ORPHEUS AND THE WINDING LEAF-CLOGGED SILENT LANES OF HE+   281   16
    IN SIGN OF DAUNTLESS SILENT VIOLETS   317   18
    WHO LIES WITH THE WATERS OF HIS SILENT PASSION WOMB-ELE+   335   28
    SILENT   344   31
    HE WAS HAVING A SILENT REST   344   32
    AGELESSLY SILENT   360   13
    ONLY AGELESSLY SILENT WITH A REPTILE'S AWFUL PERSISTENCY   362   25
    DRAGGED OUT OF AN ETERNITY OF SILENT ISOLATION   362   27
    INSTEAD OF WHICH THE SILENT FATAL EMISSION FROM THAT PA+   390   25
    EMPTY DAWNS IN SILENT AUSTRALIA   393   13
    FOR A NEW SIGNAL FROM LIFE IN THAT SILENT LOST LAND OF +   394   12
    BUT ALL WAS SILENT SAVE FOR PARROTS OCCASIONALLY IN THE   394   18
    AND HE LIES LIKE A LOG AND SCREAMS AND HIS SCREAM IS SI+   407   20
    WATCH SILENT THE LOOMING OF THE HOARY FAR-GONE AGES   426   21
    AND IN SOME STRANGE AND SILENT WAY   472   4
    AND EVEN THE SEA IS SILENT IN THE SUN   605   25
    AND NOON IS SUDDENLY DARK IS LUSTROUS IS SILENT AND DARK   606   4
    THE UNHAPPY SOULS ARE THOSE THAT CAN'T DIE AND BECOME S+   612   19
    OCCASIONALLY I SEE HIM SILENT A LITTLE WONDERING   645   18
    AND SILENT   646   11
    WHEN I AM ALONE WITH THE SILENT GREAT COSMOS   646   15
    AND THE LIME-TREE LOVELY AND TALL EVERY LEAF SILENT   646   21
    THEY ARE SO SILENT THEY ARE IN ANOTHER WORLD   683   21
    AND THE SHOULDERS PALLID WITH LIGHT FROM THE SILENT SKY+   693   11
    AND A SILENT SHEER CESSATION OF ALL AWARENESS   724   22
    AND THERE OBLIVION DWELLS AND THE SILENT SOUL   726   10
    SILENT REACH OUT LET US TOUCH   764   32
    TOWARDS THE SILENT DOORS OF THE WEST   769   31
    WHICH ELSE WERE A SILENT GRASP THAT HELD THE SKIES   773   9
    WITH THE GOD-THRUST THRUSTING YOU SILENT FROM BELOW   781   28
    THE GOD-THRUST THRUSTING YOU SILENT AND DARK FROM BENEA+   782   9
    SILENT UPON THE AMERICAN CEDAR-BUSH   783   13
    THEN DRIVEN BACK IN A NEW SILENT RUSH   784   14
    THEN BE SILENT   803   15
    THEN BE SILENT   803   22
    AND IS SILENT WITH A SENSE OF JUSTICE THE FIERY PRIMORD+   844   26
    OUT OF EDEN WEARY WITH THE WISTFULNESS OF HER SILENT TO+   864   24
    LYING RIGID AND SILENT WITH YOUR FACE ON THE SHORT SEA +   871   34
    SOMETHING HAS GONE DOWN THE SILENT RIVER   887   24

SILENT
    AS A SILENT BEE AT THE END OF A SHOWER   *913   20
    ALL THE BIRDS ARE FOLDED IN A SILENT BALL OF SLEEP   *917   27
    THIRTEEN WERE THE SLITHERING SILENT JOURNEYS   *933   2
    SILENT TONGUED I AM ASHAMED   *946   6
    RIGGING ITS MAST WITH THE SILENT INVISIBLE SAIL   *961   1

SILENTLY
    OF STARS GREW SILENTLY   35   20
    AS IT SILENTLY SWEEPS TO ITS SOMEWHERE ITS GOAL   68   15
    THE ROUND DARK HEADS OF MEN CROWD SILENTLY   232   21
    SILENTLY   349   18
    HARK HARK STEP ASIDE SILENTLY AND SWIFTLY   642   19
    BE ALONE AND FEEL THE TREES SILENTLY GROWING   646   9
    AND THERE ARE THE DARK DOORS WHERE SOULS PASS SILENTLY   711   4
    AND GOES HIS WAY SILENTLY UNASSERTING   768   20
    SILENTLY SWIMMING AND SLEEPING AND PRESSING THE FLOOD   841   4
    AND WELL I KNOW TO OPEN SILENTLY   878   2
    AS HE SILENTLY SWEEPS TO HIS SOMEWHERE HIS GOAL   *914   30

SILHOUETTE
    SHE STANDS IN SILHOUETTE AGAINST THE WINDOW   *942   21

SILK
    NO LONGER HURT WHERE THE SILK SAILS FILL   53   12
    SCRAMBLE SEVEN TOADS ACROSS SILK OBSCURE LEAVES   126   18
    HER PROUD HEAD HELD IN ITS BLACK SILK SCARF   228   14
    AND TURN THE POOR SILK GLOVE INTO A LUSTY SOW'S EAR   538   22
    AND THE POOR WILLY WET-LEGS THE SOFT SILK GLOVES   538   23
    KILOSSA SWEET WELL OF MY STRENGTH THOU CORDED WITH SILK   759   14
    LIKE SILK THEY ARE FLESH SHEER FLESH   827   3
    THIS IS COMFORTLESS AND UNLOVELY WITH CUSHIONS AND THOS+   856   9
    SHONE SWEETLY THROUGH YELLOW SILK A MAN FULL IN THE LIG+   865   2
    NO LONGER SHAKE WHERE THE SILK SAIL FILLS   *906   4
    THAT STOOD CLOSE TO THE WALL AND THE FRONT'S FADED SILK+   *940   3

SILKEN
    OR FIRM AND SILKEN AS YOUNG PEONY FLOWERS   65   10
    THE SILKEN SHRIEK OF THE SOUL'S TORN MEMBRANE   364   24
    STRAYED DOWN THE HILL CRUSHING THE SILKEN MOSS   863   22
    WITH HER SILKEN STEAM LIKE A BANNER BEHIND HER AFLOW   *894   30
    BLUE SILKEN SKY BEFORE THEY BEND ANEW   *895   4
    COOL AND FIRM AND SILKEN AS PINK YOUNG PEONY FLOWERS   *913   11
    FIRM AND SILKEN LIKE PINK YOUNG PEONY FLOWERS   *914   11

SILK-FLOATING
    THE LAST SILK-FLOATING THOUGHT HAS GONE FROM THE DANDEL+   97   7

SILKILY
    AND SHARES BEING WITH ME SILKILY   656   3

SILKY
    SILKY WITH OIL OF DISTILLED EXPERIENCE   505   8
    WILL SWEEP ROUND AND UP TO GREET THE SUN WITH A SILKY G+   625   4
    OUT OF THE WINTER'S SILKY FUR   814   13

SILL
    I HAVE OPENED THE WINDOWS TO WARM MY HANDS ON THE SILL   52   12
    I HAVE OPENED THE WINDOW TO WARM MY HANDS ON THE SILL   *905   1

SILLY
    YOU ARE SHY YOU SILLY YOU SILLY SHY THING   254   13
    WITH A PINCH OF SNOW IN THE GROOVE OF YOUR SILLY SNUB N+   375   17
    ALL THE SILLY BUNK   556   18
    IT'S A SILLY SHAME   564   30
    SAID GROSS COARSE HIDEOUS AND I LIKE A SILLY   579   18
    SUCH SILLY HYSTERICS   581   25
    COLD SUPERIORITY NOR SILLY   709   31
    BECOMES POINTLESS AND SILLY   723   28
    BECOMES POINTLESS AND SILLY   *961   10

SILTS
    INTO THE SHADOW-WHITE CHAMBER SILTS THE WHITE   154   27

SILVER
    TAKE THEM AND BUY THEE A SILVER RING   44   4
    THE SILVER MOON   54   8
    IT IS STORMY AND RAINDROPS CLING LIKE SILVER BEES TO TH+   92   1
    BUT THREADED WITH FILIGREE SILVER   101   5
    A SILVER WIND IS HASTILY WIPING   150   15
    GO BY WITH THEIR LOADS OF GREEN AND SILVER BIRCH-TREES   209   17
    GLISTEN AS SILVER THEY CRUMPLE UP   217   20
    OF SILVER SINGING AFLOAT   253   2
    I SHALL BE CLEARED DISTINCT SINGLE AS IF BURNISHED IN S+   267   18
    MADE OF THICK SMOOTH SILVER   298   20
    MADE OF SWEET UNTARNISHED SILVER IN THE SEA-SOUTHERN AIR   298   21
    THICK SMOOTH-FLESHED SILVER DULL ONLY AS HUMAN LIMBS ARE   298   23
    TAKE AWAY ALL THIS CRYSTAL AND SILVER   427   11
    AND LET ME COME PAST THE SILVER BELLS OF YOUR FLOWERS A+   696   2
    AND RUBS THE SILVER CLEAN WITH HIS THICK BROWN FINGERS   734   2
    THOU SILVER BEAM IN THE PRESENCE   753   16
    THOU WELL OF KILOSSA THY WELL-CHORDS ARE OF SILVER   759   12
    THEY WANT GOLD THEY WANT SILVER FROM THE MOUNTAINS   793   18
    THEY GIVE US PESOS MADE OF MEXICAN SILVER   794   3
    TAKE BACK OUR LANDS AND SILVER AND OIL TAKE THE TRAINS +   794   21
    FLOATING ABOVE MY SILVER SO THAT THE ADEPT   874   5
    WITH DIM LIGHT SHOWING THE HEADS OF THE SILVER NAILS   876   14
    SILVER SLOW GOES BY THE RIVER   887   26
    IT IS STORMY AND RAIN-DROPS CLING LIKE SILVER BEES TO T+   *926   1
    GLISTEN AS SILVER THEY CRUMPLE UP   *943   3

SILVERILY
    TWITCHES AND EBBS HITTING WASHING INWARDLY SILVERILY   453   20

SILVER-MOIST
  MOVES IN SILVER-MOIST FLASHES IN MUSICAL TRIM   147 20

SILVER-PINK
  SILVER-PINK PEACH VENETIAN GREEN GLASS OF MEDLARS AND S+   283 5

SILVERY
  SHE'S A SILVERY DOVE WORTH MORE THAN ALL I'VE GOT   238 22
  WHY FROM SILVERY PEACH-BLOOM   279 10
  IN THE DISTANCE LIKE HOAR-FROST LIKE SILVERY GHOSTS COM+   306 26
  GUARD MY SHEEP CAME THE SILVERY VOICE FROM THE PINNACLE   324 23
  HIMSELF ALL SILVERY HIMSELF   336 1
  EVEN THE OLD PRIEST IN HIS LONG BLACK ROBE AND SILVERY +   618 16
  AND OIL ME WITH THE LYMPH OF SILVERY TREES   652 23
  AND SUBTLE SILVERY TINKLING AND RIPPLING   667 29
  NOW LADY OF THE MOON NOW OPEN THE GATE OF YOUR SILVERY +   696 1
  AND SILVERY CITY OF THE NOW HOPELESS BODY   721 12
  AGAINST THE SILVERY ADAMANT WALLS OF LIFE'S EXCLUSIVE C+   722 3
  THAT LIE OUTSIDE THE SILVERY WALLS OF OUR BODY'S BUILDE+ *957 17
  IT IS EASY TO BE PUSHED OUT OF THE SILVERY CITY OF THE + *957 20
  ONCE OUTSIDE THE GATE OF THE WALLED SILVERY LIFE OF DAYS *957 27
  AGAINST THE SILVERY ADAMANT WALLS OF THIS OUR EXCLUSIVE+ *958 3

SILVERY-SIDED
  SILVERY-SIDED FISH-FANGED FIERCE-FACED WHISKERED MOTTLED   409 3

SIMILAR
  MILLIONS OF SIMILAR HONEST PENCE   488 19
  YOU A SIMILAR GLORY SINCE YOU'D RISEN   555 23

SIMILARITY
  NOT IN MIXING MERGING NOT IN SIMILARITY   267 5

SIMMERING
  HANGING RED AT THE RIVER AND SIMMERING   217 3
  HERE IN THIS SIMMERING MARSH   217 8
  HANGING RED AT THE RIVER AND SIMMERING   *942 14

SIMPER
  BEFORE THE ROSE BEGAN TO SIMPER SUPREME   285 16

SIMPERING
  NEITHER CAN A YOUNG COCK-EAGLE SIT SIMPERING   413 30

SIMPLE
  THE PAIN THAT IS HER SIMPLE ACHE FOR ME   128 26
  HOW I ADORE YOU FOR YOUR SIMPLE PRIDE   221 14
  THE MONEY-MUCK YOU SIMPLE FLOWERS   456 18
  WE MUST HAVE THE MODESTY OF SIMPLE LIVING   487 22
  COUNTERSIGN YOUR DECLARATION IT'S SO SIMPLE AND REALLY +   546 17
  OR GLOATED OR PEEPED AT THE SIMPLE SPOT   579 3
  AH BUT THE SIMPLE ASK FOR IMAGES   651 10
  THEY MAY EVEN ONE DAY DISCOVER SIMPLE AFFECTION AS A GR+   832 18
  HOW I ADORE YOU FOR YOUR SIMPLE PRIDE   *944 28

SIMPLEST
  ANGRY AT THE SIMPLEST DOOR   95 13

SIMPLICITY
  KILLS SEX IN A MAN THE SIMPLICITY   485 2

SIMPLY
  IT WOULD BE SIMPLY THE SAME   214 15
  ANYHOW THE TOLSTOYAN LOT SIMPLY ASKED FOR EXTINCTION   533 24
  PROVES IT QUITE THANK YOU SO MUCH WE'RE GETTING ON SIMP+   546 20
  OR MUST ONE SIMPLY SAY   548 6
  THEY CAN'T THEY'RE SIMPLY FUSED   553 18
  AND I SIMPLY DAREN'T THINK OF AUNT LOU   571 30
  SO THEY SIMPLY ADORED ONE ANOTHER   605 15
  PERHAPS WHAT'S WRONG IS SIMPLY LACK OF VITALITY   842 28

SIMULACRUM
  IT WAS A SIMULACRUM SOMETHING   601 19

SIN
  MY WINDOWS OF DISCOVERY AND SHRILL SIN   122 30
  WHAT ABOUT SIN FOR IT SEEMS   223 22
  OUT ALL THE SIN   254 7
  NO SIN IS IT TO DRINK AS MUCH AS A MAN CAN TAKE AND GET+   277 10
  SEX ISN'T SIN AH NO SEX ISN'T SIN   463 24
  WE SHALL DO AS WE LIKE SIN IS OBSOLETE THE YOUNG ASSERT   463 26
  SIN IS OBSOLETE SIN IS OBSOLETE BUT NOT SO DIRT   463 27
  AND DIRT IF IT ISN'T SIN IS WORSE ESPECIALLY DIRT INSIDE   464 5
  SEX ISN'T SIN BUT DIRTY SEX IS WORSE SO THERE YOU ARE 464 8
  SEX ISN'T SIN IT'S A DELICATE FLOW BETWEEN WOMEN AND MEN   464 14
  AND THE SIN IS TO DAMAGE THE FLOW FORCE IT OR DIRTY IT +   464 15
  WITH HELLO BOY WHAT ABOUT SIN   493 12
  LET ME SIN MY WAY TO JESUS SO THEY SINNED THEMSELVES   533 27
  WE COULD SIN TOGETHER   618 3
  SHE CAN KEEP HER SIN   618 6
  SHE CAN SIN WITH SOME THICK-SET SPANIARD   618 7
  SIN DOESN'T INTEREST ME   618 8
  SO THEY GO ON SINNING THOUGH SIN IS OBSOLETE   618 14
  THE SIN AGAINST THE HOLY GHOST   620 23
  AND ALL ARE ENCOURAGED INTO THE SIN   620 24
  THERE IS NO SINNING AGAINST GOD WHAT DOES GOD CARE ABOU+   621 1
  NOWADAYS TO TALK OF HUMILITY IS A SIN AGAINST THE HOLY +   621 12
  WITHOUT SHEDDING OF BLOOD THERE IS NO REMISSION OF SIN   678 18
  DOES IT MEAN THAT LIFE WHICH HAS GONE UGLY AND UNLIVING+   678 20
  THERE IS NO SUCH THING AS SIN   679 18
  MY WINDOWS OF DISCOVERY AND SHRILL SIN   *934 6

SINCERE
  ARE PERFECTLY SINCERE   659 9
  IF IT IS PERFECTLY SINCERE TO DENY YOUR OWN MAKE-UP   659 11

SINCEREST
  WITHIN HIS EYES' SINCEREST PUPILS THERE   876 36

SINEW
  TO HIS GUEST CHAMBER KNOWING EACH SINEW AND VEIN   877 37

SING
  SING THROUGH AND EACH WITH A FLOOR-LIGHT RACING ALONG 144 9
  OH AND I WANT TO SING   216 1
  YOU SHALL KNOW A BIRD BY HIS CRY AND GREAT BIRDS CRY LO+   368 9
  IN THE NORTH TO HIDE WHERE THE TURTLES SING   580 6
  THOUGH THEY NEVER SING THEY NEVER SING   580 7
  AND SO I SING A DEMOCRACY   627 5
  SOME YOU MAY SING THROUGH AND ALL MEN HEAR   711 8
  SING THE SONG OF DEATH O SING IT   723 26
  SING THEN THE SONG OF DEATH AND THE LONGEST JOURNEY   724 1
  SING THEN THE CORE OF DARK AND ABSOLUTE   724 8
  SING THE SONG OF DEATH O SING IT   724 11
  TO SING IN THE SHELL OF MY HEART THE LULL AND INCREASE   747 22
  SING SOOTHINGLY   758 18
  HIS THROAT TO SING GLANCES DOWN   771 4
  SHALL SING OF HEAVEN ACHIEVED WHERE EVERY BRIGHT   872 15
  AND SING IN THIS SPACE THAT THE BUILDER NOW DEMANDS   *896 16
  SING LIKE A CHORUS SOME DAY   *938 20
  I SING OF AUTUMN AND THE FALLING FRUIT   *956 24
  SING THE SONG OF DEATH OH SING IT   *961 8
  SING THEN THE SONG OF DEATH AND THE LONGEST JOURNEY   *961 11

SINGED
  WITH SINGED HOT EYES AND RELENTLESSNESS   769 5

SINGEING
  FEATHERS ARE SINGEING   330 7

SINGER
  SO NOW IT IS VAIN FOR THE SINGER TO BURST INTO CLAMOUR   148 15

SINGERS
  IN THE NOISE OF THE TOM-TOMS AND SINGERS   387 37

SINGES
  AND SINGES US AND BURNS THE HOUSE DOWN   506 10

SINGING
  FLUSHED WITH THE SONGS OF SEVEN LARKS SINGING AT ONCE G+   34 14
  AND MORNING SINGING WHERE THE WOODS ARE SCROLLED   135 27
  OH THE SINGING MANSIONS   146 11
  IN THE CHOIR THE BOYS ARE SINGING THE HYMN   147 18
  SOFTLY IN THE DUSK A WOMAN IS SINGING TO ME   148 4
  THE SEA IN THE STONES IS SINGING   200 17
  WE WERE WANDERING AND SINGING   216 20
  FROGS WERE SINGING AND OVER THE RIVER CLOSES   217 4
  OF SILVER SINGING AFLOAT   253 2
  SINGING AGAINST THE BLACK BIRD   272 26
  THAT MY HEART WHICH LIKE A LARK AT HEAVEN'S GATE SINGIN+   322 30
  AND MY MOTHER SINGING TO HERSELF   366 16
  AND THE FIRST TENOR SINGING OF THE PASSIONATE THROAT OF+   366 17
  SINGING AND CALLING AND SINGING AGAIN BEING ANSWERED   366 36
  THE JUNGLE SINGING   388 36
  WILL THE SINGING OF SWANS HIGH UP HIGH UP INVISIBLE   439 8
  A NIGHTINGALE SINGING AT THE TOP OF HIS VOICE   523 8
  SINGING BETWEEN THE SUN AND THE MARSH   623 18
  ON AND ON LIKE A DARK-FACED BIRD SINGING ALONE   623 19
  SINGING TO THE MEN BELOW THE FELLOW-TRIBESMEN   623 20
  AND THE WILD SWANS FLOWN AWAY SINGING THE SWAN-SONG OF +   624 2
  CLASS-CHILDREN ARE SINGING IN SCHOOL   657 11
  PEOPLE GO ON SINGING WHEN THEY HAVE NO SONG IN THEM   657 17
  MEN SINGING SONGS AND WOMEN BRUSHING THEIR HAIR IN THE +   691 24
  SINGING DARKER THAN THE NIGHTINGALE ON ON TO THE SOLSTI+   727 12
  AND THE SINGING IS LOW AND SENSITIVE   768 17
  WHOM THE MEADOW-LARK SINGING SPEAKS TO   769 28
  SINGING MY STAVE   772 21
  I HEARD THE STAR SINGING LIKE A DYING BIRD   786 15
  THEY HAD RED LILY AND PEOPLE SINGING SONGS   846 8
  WHO IS IT SINGING   861 13
  AND HIS SINGING SOUND AS THEY ALWAYS DO AT THE BEGINNIN+   865 17
  AND SHUFFLE OF BROKEN SODDENED BOOTS YET SINGING GOES R+   866 14
  BEING TOO MIRTHLESS TO MOVE THE LILT OF SINGING   884 13
  RICH WITH THE SONGS OF SEVEN LARKS SINGING AT ONCE GOES+ *892 2
  BY NOISE OF SMALL BIRDS SINGING FIFE   *914 22
  AND MORNING SINGING WHERE THE WOODS WERE SCROLLED   *939 19
  SOFTLY IN THE SHADOWS A WOMAN IS SINGING TO ME   *940 8
  SINGING LOVE'S FIRST SURPRISED GLADNESS ALONE IN THE GL+ *940 15
  A WOMAN IS SINGING ME A WILD HUNGARIAN AIR   *940 19
  WE WERE WANDERING AND SINGING   *942 6
  FROGS WERE SINGING AND OVER THE RIVER CLOSES   *942 15
  AND THE WILD SWANS FLOWN AWAY SINGING THE SWAN-SONG OF + *953 20

SINGLE
  A SINGLE STAR IN A VEIL OF LIGHT   41 29
  A TINY MOON AS SMALL AND WHITE AS A SINGLE JASMINE FLOW+   67 18
  AND ONLY IN HARMONY WITH OTHERS THE SINGLE SOUL CAN BE +   93 10
  OVER EVERY SINGLE BEAUTY   95 20
  YOU ARE CELIBATE AND SINGLE SCORNING A COMRADE EVEN   197 3
  YOU ARE SINGLE YOU ARE FRUITLESS PHOSPHORESCENT COLD AND   197 12
  IN A GREAT SWARM CLOTTED AND SINGLE   205 25
  AND SINGLE ME PERFECTED FROM MY FELLOW   218 8
  SINGLE AND PERFECTLY DISTINCT FROM EVERYTHING ELSE   254 25
  I SHALL BE CLEARED DISTINCT SINGLE AS IF BURNISHED IN S+   267 18
  CONDITIONED ONLY BY OUR OWN PURE SINGLE BEING   267 28
  AND THEN YOUR SINGLE RESURRECTION   290 24
  WITH MARVELLOUS NAKED ASSURANCE EACH SINGLE TWIG   299 26
  AZALEA AND CAMELLIA SINGLE PEONY   313 28
  SEX WHICH BREAKS UP OUR INTEGRITY OUR SINGLE INVIOLABIL+   366 31
  YOU DON'T NEED ONE SINGLE SOCIAL INFERIOR TO EXALT YOU   526 26
  OH THE ROSE OF ENGLAND IS A SINGLE ROSE   534 23
  CHANGE FROM BEING SINGLE AND BECOME GRADUALLY DOUBLE   534 26
  OH THE ROSE OF ENGLAND IS A SINGLE ROSE   535 13

SINGLE
  I NEVER MET A SINGLE   555   9
  THAT THEY STARED AND LEERED AT THE SINGLE SPOT   578 22
  GIVE US BACK OUR BODIES FOR A DAY FOR A SINGLE DAY   585   3
  THEN WHAT IS A SINGLE MAN TO DO   631 23
  FOR MANKIND IS A SINGLE CORPUS WE ARE ALL ONE FLESH   631 24
  THEN MUST A SINGLE MAN DIE WITH THEM IN THE CLUTCH OF   632   1
  A SINGLE EGO STRIVING FOR ITS OWN ENDS   714 27
  OR VOICE OR ANY SINGLE SPARK   738   4
  TO GIVE THE INDIANS ONE SINGLE THING NOT ONE CENT   778 25
  LIFS THE LIVING ROCK OF A SINGLE CREATURE'S PRIDE   844   9
  FILLING HIS SINGLE MEASURE WITH MUSIC FULL   877 27
  EVERY SINGLE ERECTION OF HIS IS AN ERECTION OF MEAN SPI+ *949 15

SINGLED
  SHE IS MARKED SHE IS SINGLED OUT   228 21
  LOOK YOU ARE CLEAN AND FINE AND SINGLED OUT   255 10

SINGLENESS
  EVERY MAN HIMSELF AND THEREFORE A SURPASSING SINGLENESS+   268   1
  YOUR SINGLENESS WITHIN THE UNIVERSE   290 14
  IN A NEW PROUD SINGLENESS AMERICA   290 20
  DRIVEN AFTER AEONS OF PRISTINE FORE-GOD-LIKE SINGLENESS+   363 14
  WHEN THE MAN WAS HIMSELF SO A GOD IN HIS SINGLENESS   676 12

SINGS
  HER WOES HER LOVER WOOS AND SINGS WITHIN ANOTHER WOOD   65 26
  AND HER DEAD MOUTH SINGS   101 15
  THE LARK SINGS LOUD AND GLAD   110   9
  AS SHE SINGS   148   9
  SINGS ITSELF OVER AND SO THE GAME   151 23
  THE DAWN ROOKS CALL AT EVENING WHEN THE NIGHTINGALE SIN+   368 11
  REJECT NOTHING SINGS WALT WHITMAN   399   1
  A LITTLE MOON QUITE STILL LEANS AND SINGS TO HERSELF   656   8
  PRESSING THE LITTLE POISED FEET OF THE MOTHER WHO SMILE+ *940   8

SINISTER
  DOWN THE LABYRINTH OF THE SINISTER FLOWER   166 23
  THEIR RHYTHMS ON LONG-DRAWN HOLLOW SINISTER DRUMS   371   5
  IN ALL THE SINISTER SPLENDOUR OF THEIR RED BLOOD-SACRIF+   371 35
  THEIR BELLS SOUNDING FRUSTRATE AND SINISTER   391   4
  AND SINISTER BEINGS WILL BECKON BETWEEN   748   4
  OH SINISTER INDIAN EAGLE   783 22

SINK
  WHEN SHALL I SEE THE HALF-MOON SINK AGAIN   62 25
  THROW 'IMSELF DOWN THAT SINK   81 20
  WITH SOUNDS THAT ENDLESSLY SWELL AND SINK LIKE THE STOR+   97 24
  AND ALL THE LOTUS BUDS OF LOVE SINK OVER   113 14
  SUPPOSE YOU DIDN'T WANT ME I SHOULD SINK DOWN   246   7
  TO SINK AND HAVE DONE   253 30
  TO SINK AND RISE AND GO TO SLEEP WITH THE WATERS   336 28
  FALL SINK LURCH AND ROUND AND ROUND   345 20
  STONE THAT CAN SINK NO FURTHER   383 12
  REMEMBERING I TOLD THEM TO DIE TO SINK INTO THE GRAVE IN   410 30
  DOWN THE SINK OF THE MALE CONCEIT   457 24
  THAT PUT TO SEA AND BOLDLY SINK ARMADAS   542   9
  THEY SINK   542 25
  MAY SINK INTO GOD AT LAST HAVING PASSED THE VEILS   726 11
  IN SLEEP AND SINK IN GOOD OBLIVION   726 23
  TO SINK UNCONSCIOUS IN THE ROCKING DARK   771 28
  SHAKE AND SINK DOWN TO REST THEN SHAKE AGAIN   878 26
  THROW HISSELF IN THAT SINK   *923 20

SINKING
  MY KISSES ARE SINKING SOON   37 21
  CLOTTING TO ONE DEAD MASS IN THE SINKING FIRE   47   5
  OUR PALE DAY IS SINKING INTO TWILIGHT   286 21
  AND I MUST RESUME MY NAKEDNESS LIKE A FISH SINKING DOWN   321 29
  CAN PIERCE FOR THAT IS WHERE WILL GIVES OUT LIKE A SINK+   383 11
  THAT AWFUL AND SICKENING ENDLESS SINKING   699 21
  AND SINKS SEETHING AND SINKING CORRUPT   699 24
  AND SINKING STILL IN DEPTH AFTER DEPTH OF DISINTEGRATIV+   699 25
  SINKING IN THE ENDLESS UNDOING THE AWFUL KATABOLISM INT+   699 26
  THE MIDNIGHT SHADOW SINKING DOWN HAS SLUNG   750 14
  HE CAME LIKE A SEA-GULL SINKING WITH UPLIFTED WINGS DOW+   860   2
  THE PLANE-LEAVES FALL THROUGH THE LAMP-LIGHT LIKE TIRED+ *917   9

SINKS
  PLAYS WITH ME SWAYS ME LIFTS ME AND SINKS ME MURMURS OH   34 20
  EVEN HER FLOATING HAIR SINKS HEAVILY   74   3
  HOW STRANGELY SHE TRIES TO DISOWN IT AS IT SINKS   128 15
  IN ONE RICH DRIP IT SINKS TO ANOTHER SLEEP   195 15
  AND SINKS LOW   246   9
  WHERE THE SEED SINKS IN   254   3
  SINKS TO SETTING AND THE WINTER SOLSTICE   455 27
  SINKS AND IS GONE LIKE A COMET CURVING INTO THE INVISIB+ 476 11
  AND SINKS DOWN WITH A SWIFT RUSTLE AND A STRANGE FALLING   651 15
  AND SINKS SEETHING AND SINKING CORRUPT   699 24
  BLUE DAYLIGHT SINKS IN MY HAIR   802 26
  AND STILL THE LONG HARSH BREATH SINKS HOARSELY OUT   878 27
  PLAYS WITH ME SWAYS ME LIFTS ME AND SINKS ME AS THOUGH + *892   8
  EVEN HER FLOATING HAIR SINKS LIKE STORM-BRUISED YOUNG L+ *913 24

SINLESS
  THERE SURE IN SINLESS BEING   243   5
  SINLESS AND STAINLESS GOING ROUND AND ROUND   714   2

SIN-MOUSE
  EVERY SIN-MOUSE YOU COULD CAPTURE   95 23

SINNED
  LET ME SIN MY WAY TO JESUS SO THEY SINNED THEMSELVES   533 27

SINNERS
  ARE SINNERS STRANGE THE BEE THAT BLUNDERS   223 19
  SINNERS   531   2
  WHY SHOULD OUR LATTER-DAY SINNERS EXPECT SUCH A LONG   531 16

SINNING
  BUT HE CAN'T STOP ME FROM SINNING AGAINST HIM IF I WANT+   618 11
  SO THEY GO ON SINNING THOUGH SIN IS OBSOLETE   618 14
  THERE IS NO SINNING AGAINST GOD WHAT DOES GOD CARE ABOU+   621   1
  BUT THERE IS SINNING AGAINST THE HOLY GHOST SINCE THE H+   621   2

SINS
  AN' ALL THEY CAN THINK OF IS SINS   553 12
  FOR THE SINS OF OMISSION   562 12
  EXPIATING THEIR SINS   627 23

SINUOUS
  AMONG THE SINUOUS FLAME-TALL CYPRESSES   296 17

SIN'
  AN' THERE'S COMPENSATION SIN' IT'S ACCIDENT   45 32
  GO THEN SIN' THA MAUN   139 27

SIP
  TO SIP THEM ALL UP AGAIN   109 26
  I SEE THE SILENCE EASILY SIP THEM   110   7
  AND SIPPED DOWN PERHAPS WITH A SIP OF MARSALA   281 24
  AND IF WE SIP THE WINE WE FIND DREAMS COMING UPON US   286 22
  AS WE SIP THE WINE   286 31
  BUTTERFLY WHY DO YOU SETTLE ON MY SHOE AND SIP THE DIRT+   696 13
  AS HE DID SIP THE BITTER MILK OF SLEEP   878 14

SIPPED
  AND SIPPED DOWN PERHAPS WITH A SIP OF MARSALA   281 24
  HE SIPPED WITH HIS STRAIGHT MOUTH   349 15

SIPPING
  AND KISSES PALE AND SIPPING THE TOLL   151 29
  SIPPING TO NOTHINGNESS EVEN THOUGHT   824 12

SIPS
  THOU SIPS THEM UP AND 'TIS ALL THE SAME   824 15

SIR
  VERY BRAVE OF YOU SIR   80 32
  OH I'M A BRITISH BOY SIR   576 16
  FOR I'M A BRITISH BOY SIR   576 22
  CREDENTIALS SIR   582   8
  APPLICANT I DON'T THINK SO SIR I'M AFRAID NOT   582 18
  YES SIR YES SIR   669 21
  BRISTLING WITH ANIMATION OH PLEASE SIR HOW D'YOU LIKE T+   865 21
  PLEASE SIR I WAS SWEEPING SNOW AN' I NEVER HEARD THE BE+   866   9
  I DIDN'T KNOW IT WAS SO LATE NO SIR I 'AD TO BECAUSE   866 10
  HE HE'S IN PRISON MY FATHER YES SIR ONE AND SIX WITH   866 11
  TILL HE SAW ME BUT PLEASE SIR MY MOVVER SAID I COULD AN'   866 19
  CLEANIN' YES SIR A SHILLN BY MYSELF ALL RIGHT SIR   866 21
  VERY NICE ON YOU SIR   *922 32

SIR CLIFFORD
  IS EKKE SIR CLIFFORD IT'S REALLY FUNNY   669   1

SIRIUS
  GREEN STAR SIRIUS   229   5
  IN THE LONG DARK NIGHTS OF THE EVENING STAR AND SIRIUS +   305 23
  VEGA AND SIRIUS AND ALTAIR   713 21

SIR JESSE BOOT
  BY GOOD SIR JESSE BOOT   488 14
  VERY SUMPTUOUS WITH THE MONEY OF SIR JESSE BOOT OF CASH+ *950 14

SIRS
  WHAT OH MY SIRS 'E NEVER SAYS THAT   44 24
  MY SIRS BUT I SAY 'TWAS FOR A BLITHER   60 30
  AS STOUT AS THE TRUTH MY SIRS AN' 'IS FACE   79   6
  ROUND-SHOULDERED HAG MY SIRS TO THINK   81 18
  AS STOUT AS THE TRUTH MY SIRS AN' 'IS FACE   *921   2
  ROUND-SHOULDERED HAG MY SIRS TO THINK   *923 18

SISTER
  SISTER THA KNOWS WHILE WE WAS ON TH' PLANKS   60 11
  SISTER THE WHOLE DAY LONG   628   2
  NO SISTER   751 22
  SISTER OH HOLY SISTER   753 12
  THOU DOOR INTO HEAVEN SISTER   753 13
  SO LONG AS WE'RE HERE IN LIFE OUR SISTER WE COME   753 17
  DID TER NOTICE THAT LASS SISTER AS STOOD AWAY BACK   909 29
  SISTER THA KNOWS WHILE WE WAS ON THE PLANKS   910 26
  ME LEST YOU MY SISTER SHOULD GO HEAPED WITH SUCH SHADOW+ *937 33
  OR THIS IS MY SISTER AT HOME IN THE OLD FRONT ROOM   *940 14

SISTERLESS
  FATHERLESS MOTHERLESS BROTHERLESS SISTERLESS   357 24

SISTERS
  SISTERS THE SEARCHLIGHT'S SWINGING FAN   758 13
  SISTERS THE GUNS ARE SPEAKING LET ALL   758 17

SISTER'S
  HE HE'S IN PRISON MY FATHER YES SIR ONE AND SIX WITH MY+   866 11

SIT
  I SIT ABSOLVED ASSURED I AM BETTER OFF   36   7
  I MUST SIT ALONE AND WAIT AND NEVER KNOW   48   7
  AS I SIT ON THE SHORES OF THE CLASS ALONE   51 10
  IN THE RIPENING MORNING TO SIT ALONE WITH THE CLASS   51 22
  OF EACH OTHER I SHALL SIT AND WAIT FOR THE BELL   75   6
  SIT NODDIN' THY HEAD AT ME   78 22
  NOW HERE I SIT WHILE YOU BREAK THE MUSIC BENEATH   85 21

SIT
    HOW I SIT AND LAUGH AT YOU   95 10
    AND SO I SIT AND SCAN THE BOOK OF GREY   135 17
    I WHO SIT IN TEARS   169 9
    WHERE ALL THE MOUNTAINS SIT   196 8
    AS WE SIT IN THE SUNSHINE ON THE SEAT BY THE LITTLE SHR+   204 12
    THE BIG MOUNTAINS SIT STILL IN THE AFTERNOON LIGHT   223 13
    HOW YOU SIT IN THE THRONE OF MY EYES   227 30
    BECAUSE WHEN I SIT IN THE ROOM   235 26
    AND SIT BY FIRELIGHT   237 22
    AND SIT BESIDE THE STEEL-STRAIGHT ARMS OF YOUR FAIR WOM+   291 5
    LET ME SIT DOWN BENEATH THE MANY-BRANCHING CANDELABRUM   299 9
    LET ME SIT DOWN BENEATH THIS MANY-BRANCHING CANDELABRUM   299 19
    YOU GO DOWN SHADE TO THE RIVER WHERE NAKED MEN SIT ON   386 23
    INSTEAD OF WHICH YOU SIT THERE AND ROLL YOUR HEAD LIKE A   398 9
    I'M GOING TO SIT DOWN ON MY TAIL RIGHT HERE   405 29
    AND I I SIT ON THIS HIGH AMERICAN DESERT   410 27
    NEITHER CAN A YOUNG COCK-EAGLE SIT SIMPERING   413 30
    YET THEY SIT UP   425 21
    YOU CAN'T SIT ON A BUS NOR IN THE TUBE   434 2
    THE UPHOLSTERED DEAD THAT SIT IN DEEP ARM-CHAIRS   440 20
    IF YOU CAN ONLY SIT WITH A MIRROR IN YOUR HAND AN AGEING   478 20
    I WOULD RATHER SIT STILL IN A STATE OF PEACE ON A STONE   498 1
    I WISH PEOPLE WHEN YOU SIT NEAR THEM   506 20
    REFUSING TO SIT STILL AND BE MEASURED   524 25
    WHICH ARE VERY LIKE TO HIT YOU ON THE HEAD AS YOU SIT   541 5
    YOU SIT IN THE BOUGHS AND GIBBER   549 17
    I HAD TO SIT DOWN AND CRY   554 12
    SIT SIT SIT CORPSE-BODY IN THE CAR   584 13
    SIT SIT SIT   584 25
    FOR TODAY THE BASE THE ROBOTS SIT ON THE THRONES OF THE   637 17
    HAVE A GAME OF TENNIS GO OUT IN THE CAR DO SOME SHOPPIN+   651 21
    YOU SIT TALKING IN ALL EARNESTNESS TO A WOMAN   655 1
    BUT TO THOSE THAT CAN SIT STILL   658 6
    AND MEN THAT SIT IN MACHINES   711 26
    SIT IN THE GREY MIST OF MOVEMENT WHICH MOVES NOT   711 28
    THAT IS THEY SIT AND ARE EVIL IN EVIL   712 1
    YOU SIT NEXT TO ME ON THE PERCH   761 29
    I AM HERE UNDEPARTING I SIT TIGHT   788 15
    HOW NICE TO SIT IN THE CINE WHERE THE PICTURE OF ALL TH+   794 17
    THERE ARE DEAD THAT SIT UNDER THE TREES WATCHING WITH A+   795 26
    MIGHT FOLLOW WARM AND GLAD WHO SIT HERE COLD   879 15
    SIT AND MAKE LOVE TO EACH OTHER   887 11
    AS YOU SIT ON THE TRESTLE I ON THE GROUND   887 12
    I WILL SIT AND WAIT FOR THE BELL   *896 5
    AS I SIT ON THE BEACH OF THE CLASS ALONE   *898 22
    AS I SIT ON THE BEACH OF THE CLASS ALONE   *902 6
    I WILL SIT AND WAIT FOR THE BELL   *904 26
    SIT NODDIN' THY HEAD AT ME   *920 14
    STILL I MUST SIT IN AGONY   *931 1
    AND SO I SIT AND TURN THE BOOK OF GRAY   *939 1
    AND WIDE IN ECSTASY I SIT AND WATCH   *943 20
    NOW IN THE TWILIGHT SIT BY THE INVISIBLE SEA   *960 12

SITHEE
    NOW SITHEE THEER AT TH' REELROAD CROSSIN'   79 1
    NOW SITHEE THEER AT TH' RAILROAD CROSSIN'   *920 25

SITS
    AND SITS WITH A SMOOTH BLAND SMILE UP THERE IN THE SKY   54 12
    SITS INDIFFERENT HUGGED IN HER RAGS   54 18
    COLOSSAL IN NEARNESS A BLUE POLICE SITS STILL ON HIS HO+   66 9
    AND SITS IN HER OWN DARK NIGHT OF HER BITTER HAIR   129 1
    SAD AS HE SITS ON THE WHITE SEA-STONE   130 1
    HE SITS LIKE A SHADE BY THE FLOOD ALONE   130 5
    SHE SITS ON THE RECREATION GROUND   152 26
    WHILE THE DRIVER ON THE SHAFT SITS CROUCHED IN DREAMS   225 16
    THAT VEXES ME WITH WONDER HE SITS SO STILL   225 18
    THERE HE SITS THE LONG LOUD ONE   347 21
    BUT THE YELLOW ANTIPODAL KANGAROO WHEN SHE SITS UP   392 27
    THE LITTLE SLENDER SOUL SITS SWIFTLY DOWN AND TAKES THE+   723 20
    THERE HE SITS IN THE SADDLE OF THIS THE FIVE   733 11
    SITS AN EAGLE ERECT AND SCORCH-BREASTED   780 27
    AND IN WHOM THE DREAM SITS UP LIKE A RABBIT LIFTING LON+   807 8
    HAS CONVEYED THIS THING THAT SITS AND WRITES   887 6
    THE LITTLE SLENDER SOUL SITS SWIFTLY DOWN AND TAKES THE+   *958 32

SITTING
    ALL THE LONG YEARS OF SITTING IN MY HUSBAND'S HOUSE   47 30
    YOU SITTING IN THE COWSLIPS OF THE MEADOW ABOVE   90 14
    SITTING HUDDLED AGAINST THE CERULEAN ON FLESH WITH THE+   142 11
    A CHILD SITTING UNDER THE PIANO IN THE BOOM OF THE TING+   148 6
    SO SITTING UNDER THE KNOTTED CANOPY   153 1
    WE SITTING HERE AMONG THE CRANBERRIES   223 16
    BUT SITTING IN A BOAT ON THE ZELLER LAKE   337 28
    AT EVENING SITTING IN THIS TERRACE   340 17
    SITTING UP THERE RABBIT-WISE BUT HUGE PLUMB-WEIGHTED   393 5
    OR SITTING WITH OUR TAILS CURLED   450 14
    AND WEARING OUR SEATS OUT SITTING ON MONEY   485 26
    I SEE THE TIN-MAN THE TINKER SITTING DAY AFTER DAY ON T+   520 13
    THE SAME WITH THE FISHERMEN SITTING DARNING THEIR NETS   520 17
    OR SITTING STUCK LIKE AUTOMATA IN AUTOMOBILES   530 17
    ARE ONLY SITTING TIGHT ON THE CRATERS OF THEIR VOLCANO   539 25
    OF SITTING THERE ON THE FENCE AND LETTING   560 3
    OF SITTING ON THE FENCE   560 10
    WHEN I WAS WAITING AND NOT THINKING SITTING AT A TABLE +   672 18
    AND STILL THIS IS THE GOD HERMES SITTING BY MY HEARTH   692 21
    AS OF THE MASTER SITTING AT THE BOARD   700 14
    AND A SOLDIER IN THE SADDLE OF THE LEFT-HAND DRAUGHT-HO+   733 8
    SITTING THERE TOGETHER FOR A LITTLE WHILE   756 16
    I AM HUITZILOPOCHTLI SITTING IN THE DARK   804 15
    HE IS HUITZILOPOCHTLI SITTING IN THE DARK   805 23
    TO HAVE YOU SITTING AVERTED THERE   *931 13
    A CHILD SITTING UNDER THE PIANO IN THE BOOM OF THE SHAK+   *940 7

SITTIN'
    SITTIN' THERE IN ROWS ON YOUR SHELVES   553 24

SIVA
    OR SIVA   674 5
    BUT PERHAPS ASHTAROTH PERHAPS SIVA PERHAPS HUITZILOPOCH+   674 25

SIX
    SIX TIMES WIDE OPEN   307 13
    AND HENCE SIX TIMES MORE SOLITARY   354 11
    AT SIX IN THE MORNING THEY TURNED HIM DOWN   490 11
    AT THE WHIM OF SIX POLICEMEN AND A MAGISTRATE WHOSE STA+   633 5
    A MAGISTRATE AND SIX FAT SMALLER FRY   633 15
    SIX FAT SMALLER BOBBIES ARE THE INQUISITORS MINOR   633 16
    AND SIX HAVE GIVEN ME GIFTS AND KISSED ME GOD-SPEED   695 28
    HE HE'S IN PRISON MY FATHER YES SIR ONE AND SIX WITH MY+   866 11

SIX HUNDRED
    SHE WAS BOUGHT AT GIARDINI FAIR ON THE SANDS FOR SIX HU+   385 7

SIXTEEN
    SUCH ON THE VIRGIN HAIR OF DEAD SIXTEEN   854 24

SIXTY
    BECAUSE OF THEIR OWN FIFTY OR SIXTY OR SEVENTY OR   502 20
    AND TAKE SIXTY SLASHES   563 11
    THE LITTLE-BOY OF THIRTY OR FORTY OR FIFTY OR SIXTY   841 19

SIZE
    THE OLD DRAGON WILL DWINDLE DOWN TO THE SIZE OF A STRAY+   665 14

SKEIN
    MESHED AND TANGLED TOO MUCH IN THE SKEIN OF GUILT   884 14

SKELETON
    LIKE A BE-AUREOLED BLEACHED SKELETON HOVERING   290 22
    EVEN THE WINGED SKELETON OF YOUR BLEACHED IDEAL   290 26
    YOUR HORRIBLE SKELETON AUREOLED IDEAL   292 7

SKI'D
    AND WE SLID AND YOU SKI'D AND WE CAME IN TO TEA   550 31

SKIES
    IN ONE BLUE STOOP FROM OUT THE SKIES   42 30
    IS LOST IN THIS SHADOWED SILENCE THE SKIES DISTIL   76 19
    BLACKENED EDGE OF THE SKIES   103 27
    AND SKIES OF GOLD AND LADIES IN BRIGHT TISSUE   135 4
    OF QUEENS IN HYACINTH AND SKIES OF GOLD   135 26
    THE RAINBOW ARCHING YOUR IN THE SKIES   136 15
    AND NOW THAT THE SKIES ARE FALLING THE WORLD IS SPOUTIN+   160 1
    I THINK IN MY CONVULSION THE SKIES WOULD BREAK   213 20
    AGAIN ON THE WONTED SKIES   253 22
    SKIES TREES FLOWERS BIRDS WATER   256 25
    PILLARS OF WHITE BRONZE STANDING RIGID LEST THE SKIES F+   287 16
    WHEN THE SKIES ARE GOING TO FALL FALL THEY WILL   287 20
    SEE IF YOUR SKIES AREN'T FALLING   289 16
    WHEN YOUR WORLD IS IN RUINS UNDER YOUR FALLEN SKIES   289 20
    BIRDS ARE THE LIFE OF THE SKIES AND WHEN THEY FLY THEY +   368 1
    THE THOUGHTS OF THE SKIES THE EAGLE FLIES NEAREST TO TH+   368 2
    OUT OF FATHOMLESS SKIES AND SEAS   438 32
    MY DEARS IF YOU WANT THE SKIES TO FALL   541 23
    THEY ARE OPEN TO THE RESTLESS SKIES AND STREAMS FLOW IN+   675 10
    THE SKIES FALL   748 27
    WHICH ELSE WERE A SILENT GRASP THAT HELD THE SKIES   773 9
    WILD SKIES   816 27
    IS LOST IN THE SHADOWED SILENCE THE SKIES DISTIL   *898 13
    THAT BEARS ALOFT TOWARD RARER SKIES   *899 28
    IS LOST IN THE SHADOWED SILENCE THE SKIES DISTIL   *901 22
    THAT BEARS ALOFT TOWARDS RARER SKIES   *903 7
    OF CLOUD THE MORN SKIES YIELD   *915 4
    SHE WATCHED MY HAND AND THE SKIES BEGAN TO THRILL   *935 28
    AND PALE HOT SKIES HAVE DARKENED AND GONE COLD   *939 15
    OF QUEENS IN HYACINTH 'NEATH SKIES OF GOLD   *939 18

SKILFUL
    HE'S MOST FRIGHTFULLY SKILFUL IN HIS LOVE-MAKING   *948 11

SKILL
    COMPELLED TO SEE THE DELICATE SKILL OF FLICKERING HUMAN   445 26

SKIM
    LIFE SEEMS TO LEAP AT THE AIR OR SKIM UNDER THE WIND   392 15

SKIMS
    BRUSHING THE STARS GOES MY SOUL THAT SKIMS THE BOUNDS   193 25
    SHE SKIMS HIM SENSITIVE   426 17

SKIN
    OVER MY SKIN IN THE SUNSHINE THE WARM CLINGING AIR   34 13
    WI' A BITTER DIRTY SKIN   77 14
    DO YOU MEAN IT IS WRONG THE GOLD-FILMED SKIN INTEGUMENT   278 29
    THEN YOU THROW AWAY THE SKIN   282 5
    BUT HE CATCHES THE FOLDS OF VULNERABLE LEATHERY SKIN   362 6
    ONLY HE SENSES THE VULNERABLE FOLDS OF SKIN   362 15
    HER FOLDS OF SKIN THAT WORK AND ROW   362 18
    SKIN   369 26
    UNDER A SMOOTH SKIN AND AN UPRIGHT APPEARANCE   431 21
    THE CONFORMING WORM STAYS JUST INSIDE THE SKIN   432 6
    WASH YOURSELF AND RUB OIL IN YOUR SKIN   791 21
    SKIN LET EVERY WOMAN   791 23
    OVER MY SUNLIT SKIN THE WARM CLINGING AIR   *892 1
    WITH A BITTER SWARTHY SKIN   *919 2

SKINNY
    WINGS DARK SKINNY AND FLAPPING THE AIR   346 23
    AND REACH YOUR SKINNY LITTLE NECK   352 13
    HIS LOW FOREHEAD HIS SKINNY NECK HIS LONG SCALED STRIVI+   360 2
    SUDDENLY OR HER SKINNY LIMB   362 22

SKINNY
  AND SKINNY REPULSIVE   369   5

SKINS
  I LOVE TO SUCK YOU OUT FROM YOUR SKINS   280   3
  AT ALL THESE SKINS OF WILD BEASTS   409 27
  THEIR SKINS ALL NEAT   828   6

SKIN-WRAPPED
  DARKNESS AND SKIN-WRAPPED   171   2

SKIPS
  AND VENUS AMONG THE FISHES SKIPS AND IS A SHE-DOLPHIN   695   9

SKIRT
  AND THRUST HER FISTS SUPPRESSED IN THE FOLDS OF HER SKI+   128 19
  AS SHE THRUSTS THEM UPWARD UNDER THE RUFFLED SKIRT   145 30
  MY ARMS LET ME COVER HIM UP IN MY SKIRT   750 20
  AND YOUR SHRED OF A SKIRT   835 19
  THE SKIRT OF THE SPIRIT'S EXPERIENCE HAS MELTED AWAY   *959 28

SKIRTING
  AND FROM THE SICILIAN TOWNLETS SKIRTING ETNA   312 10
  SKIRTING THE POLES OF BEING AND OF NOT-BEING   542 15

SKIRTS
  WHAT THEN IS THERE HIDDEN IN THE SKIRTS OF ALL THE BLOS+   119 27
  WHAT IS PEEPING FROM YOUR SKIRTS O MOTHER HEN   119 28
  A GREAT BAY STALLION DANCES SKIRTS   126 25
  AFTER THE BLACK-GREEN SKIRTS OF A YELLOW-GREEN OLD MEXI+   395 31
  PRANCING THEIR KNEES UNDER THEIR TINY SKIRTS   537 20
  AND SPREADING THEIR SKIRTS   539 26
  SHAKEN SOFTLY FROM THE HEAVY-FOLDED SKIRTS OF NIGHT   858 14

SKIS
  ON THE LONG FLAT SKIS OF HER LEGS   393 27

SKULL
  SAY IN THE DEEP SOCKETS OF YOUR IDEALISTIC SKULL   292 27

SKUNK
  STUFF IS JUST HOLY SKUNK   556 20
  TOO GREAT A SKUNK TO ABIDE BY HIS OWN SELF   *949   2

SKY
  SKY CEASED TO QUIVER AND LOST ITS ACTIVE SHEEN   95 15
  AND SITS WITH A SMOOTH BLAND SMILE UP THERE IN THE SKY   54 12
  UNFOLDS FROM THE SKY FOR YOUR GOOD   56   9
  WITH WHITE PLUMES BLINKING UNDER THE EVENING GREY SKY   66 14
  SEE IN THE SKY BEFORE ME A WOMAN I DID NOT KNOW   67 10
  ARRIVING ACROSS THE SKY   71   6
  YOU FEET OF THE RAINBOW BALANCING THE SKY   73   9
  THE SNOW DESCENDS AS IF THE SLOW SKY SHOOK   76 14
  OBSCURES THE DARK WOOD AND THE DULL ORANGE SKY   85 10
  SO EVEN IT BEATS LIKE SILENCE AND SKY AND EARTH IN ONE +   88   3
  ITS FIGURED PAGES AND SKY AND EARTH AND ALL BETWEEN ARE+   88 10
  OF A TRAIL OF OUR SMALL FIRE ON THE DARKENED SKY   89 15
  THE SEA AND THE SKY WENT GREY AS IF THERE HAD SUNK   98 12
  OF THE SKY SAGGED DUSTY AS SPIDER CLOTH   98 14
  HOW TOWARDS THE NORTH A RED BLOTCH ON THE SKY   103 10
  WHEN ONLY THERE GLOWED ON THE DARK OF THE SKY   103 16
  ON HIGH TO THE FUMING SKY OF NIGHT   105   2
  BEYOND ME LIES ON THE LOW STILL FLOOR OF THE SKY   114 18
  SO HALF LIES ON THE SKY FOR A GENERAL SIGN   114 25
  SHAFT-GOLDEN WITH LIGHT SHEER INTO THE SKY   116 16
  IS DRUNK FROM AN AGONISED SKY BY THE EARTH   117 32
  ONCE HIS FACE WAS OPEN LIKE THE SKY   119 24
  OPEN LIKE THE SKY LOOKING DOWN IN ALL ITS LAUGHTER   119 25
  THE ROUND EARTH ROLLS LIKE A GERM IN THE SKY   126   8
  TO QUICKEN THE SPHERES SPRING-VIRGIN AGAIN IN THE SKY   127 10
  FRAIL AS A SCAR UPON THE PALE BLUE SKY   131 24
  THE CLOUDS GO DOWN THE SKY WITH A WEALTHY EASE   133 16
  SINCE I LOST YOU MY DARLING THE SKY HAS COME NEAR   134 14
  TO BE LOST IN THE HAZE OF THE SKY I WOULD LIKE TO COME   134 22
  SINCE ALL THE SKY HAS WITHERED AND GONE COLD   135 16
  THE CLEAR COLD SKY COLDLY BETHINKS ITSELF   142 13
  AND BEAUTIFULLY LAID IN BLACK ON A GOLD-GREY SKY   146 29
  A HAWK IS IN THE SKY HIS WINGS   149 27
  STILL HANGS THE HAWK WITH THE WHOLE SKY MOVING   150   1
  EASILY DOWN THE SKY THE DAISIES SENDING   150 11
  UNDER AN OAK WHOSE YELLOW BUDS DOT THE PALE BLUE SKY   152 27
  SOON THE SPACES OF THE WESTERN SKY   163 13
  FROM THE SKY THE LOW TIRED MOON FADES OUT   163 21
  A SHARP SKY BRUSHES UPON   166 19
  AND UP IN THE SKY   170 21
  THE WAN WONDERING LOOK OF THE PALE SKY   203 10
  SQUARE PICTURE-DUSK THE WINDOW OF DARK SKY   210 20
  MY FEET HAVE NO HOLD YOU TAKE THE SKY FROM ABOVE ME   211 10
  THE SKY WAS GREEN WINE HELD UP IN THE SUN   216 14
  SKY OF STONE   220 26
  DARK AND PROUD ON THE SKY LIKE A NUMBER OF KNIGHTS   221   8
  WITH HIS HEAD HELD HIGH-SERENE AGAINST THE SKY   221 11
  DARK SKY OF NIGHT A WANDERING GLITTER A SWARM   221 26
  ON THE SKY   222   8
  AGAINST THE HARD AND PALE BLUE EVENING SKY   225   1
  OF THE SKY AND THE ALMOND FLOWERS   244   6
  HE THINKS THE WHOLE BLUE SKY   244 29
  AND TAINTS AND BLACKENS THE SKY TILL AT LAST IT IS DARK+   258 12
  EACH ONE SETTING OFF STRAIGHT TO THE SKY   299 27
  BUT YOU MISTAKE IT IS NOT FROM THE SKY   304 15
  NOW THAT IT SOUNDS SELF-CONSCIOUS THROUGH THE UNLIMITED+   325   4
  AND SERRATED WINGS AGAINST THE SKY   341 12
  IN THE SKY   374 13
  AND THOUGH THE SUN LEAPS LIKE A THING UNLEASHED IN THE +   408 21
  THEY SEND AEROPLANES ACROSS THE SKY   441 18
  AH THE CLEAN WATERS OF THE SKY AH CAN YOU WASH   581   6
  THE TRILLING LARK IN A WILD DESPAIR WILL TRILL DOWN ARR+   624 14
  NOW IT IS ALMOST NIGHT FROM THE BRONZEY SOFT SKY   647   8

SKY
  AND TUMBLING WRIGGLING DOWN THE SKY   647 15
  NOW TURNED AND CAME SLOWLY BACK WITH HER BACK TO THE EV+   693   7
  AND THE SHOULDERS PALLID WITH LIGHT FROM THE SILENT SKY+   693 11
  LIKE A SHED WHITE HUSK ON THE TORRID SKY   747 29
  OUT OF THE SKY TONIGHT   748   2
  YOU NOW AS YOU TURN YOUR FACE TOWARDS THE SKY   750 14
  LOOK IN THE SKY AT THE BRIGHT   755 12
  THE SKY WITH A WEALTH OF EASE AND ASSURANCE   772   5
  TROOP INTO THE SKY   798 22
  THOSE THAT FOLLOW ME MUST CROSS THE MOUNTAINS OF THE SKY   799   8
  OUT OF THE DEPTHS OF THE SKY I CAME LIKE AN EAGLE   801   6
  ALL THINGS THAT LIFT IN THE LIFT OF LIVING BETWEEN EART+   801   8
  AND THE BRANCHES ARE MINE IN THE PATHS OF THE SKY AND T+   801 17
  BLUE IS THE DEEP SKY AND THE DEEP WATER   808 24
  ALL OVER THE SKY THEIR WINGS ARE TOSSED   823   3
  IS SWEPT FROM OUT OF THE ENDLESS SKY   823 19
  TORN WINGS OF FLAME ARE WAFTING DOWN THE SKY   855 21
  SOON THE WESTERN WINDOWS OF THE SKY   857 13
  IN THE SKY THE LOW TIRED MOON GOES OUT   857 21
  AND DARK NOW IS THE SKY THAT SHE CAME THROUGH   863 13
  UNDER AN OAK TREE WHOSE YELLOW BUDS DOTTED THE PALE BLU+   866 23
  YOU WERE ALL THE MORNING TO ME ALL THE SEA AND THE MORN+   870 25
  NO MEANING IN THE SKY THE MEANING HAS VANISHED FROM THE   871 14
  EMERGING AND CROSSING THE CLEAR SKY UNPERCEIVED   874 24
  REVEALING THE SKY THROUGH THE RAGGED EARTH AND SUDDEN   874 29
  THE NAKED SKY   874 32
  I SAW THE SKY WAS LIT   883 19
  UNDER THE COLOURED FADING-OFF OF THE SKY   884 32
  HAD UTTERLY GONE FROM OUT OF THE TREMBLING SKY   885   8
  BLUE SILKEN SKY BEFORE THEY BEND ANEW   *895   4
  DARK GLITTER OF LIFE AMID A SKY THAT TEEMS   *895   7
  THE SNOW DESCENDS AS IF THE DULL SKY SHOOK   898   8
  THE SNOW DESCENDS AS IF THE DULL SKY SHOOK   *901 17
  THE GOLDEN GRAINED NIGHT AFLOWER ACROSS THE SKY   *916 12
  ACROSS THE SKY   *917 24
  SHAFT-GOLDEN WITH LIGHT AT THE JOINT OF THE SKY   *930 15
  WITH GOLDEN CHICKS OF CLOUD AND A SKY OF RUNNING LAUGHT+ *933 15
  AND NOW THE SKY WITH DREARY DIRT IS BARKLED   *933 16
  THROUGH THE WHOLE BLUE SKY AND THE NOON   *937 11
  WITH LIFE TILL THE EARTH AND THE SKY HAVE TUMBLED   *937 18
  FRAIL AS A SCAR UPON THE PALE BLUE SKY   *937 23
  DARK AND PROUD ON THE SKY LIKE A NUMBER OF KNIGHTS   *944 21
  WITH MY HEAD HELD HIGH-SERENE AGAINST THE SKY   *944 24
  DARK SKY OF NIGHT THE WANDERING GLITTER THE SWARM   *945 12

SKY-BLUE
  COOLING TO A POWDERY PALE-OXYDISED SKY-BLUE   369 14
  OXYDISED SKY-BLUE   369 20
  THE SKY-BLUE WALLS OF OUR UNVENTILATED HEAVEN   515   5
  AND PAINTS THE INSIDE WALLS SKY-BLUE   515   8
  HE'S GOING TO WEAR THE SKY-BLUE CLOAK   797 15

SKY-DOORS
  SO TINY WHEN YOU OPEN SKY-DOORS ON ME   876   2

SKY-DROPPED
  SO THAT THE RAMBLING SKY-DROPPED GRAPE CAN ADD ITS SAVO+ 301 35

SKYLARK
  AND THE SKYLARK TWINKLES BLUE   216 10

SKY-LINE
  ON THE SKY-LINE   222   5
  ALONG THE SKY-LINE SHE   222 14

SKY'S
  SHE CREEPS PERSISTENT DOWN THE SKY'S LONG STAIRS   131 28
  AND FEARFUL TO SALLY FORTH DOWN THE SKY'S LONG RANGE   132 20
  OR ELSE RUSH HORIZONTAL TO CHARGE AT THE SKY'S HORIZON   392 18
  WHEN I SEE THE SKY'S BLUE DARKEN   869   4
  WHEN THE SKY'S BLUE DARKENS AT NIGHTFALL   869   8
  WRAPPED UP IN THE SKY'S DIM SPACE OF HOARSE SILENCE   *898 14
  WRAPPED UP IN THE SKY'S DIM SPACE OF HOARSE SILENCE   *901 24
  DOWN THE SKY'S STEEP STAIRS CHARTING NO TRACK FOR HER   *937 27

SKYWARD
  AND WHAT IS DAYLIGHT TO ME THAT I SHOULD LOOK SKYWARD   287 26

SKYWARDS
  AND SKYWARDS HIS FACE IS IMMOBILE EYELIDS ASLANT   66 11

SKYWARD-SMILING
  THE OPEN-COUNTENANCED SKYWARD-SMILING ROSE   285   9

SLACK
  SLACK   34   6
  ALONG WITH A RIPE SLACK COUNTRY LASS   198   7
  SOFTLY DRANK THROUGH HIS STRAIGHT GUMS INTO HIS SLACK L+ 349 16
  EVER AGAIN LYING PRONE LYING SLACK   827 12

SLACKNESS
  AND TRAILED HIS YELLOW-BROWN SLACKNESS SOFT-BELLIED DOWN 349 10

SLAG
  A BIT OF SLAG STILL ADHERING AFTER YOUR FIRING IN THE F+ 370   2

SLAG-WATTLED
  SLAG-WATTLED TURKEY-COCK   372   3

SLAIN
  YOU HAVE SLAIN AS WAS YOUR DUTY   95 22
  WE HAVE DIED WE HAVE SLAIN AND BEEN SLAIN   244 21
  WHEN SHE IS SLAIN AGAINST ME AND LIES IN A HEAP LIKE ON+ 267 13
  MEN THAT ARE SLAIN   269   6
  ONLY BEHOLD THE GHOSTS THE GHOSTS OF THE SLAIN   736   4
  BETWEEN ME AND THEE SO MANY GHOSTS OF THE SLAIN   739   9
  THE MORE WE SLAY AND ARE SLAIN THE MORE WE RAISE UP NEW   739 27

SLAIN
　　TILL WE ARE MAD WITH TERROR SEEING THE SLAIN   740 1
　　AND CRIMSON AND THE BLOOD-BROWN HEAPS OF SLAIN   745 26
　　MICHAEL AND GABRIEL ALL OF THEM SLAIN   823 13

SLANT
　　SMOULDERING WITH DARKENED BUSBIES BENEATH THE BAYONETS'+ 66 8
　　HOLD MY HAND TO CATCH THE RAINDROPS THAT SLANT INTO SIG+ 179 21

SLANTING
　　WHEN THEY POINT THEIR SLANTING FINGERS   731 7

SLANTS
　　OF REDDISH HERBAGE THAT BRISTLES AND SLANTS   50 21

SLAP
　　DROPPING BACK WITH A SLAP ON THE FACE OF THE FLOOD   337 4

SLARTS
　　I'M NOT 'AVIN' YOUR ORTS AN' SLARTS   82 3
　　JUST ORTS AND SLARTS BERRIES THAT SMOULDER IN THE BUSH   219 15
　　I'M NOT HAVIN' YOUR ORTS AN' SLARTS   *924 7

SLASHED
　　SHRIEKED AND SLASHED THE WIND AS A SHIP'S   36 11

SLASHES
　　AND TAKE SIXTY SLASHES   563 11

SLATE
　　THE LORD WROTE IT ALL DOWN ON THE LITTLE SLATE   356 9

SLAUGHTER
　　SLAUGHTER   827 9

SLAVE
　　HE CAN'T HELP BEING A SLAVE A WAGE-SLAVE   524 11
　　AND THE SLAVE IS THE MACHINE INCARNATE   635 15
　　DIVISION INTO SLAVE AND FREEMAN   636 14
　　WHEREIN A MAN CAN LIVE HIS LIFE WITHOUT BEING A SLAVE T+ 837 25

SLAVER
　　WRIGGLE AND WAG AND SLAVER AND GET THE MENTALITY OF A D+ 645 4

SLAVERING
　　AND SLAVERING WET AND SOGGY   492 2

SLAVERY
　　AND WAS SOLD INTO SLAVERY   378 9

SLAVES
　　THE HEART ALL CROWDED WITH SLAVES MOST WORKING SOME FEW+ 174 20
　　AND KEEP YOU IN MILLIONS AT THE MILLS SIGHTLESS PALE SL+ 441 8
　　LIKE GROSS SUCCESSFUL SLAVES MECHANICALLY WADDLING   526 15
　　AND THEIR GRANDCHILDREN ARE ONCE MORE SLAVES   535 26
　　WHAT ARE YOU GOOD FOR BUT TO BE SLAVES AND ROT AWAY   795 8
　　WE HAVE LEARNT NOT TO HAVE SLAVES NOT TO WANT THEM   832 28
　　POOR DREAM-HEAVY SLAVES AT THE MILL WHAT WE HAVE TO DO + 859 28
　　A TEACHER OF THESE YOUNG BOYS MY SLAVES   *899 6
　　ONLY AS SWALLOWS ARE SLAVES TO THE EAVES   *899 7
　　THEY BUILD UPON AS MICE ARE SLAVES   *899 8
　　A TEACHER OF THESE YOUNG BOYS MY SLAVES   *902 18
　　ONLY AS SWALLOWS ARE SLAVES TO THE EAVES   *902 19
　　THEY BUILD UPON AS MICE ARE SLAVES   *902 20

SLAY
　　AND TO-NIGHT I SLAY IT   238 18
　　AND A SICKLY PEOPLE WILL SLAY US   537 9
　　O SLAY NOT THE BEST BRIGHT PROUD LIFE THAT IS IN YOU TH+ 678 24
　　THE MORE WE SLAY AND ARE SLAIN THE MORE WE RAISE UP NEW 739 27

SLEEK
　　STANDING THERE SO SLEEK AND ERECT AND EYEABLE   431 14
　　AND SUNBURNT AND WATER-WASHED FULL-FED AND SLEEK   827 11
　　BEAUTIES SO SLEEK   861 8
　　SOMEWHERE BENEATH THAT PIANO'S SUPERB SLEEK BLACK   *940 1

SLEEKNESS
　　WITH SLEEKNESS AND FATNESS   826 15

SLEEP
　　WITH DARK SLEEP THAT ONCE COVERED THE CEILING   38 5
　　PUTS THE HARD HANDS OF MY FRIEND TO SLEEP   41 9
　　ME SO DISTINCTLY FROM SLEEPING THE SLEEP I'D LOVE BEST   48 26
　　AS IT SHOWS HIM SLEEPING A SLEEP HE GOT   59 5
　　OH AND I LONG TO SEE HIM SLEEP   59 17
　　HE WILL SLEEP OF ME   59 28
　　ON HIS SLEEP THAT IS FILLED OF ME   60 2
　　ON HIS LIMBS IN SLEEP AT LAST LAID LOW   60 7
　　ALL THE BIRDS ARE FOLDED IN A SILENT BALL OF SLEEP   71 9
　　WHO CURL LIKE KITTENS WHO MASS AS A SWARM   73 17
　　TO ESCAPE IN SLEEP THE TERROR OF THIS GREAT BIVALVE DAR+ 88 14
　　ROUNDED LIKE PEARLS FOR SLEEP AND THEN FROM BETWEEN SHU+ 88 16
　　DEADENED ME THROUGH TILL THE GREY DOWNS DULLED TO SLEEP   98 22
　　AND MEMORIES CLUSTERED ME CLOSE AND SLEEP WAS CAJOLED   98 30
　　I HEARD YOU IN YOUR SLEEP SPEAK STRANGELY TO ME   99 10
　　STILL WINSOME SLEEP SO STILL AND SO COMPOSED   101 11
　　ENDS LIKE A BROKEN LOVE THAT TURNS TO THE DARK OF SLEEP 114 28
　　WITHOUT EVER SLEEP DELIVERING US   116 18
　　US AWAY IN AN UTTER SLEEP UNTIL   117 6
　　UNEASILY IN THEIR SLEEP DISTURBING MY METTLE   128 13
　　CLOSES HER ARMS THAT SHOULD FOLD ON ME IN SLEEP   128 30
　　AND FLING MYSELF AT THE DOORS OF SLEEP FOR REST   129 22
　　THE SLEEP NO DREAM NOR DOUBT CAN UNDERMINE   129 26
　　DROPPING AND STARTING FROM SLEEP   143 3
　　SLEEP IN A ROW THE OUTCASTS   144 15
　　BEASTS THAT SLEEP WILL COVER   144 20
　　HAVE HUDDLED RAGS OR LIMBS ON THE NAKED SLEEP   144 22

SLEEP
　　WASTRELS THAT SLEEP ON THE FLAGSTONES WITHOUT ANY HURT   145 33
　　FOR A PLACE TO LIE DOWN AND STILL AS THEY STAND THEY SL+ 146 7
　　AS IT SPINS TO SLEEP ON ITS MOTION DRUGGED DENSE IN THE 149 7
　　SLEEP OF THE WHEEL   149 8
　　WITH VIOLENT ACHINGS HEAVING TO BURST THE SLEEP THAT IS+ 149 23
　　IF WE'RE GOING TO SLEEP THE SLEEP WITH THOSE   164 14
　　SLEEP TO MAKE US FORGET BUT HE UNDERSTANDS   167 19
　　SLEEP ON SPEED IN DEAD CERTAINTY   169 20
　　WE ASPHYXIATE IN A SLEEP OF DREAMS REBREATHING THE IMPU+ 174 26
　　SLEEP   175 13
　　TILL AT LENGTH THEY INDUCE ME TO SLEEP AND TO FORGET   180 36
　　YOU GREAT YOU PATIENT EFFORT AND YOU SLEEP   194 19
　　YOU SLEEP STRETCHED OUT FOR EVER EVER GIVING   194 21
　　US OUT AS DREAMS YOU AUGUST SLEEP   194 22
　　SINCE YOU VAST OUTSTRETCHED WORDLESS SLEEP   194 26
　　WE ARE AND BODY OF SLEEP LET IT NEVER BE SAID   194 28
　　OF A DAY'S EXPERIENCE SLEEP DOES SLOWLY DRAW   195 2
　　AT NIGHT I SAY WHEN I AM GONE IN SLEEP   195 5
　　THIS ME WHICH RISES FROM THE DARK OF SLEEP   195 10
　　FROM OUT THE CLOUD OF SLEEP LOOKS ROUND ABOUT   195 13
　　IN ONE RICH DRIP IT SINKS TO ANOTHER SLEEP   195 15
　　AND SLEEP THEREBY IS ONE MORE CREAM ENRICHENED   195 16
　　IF SO THE VAST THE GOD THE SLEEP THAT STILL GROWS RICHER 195 17
　　HAVE SAID THAT I THIS MOTE IN THE BODY OF SLEEP   195 18
　　LAPPED LIKE A BODY CLOSE UPON A SLEEP   195 27
　　HIDING AND COVERING IN THE ETERNAL SLEEP   195 28
　　WITH ACHE OF DREAMS THAT BODY FORTH THE SLEEP   195 30
　　AND GRIEF ARE BUT THE SAME LAST WONDER SLEEP   196 2
　　AND EVERYTHING SHUT UP AND GONE TO SLEEP   203 12
　　NOT SLEEP WHICH IS GREY WITH DREAMS   205 12
　　WHAT IS SLEEP   205 15
　　SLEEP   210 24
　　COME BACK TO BED LET US SLEEP ON OUR MYSTERIES   211 25
　　BUT NEVER MIND MY LOVE NOTHING MATTERS SAVE SLEEP   212 10
　　SAVE YOU AND ME AND SLEEP ALL THE REST WILL KEEP   212 11
　　NIGHT FOLK TUATHA DE DANAAN DARK GODS GOVERN HER SLEEP   213 25
　　IN SLEEP   213 27
　　WE MOVE WITHOUT KNOWING WE SLEEP AND WE TRAVEL ON   252 7
　　DARKNESS AND DEPTH OF SLEEP   254 1
　　SLEEP YET FIGHTING FIGHTING TO KEEP AWAKE   287 3
　　SLEEPS FOUR SLEEPS THE SLEEP OF THE LION THE SLEEP ON T+ 319 5
　　SLEEP OF THE MAN AND THE EAGLE'S SLEEP AFTER WHICH THE + 319 6
　　QUARTERS THEN SLEEP IS EMPTY TOO MAN SLEEPS NO MORE LIK+ 319 10
　　AND THE BULL NOR WAKES FROM THE LIGHT-EYED EAGLE SLEEP   319 11
　　TO SINK AND RISE AND GO TO SLEEP WITH THE WATERS   336 28
　　CREATURES THAT HANG THEMSELVES UP LIKE AN OLD RAG TO SL+ 342 1
　　AND GRINNING IN THEIR SLEEP   342 4
　　OR IS SLEEP COMING OVER YOU AGAIN   353 13
　　FAR ONE TO SLEEP AND A FORGETTING AND OFTEN THE DEAD LO+ 406 5
　　THEY CAMPED AND WENT TO SLEEP   407 7
　　IN THEIR SLEEP   407 15
　　LIKE A MAN WHEN HE SLEEPS AND HIS SLEEP IS OVER AND HE   407 18
　　SO HE LAUGHS FROM FEAR PURE FEAR IN THE GRIP OF THE SLE+ 407 22
　　A MEMBRANE OF SLEEP LIKE A BLACK BLANKET   407 25
　　WE WALK IN OUR SLEEP IN THIS LAND   407 26
　　AND OUR SCREAM IS SOUNDLESS IN THE PARALYSIS OF SLEEP   408 2
　　TO TEAR THE MEMBRANE OF THIS SLEEP   408 6
　　TO THE SLEEP OF ICE   436 7
　　WITH DREAMS AND THRUSTS THAT MAKE THEM DRY IN THEIR SLE+ 438 15
　　AND SLEEP IN MASSIVE SILENCE AND WAKE   465 17
　　SLEEP SLEEP SLEEP CORPSE-BODY FACTORY-HAND SLEEP   584 17
　　SLEEP IS THE SHADOW OF DEATH BUT NOT ONLY THAT   724 27
　　SLEEP IS A HINT OF LOVELY OBLIVION   724 28
　　IN SLEEP I AM NOT I AM GONE   725 1
　　AND NOTHING IN THE WORLD IS LOVELIER THAN SLEEP   725 3
　　DARK DREAMLESS SLEEP IN DEEP OBLIVION   725 4
　　YET THERE IS WAKING FROM THE SOUNDEST SLEEP   725 6
　　DID YOU SLEEP WELL   725 8
　　AH YES THE SLEEP OF GOD   725 9
　　FOR GOD IS DEEPER FORGETTING FAR THAN SLEEP   726 15
　　IN SLEEP AND SINK IN GOOD OBLIVION   726 23
　　AND LAY THEM DEEP IN LOVE LAY THEM TO SLEEP   736 15
　　TO SLEEP AT LAST IN IMMEMORIAL LOVE   736 21
　　WE COVER THE HOUSELESS DEAD SO THEY SLEEP IN PEACE   736 25
　　OF SWEET RETURNING FROM THE SLEEP OF DEATH   745 5
　　THE LONG SLEEP   787 10
　　SLEEP SLEEP MY BROTHER SLEEP   787 11
　　THAT I MAY HOLD THEM LIKE MEMORIES IN MY ARMS WHEN I GO+ 789 20
　　IS LASHING HIS TAIL IN HIS SLEEP THE WINDS HOWL THE COL+ 795 14
　　THERE ARE DEAD THAT SLEEP IN THE WAVES OF THE MORNING S+ 795 18
　　WHEN YOU SLEEP IT SOFTLY SHINES   800 7
　　PUT SLEEP AS BLACK AS BEAUTY IN THE SECRET OF MY BELLY   803 2
　　WHEN YOU SLEEP AND KNOW IT NOT   807 28
　　IN YOUR SLEEP YOU TWIST YOUR SOUL HURTS YOU   807 30
　　AS I WENT DOWN THE ROAD OF SLEEP   808 3
　　THAT YOUR SLEEP BE NOT AS A CEMETERY   808 15
　　TO THOSE WHO WOULD SLEEP   811 19
　　THAT WE CAN NEVER ESCAPE NOT EVEN IN SLEEP   833 32
　　AND THE ANIMALS CURL DOWN ON THE DEAR EARTH TO SLEEP   834 3
　　THERE IS NO ACTION IT IS ALMOST A SLEEP   856 23
　　AND ALONG THE SCENT AND THE COOLNESS A DROWSE OF SLEEP + 858 20
　　AND HAVING WON I WILL LIE DOWN TO SLEEP   876 4
　　AND STEALING INTO HIS SLEEP SHOULD SET HIM LONGING   877 33
　　FOR HE HAS DRUNK THE MORSELS WHITE OF SLEEP   878 11
　　AS HE DID SIP THE BITTER MILK OF SLEEP   878 14
　　AND STILL HIS LIFE SHAKES AT THE LATCH OF SLEEP   878 28
　　AND HIS CHILDREN STIRRED IN THEIR SLEEP AND WHEN THEY W+ 885 12
　　WITH THE DARK SLEEP THAT ONCE COVERED THE CEILING   *892 21
　　FOR MYSELF A HEAP OF ASHES OF WEARINESS TILL SLEEP   *896 1
　　FOR MYSELF A HEAP OF ASHES OF WEARINESS TILL SLEEP   *904 22
　　THE MOON OF SLEEP IS ALIGHT   *917 16
　　ALL THE BIRDS ARE FOLDED IN A SILENT BALL OF SLEEP   *917 27
　　WITH DREAMS AND THRUSTS THAT MAKE THEM CRY IN THEIR SLE+ *947 21

SLEEP-BOUND
    THE MOANING OF SLEEP-BOUND BEINGS IN TRAVAIL THAT TOIL +   149 19

SLEEPER
    WHEN THE SLEEPER STIRS OR TURNS ON THE EBB OF THE FLOOD   145 27

SLEEPERS
    AT THE FEET OF THE SLEEPERS WATCHING   146 5

SLEEPING
    THE GLIMMER OF THE LIMES SUN-HEAVY SLEEPING   35 26
    THEIR SLEEPING COVER THEM SOFT UNSEEN   48 22
    HARDLY A MURMUR COMES FROM THE SLEEPING BROOD   48 23
    ME SO DISTINCTLY FROM SLEEPING THE SLEEP I'D LOVE BEST   48 26
    ON HIM WHO IS SLEEPING SATIATE   58 30
    AS IT SHOWS HIM SLEEPING A SLEEP HE GOT   59 5
    AND I SHALL SEE MY SLEEPING ROD   59 11
    WITH AFTER-PAIN MY SLEEPING BABY HANGS UPON MY LIFE   73 27
    UPON ME LIKE SLEEPING BIRDS LIKE BIRDS THAT SHIFT   128 12
    OUT OF THE DARKNESS FRETTED SOMETIMES IN ITS SLEEPING   136 5
    A LITTLE BEARDED MAN PEAKED IN SLEEPING   145 8
    AND A HEAVY WOMAN SLEEPING STILL KEEPING   145 10
    IN THE AVENUES WHERE THE BAT HANGS SLEEPING UPSIDE-DOWN   322 33
    IT IS RATHER AGITATING SLEEPING WITH A LITTLE VESUVIUS   539 6
    OR LIKE THE WOMAN WHO SAT DOWN ON A SLEEPING MASTODON   540 1
    I KNOW HE IS EITHER A BED-BUG BATTENING ON SLEEPING PEO+   621 23
    SLEEPING ON THE HEARTH AND YAWNING BEFORE THE FIRE   700 7
    SLEEPING ON THE HEARTH OF THE LIVING WORLD   700 8
    DO THOU O VIRGIN AT DAY WHEN WE RISE FROM OUR SLEEPING   753 3
    FROM HEAVEN PAST THE SLEEPING SONS OF GOD   801 5
    I AM THE SLEEPING AND WAKING   805 8
    HE IS HUITZILOPOCHTLI SLEEPING OR WAKING   806 11
    CREEPING AMONG THE SLEEPING AND THE DREAMING WHO ARE LA+   807 6
    IN THE NIGHT I SEE THE GREY DOGS CREEPING OUT OF THE SL+   807 11
    SILENTLY SWIMMING AND SLEEPING AND PRESSING THE FLOOD   841 4
    MY SLEEPING BABY HANGS UPON MY LIFE   *913 19

SLEEPS
    SHE SLEEPS A RARE   101 10
    NAY BUT SHE SLEEPS LIKE A BRIDE AND DREAMS HER DREAMS   101 12
    OF DARKNESS WHEREON SHE SLEEPS ON HER PERFECT BED   133 25
    RIGID SLEEPS THE HOUSE IN DARKNESS I ALONE   140 7
    TIME SLEEPS AGAIN   169 23
    SLEEPS ON UNKNOWN UNNOTICED THERE UNTIL   176 28
    THAT SLEEPS BELOW ON THE LAKE   227 22
    THE NIGHT LIVES FOUR LIVES AND MAN THAT SLEEPS THROUGH +   319 4
    SLEEPS FOUR SLEEPS THE SLEEP OF THE LION THE SLEEP ON T+   319 5
    QUARTERS THEN SLEEP IS EMPTY TOO MAN SLEEPS NO MORE LIK+   319 10
    LIKE A MAN WHEN HE SLEEPS AND HIS SLEEP IS OVER AND HE   407 18
    WHEN IT'S LEFT ALONE AS IT STIRS AND ROUSES AND SLEEPS   464 31
    TOUCH COMES WHEN THE WHITE MIND SLEEPS   470 23
    SLEEPS IN THE HEALING WATERS   787 9
    THE DRAGON OF THE DISAPPOINTED DEAD THAT SLEEPS IN THE +   795 12
    BUT SLEEPS THE LONG WEEK OUT EMBOSOMED IN MURMURING LIM+   858 23
    HE SLEEPS AS EVER GENEROUSLY UNLOCKED   878 1
    AND WELL I KNOW HE SLEEPS TO WAKE NO MORE   878 7
    AND NOW HE SLEEPS   878 19
    A DARKNESS WITHIN ME A PRESENCE WHICH SLEEPS CONTAINED   *920 7

SLEEP-SUAVE
    SLEEP-SUAVE LIMBS OF A YOUTH WITH LONG SMOOTH THIGHS   145 18

SLEEP-TENT
    WHILE JOSEPH PITCHES THE SLEEP-TENT   201 17

SLEEPY
    PALE SLEEPY PHANTOMS ARE TOSSED ABOUT   163 23
    NAY I'M TOO SLEEPY AH YOU ARE HORRIBLE   211 7
    PALE SLEEPY FLOWERS ARE TOSSED ABOUT   857 23

SLEEVE
    THAT HAS KEPT SO MANY SECRETS UP ITS SLEEVE   299 14
    UP ITS SLEEVE   299 18
    THEY ALL OF THEM ALWAYS KEPT UP THEIR SLEEVE   554 31

SLEEVES
    THEN I AM WILLING TO FIGHT I WILL ROLL MY SLEEVES UP   430 11

SLENDER
    WITHIN THE HOUSE TWO VOICES AROSE A SLENDER LASH   36 13
    WITH A WANTON PRINCESS SLENDER AND PROUD   70 15
    THE SLENDER BARE ARMS OF THE BRANCHES YOUR TIRE-MAIDENS   86 17
    DUSKY SLIM MARROW-THOUGHT OF SLENDER FLICKERING MEN OF   297 6
    WERE THEY THEN VICIOUS THE SLENDER TENDER-FOOTED   297 14
    AND LIFTING HER BEAUTIFUL SLENDER FACE OH SO MUCH MORE   393 6
    THEY ARE LIKE SLENDER TREES PUTTING FORTH LEAVES A LONG+   451 5
    THE LITTLE SLENDER SOUL SITS SWIFTLY DOWN AND TAKES THE+   723 20
    AS A FINE GREY EGG OR A SLENDER ROD   752 10
    A SWIFT DEXTEROUS MAN PLYING THE SLENDER POLE   867 22
    THE LITTLE SLENDER SOUL SITS SWIFTLY DOWN AND TAKES THE+   *958 32

SLEPT
    AND I SLEPT TILL DAWN AT THE WINDOW BLEW IN LIKE DUST   99 1
    HAS SLEPT UNNOTICED ON A FORGOTTEN HILL   176 27
    HAVING TASTED ALL THERE WAS TO TASTE AND HAVING SLEPT H+   324 11
    HER HANDSOME THIGHS DOWN DOWN TILL SHE SLEPT HER   444 31
    SLEPT I QUETZALCOATL   786 4
    STARTLED AND FULL OF AGONY TO FIND HE HAD BUT SLEPT   859 18
    AND THE FLUSH FADED AND IT CAME DARK I SLEPT STILL IGNO+   860 7
    WHO HAD NOT SLEPT   881 17
    BUT I HAD NOT SLEPT   881 20

SLICES
    WHERE NOW THEY DEAL OUT SLICES OF PLATO-SAUSAGE TO THE +   762 27

SLID
    FROM THIS ROSY TERROR OF BIRTH THAT HAS SLID DOWN   88 24
    HER HANDS SLID IN AND SET ME FREE   262 15
    DARK BREATH OF THE EARTH THE SERPENT SLID FORTH LAY REV+   348 7
    AND WE SLID AND YOU SKI'D AND WE CAME IN TO TEA   550 31

SLIDES
    TILL THE WIND SLIDES YOU SHEER FROM THE ARCH-CREST   696 24

SLIDING
    SOMETHING FAERY AND FINE THE SHUTTLES SLIDING   72 7
    DANCE TO THE SLIDING SEA AND THE MOON   130 10
    IN THE WILD DAYS WHEN LIFE WAS SLIDING WHIRLWINDS BLUE-+   529 23

SLIGHTLY
    DONE AND SLIGHTLY SUBTLE   532 18
    WHEN REALLY YOU ARE SLIGHTLY INFERIOR   548 19

SLIM
    SLIM VOTARESSES   96 8
    AND DOWN MY SLIM   96 20
    LIKE SHARP SLIM WAGTAILS THEY FLASH A LITTLE ASIDE   269 26
    ON ONE OLD SLIM IMPERISHABLE THOUGHT WHILE YOU REMAIN   297 4
    DUSKY SLIM MARROW-THOUGHT OF SLENDER FLICKERING MEN OF   297 6
    A SLIM YOUNG PIKE WITH SMART FINS   338 1
    AND THE SLIM NAKED MAN SLIPS DOWN AND THE BEAST DEPOSITS   387 14
    SLIM LIMBS AND BREASTS   389 17
    A LONG LONG SLIM CAT YELLOW LIKE A LIONESS   401 24
    OF THAT SLIM YELLOW MOUNTAIN LION   402 33
    THE TRAPEZE MAN SLIM AND BEAUTIFUL AND LIKE A FISH IN T+   445 4
    AND LET THE SLIM BLACK SHIP OF DIONYSOS COME SAILING IN   688 4
    SLIM NAKED MEN FROM CNOSSOS SMILING THE ARCHAIC SMILE   688 13
    WITH SLIM WAISTS OF WARRIORS AND THE LONG FEET   689 3
    MY YOUNG SLIM LAD AN' I'M SORRY FOR THEE   *944 16

SLIME
    TO SPONGE AWAY THE SLIME   581 2
    THEY'LL MELT MERCILESSLY BACK INTO SLIME   828 13

SLIMLY
    MEN SLIMLY WENT LIKE FISHES AND DIDN'T CARE   688 22

SLIM-MUZZLED
    LONG PENSIVE SLIM-MUZZLED GREYHOUND BUDS   310 29

SLIMY
    AS IT FEELS THE SLIMY TAINT   500 20

SLINK
    AS WELL IN THE SCENTS THAT SLINK   107 16
    OF THE YELLOW DOGS HOW THEY SLINK AWAY   494 7

SLINKING
    REMINISCENT OF SLINKING BEASTS MAKE ME FEAR   107 6
    THAT CANNOT EMBARK ON THE SLINKING SEA BEYOND   722 23
    THAT INTERVENE BETWEEN OUR TOWER AND THE SLINKING SEA O+   *957 24

SLINKS
    IN THE BLACK WET NIGHT AS THE FURTIVE RAIN SLINKS DOWN   143 2

SLIP
    AS IF SHE WOULD SLIP THE GOLD AND GLIMMERING   106 5
    SEAL UP EACH CHANNEL OUT OF WHICH MIGHT SLIP   153 22
    OR SLIP LIKE WATER SLIPPERY TOWARDS ITS ENDS   392 20
    THEIR CHILDREN BROUGHT UP EASY LET IT SLIP AWAY AGAIN   535 24
    SLIP OUT O SLIP OUT FROM BETWEEN THE MILLSTONES   642 6
    SLIP ASIDE SLIP OUT   642 24
    SCREENS US PURELY AND WE CAN SLIP THROUGH   699 11
    CAN SLIP ENTIRELY THROUGH THE FINGERS OF THE HANDS OF G+ 701 14
    IS AN ABYSS DOWN WHICH THE SOUL CAN SLIP   701 18
    LET NOBODY BE ABOUT SLIP IN GO ALL UNSEEN   711 10
    WE LET THE WEAPONS SLIP FROM OUT OUR HANDS   736 22
    FALSE FAIR ONES CANNOT SLIP THROUGH   810 5
    AS WE SLIP IN UNSEEN   812 16
    I ASK FOR NOTHING EXCEPT TO SLIP   812 25
    THYSELF SLIP OUT THE LEASH AND HUNTS THY WAY   879 13
    AND ALL THE LESSONS LET SLIP BY   *894 13
    HE SHALL SLIP DOWN THE SHORES INVISIBLE   *958 25

SLIPPED
    REFOLDING SHE SLIPPED TO THE FLOOR AS A GHOST-WHITE PEO+ 155 23
    SLIPPED THROUGH MY ARMS ON THE THRESHING FLOOR   198 11
    THEY SLIPPED INTO THE FRAY   560 1
    SLIPPED LIKE ANYTHING BUT DON'T YOU LIKE IT AIN'T IT FI+ 865 23
    WHEN YOU'D GONE I SLIPPED BACK TER SEE WHO SHE MIGHT BE *910 5

SLIPPERED
    WE ALL MARCH OUT TO PRAYERS SOFT SLIPPERED FEET AND CLA+ 866 13

SLIPPERS
    LADS IN THEIR WARM LIGHT SLIPPERS BOUND DOWN THE HALL T+ 865 28

SLIPPERY
    YOU LEAPT ABOUT IN THE SLIPPERY ROCKS AND THREW   98 19
    ABHORRENT GREEN SLIPPERY CITY   278 10
    OR SLIP LIKE WATER SLIPPERY TOWARDS ITS ENDS   392 20
    WHITE AND SLIPPERY AS ON THE BLACK WATER IN A PORT   453 14
    THE LIES THE TREACHERY THE SLIPPERY CULTURED SQUALOR OF+ 497 4
    AND BUTTER YOUR SLIPPERY BUTS   549 12
    DOWN THE TRUNK OF THE SLIPPERY TREE   552 6

SLIPPING
    BY THE SLIPPING SHAWL OF STARS   55 27
    IF UNDER YOUR SLIPPING WORDS THAT EASILY FLOW   122 10
    THE RIVER SLIPPING BETWEEN   144 3
    SLIPPING INTO ITS BED OF DEAD LEAVES YOU HURRY INTO YOUR 254 16

SLIPS
SLIPS AWAY SO I GASP IN SURPRISE   38 33
OF A SECOND LIKE SNOW THAT SLIPS   62 10
THE PASSION SLIPS   96 19
BUT HELD MY HAND AFLOAT TOWARDS THE SLIPS   125 21
FLESH OF MY HEART ERE DOWN REBUKED IT SLIPS   127 28
SOME MONEY HER HAND SLIPS OUT OF THE BREAST OF HER   143 8
AND OVER MY FACE THE STRAY FIRE SLIPS   151 8
SLIPS   155 24
WHICH SLIPS DOWN LIKE A PENDULUM TO BALANCE THE THROBBI+   370 6
AND THE SLIM NAKED MAN SLIPS DOWN AND THE BEAST DEPOSITS   387 14
IT SLIPS OVER IT AS SHADOWS DO WITHOUT HURTING ITSELF   467 19
AND OVER MY FACE YOUR STRAY FIRE SLIPS   873 18
WHERE THE EBB OF LIFE SLIPS BY   *917 8
BUT HELD MY HAND AFLOAT STILL TOWARDS THE SLIPS   *936 20
MY TREASURE SOFTLY SLIPS UNCURLED   *943 23
SLIPS OUT THE SOUL INVISIBLE ONE WRAPPED STILL   *957 8
FRIGHTENED AND ALONE THE SOUL SLIPS OUT OF THE HOUSE   *957 12
OF THE BODY'S MEMORIES SLIPS AND IS ABSORBED   *959 25
AS THE SOUL AT LAST SLIPS PERFECT INTO THE GOAL THE CORE   *959 31

SLIT
PURPLE SLIT   283 31
AND THE SUN COMING IN THROUGH THE NARROWEST FIBRIL OF A+   324 13
AND THE COFFIN-LIFE SLIT WHERE THE INDIAN'S EYES ARE   403 30

SLITHERING
BUT NOW I AM SLITHERING DOWN AGAIN   552 5
IN PANIC IN REBELLION SLITHERING MILLIONS OF FISH   586 26
THIRTEEN WERE THE SLITHERING SILENT JOURNEYS   *933 2

SLITS
LIKE SLITS IN AN AUTOMATIC-MACHINE YOU COLUMNS OF GIVE-+   288 25
YELLOW EYES INCOMPREHENSIBLE WITH THIN SLITS   380 28

SLITTED
AND HIS SLITTED EYES SEEKING THE NEEDLE'S EYE   382 4
WHILE HIS SLITTED EYES SQUINT BACK TO THE ROOTS OF HIS +   386 22

SLIVE
THA SHOULD HA' SEED 'ER SLIVE UP WHEN YER'D GONE   61 5
TILL 'ER'S TOUGH AS WHIT-LEATHER TO SLIVE   77 19
YOU SHOULD 'A SEEN HER SLIVE UP WHEN WE'D GO   *910 9
THA SHOULD HA' SEED HER SLIVE UP WHEN WE'D GONE   *911 21
TILL 'ER'S TOUGH AS WHIT-LEATHER TO SLIVE   *919 7

S'LL
THERE'S ONE THING WE S'LL 'AVE A PEACEFUL 'OUSE   45 29
I S'LL NEVER CATCH THAT TRAIN   46 2
FOR WHENEVER I LOOK THEE I' TH' FACE I S'LL SEE   82 23
ALL AS WE S'LL WANT FOR FURNITURE WHEN THA LEAVES THIS +   83 8
SO I S'LL GO AN' LEAVE YER   84 17
FOR WHENEVER I LOOK THEE I' TH' FACE I S'LL SEE   *924 27

SLOGAN
BUT IT SOUNDS SO AMAZINGLY LIKE A SLOGAN   333 23

SLOPE
DRAWS TOWARDS THE DOWNWARD SLOPE SOME SORROW HATH   131 25
DOWN THE ENDLESS SLOPE WHERE THE LAST ROAD GOES   164 12
WHO HAD LAIN HER SHIFT ON THE SHORE ON THE SHINGLE SLOPE   693 4
SAUNTERING DOWN THE LONG SLOPE FROM THE EAST   770 21
AND STARTED DOWN THE LONG SLOPE   787 3
JESUS HAD GONE FAR UP THE DARK SLOPE WHEN HE LOOKED BACK   789 16
THE SUN HAS CLIMBED THE HILL THE DAY IS ON THE DOWNWARD+   803 5
DRAWS TOWARDS THE DOWNWARD SLOPE SOME SICKNESS HATH   *937 24

SLOPES
IS THERE SOME GREAT IACCOS OF THESE SLOPES   141 1
SLOPES ROUND THE HEAVENS IN ONE SMOOTH CURVE   172 19
STRANGE SHEER SLOPES AND WHITE LEVELS   261 9
SLOPES   300 25
CLIMBING THE SLOPES   301 16
DOWN BETWEEN THE STEEP SLOPES OF DARKNESS FUCUS-DARK SE+   321 35
BEHOLD ME TROTTING AT EASE BETWIXT THE SLOPES OF THE GO+   409 6
JAGUAR-SPLASHED PUMA-YELLOW LEOPARD-LIVID SLOPES OF   409 24
ON THE VERY SLOPES OF THE MATRIMONIAL MOUNTAIN   541 6
DOWN THE GOLDEN SLOPES TO SUNSET   769 30

SLOPING
HERE IN THE SLOPING SHADOW   227 7

SLOPPY
AT TH' SLOPPY GRAVE AN' 'ER LITTLE NECK SHONE   61 7
WHICH IS ONLY A SLOPPY WAY OF BEING IN LOVE WITH YOURSE+   508 15
AND IT'S NO GOOD MOONING FOR SLOPPY EASE   559 9
DROP YOUR SLOPPY BEHAVIOUR   564 15
AT TH' SLOPPY WET GRAVE AN' 'ER LITTLE NECK SHONE   *911 23

SLOTH
FOR A FAIRY-WIND TO WAKE THEM FROM THEIR SLOTH   *943 13

SLOUCHES
MOST OF HIS TIME THE TIGER PADS AND SLOUCHES IN A BURNI+   496 13

SLOUCHING
SLOUCHING ALONG AWAY BELOW HALF OUT OF SIGHT   338 3

SLOVENLY
OF SLOVENLY WORK THAT THEY HAVE OFFERED ME   74 15
OF SLOVENLY WORK THAT THEY HAVE OFFERED ME   *895 23
OF SLOVENLY WORK THAT THEY HAVE OFFERED ME   *904 12

SLOW
SO SLOW   33 17
WHY IS IT THE LONG SLOW STROKE OF THE MIDNIGHT BELL   63 1
THE RED RANGE HEAVES IN SLOW MAGNETIC REPLY   66 16
THE SNOW DESCENDS AS IF THE SLOW SKY SHOOK   76 14

SLOW
THE HILL IS STEEP ON THE SNOW MY STEPS ARE SLOW   85 15
AS IF FROM THE WOMB THE SLOW MOON RISES AS IF THE TWIN-+   88 18
AND DRAWING THE DARKNESS TOGETHER CRUSH FROM IT A TWILI+   92 19
NOR BE THWARTED IN LIFE'S SLOW STRUGGLE TO UNFOLD THE F+   93 18
THE NIGHT'S SLOW CARE   142 20
THROUGH THE SHROUD OF THE TOWN AS SLOW   142 26
THE FLOOD'S SLOW GAIT   146 9
SLOW BOOM   149 4
ON THE SLOW BUBBLING OF YOUR RHYTHMIC HEART   154 11
MOVED WITH SLOW FEET AND HER EYES' FLAME STEADILY BURNED   156 10
SLOW TRAINS STEAL PAST   169 3
DOES MY SLOW HEART REBEL DO MY DEAD HANDS   195 6
SO ON WITH THE SLOW MEAN JOURNEY   201 13
NO CHILD AND NO PALFREY SLOW   202 22
TO DRAW THE LOAD SO STILL AND SLOW IT MOVES   225 15
WHERE THE SLOW TOADS SAT BROODING ON THE PAST   310 15
SLOW TOADS AND CYCLAMEN LEAVES   310 16
SLOW WATERY ROTTING BACK TO LEVEL MUCK   318 2
A LIVING FOREHEAD WITH ITS SLOW WHORL OF HAIR   325 27
PROCEEDED TO DRAW HIS SLOW LENGTH CURVING ROUND   350 31
SLOW ONE   352 17
AND MOVE ON YOUR SLOW SOLITARY HUNT   352 19
UNDER ITS SLOW LID TINY BABY TORTOISE   352 22
EXCEPT THAT YOU MAKE SLOW AGELESS PROGRESS   352 31
IN THE SLOW DIGNITY OF YOUR ETERNAL PAUSE   354 9
FULFILLED OF THE SLOW PASSION OF PITCHING THROUGH IMMEM+   354 12
THIS SLOW ONE   356 18
HE VEERS ROUND THE SLOW GREAT MOUND OF HER   356 29
TO ROAM AND FEEL THE SLOW HEART BEAT   358 12
SLOW AND UNQUESTIONED   358 16
WANDERING IN THE SLOW TRIUMPH OF HIS OWN EXISTENCE   358 18
HEART-THROB SLOW HEART-THROB PERSISTENT FOR THE NEXT   365 27
AND WENT WHIZZING THROUGH THE SLOW VAST SUCCULENT   372 12
I BELIEVE HE PIERCED THE SLOW VEGETABLE VEINS WITH HIS +   372 17
AS HE CHARGES SLOW AMONG THE HERD   380 17
THE SLOW BEAST CURIOUSLY SPREADING HIS ROUND FEET FOR T+   387 12
THE ELEPHANT BELLS STRIKING SLOW TONG-TONG TONG-TONG   387 33
PERPETUAL FIRE-LAUGHING MOTION AMONG THE SLOW SHUFFLE   389 18
GOES OFF IN SLOW SAD LEAPS   393 26
WITH WHAT SHADOW-LIKE SLOW CAREFULNESS   426 16
AND MOVING ALWAYS WITH A SOFT SLOW PRECISION   445 15
INTO SLOW DEATH   456 11
LIKE THE FLAME OF A CANDLE SLOW AND QUICK   460 7
IS SLOW TO MATE   465 8
SOFT SLOW SYMPATHY   471 1
THE WONDERFUL SLOW FLOWING OF THE SAPPHIRE   476 26
THAT IS THE CRYSTAL OF PEACE THE SLOW HARD JEWEL OF TRU+   477 17
AND THE SMALL HAWK HIGH UP TURNS ROUND ON THE SLOW PIVO+   496 14
SLOW CREEPING COLD ONES   511 12
AND THE SLOW COLD FLAMES   511 15
ARE LONG SLOW VIBRATIONS OF PAIN   627 18
THE GREAT GRIND OF UNWILLINGNESS THE SLOW UNDERGRIND OF+   648 10
AND SLOW MOUNTING MARVEL OF A LITTLE TREE   667 18
IN SOFT SEPTEMBER AT SLOW SAD MICHAELMAS   697 2
THROUGH THE SLOW CORRUPTIVE LEVELS OF DISINTEGRATIVE KN+   699 22
A SLOW HEAVY PATTER OF LESSENING VIBRATION   767 20
SLOW SLOW FUNGOID CLAMMILY DECAY   784 28
THE SLOW WAY NOT THE SWIFT   784 29
AND WHERE WITH THE SLOW PATIENCE OF INTUITION   833 25
ALONG WHERE MY SLOW FEET NEVER TRODE   857 11
SLOW INFIRM DEATH HAS AT LAST GATHERED UP THE WASTE   859 21
BY A SLOW GASPING PUMP THAT HAS AWFUL INTERVALS   878 34
HEAR RE-ECHO YOUR SLOW RELUCTANT FEET   880 16
SLOW CATTLE STIR ON THE STEEP MEADOW NEAR BY   886 28
SILVER SLOW GOES BY THE RIVER   887 26
SO SLOW   *891 19
ALL THE SLOW SCHOOL HOURS ROUND THE IRREGULAR HUM OF TH+   *897 20
ALL THE SLOW SCHOOL HOURS ROUND THE IRREGULAR HUM OF TH+   *900 28
STRONG AND SLOW I LIKE TO SEE SAID SHE   *934 17
IN SOFT SEPTEMBER AT SLOW SAD MICHAELMAS   *955 26
SLOW SLOW MY SOUL IN HIS LITTLE SHIP   *959 9

SLOW-BLOODED
SLOW-BLOODED ICY-FLESHED PORTENTOUS   271 16

SLOW-BREATHING
SLOW-BREATHING SEA   860 3

SLOW-DRAGGING
AND SET FORWARD SLOW-DRAGGING ON YOUR FOUR-PINNED TOES   352 27

SLOWER
FLYING SLOWER   345 14
AS FLOWERS ARE AND WE ARE ONLY SLOWER   476 25
TIME WAS MUCH SLOWER WHEN THE ROCKS CAME FORTH   477 4

SLOWLY
AND SLOWLY BACK IN MY BLOOD   37 20
SLOWLY ROTATE TILL THEY TOUCH THE TREE   52 5
THE CLOUDS ARE PUSHING IN GREY RELUCTANCE SLOWLY NORTHW+   57 10
SLOWLY THE MOON IS RISING OUT OF THE RUDDY HAZE   67 9
DIM SELF THAT RISES SLOWLY TO LEAVES AND THE FLOWER'S G+   92 20
IS HEAVY AND MY HEART BEATS SLOWLY LABORIOUSLY   95 2
THROUGH INVISIBLE PULSES SLOWLY FILLING THE NIGHT'S DAR+   97 28
AS SLOWLY THE HOUSE OF DAY IS CLOSING ITS EASTERN SHUTT+   102 28
AND SLOWLY ALL THE BLOSSOM SHUTS IN PAIN   113 13
TWO BROWN PONIES TROTTING SLOWLY   121 28
SLOWLY INTO ANOTHER DAY SLOWLY THE ROVER   132 29
ON THE OUTER PAVEMENT SLOWLY   146 17
WAVING SLOWLY BEFORE ME PUSHED INTO THE DARK   147 1
OF MY BODY SLOWLY BEHIND   147 3
SLOWLY BEGIN TO PLASH   149 28
THE NIGHT TURNS SLOWLY ROUND   169 1
OF A DAY'S EXPERIENCE SLEEP DOES SLOWLY DRAW   195 2
THAT SLOWLY LABOURS IN A VAST TRAVAIL   195 33
OVERHANGS THE STREET WHERE THE BULLOCK-WAGONS SLOWLY   209 16
AND SLOWLY DOWN THE MOUNTAIN ROAD BELATED   225 9

SLOWLY
  SLOWLY ABOVE THE STREET   253 8
  UNFOLD SLOWLY UPWARDS BLOOD-DARK   302 17
  VEERING SLOWLY   321 34
  AND LASHED HIS TAIL SLOWLY SLOWLY   324 7
  SLOWLY TO GAPE THROUGH THE WATERS   336 26
  FISH-BLOOD SLOWLY RUNNING NEXT TO THE FLOOD EXTRACTING   336 31
  AND SLOWLY TURNED HIS HEAD   350 29
  AND SLOWLY VERY SLOWLY AS IF THRICE ADREAM   350 30
  AND AS HE SLOWLY DREW UP SNAKE-EASING HIS SHOULDERS AND   351 2
  DELIBERATELY GOING INTO THE BLACKNESS AND SLOWLY DRAWING   351 6
  YOU DRAW YOUR HEAD FORWARD SLOWLY FROM YOUR LITTLE   352 25
  ROWING SLOWLY FORWARD   352 28
  DO YOU WONDER AT THE WORLD AS SLOWLY YOU TURN YOUR   353 10
  AND SLOWLY PITCHING ITSELF AGAINST THE INERTIA   353 19
  AND YOU ARE SLOWLY MOVING PIONEER YOU ALONE   354 3
  OF THAT MUD-HOVEL OF HIS SLOWLY RAMBLING SPOUSE   361 14
  AS SHE MOVES ETERNALLY SLOWLY AWAY   363 7
  FLY SLOWLY AWAY WITH A RUST OF FIRE IN YOUR TAIL   374 30
  SLOWLY REVOLVING TOWARDS UNEXPLODED EXPLOSION   381 18
  SLOWLY SAILING IN GORGEOUS APPAREL THROUGH THE FLAME-LI+   387 30
  AND THE SPARSE-HAIRED ELEPHANTS SLOWLY FOLLOWING   389 34
  I GO SLOWLY   409 11
  TO ANOTHER BALANCE TRIPPED ROUND POISED AND SLOWLY SANK   444 30
  SLOWLY SLOWLY TO ROUSE   465 12
  SO SLOWLY THE GREAT HOT ELEPHANT HEARTS   465 19
  TOUCH COMES SLOWLY IF EVER IT SEEPS   470 25
  SLOWLY UP IN THE BLOOD OF MEN   470 26
  AND HE CAN ONLY SLOWLY DIE   474 31
  FOR A DAY FOR TWO DAYS AND WITHDRAW SLOWLY VANISH AGAIN   476 14
  SLOWLY A GEM FORMS IN THE ANCIENT ONCE-MORE-MOLTEN   477 13
  SLOWLY THE SALT OF THE EARTH BECOMES SALT OF THE SEA   495 1
  SLOWLY THE RAINDROPS OF APPRECIATION   495 2
  SLOWLY THE SALT OF THE EARTH BECOMES SALT OF THE SEA   495 9
  I SHALL SLOWLY RESURRECT   513 12
  AND SLOWLY FEEL YOURSELF DROWN   551 5
  IN ITS MUD AND ITS TALK SLOWLY SWIRLED   551 6
  THE THING TO DO IS IN SOLITUDE SLOWLY AND PAINFULLY PUT   610 16
  THE WHOLE GREAT HEAVENS HAVE SHIFTED OVER AND SLOWLY PU+   616 23
  THEY MOVE IN A GREAT GRIND OF HATE SLOWLY BUT INEVITABLY   648 7
  AND WHO NOW DRAWS SLOWLY AWAY COLD THE WISTFUL GODDESS +   675 18
  AND GOES SLOWLY DOWN THE HILL   687 14
  PAUSES NEAR THE CREST OF THE HILL CLIMBING SLOWLY LIKE +   687 17
  HE CAME IN SLOWLY AND SAT DOWN BY THE HEARTH   692 13
  NOW TURNED AND CAME SLOWLY BACK WITH HER BACK TO THE EV+   693 7
  WITH THE FULL THIGHS SLOWLY LIFTING OF THE WADER WADING+   693 10
  OH YOU WHO WALK SO SLOWLY AND MAKE ME   762 5
  TO BLANCH SLOWLY   766 20
  IT DRIPS SLOWLY AWAY   767 12
  SLOWLY INSIDIOUSLY INTO NEW PLACES   768 12
  WALKING SLOWLY WESTWARDS HOUSELESS   770 4
  AS HE SLOWLY WALKS FROM THE WESTERN DOOR TO THE WORLD   770 14
  SLOWLY THE WINGS OF DAY ARE EDDYING LOWER   855 27
  SLOWLY ROTATE TILL THEY TOUCH THE TREE   *899 19
  AND SLOWLY FINGERING UP MY STEM AND FOLLOWING ALL TINILY   *900 18
  SLOWLY ROTATE TILL THEY TOUCH THE TREE   *902 31
  AND SLOWLY FINGERING UP MY STEM AND FOLLOWING ALL TINILY   *903 30
  AND SILENCE ISSUES SLOWLY FROM THE HUSK   *929 11

SLOW-STEPPING
  MY HEART DISTURBED IN ITS DREAM SLOW-STEPPING ALARMS   *937 32

SLOW-SWIFTNESS
  ADVANCING WITH THE SLOW-SWIFTNESS OF A SHIP BACKING HER+   672 21

SLUDGED
  AS 'AS SLUDGED LIKE A HORSE ALL 'ER LIFE   77 18
  AS HAS SLUDGED LIKE A HORSE ALL HER LIFE   *919 6

SLUGGISH
  IN SLUGGISH VENICE   332 10

SLUICE
  CONSTRAINED TO POUR FORTH ALL HIS FIRE DOWN THE NARROW +   327 11
  YOUR LIFE A SLUICE OF SENSATION ALONG YOUR SIDES   335 8

SLUICES
  LIFTING AND FALLING LONG GASPS THROUGH THE SLUICES LIKE+   97 26

SLUICING
  FOR THE SLUICING OF THEIR RAIN-DISHEVELLED PETALS   217 22

SLUMBER
  SLUMBER BENEATH   172 17

SLUMBERING
  MY SOFT SLUMBERING BELLY   39 7
  A BLADE ON THE WHEEL THEN THE SLUMBERING NIGHT   773 4
  AND MY SOFT SLUMBERING BELLY   *893 20
  SENDING INTO ITS SLUMBERING FLESH   *937 16

SLUMBEROUS
  RHYTHM STARTS AND MY SILENT AND SLUMBEROUS BELLY   39 5
  NAY EVEN THE SLUMBEROUS EGG AS IT LABOURS UNDER THE SHE+   64 11

SLUNG
  THE MIDNIGHT SHADOW SINKING DOWN HAS SLUNG   750 9

SLUSH
  ARE AN AMAZING PUTRESCENT SLUSH   830 18

SLUSHY
  FULL INSIDE OF WEIRD BROWN SLUSHY CRAB-MEAT   830 20

SLY
  THE SLY BIRD OF JOHN   329 2
  AND SEE WHO WINS IN THIS SLY GAME OF BLUFF   333 8
  OR EVEN THE SLY GOLD SERPENT FATHERLY LIFTED HIS HEAD O+   437 18
  TRUTHS THAT THE SLY TROT OUT   458 19
  AND SLY WITH A LOT OF AFTER-THOUGHT   556 11

SMACK
  THOUGH EVEN THE WORD MARSALA WILL SMACK OF PRECIOSITY   280 11

SMALL-BOSOMED
  SMALL-BOSOMED GIRLS OF THE SPRING OF LOVE   179 17

SMALL-BOY'S
  AND FINDS THAT THE SUBTLE DESTRUCTIVE CYNICISM IS ONLY +   842 2

SMALLER
  HIGH AND SMALLER GOES THE MOON SHE IS SMALL AND VERY FA+   67 13
  HE IS MUCH SMALLER   359 30
  AND SMALLER MORE FRIGHTENED ELEPHANTS   389 4
  A MAGISTRATE AND SIX FAT SMALLER FRY   633 15
  SIX FAT SMALLER BOBBIES ARE THE INQUISITORS MINOR   633 16

SMALLEST
  JEALOUS OF THE SMALLEST COVER   95 12

SMALLNESS
  ASIDE TO LOSE MYSELF FOR VERY SMALLNESS I   876 7

SMART
  LEAVING A BURN AND AN UGLY SMART   151 9
  A SLIM YOUNG PIKE WITH SMART FINS   338 1
  WHERE SMART MEN WOULD DISPENSE   488 24
  DOSES OF SMART CASH-CHEMISTRY   488 25
  GULPING UP SCIENCE'S SMART ARMADA   824 11
  O SO SMART AND SO MECHANICALLY FINISHED   845 23
  THERE FOR THE HEAT OF IT CAUSES A SMART   863 19
  LEAVING A BURN AND A SMART   873 19
  FOR IT GAVE THE SMART   *897 18
  THE CARES AND THE RESTLESS SMART   *936 4

SMARTIES
  BUT IT IS HARD TO BE TOLERANT WITH THE SMARTIES   499 16

SMASH
  WITH A SMASH   289 15
  SMASH   289 18
  AND SO IT WILL BE AGAIN MEN WILL SMASH THE MACHINES   451 20
  FOR AFTER ALL HE HELPED TO SMASH A LOT OF OLD ROMAN LIES   497 3
  SMASH THEM UP THE SMOOTHED-FACED FAT-FACED PLAUSIBLES   765 29
  SMASH IT IN LIKE A FRAIL VESSEL   869 23
  IT WILL BE SO AGAIN FOR MAN WILL SMASH ALL HIS MACHINES+   *950 6

SMASHED
  SMASHED ALL OOZING WITH BLOOD AND BURNED IN HEAPS   258 3
  AMONG ALL THE SMASHED DEBRIS OF MYSELF   514 6

SMASHES
  LET EVERYTHING GO AS THE WAVE SMASHES US   514 7

SMASHING
  FOR THE RIPPING OF ARRAS AND SMASHING OF WALLS AND THE +   174 15
  OF THE ANCIENT CAVE SMASHING INTO ONE ANOTHER   544 15
  BUT OF COURSE THIS MEANS SMASHING THE PRESENT SYSTEM OF+   837 27

SMEAR
  BESIDE THE INFINITESIMAL FAINT SMEAR OF YOU   334 17

SMEARED
  WHO SMEARED THEIR DOORS WITH BLOOD   313 19

SMEARING
  OF ALL THOSE NASTY POLICE-EYES LIKE SNAIL-TRACKS SMEARI+   580 21

SMELL
  AND CARESSES ME WITH HIS FINGERS THAT STILL SMELL GRIM   43 27
  AN' WARM FOR TH' SMELL COME WAFTIN' TO ME 'ER PUT 'ER F+   61 13
  I CAN SMELL THE BOG-END GORGEOUS IN ITS BREATHLESS   90 7
  OF A ROSE-TREE MOVE TO ROSES AND THORNS AND A DELICATE +   176 9
  THIS BOUNDLESS LOVE IS LIKE THE BAD SMELL   291 17
  JUST A BAD SMELL   291 21
  THE ROSE WOULD SMELL AS SWEET   292 3
  SMELL 'EM SMELL 'EM OUT   309 8
  AND THE SMELL OF HORSES AND OTHER BEASTS   444 13
  INSTEAD OF MERELY THE SMELL OF MAN   444 14
  YOU MAY SMELL THE BREATH OF THE GODS IN THE COMMON ROSES   655 7
  LIKE A BAD SMELL   687 11
  NOR THE SMELL OF MIGNONETTE   690 21
  TO SMELL AT THE MIGNONETTE   690 24
  AND DEATH IS ON THE AIR LIKE A SMELL OF ASHES   717 5
  AH CAN'T YOU SMELL IT   717 6
  US A LITTLE WIFT AN' I KNEW THE SMELL   *910 19
  O' TH' SMELL COME WAFTIN' TO ME 'ER PUT 'ER FACE   *911 29

SMELLING
  ON SMELLING IT ALL BEFORE YOUR BIT OF VITALITY SPENT IS   462 34

SMELLS
  IT SMELLS OF BURNING SNOW OF HOT-ACHE   270 18
  SAP THAT SMELLS STRANGE ON YOUR FINGERS THAT EVEN GOATS+   283 12
  AND HE SMELLS SO RANK AND HIS NOSE GOES BACK   382 29
  IT SMELLS STRANGE LIKE THE SHOUTING OF MEN   759 2
  THIS FLESH THAT SMELLS   792 26

SMELLY
HOW SMELLY THEY MAKE THE GREAT BACK-YARD   493 27

SMELTED
SMELTED PURE   372 2

SMELTING
MY BELOVED SMELTING DOWN IN THE BLAZE   103 18

SMILE
HIS STRONG TEETH IN A SMILE AND FLASHES HIS EYES   43 20
IN A SMILE LIKE TRIUMPH UPON ME THEN CARELESS-WISE   43 21
AND SITS WITH A SMOOTH BLAND SMILE UP THERE IN THE SKY   54 12
AND I SMILE   71 23
I STAND AND SMILE   71 29
THE WAKING SMILE OF HER EYES   121 22
THE SMILE THE SUBTLE ETRUSCAN SMILE STILL LURKING   297 22
NAY LEONARDO ONLY BUNGLED THE PURE ETRUSCAN SMILE   297 26
YOU TURN YOUR HEAD TOWARDS YOUR TAIL AND SMILE   332 11
AND WE SMILE FOOLISHLY AS IF WE DIDN'T KNOW   401 21
THE INDIAN SMILE   404 4
THE WRINKLED SMILE OF COMPLETENESS THAT FOLLOWS A LIFE   503 17
AND EAT AND CACHINNATE AND EVEN SEEM TO SMILE   644 19
SEEM TO SMILE YE GODS   644 20
SLIM NAKED MEN FROM CNOSSOS SMILING THE ARCHAIC SMILE   688 13
THE SMILE OF THE LEOPARD AND THE MEADOW-LARK   770 12
THE KNOWING SMILE OF THE FINAL VIRGIN IN MAN   770 13
LOOKED UP AND THE WORDS MOVED LIKE A SMILE FROM HIS LIPS   865 3
SMILE   865 15

SMILED
BOWED AND LIFTED HER FOOT IN HER HAND SMILED SWUNG HER   444 28
WHEN SHE ROSE TILTING HER PARASOL AND SMILED AT THE   445 1
ENTERED ME I SMILED TO MYSELF SAYING HE IS GOD   692 16

SMILES
KIND ON THE WEIGHT OF SUFFERING SMILES AGAIN   113 16
AND THE MOON SIGNIFICANT SMILES AT THE CLIFFS AND THE   130 3
AND PRESSING THE SMALL POISED FEET OF A MOTHER WHO SMIL+   148 8
SO THAT THE FAITH IN HIS HEART SMILES AGAIN   306 1
HE SMILES FOOLISHLY AS IF HE WERE CAUGHT DOING WRONG   401 20
AND SMILES THE VASTNESS OF HER ELEPHANT ANTIQUITY   426 6
AND SMILES AT MY FURTIVE SHADOW   731 11
PRESSING THE LITTLE POISED FEET OF THE MOTHER WHO SMILE+   *940 8

SMILING
SERENELY SMILING AT NAUGHT   54 13
IN TEDIUM AND MOUTH RELAXED AS IF SMILING INEFFABLE TED+   66 12
THINK TO STAND THERE IN FULL-UNFOLDED NUDITY SMILING   306 17
WHILE SHE WITH HER GOATY MOUTH STANDS SMILING THE WHILE   382 18
SHE SMILING WITH GOATY MUNCH-MOUTH MONA LISA ARRANGES   382 26
HE TRAPPED HER THIS MORNING HE SAYS SMILING FOOLISHLY   401 26
COME TALL OLD DEMONS SMILING   404 3
DON'T EVER BE KIND TO THE SMILING TOOTH-MOUTHED DEAD   441 32
SLIM NAKED MEN FROM CNOSSOS SMILING THE ARCHAIC SMILE   688 13
WITH FACES IN SHADOW BUT SMILING   770 11
AND SMILING CURIOUSLY WITH WATCHFUL EYES   878 13
AND CURIOUS SMILING EYES   878 18

SMILINGLY
THE SEA HAS ITS BUD-LIPS SMILINGLY CURLED   814 26

SMITE
AS SOME SHOULD HA'E HARDLY A SMITE O' TROUBLE   45 23
AND I WANT TO SMITE IN ANGER THE BARREN ROCK OF EACH WA+   57 30
MADE TO SMITE THE WATERS BEHIND IT   438 30
OF THOSE THAT CAN USE IT SMITE WITH IT   843 6

SMITES
AS THE LEOPARD SMITES THE SMALL CALF WITH A SPANGLED PA+   683 9

SMITING
TOWARDS A SHOCK AND A CRASH AND A SMITING OF HORNS AHEAD   381 22
THUS HAMMERING THE METTLE OF GOATS INTO PROOF AND SMITI+   381 28

SMITTEN
UNTIL HER PRIDE'S FLAG SMITTEN CLEAVED DOWN TO THE STAFF   125 18
SMITTEN WITH REVERENT SURPRISE   234 12
I HAVE NEVER YET BEEN SMITTEN THROUGH THE BELLY WITH THE   263 9
THE SWAN WILL LIFT UP AGAIN HIS FLATTENED SMITTEN HEAD   625 2
YOU WHO CAME BEFORE ROCK WAS SMITTEN INTO WEEPING   783 10

SMOCK-RAVELLED
THA ART SMOCK-RAVELLED BUNNY   78 29
THA ART SMOCK-RAVELLED BUNNY   *920 21

SMOKE
IN THE FLAPPING OF RED-ROOF SMOKE AND THE SMALL   68 22
WHEREIN WE FAINTED LIKE A SMOKE OR DEW   90 30
THORN-BLOSSOM LIFTING IN WREATHS OF SMOKE BETWEEN   116 3
NOT EVEN PALISH SMOKE LIKE THE REST OF THE THRONG   116 12
IN THE SHADY SMOKE   131 16
GOING UP IN A FOETID SMOKE TO GET RID OF THEM   258 4
SMOKE THAT ROLLS   258 11
OF MANY-STEMMED MACHINES AND CHIMNEYS THAT SMOKE LIKE   293 3
WHAT VOICE OF THE LORD IS THAT FROM THE TREE OF SMOKE   375 15
IS LEAVING A LONG THREAD OF DARK SMOKE   687 10
THE BITTER WORLD AMID THE SMOKE   744 23
THROUGH SMOKE THROUGH SMOKINESS   769 4
THEY PUT UP TALL CHIMNEYS THAT SMOKE   793 23
DON RAMON DON'T DRINK DON'T SMOKE   797 13
SO THAT WITHIN A PILLAR OF PURPLE SMOKE   881 11
IN THE FLAPPING RED-ROOF SMOKE AND THE SMALL   *915 6
STREAM GOLDEN SMOKE   *916 20

SMOKED
IF YOU HAVEN'T SMOKED THEM ALL   540 28

SMOKELESS
SMOKELESS HOUSELESS HOMELESS   768 28

SMOKE-PUFFS
OF GROWING THESE SMOKE-PUFFS THAT PUFF IN WILD GYRATION   116 8

SMOKES
TILL ALL YOUR BEING SMOKES WITH FINE DESIRE   219 4
EARTH SMOKES BLUE   467 8

SMOKE-SODDEN
AND I AM DEAD AND TRODDEN TO NOUGHT IN THE SMOKE-SODDEN   258 14

SMOKE-WAVES
AND ROOKS AND THE RISING SMOKE-WAVES SCATTER AND WHEEL   148 22

SMOKE-WREATHS
TO-DAY A THICKET OF SUNSHINE WITH BLUE SMOKE-WREATHS   72 15

SMOKINESS
THROUGH SMOKE THROUGH SMOKINESS   769 4

SMOKING
ON THE DAY OF SICILIAN JULY WITH ETNA SMOKING   349 28
HIGH HIGH FLAMBEAUX SMOKING OF THE EAST   388 29
WHAT DO I CARE IF THE SMOKING SHIPS   688 6
DARKENING THE DAY-TIME TORCH-LIKE WITH THE SMOKING BLUE+ 697 4
DARKENING THE DAYTIME TORCH-LIKE WITH THE SMOKING BLUEN+ *956 2
BLACK LAMPS FROM THE HALLS OF DIS SMOKING DARK BLUE   *956 7

SMOKY
WHEN YOU PICK THE RED SMOKY HEART FROM A RABBIT OR A   374 5
AND FEAR IN THE SMOKY WHITES OF YOUR EYES YOU NIGGER   400 26
BUT OVER THE MIDDLE OF THE EARTH WILL BE THE SMOKY RUIN+ 625 8

SMOOTH
AND SITS WITH A SMOOTH BLAND SMILE UP THERE IN THE SKY   54 12
IS SMOOTH AND FAIR   101 8
SLEEP-SUAVE LIMBS OF A YOUTH WITH LONG SMOOTH THIGHS   145 18
SLOPES ROUND THE HEAVENS IN ONE SMOOTH CURVE   172 19
THOSE SHOULDERS SO WARM AND SMOOTH I FEEL THAT I   245 18
IS NOT SO FRIGHTENING AS THAT CLEAN SMOOTH   290 27
MADE OF THICK SMOOTH SILVER   298 20
UNDER A SMOOTH SKIN AND AN UPRIGHT APPEARANCE   431 21
SMOOTH RUN   531 17
OH YOU GODLY AND SMOOTH MACHINE SPINNING ON IN YOUR   643 19
SMOOTH OCEAN WHERE THE FISHES REST ON EDGE   652 10
SHE LEANS FORWARD HER SMOOTH PALE FACE   731 10

SMOOTHED-FACED
THE SMOOTHED-FACED FAT-HAMMED FUNGUSSY FAT ONE   765 24
SMASH THEM UP THE SMOOTHED-FACED FAT-FACED PLAUSIBLES   765 29

SMOOTH-FLESHED
THICK SMOOTH-FLESHED SILVER DULL ONLY AS HUMAN LIMBS ARE 298 23

SMOOTHLY
THOUGH NOT SO SMOOTHLY SPOKEN   575 17

SMOOTHNESS
YOUR YOUTHFUL SMOOTHNESS I FLEECED WHERE FLEECE WAS NONE 156 26

SMOOTH-ROUNDED
WE ARE ONE SMOOTH-ROUNDED   117 7

SMOOTHS
WHO IS IT SMOOTHS THE BED-SHEETS LIKE THE COOL   652 9

SMOTE
A PALE STROKE SMOTE   165 12

SMOTHER
NOT SMOTHER   93 21
OR I'LL SMOTHER THEM ALL   792 3
I'LL SEND FIRE AND ASHES UPON THEM AND SMOTHER THEM ALL 792 5

SMOTHERED
THE SUN FROM THEIR NEIGHBOUR EITHER NOR BE SMOTHERED IN+ 93 22
AND LET THE LIGHTNING OUT OF YOUR SMOTHERED DUSK   383 19

SMOULDER
JUST ORTS AND SLARTS BERRIES THAT SMOULDER IN THE BUSH 219 15

SMOULDERING
SMOULDERING WITH DARKENED BUSBIES BENEATH THE BAYONETS'+ 66 8
A SODOM SMOULDERING IN THE DENSE SOILED AIR   72 14
NOW VERDIGRIS SMOULDERING SOFTLY SPREAD   142 25
AND IN HIS BELLY THE SMOULDERING HATE OF ME   226 8
UPON THE SMOULDERING AIR   317 10
IT IS VERY UNNERVING MOVING IN A WORLD OF SMOULDERING   539 4
FROM BURNING FIRES OF MANY SMOULDERING LIVES   744 24

SMUDGE
QUEER WHAT A DIM DARK SMUDGE YOU HAVE DISAPPEARED   334 18

SMUG
YET THE MOMENT I HATE HER SHE TRIPS MILD AND SMUG LIKE A 385 12

SMUSH
AND TRAMPLED ALL THE LISTENERS TO A SMUSH   540 6

SNAIL
   AND CRAWL AWAY LIKE A BLACK SNAIL   400 11
   MEN MIGHT PUT THEM FORTH AS A SNAIL ITS SHELL AS A BIRD+   451 12

SNAIL-NACREOUS
   SNAIL-NACREOUS   310 24

SNAILS
   PICKS UP ITS SEEDS OR LITTLE SNAILS   443 13

SNAIL-TRACKS
   OF ALL THOSE NASTY POLICE-EYES LIKE SNAIL-TRACKS SMEARI+   580 21

SNAKE
   FOR MY HAND LIKE A SNAKE WATCHED HERS THAT COULD NOT FLY   125 24
   LIKE A SNAKE WE THRESH ON THE LONG FORLORN   163 19
   LET IT BE AS THE SNAKE DISPOSES   217 1
   OUT OF THEIR COVERS LIKE ANY SNAKE   254 15
   WALKING LIKE A ROYAL SNAKE DOWN THE MOUNTAIN   293 20
   THAT KNOWS THE DEADLIEST POISON LIKE A SNAKE   304 10
   A SNAKE CAME TO MY WATER-TROUGH   349 1
   AND I WISHED HE WOULD COME BACK MY SNAKE   351 23
   FOOT IN THE MOUTH OF AN UP-STARTING SNAKE   365 31
   AND REACHES HER BLACK-STRIPED FACE UP LIKE A SNAKE FAR +   385 26
   STEERED AND PROPELLED BY THAT STEEL-STRONG SNAKE OF A T+   393 28
   A STILL BRIGHTER WHITE SNAKE WRIGGLES AMONG IT SPILLED   647 14
   THE PATH LIKE A SNAKE THAT IS GONE LIKE THE LENGTH OF A   788 11
   I AM QUETZALCOATL OF THE EAGLE AND THE SNAKE   800 36
   OUT OF THE BOWELS OF THE EARTH LIKE A SNAKE   801 7
   THE ROOTS ARE MINE DOWN THE DARK MOIST PATH OF THE SNAKE   801 16
   THE SNAKE OF MY LEFT-HAND OUT OF THE DARKNESS IS KISSIN+   801 22
   FOR I AM QUETZALCOATL THE FEATHERED SNAKE   801 27
   THE SNAKE HAS KISSED MY HEEL   802 23
   AND I KEPT THE CHOKED SNAKE FLOWER IN ITS PANGS   *936 15
   AND MY HAND LIKE A SNAKE WATCHED HERS THAT COULD NOT FLY   *936 23

SNAKE-BITES
   WITH SNAKE-BITES OF TANGLED UNCONSCIOUS EMOTION   833 31

SNAKE-EASING
   AND AS HE SLOWLY DREW UP SNAKE-EASING HIS SHOULDERS AND   351 2

SNAKE-LIKE
   SNAKE-LIKE SHE DRAWS AT MY FINGER WHILE I DRAG IN HORROR   359 26

SNAKE-MARKS
   BUT IN THE ODD PATTERN LIKE SNAKE-MARKS ON THE SAND   448 26

SNAKES
   LIKE THE SNAKES ON MEDUSA'S HEAD   300 10
   AND LONG SNAKES QUICKLY GLIDE INTO THE DARK HOLE IN THE+   321 24
   EVEN SNAKES LIE TOGETHER   335 13
   FOR IN SICILY THE BLACK BLACK SNAKES ARE INNOCENT THE G+   350 3
   WHERE NOTHING BITES BUT INSECTS AND SNAKES AND THE SUN   394 14
   LIKE SNAKES OF HATE AGAINST THE MAN IN THE MACHINE   624 17
   STRANGLING ON ONE ANOTHER LIKE SNAKES   833 28

SNAKE-TANGLE
   WE CAN UNCOIL THE GHASTLY SNAKE-TANGLE OF OUR UNCONSCIO+   833 26

SNAP
   AS THEIR NERVES ARE STRETCHED TILL THEY TWANGLE AND SNAP   616 8

SNAPDRAGON
   THE SNAPDRAGON PUT OUT HIS TONGUE AT ME   *934 18

SNAP-DRAGON
   THE SNAP-DRAGON PUT OUT HIS TONGUE AT ME   123 12

SNAPPED
   SNAPPED SUDDEN OUT OF ALL   *911 10

SNAPPING
   ALL THE SPORT OF SUMMER AND SPRING AND FLOWERS SNAPPING   309 18
   SNAPPING OUT OF FEAR   535 18

SNAPS
   HE SNAPS WHEN I OFFER HIM HIS OFFSPRING   357 12
   JUST AS HE SNAPS WHEN I POKE A BIT OF STICK AT HIM   357 13
   SHE SNAPS THE SOFT BREAD FROM MY HAND IN GREAT MOUTHFULS   359 1
   AND SNAPS THEM SHARP WITH A LITTLE TWIST OF HER ANACONDA   385 28

SNARE
   OF THE RABBIT'S FUR GOD I AM CAUGHT IN A SNARE   43 28
   IN A PURITAN FILLET A CHASTE WHITE SNARE   178 9
   LIKE A SNARE   813 4

SNARLING
   WITH SNARLING RED JAWS AND I HEARD THE CRIES   38 10
   WITH RED SNARLING JAWS LET YOURSELF LISTEN TO THE CRIES   *892 25

SNATCH
   FOR A MOMENT THE MIGHTY DIRECTION SNATCH   68 27
   A YELL OF TRIUMPH AS YOU SNATCH MY SCALP   333 24
   THEY DO NOT SNATCH THEY DO NOT TEAR   465 27
   SWAYING I SNATCH AND LOOT   861 7

SNATCHES
   AND STILL AMONG IT ALL SNATCHES OF LOVELY OBLIVION AND +   727 22

SNATCHING
   MAKES IN ITS SNATCHING   334 9

SNEAKING
   SNEAKING COURT OF RAVENNA   497 5
   OF SNEAKING EXULTANCE   500 6
   IT IS A SNEAKING EVASION OF THE RESPONSIBILITY   621 13

SNEAK-THIEFED
   BUT MY GOD THEY SNEAK-THIEFED HIS VERY GENITALS AWAY FR+   659 15

SNEAK-THIEF
   AND MOST LOVE-AFFAIRS JUST SNEAK-THIEF POCKET-PICKING   607 22

SNEERED
   OR THEY BOILED AND THEY FUMED IN FURY THEY SNEERED   578 9

SNIFF
   HE DOES NOT LOOK AT HER NOR SNIFF AT HER   362 13
   NO NOT EVEN SNIFF AT HER HIS NOSE IS BLANK   362 14
   HIS NOSTRILS TURNING BACK TO SNIFF AT EVEN HIMSELF   382 3

SNIFFING
   SNIFFING FOREVER AHEAD OF HIM AT THE REAR OF THE GOATS +   380 21
   YOU CAN'T IMAGINE THE HOLY GHOST SNIFFING AT CHERRY-PIE+   690 25

SNIFFS
   WHO SNIFFS WITH JOY BEFORE HE DRINKS THE BLOOD   43 32
   SO SHE WISTFULLY SENSITIVELY SNIFFS THE AIR AND THEN TU+   393 25
   SNIFFS ROUND YOUR PLACE   405 10

SNIGGERED
   AND THEY BLUSHED THEY GIGGLED THEY SNIGGERED THEY   578 7

SNORE
   AND THE SNORE OF THE NIGHT IN MY EAR   107 8
   INTERIOR A HOUSE OF DREAMS WHERE THE DREAMERS WRITHE AN+   174 24

SNORING
   SO MEAN AND SELF-CONSCIOUS BLOWING AND SNORING   494 20

SNORTING
   SNORTING DEFIANCE   325 31

SNOT
   PASTY LITTLE SNOT   552 24

SNOUT-FACE
   BUT YOU YOU SNOUT-FACE YOU REJECT NOTHING YOU MERGE SO   399 9

SNOW
   OF A SECOND LIKE SNOW THAT SLIPS   62 10
   A MOMENT THERE LIKE SNOW IN THE DARK   62 13
   HOW DIFFERENT IN THE MIDST OF SNOW THE GREAT SCHOOL RIS+   75 7
   AND LAID THE DESERT HORRIFIC OF SILENCE AND SNOW ON THE+   75 16
   MUFFLING MY MIND AS SNOW MUFFLES THE SOUNDS THAT PASS   75 22
   THE THICK SNOW IS CRUMPLED ON THE ROOF IT PLUNGES DOWN   76 6
   THE SNOW DESCENDS AS IF THE SLOW SKY SHOOK   76 14
   YOU'RE STOUT TO BRAVE THIS SNOW MISS STAINWRIGHT   78 1
   I' TH' SNOW BUT I'S WARRANT THERE   78 31
   IN A' THIS DEPTH O' SNOW   79 14
   YESTERDAY THE FIELDS WERE ONLY GREY WITH SCATTERED SNOW   85 5
   YET HER DEEP FOOTSTEPS MARK THE SNOW AND GO   85 7
   THE HILL IS STEEP ON THE SNOW MY STEPS ARE SLOW   85 15
   LIKE A STORM OF EMERALD SNOW NOW SEE   126 24
   BEYOND THE WITHERING SNOW OF THE SHORN FIELDS   135 6
   T' SNOW IS WITHERIN' OFF'N TH' GRESS   137 18
   T' SNOW IS WITHERIN' OFF'N TH' GRESS   137 20
   AN' MIST IS SUCKIN' AT TH' SPOTS O' SNOW   137 21
   A WHIRL LIKE SNOW FROM THE PLUM-TREES AND THE PEAR   154 30
   OF A SHIP THAT STANDS IN A SHADOWY SEA OF SNOW   155 21
   LIKE ANY FIELD OF SNOW   165 5
   BECAUSE OF THE SILENT SNOW WE ARE ALL HUSHED   165 29
   SNOW OF SALT WHITE BURNING EATING SALT   207 31
   STAND IN THEIR BLUENESS FLASHING WITH SNOW AND THE   209 24
   THE MOUNTAIN'S NEW-DROPPED SUMMER SNOW IS CLEAR   225 2
   WHITE PEAKS OF SNOW AT THE FOOT OF THE SUNKEN CHRIST   225 30
   WHEN SNOW FELL ON THE APPLE-TREES   248 17
   IT SMELLS OF BURNING SNOW OF HOT-ACHE   270 18
   ODD FLAKES AS IF OF SNOW ODD BITS OF SNOW   304 13
   ODD CRUMBS OF MELTING SNOW   304 14
   IN ROSE-HOT TIPS AND FLAKES OF ROSE-PALE SNOW   304 20
   COMES ROUND THE CABIN IN THE SNOW   375 2
   HE RUNS IN THE SNOW LIKE A BIT OF BLUE METAL   375 3
   SNOW   375 11
   OH BIBBLES LITTLE BLACK BITCH IN THE SNOW   375 16
   WITH A PINCH OF SNOW IN THE GROOVE OF YOUR SILLY SNUB N+   375 17
   EVERY DAY SINCE THE SNOW IS HERE   375 22
   AND BOBBING HIS THICK DARK CREST ABOUT THE SNOW AS IF   375 26
   LOBBING WILDLY THROUGH DEEP SNOW LIKE A RABBIT   397 7
   HURTLING LIKE A BLACK BALL THROUGH THE SNOW   397 8
   CLIMBING THROUGH THE JANUARY SNOW INTO THE LOBO CANYON   401 1
   SNOW AND INWARDNESS OF THE LOBO VALLEY   401 13
   TO THE SNOW OF THE SANGRE DE CRISTO MOUNTAINS THE ICE OF   402 23
   AND NEAR ACROSS AT THE OPPOSITE STEEP OF SNOW GREEN TRE+   402 25
   MOTIONLESS STANDING IN SNOW LIKE A CHRISTMAS TOY   402 26
   AND THE WHITE SNOW GLISTENED THE WHITE WORLD WAS GAY   550 29
   AND HOW JOLLY IT WAS WITH US UP IN THE SNOW   551 1
   UP THERE IN THE SNOW   557 21
   UP THERE IN THE SNOW   557 30
   FROM THE HILLS WHERE SNOW MUST HAVE FALLEN THE WIND IS +   696 16
   WITH SNOW   696 17
   WHEN ANAXAGORAS SAYS EVEN THE SNOW IS BLACK   708 12
   THAT ALL THINGS ARE MIXED AND THEREFORE THE PUREST WHIT+   708 15
   AND NONSENSE FOR PURE SNOW IS WHITE TO US   708 19
   FROM OFF THE SHEER WHITE SNOW OR THE POISED MOON   708 27
   AND IN THE SHADOW OF THE SUN THE SNOW IS BLUE SO BLUE-A+   708 28
   LIKE SAYING SNOW IS BLACK OR DESIRE IS EVIL   709 34
   SNOW AND THE SILENCE OF SNOW HEAVY ON THE ROUSING DAY   865 11
   PLEASE SIR I WAS SWEEPING SNOW AN' I NEVER HEARD THE BE+   866 9
   COMING HOME OVER THE WASTE-LANDS WIDE AND LONELY WITH S+   866 16
   MUFFLING MY MIND AS SNOW MUFFLES THE SOUNDS THAT PASS   *897 22
   THE THICK SNOW IS CRUMPLED ON THE ROOF IT PLUNGES DOWN   *898 1
   THE SNOW DESCENDS AS IF THE DULL SKY SHOOK   *898 8
   MUFFLING MY MIND AS SNOW MUFFLES THE SOUNDS THAT PASS   *900 30
   THE THICK SNOW IS CRUMPLED ON THE ROOF IT PLUNGES DOWN   *901 10

SNOW
    THE SNOW DESCENDS AS IF THE DULL SKY SHOOK   *901 17
    PALE LOVE LOST IN A SNOW OF FEAR   *912 21
    YOU'RE STOUT TO BRAVE THIS SNOW MISS STAINWRIGHT   *919 21
    I' TH' SNOW BUT I'S WARANT THEE BUNNY   *920 23
    IN A' THIS DEPTH O' SNOW   *921 10
    BEYOND THE WITHERING SNOW OF THE SHORN FIELDS   *939 6

SNOWBALL
    IN THE PLAYGROUND A SHAGGY SNOWBALL STANDS HUGE AND STI+   76 17
    THE ROUGH SNOWBALL IN THE PLAYGROUND STANDS HUGE AND ST+   *898 11
    THE ROUGH SNOWBALL IN THE PLAYGROUND STANDS HUGE AND ST+   *901 20

SNOW-BERRIES
    AMONG SNOW-BERRIES   134 17

SNOWDROPS
    HERE LAMPS ARE WHITE LIKE SNOWDROPS IN THE GRASS   136 1
    LIKE LAVENDER CROCUSES SNOWDROPS LIKE ROMAN HYACINTHS   270 6
    SNOWDROPS STRAIGHT DEATH-VEINED EXHALATIONS OF WHITE AND   271 6
    I TRAMPLE ON THE SNOWDROPS IT GIVES ME PLEASURE TO TREA+   271 12
    THE LAMPS ARE WHITE LIKE SNOWDROPS IN THE GRASS   *938 29

SNOWED
    THA'S BIN SNOWED UP I' THIS COTTAGE WI' ME   137 25
    THA'S BIN SNOWED UP I' THIS COTTAGE WI' ME   137 27
    IT SNOWED AND HIS HELMET WAS LOST HE FORGOT ME HE DID N+   732 17

SNOW-EDGED
    TO THE GREEN NIGHT-BAYING OF THE DOG-STAR ETNA'S SNOW-E+   306 11

SNOW-LEOPARDS
    AND SPURTING SUDDENLY UP SNOW-WHITE LIKE SNOW-LEOPARDS   454 7

SNOW-REMEMBERING
    FROM THE SNOW-REMEMBERING HEART   305 21

SNOWS
    NIGHT BLENCHED WITH A THOUSAND SNOWS   104 28
    TO GAZE ANY MORE AT THE CHRIST WHOM THE MOUNTAIN SNOWS   225 11
    WITH THE MOUNTAIN SNOWS ACROSS THE LAKE   228 10
    THE SUMMER AND THE SNOWS THE WILD WELTER OF EARTH   707 29
    HOW DIFFERENT IN THE MIDDLE OF SNOWS THE GREAT SCHOOL R+   865 18

SNOW'S
    AND ASLEEP ON THE SNOW'S LAST SHADOW   226 19

SNOW-TOPS
    THE SNOW-TOPS SHINING ROSY   226 14

SNOW-WHITE
    AND SPURTING SUDDENLY UP SNOW-WHITE LIKE SNOW-LEOPARDS   454 7
    THE DRAGON OF THE DISAPPOINTED DEAD THAT SLEEPS IN THE +   795 12

SNOW-WIND
    THE ETNA SNOW-WIND THROUGH THE LONG NIGHT   305 24
    STAR AND THE SNOW-WIND AND THE LONG LONG NIGHTS   305 32
    WITH ALL THE SNOW-WIND AND THE SUN-GLARE AND THE DOG-ST+   306 18

SNOWY
    WE ARE FOLDED TOGETHER MEN AND THE SNOWY GROUND   166 11
    NO SHADOW OF US ON THEIR SNOWY FOREHEAD OF DREAMS   223 24

SNUB
    WITH A PINCH OF SNOW IN THE GROOVE OF YOUR SILLY SNUB N+   375 17

SNUBBED
    SEE HIS BLACK NOSE SNUBBED BACK PRESSED OVER LIKE A WHA+   380 13

SNUB-NOSED
    LITTLE BLACK SNUB-NOSED BITCH WITH A SHOVED-OUT JAW   394 29

SNUFFING
    OR GREEDILY SNUFFING BEHIND THE COWS   325 32

SNUFFIN'
    AFTER LICKIN' AND SNUFFIN' AT ME THA COULD   *922 18

SNUFFS
    AND THE WHITE DOG SNUFFS THE WARMTH APPEALING   41 10

SNUGGLE
    THE WORLD TO SNUGGLE DOWN IN THE WARMTH   394 3

SNUGGLES
    SEE HOW SHE SNUGGLES AGAINST MY NECK   863 1

SOAK
    WHILE HER TEARS SOAK THROUGH TO MY BREAST   64 18
    ARE BORN DEAD THEY ARE SHROUDS THEY SOAK LIFE OUT OF US   448 9

SOAKED
    WHEN HE LIFTS HIS FOOT I SEE THE PAD OF HIS SOAKED STOC+   866 7
    AND DRINKS HIMSELF LIKE A SOAKED GORGED CREATURE DULL   877 9

SOAKS
    WHERE THE SUNLIGHT SOAKS IN THE STONE THE AFTERNOON   52 13
    HOW THIS DARKNESS SOAKS ME THROUGH AND THROUGH   131 2
    WHEN DESTRUCTION SOAKS THROUGH THE MORTIFIED DECOMPOSING   270 21
    WHERE THE SUNLIGHT SOAKS IN THE STONE THE AFTERNOON   *905 2

SOAR
    BUT YOU FLY YOU SOAR YOU SWEEP AWAY   783 31
    NEVER AN ANGEL WILL SOAR AGAIN   823 11

SOARING
    OR A SOARING CONSCIOUSNESS   323 29
    AND BEYOND THE EAGLE ROSE AND THE PHOENIX PARENT SOARIN+   *946 23

SOB
    TO PUT HER EARS TO THE PAINFUL SOB OF MY BLOOD   64 17
    ASLEEP STILL SHAKES IN THE CLUTCH OF A SOB   136 25
    AND JUST LOVES TO HEAR YOU SOB AND GROAN   572 8

SOBBING
    THE SUN WARMS THE SEA LITTLE LONELY AND SAD SIFTING THE+   180 3
    SOBBING IN DARK SWEAT-SHINING BREASTS   389 12
    AND HEARD THE AUDIENCE SIGHING AND SOBBING WITH ALL THE   443 24

SOBBIN'
    BY A HEAD-STUN SOBBIN' AN' SOBBIN' AGAIN   *911 4

SOBER
    LET US GO TO THE SODA-FOUNTAIN TO GET SOBER   286 37

SOBERNESS
    SOBERNESS SOBRIETY   287 1
    SOBERNESS SOBRIETY WITH HEAVY EYES PROPPED OPEN   287 4

SOBRIETY
    SOBERNESS SOBRIETY   287 1
    SOBERNESS SOBRIETY WITH HEAVY EYES PROPPED OPEN   287 4

SOBS
    SOBS STRUGGLING INTO HER FROSTY SIGH   85 12
    BREAKS AND SOBS IN THE BLIND   140 18
    BEATING LIKE SOBS I COME TO MYSELF AND STAND   143 21
    POOR SIEGMUND TAKE THE SOBS FROM OUT OF YOUR VOICE   871 17
    THERE I CANNOT BEAR TO SEE THE SOBS IN YOUR THROAT   871 19
    AND TERRIBLY STRANGE IS THE THROAT THAT IS WORKING WITH+   871 26
    WI' LITTLE SOBS AS YOU SCARCE COULD HEAR   *910 14

SOB-STUFF
    IF WE TOUCH THE SOB-STUFF CROWN   537 10

SO-CALLED
    I REALISED WHAT A LUST THERE WAS IN HIM TO WREAK HIS SO+   620 6

SOCIAL
    ITS CAGE-RIBS IN THE SOCIAL HEAVEN BENEFICENT   290 23
    BUT HE INSISTS ON GNAWING A LITTLE HOLE IN THE SOCIAL   432 13
    IS SOCIAL INSANITY   514 26
    TODAY THE SOCIAL CONSCIOUSNESS IS MUTILATED   516 1
    A FEARFUL THING IS THE MUTILATED SOCIAL CONSCIOUSNESS   516 6
    THE GREAT SOCIAL IDIOT IT MUST BE CONFESSED   522 6
    YOU DON'T NEED ONE SINGLE SOCIAL INFERIOR TO EXALT YOU   526 26
    WE NEED HAVE NO DEAD PEOPLE MONEY-SLAVES AND SOCIAL   527 7
    AS LITTLE SOCIAL ANTS PERHAPS WE FUNCTION ALL RIGHT   544 11
    IT IS WELL TO BE DISCIPLINED IN ALL THE SOCIAL USAGES   608 8
    IT SHOWS AGAIN HOW HIGHLY DEVELOPED THE SOCIAL CONSCIEN+   829 16
    WHICH SHOWS ONCE MORE THAT OUR SOCIAL CONSCIENCE IS DEV+   829 22
    FAR BEYOND THE PRESENT SOCIAL FORM   829 23
    IS FOR SOME MORE NATURAL MORE DECENT SOCIAL ARRANGEMENT   837 24

SOCIALISTS
    IT'S THE SOCIALISTS COME TO TOWN   312 6
    THE SOCIALISTS HAVE GATHERED UPON US TO LOOK AT US   312 11
    IT'S THE SOCIALISTS IN THE TOWN   312 27
    SOCIALISTS   313 8
    IS THIS HOW YOU'LL HAVE IT RED-DECKED SOCIALISTS   314 21
    YOU SOCIALISTS   314 31

SOCIALIZATION
    IT SEEMS TO ME THAT SOME SORT OF DECENT SOCIALIZATION E+   829 8

SOCIALLY
    HOW HIGHLY AWARE WE ARE OF ONE ANOTHER SOCIALLY   829 17
    HOW DECENT IS OUR DESIRE TOWARDS ONE ANOTHER SOCIALLY   829 18

SOCIETY
    THE PROPER WAY TO EAT A FIG IN SOCIETY   282 1
    THAT SOCIETY MUST ESTABLISH ITSELF UPON A DIFFERENT PRI+   487 19
    AND OUR SOCIETY IS ONLY PART CONSCIOUS LIKE AN IDIOT   515 2
    TODAY SOCIETY HAS SANCTIFIED   620 22
    ON OUR CASTRATED SOCIETY   628 12
    MODERN SOCIETY IS A MILL   641 22
    FOR OUR SOCIETY IS BASED ON GRAB AND DEVIL TAKE THE HIN+   829 24
    IS A NEW FRAME OF SOCIETY   833 13

SOCKET
    SOCKET   245 15

SOCKETS
    SAY IN THE DEEP SOCKETS OF YOUR IDEALISTIC SKULL   292 27
    SHALL GREAT WINGS FLAME FROM HIS SHOULDER SOCKETS   326 6
    SOCKETS AMONG BARE FEET OF ELEPHANTS AND MEN ON THE   388 31

SOCKET-TIP
    INTENT TO HOLD THE CANDLE OF THE SUN UPON ITS SOCKET-TIP   299 29
    SOCKET-TIP   299 35

SOCKS
    'E'LL GIE THEE SOCKS   44 17

SOD
    I ONLY KNOW THAT LIKE A SOD   881 21
    AND LIKE A SOD IN A MEADOW   881 29
    IS HEARD IN THE GRASS OF THE SOD   *914 31

SODA-FOUNTAIN
    LET US GO TO THE SODA-FOUNTAIN TO GET SOBER   286 37

SODDEN
    I FORCE MY CART THROUGH THE SODDEN FILTH THAT IS PRESSED   167 5

SODDENED
    AND SHUFFLE OF BROKEN SODDENED BOOTS YET SINGING GOES R+   866 14

SODOM
    A SODOM SMOULDERING IN THE DENSE SOILED AIR   72 14
    IS IT MORE THAN THE APPLES OF SODOM YOU SCORN SO THE MEN   235 7
    OF SODOM THAT COVERS THE EARTH BRING THEM FORTH   235 11
    QUITE APART FROM SODOM   562 23

SODOMIST
    BY INSTINCT HE'S A SODOMIST   446 29
    DON JUAN WAS NEVER ANYTHING BUT A SELF-THWARTED SODOMIST   *949 17

SODOMITICAL
    EVEN THAT ISN'T SODOMITICAL SAID I   447 5
    AND LOOK AT THE SODOMITICAL AND LESBIAN STUFF WEARING   532 6

SODOMY
    EVEN SODOMY CAN BE SANE AND WHOLESOME   845 4
    AND SODOMY ON THE BRAIN BECOMES A MISSION   845 9
    SODOMY   *949 5
    EVEN AT THE RIGHT TIMES SODOMY CAN BE SANE AND WHOLESOME   *952 16
    IN FACT IT MAY BE THAT A LITTLE SODOMY IS NECESSARY TO +   *952 18
    AND SODOMY ON THE BRAIN IS A SORT OF MISSION AND WHAT I+   *952 21

SODS
    ROAMING OVER THE SODS   361 19

SOFT
    NAKED ON THE STEEP SOFT LIP   33 18
    BELOW THE LAWN IN SOFT BLUE SHADE IS KEEPING   35 28
    MY SOFT SLUMBERING BELLY   39 7
    LIGHTS THE SOFT HAIR OF A GIRL AS SHE READS   41 7
    HE FLINGS THE RABBIT SOFT ON THE TABLE BOARD   43 22
    THEIR SLEEPING COVER THEM SOFT UNSEEN   48 22
    SOFT AS A SUMMERING TREE   56 8
    CUP FOR A MOMENT SOFT LITTLE WING-BEATS UTTERING   65 4
    LIQUID AS LIME-TREE BLOSSOM SOFT AS BRILLIANT WATER OR +   67 20
    HER SOFT WHITE LEGS HANGING HEAVILY OVER MY ARM   73 25
    LIKE SOFT HOT ASHES ON MY HELPLESS CLAY   87 13
    SOFT GLIMMERS OF DESIRE ESCAPED FROM PRISON   113 4
    OF YOUR SOFT WHITE BODY AS LIGHTNING   117 31
    AND SHE SETTLED SOFT   124 5
    LIKE A SOFT FULL DROP OF DARKNESS IT SEEMS TO SWAY   148 1
    SOFT SHE LAY AS A SHED FLOWER FALLEN NOR HEARD   155 26
    IS SOFT THOUGH IT IS COLD DO NOT DARE   158 20
    THE SOFT WIND BLOWING COOL   194 7
    THE BIG SOFT COUNTRY LASS   198 9
    THE WARM SOFT COUNTRY LASS   198 13
    ONLY THE TWILIGHT NOW AND THE SOFT SH OF THE RIVER   203 15
    MY DEAR THE NIGHT IS SOFT AND ETERNAL NO DOUBT   211 11
    YOU ARE LOVELY YOUR FACE IS SOFT   240 16
    A SOFT MOST UNWARRANTABLE BURNING   241 11
    NOW WINNOWED SOFT   269 7
    SO BROWN AND SOFT AND COMING SUAVE   280 4
    TO ME MEN'S FOOTFALLS FALL WITH A DULL SOFT RUMBLE   288 28
    AND WRAPT INVIOLABLE IN SOFT CYPRESS-TREES   298 13
    OUT OF THE DEEP SOFT FLEDGE OF SICILIAN WINTER-GREEN   300 22
    OF UNEATABLE SOFT GREEN   301 17
    COLUMNS DARK AND SOFT   301 27
    SOFT SHAFTS SUNBREATHING MOUTHS   301 29
    AND BREATHING SOFT UNWILLING TO WAKE TO THE NEW DAY   311 12
    SOFT RED TONGUE AND HARD THIN GUMS   359 7
    SHE SNAPS THE SOFT BREAD FROM MY HAND IN GREAT MOUTHFULS   359 1
    HER THICK SOFT TONGUE   359 6
    THE SOFT WELLING OF BLOOD INVINCIBLE EVEN BEYOND BONE OR   383 4
    THE SOFT THE SECRET THE UNFATHOMABLE BLOOD   383 6
    GET OUT YOU LITTLE SOFT FOOL   400 8
    SOFT GRASS RUNS UPON A PATH THAT IS PATHLESS TO MEN SO +   406 3
    AND MOVING ALWAYS WITH A SOFT SLOW PRECISION   445 15
    THINGS MEN HAVE MADE WITH WAKENED HANDS AND PUT SOFT   448 1
    AMONG SOFT AMENITIES   462 26
    SOFT SLOW SYMPATHY   471 1
    WITH A SOFT ONE WARMTH AND A GENEROUS   471 6
    THE SOFT BLOOD SOFTLY FLOWS TOGETHER   471 15
    AND THERE SHALL BE THE SOFT SOFT TREMOR AS OF UNHEARD B+   479 4
    FRAGRANT LIKE YELLOWING LEAVES AND DIM WITH THE SOFT   503 24
    AND THE POOR WILLY WET-LEGS THE SOFT SILK GLOVES   535 23
    AND FALL INTO SHARP SELF-CENTRED SELF-ASSERTION SHARP O+   616 6
    THE SOFT THUDDING OF DRUMS   623 5
    NOW IT IS ALMOST NIGHT FROM THE BRONZEY SOFT SKY   647 8
    OF THE UNKNOWN AIR AND EYES SO SOFT   667 8
    IN THE CLASP AND THE SOFT WILD CLUTCH OF A SHE-WHALE'S +   694 19
    WILL YOU CLIMB ON YOUR BIG SOFT WINGS BLACK-DOTTED   696 22
    IN SOFT SEPTEMBER AT SLOW SAD MICHAELMAS   697 2
    CUFFING THEM WITH SOFT PAWS   709 11
    SET A PLACE FOR THE DEAD WITH A CUSHION AND SOFT SEAT   723 9
    MY SPIRIT DARKENS AND GOES OUT AND SOFT STRANGE GLOOM   727 2
    TO START MY HEART AFRESH GIVE ME THE SOFT SMALL STRESS   738 31
    STRANGER SOFT ARE THE TEARS THAT FALL   758 15
    AS FIRE BUT SOFT AS SUNSHINE SOFT AS KISSES   784 16
    SOFT AS A KIND HEART'S KINDNESS TREMULOUS   784 17
    THE SOFT GULF BE WISE   818 4
    YET ARE FLEECED WITH SOFT HAIR   827 20
    THE SOFT CLUSTERED SHOULDER-FEATHERS IN ROSY CONFUSION + 855 23
    SOFT TICKLING BROWN   863 8
    HER FRUIT IS UNRIPE AND HER SOFT MOUTH IS BITTER AND RO+ 864 18
    WE ALL MARCH OUT TO PRAYERS SOFT SLIPPERED FEET AND CLA+ 866 13
    WHILE THE SOFT CARESS OF HER HIDDEN LAUGHTER   868 10
    THAT MADE SHADOWS AND SHIMMERING RIPPLES THE SOFT NOTES+ 868 14
    OUT OF THE SOFT MATRIX   870 8
    NAKED ON THE STEEP SOFT LIP   *891 20

SOFT
    GATHERING THE SOFT RIPPLES BELOW MY BREASTS   *893 18
    AND MY SOFT SLUMBERING BELLY   *893 20
    WHERE THE GLASS IS DOMED BY THE BLUE SOFT DAY   *905 8
    INTO FORGETFULNESS SOFT SAILING WATERS WHERE FEARS   *906 3
    WHITE WHEN THE WIND SHIFTED HER HAIR THAT WAS SOFT AN' + *910 12
    HER SOFT WHITE LEGS HANGING HEAVILY OVER MY ARM   *913 17
    OH I TORE THEM UP THOUGH THE WISTFUL LEAVES WERE FRAGRA+ *926 15
    SO SHE SETTLED SOFT   *936 11
    WHENCE ISSUE UNBLEMISHED THE ATOMS WHICH SOFT BESTOWED *938 17
    TILL HE'S GOT A WOMAN A BIT SOFT AND TRUSTFUL   *948 15
    IN SOFT SEPTEMBER AT SLOW SAD MICHAELMAS   *955 26

SOFT-BALLED
    KISSES OF THE SOFT-BALLED PAWS WHERE THE TALONS ARE   709 13

SOFT-BELLIED
    AND TRAILED HIS YELLOW-BROWN SLACKNESS SOFT-BELLIED DOWN 349 10

SOFT-BOILED
    O YOU HARD-BOILED CONSERVATIVES AND YOU SOFT-BOILED LIB+ 664 12

SOFTEN
    WAS ALWAYS SOONER TO SOFTEN   55 14
    COME AND SOFTEN THE WILLOW BUDS TILL THEY ARE PUFFED AN+ 273 2
    I NEVER SAW THEM HOW THEY MUST SOFTEN   460 13
    IF THEY DIDN'T IF THEY DID NOT SOFTEN   460 17

SOFTENED
    TILL THEY ARE SOFTENED BACK TO LIFE-STUFF AGAIN AGAINST+ 663 7
    IN ANOTHER SOFTENED SPRINGTIME   769 10

SOFTENING
    IS BRITISH HYPOCRISY A FORM OF SOFTENING OF THE BRAIN   659 22

SOFTENS
    WHERE HER BOSOM SOFTENS TOWARDS ME AND THE TURMOIL HAS 250 7
    AND IT NEVER SOFTENS   359 11

SOFTER
    SOFTER THAN THE SPACE BETWEEN THE STARS   667 9

SOFT-FOOTED
    SOFT-FOOTED DEAD   171 4
    AND ON THE MARGIN MEN SOFT-FOOTED AND PRISTINE   285 24
    THE INVOLVED VOLUPTUOUSNESS OF THE SOFT FOOTED CAT   382 1

SOFT-FOOT
    OF HER SOFT-FOOT MALADY   106 30
    WHO GO BY WITHOUT PAUSING SOFT-FOOT WITHOUT LISTENING Y+ 623 21

SOFTLY
    THE DAISY-FROTH QUIESCENT SOFTLY IN THRALL   35 29
    LOW FROM THE ROOF AND THE WET DUST FALLING SOFTLY FROM + 112 26
    LIKE HEAVY BIRDS AT REST THERE SOFTLY STIRRED   123 10
    LAST EVENING AND SHE WHO WAS SOFTLY IN BLOOM   141 7
    NOW VERDIGRIS SMOULDERING SOFTLY SPREAD   142 25
    SOFTLY IN THE DUSK A WOMAN IS SINGING TO ME   149 6
    SHE SOFTLY PASSED THE SORROWFUL FLOWER SHED   156 7
    SOFTLY I KNEW IT WOULD COME TO THIS SHE SAID   156 13
    MOAN SOFTLY WITH AUTUMNAL PARTURITION   160 9
    OF SEED-SPECKS KINDLED LATELY AND SOFTLY BLOWN   218 16
    MY MOUTH ON HERS IN KISSES AND SO SOFTLY   218 19
    THAT SOFTLY PACE   268 25
    SOFTLY DRANK THROUGH HIS STRAIGHT GUMS INTO HIS SLACK L+ 349 16
    FLUTTERING AND SOFTLY UNRAVELLING   460 8
    WELL SOFTLY UP FOR A NEW INCREASE   461 26
    THE SOFT BLOOD SOFTLY FLOWS TOGETHER   471 15
    SOFTLY FLUTTERING THE SENSES IN THE EXQUISITE ORGASM OF 481 24
    SOFTLY BLOWS OUT ITS THIN LITTLE MALE STAMENS   535 3
    SOFTLY SUBTLY SECRETLY IN SOUL FIRST THEN IN SPIRIT THE+ 642 22
    SOFTLY SUBTLY SECRETLY SAYING NOTHING   642 27
    BE QUITE ALONE AND FEEL THE LIVING COSMOS SOFTLY ROCKING 646 12
    WHO IS IT THAT SOFTLY TOUCHES THE SIDES OF MY BREAST   652 6
    ARE HEARD SOFTLY LAUGHING AND CHATTING AS EVER   688 18
    BUT SOFTLY SOFTLY   766 1
    BUT SOFTLY SOFTLY AND RUTHLESSLY   766 5
    WHEN YOU SLEEP IT SOFTLY SHINES   800 7
    WAVES SOFTLY   811 21
    DREW HER LIPS OVER THE MOON-PALE PETALS SOFTLY BENT   856 20
    SHAKEN SOFTLY FROM THE HEAVY-FOLDED SKIRTS OF NIGHT   858 14
    IT SETTLED SO SOFTLY I WAS ALL UNAWARE   860 6
    WHEN SOFTLY I CALL AT HER DOOR AND ENTER THE ROOM   868 25
    OR SOFTLY TAPPING AT MY STUDY DOOR   875 10
    SOFTLY IN THE SHADOWS A WOMAN IS SINGING TO ME   *940 5
    WHEN SOFTLY I CALL AT HER DOOR AND ENTER THE ROOM   *941 25
    MY TREASURE SOFTLY SLIPS UNCURLED   *943 23
    TO SET SOFTLY FORTH ON THE LONGEST JOURNEY THE LONGEST + *957 19

SOFTLY-IMPULSIVE
    SOFTLY-IMPULSIVE ADVANCING AS WATER TOWARDS A WEIR FROM+ 66 19

SOFTLY-STIRRING
    ITS SOFTLY-STIRRING CRIMSON WELLING-UP   153 27

SOFTLY-SWAYING
    VICIOUS YOU SUPPLE BROODING SOFTLY-SWAYING PILLARS OF   297 10

SOFTNESS
    ALL THAT I AM-NOT IN SOFTNESS SWEET SOFTNESS FOR SHE IS+ 250 3
    AND THEN THE SOFTNESS OF DEEP SHADOWS FOLDING FOLDING   727 9
    AND THE WOOD LIKE A MANLY HUSBAND SPREADS SOFTNESS AND + 854 9
    COMES OVER THE SOFTNESS AND SILENCE OF MORNING I PASS *895 11

SOFT-SAILING
  TO FORGETFULNESS SOFT-SAILING WATERS WHERE FEARS   53 11

SOFT-SKINNED
  AND GIVE ME SOFT-SKINNED WOOD   427 12
  OF FINGER OR FIST OR SOFT-SKINNED STICKS UPON THE STRET+   623 6

SOFT-SKIRTED
  OF SOFT-SKIRTED WOMEN   410 22

SOFT-SLIPPING
  PLAYING WITH THE SOFT-SLIPPING WATER   867 19

SOFT-THROATED
  SHE IS SWEET AND SOFT-THROATED   862 6

SOFT-TONED
  THE OLD DREAMS ARE BEAUTIFUL BELOVED SOFT-TONED AND SURE   174 21
  THE OLD DREAMS ARE BELOVED BEAUTIFUL SOFT-TONED AND SURE   *907 4
  THE OLD DREAMS ARE BEAUTIFUL BELOVED SOFT-TONED AND SURE   *909 1

SOFT-WORN
  SUBTLER THAN AN OLD SOFT-WORN FIDDLE-BOW   254 33

SOFTY
  NOT THAT YOU'RE MERELY A SOFTY OH DEAR ME NO   396 16

SOGGY
  AND THEN WATCH HIM GO SOGGY LIKE A WET MERINGUE   431 6
  AND SLAVERING WET AND SOGGY   492 2

SOIL
  I HAVE PUSHED MY HANDS IN THE DARK SOIL UNDER THE FLOWE+   92 8
  OF GREEN FIRES LIT ON THE SOIL OF EARTH THIS BLAZE   116 7
  I AM BURROWING MY BODY INTO THE SOIL   259 32
  PUT ME DOWN AGAIN ON THE EARTH JESUS ON THE BROWN SOIL   321 10
  HIS MOTHER DEPOSITED HIM ON THE SOIL AS IF HE WERE NO M+   356 24
  INTO THE SOIL OF ENGLAND   431 29
  AND TREADS THE EARTH TO FEEL THE SOIL   459 23

SOILED
  A SODOM SMOULDERING IN THE DENSE SOILED AIR   72 14
  DOWN THE SOILED STREET WE HAVE PATTERED THE LESSONS   75 23
  BLOTCHING THE THICK SOILED AIR   142 18
  DOWN THE SOILED STREET WE HAVE PATTERED THE LESSONS CEA+   *897 23
  DOWN THE SOILED STREET WE HAVE PATTERED THE LESSONS   *900 31

SOILING
  SOILING THE CLEAN WHITE DUST HE RUBS THE BELLY   734 9

SOIL'S
  FIXED IN THE DARKNESS GRAPPLING FOR THE DEEP SOIL'S CRO+   92 11
  FIXED IN THE DARKNESS GRAPPLING FOR THE DEEP SOIL'S LIT+   *926 11

SOJOURNER
  AH YES I KNOW YOU WELL A SOJOURNER   234 1

SOLACE
  WAFTING LIKE SOLACE DOWN THEIR LENGTH OF DAYS   *941 16

SOLD
  THEY ARE ALWAYS SOLD   309 29
  AND WAS SOLD INTO SLAVERY   378 9
  AND SOLD   442 9
  THEY FIND HE HAS SOLD THEM TO HIS FATHER   442 13
  SOLD TO THE DEVIL   483 5
  JESUS YOU'VE NOT ONLY SOLD JESUS   762 15
  YOU'VE SOLD EVERY MAN THERE WAS TO BE SOLD   762 16
  YOU'VE SOLD EVERY GREAT MAN THAT EVER APPEARED   762 18
  THEY'VE SOLD EVERYTHING BUT EVERYTHING   762 24
  THEY SOLD PLATO TO THE SAUSAGE FACTORIES OF UNIVERSITIES   762 26
  AND ALL THE HEROES OF THE BIBLE THEY SOLD FOR CATS-MEAT+   763 1
  NAPOLEON THEY SOLD TO MADAME TUSSAUDS AND TO THE ARTIFI+   763 4
  SHAKESPEARE THEY SOLD TO CROSSE AND BLACKWELLS TO BE JA+   763 6
  AND BEETHOVEN THEY SOLD TO CERTAIN CONDUCTORS TO BE CON+   763 8
  HAS BEEN SUCCESSFULLY SOLD   763 11
  AND WHATEVER NEW COMES ALONG WILL BE SUCCESSFULLY SOLD   763 12
  AND A MAN WHEN HE ISN'T BOUGHT FEELS SOLD   814 12

SOLDIER
  SHUT-UP COFFIN OF A THING WITH A SOLDIER WEARY   733 6
  AND A SOLDIER IN THE SADDLE OF THE LEFT-HAND DRAUGHT-HO+   733 8
  HE WAS A SOLDIER ONCE OUR FIERCE LITTLE BARON A POLE   859 5
  HE WAS A SOLDIER ALWAYS IN CHURCH IT WAS A SIGHT   859 7

SOLDIER-ERECT
  OH SOLDIER-ERECT BIG BIRD   781 13
  SOLDIER-ERECT FROM THE GOD-THRUST EAGLE   783 8

SOLDIERS
  RESTS A STILL LINE OF SOLDIERS RED MOTIONLESS RANGE OF +   66 7
  THE WAVE OF SOLDIERS THE COMING WAVE THE THROBBING RED +   66 23
  MOUTH-HAIR OF SOLDIERS PASSING ABOVE US OVER THE WRECK +   66 29
  AND HUNDREDS OF SOLDIERS ON HORSEBACK HAVE FILED BETWEEN   732 6
  THIS PLACE TODAY THESE SOLDIERS WEAR THE SAME   732 11
  THE SUN IS GONE FROM MID-HEAVEN THE SOLDIERS ARE GONE F+   757 1

SOLE
  WE CAN DO WITHOUT THE SOLE OF THE SHOE   774 10

SOLEDAD
  PURISIMA REFUGIO AND SOLEDAD   798 15

SOLEMN
  SOLEMN IN GROUPS   196 9

SOLEMNLY
  SOLEMNLY AND DISTINCTLY CRIES DOWN THE BABEL OF CHILDREN   48 15
  SOLEMNLY USED TO APPROVE CHIME CHIMING   170 23

SOLES
  AND SAT UP TAKING STRANGE POSTURES SHOWING THE PINK SOL+   445 12
  WE ALL MARCH OUT TO PRAYERS SOFT SLIPPERED FEET AND CLA+   866 13

SOLID
  SOLID   486 2
  DENIED A SIGNATURE WE ENGLISH ARE A SOLID PEOPLE AFTER +   546 19
  YOU'VE NO MORE USE FOR THE SOLID EARTH   549 15
  AND ENGINES WILL RUSH AT THE SOLID HOUSES THE EDIFICE O+   624 28
  THIS IS THE MASSIVE SOLID FLY-WHEEL WHICH SAVES MAN FRO+   838 19
  MY HEART IS FIRM AND SOLID IT NEEDS   888 9

SOLITARY
  OF LIGHTS EACH SOLITARY ROSE   104 25
  TO TAKE YOUR FIRST SOLITARY BITE   352 18
  AND MOVE ON YOUR SLOW SOLITARY HUNT   352 19
  AND HENCE SIX TIMES MORE SOLITARY   354 11
  I SAW A DARK FIGURE APPROACHING A RAGGED SOLITARY CROW   866 17

SOLITUDE
  THE THING TO DO IS IN SOLITUDE SLOWLY AND PAINFULLY PUT   610 16

SOLOMON
  NOW IF THE LILIES OF FRANCE LICK SOLOMON IN ALL HIS GLO+   413 27

SOLOMON'S
  PROPERTY IS NOW SOLOMON'S BABY   664 14

SOLSTICE
  THE SUN IN ME DECLINES TO HIS WINTER SOLSTICE   455 17
  SINKS SINKS TO SETTING AND THE WINTER SOLSTICE   455 27
  SINGING DARKER THAN THE NIGHTINGALE ON ON TO THE SOLSTI+   727 12

SOLUTION
  THE SOLUTION THAT EVER IS MUCH TOO DEEP FOR THE MIND   118 29
  OF YOUR LAST SOLUTION   235 16
  YOU ARE NO SOLUTION   346 30

SOLVE
  SOLVE THE INDIAN QUESTION FINALLY   780 1

SOLVES
  THAT THE PROPERTY PROBLEM SOLVES ITSELF BY THE WAY   665 9

SOLVET SAECLUM IN FAVILLA
  SOLVET SAECLUM IN FAVILLA   511 7

SOMARO
  SOMARO   379 3
  NOW HE'S A JACKASS A PACK-ASS A DONKEY SOMARO BURRO   379 9

SOMBRE
  WITH SHUTTERS OF SOMBRE CLOUD WILL CLOSE   163 14
  BEAT AFTER BEAT FALLS SOMBRE AND DULL   164 1
  INTO OOZE AND THE SOMBRE DIRT SPOUTS UP AT MY HANDS   167 6
  IN FRONT OF THE SOMBRE MOUNTAINS A FAINT LOST RIBBON OF   208 23
  AND A BULL'S LARGE SOMBRE GLANCING EYE   325 28
  THE PONDEROUS SOMBRE SOUND OF THE GREAT DRUM OF   371 6
  AND THOSE SOMBRE DEAD FEATHER-LUSTROUS AZTECS   371 33

SOMEBODY
  THAT SOMEBODY HAS SPUN SO HIGH   54 9
  THEN WILL SOMEBODY SQUARE THIS SHADE WITH THE BEING I   141 22
  IT IS SOMEBODY WANTS TO DO US HARM   250 30
  SOMEBODY IS COMING   309 10
  AHA THERE'S SOMEBODY IN THE KNOW   338 5
  AND YOU LOVE TO MAKE SOMEBODY LOVE YOU INDISCRIMINATE   396 21
  YOU RUN STRAIGHT AWAY TO LIVE WITH SOMEBODY ELSE   399 13
  O START A REVOLUTION SOMEBODY   453 6
  O START A REVOLUTION SOMEBODY   453 9
  AN' THEN SOMEBODY HAS TER MARRY YOU   493 17
  FOR EVERYDAY USE GIVE ME SOMEBODY WHIMSICAL WITH NOT   496 3
  HE FEELS MUCH GAYER THAN IF SOMEBODY HAD LEFT HIM A FOR+   496 7
  YET I CAN'T BE ALONE I WANT SOMEBODY TO KEEP ME WARM   603 20
  USUALLY WANT TO FORCE SOMEBODY TO AGREE WITH THEM   626 5
  O SOMEBODY BAIL THEM OUT   632 29
  WHEN I HEAR SOMEBODY COMPLAIN OF BEING LONELY   646 1
  LIES IN FORCING YOURSELF OR SOMEBODY ELSE   836 18

SOMEBODY'S
  SOMEBODY'S KNOCKIN' AT TH' DOOR   44 10
  IT'S SOMEBODY'S LIES   77 10
  SOMEBODY'S POUND OF FLESH RENDERED UP   279 7
  IT'S SOMEBODY'S LIES   *918 28

SOMEHOW
  AN' WI' 'ER SOMEHOW IT ISN'T RIGHT   85 3
  SOMEHOW ALAS HE FELL IN LOVE   378 4
  SOMEHOW THEY ARE A LIE   505 24
  HER LETTER SOMEHOW   748 14
  SOMEHOW SO SAD SO INTRINSIC SO SPIRITUAL YET SO CAUTIOU+   *932 13

SOMEONE
  SOMEONE WAS BEFORE ME AT MY WATER-TROUGH   349 19
  WE SCREAM FOR SOMEONE TO WAKE US   408 1
  BUT I'M ALWAYS LONGING FOR SOMEONE TO SAY   490 27
  SOMEONE WILL ENTER BETWEEN THE GATES   788 26
  SOMEONE WILL COME TO THE PLACE OF FIRE   789 1

SOMERS
  ME AND EKKERHART AND SOMERS AND PAMELIE   668 21

SOMERSAULTS
    AND DOGS JUMPED THROUGH HOOPS AND TURNED SOMERSAULTS   444 18

SOMETHING
    AND STRUCK AT ME WITH SOMETHING DARK   46 22
    ASKING SOMETHING MORE OF ME   64 27
    SOMETHING FAERY AND FINE THE SHUTTLES SLIDING   72 7
    SOMETHING WHICH SETS THE BLACK POPLARS ASHAKE WITH HYST+   102 26
    FOR SOMETHING MUST COME SINCE WE PASS AND PASS   164 5
    TRACK OF THE RAILWAY ALIVE AND WITH SOMETHING TO DO   174 8
    THERE IS SOMETHING I WANT TO FEEL IN MY RUNNING BLOOD   180 30
    SOMETHING I WANT TO TOUCH I MUST HOLD MY FACE TO THE RA+   180 31
    SOMETHING IN ME REMEMBERS   199 17
    AND SOMETHING IN ME HAS FORGOTTEN   199 21
    THERE IS SOMETHING IN YOU DESTROYS ME   210 28
    SURELY ABOUT HIS SUNBURNT FACE IS SOMETHING   225 17
    SOMETHING FROZEN IN THE SILENCE THAT DARE NOT BE   225 27
    IF SOMETHING STIRS IN THE BRANCHES   231 16
    THERE WAS SOMETHING I OUGHT TO REMEMBER AND YET   243 26
    AND THINK THERE WILL SOMETHING COME FORTH FROM US   247 18
    THERE WILL SOMETHING COME FORTH FROM US   247 20
    SOMETHING THAT STANDS OVER   248 7
    SOMETHING I SHALL NEVER BE   248 8
    SOMETHING SEEMED TO SURGE THROUGH ME WHEN I TOUCHED   255 5
    YET SOMETHING REMAINS   265 28
    SOMETHING SHALL NOT ALWAYS REMAIN   265 29
    AND SOMETHING BEYOND QUITE BEYOND IF YOU UNDERSTAND WHAT   266 18
    AND BECAUSE I SAY SO YOU WOULD LIKE TO THROW SOMETHING   279 26
    SOMETHING OF THE SAME FLAVOUR OF SYRACUSAN MUSCAT WINE   280 9
    OF SOMETHING GONE WRONG IN THE MIDDLE   291 18
    SOMETHING IN YOU WHICH CARRIES ME BEYOND   291 27
    SOMETHING MUST BE REASSURING TO THE ALMOND IN THE EVENI+   305 31
    SOMETHING SEEMED TO BLOW HIM BACK FROM THE WINDOW   344 11
    HE SQUATTED THERE LIKE SOMETHING UNCLEAN   346 2
    AND I HAVE SOMETHING TO EXPIATE   351 29
    SOMETHING LIKE AN OWL WHOOING   366 13
    OR PERHAPS IT IS SOMETHING UNFINISHED   370 1
    OF PERHAPS THERE IS SOMETHING IN YOUR WATTLES OF A BULL+   370 4
    HE REGRETS SOMETHING THAT HE REMEMBERS   377 30
    WHILE SOMETHING STIRS QUICKLY IN HER BELLY AND A LEAN   393 30
    UNTOLD CENTURIES OF WATCHING FOR SOMETHING TO COME   394 11
    THEY WANT SOMETHING OF YOU SO YOU SQUEAK AND COME   400 2
    SOMETHING YELLOW   401 16
    AND SOMETHING HAS COME   403 19
    THINKING DEATH WILL AWAKEN SOMETHING   408 13
    LIFTING THE RABBIT-BLOOD OF THE MYRIADS UP INTO SOMETHI+   414 22
    GIVE US SOMETHING ELSE   437 9
    SEX ISN'T SOMETHING YOU'VE GOT TO PLAY WITH SEX IS YOU   464 17
    AND LOVE LIKE A FLOWER WILL FADE WILL CHANGE INTO SOMET+   476 3
    WE ARE SOMETHING ELSE   480 2
    FOR OF COURSE IF YOU REALLY FEEL SOMETHING   500 24
    SO I AM JUST GOING TO GO ON BEING A BLANK TILL SOMETHIN+   501 23
    THE TINY GRAIN OF SOMETHING THAT NO WAVE CAN WASH AWAY   514 4
    AND HAS SOMETHING COMPARABLE TO THAT WHICH   515 21
    WHY DON'T WE DO SOMETHING ABOUT THE MONEY SYSTEM   518 6
    IF WE BRACE OURSELVES UP IT SHOULD BE FOR SOMETHING WE   520 6
    PURE IMPULSE TO MAKE SOMETHING TO PUT SOMETHING FORTH   520 11
    I IMMEDIATELY WANT TO GO AND DO SOMETHING JOLLY TOO   520 25
    ONLY IS MAN AGONISED IN FRONT OF THE NECESSITY TO BE SO+   529 14
    IT'S SOMETHING ELSE YOU ARE AFTER IF YOU COULD BUT   541 15
    SOMETHING IS LEFT BEHIND LOST AND HOWLING AND WE KNOW IT   543 25
    THEY ARE STILL SUPERIOR SO THERE MUST BE SOMETHING THEY   548 1
    LIKE MONKEYS OR ANGELS OR SOMETHING IN A LIMITED   550 3
    AS IF THEY'D GOT SOMETHING TO LOSE   555 12
    IT WAS SOMETHING I NEVER COULD FATHOM   555 17
    STAND UP FOR SOMETHING DIFFERENT   560 25
    FIGHTING FOR SOMETHING WORTH FIGHTING FOR   560 27
    OR IS SOMETHING MISSING OR WHAT'S WRONG WITH THEM   578 20
    I TELL YOU THERE MUST BE SOMETHING WRONG   579 5
    IT WAS A SIMULACRUM SOMETHING   601 19
    PEOPLE WHO COMPLAIN OF LONELINESS MUST HAVE LOST SOMETH+   610 8
    PUSHED THEM ALL ASIDE DISCARDED THEM MAKE WAY NOW FOR S+   616 26
    BUT TO SOMETHING UNSEEN UNKNOWN CREATIVE   622 11
    TODAY IF A MAN DOES SOMETHING PRETENTIOUS AND DELIBERATE   634 10
    BUT IF HE PRODUCES SOMETHING BEAUTIFUL WITH THE FRAIL   634 13
    YOU TO WHOM THE SUN IS MERELY SOMETHING THAT MAKES THE   643 13
    YOU WERE ONLY SEEKING TO LOSE SOMETHING   661 3
    NOT TO FIND SOMETHING   661 4
    SOMETHING ELSE   665 8
    WHEREAS IF YOU RIDE AWAY AND BECOME DEEPLY CONCERNED IN+   665 12
    INTO SOMETHING NEW AND STRANGE   667 25
    TO SOMETHING FLOWERY AND FULFILLED AND WITH A STRANGE S+   677 16
    OF SOMETHING COMING SHIPS A-SAIL FROM OVER THE RIM OF T+   687 3
    GOAL TO TRAVEL TOWARDS YET IT'S SOMETHING TO ATTAIN YOU+   761 15
    I WANT MY SON TO BE SOMETHING BETTER THAN HIS FATHER WAS   773 26
    THE WORD STANDS FOR SOMETHING   774 20
    BUT TO BE FAITHFUL TO SOMETHING THAT HAS NOT YET   775 20
    DO ANYTHING BUT DO SOMETHING TO DRAW THIS ONE   780 11
    SENT OUT THE SUN SO THAT SOMETHING SHOULD FLUTTER IN HE+   783 4
    SEEM ALWAYS TO BE ASKING ASKING SOMETHING   816 4
    THEY AREN'T AFRAID OF LOSING SOMETHING AS THE OLDER ONE+   828 25
    NEW LIFE BUBBLES IN WE BECOME SOMETHING ELSE   832 22
    SOMETHING WE HAVE NOT BEEN AND THEREFORE CANNOT YET KNOW   832 23
    SOMETHING THRILLS IN ME AND I KNOW   841 8
    ITS MOTHER DID SOMETHING TO IT AT ABOUT THE AGE OF TWEL+   841 13
    THERE IS SOMETHING ABOUT THAT THEY CALL THE WIND   882 16
    IN THE CITY SOMETHING OF YOU   887 8
    SOMETHING HAS GONE DOWN THE SILENT RIVER   887 24
    THERE IS SOMETHING STIRS IN ME FROM THE FLOW OF THEIR L+   *906 17

SOMETHING'S
    I TELL YOU SOMETHING'S BEEN DONE TO 'EM   550 13

SOMETIME
    YET SOMETIME STOPPING   861 29

SOMETIMES
    BUT SOMETIMES THE OPENING PETALS ARE FIRE AND THE SCARL+   93 31
    AND SOMETIMES HOW SHE GRASPS HER ARMS WITH HER   128 20
    OUT OF THE DARKNESS FRETTED SOMETIMES IN ITS SLEEPING   136 5
    SOMETIMES THE DARKNESS TRAPPED WITHIN A WHEEL   136 8
    SOMETIMES HE TURNS WITH A START TO FIGHT TO CHALLENGE TO   381 8
    THEN SOMETIMES I FEEL DEFEATED AND THEN AGAIN I KNOW   508 22
    BUT SOMETIMES WE RUN AHEAD TOO FAST   543 16
    YOU MUST SOMETIMES PRAY   558 3
    AND SOMETIMES THEY GIVE IT AS LOVE   559 4
    BUT SOMETIMES THEY GIVE IT AS LIGHTNING   559 6
    SOMETIMES THE SUN TURNS HOSTILE TO MEN   608 20
    SOMETIMES I SEE HER LIKE A FLOWER NODDING HER WAY AND   645 22
    AND AS THE ELECTRIC LIQUID POURS OUT SOMETIMES   647 13
    SOMETIMES THEY COME TO TELL US THINGS   793 15
    MY CHEST GAPES OPEN SOMETIMES   869 1
    I THINK SOMETIMES IT WILL CRUSH MY HEART INWARD   869 22

SOMEWHAT
    IS THE BLOOD OF YOUR CONTINENT SOMEWHAT REPTILIAN STILL   374 23
    THE SUPERIOR PERSONS SOMEWHAT INFERIOR   547 30

SOMEWHERE
    SOMEWHERE THE LONG MELLOW NOTE OF THE BLACKBIRD   40 25
    SOMEWHERE THE WIND-FLOWERS FLING THEIR HEADS BACK   40 27
    SOMEWHERE THE LAMP HANGING LOW FROM THE CEILING   41 6
    AS IT SILENTLY SWEEPS TO ITS SOMEWHERE ITS GOAL   68 15
    WITH HIS WAN SPIRIT SOMEWHERE IN THE AIR   158 23
    AND SOMEWHERE THERE IS A LIONESS   325 12
    SETTING OFF SOMEWHERE APPARENTLY   356 22
    THAT SHINES SOMEWHERE IN THE ATOM SOMEWHERE PIVOTS THE   481 14
    AND SOMEWHERE IT HAS A WILD HEART   525 4
    THERE MUST BE A NADIR SOMEWHERE   547 27
    THERE MUST BE A BED-ROCK SOMEWHERE OF PEOPLE WHO ARE   548 3
    ONE MUST COME DOWN TO TERRA FIRMA SOMEWHERE   548 5
    WE MUST DRAW A LINE SOMEWHERE   548 28
    SOMEWHERE INSIDE YOU   563 23
    SOMEWHERE SHE IS THERE   719 18
    THE ANGELS HAVE SOMEWHERE FOUGHT AND LOST   823 1
    AND TREMBLING SOMEWHERE DEEP IN THEIR SUNKIST GLOOM   868 27
    AS HE SILENTLY SWEEPS TO HIS SOMEWHERE HIS GOAL   *914 30
    SOMEWHERE BENEATH THAT PIANO'S SUPERB SLEEK BLACK   *940 1
    WHILE TREMBLING SOMEWHERE IN THEIR WONDROUS GLOOM   *941 27

SOMNAMBULE
    SOMNAMBULE   149 10

SOMNAMBULISM
    AND SHOOT ONE ANOTHER AMAZED AND MAD WITH SOMNAMBULISM   408 12

SOMNAMBULIST
    SOMNAMBULIST WIDE-EYED AFRAID   407 27

SON
    STRANGE HE IS MY SON FOR WHOM I HAVE WAITED LIKE A LOVER   47 8
    IT WILL NOT BE ANY MORE NO MORE MY SON MY SON   48 2
    THIS LAST ONE TO CLAIM ME AND NOW MY SON O MY SON   48 6
    BECAUSE I AM THE SON OF MAN   283 31
    HE WAS THE SON OF MAN   320 7
    HE SERVES THE SON OF MAN   327 7
    THE SON OF MAN   327 9
    THE WEEPING MOTHER OF GOD INCONSOLABLE OVER HER SON   439 29
    I WANT MY SON TO BE SOMETHING BETTER THAN HIS FATHER WAS 773 26
    AND BORN HIM A SON OR SO WHO AT THE AGE OF SEVEN IS SO + 842 7

SONG
    THINK OF ME HERE IN THE LIBRARY TRYING AND TRYING A SON+   57 21
    IS WINSOME AS A ROBIN'S SONG SO FLUTTERING   65 2
    SONG FIERILY   108 28
    THAT SILENCE SHOULD TAKE THE SONG AND THE BIRD   110 11
    IN SPITE OF MYSELF THE INSIDIOUS MASTERY OF SONG   148 10
    WAS SET TO SONG AND NEVER YOUR SONG DENIES   156 23
    SONG AND CHIRRUPING GAY FEATHERS FLUFF-SHADOWED   443 17
    THEY HAVE NO SONG IN THEIR SOULS NONE IN THEIR SPIRITS 657 13
    PEOPLE GO ON SINGING WHEN THEY HAVE NO SONG IN THEM   657 17
    SING THE SONG OF DEATH O SING IT   723 26
    FOR WITHOUT THE SONG OF DEATH THE SONG OF LIFE   723 27
    SING THEN THE SONG OF DEATH AND THE LONGEST JOURNEY   724 1
    SING THE SONG OF DEATH O SING IT   724 11
    SO SWEET LIKE A SWOON OR MORE LIKE THE DROWSE OF A LOW + 727 11
    ON HIS THROAT BELOW HIS SONG   768 22
    FORGOTTEN LIKE LAST YEAR'S LINNET SONG   855 14
    HIS FULL FINE BODY BENDING AND URGING LIKE THE STRESS O+867 24
    THAT MADE SHADOWS AND SHIMMERING RIPPLES THE SOFT NOTES+868 14
    CARRIES A DIM LOW SONG THAT STIRS   868 30
    LIFTING HIS HAUNTED EYES TO ME I AM WANTING IN SONG   884 11
    IS LIKE A LITTLE LINNET SONG WINSOME   *913 2
    IS LIKE A LITTLE ROBIN'S SONG WINSOME   *914 3
    THE FIGURE OF SONG AFLUTTER IN A BLACK-WINGED REVELRY *918 2
    THE FULL THROATED WOMAN HAS CHOSEN A WINNING LIVING SONG *940 9
    SING THE SONG OF DEATH OH SING IT   *961 8
    FOR WITHOUT THE SONG OF DEATH THE SONG OF LIFE   *961 9
    SING THEN THE SONG OF DEATH AND THE LONGEST JOURNEY   *961 11

SONGLESS
    IN A GREEN MUDDY WEB-FOOT UNUTTERLY SONGLESS WORLD   286 1
    AND I WAS SONGLESS AS HE WAS AND LOOKED AT HIM   884 20

SONG-MEASURE
    HIS OWN SONG-MEASURE MANY MONTHS AGO   877 24

SONGS
    FLUSHED WITH THE SONGS OF SEVEN LARKS SINGING AT ONCE G+ 34 14
    MEN SINGING SONGS AND WOMEN BRUSHING THEIR HAIR IN THE + 691 24
    THEY HAD RED LILLY AND PEOPLE SINGING SONGS   846 8
    YOU MUST MAKE MY SONGS FOR ME LOVE I HAVE NONE   884 12
    WITHOUT THE PULSING WATERS WHERE WERE THE MARIGOLDS AND+*891 24
    RICH WITH THE SONGS OF SEVEN LARKS SINGING AT ONCE GOES+*892 2

SONGS
  AS MY WILD SOUL SHRINKS AND THE SONGS ARE DRIVEN FROM M+   *896 12
  BLACK BIRDS WHOSE SONGS ARE UNUTTERABLE SPINNING FANTAS+   *918 14

SON OF A BITCH
  WHO HINDER ME MAMMON GREAT SON OF A BITCH   584 8

SON OF GOD
  JESUS THE SON OF GOD BIDS YOU FAREWELL   798 29

SON OF MAN
  TO THE SON OF MAN   320 16
  WILT THOU LIFT ME UP SON OF MAN   320 18
  NAY SON OF MAN I HAVE BEEN LIFTED UP   322 7
  BUT EVEN THOU SON OF MAN CANST NOT QUAFF OUT THE DREGS +   322 9
  AND THOU ART JESUS SON OF MAN   323 7
  GOD MAY STAY IN MID-HEAVEN THE SON OF MAN HAS CLIMBED TO   323 14
  THE SON OF MAN GOES FORTH TO WAR   541 19
  OR THE SON OF MAN THAT THOU PITIEST HIM   548 32
  AND THE SON OF MAN THAT THOU PITIEST HIM NOT   629 13

SON OF THE MORNING
  IT IS LUCIFER'S TURN THE TURN OF THE SON OF THE MORNING   614 9
  I AM THE SON OF THE MORNING STAR AND CHILD OF THE DEEPS   799 14

SONO IO
  THE SONO IO OF PERFECT DRUNKENNESS   281 29

SONS
  BRING FORTH THE SONS OF YOUR WOMB THEN AND PUT THEM   235 9
  SONS OF EARTH SONS OF FIRE SONS OF AIR AND WATER   635 3
  SONS OF THE LIVING ELEMENTS SONS OF THE UNTHINKING GODS   635 4
  SONS OF THE ELEMENTS AND THE UNSPEAKING GODS   635 24
  SONS OF THE WIND AND RAIN SONS OF THE FIRE AND ROCK   635 25
  AND THE SONS OF MEN WITH THE WIND AND THE FIRE OF LIFE   635 30
  SONS OF MEN FROM THE WOMBS OF WISTFUL WOMEN   642 16
  SONS OF MEN WITH THE WONDERING EYES OF LIFE   642 18
  O STEP ASIDE WITH DECISION SONS OF MEN WITH DECISION   642 29
  FROM HEAVEN PAST THE SLEEPING SONS OF GOD   801 5

SONS OF GOD
  BUT THE SONS OF GOD COME AND GO   799 2

SON'S
  THE FATHER EATS THE PEAR AND THE SON'S TEETH ARE SET ON+   530 22

SOON
  MY KISSES ARE SINKING SOON   37 21
  AH SOON IN HIS LARGE HARD HANDS SHE DIES   43 12
  WHAT THEN LOVE IF SOON   49 17
  PRESSING ROUND AND LOW AT FIRST BUT SOON   50 4
  SHALL GET MY THROAT AT LAST SHALL GET IT SOON   126 2
  YET SOON TOO SOON SHE HAD HIM HOME AGAIN   155 9
  I KNEW THAT SOME DAY SOON I SHOULD FIND YOU THUS   156 14
  SOON THE SPACES OF THE WESTERN SKY   163 13
  SOON STREWS ITSELF ON THE FLOOR AND KEEP THE RADIANCE O+   179 4
  SO SOON   214 5
  O SOON SOON   273 22
  SOON IN THE PUSSYFOOT WEST   280 12
  AND ROTTENNESS SOON SETS IN   284 5
  DOESN'T SOON GO BUST   519 20
  TO SEE THAT A CHILD AS SOON AS IT IS BORN   521 26
  AS SOON AS YOU LET PEOPLE BE YOUR MEASURE   527 18
  WE'RE GETTING TO BE BIG LADS NOW AN' SOON   573 19
  IF YOU'RE NOT NICE THEY SOON MAKE YOU FEEL IT   660 3
  AND SOON EVEN GOD WON'T BE BIG ENOUGH TO HANDLE THAT IN+   670 20
  AND SOON IT WILL RISE ON THE WORLD ON THE OUTSIDE WORLD   718 16
  VERY SOON   755 19
  SOON THE WESTERN WINDOWS OF THE SKY   857 13
  AND SOON THE OWL WINGED WITH STILLNESS WILL FLOAT OUT T+   858 16
  TWAS A TALE SOON TOLD   863 12
  THAT HOLDS IT BACK MIGHT FOLLOW SOON TO THEE   879 17
  WHERE OUR TED 'UD SOON BE SANK   *911 8
  SHALL GET MY THROAT AT LAST SHALL GET IT SOON   *937 2

SOONER
  WAS ALWAYS SOONER TO SOFTEN   55 14
  SOONER THAN OUR FULL CONSUMMATION HERE   193 12
  NO SOONER ISSUED SIDEWAYS FROM THE THIGH OF HIS PREDECE+   299 32
  HE SAYS THE SOONER WILL YOU EAT IMAGINARY CAKE IN THE   442 15

SOOT
  THEY ALL SHOULD BE UNDERGROUND SIFTED WITH SOOT   827 28

SOOTHE
  SPURTING TO SOOTHE THE WOMB'S UNSLAKED DESIRE   89 21
  SOOTHE THEM WITH SERVICE AND HONOUR AND SILENCE MEET   740 17
  THE WILLOW SHALL LIFT HER LEAVES TO SOOTHE THY DISTRESS   749 24
  AS IF THE SOUTHERN-WOOD SHOULD SOOTHE HIS DREAMS   877 32

SOOTHED
  THEY BEGIN TO BE SOOTHED AND SOOTHING THEN WE THROW   448 12
  IT HAS ALL THE TIME TO BE SOOTHED AND CONSOLED BY   641 20
  SOOTHED RESTORED AND HEALED   646 14
  SO THAT MY HEART BEATS SOOTHED SOOTHED SOOTHED AND AT P+ 652 8
  SO HE TOO MAY BE HEALED BE SOOTHED TO PEACE   736 27

SOOTHES
  AND SOOTHES THEM QUITE QUITE OR NOT QUITE   824 27

SOOTHING
  WITH THE OLD SWEET SOOTHING TEARS AND LAUGHTER THAT   53 5
  THEY BEGIN TO BE SOOTHED AND SOOTHING THEN WE THROW   448 12
  SOOTHING OLD PEOPLE SHOULD BE LIKE APPLES   503 22
  SOOTHING AND RESTORING AND HEALING   646 13
  WITH THE OLD SWEET SOOTHING TEARS AND LAUGHTER THAT SHA+ *905 19
  AND DRUNK WITH THE DEATH OF THE SOOTHING GREY-WINGED CR+ *918 11

SOOTHINGLY
  SPEAK SOOTHINGLY FOR US TO GOD AND WHEN IN DISTRESS WE   753 4
  SING SOOTHINGLY   758 18

SOOTY
  INTO OUR SOOTY GARDEN HE DRAGS AND BEATS   47 16

SOPHISTICATED
  SEA ONLY YOU ARE FREE SOPHISTICATED   197 18

SORB-APPLES
  SORB-APPLES MEDLARS WITH DEAD CROWNS   280 23
  SO IN THE STRANGE RETORTS OF MEDLARS AND SORB-APPLES   281 12
  MEDLARS SORB-APPLES   281 20
  SILVER-PINK PEACH VENETIAN GREEN GLASS OF MEDLARS AND S+ 283 5

SORB-APPLE
  IN THE MEDLAR IN THE SORB-APPLE   280 15

SORCERER
  BUT I KNOW YOUR GAME NOW STREAKY SORCERER   332 24

SORDID
  TO SEE YOU ALL SORDID OR RADIANT-TISSUED   73 7
  OF ALL THE SORDID PEOPLE THAT HAVE STARED AT THEM UNCLE+ 580 25
  BECAUSE THEY WERE SUCH BASE AND SORDID OPTIMISTS   627 26
  HOW DISGUSTING HOW INFINITELY SORDID THIS HUMANITY IS   628 4

SORE
  SEE IN HIM YOUR SELF'S DREAM IN HIS SORE   157 31
  MY BREAST WHICH IS SO SORE   230 13
  THESE ARE NO SPIRITS CAUGHT AND SORE   460 3
  WILL GET TIRED AND SORE AT LAST   560 2
  THEN WITH A SORE   563 13
  OF FREEDOM SHRIEKING TILL HER THROAT WAS SORE   574 23

SORE-HEARTED-LOOKING
  SORE-HEARTED-LOOKING   307 16

SORE-HEARTEDNESS
  AND RED AT THE CORE WITH THE LAST SORE-HEARTEDNESS   307 15

SORES
  DEVOURING THE EARTH INTO SORES   793 2

SORREL
  AND ALL THE SORREL SPEARS IN THE LUSH LONG GRASS   884 25

SORREL'S
  OF THE SORREL'S CRESSET A GREEN BRAVE TOWN   49 27

SORRIER
  ME FOR ANOTHER LESSER SORRIER LOVE   877 4

SORROW
  YOURS IS THE SULLEN SORROW   111 8
  AND TURGID SORROW   116 20
  DRAWS TOWARDS THE DOWNARD SLOPE SOME SORROW HATH   131 25
  IN SORROW SINCE WE STAND IN BEWILDERMENT STRANGE   132 19
  OF HORRID SORROW   207 16
  OLD SORROW AND NEW HAPPINESS   247 24
  BELIEF IN LOVE AND SORROW OF SUCH BELIEF   410 12
  I TEAR BUT NEWS OF SORROW AND PAIN   772 23
  I TELL YOU SORROW UPON YOU YOU SHALL ALL DIE   796 2
  NOW THE WORLD IS ENDING IN DUST AND IN SORROW   815 1
  WE'LL SEE THE JOKE AND HOW FUNNY IS SORROW   815 5
  FORLORN ENJOYMENTS FORLORNER SORROW   825 5
  NOR IS HE A WOMAN WITH A BOSOM OF SORROW AND CONSOLATION 840 21
  TO ITS SORROW   841 11
  OR SORROW TO WEEP   856 25
  I THINK IT IS THE HAND OF SORROW   869 20
  AN' ANSWER ME FOR I'VE SAID MY SAY AN' THERE'S NO MORE + *925 22
  IT IS YOU WHO HAVE BORNE THE SHAME AND SORROW   *927 1
  YOURS IS THE SHAME AND SORROW   *928 1

SORROW-CLOSED
  ALONG HER FOOT-SEARCHED WAY HER SORROW-CLOSED EYE   *937 26

SORROWED
  I HAVE NO DESIRE IN THE LEAST TO BE SORROWED OVER OR CO+ 840 22

SORROWFUL
  SHE SOFTLY PASSED THE SORROWFUL FLOWER SHED   156 7
  IN A CASCADE OF SOULS TO SORROWFUL DEATH   743 31
  WITH SORROWFUL FINGERS STROKED HER EYELIDS SHUT   881 2
  SWAYS ON MY ARM LIKE SORROWFUL STORM-HEAVY BOUGHS   *913 23

SORROWS
  OF LIVES WHICH SORROWS LIKE MISCHIEVOUS DARK MICE CHAVEL 132 13
  STRONG WITH EYES OF DEFIANCE EVE WALKS WITH SORROWS   864 23
  OF LIVES THAT SORROWS LIKE MISCHIEVOUS STRANGE MICE CHA+ *938 5

SORRY
  SORRY I AM FOR THIS BUSINESS AN' SORRY IF EVER I'VE DRI+ 83 6
  LOOK UP AN' SAY THA'RT SORRY THA DID IT SAY THA'RT SORR+ 83 15
  IF MY FATHER CAN GET THEE A JOB ON T' BANK SAY THA'RT S+ 83 17
  AY I'M SORRY I'M SORRY   83 18
  AY I'M SORRY THA NEDNA WORRY   83 20
  I'M SORRY FOR THEE I'M SORRY F'R 'ER   83 22
  I'M SORRY F'R US A'   83 23
  I'M SORRY FOR TH' TROUBLE AY   84 9
  BUT SORRY FOR WHAT I HAD WHY   84 11
  AM SORRY FOR WHAT'S IN STORE   219 24
  THOUGH IT'S SORRY I AM ON HIS YOUNG FEET KNOWING   219 27
  YEA THOUGH I'M SORRY FOR THEE   220 8
  SORRY PLIGHT   363 21
  SORRY FOR ITSELF   467 2
  WITHOUT EVER HAVING FELT SORRY FOR ITSELF   467 4

SORRY
  YET EVEN WASTE GREY FORESHORES AND SORRY FAR-OUT   509 17
  O SMALL FLOTILLA OF SORRY SOULS   542 11
  WITH MY THIRTEEN SORRY PICTURES THAT HAVE JUST BEEN RES+ 580 17
  SISTERS I AM SORRY FOR THIS FOREIGN MAN   758 11
  AWFULLY SORRY DEAR BUT I CAN'T COME BECAUSE OF THE CHIL+ 832 11
  SORRY I AM FOR THIS BUSINESS AN' SORRY IF I HA'E DRIVEN+ *925 10
  AM SORRY FOR WHAT'S I' STORE   *944 4
  BUT I'M SORRY FOR HIM ON HIS YOUNG FEET KNOWIN'   *944 7
  MY YOUNG SLIM LAD AN' I'M SORRY FOR THEE   *944 16

SORT
  AND I WHAT SORT OF FIRE AM I AMONG   116 10
  BUT IT'S MY SORT O' WOMAN   140 2
  SORT O' WOMAN FOR ANY LAD   140 5
  LET THE DEAD SORT   168 10
  A SORT OF HORROR A SORT OF PROTEST AGAINST HIS WITHDRAW+ 351 4
  YOUR SORT OF GORGEOUSNESS   369 3
  PERHAPS IT IS A SORT OF UNCANNY DECORATION A VEIL OF LO+ 369 25
  SHE TURNS HER HEAD AWAY WITH AN OBTUSE FEMALE SORT OF   385 1
  BUT A DIFFERENT SORT A COLD REBELLIOUS JEERING DEVIL   390 4
  LITTLE BLACK FEMALE PUP SORT OF FRENCH BULL THEY SAY   395 1
  IN A SORT OF WORSHIP   403 27
  OR A SORT OF PROSPERITY-GANDER   414 11
  THAT SORT   446 21
  SO HE VERY CLEVERLY TORTURES WOMEN WITH HIS SORT OF LOVE 447 15
  SORT   452 19
  WHAT WE WANT IS SOME SORT OF COMMUNISM   483 25
  NOT BASED ON WAGES NOR PROFITS NOR ANY SORT OF BUYING A+ 483 26
  OLD TRUTH OLD TEACHING OF ANY SORT   495 14
  INHERITING A SORT OF CONFINEMENT   518 11
  WE LOATHE THE THOUGHT OF ANY SORT OF TRIUMPH   519 8
  AND A WAGE-EARNER IS A SORT OF GAOL-BIRD   521 8
  REALLY PATRIOTIC PEOPLE THE RIGHT SORT OF PEOPLE YOU KN+ 546 8
  SOME MYSTERIOUS SORT OF PRESTIGE   555 14
  NO MATTER OF WHAT SORT THE CABBAGE BE   569 14
  ONLY THE BRAINY SORT   637 22
  UNLESS SHE'S A GLIMPSE OF A GODDESS OF SOME SORT   671 12
  THERE'S ALL SORTS OF GODS ALL SORTS AND EVERY SORT   671 13
  SOME SUGAR OF THE SAME WHITE SORT   751 6
  WHAT SORT OF TIMOROUS POTION OF LOVE HAVE YOU DRUNK   755 2
  IT SEEMS TO ME THAT SOME SORT OF DECENT SOCIALIZATION E+ 829 8
  THEY DON'T MIND BEING DEPRAVED IMMORAL OR ANYTHING OF T+ 829 12
  AND A GOO-GOO SORT OF VOICE-BOX   830 31
  WAS TH' LITTLE LOVIN' SORT AS 'AS NOWT TER SCREEN 'EM   *910 25
  BUT BAWDY ON THE BRAIN IS LEWD AND NAUSEOUS A SORT OF I+ *952 19
  AND SODOMY ON THE BRAIN IS A SORT OF MISSION AND WHAT I+ *952 21

SORTS
  FROM ALL SORTS OF MEN DON'T BE BEHOLDEN   458 28
  FOR THERE ARE ALL SORTS OF FLAME   511 11
  THERE'S ALL SORTS OF GODS ALL SORTS AND EVERY SORT   671 13

SO'S
  CLEAN AN' NEW AN' NICE SO'S WHEN   77 27
  BUT THA WANTED ME MORE TER WANT THEE SO'S   138 22
  CLEAN AN' NEW AN' NICE SO'S WHEN   *919 15

SOUGH
  LIKE THE SOUGH OF A WIND THAT IS CAUGHT UP HIGH IN THE +   58 1
  IN THE WIND'S SAD SOUGH   252 19

SOUGHT
  WE SOUGHT YOU SUBSTANTIAL YOU TOUCHSTONE OF CARESSES YO+   34 17
  SOUGHT HER AFRESH   120 31
  ALL EYES SOUGHT THE SAME OLD SPOT   578 2
  AH I KNOW HOW YOU HAVE SOUGHT ME   880 9

SOUL
  ALWAYS ON THE DISTANCE AS IF HIS SOUL WERE CHAUNTING   47 12
  IN MY SOUL FROM UNDER THE SUDDEN FROWN OF HIS BROW   47 26
  HOW MANY SHADOWS IN YOUR SOUL   49 3
  OF THE SHIP OF THE SOUL OVER SEAS WHERE DREAMED DREAMS   53 7
  AND I SHED MY VERY SOUL DOWN INTO YOUR   56 15
  A SUDDEN CAR GOES SWEEPING PAST AND I STRAIN MY SOUL TO+   58 3
  MY LAST DEAR FUEL OF LIFE TO HEAP ON MY SOUL   74 19
  I WILL NOT WASTE MY SOUL AND AND MY STRENGTH FOR THIS   74 23
  YOU YOUR SOUL LIKE A LADY-SMOCK LOST EVANESCENT   90 17
  AND WHEN YOUR STIFLING SOUL WOULD SUMMON   91 10
  SOUL   92 9
  AND TRIED TO BREAK THE VESSEL AND VIOLATE MY SOUL   92 24
  AND ONLY IN HARMONY WITH OTHERS THE SINGLE SOUL CAN BE +   93 10
  ALL THE CHAMBERS OF MY SOUL   95 9
  COLD THAT HAD SUNK TO MY SOUL AND THERE KEPT HOLD   98 25
  ONCE FROM YOUR SOUL TO BE   101 26
  I MUST GO BUT MY SOUL LIES HELPLESS   102 23
  MY SOUL ALONG WITH THE ROUT   107 22
  WITHIN HER SPACIOUS SOUL TO FIND DELIGHT   125 35
  WHEN I HOLD THEM MY SPENT SOUL UNDERSTANDS   128 8
  OF THE NIGHT IN HIS SOUL AND NONE OF THE TUNE   130 14
  THA COULD LET THY VERY SOUL OUT A MAN   138 23
  WHY DOES MY SOUL CONTRACT WITH UNNATURAL FEAR   140 21
  I WAS LAST NIGHT WHEN MY SOUL RANG CLEAR AS A BELL   141 24
  I KNOW NOT MY SOUL IS IN STRIFE   143 24
  MOANS AND BOOMS THE SOUL OF A PEOPLE IMPRISONED ASLEEP   149 11
  YOUR PASSION IN THE BASKET OF YOUR SOUL   151 13
  CAN WARM HER HANDS AND INVITE HER SOUL   151 27
  I WOULD GIVE MY SOUL FOR THE HOMESTEAD TO FALL WITH ME + 160 3
  A POOL PUT OFF THE SOUL YOU'VE GOT OH LACK   161 27
  AND A GASP OF RELIEF BUT THE SOUL IS STILL COMPRESSED   167 15
  MATE MY HUNGRY SOUL WITH A GERM OF ITS WOMB   179 27
  OF FLOTSAM UNTIL MY SOUL IS TIRED OR SATISFIED   180 7
  BEND OVER THEM WITH MY SOUL TO CHERISH THE WET   180 10
  BRUSHING THE STARS GOES MY SOUL THAT SKIMS THE BOUNDS   193 25
  WITHIN MY BODY CRY OUT TO THE DREAMING SOUL   195 32
  THE INNERMOST FIRE OF MY OWN DIM SOUL OUT-SPINNING   218 22
  MY SOUL TO SEE YOU SETTLING AND TRYING TO CLIMB   221 23
  MY POOR MY PERISHED SOUL WITH THE SIGHT OF YOU   221 29

SOUL
  AND NOW IN THE DARK MY SOUL TO YOU   226 23
  HOW MY SOUL CLEAVES TO YOUR BOSOM AS I CLASP YOU   246 5
  OH FOR THE WONDER THAT BUBBLES INTO MY SOUL   250 25
  IT ALL IN YOUR SOUL   257 12
  AND YET THE SOUL CONTINUING NAKED-FOOTED EVER MORE VIVI+ 281 7
  EACH SOUL DEPARTING WITH ITS OWN ISOLATION   281 17
  SAVE IT HAD FIRST APPROACHED HIM AND CAJOLED HIS SOUL   290 3
  WHY WON'T YOU CAJOLE MY SOUL   290 6
  MY SOUL IS HALF-CAJOLED HALF-CAJOLED   291 26
  OF A PEERLESS SOUL   314 15
  I MIGHT BE A SOUL IN BLISS AN ANGEL APPROXIMATING TO THE 321 2
  WHERE MY SOUL FALLS IN THE LAST THROES OF BOTTOMLESS CO+ 322 3
  IS NOT EACH SOUL A VIVID THOUGHT IN THE GREAT CONSCIOUS+ 328 27
  THIS GREY MONOTONOUS SOUL IN THE WATER   338 11
  AND THE HUMAN SOUL IS FATED TO WIDE-EYED RESPONSIBILITY   347 2
  DEPTHS OF MY SOUL   366 3
  BEFORE ANYTHING HAD A SOUL   372 9
  HE SPOKE THIS WORD STOP DON'T BEAT IT FOR IT IS THE SOU+ 376 6
  ALL HIS SOUL IN HIS GALLANT MEMBER   378 13
  SOFT GRASS RUNS UPON A PATH THAT IS PATHLESS TO MEN SO + 406 3
  LINGER FOR NOW THEY REALISE ALL THAT IS LOST THEN THE L+ 406 6
  AND ALLOW THE SOUL TO FIND ITS LEVEL   428 7
  THERE'LL BE BABIES BORN THAT ARE CYGNETS O MY SOUL   438 21
  SO THAT HER SOUL CAN COME OUT BACK TO HER   448 25
  ON HIS SOUL THAT IS DARK OCEAN WITHIN HIM   453 22
  HIGH AND CLAWING WITH RAGE AT THE CLIFFS OF THE SOUL   454 9
  AS THE SUN OF MY SOUL IS SETTING   455 21
  WINTER AND THE GREAT DAY-SUN AND THE SUN IN MY SOUL   455 26
  OLDER THAN PLASM ALTOGETHER IS THE SOUL OF A MAN UNDERN+ 477 11
  GO DEEPER THAN LOVE FOR THE SOUL HAS GREATER DEPTHS   477 21
  PIVOTAL CORE OF THE SOUL HEAVIER THAN IRON   480 10
  THE SOUL OF MAN ALSO LEANS IN THE UNCONSCIOUS INCLINATI+ 487 17
  SOUL   490 13
  MY MOTHER WAS A SUPERIOR SOUL   490 14
  A SUPERIOR SOUL WAS SHE   501 20
  MY SOUL IS ALMOST BLANK MY SPIRIT QUITE   514 12
  AND GUARD THE LAST TREASURE OF THE SOUL OUR SANITY   545 5
  SOUL SOUL SOUL   545 12
  HE'S GOT A SOUL SOUL SOUL   545 21
  AND HIS SOUL SOUL SOUL   546 1
  BODY AND SOUL   580 19
  LEAVE ME ALONE NOW FOR MY SOUL IS BURNING   586 3
  THEN I SCREAM IN MY SOUL FOR I KNOW I CANNOT   601 3
  IS TO BE ALONE TO POSSESS ONE'S SOUL IN SILENCE   608 11
  IT IS ABSURD FOR ME TO DISPLAY MY NAKED SOUL AT THE TEA+ 608 16
  BUT WHEN EVERYBODY GOES ROUND WITH SOUL HALF-BARED OR Q+ 609 5
  WE FEEL HIM STRANGLING EVEN MORE THE ISSUES OF OUR SOUL   616 14
  TILL THE SOUL OF THE STIFF-NECKED IS GROUND TO DUST TO + 620 13
  I AM ILL BECAUSE OF WOUNDS TO THE SOUL TO THE DEEP EMOT+ 620 15
  AND THE WOUNDS TO THE SOUL TAKE A LONG LONG TIME ONLY   622 18
  YET FOREVER FELT IN THE SOUL   624 12
  INTO THE UTTERMOST CORNERS OF THE SOUL   624 20
  AND AGAINST THIS INWARD REVOLT OF THE NATIVE CREATURES + 629 6
  AND NOW THE IRON HAS ENTERED INTO THE SOUL   632 18
  I SCREAM IN MY SOUL FOR I KNOW I CANNOT   638 15
  YOU TELL ME EVERY MAN HAS A SOUL TO SAVE   638 17
  A SOUL TO LOSE   638 10
  THE AUTOMAT HAS NO SOUL TO LOSE   640 1
  IN THE MOMENT OF CHOICE THE SOUL ROLLS BACK   640 7
  AND THEN WHEN THE SOUL OF LIVING MEN REPUDIATES THEM   642 22
  SOFTLY SUBTLY SECRETLY IN SOUL FIRST THEN IN SPIRIT THE+ 696 26
  FAREWELL FAREWELL LOST SOUL   699 27
  EVEN OF THE SOUL FALLEN FROM THE HANDS OF GOD   701 18
  IS AN ABYSS DOWN WHICH THE SOUL CAN SLIP   708 22
  IN WHICH THE SOUL DELIGHTS AND THE SENSES   712 10
  BUT IN THE WORLD OF THE SOUL OF MAN   712 12
  ONLY IN THE SOUL OF MAN WHEN IT PIVOTS UPON THE EGO   712 24
  BUT IT IS THE SOUL OF MAN ONLY AND HIS MACHINES   713 1
  DO NOT THINK THAT A MACHINE IS WITHOUT A SOUL   713 2
  EVERY WHEEL ON ITS HUB HAS A SOUL EVIL   717 7
  AND IN THE BRUISED BODY THE FRIGHTENED SOUL   718 12
  PIECEMEAL THE BODY DIES AND THE TIMID SOUL   718 19
  AND OUR SOUL COWERS NAKED IN THE DARK RAIN OVER THE FLO+ 718 23
  OF DEATH TO CARRY THE SOUL ON THE LONGEST JOURNEY   718 26
  FITTING AND READY FOR THE DEPARTING SOUL   719 2
  AND LIFE DEPARTS LAUNCH OUT THE FRAGILE SOUL   720 10
  AND STRANGELY O CHILLED WAN SOUL A FLUSH OF ROSE   720 16
  AND THE FRAIL SOUL STEPS OUT INTO HER HOUSE AGAIN   721 4
  SO BUILD YOUR SHIP OF DEATH AND LET THE SOUL DRIFT   721 20
  FOR THE SOUL HAS A LONG LONG JOURNEY AFTER DEATH   723 20
  THE LITTLE SLENDER SOUL SITS SWIFTLY DOWN AND TAKES THE+ 724 2
  AND WHAT THE SOUL TAKES WITH HIM AND WHAT HE LEAVES BEH+ 724 7
  WHERE THE SOUL COMES AT LAST AND HAS UTTER PEACE   724 9
  OBLIVION WHERE THE SOUL AT LAST IS LOST   724 16
  THE SOUL HAS PEACE INWARD AND LOVELY PEACE   725 11
  MY SOUL HAS HAD A LONG HARD DAY   725 15
  THERE IS NO PLACE FOR THE SOUL TO FIND HER OBLIVION   726 10
  AND THERE OBLIVION DWELLS AND THE SILENT SOUL   726 22
  AND IF TONIGHT MY SOUL MAY FIND HER PEACE   727 10
  AROUND MY SOUL AND SPIRIT AROUND MY LIPS   744 5
  MY SOUL COMES LAMBENT FROM THE ENDLESS NIGHT   746 15
  OUR SOUL NOTHING BUT THE MAD MONOTONOUS   747 14
  OF NERVES THAT GRIND AND A SOUL THAT STINGS   750 12
  THE FLAME OF MY SOUL LIKE A TREMBLING STAR IS HUNG   757 2
  OH OUT-LANDER WEARY SOUL   759 13
  AND A DRAUGHT OF THEE IS STRENGTH TO A SOUL IN HELL   759 15
  HEAL ME FOR BODY AND SOUL I AM NOT WELL   803 6
  BETWEEN THE MORNING AND THE AFTERNOON STAND I HERE WITH+ 803 8
  MY SOUL IS HEAVY WITH SUNSHINE AND STEEPED WITH STRENGTH 807 4
  IN THE NIGHT THE SOUL OF A COWARD CREEPS OUT OF HIM   807 30
  IN YOUR SLEEP YOU TWIST YOUR SOUL HURTS YOU   824 13
  SOUL AND BODY BONE AND BLOOD   859 8
  TO SEE HIM FLASH AND TREMBLE WITH THE FIRE OF HIS SOUL   859 19
  EYES WHERE HIS HOT IMPRISONED SOUL HAS KEPT   861 28
  THE SOUL BESEECHING   865 8
  SHE TURNED AND KISSED HIM AND HIS EYES WERE THE SOUL OF+ 870 28
  OH WHAT WERE YOU WHAT WERE YOU BUT THE STUFF OF MY SOUL

SOUL
    AND NOW WITH THE KNOCKING OF HIS HEART AGAINST MY SOUL   871   8
    I RUN AWAKE TO THE HOUSE OF MY SOUL AND FIND IT EMPTY   871   9
    YOUR BEAUTY IN THE BASKET OF YOUR SOUL   873   23
    WATCHING THY GREAT SOUL TUG WITHIN THE LEASH   879   16
    HER NAKED SOUL OF FEAR   880   30
    THEN UP FROM OUT HER VERY SOUL THERE SEEMED   881   6
    HER SOUL TO ME AND SHE WAS VERY GLAD   881   13
    BUT WHETHER IT CALLED IN MY SOUL   881   24
    TO FIND YOU AND FILL MY SOUL WITH YOU   887   17
    WITHERED MY INSOLENT SOUL WOULD BE GONE LIKE FLOWERS TH+   *891   27
    SO MY SOUL LIKE A PASSIONATE WOMAN TURNS   *891   29
    AND THE SOUL OF THE WIND AND MY BLOOD COMPARE   *892   4
    THE LAST DEAR FUEL AND HEAP IT ON MY SOUL   *895   27
    AS MY WILD SOUL SHRINKS AND THE SONGS ARE DRIVEN FROM M+   *896   12
    THEY KEEP ME ASSURED AND WHEN MY SOUL FEELS LONELY   *900   20
    THEY KEEP ME ASSURED AND WHEN MY SOUL FEELS LONELY   *903   32
    THE LAST DEAR FUEL AND HEAP IT ON MY SOUL   *904   16
    OF THE SHIP OF THE SOUL OVER SEAS WHERE DREAMED DREAMS +   *905   20
    THE HALLS OF MY LIFE AND COMPELS MY SOUL TO CONFORM   *906   14
    THE HALLS OF MY LIFE COMPELLING MY SOUL TO CONFORM   *908   8
    AND DO I NOT SEEK TO MATE MY GROWN DESIROUS SOUL   *926   22
    THE HATE OF TERROR OR DENY THE FECUND SOUL HER EMBRACES   *926   25
    MY SOUL AGAIN   *929   29
    IN HER BARBAROUS SOUL TO GROPE WITH ECSTASY   *936   35
    FOR OUT IN THE WASTE WILD SOUL SPACE THAT SHALL   *938   19
    AND HER ARMS AND HER BOSOM AND THE WHOLE OF HER SOUL IS+   *940   20
    I SEE THE WOMAN'S SOUL STEAL IN HER EYES   *943   19
    MY POOR AND PERISHED SOUL AT THE JOY OF YOU   *945   15
    I NEED NOT LOOK AFTER MY SOUL BEGUILE MY FEAR   *945   27
    I'M A RELIGIOUS SOUL   *947   15
    THERE'LL BE BABIES BORN THAT ARE YOUNG WILD SWANS O MY +   *947   24
    CENTRAL PRIMORDIAL FIRE OF THE SOUL HEAVIER THAN IRON   *951   24
    CENTRAL PRIMORDIAL FIRE OF THE SOUL HEAVIER THAN IRON   *952   1
    CENTRAL PRIMORDIAL FIRE OF THE SOUL THAT LEANS AND YEAR+   *952   6
    THE SOUL   *954   15
    BLUE JOY OF MY SOUL   *954   23
    WHAT A JOURNEY FOR MY SOUL   *955   1
    SLIPS OUT THE SOUL INVISIBLE ONE WRAPPED STILL   *957   8
    FRIGHTENED AND ALONE THE SOUL SLIPS OUT OF THE HOUSE   *957   12
    AND BUILD IT LOVINGLY AND PUT IT BETWEEN THE HANDS OF Y+   *957   26
    WHAT WILL YOU DO IF YOU HAVE NO SHIP OF THE SOUL   *957   33
    BUT FOR MYSELF BUT FOR MY SOUL DEAR SOUL   *958   17
    DAINTY AND READY FOR THE DEPARTING SOUL   *958   22
    AND PUT IT BETWEEN THE HANDS OF THE TREMBLING SOUL   *958   23
    THE LITTLE SLENDER SOUL SITS SWIFTLY DOWN AND TAKES THE+   *958   32
    SLOW SLOW MY SOUL IN HIS LITTLE SHIP   *959   9
    ROW LITTLE SOUL ROW ON   *959   15
    DRIFT ON DRIFT ON MY SOUL TOWARDS THE MOST PURE   *959   22
    AS THE SOUL AT LAST SLIPS PERFECT INTO THE GOAL THE CORE   *959   31
    OF THIS MY SOUL INTO THE PLASM OF PEACE   *960   2
    OF DEATH THAT WILL CARRY THE SOUL   *960   14
    THE LITTLE SHIP WITH ITS SOUL TO THE WONDER-GOAL   *961   4
    AND WHAT THE SOUL CARRIES WITH HIM AND WHAT HE LEAVES B+   *961   12

SOULLESS
    A SOULLESS NECKAR WITH WINKING SEAS IN HIS EYES   130   19
    ON HIS LIPS I LONG TO BE SOULLESS I TINGLE   130   21

SOULLESSLY
    YOU UNDINE-CLEAR AND PEARLY SOULLESSLY COOL   161   15

SOULS
    FROM ME TO THE BOYS WHOSE BRIGHTENING SOULS IT LAVES   51   24
    SOME FEW DARK-CLEAVING THE DOORWAY SOULS THAT CLING AS +   75   10
    I MUST NOT WIN THEIR SOULS NO NEVER I ONLY MUST WIN   93   7
    THE AIR IS ALL CLOSE AND POISONOUS IT HAS DRUGGED OUR S+   175   12
    TINY LIGHTHOUSES LITTLE SOULS OF LANTERNS COURAGE BURST+   206   16
    OF QUESTING BRILLIANT SOULS GOING OUT WITH THEIR TRUE   221   27
    YOU HAVE CAJOLED THE SOULS OF MILLIONS OF US   290   4
    AND THEN TO SEE THE NEW REAL SOULS SPROUT UP   315   31
    NEW WILD SOULS   315   34
    THEIR STILL SOULS ABSORBED   451   15
    O SMALL FLOTILLA OF SORRY SOULS   542   11
    THE GENTLE SOULS THAT FIGURE IN THE PAINT   580   22
    THE UNHAPPY SOULS ARE THOSE THAT CAN'T DIE AND BECOME S+   612   19
    GENITALS BRAINS AND SOULS   631   22
    THEY HAVE NO SONG IN THEIR SOULS NONE IN THEIR SPIRITS   657   13
    THEIR HARDENED SOULS ARE WASHED WITH FIRE AND WASHED AN+   663   6
    SO THAT LOST SOULS MAY EAT GRAPES   710   17
    AND THERE ARE THE BRIGHT DOORS WHERE SOULS GO GAILY IN   711   3
    AND THERE ARE THE DARK DOORS WHERE SOULS PASS SILENTLY   711   4
    HELL IS THE HOME OF SOULS LOST IN DARKNESS   711   15
    EVEN AS HEAVEN IS THE HOME OF SOULS LOST IN LIGHT   711   16
    THERE ARE SOULS THAT ARE AT HOME IN BOTH HOMES   711   18
    ALREADY OUR SOULS ARE OOZING THROUGH THE EXIT   718   4
    THE EARTH'S LONG CONICAL SHADOW IS FULL OF SOULS   721   15
    ARE CROWDED WITH LOST SOULS THE UNEASY DEAD   722   22
    WE LET OUR SOULS BE PURE AND VULNERABLE   736   24
    IN A CASCADE OF SOULS TO SORROWFUL DEATH   743   31
    TO ROLL THE GRAVE-STONE OFF THEIR SOULS FROM THE CAVE O+   793   7
    LIES LATENT IN THE SOULS OF THE YOUNG A LATENT DESIRE   829   10
    THERE ARE ENOUGH OF GREAT SOULS TO COMPLETE AN EFFICIEN+   859   23
    BY NATURE THAN BY BOOTS AND WET FEET OFTEN CARRY MERRY +   866   15
    ON THE LITTLE BANK OUR TWO SOULS   887   1
    WITH THE LUSTY SOULS OF MY BOYS YET THEY HIDE THEIR FAC+ *926   23
    STREWN WITH DIM WRECKAGE AND CROWDED WITH CRYING SOULS   *957   16
    THE LONG MARGINAL STRETCHES OF EXISTENCE CROWDED WITH L+ *957   23
    ONCE OUTSIDE UPON THE GREY MARSH BEACHES WHERE LOST SOU+ *957   28
    THEY FALL UPON THE NEW OUTCOMING SOULS WITH RAGE   *958   5

SOUL-STAR
    BETWEEN NIGHT AND DAY MY SOUL-STAR IN ONE   799   23

SOUL'S
    SOUL'S NAKED LIGHTNING WHICH SHOULD SURE ATTEST   87   24
    THOUGH SURELY MY SOUL'S BEST DREAM IS STILL   117   4
    AND FALLING WAVES IN HIS ARMS AND THE LOST SOUL'S KISS   130   20
    OF FIERY COLDNESS TO BE GONE IN A LOST SOUL'S BLISS   130   23
    BENEATH THIS POWERFUL TREE MY WHOLE SOUL'S FLUID   131   8
    THE POOL FOR MY LIMBS TO FATHOM MY SOUL'S LAST SCHOOL   161   17
    THE SILKEN SHRIEK OF THE SOUL'S TORN MEMBRANE   364   24
    THE MALE SOUL'S MEMBRANE   364   25
    OUT OF THE SOUL'S MIDDLE TO THE MIDDLE-MOST SUN WAY-OFF   480   26
    THE SOUL'S FIRST PASSION IS FOR SHEER LIFE   482   1
    AND THE SOUL'S NEXT PASSION IS TO REFLECT   482   3
    ACCORDING TO THE SOUL'S DESIRE   652   17
    OH THINK OF THEM AND WITH THE SOUL'S DEEP SIGH   722   12
    AND MY SOUL'S DESIRE AND MADE YOU REAL   871   5
    OF HER SOUL'S PAINED PERFUME   881   9
    HER SOUL'S FLAG SANK AND HER PRIDE PUT OFF ITS CROWN   *936   17
    WHEN MEN WOVE WITH THEIR HANDS AND THEIR SOUL'S ATTENTI+ *949   26
    AND THINK OF THEM AND WITH THE SOUL'S DEEP SIGH   *958   17

SOUND
    WHISTLING SHE-DELIRIOUS RAGE AND THE DREADFUL SOUND   36   14
    AND I WOKE TO THE SOUND OF THE WOOD-PIGEON AND LAY AND +   38   12
    HOW BEAUTIFUL HE IS WITHOUT SOUND   39   19
    STRANGE VOICE HAS NO SOUND   40   12
    AND STRANGE IN MY BLOOD-SWEPT EARS WAS THE SOUND   61   24
    LISTENING FOR THE SOUND OF HER FEET ACROSS THE FLOOR   121   16
    AND THE SOUND OF HER GENTLY RUSTLING IN HEAVEN LIKE A   134   18
    AND A CURIOUS DEARTH OF SOUND   145   31
    THE YOUNG GRASS TWINKLES IN THE WIND AND THE SOUND   152   28
    NOR SOUND ONLY INTERMITTENT MACHINERY WHIRRING   153   8
    WILL SOUND IN HEAVEN BEFORE IT IS UNDONE   154   17
    NO SOUND OF GUNS NOR OVERHEAD NO RUSHED   165   31
    THERE IS SILENCE ONLY THE SILENCE NEVER A SOUND   166   13
    SOUND OF ARTILLERY AEROPLANES PRESENCES   169   15
    NO SOUND FROM ST STEPHEN'S   170   27
    NO SOUND FROM THE STRANGERS THE PLACE IS DARK AND FEAR   173   3
    SOUND   205   7
    A SOUND SUBDUED IN THE DARKNESS TEARS   210   21
    LIKE THE SEETHING SOUND IN A SHELL   216   7
    WITHOUT A SOUND   229   9
    FIND OUT IF I'M SOUND OR BANKRUPT   237   3
    IN THE WINDOW HIS BODY BLACK FUR AND THE SOUND OF   243   24
    UNHEARD AND SUBTLE NEVER A SOUND   262   8
    SAY IN THE SOUND OF ALL YOUR MACHINES   292   31
    HAVING SHED THEIR SOUND AND FINISHED ALL THEIR ECHOING   296   27
    NOR SOUND OF STILL MORE FOUL HUMAN PERFECTION   316   8
    OR DID IT SOUND ON THE PLASM DIRECT   320   4
    I REMEMBER WHEN I FIRST HEARD BULL-FROGS BREAK INTO SOU+   365   32
    AND RUNNING AWAY FROM THE SOUND OF A WOMAN IN LABOUR   366   12
    THE PONDEROUS SOMBRE SOUND OF THE GREAT DRUM OF   371   6
    AND ROUND THE RING THEY WENT TO THE SOUND OF THE WHIP   444   20
    WHAT WAS WOUNDED IS SOUND   461   22
    BE SWEET AND SOUND   504   9
    MAKES OF HIMSELF A BELFRY OF THROBBING SOUND   530   10
    THE MOHAMMEDANS SAY THAT THE SOUND OF BELLS   622   19
    OF SOUND   623   7
    WHERE TISSUE PLUNGES INTO BRONZE WITH WIDE WILD CIRCLES+   623   10
    AND THE SOUND OF A BLAST THROUGH THE SEA-CURVED CORE OF+   623   13
    SWIFT WIND OR SOUND RINGING ROCK   637   11
    AND WHAT AN AWFUL CONCATENATION OF SOUND IT IS   657   12
    AND THE SOUND OF ITS HOWLING GETS BIGGER AND BIGGER AND+   670   14
    LET THE SEA HEAVE NO MORE IN SOUND   698   10
    FOR THE SOUND OF THE SEA AS IT FURLS AND UNFURLS   747   21
    WITHOUT A SOUND   824   31
    I START FROM THE DROOP OF FORGETFULNESS AS THE SOUND OF+   858   21
    AND HIS SINGING SOUND AS THEY ALWAYS DO AT THE BEGINNIN+   865   17
    THE YOUNG GRASS TWINKLED IN THE WIND AND THE SOUND   866   24
    AND WHAT WAS THE SOUND OF THE BIRDS AND THE WATER BUT S+   870   26
    YOU SOUND SO DREADFUL SO CRUELLY HURT MY DEAR   871   18
    I SEE THE STRONG SOUND EARTH BETRAYED AS A FLOATING   874   30
    NEVER A SOUND WAS HEARD   887   23
    AND WAKE TO THE SOUND OF THE WOODPIGEONS AND LIE AND LI+ *912   4
    AND STRANGE IN MY BLOOD-SWEPT EARS WAS THE SOUND   *912   4
    THE STREET THAT IS FULL OF THE RUSTLING SOUND OF A SHELL *917   2
    SURGEON ME SOUND   *929   17
    I CAN HEAR THE SOUND OF THE SCYTHE STROKES FOUR   *944   2

SOUNDED
    AS THE ELEPHANT BELLS SOUNDED TONG-TONG-TONG BELL OF THE   390   32
    A TINY BELL OF CONCLUSION HAS SOUNDED   512   7

SOUNDER
    AND SOUNDER THAN ALL INSURANCE IS A SHINY MENTAL CONCEIT   543   3

SOUNDEST
    YET THERE IS WAKING FROM THE SOUNDEST SLEEP   725   6

SOUNDING
    I DO FORGET THE SOUNDING OF YOUR VOICE   129   8
    TORTOISE-WISE THE FIRST BELL SOUNDING   358   13
    THEIR BELLS SOUNDING FRUSTRATE AND SINISTER   391   4
    BUT SETTING SETTING BEHIND THE SOUNDING SEA BETWEEN   455   23
    NO DOUBT TO THE SOUNDING OF THE SPHERES   524   14

SOUNDLESS
    ON THE FLOOD THAT SOUNDLESS SWINGS   109   16
    THE SOUNDLESS NIGHT WHEREON OUR DAYS ARE SHIPPED   133   4
    SOUNDLESS BLISS-FULL WIDE-RAYED HONEY-BODIED   307   6
    FOLDING BACK THEIR SOUNDLESS PETALLED EARS   311   9
    OVER THE EDGE OF THE SOUNDLESS CATARACT   322   1
    BUT SOUNDLESS AND OUT OF CONTACT   337   17
    RINGING THE SOUNDLESS BELL OF HIS PRESENCE IN CHAOS   358   19
    AND OUR SCREAM IS SOUNDLESS IN THE PARALYSIS OF SLEEP   408   2
    TILL ALL IS SOUNDLESS AND SENSELESS A TREMENDOUS BODY O+   698   22
    BLACKER UPON THE SOUNDLESS UNGURGLING FLOOD   719   12
    WHOSE WHORLS FOLD ROUND TO THE CORE OF SOUNDLESS SILENC+   724   5
    AND LET THE DARK BE SOUNDLESS WITHOUT FACE   738   3

SOUNDLESS
   HAVING NO BOAT TO LAUNCH UPON THE SHAKEN SOUNDLESS   *957 30
   ON THE MOST SOUNDLESS OF ALL SEAS   *959 10

SOUNDLESSLY
   SOUNDLESSLY DOWN ACROSS THE COUNTIES OUT OF THE RESONANT   149 1
   OUT OF THE SLEEP FROM THE GLOOM OF MOTION SOUNDLESSLY   149 9
   SOUNDLESSLY MOVING IN HEAVEN'S OTHER DIRECTION   161 23

SOUNDS
   SUCCEEDING SHARP LITTLE SOUNDS DROPPING INTO SILENCE   63 10
   MUFFLING MY MIND AS SNOW MUFFLES THE SOUNDS THAT PASS   75 22
   WITH SOUNDS THAT ENDLESSLY SWELL AND SINK LIKE THE STOR+   97 24
   SOUNDS WAVE THEIR LITTLE WINGS   109 14
   NOW THAT IT SOUNDS SELF-CONSCIOUS THROUGH THE UNLIMITED+   325 4
   BUT IT SOUNDS SO AMAZINGLY LIKE A SLOGAN   333 23
   SOUNDS STILL UNFROZEN AND THE TRAIL IS STILL EVIDENT   401 3
   AND THEN THE HEAVENS CACKLE WITH UNCOUTH SOUNDS   647 16
   ONLY THEY ARE MADE TO UTTER THESE COG-WHEEL SOUNDS   657 15
   FOLD UP ALL SOUNDS   698 13
   BREATHLESS SOUNDS OF SATISFACTION CLAMOUR OF DELIGHT   865 27
   MUFFLING MY MIND AS SNOW MUFFLES THE SOUNDS THAT PASS   *897 22
   MUFFLING MY MIND AS SNOW MUFFLES THE SOUNDS THAT PASS   *900 30

SOUP
   TILL HE WAS BORN FROM A WOMB AND ATE SOUP AND BREAD   689 28

SOUR
   DEAD AND TRODDEN TO NOUGHT IN THE SOUR BLACK EARTH   258 16
   TRODDEN TO NOUGHT IN SOUR DEAD EARTH   258 19
   I IN THE SOUR BLACK TOMB TRODDEN TO ABSOLUTE DEATH   259 1
   IS SOUR BITTER FRUITS CANKERED BY LIES   504 14
   MEANING SOUR MAKE YOU PULL A FACE AFTER   530 19
   THOUGH SOME APPLES TASTE PREPONDERANTLY OF WATER WET AN+ 708 2
   I'LL TURN THEIR BLOOD LIKE SOUR MILK ROTTEN WITH THUNDER 792 6

SOURCE
   OF KISSES OH HELP ME GOD HERE AT THE SOURCE   153 28
   WE ARE THE SOURCE   204 27
   FROM THE NIGHT TO THE SOURCE OF YOU   240 5
   SHE FOUND THE SOURCE OF MY SUBJECTION   262 17
   FROM THE SOURCE NOT OUT OF BOTTLES AND BOTTLED PERSONAL   481 4
   LIFE FROM THE SOURCE UNADULTERATED   481 11
   SOURCE   481 29
   THE SOURCE AND THE END OF WHICH WE KNOW   811 7

SOURCES
   TO THE SOURCES OF MYSTERY IN THE DEPTHS   261 14
   WHEN SHE HAS PUT HER HAND ON MY SECRET DARKEST SOURCES + 267 6

SOUTH
   THE VERY MOON IN THE SOUTH   37 14
   SOUTH WITH FLYING CURDS   99 21
   A TRAIN GOES ROARING SOUTH   110 13
   MY LOVE TILL YOU WENT SOUTH   156 24
   THE SOUTH   284 27
   SOUTH   394 13
   EMBEDDED IN THEM I LOOK OUT ON THE SUNSHINE OF THE SOUTH 620 31
   TAKE ME SOUTH AGAIN TO THE OLIVE TREES   652 22
   AS THE WIND RACES SOUTH   861 2
   FLAPS UP FROM THE PLAYGROUND AS A GREAT TRAIN STEAMS SO+ *894 29

SOUTHERN
   HAVE YOU NOT SEEN IN THE WILD WINTER SUN OF THE SOUTHER+ 303 4
   THIS IS THE ANCIENT SOUTHERN EARTH WHENCE THE VASES WERE 305 12

SOUTHERN-WOOD
   AS IF THE SOUTHERN-WOOD SHOULD SOOTHE HIS DREAMS   877 32

SOUTHRON
   HE LEAVES ME GOES DOWN TO THE SOUTHRON FOLK   877 14

SOUTHWARDS
   SOUTHWARDS ALAS   50 18

SOUTH-WESTWARD
   EAGLE SOUTH-WESTWARD FACING   781 6

SOUTH-WEST
   TOWARDS THE SUN TOWARDS THE SOUTH-WEST   372 25
   TOWARDS THE SUN TO SOUTH-WEST   781 1

SOVIET
   YOU ARE ITEMS IN THE SOVIET STATE   443 3
   BUT IT IS THE SOVIET STATE ALONE WHICH COUNTS   443 5
   WHY HAVE A SOVIET THAT ONLY WANTS TO SCREW US ALL IN AS   452 3

SOVIETS
   INDUSTRIAL AND FINANCIAL SYSTEMS MACHINES AND SOVIETS   452 10
   SUCCESS FAILURE LOVE CHASTITY DEBAUCHERY MONEY OR SOVIE+ 839 19

SOW
   LAST NIGHT WHEN I WENT WITH THE LANTERN THE SOW WAS GRA+   38 8
   TAKE THE LANTERN AND WATCH THE SOW FOR FEAR SHE GRAB HE+ *892 24

SOWN
   AND HE IS THE BRIDE I HAVE SOWN HIM WITH THE SEED   742 13

SOWS
   TO THE MAN WHO THRESHES AND SOWS THE SHEAVES   *899 9
   TO THE MAN WHO THRESHES AND SOWS THE SHEAVES   *902 21

SOW'S
   AND TURN THE POOR SILK GLOVE INTO A LUSTY SOW'S EAR   538 22
   INTO SOW'S EARS   538 25

SPACE
   AND I SAW HER FOR THE FLARING SPACE   62 9
   SO SO GAILY A GENERAL CANTERS ACROSS THE SPACE   66 13
   ACROSS THE SPACE ON THE CAT IN HEAVEN'S HOSTILE EMINENCE   97 22
   OF HER FEET AS THEY FLEW FOR A SPACE THEN PAUSED TO PRE+ 123 4
   BACKWARD INTO SPACE TO ALIGHT   162 27
   THE SAME INSANITY OF SPACE   214 19
   THE SPACE OF THE WORLD IS IMMENSE BEFORE ME AND AROUND + 222 22
   IF I TURN QUICKLY I AM TERRIFIED FEELING SPACE SURROUND+ 222 23
   LIKE A MAN IN A BOAT ON VERY CLEAR DEEP WATER SPACE FRI+ 222 24
   WITH AN INTERVAL OF SPACE BETWEEN   228 2
   AND I COVERED THE EARTH AND ALL SPACE   248 27
   THREE SIDES SET ON ME SPACE AND FEAR BUT THE FOURTH SIDE 249 10
   AT THE CORE OF SPACE   435 22
   BEYOND THE GREAT BULL THAT BELLOWED THROUGH SPACE AND   437 10
   SPACE   440 3
   SWUNG GREAT CURVES THROUGH THE UPPER SPACE AND CAME   445 6
   CURVED SPACE   481 15
   PEACE I HAVE FROM THE CORE OF THE ATOM FROM THE CORE OF+ 499 4
   THE VEINS OF LIVING SPACE AND ADDS A GLISTEN   505 5
   FOR SPACE IS ALIVE   505 5
   INTO HOLLOW SPACE   506 7
   IN THE MIDDLE OF VOLUTED SPACE   512 4
   AT THE CORE OF SPACE THE FINAL KNELL   512 16
   WITHIN THE GENITALS OF LIVING SPACE   513 18
   NOTHING AND NOBODY IN THE WHOLE VAST REALM OF SPACE   514 20
   AND FRESHEN THE PUTRID LITTLE SPACE IN WHICH WE ARE CRI+ 515 4
   THE SANITY OF SPACE   515 17
   AND THEY MAKE ME FEEL AS IF SPACE SHIFTED   524 21
   SPACE OF COURSE IS ALIVE   525 1
   FROM THE WILD HEART OF SPACE THAT I CALL THE SUN OF SUNS 525 9
   SWEEPING THE CURVE OF SPACE AND MOVING THE SILENCE   609 12
   SOFTER THAN THE SPACE BETWEEN THE STARS   667 9
   AND BEHIND ME NOW IN THE GULFS OF SPACE LIES THE GOLDEN+ 695 26
   BUT A STEP ONWARDS IN UNTRAVELLED SPACE   713 15
   FOR ONE YEAR'S SPACE ATTEND ON OUR ANGRY DEAD   740 16
   SET OFF IN DIFFERENT DIRECTIONS NOT DIFFERENT DIRECTION+ 760 24
   FAR IN THE HOLLOW OF SPACE   787 22
   YET I HAVE LAIN IN HIS LOINS ERE HE BEGOT ME IN MOTHER + 801 14
   ASK IN THE SPACE OF THEIR EYES   816 10
   AND MORE SPACE THAN IN LIFE   816 23
   UNINHABITED SPACE NOW RUNS   823 25
   FAR OFF UPON THE MISTY WATERS OF THE DEPTHS OF SPACE   841 3
   LIKE A LONELY STAR DROPPING THROUGH SPACE   867 24
   TO THE VAST OF SPACE WHERE BRIGHTNESS RACES THE BLUE   875 14
   HE DRAWS A DEEP HARD BREATH FROM SPACE TO SPACE   878 23
   FROM SPACE TO LONGER SPACE LIFTS A HARSH BREATH   878 24
   INTO MUD THE SPACE FAST SHRINKS IN THE BUILDER'S HANDS   *896 11
   AND SING IN THIS SPACE THAT THE BUILDER NOW DEMANDS   *896 16
   WRAPPED UP IN THE SKY'S DIM SPACE OF HOARSE SILENCE   *898 15
   WRAPPED UP IN THE SKY'S DIM SPACE OF HOARSE SILENCE   *901 24
   AND I SAW HER FOR THE FLARING SPACE   *912 16
   OF HER FEET AS THEY LEPT FOR A SPACE THEN PAUSE TO PRESS *934 10
   FOR OUT IN THE WASTE WILD SOUL SPACE THAT SHALL   *938 19
   THREE SIDES SET ON ME SPACE AND FEAR BUT THE FOURTH SID+ *945 22
   A GREAT BULL BELLOWED THROUGH SPACE CALLING TO THE MILK+ *946 21

SPACES
   HAVE PRESSED IMMEASURABLE SPACES OF HOARSE SILENCE   75 21
   SOON THE SPACES OF THE WESTERN SKY   163 13
   NOW FROM THE DARKENED SPACES   242 20
   FOLLOW THE TRAIL OF THE DEAD ACROSS GREAT SPACES FOR TH+ 406 4
   BUT IN THE GREAT SPACES OF DEATH   677 18
   IN SPACES WIDE WITH MISTRUST   823 22
   HAVE PRESSED THE IMMEASURABLE SPACES OF HOARSE SILENCE   *897 21
   HAVE PRESSED IMMEASURABLE SPACES OF HOARSE SILENCE   *900 29

SPACIOUS
   WITHIN HER SPACIOUS SOUL TO FIND DELIGHT   125 35
   AND THAT'S WHAT MAKES IT ETERNALLY SPACIOUS AND UNSTUFFY 525 3
   WITHIN THE SPACIOUS GLOOM OF MYSTERY   *936 34

SPADE
   SUCH AN INSTRUMENT A SPADE LIKE A SPEAR OR AN OAR   254 20

SPAN
   WHERE I SHOULD BE AND WITH HER OWN STRONG SPAN   128 29

SPANGLED
   THAT SPANGLED GLISTEN IS GONE THAT AT-ONENESS WITHOUT A+ 656 16
   AS THE LEOPARD SMITES THE SMALL CALF WITH A SPANGLED PA+ 683 9
   THERE IS THE SPANGLED DRAGON OF THE STARS AT LARGE   796 20

SPANGLES
   WITH A FEW GOLD SPANGLES   444 25

SPANGLING
   AND FOAL-FOOTS SPANGLING THE PATHS   152 11

SPANIARD
   SHE CAN SIN WITH SOME THICK-SET SPANIARD   618 7
   THE INWARD COCKY ASSERTIVENESS OF THE SPANIARD SEEMS TO+ 618 9

SPANIELS
   HIM TO PIECES THE GOOD-HEARTED SPANIELS   494 4

SPANISH
   I REALISED THE SECRET JOY HER YOUNG SPANISH HUSBAND HAD   618 22

SPARE
   WE ARE NOT LOVERS MY DARLING WE FIGHT AND WE DO NOT SPA+   92 16
   SPARE ME THE STRENGTH TO LEAVE YOU   102 21
   THAT CARRIES MOONS ALONG AND SPARE THE STRESS   195 35
   SPARE A MILLION OR TWO OF HUMANS   402 30
   DEATH DEATH TAKE ME WITH YOU TO SPARE ME THIS LAST   767 27

SPARETH
    SO MUCH MORE ROOM FOR RIOT THE GREAT GOD SPARETH NOT   *926 28

SPARK
    SPARK FLIES   47 25
    THAT SPARK FLY UP AT US EVEN   49 14
    A SPARK BENEATH THE WHEEL   68 28
    THE REST HAD DOORWAY TO THEE THROUGH THAT SPARK   69 21
    FLY LIKE A SPARK INTO THE WOMB OF PASSION   89 6
    EVEN THERE I SEE A BLUE SPARK THAT WILL FLY   89 34
    DIM SELF THAT RISES SLOWLY TO LEAVES AND THE FLOWER'S G+   92 20
    THE LENGTH OF A SPARK   110 6
    EXTINCT ONE YELLOW-FLUFFY SPARK   119 22
    THE SPARK INTENSE WITHIN IT ALL WITHOUT   160 22
    THE SPARK FROM STORMS OF CORROSION AS SEEDS   160 28
    TO BE BLOWN OUT TO LET NIGHT DOWSE THE SPARK   212 9
    WHAT IS THAT SPARK   241 5
    THE FINEST SPLINTER OF A SPARK   241 8
    WITH THAT FINE DEMONIACAL SPARK   241 15
    TO BURY ITS WEARY SPARK   253 32
    IS THERE A SAPPHIRE OF MUTUAL TRUST A BLUE SPARK   478 6
    IS THAT UNBROKEN SPARK IN HIM   524 2
    AND ALL I WANT IS TO SEE THE SPARK FLICKER   524 5
    WITH LUST CRUSHES OUT THE SPARK   524 8
    BECAUSE WHEN THE SPARK IS CRUSHED IN A MAN   524 10
    THE SPARK FELL AND KINDLED INSTANTLY ON MY BLOOD   618 4
    OR VOICE OR ANY SINGLE SPARK   738 4
    BUT THE SPARK OF ME THAT IS ME IS MORE THAN MINE OWN   801 18
    THE QUICK KINDLING SPARK OF A GENEROUS TRUST   855 8
    A MOMENT LIKE A WAVERING SPARK   *912 19
    A SPARK BENEATH HIS WHEEL   *915 12
    HE MADE HAD DOORWAY TO THEE THROUGH THAT SPARK   *916 4
    EXTINCT ONE YELLOW BLOODY SPARK   *932 31

SPARKING
    AND IN HER HANDS THE SPARKING NEEDLES FLY   752 10
    THE MINUTE SPARKING OF DARKNESS WHICH   772 29

SPARKLE
    SPARKLE BENEATH LUMINOUS HILLS   162 7
    ARE THOSE THAT GIVE THEMSELVES AWAY IN FLASH AND SPARKLE   523 22
    IF YOU SEE MY RINGS HOW THEY SPARKLE WITHIN MY EARS   755 3

SPARKLED
    AND I DON'T SUPPOSE THE ICHTHYOSAURUS SPARKLED LIKE THE   523 16
    ONCE I KNEW A SUMMER THAT SPARKLED   *933 14

SPARKLES
    LIKE A CAT'S DISTENDED PUPIL THAT SPARKLES WITH LITTLE +   97 15
    O THE GOLDEN SPARKLES LAID EXTINCT   120 6

SPARKS
    THE QUICK SPARKS ON THE GORSE-BUSHES ARE LEAPING   33 1
    GO MYRIAD SPARKS OF PEOPLE FILLING   110 19
    YOU WATCH THE RED SPARKS WHIRL AND FLEE   116 23
    JETS OF SPARKS IN FOUNTAINS OF BLUE COME LEAPING   136 6
    NEW SPARKS OF WONDER OPENING IN SURPRISE   136 16
    TO BRING TOGETHER TWO STRANGE SPARKS BEGET   218 20
    CUNNINGLY BLOWING ON THE FALLEN SPARKS ODDS AND ENDS OF+   271 31
    AND SENDS OFF MILLIONS OF SPARKS OF NEW ATOMS   506 9
    SEND ME THEM BY THE SWIFT WAY THE WAY OF THE SPARKS   789 19
    FOLLOW ME NOW UP THE LADDERS OF SPARKS   798 11
    RUN UP THE FLAMES AND WITH FEET ON THE SPARKS   798 21
    THE QUICK SPARKS ON THE GORSE BUSHES ARE LEAPING   *891 1
    YOU WATCH THE FIRE SPARKS SWIRL AND FLEE   *930 22

SPARROW
    A SPARROW FLUTTERS   244 7
    MY BIRD MY BROWN SPARROW IN MY BREAST   246 18

SPARROW-BUBS
    SPARROW-BUBS   271 35

SPARROWS
    WANTON SPARROWS THAT TWITTERED WHEN MORNING LOOKED IN   71 13
    LEST HER BRIGHT EYES LIKE SPARROWS SHOULD FLY IN   122 29
    IT IS ONLY THE SPARROWS LIKE DEAD BLACK LEAVES ON THE   142 9
    LEST HER BRIGHT EYES LIKE SPARROWS SHOULD FLY IN   *934 5

SPARS
    WITH MASTS ERECT AND SPARS ALL SET AND SAILS SPREAD   542 2

SPARSE-HAIRED
    AND THE SPARSE-HAIRED ELEPHANTS SLOWLY FOLLOWING   389 34

SPASM
    ENCROACHING TOWARDS A CRISIS A MEETING A SPASM AND THRO+   66 22
    A KISS AND A SPASM OF FAREWELL A MOMENT'S ORGASM OF   280 27
    THEY EXCHANGE NO WORD NO SPASM NOT EVEN ANGER   337 18
    TILL SUDDENLY IN THE SPASM OF COITION TUPPING LIKE A JE+   365 7
    SPASM   365 28

SPATTERING
    LIKE SPATTERING SHOUTS OF AN ORATOR ENDLESSLY DROPPING   54 6

SPAWN
    AND THEN THE HORDES OF THE SPAWN OF THE MACHINE   635 6
    AND LIVED TO SEE THEM SPAWN INTO MACHINE-ROBOTS   644 6

SPEAK
    SPEAK YOU MY HOME WHAT IS IT I DON'T DO WELL   63 7
    THAT SPEAK NO WORD OF THEIR RAPTURE BUT ONLY   69 7
    SPEAK UP YOU NEDN'T BE FEARED   78 8
    WHY EVEN NOW YOU SPEAK THROUGH CLOSE-SHUT TEETH   87 5
    I HEARD YOU IN YOUR SLEEP SPEAK STRANGELY TO ME   99 10
    AND SHE STARTED TO SPEAK   156 12
    WHY DON'T THEY OPEN WITH VISION AND SPEAK TO ME WHAT HA+   180 21
    HOW CAN ONE SPEAK WHERE THERE IS A DUMBNESS ON ONE'S MO+   266 10

SPEAK
    NOT TO SPEAK OF BABYLON'S WHOREDOM   328 6
    TO SPEAK ENDLESS INAUDIBLE WAVELETS INTO THE WAVE   336 29
    THAT BEING HER WAY OF ANSWER IF I SPEAK TO HER SELF-CON+   385 5
    AND EMERGE AS SQUEAKY GLOBULES WITH NO BODIES TO SPEAK +   501 2
    AND THEY TAUGHT YOU TO SPEAK KING'S ENGLISH   549 11
    AND STILL SPEAK HIS NATIVE LANGUAGE THE BEST   575 23
    SPEAK WITH THEM AND GIVE THEM PEACE AND DO THEM HONOUR   723 13
    HE KNOWS ME BUT DOES NOT SPEAK INSTEAD   734 28
    AND SPEAK NO SYLLABLE AND NEVER BE   737 17
    OF LIVES I SPEAK TO ALL WHO CANNOT HEAR   745 23
    I SPEAK ALOUD TO FLEETING HOSTS OF RED   745 25
    I SPEAK WITH A VAIN MOUTH   745 29
    AND KILL APHRODITE DON'T SPEAK DO NOT TALK   750 23
    SPEAK SOOTHINGLY FOR US TO GOD AND WHEN IN DISTRESS WE   753 4
    I AM GOING TO SPEAK TO THE DRAGON OF THE INNER FIRES   797 1
    WHEN YOU SPEAK TRUE AND TRUE IT IS BRIGHT ON YOUR LIPS +   800 8
    THE YOUNGER INTELLIGENTSIA SO TO SPEAK   829 6
    I SPEAK OF THE YOUNGER GENERATIONS   833 6
    SPEAK IN HALF-BITTER SCENT YOUR DREAM OF ME   880 12
    THAT SPEAK NO WORD OF THEIR RAPTURE BUT ONLY   *915 19
    SPEAK UP YOU NEDNA BE FEARED   *919 28

SPEAKING
    COME NOW SPEAKING OF RIGHTS WHAT RIGHT HAVE YOU TO THIS   314 12
    THIS BUSINESS OF SPEAKING FROM HEART TO HEART   575 25
    OF SPEAKING PLAIN ENGLISH TO AN ENGLISHMAN YOU'LL SEEM   576 7
    AND CROUCHING AND SPEAKING THE MUSIC OF LOST LANGUAGES   688 16
    SISTERS THE GUNS ARE SPEAKING LET ALL   758 17
    SPEAKING OF PERVERTS HE TAKES ON AN AMUSED BUT ICY   *948 4

SPEAKS
    THE MOON-MIST IS OVER THE VILLAGE OUT OF THE MIST SPEAK+   63 4
    I DIED AND DEATH IS NEUTER IT SPEAKS NOT IT GIVES   461 13
    YET WHEN IT SPEAKS FROM HEART TO HEART   575 19
    WHOM THE MEADOW-LARK SINGING SPEAKS TO   769 28
    THE MAN SPEAKS   874 22
    THE WOMAN SPEAKS   876 22

SPEAR
    SUCH AN INSTRUMENT A SPADE LIKE A SPEAR OR AN OAR   254 20
    ALAS THE SPEAR IS THROUGH THE SIDE OF HIS ISOLATION   361 1

SPEARS
    PASSING WITH SPEARS AND PENNANTS AND MANLY SCORN   221 9
    THE CORN-STALKS TIPPING WITH FIRE THE SPEARS   221 24
    AND ALL THE SORREL SPEARS IN THE LUSH LONG GRASS   884 25
    PASSING WITH SPEARS AND PENNANTS AND MANLY SCORN   *944 22
    THE CORN-STALKS TIPPING WITH FIRE THEIR SPEARS   *945 10

SPECIES
    ESPECIALLY THE MALE OF THE SPECIES   430 16
    ESPECIALLY THE MALE OF THE SPECIES   431 12
    HIS SPECIES   523 10

SPECIMEN
    SPECIMEN   430 20

SPECIMENS
    SPECIMENS TO BE ANATOMISED   619 23

SPECK
    SPECK   62 5
    TO ALTER MY ONE SPECK OF DOOM WHEN ROUND ME BURNS   195 25
    GOLD WITH AN INNERMOST SPECK   253 1
    YOU SPECK   333 4
    AND IN A STRANGE LEVEL FLUTTERING YOU GO OUT TO SEA-WAR+   696 25
    AND YET THERE IS A SPECK A GERM OF AMERICAN FUTURE   775 7
    THAT DRINKS ME UP AS IF I WERE A SPECK   876 18
    THAT THE BLACK NIGHT HID HER FROM ME BLOTTED OUT EVERY +   *912 12

SPECKS
    THE HEAVENS LIKE SPECKS OF DUST THAT ARE FLOATING ASUND+   223 3

SPECS
    SHE'LL TAKE OFF HER SPECS AND SHE'LL PUT DOWN THE PAPER   583 12

SPECTACLES
    CLEVER LITTLE ANTS IN SPECTACLES WE ARE   544 1
    FOR SPECTACLES AND BULGING CLEVER ANT-EYES ARE NO GOOD +   544 7
    FOR A MOMENT AS HE LOOKED AT ME THROUGH HIS SPECTACLES   672 25

SPECTRES
    TWO SPECTRES   292 9

SPED
    AND CLEAN AS ARROWS THEY SPED AT THE MARK   688 24
    EVE WITH A HEART OF RESENTMENT IS QUICKLY SPED   864 21

SPEECH
    DEAD WITH A DEAD RACE AND A DEAD SPEECH AND YET   296 9
    THE FIRST ELEMENTS OF FOREIGN SPEECH   366 20
    IN PLACE OF SPEECH   629 11
    ANOTHER RACE ANOTHER SPEECH AMONG   746 5
    SO THE SPEECH IN THE PUEBLO ON GOOD FRIDAY   778 31
    SAYING WITHOUT SPEECH LOOK YOU   802 29
    IN THE PULPIT WHERE SHRIVELLED AND GHASTLY IN UNINTELLI+   859 14
    AH COIN ME SPEECH OF YOUR HEART'S GOLD FURNACE HEAT   872 27
    I DIDN'T LEARN IT FROM HER SPEECH   *893 6

SPEECHES
    HIS WONDERFUL SPEECHES FULL OF OTHER FOLKS' WHORING   494 21

SPEED
    RUNS INTO SPEED LIKE A DREAM THE BLUE OF THE STEEL   136 9
    SLEEP ON SPEED IN DEAD CERTAINTY   169 20
    THE FLAMES' STIFF SPEED   242 15
    THE DIVIDERS THE THUNDERERS THE SWIFT ONES BLIND WITH S+   707 20

SPEED
  AND THE WILL THE LIVING DYNAMO GIVES THE MOTION AND THE+   712 14

SPEEDS
  OF SPRING UPON IT AND IT SPEEDS   888 11

SPELL
  SPELL OF ITS WORD   149 14
  SINCE I AM HERE FOR SO SHORT A SPELL   152 7
  HAS BROKEN HER SPELL   171 16
  THE SPELL IS NEVER BROKEN   575 20
  THE SPELL IS NEVER BROKEN   575 21
  IF YOU DON'T WANT TO BREAK THE SWEET ENGLISH SPELL   576 11
  CAN'T LIVE ANY MORE EXCEPT FOR A SPELL WHEN THE LIVING   639 4
  AND OUT OF THE STRUGGLE WITH HIS MATERIAL IN THE SPELL +   690 6

SPELLBOUND
  IN THE SPELLBOUND NORTH CONVULSIVE NOW WITH A DREAM NEAR   149 21
  AND THAT HELD HER SPELLBOUND FOR TWO SECONDS   604 22

SPEND
  THE GHASTLY DREAM OF RICHES OF MASSES OF MONEY TO SPEND   175 7
  SO I HOPE I SHALL SPEND ETERNITY   250 9
  AND I HOPE TO SPEND ETERNITY   *946 7

SPENDING
  THE HAWK HAS DROPPED THE WIND IS SPENDING   150 5

SPENT
  WAKE OF A TUMULT NOW SPENT AND GONE   53 17
  LIFE WOULD HAVE BEEN SHOULD I HAVE SPENT   104 18
  WHEN I HOLD THEM MY SPENT SOUL UNDERSTANDS   128 8
  TO HAVE MY SUBSTANCE SO SUBTLY SPENT   152 2
  OF OLD SPENT LIVES LINGER BLURRED AND WARM   173 18
  THE HARVEST THE SPENT ACTION TO ITSELF   195 3
  OF SUDDEN ANGUISH SUDDEN OVER AND SPENT   196 4
  TILL HE FELL IN A CORNER PALPITATING SPENT   345 27
  SPENT   346 25
  OF THE WALLS WITHIN WHICH OUR LIVES ARE SPENT   462 12
  ON SMELLING IT ALL BEFORE YOUR BIT OF VITALITY SPENT IS   462 34
  OH AREN'T THEY GREEN OH HAVEN'T WE HAVEN'T WE SPENT   569 11
  WHEN ALL MY SUBSTANCE IS BEING SPENT   874 16
  TILL IT HAS SPENT ITSELF   *893 28
  WAKE OF THE HUSHED TUMULT NOW SPENT AND GONE   *906 8

SPERM
  WHO IS IT EJECTS HIS SPERM TO THE NAKED FLOOD   335 25
  LIKE SPERM OF WHALES LIKE GERMS OF THE GREAT DEAD PAST   428 28
  IS THE BEST THAT WE ARE BUT SPERM LOOSE SPERM LIKE THE   429 3
  SPERM OF FISHES   429 4
  TO USE THE SPERM OF WHAT'S WORTH WHILE IN US   429 20
  THAT CASTS ITS SPERM UPON THE WATERS AND KNOWS NO INTER+ 616 25

SPERM-WHALES
  THE RIGHT WHALES THE SPERM-WHALES THE HAMMER-HEADS THE + 694 5

SPHERE
  WHY THE RIPPLE DOWN THE SPHERE   £79 19

SPHERES
  TO QUICKEN THE SPHERES SPRING-VIRGIN AGAIN IN THE SKY   127 10
  IN THE MIDST OF THE SPHERES   253 23
  NO DOUBT TO THE SOUNDING OF THE SPHERES   524 14

SPHINXES
  AND SPHINXES OF SELF-CONSCIOUSNESS   603 25

SPICES
  WITH HER SUAVE FORM DUSTY WITH SPICES HONEY SWEET STRAY+ 864 4

SPICILY
  SPICILY NASTY OF COURSE   491 6

SPICY
  SUGGEST THAT THEY'RE SPICY YET HOW PURE THEY ARE   583 20

SPIDER
  OF THE SKY SAGGED DUSTY AS SPIDER CLOTH   98 14
  SCOOPED OUT AND BARE WHERE A SPIDER   112 20
  BUT IT MIGHT AS WELL HAVE BEEN HAIR ON A SPIDER THING   345 34

SPIDER-CLOTHS
  BUT A GREY CAVE WITH GREAT GREY SPIDER-CLOTHS HANGING   112 25

SPIDERS
  THE SPIDERS WITH WHITE FACES THAT SCUTTLE ON THE FLOOR + 112 28

SPIDER-WEB
  UNDER THE SPIDER-WEB NETS   797 8

SPIED
  THEN SUDDENLY HE SPIED THE OLD LAKE AND HE THREW IT IN   791 7

SPIKE
  A FINE PROUD SPIKE OF PURPLE IRISES   90 3

SPIKED
  OH CROWN OF SPIKED GREEN METAL   278 15

SPILL
  THE POOR WATERS SPILL   49 9
  GLITTER AND SPILL   94 15
  SURELY AH NOT IN WORDS ALONE I'D SPILL   127 16
  O SPILL THE BLOOD NOT OF YOUR FIRSTLING LAMB WITHOUT SP+ 678 22
  DON'T SPILL THE SALT FOR IT IS THE LAND MARK   706 15
  TIP THE MORNING LIGHT ON EDGE AND SPILL IT WITH DELIGHT 709 6
  GLITTER AND SPILL   *897 3

SPILLED
  IN THE STREET SPILLED OVER SPLENDIDLY   143 22
  THE PORTION TO THE GODS IS SPILLED   177 7
  A STILL BRIGHTER WHITE SNAKE WRIGGLES AMONG IT SPILLED   647 14

SPILLS
  TIPPLES OVER AND SPILLS DOWN   647 10

SPILT
  LIKE A LOVING-CUP LIKE A GRAIL BUT THEY SPILT IT TRIUMP+ 92 23
  THEY LIE SPILT ROUND THE CUP   216 4
  AND THE BLOOD OF IT MUST BE SPILT   678 21

SPIN
  YOU WHO TOIL NOT YOU WHO SPIN NOT   197 19
  AND THOU SHALT BEGIN TO SPIN ROUND ON THE HUB OF THE   714 17
  FAINT-FASHIONED WONDER WHEREIN LOST WE SPIN   875 4

SPINE
  CALLED THE ALMOND BONE IN THE BODY THE LAST BONE OF THE+ 303 9
  AND STRONG SPINE URGING DRIVING   336 10
  WHICH QUIVERS INDRAWN AS YOU CLENCH YOUR SPINE   370 13

SPINES
  THE WORN ARCHES OF THEIR SPINES SUPPORT   426 3

SPINNING
  MY LOVE THAT SPINNING COIN LAID STILL   59 21
  OH EARTH YOU SPINNING CLOD OF EARTH   73 1
  STAR-SPIDERS SPINNING THEIR THREAD   113 18
  LIKE A BREATH IN A BUBBLE SPINNING   193 24
  WERE NOT WORTH WHILE NOR SPINNING WORTH THE EFFORT   197 21
  SPINNING AND DANCING LIKE FLAMEY FIRE-SPOUTS IN THE DARK 440 10
  SPINNING A GLAMOUR ROUND MONEY AND CLERGYMEN   456 24
  SPINNING WITH THE HEAVINESS OF BALANCE   480 16
  OH YOU GODLY AND SMOOTH MACHINE SPINNING ON IN YOUR   643 19
  AMONG SPINNING WHEELS IN AN APOTHEOSIS OF WHEELS   711 27
  IT IS PART OF THE EVIL WORLD-SOUL SPINNING   713 3
  BLACK BIRDS WHOSE SONGS ARE UNUTTERABLE SPINNING FANTAS+ *918 14
  STAR-SPIDERS SPINNING THEIR THREAD   *929 7

SPINS
  LIKE VIVID THOUGHT THE AIR SPINS BRIGHT AND ALL   142 14
  AS IF SPINS TO SLEEP ON ITS MOTION DRUGGED DENSE IN THE 149 7
  LIKE A RATTLE A CHILD SPINS ROUND FOR JOY THE NIGHT RAT+ 206 31
  AND THE WHEEL OF THE CONSCIOUS SELF SPINS ON IN ABSOLUT+ 712 15

SPINY
  TO ROW FORWARD AND REACH HIMSELF TALL ON SPINY TOES   358 1

SPIRAL
  THERE IS A SPIRAL FLAME-TIP THAT CAN LICK OUR LITTLE AT+ 440 5

SPIRALS
  LOOK HE HATH MOVEMENT UPWARD HE SPIRALS   682 18

SPIRES
  PIERCING THE BLUE WITH THEIR CROCKETED SPIRES   49 25

SPIRIT
  HAS FLUTTERED HER SPIRIT TO STUMBLING FLIGHT   46 15
  THE SPIRIT FROM EACH LEAF'S FRAME   68 4
  AND OUT OF THE CHAMBERED WILDERNESS WANDERS A SPIRIT AB+ 70 6
  MY SPIRIT IS DEAD   95 3
  HAS DRAWN MY SPIRIT OUTSIDE   107 26
  YOU WOKE MY SPIRIT AND BORE ME   111 15
  OF HER SPIRIT WAVERED LIKE WATER THRILLED WITH LIGHT   125 32
  WITH HIS WAN SPIRIT SOMEWHERE IN THE AIR   158 23
  MY SPIRIT HEARS   169 13
  I AM SO SICK OF THE PRETENSIONS OF THE SPIRIT   200 15
  AND AT EVENING I MUST LEAVE OFF MY WINGS OF THE SPIRIT   321 27
  OF MY SPIRIT   322 27
  I CAN NO MORE DENY THE BAT-WINGS OF MY FATHOM-FLICKERIN+ 323 2
  OR A SPIRIT   323 27
  THE LION OF THE SPIRIT   323 31
  THE LION OF THE SPIRIT   324 4
  THE POOR OLD GOLDEN EAGLE OF THE WORD-FLEDGED SPIRIT   329 30
  PLENTY OF GAME OLD SPIRIT IN YOU BIBBLES   397 28
  THE HEART IS FROZEN THE SPIRIT DEAD   456 2
  WIDE EYES AND WONDERING SPIRIT NOT   461 7
  LOFTY SPIRIT   473 11
  MY SOUL IS ALMOST BLANK MY SPIRIT QUITE   501 20
  BECAUSE THEIR SPIRIT CAN'T MOVE   558 27
  THE MIND IS TOUCHLESS SO IS THE WILL SO IS THE SPIRIT   611 11
  AND THE HUMAN SPIRIT IS SO MUCH GAS TO KEEP IT ALL GOING 641 8
  SOFTLY SUBTLY SECRETLY IN SOUL FIRST THEN IN SPIRIT THE+ 642 22
  THEY SAY THAT REALITY EXISTS ONLY IN THE SPIRIT   689 14
  WITH A BODY AND WITH NEEDS AND A LOVELY SPIRIT   689 30
  MY SPIRIT DARKENS AND GOES OUT AND SOFT STRANGE GLOOM   727 2
  AROUND MY SOUL AND SPIRIT AROUND MY LIPS   727 10
  THAT IS MY SPIRIT HOVERING CLOSE ABOVE   750 13
  SULKY IN SPIRIT AND INERT   795 7
  MIND AND SPIRIT BAD AND GOOD   824 14
  WHERE SHAPE ON SPIRIT IN SUPERB DEGREE   872 10
  ALL MATTER AND ALL SPIRIT STANDING UPRIGHT   872 13
  THE SPIRIT FROM EACH LEAF'S FRAME   *914 19
  OF HER SPIRIT WAVERED LIKE WATER THREADED WITH LIGHT   *936 31
  SPIRIT OF CARELESS JOY AH HOW I WARM   *945 14

SPIRITS
  HE SAID DO YOU SEE THE SPIRITS   201 25
  BUT I INVOKE THE SPIRITS OF THE LOST   298 9
  THESE ARE NO SPIRITS CAUGHT AND SORE   460 3
  THEY HAVE NO SONG IN THEIR SOULS NONE IN THEIR SPIRITS   657 13
  THE SPIRITS OF THE COLD DEAD WHISTLE IN THE EARS OF THE+ 795 15

SPIRIT'S
    THE SKIRT OF THE SPIRIT'S EXPERIENCE HAS MELTED AWAY   *959 28

SPIRITUAL
    HE IS CEREBRAL INTELLECTUAL MENTAL SPIRITUAL   473 17
    SOMEHOW SO SAD SO INTRINSIC SO SPIRITUAL YET SO CAUTIOU+   *932 13

SPIT
    SPIT IT OUT   441 27
    DO IT JUST TO SPIT IN THEIR EYE   517 6
    AND EVEN THEN THEY SHALL SPIT YOU OUT AS BROKEN-HAUNCHE+   796 27

SPITE
    IN SPITE OF MYSELF THE INSIDIOUS MASTERY OF SONG   148 10
    STRANGE HOW WE SUFFER IN SPITE OF THIS   203 29
    I HAVE STEPPED ACROSS MY PEOPLE AND HURT THEM IN SPITE   209 10
    IN THE LONG RUN IN SPITE OF THEMSELVES   317 5
    FOOL IN SPITE OF YOUR PRETTY WAYS AND QUAINT KNOW-ALL   400 18
    HOW THEY WREAK THEIR SPITE ON WOMEN   447 9
    AND THEY CAN'T HELP WANTING TO SPITE IT ON THEM   502 25
    AND STILL IN SPITE OF ALL THEY DO I LOVE THE ROSE OF EN+   569 1
    IN SPITE OF MY ASCENT   626 14
    AND GOING BLANDLY ON TO HIS NEXT SPITE   *949 14
    EVERY SINGLE ERECTION OF HIS IS AN ERECTION OF MEAN SPI+   *949 15
    TAKING IT OUT IN SPITE ON WOMEN   *949 18

SPLASH
    ARE TORN AWAY AND A SPLASH   149 30
    WASH OVER OUR KNEES AND SPLASH BETWEEN OUR THIGHS   425 4

SPLASHED
    SOME DEWDROP MAYBE SPLASHED MY FACE DOWN HERE   87 4

SPLASHES
    YET THE SPLASHES OF DAY AND NIGHT   37 26
    AND SPLASHES WARM BETWEEN THE BUTTOCKS   427 6
    HE SPLASHES WATER FROM THE PAIL UPON THEM   734 1
    YET THE SPLASHES OF DAY AND NIGHT   *892 14

SPLASHING
    AND THE ACCUMULATED SPLASHING OF A GONG   623 9

SPLAY
    RUNNING BESIDE HER LIKE A DOG BITING HER EARTHY SPLAY   360 8
    THEIR SPLAY FEET RAMBLING AND ROWING LIKE PADDLES   361 24

SPLENDID
    BUT HOW SPLENDID IT IS TO BE SUBSTANCE HERE   34 7
    SWORN TO A HIGH AND SPLENDID PURPOSELESSNESS   197 16
    GENTLE NURTURED FRAIL AND SPLENDID   313 32
    FLAME-FLUSHED ENRAGED SPLENDID SALVIA   314 27
    SPLENDID   414 23
    SPLENDID BODY ON THE ROPE   444 32
    ANTHONY MIGHT HAVE MADE A SPLENDID THING OF THE EAST   479 24
    AND DOWN THE SHAFTS OF HIS SPLENDID PINIONS   496 11
    AND PLUME FORTH AND BE SPLENDID   498 25
    OR THE SPLENDID GROWING OF AN ASH-TREE   610 22
    IT WAS TO THE GODS WHO MAKE US SPLENDID   679 12
    AS THE PEACOCK TURNS TO THE SUN AND COULD NOT BE MORE S+   683 8
    OUT OF SHEER DESIRE TO BE SPLENDID AND MORE SPLENDID   831 4

SPLENDIDLY
    IN THE STREET SPILLED OVER SPLENDIDLY   143 22
    USED TO WEAR HER LIGHTS SPLENDIDLY   170 18
    SPLENDIDLY PLANTING HIS FEET ONE ROCKY FOOT STRIKING THE   381 13
    SPLENDIDLY AND IT IS A COMFORT ISN'T IT   546 21

SPLENDOUR
    EXQUISITE SPLENDOUR   305 28
    IN ALL THE SINISTER SPLENDOUR OF THEIR RED BLOOD-SACRIF+   371 35
    SERVE VAST MOUNTAINOUS BLOOD IN SUBMISSION AND SPLENDOUR   390 23
    WITH A BIT OF SPLENDOUR   523 25
    ONLY MAN IS TERRIFIED OF HIS OWN POSSIBLE SPLENDOUR AND   529 12
    AND THINK HOW ALL ANIMALS TROT WITH SPLENDOUR   530 12
    IN ITS OWN SPLENDOUR AND ITS OWN FEATHERY MALENESS   587 14
    AND FEEL THE SPLENDOUR OF THE GODS GO THROUGH YOU EVEN +   655 8
    ON A DAY OF SPLENDOUR FOR THE FURTHER SPLENDOUR OF BEIN+   679 14
    INTO THE DANCE AND SPLENDOUR OF A BIGGER LIFE   679 17
    AMONG THE SPLENDOUR OF TORCHES OF DARKNESS SHEDDING DAR+   697 21
    AMONG THE SPLENDOUR OF BLACK-BLUE TORCHES SHEDDING FATH+   *956 19

SPLINTER
    THE FINEST SPLINTER OF A SPARK   241 8
    IN WHICH IS HEARD THE CRASHING SPLINTER OF MACHINES   640 11

SPLINTERED
    THE SPLINTERED STREETS HEAR NOISES   159 17

SPLINTERS
    AND SMALL FISH FLY LIKE SPLINTERS   338 20
    OR FIGHT AND MAKE THE SPLINTERS FLY   458 6
    QUICK LITTLE SPLINTERS OF LIFE   466 15
    EVEN THE SHAKING WHITE POPLAR WILL DAZZLE LIKE SPLINTER+   624 18
    LOVE CANNOT LIVE BUT ONLY BARE SALT SPLINTERS   693 22

SPLIT
    THE ROCK WILL SPLIT WE SHALL COME AT THE WONDER WE SHALL   250 23
    IS TO SPLIT IT IN FOUR HOLDING IT BY THE STUMP   282 2
    AND PANTING WITH THAT SPLIT GRIN   397 25
    MY IVORY AND IDOLS SPLIT IN TWAIN   873 30

SPLIT-FACE
    YOU SPLIT-FACE   397 21

SPOIL
    WOULD BLUR NO WHISPER SPOIL NO EXPRESSON   250 27
    WILL DEFILE IT AND SPOIL ITS BEAUTY   634 17

SPOILED
    SAINT FRANCIS HIMSELF WAS A RICH AND SPOILED YOUNG MAN   498 11

SPOKE
    SHE SPOKE AND I CLOSED MY EYES   124 18
    TILL A BEGGAR SPOKE TO JOSEPH   202 9
    STILL THE JOY WAS THERE ALSO YOU SPOKE TRULY   207 10
    HE SPOKE THIS WORD STOP DON'T BEAT IT FOR IT IS THE SOU+   376 6
    SO SPOKE THE BRITISH GENTLEMAN   433 14
    SHE SPOKE AND I CLOSED MY EYES   *935 18

SPOKEN
    THAT'S SPOKEN LIKE A MAN TIMMY   81 5
    THAT'S SPOKEN LIKE A MAN   81 6
    NOT TO BE SPOKEN ALOUD   264 17
    THOUGH NOT SO SMOOTHLY SPOKEN   575 17
    HAVE LENT YOU VOICE NOR SPOKEN OF THE FACE   737 21
    BEYOND SPOKEN DAY   810 25
    THAT'S SPOKEN LIKE A MAN TIMMY   *923 5
    THAT'S SPOKEN LIKE A MAN   *923 6

SPOKES
    HOW THOU DOST POKE UP AMONG THE SPOKES OF MY   760 4

SPONGE
    SHE STOOPS TO THE SPONGE AND HER SWUNG BREASTS   217 16
    GIVE ME A SPONGE AND SOME CLEAR CLEAN WATER   580 15
    AH MY NICE PICTURES LET ME SPONGE YOU VERY GENTLY   581 1
    TO SPONGE AWAY THE SLIME   581 2

SPONGED
    ARE YOU WILLING TO BE SPONGED OUT ERASED CANCELLED   728 1

SPONTANEITY
    AND WE HAVE LOST OUR NATURAL SPONTANEITY   833 11

SPONTANEOUS
    ABOUT YOUR FEET SPONTANEOUS ACONITE   308 30
    WOULD BE LOVELY IF THEY ROSE FROM THE MAN HIMSELF SPONT+   520 10
    MORE SPONTANEOUS AND WE   557 28
    O SACRIFICE NOT THAT WHICH IS NOBLE AND GENEROUS AND SP+   679 1

SPOOLS
    THE RED-GOLD SPOOLS OF THEIR HANDS AND THEIR FACES SWIN+   72 8
    SWALLOWS WITH SPOOLS OF DARK THREAD SEWING THE SHADOWS   340 29

SPOON
    AN' A FORK AN' A SPOON 'E'LL WANT AN' WHAT ELSE   46 1

SPORT
    ALL THE SPORT OF SUMMER AND SPRING AND FLOWERS SNAPPING   309 18
    BUT THE PLUCKY LITTLE SPORT IT GIVES TO LIFE   443 16
    TO MAKE SPORT OF ME WHEN THE DAYS OF MY HEART   731 16
    CURVING THEIR FEET AND DANCING AND FLUTTERING IN SPORT   751 4
    SPORT ON HER LITTERED PIANO AND MOCK AT THE SIGHT   856 17

SPORTFULLY
    DANCING SPORTFULLY   272 15

SPORTING
    SHE IS THE GAY DELIGHTED PORPOISE SPORTING WITH LOVE AN+   695 10

SPOT
    LOOK SHE'S A WONDERFUL DOVE WITHOUT BLEMISH OR SPOT   239 1
    LITTLE BLACK SPOT IN THE LANDSCAPE   397 10
    SO PERHAPS SHE'LL BE MORE ON THE SPOT   571 22
    THE SPOT I SHOULD HIT ON WOULD BE LITTLE BRITAIN   574 13
    ALL EYES SOUGHT THE SAME OLD SPOT   578 2
    AT THE SPOT WHERE THE FIG-LEAF JUST WAS NOT   578 13
    THAT THEY STARED AND LEERED AT THE SINGLE SPOT   578 22
    OR GLOATED OR PEEPED AT THE SIMPLE SPOT   579 3
    AND OUR CONSCIOUSNESS IS A SPOT OF LIGHT IN A GREAT BUT   636 31
    O SPILL THE BLOOD NOT OF YOUR FIRSTLING LAMB WITHOUT SP+   678 22

SPOTS
    AN' MIST IS SUCKIN' AT TH' SPOTS O' SNOW   137 21
    AND THE LEOPARD CANNOT CHANGE HIS SPOTS   413 28

SPOTTED
    TIE MY SPOTTED SHOES FOR DANCING   802 22
    NO SPOTTED TRAITORS CRAWL BY   810 4

SPOUSE
    NOT LIKE THE EARTH THE SPOUSE ALL FULL OF INCREASE   197 10
    OF THAT MUD-HOVEL OF HIS SLOWLY RAMBLING SPOUSE   361 14

SPOUTING
    AND NOW THAT THE SKIES ARE FALLING THE WORLD IS SPOUTIN+ 160 1
    WHEN I HEAR MAN SPOUTING ABOUT HUMILITY TODAY   621 22

SPOUTS
    INTO OOZE AND THE SOMBRE DIRT SPOUTS UP AT MY HANDS   167 6

SPRANG
    A DOE SPRANG OUT OF THE CORN   222 2
    THE ROSY RIVER THAT SPRANG   766 17
    AND ONE GREEN LEAF SPRANG AMONG THE BLACK   809 20

SPRAWLS
    THAT WORK BENEATH HER WHILE SHE SPRAWLS ALONG   362 16
    THAT SPRAWLS ACROSS THE EARTH IN IRON IMBECILITY   642 26

SPRAY
　LEAPING LIKE SPRAY IN THE RETURN OF PASSION　　　　89　17
　LIKE SPRAY ACROSS THE TOWN　　　　　　　　　　　　99　18
　ALL THESE PURE THINGS COME FOAM AND SPRAY OF THE SEA　136　17
　WITH A BODY LIKE SPRAY DAWN-TENDER AND LOOKING ABOUT　306　30
　IN WILD WHITE SIBILANT SPRAY　　　　　　　　　　467　13

SPRAYS
　IN SPRAYS AND SPURTS OF FOAM　　　　　　　　　　885　30

SPREAD
　PRESSING HER SPREAD HANDS OVER HER BREASTS AS SHE　128　24
　NOW VERDIGRIS SMOULDERING SOFTLY SPREAD　　　　　142　25
　SPREAD OUT AND KNOWN AT LAST AND WE ARE SURE　　193　8
　HER FLAKE BY FLAKE AND SPREAD HER MEANING OUT　197　23
　I SPREAD OVER YOU HOW LOVELY YOUR ROUND HEAD YOUR　245　21
　BEFORE PETALS SPREAD BEFORE COLOUR MADE ITS DISTURBANCE　285　31
　OUT OF THE EARTH BEFORE THE SUN WAS SPREAD OUT AND BEFO+　295　5
　SO HALTS THE LITTLE BLACK BITCH ON FOUR SPREAD PAWS IN +　375　10
　WITH MASTS ERECT AND SPARS ALL SET AND SAILS SPREAD　542　2
　SPREAD YOUR SMALL SAILS IMMUNE LITTLE SHIPS　　543　10
　WHO HAD SPREAD WHITE WASHING ON THE GRAVEL BANKED ABOVE+　693　3
　RIBBED AND TORCH-LIKE WITH THEIR BLAZE OF DARKNESS SPRE+　697　6
　HAS THE WARMTH OF A NIGHT KISS SPREAD THROUGH THEIR BLO+　860　22
　SHE WILL START WHEN SHE SEES ME AND BLUSHING SPREAD OUT+　*940　16
　RIBBED HELLISH FLOWERS ERECT WITH THEIR BLAZE OF DARKNE+　*956　4
　THAT WILL SPREAD IN DEATH TO THE BREEZE　　　　*961　2

SPREAD-EAGLE
　MOUNTED AND TENSE SPREAD-EAGLE OUT-REACHING OUT OF THE　364　30
　LONG NECK AND LONG VULNERABLE LIMBS EXTRUDED SPREAD-EAG+　365　1

SPREADING
　THE SLOW BEAST CURIOUSLY SPREADING HIS ROUND FEET FOR T+　387　12
　AND A BLACK CRUCIFIX LIKE A DEAD TREE SPREADING WINGS　403　24
　AND SPREADING THEIR SKIRTS　　　　　　　　　　539　26

SPREADS
　SHE SPREADS THE BATH-CLOTH UNDERNEATH THE WINDOW　217　11
　BUT KILL THE SCABBED AND UGLY LAMB THAT SPREADS CONTAGI+　678　23
　AND THE WOOD LIKE A MANLY HUSBAND SPREADS SOFTNESS AND +　854　9

SPREE
　THINKING OLD NEPTUNE WAS OFF ON A SPREE　　　575　9

SPRIG
　HAPPY AM I A NAKED SPRIG　　　　　　　　　　888　13

SPRIGHTLY
　THEN GAY FEAR THAT TURNS THE TAIL SPRIGHTLY FROM A SHAD+　336　18

SPRIGS
　THAT HAS STRIPPED THEIR SPRIGS　　　　　　　　51　4
　SPRIGS　　　　　　　　　　　　　　　　　　142　10

SPRING
　AND CROUCHES LOW THEN WITH WILD SPRING　　　　43　7
　THE NEW RED HOUSES SPRING LIKE PLANTS　　　　50　19
　THIS SPRING AS IT COMES BURSTS UP IN BONFIRES GREEN　116　1
　I AM AMAZED AT THIS SPRING THIS CONFLAGRATION　116　6
　THIS CONFLAGRATION OF SPRING THE GAP IN IT ALL　116　11
　DIM SPRING THAT INTERWEAVES　　　　　　　　126　20
　GOING OUT IN SPRING TO THE ROUND OF HIS TAME DESERTS　126　27
　COULD I BUT SEAL ITS RUDDY SHINING SPRING　　153　25
　TO THIS SPRING OF COSMIC GOLD　　　　　　　162　10
　SOON STREWS ITSELF ON THE FLOOR AND KEEP THE RADIANCE O+　179　4
　SMALL-BOSOMED GIRLS OF THE SPRING OF LOVE　　179　17
　IT IS REALLY SPRING SEE　　　　　　　　　　244　9
　IT IS FINISHED THE SPRING IS HERE　　　　　244　18
　THE BLAZING TIGER WILL SPRING UPON THE DEER UNDIMMED　268　3
　WHAT IS IT THAT FROM THEIR FACES FRESH AS SPRING　270　4
　I WISH IT WERE SPRING IN THE WORLD　　　　　270　29
　LET IT BE SPRING　　　　　　　　　　　　　270　30
　COME SPRING MAKE HAVOC OF THEM　　　　　　271　11
　I WANT THE FINE KINDLING WINE-SAP OF SPRING　271　17
　I WISH IT WERE SPRING　　　　　　　　　　271　30
　I WISH THAT SPRING　　　　　　　　　　　　272　1
　I WISH IT WERE SPRING THUNDERING　　　　　　272　4
　DELICATE TENDER SPRING　　　　　　　　　　272　5
　OH IN THE SPRING THE BLUEBELL BOWS HIM DOWN FOR VERY　272　9
　OH YES THE GUSH OF SPRING IS STRONG ENOUGH　272　13
　THE GUSH OF SPRING IS STRONG ENOUGH　　　　272　18
　AH COME COME QUICKLY SPRING　　　　　　　272　30
　ON THE THRESHOLD OF SPRING I FEAR I SHALL DIE　273　29
　WE SHALL HAVE SPRING　　　　　　　　　　　273　35
　IT WILL BE SPRING IN THE WORLD　　　　　　274　3
　IT WILL BE SPRING IN THE WORLD OF THE LIVING　274　4
　ALL THE SPORT OF SUMMER AND SPRING AND FLOWERS SNAPPING　309　18
　IT IS SPRING　　　　　　　　　　　　　　309　22
　IT IS SPRING　　　　　　　　　　　　　　309　30
　AND TO SPRING AWAY WITH A CURVETTING CLICK IN THE AIR　337　2
　IN THE SPRING　　　　　　　　　　　　　　365　33
　HE IS ALIVE LIKE A TREE IN SPRING　　　　　450　25
　THE EFFORTS OF MEN LIKE THE EFFORTS OF BIRDS IN SPRING　520　9
　ANOTHER SPRING OF YET ANOTHER YEAR　　　　　745　32
　LET US HAVE A SPRING CLEANING IN THE WORLD　792　33
　THOUGH THE PURPLE DREAMS OF THE INNOCENT SPRING HAVE GO+　854　6
　AT THE END OF A SWEET SPRING DAY THEY WILL VANISH　855　5
　AT THE END OF THE SWEET SPRING DAY THEY ARE YOURS　855　13
　OF SPRING UPON IT AND IT SPEEDS　　　　　　888　11

SPRINGING
　BUT THE UTTER ANGUISHED SPRINGING FORTH OF ME　880　5

SPRINGS
　ABOVE ME SPRINGS THE BLOOD-BORN MISTLETOE　　131　15
　SO THAT STRENGTH WELLS UP IN ME LIKE WATER IN HOT SPRIN+　799　21
　ALL MY BODY SPRINGS ALIVE　　　　　　　　　*893　12

SPRINGTIME
　IN ANOTHER SOFTENED SPRINGTIME　　　　　　769　10

SPRING-VIRGIN
　TO QUICKEN THE SPHERES SPRING-VIRGIN AGAIN IN THE SKY　127　10

SPRINGY
　LIKE STAGS ON ROCKY GROUND OR PAWING HORSES OR SPRINGY　392　16

SPRINKLE
　SO DO FORGIVE ME I SPRINKLE MY HAIR　　　　492　29
　AT LOVE SHOULD SPRINKLE ME DAILY WITH A RARE　874　6

SPRINKLING
　SPRINKLING INCENSE AND SALT OF WORDS　　　　151　28
　AMONG SQUAT TOAD-LEAVES SPRINKLING THE UNBORN　312　2

SPRITE
　HAS OPENED THE WINGS OF THE WILD YOUNG SPRITE　46　14
　AFTER THEM ISSUES A DARK-WINGED FLUTTERING SPRITE　858　15

SPROTTLE
　WHY DO YOU SPURT AND SPROTTLE　　　　　　240　22

SPROTTLING
　IT GOES RIGHT THROUGH HIM THE SPROTTLING INSECT　356　2

SPROUT
　AND THEN TO SEE THE NEW REAL SOULS SPROUT UP　315　31
　NETTLES AND A ROSE SPROUT　　　　　　　　　316　1
　WHERE FLOWERS SPROUT IN THE ACRID HUMUS AND FADE INTO H+　321　11

SPROUTING
　AND THE CROSS SPROUTING ITS SUPERB AND FEARLESS FLOWERS　305　30

SPROUTS
　AS THE HORNBEAM PUSHES UP HIS SPROUTS　　　*954　9

SPRUCE-TREES
　DARK GROW THE SPRUCE-TREES BLUE IS THE BALSAM WATER　401　2

SPRUNG
　PLANT OF YOUR BODY TO ME YOU LOOKED ERE SPRUNG　156　20
　THE MUCK FROM WHICH YOU'VE SPRUNG　　　　　456　17
　OUTSIDER SPRUNG UP FROM SOME HORRIBLE GUTTER　576　9
　WE LEAK LIKE A BARREL THAT IS SPRUNG BUT YET　750　6

SPRY
　WHEN OUR PARENTS FELT SPRY　　　　　　　　562　26

SPUE
　AND SPUE OUT CORROSIONS INTO YOUR STREAMS ON YOUR RAINS　797　6

SPUME
　SEE THE MILK OF NORTHERN SPUME　　　　　　301　24

SPUMED
　SPUMED WITH MUD　　　　　　　　　　　　310　23

SPUN
　THAT SOMEBODY HAS SPUN SO HIGH　　　　　　54　9
　SPUN LIKE A TOY　　　　　　　　　　　　121　6
　FOOTED CAUTIOUSLY OUT ON THE ROPE TURNED PRETTILY SPUN　444　26
　THAT THE TIME-THREADS SPUN ACROSS MY FACE　860　13
　LAPPED PRISONER IN THE CORDS OF LOVE I HAVE SPUN　884　16

SPUNK
　LIKE THEE CAN'T REST TILL HIS LAST SPUNK GOES　138　24
　O' THY SPUNK AN' THA'RT EMPTY AN' MORTIFIED　139　12
　PLENTY OF GAME OLD SPUNK LITTLE BITCH　　　397　29
　THEY HAVEN'T THE SPUNK OF A BATTLE-TWIG　　553　11
　IF YOU'VE NONE OF YOU GOT MORE SPUNK　　　553　26

SPUR
　AND LOOKS AROUND AGAIN AT HIS HEEL THE BRIGHT SPUR　734　14

SPURS
　JESUS HIS SPURS ARE RED WITH SHINING BLOOD　733　34

SPURT
　LIKE A SPURT OF WHITE FOAM RENT　　　　　　200　22
　WHY DO YOU SPURT AND SPROTTLE　　　　　　240　22

SPURTING
　LIFT MY ARMS THE HILL BURSTS AND HEAVES UNDER THEIR SPU+　33　9
　SPURTING TO SOOTHE THE WOMB'S UNSLAKED DESIRE　89　21
　AND SPURTING SUDDENLY UP SNOW-WHITE LIKE SNOW-LEOPARDS　454　7
　MOVE MY ARMS THE HILL BURSTS AND HEAVES UNDER THEIR SPU+　*891　10

SPURTS
　SPURTS FROM THE TERROR OF HIS ONCOMING　　43　8
　SPURTS　　　　　　　　　　　　　　　　　126　23
　YET SHE HAS SUCH ADORABLE SPURTY KIDS LIKE SPURTS OF BL+　386　17
　IN SPRAYS AND SPURTS OF FOAM　　　　　　　885　30

SPURTY
　YET SHE HAS SUCH ADORABLE SPURTY KIDS LIKE SPURTS OF BL+　386　17

SPY
　HERE NOT EVEN THE STARS CAN SPY US　　　　114　5
　HERE NOT EVEN THE STARS CAN SPY US　　　　*929　22

SPY-GOVERNMENT
    AND SPY-GOVERNMENT EVERYWHERE   536 17

SPYING
    START A SYSTEM OF OFFICIAL SPYING   536 4

SQUALID
    BUT HOW PALTRY MINGY AND DINGY AND SQUALID PEOPLE LOOK   530 15
    THEY SAVED YOU FROM SQUALID COTTAGES AND POVERTY OF HAND   630 17
    BUT THAT WHICH IS MEAN AND BASE AND SQUALID AND DEGENER+   679 3

SQUALOR
    THE LIES THE TREACHERY THE SLIPPERY CULTURED SQUALOR OF+   497 4

SQUARE
    ITS SQUARE SHADOWS   50 22
    THEN WILL SOMEBODY SQUARE THIS SHADE WITH THE BEING I   141 22
    SQUARE PICTURE-DUSK THE WINDOW OF DARK SKY   210 20

SQUASH-BLOSSOM
    THE FIG THE HORSE-SHOE THE SQUASH-BLOSSOM   282 25

SQUAT
    AMONG SQUAT TOAD-LEAVES SPRINKLING THE UNBORN   312 2
    NO HE MUST NOT SQUAT NOR HANG OBSCENE IN MY ROOM   346 3
    YOU DO NOTHING BUT SQUAT ON YOUR HAMS AND STARE WITH VA+   795 2

SQUATTED
    AND THERE A CLOT HE SQUATTED AND LOOKED AT ME   345 28
    HE SQUATTED THERE LIKE SOMETHING UNCLEAN   346 2

SQUATTING
    AND THEN TO LOOK BACK TO THE ROUNDED SIDES OF THE SQUAT+   409 21
    WITH DARK-WRAPPED ROCKY MOUNTAINS MOTIONLESS SQUATTING   410 28
    DID THEY DO IT BY SQUATTING ON THEIR HAMS   795 1

SQUAWK
    A BIT AWKWARD AND WITH A FUNNY SQUAWK IN HIS VOICE   413 21

SQUEAK
    THEY WANT SOMETHING OF YOU SO YOU SQUEAK AND COME   400 2
    THEY WILL STILL SQUEAK INTENSELY ABOUT THEIR FEELINGS   501 4
    GOING SQUEAK SQUEAK I AM ALL THINGS UNTO MYSELF   603 19

SQUEAKILY
    SQUEAKILY BELLOWING FOR ALL HE WAS WORTH   492 1

SQUEAKY
    AND EMERGE AS SQUEAKY GLOBULES WITH NO BODIES TO SPEAK +   501 2

SQUEEZE
    AND ALL BUT SQUEEZE THE LIFE OUT OF HIM   674 21

SQUEEZED
    OF ALL THE THINGS THEY SQUEEZED OUT OF YOU   549 5
    THEY SQUEEZED OUT MOST OF YOUR GUTS   549 8

SQUINT
    WHILE HIS SLITTED EYES SQUINT BACK TO THE ROOTS OF HIS +   386 22
    YET IT MAKES YOU SQUINT   551 11

SQUIRM
    DOES HE JUST SQUIRM   558 18

SQUIRMING
    AND GLUTTED SQUIRMING POPULOUSNESS ON FIRE   315 28

SQUIRREL
    A SQUIRREL COCKS HIS HEAD ON THE FENCE AND WONDERS   223 21
    OVERHEAD IT WILL BE A SQUIRREL MOVING   231 17
    MY SQUIRREL CLUTCHING IN TO ME   246 19
    MY WEE SQUIRREL   863 10

SQUIRRELS
    AND WHEN WE ESCAPE LIKE SQUIRRELS FROM TURNING IN THE   482 16

SQUIRT
    AS YOU SEE A TINY CELLULOID BALL TOSSING ON A SQUIRT OF+   272 16
    OR A DUNG SQUIRT   463 4

STAB
    AND DRINK FIRE-WATERS AND QUARREL AND STAB   795 3

STABS
    WITH A NEEDLE OF LONG RED FLINT HE STABS IN THE DARK   382 16

STACCATO
    AND JUMPS STACCATO TO EARTH A SHARP DRY JUMP STILL   384 30

STACK
    AH YOU STACK OF WHITE LILIES ALL WHITE AND GOLD   86 9
    ARE NOT A STACK OF WHITE LILIES NOW BUT A WHITE   86 14
    MY STACK OF LILIES ONCE WHITE INCANDESCENT   86 23
    SOME STREET-ENDS THRUST FORWARD THEIR STACK   164 20

STACKYARD
    O THE WET WALK OF MY BROWN HEN THROUGH THE STACKYARD   119 9
    OH THE WET WALK OF MY BROWN HEN THROUGH THE STACKYARD   *932 18

STAFF
    UNTIL HER PRIDE'S FLAG SMITTEN CLEAVED DOWN TO THE STAFF 125 18

STAG
    WHERE NO BULL ROARED NO COW EVER LOWED NO STAG CRIED   394 16

STAGES
    COMES OUT OF YOUR FALLING THROUGH THE STAGES OF DECAY   280 7
    WHICH GOES THROUGH ALL THE STAGES OF STEAM AND STREAM A+ 505 21
    FLOWERS NOW AS WE'RE CROSSING THE DREARY STAGES   814 6

STAGGER
    YOU STAGGER   334 4
    CLUTCH CLEAVE STAGGER   344 8
    WE WADE WE WADE WE STAGGER DARKNESS RUSHED   425 6

STAGGERING
    THE HUM OF HIS HEAVY STAGGERING WINGS   46 18
    STAGGERING   345 3
    OUT OF THE SADDLE AND STAGGERING   733 16
    HAVE POURED FOR THE HORSES A DARK-BLUE STAGGERING   733 18
    STAGGERING WORDS   *893 7

STAGNANT
    AND THE STAGNANT TEARS   240 3

STAGS
    LIKE STAGS ON ROCKY GROUND OR PAWING HORSES OR SPRINGY   392 16

STAIN
    MY IVORY AND MARBLE BLACK WITH STAIN   151 18
    DRAWS DOWN THE BLINDS WHOSE SHADOWS SCARCELY STAIN   155 2
    TILL NIGHT WHEN BY THE FIRE'S RED STAIN   202 26
    QUEER WHAT A BIG STAIN MY SUCKED BLOOD MAKES   334 16
    AND KICKS DUST OVER THE RED STAIN IN THE ROAD   734 16
    THAT NOTHING NOT LIFE CAN STAIN   772 27
    THE NIGHT A BIG BLACK STAIN   862 20
    A PRIESTESS EXECRATED FULL OF STAIN   874 1
    AND AH WITH ALL HIS BLOOD FOR ERE THE STAIN   885 4
    OF MY BREAKING HAD DIED UPON HIM ERE THE STAIN   885 5

STAINED
    STAINED WITH RED DYE   36 26

STAINING
    WITH MY REDNESS STAINING THE BODY OF THE DARK   804 16
    WITH HIS REDNESS STAINING THE BODY OF THE NIGHT   805 24

STAINLESS
    SINLESS AND STAINLESS GOING ROUND AND ROUND   714 2

STAINS
    STAINS   92 5
    THE BREATH OF THE BULLOCK STAINS THE HARD CHILL AIR   225 13
    STAINS   *926 5

STAIR
    PALPITATING DOWN THE STAIR   37 10

STAIRS
    DOWN THE STONE STAIRS   71 20
    SHE CREEPS PERSISTENT DOWN THE SKY'S LONG STAIRS   131 28
    AND CLIMB THE STAIRS TO FIND THE GROUP OF DOORS   140 9
    DOWN THE DARKER AND DARKER STAIRS WHERE BLUE IS DARKENE+ 697 15
    DOWN THE SKY'S STEEP STAIRS CHARTING NO TRACK FOR HER   *937 27
    DOWN THE DARKER AND DARKER STAIRS WHERE BLUE IS DARKENE+ *956 12

STALE
    AND MAKE A JOKE OF STALE INFINITY   299 12
    AND EVEN SO HE'S STALE HE'S BEEN THERE TOO LONG   431 18
    O THE STALE OLD DOGS WHO PRETEND TO GUARD   493 25
    EVEN AS TRIMMINGS THEY'RE STALE   557 6
    AT THE WHIM OF SIX POLICEMEN AND A MAGISTRATE WHOSE STA+ 633 5
    BUT THE GRAND INQUISITOR IS A STALE MAGISTRATE   633 18
    FRAGRANCE OF ROSES IN A STALE STINK OF LIES   634 28
    LEAVE THEM TO STALE ON EARTH   662 19
    THAT NOTHING CAN STALE OR PROFANE   772 15

STALENESS
    OF INFINITE STALENESS   478 29

STALK
    AND THE FLESH OF THE STALK HOLDS UP FOR NOTHING A BLANK+ 97 8
    LIKE AN EMPTY DANDELION STALK BEREFT OF CONNECTION SMALL 98 3
    BLOSSOM ME STALK BY STALK   111 14
    AND LEANING TO ME LIKE A FLOWER ON ITS STALK   178 29
    QUEER HOW YOU STALK AND PROWL THE AIR   332 25
    INTO ONE BUD ON THE STALK OF ETERNITY   *908 3
    BLOSSOM YOU STALK BY STALK   *927 7
    BLOSSOM YOU STALK BY STALK   *928 7

STALKER
    THE LONELY RAMBLER THE STOIC DIGNIFIED STALKER THROUGH 360 28

STALKS
    THEN THE PROUD LION STALKS ABROAD ALONE   325 19

STALL
    A LOOK AS HE STANDS ON THE EDGE OF THIS NAKED STALL   144 19
    NONE OF THE TROUBLE HE'S LED TO STALL   219 28
    PRETENDING TO LOOK ROUND THE STALL   384 32
    FULL-FED IN STALL   827 33
    NONE O' THE TROUBLE HE'S LED TO STALL   *944 8

STALLING
    STALLING   65 28

STALLION
    A GREAT BAY STALLION DANCES SKIRTS   126 25

STALLS
    I CAN ALWAYS LINGER OVER THE HUDDLED BOOKS ON THE STALLS   180 24

STAMENS
    SOFTLY BLOWS OUT ITS THIN LITTLE MALE STAMENS   535 3
    PUFFING ITS LITTLE MALE STAMENS OUT INTO STERILE PETAL + 535 6

STAMP
    AND I SHALL COUNT THE STAMP AND WORTH   59 13
    INDIANS DANCE AND RUN AND STAMP   407 11
    WE SHALL STAMP OUR FEET WITH NEW POWER   482 24
    TO STAMP THE EARTH AND FEEL THE WIND LIKE WAKEFUL   585 4

STAMPEDING
    RUSHES STAMPEDING DOWN   99 20
    STAMPEDING OVER EVERYBODY   502 9

STAMPING
    THAT WE'VE NEVER SEEN COMING STAMPING AND SWEARING   572 13
    THE INRUSH THE CLATTER THE STAMPING EYES LAUGHING WIDE + 865 25

STAMPS
    AND STAMPS HIS BLACK MARSH-FEET ON THEIR WHITE AND   436 18

STANCHIONS
    THE BRIDGE ON ITS STANCHIONS   146 14

STAND
    ON THE TURF I STAND WATCHING MY OWN WHITE SHADOW QUIVER+ 33 19
    ITS STARS STAND STILL   49 12
    BARE STEMS OF STREET LAMPS STIFFLY STAND   51 1
    SUCH A ONE IN THE NORTH IT FLOWERS ON THE STREET AND I + 58 13
    LIKE A WIND-SHADOW RUNNING ON A POND SO SHE COULD STAND   65 6
    I STAND AND SMILE   71 29
    WHO STAND ALONE IN DESPAIR LIKE A GUTTERING LIGHT   73 13
    AS I STAND ON THIS HILL WITH THE WHITENING CAVE OF THE + 97 11
    WHITE STAND NAKED OF GOWN   106 6
    AT THE SAME TIME STAND EXPOSED   108 1
    WHY SHOULD I START AND STAND STILL   110 27
    AND I HAVE SEEN HER STAND ALL UNAWARE   128 23
    SINCE THE MONTH OF CHILDHOOD IS OVER AND WE STAND ALONE 132 16
    IN SORROW SINCE WE STAND IN BEWILDERMENT STRANGE   132 19
    THE TREES STAND THE BOULEVARD STAND NAKED IN THOUGHT   142 1
    BEATING LIKE SOBS I COME TO MYSELF AND STAND   143 21
    STAND THOSE THAT WAIT   146 6
    FOR A PLACE TO LIE DOWN AND STILL AS THEY STAND THEY SL+ 146 7
    STAND A WAY OFF AND IF YOU LIKE COMMUNE   158 22
    STAND YOU FAR OFF AND TRIUMPH LIKE A JEW   158 28
    THAT HE IS DEAD AND YOU ARE NOT BUT STAND   158 29
    FAR-OFF THE LILY-STATUES STAND WHITE-RANKED IN THE GARD+ 159 19
    BUT WORN OUT THEY HIDE NO MORE THE WALLS THEY STAND BEF+ 174 22
    AT THE OPEN DOOR OF THE ROOM I STAND AND LOOK AT THE NI+ 179 20
    THEY STAND UPRIGHT ON OUR LOVE   204 25
    STAND LIKE DARK STUMPS STILL IN THE GREEN WHEAT   208 23
    STAND IN THEIR BLUENESS FLASHING WITH SNOW AND THE   209 24
    YOU STAND BEFORE ME LIKE GHOSTS LIKE A DARKNESS UPRIGHT 211 8
    STAND STILL AND BIND AND BLIND MYSELF   215 1
    YOU STAND AND THE NIGHT COMES THROUGH   215 18
    I STAND ASIDE ON THE GRASS TO LET THEM GO   225 21
    I STAND IN A CHILL OF ANGUISH TRYING TO SAY   225 31
    AND I AS I STAND IN THE COLD AVERTED FLOWERS   226 9
    DOES NOT THAT PASSION STAND IN YOUR WAY LIKE A BALAAM'S+ 236 8
    I SAW HER STAND AND WAIT   261 24
    IT IS EASIER TO STAND STOCK RIGID THAN TO MOVE   288 7
    AND MY HEAD AT LEAST IS THICK ENOUGH TO STAND IT THE   289 17
    THINK TO STAND THERE IN FULL-UNFOLDED NUDITY SMILING   306 17
    TO BE ABLE TO STAND FOR ALL THESE   317 26
    WHAT DO YOU STAND ON SUCH HIGH LEGS FOR   332 3
    STAND UPON ME WEIGHTLESS YOU PHANTOM   332 8
    SETTLE AND STAND ON LONG THIN SHANKS   333 1
    I BEHOLD YOU STAND   333 28
    I STAND AT THE PALE OF MY BEING   338 28
    AND FOUND HIS FEET SO HE IS THE FIRST OF CREATURES TO S+ 348 14
    AND MUST WAIT MUST STAND AND WAIT FOR THERE HE WAS AT   349 6
    DO THEY STAND UNDER THE DAWN HALF-GODLY HALF-DEMON   371 36
    TO STAND ON THE HIGHEST PEAK   382 13
    THE STAND UPON THE GRASS BELOW AND OPPOSITE   387 24
    TO STAND AND HOLD FEATHERS THREE FEATHERS ABOVE THE WOR+ 392 4
    STAND THEY AND GOD HOW THEY STINK   457 2
    ONE CAN'T STAND PEACELESS PEOPLE ANY MORE   499 19
    AND YOU STAND THERE AND EXPECT ME TO TREAT YOU LIKE AN 547 8
    AND THERE YOU STAND WITH NOTHING AND EXPECT ME TO HAND 547 13
    I CAN'T STAND WILLY WET-LEG   559 17
    CAN'T STAND HIM AT ANY PRICE   559 11
    STAND UP BUT NOT FOR JESUS   560 13
    STAND UP FOR JUSTICE AND A JOLLY LIFE   560 15
    STAND UP STAND UP FOR JUSTICE   560 17
    STAND UP AND DO SOME PUNCHING   560 19
    STAND UP FOR JOLLY JUSTICE   560 21
    STAND UP FOR SOMETHING DIFFERENT   560 25
    STAND UP FOR A NEW ARRANGEMENT   560 29
    IDLE WE STAND BY THE KERB-EDGE AUNTIE   572 25
    WHEN I STAND IN MY SHIRT I HAVE NO POCKETS   607 24
    HOW STILL THEY ARE TOGETHER THEY STAND SO STILL   647 5
    IT GONE BY OUR FARM TO THE MOUNTAINS THAT STAND BACK BL+ 732 7
    DOWN TO THE GATE AND STAND AND WAIT   734 25
    WHEN I STAND IN THE DOORWAY SHAMEFULLY   735 28
    THEY DEMAND AS THEY STAND IN MENACE OVER AGAINST US   740 8
    OH AS YOU STAND LOOKING UP DO YOU KNOW IT IS I   750 15
    FOR GOD'S SAKE LET US STOP OH YOU WHO STAND BEHIND US   756 1
    MUST WE GO ON TILL WE DROP OH YOU WHO STAND BEHIND US   756 3
    THE BLOOD FROM OUR HEARTS OH YOU WHO STAND BEHIND US   756 7
    THERE ARE DEAD THAT STAND UPON YOU WHEN YOU GO IN TO YO+ 795 30
    BETWEEN THE MORNING AND THE AFTERNOON STAND I HERE WITH+ 803 6
    AND STAND UP AND LOOK ABOUT HIM   809 17
    AND WHERE HE STOOD I SEE MY OWN SHADOW STAND   871 11
    RETURN WHERE ALL IN BEAUTY STAND ERECT   872 9
    OF THE BANK I STAND WATCHING MY OWN WHITE SHADOW QUIVER+ *891 21

STAND
    I STAND RELUCTANT TO ENTER TO DREAM NO MORE BUT TO BOW *894 21
    THE MEN UPLIFTED ON THE NEW WHITE WOODSTACK STAND   *895 1
    SO SHE MAY STAND ON MY KNEE   *913 8
    SO THAT SHE CAN STAND ON MY KNEE   *914 8
    OF ALL US FLESH AND WE STAND IN OUR NAKEDNESS NESH   *938 11

STANDING
    STANDING ANGEL-STERN AND TALL   140 10
    AND STANDING THERE   176 22
    I SEE THE GREAT ORION STANDING   198 19
    ONE MOMENT THE HATE LEAPS AT ME STANDING THERE   225 25
    AND MY NAKED BODY STANDING ON YOUR GRAVE   233 14
    AS YOU SEE IT STANDING GROWING YOU FEEL AT ONCE IT IS S+ 282 13
    THERE NEVER WAS ANY STANDING ALOFT AND UNFOLDED ON A BO+ 283 3
    LOOK AT THEM STANDING THERE IN AUTHORITY   287 11
    PILLARS OF WHITE BRONZE STANDING RIGID LEST THE SKIES F+ 287 16
    ALL STANDING IN CLOUDS OF GLORY   303 6
    SEE HIM STANDING WITH HIS HEAD DOWN NEAR THE PORTA CAPP+ 379 1
    WHAT DO I CARE FOR HER THE UGLY FEMALE STANDING UP THERE 384 25
    TO CATCH SIGHT OF HER STANDING LIKE SOME HUGE GHOULISH 385 16
    AND THE FLAT FLACCID MOUNTAINS OF THE ELEPHANTS' STANDI+ 390 13
    MOTIONLESS STANDING IN SNOW LIKE A CHRISTMAS TOY   402 26
    STANDING WITHOUT FEET ON THE RIM OF THE FAR-OFF MESA   403 5
    COULD ONE AT NIGHT RUN UP AGAINST THE STANDING FLESH   428 2
    STANDING THERE SO SLEEK AND ERECT AND EYEABLE   431 14
    STANDING IN THEIR THOUSANDS THESE APPEARANCES IN DAMP 431 25
    THE ANGELS ARE STANDING BACK THE ANGELS OF THE KISS   707 6
    AND THE ANGELS ARE STANDING BACK   707 25
    ALL MATTER AND ALL SPIRIT STANDING UPRIGHT   872 13

STANDIN'
    AN' ME STANDIN' THERE ON TH' PLANK   60 20
    AN' ME STANDIN' ON THE PLANK   *911 6

STANDS
    AGAINST THE HAYSTACK A GIRL STANDS LAUGHING AT ME   37 1
    HE STANDS AND I TREMBLE BEFORE HIM   39 13
    HE STANDS THE COLUMN OF FIRE BY NIGHT   39 22
    HE STANDS LIKE A LIGHTHOUSE NIGHT CHURNS   39 31
    AS HE BLENCHES AND TURNS AWAY AND MY HEART STANDS STILL 47 27
    WHILE NORTH OF THEM ALL AT THE FARTHEST ENDS STANDS ONE+ 57 11
    IN THE PLAYGROUND A SHAGGY SNOWBALL STANDS HUGE AND STI+ 76 17
    AND MY HOLLOW FLESH STANDS UP IN THE NIGHT LIKE VANITY 97 10
    OF FLESH THAT STANDS DISMAYED ON THE BUSH   107 18
    BUT MY HEART STANDS STILL AS A NEW STRONG BREAD ALARMS 133 6
    THE EDGE OF THE BLUE AND THE SUN STANDS UP TO SEE US GL+ 132 28
    STANDS RUBBLE OF STUNTED HOUSES ALL IS REAPED   135 7
    A LOOK AS HE STANDS ON THE EDGE OF THIS NAKED STALL   144 19
    OF A SHIP THAT STANDS IN A SHADOWY SEA OF SNOW   155 21
    IT STANDS SO STILL IN THE HUSH COMPOSED OF TREES AND IN+ 159 27
    A TWISTED THORN-TREE STILL IN THE EVENING STANDS   167 9
    STANDS WATCHING EVERMORE   200 16
    WHO DO YOU THINK STANDS WATCHING   226 13
    AND AT THE FOOT OF A GRAVE A FATHER STANDS   232 24
    SOMETHING THAT STANDS OVER   248 7
    THE ITALIANS VULGARLY SAY IT STANDS FOR THE FEMALE PART+ 282 17
    AS ONE STANDS ON A BANK AND LOOKS IN   338 31
    HIS GOD STANDS OUTSIDE MY GOD   339 14
    WHILE SHE WITH HER GOATY MOUTH STANDS SMILING THE WHILE 382 18
    STANDS SAYING SEE I'M INVISIBLE   403 11
    A RED WOLF STANDS ON THE SHADOW'S DARK RED RIM   403 20
    HE STANDS WITH HIS FOREFEET ON THE DRUM   426 8
    WHILE HE STANDS ASIDE WATCHING WITH A SUPERIOR LITTLE G+ 447 30
    AND STANDS THERE A PIECE OF DUNG   450 4
    THE WHEAT ON BOTH SIDES OF THE ROAD STANDS GREEN   732 5
    IF HE ONLY STANDS   754 9
    THE WORD STANDS FOR SOMETHING   774 20
    AS A BIRD THAT LIFTS ITS WINGS AND STANDS   787 17
    OF WAITING AND THE ROOM STANDS STILL WITH FRIGHT   878 35
    ONE BROKEN THORN-TREE STILL IN THE TWILIGHT STANDS   *896 14
    THE ROUGH SNOWBALL IN THE PLAYGROUND STANDS HUGE AND ST+ *898 11
    THE ROUGH SNOWBALL IN THE PLA'GROUND STANDS HUGE AND ST+ *901 20
    A RUBBLE OF STUNTED HOUSES STANDS UNREAPED   *939 7
    SHE STANDS IN SILHOUETTE AGAINST THE WINDOW   *942 21

STAN'S
    MAUN THA CLING TO THE WA' AS THA STAN'S   139 21

STAR
    A SINGLE STAR IN A VEIL OF LIGHT   41 29
    YOUR STAR BE TOSSED OVER A WAVE   49 18
    UNLESS THE LITTLE STAR THAT KEEPS HER COMPANY   54 14
    OF GOLDEN DUST WITH STAR AFTER STAR   70 18
    WHEN DAWN IS FAR BEHIND THE STAR THE DUST-LIT TOWN HAS 71 7
    AND CLUSTERED STAR CALLED DOWN TO ME TO-NIGHT   86 15
    LIGHTING THESE AUTUMN LEAVES LIKE A STAR DROPPED THROUGH 86 16
    MY FALLEN STAR AMONG THE LEAVES MY DEAR   86 24
    OVERHEAD AT HOME AND HAD NOT ONE STAR   103 6
    THE STAR ABOVE THE HOUSE-TOPS GREETS   108 26
    THE PLACE WHERE A STAR USED TO BE   115 18
    THE HOURS HAVE CEASED TO FALL AND A STAR COMMANDS   167 17
    HE'S THE STAR OF MY FIRST BELOVED   198 21
    GREEN STAR SIRIUS   229 5
    THE GREAT STAR GOES   229 21
    UNDER MINE LIKE A STAR ON THE LAKE   248 26
    IN THE LONG DARK NIGHTS OF THE EVENING STAR AND SIRIUS + 305 23
    STAR AND THE SNOW-WIND AND THE LONG LONG NIGHTS   305 32
    DOWN LIKE A STAR   445 7
    THE FLAME OF MY SOUL LIKE A TREMBLING STAR IS HUNG   750 12
    I ROSE AGAIN TO SEE A STAR FALLING AND FEEL A BREATH ON 786 10
    THE STAR THAT WAS FALLING WAS FADING WAS DYING   786 14
    I HEARD THE STAR SINGING LIKE A DYING BIRD   786 15
    LIKE A STAR LIKE A POND   788 24
    A FALLING STAR WAS RUNNING LIKE A WHITE DOG OVER A PLAIN 791 1
    NIGHT TURNS UPON ME AND DAY WHO AM THE STAR BETWEEN 800 1
    BETWEEN YOUR BREAST AND BELLY IS A STAR   800 2
    WHEN YOU WALK THE STAR WALKS WITH YOU BETWEEN YOUR BREA+ 800 5

STAR
    THE STAR OF THE BEYOND IS WITHIN YOU   800 17
    BUT HAVE YOU SEEN A DEAD MAN HOW HIS STAR HAS GONE OUT +   800 18
    SO THE STAR WILL GO OUT OF YOU EVEN AS A WOMAN WILL LEA+   800 19
    SHOULD YOU SAY I HAVE NO STAR I AM NO STAR   800 21
    IF THE STAR SHONE THEY DARE NOT THEY COULD NOT   800 28
    IF THE STAR SHONE WITHIN YOU   800 30
    BUT I AM THE INWARD STAR INVISIBLE   801 10
    AND THE STAR IS THE LAMP IN THE HAND OF THE UNKNOWN MOV+   801 11
    THE STAR COMES OUT BETWEEN THE TWO   802 27
    BEYOND THE STAR   811 17
    BUT THE STAR IS THE SAME FOR BOTH OF US   812 7
    AWAY ON THE HILLSIDE WAKES A STAR   857 25
    LIKE A LONELY STAR DROPPING THROUGH SPACE   862 24
    DEEP INTO THE HEART OF THE LIGHT THE CENTRE OF A STAR   865 6
    THERE IN THE HEART OF A STAR SET FAR OFF IN THE NIGHT   865 7
    SHE TURNED AND KISSED HIM AND HIS EYES WERE THE SOUL OF+   865 8
    AND THE WHITE NAPE OF HER NECK WAS THE BEAUTY OF THE ST+   865 9
    THE HOURS HAVE CEASED TO FALL AND A STAR COMMANDS   *896 22
    OUT OF EACH STAR DARK STRANGE BEAMS THAT DISQUIET   *897 28
    OUT OF EACH STAR DARK STRANGE BEAMS THAT DISQUIET   *901 5
    WHEN THE DAWN IS FAR BEHIND THE STAR THAT THE LAMP-LIT +   *917 25

STARE
    THA CAN STARE AT ME WI' THY FIERCE BLUE EYES   79 11
    THA WON'T STARE ME OUT I GUESS   79 12
    STARE   386 5
    STARE STARE STARE CORPSE-BODY AT THE FILM   584 14
    ONLY OH MAN STARE STARE INTO THE GULF   637 33
    YOU ONLY STARE AT THE SUN WITH THE ONE BROAD EYE OF YOUR   781 29
    YOU DO NOTHING BUT SQUAT ON YOUR HAMS AND STARE WITH VA+   795 2
    THA CAN STARE AT ME WI' THY FIERCE BLUE EYES   *921 7
    BUT THA DOESNA STARE ME OUT I GUESS   *921 8

STARED
    AT WHICH IN THE INTENSE STILL NOON I STARED WITH FASCIN+   351 17
    AND THEY STARED AND THEY STARED THE HALF-WITTED LOT   578 12
    THAT THEY STARED AND LEERED AT THE SINGLE SPOT   578 22
    OF ALL THE SORDID PEOPLE THAT HAVE STARED AT THEM UNCLE+   580 25

STARES
    AND THE RED-GOLD MIRROR-EYE STARES AND DIES   339 17
    AND IMMEDIATELY SHE SEES ME SHE BLINKS STARES DOESN'T   384 22
    AND STARES IN SURPRISE   754 10
    WHERE HE STARES AT THE SUN   782 24

STARING
    WE WENT IN SILENCE AND YOU STARING TO ENGLAND   206 7
    STARING AT WHAT HE SEES   227 10
    YOU STARING CARYATIDS   289 10
    STROLLING IN GANGS AND STARING ALONG THE CORSO   312 19
    STARING CREATION OUT OF COUNTENANCE   328 20
    AS AN EAGLE STARING DOWN ON THE SUN   328 22
    STARING TWO WAYS AT ONCE TO RIGHT AND LEFT   373 13
    OR THE ROUND WILD VIVID EYE OF A WILD-GOOSE STARING   438 31
    STARING TWO WAYS AT ONCE TO RIGHT AND LEFT   781 19

STARINGS
    AWAY THE EVIL STARINGS AND THE BREATH   581 7

STARK
    I LAY DUMB AND STARK   46 24
    AND MY HEART LEAPED UP IN LONGING TO PLUNGE ITS STARK   125 33
    STARK ON THE HEAP   146 2
    SHE FARES IN THE STARK IMMORTAL   199 13
    IN THE SHEER COITION OF THE LIFE-FLOW STARK AND UNLYING   482 14
    AS STRIPS YOU STARK AS A MONKEY NUT   493 15
    ONLY WHEN I AM STRIPPED STARK NAKED I AM ALONE   607 30
    AND IF STARK NAKED I APPROACH A FELLOW-MAN OR FELLOW-WO+   608 1
    OFFER ME NOTHING BUT THAT WHICH YOU ARE STARK AND   608 5
    THE THICK RANK STREETS AND A STARK WHITE LIGHT   748 5
    ONLY STARK WITHOUT CLOTHING   825 10
    STARK ASUNDER   839 9
    AND MY HEART LEAPED UP IN LONGING TO PLUNGE ITS STARK   *936 32

STARK-CLEAR
    IN STARK-CLEAR ROSES THAN I TO MYSELF AM BROUGHT   218 12

STARLIGHT
    ALL THE LEAVES ARE FALLEN AND THE STARLIGHT SHINES THRO+ *917 28

STARLING
    THE STARLING SHAKING ITS HEAD AS IT WALKS IN THE GRASS   137 11
    NO LOOK AT THE WET STARLING   137 17
    AS A COLUMBINE FLOWER HAS OR EVEN A STARLING WALKING AN+   621 16

STARLINGS
    YOU FLUTTER IN A HOST OF FLAMES LIKE WINTER STARLINGS R+   784 1

STAR-LIT
    THE STAR-LIT RUSH OF A HARE   152 17

STAR OF EVENING
    AND WOMAN IS THE STAR OF EVENING   800 15

STAR-OIL
    PUT STAR-OIL OVER ME   803 3

STAR-ROAD
    HE SAYS HOWEVER HE IS STAR-ROAD   405 23

STARS
    OF STARS GREW SILENTLY   35 20
    SEE THE STARS LOVE   48 27
    HOW MANY STARS IN YOUR BOWL   49 2
    HOW THE STARS ARE TOSSED   49 6
    THE STARS WATERS TROUBLED FORSAKEN   49 10
    ITS STARS STAND STILL   49 12

STARS
    STARS ARE NOT SAFE IN HEAVEN   49 15
    AND THE STARS CAN CHAFF   54 29
    BY THE SLIPPING SHAWL OF STARS   55 27
    COULD SEE THE SMALL STARS TREMBLE   55 28
    HAVE BEEN FOR ME LIKE A DAZED CONSTELLATION OF STARS   75 26
    SILENCE THAT RUSTLES BEYOND THE STARS THERE   76 11
    YOU HELEN WHO SEE THE STARS   86 1
    LIKE A CAT'S DISTENDED PUPIL THAT SPARKLES WITH LITTLE +   97 15
    EVERYTHING TEAR-TREMBLING STARS OF AUTUMN   107 7
    FOR THE STARS TO PROBE   108 4
    THE STARS ARE BUOYS   110 24
    HERE NOT EVEN THE STARS CAN SPY US   114 5
    AND CITY STARS SO DIM AND HOLY   121 31
    FINE THRILLS TO THE NEIGHBOUR STARS FINE HIDDEN BEAMS   127 7
    WHEN I TELL YOU THE STARS FLASH SIGNALS EACH ONE   130 25
    STREWN STARS OF UNKNOWN PEOPLE AND LUMINOUS LITTER   132 12
    AND I AM OF IT THE SMALL SHARP STARS ARE QUITE NEAR   134 15
    RIPE LITTLE STARS COME ROLLING FROM THEIR HUSK   135 12
    THE MUD-WEED OPENING TWO PALE SHADOWLESS STARS   145 3
    BRUSHING THE STARS GOES MY SOUL THAT SKIMS THE BOUNDS   193 25
    THE STARS THAT OPEN AND SHUT   194 4
    LIKE STARS ON A POOL   194 6
    YOU WHO ROLL THE STARS LIKE JEWELS IN YOUR PALM   197 24
    BENEATH BARE JUDGMENT STARS   202 14
    STARS COME LOW AND WANDERING HERE FOR LOVE   221 18
    THE STARS HAVE GONE SO FAR ON THEIR ROAD   229 7
    A DISARRAY OF FALLING STARS COMING TO NOUGHT   236 23
    THE STARS IN THEIR SUN-DIMMED CLOSES   242 29
    THERE'S THIS OTHER BEAUTY THE WAY OF THE STARS   251 20
    HOW THE STARS ARE MOVING IN SURETY   252 5
    AND HEAVE IT OFF AMONG THE STARS INTO THE INVISIBLE   272 24
    BURST THE NIGHT'S MEMBRANE OF TRANQUIL STARS   302 18
    WINGS FULL OF STARS THEY RULE THE NIGHT AND MAN THAT WA+ 319 3
    TROPICAL STARS   387 20
    TOWARDS THE BREATHING STARS AND THE CENTRAL OF ALL SUNN+ 480 18
    STARS AND SUNS   482 7
    IN TERRIBLE RIPPLING CIRCLES BETWEEN THE STARS   512 18
    SOFTER THAN THE SPACE BETWEEN THE STARS   667 9
    AT LAST THE NARCISSUS LIFTED A TUFT OF FIVE-POINT STARS   683 2
    LADY LADY OF THE LAST HOUSE DOWN THE LONG LONG STREET O+ 696 8
    HOLD THE STARS STILL LEST WE HEAR THE HEAVENS DIMLY RIN+ 698 11
    IF I STRING THE PLANETS AND THE BEADY STARS   735 18
    THE STARS AND THE EARTH AND THE SUN AND THE MOON AND TH+ 792 17
    FOR SUN AND STARS AND EARTH AND THE VERY RAINS ARE WEARY 792 20
    THIS IS WHAT STARS AND SUN AND EARTH AND MOON AND WINDS+ 793 3
    THERE IS THE SPANGLED DRAGON OF THE STARS AT LARGE   796 20
    AND SHALL PASS THE HOUSES OF THE STARS BY NIGHT   799 9
    SAVE FOR THE MORNING AND EVENING STARS UPON WHICH THEY + 799 27
    AND THE PALE STARS OF FORGET-ME-NOTS HAVE CLIMBED TO TH+ 854 2
    OF DUSTY GRASSES LIKE THE STARS THAT DAWN   884 31
    HAVE SHONE FOR ME LIKE A CROWDED CONSTELLATION OF STARS *897 25
    THAT RUSTLES BEYOND THE STARS TO ME THERE   *898 5
    HAVE SHONE FOR ME LIKE A CROWDED CONSTELLATION OF STARS *901 2
    THAT RUSTLES BEYOND THE STARS TO ME THERE   *901 14
    HERE NOT EVEN THE STARS CAN SPY US   *929 22
    AND WHAT HAS BECOME OF THE FLUFFY YELLOW STARS   *933 24
    STREWN STARS OF PALLID PEOPLE AND THROUGH LUMINOUS LITT+ *938 4
    STARS COME LOW AND WANDERING HERE FOR LOVE   *945 4

STAR-SHADOWS
    STAR-SHADOWS SHINE LOVE   49 1

STAR-SPIDERS
    STAR-SPIDERS SPINNING THEIR THREAD   113 18
    STAR-SPIDERS SPINNING THEIR THREAD   *929 7

STAR'S
    TO NOUGHT DIMINISHING EACH STAR'S GLITTER   132 14
    TO STREW ROUND OUR WAY TO DIMINISH EACH FULL STAR'S GLI+ *938 6

START
    UP THE WARM GRASS WHERE THE SUNBEAMS START   46 8
    MY PACK OF UNRULY HOUNDS I CANNOT START   74 9
    TO START A BIRTH FROM JOY OF THE BEGETTING   89 7
    I SEE EACH SHADOW START   108 7
    WHY SHOULD I START AND STAND STILL   110 27
    TO START AGAIN   244 24
    IF YOU START AWAY FROM MY BREAST AND LEAVE ME   246 24
    IT WAS ALL TAINTED WITH MYSELF I KNEW IT ALL TO START W+ 256 29
    WOULD START THE THUNDERING TRAFFIC OF FEET   272 2
    BUT WE AS WE START AWAKE CLUTCH AT OUR VISTAS DEMOCRATIC 286 34
    WHEN DID YOU START YOUR TRICKS   332 1
    SOMETIMES HE TURNS WITH A START TO FIGHT TO CHALLENGE TO 381 8
    AND START PRANCING AND LICKING AND CUDDLING AGAIN   396 24
    OF A SWAMPED CIVILISATION AND START A NEW WORLD OF MAN   429 12
    AND START IN   430 12
    O START A REVOLUTION SOMEBODY   453 6
    O START A REVOLUTION SOMEBODY   453 9
    START IN AND BUST IT ALL   457 10
    DON'T SAY YOU CAN'T START IN AND TRY   458 9
    BREAK THE CAGE THEN START IN AND TRY   485 9
    BEFORE WE START KILLING ONE ANOTHER ABOUT IT   487 12
    WE SHOULD START AN' KICK THEIR -SES FOR 'EM   491 3
    START A SYSTEM OF OFFICIAL SPYING   536 4
    WOMEN START IN TO MAKE CHANGES   538 19
    AND START IN TO SHOW   564 16
    BUT DON'T TRY IT ON OH NEVER START   575 24
    SUPERIOR TO EVERYONE ELSE SO DON'T START   576 13
    TO START THE YEAR ON EASTER SUNDAY   609 19
    SUDDENLY HIS HORSES BEGAN TO START   735 7
    TO START MY HEART AFRESH GIVE ME THE SOFT SMALL STRESS   738 31
    TO START THE GLORY OF ANOTHER YEAR   746 2
    SAW MY LAST HOPE START   748 24
    WHEN I SAY THE WORD THEY WILL START   792 19
    ARE DISCUSSING WITH ONE ANOTHER THEY ARE MAKING READY T+ 793 4
    THE THING FOR MEN TO DO IS TO START TO PULL DOWN MONEY   838 11
    I START FROM THE DROOP OF FORGETFULNESS AS THE SOUND OF+ 858 21

START
    MY PACK OF UNRULY HOUNDS I CANNOT START   *895 17
    MY PACK OF UNRULY HOUNDS I CANNOT START   *904 6
    SINCE THE MONTH OF CHILDHOOD IS OVER AND WE START AFRESH   *938 8
    SHE WILL START WHEN SHE SEES ME AND BLUSHING SPREAD OUT+   *940 16

STARTED
    THE STREET-LAMPS IN THE TWILIGHT HAVE SUDDENLY STARTED +   102 31
    AND SHE STARTED TO SPEAK   156 12
    PERHAPS IF WE STARTED RIGHT ALL THE CHILDREN COULD GROW+   527 4
    I SUPPOSE WHEN THE MEN ALL STARTED BEING WILLY WET-LEGS   537 28
    SO UP I STARTED CLIMBING   554 9
    AND THE COFFEE-PLANT STARTED COFFING THREE VERY DISTINC+   760 27
    INTO TANTRUMS AND STARTED THEIR HULLABALOO   761 6
    YET THE CLASH HAS BEEN STARTED THE INDIAN IS ABOUT TO BE   777 20
    AND STARTED DOWN THE LONG SLOPE   787 3
    AND I STARTED WITH PLEASURE FOR IN THE NIGHT IT HAD COM+   860 12

STARTING
    DROPPING AND STARTING FROM SLEEP   143 3
    AT STARTING OTHER LIFE FULFILLED MY OWN   218 14
    AND STARTING FORWARD IN THE DUSK WITH YOUR LITTLE BLACK   396 31

STARTLE
    BECAUSE WHEN YOUR EYES LOOK UP AT ME THEY STARTLE   874 27
    YOU STARTLE ME WITH REMINISCENCE OF THE GREAT   875 3

STARTLED
    SHE GLANCES QUICK HER STARTLED EYES   42 24
    STARTLED UPON YOUR EYES NOW SO WIDE WITH HEREAFTER   58 22
    I HAVE STARTLED A HUNDRED EYES AND NOW I MUST LOOK   76 12
    I ON THE DECK AM STARTLED BY THIS DAWN CONFRONTING   133 1
    THRONG OF STARTLED BEINGS SUDDENLY THROWN   140 12
    YOU FROM THOSE STARTLED HILLS   178 16
    OVER HER STARTLED EYES   201 2
    WHEN SHE LIFTED HER HEAD IN DELICATE STARTLED WONDER   255 28
    AND HE WAS THOROUGHLY STARTLED   324 18
    NIGHTINGALE'S PIERCING CRIES AND GURGLES STARTLED THE   366 2
    THEY STARTLED CREATION AND WHEN THEY WERE THROUGH   761 7
    STARTLED AND FULL OF AGONY TO FIND HE HAD BUT SLEPT   859 14
    I HAVE STARTLED A HUNDRED EYES AND I MUST LOOK   *898 6
    I HAVE STARTLED A HUNDRED EYES AND I MUST LOOK   *901 15

STARTLES
    THAT STARTLES ME ALARMS ME STIRS UP A REPULSION   270 14

STARTLING
    STARTLING A FEAR UNSPEAKABLE AS THE SHUDDERING WIND   140 17
    YET UNRELEASED AND AFTER THE MOMENT THE SUDDEN STARTLING   365 17
    STARTLING BIG BIRD   413 19
    STARTLING THE THICK-SPUN TWILIGHT THE BELLS SHAKE OUT   858 25
    STARTLING MY HORSE WHO STIRS AND WOULD TURN HER ABOUT   858 28

STARTS
    RHYTHM STARTS AND MY SILENT AND SLUMBEROUS BELLY   39 5
    RELIEF THAT STARTS IN MY BREAST   100 10
    GOD HOW SHE STARTS   143 14
    EVERYTHING STARTS FROM US   204 26
    THE DARKNESS STARTS UP WHERE   215 17
    FULL IN MY OWN AND THE TORMENT STARTS AGAIN   225 24
    ARE PROPPED ON END THERE WHERE THE MYSTERY STARTS   233 8
    THAN OFF HE STARTS WITHOUT A QUALM   299 33
    WHEN A LOW BULL-MONGREL STARTS DECLAIMING   494 9
    WHEN SCIENCE STARTS TO BE INTERPRETIVE   523 1
    AND YOUR DEMON STARTS LASHING OUT   564 3
    AND THE WHEEL STARTS THE PRINCIPLE OF ALL EVIL   712 7
    A FLUSH OF ROSE AND THE WHOLE THING STARTS AGAIN   720 11

STARVE
    I LOST AT LAST THE FIERCENESS THAT FEARS IT WILL STARVE   265 3
    THAT I SHOULD NEVER STARVE   265 6
    OR PRACTICALLY STARVE   831 11

STARVED
    I NEW-RISEN RESURRECTED STARVED FROM THE TOMB   259 14
    STARVED FROM A LIFE OF DEVOURING ALWAYS MYSELF   259 15

STARVING
    THEY SAY WE ARE SAVED BUT WE ARE STARVING   442 14

STATE
    TO YOUR DUBIOUS STATE   237 6
    THE FULL MOON SANK IN STATE   261 23
    YOU ARE ITEMS IN THE SOVIET STATE   443 3
    BUT IT IS THE SOVIET STATE ALONE WHICH COUNTS   443 5
    THE STATE HAVING SAVED THEM ALL   443 7
    SEX IS A STATE OF GRACE   472 1
    SEX IS A STATE OF GRACE   485 7
    I WOULD RATHER SIT STILL IN A STATE OF PEACE ON A STONE   498 1
    THAT A MAN OR A WOMAN IN A STATE OF GRACE   578 25
    REMEMBER THE STATE OF MIND OF THE BRITISH PUBLIC   669 27

STATELY
    AND BID FAREWELL OF STATELY TRAVELLERS   740 20

STATEMENT
    FALTERS A STATEMENT ABOUT AN ABSTRACT NOUN   76 8

STATEMENTS
    THOUGHT IS THE TESTING OF STATEMENTS ON THE TOUCHSTONE +   673 11

STATES
    THESE STATES AS WHITMAN SAID   293 11
    MANY VIVID SMALL STATES LIKE A KALEIDOSCOPE ALL COLOURS   611 19

STATIC
    ARRESTED STATIC   255 36

STATICALLY
    SO NINE-TENTHS ASLEEP MOTIONLESS BORED AND STATICALLY A+   324 15

STATION
    A BRILLIANT STATION THE CHASE   862 28

STATUES
    WHEN PEOPLE POSE AS GODS THEY ARE CRYSTAL PALACE STATUES   673 2

STATURE
    MY FACE MAY NOT PLEASE YOU NOR MY STATURE YET IF YOU   251 9
    STATURE   841 15

STAVE
    SINGING MY STAVE   772 21

STAVROGINS
    AND THE ALYOSHAS AND DMITRIS AND MYSHKINS AND STAVROGINS   533 14

STAY
    WILL ENTER AND SHUT THE DOOR TO STAY   91 9
    THE DANDELION SEEDS STAY HALF-SUBMERGED IN THE GRASS   204 21
    GOD MAY STAY IN MID-HEAVEN THE SON OF MAN HAS CLIMBED TO   323 14
    O YOU WITH MENTAL BODIES STAY A LITTLE DISTANCE FROM ME   468 25
    THE BODY INTO IT LET US STAY APART   469 5
    WE ARE GOING TO STAY ON AND ON AND ON AND ON AND ON   503 3
    AN EARL ONCE ASKED ME DOWN TO STAY   551 27
    I DIDN'T STAY VERY LONG WITH THE EARL   552 1
    YET ONCE MORE I MET A MAN AND I HAD TO STAY   569 21
    IF YOU STAY IN MY OFFICE YOU'VE GOT TO BE KITH   583 27
    EITHER TO STAY CONNECTED WITH THE TREE OF LIFE AND SUBM+   617 13
    THEY'VE GOT TO STAY UP   667 23
    AND NOTHING WILL STAY THE DEATH-FLOOD RISING WITHIN US   718 15
    NOR CEASE TO BE DARK ON THE DARKNESS STAY   738 20
    SHE SAID TO ME STAY THREE HOURS TO COMFORT ME SUCH IS A+   749 19
    THAT THE BOYS MUST STAY AT SCHOOL NOT BE KEPT AWAY   777 33
    THAT OUR BOYS MUST STAY AT SCHOOL TILL THEY ARE EIGHTEEN   779 2
    AND WILL SHINE IF I STAY OR I GO AWAY   815 20
    PERSUADES ME TO STAY SINCE STAY I MAY   815 21
    WHY NOT STAY OUT AND LEARN TO CONTAIN ONESELF   839 22

STAYED
    THE ANGELS CAME TO ABRAHAM AND THEY STAYED   234 5
    HE STAYED WITH THE HORSES SULKILY   735 11
    DOWN TO THE LEVELS WHERE YOU HAVE STAYED   763 19

STAYS
    THAT STAYS WITH STEADY JOY OF ITS OWN FIRE   151 15
    THE CONFORMING WORM STAYS JUST INSIDE THE SKIN   432 6
    AND THE MORTAL RESERVE OF YOUR SEX AS IT STAYS IN YOUR   464 26
    BUT IF HE STAYS FAR FROM ME AND DOES NOT TOUCH ME   468 9
    IT STAYS ON ITS HUB   713 26
    THAT STEADY STAYS WITH JOY OF ITS OWN FIRE   873 25

STEAD
    TO STEAD HER WOMB AROUND US BEYOND THE SWOON   *938 15

STEADFAST
    GLISTENING IN STEADFAST STILLNESS LIKE TRANSCENDENT   225 3

STEADFASTLY
    LIKE A NEEDLE STEADFASTLY   99 24

STEADFASTNESS
    FRIGHTENED ME WITH THE STEADFASTNESS OF THEIR LOOKING   884 33

STEADIER
    THE TRAIN IN RUNNING ACROSS THE WEALD HAS FALLEN INTO A+   88 1

STEADILY
    AND THE RED FIRELIGHT STEADILY REELING   41 8
    MOVED WITH SLOW FEET AND HER EYES' FLAME STEADILY BURNED 156 10
    OF DARKNESS ADVANCING STEADILY OVER US ALL   164 24
    BUT STEADILY SURELY AND NOTWITHSTANDING   209 12
    THE GOD-THRUST ENTERING YOU STEADILY FROM BELOW   373 22

STEADY
    THE SUBTLE STEADY RUSH OF THE WHOLE   68 13
    THEIR PALE-GOLD PETALS BACK WITH STEADY WILL   91 13
    TO STEADY MY BRAIN IN THIS PHANTOM SHOW   105 10
    THAT STAYS WITH STEADY JOY OF ITS OWN FIRE   151 15
    THE STEADY GLOW FOR OIL THE CHARM   873 11
    THAT STEADY STAYS WITH JOY OF ITS OWN FIRE   873 25
    WITH A STEADY RUSH OF LIVING A FOAM   888 7
    THE SUBTLE STEADY RUSH OF THE WHOLE   *914 28

STEAL
    DISCOVERY LIKE BIRDS THAT STEAL AND FLEE   51 30
    SLOW TRAINS STEAL PAST   169 3
    SHADOWS STEAL OUT OF THE EARTH   425 2
    WHY SHOULDN'T WE STEAL THE JAM IN THE CUPBOARD   573 11
    WHY SHOULDN'T I STEAL THE JAM IN THE CUPBOARD   670 26
    BUT YOU WOULD STEAL   756 6
    I STEAL ACROSS THE HUSHED CORRIDOR   877 36
    AND LAMPS LIKE VENTUROUS GLOW-WORMS STEAL AMONG   *939 9
    I SEE THE WOMAN'S SOUL STEAL IN HER EYES   *943 19

STEALING
    HER HAND GO STEALING   35 23
    ITSELF AMONG EVERYTHING ELSE HERE HUNGRILY STEALING   141 18
    AND STEALING INTO HIS SLEEP SHOULD SET HIM LONGING   877 33
    SHOWED ME SOME OTHER LOVERS STEALING DOWN THE OTHER HED+ 882 21
    AS BIRDS WHO ARE STEALING TURN AND FLEE   *899 13
    AS BIRDS WHO ARE STEALING TURN AND FLEE   *902 25

STEALS
AND ASKING NOTHING PATIENTLY STEALS BACK AGAIN   63 29
THE DARKNESS STEALS THE FORMS OF ALL THE QUEENS   135 21
YET THROUGH THE TEARS STEALS A SENSE OF PEACE AND GREAT+   768 1
AND THEN ONE STEALS   825 11
THE DARKNESS STEALS THE FORMS OF ALL THE QUEENS   *938 25
THE DARKNESS STEALS THE FORMS OF ALL THE QUEENS   *939 21

STEALTHILY
TOMORROW COMES STEALTHILY OUT OF THE MOULD   815 7

STEALTHY
AND I IN THE STEALTHY BRINDLED ODOURS   107 19
I SEE THE STEALTHY SHADOW OF SILENCE   110 15

STEAM
HELEN YOU LET MY KISSES STEAM   86 5
OF STEAM FROM THE DARKENING NORTH   99 22
THE CRISPING STEAM OF A TRAIN   100 2
OOZES AWAY FROM ME AS A SACRIFICE STEAM   131 9
IN STEAM   175 25
HER FACE IS BENT IN THE BITTER STEAM   202 27
DOES THE SUN NEED STEAM OF BLOOD DO YOU THINK   374 9
WHICH GOES THROUGH ALL THE STAGES OF STEAM AND STREAM A+   505 21
NOW BEGIN TO STEAM OMINOUSLY   541 3
DRIVEN BY STEAM   631 16
USING ALL LIFE ONLY AS POWER AS AN ENGINE USES STEAM OR+   635 11
HAS EVAPORATED FROM YOU LIKE STEAM FROM GLASS   871 6
AND BROKEN BY MY WEIGHT AND THE PURPLE STEAM   881 8
WITH HER SILKEN STEAM LIKE A BANNER BEHIND HER AFLOW   *894 30

STEAMER
BEHIND ME ON THE LAKE I HEAR THE STEAMER DRUMMING   231 5

STEAM-FLAG
THE STEAM-FLAG FLOWING   110 14

STEAMING
A MANGO-FLESHED AURA NAUSEOUSLY STEAMING   760 9

STEAMS
THE EARTH AGAIN LIKE A SHIP STEAMS OUT OF THE DARK SEA +   132 27
FLAPS UP FROM THE PLAYGROUND AS A GREAT TRAIN STEAMS SO+   *894 29

STEEL
WITH BOWELS OF STEEL   56 28
OF MY STEEL LOVELY WHITE FLINT OF DESIRE   118 5
HEAVIER THAN MINE YET LIKE LEVERETS CAUGHT IN STEEL   128 7
RUNS INTO SPEED LIKE A DREAM THE BLUE OF THE STEEL   136 9
PURPLED STEEL   149 6
OF IRON KISSES KISSES LINKED LIKE STEEL   154 20
WEBBING OF STEEL ON YOUR FEET SO YOU SHALL FEEL   154 22
THE GHASTLY DREAM OF LABOUR AND THE STENCH OF STEEL AND+   175 1
LIKE STEEL LIKE SENSITIVE STEEL IN THE AIR   300 29
GREY LAVENDER SENSITIVE STEEL CURVING THINLY AND BRITTLY   300 30
HAVE YOU A STRANGE ELECTRIC SENSITIVENESS IN YOUR STEEL+   301 2
UPON THE IRON AND UPON THE STEEL   304 12
FROM OUT THE IRON AND FROM OUT THE STEEL   304 16
ALONG THE IRON TO THE LIVING STEEL   304 19
SHE HAS NO QUALM WHEN SHE CATCHES MY FINGER IN HER STEEL   359 20
THINGS MADE BY IRON AND HANDLED BY STEEL   448 8
NOR CUT THE INVISIBLE WIRES OF STEEL THAT PULL THEM   586 6
AND STEEL HAS TWISTED THE LOINS OF MAN ELECTRICITY HAS   629 8
NOR CUT THE INVISIBLE WIRES OF STEEL THAT PULL THEM   632 21
ARE THE GUNS AND THE STEEL THE BRIDEGROOM   742 25
THE DEAD OF THE STEEL MACHINES GO UP IN MOTION AWAY   796 9

STEEL-SLAG
YOUR WATTLES ARE THE COLOUR OF STEEL-SLAG WHICH HAS BEE+   369 12

STEEL-STRAIGHT
AND SIT BESIDE THE STEEL-STRAIGHT ARMS OF YOUR FAIR WOM+   291 5

STEEL-STRONG
STEERED AND PROPELLED BY THAT STEEL-STRONG SNAKE OF A T+   393 28

STEEL-TRAP
PARTING HIS STEEL-TRAP FACE SO SUDDENLY AND SEIZING HER   360 20
AND CLOSING HIS STEEL-TRAP FACE   360 24
HIS STEEL-TRAP STOIC AGELESS HANDSOME FACE   360 25

STEELY
AND WITH HIDEOUS SHRIEKS OF STEELY RAGE AND FRUSTRATION   676 3

STEEP
NAKED ON THE STEEP SOFT LIP   33 18
IS HE MOVING INVISIBLY DOES HIS STEEP   40 3
THE HILL IS STEEP ON THE SNOW MY STEPS ARE SLOW   85 15
OF EGRESS FROM YOU I WILL SEAL AND STEEP   154 14
AND ROLLS DOWN THE STEEP   162 24
YOU WHO STEEP FROM OUT THE DAYS THEIR COLOUR   197 26
STILL AND THE DARKNESSES STEEP   254 6
DOWN BETWEEN THE STEEP SLOPES OF DARKNESS FUCUS-DARK SE+   321 35
AND NEAR ACROSS AT THE OPPOSITE STEEP OF SNOW GREEN TRE+   402 25
WE CLIMBED THE STEEP ASCENT TO HEAVEN   554 1
SLOW CATTLE STIR ON THE STEEP MEADOW NEAR BY   886 28
NAKED ON THE STEEP SOFT LIP   *891 20
DOWN THE SKY'S STEEP STAIRS CHARTING NO TRACK FOR HER   *937 27

STEEPED
IN WHAT STRONG AQUA REGIA NOW ARE YOU STEEPED   53 27
TILL AFTER A LONG TIME WHEN THEY ARE OLD AND HAVE STEEP+   448 10
STEEPED ENOUGH TELL HIM TO COME ACROSS   759 8
MY SOUL IS HEAVY WITH SUNSHINE AND STEEPED WITH STRENGTH   803 8

STEEPLE
A STEEPLE   162 5

STEEPS
THE PATH BETWEEN GULFS OF THE DARK AND THE STEEPS OF   788 9

STEER
DARKLY FOR WE CANNOT STEER AND HAVE NO PORT   719 9
AND STEER ACCORDING TO THE CURRENTS AND WINDS AND TIDES+   *953 10

STEERED
STEERED AND PROPELLED BY THAT STEEL-STRONG SNAKE OF A T+   393 28

STEERING
WITH HIS HEAD UP STEERING LIKE A BIRD   337 26
THEN SWERVING AND STEERING AFRESH   380 25

STEERS
AS IF A BIRD IN DIFFICULTY UP THE VALLEY STEERS   210 22
OF DOVES FOR VENUS OR STEERS FOR HERMES   678 5
ODYSSEUS CALLS THE COMMANDS AS HE STEERS PAST THOSE FOA+   687 20

STEM
THE LAST SILK-FLOATING THOUGHT HAS GONE FROM THE DANDEL+   97 7
FROM THAT SHALLOW-SILVERY WINE-GLASS ON A SHORT STEM   279 11
AS FROM THE STEM OF HIS BRISTLING LIGHTNING-CONDUCTOR T+   381 19
FLOWERS OFF THEIR FIVE-FOLD STEM   451 27
LEAPS UP TO THE SUMMIT OF THE STEM GLEAMS TURNS OVER   474 4
TELL ME IS THE GENTIAN SAVAGE AT THE TOP OF ITS COARSE +   684 2
ODD WINTRY FLOWERS UPON THE WITHERED STEM YET NEW STRAN+   727 24
THE LOWEST STEM OF THIS LIFE OF MINE   *899 26
THE OLD HARD STEM OF MY LIFE   *899 27
AND SLOWLY FINGERING UP MY STEM AND FOLLOWING ALL TINILY   *900 18
THE LOWEST STEM OF THIS LIFE OF MINE   *903 5
THE OLD HARD STEM OF MY LIFE   *903 6
AND SLOWLY FINGERING UP MY STEM AND FOLLOWING ALL TINILY   *903 30
GIVE ME A FLOWER ON A TALL STEM AND THREE DARK FLAMES   *956 21

STEMLESS
GREAT COMPLICATED NUDE FIG-TREE STEMLESS FLOWER-MESH   299 3

STEMS
BARE STEMS OF STREET LAMPS STIFFLY STAND   51 1
THE BLUE-GLEAMED DRAKE STEMS PROUD   126 15
SHALLOW WINE-CUPS ON SHORT BULGING STEMS   283 6
YOU HAVE WELDED YOUR THIN STEMS FINER   300 28
STEMS   372 13
AS HE BITES AT THE STEMS OF LEAVES IN AUTUMN TO MAKE TH+   609 3
THE GREEN-FLY ON THE STEMS   655 9
I FEEL THE PAIN OF FALLING LEAVES AND STEMS THAT BREAK +   727 7
NOT ON THE STEMS OF VIRGINITY LOVELY AND MUTE   855 11
SWINGS ROUND THE STEMS OF THE MANY INSIGNIFICANT MUTE   855 19

STENCH
THE GHASTLY DREAM OF LABOUR AND THE STENCH OF STEEL AND+   175 1
AND THE NOISE AND THE STENCH AND THE DREARINESS   510 28

STEP
I SAW HER STEP TO THE KERB AND FAST   122 3
SO YOU STEP DOWN THE BANK TO MAKE WAY   387 9
THE LAST STEP OUT OF THE EAST   404 28
HARK HARK STEP ASIDE SILENTLY AND SWIFTLY   642 19
STEP ASIDE STEP OUT OF IT IT IS EATING YOU UP   642 28
O STEP ASIDE WITH DECISION SONS OF MEN WITH DECISION   642 29
AND WATCHING OUR EVERY STEP   707 4
BUT A STEP ONWARDS IN UNTRAVELLED SPACE   713 15
THEIR GOING ROUND EACH TIME IS A STEP   713 17
PERHAPS ONE COULD STEP ACROSS   763 24
NOR A WOMAN STEP OUT LIKE A MAN   812 18
BUT WATCH YOUR SEXUAL STEP OH DEAR MY DEAR   829 29

STEPPED
LAD NEVER STEPPED TILL 'E GOT IN WITH YOUR LOT   60 31
YOU HAVE STEPPED ACROSS YOUR PEOPLE CARELESSLY HURTING   209 8
I HAVE STEPPED ACROSS MY PEOPLE AND HURT THEM IN SPITE   209 10
FURTHER STILL BEFORE THE CURLED HORNS OF THE RAM STEPPED   437 14
OH HE HAS PUT HIS PINCE-NEZ ON AND STOUTLY HAS STEPPED   633 20
FOR A MOMENT AT EVENING TIRED AS HE STEPPED OFF THE TRA+   672 7
MUNDANE EGG AT VARIOUS POINTS THEY STEPPED OUT AND IMME+   760 23
WONDERING HE STEPPED NEARER AND LOOKED AT HER   790 6
AND FURTHER STILL BEFORE THE CURLED HORNS OF THE RAM ST+   *946 25

STEPPES OF TARTARY
THE STEPPES OF TARTARY   378 1
THE STEPPES OF TARTARY   380 1

STEPPING
STEPPING LIKE BIRDS WITH THEIR BRIGHT AND POINTED FEET   71 25
GOD STEPPING THROUGH OUR LOINS IN ONE BRIGHT STRIDE   87 25
STEPPING WEE MITE IN HIS LOOSE TROUSERS   355 21
AND THE HUGE FRONTAL OF THREE GREAT ELEPHANTS STEPPING   387 28
AND STEPPING IN HOMAGE STUBBORN TO THAT NERVOUS PALE   388 24
HEAVILY STEPPING WEARY ON OUR HEARTS   704 10

STEPS
SERENELY WITH STEPS UNSWERVING   63 32
THE HILL IS STEEP ON THE SNOW MY STEPS ARE SLOW   85 15
THE YELLOW SUN STEPS OVER THE MOUNTAIN-TOP   230 5
AND FALTERS A FEW SHORT STEPS ACROSS THE LAKE   230 6
AND IN A GREAT AND SACRED FORTHCOMING STEPS FORTH STEPS   306 6
I CAME DOWN THE STEPS WITH MY PITCHER   349 5
AND THE FRAIL SOUL STEPS OUT INTO HER HOUSE AGAIN   720 16
BENEATH THE STEPS OF ST PAUL'S CATCH SEVERAL   750 22

STERILE
  HOW I KNOW THAT GLITTER OF SALT DRY STERILE SHARP CORRO+   207 17
  PUFFING ITS LITTLE MALE STAMENS OUT INTO STERILE PETAL +   535 6
  IT IS LIKE A VAST GREAT TREE WITH A VAST GREAT LOT OF S+   677 21

STERILISED
  STERILISED   582 17

STERILITY
  SUCH PEARLED ZONES OF FAIR STERILITY   855 1

STERN
  AH STERN COLD MAN   55 1
  LIKE THE PROW OF A BOAT HIS HEAD LAID BACK LIKE THE STE+   155 20
  HAVE A STERN EYE ON LIFE   528 15
  GREY STERN ANGRY UNSATISFIED   739 26

STERNLY
  EDITOR STERNLY HAVE YOU BEEN MADE SAFE FOR THE GREAT   582 12

STERTOROUS
  YOU HEAR THE STERTOROUS SELF-RIGHTEOUS HEAVY   528 19

ST GEORGE
  AND TURN ONCE MORE TO MEN TO SAVE THEM PERSEUS ST GEORGE   619 26

STICK
  WOULDN'T I STICK THE SALVIA IN MY COAT   315 12
  YOU WOULD TAKE A STICK AND BREAK HIM NOW AND FINISH   350 6
  JUST AS HE SNAPS WHEN I POKE A BIT OF STICK AT HIM   357 13
  A HOLE IN THE BLOOD-ORANGE BRILLIANT ROCKS THAT STICK U+   402 12
  RED MEN STILL STICK THEMSELVES OVER WITH BITS OF HIS FL+   414 3

STICKILY
  STICKILY GLISTENING WITH ETERNAL SHADOW   310 17

STICKING
  LIKE IRON STICKING GRIMLY OUT OF EARTH   300 19
  DECEMBER'S BARE IRON HOOKS STICKING OUT OF EARTH   304 8
  AND HIM FROM STICKING HIMSELF LIKE A PIG   479 26

STICKING-OUT
  WITH STICKING-OUT DEAD BERRY EYES BLACK   345 29

STICKS
  OF FINGER OR FIST OR SOFT-SKINNED STICKS UPON THE STREE+   629 0
  MADE OF CEMENT POURED INTO A MOULD AROUND IRON STICKS   673 3
  AND LO IT STICKS BETWEEN THE RIBS OF A MAN   807 21

STIFF
  OH YOU STIFF SHAPES SWIFT TRANSFORMATION SEETHES   72 12
  IS THIS ARMOUR OF STIFF RELUCTANCY   117 9
  THE LONELINESS DAUNTS THEM THEIR STIFF THROATS ACHE   228 12
  THE FLAMES' STIFF SPEED   242 15
  AND ALL THESE HUMAN PILLARS OF LOFTINESS GOING STIFF ME+   288 1
  STIFF GALLANT IRASCIBLE CROOK-LEGGED REPTILE   363 19
  WHEN THOUGHTS ARE STIFF LIKE OLD LEAVES   608 22
  STIFF AND DESPAIRING   662 1

STIFFEN
  MUST BE EXCRUCIATING UNLESS YOU STIFFEN INTO METAL WHEN   288 6

STIFFENED
  IS WOMB-FIRE IN THE STIFFENED CLAY OF US   89 3

STIFFLY
  BARE STEMS OF STREET LAMPS STIFFLY STAND   51 1
  O STIFFLY SHAPEN HOUSES THAT CHANGE NOT   53 20

STIFF-NECKED
  AND THE STIFF-NECKED PEOPLE AND THE SELF-WILLED PEOPLE +   616 2
  TILL THE SOUL OF THE STIFF-NECKED IS GROUND TO DUST TO +   616 14

STIFFNESS
  WITH STIFFNESS COMES FOR THE WATER THAT I   733 17

STIFLE
  I STIFLE A CRY OF DESPAIR   883 18

STIFLING
  AND WHEN YOUR STIFLING SOUL WOULD SUMMON   91 10
  THINK OF THE WORLD THAT YOU'RE STIFLING IN   457 5

STILLED
  IN BATTLE OF HEATED WORDS HARDLY STILLED BY MY REITERAT+   865 32

STILL-FLICKERING
  WERE NOT YET TO COME STILL MORE FROM THE STILL-FLICKERI+   272 8

STILL-LIVING
  HOVERING TO PECK OUT THE EYES OF THE STILL-LIVING CREAT+   500 17
  WAFTING WITH WARM LOVE FROM STILL-LIVING HEARTS   723 22

STILLNESS
  I LISTEN TO THE STILLNESS OF YOU   110 1
  GLISTENING IN STEADFAST STILLNESS LIKE TRANSCENDENT   225 3
  ONE MOMENT I SEE THE STILLNESS OF AGONY   225 26
  FULL OF SWEET STILLNESS   261 20
  IN THAT MOST AWFUL STILLNESS THAT ONLY GASPED AND HUMMED   372 7
  AS IF SWAYING WERE ITS FORM OF STILLNESS   467 17
  STILLNESS AND SATISFACTION OF AUTUMN   503 25
  IN THE RED STILLNESS OF THE DUSK   506 15
  AT THE STILLNESS OF THE AIR   646 18
  AH THE FALLEN STILLNESS OF GOD AUTUMNUS AND IT IS ONLY +   651 18
  BUT A TINY CORE OF STILLNESS IN THE HEART   658 14
  STILLNESS   672 5
  IN THE STILLNESS HE TOOK OFF HIS HELMET TO KISS ME   732 16
  OF STILLNESS AND AFTERNOON   770 26

STILLNESS
  IN THE STILLNESS WHERE WATERS ARE BORN   786 3
  IN THE STILLNESS OF MY NIGHT   804 19
  IN THE STILLNESS OF HIS NIGHT   806 1
  AND SOON THE OWL WINGED WITH STILLNESS WILL FLOAT OUT T+   858 16
  THE MUSIC OF MUSIC IS STILLNESS YOU BIRDS   *914 12

STILLY
  FOR NOW WE ARE PASSING THROUGH THE GATE STILLY   699 3

STIMULATES
  ONE FREE CHEERFUL ACTIVITY STIMULATES ANOTHER   520 26

STING
  NOR EVEN A LOVELY WOMAN FOAMY TO STING ME LIKE BRINE   840 23

STINGING
  THE STINGING NETTLES ON MY WRISTS WOKE ME   881 16
  THEN THE STINGING NETTLES ON MY WRISTS   882 20

STINGS
  OF NERVES THAT GRIND AND A SOUL THAT STINGS   747 14
  THAT STINGS DOWN TO MY HEART   863 20

STINK
  STAND THEY AND GOD HOW THEY STINK   457 2
  FRAGRANCE OF ROSES IN A STALE STINK OF LIES   634 28

STINKER
  YOU STINKER   398 30

STINKERS
  OF THE P AND O AND THE ORIENT LINE AND ALL THE OTHER ST+   688 7

STINKING
  AND SET THE STINKING RUBBISH-HEAP OF THIS FOUL WORLD   315 23
  AND FIR-WORT STINKING FOR THE CARRION WASP   316 5
  PROFITEERS HERE BEING CALLED DOG-FISH STINKING DOG-FISH+   316 25
  MONEY IS THE VAST STINKING BEAST   843 7

STINKS
  NO MORE AND MONEY STINKS NOT AND DEATH AT LAST   173 23
  OF PUTRESCENT WISDOM AND SAPIENCE THAT SUBTLY STINKS   441 3

STIR'
  ON THE GREAT BLUE PALACE AT SYDENHAM LIGHTS STIR AND SH+   52 18
  THAT STIRS WITH A STIR WHICH IS COSMIC AS EVER INVISIBLY   176 3
  THAT SHINE AS HER FINGERS STIR   200 20
  COME QUICKLY AND STIR THE ROTTEN GLOBE OF THE WORLD FROM   273 7
  AND YOU STIR UP THE MOST AMAZING MUD   830 15
  SLOW CATTLE STIR ON THE STEEP MEADOW NEAR BY   886 28
  ON THE UPLIFTED BLUE PALACE LIGHT POOLS STIR AND SHINE   *905 7
  WATCH THE STIR WHOSE RHYTHM IS SECRET WHOSE SECRET IS S+ *907 13
  WATCH THE STIR WHICH IS RHYTHMIC AND MOVES THEM ALL AS + *909 9

STIRRED
  STIRRED BY AN IMPETUOUS WIND SOME WAYS'LL   40 28
  THROUGH THE STIRRED IRIDESCENCE THAT SWIMS IN THE WARM   53 16
  LIKE HEAVY BIRDS AT REST THERE SOFTLY STIRRED   123 16
  AND HE HARDLY STIRRED IN MY HAND MUFFLED UP   347 8
  AND A SILENCE THAT STIRRED   748 23
  AND HIS CHILDREN STIRRED IN THEIR SLEEP AND WHEN THEY W+   885 12
  LIKE A HEAVY BIRD DISTURBED AND HER SHOULDERS STIRRED   *934 16

STIRRING
  STIRRING WITH EARTH-COLOURED LIFE EVER TURNING AND STIR+   153 6
  STIRRING OF NEW SEASONS   274 6
  NEW THROB LIKE A STIRRING UNDER THE FALSE DAWN THAT PRE+   292 34
  AND RUDDY-ORANGE LIMBS STIRRING THE LIMBO   667 7
  THEN THE SMALL STIRRING OF A NEW SMALL BUB IN THE NEST   728 9
  THE DRAGONS IN THE COSMOS ARE STIRRING WITH ANGER AGAIN   795 11
  STIRRING THE FIRES TO ACID OF BITTERNESS   795 25

STIRS
  HOMUNCULUS STIRS FROM HIS ROOTS AND STRIVES UNTIL   39 11
  HOW IT STIRS LIKE A SUBTLE STOAT WHATEVER SHE THINKS   128 17
  WHEN THE SLEEPER STIRS OR TURNS ON THE EBB OF THE FLOOD   145 27
  EACH WITH A SECRET WHICH STIRS IN HIS LIMBS AS THEY MOVE   174 10
  THAT STIRS WITH A STIR WHICH IS COSMIC AS EVER INVISIBLY   176 3
  AND DREAMS AS SHE STIRS THE MIXING-POT   203 7
  A BLOTCH OF PALLOR STIRS BENEATH THE HIGH   210 19
  IF SOMETHING STIRS IN THE BRANCHES   231 16
  THAT STARTLES ME ALARMS ME STIRS UP A REPULSION   270 14
  WHILE SOMETHING STIRS QUICKLY IN HER BELLY AND A LEAN   393 30
  WHEN IT'S LEFT ALONE AS IT STIRS AND ROUSES AND SLEEPS   464 31
  AND IT STIRS LIFE A SWAN   505 6
  STARTLING MY HORSE WHO STIRS AND WOULD TURN HER ABOUT   858 28
  CARRIES A DIM LOW SONG THAT STIRS   868 30
  THERE IS SOMETHING STIRS IN ME FROM THE FLOW OF THEIR L+ *906 17
  THEY HAVE A SECRET THAT STIRS IN THEIR LIMBS AS THEY MO+ *908 14
  COMES OVER TO ME WITH A COVERT MUSIC THAT STIRS   *942 2
  SHE STIRS HER GOLDEN SHADOW   *943 7

STITCH
  BUT NOW THEY STITCH TO ADORN THE BURSTEN FIG NOT TO COV+   284 14

STOAT
  MY PULSE OF LIFE AND LET HIM NOSE LIKE A STOAT   43 31
  HOW IT STIRS LIKE A SUBTLE STOAT WHATEVER SHE THINKS   128 17

STOATS
  AS FOXES STOATS AND WOLVES AND PRAIRIE DOGS   392 21

STOCK
  IT IS EASIER TO STAND STOCK RIGID THAN TO MOVE   288 7
  WOULD STOCK A MENAGERIE   489 26
  NEW STOCK   640 24

STOCK-BROKERS
    CLERGYMEN PROFESSORS BANK-DIRECTORS AND STOCK-BROKERS   774   6

STOCKING
    WHEN HE LIFTS HIS FOOT I SEE THE PAD OF HIS SOAKED STOC+   866   7

STOCKINGS
    NO MORE STOCKINGS TO DARN FOR THE FLOWER-ROOTS DOWN   309   2

STOCKIN'S
    'AVE I PUT 'IS CLEAN STOCKIN'S AN' SHIRT   45 14

STOCK-TAKING
    HAVE A REAL STOCK-TAKING   237   1

STOIC
    A SET STOIC ENDURANCE NON-EUROPEAN   292 12
    STOIC ABLE TO WAIT THROUGH AGES   292 29
    STOIC ULYSSEAN ATOM   354   5
    AND INORDINATELY THERE O STOIC   358 17
    HIS STEEL-TRAP STOIC AGELESS HANDSOME FACE   360 25
    THE LONELY RAMBLER THE STOIC DIGNIFIED STALKER THROUGH   360 28

STOLE
    THEY STOLE YOUR BODY FROM YOU AND LEFT YOU AN ANIMATED   630 26
    MY SIGHT BUT THEN WHO HAS STOLE THE BRIGHT WHITE HEN OF+ *933 23

STOLEN
    AND STOLEN KISSES SHALLOW AND GAY   42 13
    THAT HE'S STOLEN FROM THE MOTHER OF GOD   797 16
    HAVE STOLEN THE TREASURE OF AWAKENING   878 30

STOLID
    HE PREACHED TO THE STOLID FARMERS TILL AT LAST HE COULD+ 859 15

STOMACH
    THAN STOMACH OR THROAT OR EVEN THE MIND   264 12
    FROM THE PIT OF YOUR STOMACH   399   8

STONE
    WHERE THE SUNLIGHT SOAKS IN THE STONE THE AFTERNOON   52 13
    WHAT IS THIS MOUTH OF STONE   55 22
    O' WARMTH AS 'E GOT DOWN THEER TH' REST WOR STONE COLD   61 18
    DOWN THE STONE STAIRS   71 20
    TO YOU EARTH OF MY ATMOSPHERE STONE   118   4
    I FEEL THICK WALLS OF STONE BEHIND THE ARRAS   173 26
    SKY OF STONE   220 26
    AND BREATHE DESPAIR THAT TURNS MY LUNGS TO STONE   226 11
    LIKE A MOTH ON A STONE   226 20
    HEAVY AS A STONE PASSIVE   240 29
    POMEGRANATES LIKE BRIGHT GREEN STONE   278 13
    WOULD YOU LIKE TO THROW A STONE AT ME   279   3
    HERE YOU CAN HAVE MY PEACH STONE   279 28
    MY ROOM A CRASH-BOX OVER THAT GREAT STONE RATTLE   342 10
    OVER THE EDGE OF THE STONE TROUGH   349 11
    AND RESTED HIS THROAT UPON THE STONE BOTTOM   349 12
    NOT IN STONE LIKE THE JUDEAN LORD OR BRONZE BUT IN LIFE+ 355 18
    HAS HE SEEN THE GORGON'S HEAD AND TURNED TO STONE   379   7
    THE WAVE OF AGONY BURSTS IN THE STONE THAT HE WAS   379 20
    STONE THAT CAN SINK NO FURTHER   383 12
    WHICH IS JUST A STONE TO ANYONE ASKING FOR MEAT   414 31
    I WOULD RATHER SIT STILL IN A STATE OF PEACE ON A STONE   498   1
    TILL THEY GROW HOT AND BURST AS EVEN STONE CAN   642 16
    IT IS THE WHITE STONE OF LIMITS THE TERM THE LANDMARK B+ 706 11
    NOW I TAKE THE BIG STONE JUG OF WATER   734 24
    DESTROY AT LAST THE HEAVY BOOKS OF STONE   737 25
    IN THE STONE AND IRON LEAPS IN FIRE   773   5
    AT HER CITIES OF STONE AND HER HUTS OF STRAW   790   8
    STONE OF ANGER AT THE BOTTOM   790 15
    THEY HAVE GONE STONE DEAF HE SAID   790 23
    IT WAS THE STONE OF CHANGE   791   4
    THIS IS THE STONE OF CHANGE HE SAID   791   5
    WHERE THE SUNLIGHT SOAKS IN THE STONE THE AFTERNOON   *905   2
    HIS SCYTHE STONE AN' OVER THE GRASS TO ME   *944 13

STONE-BLIND
    STONE-BLIND ONES   665 27
    THE STONE-BLIND BOURGEOIS AND THE STONE-BLIND BOLSHEVIST 666   8

STONE-ENGENDERED
    SUB-DELIGHTED STONE-ENGENDERED   311   2

STONES
    AND WHAT DO I CARE THOUGH THE VERY STONES SHOULD CRY ME 133 10
    I KISS THE STONES I KISS THE MOSS ON THE WALL   173 13
    THE SEA IN THE STONES IS SINGING   200 17
    STONES WOMEN AND MEN   249 25
    AND LET IT MOULT THERE AMONG THE STONES OF THE BITTER S+ 329 20
    AND THE MONOLITHIC WATER-BUFFALOES LIKE OLD MUDDY STONES 386 29
    BETWEEN OUR STONES   425   7
    WHILE DARKNESS SUBMERGES THE STONES   427   5
    THE GUTS AND THE STONES AND THE WOMB ROTS THEM DOWN   463 21
    WHICH ROTS THE BRAIN THE BLOOD THE BONES THE STONES THE 487 16
    BENEATH ENGLAND'S GARDEN STONES   492 14
    AND IF THEY'RE OVER FORTY-FIVE HURL GREAT STONES INTO T+ 541   4
    THEY TOOK AWAY YOUR GOOD OLD STONES   549   9
    AND STONES SHALL MAKE PLACE FOR THY FOOT BECOME EASY TO+ 750   1
    WHAT DO I CARE THOUGH THE VERY STONES   771 21
    SUCH LUMPS SUCH FROGS WITH STONES IN THEIR BELLIES   791 29
    TELL THEM THEY ARE LIKE FROGS WITH STONES IN THEIR BELL+ 791 30
    TELL THEM THEY MUST GET THE STONES OUT OF THEIR BELLIES 791 31
    AND THE STARS ARE READY WITH STONES TO THROW IN THE FAC+ 792 13

STONE-SLOPES
    AND UP THE PALLID SEA-BLENCHED MEDITERRANEAN STONE-SLOP+ 311 20

STOOD
    DEED AN' I WISH I C'D 'A' STOOD AT TH' ALTAR WI' THEE A+ 83 11
    UPON THE FLOOR THAT ERST STOOD UP SO FRESH   87 29
    HOVERING ABOUT THE JUDGMENT THAT STOOD IN MY EYES   94 17
    I HAD STOOD WITH MY HAND UPLIFTED   122   5
    THE MELLOW SUNLIGHT STOOD AS IN A CUP   122 26
    THE NIGHT UPRISEN STOOD   164 27
    THIS WONDER STOOD GLISTENING   165 18
    AND YOU STOOD ALONE WATCHING THEM GO   206   1
    AT LAST AS YOU STOOD YOUR WHITE GOWN FALLING FROM YOUR   207   1
    STRONGER THAN FEAR OR DESTRUCTIVE MOTHER-LOVE IT STOOD   207 12
    SHE STOOD BEFORE ME LIKE RICHES THAT WERE MINE   264 29
    SHE LOVED ME AND STOOD BEFORE ME LOOKING TO ME   264 34
    BUT SHOULD HAVE STOOD ASIDE AND MADE THEM WAY   269 17
    HAD STOOD UP FOR THEMSELVES AND SEEN   536   9
    THE MEN STOOD AROUND LIKE CROCUSES AGAPE IN THE SUN   540   4
    AND WHEN AT LAST MAN STOOD ON TWO LEGS AND WONDERED   683 11
    HIS WORK TOOK PLACE IT CAME TO PASS IT STOOD UP AND SAL+ 690   7
    STOOD BETWEEN THE DAY AND THE NIGHT   787 16
    THE DAWN STAR STOOD INTO SIGHT   787 20
    AND WHERE HE STOOD I SEE MY OWN SHADOW STAND   871 11
    AND THE MOON STOOD OPPOSITE   883 22
    HOVERING TO PLUCK AT THE JUDGMENT WHICH STOOD IN MY EYES *897   5
    DID TER NOTICE THAT LASS SISTER AS STOOD AWAY BACK   *909 20
    DEED AN' I WISH AS I COULD STOOD AT THE ALTAR WI' THEE + *925 15
    THE HOURS PECKED PLEASURE FROM ME AND THE SUN DELIGHTED+ *933 19
    THE MELLOW SUNLIGHT STOOD AS IN A CUP   *934   2
    THAT STOOD CLOSE TO THE WALL AND THE FRONT'S FADED SILK+ *940   3

STOOL
    WARMIN' 'IS-SEN AT THE STOOL O' FIRE   79   2
    A STOOL   449 11
    GOOD IS THE STOOL   449 13
    WARMIN' HIS-SEN AT THE STOOL O' FIRE   *920 26

STOOP
    IN ONE BLUE STOOP FROM OUT THE SKIES   42 30
    TO YOU TO STOOP   96 27
    WHAT MAN WILL STOOP IN YOUR FLESH TO PLOUGH   112   9
    WHAT MAN WILL STOOP IN YOUR FLESH TO PLOUGH   *928 29

STOOPED
    AND STOOPED AND DRANK A LITTLE MORE   349 25

STOOPING
    AND BRANDISHING AND STOOPING OVER EARTH'S WINTRY FLEDGE 301 15
    OF THE LONG SCYTHE THE STOOPING MOWER WIELDS   *939   8
    STOOPING OVER HIS BRIDE   *946 13

STOOPIN'
    OF 'IM STOOPIN' TO 'ER YOU'D WONDER 'E COULD   81 19
    OF HIM STOOPIN' TO HER YOU'D WONDER HE COULD   *923 19

STOOPS
    STOOPS LIKE A PALL   146 15
    ACROSS THE INSENSIBLE VOID TILL SHE STOOPS TO SEE   153   3
    SHE STOOPS TO THE SPONGE AND HER SWUNG BREASTS   217 16
    BUT HE STOOPS NOW   436 10

STOP
    AN' STOP THY SCRAIGHTIN' CHILDT   45   3
    NOW STOP CARPING AT ME DO YOU WANT ME TO HATE YOU   119   1
    NO NOW I WISH THE SUNSHINE WOULD STOP   205   1
    HE SPOKE THIS WORD STOP DON'T BEAT IT FOR IT IS THE SOU+ 376   6
    WON'T STOP A HOLE HOLE HOLE   545 22
    WOULD STOP A HOLE TO KEEP THE WIND AWAY   545 25
    THE GREAT MOVEMENT OF CENTRALISING INTO ONENESS WILL ST+ 611 17
    BUT HE CAN'T STOP ME FROM SINNING AGAINST HIM IF I WANT+ 618 11
    THEN LET THE MILLSTONES GRIND FOR THEY CANNOT STOP   642   9
    PEOPLE KEEP IT UP BECAUSE THEY DAREN'T STOP   657 20
    STOP THAT AT ONCE   669 10
    STOP WHERE'S YOUR EDUCATION   669 16
    CAREFULLY AGAIN AND AGAIN TO STOP THE BLEEDING   734 10
    YOU'LL STOP THAT BLOOMING   755 20
    FOR GOD'S SAKE LET US STOP OH YOU WHO STAND BEHIND US   756   1
    DO THEY STOP THE FLOW   765 13
    GOD OH MAKE IT STOP   767   5
    AH BE STILL BE STILL AND STOP SHUDDERING   768   6
    NOW STOP CARPING AT ME BUT GOD HOW I HATE YOU   *932 10

STOPPED
    AH STOPPED BEHIND ON T' PAD I' T' POURIN' WET   61   3
    STOPPED AT A DIM-LIT TROUGH TO DRINK   121 29
    WHILE T' CLOCKS 'AS A' RUN DOWN AN' STOPPED   137 28
    SOME ONE STOPPED ME AND SAID YOUR LOVER IS HURT   750 18
    AROUND ITS GOLDEN STOPPED NOTES   868 22
    AH STOPPED BEHIND ON T' PAD I' TH' DRIPPIN WET   *911 19

STOPPING
    FROM THE TOWER ON THE TOWN BUT ENDLESSLY NEVER STOPPING 54   7
    YET SOMETIME STOPPING   861 29

STOPS
    BEFORE MY HEART STOPS BEATING AND I BECOME WHAT I AM NOT 321   9
    STOPS AGAIN HALF TURNS INQUISITIVE TO LOOK BACK   393 29
    LET'S HAVE NO FULL STOPS LET'S JUST MANAGE WITH COMMAS 550 28

STORE
    A TEAR WHICH I HAD HOPED THAT EVEN HELL HELD NOT AGAIN + 67 17
    ARE YOU PLEASED WITH WHAT'S IN STORE   95 15
    CREEPS UPON HER THEN AND RAVISHES HER STORE   120   4
    YOUR REPTILE FLAMES OF LUST AH STORE   151 12
    THE STORE   180   6
    AM SORRY FOR WHAT'S IN STORE   219 24
    THAT ARE HELD IN STORE   238   6
    OF TEARS THE STORE   269   1
    WITH ITS STORE OF FOOD AND THE LITTLE COOLING PANS   719   4
    AND THE PROPER STORE OF MEAL FOR THE LONGEST JOURNEY   721 23

STORE
ONLY THE WASTE NIGHT LIES IN STORE   747 27
YOUR REPTILE FLAMES OF PASSION STORE   873 22
I LONGED TO POUR THE BURNING STORE   *935 1
AM SORRY FOR WHAT'S I' STORE   *944 4

STORES
LIKE ANY PRINCE SUCH STORES OF THE WORLD'S SUPPLY   264 4

STORIES
ROMANTIC STORIES NOW NO MORE TO BE TOLD   141 30

STORM
WIERD RIGGING IN A STORM SHRIEKS HIDEOUSLY   36 12
STORM   53 14
ACROSS THE HEAVENS WHEN THE STORM LEAPS HIGHER   89 23
WITH SOUNDS THAT ENDLESSLY SWELL AND SINK LIKE THE STOR+   97 24
DEATH-DARKENED STORM AND DEATH   118 11
LIKE A STORM OF EMERALD SNOW NOW SEE   126 24
BUT WE STORM THE ANGEL-GUARDED   243 9
SHUDDERING STORM WIND OR A WATER RUSHING THROUGH   370 25
THE STORM IS WORDS THE BOTTLES NEVER BREAK   543 11
DESOLATE AND DESPOILED AM I FOR THEIR FLAMING STORM   *897 11
TO FOLLOW MY LIFE ALOFT TO THE FINE WILD AIR OF LIFE AN+ *900 8
TO FOLLOW MY LIFE ALOFT TO THE FINE WILD AIR OF LIFE AN+ *903 20
WITH THE UNFELT BREEZE THAT EBBS OVER THE SEAS WHEN THE+ *906 5

STORM-BRUISED
EVEN HER FLOATING HAIR SINKS LIKE STORM-BRUISED YOUNG L+ *913 24

STORM-HEAVY
SWAYS ON MY ARM LIKE SORROWFUL STORM-HEAVY BOUGHS   *913 23

STORMING
FLYING NOT DOWN FROM HEAVEN BUT STORMING UP   304 17
STRANGE STORMING UP FROM THE DENSE UNDER-EARTH   304 18

STORM-LIGHTNING-SLITTED
AND STORM-LIGHTNING-SLITTED EYES   381 12

STORMS
THE SPARK FROM STORMS OF CORROSION AS SEEDS   160 28
STORMS AND CUMULUS CLOUDS OF ALL IMAGINABLE BLOSSOM   271 27
AND PREPARE FOR STORMS   559 15
I FEEL THE PAIN OF FALLING LEAVES AND STEMS THAT BREAK + 727 7
OR STORMS OF TEARS OR RAGE OR BLACKENING RAIN   745 12

STORM-TOSSED
ONE LONELY BELL ONE ONLY THE STORM-TOSSED AFTERNOON IS   137 1

STORMY
IT IS STORMY AND RAINDROPS CLING LIKE SILVER BEES TO TH+ 92 1
IT IS STORMY AND RAIN-DROPS CLING LIKE SILVER BEES TO T+ *926 1

STORY
AND WAIT FOR HIM TO COME BACK WITH A NEW STORY   405 30
WHICH DESCRIBED IN A STORY   551 19
ALL THAT STORY OF MR GOD SWITCHING ON DAY   601 19

STOUT
YOU'RE STOUT TO BRAVE THIS SNOW MISS STAINWRIGHT   78 1
AS STOUT AS THE TRUTH MY SIRS AN' 'IS FACE   79 6
OR THE STOUT SWART BEETLE ROLLED THE GLOBE OF DUNG IN W+ 437 16
IN THE SHAPE OF HALF-A-DOZEN STOUT   632 32
YOU'RE STOUT TO BRAVE THIS SNOW MISS STAINWRIGHT   *919 21
AS STOUT AS THE TRUTH MY SIRS AN' 'IS FACE   *921 2
BEFORE THE STOUT SWART BEETLE HAD A BALL OF DUNG TO ROL+ *946 26

STOUTLY
OH HE HAS PUT HIS PINCE-NEZ ON AND STOUTLY HAS STEPPED   633 20

STOWED
AND WE SHALL BE SEALED AND STOWED AWAY   748 7

ST PAUL'S
BENEATH THE STEPS OF ST PAUL'S CATCH SEVERAL   750 22

ST PETERSBURG
WAYS OF ST PETERSBURG I HAVE DWELLED IN THE CORE   866 28

STRAGGLE
STRAGGLE OF A LONG THIN EAR LIKE RIBBON   393 18

STRAGGLING
YOU STRAGGLING WOMEN   251 21

STRAIGHT
HER HEAD ASIDE BUT STRAIGHT TOWARDS THE BED   156 9
IF SO LET US FORGE AHEAD STRAIGHT ON   164 13
SURELY YOU'VE TRODDEN STRAIGHT   167 21
BACK FROM THE STRAIGHT HORIZON THAT ENDS ALL ONE SEES   168 6
SURELY YOU'VE TRODDEN STRAIGHT   168 27
AH YOU YOU EAR OF CORN STRAIGHT LYING   171 18
WHAT ARE SO MANY STRAIGHT TREES TO ME   224 23
THAT YOU THROW OFF STRAIGHT ON THE TINDER OF MY NERVES 241 9
AND I LOVE YOU SO STRAIGHT AND CLEAN AND ALL OF A PIECE+ 254 18
AS IT LIFTS ITS STRAIGHT WHITE THROAT   255 24
ISSUING STRAIGHT OUT OF THE UNKNOWN   268 7
SNOWDROPS STRAIGHT DEATH-VEINED EXHALATIONS OF WHITE AND 271 6
EACH TIME STRAIGHT TO HEAVEN   299 25
EACH ONE SETTING OFF STRAIGHT TO THE SKY   299 27
GREAT HASTE AND STRAIGHT ALMOST BIRD STRAIGHT ABOVE THE 347 12
HE SIPPED WITH HIS STRAIGHT MOUTH   349 15
SOFTLY DRANK THROUGH HIS STRAIGHT GUMS INTO HIS SLACK L+ 349 16
LOOKS STRAIGHT AT THE SUN   373 25
AT THE END OF A BACK-BONE RIDGE LIKE A STRAIGHT SIERRA   381 3
STRAIGHT AS A BOARD ON THE BOUGH LOOKING DOWN LIKE SOME 385 19
RUSHING IN LIKE A LITTLE BLACK WHIRLWIND LEAPING STRAIG+ 397 2

STRAIGHT
YOU RUN STRAIGHT AWAY TO LIVE WITH SOMEBODY ELSE   399 13
STRAIGHT TO THE VERY END   471 23
EACH ONE TURNING HIS BREAST STRAIGHT TO THE SUN OF SUNS 525 12
AND LOOKED SULKY UNDER HER THICK STRAIGHT BROWS   617 20
SOME MEN LOOK STRAIGHT INTO THE EYES OF THE GODS   649 9
IS A STRAIGHT WAY TO RAVING INSANITY   845 14
NEITHER STRAIGHT NOR CROOKED NEITHER HERE NOR THERE   *959 17

STRAIGHTENS
STRAIGHTENS HIS DONKEY NECK   379 22

STRAIGHTFORWARD
ARE MUCH MORE HELLISHLY PEACELESS THAN A LITTLE STRAIGH+ 497 7
BEING CRUDE AND STRAIGHTFORWARD YOU'LL ONLY PROVE   576 14

STRAIGHTWAY
SO HE PAUSES AND IS BEHOLDEN AND STRAIGHTWAY IS GONE   403 8

STRAIN
A SUDDEN CAR GOES SWEEPING PAST AND I STRAIN MY SOUL TO+ 58 3

STRAINED
HOW LONG HAVE THEY TUGGED THE LEASH AND STRAINED APART   74 8
HOW LONG HAVE THEY TUGGED THE LEASH AND STRAINED APART *895 16
HOW LONG HAVE THEY TUGGED THE LEASH AND STRAINED APART *904 5

STRAINING
FOR YOU WERE STRAINING WITH A WILD HEART BACK BACK AGAIN 206 23
EVEN IF HE HAD ANY BRAINS STRAINING HIS MIGHTY MIND   690 27
STILL PLIES THE LOVE OF OUR MOTHER FOR US STRAINING OUR+ *938 21

STRAINS
WHITE ON THE WATER WIMPLES MY SHADOW STRAINS LIKE A DOG+ 33 25
AND SO HE STRAINS BENEATH HER HOUSEY WALLS   362 20

STRAIT
THROUGH THE STRAIT GATE OF PASSION   242 8
THROUGH THAT WHITE STRAIT OF THY THICK SHAKEN THROAT   879 7

STRAND
WHY DOES THE THIN GREY STRAND   106 23
AND I OPEN MY LIPS TO TAKE A STRAND OF KEEN HAIR   883 15
NOW I AM ON THE STRAND OF A TURBULENT SEA   *894 19

STRANDS
STRANDS OF MY EYES AND MY LIDS AND MY HANDS AND MY FEET+ 180 5
WITH STRANDS OF DOWN LIKE FLOATING ASH   728 10
SHE HAS SHOWN ME THE STRANDS THAT WEAVE   *893 4
WISE WONDERFUL STRANDS OF WINDS THAT ARE LADEN WITH RARE *938 22

STRANGE
STRANGE THROBS BEYOND LAUGHTER AND TEARS   38 22
STRANGE VOICE HAS NO SOUND   40 12
STRANGE HE IS MY SON FOR WHOM I HAVE WAITED LIKE A LOVER 47 8
STRANGE TO ME LIKE A CAPTIVE IN A FOREIGN COUNTRY HAUNT+ 47 9
AND STRANGE   52 21
AND STRANGE IN MY BLOOD-SWEPT EARS WAS THE SOUND   61 24
WITH A STRANGE NEW KNOCKING OF LIFE AT HER SIDE   64 8
OLD QUESTION WITHOUT ANSWER STRANGE AND FAIN   69 27
OUT OF EACH FACE STRANGE DARK BEAMS THAT DISQUIET   76 1
WITH COLD LIKE THE SHELL OF THE MOON AND STRANGE IT SEE+ 99 14
INTO THIS STRANGE COUNTRIE   101 20
STRANGE BEAMS MUST TRAVEL STILL FOR I FEEL THAT I   115 3
IN SORROW SINCE WE STAND IN BEWILDERMENT STRANGE   132 19
PHANTOM TO PHANTOM LEANING STRANGE WOMEN WEEP   140 15
SO LIKE TO WOMEN TALL STRANGE WOMEN WEEPING   140 19
STRANGE WHITE SIGNALS SEEM INTENDING   150 12
WHO FOR ONE STRANGE YEAR WAS AS A BRIDE TO YOU SET +   157 4
BEFORE ONWARD THE STRANGE ROAD GOES   163 12
ONWARD WHEREVER THE STRANGE ROAD GOES   163 28
WHERE STRANGE WINDS BLOW   202 24
STRANGE HOW WE SUFFER IN SPITE OF THIS   203 29
STRANGE THAT THE URGENT WILL IN ME TO SET   218 18
TO BRING TOGETHER TWO STRANGE SPARKS BEGET   218 20
I BECAME A STRANGE BEING   222 11
ARE SINNERS STRANGE THE BEE THAT BLUNDERS   223 19
IN STRANGE CONJUNCTION   236 20
IT SETS UP A STRANGE FIRE   241 10
IN YOUR STRANGE LUST   242 7
AND THEN IN A STRANGE GREY HOUR   248 24
NO NO IT IS THE THREE STRANGE ANGELS   250 31
WHO IS SO STRANGE SHOULD CORRESPOND WITH ME   251 30
THE GOLD OF THEIR STRANGE PERSISTENCE   253 12
THE OTHER SHE TOO HAS STRANGE GREEN EYES   261 1
AND STRANGE WAYS WHERE I FALL INTO OBLIVION OF UTTERMOST 261 6
STRANGE SHEER SLOPES AND WHITE LEVELS   261 9
AH WITH A FEARFUL STRANGE DETECTION   262 16
IMMORTALITY THE HEAVEN IS ONLY A PROJECTION OF THIS STR+ 265 17
GOING DOWN THE STRANGE LANES OF HELL MORE AND MORE   281 4
SO IN THE STRANGE RETORTS OF MEDLARS AND SORB-APPLES   281 12
STRANGEST OF ALL STRANGE COMPANIONS   281 18
SAP THAT SMELLS STRANGE ON YOUR FINGERS THAT EVEN GOATS+ 283 12
THE STRANGE UNACCUSTOMED GESTE OF YOUR DEMONISH NEW WOR+ 292 15
DEEP PULSING OF A STRANGE HEART   292 33
RATHER LIKE AN OCTOPUS BUT STRANGE AND SWEET-MYRIAD-LIM+ 299 5
OH MANY-BRANCHING CANDELABRUM OH STRANGE UP-STARTING   300 5
HAVE YOU A STRANGE ELECTRIC SENSITIVENESS IN YOUR STEEL+ 301 2
LIKE SOME STRANGE MAGNETIC APPARATUS   301 4
DO YOU TAKE IN MESSAGES IN SOME STRANGE CODE   301 5
STRANGE STORMING UP FROM THE DENSE UNDER-EARTH   304 18
SHUDDERING A STRANGE WAY DOWN THE BOTTOMLESS PIT   322 23
BACK ON A STRANGE PARABOLA THEN ROUND ROUND DIZZY IN   344 13
AND STRANGE AND GRIMLY DRAGS AT HER   362 23
STRANGE FAINT COITION YELL   366 25
WITH THE STRANGE DARK LAUGH IN THEIR EYES GLANCING UP 389 33
INTO WHICH THE CREATIVE FUTURE SHALL BLOW STRANGE UNKNO+ 428 29
WON'T IT BE STRANGE WHEN THE NURSE BRINGS THE NEW-BORN 438 26

STRANGE
AND SAT UP TAKING STRANGE POSTURES SHOWING THE PINK SOL+   445 12
YET THE STRANGE ALMOST FRIGHTENED SHOUT OF DELIGHT THAT   446 14
AND SEES STRANGE LOOKS ON THE FACES OF MEN   459 27
LO THERE IS WOMAN AND HER WAY IS A STRANGE WAY   461 11
AND IN SOME STRANGE AND SILENT WAY   472 4
AND SWINGING IN A STRANGE UNISON OF POWER   478 17
THAT STRANGE ESSENTIAL COMMUNICATION OF LIFE   481 7
IT HAS GOT US DOWN WE GROVEL BEFORE IT IN STRANGE TERROR   486 15
FROM THE HEART AND LEAVING STRANGE COLD STRETCHES OF SA+   509 4
HOW STRANGE IT WOULD BE IF SOME WOMEN CAME   525 22
IT IS STRANGE TO THINK OF THE ANNAS THE VRONSKYS THE   533 11
HARK THE STRANGE NOISE OF MILLIONS OF FISH IN PANIC   586 25
A STRANGE GREY DISTANCE SEPARATES   607 1
STRANGE   608 6
AND OUT OF THE LIPS OF PEOPLE JERK STRANGE MECHANICAL N+   629 10
AND SINKS DOWN WITH A SWIFT RUSTLE AND A STRANGE FALLING   651 15
THE BAFFLING LIGHT OR THE STRANGE STILL GLEAM OF THE GO+   656 13
BECAUSE THOSE FACES WERE WINDOWS TO THE STRANGE HORIZON+   656 21
INTO SOMETHING NEW AND STRANGE   667 25
UP FROM THE BOUNDING EARTH STRANGE PREGNANT STREAMS IN +   675 13
TERRIBLE AND STRANGE THE GOD LIES ON THE BED WISTFUL CO+   676 9
THERE COMES AN AFTER-GLADNES A STRANGE JOY   677 6
TO SOMETHING FLOWERY AND FULFILLED AND WITH A STRANGE S+   677 16
BUT IT IS A GREAT STRANGE URGE IT IS NOT A MIND   690 2
A STRANGE ACHE POSSESSED HIM AND HE ENTERED THE STRUGGLE   690 5
LO THERE IS A CREATURE FORMED HOW STRANGE   690 12
AND DREAMING WITH STRANGE WHALE EYES WIDE OPEN IN THE W+   694 31
AND IN A STRANGE LEVEL FLUTTERING YOU GO OUT TO SEA-WAR+   696 25
THEY WANDER THEIR STRANGE AND DIFFERENT WAYS IN HEAVEN   713 22
EMERGES STRANGE AND LOVELY   720 13
MY SPIRIT DARKENS AND GOES OUT AND SOFT STRANGE GLOOM   727 2
ODD WINTRY FLOWERS UPON THE WITHERED STEM YET NEW STRAN+   727 24
NOW LIKE A STRANGE LIGHT BREAKING FROM THE GROUND   744 10
AND DIE LIKE A DOG IN A HOLE 'TIS STRANGE WHAT A SHODDY   755 8
IT SMELLS STRANGE LIKE THE SHOUTING OF MEN   759 2
WHO ARE THESE STRANGE FACES IN MEXICO   793 10
WITH ITS STRANGE PRIMORDIAL CONSCIOUSNESS OF JUSTICE   844 13
HIS COAT AND HIS ARMS AND HIS LABOURING HEART ARE STRAN+   871 25
AND TERRIBLY STRANGE IS THE THROAT THAT IS WORKING WITH+   871 26
AND TERRIBLY STRANGE ARE HIS TEARS THAT ARE WETTING MY +   871 27
THAT LIFT UP HIGH THEN DROP HIS STRANGE HARSH BREAST   879 1
UNDER THE WILD STRANGE TYRANNY OF MY BODY   *893 27
OUT OF EACH STAR DARK STRANGE BEAMS THAT DISQUIET   *897 28
OUT OF EACH STAR DARK STRANGE BEAMS THAT DISQUIET   *901 5
AND STRANGE   *905 10
AND STRANGE IN MY BLOOD-SWEPT EARS WAS THE SOUND   *912 4
OF LIVES THAT SORROWS LIKE MISCHIEVOUS STRANGE MICE CHA+   *938 5
'TIS STRANGE WE NEVER KNEW   *941 9
PAST THE STRANGE WHIRLPOOLS OF REMEMBERED GREED   *959 7

STRANGELY
I HEARD YOU IN YOUR SLEEP SPEAK STRANGELY TO ME   99 10
HOW STRANGELY SHE TRIES TO DISOWN IT AS IT SINKS   128 15
STRANGELY HALF-SINISTERLY FLESH-FRAGRANT   280 20
INSTEAD OF WHICH SHE STRANGELY REARS ON HER PERCH IN THE   385 13
AND STRANGELY PAWS THE AIR DELICATE   385 25
BUT WHY DO I FEEL SO STRANGELY ABOUT YOU   604 6
AND STRANGELY O CHILLED WAN SOUL A FLUSH OF ROSE   720 10

STRANGE-MOUNDED
ALSO SHE WHO IS THE OTHER HAS STRANGE-MOUNDED BREASTS A+   261 8

STRANGER
SHE ALIGHTS A STRANGER WONDERING UNUSED TO THE SCENE   153 10
SO THAT HE SEEMS A STRANGER IN HIS PASSING   197 30
SUDDEN A DARK-FACED STRANGER   200 9
AND DIONYSOS YOUNG AND A STRANGER   688 19
BUT A NAKED MAN A STRANGER LEANED ON THE GATE   692 10
A FRAGILE STRANGER IN THE FLUX OF LIVES   745 18
STRANGER SOFT ARE THE TEARS THAT FALL   758 15
AND YOU STAND A STRANGER TO ME   871 7

STRANGERS
NO SOUND FROM THE STRANGERS THE PLACE IS DARK AND FEAR   173 3
TWO MEXICANS STRANGERS EMERGING OUT OF THE DARK AND   401 12
IN THE THUNDER AIR ALL STRANGERS TO ONE ANOTHER   647 6
AS THE GREEN GRASS GLOWS UPWARDS STRANGERS IN THE GARDEN   647 7
OF THIS OLD HOUSE WHOSE STRANGERS I NOW ENTERTAIN   877 38

STRANGER'S
THE STRANGER'S HAIR WAS SHORN LIKE A LAD'S DARK POLL   156 1

STRANGE-SCENTED
IN THE DEEP STRANGE-SCENTED SHADE OF THE GREAT DARK CAR+   349 4

STRANGE-SHAPEN
HOW WERT THOU SO STRANGE-SHAPEN WHAT WARM FINGER   69 13

STRANGEST
STRANGEST OF ALL STRANGE COMPANIONS   281 18

STRANGLE
WHY HAVE A FINANCIAL SYSTEM TO STRANGLE US ALL IN ITS   451 30
AND SO STRANGLE OFF THEIR CONNECTION WITH THE CEASELESS+   616 5
AND ROSE-BRIARS TO STRANGLE THE MACHINE   634 30
HAST THOU DETERMINED TO STRANGLE ME O GOD   751.14

STRANGLED
STRANGLED MY HEART SWELLED UP SO FULL   123 15
AND RUTHLESSLY STRANGLED OFF THE FANTASIES   141 28
OF EARTH WINTER-PRESSED STRANGLED IN CORRUPTION   270 19
STRANGLED MY HEART SWELLED UP SO FULL   *934 21

STRANGLING
WE FEEL HIM STRANGLING EVEN MORE THE ISSUES OF OUR SOUL   609 5
STRANGLING ON ONE ANOTHER LIKE SNAKES   833 28

STRAW
ENJOYS THE OPEN BLOSSOMS AS THEY STRAW   129 17
AND CARES NOT A STRAW FOR THE PUT-UP HUMAN FIGMENTS   481 16
AND NOW NO REALLY THE FINAL STRAW   491 21
AS TO THE LAST STRAW   558 25
AT HER CITIES OF STONE AND HER HUTS OF STRAW   790 8

STRAWBERRIES
ROUND THE HOUSE WERE LILACS AND STRAWBERRIES   152 10
ADMIT THAT APPLES AND STRAWBERRIES AND PEACHES AND PEAR+   285 5

STRAWBERRY
AND BETRAYS ITS CANDOUR IN THE ROUND WHITE STRAWBERRY F+   272 28

STRAWBERRY FAIR
WHICH ARE MEANT TO BE THE OLD FOLK-SONG STRAWBERRY FAIR   657 16

STRAY
STRAY WHITEBEAM AND HER WHITE FIRE ALL UNLADENS   86 20
AND OVER MY FACE THE STRAY FIRE SLIPS   151 8
WE TAKE NO HUNGRY STRAY FROM THE PALE-FACE   405 7
THE OLD DRAGON WILL DWINDLE DOWN TO THE SIZE OF A STRAY+   665 14
AND OVER MY FACE YOUR STRAY FIRE SLIPS   873 18

STRAYED
STRAYED DOWN THE HILL CRUSHING THE SILKEN MOSS   863 22
WITH HER SUAVE FORM DUSTY WITH SPICES HONEY SWEET STRAY+   864 4

STRAYING
WHEN I SAW HER STRAYING A LITTLE DAZED THROUGH HER UNTI+   618 21

STRAYS
OF ALL THE STRAYS OF LIFE THAT CLIMB MY LIFE   *900 27
OF ALL THE STRAYS OF LIFE THAT CLIMB MY LIFE   *904 3

STREAKED
TO SAVE THE STREAKED PANSY OF THE HEART FROM   658 11

STREAKY
BUT I KNOW YOUR GAME NOW STREAKY SORCERER   332 24

STREAM
AND FEEL THE STREAM OF AWAKENING RIPPLE AND PASS   51 23
ON OUR STREAM   70 19
BY HEAVEN AND EARTH AND HELLISH STREAM   177 18
THE STREAM OF MY LIFE IN THE DARKNESS   199 19
STREAM WITHIN STREAM   280 8
IS NOT EACH SOUL A VIVID THOUGHT IN THE GREAT CONSCIOUS+   328 27
A GREEN LIGHT ENTERS AGAINST STREAM FLUSH FROM THE WEST   340 25
CITYWARDS IN LITTLE RIVERS THAT SWELL TO A GREAT STREAM   484 3
WHICH GOES THROUGH ALL THE STAGES OF STEAM AND STREAM A+   505 21
SHIMMERS IN A STREAM OF BLUENESS AND LONG-TRESSED   530 6
THEY STREAM PAST STREAM PAST GOING TO WORK   585 25
BUT OH THE STREAMS THAT STREAM WHITE-FACED IN AND OUT   628 15
AND THE STREAM IS TOWARDS THE GODS NOT BACKWARDS TOWARD+   650 11
WHERE A STREAM CAME DOWN TO THE GRAVEL OF THE SEA AND S+   693 2
AND PUTS HIS MOUTH DOWN TO THE GUSHING STREAM   877 8
THE STREAM AND CLOAK ME OVER WITH THY RED   879 9
AND WHEN BLACK LEAVES STREAM OUT IN A TRAIL DOWN THE WI+   883 12
WHERE THE LOFTY TREES ATHWART STREAM PERCHANCE   *914 26
STREAM GOLDEN SMOKE   *916 20

STREAMED
HE COULD NOT PLUNGE INTO THE DAYLIGHT THAT STREAMED AT +   344 20
STREAMED REDNESS DOWN THE AIR SHOT RED ON HIS EYES   884 24

STREAMING
STREAMING BACK WHERE THE MISTS DISTIL   53 10
TWO STREAMING PEACOCKS GONE IN A CLOUD   70 17
TO HALT THE HEART DIVERT THE STREAMING FLOW   195 34
QUEER WITH YOUR THIN WINGS AND YOUR STREAMING LEGS   332 15
FLOWERS AND SAPPHIRES AND US DIVERSELY STREAMING   476 28
STREAMING FORTH FROM LITTLE DOORWAYS   484 2
AND FALLS WINGLESS BLOOD STREAMING THROUGH ITS YELLOW H+   855 25
STREAMING BACK WHERE THE MIST DISTILS   *906 2

STREAMLET
THERE THE LAZY STREAMLET PUSHES   33 13
THERE THE LAZY STREAMLET PUSHES   *891 14

STREAMS
AND OUT OF THE INVISIBLE STREAMS OF BRIGHT BLUE DROPS   136 11
NEW SUNNY STREAMS OF BLOOD   240 8
GREEN STREAMS THAT FLOW FROM THE INNERMOST CONTINENT OF   260 24
BLOOD FROM SIDE TO SIDE CAUSING MY MYRIAD SECRET STREAMS   320 28
THE UNIVERSE FLOWS IN INFINITE WILD STREAMS RELATED   479 9
BUT OH THE STREAMS THAT STREAM WHITE-FACED IN AND OUT   628 15
THEY ARE OPEN TO THE RESTLESS SKIES AND STREAMS FLOW IN+   675 10
UP FROM THE BOUNDING EARTH STRANGE PREGNANT STREAMS IN +   675 13
AND SPUE OUT CORROSIONS INTO YOUR STREAMS ON YOUR RAINS   797 6

STREET
BEYOND THE LEAVES THAT OVERHANG THE STREET   36 1
BARE STEMS OF STREET LAMPS STIFFLY STAND   51 1
A CAR AT THE END OF THE STREET GOES BY WITH A LAUGH   54 26
SUCH A ONE IN THE NORTH IT FLOWERS ON THE STREET AND I +   58 13
THE STREET   71 2
DOWN THE SOILED STREET WE HAVE PATTERED THE LESSONS   75 23
THE STREET PALE-PASSIONATE GOES   106 8
WHETHER THE PEOPLE IN THE STREET   109 17
OF LEAVES AND LAMPS AND THE CITY STREET MINGLED   111 6
THE LOW-HUNG LAMPS STRETCHED DOWN THE STREET   121 18
THE TIRED LIGHTS DOWN THE STREET WENT OUT   121 23
IT SHUT BEHIND HER LEAVING THE STREET AGHAST   122 8

STREET
IN THE STREET SPILLED OVER SPLENDIDLY   143 22
OVERHANGS THE STREET WHERE THE BULLOCK-WAGONS SLOWLY   209 16
MY DEAR WHEN YOU CROSS THE STREET IN THE SUNSHINE SURELY   211 13
SLOWLY ABOVE THE STREET   253 8
I MET HIM IN THE STREET   569 15
IN THE STREET   570 5
STREET   608 13
MY NEIGHBOUR IS NOT THE MAN IN THE STREET AND NEVER WAS   645 14
IT IS CURIOUS TOO THAT THOUGH THE MODERN MAN IN THE STR+   648 1
MEN IN THE STREET   648 6
LADY LADY OF THE LAST HOUSE DOWN THE LONG LONG STREET O+   696 8
AS I WENT DOWN THE STREET IN MY NOSE-RED PELERINE   750 17
IN A LITTLE HALF-BUILT STREET WHERE RED AND WHITE VILLAS   864 25
WHO PASS ALONG THE STREET   877 19
DOWN THE SOILED STREET WE HAVE PATTERED THE LESSONS CEA+   *897 23
DOWN THE SOILED STREET WE HAVE PATTERED THE LESSONS   *900 31
WHILE THE STREET LAMP CENSERS SWINGING HIGH   *916 19
THE STREET THAT IS FULL OF THE RUSTLING SOUND OF A SHELL   *917 2
AND WASH OF VOICES ALONG THE STREET   *917 7
OUR FACES FLOWER FOR A LITTLE HOUR PALE AND UNCERTAIN A+   *917 21

STREET-ENDS
SOME STREET-ENDS THRUST FORWARD THEIR STACK   164 20

STREET-LAMPS
THE STREET-LAMPS IN THE TWILIGHT HAVE SUDDENLY STARTED +   102 31

STREET-LAMP
LARGE SHADOWS FROM THE OUTSIDE STREET-LAMP BLOWN   140 14
OF THE STREET-LAMP THROUGH THE UNBLINDED WINDOW PANE   878 6

STREETS
FORM AFTER FORM IN THE STREETS   108 23
CAME NEARER TO SEARCH THROUGH THE STREETS   121 32
THE SPLINTERED STREETS HEAR NOISES   159 17
PEOPLE HOUSES STREETS VEHICLES MACHINES   256 26
STREETS   432 23
NEW HOUSES NEW FURNITURE NEW STREETS NEW CLOTHES NEW   448 14
AND STREETS AND HOUSES AND EVEN SEAS   480 5
IN THEIR RAG GARMENTS SCUTTLING THROUGH THE STREETS   530 16
WHEN IN THE STREETS OF THE WORKING QUARTERS   585 24
THE PRIESTS TO WEAR ROSE-COLOUR OR MAGENTA IN THE STREE+   609 17
IN ANCIENT ROME DOWN THE THRONGED STREETS   703 24
VICTORIOUS GREY GRISLY GHOSTS IN OUR STREETS   740 2
THE THICK RANK STREETS AND A STARK WHITE LIGHT   748 6
CRAWL LIKE MASTERLESS DOGS IN THE BACK STREETS OF THE A+   796 12
LO IN THE BACK STREETS OF THE AIR DEAD ONES ARE CRAWLIN+   796 29
DOWN THE GLAD STREETS PINCHED WAIFS IN ILL-ASSORTED CLO+   866 5

STREET'S
THE STREET'S LONG OUTSTRETCHED MILKY-WAY   115 24
HANG FROM THE STREET'S LONG BOUGH   252 14

STRENGTH
I WILL NOT WASTE MY SOUL AND AND MY STRENGTH FOR THIS   74 23
I SHALL KEEP MY STRENGTH FOR MYSELF THEY CAN KEEP   75 3
SPARE ME THE STRENGTH TO LEAVE YOU   102 31
HER FORTH FROM THE DARK MY STRENGTH HAS FAILED   106 1
I PUT MY STRENGTH UPON YOU AND I THREW   156 29
SERVE THEN I TELL YOU ADD YOUR STRENGTH TO MINE   235 1
PRIDE STRENGTH ALL THE LOT   239 3
MAKING THEM SWELL WITH TURGID UNGOVERNABLE STRENGTH   241 20
SURE AND A TOWER OF STRENGTH 'TWIXT THE WALLS OF HER BR+   249 12
A WOMAN HAS GIVEN ME STRENGTH AND AFFLUENCE   262 25
HAS NOT SO MUCH OF STRENGTH AS THE BODY OF ONE WOMAN   263 2
LIKE A WHALE RECOVERING ITS VELOCITY AND STRENGTH   428 14
HIS STRENGTH AND HIS PROMPTINGS   525 17
O GOD TO US MAY STRENGTH BE GIVEN   554 3
AND THERE THEY ARE BUT NO STRENGTH COMES FROM   660 21
STRENGTH COMES   660 25
COMES A NEW STRENGTH   662 11
AND EMOTIONS AND DESIRES AND STRENGTH GLORY OR HONOUR   691 11
AND OUR STRENGTH LEAVES US   718 18
AND STRENGTH IS GONE AND MY LIFE   727 20
AND A DRAUGHT OF THEE IS STRENGTH TO A SOUL IN HELL   759 13
KILOSSA SWEET WELL OF MY STRENGTH THOU CORDED WITH SILK   759 14
AND THROWS UP STRENGTH THAT IS LIVING STRENGTH AND REGA+   782 19
AND FILL THEM STRONG WITH STRENGTH OF WINGS   799 19
SO THAT STRENGTH WELLS UP IN ME LIKE WATER IN HOT SPRIN+   799 21
AND KNEES AND THIGHS AND LOINS AND THE BOWELS OF STRENG+   801 8
AND PUTTING HIS STRENGTH IN YOUR HEELS AND ANKLES HIS F+   801 24
MY SOUL IS HEAVY WITH SUNSHINE AND STEEPED WITH STRENGTH   803 8
STILL GAY AND LAUGHING IN MY OWN VAIN STRENGTH   875 30
KNOTTING THEMSELVES WITH WILD STRENGTH   *893 24
SOME OF MY STRENGTH FOR MYSELF FOR IF I SHOULD SELL   *896 3
SOME OF MY STRENGTH FOR MYSELF FOR IF I SHOULD SELL   *904 24
WARM IN A CITY OF STRENGTH BETWEEN HER BREASTS   *945 23

STRENGTHEN
STRENGTHEN PREPARE THEM FOR THE JOURNEY HENCE   740 18

STRENGTHENING
FOR THE FEEDING AND STRENGTHENING OF THE HANDSOMER FULL+   679 10

STRESS
OUT OF THE STRESS OF THE CROWD   70 9
THAT CARRIES MOONS ALONG AND SPARE THE STRESS   195 35
UNEASILY DISTURBED BY THE STRESS   231 18
TO START MY HEART AFRESH GIVE ME THE SOFT SMALL STRESS   738 31
STRESS OF COMPULSION REMAINS AND A BAND THAT GIRTS   746 16
A NAKED NIGHTLY THING TOO FRAIL AND WISE FOR THE STRESS   771 23
HIS FULL FINE BODY BENDING AND URGING LIKE THE STRESS O+   867 24
HAVE CLOSED IN LOVE LIKE VERY DEATH FOR STRESS   875 19

STRETCH
YOU DID NOT STRETCH FORWARD TO CARESS HER   255 29
EVEN THE LAMBS WILL STRETCH FORTH THEIR NECKS LIKE SERP+   624 16

STRETCHED
STRETCHED IN THE BRINDLED DARKNESS   111 2
THE LOW-HUNG LAMPS STRETCHED DOWN THE STREET   121 18
HER LARGE BROWN HAND STRETCHED OVER   123 20
STRETCHED OUT ON THE WAY AND A LOUT CASTS   144 18
STRETCHED OUT AT REST   155 6
YOU SLEEP STRETCHED OUT FOR EVER EVER GIVING   194 21
AS THEIR NERVES ARE STRETCHED TILL THEY TWANGLE AND SNAP   616 8
OF FINGER OR FIST OR SOFT-SKINNED STICKS UPON THE STRET+   623 6
THAT WE'VE HAD ENOUGH THE BRAIN IS STRETCHED TILL IT PA+   756 5
CAN MAKE THEM YAWN I STRETCHED MY HAND TO THE DINT   *935 25

STRETCHES
SUDDENLY SEIZING THE UGLY ANKLE AS SHE STRETCHES OUT TO   361 17
FROM THE HEART AND LEAVING STRANGE COLD STRETCHES OF SA+   509 4
THE LONG MEAN MARGINAL STRETCHES OF OUR EXISTENCE   722 21
THE LONG MARGINAL STRETCHES OF EXISTENCE CROWDED WITH L+   *957 23

STRETCHING
STRETCHING BARE   120 13
I DON'T MIND THIS CONTINENT STRETCHING THE SEA FAR AWAY   213 7
NOW HERE WAS I NEW-AWAKENED WITH MY HAND STRETCHING   259 16
STRETCHING OUT MY HAND MY HAND FLUNG LIKE A DROWNED   260 10
STRETCHING THEIR BIG FULL LIMBS TO SEEK   827 13
STRETCHING REACHING   861 26

STREW
TO STREW ROUND OUR WAY TO DIMINISH EACH FULL STAR'S GLI+   *938 6

STREWN
STREWN STARS OF UNKNOWN PEOPLE AND LUMINOUS LITTER   132 12
AND THE STREWN TAWDRY TRAPPINGS THAT LAST NIGHT'S POETR+   856 11
HAS STREWN MYRIAD TWINKLING POPPY-PETALS DOWN THE PATH +   860 18
STREWN ACROSS THE FLOOD   860 24
OVER A GIRL WHO HAS STREWN HERSELF IN A HAMMOCK   868 6
OVER HER STREWN WHITE LAUGHING FORM   868 16
STREWN STARS OF PALLID PEOPLE AND THROUGH LUMINOUS LITT+   *938 4
STREWN WITH DIM WRECKAGE AND CROWDED WITH CRYING SOULS   *957 16

STREWS
STREWS EACH SIDE THE LINES   162 4
SOON STREWS ITSELF ON THE FLOOR AND KEEP THE RADIANCE O+   179 4
ON TO THE FUR OF THE WOLF-PELT THAT STREWS THE PLAIN   409 20
AS A WHITE ROSE STREWS THE GROUND   868 7

STRICKEN
A STRICKEN WIFE SO SUNK IN OBLIVION BOWED   155 30
SHADOWS TO COVER OUR STRICKEN MANHOOD AND BLEST   167 18
WITHOUT A SERVANT'S HELP SO HE BE NOT STRICKEN IN YEARS   277 11
DARKNESS TO RAISE THE STRICKEN DIGNITY AND REST   *896 23

STRICTLY
STRICTLY DON'T FORGET IT HE IS A SAVAGE WHO HAS FOR   776 24
BUT STRICTLY HE IS A SAVAGE   776 27

STRIDE
GOD STEPPING THROUGH OUR LOINS IN ONE BRIGHT STRIDE   87 25
OUT IN ONE STRIDE   306 7
ANSWERS THE QUESTION AS HE PUTS IT IN HIS STRIDE   816 8
THE SHADOWS OF THE ASH-TREES STRIDE ACROSS THE HAY   858 9
BEFORE THE LIFE SHALL CEASE TO URGE AND STRIDE   879 6
BUT I WILL CATCH THEE UP AT A STRIDE OF DEATH   879 28

STRIDENT
COMES A STRIDENT LAUGH AS WE APPROACH THIS LITTLE BLACK   375 8

STRIDENTLY
ARE HURRYING AND STRIDENTLY CALLING   54 2

STRIDING
SHE HURRIES UP STRIDING REARED ON LONG UNCANNY LEGS   358 31

STRIFE
BY BRIGHT LEAVES UTTERED ALOUD AND STRIFE   68 7
THE NIGHT WITH STRIFE   110 20
I KNOW NOT MY SOUL IS IN STRIFE   143 24
BEATS THE NEW FRESH AIR OF LIFE THEY COME FOR STRIFE   174 14
HOMER WAS WRONG IN SAYING WOULD THAT STRIFE MIGHT PASS   348 1
THE BREATH THAT RUSHES THROUGH MY NOSE THE STRIFE   461 3
IS LIFE STRIFE IS IT THE LONG COMBAT   606 13
YET I AM NOT INTERESTED IN FIGHT IN STRIFE IN COMBAT   606 16
LIFE IS FOR KISSING AND FOR HORRID STRIFE   709 25
LIFE IS FOR KISSING AND FOR HORRID STRIFE   710 1
NOR YET THE STRIVING AND THE HORRID STRIFE   710 8
ABSOLUTE CONSCIOUSNESS ABSOLVED FROM STRIFE AND KISSES   712 17
ONLY THE HUMAN BEING ABSOLVED FROM KISSING AND STRIFE   713 27
A THING OF KISSES AND STRIFE   714 7
BUT WHEN STRIFE IS A THING OF ONE   714 26
THEN STRIFE IS EVIL BECAUSE IT IS NOT STRIFE   714 29
THE WAR WAS NOT STRIFE   715 1
IT HAS BEEN MADE A CAUSE FOR STRIFE A CASUS BELLI   777 15
THE HORIZONS OF LOVE AND STRIFE   788 23
OH FOR A DELIRIUM OF LOVE OR OF STRIFE   856 24
OF FLOWERING STRIFE   888 8
A TOSSING SEA OF TURBULENT STRIFE WHERE NOW   *894 20
TO THE RECKLESS EXTRAVAGANT TURMOIL OF LIVING THE STRIFE   *895 13
UP DIMLY FROM THEIR STRIVING IT HEARTENS MY STRIFE   *900 24
UP DIMLY FROM THEIR STRIVING IT HEARTENS MY STRIFE   *903 36

STRIKE
IS THAT IT WOMAN DOES IT STRIKE YOU SO   219 1
GIVE US OUR TURN GIVE US A CHANCE LET OUR HOUR STRIKE   273 21
HE WILL NEVER QUITE STRIKE HOME ON THE TARGET-QUICK FOR   382 20
I'M PERFECTLY WILLING TO STRIKE A DECENT BARGAIN   483 22

STRIKE
    NOW THAT THE WAVES OF OUR UNDOING HAVE BEGUN TO STRIKE   513 22
    WHEN STRIKE IS A THING OF TWO   714 22
    HOW GHASTLY IT WOULD BE TO STRIKE A MATCH AND MAKE A LI+   724 16
    TO HEAR THE LONG WAVES STRIKE THE COAST   747 11
    WILL YOU STRIKE AT THE HEART OF THE SUN WITH YOUR BLOOD+   783 17
    WILL YOU STRIKE THE SUN'S HEART OUT AGAIN   783 19
    AND STRIKE WITH A BLINDNESS OF FURY AGAINST ME CAN I CA+   *926 24

STRIKES
    THE HOUR STRIKES   323 9
    AS HE STRIKES SINCE SURE   382 19
    AND THE FLOOD STRIKES THE BELLY AND WE ARE GONE   425 18
    THOUGH IT STRIKES NO SHORE   454 15
    LIKE A HARPIST THAT STRIKES HIS DEFT   746 25
    HE STRIKES THE GUSH OF PASSION EASILY   877 7

STRIKING
    THE CHIME OF THE BELLS AND THE CHURCH CLOCK STRIKING EI+   48 14
    LIKE SAVAGE MUSIC STRIKING FAR OFF AND THERE   52 17
    SPLENDIDLY PLANTING HIS FEET ONE ROCKY FOOT STRIKING THE   381 13
    THE ELEPHANT BELLS STRIKING SLOW TONG-TONG TONG-TONG   387 33
    STRIKING US THE VIBRATIONS OF OUR FINISH   512 22
    THAT HARD CLAPPER STRIKING IN A HARD MOUTH   622 21
    LIKE SAVAGE MUSIC STRIKING FAR OFF AND AWAY   *905 6

STRING
    STRING TO RUN ON   33 26
    IF I STRING THE PLANETS AND THE BEADY STARS   735 18
    IT IS A STRING OF INSANITIES   839 20
    FROM OUT HIS FINGERS FROM THAT SUPPLE STRING   877 12

STRINGS
    HANG STRINGS OF CRIMSON CHERRIES AS IF HAD BLED   36 21
    STRINGS   148 7
    AS A HARPIST RUNNING ALONG THE STRINGS   747 12
    THE STRINGS OF MY HEART   751 18
    A CHILD SITTING UNDER THE PIANO IN THE BOOM OF THE SHAK+   *940 7

STRIP
    AND STRIP ME NAKED TOUCH ME LIGHT   117 13
    THAT STRIP US AND DESTROY US AND BREAK US DOWN   709 17
    WE SHALL STRIP TO THE FATA MORGANA THEN   748 9
    AND STRIP ME NAKED TOUCH ME ALIGHT   *931 17

STRIPE
    IS SHATTERED AT LAST BENEATH THE STRIPE   253 25

STRIPE-CHEEKED
    AHA THE STRIPE-CHEEKED WHELPS WHIPPET-SLIM CROCUSES   309 5

STRIPED
    AND HER BRIGHT STRIPED FROST-FACE WILL NEVER WATCH ANY   402 17
    A TIGER IS STRIPED AND GOLDEN FOR HIS OWN GLORY   523 13

STRIPES
    TA'E OFF THY DUTY STRIPES TIM   82 17
    AND STRIPES IN THE BRILLIANT FROST OF HER FACE SHARP FI+   402 4
    LEAVING THEM SHADOW STRIPES BARRED ON A FIELD OF GREY   858 12
    TAKE OFF THY DUTY STRIPES TIM   *924 21

STRIPPED
    THAT HAS STRIPPED THEIR SPRIGS   51 4
    SINCE DEATH HAS DELIVERED US UTTERLY STRIPPED AND WHITE   132 15
    ME WHO AM ISSUED AMAZED FROM THE DARKNESS STRIPPED   133 2
    AND STRIPPED IT BARE   507 23
    ONLY WHEN I AM STRIPPED STARK NAKED I AM ALONE   607 30

STRIPS
    AS STRIPS YOU STARK AS A MONKEY NUT   493 15

STRIVE
    AND STRIVE TO DETACH HERSELF FROM THE RAW   103 26
    STRIVE TO ESCAPE   103 28
    LISTEN EXCEPT THOSE WHO STRIVE WITH THEIR DEAD   233 3
    OUR OVERWEENING DAYS STRIVE TOO FAR TILL THE HEAT AND T+   856 1
    STRIVE WITH THE FORMLESS THINGS AND GENTLY TOUCH   872 6
    THE MYSTERY I STRIVE TOWARD HOWEVER   876 28

STRIVES
    HOMUNCULUS STIRS FROM HIS ROOTS AND STRIVES UNTIL   39 11
    IN A WORM THAT IS BLIND YET STRIVES   170 5
    CLUSTERING UPON ME REACHING UP AS EACH AFTER THE OTHER +   *900 7
    CLUSTERING UPON ME REACHING UP AS EACH AFTER THE OTHER +   *903 19

STRIVING
    HIS LOW FOREHEAD HIS SKINNY NECK HIS LONG SCALED STRIVI+   360 2
    SO STRIVING STRIVING   360 4
    NOR YET THE STRIVING AND THE HORRID STRIFE   710 8
    A SINGLE EGO STRIVING FOR ITS OWN ENDS   714 27
    UP DIMLY FROM THEIR STRIVING IT HEARTENS MY STRIFE   *900 24
    UP DIMLY FROM THEIR STRIVING IT HEARTENS MY STRIFE   *903 36
    AND STRIVING TO CATCH A GLIMPSE OF THE SHAPE OF THE COM+   *909 25

STRODE
    AS SHE STRODE HER LIMBS AMONGST IT ONCE MORE   155 14

STROKE
    WHY IS IT THE LONG SLOW STROKE OF THE MIDNIGHT BELL   63 1
    STROKE   88 2
    NO FLESH RESPONDED TO MY STROKE   111 25
    A PALE STROKE SMOTE   165 12
    LIKE A BELL THAT IS CHIMING EACH STROKE AS A STROKE FAL+   251 12
    WITH EVERY STROKE AND GO ON   512 25
    STROKE   695 19
    RED STROKE ACROSS MY LIPS   735 27
    AND YOU KILL HIM THERE WITH ONE STROKE   ,808 13
    WINROW AFTER WINROW FALLS UNDER THIS FIRST STROKE OF NI+   858 10

STROKE
    THE WATERS' RESTLESS STROKE   *916 23
    FLAWED MY DELICATE COURAGE IN ITS STROKE   *927 13
    YOUR BODY QUAILED AT MY STROKE   *928 13

STROKED
    WITH SORROWFUL FINGERS STROKED HER EYELIDS SHUT   881 2

STROKES
    I CAN HEAR THE SOUND OF THE SCYTHE STROKES FOUR   *944 2

STROLL
    ALMOST EVERY SCRAP OF THE LIVING EARTH YOU STROLL UP AND 521 15

STROLLING
    STROLLING IN GANGS AND STARING ALONG THE CORSO   312 19
    LIVING ON YOUR INCOME IS STROLLING GRANDLY OUTSIDE THE   521 11

STRONG
    HIS STRONG TEETH IN A SMILE AND FLASHES HIS EYES   43 20
    IN WHAT STRONG AQUA REGIA NOW ARE YOU STEEPED   53 27
    CURVED THY MOUTH FOR THEE AND WHAT STRONG SHOULDER   69 14
    AND THE GENTLE LEAVES AND HAVE FELT WHERE THE ROOTS ARE+   92 10
    ARE STRONG   93 6
    BEAUTIFUL PASSIVE AND STRONG AS THE BREATH   118 14
    THOUGH HER HANDS ARE STILL THE WOMAN HER LARGE STRONG   128 5
    WHERE I SHOULD BE AND WITH HER OWN STRONG SPAN   128 29
    FEELING YOUR STRONG BREAST CARRY ME ON INTO   129 25
    BUT MY HEART STANDS STILL AS A NEW STRONG DREAD ALARMS   132 5
    OF THE STRONG MACHINE THAT RUNS MESMERIC BOOMING THE   149 13
    MORNING STRONG   149 22
    THE DRINK AND A LONG STRONG PULL   177 12
    BUT ALWAYS STRONG UNREMITTING   214 26
    LIVING AS THE MOUNTAINS DO BECAUSE THEY ARE STRONG   226 2
    I WHO AM SO FIERCE AND STRONG ENFOLDING YOU   246 23
    BUT NOW I AM FULL AND STRONG AND CERTAIN   247 1
    HOW SURE I FEEL HOW WARM AND STRONG AND HAPPY   247 4
    WHY SHOULDN'T YOUR LEGS AND YOUR GOOD STRONG THIGHS   254 11
    SIGHTLESS AND STRONG OBLIVION IN UTTER LIFE TAKES POSSE+ 261 10
    THE UNKNOWN STRONG CURRENT OF LIFE SUPREME   261 12
    IT IS SO DEEP A MOLOCH RUTHLESS AND STRONG   264 15
    A MAN IS SO TERRIFIED OF STRONG HUNGER   264 32
    STRONG LIKE THE GREATEST FORCE OF WORLD-BALANCING   271 20
    OH YES THE GUSH OF SPRING IS STRONG ENOUGH   272 13
    THE GUSH OF SPRING IS STRONG ENOUGH   272 18
    AND STRONG SPINE URGING DRIVING   336 10
    A STRONG INRUSHING WIND   343 18
    YOU THICK BIRD WITH A STRONG CREST   375 30
    WREATHE STRONG WEED ROUND THE KNEES AS THE DARKNESS   425 13
    THAT STRONG ONE RULING THE UNIVERSE WITH A ROD OF IRON   439 25
    AND STRONG MEN   439 27
    GOING IT STRONG   564 4
    IS APT TO PROVE A GREAT DEAL TOO STRONG   576 2
    HER SELF-ABSORPTION IS EVEN AS STRONG AS MINE   605 8
    THAT IS THE ONLY STRONG FEELING HE IS CAPABLE OF   648 4
    THE BATTLE IS NOT TO THE STRONG   658 8
    AND ROLL WITH MASSIVE STRONG DESIRE LIKE GODS   694 12
    THE LONG TIP REACHES STRONG INTENSE LIKE THE MAELSTROM-+ 694 17
    AND OVER THE BRIDGE OF THE WHALE'S STRONG PHALLUS LINKI+ 694 21
    BUTTERFLY THE WIND BLOWS SEA-WARD STRONG BEYOND THE GAR+ 696 12
    ALREADY IT IS OCTOBER AND THE WIND BLOWS STRONG TO THE + 696 15
    BUT THE WIND BLOWS STRONG TO SEA-WARD WHITE BUTTERFLY C+ 696 19
    SO GUNS AND STRONG EXPLOSIVES   715 12
    OF A STRONG HEART AT PEACE   717 19
    STRONG YOUNG MAN HE LEANS SIGHING   733 19
    ME WANT TO CRY TO SEE HIM SO STRONG AND EASY   733 23
    SWARTHY AND STRONG WITH HIS DAMP THICK HAIR   733 24
    WAS WET WITH SWEAT AND HIS MOVEMENTS STRONG AND HEAVY   734 22
    SWUNG STRONG AND HEAVY TO SADDLE AGAIN   735 13
    AND CALLED TO HIS HORSES AND HIS STRONG BLUE BODY   735 14
    INVISIBLE YET STRONG   739 8
    AND FILL THEM STRONG WITH STRENGTH OF WINGS   799 19
    NOR IS HE A STRONG MAN RULING THE EARTH   840 16
    STRONG WITH EYES OF DEFIANCE EVE WALKS WITH SORROWS   864 23
    SIEGMUND THE STRONG BEATING OF YOUR HEART HURTS ME   870 19
    I SEE THE STRONG SOUND EARTH BETRAYED AS A FLOATING   874 30
    WONDER I CRAVE FOR THAT BURNS STRONG IN HIM   876 31
    CURVED THY MOUTH FOR THEE AND HIS STRONG SHOULDER   *915 26
    UNDER THE CARESSING LEAVES AND FELT WHERE THE ROOTS WER+ *926 10
    STRONG AND SLOW I LIKE TO SEE SAID SHE   *934 17

STRONGER
    KNOWLEDGE I SET YOUR HEART TO ITS STRONGER BEAT   156 28
    STRONGER THAN FEAR OR DESTRUCTIVE MOTHER-LOVE IT STOOD   207 12
    THEY ARE NOT STRONGER THAN I AM BLIND SAMSON   288 11
    STRONGER THAN MULTIPLICITY OF BONE ON BONE   383 9
    IT IS SO MUCH STRONGER THAN HER LOVE COULD EVER BE   475 8
    TILL THEY ARE OLD WE ARE STRONGER THAN THE YOUNG   503 5
    HIS SELF-ABSORPTION IS EVEN STRONGER THAN MINE   605 12
    WHAT FUN STRONGER THAN MINE   605 13
    TELL HIM PRAYER IS STRONGER THAN IRON FAITH   754 11

STRONGEST
    FOR THE STRONGEST LIGHT THROWS ALSO THE DARKEST SHADOW   474 4

STRUCK
    AND STRUCK AT ME WITH SOMETHING DARK   46 22
    WHEN IT HAS STRUCK HOME TO HER LIKE A DEATH THIS IS HIM   267 8
    I WOULD COME IF I FELT MY HOUR HAD STRUCK   289 28
    YOUR HOUR HAS STRUCK   473 12
    WHEN I READ SHAKESPEARE I AM STRUCK WITH WONDER   494 13
    ITS KNELL HAS STRUCK   512 5
    WHO STRUCK THE BELL   512 12
    OF OUR ERA HAS STRUCK AND IT CHIMES   512 17
    STRUCK DOWN DO THOU PART US THE DARKNESS THAT WE SEE TH+ 753 6
    IN TERRIBLE RHYTHM LIKE BLOWS THAT ARE STRUCK TILL THE + 879 2

STRUGGLE
NOR BE THWARTED IN LIFE'S SLOW STRUGGLE TO UNFOLD THE F+   93 18
OF HAVING AND GETTING AND OWNING THE STRUGGLE WHICH WRE+   175 23
SINCE I MUST SERVE AND STRUGGLE WITH THE IMMINENT   234 31
AND HE MUST STRUGGLE AFTER RECONSTRUCTION IGNOMINIOUSLY   361 12
IMBECILE STRUGGLE OF COMBAT   519 16
WHEN IT NEED STRUGGLE NO MORE   535 2
BUT MUST EVER STRUGGLE ON TO ASSERT THEMSELVES   612 20
IS THE HISTORY OF THE STRUGGLE OF BECOMING   682 2
AND IN THE GREAT STRUGGLE OF INTANGIBLE CHAOS   682 12
A STRANGE ACHE POSSESSED HIM AND HE ENTERED THE STRUGGLE   690 5
AND OUT OF THE STRUGGLE WITH HIS MATERIAL IN THE SPELL +   690 6
EACH KNOWS THE OTHER IN STRUGGLE   714 23
THEY STRUGGLE AT THE GATE YOU HAVE OPENED   795 32
BUT LOVINGS AND HATINGS STRUGGLE AND FIGHTINGS   857 7

STRUGGLED
STRUGGLED TO BE TOGETHER   206 14
STRUGGLED CONVULSED BACK AND FORTH UPON ITSELF   682 4

STRUGGLES
OF THE TIME WHEN THE GRAIN STRUGGLES DOWN IN THE DARK   63 19
THAT STRUGGLES ALONE IN THE DARK   63 28
THE TRAIN BEATS FRANTIC IN HASTE AND STRUGGLES AWAY   88 23

STRUGGLING
SOBS STRUGGLING INTO HER FROSTY SIGH   85 12
CAN MOCK MY STRUGGLING   157 20
STRUGGLING IN DOUBTFUL EMBRACES   457 15
BUT WHEN I SEE THE LIFE-SPIRIT FLUTTERING AND STRUGGLIN+   622 4
STRUGGLING   681 28
STRUGGLING GERM IN INDIVIDUAL HEARTS   775 22
BUT A SUBTLE STRUGGLING LITTLE GERM STRUGGLING HALF-UNR+   775 25

STRUT
STRUT LIKE PEG-TOPS WOUND AROUND WITH HUNDREDS OF YARDS   388 17

STRUTS
AND STRUTS BLUE-BRILLIANT OUT OF THE FAR EAST   371 2

ST STEPHEN'S
NO SOUND FROM ST STEPHEN'S   170 27

STUBBLE
LIKE HEAVY BIRDS FROM THE MORNING STUBBLE TO SETTLE   128 11
THE SHADOWY STUBBLE OF THE UNDER-DUSK   135 10
IN THE AUTUMN FIELDS THE STUBBLE   152 18
STUBBLE UPON THE GROUND   165 3
THE SCYTHE-STONE AND OVER THE STUBBLE TO ME   220 5
THE SHADOWY STUBBLE OF THE UNDER-DUSK   *939 10

STUBBORN
BRIGHT GLANCING EXQUISITE CORN OF MANY A STUBBORN   263 27
AND STEPPING IN HOMAGE STUBBORN TO THAT NERVOUS PALE   388 24
FROM WHAT I'VE ARRANGED WI' THEE EH MAN WHAT A STUBBORN+   *925 26

STUCK
OR SITTING STUCK LIKE AUTOMATA IN AUTOMOBILES   530 17

STUDY
OR SOFTLY TAPPING AT MY STUDY DOOR   875 10

STUFF
MARVELLOUS STUFF   34 21
YOUR STUFF ALL GONE YOUR MENACE ALMOST RASED   53 23
WHAT MATTER THE STUFF I LICK UP IN MY DAILY FLAME   115 10
OF THE STUFF OF THE NIGHT FINDING MYSELF ALL WRONGLY   133 7
TO DEFEAT YOUR BASER STUFF   157 8
BE COMMON STUFF   234 28
OF STUFF   451 2
AND LOOK AT THE SODOMITICAL AND LESBIAN STUFF WEARING   532 6
THE STUFF OF A MAN   534 20
STUFF IS JUST HOLY SKUNK   556 20
OH WHAT WERE YOU WHAT WERE YOU BUT THE STUFF OF MY SOUL   870 28
WHAT MATTER THE STUFF I LICK UP IN MY LIVING FLAME   *930 10

STUFFED
AND A BOARD-SCHOOL BRAIN STUFFED UP WITH THE HA'PENNY   630 30

STUFFY
AND BURN IT DOWN THE GLUTTED STUFFY WORLD   315 4
WITH EYES LIKE THE INTERIORS OF STUFFY ROOMS FURNISHED   656 24

STUMBLE
WHAT IF I SUDDENLY STUMBLE AND PUSH THE DOOR   147 8
I STUMBLE AGAINST THEM   288 3
SEEMING TO STUMBLE TO FALL IN AIR   345 15
I STUMBLE WHERE THE SHADOWS LIE   731 2

STUMBLETH
IN HER EYES AS A YOUNG BEE STUMBLETH   46 16

STUMBLING
HAS FLUTTERED HER SPIRIT TO STUMBLING FLIGHT   46 15
AND STUMBLING LUNGING AND TOUCHING THE WALLS THE BELL-W+   343 11
AND STUMBLING MIXED UP IN ONE ANOTHER   361 25

STUMBLING-BLOCKS
STUMBLING-BLOCKS PAINFUL ONES   288 4

STUMP
IS TO SPLIT IT IN FOUR HOLDING IT BY THE STUMP   282 2

STUMPS
STAND LIKE DARK STUMPS STILL IN THE GREEN WHEAT   208 27

STUNG
PERHAPS THE TINY YOUNG NETTLES HAVE STUNG HER EARS   882 26

STUNNED
SICKEN US AND WE ARE STUNNED BY THE RUSHINGS OF THE LAB+   856 2

STUNTED
STANDS RUBBLE OF STUNTED HOUSES ALL IS REAPED   135 7
A RUBBLE OF STUNTED HOUSES STANDS UNREAPED   *939 7

STUNTING
ME NOW FROM THE STUNTING BONDS OF MY CHASTITY   180 17

STUPEFACTION
BUT IN THE WEIGHT OF THEIR STUPEFACTION NONE OF THEM KN+   790 25

STUPEFIED
ALL GONE STUPEFIED   790 27

STUPEFIES
STUPEFIES ME   230 19

STUPENDOUS
BEHOLD YOU ARE LIVING THE GREAT LIFE THE STUPENDOUS LIFE   441 23

STUPID
I THINK IDIOTS TELL DULL STUPID DISGUSTING TALES   837 21
I AM TIRED OF THIS JOURNEY IT IS STUPID AND CHILL   858 1

STUPIDEST
EVEN THE STUPIDEST FARMER GATHERS HIS HAY IN BLOOM IN   587 8

STUPIDITY
AND US FROM THE DREARY INHERITANCE OF ROMAN STUPIDITY   479 27

STUPIDLY
STUPIDLY   224 18

STUPOR
IN STUPOR PERSIST AT THE GATES OF LIFE OBSTINATE DARK M+   75 12
THAT WRAPS THE NORTH IN STUPOR AND PURPLE TRAVELS THE D+   149 3
A SLEEP THAT IS WRITHING STUPOR WEIGHED DOWN SO WE CAN'+   175 14

STURDY
UNLESS HE IS A STURDY PLANT   475 1

STY
A LITTLE FRESH AIR IN THE MONEY STY   459 17

STYLE
IN GRAND AND CAKEY STYLE   488 22

SUAVE
AND THE SUAVE SEA CHUCKLES AND TURNS TO THE MOON   130 2
OF THE SUAVE SENSITIVE BODY THE HUNGER FOR THIS   263 16
SO BROWN AND SOFT AND COMING SUAVE   280 4
AND SUAVE LIKE PASSION-FLOWER PETALS   298 28
NOR EVEN THE MUSICAL SUAVE YOUNG FELLOW   437 6
WITH HER SUAVE FORM DUSTY WITH SPICES HONEY SWEET STRAY+   864 4
AND ONCE AGAIN A SUAVE YOUNG GOD   *946 18

SUBAQUEOUS
AQUEOUS SUBAQUEOUS   334 25

SUB-DELIGHTED
SUB-DELIGHTED STONE-ENGENDERED   311 2
YET SUB-DELIGHTED   311 13

SUBDUED
A SOUND SUBDUED IN THE DARKNESS TEARS   210 21

SUBJECT
AND SUBJECT REALLY TO THE DRAUGHT OF EVERY MOTOR-CAR OR+   617 17

SUBJECTION
SHE FOUND THE SOURCE OF MY SUBJECTION   262 17

SUBJUGATED
CHAINED SUBJUGATED TO HIS USE   647 19

SUBLIME
WE'LL TRY TO ACT UP SUBLIME   573 4

SUBMERGED
SUBMERGED   334 26
ON THE SEA WITH NO MESSAGE IN IT AND THE BODY SUBMERGED   428 11
AND OVER THE SUBMERGED ISLETS OF MY KNEES   705 9

SUBMERGES
WHILE DARKNESS SUBMERGES THE STONES   427 5

SUBMISSION
A SUBMISSION   364 20
SERVE VAST MOUNTAINOUS BLOOD IN SUBMISSION AND SPLENDOUR   390 23
WHERE THE MEADOW-LARK WEARS HIS COLLAR OF SUBMISSION   768 21

SUBMISSIVE
LOVE ON A SUBMISSIVE ASS   379 27

SUBMIT
BUT WE WILL LEARN TO SUBMIT   236 17
EITHER TO STAY CONNECTED WITH THE TREE OF LIFE AND SUBM+   617 13
AND THEY WILL DESTROY ALL UNLESS THEY ARE MADE TO SUBMIT   637 9
SUBMIT ABJECTLY TO THE BLIND MECHANICAL TRAFFIC-STREAMS+   666 6
IF YOU CAN SUBMIT TO IT   779 29
SUBMIT TO IT AND LET YOUR AMERICAN NOBLESSE COMPEL YOU   779 30

SUBORDINATE
  SUBORDINATE TO THIS THAT HE AND SHE   231   3

SUBSEQUENT
  FROM HER SUBSEQUENT WOES   565 22

SUBSIDENCE
  HIS SCREAM AND HIS MOMENT'S SUBSIDENCE   365 15

SUBSIDES
  THE FLOOD SUBSIDES AND THE BODY LIKE A WORN SEA-SHELL   720 12

SUBSIDING
  SUBSIDING INTO THIS NIGHT   302 13
  AND THE HOUSE COMES DOWN WITH A SUBSIDING   511 19

SUBSTANCE
  I ON THE BANK ALL SUBSTANCE MY SHADOW ALL SHADOW LOOKIN+   34   2
  BUT HOW SPLENDID IT IS TO BE SUBSTANCE HERE   34   7
  SUN BUT IN SUBSTANCE YELLOW WATER-BLOBS   34 25
  ALL THAT IS RIGHT ALL THAT IS GOOD ALL THAT IS GOD TAKE+   34 27
  FOR WHAT CAN ALL SHARP-RIMMED SUBSTANCE BUT CATCH   68 25
  OR SUBSTANCE SAVE I LIGHT ON YOU TO WARM   86 11
  SUBSTANCE OF MY INCONSISTENT BREATH   118   8
  I WHO AM SUBSTANCE OF SHADOW I ALL COMPACT   133   6
  SHINE IN CONCEIT OF SUBSTANCE UPON ME WHO AM LESS THAN   133 12
  TO HAVE MY SUBSTANCE SO SUBTLY SPENT   152   2
  LUKE THE BULL THE FATHER OF SUBSTANCE THE PROVIDENCE BU+   327 16
  TO CROP A LITTLE SUBSTANCE   358   4
  GNAWS JUST THE SAME GNAWING THE SUBSTANCE OUT OF LIFE   432 12
  SHELVING SUBSTANCE ON TO THE WOMAN MADONNA MIA   437   3
  THEY ARE SUBSTANCE ITSELF THAT FLOWS IN THICK   460   5
  SUBSTANCE   538   8
  AND MARROW AND SUBSTANCE OUT OF ALL   583   3
  AND MARROW AND SUBSTANCE ARE SURE TO BE   583 24
  AND CAN'T PASS SUCH THINGS AS SUBSTANCE AND MARROW   583 29
  SHAPE NOR SUBSTANCE   651   9
  ABROAD IN MY HANDS LIKE WAVES AMONG THE ROCKS OF SUBSTA+   705   6
  INTO SUBSTANCE AND FLAKY WHITENESS   705 20
  THE SUBSTANCE TANGLED IN THE NET   747 18
  IN CONCEIT OF SUBSTANCE UPON ME   772   2
  THE SUBSTANCE OF SHADOW THAT BURSTS AND EXPLODES   788 13
  OF TOSSING AND ROLLING THE SUBSTANCE OF LIFE TO YOUR LI+   792 21
  WHEN ALL MY SUBSTANCE IS BEING SPENT   874 16
  FOR WHAT CAN ALL THAT SHARP-RIMMED SUBSTANCE BUT CATCH   *915   9

SUBSTANCELESS
  HALF SUBSTANCELESS AND WITHOUT GRAVE WORTH   118 17

SUBSTANTIAL
  WE SOUGHT YOU SUBSTANTIAL YOU TOUCHSTONE OF CARESSES YO+   34 17
  THAT WHICH IS ELEMENTAL AND OF THE SUBSTANTIAL GODS IN +   637 12
  THE LIVING SUBSTANTIAL GODS   638 14
  THAT THE IDEA OF THE FORM PRECEDES THE FORM SUBSTANTIAL   689 17

SUBTERRANEAN
  BUT BELOW ALL ROOTS OF LOVE LIES THE BEDROCK OF NAKED P+   844 19

SUBTLE
  ON A SUBTLE RUSH OF COOL GREY FLAME   68   2
  THE SUBTLE STEADY RUSH OF THE WHOLE   68 13
  GLIMMERS WITH SUBTLE GHOSTS   109   2
  HOW IT STIRS LIKE A SUBTLE STOAT WHATEVER SHE THINKS   128 17
  IN THE SUBTLE LIFT OF THE THIGHS AS THEY COME UNMARCHING   174 13
  IF ONLY I AM SENSITIVE SUBTLE OH DELICATE A WINGED GIFT   250 16
  UNHEARD AND SUBTLE NEVER A SOUND   262   8
  THE SMILE THE SUBTLE ETRUSCAN SMILE STILL LURKING   297 22
  THE PASSION OF JUSTICE BEING PROFOUND AND SUBTLE   482   8
  DONE AND SLIGHTLY SUBTLE   532 18
  AND SUBTLE SILVERY TINKLING AND RIPPLING   667 29
  COME TO PASS THAT DOES NOT YET EXIST SAVE AS A SUBTLE   775 21
  BUT A SUBTLE STRUGGLING LITTLE GERM STRUGGLING HALF-UNR+   775 25
  ITS TREASURES OF CONSCIOUSNESS ITS SUBTLE BARBARIC   776   9
  SHE BOWS QUITE HUMBLE SUCH A SUBTLE DESTROYING MIND MUS+   841 28
  AND FINDS THAT THE SUBTLE DESTRUCTIVE CYNICISM IS ONLY +   842   2
  AND THEIR SUBTLE EAGER BOOMING   885 25
  HERE IN THE SUBTLE ROUNDED FLESH   *906 20
  AS THE SUBTLE HEAT   *907 21
  HERE IN THE SUBTLE ROUNDED FLESH   *908 16
  ON THE SUBTLE RUSH OF THE COOL GREY FLAME   *914 17
  THE SUBTLE STEADY RUSH OF THE WHOLE   *914 28

SUBTLER
  SUBTLER THAN AN OLD SOFT-WORN FIDDLE-BOW   254 33
  AND KNOWN IT SUBTLER THAN FRISSON-SHAKEN NERVES   383   8

SUBTLY
  TO HAVE MY SUBSTANCE SO SUBTLY SPENT   152   2
  THE GRAPE IS SWART THE AVENUES DUSKY AND TENDRILLED SUB+   286 32
  SUBTLY TO THE TWIGS OVERHEAD FAR UP VAST BEAST   385 27
  OF PUTRESCENT WISDOM AND SAPIENCE THAT SUBTLY STINKS   441   1
  DOMINANT WOMEN ARE AS A RULE SO SUBTLY AND FIENDISHLY D+   619 24
  SOFTLY SUBTLY SECRETLY IN SOUL FIRST THEN IN SPIRIT THE+   642 22
  SOFTLY SUBTLY SECRETLY SAYING NOTHING   642 27

SUBTLY-SMILING
  THE LONG-NOSED SENSITIVE-FOOTED SUBTLY-SMILING ETRUSCANS   296 15
  WITH SUCH INSUPERABLE SUBTLY-SMILING ASSURANCE   306 31

SUBURBAN
  SUBURBAN DISMAL   141   2
  SUCH SUBURBAN AMBITION SO MESSILY GORING   494 23

SUCCEED
  NEVER SUCCEED   382 34

SUCCEEDING
  SUCCEEDING SHARP LITTLE SOUNDS DROPPING INTO SILENCE   63 10
  AND NOT SUCCEEDING   506 27

SUCCESS
  SUCCESS IS INSANE AND FAILURE IS INSANE   516   3
  SUCCESS IS A PLAYED-OUT GAME SUCCESS SUCCESS   518 14
  THE PRAISE OF JESUS IS MY SUCCESS   749 22
  THAN WOMAN OR TRIUMPH MONEY OR SUCCESS   764   3
  OH MEN DEARER THAN SUCCESS TO ME   765   4
  SUCCESS   829   2
  OF SUCCESS MONEY   831 14
  SUCCESS FAILURE LOVE CHASTITY DEBAUCHERY MONEY OR SOVIE+   839 19

SUCCESSFUL
  OF MAKING A TRIUMPH OF ENVY THE RICH AND SUCCESSFUL ONES   175 10
  BUT WHEN I SEE THESE GREY SUCCESSFUL MEN   526 13
  LIKE GROSS SUCCESSFUL SLAVES MECHANICALLY WADDLING   526 15

SUCCESSFULLY
  HAS SUCCESSFULLY KILLED ALL DESIRE IN US WHATSOEVER   439 33
  SUCCESSFULLY CASTRATING THE BODY POLITIC   627 27
  HAS BEEN SUCCESSFULLY SOLD   763 11
  AND WHATEVER NEW COMES ALONG WILL BE SUCCESSFULLY SOLD   763 12

SUCCOUR
  MALIGNANT MALIGNANT FOR WE WILL NOT SUCCOUR THEM   723   7

SUCCULENT
  AND WENT WHIZZING THROUGH THE SLOW VAST SUCCULENT   372 12

SUCCUMB
  AND MEN OFTEN SUCCUMB LIKE WHITE MICE IN A LABORATORY A+   619 22

SUCCUMBED
  SO THE POOR MALE HAS SUCCUMBED UNDER IT   843   1

SUCH-LIKE
  NOW THAT IN ENGLAND PANSIES AND SUCH-LIKE GROW ON THE   410 19

SUCK
  I LOVE TO SUCK YOU OUT FROM YOUR SKINS   280   3
  THERE ARE DEAD THAT ATTACK THE SUN LIKE SWARMS OF BLACK+   795 28

SUCKED
  SUCKED OUT OF YOUR EMPTY BLADDERS   281 23
  QUEER WHAT A BIG STAIN MY SUCKED BLOOD MAKES   334 16
  DON'T BE SUCKED IN BY THE SU-SUPERIOR   459   9
  LIKE WATER SUCKED FROM DEEP DOWN UNDERGROUND   878 33

SUCKING
  SUCKING LIVE BLOOD   333 31
  WHETHER YOU'RE A SUCKING DOVE ROO COO OOO QUARK   414   6
  SUCKING HIS LIFE OUT OF THE DEAD LEAVES OF GREATER LIFE+   431 16
  OF THEIR DANCING BLOOD LADS SUCKING THE COLD MOISTURE F+   865 29

SUCKIN-IN
  THA'RT A GOOD-UN AT SUCKIN-IN YET TIMMY   *921 21

SUCKIN'-IN
  THA'RT A GOOD-UN AT SUCKIN'-IN YET TIMMY   79 25

SUCKIN'
  AN' MIST IS SUCKIN' AT TH' SPOTS O' SNOW   137 21
  AND SUCKIN' YOUR BLOOD   557   4

SUCKLING
  AND ENORMOUS WHALES LIE DREAMING SUCKLING THEIR WHALE-T+   694 29

SUCKS
  THAT SUCKS UP BLOOD   374 27
  EVERYTHING NEW AND MACHINE-MADE SUCKS LIFE OUT OF US   448 16

SUDDEN
  IN MY SOUL FROM UNDER THE SUDDEN FROWN OF HIS BROW   47 26
  A SUDDEN CAR GOES SWEEPING PAST AND I STRAIN MY SOUL TO+   58   3
  FOR I THOUGHT YOU WERE WARM AS A SUDDEN JET OF BLOOD   99   7
  SHE WATCHED SHE WENT OF A SUDDEN INTENSELY STILL   125 11
  LIKE A SUDDEN CHUCKLING OF MUSIC I BADE HER EYES   125 26
  WHAT SUDDEN EXPECTATION OPENS YOU   126 29
  SUDDEN OUTSIDE THE HIGH WINDOW ONE CROW   147 21
  THAT LONDON LAIR OF SUDDEN   171 14
  OF SUDDEN ANGUISH SUDDEN OVER AND SPENT   196   4
  SUDDEN A DARK-FACED STRANGER   200   9
  OF THE LONG LUSH UNDER-GRASS A GLOW-WORM'S SUDDEN   206   9
  LIKE A FLAME THAT FALLS OF A SUDDEN   246 26
  WHERE I HAD BEEN WAS A SUDDEN BLAZE   259   5
  A SUDDEN FLARING BLAZE   259   6
  WHICH SHAKES MY SUDDEN BLOOD TO HATRED OF YOU   333 16
  A SUDDEN TURNING UPON ITSELF OF A THING IN THE AIR   341   4
  LIKE SUDDEN CURVED SCISSORS   359   4
  YET UNRELEASED AND AFTER THE MOMENT THE SUDDEN STARTLING   365 17
  SUDDEN DEMONIC DAUNTLESSNESS FULL ABREAST   371 10
  GROUND WITH A SUDDEN ROCK-HAMMER ANNOUNCEMENT   381 14
  AND THE SUDDEN DRIPPING OF THE KNIFE-EDGE CLEAVAGE OF T+   707 13
  REVEALING THE SKY THROUGH THE RAGGED EARTH AND SUDDEN   874 29
  IN THE SUDDEN LIFTING MY EYES IT IS CLEARER   *908 18
  SNAPPED SUDDEN OUT OF ALL   *911 10
  SHE WATCHED SHE WENT OF A SUDDEN INTENSELY STILL   *935 27
  LIKE A SUDDEN CHUCKLING OF MUSIC I BADE HER EYES   *936 25

SUDDENLY
  I SEE A REDNESS SUDDENLY COME   42   6
  AH HOME SUDDENLY I LOVE YOU   63   8
  AND SUDDENLY AS IF THE GROUND MOVED   66 15
  SEND SUDDENLY OUT AND EVERY GESTURE DOES   89   5
  AND I DARED NOT ENTER FEELING SUDDENLY DISMAYED   99 11
  THE STREET-LAMPS IN THE TWILIGHT HAVE SUDDENLY STARTED +   102 31

SUDDENLY
  FOR SUDDENLY FLUSH-FALLEN   107 9
  THEN SUDDENLY SHE LOOKED UP   123 31
  THE RAIN-BRUISED LEAVES ARE SUDDENLY SHAKEN AS A CHILD   136 24
  THRONG OF STARTLED BEINGS SUDDENLY THROWN   140 12
  ALOUD SUDDENLY ON MY MIND   140 16
  WHAT IF I SUDDENLY STUMBLE AND PUSH THE DOOR   147 8
  LONG HAS WAITED RESTLESS SUDDENLY WAFTS   154 29
  THAT WILL NOT GO NOW SUDDENLY GOING THE PAIN   155 11
  I WISH THE ELDER-TREES IN FLOWER COULD SUDDENLY HEAVE A+   159 23
  MY FATHER SUDDENLY DIED IN THE HARVESTING CORN   173 1
  ARRIVING GREY FROM THE DARKNESS ABOVE SUDDENLY INTO THE+   179 22
  AND SUDDENLY REALIZE IN THEM AS IN ME   218 3
  HOW SUDDENLY I SHALL GO DOWN INTO NOTHING   246 25
  OH AND SUDDENLY FROM OUT OF NOWHERE WHIRLS THE PEAR-BLO+   271 25
  SUDDENLY TO DARE TO COME OUT NAKED IN PERFECTION OF   306 15
  THE HARE SUDDENLY GOES UPHILL   311 18
  AND SUDDENLY PULLED A GOLD-AND-GREENISH LUCENT FISH FROM   339 2
  BUT SUDDENLY THAT PART OF HIM THAT WAS LEFT BEHIND CONV+   351 13
  SUDDENLY BEAK-SHAPED AND VERY WIDE LIKE SOME SUDDENLY   353 5
  SUDDENLY HASTY RECKLESS ON HIGH TOES   354 6
  PARTING HIS STEEL-TRAP FACE SO SUDDENLY AND SEIZING HER   360 20
  SUDDENLY SEIZING THE UGLY ANKLE AS SHE STRETCHES OUT TO   361 17
  SUDDENLY OR HER SKINNY LIMB   362 22
  NOW SUDDENLY DISTRACTED INTO THIS MAZY SIDE-TRACK   363 3
  TILL SUDDENLY IN THE SPASM OF COITION TUPPING LIKE A JE+   365 7
  YET THE BRONZE WIND-BELL SUDDENLY CLASHING   371 16
  SUDDENLY BUTT   381 9
  AND SUDDENLY LOWERING HIS HEAD THE WHORLS OF BONE AND   381 16
  QUEER IT IS SUDDENLY IN THE GARDEN   385 15
  GLEAMING LIKE METAL WITH RUNNING SWEAT AS THEY SUDDENLY   389 9
  AND TURNING THE DAY SUDDENLY INTO A BLACK TORNADO OF JO+   397 4
  AND THE CHILDREN SUDDENLY SHOUTED OUT   444 22
  AND THEN SUDDENLY WHEN SHE'S FEELING ALL LOVELY ABOUT IT   447 26
  SUDDENLY THE GROUND GOES FROM UNDER HER FEET AND SHE   447 27
  AND SPURTING SUDDENLY UP SNOW-WHITE LIKE SNOW-LEOPARDS   454 7
  THEY WOULDN'T SUDDENLY BECOME THEMSELVES ARISTOCRATIC   527 24
  THEN SUDDENLY THE MASTODON ROSE WITH THE WONDERFUL LADY   540 5
  I SUDDENLY SAID I'VE FINISHED   556 15
  AND NOON IS SUDDENLY DARK IS LUSTROUS IS SILENT AND DARK   606 4
  SUDDENLY HER YELLOW-BROWN EYES LOOKED WITH A FLARE INTO   618 1
  I SUDDENLY SAW DEEP INTO THE EYES OF GOD   650 22
  SUDDENLY IT CURVES AS IT YIELDS THE WHITE WHEAT   651 14
  MAKES THE HEART SUDDENLY QUIVER WITH LOVE   653 17
  I SAW SUDDENLY COMING TOWARDS ME LIT UP AND UPLIFTED WI+   672 20
  KEEP SUDDENLY SHOWING A WHITENESS A FLASH AND A FURL A I   607 2
  SUDDENLY HIS HORSES BEGAN TO START   735 7
  THEN SUDDENLY HE SPIED THE OLD LAKE AND HE THREW IT IN   791 7
  WHICH YOU'VE THROWN UPON HIM SHALL SUDDENLY SHAKE WITH +   797 9
  BEATS THE ACTIVE ECSTASY SUDDENLY LIFTING MY EYES   *906 21
  THEN SUDDENLY SHE LOOKED UP   *935 3

SUFFER
  AND I AT THE FOOT OF HER CROSS DID SUFFER   103 21
  AND SUFFER UNHEEDING ONLY FORBIDDEN TO EXPIRE   161 5
  STRANGE HOW WE SUFFER IN SPITE OF THIS   203 29
  TREES SUFFER LIKE RACES DOWN THE LONG AGES   304 25
  AND SUFFER FOOLS THOUGH NOT GLADLY   499 13
  WHY AS THEY GROW OLDER DO THEY SUFFER FROM BLOOD-PRESSU+   537 24
  THEN WE SUFFER AND THOUGH THE SUN BRONZES US   609 4
  AND THOSE THAT DO DESCEND HAVE GOT TO SUFFER A SENSE-CH+   667 24
  EVER TO SUFFER LOVE'S WILD ATTACK   854 18
  WITH YOUR TIRED EYES JEANNETTE WE SUFFER THE SAME DON'T+   859 31

SUFFERANCE
  ON SUFFERANCE   329 9

SUFFERED
  AWARENESS THEN I SUFFERED A BALK   111 17
  AND I SUFFERED IT WANTING TO SYMPATHISE   206 34
  FLESH-ANGUISH THEN I SUFFERED A BALK   *927 10
  ANGUISH THEN I SUFFERED A BALK   *928 10

SUFFERING
  TO HEAL THE SUFFERING OR TO MAKE REQUITE   100 26
  KIND ON THE WEIGHT OF SUFFERING SMILES AGAIN   113 16
  SUFFERING AT SIGHT OF THE CHILDREN PLAYING AROUND   153 11
  WITH WOUNDS BETWEEN THEM AND SUFFERING LIKE A GUEST   155 10
  BUT IF YOU DON'T YOU ARE SUFFERING FROM AN AMNESIA   655 13
  OR WHAT IS IT THAT MY NATION IS SUFFERING FROM   659 23
  PERHAPS EVEN NOW YOU ARE SUFFERING FROM THE HAVOC THEY +   723 17
  LIKE A PAINTED WINDOW THAT LAST SUFFERING   *927 21
  SUFFERING BURNT THROUGH YOUR FLESH   *928 22
  EFFLUENCE FROM SUFFERING FOLK-STUFF WHICH DEATH HAS LAI+   *938 23

SUFFERINGS
  HIS SUFFERINGS   499 15

SUFFERS
  SHE TOO SUFFERS   213 21

SUFFICIENCY
  AT LAST CAME DEATH SUFFICIENCY OF DEATH   257 23

SUFFICIENT
  GRIEF GRIEF I SUPPOSE AND SUFFICIENT   199 29
  QUITE COLD-BLOODED INTELLECTUAL MURDER WITH A SUFFICIENT   532 21
  OH WONDERFUL MACHINE SO SELF-SUFFICIENT SO SUFFICIENT U+   643 8
  ENDOWED WITH A SUFFICIENT ENDOWMENT   780 6

SUFFICIENTLY
  YET NOT SUFFICIENTLY CONSCIOUS TO BE ABLE TO FORGET OUR+   496 20
  BUT I CONSIDER AS SUFFICIENTLY CIRCUMCISED LONG AGO   541 22
  THEY ARE SO HEALTHY SUFFICIENTLY WEALTHY   827 10
  SUFFICIENTLY WEALTHY   827 31

SUFFOCATE
  I SUFFOCATE IN THIS INTIMACY   116 30

SUFFOCATED
  AYE SUFFOCATED WITH A DRUNK SURFEIT   877 10

SUFFOCATING
  ENOUGH OF THE VIRGINS AND LILIES OF PASSIONATE SUFFOCAT+   273 14

SUFFUSED
  WITH SUFFUSED LIGHT   768 27

SUFFUSING
  OF OUR SABBATH SUFFUSING OUR SACRED DAY   148 3

SUGAR
  NO SAND IN MY DOUBTFUL SUGAR   236 30
  AND THE SUGAR MELTS OUT OF LIFE   455 4
  FEEDING ON PURE WHITE SUGAR   751 3
  SOME SUGAR OF THE SAME WHITE SORT   751 6
  THEY TAKE SUGAR FROM THE TALL TUBES OF THE CANE   793 20

SUGGEST
  DON'T YOU DARE TO SUGGEST SUCH A THING   580 8
  SUGGEST THAT THEY'RE SPICY YET.HOW PURE THEY ARE   583 20

SUGGESTION
  WHY THE SUGGESTION OF INCISION   279 20
  I WOULDN'T INSULT YOU WITH THE SUGGESTION   541 18

SUICIDE
  IS ABOUT AS SCIENTIFIC AS MAKING SUICIDE THE FIRST LAW +   523 5
  MURDER SUICIDE RAPE   531 4
  AFTER THAT OF COURSE THERE'S SUICIDE CERTAIN ASPECTS   532 26
  YES I SHOULD SAY THE CONTEMPLATION OF CLEVER SUICIDE IS   532 28

SUIT
  THE SAME UNREMARKABLE SUNDAY SUIT   312 16
  AND GREY-STRIPED SUIT A YOUNG CUB OF A PIKE   338 2
  IT'S SO EASY TO FOLLOW SUIT   462 18
  SO IF MAUDIE DOESN'T SUIT US   573 17

SUITES
  USUALLY IN SUITES   657 10

SUITS
  WITH HIBISCUS FLOWERS IN THE BUTTONHOLES OF YOUR SUNDAY+   314 11
  IN SUNDAY SUITS AND YELLOW BOOTS ALONG THE CORSO   314 33
  IN SUNDAY SUITS AND YELLOW SHOES   316 21
  TO THE YOUTHS IN SUNDAY SUITS AND YELLOW SHOES   317 28

SULK
  AND THE SEA IS ALIVE AND CAN SULK   625 14
  AND AH MY BITTER BREASTS THAT SULK AND FRET   *933 32

SULKED
  HIS EYES AND HE SULKED HE HAD ANOTHER LOVER   735 2

SULKILY
  HE STAYED WITH THE HORSES SULKILY   735 11

SULKING
  ALL THE FRUITS ARE SULKING IN THE WET   *933 30

SULKS
  THE EVENING SULKS ALONG THE SHORE THE REDDENING SUN   625 10

SULKY
  AND LOOKED SULKY UNDER HER THICK STRAIGHT BROWS   617 20
  WITH SAVAGE BLACK EYES IS SULKY AND ALL THE TIME   734 18
  SULKY IN SPIRIT AND INERT   795 7
  AS SULKY AN' ORMIN' AS THINE HAST OWT TO SAY OTHERWISE   *925 25

SULLEN
  YOURS IS THE SULLEN SORROW   111 8
  OVER A SULLEN SEA   201 16
  THERE'S NO RELIEF ONLY A MOMENT'S SULLEN RESPITE   486 4

SULLEN-HEARTED
  FOR YOU ARE SULLEN-HEARTED STILL AND LACK   153 18

SULLENLY
  I CARRY MY PATIENCE SULLENLY THROUGH THE WASTE LANDS   167 3
  I CARRY MY PATIENCE SULLENLY THROUGH THE WASTE LANDS   167 16
  I CARRY MY ANGER SULLENLY 'CROSS THESE WASTE LANDS   *896 21

SULLEN-STAGNATING
  RAGE OF THE SULLEN-STAGNATING ATMOSPHERE OF GOATS   381 24

SULLIED
  MY ALTARS SULLIED I BEREFT REMAIN   151 20

SULPHUR
  THE AIR IS DARK WITH NORTH AND WITH SULPHUR THE GRASS IS   148 24
  EVEN THE SULPHUR AURICULAS   270 8
  DO YOU TAKE THE WHISPER OF SULPHUR FROM THE AIR   301 8
  SULPHUR SUN-BEASTS   340 7
  OF VICTORY KNEADED WITH SULPHUR   758 21

SULTRY
  HE IS WORDLESS BUT SULTRY AND VAST   39 15

SUM
  IS THIS THE SUM OF YOU   57 4
  THIS SUM OF DELIGHT   *935 17

SUM ERGO COGITO
  SUM ERGO COGITO   840 10

SUM ERGO NON COGITO
  SUM ERGO NON COGITO   439 18

SUMMAT
  HE WED HE'D HA'E SUMMAT GOOD   77 28
  'ER GEN ME SUMMAT I SHANNA   84 7
  LAD SHOULD I TELL THEE SUMMAT   137 19
  LAD BUT I'M TELLIN' THEE SUMMAT   137 24
  'ARK THA'RT FOR HEARIN' SUMMAT   137 26
  YI BUT I'M TELLIN' THEE SUMMAT   137 31
  NOW LAD I'M AXIN' THEE SUMMAT   138 2
  AREN'T TER HEARIN' SUMMAT   138 7
  THA WERT FRIT O' SUMMAT   138 9
  YI BUT THA'RT FRIT O' SUMMAT   138 13
  THA'RT DAUNTED OR SUMMAT   138 15
  OR DEAR O' ME SAY SUMMAT   138 19
  HE WED HE'D HA'E SUMMAT GOOD   *919 16

SUMMED
  IS SUMMED UP IN A NICE NARROW-GUTTED OLD MAID   584 4

SUMMER
  WATCH THE BOYS IN THEIR SUMMER BLOUSES   51 11
  AND TRODDEN THAT THE HAPPY SUMMER YIELDS   135 8
  AND HAPPY AS RAIN IN SUMMER WHY SHOULD IT BE SO   141 25
  THE MOUNTAIN'S NEW-DROPPED SUMMER SNOW IS CLEAR   225 2
  COME AND LIFT US TO OUR END TO BLOSSOM BRING US TO OUR + 272 33
  INCIPIENT PURPLING TOWARDS SUMMER IN THE WORLD OF THE H+ 273 25
  ALL THE SPORT OF SUMMER AND SPRING AND FLOWERS SNAPPING 309 18
  AND A FLOWER IT TAKES A SUMMER   477 6
  IN SUMMER AND LOVE BUT UNDERNEATH IS ROCK   477 9
  YET LOOKING IN A GREAT FULL LIME-TREE OF SUMMER   650 21
  IN THE SUMMER MORNING   655 10
  IN COLD BLOOD I CANNOT FEEL GODDESSES IN THE SUMMER EVE+ 655 18
  AND WHEN IN THE SUMMER EVENING   655 26
  THE SUMMER AND THE SNOWS THE WILD WELTER OF EARTH 707 29
  LIKE SEALS IN SUNNY SUMMER THEY HIE   825 15
  WATCH THE BOYS IN THEIR SUMMER BLOUSES   *898 23
  WATCH THE BOYS IN THEIR SUMMER BLOUSES   *902 7
  ONCE I KNEW A SUMMER THAT SPARKLED   *933 14
  AH WHERE HIS MOUTH'S RED SUMMER AND WHERE IS NOW THE YE+ *933 27

SUMMER-HAPPY
  AND WE'RE GOING TO BE SUMMER-HAPPY   244 19

SUMMERING
  SOFT AS A SUMMERING TREE   56 8

SUMMER-KIND
  AND SUMMER-KIND   244 20

SUMMERS
  EIGHTY SUMMERS   502 21

SUMMER'S
  YOUR OWN SELF THAT HAS PASSED LIKE A LAST SUMMER'S 478 24

SUMMER-WHITE
  ALONG THE FLAGGED CLEAN PAVEMENT SUMMER-WHITE   36 2

SUMMERY
  THEIR ABUNDANT SUMMERY WORDAGE SILENCED CAUGHT   142 2
  UNDER THE SUMMERY FLOWERING OF THE ROSES OF LOVE *951 12

SUMMIT
  LEAPS UP TO THE SUMMIT OF THE STEM GLEAMS TURNS OVER 476 8

SUMMON
  AND WHEN YOUR STIFLING SOUL WOULD SUMMON   91 10

SUMMONED
  THE PUEBLO SUMMONED THE OLD INDIAN MEN AND   777 26

SUMMONS
  SILENCE FULL OF SUMMONS   40 2
  ROYAL SUMMONS DIENT IHR   390 21
  SENDS SUMMONS IN THE OLD HOLLOWS OF THE SUN   623 8
  THERE ARE OTHER WAYS OF SUMMONS CRYING LISTEN LISTEN CO+ 623 23

SUMPTUOUS
  SUMPTUOUS CENTRAL GRAIN   124 12
  MYSTERY BEYOND KNOWLEDGE OR ENDURANCE SO SUMPTUOUS 260 30
  HELL RISEN IN PURSUIT OF HER ROYAL SUMPTUOUS   308 15
  BUT IF YOU WANT TO BREATHE DEEP SUMPTUOUS LIFE   698 3
  SUMPTUOUS CENTRAL GRAIN   *935 11
  VERY SUMPTUOUS WITH THE MONEY OF SIR JESSE BOOT OF CASH+ *950 14

SUMPTUOUSLY
  THE BUSHES SUMPTUOUSLY   126 26

SUN
  SUN BUT IN SUBSTANCE YELLOW WATER-BLOBS   34 25
  TO THE SUN AND THE SWALLOWS CUT CLEAR   35 4
  INTO THE SETTING SUN IF SHE CAME TO ME HERE   35 5
  SAW WHERE MORNING SUN ON THE SHAKEN IRIS GLISTENED 38 16
  FLATLY ASSUMING THE SUN   50 24
  THE BLINDS ARE DRAWN BECAUSE OF THE SUN   51 5
  THE SUN AND THE RAIN DO NOT ASK THE SECRET   63 18
  THE SUN FROM THEIR NEIGHBOUR EITHER NOR BE SMOTHERED IN+ 93 22
  THE HOAR-FROST CRUMBLES IN THE SUN   100 1
  'TIS THE SUN THAT ASKS THE QUESTION IN A LOVELY HASTE F+ 119 29
  DID YOU SEE THE WICKED SUN THAT WINKED   120 9
  YES SAY IT FOR SURE FROM THE GOLDEN SUN   127 1
  THE EDGE OF THE BLUE AND THE SUN STANDS UP TO SEE US GL+ 132 28
  WHO FOR YEARS WAS SUN FOR YOUR SHIVERING SHADE FOR YOUR 157 2

SUN
  THE SUN SHINES   162 1
  THE SUN IS BLEEDING ITS FIRES UPON THE MIST   164 17
  THE TOWN HAS OPENED TO THE SUN   166 16
  AS SHE GENTLY EXHALES TO THE SUN   166 21
  A DARK BIRD FALLS FROM THE SUN   166 25
  THE SUN SETS OUT THE AUTUMN CROCUSES   177 1
  AND THE SUN LOOKS THROUGH   178 15
  THE SUN WARMS THE SEA LITTLE LONELY AND SAD SIFTING THE+ 180 3
  THE SUN IMMENSE AND ROSY   193 14
  THE CONSTELLATIONS YOUR GREAT HEART THE SUN   194 24
  WITH HIS BACK TO THE SUN HOLDS OUT   200 10
  NO NO I DANCE IN THE SUN I'M A THING OF LIFE   211 16
  THE SHADOWS THAT LIVE IN THE SUN   215 21
  TURNS ROUND ITS BACK TO THE SUN   215 23
  THE SKY WAS GREEN WINE HELD UP IN THE SUN   216 14
  THE YELLOW SUN STEPS OVER THE MOUNTAIN-TOP   230 5
  THEY ARE LAYING THE GOLDEN RACING-TRACK OF THE SUN 230 9
  THE SUN IS IN MY EYES I MUST GET UP   230 11
  THE SEED-BALL OF THE SUN   253 15
  NO SUN WILL EVER RISE   253 21
  THE SUN OF THEIR RIGHTEOUSNESS   288 20
  THE SUN SETS IN YOU   289 25
  OUT OF THE EARTH BEFORE THE SUN WAS SPREAD OUT AND BEFO+ 295 5
  INTENT TO HOLD THE CANDLE OF THE SUN UPON ITS SOCKET-TIP 299 29
  TO HOLD THE ONE AND ONLY LIGHTED CANDLE OF THE SUN IN H+ 299 34
  AND HOLD THE LIGHTED CANDLE OF THE SUN   300 1
  DO YOU HEAR THE CHEMICAL ACCENTS OF THE SUN   301 9
  SUN DARK SUN   301 18
  SUN OF BLACK VOID HEAT   301 19
  SUN OF THE TORRID MID-DAY'S HORRIFIC DARKNESS   301 20
  HAVE YOU NOT SEEN IN THE WILD WINTER SUN OF THE SOUTHER+ 303 4
  AND JANUARY'S LOUD-SEEMING SUN   306 13
  BUT LATER IN THE SUN OF THE AFTERNOON   324 10
  AND THE SUN COMING IN THROUGH THE NARROWEST FIBRIL OF A+ 324 13
  THE SUN COMES IN THEIR LAIR THEY ARE WELL-OFF   325 17
  AS AN EAGLE STARING DOWN ON THE SUN   328 22
  THAT THE SUN IS MORE THAN BURNING MORE THAN THE BURNING+ 331 6
  THE SUN LIVES IN HIS SHINING AND IS NOT LIKE FIRES THAT+ 331 9
  WHEN THE SUN FROM THE WEST BEYOND PISA BEYOND THE 340 18
  NOR THE GOD OF BATS WHILE THE SUN SHINES   346 17
  WAS MOIST AND COLD THE SUN IN HIM DARTED UNEASY HELD DO+ 348 8
  POISON IN HIS MOUTH FOR THE SUN IN HIM WOULD FAIN RISE + 348 10
  THE TOUCH OF SUN EXCITES YOU   353 1
  THE THOUGHTS OF THE SKIES THE EAGLE FLIES NEAREST TO TH+ 368 2
  SO HE BRINGS DOWN THE LIFE OF THE SUN AND THE POWER OF + 368 4
  THE SUN BUT ALL CREATURES OF THE SUN MUST DIP THEIR MOU+ 368 6
  THE SUN IS FOREVER THIRSTY THIRSTING FOR THE BRIGHTEST + 368 7
  NOT THE EAGLE SCREAMS WHEN THE SUN IS HIGH THE PEACOCK + 368 10
  FOR THE SUN TO RISE   371 21
  TOWARDS THE SUN TOWARDS THE SOUTH-WEST   372 25
  A SCORCHED BREAST BREASTING THE SUN LIKE AN ANSWER 372 27
  REFLECTING THE SCORCH OF THE SUN FROM HIS BREAST 373 3
  YOU NEVER LOOK AT THE SUN WITH YOUR TWO EYES   373 23
  LOOKS STRAIGHT AT THE SUN   373 25
  AS IF YOU OWED HIM AN OLD OLD GRUDGE GREAT SUN OR AN OLD 374 3
  DO YOU LIFT IT TO THE SUN AS THE AZTEC PRIESTS USED TO + 374 7
  DOES THE SUN NEED STEAM OF BLOOD DO YOU THINK   374 9
  DOES THE SUN IN NEW MEXICO SAIL LIKE A FIERY BIRD OF PR+ 374 12
  IS YOUR CONTINENT COLD FROM THE ICE-AGE STILL THAT THE + 374 21
  THAT THE SUN SHOULD BE GREEDY FOR IT   374 24
  NOR YOU NOR YOUR BLOOD-THIRSTY SUN   374 26
  EVEN THE SUN IN HEAVEN CAN BE CURBED AND CHASTENED AT L+ 374 32
  OBSTACLE TO SET HIS TEETH IN THE SUN   378 7
  IN A LEAP AT THE SUN   379 14
  FLAT BROWN ROCKS TO WATCH THE FERRY IN THE SUN   386 24
  WHERE NOTHING BITES BUT INSECTS AND SNAKES AND THE SUN 394 14
  THE SUN AS HE WAITS A MOMENT HUGE AND LIQUID   403 4
  NOW THAT THE SUN HAS GONE AND THE ASPEN LEAVES   403 14
  THAT HAS FOLLOWED THE SUN FROM THE DAWN THROUGH THE EAST 404 14
  TROTTING EAST AND EAST AND EAST TILL THE SUN HIMSELF WE+ 404 15
  SINCE I TROTTED AT THE TAIL OF THE SUN AS FAR AS EVER T+ 405 26
  WHILE THE SUN GOES ROUND   407 3
  AND THOUGH THE SUN LEAPS LIKE A THING UNLEASHED IN THE + 408 21
  NOW IN NOVEMBER NEARER COMES THE SUN   455 12
  THE SUN IN ME DECLINES TO HIS WINTER SOLSTICE   455 17
  BACK TO THE OLD YEAR'S SUN ACROSS THE SEA   455 19
  AS THE SUN OF MY SOUL IS SETTING   455 21
  WINTER AND THE GREAT DAY-SUN AND THE SUN IN MY SOUL 455 26
  MY SUN AND THE GREAT GOLD SUN   455 29
  LINGERS BEHIND AS THE YELLOW SUN GLARES AND IS GONE BEY+ 467 6
  THE EARTH LEANS ITS WEIGHT ON THE SUN AND THE SUN ON THE 480 19
  SUN OF SUNS   480 20
  TOWARDS THE SUN OF SUNS AND BACK AND FORTH GOES THE BRE+ 480 24
  OUT OF THE SOUL'S MIDDLE TO THE MIDDLE-MOST SUN WAY-OFF 480 26
  CONTACT WITH THE SUN OF SUNS   481 13
  GLORY IS OF THE SUN TOO AND THE SUN OF SUNS   496 10
  PEACE COMES FROM BEHIND THE SUN WITH THE PEREGRINE FALC+ 496 15
  AND ITS PLUMES LOOK LIKE GREEN CUPS HELD UP TO THE SUN + 498 22
  I KNOW I AM NOBLE WITH THE NOBILITY OF THE SUN   499 1
  MY BODY LIKES ITS DINNER AND THE WARM SUN BUT OTHERWISE+ 501 19
  A MEETING PLACE FOR SUN AND RAIN   504 17
  A SUN WILL RISE IN ME   513 11
  A SUN IN ME   513 14
  AND BEYOND THAT THE IMMENSE SUN BEHIND THE SUN   513 ,16
  THE SUN OF IMMENSE DISTANCES THAT FOLD THEMSELVES TOGET+ 513 17
  AND FURTHER THE SUN WITHIN THE ATOM   513 19
  AND I CALL IT THE SUN   525 6
  FROM THE WILD HEART OF SPACE THAT I CALL THE SUN OF SUNS 525 9
  EACH ONE TURNING HIS BREAST STRAIGHT TO THE SUN OF SUNS 525 12
  AND FROM HIS OWN LITTLE INWARD SUN   525 14
  BUT TO THE SUN   525 27
  WITH SUN IN HIS FACE SO THAT A WOMAN CANNOT BUT OPEN 526 4
  LIKE A MARIGOLD TO THE SUN   526 5
  I AM A DEMOCRAT IN SO FAR AS I LOVE THE FREE SUN IN MEN 526 7
  I LOVE THE SUN IN ANY MAN   526 10
  TO BE AN ARISTOCRAT OF THE SUN   526 25
  YOU DRAW YOUR NOBILITY DIRECT FROM THE SUN   526 27

SUN
  FROM THE SUN   527   2
  NOT TO GO AGAINST THE SUN   527 12
  THEY HAVE UTTERLY NO REFERENCE TO THE SUN   527 17
  NO SUN NO EARTH   528   1
  AND BUSY PUTTING OUT THE SUN   528   8
  THE MEN STOOD AROUND LIKE CROCUSES AGAPE IN THE SUN   540   4
  A TRUST OF THE SUN   561   9
  THE SUN IN ME   561 20
  A SUN TO ME   561 29
  BUT A SUN THAT SHINES   562   1
  AND EVEN THE SEA IS SILENT IN THE SUN   605 25
  SOMETIMES THE SUN TURNS HOSTILE TO MEN   608 20
  THEN THE SUN TURNS HOSTILE TO US   609   1
  THEN WE SUFFER AND THOUGH THE SUN BRONZES US   609   4
  BIRTH OF THE SUN   616 22
  SENDS SUMMONS IN THE OLD HOLLOWS OF THE SUN   623   8
  SINGING BETWEEN THE SUN AND THE MARSH   623 18
SUN   623 28
  WILL SWEEP ROUND AND UP TO GREET THE SUN WITH A SILKY G+   625   4
  THE EVENING SULKS ALONG THE SHORE THE REDDENING SUN   625 10
  LET ME TELL YOU THAT THE SUN IS ALIVE AND CAN BE ANGRY   625 13
  IN MYRIADS UNDER THE HOT AND HOSTILE SUN   628   7
  AND OLEANDER IS HOT WITH PERFUME UNDER THE AFTERNOON SUN   630   3
  YOU TO WHOM THAT THE SUN IS MERELY SOMETHING THAT MAKES THE   643 13
  DARKLY FROM THE FECUND COSMOS FROM THE ANGRY RED SUN FR+   675 11
  SUN AND MOON   675 21
  WHO MADE THE SUN   681 22
  AS THE PEACOCK TURNS TO THE SUN AND COULD NOT BE MORE S+   683   8
  FOR THE SUN IS HOSTILE NOW   684 14
  NOW THAT THE SUN LIKE A LION LICKS HIS PAWS   687 13
  IS IN HER EXALTATION AND CAN LOOK DOWN ON THE SUN   688 11
  MEN SINGING SONGS AND WOMEN BRUSHING THEIR HAIR IN THE +   691 24
  GOD IS OLDER THAN THE SUN AND MOON   692   7
  GOD IS OLDER THAN THE SUN AND MOON   692 18
SUN   695 27
  FOR THE SUN IS DEAD AND ALL THAT IS IN HEAVEN   702 23
  SALT IS SCORCHED WATER THAT THE SUN HAS SCORCHED   705 19
  AND THE INSISTENCE OF THE SUN   707 30
  AND SOME OF TOO MUCH SUN BRACKISH SWEET   708   3
  AND IN THE SHADOW OF THE SUN THE SNOW IS BLUE SO BLUE-A+   708 28
  LIKE NOW WHERE THE WHITE SUN KISSES THE SEA   709   9
  ABSOLUTE ABSOLVED FROM THE SUN AND THE EARTH AND THE MO+   712 16
  FOR EVERY REVOLUTION OF THE EARTH AROUND THE SUN   713 12
  FOR THE EARTH LIKE THE SUN IS A WANDERER   713 16
  THE MOON AND THE EARTH THE SUN SATURN AND BETELGEUSE   713 20
  HOW TERRIBLE THE SUN WOULD BE   724 15
  BUT THE VERY SUN HIMSELF IS PIVOTED   724 17
  GO FORWARD SUN DO NOT TORMENT US   750   4
  THE MOON IS NOT ANY WARMER THE SUN NO   754   5
  SALLY GO ROUND THE SUN   755 22
  THE SUN IS GONE FROM MID-HEAVEN THE SOLDIERS ARE GONE F+   757   1
  THE SUN HAS CREPT LIKE A SCARLET BEETLE IN THE HUSK   757 15
  WHO LABOURS ALL DAY IN THE SUN   758 12
  BUT MASCULINE AS THE SUN   764   6
  WAITING FOR THE SUN TO RISE ON YOU   764   7
  TOWARDS THE SUN TO SOUTH-WEST   781   1
  YOU ONLY STARE AT THE SUN WITH THE ONE BROAD EYE OF YOUR   781 29
  OH YES YOU FACE THE SUN   782   1
  AT THE TOP OF YOUR BREAST   782   6
  WHERE HE STARES AT THE SUN   782 24
  DO YOU SEE THE GOLD SUN FLUTTERING BUOYANTLY IN HEAVEN   782 29
  AND IS THE SUN YOUR FIRST-BORN ONLY-BEGOTTEN   782 33
  THE GOLD SUN SHINES IN HEAVEN ONLY BECAUSE HE'S ALLOWED   783   1
  SENT OUT THE SUN SO THAT SOMETHING SHOULD FLUTTER IN HE+   783   4
  DARK-MASKED-ONE DAY-STARER THREATENING THE SUN WITH YOUR   783 11
  WILL YOU STRIKE AT THE HEART OF THE SUN WITH YOUR BLOOD+   783 17
  BEHIND THE SUN LOOKING THROUGH HIM AS A WINDOW   786   6
  HOLD BACK THE DRAGON OF THE SUN   786 20
  I BOUND THE BRIGHT FANGS OF THE SUN   786 23
  PAST THE MOUNT OF THE SUN   787   4
  HOLD BACK THE WILD HOT SUN   789 13
  THEN HE LAUGHED SEEING THE SUN DART FIERCELY AT HIM   790   1
  HE PUT UP HIS HAND AND HELD BACK THE SUN WITH HIS SHADOW   790   2
  FOR THE SUN AND THE MOON ARE ALIVE AND WATCHING WITH GL+   792 10
  THE STARS AND THE EARTH AND THE SUN AND THE MOON AND TH+   792 17
  FOR SUN AND STARS AND EARTH AND THE VERY RAINS ARE WEARY   792 20
  THIS IS WHAT STARS AND SUN AND EARTH AND MOON AND WINDS+   793   3
  THERE ARE DEAD THAT ATTACK THE SUN LIKE SWARMS OF BLACK+   795 28
  THERE ARE DRAGONS OF SUN AND ICE DRAGONS OF THE MOON AN+   796 18
  THE SUN HAS CLIMBED THE HILL THE DAY IS ON THE DOWNWARD+   803   5
  THE DARK IS DIVIDING THE SUN IS COMING PAST THE WALL   803 12
  THE SUN IS IN THE OUTER PORCH CRY TO HIM THANKS OH THAN+   803 21
  YELLOW OF THE SUN   804   8
  SUN IN THE BLOOD   804   9
  THE GRASS FEELS WITH HIS ROOTS FOR THE OTHER SUN   804 21
  IS THE YELLOW SERPENT-YELLOW SHINING OF MY SUN   805   3
  YELLOW OF THE SUN   805 16
  SUN IN THE BLOOD   805 17
  SHINES THE YELLOW SERPENT-YELLOW SHINING OF THE SUN   806   6
  THE POWER IS IN ME FROM BEHIND THE SUN   806 19
  TODAY WHEN THE SUN IS COMPUTED OLD   814   7
  AND THIS SUN CEASE SHINING OVERHEAD   815 11
  THE HOT SUN WAXES AND HEALS   824 29
  WE FEEL THE SUN   825 28
  WITH SUN AND WITH WETNESS   826 14
  SUN AND INERTIA ON THE BELLY ON THE BACK   827 14
  THE SUN IS SO LOVELY   840   1
  IF A MAN LOOKED AT ME FOR ONE MOMENT AS THE SUN DOES   840   2
  DOWN THE RIVER IN THE GLEAM OF THE SUN   867 32
  THE SUN SETS WIDE THE YELLOW CROCUSES   868 17
  AS THE SUN COMES IN THE BATHROOM   870   3
  I FEEL THE SUN ON ME   870   6
  TOGETHER WE TRODE THE EVENING WHERE THE SUN   884 23
  ONLY YOU LIKE THE SUN   888 10
  SEE THE MORNING SUN ON THE SHAKEN IRIS GLISTEN   *892 31
  FOR THE SUN IS POURING LIKE YELLOW WINE OUTSIDE   *894 24
  STILL IN THE SUN TO WATCH AND I CAN SEE   *895   2

SUN
  THE BLINDS ARE DRAWN BECAUSE OF THE SUN   *898 17
  THE BLINDS ARE DRAWN BECAUSE OF THE SUN   *902   1
  MINE WAS THE LOVE OF THE SUN FOR THE FLOWER   *927   4
  MINE WAS THE LOVE OF THE SUN FOR A FLOWER   *928   4
  THE HOURS PECKED PLEASURE FROM ME AND THE SUN DELIGHTED+   *933 19
  WHERE IS THE SUN I CANNOT UNDERSTAND   *933 20
  THE SUN SETS WIDE THE YELLOW CROCUSES   *941 17
  AS EARTH LEANS ON THE SUN   *952   5
  THE UNROLLING OF FERNS WHILE TONGUES OF ACANTHUS LAPPIN+   *953 15

SUN-ARISTOCRATS
  AND SUN-ARISTOCRATS   527   6

SUN-AWARENESS
  IS SUN-AWARENESS   527 10

SUNBEAMS
  UP THE WARM GRASS WHERE THE SUNBEAMS START   46   8
  AND THE SUNBEAMS CATCH HER   217 12
  THE SUNBEAMS HAVE FILLED ME LIKE A HONEYCOMB   803   9
  SUNBEAMS LUSTY AND CLEAN FROM THE BATH OF NIGHT   856 16
  AND THE SUNBEAMS CATCH HER   *942 22

SUN-BEASTS
  SULPHUR SUN-BEASTS   340   7

SUNBLACK
  SUNBLACK MEN   301 28

SUN-BLAZE
  THE SUN-BLAZE OF THE DESERT   781   4

SUNBREASTER
  SUNBREASTER   781 18

SUN-BREASTER
  SUN-BREASTER   373 12

SUNBREATHING
  SOFT SHAFTS SUNBREATHING MOUTHS   301 29

SUN-BRIGHT
  OR SUN-BRIGHT APOLLO HIM SO MUSICAL   307 25
  AND FLASHES ALL HERSELF AS SUN-BRIGHT   *943   8

SUNBURNT
  SURELY ABOUT HIS SUNBURNT FACE IS SOMETHING   225 17
  AND SUNBURNT AND WATER-WASHED FULL-FED AND SLEEK   827 11

SUNDAY
  TO THE OLD SUNDAY EVENINGS AT HOME WITH WINTER OUTSIDE   148 12
  SUNDAY MORNING   312   9
  THE SAME UNREMARKABLE SUNDAY SUIT   312 16
  ALAS THE SUNDAY COATS OF SICILIAN BOLSHEVISTS   313 34
  WITH HIBISCUS FLOWERS IN THE BUTTONHOLES OF YOUR SUNDAY+   314 11
  ALONG THE CORSO ALL THIS SUNDAY MORNING   314 29
  IN SUNDAY SUITS AND YELLOW BOOTS ALONG THE CORSO   314 33
  IN SUNDAY SUITS AND YELLOW SHOES   316 21
  TO THE YOUTHS IN SUNDAY SUITS AND YELLOW SHOES   317 28
  IN HIS SUNDAY CLOTHES   552 20
  THEN WHEN SUNDAY COMES IT SHALL GO TATTAH WITH ITS AUNT+   571   5
  ON SUNDAY AFTERNOON   755 25
  SUNDAY AFTER SUNDAY THEY CARRIED HIM TREMBLING TO HIS P+   859 13
  TO THE OLD SUNDAY EVENINGS WHEN DARKNESS WANDERED OUTSI+   *940 11

SUNDAY-SCHOOL SQUIRE
  OH LONDON'S MERCURY SUNDAY-SCHOOL SQUIRE   681   1

SUNDER
  THAT SUNDER US FROM EACH OTHER   709 16

SUNDERERS
  BUT ALSO THE SUNDERERS THE ANGELS WITH BLACK SHARP WING+   706 23
  BECAUSE NOW THE SUNDERERS ARE HOVERING AROUND   707   2
  TO THE SUNDERERS TO THE SWIFT ONES   707   8
  LO WE ARE IN THE MIDST OF THE SUNDERERS   707 16
  IT IS THE DAY OF THE SUNDERERS   707 24
  FOR DOOM THAT DARKENS AND THE SUNDERERS   709 15
  THE THUNDERERS AND THE SUNDERERS HAVE THEIR TERM   709 23
  LIFE IS FOR THE ANGELS AND THE SUNDERERS   709 26
  THE ANGELS AND THE SUNDERERS   710   1

SUN-DIMMED
  THE STARS IN THEIR SUN-DIMMED CLOSES   242 29

SUNDOWN
  THE NEW MOON SETS AT SUNDOWN   816   5

SUN-EXTINCT
  SUN-EXTINCT   528   7

SUN-FLECK-SCATTERED
  ALL MY MORNING'S PLEASURE IN THE SUN-FLECK-SCATTERED WO+   65 14

SUNG
  ROCKED ON THE WAVE AND SUNG LUSTILY   575   8

SUN-GENTLER
  SOME MEMORY OF FAR SUN-GENTLER LANDS   305 33

SUN-GLARE
  WITH ALL THE SNOW-WIND AND THE SUN-GLARE AND THE DOG-ST+   306 18

SUN-GLORY
    AND WALKING EACH IN HIS OWN SUN-GLORY   525 20

SUN-HEAVY
    THE GLIMMER OF THE LIMES SUN-HEAVY SLEEPING   35 26

SUNK
    WITH A SUNK UNCONSCIOUS HEAD   58 31
    WHO SUNK HIS HANDS IN FIRMNESS DOWN THY SIDES   69 10
    THE SEA AND THE SKY WENT GREY AS IF THERE HAD SUNK   98 12
    COLD THAT HAD SUNK TO MY SOUL AND THERE KEPT HOLD   98 25
    SHE SUNK INTO MY SIGHT LIKE A SETTLING BIRD   123 8
    A STRICKEN WIFE SO SUNK IN OBLIVION BOWED   155 30
    MUST HAVE SUNK AND BECOME EXTINCT   193 15
    AND SUNK INTO DEPRESSION THAT ALMOST BLOTS ME OUT   629 21
    THE CRIME FULL-EXPIATE THE ERINNYES SUNK   743 25
    YOU GO ABOUT IN A DREAM WITH YOUR COUNTENANCE SUNK   755 4
    THE EVENING SHADOW HAS SUNK   758 3
    IS DEAD AT LAST THEN HIS POOR SUNK FLAME MUST FLICKER   859 3
    HE SUNK HIS HANDS IN FIRMNESS DOWN THY SIDES   *915 22
    SHE SUNK INTO MY SIGHT LIKE A SETTLING BIRD   *934 14

SUNKEN
    NOW THE SUNKEN SWATHS   35 2
    WITH HER WHITENESS REVEALING MY SUNKEN WORLD   103 29
    WHITE PEAKS OF SNOW AT THE FOOT OF THE SUNKEN CHRIST   225 30
    WITH SUNKEN HEAD AND FORGOTTEN FOLDED HANDS   232 25
    LIKE A SUNKEN FLAME THAT GRASPS FOR SUPPORT   246 29

SUNKIST
    AND TREMBLING SOMEWHERE DEEP IN THEIR SUNKIST GLOOM   868 27

SUNLESS
    SO HIDEOUS AND CORPSE-LIKE UTTERLY SUNLESS   526 14
    I FEEL THAT WHEN PEOPLE HAVE GONE UTTERLY SUNLESS   526 23
    ARE SUNLESS   527 14
    I AM DARK AS THE SUNLESS UNDER-EARTH   806 22

SUNLIGHT
    LITTLE JETS OF SUNLIGHT TEXTURE IMITATING FLAME   33 2
    TO LET THE SUNLIGHT IN AND I   51 9
    AND VERY SWEET IT IS WHILE THE SUNLIGHT WAVES   51 21
    WHERE THE SUNLIGHT SOAKS IN THE STONE THE AFTERNOON   52 13
    THE MELLOW SUNLIGHT STOOD AS IN A CUP   122 26
    PASSING ACROSS THE SHADOW INTO THE SUNLIGHT   210 9
    OUT OF SUNLIGHT TO SHADOW   210 10
    IN THE WINDOW FULL OF SUNLIGHT   217 23
    AM A SUNLIGHT UPON THEM THAT SHINES THEM INTO BEING   245 19
    I WAS A TIGER BURSTING INTO SUNLIGHT   259 12
    BUT IT MAKES THE SUNLIGHT BEAT   746 10
    THOUGH ALL THE CROWDED SUNLIGHT JOSTLING   771 19
    TO LET THE SUNLIGHT IN AND I   *898 21
    AND VERY SWEET WHILE THE SUNLIGHT WAVES   *899 4
    TO LET THE SUNLIGHT IN AND I   *902 5
    AND VERY SWEET WHILE THE SUNLIGHT WAVES   *902 16
    WHERE THE SUNLIGHT SOAKS IN THE STONE THE AFTERNOON   *905 2
    THE MELLOW SUNLIGHT STOOD AS IN A CUP   *934 2
    IN THE WINDOW FULL OF SUNLIGHT   *943 6

SUNLIGHT-TEXTURE
    LITTLE JETS OF SUNLIGHT-TEXTURE IMITATING FLAME   *891 2

SUNLIT
    OVER MY SUNLIT SKIN THE WARM CLINGING AIR   *892 1

SUN-LIT
    THE SUN-LIT FLIRT WHO ALL THE DAY   42 11

SUN-MEN
    OF SUN-MEN   525 11

SUNNED
    AND SUNNED HIS WHISKERS   324 6
    LIKE LAGOON-WATER THAT HAS BEEN TOO MUCH SUNNED   708 4

SUNNINESSES
    TOWARDS THE BREATHING STARS AND THE CENTRAL OF ALL SUNN+ 480 18

SUNNY
    AND I REMEMBER STILL THE SUNNY HOURS   135 25
    NEW SUNNY STREAMS OF BLOOD   240 8
    SUNNY   527 5
    FOR NO LIVE SUNNY MAN WOULD BE A CENSOR   528 12
    AND MORE SUNNY   562 7
    LIKE SEALS IN SUNNY SUMMER THEY HIE   825 15
    WE HAVE FORGOTTEN THE SUNNY APPLES OF DAY THAT WE CRAVE+*917 15
    BUT I REMEMBER STILL THE SUNNY HOURS   *939 17
    IN THE SUNNY ROOM   *954 20
    OF GENTIANS HERE IN THE SUNNY ROOM   *955 3
    OF GENTIANS HERE IN THE SUNNY ROOM   *955 24

SUNNY-SWIFT
    FRESH QUIVERING KEEP THE SUNNY-SWIFT MARCH-DAYS WAITING 179 5

SUN-PEERING
    SUN-PEERING EAGLE   328 3

SUN-RAYS
    THERE AMONG THE DARK SUN-RAYS OF DEATH   677 14

SUNRISE
    HE WAS BORN IN FRONT OF MY SUNRISE   339 20

SUN-ROUND
    THE UPSTART OF YOUR ROUND-BARRED SUN-ROUND TAIL   370 21

SUNS
    FOR ALL THAT THE SETTING SUNS ARE OPEN   278 24
    SUN OF SUNS   480 20
    TOWARDS THE SUN OF SUNS AND BACK AND FORTH GOES THE BRE+ 480 24
    CONTACT WITH THE SUN OF SUNS   481 13
    STARS AND SUNS   482 7
    GLORY IS OF THE SUN TOO AND THE SUN OF SUNS   496 10
    AND THE SUNS   514 18
    FROM THE WILD HEART OF SPACE THAT I CALL THE SUN OF SUNS 525 9
    EACH ONE TURNING HIS BREAST STRAIGHT TO THE SUN OF SUNS 525 12
    THE VAST GREAT REACHES BETWEEN THE SUNS   823 23
    INTO ROLLICKING SUNS AND THEIR LOST GOLD ROTS COMPRESSED *896 20

SUNSET
    I LOOK AT THE SWALING SUNSET   134 1
    ANOTHER TORN RED SUNSET COME TO PASS   136 4
    THEIR FINGERS IN SUNSET SHINE   168 14
    TO WHERE THE SUNSET HUNG ITS WAN GOLD CLOTHS   205 27
    THE SAME SETS THE THROSTLE AT SUNSET ON A BOUGH   272 25
    DOWN THE GOLDEN SLOPES TO SUNSET   769 30
    AND THERE BEYOND THE SUNSET QUIVERS   816 6
    OF SUNSET BUT MERGING UNNOTICED INTO THE ROSY GLIMMER   860 5
    AND FURTHER STILL 'NEATH THE SUNSET GATHER   887 28
    ANOTHER TORN RED SUNSET COME TO PASS   *938 32

SUNSHINE
    OVER MY SKIN IN THE SUNSHINE THE WARM CLINGING AIR   34 13
    TO-DAY A THICKET OF SUNSHINE WITH BLUE SMOKE-WREATHS   72 15
    FOR THE SUNSHINE   111 12
    AND QUAILING HERE IN THE SUNSHINE BETRAYED FROM HAUNTING 133 3
    AMONG CROWDS OF THINGS IN THE SUNSHINE JOSTLED AND RACK+ 133 8
    AND GLEAM AS OF SUNSHINE CROSSING THE LOW BLACK HEAP   144 25
    AS WE SIT IN THE SUNSHINE ON THE SEAT BY THE LITTLE SHR+ 204 12
    HELD STILL BENEATH THE SUNSHINE   204 18
    NO NOW I WISH THE SUNSHINE WOULD STOP   205 1
    OUT OF THE SUNSHINE INTO THE SHADOW   210 8
    YOU ARMFULS OF SUNSHINE AND YOU WON'T LET ME LIVE   211 6
    MY DEAR WHEN YOU CROSS THE STREET IN THE SUNSHINE SURELY 211 13
    NO HOW CRUEL YOU ARE YOU PEOPLE THE SUNSHINE   211 18
    WITH SHADOWS WITH YOURS I PEOPLE THE SUNSHINE   211 19
    WITH DISTANT SUNSHINE   224 11
    AND SUNSHINE FILLS ONE HIGH VALLEY BED   224 12
    THE SUNSHINE SWAM IN A SHOAL ACROSS AND ACROSS   243 22
    THEN THE SWEEPING SUNSHINE OF NOON   248 20
    CURLED UP IN THE SUNSHINE LIKE A PRINCESS   255 27
    HOW VIVID YOUR TRAVELLING SEEMS NOW IN THE TROUBLED SUN+ 354 4
    OVER THE CLODS OF THE AUTUMN WIND-CHILLED SUNSHINE   357 27
    AND HOW DELICIOUS IT IS TO FEEL SUNSHINE UPON ONE   526 1
    WITH THE SUNSHINE IN ME   562 4
    EMBEDDED IN THEM I LOOK OUT ON THE SUNSHINE OF THE SOUTH 629 31
    I CAN FEEL MYSELF UNFOLDING IN THE DARK SUNSHINE OF DEA+ 677 15
    AS FIRE BUT SOFT AS SUNSHINE SOFT AS KISSES   784 16
    MY SOUL IS HEAVY WITH SUNSHINE AND STEEPED WITH STRENGTH 803 8
    BLUSHES AND FLAUNTS IN THE SUNSHINE ABOVE   858 7
    THE AIR AND THE FLOWING SUNSHINE AND BRIGHT DUST   870 9
    NO LONGER A LARGE FLECK MOVING IN THE SUNSHINE   870 14
    BETWEEN THE DOWNS GROWS HAZY WITH SUNSHINE   886 27
    LOVED TO LIFE IN SUNSHINE   *927 5
    OH WHERE-OUT NOW HAS WANDERED THE GOLDEN HEN OF SUNSHINE *933 21
    SUNSHINE OF HIS HAIR I USED TO KISS   *933 28

SUN-SOCKET
    STILL NO DOUBT EVERY ONE OF YOU CAN BE THE SUN-SOCKET AS 300 12

SUN-STARER
    AND YOU GREAT BIRD SUN-STARER HEAVY BLACK BEAK   374 34

SUN'S
    THEIR WEB WHO SHADOW THE SUN'S GREAT GESTURES AND   197 28
    THE SUN'S DEPARTURE   347 18
    WILL YOU STRIKE THE SUN'S HEART OUT AGAIN   783 19
    IN PEACE BEYOND THE LASHING OF THE SUN'S BRIGHT TAIL   786 2

SUN-TURNED
    A SCORCHED BREAST SUN-TURNED FOREVER   781 2

SUN-WOMEN
    WE ARE SUN-WOMEN   525 24

SUP
    SUP   *925 23

SUPER-AUDIBLE
    SUPER-AUDIBLE   365 11

SUPERB
    AND THE CROSS SPROUTING ITS SUPERB AND FEARLESS FLOWERS 305 30
    HOW YOU HATE BEING LAUGHED AT MISS SUPERB   397 34
    WHERE SHAPE ON SPIRIT IN SUPERB DEGREE   872 10
    SOMEWHERE BENEATH THAT PIANO'S SUPERB SLEEK BLACK   *940 1

SUPERBLY
    TO ME THE EARTH ROLLS PONDEROUSLY SUPERBLY   288 26

SUPER-FAITH
    NAY WHAT A HEART OF DELICATE SUPER-FAITH   304 22

SUPERFICIAL
    ALL HIS EMOTIONS HIS FEELINGS THAT ARE NOT SUPERFICIAL + 830 16
    AND SUPERFICIAL ATTENTION AND CARE AND FULFILMENT OF DU+ 832 16

SUPERFLUOUS
    YES I KNOW IT'S TOO BAD OF COURSE IT'S PERFECTLY SUPERF+ 546 13

SUPER-GOTHIC
    OH AND I WISH THE HIGH AND SUPER-GOTHIC HEAVENS WOULD   287 22

SUPERIOR
    I AM THEIR SUPERIOR SALUTING THE HIBISCUS FLOWER NOT TH+   316 23
    AND OH SO SEDUCTIVELY SUPERIOR SO SEDUCTIVELY   434 5
    SUPERIOR   434 8
    SUPERIOR   434 13
    HOW NICE IT IS TO BE SUPERIOR   435 5
    BECAUSE REALLY IT'S NO USE PRETENDING ONE IS SUPERIOR   435 6
    THE TROUBLE IS EVERYBODY THINKS THEY'RE JUST AS SUPERIOR   435 10
    AS WE ARE JUST AS SUPERIOR   435 11
    AT THE BOTTOM THEY MUST KNOW WE ARE REALLY SUPERIOR   435 14
    WHILE HE STANDS ASIDE WATCHING WITH A SUPERIOR LITTLE G+   447 30
    MY MOTHER WAS A SUPERIOR SOUL   490 13
    A SUPERIOR SOUL WAS SHE   490 14
    CUT OUT TO PLAY A SUPERIOR ROLE   490 15
    SUPERIOR TO   527 21
    EXCUSE ME BUT ARE YOU A SUPERIOR PERSON   546 5
    ME YOUR WORD AND SIGNING HERE PLEASE THAT YOU ARE A SUP+   546 10
    I DECLARE I AM A SUPERIOR PERSON YES EXACTLY AND HERE I   546 16
    IF YOU WERE REALLY SUPERIOR   546 23
    REALLY SUPERIOR   546 24
    THE SUPERIOR PERSONS SOMEWHAT INFERIOR   547 30
    ARE STILL SUPERIOR   547 31
    THEY ARE STILL SUPERIOR SO THERE MUST BE SOMETHING THEY   548 1
    ARE SUPERIOR TO   548 2
    NOT SUPERIOR   548 4
    ALL MY INFERIORS ARE VERY SUPERIOR   548 7
    FORTUNATELY THOUGH SOME SUPERIOR PERSONS ARE STILL SUPE+   548 10
    TO THE QUITE SUPERIOR PERSONS WHO ARE NOT SO SUPERIOR AS   548 11
    MAY I ASK IF YOU ARE REALLY SUPERIOR   548 13
    AND IF YOU ONLY LOOK SO DISTINGUISHED AND SUPERIOR   548 18
    THERE'S A LIST KEPT OF THE TRULY SUPERIOR   548 22
    THERE ARE GREAT NUMBERS OF QUITE SUPERIOR PERSONS WHO A+   548 25
    WHO ARE VERY SUPERIOR PEOPLE   548 34
    I SAW THE WHOLE SUPERIOR   554 7
    FOR IT WASN'T A BIT SUPERIOR   554 13
    OF UPPER-CLASS SUPERIORITY THAT SUPERIOR   556 19
    THIS SUPERIOR ROT   556 24
    SUPERIOR TO EVERYONE ELSE SO DON'T START   576 13
    THE CLASSES ARE SO SUPERIOR   641 13
    AND THE MASSES ARE ALSO SUPERIOR   641 15
    THE SUPERIOR CLASSES   762 23
    WHICH THE SUPERIOR CLASSES ARE MAKING MONEY OUT OF   763 14
    ARE YOU PINING TO BE SUPERIOR   773 10
    THEY'RE ALL LOOKING SUPERIOR   773 20
    VERY SUPERIOR   774 15
    AREN'T YOU PINING TO BE CLASSY SUPERIOR UPPER   774 17
    HIMSELF SO SUPERIOR   *948 6
    HE SHOWS AN AMUSED SUPERIOR CONTEMPT AT THE PREVALENCE +   *949 4

SUPERIORITY
    I'VE NEVER GOT TO THE BOTTOM OF SUPERIORITY   435 19
    OF SUPERIORITY   547 28
    IN SUPERIORITY   548 9
    WITH SUPERIORITY   549 18
    SOME NARROW-GUTTED SUPERIORITY   555 1
    AS FAR AS ANY SUPERIORITY   556 5
    THEIR SUPERIORITY WAS MEANNESS   556 9
    OF UPPER-CLASS SUPERIORITY THAT SUPERIOR   556 19
    WITHOUT ANY DIVISION INTO INFERIORITY AND SUPERIORITY   636 4
    COLD SUPERIORITY NOR SILLY   709 31
    EVERYTHING IN THE WORLD OF CULTURE AND SUPERIORITY   763 10

SUPERIORS
    SUPERIORS   435 17

SUPER-MAGICAL
    SUPER-MAGICAL   333 26

SUPERPENETRATED
    WRITHING TWISTING SUPERPENETRATED   207 26

SUPERSCRIPTION
    LITTERING THE WAVES WITH HER OWN SUPERSCRIPTION   193 6

SUPER-SENSUAL
    YOUR BRITTLE SUPER-SENSUAL ARROGANCE   370 26

SUPERVENES
    AND A CHAOS OF IMPULSE SUPERVENES   640 10
    THEN ALL IS LOST THE ROBOT SUPERVENES   650 7

SUPPLE
    VICIOUS YOU SUPPLE BROODING SOFTLY-SWAYING PILLARS OF   297 10
    BUT PRESSING HER SUPPLE BODY INTO THE COOL DARK LEAVES   864 11
    FROM OUT HIS FINGERS FROM THAT SUPPLE STRING   877 12
    OWNING MY SUPPLE BODY A RARE GLAD THING SUPREMELY GOOD   *892 11

SUPPLIED
    SO ANOTHER HUNGER WAS SUPPLIED   265 20

SUPPLY
    LIKE ANY PRINCE SUCH STORES OF THE WORLD'S SUPPLY   264 4
    TO SUPPLY THEM WITH FARM-IMPLEMENTS   778 21
    AND IN RETURN THE GOVERNMENT WOULD SUPPLY THEM WITH   778 29

SUPPORT
    LIKE A SUNKEN FLAME THAT GRASPS FOR SUPPORT   246 29
    THE WORN ARCHES OF THEIR SPINES SUPPORT   426 3
    TO SUPPORT HER THE HYSTERICAL CAMEL   492 8
    JUST TO SUPPORT YOU AND FIND YOU MONEY   547 7
    YOU'D HAVE MONEY YOU'D HAVE IT ENOUGH TO SUPPORT YOURSE+   547 11

SUPPORTING
    HIS FULL ROUND HIPS SUPPORTING HIM ABOVE HER   868 9

SUPPOSE
    I SUPPOSE BETWEEN NOW AND THEN   199 2
    GRIEF GRIEF I SUPPOSE AND SUFFICIENT   199 29
    SUPPOSE YOU DIDN'T WANT ME I SHOULD SINK DOWN   246 7
    I SUPPOSE ULTIMATELY SHE IS ALL BEYOND ME   266 11
    WHICH I SUPPOSE IS WHY AMERICA HAS GONE DRY   286 20
    AND I DON'T SUPPOSE THE ICHTHYOSAURUS SPARKLED LIKE THE   523 16
    I SUPPOSE TARTS ARE CALLED TARTS BECAUSE THEY'RE TART   530 18
    AND I SUPPOSE MOST GIRLS ARE A BIT TARTY TODAY   530 20
    I SUPPOSE AS A MATTER OF FACT IT'S GETTING A LITTLE DIF+   532 3
    AND IN THE INTERVALS OF THEIR THRILLS I SUPPOSE   533 7
    I SUPPOSE WHEN THE MEN ALL STARTED BEING WILLY WET-LEGS   537 28
    OH WELL I SUPPOSE I SHALL HAVE SOME KNIFE-EDGED TERENCE+   835 1

SUPPOSED
    AND YET I'M SUPPOSED TO CARE WITH ALL MY MIGHT   74 30
    WITH THE HEART OF THE MAN YOU SUPPOSED TO HAVE LOVED   478 18
    WAS ME OR WHAT WAS SUPPOSED FOR ME   489 13
    THIS IS THE ELECTRICITY THAT MAN IS SUPPOSED TO HAVE MA+   647 18
    SUPPOSED TO   647 20
    FOR GOD EVEN THE RAREST GOD IS SUPPOSED TO LOVE US   691 12
    AND HE IS SUPPOSED TO BE MIGHTLY AND GLORIOUS   691 14

SUPPOSING
    SUPPOSING I SAY DOGS ARE MY NEIGHBOURS   645 1

SUPPRESS
    SUPPRESS IT AGAIN   464 16

SUPPRESSED
    AND THRUST HER FISTS SUPPRESSED IN THE FOLDS OF HER SKI+   128 19

SUPPRESSING
    WHEREAS PURITANISM IS BENT ON SUPPRESSING THE FACT   *953 4

SUPPRESSION
    AND RIGID SUPPRESSION OF ALL BAWDY WHORING OR OTHER SUC+   845 13
    AND SUPPRESSION OF SUCH FACT LEADS AS WE KNOW DIRECT TO+   *953 5

SUPREME
    GOD BOWS HIS HEAD AND GRANTS ME THIS SUPREME   157 16
    THE UNKNOWN STRONG CURRENT OF LIFE SUPREME   261 12
    BEFORE THE ROSE BEGAN TO SIMPER SUPREME   285 16
    IN SUPREME BITTERNESS   304 11
    SETTING SUPREME ANNUNCIATION TO THE WORLD   304 21
    DOES NOT A SUPREME INTELLECT IDEALLY PROCREATE THE UNIV+   328 26
    PLEASE APPROACH THE SUPREME AUTHORITY DIRECT   604 18
    GOD IS SUPREME   618 10
    MUST LEARN THE SUPREME LESSON   636 24

SUPREMELY
    IN FLAT ECSTASY SUPREMELY UNFELT   444 7
    PORTRAITS ARE NOW SUPREMELY UNINTERESTING   657 1
    OWNING MY SUPPLE BODY A RARE GLAD THING SUPREMELY GOOD   *892 11

SURCHARGE
    FOR WHEN AT NIGHT FROM OUT THE FULL SURCHARGE   195 1

SURE
    LUSTROUSLY SURE UNKNOWN   39 27
    LIKE THIS I'M SURE IT IS   45 26
    AN' WHEN I KNOW FOR SURE MISSIS   78 19
    THA ART SO SURE THA'RT RIGHT LIZ   84 1
    THAT DAMNED SURE   84 2
    SOUL'S NAKED LIGHTNING WHICH SHOULD SURE ATTEST   87 24
    YES SAY IT FOR SURE FROM THE GOLDEN SUN   127 1
    THE OLD DREAMS ARE BEAUTIFUL BELOVED SOFT-TONED AND SURE   174 21
    SPREAD OUT AND KNOWN AT LAST AND WE ARE SURE   193 8
    AND DEATH WOULD ACHE STILL I AM SURE   205 18
    SURE ON OUR SANCTITY   242 31
    THERE SURE IN SINLESS BEING   243 5
    HOW SURE I FEEL HOW WARM AND STRONG AND HAPPY   247 4
    FOR THE FUTURE HOW SURE THE FUTURE IS WITHIN ME   247 5
    AND I AM SURE OF THAT   247 27
    WE ARE SURE OF THAT   247 28
    SURE AND A TOWER OF STRENGTH 'TWIXT THE WALLS OF HER BR+   249 12
    SURE ON A HAVEN OF PEACE BETWEEN THE MOUNDS OF HER   249 29
    TO MOVE AND TO BE QUITE SURE THAT HE IS MOVING   358 5
    I AM NOT SURE   377 22
    NOT SURE   380 10
    AS HE STRIKES SINCE SURE   382 19
    THINKING THIS DOG SURE HAS TAKEN A FANCY TO ME   398 20
    IT WAS LIKE BEING IN HEAVEN WHICH I AM SURE HAS A WHITE   444 3
    WHO IS SURE HE IS A GENTLEMAN   446 20
    ARE SURE OF IT   472 22
    THE NOVEL IT SURE WAS MIGHTY FINE   489 11
    HE SURE THINKS A LOT OF LIES   489 20
    I AM NOT SURE I WOULD ALWAYS FIGHT FOR MY LIFE   497 13
    I AM NOT SURE I WOULD ALWAYS FIGHT FOR MY WIFE   497 15
    SURE THEY HAVEN'T GOT THEM   501 13
    FOR WE'RE SURE TO BRING IN A LOT OF LIES   506 4
    OH I'M SURE YOU'LL UNDERSTAND WE'RE MAKING A CENSUS OF +   546 7
    THE MORNING SMILE SURE THAT IT WILL AFFORD HER   583 15
    COMFORT AND CHEER SURE THAT IT WILL TELL HER   583 16
    AND MARROW AND SUBSTANCE ARE SURE TO BE   583 24
    SURE AND MOON-SHOD COOL AND BRIGHT-FOOTED   684 12
    SURE OF OUR DEAD IN THE PROUD HALLS OF DEATH   740 27
    WHAT THEN WOULD YOU DO THEN FOR SURE YOU WOULD GO   755 7
    IS A SURE WAY TO MEET   764 14
    IF YOU HEAR A MAN CALLED BRILLIANT YOU MAY BE PRETTY SU+   841 18
    AH SURE TO VENTURE ALL ALONE IN DEATH   879 26
    FOR I WAS NOT SURE OF MYSELF   882 29
    THE OLD DREAMS ARE BELOVED BEAUTIFUL SOFT-TONED AND SURE   *907 4
    WATCH THE STIR WHOSE RHYTHM IS SECRET WHOSE SECRET IS S+   *907 13
    THE OLD DREAMS ARE BEAUTIFUL BELOVED SOFT-TONED AND SURE   *909 1

SURE
  AN' WHEN I KNOW FOR SURE MISSIS   *920 11

SURELY
  FOR ME TO RECKON FOR SURELY HE WILL   59 23
  TREMBLING BLUE IN HER PALLOR A TEAR THAT SURELY I HAVE +   67 16
  YOU SURELY SEEING I AM A BOWL OF KISSES   86 3
  THOUGH SURELY MY SOUL'S BEST DREAM IS STILL   117 4
  SURELY AH NOT IN WORDS ALONE I'D SPILL   127 16
  BIG HANDS AS IF SURELY HER ARMS DID HURT   128 22
  FOR SURELY THIS EARNEST MAN HAS NONE   130 13
  FOR SURELY THE FRAGILE FINE YOUNG THING HAD BEEN   132 3
  SURELY YOU'VE TRODDEN STRAIGHT   167 21
  SURELY YOU TOOK YOUR FATE   167 23
  SURELY YOU'VE TRODDEN STRAIGHT   168 27
  YOU HAVE SURELY ACHIEVED YOUR FATE   168 29
  SURELY BUT FOR YOU AND YOUR LIKE TOILING   197 20
  BUT STEADILY SURELY AND NOTWITHSTANDING   209 12
  MY DEAR WHEN YOU CROSS THE STREET IN THE SUNSHINE SURELY   211 13
  SURELY ABOUT HIS SUNBURNT FACE IS SOMETHING   225 17
  SURELY IT IS BAD POLICY   333 19
  SURELY THEY ARE FLESH OF MY FLESH   585 23
  ALL OF WHICH THINGS I CAN SURELY TASTE IN A GOOD APPLE   708 1
  SURELY NOT SO FOR HOW COULD MURDER EVEN SELF-MURDER   717 15
  AND HE SAID SURELY THIS LOOKS VERY CURIOUS   790 9
  SURELY HE SAID THIS IS A CURIOUS PEOPLE I HAVE FOUND   790 16
  THE AGE IS A JOKE AND SURELY TOMORROW   815 4
  SHE BOWS QUITE HUMBLE SUCH A SUBTLE DESTROYING MIND MUS+   841 28
  SURELY I CANNOT JUST BE GOING TO SCHOOL   865 12
  AN ECSTASY SURELY SWEET TO BE HAD   *899 3
  AN ECSTASY SURELY SWEET TO BE HAD   *902 15
  BUT SURELY SURELY I KNOW THAT STILL   *931 8
  FOR SURELY THE FRAGILE FINE YOUNG THING HAD BEEN   *937 30
  AND SURELY THE HEART THAT IS IN ME MUST BELONG   *940 10
  COMES UP UNNAMED FROM HER BODY AND SURELY   *946 5

SUREST
  BECAUSE IT WAS THE SUREST WAY OF MEETING YOU AT LAST   764 24

SURETY
  HOW THE STARS ARE MOVING IN SURETY   252 5

SURF
  I WILL SIFT THE SURF THAT EDGES THE NIGHT WITH MY NET T+   180 4
  FROM THE SURF HAS ARISEN THE BOYS ARE MUTTERING   *894 16

SURFACE
  UPON THE SURFACE OF THE WATERS THERE   113 2
  THE SURFACE OF DREAMS IS BROKEN THE ARRAS IS TORN   174 5
  IF YOU WILL GO DOWN INTO YOURSELF UNDER YOUR SURFACE   481 1
  AND THAT SENT THE BLOOD RUSHING TO THE SURFACE OF THE B+   502 7
  WHEN DANGER THREATENS ON THE SURFACE OF THE CEASELESS F+   695 2
  AND ON THE SURFACE SHELL OF HIM   830 10
  OVER THE SURFACE OF A SHADOW-COLOUR FLOATS   867 14
  THE SURFACE OF DREAMS IS BROKEN   *908 9

SURFEIT
  AYE SUFFOCATED WITH A DRUNK SURFEIT   877 10

SURF'S
  TO DRAW HIS NET THROUGH THE SURF'S THIN LINE AT THE DAW+   180 2

SURF-WET
  HE PUTS HIS SURF-WET FINGERS   201 1

SURGE
  CROWDS OF GLITTERING KING-CUPS SURGE TO CHALLENGE THE B+   33 11
  A CLOUD COMES UP LIKE THE SURGE OF A FOUNTAIN   50 3
  OF FLOWERS SURGE FROM BELOW TO THEIR LADDER-TOPS   136 13
  SOMETHING SEEMED TO SURGE THROUGH ME WHEN I TOUCHED   255 5
  COME LIFE SURGE THROUGH THIS MASS OF MORTIFICATION   271 2
  CROWDS OF GLITTERING KING-CUPS SURGE TO CHALLENGE THE B+   *891 12
  THE SURGE AND TIDE OF LIFE IN THE TURBULENT CLASS   *895 10

SURGEON
  SURGEON ME SOUND   *929 17

SURGES
  SURGES THE WHITE OF THE MOON   50 2

SURGICAL
  EDITOR BY SURGICAL OPERATION DID YOUR PARENTS HAVE YOU   582 16

SURGING
  COME BUBBLING SURGING TIDE OF SAP   270 31

SURLY
  AND THEN RUN LIKE SURLY DOGS AT THE BIDDING OF PALEFACE+   795 4

SURMISE
  OR SHOULD HE MY TEARS SURMISE   43 17
  THE LAND OF HER GLAD SURMISE   201 4

SURPASS
  WHAT CAN I SAY MORE EXCEPT THAT I KNOW WHY IT IS TO SUR+   266 6
  ONLY THOSE ETERNAL FEMALES TO OVERLEAP AND SURPASS AND   382 33

SURPASSED
  DIED AS IT WERE CEASED FROM KNOWING SURPASSED MYSELF   266 5
  IT IS THE MAJOR PART OF BEING THIS HAVING SURPASSED ONE+   266 20

SURPASSING
  EVERY MAN HIMSELF AND THEREFORE A SURPASSING SINGLENESS+   268 1
  UNLESS HE HAS HIS PURE MOMENTS WHEN HE IS SURPASSING   674 19
  MOVEMENT OF MULTITUDES SURPASSING RHYTHM   872 20

SURPLICES
  ALL IN THEIR SCARLET CLOAKS AND SURPLICES   232 17
  THE CANDLE-FLAMES BESIDE THE SURPLICES   232 31

SURPLUS
  THE VIVID AH THE FIERY SURPLUS OF LIFE   127 17

SURPRISE
  SLIPS AWAY SO I GASP IN SURPRISE   38 33
  AND READY TO OPEN IN BROWN SURPRISE   43 15
  IT'S NO SURPRISE   77 12
  IS IT ANY CAUSE FOR SURPRISE   80 16
  NO CAUSE FOR SURPRISE AT ALL MY LAD   80 17
  I ECHOED WITH SURPRISE   124 20
  TO TOUCH THE SEA IN THE LAST SURPRISE   130 22
  NEW SPARKS OF WONDER OPENING IN SURPRISE   136 16
  IN GLAD SURPRISE   227 32
  SMITTEN WITH REVERENT SURPRISE   234 12
  DEPARTS AND THE WORLD IS TAKEN BY SURPRISE   340 20
  BUT THE REST WAS A REAL SURPRISE   489 16
  AND STARES IN SURPRISE   754 10
  I WAS FAINT WITH SURPRISE   886 15
  OFF IN SURPRISE   *894 10
  IT'S NO SURPRISE   *918 30
  IS IT ANY CAUSE FOR SURPRISE   *922 16
  NO CAUSE FOR SURPRISE AT ALL MY LAD   *922 17
  MY HEART RE-ECHOED IN SURPRISE   *935 20

SURPRISED
  SINGING LOVE'S FIRST SURPRISED GLADNESS ALONE IN THE GL+   *940 15

SURREPTITIOUSLY
  THEN I SAW HIM TURN TO GLANCE AGAIN SURREPTITIOUSLY   604 4

SURREY
  THE FACTORIES ON THE SURREY SIDE   146 28

SURROUND
  IF I TURN QUICKLY I AM TERRIFIED FEELING SPACE SURROUND+   222 23
  WHAT LOUSY ARCHANGELS AND ANGELS YOU HAVE TO SURROUND   643 27

SURROUNDING
  BROWN HILLS SURROUNDING   340 23

SURROUNDS
  YET WHAT AN AURA SURROUNDS YOU   332 18

SURVIVE
  THEY SAY THE FIT SURVIVE   298 8
  SO WHY DIDN'T HE SURVIVE   523 20
  AS A MATTER OF FACT THE ONLY CREATURES THAT SEEM TO SUR+   523 21

SURVIVED
  THOSE THAT HAVE NOT SURVIVED THE DARKLY LOST   298 10

SUSPENDED
  BUT THE BLOOD HAS SUSPENDED ITS TIMBRE THE HEART FROM O+   67 3
  ALL SHAPES OF WONDER WITH SUSPENDED BREATH   165 19
  SUCH SILENCE SUCH SUSPENDED TRANSPORT   334 1
  MANY SUSPENDED TOGETHER FOREVER APART   337 20
  THAT WAIT ON WHALES IN MID-OCEAN SUSPENDED IN THE WAVES+   694 26
  THE DARK DRIPS DOWN SUSPENDED   782 5
  HANG HIGH SUSPENDED WITHOUTEN RESPITE   *929 8

SUSPENDS
  SHE HAS NOT CHOSEN ME FINALLY SHE SUSPENDS HER CHOICE   213 24

SUSPENSE
  THEN THERE WAS A HUSH OF SUSPENSE AT THE CORE OF EVERY +   683 12

SUSPENSION
  IN THE SUSPENSION OF WHOLENESS IN THE MOMENT OF DIVISIO+   699 7

SUSPICION
  NOT EVEN A SUSPICION   562 14

SUSPICIOUS
  SUSPICIOUS REMARK   *929 13

SUSTAIN
  LET US NOT CRY TO HER STILL TO SUSTAIN US HERE   132 21
  SUSTAIN   *900 4
  OF LIVING MY LIFE WERE DOUBLED I STILL HAVE THIS TO COM+   *903 16

SUSTENANCE
  LIKE A LIGHT THAT HAS NO SUSTENANCE   246 8

SU-SUPERIOR
  DON'T BE SUCKED IN BY THE SU-SUPERIOR   459 9

SWABS
  ONLY THIRD-RATE SWABS ARE PUSHING TO GET ON NOWADAYS   518 17

SWAGGERING
  SWAGGERING UP AND DOWN   312 8

SWALING
  I LOOK AT THE SWALING SUNSET   134 1

SWALLOW
  WHERE THE SWALLOW HAS HUNG HER MARRIAGE BED   42 22
  LIKE A SWALLOW   193 26
  A BAT BIG AS A SWALLOW   342 25
  AND GULPING AT MORE THAN SHE CAN SWALLOW AND WORKING   359 5
  AGAINST THOSE COYOTES WHO WOULD SWALLOW YOU LIKE AN   396 33
  GOBBLE UP FILTH YOU HORROR SWALLOW UTTER ABOMINATION   398 28
  DON'T SWALLOW THE CULTURE BAIT   459 10
  AND EASY TO SWALLOW ALWAYS TELL THEM THEY'RE HAPPY   583 19

SWALLOW
  I'LL SHAKE THE EARTH AND SWALLOW THEM UP WITH THEIR CIT+   792   4
  AND EITHER RELEASE ENERGY OR SWALLOW IT UP   *947   11

SWALLOWING
  CAUTIOUSLY SWALLOWING THEIR PHLEGM   554   28

SWALLOWS
  TO THE SUN AND THE SWALLOWS CUT CLEAR   35   4
  AND SWALLOWS DIP INTO THE PALLOR OF THE WEST   41   21
  SWALLOWS WITH SPOOLS OF DARK THREAD SEWING THE SHADOWS   340   29
  THE SWALLOWS ARE FLYING SO LATE   341   7
  SWALLOWS   341   8
  NEVER SWALLOWS   341   15
  THE SWALLOWS ARE GONE   341   17
  AT A WAVERING INSTANT THE SWALLOWS GIVE WAY TO BATS   341   18
  ONLY AS SWALLOWS ARE SLAVES TO THE EAVES   *899   7
  ONLY AS SWALLOWS ARE SLAVES TO THE EAVES   *902   19

SWAM
  THE SUNSHINE SWAM IN A SHOAL ACROSS AND ACROSS   243   22
  SWAM THE STILL SWAN SWEPT THE WIDE GOOSE ABOVE THE MISTS   *947   2

SWAMPED
  OF A SWAMPED CIVILISATION AND START A NEW WORLD OF MAN   429   12

SWAN
  THE GREAT SWAN UPON THE WATERS OF ALL ENDINGS   435   27
  THE SWAN WITHIN VAST CHAOS WITHIN THE ELECTRON   435   28
  SWIMS THE WILD SWAN   437   23
  LIKE A WILD SWAN OR A GOOSE WHOSE HONK GOES THROUGH MY   438   7
  WHERE THERE IS WOMAN THERE IS SWAN   438   11
  AND IT STIRS LIFE A SWAN   505   6
  ABOUT LIKE A SWAN THAT CAN'T SETTLE   524   22
  WHOSE VOICE FLIES ON AND ON CALLING LIKE A SWAN   623   17
  AND THE WHITE SWAN SWIMS IN THE MARSHES OF HIS LOINS   624   6
  THE SWAN WILL BEAT THE WATERS IN RAGE WHITE RAGE OF AN +   624   15
  THE SWAN WILL LIFT UP AGAIN HIS FLATTENED SMITTEN HEAD   625   2
  YET WHEN I THINK OF THE WILD SWAN OR THE RIPPLE-MARKED +   841   1
  SWAM THE STILL SWAN SWEPT THE WIDE GOOSE ABOVE THE MISTS   *947   2
  LIKE A WILD SWAN OR A GOOSE WHOSE HONK GOES THROUGH MY +   *947   18

SWAN-LIKE
  THERE IS A SWAN-LIKE FLAME THAT CURLS ROUND THE CENTRE +   440   2

SWANS
  YOUNG WILD SWANS   438   22
  WILL THE SINGING OF SWANS HIGH UP HIGH UP INVISIBLE   439   8
  AND THE WILD SWANS FLOWN AWAY SINGING THE SWAN-SONG OF +   624   2
  THERE'LL BE BABIES BORN THAT ARE YOUNG WILD SWANS O MY +   *947   24
  AND THE WILD SWANS FLOWN AWAY SINGING THE SWAN-SONG OF +   *953   20

SWAN-SONG
  AND THE WILD SWANS FLOWN AWAY SINGING THE SWAN-SONG OF +   624   2
  AND THE WILD SWANS FLOWN AWAY SINGING THE SWAN-SONG OF +   *953   20

SWAN'S
  THE NEXT DAY IS THE DAY OF THE GOOSE THE WILD SWAN'S DAY   841   9

SWARM
  WHO CURL IN SLEEP LIKE KITTENS WHO MASS AS A SWARM   73   17
  IN A GREAT SWARM CLOTTED AND SINGLE   205   25
  DARK SKY OF NIGHT A WANDERING GLITTER A SWARM   221   26
  ADMITTED THEY SWARM IN COMPANIES   337   14
  DARK SKY OF NIGHT THE WANDERING GLITTER THE SWARM   *945   12

SWARMING
  I HAVE SUCH SWARMING SENSE OF LIVES AT THE BASE OF ME S+   *900   5
  I HAVE SUCH SWARMING SENSE OF LIVES AT THE BASE OF ME S+   *903   17

SWARMS
  SWARMS OF MANKIND IN THE WORLD AND WE WERE LESS LONELY   224   7
  THERE ARE DEAD THAT ATTACK THE SUN LIKE SWARMS OF BLACK+   795   28

SWART
  WHO LIFT SWART ARMS TO FEND ME OFF BUT I COME   86   18
  SEE HIM THERE THE SWART SO PALPABLY INVISIBLE   286   11
  THE GRAPE IS SWART THE AVENUES DUSKY AND TENDRILLED SUB+   286   32
  OR THE STOUT SWART BEETLE ROLLED THE GLOBE OF DUNG IN W+   437   16
  BEFORE THE STOUT SWART BEETLE HAD A BALL OF DUNG TO ROL+   *946   26

SWARTHY
  HERE IN THIS SWARTHY SECRET TENT   113   25
  SWARTHY AND STRONG WITH HIS DAMP THICK HAIR   733   24
  AND ALL THE TIME HIS HANDSOME SWARTHY RED FACE   734   17
  WITH A BITTER SWARTHY SKIN   919   2
  HERE IN THIS SWARTHY SECRET TENT   *929   14

SWATHS
  NOW THE SUNKEN SWATHS   35   2
  CAUGHT DUST FROM THE SEA'S LONG SWATHS   152   13

SWAY
  OF RED UPON THE THROAT HER TERRORS SWAY   42   27
  LIKE A SOFT FULL DROP OF DARKNESS IT SEEMS TO SWAY   148   1
  SWAY LIKE FULL-BLOWN YELLOW   217   17
  WAVES OF DARK HEAT ROCK SWAY UPWARDS   302   2
  TO SWAY THE EARTH OF MEN   614   10
  AND WHEN I SEE THE TREES SWAY CLOSE   883   8
  SWAY THE LIVE PEARLS THEIR FLOWERING PLEDGES   *941   20

SWAYED
  THAT SWAYED THEIR LENGTH OF DARKNESS ALL AROUND   296   18

SWAYING
  EARTH OF MY SWAYING ATMOSPHERE   118   7
  AND OVER THE SWAYING CORN-STALKS JUST ABOVE   221   16
  HEAVY AND SWAYING LIKE A WHALE RECOVERING   428   12
  SWAYING SWAYING O SO DEEP   454   5
  AS IF SWAYING WERE ITS FORM OF STILLNESS   467   17
  AH THE GODS THE SWAYING BODY OF GOD   651   17
  I'D HANG MY HAMS WITH PUCKERED PETTICOATS SWAYING   835   32
  SWAYING I SNATCH AND LOOT   861   7
  AND OVER THE SWAYING CORNSTALKS JUST ABOVE   *945   2

SWAYS
  PLAYS WITH ME SWAYS ME LIFTS ME AND SINKS ME MURMURS OH   34   20
  THE RED RANGE HEAVES AND COMPULSORY SWAYS AH SEE IN THE+   66   17
  THE HOUSE SWAYS   288   12
  SEA-WEED SWAYS AND SWAYS AND SWIRLS   467   16
  SWAYS THE GOLDEN PEARL OF PLEASURE   868   20
  PLAYS WITH ME SWAYS ME LIFTS ME AND SINKS ME AS THOUGH +   *892   8
  SWAYS ON MY ARM LIKE SORROWFUL STORM-HEAVY BOUGHS   *913   23

SWAY-WAVE
  SWAY-WAVE   335   23

SWEALING
  TO THE LEFT THIS GHOST LIKE A CANDLE SWEALING   141   16

SWEAR
  SWEAR IN THE PALE WINE POURED FROM THE CUPS OF THE QUEEN   177   21
  I SWEAR I'LL PULL OFF MY KNICKERS RIGHT IN THE RUE DE L+   433   20
  THE MOMENT I SWEAR TO LOVE A WOMAN A CERTAIN WOMAN   472   16
  THE MOMENT I SWEAR TO LOVE A WOMAN ALL MY LIFE THAT VER+   834   8

SWEARING
  THAT WE'VE NEVER SEEN COMING STAMPING AND SWEARING   572   13

SWEAT
  WITH SWEAT I'LL ENTER A HOUSE FOR THY SAKE   44   8
  TAKE WRITHING FORMS OF ALL BEASTS THAT SWEAT AND THAT F+   73   15
  AND SWEAT OF LABOUR AND THE MEANEST FASHION   89   13
  SWEAT   157   3
  AS IF WITH SWEAT   280   21
  AND DEVIL-DANCERS LUMINOUS WITH SWEAT DANCING ON TO THE   388   33
  WITH SWEAT AND LAUGHING   389   6
  GLEAMING LIKE METAL WITH RUNNING SWEAT AS THEY SUDDENLY   389   9
  WHAT WOULD THEY DO THOSE JUNGLE MEN RUNNING WITH SWEAT   389   32
  IT IS SET UP AS A BOUNDARY AND BLOOD AND SWEAT   706   13
  WAS WET WITH SWEAT AND HIS MOVEMENTS STRONG AND HEAVY   734   22
  AND GOD REVEALED THROUGH THE SWEAT AND THE HEAT OF LOVE   742   29
  OF THIS HOUR'S IGNOMINY AND SWEAT   747   19
  THE GREED OF THIS INFAMOUS FELLOW FOR OUR SWEAT   750   8
  WORKED WITH CLEAN SWEAT FOR YEAST   758   22
  WITH HIS BROW WIPED BRIGHT OF THE TOIL OF SWEAT   770   18
  AND LIVE FROM ITS SECONDARY SWEAT   843   9
  OUR OVERWEENING DAYS STRIVE TOO FAR TILL THE HEAT AND T+   856   1

SWEATED
  THE THORN-LEAVES CRACKLED AND TWISTED AND SWEATED IN AN+   94   26
  THE THORN-LEAVES CRACKLED AND TWISTED AND SWEATED IN AN+   *897   14

SWEATING
  SWEATING HIS DROPS OF BLOOD THROUGH THE LONG-NIGHTED   305   25
  IN THE FUME OF COCOA-NUT OIL IN THE SWEATING TROPICAL N+   387   36

SWEAT-SHINING
  SOBBING IN DARK SWEAT-SHINING BREASTS   389   12

SWEEP
  CURVE SWEEP TOWARDS A WOMAN'S   40   4
  SWEEP PAST THE WINDOW AGAIN   100   4
  I ADMIRE YOU SO YOU ARE BEAUTIFUL THIS CLEAN SWEEP OF   255   11
  COME SWEEP AWAY THESE EXQUISITE GHASTLY FIRST-FLOWERS   271   3
  NEW BROOMS SWEEP CLEAN   536   1
  WILL SWEEP ROUND AND UP TO GREET THE SUN WITH A SILKY G+   625   4
  DOWN FLATTENING INTO POINTS FLATTENED UNDER THE SWEEP O+   697   7
  OF WINDY AUTUMN WHEN THE WINDS ALL SWEEP   744   7
  THAT WHIRL AND SWEEP LIKE ANXIOUS LEAVES AWAY   744   14
  AND BLOOD-BROWN FLUX OF LIVES THAT SWEEP THEIR WAY   745   8
  SWEEP ON TO BITTER TO CORROSIVE DEATH   745   34
  BUT YOU FLY YOU SOAR YOU SWEEP AWAY   783   31
  NO LONGER THEY SWEEP THE HOURS AS THE SCYTHE OF THE MOW+   855   29
  OH THE TERROR OF LIFTING THE INNERMOST I OUT OF THE SWE+ *909   21

SWEEPER
  THAT THEY CHOKE THE SWEEPER   536   3

SWEEPING
  ABOVE THEM EXULTANT THE PEEWITS ARE SWEEPING   33   3
  A SUDDEN CAR GOES SWEEPING PAST AND I STRAIN MY SOUL TO+   58   3
  THEN THE SWEEPING SUNSHINE OF NOON   .248   20
  LIKE A KING EAGLE BIRD OF THE MOST HIGH SWEEPING THE RO+   329   4
  BUT THEY OFTEN RAISE SUCH A DUST IN THE SWEEPING   536   2
  SWEEPING THE CURVE OF SPACE AND MOVING THE SILENCE   609   12
  PINIONED LIKE SWEEPING SCYTHES NOW IDLY HANGING AT REST   855   22
  PLEASE SIR I WAS SWEEPING SNOW AN' I NEVER HEARD THE BE+   866   9
  ABOVE THEM EXULTANT THE PEEWITS ARE SWEEPING   *891   3

SWEEPS
  OF SWEET FIRE SWEEPS ACROSS ME SO I DROWN   43   36
  AS IT SILENTLY SWEEPS TO ITS SOMEWHERE ITS GOAL   68   15
  SINCE LIFE SWEEPS WHIRLING DIM AND VAST   69   1
  BETWEEN THE SCHOOLS SWEEPS ONE BLACK ROOK   76   16
  DROWNS ME AND SWEEPS ME AWAY AND HOLDS ME DOWN   261   13
  SWEEPS THE HIGH GOOSE ABOVE THE MISTS   437   24
  BETWEEN THE RUDDY SCHOOLS SWEEPS ONE BLACK ROOK   *898   10
  BETWEEN THE RUDDY SCHOOLS SWEEPS ONE BLACK ROOK   *901   19
  AS HE SILENTLY SWEEPS TO HIS SOMEWHERE HIS GOAL   *914   30
  SINCE GOD SWEEPS ONWARD DIM AND VAST   *915   13

SWEET
     ALL BE SWEET WITH WHITE AND BLUE VIOLET   40   29
     SHE WOOS THE MOTH WITH HER SWEET LOW WORD   42   15
     OF SWEET FIRE SWEEPS ACROSS ME SO I DROWN   43   36
     AND VERY SWEET IT IS WHILE THE SUNLIGHT WAVES   51   21
     THIS MORNING SWEET IT IS   51   26
     WITH THE OLD SWEET SOOTHING TEARS AND LAUGHTER THAT   53   5
     SWEET DARK PURPLE AND WHITE ONES MIXED FOR A PLEDGE   58   10
     AND THE SENSE OF HER CLINGING FLESH WAS SWEET   62   1
     OF THE SWEET   67   5
     PATIENCE LITTLE HEART I SHALL BE SWEET   91   23
     ONCE FROM YOUR WOMB SWEET MOTHER   101   25
     SWEET AND STILL ON YOUR BIER   102   16
     OVER MY HEART AND SWEET   124   26
     CAREFULLY OVER THE SWEET   143   11
     WITH THE OLD SWEET THINGS OF OUR YOUTH AND NEVER YET   157   6
     OH AND IT IS SWEET   194   13
     SWEET AS AN ARMFUL OF WHEAT   198   14
     FOR ME AND AH IT WAS SWEET   198   16
     GAVE ME SWEET LYMPH AGAINST THE SALT-BURNS   208   6
     PROUD KNIGHTS TO BATTLE SWEET HOW I WARM   221   28
     NOT AS A VISITOR EITHER NOR A SWEET   230   25
     WHICH THE SWEET BLOOD FEEDS   240   6
     ALL THAT I AM-NOT IN SOFTNESS SWEET SOFTNESS FOR SHE IS+   250   3
     FULL OF SWEET STILLNESS   261   20
     SWEET IN EAR NOR SO MUCH TO GIVE   263   3
     AND THE SWEET CONSTANT BALANCED HEAT   263   15
     MAN'S SWEETEST HARVEST OF THE CENTURIES SWEET PRINTED   263   25
     MORE THAN SWEET   281   21
     THE ROSE WOULD SMELL AS SWEET   292   3
     MADE OF SWEET UNTARNISHED SILVER IN THE SEA-SOUTHERN AIR   298   21
     HO GOLDEN-SPANIEL SWEET ALERT NARCISSUS   309   7
     SWEET FIRE OF DAY   346   5
     TO EARN THEIR LIVINGS NOR YET GIRLS SWEET JOYS   459   3
     TO DISTIL SEA-WATER INTO SWEET   495   11
     BE SWEET AND SOUND   504   9
     INTO BROAD SWEET PETALS   535   4
     BUT SWEET IN YOUR SIGHT   558   7
     AH LOVE SWEET LOVE NOT SO EASY   559   5
     IF YOU DON'T WANT TO BREAK THE SWEET ENGLISH SPELL   576   11
     TO SOMETHING FLOWERY AND FULFILLED AND WITH A STRANGE S+   677   16
     AND SOME OF TOO MUCH SUN BRACKISH SWEET   708   3
     TO THE SWEET HOME OF PURE OBLIVION   721   21
     OLD PLACES OF SWEET LIFE FROM WHICH THEY ARE THRUST OUT   723   1
     SWEET DARK OBLIVION WHEN I CEASE   726   5
     IN THE SWEET WHOLENESS OF OBLIVION   726   21
     SO SWEET LIKE A SWOON OR MORE LIKE THE DROWSE OF A LOW +   727   11
     OF SWEET RETURNING FROM THE SLEEP OF DEATH   745   5
     BUT I'LL NEVER REACH THE LONG SWEET SHORE   747   25
     AS YOU WOULD A FRESH SWEET LOCUST-POD   752   14
     KILOSSA SWEET WELL OF MY STRENGTH THOU CORDED WITH SILK   759   14
     FOR I AM SWEET I AM THE LAST AND THE BEST THE POOL OF N+   796   24
     THE BITTER AND SWEET RAW AND THE ROTTEN   825   2
     IN THE SAME WAY CHASTITY IN ITS HOUR IS SWEET AND WHOLE+   845   11
     AT THE END OF A SWEET SPRING DAY THEY WILL VANISH   855   5
     AT THE END OF THE SWEET SPRING DAY THEY ARE YOURS   855   13
     SHE IS SWEET AND SOFT-THROATED   862   6
     WITH HER SUAVE FORM DUSTY WITH SPICES HONEY SWEET STRAY+   864   4
     SWEET FRAGRANCE OF LOVE AND FEED ME WITH KISSES FAIR   874   7
     I KNOW THE SWEET RED HUTCH OF HIS MOUTH WHERE WARM   876   32
     OF LIVING AND WAVER IN SWEET EXTINGUISHMENT   879   31
     AND TWO ARE ONE IN SWEET CONNECTION   887   22
     AN ECSTASY SURELY SWEET TO BE HAD   *899   3
     AND VERY SWEET WHILE THE SUNLIGHT WAVES   *899   4
     OH SWEET IT IS   *899   10
     AN ECSTASY SURELY SWEET TO BE HAD   *902   15
     AND VERY SWEET WHILE THE SUNLIGHT WAVES   *902   16
     OH SWEET IT IS   *902   22
     WITH THE OLD SWEET SOOTHING TEARS AND LAUGHTER THAT SHA+   *905   19
     AND THE SENSE OF HER CLINGING FLESH WAS SWEET   *912   9
     SWEET WISDOM OF GRACE NOW WHO WILL FREE   *927   24
     WITH A QUIVERING SWEET WISDOM OF GRACE BUT NOW   *928   24
     CHASTITY IN ITS HOUR IS SWEET AND WHOLESOME   *952   23

SWEETEST
     MAN'S SWEETEST HARVEST OF THE CENTURIES SWEET PRINTED   263   25

SWEET-FLESHED
     LIKE A NUDE LIKE A ROCK-LIVING SWEET-FLESHED SEA-ANEMONE   299   7

SWEETHEART
     ALWAYS SWEETHEART   179   1
     A MAN CAN'T GET ANY FUN OUT OF WIFE SWEETHEART OR TART   518   4
     SWEETHEART   *925   29

SWEET JOY
     I CANNOT CALL HER SWEET JOY NOW   863   9

SWEETLY
     SHONE SWEETLY THROUGH YELLOW SILK A MAN FULL IN THE LIG+   865   2

SWEET-MYRIAD-LIMBED
     RATHER LIKE AN OCTOPUS BUT STRANGE AND SWEET-MYRIAD-LIM+   299   5

SWEETNESS
     YOU HAVE FED ME WITH YOUR SWEETNESS NOW I AM SICK   234   23
     THERE IS A NEW SWEETNESS IN HIS VOLUPTUOUSLY LICKING HI+   325   1
     ITS SWEETNESS DISTILS AND TRICKLES AWAY INTO   504   21

SWEET-SCENTED
     SWEET-SCENTED TO HOLD IN THE THROAT   165   10

SWELL
     WITH SOUNDS THAT ENDLESSLY SWELL AND SINK LIKE THE STOR+   97   24
     AND OUR BODIES MOLTEN DROPS OF DREAM-BLOOD THAT SWIRL A+   176   7
     MAKING THEM SWELL WITH TURGID UNGOVERNABLE STRENGTH   241   20
     WISE GOOD PROVISION THAT MAKES THE HEART SWELL WITH LOVE   264   7
     CITYWARDS IN LITTLE RIVERS THAT SWELL TO A GREAT STREAM   484   3

SWELL
     THE WAVES RAN LAUGHING UP THE SHORE AT THE SWELL   *917   4
     SWELL DOWN HER RICH HOT WRIST   *937   8

SWELLED
     STRANGLED MY HEART SWELLED UP SO FULL   123   15
     STRANGLED MY HEART SWELLED UP SO FULL   *934   21

SWELLING
     AND WHAT IS LIFE BUT THE SWELLING AND SHAPING THE DREAM+   176   6
     THE GREAT ACTIVITY SWELLING THROUGH THE ROUND FLESH PUL+   *907   14
     THE GREAT MYSTERIOUS ONE IS SWELLING AND SHAPING THE DR+   *907   24
     IS SWELLING AND SHAPING A BUD INTO BLOSSOM   *907   26
     IS SWELLING WITH WIDESPREAD LABOURING CONCENTRATION   *908   2
     ROUNDED AND SWELLING TOWARDS THE FRUIT OF A DREAM   *908   4
     HERE IN THE SWELLING FLESH THE GREAT ACTIVITY WORKING   *909   11
     EVERYTHING GREAT AND MYSTERIOUS IN ONE SWELLING AND SHA+   *909   15
     SWELLING MANKIND LIKE ONE BUD TO BRING FORTH THE FRUIT +   *909   20

SWELLS
     AS IT SWELLS AND SHAPES A BUD INTO BLOSSOM   *909   17

SWELTED
     TILL I WAS VERILY SWELTED   80   12
     TILL I WAS VERILY SWELTED   *922   12

SWELTERING
     OF FLOWERS AND THE SWELTERING EARTH   *937   12

SWEPT
     HOW NIGHT AFTER NIGHT SWEPT LEVEL AND LOW   103   5
     A HASTENING CAR SWEPT SHAMEFUL PAST   122   1
     OF LEAVES THAT HAVE GONE UNNOTICED SWEPT LIKE OLD   141   29
     TWO PALE CLOTS SWEPT BY THE LIGHT OF THE CARS   144   28
     AND AM SWEPT AWAY IN THE HORRIBLE DAWN AM GONE   147   12
     AND THE FLAME OF YOU SWEPT BACK IN A NEW BREATH OF LIFE   784   26
     IS SWEPT FROM OUT OF THE ENDLESS SKY   823   19
     SWAM THE STILL SWAN SWEPT THE WIDE GOOSE ABOVE THE MISTS   *947   2

SWERVE
     IF YOU KNEW HOW I SWERVE IN PEACE IN THE EQUIPOISE   251   22

SWERVED
     AT LAST HE SWERVED INTO THE WINDOW BAY   343   16
     AGAIN HE SWERVED INTO THE WINDOW BAY   344   3
     EVERY TIME HE SWERVED AT IT   344   12

SWERVING
     THEN SWERVING AND STEERING AFRESH   380   25

SWIFT
     THEN BACK IN A SWIFT BRIGHT FLUTTER TO WORK   51   28
     OH YOU STIFF SHAPES SWIFT TRANSFORMATION SEETHES   72   12
     SWIFT TRAINS GO BY IN A RUSH OF LIGHT   169   2
     ONE MOMENT SEES AND SWIFT ITS DREAM IS OVER   195   14
     AND I THE SWIFT BRACTS THAT SHEATHE IT THOSE BREASTS TH+   245   16
     FLOWERS ARE JUST A MOTION A SWIFT MOTION A COLOURED   476   18
     SWIFT WIND OR SOUND RINGING ROCK   637   11
     AND SINKS DOWN WITH A SWIFT RUSTLE AND A STRANGE FALLING   651   15
     THE RACE IS NOT TO THE SWIFT   658   5
     AND THE WATCHERS THE DIVIDERS THOSE SWIFT ONES WITH DAR+   706   17
     TO THE SUNDERERS TO THE SWIFT ONES   707   8
     THE DIVIDERS THE THUNDERERS THE SWIFT ONES BLIND WITH S+   707   20
     THE SLOW WAY NOT THE SWIFT   784   29
     SEND ME THEM BY THE SWIFT WAY THE WAY OF THE SPARKS   789   19
     EVE RUNNING WITH SWIFT LIMBS QUICKENED BY DREAD   864   19
     A SWIFT DEXTEROUS MAN PLYING THE SLENDER POLE   867   22
     IN ONE SWIFT BOUND TO THE HOUSE-BOAT   868   2
     WITH A FEW SWIFT PASSIONS WOULD I DRIFT AWAY   875   32
     MIGHT FOLLOW SWIFT BEHIND THEE WHEN THOU LETS   879   12
     THEN BACK IN A SWIFT BRIGHT FLUTTER TO WORK   *899   12
     THEN BACK IN A SWIFT BRIGHT FLUTTER TO WORK   *902   24

SWIFTER
     SWIFTER AND HIGHER AND BRIGHTER OR THE YIELDING AND THE+   680   6
     FEEL SWIFTER   762   6

SWIFTLY
     WHERE ASH ON THE DYING COALS GROWS SWIFTLY LIKE HEAVY   47   6
     THE OTHER WOMAN ROSE AND SWIFTLY SAID   157   27
     WHILE A NAKED MAN COMES SWIFTLY   200   21
     LIGHT WENT OVER THE HILL-BROW SWIFTLY WITH THEIR TAILS   391   2
     LIKE A TRUNDLING PROJECTILE SWIFTLY WHIRLING UP   397   22
     LIKE SICKENING TOADSTOOLS AND LEFT TO MELT BACK SWIFTLY   431   28
     O FLOWERS THEY FADE BECAUSE THEY ARE MOVING SWIFTLY A   476   6
     THEN DIED OUT ALMOST AS SWIFTLY   618   5
     UNLESS MEN SWIFTLY DIVIDE AGAIN AND THE BASE ARE THRUST   637   14
     HARK HARK STEP ASIDE SILENTLY AND SWIFTLY   642   19
     AND A GIRL RAN SWIFTLY LAUGHING BREATHLESS TAKING IN HE+   672   13
     THE LITTLE SLENDER SOUL SITS SWIFTLY DOWN AND TAKES THE+   723   20
     TILL THE WHISTLE WENT THEN SWIFTLY HE   735   12
     SWIFTLY I WISH I MIGHT KISS HER FINGERS BUT FULL   752   11
     AND SWIFTLY SWIFTLY   766   2
     THE LITTLE SLENDER SOUL SITS SWIFTLY DOWN AND TAKES THE+   *958   32

SWIFTNESS
     SWIFTNESS GALLOPED UPHILL IN THE NIGHT GOING BACK TO   390   30

SWIFT-STRIKING
     TEMPLE OF BLOOD IN THE NIGHT SWIFT-STRIKING   390   33

SWILL
     BACK TO THIS RAINY SWILL   111   5
     THAT A NEW NIGHT POURING DOWN SHALL SWILL   117   5
     ITS RAINY SWILL ABOUT US SHE ANSWERED ME   180   14

SWILLS
    AND SMALL ON THE SAND SWILLS   883 26

SWIM
    THE FLOWERS OF ALL MY MUD SWIM INTO SIGHT   113 8
    I SAW A WATER-SERPENT SWIM ACROSS THE ANAPO   337 24
    LIFT AND SWIM AND GO THEIR WAY   337 30
    SWIM DEEPER DEEPER TILL IT LEAVES NO PEAK EMERGING   428 25
    TILL GEESE CAN SWIM IN YOUR POOLS   754 14
    AND TAKE A SWIM WITH US HERE   759 9
    EYES WHERE I CAN WATCH THE SWIM OF OLD DREAMS REFLECTED+   *907 11
    EYES WHERE I CAN WATCH THE SWIM OF OLD DREAMS REFLECTED+   *909 7

SWIMMING
    TO-MORROW SWIMMING IN EVENING'S VAGUE DIM VAPOUR   72 16
    SILENTLY SWIMMING AND SLEEPING AND PRESSING THE FLOOD   841 4

SWIMS
    THROUGH THE STIRRED IRIDESCENCE THAT SWIMS IN THE WARM   53 16
    WHO SWIMS ENWOMBED   335 27
    NO LONGER HE SWIMS CALMLY   436 2
    SWIMS THE WILD SWAN   437 23
    WHERE THE FATHER OF ALL THINGS SWIMS IN A MIST OF ATOMS   438 4
    AND THE WHITE SWAN SWIMS IN THE MARSHES OF HIS LOINS   624 6
    THROUGH THE COLOURED IRIDESCENCE THAT SWIMS IN THE WARM   *906 7
    THE FATHER OF ALL THINGS SWIMS IN THE VAST DUSK OF ALL +   *947 17
    SWIMS THE MALLARD DUCK AT DAWN IN THAT QUICK JOY   *953 27

SWINDLE
    IT DAWNS ON THEM THAT THE WHOLE DAMN SWINDLE   560 11
    DO YOU FEAR I SHALL SWINDLE YOU   *932 11

SWINDLED
    AND I'D LET MYSELF BE SWINDLED   556 13
    YE SWINDLED LITTLE BLOKES   560 18

SWINE
    SWINE WASH IN MIRE AND BARNYARD FOWLS IN DUST   376 8
    DEMOCRATIC LITTLE BULL-BITCH DIRT-EATING LITTLE SWINE   399 26

SWING
    AND SWINGS ALL LOOSE FROM THE SWING OF HIS WALK   43 13
    SWING TO MY WALKING MOVEMENT WEAK   73 26
    I FOLLOWED FOLLOWED THE SWING OF HER WHITE DRESS   123 2
    WHICH SWING AGAINST EACH OTHER   710 22
    I FOLLOWED FOLLOWED THE SWING OF HER WHITE DRESS   *934 8
    SWING LIKE FULL-BLOWN YELLOW   *942 26

SWINGING
    THE RED-GOLD SPOOLS OF THEIR HANDS AND THEIR FACES SWIN+   72 8
    THE THIN SYCAMORE IN THE PLAYGROUND IS SWINGING WITH FL+   92 2
    HER HEART IS A SWINGING CRADLE   201 9
    WE CLIMBED THE HUNTSMAN'S LADDER AND SAT SWINGING   216 22
    A MAN WITH A LANTERN SWINGING   227 3
    THE SWINGING BEAUTY OF EQUILIBRIUM   251 18
    THE SWINGING BLISS NO SHATTERING EVER DESTROYS   251 24
    HUGE MORE TAGGED SWINGING MORE DRIPPING FIRE OF NEW   388 27
    AND SWINGING IN A STRANGE UNISON OF POWER   478 17
    AND HERS A FLOWERBELL SWINGING   742 33
    SISTERS THE SEARCHLIGHT'S SWINGING FAN   758 13
    SWINGING CHERRY-TREE   860 26
    SALLIES OF SWINGING FRUIT   861 5
    EVE SWINGING HER DUSKY LIMBS DISCONSOLATE   863 21
    SWINGING TO MY LULLABY   *913 18
    WHILE THE STREET LAMP CENSERS SWINGING HIGH   *916 19
    THE THIN SYCAMORE IN THE PLAYGROUND IS SWINGING WITH FL+   *926 2
    WE CLIMBED THE HUNTSMAN'S LADDER AND SAT SWINGING   *942 8

SWINGS
    AND SWINGS ALL LOOSE FROM THE SWING OF HIS WALK   43 13
    ON THE FLOOD THAT SOUNDLESS SWINGS   109 16
    THE TASSEL OF THE BLIND SWINGS CONSTANTLY TAPPING THE P+   112 17
    UNINTERRUPTED SILENCE SWINGS   166 3
    AH THE DEWLAP SWINGS PENDULOUS WITH EXCESS   326 17
    SWINGS THE HEART RENEWED WITH PEACE   720 18
    SWINGS ROUND THE STEMS OF THE MANY INSIGNIFICANT MUTE   855 19

SWIPE
    TO A LOT OF INFERIOR SWIPE   547 23
    IN THE WEEKLY PRESS THEIR SELF-SATISFIED SWIPE   680 23

SWIRL
    AND OUR BODIES MOLTEN DROPS OF DREAM-BLOOD THAT SWIRL A+   176 7
    AND SWIRL OF A TAIL   524 16
    ALAS TOSSED BACK IN MY HEARTS SWIRL   802 18
    YOU WATCH THE FIRE SPARKS SWIRL AND FLEE   *930 22

SWIRLED
    IN ITS MUD AND ITS TALK SLOWLY SWIRLED   551 6

SWIRLING
    AND FROM THE SWIRLING ANGRY FOLK THAT TRY   89 24
    HORSES GAY HORSES SWIRLING ROUND AND PLAITING   445 19

SWIRLS
    OPEN AND A GREAT GREY DAWN SWIRLS OVER MY FEET BEFORE   147 9
    WILDLY FLOATS SWIRLS   425 17
    SEA-WEED SWAYS AND SWAYS AND SWIRLS   467 16
    THROUGHOUT THE AEONS AS THE LIZARD SWIRLS HIS TAIL FINE+   683 7

SWISH
    I CAN HEAR THE SWISH OF THE SCYTHE-STROKES FOUR   219 22

SWISHING
    SHARP BREATHS SWISHING YEA BUT I   *944 3

SWITCH
    AND A JUNIPER SWITCH   400 23

SWITCHED
    SO I SWITCHED ON THE ELECTRIC LIGHT THINKING NOW   344 26

SWITCHING
    ALL THAT STORY OF MR GOD SWITCHING ON DAY   681 19

SWITZERLAND
    OVER THERE IS RUSSIA AUSTRIA SWITZERLAND FRANCE IN A   213 1

SWOLLEN
    WITH SWOLLEN VEINS THAT MET IN THE WRIST   123 25
    AND THE EGO WILL HAVE TO BURST LIKE THE SWOLLEN FROG   472 12
    SO OF COURSE THE NATION IS SWOLLEN WITH INSOLUBLE PROBL+   535 21
    WITH SWOLLEN VEINS THAT MET IN THE WRIST   *934 31

SWOON
    WOULD YOU SWOON LOVE SWOON   49 20
    AND WE SWOON WITH KISSES SWOON TILL WE SEEM   70 16
    SO SWEET LIKE A SWOON OR MORE LIKE THE DROWSE OF A LOW +   727 11
    AND LIFTED IN THE LONG SEEPING SWOON   769 14
    AND I IN A SWOON   *937 13
    TO STEAD HER WOMB AROUND US BEYOND THE SWOON   *938 15

SWOOP
    EVER THE LONG BLACK FIGURES SWOOP BY THE BED   140 23
    A CIRCLE SWOOP AND A QUICK PARABOLA UNDER THE BRIDGE   341 1
    AS THE BATS SWOOP OVERHEAD   341 22

SWOOPED
    SHE SWOOPED HER HAND AND THE ROVER   *936 1

SWOOPING
    ALL ALL ON THE ALTAR AND DEATH SWOOPING DOWN   239 4
    AND THEY GRUDGE THE CIRCUS PEOPLE THE SWOOPING GAY   446 8

SWORD
    AND COMES TOWARDS ME AH THE UPLIFTED SWORD   43 23
    THE PEACEFUL FLOOR WHEN FELL THE SWORD ON THEIR REST   155 8
    THAT MOON-LIKE SWORD THE ASCENDANT DEAD UNSHEATHE   168 23
    AGAINST US SWORD THAT NO MAN WILL   168 24
    SWORD THAT SEVERS THE QUESTION FROM US WHO BREATHE   168 26
    LIKE A SWORD OF DAMOCLES   373 31

SWORD-BLADE
    SWORD-BLADE BORN   306 32

SWORD OF DAMOCLES
    LIKE A DOWN-CURVED SWORD OF DAMOCLES   782 7

SWORD-RUST
    BLOSSOM BEYOND THE SWORD-RUST   306 16

SWORDS
    TEARS AND SWORDS TO MY HEART ARROWS NO ARMOUR WILL TURN+   57 23
    THE RUSTY SWORDS OF ALMOND-TREES   304 24
    PAST SALUTING SWORDS OF THE ANGELS   770 16

SWORE
    YER NEDN'T 'AVE SWORE   81 12
    IN THE SAME WAY IF I SWORE TO HATE A WOMAN ALL MY LIFE + 834 10
    YOU NEDN'T HAVE SWORE   *923 12

SWORN
    SWORN TO A HIGH AND SPLENDID PURPOSELESSNESS   197 16

SWOUND
    OF ALL IN A SWOUND   120 23

SWUNG
    AS FARTHER OFF THE SCYTHE OF NIGHT IS SWUNG   135 11
    SHE STOOPS TO THE SPONGE AND HER SWUNG BREASTS   217 16
    BOWED AND LIFTED HER FOOT IN HER HAND SMILED SWUNG HER 444 28
    SWUNG GREAT CURVES THROUGH THE UPPER SPACE AND CAME   445 6
    SWUNG STRONG AND HEAVY TO SADDLE AGAIN   735 13
    TO PULL DOWN THE BOUGH THE LEAVES BROKE AND THE FRUIT S+ 864 10
    WHEN HE SWUNG LIKE THE RHYTHM OF A POEM OVER THE RIVER 868 13
    AS FURTHER OFF THE SCYTHE OF NIGHT IS SWUNG   *939 12

SYCAMORE
    BEHIND THE BLACK SYCAMORE AT THE END OF THE GARDEN   62 26
    THE THIN SYCAMORE IN THE PLAYGROUND IS SWINGING WITH FL+ 92 2
    THE THIN SYCAMORE IN THE PLAYGROUND IS SWINGING WITH FL+ *926 2

SYDENHAM
    ON THE GREAT BLUE PALACE AT SYDENHAM LIGHTS STIR AND SH+ 52 18

SYLLABLE
    THAT EVERY SYLLABLE EVERY ACCENT EVERY INTONATION AND E+ 655 4
    AND SPEAK NO SYLLABLE AND NEVER BE   737 17

SYLLABLES
    ETRUSCAN SYLLABLES   296 28

SYMBOL
    AND LONG AGO THE ALMOND WAS THE SYMBOL OF RESURRECTION 303 1
    BUT TELL ME WHY SHOULD THE ALMOND BE THE SYMBOL+   303 2
    IN CHINA THE BAT IS SYMBOL OF HAPPINESS   342 6
    AND THE SYMBOL OF THE ROBOT IS THE WHEEL REVOLVING   713 10

SYMBOLIC
    AS YOU SEE IT STANDING GROWING YOU FEEL AT ONCE IT IS S+ 282 13

SYMBOLS
  SYMBOLS   282 26
  BEAN WAS ONE OF THE OLDEST SYMBOLS OF THE MALE ORGAN FO+   303 19

SYMMETRY
  NIGHT WERE DISTINGUISHED FROM THE SYMMETRY OF THEIR MIX+   295 6

SYMPATHISE
  AND I SUFFERED IT WANTING TO SYMPATHISE   206 34
  DON'T SYMPATHISE OR YOU TAINT THE UNBORN BABIES   442 5

SYMPATHY
  FOR THE SYMPATHY IN THEIR VAST SHY HEARTS   465 11
  SOFT SLOW SYMPATHY   471 1
  AND WHOEVER WALKS A MILE FULL OF FALSE SYMPATHY   653 1
  THAT CONVULSES AND TREMBLES AGAIN WITH THE SYMPATHY OF +   *952 7

SYNDICATES
  NOT IN DOLLARS NOR IN BANKS NOR IN SYNDICATES   774 29

SYPHILIS
  AND WHORING ON THE BRAIN AS BAD AS SYPHILIS INCIPIENT I+   *952 20

SYPHILITIC
  WHORING ON THE BRAIN BECOMES REALLY SYPHILITIC   845 8

SYRACUSAN
  SOMETHING OF THE SAME FLAVOUR OF SYRACUSAN MUSCAT WINE   280 9

SYRACUSE
  IN SYRACUSE ROCK LEFT BARE BY THE VICIOUSNESS OF GREEK   278 4

SYRINGA
  COOL AS SYRINGA BUDS IN MORNING HOURS   65 9
  COOL AS SYRINGA BUDS   *913 10
  COOL LIKE SYRINGA BUDS   *914 10

SYSTEM
  I THINK I COULD BREAK THE SYSTEM WITH MY HEART   213 19
  WHY HAVE A FINANCIAL SYSTEM TO STRANGLE US ALL IN ITS   451 30
  WHY HAVE THE INDUSTRIAL SYSTEM   452 1
  WHY DON'T WE DO SOMETHING ABOUT THE MONEY SYSTEM   518 6
  WE FEEL THAT IF THE WHOLE COMBATIVE COMPETITIVE SYSTEM   519 19
  MEN ARE MADE MEAN BY FEAR AND A SYSTEM OF GRAB   520 28
  THE SYSTEM ALLOWS US TO BE   520 32
  AND UNDER A COMPETITIVE SYSTEM THAT IS IMPOSSIBLE REALLY   522 25
  WE MUST CHANGE THE SYSTEM AND MAKE LIVING FREE TO ALL   522 29
  START A SYSTEM OF OFFICIAL SPYING   536 4
  BECAUSE THEIR HOPE IS PINNED DOWN BY THE SYSTEM   558 28
  SYSTEM OF THE ROBOT   649 5
  BUT WHAT CAN YOU DO IN A SYSTEM WHICH FORCES YOU TO GO +   831 9
  BUT OF COURSE THIS MEANS SMASHING THE PRESENT SYSTEM OF+   837 27

SYSTEMS
  INDUSTRIAL AND FINANCIAL SYSTEMS MACHINES AND SOVIETS   452 10

SYSTOLE
  SYSTOLE DIASTOLE   55 30

'S
  'S LESS GRASPIN' IF 'ER'S POOR   84 4
  'S ALL I GOT OUT OF IT   84 30

TABERNACLE
  OF DEATH BUT I WAIT AWHILE IN THIS TABERNACLE   772 20

TABLE
  HE FLINGS THE RABBIT SOFT ON THE TABLE BOARD   43 22
  PERSISTS ALL MORNING HERE IN A JAR ON THE TABLE   90 2
  SHE LAUGHS AT ME ACROSS THE TABLE SAYING   218 1
  WHEN I WAS WAITING AND NOT THINKING SITTING AT A TABLE +   672 18
  AND BESIDE IT ON THE TABLE HER GLOVES AND MY WILTED WIL+   856 15
  ALONG THE TABLE AT NOON OR WHEN YOU BRING   875 8
  SHE LAUGHS AT ME ACROSS THE TABLE SAYING   *943 14

TABLET
  LIFE ESTABLISHING THE FIRST ETERNAL MATHEMATICAL TABLET   355 17

TABOO
  YET THE NAME IS TABOO   551 24

TACE TU CRAPA BESTIA
  TACE TU CRAPA BESTIA   384 13

TACITLY
  IT SHOULD ALWAYS BE TACITLY UNDERSTOOD BETWEEN ALL OF US   *953 2

TACK
  AND I WISH THAT THE BABY WOULD TACK ACROSS HERE TO ME   65 5

TACKLE
  AND TACKLE THE BLOWSY BIG BLOW-FLY   458 11
  THEREFORE BE PREPARED TO TACKLE THE CAGE   486 6
  THE MORE YOU TACKLE THE PROPERTY DRAGON   665 10
  MANLY AND TACKLE THE OUTSIDE WORLD   843 3

TACTILE
  AUDILE TACTILE SENSITIVENESS AS OF A TENDRIL WHICH ORIE+   285 26

TA'EIN'
  AN' THEY TA'EIN' 'IM I' TH' AMBULANCE   45 6

TA'EN
  IT'S TA'EN THEE SEVEN DAYS TER SAY IT TER ME   139 30

TA'E
  I'LL TA'E THY WORD GOOD-BYE LIZ   80 29
  T' CHILDT MAUN TA'E ITS LUCK IT MUN   81 1
  AN' 'ER MAUN TA'E 'ER LUCK   81 2
  TA'E OFF THY DUTY STRIPES TIM   82 17
  TA'E OFF THY P'LICEMAN'S HELMET   82 19
  AFORE I CAN TA'E THEE I'VE GOT A WIDDER O' FORTY-FIVE T+   83 8
  I'LL TA'E THY WORD GOOD-BYE LIZ   *922 29
  THE CHILDT MAUN TA'E ITS LUCK IT MAUN   *923 1
  AN' SHE MAUN TA'E HER LUCK   *923 2
  TA'E OFF THY P'LICE-MAN'S HELMET   *924 23
  BEFORE I CAN TA'E THEE I'VE GOT A WIDOW OF FORTY-FIVE T+   *925 12

TAGS
  NONE IN RAGS AND NONE IN TAGS   312 7
  NOT BY THEIR RAGS AND NOT BY THEIR TAGS   312 14
  SANS RAGS SANS TAGS   313 1

TAIL
  STILL YOUR QUICK TAIL LIE STILL AS DEAD   43 3
  AND LASHED HIS TAIL SLOWLY SLOWLY   324 7
  AND LASHING HIS TAIL ABOVE THE WORLD   324 31
  PUT SALT ON HIS TAIL   329 1
  YET PUT SALT ON THE TAIL OF THE JOHANNINE BIRD   329 14
  PUT SALT ON ITS TAIL   329 15
  YOU TURN YOUR HEAD TOWARDS YOUR TAIL AND SMILE   332 11
  TAIL   335 10
  THEN GAY FEAR THAT TURNS THE TAIL SPRIGHTLY FROM A SHAD+   336 18
  FEAR CRAVEN IN HIS TAIL   347 11
  WITH YOUR TAIL TUCKED A LITTLE ON ONE SIDE   354 19
  AND SO BEHOLD HIM FOLLOWING THE TAIL   361 13
  LIKE SOME UNHAPPY BULL AT THE TAIL OF A COW   361 15
  OR IF IT HAPPEN TO SHOW AT HER POINTED HEAVY TAIL   361 20
  AND THE DEEP SECRET ALL-PENETRATING TAIL CURVED BENEATH   365 3
  TO THE ROOT-RISING OF YOUR ERECTED TAIL   370 15
  THE UPSTART OF YOUR ROUND-BARRED SUN-ROUND TAIL   370 21
  FLY SLOWLY AWAY WITH A RUST OF FIRE IN YOUR TAIL   374 30
  HIS TAIL   380 16
  AS FROM THE STEM OF HIS BRISTLING LIGHTNING-CONDUCTOR T+   381 19
  AT SEASONS SHE CURLS BACK HER TAIL LIKE A GREEN LEAF IN+   385 31
  DEFIANT CURLING THE LEAF OF HER TAIL AS IF SHE WERE CUR+   386 13
  TOWARDS THE TAIL OF THE EVERLASTING PROCESSION   389 1
  TAIL   393 20
  STEERED AND PROPELLED BY THAT STEEL-STRONG SNAKE OF A T+   393 28
  WITH YOUR IMBECILE BIT OF A TAIL IN A LOVE-FLUTTER   396 14
  AND THEN TURN TAIL TO THE NEXT COMER FOR A NEW DOLLOP   396 23
  THEY'RE AFTER WHAT THEY CAN GET AND DON'T YOU TURN TAIL   399 30
  SINCE I TROTTED AT THE TAIL OF THE SUN AS FAR AS EVER T+   405 26
  I'M GOING TO SIT DOWN ON MY TAIL RIGHT HERE   405 29
  WHEN A BIRD FLIPS HIS TAIL IN GETTING HIS BALANCE ON A +   496 6
  AND SWIRL OF A TAIL   524 16
  THROUGHOUT THE AEONS AS THE LIZARD SWIRLS HIS TAIL FINE+   683 7
  IN PEACE BEYOND THE LASHING OF THE SUN'S BRIGHT TAIL   786 2
  IS LASHING HIS TAIL IN HIS SLEEP THE WINDS HOWL THE COL+   795 14

TAILOR
  EKED OUT BY HIS TAILOR AND HIS HATTER   *947 30

TAILORED
  WITH YOUR TAILORED CUT-AWAY COAT   835 18

TAILS
  HANGING HAIRY PIGS' TAILS   390 12
  LIGHT WENT OVER THE HILL-BROW SWIFTLY WITH THEIR TAILS   391 2
  OR SITTING WITH OUR TAILS CURLED   450 14
  THAT PUTS SALT ON THE TAILS   562 10

TAIL-SPIN
  AND EUROPE'S TAIL-SPIN ROLLS STILL UNROLLED   814 8

TAIL-TUFTS
  LIKE THE TWO LIONS WHO DEVOURED ONE ANOTHER AND LEFT TH+   665 2
  LET'S HOPE THERE'LL BE MORE SENSE IN TAIL-TUFTS   665 4

TAINT
  TO LEAVE BUT ONLY THE MEREST POSSIBLE TAINT   53 31
  DON'T SYMPATHISE OR YOU TAINT THE UNBORN BABIES   442 5
  WITH THE HUMAN TAINT   481 12
  AS IT FEELS THE SLIMY TAINT   580 20

TAINTED
  EVERYTHING WAS TAINTED WITH MYSELF   256 24
  IT WAS ALL TAINTED WITH MYSELF I KNEW IT ALL TO START W+   256 29
  TAINTED WITH THE EGO AND THE PERSONALITY   481 20
  THEM NOW FROM ALL THIS TOUCH OF TAINTED DEATH   581 5
  FOR MY TAINTED TRANSIENCY AS A THING UNREAL   772 7

TAINTS
  AND TAINTS AND BLACKENS THE SKY, TILL AT LAST IT IS DARK+   258 12

TAKE
  TAKE THEM AND BUY THEE A SILVER RING   44 4
  TO TAKE OFF 'IS PIT-DIRT   45 16
  TAKE COVER IN DEATH   55 24
  THEY TAKE TRAGEDY SO BECOMINGLY   71 30
  TAKE WRITHING FORMS OF ALL BEASTS THAT SWEAT AND THAT F+   73 15
  SO SHALL I TAKE   74 18
  THEIR DROSS OF INDIFFERENCE AND TAKE THE TOLL   74 21
  TAKE 'ER I'STEAD O' ME   80 28
  THAT SILENCE SHOULD TAKE THE SONG AND THE BIRD   110 11
  WHO SHALL TAKE YOU AFRESH   112 5
  HAD I KNOWN YESTERDAY YOU COULD TAKE   117 28
  WERE PRESSED CUP-SHAPE TO TAKE THIS REIVER   124 7
  SHE MAKES HER HANDS TAKE MY PART THE PART OF THE MAN   128 27
  OH LET US HERE FORGET LET US TAKE THE SHEER   132 23

TAKE
NAY TAKE THIS WEARY BOOK OF HOURS AWAY	135	20
TAKE THEM AWAY FROM THEIR VENTURE BEFORE FATE WRESTS	147	16
TAKE WHAT YOU'VE GOT YOUR MEMORY OF WORDS	158	7
TAKE THEN ETERNITY FOR WHAT IS THAT	158	13
YOUR HUMAN SELF IMMORTAL TAKE THE WATERY TRACK	161	28
I WISH I COULD TAKE IT ALL IN A LAST EMBRACE	173	15
NOW MORTALS ALL TAKE HOLD	177	8
LET NOW ALL MORTAL MEN TAKE UP	177	11
AND TAKE WITHIN THE WINE THE GOD'S GREAT OATH	177	17
YOU WHO TAKE THE MOON AS IN A SIEVE AND SIFT	197	22
YOUR EYES TAKE ALL OF ME IN AS A COMMUNICATION	210	12
MY FEET HAVE NO HOLD YOU TAKE THE SKY FROM ABOVE ME	211	10
BUT A NAME SHE MIGHT TAKE	213	6
DREAMING AND LETTING THE BULLOCK TAKE ITS WILL	225	20
FOR YOU TO TAKE	227	24
YOU WOULD TAKE ME TO YOUR BREAST BUT NO	230	21
TAKE ON THIS DOOM	235	2
TAKE MY WORDS AND FLING	236	25
TAKE OFF YOUR CLOAK AND YOUR HAT	237	17
TAKE OFF YOUR THINGS	238	9
I WANT HER THOUGH TO TAKE THE SAME FROM ME	266	23
THE POWER OF THE RISING GOLDEN ALL-CREATIVE SAP COULD T+	272	22
NO SIN IS IT TO DRINK AS MUCH AS A MAN CAN TAKE AND GET+	277	10
HERE TAKE ALL THAT'S LEFT OF MY PEACH	279	4
IS JUST TO PUT YOUR MOUTH TO THE CRACK AND TAKE OUT THE+	282	7
TAKE THE FERN-SEED ON OUR LIPS	287	8
DO YOU TAKE IN MESSAGES IN SOME STRANGE CODE	301	5
DO YOU TAKE THE WHISPER OF SULPHUR FROM THE AIR	301	8
BUT LET US TAKE HEART	304	4
THAT THEY TAKE HIBISCUS AND THE SALVIA FLOWER	318	6
AND I TAKE THE WINGS OF THE MORNING TO THEE CRUCIFIED	321	20
DROPPING TAKE WING	322	15
BUT FISHES ARE VERY FIERY AND TAKE TO THE WATER TO COOL	331	1
YOU WOULD TAKE A STICK AND BREAK HIM NOW AND FINISH	350	6
AND TAKE YOUR FIRST BITE AT SOME DIM BIT OF HERBAGE	352	14
TO TAKE YOUR FIRST SOLITARY BITE	352	18
TAKE UP THE TRAIL OF THE VANISHED AMERICAN	371	26
TAKE UP THE PRIMORDIAL INDIAN OBSTINACY	371	28
SO IT IS WHEN THEY TAKE THE ENEMY FROM US	382	6
AND HE COULDN'T TAKE IT	389	31
WE TAKE NO HUNGRY STRAY FROM THE PALE-FACE	405	7
THE FULL DOOM OF LOVING AND NOT BEING ABLE TO TAKE BACK	410	16
TAKE AWAY ALL THIS CRYSTAL AND SILVER	427	11
THEY'LL TAKE YOU FOR A WOMAN OF THE PEOPLE	433	12
DON'T TAKE IT	440	28
AND WE WE MUST TAKE THEM ON THE WING AND LET THEM GO	476	15
IN A CAGE IT CAN'T TAKE PLACE	485	8
BUT STILL ONE HAS NO RIGHT TO TAKE	492	11
AND REALLY TAKE DELIGHT IN HER	506	16
WITHOUT HAVING TO TAKE A CHILL TALKING TO HER	506	19
A THRILL RATHER EASILY EXHAUSTS ITSELF TAKE EVEN THE WAR	532	5
NATURALLY TAKE HOLD OF THE TOWN	537	12
HAD HAD TO TAKE HER FOR ONE NIGHT ONLY IN THE FLESH	538	7
REALLY I DON'T KNOW WHAT YOU TAKE ME FOR	546	12
FOR YOU TO TAKE	559	11
YOU MIGHT AS WELL TAKE THE LIGHTNING	559	13
AND TAKE SIXTY SLASHES	563	11
AND BEWARE AND TAKE CARE	565	15
DOES IT WANT TO GO TO BYE-BYE THERE THEN TAKE ITS LITTLE	570	22
TAKE ITS DUMMY GO TO BYE-BYE LIKE A MAN LITTLE MAN	570	24
HAVEN'T I TOLD YOU TO TAKE THE PITH	583	2
SHE'LL TAKE OFF HER SPECS AND SHE'LL PUT DOWN THE PAPER	583	12
I AM THAT I AM TAKE IT OR LEAVE IT	608	4
INTO THE UNKNOWN AND TAKE ROOTS BY ONESELF	610	18
AND THE WOUNDS TO THE SOUL TAKE A LONG LONG TIME ONLY	620	15
TAKE THE IRON HOOK OUT OF THEIR FACES THAT MAKES THEM SO	632	19
TAKE ME SOUTH AGAIN TO THE OLIVE TREES	652	22
THAT'S WHY ONE DOESN'T HAVE TO TAKE THEM SERIOUSLY	660	8
BUT YOU MUST NEVER TAKE THEM SERIOUSLY THEY WOULDN'T UN+	660	15
NOT TOO NICE OF COURSE THEY TAKE ADVANTAGE	660	17
AND AS IF SENSUAL EXPERIENCE COULD TAKE PLACE BEFORE TH+	690	17
BUILD THEN THE SHIP OF DEATH FOR YOU MUST TAKE	717	21
OH PITY THE DEAD THAT ARE DEAD BUT CANNOT TAKE	722	1
ALL UNEQUIPPED TO TAKE THE LONG LONG VOYAGE	722	5
I DREAD HIM COMING I WONDER HOW HE WILL TAKE IT	733	2
NOW I TAKE THE BIG STONE JUG OF WATER	734	24
THE FOE CAN TAKE OUR GOODS OUR HOMES AND LAND	736	16
LEAVE US TO TAKE OUR GHOSTS INTO OUR HEARTS	736	19
OH IT IS FINISHED I WOULD LIKE TO TAKE	738	9
TO TAKE IT OFF THIS CLOTHING OF A MAN	738	13
AND TAKE OUT MY INTESTINES TO TORTURE THEM	741	4
WE TAKE THE BRIDE O GOD AND OUR SEED OF LIFE	743	12
WOULD TAKE AWAY THE SICKENING FRET	747	13
AND TAKE A SWIM WITH US HERE	759	9
DON'T TAKE THE BLOOD OF MY BODY	767	7
DEATH DEATH TAKE ME WITH YOU TO SPARE ME THIS LAST	767	27
WILL YOU TAKE OFF YOUR THREAT	783	15
YOU WILL TAKE THE OTHER AWAY	784	27
THEY TAKE SUGAR FROM THE TALL TUBES OF THE CANE	793	20
HOW NICE IF WE COULD TAKE ALL THESE THINGS AWAY FROM TH+	794	19
TAKE BACK OUR LANDS AND SILVER AND OIL TAKE THE TRAINS +	794	21
OH MEN TAKE CARE TAKE CARE	806	7
TAKE CARE OF HIM AND IT	806	8
THEN I TAKE MY KNIFE AND THROW IT UPON THE GREY DOG	807	20
TAKE IT BRAVELY	809	5
TAKE DEATH BRAVELY	809	6
FOR OUR SOCIETY IS BASED ON GRAB AND DEVIL TAKE THE HIN+	829	24
AND DEVIL TAKE THE HINDMOST	829	28
AT THE SAME TIME THEY TAKE THE GREATEST POSSIBLE CARE O+	832	4
IT WILL TAKE AN EPOCH TWO THOUSAND YEARS AND MORE	833	29
ONE THING IS CERTAIN WE'VE GOT TO TAKE HANDS OFF LOVE	834	7
DEVIL TAKE THE HINDMOST	837	28
COME ON LET'S TAKE OFF YOUR COLLAR AND DON'T REPROACH ME	859	30
POOR SIEGMUND TAKE THE SOBS FROM OUT OF YOUR VOICE	871	17
BUT DO NOT SEEK TO TAKE ME BY DESIRE	873	26
AND I OPEN MY LIPS TO TAKE A STRAND OF KEEN HAIR	883	15
TAKE THE LANTERN AND WATCH THE SOW FOR FEAR SHE GRAB HE+	*892	24

TAKE
MYSELF IN THE ROAR OF LIFE WHICH SHALL TAKE AND OBLITER+	*894	23
AND SHALL I TAKE	*895	26
AND SHALL I TAKE	*904	15
TAKE OFF THY DUTY STRIPES TIM	*924	21
WHO SHALL TAKE YOU AFRESH	*928	25
TO THE FIRE AND RAIN WILL YOU TAKE THE FLOOD	*931	27
DO YOU THINK IF YOU TAKE ME THAT THAT WILL ABATE YOU	*932	12
WERE PRESSED CUP-SHAPE TO TAKE THIS REIVER	*935	7
NAY TAKE MY PAINTED MISSAL BOOK AWAY	*939	4
LORD TAKE HIS LOVE AWAY IT MAKES HIM WHINE	*945	18
GRANTED THERE IS A PROPER GIVE AND TAKE	*952	17
OH PITY THE DEAD THAT ARE DEAD BUT CANNOT TAKE	*958	1
SHALL TAKE THEM ABOARD TOWARDS THE GREAT GOAL OF OBLIVI+	*958	13

TAKEN
THEY HAVE TAKEN THE GATES FROM THE HINGES	40	21
TAKEN LIKE A SACRIFICE IN THE NIGHT INVISIBLE	90	26
YOU HAD TAKEN ME THEN HOW DIFFERENT	104	17
FOR THE NIGHT WITH A GREAT BREATH TAKEN	107	25
A PRIESTESS EXECRABLE TAKEN IN VAIN	151	21
LOOK IT HAS TAKEN ROOT	172	8
THEY ARE ACCURSED AND THE CURSE IS NOT TAKEN OFF	208	20
SHARP BREATHS TAKEN YEA AND I	219	23
AND EVENING HAS TAKEN ALL THE BEES FROM THE THYME	224	26
LIKE A FALCON 'TIS GOD HAS TAKEN THE VICTIM	239	5
AFTER YOU HAVE TAKEN OFF THE BLOSSOM WITH YOUR LIPS	282	7
WHICH THEY HAVE TAKEN AWAY	298	12
DEPARTS AND THE WORLD IS TAKEN BY SURPRISE	340	20
BUT THEY'VE TAKEN HIS ENEMY FROM HIM	382	1
AND EVEN THE DIRTIEST SCALLYWAG IS TAKEN IN	398	19
THINKING THIS DOG SURE HAS TAKEN A FANCY TO ME	398	20
AND THEY'RE TAKEN IN	399	16
WHILE THE POLE STAR LIES ASIDE LIKE AN OLD AXLE TAKEN F+	616	30
HE IS TAKEN BY THE SCIENTISTS VERY SERIOUSLY	708	13
BUT IF TAKEN AT ITS VERY BEST THE TITLE AMERICAN	775	34
AS IT MUST BE TAKEN AT ITS VERY BEST	775	36
TRANSMUTED THE DARK REDNESS TAKEN OUT	784	15
THEY HAVE TAKEN OFF THE BEAUTIFUL RED LILLY	845	24
AND THEN I KNEW I HAD TAKEN MY MOUTH FROM HER THROAT	882	7
KNOWING THEN I HAD TAKEN MY BOSOM FROM HER CRUSHED BREA+	882	9
HITHER HAS TAKEN AWAY TO THAT HELL	887	7
I COULD THINK O' NOWT BUT OUR TED AN' 'IM TAKEN	*910	3
A MOMENT AND SHE WAS TAKEN AGAIN IN THE MERCIFUL DARK	*912	24
TO THE UNKNOWN AND ARE TAKEN UP	*960	24

TAKES
ALL THAT IS RIGHT ALL THAT IS GOOD ALL THAT IS GOD TAKE+	34	27
DEATH IN WHOSE SERVICE IS NOTHING OF GLADNESS TAKES ME	48	9
TO THE NIGHT THAT TAKES US WILLING LIBERATES US TO THE +	70	4
WORLD WITHIN WORLDS A WOMB THAT GIVES AND TAKES	89	8
OF LOVE TAKES POSSESSION AND SETTLES HER DOWN	125	4
BETROTHED YOUNG LADY WHO LOVES ME AND TAKES GOOD	129	4
VESSEL OF DARKNESS TAKES THE RISING TIDE	132	30
HE TAKES THE FLAME-WILD DROPS	203	2
TAKES ALL BUT THE TALLEST POSY	226	16
BY THE FINE FINE WIND THAT TAKES ITS COURSE THROUGH THE	250	18
SIGHTLESS AND STRONG OBLIVION IN UTTER LIFE TAKES POSSE+	281	10
TAKES IT UP	429	6
SO HE TAKES IT OUT ON WOMEN	446	31
HE ONLY TAKES HIS BELLYFUL	466	21
TAKES POSSESSION OF IT	473	4
AND A FLOWER IT TAKES A SUMMER	477	6
AND IN THESE AWFUL PAUSES THE EVOLUTIONARY CHANGE TAKES	510	10
IN DEATH THE ATOM TAKES US UP	514	17
MY GOD IT TAKES SOME BEATING	547	18
SHE'S A HOLY TERROR SHE TAKES YOUR BEST FROCK	572	2
HIS URGE TAKES SHAPE IN FLESH AND LO	690	10
THE LITTLE SLENDER SOUL SITS SWIFTLY DOWN AND TAKES THE+	723	20
AND WHAT THE SOUL TAKES WITH HIM AND WHAT HE LEAVES BEH+	724	2
WITH HEAD AGAINST THE SHAFT AND TAKES	733	20
HIS EYES MEET MINE AS HE TAKES THE JUG OF WATER	734	27
NO WOMAN TAKES MY PART	751	20
TAKES EVERYTHING FROM YOU TOMORROW	752	19
HE TAKES HIMSELF SERIOUSLY	836	13
SPEAKING OF PERVERTS HE TAKES ON AN AMUSED BUT ICY	*948	4
WHAT A PITY HE TAKES HIMSELF SERIOUSLY AND DRAWS A	*950	28
THE LITTLE SLENDER SOUL SITS SWIFTLY DOWN AND TAKES THE+	*958	32

TAKING
THEIR BEAUTY FOR HIS TAKING BOON FOR BOON	129	18
TAKING ME BACK DOWN THE VISTA OF YEARS TILL I SEE	148	5
IS ONLY SAD MEN TAKING OFF THEIR SHIRTS	173	24
THEY FALL BACK AND LIKE A DRIPPING OF QUICKSILVER TAKIN+	322	12
TAKING A BIRD'S-EYE VIEW	328	4
TAKING BREAD IN HER CURVED GAPING TOOTHLESS MOUTH	359	19
AND THE LIVE LITTLE-ONE TAKING IN ITS PAW AT THE DOOR O+	394	23
AND SAT UP TAKING STRANGE POSTURES SHOWING THE PINK SOL+	445	12
AND TAKING IT OUT ON WOMEN	447	4
OF DELIBERATELY TAKING	469	26
ON A NARROW BEAT ABOUT THE SAME AS A PRISONER TAKING HIS	521	17
AND A GIRL RAN SWIFTLY LAUGHING BREATHLESS TAKING IN HE+	672	13
TAKING AND GIVING	825	31
AND TAKING IT OUT ON WOMEN	*949	16
TAKING IT OUT IN SPITE ON WOMEN	*949	18
TAKING THE LONGEST JOURNEY	*959	11

TAKIN'
I'M TAKIN' 'OME A WEDDIN'-DRESS	79	15
I'M TAKIN' 'OME A WEDDIN' DRESS	*921	11

TALE
THEY'LL LISTEN TO HER TALE	78	16
WELL I'M BELIEVIN' NO TALE MISSIS	78	17
TO DO SUCH A THING THOUGH IT'S A POOR TALE IT IS THAT I+	83	7
AN' 'DEED AN' I WISH AS THIS TALE O' THINE WOR NIVER MY+	83	10
OF AUTUMN TELL THE WITHERED TALE AGAIN	119	14
SO THE TALE BEGAN	379	28

TALE
MODERN LIFE IS A TALE TOLD BY AN IDIOT   522 1
O MY BOCCACCIO O HOW GOES YOUR PRETTY TALE   633 1
AND BANK-TELLERS TELL THE ONE TALE THAT IS TOLD   814 9
YESTERDAY YES IS A TALE THAT IS TOLD   815 6
OF THE DYING GRASS WITH A THRICE-TOLD TALE OF DEATH   858 27
TWAS A TALE SOON TOLD   863 12
THEY'LL LISTEN TO HER TALE   *920 8
WELL I'M BELIEVIN' NO TALE MISSIS   *920 9
TO SUCH A THING BUT IT'S A POOR TALE THAT I'M BOUND TO +   *925 11
BUT 'DEED AN' I WISH AS THIS TALE O' THINE WOR NIVER MY+   *925 14

TALES
TELLS DULL MEANINGLESS DISGUSTING TALES   522 7
I THINK IDIOTS TELL DULL STUPID DISGUSTING TALES   837 21

TALK
SHOULD I NOT ANSWER TO HIS TALK   43 16
I'LL TALK THEN   78 20
TALK ABOUT LOVE O' WOMEN   84 27
OF LINKING ELBOWS AND THEY TALK   106 13
I FEEL YOUR SILENCE TOUCH MY WORDS AS I TALK   110 3
WAS IT PERVERSITY THAT I LONGED TO TALK TO HIM   350 14
NO DON'T TALK TO ME ABOUT THE LOVE OF ENGLISHMEN   447 32
AND LET US IF YOU WILL TALK AND MINGLE   469 1
LET US TALK LET US LAUGH LET US TELL   470 4
OF TALK AND THOUGHT AND ME-AND-THEE   470 11
MEANWHILE IF WE MUST LET US THINK ABOUT IT AND TALK   471 21
BUT WHILE WE THINK OF IT AND TALK OF IT   471 25
THEN WE SHAN'T HAVE WAR AND WE NEEDN'T TALK ABOUT PEACE   496 5
THE ONLY PEOPLE I EVER HEARD TALK ABOUT MY LADY POVERTY   498 9
NOT FRIENDS NECESSARILY THEY TALK SO MUCH   499 21
BY WHICH THEY MEAN MORE TALK TALK TALK   502 2
SO LONG AS IT DIDN'T ALL FIZZLE OUT IN TALK   507 12
ONE MIGHT TALK OF THE SANITY OF THE ATOM   515 16
IN ITS MUD AND ITS TALK SLOWLY SWIRLED   551 6
TALK TALK TALK CORPSE-BODY NEWSPAPER TALK   584 16
ALL THIS TALK OF EQUALITY BETWEEN THE SEXES IS MERELY AN   620 1
NOWADAYS TO TALK OF HUMILITY IS A SIN AGAINST THE HOLY +   621 12
THEY TALK OF THE TRIUMPH OF THE MACHINE   623 24
I HAVE NOTICED THAT PEOPLE WHO TALK A LOT ABOUT LOYALTY   626 1
AND PEOPLE WHO TALK ABOUT FAITH   626 4
THESE TWO-LEGGED THINGS THAT WALK AND TALK   644 18
TALK TALK TALK   651 22
HEARING HER TALK THAT IS   655 2
O LET US TALK OF QUIET THAT WE KNOW   717 17
AND KILL APHRODITE DON'T SPEAK DO NOT TALK   750 23
AND IN THE BIGGEST HOUSES THEY KEEP THEIR MACHINES THAT+   793 24
I'LL TALK THEN   *920 12
THEY TALK OF THE TRIUMPH OF THE MACHINE   *953 12

TALKED
AND WE TALKED AND WE ROARED AND YOU TYPED LADY C   550 32
THERE WHEN YOU TALKED TO THEM   554 18
OH JESUS DIDN'T YOU SEE WHEN YOU TALKED OF SERVICE   629 1

TALKING
JOSTLING PEOPLE TOUCHING AND TALKING AND MAKING SMALL   249 18
BUT WITH THE WALKING AND TALKING AND CONVENTIONALLY PER+   442 2
ALL THIS TALKING INTIMACY   470 14
WITHOUT HAVING TO TAKE A CHILL TALKING TO HER   506 19
AND ON TALKING ABOUT IT   602 20
AND GOD THE SON A TALKING RADIO   641 4
AND LITTLE TALKING RADIOS   641 7
YOU SIT TALKING IN ALL EARNESTNESS TO A WOMAN   655 1
YET YOU GO ON TALKING IN ALL EARNESTNESS   655 6
PEOPLE GO ON TALKING WHEN THEY HAVE NOTHING TO SAY   657 18
AND NO TALKING WHATSOEVER   766 4

TALKIN'
LET ME GO WHAT'S GOOD O' TALKIN'   84 25

TALL
TALL AND DARK THE CHURCH MOVES ANXIOUS TO KEEP   48 21
DIM TREES SO HUGE AND TALL   68 24
SUCH AS THE TALL   96 7
TALL AND LOFTILY SHADOWED BUT THE MOON   103 30
STANDING ANGEL-STERN AND TALL   140 10
SO LIKE TO WOMEN TALL STRANGE WOMEN WEEPING   140 19
TALL BLACK BACCHAE OF MIDNIGHT WHY THEN WHY   140 28
GOLDEN-LIGHTED TALL   146 12
A TALL WOMAN WITH HER LONG WHITE GOWN AFLOW   155 13
OF THE MORNING THE ELMS ARE LOFTILY DIMMED AND TALL   164 22
AS IF MOVING IN AIR TOWARDS US TALL ANGELS   164 23
NOW EVERY TALL GLAD TREE   215 22
AND YOU WILL BE BEFORE ME TALL AND TOWERING   246 21
TO ROW FORWARD AND REACH HIMSELF TALL ON SPINY TOES   358 1
COME TALL OLD DEMONS SMILING   404 3
DUSTY POLLEN OF GRASS TALL GRASS IN ITS MIDSUMMER MALEN+   587 3
AND THE LIME-TREE LOVELY AND TALL EVERY LEAF SILENT   646 21
AND THE LARCH THAT IS ONLY A COLUMN IT GOES UP TOO TALL+   647 1
THE MAN WHO IS MOWING THE TALL WHITE CORN   651 13
AS THE TALL FOXGLOVES AND THE MULLEINS AND MALLOWS   709 18
A NICE ONE I LIKE IT HE'LL THINK IT'S A TALL ORDER   733 29
TALL VIRGINS OF THE AFTERWARDS   770 2
THEY TAKE SUGAR FROM THE TALL TUBES OF THE CANE   793 20
THEY PUT UP TALL CHIMNEYS THAT SMOKE   793 23
WE ARE LIKE TREES TALL AND RUSTLING   802 16
THESE TREES SO HUGE AND TALL   *915 8
OH BAVARIAN GENTIANS TALL ONES   *954 16
BAVARIAN GENTIANS TALL AND DARK BUT DARK   *956 1
GIVE ME A FLOWER ON A TALL STEM AND THREE DARK FLAMES   *956 21

TALLER
THE TREES RISE TALLER AND TALLER LIFTED   68 1
THE RYE IS TALLER THAN YOU WHO THINK YOURSELF   221 6
THE TREES RISE TALLER AND TALLER LIFTED   *914 16
THE RYE IS TALLER THAN YOU WHO THINK YOURSELF   *944 19

TALLEST
TAKES ALL BUT THE TALLEST POSY   226 16

TALLOW
AND ALL ITS TALLOW RIGHTEOUSNESS GOT RID OF   299 22

TALLOW-STINKING
THE JEWISH SEVEN-BRANCHED TALLOW-STINKING CANDLESTICK   299 20

TALLY
AND THE PALLOR OF NIGHT DOES NOT TALLY   38 4
AND CLASH AND YET SEEM TO TALLY   38 26
AND THE PALLOR OF NIGHT DOES NOT TALLY   *892 20

TALONS
FANGS AND CLAWS AND TALONS AND BEAKS AND HAWK-EYES   409 29
KISSES OF THE SOFT-BALLED PAWS WHERE THE TALONS ARE   709 13

TAME
GOING OUT IN SPRING TO THE ROUND OF HIS TAME DESERTS   126 27
NOT THIS HYENA TAME PEACE WHERE NO MAN DARE TELL ANOTHER 519 23
WHY DON'T WE LEARN TO TAME THE MIND   529 6

TANGIBLE
DIVIDED IN THE MYSTIC TANGIBLE AND INTANGIBLE DIFFERENCE 636 6

TANGLE
TRAFFIC WILL TANGLE UP IN A LONG DRAWN-OUT CRASH OF COL+ 624 27

TANGLED
WHITE AND HALOED WITH FIRE-MIST DOWN IN THE TANGLED   206 11
WITH HER LONG TANGLED SIDES LIKE AN OLD RUG THROWN   384 26
SHE WAS TANGLED UP IN HER OWN SELF-CONCEIT A WOMAN   619 1
O ARE YOU TANGLED UP IN YOURSELF   675 1
IS SHE TANGLED UP IN HERSELF THEN   675 3
THEY ARE LIKE CATS WITH UNCLEAN CLAWS TANGLED UP IN NETS 675 6
THE SUBSTANCE TANGLED IN THE NET   747 18
WITH SNAKE-BITES OF TANGLED UNCONSCIOUS EMOTION   833 31
FOR THE ANALYST IS TANGLED IN AN ESPECIALLY TANGLED BUN+ 833 34
MESHED AND TANGLED TOO MUCH IN THE SKEIN OF GUILT   884 14
AND I LIFT MY HEAD UPON THE TROUBLED TANGLED WORLD AND + *900 1
AND I LIFT MY HEAD UPON THE TROUBLED TANGLED WORLD AND + *903 14

TANGLES
LO THE UNIVERSE TANGLES ITS GREAT DRAGONS   795 10

TANGLING
TANGLING HIS CIRCLES TO BAFFLE YOU AND ME   118 25

TANK
UNDER TH' TANK AS FILLS TH' INGINES   79 3
UNDER THE TANK AS FILLS THE INGINES   *920 27

TANTRUMS
INTO TANTRUMS AND STARTED THEIR HULLABALOO   761 6

TAOS
FIRST TIME I LOST YOU IN TAOS PLAZA   395 27
OVER THE HEART OF THE WEST THE TAOS DESERT   403 1

TAP
FOOTSTEPPING TAP OF MEN BENEATH   68 23
AND WHERE THE WATER HAD DRIPPED FROM THE TAP IN A SMALL   349 13
AND THE HALF-HIDDEN PRIVATE PARTS JUST A LITTLE BRASS T+ 625 22
BUT A WOMAN SHY AND ALONE WAS WASHING HERSELF UNDER A T+ 651 4
FOOTSTEPPING TAP OF MEN BENEATH   *915 7

TAPER
THEN A GROUP OF TOADSTOOLS WAITING THE MOON'S WHITE TAP+   72 19
AND GUTTER TO EXTINCTION LIKE A TAPER ON A FORGOTTEN AL+ 859 4

TAPESTRY
AN ENDLESS TAPESTRY THE PAST HAS WOVEN DRAPES   173 19
AN ENDLESS TAPESTRY THE PAST HAS WOVEN DRAPES   *906 13
AN ENDLESS TAPESTRY THE PAST HAS WOVEN DRAPES   *908 7

TAPPING
IN THE TAPPING HASTE OF A FALLEN LEAF   68 21
THE TASSEL OF THE BLIND SWINGS CONSTANTLY TAPPING THE P+ 112 15
WITH A RHYTHM OF TAPPING COMING FEET   121 20
ARE TAPPING AT THE WINDOW-SASH   149 26
THE HAWK IS GONE A ROSE IS TAPPING   150 18
OR SOFTLY TAPPING AT MY STUDY DOOR   875 10
IN THE TAPPING HASTE OF A FALLEN LEAF   *915 5

TARA
TO FEED THE BONNY BABY AND KEEP ITS TARA DRY   570 19

TARANTELLA
WHILE I DANCE A TARANTELLA ON THE ROCKS AND THE CROON   130 6

TARDY
AT THIS MOMENT SCRAPING TARDY ARARAT   429 10

TARGET-QUICK
HE WILL NEVER QUITE STRIKE HOME ON THE TARGET-QUICK FOR   382 20

TARNISH
IN THIS ODD LIFE WILL TARNISH OR PASS AWAY   193 13

TARNISHED
YOU DULL ANGELS TARNISHED WITH CENTURIES OF CONVENTIONA+ 614 16
IN THE HEARSE OF NIGHT YOU SEE THEIR TARNISHED COFFINS   703 3
THE HOURS HAVE TUMBLED THEIR LUSTRELESS TARNISHED SANDS *896 6
THE HOURS HAVE TUMBLED THEIR LUSTRELESS TARNISHED SANDS *896 13

TARRIES
    TO THE DISTANCE THE WAVE THAT TARRIES   747 5

TART
    A MAN CAN'T GET ANY FUN OUT OF WIFE SWEETHEART OR TART   518 4
    I SUPPOSE TARTS ARE CALLED TARTS BECAUSE THEY'RE TART   530 18

TARTS
    NOR GUSTY JOVE WITH HIS EYE ON IMMORTAL TARTS   437 5
    I SUPPOSE TARTS ARE CALLED TARTS BECAUSE THEY'RE TART   530 18
    AND ONCE HE WAS GAY AND HEARTY WITH HIS EYE ON THE IMMO+ *946 17

TARTY
    AND I SUPPOSE MOST GIRLS ARE A BIT TARTY TODAY   530 20

TASK
    AT THIS MY TASK OF LIVING THIS MY DREAM   195 9

TASKS
    AYE BUSY WITH A FEW HARD TASKS AND WRATH   875 31

TASSEL
    THE TASSEL OF THE BLIND SWINGS CONSTANTLY TAPPING THE P+   112 17

TASSELS
    TASSELS IN ABANDON   170 20
    HUGE MORE TASSELS SWINGING MORE DRIPPING FIRE OF NEW   388 27

TASTE
    OF RIGOUR THEY TASTE DELIGHTEDLY   52 3
    OPEN THE CORE OF GLOAMING TASTE   114 15
    BLACKISH THEY WILL TASTE OF TEARS WHEN THE YELLOW DAPPL+ 119 13
    I LONGED TO TASTE I LONGED TO TURN   123 27
    TASTE IT   283 13
    HAVING TASTED ALL THERE WAS TO TASTE AND HAVING SLEPT H+ 324 11
    THEY DRAW NEAR TO TASTE IT AS IF SAYING NOW WHAT IS THI+ 331 5
    IT'S BAD TASTE TO BE WISE ALL THE TIME LIKE BEING A PER+ 496 1
    AS WE NEVER GET A TASTE OF REALLY   573 13
    THAT I NEVER GET A TASTE OF REALLY   671 1
    SO AN APPLE BECOMES MYSTIC WHEN I TASTE IT IN   707 28
    ALL OF WHICH THINGS I CAN SURELY TASTE IN A GOOD APPLE   708 1
    THOUGH SOME APPLES TASTE PREPONDERANTLY OF WATER WET AN+ 708 2
    IF I SAY I TASTE THESE THINGS IN AN APPLE I AM CALLED M+ 708 5
    AND TASTE NOTHING   708 8
    THE MOUTH OF THE MAN IS FULL OF THE TASTE OF PAIN   864 22
    OF RIGOUR THEY TASTE DELIGHTEDLY   *899 16
    OF RIGOUR THEY TASTE DELIGHTEDLY   *902 28
    TASTE OH TASTE AND LET ME TASTE   *930 3
    BRACKISH THEY WILL TASTE OF TEARS WHEN THE YELLOW DAPPL+ *932 22

TASTED
    HAVING TASTED ALL THERE WAS TO TASTE AND HAVING SLEPT H+ 324 11
    WE TASTED   817 18

TASTES
    THE FOOD OF THE NORTH TASTES TOO MUCH OF THE FAT   652 19

TASTING
    CLUTCHING TASTING DROPPING   861 27

TATTAH
    WANT TO GO A LITTLE TATTAH SO IT SHALL OF COURSE IT SHA+ 571 1
    GO A BANGING LITTLE TATTAH WITH ITS AUNTIE   571 2
    THEN WHEN SUNDAY COMES IT SHALL GO TATTAH WITH ITS AUNT+ 571 5
    AND TO GO A BANGING TATTAH WITH ITS AUNTIE   571 9

TATTERED
    AT HER TATTERED SILENCE AS SHE CROUCHES AND COVERS HER +   54 22
    AND TATTERED AND RED WITH THE LIFE THAT HAS BLED   823 4

TAUGHT
    THEY HAVE TAUGHT YOU TO SEE   118 21
    I HAVE BEEN TAUGHT THE LANGUAGE OF UNDERSTANDING   264 2
    AND THEY TAUGHT YOU TO SPEAK KING'S ENGLISH   549 11
    THEY HAVE TAUGHT YOU TO SEE   *931 31

TAUNTING
    AND CHILDREN BEHIND YOU TAUNTING YOU IN TEARS   755 5

TAUNTS
    A WOMAN TAUNTS HER LOVER   *944 17

TAUT
    AND PASSION WILL MAKE OUR BODIES TAUT WITH POWER   482 23
    TAUT AS A WETTED WARP   746 22

TAWDRY
    AND THE STREWN TAWDRY TRAPPINGS THAT LAST NIGHT'S POETR+ 856 11

TAWNY
    HER TAWNY EYES ARE ONYX OF THOUGHTLESSNESS   127 21
    BEHOLD MY EYES TURN TAWNY YELLOW   301 22

TAWNY-GOLD
    AND I WAS BLIND IN A TAWNY-GOLD DAY   123 32
    AND DAZED WITH A TAWNY-GOLD DISPLAY   *935 4

TAX
    AND HERE AM I PAYING INCOME TAX AND GOD-KNOWS-WHAT   547 5

TAXES
    TAXES   547 6

TCHEKOV
    AND THE TCHEKOV WIMBLY-WAMBLY WET-LEGS ALL WIPED OUT   533 17
    AND THE TCHEKOV LOT I'M TOO WEAK AND LOVABLE TO LIVE   534 1
    OF DOSTOEVSKY AND TCHEKOV   536 16

TEA
    AND THEY TURNED HIM UP FOR TEA   490 12
    AND A SERVANT-MAID BRINGS ME MY TEA   490 26
    AND WE SLID AND YOU SKI'D AND WE CAME IN TO TEA   550 31
    AND A DUCHESS ONCE CAME TO TEA   551 28

TEACH
    I WILL TEACH THEM THE BEGINNING OF THE LESSON AT THE RO+   93 24
    HIS MOTHER LIBERTY TRYING ALWAYS TO TEACH HIM TO COO   413 22
    WHEN WILT THOU TEACH THE PEOPLE   442 6
    GOD OF JUSTICE WHEN WILT THOU TEACH THEM TO SAVE THEMSE+ 443 9
    AND THEY RAN ME IN TO TEACH ME WHY   570 11
    TO TEACH THE RESURRECTION IN THE FLESH   609 18
    HOW CAN I TEACH YOU WHEN YOUR BLUE   *894 1
    IN SUCH A CASH-CHEMIST UNIVERSITY WHAT CAN THEY TEACH   *950 19

TEACHER
    A TEACHER OF THESE YOUNG BOYS MY SLAVES   *899 6
    A TEACHER OF THESE YOUNG BOYS MY SLAVES   *902 18

TEACHERS
    AND THE GREATEST OF TEACHERS WILL TELL YOU   726 3

TEACHING
    WHAT IS THE POINT OF THIS TEACHING OF MINE AND OF THIS   74 25
    OLD TRUTH OLD TEACHING OF ANY SORT   495 14

TEA-CUPS
    ROCKING DOWN THE SHOALS BETWEEN THE TEA-CUPS   *943 16

TEAR
    AND MELTED IN AN ICY TEAR   62 16
    TREMBLING BLUE IN HER PALLOR A TEAR THAT SURELY I HAVE +   67 16
    A TEAR WHICH I HAD HOPED THAT EVEN HELL HELD NOT AGAIN +   67 17
    IN HER VOICE AND A WEAK TEAR FALLS   106 2
    SOME LIMBS LIKE PARCELS AND TEAR   145 26
    THE ARRAS IS ALL ILLUSION OH COME AND TEAR IT AWAY   174 18
    TO TEAR THE MEMBRANE OF THIS SLEEP   403 6
    AND UNABLE TO TEAR IT   408 17
    THEY DO NOT SNATCH THEY DO NOT TEAR   465 27
    WHICH THREATEN TO TEAR THE WORLD IN TWO BETWEEN   516 22
    OR TEAR ME WITH THE FANGS OF DISAPPOINTMENT   604 11
    THEY WILL TEAR YOU TERRIBLY AND GIVE YOU BLOOD-POISONING 675 8
    I TEAR BUT NEWS OF SORROW AND PAIN   772 23
    AND GUARDED BY A GLITTERING TEAR   *912 22

TEARING
    WHEN TEARING THROUGH THE ANGUISH OF THIS LIFE   195 22
    TEARING A CRY FROM US   366 33
    LEFT IN THE DUST BEHIND LIKE A DUST-BALL TEARING ALONG   397 14
    COMING UP ON FIERCE LITTLE LEGS TEARING FAST TO CATCH U+ 397 15
    TEARING EACH OTHER'S FEELINGS TRAMPLING EACH OTHER'S TE+ 544 16

TEARLESS
    WITH TEARLESS EYES   783 9

TEARS
    IF SHE HAS ANY TEARS   37 4
    STRANGE THROBS BEYOND LAUGHTER AND TEARS   38 22
    TEARS AND DREAMS FOR THEM FOR ME   41 12
    OR SHOULD HE MY TEARS SURMISE   43 17
    WITH DREAD AND FILLS MY HEART WITH THE TEARS OF DESIRE   48 12
    WITH THE OLD SWEET SOOTHING TEARS AND LAUGHTER THAT   53 5
    THE SILENCE OF VANISHING TEARS AND THE ECHOES OF LAUGHT+   53 19
    THE NOISE DISTRESSES HER EARS AND TEARS   54 21
    TEARS AND SWORDS TO MY HEART ARROWS NO ARMOUR WILL TURN+   57 23
    NO TEARS OF LOVE UNNERVING   64 1
    WHILE HER TEARS SOAK THROUGH TO MY BREAST   64 18
    MY BABY HER BROWN HAIR DRUGGED WITH WET TEARS   73 23
    NOW WET WITH TEARS AND PAIN HANGS HEAVILY   74 2
    I HAVE FETCHED THE TEARS UP OUT OF THE LITTLE WELLS   94 10
    I WATCHED THE TEARS ON THE GUILTY CHEEKS OF THE BOYS   94 14
    THE TEARS ARE DRY AND THE CHEEK'S YOUNG FRUITS ARE FRESH 94 19
    O TEARS ON THE WINDOW-PANE   119 10
    BLACKISH THEY WILL TASTE OF TEARS WHEN THE YELLOW DAPPL+ 119 13
    I WHO SIT IN TEARS   169 9
    OF MIRTH THEN THE DRIPPING OF TEARS ON YOUR GLOVE   179 19
    NOT TEARS BUT WHITE SHARP BRINE   207 19
    A SOUND SUBDUED IN THE DARKNESS TEARS   210 21
    AND THE STAGNANT TEARS   240 3
    OF TEARS THE STORE   269 1
    OR STORMS OF TEARS OR RAGE OR BLACKENING RAIN   745 12
    AND CHILDREN BEHIND YOU TAUNTING YOU IN TEARS   755 5
    STRANGER SOFT ARE THE TEARS THAT FALL   758 15
    TEARS NOW FALL ON WHITE SAND   767 4
    YET THROUGH THE TEARS STEALS A SENSE OF PEACE AND GREAT+ 768 1
    TEARS WRINKLE OUR FACES LIKE RAIN IN THE HOLLY   814 24
    AND MY THROAT IS WET WITH HER TEARS   863 4
    TEARS FOR HER PAIN   863 16
    TEARS OPEN   869 10
    AND TERRIBLY STRANGE ARE HIS TEARS THAT ARE WETTING MY + 871 27
    THROUGH A PAIN OF RISING TEARS AND DID NOT REPLY   884 21
    US ALL ONE IN LAUGHTER AND TEARS   *893 5
    I HAVE FETCHED THE TEARS UP OUT OF THE LITTLE WELLS   *896 26
    I WATCHED THE TEARS ON THE FRUITED CHEEKS OF THE BOYS   *897 2
    THE TEARS ARE DRY THE CHEEKS' YOUNG FRUITS ARE FRESH   *897 7
    WITH THE OLD SWEET SOOTHING TEARS AND LAUGHTER THAT SHA+ *905 19
    THE MISTS OF RECEDING TEARS AND THE ECHO OF LAUGHTER   *906 10
    MY BABY HER BROWN HAIR BRUSHED WITH WET TEARS   *913 15
    HE WATERS OUR FACE WITH TEARS OUR YOUNG FRUITS FILLS WI+ *926 29
    OH TEARS ON THE WINDOW PAIN   *932 19
    BRACKISH THEY WILL TASTE OF TEARS WHEN THE YELLOW DAPPL+ *932 22

TEAR-TREMBLING
    EVERYTHING TEAR-TREMBLING STARS OF AUTUMN   107 7

TEA-TABLE
    IT IS ABSURD FOR ME TO DISPLAY MY NAKED SOUL AT THE TEA+ 608 11

TECHNICALLY
    OF THE FEMALE FORM TECHNICALLY BEAUTIFUL ACTUALLY A WHI+ 619 12

TED
    I COULD THINK O' NOWT BUT OUR TED AN' 'IM TAKEN   *910   3
    WHERE OUR TED 'UD SOON BE SANK   *911   8

TEDIUM
    IN TEDIUM AND MOUTH RELAXED AS IF SMILING INEFFABLE TED+ 66 12

TED'S
    AN' OUR TED'S COFFIN SET ON TH' GROUND 60 21

TEEMING
    THERE WERE NO TEEMING 224   6
    TEEMING OBEDIENCE 414 20
    HAVE PHOSPHORESCENT TEEMING WHITE WORDS 441   2
    THE WHOLE TEEMING FLESH OF MANKIND *907 27

TEEMIN'
    AN' I COME AWAY ACAUSE O' TH' TEEMIN' RAIN 61 16
    AN' I COME AWAY BECAUSE O' THE TEEMIN' RAIN *911 32

TEEMS
    TEEMS 176   5
    DARK GLITTER OF LIFE AMID A SKY THAT TEEMS *895   7

TEENS
    IN HER MAIDEN TEENS 564 26

TEETH
    HIS STRONG TEETH IN A SMILE AND FLASHES HIS EYES 43 20
    WITCH TEETH AN' 'ER BLACK HAWK-EYES AS I'VE 77 23
    WHY EVEN NOW YOU SPEAK THROUGH CLOSE-SHUT TEETH 87   5
    SHARPENING HIS TEETH ON THE WOLVES 324 29
    AND THE WIND IN HIS TEETH FOR A BIT 378   2
    AH THEN WHEN HE TORE THE WIND WITH HIS TEETH 378   4
    OBSTACLE TO SET HIS TEETH IN THE SUN 378   7
    BARES HIS LONG ASS'S TEETH FLATTENS HIS LONG ASS'S EARS 379 21
    SHOWING A GLINT OF TEETH AND GLANCING TROPICAL EYES ARO+ 391 14
    AND WHITE TEETH SHOWING IN YOUR DRAGON-GRIN AS YOU RACE 397 20
    AND SHOW A TINY BUNCH OF WHITE TEETH IN YOUR UNDERHUNG 398 11
    AND HOOING AND COOING AND SIDLING THROUGH THE FRONT TEE+ 433 22
    THOUGH MAYBE THE MAMMOTH GOT TOO BIG IN TUSK AND TEETH 529 17
    WHILE PEOPLE MINCE MEAN WORDS THROUGH THEIR TEETH 530 11
    THE FATHER EATS THE PEAR AND THE SON'S TEETH ARE SET ON+ 530 22
    TEETH 800   9
    WITH A BLADE OF GRASS BETWEEN MY TEETH 804 14
    WITH A BLADE OF GREEN GRASS BETWEEN HIS TEETH 805 22
    WITCH TEETH AN' 'ER BLACK HAWK-EYES AS I'VE *919 11
    THEN FLUTTER FOR A MOMENT AND THE RAT'S LONG TEETH ARE + *932 30
    THIRTEEN TIMES THE TEETH FLASHED IN A FIRE OF BLOOD *933   1

TEETHE
    THE BABES JUST BEGINNING TO TEETHE 553 32

TELEGRAM-BICYCLE
    TELEGRAM-BICYCLE APPROACHES I WAIT 100   6

TELEPHONE
    DO YOU TELEPHONE THE ROAR OF THE WATERS OVER THE EARTH 301 10

TELESCOPE
    WE LOOK AT HIM THROUGH THE WRONG END OF THE LONG TELESC+ 372 22

TELL
    'E SAYS TELL YOUR MOTHER AS 'ER MESTER'S 44 22
    YOU TELL ME THE LAMBS HAVE COME THEY LIE LIKE DAISIES W+ 57 25
    ME TELL ABOUT THAT LASS WHEN YOU'D ALL GONE 61   2
    ASKS TO BE HIDDEN AND WISHES NOTHING TO TELL 64 13
    DUNNA THEE TELL ME IT'S HIS'N MOTHER 76 23
    OH AY HE'LL COME AN TELL THEE HIS-SEN 76 25
    BUT TELL ME ISN'T IT TRUE 79 26
    SO THERE AN' I TELL THEE FLAT 80   2
    AS THA ALLUS 'AST BUT LET ME TELL THEE 80   5
    F'R I TELL YER I H'ARENA MARRYIN' NONE 81   3
    AN' 'DEED AN' I WISH AS THIS TALE O' THINE WOR NIVER MY+ 83 10
    WHY DOES SHE COME WHEN SHE KNOWS WHAT I HAVE TO TELL 85 16
    OF TONGUES SO THE SHADOWS TELL 108 14
    OF AUTUMN TELL THE WITHERED TALE AGAIN 119 14
    WHEN I TELL YOU THE STARS FLASH SIGNALS EACH ONE 130 25
    FOR I TELL YOU 131   7
    AGAIN I TELL YOU I BLEED I AM BOUND WITH WITHIES 131 11
    I TELL YOU MY BLOOD RUNS OUT ON THE FLOOR OF THIS OAK 131 13
    LAD SHOULD I TELL THEE SUMMAT 137 19
    AY LAD I'LL TELL THEE THY MIND 138 28
    I TELL THEE THA WON'T BE SATISFIED 139   8
    I TELL THEE THA WON'T BE SATISFIED 139 10
    SHALL I TELL YOU THEN HOW IT IS 169 26
    COMES WITH THE SIGHT OF THE ROOM I CANNOT TELL 220 14
    AND TELL YOU HOW 227 28
    SERVE THEN I TELL YOU ADD YOUR STRENGTH TO MINE 235   1
    I TELL YOU THERE IS ALL THESE 256   2
    AH NO I CANNOT TELL YOU WHAT IT IS THE NEW WORLD 260 19
    I CANNOT TELL YOU THE MAD ASTOUNDED RAPTURE OF ITS DISC+ 260 20
    YOU TELL ME I AM WRONG 278   1
    WHO ARE YOU WHO IS ANYBODY TO TELL ME I AM WRONG 278   2
    DO YOU MEAN TO TELL ME YOU WILL SEE NO FISSURE 279 22
    DO YOU MEAN TO TELL ME THERE SHOULD BE NO FISSURE 278 27
    BUT TELL ME TELL ME WHY SHOULD THE ALMOND BE THE SYMBOL+ 303   2
    AS CARPACCIO WILL TELL YOU 324 27
    YET I HAD TO TELL THEM TO DIE 410   4
    I DIDN'T TELL YOU TO DIE FOR NOTHING 412   1
    TELL ME FIRST O TELL ME 428 23
    LET US TALK LET US LAUGH LET US TELL 470   4

TELL
    WITH THE GODHEAD OF ENERGY THAT CANNOT TELL LIES 481 26
    AN' TELL 'EM TO 491   4
    BECAUSE TO TELL THE TRUTH I HAVE ENOUGH AS I AM 498   6
    I'M NOT GOING TO TELL ANY LIES ABOUT IT 507   3
    SHALL I TELL YOU AGAIN THE NEW WORD 513   1
    NOT THIS HYENA TAME PEACE WHERE NO MAN DARE TELL ANOTHER 519 23
    I TELL YOU THE PENIS WON'T DO IT 539 21
    WHEREAS LET ME TELL YOU IF YOU WERE MY EQUAL 547 10
    I TELL YOU SOMETHING'S BEEN DONE TO 'EM 550 13
    TELL ME A WORD 551   9
    TELL ME A THING 551 13
    TELL ME A THING 551 17
    TELL ME WHAT'S WRONG 551 21
    WHEN I HAD TO TELL MYSELF PLAIN 555   6
    AND TELL ME HOW THEY CAN PUT IT ACROSS 556 23
    A JOY TO TELL IT YOU 576 17
    A JOY TO TELL IT YOU 576 23
    FOR THE FLOWERS AND I'LL TELL YOU WHAT 578   1
    AND SAID OH BOY I TELL YOU WHAT 578 10
    BUT WHY I ASK YOU OH TELL ME WHY 578 14
    I TELL YOU THERE MUST BE SOMETHING WRONG 579   5
    COMFORT AND CHEER SURE THAT IT WILL TELL HER 583 16
    AND EASY TO SWALLOW ALWAYS TELL THEM THEY'RE HAPPY 583 19
    BUT TELL ME OH TELL ME WHAT IS BECOMING TO A MAN 606 10
    TELL ME FIRST WHAT I AM 606 11
    BUT TELL ME TELL ME HOW DO YOU KNOW 614 13
    LET ME TELL YOU THAT THE SUN IS ALIVE AND CAN BE ANGRY 625 13
    YOU TELL ME EVERY MAN HAS A SOUL TO SAVE 638 15
    I TELL YOU NOT ONE MAN IN A THOUSAND HAS EVEN 638 16
    I TELL YOU IT IS NO WOMAN IT IS NO MAN FOR I AM ALONE 652 14
    THEY TELL ME THAT THESE BRITISH MORAL BIRDS 659   7
    I SHALL TELL HER THE HOUSE IS MINE 671   6
    MY CHILD I CANNOT TELL A LIE 681 23
    TELL ME I$ THE GENTIAN SAVAGE AT THE TOP OF ITS COARSE + 684   2
    TELL ME TELL ME IS THERE IN YOU A BEAUTY TO COMPARE 684   5
    BUT TELL ME TELL ME HOW DO YOU KNOW 697 24
    OH DO NOT TELL ME THE HEAVENS AS WELL ARE A WHEEL 713 11
    BUT IS THAT A QUIETUS O TELL ME IS IT QUIETUS 717 14
    AND THE GREATEST OF TEACHERS WILL TELL YOU 726   3
    I FEEL TO HAVE TO TELL HIM 733 31
    IF THEY WOULD LISTEN I COULD TELL THEM NOW 744 26
    TO TELL ME 748 15
    AND TELL HIM FROM ME 754   4
    TELL HIM PRAYER IS STRONGER THAN IRON FAITH 754 11
    STEEPED ENOUGH TELL HIM TO COME ACROSS 759   8
    TELL THEM THEY ARE ALL FOOLS THAT I'M LAUGHING AT THEM 791 26
    TELL THEM THEY ARE LIKE FROGS WITH STONES IN THEIR BELL+ 791 30
    TELL THEM THEY MUST GET THE STONES OUT OF THEIR BELLIES 791 31
    TELL THEM SO FIRST MAN OF MY NAME 792   9
    SO TELL THE MEN I AM COMING TO 793   5
    SOMETIMES THEY COME TO TELL US THINGS 793 15
    FOR I TELL YOU THERE ARE NO DEAD DEAD NOT EVEN YOUR DEAD 795 17
    I TELL YOU SORROW UPON YOU YOU SHALL ALL DIE 796   2
    I AM ABOUT TO TELL THE DRAGON OF THE WATERS TO TURN ROU+ 797   5
    I TELL YOU THE DAY SHOULD NOT TURN INTO GLORY 799 25
    I TELL YOU YOU ARE NOT MEN ALONE 800 16
    DO NOT TELL ME MY FACE IS SHINING 802 18
    AND BANK-TELLERS TELL THE ONE TALE THAT IS TOLD 814   9
    I THINK IDIOTS TELL DULL STUPID DISGUSTING TALES 837 21
    I CAN'T TELL HOW IT COMES *893   8
    THEY WAS WILD ONES WHITE AND BLUE I COULD TELL *910 17
    ME TELL THEE ABOUT THIS LASS WHEN YOU HAD GONE *911 18
    DUNNA THEE TELL ME IT'S HIS'N MOTHER *918 15
    OH AY HE'LL BE COMIN' TO TELL THEE HIS-SEN *918 17
    BUT TELL ME ISN'T IT TRUE *921 22
    LIZZIE I TELL THEE THAT *922   2
    AS THA ALLERS HAST BUT LET ME TELL THEE *922   5
    FOR I TELL YE I SHONNA MARRY HER *923   3
    BUT 'DEED AN' I WISH AS THIS TALE O' THINE WOR NIVER MY+ *925 14
    BUT IS THAT A QUIETUS OH TELL ME IS IT QUIETUS *957   5
    OH IT IS NOT SO EASY I TELL YOU IT IS NOT SO EASY *957 18

TELLING
    AS AN INSOLENT MISTRESS TELLING MY PULSE'S BEAT 230 27
    THAT HAD THE TELLING 296 29
    AND TELLING IT OFF 328 21
    I DON'T MIND TELLING YOU 490   2
    AND BE A BIT MORE FIERY AS INCAPABLE OF TELLING LIES 505 18

TELLIN'
    LAD BUT I'M TELLIN' THEE SUMMAT 137 24
    YI BUT I'M TELLIN' THEE SUMMAT 137 31

TELLS
    TELLS DULL MEANINGLESS DISGUSTING TALES 522   7

TEMERITY
    O ACT OF FEARFUL TEMERITY 310   4

TEMPER
    THAT DARK FACE-WEAPON TO TEMPER IT WELL 373 34

TEMPERED
    A RAW AMERICAN WILL THAT HAS NEVER BEEN TEMPERED BY LIFE 370 34

TEMPESTS
    AND LET THE NODDING TEMPESTS OF VERBOSITY 543   8

TEMPLE
    IN A SMALL PAGODA ON THE TEMPLE SIDE 387 22
    TEMPLE OF BLOOD IN THE NIGHT SWIFT-STRIKING 390 33
    COME LET US BUILD A TEMPLE TO OBLIVION 726   7
    AND THE VEIL OF THE TEMPLE RENT AT THE KISS ON KISS 742 28

TEMPLES
  MY TEMPLES BROKEN THEN I SHOULD REMAIN   873 31

TEMPLE'S
  AND THROUGH THE TEMPLE'S   96 13

TEMPORAL
  THE UPRIGHT IS TEMPORAL IS EFFORT OUTREACH   827 15

TEMPORARILY
  AT NIGHT TEMPORARILY OF COURSE   761 30

TEMPORARY
  FRIGHTENED OF THE BARE EARTH AND THE TEMPORARY CANVAS   444 12

TEMPTINGLY
  TEMPTINGLY IN MID-AIR BETWEEN A PLAYFUL THUMB AND FINGER   271 24

TEN
  WITH A TOUCH THE DEAD AND THE LIVING WHILE TIME COUNTS +   174 12
  SAY TEN O'CLOCK   342 9
  AWAY FROM THE UPPER TEN   552 14

TENACIOUS
  MY TENACIOUS FEET FROM OFF THE DOME OF THE EARTH   134 25

TEND
  SEE THE WOMAN'S TRINKLING FINGERS TEND HIM A COIN   36 6
  AT THE MOMENT WE TEND TO RUN INSANE THE MIND HAVING BRO+   838 21

TENDED
  MACHINES OF IRON MUST BE TENDED BY HANDS OF FLESH   639 7

TENDENCY
  YOU'VE A DELICIOUS TENDENCY TO EMBONPOINT   835 26

TENDER
  FOR FLOWERS ARE TENDER FOLK AND ROOTS CAN ONLY HIDE   93 30
  THE ROSES LEAN DOWN WHEN THEY HEAR IT THE TENDER MILD   137 4
  IN THE TENDER WINE   148 2
  DELICATE TENDER SPRING   272 5
  ROSY TENDER GLITTERING WITHIN THE FISSURE   278 26
  NO TENDER MUZZLES   335 18
  THEY FEEL QUITE TENDER OVER YOU TILL YOU PLAY THE SAME   399 17
  I WANT TO SHOW ALWAYS THE HUMAN TENDER REVERENCE   622 5
  OF FULL DESPAIR I LIFT MY TENDER FLAME   745 13
  A TENDER GLEAM OF IMMORTALITY   746 1
  AND MAKES A POINT OF BEING VERY GENTLE VERY TENDER   *948 12
  AND HE IS VERY GENTLE AND TENDER   *948 14

TENDEREST
  TEARING EACH OTHER'S FEELINGS TRAMPLING EACH OTHER'S TE+   544 16

TENDER-FOOTED
  WERE THEY THEN VICIOUS THE SLENDER TENDER-FOOTED   297 14

TENDERLY
  YOU LOVE ME WHILE I HOVER TENDERLY   87 19
  LOVING HER TENDERLY   881 4

TENDERNESS
  ALL YOUR UNBEARABLE TENDERNESS YOU WITH THE LAUGHTER   58 21
  PEARLS ITSELF INTO TENDERNESS OF BUD   306 5
  A CERTAIN CARELESSNESS A CERTAIN TENDERNESS A CERTAIN   612 12
  MEN AND WOMEN SHOULD LEARN TENDERNESS TO EACH OTHER   620 3
  EITHER IN ANGER OR TENDERNESS OR DESIRE OR SADNESS OR W+   672 4
  FOR I DOTE ON THEM WITH TENDERNESS AND I HATE THEM   741 19
  THEN COMFORTS IT THE CREEPING TENDERNESS   *900 26
  THEN COMFORTS IT THE CREEPING TENDERNESS   *904 2

TEN-DOLLAR
  FATHERING ENDLESS TEN-DOLLAR GOLDEN EGGS   414 12

TENDRIL
  AUDILE TACTILE SENSITIVENESS AS OF A TENDRIL WHICH ORIE+   285 26

TENDRILLED
  OH WHAT OF THE TENDRILLED VINE   285 11
  THERE WAS ANOTHER WORLD A DUSKY FLOWERLESS TENDRILLED W+   285 22
  THE GRAPE IS SWART THE AVENUES DUSKY AND TENDRILLED SUB+   286 32
  DOWN THE TENDRILLED AVENUES OF WINE AND THE OTHERWORLD   287 10

TENDRILS
  AS TENDRILS REACH OUT YEARNINGLY   52 4
  YOUR FERVENT LIMBS WITH FLICKERS AND TENDRILS OF NEW   156 27
  AS TENDRILS REACHED OUT YEARNINGLY   *899 18
  AS TENDRILS REACHED OUT YEARNINGLY   *902 30

TENETS
  OF SUCH MARTYRS WHILE MARXIAN TENETS   537 11

TENNIS
  HAVE A GAME OF TENNIS GO OUT IN THE CAR DO SOME SHOPPIN+   651 21

TENOR
  AND THE FIRST TENOR SINGING OF THE PASSIONATE THROAT OF+   366 17

TEN-POUND
  AND A REAL TREMOR IF HE HANDS OUT A TEN-POUND NOTE   486 13

TENS
  FIVES AND TENS   355 23

TENSE
  MOUNTED AND TENSE SPREAD-EAGLE OUT-REACHING OUT OF THE   364 30
  REACHING AND GRIPPING TENSE MORE REACHING ANGUISH IN   365 5
  WHILST BETWEEN THE TWO ALONG THE TENSE ARCH OF YOUR BACK   370 22

TENSION
  ALL THINGS WOULD PASS AWAY FOR IN THE TENSION OF OPPOSI+   348 4
  UTTERMOST TENSION   365 6
  IT IS A DECLARATION OF SUCH TENSION IN WILL   370 30

TENT
  HERE IN THIS SWARTHY SECRET TENT   113 25
  UNDER THE YEW-TREE TENT   114 2
  I STILL AM NOT HOMELESS HERE I'VE A TENT BY DAY   133 24
  OVER YOUR TENT THE ONE TENT OF US ALL MY LOVE   750 10
  I HAVE A TENT OF DARKNESS BY DAY   772 14
  OH YOU IN THE TENT OF THE CLOVEN FLAME   812 11
  IN THE TENT OF THE HOLY GHOST   812 26
  HERE IN THIS SWARTHY SECRET TENT   *929 14
  UNDER THE YEW-TREE TENT   *929 19

TENT-CLOTHS
  COME THEN UNDER THIS TREE WHERE THE TENT-CLOTHS   113 21

TENT-FLAP
  WHO OPENS HIS FLAME LIKE A TENT-FLAP   812 15

TENTS
  PITCH TENTS OF FLAME   812 22

TEPIDLY
  PALE-FACE AUTHORITIES LOITERING TEPIDLY   316 27

TER
  TER NOTTINGHAM EH DEAR O' ME   45 7
  WAITIN' TER BE BURIED OUT O' TH' WET   60 14
  DID T' 'APPEN TER NOTICE A BIT OF A LASS WAY BACK   60 17
  BUT I THOWT TER MYSEN AS THAT WOR TH' ONLY BIT   61 17
  THA DOESNA MEAN TER SAY TER ME MOTHER   77 1
  THA NIVER BELIEVES IT DOES TER MOTHER   77 9
  TER LET IV'RYBODY SEE   78 28
  DOESN'T TER KNOW WHAT I MEAN TIMMY   79 23
  YI THA MUST HA' BIN 'ARD TER WEAN   79 24
  THA'S NO 'CASIONS TER HA'E ME ON   79 29
  ME GOTTEN A CHILDT TER THY LANDLADY   80 3
  HASNA TER SENT ME WHOAM WHEN I   80 6
  COULD TER HA' KILLED 'ER   80 24
  WELL NOW YER'VE GOT TER PAY FOR IT   81 29
  IF I HAN WHAT'S THAT TER THEE   81 30
  'E ISN'T GOIN' TER MARRY YER   81 31
  TO THINK I SHOULD 'AVE TER 'AFFLE AN' CAFFLE   82 9
  TER MARRY WI' CABS AN' RICE   82 12
  BUT WE'LL GO UNBEKNOWN TER TH' REGISTRAR   82 13
  BUT THA'LL HA'E TER PROMISE TER BE TRUE TER ME   82 27
  THINE SHALL GO TER PAY THE WOMAN AN' WI' MY BIT WE'LL B+   83 2
  LIFT THY FACE AN' LOOK AT ME MAN CANNA TER LOOK AT ME   83 5
  AFORE I CAN TA'E THEE I'VE GOT A WIDDER O' FORTY-FIVE T+   83 8
  THAT I COULD 'A' BIN FIRST WOMAN TER THEE AS THA'RT FIR+   83 13
  BUT WHAT THEN THA WANTS ME DOES TER   83 24
  I DON'T LIKE YER LIZ I WANT TER   84 19
  TER ME IT'S NO FUN   84 28
  AN' T' SHORT DAYS GOIN' UNKNOWN TER THEE   137 29
  AREN'T TER HEARIN' SUMMAT   138 7
  THA COME TER SAY GOOD-BYE TER ME   138 8
  THA COME TER HA' FINISHED AN' DONE WI' ME   138 10
  THA ARENA VERY FLIG TER GO   138 16
  DOST WANT ME TER WANT THEE AGAIN NAY THOUGH   138 17
  THA WANTED ME TER LEAVE ME THAT BAD THA KNOWS   138 20
  DOESN'T TER KNOW IT   138 21
  BUT THA WANTED ME MORE TER WANT THEE SO'S   138 22
  DRAW IT OUT OF 'IM DID TER KNOW IT   138 26
  AS 'UD MAKE THEE A WIFE AN' LOOK UP TER THEE   138 30
  AN' LIE FRIGHTENED TER DEATH UNDER THEE   138 33
  SHE WORN'T HARD TER FIND   138 34
  THA THOUGHT THA WANTED TER BE RID O' ME   139 1
  THA THOUGHT THA WANTED TER MARRY AN' SEE   139 3
  IF TER COULDNA BE MASTER AN' TH' WOMAN'S BOSS   139 4
  TER SAY GOOD-BYE AN' A'   139 7
  THA MUST THOUGH THA TRIES TER GET AWAY   139 18
  THA COME TER SAY GOOD-BYE TER ME   139 28
  IT'S TA'EN THEE SEVEN DAYS TER SAY IT TER ME   139 30
  AN' THEN SOMEBODY HAS TER MARRY YOU   493 31
  DOESN'T TER KNOW   540 13
  WE AIN'T GOT NO FARVER ONLY A MOVVER AN' SHE 'AS TER GO 866 20
  DID TER NOTICE THAT LASS SISTER AS STOOD AWAY BACK   *909 29
  WHEN YOU'D GONE I SLIPPED BACK TER SEE WHO SHE MIGHT BE *910 5
  WAS TH' LITTLE LOVIN' SORT AS 'AS NOWT TER SCREEN 'EM   *910 25
  DID T' 'APPEN TER NOTICE A BIT OF A LASS AWAY BACK   *911 3
  THA NIVER BELIEVES IT MOTHER DOES TER   *918 27
  DOESN'T TER KNOW WHAT I MEAN TIM YI   *921 19
  THA'S NO OCCASIONS TER HA'E ME ON   *921 25
  HASNA TER SENT ME WHOAM WHEN I   *922 6
  DID TER FIND HER GOOD   *922 20

TERENCE
  OH WELL I SUPPOSE I SHALL HAVE SOME KNIFE-EDGED TERENCE+   835 1

TERESA
  ALL MY SAINTS AND ANNA TERESA   798 7

TERM
  HAVE HAD THEIR TERM OF OFFICE THEY MUST GO   614 8
  IT IS THE WHITE STONE OF LIMITS THE TERM THE LANDMARK B+   706 11
  THE THUNDERERS AND THE SUNDERERS HAVE THEIR TERM   709 23
  HE IS BASICALLY A SAVAGE IT IS A TERM OF REPROACH   776 11
  BUT ALSO IT IS NOT A TERM OF REPROACH   776 12

TERMS
  AS RICH AS ANYBODY ELSE ON THE SAME TERMS   778 15

TERRACE
ALMOND-TREE BENEATH THE TERRACE RAIL   300 26
AT EVENING SITTING IN THIS TERRACE   340 17
TERRACE WRITING   347 20
TERRACE   672 19

TERRA FIRMA
ONE MUST COME DOWN TO TERRA FIRMA SOMEWHERE   548 5

TERRESTRIAL
HERE IN THE OTHER WORLD STILL TERRESTRIAL   258 33
TERRESTRIAL MANHOOD   322 10

TERRIBLE
OUTSIDE THE HOUSE AN ASH-TREE HUNG ITS TERRIBLE WHIPS   36 9
IN FRONT OF THE TERRIBLE RAGE THE DEATH   165 17
AVID AND TERRIBLE   241 23
THAT HAS DRAWN THIS TERRIBLE DRAUGHT OF WHITE FIRE   241 29
IT IS THE TERRIBLE OTHER   267 10
IN TERRIBLE RIPPLING CIRCLES BETWEEN THE STARS   512 18
TERRIBLE AND STRANGE THE GOD LIES ON THE BED WISTFUL CO+   676 9
HOW TERRIBLE THE SUN WOULD BE   724 15
HOW TERRIBLE LIFE WOULD BE   724 23
HOW TERRIBLE IT WOULD BE TO THINK AND KNOW TO HAVE CONS+   724 24
SO TERRIBLE NOW   748 18
BEYOND ME IS A LORD WHO IS TERRIBLE AND WONDERFUL AND D+   801 12
CONNECTION WITH STILL DEEPER STILL MORE TERRIBLE LIFE-F+   844 15
IN TERRIBLE RHYTHM LIKE BLOWS THAT ARE STRUCK TILL THE +   879 2
OH THE TERRIBLE ECSTASY OF THE CONSCIOUSNESS THAT I AM +   *909 18

TERRIBLY
ME FROM THE REST AH TERRIBLY   262 13
THEY WILL TEAR YOU TERRIBLY AND GIVE YOU BLOOD-POISONING   675 8
AND TERRIBLY STRANGE IS THE THROAT THAT IS WORKING WITH+   871 26
AND TERRIBLY STRANGE ARE HIS TEARS THAT ARE WETTING MY +   871 27

TERRIFIED
IF I TURN QUICKLY I AM TERRIFIED FEELING SPACE SURROUND+   222 23
HAS NEVER SEIZED ME AND TERRIFIED ME   263 17
A MAN IS SO TERRIFIED OF STRONG HUNGER   264 32
I AM SO TERRIFIED AMERICA   291 9
I REMEMBER THE SCREAM OF A TERRIFIED INJURED HORSE THE   366 10
BUT IT IS NOT MONEY WE ARE SO TERRIFIED OF   486 18
ONLY MAN IS TERRIFIED OF HIS OWN POSSIBLE SPLENDOUR AND   529 12
MY DEARS DON'T LOOK AT ME I AM MERELY TERRIFIED OF YOU   541 10
I AM TERRIFIED OF THE PEAR-BLOSSOM   886 16
I AM TERRIFIED YOU ARE DEAD   886 21

TERRIFYING
PROBABLY HE WAS A JABBING TERRIFYING MONSTER   372 21

TERROR
SPURTS FROM THE TERROR OF HIS ONCOMING   43 8
TO ESCAPE IN SLEEP THE TERROR OF THIS GREAT BIVALVE DAR+   88 14
FROM THIS ROSY TERROR OF BIRTH THAT HAS SLID DOWN   88 24
AND THIS TERROR IS THE ROOT OF ALL CRUELTY   264 33
BUT HE ROSE AND FROM A TERROR WORSE THAN ME HE FLEW PAST   344 5
WORSE EVEN THAN THE HIDEOUS TERROR OF ME WITH MY HANDKE+   344 23
I REMEMBER MY FIRST TERROR HEARING THE HOWL OF WEIRD   366 8
IT HAS GOT US DOWN WE GROVEL BEFORE IT IN STRANGE TERROR   486 15
IF MEN WERE FREE FROM THE TERROR OF EARNING A LIVING   488 4
IN TERROR LEST YOU HAVE TO GO IN AND SINCE THE WORK-PRI+   521 13
SHE'S A HOLY TERROR SHE TAKES YOUR BEST FROCK   572 2
TILL WE ARE MAD WITH TERROR SEEING THE SLAIN   740 1
FILLED WITH REMORSEFUL TERROR TO THE MAN SHE SCORNED AN+   *891 30
OH THE TERROR OF LIFTING THE INNERMOST I OUT OF THE SWE+   *909 21
THE HATE OF TERROR OR DENY THE FECUND SOUL HER EMBRACES   *926 25

TERRORS
OF RED UPON THE THROAT HER TERRORS SWAY   42 27
UNMINDFUL OF ITS TERRORS   875 35
THY BODY FROM ITS TERRORS AWKWARD LEASH   *927 25
FROM YOUR BODY'S TERRORS AND DROSS   *928 27
I NEED NOT GLANCE OVER MY SHOULDER IN FEAR OF THE TERRO+   *945 25

TER'S
GO THEN THALT' HA'E NO PEACE TILL TER'S HAD   140 3

TEST
IT IS YOUR TEST AMERICANS   779 21
DECIDE WHETHER YOU CAN BECAUSE IT IS A TEST   779 27
AND THAT IS A TEST OF YOU   779 34
IT IS A TEST AMERICANS   780 13

TESTIFY
TO TESTIFY TO A BLIGHT ON THE LAND   51 3

TESTING
THOUGHT IS THE TESTING OF STATEMENTS ON THE TOUCHSTONE +   673 11

TEXTS
THE PSALMS AND FURTIVELY FROM AMONG THE TEXTS   *894 17

TEXTURE
LITTLE JETS OF SUNLIGHT TEXTURE IMITATING FLAME   33 2

THA
SAY YES THA CLOWN   44 21
SISTER THA KNOWS WHILE WE WAS ON TH' PLANKS   60 11
THA SHOULD HA' SEED 'ER SLIVE UP WHEN YER'D GONE   61 5
THA SHOULD HA' SEED 'ER KNEEL AN' LOOK IN   61 6
GLADDER NOR OF THY LILIES IF THA MAUN BE TOLD   61 20
THA DOESNA MEAN TER SAY TER ME MOTHER   77 11
THA NIVER BELIEVES IT DOES TER MOTHER   77 9
NAY ROBIN RED-BREAST THA NEDNA   78 21
FLAYED RED IF THA COULD BUT SEE   78 24
THA ART SMOCK-RAVELLED BUNNY   78 29
THA CAN STARE AT ME WI' THY FIERCE BLUE EYES   79 11

THA
THA WON'T STARE ME OUT I GUESS   79 12
AS THA NE'D TRUDGE UP 'ERE   79 18
YI THA MUST HA' BIN 'ARD TER WEAN   79 24
WHEN THA BEGUN   79 32
AS THA ALLUS 'AST BUT LET ME TELL THEE   80 5
AFTER KISSIN' AN' CUDDLIN' WI' ME THA COULD   80 18
THA WANTS 'IM THY-SEN I SEE   81 32
THA WANTS 'IM THY-SEN TOO BAD   82 6
I WISH THA HADNA DONE IT TIM   82 21
TWENTY POUND O' THY OWN THA HAST AN' FIFTY POUND HA'E I   83 1
ALL AS WE S'LL WANT FOR FURNITURE WHEN THA LEAVES THIS +   83 3
LOOK UP AN' SAY THA'RT SORRY THA DID IT SAY THA'RT SORR+   83 15
AY I'M SORRY THA NEDNA WORRY   83 20
BUT WHAT THEN THA WANTS ME DOES TER   83 24
AN' THA'RT THAT RIGHT THA KNOWS 'TIS   83 28
THA ART SO SURE THA'RT RIGHT LIZ   84 1
ON THY FACE AS THA GOT MORE WHITE AN' WAN   138 5
THA COME TER SAY GOOD-BYE TER ME   138 8
THA WERT FRIT O' SUMMAT   138 9
THA COME TER HA' FINISHED AN' DONE WI' ME   138 10
AH WUNNA KISS THEE THA TREMBLES SO   138 14
THA ARENA VERY FLIG TER GO   138 16
THA WANTED TER LEAVE ME THAT BAD THA KNOWS   138 20
BUT THA WANTED ME MORE TER WANT THEE SO'S   138 22
THA COULD LET THY VERY SOUL OUT A MAN   139 23
THA THOUGHT THA WANTED A LITTLE WENCH   138 27
THA THOUGHT THA WANTED A LITTLE WENCH   138 29
THA THOUGHT THA WANTED TER BE RID O' ME   139 1
'APPEN THA DID AN' A'   139 2
THA THOUGHT THA WANTED TO MARRY AN' SEE   139 3
AN' THA KNOWED IT AY YET THA COMES ACROSS   139 6
I TELL THEE THA WON'T BE SATISFIED   139 8
THA MIGHT AS WELL LISTEN THA KNOWS   139 9
I TELL THEE THA WON'T BE SATISFIED   139 10
IT'S TRUE THA KNOWS   139 14
THA MUST THOUGH THA TRIES TER GET AWAY   139 18
THA WANTS IT AND EVERYTHING ELSE IS IN VAIN   139 19
MAUN THA CLING TO THE WA' AS THA STAN'S   139 21
AY AN' THA MAUN   139 22
YI THA CAN GO THA HATES ME NOW   139 24
GO THEN SIN' THA MAUN   139 27
THA COME TER SAY GOOD-BYE TER ME   139 28
A WOMAN'S MAN THA ART MA LAD   140 1
OUTSIDE IT WAS THA AND THEE   490 20
IF THA CANNA SAY'T COME THEN AN' SCRAIGHT IT OUT ON MY   540 14
EH MEN DOESNA HA'E BOSOMS 'APPEN NOT ON'Y THA KNOWS   540 16
COME THEN THA CAN SCRAIGHT IT OUT ON MY SHIRT-FRONT   540 18
DOST THA HEAR MY HORSE'S FEET AS HE CANTERS AWAY   664 1
THA KNOWS 'E 'D A WINSOME WAY WI 'IM AN' SHE   *910 24
SISTER THA KNOWS WHILE WE WAS ON THE PLANKS   *910 26
AH KNOW THA LIKED 'IM BETT'R NOR ME BUT LET   *911 11
THA SHOULD HA' SEED HER SLIVE UP WHEN WE'D GONE   *911 21
THA SHOULD HA' SEED HER KNEEL AN' LOOK IN   *911 22
THA DOESNA MEAN TO SAY TO ME MOTHER   *918 19
THA NIVER BELIEVES IT MOTHER DOES TER   *918 27
NAY ROBIN RED-BREAST THA NEDNA   *920 13
THA ART SMOCK-RAVELLED BUNNY   *920 21
THA CAN STARE AT ME WI' THY FIERCE BLUE EYES   *921 7
BUT THA DOESNA STARE ME OUT I GUESS   *921 8
IF THA MAUN KNOW   *921 12
AS THA NE'D TRUDGE UP HERE   *921 14
THA MUST 'A' BEEN HARD TO WEAN   *921 20
I ASK WHEN THA BEGUN   *921 28
AS THA ALLERS HAST BUT LET ME TELL THEE   *922 5
AFTER LICKIN' AND SNUFFIN' AT ME THA COULD   *922 18
THA WANTS 'IM THY-SEN TOO BAD   *924 10
I WISH THA HADNA DONE IT TIM   *924 25
I WISH THA COULD WESH 'ER OFF'N THEE   *925 1
TWENTY POUND O' THY OWN THA HAST AND FIFTY POUND HA'E I   *925 5
ALL AS WE SHALL WANT FOR FURNITURE WHEN THA LEAVES THIS+ *925 7

THA'D
THA'D NEED A WOMAN DIFFERENT FROM ME   139 5
WOR IT THA'D LIKED TO 'A KILLED HER   *922 24

THA'LL
BUT THA'LL HA'E TER PROMISE TER BE TRUE TER ME   82 27

THA'LT
BUT THA'LT COME AGAIN BECAUSE WHEN A MAN'S   139 25
HOW LONG IT'LL BE AFORE THA'LT BE   139 32
AN' THA'LT FEEL BETTER   540 19
AN' A MAN AN' A FATHER THA'LT HA'E TO BE   *944 15

THALT'
GO THEN THALT' HA'E NO PEACE TILL TER'S HAD   140 3

THANK
THANK HEAVEN FOR A PEACEFUL HOUSE   45 31
AND YES THANK GOD IT STILL IS POSSIBLE   90 28
LIKE VAPOUR DEW OR POISON NOW THANK GOD   91 1
I THANK YOU I DO YOU HAPPY CREATURES YOU DEARS   221 20
FOR SO MUCH I THANK THE GOOD GENERATIONS OF MANKIND   263 14
I THANK MANKIND WITH PASSIONATE HEART   263 29
AND FOR THIS I HAVE TO THANK ONE WOMAN   265 21
ASK BUT THE LEAGUE INSISTS THANK YOU SO MUCH NO SIGN HE+ 546 14
PROVES IT QUITE THANK YOU SO MUCH WE'RE GETTING ON SIMP+ 546 20
THANK YOU DEAR CLARINDA   550 19
THANK YOU THANK YOU   670 5
NAY NOW AT LAST THANK GOD FOR THE JEOPARDY   741 22

THANKLESS
AND DEPART PEACEFUL PACIFIED AND THANKLESS   350 11

THANKS
    SHINE LIKE FLAT COIN WHICH JOVE IN THANKS   162 3
    THE SUN IS IN THE OUTER PORCH CRY TO HIM THANKS OH THAN+   803 21

THANKSGIVINGS
    AND THERE ARE MY RED-LETTER THANKSGIVINGS   265 24

THA'RT
    EH THA'RT A MARD-ARSED KID   44 16
    THA'RT A GOOD-UN AT SUCKIN'-IN YET TIMMY   79 25
    THA'RT FOR DOIN' A LOT WI' T' LAD   82 8
    THAT I COULD 'A' BIN FIRST WOMAN TER THEE AS THA'RT FIR+   83 13
    LOOK UP AN' SAY THA'RT SORRY THA DID IT SAY THA'RT SORR+   83 15
    IF MY FATHER CAN GET THEE A JOB ON T' BANK SAY THA'RT S+   83 17
    AN' THA'RT THAT RIGHT THA KNOWS 'TIS   83 28
    THA ART SO SURE THA'RT RIGHT LIZ   84 1
    'ARK THA'RT FOR HEARIN' SUMMAT   137 26
    YI BUT THA'RT FRIT O' SUMMAT   138 15
    THA'RT DAUNTED OR SUMMAT   138 15
    O' THY SPUNK AN' THA'RT EMPTY AN' MORTIFIED   139 12
    THA'RT ONE O' TH' MEN AS HAS GOT TO DRAIN   139 15
    THA'RT A GOOD-UN AT SUCKIN-IN YET TIMMY   *921 21
    THA'RT FOR DOIN' A LOT WI' TH' LAD   *924 12
    YI' THA'RT A MAN THA'RT A FINE BIG MAN BUT NIVER A BABY+   *925 24

THA'S
    THA'S GOT IT FLAT   77 4
    THA'S NO 'CASIONS TER HA'E ME ON   79 29
    THA'S GOTTEN THY ANSWER PAT   80 4
    AN' THA'S LAID AGAINST ME AN' MELTED   80 10
    THA'S BIN SNOWED UP I' THIS COTTAGE WI' ME   137 25
    THA'S BIN SNOWED UP I' THIS COTTAGE WI' ME   137 27
    THA'S GOT IT FLAT   *918 22
    THA'S NO OCCASIONS TER HA'E ME ON   *921 21
    THA'S GOTTEN THY ANSWER PAT   *922 4
    THA'S LAIN RIGHT UP TO ME LIZZIE AN' MELTED   *922 10
    LAD THA'S GOTTEN A CHILDT IN ME   *944 14

THAT'S
    THAT'S NOT IT   44 25
    AND THAT'S ALL   75 2
    THAT'S SPOKEN LIKE A MAN TIMMY   81 5
    THAT'S SPOKEN LIKE A MAN   81 6
    I'M NOT THAT'S A'   84 12
    THE FIRST MAN OUT OF THE FOUR THAT'S MOWING   219 25
    HERE TAKE ALL THAT'S LEFT OF MY PEACH   279 4
    THAT'S HOW IT SHOULD BE THE FEMALE SHOULD ALWAYS BE SEC+   283 2
    THAT'S HOW THE FIG DIES SHOWING HER CRIMSON THROUGH THE   283 30
    THAT'S HOW WOMEN DIE TOO   283 34
    THAT'S OBVIOUS   377 31
    SEE ME SHE SAYS THAT'S ME   386 7
    THAT'S HER   386 8
    THAT'S WHY THE NIGHT FELL IN FRUSTRATION   390 28
    THAT'S WHY AS THE ELEPHANTS PONDEROUSLY WITH UNSEEMING   390 29
    THAT'S YOU PIPSEY   396 13
    THAT'S WHY I COME   405 6
    THAT'S TURNED   433 7
    THAT'S WHAT'S SO BORING PEOPLE ARE SO BORING   435 12
    GOGGLING OBSCENITIES IF THAT'S YOU AND YOUR FATE WHY TH+   463 17
    THAT'S WHAT HE SEES IN ME   489 22
    PERHAPS THAT'S WHY IT IS SO DIFFICULT   495 12
    THAT'S QUITE ENOUGH FOR ME   507 7
    THAT'S WHY WOMEN AREN'T MUCH FUN YOU'RE ALWAYS HAVING   517 27
    THAT'S WHY IT MOVES ABOUT   525 2
    AND THAT'S WHAT MAKES IT ETERNALLY SPACIOUS AND UNSTUFFY   525 3
    SO THAT'S WHY SO MANY YOUNG MEN HAVE LONG FACES   530 21
    AND THAT'S WHAT'S HAPPENED TO THE ENGLISH ROSE   534 27
    AND THAT'S WHAT WE'VE DONE TODAY   543 18
    PERSON THAT'S ALL WE NEED TO KNOW   546 11
    PLEASE AND THERE I COUNTERSIGN THAT'S RIGHT YES THAT'S +   546 15
    YOU'RE MY INFERIOR THAT'S WHAT YOU ARE YOU'RE MY INFERI+   547 21
    IT WAS NOWT BUT A DIRTY SELL THAT'S ALL   553 3
    THAT'S WHAT WE HOPE WE HOPE SHE'LL BE   571 23
    SAID FREEDOM WHY THAT'S MY OWN ISLAND   574 14
    LOOK AT THAT ONE THERE THAT'S PRETTY HOT   578 11
    SENSIBILITIES HATE EVERYTHING THAT'S WELL   633 6
    THAT'S WHY ONE DOESN'T HAVE TO TAKE THEM SERIOUSLY   660 8
    THAT'S WHY THE DOGGED RESISTANT OLD ONES DARE NOT DIE   662 26
    PROPERTY PROPERTY PROPERTY THAT'S WHAT THEY SEEM TO SAY   664 2
    I LICK THE CREAM OFF PROPERTY THAT'S WHAT IT SEEMS TO S+   664 4
    AND THERE'S A BATTLE THAT'S STILL TO BE BATTLED   669 5
    DON'T YOU KNOW THAT'S OBSCENE   669 17
    KILL OFF THE WORD THAT'S HAD SO MUCH TO SAY   737 26
    THAT'S BEEN WHETTED AND WHETTED IN BLOOD   782 3
    THAT'S SPOKEN LIKE A MAN TIMMY   *923 5
    THAT'S SPOKEN LIKE A MAN   *923 6
    THAT'S HIS COLLAR ROUND THE CANDLE-STICK   *923 13
    AN' THAT'S THE DARK BLUE TIE I BOUGHT 'IM   *923 14
    THE FIRST MAN OUT O' THE FOUR THAT'S MOWIN'   *944 5

THAT-WILL-BE-GLORY
    OR STILL MORE DISASTROUSLY REMINISCENT OF THAT-WILL-BE-+   835 7

THAULOW
    LIKE A PICTURE BY THAULOW DARK CLUSTERS OF SHOUTING LADS   865 19

THAW
    PALE LOVE LOST IN A THAW OF FEAR   62 15
    IN A THAW OF ANXIETY FOR THE BOY   100 7
    AN' OWER A' THE THAW AN' MESS   137 22
    COME THAW DOWN THEIR COOL PORTENTOUSNESS DISSOLVE THEM   271 5

THAW-COLD
    THAW-COLD ICE-CORRUPT BLOSSOMS   270 25

THEATRE
    AND AMONG THE WRECK OF THE THEATRE CROWD   71 28
    OR WHETHER THE THEATRE SIGHS AND SIGHS   109 19
    THEATRE PEOPLE PASS   146 18

THEBAID
    AND HIDE IN YOUR OWN WILD THEBAID   642 8

THEE
    WOULD WORSHIP THEE LETTING MY BUTTOCKS PRANCE   40 18
    AND BUILT UP THE WAY I SALUTE THEE   40 22
    BUT TO DEFLOWER THEE THY TOWER IMPINGES   40 23
    WILL GIVE THEE WHAT I HAVE THIS LAST WEEK'S   44 2
    TAKE THEM AND BUY THEE A SILVER RING   44 4
    I'LL WET MY BROW FOR THEE   44 7
    'E'LL GIE THEE SOCKS   44 17
    CURVED THY MOUTH FOR THEE AND WHAT STRONG SHOULDER   69 14
    PLANTED THEE UPRIGHT ART PROUD TO SEE   69 15
    THEN GAVE THEE THY DARK EYES O MAN THAT ALL   69 20
    THE REST HAD DOORWAY TO THEE THROUGH THAT SPARK   69 21
    AND KISSED THEE TO A PASSION OF LIFE AND LEFT   69 23
    LIFE COMES TO THEE ON WHICH THOU HAST NO CLAIM   69 28
    THEN LEAVES THEE AND THOU CANST NOT BUT COMPLAIN   69 29
    DUNNA THEE TELL ME IT'S HIS'N MOTHER   76 23
    DUNNA THEE DUNNA THEE   76 24
    OH AY HE'LL COME AN TELL THEE HIS-SEN   76 25
    I' TH' SNOW BUT I'S WARRANT THEE   78 31
    WHATIVER BRINGS THEE OUT SO FAR   79 13
    IT'S THEE AS 'AS DONE IT AS MUCH AS ME   80 1
    SO THERE AN' I TELL THEE FLAT   80 2
    AS THA ALLUS 'AST BUT LET ME TELL THEE   80 5
    AFTER I'D KISSED THEE AT NIGHT LIZZIE   80 9
    I HOPE IT DID THEE GOOD   80 20
    SAY NO MORE LIZ DUNNA THEE   80 25
    'ER'S AS GOOD AS THEE   80 26
    THEN I'LL SAY GOOD-BYE TO THEE TIMOTHY   80 27
    YIS I KNOWED 'E WOR COURTIN' THEE   81 26
    IF I HAN WHAT'S THAT TER THEE   81 30
    FOR WHENEVER I LOOK THEE I' TH' FACE I S'LL SEE   82 23
    I WISH I COULD WESH 'ER OFF'N THEE   82 25
    SORRY I AM FOR THIS BUSINESS AN' SORRY IF EVER I'VE DRI+   83 6
    AFORE I CAN TA'E THEE I'VE GOT A WIDDER O' FORTY-FIVE T+   83 8
    DUNNAT THEE THINK BUT WHAT I'VE LOVED THEE I'VE LOVED T+   83 9
    DEED AN' I WISH I C'D 'A' STOOD AT TH' ALTAR WI' THEE A+   83 11
    THEE   83 12
    THAT I COULD 'A' BIN FIRST WOMAN TER THEE AS THA'RT FIR+   83 13
    THEY'LL TURN THEE OUT O' TH' FORCE I DOUBT ME IF THEY D+   83 16
    IF MY FATHER CAN GET THEE A JOB ON T' BANK SAY THA'RT S+   83 17
    I'M SORRY FOR THEE I'M SORRY F'R 'ER   83 22
    BUT 'ARK THEE 'ERE THAT WIDDER WOMAN   84 3
    LAD SHOULD I TELL THEE SUMMAT   137 19
    LAD BUT I'M TELLIN' THEE SUMMAT   137 24
    AN' T' SHORT DAYS GOIN' UNKNOWN TER THEE   137 29
    YI BUT I'M TELLIN' THEE SUMMAT   137 31
    NOW LAD I'M AXIN' THEE SUMMAT   138 2
    AH WUNNA KISS THEE THA TREMBLES SO   138 14
    DOST WANT ME TER WANT THEE AGAIN NAY THOUGH   138 17
    THERE'S HARDLY OWT LEFT O' THEE GET UP AN' GO   138 18
    BUT THA WANTED ME MORE TER WANT THEE SO'S   138 22
    LIKE THEE CAN'T REST TILL HIS LAST SPUNK GOES   138 24
    AY LAD I'LL TELL THEE THY MIND   138 28
    AS 'UD MAKE THEE A WIFE AN' LOOK UP TER THEE   138 30
    AN' LIE FRIGHTENED TER DEATH UNDER THEE   138 33
    I TELL THEE THA WON'T BE SATISFIED   139 8
    I TELL THEE THA WON'T BE SATISFIED   139 10
    AN' I'VE LOVED THEE FOR IT   139 16
    AN' A WOMAN LIKE ME LOVES THEE FOR IT   139 20
    IT'S TA'EN THEE SEVEN DAYS TER SAY IT TER ME   139 30
    YEA THOUGH I'M SORRY FOR THEE   220 8
    AND I TAKE THE WINGS OF THE MORNING TO THEE CRUCIFIED   321 20
    UTTERLY BEYOND THEE DOVE OF THE SPIRIT   322 5
    TO THEE I ROSE LIKE A ROCKET ENDING IN MID-HEAVEN   322 8
    THEY FALL BACK FROM THEE   322 11
    MORNING-BRIGHT TO THEE   322 31
    THAN THE WINGS OF THE MORNING AND THEE THOU GLORIFIED   323 4
    DRAWING ALL MEN UNTO THEE BUT BOUND TO RELEASE THEM WHEN   323 8
    WOULD A WINGLESS LION LIE DOWN BEFORE THEE AS THIS WING+   324 2
    AND I WILL GIVE THEE THE WINGS OF THE MORNING   324 24
    I TO DO WITH THEE   357 4
    OF THE BLOOD IN THEE IN THE BLOOD IN THEE   471 2
    THE MIND CAN NEVER REACH THEE   473 24
    AND THE WHITE MIND SHINES ON ONE SIDE OF THEE   473 26
    OUTSIDE IT WAS THA AND THEE   490 20
    'ARK 'ERE LAD ATWEEN THEE AN' ME   490 28
    WILL NO ONE SAY HUSH TO THEE   540 7
    WHAT AILS THEE THEN WOMAN WHAT AILS THEE   540 12
    ALL THINGS THAT TURN TO THEE   704 10
    CALLING TO THEE FOR MY MANA   704 28
    BETWEEN ME AND THEE SO MANY GHOSTS OF THE SLAIN   739 9
    WHEN THOU RUNNEST THE RACE WITH THE FOREMOST GOD BLESS +   750 2
    WE PRAY FOR THEE MARY DELIGHTFUL THAT GOD MAY BLESS THEE   753 2
    CRY FOR THEE OUT OF THE NIGHT WHEREIN WE ARE PRONE   753 5
    STRUCK DOWN DO THOU PART US THE DARKNESS THAT WE SEE TH+   753 6
    FOR PITY OF THEE   758 10
    AND A DRAUGHT OF THEE IS STRENGTH TO A SOUL IN HELL   759 13
    HAIL AND BE DAMNED TO THEE EMPTY MOST EMPTILY   824 9
    NOTHING TO SELL IN THEE NOUGHT TO BE BOUGHT   824 10
    HAIL AND BE DAMNED TO THEE WINNING THE GAME   824 17
    MIGHT FOLLOW SWIFT BEHIND THEE WHEN THOU LETS   879 12
    THAT HOLDS IT BACK MIGHT FOLLOW SOON TO THEE   879 17
    BUT I WILL CATCH THEE UP AT A STRIDE OF DEATH   879 28
    AN' COS I LIKED HIM BEST YI BETT'R NOR THEE   *911 15
    ME TELL THEE ABOUT THIS LASS WHEN YOU HAD GONE   *911 18
    CURVED THY MOUTH FOR THEE AND HIS STRONG SHOULDER   *915 26
    PLANTED THEE UPRIGHT ART NOT PROUD TO SEE   *915 27
    THEN GAVE THEE THY DARK EYES O MAN THAT ALL   *916 3
    HE MADE HAD DOORWAY TO THEE THROUGH THAT SPARK   *916 4
    HE KISSED THEE O MAN IN A PASSION OF LOVE AND LEFT   *916 6

THEE
    DUNNA THEE TELL ME IT'S HIS'N MOTHER   *918 15
    DUNNA THEE DUNNA THEE   *918 16
    I' TH' SNOW BUT I'S WARANT THEE BUNNY   *920 23
    WHATIVER BRINGS THEE OUT SO FAR   *921 9
    IT'S THEE AS 'AS DONE IT AS MUCH AS ME   *922 1
    LIZZIE I TELL THEE THAT   *922 2
    AS .THA ALLERS HAST BUT LET ME TELL THEE   *922 5
    SAY NO MORE LIZ DUNNA THEE   *922 25
    I'LL ONLY SAY GOOD-BYE TO THEE TIMOTHY   *922 27
    AN' GI'E HER THEE BACK AGAIN   *922 28
    YIS I KNOWED 'E WOR COURTIN' THEE   *923 26
    AN' IF I HAN WHAT'S THAT TO THEE   *924 2
    IS IT A TOSS-UP 'TWIXT THEE AN' ME   *924 4
    IT'S NO TOSS-UP 'TWIXT THEE AN' ME   *924 5
    FOR WHENEVER I LOOK THEE I' TH' FACE I S'LL SEE   *924 27
    I WISH THA COULD WESH 'ER OFF'N THEE   *925 1
    SORRY I AM FOR THIS BUSINESS AN' SORRY IF I HA'E DRIVEN+   *925 10
    BEFORE I CAN TA'E THEE I'VE GOT A WIDOW OF FORTY-FIVE T+   *925 12
    DUNNAT THEE THINK BUT WHAT I LOVE THEE I LOVE THEE WELL   *925 13
    DEED AN' I WISH AS I COULD STOOD AT THE ALTAR WI' THEE +   *925 15
    O' THEE   *925 16
    THAT I COULD HA' BEEN FIRST WOMAN TO THEE AS THOU'RT FI+   *925 17
    FROM WHAT I'VE ARRANGED WI' THEE EH MAN WHAT A STUBBORN+   *925 26
    KISS ME THEN THERE NE'ER MIND IF I SCRAIGHT I WOR FOND +   *925 28
    AND I FAILED IN MY COWARDICE TO GIVE THEE THE LAST   *927 14
    THEE A GOD-JOY DIMINISHED   *927 30
    MY YOUNG SLIM LAD AN' I'M SORRY FOR THEE   *944 16

THEER
    O' WARMTH AS 'E GOT DOWN THEER TH' REST WOR STONE COLD   61 18
    NOW SITHEE THEER AT TH' REELROAD CROSSIN'   79 1
    A LOT O' VIOLETS FELL OUT OF 'ER BOSOM ON 'IM DOWN THEER   *910 16
    NOW SITHEE THEER AT TH' RAILROAD CROSSIN'   *920 25

THE FISH
    JESUS WAS CALLED THE FISH   340 15

THEFT
    WHENCE COMETH THIS THAT THOU MUST GUARD FROM THEFT   69 25
    KEEP THEN THE KISS FROM THE ADULTRESS' THEFT   *916 8

THEIRS
    IS HIDDEN IN THEIRS THEIR THRILLS ARE MINE   52 11
    LEARNING OF THEIRS IT ALL GOES DOWN THE SAME ABYSS   74 26
    THEIRS AS WELL   75 4

THEMSELVES
    WOUNDING THEMSELVES AGAINST HER DENYING HER FECUND   91 28
    ANY COMMUNION WHATEVER BUT THEY BIND THEMSELVES ON TO T+   92 18
    IN ANOTHER COUNTRY BLACK POPLARS SHAKE THEMSELVES OVER A   148 20
    SO THAT THEY SEEM TO UTTER THEMSELVES ALOUD   197 25
    ALL MOTHERS WHO FORTIFY THEMSELVES IN MOTHERHOOD DEVAST+   208 18
    AFTER THAT THERE WILL ONLY REMAIN THAT ALL MEN DETACH T+   267 24
    BUT THESE THEMSELVES MUST BURN THESE LOUTS   315 13
    IN THE LONG RUN IN SPITE OF THEMSELVES   317 5
    THEMSELVES   331 2
    CREATURES THAT HANG THEMSELVES LIKE AN OLD RAG TO SL+   342 1
    THE PENITENTES LASH THEMSELVES TILL THEY RUN WITH BLOOD   403 4
    RED MEN STILL STICK THEMSELVES OVER WITH BITS OF HIS FL+   414 3
    WHERE THE FORCES TIE THEMSELVFS UP INTO KNOTS OF ATOMS   437 29
    GOD OF JUSTICE TO SAVE THEMSELVES   442 7
    GOD OF JUSTICE WHEN WILT THOU TEACH THEM TO SAVE THEMSE+   443 9
    MODERN PEOPLE FEEL THEMSELVES AT A DISADVANTAGE   446 1
    YOU'VE NO IDEA WHEN MEN ARE IN LOVE WITH THEMSELVES   447 8
    MEN SHOULD DEMAND TO WORK FOR THEMSELVES OF THEMSELVES   450 8
    AND THEY CLOTHE THEMSELVES IN WHITE AS A TREE CLOTHES I+   451 8
    TO PROTECT THEMSELVFS AND THEIR GREEDY-MOUTHED GREEDY-M+   458 20
    THEMSELVES WITH OIL AND LARD   460 14
    THEMSELVES WITH OIL AND LARD   460 18
    THE TINY FISH ENJOY THEMSELVES   466 13
    MEN SELL THEMSELVES FOR A WAGE AND EMPLOYERS LOOK OUT   483 2
    LET PEOPLE BE WISE FOR THEMSELVES AND ANYHOW   495 23
    WERE RICH PEOPLE OR PEOPLE WHO IMAGINED THEMSELVES RICH   498 10
    ESPECIALLY ABOUT THEMSELVES AND THEIR OWN FEELINGS   502 3
    ELDERLY DISCONTENTED WOMEN ARE SO FULL OF THEMSELVES   502 4
    IT IS AS IF MODERN WOMEN HAD ALL GOT THEMSELVES ON THE +   502 6
    THE OLD ONES SAY TO THEMSELVES WE ARE NOT GOING TO BE O+   503 1
    THEY CARED SO EXCESSIVELY THEMSELVFS   508 18
    THE SUN OF IMMENSE DISTANCES THAT FOLD THEMSELVES TOGET+   513 17
    OR ELSE POOR THINGS THEY'RE HAVING TO PAY FOR THEMSELVES   518 1
    ARE THOSE THAT GIVE THEMSELVES AWAY IN FLASH AND SPARKLE   523 22
    MEN SHOULD GROUP THEMSELVES INTO A NEW ORDER   525 10
    THEY WOULD THEMSELVES AT ONCE COLLAPSE INTO NULLITY   527 22
    THEY WOULDN'T SUDDENLY BECOME THEMSELVES ARISTOCRATIC   527 24
    LET ME SIN MY WAY TO JESUS SO THEY SINNED THEMSELVES   533 27
    HAD STOOD UP FOR THEMSELVES AND SEEN   536 9
    WHY ARE THEY SO BURSTING FLINGING THEMSELVES ABOUT   537 23
    THREW THEMSELVES ON HIM IN INDIGNATION   575 2
    LOST SOME LIVING CONNECTION WITH THE COSMOS OUT OF THEM+   610 9
    BUT MUST EVER STRUGGLE ON TO ASSERT THEMSELVES   612 20
    ALL OF THEM WHO WIND THEIR ENERGY ROUND THE IDEA OF THE+   616 4
    AND NOBODY BUT THEMSELVES IS INTERESTED   618 15
    ARE ALWAYS THEMSELVES BY NATURE DISLOYAL   626 2
    AND RULERS OF MILLIONS OF ROBOTS BEING ROBOTS THEMSELVES   637 20
    PEOPLE WERE BATHING AND POSTURING THEMSELVES ON THE BEA+   651 1
    HOW TO EFFACE THEMSELVES   658 10
    HARDENED THEMSELVES   663 8
    BUT THEY LET THEMSELVES BE OVERWHELMED BY THOSE THAT ARE   665 18
    TO GATHER AND FORTIFY THEMSELVES IN EVERY CLASS IN EVER+   666 3
    THOSE THINGS THAT HAVE BECOME THEMSELVES   689 22
    AND RANGE THEMSELVES LIKE GREAT FIERCE SERAPHIM FACING +   695 4
    TO BRUISE THEMSELVES AN EXIT FROM THEMSELVES   716 21
    AT SEASONS TO PREPARE THEMSELVES TO PARTAKE   777 34
    AND NOT BE ALLOWED TO ABSENT THEMSELVES   779 3
    TO MAKE THEMSELVES CLEAN INSIDE AND OUT   793 6
    WANT TO PUT THEMSELVES TOGETHER   819 14
    SO THEY BLOOMED OUT AND FILLED THEMSELVES WITH COLOURED+   831 3

THEMSELVES
    WHEN I SEE WHAT MESSES MEN HAVE MADE OF THEMSELVES   837 13
    AND REPEAT THEMSELVES LIKE THE FLUSHING OF A W C   837 22
    SO THAT IN THE LONG PAUSE THE INSTINCTS CAN REASSERT TH+   839 3
    KNOTTING THEMSELVES WITH WILD STRENGTH   *893 24
    WOUNDING THEMSELVES AGAINST HER DENYING HER GREAT EMBRA+   *926 21
    AND FORCES TIE THEMSELVES UP INTO KNOTS OF ATOMS THEN C+   *947 6
    THEY LIVED THEMSELVES FORTH LIKE A TREE PUTTING OUT WOV+   *949 28
    TO BRUISE THEMSELVES AN EXIT FROM THEMSELVES   *956 27

THENCE
    ALL HOPE OF MY ATTAINMENT THENCE SERENE   877 16

THEORIES
    I LIKE RELATIVITY AND QUANTUM THEORIES   524 19

THEREBY
    AND LOOK YOU FLOATING JUST THEREBY   126 14
    AND SLEEP THEREBY IS ONE MORE CREAM ENRICHENED   195 16

THERE'D
    BUT THEY CAN'T OR THERE'D BE THE VICIOUS CIRCLE   819 15

THEREFORE
    THEREFORE EVEN IN THE HOUR OF MY DEEPEST PASSIONATE MALE   208 8
    I WAITED THEREFORE THEN I KNEW   262 1
    EVERY MAN HIMSELF AND THEREFORE A SURPASSING SINGLENESS+   268 1
    I AM MAN AND THEREFORE MY HEART BEATS AND THROWS THE DA+   320 21
    THAT LIVE BY NIGHT AND LAMPLIGHT AND FIRELIGHT DO THEM +   331 8
    TOES AND THE DOME OF HIS HOUSE IS HIS HEAVEN THEREFORE +   348 15
    THEREFORE YOU ARE OUR SAVINGS OUR CAPITAL   442 24
    AND THEREFORE THAT THOU ART FOREVER UNKNOWABLE   473 23
    THEREFORE BE PREPARED TO TACKLE THE CAGE   486 6
    AND THEREFORE NOTHING TO HAVE FEELINGS WITH   501 3
    AND YOU WILL BE AGAIN THEREFORE WHY LOOK BLUE   577 12
    THEREFORE NO MORALITY OF POCKETS   607 25
    THEREFORE I KNOW THE PEOPLE   627 1
    THEREFORE A GODDESS   676 17
    THAT ALL THINGS ARE MIXED AND THEREFORE THE PUREST WHIT+   708 15
    YOU CAN'T SAY I AM I AND THEREFORE   824 2
    THEREFORE NOTHING AND THEREFORE NOUGHT   824 3
    AND THEREFORE SINCE THE PEOPLE I MEET OF THE YOUNGER   829 4
    SOMETHING WE HAVE NOT BEEN AND THEREFORE CANNOT YET KNOW   832 23
    THE VIVIFIER EXISTS AND THEREFORE WE KNOW IT   840 9

THEREIN
    THE EXPECTANT ONE AND THEREIN TO INSTIL   127 13
    AND THEREIN LIES THE DANGER OF ROBOT-DEMOCRACY AND ALL +   648 5

THERE'LL
    THERE'LL BE BABIES BORN THAT ARE CYGNETS O MY SOUL   438 21
    LET'S HOPE THERE'LL BE MORE SENSE IN TAIL-TUFTS   665 4
    THERE'LL BE BABIES BORN THAT ARE YOUNG WILD SWANS O MY +   *947 24

THERMOMETER
    THERMOMETER RISE   643 14

THEY'D
    I WISH THEY'D BE TRUE TO THEIR OWN VARIATION AS WATER IS   505 20
    THEN THEY'D BE HAPPY FOR WE ARE ALL SO MUCH BETTER THAN   520 31
    THEY'D BE WORTH LOOKING AT   524 18
    THEY'D BECOME NOTHING   527 25
    HOW THEY'D HAVE HATED HIM   538 4
    AN' BLAST 'EM FOREVER BUT THEY'D ONLY   550 11
    TO USE THEY'D BETTER BE USED   553 20
    AS IF THEY'D GOT SOMETHING TO LOSE   555 12
    SEEMED TO THINK THEY'D GOT LIKE A HALO   555 19
    PERHAPS THEY'D SCOLD HIM   668 12
    THEY'D BE GOOD TO EAT   828 9
    THEN THEY'D BE ABLE TO LOVE DESPAIR CAN'T LOVE IT CAN O+   838 13

THEY'LL
    GOODNESS KNOWS IF THEY'LL BE ABLE   45 15
    THOUGH IF IT'S TRUE THEY'LL TURN 'IM OUT   78 13
    THEY'LL LISTEN TO HER TALE   78 16
    THEY'LL TURN THEE OUT O' TH' FORCE I DOUBT ME IF THEY D+   83 16
    A QUEEN THEY'LL SAY   176 26
    THEY'LL TAKE YOU FOR A WOMAN OF THE PEOPLE   433 13
    AND FORCED TO CLUTCH ON TO POSSESSIONS IN THE HOPE THEY+   522 15
    THEY'LL NEVER BE ABLE TO SAY   534 10
    THEY'LL NEVER DO A THING BOYS   553 17
    MAYBE THEY'LL REALISE IT'S TIME   560 7
    THEY'LL MERELY DESTROY ALL PROPERTY AND A GREAT MANY PE+   665 1
    BECAUSE THEY DON'T KNOW WHAT THEY'LL FIND WHEN THEY DO +   667 21
    THEY'LL MELT MERCILESSLY BACK INTO SLIME   828 13
    THOUGH IF IT'S TRUE THEY'LL TURN HIM OUT   *920 5
    THEY'LL LISTEN TO HER TALE   *920 8

THICK
    WHERE HER ARMS AND MY NECK'S THICK PULSE COULD MEET   62 2
    THE THICK SNOW IS CRUMPLED ON THE ROOF IT PLUNGES DOWN   76 6
    PUSHED GENTLY AWAY AND HIDDEN IN THE THICK OF HER HAIR   114 22
    AN UNCHARTED WAY AMONG THE MYRIAD THICK   132 11
    BLOTCHING THE THICK SOILED AIR   142 18
    I FEEL THICK WALLS OF STONE BEHIND THE ARRAS   173 26
    THE WALLS ARE THICK AND THE INNER ROOMS ARE SUCH THEY D+   174 19
    AND IT WOULD BE THICK BLACK DARK FOR EVER   205 11
    A THICK MIST-SHEET LIES OVER THE BROKEN WHEAT   212 12
    BEING BURNED WITH OIL AND CONSUMED IN CORRUPT THICK   258 10
    AND MY HEAD AT LEAST IS THICK ENOUGH TO STAND IT THE   289 17
    MADE OF THICK SMOOTH SILVER   298 20
    THICK SMOOTH-FLESHED SILVER DULL ONLY AS HUMAN LIMBS ARE   298 23
    HER THICK SOFT TONGUE   359 6
    AND BOBBING HIS THICK DARK CREST ABOUT THE SNOW AS IF   375 26
    YOU THICK BIRD WITH A STRONG CREST   375 30
    HOST ON THE SHORES OF THE LAKE LIKE THICK WILD RICE BY   391 9
    THICK UNDERDUSK   427 2
    THEY ARE SUBSTANCE ITSELF THAT FLOWS IN THICK   460 5

THICK
    OR THEY ARE LIKE LEAVES RUSTLING THICK IN THE CROWDS ON+   615   8
    AND THE THICK FALLEN CROWDS CRACKLE AND CRUMBLE UNDER T+   615 10
    AND LOOKED SULKY UNDER HER THICK STRAIGHT BROWS   617 20
    AND GOLD-BRONZE FLUTTERS BENT THROUGH THE THICK UPPER A+   647 12
    THICK ALMOST THUNDROUS ON THE HARDENED EARTH   717   4
    SWARTHY AND STRONG WITH HIS DAMP THICK HAIR   733 24
    BETWEEN HIS THICK LIPS I WONDER WHERE   733 26
    AND RUBS THE SILVER CLEAN WITH HIS THICK BROWN FINGERS   734   2
    TO THE THING AND RATHER FRETTED AND HIS THICK BLACK HAIR   734 21
    THE THICK RANK STREETS AND A STARK WHITE LIGHT   748   5
    THROUGH THAT WHITE STRAIT OF THY THICK SHAKEN THROAT   879   7
    AND WHEN I SEE THE THICK WHITE BODY OF TRAIN-SMOKE BREAK   883 16
    THE THICK SNOW IS CRUMPLED ON THE ROOF IT PLUNGES DOWN   *898   1
    THE THICK SNOW IS CRUMPLED ON THE ROOF IT PLUNGES DOWN   *901 10
    OUR CHARTERED WAY AMONG THE MYRIAD THICK   *938   3

THICKEN
    THICKEN MIASMA THE FUMES OF THE AUTOMOBILE   703 22
    DENSELY THICKEN IN THE CITIES   703 23

THICKENING
    A FEW GOLD RAYS THICKENING DOWN TO RED   455 20
    DOWN THE THICKENING THICKENING GLOOM   *955 13

THICKET
    TO-DAY A THICKET OF SUNSHINE WITH BLUE SMOKE-WREATHS   72 15
    LURKING AMONG THE DEEPS OF YOUR INDUSTRIAL THICKET   293   8
    BELONGS TO THE BAMBOO THICKET AND THE DRAKE IN THE AIR +   623 12

THICKETS
    THROUGH THE CLOSE THICKETS TO THE CLEAR OF DEATH   879 14

THICK-LEAVED
    THICK-LEAVED   854 10

THICKLY
    WHOSE EDGE OF HAIR CURVES THICKLY TO THE RED   878 21
    PULSED THICKLY AND I LONGED TO POUR   *934 33

THICK-SET
    SHE CAN SIN WITH SOME THICK-SET SPANIARD   618   7
    PONDERING YET EAGER THE BROAD AND THICK-SET ITALIAN WHO+   672 26

THICK-SPUN
    STARTLING THE THICK-SPUN TWILIGHT THE BELLS SHAKE OUT   858 25

THIEF
    LAST NIGHT A THIEF CAME TO ME   46 21
    THAT A GREY ONE LIKE A SHADOW LIKE A RAT A THIEF A RAIN+   120   3
    HE'S A THIEF   519 24
    A THIEF A MURDERER OF DREAMS   808 12
    TO OPEN ERE THE THIEF HAVE DONE HIS WORK   878 29

THIEVES
    NOT FOR THE THIEVES TO ENTER THE PILFERERS   742 20
    FROM THE LIARS FROM THE THIEVES FROM THE FALSE AND TREA+   807 16

THIEVING
    HER QUIVERING ANSWERS AND KISSES LIKE THIEVING BIRDS   868 31

THIGH
    GUARDING THE PATH HIS HAND RELAXED AT HIS THIGH   66 10
    NO SOONER ISSUED SIDEWAYS FROM THE THIGH OF HIS PREDECE+   299 32
    THIGH   300   2
    AND HE WINGS HIS HEAVY THIGH   733 15

THIGHS
    BETWEEN YOUR THIGHS FAR FAR FROM YOUR PEERING SIGHT   119   6
    SLEEP-SUAVE LIMBS OF A YOUTH WITH LONG SMOOTH THIGHS   145 18
    PUT GREAVES UPON YOUR THIGHS AND KNEES AND FRAIL   154 21
    IN THE SUBTLE LIFT OF THE THIGHS AS THEY COME UNMARCHING   174 13
    THIGHS AND KNEES   245 17
    WHY SHOULDN'T YOUR LEGS AND YOUR GOOD STRONG THIGHS   254 11
    BUT YOU LOVE LYING WARM BETWEEN WARM HUMAN THIGHS   396 19
    WASH OVER OUR KNEES AND SPLASH BETWEEN OUR THIGHS   425   4
    HER HANDSOME THIGHS DOWN DOWN TILL SHE SLEPT HER   444 30
    WITH THE FULL THIGHS SLOWLY LIFTING OF THE WADER WADING+   693 10
    ROLL DOWN MY THIGHS   705   8
    AND KNEES AND THIGHS AND LOINS AND THE BOWELS OF STRENG+   801 20
    BETWEEN YOUR THIGHS   818   2
    GREAT THIGHS THAT LEAD NOWHERE   827 19
    WERE BROKEN AGAINST HER THIGHS SHE SHATTERED THE HIBISC+   863 25
    AS I LAY ON THE BED AND YOU SAT WITH THE FLOWERS ON YOU+   886 11

THIN
    TO WAKE AND DOWN THE THIN   33   3
    LIKE A THIN WHITE BIRD BLOWN OUT OF THE NORTHERN SEAS   47 14
    THE REDDENED ACHING EYES OF THE BAR-MAN WITH THIN ARMS   72   2
    THE THIN SYCAMORE IN THE PLAYGROUND IS SWINGING WITH FL+   92   2
    WHY DOES THE THIN GREY STRAND   106 23
    AND CAST US FORTH LIKE THIN SHORN MOONS TO TRAVEL   132 10
    ON THE THIN BARE SHINS OF A MAN WHO UNEASILY LIES   145 14
    TO DRAW HIS NET THROUGH THE SURF'S THIN LINE AT THE DAW+   180   2
    YOU HAVE WELDED YOUR THIN STEMS FINER   300 28
    QUEER WITH YOUR THIN WINGS AND YOUR STREAMING LEGS   332 15
    SETTLE AND STAND ON LONG THIN SHANKS   333   1
    SOFT RED TONGUE AND HARD THIN GUMS   353   7
    YELLOW EYES INCOMPREHENSIBLE WITH THIN SLITS   380 28
    NUMEROUS AND WHISPERING THIN GRAINS OF RICE IN A   391   6
    WITH A THIN YOUNG YELLOW LITTLE PAW HANGING OUT AND   393 17
    STRAGGLE OF A LONG THIN EAR LIKE RIBBON   393 18
    LIKE A FUNNY TRIMMING TO THE MIDDLE OF HER BELLY THIN   393 19
    LITTLE DANGLE OF AN IMMATURE PAW AND ONE THIN EAR   393 20
    THIN RED WOLF OF A PALE-FACE   405   3
    THIN RED WOLF GO HOME   405   4
    WHEN THE HINDUS WEAVE THIN WOOL INTO LONG LONG LENGTHS   451   1
    WITH THEIR THIN DARK HANDS AND THEIR WIDE DARK EYES AND   451   3

THIN
    WITH THIN SCREAMING HATRED   500 15
    AND SEND THIN DRAUGHTS OF WORDS   506 22
    RATHER THIN   532   7
    SOFTLY BLOWS OUT ITS THIN LITTLE MALE STAMENS   535   3
    AND CLING TO THEIR THIN YOUNG WOMEN   558 24
    WE GET A PRETTY THIN TIME   573   2
    THE THIN SYCAMORE IN THE PLAYGROUND IS SWINGING WITH FL+   *926   2
    AND CAST US FORTH LIKE SHORN THIN MOONS TO TRAVEL   *938   2
    SINCE DEATH HAS DELIVERED NAKED AND THIN AND WHITE   *938   7

THINE
    MY BREAST'S AS RED AS THINE I RECKON   78 23
    THINE SHALL GO TER PAY THE WOMAN AN' WI' MY BIT WE'LL B+   83   2
    AN' 'DEED AN' I WISH AS THIS TALE O' THINE WOR NIVER MY+   83 10
    TO THE DARK ZENITH OF THINE ANTIPODES   322 19
    FOR THINE IS THE KINGDOM   704 11
    MY WAY IS NOT THY WAY AND THINE IS NOT MINE   812   1
    TRAVEL THINE AVOCATION HERE AND LEARN   872   2
    ALONG THY LIMBS DELIGHTED THINE HIS BRIDE'S   *915 24
    IN THE CURVE OF THINE EXQUISITE FORM THE JOY OF THE   *915 28
    MY BREAST'S AS RED AS THINE I RECKON   *920 15
    THINE SHALL GO TO PAY THE WOMAN AN' WI' MY BIT WE'LL BUY   *925   6
    BUT 'DEED AN' I WISH AS THIS TALE O' THINE WOR NIVER MY+   *925 14
    AS SULKY AN' ORMIN' AS THINE HAST OWT TO SAY OTHERWISE   *925 25

THING
    WHAT IS THIS THING THAT I LOOK DOWN UPON   33 24
    THERE'S ONE THING WE S'LL 'AVE A PEACEFUL 'OUSE   45 29
    TO DO SUCH A THING THOUGH IT'S A POOR TALE IT IS THAT I+   83   7
    COMMUNION OFFERING A BETTER THING   104   3
    A MUTE NEARLY BEAUTIFUL THING   112 11
    WHAT THING BETTER ARE YOU WHAT WORSE   131 19
    FOR SURELY THE FRAGILE FINE YOUNG THING HAD BEEN   132   3
    'TIS A LITTLE THING   137   6
    LIKE A THING UNWARRANTABLE CROSS THE HALL   140   8
    UNSIGHTLY ITS WAY TO THE WARMTH THIS THING WITH A LIST   141 15
    THAT BEAUTY IS A THING BEYOND THE GRAVE   193   9
    COME NO I'M A THING OF LIFE I GIVE   211   5
    NO NO I DANCE IN THE SUN I'M A THING OF LIFE   211 16
    THE THING WITH MY BODY THAT WOULD GO ON LIVING   214 28
    AT THE FOOT OF EACH GLOWING THING   215 26
    OR A POOR THING AT BEST   237   4
    YOU ARE SHY YOU SILLY YOU SILLY SHY THING   254 13
    IT IS A FEARFUL THING TO BE DOMINATED BY THE FEAR OF HU+   263   7
    AND A THING TO BE AFRAID OF   264 24
    SHE HAS NOT REALISED YET THAT FEARFUL THING THAT I AM T+   266 25
    COME UP THOU RED THING   302   7
    RISE THOU RED THING   302 16
    A SUDDEN TURNING UPON ITSELF OF A THING IN THE AIR   341   4
    BUT IT MIGHT AS WELL HAVE BEEN HAIR ON A SPIDER THING   345 34
    BIRDS HAVE THEIR VOICES EACH MEANS A DIFFERENT THING   368 12
    FIRST LIVE THING I'VE OWNED SINCE THE LOP-EARED RABBITS   395   7
    AND THOUGH THE SUN LEAPS LIKE A THING UNLEASHED IN THE +   408 21
    THING   430 25
    TOWARDS WOMAN OR MAN BIRD BEAST OR CREATURE OR THING   454 13
    I NEVER SAW A WILD THING   467   1
    THE MOMENT LOVE IS AN UNDERSTOOD THING BETWEEN US WE   472 21
    IS A FEARFUL THING TO BEHOLD   475 10
    ANTHONY MIGHT HAVE MADE A SPLENDID THING OF THE EAST   479 26
    IT'S ONE THING OR THE OTHER   487 13
    BUT THE FUNNIEST THING THAT COULD BE   489 12
    I KNOW A THING OR TWO ABOUT LOVE   490   3
    AND FOR EVERY BLOOMIN' MORTAL THING   493   3
    THE ONLY THING MEN INVARIABLY FIGHT FOR   497 19
    YET ONE THING I DO FIGHT FOR TOOTH AND NAIL ALL THE TIME   497 22
    THE ONE THING THE OLD WILL NEVER UNDERSTAND   511 21
    AND IN THE MIDDLE OF EVERY ATOM WHICH IS THE SAME THING   512   6
    THE ONLY THING TO BE DONE NOW   513 21
    AND THEN THE ONLY THING WE CAN DO IS TO KEEP QUITE STILL   514 11
    BUT THERE IS ALSO A THIRD THING THAT MAKES IT WATER   515 12
    BUT IT IS A THIRD THING PRESENT WHICH MAKES IT AN ATOM   515 15
    A FEARFUL THING IS THE MUTILATED SOCIAL CONSCIOUSNESS   516   6
    LABOUR IS THE ONE THING A MAN HAS HAD TOO MUCH OF   517 18
    AND AMOUNTS TO VERY MUCH THE SAME THING   523   7
    AND AS IF THE ATOM WERE AN IMPULSIVE THING   524 24
    SO LONG AS THE THING IS DONE NEATLY AND THE WORLD IS LE+   532 30
    TELL ME A THING   551 13
    TELL ME A THING   551 17
    THAT YOU DON'T MIND THE THING   551 23
    THERE ISN'T A DAMN THING IN 'EM   553   9
    THEY'LL NEVER DO A THING BOYS   553 17
    WE'LL SHOW 'EM A THING OR TWO NEVER YOU DOUBT   573 22
    A WREATH OF MIST IS THE USUAL THING   580   5
    DON'T YOU DARE TO SUGGEST SUCH A THING   580   8
    THE THING TO DO IS IN SOLITUDE SLOWLY AND PAINFULLY PUT   610 16
    THE ONE THING EASIEST TO LOSE IS SAVINGS   614   5
    THE BREATH OF LIFE AND THE SHARP WINDS OF CHANGE ARE IN+   615 16
    AND REDUCE ME TO THE LEVEL OF A THING   620   8
    AND IT ALL AMOUNTS TO THE SAME THING FURNITURE   657   9
    UNHAPPY KILL IT THE UNLIVING THING   678 26
    THERE IS NO SUCH THING AS SIN   679 18
    FOR THE THING THAT IS DONE WITHOUT THE GLOWING AS OF GOD   689 10
    IT IS A FEARFUL THING TO FALL INTO THE HANDS OF THE LIV+   699 12
    BUT IT IS A MUCH MORE FEARFUL THING TO FALL OUT OF THEM   699 13
    NO ANIMAL NO BEAST NOR CREEPING THING   701 12
    BUT EVIL IS A THIRD THING   710 23
    BUT EVIL EVIL IS ANOTHER THING IN ANOTHER PLACE   711 11
    WHICH HAS BROUGHT TO PASS THE FEARFUL THING CALLED EVIL   712 25
    A THING OF KISSES AND STRIFE   714   7
    A GREY VOID THING THAT GOES WITHOUT WANDERING   714 19
    WHEN STRIKE IS A THING OF TWO   714 22
    BUT WHEN STRIFE IS A THING OF ONE   714 26
    A FLUSH OF ROSE AND THE WHOLE THING STARTS AGAIN   720 11
    SHUT-UP COFFIN OF A THING WITH A SOLDIER WEARY   733   6
    A POOR ROAN THING ITS HIND LEG TWITCHES   734   6
    TO THE THING AND RATHER FRETTED AND HIS THICK BLACK HAIR   734 21
    I LET THE WHOLE THING GO STILL THERE IS ME   738 27

THING
A THING OF FEAR   747 30
A NAKED NIGHTLY THING TOO FRAIL AND WISE FOR THE STRESS   771 23
FOR MY TAINTED TRANSIENCY AS A THING UNREAL   772 7
NOT A MOB THING NOR A MASS THING NOR A CLASS THING NOR   775 23
A HUNDRED-PER-CENT THING   775 24
THAT IS A DIFFICULT THING TO BE FAITHFUL TO   775 27
HE IS THE ONE THING THAT IS ABORIGINALLY AMERICAN   776 21
TO GIVE THE INDIANS ONE SINGLE THING NOT ONE CENT   778 25
THE FIRST THING I DID WHEN I SAW THEM WAS TO LAUGH AT T+   791 27
PALLID POOR THING YET I   817 13
ONE THING THAT IS BOW-LEGGED   818 25
BUT THE ONE THING THAT IS BOW-LEGGED   820 5
THE GOOD THING ABOUT THE YOUNGER GENERATIONS   828 14
THE FUNNY THING ABOUT A GENTLEMAN   830 3
ANOTHER CURIOUS THING ABOUT THE ENGLISH MIDDLE CLASSES   831 20
A NEW THING COMES TO PASS EYES CLOSE   834 2
ONE THING IS CERTAIN WE'VE GOT TO TAKE HANDS OFF LOVE   834 7
THE THING FOR MEN TO DO IS TO START TO PULL DOWN MONEY   838 11
THE ONLY THING FOR A MAN TO DO NOW OR A WOMAN   838 14
SO THE ONLY THING TO DO IS TO KEEP STILL TO HOLD STILL +   839 1
THERE IS LOVE AND IT IS A DEEP THING   843 22
LOVE IS A THING OF TWONESS   844 5
TO TOUCH IT THAT NEW THING   861 25
HAS CONVEYED THIS THING THAT SITS AND WRITES   887 6
OWNING MY SUPPLE BODY A RARE GLAD THING SUPREMELY GOOD   *892 11
FLIES LIKE A WILD THING ACROSS MY BODY   *893 15
AND WATCHING THE GREAT THING LABOURING THROUGH THE WHOL+   *909 23
POOR THING   *910 6
FACE WAS THE FINEST THING THAT EVER   *925 3
TO SUCH A THING BUT IT'S A POOR TALE THAT I'M BOUND TO +   *925 11
A MUTE NEARLY BEAUTIFUL THING IS THY FACE   *927 24
A MUTE NEARLY BEAUTIFUL THING   *929 1
FOR SURELY THE FRAGILE FINE YOUNG THING HAD BEEN   *937 30
SO THE POOR THING IS LEFT FEELING AN UTTER WORM   *948 19
THE WHOLE THING HAS RISEN OUT OF THIS CASH-CHEMIST MONEY   *950 17
O LOVE IS A DEEP THING   *951 1
LIFE IS A THING YOU'VE GOT TO BE FLEXIBLE AND INTELLIGE+   *953 9

THINGS
SETS QUIVERING WITH WISDOM THE COMMON THINGS   46 19
RECOGNITIONS AND GREETINGS OF HALF-ACQUAINT THINGS AS I   52 22
OF GLASS PALACE ALOFT THERE AMONG MISTY INDEFINITE THIN+   52 24
THE LUMINOUS MIST WHICH THE POOR THINGS WIST WAS DAWN   71 5
AND ALL THINGS ARE IN SILENCE THEY CAN BROOD   76 20
I THOUGHT THAT LOVE WOULD DO ALL THINGS BUT NOW I KNOW +   93 1
OF PERFECT THINGS   101 13
ME THINGS AND THE SILENCES TOSS   108 15
ONLY PROBLEMS WRIT ON THE FACE OF THINGS   118 22
THINGS I WAS OUT TO FIND   123 23
AMONG CROWDS OF THINGS IN THE SUNSHINE JOSTLED AND RACK+   133 8
ALL THESE PURE THINGS COME FOAM AND SPRAY OF THE SEA   136 17
DOWN THE BRIGHT-GREY RUIN OF THINGS   150 23
THINGS I HAVE KNOWN THAT SHALL HAVE NO NAME   151 32
WITH THE OLD SWEET THINGS OF OUR YOUTH AND NEVER YET   157 6
IN WORDS AND THINGS WELL SAID BUT THE OTHER WAY   158 4
TO BE ALL THESE THINGS NOT TO BE   194 14
SEA YOU SHADOW OF ALL THINGS NOW MOCK US TO DEATH WITH   197 32
I THINK I COULD ALTER THE FRAME OF THINGS IN MY AGONY   213 18
ALL THE THINGS YOU NEVER KNEW   227 13
THE THINGS YOU NEVER KNEW   227 14
THERE ARE ONLY TWO THINGS NOW   238 1
TAKE OFF YOUR THINGS   238 9
ALL THINGS ON THE MOVE GOING THEIR OWN LITTLE WAYS AND +   249 17
THE FEAR OF THE WANT OF THESE THINGS SEEMS TO BE QUITE +   263 12
TO THOSE THINGS THAT LOVE DARKNESS THE LIGHT OF DAY IS +   331 3
THINGS OF ONE ELEMENT   340 3
LOOK UP AND YOU SEE THINGS FLYING   340 27
ALL THINGS WOULD PASS AWAY FOR IN THE TENSION OF OPPOSI+   348 6
THINGS HAVE THEIR BEING   348 5
OVER THE EDGE OF ALL THINGS   354 17
THINGS OF IRON ARE BEATEN ON THE ANVIL   381 31
I DO ALL THE THINGS THE BOURGEOIS DAREN'T DO   432 17
GOLD EGG OF ALL THINGS   437 13
WHERE THE FATHER OF ALL THINGS SWIMS IN A MIST OF ATOMS   438 4
THINGS MEN HAVE MADE WITH WAKENED HANDS AND PUT SOFT   448 1
AND FOR THIS REASON SOME OLD THINGS ARE LOVELY   449 6
THINGS MADE BY IRON AND HANDLED BY STEEL   448 8
TRUE WE'VE GOT ALL THESE THINGS   452 5
TO OTHER THINGS THAT ARE LEFT UNSAID   456 4
ALL KINDS OF THINGS TO ONE ANOTHER   470 5
A MAN IS MANY THINGS HE IS NOT ONLY A MIND   473 15
THE MIND THAT NEEDS TO KNOW ALL THINGS   473 19
FIDELITY AND LOVE ARE TWO DIFFERENT THINGS LIKE A FLOWER   476 1
BUT THINGS WILL HAPPEN TO US   482 20
AND OLD THINGS WILL FALL DOWN   482 25
AND REFUSED TO LET SO MANY THINGS HAPPEN BEHIND HIS BACK   483 17
WILD THINGS IN CAPTIVITY   484 22
IF SUCH THINGS WERE NICE AND WE NEEDN'T THINK TWICE   491 11
WITH PERFECTLY AWFUL THINGS IN IT   491 14
PEOPLE FEELING THINGS THEY INTEND TO FEEL THEY MEAN TO +   500 21
AND THE END OF ALL THINGS IS INSIDE US   510 19
WHEN THINGS GET VERY BAD THEY PASS BEYOND TRAGEDY   514 10
OR ELSE POOR THINGS THEY'RE HAVING TO PAY FOR THEMSELVES   518 1
POOR THINGS AND THEY KNOW IT   518 8
THE YOUNG KNOW THESE THINGS QUITE WELL   520 29
AND FORCED TO DO A THOUSAND MEAN THINGS MEANER THAN   522 13
IN THE CENTRE OF ALL THINGS   525 13
ONLY INSTEAD OF CHANGING THINGS THAT MIGHT BE CHANGED   538 20
BEAUTIFUL THINGS   540 3
POOR THINGS BUT WE CAN'T HELP THAT CAN WE   548 27
OF ALL THE THINGS THEY SQUEEZED OUT OF YOU   549 5
IS THE FRAME OF THINGS TOO HEAVY   558 19
FOR LEAVING THINGS OUT   562 13
THINGS OMITTED   563 6
AND ALL YOUR BEST THINGS AND JUST GIVES THEM AWAY   572 3
WHILE THEY CARRIED THE SHAMELESS THINGS AWAY   579 15
AND CAN'T PASS SUCH THINGS AS SUBSTANCE AND MARROW   583 29

THINGS
SO NOW I WANT ABOVE ALL THINGS   601 21
GOING SQUEAK SQUEAK I AM ALL THINGS UNTO MYSELF   603 19
AND IN THE POCKETS ARE THINGS I REQUIRE   607 12
WITH THE CENTRE OF ALL THINGS   610 7
AND EFFORT IS THE RUIN OF ALL THINGS   613 14
THE HUMAN WILL IS FREE ULTIMATELY TO CHOOSE ONE OF TWO +   617 12
AND THE BASE THINGS LIKE HYAENAS OR BED-BUGS HAVE LEAST+   621 18
NEITHER TO PERSONS NOR THINGS NOR IDEAS IDEALS NOR RELI+   622 7
TO THESE THINGS I FEEL ONLY RESPECT AND A TINGE OF REVE+   622 9
I DON'T KNOW WHAT THEY'VE DONE POOR THINGS BUT JUSTICE +   632 30
ARE THESE THINGS MY NEIGHBOURS   644 17
THESE TWO-LEGGED THINGS THAT WALK AND TALK   644 18
AM I TOLD THAT THESE THINGS ARE MY NEIGHBOURS   644 21
THINGS FROM THE SEA   647 3
WITH KNOWLEDGE OF THINGS THAT SHALL NEVER BE ADMITTED   656 18
AND ALL THINGS AND NOTHING AND BEING AND NOT-BEING   667 10
THE GODS ARE ALL THINGS AND SO ARE WE   673 16
THOSE THINGS THAT HAVE BECOME THEMSELVES   689 22
THE LOVELY THINGS ARE GOD THAT HAS COME TO PASS LIKE JE+   691 25
ALL THINGS THAT TURN TO THEE   704 18
ALL OF WHICH THINGS I CAN SURELY TASTE IN A GOOD APPLE   708 1
IF I SAY I TASTE THESE THINGS IN AN APPLE I AM CALLED M+   708 5
THAT ALL THINGS ARE MIXED AND THEREFORE THE PUREST WHIT+   708 15
OH IN THE WORLD OF THINGS   712 8
KNOW THYSELF IN DENIAL OF ALL THESE THINGS   714 16
I WASN'T AWARE OF THE THINGS I COULD DO   761 9
BLESSED IN ALL THINGS   768 24
THE COMING AND GOING OF THINGS   788 3
OR ELSE PREPARE FOR THE OTHER THINGS   793 9
SOMETIMES THEY COME TO TELL US THINGS   793 15
THEIR FACES ARE UGLY YET THEY MAKE WONDERFUL THINGS   794 7
I SEE DARK THINGS RUSHING ACROSS THE COUNTRY   794 10
HOW NICE IN THE GREAT CITIES WHERE ALL THINGS RUSH AND +   794 15
HOW NICE IF WE COULD TAKE ALL THESE THINGS AWAY FROM TH+   794 19
ALL THINGS THAT LIFT IN THE LIFT OF LIVING BETWEEN EART+   801 8
THE LAST TWO THINGS WE CAN STILL HOLD DEARLY   826 25
IS THAT THEY ARE NOT MEAN IN MATERIAL THINGS   828 17
THEY DON'T EVEN MIND DOING THINGS FOR YOU IN REASON   828 24
WHERE THE ATTENTION WILL BE LIFTED OFF MATERIAL THINGS   833 14
JUSTICE HUMAN DECENCY IN MATERIAL THINGS   833 24
THERE WILL ALWAYS BE A FATHER OF ALL THINGS IN SOME SHA+   840 7
BUT THE FATHER OF ALL THINGS IS HE WHO MAKES US EAGER   840 11
NOR A WISE MAN KNOWING ALL THINGS   840 18
I ONLY WANT TO KNOW SOME THINGS TO KNOW ALL THINGS WOUL+   840 19
THE FRAME OF THINGS HAS GROWN SO HEAVY IT'S JUST TOO HE+   842 29
BUT THERE ARE DEEPER THINGS THAN LOVE   843 23
OF ALL THINGS   844 23
GIRDLING WITH JEWELS THE MEANNESS OF COMMON THINGS   855 2
OLD THINGS THRICE SAID   857 4
THESE THINGS APART   870 11
STRIVE WITH THE FORMLESS THINGS AND GENTLY TOUCH   872 6
LIVE THINGS CARESS ME AND ENTREAT MY FONDLING   876 33
IN ALL THINGS TO THE LAST LIKE A RHAPSODY   877 26
I WAS EMBEDDED IN THE REST OF THINGS   881 30
FORBIDDEN THINGS AND THOUGHTS COME FLUTTERING   *894 18
AND ALL THINGS ARE POSSESSED BY SILENCE AND THEY CAN BR+   *898 14
AND ALL THINGS ARE POSSESSED BY SILENCE AND THEY CAN BR+   *901 15
RECOGNITIONS AND GREETINGS OF HALF-ACQUAINT THINGS AS I+   *905 11
THE LUMINOUS MIST WHICH THE POOR THINGS WIST WAS DAWN A+   *917 23
ONLY A MEAN ARITHMETIC ON THE FACE OF THINGS   *931 32
THINGS I WAS OUT TO FIND   *934 29
HOW I ADORE YOU YOU HAPPY THINGS YOU DEARS   *945 6
OF QUESTING BRILLIANT THINGS YOU JOY YOU TRUE   *945 13
AND RELIGION NOTHING WITHOUT THE FATHER OF ALL THINGS   *946 12
THE FATHER OF ALL THINGS SWIMS IN THE VAST DUSK OF ALL +   *947 17
AND AS WITH CLOTH SO WITH ALL THINGS HOUSES SHOES WAGON+   *950 2
BUT THERE ARE DEEPER THINGS THAN LOVE   *951 2
THAT CENTRES AND BALANCES ALL THINGS   *951 31

THING'S
THAT THING'S ALIVE IT'S DANGEROUS MAKE AWAY   528 16

THINK
I'S THINK IT'S NOBBUT A BEGGAR   44 12
I SH'D THINK 'E'LL GET RIGHT AGAIN   46 4
THINK OF ME HERE IN THE LIBRARY TRYING AND TRYING A SON+   57 21
I'D AS MUCH AS I COULD DO TO THINK   60 23
DONE I SHOULD THINK SO AN' MIGHT I ASK   79 31
ROUND-SHOULDERED HAG MY SIRS TO THINK   81 18
TO THINK I SHOULD 'AVE TER 'AFFLE AN' CAFFLE   82 9
DUNNAT THEE THINK BUT WHAT I'VE LOVED THEE I'VE LOVED T+   83 9
WHY I SHOULD THINK THAT FROM THE EARTH THERE FLY   127 6
HOW MANY DAYS DOST THINK HAS GONE   138 1
HOW MANY DAYS DOST THINK HAS GONE   138 3
WHEN I THINK OF THE PLACE   161 8
WHO CANNOT BEAR TO THINK BACK TO THE DEPARTURE   169 11
BUT NOW I THINK I HAVE SEEN IT ALL AND NOW   173 25
I THINK IF THEY TOLD ME SO   213 16
I THINK I COULD ALTER THE FRAME OF THINGS IN MY AGONY   213 18
I THINK I COULD BREAK THE SYSTEM WITH MY HEART   213 19
I THINK IN MY CONVULSION THE SKIES WOULD BREAK   213 20
WHAT SHOULD I THINK OF DEATH   214 13
THINK I DAREN'T DIE   214 21
THINK I COULDN'T LOOK TOWARDS DEATH   215 1
THE RYE IS TALLER THAN YOU WHO THINK YOURSELF   221 6
FOR EVER ONE EVEN MIGHT THINK THAT THEY LOVE US   223 27
WHO DO YOU THINK STANDS WATCHING   226 13
WHAT GHOST OF US BOTH DO YOU THINK HE SAW   227 11
WHAT ARE YOU BY YOURSELF DO YOU THINK AND WHAT   235 3
THINK YOU YOU DO NOT HATE ME   235 18
DO YOU THINK IT IS PURE WORSHIP   235 25
DO YOU THINK IT IS BLISS ALONE   235 32
AND THINK THERE WILL SOMETHING COME FORTH FROM US   247 18
YOU WOULD ENVY ME YOU WOULD THINK ME WONDERFUL   251 26
YOU WOULD THINK TWICE BEFORE YOU TOUCHED A WEASEL ON A   255 22
THINK OF IT   267 33
THEY THINK THAT WE ADORE THEM ALAS WOULD IT WERE TRUE   270 1

THINK
  PROBABLY THEY THINK ALL MEN ADORE THEM   270   2
  THINK OF IT FROM THE IRON FASTNESS   306 14
  THINK TO STAND THERE IN FULL-UNFOLDED NUDITY SMILING   306 17
  CERES KISS YOUR GIRL YOU THINK YOU'VE GOT HER BACK   309 25
  AND YOU THINK   341   6
  I THINK IT DID NOT HIT HIM   351 12
  NO NO DON'T THINK IT   357 30
  THINK OF IT IN A GARDEN OF INERT CLODS   358   8
  DOES THE SUN NEED STEAM OF BLOOD DO YOU THINK   374   9
  YOU THINK YOU'D BETTER MIND YOUR P'S AND Q'S FOR A BIT   400 28
  AND I THINK IN THIS EMPTY WORLD THERE WAS ROOM FOR ME   402 27
  AND I THINK IN THE WORLD BEYOND HOW EASILY WE MIGHT   402 29
  HO DO YOU THINK WE'LL GET ON   404 18
  OF COURSE I'M A LIDY WHAT D'YER THINK   434 25
  BUT THEY CAN'T REALLY THINK IT DO YOU THINK   435 13
  DON'T YOU THINK   435 15
  DON'T YOU THINK REALLY THEY KNOW WE'RE THEIR   435 16
  THE EARTH TO THINK   437 19
  SO YOU THINK SCIENTIFIC MAN YOU'LL BE FATHER OF YOUR OWN   438 18
  WHILE WE ARE EAGER WE THINK NOTHING OF IT   439 17
  OR IF YOU CAN'T RISE JUST THINK   457   4
  THINK OF THE WORLD THAT YOU'RE STIFLING IN   457   5
  THINK WHAT A WORLD IT MIGHT BE   457   6
  THINK OF THE RUBBISH YOU'RE TRIFLING IN   457   7
  BUT AT THE SAME TIME DON'T LET'S THINK   470   9
  MEANWHILE IF WE MUST LET US THINK ABOUT IT AND TALK   471 21
  BUT WHILE WE THINK OF IT AND TALK OF IT   471 25
  I AM I DO NOT THINK I AM   474 22
  BELOW WHAT WE THINK WE ARE   480   1
  WHO THINK THE ONLY WAY OUT OF YOUR MOURNFULNESS IS   485 11
  WELL THINK O' THAT NOW THINK O' THAT   489 21
  IF SUCH THINGS WERE NICE AND WE NEEDN'T THINK TWICE   491 11
  I THINK OF ALL THE LITTLE BRUTES   493 21
  AND A YOUNG MAN SHOULD THINK BY JOVE   503 29
  WOULDN'T THINK IT NECESSARY TO MAKE CONVERSATION   506 21
  AND WHEN I THINK OF THE GREAT TRAGEDY OF OUR MATERIAL-M+   508 19
  THINK THAT THE SAPPHIRE IS ONLY ALUMINA LIKE KITCHEN PA+   530   1
  THINK HOW A PEACOCK IN A FOREST OF HIGH TREES   530   5
  AND THINK HOW THE NIGHTINGALE WHO IS SO SHY   530   9
  AND THINK HOW WILD ANIMALS TROT WITH SPLENDOUR   530 12
  IT'S NOT SO MUCH WHAT WE THINK   531 23
  IT IS STRANGE TO THINK OF THE ANNAS THE VRONSKYS THE   533 11
  WE THINK WE'RE SUCH CLEVER LITTLE JOHNNIES   543 19
  AND DO YOU THINK IT'S MY BUSINESS TO BE HANDING OUT MON+   547 22
  YOU THINK THEY'RE THE SAME AS YOU ARE   549 28
  OR THEY THINK YOU'RE OFF YOUR DOT   549 30
  THINK YOU A LOWER-CLASS LOUT   550 12
  DON'T YOU THINK OR DON'T YOU AGREE   552   4
  AN' ALL THEY CAN THINK OF IS SINS   553 12
  SEEMED TO THINK I WAS LAYING IT SIEGE   555 16
  SEEMED TO THINK THEY'D GOT LIKE A HALO   555 19
  BUT I THINK YOU MAY TRUST   561 19
  AND I SIMPLY DAREN'T THINK OF AUNT LOU   571 30
  APPLICANT I DON'T THINK SO SIR I'M AFRAID NOT   582 18
  WHEN YOU KNOW THAT THEY'VE GOT TO THINK THAT THEY'RE   583   7
  THINK OF THE EFFECT ON MISS HARRISON   583 10
  WHAT SHALL WE THINK OF THESE   628 19
  OH WHEN I THINK OF THE INDUSTRIAL MILLIONS WHEN I SEE   629 16
  WHAT MAKES YOU THINK THAT YOU'RE ALL IN IT   668 24
  OH YOU'D THINK THE BRITISH PUBLIC   670 21
  WHEN MEN THINK THEY ARE LIKE GODS   673   4
  LET ME THINK ABOUT IT LET ME FORM AN IDEA   690 13
  TO THINK AMONG THE MOSS AND MUD OF LIZARDS AND MASTODONS   690 28
  TO THINK OUT IN THE ABSTRACT WHEN ALL WAS TWILIT GREEN +   690 29
  DO NOT THINK THAT A MACHINE IS WITHOUT A SOUL   713   1
  OH THINK OF THEM AND WITH THE SOUL'S DEEP SIGH   722 12
  HOW TERRIBLE IT WOULD BE TO THINK AND KNOW TO HAVE CONS+   724 24
  DO YOU THINK IT IS EASY TO CHANGE   727 31
  I THINK PERHAPS THE MAN THAT CAME   732   9
  A NICE ONE I LIKE IT HE'LL THINK IT'S A TALL ORDER   733 29
  WHAT DO YOU THINK I SAID   735   5
  THINK OF THAT NOW   773 27
  HEADS THAT THINK NOT   827 22
  NOT ON WHAT MEN THINK   831 18
  WE HAVE LEARNED I THINK NOT TO BE GREEDY   833   3
  OF WHOM I THINK THIS IS TRUE   833   7
  I THINK IDIOTS TELL DULL STUPID DISGUSTING TALES   837 21
  YET WHEN I THINK OF THE WILD SWAN OR THE RIPPLE-MARKED +   841   1
  I CAN NEVER EVEN THINK THAT IT'S BABY WHO LOOKS LIKE AR+   842 21
  I THINK IT IS THE HAND OF SORROW   869 20
  I THINK SOMETIMES IT WILL CRUSH MY HEART INWARD   869 22
  MY GOD TO THINK IT IS GONE FOR EVER   886 19
  TO THINK THAT YOU ARE GONE FOR EVER   886 20
  BUT I THINK THE KISSES PEACH   *893   9
  I COULD THINK O' NOWT BUT OUR TED AN' 'IM TAKEN   *910   3
  ME WATCHIN' DOST THINK THERE WAS OWT BETWEEN 'EM   *910 23
  I CANNA BIDE TO THINK WHERE HE IS GONE   *911 16
  DONE I SHOULD THINK SO DONE BUT MIGHT   *921 27
  ROUND-SHOULDERED HAG MY SIRS TO THINK   *923 18
  TO THINK I SHOULD HA'E TO HAFFLE AN' CAFFLE   *924 13
  DUNNAT THEE THINK BUT WHAT I LOVE THEE I LOVE THEE WELL   *925 13
  AN' THEN WI' THAT TWENTY POUND WE GI'E 'ER I S'D THINK +   *925 20
  DO YOU THINK IF YOU TAKE ME THAT THAT WILL ABATE YOU   *932 12
  THE RYE IS TALLER THAN YOU WHO THINK YOURSELF   *944 19
  DO YOU THINK I'D HAVE A CREATURE LIKE YOU AT MY SIDE   *944 25
  LORD DEAR LORD DO YOU THINK HE EVER CAN SHINE   *945 20
  THE FIRST EFFORT TO THINK   *946 28
  DON'T YOU THINK LITTLE MAN YOU'LL BE FATHER OF HUMAN BA+   *947 23
  AND THINK OF THEM AND WITH THE SOUL'S DEEP SIGH   *958 17
  OH THINK OF IT IN THE TWILIGHT PEACEFULLY   *960 18

THINKING
  THINKING THAT THEY PERHAPS   269 18
  I AM THINKING OF COURSE OF THE PEACH BEFORE I ATE IT   279 13
  THINKING OF VOLUPTUOUSNESS   324   8
  AND BECOMES THE FAITHFUL SHEEP-DOG OF THE SHEPHERD THIN+   325   8
  THINKING I AM NOT THE MEASURE OF CREATION   339 12

THINKING
  SO I SWITCHED ON THE ELECTRIC LIGHT THINKING NOW   344 26
  THINKING THIS DOG SURE HAS TAKEN A FANCY TO ME   398 20
  THINKING DEATH WILL AWAKEN SOMETHING   408- 13
  SO WHEN I CATCH MYSELF THINKING AH IF I WAS RICH   498   7
  OR THINKING THEY ARE LOVABLE OR WANTING TO BE LOVABLE   505 10
  ONE CANNOT NOW HELP THINKING   536   6
  THINKING HE WAS A LITTLE HILL AND SHE MURMURED SUCH   540   2
  THINKING OLD NEPTUNE WAS OFF ON A SPREE   575   9
  TO BE ALONE IS ONE OF LIFE'S GREATEST DELIGHTS THINKING+   610   3
  WHEN MEN AND WOMEN WHEN LADS AND GIRLS ARE NOT THINKING   672   1
  WHEN I WAS WAITING AND NOT THINKING SITTING AT A TABLE +   672 18
  IF IT IS MERELY VENUS OR HERMES YOU ARE THINKING OF   678   6

THINKS
  HOW IT STIRS LIKE A SUBTLE STOAT WHATEVER SHE THINKS   128 17
  WHEN HE THINKS HIMSELF ALONE   244 10
  HE THINKS THE WHOLE BLUE SKY   244 29
  SHE THINKS WE ARE ALL OF ONE PIECE   266 26
  AND HE CHERISHES VOLUPTUOUS DELIGHTS AND THINKS ABOUT T+   325   6
  IS A GENTLEMAN IF HE THINKS HIMSELF SO   434 20
  THE TROUBLE IS EVERYBODY THINKS THEY'RE JUST AS SUPERIOR   435 10
  IF THIS IS WHAT ARCHIBALD THINKS I AM   489 19
  HE SURE THINKS A LOT OF LIES   489 20
  HE THINKS I AM IF EVER HE THINKS AT ALL   733 27
  THE MODERN YOUNG WOMAN THINKS IT WONDERFUL TO BE SO BRI+   841 26

THINLY
  GREY LAVENDER SENSITIVE STEEL CURVING THINLY AND BRITTLY   300 30

THINNED
  OVER WATER WHERE THE WEEDS ARE THINNED   64 32
  AND SEE WHERE THE BUDDING HAZELS ARE THINNED   126   9

THIRD
  BUT THERE IS ALSO A THIRD THING THAT MAKES IT WATER   515 12
  BUT IT IS A THIRD THING PRESENT WHICH MAKES IT AN ATOM   515 15
  BECAUSE WE ARE THE THIRD AND FOURTH GENERATIONS   627 22
  AND WE ARE THE GELDED THIRD AND FOURTH GENERATION   627 28
  THERE IS HOWEVER THE VAST THIRD HOMOGENEOUS AMORPHOUS   649 24
  BUT EVIL IS A THIRD THING   710 23

THIRD-RATE
  ONLY THIRD-RATE SWADS ARE PUSHING TO GET ON NOWADAYS   518 17

THIRST
  YOU THIRST FOR COOLNESS WITH A HUSKY THIRST   91 16
  THIRST FOR FISH AS FOR MORE-THAN-WATER   340   8

THIRSTING
  THE SUN IS FOREVER THIRSTY THIRSTING FOR THE BRIGHTEST +   368   7

THIRSTY
  NOT BREAD ALONE NOT THE BELLY NOR THE THIRSTY THROAT   263   8
  THE SUN IS FOREVER THIRSTY THIRSTING FOR THE BRIGHTEST +   368   7

THIRTEEN
  FOR A GREY RAT FOUND THE GOLD THIRTEEN   119 19
  WITH MY THIRTEEN SORRY PICTURES THAT HAVE JUST BEEN RES+   580 17
  O MY THIRTEEN PICTURES ARE IN PRISON   632 28
  FOR THE GREY RAT FOUND THE GOLD THIRTEEN   *932 28
  THIRTEEN TIMES THE TEETH FLASHED IN A FIRE OF BLOOD   *933   1
  THIRTEEN WERE THE SLITHERING SILENT JOURNEYS   *933   2
  THIRTEEN LAY THE YELLOW CHICKS BENEATH THE JOIST OF WOOD   *933   3

THIRTEEN THOUSAND
  THIRTEEN THOUSAND PEOPLE CAME TO SEE   577 24

THIRTIES
  PEOPLE IN THEIR THIRTIES AND THE OLDER ONES HAVE GOTTEN   462 19
  DON'T LET ME LAST BEYOND YOUR THIRTIES   835 14

THIRTY
  ISN'T IT GOD'S OWN IMAGE TRAMPING HIS THIRTY MILES A DAY   430 22
  LOOK AT THE YOUNG MEN UNDER THIRTY   612   9
  THE LITTLE-BOY OF THIRTY OR FORTY OR FIFTY OR SIXTY   841 19
  AND WE STILL HAVE TO SEE WHAT BABY WILL BE LIKE AT THIR+   842 26

THISTLE
  THE REST IS A CLOUD OF THISTLE DOWN   863   7

THISTLEDOWN
  LIKE BALLS OF THISTLEDOWN   253   4

THISTLES
  WHERE PEOPLE ARE CROWDED LIKE THISTLES   101 21

THITHER
  HITHER AND THITHER ACROSS THE HIGH CRYSTALLINE FRAME   72   9
  LET THEM THITHER TO PEACE   88 31
  NIGHT-LIGHTS HITHER AND THITHER SHED   142 27
  MACHINES HAVE TRIUMPHED ROLLED US HITHER AND THITHER   623 30
  MADLY WE RUSH HITHER AND THITHER   739 21
  SO WHEN I RUN AT LENGTH THITHER ACROSS   742   5
  AND THITHER THEY RETURN FROM THE LAND OF MEN   799   4
  HITHER AND THITHER   867 17
  MACHINES HAVE TRIUMPHED ROLLED US HITHER AND THITHER   *953 17

THOMAS
  MY NAME IS THOMAS THOMAS EARP   680   9
  AND MY NAME IS THOMAS THOMAS EARP   680 15

THOMAS COOK
  OH THE GREAT ADVENTURE OF DEATH WHERE THOMAS COOK CANNO+   677   8

THOU'LT
  LADDIE A MAN THOU'LT HA'E TO BE   220   7

THOU'RT
  THAT I COULD HA' BEEN FIRST WOMAN TO THEE AS THOU'RT FI+   *925 17

THOUSAND
  NIGHT BLENCHED WITH A THOUSAND SNOWS   104 28
  AT WHOSE SIDE I HAVE LAIN FOR OVER A THOUSAND NIGHTS   260   6
  AFTER TWO THOUSAND YEARS   327 17
  AND FORCED TO DO A THOUSAND MEAN THINGS MEANER THAN   522 13
  I TELL YOU NOT ONE MAN IN A THOUSAND HAS EVEN   638 16

THOUSANDS
  THOUSANDS AND THOUSANDS OF GAPING HIDEOUS FOUL DEAD   258   8
  NAXOS THOUSANDS OF FEET BELOW THE OLIVE-ROOTS   293 24
  AND NOW THE OLIVE LEAVES THOUSANDS OF FEET BELOW   293 25
  STANDING IN THEIR THOUSANDS THESE APPEARANCES IN DAMP   431 25
  OUT OF THE THOUSANDS AND THOUSANDS OF CENTURIES OF MAN   623 26
  OUT OF THE THOUSANDS AND THOUSANDS OF CENTURIES OF MAN   *953 14

THOWT
  BUT I THOWT TER MYSEN AS THAT WOR TH' ONLY BIT   61 17

THRALL
  THE DAISY-FROTH QUIESCENT SOFTLY IN THRALL   35 29
  AND HOLD THEM IN THRALL   110   4
  AND OPENED UNDER HIS THRALL   127   4
  I AM SICK AND TIRED MORE THAN ANY THRALL   *895 24
  I AM SICK AND TIRED MORE THAN ANY THRALL   *904 13

THREAD
  STAR-SPIDERS SPINNING THEIR THREAD   113 18
  WHEN THE THREAD CLIPS   155 25
  THEY THREAD AND THRILL AND FLICKER EVER DOWNWARD   322 18
  SWALLOWS WITH SPOOLS OF DARK THREAD SEWING THE SHADOWS   340 29
  IS LEAVING A LONG THREAD OF DARK SMOKE   687 10
  HAS COME LIKE A THREAD LIKE A DOOR JUST OPENING   702 14
  AND YET OUT OF ETERNITY A THREAD   719 27
  A HORIZONTAL THREAD   719 29
  IN-WEAVING THE BRIGHT THREAD OF HIS JOY   867 27
  STAR-SPIDERS SPINNING THEIR THREAD   *929   7

THREADBARE
  I PICK MY WAY OVER THREADBARE GRASS WHICH IS PRESSED   *896 10

THREADED
  BUT THREADED WITH FILIGREE SILVER   101   5
  THE DEAD THREADED THE AIR LINGERING   704   3
  OF HER SPIRIT WAVERED LIKE WATER THREADED WITH LIGHT   *936 31

THREADING
  THREADING LIKE ANTS THAT CAN NEVER RELENT   50 29
  THREADING HIS WAY AMONG THE ROBOT MACHINE-PEOPLE   645 20
  WHEN GOLD LAY SHINING THREADING THE COOLED-OFF ROCK   682 24
  THREADING THE ROUND JOY OF HIS WHITE-FLANNELLED HIPS FU+   867 30

THREADS
  SOME DIM LITTLE EFFORTS PLACED IN THE THREADS OF THE   142   7
  THREADS AND THRILLS LIKE ORE THAT IS WEALTH TO THE EYE   146 31
  THEY GLIMMER WITH TISSUE OF GOLD AND GOLDEN THREADS ON   388 19
  THREADS OF BLUE WIND FAR AND DOWN THE ROAD   732 22
  AND HOLD MYRIAD THREADS FROM THEIR CLAWS   793 26
  CURVED CUT THE LAST THREADS   816 20

THREAD-THREADING
  AT THE LITTLE FISH THREAD-THREADING THE WATERY NOOK   161 11

THREAT
  AND BULLIED WITH THE THREAT GET MONEY OR EAT DIRT   522 12
  AND RANGE THEMSELVES LIKE GREAT FIERCE SERAPHIM FACING +   695   3
  IT IS THEIR THREAT THEIR LOUD JEERING THREAT   741 11
  WILL YOU TAKE OFF YOUR THREAT   783 15

THREATEN
  WHICH THREATEN TO TEAR THE WORLD IN TWO BETWEEN   516 22

THREATENED
  NOW LIVING WOMEN AND MEN ARE THREATENED WITH EXTINCTION   640 15

THREATENER
  THREATENER   783 14

THREATENING
  A THREATENING TORTURING PHALLIC MOLOCH   264 25
  DRONING OVER THREATENING ME   741 10
  DARK-MASKED-ONE DAY-STARER THREATENING THE SUN WITH YOUR   783 11

THREATENS
  WHEN DANGER THREATENS ON THE SURFACE OF THE CEASELESS F+   695   2

THREATS
  THREATS THAT BROACH   66 26

THREE
  THREE DEAD BIRDS LIE   36 24
  THREE TIMES HAVE I OFFERED MYSELF THREE TIMES REJECTED   48   1
  THREE OF THEM BLACK IN SHADOW TWO OF THEM BRIGHT   224 10
  THREE SIDES SET ON ME SPACE AND FEAR BUT THE FOURTH SIDE   249 10
  THREE SIDES SET ON ME CHAOS AND BOUNCE BUT THE FOURTH   249 27
  NO NO IT IS THE THREE STRANGE ANGELS   250 31
  AND THREE LITTLE BROTHERS   357 17
  AND THE HUGE FRONTAL OF THREE GREAT ELEPHANTS STEPPING   387 28
  CHIEFTAINS THREE OF THEM ABREAST ON FOOT   389 16
  I WISH THEY HAD GIVEN THE THREE FEATHERS TO ME   392   1
  TO STAND AND HOLD FEATHERS THREE FEATHERS ABOVE THE WOR+   392   4
  WE'VE RISEN IN THE WORLD ALL THREE   490 22
  THREE BAGS FULL   669 22

THREE
  FOR HOW CAN I COUNT IN YOUR THREE TIME THREE   702   3
  SHE SAID TO ME STAY THREE HOURS TO COMFORT ME SUCH IS A+   749 19
  AND THREW THE COFFEE-PLANT STARTED COFFING THREE VERY DISTINC+   760 27
  OF THE BOOKS THAT LIE OUT ON THE DESKS A FULL THREE SCO+   *895 21
  OF THE BOOKS THAT LIE OUT ON THE DESKS A FULL THREE SCO+   *904 10
  THREE SIDES SET ON ME SPACE AND FEAR BUT THE FOURTH SID+   *945 22
  GIVE ME A FLOWER ON A TALL STEM AND THREE DARK FLAMES   *956 21

THREES
  THREES AND FOURS AND TWELVES   355 24

THREESCORE
  OF THE BOOKS THAT LIE OUT ON THE DESKS A FULL THREESCORE   74 13

THRESH
  SOME OTHER WILL THRESH YOU OUT   105 23
  THROUGH THE WORLD DID THRESH   120 33
  LIKE A SNAKE WE THRESH ON THE LONG FORLORN   163 19
  AND NEVER AN ENEMY BROW-METALLED TO THRESH IT OUT WITH   382 30
  HARK HOW THEY THRESH   817 24

THRESHES
  TO THE MAN WHO THRESHES AND SOWS THE SHEAVES   *899   9
  TO THE MAN WHO THRESHES AND SOWS THE SHEAVES   *902 21

THRESHING
  THRESHING YOUR OWN PASSIONS WITH NO WOMAN FOR THE   197   4
  SLIPPED THROUGH MY ARMS ON THE THRESHING FLOOR   198 11
  NAKED MEN ARE THRESHING RICE   386 28

THRESHING-FLOOR
  THRESHING-FLOOR   197   5

THRESHING-TIME
  AT THRESHING-TIME BROKEN WAS BROKEN   198 15

THRESHOLD
  AND I LINGERED ON THE THRESHOLD WITH MY HAND   121 14
  ON THE THRESHOLD OF SPRING I FEAR I SHALL DIE   273 29
  WHAT DO THEY WANT FOREVER THERE ON OUR THRESHOLD   740 12

THREW
  YOU LEAPT ABOUT IN THE SLIPPERY ROCKS AND THREW   98 19
  YOU YIELDED WE THREW THE LAST CAST   111 21
  I PUT MY STRENGTH UPON YOU AND I THREW   156 29
  SHADOWS THE PASSING WILD-BEAST THREW   747   6
  AND THREW IT AT THE WATER-TROUGH WITH A CLATTER   351 11
  THREW THEMSELVES ON HIM IN INDIGNATION   575   2
  THEN SUDDENLY HE SPIED THE OLD LAKE AND HE THREW IT IN   791   7
  HE THREW THE FISH IN THE BOAT   802 10

THRICE
  AND SLOWLY VERY SLOWLY AS IF THRICE ADREAM   350 30
  OLD THINGS THRICE SAID   857   4

THRICE-TOLD
  SHARPLY BEATS OUT A THRICE-TOLD FUNERAL KNELL   858 24
  OF THE DYING GRASS WITH A THRICE-TOLD TALE OF DEATH   858 27

THRILL
  THRILL OF HIS WORK HE TURNS AGAIN FROM ME   51 18
  DO YOU NOT HEAR EACH MORSEL THRILL   127 11
  THEY THREAD AND THRILL AND FLICKER EVER DOWNWARD   322 18
  AND THRILL WITH GLITTERING RAYS   526   6
  IS THAT THEY CALMLY ASSERT WE ONLY THRILL TO PERVERSITY   531   3
  WHAT MATTERS IS WHAT WE THRILL TO   531 26
  WE ARE ULTIMATELY DETERMINED BY WHAT WE THRILL TO   531 27
  BUT WHAT DO YOU THRILL TO DO YOU KNOW   532   2
  HE REPLIED TO THRILL TO ANYTHING   532   4
  A THRILL RATHER EASILY EXHAUSTS ITSELF TAKE EVEN THE WAR   532   5
  AND IN THAT THRILL HE FELT   605   7
  AND IN THAT THRILL SHE FELT   605 11
  A THRILL THROUGH THE LISTENING TREES AND HOLD THE BREATH   858 26
  SHE WATCHED MY HAND AND THE SKIES BEGAN TO THRILL   *935 28

THRILLED
  OF HER SPIRIT WAVERED LIKE WATER THRILLED WITH LIGHT   125 32
  AND THE FROGS IN THE POOL BEYOND THRILLED WITH EXUBERAN+   206 29
  AND THRILLED   605   3
  AND THRILLED   605   6
  WITH A RICH A THRILLED YOUNG CLASP OF LIFE   *899 32
  WITH A RICH A THRILLED YOUNG CLASP OF LIFE   *903 11

THRILLING
  OF THRILLING RUIN IN THE FLESH OF PUNGENT PASSION OF RA+   273 19
  AND OF COURSE THRILLING IS LIKE LOVING YOU HAVE NO CHOI+   531 28
  RAPE WAS RATHER THRILLING   532 16
  YES IF IT'S A KEEN MATCH RAPE IS RATHER THRILLING   532 19
  I SHOULD SAY THAT WAS RATHER THRILLING   532 24
  RATHER THRILLING TO CONTEMPLATE   532 25
  RATHER THRILLING   532 29
  QUITE THRILLING I SHOULD SAY AT LEAST TO CONTEMPLATE   533   1
  FURTHER THRILLING POSSIBILITIES   533   3
  THE PROFOUND AND THRILLING VIBRATION OF JUSTICE SENSE O+   653 15

THRILLS
  IS HIDDEN IN THEIRS THEIR THRILLS ARE MINE   52 11
  TILL HER DARK DEEPS SHOOK WITH CONVULSIVE THRILLS AND T+   125 31
  FINE THRILLS TO THE NEIGHBOUR STARS FINE HIDDEN BEAMS   127   7
  THREADS AND THRILLS LIKE ORE THAT IS WEALTH TO THE EYE   146 31
  NO WHEN IT COMES TO THRILLS THERE ARE REALLY VERY FEW   532 14
  AND IN THE INTERVALS OF THEIR THRILLS I SUPPOSE   533   7
  AND UP THE IRON FEET OF THE EAGLE IN THRILLS OF FIERY P+   782 22
  SOMETHING THRILLS IN ME AND I KNOW   841   8
  TILL HER DARK DEEPS SHOOK WITH CONVULSIVE THRILLS AND T+   *936 30

THROAT
    OF RED UPON THE THROAT HER TERRORS SWAY   42 27
    I KNOW NOT WHAT FINE WIRE IS ROUND MY THROAT   43 29
    THROAT WAS FOUND   120 19
    CLOSING ITS CRIMSON THROAT MY OWN THROAT IN HER POWER   123 14
    AS IF IT WOULD BURST ITS WINE-SKIN IN MY THROAT   123 16
    IN THE FLOWER'S THROAT AND THE FLOWER GAPED WIDE WITH W+   125 10
    SHALL GET MY THROAT AT LAST SHALL GET IT SOON   126 2
    SWEET-SCENTED TO HOLD IN THE THROAT   165 10
    I HAVE SEEN IT FELT IT IN MY MOUTH MY THROAT MY CHEST MY   207 21
    WHAT YOUR THROAT IS BRUISED BRUISED WITH MY KISSES   230 14
    YOUR SHOULDERS YOUR BRUISED THROAT   238 10
    IN THE BLOOD-JETS OF YOUR THROAT   242 4
    AS IT LIFTS ITS STRAIGHT WHITE THROAT   255 24
    NOT BREAD ALONE NOT THE BELLY NOR THE THIRSTY THROAT   263 8
    THAN STOMACH OR THROAT OR EVEN THE MIND   264 12
    OR DRAGON-MOUTHED SALVIA WITH GOLD THROAT OF WRATH   314 26
    HOT IN THE THROAT   315 21
    AND THROAT OF BRIMSTONE-MOLTEN ANGRY GOLD   317 11
    AND RESTED HIS THROAT UPON THE STONE BOTTOM   349 12
    I REMEMBER HEARING A WILD GOOSE OUT OF THE THROAT OF NI+   365 34
    AND THE FIRST TENOR SINGING OF THE PASSIONATE THROAT OF+   366 17
    SO HE CLEARS HIS THROAT THE YOUNG COCK-EAGLE   413 26
    GOT HIS THROAT CUT   437 11
    OF FREEDOM SHRIEKING TILL HER THROAT WAS SORE   574 23
    THEIR ROBOT CACHINNATION COMES RATTLING OUT OF MY THROAT   645 8
    I SAW AN ANGRY ITALIAN SEIZE AN IRRITATING LITTLE OFFIC+   674 20
    OH YOU WHOSE CACKLE MAKES MY THROAT GO   762 3
    ON HIS THROAT BELOW HIS SONG   768 22
    HIS THROAT TO SING GLANCES DOWN   771 4
    WITH FIRE AND MY THROAT IS FULL   802 25
    AND MY THROAT IS WET WITH HER TEARS   863 4
    THERE I CANNOT BEAR TO SEE THE SOBS IN YOUR THROAT   871 19
    HOW HE HURTS ME WITH HIS HEART AND HIS THROAT SO NEAR T+   871 22
    AND TERRIBLY STRANGE IS THE THROAT THAT IS WORKING WITH+   871 26
    AND I CAN SEE THE PULSE WITHIN HIS THROAT   878 25
    THROUGH THAT WHITE STRAIT OF THY THICK SHAKEN THROAT   879 7
    AND THEN I KNEW I HAD TAKEN MY MOUTH FROM HER THROAT   882 7
    CLOSING ITS CRIMSON THROAT MY OWN THROAT IN HER POWER   *934 20
    AS IF IT WOULD BURST ITS WINESKIN IN MY THROAT   *934 22
    IN THE FLOWER'S THROAT AND THE FLOWER GAPED WIDE WITH W+   *935 26
    SHALL GET MY THROAT AT LAST SHALL GET IT SOON   *937 2

THROATED
    THE FULL THROATED WOMAN HAS CHOSEN A WINNING LIVING SONG *940 9

THROATS
    TO FEEL FRESH AIR IN OUR THROATS TO HAVE FRESH BREATH I+   175 21
    THROATS TO THE HEAVENS INCLINE   177 16
    THE LONELINESS DAUNTS THEM THEIR STIFF THROATS ACHE   228 12
    THROATS   437 26
    AND BITES AT OUR THROATS AND CHESTS   609 2
    NONE IN THEIR LITTLE THROATS OR CLASS-ROOM BODIES   657 14
    JUST AS IT CANNOT BE ANYTHING BUT WRONG TO CUT THE THRO+   678 4
    HONKED IN THE GLOOM THE HONK OF PROCREATION FROM SUCH T+ *947 3

THROB
    ENCROACHING TOWARDS A CRISIS A MEETING A SPASM AND THRO+   66 22
    FLOWERS OF THE BLEEDING-HEART FALL TO THE THROB   137 5
    NEW THROB LIKE A STIRRING UNDER THE FALSE DAWN THAT PRE+   292 34
    THROB THROB THROB   782 18
    THE FRANTIC THROB OF THE TRAIN   862 18

THROBBING
    THE WAVE OF SOLDIERS THE COMING WAVE THE THROBBING RED +   66 23
    WHICH SLIPS DOWN LIKE A PENDULUM TO BALANCE THE THROBBI+   370 6
    MAKES OF HIMSELF A BELFRY OF THROBBING SOUND   530 10
    ALONG THE NERVES A LOW THROBBING   767 19
    SETS MY HEART ALSO THROBBING WITH PAIN   862 22

THROBS
    STRANGE THROBS BEYOND LAUGHTER AND TEARS   38 22
    THROBS OF INVITATION   289 3
    BLUNDERING MORE INSANE AND LEAPING IN THROBS TO CLUTCH +   343 20
    THAT IS LIVING THROBS   782 17

THROES
    ALONG IN THE COILED CONVULSIVE THROES   164 6
    WHERE MY SOUL FALLS IN THE LAST THROES OF BOTTOMLESS CO+   322 3
    AND THE YOUNG ARE FLOWING IN THE THROES OF A GREAT   511 24

THRONE
    HOW YOU SIT IN THE THRONE OF MY EYES   227 30
    AND THE GLOWING THRONE OF THE ABSOLUTE ONE   823 14

THRONES
    FOR TODAY THE BASE THE ROBOTS SIT ON THE THRONES OF THE   637 17

THRONG
    NOT EVEN PALISH SMOKE LIKE THE REST OF THE THRONG   116 12
    THRONG OF STARTLED BEINGS SUDDENLY THROWN   140 12
    IN A LITTLE THRONG AT YOUR DOOR AND ADMIT THE ONE WHO IS   179 6
    OH NOW THEY MOAN AND THRONG IN ANGER AND PRESS BACK   722 24
    OF GHOSTS THAT THRONG ABOUT OUR MUFFLED HEARTS   736 3
    OF THEIR PATIENT WAITING UPON US THE THRONG OF THE GHOS+   736 6
    FOR NOW THE HOSTS OF HOMELESS GHOSTS DO THRONG   737 1
    LEFT OF THEIR LIGHT AMONG THE MEAN FLOWERS' THRONG   855 16

THRONGED
    IN ANCIENT ROME DOWN THE THRONGED STREETS   703 24

THRONGS
    WHERE THRONGS OF ANGELS HASTENING UPON   872 18

THROSTLE
    THE SAME SETS THE THROSTLE AT SUNSET ON A BOUGH   272 25

THROSTLES
    PALE-BREASTED THROSTLES AND A BLACKBIRD ROBBERLINGS   36 25

THROTTLE
    WHY SHOULD I WANT TO THROTTLE   240 24

THROTTLED
    I PRESSED THE WRETCHED THROTTLED FLOWER BETWEEN   125 13
    I PRESSED THE WRETCHED THROTTLED FLOWER BETWEEN   *936 12

THROTTLING
    HER FRANTIC EFFORT THROTTLING   43 10

THROUGHOUT
    WHERE THE FIGHT THAT IS FIGHT FOR BEING IS FOUGHT THROU+   93 4
    THAT WHICH IS IN PART FINDING ITS WHOLE AGAIN THROUGHOUT   367 6
    AND WHEN THROUGHOUT ALL THE WILD ORGASMS OF LOVE   477 12
    THAT SHE HAS IN TRAVELLING BY HERSELF THROUGHOUT TIME   610 21
    THROUGHOUT THE AEONS AS THE LIZARD SWIRLS HIS TAIL FINE+   683 7
    AND THERE IS NOTHING ELSE THROUGHOUT TIME AND ETERNITY   701 1

THROW
    THROW 'IMSELF DOWN THAT SINK   81 20
    I THROW FROM OUT OF THE DARKNESS MYSELF LIKE A FLOWER I+   93 26
    MYSELF BUT A KNOWLEDGE OF ROOTS OF ROOTS IN THE DARK TH+   94 3
    OF FINISHED BRIDEGROOM SEEN HER RISE AND THROW   193 4
    AT LAST I CAN THROW AWAY WORLD WITHOUT END AND MEET YOU   210 1
    AT LAST YOU CAN THROW IMMORTALITY OFF AND I SEE YOU   210 3
    THAT YOU THROW OFF STRAIGHT ON THE TINDER OF MY NERVES   241 9
    WOULD YOU LIKE TO THROW A STONE AT ME   279 3
    AND BECAUSE I SAY SO YOU WOULD LIKE TO THROW SOMETHING   279 26
    THEN YOU THROW AWAY THE SKIN   282 5
    AND THROWING HIMSELF UPON IT THROW OFF THE MADNESS OF H+   327 26
    HIT HIM AND KILL HIM AND THROW HIM AWAY   346 7
    THEY BEGIN TO BE SOOTHED AND SOOTHING THEN WE THROW   448 12
    THEN DESTROY THEM THROW THEM OUT INTO THE CITIES   780 16
    AND THE STARS ARE READY WITH STONES TO THROW IN THE FAC+   792 13
    THEN I TAKE MY KNIFE AND THROW IT UPON THE GREY DOG   807 20
    THROW HISSELF IN THAT SINK   *923 20

THROWING
    AND THROWING HIMSELF UPON IT THROW OFF THE MADNESS OF H+   327 26

THROWN
    WHAT CONJURER'S CLOTH WAS THROWN ACROSS YOU AND RAISED   53 21
    THROWN LUSTILY OFF FROM OUR FULL-SAPPY HIGH   127 8
    THRONG OF STARTLED BEINGS SUDDENLY THROWN   140 12
    BALANCES EVERYTHING THROWN   251 5
    I AM THROWN UPON THE SHORE   259 29
    LIKE A GLOVE A BLACK GLOVE THROWN UP AT THE LIGHT   341 13
    BUT ONLY YOU HAVE THROWN THIS AMAZING MANTILLA OF   369 19
    WITH HER LONG TANGLED SIDES LIKE AN OLD RUG THROWN   384 26
    WHICH YOU'VE THROWN UPON HIM SHALL SUDDENLY SHAKE WITH +   797 9
    HUITZILOPOCHTLI HAS THROWN HIS BLACK MANTLE   811 18
    OF GODHEAD IN MAN DESPISED CARELESSLY THROWN OVER   859 22
    WITH HEAD THROWN BACK AND PARTLY OPENED MOUTH   873 20

THROWS
    DO THEY WIPE AWAY THE GLOOM THE GULF THROWS UP   90 24
    I AM MAN AND THEREFORE MY HEART BEATS AND THROWS THE DA+   320 21
    THROWS STILL THE DARK BLOOD BACK AND FORTH   322 32
    FOR THE STRONGEST LIGHT THROWS ALSO THE DARKEST SHADOW   474 4
    SHE GROWS AND THROWS   565 19
    AND THROWS UP STRENGTH THAT IS LIVING STRENGTH AND REGA+   782 19

THRUSH
    PERHAPS WOULD YOU SAY A THRUSH WAS A PROFESSIONAL   453 1

THRUSHES
    BY ITS SHAPE LIKE THRUSHES IN CLEAR EVENINGS   101 16

THRUST
    AND THRUST HER FISTS SUPPRESSED IN THE FOLDS OF HER SKI+   128 19
    SOME STREET-ENDS THRUST FORWARD THEIR STACK   164 20
    I HAVE BEEN THRUST INTO WHITE SHARP CRYSTALS   207 25
    WITH YOUR LIFE AND AFFAIRS DON'T THRUST   561 16
    UNLESS MEN SWIFTLY DIVIDE AGAIN AND THE BASE ARE THRUST   637 14
    BEWARE THE UNHAPPY DEAD THRUST OUT OF LIFE   722 16
    OLD PLACES OF SWEET LIFE FROM WHICH THEY ARE THRUST OUT   723 1
    THAT WERE THRUST OUT OF LIFE AND NOW COME BACK AT US   723 6
    OH DO NOT SEEK TO THRUST IN ME YOUR FIRE   873 27
    INTO DARKNESS OPEN AND EAGER FOR THE THRUST OF THE   *937 20
    THRUST OUT ON TO THE GREY GREY BEACHES OF SHADOW   *957 22

THRUSTING
    WITH THE THRUSTING EMBRACE OF NEW JUSTICE NEW JUSTICE   482 5
    WITH THE GOD-THRUST THRUSTING YOU SILENT FROM BELOW   781 28
    THE GOD-THRUST THRUSTING YOU SILENT AND DARK FROM BENEA+ 782 9
    ALL MISTRUSTFUL OF THRUSTING ITS SHOOTS WHERE ONLY   *900 21
    ALL MISTRUSTFUL OF THRUSTING ITS SHOOTS WHERE ONLY   *903 33

THRUSTS
    AS SHE THRUSTS THEM UPWARD UNDER THE RUFFLED SKIRT   145 30
    THRUSTS WARM THROUGH THE LOINS SO THE LITTLE ONE   425 16
    WITH DREAMS AND THRUSTS THAT MAKE THEM DRY IN THEIR SLE+ 435 15
    WITH DREAMS AND THRUSTS THAT MAKE THEM CRY IN THEIR SLE+ *947 21

THUD
    THUD THUD THUD   326 14
    HE FELL AGAIN WITH A LITTLE THUD   346 26

THUDDING
  THE SOFT THUDDING OF DRUMS   623 5

THUMB
  TEMPTINGLY IN MID-AIR BETWEEN A PLAYFUL THUMB AND FINGER 271 24

THUMB-MARK
  NOR A THUMB-MARK LIKE A CLUE   430 8

THUMB-MOUND
  THUMB-MOUND INTO THE PALM'S DEEP POUCHES   143 12

THUMB-NAIL
  NO BIGGER THAN MY THUMB-NAIL   353 30

THUMB-PIECE
  FOUR PIN-POINT TOES AND A PROBLEMATICAL THUMB-PIECE   356 6

THUMBS
  IF I COULD SEE YOUR HAND AND IT WERE THUMBS DOWN   430 4
  BUT IF IT IS THUMBS UP AND MANKIND MUST GO ON BEING MAN+   430 10

THUNDER
  AND I HEARD THE THUNDER AND FELT THE RAIN   62 19
  WAVES CRASH LIKE THUNDER THROUGH   159 16
  AND BETWEEN US AND IT THE THUNDER   208 25
  THE THUNDER ROARS BUT STILL WE HAVE EACH OTHER   209 3
  KNOWING THE THUNDER OF HIS HEART   326 9
  THE MASSIVE THUNDER OF HIS DEW-LAPPED CHEST   326 10
  THAT SUCH TRIVIAL PEOPLE SHOULD MUSE AND THUNDER   494 14
  AH IN THE THUNDER AIR   646 19
  IN THE THUNDER AIR ALL STRANGERS TO ONE ANOTHER   647 6
  AND THE DRUMMING OF PINIONS OF THUNDER   707 11
  I'LL TURN THEIR BLOOD LIKE SOUR MILK ROTTEN WITH THUNDER   792 6
  DRAGONS OF SALTY WATERS DRAGONS OF THUNDER   796 19
  AND I WAIT FOR THE FINAL DAY WHEN THE DRAGON OF THUNDER+   797 7

THUNDERBOLT
  LIKE A THUNDERBOLT HURLED   163 4
  WHEN THEY'RE HOLDING OUT THE THUNDERBOLT   559 10
  YOU MIGHT AS WELL ACCEPT THE THUNDERBOLT   559 14

THUNDER-BOLT
  TILL YOU PRAY TO THE RIGHT GODS FOR THE THUNDER-BOLT IN+   484 16

THUNDERERS
  THE DIVIDERS THE THUNDERERS THE SWIFT ONES BLIND WITH S+   707 20
  THE THUNDERERS AND THE SUNDERERS HAVE THEIR TERM   709 23

THUNDERING
  WOULD START THE THUNDERING TRAFFIC OF FEET   272 2
  I WISH IT WERE SPRING THUNDERING   272 4

THUNDERS
  THUNDERS IN HEAVEN TILL THE BRAVE WORLDS REEL   773 8

THUNDROUS
  HUGE HUGE ROLL THE PEALS OF THE THUNDROUS LAUGH   698 18
  FOR THE SILENCE OF THE LAST GREAT THUNDROUS LAUGH   699 10
  THICK ALMOST THUNDROUS ON THE HARDENED EARTH   717 4

THUS
  TO SHOW YOU THUS TRANSFIGURED CHANGED   53 22
  HOLDING HER THUS COULD I CARE   62 3
  A SIGH AMONG THE SHADOWS THUS RETRIEVING   66 3
  THE DARK THE GRAVE-EYED MISTRESS WHO THUS DARED   155 28
  I KNEW THAT SOME DAY SOON I SHOULD FIND YOU THUS   156 14
  THUS HAMMERING THE METTLE OF GOATS INTO PROOF AND SMITI+   381 28
  THUS SAY A FEW WORDS TO EACH OTHER   405 20
  AND THUS ELIMINATE US   429 21
  THUS TO GREET   570 4
  THEIR LIMIT THEIR THUS FAR AND NO FURTHER   709 24
  WE EXPIATE IT THUS THE UNKNOWABLE CRIME   743 14
  THUS BEFOREHAND   749 7
  OF GAIETY TOO OFTEN PAY ME THUS   872 24
  HOLDING HER THUS DID I CARE   *912 11

THWART
  THEY ARE HERE TO LEARN BUT ONE LESSON THAT THEY SHALL N+   93 16

THWARTED
  NOR BE THWARTED IN LIFE'S SLOW STRUGGLE TO UNFOLD THE F+   93 18

THY
  THE GLOW OF THY FULL DESIRE   40 7
  TO THE ROCK OF VIRGINITY THY   40 11
  THY TWOFOLD DANCE   40 16
  BUT TO DEFLOWER THEE THY TOWER IMPINGES   40 23
  WITH SWEAT I'LL ENTER A HOUSE FOR THY SAKE   44 8
  AN' STOP THY SCRAIGHTIN' CHILDT   45 3
  DO SHUT THY FACE   45 4
  GLADDER NOR OF THY LILIES IF THA MAUN BE TOLD   61 20
  WHO SHOOK THY ROUNDNESS IN HIS FINGER'S CUP   69 9
  WHO SUNK HIS HANDS IN FIRMNESS DOWN THY SIDES   69 10
  ALONG THY LIMBS DELIGHTED AS A BRIDE'S   69 12
  CURVED THY MOUTH FOR THEE AND WHAT STRONG SHOULDER   69 14
  IN THE CURVES OF THY FORM THE TRACE OF THE UNKNOWN   69 16
  THEN GAVE THEE THY DARK EYES O MAN THAT ALL   69 20
  LIFE IN THY MOUTH AND DIM BREATH'S HASTENING HISS   69 24
  SIT NODDIN' THY HEAD AT ME   78 22
  THA CAN STARE AT ME WI' THY FIERCE BLUE EYES   79 11
  ME GOTTEN A CHILDT TER THY LANDLADY   80 4
  THA'S GOTTEN THY ANSWER PAT   80 4
  TURN THY MOUTH ON A WOMAN LIKE THAT   80 19
  I'LL TA'E THY WORD GOOD-BYE LIZ   80 29
  TA'E OFF THY DUTY STRIPES TIM   82 17
  TA'E OFF THY P'LICEMAN'S HELMET   82 19
  TWENTY POUND O' THY OWN THA HAST AN' FIFTY POUND HA'E I   83 1

THY
  AN' WE'LL BE MARRIED AT TH' REGISTRAR NOW LIFT THY FACE   83 4
  LIFT THY FACE AN' LOOK AT ME MAN CANNA TER LOOK AT ME   83 5
  NOR FRET THY FAT   83 21
  ON THY FACE AS THA GOT MORE WHITE AN' WAN   138 5
  THA COULD LET THY VERY SOUL OUT A MAN   138 23
  AY LAD I'LL TELL THEE THY MIND   138 28
  O' THY SPUNK AN' THA'RT EMPTY AN' MORTIFIED   139 12
  AND THY DARKNESS IS FOREVER INVISIBLE   474 3
  HALLOWED BE THY NAME THEN   704 13
  CHILD DEAR TO MY EYE GOD'S BLESSING IS ON THY SERVICE   749 21
  THE WILLOW SHALL LIFT HER LEAVES TO SOOTHE THY DISTRESS   749 24
  AND STONES SHALL MAKE PLACE FOR THY FOOT BECOME EASY TO+   750 1
  HERE BY THY TOMB   753 19
  THOU WELL OF KILOSSA THY WELL-CHORDS ARE OF SILVER   759 12
  I AM INCLINED TO HEAP THY COALS OF FIRE ON MY OWN   760 15
  AND LICK UP THY ASHES WITH A REPENTANT TONGUE   760 17
  MY WAY IS NOT THY WAY AND THINE IS NOT MINE   812 1
  AH WITH HIS BLESSING BRIGHT ON THY MOUTH AND THY BROW   872 1
  THROUGH THAT WHITE STRAIT OF THY THICK SHAKEN THROAT   879 7
  THE STREAM AND CLOAK ME OVER WITH THY RED   879 9
  THE FIERY MIXTURE OF THY LIFE SO I   879 11
  THYSELF SLIP OUT THE LEASH AND HUNTS THY WAY   879 13
  WATCHING THY GREAT SOUL TUG WITHIN THE LEASH   879 16
  TILL OFF THY MOUTH HAS LEAPT THE FLAME OF LIFE   879 22
  THY FLAME LEAP FREE WHAT IF I AM LEFT BEHIND   879 25
  GOD SHOOK THY ROUNDNESS IN HIS FINGER'S CUP   *915 21
  HE SUNK HIS HANDS IN FIRMNESS DOWN THY SIDES   *915 22
  ALONG THY LIMBS DELIGHTED THINE HIS BRIDE'S   *915 24
  CURVED THY MOUTH FOR THEE AND HIS STRONG SHOULDER   *915 26
  THEN GAVE THEE THY DARK EYES O MAN THAT ALL   *916 3
  THE VIVID LIFE OF HIS LOVE IN THY MOUTH AND THY NOSTRILS   *916 7
  SIT NODDIN' THY HEAD AT ME   *920 14
  THA CAN STARE AT ME WI' THY FIERCE BLUE EYES   *921 7
  ME GOTTEN A CHILDT TO THY LANDLADY   *922 3
  THA'S GOTTEN THY ANSWER PAT   *922 4
  AFTER THY KISSES LIZZIE AFTER   *922 9
  TURN THY MOUTH ON A WOMAN LIKE HER   *922 19
  I'LL TA'E THY WORD GOOD-BYE LIZ   *922 29
  TAKE OFF THY DUTY STRIPES TIM   *924 21
  TA'E OFF THY P'LICE-MAN'S HELMET   *924 23
  TWENTY POUND O' THY OWN THA HAST AND FIFTY POUND HA'E I   *925 5
  AN' WE'LL BE MARRIED AT TH' REGISTRAR NOW LIFT THY FACE   *925 8
  LIFT THY FACE AN' LOOK AT ME MAN UP AN' LOOK AT MF   *925 9
  BUT WE MAUN MA'E THE BEST ON'T I'LL REAR THY CHILDT IF +   *925 18
  TILL THY FULL-FED FIRE OF CURIOSITY BORE YOU   *927 8
  I HEARD THY CRIES OF PAIN AND THEY BROKE   *927 11
  WOULD HAVE WITHERED THROUGH THY FLESH   *927 22
  THY BODY FROM ITS TERRORS AWKWARD LEASH   *927 25
  A MUTE NEARLY BEAUTIFUL THING IS THY FACE   *927 28

THYME
  AND EVENING HAS TAKEN ALL THE BEES FROM THE THYME   224 26

THYSELF
  KNOW THYSELF AND THAT THOU ART MORTAL   473 22
  UNDER THE GREAT COMMAND KNOW THYSELF AND THAT THOU ART +   674 8
  KNOW THYSELF AND THAT THOU ART MORTAL   714 5
  BUT KNOW THYSELF DENYING THAT THOU ARE MORTAL   714 8
  KNOW THYSELF IN DENIAL OF ALL THESE THINGS   714 16
  THYSELF SLIP OUT THE LEASH AND HUNTS THY WAY   879 13

THY-SEN
  AX 'IM THY-SEN WENCH A WIDDER'S LODGER   77 11
  THA WANTS 'IM THY-SEN I SEE   81 32
  THA WANTS 'IM THY-SEN TOO BAD   82 6
  AX HIM THY-SEN WENCH A WIDDER'S LODGER   *918 29
  THA WANTS 'IM THY-SEN TOO BAD   *924 10

TH'
  SOMEBODY'S KNOCKIN' AT TH' DOOR   44 10
  GOT HURT I' TH' PIT   44 23
  COME OUT O' TH' WAY AN' LET ME SEE   45 1
  AN' THEY TA'EIN' 'IM I' TH' AMBULANCE   45 6
  SISTER THA KNOWS WHILE WE WAS ON TH' PLANKS   60 11
  ASIDE O' T' GRAVE AN' TH' COFFIN SET   60 12
  ON TH' YALLER CLAY WI' TH' WHITE FLOWERS TOP OF IT   60 13
  WAITIN' TER BE BURIED OUT O' TH' WET   60 14
  AN' ME STANDIN' THERE ON TH' PLANK   60 20
  AN' OUR TED'S COFFIN SET ON TH' GROUND   60 21
  LET THAT BE 'APPEN IT WORNA TH' DRINK NEITHER   60 27
  NOR TH' CARRYIN' ON AS KILLED 'IM   60 28
  AT TH' SLOPPY GRAVE AN' 'ER LITTLE NECK SHONE   61 7
  JACKET AT TH' BOSOM AN' TOOK OUT   61 10
  AN' WARM FOR TH' SMELL COME WAFTIN' TO ME 'ER PUT 'ER F+   61 13
  AN' I COME AWAY ACAUSE O' TH' TEEMIN' RAIN   61 16
  BUT I THOWT TER MYSEN AS THAT WOR TH' ONLY BIT   61 17
  O' WARMTH AS 'E GOT DOWN THEER TH' REST WOR STONE COLD   61 18
  MY GEL OWT'LL DO FOR A MAN I' TH' DARK   77 3
  AY AN' YALLER AS A CROWFLOWER AN' YET I' TH' DARK   77 7
  AS ANY MAN I' TH' FORCE   77 30
  I'M FURTHER UP TH' LINE TO UNDERWOOD   78 3
  O' TH' P'LICE FORCE WITHOUT FAIL   78 14
  I' TH' SNOW BUT I'S WARRANT THEE   78 31
  I'M FURTHER OWER TH' TOP   78 32
  NOW SITHEE THEER AT TH' REELROAD CROSSIN'   79 1
  UNDER TH' TANK AS FILLS TH' INGINES   79 3
  THERE'S 'IS COLLAR ROUND TH' CANDLESTICK   81 13
  BUT WE'LL GO UNBEKNOWN TER TH' REGISTRAR   82 13
  FOR WHENEVER I LOOK THEE I' TH' FACE I S'LL SEE   82 23
  AN' WE'LL BE MARRIED AT TH' REGISTRAR NOW LIFT THY FACE   83 4
  DEED AN' I WISH I C'D 'A' STOOD AT TH' ALTAR WI' THEE A+   83 11
  THEY'LL TURN THEE OUT O' TH' FORCE I DOUBT ME IF THEY D+   83 16
  AH'N PUT MY-SEN I' TH' WRONG LIZ   83 26
  I'M SORRY FOR TH' TROUBLE AY   84 9
  YER TOO MUCH I' TH' RIGHT FOR ME   85 2
  T' SNOW IS WITHERIN' OFF'N TH' GRESS   137 18
  T' SNOW IS WITHERIN' OFF'N TH' GRESS   137 20

TH'
   AN' MIST IS SUCKIN' AT TH' SPOTS O' SNOW   137 21
   IF TER COULDNA BE MASTER AN' TH' WOMAN'S BOSS   139 4
   THA'RT ONE O' TH' MEN AS HAS GOT TO DRAIN   139 15
   NAY I SAW NOWT BUT TH' COFFIN AN' TH' YELLER CLAY AN' '+ *909 31
   WHILE TH' PARSON WAS PRAYIN' I WATCHES 'ER AN' SHE WOR + *910 1
   WAS TH' LITTLE LOVIN' SORT AS 'AS NOWT TER SCREEN 'EM *910 25
   ASIDE O' TH' GRAVE WHILE TH' COFFIN WOR LYIN' YET   *910 27
   ON TH' YALLER CLAY AN' TH' WHITE FLOWERS TOP OF IT   *910 28
   TRYIN' TO KEEP OFF 'N HIM A BIT O' TH' WET   *910 29
   HUDDLIN' CLOSE TOGETHER A CAUSE O' TH' RAIN   *911 2
   LET BE THAT THERE'S SOME O' TH' BAD AS WE   *911 13
   AH STOPPED BEHIND ON T' PAD I' TH' DRIPPIN WET   *911 19
   AT TH' SLOPPY WET GRAVE AN' 'ER LITTLE NECK SHONE   *911 23
   JACKET AT TH' BOSOM AN' TOOK FROM OUT OF IT   *911 26
   O' TH' SMELL COME WAFTIN' TO ME 'ER PUT 'ER FACE   *911 29
   I'M OFF UP TH' LINE TO UNDERWOOD   *919 23
   O' TH' P'LICE FORCE WITHOUT FAIL   *920 1
   I' TH' SNOW BUT I'S WARANT THEE BUNNY   *920 23
   I'M FURTHER OWER TH' TOP   *920 24
   NOW SITHEE THEER AT TH' RAILROAD CROSSIN'   *920 25
   THA'RT FOR DOIN' A LOT WI' TH' LAD   *924 12
   FOR WHENEVER I LOOK THEE I' TH' FACE I S'LL SEE   *924 27
   AN' WE'LL BE MARRIED AT TH' REGISTRAR NOW LIFT THY FACE *925 8
   SHOULDER-DEEP OUT O' TH' CORN AND WIPES   *944 11

TIBERIUS
   THEN I WISH LIKE TIBERIUS THE MULTITUDE HAD ONLY ONE HE+ 526 21

'TICED
   TO HA' 'TICED A LAD O' TWENTY-FIVE   77 15
   TO HA' 'TICED A LAD O' TWENTY-FIVE   *919 3

TICKLING
   SOFT TICKLING BROWN   863 8

TICK-TICK-TICKING
   TICK-TICK-TICKING OF MACHINES   585 17

TIDAL-HEAP
   THE LONG LOW TIDAL-HEAP   145 2

TID-BIT
   HE SHAKES THE TID-BIT FOR HER WITH A MOST WOOING NOISE + 761 18

TIDE
   VESSEL OF DARKNESS TAKES THE RISING TIDE   132 30
   THE NIGHT WITH SILENCE CROSSING THE LAMP-TOUCHED TIDE 144 13
   THE RIVER'S INVISIBLE TIDE   146 30
   DOWN THE TIDE   147 13
   NOW AS THE TIDE RISES   159 14
   WILL YOU COME BACK WHEN THE TIDE TURNS   171 24
   THE SUN WARMS THE SEA LITTLE LONELY AND SAD SIFTING THE+ 180 3
   COME BUBBLING SURGING TIDE OF SAP   270 31
   ALL DAY LONG I FEEL THE TIDE ROCKING ROCKING   454 12
   THE TIDE IN MY ARMS   705 4
   THE SURGE AND TIDE OF LIFE IN THE TURBULENT CLASS *895 10
   WHEN THE TIDE WAS HIGH   *917 5

TIDES
   THE MOON'S AS SHE FEELS FOR THE TIDES   285 29
   INTO EACH OTHER AS TIDES FLOW   471 3
   AND THE DARK MOON DRAWS THE TIDES ALSO   473 28
   IN THE LAPSE OF THE LOWEST TIDE   509 15
   IT IS THE MOON THAT TURNS THE TIDES   509 20
   AND STEER ACCORDING TO THE CURRENTS AND WINDS AND TIDES+ *953 10

TIE
   AN' THERE'S THE DARK-BLUE TIE I BOUGHT 'IM   81 14
   OUR OLD GOAT WE TIE UP AT NIGHT IN THE SHED AT THE BACK+ 384 4
   WHERE THE FORCES TIE THEMSELVES UP INTO KNOTS OF ATOMS 437 29
   TIE MY SPOTTED SHOES FOR DANCING   802 22
   AN' THAT'S THE DARK BLUE TIE I BOUGHT 'IM   *923 14
   AND FORCES TIE THEMSELVES UP INTO KNOTS OF ATOMS THEN C+ *947 6

TIED
   TIED BY THE NOSE AT THE PORTA CAPPUCCINI   379 11
   AND TIED IN A KNOT INSIDE DEAD-LOCKED BETWEEN TWO DESIR+ 379 12

TIES
   THAT EVERYTHING TIES ITSELF UP INTO COMPLICATED LITTLE + *947 8

TIFF
   AND SHE SHUTS YOU IN THE CELLAR FOR THE LEAST LITTLE TI+ 572 7

TIGER
   I WAS A TIGER BURSTING INTO SUNLIGHT   259 12
   THE BLAZING TIGER WILL SPRING UPON THE DEER UNDIMMED 268 3
   MOST OF HIS TIME THE TIGER PADS AND SLOUCHES IN A BURNI+ 496 13
   A TIGER IS STRIPED AND GOLDEN FOR HIS OWN GLORY   523 13

TIGER-LILIES
   LEANING IN YOUR ROOM LIKE TWO TIGER-LILIES CURVING   91 12

TIGER-STRIPES
   TIGER-STRIPES AND WASP-BANDS   355 6

TIGER'S
   AN' IF 'ER CLAWKIN' TIGER'S EYES   *922 14

TIGHT
   AND OFTEN I SEE HER CLENCH HER FINGERS TIGHT   128 18
   ARE ONLY SITTING TIGHT ON THE CRATERS OF THEIR VOLCANO 539 25
   A RIGHT LITTLE TIGHT LITTLE ISLAND   574 16
   A RIGHT LITTLE TIGHT LITTLE ISLAND   575 12
   AH WHEN HE BEGINS TO DRAW THE LINE IN TIGHT TO LAND HIS 586 21
   I AM HERE UNDEPARTING I SIT TIGHT   788 15

TIGHTEN
   NERVES DIDN'T TIGHTEN AGAINST ME   555 11

TIGHTENED
   REPEATING WITH TIGHTENED ARMS AND THE HOT BLOOD'S BLIND+ 61 26
   TO WAKE WITH A TIGHTENED HEART   220 10
   REPEATING WITH TIGHTENED ARMS AND THE HOT BLOOD'S BLIND+ *912 6

TIGHTLY
   FIXING THE HOOK MORE TIGHTLY GETTING IT MORE FIRMLY IN 586 20

TIGHT-ROPE
   THE TIGHT-ROPE LADY PINK AND BLONDE AND NUDE-LOOKING 444 24

TIGRESS
   LIKE YELLOW HAIR OF A TIGRESS BRINDLED WITH PINES   408 26
   TIGRESS BRINDLED WITH ASPEN   409 23

TILLED
   HEATHEN DANCES AND CEREMONIES AND TILLED THEIR   777 31
   MY FLESH IS READY LIKE TILLED LOAM   888 5

TILTED
   TILL THE HEAD FLOATS TILTED LIKE A BOTTLE FORWARD TILTED 428 10

TILTING
   AND CROWNS KINGLY GENEROUS TILTING CROWNS   278 19
   WHEN SHE ROSE TILTING HER PARASOL AND SMILED AT THE 445 1

TILTS
   TRAVELS THE LIGHT AS IT TILTS IN ITS PACES   146 3

TIM
   ER'D DO FOR TIM   77 8
   TA'E OFF THY DUTY STRIPES TIM   82 17
   I WISH THA HADNA DONE IT TIM   82 21
   ER'D DO FOR TIM   *918 26
   DOESN'T TER KNOW WHAT I MEAN TIM YI   *921 19
   TAKE OFF THY DUTY STRIPES TIM   *924 21
   I WISH THA HADNA DONE IT TIM   *924 25

TIMBER
   A GANG OF LABOURERS ON THE PILED WET TIMBER   72 4
   AND THROUGH THE SCENT OF THE BALCONY'S NAKED TIMBER 208 29

TIMBERS
   PUTTING ITS TIMBERS TOGETHER IN THE DUSK   *960 29

TIMBRE
   BUT THE BLOOD HAS SUSPENDED ITS TIMBRE THE HEART FROM O+ 67 3

TIMBUCTOOT
   IF HIS BLOOD WAS BRITISH OR TIMBUCTOOT   577 2

TIME
   WHEER'S 'E HURT THIS TIME LAD   45 9
   MY LIFE WITH OTHER LEAVES MY TIME   52 10
   OF THE TIME WHEN THE GRAIN STRUGGLES DOWN IN THE DARK 63 19
   GREY FOAM-MIST OF ADVANCING TIME   68 14
   TIME WITH TRUE LONGING WHAT I WAS TO YOU   91 18
   FEELING THE RAW COLD DUN ME AND ALL THE TIME   98 18
   AT THE SAME TIME STAND EXPOSED   108 1
   AND LET ME LOVE YOU A LONG TIME ERE YOU GO   153 17
   TIME SLEEPS AGAIN   169 23
   WITH A TOUCH THE DEAD AND THE LIVING WHILE TIME COUNTS + 174 12
   THE TIME IS NOW THE WINE-CUP FULL AND FULL   177 9
   TO NOTHINGNESS AND TIME WILL DIM THE MOON   193 11
   COURSED ROUND BY RHYTHMIC MOVEMENT OF ALL TIME   194 23
   I LONG FOR THE TIME TO COME WHEN THE CURSE AGAINST YOU + 208 1
   FOR THE FIRST TIME NOW FOR THE FIRST TIME SEEN   216 18
   RIDING THE AIR AND CARRYING ALL THE TIME   221 21
   BUT THIS TIME WE BEGIN TO DO RIGHT   232 11
   I SEE YOU ALL THE TIME YOU BIRD-BLITHE LOVELY   234 9
   A FINE WIND IS BLOWING THE NEW DIRECTION OF TIME   250 14
   OF TIME   260 18
   OF TIME FROM OUT OF WHICH I COME   262 24
   PRETENDING TO AVOID US YET ALL THE TIME   269 27
   AT THE SAME TIME IT OPENS THE TINY HANDS OF THE HAZEL 272 20
   AND LAUGH AT TIME AND LAUGH AT DULL ETERNITY   299 11
   AND WATCH IT PUTTING FORTH EACH TIME TO HEAVEN   299 24
   EACH TIME STRAIGHT TO HEAVEN   299 25
   MORE FEARLESS THAN IRON ALL THE TIME   306 24
   FOR THE FIRST TIME   310 13
   ALL THE TIME I AM LIFTED UP   320 23
   BUT PUT ME DOWN AGAIN IN TIME MASTER   321 8
   HUNG ALL THE TIME DID WE BUT KNOW IT THE ALL-KNOWING SH+ 328 8
   EVERY TIME HE SWERVED AT IT   344 12
   TIME AFTER TIME THAT FRAIL TORN SCREAM   365 23
   I REMEMBER THE FIRST TIME OUT OF A BUSH IN THE DARKNESS+ 366 1
   AS TIME HAS NOT DARED TO AVOUCH NOR ETERNITY BEEN ABLE + 370 31
   OF TIME   372 23
   I NEVER DREAMED TILL NOW OF THE AWFUL TIME THE LORD MUST 395 17
   FIRST TIME I LOST YOU IN TAOS PLAZA   395 27
   SAYS LOOK FOR A LAST LONG TIME THEN LOOK LOOK WELL 403 6
   TIME   414 10
   AND WHAT AGES OF TIME   426 2
   THAT DRIFTS UPON TIME AND CHAOS TILL SOME UNKNOWN FUTURE 429 5
   IS THE TIME COME FOR HUMANS   429 22
   OF TIME   435 24
   TILL AFTER A LONG TIME WHEN THEY ARE OLD AND HAVE STEEP+ 448 10
   IT MOVES IT RIPPLES AND ALL THE TIME   460 9
   BUT AT THE SAME TIME DON'T LET'S THINK   470 9
   O FLOWERS THEY ARE ALL THE TIME TRAVELLING   476 12
   TIME WAS MUCH SLOWER WHEN THE ROCKS CAME FORTH   477 4
   AS TIME WENT ON   479 23
   BUT TIME HAS FLED OUR PARENTS ARE DEAD   490 21
   IT'S BAD TASTE TO BE WISE ALL THE TIME LIKE BEING A PER+ 496 1
   MOST OF HIS TIME THE TIGER PADS AND SLOUCHES IN A BURNI+ 496 13

TIME
    YET ONE THING I DO FIGHT FOR TOOTH AND NAIL ALL THE TIME   497 22
    YET WHEN THE TIME HAS COME TO BE NOTHING HOW GOOD IT IS   509 10
    EACH TIME THEY TOUCH US   512 20
    AND AT THE SAME TIME EXPECT TO GO ON CALMLY EATING GOOD   531 6
    THE WHOLE OF THE TIME AND NOTHING   552 11
    AND EVERY TIME THE SAME   554 30
    MAYBE THEY'LL REALISE IT'S TIME   560 7
    WE GET A PRETTY THIN TIME   573 2
    IN EVERY PICTURE EVERY TIME   578 3
    NOT BY TIME BUT BY UNCLEAN BREATH AND EYES   580 24
    LEAVING NASTY FILMS UPON YOU EVERY TIME   581 5
    YES IT IS TRUE I FIGHT ALL THE TIME   606 14
    THAT SHE HAS IN TRAVELLING BY HERSELF THROUGHOUT TIME   610 21
    AND MADE HIM PAINT HER NUDE TIME AFTER TIME   619 9
    AND EACH TIME IT CAME OUT THE SAME A HORRIBLE SEXLESS L+   619 10
    AND THE WOUNDS TO THE SOUL TAKE A LONG LONG TIME ONLY   620 15
    TIME CAN HELP   620 16
    AND THE TIME HAS COME TO CEASE TO BE KIND ANY MORE   640 16
    IT HAS ALL THE TIME TO BE SOOTHED AND CONSOLED BY   641 20
    THEN FOR A TIME AT LEAST THEY MUST DO WITHOUT   651 11
    BUT ALL THE TIME I SEE THE GODS   651 12
    GIVE WAY ALL THE TIME BEFORE THE MECHANICAL RUSHING OF +   665 26
    NOW ABOVE ALL IS THE TIME FOR THE MINORITIES OF MEN   666 1
    BUT WHEN LIVING PEOPLE DIE IN THE RIPENESS OF THEIR TIME   676 8
    FROM TIME TO TIME THE WILD CRYING OF EVERY ELECTRON   682 20
    AND EVERY TIME IT IS SHIPS IT IS SHIPS   687 4
    IT IS CREATION GOD LOOKS HIMSELF ON IT IN WONDER FOR TH+   690 10
    IT IS A LONG TIME BEFORE A MAN CAN GET HIMSELF AWAY   700 19
    AND THERE IS NOTHING ELSE THROUGHOUT TIME AND ETERNITY   701 11
    FOR HOW CAN I COUNT IN YOUR THREE TIME THREE   702 3
    THEIR GOING ROUND EACH TIME IS A STEP   713 17
    AND IT IS TIME TO GO TO BID FAREWELL   716 22
    AND ALL THE TIME HIS HANDSOME SWARTHY RED FACE   734 17
    WITH SAVAGE BLACK EYES IS SULKY AND ALL THE TIME   734 18
    NOW LIKE A CROCUS IN THE AUTUMN TIME   744 4
    THE CATTLE RUN ANXIOUS IN QUEST AS THE TIME DRAWS NIGH   749 25
    TIME BUT DIFFERENT DIRECTIONS IN CREATION WITHIN THE FO+   760 25
    LAND BETTER INSTEAD OF WASTING TIME   777 32
    AND PLAY WITH THEM ALL THE TIME   794 23
    LOOK BACK THE LAST TIME MARY MOTHER   798 3
    FOR THE LAST TIME THEY BLESS YOU AS THEY LEAVE YOU   798 31
    LAST TIME WE WERE BOTH   817 31
    THE TIME WITHOUT CLOCKS   825 23
    TIME WITHOUT END AMEN AMEN   826 7
    AS IF THE BUTCHER WERE BIDING HIS TIME   828 1
    AT THE SAME TIME THEY TAKE THE GREATEST POSSIBLE CARE O+   832 4
    AT THE SAME TIME WE LEARN A LOT   832 26
    IT IS TIME MEN TOOK THEIR THOUGHTS OFF WOMEN   838 5
    AFTER ALL THIS TIME OF PATIENCE AND PAIN   873 7
    AFTER ALL THIS TIME IT SHOULD BE THE SAME   874 11
    AND ONCE AGAIN AS MANY A TIME BEFORE   877 35
    AND FEARFUL TO FILE FORTH NOW FOR THE FIRST TIME ALONE   *938 12
    RIDING THE AIR AND CARRYING ALL THE TIME   *945 7
    LIVES WHILE HE LIVES MOST OF HIS TIME ALONE   *951 5
    OH BUILD YOUR SHIP OF DEATH OH BUILD IT IN TIME   *957 25

TIMELESS
    TIMELESS AS BRANCHING LICHENS PALE AS MUST   135 15

TIMELESSLY
    TIMELESSLY   215 8

TIMELESSNESS
    IN TIMELESSNESS LAID BY IN NOISELESS DEATH   744 3

TIME-LONG
    HARDENED THEY ARE LIKE GEMS IN TIME-LONG PRUDERY   127 22

TIMES
    THREE TIMES HAVE I OFFERED MYSELF THREE TIMES REJECTED   48 1
    AFTERWARDS HOW MANY TIMES AFTERWARDS   80 23
    A FEW TIMES ONLY AT THE BEGINNING   106 29
    HOW MANY TIMES LIKE LOTUS LILIES RISEN   113 1
    HOW MANY TIMES HAS T' CANDLE-LIGHT SHONE   138 4
    MANY TIMES   232 10
    FIVE TIMES WIDE OPEN   307 12
    SIX TIMES WIDE OPEN   307 13
    AND HENCE SIX TIMES MORE SOLITARY   354 10
    YOU'VE DIPPED IT IN BLOOD SO MANY TIMES   373 33
    IT SHALL BE IT SHALL BE ASSENTED SEVEN TIMES   702 7
    THIRTEEN TIMES THE TEETH FLASHED IN A FIRE OF BLOOD   *933 1
    EVEN AT THE RIGHT TIMES SODOMY CAN BE SANE AND WHOLESOME   *952 16

TIME-THREADS
    THAT THE TIME-THREADS SPUN ACROSS MY FACE   860 13

TIMID
    PIECEMEAL THE BODY DIES AND THE TIMID SOUL   718 12
    HISSES THROUGH THE FLOWERS THE TIMID NIGHT-AIRS BLOW   855 30
    WHEREIN THE TIMID WONDERS FLY   *894 9

TIMIDLY
    SHE GLANCED AT ME TIMIDLY   869 11
    LOOKING TIMIDLY UPON ME   869 15

TIM MERFIN
    YER KNOWED AS I WAS COURTIN' TIM MERFIN   81 25
    YOU KNOWED AS I WAS COURTIN' TIM MERFIN   *923 25

TIMMY
    DOESN'T TER KNOW WHAT I MEAN TIMMY   79 23
    THA'RT A GOOD-UN AT SUCKIN'-IN YET TIMMY   79 25
    THAT'S SPOKEN LIKE A MAN TIMMY   81 5
    IF MY FATHER CAN GET THEE A JOB ON T' BANK SAY THA'RT S+   83 17
    THA'RT A GOOD-UN AT SUCKIN-IN YET TIMMY   *921 21
    THAT'S SPOKEN LIKE A MAN TIMMY   *923 5

TIMON
    OF LEAR AND MACBETH AND HAMLET AND TIMON   508 17

TIMOROUS
    WHAT SORT OF TIMOROUS POTION OF LOVE HAVE YOU DRUNK   755 2

TIMOTHY
    THEN I'LL SAY GOOD-BYE TO THEE TIMOTHY   80 27
    I'LL ONLY SAY GOOD-BYE TO THEE TIMOTHY   *922 27

TIN
    CURVETTING BITS OF TIN IN THE EVENING LIGHT   335 24
    RUSTY TIN   356 27
    EVEN IF IT WAS ONLY A TIN PAN   520 12

TINCTURE
    WITH TOO MUCH TINCTURE OF ME INSTEAD OF THE DARK'S DEEP+   92 29

TINDER
    THAT YOU THROW OFF STRAIGHT ON THE TINDER OF MY NERVES   241 9

TINGE
    WITH A TINGE OF MISGIVING   375 13
    TO THESE THINGS I FEEL ONLY RESPECT AND A TINGE OF REVE+   622 9

TINGLE
    ON HIS LIPS I LONG TO BE SOULLESS I TINGLE   130 21

TINGLING
    AND CAME BACK TINGLING CLEAN BUT WORN AND FRAYED   99 13
    A CHILD SITTING UNDER THE PIANO IN THE BOOM OF THE TING+   148 6

TINIEST
    NEVER NOT THE TINIEST SHRED   500 10

TINILY
    TINILY   221 2
    AND NOW HE SCUFFLES TINILY PAST HER AS IF SHE WERE AN O+   356 26
    AND SLOWLY FINGERING UP MY STEM AND FOLLOWING ALL TINILY *900 18
    AND SLOWLY FINGERING UP MY STEM AND FOLLOWING ALL TINILY *903 30

TINKER
    I SEE THE TIN-MAN THE TINKER SITTING DAY AFTER DAY ON T+   520 13
    AS A MATTER OF FACT WHEN THE TINKER LOOKS SO HAPPY   520 23

TINKERING
    TINKERING   520 24

TINKLED
    TINKLED THE MUSIC OF GLEANING   152 19

TINKLE-WINKLE
    WITH ITS TINKLE-WINKLE AND TWEEDLE-DEE   681 3

TINKLING
    AND HYMNS IN THE COSY PARLOUR THE TINKLING PIANO OUR   148 13
    AND SUBTLE SILVERY TINKLING AND RIPPLING   667 29

TIN-MAN
    I SEE THE TIN-MAN THE TINKER SITTING DAY AFTER DAY ON T+   520 13

TINNING
    MENDING AND TINNING THE PANS OF ALL THE VILLAGE   520 15

TIN-POT
    THEY ARE AFRAID OF CLIMBING DOWN FROM THIS IDIOTIC TIN-+   667 19

TINS
    NOT KNOWING EACH OTHER FROM BITS OF EARTH OR OLD TINS   357 20
    THEY'RE AS EMPTY AS EMPTY TINS   553 10

TINT
    REVEAL THE UNIVERSAL TINT THAT DYES   197 27

TINTORET
    HOLBEIN AND TITIAN AND TINTORET COULD NEVER PAINT FACES+   656 20

TINY
    A TINY MOON AS SMALL AND WHITE AS A SINGLE JASMINE FLOW+   67 18
    TINY LIGHTHOUSES LITTLE SOULS OF LANTERNS COURAGE BURST+   206 16
    THE GREAT BREATH BLOWING A TINY SEED OF FIRE   219 2
    CHERISH ME MY TINY ONE CHERISH ME WHO ENFOLD YOU   246 10
    AS YOU SEE A TINY CELLULOID BALL TOSSING ON A SQUIRT OF+   272 16
    AT THE SAME TIME IT OPENS THE TINY HANDS OF THE HAZEL   272 20
    AND THE TINY VINE-FLOWER ROSE OF ALL ROSES PERFUMED   286 27
    THEY SAW TINY ROSE CYCLAMENS BETWEEN THEIR TOES GROWING   310 14
    A TINY FRAGILE HALF-ANIMATE BEAN   352 8
    TO OPEN YOUR TINY BEAK-MOUTH THAT LOOKS AS IF IT WOULD   352 9
    TINY BRIGHT-EYE   352 16
    UNDER ITS SLOW LID TINY BABY TORTOISE   352 22
    AND THE FINE BRILLIANCE OF YOUR SO TINY EYE   353 22
    THEN TWENTY-FOUR AND A TINY LITTLE KEYSTONE   355 13
    ALL TINY FAR AWAY REPTILE UNDER THE FIRST DAWN   364 21
    TINY FROM UNDER THE VERY EDGE OF THE FARTHEST FAR-OFF   366 27
    AND SHOW A TINY BUNCH OF WHITE TEETH IN YOUR UNDERHUNG   398 11
    MUSHY AND TREACHEROUS TINY   457 17
    THE TINY FISH ENJOY THEMSELVES   466 13
    RUN TINY RIVERS OF PEACE   496 12
    A TINY BELL OF CONCLUSION HAS SOUNDED   512 7
    THE TINY GRAIN OF SOMETHING THAT NO WAVE CAN WASH AWAY   514 4
    CLEAR AND FEARLESS EVEN IF TINY   526 12
    PRANCING THEIR KNEES UNDER THEIR TINY SKIRTS   537 20
    AND EXHAUSTING PENETRATING THE LAVA-CRATER OF A TINY   539 7
    HAY-SEED AND TINY GRAIN OF GRASS GRAMINIFERAE   587 4
    BUT A TINY CORE OF STILLNESS IN THE HEART   658 14
    AS NOW WHEN THE TINY WAVELETS OF THE SEA   709 5
    TINY BLACK MOTHS FLUTTER OUT AT THE TOUCH OF THE FORK   858 13
    TINY FINGERS OUTSPREAD   861 21

TINY
SO TINY WHEN YOU OPEN SKY-DOORS ON ME   876 .2
PERHAPS THE TINY YOUNG NETTLES HAVE STUNG HER EARS   882 26

TIP
IF ONLY I AM KEEN AND HARD LIKE THE SHEER TIP OF A WEDGE   250 21
FIGHT TO BE THE DEVIL ON THE TIP OF THE PEAK   383 24
AND SEA-TOUCH TIP OF A BEAK   436 24
THE LONG TIP REACHES STRONG INTENSE LIKE THE MAELSTROM-+   694 17
TIP THE MORNING LIGHT ON EDGE AND SPILL IT WITH DELIGHT   709 6

TIPPED
AND IN WHOM THE DREAM SITS UP LIKE A RABBIT LIFTING LON+   807 8

TIPPING
THE CORN-STALKS TIPPING WITH FIRE THE SPEARS   221 24
THE CORN-STALKS TIPPING WITH FIRE THEIR SPEARS   *945 10

TIPPLES
TIPPLES OVER AND SPILLS DOWN   647 10

TIPS
HAVE YOU A STRANGE ELECTRIC SENSITIVENESS IN YOUR STEEL+   301 2
IN ROSE-HOT TIPS AND FLAKES OF ROSE-PALE SNOW   304 20
TO THE TIPS OF HER TOES   565 26

TIPTOE
WILL TIPTOE INTO MY ROOM   106 20

TIP-TOE
EVEN IF IT IS ONLY A LOBSTER ON TIP-TOE   689 25
NOW LIKE A ROSE COME TIP-TOE OUT OF BUD   *943 18

TIRED
THE TIRED LIGHTS DOWN THE STREET WENT OUT   121 23
FOR I AM TIRED MY DEAR AND IF I COULD LIFT MY FEET   134 24
FROM THE SKY THE LOW TIRED MOON FADES OUT   163 21
PERHAPS WE SHALL MARCH TILL OUR TIRED TOES   164 10
OF FLOTSAM UNTIL MY SOUL IS TIRED OR SATISFIED   180 7
I AM SO TIRED OF THE LIMITATIONS OF THEIR INFINITE   288 14
WHEN THE TIRED FLOWER OF FLORENCE IS IN GLOOM BENEATH T+   340 21
GETTING TIRED   344 10
NERVES TIRED OUT   388 8
TO THAT TIRED REMNANT OF ROYALTY UP THERE   389 26
WE ARE SO TIRED OF MEN   436 29
THE ALL-WISE HAS TIRED US OF WISDOM   439 28
I AM SO TIRED OF VIOLENT WOMEN LASHING OUT AND INSISTING   479 7
WHEN ONE IS TIRED OF LOVE   503 23
WILL GET TIRED AND SORE AT LAST   560 2
MAYBE THEY'RE GETTING TIRED   560 9
FOR A MOMENT AT EVENING TIRED AS HE STEPPED OFF THE TRA+   672 7
SHE IS TIRED   725 12
IN THE SKY THE LOW TIRED MOON GOES OUT   857 21
I AM TIRED OF THIS JOURNEY IT IS STUPID AND CHILL   858 1
THEY ARE TOLLING HIS FAILURE AFTER ALL THESE YEARS TO T+   859 9
WITH YOUR TIRED EYES JEANNETTE WE SUFFER THE SAME DON'T+   859 31
TIRED AND UNSATISFIED   *893 32
I AM SICK AND TIRED MORE THAN ANY THRALL   *895 24
I AM SICK AND TIRED MORE THAN ANY THRALL   *904 13
NOW AT LAST THE CLOSED CALYX OPENS FROM OUR TIRED EYES   *916 13
THE PLANE-LEAVES FALL THROUGH THE LAMP-LIGHT LIKE TIRED+   *917 9

TIREDNESS
ROUND AND ROUND AND DITHERING WITH TIREDNESS AND HASTE   343 25

TIRELESS
AND FLARE OF A TROPICAL ENERGY TIRELESS AFIRE IN THE DA+   389 16

TIRE-MAIDENS
THE SLENDER BARE ARMS OF THE BRANCHES YOUR TIRE-MAIDENS   86 17

TISSUE
AND SKIES OF GOLD AND LADIES IN BRIGHT TISSUE   135 4
IN A TISSUE AS ALL THE MOLTEN CELLS IN THE LIVING MESH   176 8
ON FANS OF UNSUSPECTED TISSUE LIKE BATS   322 17
THEY GLIMMER WITH TISSUE OF GOLD AND GOLDEN THREADS ON   388 19
THE TISSUE THEY WEAVE   451 7
AND IRRITATION SEETHES SECRETLY THROUGH THEIR GUTS AS T+   616 9
WHERE TISSUE PLUNGES INTO BRONZE WITH WIDE WILD CIRCLES+   623 10
THE LOINS OF THIS OUR TISSUE OF TRAVAIL OUR LIFE'S   880 3

TISSUED
TISSUED FROM HIS LIFE   451 23
TISSUED FROM HIS LIFE   *950 8

'TIS
'TIS THE WOUND OF LOVE GOES HOME   42 8
AN' THA'RT THAT RIGHT THA KNOWS 'TIS   83 28
OR RATHER 'TIS I AM NOTHING HERE IN THE FUR OF THE HEAT+   98 2
DISCLOSED BUT 'TIS I WHO AM PROWLING   107 15
'TIS THE SUN THAT ASKS THE QUESTION IN A LOVELY HASTE F+   119 29
'TIS A LITTLE THING   137 6
KNOCK KNOCK 'TIS NO MORE THAN A RED ROSE RAPPING   150 20
THEN THEY WILL SAY 'TIS LONG SINCE SHE IS DEAD   176 20
LIKE A FALCON 'TIS GOD HAS TAKEN THE VICTIM   239 5
'TIS NOT OF ME BUNNY   241 13
'TIS LIKE THE UNUTTERABLE NAME OF THE DREAD LORD   264 16
I SERVE I SERVE IN ALL THE WEARY IRONY OF HIS MIEN 'TIS+   391 34
AND DIE LIKE A DOG IN A HOLE 'TIS STRANGE WHAT A SHODDY   755 8
THOU SIPS THEM UP AND 'TIS ALL THE SAME   824 15
AND I SAID 'TIS I   882 32
'TIS STRANGE WE NEVER KNEW   *941 9

TITAN
SET FORTH LITTLE TITAN UNDER YOUR BATTLE-SHIELD   353 33

TITIAN
HOLBEIN AND TITIAN AND TINTORET COULD NEVER PAINT FACES+   656 20

TITLE
BUT IF TAKEN AT ITS VERY BEST THE TITLE AMERICAN   775 34

TITTER
THEY MAKE TRAINS CHUFF MOTOR-CARS TITTER SHIPS LURCH   441 6
AND THEY WHISPER IT OUT AND THEY TITTER IT OUT BREATHING   462 25
LEAVES WHISPER AND TITTER   861 1

TITTERING
MAKES TITTERING JESTS AT THE BELLS' OBSCENITY   54 15
DIPPING WITH PETTY TRIUMPHANT FLIGHT AND TITTERING OVER   347 17

TOAD-FILMY
TOAD-FILMY EARTH-IRIDESCENT   310 20

TOAD-LEAVES
AMONG SQUAT TOAD-LEAVES SPRINKLING THE UNBORN   312 2

TOADS
SCRAMBLE SEVEN TOADS ACROSS SILK OBSCURE LEAVES   126 18
SEVEN TOADS THAT MOVE IN THE DUSK TO SHARE   126 19
WHERE THE SLOW TOADS SAT BROODING ON THE PAST   310 15
SLOW TOADS AND CYCLAMEN LEAVES   310 16

TOADSTOOL
SO NOW YOU'RE A GLISTENING TOADSTOOL SHINING HERE   86 21

TOADSTOOLS
THEN A GROUP OF TOADSTOOLS WAITING THE MOON'S WHITE TAP+   72 19
LIKE SICKENING TOADSTOOLS AND LEFT TO MELT BACK SWIFTLY   431 28
KICK THEM OVER THE TOADSTOOLS   765 28

TOAST
AND LANDED THEM ALL ON TOAST   536 23

TOASTING-FORK
HENCEFORTH HE'LL KEEP CLEAR OF HER TOASTING-FORK   577 22

TO BE OR NOT TO BE
TO BE OR NOT TO BE IS STILL THE QUESTION   265 25

TOCSIN
COCK-CRESTED CROWING YOUR ORANGE SCARLET LIKE A TOCSIN   314 28
THE TOCSIN OF THIS OUR CIVILISATION   512 11

TODAY
TODAY THE SOCIAL CONSCIOUSNESS IS MUTILATED   516 1
NOTHING IS REALLY ANY FUN TODAY   517 23
THE YOUNG TODAY ARE BORN PRISONERS   518 7
AND I SUPPOSE MOST GIRLS ARE A BIT TARTY TODAY   530 20
YOUR SELF MOVES ON AND IS NOT TODAY WHAT IT WAS YESTERD+   543 14
AND THAT'S WHAT WE'VE DONE TODAY   543 18
IF IT'S GOOD TODAY AND TOMORROW-DAY AS WELL   571 4
THE ONLY QUESTION TO ASK TODAY ABOUT MAN OR WOMAN   603 15
MOST PEOPLE TODAY ARE CHIMAERA   603 21
TODAY SOCIETY HAS SANCTIFIED   620 22
WHEN I HEAR MAN SPOUTING ABOUT HUMILITY TODAY   621 22
TODAY IF A MAN DOES SOMETHING PRETENTIOUS AND DELIBERATE   634 10
FOR TODAY THE BASE THE ROBOTS SIT ON THE THRONES OF THE   637 17
WHEN MOST MEN DIE TODAY   638 20
HOW THE GODS MUST HATE MOST OF THE OLD OLD MEN TODAY   662 15
AND EVERY GOD THAT HUMANITY HAS EVER KNOWN IS STILL A G+   671 14
ALL THE GODS AND YOU SEE THEM ALL IF YOU LOOK ALIVE AND+   671 20
AND WORSTED BY THE EVIL WORLD-SOUL OF TODAY   709 2
THIS PLACE TODAY THESE SOLDIERS WEAR THE SAME   732 11
TO LET US HAVE DONE FOR TODAY WE ARE   759 7
TODAY IS EASTER SUNDAY CHRIST RISEN TWO DAYS AGO WAS   777 22
TODAY WHEN THE SUN IS COMPUTED OLD   814 7
THE LATENT DESIRE IN ALL DECENT MEN TODAY   837 23
IF WE RALLY AT ALL TODAY INSTEAD OF KEEPING   839 8
TODAY LIFE IS A CHOICE OF INSANITIES   839 18
WI' A DRESS AS IS WANTED TODAY   *919 24

TO-DAY
TO-DAY A THICKET OF SUNSHINE WITH BLUE SMOKE-WREATHS   72 15
WI' A DRESS AS IS WANTED TO-DAY   78 4
OH COME AND WAKE US UP FROM THE GHASTLY DREAM OF TO-DAY   174 25
TO-DAY WE'VE GOT NO SEX   472 9

TO-DO
A RARE TO-DO   244 28

TOES
THE BALLS OF FIVE RED TOES   145 22
PERHAPS WE SHALL MARCH TILL OUR TIRED TOES   164 10
THEY SAW TINY ROSE CYCLAMENS BETWEEN THEIR TOES GROWING   310 14
AT HIS TOES   310 32
TOES AND THE DOME OF HIS HOUSE IS HIS HEAVEN THEREFORE +   348 15
AND SET FORWARD SLOW-DRAGGING ON YOUR FOUR-PINNED TOES   352 27
SUDDENLY HASTY RECKLESS ON HIGH TOES   354 6
SO TURN HIM OVER ON HIS TOES AGAIN   356 5
FOUR PIN-POINT TOES AND A PROBLEMATICAL THUMB-PIECE   355 6
TO ROW FORWARD AND REACH HIMSELF TALL ON SPINY TOES   358 1
HIS SMALL TOES   377 26
SHE TROTS ON BLITHE TOES   386 3
TO THE TIPS OF HER TOES   565 26
HIS TOES   866 8

TOGETHER
AND WATCH MY DEAD DAYS FUSING TOGETHER IN DROSS   47 3
AND DRAWING THE DARKNESS TOGETHER CRUSH FROM IT A TWILI+ 92 19
TOGETHER   98 5
BUT WE'LL STILL BE TOGETHER THIS ROAD AND I   163 15
TOGETHER WHEREVER THE LONG ROAD GOES   163 16
WE ARE FOLDED TOGETHER MEN AND THE SNOWY GROUND   166 11

TOGETHER
    THE GHOSTS AND I WE MOURN TOGETHER AND SHRINK   173 6
    TO BE FAITHLESS AND FAITHFUL TOGETHER   199 31
    YOU AND I TOGETHER   204 22
    STRUGGLED TO BE TOGETHER   206 14
    OUT OF MOCKERY WE DANCE TOGETHER   210 7
    ONLY TO DANCE TOGETHER IN TRIUMPH OF BEING TOGETHER   210 15
    TO BRING TOGETHER TWO STRANGE SPARKS BEGET   218 20
    ARE JOINED TOGETHER FOR EVER AS IS BEST   231 4
    WE TWO FOLDED SO SMALL TOGETHER   247 19
    ONE ON ANOTHER AND THEN IN CLUSTERS TOGETHER   258 2
    MUZZLES TOGETHER EAR-APRICK   311 24
    EVEN SNAKES LIE TOGETHER   335 13
    MANY SUSPENDED TOGETHER FOREVER APART   337 20
    TOGETHER   340 30
    SEIZES YOU AS YOU CLENCH YOURSELF TOGETHER   370 17
    LIKE SOME FIERCE MAGNET BRINGING ITS POLES TOGETHER   370 18
    GATHER HIS WILL AND HIS ENERGY TOGETHER   428 20
    DO HOLD YOURSELF TOGETHER AND FIGHT   459 13
    TOGETHER WITHOUT A WORD   465 18
    GAY AND AMUSING TOGETHER AND FREE   470 7
    THE SOFT BLOOD SOFTLY FLOWS TOGETHER   471 15
    IS NOT TO ADD OUR LOVE TOGETHER OR OUR GOOD-WILL   506 2
    THE SUN OF IMMENSE DISTANCES THAT FOLD THEMSELVES TOGET+   513 17
    WE COULD SIN TOGETHER   618 15
    SO THAT ALL MAY BE LOST TOGETHER EN MASSE THE GREAT   620 25
    HOW STILL THEY ARE TOGETHER THEY STAND SO STILL   647 5
    TOGETHER   680 7
    WITH GOD WE ARE CLOSE TOGETHER NOW THE MOON'S IN SHADOW   727 5
    I AND MY BETROTHED ARE TOGETHER IN THE SHED   756 15
    SITTING THERE TOGETHER FOR A LITTLE WHILE   756 16
    THE MORNING STAR AND THE EVENING STAR SHINE TOGETHER   800 13
    AND CAN'T PUT ITS FEET TOGETHER   818 26
    IT COULDN'T PUT ITS FEET TOGETHER   818 30
    WANT TO PUT THEMSELVES TOGETHER   819 14
    AND CAN'T PUT ITS FEET TOGETHER   820 6
    AND RALLY TOGETHER   839 16
    AND WE STILL BE TOGETHER THE ROAD AND I   857 15
    TOGETHER WHEREVER THE DUMB ROAD GOES   857 16
    HOW AM I CLOTTED TOGETHER   870 7
    WHAT IS IT THAT CLOTS ME HOLDS ME TOGETHER OUT OF THESE   870 10
    TOGETHER   870 13
    THOUGH WE HAVE CLOSED TOGETHER THROUGH THE NIGHTS   875 21
    AND WE WILL PASS TOGETHER LIKE ONE RED FLAME   879 29
    THAT LEAP AND MEET TOGETHER AT THE MOUTH   879 34
    LEAN TOGETHER AND LIFT WILD ARMS TO EMBRACE   883 7
    TOGETHER WE TRODE THE EVENING WHERE THE SUN   884 23
    GATHERS ITSELF FIERCELY TOGETHER   *893 22
    HUDDLIN' CLOSE TOGETHER A CAUSE O' TH' RAIN   *911 2
    PUTTING ITS TIMBERS TOGETHER IN THE DUSK   *960 29

TOGETHERNESS
    KINDLED TOGETHERNESS SO WE GO   471 7

TOIL
    THE MOANING OF SLEEP-BOUND BEINGS IN TRAVAIL THAT TOIL +   149 19
    AND GIVING OFF DREADFUL EFFLUVIA IN A GHASTLY EFFORT OF+   175 4
    YOU WHO TOIL NOT YOU WHO SPIN NOT   197 19
    THROUGH PERIL TOIL AND PAIN   554 2
    WITH HIS BROW WIPED BRIGHT OF THE TOIL OF SWEAT   770 18

TOILING
    SURELY BUT FOR YOU AND YOUR LIKE TOILING   197 20

TOILS
    NOW YOU ARE FREE OF THE TOILS OF A WOULD-BE-PERFECT LOVE   411 16

TOILSOME
    WITHIN THE IMMENSE AND TOILSOME LIFE-TIME HEAVED   195 29
    LIFE'S TOILSOME JOURNEY THROUGH   576 19

TOLD
    ARE YOU ALL TOLD   57 7
    GLADDER NOR OF THY LILIES IF THA MAUN BE TOLD   61 20
    FOR YOU TOLD ME NO   104 1
    ROMANTIC STORIES NOW NO MORE TO BE TOLD   141 30
    FOR I HAVE TOLD YOU PLAINLY HOW IT IS   170 16
    I THINK IF THEY TOLD ME SO   213 16
    AND TOLD TO DIE   410 10
    WHO UNDERSTOOD AT LAST WHAT IT WAS TO BE TOLD TO DIE   410 17
    REMEMBERING I TOLD THEM TO DIE TO SINK INTO THE GRAVE IN   410 30
    WOMEN WHOM I LOVED AND TOLD TO DIE   411 4
    COME BACK THEN MOTHER MY LOVE WHOM I TOLD TO DIE   411 21
    SO I TOLD YOU TO DIE   412 13
    MODERN LIFE IS A TALE TOLD BY AN IDIOT   522 1
    AND TOLD HER NOT TO BE   550 22
    HAVEN'T I TOLD YOU TO TAKE THE PITH   583 2
    YOU'VE TOLD THEM THAT LIFE ISN'T REALLY MUCH FUN   583 6
    AM I TOLD THAT THESE THINGS ARE MY NEIGHBOURS   644 21
    WHEN YOU TOLD HIM   668 11
    BEFORE PLATO TOLD THE GREAT LIE OF IDEALS   688 21
    TOLD THE OLD AMERICAN ABORIGINES THAT IT WOULD   777 29
    AND BANK-TELLERS TELL THE ONE TALE THAT IS TOLD   814 9
    WHEN THE END OF THE WORLD WE ARE TOLD IS SCROLLED   814 11
    YESTERDAY YES IS A TALE THAT IS TOLD   815 6
    WE ARE TOLD   819 4
    TWAS A TALE SOON TOLD   863 12

TOLERANT
    ONE CAN BE TOLERANT WITH A BORE   499 12
    BUT IT IS HARD TO BE TOLERANT WITH THE SMARTIES   499 16

TOLL
    THEIR DROSS OF INDIFFERENCE AND TAKE THE TOLL   74 21
    AND KISSES PALE AND SIPPING THE TOLL   151 29

TOLLING
    THEY ARE TOLLING HIS FAILURE AFTER ALL THESE YEARS TO T+   859 9

TOLSTOI
    BUT TOLSTOI WAS A TRAITOR   536 18

TOLSTOYAN
    PIERRES ALL THE TOLSTOYAN LOT   533 12
    ANYHOW THE TOLSTOYAN LOT SIMPLY ASKED FOR EXTINCTION   533 24

TOM
    THE SIGHT OF AN ORDINARY TOM WOULDN'T SEND THEM INTO   581 24

TOMB
    TOMB   258 15
    OF THE TOMB DEAD AND TRODDEN TO NOUGHT TRODDEN TO NOUGHT   258 17
    I IN THE SOUR BLACK TOMB TRODDEN TO ABSOLUTE DEATH   259 1
    I NEW-RISEN RESURRECTED STARVED FROM THE TOMB   259 14
    RISING NEW-AWAKENED FROM THE TOMB   260 3
    YET RISING FROM THE TOMB FROM THE BLACK OBLIVION   260 9
    SHALL I COME TO YOU THE OPEN TOMB OF MY RACE   289 27
    THE BROKEN GREEK TOMB IN THE GARDEN   384 5
    IN THE TOMB AND WAS NOT I HAVE RISEN AGAIN   460 23
    AND I AM JUST AWAKENED FROM THE TOMB   744 1
    HE WHO RETURNS AGAIN FROM OUT THE TOMB   745 16
    THOU OF THE DARK CLENCHED TOMB   753 14
    HERE BY THY TOMB   753 19

TOMBS
    AND TOMBS   297 21
    WITHIN THE TOMBS   297 23

TOMBSTONES
    FARTHER DOWN THE VALLEY THE CLUSTERED TOMBSTONES RECEDE   102 29

TOMLETS
    TOMLETS DICKLETS HARRYLETS WHINEY   457 19

TOMORROW
    SHE WILL CALVE TOMORROW   38 7
    THE TRUTH OF YESTERDAY BECOMES A LIE TOMORROW   661 17
    AND ALIVE AND MOVING TOMORROW MANY TOMORROWS AS YESTERD+   671 21
    TAKES EVERYTHING FROM YOU TOMORROW   752 19
    TOMORROW SWIMMING IN EVENING'S VAGUE DIM VAPOUR   797 19
    THE AGE IS A JOKE AND SURELY TOMORROW   815 4
    TOMORROW COMES STEALTHILY OUT OF THE MOULD   815 7
    TOMORROW MARRIES TOMORROW FETTERS HIMSELF   817 5
    SHE WILL CALVE TOMORROW   *892 26
    FOR TOMORROW WILL POUR THEM ALL BACK THE SCHOOL HOURS I+   *896 9
    TOMORROW WILL POUR THEM ALL BACK THE DULL HOURS I DETEST   *896 25
    COME ANOTHER NIGHT COME TOMORROW SAY   *931 24

TOMORROW-DAY
    IF IT'S GOOD TODAY AND TOMORROW-DAY AS WELL   571 4

TOMORROWS
    AND ALIVE AND MOVING TOMORROW MANY TOMORROWS AS YESTERD+   671 21
    BAD YESTERDAYS UNSURE TOMORROWS   825 3
    OUT OF EDEN WEARY WITH THE WISTFULNESS OF HER SILENT TO+   864 24

TO-MORROW
    AH WHEN TO-MORROW THE DAWN COMES LATE   58 26
    TO-MORROW SWIMMING IN EVENING'S VAGUE DIM VAPOUR   72 16
    OF A DAWNED TO-MORROW   116 17
    TO-MORROW WILL POUR THEM ALL BACK THE DULL HOURS I DETE+   167 4
    TO-MORROW WILL POUR THEM ALL BACK THE DULL HOURS I DETE+   167 20

TOM-TOMS
    IN THE NOISE OF THE TOM-TOMS AND SINGERS   387 37
    TOM-TOMS WEIRD MUSIC OF THE DEVIL VOICES OF MEN FROM   388 35

TOM-TOM'S
    FORTH TO THE TOM-TOM'S BEAT IN THE TORCH-LIGHT   387 29

TONES
    IN TONES OF THE AFTERWARDS PARADISAL   769 29

TONG
    MORE ELEPHANTS TONG TONG-TONG LOOM UP   388 26

TONG-TONG-TONG
    AS THE ELEPHANT BELLS SOUNDED TONG-TONG-TONG BELL OF THE   390 32

TONG-TONG
    THE ELEPHANT BELLS STRIKING SLOW TONG-TONG TONG-TONG   387 33
    MORE ELEPHANTS TONG TONG-TONG LOOM UP   388 26

TONGUE
    AND THE FLOWER THAT PUTS ITS TONGUE OUT AND FERN THAT P+   89 27
    THE SNAP-DRAGON PUT OUT HIS TONGUE AT ME   123 12
    LIKE A TONGUE OF DARKENED FLAME   169 28
    AND FLICKERED HIS TWO-FORKED TONGUE FROM HIS LIPS AND   349 23
    AND FLICKERED HIS TONGUE LIKE A FORKED NIGHT ON THE AIR+   350 25
    SOFT RED TONGUE AND HARD THIN GUMS   353 7
    HER THICK SOFT TONGUE   359 6
    OF EVERY TONGUE OR EAST OR WEST   575 15
    I LOVE MY NATIVE TONGUE THE BEST   575 16
    FOR OUR HONEST AND HEALTHY ENGLISH TONGUE   576 1
    AND LICK UP THY ASHES WITH A REPENTANT TONGUE   760 17
    NOT TO REACH ONE TONGUE OF FIRE   874 19
    THE SNAPDRAGON PUT OUT HIS TONGUE AT ME   *934 18

TONGUED
    SILENT TONGUED I AM ASHAMED   *945 6

TONGUES
    OF TONGUES SO THE SHADOWS TELL   108 14
    NAY TONGUES ARE DEAD AND WORDS ARE HOLLOW AS HOLLOW   296 25
    ESPECIALLY CLAPPER BELLS HARD TONGUES WAGGING IN HARD M+   623 2
    THE UNROLLING OF FERNS WHITE TONGUES OF THE ACANTHUS LA+   623 27
    THE UNROLLING OF FERNS WHILE TONGUES OF ACANTHUS LAPPIN+   *953 15

TONIGHT
    THE LITTLE RED HEIFER TONIGHT I LOOKED IN HER EYES   38 6
    AND OH MY LOVE AS I ROCK FOR YOU TONIGHT   100 24
    I OWN THAT SOME OF ME IS DEAD TONIGHT   100 28
    MY LOVE LOOKS LIKE A GIRL TONIGHT   101 1
    TONIGHT PROFANE   558 6
    TONIGHT AND REFRAIN   558 13
    AND IF TONIGHT MY SOUL MAY FIND HER PEACE   726 22
    OUT OF THE SKY TONIGHT   748 2
    TONIGHT THEY'RE COMING   755 16
    AFTER TONIGHT FOR SEE I SAID TO HIM   878 8
    TONIGHT THIS VERY LAST OF OUR NIGHTS WE   878 9

TO-NIGHT
    AND CLUSTERED STAR CALLED DOWN TO ME TO-NIGHT   86 15
    I AM ASHAMED YOU WANTED ME NOT TO-NIGHT   87 14
    HOW WE HATE ONE ANOTHER TO-NIGHT HATE SHE AND I   98 7
    TO-NIGHT I HAVE LEFT HER ALONE   212 17
    NOW YOU ARE MINE TO-NIGHT AT LAST I SAY IT   238 16
    AND TO-NIGHT I SLAY IT   238 18
    TO-NIGHT IS A WOMAN BORN   240 20
    THE MOSQUITOES ARE BITING TO-NIGHT   302 9

TONS
    AND ROCKS IT TONS OF GRAIN ON THE RIPENING WIND   271 22

TOOK
    JACKET AT TH' BOSOM AN' TOOK OUT   61 10
    WHO TOOK A HANDFUL OF LIGHT AND ROLLED A BALL   69 18
    AN' 'IM TO 'AVE BEEN TOOK IN   77 16
    ON YER YO'N GOT WHAT YER TOOK   81 4
    TILL SHE TOOK HER EYES AWAY   123 33
    TOOK PLEASURE IN TOUCHING YOU MORTALITY   158 16
    SURELY YOU TOOK YOUR FATE   167 23
    IT TOOK AEONS TO MAKE A SAPPHIRE AEONS FOR IT TO PASS A+   477 5
    WHEN THEY TOOK YOU AND REFINED YOU   549 6
    WHEN THEY TOOK YOU AND REFINED YOU   549 7
    THEY TOOK AWAY YOUR GOOD OLD STONES   549 9
    WITH HANDCUFFS AND TOOK HIM TO THE POLICE-STATION   575 3
    AND TOOK FOR ME   601 16
    I TOOK TO MY HEELS AND RAN   604 8
    THEY TOOK AWAY OH THEY TOOK AWAY YOUR MAN'S NATIVE   630 22
    HIS WORK TOOK PLACE IT CAME TO PASS IT STOOD UP AND SAL+   690 7
    IN THE STILLNESS HE TOOK OFF HIS HELMET TO KISS ME   732 16
    LIKE A BRIDE HE TOOK MY BAYONET WANTING IT   742 9
    SO I TOOK THE SANDALS OF THE SAVIOUR   787 2
    IT FLOWERED BEFORE MEN TOOK TO FLOWERING FOR WAGES   814 5
    IT IS TIME MEN TOOK THEIR THOUGHTS OFF WOMEN   838 5
    AND I TOOK HER EAR LIKE THE LEAF OF A WATER-FLOWER BETW+   882 27
    WIND TOOK   *891 28
    JACKET AT TH' BOSOM AN' TOOK FROM OUT OF IT   *911 26
    HE TOOK A HANDFUL OF LIGHT AND ROLLED A BALL   *916 1
    AN' 'IM TO HAVE BEEN TOOK IN   *919 4
    WHAT HER'S GOT HER TOOK   *923 4
    WAS I TILL SHE TOOK HER EYES AWAY   *935 5

TOOL
    WHAT A TOOL IN THE HANDS OF THE LORD   254 26
    NOW I SAY TO HER NO TOOL NO INSTRUMENT NO GOD   255 19
    AN ENGINE OF FLESH USELESS UNLESS HE IS A TOOL   635 17
    AND IN THE UNFINISHED HOUSES THE RING OF THE JOINER'S T+   865 16

TOOLS
    HANDLED ALL MY TOOLS AND MEASURES   95 18

TOOTH
    YET ONE THING I DO FIGHT FOR TOOTH AND NAIL ALL THE TIME   497 22

TOOTHLESS
    LIKE A TOOTHLESS HOUND PURSUING HIM WITH MY WILL   47 23
    TAKING BREAD IN HER CURVED GAPING TOOTHLESS MOUTH   359 19

TOOTH-MOUTHED
    DON'T EVER BE KIND TO THE SMILING TOOTH-MOUTHED DEAD   441 32

TOP
    ON TH' YALLER CLAY WI' TH' WHITE FLOWERS TOP OF IT   60 13
    I'M FURTHER OWER TH' TOP   78 32
    EMPTY AN' EMPTY FROM BOTTOM TO TOP   139 13
    AND LIGHTS ON A WITHERED OAK-TREE'S TOP OF WOE   147 23
    ONE BIRD ONE BLOT FOLDED AND STILL AT THE TOP   147 24
    AN EAGLE AT THE TOP OF A LOW CEDAR-BUSH   373 1
    OUT INTO THE OPEN WHERE THE PATH RUNS ON THE TOP OF A   387 4
    A NIGHTINGALE SINGING AT THE TOP OF HIS VOICE   523 8
    ABOUT TO THE GIDDY TOP   552 22
    FROM THE TOP OF HER HEAD   565 25
    HUSHABY BABY ON A TREE TOP   669 7
    TELL ME IS THE GENTIAN SAVAGE AT THE TOP OF ITS COARSE +   684 2
    FROM THE TOP OF A DARK-HAIRED CEDAR-BUSH   780 28
    AND THE TOP OF THE MORNING   803 11
    MY TOP OF LIFE THAT BUDS ON HIGH   *899 29
    MY TOP OF LIFE THAT BUDS ON HIGH   *903 8
    ON TH' YALLER CLAY AN' TH' WHITE FLOWERS TOP OF IT   *910 28
    I'M FURTHER OWER TH' TOP   *920 24

TOPPING
    YOU LOOK LIKE THE TOPPINGEST TOPPING FIFTH-FORM ETON BO+   835 17

TOPPINGEST
    YOU LOOK LIKE THE TOPPINGEST TOPPING FIFTH-FORM ETON BO+   835 17

TOPPLES
    HIE HIE FRUIT TOPPLES   817 1

TOPS
    YOU GLOW AT LAST LIKE THE MOUNTAIN TOPS WHEN THEY CATCH   209 29

TORCH
    LET ME GUIDE MYSELF WITH THE BLUE FORKED TORCH OF THIS +   697 14
    REACH ME A GENTIAN GIVE ME A TORCH   *956 10
    LET ME GUIDE MYSELF WITH THE BLUE FORKED TORCH OF A FLO+   *956 11

TORCHES
    WHERE THE BRANDS OF THE ANGELS LIKE TORCHES   242 25
    THE TORCHES   388 4
    AND SCARLET HOT EMBERS OF TORCHES KNOCKED OUT OF THE   388 30
    AMONG THE SPLENDOR OF TORCHES OF DARKNESS SHEDDING DAR+   697 21
    AMONG THE SPLENDOUR OF BLACK-BLUE TORCHES SHEDDING FATH+   *956 19

TORCHES'
    TORCHES' FIRE   *937 21

TORCH-FLOWERS
    TORCH-FLOWERS OF THE BLUE-SMOKING DARKNESS PLUTO'S DARK+   *956 6

TORCH-FLOWER
    TORCH-FLOWER OF THE BLUE-SMOKING DARKNESS DARK-BLUE DAZE   697 8

TORCH-LIGHT
    FORTH TO THE TOM-TOM'S BEAT IN THE TORCH-LIGHT   387 29

TORCH-LIKE
    DARKENING THE DAY-TIME TORCH-LIKE WITH THE SMOKING BLUE+   697 4
    RIBBED AND TORCH-LIKE WITH THEIR BLAZE OF DARKNESS SPRE+   697 6
    DARKENING THE DAYTIME TORCH-LIKE WITH THE SMOKING BLUEN+   *956 2

TORCH-MEN
    OF JUNGLE TORCH-MEN   389 30

TORE
    TO DIE AND THE QUICK LEAF TORE ME   111 4
    THE MYSTERIOUS BULL TORE HIM AT ADOLESCENCE INTO PIECES   361 11
    AH THEN WHEN HE TORE THE WIND WITH HIS TEETH   378 4
    OH I TORE THEM UP THOUGH THE WISTFUL LEAVES WERE FRAGRA+   *926 15

TORMENT
    FULL IN MY OWN AND THE TORMENT STARTS AGAIN   225 24
    AH THAT WAS TORMENT HARD ENOUGH   264 23
    IN THE EXCRUCIATING TORMENT OF HOPELESSNESS HELPLESSNESS   627 24
    GO FORWARD SUN DO NOT TORMENT US   750 4

TORMENTED
    HOW MUCH MORE IS HE PESTERED AND TORMENTED SAY I   361 34

TORMENTS
    HE PESTERS HER AND TORMENTS HER SAID THE WOMAN   361 33

TORN
    ANOTHER TORN RED SUNSET COME TO PASS   136 4
    ARE TORN AWAY AND A SPLASH   149 30
    I WHOSE HEART IS TORN WITH PARTING   169 10
    OPENS MY EYES TILL THE ROOTS OF MY VISION SEEM TORN   173 4
    THE SURFACE OF DREAMS IS BROKEN THE ARRAS IS TORN   174 5
    WHERE AN ARCHWAY TORN AND GLITTERING   201 23
    WHEN I SAW THE TORN DEAD I KNEW IT WAS MY OWN TORN DEAD   257 7
    WHY WAS THE VEIL TORN   364 23
    THE SILKEN SHRIEK OF THE SOUL'S TORN MEMBRANE   364 24
    TORN WITH A SHRIEK HALF MUSIC HALF HORROR   364 26
    TIME AFTER TIME THAT FRAIL TORN SCREAM   365 23
    TORN TO BECOME WHOLE AGAIN AFTER LONG SEEKING FOR WHAT   367 1
    THAT WHICH IS WHOLE TORN ASUNDER   367 5
    THE WORLD WILL BE TORN IN TWO   663 27
    ARE TORN DOWN BY DISMEMBERING AUTUMN   709 19
    TORN WINGS OF FLAME ARE WAFTING DOWN THE SKY   855 21
    AT THESE WIDE-SPACED TORN ENORMOUS BREATHS   878 36
    I'D HAVE TORN THEM UP HAD THEY BORNE AWAY THE PATIENT B+   *926 13
    ANOTHER TORN RED SUNSET COME TO PASS   *938 32
    THAT STOOD CLOSE TO THE WALL AND THE FRONT'S FADED SILK+   *940 3

TORNADO
    AND TURNING THE DAY SUDDENLY INTO A BLACK TORNADO OF JO+   397 4

TORRENT
    LITTLE TORRENT OF LIFE   476 7

TORRID
    SUN OF THE TORRID MID-DAY'S HORRIFIC DARKNESS   301 20
    LIKE A SHED WHITE HUSK ON THE TORRID SKY   747 29

TORTOISE
    WISE TORTOISE LAID HIS EARTHY PART AROUND HIM HE CAST I+   348 13
    BABY TORTOISE   352 2
    UNDER ITS SLOW LID TINY BABY TORTOISE   352 22
    YOUR FACE BABY TORTOISE   353 9
    ALONG THE BACK OF THE BABY TORTOISE   355 1
    THE SECTIONS OF THE BABY TORTOISE SHELL   355 9
    OF THE BABY TORTOISE   355 16
    LIVE-ROSY TORTOISE SHELL   355 19
    OF THE BABY TORTOISE   356 10
    BECAUSE HE IS IRASCIBLE THIS MORNING AN IRASCIBLE TORTO+   357 14
    LITTLE TORTOISE   357 25
    TO BE A TORTOISE   358 7
    A BRISK BRINDLED LITTLE TORTOISE ALL TO HIMSELF   358 9
    TORTOISE IN EXTREMIS   364 6
    MALE TORTOISE CLEAVING BEHIND THE HOVEL-WALL OF THAT DE+   364 28
    THE TORTOISE ETERNITY   365 25

TORTOISE
    OF THE MALE TORTOISE AT EXTREMITY   366 26
    THE SAME CRY FROM THE TORTOISE AS FROM CHRIST THE OSIRI+   367 3
    HAS THE SHELL GROWN TOO HEAVY FOR THE TORTOISE   558 17

TORTOISE-NAKEDNESS
    IN TORTOISE-NAKEDNESS   364 32

TORTOISES
    TORTOISES ALWAYS FORESEE OBSTACLES   356 30
    TWO TORTOISES   361 27

TORTOISE-WISE
    TORTOISE-WISE THE FIRST BELL SOUNDING   358 13

TORTURE
    FINE TORTURE YOU DID DESERVE   111 27
    AND TAKE OUT MY INTESTINES TO TORTURE THEM   741 4
    AND LEAVE ME TORTURE AND WRATH AND A DROSSED DESPAIR   874 9
    BRIGHT TORTURE THOU DIDST DESERVE   *927 15
    FINE TORTURE YOU DID DESERVE   *928 15
    IN TORTURE OF YOUR PROXIMITY   *931 3

TORTURED
    NAY BUT HOW TORTURED IS THE FRIGHTFUL SEED   160 21
    EVEN THEN IN THE DARK I WAS TORTURED RAVENING UNFREE   264 30
    A FRENZY OF TORTURED POSSESSION   475 19
    AND A MILLION FRENZIES OF TORTURED JEALOUSY   475 20

TORTURES
    SO HE VERY CLEVERLY TORTURES WOMEN WITH HIS SORT OF LOVE   447 15

TORTURING
    A THREATENING TORTURING PHALLIC MOLOCH   264 25

TOSS
    ME THINGS AND THE SILENCES TOSS   108 15
    AND I DO TOSS THROUGH THE TROUBLED NIGHT FOR YOU   129 23
    TO TOSS THE GLOBE OF EARTH LIKE A BALL ON A WATER-JET   272 14
    AS I AM IF MY HEART IN UPLIFTING CEASED TO BEAT TO TOSS+   320 27
    AND WHAT A DANDY FELLOW THE RIGHT TOSS OF A CHIN FOR YOU   524 15
    AND THE BOUGHS OF THE LIME TREE SHAKE AND TOSS THE LIGHT   878 5

TOSSED
    HOW THE STARS ARE TOSSED   49 6
    YOUR STAR BE TOSSED OVER A WAVE   49 18
    TOSSED BACK IN A SCARE   120 15
    TOSSED ON THE LOW BLACK RUFFLED HEAP   145 13
    PALE SLEEPY PHANTOMS ARE TOSSED ABOUT   163 23
    SO HE TOSSED IT AWHILE IN HIS HAND AND PLAYED WITH IT   791 6
    ALL OVER THE SKY THEIR WINGS ARE TOSSED   823 3
    PALE SLEEPY FLOWERS ARE TOSSED ABOUT   857 23
    ALAS TOSSED BACK IN MY HEARTS SWIRL   862 16

TOSSES
    TOSSES THE CRAPE OF RED ACROSS YOUR BROW AND DOWN YOUR   370 27

TOSSING
    AS YOU SEE A TINY CELLULOID BALL TOSSING ON A SQUIRT OF+   272 16
    CHAMPING IT TOSSING A MOUTHFUL   397 9
    IN RAPID ARMFULS FROM THE LINE TOSSING IT IN THE BASKET   672 15
    OF TOSSING AND ROLLING THE SUBSTANCE OF LIFE TO YOUR LI+   792 21
    A TOSSING SEA OF TURBULENT STRIFE WHERE NOW   *894 20

TOSS-UP
    IS IT A TOSS-UP 'TWIXT THEE AN' ME   *924 4
    IT'S NO TOSS-UP 'TWIXT THEE AN' ME   *924 5

T'OTHER
    A GO AT T'OTHER FOR I'M A BAD   140 4

TOTTERING-GRASS
    COCK'S-FOOT FOX-TAIL FESCUE AND TOTTERING-GRASS   587 20

TOUCH
    TOUCH ME ENOUGH   34 24
    TOUCH AFTER TOUCH I FEEL ON ME   52 1
    SLOWLY ROTATE TILL THEY TOUCH THE TREE   52 5
    YOUR FACE IN THE MARIGOLD BUNCH TO TOUCH AND CONTRAST Y+   90 10
    SO DISTANT THEY CANNOT TOUCH ME WHOM NOW NOTHING MARS   97 17
    I FEEL YOUR SILENCE TOUCH MY WORDS AS I TALK   110 3
    AND STRIP ME NAKED TOUCH ME LIGHT   117 13
    FOR I ACHE MOST EARNESTLY FOR YOUR TOUCH   117 15
    FROM OFF MY MEASURE TO TOUCH YOU DEEP AND FILL   127 18
    TO TOUCH THE SEA IN THE LAST SURPRISE   130 22
    THE TOUCH WAS ON THE QUICK I WANT TO FORGET   143 25
    MY HANDS SHOULD TOUCH THE DOOR   147 7
    TO TOUCH ITS FELLOW ON EITHER SIDE   154 6
    BETWEEN YOU BUT HIS TOUCH YOU NEVER KNEW   158 8
    BUT DO NOT TOUCH THIS MAN WHO NEVER YET   158 15
    TO TOUCH HIM WHILE HE STILL IS LYING THERE   158 21
    BUT DO NOT TOUCH HIM FOR HE HATED YOU   158 25
    TO TOUCH HIM AND HE SAID SO AND YOU KNEW   158 26
    WITH A TOUCH THE DEAD AND THE LIVING WHILE TIME COUNTS +   174 12
    AND RELEASE US POOR ONES AND RICH ONES LET US BREATHE A+   175 28
    ALWAYS GLADDEN MY AMOROUS FINGERS WITH THE TOUCH OF THE+   180 25
    SOMETHING I WANT TO TOUCH I MUST HOLD MY FACE TO THE RA+   180 31
    TILL MY HANDS ARE FULL OF THE CHILLNESS AND TOUCH OF LE+   182 35
    THROUGH THE FILM I CAN ALMOST TOUCH YOU   194 3
    STILL THE KISS WAS A TOUCH OF BITTERNESS ON MY MOUTH   206 20
    REACHING OUT IN ANGUISH YET UNABLE QUITE TO TOUCH THEM   233 4
    WHERE I TOUCH YOU I FLAME INTO BEING BUT IS IT ME OR   245 12
    I AM NOR WILL I BE BOUNCED OUT OF IT SO AT LAST I TOUCH   250 2
    DON'T TOUCH ME AND APPRECIATE ME   255 20
    I TOUCH I FEEL THE UNKNOWN   259 21
    A CURIOUS AGONY AND A RELIEF WHEN I TOUCH THAT WHICH IS+   266 14
    I WANT HER TO TOUCH ME AT LAST AH ON THE ROOT AND QUICK   266 28
    TOUCH   270 10

TOUCH
    ONE TOUCH   335 16
    NOT ONE TOUCH   337 19
    THE TOUCH OF SUN EXCITES YOU   353 1
    TOUCH ME CAREFULLY OLD FATHER   405 1
    DO YOU EXIST AND CAN A MAN TOUCH YOUR HAND   430 2
    TOUCH HIM AND YOU'LL FIND HE'S ALL GONE INSIDE   431 19
    ARE AWAKE THROUGH YEARS WITH TRANSFERRED TOUCH AND GO   448 3
    TILL THEY TOUCH IN FLOOD   465 30
    BUT IF HE STAYS FAR FROM ME AND DOES NOT TOUCH ME   468 9
    WE CAN'T BEAR TO TOUCH OR BE TOUCHED   468 13
    WE ARE HUMANLY OUT OF TOUCH   468 15
    FOR IF CEREBRALLY WE FORCE OURSELVES INTO TOUCH   468 17
    NOLI ME TANGERE TOUCH ME NOT   468 22
    O YOU CREATURES OF MIND DON'T TOUCH ME   468 23
    TOUCH COMES WHEN THE WHITE MIND SLEEPS   470 23
    TOUCH COMES SLOWLY IF EVER IT SEEPS   470 25
    TOUCH IS OF THE BLOOD   471 12
    TOWARDS TOUCH THEN THIS DELIRIOUS   471 16
    BUT ALSO HE IS INSTINCTIVE INTUITIVE AND IN TOUCH   473 18
    IN TOUCH BY INTUITION INSTINCTIVELY   474 6
    TILL YOU LOOK TO THE RIGHT MAN TO PUT YOU INTO TOUCH   484 18
    HOT HURRYING YET IT BURNS IF YOU TOUCH IT   505 26
    EACH TIME THEY TOUCH US   512 20
    IF WE TOUCH THE SOB-STUFF CROWN   537 10
    AND THE HOLY CAN'T-HELP-IT TOUCH   537 14
    SO LEAVE OFF TRYING TO PUT THE ROBBIE BURNS TOUCH   540 25
    OH TOUCH THE HARP TOUCH THE HARP GENTLY MY DEARS   576 4
    THEM NOW FROM ALL THIS TOUCH OF TAINTED DEATH   581 9
    OH COME COME NEARER COME INTO TOUCH   602 12
    BUT A DEMOCRACY OF MEN A DEMOCRACY OF TOUCH   611 9
    THE FUTURE OF RELIGION IS IN THE MYSTERY OF TOUCH   611 10
    THEN THE RESURRECTION INTO TOUCH   611 13
    ONCE MEN TOUCH ONE ANOTHER THEN THE MODERN INDUSTRIAL   611 14
    TOUCH HAS BEGUN   612 2
    A WAITING FOR THE PROPER TOUCH NOT FOR ANY WORD OR DEED   612 16
    WILL EVER COME INTO TOUCH   612 18
    WE DON'T EXIST UNLESS WE ARE DEEPLY AND SENSUALLY IN TO+   613 6
    UNLESS WE ARE IN TOUCH WITH THAT WHICH LAUGHS AT ALL OU+   613 10
    WE CAN BUT TOUCH AND WONDER AND PONDER AND MAKE OUR EFF+   667 14
    WHICH HE CAN NEVER REACH TILL HE TOUCH THE BOTTOM OF TH+   700 25
    WHICH HE CAN NEVER TOUCH FOR THE ABYSS IS BOTTOMLESS   700 29
    YOUR NOTHING AND MY NOTHINGNESS TOUCH ME   737 19
    TOUCH ME OH TOUCH ME GIVE ME DESTINIES   733 23
    BY TOUCH AND A NEW NAKEDNESS   738 24
    TOUCH ME THEN TOUCH ME TOUCH ME I DID NOT DIE   738 28
    THAT I AM NOW AH LAY ONE LITTLE TOUCH   790 00
    OF JUST ONE TOUCH EVEN SO DO I ASK TOO MUCH   738 32
    BUT SHALL I TOUCH HANDS WITH DEATH IN KILLING THAT OTHER   743 17
    TOUCH HIM ON THE SHOULDER   754 2
    SILENT REACH OUT LET US TOUCH   764 32
    DO THEY PREVENT THE TOUCH   765 14
    BUT THE FINGERS OF ALL TOUCH THE FINGERS OF ALL   811 29
    THEY TOUCH IN MID-HEAVEN LIKE AN ACROBAT   820 15
    IN SHUT-EYED TOUCH   834 6
    TINY BLACK MOTHS FLUTTER OUT AT THE TOUCH OF THE FORK   858 13
    TO TOUCH IT THAT NEW THING   861 25
    NO DO NOT TOUCH ME LEAVE ME ON THE GREY SEA-TURF   870 23
    STRIVE WITH THE FORMLESS THINGS AND GENTLY TOUCH   872 6
    TOUCH AFTER TOUCH I FEEL ON ME   *899 14
    SLOWLY ROTATE TILL THEY TOUCH THE TREE   *899 19
    TOUCH AFTER TOUCH I FEEL ON ME   *902 26
    SLOWLY ROTATE TILL THEY TOUCH THE TREE   *902 31
    TOUCH CUPS AND DRINK   *931 11
    AND STRIP ME NAKED TOUCH ME ALIGHT   *931 17
    FOR I ACHE MOST EARNESTLY FOR YOUR TOUCH   *931 19

TOUCHED
    AS 'UD WINCE WHEN THAT TOUCHED 'ER CLOSE AN'   138 31
    TOUCHED YOU TO FIRE   158 6
    SOMETHING SEEMED TO SURGE THROUGH ME WHEN I TOUCHED   255 5
    YOU WOULD THINK TWICE BEFORE YOU TOUCHED A WEASEL ON A   255 22
    TOUCHED THAT WHICH WAS VERILY NOT ME   259 3
    I TOUCHED WITH MY HAND I CLUTCHED WITH MY HAND   260 2
    I TOUCHED HER IT WAS I WHO TOUCHED AND I WHO WAS TOUCHED   260 8
    I TOUCHED HER FLANK AND KNEW I WAS CARRIED BY THE CURRE+   260 12
    THIS HAVING TOUCHED THE EDGE OF THE BEYOND AND PERISHED+   266 21
    BEING TOUCHED WITH LOVE AND DEVOID OF FATHERLINESS   357 15
    WE CAN'T BEAR TO TOUCH OR BE TOUCHED   468 13
    WITH THAT WHICH CAN BE TOUCHED BUT NOT KNOWN   613 7
    BUT I TOUCHED THE HAND OF QUETZALCOATL   806 26
    I TOUCHED THE HAND OF QUETZALCOATL   806 28
    BUT HUITZILOPOCHTLI TOUCHED THE HAND OF QUETZALCOATL   809 19
    AND I WOKE WONDERING WHO TOUCHED ME WITH SUCH FEAR AND +   860 10
    THE BOOKS THAT YOU HAVE TOUCHED CLEAVE CLOSE TO ME   880 10

TOUCHES
    CLOSE AND IT ROLLS ME ENFOLDS ME TOUCHES ME AS IF NEVER+   34 23
    TOUCHES THE CLASP WITH TREMBLING FINGERS AND TRIES   64 16
    SHE TOUCHES ME AS IF I WERE HERSELF HER OWN   266 24
    UNTIL YOUR VEILED HEAD ALMOST TOUCHES BACKWARD   370 14
    JUST TOUCHES EARTH   392 29
    A FEW OF THE TOUCHES LIKE A LOW-BORN JAKE   489 15
    WHO IS IT THAT SOFTLY TOUCHES THE SIDES OF MY BREAST   652 6
    AND TOUCHES ME OVER THE HEART   652 7
    HER BREASTS UPLIFTED IN ENDEAVOR SHE TOUCHES SHE REEVES   864 12
    TOUCHES THE MARGINS OF OUR LIFE'S EXISTENCE   *958 28

TOUCHING
    TOOK PLEASURE IN TOUCHING YOU MORTALITY   158 16
    SHINING AND TOUCHING   210 17
    JOSTLING PEOPLE TOUCHING AND TALKING AND MAKING SMALL   249 18
    AND TOUCHING THE UNKNOWN THE REAL UNKNOWN THE UNKNOWN   259 18
    AND STUMBLING LUNGING AND TOUCHING THE WALLS THE BELL-W+   343 11
    IN TOUCHING HIM AND PLANTING HER ROUND FEET   426 19
    YOUR FEET AND TOUCHING YOUR ANKLES TRY   887 16

TOUCHLESS
  TOUCHLESS   446 7
  THE MIND IS TOUCHLESS SO IS THE WILL SO IS THE SPIRIT   611 11

TOUCHSTONE
  WE SOUGHT YOU SUBSTANTIAL YOU TOUCHSTONE OF CARESSES YO+   34 17
  THOUGHT IS THE TESTING OF STATEMENTS ON THE TOUCHSTONE +   673 11

TOUGH
  TILL 'ER'S TOUGH AS WHIT-LEATHER TO SLIVE   77 19
  THE TOUGH OLD ENGLAND THAT MADE US   534 13
  TILL 'ER'S TOUGH AS WHIT-LEATHER TO SLIVE   *919 7
  A TOUGH OLD OTCHEL WI' LONG   *919 10

TOWARD
  MY MAN IS MADE TOWARD   59 10
  IN HIS EFFORT TOWARD COMPLETION AGAIN   361 9
  THE MYSTERY I STRIVE TOWARD HOWEVER   876 28
  I BEAT MY WINGS TOWARD IT NEVER   876 29
  THAT BEARS ALOFT TOWARD RARER SKIES   *899 28
  YOUR FACE TOWARD MY AGONY   *930 19
  PUT FORTH TOWARD HER SHE DID NOT MOVE NOR I   *936 22

TOWD
  THEY ON'Y TOWD ME IT WOR BAD   45 11

TOWEL
  I FORGET THE TOWEL AND MY WET LIMBS   870 5

TOWER
  BUT TO DEFLOWER THEE THY TOWER IMPINGES   40 23
  FROM THE TOWER ON THE TOWN BUT ENDLESSLY NEVER STOPPING   54 7
  SURE AND A TOWER OF STRENGTH 'TWIXT THE WALLS OF HER BR+   249 12
  THAT INTERVENE BETWEEN OUR TOWER AND THE SLINKING SEA O+   *957 24

TOWERING
  AND YOU WILL BE BEFORE ME TALL AND TOWERING   246 27
  IN FRONT OF A TOWERING GRIMACING WHITE IMAGE OF   387 31

TOWERS
  FROM THE PINE-TREE THAT TOWERS AND HISSES LIKE A PILLAR+   375 5

TOWN
  OF THE SORREL'S CRESSET A GREEN BRAVE TOWN   49 27
  FROM THE TOWER ON THE TOWN BUT ENDLESSLY NEVER STOPPING   54 7
  WHEN DAWN IS FAR BEHIND THE STAR THE DUST-LIT TOWN HAS   71 7
  WITH FAIR FLAKES LIGHTING DOWN ON IT BEYOND THE TOWN   76 18
  LIKE SPRAY ACROSS THE TOWN   99 18
  AND ALL DAY LONG THE TOWN   109 1
  THE TOWN IS LIKE A CHURCHYARD ALL SO STILL   136 2
  THROUGH THE SHROUD OF THE TOWN AS SLOW   142 26
  AND ALL HOURS LONG THE TOWN   159 1
  THE TOWN HAS OPENED TO THE SUN   166 16
  TO THE TOWN AND TRIES TO SELL THEM   203 3
  OVER THE WHISPERING TOWN   253 6
  DRIFTS OVER THE TOWN IN ITS NEED   253 29
  IT'S THE SOCIALISTS COME TO TOWN   312 6
  IT'S THE SOCIALISTS IN THE TOWN   312 27
  IN NOTTINGHAM THAT DISMAL TOWN   488 7
  NATURALLY TAKE HOLD OF THE TOWN   537 12
  OF LONDON TOWN   551 8
  THE WEATHER IN TOWN IS ALWAYS BENZINE OR ELSE PETROL   703 18
  THE TOWN GROWS FIERCER WITH HEAT   746 8
  THE TOWN WILL CLUSTER HER HERBAGE THEN   748 3
  WITH FAIR FLAKES SETTLING DOWN ON IT BEYOND THE TOWN   *898 12
  WITH FAIR FLAKES SETTLING DOWN ON IT BEYOND THE TOWN   *901 21
  WHEN THE DAWN IS FAR BEHIND THE STAR THAT THE LAMP-LIT +   *917 25
  THE TOWN IS LIKE A CHURCHYARD ALL SO STILL   *933 30
  AND ALL THE TOWN IS GONE INTO A DUST   *939 13

TOWN-DARK
  TOWN-DARK SEA   71 19

TOWNFOLK
  I MOVE AMONG A TOWNFOLK CLAD   109 10

TOWNLETS
  AND FROM THE SICILIAN TOWNLETS SKIRTING ETNA   312 10

TOWNS
  ABOVE THE TOWNS   70 21
  TWO TOWNS   97 19
  TOWNS CONSTELLATIONS RACE   862 26
  TOWNS   *917 18

TOWNWARD
  DOWN THE VALLEY ROARS A TOWNWARD TRAIN   50 15

TOY
  SPUN LIKE A TOY   121 6
  MOTIONLESS STANDING IN SNOW LIKE A CHRISTMAS TOY   402 26

TOYS
  LIKE TOYS   846 6

TRACE
  I COULD FIND NO TRACE   46 26
  IN THE CURVES OF THY FORM THE TRACE OF THE UNKNOWN   69 16
  WHERE THE MINNOWS TRACE   161 6
  BUT NOT A TRACE OF FOUL EQUALITY   316 7
  TILL NOT A VESTIGE IS LEFT AND BLACK WINTER HAS NO TRACE   709 20
  NOW LET IT ALL BE FINISHED LEAVE NO TRACE   737 23
  GO GO AWAY AND LEAVE US NOT A TRACE   738 1

TRACES
  AND EVER I SEE YOUR TRACES BROKEN-HEARTED   880 15

TRACING
  OVER MY HAIR AND TRACING MY BROWS   104 7

TRACK
  YOUR HUMAN SELF IMMORTAL TAKE THE WATERY TRACK   161 28
  TRACK OF THE RAILWAY ALIVE AND WITH SOMETHING TO DO   174 8
  SO HE COULD TRACK HER DOWN AGAIN WHITE VICTIM   308 23
  TO TRACK HER DOWN   309 17
  DOWNWARD TRACK   322 13
  BUT NOW MY LASS YOU'VE GOT NEMESIS ON YOUR TRACK   399 27
  LOOK OUT MY LAD YOU'VE GOT 'EM ON YOUR TRACK   634 9
  LO THE GREAT ONE ANSWERS TRACK HIM DOWN   808 7
  YOU TRACK THE GREY DOG HOME   808 10
  IS A TRACK OF CLOUDS ACROSS THE MOON   882 18
  DOWN THE SKY'S STEEP STAIRS CHARTING NO TRACK FOR HER   *937 27

TRACKING
  AND AS THE DOG WITH ITS NOSTRILS TRACKING OUT THE FRAGM+   406 1

TRACKS
  DRIVEN AWAY FROM HIMSELF INTO HER TRACKS   363 17

TRADITION
  WE TRAIL BEHIND US AN ENDLESS TRADITION OF COMBAT   519 11
  TRADITION TRADITION TRADITION IT IS EASY ENOUGH   775 18
  TO BE FAITHFUL TO A TRADITION   775 19

TRAFFIC
  WOULD START THE THUNDERING TRAFFIC OF FEET   272 2
  TRAFFIC WILL TANGLE UP IN A LONG DRAWN-OUT CRASH OF COL+   624 27

TRAFFICKING
  TRAFFICKING MYSTERIOUSLY THROUGH THE AIR   655 19
  I FEEL GODDESSES TRAFFICKING MYSTERIOUSLY THROUGH THE A+   655 27

TRAFFIC-STREAMS
  SUBMIT ABJECTLY TO THE BLIND MECHANICAL TRAFFIC-STREAMS+   666 6

TRAGEDIES
  I CAN'T VERY MUCH CARE ABOUT THE WOES AND TRAGEDIES   508 16
  AFTER ALL THE TRAGEDIES ARE OVER AND WORN OUT   508 25

TRAGEDY
  GIRLS WITH THEIR LARGE EYES WIDE WITH TRAGEDY   71 21
  THEY TAKE TRAGEDY SO BECOMINGLY   71 30
  TRAGEDY SEEMS TO ME A LOUD NOISE   508 11
  TRAGEDY LOOKS TO ME LIKE MAN   508 13
  AND WHEN I THINK OF THE GREAT TRAGEDY OF OUR MATERIAL-M+   508 19
  WHEN LOVE IS GONE AND DESIRE IS DEAD AND TRAGEDY HAS LE+   509 1
  THE TRAGEDY IS OVER IT HAS CEASED TO BE TRAGIC THE LAST+   510 13
  WHEN THINGS GET VERY BAD THEY PASS BEYOND TRAGEDY   514 10

TRAGIC
  THE TRAGEDY IS OVER IT HAS CEASED TO BE TRAGIC THE LAST+   510 13

TRAIL
  OF A TRAIL OF OUR SMALL FIRE ON THE DARKENED SKY   89 15
  I WILL TRAIL MY HANDS AGAIN THROUGH THE DRENCHED COLD L+   180 34
  GONE AGAIN IN THE BRIGHT TRAIL OF LAVA   293 23
  TAKE UP THE TRAIL OF THE VANISHED AMERICAN   371 26
  LEAVING THE TRAIL OF A DIFFERENT PAW HANGING OUT   394 4
  PELTING BEHIND ON THE DUSTY TRAIL WHEN THE HORSE SETS O+   397 12
  SOUNDS STILL UNFROZEN AND THE TRAIL IS STILL EVIDENT   401 3
  WHAT ARE THEY DOING HERE ON THIS VANISHING TRAIL   401 14
  FOLLOW THE TRAIL OF THE DEAD ACROSS GREAT SPACES FOR TH+   406 4
  NOR CLACKS ACROSS THE FORCES FURROWING A GREAT GAY TRAIL   436 3
  IT LEAVES ITS TRAIL   448 27
  WE TRAIL BEHIND US AN ENDLESS TRADITION OF COMBAT   519 11
  AND WHEN BLACK LEAVES STREAM OUT IN A TRAIL DOWN THE WI+   883 12

TRAILED
  THE LAST CAR TRAILED THE NIGHT BEHIND   121 24
  AND TRAILED HIS YELLOW-BROWN SLACKNESS SOFT-BELLIED DOWN   349 10

TRAILING
  FOR THE TRAILING LEISURELY RAPTURE OF LIFE   68 5
  THROUGH THE FLOWER-VINE TRAILING SCREEN   179 11
  FOR THE TRAILING LEISURELY RAPTURE OF LIFE   *914 20

TRAIN
  I S'LL NEVER CATCH THAT TRAIN   46 2
  DOWN THE VALLEY ROARS A TOWNWARD TRAIN   50 15
  CLEAR UPON THE LONG-DRAWN HOARSENESS OF A TRAIN ACROSS +   63 11
  THE TRAIN IN RUNNING ACROSS THE WEALD HAS FALLEN INTO A+   88 1
  THE TRAIN BEATS FRANTIC IN HASTE AND STRUGGLES AWAY   88 23
  MY FEAR IN ACCEPTING THE PORTENT THE TRAIN CAN NOW   88 27
  AND A TRAIN ROARING FORTH   99 19
  THE CRISPING STEAM OF A TRAIN   100 2
  A TRAIN GOES ROARING SOUTH   110 13
  HOW I HAVE LONGED FOR THIS NIGHT IN THE TRAIN   117 1
  AS THE TRAIN FALLS LEAGUE AFTER LEAGUE   162 15
  IS IT THE TRAIN   162 25
  THIS TRAIN BEATS ANXIOUSLY OUTWARD BOUND   169 4
  NOURISH HER TRAIN HER HARDEN HER   228 29
  WHEN I WENT IN A TRAIN I KNEW IT WAS MYSELF TRAVELLING +   257 3
  HOW NICE SAYS THE PEON TO GO RUSHING IN A TRAIN   794 13
  THE FRANTIC THROB OF THE TRAIN   862 18
  FLAPS UP FROM THE PLAYGROUND AS A GREAT TRAIN STEAMS SO+   *894 29
  TO SHARE THE TRAIN WITH YOU   *930 26
  HOW I HAVE LONGED FOR THIS NIGHT IN THE TRAIN   *931 5

TRAINS
  SWIFT TRAINS GO BY IN A RUSH OF LIGHT   169 2
  SLOW TRAINS STEAL PAST   169 3
  THEY MAKE TRAINS CHUFF MOTOR-CARS TITTER SHIPS LURCH   441 6
  AT HER TRAINS AT HER RAILWAYS AND HER AUTOMOBILES   790 7
  YEA LORD EVEN TRAINS AND CAMIONS AND AUTOMOBILES   794 11
  TRAINS AND CAMIONS AUTOMOBILES AND AEROLANES   794 12
  TAKE BACK OUR LANDS AND SILVER AND OIL TAKE THE TRAINS +   794 21

TRAIN-SMOKE
  AND WHEN I SEE THE THICK WHITE BODY OF TRAIN-SMOKE BREAK   883 16

TRAIPSE
  WHAT A TRAIPSE IT IS IF A MAN GETS HURT   46 3

TRAITOR
  BUT TOLSTOI WAS A TRAITOR   536 18
  TO HIS HOUSE IN THE HEART OF A TRAITOR   808 11

TRAITORS
  TRAITORS OH LIARS YOU JUDAS LOT   762 14
  WHO ARE COWARDS WHO ARE LIARS WHO ARE TRAITORS WHO HAVE+   807 12
  NO SPOTTED TRAITORS CRAWL BY   810 4

TRAM
  PASSES THE LIGHT OF THE TRAM AS IT RACES   145 14
  THEY HAVE GREEN TRAM IN FLORENCE NOW   845 22

TRAM-CARS
  SAVE AS THE TRAM-CARS HOVER   144 23
  BOULEVARDS TRAM-CARS POLICEMEN   286 35

TRAM-CAR
  FOR A MOMENT AT EVENING TIRED AS HE STEPPED OFF THE TRA+   672 7

TRAM-CONDUCTOR
  THE YOUNG TRAM-CONDUCTOR IN A BLUE UNIFORM TO HIMSELF F+   672 8

TRAMMELLED
  MY HEART IS TRAMMELLED   56 24
  FEELING TRAMMELLED AND HURT   255 17

TRAMP
  THEY COME NO NEARER AND STILL WE TRAMP   163 27

TRAMPING
  ISN'T IT GOD'S OWN IMAGE TRAMPING HIS THIRTY MILES A DAY   430 22

TRAMPLE
  I TRAMPLE ON THE SNOWDROPS IT GIVES ME PLEASURE TO TREA+   271 12

TRAMPLED
  AND TRAMPLED ALL THE LISTENERS TO A SMUSH   540 6
  BEING TRAMPLED TO MUD   658 12

TRAMPLING
  TEARING EACH OTHER'S FEELINGS TRAMPLING EACH OTHER'S TE+   544 16

TRAMS
  PASSES THE GALLIVANT BEAM OF THE TRAMS   145 5
  TRAMS THAT PASS BLOWN RUDDILY DOWN THE NIGHT   146 13

TRANQUIL
  BURST THE NIGHT'S MEMBRANE OF TRANQUIL STARS   302 18

TRANSCENDENT
  GLISTENING IN STEADFAST STILLNESS LIKE TRANSCENDENT   225 3

TRANSCENDS
  NOTHING THAT TRANSCENDS THE BOURGEOIS MIDDLINGNESS   528 2

TRANSFER
  OR TRANSFER THE CONTROL TO THE AMERICAN INSTITUTE   780 9

TRANSFERRED
  ARE AWAKE THROUGH YEARS WITH TRANSFERRED TOUCH AND GO   448 3

TRANSFIGURATION
  I SAW THE TRANSFIGURATION   165 25

TRANSFIGURED
  TO SHOW YOU THUS TRANSFIGURED CHANGED   53 22

TRANSFORMATION
  OH YOU STIFF SHAPES SWIFT TRANSFORMATION SEETHES   72 12

TRANSGRESS
  THAT NO NOISE CAN TRANSGRESS   261 21

TRANSIENCE
  FROM THE RED ROSE-FLOWERS' FIERY TRANSIENCE   219 14

TRANSIENCY
  MUST IN MY TRANSIENCY PASS ALL THROUGH PAIN   195 19
  FOR MY TAINTED TRANSIENCY AS A THING UNREAL   772 7

TRANSIT
  AT THE TRASHY MOTOR-DRIVEN TRANSIT OF DIRTY DAY   453 27

TRANSLUCENT
  INTO THAT TRANSLUCENT PHANTOM SHRED   332 13

TRANSMIT
  AND WHEN WE FAIL TO TRANSMIT LIFE LIFE FAILS TO FLOW   449 2
  SEXLESS PEOPLE TRANSMIT NOTHING   449 5
  AND IF AS WE WORK WE CAN TRANSMIT LIFE INTO OUR WORK   449 6

TRANSMITTED
  BY THE TRANSMITTED GLEAM FROM THE FACES OF VIVIDER MEN   649 14

TRANSMITTERS
  AS WE LIVE WE ARE TRANSMITTERS OF LIFE   449 1

TRANSMUTED
  TRANSMUTED THE DARK REDNESS TAKEN OUT   784 13

TRANSPORT
  SUCH SILENCE SUCH SUSPENDED TRANSPORT   334 1

TRANSUBSTANTIATION
  TRANSUBSTANTIATION   165 27

TRAP
  GNAWING IN A WOODEN TRAP TRAPPED IN   656 11

TRAPEZE
  THE TRAPEZE MAN SLIM AND BEAUTIFUL AND LIKE A FISH IN T+   445 4

TRAPPED
  SOMETIMES THE DARKNESS TRAPPED WITHIN A WHEEL   135 8
  HE TRAPPED HER THIS MORNING HE SAYS SMILING FOOLISHLY   401 26
  AND ONE TRAPPED ONE'S FINGERS IN THEIR BRASSY POLISHED   644 13
  GNAWING IN A WOODEN TRAP TRAPPED IN   656 11

TRAPPINGS
  AND THE STREWN TAWDRY TRAPPINGS THAT LAST NIGHT'S POETR+   856 11

TRASHY
  AT THE TRASHY MOTOR-DRIVEN TRANSIT OF DIRTY DAY   453 27

TRAVAIL
  THE MOANING OF SLEEP-BOUND BEINGS IN TRAVAIL THAT TOIL +   149 19
  THAT SLOWLY LABOURS IN A VAST TRAVAIL   195 33
  THE LOINS OF THIS OUR TISSUE OF TRAVAIL OUR LIFE'S   880 3

TRAVEL
  STRANGE BEAMS MUST TRAVEL STILL FOR I FEEL THAT I   115 3
  CAN THIS SHOT ARROW OF TRAVEL FLY   116 15
  AND CAST US FORTH LIKE THIN SHORN MOONS TO TRAVEL   132 10
  BITTERLY INTO CORROSION BITTERLY TRAVEL   160 16
  FIELD AND AS VICTORS WE TRAVEL   243 15
  WE MOVE WITHOUT KNOWING WE SLEEP AND WE TRAVEL ON   252 7
  TO TRAVEL TO BURROW INTO A LITTLE LOOSE EARTH AFRAID OF+   358 2
  OR A MAN MAY TRAVEL BOTH EAST AND WEST   575 22
  GOAL TO TRAVEL TOWARDS YET IT'S SOMETHING TO ATTAIN YOU+   761 15
  THEY SAY YOU DO NOT TRAVEL   783 30
  TRAVEL THINE AVOCATION HERE AND LEARN   872 2
  CAN THIS SHOT ARROW OF TRAVEL FLY   *930 14
  AND CAST US FORTH LIKE SHORN THIN MOONS TO TRAVEL   *938 2

TRAVELLED
  I HAVE TRAVELLED AND LOOKED AT THE WORLD AND LOVED IT   662 7
  HAVE YOU TRAVELLED   764 25
  HAVE YOU TRAVELLED YOUR DOWNWARD ARC   764 26
  ARE YOU NEAR HAVE YOU TRAVELLED YOUR PORTION   764 30
  NAKED HAVE I TRAVELLED THE LONG WAY ROUND   801 4
  I HAVE TRAVELLED IN RUSSIA TWO HOURS OR MORE   866 26

TRAVELLER
  TRAVELLER COLUMN OF FIRE   40 5
  LIKE LUGGAGE OF SOME DEPARTED TRAVELLER   134 9
  TO SAY YOUR SAY AS A TRAVELLER SAYS   171 28
  AM A TRAVELLER BACK AND FORTH   323 17
  TRAVELLER   354 18

TRAVELLERS
  AND THE FIVE OTHERS THE TRAVELLERS   703 1
  AND BID FAREWELL OF STATELY TRAVELLERS   740 20

TRAVELLING
  WITH JOY AT TRAVELLING TO PLANT ITSELF WITHIN   127 12
  WHEN I WENT IN A TRAIN I KNEW IT WAS MYSELF TRAVELLING +   257 3
  GREEN AND ILLUMINED AND TRAVELLING FOR EVER   260 27
  UPON ME TRAVELLING TO REEVE   262 11
  HOW VIVID YOUR TRAVELLING SEEMS NOW IN THE TROUBLED SUN+   354 4
  FLAME OF FLESH FOREVER TRAVELLING   460 6
  O FLOWERS THEY ARE ALL THE TIME TRAVELLING   476 12
  THAT SHE HAS IN TRAVELLING BY HERSELF THROUGHOUT TIME   610 21
  TRAVELLING TRAVELLING STILL STILL TRAVELLING   703 4
  ALL THE WHILE TRAVELLING TRAVELLING   784 4
  DO THOU OH TRAVELLING APPRENTICE LIKEWISE   872 5

TRAVELS
  TRAVELS THE LIGHT AS IT TILTS IN ITS PACES   146 3
  THAT WRAPS THE NORTH IN STUPOR AND PURPLE TRAVELS THE D+   149 3

TRAVERSED
  FOR I HAVE TRAVERSED MY UPWARD CURVE   764 28

TRAY
  SET DOWN THE TRAY BEFORE ME AS I WORK   875 11

TREACHEROUS
  RANK AND TREACHEROUS PROWLING   107 23
  MUSHY AND TREACHEROUS TINY   457 17
  FROM THE LIARS FROM THE THIEVES FROM THE FALSE AND TREA+   807 16

TREACHERY
  THE LIES THE TREACHERY THE SLIPPERY CULTURED SQUALOR OF+   497 4
  AND AFTER ALL LYING AND BASE HYPOCRISY AND TREACHERY   497 6
  IS THE VILEST COWARDICE AND TREACHERY   680 2

TREACLE
  TREACLE   763 9

TREAD
  TILL THE DISTANCE FOLDS OVER HIS OMINOUS TREAD   43 4
  HER CONSTANT TREAD   64 2
  AND GLADLY I'D OFFERED MY BREAST TO THE TREAD OF HER   123 6
  TREAD THEM OUT IN THE LOAM   159 22
  TREAD OVER THE EDGE OF THE PIT AND WE'RE GONE   164 11
  THE WINDS THAT TREAD   268 27
  I TRAMPLE ON THE SNOWDROPS IT GIVES ME PLEASURE TO TREA+   271 12
  BUT STILL WE ARE IN-BETWEENS WE TREAD   490 23
  TREAD OF EVERY PASSER-BY   617 18
  HENCE THE RIDICULOUS WAY THEY RUSH IN WHERE ANGELS FEAR+   665 20
  THE DEAD TREAD HEAVILY THROUGH THE MUDDY AIR   704 8
  THEY RETURN RELENTLESSLY IN THE SILENCE ONE KNOWS THEIR+   739 14
  A MAN CANNOT TREAD LIKE A WOMAN   812 17
  WOULD GLADLY HAVE OFFERED MY BREAST FOR HER TREAD TO TRY   *934 12
  BRUSH OVER MY FACE AS HE GOES TO TREAD OUR WEIRD WOMEN   *947 20

TREADING
  HE IS TREADING OUR WOMEN   436 13
  AND TREADING OF WET WEBBED WAVE-WORKING FEET   436 25

TREADS
  WOMEN WHOM HE TREADS   438 14
  AND TREADS THE EARTH TO FEEL THE SOIL   459 23
  HE TREADS   818 11
  WHICH TREADS OUT THE GLOW OF FUGITIVE ORANGE LIGHT   858 11

TREASURE
  OF DEATH-PRODUCING WINE TILL TREASURE   177 3
  AND GUARD THE LAST TREASURE OF THE SOUL OUR SANITY   514 12
  IN HERSELF A SMALL TREASURE   565 11
  WHAT IS HER TREASURE   565 18
  THE TREASURE AND THE VAUNT WE EVER HAD   737 14
  HAVE STOLEN THE TREASURE OF AWAKENING   878 30
  MY TREASURE SOFTLY SLIPS UNCURLED   *943 23

TREASURES
  YOU HAVE FINGERED ALL MY TREASURES   95 16
  ITS TREASURES OF CONSCIOUSNESS ITS SUBTLE BARBARIC   776 9

TREASURY
  OR AT LEAST WORTH TREASURY NOTES   458 27

TREAT
  I HOW CAN YOU TREAT ME SO AND LOVE ME   211 9
  YOUR OWN SMALL NIGHT GOES WITH YOU WHY TREAT IT SO   211 14
  DIDN'T TREAT HIM ROUGHER   494 17
  AND YOU STAND THERE AND EXPECT ME TO TREAT YOU LIKE AN   547 8
  TO SEE THE WAY THEY TREAT IT   670 23

TREE
  AND AT NIGHT WHEN THE WIND ROSE THE LASH OF THE TREE   36 10
  SLOWLY ROTATE TILL THEY TOUCH THE TREE   52 5
  NO TREE IN BLOOM   56 4
  SOFT AS A SUMMERING TREE   56 8
  SHEDDING YOU DOWN AS A TREE   56 11
  AS MISTLETOE BERRIES BURNING IN A BLACK TREE   86 2
  COME THEN UNDER THIS TREE WHERE THE TENT-CLOTHS   113 21
  PUT TRUST THEN NOW IN THE BLACK-BOUGHED TREE   114 9
  BE PENETRATE LIKE THE TREE   114 12
  BENEATH THIS POWERFUL TREE MY WHOLE SOUL'S FLUID   131 8
  OF THE WITHERED TREE IN THE GRAIL   147 25
  WITH WONDER EVERY BLACK TREE   165 23
  BUT LET ME BE MYSELF NOT A RIVER OR A TREE   212 5
  NOW EVERY TALL GLAD TREE   215 22
  ONE ROSE OF WONDERMENT UPON THE TREE   219 6
  THIS MAY BE A WITHERING TREE THIS EUROPE   291 7
  WITHIN THE FLESH-SCENT OF THIS WICKED TREE   299 13
  IN JANUARY AND IN FEBRUARY THE RE-BIRTH OF THE ALMOND T+   303 5
  OH GIVE ME THE TREE OF LIFE IN BLOSSOM   305 29
  A NAKED TREE OF BLOSSOM LIKE A BRIDEGROOM BATHING IN DEW   306 8
  THE TREE BEING LIFE-DIVINE   307 1
  CA-A-A COMES THE SCRAPE OF RIDICULE OUT OF THE TREE   375 14
  WHAT VOICE OF THE LORD IS THAT FROM THE TREE OF SMOKE   375 15
  AND A BLACK CRUCIFIX LIKE A DEAD TREE SPREADING WINGS   403 24
  HE IS ALIVE LIKE A TREE IN SPRING   450 25
  AND THEY CLOTHE THEMSELVES IN WHITE AS A TREE CLOTHES I+   451 8
  WHEN A BIRD FLIPS HIS TAIL IN GETTING HIS BALANCE ON A +   496 6
  I WOULD SAY THE SAME IF I WERE A CHAFFINCH OR TREE   499 3
  AS IN A WINTRY TREE   504 19
  IF YOU CLIMB UP THE TREE   549 14
  DOWN THE TRUNK OF THE SLIPPERY TREE   552 6
  THERE IS THE ORGANIC CONNECTION LIKE LEAVES THAT BELONG+   615 1
  WINDS OF HEAVEN FAN THE LEAVES OF THE TREE LIKE FLAMES +   615 4
  NO ONE NOT EVEN GOD CAN PUT BACK A LEAF ON TO A TREE   617 1
  THROUGH THE DARK HADES AT THE ROOTS OF THE TREE   617 10
  THE HUMAN WILL TO THE FLUSH OF THE VASTER IMPULSION OF +   617 14
  OH IF THE HUGE TREE DIES   640 18
  TO GRAFT ON ANOTHER TREE   640 20
  AND SLOW MOUNTING MARVEL OF A LITTLE TREE   667 18
  HUSHABY BABY ON A TREE TOP   669 7
  IT IS LIKE A VAST GREAT TREE WITH A VAST GREAT LOT OF S+   677 21
  THE TREE OF HUMANITY NEEDS PRUNING BADLY   677 24
  THE TREE OF HUMAN EXISTENCE NEEDS BADLY PRUNING   677 28
  OR THE WHOLE TREE MAY FALL ROTTEN   677 29
  A ROSE TREE BRONZEY WITH THORNS   714 10
  COWERING IN THE LAST BRANCHES OF THE TREE OF OUR LIFE   718 20
  DEEPER THAN THE ROOTS OF THE MANGO TREE   805 1
  DEEPER THAN THE ROOTS OF THE MANGO TREE   806 4
  LIKE A TREE IN NEW LEAF   811 14
  FROM THE TREE   817 6
  LIE DOWN BENEATH THE TREE   818 13
  UNDER AN OAK TREE WHOSE YELLOW BUDS DOTTED THE PALE BLU+   866 23
  HOW LONELY UNDER THE TREE UNNOTICED   867 7
  AND AH I KNOW THE SHADOWS THAT THE TREE   878 3

TREE
  AND THE BOUGHS OF THE LIME TREE SHAKE AND TOSS THE LIGHT   878 5
  SLOWLY ROTATE TILL THEY TOUCH THE TREE   *899 19
  SLOWLY ROTATE TILL THEY TOUCH THE TREE   *902 31
  ALL THE LEAVES ARE FALLEN AND THE STARLIGHT SHINES THRO+   *917 28
  THE BATS DEPRAVED ARE DROPPING GAILY FROM OFF THE TREE   *918 13
  THEY LIVED THEMSELVES FORTH LIKE A TREE PUTTING OUT WOV+   *949 28
  CAME FROM THEM LIVING LIKE LEAVES FROM THE TREE OF THEI+   *949 45
  AND THE ROOTS OF THE GREAT TREE OF FAMILY AND THE FORES+   *951 13

TREE OF LIFE
  AND SO STRANGLE OFF THEIR CONNECTION WITH THE CEASELESS+   616 5
  WITH WHICH TO MANURE AFRESH THE ROOTS OF THE TREE OF LI+   616 15
  INTO THE CIRCULATING SAP ONCE MORE OF THE TREE OF LIFE   617 11
  EITHER TO STAY CONNECTED WITH THE TREE OF LIFE AND SUBM+   617 13
  ON THE TREE OF LIFE   800 27
  FROM THEIR TREE OF LIFE AND VILLAGES WHOLE CITIES LIVED+   *950 4

TREES
  THE WISE OLD TREES   54 24
  THE BUDDING TREES   58 2
  WHERE THE TREES RISE LIKE CLIFFS PROUD AND BLUE-TINTED +   66 5
  BETWEEN THE CLIFFS OF THE TREES ON THE GREY-GREEN PARK   66 6
  THE TREES RISE TALLER AND TALLER LIFTED   68 1
  WHERE LOFTY TREES ATHWART-STREAM CHANCE   68 11
  DIM TREES SO HUGE AND TALL   68 24
  IMITATE THE MAGNIFICENT TREES   69 6
  AND LITTERED LETTERING OF TREES AND HILLS AND HOUSES CL+   88 6
  OF HAWTHORN AND OF LILAC TREES   104 29
  THE ENORMOUS CLIFF OF HORSE-CHESTNUT TREES   105 13
  THE PAGEANT OF FLOWERY TREES ABOVE   106 7
  WILD PUFFING OF GREEN-FIRE TREES AND FLAME-GREEN BUSHES   115 2
  MOURNFULLY TO AND FRO TO AND FRO THE TREES ARE WAVING   136 22
  THE FROST HAS SETTLED DOWN UPON THE TREES   141 27
  -THE TREES DOWN THE BOULEVARD STAND NAKED IN THOUGHT   142 1
  IN THE GRIM UNDERTOW NAKED THE TREES CONFRONT   142 3
  TREES BIRDS AND EARTH ARRESTED IN THE AFTER-THOUGHT   142 15
  IT STANDS SO STILL IN THE HUSH COMPOSED OF TREES AND IN+   159 27
  THE TREES IN TROUBLE BECAUSE OF AUTUMN   160 5
  HERE THE TREES AND TROOPS   196 12
  IN THE DARKNESS WE ALL ARE GONE WE ARE GONE WITH THE TR+   211 21
  WHAT ARE SO MANY STRAIGHT TREES TO ME   224 23
  IT IS WE WHO WALK IN THE TREES   231 28
  SKIES TREES FLOWERS BIRDS WATER   256 25
  IT IS SAID A DISEASE HAS ATTACKED THE CYPRESS TREES OF +   295 1
  EMPEDOKLES SAYS TREES WERE THE FIRST LIVING CREATURES T+   295 4
  TREES SUFFER LIKE RACES DOWN THE LONG AGES   304 25
  THE ALIEN TREES IN ALIEN LANDS AND YET   305 1
  AND THROUGH THE SHADOW OF BREAD-FRUIT TREES WITH THEIR   383 30
  AND THROUGH THE SHADOW OF BREAD-FRUIT TREES WITH THEIR   387 1
  AND ABOVE AND ABOVE THE TREES I FOUND HER LAIR   402 11
  ABOVE THE TREES OF THE LOBO DARK VALLEY-MOUTH   402 20
  AND NEAR ACROSS AT THE OPPOSITE STEEP OF SNOW GREEN TRE+   402 25
  THEY ARE LIKE SLENDER TREES PUTTING FORTH LEAVES A LONG+   451 5
  BELOW THE GRASS AND TREES   480 4
  THINK HOW A PEACOCK IN A FOREST OF HIGH TREES   530 5
  INTO SERVICE LIKE THE ROOTS OF TREES   637 16
  TREES RAISED FROM SEED HAVE WILD AND BITTER FRUITS   640 21
  BE ALONE AND FEEL THE -TREES SILENTLY GROWING   646 9
  HOW STILL THE TREES ARE   646 20
  AND THE GHOSTLY CREAMY COLOURED LITTLE TREES OF LEAVES   646 23
  TAKE ME SOUTH AGAIN TO THE OLIVE TREES   652 22
  AND OIL ME WITH THE LYMPH OF SILVERY TREES   652 23
  OIL ME WITH THE LYMPH OF TREES   652 24
  AWAY AWAY THROUGH THE TREES   769 15
  WALK THROUGH THE TREES AS VIRGINS   769 25
  SHE SEES MEN WALKING TOWARDS HER UNDER THE TREES   770 1
  AND ON THE TREES HANG THE APPLES OF GOLD   770 22
  THERE ARE DEAD THAT SIT UNDER THE TREES WATCHING WITH A+   795 26
  QUETZALCOATL LOVES THE SHADE OF TREES   802 14
  GIVE HIM TREES CALL BACK THE TREES   802 15
  WE ARE LIKE TREES TALL AND RUSTLING   802 16
  QUETZALCOATL IS AMONG THE TREES   802 17
  NOW THE TREES WITH INTERLOCKED HANDS AND ARMS UPLIFTED +   854 4
  A THRILL THROUGH THE LISTENING TREES AND HOLD THE BREATH   858 26
  EVE ALONE UNSATISFIED AMONG THE ORANGE AND GUAVA TREES   864 1
  THE GLOW OF RED IN A GREY-GREEN SHADOW OF TREES   867 10
  PLAYING WITH THE SHADOW COLOURS AND THE WAVING REFLECTE+   867 20
  AMONG THE SHADOWS OF BLOSSOMS AND TREES AND RUSHES   867 26
  HIS BLUE SHIRT GLIMMERING ON THE WATER AMONG THE SHADOW+   867 29
  UP THE RIVER UNDER THE TREES   867 31
  AND WHEN I SEE THE TREES SWAY CLOSE   883 8
  THE TREES RISE TALLER AND TALLER LIFTED   *914 8
  WHERE THE LOFTY TREES ATHWART STREAM PERCHANCE   *914 26
  THESE TREES SO HUGE AND TALL   *915 8
  IMITATE THE MAGNIFICENT TREES   *915 18
  COME THEN UNDER THE TREES WHERE THE LEAF-CLOTHS   *929 10
  ALL THE TREES ARE HANGING WITH DISHONOURED FLAGS' DISGR+   *933 29
  WHICH CLOTHES OUR NAKEDNESS LIKE GRASS THE PLAINS AND T+   *951 8

TREE'S
  OVER THE TREE'S EDGE AS OVER A MOUNTAIN   50 1

TREES'
  IN CONFUSION AGAINST MY ENTRY IS IT ONLY THE TREES'   140 13

TREMBLE
  HE STANDS AND I TREMBLE BEFORE HIM   39 13
  I TREMBLE IN HIS SHADOW AS HE BURNS   39 29
  COULD SEE THE SMALL STARS TREMBLE   55 28
  STILL YOU TREMBLE FAINT REPROACH   95 25
  I SEE OUR SHADOW TREMBLE   170 11
  WHERE FLAMES OF FIERCE LOVE TREMBLE   242 10
  SHOW ME I TREMBLE SO MUCH TO HEAR IT THAT EVEN NOW   273 28
  DO TREMBLE UNDER MY COMPLAINT   680 13
  AND IN THE TROPICS TREMBLE THEY WITH LOVE   694 11
  TO SEE HIM FLASH AND TREMBLE WITH THE FIRE OF HIS SOUL   859 8
  THEN I TREMBLE AND GO TREMBLING   *893 26

TREMBLED
THEN EVERY ATOM OF THE COSMOS TREMBLED WITH DELIGHT   682   8
YOU WEPT AND THE BED TREMBLED UNDER ME   886 14

TREMBLES
AH WUNNA KISS THEE THA TREMBLES SO   138 14
THE UNIVERSE TREMBLES GOD IS BORN GOD IS HERE   683 10
AND TREMBLES WITH A SENSE OF TRUTH PRIMORDIAL CONSCIOUS+   844 25
THAT CONVULSES AND TREMBLES AGAIN WITH THE SYMPATHY OF +   *952   7

TREMBLING
GOES TREMBLING PAST ME UP THE COLLEGE WALL   35 27
TOUCHES THE CLASP WITH TREMBLING FINGERS AND TRIES   64 16
TREMBLING BLUE IN HER PALLOR A TEAR THAT SURELY I HAVE +   67 16
THE SHORN MOON TREMBLING INDISTINCT ON HER PATH   131 23
AND A TREMBLING FLOWER ENCLOSES   178 25
AS LIGHTNING COMES ALL WHITE AND TREMBLING   195 12
THE FLAME OF MY SOUL LIKE A TREMBLING STAR IS HUNG   750 12
SUNDAY AFTER SUNDAY THEY CARRIED HIM TREMBLING TO HIS P+   859 13
TILL A DREAM CAME TREMBLING THROUGH MY FLESH IN THE NIG+   860   9
EVE PUSHING THE FESTOONED VANILLA TREMBLING ASIDE   864   7
AND TREMBLING SOMEWHERE DEEP IN THEIR SUNKIST GLOOM   868 27
HAD UTTERLY GONE FROM OUT OF THE TREMBLING SKY   885   8
THEN I TREMBLE AND GO TREMBLING   *893 26
IN YOU IS TREMBLING AND FUSING   *907   2
IS IN ME A TREMBLING GLADNESS   *907 20
IN YOU IS TREMBLING AND FUSING   *908 23
THE SHORN MOON TREMBLING INDISTINCT ON HER PATH   *937 22
WHILE TREMBLING SOMEWHERE IN THEIR WONDROUS GLOOM   *941 27
AND PUT IT BETWEEN THE HANDS OF THE TREMBLING SOUL   *958 23

TREMENDOUS
AND OUR NAKED CONTACT WILL BE RARE AND VIVID AND TREMEN+   608 15
GOD SIGHING AND YEARNING WITH TREMENDOUS CREATIVE YEARN+   691   2
TILL ALL IS SOUNDLESS AND SENSELESS A TREMENDOUS BODY O+   698 22

TREMOR
COMES OUT IN THE HESITATING TREMOR OF THE PRIMROSE   272 27
AND THERE SHALL BE THE SOFT SOFT TREMOR AS OF UNHEARD B+   479   4
AND A REAL TREMOR IF HE HANDS OUT A TEN-POUND NOTE   486 13

TREMORS
THE TREMORS OF NIGHT AND THE DAY   788   6

TREMULOUS
SOFT AS A KIND HEART'S KINDNESS TREMULOUS   784 17

TRENCHES
TO THE TRENCHES I SEE AGAIN A FACE WITH BLUE EYES   742   6

TREND
I MUST FOLLOW ALSO HER TREND   461 12

TRESPASS
LET THEM LIVE THE BOYS AND LEARN NOT TO TRESPASS I HAD +   93 11
NOT TO TRESPASS ON THEM WITH LOVE THEY MUST LEARN NOT T+   93 12
FROM THIS UNKNOWN THAT I WOULD TRESPASS ON   256   6
SUCH OBSCENITY OF TRESPASS   336   3

TRESPASSED
FROM TRESPASSED CONTACTS FROM RED-HOT FINGER   601 10

TRESS
LIKE A TRESS OF BLACK HAIR   883 14

TRESTLE
AS YOU SIT ON THE TRESTLE I ON THE GROUND   887 12

TRIBES
OF THOSE ILL-SMELLING TRIBES OF MEN THESE FROGS THAT CA+   792 23

TRICK
THAT IS YOUR TRICK YOUR BIT OF FILTHY MAGIC   332 21
TRICK ON THEM DIRTY BITCH   399 18
WHEN HER TRICK IS TO CLIMB OVER HIM   426 15
EVEN IT IS A TRICK BUT SHE IS NOT ASHAMED   654 12
THOUGHT IS NOT A TRICK OR AN EXERCISE OR A SET OF DODGES   673 14
BUT IT'S ALL A TRICK   *948 21
I'VE REALISED IT IS ALL A TRICK ON HIS PART   *948 22

TRICKLES
TRICKLES THE DEW   178 13
ITS SWEETNESS DISTILS AND TRICKLES AWAY INTO   504 21

TRICKLING
RUNNING DOWN RUNNING DOWN TRICKLING   454   2

TRICKS
WHEN DID YOU START YOUR TRICKS   332   1

TRIDENT
AND SHE JABBED HER BRITISH TRIDENT CLEAN   577 17
FOR THE TRIDENT WAS LEVELLED AT HIS HEAD   577 21

TRIED
AND TRIED TO BREAK THE VESSEL AND VIOLATE MY SOUL   92 24
TRIED   93 33
YOU TRIED TO LOOK BACK TO IT AND COULDN'T   381   7
TRIED   464 13
OVERHEAD THE REDDEST SHE LIFTED HER LONG ARMS AND TRIED   864   9

TRIES
TOUCHES THE CLASP WITH TREMBLING FINGERS AND TRIES   64 16
HOW STRANGELY SHE TRIES TO DISOWN IT AS IT SINKS   128 15
THA MUST THOUGH THA TRIES TER GET AWAY   139 18
TO THE TOWN AND TRIES TO SELL THEM   203   3
ONLY MAN TRIES NOT TO FLOW   479 16

TRIFLING
THINK OF THE RUBBISH YOU'RE TRIFLING IN   457   7

TRILL
THE TRILLING LARK IN A WILD DESPAIR WILL TRILL DOWN ARR+   624 14

TRILLING
THE TRILLING LARK IN A WILD DESPAIR WILL TRILL DOWN ARR+   624 14
AND THE LARK WILL FOLLOW TRILLING ANGERLESS AGAIN   625   6

TRIM
MOVES IN SILVER-MOIST FLASHES IN MUSICAL TRIM   147 20

TRIMMED
CAN IT BE THEY'VE BEEN TRIMMED SO THEY'VE NEVER SEEN   578 16

TRIMMING
LIKE A FUNNY TRIMMING TO THE MIDDLE OF HER BELLY THIN   393 19

TRIMMINGS
EVEN AS TRIMMINGS THEY'RE STALE   557   6

TRIMMIN'
AN' LEAVES YOU NEVER A TRIMMIN'   493 16

TRINKLING
SEE THE WOMAN'S TRINKLING FINGERS TEND HIM A COIN   36   6

TRIP
AND TRIP IT FOR ALL SHE WAS WORTH   550 24

TRIPPED
TO ANOTHER BALANCE TRIPPED ROUND POISED AND SLOWLY SANK   444 30

TRIPPING
TRIPPING ABOUT WITH THEIR LADYLIKE HAMS   765 11

TRIPS
YET THE MOMENT I HATE HER SHE TRIPS MILD AND SMUG LIKE A   385 12

TRIUMPH
IN A SMILE LIKE TRIUMPH UPON ME THEN CARELESS-WISE   43 21
NOW YOU CAN TRIUMPH NOW HE IS NO MORE   157 29
STAND YOU FAR OFF AND TRIUMPH LIKE A JEW   158 28
OF MAKING A TRIUMPH OF ENVY THE RICH AND SUCCESSFUL ONES   175 10
GREEN LANTERN OF PURE LIGHT A LITTLE INTENSE FUSING TRI+   206 10
ONLY TO DANCE TOGETHER IN TRIUMPH OF BEING TOGETHER   210 15
TO CROWN THE TRIUMPH OF THIS NEW DESCENT   218 28
A YELL OF TRIUMPH AS YOU SNATCH MY SCALP   333 24
WANDERING IN THE SLOW TRIUMPH OF HIS OWN EXISTENCE   358 18
WAR-CRY TRIUMPH ACUTE-DELIGHT DEATH-SCREAM REPTILIAN   364 22
TRIUMPH THE ANCIENT PIG-TAILED MONSTER   426 14
GLITTERS IN SALTY TRIUMPH   455   9
LET US TRIUMPH AND LET THE YOUNG BE LISTLESS   503   7
MEN HAVE BEEN WANTING TO TRIUMPH TRIUMPH TRIUMPH   519   2
TRIUMPH OVER THEIR FELLOW-MEN TRIUMPH OVER OBSTACLES   519   3
TRIUMPH OVER EVIL   519   4
WE LOATHE THE THOUGHT OF ANY SORT OF TRIUMPH   519   8
TRIUMPH CONQUEST   519 12
THEY TALK OF THE TRIUMPH OF THE MACHINE   623 24
BUT THE MACHINE WILL NEVER TRIUMPH   623 25
MECHANICAL MAN IN TRIUMPH SEATED UPON THE SEAT OF HIS M+   624 21
SO MECHANICAL MAN IN TRIUMPH SEATED UPON THE SEAT OF HI+   624 24
THE TRIUMPH OF THE MACHINE   625   9
ON AND ON AND THEIR TRIUMPH IN MERE MOTION   675 26
ANOTHER TRIUMPH ON THE FACE OF EARTH   746   4
THAN WOMAN OR TRIUMPH MONEY OR SUCCESS   764   3
DEARER THAN TRIUMPH   765   7
YOUR TRIUMPH OF ANGUISH ABOVE YOU THEY WOULD SAY   *941   8
THEY TALK OF THE TRIUMPH OF THE MACHINE   *953 12
BUT THE MACHINE WILL NEVER TRIUMPH   *953 13
AH NO THE MACHINE WILL NEVER TRIUMPH   *954   1

TRIUMPHANCE
TO HEAR ON ITS MOCKING TRIUMPHANCE UNWITTING THE AFTER-+   58   6
WITH THE WHITE TRIUMPHANCE OF LIGHTNING AND ELECTRIC DE+   707 19

TRIUMPHANT
THE VOICE OF THE FURTIVE TRIUMPHANT ENGINE AS IT RUSHES+   58   4
DIPPING WITH PETTY TRIUMPHANT FLIGHT AND TITTERING OVER   347 17
HENCE JESUS RODE HIM IN THE TRIUMPHANT ENTRY   378 20
ON AND ON WITH THE TRIUMPHANT SENSE OF POWER LIKE MACHI+   675 25
THE DEAD TRIUMPHANT AND THE QUICK CAST DOWN   740   4

TRIUMPHANTLY
LIKE A LOVING-CUP LIKE A GRAIL BUT THEY SPILT IT TRIUMP+   92 23

TRIUMPHED
THEY HAVE TRIUMPHED AGAIN O'ER THE AGES THEIR SCREAMING+   33   4
MACHINES HAVE TRIUMPHED ROLLED US HITHER AND THITHER   623 30
MACHINES HAVE TRIUMPHED ROLLED US HITHER AND THITHER   *953 17

TRIUMPHING
TRIUMPHING CONQUERING   519 14

TRIVIAL
THAT SUCH TRIVIAL PEOPLE SHOULD MUSE AND THUNDER   494 14

TROD
AND TROD WOLVES UNDERFOOT   378   5
WAS FUME AS I TROD   404 27

TRODDEN
BUT NOW I AM TRODDEN TO EARTH AND MY FIRES ARE LOW   94   1
AND TRODDEN THAT THE HAPPY SUMMER YIELDS   135   8
SURELY YOU'VE TRODDEN STRAIGHT   167 21
SURELY YOU'VE TRODDEN STRAIGHT   168 27
AND I AM DEAD AND TRODDEN TO NOUGHT IN THE SMOKE-SODDEN   258 14

TRODDEN
    DEAD AND TRODDEN TO NOUGHT IN THE SOUR BLACK EARTH   258 16
    OF THE TOMB DEAD AND TRODDEN TO NOUGHT TRODDEN TO NOUGHT   258 17
    GOD BUT IT IS GOOD TO HAVE DIED AND BEEN TRODDEN OUT   258 18
    TRODDEN TO NOUGHT IN SOUR DEAD EARTH   258 19
    WHEN I AM TRODDEN QUITE OUT QUITE OUT   258 26
    I IN THE SOUR BLACK TOMB TRODDEN TO ABSOLUTE DEATH   259 1

TRODE
    ON THE FLOOR WHERE NEVER MY NUMB FEET TRODE   163 11
    THAN THE EARTH THE PALFREY TRODE   202 8
    ALONG WHERE MY SLOW FEET NEVER TRODE   857 11
    TOGETHER WE TRODE THE EVENING WHERE THE SUN   884 23

TROLLS
    OF DAY TROLLS AT THE CAVE OF RINGING CERULEAN MINING   72 10

TROOP
    TROOP OUT OF YOUR SHRINES   798 18
    TROOP INTO THE SKY   798 22

TROOPING
    INVISIBLE TROOPING HOME THE UNASSUAGED GHOSTS   739 11

TROOPS
    HERE THE TREES AND TROOPS   195 12

TROPICAL
    TROPICAL LANE   386 26
    TROPICAL STARS   387 20
    THE TROPICAL NIGHT OF BLAZING COCOA-NUT   387 26
    IN THE FUME OF COCOA-NUT OIL IN THE SWEATING TROPICAL N+   387 36
    AND LUSTROUS GREAT TROPICAL EYES UNVEILED NOW GLEAMING   389 13
    AND FLARE OF A TROPICAL ENERGY TIRELESS AFIRE IN THE DA+   389 16
    APPROACHING UNDER THAT SMALL PAVILION AND TROPICAL EYES   389 22
    SHOWING A GLINT OF TEETH AND GLANCING TROPICAL EYES ARO+   391 14
    O FACES UPTURNED TO THE GLARE O TROPICAL WONDER WONDER   391 20

TROPICS
    AND IN THE TROPICS TREMBLE THEY WITH LOVE   694 11

TROT
    AS I HEAR THE SHARP CLEAN TROT OF A PONY DOWN THE ROAD   63 9
    WHEN I TROT MY LITTLE PONY THROUGH THE ASPEN-TREES OF T+   409 4
    TRUTHS THAT THE SLY TROT OUT   458 19
    AND THINK HOW WILD ANIMALS TROT WITH SPLENDOUR   530 12
    TROT TROT TROT CORPSE-BODY TO WORK   584 11

TROTH
    THE OTHER HALF OF THE BROKEN COIN OF TROTH   114 19
    OF THE TROTH WITH THE DEAD THAT WE ARE PLEDGED TO KEEP   114 26

TROTS
    SHE TROTS ON BLITHE TOES   386 3

TROTTED
    HAS THE RED WOLF TROTTED EAST AND EAST AND EAST   405 15
    SINCE I TROTTED AT THE TAIL OF THE SUN AS FAR AS EVER T+   405 26

TROTTING
    TWO BROWN PONIES TROTTING SLOWLY   121 28
    HER NIMBLE SHADOW TROTTING   222 13
    TROTTING EAST AND EAST AND EAST TILL THE SUN HIMSELF WE+   404 15
    BEHOLD ME TROTTING AT EASE BETWIXT THE SLOPES OF THE GO+   409 6
    AND THE GENTLE TROTTING OF THE LITTER-BEARERS   703 28

TROT-TROT
    TROT-TROT TO THE MOTTLED FOOT-HILLS CEDAR-MOTTLED AND P+   409 1

TROUBLE
    AS SOME SHOULD HA'E HARDLY A SMITE O' TROUBLE   45 23
    I'M SORRY FOR TH' TROUBLE AY   84 9
    WHY DOES IT TROUBLE ME   106 26
    AT A MOTHER'S KNEES THE TROUBLE   152 20
    THE TREES IN TROUBLE BECAUSE OF AUTUMN   160 5
    NONE OF THE TROUBLE HE'S LED TO STALL   219 28
    HE DOES NOT EVEN TROUBLE TO ANSWER WOMAN WHAT HAVE   357 3
    THE TROUBLE IS EVERYBODY THINKS THEY'RE JUST AS SUPERIOR   435 10
    EDITOR GOOD MORNING DON'T TROUBLE TO CALL AGAIN WE   582 19
    AND TROUBLE AND DISSOLUTION AND DISTRESS   727 8
    THE TROUBLE ABOUT THOSE THAT SET UP TO BE MORAL JUDGES   836 20
    WHY TROUBLE ABOUT PEOPLE   839 24
    NO GOOD I WARRANT THIS TROUBLE IS SUCH AS SHE   *910 7
    NONE O' THE TROUBLE HE'S LED TO STALL   *944 8

TROUBLED
    THE STARS WATERS TROUBLED FORSAKEN   49 10
    AND I DO TOSS THROUGH THE TROUBLED NIGHT FOR YOU   129 23
    HOW VIVID YOUR TRAVELLING SEEMS NOW IN THE TROUBLED SUN+   354 4
    AND I LIFT MY HEAD UPON THE TROUBLED TANGLED WORLD AND +   *900 1
    AND I LIFT MY HEAD UPON THE TROUBLED TANGLED WORLD AND +   *903 14

TROUBLES
    ALL THE TROUBLES AND ANXIETIES AND PAIN   203 13
    TROUBLES ANXIETIES AND PAINS   203 21

TROUGH
    STOPPED AT A DIM-LIT TROUGH TO DRINK   121 29
    THE TROUGH BEFORE ME   349 7
    OVER THE EDGE OF THE STONE TROUGH   349 11

TROUSER-LEGS
    AND CATCHES HER TROUSER-LEGS IN HIS BEAK   362 21

TROUSERS
    OF TROUSERS FRAY   145 20
    STEPPING WEE MITE IN HIS LOOSE TROUSERS   355 21

TRUCK
    THE INVISIBLE GODS HAVE NO MORAL TRUCK WITH US   607 32

TRUDGE
    AS THA NE'D TRUDGE UP 'ERE   79 18
    AS THA NE'D TRUDGE UP HERE   *921 14

TRUE
    THOUGH IF IT'S TRUE THEY'LL TURN 'IM OUT   78 13
    AN' IF IT'S NOT TRUE YOU MAY BACK YOUR LIFE   78 15
    BUT TELL ME ISN'T IT TRUE   79 26
    BUT THA'LL HA'E TER PROMISE TER BE TRUE TER ME   82 27
    TIME WITH TRUE LONGING WHAT I WAS TO YOU   91 18
    I SHALL ALWAYS BE TRUE TO YOU   102 2
    WHEREIN I AM TRUE   102 6
    IT'S TRUE THA KNOWS   139 14
    IS IT TRUE THAT THE LITTLE WEED   172 15
    OF QUESTING BRILLIANT SOULS GOING OUT WITH THEIR TRUE   221 27
    HOW HAPPY I AM HOW MY HEART IN THE WIND RINGS TRUE   251 11
    THEY THINK THAT WE ADORE THEM ALAS WOULD IT WERE TRUE   270 1
    OH IF IT BE TRUE AND THE LIVING DARKNESS OF THE BLOOD O+   273 31
    TRUE WE'VE GOT ALL THESE THINGS   452 9
    TO BE TRUE TO THE NATURE OF IT ITS RESERVE ITS SENSITIV+   464 20
    AND THEN PERHAPS WE SHALL KNOW TRUE SEX IN OURSELVES   472 13
    AND IT IS TRUE   503 11
    I WISH THEY'D BE TRUE TO THEIR OWN VARIATION AS WATER IS   505 20
    AND THEIR TRUE MALENESS IS GONE   535 12
    AND WHAT A SENSE OF TRUE HUMOUR THEY'VE GOT HA-HA   583 21
    YES IT IS TRUE I FIGHT ALL THE TIME   606 14
    THOSE WHO ARE NEITHER BOURGEOIS NOR BOLSHEVIST BUT TRUE+   666 2
    TRUE YOU CAN'T PRODUCE THE BEST WITHOUT ATTENDING TO TH+   668 2
    IT IS TRUE I SAID   735 3
    AND THIS I HOLD IS THE TRUE HISTORY OF EVOLUTION   761 13
    AND IT IS MUCH MORE DIFFICULT AND DELICATE TO BE TRUE   775 16
    TO GROW UP TRUE HUNDRED-PER-CENT AMERICAN   778 2
    WHEN YOU SPEAK TRUE AND TRUE IT IS BRIGHT ON YOUR LIPS +   800 8
    TRUE MEN LOOK UP AT THE DAWN   810 8
    OF WHOM I THINK THIS IS TRUE   833 7
    AND TRUE ENOUGH HE WAS INFINITELY THE MORE MANLY FELLOW   842 24
    KILLS ENTIRELY THE TRUE EXPERIENCE OF SEX   843 18
    SOME OF THEM WERE QUITE TRUE   845 19
    THOUGH IF IT'S TRUE THEY'LL TURN HIM OUT   *920 5
    AN' IF IT'S NOT TRUE I'D BACK MY LIFE   *920 7
    BUT TELL ME ISN'T IT TRUE   *921 22
    OF QUESTING BRILLIANT THINGS YOU JOY YOU TRUE   *945 13
    TOO GREAT A BOOR TO REALISE HIS TRUE FEELINGS   *949 1
    FROM THEIR TREE OF LIFE AND VILLAGES WHOLE CITIES LIVED+   *950 4

TRUE-LOVE
    MESSAGES OF TRUE-LOVE DOWN THE DUST OF THE HIGHROAD   65 18

TRUELY
    IT TRUELY A GOD-THOUGHT DIMINISHED   *927 31

TRUISM
    AN OLD FRENCHMAN UTTERED THE TRUISM   641 17

TRULY
    DID I SHIVER NAY TRULY I DO NOT KNOW   87 3
    STILL THE JOY WAS THERE ALSO YOU SPOKE TRULY   207 10
    AND TRULY I WAS AFRAID I WAS MOST AFRAID   350 19
    EXISTS NO MORE NOR EVER TRULY EXISTED   453 17
    FOR WHILE WE HAVE SEX IN THE MIND WE TRULY HAVE NONE IN   471 24
    THERE'S A LIST KEPT OF THE TRULY SUPERIOR   548 22
    THAT WHICH IS TRULY MAN AND THAT WHICH IS ROBOT   636 11

TRUMP
    IT IS YOUR TRUMP   333 13
    IT IS YOUR HATEFUL LITTLE TRUMP   333 14

TRUNDLING
    LIKE A TRUNDLING PROJECTILE SWIFTLY WHIRLING UP   397 22

TRUNK
    BLACK RUSTED IRON TRUNK   300 27
    ELEPHANT ADVANCING HIS FRONTAL BONE HIS TRUNK CURLED   387 7
    ALL AGOG AND CURLING UP HER TRUNK   426 12
    DOWN THE TRUNK OF THE SLIPPERY TREE   552 6
    THE BRAIN OF THE MACHINE KNOWS THE LIMBS AND TRUNK OF   635 21

TRUNK-CURL
    WATCHING AND HARDLY SEEING THE TRUNK-CURL APPROACH AND   388 9

TRUNK-LIPPED
    AND TRUNK-LIPPED IN THE NIGHT   383 15

TRUNKS
    WHEN THEY LIFT THEIR TRUNKS AND SCREAM ALOUD   70 11
    BLACK ALMOND TRUNKS IN THE RAIN   300 20
    ALMOND TRUNKS CURVING BLACKLY IRON-DARK CLIMBING THE   300 24
    ELEPHANTS AFTER ELEPHANTS CURL THEIR TRUNKS VAST SHADOWS   388 1
    AND CURLING THEIR PRECIOUS LIVE TRUNKS LIKE AMMONITES   445 14

TRUST
    PUT TRUST THEN NOW IN THE BLACK-BOUGHED TREE   114 9
    O RIPPLING HARD FIRE OF COURAGE O FUSING OF HOT TRUST   440 13
    TRUST THE MILLS OF GOD THOUGH THEY GRIND EXCEEDING SMALL   441 14
    IF YOU WANT TO HAVE SEX YOU'VE GOT TO TRUST   466 1
    TRUST IT YOU MUST YOU MUST   466 6
    THAT IS THE CRYSTAL OF PEACE THE SLOW HARD JEWEL OF TRU+   477 17
    IS THERE A SAPPHIRE OF MUTUAL TRUST A BLUE SPARK   478 6
    WE MUST HAVE THE COURAGE OF MUTUAL TRUST   487 21
    WITHOUT A BIT OF COMMON TRUST IN ONE ANOTHER WE CAN'T   522 19
    OH WE'VE GOT TO TRUST   561 1

TRUST
  BARGAINING TRUST   561   5
  BUT A BIGGER TRUST   561   8
  A TRUST OF THE SUN   561   9
  OH DON'T YOU TRUST ME   561 14
  BUT I THINK YOU MAY TRUST   561 19
  WHY THEN TRUST IT IT FORMS   561 26
  HE SAID TO ME YOU DON'T TRUST ME   603   1
  SINCE THERE WAS NO CIRCUMSTANCE REQUIRING TRUST BETWEEN   603   7
  IN WHOM I CAN TRUST   672 29
  THAT THE OLD DARK FATHERS SHOULD NOT TRUST THESE ARTISTS   778   4
  THE QUICK KINDLING SPARK OF A GENEROUS TRUST   855   8

TRUSTED
  WHEN WE HAVE TRUSTED OURSELVES ENTIRELY   *960 23

TRUSTFUL
  TILL HE'S GOT A WOMAN A BIT SOFT AND TRUSTFUL   *948 15

TRUTH
  HIS TRUTH TO ME AND I   59 30
  AS STOUT AS THE TRUTH MY SIRS AN' 'IS FACE   79   6
  I'LL WHISPER THE GHOSTLY TRUTH TO YOU   227 27
  IS STILL THE TRUTH ABOUT LIFE   449 17
  AND HAVE A COOL SENSE OF TRUTH INHUMAN TRUTH AT LAST   481 23
  THE COOL COOL TRUTH OF PURE VITALITY   481 27
  ENTERING IN SHOCKS OF TRUTH UNFOULED BY LIES   482   2
  AND THE PASSION OF TRUTH IS THE EMBRACE BETWEEN MAN AND   482 12
  OLD TRUTH OLD TEACHING OF ANY SORT   495 14
  BECAUSE TO TELL THE TRUTH I HAVE ENOUGH AS I AM   498   6
  PONDERING THIS NEW TRUTH OF THE SENSATIONAL YOUNG I SAID   532   1
  THEN I SAY TO MYSELF AM I ALSO DEAD IS THAT THE TRUTH   629 22
  AND THEN TRUTH MUCH MORE BITTER TO ACCEPT   636   7
  IS THE SENSE OF TRUTH   653   6
  BEFORE YOU CAN FEEL TRUTH   653 10
  AND IF YOU CAN'T FEEL TRUTH YOU CAN'T HAVE ANY OTHER   653 11
  THE PROFOUND SENSUAL EXPERIENCE OF TRUTH YEA THIS IS   653 13
  EXCEPT TRUTH   661 12
  BE VERY STILL AND TRY AND GET AT THE TRUTH   661 13
  THE TRUTH OF YESTERDAY BECOMES A LIE TOMORROW   661 17
  AND WE LIVE BY THE LETTER OF TRUTH   661 19
  AND TREMBLES WITH A SENSE OF TRUTH PRIMORDIAL CONSCIOUS+   844 25
  AS STOUT AS THE TRUTH MY SIRS AN' 'IS FACE   *921   2
  COILS AND RECOILS SENSITIVE TO LIFE AND CONSCIOUS OF TR+   *952   8

TRUTHS
  TRUTHS THAT THE SLY TROT OUT   458 19

TRY
  'APPEN I CAN IF I TRY   82 26
  HUSH WE TRY   88 13
  AND FROM THE SWIRLING ANGRY FOLK THAT TRY   89 24
  I TRY TO REMEMBER IT IS ALSO WELL BETWEEN US   208 10
  AND I JUT AGAINST YOU IF I TRY TO MOVE FOR YOU ARE EVER+   289   7
  MIGHTN'T WE TRY   404 23
  DON'T SAY YOU CAN'T START IN AND TRY   458   9
  DONE YOUR OWN LITTLE BIT MADE YOUR OWN LITTLE TRY   459 19
  BREAK THE CAGE THEN START IN AND TRY   485   9
  AS THEY TRY TO SCREW EVERYBODY ELSE DOWN WITH THEIR WILL   502 12
  WE'LL TRY TO ACT UP SUBLIME   573   4
  BUT DON'T TRY IT ON OH NEVER START   575 24
  I'M YOUR BRITISH BOY AND I DID BUT TRY   577 10
  THOUGH YOU BLOODY OUTSIDERS HAD BETTER NOT TRY IT ON   618 13
  OR MUST HE TRY TO AMPUTATE HIMSELF FROM THE IRON-ENTANG+   632   3
  IF I TRY LOVING THEM I FALL INTO THEIR ROBOT JIG-JIG-JIG   645   7
  BE VERY STILL AND TRY AND GET AT THE TRUTH   661 13
  AND IF YOU TRY TO GET THEM OUT   675   7
  BECAUSE THEY ONLY TRY TO MAKE WOMEN AND LOVE AND SEX   838   7
  YOUR FEET AND TOUCHING YOUR ANKLES TRY   887 16
  WITH THEIR LITTLE PALE SIGNS ON THE WALL TO TRY US   *929 24
  WOULD GLADLY HAVE OFFERED MY BREAST FOR HER TREAD TO TRY   *934 12

TRYING
  THINK OF ME HERE IN THE LIBRARY TRYING AND TRYING A SON+   57 21
  MY SOUL TO SEE YOU SETTLING AND TRYING TO CLIMB   221 23
  I STAND IN A CHILL OF ANGUISH TRYING TO SAY   225 31
  TRYING TO DRIVE HIM THROUGH THE WINDOW   344   2
  IN VAIN TRYING TO WAKE THE MORROW   371 23
  TRYING TO LOOK LIKE A PELICAN   413 13
  HIS MOTHER LIBERTY TRYING ALWAYS TO TEACH HIM TO COO   413 22
  THEN TRYING AGAIN   457 16
  I AM TRYING NOW TO LEARN NEVER   500   8
  WITH THE EFFORT OF TRYING TO LOVE PEOPLE   506 26
  SO LEAVE OFF TRYING TO PUT THE ROBBIE BURNS TOUCH   540 25
  AND TRYING TO MAKE YOU AGREE   555   2
  EACH SIDE TRYING TO MURDER THE OTHER SIDE   715   3
  HIS HELMET OFF AND WIPES HIS HAIR TRYING   733 21
  MY HEART TO SEE YOU SETTLING AND TRYING TO CLIMB   *945   9

TRYIN'
  TRYIN' TO KEEP OFF 'N HIM A BIT O' TH' WET   *910 29

TUATHA DE DANAAN
  NIGHT FOLK TUATHA DE DANAAN DARK GODS GOVERN HER SLEEP   213 25

TUBE
  YOU CAN'T SIT ON A BUS NOR IN THE TUBE   434   2

TUBES
  THEY TAKE SUGAR FROM THE TALL TUBES OF THE CANE   793 20

TUBING
  AND THE REDDENED LIMBS RED INDIA-RUBBER TUBING INFLATED   625 21

TUBS
  ARE DUCKING THEIR HEADS IN THE WATER TUBS AT THE GATE   732 19

TUCKED
  WITH YOUR TAIL TUCKED A LITTLE ON ONE SIDE   354 19

TUFT
  AT LAST THE NARCISSUS LIFTED A TUFT OF FIVE-POINT STARS   683   2

TUFTS
  HE CLOUTS THE TUFTS OF FLOWERS   244 14

TUG
  THIS IS WHY I TUG AT THEM INDIVIDUALLY WITH MY ARM ROUND   288   8
  WATCHING THY GREAT SOUL TUG WITHIN THE LEASH   879 16

TUGGED
  HOW LONG HAVE THEY TUGGED THE LEASH AND STRAINED APART   74   8
  HOW LONG HAVE THEY TUGGED THE LEASH AND STRAINED APART   *895 16
  HOW LONG HAVE THEY TUGGED THE LEASH AND STRAINED APART   *904   5

TULIPS
  HURT AT THE CHALK-COLOURED TULIPS AND THE EVENING-GREEN   153 12
  FROM THE TULIPS COLOURED WITH CHALK AND THE DULL GRASS'+   867   4

TUMBLED
  THE HOURS HAVE TUMBLED THEIR LEADEN MONOTONOUS SANDS   167   1
  THE HOURS HAVE TUMBLED THEIR LEADEN MONOTONOUS SANDS   167   8
  THE HOURS HAVE TUMBLED THEIR LUSTRELESS TARNISHED SANDS   *896   6
  THE HOURS HAVE TUMBLED THEIR LUSTRELESS TARNISHED SANDS   *896 13
  WITH LIFE TILL THE EARTH AND THE SKY HAVE TUMBLED   *937 18

TUMBLING
  FLESH FLAMEY AND A LITTLE HEROIC EVEN IN A TUMBLING CLO+   445 28
  AND TUMBLING WRIGGLING DOWN THE SKY   647 15

TUM-TIDDLY-UM
  NOW THERE SHALL BE TUM-TIDDLY-UM AND TUM-TIDDLY-UM   690 30

TUMULT
  WAKE OF A TUMULT NOW SPENT AND GONE   53 17
  WAKE OF THE HUSHED TUMULT NOW SPENT AND GONE   *906   8

TUNE
  OF THE NIGHT IN HIS SOUL AND NONE OF THE TUNE   130 14
  LIKE A LOST TUNE   158 24
  SO LONG AS YOU TUNE YOUR TURN-TURN LYRE   681   2
  TUNE   755 21
  PASS LIKE A TUNE THE SALLOW'S GOLDEN NOTES   *941 24

TUNES
  WINDS OF HEAVEN FAN THE LEAVES OF THE TREE LIKE FLAMES +   615   4
  TUNES HER VOICE MANY NOTED   862   8
  AND MY MOTHER'S TUNES ARE DEVOURED OF THIS MUSIC'S RAVA+   940 23

TUNNY-FISH
  SHE IS THE FEMALE TUNNY-FISH ROUND AND HAPPY AMONG THE +   695 11

TUPPENNY
  EVERY LORDLY TUPPENNY FOREIGNER FROM THE HOTELS FATTENI+   312 23

TUPPING
  TILL SUDDENLY IN THE SPASM OF COITION TUPPING LIKE A JE+   365   7

TUPS
  SO HE TUPS AND SCREAMS   365 22

TURBULENT
  AND UNDERNEATH THE GREAT TURBULENT EMOTIONS OF LOVE THE+   844   7
  NOW I AM ON THE STRAND OF A TURBULENT SEA   *894 19
  A TOSSING SEA OF TURBULENT STRIFE WHERE NOW   *894 20
  THE SURGE AND TIDE OF LIFE IN THE TURBULENT CLASS   *895 10

TURBULENTLY
  AND LOSE SIGHT OF ME THE ME WHOM YOU TURBULENTLY LOVED   477 26

TURD
  NOT JUST A GOOD TURD   564 10

TURDS
  AND BE USED TO THE TURDS   565   8

TURF
  LOW-ROUNDED ON THE MOURNFUL TURF THEY HAVE BITTEN DOWN +   33   6
  ON THE TURF I STAND WATCHING MY OWN WHITE SHADOW QUIVER+   33 19
  THEIR DROPPINGS AMONG THE TURF   321 14
  NOW THAT THE GRAVE IS MADE AND LIDDED OVER WITH TURF   411 28
  SIEGMUND DEAR WHAT ARE YOU DOING LYING WITH YOUR FACE O+   871 33
  LYING RIGID AND SILENT WITH YOUR FACE ON THE SHORT SEA +   871 34
  SIEGMUND LIFT UP YOUR FACE AGAIN OFF THE TURF   871 36

TURGID
  AND TURGID SORROW   116 20
  THE TURGID ELECTRIC ACHE AWAY   117 29
  MAKING THEM SWELL WITH TURGID UNGOVERNABLE STRENGTH   241 20
  BUT DRAW THE TURGID PAIN   *929 27

TURKEY
  BUT WATCH A TURKEY PRANCING LOW ON EARTH   371   3
  DRUM AND THE TURKEY ONRUSH   371   9
  OR A GIZZARD LIKE A TURKEY   837 16

TURKEY-COCK
  TURKEY-COCK TURKEY-COCK   371 18
  AWAITING THE CRY OF THE TURKEY-COCK   371 37
  SLAG-WATTLED TURKEY-COCK   372   3

TURMOIL
  WHERE HER BOSOM SOFTENS TOWARDS ME AND THE TURMOIL HAS   250   7
  TO THE RECKLESS EXTRAVAGANT TURMOIL OF LIVING THE STRIFE   *895 13

TURN
  I MUST FOLD MY HANDS AND TURN MY FACE TO THE FIRE   47   2
  TEARS AND SWORDS TO MY HEART ARROWS NO ARMOUR WILL TURN+   57 23
  OF THE DARK-GREEN HILLS NEW CALVES IN SHED PEEWITS TURN+   57 27
  CROUCHING AS LITTLE HOUSES CROUCH UNDER THE MIST WHEN I+   63 23
  AND SO IT IS EBB-TIME THEY TURN THE EYES BENEATH THE BU+   67   1
  THOUGH IF IT'S TRUE THEY'LL TURN 'IM OUT   78 13
  TURN THY MOUTH ON A WOMAN LIKE THAT   80 19
  THEY'LL TURN THEE OUT O' TH' FORCE I DOUBT ME IF THEY D+   83 16
  THE SUN FROM THEIR NEIGHBOUR EITHER NOR BE SMOTHERED IN+   93 22
  WHITHER I TURN AND SET   99 23
  I LONGED TO TASTE I LONGED TO TURN   123 27
  YOU WOULD NOT TURN AND ANSWER ME   130 27
  I CEASE I TURN PALE   133 28
  I CEASE I TURN PALE   133 33
  THEN I WOULD TURN ROUND   134 11
  I TURN AND RUN   143 17
  TURN AWAY   178 28
  STILL IN FULL FLIGHT EXTINCT SHALL I THEN TURN   195 23
  TURN AND ABOUT   199   8
  EVEN THEN IT IS DARK BEHIND YOU TURN ROUND MY WIFE   211 17
  I DARE NOT TURN ROUND   212 16
  IF I TURN QUICKLY I AM TERRIFIED FEELING SPACE SURROUND+   222 23
  THAT MY FINGERS SHOULD TURN INTO THESE FLAMES   241 22
  BUT COME GIVE US OUR TURN   273 13
  GIVE US OUR TURN GIVE US A CHANCE LET OUR HOUR STRIKE   273 21
  LET THE DARKNESS TURN VIOLET WITH RICH DAWN   273 23
  BEHOLD MY EYES TURN TAWNY YELLOW   301 22
  HIS HORNS TURN AWAY FROM THE ENEMY   327   6
  YOU TURN YOUR HEAD TOWARDS YOUR TAIL AND SMILE   332 11
  DO YOU WONDER AT THE WORLD AS SLOWLY YOU TURN YOUR   353 10
  TURN HIM ON HIS BACK   355 27
  SO TURN HIM OVER ON HIS TOES AGAIN   356   5
  TURN FEET APART   389 10
  AND THEN TURN TAIL TO THE NEXT COMER FOR A NEW DOLLOP   396 23
  THEY'RE AFTER WHAT THEY CAN GET AND DON'T YOU TURN TAIL   399 30
  AND DIDN'T YOU TURN YOUR EYES UP AT ME THEN   400   9
  WATCH HIM TURN INTO A MESS EITHER A FOOL OR A BULLY   431   7
  THE WORM THAT IS TOO CUNNING TO TURN   432 36
  AND THEN TURN ROUND AND EMBRACE THE EXTANT BODY OF LIFE   482   4
  OF ENGLAND WITH THE GUTS TO TURN ROUND ON HIM AIMING   494 11
  BUT WHEN MEN TURN WILLY WET-LEGS   538 18
  AND TURN THE POOR SILK GLOVE INTO A LUSTY SOW'S EAR   538 22
  HOW THEY HATE THE WOMEN'S EFFORTS TO TURN THEM   538 24
  IT MAKES YOU TURN GREEN   551 16
  THEN I SAW HIM TURN TO GLANCE AGAIN SURREPTITIOUSLY   604   4
  IT IS LUCIFER'S TURN THE TURN OF THE SON OF THE MORNING   614   9
  AND TURN ONCE MORE TO MEN TO SAVE THEM PERSEUS ST GEORGE   619 26
  THE MACHINES WILL TURN TO RUN INTO ONE ANOTHER   624 26
  IN MARLBOROUGH ROAD AND IT IS NOW HIS TURN   633 19
  TURN AWAY O TURN AWAY MAN OF FLESH   642   5
  WHICH HE WAS GOING TO TURN ROUND   672 10
  TURNING TO DEATH AS I TURN TO BEAUTY   676 22
  ALL THINGS THAT TURN TO THEE   704 18
  LET US TURN BACK LEST WE SHOULD ALL BE LOST   737 12
  THEN WE SHALL TURN US HOME AGAIN TO LIFE   740 22
  I TURN TOWARDS THE BITTER BLACKENING WIND   745 24
  YOU NOW AS YOU TURN YOUR FACE TOWARDS THE SKY   750 14
  BE CAREFUL HOW YOU TURN HIM INTO A HUNDRED-PER-CENT   776 19
  TURN THE POLES THE GERMS THE ENGLISH THE ITALIANS   777   1
  TURN THEM INTO HUNDRED-PER-CENT AMERICANS   777   3
  JUST TURN YOUR EYES THIS WAY MEXICANOS   790 20
  I'LL TURN THEIR BLOOD LIKE SOUR MILK ROTTEN WITH THUNDER   792   6
  TO WITHDRAW HIS WARMTH FROM YOUR FEET SO YOUR FEET TURN+   797   3
  I AM ABOUT TO TELL THE DRAGON OF THE WATERS TO TURN ROU+   797   5
  I TELL YOU THE DAY SHOULD NOT TURN INTO GLORY   799 25
  AND THE NIGHT SHOULD NOT TURN DEEP   799 26
  SAVE FOR THE MORNING AND EVENING STARS UPON WHICH THEY +   799 27
  WHEN YOU TURN TO YOUR WIVES AS BRAVE MEN TURN TO THEIR +   800 12
  STARTLING MY HORSE WHO STIRS AND WOULD TURN HER ABOUT   858 28
  COME ON TURN HOME OLD LASS ARE WE WASTED TOO   859 25
  NOW SEE HER TURN TO FLEE   861 19
  TO HELP HIM LIFT THE WELTERING DARKNESS TURN   872   3
  AND I WILL LEAVE YOU WHO WOULD MAKE ME TURN   876   6
  AND SHALL I SEE HIM NEVER NOR WILL HE TURN   876 23
  THEY SHOULD FLUTTER AND TURN HIS WAY AND SAVING THE FRE+   877 30
  AS BIRDS WHO ARE STEALING TURN AND FLEE   *899 13
  AS BIRDS WHO ARE STEALING TURN AND FLEE   *902 25
  THOUGH IF IT'S TRUE THEY'LL TURN HIM OUT   *920   5
  TURN THY MOUTH ON A WOMAN LIKE HER   *922 19
  AS YOU CROUCH AND TURN AWAY FROM ME   *931   2
  AND SO I SIT AND TURN THE BOOK OF GRAY   *939   1

TURNED
  I CAME TO THE BOYS WITH LOVE DEAR AND ONLY THEY TURNED +   92 21
  SHE TURNED HER FLUSHED FACE TO ME FOR THE GLINT   125   7
  IN BLONDE AND WHITE ON THE FLOOR NOR EVEN TURNED   156   8
  I QUAILED AT MY APPOINTED FUNCTION TURNED POLTROON   194 29
  SO SHE TURNED AND SAID TO HER HUSBAND   202 11
  THE LITTLE PANSIES BY THE ROAD HAVE TURNED   224 24
  AND SLOWLY TURNED HIS HEAD   350 29
  OVERCAME ME NOW HIS BACK WAS TURNED   351   8
  HAS HE SEEN THE GORGON'S HEAD AND TURNED TO STONE   379   7
  THEN YOU'RE JUST THE WORM THAT HAS TURNED   432   4
  TURNED   432 11
  BUT WHY SHOULD THE WORM THAT HAS TURNED PROTEST SO   432 20
  SO I CAN'T SEE WHERE THE WORM THAT HAS TURNED PUTS ANYT+   432 34
  THE TURNED WORM SHOUTS I BRAVELY BOOZE   433   2
  THE TURNED WORM BOASTS I COPULATE   433   4
  THAT'S TURNED   433   7
  AND DOGS JUMPED THROUGH HOOPS AND TURNED SOMERSAULTS   444 18
  FOOTED CAUTIOUSLY OUT ON THE ROPE TURNED PRETTILY SPUN   444 26
  AND TURNED MY MODEST PENNY   488 16
  AT SIX IN THE MORNING THEY TURNED HIM DOWN   490 11

TURNED
  AND THEY TURNED HIM UP FOR TEA   490 12
  THAT EVER TURNED MEN INTO FIENDS   521   6
  THAT THE DELUGE WILL NEVER BE TURNED ON THEM ONLY AFTER   531   9
  IMMORTAL CAESAR DEAD AND TURNED TO CLAY   545 24
  BUT THEN HE TURNED AND SAID   570   2
  BUT BRITANNIA TURNED PALE AND BEGAN TO FAINT   577   7
  BUT THE BRITISH BOY HE TURNED AND FLED   577 20
  TURNED ON FOR DIFFERENT PURPOSES   625 23
  NOW TURNED AND CAME SLOWLY BACK WITH HER BACK TO THE EV+   693   7
  WHAT IS THE CRIME THAT MY SEED IS TURNED TO BLOOD   742 37
  WHAT IF TURNED AROUND AND SAW ME HERE   752   4
  OF EXPIRATION TURNED INTO THE WORLD AGAIN   784 15
  THEY TURNED NOT AT ALL THEY GLANCED NOT ONE HIS WAY   790 21
  THEN TURNED AWAY AND FORGOT   836 16
  THEN SHE TURNED TO THE OTHER MAN THERE WAS USUALLY ANOT+   842 19
  SHE TURNED AND KISSED HIM AND HIS EYES WERE THE SOUL OF+   865   8
  SHE TURNED HER FLUSHED FACE TOWARDS ME FOR THE GLINT   *935 23

TURNING
  TURNING ITS BROKEN EDGE TO THE DARK ITS SHINE   114 27
  STIRRING WITH EARTH-COLOURED LIFE EVER TURNING AND STIR+   153   6
  I AM AWAY BEYOND THE SCOPE OF THIS TURNING   169   6
  WHAT IS IT IN THE GRAPE TURNING RAISIN   280 14
  THEN ALONG THE DAMP ROAD ALONE TILL THE NEXT TURNING   280 29
  A SUDDEN TURNING UPON ITSELF OF A THING IN THE AIR   341   4
  TURNING HIS BACK ON EVERYTHING   375   4
  TURNING HIS BACK ON US ALL   375 25
  HIS NOSTRILS TURNING BACK TO SNIFF AT EVEN HIMSELF   382   3
  AND TURNING THE DAY SUDDENLY INTO A BLACK TORNADO OF JO+   397   4
  AND WHEN WE ESCAPE LIKE SQUIRRELS FROM TURNING IN THE   482 16
  THAT JESSE BY TURNING MANY   488 18
  EACH ONE TURNING HIS BREAST STRAIGHT TO THE SUN OF SUNS   525 12
  THE MACHINE HAS GOT YOU IS TURNING YOU ROUND AND ROUND   642 20
  TURNING THE BLUE WHEELS OF YOUR OWN HEAVEN   643 21
  TURNING TO DEATH AS I TURN TO BEAUTY   676 22
  A GOD-LOST CREATURE TURNING UPON HIMSELF   700 25
  AND THE TURNING DOWN PLUNGE OF WRITHING OF SELF-KNOWLED+   701   5
  HIM OF THE DISAPPOINTED DEAD HE IS LASHING AND TURNING +   796 31
  SOME TURNING PINK SOME TURNING PURPLE DUSK   824 23
  YOU LOOK LIKE THE TOPPINGEST TOPPING FIFTH-FORM ETON BO+   835 17
  THEIR FEATHERS LIFELESS AND THE ROSE LIGHTS TURNING TO +   855 28
  AND TURNING ROUND IN PAIN FROM THE MUSIC HE   884   9
  FROM SIGHT OF ME WITHOUT ONCE YOUR TURNING   *930 18

TURNIP
  AS THE TURNIP MODELS HIS ROUND ROOT AS THE BUSH MAKES   451 15

TURNS
  TOWARDS HIM THEN SHE TURNS AWAY   42 25
  TURNS BACK HER LIQUID ANGUISHED EYES   43   6
  HIS COMING WITH HIS HAND HE TURNS MY FACE TO HIM   43 26
  AS HE BLENCHES AND TURNS AWAY AND MY HEART STANDS STILL   47 27
  AND THEN HE TURNS AGAIN WITH A LITTLE GLAD   51 17
  THRILL OF HIS WORK HE TURNS AGAIN FROM ME   51 18
  THIS WOMAN WHO LIKES TO LOVE ME BUT SHE TURNS   113 10
  ENDS LIKE A BROKEN LOVE THAT TURNS TO THE DARK OF SLEEP   114 28
  AND THE SUAVE SEA CHUCKLES AND TURNS TO THE MOON   130   2
  WHEN THE SLEEPER STIRS OR TURNS ON THE EBB OF THE FLOOD   145 27
  THE NIGHT TURNS SLOWLY ROUND   169   1
  WILL YOU COME BACK WHEN THE TIDE TURNS   171 24
  AND TURNS HER ROUND ABOUT   200 12
  TURNS ROUND ITS BACK TO THE SUN   215 23
  AND BREATHE DESPAIR THAT TURNS MY LUNGS TO STONE   226 11
  TURNS BACK   226 24
  THEN GAY FEAR THAT TURNS THE TAIL SPRIGHTLY FROM A SHAD+   336 18
  SOMETIMES HE TURNS WITH A START TO FIGHT TO CHALLENGE TO   381   8
  KNOW ME TURNS HER HEAD AND IGNORES ME VULGARLY WITH   384 23
  SHE TURNS HER HEAD AWAY WITH AN OBTUSE FEMALE SORT OF   385   1
  SO SHE WISTFULLY SENSITIVELY SNIFFS THE AIR AND THEN TU+   393 25
  STOPS AGAIN HALF TURNS INQUISITIVE TO LOOK BACK   393 29
  LEAPS UP TO THE SUMMIT OF THE STEM GLEAMS TURNS OVER   476   8
  AND THE SMALL HAWK HIGH UP TURNS ROUND ON THE SLOW PIVO+   496 14
  IT IS THE MOON THAT TURNS THE TIDES   509 20
  ANOTHER LITTLE RUN FOR THEIR MONEY A FEW MORE TURNS OF +   586 18
  SOMETIMES THE SUN TURNS HOSTILE TO MEN   608 20
  THEN THE SUN TURNS HOSTILE TO US   609   1
  WHICH TURNS ON AND ON THE SAME AND IS HELL ON EARTH   662 24
  AS THE PEACOCK TURNS TO THE SUN AND COULD NOT BE MORE S+   683   8
  WHEN THE MIND MAKES A WHEEL WHICH TURNS ON THE HUB OF T+   712 13
  HE DRINKS AND DRINKS THEN TURNS AWAY HIS HEAD   734 29
  BE BRIDEGROOM OR BEST MAN AS THE CASE TURNS OUT   743 20
  NIGHT TURNS UPON ME AND DAY WHO AM THE STAR BETWEEN   800   1
  YET IN THE LITTLE NEW ROAD THE YOUNG WIFE TURNS AWAY   865 13
  SO MY SOUL LIKE A PASSIONATE WOMAN TURNS   *891 29
  THEN HE TURNS AGAIN TO HIS WORK WITH GLEE   *898 28
  WITH GLEE HE TURNS WITH A LITTLE GLAD   *899   1
  ECSTASY OF WORK HE TURNS FROM ME   *899   2
  THEN HE TURNS AGAIN TO HIS WORK WITH GLEE   *902 12
  WITH GLEE HE TURNS WITH A LITTLE GLAD   *902 13
  ECSTASY OF WORK HE TURNS FROM ME   *902 14
  THEN HE TURNS AWAY AND WIPES HER FROM HIS CONSCIOUSNESS   *948 16

TURN-TURN
  SO LONG AS YOU TUNE YOUR TURN-TURN LYRE   681   2

TURRETS
  MY BOOK OF TURRETS AND OF RED-THORN BOWERS   135   3

TURTLES
  IN THE NORTH TO HIDE WHERE THE TURTLES SING   580   6

TUSCAN
  TUSCAN CYPRESSES   296   1
  TUSCAN CYPRESSES   296   5
  TUSCAN CYPRESSES   297   2

TUSCANS
    I DON'T RECOGNIZE MY TUSCANS   846 5
    OH DEAR WHAT'S HAPPENING TO TUSCANS   846 12

TUSCANY
    NOW IN TUSCANY   278 17

TUSK
    THOUGH MAYBE THE MAMMOTH GOT TOO BIG IN TUSK AND TEETH   529 17

TWAIN
    THE MOON IS BROKEN IN TWAIN AND HALF A MOON   114 17
    MY VEIL OF SENSITIVE MYSTERY RENT IN TWAIN   151 19
    INTO TWAIN   280 31
    MY IVORY AND IDOLS SPLIT IN TWAIN   873 30

TWANGED
    WHEN THE BOW-CORD TWANGED   688 25

TWANGLE
    AS THEIR NERVES ARE STRETCHED TILL THEY TWANGLE AND SNAP   616 8

TWAS
    TWAS A TALE SOON TOLD   863 12

'TWAS
    PERHAPS 'TWAS A DREAM OF WARNING   46 27
    MY SIRS BUT I SAY 'TWAS FOR A BLITHER   60 30
    'TWAS I WHOSE FINGERS DID DRAW UP THE YOUNG   156 19
    'TWAS I WHO PLACED THE BLOOM OF MANHOOD ON   156 25
    THAN A DREAM OF YOURS 'TWAS ALL YOU EVER COULD   157 30
    'TWAS YOU WHO KILLED HIM WHEN YOU BOTH CAROUSED   158 3
    'TWAS NOT THAT I WISHED IT   241 21
    WHERE 'TWAS GIVEN US TO REPOSE US   242 30
    WHY 'TWAS ONLY YESTERDAY EVERY MAN TWIRLED   814 28

TWEEDLE-DEE
    WITH ITS TINKLE-WINKLE AND TWEEDLE-DEE   681 3

TWELVE
    WILL IT NEVER FINISH THE TWELVE   63 2
    ITS MOTHER DID SOMETHING TO IT AT ABOUT THE AGE OF TWEL+   841 13

TWELVES
    THREES AND FOURS AND TWELVES   355 24

TWENTIES
    TWENTIES   462 30
    MOURNFUL YOUNG MAN IN YOUR TWENTIES   485 10

TWENTIETH
    AND TWENTIETH WAGON AND HE WILL NOT DRIVE PAST   733 12

TWENTY
    'E'S 'AD TWENTY ACCIDENTS IF 'E'S 'AD ONE   45 27
    BUT 'ER'S OLD MOTHER 'ER'S TWENTY YEAR   77 5
    TWENTY POUND O' THY OWN THA HAST AN' FIFTY POUND HA'E I   83 1
    DECIDES SHE'S HAD TWENTY LOVERS ONLY TO FIND SHE DIDN'T   539 16
    THE SERGEANT SAYS THAT EIGHT AND TWENTY WAGONS   732 1
    HOW NICE TO GET IN THE CAMION AND FOR TWENTY CENTAVOS T+   794 14
    BUT 'ER'S OLD MOTHER 'ER'S TWENTY YEAR   *918 23
    TWENTY POUND O' THY OWN THA HAST AND FIFTY POUND HA'E I   *925 5
    AN' THEN WI' THAT TWENTY POUND WE GI'E 'ER I S'D THINK +   *925 20

TWENTY-FIRST
    SO WHY SHOULD I OR YOU BE THE TWENTY-FIRST   539 18

TWENTY-FIVE
    TO HA' 'TICED A LAD O' TWENTY-FIVE   77 15
    AND ROUND THE EDGES TWENTY-FIVE LITTLE ONES   355 8
    TO HA' 'TICED A LAD O' TWENTY-FIVE   *919 3

TWENTY-FOUR
    THEN TWENTY-FOUR AND A TINY LITTLE KEYSTONE   355 13

TWICE
    TWICE YOU HAVE ISSUED ME   101 24
    TWICE I AM BORN MY DEAREST   102 3
    AND TWICE AFTER WILD KISSES I SAW   103 24
    YOU WOULD THINK TWICE BEFORE YOU TOUCHED A WEASEL ON A   255 22
    IF SUCH THINGS WERE NICE AND WE NEEDN'T THINK TWICE   491 11
    HE LETS YOU HIT HIM TWICE   559 20
    HE WHISTLED TO IT LOUDLY TWICE TILL IT FELL TO HIS HAND   791 2

TWICE-WEEKLY
    WEEKLY OR TWICE-WEEKLY WHISTLE ROUND YOUR BOTTLES   843 9

TWIG
    WITH MARVELLOUS NAKED ASSURANCE EACH SINGLE TWIG   299 26
    EVERY YOUNG TWIG   299 31
    OH WEIRD DEMOS WHERE EVERY TWIG IS THE ARCH TWIG   300 7
    THEN WHEN I DUST YOU A BIT WITH A JUNIPER TWIG   399 12
    PROLIFIC I AM A BLOSSOMING TWIG   888 17

TWIGS
    AT RANDOM DESOLATE TWIGS   51 2
    TWIGS   142 6
    SUBTLY TO THE TWIGS OVERHEAD FAR UP VAST BEAST   385 27
    AND BONES AND TWIGS AND A PERILOUS ASCENT   402 14
    OH WITHERED CRACKLING TWIGS OF BRUSHWOOD PEOPLE   784 20
    MYRIAD MYRIAD DEAD TWIGS OF PALLID AND CHAFING PEOPLE   784 21

TWILIGHT
    OR THERE IN THE WOODS OF THE TWILIGHT WITH NORTHERN WIN+   57 19
    AND DRAWING THE DARKNESS TOGETHER CRUSH FROM IT A TWILI+   92 19
    THE STREET-LAMPS IN THE TWILIGHT HAVE SUDDENLY STARTED +   102 31
    A GIBBOUS MOON HANGS OUT OF THE TWILIGHT   113 17
    FERVOUR WITHIN THE POOL OF HER TWILIGHT   125 34

TWILIGHT
    AND UNDERNEATH A BLUE-GREY TWILIGHT HEAPED   135 5
    GLIMMERED AS FLOWERS THAT IN PERFUME AT TWILIGHT UNFOLD   141 8
    THE HOPELESS WINTRY TWILIGHT FADES   142 21
    AS I MAKE MY WAY IN TWILIGHT NOW TO REST   167 7
    THE LITTLE RIVER TWITTERING IN THE TWILIGHT   203 9
    GONE UNDER THE TWILIGHT   203 14
    ONLY THE TWILIGHT NOW AND THE SOFT SH OF THE RIVER   203 15
    I CAN SEE IT ALL IT IS WHOLE LIKE THE TWILIGHT   203 18
    BY THE ISAR IN THE TWILIGHT   216 19
    BY THE ISAR IN THE TWILIGHT   217 1
    FROM THE TWILIGHT LIKE HALF-SHUT LILIES   227 19
    OUR PALE DAY IS SINKING INTO TWILIGHT   286 21
    IN THE SICILIAN TWILIGHT   377 2
    THROUGH THE SICILIAN TWILIGHT   377 21
    HE FELL TO DUST AS THE TWILIGHT FELL   404 26
    IN THE LAST TWILIGHT   407 8
    TWILIGHT   427 1
    NOR HONKING HORN-LIKE INTO THE TWILIGHT   436 9
    HE MIGHT SAY INTO THE TWILIGHT WHAT IS IT   509 6
    ALL OF TWILIGHT   656 4
    TWILIGHT BETWEEN THEM   693 13
    LO GOD IS ONE GOD BUT HERE IN THE TWILIGHT   693 18
    OF THE TWILIGHT   695 32
    LIKE THE KINGDOM OF THE NIGHTINGALE AT TWILIGHT   704 20
    WHERE THE GREY TWILIGHT OF EVIL SETS IN   711 25
    LAST TWILIGHT OF THE GODS TO FIND AGAIN   737 8
    MAN IN THE TWILIGHT   803 17
    MAN IN THE TWILIGHT   803 20
    IF TWILIGHT CAME IN THE EYES OF WOMEN   840 4
    STARTLING THE THICK-SPUN TWILIGHT THE BELLS SHAKE OUT   858 25
    ONE BROKEN THORN-TREE STILL IN THE TWILIGHT STANDS   *896 14
    A BIG BUD OF MOON HANGS OUT OF THE TWILIGHT   *929 6
    DRY FEVER IN HER POOL OF FULL TWILIGHT   *936 33
    UNDER THE BLUE-GREY TWILIGHT HEAPED   *939 5
    BY THE ISAR IN THE TWILIGHT   *942 5
    BY THE ISAR IN THE TWILIGHT   *942 12
    IN THE TWILIGHT OUR KISSES ACROSS THE ROSES   *942 17
    NOW IN THE TWILIGHT SIT BY THE INVISIBLE SEA   *960 12
    OH THINK OF IT IN THE TWILIGHT PEACEFULLY   *960 18

TWILIGHT'S
    INTO THE TWILIGHT'S EMPTY HALL   42 31

TWILIT
    FIRE HORIZONTAL DECLINING AND EBBING THE TWILIT EBB OF +   67 6
    TO DUST TO ASH ON THE TWILIT FLOOR OF THE DESERT   403 23
    TO THINK OUT IN THE ABSTRACT WHEN ALL WAS TWILIT GREEN +   690 29

'TWILL
    'TWILL NOT BE TOO MANY PRAYERS TO SAY   735 20

TWIN
    ALL ROUND ME ABOVE AND BELOW THE NIGHT'S TWIN CONSCIOUS+   97 23
    TWIN FLESH AND WHAT IS DEATH FOR ME WHAT IS IT   880 4
    TWIN BUBBLES SHADOW-FULL OF MYSTERY AND CHALLENGE IN TH+   *897 30
    TWIN BUBBLES SHADOW-FULL OF MYSTERY AND CHALLENGE IN TH+   *901 7

TWIN-BUBBLING
    TWIN-BUBBLING CHALLENGE AND MYSTERY IN THE FOAM'S   76 3

TWINE
    AS VINES GOING EAGERLY UP THEY TWINE   52 9
    ON HIS BROW WHERE THE CURVED WISPS CLOT AND TWINE   60 3
    SO I LEAD THEM UP SO DO THEY TWINE   *899 23
    SO I LEAD THEM UP SO DO THEY TWINE   *903 2

TWINED
    MY GRAIL A BROWN BOWL TWINED   123 24
    MY GRAIL WHOSE BOWL WAS TWINED   *934 30

TWINKLED
    THE YOUNG GRASS TWINKLED IN THE WIND AND THE SOUND   866 24

TWINKLES
    THE YOUNG GRASS TWINKLES IN THE WIND AND THE SOUND   152 28
    AND THE SKYLARK TWINKLES BLUE   215 10
    ACH ACH NOW INDEED GOD IS BORN HE TWINKLES WITHIN   682 28
    I SAID THIS IS GRASS THAT TWINKLES IN THE DARK   882 15

TWINKLING
    YOUR DEMON RUMP TWINKLING   564 17
    LIKE A GIRL'S TWINKLING MERRIMENT AT NIGHT WHEN THE SEA+   860 16
    HAS STREWN MYRIAD TWINKLING POPPY-PETALS DOWN THE PATH +   860 18

TWINKLIN'
    IS QUIETLY TWINKLIN'   562 18

TWIN-WALLED
    AS IF FROM THE WOMB THE SLOW MOON RISES AS IF THE TWIN-+   88 18

TWIRLED
    WHY 'TWAS ONLY YESTERDAY EVERY MAN TWIRLED   814 28

TWIST
    DART AND TWIST STILL HE MUST GO WITH HIS BELLY ON THE G+   348 12
    AND SNAPS THEM SHARP WITH A LITTLE TWIST OF HER ANACONDA   385 28
    THERE WAS THE FAINTEST TWIST OF MOCKERY IN EVERY FACE   391 16
    TO TWIST AND GROVEL AND BECOME A HEAP OF DIRT   742 2
    IN YOUR SLEEP YOU TWIST YOUR SOUL HURTS YOU   807 30
    HER FINGERS AS IF IT WOULD TWIST   *937 10

TWISTED
    YOU WHO ARE TWISTED IN GRIEF LIKE CRUMPLING BEECH-LEAVES   73 16
    THE THORN-LEAVES CRACKLED AND TWISTED AND SWEATED IN AN+   94 26
    A TWISTED THORN-TREE STILL IN THE EVENING STANDS   167 9
    LIKE IRON IMPLEMENTS TWISTED HIDEOUS OUT OF THE EARTH   300 21
    WITH IRON BRANCHING BLACKLY RUSTED LIKE OLD TWISTED   301 13

TWISTED
  LO I SEE FEAR IN THE TWISTED FACES   460 27
  OF DESIRE IS DISTORTED AND TWISTED AWRY   485 3
  AND STEEL HAS TWISTED THE LOINS OF MAN ELECTRICITY HAS   629 8
  THE THORN-LEAVES CRACKLED AND TWISTED AND SWEATED IN AN+   *897 14
  AND I TWISTED THEM OVER THE BROKEN LEAVES INTO UNBREAKA+   *926 17

TWISTING
  WRITHING TWISTING SUPERPENETRATED   207 26
  BEHOLD MY HAIR TWISTING AND GOING BLACK   301 21
  BUT NOT THE JAGGLING AND TWISTING OF ALREADY EXISTENT I+   673 8
  WRITHING AND TWISTING IN ALL THE REVOLUTIONS   701 19
  LIFE TWISTING ITS CRAZED MACHINERY   887 5

TWISTS
  OF DESIRES IN THE LOINS' DARK TWISTS   461 4

TWITCH
  A TWITCH A TWITTER AN ELASTIC SHUDDER IN FLIGHT   341 11

TWITCHES
  TWITCHES AND EBBS HITTING WASHING INWARDLY SILVERILY   453 20
  A POOR ROAN THING ITS HIND LEG TWITCHES   734 6

TWITCHING
  TWITCHING REMARK   113 24

TWITCHY
  WITH A TWITCHY NERVOUS INTOLERABLE FLIGHT   342 22

TWITTER
  A TWITCH A TWITTER AN ELASTIC SHUDDER IN FLIGHT   341 11

TWITTERED
  WANTON SPARROWS THAT TWITTERED WHEN MORNING LOOKED IN   71 13

TWITTERING
  IN SCARLET ALIVE WITH THE BIRDS' BRIGHT TWITTERING   72 22
  BUT WHO ARE YOU TWITTERING TO AND FRO   131 17
  THE LITTLE RIVER TWITTERING IN THE TWILIGHT   203 9

'TWIXT
  WITH GENTLENESS CAME I WITH MY HEART 'TWIXT MY HANDS LI+   92 22
  AND NAKEDLY NOTHING 'TWIXT WORLD AND HEAVEN TWO CREATUR+   98 4
  SURE AND A TOWER OF STRENGTH 'TWIXT THE WALLS OF HER BR+   249 12
  IS IT A TOSS-UP 'TWIXT THEE AN' ME   *924 4
  IT'S NO TOSS-UP 'TWIXT THEE AN' ME   *924 5

TWO
  WITHIN THE HOUSE TWO VOICES AROSE A SLENDER LASH   36 13
  SIGNALLING THOSE TWO KISSES   37 17
  OR LIKE TWO BUTTERFLIES THAT SETTLE ON A GLASS   65 3
  WITH TWO LITTLE BARE WHITE FEET UPON MY KNEE   65 7
  TWO STREAMING PEACOCKS GONE IN A CLOUD   70 17
  IN A WIK OR TWO   79 28
  LEANING IN YOUR ROOM LIKE TWO TIGER-LILIES CURVING   91 12
  TWO TOWNS   97 19
  AND NAKEDLY NOTHING 'TWIXT WORLD AND HEAVEN TWO CREATUR+   98 4
  MELTS IN THE AIR WHILE TWO BLACK BIRDS   100 3
  TWO AND TWO ARE THE FOLK THAT WALK   106 11
  LOST AND YET STILL CONNECTED AND BETWEEN THE TWO   115 2
  TWO BROWN PONIES TROTTING SLOWLY   121 28
  TWO HARD CRUDE PAWS IN HUNGER ON THE LONELY   127 27
  BUT OH THE PALMS OF HIS TWO BLACK HANDS ARE RED   135 22
  PALE-BLURRED WITH TWO ROUND BLACK DROPS AS IF IT MISSED   141 17
  TWO NAKED FACES ARE SEEN   144 26
  TWO PALE CLOTS SWEPT BY THE LIGHT OF THE CARS   144 28
  THE MUD-WEED OPENING TWO PALE SHADOWLESS STARS   145 3
  OVER THE PALLOR OF ONLY TWO FACES   145 4
  SHOWS IN ONLY TWO SAD PLACES   145 6
  OVER THE PALLOR OF ONLY TWO PLACES   145 12
  OVER TWO SHADOWLESS SHAMELESS FACES   146 1
  OF COMING MINE AND OF THE TWO OF US   156 16
  BETWEEN TWO VALVES OF DARKNESS   205 5
  TWO WHITE ONES SHARP VINDICATED   210 16
  TO BRING TOGETHER TWO STRANGE SPARKS BEGET   218 20
  TWO GREAT DRAGON-FLIES WRESTLING   224 2
  THREE OF THEM BLACK IN SHADOW TWO OF THEM BRIGHT   224 10
  THERE ARE ONLY TWO THINGS NOW   238 1
  AND WE THE TWO RIPE PIPS   238 5
  WE TWO FOLDED SO SMALL TOGETHER   247 19
  IN A MOTION HUMAN INHUMAN TWO AND ONE   252 10
  TWO PRIMARY INSTANCES   263 19
  THEN WE SHALL BE TWO AND DISTINCT WE SHALL HAVE EACH OUR   266 31
  TWO OF US UNUTTERABLY DISTINGUISHED AND IN UNUTTERABLE +   267 22
  TWO SPECTRES   292 9
  THOSE TWO ENFRANCHISED WOMEN   309 9
  AFTER TWO THOUSAND YEARS   327 19
  ON TWO WINGS LIKE A PAIR OF COMPASSES   329 7
  ON EACH SIDE TWO ABOVE ON EACH SIDE TWO BELOW   355 32
  THEIR TWO SHELLS LIKE DOMED BOATS BUMPING   361 22
  TWO TORTOISES   361 27
  WHILST BETWEEN THE TWO ALONG THE TENSE ARCH OF YOUR BACK   370 22
  STARING TWO WAYS AT ONCE TO RIGHT AND LEFT   373 13
  WITH IRON BETWEEN YOUR TWO EYES   373 17
  YOU NEVER LOOK AT THE SUN WITH YOUR TWO EYES   373 23
  AND TIED IN A KNOT INSIDE DEAD-LOCKED BETWEEN TWO DESIR+   379 12
  IN ELEPHANTS AND THE EAST ARE TWO DEVILS IN ALL MEN MAY+   390 5
  AND A KICK OR TWO   400 21
  TWO MEN   401 5
  TWO MEXICANS STRANGERS EMERGING OUT OF THE DARK AND   401 12
  HER ROUND FINE-FASHIONED HEAD WITH TWO DEAD EARS   402 3
  SPARE A MILLION OR TWO OF HUMANS   402 30
  EAGLES WITH TWO HEADS EAGLES WITH ONE PRESENTLY EAGLES   413 7
  FLAT PERSONALITIES IN TWO DIMENSIONS IMPONDERABLE AND   446 6
  FIDELITY AND LOVE ARE TWO DIFFERENT THINGS LIKE A FLOWER   476 1
  FOR A DAY FOR TWO DAYS AND WITHDRAW SLOWLY VANISH AGAIN   476 14
  OF TWO HUMAN HEARTS TWO ANCIENT ROCKS A MAN'S HEART   477 15

TWO
  I KNOW A THING OR TWO ABOUT LOVE   490 3
  WATER IS H2O HYDROGEN TWO PARTS OXYGEN ONE   515 11
  THE ATOM LOCKS UP TWO ENERGIES   515 14
  WHICH THREATEN TO TEAR THE WORLD IN TWO BETWEEN   516 22
  THEY HAVE ONLY TWO MEASURES   527 15
  FOR THEIR MIDDLENESS IS ONLY AN UNREALITY SEPARATING TWO   527 26
  WE'LL SHOW 'EM A THING OR TWO NEVER YOU DOUBT   573 22
  AND THAT HELD HER SPELLBOUND FOR TWO SECONDS   604 22
  THE HUMAN WILL IS FREE ULTIMATELY TO CHOOSE ONE OF TWO +   617 12
  AT TWO POUNDS A WEEK   643 25
  THERE ARE TWO CLASSES OF MEN   649 19
  AND BETWEEN THE TWO BLADES OF THIS PAIR OF SHEARS PROPE+   663 16
  THE WORLD WILL BE TORN IN TWO   663 27
  LIKE THE TWO LIONS WHO DEVOURED ONE ANOTHER AND LEFT TH+   665 2
  AND WHEN AT LAST MAN STOOD ON TWO LEGS AND WONDERED   683 11
  IN THE FLAT RECURRENT BREAKERS OF MY TWO FEET   705 13
  TO THE WHITE-TREADING WAVES OF TWO SALT FEET   705 17
  BETWEEN THE TWO GREAT ONES FIRE AND THE WET   705 22
  THE TWO GREAT AND MOVING ONES FIRE AND THE YIELDING WET   706 12
  WITH HIS KEY TO THE TWO DARK DOORS   710 26
  WHEN STRIKE IS A THING OF TWO   714 22
  TODAY IS EASTER SUNDAY CHRIST RISEN TWO DAYS AGO WAS   777 22
  STARING TWO WAYS AT ONCE TO RIGHT AND LEFT   781 19
  WITH IRON BETWEEN YOUR TWO EYES   781 23
  AND TWO MEN LOOKED UP   791 9
  ARE THERE TWO OF YOU AWAKE   791 11
  THE STAR COMES OUT BETWEEN THE TWO   802 27
  THE LIGHT WHICH IS FED FROM TWO VESSELS   810 27
  YET IT'S GOT TWO FEET   819 1
  AND TWO POTS OF GOLD   819 3
  THE TWO FEET OF THE RAINBOW   819 13
  AND THESE TWO AS YOU KNOW   820 10
  THE LAST TWO THINGS WE CAN STILL HOLD DEARLY   826 25
  A YEAR OR TWO   842 6
  BETTER MAN OF THE TWO   842 8
  ABOUT ONE OR TWO   845 20
  SHE IS NO LONGER TWO DAYS OLD   863 11
  I HAVE TRAVELLED IN RUSSIA TWO HOURS OR MORE   866 26
  AND THOUGH WE TWO   875 18
  THE TWO IMMENSITIES WOULD FLOAT UNWILLING   875 29
  WE LEAP LIKE TWO CLASPED FLAMES FROM OFF THE FIRE   879 30
  THAN WHO CAN SEPARATE TWO LITHE RICH FLAMES   879 33
  ON THE LITTLE BANK OUR TWO SOULS   887 1
  AND TWO ARE ONE IN SWEET CONNECTION   887 22
  LIKE IVORY AND GOLDEN MARBLE TWO BLACK CROWS HOLD   *894 27
  IS LIKE WHEN TWO WHITE BUTTERFLIES SETTLE IN THE ARMS O+   *913 3
  WITH HER TWO BARE FEET ON MY HANDS   *913 9
  OR AS TWO WHITE BUTTERFLIES SETTLE IN THE CUP OF ONE FL+   *914 4
  IN A WEEK OR TWO   *921 24
  BUT OH THE PALMS OF HER TWO BLACK HANDS ARE RED   *938 26

TWO-EYED
  A TWO-EYED CLOCK LIKE AN OWL   170 22

TWOFOLD
  THY TWOFOLD DANCE   40 16

TWO-FOLD
  BUT IN HIS CONSCIOUSNESS HE IS TWO-FOLD AT LEAST   473 16

TWO-FORKED
  AND FLICKERED HIS TWO-FORKED TONGUE FROM HIS LIPS AND   349 23

TWO-LEGGED
  THESE TWO-LEGGED THINGS THAT WALK AND TALK   644 18

TWONESS
  A TWONESS   714 25
  LOVE IS A THING OF TWONESS   844 5
  BUT UNDERNEATH ANY TWONESS MAN IS ALONE   844 6
  LOVE IS OF TWONESS AND IS LOVELY   844 17

TWO THOUSAND
  YOUR TWO THOUSAND YEARS ARE UP   616 20
  IT WILL TAKE AN EPOCH TWO THOUSAND YEARS AND MORE   833 29

TWO-WINGED
  WHO THEN SEES THE TWO-WINGED   226 17
  AND NEVER THE TWO-WINGED VESSEL   227 21

TYPE
  ANOTHER TYPE THAT ENGLAND HAS PRODUCED   841 10

TYPED
  AND WE TALKED AND WE ROARED AND YOU TYPED LADY C   550 32

TYRANNY
  TO ABOLISH THE TYRANNY OF MONEY   838 4
  UNDER THE WILD STRANGE TYRANNY OF MY BODY   *893 27

TYRE
  THE MAN OF TYRE WENT DOWN TO THE SEA   692 22

T'
  ASIDE O' T' GRAVE AN' TH' COFFIN SET   60 12
  AN' T' PARSON MAKIN' HASTE AN' A' T' BLACK   60 15
  HUDDLIN' UP I' T' RAIN   60 16
  DID T' 'APPEN TER NOTICE A BIT OF A LASS WAY BACK   60 17
  AH STOPPED BEHIND ON T' PAD I' T' POURIN' WET   61 3
  T' CHILDT MAUN TA'E ITS LUCK IT MUN   81 1
  THA'RT FOR DOIN' A LOT WI' T' LAD   82 8
  IF MY FATHER CAN GET THEE A JOB ON T' BANK SAY THA'RT S+   83 17
  T' SNOW IS WITHERIN' OFF'N TH' GRESS   137 18
  T' SNOW IS WITHERIN' OFF'N TH' GRESS   137 20
  WHILE T' CLOCKS 'AS A' RUN DOWN AN' STOPPED   137 28
  AN' T' SHORT DAYS GOIN' UNKNOWN TER THEE   137 29
  HOW MANY TIMES HAS T' CANDLE-LIGHT SHONE   138 4

UNCANNINESS
  YOUR NEW ENGLAND UNCANNINESS   291 24

UNCANNY
  AND UNCANNY COLD   101 6
  MODERN UNISSUED UNCANNY AMERICA   293 6
  SHE HURRIES UP STRIDING REARED ON LONG UNCANNY LEGS   358 31
  PERHAPS IT IS A SORT OF UNCANNY DECORATION A VEIL OF LO+   369 25

UNCEASING
  DOWN ON THE DAMP UNCEASING GROUND WHERE MY FEET BELONG   321 16

UNCERTAIN
  OUR FACES FLOWER FOR A LITTLE HOUR PALE AND UNCERTAIN A+   71 1
  AND I SHALL BE WAVERING UNCERTAIN   246 28
  OUR FACES FLOWER FOR A LITTLE HOUR PALE AND UNCERTAIN A+   *917 21

UNCHALLENGED
  UNCHALLENGED INTACT UNABRIDGED HENCEFORTH A HOST   743 27

UNCHANGING
  THE WIND IS UNCHANGING NOT ONE OF US KNOWS   164 2

UNCHARTED
  AN UNCHARTED WAY AMONG THE MYRIAD THICK   132 11

UNCHECKED
  THE LIGHTNING AND THE RAINBOW APPEARING IN US UNBIDDEN +   268 8

UNCHEQUERED
  THE COOL OF AN OAK'S UNCHEQUERED SHADE   49 21

UNCHIDDEN
  OF ROSES UNCHIDDEN AND PURPOSELESS A ROSE   219 18

UNCLASPING
  QUICKENS THE UNCLASPING HANDS OF HAZEL   40 26

UNCLE
  SO BE A NICE UNCLE BE GOOD TO US GIRLS   574 5
  WE'LL BACK YOU UP UNCLE WE'RE YOUNG AND WE'RE   574 9

UNCLEAN
  HE SQUATTED THERE LIKE SOMETHING UNCLEAN   346 2
  THEIR UNCLEAN CORNERS   346 14
  NOT BY TIME BUT BY UNCLEAN BREATH AND EYES   580 24
  ARE DEFLOWERED BY BEING LOOKED AT BY SO MANY UNCLEAN   634 19
  THEY ARE LIKE CATS WITH UNCLEAN CLAWS TANGLED UP IN NETS   675 6
  DESTROY IT SHED ITS UNCLEAN BLOOD KILL IT PUT IT OUT OF+   679 4
  O SHED THE UNCLEAN MEAN COWARDLY GREEDY EGOISTIC DEGENE+   679 5
  KILL HIM IN HIS UNCLEAN HOUSE   808 8
  WHERE DOGS CREEP UNCLEAN   808 16

UNCLEANLY
  OF ALL THE SORDID PEOPLE THAT HAVE STARED AT THEM UNCLE+   580 25

UNCLES
  WE'LL SHOW THESE OLD UNCLES WHO'S GOING TO BE BOSSY   573 24

UNCLOSE
  FOR ME IT IS MORE THAN ENOUGH IF THE FLOWER UNCLOSE   219 20

UNCLOSED
  AND HER MOUTH UNCLOSED IN A LAST LONG KISS   198 3
  AND HER MOUTH UNCLOSED IN THE LAST LONG KISS   199 11

UNCLOSES
  WHEN THE BLUE MIST UNCLOSES   178 14

UNCLOTHED
  AND UNCLOTHED THE WORD HAS NO MEANING FOR ME   607 10

UNCLOUDED
  THE UNCLOUDED SEAS OF BLUEBELLS HAVE EBBED AND PASSED   854 1

UNCOIL
  WE CAN UNCOIL THE GHASTLY SNAKE-TANGLE OF OUR UNCONSCIO+   833 26

UNCOMFORTABLE
  FLUSHING THE AFTERNOON THEY ARE UNCOMFORTABLE   223 11

UNCOMFORTABLENESSES
  AT MAN AND HIS UNCOMFORTABLENESSES   299 16

UNCONCEIVED
  FOREVER UNCONCEIVED   622 16

UNCONCERN
  INTO RUBBER-LIKE DEADNESS DUNLOP INFLATED UNCONCERN   625 18

UNCONCERNED
  THEN ONLY UNDER THE MOON COOL AND UNCONCERNED   609 10

UNCONFORMING
  THE UNCONFORMING WORM THAT IS THE WORM THAT HAS   432 10

UNCONQUERABLE
  ALL THE WORLD GLEAMS WITH THE LILIES OF DEATH THE UNCON+   273 12

UNCONSCIOUS
  WITH A SUNK UNCONSCIOUS HEAD   58 31
  THE SOUL OF MAN ALSO LEANS IN THE UNCONSCIOUS INCLINATI+   480 22
  TO SINK UNCONSCIOUS IN THE ROCKING DARK   771 28
  WE CAN UNCOIL THE GHASTLY SNAKE-TANGLE OF OUR UNCONSCIO+   833 26
  WITH SNAKE-BITES OF TANGLED UNCONSCIOUS EMOTION   833 31
  THEN TO FALL BACK EXHAUSTED INTO THE UNCONSCIOUS MOLTEN+   *909 28
  LEANING IN THE MASSIVE UNCONSCIOUS INCLINATION WE CALL +   *952 4

UNCONSCIOUSLY
  UNCONSCIOUSLY   60 6

UNCONSENTING
  MANY HAVE DIED UNCONSENTING   739 5

UNCONTAMINATED
  UNCONTAMINATED THE UNMENTAL FLOOD   471 13
  UNCONTAMINATED BY EVEN THE BEGINNINGS OF A LIE   481 30

UNCOUTH
  BUSHED IN AN UNCOUTH ARDOUR COILED AT CORE   160 13
  IT IS THE MIND WHICH IS UNCOUTH AND OVERWEENING   529 9
  AND THEN THE HEAVENS CACKLE WITH UNCOUTH SOUNDS   647 16

UNCOVER
  THEN HER BRIGHT BREAST SHE WILL UNCOVER   42 17

UNCOVERED
  FRAIL-NAKED UTTERLY UNCOVERED   306 10
  PELASGIC FACES UNCOVERED   311 16

UNCOVERS
  AND UNCOVERS HER LAUGHTER   133 27
  HENCE HE UNCOVERS HIS BIG ASS-TEETH AND HOWLS IN THAT A+   378 24

UNCRINGING
  WITH BRIGHT LEGS AND UNCRINGING BUTTOCKS   525 21

UNCROWNED
  LIKE A KING IN EXILE UNCROWNED IN THE UNDERWORLD   351 25

UNCTION
  THE PROPER UNCTION ABOUT IT   555 27

UNCURLED
  AN' MAKING US COME UNCURLED   493 8
  MY TREASURE SOFTLY SLIPS UNCURLED   *943 23

UNDAUNTED
  OR WHEN IT UTTERS THAT UNDAUNTED LITTLE BIRD-CRY   439 1
  SETTING FIERCE AND UNDAUNTED WINTRY   455 22
  LIVED UNDAUNTED AND UNSOURED WITH ACCEPTED LIES   503 18
  BUT REMEMBER THE UNDAUNTED GODS   559 2

UNDAUNTEDLY
  UNDAUNTEDLY   524 4

UNDAWNING
  FEELING MYSELF UNDAWNING THE DAY'S LIGHT PLAYING UPON ME   133 5

UNDEFILED
  AGAIN UNDEFILED   239 18

UNDELIVERABLE
  THE UNDELIVERABLE SECRET   296 8

UNDENIABLE
  AND TO ME UNDENIABLE JESUS   322 34
  AND UNDENIABLE NEW GODS SHARE THEIR LIFE WITH US WHEN WE   662 12

UNDEPARTING
  I AM HERE UNDEPARTING I SIT TIGHT   788 15

UNDER-DEEPS
  DOZING IN THE UNDER-DEEPS THEN REACHING OUT A SAVAGE AN+   689 20

UNDERDUSK
  THICK UNDERDUSK   427 2

UNDER-DUSK
  THE SHADOWY STUBBLE OF THE UNDER-DUSK   135 10
  AND I WAS HERE IN THE UNDER-DUSK OF THE ISAR   206 26
  THE SHADOWY STUBBLE OF THE UNDER-DUSK   *939 10

UNDER-EARTH
  AND LOVE WOULD ONLY WEAKEN THEIR UNDER-EARTH GRIP MAKE +   92 27
  STRANGE STORMING UP FROM THE DENSE UNDER-EARTH   304 18
  AND IMPUDENT NETTLES GRABBING THE UNDER-EARTH   317 19
  I AM DARK AS THE SUNLESS UNDER-EARTH   806 22

UNDERFOOT
  AND TROD WOLVES UNDERFOOT   378 5

UNDER-GOLD
  WITH THEIR GOLD RED EYES AND GREEN-PURE GLEAM AND UNDER+   339 26

UNDER-GRASS
  OF THE LONG LUSH UNDER-GRASS A GLOW-WORM'S SUDDEN   206 9

UNDERGRIND
  THE GREAT GRIND OF UNWILLINGNESS THE SLOW UNDERGRIND OF+   648 10

UNDERGROUND
  MY LOVE LIES UNDERGROUND   198 1
  MY LOVE LIES UNDERGROUND   199 9
  THEY ALL SHOULD BE UNDERGROUND SIFTED WITH SOOT   827 28
  LIKE WATER SUCKED FROM DEEP DOWN UNDERGROUND   878 33

UNDERGROWTH
  DEMONISH LURKING AMONG THE UNDERGROWTH   293 2
  THE SHAGGY UNDERGROWTH OF THEIR OWN HAIR   310 12

UNDERHUNG
  WRINKLED UNDERHUNG PHYSIOG THAT LOOKS AS IF IT HAD DONE   398 6
  AND SHOW A TINY BUNCH OF WHITE TEETH IN YOUR UNDERHUNG   398 11

UNDERLIES
THEIR FEAR THEIR SHAME THEIR JOY THAT UNDERLIES 125 28
THEIR FEAR THEIR SHAME THEIR JOY THAT UNDERLIES *936 27

UNDERLINED
A DAMN FRAUD UNDERLINED 553 4

UNDERMINE
THE SLEEP NO DREAM NOR DOUBT CAN UNDERMINE 129 26

UNDER-MIRE
ALIVE WITHIN THE OOZY UNDER-MIRE 89 19

UNDERMIST
AND WHAT IS THIS THAT FLOATS ON THE UNDERMIST 141 13
I HERE IN THE UNDERMIST ON THE BAVARIAN ROAD 213 3

UNDERNEATH
THE EAR PERHAPS IS CHILLY UNDERNEATH 87 8
WITH PEOPLE PASSING UNDERNEATH 121 19
AND UNDERNEATH A BLUE-GREY TWILIGHT HEAPED 135 5
SHE SPREADS THE BATH-CLOTH UNDERNEATH THE WINDOW 217 11
AND THE SHADOW OF A JEER OF UNDERNEATH DISAPPOINTMENT 391 22
IN SUMMER AND LOVE BUT UNDERNEATH IS ROCK 477 9
OLDER THAN PLASM ALTOGETHER IS THE SOUL OF A MAN UNDERN+ 477 11
BUT UNDERNEATH ARE THE DEEP ROCKS THE LIVING ROCK THAT + 844 2
BUT UNDERNEATH ANY TWONESS MAN IS ALONE 844 6
AND UNDERNEATH THE GREAT TURBULENT EMOTIONS OF LOVE THE+ 844 7
AND MOONY-DAISIES UNDERNEATH THE MIST 884 30
BUT UNDERNEATH MAN IS ALONE EACH ONE A ROCK TO HIMSELF *951 10
UNDER IT ALL UNDERNEATH *951 14

UNDER-NIGHT
TO THE EARTH OF THE UNDER-NIGHT 254 4

UNDERSOIL
A NET ON THE UNDERSOIL THAT LIES PASSIVE AND QUICKENED + 94 4

UNDERSTAND
AH YOU WILL UNDERSTAND 106 27
BACK YOU UNDERSTAND 158 30
OUR DARKNESS DO YOU UNDERSTAND 170 15
THEY WILL NEVER UNDERSTAND MY WEEPING FOR JOY TO BE 256 16
WHICH THEY WILL NOT UNDERSTAND BECAUSE IT IS QUITE QUITE 256 20
SILENCE HARD TO UNDERSTAND 261 28
AND SOMETHING BEYOND QUITE BEYOND IF YOU UNDERSTAND WHAT 266 18
THEY BEGIN TO UNDERSTAND 390 1
THE RICKSHAW BOYS BEGIN TO UNDERSTAND 390 2
THEN IT'S QUITE ALL RIGHT WE UNDERSTAND 491 7
THE ONE THING THE OLD WILL NEVER UNDERSTAND 511 21
BECAUSE I DON'T UNDERSTAND THEM 524 20
OH I'M SURE YOU'LL UNDERSTAND WE'RE MAKING A CENSUS OF + 546 7
COURSE YOU UNDERSTAND WHAT I MEAN SO WOULD YOU MIND GIV+ 546 9
AND YOU DON'T SEEM TO UNDERSTAND 572 20
AND YOU DON'T SEEM TO UNDERSTAND 573 8
FIXED ARRANGE YOU UNDERSTAND WHAT I MEAN 582 10
THEY DON'T REALLY UNDERSTAND 660 12
BUT YOU MUST NEVER TAKE THEM SERIOUSLY THEY WOULDN'T UN+ 660 16
WHERE IS THE SUN I CANNOT UNDERSTAND *933 20

UNDERSTANDING
I HAVE BEEN TAUGHT THE LANGUAGE OF UNDERSTANDING 264 2
HIM WITH A NEW DEMAND ON HIS UNDERSTANDING 431 5
AND THEY GRUDGE THEM THE IMMEDIATE PHYSICAL UNDERSTANDI+ 446 11
PASSES UNDERSTANDING 497 10

UNDERSTANDS
ALONE UNDERSTANDS 39 24
UNDERSTANDS AND KNOWS 39 26
WHEN I HOLD THEM MY SPENT SOUL UNDERSTANDS 128 8
SLEEP TO MAKE US FORGET BUT HE UNDERSTANDS 167 19
THAT AUNTIE UNDERSTANDS 572 29
IF HE UNDERSTANDS 754 7

UNDERSTAN'S
AN' THA LOOKS AT ME AN' THA UNDERSTAN'S 139 23

UNDERSTOOD
IT IS UNDERSTOOD 323 6
WHO UNDERSTOOD AT LAST WHAT IT WAS TO BE TOLD TO DIE 410 17
THE MOMENT LOVE IS AN UNDERSTOOD THING BETWEEN US WE 472 21
AND WHAT I'VE UNDERSTOOD AND THEN THE UTTER ACHE 738 11
IT SHOULD ALWAYS BE TACITLY UNDERSTOOD BETWEEN ALL OF US *953 2

UNDERTOW
IN THE GRIM UNDERTOW NAKED THE TREES CONFRONT 142 9

UNDERWATER
OF UNDERWATER FLOAT BRIGHT RIPPLES RUN 51 7

UNDER-WATER
OF UNDER-WATER FLOAT BRIGHT RIPPLES RUN *898 19
OF UNDER-WATER FLOAT BRIGHT RIPPLES RUN *902 3

UNDERWOOD
I'M OFF UP TH' LINE TO UNDERWOOD 78 3
OH ARE YOU GOIN' TO UNDERWOOD 78 5
WHY IS THERE A WEDDIN' AT UNDERWOOD 79 17
I'M OFF UP TH' LINE TO UNDERWOOD *919 23
OH ARE YOU GOIN' TO UNDERWOOD *919 25
WHY IS THERE A WEDDIN' AT UNDERWOOD *921 13

UNDERWORLD
LIKE A KING IN EXILE UNCROWNED IN THE UNDERWORLD 351 25
AND ALL THE DARK GREAT ONES OF THE UNDERWORLD *955 17

UNDESIRABLE
MANY UNDESIRABLE ASSOCIATIONS 581 13
IT SAVES HIM FROM SO MANY UNDESIRABLE ASSOCIATIONS 581 16
TO SAVE THEM FROM UNDESIRABLE ASSOCIATIONS 581 22

UNDID
SCRAIGHTIN' MYSEN AS WELL 'ER UNDID 'ER BLACK 61 9
AN' SHE UNDID 'ER JACKET NECK AN' THEN *910 15
SCRAIGHTIN' MY-SEN AS WELL 'EN UNDID HER BLACK *911 25

UNDIGNIFIED
IN UNDIGNIFIED HASTE 351 14
HOW YOU HATE BEING MADE TO LOOK UNDIGNIFIED MA'AM 397 33

UNDIMMED
THE BLAZING TIGER WILL SPRING UPON THE DEER UNDIMMED 268 3
OF LIFE UNDIMMED DELIGHTS HIM SO EVEN HE IS LIT UP 648 21

UNDINE
UNDINE TOWARDS THE WATERS MOVING BACK 161 25

UNDINE-CLEAR
YOU UNDINE-CLEAR AND PEARLY SOULLESSLY COOL 161 15

UNDISCOVERABLE
THE REST THE UNDISCOVERABLE IS THE DEMI-URGE 691 26

UNDOING
NOW THAT THE WAVES OF OUR UNDOING HAVE BEGUN TO STRIKE 513 22
SINKING IN THE ENDLESS UNDOING THE AWFUL KATABOLISM INT+ 699 26

UNDONE
US CREATURES PEOPLE AND FLOWERS UNDONE 127 3
WILL SOUND IN HEAVEN BEFORE IT IS UNDONE 154 17
SHE UNFOLDS SHE COMES UNDONE 165 18
THEY SHONE CLEAR LIKE FLOWERS UNDONE 216 17
FOR THE JOY LIKE A FOUNT UNDONE 888 12

UNDREAMED
THERE ARE VAST REALMS OF CONSCIOUSNESS STILL UNDREAMED + 666 24

UNDRESSED
YEA BUT IT IS CRUEL WHEN UNDRESSED IS ALL THE BLOSSOM 120 1

UNDROSSED
UNDROSSED IT AND LEFT IT BLEST 112 3
UNDROSSED IT AND BLESSED IT WITH A QUIVERING *927 23
UNDROSSED IT AND LEFT IT BLEST *928 23

UNDULATING
IN UNDULATING SHIVERS BENEATH THE WIND 126 11

UNDYING
EARNS MY UNDYING DETESTATION 507 15
IS THIS ILLUSION OF THE DEATH OF THE UNDYING 703 15

UNEASILY
UNEASILY IN THEIR SLEEP DISTURBING MY METTLE 128 13
ON THE THIN BARE SHINS OF A MAN WHO UNEASILY LIES 145 21
UNEASILY DISTURBED BY THE STRESS 231 18

UNEASINESS
YOU WHO DON'T HEAR THE SEA'S UNEASINESS 643 12

UNEASY
IT WOULD BE LAMBENT UNEASY 205 19
ROCKS SEEM AND EARTH AND AIR UNEASY AND WATERS STILL 249 15
BATS AND AN UNEASY CREEPING IN ONE'S SCALP 341 21
WAS MOIST AND COLD THE SUN IN HIM DARTED UNEASY HELD DO+ 348 8
IT WAS FULL OF UNEASY PEOPLE 444 11
ARE CROWDED WITH LOST SOULS THE UNEASY DEAD 722 22
ENDLESSLY RETURNING ON THE UNEASY SEA 739 12
AND CROSSED THE ROAD OF THE UNEASY 808 4
DOWN THE ROAD OF THE UNEASY 808 9

UNEATABLE
EARTH-GRASS UNEATABLE 300 23
OF UNEATABLE SOFT GREEN 301 17

UNENDING
ALL THE ROSES AND UNENDING 150 6

UNEQUIPPED
ALL UNEQUIPPED TO TAKE THE LONG LONG VOYAGE 722 5

UNEXPLAINED
DEEP UNEXPLAINED 369 9

UNEXPLODED
SLOWLY REVOLVING TOWARDS UNEXPLODED EXPLOSION 381 18

UNEXPLORED
AND WE WE ARE MOSTLY UNEXPLORED HINTERLAND 636 30

UNEXTRICATED
TILL THEN WE ARE CONFUSED A MIXTURE UNRESOLVED UNEXTRIC+ 267 1

UNFAIR
BUT THEY DO MIND BEING UNJUST UNFAIR 829 13

UNFALLEN
MOST MEN EVEN UNFALLEN CAN ONLY LIVE 649 13

UNFATHOMABLE
WHEN SHE KNOWS THE FEARFUL OTHER FLESH AH DARKNESS UNFA+ 267 11
OUT OF LIFE'S UNFATHOMABLE DAWN 364 2
THE SOFT THE SECRET THE UNFATHOMABLE BLOOD 383 6

UNFATHOMED
A DARK UNFATHOMED WILL THAT IS NOT UN-JEWISH 292 11

UNFELT
WITH THAT UNFELT BREEZE THAT EBBS OVER THE SEAS WHERE T+ 53 13
IN FLAT ECSTASY SUPREMELY UNFELT 444 7
WITH THE UNFELT BREEZE THAT EBBS OVER THE SEAS WHEN THE+ *906 5

UNFINISHED
PERFECTING NOW OUR UNFINISHED FIRST EMBRACE 157 22
UNFINISHED FOR EVER BUT GASPING FOR MONEY AS THEY DREAM+ 175 5
YOUR IMPASSIONED UNFINISHED HATE 236 5
LIKE A RED INDIAN DARKLY UNFINISHED AND ALOOF 369 10
OR PERHAPS IT IS SOMETHING UNFINISHED 370 1
OF THE UNFINISHED PLUNGE 701 20
AND IN THE UNFINISHED HOUSES THE RING OF THE JOINER'S T+ 865 16
OF A LIVE SAD WORK UNFINISHED *927 27

UNFOLD
NOR BE THWARTED IN LIFE'S SLOW STRUGGLE TO UNFOLD THE F+ 93 18
GLIMMERED AS FLOWERS THAT IN PERFUME AT TWILIGHT UNFOLD 141 8
UNFOLD SLOWLY UPWARDS BLOOD-DARK 302 17
WHO IS IT THAT CLASPS AND KNEADS MY NAKED FEET TILL THE+ 652 12
THE GOLD-BROWN FLOWERS OF HER EYES UNFOLD 868 26
GOLD GOLD DEEP GOLD HER GLOWING EYES UNFOLD *941 26

UNFOLDED
UNFOLDED WOMANHOOD 56 10
THERE NEVER WAS ANY STANDING ALOFT AND UNFOLDED ON A BO+ 283 3
FROM THE UNFOLDED ROSE 285 3
OURS IS THE UNIVERSE OF THE UNFOLDED ROSE 285 12

UNFOLDING
UNFOLDING ALL HER COILED AND LOVELY SELF 317 23
TO THE BREATH THAT IS OF NEW BEAUTY UNFOLDING IN DEATH 676 23
I CAN FEEL MYSELF UNFOLDING IN THE DARK SUNSHINE OF DEA+ 677 15
FOR THE RUSTLING OF THEIR WHITE UNFOLDING PETALS *943 5

UNFOLDS
UNFOLDS FROM THE SKY FOR YOUR GOOD 56 9
SHE UNFOLDS SHE COMES UNDONE 166 18
AND THE GETHSEMANE BLOOD AT THE IRON PORES UNFOLDS UNFO+ 306 4

UNFORGIVING
THEY FALL VICTIM AT ONCE TO THE VENGEANCE OF THE UNFORG+ 616 7

UNFORGOTTEN
IRON BUT UNFORGOTTEN 305 16

UNFORMED
WHEN THE DIM FLUX OF UNFORMED LIFE 682 3

UNFOULED
ENTERING IN SHOCKS OF TRUTH UNFOULED BY LIES 482 2

UNFREE
EVEN THEN IN THE DARK I WAS TORTURED RAVENING UNFREE 264 30

UNFROZEN
SOUNDS STILL UNFROZEN AND THE TRAIL IS STILL EVIDENT 401 3

UNFULFILMENT
UNFULFILMENT 214 18

UNFURLED
NEVER MAGNOLIA-LIKE UNFURLED 103 31

UNFURLS
FOR THE SOUND OF THE SEA AS IT FURLS AND UNFURLS 747 21

UNFUSED
THE MULTITUDINOUS PEOPLE UNFUSED 746 6

UNFUSING
AND THERE A NEW PARTNER A NEW PARTING A NEW UNFUSING 280 30

UNGAINLY
IN HER UNGAINLY PACE 362 17

UNGODLY
SAVE ME O GOD FROM FALLING INTO THE UNGODLY KNOWLEDGE 699 16

UNGOVERNABLE
MAKING THEM SWELL WITH TURGID UNGOVERNABLE STRENGTH 241 20

UNGROWING
THEY ALL DO CLOTHE MY UNGROWING LIFE *899 31
THEY ALL DO CLOTHE MY UNGROWING LIFE *903 10

UNGURGLING
BLACKER UPON THE SOUNDLESS UNGURGLING FLOOD 719 12

UNHAMPERED
SO UNHAMPERED IN THEIR LIVING AND DYING 677 11

UNHAPPINESS
BUT THE UNHAPPINESS OF A WIFE WITH A GOOD HUSBAND 456 7
THAN THE UNHAPPINESS OF A WIFE WITH A BAD HUSBAND 455 9

UNHAPPY
LIKE SOME UNHAPPY BULL AT THE TAIL OF A COW 361 15
GOOD HUSBANDS MAKE UNHAPPY WIVES 456 5
THE UNHAPPY SOULS ARE THOSE THAT CAN'T DIE AND BECOME S+ 612 19
BUT IT IS ONLY UNHAPPY MEN MAKING A NOISE 656 6
UNHAPPY KILL IT THE UNLIVING THING 678 26
BEWARE THE UNHAPPY DEAD THRUST OUT OF LIFE 722 16

UNHEALTHY
ALL THE LOT OF THEM VICE MISSIONS ETC INSANELY UNHEALTHY 845 10

UNHEARD
UNHEARD AND SUBTLE NEVER A SOUND 262 8
AND THERE SHALL BE THE SOFT SOFT TREMOR AS OF UNHEARD B+ 479 4

UNHEEDING
AND SUFFER UNHEEDING ONLY FORBIDDEN TO EXPIRE 161 5

UNHOLY
UNHOLY FEAR IN MY ESSENCE YOU WOULD PAUSE TO 131 4

UNHOLY INQUISITION
AN UNHOLY INQUISITION HAS ARRESTED ALL MY PICTURES 633 14

UNHOOKED
UNHOOKED HIS GORPING WATER-HONEY MOUTH 339 6

UNHOOKS
HIS SCYTHE-BLADE BRIGHT UNHOOKS 220 4
HIS SCYTHE BLADE BRIGHT UNHOOKS *944 12

UNHOUSELED
HOME AT LAST IN THE OPEN AGAIN AND UNHOUSELED 770 8

UNIFORM
THE YOUNG TRAM-CONDUCTOR IN A BLUE UNIFORM TO HIMSELF F+ 672 8

UNIFORMS
AND THEIR UNIFORMS ARE THE SAME OF WHITE AND BLUE 732 13

UNINHABITED
UNINHABITED SPACE NOW RUNS 823 25

UNINTELLIGENT
WITH UNINTELLIGENT AND EVIL DESTRUCTION 677 26

UNINTELLIGIBLE
IN THE PULPIT WHERE SHRIVELLED AND GHASTLY IN UNINTELLI+ 859 14

UNINTERESTING
PORTRAITS ARE NOW SUPREMELY UNINTERESTING 657 1

UNINTERRUPTED
UNINTERRUPTED SILENCE SWINGS 166 3
AND FEELING ONESELF UNINTERRUPTED IN THE ROOTED CONNECT+ 610 6

UNIQUE
ONE CLEAR BURNISHED ISOLATED BEING UNIQUE 267 20
AND BECOME UNIQUE 267 25
YOUR UNIQUE DAY IS OVER 473 13

UNISON
AND SWINGING IN A STRANGE UNISON OF POWER 478 17
UNDER THE GREEN GRASSY UNISON OF ALL OUR FRIENDLINESS *951 11

UNISSUED
MODERN UNISSUED UNCANNY AMERICA 293 6

UNIT
THE ROBOT IS THE UNIT OF EVIL 713 9

UNITY
IN A UNITY 157 26

UNIVERSAL
REVEAL THE UNIVERSAL TINT THAT DYES 197 27
BORN IN A UNIVERSAL WORKHOUSE 518 9
THIS IS CALLED UNIVERSAL FREEDOM 521 19

UNIVERSALISM
AND UNIVERSALISM AND COSMOPOLITANISM WILL CEASE 611 16

UNIVERSE
I SEE MYSELF ISOLATED IN THE UNIVERSE AND WONDER 223 1
OURS IS THE UNIVERSE OF THE UNFOLDED ROSE 285 12
YOUR SINGLENESS WITHIN THE UNIVERSE 290 14
DOES NOT A SUPREME INTELLECT IDEALLY PROCREATE THE UNIV+ 328 26
FOR THE DESTRUCTION OF THE UNIVERSE FOR IF HIS PRAYER W+ 348 3
INANIMATE UNIVERSE 354 2
BUD OF THE UNIVERSE 356 20
THE UNIVERSE 367 7
THAT STRONG ONE RULING THE UNIVERSE WITH A ROD OF IRON 439 25
THE UNIVERSE FLOWS IN INFINITE WILD STREAMS RELATED 479 9
IF ONCE FOR A SECOND THE UNIVERSE CEASED TO FLOW 479 13
BETWEEN MAN AND ALL HIS KNOWN UNIVERSE 482 11
THERE IS THE OTHER UNIVERSE OF THE HEART OF MAN 606 21
THE UNIVERSE TREMBLES GOD IS BORN GOD IS HERE 683 10
LO THE UNIVERSE TANGLES ITS GREAT DRAGONS 795 10
UNIVERSE ANY MORE *947 13

UNIVERSITIES
THEY SOLD PLATO TO THE SAUSAGE FACTORIES OF UNIVERSITIES 762 26

UNIVERSITY
THEY'VE BUILT A NEW UNIVERSITY 488 9
INTO A UNIVERSITY 488 23
THEY HAVE BUILT A NEW AND CAKEY UNIVERSITY *950 13
IN SUCH A CASH-CHEMIST UNIVERSITY WHAT CAN THEY TEACH *950 19
AND WHEN THIS CASH-CHEMIST UNIVERSITY GRANTS DEGREES LI+ *950 22

UN-JEWISH
A DARK UNFATHOMED WILL THAT IS NOT UN-JEWISH 292 11

UNJUST
    BUT THEY DO MIND BEING UNJUST UNFAIR   829 13

UNKNOWABLE
    AND THEREFORE THAT THOU ART FOREVER UNKNOWABLE   473 23
    WE EXPIATE IT THUS THE UNKNOWABLE CRIME   743 14
    WHICH RESTS IN CONNECTION WITH THE FURTHER FOREVER UNKN+   844 22
    BALANCE WITH THE OTHER THE VAST UNKNOWABLE FIRE   *951 30

UNKNOWN
    MY UNKNOWN BREASTS BEGIN   39 2
    LUSTROUSLY SURE UNKNOWN   39 27
    IN THE CURVES OF THY FORM THE TRACE OF THE UNKNOWN   69 16
    INTO THE WOMB TO KINDLE AN UNKNOWN FIRE   89 35
    STREWN STARS OF UNKNOWN PEOPLE AND LUMINOUS LITTER   132 12
    UNKNOWN THAT LIES BEFORE US BEARING THE ARK OF THE COVE+   132 24
    AN' T' SHORT DAYS GOIN' UNKNOWN TER THEE   137 29
    SLEEPS ON UNKNOWN UNNOTICED THERE UNTIL   176 28
    FROM THIS UNKNOWN THAT I WOULD TRESPASS ON   256 6
    AND WHOSOEVER THE UNKNOWN PEOPLE OF THIS UNKNOWN   256 14
    IT WAS THE UNKNOWN   259 10
    I WAS GREEDY I WAS MAD FOR THE UNKNOWN   259 13
    AND TOUCHING THE UNKNOWN THE REAL UNKNOWN THE UNKNOWN   259 18
    UNKNOWN   259 19
    I TOUCH I FEEL THE UNKNOWN   259 21
    THE UNKNOWN THE UNKNOWN   259 28
    THE UNKNOWN THE NEW WORLD   259 33
    WHITE SANDS AND FRUITS UNKNOWN AND PERFUMES THAT NEVER   261 2
    THE UNKNOWN STRONG CURRENT OF LIFE SUPREME   261 12
    ISSUING STRAIGHT OUT OF THE UNKNOWN   268 7
    INTO WHICH THE CREATIVE FUTURE SHALL BLOW STRANGE UNKNO+   428 29
    THAT DRIFTS UPON TIME AND CHAOS TILL SOME UNKNOWN FUTURE   429 5
    WITH UNKNOWN SHOCKS   436 17
    OUT OF FEAR OF THE UNKNOWN ENEMY   529 19
    INTO THE UNKNOWN AND TAKE ROOTS BY ONESELF   610 18
    TO FERTILISE THE ROOTS OF UNKNOWN MEN WHO ARE STILL TO +   614 24
    BUT TO SOMETHING UNSEEN UNKNOWN CREATIVE   622 11
    FOREVER UNKNOWN   622 15
    IN THE SIGHT OF GOD AND THE UNKNOWN GODS   638 10
    OF THE UNKNOWN AIR AND EYES SO SOFT   667 8
    THOUGHT IS THE WELLING UP OF UNKNOWN LIFE INTO CONSCIOU+   673 10
    AND PERHAPS IN UNKNOWN DEATH WE PERHAPS SHALL KNOW   710 3
    UNKNOWN WITHIN YOUR BREAST AND YOUR DEADENED LOINS   723 18
    I AM IN THE HANDS OF THE UNKNOWN GOD   727 28
    THEN LEAD THEM TO THE GATES OF THE UNKNOWN   740 19
    THERE IS A BREAST OF A VAST AND UNKNOWN BODY   784 9
    AND DEEPER STILL THE UNKNOWN FIRE UNKNOWN AND HEAVY HEA+   844 3
    INTO THE PASSIVE UNKNOWN MONSTROUS WOMB   880 7
    THE UNKNOWN FLOWER ISSUED MAGIC-WISE   *943 21
    TO THE UNKNOWN AND ARE TAKEN UP   *960 24

UNKNOWN MOVER
    AND THE STAR IS THE LAMP IN THE HAND OF THE UNKNOWN MOV+   801 11

UNLADE
    YOU UNLADE YOUR RICHES INTO DEATH   168 8

UNLADENS
    STRAY WHITEFOAM AND HER WHITE FIRE ALL UNLADENS   86 20

UNLEASHED
    AND THOUGH THE SUN LEAPS LIKE A THING UNLEASHED IN THE +   408 21

UNLESS
    UNLESS THE LITTLE STAR THAT KEEPS HER COMPANY   54 14
    UNLESS THERE WERE A MORPHINE OR A DRUG   214 24
    MUST BE EXCRUCIATING UNLESS YOU STIFFEN INTO METAL WHEN   288 6
    UNLESS YOU'RE A WAGE-SLAVE   450 2
    UNLESS IT ABSORBS YOU   450 19
    UNLESS HE IS A STURDY PLANT   475 1
    NO MAN UNLESS HE HAS DIED AND LEARNED TO BE ALONE   612 17
    A MAN CAN'T FULLY LIVE UNLESS HE DIES AND CEASES TO CARE   613 1
    WE DON'T EXIST UNLESS WE ARE DEEPLY AND SENSUALLY IN TO+   613 6
    UNLESS WE ARE IN TOUCH WITH THAT WHICH LAUGHS AT ALL OU+   613 10
    UNLESS GOGGLING EYES TO GOGGLE AT THE FILM   630 29
    AN ENGINE OF FLESH USELESS UNLESS HE IS A TOOL   635 17
    AND THEY WILL DESTROY ALL UNLESS THEY ARE MADE TO SUBMIT 637 9
    UNLESS MEN SWIFTLY DIVIDE AGAIN AND THE BASE ARE THRUST   637 14
    UNLESS THEY HAVE FALLEN AND BECOME ROBOTS   649 2
    UNLESS THERE'S THE GLIMPSE OF A GOD IN HIM   671 10
    UNLESS SHE'S A GLIMPSE OF A GODDESS OF SOME SORT   671 12
    UNLESS HE HAS HIS PURE MOMENTS WHEN HE IS SURPASSING   674 19
    UNLESS GOD HAS A BODY HOW CAN HE HAVE A VOICE   691 10
    UNLESS IT PRE-OCCUPIES YOU AS WELL AS OCCUPIES YOU   *949 20

UNLICKED
    WHERE BEASTS DROP THEIR UNLICKED YOUNG AND PASTURE AND +   321 13

UNLIMITED
    NOW THAT IT SOUNDS SELF-CONSCIOUS THROUGH THE UNLIMITED+   325 4

UNLIVING
    I KNOW THE UNLIVING FACTORY-HAND LIVING-DEAD MILLIONS   629 26
    IS UNLIVING ME LIVING-DEAD ME   629 27
    DOES IT MEAN THAT LIFE WHICH HAS GONE UGLY AND UNLIVING+ 678 20
    UNHAPPY KILL IT THE UNLIVING THING   678 26

UNLOCKED
    YOU COULD HAVE UNLOCKED THE MOON ON THE NIGHT   104 12
    HE SLEEPS AS EVER GENEROUSLY UNLOCKED   878 1

UNLOCKS
    UNLOCKS THE FOUNTAINS OF PEACE AGAIN   461 24

UNLOVELY
    THIS IS COMFORTLESS AND UNLOVELY WITH CUSHIONS AND THOS+   856 9

UNLOVING
    YOU YOU ARE ALL UNLOVING LOVELESS YOU   197 1

UNLYING
    IN THE SHEER COITION OF THE LIFE-FLOW STARK AND UNLYING   482 14
    COOL UNLYING LIFE WILL RUSH IN   482 22

UNMAKE
    WHITE MEN MAKE GOLD-MINES AND THE MOUNTAINS UNMAKE   407 13

UNMARCHING
    IN THE SUBTLE LIFT OF THE THIGHS AS THEY COME UNMARCHING 174 13

UNMECHANISED
    BUT OH MEN MEN STILL UNMECHANISED   635 23

UNMENTAL
    UNCONTAMINATED THE UNMENTAL FLOOD   471 13

UNMENTALISED
    ONLY THAT EXISTS WHICH EXISTS DYNAMICALLY AND UNMENTALI+ 474 19

UNMENTIONABLE
    SO YOU YOU GO OUT AT LAST AND EAT THE UNMENTIONABLE   399 2

UNMINDFUL
    UNMINDFUL OF ITS TERRORS   875 35

UNNAMED
    COMES UP UNNAMED FROM HER BODY AND SURELY   *946 5

UNNATURAL
    WHY DOES MY SOUL CONTRACT WITH UNNATURAL FEAR   140 21
    THAT UNNATURAL BARREL BODY THAT LONG GHOUL NOSE   338 8

UNNERVING
    NO TEARS OF LOVE UNNERVING   64 1
    KILLING THE BLUE DUSK WITH HARSH SCENT UNNERVING   91 14
    IT IS VERY UNNERVING MOVING IN A WORLD OF SMOULDERING   539 4

UNNOTICED
    OF LEAVES THAT HAVE GONE UNNOTICED SWEPT LIKE OLD   141 29
    UNNOTICED AMONG THEM A STILL QUEEN LOST IN THE MAZE   176 24
    HAS SLEPT UNNOTICED ON A FORGOTTEN HILL   176 27
    SLEEPS ON UNKNOWN UNNOTICED THERE UNTIL   176 28
    OF SUNSET BUT MERGING UNNOTICED INTO THE ROSY GLIMMER   860 5
    HOW LONELY UNDER THE TREE UNNOTICED   867 7

UNOCEANED
    LURE THE UNOCEANED EXPLORER   53 8
    UNOCEANED EXPLORER   *905 21

UNOPENED
    TO DIE UNOPENED WHEN THIS MOON-FACED LOVER   113 15

UNPEOPLED
    ARE ALL UNPEOPLED OF GOD   823 24

UNPERCEIVED
    EMERGING AND CROSSING THE CLEAR SKY UNPERCEIVED   874 24

UNPERVERTED
    BUT BY THE HEAVY DRIFT OF HIS UNPERVERTED INSTINCTS   838 17

UNPLEASANTLY
    UNPLEASANTLY   369 31

UNPOPULAR
    UNPOPULAR PLACE   632 6

UNPREPARED
    UNREADY UNPREPARED UNWILLING UNABLE   722 17

UNPRODUCED
    UNBORN AND UNPRODUCED YET TO BE BORN   746 7

UNPROMISED
    FLAKED OUT AND COME UNPROMISED   306 35

UNQUENCHABLE
    THE UNQUENCHABLE HEART OF BLOSSOM   305 3
    THAT IS HALF INSATIABLE DESIRE AND HALF UNQUENCHABLE   378 25
    UNQUENCHABLE OF WIND OR HOSTS OF DEATH   745 11
    WITH ALL THE UNQUENCHABLE DARKNESS   772 26

UNQUESTIONED
    SLOW AND UNQUESTIONED   358 16

UNRAVEL
    WITH A KNOT OF LIFE THAT ONLY BLISS CAN UNRAVEL   160 14

UNRAVELLING
    FLUTTERING AND SOFTLY UNRAVELLING   460 8

UNREADY
    UNREADY UNPREPARED UNWILLING UNABLE   722 17

UNREAL
    UNREAL THOUGH THE CLOUDS   133 11
    FOR MY TAINTED TRANSIENCY AS A THING UNREAL   772 7

UNREALITY
    FOR THEIR MIDDLENESS IS ONLY AN UNREALITY SEPARATING TWO   527 26

UNREAPED
    A RUBBLE OF STUNTED HOUSES STANDS UNREAPED   *939 7

UNRELEASED
    YET UNRELEASED AND AFTER THE MOMENT THE SUDDEN STARTLING   365 17

UNREMARKABLE
    THE SAME UNREMARKABLE SUNDAY SUIT   312 16

UNREMITTING
    BUT ALWAYS STRONG UNREMITTING   214 26
    IT IS THE VENGEANCE OF THE LORD LONG AND UNREMITTING   616 13

UNREPRESENTED
    FOREVER UNREPRESENTED   622 17

UNRESOLVED
    TILL THEN WE ARE CONFUSED A MIXTURE UNRESOLVED UNEXTRIC+   267 1

UNREVEALED
    AMERICA STILL HAS ONLY AN UNREVEALED FUTURE   775 15

UNRIPE
    HER FRUIT IS UNRIPE AND HER SOFT MOUTH IS BITTER AND RO+   864 18

UNROLLED
    AND EUROPE'S TAIL-SPIN ROLLS STILL UNROLLED   814 8

UNROLLING
    THE UNROLLING OF FERNS WHITE TONGUES OF THE ACANTHUS LA+   623 27
    THE UNROLLING OF FERNS WHILE TONGUES OF ACANTHUS LAPPIN+ *953 15

UNROLLS
    OF MEMORY UNROLLS AGAIN TO ME   100 17

UNRULY
    MY PACK OF UNRULY HOUNDS I CANNOT START   74 9
    MY PACK OF UNRULY HOUNDS I CANNOT START   *895 17
    MY PACK OF UNRULY HOUNDS I CANNOT START   *904 6

UNSAID
    TO OTHER THINGS THAT ARE LEFT UNSAID   456 4

UNSALTED
    INSIPID UNSALTED RABBITY ENDLESSLY HOPPING   606 19

UNSATISFACTORILY
    AND WHEN SHE HAS MOST UNSATISFACTORILY SHARED HIS LITTL+   842 5

UNSATISFIED
    UNSATISFIED IS THERE NO HOPE   119 5
    WHAT MAKES PEOPLE UNSATISFIED   504 1
    GREY STERN ANGRY UNSATISFIED   739 26
    EVE ALONE UNSATISFIED AMONG THE ORANGE AND GUAVA TREES   864 1
    TIRED AND UNSATISFIED   *893 32

UNSCIENTIFIC
    AND IN THE DARK UNSCIENTIFIC I FEEL THE DRUM-WINDS OF H+   438 9
    IT IS MORE UNSCIENTIFIC EVEN THAN MYSTICISM   523 2

UNSEALS
    AN INVISIBLE WOE UNSEALS   159 7

UNSEAT
    WHO CAN UNSEAT HER LIKE A LIQUID DROP THAT IS HEAVY AND   392 28

UNSEEING
    AND LOOKED AROUND LIKE A GOD UNSEEING INTO THE AIR   350 28

UNSEEMING
    THAT'S WHY AS THE ELEPHANTS PONDEROUSLY WITH UNSEEMING   390 29

UNSEEN
    THEIR SLEEPING COVER THEM SOFT UNSEEN   43 22
    THE NIGHT RAIN DRIPPING UNSEEN   144 1
    UNSEEN MY HANDS EXPLORE THE SILENCE DRAWING THE BARK   147 2
    THAT CRUSHES ME TO AN UNSEEN ATOM OF FIRE   195 36
    ITS NAKEDNESS ALL WITHIN-WALLS ITS FLOWERING FOREVER UN+ 283 15
    RESPECTABLY UNSEEN AND CHEERFULLY GNAWS AWAY AT THE   432 7
    HITTING OURSELVES AGAINST UNSEEN ROCK CRASHING OUR HEAD   544 13
    BY SOME MALIGNANT FISHERMAN ON AN UNSEEN SAFE SHORE   586 10
    NAKEDLY TO BE ALONE UNSEEN   601 4
    MEN ARE UNSEEN BENEATH THE SHADING HATS   606 5
    BUT TO SOMETHING UNSEEN UNKNOWN CREATIVE   622 11
    BY SOME MALIGNANT FISHERMAN ON AN UNSEEN SHORE   632 25
    VAST RANGES OF EXPERIENCE LIKE THE HUMMING OF UNSEEN HA+ 666 25
    FOR THE UNSEEN WITNESSES ARE THE ANGELS OF CREATION   706 22
    LET NOBODY BE ABOUT SLIP IN GO ALL UNSEEN   711 10
    THEY LET DEATH UPON UNSEEN MEN   715 14
    FOR YOUR DEAD YOUR UNSEEN DEAD AND WITH YOUR HEARTS   723 12
    THE UNSEEN CLOUD   748 28
    BUT INTO THE INWARDS OF THE UNSEEN   784 6
    UNSEEN   788 8
    BEFORE THE UNSEEN   811 10
    AS WE SLIP IN UNSEEN   812·16
    FLOCK UNSEEN FROM MY LIPS TO HERS   868 32
    OH THE GREAT MYSTERY AND FASCINATION OF THE UNSEEN SHAP+ *909 13
    PASS UNSEEN FROM MY LIPS TO HERS   *942 4
    AND FOLDED IN THE DARK-RED UNSEEN   *957 10

UNSEEN SHAPER
    THE RADIANCE OF THE UNSEEN SHAPER   *907 19

UNSETTLED
    UNSETTLED SEAS AND WINDS   285 20

UNSHEATHE
    THAT MOON-LIKE SWORD THE ASCENDANT DEAD UNSHEATHE   168 23

UNSHEATHED
    UNSHEATHED AND NAKED AND NARROW AND WHITE   210 2

UNSHOWING
    AND LIKE A MOON UNSHOWING IT MUST STILL SHINE THERE   114 24

UNSIGHTLY
    UNSIGHTLY ITS WAY TO THE WARMTH THIS THING WITH A LIST   141 15

UNSLAKED
    SPURTING TO SOOTHE THE WOMB'S UNSLAKED DESIRE   89 21

UNSMELTED
    ONLY YOURS WOULD BE A RAW UNSMELTED PASSION THAT WILL   370 9

UNSOURED
    LIVED UNDAUNTED AND UNSOURED WITH ACCEPTED LIES   503 18

UNSPEAKABLE
    STARTLING A FEAR UNSPEAKABLE AS THE SHUDDERING WIND   140 17
    AND ALL THE UNSPEAKABLE CHARM OF BIRDS HOPPING   443 19

UNSPEAKING
    SONS OF THE ELEMENTS AND THE UNSPEAKING GODS   635 24

UNSPOKEN
    BEYOND THE UNSPOKEN PASSION OF NIGHT   810 26

UNSTABLE
    MAN IS KEPT SANE NOT BY HIS MIND WHICH BY NATURE IS UNS+ 838 16

UNSTRAIN
    WE LOOSE OUR GRIP AND WE UNSTRAIN OUR EYES   736 23

UNSTUFFY
    AND THAT'S WHAT MAKES IT ETERNALLY SPACIOUS AND UNSTUFFY 525 3

UNSURE
    BAD YESTERDAYS UNSURE TOMORROWS   825 3

UNSUSPECTED
    ON FANS OF UNSUSPECTED TISSUE LIKE BATS   322 17

UNSWEPT
    OF THE UNSWEPT SEA A GREY PALE LIGHT LIKE MUST   99 3

UNSWERVING
    OF UNSWERVING INDIFFERENCE TO ME   55 9
    SERENELY WITH STEPS UNSWERVING   63 32

UNTACKLED
    THE HORSES ARE UNTACKLED THE CHATTERING MACHINE   35 11

UNTARNISHED
    MADE OF SWEET UNTARNISHED SILVER IN THE SEA-SOUTHERN AIR 298 21
    I SAY UNTARNISHED BUT I MEAN OPAQUE   293 22

UNTELLABLE
    AND HIS BLOOD RIPPLES WITH THAT UNTELLABLE DELIGHT OF O+ 306 2

UNTHINKABLE
    YOU HAVE A HOT UNTHINKABLE DESIRE OF ME BUNNY   241 4
    THE THOUGHT IS UNTHINKABLE ANYHOW   479 15

UNTHINKING
    SONS OF THE LIVING ELEMENTS SONS OF THE UNTHINKING GODS   635 4

UNTHREADED
    HIS OWN UNTHREADED FOREVER   382 5

UNTIDY
    WHEN I SAW HER STRAYING A LITTLE DAZED THROUGH HER UNTI+ 618 21

UNTIE
    ME TO COME DOWN AND UNTIE HER   384 7

UNTIED
    KNOT IS UNTIED   384 29
    AND COME UNTIED   437 30
    AND FORCES TIE THEMSELVES UP INTO KNOTS OF ATOMS THEN C+ *947 6
    AND BUMP ON ONE ANOTHER AND COME UNTIED   *947 10

UNTIL
    OVER MY FACE AND MY HEAD UNTIL   35 24
    OF A MALE THONG BOOMING AND BRUISING UNTIL IT HAD   36 15
    HOMUNCULUS STIRS FROM HIS ROOTS AND STRIVES UNTIL   39 11
    YOUR BODY WITH THEIR NIPPLE-THRUST UNTIL   91 15
    US AWAY IN AN UTTER SLEEP UNTIL   117 6
    UNTIL HER PRIDE'S FLAG SMITTEN CLEAVED DOWN TO THE STAFF 125 18
    HIS MIND UNTIL IT BURNT HIS HEART AWAY   158 2
    SLEEPS ON UNKNOWN UNNOTICED THERE UNTIL   176 28
    OF FLOTSAM UNTIL MY SOUL IS TIRED OR SATISFIED   180 7
    FOLD ON FOLD UNTIL IT GLOWS AS   217 25
    UNTIL THEY GLOW   237 26
    UNTIL YOUR VEILED HEAD ALMOST TOUCHES BACKWARD   370 14
    NOR IS IT DIRTY NOT UNTIL THE DIRTY MIND POKES IN   463 25
    UNTIL THEY COLLAPSE INTO EGOISM THE MECHANICAL SELF-CEN+ 649 4
    UNTIL HE IS BORN   683 16
    RIGHT UNTIL 'EM AND SCRAIGHTED OUT AGAIN   *911 30
    THEY HAVE ADDED BLUENESS TO BLUENESS UNTIL   *954 21

UNTIMELY
      LEST OUR FACES BETRAY US TO SOME UNTIMELY FIEND   267 34

UNTO
      THAT THEY CLEAVE UNTO AND UP WHICH THEY CLIMB   52 6
      AND THEN I OFFER ALL MYSELF UNTO   113 9
      IN US LIFE UNTO DEATH AGREEING   243 7
      A MAN BALANCES BONE UNTO BONE   251 4
      AND I IF I BE LIFTED UP WILL DRAW ALL MEN UNTO ME   320 4
      TO DRAW ALL MEN UNTO ME   320 12
      DRAWING ALL MEN UNTO THEE BUT BOUND TO RELEASE THEM WHEN   323 8
      DRINK A LITTLE BLOOD AND LOSING ANOTHER ROYALTY UNTO   414 27
      GIVE AND IT SHALL BE GIVEN UNTO YOU   449 16
      THE BODY OF ANOTHER UNTO MINE   469 27
      GOING SQUEAK SQUEAK I AM ALL THINGS UNTO MYSELF   603 19
      OH WONDERFUL MACHINE SO SELF-SUFFICIENT SO SUFFICIENT U+   643 8
      I LIFT UP MINE EYES UNTO THE HILLS   660 20
      NOTHING REMAINS NOW BUT MOULD UNTO MOULD   814 17
      THAT THEY CLEAVE UNTO THAT THEY LEAP ALONG   *899 20
      THAT THEY CLEAVE UNTO THAT THEY LEAP ALONG   *902 32
      LET US SEEK TO WIN HER BACK UNTO US THE MOON   *938 13
      A ROSE-BUSH UNTO YOU IN ALL THEIR HEARTS   *941 14
      AND EACH MAN A ROCK UNTO HIMSELF   *951 16

UNTOLD
      UNTOLD CENTURIES OF WATCHING FOR SOMETHING TO COME   394 11

UNTOUCHED
      GREAT IS MY NEED TO BE UNTOUCHED   469 8
      UNTOUCHED   469 9
      VIBRATES UNTOUCHED AND VIRILE IN LIFE UNUTTERABLE RICH   772 30
      ARE QUITE UNTOUCHED   *954 3

UNTOWARDS
      FOOD UNTOWARDS   171 23

UNTRAMMELLED
      EVERY HUMAN BEING WILL THEN BE LIKE A FLOWER UNTRAMMELL+   267 30

UNTRAVELLED
      BUT A STEP ONWARDS IN UNTRAVELLED SPACE   713 15

UNTRUE
      IT IS PAINFULLY UNTRUE   266 27

UNTURNED
      THE UNTURNED SAYS YOU LOOK IT   433 5

UNUSED
      SHE ALIGHTS A STRANGER WONDERING UNUSED TO THE SCENE   153 10

UNUTTERABLE
      GLITTERING AT ME ON THE UNUTTERABLE DARKNESS   241 6
      'TIS LIKE THE UNUTTERABLE NAME OF THE DREAD LORD   264 16
      IT IS IN PURE UNUTTERABLE RESOLVEDNESS DISTINCTION OF B+   267 3
      TWO OF US UNUTTERABLY DISTINGUISHED AND IN UNUTTERABLE +   267 22
      FOLDED UPON ITSELF AND SECRET UNUTTERABLE   283 10
      VIBRATES UNTOUCHED AND VIRILE IN LIFE UNUTTERABLE RICH   772 30
      NO MORE AND HE LAY AT HOME UNUTTERABLE DESPAIR IN HIS F+   859 16
      BLACK BIRDS WHOSE SONGS ARE UNUTTERABLE SPINNING FANTAS+   *918 14

UNUTTERABLY
      TWO OF US UNUTTERABLY DISTINGUISHED AND IN UNUTTERABLE +   267 22

UNUTTERLY
      IN A GREEN MUDDY WEB-FOOT UNUTTERLY SONGLESS WORLD   286 1

UNVEILED
      AND LUSTROUS GREAT TROPICAL EYES UNVEILED NOW GLEAMING   389 13

UNVENTILATED
      THE SKY-BLUE WALLS OF OUR UNVENTILATED HEAVEN   515 5

UNWARRANTABLE
      LIKE A THING UNWARRANTABLE CROSS THE HALL   140 8
      A SOFT MOST UNWARRANTABLE BURNING   241 11

UNWEARIEDLY
      UNWEARIEDLY UNWEARIEDLY   64 26

UNWILLING
      AND BREATHING SOFT UNWILLING TO WAKE TO THE NEW DAY   311 12
      EVEN WORK IS UNWILLING THE WORKER IS UNWILLING UNWILLING   648 9
      UNREADY UNPREPARED UNWILLING UNABLE   722 17
      THE TWO IMMENSITIES WOULD FLOAT UNWILLING   875 29
      WITH WINCING UNWILLING WAVES   *953 29

UNWILLINGNESS
      THE GREAT GRIND OF UNWILLINGNESS THE SLOW UNDERGRIND OF+   648 10

UNWINKING
      LAYING BACK HER LONG EARS WITH UNWINKING BLISS   311 19

UNWITTING
      TO HEAR ON ITS MOCKING TRIUMPHANCE UNWITTING THE AFTER-+   58 6
      WHAT IF UNWITTING I SET THE DOOR OF ETERNITY WIDE   147 11

UNWONTEDLY
      SUCH ANGER AS SETS YOUR MOUTH UNWONTEDLY   85 20

UPBORNE
      FLUENT FIGURES OF MEN GO DOWN THE UPBORNE   174 7

UPBRAID
      THE OLD ENGLAND THAT DOESN'T UPBRAID ME   534 21

UP-FLUTTER
      THEN DOUBLED AND BACK WITH A FUNNY UP-FLUTTER OF WINGS   444 21

UPHILL
      THE HARE SUDDENLY GOES UPHILL   311 18
      SWIFTNESS GALLOPED UPHILL IN THE NIGHT GOING BACK TO   390 30

UPHOLSTERED
      THE UPHOLSTERED DEAD THAT SIT IN DEEP ARM-CHAIRS   440 20

UPLIFTED
      AND COMES TOWARDS ME AH THE UPLIFTED SWORD   43 23
      I HAD STOOD WITH MY HAND UPLIFTED   122 5
      AM DRAWN TO THE UPLIFTED AS ALL MEN ARE DRAWN   320 15
      UPLIFTED   321 3
      I SAW SUDDENLY COMING TOWARDS ME LIT UP AND UPLIFTED WI+   672 20
      YET IS UPLIFTED IN ME THE PURE BEAM   745 30
      NOW THE TREES WITH INTERLOCKED HANDS AND ARMS UPLIFTED +   854 4
      HE CAME LIKE A SEA-GULL SINKING WITH UPLIFTED WINGS DOW+   860 2
      HER BREASTS UPLIFTED IN ENDEAVER SHE TOUCHES SHE REEVES   864 12
      THE MEN UPLIFTED ON THE NEW WHITE WOODSTACK STAND   *895 1
      ON THE UPLIFTED BLUE PALACE LIGHT POOLS STIR AND SHINE   *905 7

UPLIFTING
      YES EVEN DURING MY UPLIFTING   320 24
      AS I AM IF MY HEART IN UPLIFTING CEASED TO BEAT TO TOSS+   320 27
      AND EVEN MY HEART LORD FOREVER AFTER ALL UPLIFTING   321 17

UPPER
      HERE IN THIS UPPER ROOM   209 14
      TO THE FREE CALM UPPER AIR   343 2
      TO LIFT THE UPPER HAWK-BEAK FROM THE LOWER BASE   352 12
      SWUNG GREAT CURVES THROUGH THE UPPER SPACE AND CAME   445 6
      AWAY FROM THE UPPER TEN   552 14
      THE UPPER MILLSTONE OF THE ROBOT-CLASSES   642 1
      AND GOLD-BRONZE FLUTTERS BENT THROUGH THE THICK UPPER A+   647 12
      THE UPPER DARKNESS IS HEAVY AS THE LOWER   719 22
      CIRCLE WHILE I PRANCE IN THE UPPER   762 10
      AND OH SO UPPER   765 19
      FROM THE EAST TO THE WEST IN THE UPPER VALLEY   770 25
      THE LOWER CLASSES SHALL BE MADE UPPER   774 9
      AREN'T YOU PINING TO BE CLASSY SUPERIOR UPPER   774 17

UPPER CLASSES
      AND IF THEY HAD NO UPPER CLASSES EITHER TO BE INFERIOR +   527 23
      THE UPPER CLASSES THEY'RE WORSE   553 6
      NO THERE'S NOWT IN THE UPPER CLASSES   553 13
      THAN THEY'VE GOT IN THE UPPER CLASSES   553 27
      THE UPPER CLASSES ARE JUST A FRAUD   555 7

UPPER-CLASS
      OF UPPER-CLASS SUPERIORITY THAT SUPERIOR   556 19
      LET THEM GRIND ON ONE ANOTHER UPPER-CLASS ROBOT   642 12

UPPERS
      LET US WALK ABOUT IN UPPERS   774 12
      VERY HANDSOME UPPERS   774 13
      VERY REFINED UPPERS   774 14

UPRAISED
      UPRAISED TO KNOCK AND KNOCK ONCE MORE   121 15
      UPRAISED ON THE BED WITH FEET ERECT AS A BOW   155 19

UPREAR
      HEAVY TO BEAR EVEN HEAVY TO UPREAR   87 27

UPRIGHT
      PLANTED THEE UPRIGHT ART PROUD TO SEE   69 15
      THEY STAND UPRIGHT ON OUR LOVE   204 25
      YOU STAND BEFORE ME LIKE GHOSTS LIKE A DARKNESS UPRIGHT   211 8
      UPRIGHT TOWARDS HEAVEN IS BURNING OFF TO YOU   299 15
      THE LONE CLEAVAGE OF DIVISION UPRIGHT OF THE ETERNAL CR+   355 30
      UNDER A SMOOTH SKIN AND AN UPRIGHT APPEARANCE   431 21
      WITH THE UPRIGHT DIVISION INTO SEX   636 2
      THAT SEX IS AN ETERNAL UPRIGHT DIVISION BEFORE WHICH WE   636 25
      THE UPRIGHT IS TEMPORAL IS EFFORT OUTREACH   827 15
      ALL MATTER AND ALL SPIRIT STANDING UPRIGHT   872 13
      PLANTED THEE UPRIGHT ART NOT PROUD TO SEE   *915 27

UPRISEN
      THE NIGHT UPRISEN STOOD   164 27
      AUTOMATON OF YOUR UPRISEN SELF   290 28

UPROAR
      AND INSTANTLY ROSE A GREAT UPROAR   574 22

UPSET
      AND IT WOULD BE FUN TO UPSET THE APPLE-CART   517 11

UPSETTING
      SHE EDGES THROUGH WITHOUT UPSETTING HIM   426 13

UPSHOT
      THE UPSHOT WAS MY PICTURE MUST BURN   579 23

UPSIDE
      AND DISGUSTINGLY UPSIDE DOWN   342 2
      HANGING UPSIDE DOWN LIKE ROWS OF DISGUSTING OLD RAGS   342 3
      EVEN ITS BRAIN SEEMS UPSIDE DOWN   830 29

UPSIDE-DOWN
      IN THE AVENUES WHERE THE BAT HANGS SLEEPING UPSIDE-DOWN   322 33

UPSTAIRS
      UPSTAIRS DOWNSTAIRS   669 14

UPSTART
   THE UPSTART OF YOUR ROUND-BARRED SUN-ROUND TAIL   370 21
   NOT MERELY THE PERSONAL UPSTART   466 4

UP-STARTING
   OH MANY-BRANCHING CANDELABRUM OH STRANGE UP-STARTING   300 5
   FOOT IN THE MOUTH OF AN UP-STARTING SNAKE   365 31

UP-STRIVING
   OF THEIR VAIN UP-STRIVING AND NIGHT REMAINS FOR REGRET   856 4

UPTURNED
   WITH HER FACE UPTURNED TO MINE   198 2
   WITH HER FACE UPTURNED TO MINE   199 10
   GLEBE IN THE UPTURNED DARKNESS   263 28
   O FACES UPTURNED TO THE GLARE O TROPICAL WONDER WONDER   391 20

UPWARD
   WHICH RUSHES UPWARD BLADE BEYOND BLADE   49 23
   AS SHE THRUSTS THEM UPWARD UNDER THE RUFFLED SKIRT   145 30
   THE WANING MOON LOOKS UPWARD THIS GREY NIGHT   172 18
   AND THE OLD UPWARD FLOWING OF OUR SAP THE PRESSURE OF O+   609 7
   UPWARD FLOW OF FEELING   609 8
   LOOK HE HATH MOVEMENT UPWARD HE SPIRALS   682 18
   FOR I HAVE TRAVERSED MY UPWARD CURVE   764 28

UPWARDS
   AS THE BREATH WHICH UPWARDS FROM THE NOSTRILS OF AN IMM+   97 20
   WAVES OF DARK HEAT ROCK SWAY UPWARDS   302 2
   COMPARED TO THE FLOOD OF BLACK HEAT THAT ROLLS UPWARDS   302 5
   UNFOLD SLOWLY UPWARDS BLOOD-DARK   302 17
   IS IT SO THAT YOU SHALL LIFT YOUR CENTRE OF GRAVITY UPW+   332 6
   SUCH A CANNY LISTENER FROM A DISTANCE LOOKING UPWARDS   384 17
   AS THE GREEN GRASS GLOWS UPWARDS STRANGERS IN THE GARDEN   647 7
   AS HE RIPPLES UPWARDS   689 7

URANUS
   PAST VENUS AND URANUS AND THE SIGNS   713 23

URGE
   I CAN HAUL THEM AND URGE THEM NO MORE   74 11
   THE URGE THE MASSIVE BURNING ACHE   326 20
   THE MYSTERY OF CREATION IS THE DIVINE URGE OF CREATION   690 1
   BUT IT IS A GREAT STRANGE URGE IT IS NOT A MIND   690 2
   AND OUT OF THE STRUGGLE WITH HIS MATERIAL IN THE SPELL +   690 6
   GOD IS A GREAT URGE WONDERFUL MYSTERIOUS MAGNIFICENT   690 8
   HIS URGE TAKES SHAPE IN FLESH AND LO   690 10
   GOD IS THE GREAT URGE THAT HAS NOT YET FOUND A BODY   691 1
   BUT URGES TOWARDS INCARNATION WITH THE GREAT CREATIVE U+   691 16
   ALL THE WHALES IN THE WIDER DEEPS HOT ARE THEY AS THEY +   694 3
   BEFORE THE LIFE SHALL CEASE TO URGE AND STRIDE   879 6
   I CAN HAUL THEM AND URGE THEM NO MORE   *895 19
   I CAN HAUL THEM AND URGE THEM NO MORE   *904 8

URGENT
   RIPPLES BELOW THE BREAST AN URGENT   39 4
   STRANGE THAT THE URGENT WILL IN ME TO SET   218 18
   THE HOTTEST BLOOD OF ALL AND THE WILDEST THE MOST URGENT   694 2
   INTO URGENT PASSIONATE WAVES   *893 19

URGES
   BUT URGES TOWARDS INCARNATION WITH THE GREAT CREATIVE U+   691 16

URGING
   AND STRONG SPINE URGING DRIVING   336 10
   AND NERVES URGING FORWARD TO THE WALL YOU'D HAVE EYES   381 4
   HIS FULL FINE BODY BENDING AND URGING LIKE THE STRESS O+   867 24

URINAL
   THE DIRTY MIND LIKE A URINAL AGAIN   463 3

USAGE
   AND EXULTS IN ITS BITTER USAGE OF US ALL   746 12
   AND BEHOLD THEM DEPLORABLY DEAD BY WRONG USAGE DEFACED   859 24

USAGES
   IT IS WELL TO BE DISCIPLINED IN ALL THE SOCIAL USAGES   608 8

USE
   CAN USE   88 7
   LISTEN I HAVE NO USE   234 13
   RISE UP AND GO I HAVE NO USE FOR YOU   234 17
   IT IS NO USE MY SAYING TO HIM IN AN EMOTIONAL VOICE   357 1
   TO USE THE SPERM OF WHAT'S WORTH WHILE IN US   429 20
   I BOOZE AND FORNICATE AND USE FOUL LANGUAGE AND DESPISE   432 18
   IF YOU DON'T USE ROUGE AND A LIP-STICK IN PARIS   433 12
   BECAUSE REALLY IT'S NO USE PRETENDING ONE IS SUPERIOR   435 6
   WHAT WOULD BE THE USE   491 12
   AND HENCEFORTH I WILL NEVER USE   492 27
   FOR EVERYDAY USE GIVE ME SOMEBODY WHIMSICAL WITH NOT   496 3
   WOMEN FELT IT WAS NO LONGER ANY USE BEING A LINGER-LONG+   537 29
   NO MY POOR LITTLE PENIS WOULD BE OF NO USE TO YOU   541 13
   YOU'VE NO MORE USE FOR THE SOLID EARTH   549 15
   TO USE THEY'D BETTER BE USED   553 20
   CHAINED SUBJUGATED TO HIS USE   647 19
   THEY KNEW IT WAS NO USE KNOWING   688 26
   OF THOSE THAT CAN USE IT SMITE WITH IT   843 6

USED
   THE PLACE WHERE A STAR USED TO BE   115 18
   USED TO WEAR HER LIGHTS SPLENDIDLY   170 18
   SOLEMNLY USED TO APPROVE CHIME CHIMING   170 23
   THE SHADOW IT USED TO SHUN   215 25
   THAT HE USED SO OFTEN   255 2
   DO YOU LIFT IT TO THE SUN AS THE AZTEC PRIESTS USED TO +   374 7
   COMMUNION WITH THE GODHEAD THEY USED TO SAY IN THE   481 17
   HAPPY AS PERHAPS KINGS USED TO BE BUT CERTAINLY AREN'T   520 18
   AND CAN'T GET USED TO THE FACT   529 2
   AND THE LAD YOU USED TO BE   549 16
   TO USE THEY'D BETTER BE USED   553 20
   YOU'VE GOT USED TO IT   557 17
   AND BE USED TO THE TURDS   565 8
   HE USED TO GIVE KIND ADVICE TO THE PROSTITUTES ON PICCA+   582 2
   I USED TO SAY THIS IN THE PAST BUT NOW NO MORE   602 17
   WHERE THE ANGELS USED TO ALIGHT   725 19
   DEFENDING THE MEMORY OF BIRDS THAT USED TO NEST   *896 15
   FOR I USED TO THINK THAT THY   *925 2
   SUNSHINE OF HIS HAIR I USED TO KISS   *933 28
   MEN USED TO PUT THEM FORTH SENSITIVELY LIKE BOUGHS LEAV+   *950 2

USEFUL
   THEY KNEW THE USEFUL GODHEAD OF PROVIDENCE   609 24

USELESS
   DANGLING OUR USELESS HANDS   572 26
   I KNOW THERE IS NO HOPE FOR US DEATH WAITS IT IS USELES+   632 12
   AN ENGINE OF FLESH USELESS UNLESS HE IS A TOOL   635 17
   IN THESE USELESS PRACTICES OF CEREMONIAL   777 35

USES
   USING ALL LIFE ONLY AS POWER AS AN ENGINE USES STEAM OR+   635 11

USING
   AND USING HIS MOST MELODIOUS WOULD-BE-OXFORD VOICE   433 16
   FOR USING WORDS THEY PRIVATELY KEEP   492 25
   USING ALL LIFE ONLY AS POWER AS AN ENGINE USES STEAM OR+   635 11

USUAL
   CAN BLOW ACROSS THE DARK SEAS TO OUR USUAL WORLD   261 3
   A WREATH OF MIST IS THE USUAL THING   580 5

USUALLY
   USUALLY WANT TO FORCE SOMEBODY TO AGREE WITH THEM   626 5
   USUALLY IN SUITES   657 10
   THEY ARE USUALLY MUCH LESS THAN MEN   673 5
   THEN SHE TURNED TO THE OTHER MAN THERE WAS USUALLY ANOT+   842 19

UTERUS
   ARE PARTS OF THE EARTH JUST AS EMBRYOS ARE PARTS OF THE+   295 9

UTMOST
   EACH WITH THE UTMOST APATHY   357 7
   ON HER KNEES IN UTMOST CAUTION   426 11

UTTER
   THE LEAVES FLY OVER THE WINDOW AND UTTER A WORD AS THEY+   103 1
   US AWAY IN AN UTTER SLEEP UNTIL   117 6
   SO THAT THEY SEEM TO UTTER THEMSELVES ALOUD   197 25
   SIGHTLESS AND STRONG OBLIVION IN UTTER LIFE TAKES POSSE+   261 10
   AND KINDLES IT FURTHER AT THE CORE OF UTTER MYSTERY   261 16
   WRETCHES UTTER WRETCHES KEEP YOUR HANDS FROM BEANS SAITH   303 15
   AND UTTER LOVABLENESS YOU UGLY-MUG   398 4
   GOBBLE UP FILTH YOU HORROR SWALLOW UTTER ABOMINATION   398 28
   TO HIM WORSE THAN A BOLSHEVIST JEW OR AN UTTER   576 8
   WITH ASHES OF UTTER BOREDOM ENNUI AND DISGUST   616 12
   ONLY THEY ARE MADE TO UTTER THESE COG-WHEEL SOUNDS   657 15
   WHERE THE SOUL COMES AT LAST AND HAS UTTER PEACE   724 7
   IN UTTER PEACE   724 10
   IF THERE WERE NOT AN UTTER AND ABSOLUTE DARK   724 12
   AND IF THERE WERE NOT AN ABSOLUTE UTTER FORGETTING   724 20
   AND WHAT I'VE UNDERSTOOD AND THEN THE UTTER ACHE   738 11
   TO HAVE NO REST SAVE IN THE UTTER NIGHT   744 15
   THE SECRET OF THE NOISELESS UTTER GRACE   744 27
   INTO THE UTTER DARK THEY CANNOT HEAR   744 31
   FROM SEEKING THE UTTER DROWNING   772 18
   NOT TO UTTER ONE CRY TO HER   874 21
   BUT THE UTTER ANGUISHED SPRINGING FORTH OF ME   880 5
   SO THE POOR THING IS LEFT FEELING AN UTTER WORM   *948 19
   THAT CONVULSES AND TREMBLES AGAIN WITH THE SYMPATHY OF +   *952 7
   AND PIERCES HER ONCE MORE WITH HIS PASSION OF THE UTTER+   *956 18
   OF SHEER OBLIVION AND OF UTTER PEACE   *959 32
   AND HOW HE FINDS THE DARKNESS THAT ENFOLDS HIM INTO UTT+   *961 13

UTTERANCE
   CHILDREN ACTS UTTERANCE   247 21
   BUT IT WILL BE LIKE MUSIC SHEER UTTERANCE   268 6
   HERE'S TO THE THORN IN FLOWER HERE IS TO UTTERANCE   283 8

UTTERED
   BY BRIGHT LEAVES UTTERED ALOUD AND STRIFE   68 7
   IS THE LAST WORD NOW UTTERED   102 19
   AND THE CHILDREN UTTERED A LITTLE CRY   444 17
   AN OLD FRENCHMAN UTTERED THE TRUISM   641 17

UTTERING
   CUP FOR A MOMENT SOFT LITTLE WING-BEATS UTTERING   65 4

UTTERLY
   IN MY POWER UTTERLY   59 18
   AND CLAIM HER UTTERLY IN A KISS   62 7
   SINCE DEATH HAS DELIVERED US UTTERLY STRIPPED AND WHITE   132 15
   UTTERLY   205 22
   HOW I DEPEND ON YOU UTTERLY   247 13
   MORE UTTERLY THAN WE WHO HAVE NEVER KNOWN   286 18
   FRAIL-NAKED UTTERLY UNCOVERED   306 10
   UTTERLY BEYOND THEE DOVE OF THE SPIRIT   322 5
   SO UTTERLY WITHOUT MISGIVING   337 7
   I AM HERE YET MY HEART IS BARE AND UTTERLY EMPTY   509 7
   THE HOWL OF THE UTTERLY LOST   514 23
   SO HIDEOUS AND CORPSE-LIKE UTTERLY SUNLESS   526 14
   I FEEL THAT WHEN PEOPLE HAVE GONE UTTERLY SUNLESS   526 23
   THEY HAVE UTTERLY NO REFERENCE TO THE SUN   527 17
   CRUSHED UTTERLY AND BREATHED THROUGH AND THROUGH   530 2
   AWARE AT LAST THAT OUR MANHOOD IS UTTERLY LOST   585 7
   BUT UTTERLY FAILS TO RECOGNISE ANY MORE THE GREY RAT-HO+   640 5

UTTERLY
    TILL ALL IS WELL TILL ALL IS UTTERLY WELL THE LOTUS-LIL+   652 13
    AND SIDEWAYS UTTERLY DARK SO THERE IS NO DIRECTION ANY +   719 14
    AND LONGING UTTERLY TO DIE   721 2
    OF WHAT WAS GOD BE GONE BE UTTERLY GONE   738 5
    UTTERLY GONE AWAY ON ANOTHER ERRAND   767 25
    BUT BE CAREFUL HOW YOU UTTERLY QUASH THEM   776 32
    UTTERLY DEAD WHO LIVED BUT TO BANISH   855 7
    HAD UTTERLY GONE FROM OUT OF THE TREMBLING SKY   885 8
    AND CLAIM HER UTTERLY IN A KISS   *912 14

UTTERMOST
    AND STRANGE WAYS WHERE I FALL INTO OBLIVION OF UTTERMOST   261 6
    UTTERMOST TENSION   365 6
    INTO THE UTTERMOST CORNERS OF THE SOUL   624 12
    ALL THE CREATURES THAT WERE DRIVEN BACK INTO THE UTTERM+   *954 14

UTTERS
    OR WHEN IT UTTERS THAT UNDAUNTED LITTLE BIRD-CRY   439 1

VACANT
    ALONG THE VACANT ROAD A RED   100 5
    YOU DO NOTHING BUT SQUAT ON YOUR HAMS AND STARE WITH VA+   795 2

VACUOUS
    I MUST BE RECIPROCATING YOUR VACUOUS HIDEOUS PASSION   241 27

VAGUE
    TO-MORROW SWIMMING IN EVENING'S VAGUE DIM VAPOUR   72 16

VAGUELY
    AND LOOKED AT ME VAGUELY AS DRINKING CATTLE DO   349 22
    SHOWS THAT THE CHILDREN VAGUELY KNOW HOW CHEATED THEY   446 16

VAIN
    IT IS VAIN   40 6
    SHE SHINES THE FIRST WHITE LOVE OF MY YOUTH PASSIONLESS+   67 21
    I'LL SAY YOUR BOND OF UGLINESS IS VAIN   72 23
    THA WANTS IT AND EVERYTHING ELSE IS IN VAIN   139 19
    SO NOW IT IS VAIN FOR THE SINGER TO BURST INTO CLAMOUR   148 15
    A PRIESTESS EXECRABLE TAKEN IN VAIN   151 1
    HAS THE PEACOCK HAD HIS DAY DOES HE CALL IN VAIN SCREECH   371 20
    IN VAIN TRYING TO WAKE THE MORROW   371 23
    IN VAIN IN VAIN IN VAIN OH VASTLY IN VAIN   636 20
    I SPEAK WITH A VAIN MOUTH   745 29
    IN VAIN   748 25
    SO HE PASSED THE YELLOW LINE WHO LASHED LIKE A DRAGON I+   790 3
    OF THEIR VAIN UP-STRIVING AND NIGHT REMAINS FOR REGRET   856 4
    STILL GAY AND LAUGHING IN MY OWN VAIN STRENGTH   875 30

VALLEY
    THE SAME VALLEY WITH PURPLE AND WHITE   37 28
    THIS IS OUR OWN STILL VALLEY   38 1
    AND I KNEW THAT HOME THIS VALLEY WAS WIDER THAN PARADISE   38 17
    SO NOW I KNOW THE VALLEY   38 23
    IN THE WOMANLY VALLEY AND PLY   40 15
    DOWN THE VALLEY ROARS A TOWNWARD TRAIN   50 15
    CLEAR UPON THE LONG-DRAWN HOARSENESS OF A TRAIN ACROSS +   63 11
    IN THE VALLEY A CORNCRAKE CALLS   64 21
    FARTHER DOWN THE VALLEY THE CLUSTERED TOMBSTONES RECEDE   102 29
    AS IF A BIRD IN DIFFICULTY UP THE VALLEY STEERS   210 22
    AND SUNSHINE FILLS ONE HIGH VALLEY BED   224 12
    SNOW AND INWARDNESS OF THE LOBO VALLEY   401 13
    THE ISAR WHISPERS AGAIN IN THE VALLEY THE CHILDREN   732 18
    THE HIGH VIRGIN VALLEY   768 26
    TO A VIRGIN VALLEY HIGH UP   769 17
    FROM THE EAST TO THE WEST IN THE UPPER VALLEY   770 25
    THIS IS OUR OWN STILL VALLEY   *892 17
    AND SAY THAT THIS HOME THIS VALLEY IS WIDER THAN PARADI+   *892 32
    THE ASH-TREES OF THE VALLEY ROAD SHOULD RAISE   *941 2

VALLEY-MOUTH
    ABOVE THE TREES OF THE LOBO DARK VALLEY-MOUTH   402 20

VALLEY-ROAD
    THE ASH-TREES OF THE VALLEY-ROAD WILL RAISE   176 15

VALLEYS
    FIVE VALLEYS GO FIVE PASSES LIKE GATES   224 9
    AND VALLEYS THAT DRAW CLOSE IN LOVE   261 5
    VALLEYS OF THE WATERS UNDER THE SEA   321 36
    WANDERING INTO NEW VALLEYS   768 14

VALUE
    AS IF IT WERE COIN WITH A FIXED VALUE   662 5

VALUES
    FOR OLD VALUES AND OLD PEOPLE   612 14

VALVED
    ALL LIPS ARE DUSKY AND VALVED   288 22

VALVES
    BETWEEN TWO VALVES OF DARKNESS   205 5
    HE OPENED THE VALVES OF LIFE AND HIS LIFE SIGHED OUT   885 9

VAN
    THE DARK VAN DRUMMED DOWN THE DISTANCE LOWLY   121 30

VANILLA
    EVE PUSHING THE FESTOONED VANILLA TREMBLING ASIDE   864 7

VANISH
    I WOULD BE WILLING TO VANISH COMPLETELY COMPLETELY   430 9
    FOR A DAY FOR TWO DAYS AND WITHDRAW SLOWLY VANISH AGAIN   476 14
    IT IS ENOUGH I SAW YOU VANISH INTO AIR   696 28
    AT THE END OF A SWEET SPRING DAY THEY WILL VANISH   855 5

VANISHED
    TAKE UP THE TRAIL OF THE VANISHED AMERICAN   371 26
    NO MEANING IN THE SKY THE MEANING HAS VANISHED FROM THE   871 14

VANISHING
    THE SILENCE OF VANISHING TEARS AND THE ECHOES OF LAUGHT+   53 19
    NOW EVEN THE SHADOW OF THE LOST SECRET IS VANISHING FRO+ 295 3
    WHAT ARE THEY DOING HERE ON THIS VANISHING TRAIL   401 14

VANITY
    AND MY HOLLOW FLESH STANDS UP IN THE NIGHT LIKE VANITY   97 10
    BUT ANOTHER WORD CONCEIT AND VANITY   158 14
    FOR THE DEAD VANITY OF KNOWING BETTER NOR THE BLANK   709 30
    THE VANITY OF LIFE   762 2

VANQUISHED
    AND VANQUISHED EVAPORATE AWAY   53 30

VANTAGE
    YEA THOUGH THE VERY CLOUDS HAVE VANTAGE OVER ME   133 22
    YEA THOUGH THE VERY CLOUDS HAVE VANTAGE OVER ME   772 9

VAPOUR
    TO-MORROW SWIMMING IN EVENING'S VAGUE DIM VAPOUR   72 16
    LIKE VAPOUR DEW OR POISON NOW THANK GOD   91 1
    A VAPOUR OF ROTTENNESS OUT OF THEIR MOUTHS LIKE SEWER-S+ 462 27
    AS IF IT WAS GIVING OFF POISON VAPOUR   583 13
    AND A BREATH OF VAPOUR BEGAN TO WREATHE UP   682 14

VARIATION
    I WISH THEY'D BE TRUE TO THEIR OWN VARIATION AS WATER IS 505 20

VARIEGATED
    HOW EVANESCENT VARIEGATED ELDER SHE HESITATES ON THE GR+ 646 25

VARIEGATION
    AND BUDDING TOWARDS INFINITE VARIETY VARIEGATION   612 5

VARIETY
    AND BUDDING TOWARDS INFINITE VARIETY VARIEGATION   612 5
    AND WHERE THERE IS INFINITE VARIETY THERE IS NO INTERES+ 612 6
    TO KEEP THE REFLECTED VARIETY OF THE HOUSEBOATS   867 9

VARIOUS
    THAT DOES INFORM THIS VARIOUS DREAM OF LIVING   194 20
    I AM NOT A MECHANISM AN ASSEMBLY OF VARIOUS SECTIONS   620 10
    MUNDANE EGG AT VARIOUS POINTS THEY STEPPED OUT AND IMME+ 760 23

VASES
    THIS IS THE ANCIENT SOUTHERN EARTH WHENCE THE VASES WERE 305 12

VAST
    HE IS WORDLESS BUT SULTRY AND VAST   39 15
    SINCE LIFE SWEEPS WHIRLING DIM AND VAST   69 1
    IT CURVES IN A RUSH TO THE HEART OF THE VAST   166 26
    WALLED IN WALLED IN THE WHOLE WORLD IS A VAST IMPURE   174 23
    STILL IN THE VAST HOLLOW   193 23
    SINCE YOU VAST OUTSTRETCHED WORDLESS SLEEP   194 26
    IF SO THE VAST THE GOD THE SLEEP THAT STILL GROWS RICHER 195 17
    THAT SLOWLY LABOURS IN A VAST TRAVAIL   195 33
    SEE IF I DON'T MOVE UNDER A DARK AND NUDE VAST HEAVEN   289 19
    NOT THIS VAST ROTTING CABBAGE PATCH WE CALL THE WORLD   315 32
    NAY ONCE IT WAS ALSO A FORTRESS WALL AND THE WEIGHT OF + 326 25
    IS HE NOT OVER-FULL OF OFFERING A VAST VAST OFFER OF HI+ 327 18
    THE VAST INANIMATE   353 21
    WHAT A HUGE VAST INANIMATE IT IS THAT YOU MUST ROW   353 25
    AND WENT WHIZZING THROUGH THE SLOW VAST SUCCULENT   372 12
    AIR VAST BEAST   385 24
    SUBTLY TO THE TWIGS OVERHEAD FAR UP VAST BEAST   385 27
    THE KEEPER HOODS THE VAST KNEE THE CREATURE SALAAMS   387 16
    ELEPHANTS AFTER ELEPHANTS CURL THEIR TRUNKS VAST SHADOWS 388 1
    SERVE VAST MOUNTAINOUS BLOOD IN SUBMISSION AND SPLENDOUR 390 14
    AND THEN HER GREAT WEIGHT BELOW THE WAIST HER VAST PALE 393 15
    AND SHOW VAST BELLIES TO THE CHILDREN   425 22
    LEAVING IT TO THE VAST REVOLUTIONS OF CREATIVE CHAOS   429 24
    THE SWAN WITHIN VAST CHAOS WITHIN THE ELECTRON   435 28
    AS THE VAST WHITE BIRD   436 15
    FOR THE SYMPATHY IN THEIR VAST SHY HEARTS   465 11
    MONEY IS OUR MADNESS OUR VAST COLLECTIVE MADNESS   486 7
    WE LIVE IN A VAST HOUSE   510 26
    AND YET AS WE DIE WHY SHOULD NOT OUR VAST MECHANISED   512 27
    NOTHING AND NOBODY IN THE WHOLE VAST REALM OF SPACE   514 20
    AND ENSHROUDED IN THE VAST CORPSE OF THE INDUSTRIAL MIL+ 629 30
    AND DEVOURED YOU WITH THE MACHINE THE VAST MAW OF IRON 630 16
    WHEN THE VAST MASSES OF MEN HAVE BEEN CAUGHT BY THE   631 11
    THERE IS HOWEVER THE VAST THIRD HOMOGENEOUS AMORPHOUS   649 24
    THERE ARE VAST REALMS OF CONSCIOUSNESS STILL UNDREAMED + 666 24
    VAST RANGES OF EXPERIENCE LIKE THE HUMMING OF UNSEEN HA+ 666 25
    IT IS LIKE A VAST GREAT TREE WITH A VAST GREAT LOT OF S+ 677 21
    THERE IS A BREAST OF A VAST AND UNKNOWN BODY   784 9
    THE VAST GREAT REACHES BETWEEN THE SUNS   823 23
    MONEY IS THE VAST STINKING BEAST   843 7
    CREEP ON THE VAST MONEY-BEAST   843 11
    TO THE VAST OF SPACE WHERE BRIGHTNESS RACES THE BLUE   875 14
    SINCE GOD SWEEPS ONWARD DIM AND VAST   *915 13
    THE FATHER OF ALL THINGS SWIMS IN THE VAST DUSK OF ALL *947 17
    BALANCE WITH THE OTHER THE VAST UNKNOWABLE FIRE   *951 30

VAST-BLOODED
  VAST-BLOODED BEASTS   390 15

VASTER
  THE HUMAN WILL TO THE FLUSH OF THE VASTER IMPULSION OF +   617 14
  THE VASTER FIRE   *952 3

VASTLY
  IN VAIN IN VAIN IN VAIN OH VASTLY IN VAIN   636 20
  THEY DON'T REALLY CARE VASTLY   828 23

VASTNESS
  AND SMILES THE VASTNESS OF HER ELEPHANT ANTIQUITY   426 6
  THE VASTNESS IS EMPTY EXCEPT THAT THERE PLY   823 20

VAT
  IN A VAT   129 31

VAULTED
  HOW HAVE I WANDERED HERE TO THIS VAULTED ROOM   141 5
  DRUMMING HIS VAULTED WINGS AS SAVAGES DRUM   371 4

VAULTS
  AND LOOK ROUND AND RISE AND ON THE GREAT VAULTS OF HIS +   625 3

VAUNT
  THE TREASURE AND THE VAUNT WE EVER HAD   737 14

VEAL
  THE ROAST VEAL I AM SHAKING IT FOR YOU   762 13

VEERING
  VEERING SLOWLY   321 34

VEERS
  OF THE WIND AND ITS ONENESS VEERS   253 26
  HE VEERS ROUND THE SLOW GREAT MOUND OF HER   356 29

VEGA
  VEGA AND SIRIUS AND ALTAIR   713 21

VEGETABLE
  VEGETABLE NEW IN RENOWN   49 28
  I BELIEVE HE PIERCED THE SLOW VEGETABLE VEINS WITH HIS +   372 16
  LIKE A WELL-WASHED VEGETABLE   828 5

VEHICLES
  PEOPLE HOUSES STREETS VEHICLES MACHINES   256 26

VEIL
  A SINGLE STAR IN A VEIL OF LIGHT   41 29
  FOR THE LIPS AND THE EYES OF GOD ARE BEHIND A VEIL   48 10
  VEIL   53 2
  WHEN THE WIND BLOWS HER VEIL   133 26
  WHEN THE WIND BLOWS HER VEIL   133 29
  WHEN THE WIND BLOWS HER VEIL   133 32
  MY VEIL OF SENSITIVE MYSTERY RENT IN TWAIN   151 19
  WHY WAS THE VEIL TORN   364 23
  PERHAPS IT IS A SORT OF UNCANNY DECORATION A VEIL OF LO+   369 25
  IN THE PURPLE VEIL   742 16
  YOU ARE MISTAKEN THE VEIL OF THE FLESH IS RENT   742 18
  AND THE VEIL OF THE TEMPLE RENT AT THE KISS ON KISS   742 28
  I HAVE A CHARM LIKE LAUGHTER THROUGH A VEIL   860 15
  UP THROUGH THE VEIL AS WE PASSED   884 34
  OVER THE NEARNESS OF NORWOOD HILL THROUGH THE MELLOW VE+   *905 17

VEILED
  AND ANOTHER LILAC IN PURPLE VEILED   105 31
  UNTIL YOUR VEILED HEAD ALMOST TOUCHES BACKWARD   370 14

VEILS
  WITH SEVEN VEILS AND AN INNERMOST   726 8
  MAY SINK INTO GOD AT LAST HAVING PASSED THE VEILS   726 11

VEIN
  CREATING THE CHANNELLED VEIN OF MAN   69 2
  THROUGH INVISIBLE PULSES SLOWLY FILLING THE NIGHT'S DAR+   97 28
  THEIR BLOOD IN A WOMAN TO THE VERY LAST VEIN   139 17
  I THE GREAT VEIN THAT LEADS   240 4
  TO HIS GUEST CHAMBER KNOWING EACH SINEW AND VEIN   877 37
  DOWN EVERY CHANNELLED VEIN OF MAN   *915 14
  FOR I HAVE SEEN THE VEIN   *937 7

VEINED
  LIFTING YOUR VEINED WINGS LIFTING THEM BIG WHITE BUTTER+   696 14

VEINS
  WITH SWOLLEN VEINS THAT MET IN THE WRIST   123 25
  I ADAM FORM THE VEINS OF ME   240 11
  UP MY VEINS AS UP A CHIMNEY   241 30
  COAGULATING AND GOING BLACK IN MY VEINS   301 25
  PURE BLOOD AND NOBLE BLOOD IN THE FINE AND ROSE-RED VEI+   314 1
  I BELIEVE HE PIERCED THE SLOW VEGETABLE VEINS WITH HIS +   372 17
  O RUDDY GOD IN OUR VEINS O FIERY GOD IN OUR GENITALS   440 12
  POURING INTO THE VEINS FROM THE DIRECT CONTACT WITH THE   481 28
  THE VEINS OF THE EARTH   504 22
  THE VEINS OF LIVING SPACE AND ADDS A GLISTEN   505 3
  IF MY VEINS AND MY BREASTS WITH LOVE EMBOSSED   *891 26
  WITH SWOLLEN VEINS THAT MET IN THE WRIST   *934 31

VELOCITY
  LIKE A WHALE RECOVERING ITS VELOCITY AND STRENGTH   428 14

VELVET
  WE HAVE SHUT THE DOORS BEHIND US AND THE VELVET FLOWERS+   70 1
  A JACKET OF VELVET   388 20
  WE HAVE SHUT THE DOORS BEHIND US AND THE VELVET FLOWERS+   *916 9

VELVETY
  WHY SO VELVETY WHY SO VOLUPTUOUS HEAVY   279 14

VENDOR
  AS A VENDOR OF FRIED FISH ONCE MORE YELLOW   760 21

VENETIAN
  SILVER-PINK PEACH VENETIAN GREEN GLASS OF MEDLARS AND S+   283 5
  THE VENETIAN SHUTTERS I PUSH WIDE   343 1

VENGEANCE
  VENGEANCE IS MINE SAITH THE LORD   541 8
  VENGEANCE IS MINE SAITH THE LORD I WILL REPAY   616 1
  THEY FALL VICTIM AT ONCE TO THE VENGEANCE OF THE UNFORG+   616 7
  IT IS THE VENGEANCE OF THE LORD LONG AND UNREMITTING   616 13
  AND SO THE LORD OF VENGEANCE PAYS BACK REPAYS LIFE   616 16

VENICE
  WHEREAS AT VENICE   278 9
  AT LEAST AT VENICE   323 23
  AT VENICE AND ELSEWHERE   325 24
  IN SLUGGISH VENICE   332 10

VENOM
  THE FEMALE WHOSE VENOM CAN MORE THAN KILL CAN NUMB AND +   98 9
  LIKE MILK WITH ELECTRIC VENOM   797 11

VENOMOUS
  ARE VENOMOUS   350 4
  CREEPING FOR THE GARBAGE OF LIFE AND BITING WITH VENOMO+   796 13

VENOMOUSLY
  VENOMOUSLY   502 26

VENT
  WHICH MUST BE POURED THROUGH SO SMALL A VENT   327 19
  TOO SMALL A VENT   327 20
  OF OBSCENITY AND LIFT YOUR NOSES WHERE THE VENT IS   462 32

VENTURE
  TAKE THEM AWAY FROM THEIR VENTURE BEFORE FATE WRESTS   147 16
  I VENTURE FROM THE HALLS OF SHADOWY DEATH   744 11
  AH SURE TO VENTURE ALL ALONE IN DEATH   879 26

VENTURED
  VENTURED SO LONG AGO IN THE DEEPS OF REFLECTION   161 19
  VENTURED IN   256 11

VENTURESOME
  FOR YOU SET WIDE THE DOORS OF MY VENTURESOME ARK   875 23

VENTUROUS
  AND LAMPS LIKE VENTUROUS GLOW-WORMS STEAL AMONG   *939 9

VENUS
  WHAT DOES SHE WANT VOLCANIC VENUS AS SHE GOES FUMING   539 10
  OF DOVES FOR VENUS OR STEERS FOR HERMES   678 5
  IF IT IS MERELY VENUS OR HERMES YOU ARE THINKING OF   678 6
  VENUS WOULD RATHER HAVE LIVE DOVES THAN DEAD IF YOU WAN+   673 7
  AND VENUS AMONG THE FISHES SKIPS AND IS A SHE-DOLPHIN   695 9
  FAR AND FORGOTTEN IS THE VILLA OF VENUS THE GLOWING   695 25
  PAST VENUS AND URANUS AND THE SIGNS   713 23

VERB
  THERE WAS NO VERB   681 14

VERBOSITY
  AND LET THE NODDING TEMPESTS OF VERBOSITY   543 8

VERDIGRIS
  NOW VERDIGRIS SMOULDERING SOFTLY SPREAD   142 25

VERGE
  ON TOWARDS THE PINES AT THE HILL'S WHITE VERGE   85 8

VERILY
  TILL I WAS VERILY SWELTED   80 12
  TOUCHED THAT WHICH WAS VERILY NOT ME   259 3
  VERILY IT WAS NOT ME   259 4
  IT VERILY WAS NOT I   259 9
  TILL I WAS VERILY SWELTED   *922 12

VERITIES
  OF VERITIES   236 31

VERITY
  NOR A VERITY   166 14
  INTO THE VERITY OF THE ONLY ONE   784 7

VERMILION
  FAR-OFF KINGS PAINTED THEIR FACES VERMILION AND WERE AL+   303 22
  THIS QUEER DROSS SHAWL OF BLUE AND VERMILION   369 22
  LO THE LOVELIEST IS RED ALL OVER RIPPLING VERMILION   689 6
  VERMILION   689 11

VERMIN
  THESE MONEY VERMIN   792 28

VERSE
  DARTING HIS LIGHT PUNT WITH THE QUICK-SHIFTING FANCY OF+   867 25

VERTEBRAL
  IN A RUSH UP THE SHRIEKING DUCT OF HIS VERTEBRAL WAY   381 20

VERY-YOUNG
    LIKE DELICATE VERY-YOUNG GREYHOUND BITCHES   311 6

VESSEL
    OUR BEACHED VESSEL DARKENED RENCONTRE INHUMAN AND CLOSE+   65 27
    AND TRIED TO BREAK THE VESSEL AND VIOLATE MY SOUL   92 24
    VESSEL OF DARKNESS TAKES THE RISING TIDE   132 30
    NOW LIKE A VESSEL IN PORT   168 7
    AND NEVER THE TWO-WINGED VESSEL   227 21
    SMASH IT IN LIKE A FRAIL VESSEL   869 23
    VESSEL ITSELF   *953 11

VESSELS
    LIPS TO THE VESSELS NEVER SHRINK   177 15
    VESSELS   481 5
    BUT THE WOMEN ARE MY FAVOURITE VESSELS OF WRATH   541 9
    THE LIGHT WHICH IS FED FROM TWO VESSELS   810 27

VESTIGE
    EVERY VESTIGE GONE THEN I AM HERE   258 27
    TILL NOT A VESTIGE IS LEFT AND BLACK WINTER HAS NO TRACE   709 20

VESUVIUS
    IT IS RATHER AGITATING SLEEPING WITH A LITTLE VESUVIUS   539 6

VETCH-CLUMP
    WHILE THAT VETCH-CLUMP STILL BURNS RED   35 8

VEXES
    THAT VEXES ME WITH WONDER HE SITS SO STILL   225 18

VIA DE' BARDI
    THE VIA DE' BARDI   342 11
    ABOVE THAT CRASH-GULF OF THE VIA DE' BARDI   343 14
    VIA DE' BARDI   347 13

VIBRATE
    OF BEES THAT VIBRATE WITH REVOLT WHO FALL TO EARTH   73 18

VIBRATES
    VIBRATES UNTOUCHED AND VIRILE IN LIFE UNUTTERABLE RICH   772 30
    AND DAY BY DAY MY HAPPINESS VIBRATES   *943 24

VIBRATING
    MOVING VIBRATING ENDLESSLY IN THE ROUNDED FLESH   *906 24
    OF MEN VIBRATING IN ECSTASY THROUGH THE ROUNDED FLESH   *908 21

VIBRATION
    VIBRATION TO DRAW   165 32
    COMES LIKE A PUNGENT SCENT A VIBRATION BENEATH   270 13
    THE VIBRATION OF THE MOTOR-CAR HAS BRUISED THEIR INSENS+   625 17
    THE PROFOUND AND THRILLING VIBRATION OF JUSTICE SENSE O+   653 15
    A SLOW HEAVY PATTER OF LESSENING VIBRATION   767 20

VIBRATIONS
    SENDING OUT MAGNETIC VIBRATIONS OF WARNING PITCH-DARK   289 2
    TILL IT REACHES US AND ITS VIBRATIONS SHATTER US   512 19
    STRIKING US THE VIBRATIONS OF OUR FINISH   512 22
    ARE LONG SLOW VIBRATIONS OF PAIN   627 18

VICAR
    THE BURDENED AGE SEVENTY-NINE THE VICAR   859 2

VICE
    ALL THE LOT OF THEM VICE MISSIONS ETC INSANELY UNHEALTHY   845 10
    BUT CHASTITY ON THE BRAIN IS A VICE A PERVERSION   845 12
    BUT CHASTITY ON THE BRAIN IS ANOTHER VICE IT ENDS IN LU+   *952 26

VICES
    THEY ARE DEAD WITH ALL THEIR VICES   297 18

VICIOUS
    ASHAMED AND SHAMEFUL AND VICIOUS   264 31
    WHOM ROME CALLED VICIOUS   297 8
    VICIOUS DARK CYPRESSES   297 9
    VICIOUS YOU SUPPLE BROODING SOFTLY-SWAYING PILLARS OF   297 10
    WERE THEY THEN VICIOUS THE SLENDER TENDER-FOOTED   297 14
    WE BECOME VICIOUS   468 21
    THE WAGES OF WANT MORE CASH IS VICIOUS COMPETITION   521 3
    THE WAGES OF VICIOUS COMPETITION IS THE WORLD WE LIVE IN   521 4
    BUT THEY CAN'T OR THERE'D BE THE VICIOUS CIRCLE   819 15
    BAWDY ON THE BRAIN BECOMES OBSCENITY VICIOUS   845 7

VICIOUSEST
    THE WORK-CASH-WANT CIRCLE IS THE VICIOUSEST CIRCLE   521 5

VICIOUSNESS
    IN SYRACUSE ROCK LEFT BARE BY THE VICIOUSNESS OF GREEK   278 4

VICTIM
    LIKE A FALCON 'TIS GOD HAS TAKEN THE VICTIM   239 5
    SO HE COULD TRACK HER DOWN AGAIN WHITE VICTIM   308 23
    THEY FALL VICTIM AT ONCE TO THE VENGEANCE OF THE UNFORG+   616 7
    TO ITS VICTIM   765 25

VICTIMS
    FOR THEIR VICTIMS   795 27

VICTORIAN
    HER LITTLE LOOSE HANDS AND DROOPING VICTORIAN SHOULDERS   393 14

VICTORIANS
    WE HATE THE VICTORIANS SO MUCH   627 21
    HAVE ALL BY MR WATTS AND THE VICTORIANS BEEN CAREFULLY   658 18

VICTORIOUS
    VICTORIOUS GREY GRISLY GHOSTS IN OUR STREETS   740 2

VICTORS
    FIELD AND AS VICTORS WE TRAVEL   243 15

VICTORY
    OF VICTORY KNEADED WITH SULPHUR   758 21

VIEW
    TAKING A BIRD'S-EYE VIEW   328 4

VIEWED
    IN VIRGIN OUTRAGE AS THEY VIEWED   680 18

VIGOROUSLY
    WHEN YOU WENT FORTH SO VIGOROUSLY IN SEARCH   661 5

VILE
    CONDESCEND TO BE VILE   234 8
    WHY SHOULD ONE LOVE PEACE IT IS SO OBVIOUSLY VILE TO MA+   495 18
    FROM DURANCE VILE   580 18
    ORDER YOU DESTROY THE WHOLE VILE PACK   633 29

VILEST
    SELF-SACRIFICE IS PERHAPS THE VILEST DEED A MAN CAN DO   679 23
    IS THE VILEST COWARDICE AND TREACHERY   680 2

VILLA
    FAR AND FORGOTTEN IS THE VILLA OF VENUS THE GLOWING   695 25

VILLAGE
    THE MOON-MIST IS OVER THE VILLAGE OUT OF THE MIST SPEAK+   63 4
    AND ALL THE LITTLE ROOFS OF THE VILLAGE BOW LOW PITIFUL+   63 5
    AND THE VILLAGE FOLK OUTSIDE IN THE BURYING-GROUND   233 2
    BUT IF OBSCENE VILLAGE IDIOTS YOU WANT TO BE THEN BE IT   463 13
    MENDING AND TINNING THE PANS OF ALL THE VILLAGE   520 15

VILLAGE-IDIOT
    IT'S THE VILLAGE-IDIOT MIND   463 8

VILLAGERS
    THE PRIESTS IN GOLD AND BLACK THE VILLAGERS   232 19
    THE SILENCE OF THE MANY VILLAGERS   232 30
    THOSE VILLAGERS ISOLATED AT THE GRAVE   233 5

VILLAGES
    VILLAGES   389 3
    MEN-PEASANTS FROM JUNGLE VILLAGES DANCING AND RUNNING   389 5
    THE JUNGLE VILLAGES   390 31
    FROM THEIR TREE OF LIFE AND VILLAGES WHOLE CITIES LIVED+   *950 4

VILLAS
    IN A LITTLE HALF-BUILT STREET WHERE RED AND WHITE VILLAS   864 25

VINDICATE
    COME QUICKLY AND VINDICATE US   273 5

VINDICATED
    TWO WHITE ONES SHARP VINDICATED   210 16

VINDICTIVE
    VINDICTIVE   341 27
    OH VINDICTIVE EAGLE OF AMERICA   783 21

VINDICTIVENESS
    WITH POSSESSIVE VINDICTIVENESS   475 23

VINE
    WHAT THEN OF THE VINE   285 10
    OH WHAT OF THE TENDRILLED VINE   285 11
    OF WHICH WORLD THE VINE WAS THE INVISIBLE ROSE   285 30
    THE VINE WAS ROSE OF ALL ROSES   286 2
    WHEN THE VINE WAS ROSE GODS WERE DARK-SKINNED   286 14
    LOOK AT THE MANY-CICATRISED FRAIL VINE NONE MORE SCARRED   305 4
    SO IT WILL LEAVE YOU AND YOU WILL HAND LIKE A GOURD ON +   800 22

VINE-FLOWER
    AND THE TINY VINE-FLOWER ROSE OF ALL ROSES PERFUMED   286 27

VINES
    AS VINES GOING EAGERLY UP THEY TWINE   52 9
    GREEN DIM INVISIBLE FLOURISHING OF VINES   286 5
    WHOSE MASTS HAVE PURPLE VINES   693 26
    WITH VINES AND POPPIES AND FIG-TREES   710 16

VINGONE
    THE ONE THAT WENT TO VINGONE   846 7

VIOLATE
    AND TRIED TO BREAK THE VESSEL AND VIOLATE MY SOUL   92 24
    WE VIOLATE OURSELVES   468 20
    THEN THEY'D BE ABLE TO LOVE DESPAIR CAN'T LOVE IT CAN O+   838 13
    WE VIOLATE OURSELVES EVERY MOMENT AND VIOLATE EVERYBODY+   839 6

VIOLATED
    AND AREN'T YOUR FEELINGS VIOLATED YOU HIGH-BRED LITTLE +   400 13

VIOLATION
    AND REALLY A NASTY VIOLATION   470 20
    IN A COG-WHEEL CLATTER OF VIOLATION   839 7

VIOLENT
    YOUR VIOLENT HEART BEATS TO AND FRO   122 12
    WITH VIOLENT ACHINGS HEAVING TO BURST THE SLEEP THAT IS+   149 23
    I AM SO TIRED OF VIOLENT WOMEN LASHING OUT AND INSISTING   479 7
    AND STILL AGAINST THE DARK AND VIOLENT WIND   745 6
    AND UNDERNEATH THE GREAT TURBULENT EMOTIONS OF LOVE THE+   844 7

VIOLENTEST
    AND DARKER THAN EVEN THE ARROWS OF VIOLENTEST WILL   383 10

VIOLET
    ALL BE SWEET WITH WHITE AND BLUE VIOLET   40 29
    VIOLET AIR   149 18
    LET THE DARKNESS TURN VIOLET WITH RICH DAWN   273 23
    LET THE DARKNESS BE WARMED WARMED THROUGH TO A RUDDY VI+   273 24
    SHE FANNED HERSELF WITH A VIOLET FAN   617 19
    LIKE THE EYE OF A VIOLET   658 15
    FROM THE HIPS A VIOLET   819 22

VIOLET-HEADS
    HUNDREDS OF VIOLET-HEADS IN A SHOWER   880 19

VIOLETS
    YOU SHOULD BE OUT BY THE ORCHARD WHERE VIOLETS SECRETLY+   57 17
    YOU PROMISED TO SEND ME SOME VIOLETS DID YOU FORGET   58 8
    OVER A DOUBLE 'ANDFUL O' VIOLETS A' IN A PACK   61 11
    ARE THE VIOLETS ALREADY HERE   273 27
    SHOW ME THE VIOLETS THAT ARE OUT   273 30
    IS 'PURPLING WITH VIOLETS   273 32
    IF THE VIOLETS ARE COMING OUT FROM UNDER THE RACK OF MEN   273 33
    PRAY NOT TO DIE ON THIS PISGAH BLOSSOMING WITH VIOLETS   273 36
    IF YOU CATCH A WHIFF OF VIOLETS FROM THE DARKNESS OF TH+   274 1
    WONDERMENT ORGANISING ITSELF HERALDING ITSELF WITH THE +   274 5
    VIOLETS   311 30
    IN SIGN OF DAUNTLESS SILENT VIOLETS   317 18
    I SAW THE BROKEN VIOLETS   880 23
    TO RISE AN ODOUR OF PURPLE VIOLETS CRUSHED   881 7
    A LOT O' VIOLETS FELL OUT OF 'ER BOSOM ON 'IM DOWN THEER *910 16
    OVER A DOUBLE 'ANDFUL OF VIOLETS ALL IN A PACK   *911 27

VIOLIN
    THEN HE LAID DOWN THE BOW OF HIS VIOLIN   884 8

VIRGIN
    IT WAS ONLY I WHO SAW THE VIRGIN YOU   411 22
    THE OVERLOOKED VIRGIN   411 24
    COME DELICATE OVERLOOKED VIRGIN COME BACK TO ME   411 29
    I WANTED THE VIRGIN YOU TO BE HOME AT LAST   412 2
    WHERE THE VIRGIN IN WOMAN COMES HOME TO A MAN   412 5
    THE HOMELESS VIRGIN   412 6
    SHABBY VIRGIN   437 4
    THE CROSS THE VIRGIN PISCES THE SACRED FISH   616 24
    IN VIRGIN OUTRAGE AS THEY VIEWED   680 18
    LIKE A VIRGIN THE BLADE OF MY BAYONET WANTING IT   742 10
    DO THOU O VIRGIN ART DAY WHEN WE RISE FROM OUR SLEEPING   753 3
    WHERE THE WORLD IS VIRGIN AND HOUSELESS   768 16
    THE HIGH VIRGIN VALLEY   768 26
    TO A HIGHER PLACE THAT IS VIRGIN   769 16
    TO A VIRGIN VALLEY HIGH UP   769 17
    THE KNOWING SMILE OF THE FINAL VIRGIN IN MAN   770 13
    WHERE THE FIRE-BURNT VIRGIN IN MAN AND THE VIRGIN IN FI+ 770 27
    THAT ARE VIRGINS AT LAST FROM THE FURNACE WITH VIRGIN   771 6
    SUCH ON THE VIRGIN HAIR OF DEAD SIXTEEN   854 24
    LEAVING ALL TO THE WOMAN MADONNA MIA POOR VIRGIN   *946 16

VIRGINAL
    FOR THE VIRGINAL YOU   412 11
    VIRGINAL FIRST AND LAST   412 14
    VIRGINAL PURE POLICEMEN CAME   579 13

VIRGIN-BUDDED
    EVE WITH HER RESISTLESS VIRGIN-BUDDED BREAST   864 13

VIRGINITY
    TO THE ROCK OF VIRGINITY THY   40 11
    WHO HAVE KEPT INTACT FOR YOU YOUR VIRGINITY   157 10
    BUT IN VIRGINITY JEALOUSY DOES NOT ENTER   412 31
    NOT ON THE STEMS OF VIRGINITY LOVELY AND MUTE   855 11

VIRGINS
    ENOUGH OF THE VIRGINS AND LILIES OF PASSIONATE SUFFOCAT+ 273 14
    AND ALWAYS VIRGINS   411 19
    THE VIRGINS   412 21
    FOR VIRGINS ARE NOT EXCLUSIVE OF VIRGINS   412 28
    GODDESSES OF LOVE GODDESSES OF DIRT EXCREMENT-EATERS OR+ 671 18
    WALK THROUGH THE TREES AS VIRGINS   769 25
    TALL VIRGINS OF THE AFTERWARDS   770 2
    TOWARDS THE WOMEN WHO ARE VIRGINS OF THE AFTERWARDS   770 20
    THAT ARE VIRGINS AT LAST FROM THE FURNACE WITH VIRGIN   771 6
    HO ALL MY SAINTS AND MY VIRGINS   798 17

VIRILE
    VIBRATES UNTOUCHED AND VIRILE IN LIFE UNUTTERABLE RICH   772 30

VIRTUE
    OF HER MAIDENLY VIRTUE AND OF MY GOOD NAME   129 6
    WHICH I BEING A LITTLE WEARY OF ROMAN VIRTUE   297 32

VISIBLE
    OUTWARD AND VISIBLE INDICATION OF THE PLAN WITHIN   356 11
    VISIBLE UNDER THE CHANGING EYES   *907 16
    VISIBLE THERE IN THE CHANGE OF EYES AND THE MOBILE FEAT+ *909 12

VISION
    OPENS MY EYES TILL THE ROOTS OF MY VISION SEEM TORN   173 .4
    WHY DON'T THEY OPEN WITH VISION AND SPEAK TO ME WHAT HA+ 180 21
    THE VISION   208 19
    CLOTHED VISION CAN NEVER COMMUNICATE   286 29
    AND GLEAMS ON THE WORLD WITH THE WARM DARK VISION OF   544 24
    TILL MY PARCHED VISION COOLS   754 15
    WITH VISION   802 2

VISIONLESS
    SIGHTFUL SIGHTLESS SEEING AND VISIONLESS   359 17
    HE IS DUMB HE IS VISIONLESS   362 2

VISIT
    FOR SO RARE A VISIT   234 14

VISITOR
    NOT AS A VISITOR EITHER NOR A SWEET   230 25

VISTA
    TAKING ME BACK DOWN THE VISTA OF YEARS TILL I SEE   148 5
    VISTA OF DAY   311 8

VISTAS
    VISTAS DOWN DARK AVENUES   286 30
    BUT WE AS WE START AWAKE CLUTCH AT OUR VISTAS DEMOCRATIC 286 34

VISUALITY
    SIGHTLESS AMONG ALL YOUR VISUALITY   289 9

VITAL
    FOR THESE MOST VITAL   563 5

VITALITY
    SO WE ROAR UP LIKE BONFIRES OF VITALITY   440 7
    WITH ENFEEBLED VITALITY   457 8
    ON SMELLING IT ALL BEFORE YOUR BIT OF VITALITY SPENT IS 462 34
    THE COOL COOL TRUTH OF PURE VITALITY   481 27
    I SAY TO MYSELF HELLO I'M NOT WELL MY VITALITY IS LOW   498 8
    DO YOU LACK VITALITY   558 16
    GIVE VITALITY STILL TO THE DAUNTLESS   559 3
    YOU'LL NOT GET VITALITY ANY OTHER WAY   559 16
    PERHAPS WHAT'S WRONG IS SIMPLY LACK OF VITALITY   842 28
    THE WILD GODS SEND VITALITY THEY PUT THE LIGHTNING INTO+ 843 5

VITALLY
    THE YOUNG AREN'T VITALLY INTERESTED IN IT ANY MORE   513 16

VIVID
    BUT DAY SHOWS IT VIVID WITH FEELING   38 3
    THE VIVID AH THE FIERY SURPLUS OF LIFE   127 17
    LIKE VIVID THOUGHT THE AIR SPINS BRIGHT AND ALL   142 14
    IS NOT EACH SOUL A VIVID THOUGHT IN THE GREAT CONSCIOUS+ 328 27
    HOW VIVID YOUR TRAVELLING SEEMS NOW IN THE TROUBLED SUN+ 354 4
    OR THE ROUND WILD VIVID EYE OF A WILD-GOOSE STARING   438 31
    VIVID AND CLEAN   524 6
    AND OUR NAKED CONTACT WILL BE RARE AND VIVID AND TREMEN+ 608 15
    AND THERE WILL BE A VIVID RECOIL INTO SEPARATENESS   611 18
    MANY VIVID SMALL STATES LIKE A KALEIDOSCOPE ALL COLOURS 611 19
    OH MEN LIVING MEN VIVID MEN OCEAN AND FIRE   639 1
    VIVID LIFE   639 9
    FLINGS OUT ITS VIVID BLACK NOTES   772 32
    BUT THE DAY SHOWS IT VIVID WITH FEELING   *892 19
    THE VIVID LIFE OF HIS LOVE IN THY MOUTH AND THY NOSTRILS *916 7

VIVIDER
    BY THE TRANSMITTED GLEAM FROM THE FACES OF VIVIDER MEN 649 14

VIVIDLY
    AND YET THE SOUL CONTINUING NAKED-FOOTED EVER MORE VIVI+ 281 7
    HOW VIVIDLY THEY MAKE THEIR ASSERTION OF LIFE   530 14

VIVIFIER
    YET O MY YOUNG MEN THERE IS A VIVIFIER   439 15
    YET O MY YOUNG MEN THERE IS A VIVIFIER   440 1
    THE VIVIFIER EXISTS AND THEREFORE WE KNOW IT   840 9
    THE VIVIFIER EXISTS BUT FOR ME IS NEITHER MAN-LIKE NOR + 840 25

VOICE
    THE OTHER VOICE IN A SILENCE OF BLOOD 'NEATH THE NOISE 36 17
    STRANGE VOICE HAS NO SOUND   40 12
    BUT THE HOSTS OF MEN WITH ONE VOICE DENY   40 19
    LOVE MAKES THE BURDEN OF HER VOICE   46 17
    AND THE THOUGHT OF THE LIPLESS VOICE OF THE FATHER SHAK+ 48 11
    THE VOICE OF THE FURTIVE TRIUMPHANT ENGINE AS IT RUSHES+ 58 4
    WITH A PLAINTIVE UNALTERABLE VOICE THAT DEADENS   64 23
    AWFULLY MUST I CALL BACK A HUNDRED EYES A VOICE   76 7
    IN HER VOICE AND A WEAK TEAR FALLS   106 2
    SO WITH A DOWNCAST MIEN AND LAUGHING VOICE   123 1
    I DO FORGET THE SOUNDING OF YOUR VOICE   129 8
    WHO VOICE THE DUMB NIGHT FITTINGLY   197 31
    GUARD MY SHEEP CAME THE SILVERY VOICE FROM THE PINNACLE 324 23
    THE VOICE OF MY EDUCATION SAID TO ME   350 1
    IT IS NO USE MY SAYING TO HIM IN AN EMOTIONAL VOICE   357 1
    SEX WHICH BREAKS US INTO VOICE SETS US CALLING ACROSS T+ 366 34
    WHAT VOICE OF THE LORD IS THAT FROM THE TREE OF SMOKE 375 15
    I RECOGNISED WHEN I HEARD ITS VOICE   376 7
    LIFTS UP HIS VOICE AND HOWLS TO THE WALLS OF THE PUEBLO 405 11
    A BIT AWKWARD AND WITH A FUNNY SQUAWK IN HIS VOICE   413 21
    AND A HIDDEN VOICE LIKE WATER CLUCKING   427 3
    AND USING HIS MOST MELODIOUS WOULD-BE-OXFORD VOICE   433 16
    THE OXFORD VOICE   433 23
    THE WOULD-BE OXFORD VOICE   433 25
    FOR MANKIND SAYS WITH ONE VOICE HOW MUCH IS HE WORTH   486 20
    LIFE'S VOICE EVEN WHEN SHE'S HOARSE   491 8
    A NIGHTINGALE SINGING AT THE TOP OF HIS VOICE   523 8
    SOME SMALL VOICE WENT AHEM   554 20
    WHOSE VOICE FLIES ON AND ON CALLING LIKE A SWAN   623 17
    NO VOICE   681 15
    UNLESS GOD HAS A BODY HOW CAN HE HAVE A VOICE   691 10
    NOR VOICE DESCRIBE HIM   692 9
    NOR THE VOICE DESCRIBE HIM   692 20
    AND PERSEPHONE HERSELF IS BUT A VOICE   697 18
    HAVE LENT YOU VOICE NOR SPOKEN OF THE FACE   737 21
    OR VOICE OR ANY SINGLE SPARK   738 4
    HEAR A VOICE SAYING I KNOW YOU NOT   789 7
    I HEAR THE VOICE OF MY FIRST MAN ASK ME WHY I AM LAUGHI+ 791 14

VOICE
     IS WHERE DOES IT COME FROM THIS LOVELY ENGLISH VOICE   830 23
     THIS MANLY VOICE   830 27
     THE LOVELY ENGLISH VOICE   830 32
     TUNES HER VOICE MANY NOTED   862 8
     POOR SIEGMUND TAKE THE SOBS FROM OUT OF YOUR VOICE   871 17
     AWFULLY MUST I CALL BACK THOSE HUNDRED EYES A VOICE   *898 2
     AWFULLY MUST I CALL BACK THOSE HUNDRED EYES A VOICE   *901 11
     SO WITH A DOWNCAST MIEN AND LAUGHING VOICE   *934 7
     AND PERSEPHONE HERSELF IS BUT A VOICE AS A BRIDE   *956 15

VOICE-BOX
     AND A GOO-GOO SORT OF VOICE-BOX   830 31

VOICELESS
     VOICELESS LITTLE BIRD   354 7
     COLD VOICELESS AGE-AFTER-AGE BEHIND HIM SERPENTS' LONG   360 15
     ELOQUENT PURITY VOICELESS IN THE DUST   855 6

VOICES
     WITHIN THE HOUSE TWO VOICES AROSE A SLENDER LASH   36 13
     VOICES OF MEN   169 14
     LITTLE LUMPS THAT FLY IN AIR AND HAVE VOICES INDEFINITE+   341 26
     AND VOICES IN ME SAID IF YOU WERE A MAN   350 5
     AND YET THOSE VOICES   350 17
     I DESPISED MYSELF AND THE VOICES OF MY ACCURSED HUMAN   351 20
     BIRDS HAVE THEIR VOICES EACH MEANS A DIFFERENT THING   368 12
     TOM-TOMS WEIRD MUSIC OF THE DEVIL VOICES OF MEN FROM   388 35
     VOICES GURGLING LIKE WATER   425 12
     AND THEIR VOICES ARE LIKE SCREW-DRIVERS   502 11
     ROBOT VOICES ROBOT EVEN THE GAY UMBRELLAS   651 3
     SO LONG WILL THEY LIFT THEIR IMPERTINENT VOICES   681 5
     AND WASH OF VOICES ALONG THE STREET   *917 7

VOID
     IN VOID AND NULL PROFUSION HOW IS THIS   53 26
     ACROSS THE INSENSIBLE VOID TILL SHE STOOPS TO SEE   153 3
     OUR ATTENTION OUT OF THE VOID WHEREIN WE ARE CRUSHED   165 33
     SUN OF BLACK VOID HEAT   301 19
     A GREY VOID THING THAT GOES WITHOUT WANDERING   714 19
     WITHIN THE SILENCE VOID OF ECHOES EVEN   738 8

VOLCANIC
     WHAT DOES SHE WANT VOLCANIC VENUS AS SHE GOES FUMING   539 10

VOLCANO
     SHE'S SEETHING LIKE A VOLCANO AND VOLCANOS DON'T WANT   539 14
     NOW A VOLCANO OF RAGE   539 20
     ARE ONLY SITTING TIGHT ON THE CRATERS OF THEIR VOLCANO   539 25
     LIKE A VOLCANO MY HIPS ARE MOVING   802 24

VOLCANOES
     THE WOMEN ARE LIKE LITTLE VOLCANOES   539 2
     VOLCANOES   539 5

VOLCANOS
     SHE'S SEETHING LIKE A VOLCANO AND VOLCANOS DON'T WANT   539 14

VOLTE FACE
     ALL THE VOLTE FACE OF DECIMALS   355 25

VOLUPTUOUS
     WHY SO VELVETY WHY SO VOLUPTUOUS HEAVY   279 14
     VOLUPTUOUS WRATH   324 33
     AND HE CHERISHES VOLUPTUOUS DELIGHTS AND THINKS ABOUT T+   325 6
     OF HIS VOLUPTUOUS PLEASURE OF CHASING THE SHEEP TO THE +   325 9

VOLUPTUOUSLY
     THERE IS A NEW SWEETNESS IN HIS VOLUPTUOUSLY LICKING HI+   325 1

VOLUPTUOUSNESS
     THINKING OF VOLUPTUOUSNESS   324 8
     THE INVOLVED VOLUPTUOUSNESS OF THE SOFT-FOOTED CAT   383 1

VOLUTED
     IN THE MIDDLE OF VOLUTED SPACE   512 4

VOMIT
     AND THEN YOU RUN IN TO VOMIT IT IN MY HOUSE   399 4

VOMITING
     AND A FEW VOMITING BOUTS   400 22

VORACIOUS
     BEING MAD WITH VORACIOUS DESIRE   264 36

VOTARESSES
     SLIM VOTARESSES   96 8

VOTE
     WE VOTED 'EM IN AND WE'LL VOTE 'EM OUT   573 21
     JUST VOTE US SOME PIN-MONEY TO ENCOURAGE OUR   574 6

VOTED
     WE VOTED 'EM IN AND WE'LL VOTE 'EM OUT   573 21
     REMEMBER WHO VOTED YOU INTO YOUR SEAT   573 26

VOTES
     FOR ACCORDING TO SOME THE BEANS WERE THE BEANS OF VOTES+   303 17

VOYAGE
     A VOYAGE TO SAIL BEYOND THE CHARTED SEAS   168 3
     FOR THE VOYAGE OF OBLIVION AWAITS YOU   720 22
     ALL UNEQUIPPED TO TAKE THE LONG LONG VOYAGE   722 5

VRONSKY
     IF VRONSKY AND ANNA KARENIN   536 8
     OF REBELS LIKE ANNA AND VRONSKY   536 14

VRONSKYS
     IT IS STRANGE TO THINK OF THE ANNAS THE VRONSKYS THE   533 11

VULGAR
     OR VULGAR MARSALA   280 10
     BUT THE VULGAR WAY   282 8
     I THOUGHT HOW PALTRY HOW VULGAR WHAT A MEAN ACT   351 19

VULGARLY
     THE ITALIANS VULGARLY SAY IT STANDS FOR THE FEMALE PART+   282 17
     KNOW ME TURNS HER HEAD AND IGNORES ME VULGARLY WITH   384 23

VULNERABLE
     BUT HERE EVEN A CUSTOMS-OFFICIAL IS STILL VULNERABLE   291 8
     BUT HE CATCHES THE FOLDS OF VULNERABLE LEATHERY SKIN   362 6
     ONLY HE SENSES THE VULNERABLE FOLDS OF SKIN   362 15
     LONG NECK AND LONG VULNERABLE LIMBS EXTRUDED SPREAD-EAG+   365 1
     WE LET OUR SOULS BE PURE AND VULNERABLE   736 24
     LEAVING THIS NAKED PALLID HELPLESS VULNERABLE REMAINS   767 26

VULTURE
     THE VULTURE IS BALD SO IS THE CONDOR OBSCENELY   369 18
     AS THE VULTURE THAT SCREAMS HIGH UP ALMOST INAUDIBLE   500 16
     THE GREY VULTURE THE GREY HYAENA CORPSE-EATERS   711 23

WADDLING
     LIKE GROSS SUCCESSFUL SLAVES MECHANICALLY WADDLING   526 15

WADE
     WE WADE WE WADE WE STAGGER DARKNESS RUSHED   425 6

WADED
     WHO HAD WADED TO THE PALE GREEN SEA OF EVENING OUT OF A+   693 5

WADER
     WITH THE FULL THIGHS SLOWLY LIFTING OF THE WADER WADING+   693 10

WADING
     WITH THE FULL THIGHS SLOWLY LIFTING OF THE WADER WADING+   693 10

WAFT
     TO THE FACE THAT GAZES OUTWARDS WATCHING FOR NIGHT TO W+   103 2
     OF THE MOURNFUL TILL PEOPLE WAFT   108 21
     WAFT NEARER TO THEM THE BARK OF DELIVERY   *958 18
     OF THE KINDNESS OF THE COSMOS THAT WILL WAFT   *961 3

WAFTING
     AND THE DEAR DEAR FIREFLIES WAFTING IN BETWEEN   221 15
     WAFTING WITH WARM LOVE FROM STILL-LIVING HEARTS   723 22
     TORN WINGS OF FLAME ARE WAFTING DOWN THE SKY   855 21
     WAFTING LIKE SOLACE DOWN THEIR LENGTH OF DAYS   *941 16
     THEN DOWN THE BREEZE LIGHT WAFTING O'ER THE FALLOW   *941 23
     AND THOSE BRIGHT FIREFLIES WAFTING IN BETWEEN   *945 1

WAFTIN'
     AN' WARM FOR TH' SMELL COME WAFTIN' TO ME 'ER PUT 'ER F+   61 13
     O' TH' SMELL COME WAFTIN' TO ME 'ER PUT 'ER FACE   *911 29

WAFTS
     LONG HAS WAITED RESTLESS SUDDENLY WAFTS   154 29
     SAVES YOU WAFTS YOU AWAY ON THE VERY DRAUGHT MY ANGER   334 8

WAG
     WRIGGLE AND WAG AND SLAVER AND GET THE MENTALITY OF A D+   645 4

WAGE
     MEN SELL THEMSELVES FOR A WAGE AND EMPLOYERS LOOK OUT   483 2
     EARNING A WAGE IS A PRISON OCCUPATION   521 7
     YOUR WAGE IS THE DOLE OF WORK AND THE DOLE IS YOUR   630 20
     WAGE OF NULLITY   630 21

WAGE-EARNER
     AND A WAGE-EARNER IS A SORT OF GAOL-BIRD   521 8

WAGE-EARNING
     MEN SHOULD REFUSE TO BE HEAPS OF WAGE-EARNING DUNG   450 6

WAGE-PAID
     WAGE-PAID WORK   631 14

WAGES
     NOT BASED ON WAGES NOR PROFITS NOR ANY SORT OF BUYING A+   483 26
     THE WAGES OF WORK IS CASH   521 1
     THE WAGES OF CASH IS WANT MORE CASH   521 2
     THE WAGES OF WANT MORE CASH IS VICIOUS COMPETITION   521 3
     THE WAGES OF VICIOUS COMPETITION IS THE WORLD WE LIVE IN   521 4
     BUT WAGES GO DOWN AND REALLY AUNTIE   573 1
     IT FLOWERED BEFORE MEN TOOK TO FLOWERING FOR WAGES   814 5

WAGE-SLAVES
     MEN SHOULD REFUSE TO WORK AT ALL AS WAGE-SLAVES   450 7

WAGE-SLAVE
     UNLESS YOU'RE A WAGE-SLAVE   450 2
     WHILE A WAGE-SLAVE WORKS HE LEAVES LIFE ASIDE   450 3
     HE CAN'T HELP BEING A SLAVE A WAGE-SLAVE   524 11

WAGE-SYSTEM
     IT BEGAN WITH JUDAS AND GOES ON IN THE WAGE-SYSTEM   483 1

WAGGING
  ESPECIALLY CLAPPER BELLS HARD TONGUES WAGGING IN HARD M+   623   2
  WAGGING   665   3

WAGGLE
  SUCH A WAGGLE OF LOVE YOU CAN HARDLY DISTINGUISH ONE   399   22

WAGING
  FOR WITH THE REDNESS OF LAUGHTER THE BATTLE IS WAGING I+   854   19

WAGON
  A BULLOCK WAGON COMES SO I AM ASHAMED   225   10
  SO THERE'S AN OXEN WAGON   227   1
  AND TWENTIETH WAGON AND HE WILL NOT DRIVE PAST   733   12

WAGONS
  AS WITH CLOTH SO WITH HOUSES SHIPS SHOES WAGONS OR CUPS   451   10
  THE SERGEANT SAYS THAT EIGHT AND TWENTY WAGONS   732   1
  I WAIT FOR THE EIGHT AND TWENTY WAGONS TO COME   732   23
  HERE COMES THE FIRST OF THE WAGONS A GREY A DREARY   733   5
  AND AWAY WENT THE LAST OF THE WAGONS   735   16
  AND AS WITH CLOTH SO WITH ALL THINGS HOUSES SHOES WAGON+   *950   1

WAGTAIL
  AND HAPPY AS A WAGTAIL BY A POOL   520   16

WAGTAILS
  BEFORE THE SHOPS LIKE WAGTAILS ON THE EDGE OF A POOL   269   24
  LIKE SHARP SLIM WAGTAILS THEY FLASH A LITTLE ASIDE   269   26

WAIFS
  DOWN THE GLAD STREETS PINCHED WAIFS IN ILL-ASSORTED CLO+   865   5

WAIL
  THE FIRST WAIL OF AN INFANT   366   15

WAILING
  IS PEOPLED WITH SHADOWS AND WAILING AND LAST GHOSTS LUR+   54   31
  AND IT'S NO GOOD WAILING FOR LOVE   559   7

WAIST
  THEIR WAIST   288   9
  AND THEN HER GREAT WEIGHT BELOW THE WAIST HER VAST PALE   393   15

WAISTS
  WITH SLIM WAISTS OF WARRIORS AND THE LONG FEET   689   3

WAIT
  I WISH YOU DID NOT WAIT MY DEAR   41   15
  I MUST SIT ALONE AND WAIT AND NEVER KNOW   48   7
  OF EACH OTHER I SHALL SIT AND WAIT FOR THE BELL   75   6
  YET WAIT AWHILE FOR HENCEFORTH I WILL LOVE WHEN A BLOSS+   94   5
  MY LOVE WHERE IT IS WANTED YET WAIT AWHILE MY FALL   94   7
  IS COMPLETE FOR THE MOMENT YET WAIT AND YOU'LL SEE THAT+   94   8
  TELEGRAM-BICYCLE APPROACHES I WAIT   100   6
  STAND THOSE THAT WAIT   146   6
  WITHIN ITS QUICK COMMITTED TO HOLD AND WAIT   161   4
  OUR EXISTENCE WE WAIT AND ARE STILL DENIED   166   10
  WAIT AMONG THE BEECHES   178   30
  WHITELY CONFRONT I WAIT ON THE GRASS AM LAMED   225   12
  THAT I SHALL ALWAYS WONDER OVER AND WAIT FOR   248   9
  I SAW HER STAND AND WAIT   261   24
  STOIC ABLE TO WAIT THROUGH AGES   292   29
  AND MUST WAIT MUST STAND AND WAIT FOR THERE HE WAS AT   349   6
  WAIT WAIT A BIT I'LL COME WHEN I'VE LIT THE FIRE   384   9
  AND MAKE ME WAIT   385   11
  AND WAIT FOR HIM TO COME BACK WITH A NEW STORY   405   30
  OH BUT WAIT   431   1
  THEY WAIT   465   10
  HOW TO WAIT FOR THE LONELIEST OF FEASTS   465   25
  AND YOU'LL HAVE TO WAIT   472   2
  AND WAIT   508   9
  KEEP QUIET AND WAIT   514   7
  WHY SHOULD THE DELUGE WAIT WHILE THESE YOUNG GENTRY GO   531   13
  YOU MUSTN'T EXPECT IT ALSO TO WAIT FOR YOUR CONVENIENCE   531   21
  WAIT DEAR LADY JEAN WAIT A MINUTE   668   23
  WAIT WAIT DON'T BRING THE COFFEE YET NOR THE PAIN GRILLE   687   21
  THAT WAIT ON WHALES IN MID-OCEAN SUSPENDED IN THE WAVES+   694   26
  THEY WAIT THEY GIVE WAY NOW   707   7
  AH WAIT WAIT FOR THERE'S THE DAWN   720   3
  WAIT WAIT THE LITTLE SHIP   720   6
  WAIT WAIT EVEN SO A FLUSH OF YELLOW   720   9
  I WAIT FOR THE EIGHT AND TWENTY WAGONS TO COME   732   23
  DOWN TO THE GATE AND STAND AND WAIT   734   25
  AND WAIT TILL THEY ARE LOST UPON OUR SIGHT   740   21
  WE ARE SO LET US HAVE DONE AH MASTER WE WAIT   757   18
  OF DEATH BUT I WAIT AWHILE IN THIS TABERNACLE   772   20
  AND I WAIT FOR THE FINAL DAY WHEN THE DRAGON OF THUNDER+   797   7
  WAIT ONLY WAIT LITTLE BY LITTLE IT ALL SHALL COME UPON +   797   12
  I WAIT BEHIND MEN   804   18
  I HOLD HER STILL AND WAIT TILL THE BELL SHALL FALTER   859   1
  AND I MUST WAIT   879   21
  I WILL SIT AND WAIT FOR THE BELL   *896   5
  I WILL SIT AND WAIT FOR THE BELL   *904   26
  I WAIT FOR THE BABY TO WANDER HITHER TO ME   *913   6
  AND WAIT WAIT AWHILE   *947   22

WAITED
  STRANGE HE IS MY SON FOR WHOM I HAVE WAITED LIKE A LOVER   47   8
  LONG HAVE I WAITED NEVER ONCE CONFESSED   122   13
  LONG HAS WAITED RESTLESS SUDDENLY WAFTS   154   29
  I WAITED THEREFORE THEN I KNEW   262   1
  I HAVE WAITED WITH A LONG ROD   339   1
  I WAITED BUT HE WOULD NOT COME BACK TO ME   735   10
  I BROUGHT FOR HIM AND WAITED WHILE HE DRANK   878   15
  I WAITED AND MY SILENCE CHALLENGED HIM   878   16

WAITING
  AND WAITING WHILE LIGHT IS SHED   58   29
  THEN A GROUP OF TOADSTOOLS WAITING THE MOON'S WHITE TAP+   72   19
  BUT SHE'S WAITING I KNOW IMPATIENT AND COLD HALF   85   11
  AND WAITING THROUGH THE BLUE   91   20
  WAITING EVER TO GET   99   25
  I FEEL THE SILENCE WAITING   109   25
  WASTE NOT THE YEW-TREE'S WAITING WASTE   114   13
  FRESH QUIVERING KEEP THE SUNNY-SWIFT MARCH-DAYS WAITING   179   5
  THEN JOSEPH GREY WITH WAITING   202   1
  YET HOT WAITING   240   30
  WHAT ARE YOU WAITING FOR   241   1
  WHAT ARE YOU WAITING FOR   241   2
  STILL WAITING FOR YOU HOWEVER OLD YOU ARE AND I AM   248   11
  FROM THE WOMB OF THE ALL I AM WAITING DAZED   262   20
  MOULTING AND MOPING AND WAITING WILLING AT LAST   329   31
  AND I LIKE A SECOND COMER WAITING   349   20
  WAITING FOR THE FIREWORKS OF THE AFTER-SHOW   391   11
  THE WORLD IS WAITING FOR A NEW GREAT MOVEMENT OF   522   26
  A WAITING FOR THE PROPER TOUCH NOT FOR ANY WORD OR DEED   612   16
  WHEN I WAS WAITING AND NOT THINKING SITTING AT A TABLE +   672   18
  WITH HIS CLOAK OVER HIS ARM WAITING TO BE ASKED IN   692   11
  OF THEIR PATIENT WAITING UPON US THE THRONG OF THE GHOS+   736   6
  WAITING AND I KNEW HE WANTED IT   742   8
  WAITING FOR THE SUN TO RISE ON YOU   764   7
  WAITING FOR THE RATS OF THE DARK TO COME AND GNAW YOUR +   800   24
  WAITING BEHIND MEN   805   26
  OF WAITING AND THE ROOM STANDS STILL WITH FRIGHT   878   35
  I KNEW THAT SHE WAS WAITING   885   18
  FLOAT LIKE BOATS ON A RIVER WAITING   *943   12
  WAITING WAITING TILL AT LAST THE ANCIENT BOATMAN WITH T+   *958   11

WAITIN'
  WAITIN' TER BE BURIED OUT O' TH' WET   60   14
  WAITIN' TO BE SANK   60   22

WAITS
  WAITS WITH A LIFTED OAR   201   20
  THE SUN AS HE WAITS A MOMENT HUGE AND LIQUID   403   4
  I KNOW THERE IS NO HOPE FOR US DEATH WAITS IT IS USELES+   632   12
  SEE THE LIGHT ON THE MAN THAT WAITS   788   28

WAKE
  TO WAKE AND DOWN THE THIN   39   3
  WAKE OF A TUMULT NOW SPENT AND GONE   53   17
  AND WHEN I WAKE IN THE MORNING AFTER RAIN   72   20
  FROM THE DROWSE OF LIFE WAKE UP ANOTHER WILL   127   15
  OH COME AND WAKE US UP FROM THE GHASTLY DREAM OF TO-DAY   174   15
  A SLEEP THAT IS WRITHING STUPOR WEIGHED DOWN SO WE CAN'+   175   14
  LET US BREATHE FRESH AIR AND WAKE FROM FOUL DREAMS IN W+   175   19
  ONE ANOTHER IN WONDER OF WAKING LET US WAKE TO THE GLEAM   175   29
  OF HELL TO WAKE AND BE FREE   177   22
  WHAT PAIN TO WAKE AND MISS YOU   220   9
  TO WAKE WITH A TIGHTENED HEART   220   10
  AND BREATHING SOFT UNWILLING TO WAKE TO THE NEW DAY   311   12
  YOU ARE SO HARD TO WAKE   353   15
  IN VAIN TRYING TO WAKE THE MORROW   371   23
  THEY CAN'T THEY CAN'T WAKE   407   6
  AND THEY CAN'T WAKE   407   10
  CAN'T WAKE UP   407   19
  BECAUSE HIS BODY CAN'T WAKE UP   407   21
  WE SCREAM FOR SOMEONE TO WAKE US   408   1
  AND SLEEP IN MASSIVE SILENCE AND WAKE   465   17
  AND IN THE MORNING WAKE LIKE A NEW-OPENED FLOWER   726   24
  WILL WAKE AT LAST FROM THE CLEAN FORGETTING   809   16
  THAT BASK AND WAKE OH HIGH AND DRY   824   19
  WITH BEAUTY SHINE AND BOW IN GOD'S GREAT WAKE   872   22
  AND WELL I KNOW HE SLEEPS TO WAKE NO MORE   878   7
  SO HE WILL WAKE NO MORE   878   31
  AND WAKE TO THE SOUND OF THE WOODPIGEONS AND LIE AND LI+   *892   28
  WAKE OF THE HUSHED TUMULT NOW SPENT AND GONE   *906   8
  FOR A FAIRY-WIND TO WAKE THEM FROM THEIR SLOTH   *943   13

WAKEFUL
  TO STAMP THE EARTH AND FEEL THE WIND LIKE WAKEFUL   585   4

WAKEN
  DAISIES THAT WAKEN ALL MISTAKEN WHITE-SPREAD IN EXPECTA+   71   3
  DAISIES THAT WAKEN ALL MISTAKEN WHITE-SPREAD IN EXPECTA+ *917   22

WAKENED
  HOW YOU HAVE WAKENED ME BUT WHY WHY DO YOU   210   25
  NO I HAVE WAKENED IT IS YOU YOU ARE CRUEL TO ME   211   2
  WAKENED NOT TO THE OLD KNOWLEDGE   260   16
  THINGS MEN HAVE MADE WITH WAKENED HANDS AND PUT SOFT   448   1
  THROUGH THE WAKENED AFTERNOON RIDING DOWN MY DREAMS   *906   15

WAKES
  HIS BENT COURSE MILDLY HERE WAKES AGAIN LEAPS LAUGHS AN+   33   14
  THE SEED OF LIFE INCARNATE THAT FALLS AND WAKES   89   10
  AWAY IN THE DISTANCE WAKES A LAMP   163   25
  SLEEP OF THE MAN AND THE EAGLE'S SLEEP AFTER WHICH THE +   319   6
  AND THE BULL NOR WAKES FROM THE LIGHT-EYED EAGLE SLEEP   319   11
  AWAY ON THE HILLSIDE WAKES A STAR   857   25
  THE BREEZE WAKES UP A MUSIC IN THE SALLOW   863   21
  ITS CURIOUS COURSE MILDLY HERE IT WAKES AGAIN LEAPS LAU+ *891   15
  WAKES FROM THE HUM FALTERING ABOUT A NOUN   *898   3
  WAKES FROM THE HUM FALTERING ABOUT A NOUN   *901   12
  THE BREEZE WAKES UP A MUSIC IN THE SALLOW   *941   21

WAKING
  THE WAKING SMILE OF HER EYES   121   22
  ONE ANOTHER IN WONDER OF WAKING LET US WAKE TO THE GLEAM   175   29
  WAKING PRICKING THEIR EARS   311   5
  YET THERE IS WAKING FROM THE SOUNDEST SLEEP   725   6
  WAKING AND WAKING NEW   725   7
  AND I WAIT FOR THE FINAL DAY WHEN THE DRAGON OF THUNDER+   797   7
  I AM THE SLEEPING AND WAKING   805   8

WAKING
   HE IS HUITZILOPOCHTLI SLEEPING OR WAKING   805 11

WALK
   AND SWINGS ALL LOOSE FROM THE SWING OF HIS WALK   43 13
   TO WALK THE LONELY DUSKY HEIGHTS   63 31
   TWO AND TWO ARE THE FOLK THAT WALK   106 11
   O THE WET WALK OF MY BROWN HEN THROUGH THE STACKYARD   119 9
   WHO FOR THE REST OF LIFE WALK OUT OF CARE   157 11
   WALK NOW AS ONE   157 14
   WALK INNOCENT IN THE DAFFODILS   178 7
   YOU FROM YOUR LONELY WALK   178 27
   I WALK UP TO MY NECK IN MIST HOLDING MY MOUTH UP   212 13
   I WALK IN FEAR OF YOU   215 16
   IT IS WE WHO WALK IN THE TREES   231 28
   WALK   361 18
   BORN TO WALK ALONE   363 1
   THE MOUNTAINS NEVER GET UP AND WALK ABOUT   407 5
   WE WALK IN OUR SLEEP IN THIS LAND   407 26
   JUST YOU WALK AROUND THEM   556 21
   THESE TWO-LEGGED THINGS THAT WALK AND TALK   644 18
   WALK WARILY WALK WARILY BE CAREFUL WHAT YOU SAY   707 1
   I WALK THE EARTH INTACT HEREAFTERWARDS   743 24
   LIKE BLOOD IN THE EARTH AGAIN WE WALK THE EARTH   743 26
   AND YOU SEE THE MYRIAD DOVES THAT WALK   750 21
   OH YOU WHO WALK SO SLOWLY AND MAKE ME   762 5
   WALK THROUGH THE TREES AS VIRGINS   769 25
   LET US WALK ABOUT IN UPPERS   774 12
   LET HIM HAVE NO ANIMAL WALK ON HIS BODY NOR THROUGH THE+   791 24
   WHEN YOU WALK THE STAR WALKS WITH YOU BETWEEN YOUR BREA+   800 5
   OF THE MEN AND THE WOMEN WHO WALK AMONG YOU   807 24
   MEN IN THEIR MANHOOD WALK OUT   810 9
   OH THE WET WALK OF MY BROWN HEN THROUGH THE STACKYARD   *932 18

WALKED
   ITS HEAD AS IT WALKED I CAN NEVER CALL HIM TO ME   137 15
   HAVING WALKED HIMSELF IN THE THORNY DIFFICULT   199 3
   SO FATHER NEPTUNE WALKED UP THE SHORE   574 19
   AND WE WALKED DARK SO HE HELD HIS ARM CLOSE ROUND ME   732 15

WALKING
   SWING TO MY WALKING MOVEMENT WEAK   73 26
   UP THE WOLDS THE WOODS WERE WALKING   152 14
   OF WALKING OVER THE FACES OF MEN LIKE COBBLE-STONES   175 8
   IF I GO ON WALKING THROUGH THE WHOLE BREADTH OF GERMANY   212 24
   WALKING LIKE A ROYAL SNAKE DOWN THE MOUNTAIN   293 20
   BUT WITH THE WALKING AND TALKING AND CONVENTIONALLY PER+   442 2
   AND WALKING EACH IN HIS OWN SUN-GLORY   525 20
   AS A COLUMBINE FLOWER HAS OR EVEN A STARLING WALKING AN+   621 16
   PEOPLE GO ON WALKING WHEN THEY HAVE NOWHERE TO GO   657 19
   AND AN OCEAN LINER GOING EAST LIKE A SMALL BEETLE WALKI+   687 9
   THEN I SHALL KNOW THAT I AM WALKING STILL   727 4
   SHE SEES MEN WALKING TOWARDS HER UNDER THE TREES   770 1
   WALKING SLOWLY WESTWARDS HOUSELESS   770 4
   WITH MEN OF THE AFTERWARDS WALKING TO MEET US FROM   770 9
   AN INDIAN WALKING WRAPT IN HIS WINDING SHEET   816 7
   WHILE SHE WAS HERE AND WALKING IN OUR WAYS   *941 10

WALKIN'
   AN' WALKIN' IN AGONY   80 8
   AN' WALKIN' IN AGONY   *922 8

WALKS
   THE MOON WALKS HER LONELY WAY WITHOUT ANGUISH   63 20
   A WET BIRD WALKS ON THE LAWN CALL TO THE BOY TO COME   137 7
   THE STARLING SHAKING ITS HEAD AS IT WALKS IN THE GRASS   137 11
   AND WHOEVER WALKS A MILE FULL OF FALSE SYMPATHY   653 1
   WALKS TO THE FUNERAL OF THE WHOLE HUMAN RACE   653 2
   THE YOUTH WALKS UP TO THE WHITE HORSE TO PUT ITS HALTER+   683 19
   AS HE SLOWLY WALKS FROM THE WESTERN DOOR TO THE WORLD   770 14
   WHEN YOU WALK THE STAR WALKS WITH YOU BETWEEN YOUR BREA+   800 5
   STRONG WITH EYES OF DEFIANCE EVE WALKS WITH SORROWS   864 23

WALL
   GOES TREMBLING PAST ME UP THE COLLEGE WALL   35 27
   THE BIRD LIES WARM AGAINST THE WALL   42 23
   CREEP UP THE WALL TO ME AND IN AT MY OPEN WINDOW   62 28
   WHY SHOULD WE BEAT OUR HEADS AGAINST THE WALL   75 5
   AH AND SHE PUTS HER HANDS UPON THE WALL   128 31
   PACKED IN A LINE WITH THEIR HEADS AGAINST THE WALL   144 16
   I KISS THE STONES I KISS THE MOSS ON THE WALL   173 13
   WHEN I WOKE THE LAKE-LIGHTS WERE QUIVERING ON THE WALL   243 21
   AND LONG SNAKES QUICKLY GLIDE INTO THE DARK HOLE IN THE+   321 24
   A WALL A BASTION   325 26
   IS HIS BREAST A WALL   326 24
   NAY ONCE IT WAS ALSO A FORTRESS WALL AND THE WEIGHT OF I   326 25
   THE WALL   343 30
   WALL   381 2
   AND NERVES URGING FORWARD TO THE WALL YOU'D HAVE EYES   381 4
   BUT THEY BUBBLE UNDER THE HEAVY WALL   461 27
   THEY BUBBLE UNDER THE HEAVY WALL   462 1
   IN SECRET UNDER THE SICKENING WALL   462 7
   AROUND THEM AN INVISIBLE WALL   555 20
   BUTTERFLY THE WIND BLOWS SEA-WARD STRONG BEYOND THE GAR+   696 12
   BACKWARD AND FORWARD FROM WALL TO WALL   746 11
   THE DARK IS DIVIDING THE SUN IS COMING PAST THE WALL   803 12
   WITH THEIR LITTLE PALE SIGNS ON THE WALL TO TRY US   *929 24
   THAT STOOD CLOSE TO THE WALL AND THE FRONT'S FADED SILK+   *940 3
   THROUGH ANY BREACH IN THE WALL   *957 21

WALLED
   WALLED IN WALLED IN THE WHOLE WORLD IS A VAST IMPURE   174 23
   AND THE POOR DEAD WHEN THEY HAVE LEFT THE WALLED   721 11
   ONCE OUTSIDE THE GATE OF THE WALLED SILVERY LIFE OF DAYS   *957 27

WALLET-CARRYING
   AND A MINGLING OF WALLET-CARRYING WOMEN   484 5

WALL-FACE
   AND CLIMB AGAIN THE BROKEN BANK OF MY WALL-FACE   350 32

WALL-FRONT
   INTO THE BLACK HOLE THE EARTH-LIPPED FISSURE IN THE WAL+   351 16

WALLOW
   YOU LOVE TO LAP UP AFFECTION TO WALLOW IN IT   396 22

WALLOWED
   AND THE DOSTOEVSKY LOT WALLOWED IN THE THOUGHT   533 26

WALLS
   ACROSS THE WALLS AS THE BLINDS ARE BLOWN   51 8
   WALLS   112 23
   BETWEEN THE OLD GREY WALLS I DID NOT DARE   122 27
   THE WALLS OF THE HOUSE AND NETTLES PUFF OUT FROM THE HE+   159 25
   I FEEL THICK WALLS OF STONE BEHIND THE ARRAS   173 26
   THERE'S A BREACH IN THE WALLS OF THE PAST LETS THE DAYL+   174 6
   FOR THE RIPPING OF ARRAS AND SMASHING OF WALLS AND THE +   174 15
   THE WALLS ARE THICK AND THE INNER ROOMS ARE SUCH THEY D+   174 19
   BUT WORN OUT THEY HIDE NO MORE THE WALLS THEY STAND BEF+   174 22
   AND BREAK THE WALLS OF POSSESSION OF ALL THE WIDE WORLD   175 17
   OH MEN WITH THE AXE AND THE PICK-AXE BREAK THE WALLS OF+   175 26
   WALLS OF BLUE SHADOW   204 14
   I WISH THAT WHATEVER PROPS UP THE WALLS OF LIGHT   205 9
   SURE AND A TOWER OF STRENGTH 'TWIXT THE WALLS OF HER BR+   249 12
   AND STUMBLING LUNGING AND TOUCHING THE WALLS THE BELL-W+   343 11
   AND SO HE STRAINS BENEATH HER HOUSEY WALLS   362 20
   HER WALLS   365 4
   LIFTS UP HIS VOICE AND HOWLS TO THE WALLS OF THE PUEBLO   405 11
   OF THE WALLS WITHIN WHICH OUR LIVES ARE SPENT   462 12
   TILL THE WALLS BEGIN TO LOOSEN AND CRACK   462 13
   THE SKY-BLUE WALLS OF OUR UNVENTILATED HEAVEN   515 5
   AND PAINTS THE INSIDE WALLS SKY-BLUE   515 8
   AGAINST THE SILVERY ADAMANT WALLS OF LIFE'S EXCLUSIVE C+   722 3
   THROUGH BREACHES IN THE WALLS OF THIS OUR BY-NO-MEANS I+   722 25
   WITHIN YOUR WALLS WITHIN YOUR VERY HEART   723 15
   SHAKES O'ER HIS WALLS WHEN THE WIND DISTURBS THE NIGHT   878 4
   BRISTLE AND FLY IN SHADOWS ACROSS THE WALLS   879 3
   CLEAVES FROZEN TO THE WALLS OF MY COLD BREAST   879 4
   ACROSS THE WALLS AS THE BLINDS ARE BLOWN   *898 20
   ACROSS THE WALLS AS THE BLINDS ARE BLOWN   *902 4
   BETWEEN THE OLD RED WALLS I DID NOT DARE   *934 3
   THAT LIE OUTSIDE THE SILVERY WALLS OF OUR BODY'S BUILDE+   *957 17
   AGAINST THE SILVERY ADAMANT WALLS OF THIS OUR EXCLUSIVE+   *958 3
   OVER THE ADAMANT WALLS OF THIS OUR BY-NO-MEANS IMPREGNA+   *958 7

WALT-WHITMANESQUE
   YOU LITTLE WALT-WHITMANESQUE BITCH   395 26

WALT WHITMAN
   REJECT NOTHING SINGS WALT WHITMAN   399 1

WALY
   BLACK FOR THE FUNERAL WOW WALY AND WORROW   819 3

WAN
   AND AS I WATCH THE WAN LIGHT SHINE   60 1
   ON THY FACE AS THA GOT MORE WHITE AN' WAN   138 5
   WITH HIS WAN SPIRIT SOMEWHERE IN THE AIR   158 23
   AS THE WIND ASKS WHITHER THE WAN ROAD GOES   163 24
   GREY DAYS AND WAN DREE DAWNINGS   193 17
   THE WAN WONDERING LOOK OF THE PALE SKY   293 10
   TO WHERE THE SUNSET HUNG ITS WAN GOLD CLOTHS   205 27
   ASH FLUTTERS FLOCCULENT LIKE DOWN ON A BLUE WAN FLEDGEL+   330 8
   AND STRANGELY O CHILLED WAN SOUL A FLUSH OF ROSE   720 10
   AND THE GLIMMERING DREAMLETS OF THE MORNING ARE PALLID +   854 7

WANDER
   WHY DO I WANDER AIMLESS AMONG THEM DESIROUS FOOL   180 23
   THEY WANDER AND ARE EXILED THEY LIVE IN EXILE THROUGH   304 26
   WHITHER DO YOU WANDER   669 13
   THEY WANDER THEIR STRANGE AND DIFFERENT WAYS IN HEAVEN   713 22
   TO MANY ABOUT US SO WE WANDER ABOUT   737 2
   AND THE SERPENTS WANDER THEIR OWN WAYS RECONCILED   771 8
   FLARE BRIGHT TO WANDER AND DO NOTHING   794 16
   I WAIT FOR THE BABY TO WANDER HITHER TO ME   *913 6
   I LONG FOR THE BABY TO WANDER HITHER TO ME   *914 6

WANDERED
   AND I IN THE DARKNESS WANDERED ABOUT   121 25
   HOW HAVE I WANDERED HERE TO THIS VAULTED ROOM   141 5
   OH WHERE-OUT NOW HAS WANDERED THE GOLDEN HEN OF SUNSHINE   *933 21
   TO THE OLD SUNDAY EVENINGS WHEN DARKNESS WANDERED OUTSI+   *940 11

WANDERER
   FOR THE EARTH LIKE THE SUN IS A WANDERER   713 16

WANDERING
   AND ALL THE HEAVENS ARE WANDERING IN DISARRAY   115 21
   WE WERE WANDERING AND SINGING   216 20
   STARS COME LOW AND WANDERING HERE FOR LOVE   221 18
   DARK SKY OF NIGHT A WANDERING GLITTER A SWARM   221 26
   WANDERING UP AND DOWN   253 5
   FROM HEAVEN'S WOLFISH WANDERING ELECTRICITY THAT PROWLS   301 6
   WANDERING IN THE SLOW TRIUMPH OF HIS OWN EXISTENCE   358 18
   GONE DEAD OR WANDERING IN EXILE WITH THEIR FEATHERS   533 18
   BUT ONWARDS ONWARDS FOR THE HEAVENS ARE WANDERING   713 19
   FOR LIFE IS A WANDERING WE KNOW NOT WHITHER BUT GOING   713 24
   GOES ON AND ON AND ON WITHOUT WANDERING   713 28
   GOING YET NEVER WANDERING FIXED YET IN MOTION   713 30
   A GREY VOID THING THAT GOES WITHOUT WANDERING   714 19
   WANDERING INTO NEW VALLEYS   768 14
   THEIR WANDERING HAPPINESS AND THE WIND WASTED IN LIBERT+   *892 5

WANDERING
  LIKE A WIND-SHADOW WANDERING OVER THE WATER   *913 7
  LIKE A WIND-SHADOW WANDERING OVER THE WATER   *914 7
  WE WERE WANDERING AND SINGING   *942 6
  STARS COME LOW AND WANDERING HERE FOR LOVE   *945 4
  OF THIS DARK EARTH AND WANDERING ALL SERENE   *945 5
  DARK SKY OF NIGHT THE WANDERING GLITTER THE SWARM   *945 12

WANDERINGS
  SHE FOLLOWS HIS RESTLESS WANDERINGS   202 25

WANDERS
  AND OUT OF THE CHAMBERED WILDERNESS WANDERS A SPIRIT AB+   70 6
  ONLY THE WHEEL GOES ROUND BUT IT NEVER WANDERS   713 25
  AND OUT OF THE CHAMBERED WEARINESS WANDERS A PERFUME AB+   *916 14

WANES
  WANES THE OLD PALIMPSEST   41 23

WANING
  THE WANING MOON LOOKS UPWARD THIS GREY NIGHT   172 18

WANT
  BEYOND A WORLD I NEVER WANT TO JOIN   36 8
  AN' A FORK AN' A SPOON 'E'LL WANT AN' WHAT ELSE   46 1
  YOU WANT AT LAST AH ME   55 10
  AND I WANT TO SMITE IN ANGER THE BARREN ROCK OF EACH WA+   57 30
  'ER DOESNA WANT NO WEDDIN'-DRESS   79 21
  BUT I WANT YOU TO KNOW 'E'S NOT MARRYIN' YOU   82 5
  ALL AS WE S'LL WANT FOR FURNITURE WHEN THA LEAVES THIS +   83 3
  I DON'T LIKE YER LIZ I WANT TER   84 19
  THEN PERHAPS IN THE DARK YOU'D GET WHAT YOU WANT TO FIND   118 29
  NOW STOP CARPING AT ME DO YOU WANT ME TO HATE YOU   119 1
  DOST WANT ME TER WANT THEE AGAIN NAY THOUGH   138 17
  BUT THA WANTED ME MORE TER WANT THEE SO'S   138 22
  I WANT MY OWN ROOM'S SHELTER BUT WHAT IS THIS   140 11
  I WANT TO GIVE HER   143 7
  THE TOUCH WAS ON THE QUICK I WANT TO FORGET   143 25
  THERE IS SOMETHING I WANT TO FEEL IN MY RUNNING BLOOD   180 30
  SOMETHING I WANT TO TOUCH I MUST HOLD MY FACE TO THE RA+   180 31
  THE SAME WANT LIFE OR DEATH   214 17
  OH AND I WANT TO SING   216 1
  AND HIS HANDS ARE AWKWARD AND WANT TO HIDE   228 3
  I WANT TO GO THERE'S A GOLD ROAD BLAZES BEFORE   230 12
  AND YOU WANT TO ENLARGE YOURSELF WITH THIS FRIEND OF MI+   235 28
  WHY SHOULD I WANT TO THROTTLE   240 24
  I DID NOT WANT IT   241 17
  IT MUST BE THE WANT IN YOU   241 28
  SUPPOSE YOU DIDN'T WANT ME I SHOULD SINK DOWN   246 7
  BUT THAT IS ALL I WANT   247 26
  THE FEAR OF THE WANT OF THESE THINGS SEEMS TO BE QUITE +   263 12
  I WANT HER THOUGH TO TAKE THE SAME FROM ME   266 23
  I WANT HER TO TOUCH ME AT LAST AH ON THE ROOT AND QUICK   266 28
  I WANT THE FINE KINDLING WINE-SAP OF SPRING   271 17
  CARRIES ME WHERE I WANT TO BE CARRIED   291 30
  I DON'T AT ALL WANT TO ANNIHILATE THEM   316 14
  ACHE AND WANT OF BEING   362 29
  WANT   362 30
  THEY WANT SOMETHING OF YOU SO YOU SQUEAK AND COME   400 2
  I WANT TO DRINK OUT OF DARK CUPS THAT DRIP DOWN ON   427 9
  WOMEN DON'T WANT WISTFUL   457 13
  WOMEN WANT FIGHTERS FIGHTERS   457 25
  WHAT DO YOU WANT WILD LOINS AND WHAT   461 5
  DO YOU WANT WARM HEART AND WHAT   461 6
  BUT IF OBSCENE VILLAGE IDIOTS YOU WANT TO BE THEN BE IT   463 13
  IF YOU WANT TO HAVE SEX YOU'VE GOT TO TRUST   466 1
  I DO NOT WANT A WOMAN WHOM AGE CANNOT WITHER   478 27
  WHAT WE WANT IS SOME SORT OF COMMUNISM   483 25
  THE YOUNG ONES COPULATE HATE IT AND WANT TO CRY   485 6
  HOW THEY RUSH OUT AND WANT TO RIVE   494 3
  I DON'T WANT TO BE POOR IT MEANS I AM PINCHED   498 16
  BUT NEITHER DO I WANT TO BE RICH   498 17
  I WANT TO BE LIKE THAT TO HAVE A NATURAL ABUNDANCE   498 24
  SO IF YOU WANT EITHER OF US TO FEEL ANYTHING AT ALL   501 14
  THE OLD ONES WANT TO BE YOUNG AND THEY AREN'T YOUNG   502 23
  WE WANT A NEW WORLD OF WILD PEACE WHERE LIVING IS FREE   519 22
  WANT TO DO   520 7
  I IMMEDIATELY WANT TO GO AND DO SOMETHING JOLLY TOO   520 25
  THE WAGES OF CASH IS WANT MORE CASH   521 2
  THE WAGES OF WANT MORE CASH IS VICIOUS COMPETITION   521 3
  AND ALL I WANT IS TO SEE THE SPARK FLICKER   524 5
  THEN I AM MORE THAN RADICAL I WANT TO WORK A GUILLOTINE   526 16
  FINALLY OUR LITTLE LOT I DON'T WANT TO DIE BUT BY JINGO+   534 6
  AND WANT TO BE COLD AND DEVILISH HARD   537 17
  THEY WANT TO CHANGE THE MAN HIMSELF   538 21
  WHAT DOES SHE WANT VOLCANIC VENUS AS SHE GOES FUMING   539 10
  WHAT DOES SHE WANT   539 12
  SHE'S SEETHING LIKE A VOLCANO AND VOLCANOS DON'T WANT   539 14
  REALLY WANT THEM   539 17
  I DON'T KNOW WHAT YOU WANT BUT I CERTAINLY HAVEN'T GOT   541 11
  MY DEARS IF YOU WANT THE SKIES TO FALL   541 23
  IF YOU WANT TO KNOW YOURSELF   543 12
  WANT TO GET UP AN' SHOUT   550 10
  STILL IF YOU DON'T WANT TO BOTHER   557 7
  IF YOU WANT JUSTICE   562 8
  DOES IT WANT TO GO TO BYE-BYE THERE THEN TAKE ITS LITTLE   570 22
  WANT TO GO A LITTLE TATTAH SO IT SHALL OF COURSE IT SHA+   571 1
  WE WANT TO BE LOVED ESPECIALLY AUNTIE   572 23
  IF YOU DON'T WANT TO BREAK THE SWEET ENGLISH SPELL   576 11
  WHEN YOU WANT ONE SO I DID WITHOUT   579 11
  SO NOW I WANT ABOVE ALL THINGS   601 21
  YET I DON'T WANT THEM TO COME NEAR   602 6
  YET I CAN'T BE ALONE I WANT SOMEBODY TO KEEP ME WARM   603 20
  IF YOU WANT TO GET A GLIMPSE OF FUTURE POSSIBILITIES   612 8
  BUT HE CAN'T STOP ME FROM SINNING AGAINST HIM IF I WANT+   618 11
  AND WHEN I WANT TO I'M GOING TO   618 12
  AND I WANT NO MAN TO BE HUMBLE BEFORE ME   622 3
  I WANT TO SHOW ALWAYS THE HUMAN TENDER REVERENCE   622 5

WANT
  USUALLY WANT TO FORCE SOMEBODY TO AGREE WITH THEM   626 5
  AND WANT TO PUT ME DOWN   626 22
  HELP HELP THEY WANT TO BURN MY PICTURES   633 7
  THEY WANT TO MAKE AN AUTO-DA-FE   633 8
  THEY WANT TO MAKE AN ACT OF FAITH AND BURN MY PRETTY   633 9
  HELP OH HELP THEY WANT TO BURN MY PICTURES   634 6
  NOW I DON'T WANT TO LOOK AT THE WORLD ANY MORE   662 8
  BECAUSE THE GODS DON'T WANT THEM   662 17
  VENUS WOULD RATHER HAVE LIVE DOVES THAN DEAD IF YOU WAN+   678 7
  IF YOU WANT TO MAKE HER AN OFFERING LET THE DOVES FLY F+   678 9
  ALL I WANT OF YOU MEN AND WOMEN   683 24
  ALL I WANT OF YOU   683 25
  OH LEAVE OFF SAYING I WANT YOU TO BE SAVAGES   684 1
  I WANT YOU TO BE AS SAVAGE AS THE GENTIAN AND THE DAFFO+   684 4
  BUT IF YOU WANT TO BREATHE DEEP SUMPTUOUS LIFE   698 3
  OH WHAT WE WANT ON EARTH   726 17
  ME WANT TO CRY TO SEE HIM SO STRONG AND EASY   733 24
  AND WHAT DO YOU WANT   735 4
  I WANT TO KNOW NO MORE I WANT TO SEE   738 25
  WHAT DO THEY WANT   739 19
  WHAT DO THEY WANT THE GHOSTS WHAT IS IT   740 7
  WHAT DO THEY WANT FOREVER THERE ON OUR THRESHOLD   740 12
  DO YOU WANT TO RISE IN THE WORLD   773 12
  RISE DO YOU WANT TO RISE   773 14
  DO YOU WANT TO LOOK LIKE A BANK-CLERK   773 16
  DO YOU WANT TO LOOK LIKE A BANK-MANAGER   773 18
  I WANT MY SON TO BE SOMETHING BETTER THAN HIS FATHER WAS   773 26
  PEOPLE WANT TO KEEP THE INDIAN BACK WANT TO   778 7
  SO NATURALLY THEY WANT TO KEEP HIM BACK DOWN POOR   778 12
  WHAT THEN DO THEY WANT   793 16
  THEY WANT GOLD THEY WANT SILVER FROM THE MOUNTAINS   793 18
  WANT APPLES   817 5
  WANT TO PUT THEMSELVES TOGETHER   819 14
  WE WANT TO BE FAIR   829 19
  WE HAVE LEARNT NOT TO HAVE SLAVES NOT TO WANT THEM   832 28
  NOT TO WANT TO PILE UP POSSESSIONS   833 4
  NOT TO WANT TO BULLY THOSE WEAKER THAN OURSELVES   833 5
  I ONLY WANT TO KNOW SOME THINGS TO KNOW ALL THINGS WOUL+   840 19
  STILL TO SAY I WANT NO FLAME   873 9
  'ER DOESNA WANT NO WEDDIN'-DRESS   *921 17
  I WANT YOU TO KNOW 'E'S NON MARRYIN' YOU   *924 9
  ALL AS WE SHALL WANT FOR FURNITURE WHEN THA LEAVES THIS+   *925 7
  THEN PERHAPS IN THE DARK YOU'LL HAVE GOT WHAT YOU WANT +   *932 6
  AND I GIVE YOU EVERYTHING THAT YOU WANT ME TO   *945 19
  AH IF YOU WANT TO LIVE IN PEACE ON THE FACE OF THE EARTH   *961 5

WANTED
  HAVING FOUND WHAT HE WANTED HAVING GOT WHAT WAS   51 19
  WI' A DRESS AS IS WANTED TO-DAY   78 4
  I AM ASHAMED YOU WANTED ME NOT TO-NIGHT   87 14
  MY LOVE WHERE IT IS WANTED YET WAIT AWHILE MY FALL   94 7
  THA WANTED TER LEAVE ME THAT BAD THA KNOWS   138 20
  BUT THA WANTED ME MORE TER WANT THEE SO'S   138 22
  THA THOUGHT THA WANTED A LITTLE WENCH   138 27
  THA THOUGHT THA WANTED A LITTLE WENCH   138 29
  THA THOUGHT THA WANTED TER BE RID O' ME   139 1
  THA THOUGHT THA WANTED TER MARRY AN' SEE   139 3
  FOR WHICH I WANTED THE NIGHT TO RETREAT   220 20
  I WANTED TO GATHER THEM ONE BY ONE   227 15
  I WANTED THE VIRGIN YOU TO BE HOME AT LAST   412 2
  AND I THOUGHT YOU WANTED LIFE AND EXPERIENCE DEAR YOUNG   463 5
  THAT WAS JUST WHAT SATAN WANTED TO DO   483 7
  MEN WANTED TO BE LIKE GODS   640 25
  I HAVE ALWAYS WANTED TO BE AS THE FLOWERS ARE   677 10
  AND GOD IS GOOD FOR I WANTED HIM TO DIE   742 1
  WAITING AND I KNEW HE WANTED IT   742 8
  THAT THE INDIANS WANTED THE WHITE MAN'S GOVERNMENT   778 20
  WI' A DRESS AS IS WANTED TODAY   *919 24

WANTIN
  AN' 'ER'S WANTIN IT I HEAR   *921 16

WANTING
  AND I SUFFERED IT WANTING TO SYMPATHISE   206 34
  AND THEY CAN'T HELP WANTING TO SPITE IT ON THEM   502 34
  OR THINKING THEY ARE LOVABLE OR WANTING TO BE LOVABLE   505 10
  MEN HAVE BEEN WANTING TO TRIUMPH TRIUMPH TRIUMPH   519 2
  LIKE A BRIDE HE TOOK MY BAYONET WANTING IT   742 9
  LIKE A VIRGIN THE BLADE OF MY BAYONET WANTING IT   742 10
  LIFTING HIS HAUNTED EYES TO ME I AM WANTING IN SONG   884 11

WANTIN'
  'ER'LL BE WANTIN' IT I 'EAR   79 20
  AS 'ER'LL BE WANTIN' MY WEDDIN'-DRESS   79 27
  AS 'ER'LL BE WANTIN' MY WEDDIN' DRESS   *921 23

WANTON
  WITH A WANTON PRINCESS SLENDER AND PROUD   70 15
  WANTON SPARROWS THAT TWITTERED WHEN MORNING LOOKED IN   71 13

WANTON-HEADED
  BY-PATHS WHERE THE WANTON-HEADED FLOWERS DOFF THEIR HOOD   65 30

WANTS
  SHOUT AN' AX WHAT 'E WANTS   44 18
  THA WANTS 'IM THY-SEN I SEE   81 32
  THA WANTS 'IM THY-SEN TOO BAD   82 6
  BUT WHAT THEN THA WANTS ME DOES TER   83 24
  THA WANTS IT AND EVERYTHING ELSE IS IN VAIN   139 19
  IT IS SOMEBODY WANTS TO DO US HARM   250 30
  WHY HAVE A SOVIET THAT ONLY WANTS TO SCREW US ALL IN AS   452 21
  THAT NOBODY EATS AND NOBODY WANTS SO IT ROTS BUT IS NOT   462 21
  NOWADAYS EVERYBODY WANTS TO BE YOUNG   502 13
  WANTS US OR CAN HAVE ANYTHING TO DO WITH US   514 21
  SHE SAYS SHE WANTS A LOVER BUT DON'T YOU BELIEVE HER   539 13
  HE WANTS HIS ONE GREAT WONDERING EYE THE EYE OF THE   544 9
  OH BUT A MAN WANTS TO GET ON IN THE WORLD   773 21

WANTS
    THA WANTS 'IM THY-SEN TOO BAD   *924 10
    HE NEVER WANTS A WOMAN HE DOESN'T LIKE WOMEN   *948 23

WAR
    NATIONS ARMIES WAR PEACE-TALKING   256 27
    WHEN I HEARD THE CANNON OF THE WAR I LISTENED WITH MY   257 7
    WAR CAME AND EVERY HAND RAISED TO MURDER   257 27
    LET IT BE WAR   327 28
    AND SO IT IS WAR   327 29
    PEOPLE ALWAYS MAKE WAR WHEN THEY SAY THEY LOVE PEACE   495 19
    WAR   495 19
    LOUD PEACE PROPAGANDA MAKES WAR SEEM IMMINENT   495 20
    IT IS A FORM OF WAR EVEN SELF-ASSERTION AND BEING WISE +   495 21
    THEN WE SHAN'T HAVE WAR AND WE NEEDN'T TALK ABOUT PEACE   496 5
    A THRILL RATHER EASILY EXHAUSTS ITSELF TAKE EVEN THE WAR   532 5
    THE SON OF MAN GOES FORTH TO WAR   541 19
    WAR WILL CEASE THERE WILL BE NO MORE WARS   612 3
    AND WHERE THERE IS INFINITE VARIETY THERE IS NO INTERES+   612 6
    ONENESS MAKES WAR AND THE OBSESSION OF ONENESS   612 7
    IT NEEDS THOROUGHLY PRUNING NOT AS IN THE LATE WAR BLAS+   677 25
    THE WAR WAS NOT STRIFE   715 1
    WHY AM I BRIDEGROOM OF WAR WAR'S PARAMOUR   742 36
    THE MAN ANDREW KEEP HIM SAFE IN THE WAR   751 10
    ARE ABOUT TO DANCE THE WAR DANCE ROUND YOU MEN   792 18

WARANT
    I' TH' SNOW BUT I'S WARANT THEE BUNNY   *920 23

WAR-CRY
    WAR-CRY TRIUMPH ACUTE-DELIGHT DEATH-SCREAM REPTILIAN   364 22

WARD
    ONE FROM THE WARD   146 27
    I WATCH HER WARD AWAY THE FLAME   151 34
    THE AMERICAN INDIAN LINGERS HERE WARD OF THE   776 5
    THAT SHE SHOULD WARD AWAY THE FLAME   874 12

WAR-HORSES
    LIKE WAR-HORSES OR WAR-PONIES AT LAST   537 21

WARILY
    WALK WARILY WALK WARILY BE CAREFUL WHAT YOU SAY   707 1

WARLESS
    THE HEART OF MAN IN SO FAR AS IT IS BUDDING IS BUDDING +   612 4

WARLESSNESS
    A CERTAIN WARLESSNESS EVEN MONEYLESSNESS   612 15

WAR-LESS
    WHAT WE NEED IS A LONG LONG WAR-LESS EPOCH   833 22

WARM
    OVER MY SKIN IN THE SUNSHINE THE WARM CLINGING AIR   34 13
    SHE KISSED ME WARM ON THE MOUTH   37 13
    IS WARM WITH A RUDDY GLOW   37 15
    THE WARM DUMB WISDOM   50 19
    THE BIRD LIES WARM AGAINST THE WALL   42 23
    HER SMALL HEAD MAKING WARM DISPLAY   42 26
    HER OUT OF THE NEST'S WARM BUSY BALL   42 28
    UP THE WARM GRASS WHERE THE SUNBEAMS START   46 8
    I HAVE OPENED THE WINDOWS TO WARM MY HANDS ON THE SILL   52 12
    THROUGH THE STIRRED IRIDESCENCE THAT SWIMS IN THE WARM   53 16
    AN' WARM FOR TH' SMELL COME WAFTIN' TO ME 'ER PUT 'ER F+   61 13
    HER BREATH FLEW WARM AGAINST MY NECK   61 28
    WARM AS A FLAME IN THE CLOSE NIGHT AIR   61 29
    OUR BEACHED VESSEL DARKENED RENCONTRE INHUMAN AND CLOSE+   66 27
    HOW WERT THOU SO STRANGE-SHAPEN WHAT WARM FINGER   69 13
    OR SUBSTANCE SAVE I LIGHT ON YOU TO WARM   86 11
    AND DIM HOPES CROWDED ME WARM WITH COMPANIONSHIP   98 29
    FOR I THOUGHT YOU WERE WARM AS A SUDDEN JET OF BLOOD   99 7
    AND YOU MY LASS WITH YOUR RICH WARM FACE AGLOW   126 28
    CAN WARM HER HANDS AND INVITE HER SOUL   151 27
    YET WARM HERSELF AT THE FIRE THEN BLAME   151 35
    YET WARM THE CHASE   165 6
    WHITE-BODIED AND WARM THE NIGHT WAS   165 9
    OF OLD SPENT LIVES LINGER BLURRED AND WARM   173 18
    THE WARM SOFT COUNTRY LASS   198 13
    PROUD KNIGHTS TO BATTLE SWEET HOW I WARM   221 28
    THE WINE IS WARM IN THE HEARTH   237 23
    I WILL WARM YOUR LIMBS WITH KISSES   237 25
    THOSE SHOULDERS SO WARM AND SMOOTH I FEEL THAT I   245 18
    MY PIGEON MY LITTLE ONE SO WARM   246 20
    HOW SURE I FEEL HOW WARM AND STRONG AND HAPPY   247 4
    HAS FOR ME A DOOR INTO PEACE WARM DAWN IN THE EAST   250 6
    EXULTING WITH SECRET WARM EXCESS   272 11
    POMEGRANATES TO WARM YOUR HANDS AT   278 18
    FROM THE WARM BLOOD IN THE DARK-CREATION MORNING   358 14
    BUT YOU LOVE LYING WARM BETWEEN WARM HUMAN THIGHS   396 19
    THRUSTS WARM THROUGH THE LOINS SO THE LITTLE ONE   425 16
    AND SPLASHES WARM BETWEEN THE BUTTOCKS   427 4
    WARM STILL WITH THE LIFE OF FORGOTTEN MEN WHO MADE THEM   448 7
    DO YOU WANT WARM HEART AND WHAT   461 6
    MY BODY LIKES ITS DINNER AND THE WARM SUN BUT OTHERWISE+   501 16
    AND GLEAMS ON THE WORLD WITH THE WARM DARK VISION OF   544 24
    YET I CAN'T BE ALONE I WANT SOMEBODY TO KEEP ME WARM   603 20
    SHE WHO AT HER BEST HOURS WAS HERSELF WARM FLICKERING H+   675 16
    AND ONE WARM KIND KISS OF THE LION WITH GOLDEN PAWS   695 33
    HERE IN THE GARDEN WITH RED GERANIUMS IT IS WARM IT IS +   696 18
    WILL YOU GO WILL YOU GO FROM MY WARM HOUSE   696 21
    WRAPPED IN THE DARK-RED MANTLE OF WARM MEMORIES   723 19
    WAFTING WITH WARM LOVE FROM STILL-LIVING HEARTS   723 22
    WARM OF ME FADING TO WHITE   766 24
    HER WARM RED LIPS   862 10
    LADS IN THEIR WARM LIGHT SLIPPERS BOUND DOWN THE HALL T+   865 28
    TO LICK ME UP BUT ONLY THE WARM   873 10
    YET WARM HERSELF AT THE FIRE AND BLAME   874 13

WARM
    I KNOW THE SWEET RED HUTCH OF HIS MOUTH WHERE WARM   876 32
    MIGHT FOLLOW WARM AND GLAD WHO SIT HERE COLD   879 15
    OVER MY SUNLIT SKIN THE WARM CLINGING AIR   *892 1
    THIS WARM DUMB WISDOM   *893 2
    I HAVE OPENED THE WINDOW TO WARM MY HANDS ON THE SILL   *905 1
    THROUGH THE COLOURED IRIDESCENCE THAT SWIMS IN THE WARM   *906 7
    OF OLD INEFFECTUAL LIVES LINGER BLURRED AND WARM   *906 12
    OF OLD INEFFECTUAL LIVES LINGER BLURRED AND WARM   *908 6
    BECAUSE THEY WAS WARM AN' THE WIND BLEW   *910 18
    RAVELLED BLUE AND WHITE WARM FOR A BIT   *911 28
    HER BREATH FLEW WARM AGAINST MY NECK   *912 7
    WARM AS A FLAME IN THE CLOSE NIGHT AIR   *912 8
    AND HYMNS GLEAMED ON OUR WARM LIPS AS WE WATCHED MOTHER+   *940 12
    WE FOUND OUR WARM WILD ROSES   *942 13
    SPIRIT OF CARELESS JOY AH HOW I WARM   *945 14
    WARM IN A CITY OF STRENGTH BETWEEN HER BREASTS   *945 23

WARMED
    I HAVE EATEN AND DRUNK AND WARMED AND CLOTHED MY BODY   264 1
    LET THE DARKNESS BE WARMED WARMED THROUGH TO A RUDDY VI+   273 24
    WHO WARMED THE COCKLES OF MY HEART   507 9
    I'D REJOICE OVER THE WOMAN AND THE WARMED COCKLES OF MY   507 10

WARMER
    THE MOON IS NOT ANY WARMER THE SUN NO   754 5

WARMIN'
    WARMIN' 'IS-SEN AT THE STOOL O' FIRE   79 2
    WARMIN' HIS-SEN AT THE STOOL O' FIRE   *920 26

WARMS
    THE SUN WARMS THE SEA LITTLE LONELY AND SAD SIFTING THE+   180 3
    BUT IF IT WARMS   561 24
    HIS WARMTH NEVER WARMS HER   800 20

WARMTH
    AND THE WHITE DOG SNUFFS THE WARMTH APPEALING   41 10
    O' WARMTH AS 'E GOT DOWN THEER TH' REST WOR STONE COLD   61 18
    THAT MY LOVE CAN DAWN IN WARMTH AGAIN UNAFRAID   99 15
    UNSIGHTLY ITS WAY TO THE WARMTH THIS THING WITH A LIST   141 15
    HUTCHED UP FOR WARMTH THE MUDDY RIMS   145 19
    FULL OF FINE WARMTH I ISSUE FORTH IN CLEAR   218 7
    UP WITH MYSELF AND MY WARMTH LIKE A FLAME ROUND THE   245 8
    THE WORLD TO SNUGGLE DOWN IN THE WARMTH   394 3
    WARMTH   443 18
    WITH A SOFT ONE WARMTH AND A GENEROUS   471 6
    TO WITHDRAW HIS WARMTH FROM YOUR FEET SO YOUR FEET TURN+   797 3
    HIS WARMTH NEVER WARMS HER   800 20
    MY HEART HAS A WARMTH LIKE THIS SEA WHERE THE DAWN   860 17
    HAS THE WARMTH OF A NIGHT KISS SPREAD THROUGH THEIR BLO+   860 22
    THE POOR SHUT DANDELIONS WHOM SMALL WARMTH EXPANDS   *896 19
    ME COMFORTED TO FEEL THE WARMTH THAT CREEPS   *900 23
    ME COMFORTED TO FEEL THE WARMTH THAT CREEPS   *903 35

WARN
    I WOULD WARN ANYBODY AGAINST A CULTURE   763 13

WARNING
    PERHAPS 'TWAS A DREAM OF WARNING   46 27
    SENDING OUT MAGNETIC VIBRATIONS OF WARNING PITCH-DARK   289 2
    DAY OF WRATH O DAY OF WARNING   511 8

WARP
    TAUT AS A WETTED WARP   746 22

WARPING
    WARPING THE PERFECT IMAGE OF GOD   *929 4

WAR-PONIES
    LIKE WAR-HORSES OR WAR-PONIES AT LAST   537 21

WARRANT
    I' TH' SNOW BUT I'S WARRANT THEE   78 31
    NO GOOD I WARRANT THIS TROUBLE IS SUCH AS SHE   *910 7

WARRIOR-LIKE
    WARRIOR-LIKE DAWN-COCK'S-COMB FLARING FLOWER   315 1

WARRIORS
    WITH SLIM WAISTS OF WARRIORS AND THE LONG FEET   689 3

WARS
    WAR WILL CEASE THERE WILL BE NO MORE WARS   612 3

WAR'S
    WHY AM I BRIDEGROOM OF WAR WAR'S PARAMOUR   742 36

WASH
    WHILE I WASH YOU WITH WEEPING WATER   55 3
    LAMPS IN A WASH OF RAIN   119 8
    AND WASH QUITE CLEAN   229 18
    THE WATERS WASH   335 3
    YOU WASH IN ONENESS   335 4
    SWINE WASH IN MIRE AND BARNYARD FOWLS IN DUST   376 8
    WASH OVER OUR KNEES AND SPLASH BETWEEN OUR THIGHS   425 4
    THE TINY GRAIN OF SOMETHING THAT NO WAVE CAN WASH AWAY   514 4
    AH THE CLEAN WATERS OF THE SKY AH CAN YOU WASH   581 6
    HE WATERS THE HORSES DOES HE WASH HIS HEEL   733 30
    OF THE WAVES THAT WASH   747 4
    WOULD WASH AWAY THIS IGNOMINY   747 9
    WASH YOURSELF AND RUB OIL IN YOUR SKIN   791 21
    ON THE SEVENTH DAY LET EVERY MAN WASH HIMSELF AND PUT O+   791 22
    AND WASH OF VOICES ALONG THE STREET   *917 7
    LAMPS IN A WASH OF RAIN   *932 17

WASHED
  SO I WENT AND WASHED MY DEADENED FLESH IN THE SEA   99 12
  IS WASHED FROM THE BLUE   118 12
  I AM WASHED QUITE CLEAN   229 22
  EVEN IF IT'S ONLY IN THE WHITENESS OF A WASHED POCKET-M+   449 22
  THEIR HARDENED SOULS ARE WASHED WITH FIRE AND WASHED AN+   663 6
  HAS HER FOOTING WASHED AWAY AS THE DARK FLOOD RISES   718 13
  IS WASHED BONE   810 18

WASHES
  RUSTLE OF LEAVES WASHES OUT THE RENDING   150 7
  IRON WASHES-AWAY LIKE AN OLD BLOOD-STAIN   455 5
  AND HE GOES AND WASHES THE BELLY OF THE HORSE   734 5
  HE COMES TO THE SIDE OF THE ROAD AND WASHES HIS HAND   734 13
  THAT WASHES THE LORDS OF LIFE   788 25

WASHING
  WASHING YOU THROUGH   240 9
  TWITCHES AND EBBS HITTING WASHING INWARDLY SILVERILY   453 20
  BUT A WOMAN SHY AND ALONE WAS WASHING HERSELF UNDER A T+   651 4
  WASHING   672 14
  AND A WOMAN WHO HAS BEEN WASHING CLOTHES IN THE POOL OF+   693 1
  WHO HAD SPREAD WHITE WASHING ON THE GRAVEL BANKED ABOVE+   693 3
  IS WASHING IN THROUGH THE BREACHES OF OUR WOUNDS   718 7

WASHINGTON
  NOR IN WASHINGTON   774 30
  AND THE BIG WHITE MEN FROM WASHINGTON DROVE OUT TO   777 25

WASH-OUTS
  AND YOUNG WASH-OUTS PRETENDING TO BE IN LOVE WITH DEATH   535 19

WAS-IT-AUDIBLE
  A FAR WAS-IT-AUDIBLE SCREAM   364 11

WASN'T
  BUT IT WASN'T ROUND AND FINISHED LIKE A BILLIARD BALL   279 25
  IT DAMN WELL WASN'T WORTH IT   553 1
  FOR IT WASN'T A BIT SUPERIOR   554 13
  I WASN'T AWARE OF THE THINGS I COULD DO   761 9

WASP
  AND FIR-WORT STINKING FOR THE CARRION WASP   316 5

WASP-BANDS
  TIGER-STRIPES AND WASP-BANDS   355 6

WASTE
  I WILL NOT WASTE MY SOUL AND AND MY STRENGTH FOR THIS   74 23
  THIS NEW RED ROCK IN A WASTE OF WHITE RISES AGAINST THE+   75 13
  WASTE NOT THE YEW-TREE'S WAITING WASTE   114 13
  SHE KNOWS THE WASTE ALL DRY BENEATH HER IN ONE PLACE   153 5
  ON THE MISTY WASTE LANDS AWAY FROM THE FLUSHING GREY   164 21
  I CARRY MY PATIENCE SULLENLY THROUGH THE WASTE LANDS   167 3
  I CARRY MY PATIENCE SULLENLY THROUGH THE WASTE LANDS   167 16
  RUNS WASTE DOWN THEIR CHALICES   177 4
  OVER THE WASTE WHERE NO HOPE IS SEEN   179 14
  WHEN I WENT TO THE CIRCUS THAT HAD PITCHED ON THE WASTE   444 9
  A WASTE EXPANSE OF NOTHING LIKE WIDE FORESHORES WHERE N+   509 12
  YET EVEN WASTE GREY FORESHORES AND SORRY FAR-OUT   509 17
  THEIR GOOD YOUTH GO TO WASTE   560 4
  UPON THE FLOOD'S BLACK WASTE   719 6
  OH THEY CAN LAY YOU WASTE THE ANGRY DEAD   723 16
  ONLY THE WASTE NIGHT LIES IN STORE   747 27
  SLOW INFIRM DEATH HAS AT LAST GATHERED UP THE WASTE   859 21
  I WILL NOT WASTE MYSELF TO EMBERS FOR THEM   *895 31
  I CARRY MY ANGER SULLENLY 'CROSS THESE WASTE LANDS   *896 21
  I WILL NOT WASTE MYSELF TO EMBERS FOR THEM   *904 20
  WASTE ME NOT.I BEG YOU WASTE   *930 1
  FOR OUT IN THE WASTE WILD SOUL SPACE THAT SHALL   *938 19

WASTED
  WE ARE NOT WASTED WE ARE NOT LEFT OUT   802 6
  AND WASTED   817 19
  A FIERY SIGN OF THE CHAINED POWER THAT WASTED HIM TO TH+   859 20
  COME ON TURN HOME OLD LASS ARE WE WASTED TOO   859 25
  THEIR WANDERING HAPPINESS AND THE WIND WASTED IN LIBERT+   *892 5
  IS HEAVY IS CLOGGED AND HEAVY WITH WASTED ASH   *897 17

WASTEFUL
  WASTEFUL INTO THE NIGHT'S BLACK NOSTRILS DRINK   86 6

WASTE-LANDS
  COMING HOME OVER THE WASTE-LANDS WIDE AND LONELY WITH S+   866 16

WASTE-PAPER
  ALL THAT WE KNOW IS NOTHING WE ARE MERELY CRAMMED WASTE+   613 8

WASTES
  WASTES LIKE A LIE   41 27
  THEY ARE LORDS OF THE DESOLATE WASTES OF SADNESS THEIR + *891 4

WASTING
  LAND BETTER INSTEAD OF WASTING TIME   777 32

WASTRELS
  WASTRELS THAT SLEEP ON THE FLAGSTONES WITHOUT ANY HURT   145 33

WATCH
  AND WATCH MY DEAD DAYS FUSING TOGETHER IN DROSS   47 3
  WATCH THE BOYS IN THEIR SUMMER BLOUSES   51 11
  MYSELF TO WATCH THE DAYLIGHT WIN   59 3
  SHALL WATCH THE DAWN LIGHT UP FOR ME   59 31
  AND AS I WATCH THE WAN LIGHT SHINE   60 1
  YOU WATCH THE RED SPARKS WHIRL AND FLEE   116 23
  SO WIDE AS YOU WATCH THE CATKINS BLOW   126 30
  I WATCH HER WARD AWAY THE FLAME   151 34
  TO WATCH THE WORLD THAT LINGERS   162 19

WATCH
  I LINGER TO WATCH HER   217 10
  SHE MOVED ROUND TO WATCH   222 6
  WATCH AT THE BANNER OF DEATH AND THE MYSTERY   232 23
  YOU MUST COME TO THE WINDOW TO WATCH ME GO   235 24
  NOW I SEE THEM JUST THE SAME AND WATCH THEM   269 20
  AND WATCH IT PUTTING FORTH EACH TIME TO HEAVEN   299 24
  LET THE GOD WHO IS MAKER OF BATS WATCH WITH THEM IN   346 15
  ALTHOUGH YOU WATCH   359 12
  BUT WATCH A TURKEY PRANCING LOW ON EARTH   371 3
  AND UP THE HILL LIKE A RIVER IF YOU WATCH   383 29
  FLAT BROWN ROCKS TO WATCH THE FERRY IN THE SUN   386 24
  AND HER BRIGHT STRIPED FROST-FACE WILL NEVER WATCH ANY   402 17
  WATCH SILENT THE LOOMING OF THE HOARY FAR-GONE AGES   425 21
  AND THEN WATCH HIM GO SOGGY LIKE A WET MERINGUE   431 6
  WATCH HIM TURN INTO A MESS EITHER A FOOL OR A BULLY   431 7
  JUST WATCH THE DISPLAY OF HIM CONFRONTED WITH A NEW   431 8
  WHILE YOU LISTEN IN WHILE YOU WATCH THE FILM WHILE YOU   441 20
  AND FORCED TO WATCH EVERYONE THAT COMES NEAR YOU LEST   522 17
  HAVE NOT YET PASSED THE ISLANDS I MUST WATCH THEM STILL   687 23
  PROMISE YOU WILL NOT WATCH THE SCAR'S   735 26
  THEY WATCH US THEY PRESS ON US   739 16
  I WATCH BY THE FIRE   804 17
  WATCH THE NEW MOON   816 19
  BUT WATCH YOUR SEXUAL STEP OH DEAR MY DEAR   829 29
  AND I HAVE COME TO WATCH   879 4
  TAKE THE LANTERN AND WATCH THE SOW FOR FEAR SHE GRAB HE+ *892 24
  DO WATCH YOUR EYES   *894 8
  STILL IN THE SUN TO WATCH AND I CAN SEE   *895 2
  WATCH THE BOYS IN THEIR SUMMER BLOUSES   *898 23
  WATCH THE BOYS IN THEIR SUMMER BLOUSES   *902 7
  EYES WHERE I CAN WATCH THE SWIM OF OLD DREAMS REFLECTED+ *907 11
  WATCH THE STIR WHOSE RHYTHM IS SECRET WHOSE SECRET IS S+ *907 13
  AND I WATCH TO SEE THE CREATOR THE POWER THAT PATTERNS   *908 25
  EYES WHERE I CAN WATCH THE SWIM OF OLD DREAMS REFLECTED+ *909 7
  WATCH THE STIR WHICH IS RHYTHMIC AND MOVES THEM ALL AS + *909 9
  YOU WATCH THE FIRE SPARKS SWIRL AND FLEE   *930 22
  I LINGER TO WATCH HER   *942 20
  AND WIDE IN ECSTASY I SIT AND WATCH   *943 20

WATCHED
  AND WATCHED WHAT 'ER 'AD ON   61 4
  I WATCHED THE TEARS ON THE GUILTY CHEEKS OF THE BOYS   94 14
  I WATCHED THEM FLOAT UP THE DARK CHIMNEY   107 4
  THAT ROCKED IN A LILT ALONG I WATCHED THE POISE   123 3
  CHOKE ME IN MY OWN CRIMSON I WATCHED HER PULL   123 17
  SHE WATCHED SHE WENT OF A SUDDEN INTENSELY STILL   125 11
  SHE WATCHED MY HAND TO SEE WHAT IT WOULD FULFILL   125 12
  FOR MY HAND LIKE A SNAKE WATCHED HERS THAT COULD NOT FLY   125 24
  ON AND ON WATCHED RELENTLESS BY ME ROUND AND ROUND IN   343 23
  SO BIG AND QUIET AND REMOTE HAVING WATCHED SO MANY   393 12
  THE PEOPLE WATCHED AND WONDERED AND SEEMED TO RESENT   445 17
  AND WATCHED FOR YOUR GLISTENING FEET DOWN THE GARDEN PA+   695 11
  I WATCHED THE TEARS ON THE FRUITED CHEEKS OF THE BOYS   *897 2
  AN' WATCHED WHAT 'ER 'AD ON   *911 20
  THAT ROCKED IN A LILT ALONG I WATCHED THE POISE   *934 9
  AND CHOKE ME IN MY OWN CRIMSON I WATCHED HER PULL   *934 23
  SHE WATCHED SHE WENT OF A SUDDEN INTENSELY STILL   *935 27
  SHE WATCHED MY HAND AND THE SKIES BEGAN TO THRILL   *935 28
  AND MY HAND LIKE A SNAKE WATCHED HERS THAT COULD NOT FLY *936 23
  AND HYMNS GLEAMED ON OUR WARM LIPS AS WE WATCHED MOTHER+ *940 12

WATCHER
  I AM THE WATCHER AND MASTER OF THE DREAM   807 1

WATCHERS
  FOR HER WATCHERS TO SHUT THE GATE   261 25
  AND THE WATCHERS THE DIVIDERS THOSE SWIFT ONES WITH DAR+   706 17

WATCHES
  WINGS FULL OF STARS THEY RULE THE NIGHT AND MAN THAT WA+   319 3
  STILL SHE WATCHES WITH ETERNAL COCKED WISTFULNESS   394 5
  SHE WATCHES WITH INSATIABLE WISTFULNESS   394 10
  LO I AM LORD OF THE WATCHES OF THE NIGHT   806 29
  WHILE TH' PARSON WAS PRAYIN' I WATCHES 'ER AN' SHE WOR + *910 1

WATCHFUL
  ACQUIESCENCE OF WATCHFUL LIONS   770 17
  AND SMILING CURIOUSLY WITH WATCHFUL EYES   878 13

WATCHING
  ON THE TURF I STAND WATCHING MY OWN WHITE SHADOW QUIVER+   33 19
  WATCHING THE DOOR OPEN HE FLASHES BARE   43 19
  IT WILL FIND ME WATCHING AT THE MARRIAGE GATE   58 28
  WISTFUL AND CANDID WATCHING ME WISTFULLY FROM HER DISTA+   67 14
  TO THE FACE THAT GAZES OUTWARDS WATCHING FOR NIGHT TO W+   103 2
  I WAS WATCHING THE WOMAN THAT BORE ME   111 1
  LIES ON THE DUST WATCHING WHERE THERE IS NOTHING TO SEE+   112 22
  WATCHING US OVERHEAD   113 20
  AT THE FEET OF THE SLEEPERS WATCHING   146 5
  AND THE PLACE IS NO LONGER OURS WATCHING I HEAR   173 2
  STANDS WATCHING EVERMORE   200 16
  AND YOU STOOD ALONE WATCHING THEM GO   206 1
  AND FELT HER WATCHING   222 10
  WHO DO YOU THINK STANDS WATCHING   226 13
  AND WATCHING THE FISHES IN THE BREATHING WATERS   337 29
  BUT WATCHING CLOSER   338 6
  WATCHING AND HARDLY SEEING THE TRUNK-CURL APPROACH AND   388 9
  UNTOLD CENTURIES OF WATCHING FOR SOMETHING TO COME   394 11
  WISTFULLY WATCHING WITH WONDERFUL LIQUID EYES   394 20
  WHILE HE STANDS ASIDE WATCHING WITH A SUPERIOR LITTLE G+   447 36
  AND WATCHING OUR EVERY STEP   707 4
  AND HIS FATHER WATCHING HIM   782 31
  FOR THE SUN AND THE MOON ARE ALIVE AND WATCHING WITH GL+   792 10
  THERE ARE DEAD THAT SIT UNDER THE TREES WATCHING WITH A+   795 26
  HE IS WATCHING BY THE FIRE   805 29
  WATCHING THY GREAT SOUL TUG WITHIN THE LEASH   879 16
  FOR WATCHING I AM FROZEN AS IN ICE   879 18

WATCHING
    OF THE BANK I STAND WATCHING MY OWN WHITE SHADOW QUIVER+   *891 21
    AND WATCHING THE GREAT THING LABOURING THROUGH THE WHOL+   *909 23
    WATCHING US OVERHEAD   *929 9

WATCHIN'
    ME WATCHIN' DOST THINK THERE WAS OWT BETWEEN 'EM   *910 23

WATER
    WHITE ON THE WATER WIMPLES MY SHADOW STRAINS LIKE A DOG+   33 25
    AND THE WATER RUNS AND RUNS FASTER RUNS FASTER   34 4
    OH BUT THE WATER LOVES ME AND FOLDS ME   34 19
    IN THE WATER MUCH CLEARER AND BRIGHTER   48 28
    WHILE I WASH YOU WITH WEEPING WATER   55 3
    OVER WATER WHERE THE WEEDS ARE THINNED   64 32
    SOFTLY-IMPULSIVE ADVANCING AS WATER TOWARDS A WEIR FROM+   66 19
    LIQUID AS LIME-TREE BLOSSOM SOFT AS BRILLIANT WATER OR+   67 20
    ONCE I HAD A LOVER BRIGHT LIKE RUNNING WATER   119 23
    OF HER SPIRIT WAVERED LIKE WATER THRILLED WITH LIGHT   125 32
    IN THE LUSTROUS GLEAM OF THE WATER THERE   126 17
    OF THEIR PALE-GREEN GLACIER WATER FILLED THE EVENING   216 25
    SHE DRIPS HERSELF WITH WATER AND HER SHOULDERS   217 19
    LIKE A MAN IN A BOAT ON VERY CLEAR DEEP WATER SPACE FRI+   222 24
    SKIES TREES FLOWERS BIRDS WATER   256 25
    AS YOU SEE A TINY CELLULOID BALL TOSSING ON A SQUIRT OF+   272 16
    FIRE AND WATER THEY CONTAIN THE PROPORTION OF MALE AND+   295 7
    ARE EXCRETIONS OF THE WATER AND FIRE IN PLANTS   295 10
    WHAT IS THE HORIZONTAL ROLLING OF WATER   302 4
    BUT FISHES ARE VERY FIERY AND TAKE TO THE WATER TO COOL   331 1
    AND WATER WETLY ON FIRE IN THE GRATES OF YOUR GILLS   335 11
    BUT OH FISH THAT ROCK IN WATER   335 14
    A MAGNETISM IN THE WATER BETWEEN THEM ONLY   337 13
    THIS GREY MONOTONOUS SOUL IN THE WATER   338 11
    A DIP TO THE WATER   341 5
    AND WHERE THE WATER HAD DRIPPED FROM THE TAP IN A SMALL   349 13
    SHUDDERING STORM WIND OR A WATER RUSHING THROUGH   370 25
    WATER   385 4
    BOW DEEP FOR IT'S GOOD AS A DRAUGHT OF COOL WATER TO BOW   391 30
    OR SLIP LIKE WATER SLIPPERY TOWARDS ITS ENDS   392 20
    DARK GROW THE SPRUCE-TREES BLUE IS THE BALSAM WATER   401 2
    VOICES GURGLING LIKE WATER   425 12
    AND A HIDDEN VOICE LIKE WATER CLUCKING   427 3
    WHITE AND SLIPPERY AS ON THE BLACK WATER IN A PORT   453 14
    I WISH THEY'D BE TRUE TO THEIR OWN VARIATION AS WATER IS   505 20
    WATER IS H2O HYDROGEN TWO PARTS OXYGEN ONE   515 11
    BUT THERE IS ALSO A THIRD THING THAT MAKES IT WATER   515 12
    THE SANITY OF WATER   515 19
    GIVE ME A SPONGE AND SOME CLEAR CLEAN WATER   580 15
    SONS OF EARTH SONS OF FIRE SONS OF AIR AND WATER   635 3
    WHEN AT A CERTAIN POINT A DROP OF WATER BEGAN TO DRIP D+   682 13
    THROUGHOUT THE AEONS AS THE LIZARD SWIRLS HIS TAIL FINE+   683 7
    POURING SEA WATER OVER HERSELF   693 6
    SALT IS SCORCHED WATER THAT THE SUN HAS SCORCHED   705 19
    THOUGH SOME APPLES TASTE PREPONDERANTLY OF WATER WET AN+   708 2
    THE WATER WE CAN AT THE GATES FOR THE HORSES HE GALLOPS   732 3
    ARE DUCKING THEIR HEADS IN THE WATER TUBS AT THE GATE   732 19
    HE PULLS UP FOR OUR WATER WOULD HE DRIVE   733 13
    WITH STIFFNESS COMES FOR THE WATER THAT I   733 17
    HE SPLASHES WATER FROM THE PAIL UPON THEM   734 1
    AND BLOODY WATER FALLS UPON THE ROAD   734 8
    NOW I TAKE THE BIG STONE JUG OF WATER   734 24
    HIS EYES MEET MINE AS HE TAKES THE JUG OF WATER   734 27
    SO THAT STRENGTH WELLS UP IN ME LIKE WATER IN HOT SPRIN+   799 21
    BLUE IS THE DEEP SKY AND THE DEEP WATER   808 24
    WHEN THE WATER OF MALINTZI FALLS   811 22
    TO THE WATER AND IS GONE   825 12
    THEY MOW AND THEY PLASH IN THE WATER   827 6
    CRAWL OUT OF THE WATER AND LIE ON THE BEACH   827 17
    A LIGHT LIKE MELLOW MOONLIGHT GLEAMED ON THIS WATER   864 29
    PLAYING WITH THE SOFT-SLIPPING WATER   867 19
    HIS BLUE SHIRT GLIMMERING ON THE WATER AMONG THE SHADOW+   867 29
    AND WHAT WAS THE SOUND OF THE BIRDS AND THE WATER BUT S+   870 26
    ME AS A DARK BLUE WATER BETWEEN THE HILLS   874 28
    LIKE WATER SUCKED FROM DEEP DOWN UNDERGROUND   878 33
    IT LAY ON ME AS ON WATER   881 33
    OH BUT THE WATER LOVES ME AND FOLDS ME   *892 7
    AND RIPPLES POISE AND RUN LAPPING ACROSS THE WATER   *912 27
    LIKE A WIND-SHADOW WANDERING OVER THE WATER   *913 7
    THEY POISE AND RUN LIKE RIPPLES LAPPING ACROSS THE WATER *914 1
    LIKE A WIND-SHADOW WANDERING OVER THE WATER   *914 7
    ONCE I HAD A LOVER BRIGHT LIKE RUNNING WATER   *933 13
    OF HER SPIRIT WAVERED LIKE WATER THREADED WITH LIGHT   *936 31
    SHE DRIPS HERSELF WITH WATER   *943 1
    DRINKING THE CONFIDENT WATER FROM THE LITTLE JUG   *959 13

WATER-ALIVE
    WATER-ALIVE   340 9

WATER-BLOBS
    SUN BUT IN SUBSTANCE YELLOW WATER-BLOBS   34 25

WATER-BUFFALOES
    AND THE MONOLITHIC WATER-BUFFALOES LIKE OLD MUDDY STONES   386 29

WATER-EAGER
    WATER-EAGER EYES   336 8

WATER-EYES
    FIXED WATER-EYES   335 12
    WATER-EYES CRANING   336 14

WATER-FLOWER
    AND I TOOK HER EAR LIKE THE LEAF OF A WATER-FLOWER BETW+   882 27

WATER-HEN
    OH WATER-HEN BESIDE THE RUSHES   43 1

WATER-HONEY
    UNHOOKED HIS GORPING WATER-HONEY MOUTH   339 6

WATERING-CAN
    AS FULL OF WET AS A WATERING-CAN   434 15

WATER-IN-THE-BRAIN
    WAS A GREAT BIG HYDROCEPHALOUS WATER-IN-THE-BRAIN INFANT 670 22

WATER-JAR
    OH THE MOIST FULL WATER-JAR   759 5

WATER-JET
    TO TOSS THE GLOBE OF EARTH LIKE A BALL ON A WATER-JET   272 14

WATERLESS
    AND I WANT TO SMITE IN ANGER THE BARREN ROCK OF EACH WA+   57 30

WATER-LILIES
    AND LIKE WATER-LILIES   651 6

WATER-LORDS
    THE DEAD OF THE WATER-LORDS ROCK AND GLIMMER IN THE SEAS 796 8

WATERLY
    AND WATERLY   161 16

WATER-PRECIOUS
    HIS RED-GOLD WATER-PRECIOUS MIRROR-FLAT BRIGHT EYE   339 8

WATER-RIGHTS
    TO MAKE THIS BIT OF LAND AND WATER-RIGHTS   779 18

WATERS
    WHAT IF THE WATERS CEASED WHERE WERE THE MARIGOLDS THEN+   33 22
    THE POOR WATERS SPILL   49 9
    THE STARS WATERS TROUBLED FORSAKEN   49 10
    TO FORGETFULNESS SOFT-SAILING WATERS WHERE FEARS   53 11
    UPON THE SURFACE OF THE WATERS THERE   113 2
    OF THE WATERS WITHIN HIM ONLY THE WORLD'S OLD WISDOM   130 15
    UNDINE TOWARDS THE WATERS MOVING BACK   161 25
    WHAT BREAD AFLOAT ON THE WATERS   171 21
    ROCKS SEEM AND EARTH AND AIR UNEASY AND WATERS STILL   249 15
    DO YOU TELEPHONE THE ROAR OF THE WATERS OVER THE EARTH   301 10
    VALLEYS OF THE WATERS UNDER THE SEA   321 36
    WHETHER THE WATERS RISE AND COVER THE EARTH   334 22
    OR WHETHER THE WATERS WILT IN THE HOLLOW PLACES   334 23
    AS THE WATERS ROLL   335 1
    THE WATERS WASH   335 3
    YOU LIE ONLY WITH THE WATERS   335 15
    WHO LIES WITH THE WATERS OF HIS SILENT PASSION WOMB-ELE+ 335 28
    FISH IN THE WATERS UNDER THE EARTH   335 29
    WHAT PRICE HIS BREAD UPON THE WATERS   335 30
    SLOWLY TO GAPE THROUGH THE WATERS   336 26
    TO SINK AND RISE AND GO TO SLEEP WITH THE WATERS   336 28
    IN THE WATERS   337 9
    EACH ONE ALONE WITH THE WATERS UPON ONE WAVE WITH THE   337 21
    AND WATCHING THE FISHES IN THE BREATHING WATERS   337 29
    CRY LOUDLY BEYOND THE LAKE OF WATERS   365 35
    THE GREAT SWAN UPON THE WATERS OF ALL ENDINGS   435 27
    WHERE THE WATERS END IN MARSHES   437 22
    MADE TO SMITE THE WATERS BEHIND IT   438 30
    KNOWS THAT THE WATERS HAVE RISEN   462 4
    TILL THE SECRET WATERS OVERFLOW   462 10
    AH THE CLEAN WATERS OF THE SKY AH CAN YOU WASH   581 6
    THAT CASTS ITS SPERM UPON THE WATERS AND KNOWS NO INTER+ 616 25
    THE SWAN WILL BEAT THE WATERS IN RAGE WHITE RAGE OF AN+   624 15
    GREAT HEAVEN OF WHALES IN THE WATERS OLD HIERARCHIES   694 28
    AND DREAMING WITH STRANGE WHALE EYES WIDE OPEN IN THE W+ 694 31
    UPON THE WATERS OF THE END   719 7
    IT MEANS PASSING THROUGH THE WATERS OF OBLIVION   727 33
    HE WATERS THE HORSES DOES HE WASH HIS HEEL   733 33
    IN THE STILLNESS WHERE WATERS ARE BORN   786 3
    IS THE PLACE THERE THE WATERS RISE   786 7
    ON THE WATERS OF THE AFTER-LIFE   786 9
    SLEEPS IN THE HEALING WATERS   787 9
    HOW GAVE THESE PALEFACES YELLOWFACES CROSSED THE WATERS+ 794 30
    DRAGONS OF SALTY WATERS DRAGONS OF THUNDER   796 19
    I AM ABOUT TO TELL THE DRAGON OF THE WATERS TO TURN ROU+ 797 5
    THE COCK ROSE AND CREW OVER THE WATERS   802 11
    FAR OFF UPON THE MISTY WATERS OF THE DEPTHS OF SPACE   841 3
    UPON THESE AWFUL WATERS OF LIFE AND DEATH   875 27
    WITHOUT THE PULSING WATERS WHERE WERE THE MARIGOLDS AND+ *891 24
    MYSELF AND GATHER THE WATERS BENEATH ME AND LOSE   *894 22
    INTO FORGETFULNESS SOFT SAILING WATERS WHERE FEARS   *906 3
    HE WATERS OUR FACE WITH TEARS OUR YOUNG FRUITS FILLS WI+ *926 20
    UPON THE WATERS THAT ENDED IN MARSHES   *947 1

WATER-SERPENT
    I SAW A WATER-SERPENT SWIM ACROSS THE ANAPO   337 24

WATERSPOUT
    A WATERSPOUT   207 29

WATER-SUAVE
    AND THE WATER-SUAVE CONTOUR DIMS   339 18

WATER'S
    THE WATER'S EDGE   391 10

WATERS'
    THE WATERS' RESTLESS STROKE   *916 23

WATER-TROUGH
    A SNAKE CAME TO MY WATER-TROUGH   349   1
    SOMEONE WAS BEFORE ME AT MY WATER-TROUGH   349 19
    AT MY WATER-TROUGH   350 10
    AND THREW IT AT THE WATER-TROUGH WITH A CLATTER   351 11

WATER-WASHED
    AND SUNBURNT AND WATER-WASHED FULL-FED AND SLEEK   827 11

WATER-WAYFARERS
    WATER-WAYFARERS   340   2

WATERY
    AND EVEN IN THE WATERY SHELLS THAT LIE   89 18
    WHERE THE WOOD FUMES UP AND THE FLICKERING WATERY   116   4
    AT THE LITTLE FISH THREAD-THREADING THE WATERY NOOK   161 11
    YOUR HUMAN SELF IMMORTAL TAKE THE WATERY TRACK   161 28
    HARDLY A GREENISH LILY WATERY FAINT   286   4
    SLOW WATERY ROTTING BACK TO LEVEL MUCK   318   2
    PISCES OH FISH JESUS OF THE WATERY WAY   616 19
    AND TO SERVE THAT WHICH IS FLAMEY OR PURE AND WATERY OR   637 10

WATERY-HEARTED
    WATERY-HEARTED WITH WISHY-WASHY KNEES   795   6

WATTLED
    WHY DO YOU HAVE WATTLES AND A NAKED WATTLED HEAD   369 15
    BURNING PALE POSITIVE POLE OF YOUR WATTLED HEAD   370 19
    AND DO YOU AWAIT US WATTLED FATHER WESTWARD   371 24

WATTLES
    YOUR WATTLES ARE THE COLOUR OF STEEL-SLAG WHICH HAS BEE+   369 12
    WHY DO YOU HAVE WATTLES AND A NAKED WATTLED HEAD   369 15
    YOUR WATTLES DRIP DOWN LIKE A SHAWL TO YOUR BREAST   369 19
    OF PERHAPS THERE IS SOMETHING IN YOUR WATTLES OF A BULL+   370   4

WAVE
    WAVE FRIGHTENED WHO COMES A LABOURER ALAS   41   4
    YOUR STAR BE TOSSED OVER A WAVE   49 18
    THE WAVE OF SOLDIERS THE COMING WAVE THE THROBBING RED +   66 23
    SOUNDS WAVE THEIR LITTLE WINGS   109 14
    WHILE DAYS RUSH WAVE AFTER WAVE   159   5
    CONFESSION OF DELIGHT UPON THE WAVE   193   5
    WHAT EFFECT I CAN HAVE MY HANDS WAVE UNDER   223   2
    TO SPEAK ENDLESS INAUDIBLE WAVELETS INTO THE WAVE   336 29
    EACH ONE ALONE WITH THE WATERS UPON ONE WAVE WITH THE   337 21
    THE WAVE OF AGONY BURSTS IN THE STONE THAT HE WAS   379 20
    FROM WOUNDS BELOW THE DEEP BLACK WAVE   428 13
    UNDER THE COLD BLACK WAVE   428 15
    A WAVE BURSTS IN ANGER ON A ROCK BROKEN UP   467 12
    LET EVERYTHING GO AS THE WAVE SMASHES US   514   2
    THE TINY GRAIN OF SOMETHING THAT NO WAVE CAN WASH AWAY   514   4
    NOT EVEN THE MOST MASSIVE WAVE OF DESTINY   514   5
    OR FOR A GREAT WAVE OF DEATH   522 28
    ROCKED ON THE WAVE AND SUNG LUSTILY   575   8
    SEE THEM WAVE SEE THEM WAVE PLUMES   587 21
    TO THE DISTANCE THE WAVE THAT TARRIES   747   5
    TO SHARE THE RHYTHM OF THE DEATHLESS WAVE   772 19
    WAVE THEM   783 25

WAVE-LENGTH
    IN A BACKWARD RIPPLE THE WAVE-LENGTH REVEAL   68 26

WAVELETS
    TO SPEAK ENDLESS INAUDIBLE WAVELETS INTO THE WAVE   336 29
    WENT UP IN WAVELETS TO HIM FROM THE BREASTS AND EYES   389 29
    AS NOW WHEN THE TINY WAVELETS OF THE SEA   709   5
    AND PLAYS WITH THE WAVELETS LIKE A PANTHER PLAYING WITH+   709 10

WAVE-MOTHER
    IN THE WAVE-MOTHER   335 26

WAVER
    WAVER PERPENDICULAR   302   3
    OF LIVING AND WAVER IN SWEET EXTINGUISHMENT   879 31

WAVERED
    OF HER SPIRIT WAVERED LIKE WATER THRILLED WITH LIGHT   125 32
    OF HER SPIRIT WAVERED LIKE WATER THREADED WITH LIGHT   *936 31

WAVERING
    FACE FREED OF THE WAVERING BLAZE   59   8
    BUT I AM ALONE AND WAVERING HOME   106 15
    AND I SHALL BE WAVERING UNCERTAIN   246 28
    ETRUSCAN-DUSKY WAVERING MEN OF OLD ETRURIA   296 19
    AT A WAVERING INSTANT THE SWALLOWS GIVE WAY TO BATS   341 18
    AND HARDLY DISTURBING WAVERING SHIMMER   860   4
    A MOMENT LIKE A WAVERING SPARK   *912 19

WAVES
    AND VERY SWEET IT IS WHILE THE SUNLIGHT WAVES   51 21
    KNOWS BUT THE RETREAT OF THE BURNING SHOULDERS THE RED-+   67   4
    WAVES LIKE A GHOST ALONG   108 24
    AND FALLING WAVES IN HIS ARMS AND THE LOST SOUL'S KISS   130 20
    WAVES CRASH LIKE THUNDER THROUGH   159 16
    LITTERING THE WAVES WITH HER OWN SUPERSCRIPTION   193   6
    ROCK WAVES OF DARK HEAT   302   1
    WAVES OF DARK HEAT ROCK SWAY UPWARDS   302   2
    NOW THAT THE WAVES OF OUR UNDOING HAVE BEGUN TO STRIKE   513 22
    LOST BETWEEN GREAT WAVES OF ULTIMATE IDEAS   542 30
    WHAT ARE THE WILD WAVES SAYING   628   1
    WHAT ARE THE WILD WAVES SAYING   628   9
    AND LET THE WAVES GO OVER THEM   658   7
    THAT WAIT ON WHALES IN MID-OCEAN SUSPENDED IN THE WAVES+   694 26
    ABROAD IN MY HANDS LIKE WAVES AMONG THE ROCKS OF SUBSTA+   705   6
    TO THE WHITE-TREADING WAVES OF TWO SALT FEET   705 17
    AND THE LONG WAVES RUSH AND PLY   746 23
    OH TO SEE THE LONG WAVES RUSH   747   1

WAVES
    OF THE WAVES THAT WASH   747   4
    TO HEAR THE LONG WAVES STRIKE THE COAST   747 11
    THERE ARE DEAD THAT SLEEP IN THE WAVES OF THE MORNING S+   795 18
    WAVES SOFTLY   811 21
    INTO URGENT PASSIONATE WAVES   *893 19
    AND VERY SWEET WHILE THE SUNLIGHT WAVES   *899   4
    AND VERY SWEET WHILE THE SUNLIGHT WAVES   *902 16
    THE WAVES RAN LAUGHING UP THE SHORE AT THE SWELL   *917   4
    WITH WINCING UNWILLING WAVES   *958 29

WAVES'
    OF MY MOCKERY MOCKS AT HIM OVER THE WAVES' BRIGHT   130   7

WAVE-THRILLED
    AND WAVE-THRILLED   334 27

WAVE-WORKING
    AND TREADING OF WET WEBBED WAVE-WORKING FEET   436 25

WAVING
    AND WAVING FLAGS AND THE RAGGED FIRES   49 26
    MOURNFULLY TO AND FRO TO AND FRO THE TREES ARE WAVING   136 22
    WAVING SLOWLY BEFORE ME PUSHED INTO THE DARK   147   1
    AND POKING HIS HEAD OUT AND WAVING HIMSELF   432 15
    THEY SEE ONLY THE WAVING OF WINGS   788   2
    PLAYING WITH THE SHADOW COLOURS AND THE WAVING REFLECTE+   867 20
    DARK WAVING OF THEIR ARMS AGAINST THE BLAND   *895   3

WAX
    SETTLE UPON US MAGNETIC SO WE WAX AND BLOOM   *938 18

WAXES
    AS A BEE WAXES OVER A WOUND   824 28
    THE HOT SUN WAXES AND HEALS   824 29
    WAXES THEM OVER TILL ALL IS FORGOTTEN   825   1

WAY-OFF
    OUT OF THE SOUL'S MIDDLE TO THE MIDDLE-MOST SUN WAY-OFF   480 26

WAYS
    OUR WAYS ARE DIFFERENT NOW   102   8
    THEY WILL CONSIDER HOW YOU WENT YOUR WAYS   176 23
    WAYS OF MEN   199   4
    WE HAVE COME OUR WAYS AND MET AT LAST   209 13
    ALL THINGS ON THE MOVE GOING THEIR OWN LITTLE WAYS AND +   249 17
    AND STRANGE WAYS WHERE I FALL INTO OBLIVION OF UTTERMOST   261   6
    STARING TWO WAYS AT ONCE TO RIGHT AND LEFT   373 13
    IN MANY WAYS VERY FINELY BRED   400 15
    FOOL IN SPITE OF YOUR PRETTY WAYS AND QUAINT KNOW-ALL   400 27
    THERE ARE OTHER WAYS OF SUMMONS CRYING LISTEN LISTEN CO+   623 23
    THEY WANDER THEIR STRANGE AND DIFFERENT WAYS IN HEAVEN   713 22
    THEY WENT THEIR WAYS AS CREATURES DO   761   2
    OPPOSITE WAYS ROUND THE CIRCLE   764 13
    AND THE SERPENTS WANDER THEIR OWN WAYS RECONCILED   771   8
    CERTAIN WAYS PERFORM CERTAIN SACRIFICES   775 30
    STARING TWO WAYS AT ONCE TO RIGHT AND LEFT   781 19
    WAYS OF ST PETERSBURG I HAVE DWELLED IN THE CORE   866 28
    WHILE SHE WAS HERE AND WALKING IN OUR WAYS   *941 10

WAYS'LL
    STIRRED BY AN IMPETUOUS WIND SOME WAYS'LL   40 28

WA'
    MAUN THA CLING TO THE WA' AS THA STAN'S   139 21

W C
    IN THE W C WRIT LARGE   492 18
    AND REPEATS HIMSELF LIKE THE FLUSHING OF A W C   522   8
    AND REPEAT THEMSELVES LIKE THE FLUSHING OF A W C   837 22

WEAK
    SWING TO MY WALKING MOVEMENT WEAK   73 26
    IN HER VOICE AND A WEAK TEAR FALLS   106   2
    AND THE TCHEKOV LOT I'M TOO WEAK AND LOVABLE TO LIVE   534   1

WEAKEN
    AND LOVE WOULD ONLY WEAKEN THEIR UNDER-EARTH GRIP MAKE +   92 27

WEAKER
    NOT TO WANT TO BULLY THOSE WEAKER THAN OURSELVES   833   5

WEAKNESS
    WEAKNESS   525 19

WEALD
    THE TRAIN IN RUNNING ACROSS THE WEALD HAS FALLEN INTO A+   88   1
    THE WEALD THE ENORMOUS BED   886 26

WEALS
    LIKE BEES ABOVE THEM AND FEELS FOR THEIR WEALS   824 26

WEALTH
    BE WEALTH OF LIFE TO ME   59 24
    THREADS AND THRILLS LIKE ORE THAT IS WEALTH TO THE EYE   146 31
    THE SKY WITH A WEALTH OF EASE AND ASSURANCE   772   5
    TO HAVE HEALTH WEALTH HEALTH WEALTH HEALTH   826 24

WEALTHY
    THE CLOUDS GO DOWN THE SKY WITH A WEALTHY EASE   133 16
    THE WEALTHY ARE INSANE   516 14
    THE WEALTHY ARE AFRAID   516 19
    THIS FOREIGN WOMAN OF THE WEALTHY NORTH   618 24
    ALL OF THEM HEALTHY MORE OR LESS WEALTHY   826 27
    THEY ARE SO HEALTHY SUFFICIENTLY WEALTHY   827 10
    SUFFICIENTLY WEALTHY   827 31
    MORE OR LESS WEALTHY   828   3

WEAN
    YI THA MUST HA' BIN 'ARD TER WEAN   79 24
    THA MUST 'A' BEEN HARD TO WEAN   *921 20

WEAPON
    POISED AT HER LIKE A WEAPON MY HAND WAS WHITE AND KEEN   125 15
    NOW THAT IT IS A WEAPON OF HEAVEN   325   2
    THE WEAPON OF YOUR FACE   781 33
    POISED AT HER LIKE A WEAPON MY HAND WAS WHITE AND KEEN   *936 14

WEAPON-HARD
    AND DARK CLEAVES DOWN AND WEAPON-HARD DOWNWARD   373 28
    THE DARK CLEAVES DOWN AND WEAPON-HARD DOWNWARDS CURVING 782   4

WEAPONS
    WE LET THE WEAPONS SLIP FROM OUT OUR HANDS   736 22

WEAR
    WEAR   154   3
    USED TO WEAR HER LIGHTS SPLENDIDLY   170 18
    I KNOW RIGHT WELL THE MARRIAGE RING YOU WEAR   234   3
    THE PRIESTS TO WEAR ROSE-COLOUR OR MAGENTA IN THE STREE+ 609 17
    THIS PLACE TODAY THESE SOLDIERS WEAR THE SAME   732 11
    YOU WEAR ON YOUR FINGER SO GLADLY FOR GOD   752 18
    I WEAR FRAILITY AS A CROWN   772   8
    HE'S GOING TO WEAR THE SKY-BLUE CLOAK   797 15

WEARIEDLY
    UPON THE WOODSTACKS WORKING WEARIEDLY   *895 25
    UPON THE WOODSTACKS WORKING WEARIEDLY   *904 14

WEARIES
    DAY WEARIES ME WITH ITS OSTENTATION AND FAWNINGS   193 19

WEARILY
    WEARILY CATCHING   146   8
    HE WEARILY LOOKS THE OTHER WAY   357   5
    AND SHE EVEN MORE WEARILY LOOKS ANOTHER WAY STILL   357   6
    THE FRIZZLING FALLING FIRE THAT CANNOT GO OUT DROPPING + 701 27
    WEARILY   733   9
    WEARILY THROUGH THE OAKS THE NIGHT WIND BLOWS   857 22

WEARINESS
    ARE A HEAVINESS AND A WEARINESS   74   6
    WHEN WILL THE BELL RING AND END THIS WEARINESS   74   7
    A MOMENT THEN IN WEARINESS SETTLE   109 15
    IMPURE EVEN IN WEARINESS   346 22
    HAVE AEONS OF WEARINESS ROUND THEIR EYES   425 20
    WITH WEARINESS FAINT AS FLUFF   757 17
    WHEN WILL THE BELL RING AND END THIS WEARINESS   *895 15
    FOR MYSELF A HEAP OF ASHES OF WEARINESS TILL SLEEP   *896   1
    WHEN WILL THE BELL RING AND END THIS WEARINESS   *904   4
    FOR MYSELF A HEAP OF ASHES OF WEARINESS TILL SLEEP   *904 22
    ARE A HEAVINESS AND A WEARINESS   *913 27
    AND OUT OF THE CHAMBERED WEARINESS WANDERS A PERFUME AB+ *916 14
    NARCOTIC OF WEARINESS   *917 12

WEARING
    IT FEELS AS IF HIS HANDGRASP WEARING YOU   254 28
    AND WEARING OUR SEATS OUT SITTING ON MONEY   485 26
    AND LOOK AT THE SODOMITICAL AND LESBIAN STUFF WEARING   532   6
    WEARING NO BOOT MY CHILDREN   757 11

WEARISOME
    AND WEARISOME   731 18

WEARS
    BUT ON AND ON ON AND ON TILL THE FRICTION WEARS THEM OUT 676   1
    WHERE THE MEADOW-LARK WEARS HIS COLLAR OF SUBMISSION   768 21

WEARY
    BENT IF WE DID BUT KNOW IT ON A WEARY AND BITTER GRIMACE 54 23
    BUT WHEN I MEET THE WEARY EYES   72   1
    SCHOOL NOW IS THE ROCK IN THIS WEARY LAND THE WINTER BU+ 75 18
    BIRD WHO WAS WEARY TO HAVE FURLED   124   8
    AS WE WERE WEARY TO RECEIVE HER   124 10
    NAY TAKE THIS WEARY BOOK OF HOURS AWAY   135 20
    WEARY AN' SICK O' THE LIKES O' SHE   139 33
    BUT MUD HAS FLOODED THE HOMES OF THESE WEARY LANDS   167 11
    I AM WEARY OF MYSELF   194 17
    DISSATISFIED AND WEARY   200   5
    MY FLESH IS WEARY WITH BOUNCE ON THEM AND   249 21
    MY EARS ARE WEARY WITH WORDS THAT BOUNCE ON THEM AND   249 22
    TO BURY ITS WEARY SPARK   253 32
    I WAS SO WEARY OF THE WORLD   256 22
    I AM SO WEARY OF PALE-FACE IMPORTANCE   288 18
    WHICH I BEING A LITTLE WEARY OF ROMAN VIRTUE   297 32
    THAT THE OLD BIRD IS WEARY AND ALMOST WILLING   329 27
    AND ALL THERE WAS TO BOW TO A WEARY DIFFIDENT BOY WHOSE 391 32
    I SERVE I SERVE IN ALL THE WEARY IRONY OF HIS MIEN 'TIS+ 391 34
    HAS WORN US WEARY OF RENUNCIATION AND LOVE AND EVEN PAIN 439 24
    NOT A WEARY INSISTENT   561 30
    HEAVILY STEPPING WEARY ON OUR HEARTS   704 10
    SHUT-UP COFFIN OF A THING WITH A SOLDIER WEARY   733   6
    OH OUT-LANDER WEARY SOUL   757   2
    FOR SUN AND STARS AND EARTH AND THE VERY RAINS ARE WEARY 792 20
    OUT OF EDEN WEARY WITH THE WISTFULNESS OF HER SILENT TO+ 864 24
    WILL YOU LOOSE THE HEAVY WEARY BUD   *931 26
    BIRD WHO WAS WEARY TO HAVE FURLED   *935   8
    HER WINGS AS WE WERE WEARY TO RECEIVE HER   *935   9

WEASEL
    YOU WOULD THINK TWICE BEFORE YOU TOUCHED A WEASEL ON A 255 22

WEATHER
    YOU'RE AS MIXED AS THE WEATHER   564   9
    THERE IS EVEN NO MORE ANY WEATHER   703 17
    THE WEATHER IN TOWN IS ALWAYS BENZINE OR ELSE PETROL   703 18

WEATHERS
    MY FATHER HAS FACED ALL WEATHERS BUT IT'S BEEN A LIFE 503 30

WEAVE
    WHEN THE HINDUS WEAVE THIN WOOL INTO LONG LONG LENGTHS 451   1
    THE TISSUE THEY WEAVE   451   7
    SHE HAS SHOWN ME THE STRANDS THAT WEAVE   *893   4
    ON THE AIR FOR OUR NOURISHMENT WHO FROM THESE WEAVE FAI+ *938 24

WEAVES
    WHICH WEAVES ITS WAY THROUGH THE EVENING WIND   42   3
    THE CLASS OVER THEM ALL THE DARK NET OF MY DISCIPLINE W+ 97   6
    LIKE A FLY THAT WEAVES THROUGH THE SHADOWS   867 11
    THE CLASS OVER THEM ALL THE DARK NET OF MY DISCIPLINE W+ *926   6

WEAVING
    OF THE MOURNFUL CONSTANT HEART THAT WHILE SHE'S WEAVING 65 25
    AND A NAVAJO WOMAN WEAVING HER RUG IN THE PATTERN OF   448 22

WEB
    AND DAMP OLD WEB OF MISERY'S HEIRLOOM   141 11
    A GLINTING WEB QUICK HID IN THE GLOOM OF THE BROOK   161   7
    THEIR WEB WHO SHADOW THE SUN'S GREAT GESTURES AND   197 28
    NEAR THE CEILING AS IF IN A WEB   345   2
    PLUNGING FALLING OUT OF THE WEB   345   4
    WEB OF LIVING LEAF   451   6
    DOWN WHERE THE LIVE WEB HUMS   *893 10

WEBBED
    AND CREATURES WEBBED AND MARSHY   285 23
    AND TREADING OF WET WEBBED WAVE-WORKING FEET   436 25
    AND THE DRIP OF HIS COLD WEBBED FEET MUD-BLACK   438 11
    TO THE PROUD FATHER AND SHOWS ITS LITTLE WEBBED GREENISH 438 28
    WITH WEBBED FECUNDITY PLUNGING THE SEED OF LIFE IN THE + 841   5
    AND IN THE DARK I FEEL HIS COLD WEBBED FEET MUD BLACK *947 19

WEBBING
    WEBBING OF STEEL ON YOUR FEET SO YOU SHALL FEEL   154 22

WEB-FOOT
    IN A GREEN MUDDY WEB-FOOT UNUTTERLY SONGLESS WORLD   286   1

WED
    AND WED ME TO EASE MY YEARNINGS   44   5
    HE WED HE'D HA'E SUMMAT GOOD   77 28
    HE WED HE'D HA'E SUMMAT GOOD   *919 16

WEDDED
    FOR THE REST WHEN THOU ART WEDDED   44   6

WEDDING
    ARE GATHERING TO A WEDDING IN THE WINTER DARK   *955 21
    FOR I WILL GO TO THE WEDDING AND BE WEDDING-GUEST   *956 22

WEDDING-GUEST
    FOR I WILL GO TO THE WEDDING AND BE WEDDING-GUEST   *956 22

WEDDIN'-DRESS
    I'M TAKIN' 'OME A WEDDIN'-DRESS   79 15
    IT'S WIDDER NAYLOR'S WEDDIN'-DRESS   79 19
    'ER DOESNA WANT NO WEDDIN'-DRESS   79 21
    AS 'ER'LL BE WANTIN' MY WEDDIN'-DRESS   79 27
    IT'S WIDOW NAYLOR'S WEDDIN'-DRESS   *921 15
    'ER DOESNA WANT NO WEDDIN'-DRESS   *921 17

WEDDIN'
    WHY IS THERE A WEDDIN' AT UNDERWOOD   79 17
    I'M TAKIN' 'OME A WEDDIN' DRESS   *921 11
    WHY IS THERE A WEDDIN' AT UNDERWOOD   *921 13
    AS 'ER'LL BE WANTIN' MY WEDDIN' DRESS   *921 23

WEDGE
    IF ONLY I AM KEEN AND HARD LIKE THE SHEER TIP OF A WEDGE 250 21
    THEN CLOSE THE WEDGE OF YOUR LITTLE MOUNTAIN FRONT   353   8
    OPENING HER RATHER PRETTY WEDGE OF AN IRON PRISTINE FACE 359   2
    A WEDGE   781 32

WEDGE-BALANCING
    FOUR ROWING LIMBS AND ONE WEDGE-BALANCING HEAD   356   7

WEDGE-BLADE
    LIKE A FINE AN EXQUISITE CHISEL A WEDGE-BLADE INSERTED 250 20

WE'D
    WE'D BETTER GET OUT AN' MAKE WAY FOR   553 31
    WE THOUGHT WE'D ELECT YOU TO KEEP YOU ALL BUSY   574   4
    YOU SHOULD 'A SEEN HER SLIVE UP WHEN WE'D GO   *910   9
    THA SHOULD HA' SEED HER SLIVE UP WHEN WE'D GONE   *911 21

WEE
    STEPPING WEE MITE IN HIS LOOSE TROUSERS   355 21
    MY WEE MOUSE   863   2
    MY WEE SQUIRREL   863 10

WEED
    OF WEED THAT BLACKENED THE SHORE SO THAT I RECOILED   98 17
    IS IT TRUE THAT THE LITTLE WEED   172 15
    WREATHE STRONG WEED ROUND THE KNEES AS THE DARKNESS   425 13
    AND GONE LIKE WEED LIKE WEED LIKE EGGS OF FISHES   428 27
    THROUGH THE DEAD WEED OF A LIFE-TIME'S FALSITY   *959   8

WEEDED
    LIKE A WEEDED CITY IN SHADOW UNDER THE SEA   72 17

WEEDS
    OVER WATER WHERE THE WEEDS ARE THINNED   64 32
    ON YOUR GRAVE IN ENGLAND THE WEEDS GROW   233 10
    LIKE A FIELD OF FILTHY WEEDS   315 29
    LET ME FIGHT THE WICKED OBSTREPEROUS WEEDS MYSELF AND P+   316 11
    AND FERTILISE THE WEEDS ON EVERY MEAD   634 5

WEEK
    AT TWO POUNDS A WEEK   643 25
    COME IN A WEEK   702 1
    YES YES IN THE SEVEN-DAY WEEK   702 2
    OF THE SEA-BLOWN WEEK OF NINE   702 4
    IN A WEEK   702 19
    BUT SLEEPS THE LONG WEEK OUT EMBOSOMED IN MURMURING LIM+   858 23
    IN A WEEK OR TWO   *921 24

WEEKLY
    WEEKLY OR TWICE-WEEKLY WHISTLE ROUND YOUR BOTTLES   543 9
    IN THE WEEKLY PRESS THEIR SELF-SATISFIED SWIPE   680 23

WEEKS
    AND IF AS WEEKS GO ROUND IN THE DARK OF THE MOON   727 1

WEEK'S
    WILL GIVE THEE WHAT I HAVE THIS LAST WEEK'S   44 2

WEEP
    FOR THE MAN TO HEED LEST THE GIRL SHALL WEEP   41 11
    I SHALL WEEP OH I SHALL WEEP I KNOW   60 9
    AND I DO WEEP FOR VERY PAIN OF YOU   129 21
    PHANTOM TO PHANTOM LEANING STRANGE WOMEN WEEP   140 15
    DOWN IN THE FLOOD OF REMEMBRANCE I WEEP LIKE A CHILD FOR   148 18
    WEEP   210 26
    WEEP THEN YEA   232 7
    WEEP THEN WEEP   232 12
    YOU WOULD WEEP TO BE LAPSING ON SUCH HARMONY   251 28
    NOTHING TO KNOW OR TO WEEP   254 2
    THERE ARE DEAD THAT WEEP IN BITTER RAINS   795 20
    OR SORROW TO WEEP   856 25

WEEPING
    WHILE I WASH YOU WITH WEEPING WATER   55 3
    FROM A ROOF INERT WITH DEATH WEEPING NOT THIS NOT   62 11
    SO LIKE TO WOMEN TALL STRANGE WOMEN WEEPING   140 19
    LET US MAKE FOR THE WEEPING WILLOW   237 15
    THEY WILL NEVER UNDERSTAND MY WEEPING FOR JOY TO BE   256 16
    THE WEEPING MOTHER OF GOD INCONSOLABLE OVER HER SON   439 29
    YOU WHO CAME BEFORE ROCK WAS SMITTEN INTO WEEPING   783 10

WEEPS
    BETRAYS ME BACK TILL THE HEART OF ME WEEPS TO BELONG   148 11
    NO MOTHER WEEPS FOR ME   751 21
    THE WOMAN WEEPS HER CHANGE OF LIFE   766 7
    SHE WEEPS AND CANNOT BE COMFORTED   767 8

WEFT
    LIKE A SHUTTLE THAT CARRIES THE WEFT   746 24

WEHMUT IST DIR WEH
    IS IT WEHMUT IST DIR WEH   232 6

WEIGH
    AND WEIGH NO MORE THAN AIR AS YOU ALIGHT UPON ME   332 7
    THEN WEIGH AND OUT TO THE INFINITIES   542 14

WEIGHED
    A SLEEP THAT IS WRITHING STUPOR WEIGHED DOWN SO WE CAN+   175 14
    AND I ALMOST CEASE TO EXIST WEIGHED DOWN TO EXTINCTION   629 20

WEIGHING
    AND KNOW THE DEAD CHRIST WEIGHING ON MY BONE   226 12

WEIGHS
    AND MOVE ON FEET BUT MOIST EARTH WEIGHS HIM DOWN THOUGH+   348 11

WEIGHT
    KIND ON THE WEIGHT OF SUFFERING SMILES AGAIN   113 16
    HIS BODY DOWN IN WEIGHT TO REST IN YOU   158 11
    LIE ON ME WITH A HOT PLUMB LIVE WEIGHT   240 28
    WHAT IS THE HOT PLUMB WEIGHT OF YOUR DESIRE ON ME   241 3
    WHY HANGING WITH SUCH INORDINATE WEIGHT   279 15
    WITH THE WEIGHT OF THEIR RESPONSIBILITY   288 2
    DON'T HANG MUCH WEIGHT ON   297 33
    THE GREAT ROARING WEIGHT ABOVE   326 18
    NAY ONCE IT WAS ALSO A FORTRESS WALL AND THE WEIGHT OF +   326 25
    AND THEN HER GREAT WEIGHT BELOW THE WAIST HER VAST PALE   393 15
    AND ALL HER WEIGHT ALL HER BLOOD DRIPPING SACK-WISE DOWN   394 21
    WEIGHT OF LIMBS   446 9
    THE EARTH LEANS ITS WEIGHT ON THE SUN AND THE SUN ON THE   480 19
    BENEATH THE WEIGHT OF MUCK   491 24
    WITH FIERY WEIGHT AND WILD LIFE AND COMING OUT   530 3
    A WEIGHT COMES OVER ME HEAVIER THAN LEADEN LININGS OF   629 18
    WEIGHT UPON LOWER-CLASS ROBOT WEIGHT   642 13
    BUT IN THE WEIGHT OF THEIR STUPEFACTION NONE OF THEM KN+   790 25
    ITS COOL WEIGHT LAY FULL ON HER BOSOM NOW IT ROLLS TO R+   864 15
    AND BROKEN BY MY WEIGHT AND THE PURPLE STEAM   881 8
    SO PONDEROUSLY CENTRAL YET LEANING ITS WEIGHT TOWARDS   *952 2

WEIGHTLESS
    STAND UPON ME WEIGHTLESS YOU PHANTOM   332 8

WEIGHTLESSNESS
    YOUR OWN IMPONDERABLE WEIGHTLESSNESS   334 7

WEIGHTS
    WEIGHTS   529 24

WEIR
    SOFTLY-IMPULSIVE ADVANCING AS WATER TOWARDS A WEIR FROM+   66 19

WEIRD
    A MONOTONOUS WEIRD OF DEPARTURE AWAY FROM ME   47 13
    AM LIT BENEATH MY HEART WITH A HALF-MOON WEIRD AND BLUE   115 4
    YOUR WEIRD BRIGHT MOTOR-PRODUCTIVE MECHANISM   292 8
    FIG-TREES WEIRD FIG-TREES   298 19
    OH WEIRD DEMOS WHERE EVERY TWIG IS THE ARCH TWIG   300 7
    I REMEMBER MY FIRST TERROR HEARING THE HOWL OF WEIRD   366 8
    TOM-TOMS WEIRD MUSIC OF THE DEVIL VOICES OF MEN FROM   388 35
    TO SEEK THE WOMEN IN THE DARK OUR WOMEN OUR WEIRD   438 13
    FULL INSIDE OF WEIRD BROWN SLUSHY CRAB-MEAT   830 20
    BRUSH OVER MY FACE AS HE GOES TO TREAD OUR WEIRD WOMEN   *947 20

WELCOME
    TO MY ARMS WITH HER WELCOME LOAD   106 18
    I HAVE COME I FEEL THEM WHIMPER IN WELCOME AND MOURN   172 25
    HOW WELCOME DEATH WOULD BE   628 10
    AND IN THE SILENCE REVERENTLY WELCOME THEM   740 14
    AND SAY BE WELCOME DEAREST FRIEND   754 25
    LIFT YOUR HAND SAY FAREWELL SAY WELCOME   803 14
    LIFT YOUR HAND SAY FAREWELL SAY WELCOME   803 19

WELDED
    YOU HAVE WELDED YOUR THIN STEMS FINER   300 28

WELFARE
    HAVE THE WELFARE OF THE BRITISH PUBLIC AT HEART   582 20

WELKIN
    AWAITING THE SENTENCE OUT FROM THE WELKIN BROUGHT   142 16

WELL-BELOVED
    JOIN ME TO MY WELL-BELOVED FRIEND   754 22

WELL-CHORDS
    THOU WELL OF KILOSSA THY WELL-CHORDS ARE OF SILVER   759 12

WELL-CORKED
    OH SAFER THAN ANYTHING ELSE IN A WELL-CORKED GLASSY EGO   543 2

WELLED
    RIPENESS WELLED THROUGH ME AT HIS KISS   *933 26

WELL-EDUCATED
    AS HUNDRED-PER-CENT AMERICANS WELL-EDUCATED   780 18

WELL-GROOMED
    FRESH CLEAN WELL-GROOMED ENGLISHMAN   830 9
    HE HAS FRESH CLEAN WELL-GROOMED EMOTIONS   830 11
    WELL-GROOMED   830 17

WELL-GROWN
    WELL-GROWN LIKE POTATOES ON A LIFTED ROOT   827 27

WELL-HEADS
    OUT OF THE WELL-HEADS OF THE NEW WORLD   260 31

WELL-HEAD
    I WOULD BE A GOOD FOUNTAIN A GOOD WELL-HEAD   250 26

WELLING
    THE SOFT WELLING OF BLOOD INVINCIBLE EVEN BEYOND BONE OR   383 4
    THE WELLING OF PEACE WHEN IT RISES AND FLOWS   462 6
    THOUGHT IS THE WELLING UP OF UNKNOWN LIFE INTO CONSCIOU+   673 10

WELLING-UP
    ITS SOFTLY-STIRRING CRIMSON WELLING-UP   153 27

WELL-OFF
    THE SUN COMES IN THEIR LAIR THEY ARE WELL-OFF   325 17

WELL-REMEMBERED
    FROM HER FLUTTERED FAREWELLS AT THE APPROACH OF MY WELL+   865 14

WELLS
    I HAVE FETCHED THE TEARS UP OUT OF THE LITTLE WELLS   94 10
    SO THAT STRENGTH WELLS UP IN ME LIKE WATER IN HOT SPRIN+   799 21
    I HAVE FETCHED THE TEARS UP OUT OF THE LITTLE WELLS   *896 26

WELL-SHOT
    THE ROCKS WHERE RAVENS FLYING TO WINDWARD MELT AS A WEL+   57 15

WELL-TO-DO
    A WELL-TO-DO FAMILY   325 18
    IF I WERE WELL-TO-DO   *940 25

WELL-WASHED
    LIKE A WELL-WASHED VEGETABLE   828 5

WE'LL
    BUT WE'LL GO UNBEKNOWN TER TH' REGISTRAR   82 13
    THINE SHALL GO TER PAY THE WOMAN AN' WI' MY BIT WE'LL B+   83 2
    AN' WE'LL BE MARRIED AT TH' REGISTRAR NOW LIFT THY FACE   83 4
    BUT WE'LL STILL BE TOGETHER THIS ROAD AND I   163 15
    HOW HAPPY WE'LL BE SEE HIM   244 13
    HE'S GOT IN HIS NEST WE'LL BE HAPPY   244 31
    HO DO YOU THINK WE'LL GET ON   404 18
    WE'LL TRY TO ACT UP SUBLIME   573 4
    WE VOTED 'EM IN AND WE'LL VOTE 'EM OUT   573 21
    WE'LL SHOW 'EM A THING OR TWO NEVER YOU DOUBT   573 22

WE'LL
WE'LL SHOW THESE OLD UNCLES WHO'S GOING TO BE BOSSY   573 24
WE'LL BACK YOU UP UNCLE WE'RE YOUNG AND WE'RE   574   9
WE'LL SEE THE JOKE AND HOW FUNNY IS SORROW   815   5
BUT WE'LL GO UNBEKNOWN TO THE REGISTRAR   *924 17
THINE SHALL GO TO PAY THE WOMAN AN' WI' MY BIT WE'LL BUY *925   6
AN' WE'LL BE MARRIED AT TH' REGISTRAR NOW LIFT THY FACE *925   8

WELTER
DAY OF THE MENTAL WELTER AND BLETHER   471 17
THE SUMMER AND THE SNOWS THE WILD WELTER OF EARTH   707 29

WELTERING
TO HELP HIM LIFT THE WELTERING DARKNESS TURN   872   3

WENCH
WENCH WUNNA HE   76 26
AX 'IM THY-SEN WENCH A WIDDER'S LODGER   77 11
THA THOUGHT THA WANTED A LITTLE WENCH   138 27
THA THOUGHT THA WANTED A LITTLE WENCH   138 29
NOW GO AN' MARRY THAT WENCH AN' SEE   139 31
POOR LASS POOR BIT OF A WENCH   540   8
COME AN' BE STILL WI' ME MY OWN BIT OF A WENCH   540 10
WENCH WUNNA HE   *918 18
AX HIM THY-SEN WENCH A WIDDER'S LODGER   *918 29

WENCH'S
FROM THAT BIT OF A WENCH'S BOSOM 'E'D BE GLAD OF IT   61 19

WENDING
THE HAWK HIS WINDSWEPT WAY IS WENDING   150 10
BUT THE MOON IS WENDING HER WAY ATTENDING   456   3

WENDS
SEED AFTER DAY-SEED WENDS   253 19

WENT
LAST NIGHT WHEN I WENT WITH THE LANTERN THE SOW WAS GRA+ 38   8
THE ANGEL OF CHILDHOOD KISSED ME AND WENT I EXPECTED   48   5
WENT THROUGH ME AS THE LIGHT WENT OUT   80 15
THE SEA AND THE SKY WENT GREY AS IF THERE HAD SUNK   98 12
SO I WENT AND WASHED MY DEADENED FLESH IN THE SEA   99 12
THE WORLD WENT ROUND   120 17
THE TIRED LIGHTS DOWN THE STREET WENT OUT   121 23
SHE WATCHED SHE WENT OF A SUDDEN INTENSELY STILL   125 11
WHEN YOU WENT HOW WAS IT YOU CARRIED WITH YOU   135   1
SO I DID NOT FIGHT YOU WENT YOUR WAY INSTEAD   156 15
MY LOVE TILL YOU WENT SOUTH   156 24
A PULSE THAT STILL WENT FLEETING   165 15
THEY WILL CONSIDER HOW YOU WENT YOUR WAYS   176 23
SHE SAYS I WENT TO CYTHERA   201   7
WENT ROLLING IN THE DUSK TOWARDS THE RIVER   205 26
WE WENT IN SILENCE AND YOU STARING TO ENGLAND   206   7
AND THE LITTLE ELECTRIC FLASHES WENT WITH US IN THE GRA+ 206 15
AS I WENT THROUGH THE MARSHES   222   1
WHEN I WENT IN A TRAIN I KNEW IT WAS MYSELF TRAVELLING + 257   3
MAHOMET NEVER WENT TO ANY MOUNTAIN   290   2
WHEN I WENT INTO MY ROOM AT MID-MORNING   342 12
WHEN I WENT INTO MY ROOM AT MID-MORNING   342 12
AND AWAY HE WENT   347 10
I REMEMBER THE SCREAM OF A RABBIT AS I WENT THROUGH A   366   4
AND WENT WHIZZING THROUGH THE SLOW VAST SUCCULENT   372 12
WENT UP IN WAVELETS TO HIM FROM THE BREASTS AND EYES   389 29
LIGHT WENT OVER THE HILL-BROW SWIFTLY WITH THEIR TAILS   391   2
AS THE ROCKETS WENT UP AND THE GLARE PASSED OVER COUNTL+ 391 12
TROTTING EAST AND EAST AND EAST TILL THE SUN HIMSELF WE+ 404 15
CREATURE WENT EAST   405 27
THEY CAMPED AND WENT TO SLEEP   407   7
WHEN I WENT TO THE FILM AND SAW ALL THE BLACK-AND-WHITE 443 22
WHEN I WENT TO THE CIRCUS THAT HAD PITCHED ON THE WASTE 444   9
AND ROUND THE RING THEY WENT TO THE SOUND OF THE WHIP   444 20
AS TIME WENT ON   479 23
WHERE I WENT TO SCHOOL AND COLLEGE   488   8
SO THEY WENT   534   2
AND HAD A BRAVE DESTINY EVEN WHEN SHE WENT WRONG   535 16
SOME SMALL VOICE WENT AHEM   554 20
AHEM THEY WENT THIS FELLOW   554 21
OR HALO OR PRESTIGE WENT   556   6
I SADLY WENT MY WAY   569 19
MY PICTURES AND ON THE PROCEEDINGS WENT   579 22
WHEN I WENT TO THE SCIENTIFIC DOCTOR   620   5
WHEN YOU WENT FORTH SO VIGOROUSLY IN SEARCH   661   5
BUT OFF SHE WENT BEING REALLY RATTLED   669   4
MEN SLIMLY WENT LIKE FISHES AND DIDN'T CARE   688 22
THEY ARE DANCING THEY RETURN AS THEY WENT DANCING   689   9
THE MAN OF TYRE WENT DOWN TO THE SEA   692 22
OH LOVELY LOVELY WITH THE DARK HAIR PILED UP AS SHE WEN+ 693   8
AND THE MOON THAT WENT   702 25
TILL THE WHISTLE WENT THEN SWIFTLY HE   735 12
AND AWAY WENT THE LAST OF THE WAGONS   735 16
AS I WENT DOWN THE STREET IN MY NOSE-RED PELERINE   750 17
DIMENSION THE CUCKOO WENT CUCKOO-WARDS THE COW WENT COW+ 760 26
THEY WENT THEIR WAYS AS CREATURES DO   761   2
I WENT THE OPPOSITE WAY ROUND THE CIRCLE   764 23
IN HIS HAND IT LAY AND WENT DARK   791   6
AS I WENT DOWN THE ROAD OF SLEEP   808   3
THE ONE THAT WENT TO VINGONE   846   7
AND I WENT BACK WITH MY MOUTH TO HER MOUTH   882 10
WENT THROUGH ME JUST AS THE LIGHT WENT OUT   *922 15
SHE WATCHED SHE WENT OF A SUDDEN INTENSELY STILL   *935 27
IN NOTTINGHAM WHERE I WENT TO SCHOOL AND COLLEGE   *950 12

WEPT
MAKES US PREFER TO BE WOMANLESS RATHER THAN BE WEPT OVER 439 30
SHE WEPT BITTERLY HIDING HER FACE IN HER KERCHIEF I SAI+ 749 16
YOU WEPT AND THE BED TREMBLED UNDER ME   886 14

WEREN'T
HE MIGHT POSSIBLY LIKE MEN IF HE WEREN'T TOO FRIGHTENED 447 13
WERE HAPPY WEREN'T WE   557 29

WE'RE
THAT HERE WE'RE SAFE FROM EVEN THE ERMINE MOTH'S   113 23
TREAD OVER THE EDGE OF THE PIT AND WE'RE GONE   164 11
IF WE'RE GOING TO SLEEP THE SLEEP WITH THOSE   164 14
YET WE'RE AWAKE   229   8
AND WE'RE GOING TO BE SUMMER-HAPPY   244 19
DON'T YOU THINK REALLY THEY KNOW WE'RE THEIR   435 16
FOR WE'RE ALL SELF-CONSCIOUSLY AWARE OF OURSELVES   496 19
FOR WE'RE SURE TO BRING IN A LOT OF LIES   506   4
WE THINK WE'RE SUCH CLEVER LITTLE JOHNNIES   543 19
OH I'M SURE YOU'LL UNDERSTAND WE'RE MAKING A CENSUS OF + 546   7
PROVES IT QUITE THANK YOU SO MUCH WE'RE GETTING ON SIMP+ 546 20
WE'RE NOT FIT FOR THE EARTH WE LIVE ON   553 29
WE'RE NOT FIT FOR THE AIR WE BREATHE   553 30
WE'RE GETTING TO BE BIG LADS NOW AN' SOON   573 19
WE'LL BACK YOU UP UNCLE WE'RE YOUNG AND WE'RE   574   9
WE'RE ALL IN IT ALL MY FAMILY   668 20
SO LONG AS WE'RE HERE IN LIFE OUR SISTER WE COME   753 17
FLOWERS NOW AS WE'RE CROSSING THE DREARY STAGES   814   6
TO LAUGH WHEN WE'RE FEELING MELANCHOLY   814 23
PAST AND WE'RE BRUSHING   862 27
THAT HERE WE'RE SAFE FROM EVEN THE ERMINE MOTH'S   *929 12

WERT
HOW WERT THOU SO STRANGE-SHAPEN WHAT WARM FINGER   69 13
THA WERT FRIT O' SUMMAT   138   9
AND SO THOU WERT GOD-SHAPEN HIS FINGER   *915 25

WESH
I WISH I COULD WESH 'ER OFF'N THEE   82 25
I WISH THA COULD WESH 'ER OFF'N THEE   *925   1

WEST
AND SWALLOWS DIP INTO THE PALLOR OF THE WEST   41 21
AH ONLY THE LEAVES BUT IN THE WEST   42   5
THE ROSES WITH THE WEST WIND RAPPING   149 29
THE WINDOW-SASH AS THE WEST WIND BLOWS   150 19
THROUGH THE LOW WEST WINDOW A COLD LIGHT FLOWS   163 10
AND PILED THEM UP IN A DULL GREY HEAP IN THE WEST   167   2
AND PILED THEM UP IN A DULL GREY HEAP IN THE WEST   167 12
EBBING WEST   249 16
SOON IN THE PUSSYFOOT WEST   280 12
WHEN THE SUN FROM THE WEST BEYOND PISA BEYOND THE   340 18
A GREEN LIGHT ENTERS AGAINST STREAM FLUSH FROM THE WEST 340 25
OVER THE HEART OF THE WEST THE TAOS DESERT   403   1
COME AWAY FROM THE PLACE OF GRAVES COME WEST   411   2
NOW COME WEST COME HOME   412   9
COME WEST TO ME   412 27
OF EVERY LAND OR EAST OR WEST   575 13
OF EVERY TONGUE OR EAST OR WEST   575 15
OH A MAN MAY TRAVEL BOTH EAST AND WEST   575 22
THERE IS A BAND OF DULL GOLD IN THE WEST AND SAY WHAT Y+ 656   1
TOWARDS THE SILENT DOORS OF THE WEST   769 31
THE DOORS OF THE WEST   770 10
FROM THE EAST TO THE WEST IN THE UPPER VALLEY   770 25
THE MEN COME IN BY THE FURNACE-GATE OF THE WEST   771 10
IN THE PLACE OF THE WEST   786   1
WHAT HAVE WE LOST IN THE WEST   816 12
WE WHO HAVE GONE WEST   816 13
INTO THE WEST   855 26
FROM THE LOW WEST WINDOWS THE COLD LIGHT FLOWS   857 10
THE CRIMSON SHEAF OF THE WEST THE DEEP FETCHED SIGH   885   6
THERE LIES THE DULL RED HEAP OF THEIR SAND IN THE WEST *896   7
THERE LIES A DULL RED HEAP OF HIS SAND IN THE WEST   *896 17

WESTERN
SOON THE SPACES OF THE WESTERN SKY   163 13
YOUR WESTERN BRUTAL FAERY QUALITY   291 25
AS HE SLOWLY WALKS FROM THE WESTERN DOOR TO THE WORLD   770 14
SOON THE WESTERN WINDOWS OF THE SKY   857 13

WESTWARD
AND DO YOU AWAIT US WATTLED FATHER WESTWARD   371 24

WESTWARDS
WALKING SLOWLY WESTWARDS HOUSELESS   770   4

WET
I'LL WET MY BROW FOR THEE   44   7
WAITIN' TER BE BURIED OUT O' TH' WET   60 14
AH STOPPED BEHIND ON T' PAD I' T' POURIN' WET   61   3
OH BUT THE RAIN CREEPS DOWN TO WET THE GRAIN   63 27
A GANG OF LABOURERS ON THE PILED WET TIMBER   72   4
MY BABY HER BROWN HAIR BRUSHED WITH WET TEARS   73 23
NOW WET WITH TEARS AND PAIN HANGS HEAVILY   74   2
AND THOUGH IT BE LOVE'S WET BLUE EYES THAT CRY   89 32
LIKE FLAGS IN PALE BLOOD NEWLY WET   105   3
LOW FROM THE ROOF AND THE WET DUST FALLING SOFTLY FROM + 112 26
OVER THE WET DARK ROCKS THE HOUSES AND OVER   112 27
O THE WET WALK OF MY BROWN HEN THROUGH THE STACKYARD   119   9
A WET BIRD WALKS ON THE LAWN CALL TO THE BOY TO COME   137   7
NO LOOK AT THE WET STARLING   137 17
IN THE BLACK WET NIGHT AS THE FURTIVE RAIN SLINKS DOWN   143   2
WITH WET FLAT LIGHTS WHAT I'VE DONE   143 23
BEND OVER THEM WITH MY SOUL TO CHERISH THE WET   180 10
LIKE WET AND FALLING ROSES AND I LISTEN   217 21
FALL BLACK AND WET   268 15
WET ALMOND-TREES IN THE RAIN   300 18
THE HOT DARK BLOOD OF ITSELF A-LAUGHING WET HALF-DEVILI+ 389 20
AND THEN WATCH HIM GO SOGGY LIKE A WET MERINGUE   431   6
AS FULL OF WET AS A WATERING-CAN   434 15
AND TREADING OF WET WEBBED WAVE-WORKING FEET   436 25
THIS WET WHITE GLEAM   453 19
THE IDIOT WITH HIS CHIN ALL WET   463 16

WET
    AND SLAVERING WET AND SOGGY   492   2
    BEHOLD HE IS BORN WET   682 17
    BETWEEN THE TWO GREAT ONES FIRE AND THE WET   705 22
    OF FIRE AND THE WET EARTH AND THE WIDE AIR OF THE WORLD   705   5
    SO SALT IS THE BOUNDARY MARK BETWEEN FIRE THAT BURNS AN+   706 10
    THE TWO GREAT AND MOVING ONES FIRE AND THE YIELDING WET   706 12
    ARE MARKED OUT WITH THE BOUNDARY OF SALT BETWEEN FIRE A+   706 14
    THOUGH SOME APPLES TASTE PREPONDERANTLY OF WATER WET AN+   708   2
    WAS WET WITH SWEAT AND HIS MOVEMENTS STRONG AND HEAVY   734 22
    THE SEA ALL WET   747   8
    WET AND DRY WET AND DRY   825 14
    NOW WET NOW DRY   825 17
    FROM WET TO DRY   826   3
    WITH WEBBED FECUNDITY PLUNGING THE SEED OF LIFE IN THE +   841   5
    AND MY THROAT IS WET WITH HER TEARS   863   4
    MY PALE WET BUTTERFLY FLUFFY CHICKEN   863   6
    BY NATURE THAN BY BOOTS AND WET FEET OFTEN CARRY MERRY +   866 15
    I FORGET THE TOWEL AND MY WET LIMBS   870   5
    TRYIN' TO KEEP OFF 'N HIM A BIT O' TH' WET   *910 29
    AH STOPPED BEHIND ON T' PAD I' TH' DRIPPIN WET   *911 19
    AT TH' SLOPPY WET GRAVE AN' 'ER LITTLE NECK SHONE   *911 23
    MY BABY HER BROWN HAIR BRUSHED WITH WET TEARS   *913 15
    OH THE WET WALK OF MY BROWN HEN THROUGH THE STACKYARD   *932 18
    IS IT ONLY THAT THE GREAT WET HAYSTACKS MARS   *933 22
    ALL THE FRUITS ARE SULKING IN THE WET   *933 30
    AH AND MY HAIR IS HANGING WET AND BITTER ON MY FACE   *933 31
    LIKE WET AND SHAKEN ROSES AND I LISTEN   *943   4

WET-LEGS
    AND THE TCHEKOV WIMBLY-WAMBLY WET-LEGS ALL WIPED OUT   533 17

WETLY
    WETLY BOBBING AND DRIFTING AWAY ON OUR SIGHT   146 22
    AND WATER WETLY ON FIRE IN THE GRATES OF YOUR GILLS   335 11

WETNESS
    WITH SUN AND WITH WETNESS   826 14

WETTED
    TAUT AS A WETTED WARP   746 22

WETTING
    WETTING AFTER EVERYONE THAT PASSES   493 28
    AND TERRIBLY STRANGE ARE HIS TEARS THAT ARE WETTING MY +   871 27

WE'VE
    TRUE WE'VE GOT ALL THESE THINGS   452   9
    LET'S BE HONEST AT LAST ABOUT SEX OR SHOW AT LEAST THAT+   464 12
    TO-DAY WE'VE GOT NO SEX   472   9
    WE'VE MADE A GREAT MESS OF LOVE   472 14
    AND WE'VE MADE A GREAT MESS OF LOVE MIND-PERVERTED WILL+   473   6
    FROM THE ONE WE'VE GOT NOW   487 20
    WE'VE RISEN IN THE WORLD ALL THREE   490 22
    DO IT BECAUSE WE'VE GOT TOO MUCH EQUALITY   517 10
    AND WE FEEL WE'VE GOT TO KEEP IT UP KEEP ON COMBATING   519 13
    AND THAT'S WHAT WE'VE DONE TODAY   543 18
    OH WE'VE GOT TO TRUST   561   1
    SO WE'VE GOT A LOT OF NURSES OF NURSES OF NURSES   570 18
    WE'VE GOT A CHANGE OF GOVERNMENT   571 15
    THAT WE'VE NEVER SEEN COMING STAMPING AND SWEARING   572 13
    WE'VE GOT THE INQUISITION BACK   634   7
    THAT WE'VE HAD ENOUGH THE BRAIN IS STRETCHED TILL IT PA+   756   5
    ONE THING IS CERTAIN WE'VE GOT TO TAKE HANDS OFF LOVE   834   7

WHALE
    HEAVY AND SWAYING LIKE A WHALE RECOVERING   428 12
    LIKE A WHALE RECOVERING ITS VELOCITY AND STRENGTH   428 14
    I DON'T CARE MYSELF A WHALE   557   8
    AND OUT OF THE INWARD ROARING OF THE INNER RED OCEAN OF+   694 16
    AND DREAMING WITH STRANGE WHALE EYES WIDE OPEN IN THE W+   694 31

WHALE-CALVES
    AND BULL-WHALES GATHER THEIR WOMEN AND WHALE-CALVES IN +   695   1

WHALES
    LIKE SPERM OF WHALES LIKE GERMS OF THE GREAT DEAD PAST   428 28
    IN THE BOUNCING OF THESE SMALL AND HAPPY WHALES   693 30
    ALL THE WHALES IN THE WIDER DEEPS HOT ARE THEY AS THEY +   694   3
    THE RIGHT WHALES THE SPERM-WHALES THE HAMMER-HEADS THE +   694   5
    WONDER OF WHALES   694 22
    THAT WAIT ON WHALES IN MID-OCEAN SUSPENDED IN THE WAVES+   694 26
    GREAT HEAVEN OF WHALES IN THE WATERS OLD HIERARCHIES   694 28
    AND ENORMOUS WHALES LIE DREAMING SUCKLING THEIR WHALE-T+   694 29
    AND APHRODITE IS THE WIFE OF WHALES   695   7

WHALE'S
    SEE HIS BLACK NOSE SNUBBED BACK PRESSED OVER LIKE A WHA+   380 13
    AND OVER THE BRIDGE OF THE WHALE'S STRONG PHALLUS LINKI+   694 21

WHALE-TENDER
    AND ENORMOUS WHALES LIE DREAMING SUCKLING THEIR WHALE-T+   694 29

WHARF
    THE MEN THAT LOUNGE IN A GROUP ON THE WHARF   228 16

WHATEVER
    ANY COMMUNION WHATEVER BUT THEY BIND THEMSELVES ON TO T+   92 18
    HOW IT STIRS LIKE A SUBTLE STOAT WHATEVER SHE THINKS   128 17
    NEVER HE IS NOT WHATEVER SHALL COME TO PASS   137 16
    I WISH THAT WHATEVER PROPS UP THE WALLS OF LIGHT   205   9
    SHE HAS NO PART IN IT NO PART WHATEVER   267   9
    OF NO ACCOUNT WHATEVER   269 16
    WHATEVER HE MEANT   293 12
    WHATEVER MAN MAKES AND MAKES IT LIVE   448 19
    AND WHATEVER COSTS YOU MONEY MONEY MONEY IS REALLY   517 10
    WHATEVER ELSE THEY SAY OF ME   534   9
    AND WHATEVER NEW COMES ALONG WILL BE SUCCESSFULLY SOLD   763 12

WHATEVER
    IN JAPANESE HENNA OR WHATEVER IT IS CHEAP AT THE PRICE   835   8

WHATIVER
    WHATIVER BRINGS THEE OUT SO FAR   79 13
    WHATIVER BRINGS THEE OUT SO FAR   *921   9

WHATSOEVER
    HAS SUCCESSFULLY KILLED ALL DESIRE IN US WHATSOEVER   439 33
    DEAR LADIES NONE WHATSOEVER   541 14
    AND TO SACRIFICE THAT TO ANYTHING OR ANYBODY WHATSOEVER   680   1
    AND NO TALKING WHATSOEVER   766   4

WHAT'S
    IS THIS WHAT'S BECOME OF YOU   57   9
    WHAT'S THAT AS 'APPEN I'VE 'EERED ON MISSIS   78   7
    LIZZIE WHAT'S DONE IS DONE   79 30
    IF I HAN WHAT'S THAT TER THEE   81 30
    THOUGH I'LL SEE AS 'E PAYS YOU AN' DOES WHAT'S RIGHT   82   7
    LET ME GO WHAT'S GOOD O' TALKIN'   84 25
    WHAT'S BEYOND THEM AND FIGHT WITH ME IN DISCIPLINE'S LI+   93 28
    ARE YOU PLEASED WITH WHAT'S IN STORE   95 15
    AM SORRY FOR WHAT'S IN STORE   219 24
    TO USE THE SPERM OF WHAT'S WORTH WHILE IN US   429 20
    THAT'S WHAT'S SO BORING PEOPLE ARE SO BORING   435 12
    WHY DON'T YOU KNOW WHAT'S WHAT YOUNG PEOPLE SEEMS   464   9
    AND THAT'S WHAT'S HAPPENED TO THE ENGLISH ROSE   534 27
    TELL ME WHAT'S WRONG   551 21
    WHEN SHE KNOWS WHAT'S WHAT   565 24
    ARREST HIM HE'S INDECENT HE'S OBSCENE WHAT'S MORE   574 24
    WHAT'S THE MATTER WITH THEM AREN'T THEY WOMEN AND   578 18
    OR IS SOMETHING MISSING OR WHAT'S WRONG WITH THEM   578 20
    AND WHAT'S MORE THEY'RE VERY NICE ABOUT BEING NICE   660   1
    WHAT'S THE GOOD OF A MAN   671   9
    AND WHAT'S THE GOOD OF A WOMAN   671 11
    NULLUS NOTHINGNESS WHAT'S IN A NAME   824 16
    PERHAPS WHAT'S WRONG IS SIMPLY LACK OF VITALITY   842 28
    OH DEAR WHAT'S HAPPENING   846   2
    OH DEAR WHAT'S HAPPENING TO TUSCANS   846 12
    WHAT'S THAT AS 'APPEN I'VE 'EERED-ON MISSIS   *919 27
    LIZZIE WHAT'S DONE IS DONE   *921 26
    AN' IF I HAN WHAT'S THAT TO THEE   *924   2
    AM SORRY FOR WHAT'S I' STORE   *944   4

WHEAT
    LIKE A LOOSE SHEAF OF WHEAT   198 10
    SWEET AS AN ARMFUL OF WHEAT   198 14
    AND DOWN BELOW IN THE GREEN WHEAT THE LABOURERS   208 26
    STAND LIKE DARK STUMPS STILL IN THE GREEN WHEAT   208 27
    WE LOOK OVER THE GROWING WHEAT WHERE THE JADE-GREEN   209 20
    A THICK MIST-SHEET LIES OVER THE BROKEN WHEAT   212 12
    ALL THE ROCKING WHEAT OF CANADA RIPENING NOW   263   1
    THIS IS THE SAME THAT PICKS UP THE HARVEST OF WHEAT   271 21
    THE PEASANTS ARE BENDING CUTTING THE BEARDED WHEAT   605 22
    LIKE BEARDED WHEAT IN EAR   627   8
    SUDDENLY IT CURVES AS IT YIELDS THE WHITE WHEAT   651 14
    THE WHEAT ON BOTH SIDES OF THE ROAD STANDS GREEN   732   5
    WHEAT FROM THE HIGH LANDS AND MAIZE   793 21

WHEEL
    A SPARK BENEATH THE WHEEL   68 28
    SOMETIMES THE DARKNESS TRAPPED WITHIN A WHEEL   136   8
    AND ROOKS AND THE RISING SMOKE-WAVES SCATTER AND WHEEL   148 22
    SLEEP OF THE WHEEL   149   8
    THE WHEEL ON WHICH OUR SILENCE FIRST IS BROKEN   366 30
    WHILE THE POLE STAR LIES ASIDE LIKE AN OLD AXLE TAKEN F+   616 30
    ARE THEIR HEARTS THE HUB OF THE WHEEL   631 29
    AND THE WHEEL STARTS THE PRINCIPLE OF ALL EVIL   712   7
    THE WHEEL IS THE FIRST PRINCIPLE OF EVIL   712   9
    WHEN THE MIND MAKES A WHEEL WHICH TURNS ON THE HUB OF T+   712 13
    AND THE WHEEL OF THE CONSCIOUS SELF SPINS ON IN ABSOLUT+   712 15
    EVERY WHEEL ON ITS HUB HAS A SOUL EVIL   713   2
    AND THE SYMBOL OF THE ROBOT IS THE WHEEL REVOLVING   713 10
    OH DO NOT TELL ME THE HEAVENS AS WELL ARE A WHEEL   713 11
    ONLY THE WHEEL GOES ROUND BUT IT NEVER WANDERS   713 25
    A BLADE ON THE WHEEL THEN THE SLUMBERING NIGHT   773   4
    AND DARKNESS RUNS THE RACING WHEEL   773   6
    WHERE FLAMES WHEEL IN LIKE BREATH   784 10
    ALL THESE GLITTERING SEA-BIRDS WHEEL AND FRET   860 20
    A SPARK BENEATH HIS WHEEL   *915 12

WHEELED
    IS DEAD TOO A DEAD ORB WHEELED ONCE A MONTH ROUND THE P+   702 27

WHEELING
    WINGS AND FEATHERS ON THE CRYING MYSTERIOUS AGES PEEWIT+   34 26
    WHERE WHEELING AND SCREAMING THE PETULANT PLOVERS   41   3
    WINGS AND MEN WHO SEE HIM WHEELING ARE FILLED WITH THE +   368   5
    WHEELING TO LACERATE AND RIP UP THIS MY BODY   741 13

WHEELS
    TURNING THE BLUE WHEELS OF YOUR OWN HEAVEN   643 21
    IS DEAD WE RUN WHEELS ACROSS HER CORPSE   703   8
    NO WHEELS MIGHT RUN NO INSOLENT CHARIOTS   703 25
    AMONG SPINNING WHEELS IN AN APOTHEOSIS OF WHEELS   711 27
    WHEELS ARE EVIL   716   4

WHEER
    OUT O' MY WAY CHILDT DEAR O' ME WHEER   45 13
    I DUNNO WHEER 'IS EYES WAS A GRET   81 17

WHEER'S
    WHEER'S 'E HURT THIS TIME LAD   45   9

WHELMED
    WHELMED IN PROFUNDITIES OF PROFOUND CONVERSATION   542 29

WHELPED
    WHICH WHELPED AND WAS MARK   323 20

WHELPS
    AHA THE STRIPE-CHEEKED WHELPS WHIPPET-SLIM CROCUSES   309 5
    WHELPS PLAY BETWEEN THE PAWS OF THE LION   325 14

WHENCE
    WHENCE COMETH THIS THAT THOU MUST GUARD FROM THEFT   69 25
    WHENCE COMETH WHITHER GOETH STILL THE SAME   69 26
    THE WORLD WITHIN WORLDS IS A WOMB WHENCE ISSUES ALL   89 33
    TO SHOW THE PLACE WHENCE THE SCREAM WAS HEARD   150 13
    PURE LOOK OF YOUR LAST DEAD FACE WHENCE NOW IS GONE   157 17
    WHENCE HE DREW THE CURIOUS LIQUORS   202 19
    THIS IS THE ANCIENT SOUTHERN EARTH WHENCE THE VASES WERE   305 12
    WHENCE THE RE-START   318 4
    ALAS MY LAND IS ENGLAND AND I KNOW NOT HOW NOR WHENCE   757 3
    MY FATHER IS DEEP WITHIN THE DEEPS WHENCE HE SENT ME FO+   799 16
    INWARDS I CAN SEE WHENCE THE THORNS WERE RENT   856 21
    UPON A ROCK FROM WHENCE AH CHARLATAN   877 6
    WHENCE ISSUE UNBLEMISHED THE ATOMS WHICH SOFT BESTOWED   *938 17
    THAT SHE WAS AS THE WINE-JAR WHENCE WE DREW   *941 11

WHENEVER
    FOR WHENEVER I LOOK THEE I' TH' FACE I S'LL SEE   82 23
    FOR WHENEVER I LOOK THEE I' TH' FACE I S'LL SEE   *924 27

WHEREAS
    FOR THE FLUSH OF THE NIGHT WHEREAS NOW THE GLOOM   141 9
    WHEREAS AT VENICE   278 9
    WHEREAS THE PEACOCK HAS A DIADEM   369 23
    WHEREAS LET ME TELL YOU IF YOU WERE MY EQUAL   547 10
    WHEREAS FACES NOW ARE ONLY HUMAN GRIMACES   656 23
    WHEREAS LETTERS ARE FIXED   661 18
    WHEREAS IF YOU RIDE AWAY AND BECOME DEEPLY CONCERNED IN+   665 12
    WHEREAS TO THE ORDINARY MORAL HUMAN BEING THE WORD   837 3
    WHEREAS PURITANISM IS BENT ON SUPPRESSING THE FACT   *953 4

WHEREFORE
    THERE IS NOW NO WHY THERE IS NOW NO WHEREFORE   824 1
    WITHOUT WHEREFORE OR WHY   825 18

WHEREIN
    WHEREIN WE FAINTED LIKE A SMOKE OR DEW   90 30
    WHEREIN I AM TRUE   102 6
    RESTARTS ITSELF WHEREIN I AM KEPT   151 24
    OUR ATTENTION OUT OF THE VOID WHEREIN WE ARE CRUSHED   165 33
    WHEREIN WE CIRCLE ON OUR FATE   236 19
    WHEREIN WE KNOW OURSELF FOR WHAT WE ARE   621 6
    CRY FOR THEE OUT OF THE NIGHT WHEREIN WE ARE PRONE   753 5
    WHEREIN WE ARE NOW BLIND UGLY BOORS   833 17
    WHEREIN A MAN CAN LIVE HIS LIFE WITHOUT BEING A SLAVE T+   837 25
    FAINT-FASHIONED WONDER WHEREIN LOST WE SPIN   875 4
    WHEREIN THE TIMID WONDERS FLY   *894 9

WHEREON
    THE SOUNDLESS NIGHT WHEREON OUR DAYS ARE SHIPPED   133 4
    OF DARKNESS WHEREON SHE SLEEPS ON HER PERFECT BED   133 25
    OF THIS LAND WHEREON THE WRONG ROAD GOES   164 16

WHERE-OUT
    OH WHERE-OUT NOW HAS WANDERED THE GOLDEN HEN OF SUNSHINE   *933 21

WHERE'S
    WHERE'S YOUR GOD YOU WHITE ONE   404 24
    WHERE'S YOUR WHITE GOD   404 25
    STOP WHERE'S YOUR EDUCATION   669 16

WHEREVER
    TOGETHER WHEREVER THE LONG ROAD GOES   163 16
    ONWARD WHEREVER THE STRANGE ROAD GOES   163 28
    THAT GOES WHEREVER THIS OLD ROAD GOES   164 8
    WHEREVER IS IT PRODUCED   830 26
    TOGETHER WHEREVER THE DUMB ROAD GOES   857 16

WHEREWITHAL
    THE WHEREWITHAL   826 23

WHETHER
    WHETHER THE PEOPLE IN THE STREET   109 17
    OR WHETHER THE THEATRE SIGHS AND SIGHS   109 19
    AS TO WHETHER YOU'VE FOUND A FORTUNE   237 7
    I DON'T CARE WHETHER I AM BEAUTIFUL TO YOU   251 1
    WHETHER THE WATERS RISE AND COVER THE EARTH   334 22
    OR WHETHER THE WATERS WILT IN THE HOLLOW PLACES   334 23
    WHETHER YOU'RE A SUCKING DOVE ROO COO OOO QUARK   414 6
    OR WHETHER IT ACTUALLY IS AN EAGLE YOU ARE   414 13
    THAT EVERY MAN WHETHER HIGH OR LOW   434 19
    IT ALL DEPENDS WHETHER I FOUND THEM WORTH FIGHTING FOR   497 18
    IN THE HEART OF EVERY INTELLIGENT AMERICAN WHETHER   775 8
    DECIDE WHETHER YOU CAN BECAUSE IT IS A TEST   779 27
    FOR WHETHER I SEE YOU SET THE DAFFODILS   875 7
    BUT WHETHER IT CALLED IN MY SOUL   881 24
    OR WHETHER IT RANG IN THE AIR   881 25
    OR WHETHER MY HEART WAS ITS NEST   881 26
    FOR THE FULL MOON SHONE BUT WHETHER   881 32
    OR WHETHER I WAS THE DARKNESS WITH ARCHED WINGS   882 1

WHETTED
    BLUE AT THE CORE AND WHEN IS WHETTED   773 3
    THAT'S BEEN WHETTED AND WHETTED IN BLOOD   782 3

WHIFF
    IF YOU CATCH A WHIFF OF VIOLETS FROM THE DARKNESS OF TH+   274 1

WHILST
    HIS HAPPINESS WHILST HE IN DISPLEASURE RETREATS   47 20
    WHILST BETWEEN THE TWO ALONG THE TENSE ARCH OF YOUR BACK   370 22

WHIM
    AT THE WHIM OF SIX POLICEMEN AND A MAGISTRATE WHOSE STA+   633 5

WHIMPER
    I HAVE COME I FEEL THEM WHIMPER IN WELCOME AND MOURN   172 25

WHIMPERING
    AND RESTLESS WERE THE WHIMPERING RAT-BAIRNIES   *933 4

WHIMSICAL
    FOR EVERYDAY USE GIVE ME SOMEBODY WHIMSICAL WITH NOT   496 3

WHIMSICALLY
    AND BE WHIMSICALLY AT HOME IN OURSELVES   496 21

WHINE
    LORD TAKE HIS LOVE AWAY IT MAKES HIM WHINE   *945 18

WHINEY
    TOMLETS DICKLETS HARRYLETS WHINEY   457 19

WHIP
    AND ROUND THE RING THEY WENT TO THE SOUND OF THE WHIP   444 20

WHIP-LASH
    AND UNDER THE FLICKING OF THE WHITE WHIP-LASH OF THE   453 23

WHIPPET-SLIM
    AHA THE STRIPE-CHEEKED WHELPS WHIPPET-SLIM CROCUSES   309 5

WHIPS
    OUTSIDE THE HOUSE AN ASH-TREE HUNG ITS TERRIBLE WHIPS   36 9
    ABOVE THAT CRASH-GULF OF EXPLODING WHIPS   347 14

WHIRL
    YOU WATCH THE RED SPARKS WHIRL AND FLEE   116 23
    A WHIRL LIKE SNOW FROM THE PLUM-TREES AND THE PEAR   154 30
    ROSE-LEAVES THAT WHIRL IN COLOUR ROUND A CORE   218 15
    WHIRL IN THESE PERILOUS MARCHES   242 26
    THAT WHIRL AND SWEEP LIKE ANXIOUS LEAVES AWAY   744 14

WHIRLED
    EXPLOSIONS HAVE WHIRLED   748 22

WHIRLIGIG
    THE WHIRLIGIG OF DOZENS AND THE PINNACLE OF SEVEN   355 26

WHIRLING
    SINCE LIFE SWEEPS WHIRLING DIM AND VAST   69 1
    WHIRLING A FLAME   94 18
    WHIRLING IN THE DRAUGHT OF LIFE   110 18
    AND THE WORLD ALL WHIRLING   121 1
    THE PILLAR OF SALT THE WHIRLING HORRIBLE COLUMN OF SALT+   207 28
    AND WHIRLING IN BLOSSOM OF FLAME AND BEING UPON ME   218 23
    LIKE A TRUNDLING PROJECTILE SWIFTLY WHIRLING UP   397 22
    WHIRLING A FLAME   *897 6

WHIRLPOOLS
    PAST THE STRANGE WHIRLPOOLS OF REMEMBERED GREED   *959 7

WHIRLS
    OH AND SUDDENLY FROM OUT OF NOWHERE WHIRLS THE PEAR-BLO+   271 25

WHIRLWIND
    RUSHING IN LIKE A LITTLE BLACK WHIRLWIND LEAPING STRAIG+   397 2

WHIRLWINDS
    IN THE WILD DAYS WHEN LIFE WAS SLIDING WHIRLWINDS BLUE-+   529 23

WHIRLY-BURLY
    AND EVEN MORE WHIRLY-BURLY   834 22

WHIRRING
    NOR SOUND ONLY INTERMITTENT MACHINERY WHIRRING   153 8
    THE FROGS HELPED ALSO WHIRRING AWAY   207 14
    FOR AT PRESENT IN THE WHIRRING INSANITY OF THE MENTAL C+   839 5

WHISKERED
    SILVERY-SIDED FISH-FANGED FIERCE-FACED WHISKERED MOTTLED   409 3

WHISKERS
    AND SUNNED HIS WHISKERS   324 6
    PAST THE OTTER'S WHISKERS   409 19

WHISKEY
    DROP OF WHISKEY IN ITS MINKY WELL IT SHALL YET IT SHALL   570 25
    TO HAVE WHISKEY IN ITS MINKY   571 8

WHISPER
    IS HEARD IN THE WINDLESS WHISPER OF LEAVES   68 17
    I'LL WHISPER THE GHOSTLY TRUTH TO YOU   227 27
    WOULD BLUR NO WHISPER SPOIL NO EXPRESSON   250 27
    DO YOU TAKE THE WHISPER OF SULPHUR FROM THE AIR   301 8
    SO NOW I WHISPER COME AWAY   411 1
    AND THEY WHISPER IT OUT AND THEY TITTER IT OUT BREATHING   462 25
    I SHOULD LEAN AND WHISPER IN HIS EAR   752 5
    LEAVES WHISPER AND TITTER   861 1
    THE HUM AND WHISPER OF THE CLASS LIKE A LITTLE WIND   *894 15
    IS HEARD IN THE WINDLESS WHISPER OF LEAVES   *915 1
    ENDLESS WHISPER OF PASSING FEET   *917 6

WHISPERED
  FEAR WAS ABROAD WE WHISPERED NO ONE KNOWS US   217 6

WHISPERING
  WHISPERING RIOT   76 4
  HE SAID DO YOU HEAR THEM WHISPERING   201 27
  OVER THE WHISPERING TOWN   253 6
  WHISPERING WITCHCRAFT   311 25
  NUMEROUS AND WHISPERING THIN GRAINS OF RICE IN A   391 6
  THEY WERE FOILED THE MYRIAD WHISPERING DARK-FACED   391 25
  ORTHODOX MICHAEL AND THAT WHISPERING GABRIEL   614 7
  IN THE WHISPERING WHORLS   747 24
  WHISPERING RIOT   *897 31
  WHISPERING RIOT   *901 8
  HOARSELY WHISPERING US HOW   *917 3

WHISPERS
  THE ISAR WHISPERS AGAIN IN THE VALLEY THE CHILDREN   732 18

WHISTLE
  WILL THERE BE A WHISTLE OF WINGS IN THE AIR AND AN ICY   439 6
  WEEKLY OR TWICE-WEEKLY WHISTLE ROUND YOUR BOTTLES   543 9
  TILL THE WHISTLE WENT THEN SWIFTLY HE   735 12
  THE SPIRITS OF THE COLD DEAD WHISTLE IN THE EARS OF THE+   795 15

WHISTLED
  HE WHISTLED TO IT LOUDLY TWICE TILL IT FELL TO HIS HAND   791 2

WHISTLING
  WHISTLING SHE-DELIRIOUS RAGE AND THE DREADFUL SOUND   36 14
  WHISTLING AND SEETHING AND PULLING THE ANGLER DOWN INTO   586 27

WHITE
  ON THE TURF I STAND WATCHING MY OWN WHITE SHADOW QUIVER+   33 19
  WHITE ON THE WATER WIMPLES MY SHADOW STRAINS LIKE A DOG+   33 25
  HOW IT LOOKS BACK LIKE A WHITE DOG TO ITS MASTER   34 1
  AND THE WHITE DOG DANCES AND QUIVERS I AM HOLDING HIS C+   34 5
  THE SAME VALLEY WITH PURPLE AND WHITE   37 28
  ALL BE SWEET WITH WHITE AND BLUE VIOLET   40 29
  AND THE WHITE DOG SNUFFS THE WARMTH APPEALING   41 10
  WHITE AND GAUNT WITH WISTFUL EYES THAT HOVER   47 11
  LIKE A THIN WHITE BIRD BLOWN OUT OF THE NORTHERN SEAS   47 14
  SURGES THE WHITE OF THE MOON   50 2
  HEAVING AND PILING A ROUND WHITE DOME   50 5
  THE WHITE MOON SHOW LIKE A BREAST REVEALED   55 26
  WHITE BOSOM   56 6
  YOU TELL ME THE LAMBS HAVE COME THEY LIE LIKE DAISIES W+   57 25
  WHITE ONES AND BLUE ONES FROM UNDER THE ORCHARD HEDGE   58 9
  SWEET DARK PURPLE AND WHITE ONES MIXED FOR A PLEDGE   58 10
  ON TH' YALLER CLAY WI' TH' WHITE FLOWERS TOP OF IT   60 13
  THAT WHITE AN' 'ER CRIED THAT MUCH I'D LIKE TO BEGIN   61 8
  AN' WHITE AN' BLUE IN A RAVEL LIKE A CLOUT   61 12
  WHEN WILL THE SCENT OF THE DIM WHITE PHLOX   62 27
  WHEN THE WHITE FEET OF THE BABY BEAT ACROSS THE GRASS   64 29
  THE LITTLE WHITE FEET NOD LIKE WHITE FLOWERS IN A WIND   64 30
  AND THE SIGHT OF THEIR WHITE PLAYING IN THE GRASS   65 1
  WITH TWO LITTLE BARE WHITE FEET UPON MY KNEE   65 7
  WITH WHITE PLUMES BLINKING UNDER THE EVENING GREY SKY   66 14
  EMERGING WHITE AND EXQUISITE AND I IN AMAZE   67 9
  A TINY MOON AS SMALL AND WHITE AS A SINGLE JASMINE FLOW+   67 18
  SHE SHINES THE FIRST WHITE LOVE OF MY YOUTH PASSIONLESS+   67 21
  THEN A GROUP OF TOADSTOOLS WAITING THE MOON'S WHITE TAP+   72 19
  HER SOFT WHITE LEGS HANGING HEAVILY OVER MY ARM   73 25
  THIS NEW RED ROCK IN A WASTE OF WHITE RISES AGAINST THE+   75 13
  YI AN' 'IS FACE GOES WHITE OH YES   79 10
  ON TOWARDS THE PINES AT THE HILL'S WHITE VERGE   85 8
  AH YOU STACK OF WHITE LILIES ALL WHITE AND GOLD   86 9
  WHITE PETALS INCANDESCENT SO THAT YOU   86 13
  ARE NOT A STACK OF WHITE LILIES NOW BUT A WHITE   86 14
  STRAY WHITEBEAM AND HER WHITE FIRE ALL UNLADENS   86 20
  MY STACK OF LILIES ONCE WHITE INCANDESCENT   86 23
  WHITE BODY DRIPS   96 21
  HER WHITE HER LAMP-LIKE SHAPE   103 32
  WHITE LILAC SHOWS DISCOLOURED NIGHT   104 30
  WHITE LITTLE SHEAVES OF NIGHTGOWNED MAIDS   105 22
  HER WHITE MANTILLA ABOUT   105 26
  GRACEFULLY SIGHING THROUGH THE WHITE   105 29
  WHITE STAND NAKED OF GOWN   106 6
  THE SPIDERS WITH WHITE FACES THAT SCUTTLE ON THE FLOOR +   112 28
  COMES ON US LIFT YOUR FINGERS WHITE   117 12
  OF YOUR SOFT WHITE BODY AS LIGHTNING   117 31
  OF MY STEEL LOVELY WHITE FLINT OF DESIRE   118 5
  AND HER SHIFT IS LYING WHITE UPON THE FLOOR   120 2
  I FOLLOWED FOLLOWED THE SWING OF HER WHITE DRESS   123 2
  POISED AT HER LIKE A WEAPON MY HAND WAS WHITE AND KEEN   125 15
  WHITE DUCKS A QUACKING FLOTILLA OF CLOUD   126 13
  SAD AS HE SITS ON THE WHITE SEA-STONE   130 1
  SINCE DEATH HAS DELIVERED US UTTERLY STRIPPED AND WHITE   132 15
  THE WHITE MOON GOING AMONG THEM LIKE A WHITE BIRD   134 16
  HERE LAMPS ARE WHITE LIKE SNOWDROPS IN THE GRASS   136 1
  ON THY FACE AS THA GOT MORE WHITE AN' WAN   138 5
  THE WHITE BARE BONE OF OUR SHAMS   145 7
  STRANGE WHITE SIGNALS SEEM INTENDING   150 12
  INTO THE SHADOW-WHITE CHAMBER SILTS THE WHITE   154 27
  A NURSE IN WHITE AT THE DAWNING FLOWER-FOAMED PANE   155 1
  THE WHITE RUGS ON THE FLOOR NOR THE SILENT BED   155 3
  A TALL WOMAN WITH HER LONG WHITE GOWN AFLOW   155 13
  IN BLONDE AND WHITE ON THE FLOOR NOR EVEN TURNED   156 8
  IN WHITE   164 28
  SHONE WHITE   165 4
  WHITE AND ALIGHT THE NIGHT WAS   165 11
  THE WHOLE WHITE NIGHT   165 22
  WHITE EARTH AND RUINS OURSELVES AND NOTHING BESIDE   166 8
  WITH MULTITUDE OF WHITE ROSES AND SINCE YOU WERE BRAVE   176 12
  IS BLAZONED HERE SO WHITE AND SO BLOODILY RED   176 19
  IN A PURITAN FILLET A CHASTE WHITE SNARE   178 9
  IN WHITE FLESH ROBED TO DRAPE ANOTHER DREAM   195 11
  AS LIGHTNING COMES ALL WHITE AND TREMBLING   195 12

WHITE
  LIKE A SPURT OF WHITE FOAM RENT   200 22
  AND THE WHITE SHINING HOUSES AND THE GAY RED FLOWERS ON   205 2
  WHITE AND HALOED WITH FIRE-MIST DOWN IN THE TANGLED   206 11
  AT LAST AS YOU STOOD YOUR WHITE GOWN FALLING FROM YOUR   207 1
  NOT TEARS BUT WHITE SHARP BRINE   207 19
  I HAVE BEEN THRUST INTO WHITE SHARP CRYSTALS   207 25
  SNOW OF SALT WHITE BURNING EATING SALT   207 31
  BREEZE OF THE MORNING THROUGH A NARROW WHITE BIRCH   209 28
  UNSHEATHED AND NAKED AND NARROW AND WHITE   210 2
  TWO WHITE ONES SHARP VINDICATED   210 16
  GLISTENING WHITE ON THE SHOULDERS   217 13
  CAN SEE THE WHITE   220 24
  GREEN GRASS SHINING AND LITTLE WHITE HOUSES   224 13
  WHITE AND LOOSE AT LAST WITH ALL THE PAIN   225 7
  WHITE PEAKS OF SNOW AT THE FOOT OF THE SUNKEN CHRIST   225 30
  THAT HAS DRAWN THIS TERRIBLE DRAUGHT OF WHITE FIRE   241 29
  MAKES SICKENING THE WHITE   252 22
  AS IT LIFTS ITS STRAIGHT WHITE THROAT   255 24
  WHITE SANDS AND FRUITS UNKNOWN AND PERFUMES THAT NEVER   261 2
  STRANGE SHEER SLOPES AND WHITE LEVELS   261 9
  SNOWDROPS STRAIGHT DEATH-VEINED EXHALATIONS OF WHITE AND   271 6
  AND BETRAYS ITS CANDOUR IN THE ROUND WHITE STRAWBERRY F+   272 28
  WHAT IS THAT REMINDS US OF WHITE GODS   280 18
  PILLARS OF WHITE BRONZE STANDING RIGID LEST THE SKIES F+   287 16
  AND WHITE WORDS WHITE-WASH AMERICAN   292 32
  BITTER-STINGING WHITE WORLD THAT BORE US   302 12
  HEAVEN THE WHITE GOD   307 18
  AT HER WHITE ANKLES   308 19
  SO HE COULD TRACK HER DOWN AGAIN WHITE VICTIM   308 23
  SMALL INTERSPERSED WITH JEWELS OF WHITE GOLD   314 2
  AND WHITE MEAT   339 29
  SO TO DRIVE HIM OUT FLICKING WITH MY WHITE HANDKERCHIEF   343 5
  WAS THE HORROR OF WHITE DAYLIGHT IN THE WINDOW   344 25
  DELICATE FRAIL CRESCENT OF THE GENTLE OUTLINE OF WHITE   371 13
  IN SCORCHED WHITE FEATHERS   373 8
  WHITE MAN YOU ARE SALUTED   387 17
  AND WHITE PEOPLE IN EVENING DRESS BUZZING AND CROWDING   387 23
  IN FRONT OF A TOWERING GRIMACING WHITE IMAGE OF   387 31
  LIFTING HER FACE TO NIBBLE AT A ROUND WHITE PEPPERMINT   393 8
  AND THOSE OVER-PROLIFIC WHITE MICE AND ADOLPH AND REX   395 9
  AND WHITE TEETH SHOWING IN YOUR DRAGON-GRIN AS YOU RACE   397 20
  AND SHOW A TINY BUNCH OF WHITE TEETH IN YOUR UNDERHUNG   398 11
  YET WHAT A GAP IN THE WORLD THE MISSING WHITE FROST-FACE   402 32
  AND THE INDIAN IN A WHITE SHEET   403 9
  LIKE A WHITE CHRISTUS FALLEN TO DUST FROM A CROSS   403 22
  WHERE'S YOUR GOD YOU WHITE ONE   404 24
  WHERE'S YOUR WHITE GOD   404 25
  THEN YOU'RE A LOST WHITE DOG OF A PALE-FACE   404 29
  ROUND A WHITE HEARTH OF DESERT   407 2
  WHITE MEN MAKE GOLD-MINES AND THE MOUNTAINS UNMAKE   407 13
  THE INDIANS THOUGHT THE WHITE MAN WOULD AWAKE THEM   408 8
  AND INSTEAD THE WHITE MEN SCRAMBLE ASLEEP IN THE   408 9
  AS THE VAST WHITE BIRD   436 15
  AND STAMPS HIS BLACK MARSH-FEET ON THEIR WHITE AND   436 18
  THAT PALE ONE FILLED WITH RENUNCIATION AND PAIN AND WHI+   439 22
  HAVE PHOSPHORESCENT TEEMING WHITE WORDS   441 2
  IT WAS LIKE BEING IN HEAVEN WHICH I AM SURE HAS A WHITE   444 3
  ARE CAST IN BLACK AND WHITE AND MOVE   444 6
  THEY ARE LIKE SLENDER TREES PUTTING FORTH LEAVES A LONG+   451 5
  AND THEY CLOTHE THEMSELVES IN WHITE AS A TREE CLOTHES I+   451 8
  WHITE AND SLIPPERY AS ON THE BLACK WATER IN A PORT   453 14
  THIS WET WHITE GLEAM   453 19
  AND UNDER THE FLICKING OF THE WHITE WHIP-LASH OF THE   453 23
  IN WILD WHITE SIBILANT SPRAY   467 13
  FROM ALL THE WHITE SELF-CONSCIOUS LECHERY   469 21
  TOUCH COMES WHEN THE WHITE MIND SLEEPS   470 23
  AND THE WHITE MIND SHINES ON ONE SIDE OF THEE   473 26
  BUT TO MY WHITE MIND   474 12
  AND DAMASKED RED AND WHITE   534 24
  AND THE WHITE SNOW GLISTENED THE WHITE WORLD WAS GAY   550 29
  OF THE FEMALE FORM TECHNICALLY BEAUTIFUL ACTUALLY A WHI+   619 12
  THAT SHE EXUDES LIKE PEARLY WHITE POISON GAS   619 21
  AND MEN OFTEN SUCCUMB LIKE WHITE MICE IN A LABORATORY A+   619 22
  THE UNROLLING OF FERNS WHITE TONGUES OF THE ACANTHUS LA+   623 27
  AND THE WHITE SWAN SWIMS IN THE MARSHES OF HIS LOINS   624 6
  THE SWAN WILL BEAT THE WATERS IN RAGE WHITE RAGE OF AN +   624 15
  EVEN THE SHAKING WHITE POPLAR WILL DAZZLE LIKE SPLINTER+   624 18
  BE ALONE AND SEE THE MOONLIGHT OUTSIDE WHITE AND BUSY   646 10
  WHITE IVORY WHITE AMONG THE RAMBLING GREENS   646 24
  JUGFULL AFTER JUGFULL OF PURE WHITE LIQUID FIRE BRIGHT +   647 9
  A STILL BRIGHTER WHITE SNAKE WRIGGLES AMONG IT SPILLED   647 14
  THE MAN WHO IS MOWING THE TALL WHITE CORN   651 12
  SUDDENLY IT CURVES AS IT YIELDS THE WHITE WHEAT   651 14
  AND A GIRL RAN SWIFTLY LAUGHING BREATHLESS TAKING IN HE+   672 13
  ADVANCING WITH THE SLOW-SWIFTNESS OF A SHIP BACKING HER+   672 21
  THE YOUTH WALKS UP TO THE WHITE HORSE TO PUT ITS HALTER+   683 19
  WHO HAD SPREAD WHITE WASHING ON THE GRAVEL BANKED ABOVE+   693 3
  THERE THEY BLOW THERE THEY BLOW HOT WILD WHITE BREATH O+   694 6
  AND MY LOST WHITE FEARLESS BREAST   696 5
  LIFTING YOUR VEINED WINGS LIFTING THEM BIG WHITE BUTTER+   696 14
  BUT THE WIND BLOWS TO SEA-WARD WHITE BUTTERFLY C+   696 19
  AND IN A STRANGE LEVEL FLUTTERING YOU GO OUT TO SEA-WAR+   696 25
  DOWN FLATTENING INTO POINTS FLATTENED UNDER THE SWEEP O+   697 7
  NO COBRA NOR HYAENA NOR SCORPION NOR HIDEOUS WHITE ANT   701 13
  BY HERMES AND APHRODITE FLASHING WHITE GLITTERING WORDS   702 10
  OPENING TILL THE ROUND WHITE DOORWAY OF DELIGHT   702 15
  IT IS THE WHITE STONE OF LIMITS THE TERM THE LANDMARK B+   706 11
  WITH THE WHITE TRIUMPHANCE OF LIGHTNING AND ELECTRIC DE+   707 19
  THAT ALL THINGS ARE MIXED AND THEREFORE THE PUREST WHIT+   708 15
  AND NONSENSE FOR PURE SNOW IS WHITE TO US   708 19
  WHITE AND WHITE AND ONLY WHITE   708 20
  WITH A LOVELY BLOOM OF WHITENESS UPON WHITE   708 21
  FROM OFF THE SHEER WHITE SNOW OR THE POISED MOON   708 27
  LIKE NOW WHERE THE WHITE SUN KISSES THE SEA   709 9
  AND THE WHITE SHORES OF LIFE   722 15
  HOW BIG AND WHITE THE NIGHT IS   731 1
  WITH THE WHITE OF THE MOON BETWEEN   731 8

WHITE
AND THEIR UNIFORMS ARE THE SAME OF WHITE AND BLUE 732 13
BUT HIS HANDKERCHIEF IS WHITE WITH A BROAD BLUE BORDER 733 28
SOILING THE CLEAN WHITE DUST HE RUBS THE BELLY 734 9
THEY COME BACK OVER THE WHITE SEA IN THE MIST 739 10
A FRAIL WHITE GLEAM OF RESURRECTION 744 12
LIKE A SHED WHITE HUSK ON THE TORRID SKY 747 29
THE THICK RANK STREETS AND A STARK WHITE LIGHT 748 5
FEEDING ON PURE WHITE SUGAR 751 3
SOME SUGAR OF THE SAME WHITE SORT 751 6
LOOK AT THE SHAKING WHITE 755 14
WHERE WHITE MAID ARE THE MEN YOU HAVE LOVED 759 18
BECAUSE FLAT-FOOT IS THE FAVOURITE OF THE WHITE LEGHORN+ 761 17
SHE LAYS AN EGG HE BRISTLES LIKE A DOUBLE WHITE POPPY A+ 761 19
WARM OF ME FADING TO WHITE 766 24
GOD WHAT SHALL I DO IN THE WHITE DAYS 766 25
TEARS NOW FALL ON WHITE SAND 767 4
WHAT DO I CARE THOUGH FROM THE DAY'S WHITE ENVELOPE 772 22
ON GOOD FRIDAY THE BIG WHITE MEN OF THE INDIAN BUREAU 777 24
AND THE BIG WHITE MEN FROM WASHINGTON DROVE OUT TO 777 25
WITH THE WHITE MEN HIS BROTHERS 778 16
FURTHERMORE THE WHITE BIG-MEN SAID TO THE OLD INDIANS 778 17
THE WHITE MEN DROVE AWAY 778 34
IN SCORCHED WHITE FEATHERS 781 14
FLAP WHITE WINGS AND YELLOW PINIONS 783 26
WHITE BREAST-TIPS OF MY MEXICO 787 6
AND HE SAW MEXICO LYING LIKE A DARK WOMAN WITH WHITE BR+ 790 4
A FALLING STAR WAS RUNNING LIKE A WHITE DOG OVER A PLAIN 791 1
THESE WHITE MEN AND RED MEN AND YELLOW MEN AND BROWN MEN 792 29
THAT ARE NEITHER WHITE NOR RED NOR YELLOW NOR BROWN NOR+ 792 31
LO I RELEASE THE DRAGONS THE GREAT WHITE ONE OF THE NOR+ 796 30
WHITE OF THE BONE 804 11
WHITE OF THE BONE 805 19
AND WHITE AS BONE 806 24
THE BONE IS WHITE AND ALIVE 808 27
WHITE HUITZILOPOCHTLI 810 17
BEYOND THE WHITE OF WHITENESS 810 23
FROM THE BLACK OIL AND THE WHITE 811 1
NAKED AND WHITE NOT QUITE NOT QUITE 824 22
IN THE WHITE AIR 827 24
IN THE WHITE MORNING WHERE IS THE ENCHANTED ROOM OF THE+ 856 7
OF MY WILTED WILD ROSES PINK AND IVORY WHITE 856 18
I CAN JUST SEE THE NAPE OF HER WHITE LITTLE NECK 863 5
MY WHITE BIRD 863 14
IN A LITTLE HALF-BUILT STREET WHERE RED AND WHITE VILLAS 864 25
AND THE WHITE NAPE OF HER NECK WAS THE BEAUTY OF THE ST+ 865 9
AS A WHITE ROSE STREWS THE GROUND 868 7
OVER HER STREWN WHITE LAUGHING FORM 868 16
OF MY OLD WHITE METAL OF MEANING YOU FINE 873 4
THOUGH WHITE YOU ARE COOL-DROOPING AND RICH 874 25
AS WILD WHITE FOX GLOVES DROOPING WITH FULNESS 874 26
FOR HE HAS DRUNK THE MORSELS WHITE OF SLEEP 878 11
THROUGH THAT WHITE STRAIT OF THY THICK SHAKEN THROAT 879 7
AND THAT WHITE SCUD OF HEAVEN 882 17
AND WHEN I SEE THE THICK WHITE BODY OF TRAIN-SMOKE BREAK 883 16
YOUR SMALL BREASTS CLUMPS OF WHITE 886 6
TO THE WINDOW AND THE WHITE PEAR-TREE 886 9
ROUND AND WHITE AS A SMALL BOSOM 886 17
OF THE BANK I STAND WATCHING MY OWN WHITE SHADOW QUIVER+ *891 21
THE SAME EDEN WITH PURPLE AND WHITE *892 16
THE MEN UPLIFTED ON THE NEW WHITE WOODSTACK STAND *895 1
TO HOIST THE NEXT WHITE PLANK THEIR MOVEMENT SEEMS *895 5
WHITE WHEN THE WIND SHIFTED HER HAIR THAT WAS SOFT AN' + *910 12
THEY WAS WILD ONES WHITE AND BLUE I COULD TELL *910 17
ON TH' YALLER CLAY AN' TH' WHITE FLOWERS TOP OF IT *910 28
THAT WHITE AN' 'ER SHOOK THAT MUCH I'D LIKE TO BEGIN *911 24
RAVELLED BLUE AND WHITE WARM FOR A BIT *911 28
WHEN THE WHITE FEET OF THE BABY BEAT ACROSS THE GRASS *912 25
WHITE FLOWERS IN THE WIND BOB UP AND DOWN *912 26
THE SIGHT OF THEIR WHITE PLAY AMONG THE GRASS *913 1
IS LIKE WHEN TWO WHITE BUTTERFLIES SETTLE IN THE ARMS O+ *913 3
HER SOFT WHITE LEGS HANGING HEAVILY OVER MY ARM *913 17
THE LITTLE WHITE FEET NOD LIKE WHITE FLOWERS IN THE WIND *913 29
AND THE SIGHT OF THEIR WHITE PLAY AMONG THE GRASS *914 2
OR AS TWO WHITE BUTTERFLIES SETTLE IN THE CUP OF ONE FL+ *914 4
TO HA'E GONE AN' GIVEN HIS WHITE YOUNG FLESH *919 19
YES AN' 'IS FACE GOES WHITE OH YES *921 6
NOT EVEN THE WHITE MOTHS WHITE *929 23
COMES ON US YOU'LL LIFT YOUR FINGERS WHITE *931 16
THE WHITE DOG NIPPED THE MOTHER RAT THE FATHER RAT BESI+ *933 7
MY SIGHT BUT THEN WHO HAS STOLE THE BRIGHT WHITE HEN OF+ *933 23
I FOLLOWED FOLLOWED THE SWING OF HER WHITE DRESS *934 8
POISED AT HER LIKE A WEAPON MY HAND WAS WHITE AND KEEN *936 14
SINCE DEATH HAS DELIVERED NAKED AND THIN AND WHITE *938 7
THE LAMPS ARE WHITE LIKE SNOWDROPS IN THE GRASS *938 29
WITH MULTITUDE OF WHITE ROSES AND JUST A FEW *940 27
THEY WOULD SAY SEEING EACH MOUTH OF WHITE ROSE PRAISE *941 6
GLISTENING WHITE ON THE SHOULDERS *942 23
FOR THE RUSTLING OF THEIR WHITE UNFOLDING PETALS *943 5
BLOWN FLAT INTO POINTS BY THE HEAVY WHITE DRAUGHT OF TH+ *956 5
IN THE WHITE SHIRT OF THE MIND'S EXPERIENCES *957 9

WHITE AMERICANS
THEN THE BIG MEN OF THE WHITE AMERICANS 777 28

WHITEBEAM
STRAY WHITEBEAM AND HER WHITE FIRE ALL UNLADENS 86 20

WHITE-BODIED
WHITE-BODIED AND WARM THE NIGHT WAS 165 9

WHITE-CAST
WHOM HAVE YOU COME FOR HERE IN THE WHITE-CAST DAY *956 9

WHITE-ENAMELLED
WITH A HARD FACE WHITE-ENAMELLED 56 21

WHITE-FACED
BUT OH THE STREAMS THAT STREAM WHITE-FACED IN AND OUT 628 15
IN AND OUT WHEN THE HOOTER HOOTS WHITE-FACED WITH A 628 16
WHAT HAVE THEY DONE TO YOU WHITE-FACED MILLIONS 628 22

WHITE-FLANNELLED
THREADING THE ROUND JOY OF HIS WHITE-FLANNELLED HIPS FU+ 867 30

WHITE-HANDED
CRINGING PITY AND LOVE WHITE-HANDED CAME 94 16
CRINGING PITY AND MY SELF WHITE-HANDED CAME *897 4

WHITE-HOT
WITHIN WHITE-HOT LAVA NEVER AT PEACE 294 2
ANY MORE THAN I COULD ENTER THE WHITE-HOT DOOR OF A BLA+ 344 18
QUICKENS THE HASTENING WHITE-HOT METAL *907 22
AS IT QUICKENS WITHIN THE LABOURING WHITE-HOT METAL *909 26

WHITELY
WHITELY CONFRONT I WAIT ON THE GRASS AM LAMED 225 12

WHITE MAN'S GOVERNMENT
THAT THE INDIANS WANTED THE WHITE MAN'S GOVERNMENT 778 20
THE WHITE MAN'S GOVERNMENT WAS UNDER NO OBLIGATION 778 24

WHITENED
NOT BLEEDING AWAY TO LEAVE ME WITH WHITENED GUMS 768 10

WHITENESS
WITH HER WHITENESS REVEALING MY SUNKEN WORLD 103 29
YET NEVER ABLE TO PASS THE WHITENESS OF LIGHT INTO 345 17
EVEN IF IT'S ONLY IN THE WHITENESS OF A WASHED POCKET-H+ 449 22
ALREADY THE WHITENESS OF FALSE DAWN IS ON MY INNER OCEAN 513 13
KEEP SUDDENLY SHOWING A WHITENESS A FLASH AND A FURL A + 687 2
INTO SUBSTANCE AND FLAKY WHITENESS 705 20
WITH A LOVELY BLOOM OF WHITENESS UPON WHITE 708 21
BEYOND THE WHITE OF WHITENESS 810 23
SCATTER OVER THE WHITENESS ONE BOY ALONE IN THE CLASSRO+ 865 20

WHITE-NIGHTGOWNED
WHITE-NIGHTGOWNED LITTLE CHITS I SEE 105 16

WHITENING
WHITENING ACROSS THE BED 69 27
AS I STAND ON THIS HILL WITH THE WHITENING CAVE OF THE + 97 11

WHITER
THAN THOSE ABOVE US AND WHITER 48 29
BREAKS LIGHT INTO GEMS AND DEAD BREASTS WHITER 168 17
LIKE A FLAME BLOWN WHITER AND WHITER 281 9

WHITE-RANKED
FAR-OFF THE LILY-STATUES STAND WHITE-RANKED IN THE GARD+ 159 19

WHITES
WHITES OF THEIR EYES 389 22
AND FEAR IN THE SMOKY WHITES OF YOUR EYES YOU NIGGER 400 26

WHITE-SPREAD
DAISIES THAT WAKEN ALL MISTAKEN WHITE-SPREAD IN EXPECTA+ 71 3
DAISIES THAT WAKEN ALL MISTAKEN WHITE-SPREAD IN EXPECTA+ *917 22

WHITEST
AND BY ARTEMIS THE WHITEST 702 9

WHITE-TREADING
TO THE WHITE-TREADING WAVES OF TWO SALT FEET 705 17

WHITE-WASH
AND WHITE WORDS WHITE-WASH AMERICAN 292 32

WHITHER
WHENCE COMETH WHITHER GOETH STILL THE SAME 69 26
WHITHER I TURN AND SET 99 23
GONE ONE KNOWS NOT WHITHER 134 10
WHITHER THEN WHITHER WHAT IS IT SAY 140 26
AS THE WIND ASKS WHITHER THE WAN ROAD GOES 163 24
A DARK BOAT THROUGH THE GLOOM AND WHITHER 209 2
WHITHER OR WHY OR EVEN HOW I AM GOING 223 6
WHITHER AWAY SMALL BIRD 352 29
WHITHER AWAY BRISK EGG 356 23
WHITHER DO YOU WANDER 669 13
IS A FOOTSTEP ONWARDS ONWARDS WE KNOW NOT WHITHER 713 13
ONWARDS WE KNOW NOT WHITHER 713 18
FOR LIFE IS A WANDERING WE KNOW NOT WHITHER BUT GOING 713 24
YOU ARE OFF YOU ARE ON THE WING WHITHER WHITHER 784 2
FOR NONE GO WHITHER THIS LONG ROAD GOES 857 20
AS THE WIND ASKS WHITHER THE DARK ROAD GOES 857 24

WHITISH
HOW CAN MY HEART KEEP BEATING IN THIS PALLOR OF WHITISH 766 28

WHIT-LEATHER
TILL 'ER'S TOUGH AS WHIT-LEATHER TO SLIVE 77 19
TILL 'ER'S TOUGH AS WHIT-LEATHER TO SLIVE *919 7

WHITMAN
THESE STATES AS WHITMAN SAID 293 11

WHITSUN
THE WHITSUN ZENITH 323 15

WHIZZING
    AND WENT WHIZZING THROUGH THE SLOW VAST SUCCULENT   372 12

WHOAM
    HASNA TER SENT ME WHOAM WHEN I   80   6
    HASNA TER SENT ME WHOAM WHEN I   *922 6

WHO'D
    WHO'D EVER HAVE THOUGHT IT OF THAT LAD A   552 23

WHOEVER
    BUT WHOEVER WOULD PLUCK APART MY FLOWERING WILL BURN TH+   93 29
    I GIVE WHOEVER DENIES   202 12
    TO YOU WHOEVER YOU ARE WITH ENDLESS EMBRACE   396 12
    AND WHOEVER SAYS SHE ISN'T IS A LIAR   498 15
    AND WHOEVER WALKS A MILE FULL OF FALSE SYMPATHY   653 1
    AND WHOEVER FORCES HIMSELF TO LOVE ANYBODY   653 3
    AND WHOEVER GETS IT IT'LL BE A DEAD BABY   664 15

WHOLE
    THE SUBTLE STEADY RUSH OF THE WHOLE   68 13
    BENEATH THIS POWERFUL TREE MY WHOLE SOUL'S FLUID   131 8
    THE WHOLE OF THE DAY TO EXTINGUISH THE SHADOW I LIFT ON+   133 20
    STILL HANGS THE HAWK WITH THE WHOLE SKY MOVING   150 1
    IN SILENCE WHEN SHE LOOKED FOR ALL THE WHOLE   156 3
    THE PULSE THROUGH THE WHOLE BLAND BEING   165 13
    THE WHOLE WHITE NIGHT   165 22
    WALLED IN WALLED IN THE WHOLE WORLD IS A VAST IMPURE   174 23
    THE WHOLE WIDE WORLD IS INTERIOR NOW AND WERE ALL SHUT +   175 11
    THE WHOLE GREAT CONFLAGRATION OF ALL LIFE   195 26
    I CAN SEE IT ALL IT IS WHOLE LIKE THE TWILIGHT   203 18
    IF I GO ON WALKING THROUGH THE WHOLE BREADTH OF GERMANY   212 24
    HE THINKS THE WHOLE BLUE SKY   244 29
    JOHN KNEW THE WHOLE PROPOSITION   328 10
    JOHN KNEW THE WHOLE PROPOSITION   328 16
    TORN TO BECOME WHOLE AGAIN AFTER LONG SEEKING FOR WHAT   367 1
    THAT WHICH IS WHOLE TORN ASUNDER   367 5
    THAT WHICH IS IN PART FINDING ITS WHOLE AGAIN THROUGHOUT   367 6
    WHOLE   378 29
    SO FIERCE WHEN THE COYOTES HOWL BARKING LIKE A WHOLE   396 29
    THAT WILL BLOSSOM FORTH THE WHOLE OF HUMAN NATURE   429 13
    THERE'S NOT A YOUNG MAN IN THE WHOLE   494 10
    MY WHOLE CONSCIOUSNESS IS CLICHE   510 1
    NOTHING AND NOBODY IN THE WHOLE VAST REALM OF SPACE   514 20
    WE FEEL THAT IF THE WHOLE COMBATIVE COMPETITIVE SYSTEM   519 19
    ON THE WHOLE WHOLE WHOLE   545 14
    NOT ONE OF THE WHOLE JOB LOT   549 28
    THE WHOLE OF THE TIME AND NOTHING   552 11
    I SAW THE WHOLE SUPERIOR   554 7
    IT DAWNS ON THEM THAT THE WHOLE DAMN SWINDLE   560 11
    AS A CACHE SEXE I'D HAVE PUT A WHOLE FOG   580 12
    THE WHOLE GREAT HEAVENS HAVE SHIFTED OVER AND SLOWLY PU+   616 23
    THAT POSSESS THE WHOLE BODY   627 19
    SISTER THE WHOLE DAY LONG   628 2
    ORDER YOU DESTROY THE WHOLE VILE PACK   633 29
    WALKS TO THE FUNERAL OF THE WHOLE HUMAN RACE   653 2
    TRUE YOU CAN'T PRODUCE THE BEST WITHOUT ATTENDING TO TH+   668 2
    OR THE WHOLE TREE MAY FALL ROTTEN   677 29
    A HEALED WHOLE MAN O MOON   696 7
    THE WHOLE   699 8
    A FLUSH OF ROSE AND THE WHOLE THING STARTS AGAIN   720 11
    I LET THE WHOLE THING GO STILL THERE IS ME   738 27
    THE WHOLE APPLE   817 30
    DARK BLUE THE WHOLE DESIRE LEAPS   819 24
    THE WHOLE TEEMING FLESH OF MANKIND   *907 27
    OH THE MIRACLE OF THE WHOLE THE WIDESPREAD LABOURING CO+ *909 19
    AND WATCHING THE GREAT THING LABOURING THROUGH THE WHOL+ *909 23
    THE SUBTLE STEADY RUSH OF THE WHOLE   *914 28
    THROUGH THE WHOLE BLUE SKY AND THE NOON   *937 11
    AND HER ARMS AND HER BOSOM AND THE WHOLE OF HER SOUL IS+ *940 20
    FROM THEIR TREE OF LIFE AND VILLAGES WHOLE CITIES LIVED+ *950 4
    THE WHOLE THING HAS RISEN OUT OF THIS CASH-CHEMIST MONEY *950 17

WHOLENESS
    SANITY MEANS THE WHOLENESS OF THE CONSCIOUSNESS   515 1
    THOUGHT IS A MAN IN HIS WHOLENESS WHOLLY ATTENDING   673 15
    IN THE SUSPENSION OF WHOLENESS IN THE MOMENT OF DIVISIO+   699 7
    IN THE SWEET WHOLENESS OF OBLIVION   726 21

WHOLESALE
    OR LENIN SAYS YOU ARE SAVED BUT YOU ARE SAVED WHOLESALE   443 1

WHOLESOME
    BAWDY CAN BE SANE AND WHOLESOME   844 29
    TO KEEP IT SANE AND WHOLESOME   844 31
    AND A LITTLE WHORING CAN BE SANE AND WHOLESOME   845 1
    TO KEEP IT SANE AND WHOLESOME   845 3
    EVEN SODOMY CAN BE SANE AND WHOLESOME   845 4
    IN THE SAME WAY CHASTITY IN ITS HOUR IS SWEET AND WHOLE+   845 11
    BAWDY CAN BE SAND AND WHOLESOME   *952 10
    TO KEEP IT SANE AND WHOLESOME   *952 15
    EVEN AT THE RIGHT TIMES SODOMY CAN BE SANE AND WHOLESOME *952 16
    CHASTITY IN ITS HOUR IS SWEET AND WHOLESOME   *952 23
    WHOLESOME   *952 25
    PURITY HOWEVER IS NEVER SANE AND NEVER WHOLESOME   *953 1
    AND EATING THE BRAVE BREAD OF A WHOLESOME KNOWLEDGE   *959 14

WHOLLY
    THOUGHT IS A MAN IN HIS WHOLENESS WHOLLY ATTENDING   673 15

WHOOING
    SOMETHING LIKE AN OWL WHOOING   366 13
    WHOOING AND COOING AND FADING AWAY WITH WONDERFUL   830 24

WHORE
    AS IF SHE WERE A WORM OR A HIRED WHORE WHO BORED HIM   *948 17

WHOREDOM
    NOT TO SPEAK OF BABYLON'S WHOREDOM   328 6

WHORING
    HIS WONDERFUL SPEECHES FULL OF OTHER FOLKS' WHORING   494 21
    AND A LITTLE WHORING CAN BE SANE AND WHOLESOME   845 1
    IN FACT A LITTLE WHORING IS NECESSARY IN EVERY LIFE   845 2
    WHORING ON THE BRAIN BECOMES REALLY SYPHILITIC   845 8
    AND RIGID SUPPRESSION OF ALL BAWDY WHORING OR OTHER SUC+   845 13
    AND A LITTLE WHORING CAN BE SANE AND HEALTHY   *952 13
    IN FACT A LITTLE WHORING IS NECESSARY IN EVERY LIFE   *952 14
    AND WHORING ON THE BRAIN AS BAD AS SYPHILIS INCIPIENT I+ *952 20

WHORL
    A LIVING FOREHEAD WITH ITS SLOW WHORL OF HAIR   325 27
    A FLUSH AT THE FLAILS OF YOUR FINS DOWN THE WHORL OF YO+   335 9

WHORLED
    YET IF YOU HAD WHORLED HORNS OF BRONZE IN A FRONTAL DARK   381 1
    FOR THE COSMOS EVEN IN DEATH IS LIKE A DARK WHORLED SHE+   724 4

WHORLS
    AND SUDDENLY LOWERING HIS HEAD THE WHORLS OF BONE AND   381 16
    WHOSE WHORLS FOLD ROUND TO THE CORE OF SOUNDLESS SILENC+   724 5
    IN THE WHISPERING WHORLS   747 24

WHOSOEVER
    AND WHOSOEVER THE UNKNOWN PEOPLE OF THIS UNKNOWN   256 14
    AND WHOSOEVER COMES AFTER WILL FIND ME IN THE NEW WORLD   260 22

WHO'S
    TO THE CHAR WHO'S AS GOOD AS YOU ARE ANY DAY   572 4
    WE'LL SHOW THESE OLD UNCLES WHO'S GOING TO BE BOSSY   573 24

WHO'VE
    IT'S YOU WHO'VE BEEN WRONG   564 6
    WHO'VE DECIDED THAT BOCCACCIO MUST BURN   633 17

WI
    THA KNOWS 'E 'D A WINSOME WAY WI 'IM AN' SHE   *910 24
    HE'S GONE WI THAT   *918 20

WICK
    WICK   245 9
    LIKE A FLAME ON A WICK   246 3

WICKED
    DID YOU SEE THE WICKED SUN THAT WINKED   120 9
    WITHIN THE FLESH-SCENT OF THIS WICKED TREE   299 13
    WICKED FIG-TREE EQUALITY PUZZLE WITH YOUR SELF-CONSCIOUS 300 16
    LET ME FIGHT THE WICKED OBSTREPEROUS WEEDS MYSELF AND P+ 316 11
    SHUFFLE SHUFFLE AND HIS LITTLE WICKED EYE HAS SEEN YOU + 387 10

WICKEDNESS
    HIS WICKEDNESS AMONG   *911 11

WICKS
    OF EASY SAILING ODD RED WICKS SERVE   172 20

WIDDER
    AFORE I CAN TA'E THEE I'VE GOT A WIDDER O' FORTY-FIVE T+   83 8
    BUT 'ARK THEE 'ERE THAT WIDDER WOMAN   84 3

WIDDER NAYLOR'S
    IT'S WIDDER NAYLOR'S WEDDIN'-DRESS   79 19

WIDDER'S
    AX 'IM THY-SEN WENCH A WIDDER'S LODGER   77 11
    AX HIM THY-SEN WENCH A WIDDER'S LODGER   *918 29

WIDE
    STARTLED UPON YOUR EYES NOW SO WIDE WITH HEREAFTER   58 22
    GIRLS WITH THEIR LARGE EYES WIDE WITH TRAGEDY   71 21
    IN THE FLOWER'S THROAT AND THE FLOWER GAPED WIDE WITH W+ 125 10
    SO WIDE AS YOU WATCH THE CATKINS BLOW   126 30
    BUT WHEN THE APPLE-BLOSSOM OPENS WIDE   129 11
    WHAT IF UNWITTING I SET THE DOOR OF ETERNITY WIDE   147 11
    THE WHOLE WIDE WORLD IS INTERIOR NOW AND WERE ALL SHUT + 175 11
    AND BREAK THE WALLS OF POSSESSION OF ALL THE WIDE WORLD   175 17
    FIVE TIMES WIDE OPEN   307 12
    SIX TIMES WIDE OPEN   307 13
    THE VENETIAN SHUTTERS I PUSH WIDE   343 1
    SUDDENLY BEAK-SHAPED AND VERY WIDE LIKE SOME SUDDENLY   353 5
    SHE IS SUCH AN ALERT LISTENER WITH HER EARS WIDE TO KNOW 384 15
    WITH THEIR THIN DARK HANDS AND THEIR WIDE DARK EYES AND   451 3
    THE WIDE SEA WINS AND THE DARK   455 25
    WIDE EYES AND WONDERING SPIRIT NOT   461 7
    A WASTE EXPANSE OF NOTHING LIKE WIDE FORESHORES WHERE N+ 509 12
    WHERE TISSUE PLUNGES INTO BRONZE WITH WIDE WILD CIRCLES+ 623 10
    AND THROUGH THE WIDE PRAIRIES OF HIS BREAST A YOUNG BUL+ 624 7
    AND DREAMING WITH STRANGE WHALE EYES WIDE OPEN IN THE W+ 694 31
    OF FIRE AND THE WET EARTH AND THE WIDE AIR OF THE WORLD   706 5
    HE SENDS THE EAGLE OF SILENCE DOWN ON WIDE WINGS   799 17
    AND WIDE WIDE APART   819 11
    IN SPACES WIDE WITH MISTRUST   823 22
    THE INRUSH THE CLATTER THE STAMPING EYES LAUGHING WIDE + 865 25
    COMING HOME OVER THE WASTE-LANDS WIDE AND LONELY WITH S+ 866 16
    OF RUSSIA THROUGH THE NEW GREAT NAIVETE OF RUSSIA HER W+ 866 29
    HOW LONELY IN THE WIDE WORLD IS THIS PLAYGROUND   867 6
    THE SUN SETS WIDE THE YELLOW CROCUSES   868 17
    FOR YOU SET WIDE THE DOORS OF MY VENTURESOME ARK   875 23
    FAR AND WIDE RUN THE EASY ROOTS THAT BEAR THE LEAVES OF+ *926 12
    IN THE FLOWER'S THROAT AND THE FLOWER GAPED WIDE WITH W+ *935 26
    THE SUN SETS WIDE THE YELLOW CROCUSES   *941 17
    AND WIDE IN ECSTASY I SIT AND WATCH   *943 20

WIDE
IN WIDE AND WIDER CIRCLES ROUND THE WORLD *943 25
SWAM THE STILL SWAN SWEPT THE WIDE GOOSE ABOVE THE MISTS *947 2

WIDE-EARED
CURIOUS LONG-LEGGED FOALS AND WIDE-EARED CALVES AND NAK+ 271 34

WIDE-EYED
AND THE HUMAN SOUL IS FATED TO WIDE-EYED RESPONSIBILITY 347 2
SOMNAMBULIST WIDE-EYED AFRAID 407 27

WIDER
AND I KNEW THAT HOME THIS VALLEY WAS WIDER THAN PARADISE 38 17
ALL THE WHALES IN THE WIDER DEEPS HOT ARE THEY AS THEY + 694 3
AND SAY THAT THIS HOME THIS VALLEY IS WIDER THAN PARADI+ *892 32
IN WIDE AND WIDER CIRCLES ROUND THE WORLD *943 25

WIDE-RAYED
SOUNDLESS BLISS-FULL WIDE-RAYED HONEY-BODIED 307 6

WIDE-SPACED
AT THESE WIDE-SPACED TORN ENORMOUS BREATHS 878 36

WIDESPREAD
IS SWELLING WITH WIDESPREAD LABOURING CONCENTRATION *908 2
OH THE MIRACLE OF THE WHOLE THE WIDESPREAD LABOURING CO+ *909 19

WIDOW
A WIDOW O' FORTY-FIVE 77 13
A WIDOW OF FORTY-FIVE 77 17
A WIDOW OF FORTY-FIVE 77 21
YOUR WIDOW AM I AND ONLY I I DREAM 157 15
A WIDOW OF FORTY-FIVE *919 1
A WIDOW O' FORTY-FIVE *919 5
A WIDOW OF FORTY-FIVE *919 9
BEFORE I CAN TA'E THEE I'VE GOT A WIDOW OF FORTY-FIVE T+ *925 12

WIDOW NAYLOR'S
IT'S WIDOW NAYLOR'S WEDDIN'-DRESS *921 15

WIDOW NAYLOR
WHY YOUR YOUNG MAN AN' WIDOW NAYLOR 78 9
WHY YOUR YOUNG MAN AN' WIDOW NAYLOR *920 1

WIELD
AS THE HEART BENEATH DID WIELD 55 29

WIELDING
MY HAND IS HEAVY AND HELPLESS SINCE WIELDING THE LASH *897 19

WIELDS
OF THE LONG SCYTHE THE STOOPING MOWER WIELDS *939 8

WIERD
WIERD RIGGING IN A STORM SHRIEKS HIDEOUSLY 36 12

WIFE
ATWEEN A LAD AN' 'IS WIFE 77 20
OF KISSES LONG SEEKING FOR A WIFE 105 7
AS 'UD MAKE THEE A WIFE AN' LOOK UP TER THEE 138 30
A STRICKEN WIFE SO SUNK IN OBLIVION BOWED 155 30
AM NOW YOUR WIFE 156 18
AH LOT'S WIFE LOT'S WIFE 207 27
LOT'S WIFE NOT WIFE BUT MOTHER 207 33
EVEN THEN IT IS DARK BEHIND YOU TURN ROUND MY WIFE 211 17
IT WAS THE FLANK OF MY WIFE 260 1
IT WAS THE FLANK OF MY WIFE 260 4
NOW THAT THE GRAVE IS MADE OF MOTHER AND WIFE 411 27
NOW THAT THE WIFE AND MOTHER AND MISTRESS IS BURIED IN 412 23
BUT THE UNHAPPINESS OF A WIFE WITH A GOOD HUSBAND 456 7
THAN THE UNHAPPINESS OF A WIFE WITH A BAD HUSBAND 456 9
IT'S YOUR WIFE WI' HER AIRS AN' GRACES 493 20
I AM NOT SURE I WOULD ALWAYS FIGHT FOR MY WIFE 497 15
A WIFE ISN'T ALWAYS WORTH FIGHTING FOR 497 16
A MAN CAN'T GET ANY FUN OUT OF WIFE SWEETHEART OR TART 518 4
HIS CREDIT HIS NAME HIS WIFE EVEN MAY BE JUST ANOTHER 607 17
AND APHRODITE IS THE WIFE OF WHALES 695 7
WHY THE MODERN YOUNG WIFE OF THE LITTLE-BOY BRILLIANT B+ 842 9
YET IN THE LITTLE NEW ROAD THE YOUNG WIFE TURNS AWAY 865 13
WAS UNAWARE BUT HIS WIFE CRIED IN HER DREAM 885 11
ATWEEN A LAD AN' 'IS WIFE *919 8

WIFE'S
OH MY WIFE'S BRASS INCENSE-BOWL 760 12

WIFT
US A LITTLE WIFT AN' I KNEW THE SMELL *910 19

WIK
IN A WIK OR TWO 79 28

WILD
AND CROUCHES LOW THEN WITH WILD SPRING 43 7
HAS OPENED THE WINGS OF THE WILD YOUNG SPRITE 46 14
WITH FIRE AS IT GUARDS THE WILD NORTH-COASTS RED-FIRE S+ 57 13
THE WILD YOUNG HEIFER GLANCING DISTRAUGHT 64 7
LIKE A WILD DAFFODIL DOWN-DREAMING 91 19
IN WILD CARESSES 96 16
AND TWICE AFTER WILD KISSES I SAW 103 24
WILD PUFFING OF GREEN-FIRE TREES AND FLAME-GREEN BUSHES 116 2
OF GROWING THESE SMOKE-PUFFS THAT PUFF IN WILD GYRATION 116 8
THE WILD ANEMONES LIE 126 10
I WISH A WILD SEA-FELLOW WOULD COME DOWN THE GLITTERING 130 17
FOR YOU WERE STRAINING WITH A WILD HEART BACK BACK AGAIN 206 23
WE FOUND THE DARK WILD ROSES 217 2
HAVE YOU NOT SEEN IN THE WILD WINTER SUN OF THE SOUTHER+ 303 4
IN LITTLE BUNCHES LIKE BUNCHES OF WILD HARES 311 23
NEW WILD SOULS 315 34

WILD
I REMEMBER HEARING A WILD GOOSE OUT OF THE THROAT OF NI+ 365 34
ON WILD DARK LIPS 366 21
HOST ON THE SHORES OF THE LAKE LIKE THICK WILD RICE BY 391 9
LIKE BULLS OR BISONS OR WILD PIGS 392 19
OF WOLF ALL HAIRY AND LEVEL A WOLF'S WILD PELT 408 29
AT ALL THESE SKINS OF WILD BEASTS 409 27
SWIMS THE WILD SWAN 437 23
LIKE A WILD SWAN OR A GOOSE WHOSE HONK GOES THROUGH MY 438 7
YOUNG WILD SWANS 438 22
OR THE ROUND WILD VIVID EYE OF A WILD-GOOSE STARING 438 31
WHILE YOU READ ABOUT THE AIR-SHIP CROSSING THE WILD ATL+ 441 22
IN THE BRIGHT WILD CIRCUS FLESH 446 18
WHAT DO YOU WANT WILD LOINS AND WHAT 461 5
I NEVER SAW A WILD THING 467 1
IN WILD WHITE SIBILANT SPRAY 467 13
DURING THE WILD ORGASMS OF CHAOS 477 3
AND WHEN THROUGHOUT ALL THE WILD ORGASMS OF LOVE 477 12
THE GEM OF MUTUAL PEACE EMERGING FROM THE WILD CHAOS 477 19
LOVE IS LIKE THE GRASS BUT THE HEART IS DEEP WILD ROCK 477 22
BUT SAY IN THE DARK WILD METAL OF YOUR HEART 478 4
HAVE YOU NO DEEP OLD HEART OF WILD WOMANHOOD 478 15
THE UNIVERSE FLOWS IN INFINITE WILD STREAMS RELATED 479 9
THE HOT WILD CORE OF THE EARTH HEAVIER THAN WE CAN EVEN 480 8
WHAT EVEN THE WILD WITCHCRAFT OF THE PAST WAS SEEKING 481 9
WILD THINGS IN CAPTIVITY 484 22
WHILE THEY KEEP THEIR OWN WILD PURITY 484 23
WE WANT A NEW WORLD OF WILD PEACE WHERE LIVING IS FREE 519 22
AND SOMEWHERE IT HAS A WILD HEART 525 4
FROM THE WILD HEART OF SPACE THAT I CALL THE SUN OF SUNS 525 9
IN THE WILD DAYS WHEN LIFE WAS SLIDING WHIRLWINDS BLUE-+ 529 23
WITH FIERY WEIGHT AND WILD LIFE AND COMING OUT 530 3
AND THINK HOW WILD ANIMALS TROT WITH SPLENDOUR 530 12
THE WILD ROSE IN A SHELTERED GARDEN 535 1
OH EVEN TO KNOW THE LAST WILD WINCING OF DESPAIR 585 6
WHERE TISSUE PLUNGES INTO BRONZE WITH WIDE WILD CIRCLES+ 623 10
AND THE WILD SWANS FLOWN AWAY SINGING THE SWAN-SONG OF + 624 2
WILL SEND UP THE WILD CRY OF DESPAIR 624 13
THE TRILLING LARK IN A WILD DESPAIR WILL TRILL DOWN ARR+ 624 14
WHAT ARE THE WILD WAVES SAYING 628 1
WHAT ARE THE WILD WAVES SAYING 628 9
WILD ROSES OF ENGLAND 634 23
MEN WHO ARE WILD ROSES OF ENGLAND 634 24
TREES RAISED FROM SEED HAVE WILD AND BITTER FRUITS 640 21
AND HIDE IN YOUR OWN WILD THEBAID 642 8
FROM TIME TO TIME THE WILD CRYING OF EVERY ELECTRON 682 20
THERE THEY BLOW THERE THEY BLOW HOT WILD WHITE BREATH O+ 694 6
IN THE CLASP AND THE SOFT WILD CLUTCH OF A SHE-WHALE'S + 694 19
THE SUMMER AND THE SNOWS THE WILD WELTER OF EARTH 707 29
HOLD BACK THE WILD HOT SUN 789 13
WILD SKIES 816 27
YET WHEN I THINK OF THE WILD SWAN OR THE RIPPLE-MARKED + 841 1
THE NEXT DAY IS THE DAY OF THE GOOSE THE WILD SWAN'S DAY 841 9
THE WILD GODS SEND VITALITY THEY PUT THE LIGHTNING INTO+ 843 5
EVER TO SUFFER LOVE'S WILD ATTACK 854 18
AND BESIDE IT ON THE TABLE HER GLOVES AND MY WILTED WIL+ 856 15
OF MY WILTED WILD ROSES PINK AND IVORY WHITE 856 18
AND I'LL LIE IN HER LAP WHERE THE WORLD'S WILD ROSE 858 6
A LITTLE WILD BUBBLE IS LOOSENING HOLD 868 28
AS WILD WHITE FOX GLOVES DROOPING WITH FULNESS 874 26
LEAN TOGETHER AND LIFT WILD ARMS TO EMBRACE 883 9
FLIES LIKE A WILD THING ACROSS MY BODY *893 15
KNOTTING THEMSELVES WITH WILD STRENGTH *893 24
UNDER THE WILD STRANGE TYRANNY OF MY BODY *893 27
AS MY WILD SOUL SHRINKS AND THE SONGS ARE DRIVEN FROM M+ *896 12
TO FOLLOW MY LIFE ALOFT TO THE FINE WILD AIR OF LIFE AN+ *900 8
TO FOLLOW MY LIFE ALOFT TO THE FINE WILD AIR OF LIFE AN+ *903 20
IN HIS WILD FITS *910 4
THEY WAS WILD ONES WHITE AND BLUE I COULD TELL *910 17
FOR OUT IN THE WASTE WILD SOUL SPACE THAT SHALL *938 19
A WOMAN IS SINGING ME A WILD HUNGARIAN AIR *940 19
A LITTLE WILD BUBBLE IS LOOSING HOLD *941 28
WE FOUND OUR WARM WILD ROSES *942 13
LIKE A WILD SWAN OR A GOOSE WHOSE HONK GOES THROUGH MY + *947 18
THERE'LL BE BABIES BORN THAT ARE YOUNG WILD SWANS O MY + *947 24
AND WILD GEESE O MY HEART *947 25
AND THE WILD SWANS FLOWN AWAY SINGING THE SWAN-SONG OF + *953 20
IN SOME HEARTS STILL THE SANCTUARIES OF WILD LIFE *954 2
SEND UP THE LAST WILD CRY OF DESPAIR *954 11

WILD-BEAST
SHADOWS THE PASSING WILD-BEAST THREW 262 6

WILDERNESS
WE CRY IN THE WILDERNESS FORGIVE ME I 40 13
AND OUT OF THE CHAMBERED WILDERNESS WANDERS A SPIRIT AB+ 70 6
WITH WEBBED FECUNDITY PLUNGING THE SEED OF LIFE IN THE I 841 5

WILDEST
THE HOTTEST BLOOD OF ALL AND THE WILDEST THE MOST URGENT 694 2

WILD-FLOWER
THE WILD-FLOWER SHAKES ITS BELL 216 9

WILD-GOOSE
OR THE ROUND WILD VIVID EYE OF A WILD-GOOSE STARING 438 31

WILDLY
LITTLE LUMPS THAT FLY IN AIR AND HAVE VOICES INDEFINITE+ 341 26
LOBBING WILDLY THROUGH DEEP SNOW LIKE A RABBIT 397 7
WILDLY FLOATS SWIRLS 425 17

WILDNESS
WITH A LAUGH AND A MERRY WILDNESS THAT IT WAS SHE 180 15

WILD-THYME
    THE BEES ROLL ROUND IN THE WILD-THYME WITH DELIGHT   223 15

WILFUL
    EVEN THE WILFUL OBSTINATE GUMMY FIG-TREE   305 8

WILLIAM BLAKE
    HAIRY HORRID GOD THE FATHER IN A WILLIAM BLAKE   385 20

WILLING
    TO THE NIGHT THAT TAKES US WILLING LIBERATES US TO THE +   70 4
    AND I AM WILLING TO COME TO YOU NOW MY DEAR   134 20
    THAT THE OLD BIRD IS WEARY AND ALMOST WILLING   329 27
    MOULTING AND MOPING AND WAITING WILLING AT LAST   329 31
    I WOULD BE WILLING TO GIVE WAY LIKE THE PTERODACTYL   430 5
    I WOULD BE WILLING TO VANISH COMPLETELY COMPLETELY   430 9
    THEN I AM WILLING TO FIGHT I WILL ROLL MY SLEEVES UP   430 11
    I'M PERFECTLY WILLING TO STRIKE A DECENT BARGAIN   483 22
    IF YOU WERE WILLING TO SEE IT   555 21
    IN A ROBOT-DEMOCRACY NOBODY IS WILLING TO SERVE   643 8
    IS NOW TO BE WILLING TO DIE AND TO BUILD THE SHIP   718 22
    ARE YOU WILLING TO BE SPONGED OUT ERASED CANCELLED   728 1

WILLINGLY
    I WISH I DID IT MORE WILLINGLY   41 14

WILL-LESS
    ARE WILL-LESS THERE   149 20

WILLOW
    LET US MAKE FOR THE WEEPING WILLOW   237 15
    COME AND SOFTEN THE WILLOW BUDS TILL THEY ARE PUFFED AN+   273 2
    THE WILLOW SHALL LIFT HER LEAVES TO SOOTHE THY DISTRESS   749 24

WILLOWS
    DARK OVERGROWN WITH WILLOWS COOL WITH THE BROOK EBBING +   33 16
    FAR OFF IN GOLD THE WILLOWS QUIVER   887 27
    DARK OVERGROWN WITH WILLOWS COOL WITH THE BROOK EBBING + *891 18

WILL-PERVERTED
    AND WE'VE MADE A GREAT MESS OF LOVE MIND-PERVERTED WILL+   473 6

WILLS
    AND THEIR WILLS ARE LIKE THEIR MACHINES OF IRON   794 8

WILL-TENSE
    YOU BRITTLE WILL-TENSE BIRD WITH A FOOLISH EYE   370 35

WILL-TO-LIVE
    NO BATTLE NO WILL-TO-LIVE   769 20

WILLY
    THEN WILLY NILLY   39 9

WILLY WET-LEGS
    I SUPPOSE WHEN THE MEN ALL STARTED BEING WILLY WET-LEGS   537 28
    BUT WHEN MEN TURN WILLY WET-LEGS   538 18
    AND THE POOR WILLY WET-LEGS THE SOFT SILK GLOVES   538 23

WILLY WET-LEG
    TOO MUCH OF THE HUMBLE WILLY WET-LEG   537 13
    I CAN'T STAND WILLY WET-LEG   559 17

WILT
    WILT THOU LIFT ME UP SON OF MAN   320 18
    OR WHETHER THE WATERS WILT IN THE HOLLOW PLACES   334 23
    WHEN WILT THOU TEACH THE PEOPLE   442 6
    GOD OF JUSTICE WHEN WILT THOU TEACH THEM TO SAVE THEMSE+   443 9

WILTED
    AND BESIDE IT ON THE TABLE HER GLOVES AND MY WILTED WIL+   856 15
    OF MY WILTED WILD ROSES PINK AND IVORY WHITE   856 18
    OF MY ARMS INERT WITH DREAD WILTED IN FEAR OF MY KISS   *912 18

WIMBLY-WAMBLY
    AND WIMBLY-WAMBLY YOUNG MEN OF SEX STILL MORE INDETERMI+   522 4
    AND THE TCHEKOV WIMBLY-WAMBLY WET-LEGS ALL WIPED OUT   533 17

WIMPLE
    WIMPLE   352 26
    HEAD IN ITS WIMPLE   353 11
    RESTING YOUR HEAD HALF OUT OF YOUR WIMPLE   354 8
    HIS WIMPLE HIS BLUNT-PROWED FACE   360 1

WIMPLES
    WHITE ON THE WATER WIMPLES MY SHADOW STRAINS LIKE A DOG+   33 25

WIN
    MYSELF TO WATCH THE DAYLIGHT WIN   59 3
    YOUNG YEARS AND THE OLD MUST NOT WIN NOT EVEN IF THEY L+   93 5
    I MUST NOT WIN THEIR SOULS NO NEVER I ONLY MUST WIN   93 7
    NEWNESS NEW SHAPE TO WIN   127 14
    MEN FIGHT FOR LIBERTY AND WIN IT WITH HARD KNOCKS   535 23
    I PLAY MY RECKLESS GAME TO WIN MY POINT   876 1
    LET US SEEK TO WIN HER BACK UNTO US THE MOON   *938 13

WINCE
    AS 'UD WINCE WHEN THAT TOUCHED 'ER CLOSE AN'   133 31

WINCING
    OH EVEN TO KNOW THE LAST WILD WINCING OF DESPAIR   585 6
    WITH HIS EARS PRICKED AND HIS BODY WINCING   645 19
    FINDS ITSELF SHRINKING WINCING FROM THE COLD   717 8
    WITH WINCING UNWILLING WAVES   *958 29

WINCINGLY
    AND ROSY-RED HIBISCUS WINCINGLY   317 22

WINCINGNESS
    UPON THE WINCINGNESS OF NEXT TO NOTHINGNESS   733 29

WIND
    AND AT NIGHT WHEN THE WIND ROSE THE LASH OF THE TREE   36 10
    SHRIEKED AND SLASHED THE WIND AS A SHIP'S   36 11
    STIRRED BY AN IMPETUOUS WIND SOME WAYS'LL   40 28
    WHICH WEAVES ITS WAY THROUGH THE EVENING WIND   42 3
    LIKE THE SOUGH OF A WIND THAT IS CAUGHT UP HIGH IN THE +   58 1
    THE LITTLE WHITE FEET NOD LIKE WHITE FLOWERS IN A WIND   64 30
    THEY POISE AND RUN LIKE PUFFS OF WIND THAT PASS   64 31
    OF SHAPES BY A HARD WIND RIDDEN   68 8
    UPON YOU AS AN AUTUMN WIND ON SOME   86 19
    AND CHITTER AND WIND THAT SHAKES AND CUFFS   89 29
    THE HARSH COLD WIND OF MY WORDS DROVE ON AND STILL   94 13
    THE WIND COMES FROM THE NORTH   99 16
    THE PINE-TREES BEND TO LISTEN TO THE AUTUMN WIND AS IT +   102 25
    TILL I KNEW YOU NOT FROM A LITTLE WIND   104 8
    OR THE WIND SHAKES A RAVEL OF LIGHT   109 21
    LESS THAN THE WIND THAT RUNS TO THE FLAMY CALL   116 13
    ROUND CLOUDS ROLL IN THE ARMS OF THE WIND   126 7
    IN UNDULATING SHIVERS BENEATH THE WIND   126 11
    LIFT OF THE PULSING WIND AH SAY THAT YOU KNOW   126 32
    WHEN THE WIND BLOWS HER VEIL   133 26
    WHEN THE WIND BLOWS HER VEIL   133 29
    WHEN THE WIND BLOWS HER VEIL   133 32
    TO FALL LIKE A BREATH WITHIN THE BREATHING WIND   134 26
    STARTLING A FEAR UNSPEAKABLE AS THE SHUDDERING WIND   140 17
    MANY ROSES IN THE WIND   149 25
    THE ROSES WITH THE WEST WIND RAPPING   149 29
    THE HAWK HAS DROPPED THE WIND IS SPENDING   150 5
    A RED ROSE GOES ON THE WIND ASCENDING   150 9
    A SILVER WIND IS HASTILY WIPING   150 15
    THE WINDOW-SASH AS THE WEST WIND BLOWS   150 19
    THE YOUNG GRASS TWINKLES IN THE WIND AND THE SOUND   152 28
    OF THE WIND IN THE KNOTTED BUDS MAKES A CANOPY   152 29
    OF THE WIND SHE IS LIFTED AND CARRIED AWAY AS IN A BALL+   153 2
    FLUX OF ANOTHER DAWN THE WIND THAT ALL NIGHT   154 28
    THE WIND CHASES BY US AND OVER THE CORN   163 17
    AS THE WIND ASKS WHITHER THE WAN ROAD GOES   163 24
    THE WIND IS UNCHANGING NOT ONE OF US KNOWS   164 2
    AGAINST THE WIND AND IF WHERE THE LAMPLIGHT BLEW   180 13
    I MUST HOLD MY FACE TO THE WIND AND LET IT EXPLAIN   180 32
    THE SOFT WIND BLOWING COOL   194 7
    HAS SHE NOT FLED ON THE SAME WIND WITH ME   222 20
    I HOLD MYSELF UP AND FEEL A BIG WIND BLOWING   223 4
    LITTLE TO COUNT IN THE WIND THAT DRIFTS ME THROUGH   223 12
    NOT I NOT I BUT THE WIND THAT BLOWS THROUGH ME   250 13
    A FINE WIND IS BLOWING THE NEW DIRECTION OF TIME   250 14
    BY THE FINE FINE WIND THAT TAKES ITS COURSE THROUGH THE   250 18
    HOW HAPPY I AM HOW MY HEART IN THE WIND RINGS TRUE   251 11
    OF THE WIND AND ITS ONENESS VEERS   253 26
    AND ROCKS IT TONS OF GRAIN ON THE RIPENING WIND   271 22
    CYPRESS-TREES IN A WIND   297 17
    WIND   306 12
    BUT BLEW BACK AS IF AN INCOMING WIND BLEW HIM IN AGAIN   343 17
    A STRONG INRUSHING WIND   343 18
    YOU GLOSSY DARK WIND   369 2
    SHUDDERING STORM WIND OR A WATER RUSHING THROUGH   370 25
    AND THE WIND IN HIS TEETH FOR A BIT   378 2
    AH WHEN HE TORE THE WIND WITH HIS TEETH   378 4
    LIFE SEEMS TO LEAP AT THE AIR OR SKIM UNDER THE WIND   392 15
    WOULD STOP A HOLE TO KEEP THE WIND AWAY   545 25
    TO STAMP THE EARTH AND FEEL THE WIND LIKE WAKEFUL   585 4
    ALONE ON A HILL-SIDE IN THE NORTH HUMMING IN THE WIND   610 23
    BUT THE LIVING LEAVES IN THE BREATH OF THE WIND ARE MOR+   615 14
    ALL OF THEM WHO WIND THEIR ENERGY ROUND THE IDEA OF THE+   616 4
    SONS OF THE WIND AND RAIN SONS OF THE FIRE AND ROCK   635 25
    AND THE SONS OF MEN WITH THE WIND AND THE FIRE OF LIFE   635 30
    SWIFT WIND OR SOUND RINGING ROCK   637 11
    HOW THEN ARE THE FEW MEN MEN OF THE WIND AND RAIN   637 27
    WHEN THE WIND BLOWS THE CRADLE SHALL ROCK   669 8
    BUTTERFLY THE WIND BLOWS SEA-WARD STRONG BEYOND THE GAR+   696 12
    ALREADY IT IS OCTOBER AND THE WIND BLOWS STRONG TO THE +   696 15
    FROM THE HILLS WHERE SNOW MUST HAVE FALLEN THE WIND IS +   696 16
    BUT THE WIND BLOWS STRONG TO SEA-WARD WHITE BUTTERFLY C+   696 19
    TILL THE WIND SLIDES YOU SHEER FROM THE ARCH-CREST   696 24
    A WIND THAT BLOWS BACK AND FORTH   714 13
    THE WIND THE RASCAL KNOCKED AT MY DOOR AND I SAID   731 13
    BUT OH WIND WHAT A KNAVE THOU ART   731 15
    THREADS OF BLUE WIND FAR AND DOWN THE ROAD   732 22
    THE DEAD ARE BURNING IN THE FUNERAL WIND   744 9
    BUT ON THEY GO LIKE LEAVES WITHIN A WIND   744 29
    AND STILL AGAINST THE DARK AND VIOLENT WIND   745 6
    UNQUENCHABLE OF WIND OR HOSTS OF DEATH   745 11
    THAT POUR CASCADE-LIKE DOWN THE BLACKENING WIND   745 19
    I TURN TOWARDS THE BITTER BLACKENING WIND   745 24
    YOU ARE EMPTY GOURD-SHELLS FILLED WITH DUST AND WIND   800 4
    WHEN THE BLUE WIND OF QUETZALCOATL   811 20
    THE WIND CHASES BY ME AND OVER THE CORN   857 17
    WEARILY THROUGH THE OAKS THE NIGHT WIND BLOWS   857 22
    AS THE WIND ASKS WHITHER THE DARK ROAD GOES   857 24
    AS THE WIND RACES SOUTH   861 2
    THE YOUNG GRASS TWINKLED IN THE WIND AND THE SOUND   866 24
    OF THE WIND HUNG ROUND THE KNOTTED BUDS LIKE A CANOPY   866 25
    SHAKES O'ER HIS WALLS WHEN THE WIND DISTURBS THE NIGHT   878 4
    THERE IS SOMETHING ABOUT THAT THEY CALL THE WIND   882 16
    LIFT AND RUFFLE IN THE WIND   883 3
    AND ITS BEAT OF PAIN IS DISTRIBUTED ON THE WIND   883 7
    AND WHEN BLACK LEAVES STREAM OUT IN A TRAIL DOWN THE WI+   883 12
    WIND TOOK   *891 28
    AND THE SOUL OF THE WIND AND MY BLOOD COMPARE   *892 4
    THEIR WANDERING HAPPINESS AND THE WIND WASTED IN LIBERT+ *892 5
    THE HUM AND WHISPER OF THE CLASS LIKE A LITTLE WIND   *894 15
    WHITE WHEN THE WIND SHIFTED HER HAIR THAT WAS SOFT AN' + *910 12

WIND
BECAUSE THEY WAS WARM AN' THE WIND BLEW   *910 18
WHITE FLOWERS IN THE WIND BOB UP AND DOWN   *912 26
THE LITTLE WHITE FEET NOD LIKE WHITE FLOWERS IN THE WIND   *913 29

WIND-BELL
YET THE BRONZE WIND-BELL SUDDENLY CLASHING   371 16

WIND-CHILLED
OVER THE CLODS OF THE AUTUMN WIND-CHILLED SUNSHINE   357 27

WIND-FLOWERS
SOMEWHERE THE WIND-FLOWERS FLING THEIR HEADS BACK   40 27
OR THERE IN THE WOODS OF THE TWILIGHT WITH NORTHERN WIN+   57 19

WINDING
WINDING ABOUT THEIR DIMNESS THE MIST'S GREY CEREMENTS A+   102 30
ORPHEUS AND THE WINDING LEAF-CLOGGED SILENT LANES OF HE+   281 16
AN INDIAN WALKING WRAPT IN HIS WINDING SHEET   816 7

WINDING-SHEET
THE WINDING-SHEET OF YOUR SELF-LESS IDEAL LOVE   291 12

WINDLESS
IS HEARD IN THE WINDLESS WHISPER OF LEAVES   68 17
IS HEARD IN THE WINDLESS WHISPER OF LEAVES   *915 1

WINDOW
AT THE WINDOW SO BIG AND RED   37 6
OR A BEAT OF WINGS AT THE WINDOW THERE   37 11
WHAT LARGE DARK HANDS ARE THOSE AT THE WINDOW   42 1
CREEP UP THE WALL TO ME AND IN AT MY OPEN WINDOW   62 28
LEANS ALL ALONE ABOVE MY WINDOW ON NIGHT'S WINTRY BOWER   67 19
AND I SLEPT TILL DAWN AT THE WINDOW BLEW IN LIKE DUST   99 1
SWEEP PAST THE WINDOW AGAIN   100 4
THE LEAVES FLY OVER THE WINDOW AND UTTER A WORD AS THEY+   103 1
MEANING OR A MESSAGE OVER THE WINDOW GLASS   103 3
LIKE A PAINTED WINDOW THE BEST   112 1
THE SICK GRAPES ON THE CHAIR BY THE BED LIE PRONE AT TH+   112 16
THAT AT THE WINDOW ENDLESSLY   116 22
SUDDEN OUTSIDE THE HIGH WINDOW ONE CROW   147 21
THROUGH THE LOW WEST WINDOW A COLD LIGHT FLOWS   163 10
THE GREAT DARK GLITTERY WINDOW   193 21
WITH THE PALE DAWN SEETHING AT THE WINDOW   204 4
AT HOME WE LEANED IN THE BEDROOM WINDOW   206 27
SQUARE PICTURE-DUSK THE WINDOW OF DARK SKY   210 20
WHY HAVE YOU GONE TO THE WINDOW WHY DON'T YOU   210 22
SHE SPREADS THE BATH-CLOTH UNDERNEATH THE WINDOW   217 11
IN THE WINDOW FULL OF SUNLIGHT   217 23
YOU MUST COME TO THE WINDOW TO WATCH ME GO   235 24
IN THE WINDOW HIS BODY BLACK FUR AND THE SOUND OF   243 24
AT LAST HE SWERVED INTO THE WINDOW BAY   343 16
TRYING TO DRIVE HIM THROUGH THE WINDOW   344 2
AGAIN HE SWERVED INTO THE WINDOW BAY   344 3
SOMETHING SEEMED TO BLOW HIM BACK FROM THE WINDOW   344 11
WINDOW   344 21
WAS THE HORROR OF WHITE DAYLIGHT IN THE WINDOW   344 25
HASTILY I SHOOK HIM OUT OF THE WINDOW   347 9
IN THE DARK AGAINST A WINDOW   363 9
LIKE A BELLE AT HER WINDOW   384 21
LITTLE FACE COMES OUT AS FROM A WINDOW   393 31
WINDOW   630 2
BEHIND THE SUN LOOKING THROUGH HIM AS A WINDOW   786 6
OF THE STREET-LAMP THROUGH THE UNBLINDED WINDOW PANE   878 6
THE FLOWERS AGAINST YOUR WINDOW PANE   886 1
TO THE WINDOW AND THE WHITE PEAR-TREE   886 9
I HAVE OPENED THE WINDOW TO WARM MY HANDS ON THE SILL   *905 1
LIKE A PAINTED WINDOW THAT LAST SUFFERING   *927 21
LIKE A PAINTED WINDOW THE BEST   *928 21
AS AT THE WINDOW ENDLESSLY   *930 21
OH TEARS ON THE WINDOW PAIN   *932 19
SHE STANDS IN SILHOUETTE AGAINST THE WINDOW   *942 21
IN THE WINDOW FULL OF SUNLIGHT   *943 6

WINDOW-PANE
O TEARS ON THE WINDOW-PANE   119 10

WINDOWS
I HAVE OPENED THE WINDOWS TO WARM MY HANDS ON THE SILL   52 12
MY WINDOWS OF DISCOVERY AND SHRILL SIN   122 30
THE WINDOWS OF MY MIND   123 21
AT PEACE AND LOOK OUT OF THE WINDOWS   227 31
BECAUSE THOSE FACES WERE WINDOWS TO THE STRANGE HORIZON+   656 21
FROM THE LOW WEST WINDOWS THE COLD LIGHT FLOWS   857 10
SOON THE WESTERN WINDOWS OF THE SKY   857 13
YEA I WOULD SHUT MY EYES I WOULD CLOSE MY WINDOWS   875 26
MY WINDOWS OF DISCOVERY AND SHRILL SIN   *934 6
THE WINDOWS OF MY MIND   *934 27

WINDOW-SASH
ARE TAPPING AT THE WINDOW-SASH   149 26
THE WINDOW-SASH AS THE WEST WIND BLOWS   150 19

WINDOW-SHAFTS
TILL PETALS HEAPED BETWEEN THE WINDOW-SHAFTS   154 31

WINDS
THE CONFINES GAZING OUT BEYOND WHERE THE WINDS GO FREE   47 10
WITH SHELTER NOW AND WITH BLANDISHMENT SINCE THE WINDS +   75 14
I SEE MYSELF AS THE WINDS THAT HOVER   118 16
WHERE STRANGE WINDS BLOW   202 24
THE WINDS THAT TREAD   268 27
UNSETTLED SEAS AND WINDS   285 20
AND IT IS DAY THEN FROM THE FOUR QUARTERS THE FOUR WIND+   319 7
FOUR GREAT BEASTS THE FOUR NATURES THE FOUR WINDS THE F+   319 9
WITH CAVERNOUS NOSTRILS WHERE THE WINDS RUN HOT   325 30
AND THE MILLS OF GOD GRIND OTHERWISE WITH THE WINDS OF   441 12
WINDS OF HEAVEN FAN THE LEAVES OF THE TREE LIKE FLAMES +   615 4

WINDS
BUT WINDS OF HEAVEN ARE MILLS OF GOD TO THE FALLEN LEAV+   615 5
OF THE WINDS   615 11
THE BREATH OF LIFE AND THE SHARP WINDS OF CHANGE ARE TH+   615 16
FEEL THE WINDS OF CHANGE GRIND THEM DOWN   615 19
THE WINDS OF THE AFTERWARDS KISS US INTO BLOSSOM OF MAN+   677 19
THE BREATH OF LIFE IS IN THE SHARP WINDS OF CHANGE   698 1
OF WINDY AUTUMN WHEN THE WINDS ALL SWEEP   744 7
THERE THE WINDS ARE BORN   786 8
THE STARS AND THE EARTH AND THE SUN AND THE MOON AND TH+   792 17
THIS IS WHAT STARS AND SUN AND EARTH AND MOON AND WINDS+   793 3
IS LASHING HIS TAIL IN HIS SLEEP THE WINDS HOWL THE COL+   795 14
THE ROAD WINDS FOREVER AND WHICH OF US KNOWS   858 2
WISE WONDERFUL STRANDS OF WINDS THAT ARE LADEN WITH RARE   *933 22
AND STEER ACCORDING TO THE CURRENTS AND WINDS AND TIDES+   *953 10

WIND-SHADOW
LIKE A WIND-SHADOW RUNNING ON A POND SO SHE COULD STAND   65 6
LIKE A WIND-SHADOW WANDERING OVER THE WATER   *913 7
LIKE A WIND-SHADOW WANDERING OVER THE WATER   *914 7

WIND-SNATCHED
THROUGH WIND-SNATCHED HAIR   861 18

WINDSWEPT
THE HAWK HIS WINDSWEPT WAY IS WENDING   150 10

WIND'S
LOOSING HOLD IN THE WIND'S INSISTENT PUSH   160 8
IN THE WIND'S SAD SOUGH   252 19
AMID THE HIGH WIND'S ENTERPRISE   *899 30
AMID THE HIGH WIND'S ENTERPRISE   *903 9

WINDWARD
THE ROCKS WHERE RAVENS FLYING TO WINDWARD MELT AS A WEL+   57 15

WINDY
OF WINDY AUTUMN WHEN THE WINDS ALL SWEEP   744 7

WINE
LIKE WINE THAT IS STILL   96 33
IN THE TENDER WINE   148 2
OF DEATH-PRODUCING WINE TILL TREASURE   177 3
OUT OF THE HELL-QUEEN'S CUP THE HEAVEN'S PALE WINE   177 13
AND TAKE WITHIN THE WINE THE GOD'S GREAT OATH   177 17
SWEAR IN THE PALE WINE POURED FROM THE CUPS OF THE QUEEN   177 21
THE SKY WAS GREEN WINE HELD UP IN THE SUN   216 16
HIS EVENING IS A FLAME OF WINE   228 17
THE WINE IS WARM IN THE HEARTH   237 23
SOMETHING OF THE SAME FLAVOUR OF SYRACUSAN MUSCAT WINE   280 9
AND IF WE SIP THE WINE WE FIND DREAMS COMING UPON US   286 22
AS WE SIP THE WINE   286 31
DUSKY ARE THE AVENUES OF WINE   287 5
DOWN THE TENDRILLED AVENUES OF WINE AND THE OTHERWORLD   287 10
AND FULL OF WINE   498 23
AND FURNISH IT WITH FOOD WITH LITTLE CAKES AND WINE   718 10
AND SERVE THE BEST OF FOOD THE FONDEST WINE   723 11
FOR THE SUN IS POURING LIKE YELLOW WINE OUTSIDE   *894 24
THE MIST IS A CUP OF WINE AND THE NEW AND OLD   *894 25
AND DEEP IN THE GOLDEN WINE OF THEIR CHALICES   *941 19

WINE-CUPS
SHALLOW WINE-CUPS ON SHORT BULGING STEMS   283 6

WINE-CUP
THE TIME IS NOW THE WINE-CUP FULL AND FULL   177 9

WINE-FILLED
AND DEEP IN THE GLOWING WINE-FILLED CHALICES   868 19

WINE-GLASS
FROM THAT SHALLOW-SILVERY WINE-GLASS ON A SHORT STEM   279 11
AND PUT A PLATE AND PUT A WINE-GLASS OUT   723 10

WINE-JAR
THAT SHE WAS AS THE WINE-JAR WHENCE WE DREW   *941 11

WINES
COMMINGLED WINES   97 3

WINE-SAP
I WANT THE FINE KINDLING WINE-SAP OF SPRING   271 17

WINESKIN
AS IF IT WOULD BURST ITS WINESKIN IN MY THROAT   *934 22

WINESKINS
WINESKINS OF BROWN MORBIDITY   280 16

WINE-SKIN
AS IF IT WOULD BURST ITS WINE-SKIN IN MY THROAT   123 16

WING
LIKE A BIRD FROM THE FAR NORTH BLOWN WITH A BROKEN WING   47 15
DROPPING TAKE WING   322 15
AND WE MUST TAKE THEM ON THE WING AND LET THEM GO   476 15
YOU ARE OFF YOU ARE ON THE WING WHITHER WHITHER   784 2
WITH THE BRIGHT WING ON THE RIGHT   787 18
AND THE WING OF THE DARK ON THE LEFT   787 19
I BRUSH THE WING OF THE DAY   787 23
THE OTHER WING BRUSHES THE DARK   787 25

WING-BEAT
PAST HIM ONLY A WING-BEAT PROVING   150 2

WING-BEATS
    CUP FOR A MOMENT SOFT LITTLE WING-BEATS UTTERING   65   4

WINGED
    IF ONLY I AM SENSITIVE SUBTLE OH DELICATE A WINGED GIFT   250   16
    EVEN THE WINGED SKELETON OF YOUR BLEACHED IDEAL   290   26
    BUT WINGED   323   21
    OR A WINGED THOUGHT   323   28
    WOULD A WINGLESS LION LIE DOWN BEFORE THEE AS THIS WING+   324   2
    YOU WINGED BLOOD-DROP   334   11
    AND SOON THE OWL WINGED WITH STILLNESS WILL FLOAT OUT T+   858   16

WINGED VICTORY
    I HEARD A WOMAN CALL YOU THE WINGED VICTORY   332   9
    WINGED VICTORY   332   28
    WINGED VICTORY   334   14

WINGING
    GO WINGING GLAD THE YELLOW MOTES   868   24

WINGLESS
    WOULD A WINGLESS LION LIE DOWN BEFORE THEE AS THIS WING+   324   2
    AND FALLS WINGLESS BLOOD STREAMING THROUGH ITS YELLOW H+   855   25

WINGS
    WINGS AND FEATHERS ON THE CRYING MYSTERIOUS AGES PEEWIT+   34   26
    UNDER THE GLISTENING CHERRIES WITH FOLDED WINGS   36   23
    OR A BEAT OF WINGS AT THE WINDOW THERE   37   11
    SUCH AS LIES ALONG THE FOLDED WINGS   46   11
    HAS OPENED THE WINGS OF THE WILD YOUNG SPRITE   46   14
    THE HUM OF HIS HEAVY STAGGERING WINGS   46   18
    AS THE WINGS OF A DRENCHED DROWNED BEE   74   5
    SOUNDS WAVE THEIR LITTLE WINGS   109   14
    CLUCK AND THE RAIN-WET WINGS   119   16
    HER WINGS IN US   124   9
    WITH HER WINGS AND HER FEATHERS TO DROWN   125   5
    A HAWK IS IN THE SKY HIS WINGS   149   27
    AND FEAR IS A PLASH OF WINGS   150   21
    A CROW FLOATS PAST ON LEVEL WINGS   166   1
    WINGS FULL OF STARS THEY RULE THE NIGHT AND MAN THAT WA+   319   3
    AND I TAKE THE WINGS OF THE MORNING TO THEE CRUCIFIED   321   20
    AND AT EVENING I MUST LEAVE OFF MY WINGS OF THE SPIRIT   321   27
    MEMBRANED BLOOD-VEINED WINGS   322   16
    MORNING COMES AND I SHAKE THE DEWS OF NIGHT FROM THE WI+ 322   26
    THAN THE WINGS OF THE MORNING AND THEE THOU GLORIFIED   323   4
    I HAVE MOUNTED UP ON THE WINGS OF THE MORNING AND I HAVE 323   11
    A LION WITH WINGS   323   22
    WHY SHOULD HE HAVE WINGS   323   25
    AND I WILL GIVE THEE THE WINGS OF THE MORNING   324   24
    SHALL GREAT WINGS FLAME FROM HIS SHOULDER SOCKETS   326   6
    IT WOULD BE NO WONDER IF GREAT WINGS LIKE FLAMES FANNED+ 326   12
    ON TWO WINGS LIKE A PAIR OF COMPASSES   329   7
    QUEER WITH YOUR THIN WINGS AND YOUR STREAMING LEGS   332   15
    GHOUL ON WINGS   332   27
    AND SERRATED WINGS AGAINST THE SKY   341   12
    WINGS LIKE BITS OF UMBRELLA   341   28
    EVEN WINGS HEAVY   345   22
    AND SHUT WINGS   345   31
    WINGS   346   21
    WINGS DARK SKINNY AND FLAPPING THE AIR   346   23
    WINGS AND MEN WHO SEE HIM WHEELING ARE FILLED WITH THE + 368   5
    DRUMMING HIS VAULTED WINGS AS SAVAGES DRUM   371   4
    DOES HE FAN GREAT WINGS ABOVE THE PRAIRIE LIKE A HOVERI+ 374   16
    AND A BLACK CRUCIFIX LIKE A DEAD TREE SPREADING WINGS   403   24
    MAYBE A BLACK EAGLE WITH ITS WINGS OUT   403   25
    OF THE EAGLE'S WINGS   403   29
    OPENING GREAT WINGS IN THE FACE OF THE SHEEP-FACED EWE   414   25
    COME WITH A HISS OF WINGS   436   23
    WINGS   438   10
    WILL THERE BE A WHISTLE OF WINGS IN THE AIR AND AN ICY   439   6
    THEN DOUBLED AND BACK WITH A FUNNY UP-FLUTTER OF WINGS   444   21
    AND LOOK ROUND AND RISE AND ON THE GREAT VAULTS OF HIS + 625   3
    LIFTING YOUR VEINED WINGS LIFTING THEM BIG WHITE BUTTER+ 696   14
    WILL YOU CLIMB ON YOUR BIG SOFT WINGS BLACK-DOTTED   696   22
    WINGS   706   18
    AND BEATING THEIR GREAT WINGS IN OUR PANTING FACES   707   7
    THE ONES WITH THE SHARP BLACK WINGS   707   9
    AND THE LITTLE SHIP WINGS HOME FALTERING AND LAPSING   720   14
    AND HE WINGS HIS HEAVY THIGH   733   15
    FLAP WHITE WINGS AND YELLOW PINIONS   783   26
    YOU WILL NEVER FLY ON YELLOW KINDLED WINGS   784   23
    AS A BIRD THAT LIFTS ITS WINGS AND STANDS   787   17
    SEE ME THROUGH THE FLASHING OF WINGS   787   29
    THEY SEE ONLY THE WAVING OF WINGS   788   2
    BETWEEN THE WINGS OF THE ENDLESS FLIGHT   788   16
    HE SENDS THE EAGLE OF SILENCE DOWN ON WIDE WINGS   799   17
    AND FILL THEM STRONG WITH STRENGTH OF WINGS   799   19
    ALL OVER THE SKY THEIR WINGS ARE TOSSED   823   3
    TORN WINGS OF FLAME ARE WAFTING DOWN THE SKY   855   21
    SLOWLY THE WINGS OF DAY ARE EDDYING LOWER   855   27
    SICKEN US AND WE ARE STUNNED BY THE RUSHINGS OF THE LAB+ 856   2
    HE CAME LIKE A SEA-GULL SINKING WITH UPLIFTED WINGS DOW+ 860   2
    I BEAT MY WINGS TOWARD IT NEVER   876   29
    OR WHETHER I WAS THE DARKNESS WITH ARCHED WINGS   882   1
    FOR A MOMENT THEN AWAY WITH A FLUTTER OF WINGS   *913   5
    AS THE WINGS OF A DRENCHED DROWNED BEE   *913   26
    FOR A MOMENT THEN AWAY WITH A FLUTTER OF WINGS   *914   5
    CLUCK AND THE RAIN-WET WINGS   *932   25
    HER WINGS AS WE WERE WEARY TO RECEIVE HER   *935   9
    ON MY BREAST WITH HER WINGS AND HER FEATHERS TO DROWN   *936   7

WING-TIPS
    BUT ALSO THE SUNDERERS THE ANGELS WITH BLACK SHARP WING+   706   23

WINK
    UP JUST A WINK   434   29
    BREASTS THAT WINK NOT   827   21

WINKED
    DID YOU SEE THE WICKED SUN THAT WINKED   120   9

WINKING
    A SOULLESS NECKAR WITH WINKING SEAS IN HIS EYES   130   19

WINNING
    HAIL AND BE DAMNED TO THEE WINNING THE GAME   824   17
    THE FULL THROATED WOMAN HAS CHOSEN A WINNING LIVING SONG *940   9

WINNOWED
    NOW WINNOWED SOFT   269   7

WINROW
    WINROW AFTER WINROW FALLS UNDER THIS FIRST STROKE OF NI+   858   10

WINS
    AND SEE WHO WINS IN THIS SLY GAME OF BLUFF   333   8
    THE WIDE SEA WINS AND THE DARK   455   25

WINSOME
    IS WINSOME AS A ROBIN'S SONG SO FLUTTERING   65   2
    STILL WINSOME SLEEP SO STILL AND SO COMPOSED   101   11
    AND WINSOME CHILD OF INNOCENCE NOR   230   26
    WINSOME   812   8
    I KNOW I KNOW YOU ARE WINSOME SO BUT YOU CHEAT   872   25
    THA KNOWS 'E 'D A WINSOME WAY WI 'IM AN' SHE   *910   24
    IS LIKE A LITTLE LINNET SONG WINSOME   *913   2
    IS LIKE A LITTLE ROBIN'S SONG WINSOME   *914   3

WINTER
    SCHOOL NOW IS THE ROCK IN THIS WEARY LAND THE WINTER BU+   75   18
    NOW I AM BROKEN DOWN LIKE A PLANT IN WINTER AND ALL   94   2
    TO THE OLD SUNDAY EVENINGS AT HOME WITH WINTER OUTSIDE   148   12
    THEY ARE THE ISSUE OF ACRID WINTER THESE FIRST-FLOWER Y+ 270   15
    WE WHO ARE WINTER-WEARY IN THE WINTER OF THE WORLD   272   34
    HAVE YOU NOT SEEN IN THE WILD WINTER SUN OF THE SOUTHER+ 303   4
    THE SUN IN ME DECLINES TO HIS WINTER SOLSTICE   455   17
    WINTER AND THE GREAT DAY-SUN AND THE SUN IN MY SOUL   455   26
    SINKS SINKS TO SETTING AND THE WINTER SOLSTICE   455   27
    NOW THAT THE WINTER OF OUR DISCONTENT   569   7
    TILL NOT A VESTIGE IS LEFT AND BLACK WINTER HAS NO TRACE 709   20
    YOU FLUTTER IN A HOST OF FLAMES LIKE WINTER STARLINGS R+ 784   1
    LIKE A MUD FROM WINTER DISGUISED IN GREY   815   8
    ARE GATHERING TO A WEDDING IN THE WINTER DARK   *955   21

WINTER-CELL
    BREAKS FROM THE WINTER-CELL TO CLAMBER   46   7

WINTER-GREEN
    OUT OF THE DEEP SOFT FLEDGE OF SICILIAN WINTER-GREEN   300   22

WINTER-PRESSED
    OF EARTH WINTER-PRESSED STRANGLED IN CORRUPTION   270   19

WINTER-ROTTEN
    WINTER-ROTTEN AND FALLEN   273   34

WINTER'S
    IMPLACABLE WINTER'S LONG CROSS-QUESTIONING BRUNT   142   4
    TO WOLFRATSHAUSEN LAST WINTER'S END COMES THROUGH   732   10
    OUT OF THE WINTER'S SILKY FUR   814   13

WINTER-WEARY
    WE WHO ARE WINTER-WEARY IN THE WINTER OF THE WORLD   272   34

WINTRY
    LEANS ALL ALONE ABOVE MY WINDOW ON NIGHT'S WINTRY BOWER   67   19
    THE HOPELESS WINTRY TWILIGHT FADES   142   21
    AND BRANDISHING AND STOOPING OVER EARTH'S WINTRY FLEDGE 301   15
    SETTING FIERCE AND UNDAUNTED WINTRY   455   22
    AS IN A WINTRY TREE   504   19
    ODD WINTRY FLOWERS UPON THE WITHERED STEM YET NEW STRAN+ 727   24

WIPE
    DO THEY WIPE AWAY THE GLOOM THE GULF THROWS UP   90   24
    TO WIPE AWAY THE MYSTIC BARRIERS OF SEX   636   19

WIPED
    WIPED OUT   533   13
    ALL WIPED OUT   533   16
    AND THE TCHEKOV WIMBLY-WAMBLY WET-LEGS ALL WIPED OUT   533   17
    IT CAN NEVER BE WIPED OUT   636   28
    WITH HIS BROW WIPED BRIGHT OF THE TOIL OF SWEAT   770   18
    AND HIS MOUTH WIPED CLEAN OF THE BITTERNESS OF REPROACH 770   19

WIPES
    SHOULDER-DEEP OUT OF THE CORN AND WIPES   220   3
    HIS HELMET OFF AND WIPES HIS HAIR TRYING   733   21
    SHOULDER-DEEP OUT O' TH' CORN AND WIPES   *944   11
    THEN HE TURNS AWAY AND WIPES HER FROM HIS CONSCIOUSNESS *948   16

WIPING
    A SILVER WIND IS HASTILY WIPING   150   15

WIRE
    TO BE CHOKED BACK THE WIRE RING   43   9
    I KNOW NOT WHAT FINE WIRE IS ROUND MY THROAT   43   29
    AT A WIRE AT A BELL-ROPE   343   22
    HIS BODY THAT DOES SHAKE LIKE THE WIRE OF A HARP   877   13

WIRELESS
  LISTEN LISTEN LISTEN CORPSE-BODY TO THE WIRELESS   584 15
  JAZZ AND FILM AND WIRELESS   716 11

WIRES
  SO IF ANY OF YOU'S LIVE WIRES WITH WITS   553 19
  NOR CUT THE INVISIBLE WIRES OF STEEL THAT PULL THEM   586 6
  NOR CUT THE INVISIBLE WIRES OF STEEL THAT PULL THEM   632 21

WISDOM
  THE WARM DUMB WISDOM   38 19
  SETS QUIVERING WITH WISDOM THE COMMON THINGS   46 19
  WISDOM   119 30
  WHAT A LOVELY HASTE FOR WISDOM IS IN MEN   119 31
  OF THE WATERS WITHIN HIM ONLY THE WORLD'S OLD WISDOM   130 15
  WERE OPEN TO ME IN THE WISDOM AND GOODNESS OF MAN   264 5
  THE ALL-WISE HAS TIRED US OF WISDOM   439 28
  OF PUTRESCENT WISDOM AND SAPIENCE THAT SUBTLY STINKS   441 1
  CARRY THE SALT OF THE EARTH THE WISDOM OF WISE MEN   495 3
  TO GET A REFRESHING DRINK OUT OF OLD WISDOM   495 13
  THE DIRTY DOGS OF WISDOM   762 21
  THE WISDOM OF AGES DROOPS IT IS FOLLY   814 22
  THE WISDOM OF AGES DROOPS AIN'T IT JOLLY   814 25
  THIS WARM DUMB WISDOM   *893 2
  SWEET WISDOM OF GRACE NOW WHO WILL FREE   *927 24
  WITH A QUIVERING SWEET WISDOM OF GRACE BUT NOW   *928 24

WISE
  THE WISE OLD TREES   54 24
  AND COILING IT ROUND THE WISE BROWS OF A MAID   178 21
  WISE GOOD PROVISION THAT MAKES THE HEART SWELL WITH LOVE 264 7
  WISE TORTOISE LAID HIS EARTHY PART AROUND HIM HE CAST I+ 348 13
  CARRY THE SALT OF THE EARTH THE WISDOM OF WISE MEN   495 3
  IT IS A FORM OF WAR EVEN SELF-ASSERTION AND BEING WISE + 495 21
  LET PEOPLE BE WISE FOR THEMSELVES AND ANYHOW   495 23
  NOBODY CAN BE WISE EXCEPT ON RARE OCCASIONS LIKE GETTING 495 24
  IT'S BAD TASTE TO BE WISE ALL THE TIME LIKE BEING A PER+ 496 1
  I AM MORE ALIVE MORE AWARE AND MORE WISE   655 24
  FOR A MOMENT HE WAS THE CENTAUR THE WISE YET HORSE-HOOF+ 672 28
  A NAKED NIGHTLY THING TOO FRAIL AND WISE FOR THE STRESS 771 23
  THE SOFT GULF BE WISE   818 4
  HE IS WISE IS HE   818 17
  NOR A WISE MAN KNOWING ALL THINGS   840 18
  FOR YOU ARE WISE   *894 18
  WISE WONDERFUL STRANDS OF WINDS THAT ARE LADEN WITH RARE *938 22

WISEST
  OLDEST THEY ARE AND THE WISEST OF BEASTS   465 23

WISH
  I WISH I DID IT MORE WILLINGLY   41 14
  I WISH YOU DID NOT WAIT MY DEAR   41 15
  I WISH I WAS ONLY A BUST   41 18
  I WISH THE CHURCH HAD COVERED ME UP WITH THE REST   48 24
  AND I WISH THAT THE BABY WOULD TACK ACROSS HERE TO ME   65 5
  I WISH THA HADNA DONE IT TIM   82 21
  I WISH I COULD WESH 'ER OFF'N THEE   82 25
  AN' 'DEED AN' I WISH AS THIS TALE O' THINE WOR NIVER MY+ 83 10
  DEED AN' I WISH I C'D 'A' STOOD AT TH' ALTAR WI' THEE A+ 83 11
  I WISH I COULD PUT YOU AWAY FROM ME   116 29
  I WISH A WILD SEA-FELLOW WOULD COME DOWN THE GLITTERING 130 17
  AND WISH I COULD GO ALSO   134 2
  I WISH THAT I COULD GO   134 4
  I WISH THE ELDER-TREES IN FLOWER COULD SUDDENLY HEAVE A+ 159 23
  AND WISH I COULD PASS IMPREGNATE INTO THE PLACE   173 14
  I WISH I COULD TAKE IT ALL IN A LAST EMBRACE   173 15
  I WISH WITH MY BREAST I HERE COULD ANNIHILATE IT ALL   173 16
  YOU ARE THE WISH AND I THE FULFILMENT   203 23
  NO NOW I WISH THE SUNSHINE WOULD STOP   205 1
  I WISH THAT WHATEVER PROPS UP THE WALLS OF LIGHT   205 9
  I WISH IT WOULD BE COMPLETELY DARK EVERYWHERE   205 20
  AND OH I WISH IT WAS BETTER   208 22
  YOU WOULD DRAW YOUR MIRROR TOWARDS YOU YOU WOULD WISH   251 14
  I WISH I COULD GRIP YOU LIKE THE FIST OF THE LORD   255 14
  I WISH IT WERE SPRING IN THE WORLD   270 29
  I WISH IT WERE SPRING   271 30
  I WISH THAT SPRING   272 1
  I WISH IT WERE SPRING THUNDERING   272 4
  I WISH THESE BRITTLE FROST-LOVELY FLOWERS OF PASSIONATE+ 272 6
  OH AND I WISH THE HIGH AND SUPER-GOTHIC HEAVENS WOULD   287 22
  I WISH YOU WOULD   290 7
  I WISH THEY HAD GIVEN THE THREE FEATHERS TO ME   392 1
  I WISH YOU'D SHOW YOUR HAND   430 14
  I WISH I WAS A GENTLEMAN   434 14
  WHEN I WISH I WAS RICH THEN I KNOW I AM ILL   498 5
  I WISH MEN WOULD GET BACK THEIR BALANCE AMONG THE ELEME+ 503 17
  I WISH THEY'D BE TRUE TO THEIR OWN VARIATION AS WATER IS 505 20
  I WISH I KNEW A WOMAN   506 11
  I WISH PEOPLE WHEN YOU SIT NEAR THEM   506 20
  THEN I WISH LIKE TIBERIUS THE MULTITUDE HAD ONLY ONE HE+ 526 21
  SO I WISH NO MAN TO PICK MY POCKET   607 13
  AND WISH US TO BE THIS THAT AND THE OTHER   691 13
  OH AND I WISH THAT I   746 19
  I WISH I COULD HAVE SOME TOO   751 5
  SWIFTLY I WISH I MIGHT KISS HER FINGERS BUT FULL   752 11
  I WISH I HAD FINS AND GILLS   837 15
  I WISH I KNEW WHERE THIS PALE ROAD GOES   857 12
  I WISH TO DROWN MYSELF   877 2
  I WISH THAT I MIGHT DIP MYSELF WITHIN   879 8
  I WISH THA HADNA DONE IT TIM   *924 25
  I WISH THA COULD WESH 'ER OFF'N THEE   *925 1
  BUT 'DEED AN' I WISH AS THIS TALE O' THINE WOR NIVER MY+ *925 14
  DEED AN' I WISH AS I COULD STOOD AT THE ALTAR WI' THEE + *925 15

WISHED
  'TWAS NOT THAT I WISHED IT   241 21
  AND I WISHED HE WOULD COME BACK MY SNAKE   351 23
  IT IS A CONSUMMATION DEVOUTLY TO BE WISHED   511 4
  DONA CARLOTA WISHED HE WOULD   797 14

WISHES
  ASKS TO BE HIDDEN AND WISHES NOTHING TO TELL   64 13
  WHICH WISHES TO BLASPHEME THE WORLD INTO GREYNESS   713 7

WISHFUL
  IN A WISHFUL DREAM OF LORNA DOONE   *905 4

WISHY-WASHY
  WATERY-HEARTED WITH WISHY-WASHY KNEES   795 6

WISP
  WITH A PALE LITTLE WISP OF A PRINCE OF WALES DIFFIDENT + 387 21
  THE WISP OF MODERN BLACK MANTILLA   617 21

WISPS
  ON HIS BROW WHERE THE CURVED WISPS CLOT AND TWINE   60 3

WISPY
  WHILE THE WISPY MODERN CHILDREN HALF-AFRAID   426 20

WIST
  THE LUMINOUS MIST WHICH THE POOR THINGS WIST WAS DAWN   71 5
  THE LUMINOUS MIST WHICH THE POOR THINGS WIST WAS DAWN A+ *917 23

WISTFUL
  WHITE AND GAUNT WITH WISTFUL EYES THAT HOVER   47 11
  IN A WISTFUL DREAM OF LORNA DOONE   52 15
  WISTFUL AND CANDID WATCHING ME WISTFULLY FROM HER DISTA+ 67 14
  THOUGH HE IS ALL WISTFUL AND PATHETIC LIKE A MONOLITH   255 35
  NO WISTFUL BELLIES   335 19
  WOMEN DON'T WANT WISTFUL   457 13
  SAID THE LOVELY YOUNG LADY HALF WISTFUL HALF MENACING   604 7
  SONS OF MEN FROM THE WOMBS OF WISTFUL WOMEN   642 16
  TERRIBLE AND STRANGE THE GOD LIES ON THE BED WISTFUL CO+ 676 9
  AND WHO NOW DRAWS SLOWLY AWAY COLD THE WISTFUL GODDESS + 676 18
  THIS IS NO WISTFUL ALLURE   *907 6
  OH I TORE THEM UP THOUGH THE WISTFUL LEAVES WERE FRAGRA+ *926 15

WISTFULLY
  DRIFTS MY BOAT WISTFULLY LAPSING AFTER   53 18
  WISTFUL AND CANDID WATCHING ME WISTFULLY FROM HER DISTA+ 67 14
  AND BLACK-SCARVED FACES OF WOMEN FOLK WISTFULLY   393 18
  SO SHE WISTFULLY SENSITIVELY SNIFFS THE AIR AND THEN TU+ 393 25
  WISTFULLY WATCHING WITH WONDERFUL LIQUID EYES   394 20
  DRIFTS MY BOAT WISTFULLY LAPSING AFTER   *906 9

WISTFULNESS
  THERE LIES THE WORLD MY DARLING FULL OF WONDER AND WIST+ 52 20
  STILL SHE WATCHES WITH ETERNAL COCKED WISTFULNESS   394 5
  SHE WATCHES WITH INSATIABLE WISTFULNESS   394 10
  OUT OF EDEN WEARY WITH THE WISTFULNESS OF HER SILENT TO+ 864 24
  THERE LIES THE WORLD MY DARLING FULL OF WONDER AND WIST+ *905 9

WIT
  YOU MUST FUSE MIND AND WIT WITH ALL THE SENSES   653 9

WITCH
  WITCH TEETH AN' 'ER BLACK HAWK-EYES AS I'VE   77 23
  THIS MUTABLE WITCH   124 13
  AN OBSTINATE OLD WITCH ALMOST JERKING THE ROPE FROM MY 385 9
  WITCH TEETH AN' 'ER BLACK HAWK-EYES AS I'VE   *919 11
  THIS MUTABLE WITCH   *935 12

WITCHCRAFT
  WHISPERING WITCHCRAFT   311 25
  WHAT EVEN THE WILD WITCHCRAFT OF THE PAST WAS SEEKING   481 9

WITHAL
  ONE OF YOU KINDLE A FIRE TO CONSUME THEM WITHAL   750 24

WITHDRAW
  FOR A DAY FOR TWO DAYS AND WITHDRAW SLOWLY VANISH AGAIN 476 14
  WITHDRAW WITHDRAW YOUR FLOW   639 12
  TO WITHDRAW HIS WARMTH FROM YOUR FEET SO YOUR FEET TURN+ 797 3

WITHDRAWING
  A SORT OF HORROR A SORT OF PROTEST AGAINST HIS WITHDRAW+ 351 4
  THEN GRIEF AND PAIN GO TOO WITHDRAWING   509 3

WITHDRAWN
  AS IF WITHDRAWN FROM LIVING WOUNDS RAN RED   884 26

WITHDRAWS
  AND WITHDRAWS ITSELF AND RECOGNISES A FLOWER OR THE   640 3

WITHER
  I DO NOT WANT A WOMAN WHOM AGE CANNOT WITHER   478 27
  AND WITHER THEY ARE GOING I HAVE BEEN   744 2
  TO WITHER ON THE BOSOM OF THE MERCIFUL SO MANY SEEDS TH+ *926 27

WITHERED
  UNBLOWN AND UNBLOSSOMED HAS WITHERED AWAY   117 19
  OF AUTUMN TELL THE WITHERED TALE AGAIN   119 14
  SINCE ALL THE SKY HAS WITHERED AND GONE COLD   135 16
  AND LIGHTS ON A WITHERED OAK-TREE'S TOP OF WOE   147 23
  OF THE WITHERED TREE IN THE GRAIL   147 25
  AND MY HAND WITHERED IN YOUR HAND   206 22
  IN LOVE WITH A SELF THAT NOW IS SHALLOW AND WITHERED   478 23
  ODD WINTRY FLOWERS UPON THE WITHERED STEM YET NEW STRAN+ 727 24
  OH WITHERED CRACKLING TWIGS OF BRUSHWOOD PEOPLE   784 26
  STILL YEARNING BUT WITHERED AND NUMB   862 2
  OVER THE WITHERED MOSSES AND RED EARTH   880 20

WITHERED
  WITHERED MY INSOLENT SOUL WOULD BE GONE LIKE FLOWERS TH+   *891 27
  WOULD HAVE WITHERED THROUGH THY FLESH   *927 22
  UNBLOWN AND UNBLOSSOMED HAS WITHERED AWAY   *931 23

WITHERING
  BEYOND THE WITHERING SNOW OF THE SHORN FIELDS   135 6
  OUT OF THE WITHERING DAFFODILS   178 18
  WE LOOK BACK ON THE WITHERING ROSES   242 28
  THIS MAY BE A WITHERING TREE THIS EUROPE   291 7
  TILL IT BURST FORTH BLINDING WITHERING THE EARTH   294 3
  IN MY BROOD-SOUL WITHERING   766 18
  THE WITHERING FLOWERS THAT DAYS AGO YOU BROUGHT ME   880 11
  BEYOND THE WITHERING SNOW OF THE SHORN FIELDS   *939 6

WITHERIN'
  T' SNOW IS WITHERIN' OFF'N TH' GRESS   137 18
  T' SNOW IS WITHERIN' OFF'N TH' GRESS   137 20

WITHHOLD
  YEA BUT I LOATHE YOU THAT YOU SHOULD WITHHOLD   122 23

WITHIES
  AGAIN I TELL YOU I BLEED I AM BOUND WITH WITHIES   131 11

WITHIN
  WITHIN THE HOUSE TWO VOICES AROSE A SLENDER LASH   36 13
  HER WOES HER LOVER WOOS AND SINGS WITHIN ANOTHER WOOD   65 26
  ALONE WITHIN THE DIM AND HOARSE SILENCE   76 21
  THE WORLD WITHIN WORLDS IS A WOMB WHENCE ISSUES ALL   88 33
  AND THE SAME FIRE THAT BOILS WITHIN THIS BALL   89 1
  WORLD WITHIN WORLDS A WOMB THAT GIVES AND TAKES   89 8
  WITHIN THE WOMB NEW SHAPES AND THEN NEW MEN   89 11
  ALIVE WITHIN THE OOZY UNDER-MIRE   89 19
  WITHIN YOUR CUP   96 31
  BLUE SHADOW WITHIN ME A PRESENCE WHICH LIVES CONTAINED   115 7
  FERVOUR WITHIN THE POOL OF HER TWILIGHT   125 34
  WITHIN HER SPACIOUS SOUL TO FIND DELIGHT   125 35
  WITH JOY AT TRAVELLING TO PLANT ITSELF WITHIN   127 12
  OF THE WATERS WITHIN HIM ONLY THE WORLD'S OLD WISDOM   130 15
  THE DEAD MOON HEAPED WITHIN THE NEW MOON'S ARMS   132 2
  DO I NOT KNOW THE DARKNESS WITHIN THEM WHAT ARE THEY   133 14
  TO FALL LIKE A BREATH WITHIN THE BREATHING WIND   134 26
  SOMETIMES THE DARKNESS TRAPPED WITHIN A WHEEL   136 8
  THE SECRET OF THE MOON WITHIN YOUR EYES   156 21
  WITHIN THE RAGE WE SHALL NOT KNOW TILL IT BURST   160 19
  THE SPARK INTENSE WITHIN IT ALL WITHOUT   160 22
  WITHIN ITS QUICK COMMITTED TO HOLD AND WAIT   161 4
  AND TAKE WITHIN THE WINE THE GOD'S GREAT OATH   177 17
  WITHIN THE IMMENSE AND TOILSOME LIFE-TIME HEAVED   195 29
  WITHIN MY BODY CRY OUT TO THE DREAMING SOUL   195 32
  SO THEN THERE SHONE WITHIN THE JUNGLE DARKNESS   206 8
  IT BURNS WITHIN ME LIKE A DEEP OLD BURN   208 21
  FOR THE FUTURE HOW SURE THE FUTURE IS WITHIN ME   247 5
  WITHIN   273 8
  ROSY TENDER GLITTERING WITHIN THE FISSURE   273 26
  IT IS SO LOVELY DAWN-KALEIDOSCOPIC WITHIN THE CRACK   279 2
  STREAM WITHIN STREAM   280 8
  YOUR SINGLENESS WITHIN THE UNIVERSE   290 14
  WITHIN WHITE-HOT LAVA NEVER AT PEACE   294 2
  WITHIN THE TOMBS   297 23
  WITHIN THE FLESH-SCENT OF THIS WICKED TREE   299 13
  WITHIN IRON AND EARTH   307 3
  HELL ON EARTH AND DIS WITHIN THE DEPTHS   309 14
  OUTWARD AND VISIBLE INDICATION OF THE PLAN WITHIN   356 11
  THIS GRIM NECESSITY FROM WITHIN   363 5
  THE SWAN WITHIN VAST CHAOS WITHIN THE ELECTRON   435 28
  ON HIS SOUL THAT IS DARK OCEAN WITHIN HIM   453 22
  OF ETERNAL SALT RAGE ANGRY IS OLD OCEAN WITHIN A MAN   454 11
  OF THE WALLS WITHIN WHICH OUR LIVES ARE SPENT   462 12
  FROM WITHIN   501 24
  WITHIN THE GENITALS OF LIVING SPACE   513 18
  AND FURTHER THE SUN WITHIN THE ATOM   513 19
  WITHIN IT UPON IT   656 14
  WE KNOW NOTHING OF WITHIN US   666 26
  THE KNOWLEDGE IS WITHIN ME WITHOUT BEING A MATTER OF FA+   677 3
  ACH ACH NOW INDEED GOD IS BORN HE TWINKLES WITHIN   682 28
  I SEE HIM MORE LIKE THE RUBY A GLEAM FROM WITHIN   697 28
  IN THE SUSPENSION OF WHOLENESS IN THE MOMENT OF DIVISIO+   699 7
  AND NOTHING WILL STAY THE DEATH-FLOOD RISING WITHIN US   718 15
  WITHIN YOUR WALLS WITHIN YOUR VERY HEART   723 15
  UNKNOWN WITHIN YOUR BREAST AND YOUR DEADENED LOINS   723 18
  WITHIN THE SILENCE VOID OF ECHOES EVEN   738 8
  AND THEN WITHIN THE NIGHT WHERE NOTHING IS   738 21
  BUT ON THEY GO LIKE LEAVES WITHIN A WIND   744 29
  IF YOU SEE MY RINGS HOW THEY SPARKLE WITHIN MY EARS   755 3
  OF THE HILLS AND THE HEARTS WITHIN US DITHER   757 16
  TIME BUT DIFFERENT DIRECTIONS IN CREATION WITHIN THE FO+   760 25
  I HAVE A DARKNESS INTACT WITHIN ME GLOWING SECURE   772 10
  WITHIN KEN   787 32
  HE SAT WITHIN THE HOLLOW OF A CLOUD AND SAW THE MEN THA+   790 10
  MY FATHER IS DEEP WITHIN THE DEEPS WHENCE HE SENT ME FO+   799 16
  THE STAR OF THE BEYOND IS WITHIN YOU   800 17
  IF THE STAR SHONE WITHIN YOU   800 30
  WITHIN THE NOISELESS   811 12
  TO FOUNDER AT LAST WITHIN THE DREADFUL FLOOD   875 33
  I GO TO PLAY MY GAME OF LIFE WITHIN   876 9
  BUT THERE WITHIN THE BLUE-SKY RIMS THAT COPE   876 34
  WITHIN HIS EYES' SINCEREST PUPILS THERE   876 36
  AH THERE WITHIN THAT BLUE-COPED WELL AH THERE   877 1
  LINEN WITHIN MY OWN OLD FRAGRANT CHEST   877 31
  AND I CAN SEE THE PULSE WITHIN HIS THROAT   878 25
  I WISH THAT I MIGHT DIP MYSELF WITHIN   879 8
  WATCHING THY GREAT SOUL TUG WITHIN THE LEASH   879 16
  WHAT ARE WE BUT AS SEED RIPENED WITHIN   880 2
  THEN LOOKED AGAIN WITHIN HER EYES   881 3
  SO THAT WITHIN A PILLAR OF PURPLE SMOKE   881 11
  LIKE A GLITTERING OF SHADOWS WITHIN THE MORNING AIR   *895 6

WITHIN
  AS IT QUICKENS WITHIN THE LABOURING WHITE-HOT METAL   *909 26
  A DARKNESS WITHIN ME A PRESENCE WHICH SLEEPS CONTAINED   *930 7
  IN MY FLAME OF LIVING A SHADOW WITHIN THE SHINE   *930 8
  WITHIN THE SPACIOUS GLOOM OF MYSTERY   *936 34
  THE DEAD MOON HEAPED WITHIN THE YOUNG MOON'S ARMS   *937 29

WITHIN-WALLS
  ITS NAKEDNESS ALL WITHIN-WALLS ITS FLOWERING FOREVER UN+   283 15

WITHOUTEN
  DROP A LITTLE LOWER WITHOUTEN RESPITE   113 19
  HANG HIGH SUSPENDED WITHOUTEN RESPITE   *929 8

WITNESS
  THE WITNESS OF ALL THAT BITTER-SWEET   198 23

WITNESSES
  THEY WERE BUT WITNESSES   196 20
  FOR THE UNSEEN WITNESSES ARE THE ANGELS OF CREATION   706 22
  BEFORE THE EVERLASTING WITNESSES   779 28

WITS
  SO IF ANY OF YOU'S LIVE WIRES WITH WITS   553 19

WIVE
  I'LL WORK AND I'LL WIVE   857 8

WIVES
  COME BACK THEN YOU WHO WERE WIVES AND MOTHERS   411 18
  AS WIVES ARE OF WIVES   412 29
  GOOD HUSBANDS MAKE UNHAPPY WIVES   456 5
  WHEN YOU TURN TO YOUR WIVES AS BRAVE MEN TURN TO THEIR +   800 12

WIZENED
  MONKEYS RODE RATHER GREY AND WIZENED   444 15

WI'
  ON TH' YALLER CLAY WI' TH' WHITE FLOWERS TOP OF IT   60 13
  HE'S GONE WI' THAT   77 2
  WI' A BITTER DIRTY SKIN   77 14
  A GLUM OLD OTCHEL WI' LONG   77 22
  WI' A DRESS AS IS WANTED TO-DAY   78 4
  'ER AS 'E LODGES WI'   78 10
  THEY SAY HE'S GOT 'ER WI' CHILDT BUT THERE   78 11
  IT'S NOTHING TO DO WI' ME   78 12
  MY CONSTABLE WI' 'IS BUTTONED BREAST   79 5
  THA CAN STARE AT ME WI' THY FIERCE BLUE EYES   79 11
  AFTER KISSIN' AN' CUDDLIN' WI' ME THA COULD   80 18
  AN' YET YER'VE BIN CARRYIN' ON WI' 'IM   81 27
  AY AN' 'IM WI' ME   81 28
  THA'RT FOR DOIN' A LOT WI' T' LAD   82 8
  WI' A WOMAN AN' NAME 'ER A PRICE   82 10
  TER MARRY WI' CABS AN' RICE   82 12
  AN' COME IN 'ERE WI' ME   82 18
  THINE SHALL GO TER PAY THE WOMAN AN' WI' MY BIT WE'LL B+   83 2
  DEED AN' I WISH I CID 'A' STOOD AT TH' ALTAR WI' THEE A+   83 11
  WHAT BIT O' CUNT I HAD WI' 'ER   84 29
  AN' WI' 'ER SOMEHOW IT ISN'T RIGHT   85 3
  THA'S BIN SNOWED UP I' THIS COTTAGE WI' ME   137 25
  THA'S BIN SNOWED UP I' THIS COTTAGE WI' ME   137 27
  THA COME TER HA' FINISHED AN' DONE WI' ME   138 10
  AN' FRESH AN' MORE NICER FOR MARRYIN' WI'   138 12
  IT'S YOUR WIFE WI' HER AIRS AN' GRACES   493 20
  COME AN' BE STILL WI' ME MY OWN BIT OF A WENCH   540 10
  WI' LITTLE SOBS AS YOU SCARCE COULD HEAR   *910 14
  A TOUGH OLD OTCHEL WI' LONG   *919 10
  WI' A DRESS AS IS WANTED TODAY   *919 24
  HER AS HE LODGES WI'   *920 2
  THEY SAY HE'S GOT HER WI' CHILDT BUT THERE   *920 3
  IT'S NOTHING TO DO WI' ME   *920 4
  MY CONSTABLE WI' 'IS BUTTONED BREAST   *921 1
  THA CAN STARE AT ME WI' THY FIERCE BLUE EYES   *921 7
  AN' YET YOU'VE BEEN CARRYIN' ON WI' HIM   *923 27
  AY AN' 'IM WI' ME   *923 28
  THA'RT FOR DOIN' A LOT WI' TH' LAD   *924 12
  WI' A WOMAN AN' PAY 'ER A PRICE   *924 14
  TO MARRY WI' CABS AN' RICE   *924 16
  AN' COME WI' ME IN HERE   *924 22
  THINE SHALL GO TO PAY THE WOMAN AN' WI' MY BIT WE'LL BUY   *925 6
  DEED AN' I WISH AS I COULD STOOD AT THE ALTAR WI' THEE +   *925 15
  AN' THEN WI' THAT TWENTY POUND WE GI'E 'ER I S'D THINK +   *925 20
  FROM WHAT I'VE ARRANGED WI' THEE EH MAN WHAT A STUBBORN+   *925 26

WOBBLE
  AND THE MACHINE BEGINS TO WOBBLE   676 2

WOE
  IN THE FLOWER'S THROAT AND THE FLOWER GAPED WIDE WITH W+   125 10
  WOE   132 7
  AND LIGHTS ON A WITHERED OAK-TREE'S TOP OF WOE   147 23
  AN INVISIBLE WOE UNSEALS   159 7
  MORE MARVEL THAN WOE   171 29
  AND WOE BETIDE   201 8
  IF YOU'RE DIRTY INSIDE YOU GO ROTTEN AND ONCE ROTTEN WOE   464 6
  WOE WOE TO THE WORLD   496 18
  AND WOE BETIDE YOU   563 25
  THE FIG-LEAF THAT WAS NOT WOE IS ME   578 6
  WHO KNOWS WHO KNOWS HOW MUCH OUR MODERN WOE   723 4
  IN THE FLOWER'S THROAT AND THE FLOWER GAPED WIDE WITH W+   *935 26
  ME LEST YOU MY SISTER SHOULD GO HEAPED WITH SUCH SHADOW+   *937 33

WOES
  HER WOES HER LOVER WOOS AND SINGS WITHIN ANOTHER WOOD   65 26
  FROM THE WOES I BEWAIL   133 30
  I CAN'T VERY MUCH CARE ABOUT THE WOES AND TRAGEDIES   508 16
  FROM HER SUBSEQUENT WOES   565 22

WOKE
AND I WOKE TO THE SOUND OF THE WOOD-PIGEON AND LAY AND +   38 12
YOU WOKE MY SPIRIT AND BORE ME   111 15
AND SHE WOKE TO DISTIL THE BERRIES   202 17
WHEN I WOKE THE LAKE-LIGHTS WERE QUIVERING ON THE WALL   243 21
AND I WOKE WONDERING WHO TOUCHED ME WITH SUCH FEAR AND +   860 10
THE STINGING NETTLES ON MY WRISTS WOKE ME   881 16
AND HIS CHILDREN STIRRED IN THEIR SLEEP AND WHEN THEY W+   885 12

WOKEN
FLUENT ACTIVE FIGURES OF MEN PASS ALONG THE RAILWAY AND+   *908 11

WOLDS
UP THE WOLDS THE WOODS WERE WALKING   152 14

WOLF
A RED WOLF STANDS ON THE SHADOW'S DARK RED RIM   403 20
THIN RED WOLF OF A PALE-FACE   405 3
THIN RED WOLF GO HOME   405 4
HAS THE RED WOLF TROTTED EAST AND EAST AND EAST   405 15
AND WOLF HE CALLS ME AND RED   405 21
I'M THE RED WOLF SAYS THE DARK OLD FATHER   405 31
OF WOLF ALL HAIRY AND LEVEL A WOLF'S WILD PELT   408 29

WOLFISH
FROM HEAVEN'S WOLFISH WANDERING ELECTRICITY THAT PROWLS   301 6

WOLF-PELT
ON TO THE FUR OF THE WOLF-PELT THAT STREWS THE PLAIN   409 20

WOLFRATSHAUSEN
TO WOLFRATSHAUSEN LAST WINTER'S END COMES THROUGH   732 10
MARIA OF THE GASTHAUS GREEN HAT WOLFRATSHAUSEN   734 33

WOLF'S
OF WOLF ALL HAIRY AND LEVEL A WOLF'S WILD PELT   408 29

WOLF-WRAPPED
ORIGINAL WOLF-WRAPPED   171 6

WOLVES
IN PELTS OF WOLVES ALL HER LUMINOUS   171 7
SHARPENING HIS TEETH ON THE WOLVES   324 29
AND ROARS TO ANNOUNCE HIMSELF TO THE WOLVES   325 20
AND TROD WOLVES UNDERFOOT   378 5
AS FOXES STOATS AND WOLVES AND PRAIRIE DOGS   392 21

WOMAN
WAS WOMAN ONCE TO YOU   56 2
SEE IN THE SKY BEFORE ME A WOMAN I DID NOT KNOW   67 10
TO A WOMAN THAT COARSE   77 32
TURN THY MOUTH ON A WOMAN LIKE THAT   80 19
WI' A WOMAN AN' NAME 'ER A PRICE   82 10
THINE SHALL GO TER PAY THE WOMAN AN' WI' MY BIT WE'LL B+   83 2
THAT I COULD 'A' BIN FIRST WOMAN TER THEE AS THA'RT FIR+   83 13
BUT 'ARK THEE 'ERE THAT WIDDER WOMAN   84 3
AND THE GULF THAT CAME BETWEEN YOU WOMAN AND ME MAN   91 3
ONE DAY A HEAVY-BREASTED JUNE HOT WOMAN   91 8
AND NEVER A BLOSSOMING WOMAN WILL ROAM   106 17
I WAS WATCHING THE WOMAN THAT BORE ME   111 1
THIS WOMAN WHO LIKES TO LOVE ME BUT SHE TURNS   113 10
THOUGH HER HANDS ARE STILL THE WOMAN HER LARGE STRONG   128 5
OUT OF 'IM INTO A WOMAN AS CAN   138 25
THA'D NEED A WOMAN DIFFERENT FROM ME   139 5
TILL A WOMAN HAS DRAWN THE LAST LAST DROP   139 11
THEIR BLOOD IN A WOMAN TO THE VERY LAST VEIN   139 17
AN' A WOMAN LIKE ME LOVES THEE FOR IT   139 20
BUT IT'S MY SORT O' WOMAN   140 2
SORT O' WOMAN FOR ANY LAD   140 5
A WOMAN CROUCHES   143 5
AND A HEAVY WOMAN SLEEPING STILL KEEPING   145 10
SOFTLY IN THE DUSK A WOMAN IS SINGING TO ME   148 4
A TALL WOMAN WITH HER LONG WHITE GOWN AFLOW   155 13
THE OTHER WOMAN ROSE AND SWIFTLY SAID   157 27
THE WOMAN YOU ARE SHOULD BE NIXIE THERE IS A POOL   161 13
THRESHING YOUR OWN PASSIONS WITH NO WOMAN FOR THE   197 4
A WOMAN BINDS HER HAIR   200 18
IS THAT IT WOMAN DOES IT STRIKE YOU SO   219 1
COME TO ME LIKE A WOMAN COMING HOME   231 1
AND SERVE NOW WOMAN SERVE AS A WOMAN SHOULD   234 29
WHERE NEVER WOMAN SAT   237 19
AND YET A WOMAN KNOWING   239 19
TO-NIGHT IS A WOMAN BORN   240 20
I WAS A LOVER I KISSED THE WOMAN I LOVED   257 18
A WOMAN HAS GIVEN ME STRENGTH AND AFFLUENCE   262 25
HAS NOT SO MUCH OF STRENGTH AS THE BODY OF ONE WOMAN   263 2
THE HUNGER FOR THE WOMAN ALAS   264 14
I THOUGHT IT WAS WOMAN INDISCRIMINATE WOMAN   264 21
A WOMAN FED THAT HUNGER IN ME AT LAST   264 26
WHAT MANY WOMEN CANNOT GIVE ONE WOMAN CAN   264 27
AND FOR THIS I HAVE TO THANK ONE WOMAN   265 21
BUT ONE WOMAN   265 23
WOMAN'S BUT THE APPLES OF LIFE THE DRAGON GUARDS AND NO+   277 8
FOLDED UPON ITSELF ENCLOSED LIKE ANY MOHAMMEDAN WOMAN   283 14
I HEARD A WOMAN CALL YOU THE WINGED VICTORY   332 9
HE DOES NOT EVEN TROUBLE TO ANSWER WOMAN WHAT HAVE   357 3
I HEARD A WOMAN PITYING HER PITYING THE MERE TORTUE   361 31
HE PESTERS HER AND TORMENTS HER SAID THE WOMAN   361 33
AND RUNNING AWAY FROM THE SOUND OF A WOMAN IN LABOUR   366 12
WOMAN GOING TO MASS   385 13
WOMAN   395 32
WHERE THE VIRGIN IN WOMAN COMES HOME TO A MAN   412 5
IS WOMAN   412 15
TO THE WOMAN RATHER OLDER THAN HIMSELF   433 11
THEY'LL TAKE YOU FOR A WOMAN OF THE PEOPLE   433 13
AND THE WOMAN SAID DEAR ME   433 17
SHELVING SUBSTANCE ON TO THE WOMAN MADONNA MIA   437 3
WHERE THERE IS WOMAN THERE IS SWAN   438 17

WOMAN
WOMAN WHERE GOT YOU THIS LITTLE BEAST   439 5
THEN MORE THAN THAT HE MAKES A WOMAN FEEL HE IS SERVING   447 22
AND A NAVAJO WOMAN WEAVING HER RUG IN THE PATTERN OF   448 22
EVEN IF IT IS A WOMAN MAKING AN APPLE DUMPLING OR A MAN   449 10
CONTENT IS THE WOMAN WITH FRESH LIFE RIPPLING IN TO HER   449 14
TOWARDS WOMAN OR MAN BIRD BEAST OR CREATURE OR THING   454 13
LO THERE IS WOMAN AND HER WAY IS A STRANGE WAY   461 11
THE MOMENT I SWEAR TO LOVE A WOMAN A CERTAIN WOMAN   472 16
THE MOMENT I EVEN SAY TO A WOMAN I LOVE YOU   472 19
THE JEALOUSY OF AN EGO-BOUND WOMAN   475 6
THE JEALOUSY OF AN EGO-BOUND WOMAN   475 9
GENTLE WOMAN GONE MAD   475 22
AND MAN AND WOMAN ARE LIKE THE EARTH THAT BRINGS FORTH   477 7
GO DOWN TO YOUR DEEP OLD HEART WOMAN AND LOSE SIGHT OF   477 24
WOMAN   478 21
I DO NOT WANT A WOMAN WHOM AGE CANNOT WITHER   478 27
ALL I ASK OF A WOMAN IS THAT SHE SHALL FEEL GENTLY TOWA+   479 1
THROUGH A WOMAN   485 12
YET YOU FAIL TO FIND THE WOMAN WHEN THERE ARE SO MANY   485 13
THAT NO WOMAN WILL EVER DESIRE YOU AS YOU ARE   485 17
IF YOU COPULATE WITH THE FINEST WOMAN ON EARTH   486 3
YET MY ROOTS ARE IN A WOMAN TOO   499 10
I WISH I KNEW A WOMAN   506 11
IF THERE'S A MAN HERE AND THERE OR A WOMAN   507 5
AND IF BY A MIRACLE A WOMAN HAPPENED TO COME ALONG   507 8
I'D REJOICE OVER THE WOMAN AND THE WARMED COCKLES OF MY   507 10
ANY WOMAN WHO SAYS TO ME   507 13
WITH SUN IN HIS FACE SO THAT A WOMAN CANNOT BUT OPEN   526 4
OR LIKE THE WOMAN WHO SAT DOWN ON A SLEEPING MASTODON   540 1
WHAT AILS THEE THEN WOMAN WHAT AILS THEE   540 12
THAT A WOMAN IS ALWAYS   563 1
IF YOU'RE A WOMAN   563 19
THAT A MAN OR A WOMAN IN A STATE OF GRACE   578 25
THE ONLY QUESTION TO ASK TODAY ABOUT MAN OR WOMAN   603 15
A MAN A WOMAN THERE   606 8
AND NO MAN KNOWS NO WOMAN KNOWS   607 5
THIS FOREIGN WOMAN OF THE WEALTHY NORTH   618 24
SHE WAS TANGLED UP IN HER OWN SELF-CONCEIT A WOMAN   619 1
WHEN A WOMAN CAN ONLY LOVE FLAMILY THOSE OF HER OWN SEX   619 19
AND THE AIR IS ALIVE AND CAN DENY US AS A WOMAN CAN   625 15
OR THAT HARD-BOILED YOUNG WOMAN BESIDE HIM   645 12
BUT A WOMAN SHY AND ALONE WAS WASHING HERSELF UNDER A T+   651 4
I TELL YOU IT IS NO WOMAN IT IS NO MAN FOR I AM ALONE   652 14
YOU HEAR A WOMAN SAY I LOVE MY HUSBAND DEARLY   654 10
YOU SIT TALKING IN ALL EARNESTNESS TO A WOMAN   655 1
AND WHAT'S THE GOOD OF A WOMAN   671 11
THE WOMAN WHO LOOKS FOR ME IN THE WORLD   672 23
POOR WOMAN POOR WOMAN   675 4
AND THE WOMAN WAS HERSELF NEVER TO BE DUPLICATED A GODD+   675 13
YET A WOMAN CAN ADD HER FLAME TO A MAN'S   680 3
WOMAN   691 19
AND A WOMAN WHO HAS BEEN WASHING CLOTHES IN THE POOL OF+   693 1
AND WHAT ARE YOU WOMAN PEERING THROUGH THE RENTS   742 15
NO WOMAN TAKES MY PART   751 20
THAN WOMAN OR TRIUMPH MONEY OR SUCCESS   764 3
THE WOMAN WEEPS HER CHANGE OF LIFE   766 7
WOMAN   770 28
AND HE SAW MEXICO LYING LIKE A DARK WOMAN WITH WHITE BR+   790 5
SKIN LET EVERY WOMAN   791 23
AND WOMAN IS THE STAR OF EVENING   800 15
SO THE STAR WILL GO OUT OF YOU EVEN AS A WOMAN WILL LEA+   800 19
A MAN CANNOT TREAD LIKE A WOMAN   812 17
NOR A WOMAN STEP OUT LIKE A MAN   812 18
BE WITH ME THERE MY WOMAN   813 1
AND LAUGH WITH ME WHILE THE WOMAN RESTS   813 7
EAT WOMAN EAT MORE   817 26
IS ONE FOOT IN THE LAP OF A WOMAN   819 7
AND THE OTHER IS THE HEART OF A WOMAN   820 9
THE MOMENT I SWEAR TO LOVE A WOMAN ALL MY LIFE THAT VER+   834 8
IN THE SAME WAY IF I SWORE TO HATE A WOMAN ALL MY LIFE +   834 10
THE ONLY THING FOR A MAN TO DO NOW OR A WOMAN   838 14
NOR IS HE A WOMAN WITH A BOSOM OF SORROW AND CONSOLATION   840 21
NOR EVEN A LOVELY WOMAN FOAMY TO STING ME LIKE BRINE   840 23
THE MODERN YOUNG WOMAN THINKS IT WONDERFUL TO BE SO BRI+   841 26
THOUGH THE YEAR IS RIPENING LIKE A WOMAN WHO HAS CONCEI+   854 8
A WOMAN CAME INTO THE GLOW FROM OUT OF THE SHADOWY LIGHT   865 4
THE WOMAN SPEAKS   876 22
SO MY SOUL LIKE A PASSIONATE WOMAN TURNS   *891 29
BLOOD OF A HEAVING WOMAN WHO HOLDS ME   *892 10
TO A WOMAN THAT COARSE   *919 20
TURN THY MOUTH ON A WOMAN LIKE HER   *922 19
WI' A WOMAN AN' PAY 'ER A PRICE   *924 14
THINE SHALL GO TO PAY THE WOMAN AN' WI' MY BIT WE'LL BUY   *925 6
THAT I COULD HA' BEEN FIRST WOMAN TO THEE AS THOU'RT FI+   *925 17
SOFTLY IN THE SHADOWS A WOMAN IS SINGING TO ME   *940 5
THE FULL THROATED WOMAN HAS CHOSEN A WINNING LIVING SONG   *940 9
A WOMAN IS SINGING ME A WILD HUNGARIAN AIR   *940 19
A WOMAN TAUNTS HER LOVER   *944 17
YOU'RE A FOOL WOMAN I LOVE YOU AND YOU KNOW I DO   *945 17
LEAVING ALL TO THE WOMAN MADONNA MIA POOR VIRGIN   *946 16
TILL HE'S GOT A WOMAN A BIT SOFT AND TRUSTFUL   *948 15
HE NEVER WANTS A WOMAN HE DOESN'T LIKE WOMEN   *948 23

WOMANHOOD
UNFOLDED WOMANHOOD   56 10
HER HAIR FOR WOMANHOOD AND PLAY AWHILE WITH HER THEN   179 8
HAVE YOU NO DEEP OLD HEART OF WILD WOMANHOOD   478 15

WOMANLESS
MAKES US PREFER TO BE WOMANLESS RATHER THAN BE WEPT OVER   439 30
WOMANLESS SHOUTING IN ANGER   759 3

WOMAN-LIKE
THE VIVIFIER EXISTS BUT FOR ME IS NEITHER MAN-LIKE NOR +   840 25

WOMANLY
   IN THE WOMANLY VALLEY, AND PLY   40 15

WOMAN'S
   SEE THE WOMAN'S TRINKLING FINGERS TEND HIM A COIN   36   6
   CURVE SWEEP TOWARDS A WOMAN'S   40   4
   AN' THESE IS THE WOMAN'S KIDS 'E'S SO FOND ON   81 15
   IF TER COULDNA BE MASTER AN' TH' WOMAN'S BOSS   139   4
   A WOMAN'S MAN THA ART MA LAD   140   1
   OF A WOMAN'S KNEES   145 29
   INTO THE WOMAN'S FERTILE FATHOMLESS LAP   172   7
   WOMAN'S BUT THE APPLES OF LIFE THE DRAGON GUARDS AND NO+   277   8
   AND A WOMAN'S   477 16
   AN' THESE IS THE WOMAN'S KIDS HE'S SO FOND ON   *923 15
   I SEE THE WOMAN'S SOUL STEAL IN HER EYES   *943 19

WOMB
   AS IF FROM THE WOMB THE SLOW MOON RISES AS IF THE TWIN+   88 18
   THE WORLD WITHIN WORLDS IS A WOMB WHENCE ISSUES ALL   88 33
   FLY LIKE A SPARK INTO THE WOMB OF PASSION   89   6
   WORLD WITHIN WORLDS A WOMB THAT GIVES AND TAKES   89   8
   WITHIN THE WOMB NEW SHAPES AND THEN NEW MEN   89 11
   INTO THE WOMB OF THE WORLDS THAT NOTHING KNOWS   89 31
   INTO THE WOMB TO KINDLE AN UNKNOWN FIRE   89 35
   ONCE FROM YOUR WOMB SWEET MOTHER   101 31
   MATE MY HUNGRY SOUL WITH A GERM OF ITS WOMB   179 27
   THE MERE FRUIT OF YOUR WOMB   235   4
   WHAT IS THE FRUIT OF YOUR WOMB THEN YOU MOTHER YOU QUEEN   235   5
   BRING FORTH THE SONS OF YOUR WOMB THEN AND PUT THEM   235   9
   FROM THE WOMB OF YOUR PRECIOUS DESIRE   235 12
   THIS FIREGLOW IS A RED WOMB   239 22
   FROM THE WOMB OF THE ALL I AM WAITING DAZED   262 20
   THAT LIES OUTSIDE THE MONSTROUS WOMB   262 23
   WHEN THEY BREAK AND SHOW THE SEED THEN WE LOOK INTO THE+   277   2
   NOW THERE IS A FRUIT LIKE A RIPE WOMB   282 28
   THE GUTS AND THE STONES AND THE WOMB ROTS THEM DOWN   463 21
   TILL HE WAS BORN FROM A WOMB AND ATE SOUP AND BREAD   689 28
   INTO THE WOMB OF REFRESHMENT   786 27
   AND THEY DART TO HER WOMB THEY FIGHT FOR THE CHANCE TO +   795 31
   AND LOSING MINGLE IN THE PROCREANT WOMB   876 20
   INTO THE PASSIVE UNKNOWN MONSTROUS WOMB   880   7
   TO STEAD HER WOMB AROUND US BEYOND THE SWOON   *938 15
   OR DEEPER LIKE THE FOLDINGS AND INVOLVINGS OF A WOMB   *959 21
   THE WOMB OF SILENCE IN THE LIVING NIGHT   *959 33

WOMB-ELEMENT
   WHO LIES WITH THE WATERS OF HIS SILENT PASSION WOMB-ELE+   335 28

WOMB-FIBRILLED
   THE FLOWERING ALL INWARD AND WOMB-FIBRILLED   282 23

WOMB-FIRE
   IS WOMB-FIRE IN THE STIFFENED CLAY OF US   89   3

WOMB-LIKE
   INTO THE SHELL-LIKE WOMB-LIKE CONVOLUTED SHADOW   *959 26

WOMBS
   SONS OF MEN FROM THE WOMBS OF WISTFUL WOMEN   642 16

WOMB'S
   SPURTING TO SOOTHE THE WOMB'S UNSLAKED DESIRE   89 21

WOMB-WARD
   THERE WAS A FLOWER THAT FLOWERED INWARD WOMB-WARD   282 27

WOMEN
   TALK ABOUT LOVE O' WOMEN   84 27
   PHANTOM TO PHANTOM LEANING STRANGE WOMEN WEEP   140 15
   SO LIKE TO WOMEN TALL STRANGE WOMEN WEEPING   140 19
   AND THE BODIES OF MEN AND WOMEN ARE MOLTEN MATTER OF DR+   176   2
   THE FACES OF ALL THE WOMEN AS THEY GO PAST   180   9
   AND SHE WITH HER WOMEN HOT AND HARD   228 19
   CHAMPION HER ALL YOU WOMEN MEN MENFOLK   223 27
   WOMEN ALL   228 30
   WOMEN ANOTHER CHAMPION   229   1
   AND BLACK-SCARVED FACES OF WOMEN FOLK WISTFULLY   232 22
   QUEENS LADIES ANGELS WOMEN RARE   234 25
   YOU WOMEN MOST HOLY YOU MOTHER YOU BEING BEYOND   235 13
   STONES WOMEN AND MEN   249 25
   YOU OTHER WOMEN   251   2
   IN THE SCALE YOU OTHER WOMEN   251   6
   YOU OTHER WOMEN   251 13
   YOU OTHER WOMEN   251 19
   YOU STRAGGLING WOMEN   251 21
   YOU OTHER WOMEN   251 25
   YOU OTHER WOMEN   252   8
   YOU OTHER WOMEN   252 12
   WHAT MANY WOMEN CANNOT GIVE ONE WOMAN CAN   264 27
   ESPECIALLY THE YOUNG WOMEN I LOOK AT THEM   269 22
   WHAT IS IT THAT FROM THE FACES OF THE FAIR YOUNG WOMEN   270 12
   WOMEN   270 16
   WOMEN   278   5
   THAT'S HOW WOMEN DIE TOO   283 34
   THE YEAR OF OUR WOMEN   284   2
   THE YEAR OF OUR WOMEN IS FALLEN OVER-RIPE   284   3
   THE YEAR OF OUR WOMEN IS FALLEN OVER-RIPE   284   6
   AND WOMEN HAVE BEEN SEWING EVER SINCE   284 13
   WHAT THEN GOOD LORD CRY THE WOMEN   284 20
   WHAT THEN WHEN WOMEN THE WORLD OVER HAVE ALL BURSTEN IN+   284 29
   AND SIT BESIDE THE STEEL-STRAIGHT ARMS OF YOUR FAIR WOM+   291   5
   THOSE TWO ENFRANCHISED WOMEN   309   9
   POOR PERSEPHONE AND HER RIGHTS FOR WOMEN   309 20
   LIKE WOMEN AT A WELL THE DAWN-FOUNTAIN   311 26
   WOMEN I LOVED AND CHERISHED LIKE MY MOTHER   410   3
   WOMEN WHO WERE GENTLE   410   7
   WOMEN WITH THE BEAUTIFUL EYES OF THE OLD DAYS   410 11
   WOMEN OF THE OLDER GENERATION WHO KNOW   410 15

WOMEN
   GRAVES OF WOMEN   410 20
   OF SOFT-SKIRTED WOMEN   410 22
   WOMEN WITH EYES THAT WERE GENTLE IN OLDEN BELIEF IN LOVE   410 23
   THE GENTLE-KNEED WOMEN   410 32
   WOMEN   411   3
   WOMEN WHOM I LOVED AND TOLD TO DIE   411   4
   WOMEN I'VE LOVED FOR GENTLENESS   412 10
   HE IS TREADING OUR WOMEN   436 13
   FURROWS OUR FEATHERLESS WOMEN   436 16
   TO SEEK THE WOMEN IN THE DARK OUR WOMEN OUR WEIRD   438 13
   WOMEN WHOM HE TREADS   438 14
   AND BABIES OF WOMEN WILL COME OUT YOUNG WILD GEESE   438 23
   SO HE TAKES IT OUT ON WOMEN   446 31
   AND TAKING IT OUT ON WOMEN   447   4
   HOW THEY WREAK THEIR SPITE ON WOMEN   447   9
   RONALD SHE RESUMED DOESN'T LIKE WOMEN JUST ACUTELY   447 11
   SO HE VERY CLEVERLY TORTURES WOMEN WITH HIS SORT OF LOVE   447 15
   WOMEN DON'T WANT WISTFUL   457 13
   WOMEN ARE SICK OF CONSOLING   457 21
   WOMEN WANT FIGHTERS FIGHTERS   457 25
   NEW LIFE FOR YOURSELVES AND YOUR WOMEN COMPLEMENTAL   463 12
   SEX ISN'T SIN IT'S A DELICATE FLOW BETWEEN WOMEN AND MEN   464 14
   MEN AND WOMEN LET US BE   470   6
   AND WOMEN   470 27
   EGO-BOUND WOMEN ARE OFTEN LESBIAN   475 12
   I AM SO TIRED OF VIOLENT WOMEN LASHING OUT AND INSISTING   479   7
   BETWEEN MEN AND MEN AND WOMEN AND EARTH AND   482   6
   AND A MINGLING OF WALLET-CARRYING WOMEN   484   5
   WOMEN ABOUT   485 14
   THE WOMEN ARE IN THE CAGE AS MUCH AS YOU ARE   485 19
   AFTER A LOT O' WOMEN   493 14
   ELDERLY DISCONTENTED WOMEN ASK FOR INTIMATE COMPANIONSH+   502   1
   ELDERLY DISCONTENTED WOMEN ARE SO FULL OF THEMSELVES   502   4
   IT IS AS IF MODERN WOMEN HAD ALL GOT THEMSELVES ON THE +   502   6
   THAT'S WHY WOMEN AREN'T MUCH FUN YOU'RE ALWAYS HAVING   517 27
   FLAT-CHESTED CROP-HEADED CHEMICALISED WOMEN OF INDETERM+   522   2
   HOW STRANGE IT WOULD BE IF SOME WOMEN CAME   525 22
   AND WOMEN EVEN CUT THEIR SHIMMERY HAIR   530   8
   WHY ARE WOMEN SO ENERGETIC   537 19
   WOMEN FELT IT WAS NO LONGER ANY USE BEING A LINGER-LONG+   537 29
   ALL THE WOMEN WHO ADORED THE SHADOW OF THE MAN ON   538 10
   WOMEN MIGHT BE DEVOTED AND GENTLE   538 16
   WOMEN START IN TO MAKE CHANGES   538 19
   THE WOMEN ARE LIKE LITTLE VOLCANOES   539   2
   THE WONDERFUL THOUGHTFUL WOMEN WHO MAKE SUCH GOOD   539 23
   IT'S NO GOOD THE WOMEN ARE IN ERUPTION   541   1
   BUT THE WOMEN ARE MY FAVOURITE VESSELS OF WRATH   541   9
   AND CLING TO THEIR THIN YOUNG WOMEN   558 24
   WHAT'S THE MATTER WITH THEM AREN'T THEY WOMEN AND   578 18
   TOWARDS OTHER WOMEN IN COMMUNION   619   3
   DOMINANT WOMEN ARE AS A RULE SO SUBTLY AND FIENDISHLY D+   619 24
   MEN AND WOMEN SHOULD LEARN TENDERNESS TO EACH OTHER   620   3
   WOMEN WOMEN THE SAME   635   5
   MEN ON THIS SIDE WOMEN ON THAT SIDE   636   3
   WHEN MOST WOMEN DIE   638 21
   BY THE KINDNESS OF LIVING WOMEN AND MEN   640 14
   NOW LIVING WOMEN AND MEN ARE THREATENED WITH EXTINCTION   640 15
   SONS OF MEN FROM THE WOMBS OF WISTFUL WOMEN   642 16
   SOME WOMEN LIVE FOR THE IDIOTIC FURNITURE OF THEIR HOUS+   657   6
   OLD MEN OLD OBSTINATE MEN AND WOMEN   663   4
   AND ME AND YOU AND OTHER MEN AND WOMEN   667   5
   WHEN MEN AND WOMEN WHEN LADS AND GIRLS ARE NOT THINKING   672   1
   ALL I WANT OF YOU MEN AND WOMEN   683 24
   MEN SINGING SONGS AND WOMEN BRUSHING THEIR HAIR IN THE +   691 24
   AND BULL-WHALES GATHER THEIR WOMEN AND WHALE-CALVES IN +   695   1
   EVERYWHERE MEN AND WOMEN ALIGHT WITH GOD   742 31
   AND WHY DO THE WOMEN FOLLOW US SATISFIED   743   3
   WHERE ONLY THE WOMEN OF THE AFTERWARDS   769 24
   TOWARDS THE WOMEN WHO ARE VIRGINS OF THE AFTERWARDS   770 20
   WOMEN THE SAME   771   7
   THE WOMEN BY THE GATE OF THE EAST   771 11
   THE WOMEN WITH LIGHT ON THEIR FACES   771 12
   BUT A GERM IN THE HEARTS OF MEN AND WOMEN AMERICANS   774 31
   HE SAW THE WOMEN THAT WERE NOT CLEAN   790 13
   OF HIS HAIR SAY THE SAME TO THE WOMEN   791 25
   THERE ARE DEAD THAT STAND UPON YOU WHEN YOU GO IN TO YO+   795 30
   WHEN YOU TURN TO YOUR WIVES AS BRAVE MEN TURN TO THEIR +   800 12
   AND THE FEET OF MEN AND THE HANDS OF THE WOMEN KNOW ME   801 19
   OF THE MEN AND THE WOMEN WHO WALK AMONG YOU   807 24
   MEN THAT SEEM HARMLESS WOMEN WITH FAIR WORDS   807 26
   WHEN I SEE THE MESSED-UP CHEMICALISED WOMEN   837 14
   IT IS TIME MEN TOOK THEIR THOUGHTS OFF WOMEN   838   5
   BECAUSE THEY ONLY TRY TO MAKE WOMEN AND LOVE AND SEX   838   7
   AND SINCE WOMEN ARE INSIDE THE PRISON JUST AS MUCH AS M+   838   9
   IF TWILIGHT CAME IN THE EYES OF WOMEN   840   4
   OH LOVELY WOMEN   840   6
   AND WOMEN FALL FOR THESE LITTLE-BOY MINDS THEY FEEL QUI+   841 24
   THAN HE WILL NOTE THE OTHER ORDINARY WOMEN   877 18
   OTHER WOMEN HAVE REARED IN ME   888   1
   BRUSH OVER MY FACE AS HE GOES TO TREAD OUR WEIRD WOMEN   *947 20
   HE NEVER WANTS A WOMAN HE DOESN'T LIKE WOMEN   *948 23
   AND IS HIMSELF NORMAL A LOVER OF WOMEN   *949   6
   BUT ASK THE WOMEN   *949   7
   ASK ALL THE WOMEN HE'S EVER HAD   *949   8
   AND TAKING IT OUT ON WOMEN   *949 12
   TAKING IT OUT IN SPITE ON WOMEN   *949 18

WOMEN'S
   WOMEN'S GRAVES   410   6
   HOW THEY HATE THE WOMEN'S EFFORTS TO TURN THEM   538 24

WON
   TO HAVE WON ONCE MORE   168 31
   I HAVE WON MY RENOWN   239   6
   IT WAS WON BY THE ONE ALMIGHTY NULLUS   824   6
   AND HAVING WON I WILL LIE DOWN TO SLEEP   876   4

WONDER
    THERE LIES THE WORLD MY DARLING FULL OF WONDER AND WIST+   52 20
    AT REST IN THE BLUE AND WONDER AT WHAT THEY MEAN   58 15
    OF 'IM STOOPIN' TO 'ER YOU'D WONDER 'E COULD   81 19
    I WONDER IF GOD ALLOWS   104   9
    I WONDER IF ONLY   104 16
    I WONDER CAN THE NIGHT GO BY   116 14
    I WONDER IF WITH YOU AS IT IS WITH ME   122   9
    NEW SPARKS OF WONDER OPENING IN SURPRISE   136 16
    THIS WONDER STOOD GLISTENING   165 18
    ALL SHAPES OF WONDER WITH SUSPENDED BREATH   165 19
    WITH WONDER EVERY BLACK TREE   165 23
    ONE ANOTHER IN WONDER OF WAKING LET US WAKE TO THE GLEAM   175 29
    THEIR EYES AND LOOK AT THE GRAVE ON THE HILL IN WONDER   176 16
    AND GRIEF ARE BUT THE SAME LAST WONDER SLEEP   196   2
    MY VERY SELF I WITH THE WONDER MELLOW   218   6
    I WONDER WHERE   221   3
    I SEE MYSELF ISOLATED IN THE UNIVERSE AND WONDER   223   1
    THAT VEXES ME WITH WONDER HE SITS SO STILL   225 18
    THERE IS NOTHING TO WONDER OR CAVIL AT   228   8
    I WONDER WHAT IT WILL BE   247   7
    THAT I SHALL ALWAYS WONDER OVER AND WAIT FOR   248   9
    I SHALL ALWAYS WONDER OVER YOU AND LOOK FOR YOU   248 12
    THE ROCK WILL SPLIT WE SHALL COME AT THE WONDER WE SHALL   250 23
    OH FOR THE WONDER THAT BUBBLES INTO MY SOUL   250 25
    AS CARRIES ME YOU WOULD WONDER ALOUD THAT HE   251 29
    SO THAT I BEGAN TO WONDER OVER MYSELF AND WHAT I WAS   254 23
    WHEN SHE LIFTED HER HEAD IN DELICATE STARTLED WONDER   255 28
    NOISELESS THEIR WONDER NOISELESS BLEW   262   3
    DO YOU WONDER THAT I AM AFRAID TO COME   291   1
    IT WOULD BE NO WONDER   326   8
    IT WOULD BE NO WONDER IF GREAT WINGS LIKE FLAMES FANNED+   326 12
    BUT I I ONLY WONDER   340 11
    DO YOU WONDER AT THE WORLD AS SLOWLY YOU TURN YOUR   353 10
    ARE YOU ABLE TO WONDER   353 16
    I WONDER WHY   369 24
    O FACES UPTURNED TO THE GLARE O TROPICAL WONDER WONDER   391 20
    BUT THE AUDIENCE COMPELLED TO WONDER   445 24
    IT IS A WONDER FOAM IS SO BEAUTIFUL   467 11
    AND NO WONDER FOR MONEY HAS A FEARFUL CRUEL POWER   486 16
    WHEN I READ SHAKESPEARE I AM STRUCK WITH WONDER   494 13
    LEAR THE OLD BUFFER YOU WONDER HIS DAUGHTERS   494 16
    WONDER OUTWAITING PAIN   504   8
    LIKE MACHINES AND YOU CAN'T WONDER MUCH   537 18
    I REALLY WONDER AND WONDER WHAT THEY MEAN   646   3
    ALL MEN WORSHIP THE WONDER OF LIFE   649   8
    WE CAN BUT TOUCH AND WONDER AND PONDER AND MAKE OUR EFF+   667 14
    EITHER IN ANGER OR TENDERNESS OR DESIRE OR SADNESS OR W+   672   4
    AND GREW UP AND BECAME IN THE WONDER OF CREATION JESUS   689 29
    IT IS CREATION GOD LOOKS HIMSELF ON IT IN WONDER FOR TH+   690 11
    WONDER OF WHALES   694 22
    I DREAD HIM COMING I WONDER HOW HE WILL TAKE IT   733   2
    BETWEEN HIS THICK LIPS I WONDER WHERE   733 26
    I WONDER WILL HE CARE   734 23
    FAINT-FASHIONED WONDER WHEREIN LOST WE SPIN   875   4
    I WOULD NOT MISS IT FOR YOUR ACHE OF WONDER   876 16
    BLUE DARKNESSES OF WONDER THAT HOLD ALL   876 27
    WONDER I CRAVE FOR THAT BURNS STRONG IN HIM   876 31
    AND ALL THE WONDER LOST FROM OUT HIS EYES   877 11
    THERE LIES THE WORLD MY DARLING FULL OF WONDER AND WIST+ *905   9
    OF HIM STOOPIN' TO HER YOU'D WONDER HE COULD   *923 19
    I WONDER CAN THE NIGHT GO BY   *930 13
    THEIR EYES TO YOUR BRIGHT PLACE AND THEN IN WONDER   *941   3
    TO THE LAST WONDER OF OBLIVION   *960 21
    OBLIVION THE LAST WONDER   *960 22

WONDERED
    I WONDERED I LOOKED AROUND   165   1
    SO SHE SAID AND I WONDERED   255 16
    THE PEOPLE WATCHED AND WONDERED AND SEEMED TO RESENT   445 17
    AND WHEN AT LAST MAN STOOD ON TWO LEGS AND WONDERED   683 11
    AND ROSES WONDERED AT HER PRAYER   753 11

WONDERFUL
    YOU THAT I LOVED YOU WONDERFUL   56 33
    THE NIGHT IS WONDERFUL   130 28
    LOOK SHE'S A WONDERFUL DOVE WITHOUT BLEMISH OR SPOT   239   1
    YOU WOULD ENVY ME YOU WOULD THINK ME WONDERFUL   251 26
    I SAY WONDERFUL ARE THE HELLISH EXPERIENCES   280 24
    THE WONDERFUL MOIST CONDUCTIVITY TOWARDS THE CENTRE   282 20
    WISTFULLY WATCHING WITH WONDERFUL LIQUID EYES   394 20
    THE WONDERFUL SLOW FLOWING OF THE SAPPHIRE   476 26
    HIS WONDERFUL SPEECHES FULL OF OTHER FOLKS' WHORING   494 21
    IT MUST BE WONDERFUL TO LIVE AND GROW OLD   503 27
    WHAT A PITY HE SEES HIMSELF SO WONDERFUL   528 25
    THE WONDERFUL THOUGHTFUL WOMEN WHO MAKE SUCH GOOD   539 13
    THEN SUDDENLY THE MASTODON ROSE WITH THE WONDERFUL LADY   540   5
    SOME WONDERFUL LEADER   564 21
    OH WONDERFUL MACHINE SO SELF-SUFFICIENT SO SUFFICIENT U+   643   8
    OH WONDERFUL MACHINE YOU ARE MAN'S IDEA OF GODLINESS   643 15
    TERRIBLE AND STRANGE THE GOD LIES ON THE BED WISTFUL CO+   676   9
    GOD IS A GREAT URGE WONDERFUL MYSTERIOUS MAGNIFICENT   690   8
    BECAUSE NAKED YOU ARE MORE WONDERFUL THAN ANYTHING WE C+   695 18
    WONDERFUL ARE THE MACHINES OF THE GREEDY ONES   793 27
    THEIR FACES ARE UGLY YET THEY MAKE WONDERFUL THINGS   794   7
    BEYOND ME IS A LORD WHO IS TERRIBLE AND WONDERFUL AND D+   801 12
    WHOOING AND COOING AND FADING AWAY WITH WONDERFUL   830 24
    THE MODERN YOUNG WOMAN THINKS IT WONDERFUL TO BE SO BRI+   841 26
    WISE WONDERFUL STRANDS OF WINDS THAT ARE LADEN WITH RARE *938 22

WONDERFULLY
    OR IF YOU ONLY LOOK IT SO WONDERFULLY   548* 14

WONDER-GOAL
    THE LITTLE SHIP WITH ITS SOUL TO THE WONDER-GOAL   *961   4

WONDERING
    SHE ALIGHTS A STRANGER WONDERING UNUSED TO THE SCENE   153 10
    WONDERING MOUNT AND PUT THE FLOWERS ASUNDER   176 17
    THE WAN WONDERING LOOK OF THE PALE SKY   203 10
    WIDE EYES AND WONDERING SPIRIT NOT   461   7
    HE WANTS HIS ONE GREAT WONDERING EYE THE EYE OF THE   544   9
    YOU NEED YOUR OWN GREAT WONDERING EYE THAT FLASHES WITH   544 22
    SONS OF MEN WITH THE WONDERING EYES OF LIFE   642 18
    OCCASIONALLY I SEE HIM SILENT A LITTLE WONDERING   645 18
    WONDERING HE STEPPED NEARER AND LOOKED AT HER   790   6
    AND I WOKE WONDERING WHO TOUCHED ME WITH SUCH FEAR AND +   860 10
    I AM COME BACK A FOREIGNER WONDERING AND SHRINKING FROM+   867   2

WONDERLAND
    THEN I FOUND MYSELF IN A WONDERLAND   261 26

WONDERMENT
    ONE ROSE OF WONDERMENT UPON THE TREE   219   6
    WONDERMENT ORGANISING ITSELF HERALDING ITSELF WITH THE +   274   5

WONDER-RIDDEN
    AM WONDER-RIDDEN   108 10

WONDERS
    A SQUIRREL COCKS HIS HEAD ON THE FENCE AND WONDERS   223 21
    ACROSS THE HISS OF WONDERS AS THE ROCKET BURST   391 17
    WONDERS SHINES OUT OF EVERYWHERE   802 28
    AND WONDERS IF A PARROT HASN'T MORE TO IT   842 11
    WHEREIN THE TIMID WONDERS FLY   *894   9

WONDROUS
    COMPRESSED IT TILL ITS BEAM GREW WONDROUS DARK   69 19
    COMPRESSED IT TILL ITS BEAM GREW WONDROUS DARK   *916   2
    WHILE TREMBLING SOMEWHERE IN THEIR WONDROUS GLOOM   *941 27

WONTED
    AGAIN ON THE WONTED SKIES   253 22

WOO
    SHY OF YOUR FACE STILL BEND TO WOO   887 15

WOOD
    ALL MY MORNING'S PLEASURE IN THE SUN-FLECK-SCATTERED WO+   65 14
    HER WOES HER LOVER WOOS AND SINGS WITHIN ANOTHER WOOD   65 26
    OBSCURES THE DARK WOOD AND THE DULL ORANGE SKY   85 10
    WHERE THE WOOD FUMES UP AND THE FLICKERING WATERY   116   4
    LOOK NOW THROUGH THE WOOD WHERE THE BEECH-GREEN   126 22
    WHEN WE CAME OUT OF THE WOOD   164 25
    WOOD AT MIDNIGHT   366   5
    ROUND A LOG OF WOOD   387   8
    THE LUMP OF WOOD CAREFULLY   387 15
    WOOD   387 32
    ME OR THE MEXICAN WHO COMES TO CHOP WOOD   398 23
    AND GIVE ME SOFT-SKINNED WOOD   427 12
    ROTTING WOOD   677 22
    HELMETS AS HIS HE LOST IN THE WOOD THAT NIGHT   732 12
    AND THE WOOD LIKE A MANLY HUSBAND SPREADS SOFTNESS AND +   854   9
    THIRTEEN LAY THE YELLOW CHICKS BENEATH THE JOIST OF WOOD *933   3

WOOD-ASH
    AND THE WOOD-ASH GATHERED IN THE FIRE   248 18

WOODBINE
    THE WOODBINE CREEPS ABROAD   42   9

WOODEN
    A WOODEN BLANK ON HER FACE   384 24
    GNAWING IN A WOODEN TRAP TRAPPED IN   653 11

WOODPIGEONS
    AND WAKE TO THE SOUND OF THE WOODPIGEONS AND LIE AND LI+ *892 28

WOODPIGEON'S
    A FEW QUICK BEATS OF A WOODPIGEON'S HEART THEN RISE   *892 30

WOOD-PIGEON'S
    A FEW QUICK BEATS FROM A WOOD-PIGEON'S HEART AND WHEN I+   38 14

WOOD-PIGEON
    AND I WOKE TO THE SOUND OF THE WOOD-PIGEON AND LAY AND +   38 12

WOODS
    OR THERE IN THE WOODS OF THE TWILIGHT WITH NORTHERN WIN+   57 19
    AND MORNING SINGING WHERE THE WOODS ARE SCROLLED   135 27
    UP THE WOLDS THE WOODS WERE WALKING   152 14
    AND MORNING SINGING WHERE THE WOODS WERE SCROLLED   *939 19
    SO SHE CLOSES HER EYES BUT THE AIMLESS BREEZE OF THE WO+ *942   1

WOODSTACK
    THE MEN UPLIFTED ON THE NEW WHITE WOODSTACK STAND   *895   1

WOODSTACKS
    WOODSTACKS BESIDE THE RAILWAY GLISTEN AND GLOW   *894 26
    UPON THE WOODSTACKS WORKING WEARIEDLY   *895 25
    UPON THE WOODSTACKS WORKING WEARIEDLY   *904 14

WOOD'S
    ON THE GREEN WOOD'S EDGE A SHY GIRL HOVERS   41   1

WOOD-WORK
    AND PAINTING THE WOOD-WORK RED   572 14

WOOED
    LONG AGO LONG AGO WOOED   105   8

WOOF
    LIKE THE WOOF THE SHUTTLE CARRIES   747   2

WOOING
    WOOING BOYS AND BEAUTY   437   7
    HE SHAKES THE TID-BIT FOR HER WITH A MOST WOOING NOISE +   761 18
    WOOING BOYS AND BEAUTY   *946 19

WOOL
    WHEN THE HINDUS WEAVE THIN WOOL INTO LONG LONG LENGTHS   451   1
    HAVE YOU ANY WOOL   669 20
    THE DAUGHTER OF THE GREAT MAN ROLLS HER KHAKI WOOL   752   9

WOOS
    SHE WOOS THE MOTH WITH HER SWEET LOW WORD   42 15
    HER WOES HER LOVER WOOS AND SINGS WITHIN ANOTHER WOOD   65 26

WOR
    THEY ON'Y TOWD ME IT WOR BAD   45 11
    BUT I THOWT TER MYSEN AS THAT WOR TH' ONLY BIT   61 17
    O' WARMTH AS 'E GOT DOWN THEER TH' REST WOR STONE COLD   61 18
    YIS I KNOWED 'E WOR COURTIN' THEE   81 26
    WHICH ON US SAID YOU WOR   82   4
    AN' 'DEED AN' I WISH AS THIS TALE O' THINE WOR NIVER MY+   83 10
    SAY IT WOR NOUGHT   84   8
    AN' OFF TO A GEL AS WOR YOUNGER THAN ME   138 11
    WHILE TH' PARSON WAS PRAYIN' I WATCHES 'ER AN' SHE WOR +   *910 16
    ASIDE O' TH' GRAVE WHILE TH' COFFIN WOR LYIN' YET   *910 27
    WOR IT THA'D LIKED TO 'A KILLED HER   *922 24
    YIS I KNOWED 'E WOR COURTIN' THEE   *923 26
    WHICH ON US SAID YOU WOR   *924   8
    BUT 'DEED AN' I WISH AS THIS TALE O' THINE WOR NIVER MY+   *925 11
    SO VERY MUCH WORSER OFF THAN 'ER WOR BEFORE AN' NOW LOO+   *925 21
    KISS ME THEN THERE NE'ER MIND IF I SCRAIGHT I WOR FOND +   *925 28

WORD
    SHE WOOS THE MOTH WITH HER SWEET LOW WORD   42 15
    THAT SPEAK NO WORD OF THEIR RAPTURE BUT ONLY   69   7
    I'LL TA'E THY WORD GOOD-BYE LIZ   80 29
    IS THE LAST WORD NOW UTTERED   102 19
    THE LEAVES FLY OVER THE WINDOW AND UTTER A WORD AS THEY+   103   1
    THE LOW WORD DON'T I LET THE FLOWER FALL   125 20
    SPELL OF ITS WORD   149 14
    BUT ANOTHER WORD CONCEIT AND VANITY   158 14
    HE SAYS NOT A WORD BUT PASSES   227   9
    THOUGH EVEN THE WORD MARSALA WILL SMACK OF PRECIOSITY   280 11
    AND TO BE LIMITED BY A MERE WORD IS TO BE LESS THAN A H+   292   4
    WE HAVE ONLY ROMAN WORD FOR IT   297 31
    IN THE BEGINNING WAS THE WORD   328 12
    AND THE WORD WAS GOD   328 13
    AND THE WORD WAS WITH GOD   328 14
    IN THE BEGINNING WAS THE WORD   328 24
    IN THE BEGINNING WAS THE WORD OF COURSE   329 10
    AND THE WORD WAS THE FIRST OFFSPRING OF THE ALMIGHTY JO+   329 11
    THEY EXCHANGE NO WORD NO SPASM NOT EVEN ANGER   337 18
    HE SPOKE THIS WORD STOP DON'T BEAT IT FOR IT IS THE SOU+   376   6
    TOGETHER WITHOUT A WORD   465 18
    FOR OUR WORD IS DEAD   510 24
    FOR THE NEW WORD IS RESURRECTION   512 31
    SHALL I TELL YOU AGAIN THE NEW WORD   513   1
    THE NEW WORD OF THE UNBORN DAY   513   2
    AND THE NEW WORD MEANS NOTHING TO US   513   7
    IT IS SUCH AN OLD WORD   513   8
    FOR THE WORD IS RESURRECTION   514   8
    TILL NOW THE VERY WORD IS NAUSEATING WE CAN'T HEAR IT A+   519   5
    HE IS GIVING HIMSELF AWAY IN EVERY SENSE OF THE WORD   523 11
    ME YOUR WORD AND SIGNING HERE PLEASE THAT YOU ARE A SUP+   546 10
    AND NEVER A WORD THEY SAY   549 20
    TELL ME A WORD   551   9
    AND UNCLOTHED THE WORD HAS NO MEANING FOR ME   607 10
    A WAITING FOR THE PROPER TOUCH NOT FOR ANY WORD OR DEED   612 16
    WORD OF OUR CIVILISATION   620 26
    THEY'RE NOT NICE IN OUR SENSE OF THE WORD ARE THEY NOW   660   7
    NO WORD   681 16
    FOR A WORD HE IS COMING TOWARDS THE GATE   734 26
    KILL OFF THE WORD THAT'S HAD SO MUCH TO SAY   737 26
    AND NEVER A WORD   748 20
    FOR THE WORD NOW LET US GO THROUGH THE GATE   757 19
    REACH OUT REACH OUT SAY NOT A WORD   764 31
    HEART THERE IS NO WORD TO SAY   767   1
    THE WORD STANDS FOR SOMETHING   774 20
    WHEN I SAY THE WORD THEY WILL START   792 19
    CAMBREE MY WORD CAMBREE   835 12
    THEY ARE EITHER IMMORALLY GOOD THE WORD DOES NOT AND   836 22
    OR ELSE THEY ARE IMMORALLY NASTY AND THE WORD LOOMS   837   1
    WHEREAS TO THE ORDINARY MORAL HUMAN BEING THE WORD   837   3
    LIKE ANY OTHER WORD OF FOUR LETTERS   837   5
    AFTER ALL IT IS IMMORAL FOR A WORD TO MEAN LESS THAN IT+   837   6
    IN ALL HONESTY A WORD IS NEITHER A GAP IN THE CONSCIOUS+   837   8
    AND QUITE CLEVER BRILLIANT IS THE MODERN WORD   841 19
    HUSH THEN NEVER A WORD   887 19
    THAT SPEAK NO WORD OF THEIR RAPTURE BUT ONLY   *915 19
    I'LL TA'E THY WORD GOOD-BYE LIZ   *922 29
    THE LOW WORD DON'T I LET THE FLOWER FALL   *936 19
    ALL FEARFUL LEST I FIND SOME NEXT WORD BLEEDING   *939   3

WORDAGE
    THEIR ABUNDANT SUMMERY WORDAGE SILENCED CAUGHT   142   2

WORD-FLEDGED
    THE POOR OLD GOLDEN EAGLE OF THE WORD-FLEDGED SPIRIT   329 30

WORDLESS
    HE IS WORDLESS BUT SULTRY AND VAST   39 15
    SINCE YOU VAST OUTSTRETCHED WORDLESS SLEEP   194 26
    AND WE KNOW NOT HOW TO LIVE WORDLESS   510 25

WORDS
    AND QUIVERS IN WORDS THROUGH MY MOUTH   38 31
    THAT SHE SAYS AND HER WORDS REJOICE   46 20
    OF THE WORDS I KEPT REPEATING   61 25
    SCOOPED THEM UP WITH SMALL IRON WORDS   94 11
    THE HARSH COLD WIND OF MY WORDS DROVE ON AND STILL   94 13
    ME WORDS THAT RANG WITH A BRASSY SHALLOW CHIME   98 20
    WITH WORDS BUT THE NIGHT SHOWS THROUGH   109 11
    THEIR WORDS AS THEY MOVE   109 12
    I FEEL YOUR SILENCE TOUCH MY WORDS AS I TALK   110   3
    MY WORDS FLY OFF A FORGE   110   5
    AM I DOOMED IN A LONG COITION OF WORDS TO MATE YOU   119   4
    IF UNDER YOUR SLIPPING WORDS THAT EASILY FLOW   122 10
    SURELY AH NOT IN WORDS ALONE J'D SPILL   127 16
    MEANS EVEN LESS THAN HER MANY WORDS TO ME   127 24
    ALL FEARFUL LEST I FIND THE LAST WORDS BLEEDING   135 19
    SPRINKLING INCENSE AND SALT OF WORDS   151 28
    IN WORDS AND THINGS WELL SAID BUT THE OTHER WAY   158   4
    TAKE WHAT YOU'VE GOT YOUR MEMORY OF WORDS   158   7
    TO MAKE NEW WORDS WITH OUR LIPS TO ESCAPE THE FOUL DREAM   175 22
    TAKE MY WORDS AND FLING   236 25
    MY EARS ARE WEARY WITH WORDS THAT BOUNCE ON THEM AND   249 22
    AND WHITE WORDS WHITE-WASH AMERICAN   292 30
    ARE OUR WORDS NO GOOD   296   7
    NAY TONGUES ARE DEAD AND WORDS ARE HOLLOW AS HOLLOW   296 25
    THUS SAY A FEW WORDS TO EACH OTHER   405 20
    HAVE PHOSPHORESCENT TEEMING WHITE WORDS   441   2
    PUTTING IN ALL THE IMPOSSIBLE WORDS   491 15
    WAS WORDS LIKE SH- AND F-   491 22
    SUCH WORDS TO THE CAMEL'S CHARGE   492 16
    POOR HOMELY WORDS I MUST GIVE YOU BACK   492 19
    FOR USING WORDS THEY PRIVATELY KEEP   492 25
    AND SEND THIN DRAUGHTS OF WORDS   506 22
    WHILE PEOPLE MINCE MEAN WORDS THROUGH THEIR TEETH   530 11
    THE STORM IS WORDS THE BOTTLES NEVER BREAK   543 11
    WITH WORDS OR WITH YOU   551 22
    SHOULD HEAR ALL THE ROUGH WORDS   565   6
    OH MINCE YOUR WORDS AND MINCE THEM WELL   575 10
    FOR PRINTING THOSE NAUGHTY WORDS   668 13
    WHERE GOD IS ALSO LOVE BUT WITHOUT WORDS   695   6
    BY HERMES AND APHRODITE FLASHING WHITE GLITTERING WORDS   702 10
    PERVADES MY MOVEMENTS AND MY THOUGHTS AND WORDS   727   3
    AND HARK TO THE WORDS OF THEIR HEART'S DESIRE   789   3
    THESE WORDS THAT ARE ALL FLAT   792 27
    MEN THAT SEEM HARMLESS WOMEN WITH FAIR WORDS   807 26
    REFUSED TO BE MOULDED IN ARROWS OF ENGLISH WORDS   859 12
    LOOKED UP AND THE WORDS MOVED LIKE A SMILE FROM HIS LIPS   865   3
    IN BATTLE OF HEATED WORDS HARDLY STILLED BY MY REITERAT+   865 32
    SHE MAY COVER HER EYES YET THE AIMLESS BREEZE OF MY WOR+   868 29
    STAGGERING WORDS   *893   7
    SCOOPED THEM UP WITH SMALL IRON WORDS   *896 27
    THE HARSH COLD WRATH OF MY WORDS DROVE ON AND STILL   *897   1
    OF THE WORDS I KEPT REPEATING   *912   5
    AND LISTEN OH EVERYTHING LISTEN FOR WORDS   *914 14

WORE
    HE WORE US OUT SO NOW WE ARE GODLESS AND UNBELIEVING   439 14
    AND THE STREWN TAWDRY TRAPPINGS THAT LAST NIGHT'S POETR+   856 11
    CLOTH THEY WORE   *949 27

WORK
    WORK WORK YOU FOOL   41   5
    FOR ME TO COME SINCE WORK I MUST   41 16
    THRILL OF HIS WORK HE TURNS AGAIN FROM ME   51 18
    THEN BACK IN A SWIFT BRIGHT FLUTTER TO WORK   51 28
    IT IS WELL FOR YOU FOR ME THE NAVVIES WORK IN THE ROAD +   57 29
    AND LAUGHING WITH LABOUR LIVING THEIR WORK LIKE A GAME   72 11
    WHO GRAPPLING DOWN WITH WORK OR HATE OR PASSION   73 14
    OF SLOVENLY WORK THAT THEY HAVE OFFERED ME   74 15
    ONLY I AND THE CLASS MUST WRANGLE THIS WORK IS A BITTER+   76 22
    MY EYES FROM DUTEOUS WORK MALINGERING   129 14
    NAY LET ME WORK A DELICATE CHAIN OF KISSES   154   4
    WORK RECREATION GOVERNING ANARCHY   256 28
    THAT WORK BENEATH HER WHILE SHE SPRAWLS ALONG   362 16
    HER FOLDS OF SKIN THAT WORK AND ROW   362 18
    WORK FOR ME   442 22
    AND IF AS WE WORK WE CAN TRANSMIT LIFE INTO OUR WORK   449   6
    AND WORK IS LIFE AND LIFE IS LIVED IN WORK   450   1
    MEN SHOULD REFUSE TO BE LIFELESSLY AT WORK   450   5
    MEN SHOULD REFUSE TO WORK AT ALL AS WAGE-SLAVES   450   7
    MEN SHOULD DEMAND TO WORK FOR THEMSELVES OF THEMSELVES   450   8
    FOR IF A MAN HAS NO LIFE IN HIS WORK HE IS MOSTLY A HEAP   450 10
    THERE IS NO POINT IN HIM   450 13
    WHEN A MAN GOES OUT INTO HIS WORK   450 24
    WHY NOT HAVE MEN AS MEN AND THE WORK AS MERELY PART   452   7
    OH QUITE BUT HE MUST WORK HE MUST HAVE A JOB OF SOME   452 18
    AND MEN WOULD WORK GAILY   488   6
    WORK CAN BE FUN AND MEN CAN ENJOY IT THEN IT'S NOT   517 20
    WORK AND PRISONERS' ROUTINE   518 12
    WORK IS THE CLUE TO A MAN'S LIFE   520 19
    BUT IT MUST BE FREE WORK NOT DONE JUST FOR MONEY BUT FOR   520 20
    THE WAGES OF WORK IS CASH   521   1
    THEN I AM MORE THAN RADICAL I WANT TO WORK A GUILLOTINE   526 16
    AND SHE MAKES YOU GO TO WORK EVEN IF   572   5
    PLEASING BRITANNIA IS NO LIGHT WORK   577 23
    TROT TROT TROT CORPSE-BODY TO WORK   584 11
    CORPSE-ANATOMIES THAT CAN WORK   584 22
    WORK WORK WORK   584 23
    CREEPING BACK AND FORTH TO WORK   585 10
    THEY STREAM PAST STREAM PAST GOING TO WORK   585 25
    BACK AND FORTH TO WORK   586   7
    BACK AND FORTH TO WORK   586   8
    BACK AND FORTH TO WORK   630 10
    YOUR WAGE IS THE DOLE OF WORK AND THE DOLE IS YOUR   630 20
    TO WORK WITH AND NOTHING ELSE   630 28
    WAGE-PAID WORK   631 14
    BACK AND FORTH TO WORK   632 22
    BACK AND FORTH TO WORK   632 23

WORK

EVEN WORK IS UNWILLING THE WORKER IS UNWILLING UNWILLING   648   9
EVEN AN ARTIST KNOWS THAT HIS WORK WAS NEVER IN HIS MIND   690   3
HIS WORK TOOK PLACE IT CAME TO PASS IT STOOD UP AND SAL+   690   7
WORK HAS MADE US BLIND AND NOW THE DUSK   757   13
AND WORK IRON ELBOWS UP AND DOWN   793   25
WE WORK WITH THEIR MACHINES WE WORK IN THEIR FIELDS   794   2
SEX WON'T WORK IN CAPTIVITY   843   13
I'LL WORK AND I'LL WIVE   857   8
LEANS OVER TO READ HIS WORK AND HER DARK HEAD DIPS   865   5
SET DOWN THE TRAY BEFORE ME AS I WORK   875   11
TO OPEN ERE THE THIEF HAVE DONE HIS WORK   878   29
OF SLOVENLY WORK THAT THEY HAVE OFFERED ME   *895   23
THEN HE TURNS AGAIN TO HIS WORK WITH GLEE   *898   28
ECSTASY OF WORK HE TURNS FROM ME   *899   2
THEN BACK IN A SWIFT BRIGHT FLUTTER TO WORK   *899   12
THEN HE TURNS AGAIN TO HIS WORK WITH GLEE   *902   12
ECSTASY OF WORK HE TURNS FROM ME   *902   14
THEN BACK IN A SWIFT BRIGHT FLUTTER TO WORK   *902   24
OF SLOVENLY WORK THAT THEY HAVE OFFERED ME   *904   12
OF A LIVE SAD WORK UNFINISHED   *927   27
ALL DAY LONG I AM BUSY AND HAPPY AT MY WORK   *945   24
BEHIND I AM FORTIFIED I AM GLAD AT MY WORK   *945   26
THERE IS NO POINT IN WORK   *949   19
A MAN NEEDS TO BE INDEPENDENT AT HIS WORK SO THAT HE CA+ *949   22
WHEN A MAN FREES HIS OWN SELF INTO HIS WORK   *949   24

WORK-CASH-WANT
THE WORK-CASH-WANT CIRCLE IS THE VICIOUSEST CIRCLE   521   5

WORKED
THEY ARE SO GREEDY YET SO HELPLESS IF NOT WORKED FOR   441   31
AND SEX ALAS GETS DIRTIER AND DIRTIER WORKED FROM THE   464   1
WORKED WITH CLEAN SWEAT FOR YEAST   758   22
HE SAT WITHIN THE HOLLOW OF A CLOUD AND SAW THE MEN THA+   790   10

WORKER
EVEN WORK IS UNWILLING THE WORKER IS UNWILLING UNWILLING   648   9

WORKHOUSE
BORN IN A UNIVERSAL WORKHOUSE   518   9

WORKING
THE HEART ALL CROWDED WITH SLAVES MOST WORKING SOME FEW+   174   20
WORKING IN MOTION   288   33
RATHER LIKE A BABY WORKING ITS LIMBS   352   30
AND GULPING AT MORE THAN SHE CAN SWALLOW AND WORKING   359   5
HE IS LIVING NOT MERELY WORKING   450   26
WHY HAVE WORKING CLASSES AT ALL AS IF MEN WERE ONLY   452   5
WORKING CLASSES   452   11
NOT TO INSTALL THE WORKING CLASSES   453   10
BUT TO ABOLISH THE WORKING CLASSES FOR EVER   453   11
MY FATHER WAS A WORKING MAN   490   9
BEING BORN AMONG THE WORKING PEOPLE   498   12
DON'T DO IT FOR THE WORKING CLASSES   517   13
AND WHEN I SEE WORKING MEN   526   17
WHEN IN THE STREETS OF THE WORKING QUARTERS   585   24
AND IT IS NOT BECAUSE THE MECHANISM IS WORKING WRONGLY   620   11
OH I HAVE LOVED THE WORKING CLASS   644   6
AND TERRIBLY STRANGE IS THE THROAT THAT IS WORKING WITH+   871   26
UPON THE WOODSTACKS WORKING WEARIEDLY   *895   25
UPON THE WOODSTACKS WORKING WEARIEDLY   *904   14
HERE IN THE SWELLING FLESH THE GREAT ACTIVITY WORKING   *909   11
COMPLETING HIS CIRCLES AND WORKING CLEVERLY   *932   3
HE IS LIVING NOT MERELY WORKING   *949   25

WORKING-MAN
DEAR DEAR WORKING-MAN   773   15

WORKMEN
THE WRITHING OF MYRIADS OF WORKMEN ALL DREAMING THEY AR+   175   2

WORKMEN'S
AND EMBEDDED YOU IN THE WORKMEN'S DWELLINGS WHERE   630   19

WORK-PRISON
IN TERROR LEST YOU HAVE TO GO IN AND SINCE THE WORK-PRI+   521   13

WORKS
FROM THE WORKS BEYOND   148   23
THEIR HANDS AND PRODUCE WORKS OF ART AS MEN DO HORSES W+ 376   2
WHILE A WAGE-SLAVE WORKS HE LEAVES LIFE ASIDE   450   3
WORKS   644   14
PONDERING YET EAGER THE BROAD AND THICK-SET ITALIAN WHO+ 672   26

WORLD
PASSES THE WORLD WITH SHADOWS AT THEIR FEET   36   3
BEYOND A WORLD I NEVER WANT TO JOIN   36   8
THERE LIES THE WORLD MY DARLING FULL OF WONDER AND WIST+   52   20
AND LAID THE DESERT HORRIFIC OF SILENCE AND SNOW ON THE+   75   16
THE WORLD WITHIN WORLDS IS A WOMB WHENCE ISSUES ALL   88   33
WORLD WITHIN WORLDS A WOMB THAT GIVES AND TAKES   89   8
AND NAKEDLY NOTHING 'TWIXT WORLD AND HEAVEN TWO CREATUR+   98   4
I IN THE FUR OF THE WORLD ALONE BUT THIS HELEN CLOSE BY   98   6
A FLOCCULENT DUST ON THE FLOOR OF THE WORLD THE FESTOON   98   13
WITH HER WHITENESS REVEALING MY SUNKEN WORLD   103   29
AND OFF THE FORGE OF THE WORLD   110   17
THE WORLD WENT ROUND   120   17
THROUGH THE WORLD DID THRESH   120   33
AND THE WORLD ALL WHIRLING   121   1
IT SEEMED THAT I AND THE MORNING WORLD   124   5
AND NOW THAT THE SKIES ARE FALLING THE WORLD IS SPOUTIN+ 160   1
INTO THE WORLD OF SHADOW CARRIED DOWN   160   11
TO WATCH THE WORLD THAT LINGERS   162   19
OR IS IT THE ILLUSORY WORLD   163   1
IN ONE WORLD WITH ME   170   3
THE WORLD IS A PAINTED MEMORY WHERE COLOURED SHAPES   173   17
WALLED IN WALLED IN THE WHOLE WORLD IS A VAST IMPURE   174   23

WORLD
THE WHOLE WIDE WORLD IS INTERIOR NOW AND WERE ALL SHUT + 175   11
AND BREAK THE WALLS OF POSSESSION OF ALL THE WIDE WORLD   175   17
THE HEART OF THE LIVE WORLD PULSES AND THE BLOOD OF THE+ 176   4
PLAYING YOUR GREAT GAME AROUND THE WORLD ALONE   197   7
AT LAST I CAN THROW AWAY WORLD WITHOUT END AND MEET YOU   210   1
THE SPACE OF THE WORLD IS IMMENSE BEFORE ME AND AROUND + 222   22
SWARMS OF MANKIND IN THE WORLD AND WE WERE LESS LONELY   224   7
FROM AUSTRIA THERE LIES THE WORLD AND HERE   231   6
THE WORLD IS YOUR GRAVE   233   13
TO THE OTHER WORLD WHERE YOU ARE NOW   233   23
YOU ARE HELD BACK BY MY BEING IN THE SAME WORLD WITH YOU 235   31
I SACRIFICE ALL IN HER MY LAST OF THE WORLD   239   2
SEE HOW GORGEOUS THE WORLD IS   245   3
HAVING KNOWN THE WORLD SO LONG I HAVE NERVER CONFESSED   249   13
CHAOS OF THE WORLD   250   19
AND SO I CROSS INTO ANOTHER WORLD   256   4
I AM VERY GLAD AND ALL ALONE IN THE WORLD   256   7
ALL ALONE AND VERY GLAD IN A NEW WORLD   256   8
I COULD CRY WITH JOY BECAUSE I AM IN THE NEW WORLD JUST   256   10
WORLD MAY BE   256   15
BECAUSE IT WILL STILL BE A GESTURE OF THE OLD WORLD I AM 256   18
I WAS SO WEARY OF THE WORLD   256   22
HERE IN THE OTHER WORLD STILL TERRESTRIAL   258   33
I HAVE FOUND THE OTHER WORLD   259   27
THE UNKNOWN THE NEW WORLD   259   33
OVER TO THE NEW WORLD AND WAS CLIMBING OUT ON THE SHORE   260   14
RISEN NOT TO THE OLD WORLD THE OLD CHANGELESS I THE OLD+ 260   15
BUT TO A NEW EARTH A NEW I A NEW KNOWLEDGE A NEW WORLD   260   17
AH NO I CANNOT TELL YOU WHAT IT IS THE NEW WORLD   260   19
AND WHOSOEVER COMES AFTER WILL FIND ME IN THE NEW WORLD   260   22
THE NEW WORLD   260   25
OUT OF THE WELL-HEADS OF THE NEW WORLD   260   31
CAN BLOW ACROSS THE DARK SEAS TO OUR USUAL WORLD   261   3
I WISH IT WERE SPRING IN THE WORLD   270   29
WE WHO ARE WINTER-WEARY IN THE WINTER OF THE WORLD   272   34
COME QUICKLY AND STIR THE ROTTEN GLOBE OF THE WORLD FROM 273   7
BURST IT WITH GERMINATION WITH WORLD ANEW   273   9
ALL THE WORLD GLEAMS WITH THE LILIES OF DEATH THE UNCON+ 273   12
INCIPIENT PURPLING TOWARDS SUMMER IN THE WORLD OF THE H+ 273   25
IT WILL BE SPRING IN THE WORLD   274   3
IT WILL BE SPRING IN THE WORLD OF THE LIVING   274   4
WHAT THEN WHEN WOMEN THE WORLD OVER HAVE ALL BURSTEN IN+ 284   29
ROSE OF ALL THE WORLD   285   4
BEFORE THE ROSE OF ALL ROSES ROSE OF ALL THE WORLD WAS + 285   17
THERE WAS ANOTHER WORLD A DUSKY FLOWERLESS TENDRILLED W+ 285   22
OF WHICH WORLD THE VINE WAS THE INVISIBLE ROSE   285   30
IN A GREEN MUDDY WEB-FOOT UNUTTERLY SONGLESS WORLD   286   1
OF THE WORLD BEFORE THE FLOODS WHERE MAN WAS DARK AND   286   25
OF THE LOST FERN-SCENTED WORLD   287   7
WHEN YOUR WORLD IS IN RUINS UNDER YOUR FALLEN SKIES   289   20
BITTER-STINGING WHITE WORLD THAT BORE US   302   12
SETTING SUPREME ANNUNCIATION TO THE WORLD   304   21
AH MEDITERRANEAN MORNING WHEN OUR WORLD BEGAN   311   14
SHOUTING FORTH FLAME TO SET THE WORLD ON FIRE   315   2
THE DUST-HEAP OF MAN'S FILTHY WORLD ON FIRE   315   3
AND BURN IT DOWN THE GLUTTED STUFFY WORLD   315   4
TO BURN THE WORLD BACK TO MANURE-GOOD ASH   315   11
AND SET THE STINKING RUBBISH-HEAP OF THIS FOUL WORLD   315   23
TO LICK THE WORLD WITH FLAME THAT LICKS IT CLEAN   315   26
NOT THIS VAST ROTTING CABBAGE PATCH WE CALL THE WORLD   315   32
YOU NEED NOT CLEAR THE WORLD LIKE A CABBAGE PATCH FOR ME 316   9
IN A DOUBTFUL WORLD   317   24
IF THEY PULL ALL THE WORLD DOWN   317   34
AND LASHING HIS TAIL ABOVE THE WORLD   324   31
AND ALSO TO ENSURE A GOODLY INCREASE IN THE WORLD   325   22
LOOK AT HIM WITH HIS PAW ON THE WORLD   325   23
BUT ALSO IT WAS A FIERY FORTRESS FROWNING SHAGGILY ON T+ 327   1
LET HIM ROAR OUT CHALLENGE ON THE WORLD   327   25
DEPARTS AND THE WORLD IS TAKEN BY SURPRISE   340   20
OUT AND IS THE FOUNDATION OF THE WORLD   348   16
DO YOU WONDER AT THE WORLD AS SLOWLY YOU TURN YOUR   353   10
IN THE WORLD WHERE THE HUMMING-BIRD FLASHED AHEAD OF   372   15
LIKE THE DEVIL AND LOOK ON THE WORLD AS HIS OWN   382   14
AND FIGHT TO BE BOSS OF THE WORLD   383   21
OVERLOOKING THE WORLD FOR HIS OWN   383   25
TO STAND AND HOLD FEATHERS THREE FEATHERS ABOVE THE WOR+ 392   4
THE WORLD TO SNUGGLE DOWN IN THE WARMTH   394   3
BUT BRED IN CONCEIT THAT THE WORLD IS ALL FOR LOVE   400   16
MEN THE ONLY ANIMAL IN THE WORLD TO FEAR   401   6
AND I THINK IN THIS EMPTY WORLD THERE WAS ROOM FOR ME   402   27
AND I THINK IN THE WORLD BEYOND HOW EASILY WE MIGHT   402   29
YET WHAT A GAP IN THE WORLD THE MISSING WHITE FROST-FACE 402   32
NO MORE CHILDREN TO LAUNCH IN A WORLD YOU MISTRUST   411   10
WORLD   413   11
THE NEW NAKED LITTLE REPUBLICS COME INTO THE WORLD   413   16
ON THE ROOF OF THE WORLD   413   20
THE WORLD   414   28
AND GO FORTH TO CHANGE THE WORLD   428   19
UPON THE WORLD TO BRING A CHANGE TO PASS   428   22
OF A SWAMPED CIVILISATION AND START A NEW WORLD OF MAN   429   12
AND MAKE A NEW JOB OF THE HUMAN WORLD   429   16
AND HAVE A WORLD OF MEN   453   12
THINK OF THE WORLD THAT YOU'RE STIFLING IN   457   5
THINK WHAT A WORLD IT MIGHT BE   457   6
AND SEE SATAN BARGAINING THE WORLD AWAY   483   12
TO ALL AND ANYBODY ALL AND ANYBODY ALL OVER THE WORLD   487   10
THERE WOULD BE ABUNDANCE IN THE WORLD   488   5
WE'VE RISEN IN THE WORLD ALL THREE   490   22
OF PUTTING US IN THE WORLD   493   6
WOE WOE TO THE WORLD   496   18
DEEP BEYOND THE WORLD OF MAN   499   7
IN THIS WORLD OF MECHANICAL SELF-ASSERTION   511   5
FLAME DEVOURS THE WORLD   511   9
WORLD   512   30
AND THEY DIVIDE THE WORLD   516   13
AND THE WORLD IS GOING TO PIECES BETWEEN THEM   516   16
WHICH THREATEN TO TEAR THE WORLD IN TWO BETWEEN   516   22

WORLD
    WE WANT A NEW WORLD OF WILD PEACE WHERE LIVING IS FREE   519 22
    THE WAGES OF VICIOUS COMPETITION IS THE WORLD WE LIVE IN   521 4
    THE WORLD IS WAITING FOR A NEW GREAT MOVEMENT OF   522 26
    SO LONG AS THE THING IS DONE NEATLY AND THE WORLD IS LE+   532 30
    IF MEN ONLY FOUGHT OUTWARDS INTO THE WORLD   538 15
    WHAT HAS HAPPENED IN THE WORLD   539 1
    IT IS VERY UNNERVING MOVING IN A WORLD OF SMOULDERING   539 4
    AND GLEAMS ON THE WORLD WITH THE WARM DARK VISION OF   544 24
    AFRAID OF THE WORLD BUT TO SALLY FORTH   550 23
    AND THE WHITE SNOW GLISTENED THE WHITE WORLD WAS GAY   550 29
    WITH THE CREST OF THE DIRTY DRAB WORLD DOWN BELOW   551 2
    TO THE DIRTY DRAB WORLD   551 4
    I ROSE UP IN THE WORLD OOPAY   551 25
    BUT STILL I ROSE QUITE HIGH IN THE WORLD   552 3
    YOU'LL NONE OF YOU RISE IN THE WORLD LIKE I DID   552 27
    WORLD SHINE LIKE THE PROMISED LAND   554 8
    WITH THE WORLD BELOW   557 31
    SEEK ALL THE WORLD ROUND THERE'S NONE CAN BE FOUND   574 17
    MY BRITISH BLOOD THE WORLD SHALL KNOW   576 21
    AND HIS BRITISH BLOOD THE WORLD IT KNEW   576 25
    AND THE WORLD IT DIDN'T GIVE A HOOT   577 1
    OF THE FACTORY WORLD   586 12
    IS BETTER THAN ANYTHING ELSE IN THE WORLD   601 5
    IN THE WORLD   602 9
    DOING ONE'S OWN LITTLE JOBS SEEING THE WORLD BEYOND   610 5
    THE WORLD IS MOVING MOVING STILL TOWARDS FURTHER DEMOCR+   611 6
    OH WHEN THE WORLD IS HOPELESS   631 9
    OF THE FACTORY WORLD   632 27
    THE COURAGE OF ROSINESS IN A CABBAGE WORLD   634 27
    WORLD   637 18
    THEY ARE THE NICEST PEOPLE IN THE WORLD   659 26
    I HAVE TRAVELLED AND LOOKED AT THE WORLD AND LOVED IT   662 7
    NOW I DON'T WANT TO LOOK AT THE WORLD ANY MORE   662 8
    THE WORLD WILL BE TORN IN TWO   663 27
    THERE IS A MARVELLOUS RICH WORLD OF CONTACT AND SHEER F+   667 3
    THE WOMAN WHO LOOKS FOR ME IN THE WORLD   672 23
    O WHEN THE OLD WORLD SACRIFICED A RAM   679 11
    WHEN FROM A WORLD OF MOSSES AND OF FERNS   683 1
    THEY ARE SO SILENT THEY ARE IN ANOTHER WORLD   683 21
    SLEEPING ON THE HEARTH OF THE LIVING WORLD   700 8
    OF FIRE AND THE WET EARTH AND THE WIDE AIR OF THE WORLD   706 5
    BUT THE FOUR WE HAVE ALWAYS WITH US THEY ARE OUR WORLD   706 8
    OH IN THE WORLD OF THE FLESH OF MAN   712 5
    OH IN THE WORLD OF THINGS   712 8
    BUT IN THE WORLD OF THE SOUL OF MAN   712 10
    WHICH WISHES TO BLASPHEME THE WORLD INTO GREYNESS   713 7
    A CENTRE OF THE EVIL WORLD   714 21
    TO REDUCE THE WORLD TO GREY ASH   716 3
    AND SOON IT WILL RISE ON THE WORLD ON THE OUTSIDE WORLD   718 16
    AND NOTHING IN THE WORLD IS LOVELIER THAN SLEEP   725 3
    THE WORLD IS CREATED AFRESH   725 10
    O AND IN THE WORLD   725 14
    THE BITTER WORLD AMID THE SMOKE   744 23
    OF IMMORTALITY INTO THE WORLD   745 3
    RAIN AND A FALLING WORLD   748 19
    EVERYTHING IN THE WORLD OF CULTURE AND SUPERIORITY   763 10
    WE WOULDN'T HURT YOU FOR THE WORLD SAYS THE PARASITE   765 23
    WHERE THE WORLD IS VIRGIN AND HOUSELESS   768 16
    AS HE SLOWLY WALKS FROM THE WESTERN DOOR TO THE WORLD   770 14
    DO YOU WANT TO RISE IN THE WORLD   773 12
    OH BUT A MAN WANTS TO GET ON IN THE WORLD   773 21
    AND SO WHEN THE OUTSIDE WORLD CALLS UPON AMERICA TO ACT+   775 29
    HE LINGERS ON FROM AN OLD SAVAGE WORLD THAT STILL HAS   776 8
    HE WOULD GO OUT INTO THE WORLD AND BECOME   778 14
    FROM THE FIRE THAT BOILS IN THE MOLTEN HEART OF THE WOR+   782 15
    THE HEART OF THE WORLD IS THE HEART OF THE EARTH WHERE +   782 16
    THE OLD FATHER OF LIFE AT THE HEART OF THE WORLD LIFE-F+   783 2
    OF EXPIRATION TURNED INTO THE WORLD AGAIN   784 15
    LET US HAVE A SPRING CLEANING IN THE WORLD   792 33
    HOW NICE TO SIT IN THE CINE WHERE THE PICTURE OF ALL TH+   794 17
    WORLD   794 31
    THE SPIRITS OF THE COLD DEAD WHISTLE IN THE EARS OF THE+   795 15
    THOSE THAT HAVE MASTERED THE FORCES OF THE WORLD DIE IN+   796 14
    BUT THE GREY DOG BELONGS TO THE ASH OF THE WORLD   808 20
    WHEN THE END OF THE WORLD WE ARE TOLD IS SCROLLED   814 11
    WHAT YET ANOTHER BAD END OF THE WORLD   814 27
    BRAGGADOCCIOS AROUND THE BLUE RIMS OF THE WORLD   814 30
    NOW THE WORLD IS ENDING IN DUST AND IN SORROW   815 1
    THE WORLD IS ENDING LET'S HURRY TO BORROW   815 2
    IN THE WORLD WITHOUT END AMEN   823 12
    WHEN I SEE WHAT A MESS MEN HAVE MADE OF THE WORLD   837 12
    MANLY AND TACKLE THE OUTSIDE WORLD   843 3
    CAVES INWARD KNOWING THE OUTSIDE WORLD   843 4
    HOW LONELY IN THE WIDE WORLD IS THIS PLAYGROUND   867 6
    THE BONNY FLOATING ARK OF THIS FAIR WORLD   876 10
    AND THE WORLD WAS ALIGHT   884 7
    AND I LIFT MY HEAD UPON THE TROUBLED TANGLED WORLD AND +   *900 1
    AND I LIFT MY HEAD UPON THE TROUBLED TANGLED WORLD AND +   *903 14
    THERE LIES THE WORLD MY DARLING FULL OF WONDER AND WIST+   *905 9
    MY WORLD IS A PAINTED FRESCO WHERE COLOURED SHAPES   *906 11
    THE GIGANTIC FLESH OF THE WORLD   *908 1
    MY WORLD IS A PAINTED FRESCO WHERE COLOURED SHAPES   *908 5
    OUT OF THE DISTANCE NEARER COMMANDING MY DREAMY WORLD   *908 15
    FLESH OF THE WORLD   *909 24
    IT SEEMED THAT I AND THE WOVEN WORLD   *935 6
    IN WIDE AND WIDER CIRCLES ROUND THE WORLD   *943 25

WORLD-BALANCING
    STRONG LIKE THE GREATEST FORCE OF WORLD-BALANCING   271 20

WORLDLY
    ALL THAT THE WORLDLY DAY HAS MEANT   41 26

WORLDS
    THE WORLD WITHIN WORLDS IS A WOMB WHENCE ISSUES ALL   88 33
    WORLD WITHIN WORLDS A WOMB THAT GIVES AND TAKES   89 8
    INTO THE WOMB OF THE WORLDS THAT NOTHING KNOWS   89 31
    THUNDERS IN HEAVEN TILL THE BRAVE WORLDS REEL   773 8
    THAT THE LORD GOD RESTED THE WORLDS ON   819 10
    WORLDS WITHOUT END WITHOUT REASON WHY   823 21
    IN CURLS AND FLAPS BETWEEN WORLDS THAT PLOD   823 26
    AND POISED WITH A SENSE OF JUSTICE AS WORLDS ARE POISED   *952 9

WORLD-SOUL
    AND WORSTED BY THE EVIL WORLD-SOUL OF TODAY   709 2
    OH THERE IS EVIL THERE IS AN EVIL WORLD-SOUL   712 23
    IT IS PART OF THE EVIL WORLD-SOUL SPINNING   713 3
    IS EVIL EVIL PART OF THE EVIL WORLD-SOUL   713 6
    MAKES AN EVIL WORLD-SOUL WHICH PURPOSES   716 2

WORLD'S
    OF THE WATERS WITHIN HIM ONLY THE WORLD'S OLD WISDOM   130 15
    LIKE ANY PRINCE SUCH STORES OF THE WORLD'S SUPPLY   264 4
    GREECE AND THE WORLD'S MORNING   311 27
    AND I'LL LIE IN HER LAP WHERE THE WORLD'S WILD ROSE   858 6
    THAT FRINGE WITH SHADOW ALL THIS WORLD'S EXISTENCE   *959 2

WORM
    IN A WORM THAT IS BLIND YET STRIVES   170 5
    YOU'RE JUST A WORM   431 32
    THEN YOU'RE JUST THE WORM THAT HAS TURNED   432 4
    IN EITHER CASE A WORM   432 5
    THE CONFORMING WORM STAYS JUST INSIDE THE SKIN   432 6
    THE UNCONFORMING WORM THAT IS THE WORM THAT HAS   432 10
    BUT WHY SHOULD THE WORM THAT HAS TURNED PROTEST SO   432 20
    SO I CAN'T SEE WHERE THE WORM THAT HAS TURNED PUTS ANYT+ 432 34
    THE WORM THAT IS TOO CUNNING TO TURN   432 36
    THE TURNED WORM SHOUTS I BRAVELY BOOZE   433 2
    THE TURNED WORM BOASTS I COPULATE   433 4
    YOU'RE A D B B P BB SAYS THE WORM   433 6
    POOR MENTAL WORM   529 16
    LIKE THE WORM I AM SO HE WRIGGLED AND GOT THERE   534 5
    THE SECRET IN THE BLIND MOUTH OF THE WORM   744 28
    AS IF SHE WERE A WORM OR A HIRED WHORE WHO BORED HIM   *948 17
    SO THE POOR THING IS LEFT FEELING AN UTTER WORM   *948 19

WORMS
    WORMS   527 8
    TO MAKE THEM FEEL ABSOLUTE WORMS   *948 26
    LEAVING THEM CRUSHED WORMS   *949 13

WORMY
    JUST LIKE AN OLD MUSHROOM ALL WORMY INSIDE AND HOLLOW   431 20
    FULL OF SEETHING WORMY HOLLOW FEELINGS   431 22

WORN
    AND CAME BACK TINGLING CLEAN BUT WORN AND FRAYED   99 13
    WORN HER AWAY TO THE QUICK SO SHE FAINTLY FARES   131 26
    BUT WORN OUT THEY HIDE NO MORE THE WALLS THEY STAND BEF+ 174 22
    I WHO AM WORN AND CAREFUL   199 25
    YET NO PATHWAY WORN   249 4
    THE WORN ARCHES OF THEIR SPINES SUPPORT   426 3
    WE HAVE WORN OUT THE GODS AND THEY US   439 21
    HAS WORN US WEARY OF RENUNCIATION AND LOVE AND EVEN PAIN 439 24
    I AM WORN OUT   506 25
    AFTER ALL THE TRAGEDIES ARE OVER AND WORN OUT   508 25
    WE HAVE WORN THEM OUT   510 17
    THE FLOOD SUBSIDES AND THE BODY LIKE A WORN SEA-SHELL   720 12
    WORN HER AWAY TO THE QUICK SO SHE FAINTLY FACES   *937 25
    AND THE KEYS WITH LITTLE HOLLOWS THAT MY MOTHER'S FINGE+ *940 4

WORNA
    LET THAT BE 'APPEN IT WORNA TH' DRINK NEITHER   60 27

WORN-OUT
    THE WORN-OUT MACHINE AT LAST BREAKS DOWN   676 4
    THE DEATH OF NOTHINGNESS WORN-OUT MACHINES KAPUT   676 7

WORN'T
    SHE WORN'T HARD TER FIND   138 34

WORRIED
    SO WORRIED BY THE HOLY GHOST   536 21
    AND IT WORRIED ME A GOOD DEAL   555 28
    HE FROWNS AS IF HE WERE WORRIED AS IF THE PLACE   734 19

WORROW
    BLACK FOR THE FUNERAL WOW WALY AND WORROW   815 3

WORRY
    AY I'M SORRY THA NEDNA WORRY   83 20
    THEN WHEN JOHN THOMAS DON'T WORRY YOU   493 19

WORSE
    WHAT THING BETTER ARE YOU WHAT WORSE   131 19
    WORSE LET ME NOT DECEIVE MYSELF   274 8
    BUT HE ROSE AND FROM A TERROR WORSE THAN ME HE FLEW PAST 344 5
    WORSE EVEN THAN THE HIDEOUS TERROR OF ME WITH MY HANDKE+ 344 23
    WORSE THAN THE CRY OF THE NEW-BORN   364 13
    YOU WORSE THAN A CARRION-CROW   398 31
    OR WORSE STILL   433 24
    AND DIRT IF IT ISN'T SIN IS WORSE ESPECIALLY DIRT INSIDE 464 5
    SEX ISN'T SIN BUT DIRTY SEX IS WORSE SO THERE YOU ARE   464 8
    WHICH IS PERHAPS WORSE   518 2
    WORSE THAN THE EVIL EYE   538 14
    THE UPPER CLASSES THEY'RE WORSE   553 6
    A WORSE LOT O' JUJUBEY ASSES   553 15
    TO HIM WORSE THAN A BOLSHEVIST JEW OR AN UTTER   576 8
    OF DANGER I FIND HER EVEN WORSE THAN THE FIELDS WHERE W+ 752 12
    THE INDIAN QUESTION HAS WORSE LUCK BECOME A POLITICAL   777 13
    WERE WORSE THAN BEING LEFT ALONE IN LIFE   879 27

WORSE
  PALS WORSE N'R ONY NAME AS YOU COULD CALL   *911 12

WORSER
  SO VERY MUCH WORSER OFF THAN 'ER WOR BEFORE AN' NOW LOO+   *925 21

WORSHIP
  WOULD WORSHIP THEE LETTING MY BUTTOCKS PRANCE   40 18
  NAKED OF WORSHIP OF LOVE OR OF ADORNMENT   197 14
  DO YOU THINK IT IS PURE WORSHIP   235 25
  THOUGH WE DO NOT WORSHIP   271 29
  IN A SORT OF WORSHIP   403 27
  ALL MEN WORSHIP THE WONDER OF LIFE   649 9
  AND WORSHIP IS THE JOY OF THE GLEAM FROM THE EYES OF TH+   649 16

WORSHIPPERS
  ALL MEN ARE WORSHIPPERS   649 1

WORST
  THAT LITTLE COD'S THE HOLY WORST   493 23
  THE WORST OF THE YOUNGER GENERATION THOSE LATTER-DAY   531 1
  AT THE WORST YOU CAN ONLY SAVE IT UP   614 2
  THE WORST OF IT IS   619 18

WORSTED
  AND I MUST SAY I AM OFTEN WORSTED   497 25
  AND WORSTED BY THE EVIL WORLD-SOUL OF TODAY   709 2

WORTH
  WORTH   57 22
  AND I SHALL COUNT THE STAMP AND WORTH   59 13
  HALF SUBSTANCELESS AND WITHOUT GRAVE WORTH   118 17
  WERE NOT WORTH WHILE NOR SPINNING WORTH THE EFFORT   197 21
  AND WHAT IT'S WORTH   234 4
  AND THEN IF IT'S WORTH IT BE GRATEFUL   237 11
  SHE'S A SILVERY DOVE WORTH MORE THAN ALL I'VE GOT   238 22
  SO THE LION OF THE SENSES THOUGHT IT WAS WORTH IT   324 25
  TO USE THE SPERM OF WHAT'S WORTH WHILE IN US   429 20
  OR AT LEAST WORTH TREASURY NOTES   458 27
  FOR MANKIND SAYS WITH ONE VOICE HOW MUCH IS HE WORTH   486 20
  SQUEAKILY BELLOWING FOR ALL HE WAS WORTH   492 1
  LIFE MIGHT NOT BE WORTH FIGHTING FOR   497 14
  A WIFE ISN'T ALWAYS WORTH FIGHTING FOR   497 16
  IT ALL DEPENDS WHETHER I FOUND THEM WORTH FIGHTING FOR   497 18
  AND WE FEEL IS WORTH DOING   520 8
  THEY'D BE WORTH LOOKING AT   524 18
  AND TRIP IT FOR ALL SHE WAS WORTH   550 24
  IT DAMN WELL WASN'T WORTH IT   553 1
  FIGHTING FOR SOMETHING WORTH FIGHTING FOR   560 27
  YOU ARE NOT WORTH A GOD   795 9
  FOR ALL WE ARE WORTH   813 8
  AND MAKE THE CONSIDERABLE MESS THAT ISN'T EVEN WORTH TH+   *947 12

WORTHY
  GOD MAKE ME OF IT WORTHY   576 18
  SO BIG AND WORTHY IN MY OWN SMALL ARK   876 3

WOULD-BE-OXFORD
  AND USING HIS MOST MELODIOUS WOULD-BE-OXFORD VOICE   433 16

WOULD-BE-PERFECT
  NOW YOU ARE FREE OF THE TOILS OF A WOULD-BE-PERFECT LOVE   411 16

WOULD-BE
  THE WOULD-BE OXFORD VOICE   433 25

WOULDN'T
  WOULDN'T I STICK THE SALVIA IN MY COAT   315 12
  WOULDN'T YOU LIKE TO BE LIKE THAT WELL OFF AND QUITE THE   430 24
  WE WOULDN'T INSIST ON IT FOR A MOMENT   434 9
  WOULDN'T THINK IT NECESSARY TO MAKE CONVERSATION   506 21
  THEY WOULDN'T SUDDENLY BECOME THEMSELVES ARISTOCRATIC   527 24
  I WOULDN'T INSULT YOU WITH THE SUGGESTION   541 18
  THE SIGHT OF AN ORDINARY TOM WOULDN'T SEND THEM INTO   581 24
  BUT YOU MUST NEVER TAKE THEM SERIOUSLY THEY WOULDN'T UN+   660 15
  WE WOULDN'T HURT YOU FOR THE WORLD SAYS THE PARASITE   765 23

WOUND
  'TIS THE WOUND OF LOVE GOES HOME   42 8
  AND BLESS THE WOUND   113 28
  OUT OF THE WOUND   117 27
  OR IF ONLY YOU WOULD REPULSE ME A WOUND WOULD BE   122 19
  LIKE A WOUND THE EXPOSURE OF HER SECRET ON THE OPEN DAY   283 32
  STRUT LIKE PEG-TOPS WOUND AROUND WITH HUNDREDS OF YARDS   388 17
  IRON GIVES THE DEADLY WOUND   712 6
  FORWARDS AS HE RUBS THE WOUND   734 7
  AS A BEE WAXES OVER A WOUND   824 28

WOUNDED
  THAT IS WOUNDED THERE   159 3
  WHAT WAS WOUNDED IS SOUND   461 22

WOUNDING
  WOUNDING THEMSELVES AGAINST HER DENYING HER FECUND   91 28
  WOUNDING THEMSELVES AGAINST HER DENYING HER GREAT EMBRA+   *926 21

WOUNDS
  WITH WOUNDS BETWEEN THEM AND SUFFERING LIKE A GUEST   155 10
  IT WOUNDS ME TO DEATH WITH MY OWN NOT-BEING DEFINITE IN+   266 16
  FROM WOUNDS BELOW THE DEEP BLACK WAVE   428 13
  I AM ILL BECAUSE OF WOUNDS TO THE SOUL TO THE DEEP EMOT+   620 13
  AND THE WOUNDS TO THE SOUL TAKE A LONG LONG TIME ONLY   620 15
  IS WASHING IN THROUGH THE BREACHES OF OUR WOUNDS   718 7
  MY KISS TO WOUNDS   743 1
  FEED ON OUR WOUNDS LIKE BREAD RECEIVE OUR BLOOD   743 4
  IN OUR SHEAF OF SELF-GATHERED WOUNDS WE GO TO MEET   743 8
  AS IF WITHDRAWN FROM LIVING WOUNDS RAN RED   884 26

WOUND-STUMP
  FROM THE SMALL WOUND-STUMP   305 7

WOUND'S
  AT THE WOUND'S ACHING CICATRICE   869 2

WOVE
  WHEN MEN WOVE WITH THEIR HANDS AND THEIR SOUL'S ATTENTI+   *949 26

WOVEN
  GREAT SEALS UPON YOUR OUTGOINGS AND WOVEN   154 24
  AN ENDLESS TAPESTRY THE PAST HAS WOVEN DRAPES   173 19
  NOR WOVEN WITH ITALIAN ART   575 18
  A HAT QUAINTLY CURIOUSLY WOVEN LUXURIOUS WITH BIG ROSES   856 12
  HAD BEEN WOVEN INTO A GLORIOUS MESH LIKE A BRIDAL LACE   860 14
  AN ENDLESS TAPESTRY THE PAST HAS WOVEN DRAPES   *906 13
  AN ENDLESS TAPESTRY THE PAST HAS WOVEN DRAPES   *908 7
  IT SEEMED THAT I AND THE WOVEN WORLD   *935 6
  THEY LIVED THEMSELVES FORTH LIKE A TREE PUTTING OUT WOV+ *949 28
  AND IT MADE THEM HAPPY AND THE WOVEN CLOTH OF THEIR HAN+ *949 29

WOW
  BLACK FOR THE FUNERAL WOW WALY AND WORROW   815 3

WOWSER
  THERE IS A LITTLE WOWSER   493 1

WRACK
  TO GAPE AND OUR HOUSE IS GOING TO WRACK   462 14
  ROSY WRACK   854 20

WRANGLE
  ONLY I AND THE CLASS MUST WRANGLE THIS WORK IS A BITTER+   76 22

WRAP
  HOW I LOVE ALL OF YOU DO YOU FEEL ME WRAP YOU   245 7
  THEN LET THE FLAME WRAP ROUND US   813 3

WRAPPED
  IF BUT I COULD HAVE WRAPPED YOU IN MYSELF   100 14
  CHAIN OF MY MYSTIC WILL WRAPPED PERFECTLY   154 25
  UPON YOU WRAPPED IN INDOMITABLE ME   154 26
  WRAPPED TO THE EYES THE SHEET BOUND CLOSE ON HIS BROWS   403 10
  AND I AM WRAPPED IN THE LEAD OF A COFFIN-LINING THE LIV+   630 7
  WRAPPED IN THE DARK-RED MANTLE OF WARM MEMORIES   723 19
  WRAPPED UP IN THE SKY'S DIM SPACE OF HOARSE SILENCE   *898 15
  WRAPPED UP IN THE SKY'S DIM SPACE OF HOARSE SILENCE   *901 24
  SLIPS OUT THE SOUL INVISIBLE ONE WRAPPED STILL   *957 6
  WRAPPED IN THE DARK-RED MANTLE OF THE BODY'S MEMORIES   *958 31

WRAPS
  THAT WRAPS THE NORTH IN STUPOR AND PURPLE TRAVELS THE D+   149 3

WRAPT
  AND WRAPT INVIOLABLE IN SOFT CYPRESS-TREES   298 13
  AN INDIAN WALKING WRAPT IN HIS WINDING SHEET   816 7

WRATH
  FOR YOUR WRATH AND YES I OPINE   168 18
  OR DRAGON-MOUTHED SALVIA WITH GOLD THROAT OF WRATH   314 26
  IS YOUR WRATH RED AS SALVIAS   314 30
  OF YELLOW-RED OUTREACHING LIVING WRATH   317 9
  VOLUPTUOUS WRATH   324 33
  HIS FIRES OF WRATH ARE BANKED DOWN   327 5
  DAY OF WRATH O DAY OF WARNING   511 8
  BUT THE WOMEN ARE MY FAVOURITE VESSELS OF WRATH   541 9
  FLASHING OF DELICATE WRATH   735 23
  AND LEAVE ME TORTURE AND WRATH AND A DROSSED DESPAIR   874 9
  AYE BUSY WITH A FEW HARD TASKS AND WRATH   875 31
  THE HARSH COLD WRATH OF MY WORDS DROVE ON AND STILL   *897 1
  THEN UP WITH WRATH THE RED-EYED MORNING QUICKENS   *933 12

WREAK
  HOW THEY WREAK THEIR SPITE ON WOMEN   447 9
  I REALISED WHAT A LUST THERE WAS IN HIM TO WREAK HIS SO+   620 6

WREATH
  A WREATH OF MIST WITH NOTHING BEHIND IT   580 4
  A WREATH OF MIST IS THE USUAL THING   580 5
  A WREATH OF ENGLISH MIST WOULD DO   580 11

WREATHE
  WREATHE AND ENLAP AND ANOINT THEM   229 3
  WREATHE STRONG WEED ROUND THE KNEES AS THE DARKNESS   425 13
  AND A BREATH OF VAPOUR BEGAN TO WREATHE UP   682 14
  I RAISE MY FACE SO IT SHALL WREATHE ME   883 13

WREATHED
  WITH LONG PINS LEANING OUT THEIR PORCELAIN GLOBES WREAT+   856 13

WREATHING
  MISTS WREATHING MISTS   438 6
  WREATHING   462 28

WREATHS
  THORN-BLOSSOM LIFTING IN WREATHS OF SMOKE BETWEEN   116 3
  WREATHS   233 7

WRECK
  MOUTH-HAIR OF SOLDIERS PASSING ABOVE US OVER THE WRECK +   66 29
  AND AMONG THE WRECK OF THE THEATRE CROWD   71 28
  ONLY TO WRECK ON THE SHORES OF NIGHT AGAIN   771 26
  ONE OF HIS BELOVEDS LOOKING RATHER A WRECK   *948 8

WRECKAGE
    THE WRECKAGE   71 27
    TO KEEP STILL AND LET THE WRECKAGE OF OURSELVES GO   514 1
    STREWN WITH DIM WRECKAGE AND CROWDED WITH CRYING SOULS   *957 16

WRECKED
    WRECKED CHIEFLY ME   *897 12

WRECKS
    THEY WERE BOTH NERVOUS WRECKS BECAUSE   605 17

WRENCH
    BUT HORRIBLE AS IF YOUR HEART WOULD WRENCH OUT   447 29

WRESTLE
    AND WRESTLE WITH FOR THE PRIZE OF PERFECT LOVE   411 9

WRESTLING
    TWO GREAT DRAGON-FLIES WRESTLING   224 2

WRESTS
    TAKE THEM AWAY FROM THEIR VENTURE BEFORE FATE WRESTS   147 16
    OF HAVING AND GETTING AND OWNING THE STRUGGLE WHICH WRE+   175 23

WRETCH
    AND SHE SAID DON'T DARE YOU WRETCH TO BE LEWD   577 15
    WRETCH   643 24

WRETCHED
    POINTING MY EYES IN WRETCHED DEFIANCE WHERE LOVE HIDES +   63 25
    I PRESSED THE WRETCHED THROTTLED FLOWER BETWEEN   125 13
    FOR POOR YOUNG WRETCHED MEN   558 20
    I PRESSED THE WRETCHED THROTTLED FLOWER BETWEEN   *936 12

WRETCHES
    WRETCHES UTTER WRETCHES KEEP YOUR HANDS FROM BEANS SAITH   303 15

WRIGGLE
    NOW THE PROUSTIAN LOT DEAR DARLING DEATH LET ME WRIGGLE   534 3
    DO THEY JAZZ AND JUMP AND WRIGGLE   558 21
    WRIGGLE AND WAG AND SLAVER AND GET THE MENTALITY OF A D+   645 4

WRIGGLED
    LIKE THE WORM I AM SO HE WRIGGLED AND GOT THERE   534 5

WRIGGLES
    A STILL BRIGHTER WHITE SNAKE WRIGGLES AMONG IT SPILLED   647 14
    SO IT WRIGGLES ITS WAY EVEN FURTHER DOWN FURTHER DOWN   701 30

WRIGGLING
    AND YOUR BLACK LITTLE BODY BOUNCING AND WRIGGLING   396 5
    AND TUMBLING WRIGGLING DOWN THE SKY   647 15
    FATHOMLESS FATHOMLESS SELF-CONSCIOUSNESS WRIGGLING   701 22

WRING
    WHICH IS PERHAPS THE LAST ADMISSION THAT LIFE HAS TO WR+   338 16

WRINGS
    YOU LOOK SO LIKE BABY IT WRINGS MY HEART   842 15

WRINKLE
    TEARS WRINKLE OUR FACES LIKE RAIN IN THE HOLLY   814 24

WRINKLED
    AND THE YOUNG BULL IN THE FIELD WITH HIS WRINKLED SAD F+   255 33
    WRINKLED WITH SECRETS   279 8
    WRINKLED PILLARS OF THEIR LEGS AS THEY WERE BEING   390 17
    AND A WRINKLED REPROACHFUL LOOK   394 30
    ALL YOUR WRINKLED MISERERE CHINESE BLACK LITTLE FACE   396 3
    ALL THAT DUST OUT OF YOUR WRINKLED FACE   397 31
    WRINKLED UNDERHUNG PHYSIOG THAT LOOKS AS IF IT HAD DONE   398 6
    WRINKLED OLD AUNTY'S FACE   400 19
    AND WRINKLED RIPE FULFILMENT   503 16
    THE WRINKLED SMILE OF COMPLETENESS THAT FOLLOWS A LIFE   503 17

WRIST
    WITH SWOLLEN VEINS THAT MET IN THE WRIST   123 25
    AND FEEL HIM GRIPPING MY WRIST AS IF HE WOULD BREAK IT   733 4
    WITH SWOLLEN VEINS THAT MET IN THE WRIST   *934 31
    SWELL DOWN HER RICH HOT WRIST   *937 8

WRISTS
    IS ME IN THE NARROWS OF MY WRISTS   460 26
    THE KNOCK OF THE BLOOD IN MY WRISTS   461 2
    THAT RUNS DOWN TO THE SHALLOWS OF MY WRISTS AND BREAKS   705 5
    MY WRISTS SEEM BROKEN AND MY HEART SEEMS DEAD   727 19
    THE STINGING NETTLES ON MY WRISTS WOKE ME   881 16
    I AWOKE WITH THE YOUNG NETTLES ON MY WRISTS   882 5
    THEN THE STINGING NETTLES ON MY WRISTS   882 20

WRIT
    ONLY PROBLEMS WRIT ON THE FACE OF THINGS   118 22
    OR THE BURDEN OF MAN WRIT LARGE   411 13
    IN THE W C WRIT LARGE   492 18

WRITE
    AS THEY WRITE THEIR ROUND HEADS BUSILY BOWED   51 12
    WHAT DOES IT MATTER TO ME IF THEY CAN WRITE   74 27
    AND I CAN NEITHER PAINT NOR WRITE   680 10
    ALL PEOPLE THAT CAN WRITE OR PAINT   680 12
    AS THEY WRITE THEIR ROUND HEADS BUSILY BOWED   *898 24
    AS THEY WRITE THEIR ROUND HEADS BUSILY BOWED   *902 8
    NOT EVEN THE WHITE MOTHS WRITE   *929 23

WRITES
    HAS CONVEYED THIS THING THAT SITS AND WRITES   887 6

WRITHE
    INTERIOR A HOUSE OF DREAMS WHERE THE DREAMERS WRITHE AN+   174 24
    WE WRITHE AND LUST IN BOTH   177 20
    FROM THIS NIGHTMARE WE WRITHE IN   177 23
    IN THE ENDLESS WRITHE OF THE LAST THE LAST SELF-KNOWLED+   700 27

WRITHED
    IN WHICH I HAVE WRITHED   207 32
    WRITHED LIKE LIGHTNING AND WAS GONE   351 15

WRITHING
    TAKE WRITHING FORMS OF ALL BEASTS THAT SWEAT AND THAT F+   73 15
    THE WRITHING OF MYRIADS OF WORKMEN ALL DREAMING THEY AR+   175 2
    A SLEEP THAT IS WRITHING STUPOR WEIGHED DOWN SO WE CAN+   175 14
    THE RICH AND THE POOR ALIKE DREAMING AND WRITHING ALL I+   175 15
    WRITHING TWISTING SUPERPENETRATED   207 26
    AND THE TURNING DOWN PLUNGE OF WRITHING OF SELF-KNOWLED+   701 5
    WRITHING AND TWISTING IN ALL THE REVOLUTIONS   701 19
    WRITHING DEEPER AND DEEPER IN ALL THE MINUTIAE OF SELF-+   701 23

WRITING
    TERRACE WRITING   347 20
    LONG-HAIRED PEOPLE PAINTING THE INDIAN AND WRITING   778 10

WRITINGS
    NO READINGS AND WRITINGS   857 5

WRITTEN
    PEACE IS WRITTEN ON THE DOORSTEP   293 13
    BUT I CAN'T FOR IT IS WRITTEN AGAINST ME I MUST NOT   741 5

WRONG
    AH'N PUT MY-SEN I' TH' WRONG LIZ   83 26
    I THOUGHT THAT LOVE WOULD DO ALL THINGS BUT NOW I KNOW +   93 1
    OF THIS LAND WHEREON THE WRONG ROAD GOES   164 16
    AND BREATHING THE FROZEN MEMORY OF HIS WRONG   226 4
    WE HAVE DONE WRONG   232 9
    YOU TELL ME I AM WRONG   278 1
    WHO ARE YOU WHO IS ANYBODY TO TELL ME I AM WRONG   278 2
    I AM NOT WRONG   278 3
    DO YOU MEAN IT IS WRONG THE GOLD-FILMED SKIN INTEGUMENT   278 29
    WRONG   289 13
    OF SOMETHING GONE WRONG IN THE MIDDLE   291 18
    HOMER WAS WRONG IN SAYING WOULD THAT STRIFE MIGHT PASS   348 1
    WE LOOK AT HIM THROUGH THE WRONG END OF THE LONG TELESC+   372 22
    OR LIKE A LIFTED HAND HAILING AT HER WRONG END   385 33
    HE SMILES FOOLISHLY AS IF HE WERE CAUGHT DOING WRONG   401 20
    AND THIS IS ALL WRONG   487 6
    AND HAD A BRAVE DESTINY EVEN WHEN SHE WENT WRONG   535 16
    TELL ME WHAT'S WRONG   551 21
    IT'S YOU WHO'VE BEEN WRONG   564 6
    OR IS SOMETHING MISSING OR WHAT'S WRONG WITH THEM   578 20
    I TELL YOU THERE MUST BE SOMETHING WRONG   579 5
    WRONG   663 21
    THE WRONG   663 23
    THE WRONG   663 25
    SELF-SACRIFICE AFTER ALL IS A WRONG AND MISTAKEN IDEA   678 1
    IT CANNOT BE ANYTHING BUT WRONG TO SACRIFICE   678 2
    JUST AS IT CANNOT BE ANYTHING BUT WRONG TO CUT THE THRO+   678 4
    PERHAPS WHAT'S WRONG IS SIMPLY LACK OF VITALITY   842 28
    AND BEHOLD THEM DEPLORABLY DEAD BY WRONG USAGE DEFACED   859 24

WRONGED
    AND WHAT I HAVE FAILED IN WHAT I HAVE WRONGED   *946 4

WRONGLY
    OF THE STUFF OF THE NIGHT FINDING MYSELF ALL WRONGLY   133 7
    AND IT IS NOT BECAUSE THE MECHANISM IS WORKING WRONGLY   620 11

WROTE
    THE LORD WROTE IT ALL DOWN ON THE LITTLE SLATE   355 9
    THEY SAY I WROTE A NAUGHTY BOOK   491 13
    A MAN WROTE TO ME WE MISSED IT YOU AND I   603 9

WUNNA
    WENCH WUNNA HE   76 26
    AH WUNNA KISS THEE THA TREMBLES SO   138 14
    WENCH WUNNA HE   *918 18
    AN' THEN WI' THAT TWENTY POUND WE GI'E 'ER I S'D THINK +   *925 20

YACHTS
    WHO IN LASSITUDE LEAN AS YACHTS ON THE SEA-WIND LIE   73 11

YALLER
    ON TH' YALLER CLAY WI' TH' WHITE FLOWERS TOP OF IT   60 13
    AY AN' YALLER AS A CROWFLOWER AN' YET I' TH' DARK   77 7
    ON TH' YALLER CLAY AN' TH' WHITE FLOWERS TOP OF IT   *910 28
    AY AN' YALLER AS A CROWFLOWER AN' YET I' THE DARK   *918 25

YANKEE
    YANKEE YANKEE   291 28

YAPPING
    YAPPING IN HIS POWER AND HIS GLORY   704 23

YARD
    A YARD OF INDIA MUSLIN IS ALIVE WITH HINDU LIFE   448 21
    ALL ROUND THE YARD IT IS CLUCK MY BROWN HEN   *932 24

YARDS
STRUT LIKE PEG-TOPS WOUND AROUND WITH HUNDREDS OF YARDS   388 17
FOURTH DIMENSION NOT IN YARDS AND MILES LIKE THE ETERNA+   761 16

YARD-WAY
THROUGH THE OPEN YARD-WAY CAN I NOT GO PAST THE SHEDS   173 10

Y'ARE
WHO Y'ARE YIS YOU'RE LIZZIE STAINWRIGHT   81 22

YAWLS
FRIGATES BARKS AND PINNACES YAWLS   542 7

YAWN
CAN MAKE THEM YAWN I PUT MY HAND TO THE DINT   125 9
MAKE YOU PAUSE TO YAWN   353 3
CAN MAKE THEM YAWN I STRETCHED MY HAND TO THE DINT   *935 25

YAWNING
SLEEPING ON THE HEARTH AND YAWNING BEFORE THE FIRE   700 7
YAWNING AT HOME BEFORE THE FIRE OF LIFE   700 9

YAWP
AND HIM ALWAYS ENDING WITH A YAWP   413 23
YAWP   413 25
YAWP   414 7

YE
YE SWINDLED LITTLE BLOKES   560 18
SEEM TO SMILE YE GODS   644 20
LIFT UP YOUR HEADS O YE GATES   699 9
BUT YE THAT PERCEIVE ME BETWEEN   788 5
O YE GATES EVEN LIFT THEM UP   818 6
YE EVERLASTING DOORS   818 7
LIFT UP YOUR HEADS O YE GATES   818 10
FOR I TELL YE I SHONNA MARRY HER   *923 3

YEA
YEA BUT IT IS CRUEL WHEN UNDRESSED IS ALL THE BLOSSOM   120 1
YEA BUT I LOATHE YOU THAT YOU SHOULD WITHHOLD   122 23
YEA AND HER MOUTH'S PRUDENT AND CRUDE CARESS   127 23
YEA THOUGH THE VERY CLOUDS HAVE VANTAGE OVER ME   133 22
YEA WHAT GOOD BEGINNINGS   152 22
SHARP BREATHS TAKEN YEA AND I   219 23
YEA THOUGH I'M SORRY FOR THEE   220 8
WEEP THEN YEA   232 7
THE PROFOUND SENSUAL EXPERIENCE OF TRUTH YEA THIS IS   653 13
A MIXTURE OF YEA AND NAY   714 11
YEA THOUGH THE VERY CLOUDS HAVE VANTAGE OVER ME   772 9
YEA I AM ALWAYS HERE I AM LORD   787 27
YEA LORD EVEN TRAINS AND CAMIONS AND AUTOMOBILES   794 11
YEA I WOULD SHUT MY EYES I WOULD CLOSE MY WINDOWS   875 26
YEA AND HE LEAVES   877 3
YEA I WAS FINE ENOUGH TO EXPLORE YOU   *927 6
SHARP BREATHS SWISHING YEA BUT I   *944 3

YEAR
BUT 'ER'S OLD MOTHER 'ER'S TWENTY YEAR   77 5
ALL ROUND THE YEAR IT IS CLUCK MY BROWN HEN   119 15
LESS THAN A YEAR THE FOURFOLD FEET HAD PRESSED   155 7
WHO FOR ONE STRANGE YEAR WAS AS A BRIDE TO YOU YOU SET +   157 4
THE NEW YOUNG YEAR COMES IN   229 10
AND THE YEAR IS OVER   283 26
AND THE FIG IS FINISHED THE YEAR IS OVER   283 29
THE YEAR IS FALLEN OVER-RIPE   284 1
THE YEAR OF OUR WOMEN   284 2
THE YEAR OF OUR WOMEN IS FALLEN OVER-RIPE   284 3
THE YEAR OF OUR WOMEN IS FALLEN OVER-RIPE   284 6
THE GARDEN ONCE A YEAR   358 22
TO START THE YEAR ON EASTER SUNDAY   609 19
WHEN YEAR BY YEAR YEAR IN YEAR OUT IN MILLIONS IN INCRE+   631 17
THE LOVE I FEEL FOR MY FRIEND THIS YEAR   662 1
IS DIFFERENT FROM THE LOVE I FELT LAST YEAR   662 2
AND THE SILENCE OF SHORT DAYS THE SILENCE OF THE YEAR T+   727 13
ANOTHER SPRING OF YET ANOTHER YEAR   745 32
TO START THE GLORY OF ANOTHER YEAR   746 2
ANOTHER EPOCH IN ANOTHER YEAR   746 3
A YEAR OR TWO   842 6
THOUGH THE YEAR IS RIPENING LIKE A WOMAN WHO HAS CONCEI+   854 8
THAT YEAR WHEN THE PEAR WAS OUT MY DELIGHT   886 4
BUT 'ER'S OLD MOTHER 'ER'S TWENTY YEAR   *918 23

YEARN
THE HEAVENS ABOVE THAT WE YEARN TO AND ASPIRE TO   287 24
I DO NOT YEARN NOR ASPIRE FOR I AM A BLIND SAMSON   287 25

YEARNING
OF MY YEARNING BLOWS OVER YOU   118 15
YEARNING TOWARDS ENGLAND TOWARDS YOUR YOUNG CHILDREN   207 8
NOW THEN THAT ALL THEIR YEARNING IS HUSHED AND COVERED   410 24
NOW THE DIVIDED YEARNING IS OVER   411 6
GOD SIGHING AND YEARNING WITH TREMENDOUS CREATIVE YEARN+   691 2
STILL YEARNING BUT WITHERED AND NUMB   862 2
HERE HAVE I FOUND AN ANSWER FOR MY HOLLOW YEARNING   *907 10
HERE IN MY CLASS IS THE ANSWER FOR THE GREAT YEARNING   *909 6

YEARNING-EYED
THE BEGGAR-WOMAN THE YEARNING-EYED   64 5

YEARNINGLY
AS TENDRILS REACH OUT YEARNINGLY   52 4
AS TENDRILS REACHED OUT YEARNINGLY   *899 18
AS TENDRILS REACHED OUT YEARNINGLY   *902 30

YEARNINGS
AND WED ME TO EASE MY YEARNINGS   44 5

YEARNS
AFTER MANY DAYS MY HEART YEARNS   171 25
CENTRAL PRIMORDIAL FIRE OF THE SOUL THAT LEANS AND YEAR+   *952 6

YEARS
SHE'S A QUICKER INSTRUCTRESS THAN YEARS   38 20
ALL THE LONG YEARS OF SITTING IN MY HUSBAND'S HOUSE   47 30
ALL THE BYGONE HUSHED YEARS   53 9
IN AFTER YEARS IN MEMORY TO YOU   91 24
YOUNG YEARS AND THE OLD MUST NOT WIN NOT EVEN IF THEY L+   93 5
MANY YEARS HAVE I STILL TO BURN DETAINED   115 5
TAKING ME BACK DOWN THE VISTA OF YEARS TILL I SEE   148 5
BUT I WHOM THE YEARS HAD REARED TO BE YOUR BRIDE   157 1
WHO FOR YEARS WAS SUN FOR YOUR SHIVERING SHADE FOR YOUR   157 2
AND THE UGLY BRUTAL YEARS   240 1
WHOM I MARRIED YEARS AGO   260 5
WITHOUT A SERVANT'S HELP SO HE BE NOT STRICKEN IN YEARS   277 11
AND HEAR HIM BELLOW AFTER MANY YEARS THE BULL THAT SERV+   327 8
AFTER TWO THOUSAND YEARS   327 17
ARE AWAKE THROUGH YEARS WITH TRANSFERRED TOUCH AND GO   448 3
FOR LONG YEARS   448 5
MAY BURN FOR LONG YEARS   511 16
IT SEEMS TO ME THAT FOR FIVE THOUSAND YEARS AT LEAST   519 1
DINNERS FOR THE NEXT FIFTY YEARS   531 7
GOOD DINNERS FOR FIFTY MORE LONG YEARS   531 15
WHERE YOU'VE SAT PEACEFULLY ALL THESE YEARS   541 7
FOR YEARS AND YEARS IT BOTHERED ME   556 1
YOUR TWO THOUSAND YEARS ARE UP   616 20
MY YEARS HAVE BEEN   766 26
GREATER GLOOM THAN FOR MANY YEARS   778 36
IT WILL TAKE AN EPOCH TWO THOUSAND YEARS AND MORE   833 29
THEY ARE TOLLING HIS FAILURE AFTER ALL THESE YEARS TO T+   859 9
SHE'S A FINER INSTRUCTOR THAN YEARS   *893 3
OVER THE BYGONE HUSHED YEARS   *906 1
MANY YEARS HAVE I STILL TO BURN DETAINED   *930 5
AND THROUGH THESE YEARS WHILE I BURN ON THE FUEL OF LIFE   *930 9
QUIETLY THROUGH THE YEARS I HAVE CREPT BACK TO SEE   *940 6

YEAR'S
THE LAST YEAR'S FIRE IS GONE AND YOUR FACE IS ASH   91 2
WITH THIS YEAR'S NEWNESS AND IS THAT EVIL   127 20
BACK TO THE OLD YEAR'S SUN ACROSS THE SEA   455 19
FOR ONE YEAR'S SPACE ATTEND ON OUR ANGRY DEAD   740 16
FORGOTTEN LIKE LAST YEAR'S LINNET SONG   855 14

YEAST
WORKED WITH CLEAN SWEAT FOR YEAST   758 22

YELL
A YELL OF TRIUMPH AS YOU SNATCH MY SCALP   333 24
A YELL   364 15
AND GIVING THAT FRAGILE YELL THAT SCREAM   365 10
THE INEXPRESSIBLE FAINT YELL   365 19
STRANGE FAINT COITION YELL   366 25
WILL YOUR YELL DO IT   371 25
AND YET AS HIS BRASS-RESONANT HOWLING YELL RESOUNDS   377 20

YELLER
NAY I SAW NOWT BUT TH' COFFIN AN' TH' YELLER CLAY AN' '+   *909 31

YELLING
YELLING PIPS PIPS BIBBLES   396 9

YELLOW
SUN BUT IN SUBSTANCE YELLOW WATER-BLOBS   34 25
INTO THE YELLOW EVENING GLOW   42 19
WHEN INTO THE NIGHT THE YELLOW LIGHT IS ROUSED LIKE DUST   70 20
BUT THE FACES OF THE BOYS IN THE BROODING YELLOW LIGHT   75 25
YOU AMID THE BOG-END'S YELLOW INCANTATION   90 13
THE HEADS OF THE BOYS MOVE DIMLY THROUGH A YELLOW GLOOM+   92 4
A YELLOW LEAF FROM THE DARKNESS   110 25
BLACKISH THEY WILL TASTE OF TEARS WHEN THE YELLOW DAPPL+   119 13
CLUCK FOR YOUR YELLOW DARLINGS   119 18
AND O BEHIND THE CLOUD-LEAVES LIKE YELLOW AUTUMN   120 7
NOW LAMPS LIKE YELLOW ECHOES GLIMMER AMONG   135 9
UNDER AN OAK WHOSE YELLOW BUDS DOT THE PALE BLUE SKY   152 27
WITH YELLOW FRAIL SEA-POPPIES   200 19
SWAY LIKE FULL-BLOWN YELLOW   217 17
THE YELLOW SUN STEPS OVER THE MOUNTAIN-TOP   230 5
BEHOLD MY EYES TURN TAWNY YELLOW   301 22
EYES OF YELLOW GOLDEN SAND   301 30
IN SUNDAY SUITS AND YELLOW BOOTS ALONG THE CORSO   314 33
IN SUNDAY SUITS AND YELLOW SHOES   316 21
TO THE YOUTHS IN SUNDAY SUITS AND YELLOW SHOES   317 28
AND HE DID NOT MIND THE YELLOW ELECTRIC LIGHT   344 30
YELLOW EYES INCOMPREHENSIBLE WITH THIN SLITS   380 28
VERY HANDSOME AND SOME PURE YELLOW FANGED LEAVES   387 3
BUT THE YELLOW ANTIPODAL KANGAROO WHEN SHE SITS UP   392 27
WITH A THIN YOUNG YELLOW LITTLE PAW HANGING OUT AND   393 17
SOMETHING YELLOW   401 16
A LONG LONG SLIM CAT YELLOW LIKE A LIONESS   401 24
SO SHE WILL NEVER LEAP IN THAT WAY AGAIN WITH THE YELLOW   402 15
OF THAT SLIM YELLOW MOUNTAIN LION   402 33
LIKE YELLOW HAIR OF A TIGRESS BRINDLED WITH PINES   408 26
ON THE YELLOW POINTED ASPEN-TREES LAID ONE ON ANOTHER L+   409 14
LINGERS BEHIND AS THE YELLOW SUN GLARES AND IS GONE BEY+   467 6
OF THE YELLOW DOGS HOW THEY SLINK AWAY   494 7
OH HE KNOWS ALL ABOUT IT HE CASTS A YELLOW EYE   633 26
FOR A MOMENT PURE IN THE YELLOW EVENING LIGHT HE WAS HY+   672 11
GOD IS BORN GOD IS BORN BRIGHT YELLOW AND DUCTILE HE IS+   682 25
WAIT WAIT EVEN SO A FLUSH OF YELLOW   720 9
AS A VENDOR OF FRIED FISH ONCE MORE YELLOW   760 21
FLAP WHITE WINGS AND YELLOW PINIONS   783 26
YOU WILL NEVER FLY ON YELLOW KINDLED WINGS   784 23
SO HE PASSED THE YELLOW LINE WHO LASHED LIKE A DRAGON I+   790 3

YELLOW
    AND HAVING PASSED THE YELLOW LINE HE SAW THE EARTH BENE+   790   4
    THESE WHITE MEN AND RED MEN AND YELLOW MEN AND BROWN MEN   792   29
    THAT ARE NEITHER WHITE NOR RED NOR YELLOW NOR BROWN NOR+   792   31
    YELLOW OF THE SUN   804   8
    IS THE YELLOW SERPENT-YELLOW SHINING OF MY SUN   805   3
    YELLOW OF THE SUN   805   16
    SHINES THE YELLOW SERPENT-YELLOW SHINING OF THE SUN   806   6
    AND YELLOW AS THE FIRE THAT CONSUMES   806   23
    BUT WHOSE DREAMS ARE DOGS GREY DOGS WITH YELLOW MOUTHS   807   15
    YELLOW IS THE FLAME   808   26
    AND FALLS WINGLESS BLOOD STREAMING THROUGH ITS YELLOW H+   855   25
    SHONE SWEETLY THROUGH YELLOW SILK A MAN FULL IN THE LIG+   865   2
    UNDER AN OAK TREE WHOSE YELLOW BUDS DOTTED THE PALE BLU+   866   23
    THE SUN SETS WIDE THE YELLOW CROCUSES   868   17
    GO WINGING GLAD THE YELLOW MOTES   868   24
    FOR THE SUN IS POURING LIKE YELLOW WINE OUTSIDE   *894   24
    BUT THE FACES OF THE BOYS IN THE BROODING YELLOW LIGHT   *897   24
    BUT THE FACES OF THE BOYS IN THE BROODING YELLOW LIGHT   *901   1
    WHEN INTO THE NIGHT THE YELLOW LIGHT IS ROUSED LIKE DUS+ *917   17
    THE HEADS OF MY BOYS MOVE DIMLY THROUGH THE YELLOW GLOO+ *926   4
    BRACKISH THEY WILL TASTE OF TEARS WHEN THE YELLOW DAPPL+ *932   22
    OF LEAVES LIKE YELLOW FRUITS SHOW PLAIN   *932   23
    CLUCK TO YOUR YELLOW DARLINGS   *932   27
    EXTINCT ONE YELLOW BLOODY SPARK   *932   31
    THIRTEEN LAY THE YELLOW CHICKS BENEATH THE JOIST OF WOOD *933   3
    AND WHAT HAS BECOME OF THE FLUFFY YELLOW STARS   *933   24
    AH WHERE HIS MOUTH'S RED SUMMER AND WHERE IS NOW THE YE+ *933   27
    THE SUN SETS WIDE THE YELLOW CROCUSES   *941   17
    SWING LIKE FULL-BLOWN YELLOW   *942   26

YELLOW-BROWN
    AND TRAILED HIS YELLOW-BROWN SLACKNESS SOFT-BELLIED DOWN   349   10
    SUDDENLY HER YELLOW-BROWN EYES LOOKED WITH A FLARE INTO   618   1

YELLOWFACES
    PALEFACES YELLOWFACES BLACKFACES THESE ARE NO MEXICANS   793   11
    HOW GAVE THESE PALEFACES YELLOWFACES CROSSED THE WATERS+   794   30

YELLOW-FLUFFY
    EXTINCT ONE YELLOW-FLUFFY SPARK   119   22

YELLOW-GREEN
    AFTER THE BLACK-GREEN SKIRTS OF A YELLOW-GREEN OLD MEXI+   395   31

YELLOW-HAIRED
    SCYLLAS AND YELLOW-HAIRED HELLEBORE JONQUILS DIM ANEMON+   270   7

YELLOWING
    FRAGRANT LIKE YELLOWING LEAVES AND DIM WITH THE SOFT   503   24

YELLOW-PALE
    GIVING OFF DARKNESS BLUE DARKNESS UPON DEMETER'S YELLOW+ *956   8

YELLOW-RED
    OF YELLOW-RED OUTREACHING LIVING WRATH   317   9

YER
    IF YER MUN KNOW   79   16
    F'R I TELL YER I H'ARENA MARRYIN' NONE   81   3
    ON YER YO'N GOT WHAT YER TOOK   81   4
    YER NEDN'T 'AVE SWORE   81   12
    I EXPECT YER KNOW WHO I AM MRS NAYLOR   81   21
    YER KNOWED AS I WAS COURTIN' TIM MERFIN   81   25
    'E ISN'T GOIN' TER MARRY YER   81   31
    NEITHER ON YER   84   14
    SO I S'LL GO AN' LEAVE YER   84   17
    BOTH ON YER   84   18
    I DON'T LIKE YER LIZ I WANT TER   84   19
    GET AWAY FROM YER   84   20
    I'LL SAY GOOD-BYE LIZ TO YER   85   1
    YER TOO MUCH I' TH' RIGHT FOR ME   85   2
    I BET I AM YOU CAN 'OLD YER PHIZ   434   22
    'ERE SHE'S A LIDY AREN'T YER OLD QUIZZ   434   24
    YOU MIND WHO YER SAYIN' ISN'T LIDIES   434   26
    UP I ROSE MY LADS AN' I HEARD YER   552   11
    WHO YER ARE YIS YOU'RE LIZZIE STAINWRIGHT   *923   22

YER'D
    THA SHOULD HA' SEED 'ER SLIVE UP WHEN YER'D GONE   61   5

YER'S
    OF YER'S TOO MUCH FOR THIS LAD   84   24

YER'VE
    AN' YET YER'VE BIN CARRYIN' ON WI' 'IM   81   27
    WELL NOW YER'VE GOT TER PAY FOR IT   81   29

YESTERDAY
    YESTERDAY THE FIELDS WERE ONLY GREY WITH SCATTERED SNOW   85   5
    HELEN HAD I KNOWN YESTERDAY   117   25
    HAD I KNOWN YESTERDAY YOU COULD TAKE   117   28
    OH COME AND BREAK THIS PRISON THIS HOUSE OF YESTERDAY   174   17
    OF YESTERDAY   178   6
    YOUR SELF MOVES ON AND IS NOT TODAY WHAT IT WAS YESTERD+ 543   14
    THE TRUTH OF YESTERDAY BECOMES A LIE TOMORROW   661   17
    WHY 'TWAS ONLY YESTERDAY EVERY MAN TWIRLED   814   28
    YESTERDAY YES IS A TALE THAT IS TOLD   815   6

YESTERDAYS
    AND ALIVE AND MOVING TOMORROW MANY TOMORROWS AS YESTERD+ 671   21
    BAD YESTERDAYS UNSURE TOMORROWS   825   3

YEW-TREE'S
    WASTE NOT THE YEW-TREE'S WAITING WASTE   114   13

YEW-TREE
    UNDER THE YEW-TREE TENT   114   2
    UNDER THE YEW-TREE TENT   *929   19

YI
    YI AN' 'IS FACE GOES WHITE OH YES   79   10
    YI THA MUST HA' BIN 'ARD TER WEAN   79   24
    YI BUT I'M TELLIN' THEE SUMMAT   137   31
    YI BUT THA'RT FRIT O' SUMMAT   138   13
    YI THA CAN GO THA HATES ME NOW   139   24
    YI AN' 'IM THAT YOUNG   *911   9
    AN' COS I LIKED HIM BEST YI BETT'R NOR THEE   *911   15
    DOESN'T TER KNOW WHAT I MEAN TIM YI   *921   19

YIELD
    AND YIELD HER HONEY-DROP TO HER LOVER   42   18
    OF CLOUD THE RAIN-SKIES YIELD   68   20
    IF ONLY MOST LOVELY OF ALL IS YIELD MYSELF AND AM BORRO+ 250   17
    I DON'T YIELD TO YOU BIG JOWL-FACED EAGLE   374   25
    TO BE ABLE TO FORGET IS TO BE ABLE TO YIELD   725   20
    WE YIELD THE ENEMY HIS LAST DEMANDS   736   26
    WE GIVE HATE HER DUES O GOD WE YIELD HER UP   743   15
    OF CLOUD THE MORN SKIES YIELD   *915   4
    BUT WE MAUN MA'E THE BEST ON'T I'LL REAR THY CHILDT IF + *925   18

YIELDED
    YOU YIELDED WE THREW THE LAST CAST   111   21
    DREAMING YOUR YIELDED MOUTH IS GIVEN TO MINE   129   24

YIELDING
    SWIFTER AND HIGHER AND BRIGHTER OR THE YIELDING AND THE+ 680   6
    THE TWO GREAT AND MOVING ONES FIRE AND THE YIELDING WET 706   12

YIELDS
    AND TRODDEN THAT THE HAPPY SUMMER YIELDS   135   8
    SUDDENLY IT CURVES AS IT YIELDS THE WHITE WHEAT   651   14
    WHICH YIELDS THE DAY TO DEATH ERE YET THE LIGHT   885   7

YIS
    WHO Y'ARE YIS YOU'RE LIZZIE STAINWRIGHT   81   22
    YIS I KNOWED 'E WOR COURTIN' THEE   81   26
    WHO YER ARE YIS YOU'RE LIZZIE STAINWRIGHT   *923   22
    YIS I KNOWED 'E WOR COURTIN' THEE   *923   26

YI'
    YI' THA'RT A MAN THA'RT A FINE BIG MAN BUT NIVER A BABY+ *925   24

YONI
    THE FISSURE THE YONI   282   19

YO'N
    ON YER YO'N GOT WHAT YER TOOK   81   4

YOUNG
    HAS OPENED THE WINGS OF THE WILD YOUNG SPRITE   46   14
    IN HER EYES AS A YOUNG BEE STUMBLETH   46   16
    THE PINK YOUNG HORSES SHOW ONE SIDE BRIGHT   50   23
    THAT YOUNG AN' A' THE FAULT OF DRINK   60   25
    THE WILD YOUNG HEIFER GLANCING DISTRAUGHT   64   7
    OR FIRM AND SILKEN AS YOUNG PEONY FLOWERS   65   10
    TO HA' GONE AN' GIVEN HIS CLEAN YOUNG FLESH   77   31
    WHY YOUR YOUNG MAN AN' WIDOW NAYLOR   78   9
    AND PERHAPS THEY WERE RIGHT FOR THE YOUNG ARE BUSY DEEP+ 92   25
    YOUNG YEARS AND THE OLD MUST NOT WIN NOT EVEN IF THEY L+ 93   5
    THE YOUNG   93   13
    THE TEARS ARE DRY AND THE CHEEK'S YOUNG FRUITS ARE FRESH 94   19
    SHE LOOKS LIKE A YOUNG MAIDEN SINCE HER BROW   101   7
    BETROTHED YOUNG LADY WHO LOVES ME AND TAKES GOOD   129   4
    FOR SURELY THE FRAGILE FINE YOUNG THING HAD BEEN   132   3
    ME MIGHT A YOUNG GIRL BE HEAPED WITH SUCH SHADOW OF   132   6
    YOUNG BIRDS FORSAKEN AND LEFT IN A NEST OF MUD   145   24
    THE YOUNG GRASS TWINKLES IN THE WIND AND THE SOUND   152   28
    'TWAS I WHOSE FINGERS DID DRAW UP THE YOUNG   156   19
    YOUR YOUNG HUSHED LOOK THAT THEN SAW GOD ABLAZE   157   23
    MOILED OVER WITH THE REARING OF HER MANY-MOUTHED YOUNG 197   11
    YEARNING TOWARDS ENGLAND TOWARDS YOUR YOUNG CHILDREN   207   8
    I AM BEAUTIFUL I LOOK AT THE RUMPLED YOUNG ROSES   218   2
    THOUGH IT'S SORRY I AM ON HIS YOUNG FEET KNOWING   219   27
    CHRIST ON THE CROSS HIS BEAUTIFUL YOUNG MAN'S BODY   225   5
    THE NEW YOUNG YEAR COMES IN   229   10
    AND THE YOUNG BULL IN THE FIELD WITH HIS WRINKLED SAD F+ 255   33
    ESPECIALLY THE YOUNG WOMEN I LOOK AT THEM   269   22
    WHAT IS IT THAT FROM THE FACES OF THE FAIR YOUNG WOMEN 270   12
    THEY ARE THE ISSUE OF ACRID WINTER THESE FIRST-FLOWER Y+ 270   15
    EVERY YOUNG TWIG   299   31
    HE CAUSALLY GIVES BIRTH TO ANOTHER YOUNG BUD FROM HIS   300   1
    CYCLAMENS YOUNG CYCLAMENS   311   3
    AND FEED THE YOUNG NEW FIELDS OF LIFE WITH ASH   315   5
    WHERE BEASTS DROP THEIR UNLICKED YOUNG AND PASTURE AND + 321   13
    A SLIM YOUNG PIKE WITH SMART FINS   338   1
    AND GREY-STRIPED SUIT A YOUNG CUB OF A PIKE   338   2
    YOUNG GAIETY   357   28
    YOUNG COLLIER WHO HAS LONG SINCE DRUNK HIMSELF TO   366   18
    WITH A THIN YOUNG YELLOW LITTLE PAW HANGING OUT AND   393   17
    SO HE CLEARS HIS THROAT THE YOUNG COCK-EAGLE   413   26
    NEITHER CAN A YOUNG COCK-EAGLE SIT SIMPERING   413   30
    BUT YOU SEE SAID THE HANDSOME YOUNG MAN WITH THE   433   9
    NOR YET THAT PALE YOUNG MAN AFRAID OF FATHERHOOD   437   2
    NOR EVEN THE MUSICAL SUAVE YOUNG FELLOW   437   6
    YOUNG WILD SWANS   438   22
    YET O MY YOUNG MEN THERE IS A VIVIFIER   439   15
    YET O MY YOUNG MEN THERE IS A VIVIFIER   440   1
    O PILLARS OF FLAME BY NIGHT O MY YOUNG MEN   440   9
    WHEN THE FIRE REACHES US O MY YOUNG MEN   440   14
    THIS MODERATELY YOUNG GENTLEMAN   446   22
    YOU HALF-ALIVE YOUNG   456   15
    OLD MONEY-WORMS YOUNG MONEY-WORMS   456   22
    RISE THEN MY YOUNG MEN RISE AT THEM   457   3

YOUNG
    MUSHY PATHETIC YOUNG MEN   457 14
    YOUNG GENTS YOU'VE GOT NO OPTION   458 2
    BEWARE O MY DEAR YOUNG MEN OF GOING ROTTEN   462 17
    AND IT'S FUNNY MY DEAR YOUNG MEN THAT YOU IN YOUR   462 29
    FOR OBSCENITY AFTER ALL MY DEAR YOUNG MEN   463 1
    AND I THOUGHT YOU WANTED LIFE AND EXPERIENCE DEAR YOUNG   463 5
    PLAYING WITH MUCK AND I THOUGHT YOU YOUNG GENTS   463 9
    WE SHALL DO AS WE LIKE SIN IS OBSOLETE THE YOUNG ASSERT   463 26
    WHY DON'T YOU KNOW WHAT'S WHAT YOUNG PEOPLE SEEMS   464 9
    NEVER MY YOUNG MEN   484 12
    THE YOUNG ONES COPULATE HATE IT AND WANT TO CRY   485 6
    MOURNFUL YOUNG MAN IN YOUR TWENTIES   485 10
    AND THE YOUNG THE MODERN AND JAUNTY YOUNG   494 5
    THERE'S NOT A YOUNG MAN IN THE WHOLE   494 10
    SAINT FRANCIS HIMSELF WAS A RICH AND SPOILED YOUNG MAN   498 11
    NOWADAYS EVERYBODY WANTS TO BE YOUNG   502 13
    SO MUCH SO THAT EVEN THE YOUNG ARE OLD WITH THE   502 14
    EFFORT OF BEING YOUNG   502 15
    THE OLD ONES WANT TO BE YOUNG AND THEY AREN'T YOUNG   502 23
    AND IT RANKLES THEY ACHE WHEN THEY SEE THE YOUNG   502 24
    AND MAKE THE YOUNG LOOK AFTER US   503 4
    TILL THEY ARE OLD WE ARE STRONGER THAN THE YOUNG   503 5
    LET US TRIUMPH AND LET THE YOUNG BE LISTLESS   503 7
    WE ARE YOUNGER EVEN NOW THAN THE YOUNG WE CAN PUT THEIR   503 9
    AND A YOUNG MAN SHOULD THINK BY JOVE   503 29
    AND THE YOUNG AMONG THE OLD   504 10
    AND THE YOUNG ARE FLOWING IN THE THROES OF A GREAT   511 24
    THE YOUNG TODAY ARE BORN PRISONERS   518 7
    THE YOUNG AREN'T VITALLY INTERESTED IN IT ANY MORE   518 16
    THE YOUNG KNOW THESE THINGS QUITE WELL   520 29
    YOUNG MEN HAVING NO REAL JOY IN LIFE AND NO HOPE IN THE   521 20
    AND WIMBLY-WAMBLY YOUNG MEN OF SEX STILL MORE INDETERMI+   522 4
    SO THAT'S WHY SO MANY YOUNG MEN HAVE LONG FACES   530 21
    WHY SHOULD THE DELUGE WAIT WHILE THESE YOUNG GENTRY GO   531 13
    AS ONE OF OUR BRIGHTEST YOUNG INTELLECTUALS SAID TO ME   531 22
    PONDERING THIS NEW TRUTH OF THE SENSATIONAL YOUNG I SAID   532 1
    SO ONE OF THE BRIGHTEST YOUNG INTELLECTUALS PUT IT TO ME   533 4
    AND YOUNG WASH-OUTS PRETENDING TO BE IN LOVE WITH DEATH   535 19
    EVEN OUR BRILLIANTEST YOUNG INTELLECTUALS   544 26
    ALAS MY POOR YOUNG MEN   558 15
    FOR POOR YOUNG WRETCHED MEN   558 20
    AND CLING TO THEIR THIN YOUNG WOMEN   558 24
    THE YOUNG HAVE LEARNED SOME SENSE   559 22
    WE'LL BACK YOU UP UNCLE WE'RE YOUNG AND WE'RE   574 9
    A YOUNG MAN SAID TO ME   604 1
    SAID THE LOVELY YOUNG LADY HALF WISTFUL HALF MENACING   604 7
    THE HANDSOME AND SELF-ABSORBED YOUNG MAN   605 1
    LOOKED BACK AT THE HANDSOME AND SELF-ABSORBED YOUNG MAN   605 5
    LOOK AT THE YOUNG MEN UNDER THIRTY   612 9
    I REALISED THE SECRET JOY HER YOUNG SPANISH HUSBAND HAD   618 22
    THAT THE YOUNG OF THEIR OWN SEX REVOLT AGAINST THEM AT +   619 25
    AND THROUGH THE WIDE PRAIRIES OF HIS BREAST A YOUNG BUL+   624 7
    OR THAT HARD-BOILED YOUNG WOMAN BESIDE HIM   645 12
    AND THE YOUNG COPPER BEECH ITS LEAVES RED-ROSY AT THE E+   647 4
    WHOM THE GODS LOVE DIE YOUNG   662 14
    THE YOUNG TRAM-CONDUCTOR IN A BLUE UNIFORM TO HIMSELF F+   672 8
    AND DIONYSOS YOUNG AND A STRANGER   688 19
    YOUNG   694 30
    STRONG YOUNG MAN HE LEANS SIGHING   733 19
    IF YOU MEET MY YOUNG MAN   754 1
    AH YOUNG MAN   755 1
    CHEW ALSO YOUNG HEIFERS YOUR JUICIER CUDS   814 21
    AND IT SEEMS TO ME THAT THE YOUNG ONES THOUGH THEY GRUD+   829 1
    LIES LATENT IN THE SOULS OF THE YOUNG A LATENT DESIRE   829 10
    IT IS ODD AGAIN ABOUT THE YOUNG   829 11
    AND TO THE YOUNG THIS IS REALLY IMMORAL AND DISTASTEFUL   829 25
    THE MODERN YOUNG WOMAN THINKS IT WONDERFUL TO BE SO BRI+   841 26
    WHY THE MODERN YOUNG WIFE OF THE LITTLE-BOY BRILLIANT B+   842 9
    I HEARD HER SAY TO HER BRILLIANT YOUNG HUSBAND   842 12
    AND THE BRILLIANT YOUNG HUSBAND MADE A LITTLE MOVE POUT+   842 16
    WHICH IS WHY THE YOUNG WHO COPULATE SO FREELY   843 19
    DRAW NEARER REDDEN AND LAUGH LIKE YOUNG GIRLS KISSED   854 12
    YET IN THE LITTLE NEW ROAD THE YOUNG WIFE TURNS AWAY   865 13
    THE YOUNG GRASS TWINKLED IN THE WIND AND THE SOUND   866 24
    I AWOKE WITH THE YOUNG NETTLES ON MY WRISTS   882 5
    PERHAPS THE TINY YOUNG NETTLES HAVE STUNG HER EARS   882 26
    THE TEARS ARE DRY THE CHEEKS' YOUNG FRUITS ARE FRESH   *897 7
    A TEACHER OF THESE YOUNG BOYS MY SLAVES   *899 6
    WITH A RICH A THRILLED YOUNG CLASP OF LIFE   *899 32
    A TEACHER OF THESE YOUNG BOYS MY SLAVES   *902 18
    WITH A RICH A THRILLED YOUNG CLASP OF LIFE   *903 11
    YI AN' I'M THAT YOUNG   *911 9
    COOL AND FIRM AND SILKEN AS PINK YOUNG PEONY FLOWERS   *913 11
    EVEN HER FLOATING HAIR SINKS LIKE STORM-BRUISED YOUNG L+   *913 24
    FIRM AND SILKEN LIKE PINK YOUNG PEONY FLOWERS   *916 11
    TO HA'E GONE AN' GIVEN HIS WHITE YOUNG FLESH   *919 19
    WHY YOUR YOUNG MAN AN' WIDOW NAYLOR   *920 1
    HE WATERS OUR FACE WITH TEARS OUR YOUNG FRUITS FILLS WI+   *926 29
    THE DEAD MOON HEAPED WITHIN THE YOUNG MOON'S ARMS   *937 29
    FOR SURELY THE FRAGILE FINE YOUNG THING HAD BEEN   *937 30
    BUT I'M SORRY FOR HIM ON HIS YOUNG FEET KNOWIN'   *944 7
    MY YOUNG SLIM LAD AN' I'M SORRY FOR THEE   *944 16
    AND ONCE HE WAS A YOUNG MAN PALE AND REFUSING FATHERHOOD   *946 15
    AND ONCE AGAIN A SUAVE YOUNG GOD   *946 18
    THERE'LL BE BABIES BORN THAT ARE YOUNG WILD SWANS O MY +   *947 24

YOUNGER
    AN' OFF TO A GEL AS WOR YOUNGER THAN ME   138 11
    IN WHICH TO PICKLE THE YOUNGER GENERATIONS   495 7
    WE ARE YOUNGER EVEN NOW THAN THE YOUNG WE CAN PUT THEIR   503 9
    THE WORST OF THE YOUNGER GENERATION THOSE LATTER-DAY   531 1
    THE GOOD THING ABOUT THE YOUNGER GENERATIONS   828 14
    AND THE YOUNGER ONES   828 16
    AND THEREFORE SINCE THE PEOPLE I MEET OF THE YOUNGER   829 4
    THE YOUNGER INTELLIGENTSIA SO TO SPEAK   829 6
    I SPEAK OF THE YOUNGER GENERATIONS   833 6

YOUNGEST
    THE FACE OF THE YOUNGEST ROSE   150 16

YOURS
    EVEN YOURS DO YOU SEE   49 8
    YOURS IS THE SULLEN SORROW   111 8
    THAN A DREAM OF YOURS 'TWAS ALL YOU EVER COULD   157 30
    WITH SHADOWS WITH YOURS I PEOPLE THE SUNSHINE   211 19
    YOURS AND MINE   211 20
    THIS MEN IS YOURS   229 2
    TO YOURS   281 26
    ONLY YOURS WOULD BE A RAW UNSMELTED PASSION THAT WILL   370 9
    IS THERE A RUBY OF FUSED BEING MINE AND YOURS AN INWARD   478 7
    AT THE END OF THE SWEET SPRING DAY THEY ARE YOURS   855 13
    YOURS IS THE SHAME AND SORROW   *928 1

YOURSELF
    YOU HOLD YOURSELF ALL HARD AS IF MY KISSES   87 10
    BE ALL YOURSELF FOR OH THE CHARM   151 1
    BE ALL YOURSELF ONE BONNY BURNING COAL   151 14
    THE RYE IS TALLER THAN YOU WHO THINK YOURSELF   221 6
    WHAT ARE YOU BY YOURSELF DO YOU THINK AND WHAT   235 3
    ADD YOURSELF UP AND YOUR SEED TO THE NOUGHT   235 15
    AND YOU WANT TO ENLARGE YOURSELF WITH THIS FRIEND OF MI+   235 28
    PLEASE YOURSELF HOW YOU HAVE IT   236 24
    YES BUNCH YOURSELF BETWEEN   240 26
    YOU WHO NEVER FIND YOURSELF IN LOVE   290 10
    BUT ONLY LOSE YOURSELF FURTHER DECOMPOSING   290 11
    YOU DON'T KNOW YOURSELF   292 19
    YOU MADAME CERES MIND YOURSELF THE ENEMY IS UPON   308 28
    YOU CONTRACT YOURSELF   370 11
    YOU ARCH YOURSELF AS AN ARCHER'S BOW   370 12
    SEIZES YOU AS YOU CLENCH YOURSELF TOGETHER   370 17
    AS YOU DRAW YOURSELF UPON YOURSELF IN INSISTENCE   370 29
    EVERYBODY SO DEAR AND YOURSELF SO ULTRA-BELOVED   398 26
    DO HOLD YOURSELF TOGETHER AND FIGHT   459 13
    KNOW YOURSELF O KNOW YOURSELF THAT YOU ARE MORTAL AND   464 23
    O KNOW YOURSELF O KNOW YOUR SEX YOU MUST KNOW THERE   465 1
    YOURSELF   477 25
    IF YOU WILL GO DOWN INTO YOURSELF UNDER YOUR SURFACE   481 1
    WHICH IS ONLY A SLOPPY WAY OF BEING IN LOVE WITH YOURSE+   508 15
    IF YOU WANT TO KNOW YOURSELF   543 12
    YOU'VE GOT TO KEEP UP WITH YOURSELF   543 13
    YOU'D HAVE MONEY YOU'D HAVE IT ENOUGH TO SUPPORT YOURSE+   547 11
    AND SLOWLY FEEL YOURSELF DROWN   551 5
    ALAS THEY HAVE SAVED YOU FROM YOURSELF   595 12
    YOU ARE SO INTERESTED IN YOURSELF   602 25
    ALAS THEY HAVE SAVED YOU FROM YOURSELF FROM YOUR OWN   630 14
    EXTRACT AND EXTRICATE YOURSELF   642 7
    YOURSELF   643 9
    YOURSELF WITH   643 28
    THERE ARE NO GODS AND YOU CAN PLEASE YOURSELF   651 20
    THERE ARE NO GODS AND YOU CAN PLEASE YOURSELF   652 1
    GO AND PLEASE YOURSELF   652 2
    AND THE FIRST QUESTION TO ASK YOURSELF IS   661 14
    THEN SAY TO YOURSELF WE WILL CEASE TO CARE   666 11
    FOR A MOMENT FREE FROM ALL CONCEIT OF YOURSELF AND ALL +   674 3
    O ARE YOU TANGLED UP IN YOURSELF   675 1
    WASH YOURSELF AND RUB OIL IN YOUR SKIN   791 21
    AND SEE YOURSELF AS IN A GLASS DARKLY   834 18
    LIES IN FORCING YOURSELF OR SOMEBODY ELSE   836 18
    BE ALL YOURSELF ONE BONNY BURNING COAL   873 24
    WITH RED SNARLING JAWS LET YOURSELF LISTEN TO THE CRIES   *892 25
    THE RYE IS TALLER THAN YOU WHO THINK YOURSELF   *944 19

YOURSELVES
    YOU MAY LOOK AND SAY TO YOURSELVES I DO   251 7
    NEW LIFE FOR YOURSELVES AND YOUR WOMEN COMPLEMENTAL   463 12
    GET UP AN' DO IT YOURSELVES   553 22

YOUR'S
    WAS YOUR'S A DADDY   582 5

YOU'S
    SO IF ANY OF YOU'S LIVE WIRES WITH WITS   553 19

YOUTH
    SHE SHINES THE FIRST WHITE LOVE OF MY YOUTH PASSIONLESS+   67 21
    SLEEP-SUAVE LIMBS OF A YOUTH WITH LONG SMOOTH THIGHS   145 18
    WITH THE OLD SWEET THINGS OF OUR YOUTH AND NEVER YET   157 6
    INCONSOLABLE YOUTH DEAD-BEAT   457 22
    WITH THEIR PUNY YOUTH   503 8
    YOUTH IN ABEYANCE   503 10
    THEIR GOOD YOUTH GO TO WASTE   560 4
    THE YOUTH WALKS UP TO THE WHITE HORSE TO PUT ITS HALTER+   683 19
    THE PHOENIX RENEWS HER YOUTH   728 6
    SHOWS THAT SHE IS RENEWING HER YOUTH LIKE THE EAGLE   728 11
    THAT IT WOULD BE FAR FAR BETTER FOR THE INDIAN YOUTH   778 1

YOUTHFUL
    YOUR YOUTHFUL SMOOTHNESS I FLEECED WHERE FLEECE WAS NONE   156 26

YOUTHS
    THE MUTILATED HORROR-STRUCK YOUTHS A MULTITUDE   258 1
    THE MURDERED BODIES OF YOUTHS AND MEN IN HEAPS   258 5
    THAT ARE YOUTHS AND MEN AND ME   258 9
    YET THERE THEY ARE YOUTHS LOUTISHLY   312 18
    TO THE YOUTHS IN SUNDAY SUITS AND YELLOW SHOES   317 28

YO'
    NAY YO' BLESSED PEE-WHIPS   73 25
    YO' NEDNA SCRAIGHT AT ME   78 26
    NOR YO' SO CHEW IT NO MORE   81 10

ZELLER
    BUT SITTING IN A BOAT ON THE ZELLER LAKE   337 28

ZENITH
    TO THE DARK ZENITH OF THINE ANTIPODES   322 19
    TO THE GREAT DEPTH OF ITS REVERSED ZENITH   322 24
    THE WHITSUN ZENITH   323 15
    FROM HIS LEAP AT THE ZENITH IN HER SO IT FBLLS JUST SHO+   382 23
    AND FECUNDATES THE ZENITH AND THE NADIR   506 8

ZENITH'S
    DREDGED DOWN TO THE ZENITH'S REVERSAL   323 12

ZEST
    AS MOUNTAIN PRESSING ON MOUNTAIN IN THE ZEST OF LIFE   694 15
    THAT I HAVE LAUGHED MY WAY ACROSS WITH ZEST   875 34

ZEUS
    FOR A MOMENT SHE WAS IO IO WHO FLED FROM ZEUS OR THE DA+   672 17
    BY ARES AND KRONOS AND ZEUS   702 11

ZIGZAGGING
    ZIGZAGGING DOWN LIKE THE FIZZLE FROM A FINISHED ROCKET   701 26

ZONES
    SUCH PEARLED ZONES OF FAIR STERILITY   855 1

ZOO
    SO MY PICTURES ARE IN PRISON INSTEAD OF IN THE ZOO   580 14
    TILL THEY CHANCED TO MEET IN THE LORD'S GREEN ZOO   761 3

APPENDIX I: LAWRENCE'S PERSONA

I

	Page	Line
ARE THEY ASLEEP ARE THEY LIVING NOW SEE WHEN I	33	8
ON THE TURF I STAND WATCHING MY OWN WHITE SHADOW QUIVER+	33	19
WHAT IF THE GORSE-FLOWERS SHRIVELLED AND I WERE GONE	33	21
WHAT IS THIS THING THAT I LOOK DOWN UPON	33	24
I ON THE BANK ALL SUBSTANCE MY SHADOW ALL SHADOW LOOKIN+	34	2
AND THE WHITE DOG DANCES AND QUIVERS I AM HOLDING HIS C+	34	5
MY SHADOW IS NEITHER HERE NOR THERE BUT I I AM ROYALLY +	34	8
I AM HERE I AM HERE SCREAMS THE PEEWIT THE MAY-BLOBS BU+	34	9
IN CONFIRMATION I HEAR SEVENFOLD LARK-SONGS PEALING	34	29
I SHOULD LIKE TO DROP	35	16
I SHOULD LIKE TO LIE STILL	35	21
AS IF I WAS DEAD BUT FEELING	35	22
REMOTE ALTHOUGH I HEAR THE BEGGAR'S COUGH	36	5
I SIT ABSOLVED ASSURED I AM BETTER OFF	36	7
BEYOND A WORLD I NEVER WANT TO JOIN	36	8
OFFERS ME HER SCARLET FRUIT I WILL SEE	37	3
EVE AND I	37	25
THE LITTLE RED HEIFER TONIGHT I LOOKED IN HER EYES	38	6
LAST NIGHT WHEN I WENT WITH THE LANTERN THE SOW WAS GRA+	38	8
WITH SNARLING RED JAWS AND I HEARD THE CRIES	38	10
AND I WOKE TO THE SOUND OF THE WOOD-PIGEON AND LAY AND +	38	12
TILL I COULD BORROW	38	13
A FEW QUICK BEATS FROM A WOOD-PIGEON'S HEART AND WHEN I+	38	14
AND I KNEW THAT HOME THIS VALLEY WAS WIDER THAN PARADISE	38	17
I LEARNED IT ALL FROM MY EVE	38	18
SO NOW I KNOW THE VALLEY	38	23
SLIPS AWAY SO I GASP IN SURPRISE	38	33
HE STANDS AND I TREMBLE BEFORE HIM	39	13
AND I CAN'T DEPLORE HIM	39	16
I TREMBLE IN HIS SHADOW AS HE BURNS	39	29
DARK RUDDY PILLAR FORGIVE ME I	40	9
WE CRY IN THE WILDERNESS FORGIVE ME I	40	13
THOU DARK ONE THOU PROUD CURVED BEAUTY I	40	17
AND BUILT UP THE WAY I SALUTE THEE	40	22
HUSH NOW HUSH WHERE AM I BIURET	40	30
I WISH I DID IT MORE WILLINGLY	41	14
I WISH YOU DID NOT WAIT MY DEAR	41	15
FOR ME TO COME SINCE WORK I MUST	41	16
I WISH I WAS ONLY A BUST	41	18
I SEE A REDNESS SUDDENLY COME	42	6
SHOULD I NOT ANSWER TO HIS TALK	43	16
I HEAR HIS HAND ON THE LATCH AND RISE FROM MY CHAIR	43	18
OF THE RABBIT'S FUR GOD I AM CAUGHT IN A SNARE	43	28
I KNOW NOT WHAT FINE WIRE IS ROUND MY THROAT	43	29
I ONLY KNOW I LET HIM FINGER THERE	43	30
OF SWEET FIRE SWEEPS ACROSS ME SO I DROWN	43	36
I THE MAN WITH THE RED SCARF	44	1
WILL GIVE THEE WHAT I HAVE THIS LAST WEEK'S	44	2
I CANNA COME DOWN	44	19
I DUNNA KNOW	45	10
'AVE I PUT 'IS CLEAN STOCKIN'S AN' SHIRT	45	14
I SHAN'T 'AVE 'IM TO NUSS	45	20
I DO 'OPE AS IT'S NOT VERY BAD	45	21
AN' CLUB-MONEY I WON'T GROWSE	45	33
I S'LL NEVER CATCH THAT TRAIN	46	2
I GU'D THINK 'E'LL GET RIGHT AGAIN	46	4
I CRIED BUT NO ONE HEARD ME	46	23
I LAY DUMB AND STARK	46	24
WHEN I AWOKE THIS MORNING	46	25
I COULD FIND NO TRACE	46	26
I MUST FOLD MY HANDS AND TURN MY FACE TO THE FIRE	47	2
STRANGE HE IS MY SON FOR WHOM I HAVE WAITED LIKE A LOVER	47	8
I MUST LOOK AWAY FROM HIM FOR MY FADED EYES	47	21
ALL MY LIFE I HAVE BORNE THE BURDEN OF MYSELF	47	29
NEVER HAVE I SAID TO MYSELF AS HE CLOSED THE DOOR	47	31
NOW I AM CAUGHT YOU ARE HOPELESSLY LOST O	47	32
THREE TIMES HAVE I OFFERED MYSELF THREE TIMES REJECTED	48	1
THE ANGEL OF CHILDHOOD KISSED ME AND WENT I EXPECTED	48	5
I MUST SIT ALONE AND WAIT AND NEVER KNOW	48	7
I WISH THE CHURCH HAD COVERED ME UP WITH THE REST	48	24
WHEN I MOVE THE OARS SEE	49	5
FALLS ON ME AS I LIE IN DEEP GRASS	49	22
I HEAR IT THROUGH THE GRASS	50	16
TO LET THE SUNLIGHT IN AND I	51	9
AS I SIT ON THE SHORES OF THE CLASS ALONE	51	10
TOUCH AFTER TOUCH I FEEL ON ME	52	1
I FEEL THEM CLING AND CLEAVE TO ME	52	8
I HAVE OPENED THE WINDOWS TO WARM MY HANDS ON THE SILL	52	12
RECOGNITIONS AND GREETINGS OF HALF-ACQUAINT THINGS AS I	52	22
WHILE I WASH YOU WITH WEEPING WATER	55	3
I KISS IT IN DROUTH	55	18
I SAW YOUR BROWS	56	13
AND I SHED MY VERY SOUL DOWN INTO YOUR	56	15
LIKE FLOWERS I FELL TO BE CAUGHT	56	17
YOU THAT I LOVED YOU WONDERFUL	56	33
IT IS WELL FOR YOU FOR ME THE NAVVIES WORK IN THE ROAD +	57	29
AND I WANT TO SMITE IN ANGER THE BARREN ROCK OF EACH WA+	57	30
A SUDDEN CAR GOES SWEEPING PAST AND I STRAIN MY SOUL TO+	58	3
SUCH A ONE IN THE NORTH IT FLOWERS ON THE STREET AND I +	58	13
CAUTIOUSLY I SHALL RAISE	59	2
HE GROWS DISTINCT AND I SEE HIS HOT	59	7
THEN I SHALL KNOW WHICH IMAGE OF GOD	59	11
AND I SHALL SEE MY SLEEPING ROD	59	13
AND I SHALL COUNT THE STAMP AND WORTH	59	17
OH AND I LONG TO SEE HIM SLEEP	59	17
SO I SHALL KNOW WHAT I HAVE TO KEEP	59	19
I LONG TO SEE	59	20
HIS TRUTH TO ME AND I	59	30
AND AS I WATCH THE WAN LIGHT SHINE	60	1
I SHALL WEEP OH I SHALL WEEP I KNOW	60	9
HOW SHOULD I BE LOOKIN' ROUND	60	19
I'D AS MUCH AS I COULD DO TO THINK	60	23
MY SIRS BUT I SAY 'TWAS FOR A BLITHER	60	30
AN' I COME AWAY ACAUSE O' TH' TEEMIN' RAIN	61	16
BUT I THOWT TER MYSEN AS THAT WOR TH' ONLY BIT	61	17
I FELT THE LURCH AND HALT OF HER HEART	61	21
AND I LAUGHED TO FEEL IT PLUNGE AND BOUND	61	23
OF THE WORDS I KEPT REPEATING	61	25
HOLDING HER THUS COULD I CARE	62	3
I LEANED IN THE DARKNESS TO FIND HER LIPS	62	6
AND I SAW HER FOR THE FLARING SPACE	62	9
AND I HEARD THE THUNDER AND FELT THE RAIN	62	19
AND MY ARMS FELL LOOSE AND I WAS DUMB	62	20
ALMOST I HATED HER SACRIFICED	62	21
WHEN SHALL I SEE THE HALF-MOON SINK AGAIN	62	25
SPEAK YOU MY HOME WHAT IS IT I DON'T DO WELL	63	7
AH HOME SUDDENLY I LOVE YOU	63	8
AS I HEAR THE SHARP CLEAN TROT OF A PONY DOWN THE ROAD	63	9
AND I LEAVING HER	63	15
CROUCHING AS LITTLE HOUSES CROUCH UNDER THE MIST WHEN I+	63	23
BUT WHEN I DRAW THE SCANTY CLOAK OF SILENCE OVER MY EYES	64	14
AND I WISH THAT THE BABY WOULD TACK ACROSS HERE TO ME	65	5
AND I COULD FEEL HER FEET IN EITHER HAND	65	8
I DO NOT LIKE TO HEAR THE GENTLE GRIEVING	65	19
WHEN I KNOW THAT THERE MUST EVER BE DECEIVING	65	23
EMERGING WHITE AND EXQUISITE AND I IN AMAZE	67	9
SEE IN THE SKY BEFORE ME A WOMAN I DID NOT KNOW	67	10
I LOVED BUT THERE SHE GOES AND HER BEAUTY HURTS MY HEART	67	11
I FOLLOW HER DOWN THE NIGHT BEGGING HER NOT TO DEPART	67	12
I SEE	67	15
TREMBLING BLUE IN HER PALLOR A TEAR THAT SURELY I HAVE +	67	16
A TEAR WHICH I HAD HOPED THAT EVEN HELL HELD NOT AGAIN +	67	17
SO HERE I HIDE IN THE SHALIMAR	70	14
AND I SMILE	71	23
I STAND AND SMILE	71	29
BUT WHEN I MEET THE WEARY EYES	72	1
I AM GLAD TO GO BACK TO WHERE I CAME FROM	72	3
AND WHEN I WAKE IN THE MORNING AFTER RAIN	72	20
MY PACK OF UNRULY HOUNDS I CANNOT START	74	9
I CAN HAUL THEM AND URGE THEM NO MORE	74	11
NO LONGER NOW CAN I ENDURE THE BRUNT	74	12
I AM SICK AND WHAT ON EARTH IS THE GOOD OF IT ALL	74	16
WHAT GOOD TO THEM OR ME I CANNOT SEE	74	17
SO SHALL I TAKE	74	18
OF THEIR INSULTS IN PUNISHMENT I WILL NOT	74	22
I WILL NOT WASTE MY SOUL AND AND MY STRENGTH FOR THIS	74	23
WHAT DO I CARE FOR ALL THAT THEY DO AMISS	74	24
I DO NOT AND WILL NOT THEY WON'T AND THEY DON'T	75	1
I SHALL KEEP MY STRENGTH FOR MYSELF THEY CAN KEEP	75	3
OF EACH OTHER I SHALL SIT AND WAIT FOR THE BELL	75	6
HOW CAN I ANSWER THE CHALLENGE OF SO MANY EYES	76	5
AWFULLY MUST I CALL BACK A HUNDRED EYES A VOICE	76	7
WHAT WAS MY QUESTION MY GOD MUST I BREAK THIS	76	9
I HAVE STARTLED A HUNDRED EYES AND NOW I MUST LOOK	76	12
THEM AN ANSWER BACK IT IS MORE THAN I CAN BEAR	76	13
ONLY I AND THE CLASS MUST WRANGLE THIS WORK IS A BITTER+	76	22
AN' WHEN I KNOW FOR SURE MISSIS	78	19
MY BREAST'S AS RED AS THINE I RECKON	78	23
THA WON'T STARE ME OUT I GUESS	79	12
'ER'LL BE WANTIN' IT I 'EAR	79	20
DOESN'T TER KNOW WHAT I MEAN TIMMY	79	23
DONE I SHOULD THINK SO AN' MIGHT I ASK	79	31
SO THERE AN' I TELL THEE FLAT	80	2
HASNA TER SENT ME WHOAM WHEN I	80	6
TILL I WAS VERILY SWELTED	80	12
I HOPE IT DID THEE GOOD	80	20
I COULD HA' KILLED 'ER	80	22
THOUGH I SHONNA MARRY 'ER	80	30
F'R I TELL YER I H'ARENA MARRYIN' NONE	81	3
I DAMN WELL SHANNA MARRY 'ER	81	9
AN' THERE'S THE DARK-BLUE TIE I BOUGHT 'IM	81	14
I DUNNO WHEER 'IS EYES WAS A GRET	81	17
I EXPECT YER KNOW WHO I AM MRS NAYLOR	81	21
'APPEN I MIGHTN'T 'APPEN I MIGHT	81	24
YER KNOWED AS I WAS COURTIN' TIM MERFIN	81	25
YIS I KNOWED 'E WOR COURTIN' THEE	81	26
IF I HAN WHAT'S THAT TER THEE	81	30
THA WANTS 'IM THY-SEN I SEE	81	32
BUT I WANT YOU TO KNOW 'E'S NOT MARRYIN' YOU	82	5
TO THINK I SHOULD 'AVE TER 'AFFLE AN' CAFFLE	82	9
FOR LETTIN' ME MARRY THE LAD AS I THOUGHT	82	11
FOR I WON'T BE BEHOLDEN TO SUCH AS 'ER	82	15
I WON'T OR MY NAME'S NOT LIZ	82	16
I WISH THA HADNA DONE IT TIM	82	21
I DO AN' THAT I DO	82	22
FOR WHENEVER I LOOK THEE I' TH' FACE I S'LL SEE	82	23
I WISH I COULD WESH 'ER OFF'N THEE	82	25
'APPEN I CAN IF I TRY	82	26
TILL I DIE	82	28
TWENTY POUND O' THY OWN THA HAST AN' FIFTY POUND HA'E I	83	1
SORRY I AM FOR THIS BUSINESS AN' SORRY IF EVER I'VE DRI+	83	6
AFORE I CAN TA'E THEE I'VE GOT A WIDDER O' FORTY-FIVE T+	83	8
AN' 'DEED AN' I WISH AS THIS TALE O' THINE WOR NIVER MY+	83	10
DEED AN' I WISH I C'D 'A' STOOD AT TH' ALTAR WI' THEE A+	83	11
THAT I COULD 'A' BIN FIRST WOMAN TER THEE AS THA'RT FIR+	83	13
THEY'LL TURN THEE OUT O' TH' FORCE I DOUBT ME IF THEY D+	83	16
'ER GEN ME SUMMAT I SHANNA	84	7
BUT SORRY FOR WHAT I HAD WHY	84	11
AS FOR MARRYIN' I SHANNA MARRY	84	13
AH'VE 'AD A' AS I CAN CARRY	84	15
SO I S'LL GO AN' LEAVE YER	84	17
I DON'T LIKE YER LIZ I WANT TER	84	19
AN' I REALLY LIKE 'ER NEITHER	84	21
WHAT BIT O' CUNT I HAD WI' 'ER	84	29
'S ALL I GOT OUT OF IT	84	30
I CANNOT SEE HER SINCE THE MIST'S PALE SCARF	85	9
BUT SHE'S WAITING I KNOW IMPATIENT AND COLD HALF	85	11
WHY DOES SHE COME WHEN SHE KNOWS WHAT I HAVE TO TELL	85	16
NOW I AM COME AGAIN TO YOU WHO HAVE SO DESIRED	85	17
WHY BURNS YOUR CHEEK AGAINST ME HOW HAVE I INSPIRED	85	19
NOW HERE I SIT WHILE YOU BREAK THE MUSIC BENEATH	85	21
BUT BARBED ALOOFNESS WHEN I WOULD DRAW NEAR	85	24

YOU SURELY SEEING I AM A BOWL OF KISSES   86   3
ME UP I PRAY OH YOU WHO ARE NIGHT'S BACCHANTE   86   7
I AM ADRIFT AS A MOONBEAM AND WITHOUT FORM   86 10
OR SUBSTANCE SAVE I LIGHT ON YOU TO WARM   86 11
WHO LIFT SWART ARMS TO FEND ME OFF BUT I COME   86 18
IS IT BECAUSE I HURT YOU WITH PAIN MY DEAR   87   2
DID I SHIVER NAY TRULY I DO NOT KNOW   87   3
HURT AS I GAVE THEM YOU PUT ME AWAY   87 11
NAY NEVER I PUT YOU AWAY YET EACH KISS HISSES   87 12
I AM ASHAMED YOU WANTED ME NOT TO-NIGHT   87 14
YOUR BRIGHTNESS DIMS WHEN I DRAW TOO NEAR AND MY FREE 87 16
AND NOW I KNOW SO I MUST BE ASHAMED   87 18
YOU LOVE ME WHILE I HOVER TENDERLY   87 19
LIKE A PORTENT BUT LORD I AM GLAD SO GLAD I DROWN 88 26
NOT PASS THE RED MOON RISEN AND I AM GLAD   88 28
FOR NOW I KNOW   88 32
EVEN THERE I SEE A BLUE SPARK THAT WILL FLY   89 34
I CAN SMELL THE BOG-END GORGEOUS IN ITS BREATHLESS 90   7
YOU ARE ALWAYS ASKING DO I REMEMBER REMEMBER   90 19
TIME WITH TRUE LONGING WHAT I WAS TO YOU   91 18
PATIENCE LITTLE HEART I SHALL BE SWEET   91 23
IT IS NO GOOD DEAR GENTLENESS AND FORBEARANCE I ENDURED+ 92   7
I HAVE PUSHED MY HANDS IN THE DARK SOIL UNDER THE FLOWE+ 92   8
EACH ONE FOR ITS HOLD ON THE CONCRETE DARKNESS I KNOW T+ 92 14
I CAME TO THE BOYS WITH LOVE DEAR AND ONLY THEY TURNED + 92 21
WITH GENTLENESS CAME I WITH MY HEART 'TWIXT MY HANDS LI+ 92 22
I THOUGHT THAT LOVE WOULD DO ALL THINGS BUT NOW I KNOW + 93   1
I MUST NOT WIN THEIR SOULS NO NEVER I ONLY MUST WIN   93   7
LET THEM LIVE THE BOYS AND LEARN NOT TO TRESPASS I HAD + 93 11
I WILL TEACH THEM THE BEGINNING OF THE LESSON AT THE RO+ 93 24
I THROW FROM OUT OF THE DARKNESS MYSELF LIKE A FLOWER I+ 93 26
BUT NOW I AM TRODDEN TO EARTH AND MY FIRES ARE LOW   94   1
NOW I AM BROKEN DOWN LIKE A PLANT IN WINTER AND ALL   94   2
YET WAIT AWHILE FOR HENCEFORTH I WILL LOVE WHEN A BLOSS+ 94   5
TO MY BLOSSOM IN PERFUME AND SEED-DUST AND ONLY THEN I + 94   6
I HAVE FETCHED THE TEARS UP OUT OF THE LITTLE WELLS   94 10
I WATCHED THE TEARS ON THE GUILTY CHEEKS OF THE BOYS   94 14
DESOLATE I AM AS A CHURCH WHOSE LIGHTS ARE PUT OUT   94 23
I WILL GIVE YOU ALL MY KEYS   95   4
WHEN I HEAR YOU JINGLING THROUGH   95   8
HOW I SIT AND LAUGH AT YOU   95 10
CHALLENGE ME I KEEP ASIDE   95 26
NOW I AM ALL   96   5
I LIFT TO YOU   96 11
THE ALTAR I   96 24
THAT I MAY BE   96 30
AS I STAND ON THIS HILL WITH THE WHITENING CAVE OF THE + 97 11
AND THIS HELEN BESIDE ME I AM BLANK BEING NOTHING I   97 12
OR RATHER 'TIS I AM NOTHING HERE IN THE FUR OF THE HEAT+ 98   2
I IN THE FUR OF THE WORLD ALONE BUT THIS HELEN CLOSE BY 98   6
HOW WE HATE ONE ANOTHER TO-NIGHT HATE SHE AND I   98   7
TO NUMBNESS AND NOTHINGNESS I DEAD SHE REFUSING TO DIE   98   8
OF WEED THAT BLACKENED THE SHORE SO THAT I RECOILED   98 17
THEN I LONGED FOR YOU WITH YOUR MANTLE OF LOVE TO FOLD   98 23
AND I WAS NUMB WITH A BITTER DEATHLY ACHE   98 27
AND I SLEPT TILL DAWN AT THE WINDOW BLEW IN LIKE DUST   99   1
AND I ROSE IN FEAR NEEDING YOU FEARFULLY   99   6
FOR I THOUGHT YOU WERE WARM AS A SUDDEN JET OF BLOOD   99   7
I THOUGHT I COULD PLUNGE IN YOUR LIV   99   8
I HEARD YOU IN YOUR SLEEP SPEAK STRANGELY TO ME   99 10
AND I DARED NOT ENTER FEELING SUDDENLY DISMAYED   99 11
SO I WENT AND WASHED MY DEADENED FLESH IN THE SEA   99 12
WHITHER I TURN AND SET   99 23
TELEGRAM-BICYCLE APPROACHES I WAIT   100   6
IF I COULD HAVE PUT YOU IN MY HEART   100 13
IF BUT I COULD HAVE WRAPPED YOU IN MYSELF   100 14
HOW GLAD I SHOULD HAVE BEEN   100 15
OF YOUR SEVERAL FACES I HAD NEVER SEEN   100 21
AND I CRY ALOUD IN THE MOMENTS THAT INTERVENE   100 23
AND OH MY LOVE AS I ROCK FOR YOU TONIGHT   100 24
I OWN THAT SOME OF ME IS DEAD TONIGHT   100 28
I SHALL ALWAYS BE TRUE TO YOU   102   2
TWICE I AM BORN MY DEAREST   102   3
WHEREIN I AM TRUE   102   6
I KISS YOU GOOD-BYE MY DARLING   102   7
I AM A MAN TO PLOUGH   102 10
I KISS YOU GOOD-BYE MY DEAREST   102 15
OH IF I WERE CALM AS YOU ARE   102 17
OH GOD IF I HAD NOT TO LEAVE YOU   102 23
I MUST GO BUT MY SOUL LIES HELPLESS   103 23
AND I AT THE FOOT OF HER CROSS DID SUFFER   103 24
SO I CAME TO YOU   104   4
AND TWICE AFTER WILD KISSES I SAW   104   9
SO I LAY ON YOUR BREAST FOR AN OBSCURE HOUR   104 13
TILL I KNEW YOU NOT FROM A LITTLE WIND   104 16
I WONDER IF GOD ALLOWS   104 18
AND I BAPTISED MYSELF IN THE WELL   104 21
I WONDER IF ONLY   105 16
LIFE WOULD HAVE BEEN SHOULD I HAVE SPENT   105 18
TOO FAR AWAY O LOVE I KNOW   105 24
WHITE-NIGHTGOWNED LITTLE CHITS I SEE   106 15
OF THE LEAVES AS THOUGH THEY WOULD LEAP SHOULD I CALL 106 21
BUT I SEE LEANING FROM THE SHADES   106 28
BUT I AM ALONE AND WAVERING HOME   107   1
I SHALL GET NO ANSWER IN ANY HOUR   107   4
WHEN I CARRIED MY MOTHER DOWNSTAIRS   107 13
I SHOULD FIND FOR A REPRIMAND   107 15
I WATCHED THEM FLOAT UP THE DARK CHIMNEY   107 17
I ON THE BUSH OF THE GLOBE   107 19
DISCLOSED BUT 'TIS I WHO AM PROWLING   107 27
ABROAD I IN THIS NAKED BERRY   108   2
AND I IN THE STEALTHY BRINDLED ODOURS   108   9
ME TILL I REEL WITH DISSEMINATED CONSCIOUSNESS   108 11
I SEE EACH SHADOW START   108 12
WITH RECOGNITION AND I
I AM DAZED WITH THE FAREWELL
BUT I SCARCELY FEEL YOUR LOSS

TO ME THAT I ANSWER YES   109   6
SO I AM NOT LONELY NOR SAD   109   7
I MOVE AMONG A TOWNFOLK CLAD   109 10
SINCE I LOST YOU I AM SILENCE-HAUNTED   109 13
I FEEL THE SILENCE WAITING   109 25
I LISTEN TO THE STILLNESS OF YOU   110   1
I FEEL YOUR SILENCE TOUCH MY WORDS AS I TALK   110   3
I SEE THE SILENCE EASILY SIP THEM   110   7
YET I AM NOT LOTH   110 10
I SEE THE STEALTHY SHADOW OF SILENCE   110 15
WHY SHOULD I START AND STAND STILL   110 27
I WAS WATCHING THE WOMAN THAT BORE ME   111   1
AWARENESS THEN I SUFFERED A BALK   111 17
BODY TO BODY I COULD NOT   111 18
LOVE YOU ALTHOUGH I WOULD   111 19
SO I FAILED TO GIVE YOU THE LAST   111 26
WHO HAD I BUT PIERCED WITH THE THORNED   111 30
AS I SEE IT HARDENING   112 13
I SHOULD HAVE BEEN CRUEL ENOUGH TO BRING   112 14
AH BUT I AM ILL AND IT IS STILL RAINING COLDLY RAINING 112 29
SO I AM CLOTHED ALL OVER WITH THE LIGHT   113   5
AND THEN I OFFER ALL MYSELF UNTO   113   9
THE DARKNESS IS SECRET AND I COULD SEAR   114   3
STRANGE BEAMS MUST TRAVEL STILL FOR I FEEL THAT I 115   3
MANY YEARS HAVE I STILL TO BURN DETAINED   115   5
LIKE A CANDLE-FLAME ON THIS BODY BUT I ENCLOSE   115   6
WHAT MATTER THE STUFF I LICK UP IN MY DAILY FLAME 115 10
I FORGET MY BEREAVEMENT   115 16
DEPLOYED AROUND ME AND I SEE   115 23
I FORGET MY BEREAVEMENT   115 26
I AM AMAZED AT THIS SPRING THIS CONFLAGRATION   116   6
AND I WHAT SORT OF FIRE AM I AMONG   116 10
I WONDER CAN THE NIGHT GO BY   116 14
OPPRESSES ME SO I CAN HARDLY BEAR   116 26
I WISH I COULD PUT YOU AWAY FROM ME   116 29
I SUFFOCATE IN THIS INTIMACY   116 30
IN WHICH I HALF LOVE YOU   116 31
HOW I HAVE LONGED FOR THIS NIGHT IN THE TRAIN   117   1
FOR I ACHE MOST EARNESTLY FOR YOUR TOUCH   117 15
YET I CANNOT MOVE HOWEVER MUCH   117 16
I WOULD BE YOUR LOVER   117 17
HELEN HAD I KNOWN YESTERDAY   117 25
HAD I KNOWN YESTERDAY YOU COULD TAKE   117 28
I SHOULD HAVE HATED YOU HELEN   117 33
I CANNOT BUT CLEAVE TO YOU HELEN   118   9
OF MY EYES I SEE YOU BEAUTIFUL AND DEAR   118 13
I SEE MYSELF AS THE WINDS THAT HOVER   118 16
ARE THE EARTH I HOVER OVER   118 19
I WOULD KISS YOU OVER THE EYES TILL I KISSED YOU BLIND 118 26
IF I COULD IF ANYONE COULD   118 27
THAT I AM THE HART AND YOU ARE THE GENTLE HIND   118 31
AM I A KALEIDOSCOPE   119   2
AM I DOOMED IN A LONG COITION OF WORDS TO MATE YOU 119   4
ONCE I HAD A LOVER BRIGHT LIKE RUNNING WATER   119 23
ON THE BUTTERCUPS AND THE BUTTERCUPS WAS I   119 26
I SAW THE MIDLANDS   120 10
HOLLOW RANG THE HOUSE WHEN I KNOCKED AT THE DOOR 121 13
AND I LINGERED ON THE THRESHOLD WITH MY HAND   121 14
TO QUICKEN MY HOPE AS I HASTENED TO GREET   121 21
AND I IN THE DARKNESS WANDERED ABOUT   121 25
I SAW HER HID IN THE SHADOW   122   2
I SAW HER STEP TO THE KERB AND FAST   122   3
I HAD STOOD WITH MY HAND UPLIFTED   122   5
I WONDER IF WITH YOU AS IT IS WITH ME   122   9
LONG HAVE I WAITED NEVER ONCE CONFESSED   122 13
IF I COULD CAST THIS CLOTHING OFF FROM ME   122 17
IF I COULD LIFT MY NAKED SELF TO YOU   122 18
YEA BUT I LOATHE YOU THAT YOU SHOULD WITHHOLD   122 23
BETWEEN THE OLD GREY WALLS I DID NOT DARE   122 27
TO RAISE MY FACE I DID NOT DARE LOOK UP   122 28
I FOLLOWED FOLLOWED THE SWING OF HER WHITE DRESS 123   2
THAT ROCKED IN A LILT ALONG I WATCHED THE POISE   123   3
I LIKE TO SEE SHE SAID AND SHE CROUCHED HER DOWN 123   7
BY HER MEASURED BREATHS I LIKE TO SEE SAID SHE   123 11
CHOKE ME IN MY OWN CRIMSON I WATCHED HER PULL   123 17
OVER MY EYES AND I WAS BLIND   123 19
AND THERE IN THE DARK I DID DISCOVER   123 22
THINGS I WAS OUT TO FIND   123 23
I LONGED TO TASTE I LONGED TO TURN   123 27
I LONGED TO FEEL MY HOT BLOOD BURN   123 29
AND I WAS BLIND IN A TAWNY-GOLD DAY   123 32
SO I HELD MY HEART ALOFT   124   3
IT SEEMED THAT I AND THE MORNING WORLD   124   6
SHE SPOKE AND I CLOSED MY EYES   124 18
I ECHOED WITH SURPRISE   124 20
AGAIN I SAW A BROWN BIRD HOVER   124 23
I FELT A BROWN BIRD HOVER   124 25
I THOUGHT I SAW ON THE CLOVER   124 28
I FELT THE BROWN BIRD COVER   124 33
CAN MAKE THEM YAWN I PUT MY HAND TO THE DINT   125   9
I PRESSED THE WRETCHED THROTTLED FLOWER BETWEEN   125 13
AND I HELD THE CHOKED FLOWER-SERPENT IN ITS PANGS 125 16
THE LOW WORD DON'T I LET THE FLOWER FALL   125 20
PUT FORTH TO HER SHE DID NOT MOVE NOR I   125 23
THEN I LAUGHED IN THE DARK OF MY HEART I DID EXULT 125 25
LIKE A SUDDEN CHUCKLING OF MUSIC I BADE HER EYES 125 26
MEET MINE I OPENED HER HELPLESS EYES TO CONSULT   125 27
AND I DO NOT CARE THOUGH THE LARGE HANDS OF REVENGE 126 1
AND DEATH I KNOW IS BETTER THAN NOT-TO-BE   126   6
WHY I SHOULD THINK THAT FROM THE EARTH THERE FLY 127   6
I KNOW FROM HER HARDENED LIPS THAT STILL HER HEART IS 128   1
HUNGRY FOR LOVE YET IF I LAY MY HAND IN HER BREAST 128   2
WHEN I HOLD THEM MY SPENT SOUL UNDERSTANDS   128   8
AND OFTEN I SEE HER CLENCH HER FINGERS TIGHT   128 18
AND I HAVE SEEN HER STAND ALL UNAWARE   128 23
WHERE I SHOULD BE AND WITH HER OWN STRONG SPAN   128 29
REJECT ME NOT IF I SHOULD SAY TO YOU   129   7

I DO FORGET THE SOUNDING OF YOUR VOICE 129 8
I DO FORGET YOUR EYES THAT SEARCHING THROUGH 129 9
I SEE YOUR BLANCHED FACE AT MY BREAST AND HIDE 129 13
AH THEN UPON THE BEDROOM I DO DRAW 129 15
AND I DO LIFT MY ACHING ARMS TO YOU 129 19
AND I DO LIFT MY ANGUISHED AVID BREAST 129 20
AND I DO WEEP FOR VERY PAIN OF YOU 129 21
AND I DO TOSS THROUGH THE TROUBLED NIGHT FOR YOU 129 23
WHILE I DANCE A TARANTELLA ON THE ROCKS AND THE CROON 130 6
WHAT CAN I DO BUT DANCE ALONE 130 9
I WISH A WILD SEA-FELLOW WOULD COME DOWN THE GLITTERING 130 17
ON HIS LIPS I LONG TO BE SOULLESS I TINGLE 130 21
WHEN I TELL YOU THE STARS FLASH SIGNALS EACH ONE 130 25
FOR I TELL YOU 131 7
AGAIN I TELL YOU I BLEED I AM BOUND WITH WITHIES 131 11
I TELL YOU MY BLOOD RUNS OUT ON THE FLOOR OF THIS OAK 131 13
SOME SAY THEY SEE THOUGH I HAVE NEVER SEEN 132 1
I ON THE DECK AM STARTLED BY THIS DAWN CONFRONTING 133 1
I WHO AM SUBSTANCE OF SHADOW I ALL COMPACT 133 6
I WITH THE NIGHT ON MY LIPS I SIGH WITH THE SILENCE OF + 133 9
AND WHAT DO I CARE THOUGH THE VERY STONES SHOULD CRY ME 133 10
DO I NOT KNOW THE DARKNESS WITHIN THEM WHAT ARE THEY 133 14
BUT I 133 18
THE WHOLE OF THE DAY TO EXTINGUISH THE SHADOW I LIFT ON+ 133 20
I STILL AM NOT HOMELESS HERE I'VE A TENT BY DAY 133 24
I CEASE I TURN PALE 133 28
FROM THE WOES I BEWAIL 133 30
I CEASE I TURN PALE 133 33
I LOOK AT THE SWALING SUNSET 134 1
AND WISH I COULD GO ALSO 134 2
I WISH THAT I COULD GO 134 4
THROUGH THE RED DOORS WHERE I COULD PUT OFF 134 5
THEN I WOULD TURN ROUND 134 11
I WOULD LAUGH WITH JOY 134 13
SINCE I LOST YOU MY DARLING THE SKY HAS COME NEAR 134 14
AND I AM OF IT THE SMALL SHARP STARS ARE QUITE NEAR 134 15
BIRD I HEAR 134 19
AND I AM WILLING TO COME TO YOU NOW MY DEAR 134 20
TO BE LOST IN THE HAZE OF THE SKY I WOULD LIKE TO COME 134 22
FOR I AM TIRED MY DEAR AND IF I COULD LIFT MY FEET 134 24
AND SO I SIT AND SCAN THE BOOK OF GREY 135 17
ALL FEARFUL LEST I FIND THE LAST WORDS BLEEDING 135 19
AND I REMEMBER STILL THE SUNNY HOURS 135 25
YES MY LOVE I HEAR 136 26
HE CANNOT SEE IT I CAN NEVER SHOW IT HIM HOW IT SHOOK 137 13
ITS HEAD AS IT WALKED I CAN NEVER CALL HIM TO ME 137 15
LAD SHOULD I TELL THEE SUMMAT 137 19
I TELL THEE THA WON'T BE SATISFIED 139 8
I TELL THEE THA WON'T BE SATISFIED 139 10
RIGID SLEEPS THE HOUSE IN DARKNESS I ALONE 140 7
I WANT MY OWN ROOM'S SHELTER BUT WHAT IS THIS 140 11
I AM LISTENING IS ANYTHING SAID 140 22
DO I INTRUDE ON YOUR RITES NOCTURNAL 140 30
HAVE I PROFANED SOME FEMALE MYSTERY ORGIES 141 3
HOW HAVE I WANDERED HERE TO THIS VAULTED ROOM 141 5
THEN WILL SOMEBODY SQUARE THIS SHADE WITH THE BEING I 141 22
I WAS LAST NIGHT WHEN MY SOUL RANG CLEAR AS A BELL 141 24
WHAT IS THERE GONE AGAINST ME WHY AM I IN HELL 141 26
I MUST GO BACK TO HER 143 6
I WANT TO GIVE HER 143 7
I TURN AND RUN 143 17
BEATING LIKE SOBS I COME TO MYSELF AND STAND 143 21
I KNOW NOT MY SOUL IS IN STRIFE 143 24
THE TOUCH WAS ON THE QUICK I WANT TO FORGET 143 25
WHAT IF I SUDDENLY STUMBLE AND PUSH THE DOOR 147 8
I CAN DRAW BACK 147 10
WHAT IF UNWITTING I SET THE DOOR OF ETERNITY WIDE 147 11
TAKING ME BACK DOWN THE VISTA OF YEARS TILL I SEE 148 5
DOWN IN THE FLOOD OF REMEMBRANCE I WEEP LIKE A CHILD FOR 148 10
RETURNING I FIND HER JUST THE SAME 150 24
OF YOUR HEART OF FIRE IN WHICH I LOOK 151 2
I LOVE FOR EVER THERE IT SEEMS 151 5
MY ALTARS SULLIED I BEREFT REMAIN 151 20
RESTARTS ITSELF WHEREIN I AM KEPT 151 24
THINGS I HAVE KNOWN THAT SHALL HAVE NO NAME 151 32
FORGETTING THE PLACE FROM WHICH I CAME 151 33
I WATCH HER WARD AWAY THE FLAME 151 34
ME THAT I FLICKER IN THE BASKET 151 36
ME THAT I GLOW NOT WITH CONTENT 152 1
ME THAT I INTERRUPT HER GAME 152 3
I OUGHT TO BE PROUD THAT SHE SHOULD ASK IT 152 4
SINCE I AM HERE FOR SO SHORT A SPELL 152 7
NOT TO INTERRUPT HER WHY SHOULD I 152 8
SINCE THIS IS THE LAST NIGHT I KEEP YOU HOME 153 13
COME I WILL CONSECRATE YOU FOR THE JOURNEY 153 14
RATHER I HAD YOU WOULD NOT GO NAY COME 153 15
I WILL NOT AGAIN REPROACH YOU LIE BACK 153 16
I WILL SET A SEAL UPON YOU FROM MY LIP 153 20
I KISS YOUR MOUTH AH LOVE 153 24
COULD I BUT SEAL ITS RUDDY SHINING SPRING 153 25
I CLOSE YOUR EARS WITH KISSES 154 1
I PLACE A GREAT AND BURNING SEAL OF LOVE 154 9
NAY I PERSIST AND VERY FAITH SHALL KEEP 154 12
OF EGRESS FROM YOU I WILL SEAL AND STEEP 154 14
BUT LET ME FINISH WHAT I HAVE BEGUN 154 18
SOFTLY I KNEW IT WOULD COME TO THIS SHE SAID 156 13
I KNEW THAT SOME DAY SOON I SHOULD FIND YOU THUS 156 14
SO I DID NOT FIGHT YOU YOU WENT YOUR WAY INSTEAD 156 15
I DIED THE FIRST I IN THE AFTER-LIFE 156 17
'TWAS I WHOSE FINGERS DID DRAW UP THE YOUNG 156 19
'TWAS I WHO PLACED THE BLOOM OF MANHOOD ON 156 25
YOUR YOUTHFUL SMOOTHNESS I FLEECED WHERE FLEECE WAS NONE 156 26
KNOWLEDGE I SET YOUR HEART TO ITS STRONGER BEAT 156 28
I PUT MY STRENGTH UPON YOU AND I THREW 156 29
BUT I WHOM THE YEARS HAD REARED TO BE YOUR BRIDE 157 1
HAVE I CEASED TO GRIEVE THAT I WAS NOT GREAT ENOUGH 157 7
INDIFFERENT HERE OF MYSELF SINCE I AM GONE 157 12
WHERE YOU ARE GONE AND YOU AND I OUT THERE 157 13
YOUR WIDOW AM I AND ONLY I I DREAM 157 15
AND NOW AT LAST I KISS YOUR PERFECT FACE 157 21
I WISH THE ELDER-TREES IN FLOWER COULD SUDDENLY HEAVE A+ 159 23
AT WHICH I WAS NURSED 159 26
I WOULD GIVE MY SOUL FOR THE HOMESTEAD TO FALL WITH ME + 160 3
WHEN I THINK OF THE PLACE 161 8
A COLD HAND I PEEP BETWEEN THE FINGERS 162 18
ALWAYS THERE AS I PEEP 162 21
BUT WE'LL STILL BE TOGETHER THIS ROAD AND I 163 15
I WONDERED I LOOKED AROUND 165 1
I SAW THE TRANSFIGURATION 165 25
I CARRY MY PATIENCE SULLENLY THROUGH THE WASTE LANDS 167 3
I FORCE MY CART THROUGH THE SODDEN FILTH THAT IS PRESSED 167 5
AS I MAKE MY WAY IN TWILIGHT NOW TO REST 167 7
I CARRY MY PATIENCE SULLENLY THROUGH THE WASTE LANDS 167 16
TO-MORROW WILL POUR THEM ALL BACK THE DULL HOURS I DETE+ 167 20
I IMAGINE DEAD HANDS ARE BRIGHTER 168 13
FOR YOUR WRATH AND YES I OPINE 168 18
BUT I AM NOT HERE 169 5
I AM AWAY BEYOND THE SCOPE OF THIS TURNING 169 6
I WHO SIT IN TEARS 169 9
I WHOSE HEART IS TORN WITH PARTING 169 10
SHALL I TELL YOU THEN HOW IT IS 169 26
AND SO I SEEM 170 1
I SEE OUR SHADOW TREMBLE 170 11
FOR I HAVE TOLD YOU PLAINLY HOW IT IS 170 16
THE PLACE IS PALPABLE ME FOR HERE I WAS BORN 172 22
I HAVE COME I FEEL THEM WHIMPER IN WELCOME AND MOURN 172 25
AND THE PLACE IS NO LONGER OURS WATCHING I HEAR 173 2
CAN I GO NO NEARER NEVER TOWARDS THE DOOR 173 5
THE GHOSTS AND I WE MOURN TOGETHER AND SHRINK 173 6
IS IT IRREVOCABLE CAN I REALLY NOT GO 173 9
THROUGH THE OPEN YARD-WAY CAN I NOT GO PAST THE SHEDS 173 10
I KISS THE STONES I KISS THE MOSS ON THE WALL 173 13
AND WISH I COULD PASS IMPREGNATE INTO THE PLACE 173 14
I WISH I COULD TAKE IT ALL IN A LAST EMBRACE 173 15
I WISH WITH MY BREAST I HERE COULD ANNIHILATE IT ALL 173 16
I HAVE LIVED DELIGHTED IN THE HALLS OF THE PAST 173 21
BUT NOW I THINK I HAVE SEEN IT ALL AND NOW 173 25
I FEEL THICK WALLS OF STONE BEHIND THE ARRAS 173 26
I AM SHUT IN A PRISONER I KNOW NOT HOW 173 27
I SHALL PUT ROSES ON ROSES AND COVER YOUR GRAVE 176 11
AT THE OPEN DOOR OF THE ROOM I STAND AND LOOK AT THE NI+ 179 20
I WILL ESCAPE FROM THE HOLLOW ROOM THE BOX OF LIGHT 179 24
I WILL GO OUT TO THE NIGHT AS A MAN GOES DOWN TO THE SH+ 180 1
I WILL SIFT THE SURF THAT EDGES THE NIGHT WITH MY NET T+ 180 4
I WILL CATCH IN MY EYES' QUICK NET 180 8
HOW GLAD I SHOULD BE 180 18
WHY DO I WANDER AIMLESS AMONG THEM DESIROUS FOOL 180 23
I CAN ALWAYS LINGER OVER THE HUDDLED BOOKS ON THE STALLS 180 24
THERE IS SOMETHING I WANT TO FEEL IN MY RUNNING BLOOD 180 30
SOMETHING I WANT TO TOUCH I MUST HOLD MY FACE TO THE RA+ 180 31
I MUST HOLD MY FACE TO THE WIND AND LET IT EXPLAIN 180 32
I WILL TRAIL MY HANDS AGAIN THROUGH THE DRENCHED COLD L+ 180 34
I CAN LOOK THROUGH 194 1
THROUGH THE FILM I CAN ALMOST TOUCH YOU 194 3
I AM WEARY OF MYSELF 194 17
I QUAILED AT MY APPOINTED FUNCTION TURNED POLTROON 194 29
AT NIGHT I SAY WHEN I AM GONE IN SLEEP 195 5
NEVER LET IT BE SAID I WAS POLTROON 195 8
HAVE SAID THAT I THIS MOTE IN THE BODY OF SLEEP 195 18
STILL IN FULL FLIGHT EXTINCT SHALL I THEN TURN 195 23
SHALL I LESS THAN THE LEAST RED GRAIN OF FLESH 195 31
I WAS JUST DRIVEN 196 21
I DANCE AT THE CHRISTMAS PARTY 198 5
NOW I AM GOING HOME 198 17
I SEE THE GREAT ORION STANDING 198 19
NOR DO I GET ANY LOOK 198 27
I SUPPOSE BETWEEN NOW AND THEN 199 2
HE HAS DONE AS I HAVE DONE 199 5
I IN THESE GOODLY FROZEN 199 15
I WHO AM WORN AND CAREFUL 199 25
HOW MUCH DO I CARE 199 26
HOW IS IT I GRIN THEN AND CHUCKLE 199 27
GRIEF GRIEF I SUPPOSE AND SUFFICIENT 199 29
SHE SAYS I WENT TO CYTHERA 201 7
HEARD I HAVE BEEN TO PATMOS 202 3
I GIVE WHOEVER DENIES 202 12
AND AT LAST I KNOW MY LOVE FOR YOU IS HERE 203 17
I CAN SEE IT ALL IT IS WHOLE LIKE THE TWILIGHT 203 18
IT IS LARGE SO LARGE I COULD NOT SEE IT BEFORE 203 19
YOU ARE THE CALL AND I AM THE ANSWER 203 22
YOU ARE THE WISH AND I THE FULFILMENT 203 23
YOU ARE THE NIGHT AND I THE DAY 203 24
YOU AND I 203 27
I COULD NOT BE FREE 204 6
YOU AND I TOGETHER 204 22
NO NOW I WISH THE SUNSHINE WOULD STOP 205 1
I WISH THAT WHATEVER PROPS UP THE WALLS OF LIGHT 205 9
AND DEATH WOULD ACHE STILL I AM SURE 205 18
I WISH IT WOULD BE COMPLETELY DARK EVERYWHERE 205 20
AND I WAS HERE IN THE UNDER-DUSK OF THE ISAR 206 26
AND I SUFFERED IT WANTING TO SYMPATHISE 206 34
I ACQUIESCED AGAIN 207 4
YET HOW I HAVE LEARNED TO KNOW THAT LOOK IN YOUR EYES 207 15
HOW I KNOW THAT GLITTER OF SALT DRY STERILE SHARP CORRO+ 207 17
I HAVE SEEN IT FELT IT IN MY MOUTH MY THROAT MY CHEST MY 207 21
I HAVE BEEN THRUST INTO WHITE SHARP CRYSTALS 207 25
IN WHICH I HAVE WRITHED 207 32
I HAVE LEARNED TO CURSE YOUR MOTHERHOOD 207 34
I HAVE CURSED MOTHERHOOD BECAUSE OF YOU 207 36
I LONG FOR THE TIME TO COME WHEN THE CURSE AGAINST YOU + 208 1
I TRY TO REMEMBER IT IS ALSO WELL BETWEEN US 208 10
AND OH I WISH IT WAS BETTER 208 22
I DISTINGUISH THE SCENT OF YOUR HAIR SO NOW THE LIMBER 208 30
YOU HAVE COME YOUR WAY I HAVE COME MY WAY 209 7

I HAVE STEPPED ACROSS MY PEOPLE AND HURT THEM IN SPITE 209 10
I HAVE DONE A QUIVER OF EXULTATION GOES THROUGH ME LIKE 209 26
AT LAST I CAN THROW AWAY WORLD WITHOUT END AND MEET YOU 210 1
AT LAST YOU CAN THROW IMMORTALITY OFF AND I SEE YOU 210 3
SHAMELESS AND CALLOUS I LOVE YOU 210 5
OUT OF INDIFFERENCE I LOVE YOU 210 6
I SEE YOU AH IN FULL 210 14
I AM AFRAID OF YOU I AM AFRAID AFRAID 210 27
NO I HAVE WAKENED IT IS YOU YOU ARE CRUEL TO ME 211 2
COME NO I'M A THING OF LIFE I GIVE 211 5
I HOW CAN YOU TREAT ME SO AND LOVE ME 211 9
YOU LOVE IT IT IS DARK IT KILLS ME I AM PUT OUT 211 12
NO NO I DANCE IN THE SUN I'M A THING OF LIFE 211 16
WITH SHADOWS WITH YOURS I PEOPLE THE SUNSHINE 211 19
BUT I AM MYSELF I HAVE NOTHING TO DO WITH THESE 211 24
AND I WILL BE ALL THE SHADOW YOU THE SHINE 211 27
THE PINE-WOODS HOW I LOVE THEM SO IN THEIR MYSTERY OF 212 3
I WALK UP TO MY NECK IN MIST HOLDING MY MOUTH UP 212 13
I HOLD THE NIGHT IN HORROR 212 15
I DARE NOT TURN ROUND 212 16
TO-NIGHT I HAVE LEFT HER ALONE 212 17
THEY WOULD HAVE IT I HAVE LEFT HER FOR EVER 212 18
IF I GO ON WALKING THROUGH THE WHOLE BREADTH OF GERMANY 212 24
I COME TO THE NORTH SEA OR THE BALTIC 212 25
I HERE IN THE UNDERMIST ON THE BAVARIAN ROAD 213 3
I DON'T MIND THIS CONTINENT STRETCHING THE SEA FAR AWAY 213 7
AND IF I NEVER SEE HER AGAIN 213 15
I THINK IF THEY TOLD ME SO 213 16
I COULD CONVULSE THE HEAVENS WITH MY HORRO 213 17
I THINK I COULD BREAK THE SYSTEM WITH MY HEART 213 19
I THINK IN MY CONVULSION THE SKIES WOULD BREAK 213 20
I HAVE BEEN SO INNERLY PROUD AND SO LONG ALONE 214 1
DO NOT LEAVE ME OR I SHALL BREAK 214 2
WHAT SHOULD I DO IF YOU WERE GONE AGAIN 214 4
WHAT SHOULD I LOOK FOR 214 6
WHERE SHOULD I GO 214 7
WHAT SHOULD I BE I MYSELF 214 8
I 214 9
I 214 11
WHAT SHOULD I THINK OF DEATH 214 13
IF I DIED IT WOULD NOT BE YOU 214 14
THINK I DAREN'T DIE 214 21
AND I DAREN'T LIVE 214 23
I WOULD BEAR THE PAIN 214 25
THINK I COULDN'T LOOK TOWARDS DEATH 215 1
GOD THAT I HAVE NO CHOICE 215 6
NECESSARY AND I HAVE NO CHOICE 215 12
IS ALMOST MORE THAN I CAN BEAR 215 15
I WALK IN FEAR OF YOU 215 16
AH NEVER BEFORE DID I SEE 215 20
OH AND I WANT TO SING 216 1
AND DANCE BUT I CAN'T LIFT UP 216 2
IS ALMOST MORE THAN I CAN BEAR 216 12
I LINGER TO WATCH HER 217 10
LIKE WET AND FALLING ROSES AND I LISTEN 217 21
I AM BEAUTIFUL I LOOK AT THE RUMPLED YOUNG ROSES 218 2
I AM MYSELF AT LAST NOW I ACHIEVE 218 5
MY VERY SELF I WITH THE WONDER MELLOW 218 6
FULL OF FINE WARMTH I IS 218 7
HERE I AM ALL MYSELF NO ROSE-BUSH HEAVING 218 9
IN STARK-CLEAR ROSES THAN I TO MYSELF AM BROUGHT 218 12
I AM HERE MYSELF AS THOUGH THIS HEAVE OF EFFORT 218 13
OR ARE WE KINDLED YOU AND I TO BE 219 5
I CAN HEAR THE SWISH OF THE SCYTHE-STROKES FOUR 219 22
SHARP BREATHS TAKEN YEA AND I 219 23
IS MINE I CLAIM HIM ONCE AND FOR ALL 219 26
THOUGH IT'S SORRY I AM ON HIS YOUNG FEET KNOWING 219 27
COMES WITH THE SIGHT OF THE ROOM I CANNOT TELL 220 14
FOR WHICH I WANTED THE NIGHT TO RETREAT 220 20
THE HOUSE IS SILENT IT IS LATE AT NIGHT I AM ALONE 220 21
I CAN HEAR THE ISAR MOAN 220 23
I WONDER WHERE 221 3
KNIGHTS INDEED MUCH KNIGHT I KNOW WILL RIDE 221 10
HOW I ADORE YOU FOR YOUR SIMPLE PRIDE 221 14
I THANK YOU I DO YOU HAPPY CREATURES YOU DEARS 221 20
PROUD KNIGHTS TO BATTLE SWEET HOW I WARM 221 28
AS I WENT THROUGH THE MARSHES 222 1
I LOOKED AT HER 222 9
I BECAME A STRANGE BEING 222 11
STILL I HAD MY RIGHT TO BE THERE WITH HER 222 12
AND I KNEW HER 222 16
IF I TURN QUICKLY I AM TERRIFIED FEELING SPACE SURROUND+ 222 23
I SEE MYSELF ISOLATED IN THE UNIVERSE AND WONDER 223 1
WHAT EFFECT I CAN HAVE MY HANDS WAVE UNDER 223 2
I HOLD MYSELF UP AND FEEL A BIG WIND BLOWING 223 4
WHITHER OR WHY OR EVEN HOW I AM GOING 223 6
SMALL AM I WHAT MATTER IF MINUTELY 223 8
I BEAT MY WAY TO BE LOST IMMEDIATELY 223 9
HOW SHALL I FLATTER MYSELF THAT I CAN DO 223 10
ANYTHING IN SUCH IMMENSITY I AM TOO 223 11
WHY DON'T I GO 224 16
WHY DO I CRAWL ABOUT THIS POT THIS OUBLIETTE 224 17
WHY DON'T I GO 224 19
IF I COME TO A PINE-WOOD I CAN'T SAY 224 21
NOW I AM ARRIVED 224 22
A BULLOCK WAGON COMES SO I AM ASHAMED 225 10
WHITELY CONFRONT I WAIT ON THE GRASS AM LAMED 225 12
I STAND ASIDE ON THE GRASS TO LET THEM GO 225 21
AND CHRIST I HAVE MET HIS ACCUSING EYES AGAIN 225 22
ONE MOMENT I SEE THE STILLNESS OF AGONY 225 26
I STAND IN A CHILL OF ANGUISH TRYING TO SAY 225 31
THE JOY I BOUGHT WAS NOT TOO HIGHLY PRICED 225 32
AND I AS I STAND IN THE COLD AVERTED FLOWERS 226 9
I WANTED TO GATHER THEM ONE BY ONE 227 15
CAN I GATHER THE MOUNTAIN-TIPS 227 18
CAN I CATCH LIKE A MOTH BETWEEN MY HANDS 227 23
BUT HUSH I AM NOT REGRETTING 227 25

I KNOW YOU HERE IN THE DARKNESS 227 29
I AM WASHED QUITE CLEAN 229 22
I AM CHILLED TO THE BONE 229 28
I AM PURE LIKE BONE 230 3
THE SUN IS IN MY EYES I MUST GET UP 230 11
I WANT TO GO THERE'S A GOLD ROAD BLAZES BEFORE 230 12
AH BUT IF I AM CRUEL WHAT THEN ARE YOU 230 15
I AM BRUISED RIGHT THROUGH 230 16
WHAT IF I LOVE YOU THIS 230 17
HERE I AM GET UP AND COME TO ME 230 24
BEHIND ME ON THE LAKE I HEAR THE STEAMER DRUMMING 231 5
AM I WHICH WAY ARE YOU COMING 231 7
BUT I AM YOUR NAKED CANDLE BURNING 233 11
I FORGET YOU HAVE FORGOTTEN YOU 233 18
I AM BUSY ONLY AT MY BURNING 233 19
I AM BUSY ONLY AT MY LIFE 233 20
AND WHEN I LIFT MY FACE IT IS A FLAME THAT GOES UP 233 22
BUT I AM NOT CONCERNED WITH YOU 233 24
I HAVE FORGOTTEN YOU 233 25
I AM A NAKED CANDLE BURNING ON YOUR GRAVE 233 26
AH YES I KNOW YOU WELL A SOJOURNER 234 1
I KNOW RIGHT WELL THE MARRIAGE RING YOU WEAR 234 3
SO YOU TO MINE I IMAGINE YES HAPPILY 234 7
I SEE YOU ALL THE TIME YOU BIRD-BLITHE LOVELY 234 9
I SEE RIGHT WELL HOW I OUGHT TO BE GRATEFUL 234 11
LISTEN I HAVE NO USE 234 13
RISE UP AND GO I HAVE NO USE FOR YOU 234 17
YOU HAVE FED ME WITH YOUR SWEETNESS NOW I AM SICK 234 23
AS I DESERVE 234 24
I HAVE HAD ENOUGH 234 26
SINCE I MUST SERVE AND STRUGGLE WITH THE IMMINENT 234 31
SERVE THEN I TELL YOU ADD YOUR STRENGTH TO MINE 235 1
BECAUSE WHEN I SIT IN THE ROOM 235 26
NO DOUBT IF I WERE DEAD YOU MUST 236 1
AS I FOR YOU 236 7
AND AM I NOT BALAAM'S ASS 236 9
FOR I AM QUITE INDIFFERENT 237 5
I DON'T CARE 237 16
I HAVE MADE THE FIRE UP BRIGHT 237 20
I WILL WARM YOUR LIMBS WITH KISSES 237 25
NOW YOU ARE MINE TO-NIGHT AT LAST I SAY IT 238 16
YOU'RE A DOVE I HAVE BOUGHT FOR SACRIFICE 238 17
AND TO-NIGHT I SLAY IT 238 18
DEATH DO YOU HEAR IN MY ARMS I AM BRINGING 238 20
NOW I OFFER HER UP TO THE ANCIENT INEXORABLE GOD 238 23
I SACRIFICE ALL IN HER MY LAST OF THE WORLD 239 2
I HAVE WON MY RENOWN 239 6
NOW I GATHER YOU UP 239 10
NOW I PUT YOU BACK 239 11
I THE GREAT VEIN THAT LEADS 240 4
I ADAM FORM THE VEINS OF ME 240 11
WHY SHOULD I WANT TO THROTTLE 240 24
I DID NOT WANT IT 241 11
'TWAS NOT THAT I WISHED IT 241 21
I MUST BE RECIPROCATING YOUR VACUOUS HIDEOUS PASSION 241 27
SINCE ALREADY I AM IMPLICATED WITH YOU 242 6
WHEN I WOKE THE LAKE-LIGHTS WERE QUIVERING ON THE WALL 243 21
THERE WAS SOMETHING I OUGHT TO REMEMBER AND YET 243 26
I DID NOT REMEMBER WHY SHOULD I THE RUNNING LIGHTS 243 27
I FEEL NEW AND EAGER 244 23
YOU AND I I AND YOU 244 32
HOW I LOVE ALL OF YOU DO YOU FEEL ME WRAP YOU 245 7
AND HOW I AM NOT AT ALL EXCEPT A FLAME THAT MOUNTS OFF 245 10
WHERE I TOUCH YOU I FLAME INTO BEING BUT IS IT ME OR 245 12
AND I THE SWIFT BRACTS THAT SHEATHE IT THOSE BREASTS TH+ 245 16
THOSE SHOULDERS SO WARM AND SMOOTH I FEEL THAT I 245 18
BUT HOW LOVELY TO BE YOU CREEP CLOSER IN THAT I AM MORE 245 20
I SPREAD OVER YOU HOW LOVELY YOUR ROUND HEAD YOUR 245 21
YOUR BREASTS YOUR KNEES AND FEET I FEEL THAT WE 245 23
AND OH MY LITTLE ONE YOU WHOM I ENFOLD 246 1
HOW QUAVERINGLY I DEPEND ON YOU TO KEEP ME ALIVE 246 2
I THE MAN WHO ENFOLDS YOU AND HOLDS YOU CLOSE 246 4
HOW MY SOUL CLEAVES TO YOUR BOSOM AS I CLASP YOU 246 5
SUPPOSE YOU DIDN'T WANT ME I SHOULD SINK DOWN 246 7
NOURISH ME AND ENDUE ME I AM ONLY OF YOU 246 11
I AM YOUR ISSUE 246 12
WHEN I ENFOLD YOU AND YOU CREEP INTO ME 246 14
I WHO AM SO FIERCE AND STRONG ENFOLDING YOU 246 23
HOW SUDDENLY I SHALL GO DOWN INTO NOTHING 246 25
AND I SHALL BE WAVERING UNCERTAIN 246 28
BUT NOW I AM FULL AND STRONG AND CERTAIN 247 1
HOW SURE I FEEL HOW WARM AND STRONG AND HAPPY 247 4
I AM LIKE A SEED WITH A PERFECT FLOWER ENCLOSED 247 6
I WONDER WHAT IT WILL BE 247 7
NO MATTER I AM SO HAPPY 247 10
I FEEL LIKE A FIRM RICH HEALTHY ROOT 247 11
HOW I DEPEND ON YOU UTTERLY 247 13
BUT THAT IS ALL I WANT 247 26
AND I AM SURE OF THAT 247 27
AND I AM I AM NEVER YOU 248 2
YET I AM GLAD 248 5
I AM SO GLAD THERE IS ALWAYS YOU BEYOND BY SCOPE 248 6
SOMETHING I SHALL NEVER BE 248 8
THAT I SHALL ALWAYS WONDER OVER AND WAIT FOR 248 9
STILL WAITING FOR YOU HOWEVER OLD YOU ARE AND I AM 248 11
I SHALL ALWAYS WONDER OVER YOU AND LOOK FOR YOU 248 12
I SHALL NEVER CEASE TO BE FILLED WITH NEWNESS 248 14
WERE RANKED TO BLUE BATTLE AND YOU AND I 248 22
AND I COVERED THE EARTH AND ALL SPACE 248 27
HAVING KNOWN THE WORLD SO LONG I HAVE NERVER CONFESSED 249 13
I AM THAT I AM AND NO MORE THAN THAT BUT SO MUCH 250 1
I AM NOR WILL I BE BOUNCED OUT OF IT SO AT LAST I TOUCH 250 2
ALL THAT I AM-NOT IN SOFTNESS SWEET SOFTNESS FOR SHE IS+ 250 3
SO I HOPE I SHALL SPEND ETERNITY 250 9
NOT I NOT I BUT THE WIND THAT BLOWS THROUGH ME 250 13
IF ONLY I LET IT BEAR ME CARRY ME IF ONLY IT CARRY ME 250 15
IF ONLY I AM SENSITIVE SUBTLE OH DELICATE A WINGED GIFT 250 16

IF ONLY I AM KEEN AND HARD LIKE THE SHEER TIP OF A WEDGE   250 21
I WOULD BE A GOOD FOUNTAIN A GOOD WELL-HEAD   250 26
I DON'T CARE WHETHER I AM BEAUTIFUL TO YOU   251 1
YOU MAY LOOK AND SAY TO YOURSELVES I DO   251 7
HOW HAPPY I AM HOW MY HEART IN THE WIND RINGS TRUE   251 11
IF YOU KNEW HOW I SWERVE IN PEACE IN THE EQUIPOISE   251 22
AND I LOVE YOU SO STRAIGHT AND CLEAN AND ALL OF A PIECE+   254 18
SO THAT I BEGAN TO WONDER OVER MYSELF AND WHAT I WAS   254 23
WHEN I WAS A CHILD I LOVED MY FATHER'S RIDING-WHIP   255 1
I LOVED TO HANDLE IT IT SEEMED LIKE A NEAR PART OF HIM   255 3
SO I DID HIS PENS AND THE JASPER SEAL ON HIS NECK   255 4
SOMETHING SEEMED TO SURGE THROUGH ME WHEN I TOUCHED   255 5
THE JOY I FEEL   255 8
GOD KNOWS WHAT I FEEL BUT IT IS JOY   255 9
I ADMIRE YOU SO YOU ARE BEAUTIFUL THIS CLEAN SWEEP OF   255 11
I WOULD DIE RATHER THAN HAVE IT INJURED WITH ONE SCAR   255 13
I WISH I COULD GRIP YOU LIK   255 14
SO SHE SAID AND I WONDERED   255 16
NOW I SAY TO HER NO TOOL NO INSTRUMENT NO GOD   255 19
I TELL YOU THERE IS ALL THESE   256 2
AND SO I CROSS INTO ANOTHER WORLD   256 4
FROM THIS UNKNOWN THAT I WOULD TRESPASS ON   256 6
I AM VERY GLAD AND ALL ALONE IN THE WORLD   256 7
WHERE I AM DISEMBARKED AT LAST   256 9
I COULD CRY WITH JOY BECAUSE I AM IN THE NEW WORLD JUST   256 10
I COULD CRY WITH JOY AND QUITE FREELY THERE IS NOBODY TO   256 12
BECAUSE IT WILL STILL BE A GESTURE OF THE OLD WORLD I AM   256 18
I WAS SO WEARY OF THE WORLD   256 22
I WAS SO SICK OF IT   256 23
IT WAS ALL TAINTED WITH MYSELF I KNEW IT ALL TO START W+   256 29
WHEN I GATHERED FLOWERS I KNEW IT WAS MYSELF PLUCKING MY   257 1
WHEN I WENT IN A TRAIN I KNEW IT WAS MYSELF TRAVELLING +   257 3
WHEN I HEARD THE CANNON OF THE WAR I LISTENED WITH MY   257 5
WHEN I SAW THE TORN DEAD I KNEW IT WAS MY OWN TORN DEAD   257 7
IT WAS ALL ME I HAD DONE IT ALL IN MY OWN FLESH   257 9
I SHALL NEVER FORGET THE MANIACAL HORROR OF IT ALL IN T+   257 10
WHEN EVERYTHING WAS ME I KNEW IT ALL ALREADY I ANTICIPA+   257 11
BECAUSE I WAS THE AUTHOR AND THE RESULT   257 13
I WAS THE GOD AND THE CREATION AT ONCE   257 14
CREATOR I LOOKED AT MY CREATION   257 15
CREATED I LOOKED AT MYSELF THE CREATOR   257 16
I WAS A LOVER I KISSED THE WOMAN I LOVED   257 18
AND GOD OF HORROR I WAS KISSING ALSO MYSELF   257 19
I WAS A FATHER AND A BEGETTER OF CHILDREN   257 20
AND OH OH HORROR I WAS BEGETTING AND CONCEIVING IN MY   257 21
AND THAT AT LAST RELIEVED ME I DIED   257 24
I BURIED MY BELOVED IT WAS GOOD I BURIED MYSELF AND WAS   257 25
VERY GOOD VERY GOOD I AM A MURDERER   257 29
IT IS GOOD I CAN MURDER AND MURDER AND SEE THEM FALL   257 30
TILL IT IS ALMOST ENOUGH TILL I AM REDUCED PERHAPS   258 7
AND I AM DEAD AND TRODDEN TO NOUGHT IN THE SMOKE-SODDEN   258 14
WHEN I AM TRODDEN QUITE OUT QUITE OUT   258 26
EVERY VESTIGE GONE THEN I AM HERE   258 27
I IN THE SOUR BLACK TOMB TRODDEN TO ABSOLUTE DEATH   259 1
I PUT OUT MY HAND IN THE NIGHT ONE NIGHT AND MY HAND   259 2
WHERE I HAD BEEN WAS A SUDDEN BLAZE   259 5
SO I PUT MY HAND OUT FURTHER A LITTLE FURTHER   259 7
AND I FELT THAT WHICH WAS NOT I   259 8
IT VERILY WAS NOT I   259 9
HA I WAS A BLAZE LEAPING UP   259 11
I WAS A TIGER BURSTING INTO SUNLIGHT   259 12
I WAS GREEDY I WAS MAD FOR THE UNKNOWN   259 13
I NEW-RISEN RESURRECTED STARVED FROM THE TOMB   259 14
NOW HERE WAS I NEW-AWAKENED WITH MY HAND STRETCHING   259 16
MY GOD BUT I CAN ONLY SAY   259 20
I TOUCH I FEEL THE UNKNOWN   259 21
I AM THE FIRST COMER   259 22
I AM THE FIRST COMER   259 25
I AM THE DISCOVERER   259 26
I HAVE FOUND THE OTHER WORLD   259 27
I AM THROWN UPON THE SHORE   259 29
I AM COVERING MYSELF WITH THE SAND   259 30
I AM FILLING MY MOUTH WITH THE EARTH   259 31
I AM BURROWING MY BODY INTO THE SOIL   259 32
I TOUCHED WITH MY HAND I CLUTCHED WITH MY HAND   260 2
WHOM I MARRIED YEARS AGO   260 5
AT WHOSE SIDE I HAVE LAIN FOR OVER A THOUSAND NIGHTS   260 6
AND ALL THAT PREVIOUS WHILE SHE WAS I SHE WAS I   260 7
I TOUCHED HER IT WAS I WHO TOUCHED AND I WHO WAS TOUCHED 260 8
I TOUCHED HER FLANK AND KNEW I WAS CARRIED BY THE CURRE+ 260 12
RISEN NOT TO THE OLD WORLD THE OLD CHANGELESS I THE OLD+ 260 15
BUT TO A NEW EARTH A NEW I A NEW KNOWLEDGE A NEW WORLD   260 17
AH NO I CANNOT TELL YOU WHAT IT IS THE NEW WORLD   260 19
I CANNOT TELL YOU THE MAD ASTOUNDED RAPTURE OF ITS DISC+ 260 20
I SHALL BE MAD WITH DELIGHT BEFORE I HAVE DONE   260 21
AND STRANGE WAYS WHERE I FALL INTO OBLIVION OF UTTERMOST 261 6
I HAVE FOUND A PLACE OF LONELINESS   261 17
I SAW HER STAND AND WAIT   261 24
THEN I FOUND MYSELF IN A WONDERLAND   261 26
I WAITED THEREFORE THEN I KNEW   262 1
TO LET ME KNOW THAT I WAS FOUND   262 9
FROM THE WOMB OF THE ALL I AM WAITING DAZED   262 20
THEN I SHALL KNOW THE ELYSIUM   262 22
OF TIME FROM OUT OF WHICH I COME   262 24
I HAVE NEVER YET BEEN SMITTEN THROUGH THE BELLY WITH THE 263 9
FOR SO MUCH I THANK THE GOOD GENERATIONS OF MANKIND   263 14
I THANK MANKIND WITH PASSIONATE HEART   263 29
THAT I JUST ESCAPED THE HUNGER FOR THESE   263 30
THAT THEY WERE GIVEN WHEN I NEEDED THEM   263 31
BECAUSE I AM THE SON OF MAN   263 32
I HAVE EATEN AND DRUNK AND WARMED AND CLOTHED MY BODY   264 1
I HAVE BEEN TAUGHT THE LANGUAGE OF UNDERSTANDING   264 2
I HAVE CHOSEN AMONG THE BRIGHT AND MARVELLOUS BOOKS   264 3
I THOUGHT IT WAS WOMAN INDISCRIMINATE WOMAN   264 21
MERE FEMALE ADJUNCT OF WHAT I WAS   264 22
SO I HAVE KNOWN IT   264 28
EVEN THEN IN THE DARK I WAS TORTURED RAVENING UNFREE   264 30

HOW COULD I LOOK WHEN I WAS MAD I LOOKED SIDEWAYS FURTI+ 264 35
I LOST AT LAST THE FIERCENESS THAT FEARS IT WILL STARVE   265 3
I COULD PUT MY FACE AT LAST BETWEEN HER BREASTS   265 4
THAT I SHOULD NEVER STARVE   265 6
I HAD EATEN OF THE BREAD THAT SATISFIES   265 8
AND FOR THIS I HAVE TO THANK ONE WOMAN   265 21
AND FOR MYSELF I CAN SAY ALMOST ALMOST OH VERY NEARLY   265 27
WHAT REMAINS IN ME IS TO BE KNOWN EVEN AS I KNOW   265 31
I KNOW HER NOW OR PERHAPS I KNOW MY OWN LIMITATION AGAI+ 265 32
PLUNGING AS I HAVE DONE OVER OVER THE BRINK   266 1
I HAVE DROPPED AT LAST HEADLONG INTO NOUGHT PLUNGING UP+ 266 2
I HAVE COME AS IT WERE NOT TO KNOW   266 4
WHAT CAN I SAY MORE EXCEPT THAT I KNOW WHY IT IS TO SUR+ 266 6
I SUPPOSE ULTIMATELY SHE IS ALL BEYOND ME   266 11
A CURIOUS AGONY AND A RELIEF WHEN I TOUCH THAT WHICH IS+ 266 14
I WANT HER THOUGH TO TAKE THE SAME FROM ME   266 23
SHE TOUCHES ME AS IF I WERE HERSELF HER OWN   266 24
SHE HAS NOT REALISED YET THAT FEARFUL THING THAT I AM T+ 266 25
I WANT HER TO TOUCH ME AT LAST AH ON THE ROOT AND QUICK   266 28
AND PERISH ON ME AS I HAVE PERISHED ON HER   266 30
WHEN SHE PASSES AWAY AS I HAVE PASSED AWAY   267 15
THEN I SHALL BE GLAD I SHALL NOT BE CONFUSED WITH HER   267 17
I SHALL BE CLEARED DISTI   267 18
FALLING I HEAR AGAIN   268 23
IN LONDON I SHOULD HAVE HELD MYSELF   269 15
HAD MORE RIGHT THAN I FOR WHO WAS I   269 19
NOW I SEE THEM JUST THE SAME AND WATCH THEM   269 20
BUT OF WHAT ACCOUNT DO I HOLD THEM   269 21
ESPECIALLY THE YOUNG WOMEN I LOOK AT THEM   269 22
IF I PASS THEM CLOSE OR ANY MAN   269 25
WITH A LOVELINESS I LOATHE   270 26
I WISH IT WERE SPRING IN THE WORLD   270 29
I TRAMPLE ON THE SNOWDROPS IT GIVES ME PLEASURE TO TREA+ 271 12
FOR I AM SICK OF THEM THEIR FAINT-BLOODEDNESS   271 15
I WANT THE FINE KINDLING WINE-SAP OF SPRING   271 17
I WISH IT WERE SPRING   271 30
I WISH THAT SPRING   272 1
I WISH IT WERE SPRING THUNDERING   272 4
I WISH THESE BRITTLE FROST-LOVELY FLOWERS OF PASSIONATE+ 272 6
SHOW ME I TREMBLE SO MUCH TO HEAR IT THAT EVEN NOW   273 28
ON THE THRESHOLD OF SPRING I FEAR I SHALL DIE   273 29
FOR AGES I DON'T CARE A FIG FOR IT MEN SAY BUT WHY A FI+ 277 5
YOU TELL ME I AM WRONG   278 1
WHO ARE YOU WHO IS ANYBODY TO TELL ME I AM WRONG   278 2
I AM NOT WRONG   278 3
FOR MY PART I PREFER MY HEART TO BE BROKEN   279 1
I AM THINKING OF COURSE OF THE PEACH BEFORE I ATE IT   279 13
AND BECAUSE I SAY SO YOU WOULD LIKE TO THROW SOMETHING   279 26
I LOVE YOU ROTTEN   280 1
I LOVE TO SUCK YOU OUT FROM YOUR SKINS   280 3
I SAY WONDERFUL ARE THE HELLISH EXPERIENCES   280 24
WHICH I SUPPOSE IS WHY AMERICA HAS GONE DRY   286 20
OH AND I WISH THE HIGH AND SUPER-GOTHIC HEAVENS WOULD   287 22
I DO NOT YEARN NOR ASPIRE FOR I AM A BLIND SAMSON   287 25
AND WHAT IS DAYLIGHT TO ME THAT I SHOULD LOOK SKYWARD   287 26
ONLY I GROPE AMONG YOU PALE-FACES CARYATIDS AS AMONG A   287 27
I STUMBLE AGAINST THEM   288 3
THIS IS WHY I TUG AT THEM INDIVIDUALLY WITH MY ARM ROUND 288 8
THEY ARE NOT STRONGER THAN I AM BLIND SAMSON   288 11
I SHALL BE SO GLAD WHEN IT COMES DOWN   288 13
I AM SO TIRED OF THE LIMITATIONS OF THEIR INFINITE   288 14
I AM SO SICK OF THE PRETENSIONS OF THE SPIRIT   288 15
I AM SO WEARY OF PALE-FACE IMPORTANCE   288 16
AM I NOT BLIND AT THE ROUND-TURNING MILL   288 17
THEN WHY SHOULD I FEAR THEIR PALE FACES   288 18
AND I JUT AGAINST YOU IF I TRY TO MOVE FOR YOU ARE EVER+ 289 7
AND I AM BLIND   289 8
SEE IF I DON'T BRING YOU DOWN AND ALL YOUR HIGH OPINION   289 11
SEE IF I DON'T MOVE UNDER A DARK AND NUDE VAST HEAVEN   289 19
SEE IF I AM NOT LORD OF THE DARK AND MOVING HOSTS   289 22
BEFORE I DIE   289 23
SHALL I COME TO YOU THE OPEN TOMB OF MY RACE   289 27
I WOULD COME IF I FELT MY HOUR HAD STRUCK   289 28
I WOULD RATHER YOU CAME TO ME   289 29
I WISH YOU WOULD   290 7
I CONFESS I AM AFRAID OF YOU   290 8
DO YOU WONDER THAT I AM AFRAID TO COME   291 1
I AM SO TERRIFIED AMERICA   291 9
CARRIES ME WHERE I WANT TO BE CARRIED   291 30
OR DON'T I   291 31
AND I WHO AM HALF IN LOVE WITH YOU   292 20
WHAT AM I IN LOVE WITH   292 21
ALLURE ME TILL I AM BESIDE MYSELF   293 9
AH HOW I ADMIRE YOUR FIDELITY   296 12
YET MORE I SEE YOU DARKLY CONCENTRATE   297 1
WHAT WOULD I NOT GIVE   297 27
WHICH I BEING A LITTLE WEARY OF ROMAN VIRTUE   297 32
FOR OH I KNOW IN THE DUST WHERE WE HAVE BURIED   298 1
BUT I INVOKE THE SPIRITS OF THE LOST   298 9
I SAY UNTARNISHED BUT I MEAN OPAQUE   298 22
AH YES AH YES WOULD I MIGHT SEE IT AGAIN   303 7
NO NO I KNOW NOTHING OF THAT   303 12
IF IT BE SO I FLY TO JOIN YOU   314 23
YOU LOOK WELL WITH YOUR SALVIA FLOWERS I MUST SAY   314 34
WITH ASH I SAY   315 6
WOULDN'T I STICK THE SALVIA IN MY COAT   315 12
UGH HOW I LOVE ITS FANGS OF PERFECT RAGE   315 18
I LONG TO BE A BOLSHEVIST   315 22
I LONG TO SEE ITS CHOCK-FULL CROWDEDNESS   315 27
I DON'T AT ALL WANT TO ANNIHILATE THEM   316 14
I LIKE A ROW WITH THEM   316 15
BUT I WON'T BE PUT ON A CABBAGE-IDEALISTIC LEVEL OF EQU+ 316 16
I AM THEIR SUPERIOR SALUTING THE HIBISCUS FLOWER NOT TH+ 316 23
THE SAME I SAY TO THE PROFITEERS FROM THE HOTELS THE MO+ 316 24
THE SAME I SAY TO THE PALE AND ELEGANT PERSONS   316 26
THAT I SALUTE THE RED HIBISCUS FLOWERS   316 28
AND I SALUTE HIBISCUS AND THE SALVIA FLOWER   317 1

ALAS ALAS I HAVE GOT TO LEAVE IT ALL	317	27
AND STILL I CANNOT BEAR IT	318	5
I MATTHEW AM A MAN	320	3
AND I IF I BE LIFTED UP WILL DRAW ALL MEN UNTO ME	320	4
I MATTHEW BEING A MAN	320	10
SEEING I AM ON A PAR WITH ALL MEN	320	13
I ON THE OTHER HAND	320	14
I AM MAN	320	20
I AM MAN AND THEREFORE MY HEART BEATS AND THROWS THE DA+	320	21
ALL THE TIME I AM LIFTED UP	320	23
IF IT CEASED I SHOULD BE NO LONGER MAN	320	26
AS I AM IF MY HEART IN UPLIFTING CEASED TO BEAT TO TOSS+	320	27
I MIGHT BE A SOUL IN BLISS AN ANGEL APPROXIMATING TO THE	321	2
I AM MATTHEW THE MAN	321	5
AND I AM NOT THAT OTHER ANGELIC MATTER	321	6
SO I WILL BE LIFTED UP SAVIOUR	321	7
BEFORE MY HEART STOPS BEATING AND I BECOME WHAT I AM NOT	321	9
MATTHEW I AM THE MAN	321	19
AND I TAKE THE WINGS OF THE MORNING TO THEE CRUCIFIED	321	20
I MUST BE PUT DOWN LORD IN THE AFTERNOON	321	26
AND AT EVENING I MUST LEAVE OFF MY WINGS OF THE SPIRIT	321	27
AS I LEAVE OFF MY BRACES	321	28
AND I MUST RESUME MY NAKEDNESS LIKE A FISH SINKING DOWN+	321	29
NAY SON OF MAN I HAVE BEEN LIFTED UP	322	7
TO THEE I ROSE LIKE A ROCKET ENDING IN MID-HEAVEN	322	8
MORNING COMES AND I SHAKE THE DEWS OF NIGHT FROM THE WI+	322	26
I CAN NO MORE DENY THE BAT-WINGS OF MY FATHOM-FLICKERIN+	323	2
I AM MATTHEW THE MAN	323	5
I HAVE BEEN AND I HAVE RETURNED	323	10
I HAVE MOUNTED UP ON THE WINGS OF THE MORNING AND I HAVE	323	11
BUT I MATTHEW BEING A MAN	323	16
AND I WILL GIVE THEE THE WINGS OF THE MORNING	324	24
I HEARD A WOMAN CALL YOU THE WINGED VICTORY	332	9
BUT I KNOW YOUR GAME NOW STREAKY SORCERER	332	24
EYEING ME SIDEWAYS AND CUNNINGLY CONSCIOUS THAT I AM	333	2
I HATE THE WAY YOU LURCH OFF SIDEWAYS INTO THE AIR	333	5
YOU DON'T KNOW THAT I EXIST AND I DON'T KNOW THAT YOU	333	10
IF THAT IS SO THEN I BELIEVE A LITTLE IN PROVIDENCE PRO+	333	21
I BEHOLD YOU STAND	333	28
CAN I NOT OVERTAKE YOU	334	12
AM I NOT MOSQUITO ENOUGH TO OUT-MOSQUITO YOU	334	15
I SAW A WATER-SERPENT SWIM ACROSS THE ANAPO	337	24
AND I SAID TO MY HEART LOOK LOOK AT HIM	337	25
I SAID TO MY HEART WHO ARE THESE	337	31
I LEFT OFF HAILING HIM	338	9
I HAD MADE A MISTAKE I DIDN'T KNOW HIM	338	10
I DIDN'T KNOW HIS GOD	338	14
I DIDN'T KNOW HIS GOD	338	15
I SAW DIMLY	338	18
AND I SAID TO MY HEART THERE ARE LIMITS	338	21
I STAND AT THE PALE OF MY BEING	338	28
I HAVE WAITED WITH A LONG ROD	339	1
THINKING I AM NOT THE MEASURE OF CREATION	339	12
BUT NOT BEFORE I HAVE HAD TO KNOW	339	19
AND I A MANY-FINGERED HORROR OF DAYLIGHT TO HIM	339	23
BUT I I ONLY WONDER	340	11
I DON'T KNOW FISHES	340	13
WHEN I WENT INTO MY ROOM AT MID-MORNING	342	8
WHEN I WENT INTO MY ROOM AT MID-MORNING	342	12
THE VENETIAN SHUTTERS I PUSH WIDE	343	1
I WOULD NOT LET HIM REST	343	28
I FLICKED HIM ON	344	1
AND I RAN FORWARD TO FRIGHTEN HIM FORTH	344	4
I ALSO REALISED	344	16
ANY MORE THAN I COULD ENTER THE WHITE-HOT DOOR OF A BLA+	344	18
SO I SWITCHED ON THE ELECTRIC LIGHT THINKING NOW	344	26
AND I	345	11
NEVER I SAY	345	12
I DIDN'T CREATE HIM	346	9
ONLY IN THE BRIGHT DAY I WILL NOT HAVE THIS CLOT IN MY	346	11
I ADMIT A GOD IN EVERY CREVICE	346	15
SO I PICKED HIM UP IN A FLANNEL JACKET	347	4
FOR I WOULD HAVE HAD TO KILL HIM IF HE'D BITTEN ME THE	347	6
HASTILY I SHOOK HIM OUT OF THE WINDOW	347	9
I BELIEVE HE CHIRPS PIPISTRELLO SEEING ME HERE ON THIS	347	19
BUT I AM GREATER THAN HE	347	22
I ESCAPED HIM	347	23
ON A HOT HOT DAY AND I IN PYJAMAS FOR THE HEAT	349	2
I CAME DOWN THE STEPS WITH MY PITCHER	349	5
AND I LIKE A SECOND COMER WAITING	349	20
BUT MUST I CONFESS HOW I LIKED HIM	350	8
HOW GLAD I WAS HE HAD COME LIKE A GUEST IN QUIET TO DRI+	350	9
WAS IT COWARDICE THAT I DARED NOT KILL HIM	350	13
WAS IT PERVERSITY THAT I LONGED TO TALK TO HIM	350	14
I FELT SO HONOURED	350	16
AND TRULY I WAS AFRAID I WAS MOST AFRAID	350	19
I LOOKED ROUND I PUT DOWN MY PITCHER	351	9
I PICKED UP A CLUMSY LOG	351	10
I THINK IT DID NOT HIT HIM	351	12
AT WHICH IN THE INTENSE STILL NOON I STARED WITH FASCIN+	351	17
AND IMMEDIATELY I REGRETTED IT	351	18
I THOUGHT HOW PALTRY HOW VULGAR WHAT A MEAN ACT	351	19
I DESPISED MYSELF AND THE VOICES OF MY ACCURSED HUMAN	351	20
AND I THOUGHT OF THE ALBATROSS	351	22
AND I WISHED HE WOULD COME BACK MY SNAKE	351	23
AND SO I MISSED MY CHANCE WITH ONE OF THE LORDS	351	27
AND I HAVE SOMETHING TO EXPIATE	351	29
I TO DO WITH THEE	357	4
HE SNAPS WHEN I OFFER HIM HIS OFFSPRING	357	12
JUST AS HE SNAPS WHEN I POKE A BIT OF STICK AT HIM	357	13
I DON'T KNOW	358	29
SNAKE-LIKE SHE DRAWS AT MY FINGER WHILE I DRAG IN HORROR	359	26
YOU ARE ALMOST TOO LARGE I AM ALMOST FRIGHTENED	359	29
I HEARD A WOMAN PITYING HER PITYING THE MERE TORTUE	361	31
WHILE I I PITY MONSIEUR	361	32
HOW MUCH MORE IS HE PESTERED AND TORMENTED SAY I	361	34
I THOUGHT HE WAS DUMB	363	25
I SAID HE WAS DUMB	363	26
I REMEMBER WHEN I WAS A BOY	365	29
I HEARD THE SCREAM OF A FROG WHICH WAS CAUGHT WITH HIS	365	30
I REMEMBER WHEN I FIRST HEARD BULL-FROGS BREAK INTO SOU+	365	32
I REMEMBER HEARING A WILD GOOSE OUT OF THE THROAT OF NI+	365	34
I REMEMBER THE FIRST TIME OUT OF A BUSH IN THE DARKNESS+	366	1
I REMEMBER THE SCREAM OF A RABBIT AS I WENT THROUGH A	366	4
I REMEMBER THE HEIFER IN HER HEAT BLORTING AND BLORTING	366	6
I REMEMBER MY FIRST TERROR HEARING THE HOWL OF WEIRD	366	8
I REMEMBER THE SCREAM OF A TERRIFIED INJURED HORSE THE	366	10
I WONDER WHY	369	24
I CAN IMAGINE IN SOME OTHERWORLD	372	5
I BELIEVE THERE WERE NO FLOWERS THEN	372	14
I BELIEVE HE PIERCED THE SLOW VEGETABLE VEINS WITH HIS +	372	17
I DON'T YIELD TO YOU BIG JOWL-FACED EAGLE	374	25
DOG AND I	375	2
I IGNORE THOSE FOLK WHO LOOK OUT	375	28
I RECOGNISED WHEN I HEARD ITS VOICE	376	7
I CAN'T BEAR IT I CAN'T BEAR IT	377	8
I CAN'T	377	9
OH I CAN'T	377	10
I AM NOT SURE	377	22
OR ELSE I AM DEAD	380	6
I DON'T KNOW	380	8
I AM HERE	381	15
AM I COMING	384	16
WHAT DO I CARE FOR HER THE UGLY FEMALE STANDING UP THERE	384	25
THAT BEING HER WAY OF ANSWER IF I SPEAK TO HER SELF-CON+	385	5
YET THE MOMENT I HATE HER SHE TRIPS MILD AND SMUG LIKE A	385	12
THE MOMENT I REALLY DETEST HER	385	14
THEN I KNEW THEY WERE DEJECTED HAVING COME TO HEAR THE	390	19
I SERVE I SERVE IN ALL THE WEARY IRONY OF HIS MIEN 'TIS+	391	34
I WISH THEY HAD GIVEN THE THREE FEATHERS TO ME	392	1
THAT I HAD BEEN HE IN THE PAVILION AS IN A PEPPER-BOX A+	392	2
SERVE ME I AM MEET TO BE SERVED	392	7
WHEN I WAS A LAD	395	8
WHOM I DIDN'T OWN	395	10
APPROPRIATED ME NOT I YOU	395	12
I'D NEVER HAVE LET YOU APPROPRIATE ME HAD I KNOWN	395	16
I NEVER DREAMED TILL NOW OF THE AWFUL TIME THE LORD MUST	395	17
FIRST TIME I LOST YOU IN TAOS PLAZA	395	27
I HAD A MOMENT'S PURE DETESTATION OF YOU	396	7
AS I RUSHED LIKE AN IDIOT ROUND THE CORNER AFTER YOU	396	8
OH YES I KNOW YOUR LITTLE GAME	396	26
I'M I ON THE HORSE	397	24
I KNOW YOUR GAME	398	22
I GET MY LOVE BACK	399	5
AND I HAVE TO CLEAN UP AFTER YOU FILTH WHICH EVEN BLIND	399	6
THEN WHEN I DUST YOU A BIT WITH A JUNIPER TWIG	399	12
OH YES YOU'RE FOUND OUT I HEARD THEM KICK YOU OUT OF	400	6
AND ABOVE AND ABOVE THE TREES I FOUND HER LAIR	402	11
INSTEAD I LOOK OUT	402	21
AND I THINK IN THIS EMPTY WORLD THERE WAS ROOM FOR ME	402	27
AND I THINK IN THE WORLD BEYOND HOW EASILY WE MIGHT	402	29
I AM GOING	403	7
I AM VERY WELL OLD DEMON	404	6
OLD DEMON YOU AND I	404	19
YOU AND I YOU PALE-FACE	404	20
PALE-FACE YOU AND I	404	21
WAS FUME AS I TROD	404	27
I HAVE NO HOME OLD FATHER	405	5
THAT'S WHY I COME	405	6
I AM COME I AM HERE THE RED-DAWN-WOLF	405	9
THAT DARK OLD DEMON AND I	405	19
I CALL HIM NO NAMES	405	22
I SAY HE CAN GO BACK THE SAME GAIT	405	24
SINCE I TROTTED AT THE TAIL OF THE SUN AS FAR AS EVER T+	405	26
ALL RIGHT THE RED-DAWN-WOLF I AM	405	32
WHEN I TROT MY LITTLE PONY THROUGH THE ASPEN-TREES OF T+	409	4
I GO SLOWLY	409	11
HAWK AS I SAY OF HORUS	409	17
WOMEN I LOVED AND CHERISHED LIKE MY MOTHER	410	3
YET I HAD TO TELL THEM TO DIE	410	4
AND WHOM I LOVED	410	9
AND I SIT ON THIS HIGH AMERICAN DESERT	410	27
REMEMBERING I TOLD THEM TO DIE TO SINK INTO THE GRAVE IN	410	30
SO NOW I WHISPER COME AWAY	411	1
WOMEN WHOM I LOVED AND TOLD TO DIE	411	4
COME BACK THEN MOTHER MY LOVE WHOM I TOLD TO DIE	411	21
IT WAS ONLY I WHO SAW THE VIRGIN YOU	411	22
I DIDN'T TELL YOU TO DIE FOR NOTHING	412	1
I WANTED THE VIRGIN YOU TO BE HOME AT LAST	412	2
SO I TOLD YOU TO DIE	412	13
YOU WHOM I LOVED FOR GENTLENESS	412	17
THEY ARE MANY AND I LOVED THEM SHALL ALWAYS LOVE THEM	412	19
I WANT TO DRINK OUT OF DARK CUPS THAT DRIP DOWN ON	427	9
IF I COULD SEE YOUR HAND AND IT WERE THUMBS DOWN	430	4
I WOULD BE WILLING TO GIVE WAY LIKE THE PTERODACTYL	430	5
I WOULD NOT EVEN ASK TO LEAVE A FOSSIL CLAW EXTANT	430	7
I WOULD BE WILLING TO VANISH COMPLETELY COMPLETELY	430	9
THEN I AM WILLING TO FIGHT I WILL ROLL MY SLEEVES UP	430	11
I WISH YOU'D SHOW YOUR HAND	430	14
SHALL I MAKE YOU A PRESENT OF HIM	430	18
AND SAYING LOOK AT ME I AM NOT RESPECTABLE	432	16
I DO ALL THE THINGS THE BOURGEOIS DAREN'T DO	432	17
I BOOZE AND FORNICATE AN	432	18
SO I CAN'T SEE WHERE THE WORM THAT HAS TURNED PUTS ANYT+	432	34
THE TURNED WORM SHOUTS I BRAVELY BOOZE	433	2
THE TURNED WORM BOASTS I COPULATE	433	4
I SWEAR I'LL PULL OFF MY KNICKERS RIGHT IN THE RUE DE L+	433	20
I WISH I WAS A GENTLEMAN	434	14
I BET I AM YOU CAN 'OLD YER PHIZ	434	22
I MEAN PEOPLE LIKE YOU AND ME	435	4
QUITE I QUITE AGREE	435	9
I COULDN'T SAY	435	18
I SHOULD LIKE TO	435	20
AND IN THE DARK UNSCIENTIFIC I FEEL THE DRUM-WINDS OF H+	438	9

I SHALL TELL HER THE HOUSE IS MINE   671   6
AND I'M GOING TO DO WHAT I JOLLY WELL PLEASE   671   7
WHEN I WAS WAITING AND NOT THINKING SITTING AT A TABLE +   672 18
I SAW SUDDENLY COMING TOWARDS ME LIT UP AND UPLIFTED WI+   672 20
IN WHOM I CAN TRUST   672 20
THOUGHT I LOVE THOUGHT   673   7
I DESPISE THAT SELF-IMPORTANT GAME   673   9
AND I AM NOT INTERESTED TO KNOW ABOUT MYSELF ANY MORE   674 13
I ONLY ENTANGLE MYSELF IN THE KNOWING   674 14
I SAW AN ANGRY ITALIAN SEIZE AN IRRITATING LITTLE OFFIC+   674 20
SO LET ME LIVE THAT I MAY DIE   676 19
TURNING TO DEATH AS I TURN TO BEAUTY   676 22
ABOUT YOU I KNOW NOTHING NOTHING   676 25
ALSO I KNOW SO MUCH ABOUT YOU   677   2
AND SO I KNOW   677   4
I HAVE ALWAYS WANTED TO BE AS THE FLOWERS ARE   677 10
AND IN DEATH I BELIEVE I SHALL BE AS THE FLOWERS ARE   677 12
I SHALL BLOSSOM LIKE A DARK PANSY AND BE DELIGHTED   677 13
I CAN FEEL MYSELF UNFOLDING IN THE DARK SUNSHINE OF DEA+   677 15
I HEARD A LITTLE CHICKEN CHIRP   680   8
AND I CAN NEITHER PAINT NOR WRITE   680 10
I ONLY CAN SET OTHER PEOPLE RIGHT   680 11
FOR I AM A CHICKEN AND I CAN CHIRP   680 14
LATELY I SAW A SIGHT MOST QUAINT   680 16
MY CHILD I CANNOT TELL A LIE   681 23
I MADE IT   681 24
ALL I WANT OF YOU MEN AND WOMEN   683 24
ALL I WANT OF YOU   683 25
OH LEAVE OFF SAYING I WANT YOU TO BE SAVAGES   684   1
I WANT YOU TO BE AS SAVAGE AS THE GENTIAN AND THE DAFFO+   684   4
O LET MY ANKLES BE BATHED IN MOONLIGHT THAT I   684 10
HAVE NOT YET PASSED THE ISLANDS I MUST WATCH THEM STILL   687 23
WHAT DO I CARE IF THE SMOKING SHIPS   688   6
I SEE DESCENDING FROM THE SHIPS AT DAWN   688 12
SO I CALLED HIM COME IN IF YOU WILL   692 12
I SAID TO HIM AND WHAT IS YOUR NAME   692 14
ENTERED ME I SMILED TO MYSELF SAYING HE IS GOD   692 16
NOW I AM AT YOUR GATE YOU BEAUTY YOU LADY OF ALL NAKEDN+   695 22
NOW I MUST ENTER YOUR MANSION AND BEG YOUR GIFT   695 23
BE GOOD TO ME NOW AS I BEG YOU AS YOU'VE ALWAYS BEEN GO+   696   9
IT IS ENOUGH I SAW YOU VANISH INTO AIR   696 28
I SEE HIM MORE LIKE THE RUBY A GLEAM FROM WITHIN   697 28
OF MYSELF AS I AM WITHOUT GOD   699 17
LET ME NEVER KNOW WHAT I AM OR SHOULD BE   699 19
WHEN I HAVE FALLEN OUT OF YOUR HANDS THE HANDS OF THE L+   699 20
FOR HOW CAN I COUNT IN YOUR THREE TIME THREE   702   3
COME THEN AS I SAY IN A WEEK   702   5
WHOSE POWER AND GLORY I HAVE OFTEN HEARD AND FELT   704 21
AND I A NAKED MAN CALLING   704 27
HAVE I CAUGHT FROM IT   705   3
I AM THE SEA I AM THE SEA   705 18
SO AN APPLE BECOMES MYSTIC WHEN I TASTE IT IN   707 28
ALL OF WHICH THINGS I CAN SURELY TASTE IN A GOOD APPLE   708   1
IF I SAY I TASTE THESE THINGS IN AN APPLE I AM CALLED M+   708   5
BUT IF I EAT AN APPLE I LIKE TO EAT IT WITH ALL MY SENS+   708 10
HOGGING IT DOWN LIKE A PIG I CALL THE FEEDING OF CORPSES   708 11
I CALL IT MENTAL CONCEIT AND MYSTIFICATION   708 18
I HAVE BEEN DEFEATED AND DRAGGED DOWN BY PAIN   709   1
BUT STILL I KNOW THAT LIFE IS FOR DELIGHT   709   9
THEN I WILL FALL AND PLANT THE PATHS TO HELL   710 15
WHEN I AM NOW COMPLETELY LAPSED AND GONE   724 29
IN SLEEP I AM NOT I AM GONE   725   1
I AM GIVEN UP   725   2
SWEET DARK OBLIVION WHEN I CEASE   726   5
THEN I HAVE BEEN DIPPED AGAIN IN GOD AND NEW-CREATED   726 25
THEN I SHALL KNOW THAT I AM WALKING STILL   727   4
I FEEL THE PAIN OF FALLING LEAVES AND STEMS THAT BREAK +   727   7
THEN I SHALL KNOW THAT MY LIFE IS MOVING STILL   727 14
I FALL IN SICKNESS AND IN MISERY   727 18
THEN I MUST KNOW THAT STILL   727 27
I AM IN THE HANDS OF THE UNKNOWN GOD   727 28
I STUMBLE WHERE THE SHADOWS LIE   731   2
THE MOON IS HIGH I AM LITTLE   731   9
THE WIND THE RASCAL KNOCKED AT MY DOOR AND I SAID   731 13
I THINK PERHAPS THE MAN THAT CAME   732   9
I WAIT FOR THE EIGHT AND TWENTY WAGONS TO COME   732 23
AT LAST I HEAR A RATTLE AND THERE AWAY   732 24
I DREAD HIM COMING I WONDER HOW HE WILL TAKE IT   733   2
I CAN SEE HIS RAGING BLACK EYES BLAZE AT ME   733   3
ON IF HE KNEW THAT I WAS AT THIS FARM   733 14
WITH STIFFNESS COMES FOR THE WATER THAT I   733 17
BETWEEN HIS THICK LIPS I WONDER WHERE   733 26
HE THINKS I AM IF EVER HE THINKS AT ALL   733 27
A NICE ONE I LIKE IT HE'LL THINK IT'S A TALL ORDER   733 29
WHEN I SAY HE OUGHT TO MARRY ME AND SMALL   733 30
I FEEL TO HAVE TO TELL HIM   733 31
I WONDER WILL HE CARE   734 23
NOW I TAKE THE BIG STONE JUG OF WATER   734 24
I AM WITH CHILD BY YOU   734 34
IT IS TRUE I SAID   735   3
WHAT DO YOU THINK I SAID   735   5
I WAITED BUT HE WOULD NOT COME BACK TO ME   735 10
I HAVE MANY PRAYERS TO SAY   735 17
IF I STRING THE PLANETS AND THE BEADY STARS   735 18
FOR I HAVE INJURED YOU   735 21
I DID YOU AN INJURY   735 25
WHEN I COME HOME PROMISE ME   735 25
WHEN I STAND IN THE DOORWAY SHAMEFULLY   735 28
OH IT IS FINISHED I WOULD LIKE TO TAKE   738   9
WHICH I AM STILL AND HAVE BEEN ALL I CAN   738 15
AND I AM ONLY NEXT TO NOTHINGNESS   738 22
I WANT TO KNOW NO MORE I WANT TO SEE   738 25
I LET THE WHOLE THING GO STILL THERE IS ME   738 27
TOUCH ME THEN TOUCH ME TOUCH ME I DID NOT DIE   738 28
THAT I AM NOW AH LAY ONE LITTLE TOUCH   738 30
OF JUST ONE TOUCH EVEN SO DO I ASK TOO MUCH   738 32
HOW I HATE MYSELF THIS BODY WHICH IS ME   741   1

HOW I WOULD LIKE TO CUT OFF MY HANDS   741   3
BUT I CAN'T FOR IT IS WRITTEN AGAINST ME I MUST NOT   741   5
I MUST PRESERVE MY LIFE FROM HURT   741   6
GOD HOW GLAD I AM TO HEAR THE SHELLS   741   9
FOR I HATE THIS BODY WHICH IS SO DEAR TO ME   741 16
FOR I DOTE ON THEM WITH TENDERNESS AND I HATE THEM   741 19
I HATE THEM BITTERLY   741 20
I DO NOT DIE I AM NOT EVEN HURT   741 24
BUT I KILL MY SHADOW'S SHADOW OF ME   741 25
I SHOT MY MAN I SAW HIM CRUMBLE AND HANG   741 27
AND GOD IS GOOD FOR I WANTED HIM TO DIE   742   1
SO WHEN I RUN AT LENGTH THITHER ACROSS   742   5
TO THE TRENCHES I SEE AGAIN A FACE WITH BLUE EYES   742   6
WAITING AND I KNEW HE WANTED IT   742   8
AND I THE LOVER AM CONSUMMATE   742 12
AND HE IS THE BRIDE I HAVE SOWN HIM WITH THE SEED   742 13
WHAT I BEGET MUST I BEGET OF BLOOD   742 24
I HAD DREAMED OF LOVE OH LOVE I HAD DREAMED OF LOVE   742 27
WHY AM I BRIDEGROOM OF WAR WAR'S PARAMOUR   742 36
BUT SHALL I TOUCH HANDS WITH DEATH IN KILLING THAT OTHER   743 17
SHALL I OFFER TO HIM MY BROTHERLY BODY TO KILL   743 19
IT MAY BE I SHALL GIVE THE BRIDE   743 22
I WALK THE EARTH INTACT HEREAFTERWARDS   743 24
AND I AM JUST AWAKENED FROM THE TOMB   744   1
AND WITHER THEY ARE GOING I HAVE BEEN   744   2
I VENTURE FROM THE HALLS OF SHADOWY DEATH   744 11
I KNOW WHERE THEY ARE GOING ALL THE LIVES   744 13
OF NOISELESS DEATH I KNOW IT WELL   744 16
I WHO HAVE BEEN AND NOW AM RISEN AGAIN   744 18
FROM EMBASSY IN DEATH I ISSUE FORTH   744 21
IF THEY WOULD LISTEN I COULD TELL THEM NOW   744 26
I LIFT MY INEXTINGUISHABLE FLAME   745   2
I LIFT MY LITTLE PURE AND LAMBENT FLAME   745 10
OF FULL DESPAIR I LIFT MY TENDER FLAME   745 13
OF LIVES I SPEAK TO ALL WHO CANNOT HEAR   745 23
I TURN TOWARDS THE BITTER BLACKENING WIND   745 24
I SPEAK ALOUD TO FLEETING HOSTS OF RED   745 25
I SPEAK WITH A VAIN MOUTH   745 29
OH AND I WISH THAT I   746 19
ALREADY I SEE THE SHELLED MOON LIF   747 28
AM I LOST   749   8
HAVE I CROSSED   749 11
HAVE I NOTHING IN THIS DARK LAND   749 13
SHE WEPT BITTERLY HIDING HER FACE IN HER KERCHIEF I SAI+   749 16
WHEN IN THE MORNING I ROSE TO DEPART MY LOVE CAME TO SA+   749 17
OH AS YOU STAND LOOKING UP DO YOU KNOW IT IS I   750 15
AS I WENT DOWN THE STREET IN MY NOSE-RED PELERINE   750 17
OH BRING HIM TO ME I SAID OH LAY HIM BETWEEN   750 19
I HAVE COME TO THE HOUSE OF GOD   751   1
I WISH I COULD HAVE SOME TOO   751   5
BUT ALAS THIS IS NOT WHAT I CAME FOR I HAVE FALLEN SHORT   751   8
I AM LOSING HOPE   751 19
I SHOULD LEAN AND WHISPER IN HIS EAR   752   5
SWIFTLY I WISH I MIGHT KISS HER FINGERS BUT FULL   752 11
OF DANGER I FIND HER EVEN WORSE THAN THE FIELDS WHERE W+   752 12
FOR I AM FRAIL AS A FLASK OF GLASS   752 15
OH BROTHER AND I AM THE GOLDEN RING   752 17
NO MORE WOULD I LET HIM EAT   754 20
I AND MY BETROTHED ARE TOGETHER IN THE SHED   756 15
ALAS MY LAND IS ENGLAND AND I KNOW NOT HOW NOR WHENCE   757   3
I CAME HITHER NOR WHAT IS MY GOAL   757   4
HOW CAN I FIND MY WAY TO THE RIVER   757   5
LISTEN FOR I WILL COMPLAIN   758   7
SISTERS I AM SORRY FOR THIS FOREIGN MAN   758 11
BROTHER I LIKE YOUR FRAGRANCE   759   1
HEAL ME FOR BODY AND SOUL I AM NOT WELL   759 15
I AM INCLINED TO HEAP THY COALS OF FIRE ON MY OWN   760 15
EACH SAID TO THE OTHER TILL I CAME ACROSS YOU   761   8
I WASN'T AWARE OF THE THINGS I COULD DO   761   9
AND THIS I HOLD IS THE TRUE HISTORY OF EVOLUTION   761 13
CIRCLE WHILE I PRANCE IN THE UPPER   762 10
THE ROAST VEAL I AM SHAKING IT FOR YOU   762 13
I WOULD WARN ANYBODY AGAINST A CULTURE   763 13
I AM COMING DOWN   763 18
I AM COMING BACK   763 20
I COME BACK TO YOU   763 27
I HAVE COME BACK TO YOU FOR I NEVER LEFT YOU   764 10
I FEEL I'M COMING NEAR   764 12
I NEVER LEFT YOU   764 22
I WENT THE OPPOSITE WAY ROUND THE CIRCLE   764 23
FOR I HAVE TRAVERSED MY UPWARD CURVE   764 28
GOD WHAT SHALL I DO IN THE WHITE DAYS   766 25
I CANNOT EVEN REMEMBER MY LIFE THAT HAS BEEN   767 11
AND WHAT DO I CARE   771 18
WHAT DO I CARE THOUGH THE VERY STONES   771 21
I WEAR FRAILITY AS A CROWN   772   8
I HAVE A DARKNESS INTACT WITHIN ME GLOWING SECURE   772 10
I HAVE A TENT OF DARKNESS BY DAY   772 14
I HAVE A KNOWLEDGE OF LOVELY NIGHT   772 16
OF DEATH BUT I WAIT AWHILE IN THIS TABERNACLE   772 20
WHAT DO I CARE THOUGH FROM THE DAY'S WHITE ENVELOPE   772 22
I TEAR BUT NEWS OF SORROW AND PAIN   772 23
I BEAR THE HOPE   772 24
FOR I KNOW THE HOST   772 28
DO WE REALLY WELL I NEVER FANCY NOW FANCY THAT   773 24
I WANT MY SON TO BE SOMETHING BETTER THAN HIS FATHER WAS   773 26
THERE IS I BELIEVE SCARCELY ONE INTELLIGENT AMERICAN WHO   775 12
SLEPT I QUETZALCOATL   786   4
I ROSE AGAIN TO SEE A STAR FALLING AND FEEL A BREATH ON   786 10
I AM COMING   786 13
I HEARD THE STAR SINGING LIKE A DYING BIRD   786 15
MY NAME IS JESUS I AM MARY'S SON   786 16
I AM COMING HOME   786 17
BIND HIM WITH SHADOW WHILE I PASS   786 21
I BOUND THE BRIGHT FANGS OF THE SUN   786 23
SO I TOOK THE SANDALS OF THE SAVIOUR   787   2
TILL I SAW BENEATH ME   787   5

LO I AM ALWAYS HERE 787 21
I BRUSH THE WING OF THE DAY 787 23
BUT I I AM ALWAYS IN PLACE 787 26
YEA I AM ALWAYS HERE I AM LORD 787 27
BUT LO I AM ALWAYS HERE 787 31
I MAKE YOU THE LORDS OF THE WAY 788 7
I AM HERE UNDEPARTING I SIT TIGHT 788 15
I AM FAR BEYOND 788 22
SHALL YOU SHALL I 788 29
SHALL YOU SHALL I 789 4
HEAR A VOICE SAYING I KNOW YOU NOT 789 7
SHALL YOU SHALL I 789 8
MY NAME IS JESUS I AM MARY'S SON 789 9
I AM COMING HOME 789 10
BIND HIM WITH SHADOW WHILE I PASS 789 14
THAT I MAY HOLD THEM LIKE MEMORIES IN MY ARMS WHEN I GO+ 789 20
AND QUETZALCOATL CALLED BACK I WILL DO IT 789 21
SURELY HE SAID THIS IS A CURIOUS PEOPLE I HAVE FOUND 790 16
I WILL CALL TO THEM 790 18
I HEAR THE VOICE OF MY FIRST MAN ASK ME WHY I AM LAUGHI+ 791 14
THE FIRST THING I DID WHEN I SAW THEM WAS TO LAUGH AT T+ 791 17
WHEN I SAY THE WORD THEY WILL START 792 19
SO TELL THE MEN I AM COMING TO 793 5
I SEE DARK THINGS RUSHING ACROSS THE COUNTRY 794 10
FOR I TELL YOU THERE ARE NO DEAD DEAD NOT EVEN YOUR DEAD 795 17
I TELL YOU SORROW UPON YOU YOU SHALL ALL DIE 796 2
FOR I AM SWEET I AM THE LAST AND THE BEST THE POOL OF N+ 796 24
LO I RELEASE THE DRAGONS THE GREAT WHITE ONE OF THE NOR+ 796 30
I AM GOING TO SPEAK TO THE DRAGON OF THE INNER FIRES 797 3
I AM ABOUT TO TELL THE DRAGON OF THE WATERS TO TURN ROU+ 797 5
AND I WAIT FOR THE FINAL DAY WHEN THE DRAGON OF THUNDER+ 797 7
I AM THE SON OF THE MORNING STAR AND CHILD OF THE DEEPS 799 14
NO MAN KNOWS MY FATHER AND I KNOW HIM NOT 799 15
WHICH IS MY FATHER WHOM I KNOW NOT 799 24
I TELL YOU THE DAY SHOULD NOT TURN INTO GLORY 799 25
I TELL YOU YOU ARE NOT MEN ALONE 800 16
SHOULD YOU SAY I HAVE NO STAR I AM NO STAR 800 21
BUT I AM QUETZALCOATL OF THE MORNING STAR 800 32
I AM THE LIVING QUETZALCOATL 800 33
I AM QUETZALCOATL OF THE EAGLE AND THE SNAKE 800 36
I AM LORD OF THE TWO WAYS 800 39
I AM THE LIVING QUETZALCOATL 801 1
NAKED I COME FROM OUT OF THE DEEP 801 2
FROM THE PLACE WHICH I CALL MY FATHER 801 3
NAKED HAVE I TRAVELLED THE LONG WAY ROUND 801 4
OUT OF THE DEPTHS OF THE SKY I CAME LIKE AN EAGLE 801 6
BUT I AM THE INWARD STAR INVISIBLE 801 10
YET I HAVE LAIN IN HIS LOINS ERE HE BEGOT ME IN MOTHER + 801 14
NOW I AM ALONE ON EARTH AND THIS IS MINE 801 15
FOR I AM QUETZALCOATL THE FEATHERED SNAKE 801 27
AND I AM NOT WITH YOU TILL MY SERPENT HAS COILED HIS CI+ 801 28
AND I QUETZALCOATL THE EAGLE OF THE AIR AM BRUSHING YOU+ 802 1
I AM FANNING YOUR BREASTS WITH MY BREATH 802 3
I AM QUETZALCOATL OF THE TWO WAYS 802 5
BETWEEN THE MORNING AND THE AFTERNOON STAND I HERE WITH+ 803 6
I AM HUITZILOPOCHTLI 804 4
I AM HUITZILOPOCHTLI 804 7
I AM HUITZILOPOCHTLI 804 10
I AM HUITZILOPOCHTLI 804 13
I AM HUITZILOPOCHTLI SITTING IN THE DARK 804 15
I WATCH BY THE FIRE 804 17
I WAIT BEHIND MEN 804 18
I AM THE SLEEPING AND WAKING 805 8
I AM THE LEAPING AND QUAKING 805 10
I AM HUITZILOPOCHTLI 806 21
I AM DARK AS THE SUNLESS UNDER-EARTH 806 22
BUT I TOUCHED THE HAND OF QUETZALCOATL 806 26
I TOUCHED THE HAND OF QUETZALCOATL 806 28
LO I AM LORD OF THE WATCHES OF THE NIGHT 806 29
I AM THE WATCHER AND MASTER OF THE DREAM 807 1
IN THE DREAM OF THE NIGHT I SEE THE GREY DOGS PROWLING 807 2
IN THE NIGHT I SEE THE GREY DOGS CREEPING OUT OF THE SL+ 807 11
I SEE THE GREY DOGS CREEPING OUT WHERE MY DEER ARE BROW+ 807 18
THEN I TAKE MY KNIFE AND THROW IT UPON THE GREY DOG 807 20
AS I WENT DOWN THE ROAD OF SLEEP 808 3
I DO NOT POINT YOU TO MY ROAD NOR YET 812 5
MEET ME YOU I LIKE MOST 812 12
I ASK FOR NOTHING EXCEPT TO SLIP 812 25
WHEN I SEE THIS SEA LOOKING SHODDY AND DEAD 815 10
I SHALL COME TO NEW YORK AND LIVE ON MANHATTAN 815 14
TILL THEN I LIKE BETTER THIS SEA I MUST SAY 815 17
AND WILL SHINE IF I STAY OR I GO AWAY 815 20
PERSUADES ME TO STAY SINCE STAY I MAY 815 21
THE NIGHTFALL I 817 4
PALLID POOR THING YET I 817 13
WHAT I SEE 819 5
WHEN I LOOK AT THE RAINBOW 819 6
YOU CAN'T SAY I AM I AND THEREFORE 824 2
THAT IS THE MEN OF MY AGE AND I AM FORTY-THREE 828 15
AND THEREFORE SINCE THE PEOPLE I MEET OF THE YOUNGER 829 4
AND BY GENTLEMAN I MEAN THAT UBIQUITOUS ENGLISHMAN 830 4
BUT WHAT I WOULD LIKE TO KNOW 830 22
BUT FOR THESE CHILDREN I SHOULD BE FREE 832 9
AWFULLY SORRY DEAR BUT I CAN'T COME BECAUSE OF THE CHIL+ 832 11
WE HAVE LEARNED I THINK NOT TO BE GREEDY 833 3
I SPEAK OF THE YOUNGER GENERATIONS 833 6
OF WHOM I THINK THIS IS TRUE 833 7
THE MOMENT I SWEAR TO LOVE A WOMAN ALL MY LIFE THAT VER+ 834 4
I BEGIN TO HATE HER 834 9
IN THE SAME WAY IF I SWORE TO HATE A WOMAN ALL MY LIFE + 834 10
OH WELL I SUPPOSE I SHALL HAVE SOME KNIFE-EDGED TERENCE+ 835 1
DARLING I SEE YOUR IRON-GREY CHEVELURE 835 5
IF I WERE YOU AS I PASSED THE FORTIES 835 31
THE REAL IMMORALITY AS FAR AS I CAN SEE IT 836 17
I LOVE LIFE I LOVE LIFE SO DEARLY I COULD ALMOST DIE 837 10
WHEN I SEE WHAT A MESS MEN HAVE MADE OF THE WORLD 837 12
WHEN I SEE WHAT MESSES MEN HAVE MADE OF THEMSELVES 837 13

WHEN I SEE THE MESSED-UP CHEMICALISED WOMEN 837 14
I WISH I HAD FINS AND GILLS 837 15
I THINK IDIOTS TELL DULL STUPID DISGUSTING TALES 837 21
I COULD ACCEPT MEN 840 3
I ONLY WANT TO KNOW SOME THINGS TO KNOW ALL THINGS WOUL+ 840 19
I HAVE NO DESIRE IN THE LEAST TO BE SORROWED OVER OR CO+ 840 22
WITH SHARP DESIRE I AM NOT EAGER FOR SHARP DESIRE ANY M+ 840 24
YET WHEN I THINK OF THE WILD SWAN OR THE RIPPLE-MARKED + 841 1
SOMETHING THRILLS IN ME AND I KNOW 841 8
I HEARD HER SAY TO HER BRILLIANT YOUNG HUSBAND 842 12
SAYING YOU KNOW I ALWAYS HAVE TO SAY THAT ARCHIE LOOKS + 842 20
I CAN NEVER EVEN THINK THAT IT'S BABY WHO LOOKS LIKE AR+ 842 21
I DON'T RECOGNIZE MY TUSCANS 846 5
INWARDS I CAN SEE WHENCE THE THORNS WERE RENT 856 21
I AM QUITE SICK OF BOOKS 857 7
I AM OUT ALONE ON THE ROAD 857 9
I WISH I KNEW WHERE THIS PALE ROAD GOES 857 12
AND WE STILL BE TOGETHER THE ROAD AND I 857 15
I AM TIRED OF THIS JOURNEY IT IS STUPID AND CHILL 858 1
WHEN MORNING COMES I FIND ME A LOVE 858 5
WHY SHOULD I CARE WHERE THE OLD ROAD GOES 858 8
WE REST AT THE HEDGE MY HORSE AND I WHERE THE SCENT 858 18
I START FROM THE DROOP OF FORGETFULNESS AS THE SOUND OF+ 858 21
I HOLD HER STILL AND WAIT TILL THE BELL SHALL FALTER 859 1
I DID NOT KNOW LOVE HAD SETTLED DOWN ON ME 860 1
I SETTLED SO SOFTLY I WAS ALL UNAWARE 860 6
AND THE FLUSH FADED AND IT CAME DARK I SLEPT STILL IGNO+ 860 7
AND I WOKE WONDERING WHO TOUCHED ME WITH SUCH FEAR AND + 860 10
WITH THE FIRST DAWN I ROSE TO LOOK IN THE GLASS 860 11
AND I STARTED WITH PLEASURE FOR IN THE NIGHT IT HAD COM+ 860 12
I HAVE A CHARM LIKE LAUGHTER THROUGH A VEIL 860 15
LIKE A BIRD AM I 860 27
SWAYING I SNATCH AND LOOT 861 7
I CAN JUST SEE THE NAPE OF HER WHITE LITTLE NECK 863 5
I CANNOT CALL HER SWEET JOY NOW 863 9
AS I CAME HOME IN THE DUSK DESPOILED BY SCHOOL A MERE B+ 864 27
AND I LOOKED IN A ROOM WHERE THE LAMP AS A MOON IN MIST 865 1
AND I IN IMMEASURABLE NIGHT LOOKED ON FROM AFAR AFAR 865 10
SURELY I CANNOT JUST BE GOING TO SCHOOL 865 12
BUT I'VE HAD SUCH A JOB MY CRUTCHES I FAIRLY DRAGGED TH+ 865 22
WHEN HE LIFTS HIS FOOT I SEE THE PAD OF HIS SOAKED STOC+ 866 7
PLEASE SIR I WAS SWEEPING SNOW AN' I NEVER HEARD THE BE+ 866 9
I DIDN'T KNOW IT WAS SO LATE NO SIR I 'AD TO BECAUSE 866 10
I SAW A DARK FIGURE APPROACHING A RAGGED SOLITARY CROW 866 17
TILL HE SAW ME BUT PLEASE SIR MY MOVVER SAID I COULD AN' 866 19
I HAVE SAT IN THE RECREATION GROUND 866 22
I HAVE TRAVELLED IN RUSSIA TWO HOURS OR MORE 866 26
NO A LONG SEASON I HAVE BEEN WITH DOSTOIEVSKY IN THE DA+ 866 27
WAYS OF ST PETERSBURG I HAVE DWELLED IN THE CORE 866 28
I AM COME BACK A FOREIGNER WONDERING AND SHRINKING FROM+ 867 2
WHEN SOFTLY I CALL AT HER DOOR AND ENTER THE ROOM 868 25
WHEN I SEE THE SKY'S BLUE DARKEN 869 4
AND I COULD NOT BEAR HER LOOK UPON ME 869 7
DO YOU KNOW WHY I COULD NOT 869 12
WHY I CANNOT EVEN NOW 869 13
I ALWAYS LOVED HER 869 16
I CAN ALWAYS FEEL IT ON MY CHEST 869 19
I THINK IT IS THE HAND OF SORROW 869 20
I THINK SOMETIMES IT WILL CRUSH MY HEART INWARD 869 22
AS I PAUSE AT THE SIDE OF THE BATH 870 1
I PAUSE AND FORGET 870 4
I FORGET THE TOWEL AND MY WET LIMBS 870 5
I FEEL THE SUN ON ME 870 6
HOW AM I CLOTTED TOGETHER 870 7
WHY I SHOULD I GRIEVE THAT MY MOTHER IS NO LONGER CLOTTED 870 12
I BREATHED MY DREAMS UPON YOU I LAID MY MOUTH ON YOUR M+ 871 4
I RUN AWAKE TO THE HOUSE OF MY SOUL AND FIND IT EMPTY 871 9
AND WHERE HE STOOD I SEE MY OWN SHADOW STAND 871 11
AND THE HOUSE IS EMPTY AND I AM ALONE 871 12
I AM ALONE ALONE THERE IS NO MORE SIEGMUND FOR ME 871 13
GONE AND I AM ALONE ALONE 871 16
THERE I CANNOT BEAR TO SEE THE SOBS IN YOUR THROAT 871 19
I DARE NOT LOOK AT HIS EYES 871 28
GOD THAT I SHOULD HAVE TO REPUDIATE HIM 871 37
I KNOW I KNOW YOU ARE WINSOME SO BUT YOU CHEAT 872 25
FROM THE FIERY HAMMERING OF YOUR HEART I CAST 873 2
STILL TO SAY I WANT NO FLAME 873 9
OF YOUR HEART OF FIRE IN WHICH I LOOK 873 12
I LOVE FOR EVER AND IT SEEMS 873 15
MY TEMPLES BROKEN THEN I SHOULD REMAIN 873 31
THAT I WHO HAVE KNOWN HER A LITTLE AM KEPT 874 3
ME THAT I FLICKER IN THE BASKET 874 14
ME THAT I GLOW NOT STILL IN CONTENT 874 15
I SEE THE STRONG SOUND EARTH BETRAYED AS A FLOATING 874 30
AND I AM DAZED 875 5
FOR WHETHER I SEE YOU SET THE DAFFODILS 875 7
SET DOWN THE TRAY BEFORE ME AS I WORK 875 11
STILL I WILL LEAVE YOU STILL FORSAKE YOU TOO 875 22
AND I AM DRIFTING LIKE A SHELL DISCARDED 875 25
YEA I WOULD SHUT MY EYES I WOULD CLOSE MY WINDOWS 875 26
WITH A FEW SWIFT PASSIONS WOULD I DRIFT AWAY 875 32
THAT I HAVE LAUGHED MY WAY ACROSS WITH ZEST 875 34
I LEAVE YOU WHILE I PLAY MY GAME OF LIVING 875 37
I PLAY MY RECKLESS GAME TO WIN MY POINT 876 1
AND HAVING WON I WILL LIE DOWN TO SLEEP 876 4
AND I WILL LEAVE YOU WHO WOULD MAKE ME TURN 876 6
ASIDE TO LOSE MYSELF FOR VERY SMALLNESS I 876 7
WILL LEAVE YOU FOR I MUST FORGET MYSELF 876 8
I GO TO PLAY MY GAME OF LIFE WITHIN 876 9
I WOULD NOT MISS IT FOR YOUR ACHE OF WONDER 876 16
THAT DRINKS ME UP AS IF I WERE A SPECK 876 18
I LEAVE YOU SO I MUST 876 21
AND SHALL I SEE HIM NEVER NOR WILL HE TURN 876 23
THE MYSTERY I STRIVE TOWARD HOWEVER 876 28
I BEAT MY WINGS TOWARD IT NEVER 876 29
WONDER I CRAVE FOR THAT BURNS STRONG IN HIM 876 31
I KNOW THE SWEET RED HUTCH OF HIS MOUTH WHERE WARM 876 32

I WISH TO DROWN MYSELF   877   2
HERE IN THIS HOUSE WHERE I HAVE SERVED SO LONG   877 22
I SERVED HIM SO   877 25
I STEAL ACROSS THE HUSHED CORRIDOR   877 36
OF THIS OLD HOUSE WHOSE STRANGERS I NOW ENTERTAIN   877 38
AND WELL I KNOW TO OPEN SILENTLY   878   2
AND AH I KNOW THE SHADOWS THAT THE TREE   878   3
AND WELL I KNOW HE SLEEPS TO WAKE NO MORE   878   7
AFTER TONIGHT FOR SEE I SAID TO HIM   878   8
I BROUGHT FOR HIM AND WAITED WHILE HE DRANK   878 15
I WAITED AND MY SILENCE CHALLENGED HIM   878 16
AND I CAN SEE THE PULSE WITHIN HIS THROAT   878 25
AND I HAVE COME TO WATCH   879   4
I WISH THAT I MIGHT DIP MYSELF WITHIN   879   8
THE FIERY MIXTURE OF THY LIFE SO I   879 11
FOR WATCHING I AM FROZEN AS IN ICE   879 18
AND I MUST WAIT   879 21
UP THE DARK SHAFT TO DEATH AND WHAT IF I   879 23
THOUGH I SHALL HASTEN AFTER WHEN I SEE   879 24
THY FLAME LEAP FREE WHAT IF I AM LEFT BEHIND   879 25
BUT I WILL CATCH THEE UP AT A STRIDE OF DEATH   879 28
AH I KNOW HOW YOU HAVE SOUGHT ME   880   9
AND EVER ERE I COME YOU HAVE DEPARTED   880 13
AND EVER I SEE YOUR TRACES BROKEN-HEARTED   880 15
I SAW ON THE RED EARTH   880 18
I SAW THE BROKEN VIOLETS   880 23
I SAW THE PAIN AMONG THE IRIS THERE   880 28
AND I WAS HURT   880 31
I KISSED HER ONCE AGAIN UPON THE MOUTH   881   1
WHOM I HAD HURT   881   5
DARK INCENSE DID I FEEL HER OFFER UP   881 12
BUT I WAS AFRAID HENCEFORTH   881 14
I DO NOT KNOW WHERE I HAD BEEN   881 18
BUT I HAD NOT SLEPT   881 20
I ONLY KNOW THAT LIKE A SOD   881 21
IN A MEADOW LOST I LAY   881 22
I DO NOT KNOW   881 27
I WAS THERE THAT WAS ALL   881 28
I WAS EMBEDDED IN THE REST OF THINGS   881 30
OR WHETHER I WAS THE DARKNESS WITH ARCHED WINGS   882   1
I DO NOT KNOW   882   4
I AWOKE WITH THE YOUNG NETTLES ON MY WRISTS   882   5
AND I LIFTED MY HEAD   882   6
AND THEN I KNEW I HAD TAKEN MY MOUTH FROM HER THROAT   882   7
AND I RAISED MY BREAST   882   8
KNOWING THEN I HAD TAKEN MY BOSOM FROM HER CRUSHED BREA+   882   9
AND I WENT BACK WITH MY MOUTH TO HER MOUTH   882 10
STILL I COULD NOT DISTINGUISH MYSELF   882 14
I SAID THIS IS GRASS THAT TWINKLES IN THE DARK   882 15
BUT I WHERE AMONG THEM ALL AM I   882 19
AND I LAY CLOSE DOWN   882 22
SAYING IT IS SHE IT IS I   882 23
THIS IS I THIS IS I   882 25
AND I TOOK HER EAR LIKE THE LEAF OF A WATER-FLOWER BETW+   882 27
AND I SAID LOVE   882 28
FOR I WAS NOT SURE OF MYSELF   882 29
AND I SAID 'TIS I   882 32
I AM HERE   882 33
AND WHEN I SEE THE HEAVY RED FLEECE   883   1
I FEEL AS IF FEATHERS WERE LIFTED AND SHOOK   883   4
AND WHEN I SEE THE TREES SWAY CLOSE   883   8
I LIFT MY BREAST AND LEAN FORWARD   883 10
I RAISE MY FACE SO IT SHALL WREATHE ME   883 13
AND I OPEN MY LIPS TO TAKE A STRAND OF KEEN HAIR   883 15
AND WHEN I SEE THE THICK WHITE BODY OF TRAIN-SMOKE BREAK   883 16
I STIFLE A CRY OF DESPAIR   883 18
I SAW THE SKY WAS LIT   883 19
BUT WHEN I CROSSED THE DUNES   883 21
I WAS AFRAID   883 23
BUT I ABRUPT   884   1
LIFTING HIS HAUNTED EYES TO ME I AM WANTING IN SONG   884 11
YOU MUST MAKE MY SONGS FOR ME LOVE I HAVE NONE   884 12
LAPPED PRISONER IN THE CORDS OF LOVE I HAVE SPUN   884 16
AND I WAS SONGLESS AS HE WAS AND LOOKED AT HIM   884 20
INTO THE DARKNESS SIGHING ON DARK AND I   885 16
I LOOKED IN HER EYES THE GLOOM   885 16
I KNEW THAT SHE WAS WAITING   885 18
I KNEW THAT SHE WAS BAITING   885 20
AS I LAY ON THE BED AND YOU SAT WITH THE FLOWERS ON YOU+   886 11
AND AS I LAY AND LOOKED IN YOUR EYES   886 13
I WAS FAINT WITH SURPRISE   886 15
I AM TERRIFIED OF THE PEAR-BLOSSOM   886 16
I AM TERRIFIED YOU ARE DEAD   886 21
AM I FOR EVER MAKING LOVE TO YOU   886 25
NO I AM NOT HERE I AM NOT HERE   887   6
BUT YOU AND I YOU AND I   887   9
AS YOU SIT ON THE TRESTLE I ON THE GROUND   887 12
LAUGHS LIKE AN EYE AT ME AND I   887 14
HAPPY AM I A NAKED SPRIG   888 13
IN MY BURSTING AND BUDDING I FEEL   888 14
PROLIFIC I AM A BLOSSOMING TWIG   888 17
ARE THEY ASLEEP ARE THEY ALIVE NOW SEE WHEN I   *891   9
OF THE BANK I STAND WATCHING MY OWN WHITE SHADOW QUIVER+   *891 21
I HAVE LEARNED IT ALL FROM MY EVE   *893   1
I DIDN'T LEARN IT FROM HER SPEECH   *893   6
I CAN'T TELL HOW IT COMES   *893   8
BUT I THINK THE KISSES REACH   *893   9
THEN I TREMBLE AND GO TREMBLING   *893 26
HOW CAN I TEACH YOU WHEN YOUR BLUE   *894   1
MY MIND AND I KNOW   *894   4
THAT I PUT TO FLIGHT FROM OUT OF YOU   *894   5
ENTICING WILL RECALL WHEN I   *894   7
THEN OH I DO FORGET ALL MY   *894 19
NOW I AM ON THE STRAND OF A TURBULENT SEA   *894 19
I STAND RELUCTANT TO ENTER TO DREAM NO MORE BUT TO BOW   *894 21
STILL IN THE SUN TO WATCH AND I CAN SEE   *895   2
COMES OVER THE SOFTNESS AND SILENCE OF MORNING I PASS   *895 11

MY PACK OF UNRULY HOUNDS I CANNOT START   *895 17
I CAN HAUL THEM AND URGE THEM NO MORE   *895 19
NO MORE CAN I ENDURE TO BEAR THE BRUNT   *895 20
I AM SICK AND TIRED MORE THAN ANY THRALL   *895 24
AND SHALL I TAKE   *895 26
TILL I ROUSE MY WILL LIKE A FIRE TO CONSUME   *895 28
OF THEIR INSULTS IN PUNISHMENT I WILL NOT   *895 30
I WILL NOT WASTE MYSELF TO EMBERS FOR THEM   *895 31
SHALL HAVE RAKED THE EMBERS CLEAR I WILL KEEP   *896   2
SOME OF MY STRENGTH FOR MYSELF FOR IF I SHOULD SELL   *896   3
IT ALL FOR THEM I SHOULD HATE THEM   *896   4
I WILL SIT AND WAIT FOR THE BELL   *896   5
I CARRY MY ANGER SULLENLY 'CROSS THESE WASTE LANDS   *896   8
I PICK MY WAY OVER THREADBARE GRASS WHICH IS PRESSED   *896 10
I CARRY MY ANGER SULLENLY 'CROSS THESE WASTE LANDS   *896 21
TOMORROW WILL POUR THEM ALL BACK THE DULL HOURS I DETEST   *896 25
I HAVE FETCHED THE TEARS UP OUT OF THE LITTLE WELLS   *896 26
I WATCHED THE TEARS ON THE FRUITED CHEEKS OF THE BOYS   *897   2
FOR LAUGHTER AND GLAD THE EXONERATED EYES FOR I   *897   8
DESOLATE AND DESPOILED AM I FOR THEIR FLAMING STORM   *897 11
HOW CAN I ANSWER THE CHALLENGE OF SO MANY EYES   *897 32
AWFULLY MUST I CALL BACK THOSE HUNDRED EYES A VOICE   *898   2
MY QUESTION MY GOD I MUST BREAK FROM THIS HOARSE SILENCE   *898   4
I HAVE STARTLED A HUNDRED EYES AND I MUST LOOK   *898   6
THEM AN ANSWER BACK IT IS MORE THAN I CAN BEAR   *898   7
TO LET THE SUNLIGHT IN   *898 21
AS I SIT ON THE BEACH OF THE CLASS ALONE   *898 22
TOUCH AFTER TOUCH I FEEL ON ME   *899 14
SO I LEAD THEM UP SO DO THEY TWINE   *899 23
MOUNTS UP TO MY HEART AND I FIND IT GOOD   *899 34
AND I LIFT MY HEAD UPON THE TROUBLED TANGLED WORLD AND +   *900   1
OF LIVING MY LIFE WERE DOUBLED I STILL HAVE THIS TO COM+   *900   3
I HAVE SUCH SWARMING SENSE OF LIVES AT THE BASE OF ME S+   *900   5
AND THOUGH I SCARCELY SEE THE BOYS OR KNOW THAT THEY AR+   *900 10
AS I AM WITH LIVING MY LIFE IN EARNESTNESS STILL PROGRE+   *900 12
THE WAY THAT I HAVE GONE AND NOW AM LEADING THEY ARE DE+   *900 19
I ALONE AM LIVING THEN IT KEEPS   *900 22
HOW CAN I ANSWER THE CHALLENGE OF SO MANY EYES   *901   9
AWFULLY MUST I CALL BACK THOSE HUNDRED EYES A VOICE   *901 11
MY QUESTION MY GOD I MUST BREAK FROM THIS HOARSE SILENCE   *901 13
I HAVE STARTLED A HUNDRED EYES AND I MUST LOOK   *901 15
THEM AN ANSWER BACK IT IS MORE THAN I CAN BEAR   *901 16
TO LET THE SUNLIGHT IN AND I   *902   5
AS I SIT ON THE BEACH OF THE CLASS ALONE   *902   6
TOUCH AFTER TOUCH I FEEL ON ME   *902 26
SO I LEAD THEM UP SO DO THEY TWINE   *903   2
MOUNTS UP TO MY HEART AND I FIND IT GOOD   *903 13
AND I LIFT MY HEAD UPON THE TROUBLED TANGLED WORLD AND +   *903 14
OF LIVING MY LIFE WERE DOUBLED I STILL HAVE THIS TO COM+   *903 16
I HAVE SUCH SWARMING SENSE OF LIVES AT   *903 17
AND THOUGH I SCARCELY SEE THE BOYS OR KNOW THAT THEY AR+   *903 22
AS I AM WITH LIVING MY LIFE IN EARNESTNESS STILL PROGRE+   *903 24
THE WAY THAT I HAVE GONE AND NOW AM LEADING THEY ARE DE+   *903 31
I ALONE AM LIVING THEN IT KEEPS   *903 34
MY PACK OF UNRULY HOUNDS I CANNOT START   *904   6
I CAN HAUL THEM AND URGE THEM NO MORE   *904   7
NO MORE CAN I ENDURE TO BEAR THE BRUNT   *904   9
I AM SICK AND TIRED MORE THAN ANY THRALL   *904 10
AND SHALL I TAKE   *904 15
TILL I ROUSE MY WILL LIKE A FIRE TO CONSUME   *904 17
OF THEIR INSULTS IN PUNISHMENT I WILL NOT   *904 19
I WILL NOT WASTE MYSELF TO EMBERS FOR THEM   *904 20
SHALL HAVE RAKED THE EMBERS CLEAR I WILL KEEP   *904 23
SOME OF MY STRENGTH FOR MYSELF FOR IF I SHOULD SELL   *904 24
IT ALL FOR THEM I SHOULD HATE THEM   *904 25
I WILL SIT AND WAIT FOR THE BELL   *904 26
I HAVE OPENED THE WINDOW TO WARM MY HANDS ON THE SILL   *905   1
RECOGNITIONS AND GREETINGS OF HALF-ACQUAINT THINGS AS I+   *905 11
FOR AM I NOT ALSO DREAM-STUFF DIFFUSING MYSELF IN THE P+   *907   7
FLOWING I KNOW NOT HOW YET SERIOUSLY   *907   8
HERE HAVE I FOUND AN ANSWER FOR MY HOLLOW YEARNING   *907 10
EYES WHERE I CAN WATCH THE SWIM OF OLD DREAMS REFLECTED+   *907 11
FLUENT ACTIVE FIGURES OF MEN PASS ALONG THE RAILWAY AND+   *908 11
AND I WATCH TO SEE THE CREATOR THE POWER THAT PATTERNS +   *908 25
ALLURING MY EYES FOR I AM I NOT ALSO DREAM-STUFF   *909   3
AM I NOT QUICKENING DIFFUSING MYSELF IN THE PATTERN SHA+   *909   4
EYES WHERE I CAN WATCH THE SWIM OF OLD DREAMS REFLECTED+   *909   7
OH THE TERRIBLE ECSTASY OF THE CONSCIOUSNESS THAT I AM +   *909 18
OH THE TERROR OF LIFTING THE INNERMOST I OUT OF THE SWE+   *909 29
NAY I SAW NOWT BUT TH' COFFIN AN' TH' YELLER CLAY AN' '+   *909 31
WHILE TH' PARSON WAS PRAYIN' I WATCHES 'ER AN' SHE WOR +   *910   1
I COULD THINK O' NOWT BUT OUR TED AN' 'IM TAKEN   *910   3
WHEN YOU'D GONE I SLIPPED BACK TER SEE WHO SHE MIGHT BE   *910   5
NO GOOD I WARRANT THIS TROUBLE IS SUCH AS SHE   *910   7
I COULDNA' SEE HER FACE BUT HER LITTLE NECK SHONE   *910 11
THEY WAS WILD ONES WHITE AND BLUE I COULD TELL   *910 17
US A LITTLE WIFT AN' I KNEW THE SMELL   *910 19
I COME AWAY FOR FEAR SHE SHOULD SEE   *910 22
HOW SHOULD I BE LOOKIN' ROUND   *911   5
AN' COS I LIKED HIM BEST YI BETT'R NOR THEE   *911 15
I CANNA BIDE TO THINK WHERE HE IS GONE   *911 16
AN' I COME AWAY BECAUSE O' THE TEEMIN' RAIN   *911 32
I FELT THE LURCH AND HALT OF HER HEART   *912   1
AND I LAUGHED TO FEEL IT PLUNGE AND BOUND   *912   3
OF THE WORDS I KEPT REPEATING   *912   5
HOLDING HER THUS DID I CARE   *912 11
I LEANED ME FORWARD TO FIND HER LIPS   *912 13
AND I SAW HER FOR THE FLARING SPACE   *912 16
I WAIT FOR THE BABY TO WANDER HITHER TO ME   *913   6
I LONG FOR THE BABY TO WANDER HITHER TO ME   *914   6
AN' WHEN I KNOW FOR SURE MISSIS   *920 11
MY BREAST'S AS RED AS THINE I RECKON   *920 15
BUT THA DOESNA STARE ME OUT I GUESS   *921   8
AN' 'ER'S WANTIN IT I HEAR   *921 16
DOESN'T TER KNOW WHAT I MEAN YI   *921 21
DONE I SHOULD THINK SO DONE BUT MIGHT   *921 27
I ASK WHEN THA BEGUN   *921 28

LIZZIE I TELL THEE THAT	*922	2
HASNA TER SENT ME WHOAM WHEN I	*922	6
TILL I WAS VERILY SWELTED	*922	12
AY I DID BUT AFTERWARDS	*922	21
I SHOULD LIKE TO HA' KILLED HER	*922	22
I MIGHT LOSE MY-SEN	*922	26
BUT I SHONNA MARRY HER	*922	30
I SHONNA FOR NOBODY IT IS	*922	31
FOR I TELL YE I SHONNA MARRY HER	*923	3
I DAMN WELL SHANNA MARRY 'ER	*923	9
AN' THAT'S THE DARK BLUE TIE I BOUGHT 'IM	*923	14
I DUNNO WHERE HIS EYES WAS A GRET	*923	17
I EXPECT YOU KNOW WHO I AM MRS NAYLOR	*923	21
'APPEN I MIGHTN'T 'APPEN I MIGHT	*923	24
YOU KNOWED AS I WAS COURTIN' TIM MERFIN	*923	25
YIS I KNOWED 'E WOR COURTIN' THEE	*923	26
AN' IF I HAN WHAT'S THAT TO THEE	*924	2
I WANT YOU TO KNOW 'E'S NON MARRYIN' YOU	*924	9
TO THINK I SHOULD HA'E TO HAFFLE AN' CAFFLE	*924	13
FOR LETTIN' ME MARRY THE LAD AS I THOUGHT	*924	15
FOR I WON'T BE BEHOLDEN TO SUCH AS HER	*924	19
I WISH THA HADNA DONE IT TIM	*924	25
I DO AN' THAT I DO	*924	26
FOR WHENEVER I LOOK THEE I' TH' FACE I S'LL SEE	*924	27
I WISH THA COULD WESH 'ER OFF'N THEE	*925	1
FOR I USED TO THINK THAT THY	*925	2
TWENTY POUND O' THY OWN THA HAST AND FIFTY POUND HA'E I	*925	9
SORRY I AM FOR THIS BUSINESS AN' SORRY IF I HA'E DRIVEN+	*925	10
BEFORE I CAN TA'E THEE I'VE GOT A WIDOW OF FORTY-FIVE T+	*925	12
DUNNAT THEE THINK BUT WHAT I LOVE THEE I LOVE THEE WELL	*925	13
BUT 'DEED AN' I WISH AS THIS TALE O' THINE WOR NIVER MY+	*925	14
DEED AN' I WISH AS I COULD STOOD AT THE ALTAR WI'	*925	15
THAT I COULD HA' BEEN FIRST WOMAN TO THEE AS THOU'RT FI+	*925	17
AN' THEN WI' THAT TWENTY POUND WE GI'E 'ER I S'D THINK +	*925	20
KISS ME THEN THERE NE'ER MIND IF I SCRAIGHT I WOR FOND +	*925	28
IT IS NO GOOD DEAR MEEKNESS AND FORBEARANCE I ENDURED T+	*926	7
I HAVE PUSHED MY HANDS IN THE DARK LOAM UNDER THE FLOWE+	*926	8
OH I TORE THEM UP THOUGH THE WISTFUL LEAVES WERE FRAGRA+	*926	15
AND I TWISTED THEM OVER THE BROKEN LEAVES INTO UNBREAKA+	*926	17
AND DO I NOT SEEK TO MATE MY GROWN DESIROUS SOUL	*926	22
AND STRIKE WITH A BLINDNESS OF FURY AGAINST ME CAN I CA+	*926	24
YEA I WAS FINE ENOUGH TO EXPLORE YOU	*927	6
FLESH-ANGUISH THEN I SUFFERED A BALK	*927	10
I HEARD THY CRIES OF PAIN AND THEY BROKE	*927	11
AND I FAILED IN MY COWARDICE TO GIVE THEE THE LAST	*927	14
WHO IF I BUT PIERCED WITH THE THORNED	*927	18
I WAS DILIGENT TO EXPLORE YOU	*928	6
ANGUISH THEN I SUFFERED A BALK	*928	10
I KNEW YOUR PAIN AND IT BROKE	*928	11
WHO HAD I BUT PIERCED WITH THE THORNED	*928	18
AS I SEE IT HARDENING	*929	3
THE DARKNESS IS LOVELIEST WHERE I COULD SEAR	*929	20
WASTE ME NOT I BEG YOU WASTE	*930	1
MANY YEARS HAVE I STILL TO BURN DETAINED	*930	5
LIKE A CANDLE FLAME ON THIS BODY BUT I ENSHRINE	*930	8
AND THROUGH THESE YEARS WHILE I BURN ON THE FUEL OF LIFE	*930	9
WHAT MATTER THE STUFF I LICK UP IN MY LIVING FLAME	*930	10
SEEING I DEEP IN THE FIRE-CORE INVIOLATE	*930	11
I WONDER CAN THE NIGHT GO BY	*930	13
OPPRESSES ME I CAN SCARCELY BEAR	*930	25
STILL I MUST SIT IN AGONY	*931	1
OH I WOULD NOT LOVE YOU	*931	4
HOW I HAVE LONGED FOR THIS NIGHT IN THE TRAIN	*931	5
BUT SURELY SURELY I KNOW THAT STILL	*931	8
IT IS ONLY I FIND IT HARD TO BEAR	*931	12
FOR I ACHE MOST EARNESTLY FOR YOUR TOUCH	*931	19
I AM ASHAMED THAT I ACHE SO MUCH	*931	20
I'LL KISS YOU OVER THE EYES TILL I KISS YOU BLIND	*932	4
IF I CAN IF ANYONE COULD	*932	5
NOW STOP CARPING AT ME BUT GOD HOW I HATE YOU	*932	10
DO YOU FEAR I SHALL SWINDLE YOU	*932	11
MUST HAVE ME ALL IN YOUR WILL AND YOUR KNOWLEDGE AND I	*932	14
ONCE I HAD A LOVER BRIGHT LIKE RUNNING WATER	*933	13
ONCE I KNEW A SUMMER THAT SPARKLED	*933	14
WHERE IS THE SUN I CANNOT UNDERSTAND	*933	20
BUT I WAS ROSY FOR HIM FOR I DID FLUSH MELLOW	*933	25
SUNSHINE OF HIS HAIR I USED TO KISS	*933	28
BETWEEN THE OLD RED WALLS I DID NOT DARE	*934	3
TO RAISE MY FACE I DID NOT DARE LOOK UP	*934	4
I FOLLOWED FOLLOWED THE SWING OF HER WHITE DRESS	*934	8
THAT ROCKED IN A LILT ALONG I WATCHED THE POISE	*934	9
THE GRASS DEEP DOWN WITH HER ROYAL BURDEN AND I	*934	11
I LIKE TO SEE HER SAID AND SHE CROUCHED HER DOWN	*934	13
AND I SAW HER BOSOM COUCH IN THE NEST OF HER GOWN	*934	15
STRONG AND SLOW I LIKE TO SEE SAID SHE	*934	17
AND CHOKE ME IN MY OWN CRIMSON I WATCHED HER PULL	*934	23
OVER MY EYES AND I WAS BLIND	*934	25
AND IN THE DARK I DID DISCOVER	*934	28
THINGS I WAS OUT TO FIND	*934	29
PULSED THICKLY AND I LONGED TO POUR	*934	33
I LONGED TO POUR THE BURNING STORE	*935	1
WAS I TILL SHE TOOK HER EYES AWAY	*935	5
IT SEEMED THAT I AND THE WOVEN WORLD	*935	6
SHE SPOKE AND I CLOSED MY EYES	*935	18
CAN MAKE THEM YAWN I STRETCHED MY HAND TO THE DINT	*935	25
AND THEN I SAW A BROWN BIRD HOVER	*935	29
AGAIN AND I FELT A BROWN BIRD HOVER	*935	31
I THOUGHT I SAW ON THE CLOVER	*935	34
AND AH I HELD MY HEART ALOFT	*936	9
I PRESSED THE WRETCHED THROTTLED FLOWER BETWEEN	*936	12
AND I KEPT THE CHOKED SNAKE FLOWER IN ITS PANGS	*936	15
THE LOW WORD DON'T I LET THE FLOWER FALL	*936	19
PUT FORTH TOWARD HER SHE DID NOT MOVE NOR I	*936	22
THEN I LAUGHED IN THE DARK OF MY HEART I DID EXULT	*936	24
LIKE A SUDDEN CHUCKLING OF MUSIC I BADE HER EYES	*936	25
TO MINE I OPENED HER HELPLESS EYES TO CONSULT	*936	26
AND I DO NOT CARE THOUGH THE LARGE HANDS OF REVENGE	*937	1

FOR I HAVE SEEN THE VEIN	*937	7
AND I IN A SWOON	*937	13
SOME SAY THEY SEE THOUGH I HAVE NEVER SEEN	*937	28
IT IS DEATH I FEAR SO MUCH IT IS NOT THE DEAD	*938	27
AND SO I SIT AND TURN THE BOOK OF GRAY	*939	1
ALL FEARFUL LEST I FIND SOME NEXT WORD BLEEDING	*939	3
BUT I REMEMBER STILL THE SUNNY HOURS	*939	17
QUIETLY THROUGH THE YEARS I HAVE CREPT BACK TO SEE	*940	6
IF I WERE WELL-TO-DO	*940	25
I WOULD PUT ROSES ON ROSES AND COVER YOUR GRAVE	*940	26
WHEN SOFTLY I CALL AT HER DOOR AND ENTER THE ROOM	*941	25
I LINGER TO WATCH HER	*942	20
LIKE WET AND SHAKEN ROSES AND I LISTEN	*943	4
SHE LOVES ME AND I BLOW A LITTLE BOAT	*943	15
I SEE THE WOMAN'S SOUL STEAL IN HER EYES	*943	19
AND WIDE IN ECSTASY I SIT AND WATCH	*943	20
I CAN HEAR THE SOUND OF THE SCYTHE STROKES FOUR	*944	2
SHARP BREATHS SWISHING YEA BUT I	*944	3
IS MINE I MUN CLAIM HIM ONCE FOR ALL	*944	6
AND ALWAYS LIKELY OH IF I COULD RIDE	*944	23
HOW I ADORE YOU FOR YOUR SIMPLE PRIDE	*944	28
HOW I ADORE YOU YOU HAPPY THINGS YOU DEARS	*945	6
SPIRIT OF CARELESS JOY AH HOW I WARM	*945	14
YOU'RE A FOOL WOMAN I LOVE YOU AND YOU KNOW I DO	*945	17
AND I GIVE YOU EVERYTHING THAT YOU WANT ME TO	*945	19
ALL DAY LONG I AM BUSY AND HAPPY AT MY WORK	*945	24
I NEED NOT GLANCE OVER MY SHOULDER IN FEAR OF THE TERRO+	*945	25
BEHIND I AM FORTIFIED I AM GLAD AT MY WORK	*945	26
I NEED NOT LOOK AFTER MY SOUL BEGUILE MY FEAR	*945	27
WITH PRAYER I NEED ONLY COME HOME EACH NIGHT TO FIND TH+	*946	1
I NEED ONLY COME HOME EACH NIGHT AND LAY	*946	3
AND WHAT OF GOOD I HAVE GIVEN THE DAY MY PEACE ATTESTS	*946	4
AND WHAT I HAVE FAILED IN WHAT I HAVE WRONGED	*946	6
SILENT TONGUED I AM ASHAMED	*946	7
AND I HOPE TO SPEND ETERNITY	*947	19
AND IN THE DARK I FEEL HIS COLD WEBBED FEET MUD BLACK	*947	27
I KNOW A NOBLE ENGLISHMAN	*950	12
IN NOTTINGHAM WHERE I WENT TO SCHOOL AND COLLEGE	*950	18
AND LOOKS IT AND I PUT IT TO YOU	*954	26
HOW DEEP I HAVE GONE	*954	28
SINCE I EMBARKED ON YOUR DARK BLUE FRINGES	*955	11
OH I KNOW	*956	22
FOR I WILL GO TO THE WEDDING AND BE WEDDING-GUEST	*956	24
I SING OF AUTUMN AND THE FALLING FRUIT	*957	18
OH IT IS NOT SO EASY I TELL YOU IT IS NOT SO EASY		

I'D

ME SO DISTINCTLY FROM SLEEPING THE SLEEP I'D LOVE BEST	48	26
I'D AS MUCH AS I COULD DO TO THINK	60	23
THAT WHITE AN' 'ER CRIED THAT MUCH I'D LIKE TO BEGIN	61	8
AFTER I'D KISSED THEE AT NIGHT LIZZIE	80	9
AND GLADLY I'D OFFERED MY BREAST TO THE TREAD OF HER	123	6
SURELY AH NOT IN WORDS ALONE I'D SPILL	127	16
I'D LIE FOR EVER DRINKING AND DRAWING IN	153	29
I'D NEVER HAVE LET YOU APPROPRIATE ME HAD I KNOWN	395	16
I'D SAY IT WAS JUST A BIRD	453	3
I'D LOADED THE CAMEL'S BACK BEFORE	491	19
IS THEIR MONEY BUT I DOUBT IF I'D FIGHT FOR MINE ANYHOW	497	20
I'D REJOICE OVER THE WOMAN AND THE WARMED COCKLES OF MY	507	10
I'D BETRAY THE MIDDLE CLASSES	534	15
I FIND I'D RATHER GET BACK TO EARTH	552	7
AND I'D LET MYSELF BE SWINDLED	556	13
AS A CACHE SEXE I'D HAVE PUT A WHOLE FOG	580	12
I'D HANG MY HAMS WITH PUCKERED PETTICOATS SWAYING	835	32
AND I'D GATHER MY HAIR	836	1
THAT WHITE AN' 'ER SHOOK THAT MUCH I'D LIKE TO BEGIN	*911	24
AN' IF IT'S NOT TRUE I'D BACK MY LIFE	*920	7
I'D HAVE TORN THEM UP HAD THEY BORNE AWAY THE PATIENT B+	*926	13
AND SO I'D RAISE	*941	13
DO YOU THINK I'D HAVE A CREATURE LIKE YOU AT MY SIDE	*944	25

I'LL

I'LL WET MY BROW FOR THEE	44	7
WITH SWEAT I'LL ENTER A HOUSE FOR THY SAKE	44	8
I'LL SAY YOUR BOND OF UGLINESS IS VAIN	72	23
I'LL TALK THEN	78	20
THEN I'LL SAY GOOD-BYE TO THEE TIMOTHY	80	27
I'LL TA'E THY WORD GOOD-BYE LIZ	80	29
I'LL CHUCK THE FLAMIN' LOT O' YOU	81	11
THOUGH I'LL SEE AS 'E PAYS YOU AN' DOES WHAT'S RIGHT	82	7
I'LL SAY GOOD-BYE LIZ TO YER	85	1
AY LAD I'LL TELL THEE THY MIND	138	28
I'LL WHISPER THE GHOSTLY TRUTH TO YOU	227	27
WAIT WAIT A BIT I'LL COME WHEN I'VE LIT THE FIRE	384	9
AND I'LL PROTECT YOU	400	32
I SWEAR I'LL PULL OFF MY KNICKERS RIGHT IN THE RUE DE L+	433	20
I'LL HOLD YOUR HAT	560	16
FOR THE FLOWERS AND I'LL TELL YOU WHAT	578	1
BUT I'LL NEVER REACH THE LONG SWEET SHORE	747	25
MY CASHMERE SHAWL I'LL HANG FOR A CANOPY	754	24
OR I'LL SMOTHER THEM ALL	792	3
I'LL SHAKE THE EARTH AND SWALLOW THEM UP WITH THEIR CIT+	792	4
I'LL SEND FIRE AND ASHES UPON THEM AND SMOTHER THEM ALL	792	5
I'LL TURN THEIR BLOOD LIKE SOUR MILK ROTTEN WITH THUNDER	792	6
AND DEEP IN CENTRAL PARK I'LL FATTEN	815	15
AT HER AGE WHY I'LL BE EARNING A JOLLY GOOD SCREW	834	20
IN THE AUTUMN I'LL LOOK FOR IMMORTAL FRUIT	855	9
I'LL WORK AND I'LL WIVE	857	8
AND I'LL LIE IN HER LAP WHERE THE WORLD'S WILD ROSE	858	6
I'LL TALK THEN	*920	12
I'LL ONLY SAY GOOD-BYE TO THEE TIMOTHY	*922	27

I'LL TA'E THY WORD GOOD-BYE LIZ   *922 29
OR I'LL CHUCK THE FLAMIN' LOT OF YOU   *923 11
THOUGH I'LL SEE AS 'E PAYS YOU AN' COMES TO THE SCRATCH *924 11
BUT WE MAUN MA'E THE BEST ON'T I'LL REAR THY CHILDT IF + *925 18
I'LL KISS YOU OVER THE EYES TILL I KISS YOU BLIND   *932 4

I'M

SAY I'M BUSY   44 13
LIKE THIS I'M SURE IT IS   45 26
AND YET I'M SUPPOSED TO CARE WITH ALL MY MIGHT   74 30
I'M OFF UP TH' LINE TO UNDERWOOD   78 3
WELL I'M BELIEVIN' NO TALE MISSIS   78 17
I'M SEEIN' FOR MY-SEN   78 18
I'M SCRAIGHTIN' MY-SEN BUT ARENA GOIN'   78 27
I'M FURTHER OWER TH' TOP   78 32
I'M TAKIN' 'OME A WEDDIN'-DRESS   79 15
I'M NOT 'AVIN' YOUR ORTS AN' SLARTS   82 3
TO DO SUCH A THING THOUGH IT'S A POOR TALE IT IS THAT I+ 83 7
AY I'M SORRY I'M SORRY   83 18
AY I'M SORRY THA NEDNA WORRY   83 20
I'M SORRY FOR THEE I'M SORRY F'R 'ER   83 22
I'M SORRY F'R US A'   83 23
I'M SORRY FOR TH' TROUBLE AY   84 9
I'M NOT THAT'S A'   84 12
LAD BUT I'M TELLIN' THEE SUMMAT   137 24
YI BUT I'M TELLIN' THEE SUMMAT   137 31
NOW LAD I'M AXIN' THEE SUMMAT   138 2
A GO AT T'OTHER FOR I'M A BAD   140 4
COME NO I'M A THING OF LIFE I GIVE   211 5
NAY I'M TOO SLEEPY AH YOU ARE HORRIBLE   211 7
NO NO I DANCE IN THE SUN I'M A THING OF LIFE   211 16
YEA THOUGH I'M SORRY FOR THEE   220 8
I'M NOT AFRAID OF GOD   231 23
FIND OUT IF I'M SOUND OR BANKRUPT   237 3
BE ROUGH AND HAIRY I'M GLAD THEY'RE LIKE THAT   254 12
COME ON YOU CRAPA I'M NOT YOUR SERVANT   384 33
I'M I ON THE HORSE   397 24
STANDS SAYING SEE I'M INVISIBLE   403 11
AND I'M A PALE-FACE LIKE A HOMELESS DOG   404 13
I'M GOING TO SIT DOWN ON MY TAIL RIGHT HERE   405 29
I'M THE RED WOLF SAYS THE DARK OLD FATHER   405 31
ABAHT IT YES I'M A GENT AN' LIZ   434 23
OF COURSE I'M A LIDY WHAT D'YER THINK   434 25
I'M AMERICAN FROM NEW ORLEANS   435 2
I'M PERFECTLY WILLING TO STRIKE A DECENT BARGAIN   483 22
BUT I'M NOT HAVING ANY DODG   483 23
I'M ABOUT AS MUCH LIKE A PERSIAN CAT   489 23
BUT I'M ALWAYS LONGING FOR SOMEONE TO SAY   490 27
I SAY TO MYSELF HELLO I'M NOT WELL MY VITALITY IS LOW 498 8
I LOVE NOBODY I'M GOING TO LOVE NOBODY   507 2
I'M NOT GOING TO TELL ANY LIES ABOUT IT   507 3
AND THE TCHEKOV LOT I'M TOO WEAK AND LOVABLE TO LIVE   534 1
OH I'M SURE YOU'LL UNDERSTAND WE'RE MAKING A CENSUS OF + 546 1
THAT SAYS I'M FOR YOU   561 6
I FEEL I'M GOING TO BE NAUGHTY AUNTIE   572 19
PERHAPS I'M GOING TO BE NAUGHTY AUNTIE   573 7
OH I'M A BRITISH BOY SIR   576 16
FOR I'M A BRITISH BOY SIR   576 22
I'M YOUR BRITISH BOY AND I DID BUT TRY   577 10
APPLICANT I'M AFRAID I DON'T   582 11
APPLICANT I DON'T THINK SO SIR I'M AFRAID NOT   582 18
AND WHEN I WANT TO I'M GOING TO   618 12
AND I'M GOING TO DO WHAT I JOLLY WELL PLEASE   671 7
I FEEL I'M COMING NEAR   764 12
TELL THEM THEY ARE ALL FOOLS THAT I'M LAUGHING AT THEM 791 26
I'M OFF UP TH' LINE TO UNDERWOOD   *919 23
WELL I'M BELIEVIN' NO TALE MISSIS   *920 9
I'M SEEIN' FOR MY-SEN   *920 10
I'M SCREETIN' MY-SEN BUT ARE-NA GOIN'   *920 19
I'M FURTHER OWER TH' TOP   *920 24
I'M TAKIN' 'OME A WEDDIN' DRESS   *921 11
I'M NOT HAVIN' YOUR ORTS AN' SLARTS   *924 7
TO SUCH A THING BUT IT'S A POOR TALE THAT I'M BOUND TO + *925 11
AND I'M A KALEIDOSCOPE   *932 8
TO COVER MY MOUTH'S RAILLERY TILL I'M BOUND IN HER SHAM+ *940 17
BUT I'M SORRY FOR HIM ON HIS YOUNG FEET KNOWIN'   *944 7
MY YOUNG SLIM LAD AN' I'M SORRY FOR THEE   *944 16
I'M A RELIGIOUS SOUL   *947 15

I'VE

FOR I'VE LOST MY PEACE   46 28
OF THE MAN I'VE ACCEPTED AS MINE   59 14
WITCH TEETH AN' 'ER BLACK HAWK-EYES AS I'VE   77 23
WHAT'S THAT AS 'APPEN I'VE 'EERED ON MISSIS   78 7
AN' 'APPEN YOU'D GUESS THEN WHAT I'VE COME FOR   81 23
SORRY I AM FOR THIS BUSINESS AN' SORRY IF EVER I'VE DRI+ 83 6
AFORE I CAN TA'E THEE I'VE GOT A WIDDER O' FORTY-FIVE T+ 83 8
DUNNAT THEE THINK BUT WHAT I'VE LOVED THEE I'VE LOVED T+ 83 9
EVEN THOUGH I'VE 'AD   84 22
I STILL AM NOT HOMELESS HERE I'VE A TENT BY DAY   133 24
AN' I'VE LOVED THEE FOR IT   139 16
WITH WET FLAT LIGHTS WHAT I'VE DONE   143 23
YET I'VE FORGOTTEN IN PLAYING THIS GAME   151 31
SHE'S A SILVERY DOVE WORTH MORE THAN ALL I'VE GOT   238 22
THOUGH I'VE EATEN IT NOW   279 24
YET I'VE HEARD HIM CRY   363 27
WAIT WAIT A BIT I'LL COME WHEN I'VE LIT THE FIRE   384 9
FIRST LIVE THING I'VE OWNED SINCE THE LOP-EARED RABBITS 395 7
I'VE HAD MOMENTS OF HATRED OF YOU SINCE   396 10
WOMEN I'VE LOVED FOR GENTLENESS   412 10
I'VE NEVER GOT TO THE BOTTOM OF SUPERIORITY   435 19

I'VE CHUCKED HIM I'VE REPENTED   493 24
NOW I'VE MADE UP MY MIND   507 1
I'VE GOT TO PUT UP WITH IT   508 7
NEED TO KNOW ABOUT ANYBODY AND DO YOU KNOW I'VE NEVER B+ 546 18
I SUDDENLY SAID I'VE FINISHED   556 15
I'VE NEVER SEEN HER BUT THEY SAY   572 1
YOU MUST ADMIT I'VE RISEN   626 15
I'VE RISEN I'VE RISEN   626 16
YOU MUST ADMIT I'VE RISEN   626 17
BECAUSE I'VE RISEN CLEAR   626 26
I'VE BEEN UP TO LONDON TO SEE THE FINE QUEEN   670 2
AND WHAT I'VE UNDERSTOOD AND THEN THE UTTER ACHE   738 11
OF EVERYTHING I'VE KNOWN EVEN DREAMILY   738 12
ME NOW IF I'VE LOST MY MESS-MATES LOST THEM FOREVER   757 7
ECHO OF HER I'VE-LAID-AN-EGG CACKLE IS RICH AND RESONAN+ 761 21
I'VE LAID AN EGG   761 24
I'VE LAID AN EGG   761 26
BUT I'VE HAD SUCH A JOB MY CRUTCHES I FAIRLY DRAGGED TH+ 865 22
WITCH TEETH AN' 'ER BLACK HAWK-EYES AS I'VE   *919 11
WHAT'S THAT AS 'APPEN I'VE 'EERED-ON MISSIS   *919 27
'AN 'APPEN YOU MIGHT GUESS WHAT I'VE COME FOR   *923 23
BEFORE I CAN TA'E THEE I'VE GOT A WIDOW OF FORTY-FIVE T+ *925 12
AN' ANSWER ME FOR I'VE SAID MY SAY AN' THERE'S NO MORE + *925 22
FROM WHAT I'VE ARRANGED WI' THEE EH MAN WHAT A STUBBORN+ *925 26
I'VE REALISED IT IS ALL A TRICK ON HIS PART   *948 22

APPENDIX II: FAMILIAL

AUNT	CHILD +	FAMILY	KINDRED	SISTER
AUNTIE	CHILDT	FATHER +	KITH	SON
BABES	COUSINS	GRANDCHILDREN	MAMA	SPOUSE
BABY	DADDIES	GRANDFATHERS +	MOTHER	UNCLE
BOY +*	DADDY	GRANDMOTHERS	PA	WIFE +
BRIDE	DADDY-DO-NOTHING +	HUSBAND +	PAPA	
BRIDEGROOM	DADDYLESS	INFANT	PARENTS	
BROTHER +	DAUGHTER +	KIN	PARENTHOOD	

APPENDIX III: NATURE

A. TOPOGRAPHY

AMAZON	CRATERS	HEMISPHERE	PEAK +	SUBTERRANEAN
AMERICA	CROFT	HILL +	POND	SURFACE
ANAPO	DESERT	HORIZON	PRAIRIE	SURF'S
BAY	DIRT	ICE	PUEBLO RIVER	TOWER
BEACH +	DITCH	ICEBERGS	RANGE +	TOWN +
BERG	DUCK-POND	ISLANDS	RIDGE	TRAIL +
BOG-END	DUNES	JUNGLE	RIVER	TRENCHES
BOULDERS	DUST	LAGOON-WATER	RIVER-BEDS	TROPICS +
BRAKE	DYKE	LAKE	ROAD	TURF
BREAKER	EARTH +	LAND +	ROCK	UNDER-DEEPS
BRIDGE	EMBANKMENT	LAWN	ROCKIES	UNDER-EARTH
BROOK	EQUATOR	LEVELS	SAGE	UNDER-GRASS
BY-PATHS	EXPANSE	LINCOLNSHIRE	SAND	UNDERGROUND
CANYON	FARM	LOAM	SHORE	UNDER-MIRE
CATARACT	FIELD +	MARSH +	SLOPE +	UNDERSOIL
CAVE +	FORESHORES	MEAD	SOD	UPHILL
CAVERN +	FOREST	MEADOW	SOIL	VALLEY +
CHANNEL	GARDEN	MIDLANDS	STACKYARD	VESUVIUS
CITY	GLACIER	MOUNTAIN +	STEEP	WEALD
CLIFF +	GLEBE	OCEAN	STONE-SLOPES	WILDERNESS
COAST	GLOBE	ORCHARD	STREAM +	WOOD +
COMMON	GORSE	PADDY-FIELDS	STREET	WORLD +
CONTINENT	GRAVEL	PARK	STUBBLE	YARD-WAY
COUNTRY +	GROUND	PASTURE	STUMPS	

APPENDIX III: NATURE

B. ANIMALS

ADDER +	COCK +	GREEN-FLY	NIGHTINGALE	SHELL-BIRD
AIREDALE	COCK-EAGLE	GREY-DOGS	OCTOPUS	SHE-WHALES
ALBATROSS	CONDOR	GREYHOUND	OTTER	SKUNK
AMOEBA	COO-DOVE'S	HARE +	OWL	SKYLARK
ANACONDA	CORNCRAKE	HART	OXEN	SNAIL +
ANIMAL	COW +	HAWK +	OYSTER	SNAKE +
ANT	COYOTES	HE-GOAT	PALFREY	SNOW-LEOPARDS
ASP	CRABS	HEIFER +	PANTHER	SOW
ASS	CREATURE +	HEN	PARROT +	SPANIELS
ASS-COLT	CROW	HERD +	PARTRIDGES	SPARROW +
BADGERS	CUB +	HERON	PEACOCK	SPERM-WHALES
BAT +	CUCKOO	HIND	PEEWIT	SPIDER
BEAR	CYGNET	HOUND +	PIG	SQUIRREL
BEAST +	DEER	HUMMING-BIRD +	PIGEON	STAG
BEAVERS	DODO	HYENA +	PIKE	STALLION
BED-BUG +	DOE	ICTHYOSAURUS	PISCES	STARLING
BEE +	DOG +	INSECT +	PLOVERS	STEERS
BEETLE	DOLPHINS +	JACKAL	PONIES	STOAT
BILLY GOAT	DONKEY +	JACKASS	PORPOISE	SWALLOW
BIRD +	DOVE +	KANGAROO	POSIES	SWAN +
BISON +	DRAKE	KESTREL	PULLETS	SWINE
BITCH +	DRAUGHT-HORSE	KINGFISHERS	PUP	THROSTLE
BLACKBIRD	DUCK +	KITTENS	RABBITS +	THRUSH +
BLUE JAY	EAGLE +	LAMB	RAM	TIGER
BOVINE	ELEPHANT +	LARK +	RANCH-DOGS	TIGRESS
BULL +	ELK	LEGHORN	RAT +	TOADS
BULL-FROGS	EWE	LEOPARD	RAVENS	TORTOISE +
BULLOCK	FARM	LICE	REPTILE +	TUNNY-FISH
BULL-WHALES	FIELD-BEE	LINNET	ROAN	TURKEY
BUNNY	FIREFLIES	LION +	ROBIN	TURKEY-COCK
BURROW	FISH +	LIZARD +	ROOKS +	TURTLES
BUTTERFLY +	FLEA +	LOBSTER	ROOSTER	VULTURE
BUZZARD	FLOWER-SERPENT	LOCUSTS	SALAMANDERS	WAGTAIL
CALF +	FLY +	MALLARD	SCORPION	WAR-PONIES
CAMEL	FOALS	MARES	SEA-BIRDS	WASP
CANARY	FOWL +	MASTODON	SEA-CRAB	WATER-BUFFALOES
CAT +	FOX +	MEADOW-LARK	SEA-FOWL	WATER-HEN
CATERPILLARS	FROG +	MICE	SEA-GULL	WEASEL
CATTLE	GAD-FLIES	MINNOWS	SEAL	WHALE +
CHAFFINCH	GAZELLE-CALF	MOLES	SERPENT	WILD-BEAST
CHICK +	GEESE	MONGRELS	SHARKS	WILD-GOOSE
CHICKEN +	GLOW-WORMS +	MONKEY	SHE-DOLPHIN	WOLF +
CHOUGH	GOAT +	MOSQUITO +	SHE-DOVE	WOODPIGEONS +
CICALA	GOOSE	MOTHS	SHEEP	WORM +
COBRA	GRASSHOPPER	MOUSE	SHEEP-DOG	

APPENDIX III: NATURE

C. FRUITS, FLOWERS, AND TREES

ACANTHUS	CHICKWEED-FLOWER	GERANIUM +	MAGNOLIA-LIKE	SEED
ACONITE	CLOVE	GLOBE-FLOWERS	MAIZE	SNAPDRAGON
ACORNS	CLOVER	GLOIRE DE DIJON ROSES	MALLOW-FLOWER	SNOW-BERRIES
ALMOND	COCK'S-FOOT	GOOSEBERRIES	MANGO	SORB-APPLES
ALMOND-BLOSSOM	COCOA-NUT	GORSE-BUSHES	MARIGOLD	SORREL

*THROUGHOUT THE APPENDICES A PLUS SIGN FOLLOWING AN ENTRY INDICATES THAT THERE ARE VARIANTS, PLURALS, OR COMPOUNDS IN THE CONCORDANCE WHICH ARE NOT LISTED HERE. SEE INTRODUCTION.

APPENDIX III C (CONT.)

ALMOND-TREE
ANEMONE
APPLE
APPLE-BLOSSOM
APPLE-TREES
APRICOT-BLOSSOM
ASH-TREES
ASPEN
ASPEN-TREES
AURICULAR
AZALEA
BALSAM
BALSAM-PINES
BAMBOO
BANANA-SKIN
BAVARIAN GENTIANS
BEAN
BEAN-POD
BEECH +
BEECH-LEAF +
BERRY +
BIRCH
BIRCH-TREE +
BLACKBERRY +
BLADE
BLOSSOM +
BLUEBELL +
BLUE-GRASS
BOUGH +
BOWER +
BRANCHES
BREAD-FRUIT TREES
BUD +
BULBS
BUTTER CUP
CABAGE +
CABBAGE
CACTUS +
CALYX
CAMELLIA
CAMPION
CANE-BREAK
CARNATION
CAROB-TREE
CATKINS
CEDAR
CEDAR-BOUGHS
CEDAR-BUSH
CEDAR-MOTTLED
CEDAR-ROOTS
CHERRY
CHERRY-TREE
CHESTNUT-FLOWER

COFFEE-PLANT
COLTSFOOT FLOWERS
COLT'S-FOOT FLOWERS
COLUMBINE FLOWER
CORN +
CORNSTALKS +
COTTON
COTTON-WOOD
COWSLIPS
CRANBERRIES
CROCUS +
CROWFLOWER
CYCLAMEN +
CYPRESS +
CYPRESS-TREES
DAFFODIL +
DAISY +
DAISY-FROTH
DANDELIONS
DEWBERRIES
EARTH-GRASS
ELDER
ELDER-FLOWERS
ELDER-TREES
ELMS
ELM-TREE
ERMINE MOTH'S
FERN +
FERN-SEED
FESCUE
FESTOON
FIG +
FIG-FRUIT
FIG-LEAF +
FIG-TREE
FIRS
FIRST-FLOWER +
FIR-TREE
FIR-WORT
FLOWER +
FLOWERBELL
FLOWER-MESH
FLOWER-ROOTS
FLOWER-VINE
FOLIAGE
FORAMENIFORAE
FORGET-ME-NOTS
FOXGLOVE +
FOX-TAIL
FRUIT +
FUCHSIA
FUNGUS
GENTIAN +

GORSE-FLOWERS
GOURD +
GOURD-SHELLS
GRAIN +
GRAMINIFERAS
GRAPE +
GRAPE-VINES
GRASS +
GRASS-FLOWERS
GRASS-LEAVES
GUAVA TREES
GUELDER
GUELDER-ROSE
HAREBELLS
HAWTHORNE
HAY
HAY-SEED
HAYSTACK +
HAZEL +
HAZEL-NUTS
HAZEL-WOODS
HEATH-BELLS
HEATHER
HEDGE
HEDGEROW
HELLEBORE
HENNA
HERBAGE
HIBISCUS +
HIBISCUS TREE
HOLLY
HONEYCOMB
HONEYSUCKLE
HUMUS
HUSK
HUSK-BALL
HYACINTH +
IRIS
JASMINE
JONQUILS
JOY-BLOSSOMS
JUNIPER
KING-CUPS
LABURNUM
LARCH
LARKSPUR
LEAF
LICHENS
LILAC
LILIES
LIME-TREE
LOG
LOTUS LILIES

MAY-BLOSSOM
MIGNONETTE
MISTLETOE
MOLY
MOSS
MUD-WEED
MULBERRY
MULLEINS
MUSHROOM
MYRRH
NARCISSUS
NENUPHARS
NETTLES
OLEANDER
OLIVE +
POMPOMS
ORANGE-TREES
ORCHID-LIKE
PALM-TREES
PANSY +
PAPPUS
PASSION-FLOWER
PEACH +
PEAR
PEAR-BLOSSOM
PEAS-COD
PEE-WHIPS
PEONY
PERIWINKLES
PETALS
PINES
PIPPINS
PLANT
PLUMS
PLUM-TREES
POMEGRANATE
POPLAR
POPPIES
POTATOES
PRIMROSE
QUINCE BLOSSOM
RAISIN
RHODODENDRONS
RICE
ROOTS
ROSACEAE
ROSE +
RYE
SALVIA
SCYLLAS
SEA-ANEMONE
SEA POPPIES
SEA-WEED

SPICES
SPRUCE-TREES
SQUASH-BLOSSOM
STALK
STAMENS
STEM
STRAW
STRAWBERRIES
SYCAMORE
SYRINGA BUDS
TENDRIL +
THICKET +
THISTLE +
THISTLEDOWN
THORN +
THORN-BLOSSOM
THORN-LEAVES
THORN-TREE
THYME
TIGER-LILIES
TOAD-LEAVES
TOADSTOOL +
TORCH-FLOWER +
TOTTERING-GRASS
TREE +
TULIPS
TURF
TURNIP
TURRETS
TWIG +
UNDERGROWTH
VANILLA
VEGETABLE +
VETCH-CLUMP
VINE +
VIOLET +
WATER-FLOWER
WATER-LILIES
WEED +
WHEAT
WILD-FLOWER
WILD-THYME
WILLOW +
WIND-FLOWERS
WINTER-GREEN
WOOD-ASH
WOODBINE
WREATH +
YEW-TREE +

APPENDIX III: NATURE

D. TIME, SEASONS, AND CYCLES

AEONS
AFTER-NIGHT
AFTERNOON
AGE
AGE-AFTER-AGE
AUTUMN +
AXIS
CENTURY
CHRISTMAS
CLIME
CYCLE
DAILY
DARK
DAWN +
DAY +

DAYBREAK
DAYLIGHT
DAYTIME +
DECEMBER
DUSK
EAST
EBB-TIME
EPOCH
ERA
EVENING
EVOLUTION
FEBRUARY
FLOOD-DAWN
HARVEST +
HOUR +

ICE-AGE
JANUARY
JULY
JUNE
MARCH
MID-DAY
MID-MORNING
MIDNIGHT
MIDSUMMER +
MONTH
MORNING +
NIGHT
NOON
NORTH +
NOVEMBER

OCTOBER
RAIN
RAINBOW
SEPTEMBER
SNOW
SOLSTICE
SOUTH +
SPRING +
STORM +
SUMMER +
SUNDAY
SUNDOWN
SUNRISE
SUNSET
TEMPORAL

THRESHING-TIME
TIME +
TODAY +
TOMORROW +
TONIGHT +
TWILIGHT +
UNDERDUSK +
WEATHER
WEEK +
WEST
YEAR +
YESTERDAY +

APPENDIX III: NATURE

E. ELEMENTS AND MINERALS

AIR
ALUMINA
AMETHYST
AQUEOUS
ASH
ATMOSPHERE
ATOM
BALE-FIRE
BLAZE +
BONFIRE
BRIMSTONE
BRIMSTONE-MOLTEN +
BRONZE
BURN
CLOUD +
CLOUD REAVES
COAL
COPPER
CRYSTAL

CRYSTALLINE
CUMULUS
DIRT
DUST
EARTH
ELECTRON
ELEMENT +
EMERALD
ENERGY +
FIRE +
FLAME +
FLOOD
FOG
FROST +
GEM +
GOLD
GRAVEL
HEAT +
HOT +

HYDROGEN
H2O
IRON
JASPER
JEWEL
LAVA
LIGHTNING
LIQUID
MARBLE
METEORITE
MIST
MOON
MUD
QUARTZ
QUICKSILVER
RAIN
RAINBOW
ROCK +
RUBY

SALT
SAPPHIRE +
SEA
SILVER
SIRIUS
SKY +
SMOKE
SNOW
SPACE
STAR +
STONE
STORM +
SUBAQUEOUS
SUGAR
SULPHUR
SUN
SUNLIGHT
SUN-RAYS
SUNSHINE

TERRA FIRMA
TERRESTRIAL
THUNDER +
THUNDERBOLT +
TIDE +
TORCH +
TORRENT
UNDERMIST
UNDERWATER
UNIVERSE
URANUS
VAPOUR
VEGA
VENUS
WATER +
WAVE +
WHIRLWIND +
WIND +

APPENDIX IV: ANATOMY, PHYSIOLOGY, AND SENSES

ANKLE
APPETITE
ARM
ARSE
ATROPHY
AUDILE
BACKBONE +
BEARD +
BEGET +
BELCHING
BELLY +
BLADDER
BLIND +
BLOOD +
BLOOD-PRESSURE
BODY +
BONE +
BOSOM +
BOTTOM +
BOWELS
BRAIN +
BREAST +
BREATH
BREATHE
BROW
BUTTOCKS
BUTTS
CARCASS
CARNAL
CAUL
CELLS
CEREBRAL +
CHEEK +
CHEST +
CHEW
CHIN

COITION
COPULATE
CORPORAL (EXISTENCE)
CORPSE +
COUNTENANCE
CRANIUM
CUNT
DEAF +
DIASTOLE
DRINK +
DUMB
EAR +
EAT
ELBOW +
EMASCULATED
EMBRYOS
ENTRAILS
EYE +
EYEBROW
EYELIDS
FACE +
FEEL +
FEET
FIBRE +
FINGER +
FINGER-NAILS
FISSURE
FIST +
FLANK
FLESH +
FOOT
FOREHEAD +
FORESKINS
FORNICATE
GENITALS
GUMS

GUTS +
HAIR +
HAMS
HAND +
HAUNCHES
HEAD +
HEART +
HEEL +
HICCUP
HIPS
HUNGER +
INAUDIBLE
INDIGESTIBLE
INTESTINES
JOHN THOMAS
JOLLY LITTLE MEMBER
KATABOLISM
KISS +
KNEE
LAP
LAUGH
LEG +
LIMB +
LIP +
LISTEN +
LOINS
LOOK +
LUNGS
MAIMED
MARROW
MEMBRANED
MOUTH
MUSCULAR
MUTILATED
NAPE
NECK

NERVES
NEUROSTHENIC
NIPPLE
NOSE
NOSTRILS
ODOUR
ORGAN
ORGASM
PALM
PATE
PENIS
PHALLUS
PHLEGM
PLASM
PUDENDA
PULSE
REAR
RIBS
SCALP
SEE
SEED
SENSE +
SEX +
SHOULDER +
SIGHT +
SINEW
SKIN
SKULL
SLEEP
SMELL +
SMILE +
SNIFF
SNORE
SOB
SOCKETS
SPEAK +

SPEECH +
SPERM
SPINE
SPIT
STOMACH
SUCK
SWALLOW +
SWEAT +
SYSTOLE
TACTILE
TALK +
TASTE +
TEAR +
TEETH
TEMPLE
THIGH
THIRST +
THROAT +
THUMB
THUMB-NAIL
TOES
TONGUE +
TOOTH +
TOUCH +
TURD +
UTERUS
UTTER +
VEIN +
VISION +
VOICE +
WAIST
WHISKERS
WOMB +
WRIST +
YONI

APPENDIX V: SCIENCE AND TECHNOLOGY

ABSTRACTION
AEROPLANES
AIR-BOMBS
AIR-SHIPS
ALGEBRA
ANAESTHETIC
ANALYSIS
ANALYST
ANATOMISED
ANT-EYES
ANTHROPOLOGISTS
ANTI-LIFE
ANT-MEN
ANVIL
APOTHEOSIS
APPARATUS
AQUA REGIA
ARC-LAMP
ARITHMETIC
ARMADA
ARMOUR
ARTILLERY
ASBESTOS
ASPHALT
ASSEMBLY
ATOM
AUTOMAT
AUTOMATA
AUTOMATIC-MACHINE
AUTOMATON
AUTOMOBILE +
AXE

AXLE
BARBED-WIRE
BAYONET
BELL +
BENZENE
BODILESS
BOMBS
BOTTLES
BOWELS (OF STEEL)
BRAINS
BRAINY (ROBOT)
BRASS +
BRASS-RESONANT
BRAZIER
BRONZE
BULLETS
CACHINNATION +
CAGE
CALCULATIONS
CAMION
CANNON
CAPSICUM ESSENCE
CAR + (ELECTRIC)
CARPENTER
CELLULOID
CEMENT
CHAIN
CHEMICAL
CHEMICALISED
CHEMIST'S
CHISEL
CINEMA

CITY +
CLOCK +
COCAINE
COG-WHEEL
COILS +
COMPASSES
CORROSION +
CRAFTSMAN'S (NERVE)
CRESSET
CRUCIBLE
DECIMALS
DENTY (CARS)
DEVICES
DOCTOR
DOOR-KNOBS
DOSE +
DRUG
DYNAMO
EGO
EGO-BOUND
ELECTRICITY +
ELECTRON
ENERGY +
ENGINE +
ETHNOLOGY
EVIL +
FARM-IMPLEMENTS
FARM-MACHINERY
FILM
FLY-WHEEL
FORGE
FRICTION

FUMES
FURNACE
GAS +
GEOMETRY
GOLD-MINES
GRAMAPHONE
GRAVITY
GUN +
HOOK +
HUB
HYGIENE
IMPLEMENTS
INDUSTRIAL +
INDUSTRY
INVENTED
IRON +
LABORATORY
LAMP +
MACHINE
MAGNET
MANUFACTURING
MATTER
MECHANIC +
METAL +
MINING
MORPHINE
MOTOR +
OIL
OXYDISED
OXYGEN
PETROL
POISON

QUANTUM +
QUARTZ
QUICKSILVER
RADIO +
RAILWAY
RELATIVITIES
ROBOT +
ROCKET +
SCIENCE
SPARK
STEEL
SURGEON
SURGICAL
SYPHILITIC
TABLET (MATHEMATICAL)
TELEPHONE
TELESCOPE
THEORIES
THERMOMETER
THINK +
THOUGHT +
TRAIN +
TRAM +
TRANSMITTERS
UNGODLY (KNOWLEDGE)
URINAL (THE DIRTY MIND)
VEHICLES
VENOM
VERDIGRIS
WHEEL +
WIRE +
WIRELESS

APPENDIX VI: RELIGION, MYTHOLOGY, AND METAPHYSICS

ABSOLUTE
ABSOLUTE ONE
ABSOLUTION
ABSOLUTISM
ABSTRACTION
ABYSS
ACHILLES
ACT OF FAITH
ADAM
ADONIS
ADVENT
AEGEAN
AFRICAN
AFRICA'S
AFTER-LIFE
ALIVE
ALL-CREATIVE
ALL-FORE-ORDAINING
ALL-KNOWING
ALL-SEEING
ALL SOULS' DAY
ALL-WISE
ALMIGHTY
ALMIGHTY GOD
ALMIGHTY MAMMON

CHASTITY +
CHERUBIM
CHERUBIM OF JUDGMENT
CHERUBS
CHIMAERA +
CHOIR
CHORISTERS
CHORUS
CHRISM
CHRIST
CHRISTIANITY +
CHRISTMAS
CHRISTUS
CHURCH +
CHURCH OF ROME
CHURCH-TOWER
CHURCHYARD
CLEOPATRA
COLUMN OF FIRE
COMER
COMET +
COMMUNION
CONCEPTION
CONSCIENCE
CONSCIOUS SELF

FEAST OF CORPUS CHRISTI
FEATHERED SNAKE
FEMALE
FIRE +
FIRST BORN
FLAME +
FLOOD +
FORE-GOD-LIKE
GABRIEL
GETHSEMANE
GHOST +
GLOBE +
GLORY
GOD +
GODDESS +
GOD-GIVEN
GOD HEAD
GODHEAD IN MAN
GODLIVERS
GODS OF TIRYNS
GOOD
GOOD FRIDAY
GORGON'S HEAD
GRACE
GRAIL

LOGIC
LORD +
LOVE
LOT'S WIFE
LUCIFER
MACROCOSM
MADONNA
MAGI
MAHOMET
MAKER
MAN
MANA
MANNA
MARE
MARY +
MASS
MASTER
MASTODON
MATTHEW
MEDUSA'S
MERCURY
MICHAEL +
MIND
MINOAN +
MINOS

REPENTANCE +
RESURRECT +
RESURRECTION
RISEN MAN
ROCK OF AGES
ROSARY
SABBATH
SACKCLOTH
SACRED
SACRED FISH
SAINTS
SALT
SALVATION
SAMSON
SANDALS
SATAN
SATURN
SAVAGE
SAVIOUR
SEA-BEASTS
SEA-GOD
SEA-NYMPHS
SECRET
SELF +
SERAPHIM

ALMIGHTY NULLUS
ALTAIR
ALTAR
AMAZON
AMEN
AMERICAN INDIAN
AMERINDIAN
AM-NOT
ANAXAGORAS
ANGEL +
ANGEL OF JUDGMENT
ANIMATE
ANNIHILATE
ANNUNCIATION
ANOINT
ANTI-LIFE
ANTIPODES
APHRODITE
APOCALYPTIC
APOLLO
APOTHEOSIS
APPLE-OF-SODOM
ARARAT
ARCH
ARCHAIC
ARCHANGELS
ARES
ARGONAUTS'
ARGOSY
ARISTOCRACY
ARISTOCRAT
ARK
ARK OF THE COVENANT
ARTEMIS
ASCENT
ASHTAROTH
ASSYRIAN-WISE
ASTARTE
AS-YET-UNKNOWABLE
ATOM
ATTILA
ATTIS
AUTO-DA-FE
AUTUMNUS
AZTEC
BAAL
BABEL
BACCHAE
BACCANTE
BACCHUS
BALAAM'S ASS
BALDER
BAPTISED
BARBARIC +
BEING
BELIAL
BELIEF +
BETELGEUSE
BIBLE
BLACK PRINCE
BLASPHEMY +
BLESS +
BLOOD-SACRIFICES
BREAD
BUDDHA
BUSHMAN
CALVARY
CARNAL
CENTAUR
CEREMONIES +
CERES
CHALICES
CHANTING
CHAOS
CHAPLETS

CONSCIOUSNESS
CONSECRATE
CONSTELLATION
CONSUMMATION +
CONSUMMATUM EST
CORPUS
CORPUS CHRISTI
COSMIC
COSMOS
CREATION
CREATIVE GODHEAD
CREATOR
CROSS
CRUCIBLE
CRUCIFIED
CRUCIFIX
CRUCIFIXION
CURSE
CYCLOP +
DAIMONS
DANAE
DANCE +
DARK-CREATION
DARK-MASKED-ONE
DARKNESS
DAVID
DAWN-STAR
DAY-SUN
DEAD +
DEATH +
DELIVER
DELIVERANCE
DELUGE
DEMETER'S
DEMI-URGE
DEMOCRACY +
DEMON +
DEMOS
DESIRE
DEVIL +
DIE
DIONYSOS +
DIS
DISCOVERER
DIVES
DIVINE +
DOG-STAR
DORA
DOVE +
DOVE OF THE SPIRIT
DRAGON +
DRUID
EAST
EDEN
ELECTRON
ELEMENT +
ELYSIUM
EMPYREAN
EQUILIBRIUM
ERINNYES
ETERNAL +
ETERNITY
ETRURIA
ETRUSCAN +
EVE +
EVENING STAR
EVERLASTING
EVIL +
EXISTENCE
EXPIATION +
FAFNIR
FAITH +
FATA MORGANA
FATE +
FATHER NEPTUNE

HADES
HALO
HARMONY
HEATHEN
HEAVEN +
HEAVENLY HOST
HELIOS
HELIOTROPE
HELL +
HELL-HOUNDS
HERMES
HESPERIDES
HIERARCHY +
HINDU +
HISTORY +
HOLY
HOLY GHOST
HOLY MARY
HOLY OF HOLIES
HORIZONTAL DIVISION
HORSE +
HOST +
HORUS
HUITZILOPOCHTLI
HYACINTHUS
IACCOS
ICE-AGE
ICHTHYOSAURUS
IDEA +
IDOLS
IMAGE +
IMMACULATELY CONCEIVED
IMMORAL +
IMMORTAL
IMMORTALITY
IMPULSE
INANIMATE
INCARNATE
INCARNATION
INDIVIDUAL
INERTIA
INFINITE
INFINITY
INNOCENT
INSTINCT +
INTELLECT +
INTUITION +
INVISIBLE
IO
ISIS
ITHYPHALLIC
IXTACCIHUATL
IXTHYS
JEHOVAH
JESSE
JESUS +
JOY-IN-RESURRECTION
JUDAH
JUDAS +
JUNGLE
KINGDOM
KNOW +
KRISHNA
KRONOS
LAMB
LANGUAGE
LAOCOON
LATTER-DAY
LAW +
LEARN +
LETTER OF LAW
LETTER OF TRUTH
LIFE +
LIGHT
LIVE

MIRACLE
MISSAL
MOHAMMEDAN +
MOLOCH
MONSTER
MONTEZUMA
MOON
MORAL +
MORTAL
MOSES
MOTHER OF GOD
MYSTERY
NEIGHBOR
NEMESIS
NIHIL +
NIRVANA
NOAH'S FLOOD
NON-EXISTENCE +
NON-LIFE +
NOT-BEING
NOTHING +
NOT-ME +
NULL
NULLITY
NULLUS
OBLIVION
ODYSSEUS
ONLY-BEGOTTEN
ORION
ORPHIC
ORTHODOX
PARACLETE
PARADISE
PARTHENON
PASSION
PEACE
PELASGIC
PERSEPHONE
PERSEUS
PENTECOST
PHILANTHROPY
PHOENICIAN
PHOENIX
PINNACLE
PISCES
PISGAH
PLATO
PLUTO
POWER
PRAY
PREHENSILE
PRE-ORDAINING
PRE-WORLD
PRIAPUS
PRIEST
PRIMEVAL
PRINCIPLE
PROCREATION
PROSERPINE
PROVIDENCE
PTERODACTYL
PYRAMID
PYTHAGORAS
QUETZALCOATL +
RA
REAL
REALITY
REASON
RE-BORN
RED-CROSS
RED-DAWN-WOLF
RE-INCARNATING
RELIGION +
REMISSION
RENASCENCE

SERPENT +
SHAME-WOUNDS
SHAPER
SHIP OF DEATH +
SIN
SINLESS
SIRIUS
SIVA
SKELETON
SKIES
SLEEP
SNAKE
SODOM
SOLOMON
SON OF GOD
SON OF MAN
SON OF THE MORNING
SOUL +
SPHINXES
SPIRIT
STAR OF EVENING
STOIC
STRUGGLE
SUBSTANCE
SUN +
SUN-ARISTOCRATS
SUN-AWARENESS
SUPREME +
SURPLICES
SWORD OF DAMOCLES
SYMBOL +
SYRACUSAN
TABERNACLE
TEMPLE
TEXTS
THE FISH (JESUS)
THOUGHT +
TRANSFIGURATION
TRANSUBSTANTIATION
TREE OF LIFE
TRUTH
TUATHA DE DANAAN
ULTIMATE
UNCONSCIOUS
UNDERSTAND
UNDERWORLD
UNDINE
UNIVERSE
UNKNOWN +
UNKNOWN MOVER
UNMENTAL
UNREAL +
UNSCIENTIFIC
UNSEEN SHAPER
UNTHINKING GODS
UNUTTERABLE +
UPRIGHT DIVISION
URANUS
VEGA
VENGEANCE
VENUS
VIRGIN +
VITALITY
VIVIFIER
VOTARESSES
WATER-LORDS
WATER-SERPENT
WISDOM
WITNESSES
WOMAN +
WOMB +
WORD +
WORLD +
WORSHIP +
ZEUS

APPENDIX VII: POLITICS AND SOCIAL COMMENTARY

AMERICAN
AMERICAN GOVERNMENT
ANARCHY
ANT-LIFE
ANT-MEN
APOLLO-BELVEDERE
ARISTOCRACY
ARISTOCRAT
ARMIES
ARMOUR
ARTILLERY
ASSES (INTELLECTUAL)
ATROPHY (SENSUAL)
AUREOLED IDEAL
AUTHORITY
BACHELOR OF CASH ARTS
BANK +
BANK-BOOK
BANK-NOTES
BARBED-WIRE
BENEVOLENCE
BLUE-ARSED
BOARD-SCHOOL +

COSMOPOLITANISM
CRIPPLED
CRITICAL
CROWN
CULTURE +
CULTURED CANAILLE
CURS
CYNICISM
DANCE +
DANDY
DEAD +
DEATH +
DEBAUCHED
DECAYING
DECENT +
DEGENERATE
DEMOCRACY +
DEMONISH NEW WORLD
DEPRAVED
DESTROY
DETEST
DICKLETS.
DIE

EUNUCHS
EVANGELIST
EVIL +
EXISTENCE
FELLOW-MAN +
GARBAGE
GAS
GELDED
GELDINGS
GENERATION +
GENTLEMAN
GOD-DAMN BOURGEOISIE
GODLESS
GOLD-MINES
GOVERNMENT +
GRAND INQUISITOR
GREED +
HATE +
HUMANITY
HYPOCRISY +
ICONOCLAST
IDEALS +
IDIOT +

LONG-HAIRED
LOVE
LOVE-AFFAIRS
LOVE-BITCH
LOW-BORN
LOWER CLASSES
LUNACY +
LYING
MADAME CERES
MAGISTRATE
MAGNATE
MAMMON
MAN
MANKIND
MAN-LIFE
MARTYRS
MARXIAN
MASS +
MATERIALISTIC
MATERIAL-MECHANICAL
MATHEMATICAL
MAW
MEMBER

POSE
PRIEST +
PRIME MINISTER
PROBLEM
PROFESSOR +
PROFITEERS
PROLETARIAT
PROVIDENCE-BULL
PUBLIC
PURITAN +
PURVEYORS
PUSS PUSS
PUSSYFOOT
RADICAL
REFORM
RELIGION +
REVOLUTION +
RICH
ROBOT +
ROT +
RULERS
SANE
SCHOOL +

BOBBIES	DIRT-EATING	IDOLS	MENTAL	SCIENCE +
BOLSHEVIST +	DIRTY +	IMBECILITY +	MIDDLE-CLASS	SELF +
BOMBS	DISEASED	IMPRISONED	MILL +	SERVANT
BOURGEOIS	DISGUSTING	INCOME	MINORITIES	SEX
BOURGEOSIE	DISHONESTY	INDIAN BUREAU	MOB	SIR JESSE BOOT
BRITANNIA	DISTASTEFUL	INDUSTRIAL	MODERN	SLAVE
BRITISH	DOCTOR +	INFERIOR +	MONEY +	SMART
BRITISH PUBLIC	DOG-FISH	INHUMAN	MORE-THAN-EUROPEAN	SOCIAL +
B SC	DOGGIE (JOHN BULL)	INQUISITION	MULTIMILLIONAIRE	SOCIALISTS
BUB-EAGLE	DOLLARS	INSANITY +	MULTITUDE	SOCIETY
BULL-BITCH (DEMOCRATIC)	DOMESTICITY +	INSTITUTE +	MUNDANE EGG	SODOM
BULL-MONGREL	DOMINANT	INTELLECTUAL +	MONEY COMPULSION	SODOMY +
BUSY-BUSY BOBBIES	DOMINEERING	INTELLIGENTSIA	MURDER	SOVIET +
CABBAGE-IDEALISTIC	DON JUAN	INTERNATIONAL	NOBLE +	SPAWN
CAGE	DOOM	INVENTED +	NOBLESSE	SPY-GOVERNMENT
CAPITAL +	DRAGON +	ISLAND	NOBLESSE OBLIGE	STRANGLE
CAPTIVITY	DUMMY-TEAT	JAZZ	NO-MAN'S-LAND	SYSTEM
CARRION +	DUNG	JEW	NO-MAN'S-LIFE	TOMLETS
CARYATIDS	DUNLOP	JIG +	NORTH	TRADITION
CASH +	DYNAMO	JOHN BULL	OFFICE +	UGLY
CASTRATED SOCIETY	EARNINGS +	JOHNNIES	OVERSEER	UNHOLY INQUISITION
CAUSE +	ECZEMA	JUDGES	OXFORD +	UNIVERSALISM +
CENSOR +	EDITOR	JUSTICE	PALEFACE	UNLIVING
CHEMICALISED WOMEN	EDUCATION	KILL +	PAPACEA	UPPER-CLASS +
CHRISTIAN CANAILLE	EGO	KING	PARTIES	VICE +
CHRISTIANITY	EGO-BOUND	KING'S ENGLISH	PATENT	VOTE +
CIRCE-DOM (MODERN)	EGOCENTRIC +	KNELL	PATRIOTIC	WAGES +
CIVILISATION	EMPLOYERS	LABOUR +	PEACE-TALKING	WALLET-CARRYING-WOMEN
CLASS +	ENFRANCHISED WOMEN	LADIES	PEONS	WAR +
CLERGYMEN	ENGLISH	LECHERY	PERAMBULATOR	WEALTHY
COLLECTIVE MADNESS	ENGLISHMAN +	LENIN +	PISTON-MECHANICAL-BEGOTTEN	WILLY WET-LEG +
COMMERCE	EN MASSE	LIBERALS	PLATO	WOMEN
COMMUNISM	ENTANGLED	LIBERTY	PINCE-NEZ	WORD +
CONSERVATIVES	ENTERPRISE	LITTLE-BOY	POLICE	WORK +
CONVERSATION	EQUALITY	LIVE-BY-LOVE	POLICIES	WORLD +
CORPSE +	ETON	LIVING-DEAD	POLITICAL	
CORROSION +	ETON-ADONIS	LLOYD GEORGE	POOR	

APPENDIX VIII: DIALECT AND ARCHAISMS

ABAHT	'EAR	LASS	SCREETIN'	'TWAS
ACAUSE	'E'D	LETTIN'	S'D	'TWILL
'AD	E'EN	LICKIN'	SEED	TWINKLIN'
'AFFLE	'EERD-ON	LIDIES	SEEIN'	'TWIXT
AFORE	'EERED	LIDY	SHALT	'UD
AH'N	EH	LIETH	SHANNA	UN
AH'VE	'E'LL	LOOKIN'	SHAN'T	UNBEKNOWN
ALLERS	'EM	LOVIN'	SH'D	UNDERSTAN'S
ALLUS	'EN	LYIN'	SHILLN	UNDROSSED
A'MOST	'ER	MA	SHONNA	UNTO
AN'	ER'D	MA'AM	SIN'	VERILY
'ANDFUL	'ERE	MA'E	SITHEE	WA'
ANYTHINK	'ER'LL	MAKIN'	SITTIN'	WAFTIN'
'APPEN	'ER'S	MARD-ARSED	SKI'D	WAITIN'
'ARD	ERST	MARRYIN'	SLARTS	WALY
ARENA	'E'S	MAUN	SLIVE	WANTIN
ARE-NA	FARVER (FATHER)	MESTER'S	S'LL	WANTIN'
'ARK	FLAMIN'	MIGHTN'T	SLUDGED	WARANT
ART	FLIG	MISSIS	SNUFFIN'	WARMIN
'AS	FLOURISHETH	MOVVER	SOBBIN'	WATCHIN'
'ASN'T	FORCIN'	MOWIN'	SO'S	WEALD
'AST	F'R	MUN	SPILT	WEDDIN'
ATWEEN	GEL	MYSEN	SPUNK	WEDDIN'-DRESS
'AVE	GEN	MY-SEN	STANDIN'	WEE
'AVIN'	GENT	NA-THE	STAN'S	WELKIN
AX	GETTIN'	NAVVIES	STOCKIN'S	WENCH
AXIN'	GIE	'NEATH	STOOPIN'	WENCH'S
AY	GI'E	NE'D	STUMBLETH	WENDING
AYE	GOEST	NEDNA	SUCKIN'	WENDS
BARK	GOETH	NEDN'T	SUCKIN-IN	WERT
BEIN'	GOIN'	NIVER	SUMMAT	WESH
BELIEVIN'	GOOD-UN	NOBBUT	SWOUND	WHATIVER
BEOUT	GOTTEN	NODDIN'	T'	WHEER
BETT'R	GRASPIN'	NOTHIN'	TA'E	WHEER'S
BIDE	GRESS	NOWT	TA'EIN	WHELMED
BIN	GRET	N'R	TA'EN	WHENCE
BIT	GROWSE	NUB'DY	TAKIN'	WHILST
BLOOMIN'	GUVNOR	O'ER	TEEMIN'	WHITHER
BRINGIN'	HA'	OFF'N	TELLIN'	WHOAM
BURSTEN	HADNA	'OME	TER	WI
BURSTIN'	HA'E	ON'T	TER'S	WI'
BUSTIN'	HAFFLE	ON'Y	TH'	WIDDER
CAFFLE	HAN	'OORAY	THA	WIDDER'S
CANNA	HANKERIN'	OPE	THA'D	WIK
CANST	HA'PENNY	ORMIN'	THA'LL	WILT
CARRYIN'	H'ARENA	ORTS	THA'LT	WIST
CARRYIN'S	HASNA	OTCHEL	THALT'	WITHERIN'
'CASIONS	HAST	OUGHTER	THA'RT	WITHOUTEN
C'D	HATH	'OUSE	THA'S	WOKEN
CH'ARE	HAVIN'	'OW	THEE	WOR
CHILDT	HEAD-STUN	OWER	THEER	WORNA
CLAWKIN'	HEARIN'	OWT	THENCE	WORN'T
CLEANIN'	HIE	OWT'LL	THINE	WORROW
CLOMB	HIS'N	P'LICEMAN'S	THITHER	WORSER
COLLEYFOGLIN'	HISSELF	PRAYIN'	THOU	WORSTED
COMIN'	HIS-SEN	QUIZZ	THOU'LT	WOW
COS	HITHER	RAT BAIRNES	THOU'RT	WOWSER
COULDNA	HOVERIN'	REAVER	THOWT	WRANGLE
COULDNA'	HUDDLIN'	RECKON	THRICE	WRIT
COURTIN'	I'	REELROAD	THY	WUNNA
CROSSIN'	INGINES		THYSELF	YE

CUDDLIN'	INTIL	REMOVETH	THY-SEN	YEA
'D	IVER	RUM (ODD, QUEER)	'TICED	YER
DOESNA	IV'RYBODY	RUNNEST	'TIS	YER'D
DOIN'	I'STEAD	'S	T'OTHER	YER'VE
DOST	KEP	SAITH	TOWD	YI
DREE (TEDIOUS)	KID	SAYIN'	TRIMMIN'	YIS
DRIPPIN	KISSIN'	SAY'T	TRODE	YO'
DUNNA	KNOCKIN'	SCRAIGHT	TRUDGE	YO'N
DUNNAT	KNOWED	SCRAIGHTED	TRYIN'	YOU'S
DUNNO	KNOWIN'	SCRAIGHTIN'	T'S	
D'YER	LAD	SCRATCH	TWAIN	
'E	LARROPIN'	SCREET	TWAS	

APPENDIX IX: MISCELLANEOUS

A. NAMES

ADAM	CIUCO	ISAR	MR. GOD	SANGRE DE CRISTO
ADOLPH	CYPRIAN'S	ITALY +	MR. LAWRENCE	MOUNTAINS
ALYOSHAS	CYTHERA	JAMES	MR. MEAD	SCANDINAVIAN
AMERICA +	DAMOCLES	JANE	MR. MEADE	SHAKESPEARE
ANDREW	DANIELE MANIN	JAPAN	MR. SMITH	SICILY +
ANNA	DANTE	JEANNETTE	MR. SQUIRE	SIEGMUND
ANNA KARENIN	DAVID	JESUS	MR. WATTS	SIERRA ROQUENA
ANNAS	DIABLERETS	JOAQUIN	MRS. JUSTICE ENNIS	SIR CLIFFORD
ANTHONY	DMITRIS	JOCK'S	MRS. NAYLOR	SIR JESSE BOOT
ARAB	DONA CARLOTA	JOHANNINE	MUNCHEN	SOLOMON
ARCHIBALD	DON JUAN	JOHN	MYCENAE	SOMARO
ARCHIE	DON RAMON	JOSEPH	NAPOLEAN	SOMERS
ARNO	DORA	JOVE	NAVAJO	SOUTH WEST +
ARTHUR HOLLIDAY'S	DOSTOEVSKY +	JUDAH	NAXOS	SOVIET +
ASINELLO	DUNCAN	JUDAS +	NEW MEXICO	STAVROGINS
ATLANTIC	DUNLOP	KILOSSA	NEW ORLEANS	STEPPES OF TARTARY
ATTILA	EGYPT +	LADY C	NICHOLAS	ST. GEORGE
AUNT GWEN	EKKE	LADY JANE	NICK	ST. STEPHEN'S
AUNT GWENDOLINE	EKKERHART	LADY JEAN	NILE	SURREY
AUNT LIBBY'S	EMBABA	LAWRENCE	NORTH +	SWITZERLAND
AUNT LOU	EMPEDOKLES	LEAR	NORTH SEA	SYDENHAM
AUNT LOUIE'S	ENGLAND +	LEEDS	NORWOOD HILL	TAOS
AUNTIE MAUD	ENNA (ITALY)	LENIN	NOTTINGHAM	TAULOW
AUSTRALIA	ERECHTHEION	LEON	OKLAHOMA INDIANS	TCHEKOV
AUSTRIA	ETNA +	LEONARDO	PAMELIE	TED +
BALTIC	EUROPE +	LINCOLNSHIRE	PARIS	TERENCE
BAVARIA	EVA	LIZ	PATMOS	TERESA
BEETHOVEN	EVE	LIZZIE	PELASGIC	THEBAID
BENJAMIN FRANKLIN	FATA MORGANA	LLOYD GEORGE	PERA HERA	THOMAS COOK
BIRMINGHAM UNIVERSITY	FELIPE	LOBO CANYON	PERSIAN	THOMAS EARP
BIURET	FLORENCE (ITALY)	LONDON	PICCADILLY	TIBERIUS
BLAKE (WILLIAM)	FLOSSIE	LORNA DOONE	PICORIS	TIM
BOCCACCIO	FRANCE +	LUCY	PIERRES	TIMBUCTOOT
BORGO SAN JACOPO	FRANCIS	LUKE	PISARRO	TIMMY
BRINSLEY	CASTHAUS GREEN HAT	LYONESSE	PISGAH	TIMON
BRITAIN	GERMANY +	MABLETHORPE	PLATO	TIMOTHY
CABOT	GIARDINI FAIR	MACBETH	PLUTO	TINTORET
CAESAR	GIUNTINA	MADAME CERES	POLE	TOLSTOI +
CARPACCIO	GOETHE	MADAME TUSSAUDS	POLYNESIAN	TOM
MOUNTAINS OF CARRARA	GREECE +	MALINTZI	PONTE VECCHIO	TOMLETS
CENTRAL PARK	GUADALUPE	MANHATTAN	PORTA CAPPUCCINI	TUSCAN +
CHARING CROSS	HAMLET +	MARIA	PROVENCE	TUSCANY
CHINA +	HARRY	MARY	PUEBLO RIVER	TYRE
CHRISTINE	HARRYLETS	MAUDIE	RAVENNA	ULYSSES +
CLARINDA	HELEN	MEDITERRANEAN	REX	UNDERWOOD
CLEOPATRA	HENRIETTE	MEXICAN +	ROBBIE BURNS	VENETIAN
CNOSSOS	HENRY VIII	MISS HARRISON	ROCKY MOUNTAINS	VENICE
COLUMBUS	HOLBEIN	MISS JUPSON	ROME +	VESUVIUS
CONGO	HOMER	MISS PONSONBY	RONALD	VIA DE BARDI
CONNIE	HUICHILOBOS	MISS STAINWRIGHT	RUDOLPH VALENTINO	VILLA OF VENICE
CORSO	HUNGARIAN	MISS WILKS	RUE DE LA PAIX	VINGONE
CORTES	ICHABOD	MONA LISA	RUSSIA	WHITMAN (WALT)
CROSSE AND BLACKWELLS	ILLYSUS	MR. FORD	SAINT FRANCIS	WIDDER NAYLOR
CHRYSTAL PALACE	INDIA	MR. GLADSTONE	SAN CRISTOBAL	ZELLER LAKE

APPENDIX IX: MISCELLANEOUS

B. NUMBERS AND COLORS

ACID-BLUE	COPPER-SULPHATE	FORTY-FIVE	MAUVE-RED	TAWNY-GOLD
AMBER	CORPSE-PALE	FORTY-THREE	MILK-BLUE	TEN +
APPLE-GREEN	CRIMSON	FOUR +	MUD-BLACK	THIRD
ASH-GREY	DARK-BLUE	FOURTEEN	MUD-GREY	THIRTEEN
ASH-WHITE	DARK-GREEN	GOLD	NINE	THIRTEEN THOUSAND
ASHY GREY	DARK-RED	GOLD-AND-GREEN	NINE-TENTHS	THIRTIES
AUBURN	DAWN-PALE	GOLD-AND-GREENISH	ONE	THIRTY
AUTUMN-BROWN	DAWN-PINK	GOLD-BRONZE	ORANGE	THOUSAND +
BEECH-GREEN	DAWN-ROSE	GOLD-BROWN	PALE-GOLD	THREE
BLACK	DEAD-BLACK	GOLD-GREY	PALE-GREEN	THREESCORE
BLACK-AND-WHITE	DOZENS	GREEN +	PINK	THRICE
BLACK-BLUE	DUNG-WHITENED	GREENISH	PUMA-YELLOW	TWELVE +
BLACK-GREEN	EARTH-BROWN	GREENNESS	PURPLE	TWENTY +
BLACK-PURPLE	EARTH-GOLDEN	GREEN-PURE	RED +	TWENTY-FIRST
BLOND	EIGHT	GREY	RED-GOLD	TWENTY-FIVE
BLOOD-BROWN	EIGHT AND TWENTY	GREY-BLACK	ROSE-RED	TWENTY-FOUR
BLOOD-ORANGE	EIGHTEEN	GREY-BLUE	SABLE	TWICE
BLOOD RED	EIGHTY	GREY-GREEN	SECOND +	TWO +
BLOODY-WHITE	ELEVEN	GREYNESS	SEVEN +	TWO THOUSAND
BLUE +	EVENING-GREEN	HALF-A-DOZEN	SEVENTY	UNDER-GOLD
BLUE-BLACK	FIFTH	HELL-PURPLE	SEVENTY-NINE	VERMILION
BLUE-GREY	FIFTIES	HONEY-WHITE	SEVENTY-SEVEN	VIOLET
BLUENESS	FIFTY	HUNDRED	SILVER-PINK	WHITE +

517

BLUEY-BROWN	FIRST	HUNDRED-PER-CENT	SINGLE	YELLOW +
BLUISH	FIVE +	HUNDREDS	SIX	YELLOW-BROWN
BRIGHT-GREY	FIVE-FOLD	IRON-GREY	SIX HUNDRED	YELLOW-GREEN
BRONZE +	FIVE THOUSAND	JADE-GREEN	SIXTEEN	YELLOW-RED
BROWN	FLAME-GREEN	KHAKI +	SIXTY	
CERULEAN	FLOSS-GOLD	LAVENDER	SKY-BLUE	
CHALK-COLOURED	FORTIES	LEMON-COLOURED	SNOW-WHITE	
CLAY-COLOURED	FORTY	MAGENTA	SUN-BLACK	

APPENDIX IX: MISCELLANEOUS

C. FOREIGN WORDS AND EXPRESSIONS

ACH	CINE	FILIUS MEUS	MADONNA MIA	QUELLE JOIE DE VIVRE
ADIOS	COGITO ERGO SUM	FORESTIERE	MATER	QUE TIENE AMIGO
AGUARDIENTE	CONSUMMATUM EST	GESTE	MERE TORTUE	QUOS VULT
APPASSIONATO	COUREUR DE FEMMES	HERMOSO ES	MISERERE	PERDERE DEUS
APRE MOI LE DELUGE	CRAPA	HOLA HOLA MEXICANOS	MONSIEUR	REFUGIO
A SGHEMBO	CREPE DE CHINE	ICH DIEN	NADA	RETRO ME SATANAS
AUTO-DA-FE	DANS L'EAU	IL SIGNORE	NICHTS	ROBINETTO
BASTA	DESPEDIDA	IMORTELLE +	NIENTE RIEN	SOLEDAD
BETE	DIENT IHR	IN EXTREMIS	NOLI ME TANGERE	SONO IO
BUON VIAGGIO	DIES IRAE DIES ILLA SOLVET	IN PURIS NATURA	NON COGITO ERGO SUM	SUM ERGO COGITO
CACHE SEXE	SAECLUM IN FAVILLA	JAMQUE VALE	NULLUS	TACE TU CRAPA BESTIA
CAMION	EGO SUM	JOIE DE VIVRE	OMNES VOS OMNES SERVITE	TERRA FIRMA
CASUS BELLI	EN MASSE	KAPUT	PAIN GRILLE	VOLTE FACE
CENTAVOS	MADAME EST SI BIEN CAMBREE	LE BESTIE NON PARLANO	PER BACCO	WEHMUT IST DER WEH
CHATELAINE	FARAGLIONI	POVERINE	POST ME NIHIL	
CINCO	FATA MORGANA	LIRE	PURISIMA	

33.01-34.29 THE WILD COMMON
35.01-35.25 DOG-TIRED
35.26-36.08 FROM A COLLEGE WINDOW
36.09-36.18 DISCORD IN CHILDHOOD
36.19-37.04 CHERRY ROBBERS
37.05-37.23 DREAM-CONFUSED
37.24-38.28 RENASCENCE
38.29-40.24 VIRGIN YOUTH
40.25-41.19 STUDY
41.20-41.31 TWILIGHT
42.01-43.37 LOVE ON THE FARM
44.01-44.09 GIPSY
44.10-46.04 THE COLLIER'S WIFE
46.05-46.16 FLAPPER
46.17-46.24 THIEF IN THE NIGHT
47.01-48.13 MONOLOGUE OF A MOTHER
48.14-48.26 THE LITTLE TOWN AT EVENING
48.27-49.20 IN A BOAT
49.21-50.18 LAST HOURS
50.19-51.04 FLAT SUBURBS, S. W., IN THE MORNING
51.05-52.11 THE BEST OF SCHOOL
52.12-53.19 DREAMS OLD AND NASCENT
53.20-53.31 SUBURBS ON A HAZY DAY
54.01-54.32 WEEKNIGHT SERVICE
55.01-57.09 A MAN WHO DIED
57.10-58.07 LETTER FROM TOWN: ON A GREY MORNING IN MARCH
58.08-58.23 LETTER FROM TOWN: THE ALMOND TREE
58.24-60.10 WEDDING MORN
60.11-61.20 VIOLETS
61.21-62.24 LIGHTNING
62.25-64.28 END OF ANOTHER HOME HOLIDAY
64.29-65.10 BABY RUNNING BAREFOOT
65.11-66.04 SIGH NO MORE
66.05-67.06 GUARDS
67.07-67.12 AWARE
67.13-67.17 A PANG OF REMINISCENCE
67.18-67.21 A WHITE BLOSSOM
68.01-69.08 COROT
69.09-69.29 MICHAEL ANGELO
70.01-70.19 HYDE PARK AT NIGHT, BEFORE THE WAR
70.20-71.19 PICCADILLY CIRCUS AT NIGHT
71.20-72.03 AFTER THE OPERA
72.04-72.11 MORNING WORK
72.12-73.19 TRANSFORMATIONS
73.20-74.06 A BABY ASLEEP AFTER PAIN
74.07-75.06 LAST LESSON OF THE AFTERNOON
75.07-75.19 SCHOOL ON THE OUTSKIRTS
75.20-76.22 A SNOWY DAY IN SCHOOL
76.23-85.04 WHETHER OR NOT
85.05-85.16 A WINTER'S TALE
85.17-85.24 RETURN
86.01-86.08 THE APPEAL
86.09-87.29 LILIES IN THE FIRE
88.01-89.35 RED MOON-RISE
90.01-91.06 SCENT OF IRISES
91.07-91.24 FORECAST
91.25-91.29 PROPHET
92.01-94.02 DISCIPLINE
94.03-95.03 THE PUNISHER
95.04-96.04 TEASE
96.05-97.06 MYSTERY
97.07-98.10 REPULSED
98.11-99.15 COLDNESS IN LOVE
99.16-99.28 SUSPENSE
100.01-100.12 ENDLESS ANXIETY
100.13-100.28 THE END
101.01-101.16 THE BRIDE
101.17-102.24 THE VIRGIN MOTHER
102.25-103.03 AT THE WINDOW
103.04-104.20 REMINDER
104.21-106.22 DRUNK
106.23-107.04 SORROW
107.05-108.04 DOLOUR OF AUTUMN
108.05-109.12 THE INHERITANCE
109.13-109.28 SILENCE
110.01-110.24 LISTENING
110.25-111.07 BROODING GRIEF
111.08-112.15 LAST WORDS OF MIRIAM
112.16-112.29 MALADE
113.01-113.16 LOTUS AND FROST
113.17-114.16 THE YEW-TREE ON THE DOWNS
114.17-115.04 TROTH WITH THE DEAD
115.05-115.12 AT A LOOSE END
115.13-115.26 SUBMERGENCE
116.01-116.13 THE ENKINDLED SPRING
116.14-117.24 EXCURSION TRAIN
117.25-118.19 RELEASE
118.20-119.06 THESE CLEVER WOMEN
119.07-120.10 BALLAD OF ANOTHER OPHELIA
120.11-121.12 KISSES IN THE TRAIN
121.13-122.08 TURNED DOWN
122.09-122.24 AFTER MANY DAYS
122.25-126.06 SNAP-DRAGON
126.07-127.20 COME SPRING, COME SORROW
127.21-129.06 THE HANDS OF THE BETROTHED
129.07-129.26 A LOVE SONG
129.27-129.31 TWOFOLD
130.01-130.23 TARANTELLA
130.24-131.22 UNDER THE OAK
131.23-132.26 BROTHER AND SISTER
132.27-133.25 THE SHADOW OF DEATH
133.26-133.33 BIRDCAGE WALK
134.01-134.13 IN TROUBLE AND SHAME
134.14-134.27 CALL INTO DEATH
135.01-135.20 GREY EVENING
135.21-136.12 FIRELIGHT AND NIGHTFALL
136.13-136.29 BLUENESS

136.30-137.17 A PASSING-BELL
137.18-140.06 THE DRAINED CUP
140.07-141.04 LATE AT NIGHT
141.05-141.26 NEXT MORNING
141.27-142.16 WINTER IN THE BOULEVARD
142.17-142.28 PARLIAMENT HILL IN THE EVENING
143.01-143.25 EMBANKMENT AT NIGHT, BEFORE THE WAR /CHARITY/
144.01-146.35 EMBANKMENT AT NIGHT, BEFORE THE WAR /OUTCASTS/
147.01-147.17 SICKNESS
147.18-148.03 IN CHURCH
148.04-148.19 PIANO
148.20-149.24 THE NORTH COUNTRY
149.25-150.23 LOVE STORM
150.24-152.09 PASSING VISIT TO HELEN
152.10-152.25 TWENTY YEARS AGO
152.26-153.12 READING A LETTER
153.13-154.26 SEVEN SEALS
154.27-158.30 TWO WIVES
159.01-159.18 NOISE OF BATTLE
159.19-160.04 AT THE FRONT
160.05-161.05 REALITY OF PEACE, 1916
161.06-161.28 NARCISSUS
162.01-163.08 TOMMIES IN THE TRAIN
163.09-164.16 ON THE MARCH
164.17-164.24 RUINATION
164.25-165.28 THE ATTACK
165.29-166.15 WINTER-LULL
166.16-166.27 BOMBARDMENT
167.01-167.20 RONDEAU OF A CONSCIENTIOUS OBJECTOR
167.21-168.36 OBSEQUIAL ODE
169.01-169.25 GOING BACK
169.26-170.16 SHADES
170.17-171.16 TOWN IN 1917
171.17-172.04 BREAD UPON THE WATERS
172.05-172.17 WAR-BABY
172.18-173.16 NOSTALGIA
173.17-176.09 DREAMS OLD AND NASCENT
176.10-176.29 ON THAT DAY
177.01-177.24 AUTUMN SUNSHINE
178.01-178.33 SONG-DAY IN AUTUMN
179.01-179.19 DISAGREEABLE ADVICE
179.20-180.36 RESTLESSNESS
193.01-193.13 MOONRISE
193.14-194.03 ELEGY
194.04-194.17 NONENTITY
194.18-196.04 MARTYR A LA MODE
196.05-196.24 DON JUAN
197.01-197.33 THE SEA
198.01-199.32 HYMN TO PRIAPUS
200.01-203.08 BALLAD OF A WILFUL WOMAN
203.09-203.21 BEI HENNEF
204.01-204.27 FIRST MORNING
205.01-205.22 "AND OH--THAT THE MAN I AM MIGHT CEASE TO BE--"
205.23-208.22 SHE LOOKS BACK
208.23-209.06 ON THE BALCONY
209.07-210.18 FROHNLEICHNAM
210.19-212.11 IN THE DARK
212.12-213.29 MUTILATION
214.01-215.13 HUMILIATION
215.14-216.12 A YOUNG WIFE
216.13-216.18 GREEN
216.19-217.18 RIVER ROSES
217.19-217.36 GLOIRE DE DIJON
217.37-218.04 ROSES ON THE BREAKFAST TABLE
218.05-218.12 I AM LIKE A ROSE
218.13-219.20 ROSE OF ALL THE WORLD
219.21-220.08 A YOUTH MOWING
220.09-220.20 QUITE FORSAKEN
220.21-221.04 FORSAKEN AND FORLORN
221.05-221.29 FIREFLIES IN THE CORN
222.01-222.21 A DOE AT EVENING
222.22-223.12 SONG OF A MAN WHO IS NOT LOVED
223.13-224.07 SINNERS
224.08-224.23 MISERY
224.24-226.12 MEETING AMONG THE MOUNTAINS
226.13-227.32 EVERLASTING FLOWERS
228.01-229.04 SUNDAY AFTERNOON IN ITALY
229.05-230.04 WINTER DAWN
230.05-231.07 A BAD BEGINNING
231.08-232.15 WHY DOES SHE WEEP?
232.16-232.31 GIORNO DEI MORTI
233.01-233.26 ALL SOULS
234.01-235.16 LADY WIFE
235.17-236.23 BOTH SIDES OF THE MEDAL
236.24-237.16 LOGGERHEADS
237.17-237.26 DECEMBER NIGHT
238.01-238.15 NEW YEAR'S EVE
238.16-239.06 NEW YEAR'S NIGHT
239.07-239.21 VALENTINE'S NIGHT
239.22-240.21 BIRTH NIGHT
240.22-242.07 RABBIT SNARED IN THE NIGHT
242.08-243.20 PARADISE RE-ENTERED
243.21-243.29 COMING AWAKE
244.01-245.04 SPRING MORNING
245.05-248.15 WEDLOCK
248.16-249.08 HISTORY
249.09-250.12 SONG OF A MAN WHO IS LOVED
250.13-250.32 THE SONG OF A MAN WHO HAS COME THROUGH
251.01-252.12 ONE WOMAN TO ALL WOMEN
252.13-252.26 PEOPLE
253.01-254.07 STREET LAMPS
254.08-256.03 "SHE SAID AS WELL TO ME"
256.04-261.16 NEW HEAVEN AND EARTH
261.17-262.24 ELYSIUM
262.25-268.13 MANIFESTO
268.14-269.13 AUTUMN RAIN
269.14-270.28 FROST FLOWERS
270.29-274.08 CRAVING FOR SPRING

277.01-277.11 FRUITS
278.01-279.02 POMEGRANATE
279.03-279.28 PEACH
280.01-281.30 MEDLARS AND SORB-APPLES
282.01-284.31 FIGS
285.01-287.10 GRAPES
287.11-289.23 THE REVOLUTIONARY
289.24-293.12 THE EVENING LAND
293.13-294.06 PEACE
295.01-295.10 TREES
296.01-298.18 CYPRESSES
298.19-300.17 BARE FIG-TREES
300.18-301.17 BARE ALMOND-TREES
301.18-302.06 TROPIC
302.07-302.21 SOUTHERN NIGHT
303.01-303.22 FLOWERS
304.01-307.16 ALMOND BLOSSOM
307.17-309.50 PURPLE ANEMONES
310.01-312.03 SICILIAN CYCLAMENS
312.04-318.06 HIBISCUS AND SALVIA FLOWERS
319.01-319.11 THE EVANGELISTIC BEASTS
320.01-323.18 ST MATTHEW
323.19-325.25 ST MARK
325.26-327.30 ST LUKE
328.01-330.08 ST JOHN
331.01-331.09 CREATURES
332.01-334.19 THE MOSQUITO
334.20-340.16 FISH
340.17-342.07 BAT
342.08-347.23 MAN AND BAT
348.01-348.16 REPTILES
349.01-351.30 SNAKE
352.01-354.22 BABY TORTOISE
354.23-356.18 TORTOISE SHELL
356.19-358.21 TORTOISE FAMILY CONNECTIONS
358.22-362.11 LUI ET ELLE
362.12-363.24 TORTOISE GALLANTRY
363.25-367.07 TORTOISE SHOUT
368.01-368.12 BIRDS
369.01-372.04 TURKEY-COCK
372.05-372.24 HUMMING-BIRD
372.25-374.35 EAGLE IN NEW MEXICO
375.01-375.33 THE BLUE JAY
376.01-376.08 ANIMALS
377.01-380.12 THE ASS
380.13-383.26 HE-GOAT
383.27-386.22 SHE-GOAT
386.23-392.13 ELEPHANT
392.14-394.26 KANGAROO
394.27-400.32 BIBBLES
401.01-402.33 MOUNTAIN LION
403.01-405.32 THE RED WOLF
406.01-406.09 GHOSTS
407.01-408.22 MEN IN NEW MEXICO
408.23-409.31 AUTUMN AT TAOS
410.01-412.31 SPIRITS SUMMONED WEST
413.01-414.34 THE AMERICAN EAGLE
425.01-425.10 OUR DAY IS OVER
425.11-425.18 HARK IN THE DUSK!
425.19-425.22 ELEPHANTS IN THE CIRCUS
426.01-426.03 ELEPHANTS PLODDING
426.04-426.07 ON THE DRUM
426.08-426.22 TWO PERFORMING ELEPHANTS
427.01-427.06 TWILIGHT
427.07-427.10 CUPS
427.11-427.14 BOWLS
427.15-427.18 YOU
428.01-428.05 AFTER DARK
428.06-429.30 TO LET GO OR TO HOLD ON--?
430.01-430.14 DESTINY
430.15-431.29 HOW BEASTLY THE BOURGEOIS IS--
431.30-433.08 WORM EITHER WAY
433.09-433.20 NATURAL COMPLEXION
433.21-434.13 THE OXFORD VOICE
434.14-435.04 TRUE DEMOCRACY
435.05-435.20 TO BE SUPERIOR
435.21-436.19 SWAN
436.20-436.26 LEDA
436.27-438.25 GIVE US GODS
438.26-439.10 WON'T IT BE STRANGE--?
439.11-440.20 SPIRAL FLAME
440.21-442.05 LET THE DEAD BURY THEIR DEAD--
442.06-443.09 WHEN WILT THOU TEACH THE PEOPLE--?
443.10-443.21 A LIVING
443.22-444.08 WHEN I WENT TO THE FILM--
444.09-446.18 WHEN I WENT TO THE CIRCUS
446.19-447.32 THE NOBLE ENGLISHMAN
448.01-448.07 THINGS MEN HAVE MADE--
448.08-448.13 THINGS MADE BY IRON--
448.14-448.18 NEW HOUSES, NEW CLOTHES--
448.19-448.27 WHATEVER MAN MAKES--
449.01-449.23 WE ARE TRANSMITTERS--
449.24-450.11 ALL THAT WE HAVE IS LIFE--
450.12-450.17 LET US BE MEN--
450.18-451.28 WORK
451.29-452.13 WHY--?
452.14-453.05 WHAT IS HE?
453.06-453.12 O! START A REVOLUTION--
453.13-453.28 MOON MEMORY
454.01-454.11 THERE IS RAIN IN ME--
454.12-454.17 DESIRE GOES DOWN INTO THE SEA
454.18-455.11 THE SEA, THE SEA--
455.12-455.29 NOVEMBER BY THE SEA--
456.01-456.04 OLD SONG.
456.05-456.09 GOOD HUSBANDS MAKE UNHAPPY WIVES--
456.10-457.12 FIGHT!   O MY YOUNG MEN--
457.13-457.30 WOMEN WANT FIGHTERS FOR THEIR LOVERS

458.01-458.13 IT'S EITHER YOU FIGHT OR YOU DIE--
458.14-459.20 DON'TS
459.01-461.20 THE RISEN LORD
461.21-462.16 THE SECRET WATERS
462.17-463.18 BEWARE, O MY DEAR YOUNG MEN--
463.19-463.23 OBSCENITY
463.24-465.06 SEX ISN'T SIN--
465.07-465.30 THE ELEPHANT IS SLOW TO MATE--
466.01-466.08 SEX AND TRUST
466.09-466.12 THE GAZELLE CALF
466.13-466.17 LITTLE FISH
466.18-466.22 THE MOSQUITO KNOWS
467.01-467.04 SELF-PITY
467.05-467.10 NEW MOON
467.11-467.15 SPRAY
467.16-467.19 SEA-WEED
468.01-468.11 MY ENEMY
468.12-468.21 TOUCH
468.22-469.10 NOLI ME TANGERE--
469.11-470.03 CHASTITY
470.04-470.22 LET US TALK, LET US LAUGH--
470.23-471.18 TOUCH COMES--
471.19-472.13 LEAVE SEX ALONE--
472.14-473.07 THE MESS OF LOVE
473.08-474.22 CLIMB DOWN, O LORDLY MIND--
474.23-475.05 EGO-BOUND
475.06-475.11 JEALOUSY
475.12-475.26 EGO-BOUND WOMEN--
476.01-477.21 FIDELITY
477.22-478.29 KNOW DEEPLY, KNOW THYSELF MORE DEEPLY--
479.01-479.08 ALL I ASK--
479.09-479.27 THE UNIVERSE FLOWS--
480.01-480.27 UNDERNEATH--
481.01-482.14 THE PRIMAL PASSIONS
482.15-482.27 ESCAPE
482.28-483.28 THE ROOT OF OUR EVIL--
484.01-484.11 THE IGNOBLE PROCESSION
484.12-484.21 NO JOY IN LIFE
484.22-485.09 WILD THINGS IN CAPTIVITY
485.10-485.23 MOURNFUL YOUNG MAN--
485.24-486.06 THERE IS NO WAY OUT--
486.07-487.13 MONEY-MADNESS
487.14-487.25 KILL MONEY--
488.01-488.06 MEN ARE NOT BAD--
488.07-489.08 NOTTINGHAM'S NEW UNIVERSITY
489.09-489.28 I AM IN A NOVEL--
490.01-490.08 NO! MR LAWRENCE!
490.09-491.04 RED-HERRING
491.05-491.12 OUR MORAL AGE
491.13-492.30 MY NAUGHTY BOOK
493.01-493.24 THE LITTLE WOWSER
493.25-494.12 THE YOUNG AND THEIR MORAL GUARDIANS
494.13-494.26 WHEN I READ SHAKESPEARE
495.01-495.09 SALT OF THE EARTH
495.10-495.14 FRESH WATER
495.15-496.05 PEACE AND WAR
496.06-496.09 MANY MANSIONS
496.10-496.17 GLORY
496.18-496.23 WOE
497.01-497.12 ATTILA
497.13-497.25 WHAT WOULD YOU FIGHT FOR?
498.01-498.04 CHOICE
498.05-498.08 RICHES
498.09-498.25 POVERTY
499.01-499.03 NOBLE
499.04-499.11 WEALTH
499.12-499.19 TOLERANCE
499.20-499.25 COMPARI
500.01-500.10 SICK
500.11-500.17 DEAD PEOPLE
500.18-500.25 CEREBRAL MOTIONS
501.01-501.05 WELLSIAN FUTURES
501.06-501.15 TO WOMEN, AS FAR AS I'M CONCERNED
501.16-501.25 BLANK
502.01-502.12 EARLY DISCONTENTED WOMEN
502.13-502.22 OLD PEOPLE
502.23-503.13 THE GRUDGE OF THE OLD
503.14-503.30 BEAUTIFUL OLD AGE
504.01-504.14 COURAGE
504.15-504.19 DESIRE IS DEAD
504.20-505.08 WHEN THE RIPE FRUIT FALLS--
505.09-505.24 ELEMENTAL
505.25-506.10 FIRE
506.11-506.19 I WISH I KNEW A WOMAN
506.20-506.24 TALK
506.25-507.12 THE EFFORT OF LOVE
507.13-507.15 CAN'T BE BORNE
507.16-507.19 MAN REACHES A POINT--
507.20-507.23 GRASSHOPPER IS A BURDEN--
508.01-508.10 BASTA!
508.11-508.24 TRAGEDY
508.25-509.21 AFTER ALL THE TRAGEDIES ARE OVER--
509.22-510.15 NULLUS
510.16-511.05 DIES IRAE
511.06-511.15 DIES ILLA
511.16-511.20 STOP IT--
512.01-512.31 THE DEATH OF OUR ERA
513.01-513.10 THE NEW WORD
513.11-513.20 SUN IN ME
513.21-514.09 BE STILL!
514.10-514.24 AT LAST--
514.25-515.06 NEMESIS
515.07-515.10 THE OPTIMIST
515.11-515.15 THE THIRD THING
515.16-515.23 THE SANE UNIVERSE
516.01-516.06 FEAR OF SOCIETY IS THE ROOT OF ALL EVIL
516.07-516.10 GOD

516.11-516.23 SANE AND INSANE
517.01-517.22 A SANE REVOLUTION
517.23-518.06 ALWAYS THIS PAYING
518.07-518.13 POOR YOUNG THINGS
518.14-518.25 A PLAYED-OUT GAME
519.01-519.09 TRIUMPH
519.10-520.32 THE COMBATIVE SPIRIT
521.01-521.19 WAGES
521.20-521.27 YOUNG FATHERS
522.01-522.08 A TALE TOLD BY AN IDIOT
522.09-522.31 BEING ALIVE
523.01-523.29 SELF-PROTECTION
524.01-524.12 A MAN
524.13-524.18 LIZARD
524.19-524.25 RELATIVITY
525.01-525.09 SPACE
525.10-525.21 SUN-MEN
525.22-526.06 SUN-WOMEN
526.07-526.24 DEMOCRACY
526.25-527.08 ARISTOCRACY OF THE SUN
527.09-527.12 CONSCIENCE
527.13-528.04 THE MIDDLE CLASSES
528.05-528.09 IMMORALITY
528.10-528.21 CENSORS
528.22-528.27 MAN'S IMAGE
529.01-529.10 IMMORAL MAN
529.11-529.21 COWARDS
529.22-530.04 THINK--!
530.05-530.08 PEACOCK
530.09-530.17 PALTRY-LOOKING PEOPLE
530.18-530.22 TARTS
531.01-531.21 LATTER-DAY SINNERS
531.22-533.10 WHAT MATTERS
533.11-534.08 FATE AND THE YOUNGER GENERATION
534.09-534.22 AS FOR ME, I'M A PATRIOT
534.23-535.14 THE ROSE OF ENGLAND
535.15-535.22 ENGLAND IN 1929
535.23-535.25 LIBERTY'S OLD OLD STORY
536.01-536.03 NEW BROOMS
536.04-536.05 POLICE SPIES
536.06-537.18 NOW IT'S HAPPENED
537.19-537.29 ENERGETIC WOMEN
538.01-538.14 FILM PASSION
538.15-538.26 FEMALE COERCION
539.01-539.09 VOLCANIC VENUS
539.10-539.22 WHAT DOES SHE WANT?
539.23-540.06 WONDERFUL SPIRITUAL WOMEN
540.07-540.10 POOR BIT OF A WENCH!--
540.11-540.16 WHAT AILS THEE?--
541.01-541.09 IT'S NO GOOD!
541.10-541.25 DON'T LOOK AT ME
542.01-543.11 SHIPS IN BOTTLES
543.12-544.30 KNOW THYSELF, AND THAT THOU ART MORTAL
545.01-546.04 WHAT IS MAN WITHOUT AN INCOME?--
546.05-546.21 CANVASSING FOR THE ELECTION
546.22-547.25 ALTERCATION
547.26-548.35 FINDING YOUR LEVEL
549.01-550.18 CLIMBING UP
550.19-551.08 IO CLARINDA
551.09-551.24 CONUNDRUMS
551.25-552.16 A RISE IN THE WORLD--
552.17-553.32 UP HE GOES!--
554.01-555.08 THE SADDEST DAY
555.09-556.16 PRESTIGE
556.17-557.08 HAVE DONE WITH IT--
557.09-558.14 HENRIETTE
558.15-559.16 VITALITY
559.17-559.20 WILLY WET-LEG
559.21-560.12 MAYBE--
560.13-560.32 STAND UP!
561.01-562.07 TRUST
562.08-563.16 DEMON JUSTICE
563.17-564.24 BE A DEMON!
564.25-565.30 THE JEUNE FILLE

VOLUME II

569.01-569.14 A ROSE IS NOT A CABBAGE
569.15-570.11 THE MAN IN THE STREET
570.12-571.14 BRITANNIA'S BABY
571.15-572.16 CHANGE OF GOVERNMENT
572.17-573.08 THE BRITISH WORKMAN AND THE GOVERNMENT
573.09-573.20 CLYDESIDER
573.21-574.10 FLAPPER VOTE
574.11-575.12 SONGS I LEARNT AT SCHOOL   I. NEPTUNE'S LITTLE
                AFFAIR WITH FREEDOM
575.13-576.15 SONGS I LEARNT AT SCHOOL   II. MY NATIVE LAND
576.16-577.23 SONGS I LEARNT AT SCHOOL   III. THE BRITISH BOY
577.24-579.06 13,000 PEOPLE
579.07-580.14 INNOCENT ENGLAND
580.15-581.09 GIVE ME A SPONGE
581.10-581.13 PUSS-PUSS!
581.14-581.18 LONDON MERCURY
581.19-581.26 MY LITTLE CRITICS
582.01-582.04 DADDY-DO-NOTHING
582.05-582.06 QUESTION
582.07-582.20 EDITORIAL OFFICE
583.01-584.04 THE GREAT NEWSPAPER EDITOR TO HIS SUBORDINATE
584.05-584.08 MODERN PRAYER
584.09-585.08 CRY OF THE MASSES
585.09-585.21 WHAT HAVE THEY DONE TO YOU--?
585.22-586.12 THE PEOPLE
586.13-586.28 THE FACTORY CITIES
587.01-587.17 LEAVES OF GRASS, FLOWERS OF GRASS
587.18-587.26 MAGNIFICENT DEMOCRACY
601.01-601.23 IMAGE-MAKING LOVE
602.01-602.09 PEOPLE

602.10-602.24 DESIRE
602.25-602.28 TO A CERTAIN FRIEND
603.01-603.08 THE EMOTIONAL FRIEND
603.09-603.14 CORRESPONDENCE IN AFTER YEARS
603.15-603.20 THE EGOISTS
603.21-603.25 CHIMAERA
604.01-604.25 ULTIMATE REALITY
604.06-604.12 SPHINX
604.13-604.23 INTIMATES
605.01-605.19 TRUE LOVE AT LAST
605.20-606.08 ANDRAITX--POMEGRANATE FLOWERS
606.09-606.12 I DARE DO ALL
606.13-606.17 BATTLE OF LIFE
606.18-606.20 THERE ARE TOO MANY PEOPLE
606.21-607.08 THE HEART OF MAN
607.09-608.07 MORAL CLOTHING
608.08-608.19 BEHAVIOUR
608.20-609.13 THE HOSTILE SUN
609.14-609.21 THE CHURCH
609.22-609.27 THE PROTESTANT CHURCHES
610.01-610.07 LONELINESS
610.08-610.18 THE UPROOTED
610.19-610.23 DELIGHT OF BEING ALONE
611.01-611.05 REFUSED FRIENDSHIP
611.06-611.09 FUTURE RELATIONSHIPS
611.10-611.13 FUTURE RELIGION
611.14-611.20 FUTURE STATES
612.01-612.07 FUTURE WAR
612.08-612.16 SIGNS OF THE TIMES
612.17-612.18 INITIATION DEGREES
612.19-612.20 UNHAPPY SOULS
613.01-613.02 FULL LIFE
613.03-613.05 PEOPLE WHO CARE
613.06-613.07 NON-EXISTENCE
613.08-613.10 ALL-KNOWING
613.11-614.05 SALVATION
614.06-614.11 OLD ARCHANGELS
614.12-614.16 LUCIFER
614.17-614.20 THE MILL OF GOD
614.21-614.25 MULTITUDES
615.01-615.06 FALLEN LEAVES
615.07-615.15 THE DIFFERENCE
615.16-615.20 THE BREATH OF LIFE
616.01-616.17 VENGEANCE IS MINE
616.18-616.30 ASTRONOMICAL CHANGES
617.01-617.11 FATALITY
617.12-617.18 FREE WILL
617.19-618.08 IN A SPANISH TRAM-CAR
618.09-618.15 SPANISH PRIVILEGE
618.16-618.20 AT THE BANK IN SPAIN
618.21-618.24 THE SPANISH WIFE
619.01-619.17 THE PAINTER'S WIFE
619.18-619.23 MODERN PROBLEMS
619.24-619.27 DOMINANT WOMAN
620.01-620.04 MEN AND WOMEN
620.05-620.09 THE SCIENTIFIC DOCTOR
620.10-620.21 HEALING
620.22-620.26 EN MASSE
621.01-621.11 GOD AND THE HOLY GHOST
621.12-621.14 HUMILITY
621.15-621.21 PROPER PRIDE
621.22-621.24 HUMILITY MONGERS
622.01-622.05 TENDER REVERENCE
622.06-622.13 ABSOLUTE REVERENCE
622.14-622.18 BELIEF
622.19-623.23 BELLS
623.24-625.09 THE TRIUMPH OF THE MACHINE
625.10-625.18 FORTE DEI MARMI
625.19-625.26 SEA-BATHERS
626.01-626.03 TALK OF LOYALTY
626.04-626.06 TALK OF FAITH
626.07-627.16 AMO SACRUM VULGUS
627.17-627.20 BOREDOM, ENNUI, DEPRESSION
627.21-627.28 THE DEADLY VICTORIAN
628.01-628.09 WHAT ARE THE WILD WAVES SAYING?
628.10-628.12 WELCOME DEATH
628.13-629.15 DARK SATANIC MILLS
629.16-630.08 WE DIE TOGETHER
630.09-631.08 WHAT HAVE THEY DONE TO YOU
631.09-632.09 WHAT IS A MAN TO DO?
632.10-632.27 CITY-LIFE
632.28-633.06 13 PICTURES
633.07-634.09 AUTO-DA-FE
634.10-634.20 SHOWS
634.21-634.30 ROSE AND CABBAGE
635.01-635.31 THE GULF
636.01-637.34 THE CROSS
638.01-638.06 FELLOW-MEN
638.07-638.14 THE SIGHT OF GOD
638.15-638.19 SOULS TO SAVE
638.20-638.23 WHEN MOST MEN DIE
639.01-639.13 HOLD BACK!
639.14-640.24 IMPULSE
640.25-640.27 MEN LIKE GODS
641.01-641.10 MEN AND MACHINES
641.11-641.21 MASSES AND CLASSES
641.22-642.15 GIVE US THE THEBAID
642.16-642.29 SIDE-STEP, O SONS OF MEN!
643.01-643.07 ON AND ON AND ON
643.08-643.29 OH WONDERFUL MACHINE!
644.01-644.14 BUT I SAY UNTO YOU: LOVE ONE ANOTHER
644.15-644.22 LOVE THY NEIGHBOUR
645.01-645.26 AS THYSELF!
646.01-646.18 LONELY, LONESOME, LONEY--O!
646.19-647.07 TREES IN THE GARDEN
647.08-647.20 STORM IN THE BLACK FOREST
647.21-647.23 REVOLUTION AS SUCH!
648.01-648.07 ROBOT FEELINGS

648.08-648.13 ROBOT-DEMOCRACY
648.14-648.21 REAL DEMOCRACY
649.01-649.18 WORSHIP
649.19-649.26 CLASSES
650.01-650.05 DEMOCRACY IS SERVICE
650.06-650.11 FALSE DEMOCRACY AND REAL
650.12-650.18 SERVICE
650.19-650.23 WHAT ARE THE GODS?
651.01-650.06 THE GODS! THE GODS!
651.07-651.19 NAME THE GODS!
651.20-652.18 THERE ARE NO GODS
652.19-652.25 FOOD OF THE NORTH
653.01-653.02 RETORT TO WHITMAN
653.03-653.04 RETORT TO JESUS
653.05-653.08 THE DEEPEST SENSUALITY
653.09-653.12 SENSE OF TRUTH
653.13-653.14 SATISFACTION
653.15-653.17 VIBRATION OF JUSTICE
654.01-654.02 LIES
654.03-654.05 POISON
654.06-654.09 COMMANDMENTS
654.10-654.12 EMOTIONAL LIES
654.13-654.15 LAUGHTER
655.01-655.06 DRAWING-ROOM
655.07-655.17 CABBAGE-ROSES
655.18-655.27 COLD BLOOD
656.01-656.04 SUNSET
656.05-656.11 LISTEN TO THE BAND!
656.12-656.24 THE HUMAN FACE
657.01-657.05 PORTRAITS
657.06-657.10 FURNITURE
657.11-657.16 CHILDREN SINGING IN SCHOOL
657.17-658.04 KEEP IT UP
658.05-658.12 RACE AND BATTLE
658.13-658.15 NOTHING TO SAVE
658.16-659.06 EMASCULATION
659.07-659.23 BRITISH SINCERITY
659.24-660.19 THE ENGLISH ARE SO NICE!
660.20-660.25 THE HILLS
660.26-660.27 TOURISTS
661.01-661.05 SEEKERS
661.06-661.10 SEARCH FOR LOVE
661.11-661.15 SEARCH FOR TRUTH
661.16-662.06 LIES ABOUT LOVE
662.07-662.13 TRAVEL IS OVER
662.14-662.24 OLD MEN
662.25-663.08 DEATH
663.09-663.12 BOURGEOIS AND BOLSHEVIST
663.13-663.17 PROPERTY AND NO-PROPERTY
663.18-663.27 COWARDICE AND IMPUDENCE
664.01-664.04 LORD TENNYSON AND LORD MELCHETT
664.05-664.11 CHOICE OF EVILS
664.12-664.13 HARD-BOILED CONSERVATIVES
664.14-664.16 SOLOMON'S BABY
664.17-665.05 THE PROPERTY QUESTION
665.06-665.09 THE WAY OUT
665.10-665.18 ST GEORGE AND THE DRAGON
665.19-665.27 THE HALF-BLIND
666.01-666.09 MINORITIES IN DANGER
666.10-666.23 IF YOU ARE A MAN
666.24-667.18 TERRA INCOGNITA
667.19-667.33 CLIMBING DOWN
668.01-668.04 ONLY THE BEST MATTERS
668.05-669.06 TO PINO
669.07-670.06 BROADCASTING TO THE G. B. P.
670.07-670.20 WE CAN'T BE TOO CAREFUL
670.21-670.23 LUCKY LITTLE BRITISHER
670.24-671.08 THE WORKING MAN
671.09-671.12 GLIMPSES
671.13-672.06 ALL SORTS OF GODS
672.07-672.29 FOR A MOMENT
673.01-673.03 GOETHE AND POSE
673.04-673.06 MEN LIKE GODS
673.07-673.15 THOUGHT
673.16-673.18 /THE GODS/
674.01-674.05 BE IT SO
674.06-674.17 CONCEIT
674.18-674.26 MAN IS MORE THAN HOMO SAPIENS
675.01-675.08 SELF-CONSCIOUS PEOPLE
675.09-676.18 TWO WAYS OF LIVING AND DYING
676.19-676.23 SO LET ME LIVE
676.24-677.19 GLADNESS OF DEATH
677.20-677.29 HUMANITY NEEDS PRUNING
678.01-678.17 SELF-SACRIFICE
678.18-679.07 SHEDDING OF BLOOD
679.08-679.22 THE OLD IDEA OF SACRIFICE
679.23-680.07 SELF-SACRIFICE
680.08-680.15 /THOMAS EARP/
680.16-680.19 "GROSS, COARSE, HIDEOUS"
680.20-681.11 /MR SQUIRE/
681.12-681.29 LET THERE BE LIGHT
682.01-683.18 GOD IS BORN
683.19-683.21 THE WHITE HORSE
683.22-684.07 FLOWERS AND MEN
684.08-684.15 PRAYER
687.01-687.11 THE GREEKS ARE COMING!
687.12-687.23 THE ARGONAUTS
688.01-688.20 MIDDLE OF THE WORLD
688.21-689.13 FOR THE HEROES ARE DIPPED IN SCARLET
689.14-689.30 DEMIURGE
690.01-690.13 THE WORK OF CREATION
690.14-691.05 RED GERANIUM AND GODLY MIGNONETTE
691.06-691.14 BODILESS GOD
691.15-691.26 THE BODY OF GOD
692.01-692.06 THE RAINBOW
692.07-692.21 MAXIMUS
692.22-693.20 THE MAN OF TYRE

693.21-693.30 THEY SAY THE SEA IS LOVELESS
694.01-695.12 WHALES WEEP NOT!
695.13-696.11 INVOCATION TO THE MOON
696.12-696.28 BUTTERFLY
697.01-697.22 BAVARIAN GENTIANS
697.23-697.31 LUCIFER
698.01-698.05 THE BREATH OF LIFE
698.06-699.11 SILENCE
699.12-699.29 THE HANDS OF GOD
700.01-700.16 PAX
700.17-701.09 ABYSMAL IMMORTALITY
701.10-701.32 ONLY MAN
702.01-702.21 RETURN OF RETURNS
702.22-703.15 STOIC
703.16-704.10 IN THE CITIES
704.11-704.29 LORD'S PRAYER
705.01-705.19 MANA OF THE SEA
705.20-705.22 SALT
706.01-706.09 THE FOUR
706.10-706.14 THE BOUNDARY STONE
706.15-706.23 SPILLING THE SALT
707.01-707.25 WALK WARILY
707.26-708.11 MYSTIC
708.12-708.30 ANAXAGORAS
709.01-710.08 KISSING AND HORRID STRIFE
710.09-710.22 WHEN SATAN FELL
710.23-711.11 DOORS
711.12-712.04 EVIL IS HOMELESS
712.05-712.22 WHAT THEN IS EVIL
712.23-713.10 THE EVIL WORLD SOUL
713.11-713.26 THE WANDERING COSMOS
713.27-714.21 DEATH IS NOT EVIL, EVIL IS MECHANICAL
714.22-714.29 STRIFE
715.01-715.04 THE LATE WAR
715.05-715.11 MURDER
715.12-715.18 MURDEROUS WEAPON
715.19-716.17 DEPARTURE
716.18-720.22 THE SHIP OF DEATH
720.23-721.07 DIFFICULT DEATH
721.08-721.26 ALL SOUL'S DAY
722.01-722.15 THE HOUSELESS DEAD
722.16-723.18 BEWARE THE UNHAPPY DEAD!
723.19-723.25 AFTER ALL SAINT'S DAY
723.26-724.11 SONG OF DEATH
724.12-724.26 THE END, THE BEGINNING
724.27-724.30 SLEEP
725.01-725.10 SLEEP AND WAKING
725.11-725.19 FATIGUE
725.20-725.24 FORGET
726.01-726.06 KNOW-ALL
726.07-726.16 TABERNACLE
726.17-726.21 TEMPLES
726.22-727.30 SHADOWS
727.31-727.33 CHANGE
728.01-728.12 PHOENIX
731.01-731.12 REBUKED
731.13-731.18 THE WIND, THE RASCAL
732.01-735.16 THE YOUNG SOLDIER WITH BLOODY SPURS
735.17-735.28 AH, MURIEL!
736.01-737.15 WE HAVE GONE TOO FAR
737.16-738.32 RESURRECTION OF THE FLESH
739.01-740.27 ERINNYES
741.01-743.28 ELOI, ELOI, LAMA SABACHTHANI?
743.29-746.07 RESURRECTION
746.08-748.12 LABOUR BATTALION
748.13-749.15 NO NEWS
749.16-749.20 BITS I: THE LAST MINUTE
749.21-750.03 "   II: VICAR'S SON
750.04-750.08 "   III: DRILL IN THE HEAT
750.09-750.16 "   IV: MOTHER'S SON IN SALONIKA
750.17-750.24 "   V: CASUALTY
751.01-751.13 "   VI: MAIDEN'S PRAYER
751.14-751.25 "   VII: MAN HAULING A WAGON
752.01-752.08 "   VIII: SIGHS
752.09-752.12 "   IX: DAUGHTER OF THE GREAT MAN
752.13-752.20 "   X: THE CHILD AND THE SOLDIER
753.01-753.07 "   XI: PIETA
753.08-753.11 "   XII: THE GREY NURSE
753.12-753.19 "   XIII: LITANY OF GREY NURSES
754.01-754.12 "   XIV: MESSAGE TO A PERFIDIOUS SOLDIER
754.13-754.20 "   XV: DUST IN THE EAST
754.21-754.26 "   XVI: THE GIRL IN CAIRO
755.01-755.09 "   XVII: THE JEWESS AND THE V. C.
755.10-755.21 "   XVIII: ZEPPELIN NIGHTS
756.01-756.07 "   XIX: MUNITIONS
756.08-756.13 "   XX: LAND-WORKER
756.14-756.17 "   XXI: MOURNING
757.01-757.07 "   XXII: MESOPOTAMIA
757.08-757.11 "   XXIII: TALES
757.12-757.19 "   XXIV: FOREIGN SUNSET
758.01-758.09 "   XXV: PRISONER AT WORK IN A TURKISH GARDEN
758.10-758.18 "   XXVI: /PRISONER AT WORK IN A TURKISH GARDEN/
758.19-759.04 "   XXVII:SWING SONG OF A GIRL AND A SOLDIER
759.05-759.11 "   XXVIII: PRISONERS AT WORK IN THE RAIN
759.12-759.15 "   XXIX: THE WELL IN AFRICA
759.16-759.19 "   XXX: NEITHER MOTH NOR RUST
760.01-760.21 APOSTROPHE TO A BUDDHIST MONK
760.22-761.16 HIM WITH HIS TAIL IN HIS MOUTH
761.17-762.13 /FLAT-FOOT'S SONG/
762.14-763.14 TRAITORS
763.15-765.08 REACH OVER
765.09-766.06 SOFTLY, THEN, SOFTLY
766.07-771.17 CHANGE OF LIFE
771.18-773.09 WHAT DO I CARE?
773.10-774.18 ARE YOU PINING?
774.19-780.22 O! AMERICANS
780.23-783.24 EAGLE IN NEW MEXICO

783.25-784.31 FIRE
786.01-787.14 /THE COMING OF QUETZALCOATL/
787.15-788.25 /LORD OF THE MORNING STAR/
788.26-789.08 /SOMEONE WILL ENTER BETWEEN THE GATES/
789.09-789.15 /MY NAME IS JESUS/
789.16-793.09 QUETZALCOATL LOOKS DOWN ON MEXICO
793.10-797.12 WHAT QUETZALCOATL SAW IN MEXICO
797.13-797.16 /SONG TO THE TUNE OF LA CUCARACHA/
797.17-798.33 JESUS' FAREWELL
799.01-799.13 /THE SONG OF DON RAMON/
799.14-800.39 /SON OF THE MORNING STAR/
801.01-802.05 /THE LIVING QUETZALCOATL/
802.06-803.04 /WELCOME TO QUETZALCOATL/
803.05-803.11 /THE MID-DAY VERSE/
803.12-803.17 /THE DAWN VERSE/
803.18-803.23 /THE SUNSET VERSE/
804.01-804.03 /METAL FOR RESISTANCE/
804.04-805.11 /FIRST SONG OF HUITZILOPOCHTLI/
805.12-806.14 /SECOND SONG OF HUITZILOPOCHTLI/
806.15-807.27 /THIRD SONG OF HUITZILOPOCHTLI/
807.28-808.16 THE SONG OF THE GREY DOG
808.17-809.03 /THE LORDS OF LIFE ARE THE MASTERS OF DEATH/
809.04-809.22 /HUITZILOPOCHTLI GIVES THE BLACK BLADE OF DEATH/
809.23-810.20 /HUITZILOPOCHTLI'S WATCH/
810.21-811.12 /SONG OF THE DEAD/
811.13-811.30 /LIKE THE GREEN CANDLES OF MALINTZI/
812.01-813.08 /MY WAY IS NOT THY WAY/
814.01-815.21 MEDITERRANEAN IN JANUARY
816.01-816.23 BEYOND THE ROCKIES
816.24-818.24 THE OLD ORCHARD
818.25-820.16 RAINBOW
823.01-824.17 HYMN TO NOTHINGNESS
824.18-826.20 AUGUST HOLIDAYS
826.21-828.13 BATHING RESORT
828.14-829.10 THE YOUNG ARE NOT MEAN IN MATERIAL THINGS
829.11-829.30 THE YOUNG WANT TO BE JUST
830.01-830.33 THE GENTLEMAN
831.01-831.04 ROSES
831.05-831.19 THE YOUNG ARE NOT GREEDY
831.20-832.19 MIDDLE-CLASS CHILDREN
832.20-833.34 KNOW THYSELF
834.01-834.06 NIGHT
834.07-834.12 LOVE
834.13-836.06 SO THERE!
836.07-836.16 MORALITY
836.17-836.19 IMMORALITY
836.20-837.09 CENSORS
837.10-837.22 LIFE AND THE HUMAN CONSCIOUSNESS
837.23-837.28 THE LATENT DESIRE
838.01-838.04 FOR ALL THAT
838.05-838.13 LOVE AS AN ESCAPE
838.14-839.07 WHAT'S TO BE DONE?
839.08-839.17 RALLYING-POINT
839.18-839.22 TODAY
839.23-840.06 THE ELEMENTS
840.07-841.09 GODS
841.10-842.11 LITTLE-BOY BRILLIANT
842.12-842.27 I HEARD HER SAY
842.28-843.06 WHAT'S WRONG
843.07-843.12 MONEY
843.13-843.21 SEX WON'T WORK
843.22-844.28 DEEPER THAN LOVE
844.29-845.16 /BAWDY CAN BE SANE/
845.17-845.21 /THERE WAS A GAY BIRD NAMED CHRISTINE/
845.22-846.12 /A LA MANIERE DE D. H. LAWRENCE/
854.01-854.20 CAMPIONS
854.21-855.20 GUELDER ROSES
855.21-856.06 THE FALL OF DAY
856.07-856.21 MARRIED IN JUNE
856.22-857.08 THE WORM TURNS
857.09-858.08 ON THE ROAD
858.09-859.52 THE DEATH OF THE BARON
860.01-860.24 LOVE COMES LATE
860.25-861.20 SONG
861.21-862.05 A FAILURE
862.06-862.17 A DECISION
862.18-862.29 A TRAIN AT NIGHT
863.01-863.20 BABY SONGS TEN MONTHS OLD
863.21-864.24 EVE
864.25-865.10 AFTER SCHOOL
865.11-866.21 A SNOWY DAY AT SCHOOL
866.22-867.07 READING IN THE EVENING
867.08-868.16 A MAN AT PLAY ON THE RIVER
868.17-868.32 AMOUR
869.01-869.16 BEREAVEMENT
869.17-869.24 LOSS
870.01-870.17 GRIEF
870.18-871.37 A LOVE-PASSAGE
872.01-872.22 /AH, WITH HIS BLESSING BRIGHT ON THY MOUTH AND
                   THY BROW/
872.23-873.05 ALOOF IN GAIETY
873.06-874.21 AND JUDE THE OBSCURE AND HIS BELOVED
874.22-880.08 A DRAMA
880.09-880.16 SEPARATED
880.17-881.15 ASSUMING THE BURDEN
881.16-882.33 THE CHIEF MYSTERY
883.01-883.17 EROTIC
883.18-884.07 MOON NEW-RISEN
884.08-885.13 RED
885.14-885.27 SHE WAS A GOOD LITTLE WIFE
885.28-886.21 PEAR-BLOSSOM
886.22-887.17 AT THE CEARNE
887.18-887.29 A KISS
888.01-888.17 /OTHER WOMEN HAVE REARED IN ME/
891.01-892.11 THE WILD COMMON *
892.12-893.10 RENAISSANCE *
893.11-893.32 VIRGIN YOUTH *

894.01-900.27 THE SCHOOLMASTER /A/ *
900.28-904.26 THE SCHOOLMASTER /B/ *
905.01-908.04 DREAMS OLD AND NASCENT *
908.05-909.28 DREAMS OLD AND NASCENT *
909.29-910.25 VIOLETS FOR THE DEAD *
910.26-911.32 VIOLETS *
912.01-912.24 LIGHTNING *
912.25-913.27 BABY MOVEMENTS *
913.28-914.11 A BABY RUNNING BAREFOOT *
914.12-915.20 COROT *
915.21-916.08 MICHAEL-ANGELO *
916.09-918.14 NIGHT SONGS *
918.15-925.29 WHETHER OR NOT *
926.01-926.29 DISCIPLINE *
927.01-927.31 LAST WORDS TO MURIEL *
928.01-929.05 LAST WORDS TO MIRIAM *
929.06-930.04 LIAISON *
930.05-930.12 DISSOLUTE *
930.13-931.29 HONEYMOON *
931.30-932.15 A SPIRITUAL WOMAN *
932.16-933.32 ANOTHER OPHELIA *
934.01-937.21 SNAP-DRAGON *
937.22-938.24 TO LETTICE, MY SISTER *
938.25-939.04 GRIEF *
939.05-939.24 TWILIGHT *
940.01-940.24 THE PIANO *
940.25-941.16 BIRTHDAY *
941.17-942.04 EARLY SPRING *
942.05-943.25 ALL OF ROSES *
944.01-944.16 THE MOWERS *
944.17-945.19 FIREFLIES IN THE CORN *
945.20-946.10 SONG OF A MAN THAT IS LOVED *
946.11-947.26 RELIGION *
947.27-949.18 /I KNOW A NOBLE ENGLISHMAN/ *
949.19-950.11 WORK *
950.12-950.24 IN NOTTINGHAM *
950.25-950.29 MORALITY *
951.01-952.09 DEEPER THAN LOVE *
952.10-953.11 WHAT'S SANE AND WHAT ISN'T-- *
953.12-954.16 THE TRIUMPH OF THE MACHINE *
954.17-955.24 GLORY OF DARKNESS *
955.25-956.23 BAVARIAN GENTIANS *
956.24-960.09 SHIP OF DEATH *
960.10-961.07 THE SHIP OF DEATH *
961.08-961.14 SONG OF DEATH *